S. Pauwls Church

5. yf Waterhouse

S. Andre in Holborne

Paulus wharfe   Queene hythe   The 3. Cranes

the Eel Ships

T H

winchester house

WILLIAM SHAKESPEARE : THE COMPLETE WORKS

In memory of

Charles F. Cliame

WILLIAM SHAKESPEARE THE COMPLETE WORKS

*

GENERAL EDITOR ALFRED HARBAGE

The Pelican Text Revised

VIKING

PENGUIN BOOKS
Published by the Penguin Group
Viking Penguin Inc., 40 West 23rd Street,
New York, New York 10010, U.S.A.
Penguin Books Ltd, 27 Wrights Lane,
London W8 5TZ, England
Penguin Books Australia Ltd, Ringwood,
Victoria, Australia
Penguin Books Canada Ltd, 2801 John Street,
Markham, Ontario, Canada L3R 1B4
Penguin Books (N.Z.) Ltd, 182–190 Wairau Road,
Auckland 10, New Zealand

Penguin Books Ltd, Registered Offices:
Harmondsworth, Middlesex, England

The Pelican Text published in thirty-eight volumes
Between 1956 and 1967
This revised edition first published in 1969
By Penguin Books Inc.
Reprinted 1969, 1970, 1971 (Twice), 1972, 1974, 1975

This reprint published in 1977 by Viking Penguin Inc.

9   11   13   15   14   12   10   8

Library of Congress Catalog Card Number 69–10044

Allen Lane Edition: ISBN 0 7139-0090-3
Viking Edition: ISBN 0 140.71449 9

Manufactured in the United States of America

Designed by Hans Schmoller, R.D.I.

TABLE OF CONTENTS

THE HISTORIES

THE TRAGEDIES

THE ROMANCES

THE NON-DRAMATIC POETRY

NOTE ON THE ILLUSTRATIONS

The illustrations on pages 3, 11, 22, 33, and 43 were specially made for this volume by C. Walter Hodges. The drawing of the interior of the Swan Playhouse on page 26 is Arend van Buchel's copy of a sketch made by his friend Johannes de Witt about 1596, and is reproduced with permission from MS. 842 in the Library of the Rijksuniversiteit, Utrecht. The opening pages of the first folio, considerably reduced in size, are taken from the Capell copy in the Library of Trinity College, Cambridge, by permission of the Master and Fellows. The endpapers reproduce sections, slightly more than half the original size, from the British Museum copy of Wenceslaus Hollar's panorama of London, published by Cornelius Danckers, Amsterdam, 1647. That at the end of the volume shows the city east from London Bridge to the Tower and beyond. That at the beginning shows, at the right, St Paul's as it appeared before the Great Fire, and, at the left, the Bankside in Southwark. It includes the most trustworthy surviving picture of the exterior of an Elizabethan playhouse. I. A. Shapiro, *Shakespeare Survey*, ed. A. Nicoll, Vols. I and II (1948 and 1949), has demonstrated that the engraving was made from Hollar's sketches, drawn on the spot before he left England in 1644, and that the labels were accidentally reversed. The structure marked "Beere bayting h" is actually the Globe as rebuilt in 1614.

PREFACE

In 1953 Mr H. F. Paroissien, who had founded in Baltimore the American subsidiary of Penguin Books Ltd, invited me to edit a series corresponding to *The Penguin Shakespeare*, which could not be distributed in this country owing to contractual agreements. Since there were at the time, incredible as it may now seem, only a few of Shakespeare's plays available in soft-cover, a complete edition would obviously serve a useful purpose. However, it seemed to me that its value would be greatly enhanced if it represented a collaborative effort among American scholars rather than my personal enterprise. I was asked to draw up a plan, and I presented this to Sir Allen Lane and his directors in London in 1954. Between 1956 and 1967 the thirty-eight volumes of *The Pelican Shakespeare* appeared. That the texts might finally be assembled as a *Complete Works* in hard-cover had been considered from the start, and as the series neared completion Mr Christopher Dolley, who had assumed charge in Baltimore after Mr Paroissien became deputy managing director of the parent firm, asked me to proceed with this project. It was agreed that the collaborating editors should be encouraged to make whatever revisions in their original work they wished, and that there should be added a General Introduction, also collaborative in nature. The present volume is the result. Since the soft-cover series is being revised and retained in print, *The Pelican Shakespeare* will hereafter be available in two formats.

There are many virtuous editions of Shakespeare, but it will seem pardonable if I dwell only upon the virtues of this one as I explain its technical features. The ideal has been to serve the student and general reader by putting current advances in Shakespearean scholarship to immediate practical use. This meant that the text must be constructed from that of the original quartos and folio in the light of the new principles in bibliographical study that have evolved in recent years. (A section in the General Introduction explains the issues involved, since it seems unnecessary that these should remain a mystery to all but the experts.) Leaders in bibliographical study in this country have edited the more difficult texts, and have generously lent their counsel in the case of the less difficult ones. The practical result is that no reading has been adopted without informed consideration of alternative possibilities. At first no textual apparatus was supplied, but after the early volumes of the edition had appeared, it seemed advisable to include an essential minimum. A list of substantive departures from the copy texts is now supplied with all the works, and an explanatory appendix with those in which the textual problem is especially complex. Thus anyone interested may determine those points where emendations or readings from alternative texts appear. It is hoped that the simplicity of the textual apparatus will encourage its use; unadopted readings from unauthoritative texts are not listed.

In a modern-spelling edition, perhaps in any edition, it is impossible to indicate nuances of difference between Shakespeare's pronunciation and our own, but an attempt has been made to preserve major distinctions. Thus variant forms with important distinctions of pronunciation, such as "bankrout" which appears along with "bankrupt" in the original texts, have been preserved. On the other hand, variant spellings and even variant forms where the distinction in pronunciation is a matter of debate, as in "murther" and "murder," or is at most slight, as in "whipt" and "whip'd" or "vild" and "vile," have been normalized with a view to the comfort of the reader; thus "murder" is used throughout, and "whipped" and "vile" unless the preservation of a rhyme is involved. In verse passages, the distinction between "ed" endings which are elided and those which are not is preserved. Thus "order'd" in the original texts appears here as "ordered" while "ordered" in the original texts appears here as "orderèd," the grave accent indicating that there is textual authority for pronouncing the word as a trisyllable. When an emendation is made, that is when an editor has decided that the metre requires "orderèd" although the original text reads "order'd," the change is recorded in the textual apparatus if there is any doubt about the scansion. When the emendation is the other way about, and the editor has adopted "ordered" although the original text fails to indicate elision, he has signalled the fact in the textual apparatus by placing a grave accent over the "e" ("orderèd") in citing the quarto or folio reading although, of course, the accent does not actually appear there. When such a form as "ord'red" appears in the original text, it is retained as "ord'red" and not converted to "ordered" lest the phonetic distinction be obliterated. Except for modernization of spelling and punctuation, normalization of speech-prefixes, and occasional relineation, the features of the original copy texts are preserved. Square brackets are placed about passages supplied by alternative early texts and about additions to stage directions supplied by such texts or by the editors. By reading the unbracketed words continuously, one may determine precisely how the stage directions appear in the original most authoritative editions.

Little need be said of the critical introductions to the separate works, or the glossarial notes, since their success or failure will be self-evident. The introductions are designed for those interested primarily in theatrical and poetic art rather than in literary history. It seemed likely that they would serve best if they were brief, informative, appreciative, and humane. It was agreed that they should place the works in critical perspective, without dogmatism or eccentricity, and that they should concede defects when such appear since Shakespeare stands in no need of protective silence. In most instances a particular person was requested to edit a particular work because he was known to have a special interest in it, or in what might be called its magnetic field, but in spite of this the introductions are not specialized. So far as the glossarial notes are concerned, the ideal has been to make them "without o'erflowing full" so that they would do the necessary work of explication without inducing depression.

The present edition adds certain conveniences of arrangement not present in the original series. The lines, except for the Sonnets, are not numbered in arbitrary units. Instead all lines are numbered which contain a word, phrase, or allusion explained in the glossarial notes, so that the reader will know at a glance where assistance is offered, and will be supplied with line-numbering at the same time. In the occasional instances where there is a long stretch of unannotated text, certain lines are numbered in italics to serve the conventional reference purpose. It may be noted here that, although there may be a slight difference in the actual number of printed lines in the present as compared with the original edition (in scenes containing prose), the line-numbering has been kept identical so that the two editions will tally and citations will be equally applicable to both. As in the original series the act–scene division established by editorial tradition, and rendered essential by its use in works of reference, is retained marginally, but is corrected by the device of printing continuously those scenes improperly split in two by early editors, and by placing stars only at those points where there is actually a vacated stage signalling a change in time, place, or both. The intrusive and often inaccurate place-headings inserted by early editors are omitted here as in the original series (and as is becoming standard practise), but for the convenience of those who miss them, an indication of locale appears as first item in the annotation of each scene. "Plays within a play" are distinguished by being set in slightly reduced type. Finally, it may be observed that, in the interest of both elegance and utility, each speech-prefix is spelled out in full, and is set in a separate line when the speaker's lines are in verse except when these words form the second half of a pentameter line. Thus the verse form of the speech is kept visually intact, and turned-over lines are avoided. What is printed as verse and what is printed as prose has, in general, the authority of the original texts. Departures from the original texts in this regard have only the authority of editorial tradition and the judgment of the Pelican editors; and, in a few instances, are admittedly arbitrary.

In the General Introduction there are concise accounts of Shakespeare's life and of the transmission of his text. The only other topics treated are those having immediate relevance to the understanding and enjoyment of his mind and art. The division of labor in the preparation of this preliminary matter provides assurance that it is reliable and up to date. Brief forewords of definition have been supplied for the five categories in which the works are arranged. Since each section of the General Introduc-

tion as well as each of the five forewords is followed by a list of books, this volume incorporates a classified bibliography. Articles, specialized studies, and untranslated foreign works, valuable though they are, have of necessity been omitted; and books which have appeared in the last few decades have been favored over others. These will conduct the reader to the articles, specialized studies, foreign, and earlier books. Historical works and works of reference have been selected for inclusion because of their "standard" quality, but works of criticism have been included without a similar attempt at screening: omissions are accidental.

There remains the pleasant task of paying tribute to the co-workers upon this edition. My original intention was to edit only *Macbeth* in addition to serving as factotum. *King Lear* and *Love's Labor's Lost* were edited by me after the persons whom I first asked to do so declined, and *Henry V* so that its original editor could include the play in his own series. The remaining thirty-five works were, with only two exceptions, edited by the persons first asked to do so although the prospect of material reward was small. With no exceptions at all, these editors worked conscientiously and in the spirit of the general plan. In a word there were no balks, and with collaborative exercises of the present scope, this record may well be unique. My pleasure in the edition derives mainly from the fact that it has brought me in touch with so much good will and integrity. I wish to thank for their particular helpfulness the editors Fredson Bowers, Madeleine Doran, Richard Hosley, and Matthias Shaaber, and, for aid with the collation in time of need, my former student Anne Lancashire.

This edition is an Anglo-American product, its sponsors having a proprietary interest in it in more senses than one. The original series was the first publishing venture of the American branch of the English firm. Mr Paroissien took a personal pride in it, and himself did all the work of production and promotion usually performed by a large staff. Miss Marie Edel was our faithful and wonderfully competent ally in seeing the volumes through the press. Mr Dolley, in presiding over the transmutation to hardcover, has proved true heir to his predecessor's enthusiasm. Again the work of production has been done by a small committee rather than a large publishing staff, with a continuing gain in intimacy and ready exchange of ideas. Mr Hans Schmoller, the designer-director of Penguin Books at Harmondsworth, has designed the volume and superintended its printing, while his wife Tatyana Schmoller has seen the copy through the press. It has been a pleasure to work with them – and with Mr C. Walter Hodges, an illustrator who is himself an authority on the Elizabethan theatre. Mr Hodges, incidentally, illustrated the cover of the original series, and contributed permanently to my self-esteem by accepting my suggestion that the title *The Pelican Shakespeare* appear on a waving banner instead of on a scroll.

THE GENERAL EDITOR

THE OPENING PAGES OF THE
FOLIO OF 1623

To the Reader.

This Figure, that thou here seest put,
   It was for gentle Shakespeare cut;
Wherein the Grauer had a strife
   with Nature, to out-doo the life :
O, could he but haue drawne his wit
   As well in brasse, as he hath hit
His face ; the Print would then surpasse
   All, that was euer writ in brasse.
But, since he cannot, Reader, looke
   Not on his Picture, but his Booke.

B. I.

Mr. WILLIAM

SHAKESPEARES

COMEDIES,
HISTORIES, &
TRAGEDIES.

Published according to the True Originall Copies.

Martin Droeshout sculpsit London.

LONDON
Printed by Isaac Iaggard, and Ed. Blount. 1623.

VIRTVS VERA NOBILITAS

COLL: TRIN:
CAN- -TAB:

TO THE MOST NOBLE
Edward Duke AND
INCOMPARABLE PAIRE
OF BRETHREN.

WILLIAM
Earle of Pembroke, &c. Lord Chamberlaine to the
Kings most Excellent Maiesty.

AND

PHILIP
Earle of Montgomery, &c. Gentleman of his Maiesties
Bed-Chamber. Both Knights of the most Noble Order
of the Garter, and our singular good
LORDS.

Right Honourable,

*Hilst we studie to be thankful in our particular, for
the many fauors we haue receiued from your L.L.
we are falne vpon the ill fortune, to mingle
two the most diuerse things that can bee, feare,
and rashnesse; rashnesse in the enterprize, and
feare of the successe. For, when we valew the places your H.H.
sustaine, we cannot but know their dignity greater, then to descend to
the reading of these trifles: and, while we name them trifles, we haue
depriu'd our selues of the defence of our Dedication. But since your
L.L. haue beene pleas'd to thinke these trifles some-thing, heereto-
fore; and haue prosequuted both them, and their Authour liuing,
with so much fauour: we hope, that (they out-liuing him, and he not
hauing the fate, common with some, to be exequutor to his owne writings) you will vse the like indulgence toward them, you haue done*

A 2   vnto

unto their parent. There is a great difference, vvhether any Booke choose his Patrones, or finde them : This hath done both. For, so much were your L.L. likings of the seuerall parts, vvhen they were acted, as before they vvere published, the Volume ask'd to be yours. We haue but collected them, and done an office to the dead, to procure his Orphanes, Guardians; vvithout ambition either of selfe-profit, or fame : onely to keepe the memory of so worthy a Friend, & Fellow aliue, as was our SHAKESPEARE, *by humble offer of his playes, to your most noble patronage. Wherein, as we haue iustly obserued, no man to come neere your L.L. but vvith a kind of religious addresse ; it hath bin the height of our care, vvho are the Presenters, to make the present worthy of your H.H. by the perfection. But, there we must also craue our abilities to be considerd, my Lords. We cannot go beyond our owne powers. Country hands reach foorth milke, creame, fruites, or what they haue : and many* Nations (*we haue heard*) *that had not gummes & incense, obtained their requests with a leauened Cake. It vvas no fault to approch their Gods, by what meanes they could : And the most, though meanest, of things are made more precious, when they are dedicated to Temples. In that name therefore, we most humbly consecrate to your H.H. these remaines of your seruant* Shakespeare ; *that what delight is in them, may be euer your L.L. the reputation his, & the faults ours, if any be committed, by a payre so carefull to shew their gratitude both to the liuing, and the dead, as is*

Your Lordshippes most bounden,

IOHN HEMINGE.
HENRY CONDELL.

To the great *Variety* of *Readers*.

Rom the most able, to him that can but spell: There
you are number'd. We had rather you were weighd.
Especially, when the fate of all Bookes depends vpon your capacities : and not of your heads alone,
but of your purses. Well ! It is now publique, & you
wil stand for your priuiledges weeknow : to read,
and censure. Do so, but buy it first. That doth best
commend a Booke, the Stationer saies. Then, how odde soeuer your
braines be, or your wisedomes, make your licence the same, and spare
not. Iudge your sixe-pen'orth, your shillings worth, your fiue shillings worth at a time, or higher, so you rise to the iust rates, and welcome. But, what euer you do, Buy. Censure will not driue a Trade,
or make the Iacke go. And though you be a Magistrate of wit, and sit
on the Stage at *Black-Friers*, or the *Cock-pit*, to arraigne Playes dailie,
know, these Playes haue had their triall alreadie, and stood out all Ap-
peales ; and do now come forth quitted rather by a Decree of Court,
then any purchas'd Letters of commendation.

It had bene a thing, we confesse, worthie to haue bene wished, that
the Author himselfe had liu'd to haue set forth, and ouerseen his owne
writings ; But since it hath bin ordain'd otherwise, and he by death departed from that right, we pray you do not envie his Friends, the office
of their care, and paine, to haue collected & publish'd them ; and so to
haue publish'd them, as where (before) you were abus'd with diuerse
stolne, and surreptitious copies, maimed, and deformed by the frauds
and stealthes of iniurious impostors, that expos'd them : euen those,
are now offer'd to your view cur'd, and perfect of their limbes ; and all
the rest, absolute in their numbers, as he conceiued thé. Who, as he was
a happie imitator of Nature, was a most gentle expresser of it. His mind
and hand went together : And what he thought, he vttered with that
easinesse, that wee haue scarse receiued from him a blot in his papers.
But it is not our prouince, who onely gather his works, and giue them
you, to praise him. It is yours that reade him. And there we hope, to
your diuers capacities, you will finde enough, both to draw, and hold
you : for his wit can no more lie hid, then it could be lost. Reade him,
therefore ; and againe, and againe : And if then you doe not like him,
surely you are in some manifest danger, not to vnderstand him. And so
we leaue you to other of his Friends, whom if you need, can bee your
guides : if you neede them not, you can leade your selues, and others.
And such Readers we wish him.

A 3   *Iohn Heminge.*
                                  Henrie Condell.

To the memory of my beloued,
The AVTHOR
Mr. William Shakespeare:
And
what he hath left vs.

To draw no enuy (Shakespeare) on thy name,
    Am I thus ample to thy Booke, and Fame:
    While I confesse thy writings to be such,
As neither Man, nor Muse, can praise too much.
'Tis true, and all mens suffrage. But these wayes
Were not the paths I meant vnto thy praise:
For seeliest Ignorance on these may light,
    Which, when it sounds at best, but eccho's right;
Or blinde Affection, which doth ne're aduance
    The truth, but gropes, and vrgeth all by chance;
Or crafty Malice, might pretend this praise,
    And thinke to ruine, where it seem'd to raise.
These are, as some infamous Baud, or whore,
    Should praise a Matron. What could hurt her more?
But thou art proofe against them, and indeed
    Aboue th'ill fortune of them, or the need.
I, therefore will begin. Soule of the Age!
    The applause! delight! the wonder of our Stage!
My Shakespeare, rise; I will not lodge thee by
    Chaucer, or Spenser, or bid Beaumont lye
A little further, to make thee a roome:
    Thou art a Moniment, without a tombe,
And art aliue still, while thy Booke doth liue,
    And we haue wits to read, and praise to giue.
That I not mixe thee so, my braine excuses;
    I meane with great, but disproportion'd Muses:
For, if I thought my iudgement were of yeeres,
    I should commit thee surely with thy peeres,
And tell, how farre thou didstst our Lily out-shine,
    Or sporting Kid, or Marlowes mighty line.
And though thou hadst small Latine, and lesse Greeke,
    From thence to honour thee, I would not seeke
For names; but call forth thund'ring Æschilus,
    Euripides, and Sophocles to vs,
Paccuuius, Accius, him of Cordoua dead,
    To life againe, to heare thy Buskin tread,
And shake a Stage: Or, when thy Sockes were on,
    Loaue thee alone, for the comparison

of

Of all, that insolent Greece, or haughtie Rome
  sent forth, or since did from their ashes come.
Triumph, my Britaine, thou hast one to showe,
  To whom all Scenes of Europe homage owe.
He was not of an age, but for all time !
  And all the Muses still were in their prime,
When like Apollo he came forth to warme
  Our eares, or like a Mercury to charme !
Nature her selfe was proud of his designes,
  And ioy'd to weare the dressing of his lines !
Which were so richly spun, and wouen so fit,
  As, since, she will vouchsafe no other Wit.
The merry Greeke, tart Aristophanes,
  Neat Terence, witty Plautus, now not please ;
But antiquated, and deserted lye
  As they were not of Natures family.
Yet must I not giue Nature all : Thy Art,
  My gentle Shakespeare, must enioy a part.
For though the Poets matter, Nature be,
  His Art doth giue the fashion. And, that he,
Who casts to write a liuing line, must sweat,
  (such as thine are) and strike the second heat
Vpon the Muses anuile : turne the same,
  (And himselfe with it) that he thinkes to frame ;
Or for the lawrell, he may gaine a scorne,
  For a good Poet's made, as well as borne.
And such wert thou. Looke how the fathers face
  Liues in his issue, euen so, the race
Of Shakespeares minde, and manners brightly shines
  In his well torned, and true-filed lines :
In each of which, he seemes to shake a Lance,
  As brandish't at the eyes of Ignorance.
Sweet Swan of Auon! what a sight it were
  To see thee in our waters yet appeare,
And make those flights vpon the bankes of Thames,
  That so did take Eliza, and our Iames !
But stay, I see thee in the Hemisphere
  Aduanc'd, and made a Constellation there !
Shine forth, thou Starre of Poets, and with rage,
  Or influence, chide, or cheere the drooping Stage ;
Which, since thy flight frō hence, hath mourn'd like night,
  And despaires day, but for thy Volumes light.

BEN: IONSON.

Vpon the Lines and Life of the Famous
Scenicke Poet, Maſter WILLIAM
SHAKESPEARE.

THoſe hands, which you ſo clapt, go now, and wring
You *Britaines* braue; for done are *Shakeſpeares* dayes:
His dayes are done, that made the dainty Playes,
Which made the Globe of heau'n and earth to ring.
Dry'de is that veine, dry'd is the *Theſpian* Spring,
Turn'd all to teares, and *Phœbus* clouds his rayes:
That corp's, that coffin now beſticke thoſe bayes,
Which crown'd him *Poet* firſt, then *Poets* King.
If *Tragedies* might any *Prologue* haue,
All thoſe he made, would ſcarſe make one to this:
Where *Fame*, now that he gone is to the graue
(Deaths publique tyring-houſe) the *Nuncius* is.
    For though his line of life went ſoone about,
    The life yet of his lines ſhall neuer out.

HVGH HOLLAND.

A CATALOGVE

of the seuerall Comedies, Histories, and Tragedies contained in this Volume.

TO THE MEMORIE

of the deceased Authour Maister
W. SHAKESPEARE.

SHake-speare, *at length thy pious fellowes giue*
The world thy Workes : thy Workes, by which, out-liue
Thy Tombe, thy name must · when that stone is rent,
And Time dissolues thy Stratford Moniment,
Here we aliue shall view thee still. This Booke,
When Brasse and Marble fade, shall make thee looke
Fresh to all Ages: when Posteritie
Shall loath what's new, thinke all is prodegie
That is not Shake-speares ; eu'ry Line, each Verse
Here shall reuiue, redeeme thee from thy Herse.
Nor Fire, nor cankring Age, as Naso said,
Of his, thy wit-fraught Booke shall once inuade.
Nor shall I e're beleeue, or thinke thee dead
(Though mist) vntill our bankrout Stage be sped
(Impossible) with some new straine t'out-do
Passions of Iuliet, and her Romeo ;
Or till I heare a Scene more nobly take,
Then when thy half-Sword parlying Romans spake.
Till these, till any of thy Volumes rest
Shall with more fire, more feeling be exprest,
Be sure, our Shake-speare, thou canst neuer dye,
But crown'd with Lawrell, liue eternally.

L. Digges.

To the memorie of M. *W.* Shake-speare.

VVEE *wondred (Shake-speare) that thou went'st so soone*
From the Worlds-Stage, to the Graues-Tyring-roome.
Wee thought thee dead, but this thy printed worth,
Tels thy Spectators, that thou went'st but forth
To enter with applause. An Actors Art,
Can dye, and liue, to acte a second part.
That's but an Exit *of Mortalitie ;*
This, a Re-entrance *to a Plaudite.*

I. M.

The Workes of William Shakespeare,

containing all his Comedies, Histories, and
Tragedies: Truely set forth, according to their first
O R J G J N A L L.

The Names of the Principall Actors
in all these Playes.

William Shakespeare.	Samuel Gilburne.
Richard Burbadge.	Robert Armin.
John Hemmings.	William Ostler.
Augustine Phillips.	Nathan Field.
William Kempt.	John Underwood.
Thomas Poope.	Nicholas Tooley.
George Bryan.	William Ecclestone.
Henry Condell.	Joseph Taylor.
William Slye.	Robert Benfield.
Richard Cowly.	Robert Goughe.
John Lowine.	Richard Robinson.
Samuell Crosse.	Iohn Shancke.
Alexander Cooke.	Iohn Rice.

THE TEMPEST.

Actus primus, Scena prima.

A tempestuous noise of Thunder and Lightning heard: En-
ter a Ship-master, and a Boteswaine.

Master.

Ote-swaine.

Botes. Heere Master : What cheere ?

Mast. Good : Speake to th'Mariners : fall
too't, yarely, or we run our selues a ground,
bestirre, bestirre. *Exit.*

Enter Mariners.

Botes. Heigh my hearts, cheerely, cheerely my harts :
yare, yare : Take in the toppe-sale : Tend to th'Masters
whistle : Blow till thou burst thy winde , if roome e-
nough.

Enter Alonso, Sebastian, Anthonio, Ferdinando,
Gonzalo, and others.

Alon. Good Boteswaine haue care : where's the Master ? Play the men.

Botes. I pray now keepe below.

Anth. Where is the Master, Boson ?

Botes. Do you not heare him ? you marre our labour,
Keepe your Cabines : you do asist the storme.

Gonz. Nay, good be patient.

Botes. When the Sea is : hence, what cares these roarers for the name of King ? to Cabine ; silence : trouble
vs not.

Gon. Good, yet remember whom thou hast aboord.

Botes. None that I more loue then my selfe. You are
a Counsellor, if you can command these Elements to silence, and worke the peace of the present, wee will not
hand a rope more, vse your authoritie : If you cannot,
giue thankes you haue liu'd so long, and make your
selfe readie in your Cabine for the mischance of the
houre, if it so hap. Cheerely good hearts : out of our
way I say. *Exit.*

Gon. I haue great comfort from this fellow : methinks
he hath no drowning marke vpon him, his complexion
is perfect Gallowes : stand fast good Fate to his hanging, make the rope of his destiny our cable, for our
owne doth little aduantage : If he be not borne to bee
hang'd, our case is miserable. *Exit.*

Enter Boteswaine.

Botes. Downe with the top-Mast : yare, lower, lower,
bring her to Try with Maine-course. A plague————

A cry within. *Enter Sebastian, Anthonio & Gonzalo.*

vpon this howling : they are lowder then the weather,
or our offices : yet againe ? What do you heere ? Shal we
giue ore and drowne, haue you a minde to sinke ?

Sebas. A poxe o' your throat, you bawling, blasphe-
mous incharitable Dog.

Botes. Worke you then.

Anth. Hang cur, hang, you whoreson insolent Noyse-
maker, we are lesse afraid to be drownde, then thou art.

Gonz. I'le warrant him for drowning , though the
Ship were no stronger then a Nutt-shell, and as leaky as
an vnstanched wench.

Botes. Lay her a hold, a hold , set her two courses off
to Sea againe, lay her off.

Enter Mariners wet.

Mari. All lost, to prayers, to prayers, all lost.

Botes. What must our mouthes be cold ?

Gonz. The King, and Prince, at prayers, let's assist them,
for our case is as theirs.

Sebas. I'am out of patience.

An. We are meerly cheated of our liues by drunkards,
This wide-chopt-rascall, would thou mightst lye drowning the washing of ten Tides.

Gonz. Hee'l be hang'd yet,
Though euery drop of water sweare against it,
And gape at widst to glut him. *A confused noyse within.*
Mercy on vs.
We split, we split , Farewell my wife, and children,
Farewell brother : we split, we split, we split.

Anth. Let's all sinke with' King

Seb. Let's take leaue of him. *Exit.*

Gonz. Now would I giue a thousand furlongs of Sea,
for an Acre of barren ground : Long heath, Browne
firrs, any thing; the wills aboue be done, but I would
faine dye a dry death. *Exit.*

Scena Secunda.

Enter Prospero and Miranda.

Mira. If by your Art (my deerest father) you haue
Put the wild waters in this Rore; alay them:
The skye it seemes would powre down stinking pitch,
But that the Sea, mounting to th' welkins cheeke,
Dashes the fire out. Oh ! I haue suffered
With those that I saw suffer : A braue vessell

B

(Who

(Who had no doubt some noble creature in her)
Dash'd all to peeces : O the cry did knocke
Against my very heart : poore soules, they perish'd.
Had I byn any God of power, I would
Haue suncke the Sea within the Earth, or ere
It should the good Ship so haue swallow'd, and
The fraughting Soules within her.

  Prof. Be collected,
No more amazement : Tell your pitteous heart
there's no harme done.

  Mira. O woe, the day.

  Prof. No harme :
I haue done nothing, but in care of thee
(Of thee my deere one ; thee my daughter) who
Art ignorant of what thou art . naught knowing
Of whence I am : nor that I am more better
Then *Prospero*, Master of a full poore cell,
And thy no greater Father.

  Mira. More to know
Did neuer medle with my thoughts.

  Prof. 'Tis time
I should informe thee farther : Lend thy hand
And plucke my Magick garment from me : So,
Lye there my Art : wipe thou thine eyes, haue comfort,
The direfull spectacle of the wracke which touch'd
The very vertue of compassion in thee :
I haue with such prouision in mine Art
So safely ordered, that there is no soule
No not so much perdition as an hayre
Betid to any creature in the vessell
Which thou heardst cry, which thou saw'st sinke : Sit
For thou must now know farther.   [downe,

  Mira. You haue often
Begun to tell me what I am, but stopt
And left me to a bootelesse Inquisition,
Concluding, stay : not yet.

  Prof. The howr's now come
The very minute byds thee ope thine eare,
Obey, and be attentiue. Canst thou remember
A time before we came vnto this Cell ?
I doe not thinke thou canst, for then thou was't not
Out three yeeres old.

  Mira. Certainely Sir, I can.

  Prof. By what ? by any other house, or person ?
Of any thing the Image, tell me, that
Hath kept with thy remembrance.

  Mira. 'Tis farre off :
And rather like a dreame, then an assurance
That my remembrance warrants : Had I not
Fowre, or fiue women once, that tended me ?

  Prof. Thou hadst ; and more *Miranda* : But how is it
That this liues in thy minde ? What seest thou els
In the dark-backward and Abisme of Time ?
Yf thou rememb'rest ought ere thou cam'st here,
How thou cam'st here thou maist.

  Mira. But that I doe not.

  Prof. Twelue yere since (*Miranda*) twelue yere since,
Thy father was the Duke of *Millaine* and
A Prince of power :

  Mira. Sir, are not you my Father ?

  Prof. Thy Mother was a peece of vertue, and
She said thou wast my daughter ; and thy father
Was Duke of *Millaine*, and his onely heire,
And Princesse ; no worse Issued.

  Mira. O the heauens,
What fowle play had we, that we came from thence ?

Or blessed was't we did ?

  Prof. Both, both my Girle,
By fowle-play (as thou saist) were we heau'd thence,
But blessedly holpe hither.

  Mira. O my heart bleedes
To thinke oth' teene that I haue turn'd you to,
Which is from my remembrance, please you, farther ;

  Prof. My brother and thy vncle, call'd *Anthonio* :
I pray thee marke me, that a brother should
Be so perfidious : he, whom next thy selfe
Of all the world I lou'd, and to him put
The mannage of my state, as at that time
Through all the signories it was the first,
And *Prospero*, the prime Duke, being so reputed
In dignity ; and for the liberall Artes,
Without a paralell ; those being all my studie,
The Gouernment I cast vpon my brother,
And to my State grew stranger, being transported
And rapt in secret studies, thy false vncle
(Do'st thou attend me ?)

  Mira. Sir, most heedefully.

  Prof. Being once perfected how to graunt suites,
how to deny them : who t'aduance, and who
To trash for ouer-topping ; new created
The creatures that were mine, I say, or chang'd 'em,
Or els new form'd 'em ; hauing both the key,
Of Officer, and office, set all hearts i'th state
To what tune pleas'd his eare, that now he was
The Iuy which had hid my princely Trunck,
And suckt my verdure out on't : Thou attend'st not ?

  Mira. O good Sir, I doe.

  Prof. I pray thee marke me :
I thus neglecting worldly ends, all dedicated
To closenes, and the bettering of my mind
with that, which but by being so retir'd
Ore-priz'd all popular rate : in my false brother
Awak'd an euill nature, and my trust
Like a good parent, did beget of him
A falsehood in it's contrarie, as great
As my trust was, which had indeede no limit,
A confidence sans bound. He being thus Lorded,
Not onely with what my reuenew yeelded,
But what my power might els exact. Like one
Who hauing into truth, by telling of it,
Made such a synner of his memorie
To credite his owne lie, he did beleeue
He was indeed the Duke, out o'th' Substitution
And executing th'outward face of Roialtie
With all prerogatiue : hence his Ambition growing :
Do'st thou heare ?

  Mira. Your tale, Sir, would cure deafenesse.

  Prof. To haue no Schreene between this part he plaid,
And him he plaid it for, he needes will be
Absolute *Millanie*, Me (poore man) my Librarie
Was Dukedome large enough : of temporall roalties
He thinks me now incapable. Confederates
(so drie he was for Sway) with King of *Naples*
To giue him Annuall tribute, doe him homage
Subiect his Coronet, to his Crowne and bend
The Dukedom yet vnbow'd (alas poore *Millaine*)
To most ignoble stooping.

  Mira. Oh the heauens :

  Prof. Marke his condition, and th'euent, then tell me
If this might be a brother.

  Mira. I should sinne
To thinke but Noblie of my Grand-mother,

                             Good

GENERAL INTRODUCTION

THE INTELLECTUAL AND POLITICAL
BACKGROUND

SWilliam Shakespeare was born into a world which still lived in reasonable comfort with a philosophical synthesis inherited from the Middle Ages. A few years before Shakespeare's death John Donne could write, "And new philosophy calls all in doubt." Since Shakespeare

was fundamentally conservative in his beliefs, the old synthesis is more important for an understanding of his plays than the "new philosophy"; yet the processes of change during his lifetime, the questionings of the old verities, produced social tensions which, some critics believe, made possible the great tragedies of the early seventeenth century.

It is easier to picture the external life of the Elizabethans than to recover beliefs and ways of thought made alien to us by four centuries of accelerating change. For the external or material aspects of Elizabethan life we have the aid of paintings, drawings, descriptions by natives and by foreign visitors, arms and armor, costumes, household furnishings, and even the houses. For beliefs and ideas we must rely upon the written word. One must call upon imagination as well as knowledge to reconstruct an age which did not know Rousseau or Marx, Newton or Einstein, Lyell or Darwin. The political revolutions of England in the seventeenth century and of America and France in the eighteenth century, the vast economic and social changes of the past two hundred years, the virtual elimination of monarchial government – such innovations, in scale at least, were beyond the experience of an Elizabethan, whose political philosophers told him that of all forms of government democracy is the worst. Across the English Channel there were rebellions and civil wars, involving conflicts of religion, in which some of Shakespeare's contemporaries fought and at the same time kept a wary eye on the defense of England against subversion or attack. The Elizabethan knew well and drew moral lessons from stories of the decay of empires, but the domestic quarrels which he knew from English history were essentially dynastic, though religious conflicts had a part in his recent history: the reformation under Henry VIII, the temporary restoration of the Roman church under Mary Tudor, and a rebellion in the north in 1569. Following the Elizabethan settlement, the established church endured dissension by its members who wished to lean further toward Calvinism or who wished to maintain as much as possible of the old religion. Outside the church, dissenters were a nuisance and the Jesuit missionaries a possible threat to the safety of the Queen and the peace of England. But sixteenth-century England did not suffer the militant conflicts of religious and political beliefs that mark the seventeenth century.

Not only what they thought but how they thought makes the Elizabethans strangers to us. Logic and reason under the guidance of incontrovertible principles, rather than systematic and controlled experiment, were the conservative tests of "fact." A pre-Shakespearean example

will serve to illustrate the application of reason to known facts. When one sailed south, the climate became progressively hotter. As a logical inference, foolhardy persistence in a southward course would lead to death by extreme heat. Early explorers, and even Shakespeare's contemporaries, note the error to refute it and to praise the temperate qualities of the tropics, especially at high altitudes. Experience triumphed over reason. A more enduring example is the belief (not "unreasonable" if one has no other means of observation than unaided eyesight) in the generation of living creatures from sun-heated mud or carrion – Hamlet's "if the sun breed maggots in a dead dog" (II, ii, 181). Tradition and authority – Galen in medicine, Aristotle in natural philosophy – were as strong in the sciences as in political and social organization, and both traditional learning and learned authority were challenged in Shakespeare's lifetime. We shall see these challenges in better perspective after some account of the world order in which they operated.

Another striking difference between Shakespeare's time and our own is in the status and the state of the English language. To-day English is the native tongue of hundreds of millions and the second language of millions more. In the sixteenth century it was the language of a few million people, not even all the inhabitants of Shakespeare's "scept'red isle." Regional differences in speech had yielded to growing uniformity in writing, and the late sixteenth-century author did not have to struggle with the problems of differences in vocabulary which William Caxton describes with good humor in his preface to the translation of the *Aeneid*. Not all men of letters were confident of the future of their language. It is not surprising that Sir Francis Bacon wrote his major work in Latin, since that was still the language of scholars and assured a wider audience than any vernacular could; and Bacon saw to it that his works in English which he valued most were translated into Latin. More typical of the Elizabethan writer's attitude toward his language is Edmund Spenser's rhetorical question in a comment on classical metres: "Why a God's name may not we, as else the Greeks, have the kingdom of our own language . . . ?" Pride in the English language was one of the motives for translating classical and European works of literature, just as the spread of knowledge was the motive for translating into English a wide variety of books on geography, history, science, philosophy, and politics. Even with this growing confidence in the English language, it is startling to read the prophetic questions of Samuel Daniel in *Musophilus*, written before the first permanent English colony was established in America:

And who, in time, knows whither we may vent
The treasure of our tongue, to what strange shores
This gain of our best glory shall be sent
T' enrich unknowing nations with our stores?
What worlds in th' yet unformed occident
May come refined with th' accents that are ours?

Although the status of the English language was modest, it had reached a happy state of development for the exercise of Shakespeare's genius. It had achieved the stability necessary for a written language without loss of freedom or flexibility. The freedom could lead to the extravagant coinages of Thomas Nashe or the mannered style of John Lyly's *Euphues*. Artificially imposed rules of grammar were left for the eighteenth century to develop; the grammar which an Elizabethan schoolboy studied was Latin, and Sir Philip Sidney gave thanks that English "wants not grammar; for grammar it might have, but it needs it not, being so easy in itself, and so void of those cumbersome differences of cases, genders, moods and tenses." Such distinctions, Sir Philip thought, were part of the curse of the tower of Babel, "that a man should be put to school to learn his mother tongue." As for Shakespeare, he did not merely use the English language; he helped to create it. The readiness of composition with which his fellow-actors credited him – or even the carelessness for which Ben Jonson administered a mild reproof – led him into occasional pomposity beyond the requirements of characterization, and his early plays are marked by an exuberance that at times seems uncontrolled. Yet mastery of the newly emerged national language has contributed as much as skill in characterization to the enduring reputation of Shakespeare. The range of styles from the homely to the grand disturbed his Restoration admirers, who revised the homely metaphors he put in the mouths of princes to bring them within the pale of "decorum."

A comparatively stable political order, other ways of testing knowledge, and the state of development of the English language are a few examples of major differences between Shakespeare's age and our own. The most comprehensive difference is in the philosophical synthesis which was accepted but also challenged in Shakespeare's time. Generalization leaves little room for analysis of refinements and variations in the synthesis, and in the interest of clarity it will be better to summarize the accepted beliefs before commenting on paradoxes within the system or the ways in which it was questioned.

The distinctive characteristic of the world order is a harmony that embraces the cosmos, natural phenomena, society, and the individual. Around the earth, the center of the universe, revolve in concentric spheres the planets: the moon, Mercury, Venus, the pre-eminent Sun, Mars, Jupiter, and Saturn. Outside the planetary spheres is the sphere of the fixed stars, and beyond that the *primum mobile*, the prime mover of all. The number of spheres varies, according to the authority cited, from nine to eleven, but differences in the total number of spheres leave no doubt that beyond the last sphere God reigns in His heaven, with nine hierarchies of angels around the throne. Beyond the sphere of the moon the universe is unchanging; mutability is an earthly phenomenon, usually to be deplored. Yet on earth, too, there is order in nature: the seasons, tides, the alternation of day and night proceed with predictable regularity. As there are hierarchies in heaven and in the heavens, so there are and should be ranks and degrees in human society. "The glorious planet Sol / In noble eminence enthroned and sphered / Amidst the other" has a counterpart in the earthly monarch. God is supreme in heaven and everywhere; the Sun is the chief of planets; the king rules his earthly domain; and reason *should* rule and direct the life of man. In brief man is a microcosm with many correspondences to the great world, the macrocosm. The analogies were pursued in a detail which may seem absurd to a twentieth-century reader; for example, the veins of man are like the rivers of earth.

The parallels in universal law and order support the "doctrine of degree," which finds justification in nature for social ranks. In the "great chain of being" there are no broken links, from the inanimate clod of earth at the bottom of the scale through plants, animals, rational men, intuitive angels, to God. The reflections of some of Shakespeare's characters on the predicament of man assume his place in the chain, a little lower than the angels. In the social order the importance attached to rank was not as restrictive and frustrating as it may appear. By the grace of God and by virtue of his immortal soul, the individual did enjoy a kind of integrity and independence. A man could have dignity in his place and in his craft. Simon Eyre, the prosperous shoemaker of Thomas Dekker's *The Shoemakers' Holiday*, is unabashed by a visit from King Henry V and addresses him in a manner that is as bluff and hearty as it is respectful.

Of the various statements of the "doctrine of degree" the most widely quoted, because Shakespeare seems to have followed it closely, is a passage in *Of the Laws of Ecclesiastical Polity*, Book I. Here Richard Hooker is explaining the obedience of creation to natural law, with a passing reference to the analogy with human law.

This world's first creation, and the preservation since of things created, what is it but only so far forth a manifestation by execution, what the eternal law of God is concerning things natural? And as it cometh to pass in a kingdom rightly ordered, that after a law is once published, it presently takes effect far and wide, all states framing themselves thereunto; even so let us think it fareth in the natural course of the world: since the time that God did first proclaim the edicts of his law upon it, heaven and earth have hearkened unto his voice, and their labour hath been to do his will: He made a law for the rain; He gave his decree unto the sea, that the waters should not pass his commandment. Now if nature should intermit her course, and leave altogether, though it were but for a while, the observation of her own laws; if those principal and mother elements of the world, whereof all things in this lower world are made, should lose the qualities which now they have; if the frame of that heavenly arch erected over our heads should loosen and dissolve itself; if celestial spheres should forget their wonted motions, and by irregular volubility turn themselves any way as it might happen; if the prince of the lights of heaven, which now as a giant doth run his unwearied course, should . . . begin to stand and to rest himself; if the moon should wander from her beaten way, the times and seasons of the year blend themselves by disordered and confused mixture . . . , what would become of man himself, whom these things do now serve? See we not plainly that obedience of creatures unto the law of nature is the stay of the whole world?   (Book I, sec. iii)

Hooker completes his catalogue of derangements of natural order and their effects with the question: "See we not plainly that obedience of creatures unto the law of nature is the stay of the whole world?" Closely parallel to this statement is the long speech by Ulysses in *Troilus and Cressida* (I, iii, 75–137), from which a few lines about the "glorious planet Sol" are quoted above. It is violation of degree, a violation of the natural order, that Ulysses advances as the reason for the long stalemate in the Trojan war.

It is a pity that so perfect a world order did not work perfectly. The earth is the center of creation; man holds dominion over beast and fowl; he lives under God's

world order and the principles and methods of the learning which supported it were subjected to question, often respectful but none the less pressing. According to theory, the heavens above the moon are changeless; meteorites are assigned to the sublunary region of fire. When, in 1572, a brilliant new body was observed in the sphere of the fixed and changeless stars a fundamental "truth"

special providence. But earth, cold and dry, is also the lowest and most lumpish of the elements, subject to fall-out from the superior elements of water, air, and fire, and subject also to Mutability, who, in the incomplete seventh book of Spenser's *Faerie Queene*, dares to challenge the rule of Nature. God created the world in time and it will end in time – how soon was a subject of debate in the early years of the seventeenth century. Worst of all, and the key to most evils, was Adam's fall, which changed not only man but the earth on which he lived, changes vividly described by Milton in the tenth book of *Paradise Lost*.

Aside from inherent problems, both the traditional

became subject to doubt. The Copernican description of the solar system, advanced as a hypothesis to explain irregularities in planetary motion which became in-creasingly difficult to account for under the Ptolemaic system, was known in Shakespeare's England and was taught as an alternative theory. The telescopic observa-tions of Galileo were a more serious matter, involving physical reality, not theoretical speculation. English scientists, like Thomas Harriot, were aware of these de-velopments; indeed, Harriot's own astronomical obser-vations, which he did not publish, were contemporary with those of Galileo. It is in this context that John Donne wrote in *An Anatomy of the World* the lines so often quoted for their pithy statement of the disturbing impact of the "new" astronomy:

> And new philosophy calls all in doubt;
> The element of fire is quite put out;
> The sun is lost, and th' earth, and no man's wit
> Can well direct him where to look for it.
> And freely men confess that this world's spent,
> When in the planets and the firmament
> They seek so many new....

Donne's professed alarm may have been premature and exaggerated so far as men's daily lives were concerned. The old astronomy, based upon millenia of patient observations, had its practical uses. One could tell time by it (as the carrier does in *1 Henry IV*, II, i) and one could navigate by it. The earth necessarily remained the "center" for man; it was the only platform available to him for observing the stars, and remained the only platform until a very few years ago. The disturbing feature of changes in astronomical thought lay in the interlocking assumptions of the world order: a change in one part affected all. Oddly enough, it may be in this field of human aspiration that we come closest to the Elizabethans. Like them we have lived through radical changes in our concepts of the nature of the universe, and even without the postulate of a harmonious world order the changes have had an impact beyond a special field of scientific study.

Less sudden and startling than the discoveries in astronomy but no less effective for change were the challenges of the "principles" and the authority of the ancients. Reason was set against the principles, often metaphysical axioms applied to the study of natural philosophy; and experience was set against reason. Here change was the work of many men. Three examples within Shakespeare's lifetime will serve to illustrate the arguments. The tyranny of the principles is attacked by Agrippa in *Of the Vanity and Uncertainty of the Arts and Sciences*, translated in 1569:

For every science hath in it some certain principles, which must be believed and cannot by any means be declared: which if any will obstinately deny, the philosophers have not wherewith to dispute against him, and immediately they will say, that there is no disputation against him which denieth the principles....

(fols 4ᵇ–5ᵃ)

A word of caution may be in order here: "science" in Elizabethan usage means all kinds of knowledge, not one special branch of learning. Even so, the exemption of the principles from dispute had been an effective brake upon innovation, in what we call experimental science as in other kinds of study. Of numerous challenges to the authority accorded to Aristotle two stand out because of the eminence and influence of the authors and the vigor of their phrasing. In 1605, when Shakespeare was at the height of his career, Sir Francis Bacon declared that "knowledge derived from Aristotle, and exempted from liberty of examination, will not rise again higher than the knowledge of Aristotle" (*The Advancement of Learning*, ed. W. A. Wright, p. 37). The statement is matched by Sir Walter Raleigh's blunt assertion in the preface to *The History of the World* (1614): "But for myself, I shall never be persuaded that God hath shut up all light of learning within the lantern of Aristotle's brains."

Such utterances reflect a determination to pursue the study of nature within the limits of man's rational powers, however restricted they be. Scriptural authority remains sacrosanct in all fields, but there remains a wide area open to human curiosity, an area which Raleigh defines, in the passage just quoted, as "every question of nature and *finite* power." (The "finite" is important.) Here Raleigh speaks for his age: reason is still the prime tool, yet human reason is imperfect, and experience often teaches us what reason cannot explain. He doubts

... that God hath given invention but to the heathen; and that they only have invaded nature, and found the strength and bottom thereof; the same nature having consumed all her store and left nothing of price to after-ages. That these and these be the causes of these and these effects, time hath taught us, and not reason; and so hath experience, without art. The cheese-wife knoweth it as well as the philosopher that sour rennet doth coagulate her milk into a curd. But if we ask a reason of this cause, why the sourness doth it? whereby it doth it? and the manner how? I think that there is nothing to be found in vulgar philosophy to satisfy this and many other like vulgar questions.

The weight of authority and tradition was not the only problem faced by the Elizabethan natural philosopher. There were religious objections to prying into the secrets of nature, lest the miracles of Moses and Jesus be disparaged by comparison with merely human achievements. The common reply to such objections was to praise the study of nature as a way to know God: the book of God's work as well as the book of God's word inspires awe of the Creator. Just as Elizabethan voyagers and their great chronicler, Richard Hakluyt, found the works of the Lord and his wonders in the deep (Psalm cvii, 23 and 24) powerful persuasives to religious belief, so the study of the workings of nature under God's ordinance would buttress faith, not weaken it. To this end, natural philosophy is distinguished from other kinds of "magic"; in the definition accepted by Sir Walter Raleigh, it is "the connection of natural agents [things active] and patients [things acted upon], answerable each to other, wrought by a wise man to the bringing forth of such effects as are wonderful to those that know not their causes" (*The History of the World*, I, xi). Natural philosophy is brought into disrepute and confused with black magic, conjuring, and witchcraft by "idle ignorance, the parent of causeless admiration." Not only were the idly ignorant more inclined to find omens in the extraordinary phenomena of nature than to appreciate scientific explanations. Generally speaking, Shakespeare's characters wonder at the effects of magic and consider the aberrations of nature ominous. Thus Casca rejects a natural explanation of the strange disorders of the night preceding the assassination of Julius Caesar:

> When these prodigies
> Do so conjointly meet, let not men say
> "These are their reasons – they are natural,"
> For I believe they are portentous things
> Unto the climate that they point upon.   (I, iii, 28–32)

Some troubles of the natural philosophers were of their own making. An esoteric terminology such as the alchemists used, lack of a systematic method of experiment (a defect which Bacon hoped to remedy), and a cult of secrecy did not help the untutored to draw fine distinctions between natural philosophy and black magic. The

4

cult of secrecy derived in part from a distinction between what we call pure science and applied science and in part from disdain of the "rascal many." Both considerations go back to Plato. Abstract knowledge, like the study of divinity, was the province of learned men, not to be profaned by making it open to the populace. But humanitarian concern triumphed over the aristocracy of learning. The pragmatism of Elizabethan "science" is epitomized in the goal of Sir Francis Bacon's ambitious designs for the reform of learning : the true end of study is "the glory of the Creator and the relief of man's estate." In the same vein, when the Elizabethan reflected on the innovations of what we call the Renaissance he gave pride of place to the magnetic compass, the art of printing, and gunpowder. He might deplore the ingratitude of the masses, who were as likely to misuse the inventions of the "artist" as to appreciate his genius, but the idea of progress – of material progress – had become too strong to ignore.

For the understanding of Shakespeare's plays the importance of concepts of a world order and the questioning thereof lies chiefly in their closely linked interrelationships. Within the total complex, man and society are Shakespeare's immediate concern, as we would expect. Set speeches like that of Ulysses in *Troilus and Cressida* are exceptional ; the characters' acceptance or rejection of the order is more allusive than discursive. Yet references to it occur at moments of great tension. Gloucester, in *King Lear* (I, ii, 101–14), convinced of astrological influences, runs through a series of parallels of natural and human disorders. Contending with a storm which matches in fury his mental turmoil, Lear himself

> Strives in his little world of man to outscorn
> The to-and-fro-conflicting wind and rain,   (III, i, 10–11)

and calls upon the thunder to

> Strike flat the thick rotundity o' th' world,
> Crack Nature's moulds, all germains spill at once,
> That makes ingrateful man.   (III, ii, 7–9)

Macbeth will have his answer from the witches

> ... though the treasure
> Of Nature's germains tumble all together
> Even till destruction sicken ...   (IV, i, 58–60)

Such imprecations have a destructive force all the more meaningful because they strike at the essential order of creation. On a quieter note, just before Iago works his evil will upon him, Othello says of his love for Desdemona,

> ... when I love thee not,
> Chaos is come again.   (III, iii, 91–92)

For an Elizabethan, and for Othello, the statement is more than a metaphor.

In considering the fortunes of men and their society the Elizabethans extolled the lessons of history as illustrative of God's providence. Sir Philip Sidney is not reflecting a majority opinion when, in the *Apology for Poetry*, he calls poetry a better teacher than philosophy or history. History has a special value because God's ways do not change ; He does not overlook in one generation the sins which received just punishment in earlier generations. In Sir Walter Raleigh's statement of the prevailing belief, "The end and scope of all history" is "to teach by example of times past, such wisdom as may guide our desires and actions" (*History of the World*, II, xxi, sec. 6). This aside on the value of history, one of many in Raleigh's ambitious work, is amplified in the preface to the *History*, which has further relevance to the study of Shakespeare's plays in its running commentary on the fortunes of English kings. The moral purpose of history is pictorially summarized in the engraved title page of the first edition of *The History of the World* (1614). The central figure of the engraving is History, "the mistress of life," represented by a radiant female. This personification of history treads upon death and oblivion and lifts the globe of the world to two figures : on one side pure white Good Fame, on the other spotted Evil Fame. At the top, surveying all, is the watchful eye of Providence. Flanking History are her guides, Truth and Experience, each framed between two pillars. These pillars, supporting a platform on the edge of which, as on the fore-edge of a book, is printed "The History of the World," represent the attributes of history :

> Time's witness, herald of antiquity,
> The light of truth, and life of memory.

The lines conclude a poem by Ben Jonson facing the title page and explaining its symbolism. The phrasing, however, is from Cicero, whose statement of the attributes of history is frequently and enthusiastically quoted by Elizabethan writers. In the preface, the engraving, and in the running commentary in the text, Raleigh's book represents a summation of Tudor concepts of history and was held in high esteem for two centuries, an esteem indicated by the fact that in the seventeenth century there were twice as many editions of the *History* as of the collected works of Shakespeare.

In light of the sorry record of human affairs, one may well ask how this providential theory of history can be squared with the chronicles of kings and kingdoms. The moralists were not blind to the fact that the evil often prosper and the good often suffer, but they believed firmly in ultimate retribution for wrongdoing. God will not be mocked. Even the deeds of evil men may be retribution for unknown or forgotten sins of their victims. Thus a tyrant may be a visitation of God's wrath for the sins of a nation. If the evil man is not punished in this life, so much the worse for him : he will have to endure the judgment of the life to come. In brooding over the plan to murder Duncan, Macbeth is more willing to take his chances in the next world than to face retribution in this. If the act of assassination would be the end of the affair,

> We'ld jump the life to come. But in these cases
> We still have judgment here, that we but teach
> Bloody instructions, which, being taught, return
> To plague th' inventor. This even-handed justice
> Commends th' ingredience of our poisoned chalice
> To our own lips.   (I, vii, 7–12)

Whatever immediate causes men may assign to the falls of princes or private calamities, the ultimate cause is the working of a watchful and unforgetful providence.

This concept of history has something in common with the medieval idea of tragedy as a fall from high place. The difference lies in the degree of religious emphasis on the interpretation of events. The common element is the instability of man's fortune, represented in one early book by a crude woodcut of a primitive ferris-wheel on which some ride up while others must go down. But for historians and other moralists there is no question that even the smallest incidents of human life manifest the working of providence. Thus, speaking with a new-found wisdom, Hamlet rejects his misgivings about the fencing match with Laertes and tells the anxious Horatio, "There is special providence in the fall of a sparrow" (V, ii, 208–09). In *Richard III* statements by the three queens, Hastings, and Buckingham on the working of divine justice are like variations on a theme. Thus Buckingham goes to his execution reflecting on the justice of his suffering as he had sworn he hoped to suffer if he broke his promises to King Edward IV:

> That high All-Seer which I dallied with
> Hath turned my feignèd prayer on my head
> And given in earnest what I begged in jest.
> Thus doth He force the swords of wicked men
> To turn their own points in their masters' bosoms...
> (V, i, 20–24)

Unfortunately for the welfare of man, this moralizing, whether in history or drama, is usually *ex post facto*. Before disaster strikes, the fortunate man or prince ignores the lessons of history or pays lip service to the religious principles they illustrate. To complicate matters in Shakespeare's time, a rival philosophy was shifting the emphasis in the study of politics and history to "reasons of state," to immediate causes as understood by human intelligence. The older and still vigorous historiography had not neglected such reasons, but subordinated them to a higher cause. Now Machiavelli and other Italian writers were teaching a practical politics which shocked the godly, even if the godly were not always guiltless of practices which they ascribed, often quite inaccurately, to Italian doctrine. Although there was no English translation of *The Prince* in print until 1640, translations circulated in manuscript and the work was available in Latin and French as well as Italian. Informed Elizabethans understood the principles advanced by the Italian writers, but the unsophisticated got their knowledge of *The Prince* at second hand, in part from an attack upon "Machiavellianism" popularly known as the *Contre-Machiavel*. Two ideas thus represented were especially repugnant: that it is important for a prince to *seem* religious and that religion was devised by those in power to keep the lower orders in awe of authority. "Machiavellian" became a synonym for any kind of wrongdoing and was equated with "atheist." When the Duke of Gloucester catalogues the talents which may enable him to eliminate all obstacles on his path to the throne, one of them is that he can "set the murderous Machiavel to school" (*3 Henry VI*, III, ii, 193). In III, vii of *Richard III* he puts on a false show of religion to win popular support for his cause. On the last day of his reign he fights off a touch of conscience after a night of visitations by the ghosts of his victims and dismisses his fears with a "Machiavellian" aphorism:

> Conscience is but a word that cowards use,
> Devised at first to keep the strong in awe.   (V, iii, 310–11)

In Shakespeare's plays the Tudor concept of history, expounded by Raleigh and many other writers, governs the destinies of kings within the world order. As we have seen, monarchy on earth is a parallel to the throned eminence of the sun. The king is God's viceroy on earth, an idea sometimes elaborated into the theory of divine right. A good king rules by law, and he does not subordinate justice to an evil will, as Cornwall and Goneril do in *King Lear*. Hereditary right is justified by the law of nature

and the law of nations. The king cares for his subjects as a father cares for his children, and his subjects owe him love and obedience. The ecclesiastical authorities saw to it that the subject was informed of his duties; the homilies appointed to be read in the churches stress the virtues of obedience and the sins of sedition. Civil disobedience is so completely abhorrent that endurance of a bad king is to be preferred to any form of insurrection. In God's good time the tyrant will die, and his rule should be suffered as a punishment for the sins of the people. Insurrection, once begun, can lead to an endless train of misery and destruction. Because the king's authority is divinely sanctioned, sedition is the equivalent of atheism.

With such an official philosophy of government one can marvel at the record of rebellions, usurpations, and even assassinations of kings. A cynical explanation is found in an epigram by Sir John Harington, one of the liveliest of Shakespeare's contemporaries:

> Treason doth never prosper: what's the reason?
> For if it prosper, none dare call it treason.

A more sober explanation lies in the frailty of man, from which not even kings are exempt. Whatever the explanation or cause of insurrection, the Elizabethan wanted none of it. Aside from moral instruction, history has practical lessons in government to offer. No literate Elizabethan was allowed to forget the Wars of the Roses, from which the Tudor dynasty had emerged, and the illiterate could receive instruction in the theatre and in ceremonial pageants. When Elizabeth went through London to her coronation in January, 1559, one of the many elaborate designs set up along the route consisted of three stages, in the lowest of which sat two persons representing Henry VII, of the house of Lancaster, and his bride, Elizabeth of York. Henry held a red rose, his bride a white rose, and out of the roses two vines climbed to the next stage above, occupied by impersonators of Henry VIII and his queen, Anne Boleyn, mother of Queen Elizabeth. Still ascending, the now single vine reached a third level, where the new queen was represented. Lest the symbolism of the union of the red rose and the white be lost upon the populace, there were appropriate labels, and a child spoke verses explaining that, as the union of Henry VII and the Yorkist princess had brought peace to the land and assured a peaceful succession, so it was hoped that the reign of Queen Elizabeth would put an end to discord and establish peace and prosperity. The vigorous speech of Richmond (Henry VII) which concludes *Richard III* embodies the ideas variously presented in the coronation tableau. Richmond's speech, however, was written by Shakespeare in the perspective of more than thirty years of Elizabeth's reign, and it is marked by a patriotic assurance bred of comparative freedom from internal strife and of victories over the great enemy, Spain.

Thus history is not only a moral teacher and a dependable guide to statecraft; it is also a stimulant to patriotism. The symbolism of the coronation tableau and such utterances as the concluding speeches in *Richard III* and *King John*, or Gaunt's dying speech in *Richard II*, reflect a national pride which was celebrated in chronicles in prose and verse, in the allegories of Spenser, and in Hakluyt's collection of accounts of the English voyagers, as well as in the history plays of Shakespeare. The theme is not merely one of exuberant pride; the lessons are emphasized: national unity, an assured succession, and avoidance at all costs of civil strife are essential for a strong and peaceful England.

Elizabethan beliefs and ideas concerning the responsibilities of kings and subjects are also reflected in Shakespeare's plays, in speech and situation. Henry IV, as he nears death, and his son Henry V, before Agincourt, meditate upon the heavy responsibilities of kingship. The soldiers of the disguised Henry V debate with him the perils of dying in battle. They do not question their duty to die in the king's cause; they are troubled about the state of their souls if they are spiritually unprepared for death. Henry would exempt himself from responsibility for past misdeeds of his soldiers; if lawbreakers have escaped the penalty of the law, then war may be God's beadle, his vengeance for unpunished offenses. "Every subject's duty is the king's, but every subject's soul is his own." The conversation ends in a mild quarrel which provides the groundwork for a later jest, but the soldiers' readiness to put all responsibility upon the king makes a profound impression upon Henry. He is troubled, too, by his father's deposing of Richard II:

> Not to-day, O Lord,
> O, not to-day, think not upon the fault
> My father made in compassing the crown! (IV, i, 278–80)

The scene reduces to very human terms the interrelationships of king and subject and the importance of an unclouded title to the throne.

Of Shakespeare's plays, *Richard II* probably serves best to illustrate the dramatic treatment of history and the principles of government and law. Richard is influenced by flatterers, whereas the role of the Renaissance courtier is to give his king sound advice, such as Kent gives Lear, no matter what the cost. Richard is believed guilty of complicity in the murder of his uncle, the Duke of Gloucester, but another uncle, John of Gaunt, declines to take action against "God's substitute, / His deputy anointed in his sight" (I, ii). God's is the quarrel; let Heaven revenge the offense. Richard is arbitrary in confiscating the lands of his banished cousin, Bolingbroke. Yet despite his misdeeds Richard is the rightful king of England. When Bolingbroke returns from exile to claim his inheritance, law and hereditary right are on his side.

> If that my cousin king be King of England,
> It must be granted I am Duke of Lancaster. (II, iii, 123–24)

In an even stronger statement, which equates legal succession with the natural order of days, the Duke of York admonishes King Richard:

> Take Hereford's rights away, and take from Time
> His charters and his customary rights;
> Let not to-morrow then ensue to-day;
> Be not thyself – for how art thou a king
> But by fair sequence and succession? (II, i, 195–99)

Ideas become part of characterization and plot: Richard II stands upon an extreme interpretation of divine right; Bolingbroke at first claims only the rights of lawful inheritance; York is torn between the strong rival claims of his two nephews. But Bolingbroke violates law and degree when he deposes his cousin, ascends the throne, and plays an ambiguous role in the murder of Richard. The deposed king and others prophesy that the results of the usurpation will be a troubled reign for Henry IV and

civil war. Of course they are right: Henry had to suppress rebellions by his erstwhile supporters, and the usurpation led ultimately to the Wars of the Roses. Seven plays by Shakespeare present in historical sequence almost a century of strife which had its origin in the deposing of Richard II. Yet even a king with an imperfect title is king *de facto*; at the end of *Richard II* the ever loyal York discloses the treasonous plot of his own son to Henry IV.

The problem of legitimate succession troubled the Elizabethans even when the Queen was young and there was hope that she would marry. In her old age fears of a troubled succession were not groundless. A few men in high places were in touch with James VI of Scotland, who was to become king of England; but the country at large, knowing that there was more than one person for whom a title to the crown could be claimed, was uneasy at the possibility of strife. At the very time that there was some degree of popular unease about the succession, comparisons were made between Queen Elizabeth and Richard II, some in jest and some in earnest, on the ground that Elizabeth, like Richard, was controlled by flatterers and "caterpillars of the state." *Richard II* was performed by Shakespeare's company, under a special arrangement, on the day before the Earl of Essex made his rash attempt to seize the palace and person of the Queen.

Too much has been made of specific parallels between Elizabethan plays and contemporary politics. Some plays are clearly topical, but the known circumstances of the special performance of *Richard II* at the request of followers of Essex involve no suggestion that the author intended a contemporary parallel when he wrote the play. Shakespeare's plays are firmly rooted in the historical and political theories of his time. They invoke law and order, praise peace and deplore civil strife, present England as an island fortress, invincible as long as Englishmen are united. As in all the plays, strict historical accuracy is secondary to liveliness of characterization and action. If Shakespeare, in Edwin Arlington Robinson's happy phrase,

> Fills Ilion, Rome, or any town you like
> Of olden time with timeless Englishmen,

he no less interpreted his English history in the perspective of Elizabethan thought.

Finally in this survey we come to the individual man, a paradoxical creature endowed with an immortal soul in a body which owes its sustenance to the four elements. Corresponding to the elements, with matching qualities, are the four humours which govern the temperament of man: melancholy, cold and dry like earth; phlegm, cold and moist like water; blood, hot and moist like air; choler, hot and dry like fire. When the humours are in proper balance, man is in good temper and good health; when one of the humours is in excess, man may be – in terms which we have inherited from this system – predominantly melancholy, phlegmatic, sanguine, or choleric. Under the impact of illness or emotional stress, a humour may be burnt or, in Elizabethan phrasing, "adust," and the result was commonly called "melancholy adust," in distinction from the normal physiological melancholy. Shakespeare, unlike Ben Jonson, constructed no plays on the theory of humours, but the system so dominated medicine and what we call psychology that he could not have avoided the terminology and its application to character had he wanted to. The term "humour" is not always so strictly defined; in popular usage it came to mean merely dominant mood, or even whim or caprice. There were fashions in humours, melancholy being in the ascendant at the turn of the century when Jaques first brooded in the glades of *As You Like It*. The title page of *2 Henry IV* promises us "the humours of Sir John Falstaff and swaggering Pistol"; Shylock insolently gives his "humour" as sufficient cause for preferring the flesh of Antonio to three thousand ducats; when we are told twice, early in *As You Like It*, that the usurping Duke is "humorous" we expect trouble, not merriment. Of the self-controlled Brutus of *Julius Caesar*, on the other hand, his adversary can say in praise:

> His life was gentle, and the elements
> So mixed in him that Nature might stand up
> And say to all the world, "This was a man!"   (V, v, 73–75)

The "spirits" are as important in determining the temperament and the emotional functioning of man as the humours. The natural spirits come from the liver and reach the parts of the body in the blood. Rising to the heart, the natural spirits are changed to vital spirits. When they reach the brain through the arteries, the vital spirits are refined into animal spirits, which provide a communication system between the brain and the rest of the body, or between soul (in the comprehensive meaning which the Elizabethans gave this term) and body. The linkage of soul and body through the medium of the animal spirits explains in part the roles which the Elizabethans assign to bodily organs in describing emotional states. In *Twelfth Night*, the lovesick Duke Orsino reflects upon what the intensity of Olivia's love, now centered upon her dead brother, will be when one commanding passion takes over:

> ... when liver, brain, and heart,
> These sovereign thrones, are all supplied and filled,
> Her sweet perfections, with one self king.   (I, i, 38–40)

Three souls or, in some accounts, three parts of the soul have to function well for the proper development and government of the little world of man. The vegetable soul, common to plants, animals, and men, is responsible for reproduction, nourishment, and growth. The sensible soul, common to animals and men, provides for sense perception and feeling. The rational soul, peculiar to man, provides for knowing and judging, and, on the basis of knowledge and judgment, for the direction of the will. The rational soul marks man's special place in the chain of being: above the animals, who have only the vegetative and sensible souls, and below the angels, who know intuitively what man struggles to learn by "discourse of reason." The rational soul is the immortal part of man, and a vast literature was devoted to such questions as how one soul (or one part of the soul) could be immortal when it is linked to two souls that perish at death, or in what part of the body this immortal soul resides.

In the perfect functioning of man's body and soul, the perceptions of the senses are reported to the brain; the rational soul judges the reports and directs the will how to act; the will carries out the orders. But perfection is rarely achieved by imperfect man, the son of Adam. Physiological imbalances, in the humours or in other parts of the organism, can impair the workings of this carefully integrated system. Reason may be deceived by false appear-

ances and give the wrong commands, with tragic consequences in life or in drama. A perverse or stubborn will may disobey the commands of reason, or reason itself may yield to passion. In *Paradise Lost*, the fall of Eve and the fall of Adam are thus distinguished. Adam warns Eve:

> But God left free the will; for what obeys
> Reason is free, and Reason he made right,
> But bid her well beware, and still erect,
> Lest, by some fair appearing good surprised,
> She dictate false, and misinform the will
> To do what God expressly hath forbid.   (IX, 351–56)

The angel Raphael had warned Adam to

> take heed lest passion sway
> Thy judgment to do aught which else free will
> Would not admit; ...   (VIII, 635–37)

Both warnings went unheeded: Eve was deceived by the promises of the Serpent; Adam put his love for Eve before his love of God. The substance of Milton's few lines had been the theme of formal treatises before and during the Elizabethan period.

The many obstacles to the proper functioning of man's free will could be overcome by care of the body and sound education, especially sound religious education. But one specially vexatious problem was the influence of the stars. There was little disagreement about natural astrology, much of which is embraced in what we call meteorology; the controversy was about judicial astrology, the belief that a man's nature is determined in part by the conjunctions of planets and stars when he is born and that he is subject to planetary and stellar influences during his lifetime. The orthodox position was that the stars could not influence man's free will directly nor touch his immortal soul, but that man's physical make-up is subject to these stellar influences and hence the will could be indirectly affected. Romeo and Juliet are introduced to us as "a pair of star-crossed lovers"; in the sequence of unlucky accidents that befall them there are passing references to the stars, but no particularization of stellar influences. When Edmund, in *King Lear*, ridicules his father's belief in astrology he disclaims any "heavenly compulsion" for our follies and knaveries and calls such belief an "admirable evasion of whoremaster man, to lay his goatish disposition on the charge of a star." In rejecting the notion that the influence of the stars can excuse a man from moral responsibility Edmund is giving utterance to sound doctrine, but, like other Shakespearean villains, he is perverting good doctrine to the service of his own amoral beliefs. Thus Iago, instructing Roderigo (*Othello*, I, iii, 319–31), delivers a fine dissertation on the necessity of controlling the passions by reason and then corrupts his lesson by making love a subspecies of lust.

Elizabethan discourses on the passions, will, and reason provide a rich commentary on the language of Shakespeare's characterizations – so rich that only a few citations can be added to those already given. Two concepts are especially noteworthy for an understanding of the nature of man: that reason is his distinguishing characteristic and that man, with an immortal soul housed in a mortal body, is caught in a continuous struggle between his passions and his heavenly aspirations. The extreme of Hamlet's bitter reflections on his mother's o'er-hasty marriage is "O God, a beast that wants discourse of reason / Would have mourned longer" (I, ii, 150–51). Macbeth, hesitating to proceed with the plan to murder Duncan, answers his wife's taunts with

> I dare do all that may become a man ;
> Who dares do more is none.

Lady Macbeth is quick to make the distinction explicit :

> What beast was't then
> That made you break this enterprise to me ? (I, vii, 46–48)

The conflict in the little world of man inevitably leads to the problem of evil, on which the characters in *King Lear* express diverse opinions. Central to the problem, however, is the duality of man, further perplexed by the fact (on which poets and divines agree) that his soul is capable of knowing all things on earth save itself. At one extreme man is godlike, as in Hamlet's ascending comparisons :

What a piece of work is a man, how noble in reason, how infinite in faculties, in form and moving how express and admirable, in action how like an angel, in apprehension how like a god : the beauty of the world, the paragon of animals! (II, ii, 300–04)

At the other extreme he is the "forked animal" that Lear sees in ragged Poor Tom :

Is man no more than this? Consider him well. Thou ow'st the worm no silk, the beast no hide, the sheep no wool, the cat no perfume. Ha! here's three on's are sophisticated. Thou art the thing itself; unaccommodated man is no more but such a poor, bare, forked animal as thou art. (III, iv, 97–102)

The extremes of man's potentiality were a favorite theme of preacher, poet, and playwright. Sir John Davies brings them together in a few stanzas of *Nosce Teipsum* (1599) :

> I know my body's of so frail a kind
> As force without, fevers within, can kill ;
> I know the heavenly nature of my mind,
> But 'tis corrupted both in wit and will ;
>
> I know my soul hath power to know all things,
> Yet is she blind and ignorant in all ;
> I know I am one of nature's little kings,
> Yet to the least and vilest things am thrall.
>
> I know my life's a pain and but a span,
> I know my sense is mocked with everything ;
> And to conclude, I know myself a man,
> Which is a proud and yet a wretched thing.

Any brief survey of the dominant ideas of an age is necessarily selective. When we find in Shakespeare's plays reflections of Elizabethan concepts of world order, government, and the nature of man, we must be cautious also of two dangers of interpretation other than the familiar ones of generalization. The first is that Shakespeare's characters are usually speaking "in character," in given situations. What they say is often in close harmony with one or another prevailing Elizabethan belief; but we are reading plays, not philosophical or political tracts. A survey of Elizabethan thought with illustrative quotations from Shakespeare is not intended to be, and cannot be, an essay on "Shakespeare's philosophy," nor could such an essay be written merely by compiling a classified anthology of his characters' speeches. Even an approximate resumé of Shakespeare's personal philosophy would require a reading of all the plays and poems, consideration of recurrent ideas in the context in which they are expressed, and distinctions between the utterances of "good" and "bad" characters. The second caution, of which Professor Virgil K. Whitaker reminds us in his

book, *Shakespeare's Use of Learning*, is that Shakespeare did not begin his career with a stock of information and ideas that remained static throughout his life ; as with any intelligent person, his ideas developed as his reading widened and as he matured. With these cautions in mind, study of the background of the Elizabethan period will enrich one's understanding and enjoyment of Shakespeare, who was "of an age" as well as "for all time."

Pomona College ERNEST A. STRATHMANN

BIBLIOGRAPHY

The ideas and attitudes of the age are treated in Ernst Cassirer, *The Platonic Renaissance in England*, trans. J. E. Pettegrove (1954); Hardin Craig, *The Enchanted Glass* (1936); E. M. W. Tillyard, *The Elizabethan World Picture* (1943); Herschel Baker, *The Dignity of Man* (1947); Ernest A. Strathmann, *Sir Walter Ralegh : A Study in Elizabethan Skepticism* (1951); Paul H. Kocher, *Science and Religion in Elizabethan England* (1953); Francis R. Johnson, *Astronomical Thought in Renaissance England* (1937); Don Cameron Allen, *The Star-Crossed Renaissance* (1941) [on astrology]; Lily B. Campbell, *Shakespeare's Tragic Heroes* (1930) [section II on humoural psychology]; J. W. Allen, *A History of Political Thought in the Sixteenth Century* (1928, reprinted with revised bibliographical notes 1951), *English Political Thought 1603–1660* (1938). For the impact of the ideas on the drama, see Theodore Spencer, *Shakespeare and the Nature of Man* (1942); F. P. Wilson, *Elizabethan and Jacobean* (1945); David Bevington, *Tudor Drama and Politics* (1968); John F. Danby, *Shakespeare's Doctrine of Nature* (1949); D. G. James, *The Dream of Learning* (1951); Alfred Harbage, *Shakespeare and the Rival Traditions* (1952); Virgil K. Whitaker, *Shakespeare's Use of Learning* (1953); Roland M. Frye, *Shakespeare and Christian Doctrine* (1963). See also the bibliographies below appended to the forewords to the Histories and Tragedies. An anthology of essays on the background of ideas is *The Elizabethan Age*, ed. David L. Stevenson (1966).

Standard histories of Tudor and Stuart England are J. B. Black, *The Reign of Elizabeth 1558–1603* (2nd ed. 1959) and Godfrey Davies, *The Early Stuarts 1603–1660* (2nd ed. 1959). An excellent brief survey is S. T. Bindoff, *Tudor England* (1950). An exhaustive bibliography is Conyers Read, *Bibliography of British History ; Tudor Period 1485–1603* (2nd ed. 1959).

For social history see G. M. Trevelyan, *Illustrated English Social History*, Vol. II (1942); R. H. Tawney, *Religion and the Rise of Capitalism* (new ed. 1947); A. L. Rowse, *The England of Elizabeth* (1951); Allardyce Nicoll, *The Elizabethans* (1957); *Life and Letters in Tudor and Stuart England*, ed. L. B. Wright & V. A. La Mar (1962) ; *Shakespeare in his Own Age*, ed. A. Nicoll, *Shakespeare Survey*, Vol. XVII (1964); Louis B. Wright, *Middle-Class Culture in Elizabethan England* (1935); H. S. Bennett, *English Books and Readers 1558 to 1603* (1965); John Buxton, *Elizabethan Taste* (1963); Edwin H. Miller, *The Professional Writer in Elizabethan England* (1959).

Histories of non-dramatic literature are C. S. Lewis, *English Literature in the Sixteenth Century* (1954); Douglas Bush, *English Literature in the Earlier Seventeenth Century 1600–1660* (rev. ed. 1962).

Histories of dramatic literature are Felix E. Schelling, *Elizabethan Drama 1558–1642*, 2 vols (1908); Thomas M. Parrott & Robert H. Ball, *A Short View of Elizabethan Drama* (1943); U. M. Ellis-Fermor, *The Jacobean Drama* (rev. ed. 1953). The definitive bibliography of printed plays is Sir Walter Greg, *A Bibliography of the English Printed Drama to the Restoration*, 4 vols (1939–59). The historical facts are gathered and analyzed in Sir Edmund Chambers, *The Elizabethan Stage*, 4 vols (1923), and outlined in Alfred Harbage, *Annals of English Drama 975–1700* (1940), revised by Samuel Schoenbaum (1964).

SHAKESPEARE'S LIFE

Elizabethan England was not an age when records, private or public, were preserved with today's bureaucratic fidelity. In particular it was not an age when people cared much about preserving the life-documents of individuals who were not part of the Establishment – the

Court, the Nobility, the Military, the Church. It is a pleasant surprise, therefore, to find the records of Shakespeare's life as full as they are, for Elizabethan theatre-people did not stand high on the social ladder, and their successes and failures did not strike the age as being worthy of preservation for posterity. If the facts pertaining to the life of England's greatest writer seem meagre by present standards, they are impressively full by comparison with what we have learned about his fellow dramatists, most of whom are relatively unknown except for their work. About only one of them, Ben Jonson, are we comparably well informed.

William Shakespeare was born in Stratford-upon-Avon, a Warwickshire market-town some eighty-five miles northwest of London. The register in the parish church of Holy Trinity records his baptism on April 26, 1564 – "Gulielmus filius Johannes Shakspere." There is no record of his birth, although for reasons of sentiment it is usually celebrated on April 23, the day of England's patron, Saint George, and also the day of Shakespeare's death. His father had come from the nearby village of Snitterfield, where the family had been tenant farmers; had entered the glover's trade and become master of his own shop. Clearly a man of ambition, he enjoyed a steady rise through various civic offices until in 1568, when William was four years old, he was elected Bailiff, the equivalent of mayor and the highest civic post the town of Stratford had to offer. As several of these offices required sophisticated account-keeping, we can assume that John was intelligent, and perhaps literate, although the extant civic documents are signed only with his mark. About 1557 he had married Mary Arden, daughter of a yeoman farmer of neighboring Wilmcote who was related to the Ardens of Park Hall, a family of landed gentry which had remained faithful to Roman Catholicism. The marriage was financially as well as socially advantageous, since Mary had recently become co-heiress of her father's estate. In 1556 John himself had become a "freeholder" by purchasing two houses in Stratford, one of them on Henley Street, where it is assumed that his famous son was born and passed the first years of his life. Inevitably, in view of the upward social mobility that marked Elizabethan England, he longed to be written gentleman and so he applied to the Office of Heralds in London, probably in 1576, for the right to be granted a coat of arms. As a former Bailiff and the husband of an Arden, he was eligible for this distinction.

At this point, for reasons unknown, John Shakespeare's good fortune deserted him. He stopped appearing at meetings of the Stratford Council, and in 1586 another alderman (the post to which he had returned after his term as Bailiff) was chosen to replace him. The records that have survived of his business transactions suggest that he ran into financial difficulties, a hypothesis supported by his appearance in 1592 on a list of persons who had not been attending church "for feare of process for debtte." But there is no indication that he suffered actual bankruptcy, and the reasons for his withdrawal from civic activity remain obscure, the mystery deepened by the fact that during his long absence from the Council his fellow members made no effort to fine him for non-attendance as might have been expected. Whatever his reverses were, they had the effect of ending for the time being his attempts to acquire a coat of arms.

The record of John Shakespeare's life makes it clear that young William, with his three younger brothers and two younger sisters, grew up in a middle-class family of good local repute. The Shakespeares appear to have been quite conventional. No matter what Mary's religious heritage may have been, the family was publicly Church of England. There is no evidence that it was unusually gifted in the arts, or that its outlook was more intellectual than that of its neighbors. It is difficult to imagine seditious or skeptical conversations taking place among the members of the Shakespeare household, easy to imagine a prevalence of traditional values and accepted beliefs. Shakespeare's cultural inheritance was popular in the literal sense of the word, and it is hardly accident that as a writer he speaks for his age rather than for the minority voices that were, as in all ages, raised against it. Nor was there much in the larger society of Stratford to cause him to challenge the old verities that must have been preached at home. Stratford was a small community of some few thousand citizens. Although a medieval town, it was unwalled and had relatively broad, straight streets that cut the center into sizable blocks. The town was encircled by fields for farming and grazing, and by woods for timbering, charcoal-burning, and hunting. Its houses were half-timbered, and many had spacious gardens and outbuildings behind them. It had a market place, a guildhall, a fine Gothic church, and several inns among the public buildings and places that made Stratford a center for farmers living and working in the little villages on its periphery. The conduct of the town's citizens was carefully controlled by the men who made up the Council, and there were rules with appropriate fines for a variety of social offenses ranging from allowing one's children to roam too late at night to absence from Church on Sunday. Life in Stratford was carefully circumscribed, and it is important to remember that Shakespeare's impressionable years were spent in a family that was very much a part of this conservative, if occasionally fractious, society.

As the son of a leading citizen and public official, Shakespeare would have been expected to go to school as soon as he had learned to read and write. This early instruction might have come from the parish clerk or from some Stratford neighbor running a "petty school" which prepared students for the more rigorous world of the local

grammar school. The Stratford grammar school, one of the town's prized institutions, was a free school. Its masters, graduates of Oxford University, were well trained in Shakespeare's day, and the pay was excellent by comparison with similar schools in far larger towns. From about age seven, Shakespeare would have trudged early each morning to the guild-hall where the school was located, his normal day a strenuous one of around nine hours. School was in session summer and winter, with the three holiday seasons brief by modern standards. Discipline was strict and the rules of conduct enforced by physical punishment. The curriculum was limited, consisting almost entirely of Latin – grammar, reading, writing, and recitation. The standard text was by William Lyly, who sternly insisted that literacy depended upon cleanliness and neatness as well as hard work. It is probable, as Shakespeare became more senior and recitation more important in the curriculum, that he would have been allowed to act out scenes from Terence and Plautus; there were, too, the wonders of Ovid, particularly of the *Metamorphoses*, to reward the labors of construing. But all in all, life at the Stratford grammar school would have been hard, demanding, and dull almost beyond modern comprehension. And there is nothing in the plays or poems to suggest that young Shakespeare was lucky enough to have had one of those rare teachers, like Jonson's Camden, who could change learning from drudgery to delight.

Nevertheless, a Stratford boyhood was not wholly regimented and there were many opportunities for play. There were woods and fields to be explored on half-days and holidays. There was the Avon, with its mysterious waters where trout could be tickled if one had patience, and where, from the fine bridge that led to the road to London, one could fish more conventionally if he did not. There were market days when unsophisticated and often amusing villagers came to town. And there were the fairs, for which Stratford was well known, when the town was filled with outlandish people, some quite probably from foreign shores and speaking strange languages. Indeed there was much to stimulate the mind and imagination of an intelligent boy. Most important, there was theatrical entertainment as part of the experience of growing up. On feast days and holidays there were such popular spectacles as the pageant of Saint George and the Dragon, morris dancers, or perhaps a Robin Hood play. At other times there was more formal theatrical fare. For years, groups of entertainers had travelled about the English countryside performing rudimentary versions of the medieval morality plays. By 1569 companies of professional actors were appearing in Stratford and putting on performances at the guild-hall. Although the plays were moral in tone and subject, they were also vigorous and exciting and they could have an exhilarating effect upon the dreams and ambitions of a small boy. By the time Shakespeare was a youth, Stratford had been visited by the Earl of Warwick's men, the Earl of Worcester's men, and by England's leading adult company, that under the patronage of the Earl of Leicester. Leicester's men were headed by the actor James Burbage, who, when Shakespeare was twelve, built the first theatre in London, and was the father of Richard, Shakespeare's future colleague and friend. From civic pomp and circumstance on one hand to travelling companies of professional actors on the other,

the fantasy world of the theatre was available to William Shakespeare as he grew to manhood. If one side of Stratford life suggests the stern discipline of a colonial New England village, the other suggests equally the color and enthusiasm of the medieval world breaking through its Church-inflicted bonds into the worldly excitement of Elizabethan England. From this contrast, from this conflict, must have come eventually the impulse that sent Shakespeare to London and theatrical fame.

That Shakespeare attended the Stratford grammar school, that he saw various plays and entertainments, that he hunted and fished the local countryside are not only logical but inescapable conclusions drawn from the evidence that surrounds his documented life. Nevertheless, the first documentary reference subsequent to the notice of his baptism does not occur until November 27, 1582, when the Bishop of Worcester's register records the issuance of a marriage license. A bond of sureties issued the next day (and revealing the cavalier attitude towards English spelling that characterized the Elizabethans) allowed that "William Shagsper on thone partie, and Anne Hathwey of Stratford in the Dioces of Worcester maiden may lawfully solennize matrimony together," provided that there be no legal objection and that the banns be asked once. Normally the banns were required to be read in Church on three successive Sundays, and the waiving of this requirement has led to the assumption that Shakespeare's marriage was the hurried result of an earlier intimacy, an inference that is supported by the parish register which records the baptism of "Susanna daughter to William Shakespeare" on May 26, 1583. This suspicion has been strengthened by the fact that Anne Hathaway was eight years older than her husband, if we are to believe the inscription on her grave which states that she was sixty-seven when she died on August 6, 1623. What significance, if any, the difference in age has must be left for each reader to decide for himself. However, the circumstances of the marriage deserve comment. Elizabethan law recognized that a legal marriage contract had been made when two consenting parties agreed to marry before witnesses and it was not considered obligatory to await the public ceremony before consummating the match. Whatever its genesis the marriage continued to be fruitful, for on February 2, 1585 the register records the baptism of "Hamnet & Judeth sonne and daughter to William Shakspere." It is likely that Shakespeare's twins were named after close Stratford neighbors.

Shakespeare was eighteen when he married, almost twenty-one when the twins were born. In Michaelmas term, 1588, when he would have been twenty-four, his name appears with his mother's and father's in a suit over some property. But there is no indication that he was dwelling in Stratford at the time, or that the suit required his presence there. In fact, the years from the birth of the twins until his appearance on the London theatrical scene are quite literally lost; what he was doing, how he supported himself, is not known. In 1681 John Aubrey reported that he had learned from the son of one of Shakespeare's fellow-actors that "he had been in his younger yeares a Schoolmaster in the Countrey," but although the report has a better lineage than others first set down in the late seventeenth century, nothing has been discovered to verify it. About all that one can write with assurance is that by 1592 Shakespeare seems to have been fully immersed in the theatrical world. In that year, Philip Henslowe, proprietor of the Rose Theatre in London and a careful keeper of theatrical accounts, staged a new play called "Harey the vj." It was unusually popular, running for fifteen performances, and it is generally accepted that this was Shakespeare's *1 Henry VI*. Although Shakespeare's play did not appear in print until 1623, there is an apparent reference to its performance in Nashe's *Pierce Penilesse*, a contemporary work which was sent to press shortly after the play's successful run. Before the end of the year, further evidence had appeared to suggest that Shakespeare was making his mark in the theatre. Robert Greene, a talented but dissipated man of letters, died, leaving among his papers a letter complaining about the theatrical professionals who had ungratefully used the talents of university men like himself. He was particularly upset about

. . . an vpstart Crow, beautified with our feathers, that with his *Tygers hart wrapt in a Players hyde*, supposes he is as well able to bombast out a blanke verse as the best of you: and beeing an absolute *Iohannes fac totum*, is in his owne conceit the onely Shake-scene in a countrey.

The phrase "*Tygers hart wrapt in a Players hyde*" parodies a line in *3 Henry VI* – "O tiger's heart wrapped in a woman's hide!" – and there seems to be little reason to doubt that Greene was referring to Shakespeare, an actor who had achieved, to Greene's unhappiness, success as a playwright. When the letter was printed in Greene's *Groats-worth of Wit*, a posthumous collection put together by the playwright Henry Chettle, Shakespeare (and apparently Marlowe, who was also attacked) must have protested, for when Chettle wrote his *Kind-Harts Dreame*, registered for publication in December of that year, he apologized for the attacks, explaining that he was acquainted with neither of the persons who took offense and emphasizing that with one of them, he cared never to be. He continued:

The other, whome at that time I did not so much spare, as since I wish I had, for that as I haue moderated the heate of liuing writers, and might haue vsde my owne discretion (especially in such a case) the Author beeing dead, that I did not, I am as sory as if the originall fault had beene my fault, because my selfe haue seene his demeanor no lesse ciuill than he exelent in the qualitie he professes: Besides, diuers of worship haue reported his vprightnes of dealing, which argues his honesty, and his facetious grace in writting, that aprooues his Art.

It seems reasonable to assume, as Shakespeare scholars do, that this encomium fits more accurately with what we know about Shakespeare than with what we know about Marlowe. In any case it is clear that by 1592 Shakespeare was very much a part of the theatrical scene, both as actor and playwright. Although it is often assumed that he did not arrive in London until the beginning of the decade, there is no evidence to indicate that it might not have been earlier, and there is a certain amount of common sense in supposing that he had come to London sooner and thus had had opportunity for a more normal period of apprenticeship before scoring the hit of 1592.

In whatever year Shakespeare came to London, he would have found it excitingly different from the ordered world of Stratford-upon-Avon. London was a city caught up in economic inflation, its headiness increased by the defeat of the Spanish Armada in 1588. As a newcomer

entered one of the gates set in the site of medieval walls that once guarded the City, he would have found himself in the crowded center of a metropolitan area containing between 125 and 175 thousand people. (Most of the population of Stratford could have fitted into The Theatre, the playhouse built by James Burbage in the northern suburbs.) The community was a mixture of beauty and squalor. The Thames, still clear and the main artery of traffic, was crossed by London Bridge, an engineering marvel that led to the Surrey suburbs, the "Bankside" where much of London's entertainment was to be found and where the Globe would be erected. Downstream was the Tower of London, grim, impressive, and filled with unhappy echoes of English history. Upstream was the Royal City of Westminster beyond the Palace of Whitehall, with its church now known as Westminster Abbey, and the houses of Parliament. In the City proper the great Cathedral of St Paul towered over the many smaller churches and chapels whose bells helped to make London a city of varied if not always musical sounds. Here on Sundays Londoners came to hear sermons at "Paul's Cross," and on weekdays to buy books at the stalls and to meet business associates. The streets, mostly narrow and crooked by Stratford standards, were fronted by steep-roofed, gabled houses with shops on the ground floors and living quarters above. As with great cities today, folk from the country flocked unwanted to London, and Elizabeth found it necessary to issue an edict forbidding the building or refurbishing of houses into tenements. Traffic, sanitation, water supply were all problems, and the maintenance of law and order was difficult. With grim regularity, the normal tempo of life was upset by visitations of the plague, and the bodies of its victims, not to mention the heads of traitors rotting on pikes over the arches of London Bridge, helped to remind the spectator of the mortal frailty of mankind. To wander through these crowded streets, jostled by persons of every degree and of every nationality, must have been an eye-opening experience for a young man from the country. Equally impressive would have been London's rich and varied cultural life – not only its theatres and entertainments, but its bookstalls with volumes that the Stratford grammar school never knew, its teachers of French, Italian, and other modern languages, its artists and writers and courtiers, and its students, particularly those from the law schools known as the Inns of Court.

The theatrical life of the city will be described in the following section. It is sufficient to note here that Shakespeare was established at its center two years after the attack by Greene. Record exists of a payment for performances at Court in December, 1594, to "William Kempe, William Shakespeare, & Richard Burbage, seruantes to the Lord Chamberleyne," evidence that Shakespeare was now a sharer in one of London's two most distinguished acting companies. By this time at least five of his extant plays had been produced and probably earlier journey-work. It seems obvious that Shakespeare's rapid rise to theatrical eminence must have been the result of his several contributions, as playwright, as actor, and as company sharer. How long he remained an actor, or how talented he was, we do not know, but one can infer that he was a serious professional, for when Ben Jonson collected his own plays for publication in 1616 he added a note to *Every Man in His Humour* which listed the "principall Comoedians" for the first production of 1598; among them was "Will. Shakespeare." And when Cuthbert Burbage, Richard's brother, was describing many years later the company's reasons for leasing the Blackfriars Theatre in 1608, he identified Shakespeare as one of the "men Players" for whose use the theatre was intended. As for Shakespeare's business acumen, it is attested to not only by the financial success of his company but by his later astute dealings in Stratford.

By the end of 1594, Shakespeare had also achieved another kind of literary distinction, one quite different from his theatrical success. A serious outbreak of the plague earlier had caused the authorities to close the theatres so that from mid-summer 1592 to June 1594 few plays were produced in London. Although the companies took their repertory on the road, the usual insatiable demand for new material was temporarily abated, and Shakespeare would have had time to try his hand at a different sort of composition. He chose a popular poetic narrative form in a style designed to gain him a literary reputation that mere plays could not achieve. His first poem, *Venus and Adonis*, was published in 1593 by Richard Field, a Stratford neighbor now a London publisher. It had a dedication to the nineteen-year-old Earl of Southampton. The dedication is conventional in tone and content and does not necessarily mean that Shakespeare was personally acquainted with the glittering young courtier. *Venus and Adonis* with its rich erotic imagery was immediately popular. It was followed in 1594 by *The Rape of Lucrece*, a more sober example of narrative poetry. *The Rape of Lucrece* was also dedicated to Southampton, and it is possible to infer from the wording that the Earl had rewarded Shakespeare in some fashion for his previous dedication. The success of these two poems, which went through numerous editions during his lifetime, might well have tempted Shakespeare to join the writers who sought to live by patronage, but when the theatres reopened, he returned to the playwright's life apparently without reserve. He is remarkable among his fellow Elizabethan dramatists for his almost total concentration upon writing for the theatre.

The Shakespeare canon, thirty-seven plays plus one or two possible collaborations, is small when compared to the productivity of some of his contemporaries. Thomas Heywood claimed to have had "either an entire hand, or at the least a maine finger" in two hundred and twenty plays. But when we consider Shakespeare's many other responsibilities, the fact that he was able to provide his fellow-actors with plays at a rate that averages about two a year during his professional lifetime is impressive. It is generally agreed that by the end of 1598 he had written: *The Comedy of Errors, 1, 2, 3 Henry VI, Richard III, The Taming of the Shrew, Titus Andronicus, The Two Gentlemen of Verona, King John, A Midsummer Night's Dream, Richard II, Love's Labor's Lost, Romeo and Juliet, The Merchant of Venice,* and *1, 2 Henry IV.*

Of these sixteen plays, eight had already appeared in print: *2, 3 Henry VI* and *Romeo and Juliet* in debased versions, and *Titus Andronicus, Richard III, Richard II, Love's Labor's Lost,* and *1 Henry IV* in good versions. All but the *Henry VI* plays and *The Taming of the Shrew* had been praised in 1598 in Francis Meres' *Palladis Tamia: Wits Treasury,* a volume of literary quotations. In a critical section comparing English with Classic and Italian authors, Meres writes of "mellifluous & hony-tongued" Shakespeare's poems and sonnets, and then lists the tragedies and comedies that make him, among the English, "the most excellent in both kinds for the stage." It is comforting to observe that all the plays listed by Meres are extant, with the exception of a mysterious "Loue labours wonne" – possibly a lost play since a quarto with such a title once existed, or possibly an extant play originally published under an alternative title.

While Shakespeare was acting and writing during most months of the year in London, changes were occurring in Stratford. In August of 1596 his son Hamnet died and was buried in the parish churchyard. Ironically, two months after the death of the one to whom it would have passed, the coat of arms applied for so long ago by John Shakespeare was finally granted. William Dethick, the official who made the grant, described it thus:

I the Said Garter king of Arms have assigned, graunted, and by these presentes confirmed: This shield or cote of Arms, viz. Gould, on a Bend Sables, a Speare of the first steeled argent. And for his creast or cognizaunce a falcon his winges displayed Argent standing on a wrethe of his coullers: supporting a Speare Gould steeled as aforesaid sett vppon a helmett with mantelles & tasselles as hath ben accustomed and doth more playnely appeare depicted on this margent.

The justification for the grant, as noted in the document in the Office of Heralds, is that John Shakespeare's forbears had been rewarded by King Henry VII for "faithfull & valeant service" and the family had "continewed in those partes being of good reputacon. . . ." The Office came under attack for its readiness to grant new coats, and further justifications are appended to the document. This John was

A Justice of peace And was Baylyue The Q officer & cheff of the towne of Stratford vppon Avon xv or xvi years past. That he hath Landes & tenementes of good wealth, & substance 500^{li}. That he married a daughter and heyre of Arden, a gent. of worship.

The fact that the necessary fees had been paid by John's prospering son is not mentioned, but such was probably the case. Evidence of William's affluence is supplied by his purchase of one of the two largest dwelling places in Stratford, New Place, from William Underhill in May of 1597.

There is no question that Shakespeare considered New Place to be his home and Stratford the field for the investment of his London earnings. In addition to records of minor law suits, calculated in the manner of the times to determine amounts owed to him and by him, there are records of a number of business transactions. A Stratford survey made in February, 1598, to locate hoardings of corn and malt during a time of shortage reveals that "Wm. Shackespere" like most of his neighbors had an ample reserve, specifically ten quarters. In 1602 he bought 107 acres of farmland from William and John Combe for 320 pounds, with the deed being issued to his younger brother Gilbert "to the vse of the within named William Shakespere." Later in the same year Walter Getley transferred to him a cottage in Chapel Lane. In 1605 he paid Ralph Huband "foure hundred and fourtye poundes of lawfull Englishe money" for a half interest in the tithes (land rentals) in a number of local villages; this investment was worth about 60 pounds in annual returns. As early as 1598 he was considered sufficiently affluent to be a good prospect for a loan. On October 25 of that year Richard Quiney, whose son would ultimately marry Shakespeare's daughter Judith, addressed a letter from the Bell tavern in London "To my Loveinge good ffrend & contreymann Mr Wm. Shackespere" requesting the loan of thirty pounds, which if granted "shall ffrend me muche in helpeinge me out of all the debettes I owe in London." The formidable nature of the request is illustrated by the fact that thirty pounds equalled half the amount which Shakespeare had paid for New Place.

In 1599 the Globe Theatre was built, with Shakespeare as one of the "householders" or investors. In this year a sharp-practicing printer named William Jaggard published a small volume entitled *The Passionate Pilgrim. By W. Shakespeare*. Since most of the poems were by writers other than Shakespeare, who is represented only by two sonnets and three poems from *Love's Labor's Lost*, the name on the title page was obviously designed to capitalize upon Shakespeare's reputation. By the turn of the century he was the most popular playwright in London and his company enjoyed a unique advantage in the city's highly competitive theatrical world. In 1603 Elizabeth died, and in May of that year her successor, King James I, issued a license to Shakespeare and his fellows "freely to vse and exercise the Arte and faculty of playinge Comedies, Tragedies, histories, Enterludes, moralls, pastoralls, Stageplaies and Suche others like as theie haue alreadie studied or hereafter shall vse or studie aswell for the recreation of our lovinge Subjectes as for our Solace and pleasure when wee shall thincke good to see them duringe our pleasure." This would have relieved the sharers, who like everyone else had been victimized by the plague which, rising to frightening proportions in 1603, had delayed the King's formal entry into London. There is reason to believe that Shakespeare and his fellows went on tour that winter; although touring was arduous, it was a necessary alternative to idleness while the London theatres were closed by plague. Shakespeare was at this time still acting as well as writing, since he is named as one of the "principall Tragoedians" in Jonson's *Sejanus*, one of the few new plays brought out in 1603.

In 1604 James finally made his royal progress through the City of London, and among those in attendance were the shareholders of Shakespeare's company, now known as the King's men. As Grooms of the Chamber they were given four yards of red cloth each for liveries. Too much must not be made of their elevated state; their position as courtiers was largely technical and honorific, and there is no evidence that they had the run of the royal palace. They remained actors and theatre people, both in their own eyes and those of the Court. Nevertheless, they were very successful theatre people. Augustine Phillips, one of their original number, who died shortly after the royal progress, made liberal bequests to Shakespeare and other members of the company. Their fortunes continued to rise as their plays drew well at the Globe, and the number of command performances at Court began to double and triple. Their position as London's leading company was further consolidated when in the summer of 1608 they signed a twenty-one-year lease on the Blackfriars playhouse. The Blackfriars, small, intimate, and artificially lighted and heated, served as their winter theatre, and enabled the company to adjust to the changing character of audiences. At the time of Shakespeare's retirement, the audiences were becoming decreasingly a cross-section of the London populace, increasingly a genteel segment.

The period bounded on the one side by Meres' praises of 1598 and the building of the Globe in 1599, and on the other by the transfer of part of the company's activity to the Blackfriars in 1609, saw in Shakespeare a burst of creative activity unparalleled in literary history for its quantity, quality, and variety. It is virtually certain that within this span appeared *As You Like It*, *Henry V*, *Julius Caesar*, *Much Ado about Nothing*, *Twelfth Night*, *The Merry Wives of Windsor*, *Hamlet*, *Troilus and Cressida*, *Measure for Measure*, *Othello*, *King Lear*, *Antony and Cleopatra*, and *Pericles*. It is almost as certain that in the same period appeared *All's Well That Ends Well*, *Macbeth*, *Timon of Athens*, and *Coriolanus*. To this period also belongs the short but inimitable poem "The Phoenix and Turtle," which appeared in 1601 in a curious anthology entitled *Loves Martyr*. It may be significant that most of the great tragedies were written in the early years of the new century, a time when the nation as a whole was losing something of its earlier energetic self-confidence. Although it is tempting to see in Shakespeare's deepened seriousness a reflection of the age's disillusionment, it is better ultimately to take the plays on their own terms without trying to fit them to the Procrustean beds of either Shakespearean biography or Jacobean history. It suffices to say that, in a single decade, Shakespeare created a wealth of drama, some of it comic, some tragic, such as the world has never seen.

This harvest of genius was further enriched by the appearance in 1609 of *Shake-speares Sonnets. Neuer before Imprinted*, published by Thomas Thorpe. Thorpe's dedication of the volume "To the Onlie Begetter of these insving Sonnets Mr. W. H." has provided what is probably the greatest literary mystery of all time. In spite of centuries of energetic, if not always objective, research, the identity of "Mr. W. H." remains a secret. There have been many candidates for the honor, but all efforts have failed to make a convincing case for any particular person. This failure has been disappointing to many people, in part because of the nature of the sonnets themselves. Composed over a period of years – Meres in 1598 mentioned Shakespeare's "sugred Sonnets among his private friends" – the poems are tantalizingly obscure if read as a connected sequence. They purport to be autobiographical, but to what extent their air of self-revelation reflects a literary convention is difficult to determine. They have been searched with almost neurotic zeal by those who find the bones of Shakespeare's documented biography bare. Each interpretation seems about as plausible (or implausible) as its predecessor, and, as with the plays, it is ultimately best to take them individually on their own terms. The collection includes the finest sonnets in the language.

In 1609 Shakespeare would have been forty-five, a not inconsiderable feat in a day when the average life span was short even among those who escaped the hazard of the plague. The plays that can be assigned to the years after 1609 are distinguished by a tone that suggests a mellowing of mind; but of more obvious biographical significance is their small number. Only *Cymbeline*, *The Winter's Tale*, *The Tempest*, and *Henry VIII* followed the profusion of the preceding years. The last had its initial performance on June 29, 1613, when an unbilled fire started by a discharge of stage ordnance burned the Globe to the ground, necessitating its rebuilding the following year. The tapering-off of output raises questions about the time of Shakespeare's retirement. It has often been assumed that there was an abrupt transfer to an idyllic life in Stratford after the composition of the valedictory *Tempest*, but the facts do not quite support the assumption. Not only was *Henry VIII* first presented in 1613, but there is indication that Shakespeare had a hand in several plays by John Fletcher written in or about that year. Two other records associate him with London in 1613. He purchased, evidently as an investment, a dwelling over the great gate of the former Blackfriars priory; and he collaborated with Richard Burbage in devising the design and motto of a shield for the Earl of Rutland to be flourished in a Court tilt. Rutland's steward entered payment "to Mr Shakspeare in gold about my Lorde's impreso, xliiii^S; to Richard Burbage for paynting and making yt, in gold xliiii^S." On the other hand there is one piece of evidence suggesting, as we shall see, that he no longer kept London lodgings in 1612.

In what proportion Shakespeare divided his time between London and Stratford from 1603, when he was certainly still acting, to 1616, when he died, cannot be exactly determined. Throughout his theatrical career he could have returned to Stratford in periods when the theatres were closed, during Lent, and the warm months of certain summers. Family crises would have taken him there on other occasions. In September, 1601, his father died, and in September, 1608, his mother. On June 5, 1607, his elder daughter, Susanna, married "M. John Hall gentleman," a Stratford physician of note. Their daughter Elizabeth was baptized at the font where her mother and grandfather had been baptized. This occasion may not have been considered sufficient for a two-day journey into Warwickshire, but his first grandchild was important in Shakespeare's eyes. For most of each year, certainly until 1604 and probably until 1611, he occupied London lodgings. We have some idea of where these lodgings were, owing to the appearance of his name in lists of residents from whom taxes were due. Until 1596 he appears to have lived in the parish of St Helen's Bishopsgate (convenient to Burbage's Theatre) and in 1596 in the suburb of Southwark. Just why he moved to the Bankside before the Globe was erected there is something of a puzzle, but the move may have been related to the building of the Swan Theatre in Southwark in 1596. In November of that year one William Wayte entered sureties of the peace against Francis Langley, builder of the Swan, William Shakespeare, Dorothy Soer, and Anne Lee "for fear of death, and so forth." The nature of the contention is unknown, but a few weeks earlier Langley had entered sureties of the peace against Wayte and William Gardiner "for fear of death, and so forth," and we can be pretty sure that real estate rather than life and limb was at stake.

The most interesting record of Shakespeare's living arrangements in London, indeed the only one that affords a glimpse at the nature of the man, is contained in a lawsuit brought by Stephen Belott against his father-in-law Christopher Mountjoy. In 1604 Shakespeare was lodging with the Mountjoys, a French Huguenot family which made hair ornaments in their establishment in Cripplegate, a short distance northeast of St Paul's Cathedral. He was asked to act as intermediary in advancing a marriage between their daughter Mary and their apprentice Stephen. In 1612 the latter charged that the promised dowry had not been paid, and Shakespeare was required to testify. His deposition survives: "William Shakespeare of Stratford vpon Aven in the Countye of Warwicke gentleman of the age of xlviii yeres or thereaboutes sworne and examined . . . deposethe and sayethe": 1, That he had known the plaintiff Belott and the defendant Mountjoy for about ten years; 2, That the plaintiff was "a very good and industrious servant"; 3, That the defendant's wife "did sollicitt and entreat this deponent to move and perswade the said complainant to effect the said marriadge"; 4, That the "defendant promissed to geue the said complainant a porcion in marriadge with Marye his daughter, but what certayne porcion he rememberethe not. . . . And more he cannott depose." There is considerably more in the document, mostly circumlocution, and the general impression it conveys is that the deponent was a fair-minded man who was doing the best he could for young Belott – and would never play Cupid again. Mountjoy was apparently not a man of sterling character, but this glimpse into the home of the tire-maker, where "they had amongeste them selues manye conferences about there marriadge," suggests anything but a Bohemian milieu. The description of Shakespeare as "of Stratford vpon Aven" may mean that in 1612 he no longer retained regular London lodgings. Of course there was always the Bell, and similar inns.

Early in 1616 Shakespeare's younger daughter, Judith, married Thomas Quiney, son of his old friend Richard. Six weeks later he made his will. Written on three sheets much corrected and revised, the original is preserved in the Principal Probate Registry at Somerset House in London. The terms of the bequest are extremely detailed and are designed primarily to keep the estate together. Thus:

I Gyve Will bequeath & Devise vnto my daughter Susanna Hall for better enabling of her to performe this my will & towardes the performans thereof All that Capitall Messuage or tenemente with thappurtenaunces in Stratford aforesaied Called the newe place wherein I nowe dwell & twoe messuages or tenementes with thappurtenaunces scituat lyeing & being in Henley streete within the borough of Stratford aforesaied, And all my barnes stables Orchardes gardens landes tenementes & hereditamentes whatsoever scituat lyeing & being or to be had Receyved perceyved or taken within the townes Hamlettes villages ffieldes & groundes of Stratford vpon Avon Oldstratford Bushopton & Welcombe or in anie of them in the saied countie of Warr, And alsoe All that Messuage or tenemente with thappurtenuances wherein one John Robinson dwelleth, scituat lyeing & being in the blackfriers in London nere the Wardrobe, & all other my landes tenementes and hereditamentes whatsoever.

Susanna and her husband were also given the residue, including silver plate, jewels, and household goods, after various individual bequests had been made. Judith, the younger daughter, was given a cash bequest of one hundred and fifty pounds and another one hundred and fifty in trust; Shakespeare's sister, Joan Hart, twenty pounds, his clothing, and the life use, with token rental, of the house she was then living in. To his nephews and his granddaughter Elizabeth Hall he made specific bequests of small sums of money and silver plate respectively. There were various small bequests to other relatives and to Stratford friends. Nor did he forget the three old colleagues remaining from the great days in London: "to my ffellowes John Hemynge Richard Burbage & Henry Cundell xxvj^s viij^d A peece to buy them Ringes." Shakespeare's wife is mentioned only in the famous bequest: "I gyve vnto my wief my second best bed with the furniture." The provision must not be construed as a slight. Anne's rights as widow were provided for by law, and any direct bequest to her of property or money would have endangered the preservation of the estate intact for the male issue of the children. The specific mention of the second-best bed – presumably the family bed – like the bequest of ring money to his fellows, also an interlinear addition, was simply a token of sentiment. What Shakespeare's will reveals is his interest in carrying out his father's ambitions to establish a genteel family, the careful provisions for the future harmonizing perfectly with the history of careful investment which marked Shakespeare's own life. But his hopes were in vain, for the Halls had only the one daughter, and although she eventually became Lady Bernard she bore no sons. Judith had three boys, but the eldest lived only to twenty-one. Thus with the death of Lady Bernard in 1670 the direct line ended. Shakespeare's monument was not to be a great family.

The will, apparently written by a local scribe, was signed on each page by Shakespeare and was witnessed by five men. It was dictated soon after Judith's marriage, which probably necessitated the drawing up of a new will. In spite of the conventional claim that the maker was "in perfect health & memorie god be praysed" there is about it an air of urgency, reinforced by the many deletions and additions. That Shakespeare died within the month comes as no surprise. The monument in the Stratford Church gives the day of death as April 23, 1616. The parish register records the burial on April 25 of "Will. Shakspere, gent." and we may suppose that the last four letters would have pleased Shakespeare as much as his father. He was buried within the Church in the chancel and near the charnel house, a vault to which old bones were removed when the consecrated ground was getting overcrowded. The stone laid over Shakespeare's grave took cognizance of this possibility:

GOOD FREND FOR IESVS SAKE FORBEARE,
TO DIGG THE DVST ENCLOASED HEARE!
BLESTE BE Y^E MAN Y^T SPARES THES STONES,
AND CVRST BE HE Y^T MOVES MY BONES.

This warning has worked better than Shakespeare or his family could ever have imagined. While no one has yet had the temerity to suggest that Shakespeare's bones should make way for someone else's earthly remains, over the years the urge to peek in the tomb has been compulsive, and one can only conclude that the inscribed warning, doggerel but effective, has been a better protection than decorum and good taste.

Some years after Shakespeare's death a monument was erected on the north wall of the chancel. It contains a stylized bust of the poet which owes something of its rather lifeless quality to its having been created without fine detail in order to give scope to the painter who would finish it. Unfortunately it has since been repainted and the present colors are apparently arbitrary and without significance. The monument bears an inscription in Latin and English which likens Shakespeare to Socrates and Virgil and asks the passer-by to stay and think upon the poet whom "ENVIOVS DEATH HATH PLAST, WITH IN THIS MONVMENT."

A different and far greater testament to Shakespeare's genius was soon to come. In 1623 his old friends and fellow-actors, John Heminge and Henry Condell (Richard Burbage had died in 1619), cooperated with London stationers in publishing a collected edition of the plays. Heminge and Condell explained their motives in a prefatory note to the reader: "It had bene a thing, we confesse, worthie to haue bene wished, that the Author himselfe had liu'd to haue set forth, and ouerseen his owne writings," but this being impossible "do not envie his Friends, the office of their care, and paine, to haue collected & publish'd them." They complain of the "diuerse stolne, and surreptitious copies, maimed, and deformed" of Shakespeare's plays that have been offered to the public, and they express their own desire to offer them to the reader's view "cur'd, and perfect of their limbes; and all the rest, absolute in their numbers, as he conceiued them." If the textual purity of the plays does not always live up to the editors' promise, it does not alter the fact that for many of Shakespeare's plays the Folio is our only text, and for all of them it is an authority that commands respect. The Folio also contains an engraved portrait by Droeshout, which with the Stratford bust is the only likeness of Shakespeare with any claim to authority. In addition there are laudatory poems prefacing the plays, including an ode by Ben Jonson, "To the memory of my beloued, The AVTHOR MR. WILLIAM SHAKESPEARE: AND what he hath left vs" that contains a line justly considered to voice the ultimate tribute to Shakespeare's genius: "*He was not of an age, but for all time!*" Shakespeare, for all his modesty, had himself anticipated this verdict when with youthful bravado he wrote in one of the sonnets: "Not marble nor the gilded monuments / Of princes shall outlive this pow'rful rime."

These are the facts of William Shakespeare's life. They are fuller than we might reasonably expect, and there seems to be no reason why we should try to flesh them out with the various legends that have accrued over the years. To some these facts have seemed too commonplace – too *ordinary* – to fit their conception of a great artist. But there is another way of looking at them. One suspects that Shakespeare's humanity, his universality of appeal, could only have been possible for a man who had immersed himself fully and sympathetically in the concerns of ordinary existence. Only by living the normal life of his day could William Shakespeare have become "Shakespeare." Closet dramatists may live in closets, but playwrights who write for the theatre of the world must live in the world. They must be more than mere observers, for they must commit themselves fully to life before they can write about it with sympathy and understanding.

State University   FRANK W. WADSWORTH
of New York at Purchase

BIBLIOGRAPHY

The standard reference work on the facts about Shakespeare is Sir Edmund Chambers, *William Shakespeare : A Study of Facts and Problems*, 2 vols (1930). A fuller but less accurate collection of documents is B. Roland Lewis, *The Shakespeare Documents*, 2 vols (1941). Works on the Stratford background are Edgar I. Fripp, *Shakespeare's Stratford* (1928) and Mark Eccles, *Shakespeare in Warwickshire* (1961). Massive treatments of English educational facilities are T. W. Baldwin, *William Shakespere's petty school* (1943) and *William Shakspere's small Latine & lesse Greeke*, 2 vols (1944). The once "standard" biographies by Sir Sidney Lee (1898, enlarged edition 1915, reprinted with new preface 1925), Walter Raleigh in *E.M.L.S* (1907), and Joseph Q. Adams (1923) have been superseded, but remain highly readable. Another interesting personal treatment is J. Dover Wilson, *The Essential Shakespeare* (1932). The most objective and useful current biographies are Marchette Chute, *Shakespeare of London* (1949); Gerald E. Bentley, *Shakespeare : A Biographical Handbook* (1961); and Peter Alexander, *Shakespeare* (1964). Popular quadricentennial biographies were issued by A. L. Rowse (1963) and Peter Quennell (1964). Descriptions of attacks upon Shakespeare's authorship appear in F. E. Halliday, *The Cult of Shakespeare* (1957); Frank W. Wadsworth, *The Poacher from Stratford* (1958); and Alfred Harbage, *Conceptions of Shakespeare* (1966). Analysis of rival claims appears in William F. and Elizabeth S. Friedman, *The Shakespeare Ciphers Examined* (1957), and H. N. Gibson, *The Shakespeare Claimants* (1962). Modern interpretation of the facts about Shakespeare is considerably indebted to J. S. Smart, *Shakespeare : Truth and Tradition* (1928). An account of his reputation is Louis Marder, *His Exits and His Entrances* (1963).

THE CANON

The list of Shakespeare's authentic works – his "canon" – was virtually established in 1623 in the volume issued by Jaggard and Blount with the assistance of Heminge and Condell. (Although his narrative poems and his sonnets were not included, these had been previously mentioned as his by contemporaries, and had been published with his name on their several title pages.) Thirty-six plays were printed in the volume, eighteen of them for the first time. The reliability of the collection is indicated by external as well as internal evidence. Most of the included plays had been mentioned as Shakespeare's by Francis Meres and others, or had already appeared in print with attribution to him. None had been claimed for any other author, and none would be so claimed until 1687 when Edward Ravenscroft reported a rumor that *Titus Andronicus* was "not originally his" although he had given it some "master-touches." In contrast, the authenticity of the Beaumont and Fletcher collection of 1647 was promptly and properly challenged, in a printed statement that Beaumont had actually contributed very little to the contents and Massinger a great deal. In the Shakespeare collection the only error in content about which scholars agree is one of omission. The last three acts of *Pericles* are certainly his, and the play had been published with his name on the title page in 1609. It brings the plays of the accepted canon to a total of thirty-seven.

The authenticity of this body of work has stood up well under considerable attack. In his edition of 1723 Alexander Pope dismissed all passages that offended his taste as the interpolation of actors; and later eighteenth-century scholars (against the judgment of Samuel Johnson) initiated the tradition of classifying certain of the early plays as Shakespeare's revisions of the work of his predecessors. Such theories, carried to extreme, tend toward what has been called the "disintegration" of Shakespeare, but they should be distinguished from the eccentric variety which eliminate him entirely in favor of some other author, preferably a lord. Although much honest effort has been expended in the attempt to discover the hand of others in the thirty-seven plays, its fruits are remarkably small. Three brief passages in *Macbeth* are obvious interpolations, possibly by Thomas Middleton. The prologue, epilogue, and a few scenes of *Henry VIII* are usually assigned to John Fletcher. The hand of Shakespeare's "predecessors," especially George Peele, is still traced by some scholars in portions of the *Henry VI* plays and *Titus Andronicus*. The first two acts of *Pericles* are either non-Shakespearean or were printed from quite debased copy.

The question remains of how much Shakespearean writing may survive in addition to that in the accepted canon. There is a strong probability that he played some part in the composition of *The Two Noble Kinsmen*, published in 1634 as his and Fletcher's. On grounds partly orthographic and partly stylistic it has been cogently argued that he supplied the mob scenes in the manuscript *Book of Sir Thomas More*, a play by Antony Munday and others which failed to pass political censorship about 1595. On the basis of style and analogy with his acknowledged work, it has been argued that he wrote the episode of the wooing of the Countess of Salisbury in *Edward III*, printed anonymously in 1596; and the additional scenes depicting Hieronimo's madness printed in the 1602 edition of Kyd's *Spanish Tragedy*. There is nothing either incredible or disturbing about further possibilities – that a small fraction of non-Shakespearean writing remains unidentified among the plays of the accepted canon, or, conversely, that a small fraction of Shakespearean writing remains unidentified in anonymous plays or in ones attributed to his contemporaries. We are bound to wonder if any of his plays are lost to us in their entirety. Francis Meres lists "Loue labours wonne" among his works in 1598, and a printed play with this title was extant in the early seventeenth century, but we cannot be sure that it does not appear in the collection of 1623 under a different title. Records of lost manuscript plays from none too reliable sources yield the following titles : "The History of King Stephen," "Duke Humphrey, a Tragedy," "Iphis and Ianthe, or a Marriage Without a Man, a Comedy" by "Will: Shakespeare," "The History of Cardenio" by Fletcher and Shakespeare, and "Henry the First & Henry the Second" by Shakespeare and Davenport. The manuscripts no doubt existed, but the attributions of authorship are likely to have been as fictitious as those of a number of printed plays of the time which bore Shakespeare's name or initials on their title pages in a bid for sales. Five such plays, as well as *Pericles* and the anonymous *Sir John Oldcastle* (actually written by Drayton, Hathway, Munday, and Wilson) were added to the 1664

TABLE I: THE CANON

	First Performed	First Published	Principal Sources
Errors	1590 (? –1594)	1623 (3)	Plautus, *Menaechmi* and *Amphitruo*
1 Henry VI		1623	
2 Henry VI	1590– 1592* (? –1592)	{ 1594 (2) / 1623 }	Hall, *The Union of the Two Noble and Illustre Families of Lancaster and York*, 1548; Holinshed, *The Third Volume of Chronicles*, edition 1587
3 Henry VI		{ 1595 (2) / 1623 }	
Richard III	1593 (1592–1597)	{ 1597 (7) / 1623 }	
Shrew	1593* (? –1594)	1623	*A Shrew* or its original (?); and Gascoigne, *Supposes*, 1566
Titus	1594* ('Jan. 24')	1594 (2)	*History of Titus Andronicus* (?chapbook)
T.G.V.	1594* (? –1598)	1623	Montemayor, *Diana*, 1559; Elyot, *Governour*, 1531 (or derivatives)
John	1594* (? –1598)	1623	*The Troublesome Reign of John*, pub. 1591; Holinshed, ed. 1587
Dream	1595* (1594–1598)	1600 (1)	Miscellaneous
Richard II	1595 (1595–1597)	1597 (4)	Holinshed, ed. 1587
L.L.L.	1596* (? –1597)	1598	Miscellaneous
Romeo	1596 (? –1597)	{ 1597 / 1599 (3) }	Brooke, *Romeus and Juliet*, 1562
Merchant	1597 (1594–1598)	1600 (2)	Fiorentino, *Il Pecorone*, 1558
1 Henry IV	1597 (1595–1598)	1598 (8)	Holinshed, ed. 1587, and *The Famous Victories of Henry the Fifth*, reg. 1594 (or its predecessor)
2 Henry IV	1598 (1596–1598)	1600	
A.Y.L.	1598 (1598–1600)	1623	Lodge, *Rosalynde*, 1590
Henry V	1599 (Mar.-Sept.)	{ 1600 (2) / 1623 }	Same as for *1 & 2 Henry IV*
Caesar	1599 (1598–1599)	1623	North, *Plutarch*, 1579: Caesar, Brutus
Much Ado	1599 (1598–1600)	1600	The 'Ariodante and Genevora' tale, derived from Ariosto, 1516
Twelfth Night	1600 (1600–1602)	1623	Riche, *Farewell to Militarie Profession*, 1581, and miscellaneous
Merry Wives	1600* (1597–1602)	{ 1602 (1) / 1623 }	Miscellaneous
Hamlet	1601* (1599–1601)	{ 1603 / 1604–05 (3) }	Belleforest, *Histoires Tragiques*, 1576 (and an earlier play ?)
Troilus	1602 (1601–1603)	1609	Chaucer; Caxton, *Recuyell*, 1474; Chapman, *Homer*, 1598
All's Well	1603 (1598– ?)	1623	Boccaccio, 'Giletta of Narbona' in Painter, *Palace of Pleasure*, ed. 1575
Measure	1604 (1598–1604)	1623	Whetstone, *Promos and Cassandra*, 1578
Othello	1604 (1598–1604)	{ 1622 (5) / 1623 }	Giraldi ('Cinthio'), *Hecatommithi*, 1565
Lear	1605 (1598–1606)	{ 1608 (2) / 1623 }	Holinshed, ed. 1587; Sidney, *Arcadia*, 1590; *King Leir*, before 1594
Macbeth	1605 (1603–1611)	1623	Holinshed, ed. 1587
Timon	1606 (1598– ?)	1623	North, *Plutarch*, 1579: Antonius, Alcibiades; Lucian, *Timon* (?)
Pericles	1607* (1598–1608)	1609 (5)	Gower, *Confessio Amantis*, ed. 1554: 'Apollonius of Tyre'
Antony	1607 (1598–1608)	1623	North, *Plutarch*, 1579: Antonius
Coriolanus	1608 (1598– ?)	1623	North, *Plutarch*, 1579: Coriolanus
Cymbeline	1609 (1598–1611)	1623	Holinshed, ed. 1587; and miscellaneous
Winter's Tale	1610 (1598–1611)	1623	Greene, *Pandosto*, 1588
Tempest	1611 (1610–1611)	1623	Miscellaneous
Henry VIII	1613 (June)	1623	Holinshed, ed. 1587; Foxe, *Acts and Monuments*, ed. 1583

issue of the third edition of his collected works: *Locrine, Thomas Lord Cromwell, The London Prodigal, The Puritan,* and *A Yorkshire Tragedy.* These plays, and others which at one time or other have been mistakenly attributed to him are called collectively the "Shakespeare Apocrypha."

The thirty-seven plays accepted as authentic are listed in Table I in approximate chronological order. The date following each title is, in all but a few cases, only tentative. It represents the view of the Pelican editor on the year in which the play is most likely to have assumed its present form. When an asterisk follows a date, it means that there is some possibility that Shakespeare had revised earlier work, in most cases his own. In parentheses beside each date is given the span of years in which we would place the play if we relied solely upon a strict interpretation of external evidence. In a number of cases the only anterior limit of date is the beginning of Shakespeare's writing career, whenever that may have been, although 1587 seems a reasonable guess; and in the case of several others the only posterior limit of date is the year of Shakespeare's death. The date of first publication of each play is given in a separate column. When two dates are given, the first is that of the publication of a text which is either distinctly corrupt (a "bad" quarto) or is at least inferior to that printed in the collection of 1623. The number in parentheses beside a date indicates how often the publication of that date was reprinted. (This number is given only after the first occurrence of the date 1623. The collected works were printed four times in all before the end of the seventeenth century.) The count of reprints of the quartos does not include one quarto of *Merry Wives* reprinted from the folio of 1623, one of *Richard II* reprinted from the folio of 1632, and four of *Hamlet* (1676–1695) reprinted from the earlier quartos but with revisions. In the last column is listed the work or works from which the major action of each play was derived. The sources of incidental details are not listed. When the word "Miscellaneous" occurs, it means that the play is indebted to

earlier works only for incidental details, and that the major action appears to be Shakespeare's invention.

A. H.

BIBLIOGRAPHY

For Shakespeare's canon, as for his life, the basic reference work is Sir Edmund Chambers, *William Shakespeare*, 2 vols (1930). The plays mistakenly ascribed to Shakespeare are collected in *The Shakespeare Apocrypha*, ed. C. F. Tucker Brooke (1908), and a number of them are discussed in Baldwin Maxwell, *Studies in the Shakespeare Apocrypha* (1956).

Useful reference works are F. G. Stokes, *A Dictionary of the Characters and Proper Names in the works of Shakespeare* (1924); Karl J. Holzknecht, *The Backgrounds of Shakespeare's Plays* (1950); Oscar James Campbell & Edward G. Quinn, *The Reader's Encyclopedia of Shakespeare* (1966).

The sources of the plays are collected in *The Shakespeare Classics*, ed. Sir Israel Gollancz, 12 vols (1907–26, series not completed); *Narrative and Dramatic Sources of Shakespeare*, ed. Geoffrey Bullough, 6 vols (1957–66, series in process); *Shakespeare and his Sources*, ed. Joseph Satin (1966, sources of sixteen plays); *Shakespeare's Plutarch*, ed. T. J. B. Spencer (1964); *Elizabethan Love Stories*, ed. T. J. B. Spencer (1968, sources of eight plays).

Periodicals devoted to the study of Shakespeare are listed below, with the dates of their inception and the names of their present editors. The annuals are *Shakespeare-Jahrbuch* [Weimar], ed. A. Schlösser & A. Kuckhoff (1865–); *Shakespeare-Jahrbuch* [Heidelberg], ed. H. Heuer (1965–); *Shakespeare Survey*, ed. Kenneth Muir (1948–); *Shakespeare Studies* [Japan], ed. Jiro Ozu (1962–); *Shakespeare Studies* [U.S.A.], ed. J. L. Barroll (1965–); *Shakespearean Research Opportunities*, ed. W. R. Elton (1965–). A bi-monthly is *Shakespeare Newsletter*, ed. Louis Marder (1951–). A quarterly is *Shakespeare Quarterly*, ed. James G. McManaway (1950–).

An annual bibliography appears in *Shakespeare Quarterly*. Comprehensive bibliographies are William Jaggard, *Shakespeare Bibliography* (1911); W. Ebisch & L. L. Schücking, *A Shakespeare Bibliography* (1931, supplement 1937); *Cambridge Bibliography of English Literature*, ed. F. W. Bateson, 4 vols (1940, supplement ed. G. Watson, 1957); Gordon R. Smith, *A Classified Shakespeare Bibliography 1936–1958* (1963).

SHAKESPEARE'S THEATRE

During the quarter of a century which Shakespeare's theatrical career roughly spans, the English theatre underwent considerable change. The status of the profession, the habits of playgoing, the types of presentation responded to shifts in political and social circumstances as well as artistic accomplishment, and although we should like to know more than we do, the main outline of these changes can be discerned. As we trace the history of the London theatres during the last years of Elizabeth's reign and the first years of James's, we catch glimpses of Shakespeare both as a man of the theatre closely linked with his fellow players and as a poet somewhat apart. By examining the theatrical world of which he was a member, we gain a better understanding of his unique position in it.

At the end of the sixteenth century London was a thriving metropolis. Figures on its population are inevitably conjectural, but probably about a hundred and fifty thousand people lived in the city and its immediate environs. The municipal officials, deeply entrenched in the guilds of merchants and artisans, were jealous of their privileges and authority. At the same time, the city with its neighboring palaces comprised the capital of the kingdom. On its eastern boundary at the Thames stood a major stronghold of regal power, the Tower of London. Within the line of its former walls, precincts confiscated from the church and distributed by the crown were free from the zealous supervision of the mayor and aldermen, at least until 1608, and provided enclaves of royal prerogative. In short, London combined all the aggressiveness of a business center with all the grandeur of an ancient court.

In such a city, theatre had a turbulent existence. Pageant and spectacle enlivened streets and the halls of mansions. The city sponsored ceremonious presentations such as the annual Lord Mayor's Show, and the court sponsored chivalric mock tournaments and masques. Grammar schools and inns of court performed classical and original plays, in English as well as Latin. Professional efforts, though even more vigorous, were less uniformly acceptable than the amateur. In the stratified society of Elizabethan England, there was no place for actors in the livery companies or traditional craft guilds, but they were able to pass legal muster as the nominal household servants of members of the nobility. They used this association in becoming commercial entrepreneurs, and succeeded in producing a steady stream of new plays, but always under threat of suppression by the city or absorption by the Court.

When Shakespeare arrived in London, theatre encompassed two kinds of professional or quasi-professional activity. One kind consisted of performances of a wide assortment of romantic and historical narratives by companies of adult men. The other consisted of performances of similar material, though more classical than historical, more comic than tragic, by companies of boys. The inclusion of inter-act music and dance, and a penchant for the satirical and topical, distinguished their performances from those of the men. The men were professionals, attached in name to the Court or a noble household, but actually operating commercially as independent players. The boys were choristers attached to one of the royal chapels, the Children of St Paul's or the Children of the Chapel. Technically they were impressed into service as singers, but they were utilized as actors, supposedly for the amusement of the Queen. In the process of preparing for Court appearances, the men charged with the supervision of the choirs contrived to offer performances to a paying audience. In 1590 dramatic performances by the boys were discontinued by order of the Queen's privy council, so that only the men's companies continued to provide regular theatrical fare. In 1599 the boys' companies were revived and flourished for another decade, only to decay once more and cease to play a substantial part in the theatrical life of the city.

Meanwhile, another type of theatrical performance became fashionable, the Court masque. Under Elizabeth, the masque, more dance than spectacle, was neither literary nor opulent. With the accession of James in 1603, the masque underwent considerable alteration. Leading dramatists, notably Ben Jonson, and the Italian-trained architect and designer, Inigo Jones, expanded the theatrical features of the masque and developed its possibilities for display. Mythical and classical subjects served as convenient frames upon which to hang compliments to the sovereigns and through which to provide musical, poetic, and especially scenic, entertainment. Jones' introduction of the perspective setting and changeable scenery initiated a movement that led after 1660 to replacement of the open stage by the proscenium or picture-frame stage. Although only the first signs were apparent at the time of Shakespeare's retirement, the eventual triumph of the scenic stage was implicit in the dazzling presentations Ben Jonson and Inigo Jones prepared for King James and his court. Members of the royal family and their courtiers performed the figure dances and chose partners in the following "revels" or ballroom dancing, while professional actors and boy choristers took the introductory and interspersed speaking and singing parts. It was also left to professionals to do the comic or grotesque dancing of the "anti-masque" introduced by Jonson.

Of the three types of theatrical activity – that of the men in the public theatres, that of the boys in the chorister theatres, and that in the royal masquing halls – Shakespeare evidently wrote only for the first. Unlike his friend and rival Ben Jonson, who divided his talents among all three, Shakespeare, so far as we know, never wrote for a children's company and never penned a masque. By the time of his arrival in London the public theatre had entered a period of relative stability. In 1576 the first permanent playhouse, dubbed with the proud classical name "The Theatre," was erected to the north of the city. The following year a second permanent theatre, the Curtain, was put up in an adjacent field. Six years later, in 1583, a dozen players were selected from various companies to form the Queen's men, the only troupe to receive a patent from Elizabeth herself. At the same time, several other troupes enjoyed the protection of such

mighty lords of the realm as the Earl of Leicester. In the second half of the decade, a number of young men, educated, ambitious, some of them daring, began writing for the public theatres, unlike John Lyly, who had confined his efforts to the chorister companies. George Peele, Thomas Kyd, Christopher Marlowe, and Robert Greene are the chief of this new group of playwrights who fused the vitality of narrative drama with an extraordinary lyrical power. The existence of regular professional performances made it possible for these poets to earn a living, though not necessarily a good one. In fact, the theatre offered the writer the only practical alternative to utter dependence upon patronage.

Such stability as existed had not come easily nor did it remain unchallenged. The enmity of municipal authorities and the perils of censorship repeatedly threatened the stage. For decades the city fathers had sought to suppress all theatrical performances. Securing playing sites invariably involved pressure and counterpressure between city officials and Court councillors. Had it not been for the political support of the Queen and her nobility, the professional theatre could never have survived, and even despite this support, the first public playhouses still had to be situated beyond the limits of municipal jurisdiction.

Nor did the threat to the theatre cease after Shakespeare arrived in London. Censorship continued to exert a restrictive force, and in the course of his stay in London, was responsible for suppressing or for threatening to suppress a number of theatre companies. In 1597, a performance of the lost play, *The Isle of Dogs*, led to the temporary suspension of all performances. In 1601, Shakespeare and his fellow-players were put to interrogation when there was suspicion that the company conspired with the supporters of the Earl of Essex in reviving *Richard II*. And when censorship did not threaten, plague did. It too disrupted presentations, but more frequently and more devastatingly. Outbreaks of this disease, prevalent in the summer especially, periodically caused the closing of the theatres. In fact, the severity of the outbreak which began in June, 1592, and continued with little abatement well into 1594, brought about the complete reorganization of theatre companies. Finally, municipal antagonism, though reduced, did not disappear. To Shakespeare's good fortune, it did not present a crucial threat to the theatre during his lifetime. Eventually, however, anti-theatrical feeling surfaced with the national politico-religious eruption of the sixteen-thirties and led to the suppression of all theatre in 1642.

The likelihood of such disaster to the quality of acting would have seemed fantastic at the time of Shakespeare's retirement. In 1613 the public theatre occupied a higher status in the social scale than it had twenty-five years earlier. Gradually losing its popular, supra-class character, it was becoming increasingly narrow. In 1603, James I took the leading theatre companies under royal patronage. After 1608, men's companies began to perform in the indoor theatres formerly occupied by the children, the capacity of which was probably less than a third of that of the public playhouses. Admission fees were higher as a result. Inevitably a more exclusive clientele frequented performances of the professional companies, encouraging new tendencies in writing and perhaps in playing. These new tendencies, with their attendant effects of transforming the theatre into an aristocratic entertainment, were just manifesting themselves when Shakespeare's career came to a close. It is perhaps impossible to determine the extent to which the combination of relative stability and a multi-class public during the halcyon period of 1588 to 1613 provided Shakespeare with the fertile soil in which to plant his art. What we can merely note is the fortunate conjunction of a vigorous theatrical art which verged on fruition with an imaginative power which found in that art a supple instrument for its expression.

The core of that theatrical art was the acting company. Presentations originated with the company and were managed by it. After 1572, performances could be given regularly on weekdays in London, thus affording the basis for a stable institution. Increasingly, conditions governing rehearsal and presentation were determined by the actors' exploitation of commercial opportunities. The two other theatres of the period, those of the choristers and of the Court, operated on different assumptions and under different kinds of management. In the case of the children's companies, the manager of the boys and the freelance dramatist exploited the young actors for their own financial and artistic advantage. In the case of the Court theatre, the sovereign sponsored the masques for the glory of his reign and the delectation of his guests. In the public theatres, on the other hand, the actors exercised both financial responsibility and artistic direction through a distinctive type of theatrical organization.

This organization was essentially medieval. It consisted of three kinds of workers: sharers, journeymen, and apprentices. Responsibility and supervision were vested in the sharers, the six to ten actors who controlled the company. As sharers, they purchased plays, bought costumes, paid licensing fees, rented playhouses, and shared profits. In addition, they engaged the journeymen and other hired help such as bookholders and musicians, as well as served as masters for the apprentice boys who played the female roles. Occasionally a journeyman or an apprentice, upon reaching his majority, might be admitted to a share of the company if a place became vacant. But until such admission, the hired man, in whatever capacity, had quite a different, and lower, status from the sharer.

At first the acting company tended to be small, the proverbial "four men and a boy" of the touring group epitomized in *Hamlet*. But after 1583, when the Queen's men set the example for larger companies, nine or ten became the number of sharers in a London company. Between 1590 and 1594, internal weaknesses aggravated by the closing of the theatres due to the plague brought about the decline of the Queen's men. Other companies also succumbed to the long ban against performing in the city so that when playing finally resumed in the late spring of 1594, virtually new combinations came into existence. From 1594 through 1613, the public theatre was dominated by three companies. At first the Lord Chamberlain's and Lord Admiral's men were the major troupes. By 1602 Lord Worcester's men had achieved a position nearly equal in importance. Under James, the Lord Chamberlain's men became the King's men, the Lord Admiral's men became the Prince's men, and the Lord Worcester's men became the Queen's men, and though there were later changes, these three companies enjoyed a virtual monopoly of the public stage through the rest of Shakespeare's career.

The beginnings of Shakespeare's theatrical career

remain unknown, but by 1592 he had established himself in his profession as an actor and writer. With the emergence of the Lord Chamberlain's men in 1594, he was a leading figure of the company, a company which came to be remarkable in two respects. First, the sharers formed and maintained a well-knit group with only gradual changes during the next twenty years. One noted sharer, the comedian Will Kempe, dropped out fairly early. Several sharers died in the course of time and were succeeded by others. But a vital core, Richard Burbage, William Shakespeare, John Heminge, Henry Condell, William Sly, Augustine Phillips, Richard Cowley, Robert Armin, worked together closely over an unusually long period. Secondly, Richard Burbage and his brother Cuthbert, who together owned the building of the Theatre and a hall in Blackfriars, formed a joint partnership with five of the sharers in the construction and ownership of the Globe and later in the operation of the theatre at Blackfriars. Thus, a web of financial and artistic relationships bound the Lord Chamberlain–King's men together, and whether art served money or money art, the company prospered in both.

Under what conditions did this company perform and how did these conditions affect the art of the theatre? The diary of Philip Henslowe, owner of the Rose playhouse, gives us a clear idea of how the Lord Admiral's and the Lord Worcester's men operated between 1592 and 1602, and we have corroboratory evidence that the Lord Chamberlain's men functioned in much the same way. Added to this information are records of the royal household and occasional allusions, such as letters, which complete the picture of late Elizabethan and early Jacobean theatre practice. Performances were of three types. There were regular presentations for the public, first in the open and then later in the roofed playhouses. There were occasional performances at Court or at the home of a nobleman. There were performances in the provinces when a troupe went on tour. The three types of performance were not, however, of equal frequency. The last mentioned, that is, provincial performances, were given only as acts of necessity. A heritage of touring the country, and even the Continent, lay behind all English acting companies. But after 1576, the availability of permanent theatres in and about London together with the opportunity to perform regularly in a fixed location caused the better companies to forego touring whenever possible. Each of them became associated with particular playhouses: the Chamberlain–King's men with the Theatre, the Globe (after 1599), and Blackfriars (after 1608); the Admiral–Prince's men with the Rose, and the Fortune (after 1600); and the Worcester–Queen's men with the Red Bull (after 1605). Touring continued, but only when the plague raged during summer or some other disturbance closed the playhouses.

The total number of performances a company might give at Court varied from year to year. Christmas was the season when players were called before the sovereign, and between Christmas and Twelfth Night (January 6) revels held sway. For these appearances we have records showing the popularity of the Chamberlain–King's men under both Elizabeth and James. The number of such appearances varied from year to year, being more frequent after 1603, yet never going beyond fifteen and normally averaging seven or eight. About the number of per-

formances given in the homes of the nobility, we have too meagre evidence to arrive at any conclusion. The issue is significant only because it is sometimes assumed that Shakespeare wrote certain plays for initial presentation in a private residence. *A Midsummer Night's Dream*, it is widely suggested, was devised to celebrate a noble marriage. To this supposition, the history of the Elizabethan theatre lends little support. Whatever evidence we have indicates that the men's companies performed upon commission plays which had already been performed in their regular playhouses. Taking court and private performances all together, it is unlikely that they ever exceeded ten per cent of all performances.

A men's company derived its principal financial support from public performance before a popular audience. According to Henslowe's records, these companies performed on five or six afternoons a week except during Lent and the hottest weeks of summer, or when inhibited because of the plague or an act of indiscretion such as the performance of *The Isle of Dogs*. On an average each company gave two hundred public performances a year. To maintain this volume required extraordinary exertion. Given the playgoing population of London and the normal vagaries of theatrical popularity, a play did quite well if it achieved ten performances. Moreover, these performances were distributed over many months, for seldom did a new play, however successful, receive more than three performances in its first month. Therefore, in order to reach two hundred performances a year, a company had to offer twenty-five to thirty different plays, of which fourteen to seventeen needed to be completely new. This meant that the actors were in constant rehearsal. As soon as one play was opened, another was begun. Rarely were more than two weeks spent in rehearsing a script, and during those two weeks the actors were performing eight to ten different plays.

The constant demand for fresh material beset all companies. Though the actors bought plays in the open market, they did not wait for the dramatist, but often commissioned works on popular subjects or revived older plays that still commanded an audience. Even with the advantage of Shakespeare's pen, the Chamberlain–King's men were obliged to patronize the open market. Like the others, this company had to buy scripts from free-lance writers, some of whom we know by name, such as Ben Jonson, Thomas Dekker, and George Wilkins, and some of whom we shall never know. Once purchased, a script became the sole property of the company. The player Shakespeare knew that the writer Shakespeare had no claim to his work once it was submitted to the actors. Exactly what arrangement Shakespeare had with his fellow-sharers is unknown. He may have gradually substituted playwriting for acting as his contribution to the company or he may have received additional remuneration. Whatever the arrangement, Shakespeare never seemed to have exerted any effort to retain publishing or production rights to his work.

The close ties among the sharers may have provided Shakespeare with some compensation for the pressures to write quickly and voluminously, but perhaps more important was the manner and practice of reviving plays. Such a sense of novelty obsessed the Elizabethan theatre that a play was considered old within ten years of its presentation. Rarely were plays kept in the repertory for more than a year or two without alteration. Thereafter, they would be discontinued. At a later date, the more popular pieces would be revived, sometimes with, sometimes without, additions or deletions. A new costume or a new stage property might be introduced; a scene or a character might be cut. Since the dramatist had no proprietary interest in the script, the company could order what changes it desired, and it was not unusual for the actors to employ a writer other than the original author to add a speech or a series of scenes. On the face of it, the system seems calculated to undermine the dramatist and defeat creative effort. But quite the opposite occurred. The system afforded the writer who was strategically placed the unexcelled opportunity to refine his work. Fortunately, because he was a sharer as well as a dramatist, Shakespeare was strategically so placed to take advantage of this opportunity.

The history of *Hamlet* will illustrate the process. A play on the subject appeared on the boards of the Theatre before 1589. Unlikely to have been the work of Shakespeare in any part, the play is often, though questionably, attributed to Thomas Kyd. By 1594 this play or another one on the same subject was performed jointly by the Lord Admiral's and Lord Chamberlain's men in the first weeks after the plague abated. Again it is fairly certain that the play was not Shakespeare's though it almost certainly belonged to the Chamberlain's company. Thus, as early as 1594 Shakespeare and his colleagues possessed a script on this subject. The title is not mentioned in the list of Shakespeare's plays published by Francis Meres in 1598. Presumably Shakespeare wrote his version after that date, probably in 1600-01. To what extent he made use of the old play, we do not know. But we can be sure that he had seen it performed, and most likely himself performed a role in it. Perhaps the early play served as a source for his own. The first quarto of *Hamlet*, published in 1603, is generally regarded as a corrupt copy of the true play, yet certain features of its text, such as the use of the name Corambis for Polonius and the appearance of a Horatio–Queen scene not in the good quarto, suggest that we might have an earlier draft of the play which was "newly imprinted and enlarged" in 1604. What we can be sure of is that over a ten-year period Shakespeare had the chance to mature a conception, and whether or not he actually depended upon earlier copies, he benefited from the sustained acquaintanceship with the story.

So far I have considered the governing conditions which affected the public theatre. But what about the artistic operation? How did a company such as the Lord Chamberlain–King's men create productions? First, though this point will appear terribly obvious, the actors worked from scripts. The Italian comedy with its improvisatory technique was not unknown to the Elizabethans, but except for some of the leading comedians, the actors did not rely on improvisation. Tarleton, a famous clown of the Queen's men, was renowned for his "extemporall wit," and Will Kempe, the original Dogberry, was admired for his interpolations of comedy and dancing. But if we take Hamlet's words to be Shakespeare's thoughts, then Shakespeare is criticizing such interpolations when Hamlet bids the player prohibit the comedian from saying more than is set down for him. In fact, the actor who could not learn his part accurately was often an object of mockery in the Elizabethan theatre. This faithfulness to the text seems at odds with the company's readiness to revise it. But these were two different considerations. Privacy of authorship was not necessarily respected, but primacy of text was. Though the actors were in control of the theatrical process, they did not use plays merely as personal vehicles. Adherence to the text went beyond the mere retention of the correct words. The text itself, that is, the way in which the narrative was arranged by the dramatist, seems to have been a major organizing principle of staging.

Secondly, the actors employed a system of shared stardom. The sharers divided the principal parts, but even among them, some individuals regularly took the lead. Richard Burbage was such an actor. However varied the stage characters might be, he would usually play central roles. Within a period of four or five years, he portrayed Hamlet, Othello, and Lear, as well, no doubt, as other major characters. Oddly enough, there was little correspondence between the personality of the actor and the roles he played. Again with one exception. A comic actor could always be found on the roster of a company. No matter how serious the work, an author invariably supplied a comic role. Sometimes, as in *Othello* and *Antony and Cleopatra*, it would be generically labeled simply "clown." Aside from this special connection of actor to role, casting was determined by the recognized standing of the actor, that is, by his skills as performer. These skills were primarily three: the portrayal of character types, the expression of intense emotional states, and the rendition of heightened rhetoric. The Elizabethan acting profession had a long history of touring which required actors to double in roles, and although touring declined, it never died out completely. Doubling encouraged flexibility in the performer, stimulating him to define simply and clearly the behavior of the kings, lords, burghers, and yeomen which populated the plays. The type of acting with which we are familiar, calling upon the actor to portray not what a character says but what he leaves unsaid, was quite foreign to Elizabethan acting. Poetic expression was an exact mirror of a character's feelings. Hamlet's distraction arises because he cannot suppress his passions, and Lady Macbeth vainly abjures her husband to mask his fears. A nimble tongue and a passionate spirit were most urgently demanded and we must suppose, judging from the praise heaped upon Burbage, that he had those qualities in abundance.

Thirdly, the sharers controlled the staging of the plays. This factor is not appreciated sufficiently. Actors may be delighted by spectacle, but they will not readily permit it to overshadow themselves. Actors would never have permitted Inigo Jones to usurp the stage with scenery. Not that the King's men were impervious to changes of fashion. Being businessmen as well as actors they moved with the times. But they did not forego the primacy of acting for the delectation of scenic display. Instead they achieved spectacle through brilliant and lavish dress. They expended huge sums upon their costumes which were usually styled in the fashion of their own day, though possibly with an admixture of historical accessories.

Finally, in the case of the Chamberlain–King's men, the actors controlled the playhouses in which they performed. How did that fact influence their style of production? Considerably, according to widespread expert opinion. Scholars have long assumed that the physical structure of the playhouses determined the principles of Elizabethan staging. However, this premise needs to be examined critically through a review of what we know of the playhouses. Our concern is primarily with three : the Theatre, the Globe, and Blackfriars. The Theatre was erected in 1576 by Richard Burbage's father, James. In 1596, James purchased rooms in Blackfriars which he converted into an indoor theatre, intending to lease it to an adult company. However, he died shortly thereafter, leaving the venture to his sons Richard and Cuthbert. Like their father, they were unsuccessful in installing a men's troupe at Blackfriars and, therefore, leased the place to a boys' company, the Children of the Chapel. Concurrently, disputes with the owner of the land on which the Theatre was situated finally led the Burbages to tear down the building in 1599 and out of its frame erect a new playhouse, the Globe, across the Thames on the Bankside. The joint ownership of the Globe, which I described earlier, bound company and playhouse intimately. It was there that the major tragedies were first performed. In 1608, the children's company then occupying Blackfriars had to give up its lease which the Burbages assumed themselves. Through the creation of another joint partnership this second theatre was also tied to the fortunes of the company. This time the actors gained permission to perform at Blackfriars, thus providing themselves with an indoor and an outdoor theatre, and early in 1609 they began to use the new quarters. Four years later the Globe playhouse was accidentally set on fire and burned to the ground. Immediately, the King's men reconstructed it, thus indicating that the Globe still played a vital part in their operations. When Shakespeare concluded his career, he was not only a sharer and a dramatist but also part owner of the two most desirable theatres in London.

Insofar as we can tell, the major structural differences between the Globe and Blackfriars were two : roofing and size. Like other public playhouses, the Globe was partially roofed. The galleries in which the audience sat, the backstage areas for the actors, and a portion of the stage, were covered. The rest of the stage and the center yard, in which part of the audience stood, remained unroofed. In contrast, the private theatres, of which Blackfriars was foremost, were entirely covered, thus necessitating artificial illumination. As I mentioned previously, the outdoor theatres were considerably larger than the indoor. Estimates of capacity vary. In round figures we can assume that the public playhouses could accommodate about 2500 people, the private playhouses a third to a fifth that number.

Despite the capacity of the public playhouses, a sense of intimacy existed. The particular construction of this kind of theatre made such a paradox possible. Three floors of galleries open on one side surrounded an open yard within which a stage was set. Such a mode of vertical seating enabled a large number of people to occupy a relatively compact area. From a position at the front of the Globe stage, an actor would be no more than fifty or fifty-two feet from the furthest spectator. The theatre at Stratford, Ontario, seating over two thousand people, is a modern example of how intimacy and capacity can be combined.

Currently, there is some disagreement among scholars about the exact way in which the stage related to the play-

house frame. Except for the square Fortune, the public playhouses were either circular or polygonal. Adopting the dimensions of the Fortune theatre, for which the construction contract has survived, the open yard between galleries was fifty-five feet across. The galleries themselves were about twelve feet deep. Within the open yard, a stage platform projected from one arc or side as far as the center. Until quite recently, it was assumed that this stage was structurally connected to the frame and that the tiring house or backstage area was that part of the gallery masked by the stage. However, C. Walter Hodges has called attention to an anomaly contained in the Fortune contract. Though the Globe was circular or polygonal and the Fortune was to be square, the contract directs the carpenter to erect a stage "contrived and fashioned like unto" the Globe, within the frame of the Fortune. This suggests that the stage was not an integral part of that frame. Furthermore, there was probably a discontinuity between the appearance of the frame and that of the stage. For example, the galleries were finished in plaster and lath while, in some of the public playhouses at least, parts of the stage were painted to imitate marble. Most likely, splendid decoration set off the playing area from the rest of the playhouse, making the stage an ornament apart.

The principal features of the stage were the rectangular platform, forty-three feet wide and about twenty-seven feet deep, a two- or three-story façade, and a pair of pillars, located midway between the façade and the front of the platform to support a shadow or half-roof over the stage. These features can be seen in the accompanying sketch of the Swan playhouse, the only contemporary

view of an Elizabethan public playhouse interior to come down to us. For the moment, consider merely the main elements of this sketch since the details are open to controversy. The platform is rather large. It projects well into the yard and corroborates the evidence from the Fortune contract that the stage extended half-way into the open area. The stage is also rectangular, bearing little relationship to the frame. At the rear of the stage the *mimorum aedes* or wall of the building presents a façade pierced by two large doors or gates. In a gallery on the second level are seated figures, possibly actors, possibly auditors. Three players on the bare stage are enacting a scene. Above, in the huts, a man blowing a trumpet seems to be announcing a performance. The conjunction of this figure, the actors already performing, the figures upon the second level, and the bare galleries suggests that the sketch is a composite picture of what Johannes De Witt remembered of his visit to the theatre. Unfortunately the drawing does not adequately depict the magnificent playing place described by De Witt in his accompanying notes. To visualize its appearance we must imagine the opulence of a Renaissance structure imposed upon this rough outline.

To what extent was the façade altered for each production? Here we enter a field of controversy. About the platform, the pillars, and the shadow above, there is substantial agreement. But when we examine the façade, we encounter uncertainty and dispute. Glancing at the Swan drawing again, we note that the façade contains only the two large double doors on the stage level. Presumably these were employed for entrances and exits. The difficulty in accepting this evidence arises, however, when we try to match plays to theatre. Since we have only one extant script of a play certainly performed at the Swan playhouse and we have no extant sketch of any other public playhouse, we must match plays of one theatre with the stage of another. When we do so for plays presented at the Globe, we discover that scripts and stage do not jibe. In many plays, as in the first two scenes of *Othello*, more than two entrance points are needed. In *Hamlet* (III, i) an arras or curtain is required behind which the King and Polonius can hide. In *Pericles* an enclosure, within which the supposed corpse of Thaisa can rest, is needed together with a curtain that can be drawn across it (III, i). By way of confirmation, the non-Shakespearean plays offered at the Globe verify the recurrent use of a third place of entry and a curtained enclosure.

The discrepancy here noted is recognized by all students of the Elizabethan stage. Explanations fall into two categories. Some argue that temporary mansions or houses were placed on stage whenever such units as enclosures were required. Others attack the reliability of the Swan drawing. Any conclusion must be conjectural. But keeping in mind that the Swan stage, *as it is represented by De Witt*, cannot accommodate the plays presented at the Globe, we might consider the following facts. Two later views of indoor stages (one from the title page of *Roxana*, 1632; the other from the title page of *Messalina*, 1640) show central entrance points from curtained areas. The portable street stages, sometimes called the booth stages, which may have served as the predecessors of the Elizabethan stage, also utilized central entrance points. In essence, all explanations come to the same thing.

Either a projecting pavilion or a recessed aperture, which could be used both for discovery and entrance, often occupied the wall between the two doors of the Elizabethan stage façade. Accordingly, we can best describe Shakespeare's stage as a handsome two-story façade containing a curtained enclosure between two doors on the first level and an open gallery for acting or viewing on the second. Before this façade extended a broad expanse of platform. Binding façade and platform together was an overhanging half-roof supported by two richly-ornamented pillars.

With mention of a curtained place we are embarking upon the larger subject of scenery in the Elizabethan theatre. How much scenery was actually employed and what was its function? That there was some kind of setting or stage furniture is attested by the specific references in the plays as well as the property list contained in Philip Henslowe's *Diary*. Yet taken all in all, the number of items, either mentioned in the scripts or listed by Henslowe, is small indeed. Benches and stools, tables and beds, were introduced frequently enough. But clear evidence of more substantial units, such as steps, rocks, trees, painted cloths, and so forth, is sparse. As for representational scenery, there is virtually no sign that it was ever employed in the public playhouses. In *Troilus and Cressida* Achilles stands within the opening of his tent (II, iii). In *As You Like It* Orlando hangs verses upon a tree (III, ii). Yet the enclosure and the stage pillars could serve respectively the needs of the stage business. But even were we to accept such references as evidence of actual settings, the list would still be small. Of the many scenes composing the plays written by Shakespeare for the Globe between 1599 and 1609 only twenty per cent require any stage furniture or facility whatsoever. The rest need nothing but a bare stage, actors, and an audience.

Given these facts, it is evident that the actors could not rely on the stage façade or scenery to inform the spectator of scene location. The texts of the plays themselves illustrate why this was so. Neither in Shakespearean nor non-Shakespearean plays does the sequence of scenes depend on regular alternation of locales. Instead of being confined to a few sites which could be associated with specific entries or represented by distinctive scenery, the scenes peregrinate. *Macbeth* shifts from heaths to palaces, from Forres to Inverness to Fife to England to Dunsinane. None of the three entries presumed for the Globe stage could long retain association with any specific locale, and indeed the very effort to find correspondence between stage scenery and dramatic site betrays a misunderstanding of localization in Shakespeare's plays. Though at times Shakespeare specifies a particular place for a scene, such as the Capitol in *Julius Caesar* (III, i) or omits any localization, as in the scene between Ross and the Old Man in *Macbeth* (II, iv), the vast majority of scenes are given a *generalized* localization. When Antony meets Octavius in Rome, he meets him not in any specific part of Rome but in Rome as a whole. Cleopatra awaits him in an idea of Egypt. To apply our conception of space, in which a locale must be congruent with physical reality, would be an error. Instead we must cultivate the concept that when Macduff goes to England he goes to the image of England as it represents the alternative to hellish Scotland.

Within such a frame of reference and given the ubiquity

of the narrative Elizabethan drama, scenery·could not readily serve to indicate place. To do so consistently would have required either far more entrance points or far more scenic units than there is any indication that the London stages ever possessed. What then could have been the purpose of the objects that were introduced? First, of course, there was a utilitarian purpose. Stools must be sat on, tables must be set for banquets. Such furniture was usually brought on by servants in view of the audience. Beds, chairs, and thrones might also be carried on. What is interesting is that certain of these properties were employed conventionally. Sometimes a wounded or a sick person is carried on stage seated in a chair (*Lear*, IV, vii; *Othello*, V, ii). In addition, there are other signs, in the employment of stools, for instance, or in the entrance of ghosts at one door and exit at another, that similar types of action were staged in recurrent patterns. A second purpose begins to appear when we look closely at specific examples. A tree, as we have seen, could be represented by the stage pillars when it was needed for climbing or posting verses. But what of a tree that represents an idea such as the life of a man? Then it is no longer a mere piece of stage machinery, but an emblem. Such a tree was employed by the Lord Chamberlain's men in *A Warning for Fair Women*. That a scenic tree was actually introduced is confirmed by the stage directions for chopping it down. In *Macbeth* the cauldron, though it has a practical use, is also emblematic of the hellish forces released by the witches. In both *Macbeth* and *A Warning for Fair Women*, these scenic objects rise through the floor of the stage. In *The Devil's Charter*, also a Chamberlain–King's men play, scenic monsters rise from below the platform. Again we see that similar types of scenes employ similar staging. Both the nature of the objects and the manner of their introduction reveal that, though scenic elements were utilized sparingly, when they were utilized, they tended to have emblematic significance and were intended to excite wonder.

In the fullest sense, the stage itself was an emblem of the universe. The loft above the stage, located under the shadow or half-roof, was termed the "heavens." Out of it gods might drop. The space beneath the stage was the hell out of which devils might spring. A trap in the center of the platform provided access from below or, with need, could serve as Ophelia's grave. Between heaven and hell rose the façade of earthly life. Just as we never quite lose the sense that we are peeping into someone's home in the picture-frame theatre, so, we might suppose, the Globe audience never quite shook off the impression that it was witnessing events on a "more universal stage" than the one it sat before.

For the actors the stage and its façade served its purpose by theatricalizing and generalizing their actions. Though the façade was passive, altered minimally from play to play, its height and grandeur gave extra dimension to the dramatic narrative. Coupled with sumptuous garments, any one of which might cost more than all the scenery for a play, the façade presented a glorified pageant of life. The costumes were contemporary, yet more rich than those worn by the ordinary spectator. It was as though a new play to-day were combined with a fashion parade. The total effect of the stage must have been astonishing, intensifying the natural exuberance of the Elizabethan courtier and citizen. Would the impact of Hamlet's black garment be so striking were it not for a courtly dazzle of color? Perhaps the actors did not regard the stage so much as a dramatic instrument, but as a means for displaying their own magnificence.

The psychological impact of the Elizabethan stage can not be underestimated. However, its impact in shaping the dramatic narrative has been overestimated. The actors continued to perform elsewhere than at the Globe, and though they chiefly relied upon the Globe for their livelihood, they had not had long practice in tying their methods to a fixed stage space. Therefore, the factors that helped to shape a performance were inherent in the relations of the actors to one another and to the script. Shakespeare's plays are full of theatrical devices that do not make use of stage machinery or furniture. Observing a character without being seen (*Troilus and Cressida*, V, ii), holding a trial (*Measure for Measure*, V, i), engaging in single combat (*Hamlet*, V, ii), pleading for a boon (*Coriolanus*, V, iii) recur again and again. Hardly a story unfolds at Shakespeare's hands that does not have at least one figure in disguise. Other stage conventions, such as asides and soliloquies, help to give form to the dramatic narrative. These devices, far more than the physical stage, are instrumental in imparting theatrical life to the plays.

Underlying all of these stage conventions is the insistent impulse to juxtapose one event with another, one image with another, one character with another. Hamlet, Laertes, and Fortinbras are continual reflectors of one another. In hearing the player's speech on Priam's death, Hamlet sees the image of what he should do. The texture of a Shakespearean play is rich with such correspondence. Only rarely, however, is such juxtaposition manifested scenically. The tent of Richmond and the tent of Richard, placed simultaneously upon the stage platform, is one of the infrequent instances. Instead, theatrical juxtaposition was projected in three concurrent ways.

(1) *Poetically*. Recurrent images or phrases, like musical motifs, wind their way through the narrative, their significance not merely being in repetition but in the way in which the inner states of the characters are evoked through the images. Here the rhetorical skill of the actor was of prime importance.

(2) *Narratively*. The form of the narrative emerges from the way one scene contrasts or parallels another. For example, Banquo's and Duncan's admiration of the peaceful setting of Inverness (I, vi) contrasts with the scenes between Macbeth and Lady Macbeth which precede and follow. Lady Macbeth's invocation to the powers of darkness (I, v) is paralleled by Macbeth's later invocation (III, ii), thus stressing the transformation of Macbeth. Here the acting as well as conventional staging of recurrent devices would heighten the narrative juxtaposition.

(3) *Spatially*. The abundant use of asides, eavesdropping, and disguise give depth to the action within scenes. Events were perceived not in themselves alone, but as they were filtered through the words of a commentator or the eyes of an observer. The encounter between Hamlet and Ophelia in the so-called nunnery scene (III, i) reaches us not only directly but as it is heard by the unseen but present King and Polonius. This multi-faceted dramatic space is inherent in the structure of the plays. The use of a curtain is merely a minor contribution to the theatrical presentation.

How conscious an artist was Shakespeare? His fellow-players, Heminge and Condell, reported that they received his manuscripts of the plays with hardly a correction. Perhaps he was painstaking and made clean copies. Perhaps he wrote in such heat that his thought and hand went together. Yet neither conscious creation nor unconscious expression can be divorced. Shakespeare was steeped in his trade (and it was a trade). As we have seen, he was an actor for many years, possibly throughout his career. He was a dependable dramatist, producing an average of nearly two plays every year. He was a playhouse owner. Perhaps his very immersion in all these aspects of theatre erased the distinction between conscious and unconscious, for a man cannot work at a profession for so long and still distinguish the part of a work that is planned from the part that flows easily from his being. Shakespeare breathed drama. We are all familiar with the way he imagines the theatre and the world as embodiments of each other. "All the world's a stage." Man is "a poor player / That struts and frets his hour upon the stage." The fortunes of kings are analogous to the conditions of performing, for

> As in a theatre the eyes of men,
> After a well-graced actor leaves the stage,
> Are idly bent on him that enters next,
> Thinking his prattle to be tedious,
> Even so, or with much more contempt, men's eyes
> Did scowl on gentle Richard.

In his writing the conventional image of world-as-theatre and man-as-actor became a profound analogue of the human journey on earth. To realize that analogue Shakespeare utilized the resources of his theatre – actors especially – more fully than any other writer of his day. By being completely of the theatre, he transcended it.

Columbia University   BERNARD BECKERMAN

BIBLIOGRAPHY

The standard collection of materials on stage history until the death of Shakespeare is Sir Edmund Chambers, *The Elizabethan Stage*, 4 vols (1923). For primary materials see Sir Walter Greg, *Dramatic Documents from the Elizabethan Playhouses*, 2 vols (1931), *Henslowe's Diary*, 2 vols (1904–08), *Henslowe Papers* (1907). The *Diary* has been re-edited by R. A. Foakes and R. T. Rickert (1961). For a history of the theatres see Joseph Q. Adams, *Shakespearean Playhouses* (1917). Theatrical building is discussed in John C. Adams, *The Globe Playhouse* (rev. ed. 1961); Irwin Smith, *Shakespeare's Globe Playhouse* (1956) and *Shakespeare's Blackfriars Playhouse* (1964). The prevailing view of the stage facilities appears in C. Walter Hodges, *The Globe Restored* (1956); A. M. Nagler, *Shakespeare's Stage* (1958); Richard Southern and others in *Shakespeare Survey*, ed. Allardyce Nicoll, Vol. XII (1959). Richard Hosley has in preparation an exhaustive work on the subject. For methods of production see Ashley H. Thorndike, *Shakespeare's Theater* (1916); W. J. Lawrence, *The Physical Conditions of the Elizabethan Public Playhouse* (1927), *Pre-Restoration Stage Studies* (1927); George Reynolds, *The Staging of Elizabethan Plays at the Red Bull Theater* (1940); Alfred Harbage, *Theatre for Shakespeare* (1955); Bernard Beckerman, *Shakespeare at the Globe* (1962). The audience is described in Alfred Harbage, *Shakespeare's Audience* (1941).

SHAKESPEARE'S TECHNIQUE

$\mathscr{M}$odern plays are designed for publication as well as performance. The publication sometimes comes first. Elizabethan plays were designed only for performance, and publication, if it occurred at all, was incidental. Available to the reader is a theatrical document which was called by the actors "the book of the play." The *play* was the stage presentation of the dialogue and implied action contained in the *book*. Shakespeare's "books" (we would say "scripts") make good reading for their literary qualities alone, but they make better reading if we stage them in our minds, with awareness of the sense of theatre underlying them. The playwright's technique can be given only token treatment in a single essay: what follows is a sketch-map of territory demanding an atlas.

The most convenient approach is through the readily identifiable features of a script: its length, the structural units into which it is divided, its designated speakers, and the forms of discourse in which the speeches are composed. The comparative analysis provided in Table II* shows that a Shakespearean script may contain as many as 3776 lines or as few as 1756, as many as 37 scenes or as few as 7, as many as 46 speakers or as few as 14; and that the blank verse, rhymed verse, and prose in which the dialogue is written occurs in widely varying proportions, from as much as 95 per cent blank verse in one play to as little as 10 per cent in another, from as much as 86 per cent prose or 45 per cent rhymed verse in certain plays to as little as the vanishing point in certain others. However, the extreme figures are deceptive, since each represents an exceptional feature of a play which in other respects is normal enough. If averages are taken of all thirty-seven plays in the accepted canon, a composite picture is obtained which is representative of most of the plays in most respects. The typical Shakespearean script contains 2700 lines (67 per cent of them blank verse, 9 per cent rhymed verse, and 24 per cent prose), 19 scenes, and a cast of 23 men and 4 women, exclusive of extras. No single play conforms exactly to this pattern – *The Merchant of Venice* comes closest – but it provides a reliable basis of discussion.

A 2700-line-play could have been performed in the Elizabethan public theatres in two-and-a-half hours, with one five- or ten-minute medial interval. Although the existing evidence is not conclusive, it suggests that plays were performed by Shakespeare's company, while he was an active member of it, either without intervals or with only one, as in *Mankind*, the earliest extant play of the popular repertory. Even a good reader is rarely able to

take in a Shakespearean play in two-and-a-half hours on his first encounter. He is apt to conclude that even a good listener at the Globe could not have done so either, but it must be remembered that the original spectators were familiar with the idiom, that the actors were highly skilled elocutionists who could bring out meaning, and that in the theatre as distinct from the study no problem of visualization was entailed. The whole play was provided, not simply the spoken lines. The fact that the plays were designed for actual performances of limited duration, not for leisurely analysis, had, of course, a bearing upon the author's technique. So long as he could provide immediate interest and sustain its forward thrust, keeping the audience moving on the emotional current of the play, he need not be precise about minor points of fact and logic. Questions do not arise when there is no time to ask them.

At certain points in the plays, where a logical fallacy threatens to become too obvious to escape notice, Shakespeare cleverly diverts attention. For instance, in *Much Ado about Nothing*, Margaret could have punctured at once Don John's slander of Hero just by saying that it was she and not her mistress who conversed with Borachio from her mistress's chamber window. In other words, the whole villainous scheme is quite impractical. That Shakespeare was aware of the fact, and of the danger that the audience would detect it, is evident in his whisking Margaret out of sight during the period of the scheme's success. Out of sight, out of mind – even readers often fail to ask why Margaret does not speak up and save Hero. If our attention is called to this detail of technique, we are apt to feel that we have been tricked. (Robert Bridges complained sorrowfully of the "dishonesty of means" employed by Shakespeare even in *Macbeth*.) But we will be reconciled if we think in terms of alternatives. Shakespeare could easily have made the scheme practical by making Margaret corrupt – in fact she is somewhat so in the source story – but he preferred a bit of faulty logic covered by a bit of sleight-of-hand to widening the area of corruption in what was, after all, a comedy. Margaret is back in the play in the last scene dancing with the other innocents. We can scarcely say that her perverse silence is now forgotten if we never noticed it in the first place. In this, as in many similar instances, analysis reveals that a deliberate choice has been made – and a right one if in works of art artistic reasons should prevail. A reader who notices factual and logical discrepancies should notice as well their triviality or their artistic utility.

The general form of the Shakespearean play was the product of theatrical heredity and environment, and these were English, not Greco-Roman. It does not diminish the

* The count of lines is based upon the Pelican thirty-eight-volume edition. It would vary slightly in the present edition since the narrower column increases somewhat the number of lines in prose. The number of scenes is that determined by a cleared stage marked in the Pelican text by a star. The count of characters excludes the extras and the speakers of a line or two grouped by the editors at the foot of each *dramatis personae*. The count of songs excludes some of the ballad fragments. (In general these statistics are approximate, intended for comparative purposes only.)

TABLE II: COMPARATIVE ANALYSIS

	Total Lines	% Blank	% Rhyme	% Prose	Scenes	Casts Men	Women	Songs	Longest roles (with count for those over 500 lines)
COMEDIES									
Errors	1756	65.8	21.5	12.7	11	11	5		Antipholus S., Adriana, Dromio S.
Shrew	2584	72.5	5.8	21.7	12	19	4	2	Petruchio (549), Tranio, Kate
T.G.V	2199	68.7	5.8	25.5	19	13	3	1	Proteus, Valentine, Julia
Dream	2106	35.4	45.5	19.1	7	15	6	2	Theseus, Helena, Bottom
L.L.L.	2667	21.8	43.1	35.1	9	13	5	2	Berowne (591), Navarre, Princess
Merchant	2564	73.5	5.5	21.0	19	16	3	1	Portia (565), Shylock, Bassanio
A.Y.L.	2636	35.2	10.3	54.5	22	17	4	5	Rosalind (668), Orlando, Touchstone
Much Ado	2549	25.3	3.0	71.7	17	14	4	2	Benedick, Leonato, Don Pedro
Twelfth Night	2423	31.4	7.3	61.3	18	11	3	4	Toby, Viola, Feste
Merry Wives	2598	9.6	3.8	86.6	21	16	4	1	Falstaff, Mrs Page, Mr Ford
All's Well	2760	43.6	10.3	46.1	23	8	6		Helena, Parolles, King
Measure	2671	59.0	3.4	37.6	15	17	5	1	Vincentio (820), Isabella, Lucio
HISTORIES									
1 Henry VI	2676	88.0	11.9	0.1	19	39	3		Talbot, Joan, York
2 Henry VI	3062	82.1	3.2	14.7	18	43	4		York, Margaret, Henry
3 Henry VI	2902	95.5	4.4	0.1	22	40	3		Warwick, Edward, Richard
Richard III	3602	93.8	4.4	1.8	23	40	5		Richard (1124), Buckingham, Elizabeth
John	2560	94.9	5.1	0.0	15	18	4		Faulconbridge (520), John, Constance
Richard II	2755	80.9	19.1	0.0	18	26	5		Richard (753), Bolingbroke, York
1 Henry IV	2954	54.3	2.7	43.0	17	32	3		Falstaff (585), Hotspur (545), Hal (535)
2 Henry IV	3182	48.7	2.6	48.7	17	39	5	1	Falstaff (593), Hal, Henry
Henry V	3176	57.2	3.2	39.6	20	39	4		Henry (1025), Fluellen, Canterbury
Henry VIII	2804	95.1	2.6	2.3	16	36	4	1	Henry, Wolsey, Katherine
TRAGEDIES									
Titus	2521	93.2	5.2	1.6	13	21	3		Titus (687), Aaron, Marcus
Romeo	2964	71.0	16.6	12.4	21	21	4	1	Romeo (591), Juliet (509), Laurence
Caesar	2453	92.5	1.3	6.2	13	36	2		Brutus (701), Cassius, Antony
Hamlet	3776	66.3	5.7	28.0	20	25	2	3	Hamlet (1422), Claudius (540), Polonius
Troilus	3326	63.0	6.1	30.9	18	24	4	1	Troilus, Ulysses, Pandarus
Othello	3228	78.4	3.1	18.5	15	14	3	3	Iago (1097), Othello (860), Desdemona
Lear	3195	69.9	5.3	24.8	22	22	3	4	Lear (697), Edgar, Kent
Macbeth	2113	80.3	12.1	7.6	26	25	7		Macbeth (681), Lady Macbeth, Malcolm
Timon	2281	66.4	7.0	26.6	17	27	2		Timon (795), Apemantus, Flavius
Antony	3019	90.5	1.3	8.2	36	30	4	1	Antony (766), Cleopatra (622), Caesar
Coriolanus	3294	77.4	0.8	21.8	27	29	4		Coriolanus (809), Menenius, Volumnia
ROMANCES									
Pericles	2322	59.7	22.4	17.9	22	22	7		Pericles (592), Marina, Simonides
Cymbeline	3266	79.9	6.3	13.8	23	24	3	2	Imogen (522), Posthumus, Iachimo
Winter's Tale	2946	71.5	3.1	25.4	14	15	6	6	Leontes (648), Paulina, Autolycus
Tempest	2026	71.4	7.5	21.1	9	15	4	7	Prospero (603), Ariel, Caliban

importance of the classical influence upon English drama of the Renaissance to say that it produced not a new form but a newly-sharpened sense of form. The basic form remained native, and quite distinct from the Greco-Roman form described by Aristotle and prescribed by Horace. When the latter said that there must be no more than five acts, and that no fourth actor should speak, and when neo-classical critics formulated rules about unity of time, place, and action, they were projecting what Shakespeare's Polonius called "scene individable" as distinct from "poem unlimited." The typical Elizabethan play was "poem unlimited" – even most of those of the private theatres which deferred superficially to the five-act prescription by providing four musical interludes in the course of performance. The number of episodes was not limited to five, the number of speakers in a scene to three, the time to a single day, the place to a single town, and the action to a single tragic event or comic intrigue. In classical drama the "episode" or "act" was a continuous action originally separated from the rest by a choric ode. Any change of personnel because of an entrance or exit during this action was viewed as a signal for a new "scene" by later editors of classical texts. If we apply this terminology to Shakespearean structure, we must say that, although lacking in choric odes (as was Roman comedy), his plays contain from 7 to 36 "acts" with the average number 19, and the "acts" contain anywhere from one "scene" (as when the Herald reads a proclamation in *Othello*, II, ii) to more than a dozen (as in the remarkable succession of incidents in *Hamlet*, II, ii). If the terms are not applicable, then neither are the theoretical principles of structure habitually attached to them. There is no use discussing a Shakespearean nineteen-part play as if it were a classical or Italian five-part play, regardless of how editors have arranged and labelled the parts or critics have striven to rationalize their functions as thus arbitrarily arranged.

Shakespeare's manuscripts, on the evidence of the printed quartos and the *Sir Thomas More* manuscript, contained no structural labels whatever. They consisted of stretches of dialogue introduced by entrances and concluded by exits, with a cleared stage in between. The cleared stage signalled a shift in time or place or both. For convenience we call these "scenes," and by however much they may exceed or fall short of the average number of nineteen, they are structural units which may be intelligibly discussed, both in respect to their internal organization and their relation to each other. It is one of the curiosities of Shakespearean criticism that it has offered so little analysis of scenic structure as compared with analysis of characters in the last century, and of images in the present one. Perhaps the reason is that the subject has lain fog-bound in the exhalation of the phantom "acts" which have diverted or baffled inquiry.

A scene could present a single incident in a few lines of dialogue or monologue, or a long succession of incidents in hundreds of lines (and there is virtue in variety), but the basic problem in constructing a scene was to include as much as possible of what Hamlet calls the "necessary" matter of the play without seeming to be yielding to mere expedience. The material included must be so connected as to give the scene functional identity. In *2 Henry IV*, IV, iv, Westmoreland brings the King tidings that Bishop Scroop and his fellow-rebels have been subdued. Im-

mediately thereafter Harcourt brings tidings that the northern borders have been secured. Having heard these messengers, Henry feels the hand of death upon him – "And wherefore should these good news make me sick?" – and there follows his last poignant encounter with the son and heir he fears will fritter away the realm he has won. Now these victories mentioned by Westmoreland and Harcourt really occurred some years apart, and the second of them some years before Henry died. They are reported to him in the last moments of his reign not because there is no earlier place more convenient but because there is no place at all more meaningful. This is a most elementary illustration, but it shows that a Shakespearean scene is not a collection of historical or fictitious details but a selection of dramatic units.

The more interesting of the scenes from the standpoint of internal organization are opening ones, in which keynotes are being struck, and those great full-dress scenes involving most of the cast, usually occurring in the second half of the play and fairly far along in it – like the abdication scene in *Richard II*, the trial scene in *The Merchant of Venice*, or the mouse-trap scene in *Hamlet*. The opening scene of *Hamlet* is a stunning success in its creation of atmosphere, its immediate thrill, and its opening of future possibilities, while the mouse-trap scene is a theatrical *tour de force* unparalleled. However, since there is space for only one illustration, we may choose a scene where the principle of organization is less apparent than in these. *Hamlet*, II, ii, contains 591 lines, almost one-sixth of the play's total, and, at first glance, the strangest assortment of miscellaneous matter imaginable. King Claudius interviews Rosencrantz and Guildenstern, and then his ambassadors from Norway; Polonius proclaims to him and Gertrude that he has discovered the nature of Hamlet's "madness"; the royal couple depart as Hamlet enters and engages in elaborate mockery of Polonius; Rosencrantz and Guildenstern come to him to probe his state of mind, and are regaled with a disquisition upon "this goodly frame the earth" and "what a piece of work is a man"; a troupe of players arrives, and there is extended chit-chat about theatrical affairs; then, at Hamlet's request, a rendition of Aeneas' tale to Dido by the First Player; finally an agreement is struck for the troupe to play "The Murder of Gonzago" on the following evening, and Hamlet is left alone to soliloquize, "O, what a rogue and peasant slave am I!" How can all this be anything but a casual medley? At the very least, one might say, the scene breaks in two, since the first part belongs so clearly to Claudius and the second so clearly to Hamlet. Actually, however, the single extraneous element or "convenience" in this chain of incidents is Claudius' interview with the ambassadors, which might truly have been introduced elsewhere. The scene does not break in two. Although Claudius dominates its opening, his mind is focussed upon Hamlet, and although Hamlet dominates its close, his mind is focussed upon Claudius. Through its middle the instruments of the one (Polonius, Rosencrantz, Guildenstern) are being received and countered by the other. The only ones not sent by Claudius, the strolling players, are fastened upon by Hamlet as instruments of his own. The theatrical comment does appear casual and dilated, but there is thematic relevance in the parallel drawn between the new dispensation in the theatre and the new dispensation in the court of Denmark, and between imaginary and genuine occasions for "passion." Mark Van Doren has compared the scene to a spider's web, which will vibrate throughout if a single strand is touched. Only organic interconnectedness could be the occasion for such praise.

impression of a single entity rather than an assembly of parts. (An indication of this is the fact that even those quite familiar with one of these plays are rarely able to give even a fair estimate of the number of scenes in it.) Since Shakespeare followed the method of his day in

C. WALTER HODGES

The relation of scene to scene reveals the same kind of planning as the relation of incident to incident within scenes. In the first place, the decisions about which episodes to show, which to present by means of allusion, and which to leave to the inference of the audience, are made with an eye to maximum economy and impact; and in the second, the scenes are so interwoven that a play, however heterogeneous its materials, leaves one with an

presenting episodes in linear order, that is without chronological "flash-backs," he had to achieve suppleness by playing free with time and making the linear order more ostensible than real. He reserved the right of choice in placing an episode in one place rather than another. In the first scene of *Measure for Measure* Duke Vincentio is shown departing on a foreign mission after leaving Angelo in absolute command in Vienna. In the second scene

Claudio is shown under arrest and in danger of execution because of the new rigor with which Angelo administers the law. In the third scene the Duke is shown telling Friar Thomas that his foreign mission is a fiction, and that he will remain in Vienna disguised as a friar to watch how Angelo uses his power. Now obviously it would take less time for the Duke to establish contact with Friar Thomas than for Angelo to put into execution the reform of Vienna, so that from a logical viewpoint the second and third scenes should be transposed. To do so, however, would be to spoil the dramatic effect of Claudio's arrest. His emotions would seem excessive, and our interest in them would be languid, if we knew that Angelo was wielding only the easily-revoked power of a puppet. The present arrangement of the scenes intensifies our sense of the pain of a character's dilemma. The next time the Duke makes an appearance is in a scene interpolated between the two scenes in which Angelo receives Isabella's plea for clemency for her brother Claudio and makes the granting of the plea conditional upon her prostituting herself to him. In this case the reminder of the Duke's secret supervisory power mitigates the pain of a character's dilemma, at least for the audience, and allows us to respond with emotional approval to Isabella's rejection of Angelo's proposal.

How boldly utilitarian the scene arrangement can be is illustrated in *Antony and Cleopatra*. During the central portion of the play Antony is absent from Egypt, but Cleopatra must be kept in our view since her relationship with him governs the action even though she has no active part in it. She is shown in II, v, receiving in rage a message of Antony's marriage to Octavia, and in III, iii, a description of the bride from the same messenger. In the interim time-consuming Roman councils of state and military campaigns are shown in a succession of scenes. Analysis (such as we do not make in the theatre) reveals that a single episode has been widely split into II, v and III, iii, for good tactical reasons in defiance of chronology. To ask why two scenes are employed rather than one, or one rather than two, or why a particular scene occurs where it does rather than earlier or later in the play, or why another is included at all when at first glance it seems dispensable, is to gain a sense of the playwright's theatrical acumen, an awareness of his technique. Certainly there is more "exposition" in earlier than in later scenes, more "complication" as one scene follows another, and certainly "climax" will precede rather than follow "resolution" and "denouement," but there is small reward in discovering things which may be taken for granted in the first place. Appreciation increases as we recognize that each of his plays presented its author with a different structural problem which he solved in a different way.

Shakespeare's company of actors was sufficiently large and versatile to give him an almost completely free hand in the number and kind of characters he could employ. There had to be a part or parts for the stellar performers, of serious or comic roles, but this was the reverse of a restriction. Since each of the sharers in the company was an accomplished professional, the characters did not have to be tailored to limited skills, with a resultant reduction of diversity. The only grave restriction was that the number of women characters must be kept low since only a few actors in any given year were capable of effective female impersonation. By the time an apprentice was sufficiently

skilled, he was near the age when his voice would change and he would have to pass on to youthful male roles. Otherwise the theatrical situation was such as to offer maximum opportunity for the writer to tap the resources of his observation and imagination, and to create whatever characters his fable required.

Shakespeare's "characters" tend to induce critical intoxication, and we should try to keep our heads. Although scores of them are memorable, scores even of "minor" characters, it is an exaggeration to say that every one of the thousand who people the thirty-seven plays seems a fully-realized human being. In plays with very full casts, especially the histories and Roman tragedies, a number of characters are given only the coloration of their factions. As a matter of fact it would be an artistic flaw if there were none with the kind of neutrality possessed by walk-on characters in public life. However, in these, as in all the plays dating from about 1595 on, there is a nucleus of characters, some major and some minor, so distinct and so successfully creating the illusion that they are acting upon their own rather than the author's initiative that we have come to think of them as real people. If we ask by what means, by the use of what "technique," characters like these are created, we will get unexpected answers. Ordinarily a dramatic character may be considered the product, or at least the common denominator, of what he does in the play, what he says, the way he says things, and what others say about him. Now it has often been observed that, with Shakespeare's characterizations, there is "life-like" inconsistency within and between each of these four classes of data, and it has even been suggested that inconsistency *per se* is the Shakespearean virtue. Our minds reject this premise, and rightly, because the merest tyro in literary endeavor can achieve inconsistency, usually without trying. The fact is that, whatever the degree of consistency or inconsistency they show, the four classes of data do not account in full for the impression made by any one of the characters.

Since Shakespeare's methods were applied with more emphasis (and less subtlety) in the creation of Iago than of comparably well-known characters, they can be conveniently illustrated through him. What he does in the play, of course, is fiendish. What he says is often so "moral" that it has become proverbial – "Our bodies are our gardens . . . ," "Who steals my purse steals trash . . . ," "How poor are they that have not patience . . . ," "Jealousy! It is the green-eyed monster . . . ," etc. etc. His way of saying things is often engagingly witty, even humorous. Others keep saying about him that he is "honest" and "kind." Now we may dismiss as surplus evidence of his successful hypocrisy everything but his deeds, and say that Iago is what he does. In a sense this is true, but the statement requires a supplement. What he does is what all villains do, prey upon the well-being of others, but Iago is not like all villains. His distinction is that he preys with such relish that evil seems his good. Othello has promoted another officer above him, and he mentions (so casually as to seem scarcely to believe it himself) that Othello may have lain with his wife. We speak of such details as "motivation" of his acts, and observe that they seem strangely inadequate. At this point we begin to realize that his "character" is being determined not simply by what he does but by the "character" of the one to whom he does it. Then our eyes shift to

Desdemona, and we discern a special kind of consistency. If what he does to Othello is inadequately motivated, what he does to Desdemona is not motivated at all. From her he has suffered not even fancied wrongs. But although she trusts him so fully that she turns to him for help, he destroys her without mercy. Our conception of the "character" of Iago derives in large measure from our perception of relationships.

The loyalty of Kent is a trait of character inseparable from the character traits of the man he is loyal to. Our conception of Lear's own character derives not solely from what he does, what he says, the way he says things, and what others say about him, but also from what characters like Kent and Cordelia are willing to do for him. In a word the characterizations of Lear, Kent, and Cordelia are interwoven; and this interweaving extends into all the other characterizations, and all the actions and words of the play. We may say, then, that Shakespeare's "technique" in creating characters involves his refusal to give a character an identity extricable from the dramatic world of which he is a part. We can corral off one of his characters, a Hamlet, Falstaff, or Shylock, and say interesting things about him – his "motives," his "psychology," even his "unconscious" – but we will always feel (at least our listeners will) that the most important things are being left unsaid. It is a little like discussing a "detail" in a master painting without reference to the whole composition. There is, to be sure, a basic consistency in the plays. The total of what is said and done corresponds closely enough to the total of those who speak and do, but the impression of truth conveyed by the characters resides in no such neat equation. The characters seem real to us because, like real people, they are part of each other; and because they are never fully revealed to our view. We see, again as in real life, only their aspects which circumstance turns our way, so that a touch of mystery remains – human mystery. The tests to which they are so constantly submitted bear no resemblance to Binet tests, and they are never revolved on turntables like anatomical specimens.

An apparent "inconsistency" in *Macbeth* is the treacherousness of the Thane and his Lady to everyone else, and their devoted loyalty to each other. They betray every bond except the marriage bond. If Lady Macbeth craves for queenly state, she gives little sign of it in the play. What she seems to want is for her husband to have what he wants. He in turn seems to admire her, trust her, and yearn to live up to her "image" of him. These are loving murderers. But they destroy each other as surely as they destroy Duncan, Banquo, and the rest of their victims. The consistency of the conception lies in the fact that love can be as self-defeating and lethal as any other passion if the lovers are morally obtuse. The language of the play places in constant juxtaposition images of tenderness and callousness, of creation and destruction, so that tapestry and design seem one.

Of all the aspects of Shakespeare's technique his use of language provides the most inexhaustible subject for analysis. Although the style is predominantly monosyllabic, the vocabulary employed is the largest in any single body of creative writing extant. All the rhetorical devices used by Renaissance writers to give shape and sharpness to expression are constantly employed. The variety and aptness of the images are such that a symbolic language largely supplants the language of literal state-

ment. All these facts are easily demonstrated, but a great difficulty remains. Words can be counted, and images can be detached from a play and set down on paper. Ideas about these words and images can also be set down on paper, sometimes in a very persuasive way. The trouble is that the ideas cannot be detached from the play. What was said about the hazard involved in isolating a character from the remaining characters and the action applies with greater force to isolating details of language since the resulting distortion is apt to be more insidious. The way in which the words do things at a given moment is so closely-knit with what they do that all quotation is more or less "out of context."

To illustrate first the resourcefulness of the language a few routine lines may be cited. Malcolm asks Ross about the progress of Macbeth's bloody reign:

> MALCOLM What's the newest grief?
> ROSS That of an hour's age doth hiss the speaker;
> Each minute teems a new one. (IV, iii, 174–76)

The word 'grief' standing in place of some unspecified occurrence substitutes effect for cause in the figure known as "metonymy." Its value here is that it is economical, takes us at once to a human response, and compels us to participate in the creative process by imagining the unmentioned cause. The next line activates a more complex interpretive process, since it assumes our awareness that anyone who repeats old jokes or bits of information as if they were new will be met with contempt, just as a troupe which performs a stale play will be hissed. In Scotland outrages are occurring so fast that an account of one which occurred an hour ago is already stale news. The statement as a whole is "hyperbole," with words again used figuratively as "hiss the speaker" is substituted for "cause the speaker to be hissed." The active form of the verb is retained even though the hissers are circuited out of the statement. In the next line the word "teems" (meaning literally "brings forth"), although applying to a single outrage, suggests a whole brood or swarm of outrages. The example is useful because, without being notably beautiful or profound, it shows how the author conveys meaning through illustrative objects, actions, feelings, associations, even when there are no overt "images," and how a current of life seems to move beneath the words.

It is a style in which something is always *happening*, and especially right for drama, the root meaning of which is "happenings." Shakespeare's style is dramatic in more than a general way since the language at a particular point will seem the natural growth of the particular dramatic climate. As Nemesis approaches Macbeth, the doctor attending his lady does his duty in fear – "I think, but dare not speak." In the next scene Angus says that Macbeth's followers now "move only in command" and "nothing in love." The next scene opens with Macbeth tongue-lashing a cringing servant. Between this incident and his summoning of Seyton comes his soliloquy,

> My way of life
> Is fall'n into the sear, the yellow leaf,
> And that which should accompany old age,
> As honor, love, obedience, troops of friends,
> I must not look to have; but in their stead,
> Curses not loud but deep, mouth-honor, breath,
> Which the poor heart would fain deny, and dare not.
> (V, iii, 22–28)

The image "poor heart" is not showy, but none could seem more inevitable. It rings true because it is true to a context which has been established by visual as well as verbal means. The heart was the presumed seat of love, courage, and loyalty. In the figure known as "synecdoche" it here designates a human being, *poor* because, subservient to Macbeth, he is pitifully denied the chance to exercise his capacity for love, courage, loyalty. We have heard Angus say "nothing in love" and the doctor "I think, but dare not speak." There is always a slight sense of strain when critics cite a verbal link like "dare not" here and in the soliloquy because there are other links so strong. We have just seen Macbeth's servant obeying in fear, and we are about to see his officer obey like a cold automaton. And, of course, the words are exercising their power upon us whether or not we are aware that such things as "metonymy" or "synecdoche" are being employed.

Prospero tells Miranda that Ferdinand seems handsome to her only because she has seen no other men; compared with others he is a Caliban. She replies,

> My affections
> Are then most humble. I have no ambition
> To see a goodlier man.   (I, ii, 482–84)

The only distinction of these words (and it is enough) is that they are just right for this girl on this island at this moment. Civilly addressed to the father who has taught her civility, their contradiction seems just barely a contradiction, their rebuke just barely a rebuke, as the finality of her commitment to Ferdinand is expressed. When Juliet responds to her mother's question about her thoughts of marriage – "It is an honor that I dream not of" – we may attempt a verbal analysis, but the net we try to cast around the words will never be large enough to hold the poet's imagination. Whatever her words say, they murmur of Juliet's whole past and future, which is to say that they reverberate through the play. Mere richness does not account for the effect even of the richest passages, and when richness is not in order, the style becomes simple and spare. When Lear's face is turned up to the lord of storms, he speaks with stormy majesty:

> You sulph'rous and thought-executing fires,
> Vaunt-couriers of oak-cleaving thunderbolts,
> Singe my white head...   (III, ii, 4–6)

but when his eyes fall upon his whimpering fool, he speaks another language,

> Come on, my boy. How dost, my boy? Art cold?
> I am cold myself.   (III, ii, 68–69)

Illustrated here is the suitability of style to context – and also something of which the reader must be warned, the slight misrepresentation always occurring when we juxtapose excerpts. Although the above passages occur *near* each other in a scene, they do not appear *next* each other, and hence the style-shift is not nearly so emphatic as the quotations make it seem. There has been a realignment of the various elements that create the scene as a whole so that it is not the style alone that has changed. In hearing both passages we seem to be hearing the natural sounds of the world of the play, and this is far better than consciously hearing the wide range of the poet's voice.

There remains the subject of the formal characteristics and the various uses of the three media of expression: blank verse, rhymed verse, and prose. The prose need not be defined, but we should note that it is sufficiently rhythmic, and sufficiently rich in imagery and rhetorical design that it can appear side by side with verse without risk of incongruity. The rhymed verse is of many kinds, comic doggerel, quatrains, the various stanzaic patterns of songs, the short jingling lines of incantations, etc., but by far the greatest part of it consists of iambic pentameter couplets – that is ten-syllable lines of alternating unstressed and stressed syllables, rhyming in pairs. The following is an example from *Richard II*, which contains twice as much rhymed verse as the average 9 per cent of all lines:

> KING Give me his gage. Lions make leopards tame.
> MOWBRAY Yea, but not change his spots! Take but my shame,
>   And I resign my gage. My dear dear lord,
>   The purest treasure mortal times afford
>   Is spotless reputation. That away,
>   Men are but gilded loam or painted clay.
>   A jewel in a ten-times-barred-up chest
>   Is a bold spirit in a loyal breast.
>   Mine honor is my life, both grow in one;
>   Take honor from me, and my life is done.
>   Then, dear my liege, mine honor let me try;
>   In that I live, and for that will I die.   (I, i, 174–85)

That there are ten syllables to a line, and that the lines rhyme in pairs, anyone can see. Some of the lines are "regular" iambic lines, that is, contain five metrical feet, each containing an unstressed syllable followed by a stressed syllable –

> "The púr/est tréas/ure mór/tal tímes / affórd"

while others are only iambic in movement, with considerable variation in the accentual pattern. A common variation is inversion of accent at the beginning of a line and after the medial pause called caesura –

> "Gíve me / his gáge. // Líons / máke léo/pards táme"

or again –

> "Yéa, but / not chánge / his spóts! // Táke but / my sháme."

Although there will occasionally be a run-on line, that is one in which there is no grammatical or rhetorical stopping place at the end, most of the lines are end-stopped; and in a majority of cases a couplet contains a distinguishable unit of thought. This is illustrated in the last three couplets in the above example.

So far as basic metrical pattern is concerned, what has been said above applies equally to blank verse. It, too, consists of iambic pentameter lines. The following is also from *Richard II*:

> Alas, the part I had in Woodstock's blood
> Doth more solicit me than your exclaims
> To stir against the butchers of his life!
> But since correction lieth in those hands
> Which made the fault that we cannot correct,
> Put we our quarrel to the will of heaven,
> Who, when they see the hours ripe on earth,
> Will rain hot vengeance on offenders' heads.   (I, ii, 1–8)

Again there are "regular" iambic lines –

> "Alás, / the párt / I hád / in Wood/stock's blóod"

and ones varying the metre slightly –

"Who, when / they see / the hou / rs ripe / on earth."

(Observe that "hours" is disyllabic. In analyzing the verse or in speaking it well, one must allow for such phenomena, as well as for elided and unelided "ed" endings and the like.) Of course the obvious distinction between the two passages is that the lines of the second are "blank" – that is unrhymed. This feature carries with it, or should, the elimination of the regimentation of the thought into two-line units. In blank verse the last syllable of the line may be an unstressed tenth syllable (a "weak" ending) or an unstressed eleventh syllable (a "feminine" ending), and the meaning may "run on" from line to line, as in the first two lines and elsewhere in the above example.

There is much better blank verse in *Richard II* than the lines quoted, which have been used only because they conform so closely to the basic pattern. It is because he worked such variations upon the pattern that Shakespeare's blank verse became the remarkably expressive medium it did. Generalizations about his technique will be more intelligible if two passages are quoted in turn, the first of poor quality, the second of good quality. Both are the words of a wife urging her husband to steal a throne. Here is Eleanor speaking to Duke Humphrey in *2 Henry VI*:

> Why droops my lord like over-ripened corn
> Hanging the head at Ceres' plenteous load ?
> Why doth the great Duke Humphrey knit his brows,
> As frowning at the favors of the world ?
> Why are thine eyes fixed to the sullen earth,
> Gazing on that which seems to dim thy sight ?
> What seest thou there ? King Henry's diadem,
> Enchased with all the honors of the world ?
> If so, gaze on and grovel on thy face
> Until thy head be circled with the same.
> Put forth thy hand, reach at the glorious gold.
> What, is't too short ? I'll lengthen it with mine.   (I, ii, 1–12)

These are simply couplets with the rhymes omitted ; and the iambic beat is so regular as to seem mechanical. Compare Lady Macbeth's equivalent speech :

> Your face, my Thane, is as a book where men
> May read strange matters. To beguile the time,
> Look like the time ; bear welcome in your eye,
> Your hand, your tongue ; look like th' innocent flower,
> But be the serpent under't. He that's coming
> Must be provided for ; and you shall put
> This night's great business into my dispatch,
> Which shall to all our nights and days to come
> Give solely sovereign sway and masterdom.   (I, v, 60–68)

Although closed off with a rhyme, these lines show no vestigial trace of the couplet-making habit since the unit of thought is neither the line nor the pair of lines but the whole speech as in the way of a paragraph ; and the iambic beat is sufficiently irregular to be unobtrusive. Of course the distinction between the two passages is not metrical alone. In the first, six whole lines are expended upon Humphrey's appearance of preoccupation ; and the image of the "over-ripened corn" is ornate and inappropriate. In the second, the arresting "book" of "strange matters" not only suggests Macbeth's appearance of preoccupation in a line-and-a-half, but the image leads into the counsel to come, as the "over-ripened corn" image

does not. The literal and distracting "grovel on thy face" of the first passage is replaced in the second by the vivid "look like th' innocent flower, / But be the serpent under't."

We may examine now a brief dialogue between the Thane and his strenuous Lady which comes a little later, noting only those syllables which we would naturally stress regardless of whether we were reading verse or prose :

> LADY He has almost supped. Why have you left the chamber ?
> MACBETH Hath he asked for me ?
> LADY   Know you not he has ?
> MACBETH We will proceed no further in this business.
> He hath honored me of late, and I have bought
> Golden opinions from all sorts of people,
> Which would be worn now in their newest gloss,
> Not cast aside so soon.
> LADY   Was the hope drunk
> Wherein you dressed yourself ? Hath it slept since ?
> And wakes it now to look so green and pale
> At what it did so freely ? From this time
> Such I account thy love. Art thou afeard
> To be the same in thine own act and valor
> As thou art in desire ? Wouldst thou have that
> Which thou esteem'st the ornament of life,
> And live a coward in thine own esteem,
> Letting 'I dare not' wait upon 'I would,'
> Like the poor cat i' th' adage ?
> MACBETH   Prithee peace !
> I dare do all that may become a man ;
> Who dares do more is none.
> LADY   What beast was't then
> That made you break this enterprise to me ?   (I, vii, 29–48)

Although the iambic pentameter verse pattern is respected, neither the pauses nor the stresses are governed by it so much as by the ideas and emotions expressed. Flexibility is effected by the run-on lines, their flow often accelerated by unstressed final syllables ; by the way in which single lines are divided between two speakers ; by the number of full stops within lines ; and, finally, by the fact that the stresses are of varying degrees of strength, with one of them virtually obliterated in some part of each line.

Since the stresses fall in the right places if the lines are read with attention only to their meaning and emotional thrust, they are self-scanning. If a line sounds wrong to the ear, some word in it is not being pronounced as the author intended. The accent in certain words could shift (confíscate), an internal sound dropped by syncope (med'cine), certain sounds elided or slurred (th' unworthy), a monosyllable pronounced as a disyllable (hou-r), a disyllable as a trisyllable (mar-ri-age), and so on. Most of the instances of elision and syncope are indicated by apostrophes in the text, but not all of them, and there are no signals for shifted accent as in "confíscate" or syllabic split as in "hou-r." Hence, although the reader need have no formal knowledge of metrics and certainly need not mark off with a pencil the stressed and unstressed syllables, he must have a good ear for verse if he is to read the lines aloud with effect. The verse remains verse, however much it may work variations upon the basic pattern. That it never becomes simply rhythmic prose split into ten- and eleven-syllable lines is apparent when we compare it with the prose of the plays, even the most poetic and euphonious. If we try to rearrange this prose into blank verse lines, we discover that it cannot be done.

The advantage of the use of such blank verse is obvious. No matter what the degree of emotional intensity in a passage, a sense of form remains. The advantage of using it in combination with rhymed verse and prose is perhaps less obvious, but the plays demonstrate that it is real. A drunken porter can appear in a tragic poem without having to speak verse; and romantic young lovers can appear in a village farce without having to speak prose. The playwright has three keyboards at his disposal. Shakespeare's technique in shifting from one to another may be illustrated through *The Merchant of Venice*, where the proportion of rhymed verse (5.5 per cent), blank verse (73.5 per cent), and prose (21 per cent) is fairly representative. The rhyme appears in couplets which occasionally punctuate the end of speeches, especially the last in a scene; or where a special lyrical or gnomic quality in a speech is underlined, sometimes with parodic intent; or when an effect of ritual is desired. Most of the rhyme in this particular play appears in the casket scenes. The mottoes in the caskets are in rhymed short lines –

> All that glisters is not gold;
> Often have you heard that told –   (II, vii, 65–66)

and, having read them, the various suitors continue to speak in rhyme as if under the spell of the fateful messages. The foolish Arragon's speech is in the jingling measure of the mottoes, while Bassanio's is in dignified decasyllabic couplets – a typically Shakespearean touch. Here, as in most of the plays, the rhyme is sparingly used for special effects, not simply for decoration.

The prose also had special uses, for instance in letters and proclamations, where verse would contrast so conspicuously with familiar social custom as to call attention to itself. In the trial scene of *The Merchant of Venice*, prose appears only in Bellario's letter to the court. The most common use for prose was in realistic and comic scenes or parts of scenes, just as the most common use of blank verse was in romantic and serious ones. When Launcelot Gobbo and his clownery figure, we have prose; and when the love affair of Bassanio and Portia, and the threat of disaster to Antonio figure, we have blank verse. The distinction is normal enough, but there are areas in this as in the other plays where either media may be appropriately used. The first scene, of fairly low-pitched conversation, between Antonio, Bassanio, and their friends is in blank verse, the second scene of similar conversation between Portia and Nerissa in prose. The choice of media would have been equally appropriate if reversed. The third scene begins in prose but shifts to blank verse when Shylock stops talking business and begins to charge Antonio with injustice. This seems appropriate indeed, but blank verse does not always replace prose with the rise in the emotional temperature. In a later scene (III, i) beginning in prose, with the comic mockeries of Solanio and Salerio, the prose continues in Shylock's great speech – "I am a Jew. Hath not a Jew eyes . . . ?" Precisely the same thing happens in *Hamlet* (II, ii) where the prose of the pleasantries exchanged with Rosencrantz and Guildenstern continues in the Prince's great speech – "I

have of late – but wherefore I know not – lost all my mirth. . . ." Our conclusion must be that it is the *kind* of blank verse and the *kind* of prose that makes each appropriate to the place where it occurs. This does not mean that the playwright might as well have confined himself to either medium – the great general distinction remains. It means rather that both his prose and his blank verse have such a wide range of tone that their functions may overlap. Consequently, we cannot discuss the way he uses them in terms of hard and fast rules.

Whatever aspect of Shakespeare's technique we consider, we make an identical discovery. The way he does any particular thing cannot be adequately described in isolation from the rest of what he is doing. It is the *interconnectedness* of his way of doing things that explains his great distinction. This is only another way of saying that he is a true artist, and that his art can be represented only by itself, not by anything we write or say about it – whether we are analyzing images, scanning lines, extrapolating myths, or expounding moral messages. Even if the commentary were by a person of equal genius (surely a mere hypothesis) the commentary would not be the work of art itself. Such a statement may seem to cast suspicion upon the whole vast body of extant Shakespearean criticism, and to appear ungracious in an essay which is to be followed by a bibliography. It is intended only as a warning that a critical work should not be identified with its subject and allowed, in any measure, to displace it. Coleridge said that all comment upon Shakespeare should be "reverential." Perhaps a tone of reverence can become monotonous and even oppressive. If we reserve the right to notice that not everything that Shakespeare does is perfect, our enjoyment is enhanced. It might be better to say that all comment upon Shakespeare should be "modest." The right kind of criticism – and much of it is the right kind – can be very valuable. It can sharpen our sight and indicate what we should look for. Complaints about the superfluity of books about Shakespeare often come from those who write them. These resemble parents who view with hostility all children except their own. Actually there is something fine, or at least touching, even about the bad books. Their authors have demonstrated their yearning for association with something good. Viewed in the large, the great store of books about Shakespeare constitutes the greatest tribute human beings have ever paid to the accomplishment of one of their kind.

Harvard University   ALFRED HARBAGE

BIBLIOGRAPHY

The technicalities of construction, diction, prosody, etc., touched upon above, are treated in greater (although still insufficient) detail in A. Harbage, *Shakespeare : A Reader's Guide* (1963). For background on Elizabethan play-construction see Madeleine Doran, *Endeavors of Art* (1954); David Bevington, *From Mankind to Marlowe* (1962); W. T. Jewkes, *Act Division in Elizabethan and Jacobean Plays* (1958). Books on various aspects of Shakespeare's technique are Hereward T. Price, *Construction in Shakespeare* (1951); Henry L. Snuggs, *Shakespeare and Five Acts* (1960); F. W. Ness, *The Use of Rhyme in Shakespeare's Plays* (1941); Milton Crane, *Shakespeare's Prose* (1951); Sister Miriam Joseph, *Shakespeare's Use of the Arts of Language* (1947); Caroline

Spurgeon, *Shakespeare's Imagery and What It Tells Us* (1935); Wolfgang Clemen, *The Development of Shakespeare's Imagery* (1951); Peter Seng, *Vocal Songs in the Plays of Shakespeare* (1964); M. M. Mahood, *Shakespeare's Wordplay* (1957); William Empson, *Seven Types of Ambiguity* (1930), *The Structure of Complex Words* (1951). The following reference works aid in the study of the meaning and use of words: John Bartlett, *Complete Concordance to Shakespeare's Dramatic Works and Poems* (1894 etc.); Alexander Schmidt, *Shakespeare-Lexicon*, 2 vols (rev. ed. 1923); Charles T. Onions, *A Shakespeare Glossary* (rev. ed. 1953); Eric Partridge, *Shakespeare's Bawdy* (1948); Edwin Abbot, *A Shakespearean Grammar* (1869 etc.); Helge Kökeritz, *Shakespeare's Pronunciation* (1953).

Works of general criticism are listed here. (Works on the various dramatic types are listed with the forewords to the five sections of the present edition.) A voluminous body of past criticism is described in Augustus Ralli, *A History of Shakespearian Criticism*, 2 vols (1932); and landmarks of criticism are anthologized in *Shakespeare Criticism*, ed. D. Nichol Smith (1923). A valuable analysis of criticism, mostly of the nineteenth and twentieth centuries, is Arthur M. Eastman, *A Short History of Shakespearean Criticism* (1968). All initial commentary is printed in John Munro, *The Shakespere Allusion Book 1591 to 1700*, 2 vols (2nd ed. 1932). Works by major critics are *Johnson on Shakespeare*, ed. Arthur Sherbo, 2 vols (1968); August Wilhelm Schlegel, *A Course of Lectures on Dramatic Art and Literature*, Lecture XII, trans. John Black, 2 vols (1815); William Hazlitt, *The Characters of Shakespeare's Plays* (1817); Samuel Taylor Coleridge, *Shakespearean Criticism*, ed. T. M. Raysor, 2 vols (rev. ed. 1930); *Coleridge's Writings on Shakespeare*, ed. Terence Hawkes (1959); Henry N. Hudson, *Shakespeare: His Life, Art, and Character* (1872); Edward Dowden, *Shakespeare: A Critical Study of His Mind and Art* (1875).

Surveys of twentieth-century criticism appear in *Shakespeare Survey* by Kenneth Muir, Vol. IV (1951), and by Muriel Bradbrook, Vol. VII (1954). A very useful descriptive bibliography is Ronald Berman, *A Reader's Guide to Shakespeare's Plays* (1965). Anthologies of twentieth-century criticism are *Approaches to Shakespeare*, ed. Norman Rabkin (1964); *Shakespeare, Modern Essays in Criticism*, ed. Leonard Dean (rev. ed. 1967). Individual works are Levin L. Schücking, *Character Problems in Shakespeare's Plays* (1927); Elmer Edgar Stoll, *Art and Artifice in Shakespeare* (1933), *Shakespeare Studies* (1942); G. Wilson Knight, *The Wheel of Fire* (enlarged ed. 1954), *The Imperial Theme* (1931), *The Shakespearian Tempest* (1932); Sir Edmund Chambers, *Shakespeare, a Survey* (1925); Logan Pearsall Smith, *On Reading Shakespeare* (1933); John Middleton Murry, *Shakespeare* (1936); Derek Traversi, *An Approach to Shakespeare* (enlarged ed., 2 vols, 1968); Mark Van Doren, *Shakespeare* (1939); S. L. Bethell, *Shakespeare and The Popular Dramatic Tradition* (1944); Harley Granville-Barker, *Prefaces to Shakespeare*, ed. M. St Clare Byrne, 4 vols (1963); Alfred Harbage, *As They Liked It* (1947); Donald A. Stauffer, *Shakespeare's World of Images* (1949); J. I. M. Stewart, *Character and Motive in Shakespeare* (1949); Arthur Sewell, *Character and Society in Shakespeare* (1951); Hardin Craig, *An Interpretation of Shakespeare* (1948); Muriel C. Bradbrook, *Shakespeare and Elizabethan Poetry* (1951); L. C. Knights, *Some Shakespearean Themes* (1959); William J. Grace, *Approaching Shakespeare* (1964); Alwin Thaler, *Shakespeare and Our World* (1966); Norman N. Holland, *Psychoanalysis and Shakespeare* (1966); Norman Rabkin, *Shakespeare and the Common Understanding* (1967); Terence Eagleton, *Shakespeare and Society* (1967); J. L. Styan, *Shakespeare's Stagecraft* (1967); Anne Righter, *Shakespeare and the Idea of the Play* (1962); *Early Shakespeare*, ed. J. R. Brown & Bernard Harris, *Stratford-upon-Avon Studies*, No. 3 (1961); E. Talbert, *Elizabethan Drama and Shakespeare's Early Plays* (1963); A. C. Hamilton, *The Early Shakespeare* (1967).

THE ORIGINAL TEXTS

$\mathcal{S}$ince no manuscripts of any of Shakespeare's plays survive, the editor of his work must deal solely with printed texts, and these are of two kinds: the quarto editions of single plays published prior to the folio collection of 1623, and the edition of the folio collection itself, wherein all the plays (excluding *Pericles*) were printed together in a single volume for the first time.* Prior to 1623, nineteen plays had appeared in print: *Titus Andronicus* in 1594; *2 Henry VI* (titled *The First Part of the Contention betwixt the two famous Houses of York and Lancaster*), 1594; *3 Henry VI* (titled *The True Tragedy of Richard Duke of York*, and actually printed in octavo, not quarto), 1595; *Richard II*, 1597; *Richard III*, 1597; *Romeo and Juliet*, 1597; *Love's Labor's Lost*, 1598; *1 Henry IV*, 1598; *2 Henry IV*, 1600; *The Merchant of Venice*, 1600; *Much Ado about Nothing*, 1600; *A Midsummer Night's Dream*, 1600; *Henry V*, 1600; *The Merry Wives of Windsor*, 1602; *Hamlet*, 1603; *Lear*, 1608; *Troilus and Cressida*, 1609; *Pericles*, 1609; *Othello*, 1622. The remaining eighteen plays were printed for the first time in the 1623 folio. The editorial problem posed by this latter group of plays, which appears only in the folio, is perforce simplified; each is preserved in but a single text, of which all other editions are but reprints. But the problem posed by those plays which have both quarto and folio editions is – or can be – very much more complex.

The authority of any edition – quarto or folio – of a single play is determined by the nature of the copy from which it was printed. The printed texts of Shakespeare's plays derive from a variety of manuscript sources. Under normal circumstances, a theatrical company such as the King's men would presumably have in its archives two kinds of manuscript material for the plays in its repertory: the author's draft (his "foul papers" – so termed in Elizabethan parlance since it was bound to contain final corrections and interlineations), and the transcript (the so-called "fair copy") which would have been prepared from this either by the author himself or by a theatrical scribe or book-keeper, for use as a prompt-book. It is not to be supposed that these two manuscript categories are always readily distinguishable, or that in fact the two kinds of manuscript copy were always available for every play. Manuscripts were lost or mislaid or worn out over the years. The draft itself may have been taken over sometimes for use as a prompt-book, thereby reducing the two categories to one. Authors may have declined to deposit their drafts with the theatre company (there is some uncertainty as to whether or not they were required to do so), and preferred to keep them in their own possession. Still, to judge from the evidence of the Shakespearean quarto and folio texts, where there are two substantive editions – each printed from a separate manuscript source

– of a given play, the two manuscript sources regularly divide themselves into generally distinct categories that can appropriately be labelled author's draft and prompt-book.

Each exhibits some characteristic features, and to the extent that these are reflected in the printed texts, it is possible at least to conjecture something of the nature of the manuscript copy from which quarto and folio editions derive. An author's draft will sometimes display duplicate versions of a given passage (as in the second quarto text of *Romeo and Juliet*, III, ii, 76; V, iii, 102; V, iii, 108; or in the first quarto edition of *Love's Labor's Lost*, IV, iii, 291–349; V, ii, 807–12 and 827–41, or in the folio text of *Troilus and Cressida*, where V, x, 32–34 appears also after V, iii, 111), and in each case it is to be assumed that one version was rejected by Shakespeare but was inadequately marked for deletion in the manuscript, so that the compositor printed both versions. Often in an author's draft a character may be designated – in speech-prefixes and stage directions – by his function rather than by a proper name. Thus in *Love's Labor's Lost*, the King of Navarre is variously termed "Ferdinand," "Navarre," or "King"; in *Romeo and Juliet* (Q2), Lady Capulet, depending on her role *vis à vis* others at a given moment, is referred to as "Lady of the house," "Old Lady," "Lady," "Wife," "Capulet Wife," and "Mother." Stage directions tend to be rather more descriptive of stage business, and of the emotional stance of characters and their relation one to another, than would be strictly requisite in a prompt-book; on the other hand, they are often somewhat indefinite as concerns such details as the exact number of supernumeraries involved in a given scene, and they are often deficient in the marking of entrances and, especially, exits.

The assumption is that the prompt-book would represent the play as it was produced in the theatre. Its text would reproduce, theoretically at least, what was actually spoken on stage. Loose ends in the text of the author's draft would presumably be tidied up in the prompt-book; false starts made by the author in the process of composition would be appropriately deleted. Cuts in the text might be made as the exigencies of performance – or the demands of the censor – dictated, and these would be reflected in the prompt-book. Its stage directions would be, on the whole, straightforward and business-like, primarily concerned with bringing the proper characters on stage and getting them off at the correct moments in the action. To this end, names of characters would need to be fixed, and the inconsistent means of designating the same character noted in the draft of *Romeo and Juliet* and

---

* A "folio" was a book in the printing of which the sheets of paper had been folded once, yielding a page approximately $13^{1}/_{2}$ x $8^{1}/_{4}$ inches. In a "quarto" the sheets had been folded twice, yielding a page one-half that size.

Love's Labor's Lost would be reduced to order in the prompt-book. Directions concerning the use of necessary properties would be inserted at the appropriate points in the text.

The prompt-book would represent a document of considerable importance and considerable value to any theatrical company. It would be an indispensable guide for staging the revivals of a play that, it was to be hoped, would continue to be acted from season to season in the repertory of a company like the King's men. By no means the least measure of its importance would consist in the fact that the prompt-book bore the license of the official censor, the Master of the Revels, attesting that the text of the play in question contained no offensive matter and thereby approving it for performance. This, if nothing else, would be sufficient reason for the theatrical company to guard its prompt-books with some care. The company would, one imagines, be understandably loath to let them serve as printer's copy, and it is surely no accident that none of the nineteen Shakespearean plays published prior to 1623 was printed from one. Ten were printed from author's drafts: *Titus Andronicus, Love's Labor's Lost, Romeo and Juliet* (Q2), *Richard II, A Midsummer Night's Dream, The Merchant of Venice, 1* and *2 Henry IV, Much Ado about Nothing,* and *Hamlet* (Q2). Transcripts of author's drafts apparently served as copy for three other quarto editions – *Lear, Troilus and Cressida,* and *Othello* – though in each case there is reason to doubt that the copy was supplied by the players. It was certainly not in the case of *Troilus and Cressida,* published, according to the prefatory Epistle, against "the grand possessors' wills."

Seven quarto texts were printed from no authoritative manuscripts of any sort, neither author's drafts nor prompt-books nor transcripts of either: *2* and *3 Henry VI, Romeo and Juliet* (Q1), *Henry V, The Merry Wives of Windsor, Hamlet* (Q1), and *Pericles.* These are the famous "bad" quartos, reported texts that were put together from memory by one or more of the actors who had appeared in performances of these plays on the London stage, and who, presumably no longer members of the original producing company, sought to provide themselves and their fellows with texts of popular London theatrical successes to take on tour in the provinces. They have been termed "pirated" texts, and justly so, for even as they were compiled without authority, so too were they printed without the sanction of the theatrical company. The bad quartos share a number of features in common. All are abridged versions of the plays as we know them from the full texts that were subsequently (and authoritatively) published. All exhibit the same tricks of memory which the actors, consciously or unconsciously, fell back on to farce out the general lines of the dramatic action as they remembered it: anticipation of passages that, in fact, occur at a later point in the authoritative text, and the converse of this, the recollection of passages that have occurred at an earlier stage in the good text; repetitions and transpositions of words and phrases; borrowings from other plays in which these particular performers had acted. In the case of *Romeo and Juliet* and *Hamlet,* the texts of the bad first quartos were shortly replaced by the publication (in 1599 and 1604 respectively) of second quarto editions, each printed from Shakespeare's drafts. There is evidence to suggest that the good quarto of *Love's Labor's Lost,* printed in 1598, was similarly intended to

replace a bad quarto text (now lost) that had been published for that play one or two years before. Authoritative editions of *2* and *3 Henry VI, Henry V,* and *The Merry Wives of Windsor* were not printed until the publication of the folio collection in 1623. For *Pericles* no "authoritative" text exists.

The remaining Shakespearean play to be printed prior to 1623, *Richard III,* also originally appeared in what amounts to a memorially reconstructed text; what differentiates it from the other bad quarto texts is the apparent fact that the actors who drew upon their memories to compile the quarto text of *Richard III* were members of Shakespeare's own company. At any rate, it is a very much more accurate text than that of the usual bad quarto, though otherwise it exhibits the features – anticipations, transpositions, abridgment – characteristic of reported texts. The assumption is that the actors who put together the report of *Richard III* needed a prompt-book from which to act the play, perhaps while touring the provinces, when no prompt-book was available; so from their collective memories they drew one up as best they could to serve their purpose. When it had so served, the memorial reconstruction of *Richard III,* like the other reported texts, found its way into print. It continued in print through six editions, being indeed one of the two most frequently reprinted of all the Shakespearean quarto texts (*1 Henry IV* was the other), and an authoritative edition of *Richard III* did not appear until the publication of the folio.

When, some time around 1620, Shakespeare's former fellow-actors, headed by John Heminge and Henry Condell, embarked upon their plan to collect his plays in a single volume, one of their first and most crucial tasks was the assembling and – where there was a question of choice – the selection of copy with which to provide Jaggard, the folio printer. For the eighteen plays that had not previously been printed, the editors of the folio drew upon manuscript copy of various kinds. The author's drafts seem to have served as copy for four plays: *The Comedy of Errors, The Taming of the Shrew, All's Well That Ends Well, Timon of Athens.* Transcripts of such drafts, prepared by a professional scribe named Ralph Crane, served as copy for *Measure for Measure* and *The Winter's Tale.* Drafts annotated by the stage-adapter for use as prompt-books (or transcripts of these) served as copy for *1 Henry VI, King John, Antony and Cleopatra, Coriolanus, Cymbeline, Henry VIII, The Tempest* (this latter in a transcript prepared by Crane). Prompt-books, or transcripts thereof (as distinguished from author's drafts annotated for use in the theatre) provided copy for *As You Like It, Twelfth Night, Julius Caesar* (where the prompt-book may have been the author's fair copy), *Macbeth* (where the prompt-book was certainly not authorial, to judge from the evidences of interpolations in the folio text), *The Two Gentlemen of Verona,* and *The Merry Wives of Windsor* (the latter two in Crane transcripts).

A word should be devoted to the work of Ralph Crane. Although apparently not an official member of the King's men, he is known to have worked for them, and transcripts in his hand exist of several non-Shakespearean plays (e.g. Fletcher's *Demetrius and Enanthe,* Fletcher and Massinger's *Tragedy of Sir John van Olden Barnavelt,* Jonson's *Pleasure Reconciled to Virtue,* Middleton's *The Witch,* and three transcripts of that dramatist's *Game at Chess*). From these it is possible to draw some conclusions concerning the characteristic qualities of his work, which has some fairly distinctive features: his plentiful, somewhat fussy punctuation, with its lavish use of parentheses, and its often somewhat peculiar uses of hyphens and apostrophes; the careful division into acts and scenes which all Crane's transcripts exhibit; a tendency in some of his work to mass the names of characters at the head of each scene, rather than to name them at the point in the action where they actually enter (a practice evident in the folio texts of *The Two Gentlemen of Verona*, *The Merry Wives of Windsor*, and *The Winter's Tale*); there is a paucity of stage directions in his work, and those that are present tend to be of a literary rather than a theatrical kind. It is possible that at the outset, the folio editors planned to provide the printer with transcriptions of all the plays for use as copy; the four plays which open the volume – *The Tempest*, *The Two Gentlemen of Verona*, *The Merry Wives of Windsor*, and *Measure for Measure* – were all printed from transcripts prepared by Crane. But the plan, if it was one, was soon abandoned, and by the time work on the volume was completed, a remarkable array of assorted kinds of copy – manuscript and printed – had been brought into use.

The use of printed copy was, of course, restricted to those plays which had previously appeared in quarto. Since the compositors setting type for the folio, like all compositors, must have preferred working from printed rather than from manuscript copy, it is understandable that the folio editors, in cases where a good text of a play was already in print, should allow the folio text to be reprinted from a copy of this. The assumption would be that for such plays as *Much Ado about Nothing*, *Love's Labor's Lost*, *A Midsummer Night's Dream*, *The Merchant of Venice*, *1 Henry IV*, and *Romeo and Juliet* (as printed in Q2) – all "good" quartos, printed from Shakespeare's drafts – the theatrical archives had nothing better to offer in the way of manuscript material, and that a copy of the quarto text of each of these plays, after it had undergone some degree of comparison with a playhouse manuscript, could appropriately serve as printer's copy for the folio text. Thus the folio editions of *Much Ado about Nothing*, *Love's Labor's Lost*, and *The Merchant of Venice* were reprinted from their original quartos; *A Midsummer Night's Dream* from its second quarto (falsely dated 1600, the year of its first); *Romeo and Juliet* from its third quarto; *1 Henry IV* from its fifth quarto. Such comparison with playhouse manuscripts as these quarto prints underwent when they were made ready to serve as folio copy typically resulted in nothing more than some elaboration of the stage directions in the folio texts.

Even when the theatrical archives did have something to yield that was superior or supplementary to the text of a printed quarto, this quarto, after having been compared with and presumably corrected from the new manuscript material, none the less served as the basis for the folio printer's copy. The process varied from play to play, depending on the extent, and the nature, of the manuscript material to be incorporated into the already printed quarto text. Thus the folio text of *Titus Andronicus* was printed from a copy of Q3 which was corrected from an annotated copy of Q2 that had been used as a prompt-book, but copy for the folio incorporated as well the text of a new scene of 85 lines at the end of Act III, omitted

from all quarto editions of the play. The folio text of *Richard II* was printed in the main from a copy of Q3, though the last 151 lines of the play seem to have been printed from a copy of Q5; this was collated with the prompt-book, which contained an authentic manuscript for the deposition scene (IV, i, 154–318), missing from the first three quarto editions, though it had been supplied in Q4 in an inferior text that is usually regarded as a memorial reconstruction. The folio text of *Richard III* was printed in the main from a copy of Q6 which had been corrected by collation with a full and authoritative manuscript, presumably Shakespeare's foul papers; but the manuscript was apparently defective in two places, and its missing leaves in the middle and at the end (amounting to the first 158 lines or so of Act III and the last 345 lines of Act V) were supplied from a copy of Q3. The folio text of *Lear* was printed from a copy of Q1 that had been corrected by comparison with the prompt-book, a manuscript that had been cut for performance; in his zeal to bring his copy of Q1 into exact conformity with the manuscript, the corrector cut a number of passages that had appeared in the quarto, while supplying a number of others missing from Q1; the result is that, while the folio text of *Lear* contains some 100 lines missing from the quarto, the quarto contains nearly 300 lines missing from the folio. In the case of *Troilus and Cressida*, the folio text was printed from a copy of Q that had been collated with the author's draft, and this – if one accepts the view that Q had been printed from a manuscript containing Shakespeare's revision of the play – was a mistake, for it results in a folio text inferior in many ways to that of the quarto (though it salvaged the Prologue, missing from Q). *Othello* was printed in the folio from a copy of its 1622 quarto which had been collated with a manuscript, probably the prompt-book. Whether or not the folio texts of *Hamlet* and of *2 Henry IV* were printed from annotated quarto copy has been much disputed. The folio editions of both plays draw on independent manuscript sources; whether the folio compositors worked with these directly, or set their texts from annotated quarto copy, is not clear; both folio texts display some suspicious bibliographical links with their respective quartos (Q2 in the case of *Hamlet*). The manuscript behind the folio text of *Hamlet* was the prompt-book; like the one for *Lear*, it had been cut for performance, with the result that, while the folio edition of *Hamlet* contains about 75 lines missing from the second quarto edition, it omits over 200 lines contained in Q2. The manuscript (which may or may not have been a prompt-book) behind the folio text of *2 Henry IV*, on the other hand, restores over 150 lines omitted from the quarto edition of that play.

Just how far the practice of setting folio texts from annotated quarto copy could be – and was – extended is shown by the fact that even the bad quartos were used for folio printer's copy. The folio text of *Henry V* appears to have been printed from copy consisting of pages from Q2 and Q3 (reprints both of the bad Q1), corrected by reference to an authoritative manuscript. It has been argued that copy for the folio text of *2 Henry VI* was made up of pages from Q2 and Q3 (both reprints of *The Contention*, the bad first quarto of that play), corrected by comparison with a theatrical manuscript that was probably in the author's own hand; and that copy for the folio text of *3 Henry VI* was a similar composite of pages from its second and especially its third quarto editions (reprints of *The True Tragedy*, its bad first edition), corrected, often imperfectly, from a scribal transcript of Shakespeare's manuscript that had been annotated by the prompter.

Beyond the question of what kinds of copy were used in printing the folio text of Shakespeare's plays lies the further question of how accurately copy was followed by

make his corrupting influence felt on the folio texts of some of the greatest plays in the canon, *Romeo and Juliet*, *Hamlet, Othello, Lear*.

The quality of a compositor's work will almost certainly be affected by the degree of legibility of his copy, and so it is probably misleading to talk about the care or the carelessness of his performance in any absolute sense. The

C. Walter Hodges.

the compositors who set the type. According to Professor Hinman, the compositors were five in number, designated by him by letters from A through E. The principal workmen were Compositors A and B, whose share of the typesetting far exceeded that of Compositors C and D. A full study of the quality of the work of these four is yet to be undertaken. At present only the quality of the performance of Compositor E can be judged. Apparently he was an apprentice who was so inept that he could not be trusted to cope with the handwriting of manuscript copy, and was allowed to work only from printed copy. Since he was brought on to the job when work on the volume had reached the Tragedies, he was unfortunately present to

level of accuracy of even the most careful workman might well be lowered if he were setting type from copy prepared in a hand that was difficult to read, or contained – as in the case of the typical author's draft – a number of interlineations and marks of revision. And, conversely, a workman of fairly slovenly habits would make comparatively few errors when setting from straightforward printed copy as distinct from manuscripts or annotated quartos. Nevertheless, it is clear that some knowledge of the habits and degree of competence of particular compositors is useful to the modern editor.

The crucial editorial issue remains the treatment of plays that are preserved in two substantive texts, which is to say two independently printed from manuscript sources, and not two where one is simply a reprint of the other. As concerns the Shakespearean plays which exist in both quarto and folio editions, some can be said to possess two substantive texts, and some cannot. With plays such as *Love's Labor's Lost, Romeo and Juliet* (Q2), *1 Henry IV, Much Ado about Nothing, The Merchant of Venice*, and *A Midsummer Night's Dream*, the folio is but a reprint of the quarto; hence the quartos alone are substantive, and the folio clearly derivative. The plays with two substantive editions are those which, first printed in quarto, were reprinted in the folio in substantially different form: *Titus Andronicus, 2* and *3 Henry VI, Richard II, Richard III, Henry V, 2 Henry IV, The Merry Wives of Windsor, Hamlet, Lear, Troilus and Cressida, Othello*. But the very fact that all these plays (with the exception of *The Merry Wives*) were "reprinted" in the folio tends to put the substantive status of their folio texts in a somewhat qualified light. Each, strictly speaking, was printed in part at least from a previous quarto, but a quarto that had been so substantially altered as to acquire substantive textual status.

The use of quarto copy for these plays does, however, make for some paradoxical results so far as editorial theory is concerned. Ordinarily, in editing a work preserved in collateral substantive texts, agreement among these in the reading of any given passage would be taken as the best possible evidence that the reading in question was correct, since each text would bear independent witness that the passage read thus in the author's original manuscript, from which all the collateral texts would be independently descended. In this view it would be assumed, for example, that when the quarto and the folio texts of *Lear* were in agreement, then they must be right, for each would be a separate witness to the fact that as they read, so Shakespeare's manuscript read. But when we realize that the folio text of *Lear* was printed, not from an independent manuscript but from a copy of the quarto that had been collated with one, then agreement between the two texts tends to be suspect, theoretically at least. For agreement between the two texts, in these circumstances, raises the prospect that agreement has come about simply because a quarto reading has been left uncorrected in the copy used for printing the folio text; the person charged with the task of collating the quarto with the manuscript and correcting it accordingly may or may not have adequately carried out his assignment. When variant readings are found in two texts such as Q and F *Lear* (or in any of the other plays printed in the folio from annotated

quarto copy), then at least one can be reasonably sure (setting aside the possibility of compositorial corruption) that the person charged with preparing copy for F is on the job, introducing a reading from his manuscript to replace the reading of Q in the copy of the quarto that he is making ready for the folio printer. Agreement between two texts, in this case, far from confirming the soundness of both, may raise the suspicion that one has corrupted the other. The problem is not confined to folio texts. The authority of the second quartos of both *Romeo and Juliet* and *Hamlet* is compromised in some degree because, for all the fact that behind each edition was an authorial manuscript, each depended in some measure on its respective bad first quarto for printer's copy. These are the sorts of bibliographical relationships between editions which editors must recognize and evaluate, for it is by means of evidence of this kind that an editor establishes the authority of the copy from which a given text was printed. His conclusions on this score will determine his decision as to which of two or more substantive texts he will base his edition on, how rigorously he will adhere to that text solely, how much – and in what circumstances – he will introduce variant readings into it from other textual sources, on what scale he will resort to emendations of his own or other editors' devising.

University of Rochester   CYRUS HOY

BIBLIOGRAPHY

The quartos and folio mentioned above, with all their reprints, are fully described in Sir Walter Greg, *A Bibliography of the English Printed Drama to the Restoration*, Vol. I, *Plays to 1616* (1939), Vol. II, *Plays 1617–1689* (1951). The best facsimiles of the quartos are those issued in collotype by Greg, 14 vols (1939–1966; to be continued by Charlton Hinman). The best facsimiles of the folio are those issued in collotype by Sir Sidney Lee (1902) and by Charlton Hinman (1968), the latter a handsome and useful composite reproduction. Pioneer work in modern textual criticism appears in A. W. Pollard, *Shakespeare's Fight with the Pirates* (1917, rev. 1937); Ronald B. McKerrow, *An Introduction to Bibliography for Literary Students* (1927), *Prolegomena to the Oxford Shakespeare* (1939). For authoritative analysis of the Shakespearean textual materials see Sir Walter Greg, *The Editorial Problem in Shakespeare* (3rd ed. 1954), *The Shakespeare First Folio* (1955), *Collected Papers*, ed. J. C. Maxwell (1966); Alice Walker, *Textual Problems of the First Folio* (1953); Fredson T. Bowers, *On Editing Shakespeare and the Elizabethan Dramatists* (1955); Charlton Hinman, *The Printing and Proof-reading of the First Folio of Shakespeare*, 2 vols (1963).

EDITIONS AND CURRENT VARIANT READINGS

Mr. William Shakespeares Comedies, Histories, & Tragedies, 1623, was reprinted in 1632, in 1663 (reissued in 1664 with *Pericles* and six apocryphal plays added), and in 1685. This fourth and last folio formed the basis of the first modern edition, that by Nicholas Rowe, 6 vols (1709). Rowe's edition was succeeded by those of Alexander Pope (1723, second ed. 1728), Lewis Theobald (1733), Sir Thomas Hanmer (1743–44), William Warburton (1747), Samuel Johnson (1765), Edward Capell (1767–68), George Steevens (1773, with final revisions 1793), and

Edmond Malone (1790). The work of these eighteenth-century editors was assembled *cum notis variorum* (with notes by various editors) in the "first variorum" edited by Isaac Reed, 21 vols (1803, revised 1813) and in the "third variorum" edited by James Boswell, 21 vols (1821). The monumental *New Variorum* edited by H. H. Furness, his son, and other successors, 27 vols (1871–1955), is still in process.

The most important nineteenth-century edition was the "Cambridge Shakespeare" edited by W. G. Clark,

J. Glover, and W. A. Wright, 9 vols (1863–66), the text of which was issued in a single volume with numbered lines, the "Globe Shakespeare" (1864). Concordances, Shakespearean grammars, and other works of reference used the line-numbering of this edition, which enjoyed wide currency and is still being issued in more or less modified form. A "New Cambridge" edition has been edited by J. Dover Wilson in collaboration, on the early volumes, with Sir Arthur Quiller-Couch and, on several of the later volumes, with Alice Walker and with J. C. Maxwell, 39 vols (1931–66). The most fully annotated edition, other than the *New Variorum*, is the *Arden Shakespeare*, edited by W. J. Craig, R. H. Case, and others, 37 vols (1899–1924), succeeded by the "New Arden" under the general editorship, at first, of Una Ellis-Fermor and, at present, of Harold F. Brooks and Harold Jenkins, 20 vols (1951–58). Recent editions complete are those of George L. Kittredge (1936, revised by Irving Ribner, 1967), W. A. Neilson and C. J. Hill (1942), Peter Alexander (1951), Charles J. Sisson (1953), John Munro, 6 vols (1957), and G. Blakemore Evans (in press). Other modern-spelling editions are still in process. An old-spelling edition utilizing modern advances in textual study remains a desideratum.

The original texts in quartos and the first folio, even those set from the most authoritative manuscripts, contain numerous defects, owing to the imperfect legibility of Shakespeare's handwriting, to the absence of proof-reading by him, and to the general low standards of printing in the late sixteenth and early seventeenth centuries. Editors are compelled to correct obvious misprints as well as to cope with passages that are, or seem to be, corrupt. The emendations of the early editors were often brilliant, but the process of alteration was extended beyond legitimate bounds, owing to their competitiveness in displaying brilliance, their instinct to improve Shakespeare according to the critical standards of their day, and their imperfect knowledge of the textual problem involved. Editorial reform has been effected by the recognition that variant readings in quartos and folios reprinted from earlier quartos and folios lack authority and are themselves no more than editorial emendations; by an increased knowledge of the nature of the copy used by the printers and the methods of book-production; and by an accumulated body of lore on the Shakespearean vocabulary, orthography, and frame of reference. In recent decades some of the emendations once accepted have been rejected as unauthorized "improvements," some have yielded place to others more plausible, and some have been retained.

An edition is sometimes called "conservative" when it adheres rigidly to the copy-text in good quarto or folio, and sometimes (contradictorily) when it retains dubious emendations of which readers have grown fond. The terms "under-edited" and "over-edited" are sometimes heard. Actually the best thing an edition can be is well-informed. The ideal is to present, as nearly as the available materials permit, what Shakespeare actually wrote, regardless of precedent or sentiment, and this ideal is best served by scrupulous attention to the bibliographical evidence placed at our disposal by experts, and by equally scrupulous attention to matters of philological and artistic plausibility as argued by opposing counsel. The hard choices come when the evidence itself conflicts.

We may take for instance Juliet's

> That which we call a rose
> By any other name would smell as sweet.   (II, ii, 43–44)

The utterance has become proverbial, and it is with some dismay that we observe that the *good* quarto of 1599 actually reads "By any other *word* would smell as sweet." Since it makes perfectly good sense, and there is small likelihood ("graphic plausibility") that a compositor would mistake Shakespeare's writing of "name" for "word," an editor may feel obliged, in defiance of sentiment, to adhere to his copy-text and not to perpetuate the substitution of "name" from the *bad* quarto of 1597. However, in Juliet's speech as a whole, "name" occurs five additional times and her famous remark is immediately preceded by "What's in a name?" The editor may decide that a kind of rhetorical inevitability argues in favor of adopting the customary reading. He would be unjustified in substituting "name" for "word" on purely intuitive grounds, but the occurrence of "name" in the 1597 quarto, which has some substantive value despite its badness, may seem to him to tip the scales in favor of its being Shakespeare's actual choice. The important thing is that he be aware of what he is doing, and be willing to resist automatic austerity as well as laxity. Or to take an exactly opposite case, Gloucester, in the superior folio text of *King Lear*, says that he aided his ancient monarch because he would not see Goneril "In his anointed flesh stick boarish fangs" (III, vii, 58). But the quarto of 1608, which despite its general inferiority has considerable substantive value, reads not "stick" but "rash" meaning "rip." It seems extremely unlikely that anyone but the poet himself would employ the rare word "rash," and a departure from the copy-text of the folio appears to be indicated. However the line "In his anointed flesh rash boarish fangs" proves to be hard to enunciate, and it may seem to the editor that Shakespeare was as apt as anyone else to recognize the fact. If he decides that "stick" may be an authorial revision, he will retain, however reluctantly, this weaker but less tongue-twisting word. Second thoughts may nag him with the notion that the use of "rash" in the line requires of the speaker some rather effective lip-writhing, but he remains in doubt, and when in doubt he favors factual evidence rather than intuition.

No two editions of a Shakespearean play, conscientiously constructed from the original materials, will ever be exactly alike. Because the editorial process involves, inevitably, the exercise of individual judgment, words will vary occasionally, and punctuation will vary throughout. A responsible editor will include enough textual apparatus to signal to the interested user those places in the text where individual judgment has been exercised. Disagreement in the matter of readings has lessened somewhat, and all recent editions are more reliable than those of a generation ago. This does not mean that the older editions are *bad*. The difference in wording between any two unexpurgated editions will involve no more than a fraction of one per cent; and no one's love of Shakespeare has ever been blighted by the use of a slightly obsolete edition. We can feel a certain sympathy for readers less concerned about a punctilious text than about the appearance of the page, or even the scent of the binder's glue. Nevertheless any editor for whom the choice between "name" and "word" or between "rash" and "stick" lies in an area of indifference is not to be trusted. Areas of indifference have a way of expanding, and the question of total responsibility is involved.

Below is an illustrative sampling from each play of readings which vary in various recent good editions. The copy text is first precisely quoted in each case, with the troublesome word, phrase, or ambiguously punctuated unit italicized. Then follow the variant readings in roughly alphabetical order, with no indication of those preferred by the Pelican editors. The act–scene–line references will enable the user to turn to the Pelican readings and glosses. Of course only a small minority of the total number of variant readings are listed, but all the kinds of problems are illustrated and most of the famous cruxes are included.

A. H.

The Comedy of Errors (f 1623)

I, i, 54   A *meane woman* was deliuered   (a) mean woman   (b) meaner woman   (c) poor mean woman
I, i, 151   To seeke thy *helpe* by beneficiall *helpe*   (a) health . . . help   (b) hope . . . help   (c) help . . . means   (d) help . . . hap   (e) life . . . help
II, i, 107   Would that *alone, a loue* he would detaine   (a) alone, alone   (b) alone a love   (c) alone o' love
IV, ii, 35   A Feind, a *Fairie*, pittilesse and ruffe   (a) fairy   (b) fury
V, i, 408   After so long greefe such *Nativitie*   (a) felicity   (b) festivity   (c) Nativity

The Taming of the Shrew (f 1623)

Ind., i, 7   go by *S. Ieronimie*   (a) St Jeronimy   (b) Jeronimy
Ind., i, 15   *Brach* Meriman, the poore Curre is imbost   (a) Brach   (b) Breathe
I, ii, 109   hee'l raile in his *rope trickes*   (a) rhetricks   (b) rope-tricks
IV, i, 126   *Soud, soud, soud, soud*   (a) Food, food, food, food   (b) Soud, soud, soud, soud
V, ii, 133   Hath cost *me fiue* hundred crownes   (a) me a   (b) one

The Two Gentlemen of Verona (f 1623)

II, iii, 25   Oh that she could speake now, like *a would-woman*   (a) a wood woman   (b) an old woman
II, iv, 193   It is *mine, or Valentines*   (a) mine or Valentine's   (b) mine eye or Valentine's   (c) mine or Valentinus's
II, vii, 32   With willing sport to the *wilde* Ocean   (a) wide   (b) wild
IV, iv, 70   It seemes you lou'd not her, *not leaue* her token   (a) nor love   (b) to leave
V, iv, 67   Who should be *trusted, when ones right* hand   (a) trusted now, when one's right   (b) trusted, when one's right   (c) trusted, when one's own right

A Midsummer Night's Dream (q 1600)

II, i, 78   From *Perigenia*, whom he ravished   (a) Perigenia   (b) Perigouna
II, i, 101   The humane mortals want their winter *heere*   (a) cheer   (b) here   (c) gear
III, i, 45   *Sn.* Doth the Moone shine, that night, we play our Play   (a) Snout   (b) Snug
III, ii, 25   And *at our stampe*, here ore and ore, one falles   (a) at a stamp   (b) at our stamp   (c) at a stump

V, i, 204   Now is the *Moon vsed* between the two neighbors   (f 1623 : morall downe)   (a) Moon to see   (b) Moon used   (c) mural down   (d) mure all down   (e) wall down
V, i, 220   Then know that I, *as* Snug the Ioyner am | A *Lyon fell*   (a) as . . . lion fell   (b) one . . . lion-fell

Love's Labor's Lost (q 1598)

I, i, 104   Why should I ioy in *any* abhortiue byrth   (a) an   (b) any
I, i, 239   that base *Minow* of thy myrth   (a) minion   (b) minnow
II, i, 44   A man of soueraigne *peerelesse* he is esteemd   (f 1623 : parts)   (a) parts   (b) parts, peerless
IV, iii, 54   Disfigure not his *Shop*   (a) shop   (b) slop
IV, iii, 175   With *men like men* of inconstancie   (a) men like you, men   (b) moon-like men, men
IV, iii, 250   The hue of dungions, and the *Schoole* of night   (a) school   (b) suit
V, ii, 67   So *perttaunt like* would I ore'sway his state   (a) pertaunt-like   (b) planet-like   (c) portent-like

The Merchant of Venice (q 1600)

II, i, 35   So is Alcides beaten by his *rage*   (a) rage   (b) rogue
II, ix, 77   Paciently to beare my *wroath*   (a) roth   (b) ruth
III, i, 95   ha ha, *heere* in Genowa   (a) Heard   (b) Here
III, ii, 106   thy *palenes* moues me more then eloquence   (a) paleness   (b) plainness
III, ii, 157   but the full summe of me | is *sume of something*   (f 1623 : sum of nothing)   (a) some of something   (b) sum of nothing   (c) sum of something
IV, i, 128   O be thou damnd, *inexecrable* dogge   (a) inexecrable   (b) inexorable

As You Like It (f 1623)

II, i, 5   Heere feele we *not* the penaltie of Adam   (a) but   (b) not
II, vii, 73   Till that the *wearie* verie meanes do ebbe   (a) wearer's   (b) weary
III, ii, 149   O most gentle *Iupiter*   (a) Jupiter   (b) pulpiter
III, iii, 16   the truest poetrie is the most *faining*   (a) faining   (b) feigning
IV, iii, 87   Of femall fauour, and bestowes himselfe | Like a ripe *sister*   (a) forester   (b) sister
V, ii, 93   All puritie, all triall, all *obseruance*   (a) obedience   (b) observance

Much Ado about Nothing (q 1600)

II, i, 41   away to saint *Peter : for the heauens, he* shewes me where the Batchellers sit   (a) Peter. For the heavens, he   (b) Peter for the heavens, he
II, iii, 39   Weele fit the *kid-foxe* with a penny worth   (a) hid-fox   (b) kid-fox
IV, i, 54   Out on *thee seeming, I* wil write against it   (a) the seeming ! I   (b) thee seeming ! I   (c) thee ! Seeming ! I
V, i, 16   *And sorrow, wagge, crie* hem, when he should grone   (a) Bid sorrow wag, cry   (b) And – sorry wag – cry

Twelfth Night (f 1623)

I, iii, 121   it does indifferent well in a *dam'd colour'd* stocke   (a) damned colored   (b) flame-colored   (c) dun-colored
I, v, 194   *Vio.* . . . Some mollification for your Giant, sweete Ladie ; *tell me your minde*, I am a messenger   (a) 'Tell . . .

mind' assigned to Olivia   (b) 'Tell . . . mind' retained for Viola

II, iv, 33   More longing, wauering, sooner lost and *worne*   (a) won   (b) worn

III, iii, 15   And *thankes: and euer oft* good turnes   (a) thanks, and ever oft   (b) ever thanks, and oft   (c) thanks and ever. Oft

III, iv, 188   And laid mine honour too vnchary *on't*   (a) on't   (b) out

THE MERRY WIVES OF WINDSOR (F 1623)

I, i, 19   the salt-fish, is an old *Coate*   (a) coat   (b) cod

I, i, 223   I hope vpon familiarity will grow more *content*   (a) contempt   (b) content

I, iii, 25   The good humor is to steale at a *minutes rest*   (Q 1602: minutes rest)   (a) minim-rest   (b) minute's rest

I, iii, 49   he hath a *legend* of Angels   (a) legion   (b) legend

II, i, 195   will you goe *An-heires*   (a) Ammeers   (b) mynheers

III, iii, 144   so, now *vncape*   (a) uncape   (b) uncase   (c) uncope

V, v, 35, 53, 82, 88, speech-prefixes   *Qui. Qu. Qu. Qui.*   (a) Ann Page   (b) Quickly

ALL'S WELL THAT ENDS WELL (F 1623)

I, iii, 195   Yet in this captious, and *intemible Siue*   (a) inteemable seive   (b) intenable seive   (c) intenible seive

II, i, 173   *Seard otherwise, ne worse of worst extended*   (a) Seared otherwise; nay, worse of worst, extended   (b) Seared; otherwise – ne worse of worst – extended   (c) Seared otherwise; nay worse of worst extended

III, ii, 108   Fly with false ayme, moue the *still-peering* aire   (a) still-peering   (b) still-piecing

IV, ii, 38   I see that men *make rope's in such a scarre*   (a) make ropes in such a scar   (b) may rope's in such a snare

V, i, 6   Enter *a gentle Astringer*   (a) an Astringer   (b) a Gentleman   (c) a gentle Stranger

MEASURE FOR MEASURE (F 1623)

I, ii, 129   I had as lief haue the foppery of freedome, as the *mortality* of imprisonment   (a) morality   (b) mortality

I, ii, 145   Onely for *propogation* of a Dowre   (a) propagation   (b) prorogation

I, iii, 20   The needfull bits and curbes to headstrong *weedes*   (a) steeds   (b) weeds   (c) wills   (d) jades

I, iii, 42   And yet, my nature neuer in the *fight*   (a) fight   (b) sight

II, i, 39   Some run from *brakes of Ice*   (a) brakes of ice   (b) brakes of vice   (c) breaks of ice

IV, i, 75   Our Corne's to reape, for yet our *Tithes* to sow   (a) tilth's   (b) tithe's

1 HENRY VI (F 1623)

I, i, 50   Our Ile be made a *Nourish* of salt Teares   (a) nourish   (b) marish (i.e. marsh)

I, iv, 33   Rather then I would be so *pil'd* esteem'd   (a) pilled   (b) vile

V, iii, 10   Now ye Familiar Spirits, that are cull'd / Out of the powerfull *Regions* vnder earth   (a) legions   (b) regions

V, iii, 192   *Mad* naturall Graces that extinguish Art   (a) And   (b) Mid

V, v, 60   *Most* of all these these reasons bindeth vs   (a) It most   (b) Most   (c) Which most

2 HENRY VI (F 1623)

III, i, 140   That you will cleare your selfe from all *suspence*   (a) suspect   (b) suspence

III, i, 260   As Humfrey prou'd by *Reasons* to my Liege   (a) reasons   (b) treasons

IV, vii, 64   *Kent* to maintaine, the King, the Realme and you   (a) But   (b) Kent

IV, vii, 82   Ye shall haue a hempen *Candle then, & the help of hatchet*   (a) candle, then, and the help of hatchet   (b) caudle then and pap with a hatchet

3 HENRY VI (F 1623)

I, i, 14   And *Brother,* here's the Earle of Wiltshires blood   (a) brother   (b) cousin

I, i, 19   Such *hope* haue all the line of Iohn of Gaunt   (a) hap   (b) hope

II, v, 119   *Men* for the losse of thee, hauing no more   (a) Even   (b) Meet   (c) So

III, i, 24   Let me embrace *the sower Aduersaries*   (a) thee, sour adversity   (b) thee, sour adversities

IV, viii, 6   *King.* Let's leuie men, and beat him backe againe   (a) King   (b) Oxford

RICHARD III (F 1623)

I, i, 65   That *tempts* him to this harsh Extremity   (Q 1597: tempers)   (a) tempers   (b) tempts

I, i, 138   Now by *S. Iohn,* that Newes is bad indeed   (Q 1597: Saint Paul)   (a) Saint John   (b) Saint Paul

I, i, 142   *Where is he, in* his bed?   (Q 1597: What is he in)   (a) What, is he in   (b) Where is he? In

I, iv, 46   With that *sowre* Ferry-man which Poets write of   (Q 1597: grim)   (a) grim   (b) sour

II, iv, 65   Or let me dye to looke on *earth* no more   (Q 1597: death)   (a) death   (b) earth

IV, iv, 323   Aduantaging their *Loue,* with interest   (a) loan   (b) love

KING JOHN (F 1623)

I, i, 256   Heauen lay not my transgression to *my charge, / That art* the issue of my deere offence   (a) my charge! Thou art   (b) thy charge that art

II, i, 144   As great *Alcides shooes* vpon an Asse   (a) Alcides' shows   (b) Alcides' shoes

III, i, 259   A *cased* lion   (a) caged   (b) cased   (c) chafed

III, iii, 39   Sound on into the drowzie *race* of night   (a) ear   (b) face   (c) race

III, iii, 52   Then, in despight of *brooded* watchfull day   (a) broad-eyed   (b) brooded

IV, ii, 42   And more, more strong, *then* lesser is my feare   (a) the   (b) then   (c) when

RICHARD II (Q 1597)

I, i, 186   Coosin, throw *vp* your gage   (F 1623: down)   (a) down   (b) up

II, i, 18   As praises of whose taste *the wise are found*   (a) the wise are fond   (b) th' unwise are fond

II, i, 70   For young hot colts being *ragde,* do rage the more   (a) raged   (b) ragged   (c) reined

II, iii, 80   And fright our natiue peace with *selfeborne* armes   (a) self-born   (b) self-borne

III, iii, 119   This sweares *he, as he is princesse iust*   (F 1623: he, as he is a Prince, is iust   (a) he, as he is a prince and just   (b) he, as he is a prince, is just

1 HENRY IV (Q 1598)

I, iii, 108   Neuer did *bare* and rotten pollicy   (a) bare   (b) base

II, iv, 232   Zbloud you starueling, you *elfskin* [i.e. *elsskin*]   (a) eel-skin   (b) elf-skin

II, iv, 468   thou art essentially *made* without seeming so   (F 1623 : made)   (a) mad   (b) made

III, iii, 82   the prince is a iacke, a *sneakeup*   (F 1623 : sneak-cup)   (a) sneak-cup   (b) sneak-up

IV, ii, 30   olde *fazd* ancient   (F 1623 : fac'd)   (a) faced   (b) fazed

V, iii, 22   *Ah foole, goe* with thy soule whither it goes   (a) A fool go   (b) Ah fool, go

2 HENRY IV (Q 1600)

I, i, 102   a sullen *bell, | Remembred* tolling   (a) bell, remem'bred   (b) bell remember'd,

I, ii, 6   the braine of this foolish compoūded *clay-man is not* able to inuent   (a) clay-man is not   (b) clay, man, is not

II, iv, 313   but the diuel *blinds* him too   (F 1623 : out-bids)   (a) blinds   (b) out-bids

IV, i, 71   (not in Q ; supplied from F 1623) And are enforc'd from our most quiet *there*   (a) flow   (b) shore   (c) there

IV, v, 204   And all *thy* friends which thou must make thy friends   (a) my   (b) thy

HENRY V (F 1623)

I, ii, 173   To *tame* and hauocke more than she can eate   (a) spoil   (b) 'tame   (c) tear

II, i, 34   O welliday Lady, if he be not *hewne* now   (a) drawn   (b) hewn

II, iii, 15   for his Nose was as sharpe as a Pen, and *a Table* of greene fields   (a) 'a babbled   (b) 'a talked

II, iv, 107   the *priuy* Maidens Groanes   (a) pining   (b) privèd   (c) privy

III, i, 7   Stiffen the sinewes, *commune* vp the blood   (a) conjure   (b) summon

IV, vii, 68   To *booke* our dead, and then to bury them   (a) book   (b) look

V, ii, 77   I haue but with a *curselarie* eye   (a) cursitory   (b) cursorary

HENRY VIII (F 1623)

I, ii, 67   There is no primer *basenesse*   (a) baseness   (b) business

II, iv, 180   The *bosome* of my Conscience, enter'd me   (a) bosom   (b) bottom

II, iv, 181   Yea, with a *spitting* power   (a) spitting   (b) splitting

III, ii, 171   Yet *fill'd* with my Abilities   (a) filed   (b) filled

IV, ii, 97   How pale she lookes, | And of an earthy *cold*   (a) cold   (b) color

V, iii, 133   Then but once thinke *his* place becomes thee not   (a) his   (b) this

TITUS ANDRONICUS (Q 1594)

II, iii, 85   The King my brother shall haue *notice* of this   (a) note   (b) notice

II, iii, 88   Why *I haue* patience to indure all this   (a) have I   (b) I have

III, i, 17   That shall distill from these two auntient *ruines*   (a) ruins   (b) urns

III, i, 281   And Lauinia thou shalt be imployde in *these Armes*   (F 1623 : these thinges)   (a) these   (b) these arms   (c) these charms   (d) these things

IV, iv, 52   May this *be borne as if* his traitorous sonnes   (a) be borne as if   (b) be borne ? As if

V, iii, 124   *And* as he is to witness this is true   (a) And   (b) Damned

ROMEO AND JULIET (Q 1599)

I, i, 209   From loues weak childish bow she liues *vncharmd*   (Q 1597 : unharmed)   (a) uncharmed   (b) unharmed

I, v, 94   This holy shrine, the gentle *sin* is this   (Q 1597 : finne)   (a) fine   (b) sin

II, i, 13   Young *Abraham : Cupid*   (a) Abraham Cupid   (b) Adam Cupid

II, ii, 153   To cease thy *strife,* and leaue me to my griefe   (a) strife   (b) suit

III, i, 105   *I haue it, and soundly, to your houses*   (a) I have it, | And soundly too. Your houses !   (b) I have it | and soundly. To your houses !

III, ii, 6   That *runnawayes* eyes may wincke   (a) runagates'   (b) runway's   (c) runaways'

III, ii, 49   Or those *eyes shot,* that makes *thee* answere I   (a) eyes' shot . . . the   (b) eyes shut . . . thee

IV, i, 100   *Too many* ashes, thy eyes windowes fall   (a) To paly   (b) To waned   (c) To wanny

V, iii, 170   This is thy sheath, there *rust* and let me dye   (Q 1597 : rest)   (a) rest   (b) rust

JULIUS CAESAR (F 1623)

I, ii, 252   'Tis very *like he hath* the Falling sicknesse   (a) like he hath.   (b) like. He hath

I, iii, 128   And the Complexion of the Element | *Is Fauors,* like the Worke we haue in hand   (a) In favors   (b) Is favored   (c) Is fev'rous

III, i, 38   And turne . . . Decree | Into the *lane* of Children   (a) lane   (b) law

III, ii, 221   For I haue neyther *writ* nor words, nor worth   (a) wit   (b) writ

IV, ii, 50   *Lucillius,* do you the like   (a) Lucilius   (b) Lucius

IV, ii, 52   Let *Lucius* and Titinius guard our doore   (a) Lucilius   (b) Lucius

HAMLET (Q 1604–05)

I, ii, 129   O that this too too *sallied* flesh would melt   (F 1623 : solid)   (a) sullied   (b) solid

I, iii, 65   Of each new hatcht vnfledgd *courage*   (F 1623 : comrade)   (a) comrade   (b) courage

I, iv, 36   the dram of *eale*   (a) eale   (b) evil

I, iv, 37   Doth all the noble substance *of a doubt* | *To* his owne scandle   (a) of a doubt, | To   (b) often dout | To   (c) to a doubt | Of

I, v, 33   That *rootes* it selfe in ease on Lethe wharffe   (Q 1603 : rootes F 1623 : rots)   (a) roots   (b) rots

II, ii, 182   a *good kissing* carrion   (a) God-kissing   (b) good kissing

II, ii, 302   how like an *Angell in apprehension, how like a God*   (F 1623 : how like an Angel ? in apprehension, how like a God)   (a) angel, in apprehension how like a god   (b) angel in apprehension, how like a god

II, ii, 572   And fall a cursing like a very drabbe ; a *stallyon*   (Q 1603 : scalion F 1623 : Scullion)   (a) scullion   (b) stallion

III, i, 86   of great *pitch* and moment   (F 1623 : pith)   (a) pitch   (b) pith

III, i, 158   Like sweet bells iangled out of *time,* and harsh   (F 1623 : tune)   (a) time   (b) tune

III, iv, 162   That monster custome, who all sence doth *eate | Of habits deuill, is* angell yet in this   (a) eat, | Of habits devil, is   (b) eat | Of habits evil, is

TROILUS AND CRESSIDA (Q 1609)

I, i, 29 *So traitor then she comes when she is thence.* (a) So, traitor, then she comes when she is thence. (b) So, traitor! When she comes? When is she thence?

I, iii, 54 *Retires* to chiding fortune (a) Retorts (b) Returns

I, iii, 92 *Corrects the influence of euill Planets* (F 1623: Corrects the ill Aspects of Planets euill) (a) Q version (b) F version

III, iii, 4 That through the sight I beare in things to *loue* (a) Jove (b) love

IV, v, 59 That giue *a coasting* welcome ere it comes (a) a coasting (b) accosting

V, i, 4 How now thou *curre* of enuy (F 1623: core) (a) core (b) cur

V, x, 7 Sit gods vpon your thrones, and *smile* at Troy (a) smile (b) smite

OTHELLO (F 1623)

II, i, 12 The *chidden* Billow (Q 1622: chiding) (a) chidden (b) chiding

II, i, 13 The winde-shak'd-Surge, with high & monstrous *Maine* (a) main (b) mane

III, iii, 166 It is the greene-ey'd Monster, which doth *mocke* / The meate it feeds on (a) make (b) mock

III, iii, 170 Who dotes, yet doubts : Suspects, yet *soundly* loues (Q 1622: strongly) (a) fondly (b) soundly (c) strongly

IV, ii, 64 *I heere* looke grim as hell (a) Ay, here (b) Ay, there

V, ii, 15 Ile smell *thee* on the Tree (Q 1622: it) (a) it (b) thee

V, ii, 347 Like the base *Iudean* (Q 1622: Indian) (a) Indian (b) Judean

KING LEAR (F 1623)

I, i, 5 for *qualities* are so weigh'd (Q 1608: equalities) (a) equalities (b) qualities

I, i, 156 *nere feare* to loose it (Q 1608: nor fear) (a) ne'er fear (b) ne'er feared (c) nor fear

I, iv, 334 You are much more *at task* (Q 1608: attaskt) (a) at task (b) atasked (c) ataxed

II, i, 76 Were very pregnant and potentiall *spirits* (Q 1608: spurs) (a) spirits (b) spurs

II, i, 77 O *strange* and fastned Villaine (Q 1608: strong) (a) strange (b) strong

II, iv, 97 Would with his Daughter speake, *commands, tends, seruice* (Q 1608: commands her seruice) (a) commands her service (b) commands their service (c) commands – tends – service

II, iv, 163 To fall, and *blister* (Q 1608: To fall and blast her pride) (a) blast her pride (b) blister (c) blister her

III, vii, 63 If Wolues had at thy Gate howl'd that *sterne* time (Q 1608: dearne) (a) dearn (b) stern

IV, ii, 56 (not in F; supplied from Q 1608) France spreds his banners in our noyseles *land*, / *With plumed helme thy state begins thereat* (a) land / With plummed helm. Thy state begins to threat. (b) land. / With plumed helm thy state begins to threat.

MACBETH (F 1623)

I, ii, 56 Point against *Point, rebellious Arme* 'gainst Arme (a) point, rebellious arm (b) point rebellious, arm

I, iii, 97 as thick as *Tale* / *Can* post with post (a) hail came (b) tale came

I, vii, 59 We *faile?* (a) fail. (b) fail? (c) fail!

III, ii, 13 We haue *scorch'd* the Snake, not kill'd it (a) scorched (b) scotched

IV, i, 97 Rebellious *dead,* rise neuer (a) dead (b) head

IV, ii, 22 Each way, and *moue* (a) move (b) none

IV, iii, 14 something / You may *discerne* of him through me (a) deserve (b) discern

IV, iii, 107 By his owne interdiction stands *accust* (a) accused (b) accursed

V, iv, 11 For where there is aduantage to be *giuen* (a) given (b) gone

TIMON OF ATHENS (F 1623)

I, ii, 118 *There tast, touch all, pleas'd* from thy table rise (a) Th' ear, / Taste, touch, smell, all, pleased (b) Th' ear, / Taste, touch, smell, pleased (c) Th' ear, / Taste, touch and smell, pleased

II, ii, 38 With clamorous demands *of debt, broken Bonds* (a) of date-broke bonds (b) of debt, broken bonds (c) of broken bonds

III, v, 14 He is a Man (setting *his Fate* aside) of comely Vertues (a) his fate (b) his fault (c) this fault

IV, iii, 12 It is the *Pastour Lards, the Brothers* sides (a) pasture lards the rother's (b) pasture lards the wether's

V, iii, 4 Some Beast *reade* this ; There do's not liue a Man (a) read (b) reared

ANTONY AND CLEOPATRA (F 1623)

I, ii, 105 we bring forth weeds, / When our quicke *windes* lye still (a) minds (b) winds

I, iii, 20 *What sayes the married woman you* may goe? (a) What, says the married woman you (b) What says the married woman? You

I, iv, 46 *lacking* the varrying tyde (a) lackeying (b) lacking

III, x, 10 Yon *ribaudred* Nagge of Egypt (a) ribald-rid (b) ribaldered (c) ribaudred

IV, xv, 28 shall acquire no Honour / *Demuring* vpon me (a) demuring (b) demurring

V, ii, 7 neuer pallates more the *dung*, / The beggers Nurse, and Caesars (a) dug (b) dung

CORIOLANUS (F 1623)

I, iv, 41 wee'l beate them to their Wiues, / As they vs to our *Trenches followes* (a) trenches. Follow me (b) trenches. Follow's

I, ix, 45 Let him be made an *Ouerture* for th' Warres (a) coverture (b) overture

II, i, 243 his soaring Insolence / Shall *teach* the People (a) teach (b) touch

II, ii, 103 as *Weeds* before / A Vessell vnder sayle (a) waves (b) weeds

III, ii, 20 Lesser had bin / The *things* of your dispositions (a) taxings (b) thwartings

IV, vii, 55 *Rights by rights fouler*, strengths by strengths do faile (a) Rights by rights falter (b) Rights by rights founder (c) Right's by rights fouler

PERICLES (Q 1609)

III, Cho. 46 Hath their keele cut : but *fortune mou'd* (a) fortune moved (b) fortune's mood

III, i, 26 *Vse* honour with you (a) Use (b) Vie

III, i, 40 Tie my *pleasure* vp in silken Bagges (a) pleasure (b) treasure

IV, iii, 27 he did not flow from honourable *courses* (a) courses (b) sources

V, ii, 2 More a little, and then *dum* (a) done (b) dumb

CYMBELINE (F 1623)

III, iii, 25   Such gaine the Cap of him, that makes *him* fine   (a) him   (b) them

III, vi, 74   'Mongst *Friends? | If Brothers :* would it had bin so   (a) friends, if brothers   (b) friends ? If brothers

IV, ii, 111   For defect of iudgement / Is oft the *cause* of Feare   (a) cause   (b) cease   (c) cure

IV, ii, 170   *thou* thy selfe thou blazon'st   (a) how   (b) thou

V, v, 262   Thinke that you are vpon a *Rocke*, and now / Throw me againe   (a) lock   (b) rock

THE WINTER'S TALE (F 1623)

II, i, 143   I would *Land-damne* him   (a) lam-damn   (b) land-damn

IV, iv, 12   I should blush / To see you so attyr'd : *sworne* I thinke, / To shew my selfe a glasse   (a) swoon   (b) sworn

IV, iv, 244   *clamor* your tongues   (a) charm   (b) clammer   (c) clamor   (d) clam a'

V, i, 58   and on this Stage | (*Where we Offendors now* appeare) Soule-vext   (a) (were we offenders now   (b) (where we offenders now   (c) where we offenders move   (d) where we offend as now

V, iii, 95   then, all stand *still : | On :*   (a) still ; / Or   (b) still ; / On –

THE TEMPEST (F 1623)

I, ii, 100   Who hauing *into* truth, by telling of it   (a) into   (b) unto

III, i, 15   Most *busie lest*, when I doe it   (a) busy least   (b) busy, lest   (c) busy, least

IV, i, 164   Come with a thought ; I *thank* thee Ariell : come   (a) thank   (b) think

V, i, 290   This is *a strange thing as* ere I look'd on   (a) a strange thing as   (b) as strange a thing as

THE COMEDIES

FOREWORD

$\mathcal{U}$ntil a few years before Shakespeare began to write, the terms for the various kinds of plays were so loosely applied as to be virtually interchangeable, but by the time of *Hamlet* (c. 1601) a fair degree of consistency had been achieved. Shakespeare's own classification, which is acute although playfully assigned to Polonius, distinguishes tragedy, comedy, history, pastoral; then blurs the distinction in a scrambling of types ranging from "pastoral-comical" to "tragical-comical-historical-pastoral." Thomas Heywood in his *Apology for Actors*, written about six years later, loyally includes mention of the antiquated "morall" but otherwise gives an identical classification – "tragedyes, comedyes, historyes, pastorals." In Thomas Middleton's *Hengist King of Kent, or The Mayor of Queenborough* (c. 1618) a character called "Second Player" pays Polonius the compliment of imitation in describing the motley repertory of his company, the members of which are called "pastorists" as well as "comedians, tragedians" etc. (Since the history play had gone out of fashion, they are not "historists.")

The prominence in the system of the term "pastoral" is puzzling at first glance because the English playwrights composed few examples of the Italianate species to which it literally applies, but actually, in the references cited, the term is being used in the broader sense of our term "romance" or "romantic." When Robert Greene spoke of writing "pastorals" for the common players, he was certainly referring to plays with the kind of story material found in his romance *Pandosto* (later dramatized in Shakespeare's *The Winter's Tale*) and in his own surviving "romantic comedies." The publishers of the first folio devoted no separate section to "Pastorals," obviously because it was as difficult then as it is now to segregate those plays in which the "romantic" as distinct from the "comic" element clearly predominates. They were content to group all the plays with happy endings except the histories (and *Cymbeline*) under the inclusive heading of "comedies." Modern criticism has inadvertently restored the fourth genre by persistently referring to Shakespeare's graver "pastorals" (including *Cymbeline*) as his "romances." The type, with its relation to emergent "tragicomedy," will be briefly discussed at the relevant point in the present volume.

The lighter plays in the romantic mode, those which Polonius would have called "pastoral-comical," such as *A Midsummer Night's Dream, As You Like It*, and *Twelfth Night* not only remain among the "comedies" but tend to establish in our minds the Shakespearean norm of writing in the comic mode. They are whimsical love-tales acted out in improbable places by charming aristocrats, and hence a world removed from the ludicrous trickeries inflicted by and upon the middle-class stereotypes of classical comedy. However, the influence of the latter is perceptible in them, as is the influence of a less literary strain, the folk humor descending through medieval miracle play and early Tudor interlude, or spontaneously generated wherever the human eye perceives incongruity. It is a curious fact that the plays which we patronize as mere "farces," *The Comedy of Errors, The Taming of the Shrew*, and *The Merry Wives of Windsor*, are the most "classical" of Shakespeare's comedies – in the sense of having the most in common with the Greco-Roman school of "new comedy" practiced by Menander, Plautus, and Terence, and dearly cherished in the schools. In these plays the purists Philip Sidney and Ben Jonson would have found little to condemn so far as the characters and action are concerned; however they might have found them lacking, like all of Shakespeare's comedies, in the proper degree of satirical zeal. As a less eminent Elizabethan noted (without dissatisfaction), Shakespeare's was no "railing wit." Although there is satire in all the comedies, it never seems their *raison d'être*. The concern is with reform rather than ridicule. The theme of redemption central to the morality plays and prominent in the interludes, especially the Prodigal Son cluster, so infiltrates Shakespearean comedy as to render the satirical elements purely residual.

There remains an ingredient which can scarcely be described as either "pastoral" or "comical" – as when characters are confronted with a vengeful money-lender, as in *The Merchant of Venice*, or a malicious slanderer, as in *Much Ado about Nothing*, or an unjust judge, as in *Measure for Measure*, or a far from fortuitous barrier to marriage, as in *All's Well That Ends Well*. Such episodes often derived from the Italian novella, so that realistic as well as romantic prose fiction must be recognized as a formative influence upon Shakespearean comedy. A modern playwright handling similar material is apt to call the vehicle simply a "drama" and perhaps Shakespeare thought of some of his comedies simply as "plays." At a time when such playwrights as Brieux, Ibsen, and Shaw were revolting against the romantic tradition of serious drama, the term "problem play" came into critical currency, and it was finally applied retrospectively to *Measure for Measure, All's Well That Ends Well*, and the realistic portions of *Cymbeline* and *Troilus and Cressida*. It has since been applied to plays as various as *Hamlet* and *Antony and Cleopatra*.

Shakespeare's comedies are works of art, and therefore not alike. They balk definition, even more than works of art do generally, because their materials are so various and so variously combined. The master-key to them has been sought in the spirit of Saturnalia, in seasonal myth, and, of course, in the Freudian mystique. We need not be hostile to any of the attempts to extract a basic formula, but we must observe that each master-key, while it may work with some hypothetical master-comedy, sticks in the lock of each of Shakespeare's actual comedies – it never works with a particular play. This intransigeance is nothing to be deplored, since we are left with different plays to read instead of the same play in different disguises. If there is a unifying principle, it is a simple one. The plays *do* end happily, and in so doing seem to mark out a route to happiness. Every wise reader of Shakespearean comedy knows that the journeys end in lovers meeting – at the tempered Saturnalia of a family reunion, betrothal party, or both – after certain obstacles to this wished-for consummation have been eliminated (or leaped). The last words, whether in ribald jest or fairy blessing, are apt to allude to a "happy event" which is expected nine months hence. Thus the plays cast a vote of confidence in our kind, even though the hoped-for formation of a new society resolves itself into nothing more revolutionary than the formation of a new baby. It is pleasant to participate in a rite in which Life is welcomed.   A. H.

BIBLIOGRAPHY

Anthologies of criticism are *Shakespeare: The Comedies*, ed. K. Muir (1965); *Discussions of Shakespeare's Problem Comedies*, ed. R. Ornstein (1961); *Discussions of Shakespeare's Romantic Comedy*, ed. H. Weil, Jr (1966). For general description and criticism see H. B. Charlton, *Shakespearian Comedy* (1938); George Gordon, *Shakespearian Comedy and Other Studies* (1944); Thomas M. Parrott, *Shakespearean Comedy* (1949); E. C. Pettet, *Shakespeare and the Romance Tradition* (1949); S. C. Sen Gupta, *Shakespearian Comedy* (1951); John R. Brown, *Shakespeare and his Comedies* (1957). For particular groups see J. Dover Wilson, *Shakespeare's Happy Comedies* (1962); Derek Traversi, *Shakespeare: The Early Comedies* (1960); E. M. W. Tillyard, *Shakespeare's Early Comedies* (1966); B. O. Bonazza, *Shakespeare's Early Comedies, A Structural Analysis* (1966); W. W. Lawrence, *Shakespeare's Problem Comedies* (1931); E. M. W. Tillyard, *Shakespeare's Problem Plays* (1966). Various elements are treated in Oscar J. Campbell, *Shakespeare's Satire* (1943); John Palmer, *Comic Characters in Shakespeare* (1946); Elmer E. Stoll, *Shakespeare's Young Lovers* (1937); Robert Goldsmith, *Wise Fools in Shakespeare* (1955); William G. Meader, *Courtship in Shakespeare* (1954): and various aspects in C. L. Barber, *Shakespeare's Festive Comedy* (1959); Bertrand Evans, *Shakespeare's Comedies* (1960); Northrop Frye, *A Natural Perspective* (1965); R. G. Hunter, *Shakespeare and the Comedy of Forgiveness* (1965); Peter G. Phialas, *Shakespeare's Romantic Comedies: the Development of their Form and Meaning* (1966). For studies of particular plays see Bernard Grebanier, *The Truth About Shylock* (1962); Charles T. Prouty, *The Sources of Much Ado about Nothing* (1950); John W. Draper, *The Twelfth Night of Shakespeare's Audience* (1950); Leslie Hotson, *The First Night of Twelfth Night* (1954); Clifford Leech, *Twelfth Night and Shakespearian Comedy* (1965); R. W. Chambers, *The Jacobean Shakespeare and Measure for Measure* (1937); David L. Stevenson, *The Achievement of Shakespeare's Measure for Measure* (1966); Josephine W. Bennett, *Measure for Measure as Royal Entertainment* (1966). For a survey of twentieth-century criticism of the comedies, see J. R. Brown in *Shakespeare Survey*, ed. A. Nicoll, VIII (1955).

THE COMEDY OF ERRORS

INTRODUCTION

As the most elementally and transparently funny of Shakespeare's plays, *The Comedy of Errors* would seem to need slight introduction. Shakespeare himself wisely discarded the explanatory prologue which he found in his Latin source, Plautus' *Menaechmi* (the two Menaechmuses). He allowed the play to speak for itself, to make its incredible muddle of events its adequate explanation for being. Indeed, this play is a good beginning one for the student of Shakespeare, for ability to enjoy the madness of total bewilderment is not a tutored one; every child has it. In the chaos created by two sets of twins (not to mention some four merchants), the expert is not of much help, as painstaking plot analyses of the play have shown. In telling who is who, or where, at any one time, the expert is about as helpful and impressive a guide as a professor leading a tour through a maze of mirrors in an amusement park. One does not have much time, "in the stirring passage of the day," to speculate about the full extent of the confusion, or even to say where any two or three, of the four twins, are when they are offstage creating further embarrassments.

It is, for other reasons, a good play to begin on. Unlike Shakespeare's more mature comedies, its funniness is relatively uncomplicated by social criticism, by philosophy, or by characterization. Pure comedy of event can move more cleanly, more like a detective story, to its tidy solution. There are no lingering notes of greater problems unsolved. The value of life itself is not questioned (though the point of it all may be not too clear); all that matters is rearranging human puppets so that they can again go about their proper business. There are left over no Shylocks, no Malvolios. Indeed, there is left over nothing really to think about – except, if one wishes, the tremendously puzzling question of what so grips and amuses an audience during a play which has so little thought in it. And, again if one wishes, one can see in their most elemental form dramatic strategies that Shakespeare was to use, so skillfully that they become almost invisible, in most of his later plays, tragedies as well as comedies. It is here that the critic, if he is needed at all, can point the way toward the considerable importance of what can also be appreciated as pure fun of the most hilarious kind, but a kind of fun, perhaps, that strikes deeper into the human predicament than is at first apparent.

One could speak more confidently of the elementary nature of this comedy, and of it as a significant beginning of Shakespeare's later development in the theatre, if one knew that it is indeed an extremely early play. It would be convenient to think of it as Shakespeare's first comedy. Unfortunately, the external evidence permits of a date anywhere from the beginning of Shakespeare's career to as late as 1594, when its first recorded performance was given at the Gray's Inn Christmas Revels on December 28 before a riotous audience of learned lawyers. Of little aid in establishing the date of composition is the possibility that Shakespeare used the translation by "W. W." (?William Warner) of the *Menaechmi*. This was not published until 1595, but was entered in the Stationers' Register in 1594 and may have been available to Shakespeare considerably earlier. Warner was patronized by the Hunsdons, father and son, both of whom became patrons of Shakespeare's dramatic company; an acquaintance between Shakespeare and Warner was quite possible. But Shakespeare himself could read Plautine Latin, and he may well have gotten the strange designation of "Antipholis Sereptus," which appears inappropriately in the opening stage directions at II, i, from the Latin word "surreptus" (snatched away), used in Renaissance editions of Plautus to designate one of the twin Menaechmi.

Internal evidence suggests an earlier dating. There is the reference to Spain as having sent "whole armadoes of carracks," an allusion that would have lost some of its proud currency not long after 1588. There is also a tantalizingly specific topical allusion by Dromio of Syracuse to France as "armed and reverted, making war against her heir." This is clearly a reference to the French civil wars, which concerned England so much that Elizabeth sent over two expeditionary forces. Henry of Navarre, the "heir," had been designated such by Henry III, but he had to fight for several years to secure his full right. Even when Henry III was still alive, the Catholic League waged war against Navarre. When Henry III died on August 12, 1589, Navarre became king (Henry IV), though he did not achieve Paris until 1593. But he was technically "heir" only until 1589. It is perhaps noteworthy that another very early play, *Love's Labor's Lost*, is paired with *The Comedy of Errors* in dealing with French affairs and specifically with Henry of Navarre.

The lack of compelling characterization also suggests an early date; but this quality may just as well be artistic design as immaturity, for it permits an economical exploitation of the speed and neatness of Latin comedy. *The Comedy of Errors* is precisely the sort of play that an artistically serious young dramatist, still without too much to say about love, politics, or human nature, might design as a reaction against contemporary (and perhaps his own) dabbling in romantic comedy. A date between 1589 and 1591 would accommodate most of the essential facts that we have about the play.

Although it has been held that as sources for *The Comedy of Errors* Shakespeare drew upon every well-known Latin (not to mention Italian) comedy of mistaken identity, one play, Plautus' *Menaechmi*, is the undisputed source for the main story. But Plautus is Roman comedy at its most cynical. Elizabethans preferred a wife rather than a prostitute as the central female character, and so the Courtesan, still present, is downgraded. The English audience preferred in general some softening of the derisive, satirical spirit that constituted comedy for the Romans. Shakespeare created the attractive figure of Luciana, thus permitting a hint of the lyrical, tender, and high-spirited love interest, alien to Latin comedy, that is to distinguish his later works. He added also the "kitchen-vestal," Luce, a greasy, obese wench of the sort that Londoners would appreciate; she anticipates Touchstone's Audrey. And he enriched Plautus' Medicus into the figure of the schoolmaster, Dr Pinch, whose baleful fate and indignities may serve to warn later pedants not to deal meticulously with so robust a comedy.

Other additions are still more significant. In Plautus the father of the twins dies of grief after the loss of one twin. Shakespeare thus is responsible for the poignant, poetic role of old Egeon, whom we see only at the beginning and ending of the play. He also gives a kind of tragic overcast to the play, the sort of uneasiness in the midst of mirth that Shakespeare could never throughout his career entirely abandon. There would always be a threatened death or disaster. *The Comedy of Errors* would be slighter without this sombre background, and the reunion at the end would be less impressive if Egeon did not meet both his long-lost sons and his wife, the Abbess. For the sadness and suffering by shipwreck and the ultimate reunion – one of the major themes of Shakespearean comedy – Shakespeare was specifically indebted in this case to the Greek romance of Apollonius of Tyre (in Gower's version or in Twine's). Therein the supposedly drowned wife of Apollonius floats to Ephesus and becomes a priestess in the Temple of Diana; she is later reunited to her husband as is Egeon to the Abbess in Shakespeare. It is the Abbess who best expresses the mingled poignancy and comedy of the play: "this sympathizèd one day's error."

An even more important alteration of the *Menaechmi* was the addition of twin servants to the twin masters. Sixteenth-century Italian and Spanish versions of Plautus had experimented with more than one pair of twins, even introducing a sister; but Shakespeare was probably indebted mainly to Plautus' most popular play, *Amphitruo*. Herein – in what becomes Shakespeare's III, i, the most hilarious scene in the play – Mercury impersonates Amphitruo's servant so as to keep master and man out of the house while Jupiter (disguised as Amphitruo) is enjoying the wife within.

Shakespeare, however, needed no inspiration for the confusing quartet other than his own insight into the comic. He knew, well before Bergson brilliantly explained it, that man laughs at any imposition of the mechanical or duplicative upon the spontaneity and variety of life. Twins are, as Bergson saw, comic because they are mechanically identical. A person who looks exactly like another travesties the first by his very being; there would otherwise be no laughter at the performance of mimics. Two sets of twins increase the ludicrous trick played on man's individual ego. Shakespeare never tired of his delighted awareness that only one of a kind can have dignity. A double marriage ceremony makes a philosophical as well as ribald commentary upon a precariously civilized

institution. Four simultaneous marriages, as in *As You Like It*, are not "romantic"; the sight of four couples lined up for the ceremonious mating is inescapably farcical. Likewise *The Comedy of Errors*, by having two sets of identical twins, strips all the dignity of individuality from its participants, and even in the joyful reunion there can be no identification with any one character.

With four mistakable persons wandering in a maze, plotting rather than other dramatic skills is most needed. And perhaps the symmetry and near flawlessness of this plot make it the best work of this not contemptible kind that Shakespeare was ever to do. However, though the characterization of the play is usually not praised, it is not negligible. Shakespeare merely succeeded, for one of the rare times in his career, in not allowing any one person to outgrow his function in the story. The characters, despite their comical external likenesses, are all distinct as personalities. The two Antipholuses are remarkably dissimilar for identical twins. The Syracusian brother is melancholy, earnest, and almost tragically inclined. He speaks some of the most ardent poetry in the play and would probably, given a continued sad life, have developed into the copy of his father. The Ephesian Antipholus, on the contrary, is a prosperous, rather insensitive businessman, a respected citizen who expects his wife to behave with complete moral propriety while he himself tastes, in moderation, the pleasures of the town. He is also a realistic version of the husband with a nagging wife. His brother has no wife, and when this brother meets Luciana (who is also very different from her sister) it is with the first-love ardor of any of Shakespeare's young lovers. The two Dromios are also distinct. Both are witty, but the Syracusian has the edge; and it has been his task to cheer up his pensive master. Dromio of Ephesus, like his master, has a more prosaic nature, befitting his urban environment and the not too moral respectability of his master.

There are other interesting persons (notably Luce, who with only a few slight lines is hugely comic), but the essence of this comedy is clearly not in character. If the critic examines closely the dialogue and stage business (remembering uneasily the singed beard and fool-cut hair of the scholarly Dr Pinch), he will find that the texture of the play is made up of incessant use of a small number of low comedy elements. There are endless quibbles (mainly by the Dromios), gross accounts of the structure of Luce, tireless jokes about the cuckold's horns and the "French disease." The dialogue is animated but not memorable; this is not a comedy of subtle or even realistic language. The stage business is equally innocent of subtlety. One is aware mainly of frantic running, angry expostulation, and a rapid shifting of confusable persons on the stage. Above all one is aware of beatings, particularly blows to the head. Why this beating should be funny it is not easy to say. But Shakespeare found it merry enough to devote by large odds the greatest part of the stage business to mere blows. Each Dromio gets rewarded for his well-meaning efforts by the bloodying of the pate by both masters. Somehow the repeated act of having one's "sconce" broken is enormously satisfying to audiences. Clowns with large, artificial heads prove this to-day, taking blows growing in intensity until the thud is resonant throughout the arena. It is not, of course, funny if the victim of a mighty blow stays down. Perhaps it is the resilience of the Dromios that reassures us, even as, on a much higher (and broader) level, Falstaff rebounds from blow after blow to his ego. The blow to the head is also a blow to the pretentious part of man, gratifying the popular audience by its universally levelling virtue. One must not, incidentally, judge the length of this comedy by its scanty 1756 lines. Picture it, rather, with full stage business, dome after dome resounding from the repeated blows – domes that also suffer the added indignities of cuckold's horns and the ravages of the "French disease." It is, then, a comedy that reassures the audience that man's head is fundamentally ridiculous, not too important in any robust view of life.

But of course dialogue and stage business are secondary in this play to what it is classically famous for: mistaken identity. Mistaken identity is in itself an additional blow to the individual ego. One is seldom pleased to find that he is constantly being taken for someone else – usually, of course, someone much less impressive. There are, however, several kinds of mistaken identity. This play employs the lowest. The two higher forms of mistaken identity are mistaking the true nature of another person and mistaking one's own nature. Both lead to a re-examination of life and involve character growth. Exteriors are important only in so far as they lead to a realization of one's true nature. Of these two higher forms there are only hints in *The Comedy of Errors*. Antipholus of Syracuse asks a question that might have been all-important in a later comedy:

> Am I in earth, in heaven, or in hell?
> Sleeping or waking? mad or well advised?
> Known unto these, and to myself disguised!

This is a remote approach to the agonizing and central question which Angelo in *Measure for Measure* asks himself:

> What dost thou? or what art thou, Angelo? –

a question preparing him for a totally new understanding of his own nature. On a still higher level – and showing that mistaken identity is fundamental to Shakespearean tragedy as well – is Lear's question:

> Who is it that can tell me who I am?

There is no probing of personality in *The Comedy of Errors*. No one learns more about himself or his neighbor as a result of the errors. Confusion leads to near-madness but does not bring about the breakdown of an ego prior to self-knowledge; it leads rather to drawn swords and headblows. The resolution of the play is not the serene elevation of vision which we find in the later comedies; it is simply a recognition of who, physically, is who.

There is still another peculiar limitation in this play of mistaken identity. No actor within the play pulls the strings of the human puppets. There is no Rosalind, no Prospero to make the confusion delightfully purposeful. In no other play is the ignorance of the participants more total, nor in any play is the purpose of the confusion less apparent. Perhaps Shakespeare felt that by widening the gap in awareness between audience and participants he was giving the audience a pleasant sense of superiority. This, however, does not seem to be the way it works out. The audience grows almost as baffled and impatient as the participants. But here there is no Iago upon whom to vent one's sense

of outraged human dignity. The purposelessness of this confusion is perilously close to the purposelessness of uninstructed life. The comedy is thus elemental in a sense that may be more important than is true of the later comedies, which seem, in contrast, to be mere playacting. Here is a basic comedy of human ineptitude without a comforting presiding spirit. Man laughing at the plight of the pointlessly outraged characters in this play is man laughing, not too comfortably, at his own most painful apprehension about life; but this apprehension, it must be stressed, is never brought brilliantly to the surface of consciousness by great poetry. It is an apprehension that might have seized Antipholus of Syracuse, but never one of the Dromios.

One must not, after all, forget that the play does not lead immediately to conclusions about human life. Theatrically it is superb farce – as so many of the so-called high comedies basically are. It is the farce of high-spirited, youthful characters, not like Egeon beyond the resilience of youth, who fight back at an intolerable situation. It is a farce set in a scene faintly anticipating the magic of *A Midsummer Night's Dream*, for Ephesus had acquired the reputation from Menander and from St Paul (Acts xix:19) of being a place of sorcerers and magic. The whole experience becomes, indeed, almost a dream. As a play of "errors," thus set in a scene of witchery, it leads man into crazy antics, gives him suddenly a wife unknown to him, causes people he does not know to offer him presents – almost, as would be the case in a later play, fills the land with music at the same time one is knocked about, bound, or claimed as her own by a fat kitchen-wench.

The play is all of these things, perhaps, for in it Shakespeare was feeling his way toward many possibilities of dramatic growth. He could not write simple farce without raising questions about the meaning of farce. But he does not ask such greater questions explicitly. In his last play, *The Tempest*, Shakespeare comments with great verbal beauty upon his craft and its strategies. *The Comedy of Errors* exhibits the legerdemain of Shakespeare's art without attempting to explain it. The basic techniques, still undisguised by weightier matters, are there. They are the more valuable in that they are not the commentary of Shakespeare the dramatic critic but of Shakespeare the dramatist. To understand the full range of Shakespeare's theatrical experiments, one should no more skip *The Comedy of Errors* than *The Tempest*.

Since the prominence of the play in the rowdy "night of errors" at Gray's Inn in 1594, *The Comedy of Errors* has had a lively but not illustrious stage history. Although Macklin and Kemble have played in it, it is not a work to attract the greatest actors; it simply has no role for major interpretation. On the other hand, it has suffered less radical treatment by adapters than have some of the better plays. True, there have been operatic versions and musical comedy versions; songs from other plays have been introduced into it; the farcical quality of the Dromios has been exaggerated; and, in the last decade or so, novel settings have been used in certain productions. On the whole, however, the central features of the play have remained unchanged in revivals through the years. At present it is very popular in Germany and in Russia. Because of its brevity, it is sometimes paired with some other play. A happy inspiration prompted the Old Vic Company in 1956–57 to perform it on the same program with *Titus Andronicus*. Thereby two allegedly Shakespearean "primitives" could be seen as the classically designed, durable works that they are.

University of California PAUL A. JORGENSEN
at Los Angeles

NOTE ON THE TEXT

The Comedy of Errors was first printed in the folio of 1623 probably from the author's own draft. Except for considerable confusion of character names in the stage directions and speech-prefixes, the text is a good one. There is indication (see V, i, 9 s.d. that the folio act–division was superimposed upon the original manuscript, but this division, with a further division of the acts into scenes, is provided marginally for reference in the present edition. The following brief list of departures from the folio text is complete, except for the correction of obvious typographical errors and the normalization of speech-prefixes and of such forms as the following in the stage directions: *Antipholus Ephes.* (to *Antipholus of Ephesus*), *Antipholus Siracusia* (to *Antipholus of Syracuse*), and *S. Dromio* (to *Dromio of Syracuse*). The adopted reading in italics is followed by the folio reading in roman.

I, i, 16 *at* at any 38 *too* (om. in F) 41 (and throughout) *Epidamnum* Epidamium 42 *the* he 102 *upon* up 116 *bark* bank 123 *thee* they 151 *life* help
I, ii, s.d. *Antipholus [of Syracuse]* Antipholis Erotes 4 *arrival* a rival 30 *lose* loose 32 s.d. *Exit* Exeunt 40 *unhappy* unhappy a 66 *clock* cook 93 *God's* God 94 s.d. *Exit* Exeunt
II, i, s.d. *Antipholus [of Ephesus]* Antipholis Sereptus 11 *o'door* adore 12 *ill* thus 20 *Men* Man *masters* master 21 *Lords* Lord 45 *two* too 61 *thousand* hundred 72 *errand* arrant 107 *alone, alone* alone, a love 112 *Wear* Where
II, ii, s.d. *Antipholus [of Syracuse]* Antipholis Errotis 79 *men* them 97 *tiring* trying 101 *no time* in no time 174 *stronger* stranger 185 *offered* free'd 193 *drone* Dromio
III, i, 89 *her* your 91 *her* your
III, ii, s.d. *Luciana* Juliana 4 *building* buildings *ruinous* ruinate 16 *attaint* attaine 21 *but* not 26 *wife* wise 46 *sister's* sister 49 *bed* bud *them* thee 57 *where* when 109 *and* is
IV, i, 87 *then she* then
IV, ii, 6 *Of* Oh 34 *One* On 35 *fury* fairy 45 *he's* is 48 *That* Thus 61 *'a* I
IV, iii, 32 *ship* ships 55 *if you do* if do
V, i, 33 *God's* God 121 *death* depth 155 *whither* whether 357–62 (in F these lines follow l. 346) 404 *ne'er* are

THE COMEDY OF ERRORS

Solinus, Duke of Ephesus
Egeon, a merchant of Syracuse
Antipholus of Ephesus ⎱ twin brothers, and sons to Egeon and
Antipholus of Syracuse ⎰ Emilia, but unknown to each other
Dromio of Ephesus ⎱ twin brothers, and slaves
Dromio of Syracuse ⎰ to the two Antipholuses
Balthazar, a merchant
Angelo, a goldsmith
A Merchant, friend to Antipholus of Syracuse

A Second Merchant, to whom Angelo is a debtor
Dr Pinch, a schoolmaster and a conjurer
Emilia, wife to Egeon, an Abbess at Ephesus
Adriana, wife to Antipholus of Ephesus
Luciana, sister to Adriana
Luce, servant to Adriana
A Courtesan
Jailer, Officers, and other Attendants

Scene : Ephesus]

*

I, i *Enter the Duke of Ephesus, with the Merchant*
[Egeon] of Syracuse, Jailer, and other Attendants.

EGEON
Proceed, Solinus, to procure my fall,
And by the doom of death end woes and all.
DUKE
Merchant of Syracusa, plead no more.
4   I am not partial to infringe our laws.
The enmity and discord which of late
Sprung from the rancorous outrage of your Duke
To merchants, our well-dealing countrymen,
8   Who, wanting guilders to redeem their lives,
Have sealed his rigorous statutes with their bloods,
Excludes all pity from our threat'ning looks.
11   For since the mortal and intestine jars
'Twixt thy seditious countrymen and us,
13   It hath in solemn synods been decreed,
Both by the Syracusians and ourselves,
15   To admit no traffic to our adverse towns :
16   Nay more, if any born at Ephesus
Be seen at Syracusian marts and fairs ;
Again, if any Syracusian born
Come to the bay of Ephesus, he dies,
His goods confiscate to the Duke's dispose,
21   Unless a thousand marks be levièd,
22   To quit the penalty and to ransom him.
Thy substance, valued at the highest rate,
Cannot amount unto a hundred marks ;

Therefore, by law thou art condemned to die.
EGEON
Yet this my comfort : when your words are done,
My woes end likewise with the evening sun.
DUKE
Well, Syracusian, say in brief the cause
Why thou departed'st from thy native home,
And for what cause thou cam'st to Ephesus.
EGEON
A heavier task could not have been imposed
Than I to speak my griefs unspeakable ;
Yet that the world may witness that my end
Was wrought by nature, not by vile offense,   34
I'll utter what my sorrow gives me leave.
In Syracusa was I born, and wed
Unto a woman, happy but for me,
And by me too, had not our hap been bad.
With her I lived in joy : our wealth increased
By prosperous voyages I often made
To Epidamnum ; till my factor's death,   41
And the great care of goods at random left,
Drew me from kind embracements of my spouse ;
From whom my absence was not six months old,
Before herself (almost at fainting under
The pleasing punishment that women bear)
Had made provision for her following me,
And soon and safe arrivèd where I was.
There had she not been long but she became
A joyful mother of two goodly sons ;
And, which was strange, the one so like the other
As could not be distinguished but by names.
That very hour, and in the self-same inn,
A mean woman was delivered   54
Of such a burden male, twins both alike.
Those – for their parents were exceeding poor –
I bought, and brought up to attend my sons.
My wife, not meanly proud of two such boys,   58

I, i In Ephesus, presumably the palace of Duke Solinus   **4** *partial* inclined
8 *guilders* Dutch coins worth about 1s. 8d. apiece   **11** *intestine* (usually
means 'internal'; here, perhaps, intensifies *mortal*)   **13** *synods* councils
15 *adverse* opposed   **16** *Ephesus* (on west coast of Asia Minor)   **21** *marks*
(worth about 13s. 4d. apiece)   **22** *quit* discharge, pay   **34** *nature* natural,
i.e. fatherly, love   **41** *Epidamnum* i.e. Epidamnus, port on the east coast
of the Adriatic ('Epidamnum' was the form used by W. W. [?William
Warner] in his translation of the Latin source, 1595); *factor's* agent's
54 *mean* of low birth   **58** *not meanly* more than commonly

59 Made daily motions for our home return.
Unwilling I agreed. Alas ! too soon
We came aboard.
A league from Epidamnum had we sailed
Before the always wind-obeying deep
64 Gave any tragic instance of our harm.
But longer did we not retain much hope ;
For what obscurèd light the heavens did grant
Did but convey unto our fearful minds
68 A doubtful warrant of immediate death ;
Which, though myself would gladly have embraced,
Yet the incessant weepings of my wife,
Weeping before for what she saw must come,
72 And piteous plainings of the pretty babes,
That mourned for fashion, ignorant what to fear,
Forced me to seek delays for them and me.
And this it was, for other means was none :
The sailors sought for safety by our boat,
77 And left the ship, then sinking-ripe, to us.
78 My wife, more careful for the latter-born,
Had fast'ned him unto a small spare mast,
Such as seafaring men provide for storms ;
To him one of the other twins was bound,
Whilst I had been like heedful of the other.
The children thus disposed, my wife and I,
Fixing our eyes on whom our care was fixed,
Fast'ned ourselves at either end the mast,
And floating straight, obedient to the stream,
Was carried towards Corinth, as we thought.
At length the sun, gazing upon the earth,
Dispersed those vapors that offended us,
And by the benefit of his wishèd light
The seas waxed calm, and we discoverèd
92 Two ships from far, making amain to us :
93 Of Corinth that, of Epidaurus this.
But ere they came – O let me say no more !
Gather the sequel by that went before.

DUKE
Nay, forward, old man ; do not break off so,
For we may pity, though not pardon thee.

EGEON
O, had the gods done so, I had not now
Worthily termed them merciless to us !
For ere the ships could meet by twice five leagues,
We were encountered by a mighty rock,
Which being violently borne upon,
103 Our helpful ship was splitted in the midst ;
So that, in this unjust divorce of us,
Fortune had left to both of us alike,
What to delight in, what to sorrow for.
Her part, poor soul, seeming as burdenèd
With lesser weight, but not with lesser woe,
Was carried with more speed before the wind,
And in our sight they three were taken up
By fishermen of Corinth, as we thought.
At length another ship had seized on us,
And knowing whom it was their hap to save,
Gave healthful welcome to their ship-wracked guests,
115 And would have reft the fishers of their prey,
Had not their bark been very slow of sail ;
And therefore homeward did they bend their course.
Thus have you heard me severed from my bliss,
That by misfortunes was my life prolonged,
To tell sad stories of my own mishaps.

DUKE
And for the sake of them thou sorrowest for,
Do me the favor to dilate at full,   122
What have befall'n of them and thee till now.

EGEON
My youngest boy, and yet my eldest care,
At eighteen years became inquisitive
After his brother ; and importuned me
That his attendant – so his case was like,   127
Reft of his brother, but retained his name –
Might bear him company in the quest of him ;
Whom whilst I labored of a love to see,   130
I hazarded the loss of whom I loved.
Five summers have I spent in farthest Greece,
Roaming clean through the bounds of Asia,
And coasting homeward, came to Ephesus,
Hopeless to find, yet loath to leave unsought
Or that or any place that harbors men.   136
But here must end the story of my life ;
And happy were I in my timely death,   138
Could all my travels warrant me they live.   139

DUKE
Hapless Egeon, whom the fates have marked
To bear the extremity of dire mishap !
Now trust me, were it not against our laws,
Against my crown, my oath, my dignity,
Which princes, would they, may not disannul,   144
My soul should sue as advocate for thee.
But though thou art adjudgèd to the death,   146
And passèd sentence may not be recalled
But to our honor's great disparagement,
Yet will I favor thee in what I can.
Therefore, merchant, I'll limit thee this day
To seek thy life by beneficial help.   151
Try all the friends thou hast in Ephesus ;
Beg thou, or borrow, to make up the sum,
And live ; if no, then thou art doomed to die.
Jailer, take him to thy custody.

JAILER
I will, my lord.

EGEON
Hopeless and helpless doth Egeon wend,
But to procrastinate his lifeless end.   *Exeunt.*

*

Enter Antipholus [of Syracuse], a Merchant, and   I, ii
Dromio [of Syracuse].

MERCHANT
Therefore give out you are of Epidamnum,
Lest that your goods too soon be confiscate.

59 *motions* plea 64 *instance* clear indication 68 *doubtful warrant* disturbing omen 72 *plainings* crying 77 *sinking-ripe* ready to sink 78 *My . . . latter-born* (l. 124 indicates, puzzlingly, that not the 'latter-born,' but the elder, went with the mother) 92 *amain* speed 93 *Epidaurus* town in Argolis on the Saronic Gulf 103 *helpful ship* i.e. the mast 115 *reft* robbed 122 *dilate* relate 127–28 *attendant . . . name* (referring to the slaves, each named Dromio) 130 *of a love* out of love 136 *Or . . . or* either . . . or 138 *timely* speedy 139 *travels* (with a secondary sense of 'travails' or labors) 144 *disannul* annul 146 *the death* the sentence of death 151 *beneficial help* i.e. help by a benefactor
I, ii The mart in Ephesus s.d. (The folios have 'Antipholis Erotes,' the 'Erotes' being probably a corruption of 'Erraticus,' the wanderer. In II, i, likewise, Antipholus of Ephesus is called 'Sereptus,' for 'Surreptus,' the lost or stolen one.)

This very day a Syracusian merchant
Is apprehended for arrival here,
And not being able to buy out his life,
According to the statute of the town,
Dies ere the weary sun set in the west.
There is your money that I had to keep.

ANTIPHOLUS S.

9   Go bear it to the Centaur, where we host,
And stay there, Dromio, till I come to thee.
Within this hour it will be dinner-time;
Till that, I'll view the manners of the town,
Peruse the traders, gaze upon the buildings,
And then return and sleep within mine inn,
For with long travel I am stiff and weary.
Get thee away.

DROMIO S.

Many a man would take you at your word,
18   And go indeed, having so good a mean.

Exit Dromio [of Syracuse].

ANTIPHOLUS S.

19   A trusty villain, sir, that very oft,
When I am dull with care and melancholy,
21   Lightens my humor with his merry jests.
What, will you walk with me about the town,
And then go to my inn and dine with me?

MERCHANT

I am invited, sir, to certain merchants,
Of whom I hope to make much benefit;
26   I crave your pardon. Soon at five o'clock,
Please you, I'll meet with you upon the mart,
28   And afterward consort you till bedtime.
My present business calls me from you now.

ANTIPHOLUS S.

Farewell till then. I will go lose myself,
And wander up and down to view the city.

MERCHANT

Sir, I commend you to your own content.   *Exit.*

ANTIPHOLUS S.

He that commends me to mine own content,
Commends me to the thing I cannot get.
I to the world am like a drop of water
That in the ocean seeks another drop,
37   Who falling there to find his fellow forth,
38   Unseen, inquisitive, confounds himself.
So I, to find a mother and a brother,
In quest of them, unhappy, lose myself.

Enter Dromio of Ephesus.

41   Here comes the almanac of my true date.
What now? How chance thou art returned so soon?

DROMIO E.

Returned so soon! rather approached too late.
The capon burns, the pig falls from the spit,

The clock hath strucken twelve upon the bell;   45
My mistress made it one upon my cheek:
She is so hot because the meat is cold;
The meat is cold because you come not home;
You come not home because you have no stomach;   49
You have no stomach, having broke your fast;
But we, that know what 'tis to fast and pray,
Are penitent for your default to-day.   52

ANTIPHOLUS S.

Stop in your wind, sir; tell me this, I pray: 53
Where have you left the money that I gave you?

DROMIO E.

O, sixpence, that I had o' Wednesday last
To pay the saddler for my mistress' crupper?   56
The saddler had it, sir; I kept it not.

ANTIPHOLUS S.

I am not in a sportive humor now.
Tell me, and dally not, where is the money?
We being strangers here, how dar'st thou trust
So great a charge from thine own custody?

DROMIO E.

I pray you, jest, sir, as you sit at dinner.
I from my mistress come to you in post;   63
If I return, I shall be post indeed,   64
For she will score your fault upon my pate.
Methinks your maw, like mine, should be your clock   66
And strike you home without a messenger.

ANTIPHOLUS S.

Come, Dromio, come, these jests are out of season;
Reserve them till a merrier hour than this.
Where is the gold I gave in charge to thee?

DROMIO E.

To me, sir? Why, you gave no gold to me.

ANTIPHOLUS S.

Come on, sir knave, have done your foolishness,
And tell me how thou hast disposed thy charge.

DROMIO E.

My charge was but to fetch you from the mart
Home to your house, the Phoenix, sir, to dinner;   75
My mistress and her sister stays for you.

ANTIPHOLUS S.

Now, as I am a Christian, answer me,
In what safe place you have bestowed my money;   78
Or I shall break that merry sconce of yours   79
That stands on tricks when I am undisposed: 80
Where is the thousand marks thou hadst of me?

DROMIO E.

I have some marks of yours upon my pate,
Some of my mistress' marks upon my shoulders,
But not a thousand marks between you both.
If I should pay your worship those again,
Perchance you will not bear them patiently.

ANTIPHOLUS S.

Thy mistress' marks? What mistress, slave, hast thou?

DROMIO E.

Your worship's wife, my mistress at the Phoenix;
She that doth fast till you come home to dinner,
And prays that you will hie you home to dinner.

ANTIPHOLUS S.

What! wilt thou flout me thus unto my face,
Being forbid? There, take you that, sir knave.
[Strikes him.]

DROMIO E.

What mean you, sir? For God's sake, hold your hands!

---

9 *Centaur* (the name of an inn; houses, shops, and inns were identified, not by numbers, but by signs bearing pictures, such as that of a centaur or a phoenix)   18 *mean* means, opportunity (Dromio is a bondman)   19 *villain* servant (used good-humoredly)   21 *humor* mood (in Renaissance psychology, humor was a fluid in the body, determining disposition and temperament)   26 *Soon at five o'clock* i.e. towards evening   28 *consort* accompany   37 *forth* out   38 *confounds himself* loses itself, mingles indistinguishably   41 *alma-nac . . . date* i.e. in Dromio, Antipholus sees his own age   45 *twelve* (half an hour late for the usual dinner-time)   49 *stomach* appetite   52 *penitent* suffering (from hunger)   53 *wind* words   56 *crupper* strap attached to saddle and passing under horse's tail   63 *post* haste   64 *post* tavern pillar used for chalking up accounts   66 *maw* stomach (usually applied to ani-mals)   75 *Phoenix* i.e. the house and shop of Antipholus of Ephesus (see I, ii, 9n.)   78 *bestowed* deposited   79 *sconce* head   80 *stands on* engages in

94   Nay, an you will not, sir, I'll take my heels.

Exit Dromio [of Ephesus].

ANTIPHOLUS S.
Upon my life, by some device or other
96   The villain is o'er-raught of all my money.
97   They say this town is full of cozenage :
As, nimble jugglers that deceive the eye,
Dark-working sorcerers that change the mind,
Soul-killing witches that deform the body,
101   Disguisèd cheaters, prating mountebanks,
102   And many such-like liberties of sin :
If it prove so, I will be gone the sooner.
I'll to the Centaur to go seek this slave ;
I greatly fear my money is not safe.   *Exit.*

*

II, i   *Enter Adriana, wife to Antipholus [of Ephesus], with*
Luciana, her sister.

ADRIANA
Neither my husband nor the slave returned,
That in such haste I sent to seek his master ?
Sure, Luciana, it is two o'clock.
LUCIANA
Perhaps some merchant hath invited him,
And from the mart he's somewhere gone to dinner.
Good sister, let us dine and never fret.
A man is master of his liberty :
Time is their master, and when they see time,
They'll go or come ; if so, be patient, sister.
ADRIANA
Why should their liberty than ours be more ?
LUCIANA
11   Because their business still lies out o'door.
ADRIANA
Look, when I serve him so, he takes it ill.
LUCIANA
O, know he is the bridle of your will.
ADRIANA
There's none but asses will be bridled so.
LUCIANA
15   Why, headstrong liberty is lashed with woe.
16   There's nothing situate under heaven's eye
But hath his bound, in earth, in sea, in sky.
The beasts, the fishes, and the wingèd fowls,
Are their males' subjects, and at their controls.
Men, more divine, the masters of all these,
Lords of the wide world, and wild wat'ry seas,
22   Indued with intellectual sense and souls,
Of more pre-eminence than fish and fowls,
Are masters to their females, and their lords :
Then let your will attend on their accords.
ADRIANA
This servitude makes you to keep unwed.
LUCIANA
Not this, but troubles of the marriage-bed.
ADRIANA
But were you wedded, you would bear some sway.
LUCIANA
Ere I learn love, I'll practise to obey.
ADRIANA
30   How if your husband start some other where ?
LUCIANA
Till he come home again, I would forbear.

ADRIANA
Patience unmoved ! No marvel though she pause ;
They can be meek that have no other cause.
A wretched soul, bruised with adversity,
We bid be quiet when we hear it cry.
But were we burd'ned with like weight of pain,
As much or more we should ourselves complain :
So thou, that hast no unkind mate to grieve thee,
With urging helpless patience wouldst relieve me ;   39
But if thou live to see like right bereft,   40
This fool-begged patience in thee will be left.   41
LUCIANA
Well, I will marry one day but to try.
Here comes your man ; now is your husband nigh.

Enter Dromio of Ephesus.

ADRIANA
Say, is your tardy master now at hand ?
DROMIO E. Nay, he's at two hands with me, and that my
two ears can witness.
ADRIANA
Say, didst thou speak with him ? Know'st thou his mind ?
DROMIO E.
Ay, ay, he told his mind upon mine ear.
Beshrew his hand, I scarce could understand it.
LUCIANA Spake he so doubtfully, thou couldst not feel
his meaning ?
DROMIO E. Nay, he struck so plainly, I could too well feel
his blows ; and withal so doubtfully, that I could scarce
understand them.   54
ADRIANA
But say, I prithee, is he coming home ?
It seems he hath great care to please his wife.
DROMIO E.
Why, mistress, sure my master is horn-mad.   57
ADRIANA
Horn-mad, thou villain !
DROMIO E.   I mean not cuckold-mad ;
But, sure, he is stark mad.
When I desired him to come home to dinner,
He asked me for a thousand marks in gold.
''Tis dinner time,' quoth I : 'My gold !' quoth he.
'Your meat doth burn,' quoth I : 'My gold !' quoth he.
'Will you come ?' quoth I : 'My gold !' quoth he –
'Where is the thousand marks I gave thee, villain ?'
'The pig,' quoth I, 'is burned' : 'My gold !' quoth he.
'My mistress, sir –,' quoth I : 'Hang up thy mistress !
I know not thy mistress ; out on thy mistress !'
LUCIANA Quoth who ?
DROMIO E. Quoth my master.
'I know,' quoth he, 'no house, no wife, no mistress.'
So that my errand due unto my tongue,   72

---

94 *an* if   96 *o'er-raught* overreached, tricked out of   97 *cozenage* cheating
(Menander and St Paul, among other writers, helped establish the tradition
of Ephesus as a city of magic and trickery)   101 *mountebanks* charlatans
(peddling worthless wares)   102 *liberties of sin* licensed offenders (Steevens)
(but the right word may be 'libertines')
II, i Before the house of Antipholus of Ephesus   11 *still* always   15 *lashed*
scourged, whipped   16–24 *There's . . . lords* (Luciana here presents the
traditional idea of male supremacy in 'the great chain of being')   22–25
intellectual sense . . . will (the will, in Renaissance psychology, was supposed
to be guided by the reason, or intellectual sense)   30 *start . . . where* i.e. turn
to other women   39 *helpless* futile   40 *like right bereft* a similar injustice
41 *This . . . left* you will leave this foolish plea for patience   54 *understand*
stand under   57 *horn-mad* acting like an enraged horned beast (but
Adriana catches first the inevitable quibble on the cuckold's horns)   72
due . . . tongue which my tongue should have performed

I thank him, I bear home upon my shoulders;
For, in conclusion, he did beat me there.
ADRIANA
Go back again, thou slave, and fetch him home.
DROMIO E.
Go back again, and be new beaten home?
For God's sake send some other messenger.
ADRIANA
Back, slave, or I will break thy pate across.
DROMIO E.
79 And he will bless that cross with other beating:
80 Between you, I shall have a holy head.
ADRIANA
Hence, prating peasant! Fetch thy master home.
DROMIO E.
82 Am I so round with you as you with me,
That like a football you do spurn me thus?
You spurn me hence, and he will spurn me hither:
If I last in this service, you must case me in leather.
                                        [Exit.]
LUCIANA
86 Fie, how impatience loureth in your face!
ADRIANA
87 His company must do his minions grace,
88 Whilst I at home starve for a merry look.
Hath homely age th' alluring beauty took
From my poor cheek? Then he hath wasted it.
Are my discourses dull? barren my wit?
If voluble and sharp discourse be marred,
Unkindness blunts it more than marble hard.
94 Do their gay vestments his affections bait?
That's not my fault; he's master of my state.
What ruins are in me that can be found
By him not ruined? Then is he the ground
98 Of my defeatures. My decayèd fair
A sunny look of his would soon repair.
But, too unruly deer, he breaks the pale
101 And feeds from home; poor I am but his stale.
LUCIANA
Self-harming jealousy! fie, beat it hence!
ADRIANA
103 Unfeeling fools can with such wrongs dispense.
I know his eye doth homage otherwhere,
105 Or else what lets it but he would be here?
Sister, you know he promised me a chain;
Would that alone, alone he would detain,
108 So he would keep fair quarter with his bed!
109 I see, the jewel best enamellèd
110 Will lose his beauty; yet the gold bides still
That others touch, and often touching will

79 he . . . cross i.e. he will pay further devotion (blows) to the cross made
by the blow on my head   80 holy (pun on 'full of holes')   82 round plain-
spoken (with pun on usual meaning)   86 loureth scowls   87 minions
darlings, girl friends   88 starve die   94 his affections bait tempt him   98
defeatures disfigurements; decayèd fair lost beauty   101 from away from;
stale (1) person taken lightly and for granted, (2) harlot   103 dispense
pardon (offer dispensation for)   105 lets prevents   108 keep . . . bed remain
faithful in bed   109–13 I see . . . shame (possibly corrupt owing to omitted
line or lines; the general idea seems to be that honor, like gold, is durable
only up to a point, and must be guarded against wear by those who possess
it)   110 his its
II, ii A street in Ephesus   22 in the teeth to my face   24 earnest (1) serious,
(2) down payment to secure a bargain (see l. 25)   29 common public land
32 aspect look (basically a planet's astrological portent)   34–37 sconce
head; fort; helmet   36 An if   37 ensconce protect militarily   38 seek . . .
shoulders have to find my brains in my shoulders

Wear gold; and no man that hath a name,
By falsehood and corruption doth it shame.
Since that my beauty cannot please his eye,
I'll weep what's left away, and weeping die.
LUCIANA
How many fond fools serve mad jealousy!
                                    Exit [with Adriana].

                          *

            Enter Antipholus [of Syracuse].   II, ii
ANTIPHOLUS S.
The gold I gave to Dromio is laid up
Safe at the Centaur; and the heedful slave
Is wand'red forth, in care to seek me out
By computation and mine host's report.
I could not speak with Dromio since at first
I sent him from the mart. See, here he comes.
            Enter Dromio of Syracuse.
How now, sir! is your merry humor altered?
As you love strokes, so jest with me again.
You know no Centaur? You received no gold?
Your mistress sent to have me home to dinner?   10
My house was at the Phoenix? Wast thou mad,
That thus so madly thou didst answer me?
DROMIO S.
What answer, sir? When spake I such a word?
ANTIPHOLUS S.
Even now, even here, not half an hour since.
DROMIO S.
I did not see you since you sent me hence,
Home to the Centaur, with the gold you gave me.
ANTIPHOLUS S.
Villain, thou didst deny the gold's receipt,
And told'st me of a mistress, and a dinner;
For which, I hope, thou felt'st I was displeased.
DROMIO S.
I am glad to see you in this merry vein.
What means this jest? I pray you, master, tell me.
ANTIPHOLUS S.
Yea, dost thou jeer and flout me in the teeth?   22
Think'st thou I jest? Hold, take thou that, and that.
            Beats Dromio.
DROMIO S.
Hold, sir, for God's sake! Now your jest is earnest.   24
Upon what bargain do you give it me?
ANTIPHOLUS S.
Because that I familiarly sometimes
Do use you for my fool, and chat with you,
Your sauciness will jest upon my love,
And make a common of my serious hours.   29
When the sun shines let foolish gnats make sport,
But creep in crannies when he hides his beams.
If you will jest with me, know my aspect,   32
And fashion your demeanor to my looks,
Or I will beat this method in your sconce.   34
DROMIO S. Sconce, call you it? So you would leave bat-
tering, I had rather have it a head. An you use these   36
blows long, I must get a sconce for my head and ensconce   37
it too; or else I shall seek my wit in my shoulders. But I   38
pray, sir, why am I beaten?
ANTIPHOLUS S. Dost thou not know?
DROMIO S. Nothing, sir, but that I am beaten.
ANTIPHOLUS S. Shall I tell you why?

DROMIO S. Ay, sir, and wherefore; for they say every why hath a wherefore.

ANTIPHOLUS S. Why, first – for flouting me; and then, wherefore – for urging it the second time to me.

DROMIO S.
Was there ever any man thus beaten out of season,
When in the why and the wherefore is neither rime nor reason?
Well, sir, I thank you.

ANTIPHOLUS S. Thank me, sir, for what?

DROMIO S. Marry, sir, for this something that you gave me for nothing.

ANTIPHOLUS S. I'll make you amends next, to give you nothing for something. But say, sir, is it dinner-time?

55 DROMIO S. No, sir, I think the meat wants that I have.

56 ANTIPHOLUS S. In good time, sir; what's that?

DROMIO S. Basting.

ANTIPHOLUS S. Well, sir, then 'twill be dry.

DROMIO S. If it be, sir, I pray you eat none of it.

ANTIPHOLUS S. Your reason?

DROMIO S. Lest it make you choleric, and purchase me
62 another dry basting.

ANTIPHOLUS S. Well, sir, learn to jest in good time. There's a time for all things.

DROMIO S. I durst have denied that, before you were so choleric.

ANTIPHOLUS S. By what rule, sir?

68 DROMIO S. Marry, sir, by a rule as plain as the plain bald pate of Father Time himself.

ANTIPHOLUS S. Let's hear it.

DROMIO S. There's no time for a man to recover his hair that grows bald by nature.

73 ANTIPHOLUS S. May he not do it by fine and recovery?

DROMIO S. Yes, to pay a fine for a periwig and recover the lost hair of another man.

ANTIPHOLUS S. Why is Time such a niggard of hair,
77 being, as it is, so plentiful an excrement?

DROMIO S. Because it is a blessing that he bestows on beasts; and what he hath scanted men in hair, he hath given them in wit.

ANTIPHOLUS S. Why, but there's many a man hath more hair than wit.

DROMIO S. Not a man of those but he hath the wit to lose his hair.

ANTIPHOLUS S. Why, thou didst conclude hairy men plain dealers without wit.

87 DROMIO S. The plainer dealer, the sooner lost; yet he loseth it in a kind of jollity.

ANTIPHOLUS S. For what reason?

90 DROMIO S. For two; and sound ones too.

ANTIPHOLUS S. Nay, not sound, I pray you.

DROMIO S. Sure ones, then.

ANTIPHOLUS S. Nay, not sure, in a thing falsing.

DROMIO S. Certain ones, then.

ANTIPHOLUS S. Name them.

DROMIO S. The one, to save the money that he spends in
97 tiring; the other, that at dinner they should not drop in his porridge.

ANTIPHOLUS S. You would all this time have proved, there is no time for all things.

DROMIO S. Marry, and did, sir; namely, no time to recover hair lost by nature.

ANTIPHOLUS S. But your reason was not substantial, why there is no time to recover.

DROMIO S. Thus I mend it: Time himself is bald, and
106 therefore to the world's end will have bald followers.

ANTIPHOLUS S. I knew 'twould be a bald conclusion. But soft! who wafts us yonder?

Enter Adriana and Luciana.

ADRIANA
Ay, ay, Antipholus, look strange and frown. 109
Some other mistress hath thy sweet aspects; 110
I am not Adriana, nor thy wife.
The time was once when thou unurged wouldst vow
That never words were music to thine ear,
That never object pleasing in thine eye,
That never touch well welcome to thy hand,
That never meat sweet-savored in thy taste,
Unless I spake, or looked, or touched, or carved to thee.
How comes it now, my husband, O, how comes it,
That thou art then estrangèd from thyself?
Thyself I call it, being strange to me,
That, undividable, incorporate,
Am better than thy dear self's better part.
Ah, do not tear away thyself from me!
For know, my love, as easy mayst thou fall 124
A drop of water in the breaking gulf,
And take unmingled thence that drop again
Without addition or diminishing,
As take from me thyself and not me too.
How dearly would it touch thee to the quick,
Shouldst thou but hear I were licentious, 130
And that this body, consecrate to thee,
By ruffian lust should be contaminate!
Wouldst thou not spit at me, and spurn at me,
And hurl the name of husband in my face,
And tear the stained skin off my harlot-brow,
And from my false hand cut the wedding-ring,
And break it with a deep-divorcing vow?
I know thou canst, and therefore see thou do it.
I am possessed with an adulterate blot;
My blood is mingled with the crime of lust.
For if we two be one, and thou play false,
I do digest the poison of thy flesh,
Being strumpeted by thy contagion.
Keep then fair league and truce with thy true bed;
I live distained, thou undishonorèd. 145

ANTIPHOLUS S.
Plead you to me, fair dame? I know you not.
In Ephesus I am but two hours old,
As strange unto your town as to your talk;
Who every word by all my wit being scanned,
Wants wit in all, one word to understand.

LUCIANA
Fie, brother! how the world is changed with you!
When were you wont to use my sister thus?
She sent for you by Dromio home to dinner.

ANTIPHOLUS S. By Dromio?

DROMIO S. By me?

55 *wants ... have* lacks what I have   56 *In good time* indeed   62 *dry basting* hard beating (properly, not drawing blood)   68 *Marry* by the Virgin Mary (grown to be only a mild oath)   73 *fine and recovery* (quibble on legal procedure for gaining absolute ownership)   77 *excrement* something, like hair, that grows from the body   87–88 *The ... jollity* (alluding to loss of hair from venereal disease)   90–93 *sound ones ... falsing* (carrying out the witticism on the loss of hair and the wig)   97 *tiring* dressing (the hair)   106 *bald* paltry, lame (besides the continued reference to the head)   109 *strange* estranged (cf. ll. 119, 120)   110 *aspects* countenance (cf. l. 32)   124 *fall* let fall   145 *distained* unstained (by contagion)

ADRIANA
By thee ; and this thou didst return from him,
That he did buffet thee, and in his blows,
Denied my house for his, me for his wife.

ANTIPHOLUS S.
Did you converse, sir, with this gentlewoman ?
160 What is the course and drift of your compact ?

DROMIO S.
I, sir ? I never saw her till this time.

ANTIPHOLUS S.
Villain, thou liest ; for even her very words
Didst thou deliver to me on the mart.

DROMIO S.
I never spake with her in all my life.

ANTIPHOLUS S.
How can she thus then call us by our names ?
Unless it be by inspiration.

ADRIANA
How ill agrees it with your gravity
To counterfeit thus grossly with your slave,
Abetting him to thwart me in my mood !
170 Be it my wrong you are from me exempt,
But wrong not that wrong with a more contempt.
Come, I will fasten on this sleeve of thine :
Thou art an elm, my husband, I a vine,
Whose weakness married to thy stronger state
Makes me with thy strength to communicate.
176 If aught possess thee from me, it is dross,
177 Usurping ivy, brier, or idle moss ;
Who all for want of pruning, with intrusion
179 Infect thy sap and live on thy confusion.

ANTIPHOLUS S.
180 To me she speaks ; she moves me for her theme.
What, was I married to her in my dream ?
Or sleep I now, and think I hear all this ?
183 What error drives our eyes and ears amiss ?
Until I know this sure uncertainty,
185 I'll entertain the offered fallacy.

LUCIANA
Dromio, go bid the servants spread for dinner.

DROMIO S.
187 O, for my beads ! I cross me for a sinner.
This is the fairy land. O spite of spites,
We talk with goblins, owls, and sprites !
If we obey them not, this will ensue :
They'll suck our breath, or pinch us black and blue.

LUCIANA
Why prat'st thou to thyself and answer'st not ?
Dromio, thou drone, thou snail, thou slug, thou sot !

DROMIO S.
194 I am transformèd, master, am I not ?

ANTIPHOLUS S.
I think thou art, in mind, and so am I.

DROMIO S.
Nay, master, both in mind and in my shape.

ANTIPHOLUS S.
Thou hast thine own form.

DROMIO S.   No, I am an ape.

LUCIANA
If thou art changed to aught, 'tis to an ass.

DROMIO S.
'Tis true ; she rides me, and I long for grass.
'Tis so, I am an ass ; else it could never be
But I should know her as well as she knows me.

ADRIANA
Come, come, no longer will I be a fool,
To put the finger in the eye and weep,
Whilst man and master laughs my woes to scorn.
Come, sir, to dinner. Dromio, keep the gate.
206 Husband, I'll dine above with you to-day,
207 And shrive you of a thousand idle pranks.
208 Sirrah, if any ask you for your master,
Say he dines forth, and let no creature enter.
Come, sister. Dromio, play the porter well.

ANTIPHOLUS S.
Am I in earth, in heaven, or in hell ?
212 Sleeping or waking ? mad or well advised ?
Known unto these, and to myself disguised !
I'll say as they say, and persever so,
And in this mist at all adventures go.

DROMIO S.
Master, shall I be porter at the gate ?

ADRIANA
Ay ; and let none enter, lest I break your pate.

LUCIANA
Come, come, Antipholus, we dine too late.   *[Exeunt.]*

*

Enter Antipholus of Ephesus, his man Dromio, Angelo III, i
the Goldsmith, and Balthazar the Merchant.

ANTIPHOLUS E.
Good Signior Angelo, you must excuse us all ;
My wife is shrewish when I keep not hours.
Say that I lingered with you at your shop
4 To see the making of her carcanet,
And that to-morrow you will bring it home.
6 But here's a villain that would face me down
He met me on the mart, and that I beat him,
And charged him with a thousand marks in gold,
9 And that I did deny my wife and house.
Thou drunkard, thou, what didst thou mean by this ?

DROMIO E.
Say what you will, sir, but I know what I know ;
12 That you beat me at the mart, I have your hand to show.
If the skin were parchment and the blows you gave were
ink,
Your own handwriting would tell you what I think.

ANTIPHOLUS E.
I think thou art an ass.

DROMIO E.   Marry, so it doth appear
By the wrongs I suffer and the blows I bear.
I should kick, being kicked ; and, being at that pass,
17 You would keep from my heels and beware of an ass.

---

160 *compact* conspiracy   170 *exempt* cut off   176 *possess* take   177 *idle* worthless   179 *confusion* destruction   180 *moves* appeals to   183 *error* (here, as elsewhere in the play, the word suggests the uncanny illusions of Ephesus ; cf. ll. 188–89)   185 *entertain . . . fallacy* accept what seems to be true   187 *beads* rosary   194–98 *I . . . ass* (though influenced by Lyly here, Shakespeare was also in the mood that was to create the 'translated' Bottom of *A Midsummer Night's Dream*)   206 *dine above* (The dinner would presumably be seen 'above', i.e. on the upper stage. In Elizabethan homes the living quarters were on an upper floor, while the place of business was on the ground level.)   207 *shrive you* hear your confession   208 *Sirrah* (term of address for servants and other social inferiors)   212 *well advised* sane
III, i Before the house of Antipholus of Ephesus   4 *carcanet* necklace of gold, or set with jewels   6 *face me down* outface me (with the assertion)   9 *deny* disclaim   12 *hand* handiwork (on my body. 'Hand' could also mean handwriting.)   17 *at that pass* in that direction

ANTIPHOLUS E.

19 Y'are sad, Signior Balthazar. Pray God, our cheer
20 May answer my good will and your good welcome here.

BALTHAZAR

21 I hold your dainties cheap, sir, and your welcome dear.

ANTIPHOLUS E.

O, Signior Balthazar, either at flesh or fish,
A table-full of welcome makes scarce one dainty dish.

BALTHAZAR

24 Good meat, sir, is common; that every churl affords.

ANTIPHOLUS E.

And welcome more common, for that's nothing but
    words.

BALTHAZAR

Small cheer and great welcome makes a merry feast.

ANTIPHOLUS E.

Ay, to a niggardly host and more sparing guest.
28 But though my cates be mean, take them in good part;
Better cheer may you have, but not with better heart.
But soft! my door is locked. Go bid them let us in.

DROMIO E.

Maud, Bridget, Marian, Cicely, Gillian, Ginn!

DROMIO S. [within]

32 Mome, malt-horse, capon, coxcomb, idiot, patch!
33 Either get thee from the door or sit down at the hatch.
34 Dost thou conjure for wenches, that thou call'st for such
    store,
When one is one too many? Go get thee from the door.

DROMIO E.

What patch is made our porter? My master stays in the
    street.

DROMIO S. [within]

Let him walk from whence he came, lest he catch cold
    on's feet.

ANTIPHOLUS E.

Who talks within there? Ho, open the door!

DROMIO S. [within]

Right, sir; I'll tell you when, an you'll tell me wherefore.

ANTIPHOLUS E.

Wherefore? For my dinner: I have not dined to-day.

DROMIO S.

Nor to-day here you must not; come again when you
    may.

ANTIPHOLUS E.

42 What art thou that keep'st me out from the house I owe?

DROMIO S. [within]

The porter for this time, sir, and my name is Dromio.

DROMIO E.

O villain, thou hast stol'n both mine office and my name!
45 The one ne'er got me credit, the other mickle blame.
If thou hadst been Dromio to-day in my place,
47 Thou wouldst have changed thy face for a name, or thy
    name for an ass.

        Enter Luce [within].

LUCE [within]

48 What a coil is there, Dromio! Who are those at the gate?

DROMIO E.

Let my master in, Luce.

LUCE [within]   Faith, no; he comes too late;
And so tell your master.

DROMIO E.   O Lord, I must laugh!

51 Have at you with a proverb: Shall I set in my staff?

LUCE [within]

52 Have at you with another: that's – When? Can you tell?

DROMIO S. [within]

If thy name be called Luce – Luce, thou hast answered
    him well.

ANTIPHOLUS E.

Do you hear, you minion? You'll let us in, I hope?

LUCE [within]

I thought to have asked you.

DROMIO S. [within]   And you said no.

DROMIO E.

So come, help: well struck! There was blow for blow.

ANTIPHOLUS E.

Thou baggage, let me in.

LUCE [within]   Can you tell for whose sake?

DROMIO E.

Master, knock the door hard.

LUCE [within]   Let him knock till it ache.

ANTIPHOLUS E.

You'll cry for this, minion, if I beat the door down.   59

LUCE [within]

What needs all that, and a pair of stocks in the town?   60

        Enter Adriana [within].

ADRIANA [within]

Who is that at the door that keeps all this noise?

DROMIO S. [within]

By my troth, your town is troubled with unruly boys.

ANTIPHOLUS E.

Are you there, wife? You might have come before.

ADRIANA [within]

Your wife, sir knave! Go get you from the door.

DROMIO E.

If you went in pain, master, this 'knave' would go sore.

ANGELO

Here is neither cheer, sir, nor welcome; we would fain
    have either.

BALTHAZAR

In debating which was best, we shall part with neither.

DROMIO E.

They stand at the door, master; bid them welcome
    hither.

ANTIPHOLUS E.

There is something in the wind, that we cannot get in.

DROMIO E.

You would say so, master, if your garments were thin.
Your cake here is warm within; you stand here in the
    cold.
It would make a man mad as a buck to be so bought and   72
    sold.

ANTIPHOLUS E.

Go fetch me something; I'll break ope the gate.

---

19 *sad* serious (its usual meaning in Shakespeare); *cheer* hospitality   19-29
Y'are . . . heart (there is delightful irony in this exchange of courtesies for a
dinner that will not take place)   20 *answer* correspond to   21 *dainties*
delicacies   24 *churl* peasant   28 *cates* delicacies; *mean* plain   32 *Mome,
patch* (both words mean 'fool')   33 *hatch* half door; gate or wicket with
an open space above   34 *conjure for* bring into being by magic; *store*
quantity (of wenches)   42 *owe* own (frequent meaning)   45 *mickle* much
47 *Thou . . . ass* (obscure; Dromio E. may mean that the name brought his
face into trouble, so that, with the beatings, an ass would have been more
appropriate)   48 *Who . . . gate* (both Luce and Adriana are on the upper
stage and hence unable to see Antipholus E. and Dromio E., who are by the
rear door *under* the balcony)   51 *Have . . . proverb* I'll throw a proverb at
you; *set . . . staff* claim my home   52 *When . . . tell* (another proverb, used
to evade a question)   59 *minion* hussy   60 *What . . . town* why need we be
pestered with these ruffians when the town has stocks   72 *mad as a buck* i.e.
in mating season; *bought and sold* used

DROMIO S. *[within]*
    Break any breaking here, and I'll break your knave's pate.
DROMIO E.
    A man may break a word with you, sir, and words are
        but wind :
    Ay, and break it in your face, so he break it not behind.
DROMIO S. *[within]*
77   It seems thou want'st breaking. Out upon thee, hind !
DROMIO E.
    Here's too much 'Out upon thee !' I pray thee, let me in.
DROMIO S. *[within]*
    Ay, when fowls have no feathers, and fish have no fin.
ANTIPHOLUS E.
80   Well, I'll break in. Go borrow me a crow.
DROMIO E.
    A crow without feather ? Master, mean you so ?
    For a fish without a fin, there's a fowl without a feather :
83   If a crow help us in, sirrah, we'll pluck a crow together.
ANTIPHOLUS E.
    Go get thee gone ; fetch me an iron crow.
BALTHAZAR
    Have patience, sir ; O let it not be so !
    Herein you war against your reputation,
87   And draw within the compass of suspect
    Th' unviolated honor of your wife.
89   Once this – your long experience of her wisdom,
    Her sober virtue, years, and modesty,
    Plead on her part some cause to you unknown ;
92   And doubt not, sir, but she will well excuse
93   Why at this time the doors are made against you.
    Be ruled by me : depart in patience,
    And let us to the Tiger all to dinner ;
    And about evening come yourself alone,
    To know the reason of this strange restraint.
98   If by strong hand you offer to break in
99   Now in the stirring passage of the day,
100   A vulgar comment will be made of it,
    And that supposèd by the common rout
102   Against your yet ungallèd estimation,
    That may with foul intrusion enter in
    And dwell upon your grave when you are dead ;
105   For slander lives upon succession,
    For ever housed where it gets possession.
ANTIPHOLUS E.
    You have prevailed : I will depart in quiet,
108   And in despite of mirth mean to be merry.
    I know a wench of excellent discourse,
    Pretty and witty, wild and yet, too, gentle.

    There will we dine. This woman that I mean,
    My wife – but, I protest, without desert –   112
    Hath oftentimes upbraided me withal :
    To her will we to dinner. *[to Angelo]* Get you home
    And fetch the chain ; by this I know 'tis made.   115
    Bring it, I pray you, to the Porpentine ;   116
    For there's the house. That chain will I bestow,
    Be it for nothing but to spite my wife,
    Upon mine hostess there. Good sir, make haste.
    Since mine own doors refuse to entertain me,
    I'll knock elsewhere, to see if they'll disdain me.
ANGELO
    I'll meet you at that place some hour hence.
ANTIPHOLUS E.
    Do so. This jest shall cost me some expense.   *Exeunt.*

*

Enter Luciana, with Antipholus of Syracuse.   III, ii
LUCIANA
    And may it be that you have quite forgot
    A husband's office ? Shall, Antipholus,
    Even in the spring of love, thy love-springs rot ?   3
    Shall love, in building, grow so ruinous ?
    If you did wed my sister for her wealth,
    Then for her wealth's sake use her with more kindness :   6
    Or if you like elsewhere, do it by stealth ;
    Muffle your false love with some show of blindness :
    Let not my sister read it in your eye ;
    Be not thy tongue thy own shame's orator ;   10
    Look sweet, speak fair, become disloyalty ;   11
    Apparel vice like virtue's harbinger ;   12
    Bear a fair presence, though your heart be tainted ;
    Teach sin the carriage of a holy saint ;   14
    Be secret-false : what need she be acquainted ?
    What simple thief brags of his own attaint ?   16
    'Tis double wrong to truant with your bed,
    And let her read it in thy looks at board.   18
    Shame hath a bastard fame, well managèd ;   19
    Ill deeds is doubled with an evil word.
    Alas, poor women ! make us but believe,
    Being compact of credit, that you love us ;   22
    Though others have the arm, show us the sleeve ;
    We in your motion turn, and you may move us.   24
    Then, gentle brother, get you in again ;
    Comfort my sister, cheer her, call her wife.
    'Tis holy sport to be a little vain,
    When the sweet breath of flattery conquers strife.   27
ANTIPHOLUS S.
    Sweet mistress – what your name is else, I know not,
    Nor by what wonder you do hit of mine –   30
    Less in your knowledge and your grace you show not
    Than our earth's wonder ; more than earth divine.   32
    Teach me, dear creature, how to think and speak ;
    Lay open to my earthy-gross conceit,   34
    Smothered in errors, feeble, shallow, weak,
    The folded meaning of your words' deceit.   36
    Against my soul's pure truth why labor you
    To make it wander in an unknown field ?
    Are you a god ? Would you create me new ?
    Transform me then, and to your power I'll yield.
    But if that I am I, then well I know
    Your weeping sister is no wife of mine,
    Nor to her bed no homage do I owe.

---

77 *hind* servant **80** *crow* crowbar **83** *pluck a crow* pick a bone, settle accounts **87** *draw . . . suspect* bring under suspicion **89** *Once this* in one word (?), once you do this (?) **92** *excuse* explain **93** *made* shut **98** *offer* try **99** *stirring passage* bustle **100** *vulgar* by *the common rout* (next line ; not usually 'cheap') **102** *yet . . . estimation* hitherto untouched reputation **105** *slander . . . succession* one slander takes over, as in 'succession,' from the preceding one **108** *in . . . mirth* despite mockery (?), though lacking mirth (?) **112** *without desert* unjustly **115** *by this* by this time **116** *Porpentine* Porcupine (here the name of an inn)
III, ii The same **3** *love-springs* love-shoots (as of a plant) **6** *wealth's* welfare's **10** *orator* advocate **11** *become disloyalty* make disloyalty seem becoming (attractive) **12** *harbinger* herald, advance messenger to a court **14** *carriage* manners **16** *attaint* disgrace, crime **18** *board* table **19** *bastard fame* counterfeit reputation **22** *compact of credit* composed of credulity, i.e. made so that (we) will believe anything **24** *We . . .* our moves are governed by yours **27** *vain* false **30** *hit of* hit upon **32** *our earth's wonder* Elizabeth I (?) **34** *earthy-gross conceit* wit gross as earth **36** *folded* i.e. so as to be concealed

44 Far more, far more, to you do I decline.
45 O train me not, sweet mermaid, with thy note,
   To drown me in thy sister's flood of tears!
   Sing, siren, for thyself, and I will dote.
   Spread o'er the silver waves thy golden hairs,
   And as a bed I'll take them and there lie;
   And in that glorious supposition think
   He gains by death that hath such means to die.
52 Let Love, being light, be drownèd if she sink!
   LUCIANA
   What, are you mad, that you do reason so?
   ANTIPHOLUS S.
54 Not mad, but mated; how, I do not know.
   LUCIANA
   It is a fault that springeth from your eye.
   ANTIPHOLUS S.
   For gazing on your beams, fair sun, being by.
   LUCIANA
   Gaze where you should, and that will clear your sight.
   ANTIPHOLUS S.
58 As good to wink, sweet love, as look on night.
   LUCIANA
   Why call you me love? Call my sister so.
   ANTIPHOLUS S.
   Thy sister's sister.
   LUCIANA   That's my sister.
   ANTIPHOLUS S.   No;
   It is thyself, mine own self's better part;
   Mine eye's clear eye, my dear heart's dearer heart;
   My food, my fortune, and my sweet hope's aim;
64 My sole earth's heaven, and my heaven's claim.
   LUCIANA
   All this my sister is, or else should be.
   ANTIPHOLUS S.
66 Call thyself sister, sweet, for I am thee.
   Thee will I love, and with thee lead my life;
   Thou hast no husband yet, nor I no wife.
   Give me thy hand.
   LUCIANA   O, soft, sir! hold you still.
   I'll fetch my sister, to get her good will.   *Exit.*
        Enter Dromio of Syracuse.
   ANTIPHOLUS S. Why, how now, Dromio! Where runn'st
   thou so fast?
   DROMIO S. Do you know me, sir? Am I Dromio? Am I
   your man? Am I myself?
   ANTIPHOLUS S. Thou art Dromio, thou art my man,
   thou art thyself.
   DROMIO S. I am an ass, I am a woman's man, and besides
   myself.
   ANTIPHOLUS S. What woman's man? and how besides
80 thyself?
   DROMIO S. Marry, sir, besides myself, I am due to a
   woman: one that claims me, one that haunts me, one
   that will have me.
   ANTIPHOLUS S. What claim lays she to thee?
   DROMIO S. Marry, sir, such claim as you would lay to
86 your horse; and she would have me as a beast: not that,
   I being a beast, she would have me; but that she, being a
   very beastly creature, lays claim to me.
   ANTIPHOLUS S. What is she?
   DROMIO S. A very reverent body; aye, such a one as a
91 man may not speak of, without he say, 'Sir-reverence.'
92 I have but lean luck in the match, and yet is she a
   wondrous fat marriage.

ANTIPHOLUS S. How dost thou mean a fat marriage?
DROMIO S. Marry, sir, she's the kitchen-wench, and all
   grease; and I know not what use to put her to, but to 96
   make a lamp of her, and run from her by her own light.
   I warrant, her rags and the tallow in them will burn a
   Poland winter. If she lives till doomsday, she'll burn a
   week longer than the whole world.
ANTIPHOLUS S. What complexion is she of?
DROMIO S. Swart, like my shoe, but her face nothing like 102
   so clean kept: for why? She sweats; a man may go over 103
   shoes in the grime of it.
ANTIPHOLUS S. That's a fault that water will mend.
DROMIO S. No, sir, 'tis in grain; Noah's flood could not 106
   do it.
ANTIPHOLUS S. What's her name?
DROMIO S. Nell, sir; but her name and three quarters – 109
   that's an ell and three-quarters – will not measure her 110
   from hip to hip.
ANTIPHOLUS S. Then she bears some breadth?
DROMIO S. No longer from head to foot than from hip to
   hip: she is spherical, like a globe; I could find out coun- 114
   tries in her.
ANTIPHOLUS S. In what part of her body stands Ireland?
DROMIO S. Marry, sir, in her buttocks. I found it out by
   the bogs.
ANTIPHOLUS S. Where Scotland?
DROMIO S. I found it by the barrenness; hard in the palm
   of the hand.
ANTIPHOLUS S. Where France?   122
DROMIO S. In her forehead, armed and reverted, making
   war against her heir.
ANTIPHOLUS S. Where England?
DROMIO S. I looked for the chalky cliffs, but I could find
   no whiteness in them; but I guess it stood in her chin, 127
   by the salt rheum that ran between France and it.
ANTIPHOLUS S. Where Spain?
DROMIO S. Faith, I saw it not; but I felt it hot in her
   breath.
ANTIPHOLUS S. Where America, the Indies?
DROMIO S. O, sir, upon her nose, all o'er embellished
   with rubies, carbuncles, sapphires, declining their rich 133
   aspect to the hot breath of Spain, who sent whole arma- 134
   does of carracks to be ballast at her nose.   135

---

44 *decline* incline **45** *train* entice; *note* music **52** *light* (1) light in weight, (2) wanton **54** *mated* (1) amazed, (2) confounded, (3) married **58** *wink* close the eyes (usual meaning in Shakespeare) **64** *My . . . claim* my only heaven on earth, and my claim given me by (or to) heaven **66** *am* (often emended to 'aim' – unnecessarily, in view of l. 61) **86** *a beast* (pun on 'abased,' since 'beast' was pronounced 'baste') **91** *Sir-reverence* if you will pardon the expression (corruption of 'saving reverence') **92** *lean* poor, scanty (besides the obvious contrast with *fat*) **96** *grease* (another bad pun, 'grease' being pronounced 'grace') **102** *Swart* dark **103** *for why?* (the question mark in the folio text may be unnecessary, since 'for why' meant 'because') **106** *in grain* fast dyed, ingrained **109** *Nell* (hitherto called Luce) **110** *ell* forty-five inches (Nell *bears some breadth* – almost seven feet in circumference) **114–15** *countries in her* (a favorite Elizabethan source of humor, though perhaps Shakespeare was here indebted to Rabelais, who has Friar John map out the head and chin of Panurge) **122–24** *France . . . heir* (See Introduction for the importance of this passage in dating the play. Cowden Clarke: 'Mistress Nell's brazen forehead seemed to push back her rough and rebellious hair, as France resisted the claim of the Protestant heir to the throne.' But there is also a reference to the 'French disease' – syphilis – and its destruction of hair.) **127** *them* i.e. Nell's teeth **133–34** *declining . . . aspect* looking downward **134–35** *armadoes of carracks* armadas of great merchant ships or galleons (a topical allusion, suggesting that the date of the play was not much later than 1588) **135** *ballast* freighted

136 ANTIPHOLUS S. Where stood Belgia, the Netherlands?
DROMIO S. O, sir! I did not look so low. To conclude,
138   this drudge, or diviner, laid claim to me; called me
139   Dromio; swore I was assured to her; told me what privy
marks I had about me, as the mark of my shoulder, the
mole in my neck, the great wart on my left arm, that I,
amazed, ran from her as a witch.
And I think, if my breast had not been made of faith,
and my heart of steel,
144   She had transformed me to a curtal dog, and made me
turn i' the wheel.
    ANTIPHOLUS S.
145   Go hie thee presently post to the road;
146   And if the wind blow any way from shore,
I will not harbor in this town to-night.
If any bark put forth, come to the mart,
Where I will walk till thou return to me.
If every one knows us, and we know none,
'Tis time, I think, to trudge, pack, and be gone.
    DROMIO S.
As from a bear a man would run for life,
So fly I from her that would be my wife.   Exit.
    ANTIPHOLUS S.
There's none but witches do inhabit here,
And therefore 'tis high time that I were hence.
She that doth call me husband, even my soul
Doth for a wife abhor. But her fair sister,
Possessed with such a gentle sovereign grace,
Of such enchanting presence and discourse,
160   Hath almost made me traitor to myself.
But lest myself be guilty to self-wrong,
I'll stop mine ears against the mermaid's song.
      Enter Angelo with the chain.
· ANGELO   Master Antipholus –
    ANTIPHOLUS S.   Ay, that's my name.
    ANGELO
I know it well, sir; lo, here is the chain.
I thought to have ta'en you at the Porpentine;
The chain unfinished made me stay thus long.
    ANTIPHOLUS S.
What is your will that I shall do with this?
    ANGELO
What please yourself, sir; I have made it for you.
    ANTIPHOLUS S.
170   Made it for me, sir! I bespoke it not.
    ANGELO
Not once, nor twice, but twenty times you have.
Go home with it and please your wife withal;
And soon at supper-time I'll visit you,
And then receive my money for the chain.
    ANTIPHOLUS S.
I pray you, sir, receive the money now,
For fear you ne'er see chain nor money more.

    ANGELO
You are a merry man, sir; fare you well.   *Exit.*
    ANTIPHOLUS S.
What should I think of this, I cannot tell;
But this I think, there's no man is so vain   179
That would refuse so fair an offered chain.
I see a man here needs not live by shifts,   181
When in the streets he meets such golden gifts.
I'll to the mart, and there for Dromio stay;
If any ship put out, then straight away.   *Exit.* 184

                     *

      Enter a [second] Merchant, [Angelo, the] Goldsmith,   IV, i
      and an Officer.
    2. MERCHANT
You know since Pentecost the sum is due,
And since I have not much importuned you;
Nor now I had not, but that I am bound
To Persia, and want guilders for my voyage.
Therefore make present satisfaction,
Or I'll attach you by this officer.   6
    ANGELO
Even just the sum that I do owe to you
Is growing to me by Antipholus;   8
And in the instant that I met with you
He had of me a chain. At five o'clock
I shall receive the money for the same.
Pleaseth you walk with me down to his house,
I will discharge my bond, and thank you too.
      Enter Antipholus [of] Ephesus [and] Dromio [of
      Ephesus] from the Courtesan's.
    OFFICER
That labor may you save; see where he comes.
    ANTIPHOLUS E.
While I go to the goldsmith's house, go thou
And buy a rope's end; that will I bestow
Among my wife and her confederates,
For locking me out of my doors by day.
But soft! I see the goldsmith. Get thee gone;
Buy thou a rope, and bring it home to me.
    DROMIO E.
I buy a thousand pounds a year! I buy a rope!   21
      Exit Dromio [of Ephesus].
    ANTIPHOLUS E.
A man is well holp up that trusts to you.   22
I promisèd your presence and the chain;
But neither chain nor goldsmith came to me.
Belike you thought our love would last too long
If it were chained together, and therefore came not.
    ANGELO
Saving your merry humor, here's the note
How much your chain weighs to the utmost carat,
The fineness of the gold, and chargeful fashion,   29
Which doth amount to three odd ducats more
Than I stand debted to this gentleman.
I pray you see him presently discharged,
For he is bound to sea and stays but for it.
    ANTIPHOLUS E.
I am not furnished with the present money;
Besides, I have some business in the town.
Good signior, take the stranger to my house,
And with you take the chain, and bid my wife
Disburse the sum on the receipt thereof.
Perchance I will be there as soon as you.

---

136 *Belgia, the Netherlands* (usually called the Low Countries) 138
diviner witch, with powers of prophecy   139 *assured* betrothed   144 *curtal*
with shortened tail (hence of no value in hunting); *turn i' the wheel* (dogs
were said to be very good at turning the cooking spits)   145 *hie* hurry;
presently at once; *post* in haste; *road* roadstead or harbor   146 *And if* if
170 *bespoke* ordered   179 *vain* foolish   181 *shifts* tricks   184 *straight*
directly
IV, i *A street in Ephesus*   6 *attach* arrest (this type of financial dealing
was common in an age lacking checks and ready cash)   8 *growing* accruing
21 *I . . . rope* (a puzzling line; perhaps Dromio thinks of the rope as an
instrument for beating himself – hence his preposterous analogy)   22 *holp*
helped   29 *chargeful* costly

ANGELO

    Then you will bring the chain to her yourself?

ANTIPHOLUS E.

    No; bear it with you, lest I come not time enough.

ANGELO

    Well, sir, I will. Have you the chain about you?

ANTIPHOLUS E.

43   An if I have not, sir, I hope you have,

    Or else you may return without your money.

ANGELO

    Nay, come, I pray you, sir, give me the chain.

    Both wind and tide stays for this gentleman,

    And I, to blame, have held him here too long.

ANTIPHOLUS E.

48   Good Lord! you use this dalliance to excuse

    Your breach of promise to the Porpentine.

    I should have chid you for not bringing it,

    But, like a shrew, you first begin to brawl.

2. MERCHANT

    The hour steals on; I pray you, sir, dispatch.

ANGELO

    You hear how he importunes me: the chain!

ANTIPHOLUS E.

    Why, give it to my wife and fetch your money.

ANGELO

    Come, come, you know I gave it you even now.

56   Either send the chain or send me by some token.

ANTIPHOLUS E.

    Fie! now you run this humor out of breath.

    Come, where's the chain? I pray you, let me see it.

2. MERCHANT

59   My business cannot brook this dalliance.

    Good sir, say whe'r you'll answer me or no.

    If not, I'll leave him to the officer.

ANTIPHOLUS E.

    I answer you! What should I answer you?

ANGELO

    The money that you owe me for the chain.

ANTIPHOLUS E.

    I owe you none till I receive the chain.

ANGELO

    You know I gave it you half an hour since.

ANTIPHOLUS E.

    You gave me none; you wrong me much to say so.

ANGELO

    You wrong me more, sir, in denying it.

68   Consider how it stands upon my credit.

2. MERCHANT

    Well, officer, arrest him at my suit.

OFFICER

    I do; and charge you in the Duke's name to obey me.

ANGELO

    This touches me in reputation.

    Either consent to pay this sum for me,

    Or I attach you by this officer.

ANTIPHOLUS E.

    Consent to pay thee that I never had!

    Arrest me, foolish fellow, if thou dar'st.

ANGELO

    Here is thy fee; arrest him, officer.

    I would not spare my brother in this case,

78   If he should scorn me so apparently.

OFFICER

    I do arrest you, sir; you hear the suit.

ANTIPHOLUS E.

    I do obey thee till I give thee bail.

    But, sirrah, you shall buy this sport as dear

    As all the metal in your shop will answer.

ANGELO

    Sir, sir, I shall have law in Ephesus,

    To your notorious shame, I doubt it not.

        Enter Dromio [of] Syracuse from the bay.

DROMIO S.

    Master, there's a bark of Epidamnum

    That stays but till her owner comes aboard,

    And then she bears away. Our fraughtage, sir,   87

    I have conveyed aboard, and I have bought

    The oil, the balsamum, and aqua-vitae.   89

    The ship is in her trim; the merry wind   90

    Blows fair from land; they stay for nought at all

    But for their owner, master, and yourself.

ANTIPHOLUS E.

    How now, a madman? Why, thou peevish sheep,   93

    What ship of Epidamnum stays for me?

DROMIO S.

    A ship you sent me to, to hire waftage.   95

ANTIPHOLUS E.

    Thou drunken slave, I sent thee for a rope,

    And told thee to what purpose, and what end.

DROMIO S.

    You sent me for a rope's end as soon.   98

    You sent me to the bay, sir, for a bark.

ANTIPHOLUS E.

    I will debate this matter at more leisure,

    And teach your ears to list me with more heed.

    To Adriana, villain, hie thee straight.

    Give her this key, and tell her, in the desk

    That's covered o'er with Turkish tapestry,

    There is a purse of ducats; let her send it.

    Tell her I am arrested in the street,

    And that shall bail me. Hie thee, slave, be gone!

    On, officer, to prison till it come.

        Exeunt [all but Dromio of Syracuse].

DROMIO S.

    To Adriana – that is where we dined,

    Where Dowsabel did claim me for her husband.   110

    She is too big, I hope, for me to compass.

    Thither I must, although against my will,

    For servants must their masters' minds fulfill.   *Exit.*

                        *

        Enter Adriana and Luciana.   IV, ii

ADRIANA

    Ah, Luciana, did he tempt thee so?

    Mightst thou perceive austerely in his eye   2

    That he did plead in earnest? yea or no?

    Looked he or red or pale, or sad or merrily?

    What observation mad'st thou in this case

    Of his heart's meteors tilting in his face?   6

---

43 *An if* if   **48** *dalliance* idle delay   **56** *send . . . token* give me a token (e.g. a ring) showing my right to it   **59** *brook* endure   **68** *how . . . credit* how my credit is involved   **78** *apparently* openly   **87** *fraughtage* baggage   **89** *balsamum* balm; *aqua-vitae* spirits   **90** *in her trim* rigged and ready   **93–94** *sheep . . . ship* (pronounced similarly; a favorite Elizabethan pun)   **95** *waftage* passage by sea   **98** *You . . . soon* i.e. you just as likely sent me (for a rope's end) to be hanged   **110** *Dowsabel* i.e. Gentle and Beautiful (from French *'douce et belle'*; nicely ironic for Nell)

IV, ii Before the house of Antipholus of Ephesus   **2** *austerely* plainly   **6** *meteors tilting* passions warring

LUCIANA
First he denied you had in him no right.

ADRIANA
8   He meant he did me none; the more my spite.

LUCIANA
Then swore he that he was a stranger here.

ADRIANA
And true he swore, though yet forsworn he were.

LUCIANA
Then pleaded I for you.

ADRIANA   And what said he?

LUCIANA
That love I begged for you he begged of me.

ADRIANA
With what persuasion did he tempt thy love?

LUCIANA
14   With words that in an honest suit might move.
First, he did praise my beauty, then my speech.

ADRIANA
16   Didst speak him fair?

LUCIANA   Have patience, I beseech.

ADRIANA
I cannot, nor I will not hold me still;
18   My tongue, though not my heart, shall have his will.
19   He is deformèd, crooked, old and sere,
Ill-faced, worse bodied, shapeless everywhere;
Vicious, ungentle, foolish, blunt, unkind,
22   Stigmatical in making, worse in mind.

LUCIANA
Who would be jealous then of such a one?
No evil lost is wailed when it is gone.

ADRIANA
Ah, but I think him better than I say,
And yet would herein others' eyes were worse.
27   Far from her nest the lapwing cries away;
My heart prays for him, though my tongue do curse.
            Enter Dromio of Syracuse.

DROMIO S.
Here, go – the desk, the purse – sweet, now, make haste.

LUCIANA
How hast thou lost thy breath?

DROMIO S.   By running fast.

ADRIANA
Where is thy master, Dromio? Is he well?

DROMIO S.
32   No, he's in Tartar limbo, worse than hell.

A devil in an everlasting garment hath him;   33
One whose hard heart is buttoned up with steel;
A fiend, a fury, pitiless and rough;
A wolf, nay worse, a fellow all in buff;
A back-friend, a shoulder-clapper, one that counter-   37
    mands
The passages of alleys, creeks, and narrow lands;
A hound that runs counter and yet draws dry-foot well: 39
One that before the judgment carries poor souls to hell.   40

ADRIANA
Why, man, what is the matter?

DROMIO S.
I do not know the matter; he is 'rested on the case.   42

ADRIANA
What, is he arrested? Tell me at whose suit.

DROMIO S.
I know not at whose suit he is arrested well;
But he's in a suit of buff which 'rested him, that can I tell.
Will you send him, mistress, redemption, the money in   46
    his desk?

ADRIANA
Go fetch it, sister. – This I wonder at,   *Exit Luciana.*
That he, unknown to me, should be in debt.
Tell me, was he arrested on a band?   49

DROMIO S.
Not on a band, but on a stronger thing:
A chain, a chain. Do you not hear it ring?

ADRIANA
What, the chain?

DROMIO S.
No, no, the bell; 'tis time that I were gone.
It was two ere I left him, and now the clock strikes one.

ADRIANA
The hours come back! That did I never hear.

DROMIO S.
O yes; if any hour meet a sergeant, 'a turns back for very   56
    fear.

ADRIANA
As if time were in debt! How fondly dost thou reason!

DROMIO S.
Time is a very bankrupt, and owes more than he's worth   58
    to season.
Nay, he's a thief too: have you not heard men say,
That time comes stealing on by night and day?
If 'a be in debt and theft, and a sergeant in the way,
Hath he not reason to turn back an hour in a day?
            Enter Luciana.

ADRIANA
Go, Dromio; there's the money, bear it straight,
And bring thy master home immediately.
            [Exit Dromio of Syracuse.]
Come, sister; I am pressed down with conceit –   65
Conceit, my comfort and my injury.
            Exit [with Luciana].

                    *

            Enter Antipholus of Syracuse.   IV, iii

ANTIPHOLUS S.
There's not a man I meet but doth salute me
As if I were their well-acquainted friend;
And every one doth call me by my name.
Some tender money to me; some invite me;
Some other give me thanks for kindnesses;

8 *spite* vexation   14 *honest* virtuous, honorable   16 *Didst . . . fair* i.e. did you, in turn, speak engagingly to him   18 *his* its   19 *sere* dried up   22 *Stigmatical in making* deformed in body   27 *Far . . . away* (the lapwing protects her nest by flying about elsewhere)   32 *Tartar limbo* (limbo properly is a benign Christian place in Hell for unbaptized infants; 'Tartar' combines this with a pagan place of punishment)   33 *everlasting garment* the leather, or buff (cf. l. 36), uniform of an Elizabethan officer of the law   37 *back-friend* the type of 'friend' (police officer) who claps one on the back or shoulder; *countermands* prohibits   39 *counter* (1) opposite to the direction of the game in a hunt, (2) the name of a debtors' prison; *draws dry-foot* hunts by the scent of the foot   40 *judgment* (1) legal verdict, (2) day of judgment   42 *'rested on the case* arrested (1) in a lawsuit, (2) on his skin (case for *matter*)   46 *mistress, redemption* (possibly should be the fourth folio's 'Mistress Redemption.' Shakespeare was fond of perpetuating morality-play abstractions. This reading would carry out the idea of 'judgment'; and cf. Dromio's *Mistress Satan*, IV, iii, 44.)   49 *band* bond   56 *hour* (pun on similarly pronounced 'whore'); *'a* it, she (usually 'he')   58 *owes . . . season* (some obscure jest is intended: 'season' may have several meanings, including 'the opportunity' and 'to keep fresh')   65 *conceit* thought
IV, iii The mart

Some offer me commodities to buy.
Even now a tailor called me in his shop
And showed me silks that he had bought for me,
And therewithal took measure of my body.
10 Sure, these are but imaginary wiles,
11 And Lapland sorcerers inhabit here.
     Enter Dromio [of] Syracuse.
DROMIO S. Master, here's the gold you sent me for.
13 What, have you got the picture of old Adam new apparelled?
ANTIPHOLUS S.
What gold is this? What Adam dost thou mean?
DROMIO S. Not that Adam that kept the Paradise, but
that Adam that keeps the prison; he that goes in the
16 calf's skin that was killed for the Prodigal; he that came
behind you, sir, like an evil angel, and bid you forsake
your liberty.
ANTIPHOLUS S. I understand thee not.
DROMIO S. No? why, 'tis a plain case: he that went, like
a base-viol, in a case of leather; the man, sir, that when
22 gentlemen are tired gives them a sob, and 'rests them;
he, sir, that takes pity on decayed men and gives them
24 suits of durance; he that sets up his rest to do more ex-
25 ploits with his mace than a morris-pike.
ANTIPHOLUS S. What, thou mean'st an officer?
DROMIO S. Ay, sir, the sergeant of the band; he that
brings any man to answer it that breaks his band; one
that thinks a man always going to bed, and says, 'God
give you good rest!'
ANTIPHOLUS S. Well, sir, there rest in your foolery. Is
there any ship puts forth to-night? May we be gone?
DROMIO S. Why, sir, I brought you word an hour since
34 that the bark Expedition put forth to-night; and then
35 were you hindered by the sergeant to tarry for the hoy
36 Delay. Here are the angels that you sent for to deliver
you.
ANTIPHOLUS S.
The fellow is distract, and so am I;
And here we wander in illusions.
Some blessèd power deliver us from hence!
     Enter a Courtesan.
COURTESAN
Well met, well met, Master Antipholus.
I see, sir, you have found the goldsmith now.
Is that the chain you promised me to-day?
ANTIPHOLUS S.
43 Satan, avoid! I charge thee tempt me not!
44 DROMIO S. Master, is this Mistress Satan?
ANTIPHOLUS S. It is the devil.
46 DROMIO S. Nay, she is worse; she is the devil's dam. And
47 here she comes in the habit of a light wench, and thereof
comes that the wenches say, 'God damn me'; that's as
much as to say, 'God make me a light wench.' It is
written, they appear to men like angels of light; light is
51 an effect of fire, and fire will burn; ergo, light wenches
will burn. Come not near her.
COURTESAN
Your man and you are marvellous merry, sir.
54 Will you go with me? We'll mend our dinner here.
55 DROMIO S. Master, if you do, expect spoon-meat, or
bespeak a long spoon.
ANTIPHOLUS S. Why, Dromio?
DROMIO S. Marry, he must have a long spoon that must
eat with the devil.

ANTIPHOLUS S.
Avoid then, fiend! What tell'st thou me of supping?
Thou art, as you are all, a sorceress.
I conjure thee to leave me and be gone.
COURTESAN
Give me the ring of mine you had at dinner,
Or, for my diamond, the chain you promised,
And I'll be gone, sir, and not trouble you.
DROMIO S.
Some devils ask but the parings of one's nail,   66
A rush, a hair, a drop of blood, a pin,
A nut, a cherry-stone;
But she, more covetous, would have a chain.
Master, be wise; and if you give it her,
The devil will shake her chain and fright us with it.
COURTESAN
I pray you, sir, my ring, or else the chain.
I hope you do not mean to cheat me so?
ANTIPHOLUS S.
Avaunt, thou witch! Come, Dromio, let us go.
DROMIO S.
Fly pride, says the peacock: mistress, that you know.   75
     Exit [with Antipholus of Syracuse].
COURTESAN
Now, out of doubt, Antipholus is mad,
Else would he never so demean himself.   77
A ring he hath of mine worth forty ducats,
And for the same he promised me a chain;
Both one and other he denies me now.
The reason that I gather he is mad,
Besides this present instance of his rage,   82
Is a mad tale he told to-day at dinner,
Of his own doors being shut against his entrance.
Belike his wife, acquainted with his fits,
On purpose shut the doors against his way.
My way is now to hie home to his house,
And tell his wife that, being lunatic,
He rushed into my house and took perforce   89
My ring away. This course I fittest choose,
For forty ducats is too much to lose.   *[Exit.]*

               *

10 *imaginary wiles* tricks of the imagination   11 *Lapland* (famous for sorcery)   13–14 *What . . . apparelled* (an obscure allusion to the absence of the sergeant of law; perhaps Dromio is asking if Antipholus has obtained the sergeant a new role)   16 *calf's skin . . . Prodigal* (allusion to the fatted calf killed for the Prodigal Son. This tiresome facetiousness about the leather-clad sergeant persists through *case of leather* l. 21.)   22 *sob* (Hanmer suggested 'bob'; i.e. the sergeant's tap on the shoulder)   24 *suits of durance* clothes that last long (but Dromio, tireless punner, means also long-lasting legal suits – then very common – or cases that end in prison); *sets . . . rest* plays (at 'primero,' a card game) with all he has   25 *mace* official staff of the sergeant; *morris-pike* Moorish pike   34 *bark* seagoing vessel   35 *hoy* small coasting vessel   36 *angels* coins worth about 10s. apiece (but there are still theological overtones)   43 *avoid* be gone   44 *Mistress Satan* (another character in Dromio's miracle or morality play of the kind dealing with man's salvation)   46 *dam* mother   47 *habit* dress   51 *ergo* therefore (concluding a syllogism)   51–52 *light . . . burn* wanton girls will burn (through disease)   54 *mend* finish (i.e. the courtesan will provide 'dessert')   55 *expect spoon-meat* i.e. you will have to use a utensil   66–71 *Some . . . it* (prose in the folio text; hence irregular lines. The meaning through l. 69 is that, though most witches require only a few things belonging to a victim, this woman requires a chain.)   75 *Fly . . . know* i.e. how strange that the courtesan should, like the proud peacock, decry pride (perhaps with play on *pride* in the sense of sexual desire in the female)   77 *demean* behave   82 *rage* wild manner, madness   89 *perforce* by force

IV, iv   *Enter Antipholus [of] Ephesus, with a Jailer.*

ANTIPHOLUS E.
Fear me not, man; I will not break away.
I'll give thee, ere I leave thee, so much money,
3   To warrant thee, as I am 'rested for.
My wife is in a wayward mood to-day,
And will not lightly trust the messenger.
6   That I should be attached in Ephesus,
I tell you, 'twill sound harshly in her ears.
   Enter Dromio of Ephesus, with a rope's end.
Here comes my man; I think he brings the money.
How now, sir; have you that I sent you for?

DROMIO E.
Here's that, I warrant you, will pay them all.

ANTIPHOLUS E.
But where's the money?

DROMIO E.
Why, sir, I gave the money for the rope.

ANTIPHOLUS E.
Five hundred ducats, villain, for a rope?

DROMIO E.
14   I'll serve you, sir, five hundred at the rate.

ANTIPHOLUS E.
To what end did I bid thee hie thee home?

DROMIO E. To a rope's end, sir; and to that end am I
returned.

ANTIPHOLUS E.
And to that end, sir, I will welcome you.
   [Beats him.]

OFFICER Good sir, be patient.

DROMIO E. Nay, 'tis fŏr me to be patient; I am in
adversity.

20 OFFICER Good now, hold thy tongue.

DROMIO E. Nay, rather persuade him to hold his hands.

22 ANTIPHOLUS E. Thou whoreson, senseless villain!

DROMIO E. I would I were senseless, sir, that I might not
feel your blows.

25 ANTIPHOLUS E. Thou art sensible in nothing but blows,
and so is an ass.

DROMIO E. I am an ass indeed; you may prove it by my
28   long ears. I have served him from the hour of my nativity
to this instant, and have nothing at his hands for my
service but blows. When I am cold, he heats me with
beating; when I am warm, he cools me with beating. I
am waked with it when I sleep, raised with it when I sit,
driven out of doors with it when I go from home, welcomed home with it when I return; nay, I bear it on my
35   shoulders, as a beggar wont her brat; and, I think, when
he hath lamed me, I shall beg with it from door to door.
   *Enter Adriana, Luciana, Courtesan, and a
   Schoolmaster, called Pinch.*

ANTIPHOLUS E. Come, go along; my wife is coming
yonder.

DROMIO E. Mistress, respice finem, respect your end; or 38
rather, the prophecy like the parrot, 'Beware the rope's
end.'

ANTIPHOLUS E. Wilt thou still talk?
   Beats Dromio.

COURTESAN
How say you now? Is not your husband mad?

ADRIANA
His incivility confirms no less.
Good Doctor Pinch, you are a conjurer;   44
Establish him in his true sense again,
And I will please you what you will demand.   46

LUCIANA
Alas, how fiery and how sharp he looks!   47

COURTESAN
Mark how he trembles in his ecstasy!   48

PINCH
Give me your hand and let me feel your pulse.

ANTIPHOLUS E.
There is my hand, and let it feel your ear.
   [Strikes him.]

PINCH
I charge thee, Satan, housed within this man,
To yield possession to my holy prayers,
And to thy state of darkness hie thee straight.
I conjure thee by all the saints in heaven.

ANTIPHOLUS E.
Peace, doting wizard, peace! I am not mad.

ADRIANA
O that thou wert not, poor distressèd soul!

ANTIPHOLUS E.
You minion, you, are these your customers?   57
Did this companion with the saffron face   58
Revel and feast it at my house to-day,
Whilst upon me the guilty doors were shut
And I denied to enter in my house?

ADRIANA
O husband, God doth know you dined at home;
Where would you had remained until this time,
Free from these slanders and this open shame!

ANTIPHOLUS E.
Dined at home! Thou villain, what sayest thou?

DROMIO E.
Sir, sooth to say, you did not dine at home.

ANTIPHOLUS E.
Were not my doors locked up and I shut out?

DROMIO E.
Perdy, your doors were locked and you shut out.   68

ANTIPHOLUS E.
And did not she herself revile me there?

DROMIO E.
Sans fable, she herself reviled you there.   70

ANTIPHOLUS E.
Did not her kitchen-maid rail, taunt, and scorn me?

DROMIO E.
Certes, she did; the kitchen-vestal scorned you.   72

ANTIPHOLUS E.
And did not I in rage depart from thence?

DROMIO E.
In verity you did; my bones bear witness,
That since have felt the vigor of his rage.

IV, iv A street 3 *To warrant* as security for 6 *attached* arrested 14
I'll . . . rate I'll get you five hundred at that price (?) 20 *Good now* for
heaven's sake 22 *whoreson* (a coarse epithet with a variety of intonations;
here used to express outraged impatience) 25 *sensible* (1) intelligent,
(2) sensitive 28 *ears* (pun on 'years'; Dromio is saying that he is a fool
for having served so long) 35 *wont* is accustomed (to bear) 38 *respice
finem* remember (your) end (a pious proverb sometimes taught to parrots;
with this was associated the punning expression 'respice funem,' 'remember the rope' – or hangman) 44 *you . . . conjurer* i.e. you can expel evil
spirits (as he tries to do, ll. 51–54) 46 *please . . . demand* pay what you
ask 47 *sharp* on edge 48 *ecstasy* madness 57 *customers* paying visitors
58 *companion* fellow; *saffron* yellow 68 *Perdy* by God (*par dieu*) 70 *Sans
fable* without lying, 'no fooling' 72 *kitchen-vestal* (her job, according to
Dr Johnson, was like that of the vestal virgins of ancient Rome, to keep the
fire burning)

ADRIANA

76   Is't good to soothe him in these contraries ?

PINCH

It is no shame : the fellow finds his vein,
And yielding to him, humors well his frenzy.

ANTIPHOLUS E.

79   Thou hast suborned the goldsmith to arrest me.

ADRIANA

Alas ! I sent you money to redeem you,
By Dromio here, who came in haste for it.

DROMIO E.

Money by me ! Heart and good will you might ;

83   But surely, master, not a rag of money.

ANTIPHOLUS E.

Went'st not thou to her for a purse of ducats ?

ADRIANA

He came to me, and I delivered it.

LUCIANA

And I am witness with her that she did.

DROMIO E.

God and the rope-maker bear me witness
That I was sent for nothing but a rope !

PINCH

Mistress, both man and master is possessed ;
I know it by their pale and deadly looks.

91   They must be bound and laid in some dark room.

ANTIPHOLUS E.

Say, wherefore didst thou lock me forth to-day ?
And why dost thou deny the bag of gold ?

ADRIANA

I did not, gentle husband, lock thee forth.

DROMIO E.

And, gentle master, I received no gold ;
But I confess, sir, that we were locked out.

ADRIANA

Dissembling villain ! thou speak'st false in both.

ANTIPHOLUS E.

Dissembling harlot ! thou art false in all,

99   And art confederate with a damnèd pack
To make a loathsome abject scorn of me ;
But with these nails I'll pluck out these false eyes
That would behold in me this shameful sport.

Enter three or four, and offer to bind him. He strives.

ADRIANA

O, bind him, bind him ! Let him not come near me.

PINCH

More company ! The fiend is strong within him.

LUCIANA

Ay me, poor man, how pale and wan he looks !

ANTIPHOLUS E.

What, will you murder me ? Thou jailer, thou,
I am thy prisoner ; wilt thou suffer them
To make a rescue ?

OFFICER   Masters, let him go.
He is my prisoner, and you shall not have him.

PINCH

Go bind this man, for he is frantic too.

[They bind Dromio of Ephesus.]

ADRIANA

What wilt thou do, thou peevish officer ?
Hast thou delight to see a wretched man
Do outrage and displeasure to himself ?

OFFICER

He is my prisoner ; if I let him go,

The debt he owes will be required of me.

ADRIANA

I will discharge thee ere I go from thee.   116
Bear me forthwith unto his creditor,
And, knowing how the debt grows, I will pay it.   118
Good Master Doctor, see him safe conveyed
Home to my house. O most unhappy day !   120

ANTIPHOLUS E.

O most unhappy strumpet !

DROMIO E.

Master, I am here entered in bond for you.

ANTIPHOLUS E.

Out on thee, villain ! Wherefore dost thou mad me ?   123

DROMIO E. Will you be bound for nothing ? Be mad,
good master : cry, 'The devil !'

LUCIANA

God help, poor souls, how idly do they talk !   126

ADRIANA

Go bear him hence. Sister, go you with me.
Say now, whose suit is he arrested at ?

*Exeunt [Pinch and his company with Antipholus
and Dromio of Ephesus]. Manet Officer
[with] Adriana, Luciana, Courtesan.*

OFFICER

One Angelo, a goldsmith ; do you know him ?

ADRIANA

I know the man. What is the sum he owes ?

OFFICER

Two hundred ducats.

ADRIANA   Say, how grows it due ?   131

OFFICER

Due for a chain your husband had of him.

ADRIANA

He did bespeak a chain for me, but had it not.

COURTESAN

When as your husband all in rage to-day
Came to my house, and took away my ring –
The ring I saw upon his finger now –
Straight after did I meet him with a chain.

ADRIANA

It may be so, but I did never see it.
Come, jailer, bring me where the goldsmith is ;
I long to know the truth hereof at large.

*Enter Antipholus of Syracuse with his rapier drawn,
and Dromio of Syracuse.*

LUCIANA

God, for thy mercy ! They are loose again.

ADRIANA

And come with naked swords.   142
Let's call more help to have them bound again.   143

Run all out.

OFFICER Away ! they'll kill us.

Exeunt omnes, as fast as may be, frighted.

ANTIPHOLUS S.

I see these witches are afraid of swords.

76 *soothe* humor (cf. l. 78) 79 *suborned* instigated 83 *rag* (cant term for farthing ; also money worn thin) 91 *bound . . . room* (common treatment for madness) 99 *confederate* allied 116 *discharge* relieve of responsibility 118 *how . . . grows* the reason for the debt 120 *unhappy* unfortunate, disastrous (stronger than modern usage) 123 *mad* madden 126 *idly* senselessly 131 *grows* comes 142 *naked* drawn 143–44 (The two stage directions of the folio duplicate each other. Probably the second was the original direction, and *Run all out* was written in the margin of the prompt-copy)

DROMIO S.
She that would be your wife now ran from you.
ANTIPHOLUS S.
Come to the Centaur; fetch our stuff from thence.
I long that we were safe and sound aboard.
DROMIO S. Faith, stay here this night; they will surely do
us no harm; you saw they speak us fair; give us gold.
Methinks they are such a gentle nation that, but for the
mountain of mad flesh that claims marriage of me, I
153 could find in my heart to stay here still, and turn witch.
ANTIPHOLUS S.
I will not stay to-night for all the town;
Therefore away, to get our stuff aboard.   Exeunt.

*

V, i   Enter the [Second] Merchant and [Angelo,] the
         Goldsmith.
ANGELO
I am sorry, sir, that I have hind'red you;
But I protest he had the chain of me,
Though most dishonestly he doth deny it.
2. MERCHANT
How is the man esteemed here in the city?
ANGELO
Of very reverend reputation, sir,
Of credit infinite, highly beloved,
Second to none that lives here in the city;
8   His word might bear my wealth at any time.
2. MERCHANT
9   Speak softly; yonder, as I think, he walks.
         Enter Antipholus and Dromio [of Syracuse] again.
ANGELO
'Tis so; and that self chain about his neck
11   Which he forswore most monstrously to have.
Good sir, draw near to me, I'll speak to him.
Signior Antipholus, I wonder much
That you would put me to this shame and trouble;
And not without some scandal to yourself,
16   With circumstance and oaths so to deny
This chain which now you wear so openly.
Beside the charge, the shame, imprisonment,
19   You have done wrong to this my honest friend,
Who, but for staying on our controversy,
Had hoisted sail and put to sea to-day.
This chain you had of me; can you deny it?
ANTIPHOLUS S.
I think I had; I never did deny it.
2. MERCHANT
Yes, that you did, sir, and forswore it too.
ANTIPHOLUS S.
Who heard me to deny it or forswear it?
2. MERCHANT
These ears of mine, thou know'st, did hear thee.
Fie on thee, wretch! 'Tis pity that thou liv'st
To walk where any honest men resort.

ANTIPHOLUS S.
Thou art a villain to impeach me thus: 29
I'll prove mine honor and mine honesty
Against thee presently, if thou dar'st stand.   31
2. MERCHANT
I dare, and do defy thee for a villain.   32
         They draw. Enter Adriana, Luciana, Courtesan,
         and others.
ADRIANA
Hold, hurt him not, for God's sake! He is mad.
Some get within him, take his sword away.   34
Bind Dromio too, and bear them to my house.
DROMIO S.
Run, master, run; for God's sake, take a house!   36
This is some priory. In, or we are spoiled.
         Exeunt [Antipholus and Dromio of
                         Syracuse] to the Priory.
         Enter Lady Abbess.
ABBESS
Be quiet, people. Wherefore throng you hither?
ADRIANA
To fetch my poor distracted husband hence.
Let us come in, that we may bind him fast,
And bear him home for his recovery.
ANGELO
I knew he was not in his perfect wits.
2. MERCHANT
I am sorry now that I did draw on him.
ABBESS
How long hath this possession held the man?
ADRIANA
This week he hath been heavy, sour, sad,
And much different from the man he was;
But till this afternoon his passion
Ne'er brake into extremity of rage.
ABBESS
Hath he not lost much wealth by wrack of sea?
Buried some dear friend? Hath not else his eye
Strayed his affection in unlawful love –   51
A sin prevailing much in youthful men,
Who give their eyes the liberty of gazing?
Which of these sorrows is he subject to?
ADRIANA
To none of these, except it be the last;
Namely, some love that drew him oft from home.
ABBESS
You should for that have reprehended him.
ADRIANA
Why, so I did.
ABBESS   Ay, but not rough enough.
ADRIANA
As roughly as my modesty would let me.
ABBESS
Haply, in private.
ADRIANA   And in assemblies too.
ABBESS
Ay, but not enough.
ADRIANA
It was the copy of our conference.   62
In bed, he slept not for my urging it;   63
At board, he fed not for my urging it;
Alone, it was the subject of my theme;
In company I often glancèd it.   66
Still did I tell him it was vile and bad.   67

153 still always
V, i Before a priory 8 His . . . wealth he could have had all my wealth on
the strength of his word 9 s.d. again (an indication that the action of
'Act V' is continuous with that of 'Act IV') 11 forswore denied on oath
16 circumstance detailed argument or attempted proof 19 honest honorable
29 impeach accuse 31 presently at once; stand i.e. take your position for
fighting 32 defy challenge; villain base person 34 within him under his
guard 36 take i.e. take to 51 Strayed led astray 62 copy theme 63 for
because of 66 glancèd touched upon 67 Still always

ABBESS
And thereof came it that the man was mad.
The venom clamors of a jealous woman
Poisons more deadly than a mad dog's tooth.
It seems his sleeps were hind'red by thy railing,
And thereof comes it that his head is light.
Thou say'st his meat was sauced with thy upbraidings;
Unquiet meals make ill digestions;
Thereof the raging fire of fever bred.
And what's a fever but a fit of madness?
Thou sayest his sports were hind'red by thy brawls.
Sweet recreation barred, what doth ensue
But moody and dull melancholy,
Kinsman to grim and comfortless despair,
And at her heels a huge infectious troop
82 Of pale distemperatures and foes to life?
In food, in sport, and life-preserving rest
To be disturbed, would mad or man or beast.
The consequence is, then, thy jealous fits
Hath scared thy husband from the use of wits.
    LUCIANA
She never reprehended him but mildly
When he demeaned himself rough, rude, and wildly.
Why bear you these rebukes and answer not?
    ADRIANA
90 She did betray me to my own reproof.
Good people, enter, and lay hold on him.
    ABBESS
No, not a creature enters in my house.
    ADRIANA
Then let your servants bring my husband forth.
    ABBESS
Neither: he took this place for sanctuary,
And it shall privilege him from your hands
Till I have brought him to his wits again,
Or lose my labor in assaying it.
    ADRIANA
I will attend my husband, be his nurse,
Diet his sickness, for it is my office,
100 And will have no attorney but myself;
And therefore let me have him home with me.
    ABBESS
Be patient, for I will not let him stir
Till I have used the approvèd means I have,
With wholesome syrups, drugs, and holy prayers,
105 To make of him a formal man again.
106 It is a branch and parcel of mine oath,
A charitable duty of my order.
Therefore depart and leave him here with me.
    ADRIANA
I will not hence and leave my husband here;
And ill it doth beseem your holiness
To separate the husband and the wife.
    ABBESS
Be quiet, and depart; thou shalt not have him.   *[Exit.]*
    LUCIANA
Complain unto the Duke of this indignity.
    ADRIANA
Come, go. I will fall prostrate at his feet,
And never rise until my tears and prayers
Have won his Grace to come in person hither,
And take perforce my husband from the Abbess.
    2. MERCHANT
By this, I think, the dial points at five:

Anon, I'm sure, the Duke himself in person
Comes this way to the melancholy vale,
The place of death and sorry execution,   121
Behind the ditches of the abbey here.
    ANGELO
Upon what cause?
    2. MERCHANT
To see a reverend Syracusian merchant,
Who put unluckily into this bay
Against the laws and statutes of this town,
Beheaded publicly for his offense.
    ANGELO
See where they come. We will behold his death.
    LUCIANA
Kneel to the Duke before he pass the abbey.
    Enter the Duke of Ephesus, and [Egeon] the
    Merchant of Syracuse, bare head, with the Headsman,
    and other Officers.
    DUKE
Yet once again proclaim it publicly,
If any friend will pay the sum for him,
He shall not die; so much we tender him.   132
    ADRIANA
Justice, most sacred Duke, against the Abbess!
    DUKE
She is a virtuous and a reverend lady.
It cannot be that she hath done thee wrong.
    ADRIANA
May it please your Grace, Antipholus, my husband,
Who I made lord of me and all I had,
At your important letters, this ill day   138
A most outrageous fit of madness took him,
That desperately he hurried through the street—
With him his bondman, all as mad as he—
Doing displeasure to the citizens
By rushing in their houses, bearing thence
Rings, jewels, anything his rage did like.   144
Once did I get him bound and sent him home,
Whilst to take order for the wrongs I went   146
That here and there his fury had committed.
Anon, I wot not by what strong escape,   148
He broke from those that had the guard of him,
And with his mad attendant and himself,
Each one with ireful passion, with drawn swords
Met us again and, madly bent on us,
Chased us away, till, raising of more aid,
We came again to bind them. Then they fled
Into this abbey, whither we pursued them;
And here the Abbess shuts the gates on us,
And will not suffer us to fetch him out,
Nor send him forth that we may bear him hence.
Therefore, most gracious Duke, with thy command
Let him be brought forth and borne hence for help.   160
    DUKE
Long since thy husband served me in my wars,
And I to thee engaged a prince's word,
When thou didst make him master of thy bed,
To do him all the grace and good I could.
Go, some of you, knock at the abbey gate

82 *distemperatures* disorders 90 *She . . . reproof* she tricked me into testi-
fying against myself 100 *attorney* agent 105 *formal* in proper form, sane
106 *branch and parcel* part and parcel 121 *sorry* causing sorrow 132
tender grant 138 *important* firmly requesting 144 *rage* madness 146
take order settle 148 *wot* know; *strong* violent

And bid the Lady Abbess come to me.
I will determine this before I stir.

Enter a Messenger.

MESSENGER
O mistress, mistress, shift and save yourself!
My master and his man are both broke loose,
170 Beaten the maids a-row and bound the doctor,
Whose beard they have singed off with brands of fire;
And ever as it blazed they threw on him
Great pails of puddled mire to quench the hair.
My master preaches patience to him, and the while
175 His man with scissors nicks him like a fool;
And sure, unless you send some present help,
Between them they will kill the conjurer.

ADRIANA
Peace, fool! thy master and his man are here,
And that is false thou dost report to us.

MESSENGER
Mistress, upon my life, I tell you true;
I have not breathed almost since I did see it.
He cries for you and vows, if he can take you,
To scorch your face and to disfigure you.

Cry within.

Hark, hark! I hear him, mistress. Fly, be gone!

DUKE
185 Come, stand by me; fear nothing. Guard with halberds!

ADRIANA
Ay, me, it is my husband! Witness you,
That he is borne about invisible.
Even now we housed him in the abbey here,
And now he's there, past thought of human reason.

Enter Antipholus [of Ephesus] and Dromio of Ephesus.

ANTIPHOLUS E.
Justice, most gracious Duke! O grant me justice,
Even for the service that long since I did thee,
192 When I bestrid thee in the wars and took
Deep scars to save thy life; even for the blood
That then I lost for thee, now grant me justice.

EGEON
Unless the fear of death doth make me dote,
I see my son Antipholus and Dromio.

ANTIPHOLUS E.
Justice, sweet Prince, against that woman there!
She whom thou gav'st to me to be my wife,
That hath abusèd and dishonored me,
200 Even in the strength and height of injury!
Beyond imagination is the wrong
That she this day hath shameless thrown on me.

DUKE
203 Discover how, and thou shalt find me just.

ANTIPHOLUS E.
This day, great Duke, she shut the doors upon me,
205 While she with harlots feasted in my house.

DUKE
A grievous fault! Say, woman, didst thou so?

ADRIANA
No, my good lord. Myself, he, and my sister

To-day did dine together. So befall my soul
As this is false he burdens me withal!   209

LUCIANA
Ne'er may I look on day, nor sleep on night,
But she tells to your Highness simple truth!

ANGELO
O perjured woman! They are both forsworn;
In this the madman justly chargeth them.

ANTIPHOLUS E.
My liege, I am advisèd what I say,
Neither disturbed with the effect of wine,
Nor heady-rash, provoked with raging ire,
Albeit my wrongs might make one wiser mad.
This woman locked me out this day from dinner.
That goldsmith there, were he not packed with her,   219
Could witness it, for he was with me then;
Who parted with me to go fetch a chain,
Promising to bring it to the Porpentine,
Where Balthazar and I did dine together.
Our dinner done, and he not coming thither,
I went to seek him. In the street I met him,
And in his company that gentleman.
There did this perjured goldsmith swear me down
That I this day of him received the chain,
Which, God he knows, I saw not; for the which
He did arrest me with an officer.
I did obey, and sent my peasant home   231
For certain ducats; he with none returned.
Then fairly I bespoke the officer   233
To go in person with me to my house.
By the way we met
My wife, her sister, and a rabble more   236
Of vile confederates. Along with them
They brought one Pinch, a hungry lean-faced villain,
A mere anatomy, a mountebank,   239
A threadbare juggler, and a fortune-teller,
A needy, hollow-eyed, sharp-looking wretch,   241
A living dead man. This pernicious slave,
Forsooth, took on him as a conjurer,   243
And gazing in mine eyes, feeling my pulse,
And with no face, as 'twere, out-facing me,
Cries out, I was possessed. Then all together
They fell upon me, bound me, bore me thence,
And in a dark and dankish vault at home
There left me and my man, both bound together,
Till, gnawing with my teeth my bonds in sunder,
I gained my freedom, and immediately
Ran hither to your Grace; whom I beseech
To give me ample satisfaction
For these deep shames and great indignities.

ANGELO
My lord, in truth, thus far I witness with him,
That he dined not at home, but was locked out.

DUKE
But had he such a chain of thee, or no?

ANGELO
He had, my lord; and when he ran in here,
These people saw the chain about his neck.

2. MERCHANT
Besides, I will be sworn these ears of mine   260
Heard you confess you had the chain of him,
After you first forswore it on the mart,
And thereupon I drew my sword on you;
And then you fled into this abbey here,

---

170 *a-row* one by one (or so that they lie in a row) 175 *nicks . . . fool* cuts his hair to make him look like an Elizabethan fool 185 *halberds* long spears with a blade 192 *bestrid thee* stood over and protected you when you were down 200 *in . . . injury* to the most injurious extremes 203 *Discover* reveal 205 *harlots* vile companions 209 *he . . . withal* with which he charges me 219 *packed* in conspiracy 231 *peasant* bondman 233 *fairly* politely 236 *rabble* mob 239 *mere* sheer; *anatomy* skeleton; *mountebank* charlatan, quack 241 *sharp* hungry 243 *took . . . as* assumed the role of

From whence, I think, you are come by miracle.

ANTIPHOLUS E.

I never came within these abbey walls,
Nor ever didst thou draw thy sword on me.
I never saw the chain, so help me heaven!
And this is false you burden me withal.

DUKE

270   Why, what an intricate impeach is this!
271   I think you all have drunk of Circe's cup.
      If here you housed him, here he would have been.
273   If he were mad, he would not plead so coldly.
      You say he dined at home; the goldsmith here
      Denies that saying. Sirrah, what say you?

DROMIO E.

Sir, he dined with her there, at the Porpentine.

COURTESAN

He did, and from my finger snatched that ring.

ANTIPHOLUS E.

'Tis true, my liege; this ring I had of her.

DUKE

Saw'st thou him enter at the abbey here?

COURTESAN

As sure, my liege, as I do see your Grace.

DUKE

Why, this is strange. Go call the Abbess hither.
282   I think you are all mated or stark mad.

Exit one to the Abbess.

EGEON

Most mighty Duke, vouchsafe me speak a word.
Haply I see a friend will save my life,
And pay the sum that may deliver me.

DUKE

Speak freely, Syracusian, what thou wilt.

EGEON

Is not your name, sir, called Antipholus?
And is not that your bondman Dromio?

DROMIO E.

Within this hour I was his bondman, sir;
But he, I thank him, gnawed in two my cords.
Now am I Dromio, and his man, unbound.

EGEON

I am sure you both of you remember me.

DROMIO E.

Ourselves we do remember, sir, by you;
For lately we were bound, as you are now.
295   You are not Pinch's patient, are you, sir?

EGEON

Why look you strange on me? You know me well.

ANTIPHOLUS E.

I never saw you in my life till now.

EGEON

O, grief hath changed me since you saw me last,
299   And careful hours, with Time's deformèd hand,
300   Have written strange defeatures in my face.
      But tell me yet, dost thou not know my voice?

ANTIPHOLUS E. Neither.

EGEON Dromio, nor thou?

DROMIO E. No, trust me, sir, not I.

EGEON I am sure thou dost.

DROMIO E. Ay, sir, but I am sure I do not; and whatsoever a man denies, you are now bound to believe him.

EGEON

Not know my voice! O time's extremity,
Hast thou so cracked and splitted my poor tongue

In seven short years, that here my only son
Knows not my feeble key of untuned cares?   311
Though now this grainèd face of mine be hid   312
In sap-consuming winter's drizzled snow,
And all the conduits of my blood froze up,
Yet hath my night of life some memory,
My wasting lamps some fading glimmer left,   316
My dull deaf ears a little use to hear.
All these old witnesses – I cannot err –
Tell me thou art my son Antipholus.

ANTIPHOLUS E.

I never saw my father in my life.

EGEON

But seven years since, in Syracusa, boy,
Thou know'st we parted; but perhaps, my son,
Thou sham'st to acknowledge me in misery.

ANTIPHOLUS E.

The Duke and all that know me in the city
Can witness with me that it is not so.
I ne'er saw Syracusa in my life.

DUKE

I tell thee, Syracusian, twenty years
Have I been patron to Antipholus,
During which time he ne'er saw Syracusa.
I see thy age and dangers make thee dote.

*Enter the Abbess, with Antipholus of Syracuse and
Dromio of Syracuse.*

ABBESS

Most mighty Duke, behold a man much wronged.

All gather to see them.

ADRIANA

I see two husbands, or mine eyes deceive me!

DUKE

One of these men is genius to the other;   333
And so of these, which is the natural man,
And which the spirit? Who deciphers them?

DROMIO S.

I, sir, am Dromio; command him away.

DROMIO E.

I, sir, am Dromio; pray let me stay.

ANTIPHOLUS S.

Egeon art thou not? or else his ghost?

DROMIO S.

O, my old master! Who hath bound him here?

ABBESS

Whoever bound him, I will loose his bonds,
And gain a husband by his liberty.
Speak, old Egeon, if thou be'st the man
That hadst a wife once called Emilia,
That bore thee at a burden two fair sons.   344
O, if thou be'st the same Egeon, speak,
And speak unto the same Emilia!

EGEON

If I dream not, thou art Emilia.
If thou art she, tell me where is that son
That floated with thee on the fatal raft?

270 *intricate impeach* involved accusation   271 *Circe's cup* (the enchantress' drink turned men into animals)   273 *coldly* reasonably   282 *mated*
stupefied   295 *Pinch's patient* i.e. bound as Dromio had been while undergoing 'treatment' for madness   299 *careful* full of care   300 *defeatures*
worsenings of feature   311 *my . . . cares* my voice made feeble by discordant
cares (the image is the favorite Elizabethan one of life losing its harmony)
312 *grainèd* furrowed   316 *wasting lamps* dimming eyes   333 *genius* attendant spirit (cf. *Julius Caesar*, II, i, 66)   344 *burden* birth

ABBESS
By men of Epidamnum he and I
And the twin Dromio all were taken up;
But by and by rude fishermen of Corinth
By force took Dromio and my son from them,
And me they left with those of Epidamnum.
What then became of them, I cannot tell;
I to this fortune that you see me in.
DUKE
357 Why, here begins his morning story right:
358 These two Antipholuses, these two so like,
359 And these two Dromios, one in semblance –
360 Besides her urging of her wreck at sea –
These are the parents to these children,
Which accidentally are met together.
Antipholus, thou cam'st from Corinth first?
ANTIPHOLUS S.
No, sir, not I; I came from Syracuse.
DUKE
Stay, stand apart; I know not which is which.
ANTIPHOLUS E.
I came from Corinth, my most gracious lord –
DROMIO E.
And I with him.
ANTIPHOLUS E.
Brought to this town by that most famous warrior,
Duke Menaphon, your most renownèd uncle.
ADRIANA
370 Which of you two did dine with me to-day?
ANTIPHOLUS S.
I, gentle mistress.
ADRIANA
And are not you my husband?
ANTIPHOLUS E.
No; I say nay to that.
ANTIPHOLUS S.
And so do I; yet did she call me so;
And this fair gentlewoman, her sister here,
Did call me brother. [to Luciana] What I told you then,
I hope I shall have leisure to make good,
If this be not a dream I see and hear.
ANGELO
That is the chain, sir, which you had of me.
ANTIPHOLUS S.
380 I think it be, sir; I deny it not.
ANTIPHOLUS E.
And you, sir, for this chain arrested me.
ANGELO
I think I did, sir; I deny it not.
ADRIANA
I sent you money, sir, to be your bail,

By Dromio; but I think he brought it not.
DROMIO E.
No, none by me.
ANTIPHOLUS S.
This purse of ducats I received from you,
And Dromio, my man, did bring them me.
I see we still did meet each other's man,
And I was ta'en for him, and he for me,
And thereupon these errors are arose. 390
ANTIPHOLUS E.
These ducats pawn I for my father here.
DUKE
It shall not need; thy father hath his life.
COURTESAN
Sir, I must have that diamond from you.
ANTIPHOLUS E.
There, take it; and much thanks for my good cheer.
ABBESS
Renownèd Duke, vouchsafe to take the pains
To go with us into the abbey here,
And hear at large discoursèd all our fortunes;
And all that are assembled in this place,
That by this sympathizèd one day's error 399
Have suffered wrong, go keep us company,
And we shall make full satisfaction.
Thirty-three years have I but gone in travail 402
Of you, my sons; and till this present hour
My heavy burden ne'er deliverèd.
The Duke, my husband, and my children both,
And you the calendars of their nativity, 406
Go to a gossips' feast, and go with me; 407
After so long grief such Nativity! 408
DUKE
With all my heart I'll gossip at this feast. 409
Exeunt [all but] the two Dromios and two Brothers.
DROMIO S.
Master, shall I fetch your stuff from shipboard?
ANTIPHOLUS E.
Dromio, what stuff of mine hast thou embarked?
DROMIO S.
Your goods that lay at host, sir, in the Centaur. 412
ANTIPHOLUS S.
He speaks to me. I am your master, Dromio.
Come, go with us; we'll look to that anon.
Embrace thy brother there; rejoice with him.
Exit [with his Brother].
DROMIO S.
There is a fat friend at your master's house,
That kitchened me for you to-day at dinner; 417
She now shall be my sister, not my wife.
DROMIO E.
Methinks you are my glass, and not my brother.
I see by you I am a sweet-faced youth.
Will you walk in to see their gossiping?
DROMIO S. Not I, sir; you are my elder.
DROMIO E. That's a question; how shall we try it?
DROMIO S. We'll draw cuts for the senior; till then lead
thou first.
DROMIO E. Nay, then, thus:
We came into the world like brother and brother;
And now let's go hand in hand, not one before another.
Exeunt.

357–62 (in the folio these lines follow l. 346; the present arrangement – almost an inevitable one – is that of the Globe edition, following Capell) 358 *Antipholuses* (four syllables, the 'o' being scarcely heard) 359 *semblance* seeming, appearance 360 *urging* report 399 *sympathizèd* felt together 402 *in travail* i.e. as in giving birth 406 *you . . . nativity* i.e. the Dromios 407 *Go . . ., and go with me* (the repetition of 'go' is effective if 'me' is stressed); *gossips' feast* christening feast, at which a 'gossip' or godparent, is a sponsor 408 *Nativity* (as repeated and capitalized the word seems to carry the larger significance of a religious festivity) 409 *gossip at* take part in 412 *at host* in charge of the host 417 *kitchened* entertained in the kitchen (but the word is still too good to sacrifice to a paraphrase)

THE TAMING OF THE SHREW

INTRODUCTION

Directors of *The Taming of the Shrew* corrupt its meaning when they bring Petruchio on stage cracking a whip. Admittedly such stage business would be appropriate to an extra-Shakespearean literary tradition, conspicuous in medieval *fabliaux* and Elizabethan jestbooks, according to which the husband of a shrewish wife forced her to mend her ways by beating her or otherwise subjecting her to physical cruelty. An example is the anonymous Elizabethan ballad, *A Merry Jest of a Shrewd and Curst Wife Lapped in Morel's Skin for Her Good Behavior* (printed about 1550). In this singularly unmerry tale a wife seeks frankly to dominate her husband. When she persists in shrewish behavior, he beats her with birch rods till the blood runs on the floor and she faints. He then wraps her in the skin of an old lame ploughhorse, Morel, killed and flayed especially for the occasion. Morel's salted skin quickly "revives" the wife, and the husband threatens to keep her in it unless she yields him mastership. At this "her mood begins to sink" and she promises obedience. She becomes an exemplary wife.

Shakespeare seems to have known this bit of Elizabethan Grand Guignol, for the basic situation of *The Taming of the Shrew* closely resembles that of the *Shrewd and Curst Wife*. However, he made no use whatever of the method of wife-taming recommended in that story. He accepted rather a humanist tradition, well represented by Erasmus in *A Merry Dialogue Declaring the Properties of Shrewd Shrews and Honest Wives* (translation printed 1557), and by Vives in *The Office and Duty of an Husband* (translation printed about 1553). According to this tradition, the husband of a shrewish wife did not resort to violence, but led her, gently but firmly, to accept his rightful authority, much as he would teach a colt to go through its paces or a hawk to fly to the lure. Thus Petruchio "famishes" and "watches" his "haggard," Kate, but he always addresses her in courteous language and he never strikes her. The spanking he administers in most modern productions, like the whip he is made to carry, has no authority in the text of the play; it is a twentieth-century stage tradition, as the whip is a nineteenth-century one. The difficulty with these titillating sadistic touches, each perhaps innocent enough on the surface, is that they suggest, ultimately, a brutal domination of wife by husband. Accordingly Kate's speech on the subordination of wife to husband is sometimes misinterpreted as the blueprint for a husband's tyranny. Most spectators know better, despite what they are shown on the stage, for it is unlikely that *The Shrew* would be one of the most popular of Shakespeare's plays in the modern theatre if it really portrayed the subjugation of a wife through brutality. Incidentally, Kate's speech on subordination of the wife was probably, without

denial of the basic validity of its doctrine, as susceptible to an ironic interpretation in Shakespeare's day as in our own. Vives, in *The Instruction of a Christian Woman* (translation printed 1540), quotes the wise saw, "A good woman by lowly obeisance ruleth her husband." Certainly the Elizabethans, in their view of the marriage relationship as of other things, were much more conscious of "degree" than we are:

> Such duty as the subject owes the prince,
> Even such a woman oweth to her husband;
> And when she is froward, peevish, sullen, sour,
> And not obedient to his honest will,
> What is she but a foul contending rebel
> And graceless traitor to her loving lord?

But they too could recognize the paradox that he who is ruled can also rule.

When we first see Kate, she is a spoiled household bully who tyrannizes over her sister and openly defies her father's authority. Without provocation she strikes her sister, her music-master, and her suitor. She is, in the terms of the play, shrewd, rough, sullen, headstrong, intolerable curst, stark mad or wonderful froward, impatient, angry, envious, revengeful, proud-minded, bent on pleasing herself, a wildcat, a chider, a railer, an irksome brawling scold, a devil, the devil's dam, a fiend of hell, and a hilding of a devilish spirit. In short, she is a shrew; and Petruchio, a husband for her turn, is the man born to tame her. But "taming" is only a metaphor. We can describe the action just as well by saying that Petruchio cures Kate of chronic bad temper. And he does so by employing a therapeutic method more in favor with the Elizabethans than with us, that of driving out poison with poison. He pretends to have the same sort of bad temper that she has, and he behaves with a wanton capriciousness that out-Kates Kate. Thus, more shrew than she, he kills her in her own humor; and thus, through him as through a mirror, Kate achieves self-knowledge. Petruchio's psychology is subtle, for, besides showing her what she is through his own outrageous behavior, he keeps telling her what she may become, praising her with a fine irony for qualities precisely the opposite of her defects. He speaks to her father of her affability and bashful modesty, her wondrous qualities and mild behavior; he praises her to her face as mild, gentle, pleasant, and passing courteous; and he compares her in patience to a second Grissel. The result is that when Kate is ready to modify her personality she has at hand a model on which to pattern herself. As the ugly old woman in the medieval romance changes after her marriage into a beautiful young one, so Katherine the curst changes, after her marriage, into a young woman of congenial and wholesome disposition. Or, to suggest another aspect of her psychic metamorphosis, she comes to accept the social relationship of wife to husband.

Although countless medieval and Renaissance stories deal with conflict between husband and wife, it is now generally agreed that there is no single extant source for the Petruchio–Kate story in its entirety. The *Shrewd and Curst Wife* is not usually regarded as a source, in part perhaps because its brutality is quickly recognized as foreign to Shakespeare's conception. But if we grant that an altogether different sort of "taming" is in question, it seems not unlikely that the anonymous ballad suggested the basic framework of Shakespeare's play. In the ballad, a man with a shrewish wife has two daughters. The younger is the father's favorite, meek and gentle, sought after by many suitors. The older is the mother's favorite, and like her a shrew; she is frantic, mad, without suitors. But finally a suitor appears who wishes to marry her. The father warns him against the shrewish daughter, likening her to "a devilish fiend of hell." The suitor says he sees no evil in her, marries her, and proceeds to "tame" her, by dint of birch rods and Morel's skin. At the close of the story the father, mother, and neighbors, entertained at a dinner, marvel at the wife's "good behavior." The tale ends with the jingle, "He that can charm a shrewd wife Better than thus, Let him come to me and fetch ten pound And a golden purse." All of these details but the shrewish mother and the brutal taming crop up, transmuted, in Shakespeare.

Other elements of Shakespeare's main plot have recognizable sources or analogues. The episode of rating a tailor for cutting a gown in fantastical fashion (IV, iii) occurs in Gerard Legh's *Accidence of Armory* (1562). The business of a wife's agreeing with her husband in his assertion of what is palpably not true (IV, v) occurs in *El Conde Lucanor* of Don Juan Manuel (around 1350). And the device of three husbands wagering on their wives' obedience (V, ii) occurs in *The Book of the Knight of La Tour-Landry* (translation printed 1484). None of these stories is necessarily a direct source of the corresponding episode in Shakespeare, but in each case the general similarity is such that we may suppose Shakespeare adapted an available tradition, incorporating his adaptation within a framework suggested by the *Shrewd and Curst Wife*.

Within this framework Shakespeare also incorporated a subplot based on George Gascoigne's *Supposes*, acted at Gray's Inn in 1566 and again at Trinity College, Oxford, in 1582. This is a fairly close translation of Lodovico Ariosto's *Suppositi*, acted at Ferrara in 1509, one of the earliest extant examples of Italian Renaissance comedy in the classical tradition represented by Menander, Plautus, and Terence. Ariosto's plot is fairly typical of the tradition: a young man succeeds in possessing the girl he loves by outwitting the character who blocks his access to her. In the Greco-Roman comedies the girl is usually a sort of junior courtesan, technically a slave and hence not marriageable; and the character guarding her from access is usually a pander or courtesan possessing legal title. Generally the young man's slave conducts the necessary intrigue, and if money is also needed, as it usually is, a second intrigue may be undertaken to swindle the young man's father. Sometimes the girl is pregnant, and sometimes it is discovered that she is a citizen, stolen as a baby by pirates or otherwise victimized by circumstance, in which case the play ends with the promise of marriage. Erostrato (Lucentio) as lover, Dulipo (Tranio) as the servant who conducts an intrigue in his young master's interest, and Philogano (Vincentio) as the father who is hoaxed by his son's servant – these characters Ariosto drew straight from classical comedy. But in his, as in similar Renaissance redactions, new character-types appeared reflecting altered social customs, along with new plots drawn from the medieval *novelle*. The core of the plot, and the character of the young man, remained much the same as in classical comedy, but the girl became either the wife or daughter of a citizen instead of the chattel of a courtesan or pander, and the character to be duped out of the girl became either a husband or father. Thus Ariosto's additional characters are "modern," no one quite like them appearing in surviving classical comedy: Polinesta (Bianca), a marriageable girl of wealthy family; Damon (Baptista), a rich father wishing to marry off a daughter; Balia (expunged by Shakespeare), a chaperon-nurse; and the rival suitors Cleander (Gremio) and Dulipo-the-supposed-Erostrato (Tranio-the-supposed-Lucentio).

Shakespeare modifies these received character-types, two of them in particular. Lucentio is quite different from the young man of classical comedy or from Erostrato in the *Supposes*, for he not only wishes to marry the girl but also has no intention of seducing her. He represents a romantic tradition, that of the chaste wooer or rapturous lover. Bianca is even further from classical comedy than Polinesta, for she also represents a romantic tradition, that of the chaste heroine who can be possessed only in marriage. Not being promiscuous, she has no need of a go-between; and hence Shakespeare does not need a character corresponding to Balia. Thus he shifts the emphasis from sexual intrigue to winning the girl's hand in marriage, omitting both Polinesta's pregnancy and the slightly grim episode of the outraged father's imprisoning his daughter's lover. The character of Hortensio is a significant innovation, for in the *Supposes* the disguised lover has no competitor. Thus Shakespeare provides two *sub rosa* suitors (Lucentio and Hortensio) who appeal directly to the girl, in addition to the two open suitors (Tranio and Gremio) who appeal to the girl's father. Lucentio therefore has a potentially effective rival, and Bianca exercises choice. Though subjected to gentle mockery, Hortensio has a sympathetic character. Accordingly he must be matched with a wife at the end, and so the Widow is dragged in as a sort of *madonna ex machina*. If we expect realism this last-minute mating may seem awkward, but it is inevitable if the play is to end, as by convention a comedy should, in marriage for all the lovers, and if a genuine rivalry for the heroine is to be suggested, however briefly.

Since the *Supposes* has a "crisis" plot, with absolute unity of time and place, an important structural change is Shakespeare's adapting the story from the retrospective to the progressive mode of drama. He shows as successively occurring what Ariosto merely reports as having already occurred: the young man's falling in love with the girl upon seeing her in the street, his taking service in her father's household, his successful wooing. Another important structural change is the addition of a "stolen marriage" while the girl's father is negotiating with the fake suitor. From the point of view of plot there is a redundancy here, for Hortensio's rivalry is no longer a factor and the arrival of the lover's true father, as in the source, makes it possible, after exposure of Tranio and the fake father, for Lucentio to marry the girl – but he has taken the bit in his teeth and already married her! The point, of course, is that in proper romantic drama the lovers should effect their own marriage, without regard for the wishes of their elders. Shakespeare employed the device of a stolen marriage more effectively in *Romeo and Juliet* and *The Merry Wives of Windsor*, in each of which a stolen marriage is the only alternative to the girl's being forced to marry an undesirable suitor favored by her parents.

Shakespeare's dramaturgical skill is especially evident in his welding of two parallel actions, the construction bearing comparison with that of *The Merchant of Venice* or *Much Ado about Nothing*. A few loose ends and minor flaws in the plotting do not affect the general truth of Dr Johnson's criticism: "Of this play the two plots are so well united, that they can hardly be called two without injury to the art with which they are interwoven." Since the subplot involves only wooing and marriage, it proceeds at a slower pace than the main plot, which involves wooing, marriage, and the "taming." Throughout the first three acts the two plots run together in parallel, tightly linked by the father's insistence that the elder daughter be wed before the younger. Lucentio falls in love with Bianca (I, i), Tranio and Gremio sue to Baptista for her hand in marriage (II, i), and Lucentio and Hortensio woo her in disguise (III, i). Petruchio decides to marry Kate (I, ii), woos her (II, i), and marries her (III, ii). In the fourth act the two stories diverge. The subplot, after enlistment of the Pedant (IV, ii), forks into the gulling of Baptista and the planning of the stolen marriage (IV, iv). The main plot pursues the "taming" through the episodes of the burnt meat (IV, i) and the Tailor (IV, iii) to the meeting of Petruchio and Kate with Vincentio (IV, v). At this point the two stories, loosely connected by Hortensio's appearance in the main plot (IV, iii) after his dismissal from the subplot (IV, ii), are again united. The denouement of the "taming" action occurs in IV, v, when Kate accepts the sun as the moon and Vincentio as a young woman. This episode neatly prepares us for the denial of Vincentio's identity in V, i. The denouement of the "supposes" action occurs in this scene, with the exposure of Tranio's hoax and the reappearance of the runaway lovers as husband and wife. Technically anticlimactic, the last scene (V, ii) emphasizes the unity of the two actions by suggesting, through an exhibition of Kate's reformed nature, that Bianca and the Widow are shrews under the skin. This scene gives us also, in Lucentio's banquet, an effective symbol of the "new" society which normally "crystallizes" around the lovers when they marry at the end of a comedy.

To the parallel actions of *The Taming of the Shrew* Shakespeare added, in the form of an "induction," a third action, the gulling of Christopher Sly. This much admired sequence of comedy is an example of a widespread motif originating in the story of "The Sleeper Awakened" in *The Arabian Nights*. Early in the sixteenth century the story was retold by Vives as having actually occurred in Brussels around 1440, with Philip the Good, Duke of Burgundy, in the role of Shakespeare's Lord. Much the same version was recounted by Heuterus in *De rebus burgundicis* (1584). Up to a point, the story in

Heuterus, if we allow for variations between prose fiction and verse drama, is generally similar to that in Shakespeare. The chief difference is that the deluded artisan who corresponds to Shakespeare's Sly, having fallen asleep after a banquet, is once again dressed in his rags and returned to the street where he had been found in a drunken sleep the night before; in the morning he imagines he has dreamt what happened to him. The difficult question therefore arises whether Shakespeare concluded Sly's story with a "dramatic epilogue" which for some reason was omitted from the printed text, or whether he intended his "presenters" to disappear unobtrusively after their short "interlude" at the end of I, i. A conclusive answer may not be possible. In support of the first interpretation it can be argued that Shakespeare would not have left the Sly story up in the air after so brilliant a beginning, and that the story is "finished" in all other versions, including a dramatic one, *The Taming of a Shrew*, in some manner related to Shakespeare's play (cf. Appendix). In support of the second interpretation it can be argued that Shakespeare would have tended to avoid a dramatic epilogue as anticlimactic, that its omission would have harmonized with the Elizabethan theatrical practise of doubling roles of the induction with roles of the play proper (thus making it awkward for actors on stage at the end of the play to return to their roles of the induction), and that the thematic statement of Shakespeare's Sly material is complete as we have it – Sly's story is in effect "finished" when, like Kate, he has been persuaded to accept a new personality.

In any case, the action of Shakespeare's induction is as closely related to the parallel actions of his play proper as each of those actions is to the other – except that where the double relationship is explicit, in terms chiefly of plot, the triple one is implicit, in terms chiefly of theme. Taken together, the three actions constitute a complex of compared and contrasted poses and "supposes" – Gascoigne's word for Ariosto's *suppositi*, i.e. "assumptions." The Lord–Sly action is concerned with assumptions about identity and with how these can lead to assumptions about personality. The Lord poses as a servant and, with the aid of his servants, induces Sly to suppose himself a lord. The Lord's page poses as Sly's wife. The Petruchio–Kate action is concerned mainly with assumptions about personality, partly with assumptions about identity. Is Kate's shrewishness a pose? At any rate, Petruchio poses as a male shrew and induces Kate to accept his "supposition" that she is not a shrew but a modest and civil young woman. Together Kate and Petruchio pretend to suppose that Vincentio is a young woman. And the Lucentio–Bianca action is concerned mainly with assumptions about identity, partly with assumptions about personality. Lucentio poses as a schoolmaster, Hortensio as a music-master. Tranio poses as Lucentio, induces the Pedant to pose as Vincentio, and pretends to suppose that Vincentio is not himself – in fact, that he is a poseur. Gremio the pantaloon supposes himself a lover. Bianca and the Widow pose as models of female behavior, and Lucentio and Hortensio mistakenly suppose that their wives are obedient.

The foregoing discussion emphasizes the architectonic skill with which the component parts of *The Taming of the Shrew* were combined to make an aesthetically effective whole. That Shakespeare was the sole author of the play is now generally granted, but whether it was he who originally conceived its threefold structure is a question still open to debate. According to a view held by some scholars, Shakespeare may have used as a source a lost play consisting of the main outlines of his three inter-connected actions. One may feel skeptical about this theory of a "lost original," in part because there is no his-torical evidence for the existence of such a play (as there is in the case of *Hamlet*), in part because the theory is only a postulate to account for the relations between Shake-speare's play and the extant *The Taming of a Shrew*, an anonymous text printed in 1594. At present the probabil-ity seems to be that *A Shrew* is neither Shakespeare's source nor a version of some lost original play, but an imitation of *The Taming of the Shrew* itself (cf. Appendix). It is doubtful whether by 1594 any English dramatist other than Shakespeare was sufficiently skilled in plot-construc-tion to write such a carefully and subtly integrated triple-action play as we should have to suppose a lost original to be if *A Shrew* were derived from it in the manner envi-saged by modern textual theory.

Structural integrity and thematic unity are important aspects of the artistic excellence of *The Taming of the Shrew*. But since these qualities often go unnoticed, neither can be counted as the chief reason for the play's enduring popularity. It is a curious fact that the play rates higher with directors, actors, and spectators than it does with critics, teachers, and readers. One reason for this may be that *The Shrew* is much funnier in performance than it is on the printed page. The fun derives from many sources – for example, Sly's wary acceptance of his preposterous situation, the delicate comedy of the under-cover wooing of Bianca, Biondello's grotesque catalogue of equine ailments, the farcical business of the burnt meat, Kate's bewilderment at Petruchio's zany behavior, the efforts of the Tailor to control himself, the comic irony of the confrontation of Vincentio with the Pedant. But per-haps the chief reason for the appeal of the play is the vivid characterization of Sly, Petruchio, and Kate – the most memorable of Shakespeare's creations before Juliet, Mer-cutio, and the Nurse. These parts, when animated by good actors, can charm an audience utterly. They have this power not only because of Shakespeare's comic genius but also because of the truth to human nature which he has woven into his language. To a degree, each of us who en-gages in the War between the Sexes must cope with the sort of problem faced by Petruchio or Kate. Like other of Shakespeare's plays, *The Taming of the Shrew* deals with an archetypal situation.

University of Arizona   RICHARD HOSLEY

NOTE ON THE TEXT

This edition follows the text of the Shakespeare folio of 1623, thought to have been printed from a Shakespearean manuscript. Significant emendations are listed in the Appendix. The folio text is not divided into scenes, and its act division is unsatisfactory. In F, Induction i is labeled I, i, Acts I and II are not indicated, and Acts III, IV, and V begin, respectively, at III, i, IV, iii, and V, ii of the act–scene division of the later editors supplied marginally in the present edition.

THE TAMING OF THE SHREW

*

[INDUCTION]

Ind., i   *Enter Beggar (Christophero Sly) and Hostess.*

1 SLY I'll feeze you, in faith.

2 HOSTESS A pair of stocks, you rogue!

   SLY Y'are a baggage, the Slys are no rogues. Look in the
4 chronicles : we came in with Richard Conqueror. There-
5 fore pocas palabras, let the world slide. Sessa!

   HOSTESS You will not pay for the glasses you have burst?

7 SLY No, not a denier. Go by, St Jeronimy, go to thy cold
   bed and warm thee.

9 HOSTESS I know my remedy : I must go fetch the thirdborough.   [*Exit.*]

   SLY Third or fourth or fifth borough, I'll answer him by
   law. I'll not budge an inch, boy : let him come, and
13 kindly.
       Falls asleep.
       Wind horns. Enter a Lord from hunting, with his Train.

   LORD
14 Huntsman, I charge thee, tender well my hounds.
15 Breathe Merriman, the poor cur is embossed,
16 And couple Clowder with the deep-mouthed brach.
   Saw'st thou not, boy, how Silver made it good
18 At the hedge-corner in the coldest fault?
   I would not lose the dog for twenty pound.

   1. HUNTSMAN
   Why Bellman is as good as he, my lord.
21 He cried upon it at the merest loss
   And twice to-day picked out the dullest scent.
   Trust me, I take him for the better dog.

   LORD
   Thou art a fool. If Echo were as fleet,
   I would esteem him worth a dozen such.

But sup them well and look unto them all.
To-morrow I intend to hunt again.

1. HUNTSMAN
I will, my lord.

LORD
What's here? One dead or drunk? See, doth he breathe?

2. HUNTSMAN
He breathes, my lord. Were he not warmed with ale
This were a bed but cold to sleep so soundly.

LORD
O monstrous beast, how like a swine he lies!
Grim death, how foul and loathsome is thine image!
Sirs, I will practice on this drunken man.   34
What think you, if he were conveyed to bed,
Wrapped in sweet clothes, rings put upon his fingers,   36
A most delicious banquet by his bed,
And brave attendants near him when he wakes,   38
Would not the beggar then forget himself?

1. HUNTSMAN
Believe me, lord, I think he cannot choose.

2. HUNTSMAN
It would seem strange unto him when he waked.

Ind., i Before a country alehouse   1 *feeze you* settle your hash   2 *A pair of stocks* (she threatens him with punishment)   4 *Richard* (Sly's mistake for William)   5 *pocas palabras* few words (Spanish) ; *Sessa* (interjection of doubtful meaning, perhaps from Spanish '*cesa*', shut up)   7 *denier* copper coin of small value ; *Go by, St Jeronimy* (Sly's version of a stock phrase expressing impatience, from Kyd's *Spanish Tragedy*)   9 *thirdborough* constable (*third*, which Sly mistakes for the number, derives from the old word 'frith,' peace)   13 s.d. *Wind* sound   14 *tender* care for   15 *Breathe* rest ; *embossed* foaming at the mouth   16 *brach* bitch-hound   18 *fault* loss of scent   21 *cried* gave tongue ; *at the merest loss* when the scent was totally lost   34 *practice* play a trick   36 *sweet* perfumed   38 *brave* finely dressed

LORD

Even as a flatt'ring dream or worthless fancy.

Then take him up and manage well the jest.

Carry him gently to my fairest chamber

And hang it round with all my wanton pictures.

46   Balm his foul head in warm distillèd waters

And burn sweet wood to make the lodging sweet.

Procure me music ready when he wakes

To make a dulcet and a heavenly sound.

50   And if he chance to speak be ready straight,

And with a low submissive reverence

Say, 'What is it your honor will command?'

Let one attend him with a silver basin

Full of rose-water and bestrewed with flowers,

55   Another bear the ewer, the third a diaper,

And say, 'Will't please your lordship cool your hands?'

Some one be ready with a costly suit

And ask him what apparel he will wear,

Another tell him of his hounds and horse

And that his lady mourns at his disease.

Persuade him that he hath been lunatic,

62   And when he says he is, say that he dreams,

For he is nothing but a mighty lord.

64   This do, and do it kindly, gentle sirs.

65   It will be pastime passing excellent,

66   If it be husbanded with modesty.

1. HUNTSMAN

My lord, I warrant you we will play our part,

68   As he shall think, by our true diligence,

He is no less than what we say he is.

LORD

Take him up gently, and to bed with him,

And each one to his office when he wakes.

           [Sly is carried out.] Sound trumpets.

72   Sirrah, go see what trumpet 'tis that sounds.

                 [Exit Servingman.]

73   Belike some noble gentleman that means,

Travelling some journey, to repose him here.

         Enter Servingman.

How now, who is it?

SERVINGMAN

76   An't please your honor, players

That offer service to your lordship.

         Enter Players.

LORD

Bid them come near. – Now, fellows, you are welcome.

PLAYERS

We thank your honor.

LORD

Do you intend to stay with me to-night?

A PLAYER

81   So please your lordship to accept our duty.

LORD

With all my heart. This fellow I remember

Since once he played a farmer's eldest son.

'Twas where you wooed the gentlewoman so well.

I have forgot your name, but sure that part

Was aptly fitted and naturally performed.

A PLAYER

I think 'twas Soto that your honor means.

LORD

'Tis very true, thou didst it excellent.

Well, you are come to me in happy time,   89

The rather for I have some sport in hand

Wherein your cunning can assist me much.   91

There is a lord will hear you play to-night –

But I am doubtful of your modesties,   93

Lest, over-eyeing of his odd behavior –   94

For yet his honor never heard a play –

You break into some merry passion   96

And so offend him; for I tell you, sirs,

If you should smile he grows impatient.

A PLAYER

Fear not, my lord, we can contain ourselves

Were he the veriest antic in the world.   100

LORD

Go, sirrah, take them to the buttery   101

And give them friendly welcome every one.

Let them want nothing that my house affords.

         Exit one with the Players.

Sirrah, go you to Barthol'mew my page

And see him dressed in all suits like a lady.   105

That done, conduct him to the drunkard's chamber

And call him madam; do him obeisance.

Tell him from me – as he will win my love –

He bear himself with honorable action

Such as he hath observed in noble ladies

Unto their lords, by them accomplishèd:

Such duty to the drunkard let him do

With soft low tongue and lowly courtesy,

And say, 'What is't your honor will command

Wherein your lady and your humble wife

May show her duty and make known her love?'

And then with kind embracements, tempting kisses,

And with declining head into his bosom,

Bid him shed tears, as being overjoyed

To see her noble lord restored to health

Who for this seven years hath esteemèd him   121

No better than a poor and loathsome beggar.

And if the boy have not a woman's gift

To rain a shower of commanded tears,

An onion will do well for such a shift,   125

Which in a napkin being close conveyed   126

Shall in despite enforce a watery eye.

See this dispatched with all the haste thou canst:

Anon I'll give thee more instructions.   129

         Exit a Servingman.

I know the boy will well usurp the grace,   130

Voice, gait, and action of a gentlewoman.

I long to hear him call the drunkard husband,

And how my men will stay themselves from laughter

When they do homage to this simple peasant.

I'll in to counsel them: haply my presence

May well abate their over-merry spleen   136

Which otherwise would grow into extremes.

         [Exeunt.]

---

46 *Balm* anoint   50 *straight* immediately   55 *diaper* linen towel   62 *is* i.e. lunatic   64 *kindly* naturally   65 *passing* surpassingly   66 *husbanded* managed; *modesty* moderation   68 *As* so that   72 *Sirrah* (usual form of address to an inferior)   73 *Belike* probably   76 *An* if   81 *duty* expression of respect   89 *happy* opportune   91 *cunning* skill   93 *modesties* discretion   94 *over-eyeing* of witnessing   96 *merry passion* fit of laughter   100 *antic* buffoon   101 *buttery* room where liquor is kept   105 *suits* points   121 *this seven years* (proverbial for an indefinitely long period); *him* himself   125 *shift* purpose   126 *napkin* handkerchief; *close* secretly   129 *Anon* right away   130 *usurp* assume   136 *spleen* mood

nd., ii *Enter aloft the Drunkard [Sly] with Attendants,*
some with apparel, basin and ewer, and other
appurtenances; and Lord [as a Servant].

1 SLY For God's sake! a pot of small ale.

   1. SERVINGMAN
2 Will't please your lordship drink a cup of sack?

   2. SERVINGMAN
3 Will't please your honor taste of these conserves?

   3. SERVINGMAN
   What raiment will your honor wear to-day?

   SLY I am Christophero Sly, call not me honor nor lordship. I ne'er drank sack in my life, and if you give me any
7 conserves, give me conserves of beef. Ne'er ask me what
8 raiment I'll wear, for I have no more doublets than
   backs, no more stockings than legs, nor no more shoes
   than feet; nay, sometime more feet than shoes, or such
   shoes as my toes look through the overleather.

   LORD
12 Heaven cease this idle humor in your honor!
   O that a mighty man of such descent,
   Of such possessions and so high esteem,
   Should be infusèd with so foul a spirit!

   SLY What, would you make me mad? Am not I Chris-
17 topher Sly, old Sly's son of Burton-heath, by birth
18 a pedlar, by education a cardmaker, by transmutation a
19 bearherd, and now by present profession a tinker? Ask
20 Marian Hacket, the fat ale-wife of Wincot, if she know
21 me not. If she say I am not fourteen pence on the score
22 for sheer ale, score me up for the lyingest knave in
23 Christendom. What, I am not bestraught: here's –

   3. SERVINGMAN
   O this it is that makes your lady mourn.

   2. SERVINGMAN
   O this it is that makes your servants droop.

   LORD
   Hence comes it that your kindred shuns your house,
   As beaten hence by your strange lunacy.
   O noble lord, bethink thee of thy birth,
29 Call home thy ancient thoughts from banishment
   And banish hence these abject lowly dreams.
   Look how thy servants do attend on thee,
   Each in his office ready at thy beck.
33 Wilt thou have music? Hark, Apollo plays,
      Music.
   And twenty cagèd nightingales do sing.
   Or wilt thou sleep? We'll have thee to a couch
   Softer and sweeter than the lustful bed
37 On purpose trimmed up for Semiramis.
38 Say thou wilt walk; we will bestrew the ground.
39 Or wilt thou ride? Thy horses shall be trapped,
   Their harness studded all with gold and pearl.
   Dost thou love hawking? Thou hast hawks will soar
   Above the morning lark. Or wilt thou hunt?
43 Thy hounds shall make the welkin answer them
   And fetch shrill echoes from the hollow earth.

   1. SERVINGMAN
45 Say thou wilt course, thy greyhounds are as swift
46 As breathèd stags, ay, fleeter than the roe.

   2. SERVINGMAN
   Dost thou love pictures? We will fetch thee straight
48 Adonis painted by a running brook
49 And Cytherea all in sedges hid,
50 Which seem to move and wanton with her breath
   Even as the waving sedges play with wind.

   LORD
   We'll show thee Io as she was a maid   52
   And how she was beguilèd and surprised,
   As lively painted as the deed was done.   54

   3. SERVINGMAN
   Or Daphne roaming through a thorny wood,   55
   Scratching her legs that one shall swear she bleeds,
   And at that sight shall sad Apollo weep,
   So workmanly the blood and tears are drawn.

   LORD
   Thou art a lord and nothing but a lord.
   Thou hast a lady far more beautiful
   Than any woman in this waning age.   61

   1. SERVINGMAN
   And till the tears that she hath shed for thee
   Like envious floods o'er-run her lovely face   63
   She was the fairest creature in the world,
   And yet she is inferior to none.   65

   SLY
   Am I a lord, and have I such a lady?
   Or do I dream? Or have I dreamed till now?
   I do not sleep: I see, I hear, I speak,
   I smell sweet savors and I feel soft things.
   Upon my life, I am a lord indeed,
   And not a tinker nor Christophero Sly.
   Well, bring our lady hither to our sight,
   And once again, a pot o' th' smallest ale.   73

   2. SERVINGMAN
   Will't please your mightiness to wash your hands?
   O how we joy to see your wit restored!   75
   O that once more you knew but what you are!
   These fifteen years you have been in a dream,
   Or when you waked, so waked as if you slept.

   SLY
   These fifteen years? By my fay, a goodly nap.   79
   But did I never speak of all that time?

   1. SERVINGMAN
   O yes, my lord, but very idle words,
   For though you lay here in this goodly chamber,
   Yet would you say ye were beaten out of door
   And rail upon the hostess of the house,   84
   And say you would present her at the leet   85
   Because she brought stone jugs and no sealed quarts.   86

Ind., ii The Lord's manor house s.d. *aloft* i.e. in the tiring-house gallery
over the stage (Capell, 1768, supplied a stage direction calling for a bed
and other stage properties, but l. 35 makes clear that a bed was not used
in the original staging) 1 *small* weak (hence cheap) 2 *sack* sherry (a
gentleman's drink) 3 *conserves* candied fruit 7 *conserves of beef* salt beef
8 *doublets* coats 12 *humor* obsession 17 *Burton-heath* Barton-on-the-
Heath (a village some fifteen miles south of Stratford) 18 *cardmaker*
(a card was a comb used in preparing wool for spinning) 19 *bearherd*
keeper of a tame bear; *tinker* itinerant pot-mender (proverbially a hard
drinker) 20 *Wincot* a hamlet some four miles southwest of Stratford
(Hackets were living in the parish in 1591) 21 *on the score* chalked up as
owing 22 *sheer* unmixed; *score me up for* write me down as 23 *bestraught*
distraught, mad 29 *ancient* former 33 *Apollo* god of music 37 *Semiramis* legendary lustful queen of Assyria 38 *bestrew* spread carpets on
39 *trapped* adorned 43 *welkin* sky 45 *course* hunt the hare with greyhounds 46 *breathèd* in good wind; *roe* a kind of small deer 48 *Adonis*
(loved by Venus and killed by a wild boar while hunting; cf. Shakespeare's
Venus and Adonis) 49 *Cytherea* Venus (associated with the island of
Cythera); *sedges* water-rushes 50 *wanton* sway seductively 52 *Io* (loved
by Jupiter in the shape of a cloud and changed by him into a heifer to deceive
the jealous Juno) 54 *lively* realistically 55 *Daphne* (wooed by Apollo and
changed into a laurel tree to escape his pursuit) 61 *waning* degenerate
63 *envious* hateful 65 *yet* even now 73 *smallest* weakest 75 *wit* reason
79 *fay* faith 84 *house* inn 85 *present* accuse; *leet* manorial court 86
sealed bearing an official seal indicating capacity

Sometimes you would call out for Cicely Hacket.

SLY

Ay, the woman's maid of the house.

3 . SERVINGMAN

Why, sir, you know no house nor no such maid,
Nor no such men as you have reckoned up,
91 As Stephen Sly, and old John Naps of Greet,
And Peter Turph, and Henry Pimpernell,
And twenty more such names and men as these,
Which never were nor no man ever saw.

SLY

95 Now Lord be thankèd for my good amends!

ALL Amen.

      Enter [the Page as a] Lady, with Attendants.

SLY I thank thee, thou shalt not lose by it.

PAGE How fares my noble lord?

99 SLY Marry, I fare well, for here is cheer enough.
Where is my wife?

PAGE

Here, noble lord, what is thy will with her?

SLY

Are you my wife and will not call me husband?
103 My men should call me lord; I am your goodman.

PAGE

My husband and my lord, my lord and husband,
I am your wife in all obedience.

SLY I know it well. What must I call her?

LORD Madam.

SLY Al'ce madam or Joan madam?

LORD

Madam and nothing else, so lords call ladies.

SLY

Madam wife, they say that I have dreamed
And slept above some fifteen year or more.

PAGE

Ay, and the time seems thirty unto me,
113 Being all this time abandoned from your bed.

SLY

'Tis much. Servants, leave me and her alone.

      [Exeunt Servants.]

Madam, undress you and come now to bed.

PAGE

Thrice noble lord, let me entreat of you
To pardon me yet for a night or two,
Or if not so, until the sun be set.
For your physicians have expressly charged,
In peril to incur your former malady,
That I should yet absent me from your bed.
I hope this reason stands for my excuse.

123 SLY Ay, it stands so that I may hardly tarry so long – but

I would be loath to fall into my dreams again. I will
therefore tarry in despite of the flesh and the blood.

      Enter a Messenger.

MESSENGER

Your honor's players, hearing your amendment,
Are come to play a pleasant comedy,
For so your doctors hold it very meet,
Seeing too much sadness hath congealed your blood
And melancholy is the nurse of frenzy.   130
Therefore they thought it good you hear a play
And frame your mind to mirth and merriment,
Which bars a thousand harms and lengthens life.

SLY Marry, I will, let them play it. Is not a commonty a   134
Christmas gambol or a tumbling-trick?

PAGE

No, my good lord, it is more pleasing stuff.

SLY What, household stuff?

PAGE It is a kind of history.   138

SLY Well, we'll see't. Come, madam, wife, sit by my side
and let the world slip: we shall ne'er be younger.

      [They sit over the stage.]

      Flourish. Enter [below] Lucentio and his man Tranio.   I, i

LUCENTIO

Tranio, since for the great desire I had
To see fair Padua, nursery of arts,   2
I am arrived in fruitful Lombardy,   3
The pleasant garden of great Italy,
And by my father's love and leave am armed
With his good will and thy good company,
My trusty servant, well approved in all,   7
Here let us breathe and haply institute
A course of learning and ingenious studies.   9
Pisa, renownèd for grave citizens,
Gave me my being and my father first,   11
A merchant of great traffic through the world,
Vincentio, come of the Bentivolii.
Vincentio's son, brought up in Florence,
It shall become to serve all hopes conceived,   15
To deck his fortune with his virtuous deeds.
And therefore, Tranio, for the time I study
Virtue, and that part of philosophy
Will I apply that treats of happiness   19
By virtue specially to be achieved.
Tell me thy mind, for I have Pisa left
And am to Padua come, as he that leaves
A shallow plash to plunge him in the deep   23
And with satiety seeks to quench his thirst.

TRANIO

Mi perdonato, gentle master mine.   25
I am in all affected as yourself,   26
Glad that you thus continue your resolve
To suck the sweets of sweet philosophy.
Only, good master, while we do admire
This virtue and this moral discipline,
Let's be no stoics nor no stocks, I pray,   31
Or so devote to Aristotle's checks   32
As Ovid be an outcast quite abjured.   33
Balk logic with acquaintance that you have   34
And practice rhetoric in your common talk.
Music and poesy use to quicken you.   36
The mathematics and the metaphysics,
Fall to them as you find your stomach serves you.   38
No profit grows where is no pleasure ta'en.
In brief, sir, study what you most affect.   40

---

91 *Stephen Sly* (name of a Stratford citizen of Shakespeare's day); *Greet* a hamlet near Winchcombe, about twenty miles southwest of Stratford   95 *amends* recovery   99 *Marry* indeed (originally an oath by the Virgin Mary); *cheer* entertainment   103 *goodman* husband (a term that might be used by the wife of a yeoman or husbandman)   113 *abandoned* banished   123 *it stands so* the case is (with bawdy quibble)   130 *frenzy* madness   134 *commonty* (Sly's mistake for 'comedy')   138 *history* story
I, i A street in Padua   s.d. *man* servant; *Tranio* (name from the *Mostellaria* of Plautus connoting 'clarifier, revealer')   2 *Padua* (famous for its university)   3 *Lombardy* northern Italy   7 *approved* i.e. proved dependable   9 *ingenious* intellectual   11 *first* i.e. before me   15 *serve* fulfill   19 *apply* pursue   23 *plash* pool   25 *Mi perdonato* pardon me   26 *affected* inclined   31 *stocks* posts (i.e. incapable of feeling, punning on *stoics*)   32 *checks* restraints   33 *Ovid* the Roman love poet (cf. III, i, 28–29; IV, ii, 8); *abjured* sworn off   34 *Balk logic* bandy arguments   36 *quicken* enliven   38 *stomach* appetite   40 *affect* like

LUCENTIO

41 Gramercies, Tranio, well dost thou advise.

42 If Biondello now were come ashore,
We could at once put us in readiness
And take a lodging fit to entertain
Such friends as time in Padua shall beget.
But stay awhile, what company is this?

TRANIO

47 Master, some show to welcome us to town.

Enter Baptista with his two daughters
Kate and Bianca, Gremio a pantaloon,
[and] Hortensio suitor to Bianca.
Lucentio [and] Tranio stand by.

BAPTISTA

Gentlemen, importune me no further,
For how I firmly am resolved you know.
That is, not to bestow my youngest daughter
Before I have a husband for the elder.
If either of you both love Katherina,
Because I know you well and love you well,
Leave shall you have to court her at your pleasure.

GREMIO

55 To cart her rather, she's too rough for me.
There, there, Hortensio, will you any wife?

KATE

I pray you, sir, is it your will

58 To make a stale of me amongst these mates?

HORTENSIO

'Mates,' maid, how mean you that? No mates for you

60 Unless you were of gentler, milder mold.

KATE

I' faith, sir, you shall never need to fear:

62 Iwis it is not half way to her heart.
But if it were, doubt not her care should be
To comb your noddle with a three-legged stool

65 And paint your face and use you like a fool.

HORTENSIO

From all such devils, good Lord deliver us.

GREMIO

And me too, good Lord.

TRANIO *[aside]*

68 Hush, master, here's some good pastime toward.

69 That wench is stark mad or wonderful froward.

LUCENTIO

But in the other's silence do I see
Maid's mild behavior and sobriety.
Peace, Tranio!

TRANIO

Well said, master; mum, and gaze your fill.

BAPTISTA

Gentlemen, that I may soon make good
What I have said – Bianca, get you in,
And let it not displease thee, good Bianca,
For I will love thee ne'er the less, my girl.

KATE

78 A pretty peat! it is best

79 Put finger in the eye, an she knew why.

BIANCA

Sister, content you in my discontent.
Sir, to your pleasure humbly I subscribe.
My books and instruments shall be my company,
On them to look and practice by myself.

LUCENTIO *[aside]*

84 Hark, Tranio, thou mayst hear Minerva speak.

HORTENSIO

Signior Baptista, will you be so strange?   85
Sorry am I that our good will effects
Bianca's grief.

GREMIO   Why, will you mew her up,   87
Signior Baptista, for this fiend of hell
And make her bear the penance of her tongue?

BAPTISTA

Gentlemen, content ye, I am resolved.
Go in, Bianca.   *[Exit Bianca.]*
And for I know she taketh most delight   92
In music, instruments, and poetry,
Schoolmasters will I keep within my house,
Fit to instruct her youth. If you, Hortensio,
Or Signior Gremio, you, know any such,
Prefer them hither, for to cunning men   97
I will be very kind, and liberal
To mine own children in good bringing-up.
And so, farewell. Katherina, you may stay,
For I have more to commune with Bianca.   *Exit.* 101

KATE Why, and I trust I may go too, may I not? What,
shall I be appointed hours, as though, belike, I knew not 103
what to take and what to leave? Ha!   *Exit.*

GREMIO You may go to the devil's dam. Your gifts are so 105
good, here's none will hold you. Their love is not so 106
great, Hortensio, but we may blow our nails together 107
and fast it fairly out. Our cake 's dough on both sides. 108
Farewell – yet for the love I bear my sweet Bianca, if I
can by any means light on a fit man to teach her that
wherein she delights, I will wish him to her father. 111

HORTENSIO So will I, Signior Gremio. But a word, I
pray. Though the nature of our quarrel yet never
brooked parle, know now, upon advice, it toucheth us 114
both – that we may yet again have access to our fair
mistress and be happy rivals in Bianca's love – to labor
and effect one thing specially.

GREMIO What's that, I pray?

HORTENSIO Marry, sir, to get a husband for her sister.

GREMIO A husband? A devil.

HORTENSIO I say, a husband.

GREMIO I say, a devil. Think'st thou, Hortensio, though
her father be very rich, any man is so very a fool to be 123
married to hell?

HORTENSIO Tush, Gremio, though it pass your patience
and mine to endure her loud alarums, why, man, there 126
be good fellows in the world, an a man could light on 127
them, would take her with all her faults, and money
enough.

GREMIO I cannot tell, but I had as lief take her dowry

<hr>

41 *Gramercies* many thanks   42 *come ashore* (Padua, like Mantua and Bergamo later, is conceived of conventionally as a seaport)   47 s.d. *pantaloon* foolish old man (stock character of the '*commedia dell'arte*')   55 *cart her* i.e. have her driven through the streets in a cart, like a prostitute undergoing punishment   58 *stale* laughing-stock (playing on 'strumpet,' suggested by *cart*); *mates* low fellows (Hortensio quibbles on 'husbands')   60 *mold* character   62 *Iwis* indeed; *it* i.e. marriage; *her* i.e. Kate's   65 *paint* i.e. by drawing blood   68 *toward* in prospect   69 *froward* refractory   78 *peat* spoiled darling   79 *Put finger in the eye* i.e. weep; *an if*   84 *Minerva* goddess of wisdom and of the arts   85 *strange* unnatural   87 *mew* coop (term for caging a falcon)   92 *for* since   97 *Prefer* recommend; *cunning* well-trained   101 *commune* discuss   103 *belike* presumably   105 *dam* mother   106 *hold* endure; *Their* i.e. of women   107 *blow . . . together* i.e. be patient   108 *Our cake's dough* i.e. our expectations are disappointed (proverbial)   111 *wish* recommend   114 *brooked parle* permitted discussion; *advice* reflection   123 *so very a* such a complete   126 *alarums* calls to arms   127 *an if*

130 with this condition, to be whipped at the high-cross
every morning.

HORTENSIO Faith, as you say, there's small choice in
133 rotten apples. But come, since this bar in law makes us
friends, it shall be so far forth friendly maintained, till
by helping Baptista's eldest daughter to a husband we
136 set his youngest free for a husband, and then have
137 to't afresh. Sweet Bianca! Happy man be his dole. He
138 that runs fastest gets the ring. How say you, Signior
Gremio?

GREMIO I am agreed, and would I had given him the best
horse in Padua to begin his wooing that would thor-
oughly woo her, wed her, and bed her, and rid the house
142 of her. Come on.
Exeunt ambo. Manent Tranio and Lucentio.
TRANIO
I pray, sir, tell me, is it possible
That love should of a sudden take such hold?
LUCENTIO
O Tranio, till I found it to be true
I never thought it possible or likely.
But see, while idly I stood looking on,
148 I found the effect of love-in-idleness
And now in plainness do confess to thee,
That art to me as secret and as dear
151 As Anna to the Queen of Carthage was,
Tranio, I burn, I pine, I perish, Tranio,
153 If I achieve not this young modest girl.
Counsel me, Tranio, for I know thou canst.
Assist me, Tranio, for I know thou wilt.
TRANIO
Master, it is no time to chide you now.
157 Affection is not rated from the heart.
If love have touched you, nought remains but so,
159 'Redime te captum, quam queas minimo.'
LUCENTIO
Gramercies, lad. Go forward, this contents;
The rest will comfort, for thy counsel's sound.
TRANIO
162 Master, you looked so longly on the maid,
Perhaps you marked not what's the pith of all.
LUCENTIO
O yes, I saw sweet beauty in her face,
165 Such as the daughter of Agenor had,
That made great Jove to humble him to her hand
When with his knees he kissed the Cretan strand.
TRANIO
Saw you no more? Marked you not how her sister
Began to scold and raise up such a storm

That mortal ears might hardly endure the din?
LUCENTIO
Tranio, I saw her coral lips to move,   171
And with her breath she did perfume the air.   172
Sacred and sweet was all I saw in her.
TRANIO
Nay, then, 'tis time to stir him from his trance.
I pray, awake, sir. If you love the maid
Bend thoughts and wits to achieve her. Thus it stands:
Her elder sister is so curst and shrewd   177
That till the father rid his hands of her,
Master, your love must live a maid at home,
And therefore has he closely mewed her up,   180
Because she will not be annoyed with suitors.   181
LUCENTIO
Ah, Tranio, what a cruel father's he.
But art thou not advised he took some care   183
To get her cunning schoolmasters to instruct her?
TRANIO
Ay, marry, am I, sir, and now 'tis plotted.   185
LUCENTIO
I have it, Tranio.
TRANIO   Master, for my hand,   186
Both our inventions meet and jump in one.   187
LUCENTIO
Tell me thine first.
TRANIO   You will be schoolmaster
And undertake the teaching of the maid.
That's your device.
LUCENTIO   It is. May it be done?
TRANIO
Not possible, for who shall bear your part
And be in Padua here Vincentio's son,
Keep house and ply his book, welcome his friends,
Visit his countrymen and banquet them?
LUCENTIO
Basta, content thee, for I have it full.   195
We have not yet been seen in any house
Nor can we be distinguished by our faces
For man or master. Then it follows thus.
Thou shalt be master, Tranio, in my stead,
Keep house and port and servants as I should.   200
I will some other be, some Florentine,
Some Neapolitan or meaner man of Pisa.   202
'Tis hatched and shall be so. Tranio, at once
Uncase thee, take my colored hat and cloak.   204
When Biondello comes he waits on thee,
But I will charm him first to keep his tongue.
TRANIO
So had you need.
[They exchange cloaks and hats.]
In brief, sir, sith it your pleasure is   208
And I am tied to be obedient –
For so your father charged me at our parting,
'Be serviceable to my son,' quoth he,
Although I think 'twas in another sense –
I am content to be Lucentio
Because so well I love Lucentio.
LUCENTIO
Tranio, be so, because Lucentio loves,
And let me be a slave, t'achieve that maid
Whose sudden sight hath thralled my wounded eye.   217
Enter Biondello.
Here comes the rogue. – Sirrah, where have you been?   218

130 *high-cross* market-cross   133 *bar* obstacle   136–37 *have to't* let us set to
it   137 *Happy . . . dole* happiness be his lot (i.e. his who wins her; proverbial)   138 *ring* prize (playing on 'wedding-ring')   142 s.d. *ambo* both
(Gremio and Hortensio)   148 *love-in-idleness* the pansy (supposed to have
magical power in love)   151 *Anna* Dido's sister and confidante   153
achieve win   157 *rated* driven out by scolding   159 *Redime . . . minimo*
redeem yourself from captivity as cheaply as you can (from the *Eunuchus* of
Terence but quoted from Lily's *Latin Grammar*)   162 *longly* longingly
165 *daughter of Agenor* Europa (loved by Jupiter, who in the shape of a bull
abducted her)   171, 172 *coral, perfume* (hackneyed comparisons of the Petrarchan sonnet tradition; cf. Shakespeare's Sonnet 130)   177 *curst* bad-
tempered; *shrewd* shrewish   180 *mewed* cooped   181 *Because* so that   183
advised aware   185 *'tis plotted* I have a plan   186 *for* I'll wager   187 *inventions* plans; *jump* agree   195 *Basta* enough; *have it full* see it clearly   200
port style of living   202 *meaner* i.e. of lower than my true rank   204 *Uncase*
unclook   208 *sith* since   217 *thralled* enslaved   218 *Sirrah* (usual form of
address to an inferior)

BIONDELLO
Where have I been? Nay, how now, where are you?
Master, has my fellow Tranio stol'n your clothes,
Or you stol'n his, or both? Pray, what's the news?

LUCENTIO
Sirrah, come hither. 'Tis no time to jest,
And therefore frame your manners to the time.
Your fellow Tranio, here, to save my life,
225 Puts my apparel and my count'nance on,
And I for my escape have put on his,
For in a quarrel since I came ashore
I killed a man and fear I was descried.
Wait you on him, I charge you, as becomes,
While I make way from hence to save my life.
You understand me?

BIONDELLO   I, sir? Ne'er a whit.

LUCENTIO
And not a jot of Tranio in your mouth.
Tranio is changed into Lucentio.

BIONDELLO
The better for him, would I were so too.

TRANIO
So could I, faith, boy, to have the next wish after,
That Lucentio indeed had Baptista's youngest daughter.
But, sirrah, not for my sake but your master's, I advise
You use your manners discreetly in all kind of companies.
When I am alone, why then I am Tranio,
But in all places else, your master Lucentio.

LUCENTIO
Tranio, let's go.
242 One thing more rests, that thyself execute –
To make one among these wooers. If thou ask me why,
244 Sufficeth my reasons are both good and weighty.
                              Exeunt.

The Presenters above speak.

245 1. SERVINGMAN My lord, you nod, you do not mind the
play.

SLY Yes, by Saint Anne, do I. A good matter, surely.
Comes there any more of it?

PAGE My lord, 'tis but begun.

SLY 'Tis a very excellent piece of work, madam lady –
251 would 'twere done.
        They sit and mark.

I, ii   *Enter [below] Petruchio and his man Grumio.*

PETRUCHIO
Verona, for awhile I take my leave
To see my friends in Padua, but of all
My best belovèd and approvèd friend
4 Hortensio; and I trow this is his house.
Here, sirrah Grumio, knock, I say.

GRUMIO Knock, sir? Whom should I knock? Is there
7 any man has rebused your worship?

8 PETRUCHIO Villain, I say, knock me here soundly.

GRUMIO Knock you here, sir? Why, sir, what am I, sir,
that I should knock you here, sir?

11 PETRUCHIO Villain, I say, knock me at this gate,
And rap me well or I'll knock your knave's pate.

GRUMIO
My master is grown quarrelsome. I should knock you first,
And then I know after who comes by the worst.

PETRUCHIO
Will it not be?
16 Faith, sirrah, an you'll not knock, I'll ring it.
17 I'll try how you can sol, fa, and sing it.

He wrings him by the ears.

GRUMIO
Help, masters, help! My master is mad.   18

PETRUCHIO
Now, knock when I bid you, sirrah villain.
        Enter Hortensio.

HORTENSIO How now, what's the matter? My old friend
Grumio, and my good friend Petruchio! How do you all
at Verona?

PETRUCHIO
Signior Hortensio, come you to part the fray?
Con tutto il cuore ben trovato, may I say.   24

HORTENSIO
Alla nostra casa ben venuto,   25
Molto honorato signor mio Petruchio.
Rise, Grumio, rise, we will compound this quarrel.   27

GRUMIO Nay, 'tis no matter, sir, what he 'leges in Latin. 28
If this be not a lawful cause for me to leave his service,
look you, sir; he bid me knock him and rap him soundly,
sir. Well, was it fit for a servant to use his master so,
being perhaps, for aught I see, two and thirty, a pip out? 32
Whom would to God I had well knocked at first,
Then had not Grumio come by the worst.

PETRUCHIO
A senseless villain. Good Hortensio,
I bade the rascal knock upon your gate
And could not get him for my heart to do it.

GRUMIO Knock at the gate? O heavens! Spake you not
these words plain, 'Sirrah, knock me here, rap me here,
knock me well, and knock me soundly'? And come you
now with 'knocking at the gate'?

PETRUCHIO
Sirrah, be gone, or talk not, I advise you.

HORTENSIO
Petruchio, patience, I am Grumio's pledge.
Why, this' a heavy chance 'twixt him and you,   44
Your ancient, trusty, pleasant servant Grumio.
And tell me now, sweet friend, what happy gale
Blows you to Padua here from old Verona?

PETRUCHIO
Such wind as scatters young men through the world
To seek their fortunes farther than at home,
Where small experience grows. But in a few,   50
Signior Hortensio, thus it stands with me.
Antonio my father is deceased,
And I have thrust myself into this maze,
Haply to wive and thrive as best I may.   54
Crowns in my purse I have and goods at home,
And so am come abroad to see the world.

HORTENSIO
Petruchio, shall I then come roundly to thee   57

225 *count'nance* appearance, deportment   242 *rests* remains; *execute* arrange
244 s.d. *Presenters* choral characters of an induction who 'present' the play
proper   245 *mind* pay attention to   251 s.d. *They sit and mark* (shortly
hereafter the presenters drop unnoticed out of the action); *mark* watch
I, ii A street in Padua   s.d. *Petruchio* (diminutive of *'Pietro'*; the 'ch' is
soft, not 'Petrukio'); *Grumio* (name from the *Mostellaria* of Plautus connoting 'clodhopper')   4 *trow* believe   7 *rebused* (Grumio's mistake for
'abused')   8 *me* i.e. for me (but Grumio misunderstands, perhaps deliberately)   11 *gate* door   16 *ring* (playing on 'wring')   17 *sol, fa* (playing
on 'sowl,' pull by the ears, and 'fay,' cleanse, i.e. beat)   18 *masters* i.e. the
audience (comically considered as bystanders)   24 *Con . . . trovato* with all
my heart well met   25–26 *Alla . . . Petruchio* welcome to our house, my
much honored Signior Petruchio   27 *compound* settle   28 *'leges* alleges
32 *two . . . out* drunk (a slang expression derived from the card-game of one
and thirty; a 'pip' is a suit marking)   44 *this'* this is; *heavy chance* sad event
50 *in a few* i.e. words   54 *Haply* by chance   57 *come roundly* speak plainly

58 And wish thee to a shrewd ill-favored wife?
   Thou'ldst thank me but a little for my counsel.
   And yet I'll promise thee she shall be rich,
   And very rich – but th'art too much my friend
   And I'll not wish thee to her.
PETRUCHIO
   Signior Hortensio, 'twixt such friends as we
   Few words suffice. And therefore if thou know
   One rich enough to be Petruchio's wife –
66 As wealth is burden of my wooing dance –
67 Be she as foul as was Florentius' love,
68 As old as Sibyl, and as curst and shrewd
69 As Socrates' Xanthippe, or a worse,
   She moves me not, or not removes, at least,
   Affection's edge in me, were she as rough
   As are the swelling Adriatic seas.
   I come to wive it wealthily in Padua –
   If wealthily, then happily in Padua.
GRUMIO Nay, look you, sir, he tells you flatly what his
   mind is. Why, give him gold enough and marry him to
77 a puppet or an aglet-baby or an old trot with ne'er a
   tooth in her head, though she have as many diseases as
   two and fifty horses. Why, nothing comes amiss, so
80 money comes withal.
HORTENSIO
   Petruchio, since we are stepped thus far in,
82 I will continue that I broached in jest.
   I can, Petruchio, help thee to a wife
   With wealth enough, and young and beauteous,
   Brought up as best becomes a gentlewoman.
   Her only fault – and that is faults enough –
   Is that she is intolerable curst,
88 And shrewd and froward, so beyond all measure,
   That were my state far worser than it is
   I would not wed her for a mine of gold.
PETRUCHIO
   Hortensio, peace. Thou know'st not gold's effect.
   Tell me her father's name, and 'tis enough,
93 For I will board her though she chide as loud
   As thunder when the clouds in autumn crack.
HORTENSIO
   Her father is Baptista Minola,
   An affable and courteous gentleman.
   Her name is Katherina Minola,
   Renowned in Padua for her scolding tongue.
PETRUCHIO
   I know her father though I know not her,
   And he knew my deceasèd father well.
   I will not sleep, Hortensio, till I see her,

   And therefore let me be thus bold with you,
   To give you over at this first encounter   103
   Unless you will accompany me thither.
GRUMIO I pray you, sir, let him go while the humor lasts. 105
   A my word, an she knew him as well as I do, she would 106
   think scolding would do little good upon him. She may
   perhaps call him half a score knaves or so – why, that's
   nothing, an he begin once, he'll rail in his rope-tricks. 109
   I'll tell you what, sir, an she stand him but a little, he will 110
   throw a figure in her face and so disfigure her with it 111
   that she shall have no more eyes to see withal than a
   cat. You know him not, sir.
HORTENSIO
   Tarry, Petruchio, I must go with thee,
   For in Baptista's keep my treasure is.   115
   He hath the jewel of my life in hold,   116
   His youngest daughter, beautiful Bianca,
   And her withholds from me and other more,
   Suitors to her and rivals in my love,
   Supposing it a thing impossible,
   For those defects I have before rehearsed,
   That ever Katherina will be wooed.
   Therefore this order hath Baptista ta'en,   123
   That none shall have access unto Bianca
   Till Katherine the curst have got a husband.
GRUMIO
   Katherine the curst!
   A title for a maid of all titles the worst.
HORTENSIO
   Now shall my friend Petruchio do me grace   128
   And offer me, disguised in sober robes,
   To old Baptista as a schoolmaster
   Well seen in music, to instruct Bianca,   131
   That so I may, by this device, at last
   Have leave and leisure to make love to her
   And unsuspected court her by herself.
     Enter Gremio [with a paper] and Lucentio disguised
     [as a schoolmaster].
GRUMIO Here's no knavery! See, to beguile the old folks,
   how the young folks lay their heads together! Master,
   master, look about you. Who goes there, ha?
HORTENSIO
   Peace, Grumio, it is the rival of my love.
   Petruchio, stand by awhile.
GRUMIO
   A proper stripling, and an amorous!   140
     [They stand aside.]
GREMIO
   O very well, I have perused the note.   141
   Hark you, sir, I'll have them very fairly bound,
   All books of love, see that at any hand,   143
   And see you read no other lectures to her.   144
   You understand me. Over and beside
   Signior Baptista's liberality,
   I'll mend it with a largess. Take your paper too,   147
   And let me have them very well perfumed,   148
   For she is sweeter than perfume itself
   To whom they go. What will you read to her?
LUCENTIO
   Whate'er I read to her, I'll plead for you,
   As for my patron, stand you so assured,
   As firmly as yourself were still in place,   153
   Yea and perhaps with more successful words
   Than you – unless you were a scholar, sir.

58 *shrewd* shrewish   66 *burden* bass or undersong   67 *foul* ugly; *Florentius*
(a knight who married an old hag in return for the answer to a riddle – 'What
do women most desire?' – that would save his life; she then turned into a
beautiful maiden; cf. Gower's *Confessio Amantis*, Bk I, or Chaucer's Wife
of Bath's Tale)   68 *Sibyl* the Cumaean Sibyl (a prophetess to whom Apollo
granted as many years of life as she could hold grains of sand in her hand)
69 *Xanthippe* the philosopher's wife (reputedly a shrew)   77 *aglet-baby* tiny
doll-figure ('aglet' indicating either a spangle or the metal 'point' of a lace);
trot hag   80 *withal* at the same time   82 *that* that which   88 *froward* refractory   93 *board* (as in attacking a ship)   103 *give you over* leave you   105
humor whim   106 *A* on, by   109 *rope-tricks* (Grumio's mistake for
'rhetoric,' i.e. abusive language, with a glance at hanging)   110 *stand* withstand   111 *figure* rhetorical figure (i.e. a telling expression)   115 *keep* most
strongly fortified part of a castle   116 *hold* confinement   123 *order* measure
128 *grace* a favor   131 *seen* versed   140 *proper* handsome (ironically, of
Gremio)   141 *note* (a list of books for Bianca)   143 *at any hand* in any case
144 *read* teach; *lectures* lessons   147 *mend* increase; *largess* gift of money;
paper i.e. the note   148 *them* i.e. the books   153 *in place* present

GREMIO
O this learning, what a thing it is!

GRUMIO [aside]
157   O this woodcock, what an ass it is!

PETRUCHIO
Peace, sirrah.

HORTENSIO
Grumio, mum! [advancing] God save you, Signior
Gremio.

GREMIO
And you are well met, Signior Hortensio.
161   Trow you whither I am going? To Baptista Minola.
I promised to inquire carefully
About a schoolmaster for the fair Bianca,
And by good fortune I have lighted well
On this young man – for learning and behavior
166   Fit for her turn, well read in poetry
And other books, good ones, I warrant ye.

HORTENSIO
'Tis well, and I have met a gentleman
Hath promised me to help me to another,
170   A fine musician to instruct our mistress.
So shall I no whit be behind in duty
To fair Bianca, so beloved of me.

GREMIO
Beloved of me, and that my deeds shall prove.

GRUMIO [aside]
174   And that his bags shall prove.

HORTENSIO
175   Gremio, 'tis now no time to vent our love.
Listen to me, and if you speak me fair
177   I'll tell you news indifferent good for either.
Here is a gentleman whom by chance I met,
179   Upon agreement from us to his liking,
180   Will undertake to woo curst Katherine,
Yea and to marry her if her dowry please.

GREMIO
So said, so done, is well.
Hortensio, have you told him all her faults?

PETRUCHIO
I know she is an irksome brawling scold.
If that be all, masters, I hear no harm.

GREMIO
No, sayst me so, friend? What countryman?

PETRUCHIO
Born in Verona, old Antonio's son.
My father dead, my fortune lives for me,
And I do hope good days and long to see.

GREMIO
O sir, such a life, with such a wife, were strange.
191   But if you have a stomach, to't a God's name,
You shall have me assisting you in all.
But will you woo this wildcat?

193 PETRUCHIO   Will I live?

GRUMIO [aside]
Will he woo her? Ay, or he'll hang her.

PETRUCHIO
Why came I hither but to that intent?
Think you a little din can daunt mine ears?
Have I not in my time heard lions roar?
Have I not heard the sea, puffed up with winds,
Rage like an angry boar chafèd with sweat?
Have I not heard great ordnance in the field
And heaven's artillery thunder in the skies?

Have I not in a pitchèd battle heard
Loud 'larums, neighing steeds, and trumpets' clang?   203
And do you tell me of a woman's tongue,
That gives not half so great a blow to th' ear
As will a chestnut in a farmer's fire?
Tush, tush, fear boys with bugs.   207

GRUMIO [aside]   For he fears none.

GREMIO
Hortensio, hark.   208
This gentleman is happily arrived,
My mind presumes, for his own good and ours.

HORTENSIO
I promised we would be contributors,
And bear his charge of wooing whatsoe'er.   212

GREMIO
And so we will, provided that he win her.

GRUMIO [aside]
I would I were as sure of a good dinner.   214
      Enter Tranio brave [as Lucentio], and Biondello.

TRANIO
Gentlemen, God save you. If I may be bold,
Tell me, I beseech you, which is the readiest way
To the house of Signior Baptista Minola?

BIONDELLO He that has the two fair daughters, is't he
you mean?

TRANIO Even he, Biondello.

GREMIO
Hark you, sir; you mean not her to woo?

TRANIO
Perhaps him and her, sir, what have you to do?   221

PETRUCHIO
Not her that chides, sir, at any hand, I pray.

TRANIO
I love no chiders, sir. – Biondello, let's away.

LUCENTIO [aside]
Well begun, Tranio.

HORTENSIO   Sir, a word ere you go.
Are you a suitor to the maid you talk of, yea or no?

TRANIO
An if I be, sir, is it any offense?

GREMIO
No, if without more words you will get you hence.

TRANIO
Why, sir, I pray, are not the streets as free
For me as for you?

GREMIO   But so is not she.

TRANIO
For what reason, I beseech you?

GREMIO   For this reason, if you'll know,
That she's the choice love of Signior Gremio.

HORTENSIO
That she's the chosen of Signior Hortensio.

TRANIO
Softly, my masters. If you be gentlemen,
Do me this right, hear me with patience.
Baptista is a noble gentleman,

---

157 *woodcock* (bird easily caught, hence proverbially stupid) 161 *Trow* know 166 *turn* need 170 *mistress* beloved 174 *bags* moneybags 175 *vent* utter 177 *indifferent* equally 179 *agreement* terms (they will pay his expenses of wooing, l. 212) 180 *Will undertake* i.e. who, upon agreement, will undertake 191 *stomach* appetite; *a* in 193 *Will I live?* i.e. certainly 203 *'larums* calls to arms 207 *fear* frighten; *bugs* bogeymen 208 *hark* listen 212 *charge* expenses 214 s.d. *brave* finely dressed 221 *what . . . do* what business is it of yours

To whom my father is not all unknown,
And were his daughter fairer than she is
She may more suitors have, and me for one.
239 Fair Leda's daughter had a thousand wooers,
240 Then well one more may fair Bianca have.
And so she shall : Lucentio shall make one,
242 Though Paris came in hope to speed alone.

GREMIO
What, this gentleman will out-talk us all.

LUCENTIO
244 Sir, give him head. I know he'll prove a jade.

PETRUCHIO
Hortensio, to what end are all these words ?

HORTENSIO
Sir, let me be so bold as to ask you,
Did you yet ever see Baptista's daughter ?

TRANIO
No, sir, but I do hear that he hath two,
The one as famous for a scolding tongue
As is the other for beauteous modesty.

PETRUCHIO
Sir, sir, the first's for me, let her go by.

GREMIO
Yea, leave that labor to great Hercules,
253 And let it be more than Alcides' twelve.

PETRUCHIO
254 Sir, understand you this of me, in sooth.
255 The youngest daughter, whom you hearken for,
Her father keeps from all access of suitors
And will not promise her to any man
Until the elder sister first be wed.
The younger then is free, and not before.

TRANIO
If it be so, sir, that you are the man
261 Must stead us all, and me amongst the rest,
And if you break the ice and do this feat,
263 Achieve the elder, set the younger free
264 For our access, whose hap shall be to have her
Will not so graceless be to be ingrate.

HORTENSIO
266 Sir, you say well, and well you do conceive,
And since you do profess to be a suitor,
268 You must, as we do, gratify this gentleman,
To whom we all rest generally beholding.

TRANIO
Sir, I shall not be slack, in sign whereof,
271 Please ye we may convive this afternoon
And quaff carouses to our mistress' health,
273 And do as adversaries do in law,
Strive mightily but eat and drink as friends.

GRUMIO, BIONDELLO
O excellent motion ! Fellows, let's be gone.

HORTENSIO
The motion 's good indeed, and be it so.
Petruchio, I shall be your ben venuto.   *Exeunt.* 277

*

     Enter Kate and Bianca [with her hands tied].   II, i

BIANCA
Good sister, wrong me not, nor wrong yourself,
To make a bondmaid and a slave of me –
That I disdain. But for these other gawds,   3
Unbind my hands, I'll pull them off myself,
Yea, all my raiment, to my petticoat,
Or what you will command me will I do,
So well I know my duty to my elders.

KATE
Of all thy suitors, here I charge thee, tell
Whom thou lov'st best. See thou dissemble not.

BIANCA
Believe me, sister, of all the men alive
I never yet beheld that special face
Which I could fancy more than any other.

KATE
Minion, thou liest. Is't not Hortensio ?   13

BIANCA
If you affect him, sister, here I swear   14
I'll plead for you myself but you shall have him.

KATE
O then, belike, you fancy riches more.   16
You will have Gremio to keep you fair.   17

BIANCA
Is it for him you do envy me so ?   18
Nay, then you jest, and now I well perceive
You have but jested with me all this while.
I prithee, sister Kate, untie my hands.

KATE
If that be jest then all the rest was so.
     Strikes her.
     Enter Baptista.

BAPTISTA
Why, how now, dame, whence grows this insolence ?
Bianca, stand aside. Poor girl, she weeps.
Go ply thy needle, meddle not with her.
For shame, thou hilding of a devilish spirit,   26
Why dost thou wrong her that did ne'er wrong thee ?
When did she cross thee with a bitter word ?

KATE
Her silence flouts me and I'll be revenged.
     Flies after Bianca.

BAPTISTA
What, in my sight ? Bianca, get thee in.   *Exit [Bianca].*

KATE
Will you not suffer me ? Nay, now I see
She is your treasure, she must have a husband ;
I must dance barefoot on her wedding-day,   33
And for your love to her lead apes in hell.   34
Talk not to me, I will go sit and weep
Till I can find occasion of revenge.   *[Exit.]*

BAPTISTA
Was ever gentleman thus grieved as I ?
But who comes here ?   38
     Enter Gremio, [with] Lucentio [as a schoolmaster] in
     the habit of a mean man, Petruchio with [Hortensio
     as a music-master, and] Tranio [as Lucentio] with
     his boy [Biondello] bearing a lute and books.

239 *Leda's daughter* Helen of Troy (Leda was made love to by Jupiter in the shape of a swan)   240 *one more* i.e. than she now has   242 *Paris* Helen's lover (who took her away from her husband Menelaus) ; *came* were to come ; *speed* succeed   244 *jade* worthless horse (easily tired)   253 *Alcides* Hercules (grandson of Alcaeus)   254 *sooth* truth   255 *hearken* lie in wait   261 *stead* help   263 *Achieve* win   264 *whose hap* he whose luck   266 *well you do conceive* you have hit on a good idea   268 *gratify* recompense   271 *convive* feast together   273 *adversaries* i.e. lawyers (not their clients)   277 *ben venuto* welcome

II, i *Baptista's house*   3 *gawds* ornaments   13 *Minion* minx   14 *affect* love   16 *belike* probably   17 *fair* in finery   18 *envy* hate   26 *hilding* good-for-nothing   33 *dance . . . day* (customary for an elder unmarried sister)   34 *lead . . . hell* (proverbial fate of old maids)   38 s.d. *mean* of low social station ; *boy* page

GREMIO Good morrow, neighbor Baptista.

BAPTISTA Good morrow, neighbor Gremio. God save
you, gentlemen.

PETRUCHIO

And you, good sir. Pray, have you not a daughter
Called Katherina, fair and virtuous?

BAPTISTA

I have a daughter, sir, called Katherina.

GREMIO

You are too blunt, go to it orderly.

PETRUCHIO

You wrong me, Signior Gremio, give me leave.
I am a gentleman of Verona, sir,
That, hearing of her beauty and her wit,
Her affability and bashful modesty,
Her wondrous qualities and mild behavior,
Am bold to show myself a forward guest
Within your house, to make mine eye the witness
Of that report which I so oft have heard.
54   And for an entrance to my entertainment
I do present you with a man of mine,
     [presenting Hortensio]
Cunning in music and the mathematics,
To instruct her fully in those sciences,
Whereof I know she is not ignorant.
Accept of him or else you do me wrong.
60   His name is Litio, born in Mantua.

BAPTISTA

Y'are welcome, sir, and he for your good sake.
But for my daughter Katherine, this I know,
63   She is not for your turn, the more my grief.

PETRUCHIO

I see you do not mean to part with her,
Or else you like not of my company.

BAPTISTA

Mistake me not, I speak but as I find.
Whence are you, sir? What may I call your name?

PETRUCHIO

Petruchio is my name, Antonio's son,
A man well known throughout all Italy.

BAPTISTA

70   I know him well, you are welcome for his sake.

71 GREMIO Saving your tale, Petruchio, I pray, let us, that
72   are poor petitioners, speak too. Backare, you are marvellous forward.

PETRUCHIO

74   O pardon me, Signior Gremio, I would fain be doing.

GREMIO I doubt it not, sir, but you will curse your wooing. Neighbor, this is a gift very grateful, I am sure of it.
To express the like kindness, myself, that have been
more kindly beholding to you than any, freely give unto
you this young scholar, *[presenting Lucentio]* that hath
80   been long studying at Rheims; as cunning in Greek, Latin, and other languages as the other in music and math-
82   ematics. His name is Cambio, pray accept his service.

BAPTISTA A thousand thanks, Signior Gremio. Welcome, good Cambio. *[to Tranio]* But, gentle sir, methinks you walk like a stranger. May I be so bold to
know the cause of your coming?

TRANIO

Pardon me, sir, the boldness is mine own,
88   That, being a stranger in this city here,
Do make myself a suitor to your daughter,
Unto Bianca, fair and virtuous.

Nor is your firm resolve unknown to me
In the preferment of the eldest sister.
This liberty is all that I request,
That, upon knowledge of my parentage,
I may have welcome 'mongst the rest that woo,
And free access and favor as the rest.
And toward the education of your daughters
I here bestow a simple instrument,
And this small packet of Greek and Latin books.
If you accept them, then their worth is great.

BAPTISTA

Lucentio is your name, of whence, I pray?

TRANIO

Of Pisa, sir, son to Vincentio.

BAPTISTA

A mighty man of Pisa by report,
I know him well. You are very welcome, sir.   104
     [To Hortensio]
Take you the lute, *[to Lucentio]* and you the set of books.
You shall go see your pupils presently.   106
Holla, within!
     Enter a Servant.
Sirrah, lead these gentlemen
To my daughters, and tell them both
These are their tutors; bid them use them well.
     [Exit Servant with Hortensio,
         Lucentio, and Biondello.]
We will go walk a little in the orchard   111
And then to dinner. You are passing welcome,   112
And so I pray you all to think yourselves.

PETRUCHIO

Signior Baptista, my business asketh haste,
And every day I cannot come to woo.
You knew my father well, and in him me,
Left solely heir to all his lands and goods,
Which I have bettered rather than decreased.
Then tell me, if I get your daughter's love
What dowry shall I have with her to wife?

BAPTISTA

After my death the one half of my lands,
And in possession twenty thousand crowns.   122

PETRUCHIO

And for that dowry, I'll assure her of
Her widowhood, be it that she survive me,   124
In all my lands and leases whatsoever.
Let specialties be therefore drawn between us,   126
That covenants may be kept on either hand.

BAPTISTA

Ay, when the special thing is well obtained,
That is, her love, for that is all in all.

PETRUCHIO

Why, that is nothing, for I tell you, father,
I am as peremptory as she proud-minded,   131
And where two raging fires meet together
They do consume the thing that feeds their fury.
Though little fire grows great with little wind,

---

54 *entrance* entrance fee; *entertainment* welcome (as a suitor)   60 *Litio* (or
'*Lizio*,' an old Italian word for garlic; pronounced 'Leet-sio')   63 *turn*
purpose   70 *know him* i.e. know who he is   71 *Saving* with no disrespect
to   72 *Backare* stand back (mock Latin)   74 *fain* gladly   80 *Rheims* (here
pronounced 'reams')   82 *Cambio* (the word means 'exchange' in Italian)
88 *That* I who   104 *know him* i.e. know who he is   106 *presently* immediately   111 *orchard* garden   112 *passing* surpassingly   122 *possession*
i.e. immediate possession   124 *widowhood* income if widowed   126 *specialties* contracts   131 *peremptory* determined

Yet extreme gusts will blow out fire and all.
So I to her, and so she yields to me,
For I am rough and woo not like a babe.

BAPTISTA

138 Well mayst thou woo, and happy be thy speed,
But be thou armed for some unhappy words.

PETRUCHIO

140 Ay, to the proof, as mountains are for winds,
141 That shakes not though they blow perpetually.

Enter Hortensio [as Litio] with his head broke.

BAPTISTA

How now, my friend, why dost thou look so pale?

HORTENSIO

For fear, I promise you, if I look pale.

BAPTISTA

What, will my daughter prove a good musician?

HORTENSIO

I think she'll sooner prove a soldier.
146 Iron may hold with her but never lutes.

BAPTISTA

147 Why, then thou canst not break her to the lute?

HORTENSIO

Why, no, for she hath broke the lute to me.
149 I did but tell her she mistook her frets
150 And bowed her hand to teach her fingering,
When, with a most impatient devilish spirit,
'Frets, call you these?' quoth she, 'I'll fume with them.'
And with that word she struck me on the head,
And through the instrument my pate made way,
And there I stood amazèd for a while
As on a pillory, looking through the lute,
While she did call me rascal, fiddler,
158 And twangling Jack, with twenty such vile terms,
As had she studied to misuse me so.

PETRUCHIO

160 Now, by the world, it is a lusty wench.
I love her ten times more than e'er I did.
O how I long to have some chat with her!

BAPTISTA *[to Hortensio]*

Well, go with me, and be not so discomfited.
Proceed in practice with my younger daughter.
165 She's apt to learn and thankful for good turns.
Signior Petruchio, will you go with us
Or shall I send my daughter Kate to you?

PETRUCHIO

168 I pray you do. I will attend her here,

*Exit [Baptista with Gremio, Tranio,
and Hortensio]. Manet Petruchio.*

And woo her with some spirit when she comes.
Say that she rail, why then I'll tell her plain
She sings as sweetly as a nightingale.
Say that she frown, I'll say she looks as clear
As morning roses newly washed with dew.
Say she be mute and will not speak a word,
Then I'll commend her volubility
And say she uttereth piercing eloquence.
If she do bid me pack I'll give her thanks
As though she bid me stay by her a week.
If she deny to wed I'll crave the day   179
When I shall ask the banns, and when be marrièd. 180

Enter Kate.

But here she comes, and now, Petruchio, speak.
Good morrow, Kate, for that's your name, I hear.

KATE

Well have you heard, but something hard of hearing. 183
They call me Katherine that do talk of me.

PETRUCHIO

You lie, in faith, for you are called plain Kate,
And bonny Kate, and sometimes Kate the curst. 186
But Kate, the prettiest Kate in Christendom,
Kate of Kate-Hall, my super-dainty Kate,
For dainties are all cates, and therefore, Kate, 189
Take this of me, Kate of my consolation:
Hearing thy mildness praised in every town,
Thy virtues spoke of, and thy beauty sounded, 192
Yet not so deeply as to thee belongs,
Myself am moved to woo thee for my wife.

KATE

Moved? In good time: let him that moved you hither 195
Remove you hence. I knew you at the first,
You were a movable. 197

PETRUCHIO Why, what's a movable?

KATE A joint-stool. 199

PETRUCHIO Thou hast hit it: come sit on me.

KATE

Asses are made to bear, and so are you. 201

PETRUCHIO

Women are made to bear, and so are you.

KATE

No such jade as you, if me you mean. 203

PETRUCHIO

Alas, good Kate, I will not burden thee,
For knowing thee to be but young and light. 205

KATE

Too light for such a swain as you to catch, 206
And yet as heavy as my weight should be.

PETRUCHIO

Should be? should – buzz! 208

KATE   Well ta'en, and like a buzzard.

PETRUCHIO

O slow-winged turtle! Shall a buzzard take thee? 209

KATE

Ay, for a turtle, as he takes a buzzard. 210

PETRUCHIO

Come, come, you wasp, i' faith you are too angry.

KATE

If I be waspish best beware my sting.

PETRUCHIO

My remedy is then to pluck it out.

KATE

Ay, if the fool could find it where it lies.

---

138 *speed* fortune 140 *to the proof* in tested armor 141 s.d. *broke* i.e. with the skin broken, bleeding 146 *lutes* (playing on 'cement made of clay') 147 *break* tame 149 *frets* rings of gut, placed on the fingerboard to regulate the fingering (Kate quibbled on 'fret and fume,' be indignant) 150 *bowed* bent 158 *Jack* knave 160 *lusty* lively 165 *apt* willing 168 *attend* wait for 179 *deny* refuse 180 *ask the banns* announce in church the intent to marry 183 *hard* (playing on *heard*, pronounced similarly) 186 *bonny* strapping 189 *dainties* delicacies; *cates* choice foods (playing, of course, on 'Kates') 192 *sounded* proclaimed (with a play, in *deeply*, on 'plumbed') 195 *In good time* indeed 197 *movable* (quibbling on 'piece of furniture') 199 *joint-stool* stool made by a joiner 201 *bear* i.e. carry (Petruchio quibbles on 'bear children') 203 *jade* worthless horse (playing on *Asses* and quibbling on *bear* in the sense of 'support a male in the sexual act') 205 *For knowing* because I know; *light* (playing on a 'light' song, i.e. one without a *burden*, or bass undersong) 206 *swain* rustic lover 208 *buzz* (an expression of contempt, playing on *be*); *buzzard* fool (Petruchio quibbles on 'an inferior kind of hawk, useless for falconry') 209 *turtle* turtledove 210 *buzzard* buzzing insect (suggesting *wasp*)

PETRUCHIO
Who knows not where a wasp does wear his sting?
In his tail.
KATE In his tongue.
PETRUCHIO Whose tongue?
KATE
Yours, if you talk of tales, and so farewell.
PETRUCHIO
What, with my tongue in your tail?
Nay, come again, good Kate, I am a gentleman.
KATE That I'll try.
She strikes him.
PETRUCHIO
I swear I'll cuff you if you strike again.
KATE
224 So may you lose your arms.
If you strike me you are no gentleman,
And if no gentleman, why then no arms.
PETRUCHIO
227 A herald, Kate? O put me in thy books.
KATE
228 What is your crest, a coxcomb?
PETRUCHIO
229 A combless cock, so Kate will be my hen.
KATE
230 No cock of mine, you crow too like a craven.
PETRUCHIO
Nay, come, Kate, come, you must not look so sour.
KATE
232 It is my fashion when I see a crab.
PETRUCHIO
Why, here's no crab, and therefore look not sour.
KATE
There is, there is.
PETRUCHIO
Then show it me.
235 KATE   Had I a glass I would.
PETRUCHIO What, you mean my face?
237 KATE Well aimed of such a young one.
PETRUCHIO
Now, by Saint George, I am too young for you.
KATE Yet you are withered.
PETRUCHIO 'Tis with cares.
KATE I care not.
PETRUCHIO
242 Nay, hear you, Kate, in sooth you 'scape not so.
KATE
I chafe you if I tarry; let me go.
PETRUCHIO
No, not a whit. I find you passing gentle.
245 'Twas told me you were rough and coy and sullen,
And now I find report a very liar,
For thou art pleasant, gamesome, passing courteous,
But slow in speech, yet sweet as springtime flowers.
249 Thou canst not frown, thou canst not look askance,
Nor bite the lip as angry wenches will,
Nor hast thou pleasure to be cross in talk.
But thou with mildness entertain'st thy wooers,
With gentle conference, soft and affable.
Why does the world report that Kate doth limp?
O sland'rous world! Kate like a hazel-twig
Is straight and slender, and as brown in hue
As hazelnuts and sweeter than the kernels.
258 O let me see thee walk. Thou dost not halt.

KATE
Go, fool, and whom thou keep'st command. 259
PETRUCHIO
Did ever Dian so become a grove 260
As Kate this chamber with her princely gait?
O be thou Dian and let her be Kate.
And then let Kate be chaste and Dian sportful. 263
KATE
Where did you study all this goodly speech?
PETRUCHIO
It is extempore, from my mother-wit. 265
KATE
A witty mother, witless else her son. 266
PETRUCHIO Am I not wise?
KATE Yes, keep you warm. 268
PETRUCHIO
Marry, so I mean, sweet Katherine, in thy bed.
And therefore, setting all this chat aside,
Thus in plain terms. Your father hath consented
That you shall be my wife, your dowry 'greed upon,
And will you, nill you, I will marry you. 273
Now, Kate, I am a husband for your turn, 274
For by this light, whereby I see thy beauty –
Thy beauty that doth make me like thee well –
Thou must be married to no man but me,
Enter Baptista, Gremio, [and] Tranio [as Lucentio].
For I am he am born to tame you, Kate,
And bring you from a wild Kate to a Kate 279
Conformable as other household Kates.
Here comes your father. Never make denial,
I must and will have Katherine to my wife.
BAPTISTA
Now, Signior Petruchio, how speed you with my 283
daughter?
PETRUCHIO
How but well, sir? How but well?
It were impossible I should speed amiss.
BAPTISTA
Why, how now, daughter Katherine? In your dumps?
KATE
Call you me daughter? Now, I promise you 287
You have showed a tender fatherly regard
To wish me wed to one half lunatic,
A madcap ruffian and a swearing Jack,
That thinks with oaths to face the matter out. 291
PETRUCHIO
Father, 'tis thus. Yourself and all the world
That talked of her have talked amiss of her.
If she be curst it is for policy, 294
For she's not froward but modest as the dove.
She is not hot but temperate as the morn. 296

224 *arms* coat of arms 227 *in thy books* in your heraldic registers (playing on 'in your good graces') 228 *crest* armorial device; *coxcomb* cap of a court fool (playing on *crest*, comb; Petruchio then quibbles on 'cock's comb') 229 *combless* gentle (with 'comb' or crest cut down) 230 *craven* cock that will not fight 232 *crab* crab-apple 235 *glass* looking-glass 237 *aimed of* guessed for; *young* inexperienced 242 *sooth* truth 245 *coy* haughty 249 *askance* scornfully 258 *halt* limp 259 *whom thou keep'st* i.e. your servants 260 *Dian* Diana (goddess of virginity and of the hunt) 263 *sportful* amorous 265 *mother-wit* native intelligence 266 *witless . . . son* otherwise her son would be witless (his only wit being inherited from her) 268 *keep you warm* i.e. take care of yourself (to have the wit or wisdom to keep warm being proverbial) 273 *nill you* will you not 274 *for your turn* to suit you 279 *wild Kate* (punning on 'wild cat') 283 *speed* succeed 287 *promise* assure 291 *face* brazen 294 *policy* cunning 296 *hot* of angry disposition

297 For patience she will prove a second Grissel,
298 And Roman Lucrece for her chastity.
And, to conclude, we have 'greed so well together
That upon Sunday is the wedding-day.

KATE
I'll see thee hanged on Sunday first.

GREMIO
Hark, Petruchio, she says she'll see thee hanged first.

TRANIO
303 Is this your speeding? Nay, then good night our part!

PETRUCHIO
Be patient, gentlemen, I choose her for myself.
If she and I be pleased, what's that to you?
'Tis bargained 'twixt us twain, being alone,
That she shall still be curst in company.
I tell you, 'tis incredible to believe
How much she loves me. O the kindest Kate!
She hung about my neck, and kiss on kiss
311 She vied so fast, protesting oath on oath,
That in a twink she won me to her love.
313 O you are novices. 'Tis a world to see
How tame, when men and women are alone,
315 A meacock wretch can make the curstest shrew.
Give me thy hand, Kate, I will unto Venice
317 To buy apparel 'gainst the wedding-day.
Provide the feast, father, and bid the guests.
319 I will be sure my Katherine shall be fine.

BAPTISTA
I know not what to say – but give me your hands.
God send you joy! Petruchio, 'tis a match.

GREMIO, TRANIO
Amen, say we, we will be witnesses.

PETRUCHIO
Father, and wife, and gentlemen, adieu.
I will to Venice. Sunday comes apace.
We will have rings and things and fine array,
326 And kiss me, Kate, [sings] 'We will be married a Sunday.'
Exeunt Petruchio and Kate [severally].

GREMIO
327 Was ever match clapped up so suddenly?

BAPTISTA
Faith, gentlemen, now I play a merchant's part
329 And venture madly on a desperate mart.

TRANIO
330 'Twas a commodity lay fretting by you.
'Twill bring you gain or perish on the seas.

BAPTISTA
The gain I seek is quiet in the match.

GREMIO
No doubt but he hath got a quiet catch.
But now, Baptista, to your younger daughter.
Now is the day we long have lookèd for.
I am your neighbor and was suitor first.

TRANIO
And I am one that love Bianca more
Than words can witness or your thoughts can guess.

GREMIO
Youngling, thou canst not love so dear as I.

TRANIO
Greybeard, thy love doth freeze.

GREMIO   But thine doth fry.
341 Skipper, stand back, 'tis age that nourisheth.

TRANIO
But youth in ladies' eyes that flourisheth.

BAPTISTA
343 Content you, gentlemen, I will compound this strife.
344 'Tis deeds must win the prize, and he of both
345 That can assure my daughter greatest dower
Shall have Bianca's love.
Say, Signior Gremio, what can you assure her?

GREMIO
First, as you know, my house within the city
Is richly furnishèd with plate and gold,
350 Basins and ewers to lave her dainty hands;
351 My hangings all of Tyrian tapestry;
In ivory coffers I have stuffed my crowns;
353 In cypress chests my arras counterpoints,
354 Costly apparel, tents, and canopies,
355 Fine linen, Turkey cushions bossed with pearl,
356 Valance of Venice gold in needlework,
Pewter and brass, and all things that belongs
To house or housekeeping. Then at my farm
359 I have a hundred milch-kine to the pail,
Six score fat oxen standing in my stalls,
And all things answerable to this portion.
362 Myself am struck in years, I must confess,
And if I die to-morrow this is hers,
If whilst I live she will be only mine.

TRANIO
That 'only' came well in. Sir, list to me.
I am my father's heir and only son.
If I may have your daughter to my wife
I'll leave her houses three or four as good,
Within rich Pisa walls, as any one
Old Signior Gremio has in Padua,
371 Besides two thousand ducats by the year
372 Of fruitful land, all which shall be her jointure.
What, have I pinched you, Signior Gremio?

GREMIO
Two thousand ducats by the year of land!
[Aside]
My land amounts not to so much in all.
376 That she shall have, besides an argosy
377 That now is lying in Marseilles' road.
What, have I choked you with an argosy?

TRANIO
Gremio, 'tis known my father hath no less
380 Than three great argosies, besides two galliasses
381 And twelve tight galleys. These I will assure her
And twice as much whate'er thou off'rest next.

---

297 *Grissel* Griselda (the epitome of wifely patience and obedience; cf. Boccaccio's *Decameron*, X, 10, or Chaucer's Clerk's Tale) 298 *Lucrece* (she killed herself after being raped by Sextus Tarquinius, hence became the epitome of wifely chastity and honor; cf. Shakespeare's *Rape of Lucrece*) 303 *speeding* success 311 *vied* i.e. went me one better (cardplaying term) 313 *world* i.e. worth a world 315 *meacock* cowardly 317 *'gainst* in anticipation of 319 *fine* finely dressed 326 s.d. *severally* at different doors 327 *match* contract (with a play on 'mating'); *clapped up* shaken hands on, agreed to 329 *mart* bargain 330 *fretting* (of a stored commodity that decays, as wool 'fretted' by moths; with a play on 'chafing') 341 *Skipper* flighty youth 343 *compound* settle 344 *he of both* whichever of the two (of you) 345 *assure* guarantee 350 *lave* wash 351 *Tyrian* purple 353 *arras counterpoints* counterpanes of Arras tapestry 354 *tents* (meaning doubtful; perhaps hangings of some sort); *canopies* testers 355 *bossed* embroidered 356 *Valance* drapery round the canopy or frame of a bed 359 *milch-kine* cows; *to the pail* i.e. in a dairy 362 *struck* advanced 371 *ducats* gold coins 372 *Of* from; *jointure* settlement 376 *argosy* large merchant-ship 377 *Marseilles'* (here pronounced *Marséllus*); *road* harbor 380 *galliasses* large galleys 381 *tight* i.e. well caulked

97

GREMIO

Nay, I have off'red all, I have no more,
And she can have no more than all I have.
If you like me, she shall have me and mine.

TRANIO

387 Why, then the maid is mine from all the world
By your firm promise. Gremio is outvied.

BAPTISTA

I must confess your offer is the best,
389 And let your father make her the assurance,
She is your own, else you must pardon me.
If you should die before him, where's her dower?

TRANIO

That's but a cavil. He is old, I young.

GREMIO

And may not young men die as well as old?

BAPTISTA

Well, gentlemen, I am thus resolved.
On Sunday next, you know,
My daughter Katherine is to be married.
Now on the Sunday following shall Bianca
Be bride to you, if you make this assurance.
If not, to Signior Gremio.
And so I take my leave and thank you both.   *Exit.*

GREMIO

Adieu, good neighbor. Now I fear thee not.
402 Sirrah young gamester, your father were a fool
To give thee all and in his waning age
404 Set foot under thy table. Tut, a toy!
An old Italian fox is not so kind, my boy.   *Exit.*

TRANIO

A vengeance on your crafty withered hide!
407 Yet I have faced it with a card of ten.
'Tis in my head to do my master good.
I see no reason but supposed Lucentio
Must get a father, called supposed Vincentio;
And that's a wonder. Fathers commonly
412 Do get their children, but in this case of wooing
A child shall get a sire if I fail not of my cunning.   *Exit.*

                      *

III, i   *Enter Lucentio [as Cambio], Hortensio [as Litio], and*
          Bianca.

LUCENTIO

Fiddler, forbear, you grow too forward, sir.
Have you so soon forgot the entertainment
Her sister Katherine welcomed you withal?

HORTENSIO

But, wrangling pedant, this is
5 The patroness of heavenly harmony.
6 Then give me leave to have prerogative,
And when in music we have spent an hour
8 Your lecture shall have leisure for as much.

LUCENTIO

9 Preposterous ass, that never read so far
To know the cause why music was ordained!
Was it not to refresh the mind of man
12 After his studies or his usual pain?
13 Then give me leave to read philosophy,
And while I pause, serve in your harmony.

HORTENSIO

15 Sirrah, I will not bear these braves of thine.

BIANCA

Why, gentlemen, you do me double wrong

To strive for that which resteth in my choice.
I am no breeching scholar in the schools.   18
I'll not be tied to hours nor 'pointed times,
But learn my lessons as I please myself.
And, to cut off all strife, here sit we down.   21
Take you your instrument, play you the whiles;   22
His lecture will be done ere you have tuned.

HORTENSIO

You'll leave his lecture when I am in tune?

LUCENTIO

That will be never. Tune your instrument.

BIANCA Where left we last?

LUCENTIO Here, madam:
      [Reads.] 'Hic ibat Simois, hic est Sigeia tellus,   28
            Hic steterat Priami regia celsa senis.'

BIANCA Conster them.   30

LUCENTIO 'Hic ibat,' as I told you before; 'Simois,' I am
Lucentio; 'hic est,' son unto Vincentio of Pisa; 'Sigeia
tellus,' disguised thus to get your love; 'Hic steterat,' and
that Lucentio that comes a wooing; 'Priami,' is my man
Tranio; 'regia,' bearing my port; 'celsa senis,' that we   35
might beguile the old pantaloon.   36

HORTENSIO Madam, my instrument's in tune.

BIANCA Let's hear. *[He plays.]* O fie, the treble jars.   38

LUCENTIO Spit in the hole, man, and tune again.   39

BIANCA Now let me see if I can conster it.
'Hic ibat Simois,' I know you not; 'hic est Sigeia tellus,'
I trust you not; 'Hic steterat Priami,' take heed he hear
us not; 'regia,' presume not; 'celsa senis,' despair not.

HORTENSIO

Madam, 'tis now in tune.

LUCENTIO   All but the bass.

HORTENSIO

The bass is right, 'tis the base knave that jars.
     [Aside]
How fiery and forward our pedant is!   46
Now, for my life, the knave doth court my love.
Pedascule, I'll watch you better yet.   48

BIANCA

In time I may believe, yet I mistrust.

LUCENTIO

Mistrust it not, for sure Aeacides   50
Was Ajax, called so from his grandfather.   51

BIANCA

I must believe my master, else I promise you,
I should be arguing still upon that doubt.

---

387 *outvied* outbid   389 *assurance* guarantee   402 *Sirrah* (contemptuous to a person of equal rank); *were* would be   404 *Set... table* i.e. become your dependent; *a toy* nonsense; 407 *faced... ten* bluffed successfully with a ten-spot   412 *get* beget
III, i Baptista's house   5 *patroness* goddess (i.e. Minerva, goddess of music and inventor of musical instruments; cf. I, i, 84)   6 *prerogative* precedence   8 *lecture* lesson   9 *Preposterous* reversing the natural order of things   12 *pain* toil   13 *read* teach   15 *braves* insults   18 *breeching scholar* schoolboy liable to whipping   21 *And... down* (apparently all three sit together on a bench)   22 *the whiles* meanwhile   28–29 *Hic... senis* here flowed the Simois, here lies the Sigeian plain, here stood the lofty palace of old Priam (Ovid, *Epistolae Heroidum*, I, a letter from Penelope to Ulysses)   30 *Conster* construe (translate)   35 *bearing my port* behaving as I would   36 *pantaloon* foolish old man   38 *jars* is discordant   39 *Spit in the hole* (to make the peg hold)   46 *pedant* schoolmaster or tutor   48 *Pedascule* (Latin coinage from *pedant*, contemptuously diminutive)   50 *Aeacides* descendant of Aeacus (Lucentio explains a reference in the line of Ovid's epistle which follows immediately after the two lines already quoted)   51 *Ajax* one of the Greek heroes at Troy

But let it rest. Now, Litio, to you.
Good master, take it not unkindly, pray,
That I have been thus pleasant with you both.

HORTENSIO
You may go walk and give me leave a while.
58   My lessons make no music in three parts.

LUCENTIO
59   Are you so formal, sir? *[aside]* Well, I must wait
60   And watch withal, for but I be deceived,
Our fine musician groweth amorous.

HORTENSIO
Madam, before you touch the instrument
To learn the order of my fingering,
I must begin with rudiments of art,
65   To teach you gamut in a briefer sort,
More pleasant, pithy, and effectual
Than hath been taught by any of my trade.
And there it is in writing, fairly drawn.

BIANCA
Why, I am past my gamut long ago.

HORTENSIO
Yet read the gamut of Hortensio.

BIANCA *[reads]*
71   'Gamut I am, the ground of all accord,
A re, to plead Hortensio's passion;
B mi, Bianca, take him for thy lord,
C fa ut, that loves with all affection;
D sol re, one clef, two notes have I;
E la mi, show pity or I die.'
Call you this gamut? Tut, I like it not.
78   Old fashions please me best; I am not so nice
To change true rules for odd inventions.
        Enter a Messenger.

MESSENGER
Mistress, your father prays you leave your books
And help to dress your sister's chamber up.
You know to-morrow is the wedding day.

BIANCA
Farewell, sweet masters both, I must be gone.
            [Exeunt Bianca and Messenger.]

LUCENTIO
Faith, mistress, then I have no cause to stay. *[Exit.]*

HORTENSIO
But I have cause to pry into this pedant.
Methinks he looks as though he were in love.
Yet if thy thoughts, Bianca, be so humble
88   To cast thy wand'ring eyes on every stale,
89   Seize thee that list. If once I find thee ranging,
90   Hortensio will be quit with thee by changing. *Exit.*

                    *

58 *in three parts* for three voices   59 *formal* precise   60 *withal* at the same time; *but* unless   65 *gamut* the scale   71 s.d. *reads* (she intones each line on the note in question); *ground* lowest note; *accord* harmony   78 *nice* capricious   88 *stale* decoy, bait   89 *Seize* . . . *list* let him take you that pleases; *ranging* straying   90 *changing* i.e. to another love
III, ii Before Baptista's house   8 *forsooth* indeed   10 *rudesby* boor; *spleen* capriciousness   14 *noted for* known as   25 *withal* at the same time   29 *humor* disposition   30 *old* great, rare (Baptista misunderstands)   41 *to* about   43 *jerkin* jacket   44 *candle-cases* (worn-out boots were sometimes hung on the wall to hold candle-ends and the like)   46 *chapeless* without the metal plate on the scabbard covering the sword-point   47 *points* tagged laces for tying hose to doublet; *hipped* lamed in the hip   49 *glanders* disease affecting nose and mouth; *mose . . . chine* suffer from glanders   50 *lampass* infected mouth; *fashions* disease like glanders   51 *windgalls* leg tumors; *spavins* joint-swellings   52 *yellows* jaundice; *fives* swelling behind the ears   53 *staggers* a kind of palsy; *bots* stomach worms

Enter Baptista, Gremio, Tranio [as Lucentio], Kate,   III, ii
Bianca, [Lucentio as Cambio,] and others
(Attendants).

BAPTISTA *[to Tranio]*
Signior Lucentio, this is the 'pointed day
That Katherine and Petruchio should be married,
And yet we hear not of our son-in-law.
What will be said? What mockery will it be
To want the bridegroom when the priest attends
To speak the ceremonial rites of marriage?
What says Lucentio to this shame of ours?

KATE
No shame but mine. I must, forsooth, be forced   8
To give my hand opposed against my heart
Unto a mad-brain rudesby, full of spleen,   10
Who wooed in haste and means to wed at leisure.
I told you, I, he was a frantic fool,
Hiding his bitter jests in blunt behavior.
And to be noted for a merry man,   14
He'll woo a thousand, 'point the day of marriage,
Make friends, invite, and proclaim the banns,
Yet never means to wed where he hath wooed.
Now must the world point at poor Katherine
And say, 'Lo, there is mad Petruchio's wife,
If it would please him come and marry her.'

TRANIO
Patience, good Katherine, and Baptista too.
Upon my life, Petruchio means but well,
Whatever fortune stays him from his word.
Though he be blunt, I know him passing wise;
Though he be merry, yet withal he's honest.   25

KATE
Would Katherine had never seen him though!
                Exit weeping [with Bianca].

BAPTISTA
Go, girl, I cannot blame thee now to weep,
For such an injury would vex a very saint,
Much more a shrew of thy impatient humor.   29
            Enter Biondello.

BIONDELLO Master, master, old news! And such news   30
as you never heard of!

BAPTISTA Is it new and old too? How may that be?

BIONDELLO Why, is it not news to hear of Petruchio's
coming?

BAPTISTA Is he come?

BIONDELLO Why, no, sir.

BAPTISTA What then?

BIONDELLO He is coming.

BAPTISTA When will he be here?

BIONDELLO When he stands where I am and sees you
there.

TRANIO But say, what to thine old news?   41

BIONDELLO Why, Petruchio is coming, in a new hat and
an old jerkin; a pair of old breeches thrice turned; a pair   43
of boots that have been candle-cases, one buckled,   44
another laced; an old rusty sword ta'en out of the town
armory, with a broken hilt and chapeless; with two   46
broken points; his horse hipped – with an old mothy   47
saddle and stirrups of no kindred – besides, possessed
with the glanders and like to mose in the chine;   49
troubled with the lampass, infected with the fashions,   50
full of windgalls, sped with spavins, rayed with the   51
yellows, past cure of the fives, stark spoiled with the   52
staggers, begnawn with the bots, swayed in the back,   53

54 and shoulder-shotten; near-legged before, and with a
55 half-cheeked bit and a head-stall of sheep's leather
56 which, being restrained to keep him from stumbling,
hath been often burst and new-repaired with knots; one
58 girth six times pieced, and a woman's crupper of velure
which hath two letters for her name, fairly set down in
60 studs, and here and there pieced with packthread.

BAPTISTA Who comes with him?

BIONDELLO O sir, his lackey, for all the world caparisoned like the horse: with a linen stock on one leg and a
64 kersey boot-hose on the other, gart'red with a red and
65 blue list; an old hat and the humor of forty fancies
66 pricked in't for a feather – a monster, a very monster in
67 apparel, and not like a Christian footboy or a gentleman's lackey.

TRANIO
68 'Tis some odd humor pricks him to this fashion,
Yet oftentimes he goes but mean-apparelled.

BAPTISTA I am glad he's come, howsoe'er he comes.

BIONDELLO Why, sir, he comes not.

BAPTISTA Didst thou not say he comes?

BIONDELLO Who? That Petruchio came?

BAPTISTA Ay, that Petruchio came.

BIONDELLO No, sir, I say his horse comes, with him on
his back.

77 BAPTISTA Why, that's all one.

BIONDELLO [sings] Nay, by Saint Jamy,
79   I hold you a penny,
       A horse and a man
       Is more than one
       And yet not many.

Enter Petruchio and Grumio.

PETRUCHIO
Come, where be these gallants? Who's at home?

BAPTISTA
You are welcome, sir.

PETRUCHIO   And yet I come not well.

85 BAPTISTA And yet you halt not.

TRANIO Not so well apparelled as I wish you were.

PETRUCHIO
87 Were it better, I should rush in thus.
But where is Kate? Where is my lovely bride?
How does my father? Gentles, methinks you frown.
And wherefore gaze this goodly company
As if they saw some wondrous monument,
92 Some comet or unusual prodigy?

BAPTISTA
Why, sir, you know this is your wedding-day.
First were we sad, fearing you would not come,
95 Now sadder that you come so unprovided.
96 Fie, doff this habit, shame to your estate,
An eyesore to our solemn festival.

TRANIO
And tell us what occasion of import
Hath all so long detained you from your wife
And sent you hither so unlike yourself?

PETRUCHIO
Tedious it were to tell and harsh to hear.
Sufficeth I am come to keep my word,
103 Though in some part enforcèd to digress,
Which at more leisure I will so excuse
105 As you shall well be satisfied withal.
But where is Kate? I stay too long from her.
The morning wears, 'tis time we were at church.

TRANIO
See not your bride in these unreverent robes.
Go to my chamber; put on clothes of mine.

PETRUCHIO
Not I, believe me. Thus I'll visit her.

BAPTISTA
But thus, I trust, you will not marry her?

PETRUCHIO
Good sooth, even thus. Therefore ha' done with words. 112
To me she's married, not unto my clothes.
Could I repair what she will wear in me   114
As I can change these poor accoutrements,
'Twere well for Kate and better for myself.
But what a fool am I to chat with you
When I should bid good morrow to my bride   118
And seal the title with a lovely kiss. *Exit [with Grumio].* 119

TRANIO
He hath some meaning in his mad attire.
We will persuade him, be it possible,
To put on better ere he go to church.

BAPTISTA
I'll after him and see the event of this.   123
            Exit [with Gremio and Attendants].

TRANIO
But sir, to love concerneth us to add
Her father's liking, which to bring to pass,
As I before imparted to your worship,
I am to get a man – whate'er he be
It skills not much, we'll fit him to our turn –   128
And he shall be Vincentio of Pisa,
And make assurance here in Padua   130
Of greater sums than I have promisèd.
So shall you quietly enjoy your hope
And marry sweet Bianca with consent.

LUCENTIO
Were it not that my fellow-schoolmaster
Doth watch Bianca's steps so narrowly,
'Twere good, methinks, to steal our marriage,   136
Which once performed, let all the world say no,
I'll keep mine own despite of all the world.

TRANIO
That by degrees we mean to look into
And watch our vantage in this business.
We'll over-reach the greybeard, Gremio,
The narrow-prying father, Minola,
The quaint musician, amorous Litio –   143
All for my master's sake, Lucentio.

54 *shoulder-shotten* with dislocated shoulder; *near-legged* knock-kneed 55 *half-cheeked* with bridle attached half-way up the 'cheek' or side-piece of bit (thus giving inadequate leverage); *head-stall* part of bridle going round the head; *sheep's leather* (inferior to pigskin) 56 *restrained* drawn back 58 *pieced* patched; *crupper* strap passing under the tail to keep the saddle from working forward; *velure* velvet 60 *pieced* tied together 64 *kersey boot-hose* coarse woolen overstocking 65 *list* strip of waste cloth; *humor ... fancies* (meaning doubtful; some kind of fantastic ornament) 66 *pricked* pinned 67 *footboy* liveried attendant 68 *humor* whim; *pricks* spurs, drives 77 *all one* the same thing 79 *hold* bet 85 *halt* limp (Baptista quibbles on *come* in the sense of 'walk') 87 *it* i.e. my apparel 92 *prodigy* unnatural phenomenon 95 *unprovided* improperly equipped 96 *estate* social position 103 *digress* deviate (from his intention to dress well; cf. II, i, 317) 105 *withal* with 112 *Good sooth* indeed 114 *wear* wear out 118 *bid ... bride* (on the wedding morning it was customary for the groom to awaken the bride) 119 *seal the title* confirm my rights; *lovely* loving 123 *event* outcome 128 *skills* matters; *turn* purpose 130 *assurance* guarantee 136 *steal our marriage* i.e. marry secretly 143 *quaint* clever

Enter Gremio.

Signior Gremio, come you from the church?

GREMIO

As willingly as e'er I came from school.

TRANIO

And is the bride and bridegroom coming home?

GREMIO

148   A bridegroom, say you? 'Tis a groom indeed,
A grumbling groom, and that the girl shall find.

TRANIO

Curster than she? Why, 'tis impossible.

GREMIO

Why, he's a devil, a devil, a very fiend.

TRANIO

152   Why, she's a devil, a devil, the devil's dam.

GREMIO

153   Tut, she's a lamb, a dove, a fool to him.
I'll tell you, Sir Lucentio. When the priest
Did ask if Katherine should be his wife,
156   'Ay, by gogs-wouns,' quoth he, and swore so loud
That, all amazed, the priest let fall the book,
And as he stooped again to take it up
159   This mad-brained bridegroom took him such a cuff
That down fell priest and book, and book and priest.
161   'Now, take them up,' quoth he, 'if any list.'

TRANIO

What said the wench when he arose again?

GREMIO

163   Trembled and shook, forwhy he stamped and swore,
164   As if the vicar meant to cozen him.
But after many ceremonies done
He calls for wine. 'A health!' quoth he, as if
He had been aboard, carousing to his mates
168   After a storm; quaffed off the muscadel
169   And threw the sops all in the sexton's face,
Having no other reason
171   But that his beard grew thin and hungerly
172   And seemed to ask him sops as he was drinking.
This done, he took the bride about the neck
And kissed her lips with such a clamorous smack
That at the parting all the church did echo.
I, seeing this, came thence for very shame,
177   And after me, I know, the rout is coming.
Such a mad marriage never was before.
Hark, hark, I hear the minstrels play.

Music plays.

*Enter Petruchio, Kate, Bianca, Hortensio [as Litio],
Baptista [and Grumio, with Attendants].*

PETRUCHIO

Gentlemen and friends, I thank you for your pains.

I know you think to dine with me to-day
And have prepared great store of wedding cheer,   182
But so it is, my haste doth call me hence
And therefore here I mean to take my leave.

BAPTISTA

Is't possible you will away to-night?

PETRUCHIO

I must away to-day, before night come.
Make it no wonder. If you knew my business   187
You would entreat me rather go than stay.
And, honest company, I thank you all,
That have beheld me give away myself
To this most patient, sweet, and virtuous wife.
Dine with my father, drink a health to me,
For I must hence; and farewell to you all.

TRANIO

Let us entreat you stay till after dinner.

PETRUCHIO

It may not be.

GREMIO   Let me entreat you.

PETRUCHIO

It cannot be.

KATE   Let me entreat you.

PETRUCHIO

I am content.

KATE   Are you content to stay?

PETRUCHIO

I am content you shall entreat me stay,
But yet not stay, entreat me how you can.

KATE

Now if you love me, stay.

PETRUCHIO   Grumio, my horse!   200

GRUMIO Ay, sir, they be ready; the oats have eaten the   201
horses.

KATE

Nay then,
Do what thou canst, I will not go to-day,
No, nor to-morrow nor till I please myself.
The door is open, sir, there lies your way;
You may be jogging whiles your boots are green.   207
For me, I'll not be gone till I please myself.
'Tis like you'll prove a jolly surly groom,   209
That take it on you at the first so roundly.   210

PETRUCHIO

O Kate, content thee; prithee, be not angry.   211

KATE

I will be angry. What hast thou to do?   212
Father, be quiet, he shall stay my leisure.

GREMIO

Ay, marry, sir, now it begins to work.

KATE

Gentlemen, forward to the bridal dinner.
I see a woman may be made a fool
If she had not a spirit to resist.

PETRUCHIO

They shall go forward, Kate, at thy command.
Obey the bride, you that attend on her,
Go to the feast, revel and domineer,   220
Carouse full measure to her maidenhead,
Be mad and merry or go hang yourselves.
But for my bonny Kate, she must with me.
Nay, look not big, nor stamp, nor stare, nor fret;   224
I will be master of what is mine own.
She is my goods, my chattels; she is my house,   226

---

148 *groom* (quibbling on 'servant,' rough-mannered fellow)   152 *dam* mother   153 *to* compared with   156 *by gogs-wouns* by God's (Christ's) wounds   159 *took* gave   161 *if any list* if anyone pleases   163 *forwhy* because   164 *cozen* cheat (with an invalid ceremony)   168 *muscadel* a sweet wine (to be avoided by persons of choleric disposition)   169 *sops* dregs   171 *hungerly* sparsely   172 *ask him* ask him for; *sops* pieces of cake soaked in wine   177 *rout* mob   182 *cheer* entertainment   187 *Make* consider   200 *horse* horses (old plural)   201–02 *the oats . . . horses* (Grumio gets it backwards)   207 *You may . . . green* (proverbial for getting an early start); *green* i.e. fresh   209 *jolly* arrogant   210 *take it on you* assert yourself; *roundly* unceremoniously   211 *prithee* I pray thee   212 *What . . . do* what business is it of yours   220 *domineer* carouse   224 *big* threatening   226–28 *my house . . . ass* (echoing the Tenth Commandment, 'Thou shalt not covet thy neighbor's house, . . . nor his ox, nor his ass, . . .')

My household stuff, my field, my barn,
My horse, my ox, my ass, my anything;
And here she stands, touch her whoever dare.
230 I'll bring mine action on the proudest he
That stops my way in Padua. Grumio,
Draw forth thy weapon, we are beset with thieves.
Rescue thy mistress, if thou be a man.
Fear not, sweet wench; they shall not touch thee, Kate.
235 I'll buckler thee against a million.

Exeunt Petruchio, Kate [and Grumio].

BAPTISTA
Nay, let them go, a couple of quiet ones.

GREMIO
Went they not quickly, I should die with laughing.

TRANIO
Of all mad matches never was the like.

LUCENTIO
Mistress, what's your opinion of your sister?

BIANCA
That being mad herself, she's madly mated.

GREMIO
I warrant him, Petruchio is Kated.

BAPTISTA
Neighbors and friends, though bride and bridegroom
wants
For to supply the places at the table,
244 You know there wants no junkets at the feast.
Lucentio, you supply the bridegroom's place,
And let Bianca take her sister's room.

TRANIO
Shall sweet Bianca practice how to bride it?

BAPTISTA
She shall, Lucentio. Come, gentlemen, let's go. *Exeunt.*

*

IV, i   *Enter Grumio.*

1 GRUMIO Fie, fie, on all tired jades, on all mad masters,
2 and all foul ways! Was ever man so beaten? Was ever
3 man so rayed? Was ever man so weary? I am sent before
to make a fire, and they are coming after to warm them.
5 Now were not I a little pot and soon hot, my very lips
might freeze to my teeth, my tongue to the roof of my
mouth, my heart in my belly, ere I should come by a
fire to thaw me. But I with blowing the fire shall warm
9 myself, for considering the weather, a taller man than I
will take cold. Holla, ho! Curtis.

Enter Curtis (a Servant).

CURTIS Who is't that calls so coldly?

GRUMIO A piece of ice. If thou doubt it, thou mayst slide
from my shoulder to my heel with no greater a run but
my head and my neck. A fire, good Curtis.

CURTIS Is my master and his wife coming, Grumio?

16 GRUMIO O ay, Curtis, ay, and therefore fire, fire; cast on
no water.

CURTIS Is she so hot a shrew as she's reported?

GRUMIO She was, good Curtis, before this frost. But
thou know'st winter tames man, woman, and beast, for
it hath tamed my old master and my new mistress and
myself, fellow Curtis.

23 CURTIS Away, you three-inch fool! I am no beast.

24 GRUMIO Am I but three inches? Why, thy horn is a foot,
and so long am I at the least. But wilt thou make a fire or
shall I complain on thee to our mistress, whose hand –

she being now at hand – thou shalt soon feel, to thy cold
comfort, for being slow in thy hot office? 28

CURTIS I prithee, good Grumio, tell me, how goes the
world?

GRUMIO A cold world, Curtis, in every office but thine,
and therefore fire. Do thy duty, and have thy duty, for 32
my master and mistress are almost frozen to death.

CURTIS There's fire ready, and therefore, good Grumio,
the news.

GRUMIO Why, [*sings*] 'Jack boy, ho boy,' and as much
news as thou wilt.

CURTIS Come, you are too full of cony-catching. 38

GRUMIO Why therefore fire, for I have caught extreme
cold. Where's the cook? Is supper ready, the house
trimmed, rushes strewed, cobwebs swept, the serving- 41
men in their new fustian and white stockings, and every 42
officer his wedding-garment on? Be the jacks fair within, 43
the jills fair without, the carpets laid, and everything in 44
order?

CURTIS All ready, and therefore, I pray thee, news.

GRUMIO First, know my horse is tired, my master and
mistress fall'n out.

CURTIS How?

GRUMIO Out of their saddles into the dirt – and thereby
hangs a tale.

CURTIS Let's ha't, good Grumio.

GRUMIO Lend thine ear.

CURTIS Here.

GRUMIO There.

[Strikes him.]

CURTIS This is to feel a tale, not to hear a tale.

GRUMIO And therefore 'tis called a sensible tale, and this 56
cuff was but to knock at your ear and beseech listening.
Now I begin. Imprimis, we came down a foul hill, my 58
master riding behind my mistress –

CURTIS Both of one horse? 60

GRUMIO What's that to thee?

CURTIS Why, a horse.

GRUMIO Tell thou the tale – but hadst thou not crossed me 63
thou shouldst have heard how her horse fell, and she
under her horse; thou shouldst have heard in how miry
a place; how she was bemoiled, how he left her with the 66
horse upon her, how he beat me because her horse
stumbled, how she waded through the dirt to pluck him
off me; how he swore, how she prayed, that never prayed
before; how I cried, how the horses ran away, how her
bridle was burst; how I lost my crupper – with many
things of worthy memory, which now shall die in oblivion, and thou return unexperienced to thy grave. 73

CURTIS By this reck'ning he is more shrew than she.

230 *action* lawsuit   235 *buckler* shield   244 *junkets* delicacies
IV, i Petruchio's country house   1 *jades* worthless horses   2 *ways* roads
3 *rayed* dirtied   5 *a little . . . hot* (proverbial of a small person easily angered)
9 *taller* (playing on 'better')   16–17 *cast on no water* (Grumio misquotes
from the round, 'Scotland's Burning')   23 *three-inch* i.e. very short; *I
am no beast* (Grumio having called himself a *beast* and Curtis his *fellow*)
24 *horn* i.e. of a cuckold   28 *hot office* task of providing heat   32 *have thy
duty* have thy due, reward (proverbial)   38 *cony-catching* trickery (a 'cony'
being a rabbit; with a play on *Jack boy, ho boy*, a 'catch' or round)   41
rushes strewed i.e. on the floor   42 *fustian* coarse cotton cloth   43 *jacks*
leather drinking vessels (playing on 'fellows,' servingmen)   44 *jills* metal
measuring cups (playing on 'girls,' maidservants); *carpets* table-covers
56 *sensible* (playing on 'capable of being felt')   58 *Imprimis* first   60 *of* on
63 *crossed* interrupted   66 *bemoiled* bemired   73 *unexperienced* (hence
ignorant)

GRUMIO Ay, and that thou and the proudest of you all
76   shall find when he comes home. But what talk I of this?
Call forth Nathaniel, Joseph, Nicholas, Philip, Walter,
Sugarsop, and the rest. Let their heads be sleekly
79   combed, their blue coats brushed, and their garters of an
80   indifferent knit. Let them curtsy with their left legs and
not presume to touch a hair of my master's horsetail till
they kiss their hands. Are they all ready?

CURTIS They are.

GRUMIO Call them forth.

CURTIS Do you hear, ho! You must meet my master to
86   countenance my mistress.

GRUMIO Why, she hath a face of her own.

CURTIS Who knows not that?

GRUMIO Thou, it seems, that calls for company to
countenance her.

91 CURTIS I call them forth to credit her.

Enter four or five Servingmen.

GRUMIO Why, she comes to borrow nothing of them.

NATHANIEL Welcome home, Grumio!

PHILIP How now, Grumio?

JOSEPH What, Grumio!

NICHOLAS Fellow Grumio!

NATHANIEL How now, old lad!

GRUMIO Welcome, you; how now, you; what, you; fellow, you; and thus much for greeting. Now, my spruce
companions, is all ready and all things neat?

NATHANIEL All things is ready. How near is our master?

GRUMIO E'en at hand, alighted by this. And therefore be
103   not – Cock's passion, silence, I hear my master.

Enter Petruchio and Kate.

PETRUCHIO
Where be these knaves? What, no man at door
To hold my stirrup nor to take my horse?
Where is Nathaniel, Gregory, Philip?

ALL SERVINGMEN Here, here, sir; here, sir.

PETRUCHIO
Here, sir; here, sir; here, sir; here, sir!
You loggerheaded and unpolished grooms!
What, no attendance? No regard? No duty?
Where is the foolish knave I sent before.

GRUMIO
Here, sir, as foolish as I was before.

PETRUCHIO
113 You peasant swain, you whoreson malt-horse drudge!
114 Did I not bid thee meet me in the park
And bring along these rascal knaves with thee?

GRUMIO
Nathaniel's coat, sir, was not fully made,
117 And Gabriel's pumps were all unpinked i' th' heel.

There was no link to color Peter's hat,   118
And Walter's dagger was not come from sheathing.
There were none fine but Adam, Rafe, and Gregory;   120
The rest were ragged, old, and beggarly.
Yet, as they are, here are they come to meet you.

PETRUCHIO
Go, rascals, go, and fetch my supper in.
                  Exeunt Servants.
[Sings] 'Where is the life that late I led?'
Where are those – ? Sit down, Kate, *[They sit at table.]*   125
And welcome. Food, food, food, food!
      Enter Servants with supper.
Why, when, I say? – Nay, good sweet Kate, be merry.
Off with my boots, you rogues! You villains, when?
[Sings] 'It was the friar of orders grey,
      As he forth walkèd on his way' –
Out, you rogue! You pluck my foot awry.
     [Strikes him.]
Take that, and mend the plucking off the other.
Be merry, Kate. Some water here, what ho!
     Enter one with water.
Where's my spaniel Troilus? Sirrah, get you hence
And bid my cousin Ferdinand come hither –
                [Exit Servant.]
One, Kate, that you must kiss and be acquainted with.
Where are my slippers? Shall I have some water?
Come, Kate, and wash, and welcome heartily.
You whoreson villain, will you let it fall?
     [Strikes him.]

KATE
Patience, I pray you, 'twas a fault unwilling.

PETRUCHIO
A whoreson, beetle-headed, flap-eared knave!   141
Come, Kate, sit down; I know you have a stomach.   142
Will you give thanks, sweet Kate, or else shall I?   143
What's this, mutton?

1. SERVANT Ay.
                       145

PETRUCHIO Who brought it?

PETER I.

PETRUCHIO
'Tis burnt, and so is all the meat.
What dogs are these! Where is the rascal cook?
How durst you, villains, bring it from the dresser,   150
And serve it thus to me that love it not?
     [He throws it at them.]
There, take it to you, trenchers, cups, and all.   152
You heedless jolt-heads and unmannered slaves!
What, do you grumble? I'll be with you straight.   154
              [Exeunt Servants.]

KATE
I pray you, husband, be not so disquiet.
The meat was well if you were so contented.

PETRUCHIO
I tell thee, Kate, 'twas burnt and dried away,
And I expressly am forbid to touch it,
For it engenders choler, planteth anger,   159
And better 'twere that both of us did fast,
Since of ourselves, ourselves are choleric,
Than feed it with such over-roasted flesh.   162
Be patient. To-morrow 't shall be mended,
And for this night we'll fast in company.
Come, I will bring thee to thy bridal chamber. *Exeunt.* 165
      Enter Servants severally.

NATHANIEL Peter, didst ever see the like?

---

76 *what* why   79 *blue coats* (dark blue was the usual color of a servant's dress)   80 *indifferent* not different, the same, matching   86 *countenance* do honor to (Grumio quibbles on *face*)   91 *credit* pay respect to (Grumio quibbles)   103 *Cock's passion* by God's (Christ's) suffering   113 *swain* lout; *whoreson* contemptible; *malt-horse drudge* brewer's horse which plod-dingly turns a grain mill   114 *park* enclosed tract of land stocked with game   117 *unpinked* without ornamental pattern punched or cut in the leather   118 *link* torch (the smoke being used to blacken hats)   120 *fine* well turned out   125 *those* i.e. the servants   141 *beetle-headed* blockheaded, stupid (the 'head' of a 'beetle', the pounding tool, being usually a heavy block of wood)   142 *stomach* appetite (playing on 'temper')   143 *give thanks* i.e. say grace   145 *1. Servant* (Curtis or Peter)   150 *dresser* sideboard   152 *trenchers* wooden plates   154 *with you* even with you   159 *choler* that 'humor' (hot and dry) which produces anger (roast meat was to be avoided by persons of such disposition)   162 *it* i.e. their choler   165 s.d. *severally* at different doors

167 PETER He kills her in her own humor.

    Enter Curtis.

    GRUMIO Where is he?

    CURTIS In her chamber, making a sermon of continency
    to her,
171 And rails and swears and rates, that she, poor soul,
    Knows not which way to stand, to look, to speak,
    And sits as one new-risen from a dream.
    Away, away, for he is coming hither.   *[Exeunt.]*

    Enter Petruchio.

    PETRUCHIO
175 Thus have I politicly begun my reign,
    And 'tis my hope to end successfully.
177 My falcon now is sharp and passing empty,
178 And till she stoop she must not be full-gorged,
179 For then she never looks upon her lure.
180 Another way I have to man my haggard,
    To make her come and know her keeper's call:
182 That is, to watch her as we watch these kites
183 That bate and beat and will not be obedient.
184 She eat no meat to-day, nor none shall eat.
    Last night she slept not, nor to-night she shall not.
    As with the meat, some undeservèd fault
    I'll find about the making of the bed,
188 And here I'll fling the pillow, there the bolster,
    This way the coverlet, another way the sheets.
190 Ay, and amid this hurly I intend
    That all is done in reverent care of her.
    And in conclusion she shall watch all night,
    And if she chance to nod I'll rail and brawl
    And with the clamor keep her still awake.
195 This is a way to kill a wife with kindness,
196 And thus I'll curb her mad and headstrong humor.
197 He that knows better how to tame a shrew,
    Now let him speak: 'tis charity to show.   *Exit.*

                      *

IV, ii   *Enter Tranio [as Lucentio] and Hortensio [as Litio].*

    TRANIO
    Is't possible, friend Litio, that Mistress Bianca
    Doth fancy any other but Lucentio?
3 I tell you, sir, she bears me fair in hand.

    HORTENSIO
    Sir, to satisfy you in what I have said,
    Stand by and mark the manner of his teaching.
    [They stand aside.]

    Enter Bianca [and Lucentio as Cambio].

    LUCENTIO
6 Now mistress, profit you in what you read?

    BIANCA
7 What, master, read you? First resolve me that.

    LUCENTIO
8 I read that I profess, the Art of Love.

    BIANCA
    And may you prove, sir, master of your art.

    LUCENTIO
    While you, sweet dear, prove mistress of my heart.
    [They stand aside.]

    HORTENSIO *[advancing]*
1 Quick proceeders, marry! Now tell me, I pray,
    You that durst swear that your mistress Bianca
    Loved none in the world so well as Lucentio.

    TRANIO
    O despiteful love, unconstant womankind!   14
    I tell thee, Litio, this is wonderful.   15

    HORTENSIO
    Mistake no more: I am not Litio,
    Nor a musician, as I seem to be,
    But one that scorn to live in this disguise,
    For such a one as leaves a gentleman
    And makes a god of such a cullion.   20
    Know, sir, that I am called Hortensio.

    TRANIO
    Signior Hortensio, I have often heard
    Of your entire affection to Bianca,
    And since mine eyes are witness of her lightness   24
    I will, with you, if you be so contented,
    Forswear Bianca and her love forever.   26

    HORTENSIO
    See how they kiss and court. Signior Lucentio,
    Here is my hand and here I firmly vow
    Never to woo her more, but do forswear her,
    As one unworthy all the former favors
    That I have fondly flattered her withal.   31

    TRANIO
    And here I take the like unfeignèd oath,
    Never to marry with her though she would entreat.
    Fie on her, see how beastly she doth court him.   34

    HORTENSIO
    Would all the world but he had quite forsworn.
    For me, that I may surely keep mine oath,
    I will be married to a wealthy widow
    Ere three days pass, which hath as long loved me
    As I have loved this proud disdainful haggard.   39
    And so farewell, Signior Lucentio.
    Kindness in women, not their beauteous looks,
    Shall win my love – and so I take my leave,
    In resolution as I swore before.   *[Exit.]*

    TRANIO
    Mistress Bianca, bless you with such grace
    As 'longeth to a lover's blessed case.
    Nay, I have ta'en you napping, gentle love,
    And have forsworn you with Hortensio.

    BIANCA *[advancing]*
    Tranio, you jest. But have you both forsworn me?

    TRANIO
    Mistress, we have.

    LUCENTIO   Then we are rid of Litio.

    TRANIO
    I' faith, he'll have a lusty widow now,   50

167 *kills . . . humor* subdues her by displaying the same disposition as hers **171** *rates* berates **175** *politicly* cunningly **177** *sharp* starved **178** *stoop* fly to and seize the lure (playing on 'bow to authority') **179** *lure* feathered wicker container swung up into the air by the falconer to recall a hawk **180** *man* tame (hawking term, with a quibble); *haggard* wild female hawk **182** *watch* keep awake (as in taming a wild hawk); *kites* inferior hawks **183** *bate and beat* flutter and flap the wings **184** *She eat* she ate (pronounced 'et') **188** *bolster* long narrow cushion supporting the pillow **190** *intend* pretend **195** *kill . . . kindness* (ironically, referring to the proverb for spoiling a wife through overindulgence) **196** *humor* disposition **197** *shrow* (the pronunciation indicated by the rhyme was the normal one)
IV, ii Before Baptista's house **3** *bears . . . hand* encourages me **6** *read* study **7** *resolve* answer **8** *the Art of Love* (Ovid's *Ars Amatoria*) **11** *proceeders* candidates for a degree (playing on *master of your art*, marry indeed (originally an oath by the Virgin Mary) **14** *despitefu'* spiteful **15** *wonderful* i.e. a source of wonder **20** *cullion* base fellow **24** *lightness* wantonness **26** *Forswear* swear to renounce **31** *fondly* fooli— **34** *beastly* lasciviously **39** *haggard* wild female hawk **50** *lusty* merry

That shall be wooed and wedded in a day.

BIANCA
God give him joy.

TRANIO
Ay, and he'll tame her.

BIANCA   He says so, Tranio.

TRANIO
Faith, he is gone unto the taming-school.

BIANCA
The taming-school ? What, is there such a place ?

TRANIO
Ay, mistress, and Petruchio is the master,
57   That teacheth tricks eleven and twenty long
To tame a shrew and charm her chattering tongue.
      Enter Biondello.

BIONDELLO
O master, master, I have watched so long
That I am dog-weary, but at last I spied
61   An ancient angel coming down the hill
62   Will serve the turn.

TRANIO   What is he, Biondello ?

BIONDELLO
63   Master, a mercatante or a pedant,
I know not what ; but formal in apparel,
65   In gait and countenance surely like a father.

LUCENTIO
And what of him, Tranio ?

TRANIO
If he be credulous and trust my tale
I'll make him glad to seem Vincentio,
And give assurance to Baptista Minola
As if he were the right Vincentio.
Take in your love and then let me alone.
      [Exeunt Lucentio and Bianca.]
      Enter a Pedant.

PEDANT
God save you, sir.

TRANIO   And you, sir. You are welcome.
73   Travel you far or are you at the farthest ?

PEDANT
Sir, at the farthest for a week or two,
But then up farther and as far as Rome,
And so to Tripoli, if God lend me life.

TRANIO
What countryman, I pray ?

PEDANT   Of Mantua.

TRANIO
Of Mantua, sir ? Marry, God forbid !
And come to Padua, careless of your life ?

PEDANT
80   My life, sir ? How, I pray ? For that goes hard.

TRANIO
'Tis death for anyone in Mantua
To come to Padua. Know you not the cause ?

Your ships are stayed at Venice, and the Duke –
For private quarrel 'twixt your Duke and him –
Hath published and proclaimed it openly.
'Tis marvel, but that you are newly come,
You might have heard it else proclaimed about.

PEDANT
Alas, sir, it is worse for me than so,
For I have bills for money by exchange
From Florence and must here deliver them.   90

TRANIO
Well, sir, to do you courtesy,
This will I do and thus I will advise you –
First, tell me, have you ever been at Pisa ?

PEDANT
Ay, sir, in Pisa have I often been,
Pisa, renownèd for grave citizens.

TRANIO
Among them, know you one Vincentio ?

PEDANT
I know him not but I have heard of him,
A merchant of incomparable wealth.

TRANIO
He is my father, sir, and sooth to say,
In count'nance somewhat doth resemble you.

BIONDELLO *[aside]* As much as an apple doth an oyster,
but all one.   102

TRANIO
To save your life in this extremity
This favor will I do you for his sake,
And think it not the worst of all your fortunes
That you are like to Sir Vincentio.
His name and credit shall you undertake,   107
And in my house you shall be friendly lodged.
Look that you take upon you as you should.   109
You understand me, sir. So shall you stay
Till you have done your business in the city.
If this be court'sy, sir, accept of it.

PEDANT
O sir, I do, and will repute you ever
The patron of my life and liberty.

TRANIO
Then go with me to make the matter good.
This, by the way, I let you understand.   116
My father is here looked for every day
To pass assurance of a dower in marriage   118
'Twixt me and one Baptista's daughter here.
In all these circumstances I'll instruct you.
Go with me to clothe you as becomes you.   *Exeunt.*

         *

      Enter Kate and Grumio.   IV, iii

GRUMIO
No, no, forsooth, I dare not for my life.

KATE
The more my wrong, the more his spite appears.   2
What, did he marry me to famish me ?
Beggars that come unto my father's door,
Upon entreaty have a present alms ;   5
If not, elsewhere they meet with charity.
But I, who never knew how to entreat
Nor never needed that I should entreat,
Am starved for meat, giddy for lack of sleep,   9
With oaths kept waking and with brawling fed.

---

57 *eleven . . . long* i.e. a great many (referring to the card-game of one and thirty)   61 *angel* fellow of the good old stamp (an 'angel' being a gold coin) 62 *the turn* our purposes   63 *mercatante* merchant (the Pedant is actually a merchant, as is shown by his intention of delivering bills of exchange in Padua, ll. 89–90) ; *pedant* schoolmaster   65 *countenance* appearance   73 *at the farthest* i.e. at your destination   80 *goes hard* is serious   102 *all one* no matter   107 *credit* reputation ; *undertake* assume   109 *take upon you* play your part   116 *by the way* along the way, as we go   118 *pass* convey (legal term) ; *assurance* a guarantee
IV, iii Petruchio's house   2 *my wrong* i.e. the wrong done me   5 *present* immediate   9 *meat* food

And that which spites me more than all these wants,
He does it under name of perfect love,
13   As who should say, if I should sleep or eat
'Twere deadly sickness or else present death.
I prithee go and get me some repast,
I care not what, so it be wholesome food.

GRUMIO
17   What say you to a neat's foot?

KATE
'Tis passing good, I prithee let me have it.

GRUMIO
19   I fear it is too choleric a meat.
How say you to a fat tripe finely broiled?

KATE
I like it well, good Grumio, fetch it me.

GRUMIO
I cannot tell; I fear 'tis choleric.
What say you to a piece of beef and mustard?

KATE
A dish that I do love to feed upon.

GRUMIO
Ay, but the mustard is too hot a little.

KATE
Why then, the beef, and let the mustard rest.

GRUMIO
Nay then, I will not; you shall have the mustard
Or else you get no beef of Grumio.

KATE
Then both or one, or anything thou wilt.

GRUMIO
Why then, the mustard without the beef.

KATE
Go, get thee gone, thou false deluding slave,
         Beats him.
32   That feed'st me with the very name of meat.
Sorrow on thee and all the pack of you
That triumph thus upon my misery.
Go, get thee gone, I say.
         Enter Petruchio and Hortensio with meat.

PETRUCHIO
36   How fares my Kate? What, sweeting, all amort?

HORTENSIO
Mistress, what cheer?

KATE   Faith, as cold as can be.

PETRUCHIO
Pluck up thy spirits, look cheerfully upon me.
Here, love, thou seest how diligent I am
40   To dress thy meat myself and bring it thee.
I am sure, sweet Kate, this kindness merits thanks.
What, not a word? Nay then, thou lov'st it not,
43   And all my pains is sorted to no proof.
Here, take away this dish.

KATE   I pray you, let it stand.

PETRUCHIO
The poorest service is repaid with thanks,
And so shall mine before you touch the meat.

KATE
I thank you, sir.

HORTENSIO
Signior Petruchio, fie, you are to blame.
Come, Mistress Kate, I'll bear you company.
         [They sit at table.]

PETRUCHIO *[aside]*
Eat it up all, Hortensio, if thou lov'st me.

Much good do it unto thy gentle heart.
Kate, eat apace. And now, my honey love,   52
Will we return unto thy father's house
And revel it as bravely as the best,   54
With silken coats and caps and golden rings,
With ruffs and cuffs and farthingales and things;   56
With scarfs and fans and double change of brav'ry,   57
With amber bracelets, beads, and all this knav'ry.
What, hast thou dined? The tailor stays thy leisure,
To deck thy body with his ruffling treasure.   60
         Enter Tailor [with a gown].
Come, tailor, let us see these ornaments.
         Enter Haberdasher [with a cap].
Lay forth the gown. – What news with you, sir?

HABERDASHER
Here is the cap your worship did bespeak.   63

PETRUCHIO
Why, this was molded on a porringer: 64
A velvet dish. Fie, fie, 'tis lewd and filthy.   65
Why, 'tis a cockle or a walnut shell,   66
A knack, a toy, a trick, a baby's cap.   67
Away with it. Come, let me have a bigger.

KATE
I'll have no bigger, this doth fit the time,   69
And gentlewomen wear such caps as these.

PETRUCHIO
When you are gentle you shall have one too,
And not till then.

HORTENSIO *[aside]* That will not be in haste.

KATE
Why, sir, I trust I may have leave to speak,
And speak I will. I am no child, no babe.
Your betters have endured me say my mind,
And if you cannot, best you stop your ears.
My tongue will tell the anger of my heart
Or else my heart, concealing it, will break,
And rather than it shall, I will be free
Even to the uttermost, as I please, in words.

PETRUCHIO
Why, thou sayst true. It is a paltry cap,
A custard-coffin, a bauble, a silken pie.   82
I love thee well in that thou lik'st it not.

KATE
Love me or love me not, I like the cap,
And I will have it or I will have none.
         [Exit Haberdasher.]

PETRUCHIO
Thy gown? Why, ay – come, tailor, let us see't.
O mercy, God, what masquing stuff is here?   87
What's this, a sleeve? 'Tis like a demi-cannon.   88
What, up and down carved like an apple tart?   89
Here's snip and nip and cut and slish and slash,
Like to a censer in a barber's shop.   91

---

13 *As who* as though one   17 *neat's foot* ox's or calf's foot   19 *choleric* engendering anger (neat's foot, tripe, and beef, but not mustard, were recommended for persons of choleric disposition)   32 *very* i.e. mere   36 *sweeting* sweetheart; *all amort* spiritless, dejected   40 *dress* prepare   43 *is . . . proof* have resulted in nothing   52 *apace* quickly   54 *bravely* finely dressed   56 *farthingales* hooped petticoats   57 *brav'ry* finery   60 *ruffling* ornamented with ruffles   63 *bespeak* order   64 *porringer* bowl for soup or porridge   65 *lewd* vile   66 *cockle* cockleshell   67 *knack* trinket; *trick* trifle   69 *fit the time* accord with present fashion   82 *custard-coffin* custard-crust; *pie* i.e. meatpie (several inches deep)   87 *masquing* i.e. fit for masques   88 *demi-cannon* large cannon   89 *up and down* in every respect, exactly   91 *censer* brazier in which perfume was burned, the fumes rising through a perforated cover

Why, what a devil's name, tailor, call'st thou this?

HORTENSIO [aside]
I see she's like to have neither cap nor gown.

TAILOR
You bid me make it orderly and well,
According to the fashion and the time.

PETRUCHIO
Marry, I did. But if you be rememb'red,
I did not bid you mar it to the time.
98 Go, hop me over every kennel home,
For you shall hop without my custom, sir.
I'll none of it. Hence, make your best of it.

KATE
I never saw a better-fashioned gown,
102 More quaint, more pleasing, nor more commendable.
103 Belike you mean to make a puppet of me.

PETRUCHIO
Why, true, he means to make a puppet of thee.

TAILOR
She says your worship means to make a puppet of her.

PETRUCHIO
O monstrous arrogance!
Thou liest, thou thread, thou thimble,
108 Thou yard, three-quarters, half-yard, quarter, nail!
109 Thou flea, thou nit, thou winter-cricket thou!
110 Braved in mine own house with a skein of thread?
111 Away, thou rag, thou quantity, thou remnant,
112 Or I shall so bemete thee with thy yard
113 As thou shalt think on prating whilst thou liv'st.
I tell thee, I, that thou hast marred her gown.

TAILOR
Your worship is deceived. The gown is made
Just as my master had direction.
Grumio gave order how it should be done.

GRUMIO I gave him no order, I gave him the stuff.

TAILOR
But how did you desire it should be made?

GRUMIO Marry, sir, with needle and thread.

TAILOR
But did you not request to have it cut?
122 GRUMIO Thou hast faced many things.

TAILOR I have.
124 GRUMIO Face not me. Thou hast braved many men:
brave not me. I will neither be faced nor braved. I say
unto thee, I bid thy master cut out the gown but I did
127 not bid him cut it to pieces. Ergo, thou liest.

TAILOR Why, here is the note of the fashion to testify.

PETRUCHIO Read it.
130 GRUMIO The note lies in's throat if he say I said so.

TAILOR [reads] 'Imprimis, a loose-bodied gown –'   131
GRUMIO Master, if ever I said loose-bodied gown, sew me
in the skirts of it and beat me to death with a bottom of 133
brown thread. I said, a gown.
PETRUCHIO Proceed.
TAILOR 'With a small compassed cape –'   136
GRUMIO I confess the cape.
TAILOR 'With a trunk sleeve –'   138
GRUMIO I confess two sleeves.
TAILOR 'The sleeves curiously cut.'   140
PETRUCHIO Ay, there's the villainy.
GRUMIO Error i' th' bill, sir, error i' th' bill. I comman-
ded the sleeves should be cut out and sewed up again,
and that I'll prove upon thee, though thy little finger be 144
armed in a thimble.
TAILOR This is true that I say. An I had thee in place 146
where thou shouldst know it.
GRUMIO I am for thee straight. Take thou the bill, give 148
me thy mete-yard, and spare not me.   149
HORTENSIO God-a-mercy, Grumio, then he shall have
no odds.
PETRUCHIO Well, sir, in brief, the gown is not for me.
GRUMIO You are i' th' right, sir, 'tis for my mistress.
PETRUCHIO Go, take it up unto thy master's use.   154
GRUMIO Villain, not for thy life. Take up my mistress'
gown for thy master's use!
PETRUCHIO Why, sir, what's your conceit in that?   157
GRUMIO
O sir, the conceit is deeper than you think for.
Take up my mistress' gown to his master's use!
O, fie, fie, fie!
PETRUCHIO [aside]
Hortensio, say thou wilt see the tailor paid.
[To Tailor]
Go take it hence, be gone and say no more.
HORTENSIO
Tailor, I'll pay thee for thy gown to-morrow.
Take no unkindness of his hasty words.
Away, I say. Commend me to thy master.   Exit Tailor.
PETRUCHIO
Well, come, my Kate; we will unto your father's,
Even in these honest mean habiliments.   167
Our purses shall be proud, our garments poor,
For 'tis the mind that makes the body rich;
And as the sun breaks through the darkest clouds
So honor peereth in the meanest habit.   171
What, is the jay more precious than the lark
Because his feathers are more beautiful?
Or is the adder better than the eel
Because his painted skin contents the eye?
O no, good Kate; neither art thou the worse
For this poor furniture and mean array.   177
If thou account'st it shame, lay it on me.
And therefore frolic; we will hence forthwith   179
To feast and sport us at thy father's house.
[To Grumio]
Go call my men, and let us straight to him;
And bring our horses unto Long-lane end.
There will we mount, and thither walk on foot.
Let's see, I think 'tis now some seven o'clock,
And well we may come there by dinnertime.   185
KATE
I dare assure you, sir, 'tis almost two,
And 'twill be suppertime ere you come there.

98 *kennel* channel, gutter   102 *quaint* handsome   103 *Belike* likely; *puppet* (contemptuous term for a woman)   108 *nail* two and a quarter inches (a measure of length for cloth)   109 *nit* louse's egg   110 *Braved* defied; *with* by   111 *quantity* fragment   112 *bemete* bemeasure (i.e. beat); *yard* yard-stick   113 *think on* consider carefully before   122 *faced* trimmed (followed by a quibble, in *Face*, on 'bully')   124 *braved* dressed finely (followed by a quibble, in *brave*, on 'defy')   127 *Ergo* therefore   130 *in's throat* foully, infamously; *he* it   131 *Imprimis* first; *loose-bodied gown* (sort of dress worn by prostitutes)   133 *bottom* ball   136 *compassed* i.e. with the edge forming a circle   138 *trunk* i.e. very full   140 *curiously* elaborately   144 *prove upon* maintain by fighting with   146–47 *in place where* in a fit place   148 *bill* (playing on 'halberd')   149 *mete-yard* measuring-stick   154 *use* i.e. whatever use he can put it to (but Grumio quibbles bawdily)   157 *conceit* meaning   167 *habiliments* clothes   171 *peereth* is seen; *habit* dress   177 *furniture* clothing   179 *hence* i.e. go hence; *forthwith* immediately   185 *dinnertime* about noon

PETRUCHIO
It shall be seven ere I go to horse.
189 Look what I speak or do or think to do,
You are still crossing it. Sirs, let 't alone.
I will not go to-day, and ere I do,
It shall be what o'clock I say it is.

HORTENSIO
Why, so this gallant will command the sun.   *[Exeunt.]*

*

IV, iv   *Enter Tranio [as Lucentio] and the Pedant booted*
    and dressed like Vincentio.

TRANIO
Sir, this is the house. Please it you that I call?

PEDANT
2 Ay, what else? And but I be deceived,
3 Signior Baptista may remember me,
Near twenty years ago, in Genoa,
5 Where we were lodgers at the Pegasus.

TRANIO
'Tis well, and hold your own in any case
With such austerity as longeth to a father.
    Enter Biondello.

PEDANT
I warrant you. But sir, here comes your boy;
9 'Twere good he were schooled.

TRANIO
Fear you not him. Sirrah Biondello,
11 Now do your duty throughly, I advise you.
Imagine 'twere the right Vincentio.

BIONDELLO
Tut, fear not me.

TRANIO
But hast thou done thy errand to Baptista?

BIONDELLO
I told him that your father was at Venice,
And that you looked for him this day in Padua.

TRANIO
17 Th'art a tall fellow. Hold thee that to drink.
    [Gives money.]
18 Here comes Baptista. Set your countenance, sir.
    Enter Baptista and Lucentio [as Cambio]. Pedant
    bareheaded.
19 Signior Baptista, you are happily met.
    [To Pedant]
Sir, this is the gentleman I told you of.
I pray you, stand good father to me now,
Give me Bianca for my patrimony.

PEDANT
Soft, son.
Sir, by your leave. Having come to Padua
To gather in some debts, my son Lucentio
Made me acquainted with a weighty cause
Of love between your daughter and himself.
And – for the good report I hear of you,
And for the love he beareth to your daughter,
And she to him – to stay him not too long,
I am content, in a good father's care,
To have him matched. And if you please to like
No worse than I, upon some agreement
Me shall you find ready and willing
With one consent to have her so bestowed.
36 For curious I cannot be with you,
Signior Baptista, of whom I hear so well.

BAPTISTA
Sir, pardon me in what I have to say.
Your plainness and your shortness please me well.
Right true it is, your son Lucentio here
Doth love my daughter, and she loveth him –
Or both dissemble deeply their affections.
And therefore if you say no more than this,
That like a father you will deal with him
And pass my daughter a sufficient dower,   45
The match is made and all is done:
Your son shall have my daughter with consent.

TRANIO
I thank you, sir. Where then do you know best
We be affied and such assurance ta'en   49
As shall with either part's agreement stand?

BAPTISTA
Not in my house, Lucentio, for you know
Pitchers have ears, and I have many servants.
Besides, old Gremio is heark'ning still,   53
And happily we might be interrupted.   54

TRANIO
Then at my lodging, an it like you.   55
There doth my father lie, and there this night   56
We'll pass the business privately and well.   57
Send for your daughter by your servant here.
My boy shall fetch the scrivener presently.   59
The worst is this, that at so slender warning
You are like to have a thin and slender pittance.   61

BAPTISTA
It likes me well. Cambio, hie you home
And bid Bianca make her ready straight.
And if you will, tell what hath happenèd:
Lucentio's father is arrived in Padua,
And how she's like to be Lucentio's wife.
    [Exit Lucentio.]

BIONDELLO
I pray the gods she may with all my heart.   *Exit.*

TRANIO
Dally not with the gods, but get thee gone.
Signior Baptista, shall I lead the way?
Welcome, one mess is like to be your cheer.   70
Come, sir, we will better it in Pisa.

BAPTISTA
I follow you.   *Exeunt.*
    Enter [severally] Lucentio [as Cambio] and Biondello.

BIONDELLO Cambio!

LUCENTIO What sayst thou, Biondello?

BIONDELLO You saw my master wink and laugh upon
you?

LUCENTIO Biondello, what of that?

BIONDELLO Faith, nothing, but 'has left me here behind 77
to expound the meaning or moral of his signs and tokens. 78

LUCENTIO I pray thee, moralize them.   79

189 *Look what* whatever
IV, iv Before Baptista's house s.d. *booted* (as from travelling) 2 *but*
unless 3 *may remember me* (the Pedant is rehearsing his part) 5 *Pegasus*
(common name for an inn, after the winged horse of classical mythology)
9 *schooled* instructed how to play his part 11 *throughly* thoroughly 17 *tall*
fine 18 s.d. *bareheaded* (the Pedant doffs his cap to Baptista) 19 *happily*
luckily 36 *curious* overparticular 45 *pass* settle upon 49 *affied* betrothed 53 *heark'ning still* continually eavesdropping 54 *happily* haply,
perchance 55 *an it like you* if you please 56 *lie* lodge 57 *pass* transact
59 *scrivener* scribe specializing in legal agreements 61 *pittance* portion of
food 70 *mess* dish; *cheer* entertainment 77 *'has* he has 78 *moral* hidden
meaning 79 *moralize* explain

BIONDELLO Then thus. Baptista is safe, talking with the
deceiving father of a deceitful son.
LUCENTIO And what of him?
BIONDELLO His daughter is to be brought by you to the
supper.
LUCENTIO And then?
BIONDELLO The old priest at Saint Luke's church is at
your command at all hours.
LUCENTIO And what of all this?
90 BIONDELLO I cannot tell, except they are busied about a
counterfeit assurance. Take you assurance of her, 'cum
privilegio ad imprimendum solum.' To th' church with
the priest, clerk, and some sufficient honest witnesses.
If this be not that you look for, I have no more to say,
But bid Bianca farewell forever and a day.
LUCENTIO Hear'st thou, Biondello?
BIONDELLO I cannot tarry. I knew a wench married in an
afternoon as she went to the garden for parsley to stuff
a rabbit, and so may you, sir, and so adieu, sir. My
master hath appointed me to go to Saint Luke's, to bid
101 the priest be ready against you come with your appendix.
                                                    Exit.
LUCENTIO
I may and will, if she be so contented.
She will be pleased, then wherefore should I doubt?
104 Hap what hap may, I'll roundly go about her.
It shall go hard if Cambio go without her.   *Exit.*

*

IV, v   *Enter Petruchio, Kate, Hortensio [and Grumio, with
          Attendants].*
PETRUCHIO
1 Come on, a God's name, once more toward our father's.
Good Lord, how bright and goodly shines the moon!
KATE
The moon? The sun. It is not moonlight now.
PETRUCHIO
I say it is the moon that shines so bright.
KATE
I know it is the sun that shines so bright.
PETRUCHIO
Now by my mother's son, and that's myself,
7 It shall be moon or star or what I list,
8 Or e'er I journey to your father's house.
    [To Servants]
Go on and fetch our horses back again.
Evermore crossed and crossed, nothing but crossed.
HORTENSIO *[aside to Kate]*
Say as he says or we shall never go.
KATE
Forward, I pray, since we have come so far,

90 *assurance* agreement (the betrothal); *Take you assurance* make yourself
sure 90–91 *cum privilegio . . . solum* with sole rights of printing (copyright
formula; with a play on the husband's conjugal rights, exercise of which
will 'assure' the marriage) 101 *against you come* in anticipation of your
coming; *appendix* adjunct (i.e. bride) 104 *roundly* straightway; *go about
her* seek her out
IV, v A country road 1 *a* in 7 *list* please 8 *Or ere*, before 14 *rush-
candle* rush dipped in grease to serve as candle 22 *still* always 24 *bowl*
ball in game of bowls 25 *unluckily* unsuccessfully; *against the bias* contrary to designed course (the 'bias' being a weight in the side of the bowl
which enables the bowler to roll it in a curve) 35 *'A* he 44 *father* (respectful term of address to an old man) 46 *green* i.e. young 53 *encounter*
manner of greeting

And be it moon or sun or what you please.
An if you please to call it a rush-candle,
14 Henceforth I vow it shall be so for me.
PETRUCHIO
I say it is the moon.
KATE   I know it is the moon.
PETRUCHIO
Nay, then you lie. It is the blessèd sun.
KATE
Then God be blessed, it is the blessèd sun,
But sun it is not when you say it is not,
And the moon changes even as your mind.
What you will have it named, even that it is,
22 And so it shall be still for Katherine.
HORTENSIO
Petruchio, go thy ways, the field is won.
PETRUCHIO
24 Well, forward, forward! Thus the bowl should run,
25 And not unluckily against the bias.
But soft, what company is coming here?
    Enter Vincentio.
    [To Vincentio]
Good morrow, gentle mistress, where away?
Tell me, sweet Kate, and tell me truly too,
Hast thou beheld a fresher gentlewoman?
Such war of white and red within her cheeks!
What stars do spangle heaven with such beauty
As those two eyes become that heavenly face?
Fair lovely maid, once more good day to thee.
Sweet Kate, embrace her for her beauty's sake.
HORTENSIO *[aside]*
35 'A will make the man mad, to make a woman of him.
KATE
Young budding virgin, fair and fresh and sweet,
Whither away, or where is thy abode?
Happy the parents of so fair a child,
Happier the man whom favorable stars
Allots thee for his lovely bedfellow.
PETRUCHIO
Why, how now, Kate, I hope thou art not mad.
This is a man, old, wrinkled, faded, withered,
And not a maiden, as thou sayst he is.
KATE
44 Pardon, old father, my mistaking eyes
That have been so bedazzled with the sun
46 That everything I look on seemeth green.
Now I perceive thou art a reverend father.
Pardon, I pray thee, for my mad mistaking.
PETRUCHIO
Do, good old grandsire, and withal make known
Which way thou travell'st. If along with us,
We shall be joyful of thy company.
VINCENTIO
Fair sir, and you my merry mistress,
53 That with your strange encounter much amazed me,
My name is called Vincentio, my dwelling Pisa,
And bound I am to Padua, there to visit
A son of mine, which long I have not seen.
PETRUCHIO
What is his name?
VINCENTIO   Lucentio, gentle sir.
PETRUCHIO
Happily met, the happier for thy son.
And now by law, as well as reverend age,

I may entitle thee my loving father.
The sister to my wife, this gentlewoman,
62 Thy son by this hath married. Wonder not
63 Nor be not grieved. She is of good esteem,
Her dowry wealthy, and of worthy birth;
65 Beside, so qualified as may beseem
The spouse of any noble gentleman.
Let me embrace with old Vincentio,
And wander we to see thy honest son,
Who will of thy arrival be full joyous.

VINCENTIO
But is this true, or is it else your pleasure,
71 Like pleasant travellers, to break a jest
Upon the company you overtake?

HORTENSIO
I do assure thee, father, so it is.

PETRUCHIO
Come, go along, and see the truth hereof,
75 For our first merriment hath made thee jealous.
                              Exeunt [all but Hortensio].

HORTENSIO
Well, Petruchio, this has put me in heart.
77 Have to my widow, and if she be froward,
78 Then hast thou taught Hortensio to be untoward. *Exit.*

*

V, i   *Enter Biondello, Lucentio [as Cambio], and Bianca.*
        Gremio is out before [and stands aside].
BIONDELLO Softly and swiftly, sir, for the priest is ready.
LUCENTIO I fly, Biondello – but they may chance to need
    thee at home; therefore leave us.   *Exit [with Bianca].*
4 BIONDELLO Nay, faith, I'll see the church a your back,
    and then come back to my master as soon as I can. *[Exit.]*
GREMIO
    I marvel Cambio comes not all this while.
        Enter Petruchio, Kate, Vincentio, [and] Grumio,
        with Attendants.
PETRUCHIO
    Sir, here's the door, this is Lucentio's house.
8   My father's bears more toward the market-place.
    Thither must I, and here I leave you, sir.
VINCENTIO
    You shall not choose but drink before you go.
    I think I shall command your welcome here,
    And by all likelihood some cheer is toward.
        Knock.
GREMIO *[advancing]* They're busy within; you were best
14 knock louder.
        Pedant [as Vincentio] looks out of the window.
15 PEDANT What's he that knocks as he would beat down
    the gate?
VINCENTIO Is Signior Lucentio within, sir?
18 PEDANT He's within, sir, but not to be spoken withal.
VINCENTIO What if a man bring him a hundred pound
    or two, to make merry withal?
PEDANT Keep your hundred pounds to yourself. He shall
    need none so long as I live.
PETRUCHIO Nay, I told you your son was well beloved in
    Padua. Do you hear sir? To leave frivolous circumstan-
    ces, I pray you tell Signior Lucentio that his father is
    come from Pisa and is here at the door to speak with him.
PEDANT Thou liest. His father is come from Pisa and
    is here looking out at the window.
VINCENTIO Art thou his father?

PEDANT Ay sir, so his mother says, if I may believe her.
PETRUCHIO *[to Vincentio]* Why how now, gentleman!
    Why this is flat knavery, to take upon you another man's 32
    name.
PEDANT Lay hands on the villain. I believe 'a means to
    cozen somebody in this city under my countenance. 34
        Enter Biondello.
BIONDELLO I have seen them in the church together.
    God send 'em good shipping! But who is here? Mine 36
    old master, Vincentio! Now we are undone and brought 37
    to nothing.
VINCENTIO Come hither, crack-hemp. 39
BIONDELLO I hope I may choose, sir. 40
VINCENTIO Come hither, you rogue. What, have you
    forgot me?
BIONDELLO Forgot you? No sir. I could not forget you,
    for I never saw you before in all my life.
VINCENTIO What, you notorious villain, didst thou
    never see thy master's father, Vincentio?
BIONDELLO What, my worshipful old master? Yes,
    marry, sir, see where he looks out of the window.
VINCENTIO Is't so indeed?
        He beats Biondello.
BIONDELLO Help, help, help! Here's a madman will
    murder me.   *[Exit.]*
PEDANT Help, son! Help, Signior Baptista! *[Exit above.]*
PETRUCHIO Prithee, Kate, let's stand aside and see the
    end of this controversy.   *[They stand aside.]*
        Enter [below] Pedant [as Vincentio] with Servants,
        Baptista, [and] Tranio [as Lucentio].
TRANIO Sir, what are you that offer to beat my servant? 55
VINCENTIO What am I, sir? Nay, what are you, sir? O
    immortal gods! O fine villain! A silken doublet, a velvet
    hose, a scarlet cloak, and a copatain hat! O I am undone, 58
    I am undone! While I play the good husband at home, 59
    my son and my servants spend all at the university.
TRANIO How now, what's the matter?
BAPTISTA What, is the man lunatic?
TRANIO Sir, you seem a sober ancient gentleman by your
    habit, but your words show you a madman. Why sir, 64
    what 'cerns it you if I wear pearl and gold? I thank my 65
    good father, I am able to maintain it.
VINCENTIO Thy father! O villain, he is a sailmaker in
    Bergamo.
BAPTISTA You mistake, sir, you mistake, sir. Pray, what
    do you think is his name?
VINCENTIO His name? As if I knew not his name! I have
    brought him up ever since he was three years old, and
    his name is Tranio.
PEDANT Away, away, mad ass! His name is Lucentio.
    He is mine only son, and heir to the lands of me, Signior
    Vincentio.
VINCENTIO Lucentio? O he hath murd'red his master!
    Lay hold on him, I charge you in the Duke's name. O

---

62 *by this* by this time   63 *esteem* reputation   65 *so qualified* having such
qualities   71 *pleasant* merry   75 *jealous* suspicious   77 *Have to* now for
78 *untoward* perverse
V, i Before Lucentio's house   s.d. *out before* i.e. on stage first (he enters
before the others, whom he does not 'see')   4 *a* on   8 *bears* lies (nautical
term)   14 s.d. *looks . . . window* i.e. appears in the tiring-house gallery over
the stage   15 *What* who   18 *withal* with   32 *flat* downright   34 *cozen*
cheat; *under my countenance* by posing as me   36 *good shipping* fair sailing
37 *undone* ruined   39 *crack-hemp* fellow ripe for hanging   40 *choose* do as I
choose   55 *what* who   58 *copatain* high-crowned   59 *good husband* careful
manager   64 *habit* bearing   65 *'cerns* concerns

my son, my son! Tell me, thou villain, where is my son
Lucentio?

TRANIO *[to a Servant]* Call forth an officer.
[Enter an Officer.]
83 Carry this mad knave to the jail. Father Baptista, I
charge you see that he be forthcoming.

VINCENTIO Carry me to the jail!

GREMIO Stay, officer, he shall not go to prison.

BAPTISTA Talk not, Signior Gremio. I say he shall go to
prison.

88 GREMIO Take heed, Signior Baptista, lest you be cony-
catched in this business. I dare swear this is the right
Vincentio.

PEDANT Swear, if thou dar'st.

GREMIO Nay, I dare not swear it.

93 TRANIO Then thou wert best say that I am not Lucentio.

GREMIO Yes, I know thee to be Signior Lucentio.

BAPTISTA Away with the dotard, to the jail with him!
Enter Biondello, Lucentio, and Bianca.

96 VINCENTIO Thus strangers may be halèd and abused.
O monstrous villain!

BIONDELLO O we are spoiled, yonder he is. Deny him,
forswear him, or else we are all undone.
Exeunt Biondello, Tranio, and Pedant
as fast as may be.

LUCENTIO Pardon, sweet father.
Kneel.

VINCENTIO Lives my sweet son?

BIANCA Pardon, dear father.

BAPTISTA
How hast thou offended? Where is Lucentio?

LUCENTIO
Here's Lucentio, right son to the right Vincentio,
That have by marriage made thy daughter mine
106 While counterfeit supposes bleared thine eyne.

GREMIO
107 Here's packing, with a witness, to deceive us all!

VINCENTIO
Where is that damnèd villain Tranio,
That faced and braved me in this matter so?

BAPTISTA
Why, tell me, is not this my Cambio?

BIANCA
Cambio is changed into Lucentio.

LUCENTIO
Love wrought these miracles. Bianca's love
Made me exchange my state with Tranio
114 While he did bear my countenance in the town,
And happily I have arrivèd at the last
Unto the wishèd haven of my bliss.
What Tranio did, myself enforced him to;
Then pardon him, sweet father, for my sake.

VINCENTIO I'll slit the villain's nose that would have
sent me to the jail.

BAPTISTA *[to Lucentio]* But do you hear, sir? Have you
married my daughter without asking my good will?

VINCENTIO Fear not, Baptista, we will content you, go to. 123
But I will in, to be revenged for this villainy. *Exit.*

BAPTISTA And I, to sound the depth of this knavery.
Exit.

LUCENTIO Look not pale, Bianca, thy father will not
frown. *Exeunt [Lucentio and Bianca].*

GREMIO
My cake is dough, but I'll in among the rest, 127
Out of hope of all but my share of the feast. *[Exit.]*

KATE *[advancing]* Husband, let's follow, to see the end of
this ado.

PETRUCHIO First kiss me, Kate, and we will.

KATE What, in the midst of the street?

PETRUCHIO What, art thou ashamed of me?

KATE No sir, God forbid, but ashamed to kiss.

PETRUCHIO
Why, then let's home again.
[To Grumio] Come, sirrah, let's away.

KATE
Nay, I will give thee a kiss. Now pray thee, love, stay.

PETRUCHIO
Is not this well? Come, my sweet Kate.
Better once than never, for never's too late. *Exeunt.* 138

*

Enter Baptista, Vincentio, Gremio, the Pedant, V, ii
Lucentio, and Bianca; Tranio, Biondello, [and]
Grumio; [Petruchio, Kate, Hortensio,] and Widow;
the Servingmen with Tranio bringing in a banquet.

LUCENTIO
At last, though long, our jarring notes agree, 1
And time it is, when raging war is done,
To smile at 'scapes and perils overblown.
My fair Bianca, bid my father welcome
While I with self-same kindness welcome thine.
Brother Petruchio, sister Katherina,
And thou, Hortensio, with thy loving widow,
Feast with the best and welcome to my house.
My banquet is to close our stomachs up
After our great good cheer. Pray you, sit down, 10
For now we sit to chat as well as eat.
[They sit at table.]

PETRUCHIO
Nothing but sit and sit, and eat and eat!

BAPTISTA
Padua affords this kindness, son Petruchio.

PETRUCHIO
Padua affords nothing but what is kind.

HORTENSIO
For both our sakes I would that word were true.

PETRUCHIO
Now, for my life, Hortensio fears his widow. 16

WIDOW
Then never trust me if I be afeard. 17

PETRUCHIO
You are very sensible, and yet you miss my sense:
I mean Hortensio is afeard of you.

WIDOW
He that is giddy thinks the world turns round.

PETRUCHIO
Roundly replied. 21

---

83 *forthcoming* i.e. to stand trial 88–89 *cony-catched* duped 93 *wert best*
might as well 96 *halèd* hauled about, molested 106 *counterfeit supposes*
false assumptions (with an allusion to Gascoigne's play, the *Supposes*); *eyne*
eyes 107 *packing* plotting; *with a witness* with a vengeance 114 *bear my*
countenance pose as me 123 *go to* (expression of impatience) 127 *My cake*
is dough i.e. my hopes are dashed (proverbial) 138 *Better . . . late* i.e. better
late than never (proverbial); *once* at one time or another
V, ii Lucentio's house s.d. *bringing in* i.e. carrying onstage; *banquet*
dessert (sweetmeats, fruit, wine) 1 *long* after a long time 10 *After . . . cheer*
(Lucentio's banquet apparently follows a bridal feast given by Baptista) 16
fears is afraid of (the Widow quibbles on 'frightens') 17 *afeard* frightened
(Petruchio quibbles on 'suspicious') 21 *Roundly* straightforwardly

KATE   Mistress, how mean you that?
WIDOW
22 Thus I conceive by him.
PETRUCHIO
Conceive by me? How likes Hortensio that?
HORTENSIO
24 My widow says, thus she conceives her tale.
PETRUCHIO
Very well mended. Kiss him for that, good widow.
KATE
'He that is giddy thinks the world turns round' –
I pray you, tell me what you meant by that.
WIDOW
Your husband, being troubled with a shrow,
29 Measures my husband's sorrow by his woe –
And now you know my meaning.
KATE
31 A very mean meaning.
WIDOW   Right, I mean you.
KATE
32 And I am mean indeed, respecting you.
PETRUCHIO
To her, Kate!
HORTENSIO
To her, widow!
PETRUCHIO
35 A hundred marks, my Kate does put her down.
HORTENSIO
That's my office.
PETRUCHIO
Spoke like an officer – ha' to thee, lad.
        Drinks to Hortensio.
BAPTISTA
How likes Gremio these quick-witted folks?
GREMIO
Believe me, sir, they butt together well.
BIANCA
Head and butt! An hasty-witted body
41 Would say your head and butt were head and horn.
VINCENTIO
Ay, mistress bride, hath that awakened you?
BIANCA
Ay, but not frighted me; therefore I'll sleep again.
PETRUCHIO
Nay, that you shall not; since you have begun,
45 Have at you for a bitter jest or two.
BIANCA
Am I your bird? I mean to shift my bush,
And then pursue me as you draw your bow.
You are welcome all. *Exit Bianca [with Kate and Widow].*
PETRUCHIO
49 She hath prevented me. Here, Signior Tranio,
This bird you aimed at, though you hit her not.
Therefore a health to all that shot and missed.
TRANIO
52 O sir, Lucentio slipped me, like his greyhound,
Which runs himself and catches for his master.
PETRUCHIO
A good swift simile but something currish.
TRANIO
'Tis well, sir, that you hunted for yourself;
56 'Tis thought your deer does hold you at a bay.
BAPTISTA
O ho, Petruchio! Tranio hits you now.

LUCENTIO
I thank thee for that gird, good Tranio.   58
HORTENSIO
Confess, confess, hath he not hit you here?
PETRUCHIO
'A has a little galled me, I confess,   60
And as the jest did glance away from me,
'Tis ten to one it maimed you two outright.
BAPTISTA
Now, in good sadness, son Petruchio,   63
I think thou hast the veriest shrew of all.   64
PETRUCHIO
Well, I say no. And therefore, for assurance,   65
Let's each one send unto his wife,
And he whose wife is most obedient,
To come at first when he doth send for her,
Shall win the wager which we will propose.
HORTENSIO
Content. What's the wager?
LUCENTIO   Twenty crowns.
PETRUCHIO
Twenty crowns?
I'll venture so much of my hawk or hound,   72
But twenty times so much upon my wife.
LUCENTIO
A hundred then.
HORTENSIO   Content.
PETRUCHIO   A match, 'tis done.   74
HORTENSIO
Who shall begin?
LUCENTIO
That will I.
Go, Biondello, bid your mistress come to me.
BIONDELLO I go.   *Exit.*
BAPTISTA
Son, I'll be your half, Bianca comes.   79
LUCENTIO
I'll have no halves; I'll bear it all myself.
        Enter Biondello.
How now, what news?
BIONDELLO
Sir, my mistress sends you word
That she is busy and she cannot come.
PETRUCHIO
How? 'She's busy and she cannot come'?
Is that an answer?
GREMIO   Ay, and a kind one too.
Pray God, sir, your wife send you not a worse.
PETRUCHIO I hope better.
HORTENSIO Sirrah Biondello, go and entreat my wife to
  come to me forthwith.   *Exit Biondello.* 89

22 *conceive by* am inspired by (Petruchio quibbles on 'become pregnant by') 24 *conceives* devises 29 *Measures* judges 31 *mean* contemptible (the Widow quibbles on 'have in mind,' and Kate then quibbles on 'moderate,' i.e. in shrewishness) 32 *respecting* compared with 35 *put her down* defeat her (Hortensio quibbles bawdily) 41 *Would say . . . horn* (meaning uncertain; 'horn' may involve the common Elizabethan joke about cuckoldry or a play on 'phallus' or both) 45 *Have . . . for* let's exchange; *bitter* sharp 49 *prevented* forestalled; *Signior* (ironically) 52 *slipped* unleashed 56 *deer* (punning on 'dear'); *hold you at a bay* (like a hunted animal that turns to fight and thus keeps the hounds baying at a distance) 58 *gird* taunt 60 *galled* annoyed 63 *sadness* seriousness 64 *veriest* most perfect 65 *assurance* proof 72 *of* on 74 *match* bet 79 *be your half* take half your bet that 89 *forthwith* immediately

PETRUCHIO O ho, 'entreat her'! Nay, then she must
   needs come.
HORTENSIO I am afraid, sir, do what you can, yours will
   not be entreated. (*Enter Biondello.*) Now where's my
   wife?
BIONDELLO
   She says you have some goodly jest in hand.
   She will not come. She bids you come to her.
PETRUCHIO
   Worse and worse, 'she will not come'!
   O vile, intolerable, not to be endured!
   Sirrah Grumio, go to your mistress,
   Say I command her come to me.   *Exit [Grumio].*
HORTENSIO I know her answer.
PETRUCHIO What?
HORTENSIO She will not.
PETRUCHIO
   The fouler fortune mine, and there an end.
       Enter Kate [with Grumio].
BAPTISTA
104   Now, by my halidom, here comes Katherina!
KATE
   What is your will, sir, that you send for me?
PETRUCHIO
   Where is your sister and Hortensio's wife?
KATE
   They sit conferring by the parlor fire.
PETRUCHIO
   Go fetch them hither. If they deny to come,
109   Swinge me them soundly forth unto their husbands.
   Away, I say, and bring them hither straight. *[Exit Kate.]*
LUCENTIO
   Here is a wonder, if you talk of a wonder.
HORTENSIO
   And so it is. I wonder what it bodes.
PETRUCHIO
   Marry, peace it bodes, and love, and quiet life,
114   An awful rule and right supremacy,
   And, to be short, what not that's sweet and happy.
BAPTISTA
116   Now fair befall thee, good Petruchio.
   The wager thou hast won, and I will add
   Unto their losses twenty thousand crowns,
   Another dowry to another daughter,
   For she is changed as she had never been.
PETRUCHIO
   Nay, I will win my wager better yet
   And show more sign of her obedience,
   Her new-built virtue and obedience.
       Enter Kate, Bianca, and Widow.
   See where she comes and brings your froward wives
   As prisoners to her womanly persuasion.
   Katherine, that cap of yours becomes you not.
   Off with the bauble, throw it under foot.
       [She obeys.]

WIDOW
   Lord, let me never have a cause to sigh
   Till I be brought to such a silly pass.   129
BIANCA
   Fie, what a foolish duty call you this?
LUCENTIO
   I would your duty were as foolish too.
   The wisdom of your duty, fair Bianca,
   Hath cost me a hundred crowns since suppertime.
BIANCA
   The more fool you for laying on my duty.   134
PETRUCHIO
   Katherine, I charge thee, tell these headstrong women
   What duty they do owe their lords and husbands.
WIDOW
   Come, come, you're mocking; we will have no telling.
PETRUCHIO
   Come on, I say, and first begin with her.
WIDOW
   She shall not.
PETRUCHIO
   I say she shall – and first begin with her.
KATE
   Fie, fie, unknit that threat'ning unkind brow   141
   And dart not scornful glances from those eyes
   To wound thy lord, thy king, thy governor.   143
   It blots thy beauty as frosts do bite the meads,
   Confounds thy fame as whirlwinds shake fair buds,   145
   And in no sense is meet or amiable.
   A woman moved is like a fountain troubled,   147
   Muddy, ill-seeming, thick, bereft of beauty,
   And while it is so, none so dry or thirsty
   Will deign to sip or touch one drop of it.
   Thy husband is thy lord, thy life, thy keeper,
   Thy head, thy sovereign; one that cares for thee   152
   And for thy maintenance; commits his body
   To painful labor both by sea and land,
   To watch the night in storms, the day in cold,
   Whilst thou li'st warm at home, secure and safe;
   And craves no other tribute at thy hands
   But love, fair looks, and true obedience –
   Too little payment for so great a debt.
   Such duty as the subject owes the prince,   160
   Even such a woman oweth to her husband;
   And when she is froward, peevish, sullen, sour,   162
   And not obedient to his honest will,
   What is she but a foul contending rebel
   And graceless traitor to her loving lord?
   I am ashamed that women are so simple   166
   To offer war where they should kneel for peace,
   Or seek for rule, supremacy, and sway,
   When they are bound to serve, love, and obey.
   Why are our bodies soft and weak and smooth,
   Unapt to toil and trouble in the world,   171
   But that our soft conditions and our hearts   172
   Should well agree with our external parts?
   Come, come, you froward and unable worms,   174
   My mind hath been as big as one of yours,   175
   My heart as great, my reason haply more,
   To bandy word for word and frown for frown.   177
   But now I see our lances are but straws,
   Our strength as weak, our weakness past compare,
   That seeming to be most which we indeed least are.
   Then vail your stomachs, for it is no boot,   181

104 *by my halidom* bless my soul (originally an oath by a sacred relic)
109 *Swinge* whip   114 *awful* commanding respect   116 *fair befall thee* good
luck to you   129 *pass* predicament   134 *laying* betting   141 *unkind* un-
amiable   143 *governor* ruler   145 *Confounds thy fame* spoils your good
name   147 *moved* angry   152 *head* commander   160 *prince* monarch   162
peevish refractory, self-willed   166 *simple* foolish   171 *Unapt to* unsuited
for   172 *conditions* qualities   174 *unable* feeble; *worms* i.e. pitiful creatures
175 *big* haughty   177 *bandy* exchange (as in hitting a tennis ball back and
forth)   181 *vail your stomachs* curb your willfulness; *no boot* no use

And place your hands below your husband's foot,
In token of which duty, if he please,
184 My hand is ready, may it do him ease.

PETRUCHIO
Why, there's a wench! Come on and kiss me, Kate!

LUCENTIO
Well, go thy ways, old lad, for thou shalt ha't.

VINCENTIO
187 'Tis a good hearing when children are toward.

LUCENTIO
But a harsh hearing when women are froward.

PETRUCHIO
Come, Kate, we'll to bed.
190 We three are married, but you two are sped.

          [To Lucentio]
'Twas I won the wager, though you hit the white,   191
And being a winner, God give you good night.
                 Exit Petruchio [with Kate].

HORTENSIO
Now, go thy ways, thou hast tamed a curst shrow.

LUCENTIO
'Tis a wonder, by your leave, she will be tamèd so.
                       [Exeunt.]

184 *may it* if it may   187 *a good hearing* i.e. good news; *toward* docile   190 *sped* done for (through having disobedient wives)   191 *white* bull's-eye (playing on *Bianca*, white)

APPENDIX: THE HISTORY AND TEXT OF THE PLAY

The history of *The Taming of the Shrew* is complicated by the existence of an anonymous play entitled *The Taming of a Shrew*, printed in 1594. This was once thought to be a source of Shakespeare's *Shrew* but is now usually assumed to be a "bad" quarto, or memorial reconstruction. Because of the puzzling fact that, despite a rough agreement in plot and characterization, the scene and most of the names of *A Shrew* differ radically from those of *The Shrew*, certain textual scholars, notably G. I. Duthie (in *The Review of English Studies*, 1943), have postulated the existence of a lost Shrew play which served as a source of *The Shrew* and of which *A Shrew* is a bad quarto. But others, notably Peter Alexander (in *The Times Literary Supplement*, September 16, 1926), have assumed that *A Shrew* is simply a bad quarto of *The Shrew*, although of an unusual type. If the latter theory is correct, *A Shrew* must represent, not an attempt to reconstruct Shakespeare's play literally, but an attempt to write a play, in certain respects intentionally different from Shakespeare's, on the basis of a general knowledge, held in memory, of *The Taming of the Shrew*. The reporters responsible for *A Shrew* could not have "forgotten" Petruchio's name or that the scene was laid in Italy – but they might, for reasons that remain obscure, intentionally have altered Petruchio's name to Ferando and the scene from Italy to Greece. A reader interested in comparing the two Shrew plays will find *A Shrew* reprinted in Geoffrey Bullough's *Narrative and Dramatic Sources of Shakespeare*, vol. I (1957).

Performance by Pembroke's Men, a company active in 1592–93, is recorded on the title-page of *A Shrew*. The reference may be to either *A Shrew* or *The Shrew*. If it is to *The Shrew*, then the publisher of *A Shrew*, like the publisher of the bad quarto of *Romeo and Juliet* (1597), presumably referred, in the interests of selling his book, to the well-known company that had produced a generally similar but better play of essentially the same title. (Since for purposes of copyright *A Shrew* and *The Shrew* were regarded as one, it is clear that – contrary to modern usage – no particular significance was attached to the small variation in title; such apparent lack of discrimination is perhaps more readily understandable at a time when *The Shrew* was not yet in print.) Thus *The Shrew*, if it was originally a Pembroke's play, may be dated 1593 or earlier – probably 1593, in view of the maturity of its characterization in comparison with the characterization of other of Shakespeare's plays usually dated in or before that year. It may be added that a date of 1593 for *The Shrew* is consistent with Peter Short's registration of copyright early in May of 1594 and with his consequent publication of *A Shrew* sometime during that year. In June of 1594, according to Philip Henslowe's *Diary*, a play called *The Taming of a Shrew* was performed in the theatre at Newington Butts, about a mile to the south of London Bridge, where the Admiral's Men and the Chamberlain's Men were then playing,

whether separately or in combination is not clear. Since *The Shrew* was later the property of Shakespeare's company, we may infer that the play recorded by Henslowe was probably Shakespeare's *Shrew* and the performing company probably the Chamberlain's Men, who, organized early in 1594, may have taken it over from the disbanded Pembroke's Men. The folio speech-prefix "Sincklo" at Induction, i, 87, indicates that the part of this player was taken by John Sincklo or Sincler, a minor actor with Shakespeare's company. *The Shrew* is not mentioned by Francis Meres in *Palladis Tamia* (1598), but since Meres also failed to name *Henry VI* it is clear that he was not proposing a complete list of Shakespeare's plays.

The Shrew was first printed in the Shakespeare folio of 1623, next in a quarto of 1631. The title-page of the quarto edition alludes to performance by the King's Men, as Shakespeare's company was styled after 1603, at both the Globe and the Blackfriars. The same company, according to Sir Henry Herbert, gave a court performance of *The Shrew* ("liked") before King Charles and Queen Henrietta in November of 1633, followed shortly by a performance of *The Woman's Prize, or The Tamer Tamed* ("very well liked") before the same audience. In this sequel to Shakespeare's play, by John Fletcher, Kate has died and a second wife gets the better of Petruchio.

For nearly two centuries after the Restoration Shakespeare's *Shrew* was neglected in favor of "improved" versions. In 1667 the comedian John Lacy made an adaptation called *Sauny the Scot*, in which the induction was eliminated and his own part of Sauny (Grumio) much magnified and embellished with a sort of Scots accent. Pepys could not understand the words and pronounced it "a silly play." In 1716 the Sly material was worked up by rival dramatists, Charles Johnson and Christopher Bullock, as two farces each entitled *The Cobbler of Preston*. In 1756 Garrick adapted the main plot of Shakespeare's play as a farce called *Catherine and Petruchio*, in which induction and subplot are eliminated (Bianca being already married to Hortensio), Kate breaks a lute on the head of a real music-master, and Baptista is substituted for Vincentio in the scene corresponding to IV, v. This version continued to be produced as an afterpiece for over a century and still occasionally influences performances of the full-length *Shrew*. In 1844, J. R. Planché, encouraged by Ben Webster, finally returned to Shakespeare's version, induction and all, and in 1887 Augustin Daly mounted a much-praised production with Ada Rehan as Katherine and John Drew as Petruchio. Daly rearranged the order of scenes to accommodate his scenery, but he used the induction and strengthened the new tradition of producing Shakespeare instead of Garrick. Since then *The Shrew* has had a continual stage history, nowadays generally being produced with the subplot intact. Sometimes the induction is omitted, and sometimes when

APPENDIX

it is used Sly remains on stage throughout the play proper and is carried off asleep at the end, as in *The Taming of a Shrew*. In 1948 *The Shrew* was adapted as the successful musical comedy *Kiss Me Kate*, with music and lyrics by Cole Porter.

The present edition of *The Taming of the Shrew* follows the text of the Shakespeare folio of 1623, thought by Sir Walter Greg (*The Shakespeare First Folio*, 1955) to have been printed from Shakespeare's "foul papers" – that is, from a manuscript which was the author's last working draft before preparation of a prompt-book designed to regulate performances. The folio (F) provides a fairly good text, though in a few places probably corrupt beyond hope of successful emendation. All material departures from the folio text are listed below, with the adopted reading in italics followed by the folio reading in roman.

Ind., i, s.d. *Christophero Sly* (in F at end of s.d.) 5 *pocas palabras* Paucas pallabris 9 *thirdborough* Head-borough 15 *Breathe* Brach 20, 28 *1. Huntsman* Hunts. 81 *A Player* 2. Player 87 *A Player* Sincklo 99 *A Player* Plai 136 *their* the

Ind., ii, 2 *lordship* Lord 25 *it is* is it 71 *Christophero* Christopher 91 *Greet* Greece 134 *play it. Is not* play, it is not

I, i, 3 *in* for 13 *Vincentio* Vincentio's 42 *now were* thou wert 47 s.d. *suitor* sister 128 *her faults* faults 240 *your* you 244 s.d. *speak* speakes

I, ii, 18 *masters* mistris 71 *she* she is 118 *me and other* me. Other 132 *last* least 150 *go. What* go to : what 169 *help me* helpe one 194 *he'll* Ile 205 *th'ear* heare 210 *ours* yours 220 *to woo?* to – 246 *as to ask* as aske 248 *I do hear* heare I do 262 *feat* seeke 271 *convive* contrive

II, i, 3 *gawds* goods 8 *charge thee* charge 31 *Will* What will 75–76 *wooing. Neighbor, this* wooing neighbors : this 78–79 *unto you* vnto 168 *I will* Ile s.d. (in F after l. 167) 180 s.d. (in F after l. 181) 255 *a* the 272 *upon* on 332 *in* me 346 *have Bianca's* haue my Biancas

III, i, 46 (F heads line *Luc*.) 49 *Bianca* (F omits) 50 *Lucentio* Bian. 52 *Bianca* Hort. 79 *change* charge *odd* old 80 *Messenger* Nicke

III, ii, 29 *of thy* of 30 *master, old* master, 53 *swayed* Waid 57 *new-repaired* now repaired 124 *sir, to* sir, 126 *As I* As 145 *come* came 155 *Did* Should 162 *arose* rose 175–76 *echo. I eccho : and I* 205 *nor till* not till 245 *you supply* you shall supply

IV, i, 10 s.d. *a Servant* (in F in l. 167 s.d.) 11 *is't* is 37 *thou wilt* wilt thou 38 *too* so 42 *and white* the white 55 *is* 'tis 126 *Food, food, food, food* Soud, soud, soud, soud 164 *in* for 167 s.d. *Enter Curtis* Enter Curtis a Seruant (in F after l. 168)

IV, ii, 4 *Hortensio* Luc. 6 *Lucentio* Hor. 8 *Lucentio* Hor. *of* to 13 *none* me 31 *her* them 63 *mercatante* Mercantant 71 *Take in* Take me (F heads line *Par*.) 73 *far or* farre on, or 86 *are newly* are but newly 92 *thus* this 102 *but* &

IV, iii, 81 *is a* is 85 *I will have it* it I will haue 88 *like a* like 96 *I* and 178 *account'st* accountedst

IV, iv, s.d. *booted and* (in F in l. 18 s.d.) 1 *Sir* Sirs 6 *Tranio* (in F heads l. 5) 18 s.d. *Pedant bareheaded* Pedant booted and bare headed 19 (F heads line *Tra*.) 68 (after this line F adds *Enter Peter*) 89 *except* expect 91 *with* take 101 *ready against* readie to come against

IV, v, 18 *is* in 22 *still* so 26 *soft, what company* soft, Company 35 *a* the 37 *where* whether 77 *she be* she

V, i, 5 *master* mistris 27 *Pisa* Padua 27–28 *and is here* and here 46 *master's* Mistris 47 *my* my old 74–75 *Lucentio. He* Lucentio, and he 98 *spoiled, yonder* spoil'd, and yonder 138 *never's* neuer

V, ii, 2 *done* come 23 *Conceive* Conceiues 45 *bitter* better 57 *O ho* Oh, Oh 65 *for* sir 127 *the* that 133 *a* fiue

THE TWO GENTLEMEN OF VERONA

INTRODUCTION

The Two Gentlemen of Verona is a comedy from Shakespeare's early period, before shadows penetrated his comic world, lending it depth and perspective. Like *The Comedy of Errors* and *The Taming of the Shrew* it is two-dimensional only, unsubstantial, not intended to be taken seriously. To ask it to satisfy us intellectually is as foolish as to allow it to distress us emotionally. If we do not ask too much of it, it will provide its own kind of pleasure. It has balance of structure and charm of detail. One might say it has the grace of youth, for it is a play about the young. Its attitude and its emphasis are youthful: no specifically old people appear in it; there is no bitterness, no cynicism, no talk about the past. Fittingly, its poetry is springlike, and, without prompting from the text, we think of it all as happening in the spring. There is about it "the uncertain glory of an April day," providing we see it for itself alone. If, out of our knowledge of Shakespeare's later works, we approach it with solemn demands, we are likely to destroy it with misplaced earnestness. And if we fail to consider sympathetically the literary conventions that shape its plot, we may find ourselves more bewildered than entertained.

The play is about two subjects that much concern the young: love and friendship. The two subjects reflect what appear to have been the two principal sources of the play: *Diana*, a sixteenth-century romance in Spanish by the Portuguese Jorge de Montemayor; and one of the tales celebrating friendship, the story of Titus and Gisippus, which was available to Shakespeare in a number of versions. As these source-stories appear in the plot of *The Two Gentlemen* each is responsible for a triangle of three persons, the one composed of Julia, Proteus, and Silvia, the other of Valentine, Proteus, and Silvia. *Diana* was just such a "shallow story of deep love" as Valentine teases Proteus about in the opening scene. We can imagine the love-sick Proteus reading many such tales. It tells how a maiden, deserted by her lover, follows him and wins him back after his infatuation with a high-born lady. From it Shakespeare took the Julia–Proteus–Silvia triangle. In it there was no prototype for Valentine.

In the friendship story, Gisippus, upon discovering that his friend Titus has fallen in love with the lady he himself loves and plans to marry, not only offers the lady to Titus, but, having led her to the altar, smuggles Titus into the bridal bed in his place so that his friend becomes her legal husband. Throughout all this the lady is not consulted. Shakespeare and his audience would have been familiar with a number of such "brotherhood" stories, tales designed to demonstrate that in the noble mind the claims of friendship are superior to those of love. It is very possible that Shakespeare had read the story of Titus and Gisippus in the version included by Sir Thomas Elyot in *The Boke Named the Governour* (1531). Elyot's book is moral and didactic, its subject the education of the ruling class, and no one would accuse its author of lightness of mind. Yet he introduces his version of the story of Titus and Gisippus with:

. . . I will reherce a right goodly example of frendship. Whiche example, studiousely radde, shall ministre to the redars singuler pleasure and also incredible comforte to practise amitie.

One can imagine Valentine admiring such a tale. Shakespeare does not follow it closely, but it seems likely that from it he took the Valentine–Proteus–Silvia triangle. It contained no prototype for Julia.

Shakespeare placed the two triangles together to form a quadrilateral with interesting potentialities for plot. Proteus and Silvia are common to both stories. Proteus, the false lover of the first, is the favored friend of the second. Silvia, the rival of the heroine in the first, is the sacrifice made by the hero in the second. If Shakespeare had remained strictly faithful to his source for the second story, Proteus would have been obliged to accept the sacrifice, but Shakespeare was committed as well to the requirements of the first story. Therefore Proteus, to be available for Julia, had to reject Silvia. When we look at the plot in this way, Valentine and Julia become the hero and heroine: two people who, in what seems to be a love story, do not meet until the end, and do *not* fall in love. What we have, in fact, is a conflict between the claims of two conventions; the plot contains not only a love story, where love must be all, but a love story combined with a type of story where the whole point is to show that love is not all.

Shakespeare has attempted something that he and his contemporaries may well have found both intriguing and amusing: to show within a single plot, not the conflict between love and friendship, but the conflict between the conventions of the story that celebrated love and those of the story that celebrated friendship. To recognize that attempt is to see that the plotting, and particularly the much-debated and much-criticized ending, is far more skillful and pointed than it at first appears to the modern reader.

Valentine has been severely criticized as a lover for offering Silvia to Proteus, but within the convention from which he takes his being, he is a lover only so that he can sacrifice his love to his friend. He is not the hero of a love story but the protagonist of a brotherhood story. Silvia has met with a mixture of pity and contempt for saying nothing and doing nothing while she is being handed from man to man. But her silence is perhaps commendable if one considers that there is little that she can say. And her position is not unenviable when compared with those of her prototypes at the conclusion of each of the source stories: in *Diana* she dies, in *Titus and Gisippus* she is the victim of what strikes the modern reader as a singularly callous bed-trick. The combination of the stories seems to show up Proteus as despicable, a false lover and false friend. Yet he is not despicable in either of the source-stories, and I do not think Shakespeare intends to disparage him. He is a victim of both conventions, but he is allowed those speeches in which he struggles to escape his fate by avoiding the temptations to be untrue to both Julia and Valentine. But here literary conventions have the force of destiny, and Proteus is doomed to the roles he plays.

By his use of the two sources, Shakespeare has contrived a plot that calls for a kind of villainy without supplying a villain. Apart from minor complications provided by wrong-headed parents – and Proteus is himself the victim of one of these – the actions that threaten the happy ending must be carried out by one who is destined to participate in it. It is Proteus who is guilty of breaking his vows of love, of a calculated betrayal of his friend, of intended rape. Yet he must not put himself beyond reach of the saving grace of his own contrition and Valentine's forgiveness at the end.

From the beginning Proteus, along with Valentine, is shaped to fit the exigencies of the closing scene. And here we can see Shakespeare at an early stage in his career engaged in the craft at which he became a master: the creating of character to suit the requirements of a chosen plot in such a way as to make it credible, the attempt to provide an answer to the question, "Given these wonderful events, what sort of persons must have been involved?" To think of this ability as the main source of his greatness would be a gross oversimplification of his genius, but it was basic to the structural unity of plot and character that gives his plays their dramatic impact. By its aid he conjured *Othello* out of Cinthio's wooden narrative, perceived *Macbeth* in the sparseness of the chronicles, and established, apparently forever, the layman's conception of the characters of a line of English kings.

In *The Two Gentlemen* the friendship between the two young men is established firmly for us in the opening scene, but at the same time the difference between them is made apparent, especially as that difference concerns friendship and love. Proteus is the less self-sufficient, the weaker of the two. He has more need of both friendship and love. He has been trying to persuade Valentine not to go to Milan, and his attitude when he discovers that Valentine is firm in his intention to go has a feminine quality of resignation and implied martyrdom about it. Proteus' first speech in the play might have been spoken by the clinging-vine type of maiden. Very shortly we discover from his own words that he is the sort of young man who is unmanned by love: "I leave myself, my friends, and all for love." Julia has "metamorphosed" him, and he contrasts himself unfavorably with Valentine, who "leaves his friends to dignify them more," who hunts after honor rather than love.

Proteus is shown to be neither malign in motive nor formidable in action. The speeches in which he yields to temptation and then rationalizes his yielding are designed to reveal a nature that can be condemned only for selfishness and weakness. As a seducer he is depicted as inept. His "plot" consists of little more than informing on Valentine. When he attempts to send Silvia a dog, the outcome is

farcical; when he decides to take Silvia by force, he makes the mistake of attempting it within sight and earshot of Valentine, concealed behind the bushes. And, finally, he returns to Julia with lamblike docility. While giving us this picture of Proteus, Shakespeare at the same time has Valentine speak highly of him, shows him to be well received by the Duke and by Silvia (until she discovers his perfidy), and has Julia fall in love with him.

Whether this presentation of Proteus succeeds in making the one or the other, or both, of Shakespeare's source-stories credible as they appear in his plot must remain a question. The consensus of critical opinion suggests that it does not – or that if Shakespeare succeeded with Proteus, he failed with Valentine. And one may doubt that even genius could have succeeded in making Valentine's story plausible, especially to a modern audience. It has to be accepted within the convention of the brotherhood story or not at all. But within that convention we can see Shakespeare working to portray Valentine as a model of youthful magnanimity. From the beginning he is shown to be the stronger and the more self-reliant of the two friends. He is amused at the devastation that love has worked in Proteus, and at the same time slightly scornful about it. Not only his actions but his words as well are designed to show that friendship touches him more deeply than it does Proteus, and that, when he falls in love, he is more deeply moved. Yet he has less need than Proteus of the supports of love and friendship, and can therefore be less selfish about them. It is likely that a familiarity with the brotherhood stories had prepared many of Shakespeare's audience to accept Valentine's offer of Silvia to Proteus in the last scene, but it is also true that an examination of the part of Valentine in the play will show that Shakespeare has presented him as an uncomplicated young man of a liberal and outgoing nature from whom an audience might accept without undue shock an act of spontaneous and unreflecting generosity done in accordance with his creed.

It is when we come to Julia's actions that we realize that, in the conflict between the conventions of the two sources, the love story wins out. When Valentine tries to impose the conventions of the brotherhood tale by consigning Silvia to Proteus, Julia asserts herself, reaches into the brotherhood story, and plucks Proteus forth. In so doing she leaves Valentine no alternative but to rescue Silvia from Thurio and marry her himself. We need not draw from the victory of the love story any inferences about Shakespeare's beliefs, but that victory is worth noting as a fitting conclusion to a play that has all along been a series of variations on the theme of love. "Love's a mighty lord," says Valentine, and terminology, images, classical allusion, all reiterate the theme. There are not only the four young lovers, but also Thurio, a rival in love; Launce, a comic lover; the Duke, who pretends to be in love; Mercatio and Eglamour, who, we are told, are suitors to Julia; and the second Eglamour, who is forever faithful to a dead love. Only the fifth from the shortest of Shakespeare's plays, *The Two Gentlemen* uses the word "love" more often than do any of the others; in some of those uses it refers to friendship, but the theme of friendship, although it opens the play and produces an interesting complication at the close, and although it appears ironically in Valentine's recommendation of Proteus to the Duke and Silvia, and again inversely in Proteus' treachery to Valentine, is forced into a secondary and supporting role in the play. It is, after all, the conventions of two kinds of story that have been in conflict, and not love and friendship themselves, for it is Valentine's gesture of what must be understood as true friendship that clears the air and produces that perfect amity in which the love stories can end happily.

It is the all-pervasiveness of the theme of love that gives the play its peculiarly unadulterated romantic quality. Shakespeare has provided no sharp astringents to modify that quality. Just as there are no old men and no recollections of the past, so there are no dark figures, no dealers in death like Shylock, or in deviltry like Don John. Nor is there a bitter clown like Lavache in *All's Well*, or a melancholy Jaques, or a rogue like Parolles, or a scapegoat like Malvolio. The supremacy of love is never seriously threatened, nor are the attitudes of romance ever effectively attacked by criticism or parody throughout the play. Valentine, who in the beginning scoffs gently at love, becomes its victim. Proteus commits his treachery in the name of love. Speed's witticisms are callow and ineffective, and Thurio in renouncing love exposes only himself. As a result the play lacks vitality. It has charm and grace and even liveliness, but we miss the robust, the earthy, the vindictive, the sardonic, the malicious, the bumptious: all those qualities that serve to leaven the romantic stuff of Shakespeare's later comedies.

Happily, in the middle of Act II we come to Launce, and we are likely to welcome him as comic relief in this comedy. Even Speed improves in his company, but then no one else is ever in his company for long. For Launce, although he supplies some of the qualities otherwise missing in the comedy, and although he is in himself a triumphant comic creation, remains almost uninvolved in the action of the play. His part has about it more of the individual vaudeville turn than has any other major comic part in Shakespeare. He is not really required in the plot, yet he too is perplexed in love and distressed in friendship. His reported love affair and his relations with his dog provide mild parodies on the main themes of the play.

In its details, the play contains a number of inconsistencies and peculiarities that will puzzle the curious reader and lead him to speculation. How does one go by ship from Verona to Milan? Why do the characters, when they are in Milan, sometimes speak as if they were in Verona or Padua? Why are there two Eglamours, and what *does* happen to the second one? Why does Proteus speak as if he had only seen Silvia's picture when he has, in fact, seen her? Why does Proteus use Speed, Valentine's servant, to deliver his letter to Julia? And why do both Valentine and Proteus allow Speed such familiar pleasantries and unpleasantries – especially about the ladies they love? Why does Valentine lie to the outlaws about the reason for his banishment, and why does Shakespeare have the third outlaw banished from Verona (Valentine's city) for what was essentially Valentine's crime, plotting to steal away a lady closely related to the ruler? What is the mystery of the "wrong letter" that Julia almost delivers inadvertently to Silvia at IV, iv, 119? What is the point of having Silvia accede to Proteus' request for her picture? Was there an Emperor at Milan as well as a Duke, or are they two titles for the same role?

These questions and others like them have led to the usual speculations produced by such problems. It has been argued that the text is a patchwork of collaboration,

that it represents a first draft or a careless revision, that it is Shakespeare's hastily written "modernization" of an earlier play by another hand. This is not the place to debate such questions. It may be said only that some of these problems, together with the forms of the poetry and with the whole attitude of the play toward the story and its characters, argue an early work, but an early work by Shakespeare. The various weaknesses in the play may be accounted for by various theories. It seems to me that the only way we can account for its both containing these weaknesses and rising above them is by attributing it almost wholly to Shakespeare, a young Shakespeare, perhaps composing or revising in haste, but who in any case seems to have had a lifelong habit of negligence about a certain kind of structural detail.

The outlaws are a special problem; they are farcical from the beginning, so much so that one is reminded of W. S. Gilbert's pirates, that other band of unterrifying desperadoes who also inform us that they "are all gentlemen who have gone wrong." They are most inept, these outlaws, with their naively touching ambition to have a linguist as their king, and their inability to retain a single one of the prisoners that we hear of their taking during the play. They make Valentine their leader, Eglamour escapes them, Proteus takes Silvia from them, and when they enter delighted with their success in capturing the Duke and Thurio, Valentine makes them give up their prize with a command that is the equivalent of "Drop it, Fido." They are, of course, not outlaws but stage properties, and it is by its ability to sweep past such a weakness without losing its momentum or verve that the play shows Shakespeare's early dramatic skill.

That skill is also evident in the structural soundness of the play's conclusion. According to the conventions of his two sources and the exigencies of the plot as it has so far developed, Shakespeare must have the events of this last scene take place as they do if he is to reach the "happy ending" that is particularly his own: "One feast, one house, one mutual happiness." In its obedience to that particular kind of artistic logic, the scene is competently executed. Although we may feel that in his desire to reach the reconciliation of the conclusion, Shakespeare fails to give sufficient time, sufficient care, sufficient poetry to the business between the four lovers and the two friends to make it convincing, yet the same impatience at this point in the plot is evident, although to a lesser extent, in later and greater comedies. At the end of the play Shakespeare's interest is to tidy up the plot in order to show in broad outlines a picture of amity and happiness. With this process lengthy exchanges between Valentine and Proteus, Proteus and Silvia, Valentine and Silvia, Proteus and Julia would have been incompatible. In short, the weakness in the ending of *The Two Gentlemen*, if weakness it be, is one that remained typical of Shakespeare as a writer of comedies. Call it a method, rather than a weakness, and one can say that he became more adept at using it as he matured as a playwright. The point is that its appearance in *The Two Gentlemen* is an argument for, and not against, his authorship of the play and its ending.

The date of the play is still a subject of conjecture. Although it is first mentioned in 1598 (in the *Palladis Tamia* of Francis Meres), the existent text is usually assigned to ca. 1594, with considerable difference of opinion as to whether it was then first written or merely revised. It is, I believe, Shakespeare's first experiment with the type of romantic comedy that he later mastered and made his own. In it he is working toward the unique formula of his great comedies : the combining of the wonderful with the relentlessly real, of the marvellous event with the intractable stuff of human nature. If the potentials of human nature, ideally conceived but frustrated and deprived by the intransigence of experience, can be the material of high tragedy, the potentials of human experience, ideally conceived but diminished by the limitations of human nature, can be the material of high comedy. The happy ending can reveal an irony of its own, no less potent, but perhaps more subtle, than the irony of the tragic conclusion. The bliss of Bassanio or Claudio or Bertram at the close is as ironic as the agony of Othello. In *The Two Gentlemen of Verona* Shakespeare is still far from this effect of art, but in the juxtaposition of event and character we can see, even here, the beginning of the vision that will delight us in *As You Like It* and *Twelfth Night,* that will disturb us in *All's Well* and *Measure for Measure,* and that in *The Winter's Tale* and *The Tempest* will carry us far beyond what would seem to be the possibilities of either comedy or romance.

McMaster University BERNERS A. W. JACKSON

NOTE ON THE TEXT

The Two Gentlemen of Verona first appeared in the folio of 1623. The copy used by the printers is believed to have been a transcript made by the scrivener Ralph Crane, probably of a theatrical prompt-book. After the manner associated with Crane, the names of all characters appearing in a scene are clustered at its head in the folio text. In the present edition the names are distributed so as to appear at the points of actual entrance of the various characters. The act–scene division supplied marginally follows that of the folio. The list of characters appearing at the end of the text in the folio is here placed at the beginning, and the spellings "Protheus," "Anthonio," "Panthion" have been normalized as "Proteus," "Antonio," "Panthino." Otherwise few substantive emendations have been admitted; most of these first appeared in the later folios or in eighteenth-century editions. The following list is complete, with the adopted reading in italics followed by the folio reading in roman.

The Names of all the Actors (printed at the end of the play in F)
I, i, 65 *leave* love 77 *a sheep* Sheepe 137 *testerned* cestern'd
I, ii, 97 *your* you 122 *fearful-hanging* fearful, hanging
I, iii, 24 *whither* whether 50 *O heavenly* Pro. Oh heavenly 88 *father calls* Fathers call's 91 s.d. *Exeunt.* Exeunt. Finis.
II, iii, 26 *wood woman* would-woman 35–36 *tied...tied...tied* tide...Tide...tide 38, 49 *tied* tide
II, iv, 59 *know* knew 105 *mistress* a Mistresse 130, 137 *Love* love 163 *makes* make 193 *mine eye* mine 202 *too too* too-too 207 *dazzlèd* dazel'd 211 s.d. *Exit* Exeunt
III, i, 217, 221 *banishèd* banish'd 278 *master's ship* mastership 370 s.d. *Exit* Exeunt
IV, i, 16 *Whither* Whether 35 *been miserable* beene often miserable 49 *An heir, and near* And heir and neece
IV, ii, 17 s.d. *Musicians* Musician 113 *his* her
IV, iii, 40 *Recking* Wreaking
IV, iv, 52 *hangman's* Hangmans 66 *thou* thee 70 *to* not 203 s.d. *Exit* Exeunt
V, ii, 7 (assigned in F to Proteus) 13–14 (assigned in F to Thurio) 59 s.d. *Exit* Exeunt
V, iv, 26 *this* this ? 122 *Outlaws* Out-l

THE TWO GENTLEMEN OF VERONA

THE NAMES OF ALL THE ACTORS

Duke [of Milan], father to Silvia
Valentine } the two gentlemen
Proteus
Antonio, father to Proteus
Thurio, a foolish rival to Valentine
Eglamour, agent for Silvia in her escape
Host, where Julia lodges [in Milan]
Outlaws, with Valentine

Speed, a clownish servant to Valentine
Launce, the like to Proteus
Panthino, servant to Antonio
Julia, beloved of Proteus
Silvia, beloved of Valentine
Lucetta, waiting-woman to Julia
[Servants; Musicians

Scene: *Verona, Milan, and a forest near Mantua*]

❋

I, i   [Enter] Valentine, [and] Proteus.

VALENTINE
Cease to persuade, my loving Proteus;
2 Home-keeping youth have ever homely wits.
3 Were't not affection chains thy tender days
To the sweet glances of thy honored love,
I rather would entreat thy company
To see the wonders of the world abroad
Than, living dully sluggardized at home,
8 Wear out thy youth with shapeless idleness.
But since thou lov'st, love still, and thrive therein,
Even as I would when I to love begin.
PROTEUS
Wilt thou be gone? Sweet Valentine, adieu.
12 Think on thy Proteus, when thou haply seest
Some rare noteworthy object in thy travel.
Wish me partaker in thy happiness
15 When thou dost meet good hap; and in thy danger,
If ever danger do environ thee,
Commend thy grievance to my holy prayers,
18 For I will be thy beadsman, Valentine.
VALENTINE
19 And on a love-book pray for my success?
PROTEUS
Upon some book I love I'll pray for thee.
VALENTINE
That's on some shallow story of deep love,
22 How young Leander crossed the Hellespont.
PROTEUS
That's a deep story of a deeper love,
For he was more than over shoes in love.
VALENTINE
'Tis true, for you are over boots in love,
And yet you never swum the Hellespont.
PROTEUS
27 Over the boots? Nay, give me not the boots.
VALENTINE
28 No, I will not, for it boots thee not.

PROTEUS   What?
VALENTINE
To be in love, where scorn is bought with groans,
Coy looks with heart-sore sighs, one fading moment's
      mirth
With twenty watchful, weary, tedious nights.   31
If haply won, perhaps a hapless gain;   32
If lost, why then a grievous labor won;
However, but a folly bought with wit,   34
Or else a wit by folly vanquishèd.
PROTEUS
So, by your circumstance, you call me fool.   36
VALENTINE
So, by your circumstance, I fear you'll prove.   37
PROTEUS
'Tis Love you cavil at; I am not Love.
VALENTINE
Love is your master, for he masters you;
And he that is so yokèd by a fool
Methinks should not be chronicled for wise.
PROTEUS
Yet writers say, as in the sweetest bud
The eating canker dwells, so eating love   43
Inhabits in the finest wits of all.
VALENTINE
And writers say, as the most forward bud   45
Is eaten by the canker ere it blow,   46
Even so by love the young and tender wit
Is turned to folly, blasting in the bud,   48

I, i A street in Verona 2 *homely* dull 3 *affection* passion 8 *shapeless* aimless 12 *haply* by chance 15 *hap* fortune 18 *beadsman* one who prays for another 19 *love-book* book about love, romantic tale 22 *Leander* (in Greek legend, the lover who drowned in the Hellespont as he swam to Hero) 27 *give . . . boots* i.e. don't make fun of me 28 *boots* profits 31 *watchful* sleepless 32 *hapless* unlucky 34 *However, but* anyway, no more than 36 *circumstance* reasoning 37 *by your circumstance* in your situation 43 *canker* destructive grub 45 *most forward* earliest 46 *blow* bloom 48 *blasting* withering

120

49 Losing his verdure even in the prime,
50 And all the fair effects of future hopes.
But wherefore waste I time to counsel thee
52 That art a votary to fond desire?
53 Once more, adieu. My father at the road
Expects my coming, there to see me shipped.

PROTEUS
And thither will I bring thee, Valentine.

VALENTINE
Sweet Proteus, no; now let us take our leave.
To Milan let me hear from thee by letters
58 Of thy success in love, and what news else
Betideth here in absence of thy friend,
And I likewise will visit thee with mine.

PROTEUS
All happiness bechance to thee in Milan!

VALENTINE
As much to you at home! And so farewell.   Exit.

PROTEUS
He after honor hunts, I after love.
64 He leaves his friends to dignify them more;
65 I leave myself, my friends, and all for love.
Thou, Julia, thou hast metamorphosed me,
Made me neglect my studies, lose my time,
68 War with good counsel, set the world at nought;
Made wit with musing weak, heart sick with thought.
[Enter] Speed.

SPEED Sir Proteus, save you! Saw you my master?
PROTEUS But now he parted hence to embark for Milan.
SPEED
Twenty to one then, he is shipped already,
73 And I have played the sheep in losing him.
PROTEUS
Indeed, a sheep doth very often stray,
75 And if the shepherd be awhile away.
SPEED You conclude that my master is a shepherd then,
and I a sheep?
PROTEUS I do.
79 SPEED Why then my horns are his horns, whether I wake
or sleep.
PROTEUS A silly answer, and fitting well a sheep.
SPEED This proves me still a sheep.
PROTEUS True, and thy master a shepherd.
84 SPEED Nay, that I can deny by a circumstance.

PROTEUS It shall go hard but I'll prove it by another.
SPEED The shepherd seeks the sheep, and not the sheep
the shepherd; but I seek my master, and my master
seeks not me. Therefore I am no sheep.
PROTEUS The sheep for fodder follow the shepherd; the
shepherd for food follows not the sheep. Thou for wages
followest thy master; thy master for wages follows not
thee. Therefore thou art a sheep.
SPEED Such another proof will make me cry 'baa.'   93
PROTEUS But dost thou hear? Gav'st thou my letter to
Julia?
SPEED Ay, sir. I, a lost mutton, gave your letter to her, a
laced mutton, and she, a laced mutton, gave me, a lost 96
mutton, nothing for my labor.
PROTEUS Here's too small a pasture for such store of
muttons.
SPEED If the ground be overcharged, you were best stick 99
her.
PROTEUS Nay, in that you are astray; 'twere best pound 101
you.
SPEED Nay, sir, less than a pound shall serve me for
carrying your letter.
PROTEUS You mistake; I mean the pound – a pinfold.   104
SPEED
From a pound to a pin? Fold it over and over,   105
'Tis threefold too little for carrying a letter to your lover.
PROTEUS But what said she?
SPEED [nodding] Ay.
PROTEUS Nod, 'ay'? Why, that's noddy.   109
SPEED You mistook, sir. I say she did nod, and you ask me 110
if she did nod, and I say 'Ay.'
PROTEUS And that set together is 'noddy.'
SPEED Now you have taken the pains to set it together,
take it for your pains.
PROTEUS No, no. You shall have it for bearing the letter.
SPEED Well, I perceive I must be fain to bear with you. 116
PROTEUS Why, sir, how do you bear with me?
SPEED Marry, sir, the letter very orderly, having nothing 118
but the word 'noddy' for my pains.
PROTEUS Beshrew me, but you have a quick wit.   120
SPEED And yet it cannot overtake your slow purse.
PROTEUS Come, come, open the matter in brief. What 122
said she?
SPEED Open your purse, that the money and the matter
may be both at once delivered.
PROTEUS [giving him money] Well, sir, here is for your
pains. What said she?
SPEED Truly, sir, I think you'll hardly win her.   128
PROTEUS Why, couldst thou perceive so much from her?
SPEED Sir, I could perceive nothing at all from her: no, 130
not so much as a ducat for delivering your letter. And 131
being so hard to me that brought your mind, I fear she'll
prove as hard to you in telling your mind. Give her no 133
token but stones, for she's as hard as steel.   134
PROTEUS What, said she nothing?
SPEED No, not so much as 'Take this for thy pains.' To
testify your bounty, I thank you, you have testerned me; 137
in requital whereof, henceforth carry your letters yourself. And so, sir, I'll commend you to my master.
PROTEUS
Go, go, be gone, to save your ship from wrack,   140
Which cannot perish having thee aboard,
Being destined to a drier death on shore. [Exit Speed.] 142
I must go send some better messenger.

49 prime spring   50 all . . . hopes i.e. all promises of beauty to come   52
fond foolish   53 road anchorage   58 success progress   58–59 what . . .
Betideth news of what else happens   64 dignify honor (by improving himself)   65 leave . . . friends i.e. fail in what I owe to myself and my friends
68 War . . . counsel oppose good advice   73 sheep (with pun on shipped)
75 And if if   79 horns . . . horns (presumably a reference to cuckoldry)   84
circumstance process of reasoning   93 baa (with pun on 'bah' to signify
contempt)   96 laced mutton (slang for prostitute)   99 overcharged crowded; stick stab (as in slaughtering a sheep, but used here with sexual
innuendo)   101 pound shut up in a pen (Proteus probably intends a quibble
on 'beat,' but Speed takes one on 'pay')   104 pinfold pen for animals
105 pin i.e. something worthless   109 noddy simple-minded (perhaps a pun
on 'naughty')   110 nod (perhaps a pun on 'not' or 'nought')   116 fain
content; bear with put up with (with a pun on 'carry')   118 Marry (a
mild interjection, derived from the name of the Virgin Mary used as an
oath); orderly dutifully   120 Beshrew me curse me (mild oath)   122 open
. . . brief give the message in a few words   128 hardly only with difficulty
130 perceive receive (malapropism)   131 ducat gold coin   133 in telling
when you tell   134 stones jewels   137 testerned me given me a tester, or
sixpence, a small tip   140 wrack wreck   142 a drier . . . shore i.e. by hanging
(alluding to the proverbial 'He that is born to be hanged shall never be
drowned')

144   I fear my Julia would not deign my lines,
145   Receiving them from such a worthless post.   *Exit.*

            *

I, ii   *Enter Julia and Lucetta.*

JULIA
But say, Lucetta, now we are alone,
Wouldst thou then counsel me to fall in love?

LUCETTA
Ay, madam, so you stumble not unheedfully.

JULIA
4   Of all the fair resort of gentlemen
5   That every day with parle encounter me,
In thy opinion which is worthiest love?

LUCETTA
Please you repeat their names, I'll show my mind
According to my shallow simple skill.

JULIA
9   What think'st thou of the fair Sir Eglamour?

LUCETTA
10   As of a knight well-spoken, neat and fine;
But were I you, he never should be mine.

JULIA
What think'st thou of the rich Mercatio?

LUCETTA
Well of his wealth, but of himself, so so.

JULIA
What think'st thou of the gentle Proteus?

LUCETTA
Lord, Lord, to see what folly reigns in us!

JULIA
16   How now? What means this passion at his name?

LUCETTA
17   Pardon, dear madam, 'tis a passing shame
That I, unworthy body as I am,
19   Should censure thus on lovely gentlemen.

JULIA
Why not on Proteus, as of all the rest?

LUCETTA
Then thus: of many good I think him best.

JULIA
Your reason?

LUCETTA
I have no other but a woman's reason:
I think him so because I think him so.

JULIA
And wouldst thou have me cast my love on him?

LUCETTA
Ay, if you thought your love not cast away.

JULIA
27   Why, he, of all the rest, hath never moved me.

LUCETTA
Yet he, of all the rest, I think best loves ye.

JULIA
His little speaking shows his love but small.

LUCETTA
30   Fire that's closest kept burns most of all.

JULIA
They do not love that do not show their love.

LUCETTA
O, they love least that let men know their love.

JULIA
I would I knew his mind.

LUCETTA
Peruse this paper, madam.
    [Gives a letter.]

JULIA
'To Julia' – say from whom.

LUCETTA
That the contents will show.

JULIA
Say, say. Who gave it thee?

LUCETTA
Sir Valentine's page, and sent, I think, from Proteus.
He would have given it you, but I, being in the way,   39
Did in your name receive it. Pardon the fault, I pray.

JULIA
Now, by my modesty, a goodly broker!   41
Dare you presume to harbor wanton lines,
To whisper and conspire against my youth?
Now, trust me, 'tis an office of great worth,
And you an officer fit for the place.
There, take the paper. See it be returned,
Or else return no more into my sight.

LUCETTA
To plead for love deserves more fee than hate.

JULIA
Will ye be gone?

LUCETTA   That you may ruminate.   *Exit.*

JULIA
And yet I would I had o'erlooked the letter.   50
It were a shame to call her back again
And pray her to a fault for which I chid her.   52
What fool is she, that knows I am a maid,
And would not force the letter to my view!
Since maids, in modesty, say 'no' to that
Which they would have the profferer construe 'ay.'
Fie, fie, how wayward is this foolish love
That, like a testy babe, will scratch the nurse   58
And presently all humbled kiss the rod!   59
How churlishly I chid Lucetta hence,
When willingly I would have had her here!
How angerly I taught my brow to frown,
When inward joy enforced my heart to smile!
My penance is to call Lucetta back
And ask remission for my folly past.
What ho, Lucetta!
    [Enter Lucetta.]

LUCETTA   What would your ladyship?

JULIA
Is't near dinner-time?

LUCETTA   I would it were,
That you might kill your stomach on your meat.   68
And not upon your maid.

JULIA
What is't that you took up so gingerly?

144 *deign* i.e. accept   145 *post* messenger
I, ii Verona: Julia's house   4 *resort* group   5 *with parle . . . me* i.e. court me with their words   9 *Eglamour* (not the Eglamour who assists Silvia later in the play)   10 *neat and fine* elegant   16 *passion* show of feeling   17 *passing* surpassing   19 *censure* give an opinion   27 *moved me* i.e. made me a proposal   30 *closest* most secret   39 *being . . . way* i.e. happening to meet him   41 *broker* i.e. intermediary   50 *o'erlooked* read   52 *pray . . . chid her* ask her to commit the very wrong for which I scolded her   58 *testy* fretful   59 *presently* immediately; *kiss the rod* i.e. submit   68 *kill your stomach* (1) satisfy your hunger, (2) dispel your anger   68–69 *meat, maid* (the similarity in pronunciation continues the quibble on the two meanings of *kill your stomach*)

LUCETTA
Nothing.
JULIA
Why didst thou stoop then?
LUCETTA
To take a paper up that I let fall.
JULIA
And is that paper nothing?
LUCETTA
Nothing concerning me.
JULIA
Then let it lie for those that it concerns.
LUCETTA
77 Madam, it will not lie where it concerns,
Unless it have a false interpreter.
JULIA
Some love of yours hath writ to you in rime.
LUCETTA
That I might sing it, madam, to a tune.
81 Give me a note; your ladyship can set –
JULIA
82 As little by such toys as may be possible.
83 Best sing it to the tune of 'Light o' Love.'
LUCETTA
84 It is too heavy for so light a tune.
JULIA
85 Heavy? Belike it hath some burden then?
LUCETTA
Ay, and melodious were it, would you sing it.
JULIA
And why not you?
87 LUCETTA   I cannot reach so high.
JULIA
88 Let's see your song. [Takes the letter.] How now, minion?
LUCETTA
Keep tune there still, so you will sing it out.
90 And yet methinks I do not like this tune.
JULIA
You do not?
LUCETTA
92 No, madam; 'tis too sharp.
JULIA
You, minion, are too saucy.
LUCETTA
94 Nay, now you are too flat,

And mar the concord with too harsh a descant.   95
There wanteth but a mean to fill your song.   96
JULIA
The mean is drowned with your unruly bass.   97
LUCETTA
Indeed, I bid the base for Proteus.   98
JULIA
This babble shall not henceforth trouble me.
Here is a coil with protestation!   100
    [Tears the letter and throws it down.]
Go, get you gone, and let the papers lie –
You would be fing'ring them to anger me.
LUCETTA
She makes it strange, but she would be best pleased   103
To be so ang'red with another letter.   [Exit.]
JULIA
Nay, would I were so ang'red with the same!   105
O hateful hands, to tear such loving words!
Injurious wasps, to feed on such sweet honey,
And kill the bees that yield it with your stings!
I'll kiss each several paper for amends.   109
Look, here is writ 'kind Julia.' Unkind Julia! 110
As in revenge of thy ingratitude,   111
I throw thy name against the bruising stones,
Trampling contemptuously on thy disdain.
And here is writ 'love-wounded Proteus.'
Poor wounded name! My bosom as a bed
Shall lodge thee till thy wound be throughly healed,   116
And thus I search it with a sovereign kiss.   117
But twice or thrice was 'Proteus' written down –
Be calm, good wind, blow not a word away
Till I have found each letter in the letter,
Except mine own name; that some whirlwind bear
Unto a ragged, fearful-hanging rock,
And throw it thence into the raging sea!
Lo, here in one line is his name twice writ,
'Poor forlorn Proteus, passionate Proteus,
To the sweet Julia.' That I'll tear away –   126
And yet I will not, sith so prettily   127
He couples it to his complaining names.   128
Thus will I fold them one upon another –
Now kiss, embrace, contend, do what you will.
    [Enter Lucetta.]
LUCETTA
Madam, dinner is ready, and your father stays.   131
JULIA
Well, let us go.
LUCETTA
What, shall these papers lie like telltales here?
JULIA
If you respect them, best to take them up.   134
LUCETTA
Nay, I was taken up for laying them down.   135
Yet here they shall not lie, for catching cold. 136
JULIA
I see you have a month's mind to them.   137
LUCETTA
Ay, madam, you may say what sights you see;
I see things too, although you judge I wink.   139
JULIA
Come, come. Will't please you go?   Exeunt.

77 *concerns* is of importance 81 *note* (1) musical note, (2) letter in reply to Proteus; *set* (1) set to music, (2) write 82 *toys* trifles 83 *'Light o' Love'* (a familiar tune at the time) 84 *heavy* serious 85 *burden* bass accompaniment or refrain (with a play on 'load,' the ladies continuing to pun with musical terms) 87 *I . . . high* (1) the note is beyond me, (2) Proteus is of too high rank for me 88 *minion* hussy (with pun on 'minim,' a half-note) 90 *tune* (with second meaning 'mood') 92 *sharp* (with second meaning 'bitter') 94 *flat* (with second meaning 'outspoken') 95 *descant* improvised harmony 96 *mean* tenor part (with a play on the idea of the golden mean, and perhaps on 'man,' i.e. Proteus) 97 *unruly bass* (with second meaning 'low conduct') 98 *bid the base for* i.e. act in the interests of (the phrase is from the sixteenth-century version of the game of prisoners' base) 100 *coil with protestation* a great turmoil of vows (referring to Proteus' letter) 103 *makes it strange* pretends indifference 105 *Nay . . . same* (she wishes the cause of her anger, the letter, were intact again) 109 *several paper* separate piece 110 *Unkind* unnatural 111 *As* as if 116 *throughly* thoroughly 117 *search* cleanse; *sovereign* i.e. healing 126 *That* i.e. *sweet Julia* 127 *sith* since 128 *complaining names* i.e. his name, written several times in the letter to accompany his lover's complaints 131 *stays* waits 134 *respect* value 135 *taken up* scolded 136 *for* for fear of 137 *month's mind* to strong desire for 139 *wink* close my eyes

I, iii   *Enter Antonio and Panthino.*

ANTONIO

1   Tell me, Panthino, what sad talk was that
      Wherewith my brother held you in the cloister?

PANTHINO

      'Twas of his nephew Proteus, your son.

ANTONIO

      Why, what of him?

PANTHINO   He wond'red that your lordship
      Would suffer him to spend his youth at home,

6   While other men, of slender reputation,

7   Put forth their sons to seek preferment out:
      Some to the wars to try their fortune there,
      Some to discover islands far away,
      Some to the studious universities.
      For any or for all these exercises

12   He said that Proteus your son was meet,

13   And did request me to importune you
      To let him spend his time no more at home,

15   Which would be great impeachment to his age
      In having known no travel in his youth.

ANTONIO

      Nor need'st thou much importune me to that

18   Whereon this month I have been hammering.
      I have considered well his loss of time,
      And how he cannot be a perfect man,
      Not being tried and tutored in the world.
      Experience is by industry achieved,
      And perfected by the swift course of time.
      Then tell me, whither were I best to send him?

PANTHINO

      I think your lordship is not ignorant
      How his companion, youthful Valentine,

27   Attends the Emperor in his royal court.

ANTONIO

      I know it well.

PANTHINO

      'Twere good, I think, your lordship sent him thither.
      There shall he practise tilts and tournaments,
      Hear sweet discourse, converse with noblemen,

32   And be in eye of every exercise
      Worthy his youth and nobleness of birth.

ANTONIO

      I like thy counsel – well hast thou advised –
      And that thou mayst perceive how well I like it
      The execution of it shall make known.

37   Even with the speediest expedition
      I will dispatch him to the Emperor's court.

PANTHINO

39   To-morrow, may it please you, Don Alphonso
      With other gentlemen of good esteem
      Are journ'ying to salute the Emperor

42   And to commend their service to his will.

ANTONIO

      Good company. With them shall Proteus go
      And –
            [Enter] Proteus.

44   In good time! Now will we break with him.

PROTEUS

      Sweet love, sweet lines, sweet life!
      Here is her hand, the agent of her heart;

47   Here is her oath for love, her honor's pawn.
      O that our fathers would applaud our loves
      To seal our happiness with their consents!

      O heavenly Julia!

ANTONIO

      How now? What letter are you reading there?

PROTEUS

      May't please your lordship, 'tis a word or two
      Of commendations sent from Valentine,   53
      Delivered by a friend that came from him.

ANTONIO

      Lend me the letter. Let me see what news.

PROTEUS

      There is no news, my lord, but that he writes
      How happily he lives, how well beloved
      And daily gracèd by the Emperor,
      Wishing me with him, partner of his fortune.

ANTONIO

      And how stand you affected to his wish?   60

PROTEUS

      As one relying on your lordship's will
      And not depending on his friendly wish.

ANTONIO

      My will is something sorted with his wish.   63
      Muse not that I thus suddenly proceed,   64
      For what I will, I will, and there an end.
      I am resolved that thou shalt spend some time
      With Valentinus in the Emperor's court.
      What maintenance he from his friends receives,   68
      Like exhibition thou shalt have from me.   69
      To-morrow be in readiness to go.
      Excuse it not, for I am peremptory.   71

PROTEUS

      My lord, I cannot be so soon provided.   72
      Please you, deliberate a day or two.

ANTONIO

      Look, what thou want'st shall be sent after thee.
      No more of stay; to-morrow thou must go.
      Come on, Panthino; you shall be employed
      To hasten on his expedition.   77
                          [Exeunt Antonio and Panthino.]

PROTEUS

      Thus have I shunned the fire for fear of burning,
      And drenched me in the sea, where I am drowned.
      I feared to show my father Julia's letter,
      Lest he should take exceptions to my love;
      And with the vantage of mine own excuse
      Hath he excepted most against my love.   83
      O, how this spring of love resembleth
      The uncertain glory of an April day,
      Which now shows all the beauty of the sun,
      And by and by a cloud takes all away!
      [Enter Panthino.]

I, iii Verona: the house of Antonio   1 *sad* serious   6 *slender reputation*
less illustrious name   7 *Put forth* send abroad; *preferment* advancement
12 *meet* fitted   13 *importune* urge   15 *impeachment* detriment; *to his age*
when he is old   18 *hammering* i.e. pondering   27 *Emperor* (mentioned
five times in this scene, and only once again in the play – by Launce, who
speaks of the 'Imperial' in II, iii; his place appears to be taken by the
Duke of Milan)   32 *in eye of* in a position to witness   37 *expedition*
promptness   39 *may . . . you* if it should suit your purpose   42 *commend*
commit   44 *In good time* i.e. conveniently; *break with him* inform him (of
the plan)   47 *pawn* pledge   53 *commendations* greetings   60 *how . . .
affected to* how do you like   63 *something sorted* partly in accordance   64
Muse wonder   68 *friends* i.e. relatives   69 *exhibition* allowance   71 *Excuse
it not* make no excuses; *peremptory* resolved   72 *provided* equipped   77
hasten . . . expedition hurry him along   83 *excepted most against* i.e. most
effectively impeded

PANTHINO
Sir Proteus, your father calls for you.
He is in haste; therefore, I pray you, go.

PROTEUS
90 Why, this it is: my heart accords thereto,
And yet a thousand times it answers, 'no.'   *Exeunt.*

*

II, i   *Enter Valentine, [and] Speed.*
SPEED Sir, your glove.
VALENTINE Not mine; my gloves are on.
3 SPEED Why then this may be yours, for this is but one.
VALENTINE
Ha! Let me see. Ay, give it me, it's mine.
Sweet ornament that decks a thing divine!
Ah Silvia, Silvia!
SPEED *[calling]* Madam Silvia. Madam Silvia.
8 VALENTINE How now, sirrah?
SPEED She is not within hearing, sir.
VALENTINE Why, sir, who bade you call her?
SPEED Your worship, sir, or else I mistook.
12 VALENTINE Well, you'll still be too forward.
SPEED And yet I was last chidden for being too slow.
14 VALENTINE Go to, sir. Tell me, do you know Madam
Silvia?
SPEED She that your worship loves?
VALENTINE Why, how know you that I am in love?
SPEED Marry, by these special marks: first, you have
18 learned, like Sir Proteus, to wreathe your arms like a
19 malcontent, to relish a love-song like a robin-redbreast,
to walk alone like one that had the pestilence, to sigh
21 like a schoolboy that had lost his A B C, to weep like a
young wench that had buried her grandam, to fast like
23 one that takes diet, to watch like one that fears robbing,
24 to speak puling like a beggar at Hallowmas. You were
wont, when you laughed, to crow like a cock; when you
walked, to walk like one of the lions; when you fasted, it
27 was presently after dinner; when you looked sadly, it
was for want of money. And now you are metamor-
29 phosed with a mistress, that when I look on you, I can
hardly think you my master.
VALENTINE Are all these things perceived in me?
32 SPEED They are all perceived without ye.
VALENTINE Without me? They cannot.

SPEED Without you? Nay, that's certain, for without you 34
were so simple, none else would. But you are so without 35
these follies, that these follies are within you and shine
through you like the water in an urinal, that not an eye
that sees you but is a physician to comment on your
malady.
VALENTINE But tell me, dost thou know my lady Silvia?
SPEED She that you gaze on so as she sits at supper?
VALENTINE Hast thou observed that? Even she, I mean.
SPEED Why, sir, I know her not.
VALENTINE Dost thou know her by my gazing on her,
and yet know'st her not?
SPEED Is she not hard-favored, sir? 46
VALENTINE Not so fair, boy, as well-favored. 47
SPEED Sir, I know that well enough.
VALENTINE What dost thou know?
SPEED That she is not so fair as, of you, well-favored.
VALENTINE I mean that her beauty is exquisite, but her
favor infinite. 52
SPEED That's because the one is painted and the other out 53
of all count.
VALENTINE How painted? And how out of count?
SPEED Marry, sir, so painted to make her fair, that no
man counts of her beauty. 57
VALENTINE How esteem'st thou me? I account of her
beauty.
SPEED You never saw her since she was deformed. 59
VALENTINE How long hath she been deformed?
SPEED Ever since you loved her.
VALENTINE I have loved her ever since I saw her, and
still I see her beautiful.
SPEED If you love her, you cannot see her.
VALENTINE Why?
SPEED Because Love is blind. O, that you had mine eyes,
or your own eyes had the lights they were wont to have 67
when you chid at Sir Proteus for going ungartered! 68
VALENTINE What should I see then?
SPEED Your own present folly and her passing deformity; 70
for he, being in love, could not see to garter his hose,
and you, being in love, cannot see to put on your hose. 72
VALENTINE Belike, boy, then you are in love, for last
morning you could not see to wipe my shoes.
SPEED True, sir, I was in love with my bed. I thank you:
you swinged me for my love, which makes me the 76
bolder to chide you for yours.
VALENTINE In conclusion, I stand affected to her.
SPEED I would you were set, so your affection would cease. 79
VALENTINE Last night she enjoined me to write some
lines to one she loves.
SPEED And have you?
VALENTINE I have.
SPEED Are they not lamely writ?
VALENTINE No, boy, but as well as I can do them. Peace,
here she comes.
[Enter] Silvia.
SPEED *[aside]* O excellent motion! O exceeding puppet! 87
Now will he interpret to her. 88
VALENTINE Madam and mistress, a thousand good mor-
rows.
SPEED *[aside]* O, give ye good ev'n! Here's a million of 90
manners!
SILVIA Sir Valentine and servant, to you two thousand. 92
SPEED *[aside]* He should give her interest, and she gives it
him.

---

90 *accords thereto* is obedient to (my father's wish)
II, i A street in Milan   **3** *one* (pronounced like *on* in the line above, allowing for an easy pun)   **8** *sirrah* fellow (used in addressing inferiors)   **12**
still always   **14** *Go to* (an expression of impatience)   **18** *wreathe* fold
19 *relish* sing   **21** *A B C* primer   **23** *watch* stay awake at night   **24** *puling*
with a whine; *Hallowmas* All Saints' Day, November 1 (a day of special
alms for beggars)   **27** *presently* immediately   **29** *that* so that   **32** *without*
ye i.e. in your outward appearance   **34** *without* unless   **35** *would* i.e. perceive them   **35–36** *you are . . . follies* i.e. you are so much the walking image
of these follies   **46** *hard-favored* ugly   **47** *fair* in complexion: Julia says
of Silvia, 'Her hair is auburn, mine is perfect yellow,' IV, iv, 187); *well-*
favored good-looking   **52** *favor* charm   **53–54** *out . . . count* beyond
reckoning   **57** *counts . . . beauty* thinks her beautiful   **59** *deformed* i.e.
transformed   **67** *lights* sight   **68** *going ungartered* i.e. neglecting his appearance (a conventional sign of the lover's melancholy)   **70** *passing*
excessive   **72** *cannot . . . hose* i.e. cannot even see to put on your hose (not to
speak of your garters)   **76** *swinged* beat   **79** *set* settled (with play on *stand*)
87 *motion* i.e. puppet-show   **88** *interpret* i.e. speak the lines (like a puppet-
master)   **90** *give* (short form of 'God give')   **90–91** *a million of manners*
i.e. perfect manners (with sarcasm)   **92** *servant* i.e. lover devoted to
serving a lady without expecting a return

VALENTINE
As you enjoined me, I have writ your letter
Unto the secret, nameless friend of yours,
Which I was much unwilling to proceed in
98 But for my duty to your ladyship.
    [Gives a letter.]
SILVIA
99 I thank you, gentle servant. 'Tis very clerkly done.
VALENTINE
100 Now trust me, madam, it came hardly off,
For, being ignorant to whom it goes,
102 I writ at random, very doubtfully.
SILVIA
103 Perchance you think too much of so much pains?
VALENTINE
104 No, madam. So it stead you, I will write –
Please you command – a thousand times as much.
And yet –
SILVIA
107 A pretty period! Well, I guess the sequel –
And yet I will not name it – and yet I care not –
And yet take this again – and yet I thank you,
Meaning henceforth to trouble you no more.
SPEED *[aside]*
And yet you will; and yet another 'yet.'
VALENTINE
What means your ladyship? Do you not like it?
SILVIA
113 Yes, yes. The lines are very quaintly writ,
But since unwillingly, take them again.
Nay, take them.
    [Gives back the letter.]
VALENTINE   Madam, they are for you.
SILVIA
Ay, ay, you writ them, sir, at my request,
But I will none of them. They are for you –
I would have had them writ more movingly.
VALENTINE
Please you, I'll write your ladyship another.
SILVIA
And when it's writ, for my sake read it over,
And if it please you, so; if not, why, so.
VALENTINE
If it please me, madam, what then?
SILVIA
Why, if it please you, take it for your labor –
And so, good morrow, servant.   *Exit Silvia.*
SPEED
O jest unseen, inscrutable, invisible,
As a nose on a man's face, or a weathercock on a steeple!
My master sues to her, and she hath taught her suitor,
He being her pupil, to become her tutor.
O excellent device – was there ever heard a better? –
That my master, being scribe, to himself should write
   the letter!
VALENTINE
131 How now, sir? What, are you reasoning with yourself?
SPEED Nay, I was riming; 'tis you that have the reason.
VALENTINE To do what?
SPEED To be a spokesman from Madam Silvia.
VALENTINE To whom?
136 SPEED To yourself. Why, she woos you by a figure.
VALENTINE What figure?
SPEED By a letter, I should say.

VALENTINE Why, she hath not writ to me?
SPEED What need she, when she hath made you write to
   yourself? Why, do you not perceive the jest?
VALENTINE No, believe me.
SPEED No believing you, indeed, sir. But did you per-
   ceive her earnest?   144
VALENTINE She gave me none, except an angry word. 145
SPEED Why, she hath given you a letter.
VALENTINE That's the letter I writ to her friend.
SPEED And that letter hath she delivered, and there an
   end.
VALENTINE I would it were no worse.
SPEED I'll warrant you, 'tis as well:
   'For often have you writ to her, and she in modesty,
   Or else for want of idle time, could not again reply;
   Or fearing else some messenger that might her mind 153
     discover,
   Herself hath taught her love himself to write unto her
     lover.'
   All this I speak in print, for in print I found it.   155
   Why muse you, sir? 'Tis dinner-time.
VALENTINE I have dined.   157
SPEED Ay, but hearken, sir: though the chameleon Love 158
   can feed on the air, I am one that am nourished by my
   victuals and would fain have meat. O, be not like your 160
   mistress; be moved, be moved.   *Exeunt.*

*

       Enter Proteus, [and] Julia.   II, ii
PROTEUS
Have patience, gentle Julia.
JULIA
I must, where is no remedy.
PROTEUS
When possibly I can, I will return.
JULIA
If you turn not, you will return the sooner.   4
Keep this remembrance for thy Julia's sake.
    [Gives him a ring.]
PROTEUS
Why then, we'll make exchange. Here, take you this.
JULIA
And seal the bargain with a holy kiss.
PROTEUS
Here is my hand for my true constancy;
And when that hour o'erslips me in the day
Wherein I sigh not, Julia, for thy sake,
The next ensuing hour some foul mischance
Torment me for my love's forgetfulness!
My father stays my coming; answer not.   13
The tide is now – nay, not thy tide of tears –
That tide will stay me longer than I should.

98 *duty* (as owed by the *servant* to his lady) **99** *clerkly* in a scholarly manner **100** *came hardly off* was difficult **102** *doubtfully* uncertainly **103** *Perchance . . . pains* i.e. perhaps you find it too much trouble **104** *stead* help **107** *period* pause **113** *quaintly* cleverly **131** *reasoning with* talking to **136** *figure* device **144** *earnest* serious meaning **145** *none* (Valentine takes Speed's *earnest* to mean 'pledge') **153** *her mind discover* i.e. reveal her secret **155** *speak in print* speak by rote (the *print* in which Speed *found* the lines is probably imaginary) **157** *dined* (presumably on the sight of Silvia) **158** *chameleon* (supposedly capable of living on air) **160** *fain* gladly
II, ii Verona: the house of Julia **4** *turn* prove unfaithful **13** *stays* waits

Julia, farewell.   [Exit Julia.]
            What, gone without a word?
         Ay, so true love should do; it cannot speak,
18   For truth hath better deeds than words to grace it.
            [Enter] Panthino.
PANTHINO
         Sir Proteus, you are stayed for.
PROTEUS
         Go. I come, I come.
         Alas, this parting strikes poor lovers dumb!   Exeunt.

*

II, iii   Enter Launce [leading a dog].
     LAUNCE Nay, 'twill be this hour ere I have done weeping.
2   All the kind of the Launces have this very fault. I have
3   received my proportion, like the prodigious son, and am
4   going with Sir Proteus to the Imperial's court. I think
     Crab, my dog, be the sourest-natured dog that lives. My
     mother weeping, my father wailing, my sister crying,
     our maid howling, our cat wringing her hands, and all
     our house in a great perplexity, yet did not this cruel-
     hearted cur shed one tear. He is a stone, a very pebble
     stone, and has no more pity in him than a dog. A Jew
     would have wept to have seen our parting. Why, my
     grandam, having no eyes, look you, wept herself blind
     at my parting. Nay, I'll show you the manner of it. This
     shoe is my father. No, this left shoe is my father. No, no,
     this left shoe is my mother. Nay, that cannot be so
     neither. Yes, it is so, it is so – it hath the worser sole. This
     shoe with the hole in it is my mother, and this my father.
     A vengeance on't! There 'tis. Now, sir, this staff is my
     sister, for, look you, she is as white as a lily and as small
20   as a wand. This hat is Nan, our maid. I am the dog. No,
     the dog is himself, and I am the dog – O, the dog is me,
     and I am myself. Ay, so, so. Now come I to my father:
     'Father, your blessing.' Now should not the shoe speak a
     word for weeping. Now should I kiss my father – well,
     he weeps on. Now come I to my mother. O, that she
26   could speak now like a wood woman! Well, I kiss her –
27   why, there 'tis: here's my mother's breath up and down.
     Now come I to my sister; mark the moan she makes.
     Now the dog all this while sheds not a tear nor speaks a
     word, but see how I lay the dust with my tears.
            [Enter] Panthino.
PANTHINO Launce, away, away, aboard. Thy master is
32   shipped, and thou art to post after with oars. What's the
     matter? Why weep'st thou, man? Away, ass! You'll
     lose the tide if you tarry any longer.
     LAUNCE It is no matter if the tied were lost, for it is the
     unkindest tied that ever any man tied.

PANTHINO What's the unkindest tide?
LAUNCE Why, he that's tied here, Crab, my dog.
PANTHINO Tut, man, I mean thou'lt lose the flood; and, 39
     in losing the flood, lose thy voyage; and, in losing thy
     voyage, lose thy master; and, in losing thy master, lose
     thy service; and, in losing thy service – Why dost thou
     stop my mouth?
LAUNCE For fear thou shouldst lose thy tongue.
PANTHINO Where should I lose my tongue?
LAUNCE In thy tale.
PANTHINO In thy tail!
LAUNCE Lose the tide, and the voyage, and the master,
     and the service, and the tied! Why, man, if the river
     were dry, I am able to fill it with my tears. If the wind
     were down, I could drive the boat with my sighs.
PANTHINO Come, come away, man; I was sent to call
     thee.
LAUNCE Sir, call me what thou dar'st.
PANTHINO Wilt thou go?
LAUNCE Well, I will go.   Exeunt.

*

       Enter Valentine, Silvia, Thurio, [and] Speed.   II, iv
SILVIA Servant.
VALENTINE Mistress?
SPEED Master, Sir Thurio frowns on you.
VALENTINE Ay, boy, it's for love.
SPEED Not of you.
VALENTINE Of my mistress then.
SPEED 'Twere good you knocked him.   [Exit.]
SILVIA Servant, you are sad.
VALENTINE Indeed, madam, I seem so.
THURIO Seem you that you are not?
VALENTINE Haply I do.   11
THURIO So do counterfeits.
VALENTINE So do you.
THURIO What seem I that I am not?
VALENTINE Wise.
THURIO What instance of the contrary?
VALENTINE Your folly.
THURIO And how quote you my folly?   18
VALENTINE I quote it in your jerkin.   19
THURIO My jerkin is a doublet.   20
VALENTINE Well then, I'll double your folly.
THURIO How?
SILVIA What, angry, Sir Thurio? Do you change color?
VALENTINE Give him leave, madam; he is a kind of
     chameleon.
THURIO That hath more mind to feed on your blood than
     live in your air.   27
VALENTINE You have said, sir.   28
THURIO Ay, sir, and done too, for this time.   29
VALENTINE I know it well, sir: you always end ere you   30
     begin.
SILVIA A fine volley of words, gentlemen, and quickly
     shot off.
VALENTINE 'Tis indeed, madam. We thank the giver.
SILVIA Who is that, servant?
VALENTINE Yourself, sweet lady, for you gave the fire.
     Sir Thurio borrows his wit from your ladyship's looks,
     and spends what he borrows kindly in your company.   37
THURIO Sir, if you spend word for word with me, I shall
     make your wit bankrupt.
VALENTINE I know it well, sir. You have an exchequer of 40

18 truth … it deeds serve better than words to adorn truth
II, iii A street in Verona   2 kind family   3 proportion i.e. portion (malapropism); prodigious i.e. prodigal   4 Imperial's i.e. Emperor's   26 wood
mad (perhaps with play on 'wooden shoe'; folio reads 'would' – sometimes
emended to 'ould,' i.e. 'old')   27 up and down i.e. exactly   32 post … oars
follow in a rowboat (Proteus' ship is anchored in the harbor)   39 lose the
flood miss the tide
II, iv Milan: the palace of the Duke   11 Haply perhaps   18 quote notice
(pronounced like 'coat,' with pun following)   19 jerkin long jacket worn
over doublet or in place of it   20 doublet loose upper garment   27 your air
the air you breathe (Thurio makes play with the belief that the chameleon
lived on air)   28 You … sir so you say, sir (with the emphasis on 'say')   29
done finished (but the word implies action, in contrast to said, and veils a
threat of sword-play in the future)   30–31 end … begin i.e. stop short of a
fight   37 kindly fittingly   40 exchequer treasury

42 words and, I think, no other treasure to give your followers, for it appears by their bare liveries that they live
by your bare words.

SILVIA No more, gentlemen, no more. Here comes my
father.

[Enter] Duke.

DUKE
46 Now, daughter Silvia, you are hard beset.
Sir Valentine, your father is in good health.
What say you to a letter from your friends
Of much good news?

VALENTINE My lord, I will be thankful
50 To any happy messenger from thence.

DUKE
Know ye Don Antonio, your countryman?

VALENTINE
Ay, my good lord, I know the gentleman
To be of worth and worthy estimation,
And not without desert so well reputed.

DUKE
Hath he not a son?

VALENTINE
Ay, my good lord, a son that well deserves
The honor and regard of such a father.

DUKE
You know him well?

VALENTINE
I know him as myself, for from our infancy
60 We have conversed and spent our hours together;
And though myself have been an idle truant,
62 Omitting the sweet benefit of time
To clothe mine age with angel-like perfection,
Yet hath Sir Proteus – for that's his name –
Made use and fair advantage of his days;
His years but young, but his experience old;
67 His head unmellowed, but his judgment ripe;
And in a word – for far behind his worth
Comes all the praises that I now bestow –
He is complete in feature and in mind
With all good grace to grace a gentleman.

DUKE
72 Beshrew me, sir, but if he make this good,
He is as worthy for an empress' love
74 As meet to be an emperor's counsellor.
Well, sir, this gentleman is come to me
With commendation from great potentates,
And here he means to spend his time awhile.
I think 'tis no unwelcome news to you.

VALENTINE
Should I have wished a thing, it had been he.

DUKE
Welcome him then according to his worth.
Silvia, I speak to you – and you, Sir Thurio –
82 For Valentine, I need not cite him to it.
83 I will send him hither to you presently. *[Exit.]*

VALENTINE
This is the gentleman I told your ladyship
Had come along with me, but that his mistress
86 Did hold his eyes locked in her crystal looks.

SILVIA
87 Belike that now she hath enfranchised them
88 Upon some other pawn for fealty.

VALENTINE
Nay, sure, I think she holds them prisoners still.

SILVIA
Nay, then he should be blind, and, being blind,
How could he see his way to seek out you?

VALENTINE
Why, lady, Love hath twenty pair of eyes.

THURIO
They say that Love hath not an eye at all.

VALENTINE
To see such lovers, Thurio, as yourself;
Upon a homely object Love can wink. *[Exit Thurio.]* 95

SILVIA
Have done, have done. Here comes the gentleman.
[Enter] Proteus.

VALENTINE
Welcome, dear Proteus. Mistress, I beseech you
Confirm his welcome with some special favor.

SILVIA
His worth is warrant for his welcome hither,
If this be he you oft have wished to hear from.

VALENTINE
Mistress, it is. Sweet lady, entertain him 101
To be my fellow-servant to your ladyship.

SILVIA
Too low a mistress for so high a servant.

PROTEUS
Not so, sweet lady, but too mean a servant
To have a look of such a worthy mistress. 105

VALENTINE
Leave off discourse of disability. 106
Sweet lady, entertain him for your servant.

PROTEUS
My duty will I boast of, nothing else. 108

SILVIA
And duty never yet did want his meed. 109
Servant, you are welcome to a worthless mistress.

PROTEUS
I'll die on him that says so but yourself. 111

SILVIA
That you are welcome?

PROTEUS That you are worthless.
[Enter Thurio.]

THURIO
Madam, my lord your father would speak with you. 113

SILVIA
I wait upon his pleasure. Come, Sir Thurio,
Go with me. Once more, new servant, welcome.
I'll leave you to confer of home affairs;
When you have done, we look to hear from you.

42–43 *bare . . . bare* threadbare . . . worthless 46 *hard beset* heavily engaged
(since she entertains two suitors at one time) 50 *happy messenger* bringer
of good news 60 *conversed* associated 62 *Omitting* neglecting 67 *unmellowed* still youthful in appearance (without grey hairs) 72 *if . . . good*
i.e. if he lives up to your report 74 *meet* fit 82 *cite* urge 83 *presently*
immediately 86 *locked . . . looks* (it was believed that a spirit imprisoned
in a crystal ball might be forced to obey commands) 87 *Belike* it's likely;
enfranchised freed 88 *Upon . . . fealty* for some other pledge of loyal
service (i.e. because she has found another lover) 95 *Upon . . . wink* i.e.
Love can close his eyes to an unattractive sight 101 *entertain* engage
105 *of* from 106 *Leave . . . disability* i.e. stop this self-disparagement
108 *My duty . . . else* i.e. my only boast will be my role as Silvia's servant
109 *want* lack; *meed* reward 111 *die on him* die fighting with anyone
113 *Madam . . . you* (the folio gives this line to Thurio, and therefore
an exit must be arranged for him earlier – as above, at l. 95 – and an entrance
here. Some editors solve the problem by having a 'servant' enter to speak
this line; Thurio then may remain on stage until he leaves with Silvia at
her request.)

PROTEUS
We'll both attend upon your ladyship.

[Exeunt Silvia and Thurio.]

VALENTINE
Now tell me, how do all from whence you came?

PROTEUS
120   Your friends are well and have them much commended.

VALENTINE
And how do yours?

PROTEUS   I left them all in health.

VALENTINE
How does your lady, and how thrives your love?

PROTEUS
My tales of love were wont to weary you;
I know you joy not in a love discourse.

VALENTINE
Ay, Proteus, but that life is altered now.
126   I have done penance for contemning Love,
Whose high imperious thoughts have punished me
With bitter fasts, with penitential groans,
With nightly tears and daily heart-sore sighs;
For, in revenge of my contempt of Love,
131   Love hath chased sleep from my enthrallèd eyes,
And made them watchers of mine own heart's sorrow.
O gentle Proteus, Love's a mighty lord,
134   And hath so humbled me as I confess
135   There is no woe to his correction,
136   Nor to his service no such joy on earth.
Now no discourse, except it be of Love;
Now can I break my fast, dine, sup, and sleep,
139   Upon the very naked name of Love.

PROTEUS
Enough; I read your fortune in your eye.
Was this the idol that you worship so?

VALENTINE
Even she; and is she not a heavenly saint?

PROTEUS
No, but she is an earthly paragon.

VALENTINE
Call her divine.

PROTEUS   I will not flatter her.

VALENTINE
O, flatter me, for love delights in praises.

PROTEUS
When I was sick, you gave me bitter pills,
And I must minister the like to you.

VALENTINE
148   Then speak the truth by her: if not divine,
149   Yet let her be a principality,
150   Sovereign to all the creatures on the earth.

PROTEUS
Except my mistress.

VALENTINE   Sweet, except not any,
Except thou wilt except against my love.   152

PROTEUS
Have I not reason to prefer mine own?

VALENTINE
And I will help thee to prefer her too.   154
She shall be dignified with this high honor:
To bear my lady's train, lest the base earth
Should from her vesture chance to steal a kiss,
And, of so great a favor growing proud,
Disdain to root the summer-swelling flower,
And make rough winter everlastingly.

PROTEUS
Why, Valentine, what braggardism is this?

VALENTINE
Pardon me, Proteus, all I can is nothing   162
To her whose worth makes other worthies nothing.
She is alone.   164

PROTEUS   Then let her alone.

VALENTINE
Not for the world. Why, man, she is mine own,
And I as rich in having such a jewel
As twenty seas, if all their sand were pearl,
The water nectar, and the rocks pure gold.
Forgive me that I do not dream on thee,   169
Because thou seest me dote upon my love.
My foolish rival, that her father likes
Only for his possessions are so huge,   172
Is gone with her along, and I must after,
For love, thou know'st, is full of jealousy.

PROTEUS
But she loves you?

VALENTINE
Ay, and we are betrothed. Nay more, our marriage-hour,
With all the cunning manner of our flight,   177
Determined of: how I must climb her window,   178
The ladder made of cords, and all the means
Plotted and 'greed on for my happiness.
Good Proteus, go with me to my chamber,
In these affairs to aid me with thy counsel.

PROTEUS
Go on before; I shall inquire you forth.   183
I must unto the road to disembark   184
Some necessaries that I needs must use,
And then I'll presently attend you.   186

VALENTINE
Will you make haste?   *Exit.*

PROTEUS
I will.
Even as one heat another heat expels,   189
Or as one nail by strength drives out another,
So the remembrance of my former love
Is by a newer object quite forgotten.
It is mine eye, or Valentine's praise,
Her true perfection, or my false transgression,
That makes me reasonless to reason thus.   195
She is fair, and so is Julia that I love –
That I did love, for now my love is thawed,
Which, like a waxen image 'gainst a fire,
Bears no impression of the thing it was.
Methinks my zeal to Valentine is cold,
And that I love him not as I was wont.   201

120 *them much commended* sent many greetings   126 *contemning* despising 131 *enthrallèd* enslaved (by Silvia's beauty)   134 *as* that   135 *to* comparable to; *correction* punishment   136 *Nor . . . earth* i.e. no earthly joy is equal to that of serving Love   139 *very naked* mere   148 *by* about   149 *principality* a member of one of the nine orders of angels (Valentine is saying, 'If you won't agree that Silvia is a goddess, at least admit that she's an angel.')   150 *Sovereign* superior   152 *Except . . . against* unless you wish to disparage   154 *prefer* advance, promote (playing upon the word used by Proteus in a different sense)   162 *can* can say   164 *is alone* is peerless   169 *that I . . . thee* i.e. that I neglect you   172 *for* because   177 *cunning* ingenious   178 *Determined of* decided on   183 *inquire you forth* ask where you lodge   184 *road* anchorage   186 *presently* immediately 189 *Even . . . expels* (it was believed that exposure to fire would relieve the pain of a burn)   195 *reasonless* irrationally; *reason* argue   201 *as I was wont* as I formerly did

O, but I love his lady too too much,
And that's the reason I love him so little.
204 How shall I dote on her with more advice,
That thus without advice begin to love her!
206 'Tis but her picture I have yet beheld,
And that hath dazzlèd my reason's light,
But when I look on her perfections,
209 There is no reason but I shall be blind.
If I can check my erring love, I will;
211 If not, to compass her I'll use my skill.   *Exit.*

*

II, v   *Enter Speed and Launce.*
1 SPEED Launce, by mine honesty, welcome to Padua.
2 LAUNCE Forswear not thyself, sweet youth, for I am not
welcome. I reckon this always, that a man is never undone till he be hanged, nor never welcome to a place till
5 some certain shot be paid and the hostess say welcome.
SPEED Come on, you madcap, I'll to the alehouse with
you presently, where, for one shot of five pence, thou
shalt have five thousand welcomes. But, sirrah, how did
thy master part with Madam Julia?
10 LAUNCE Marry, after they closed in earnest, they parted
11 very fairly in jest.
SPEED But shall she marry him?
LAUNCE No.
SPEED How then? Shall he marry her?
LAUNCE No, neither.
SPEED What, are they broken?
17 LAUNCE No, they are both as whole as a fish.
SPEED Why then, how stands the matter with them?
19 LAUNCE Marry, thus: when it stands well with him, it
stands well with her.
SPEED What an ass art thou! I understand thee not.
LAUNCE What a block art thou that thou canst not! My
staff understands me.
SPEED What thou say'st?
LAUNCE Ay, and what I do too. Look thee, I'll but lean,
and my staff understands me.
SPEED It stands under thee indeed.
LAUNCE Why, stand-under and under-stand is all one.
SPEED But tell me true, will't be a match?
LAUNCE Ask my dog. If he say ay, it will. If he say no, it
will. If he shake his tail and say nothing, it will.
SPEED The conclusion is, then, that it will.
LAUNCE Thou shalt never get such a secret from me but
by a parable.
35 SPEED 'Tis well that I get it so. But Launce, how say'st
thou that, that my master is become a notable lover?
LAUNCE I never knew him otherwise.
SPEED Than how?
LAUNCE A notable lubber, as thou reportest him to be.
40 SPEED Why, thou whoreson ass, thou mistak'st me.
LAUNCE Why, fool, I meant not thee, I meant thy master.
SPEED I tell thee, my master is become a hot lover.
LAUNCE Why, I tell thee, I care not though he burn him-
self in love. If thou wilt, go with me to the alehouse; if
not, thou art an Hebrew, a Jew, and not worth the name
of a Christian.
SPEED Why?
LAUNCE Because thou hast not so much charity in thee as
49 to go to the ale with a Christian. Wilt thou go?
SPEED At thy service.   *Exeunt.*

*

Enter Proteus solus.   II, vi
PROTEUS
To leave my Julia, shall I be forsworn;
To love fair Silvia, shall I be forsworn;
To wrong my friend, I shall be much forsworn;
And ev'n that pow'r which gave me first my oath
Provokes me to this threefold perjury.
Love bade me swear, and Love bids me forswear.
O sweet-suggesting Love, if thou hast sinned,   7
Teach me, thy tempted subject, to excuse it.
At first I did adore a twinkling star,
But now I worship a celestial sun.
Unheedful vows may heedfully be broken,   11
And he wants wit that wants resolvèd will   12
To learn his wit t' exchange the bad for better.   13
Fie, fie, unreverend tongue, to call her bad,
Whose sovereignty so oft thou hast preferred   15
With twenty thousand soul-confirming oaths!   16
I cannot leave to love, and yet I do;   17
But there I leave to love where I should love.
Julia I lose and Valentine I lose.
If I keep them, I needs must lose myself;
If I lose them, thus find I by their loss:
For Valentine, myself; for Julia, Silvia.
I to myself am dearer than a friend,
For love is still most precious in itself,   24
And Silvia – witness heaven that made her fair! –
Shows Julia but a swarthy Ethiope.   26
I will forget that Julia is alive,
Rememb'ring that my love to her is dead,
And Valentine I'll hold an enemy,
Aiming at Silvia as a sweeter friend.
I cannot now prove constant to myself
Without some treachery used to Valentine.
This night he meaneth with a corded ladder
To climb celestial Silvia's chamber window,
Myself in counsel, his competitor.   35
Now presently I'll give her father notice
Of their disguising and pretended flight,   37
Who, all enraged, will banish Valentine;
For Thurio, he intends, shall wed his daughter.
But, Valentine being gone, I'll quickly cross   40
By some sly trick blunt Thurio's dull proceeding.   41
Love, lend me wings to make my purpose swift,
As thou hast lent me wit to plot this drift.   *Exit.*   43

*

204 *advice* mature consideration   206 *picture* (used figuratively for 'outer
semblance,' since he has actually seen her? or a confusion in the text?)
209 *There . . . blind* I shall certainly be blinded   211 *compass* obtain
II, v A street in Milan   1 *Padua* (a slip? the scene is Milan)   2 *Forswear*
perjure   5 *shot* tavern bill   10 *closed* embraced   11 *fairly* gently   17 *as
whole . . . fish* (proverb)   19–20 *when . . . her* (a ribald pun)   35–36 *how
say'st thou that* what do you think of this   40 *whoreson* (mildly abusive
epithet)   49 *go . . . Christian* (Launce refers to the custom of holding a
church-ale, or village drinking party, to raise money for the church)
II, vi The palace of the Duke   7 *sweet-suggesting* seductive   7–8 *if thou
. . . it* i.e. if what you tempt me to is a sin, show me how to extenuate
it (?)   11 *Unheedful* thoughtless; *heedfully* after careful thought   12
wants lacks   13 *learn* teach   15 *preferred* promoted, urged   16 *soul-
confirming* devout   17 *leave* cease   24 *still* always   26 *Shows Julia but*
makes Julia (by comparison) appear no better than   35 *Myself . . . competitor* myself taken into his confidence as his partner   37 *pretended*
intended   40 *cross* foil   41 *blunt* stupid; *proceeding* i.e. his courtship   43
drift scheme

II, vii *Enter Julia and Lucetta.*

JULIA
Counsel, Lucetta; gentle girl, assist me;
2 And ev'n in kind love I do conjure thee,
3 Who art the table wherein all my thoughts
4 Are visibly charactered and engraved,
5 To lesson me and tell me some good mean
How, with my honor, I may undertake
A journey to my loving Proteus.

LUCETTA
Alas, the way is wearisome and long!

JULIA
A true-devoted pilgrim is not weary
10 To measure kingdoms with his feeble steps;
Much less shall she that hath Love's wings to fly,
And when the flight is made to one so dear,
Of such divine perfection, as Sir Proteus.

LUCETTA
Better forbear till Proteus make return.

JULIA
O, know'st thou not his looks are my soul's food?
Pity the dearth that I have pinèd in
By longing for that food so long a time.
18 Didst thou but know the inly touch of love,
Thou wouldst as soon go kindle fire with snow
As seek to quench the fire of love with words.

LUCETTA
I do not seek to quench your love's hot fire,
But qualify the fire's extreme rage,
Lest it should burn above the bounds of reason.

JULIA
The more thou dam'st it up, the more it burns.
The current that with gentle murmur glides,
Thou know'st, being stopped, impatiently doth rage;
But when his fair course is not hinderèd,
28 He makes sweet music with th' enamelled stones,
Giving a gentle kiss to every sedge
He overtaketh in his pilgrimage.
And so by many winding nooks he strays
32 With willing sport to the wild ocean.
Then let me go and hinder not my course.
I'll be as patient as a gentle stream
And make a pastime of each weary step,
Till the last step have brought me to my love;
And there I'll rest, as after much turmoil
A blessèd soul doth in Elysium.

LUCETTA
39 But in what habit will you go along?

JULIA
40 Not like a woman, for I would prevent
The loose encounters of lascivious men.
Gentle Lucetta, fit me with such weeds   42
As may beseem some well-reputed page.   43

LUCETTA
Why then, your ladyship must cut your hair.

JULIA
No, girl, I'll knit it up in silken strings
With twenty odd-conceited true-love knots.   46
To be fantastic may become a youth   47
Of greater time than I shall show to be.   48

LUCETTA
What fashion, madam, shall I make your breeches?

JULIA
That fits as well as 'Tell me, good my lord,
What compass will you wear your farthingale?'   51
Why, ev'n what fashion thou best likes, Lucetta.

LUCETTA
You must needs have them with a cod-piece, madam.   53

JULIA
Out, out, Lucetta, that will be ill-favored!   54

LUCETTA
A round hose, madam, now's not worth a pin,   55
Unless you have a cod-piece to stick pins on.   56

JULIA
Lucetta, as thou lov'st me, let me have
What thou think'st meet, and is most mannerly.
But tell me, wench, how will the world repute me
For undertaking so unstaid a journey?   60
I fear me it will make me scandalized.   61

LUCETTA
If you think so, then stay at home and go not.

JULIA
Nay, that I will not.

LUCETTA
Then never dream on infamy, but go.
If Proteus like your journey when you come,
No matter who's displeased when you are gone.
I fear me he will scarce be pleased withal.   67

JULIA
That is the least, Lucetta, of my fear.
A thousand oaths, an ocean of his tears,
And instances of infinite of love,   70
Warrant me welcome to my Proteus.

LUCETTA
All these are servants to deceitful men.

JULIA
Base men, that use them to so base effect!
But truer stars did govern Proteus' birth;   74
His words are bonds, his oaths are oracles,
His love sincere, his thoughts immaculate,
His tears pure messengers sent from his heart,
His heart as far from fraud as heaven from earth.

LUCETTA
Pray heav'n he prove so when you come to him!

JULIA
Now, as thou lov'st me, do him not that wrong
To bear a hard opinion of his truth.
Only deserve my love by loving him,
And presently go with me to my chamber   83
To take a note of what I stand in need of
To furnish me upon my longing journey.   85
All that is mine I leave at thy dispose,
My goods, my lands, my reputation;
Only, in lieu thereof, dispatch me hence.   88

II, vii Verona: the house of Julia **2** *conjure* solemnly require **3** *table* notebook **4** *charactered* written **5** *lesson* teach **10** *measure* traverse **18** *inly* inward **28** *enamelled* shiny **32** *wild* unbounded **39** *habit* clothing **40** *prevent* forestall **42** *weeds* garments **43** *beseem* suit **46** *odd-conceited* ingeniously conceived **47** *fantastic* fanciful **48** *time* age **51** *compass* circumference, fullness **53** *cod-piece* bag-like appendage at the crotch of tight-fitting breeches; often conspicuously tailored **54** *Out, out* i.e. out upon you; *ill-favored* unsightly **55** *round hose* short, wide breeches puffed out with padding **56** *to stick pins on* (one of the methods used to decorate the cod-piece was to ornament it with pins) **60** *unstaid* reckless **61** *I . . . scandalized* I'm afraid it will get me talked about **67** *withal* with it **70** *infinite* an infinity **74** *truer . . . birth* (reference to the belief that one's character was determined by the position of the stars at one's birth) **83** *presently* now **85** *longing* love-prompted **88** *dispatch* hasten

Come, answer not, but to it presently;
I am impatient of my tarriance.   *Exeunt.*

*

III, i   *Enter Duke, Thurio, [and] Proteus.*

DUKE
1   Sir Thurio, give us leave, I pray, awhile.
We have some secrets to confer about.   *[Exit Thurio.]*
Now tell me, Proteus, what's your will with me?

PROTEUS
4   My gracious lord, that which I would discover
The law of friendship bids me to conceal;
But when I call to mind your gracious favors
Done to me, undeserving as I am,
My duty pricks me on to utter that
Which else no worldly good should draw from me.
Know, worthy prince, Sir Valentine, my friend,
This night intends to steal away your daughter.
12   Myself am one made privy to the plot.
I know you have determined to bestow her
On Thurio, whom your gentle daughter hates,
And should she thus be stol'n away from you,
It would be much vexation to your age.
Thus, for my duty's sake, I rather chose
18   To cross my friend in his intended drift
Than, by concealing it, heap on your head
A pack of sorrows which would press you down,
21   Being unprevented, to your timeless grave.

DUKE
Proteus, I thank thee for thine honest care,
23   Which to requite, command me while I live.
This love of theirs myself have often seen,
25   Haply when they have judged me fast asleep,
And oftentimes have purposed to forbid
Sir Valentine her company and my court.
But, fearing lest my jealous aim might err,
And so unworthily disgrace the man –
A rashness that I ever yet have shunned –
I gave him gentle looks, thereby to find
That which thyself hast now disclosed to me.
And, that thou mayst perceive my fear of this,
34   Knowing that tender youth is soon suggested,
I nightly lodge her in an upper tow'r,
The key whereof myself have ever kept,
And thence she cannot be conveyed away.

PROTEUS
Know, noble lord, they have devised a mean
How he her chamber window will ascend
And with a corded ladder fetch her down;
For which the youthful lover now is gone,
42   And this way comes he with it presently,
Where, if it please you, you may intercept him.
But, good my lord, do it so cunningly
45   That my discovery be not aimèd at;
For love of you, not hate unto my friend,
47   Hath made me publisher of this pretense.

DUKE
Upon mine honor, he shall never know
That I had any light from thee of this.

PROTEUS
Adieu, my lord. Sir Valentine is coming.   *[Exit.]*
     [Enter] Valentine.

DUKE
Sir Valentine, whither away so fast?

VALENTINE
Please it your Grace, there is a messenger   52
That stays to bear my letters to my friends,
And I am going to deliver them.

DUKE
Be they of much import?

VALENTINE
The tenor of them doth but signify   56
My health and happy being at your court.

DUKE
Nay then, no matter; stay with me awhile.
I am to break with thee of some affairs   59
That touch me near, wherein thou must be secret.
'Tis not unknown to thee that I have sought
To match my friend Sir Thurio to my daughter.

VALENTINE
I know it well, my lord; and sure, the match
Were rich and honorable. Besides, the gentleman
Is full of virtue, bounty, worth, and qualities
Beseeming such a wife as your fair daughter.   66
Cannot your Grace win her to fancy him?

DUKE
No, trust me, she is peevish, sullen, froward,   68
Proud, disobedient, stubborn, lacking duty,
Neither regarding that she is my child,
Nor fearing me as if I were her father.
And, may I say to thee, this pride of hers,
Upon advice, hath drawn my love from her;   73
And, where I thought the remnant of mine age   74
Should have been cherished by her childlike duty,   75
I now am full resolved to take a wife
And turn her out to who will take her in.
Then let her beauty be her wedding dow'r,
For me and my possessions she esteems not.

VALENTINE
What would your Grace have me to do in this?

DUKE
There is a lady in Verona here   81
Whom I affect, but she is nice and coy   82
And nought esteems my agèd eloquence.
Now, therefore would I have thee to my tutor –
For long agone I have forgot to court;   85
Besides, the fashion of the time is changed –
How and which way I may bestow myself   87
To be regarded in her sun-bright eye.

VALENTINE
Win her with gifts, if she respect not words.   89
Dumb jewels often in their silent kind   90
More than quick words do move a woman's mind.

DUKE
But she did scorn a present that I sent her.

III, i Milan: the palace of the Duke 1 *give us leave* (polite way of asking to be left alone) 4 *discover* reveal 12 *made privy to* let in on 18 *cross* thwart; *drift* scheme 21 *timeless* untimely 23 *Which . . . live* in return for which you may ask anything of me as long as I live 25 *Haply* by chance 34 *soon suggested* easily led astray 42 *presently* now 45 *discovery* disclosure (of Valentine's secret); *aimèd at* guessed 47 *pretense* intention 52 *Please . . . Grace* if it please your Grace 56 *tenor* theme 59 *break* i.e. broach the subject 66 *Beseeming* suited to 68 *froward* perverse 73 *Upon advice* after some thought 74 *where* whereas; *the remnant . . . age* my last years 75 *childlike* filial 81 *Verona* (an error for Milan?) 82 *affect* aspire to; *nice and coy* fastidious and shy 85 *forgot* forgotten how 87 *bestow* i.e. conduct 89 *respect not* pays no attention to 90 *kind* nature

VALENTINE
A woman sometime scorns what best contents her.
Send her another; never give her o'er,
For scorn at first makes after-love the more.
If she do frown, 'tis not in hate of you,
But rather to beget more love in you.
If she do chide, 'tis not to have you gone,
99 For why the fools are mad if left alone.
Take no repulse, whatever she doth say;
For 'get you gone,' she doth not mean 'away.'
Flatter and praise, commend, extol their graces;
103 Though ne'er so black, say they have angels' faces.
That man that hath a tongue, I say is no man,
If with his tongue he cannot win a woman.
DUKE
But she I mean is promised by her friends
Unto a youthful gentleman of worth,
108 And kept severely from resort of men,
109 That no man hath access by day to her.
VALENTINE
Why, then I would resort to her by night.
DUKE
Ay, but the doors be locked and keys kept safe,
That no man hath recourse to her by night.
VALENTINE
113 What lets but one may enter at her window?
DUKE
Her chamber is aloft, far from the ground,
And built so shelving that one cannot climb it
Without apparent hazard of his life.
VALENTINE
117 Why then a ladder, quaintly made of cords,
To cast up with a pair of anchoring hooks,
119 Would serve to scale another Hero's tow'r,
So bold Leander would adventure it.
DUKE
Now, as thou art a gentleman of blood,
Advise me where I may have such a ladder.
VALENTINE
When would you use it? Pray, sir, tell me that.
DUKE
This very night; for Love is like a child,
That longs for everything that he can come by.
VALENTINE
By seven o'clock I'll get you such a ladder.
DUKE
But hark thee, I will go to her alone;
How shall I best convey the ladder thither?
VALENTINE
It will be light, my lord, that you may bear it
130 Under a cloak that is of any length.

DUKE
A cloak as long as thine will serve the turn?
VALENTINE
Ay, my good lord.
DUKE   Then let me see thy cloak;
I'll get me one of such another length.   133
VALENTINE
Why, any cloak will serve the turn, my lord.
DUKE
How shall I fashion me to wear a cloak?   135
I pray thee, let me feel thy cloak upon me.
  [Pulls open Valentine's cloak.]
What letter is this same? What's here? 'To Silvia'!
And here an engine fit for my proceeding!   138
I'll be so bold to break the seal for once.
  [Reads.]
'My thoughts do harbor with my Silvia nightly,   140
  And slaves they are to me that send them flying.
O, could their master come and go as lightly,   142
  Himself would lodge where senseless they are lying!
My herald thoughts in thy pure bosom rest them,
  While I, their king, that thither them importune, 145
Do curse the grace that with such grace hath blessed them, 146
  Because myself do want my servants' fortune.   147
I curse myself, for they are sent by me,
That they should harbor where their lord should be.'
What's here?
'Silvia, this night I will enfranchise thee.'
'Tis so, and here's the ladder for the purpose.
Why, Phaeton – for thou art Merops' son –   153
Wilt thou aspire to guide the heavenly car   154
And with thy daring folly burn the world?
Wilt thou reach stars, because they shine on thee?
Go, base instruder, overweening slave!
Bestow thy fawning smiles on equal mates,   158
And think my patience, more than thy desert,
Is privilege for thy departure hence.   160
Thank me for this more than for all the favors
Which all too much I have bestowed on thee.
But if thou linger in my territories
Longer than swiftest expedition
Will give thee time to leave our royal court,
By heaven, my wrath shall far exceed the love
I ever bore my daughter or thyself!
Be gone; I will not hear thy vain excuse,
But, as thou lov'st thy life, make speed from hence.
                                        [Exit.]

VALENTINE
And why not death rather than living torment?
To die is to be banished from myself.
And Silvia is myself; banished from her
Is self from self, a deadly banishment.
What light is light, if Silvia be not seen?
What joy is joy, if Silvia be not by?
Unless it be to think that she is by
And feed upon the shadow of perfection.   177
Except I be by Silvia in the night,   178
There is no music in the nightingale;
Unless I look on Silvia in the day,
There is no day for me to look upon.
She is my essence, and I leave to be,   182
If I be not by her fair influence   183
Fostered, illumined, cherished, kept alive.
I fly not death to fly his deadly doom: 185

99 *For why* because 103 *black* swarthy of skin 108 *resort* the visits
109 *That* so that 113 *lets* prevents 117 *quaintly* skillfully 119–20
Hero's, Leander (see I, i, 22 n.) 130 *any length* any normal length 133
such another the same 135 *fashion . . . wear* i.e. get used to wearing
138 *engine* contrivance (i.e. the rope ladder) 140 *harbor* lodge 142 *lightly*
easily 145 *importune* command 146 *grace . . . grace* kindness . . . favor
147 *want* lack 153 *Phaeton* (mythical overreacher, slain by Zeus for
scorching the earth while trying to drive the chariot of the sun) 154 *car*
chariot 158 *equal mates* i.e. women of your own inferior rank 160 *Is
privilege for* grants the privilege of 177 *shadow* illusion 178 *Except*
unless 182 *leave* cease 183 *influence* i.e. power exerted by his ruling star
(astrological metaphor) 185 *I . . . doom* i.e. I do not avoid death by avoiding
the Duke's sentence

186   Tarry I here, I but attend on death,
187   But, fly I hence, I fly away from life.
      [Enter Proteus and] Launce.
PROTEUS Run, boy, run, run and seek him out.
189 LAUNCE Soho, soho!
PROTEUS What seest thou?
191 LAUNCE Him we go to find. There's not a hair on's head
      but 'tis a Valentine.
PROTEUS Valentine?
VALENTINE No.
PROTEUS Who then? His spirit?
VALENTINE Neither.
PROTEUS What then?
VALENTINE Nothing.
LAUNCE Can nothing speak? Master, shall I strike?
PROTEUS Who wouldst thou strike?
LAUNCE Nothing.
PROTEUS Villain, forbear.
LAUNCE Why, sir, I'll strike nothing. I pray you –
PROTEUS Sirrah, I say forbear. Friend Valentine, a word.
VALENTINE
      My ears are stopped and cannot hear good news,
      So much of bad already hath possessed them.
PROTEUS
207   Then in dumb silence will I bury mine,
      For they are harsh, untuneable, and bad.
VALENTINE
      Is Silvia dead?
PROTEUS
      No, Valentine.
VALENTINE
      No Valentine indeed, for sacred Silvia.
      Hath she forsworn me?
PROTEUS
      No, Valentine.
VALENTINE
      No Valentine, if Silvia have forsworn me.
      What is your news?
LAUNCE Sir, there is a proclamation that you are vanished.
PROTEUS
      That thou art banishèd – O, that's the news –
      From hence, from Silvia, and from me thy friend.
VALENTINE
      O, I have fed upon this woe already,
      And now excess of it will make me surfeit.
      Doth Silvia know that I am banishèd?
PROTEUS
222   Ay, ay, and she hath offered to the doom,
223   Which, unreversed, stands in effectual force,
      A sea of melting pearl, which some call tears.
      Those at her father's churlish feet she tendered;
      With them, upon her knees, her humble self,
      Wringing her hands, whose whiteness so became them
      As if but now they waxèd pale for woe.
      But neither bended knees, pure hands held up,
      Sad sighs, deep groans, nor silver-shedding tears,
      Could penetrate her uncompassionate sire;
      But Valentine, if he be ta'en, must die.
      Besides, her intercession chafed him so,
      When she for thy repeal was suppliant,
      That to close prison he commanded her
      With many bitter threats of biding there.
VALENTINE
      No more, unless the next word that thou speak'st

      Have some malignant power upon my life.
      If so, I pray thee breathe it in mine ear,
240   As ending anthem of my endless dolor.
PROTEUS
      Cease to lament for that thou canst not help,
242   And study help for that which thou lament'st.
      Time is the nurse and breeder of all good.
      Here if thou stay, thou canst not see thy love;
      Besides, thy staying will abridge thy life.
      Hope is a lover's staff; walk hence with that
247   And manage it against despairing thoughts.
      Thy letters may be here, though thou art hence,
      Which, being writ to me, shall be delivered
250   Even in the milk-white bosom of thy love.
251   The time now serves not to expostulate.
      Come, I'll convey thee through the city gate,
253   And, ere I part with thee, confer at large
      Of all that may concern thy love-affairs.
      As thou lov'st Silvia, though not for thyself,
      Regard thy danger, and along with me!
VALENTINE
257   I pray thee, Launce, and if thou seest my boy,
      Bid him make haste and meet me at the Northgate.
PROTEUS
      Go, sirrah, find him out. Come, Valentine.
VALENTINE
      O, my dear Silvia! Hapless Valentine!
      [Exeunt Valentine and Proteus.]
LAUNCE I am but a fool, look you, and yet I have the wit
      to think my master is a kind of a knave. But that's all one,
      if he be but one knave. He lives not now that knows me
      to be in love, yet I am in love. But a team of horse shall
      not pluck that from me, nor who 'tis I love. And yet 'tis
      a woman, but what woman I will not tell myself. And
      yet 'tis a milkmaid. Yet 'tis not a maid, for she hath had
268   gossips. Yet 'tis a maid, for she is her master's maid, and
269   serves for wages. She hath more qualities than a water
270   spaniel – which is much in a bare Christian. *[Pulls out a*
271   *paper.]* Here is the cate-log of her condition. 'Imprimis:
      She can fetch and carry.' Why, a horse can do no more.
      Nay, a horse cannot fetch, but only carry; therefore is
274   she better than a jade. 'Item: She can milk.' Look you, a
      sweet virtue in a maid with clean hands.
      [Enter] Speed.
SPEED How now, Signior Launce? What news with your
      mastership?
LAUNCE With my master's ship? Why, it is at sea.
SPEED Well, your old vice still: mistake the word. What
      news, then, in your paper?
LAUNCE The black'st news that ever thou heard'st.
SPEED Why, man, how black?

---

186 *attend on* wait for   **187** *life* i.e. Silvia   **189** *Soho* (hunter's cry when the game is sighted)   **191** *hair* (a pun on 'hare', i.e. one kind of game)   **207** *mine* i.e. my news   **222** *offered . . . doom* paid out against the judgment   **223** *unreversed* unless reversed; *stands . . . force* must take effect   **240** *ending anthem* funeral hymn   **242** *study* devise   **247** *manage* wield (as a weapon)   **250** *Even . . . love* i.e. directly to your love in secret   **251** *expostulate* argue   **253** *confer at large* discuss at length   **257** *and if* if   **268** *gossips* sponsors for her child   **269–70** *water spaniel* (noted for fawning)   **270** *bare* mere   **271** *cate-log* (Launce's version of 'catalogue'); *condition* qualities; *Imprimis* in the first place (the usual beginning for a list, each subsequent part of which would begin with *Item*)   **274** *jade* (term applied to an inferior horse or a worthless woman)

LAUNCE Why, as black as ink.

SPEED Let me read them.

285 LAUNCE Fie on thee, jolthead! Thou canst not read.

SPEED Thou liest; I can.

LAUNCE I will try thee. Tell me this: who begot thee?

SPEED Marry, the son of my grandfather.

289 LAUNCE O illiterate loiterer! It was the son of thy grand-
mother. This proves that thou canst not read.

SPEED Come, fool, come; try me in thy paper.

292 LAUNCE There – and Saint Nicholas be thy speed!

293 SPEED [reads] 'Imprimis: She can milk.'

LAUNCE Ay, that she can.

SPEED 'Item: She brews good ale.'

LAUNCE And thereof comes the proverb, 'Blessing of
your heart, you brew good ale.'

SPEED 'Item: She can sew.'

LAUNCE That's as much as to say, 'Can she so?'

300 SPEED 'Item: She can knit.'

301 LAUNCE What need a man care for a stock with a wench,
302 when she can knit him a stock?

SPEED 'Item: She can wash and scour.'

304 LAUNCE A special virtue, for then she need not be washed
and scoured.

SPEED 'Item: She can spin.'

307 LAUNCE Then may I set the world on wheels, when she
can spin for her living.

309 SPEED 'Item: She hath many nameless virtues.'

LAUNCE That's as much as to say bastard virtues, that
indeed know not their fathers, and therefore have no
names.

SPEED Here follow her vices.

LAUNCE Close at the heels of her virtues.

314 SPEED 'Item: She is not to be fasting, in respect of her
breath.'

LAUNCE Well, that fault may be mended with a breakfast. Read on.

318 SPEED 'Item: She hath a sweet mouth.'

LAUNCE That makes amends for her sour breath.

SPEED 'Item: She doth talk in her sleep.'

321 LAUNCE It's no matter for that, so she sleep not in her talk.

SPEED 'Item: She is slow in words.'

LAUNCE O villain, that set this down among her vices!
To be slow in words is a woman's only virtue. I pray
325 thee, out with't, and place it for her chief virtue.

SPEED 'Item: She is proud.'

327 LAUNCE Out with that too. It was Eve's legacy, and
cannot be ta'en from her.

SPEED 'Item: She hath no teeth.'

LAUNCE I care not for that neither, because I love crusts.

SPEED 'Item: She is curst.'   331

LAUNCE Well, the best is, she hath no teeth to bite.

SPEED 'Item: She will often praise her liquor.'   333

LAUNCE If her liquor be good, she shall. If she will not, I
will, for good things should be praised.

SPEED 'Item: She is too liberal.'   336

LAUNCE Of her tongue she cannot, for that's writ down
she is slow of. Of her purse she shall not, for that I'll
keep shut. Now, of another thing she may, and that
cannot I help. Well, proceed.

SPEED 'Item: She hath more hair than wit, and more 341
faults than hairs, and more wealth than faults.'

LAUNCE Stop there. I'll have her. She was mine and not
mine twice or thrice in that last article. Rehearse that
once more.

SPEED 'Item: She hath more hair than wit' –

LAUNCE More hair than wit – It may be. I'll prove it: the
cover of the salt hides the salt, and therefore it is more 348
than the salt; the hair that covers the wit is more than
the wit, for the greater hides the less. What's next?

SPEED 'And more faults than hairs' –

LAUNCE That's monstrous! O, that that were out!

SPEED 'And more wealth than faults.'

LAUNCE Why, that word makes the faults gracious. Well, 354
I'll have her; and if it be a match, as nothing is impossible –

SPEED What then?

LAUNCE Why, then will I tell thee – that thy master stays
for thee at the Northgate.

SPEED For me?

LAUNCE For thee! Ay, who art thou? He hath stayed for
a better man than thee.

SPEED And must I go to him?

LAUNCE Thou must run to him, for thou hast stayed so
long that going will scarce serve the turn.   365

SPEED Why didst not tell me sooner? Pox of your love 366
letters!   [Exit.]

LAUNCE Now will he be swinged for reading my letter – 368
an unmannerly slave, that will thrust himself into
secrets. I'll after, to rejoice in the boy's correction. Exit. 370

*

Enter Duke, [and] Thurio.   III, ii

DUKE
Sir Thurio, fear not but that she will love you
Now Valentine is banished from her sight.

THURIO
Since his exile she hath despised me most,
Forsworn my company and railed at me,
That I am desperate of obtaining her.   5

DUKE
This weak impress of love is as a figure
Trenchèd in ice, which with an hour's heat
Dissolves to water and doth lose his form.   8
A little time will melt her frozen thoughts,
And worthless Valentine shall be forgot.
    [Enter] Proteus.
How now, Sir Proteus? Is your countryman,
According to our proclamation, gone?

PROTEUS
Gone, my good lord.

---

285 *jolthead* blockhead   289 *loiterer* loafer (he is lazy, and therefore
illiterate)   292 *Saint Nicholas* (patron saint of young scholars); *be thy
speed* help you   293 *milk* (Launce perhaps takes it in its figurative meaning
of coaxing or using wiles to get everything from a person; i.e. 'milk dry')
300 *knit* (with a play on the meaning 'conceive')   301 *stock* dowry   302
stock stocking   304–05 *washed and scoured* (slang for 'knocked down and
beaten')   307 *set . . . wheels* i.e. live at ease   309 *nameless* inexpressible
314 *is . . . fasting* i.e. must avoid fasting (often emended to 'is not to be
kissed fasting')   318 *sweet mouth* sweet tooth   321 *sleep* (with pun on
'slip')   325 *out with't* strike it out   327 *Eve's legacy* (Launce could take
proud to mean 'lascivious,' or to refer to the original sin of pride)   331
curst bad-tempered   333 *praise* appraise, i.e. taste   336 *liberal* free   341
more . . . wit (proverbial)   348 *salt* salt cellar (which in Elizabethan times
had a cover)   354 *gracious* agreeable   365 *going* walking; *serve the turn*
be satisfactory   366 *Pox of* i.e. disease take (mild oath)   368 *swinged*
thrashed   370 *correction* punishment
III, ii The same   5 *desperate* hopeless   8 *his* its

DUKE
My daughter takes his going grievously.

PROTEUS
A little time, my lord, will kill that grief.

DUKE
So I believe, but Thurio thinks not so.

17 Proteus, the good conceit I hold of thee –
For thou hast shown some sign of good desert –

19 Makes me the better to confer with thee.

PROTEUS
Longer than I prove loyal to your Grace,
Let me not live to look upon your Grace.

DUKE
Thou know'st how willingly I would effect
The match between Sir Thurio and my daughter.

PROTEUS
I do, my lord.

DUKE
And also, I think, thou art not ignorant

26 How she opposes her against my will.

PROTEUS
She did, my lord, when Valentine was here.

DUKE
Ay, and perversely she persevers so.
What might we do to make the girl forget
The love of Valentine, and love Sir Thurio?

PROTEUS
The best way is to slander Valentine
With falsehood, cowardice, and poor descent,
Three things that women highly hold in hate.

DUKE
Ay, but she'll think that it is spoke in hate.

PROTEUS
35 Ay, if his enemy deliver it;
36 Therefore it must with circumstance be spoken
By one whom she esteemeth as his friend.

DUKE
Then you must undertake to slander him.

PROTEUS
And that, my lord, I shall be loath to do.
'Tis an ill office for a gentleman,
41 Especially against his very friend.

DUKE
Where your good word cannot advantage him,
Your slander never can endamage him.
Therefore the office is indifferent,
45 Being entreated to it by your friend.

PROTEUS
You have prevailed, my lord. If I can do it
By aught that I can speak in his dispraise,
She shall not long continue love to him.
But, say this weed her love from Valentine,
It follows not that she will love Sir Thurio.

THURIO
Therefore, as you unwind her love from him,
52 Lest is should ravel and be good to none,
53 You must provide to bottom it on me;
Which must be done by praising me as much
As you in worth dispraise Sir Valentine.

DUKE
And, Proteus, we dare trust you in this kind,
Because we know, on Valentine's report,
You are already Love's firm votary
And cannot soon revolt and change your mind.

Upon this warrant shall you have access
Where you with Silvia may confer at large,
For she is lumpish, heavy, melancholy,
And, for your friend's sake, will be glad of you;
Where you may temper her by your persuasion   64
To hate young Valentine and love my friend.

PROTEUS
As much as I can do I will effect.
But you, Sir Thurio, are not sharp enough.
You must lay lime to tangle her desires   68
By wailful sonnets, whose composèd rimes
Should be full-fraught with serviceable vows.   70

DUKE
Ay, much is the force of heaven-bred poesy.

PROTEUS
Say that upon the altar of her beauty
You sacrifice your tears, your sighs, your heart.
Write till your ink be dry, and with your tears
Moist it again, and frame some feeling line   75
That may discover such integrity.   76
For Orpheus' lute was strung with poets' sinews, 77
Whose golden touch could soften steel and stones,
Make tigers tame, and huge leviathans   79
Forsake unsounded deeps to dance on sands.
After your dire-lamenting elegies,
Visit by night your lady's chamber window
With some sweet consort. To their instruments   83
Tune a deploring dump; the night's dead silence   84
Will well become such sweet-complaining grievance.
This, or else nothing, will inherit her.   86

DUKE
This discipline shows thou hast been in love.   87

THURIO
And thy advice this night I'll put in practice.
Therefore, sweet Proteus, my direction-giver,
Let us into the city presently
To sort some gentlemen well skilled in music.   91
I have a sonnet that will serve the turn   92
To give the onset to thy good advice.

DUKE
About it, gentlemen!

PROTEUS
We'll wait upon your Grace till after supper,   95
And afterward determine our proceedings.

DUKE
Even now about it. I will pardon you.   *Exeunt.* 97

*

Enter Valentine, Speed, and certain Outlaws.   IV, i

I. OUTLAW
Fellows, stand fast; I see a passenger.   1

17 *conceit* opinion 19 *better* more willing 26 *opposes her* contends 35 *deliver* speak 36 *circumstance* supporting detail 41 *very* true 45 *your friend* i.e. the Duke himself 52 *ravel* tangle 53 *bottom . . . me* i.e. wind it on me (as you would wind a skein on a core, or bottom) 64 *temper* influence 68 *lime* sticky substance used for trapping birds; *tangle* capture 70 *serviceable vows* vows of service 75 *feeling* passionate 76 *discover . . . integrity* reveal such true emotion 77 *Orpheus* (the fabled musician of Thrace whose music could enthrall not only animals and trees, but also inanimate things) 79 *leviathans* whales (?), sea monsters (?) 83 *consort* group of musicians 84 *dump* mournful air 86 *inherit* win 87 *discipline* teaching 91 *sort* select 92–93 *will . . . onset to* can be used as a first step in following 95 *wait upon* attend 97 *pardon you* excuse you (from attendance on me)
IV, i A forest on the border of Mantua 1 *passenger* traveller

2 . OUTLAW
   If there be ten, shrink not, but down with 'em.
3 . OUTLAW
   Stand, sir, and throw us that you have about ye.
   If not, we'll make you sit, and rifle you.
SPEED
   Sir, we are undone. These are the villains
   That all the travellers do fear so much.
VALENTINE
   My friends –
1 . OUTLAW
   That's not so, sir; we are your enemies.
2 . OUTLAW
   Peace! We'll hear him.
3 . OUTLAW
10   Ay, by my beard, will we, for he is a proper man.
VALENTINE
   Then know, that I have little wealth to lose.
   A man I am, crossed with adversity;
   My riches are these poor habiliments,
14 Of which if you should here disfurnish me,
   You take the sum and substance that I have.
2 . OUTLAW
   Whither travel you?
VALENTINE
   To Verona.
1 . OUTLAW
   Whence came you?
VALENTINE
   From Milan.
3 . OUTLAW
   Have you long sojourned there?
VALENTINE
   Some sixteen months, and longer might have stayed,
   If crooked fortune had not thwarted me.
1 . OUTLAW
   What, were you banished thence?
VALENTINE
   I was.
2 . OUTLAW
   For what offense?
VALENTINE
26 For that which now torments me to rehearse:
   I killed a man, whose death I much repent,
   But yet I slew him manfully in fight,
   Without false vantage or base treachery.
1 . OUTLAW
   Why, ne'er repent it, if it were done so.
   But were you banished for so small a fault?
VALENTINE
32 I was, and held me glad of such a doom.
2 . OUTLAW
33 Have you the tongues?
VALENTINE
34 My youthful travel therein made me happy,

Or else I often had been miserable.
3 . OUTLAW
   By the bare scalp of Robin Hood's fat friar,   36
   This fellow were a king for our wild faction!   37
1 . OUTLAW
   We'll have him. Sirs, a word.
SPEED Master, be one of them; it's an honorable kind of
   thievery.
VALENTINE Peace, villain!
2 . OUTLAW Tell us this: have you anything to take to? 42
VALENTINE Nothing but my fortune.
3 . OUTLAW
   Know then, that some of us are gentlemen
   Such as the fury of ungoverned youth
   Thrust from the company of awful men.   46
   Myself was from Verona banishèd
   For practising to steal away a lady,   48
   An heir, and near allied unto the Duke.
2 . OUTLAW
   And I from Mantua, for a gentleman
   Who, in my mood, I stabbed unto the heart.   51
1 . OUTLAW
   And I for such like petty crimes as these.
   But to the purpose – for we cite our faults
   That they may hold excused our lawless lives;
   And partly, seeing you are beautified
   With goodly shape, and by your own report
   A linguist, and a man of such perfection
   As we do in our quality much want –   58
2 . OUTLAW
   Indeed, because you are a banished man,
   Therefore, above the rest, we parley to you.   60
   Are you content to be our general,
   To make a virtue of necessity
   And live as we do in this wilderness?
3 . OUTLAW
   What say'st thou? Wilt thou be of our consort?   64
   Say ay, and be the captain of us all.
   We'll do thee homage and be ruled by thee,
   Love thee as our commander and our king.
1 . OUTLAW
   But if thou scorn our courtesy, thou diest.
2 . OUTLAW
   Thou shalt not live to brag what we have offered.
VALENTINE
   I take your offer and will live with you,
   Provided that you do no outrages
   On silly women or poor passengers.   72
3 . OUTLAW
   No, we detest such vile, base practices.
   Come, go with us, we'll bring thee to our crews   74
   And show thee all the treasure we have got,
   Which, with ourselves, all rest at thy dispose.   *Exeunt.*

*

Enter Proteus.   IV, ii
PROTEUS
   Already have I been false to Valentine,
   And now I must be as unjust to Thurio.
   Under the color of commending him,   3
   I have access my own love to prefer.   4
   But Silvia is too fair, too true, too holy,
   To be corrupted with my worthless gifts.

---

10 *proper* handsome   14 *disfurnish* deprive   26 *rehearse* tell about   32 *doom* sentence   33 *tongues* foreign languages   34 *happy* fortunate   36 *friar* i.e. Friar Tuck   37 *This . . . faction* this is just the fellow to lead our wild band   42 *anything to take to* any means of subsistence   46 *awful* law-abiding   48 *practising* plotting   51 *mood* anger   58 *quality* profession; *want* lack   60 *above the rest* for this main reason   64 *consort* company   72 *silly* helpless   74 *crews* bands
IV, ii Before the palace of the Duke, under the window of Silvia's chamber   3 *color* pretense   4 *prefer* put forward

When I protest true loyalty to her,
She twits me with my falsehood to my friend.
9 When to her beauty I commend my vows,
She bids me think how I have been forsworn
In breaking faith with Julia whom I loved.
12 And notwithstanding all her sudden quips,
The least whereof would quell a lover's hope,
Yet, spaniel-like, the more she spurns my love,
15 The more it grows, and fawneth on her still.
But here comes Thurio. Now must we to her window,
And give some evening music to her ear.
[Enter] Thurio, Musicians.

THURIO
How now, Sir Proteus, are you crept before us?
PROTEUS
Ay, gentle Thurio, for you know that love
20 Will creep in service where it cannot go.
THURIO
Ay, but I hope, sir, that you love not here.
PROTEUS
Sir, but I do – or else I would be hence.
THURIO
Who? Silvia?
PROTEUS
Ay, Silvia – for your sake.
THURIO
I thank you for your own. Now, gentlemen,
Let's tune, and to it lustily awhile.
[Enter] Host, [with] Julia [disguised as a boy].
HOST
27 Now, my young guest, methinks you're allycholly.
I pray you, why is it?
JULIA
Marry, mine host, because I cannot be merry.
HOST Come, we'll have you merry. I'll bring you where
you shall hear music, and see the gentleman that you
asked for.
JULIA But shall I hear him speak?
HOST Ay, that you shall.
JULIA That will be music.
[Music plays.]
HOST Hark! hark!
JULIA Is he among these?
HOST Ay – but peace, let's hear 'em.

Song.

Who is Silvia? What is she,
40   That all our swains commend her?
Holy, fair, and wise is she;
   The heaven such grace did lend her,
That she might admirèd be.

Is she kind as she is fair?
   For beauty lives with kindness.
46 Love doth to her eyes repair,
   To help him of his blindness,
And, being helped, inhabits there.

Then to Silvia let us sing,
   That Silvia is excelling.
She excels each mortal thing
   Upon the dull earth dwelling.
To her let us garlands bring.

HOST How now? Are you sadder than you were before?
55 How do you, man? The music likes you not.

JULIA You mistake; the musician likes me not.
HOST Why, my pretty youth?
JULIA He plays false, father.
HOST How? Out of tune on the strings?
JULIA Not so, but yet so false that he grieves my very
heartstrings.
HOST You have a quick ear.
JULIA Ay, I would I were deaf; it makes me have a slow 63
heart.
HOST I perceive you delight not in music.
JULIA Not a whit, when it jars so.
HOST Hark, what fine change is in the music! 67
JULIA Ay, that change is the spite. 68
HOST You would have them always play but one thing?
JULIA I would always have one play but one thing.
But, host, doth this Sir Proteus that we talk on
Often resort unto this gentlewoman?
HOST I tell you what Launce, his man, told me: he loved
her out of all nick. 74
JULIA Where is Launce?
HOST Gone to seek his dog, which to-morrow, by his
master's command, he must carry for a present to his
lady.
JULIA Peace. Stand aside; the company parts.
PROTEUS
Sir Thurio, fear not you. I will so plead
That you shall say my cunning drift excels. 80
THURIO Where meet we?
PROTEUS At Saint Gregory's well.
THURIO Farewell. *[Exeunt Thurio and Musicians.]*
[Enter, at her window above,] Silvia.
PROTEUS
Madam, good ev'n to your ladyship.
SILVIA
I thank you for your music, gentlemen.
Who is that that spake?
PROTEUS
One, lady, if you knew his pure heart's truth,
You would quickly learn to know him by his voice.
SILVIA
Sir Proteus, as I take it.
PROTEUS
Sir Proteus, gentle lady, and your servant.
SILVIA
What's your will?
PROTEUS
That I may compass yours. 92
SILVIA
You have your wish. My will is even this:
That presently you hie you home to bed.
Thou subtle, perjured, false, disloyal man!
Think'st thou I am so shallow, so conceitless, 96
To be seducèd by thy flattery,
That hast deceived so many with thy vows?
Return, return, and make thy love amends.
For me, by this pale queen of night I swear, 100
I am so far from granting thy request
That I despise thee for thy wrongful suit,

9 *commend* offer   12 *quips* rebukes   15 *still* constantly   20 *go* walk   27 *allycholly* melancholy (a whimsical form of the word)   40 *swains* young men   46 *repair* pay a visit   55 *likes* pleases   63 *slow* heavy   67 *change* modulation   68 *spite* thing that hurts   74 *out . . . nick* more than can be reckoned   80 *drift* scheme   92 *compass* win   96 *conceitless* witless   100 *pale . . . night* i.e. Diana, the moon

And by and by intend to chide myself
Even for this time I spend in talking to thee.

PROTEUS
I grant, sweet love, that I did love a lady,
But she is dead.

JULIA *[aside]*   'Twere false, if I should speak it,
For I am sure she is not burièd.

SILVIA
Say that she be ; yet Valentine thy friend
Survives, to whom – thyself art witness –
I am betrothed. And art thou not ashamed
111   To wrong him with thy importunacy ?

PROTEUS
I likewise hear that Valentine is dead.

SILVIA
And so suppose am I, for in his grave
Assure thyself my love is burièd.

PROTEUS
Sweet lady, let me rake it from the earth.

SILVIA
Go to thy lady's grave and call hers thence ;
Or, at the least, in hers sepulchre thine.

JULIA *[aside]*
He heard not that.

PROTEUS
Madam, if your heart be so obdurate,
Vouchsafe me yet your picture for my love,
The picture that is hanging in your chamber.
To that I'll speak, to that I'll sigh and weep ;
For, since the substance of your perfect self
124   Is else devoted, I am but a shadow,
125   And to your shadow will I make true love.

JULIA *[aside]*
If 'twere a substance, you would, sure, deceive it.
And make it but a shadow, as I am.

SILVIA
I am very loath to be your idol, sir.
129   But, since your falsehood shall become you well
To worship shadows and adore false shapes,
131   Send to me in the morning, and I'll send it.
And so, good rest.   *[Exit.]*

PROTEUS   As wretches have o'er night
That wait for execution in the morn.   *[Exit.]*

JULIA Host, will you go ?
135 HOST By my halidom, I was fast asleep.
136 JULIA Pray you, where lies Sir Proteus ?
HOST Marry, at my house. Trust me, I think 'tis almost day.

JULIA
Not so, but it hath been the longest night
139   That e'er I watched, and the most heaviest.   *[Exeunt.]*

*

Enter Eglamour.   IV, iii

EGLAMOUR
This is the hour that Madam Silvia
Entreated me to call and know her mind.
There's some great matter she'd employ me in.
Madam, madam !
     [Enter, at her window above,] Silvia.

SILVIA   Who calls ?

EGLAMOUR   Your servant, and your friend :
One that attends your ladyship's command.

SILVIA
Sir Eglamour, a thousand times good morrow.

EGLAMOUR
As many, worthy lady, to yourself.
According to your ladyship's impose,   8
I am thus early come to know what service
It is your pleasure to command me in.

SILVIA
O Eglamour, thou art a gentleman –
Think not I flatter, for I swear I do not –
Valiant, wise, remorseful, well-accomplished.   13
Thou art not ignorant what dear good will   14
I bear unto the banished Valentine,
Nor how my father would enforce me marry
Vain Thurio, whom my very soul abhorred.
Thyself hast loved, and I have heard thee say
No grief did ever come so near thy heart
As when thy lady and thy true love died,
Upon whose grave thou vow'dst pure chastity.
Sir Eglamour, I would to Valentine,   22
To Mantua, where I hear he makes abode ;
And, for the ways are dangerous to pass,
I do desire thy worthy company,
Upon whose faith and honor I repose.   26
Urge not my father's anger, Eglamour,
But think upon my grief, a lady's grief,
And on the justice of my flying hence
To keep me from a most unholy match,
Which heaven and fortune still rewards with plagues.   31
I do desire thee, even from a heart
As full of sorrows as the sea of sands,
To bear me company and go with me.
If not, to hide what I have said to thee,
That I may venture to depart alone.

EGLAMOUR
Madam, I pity much your grievances ;
Which since I know they virtuously are placed,   38
I give consent to go along with you,
Recking as little what betideth me
As much I wish all good befortune you.
When will you go ?

SILVIA This evening coming.

EGLAMOUR Where shall I meet you ?

SILVIA At Friar Patrick's cell, where I intend holy confession.

EGLAMOUR I will not fail your ladyship. Good morrow, gentle lady.

SILVIA Good morrow, kind Sir Eglamour.   *Exeunt.*

*

Enter Launce [with his dog].   IV, iv

LAUNCE When a man's servant shall play the cur with him,
look you, it goes hard : one that I brought up of a puppy,   2

---

111 *importunacy* importunity   124 *else* elsewhere ; *shadow* lifeless person (?), inseparable follower (?)   125 *shadow* portrait   129 *since . . . well* since it suits a false lover like yourself   131 *Send* i.e. send a messenger   135 *halidom* originally, a sacred relic (mild oath)   136 *lies* lodges   139 *watched* stayed awake throughout ; *most heaviest* most unhappy

IV, iii The same   8 *impose* command   13 *remorseful* sympathetic   14 *dear* loving   22 *would to* wish to go to   26 *repose* depend   31 *still* always 38 *virtuously are placed* are not incurred through wickedness

IV, iv The same   2 *of* from

one that I saved from drowning when three or four of
4 his blind brothers and sisters went to it. I have taught
him, even as one would say precisely, 'Thus I would
teach a dog.' I was sent to deliver him as a present to
Mistress Silvia from my master, and I came no sooner
8 into the dining chamber but he steps me to her trencher
and steals her capon's leg. O, 'tis a foul thing when a cur
10 cannot keep himself in all companies! I would have, as
one should say, one that takes upon him to be a dog
12 indeed, to be, as it were, a dog at all things. If I had not
had more wit than he, to take a fault upon me that he
did, I think verily he had been hanged for't. Sure as I
live, he had suffered for't. You shall judge. He thrusts
me himself into the company of three or four gentlemanlike dogs under the Duke's table. He had not been there
18 – bless the mark – a pissing-while but all the chamber
smelt him. 'Out with the dog,' says one. 'What cur is
that?' says another. 'Whip him out,' says the third. 'Hang
him up,' says the Duke. I, having been acquainted with
the smell before, knew it was Crab, and goes me to the
fellow that whips the dogs. 'Friend,' quoth I, 'you mean
to whip the dog?' 'Ay, marry, do I,' quoth he. 'You do
him the more wrong,' quoth I; ''twas I did the thing
26 you wot of.' He makes me no more ado, but whips me
out of the chamber. How many masters would do this
for his servant? Nay, I'll be sworn, I have sat in the
29 stocks for puddings he hath stol'n, otherwise he had been
30 executed. I have stood on the pillory for geese he hath
killed, otherwise he had suffered for't. Thou think'st not
of this now. Nay, I remember the trick you served me
when I took my leave of Madam Silvia. Did not I bid
34 thee still mark me and do as I do? When didst thou see
me heave up my leg and make water against a gentle-
36 woman's farthingale? Didst thou ever see me do such a
trick?
    [Enter] Proteus, [with] Julia [disguised as a boy].
PROTEUS
Sebastian is thy name? I like thee well,
And will employ thee in some service presently.
JULIA In what you please; I'll do what I can.
PROTEUS
I hope thou wilt. *[to Launce]* How now, you whoreson
    peasant,
Where have you been these two days loitering?
LAUNCE Marry, sir, I carried Mistress Silvia the dog you
bade me.
44 PROTEUS And what says she to my little jewel?
LAUNCE Marry, she says your dog was a cur, and tells you
currish thanks is good enough for such a present.
PROTEUS But she received my dog?
LAUNCE No, indeed did she not; here have I brought
him back again.
PROTEUS What, didst thou offer her this from me?
51 LAUNCE Ay, sir, the other squirrel was stolen from me by
52 the hangman's boys in the marketplace; and then I
offered her mine own, who is a dog as big as ten of yours,
and therefore the gift the greater.
PROTEUS
Go, get thee hence and find my dog again,
Or ne'er return again into my sight.
Away, I say. Stayest thou to vex me here? *[Exit Launce.]*
58 A slave that still an end turns me to shame!
Sebastian, I have entertainèd thee,
60 Partly that I have need of such a youth,

That can with some discretion do my business –
For 'tis no trusting to yond foolish lout –
But chiefly for thy face and thy behavior,
Which, if my augury deceive me not,
Witness good bringing up, fortune, and truth. 65
Therefore, know thou, for this I entertain thee. 66
Go presently, and take this ring with thee; 67
Deliver it to Madam Silvia –
She loved me well delivered it to me. 69
JULIA
It seems you loved not her, to leave her token. 70
She is dead, belike? 71
PROTEUS
Not so; I think she lives.
JULIA
Alas!
PROTEUS
Why dost thou cry 'alas'?
JULIA
I cannot choose but pity her.
PROTEUS
Wherefore shouldst thou pity her?
JULIA
Because methinks that she loved you as well
As you do love your lady Silvia.
She dreams on him that has forgot her love;
You dote on her that cares not for your love. 80
'Tis pity love should be so contrary;
And thinking on it makes me cry 'alas.'
PROTEUS
Well, give her that ring, and therewithal
This letter. That's her chamber. Tell my lady
I claim the promise for her heavenly picture.
Your message done, hie home unto my chamber,
Where thou shalt find me sad and solitary. *[Exit.]*
JULIA
How many women would do such a message?
Alas, poor Proteus, thou hast entertained
A fox to be the shepherd of thy lambs!
Alas, poor fool, why do I pity him 91
That with his very heart despiseth me?
Because he loves her, he despiseth me;
Because I love him, I must pity him.
This ring I gave him when he parted from me
To bind him to remember my good will;
And now am I, unhappy messenger,
To plead for that which I would not obtain,
To carry that which I would have refused,
To praise his faith which I would have dispraised.
I am my master's true-confirmèd love, 101
But cannot be true servant to my master

4 *to it* to death   8 *steps me* steps; *trencher* wooden plate   10 *keep* behave
12 *a dog* at skilled at   18 *bless the mark* (a phrase used in apology for coarse
language; probably at one time a formula to turn aside an ill omen);
but when, before   26 *wot* know; *He . . . ado* i.e. he wastes no further time
29 *stocks* wooden clamp in which a seated malefactor's legs were fastened;
puddings fat meat sausages   30 *pillory* wooden clamp in which a standing
malefactor's neck and wrists were fastened   34 *mark* watch   36 *farthingale*
hooped skirt of the period   44 *jewel* (Proteus refers to the small dog he
thinks he sent to Silvia)   51 *squirrel* (Launce's word for lap-dog)   52
hangman's i.e. fit for the hangman   58 *still an end* always   60 *that* because
65 *Witness* bear witness to   66 *entertain thee* take you into service   67
presently immediately   69 *delivered* who delivered   70 *leave* part with
71 *belike* presumably   91 *poor fool* i.e. Julia herself   101 *true-confirmèd*
betrothed

Unless I prove false traitor to myself.
Yet will I woo for him, but yet so coldly
105 As, heaven it knows, I would not have him speed.
        [Enter] Silvia [with Attendants].
Gentlewoman, good day ; I pray you be my mean
107 To bring me where to speak with Madam Silvia.

SILVIA
What would you with her, if that I be she ?

JULIA
If you be she, I do entreat your patience
To hear me speak the message I am sent on.

SILVIA
From whom ?

JULIA
From my master, Sir Proteus, madam.

SILVIA
O, he sends you for a picture ?

JULIA
Ay, madam.

SILVIA
Ursula, bring my picture there –
        [Attendant brings picture.]
Go, give your master this. Tell him from me,
One Julia, that his changing thoughts forget,
118 Would better fit his chamber than this shadow.

JULIA
Madam, please you peruse this letter –
120 Pardon me, madam, I have unadvised
Delivered you a paper that I should not.
This is the letter to your ladyship.

SILVIA
I pray thee, let me look on that again.

JULIA
It may not be ; good madam, pardon me.

SILVIA
There, hold.
I will not look upon your master's lines.
I know they are stuffed with protestations
And full of new-found oaths, which he will break
As easily as I do tear his paper.

JULIA
Madam, he sends your ladyship this ring.

SILVIA
The more shame for him that he sends it me,
For I have heard him say a thousand times
His Julia gave it him at his departure.
Though his false finger have profaned the ring,
Mine shall not do his Julia so much wrong.

JULIA
She thanks you.

SILVIA
What say'st thou ?

JULIA
138 I thank you, madam, that you tender her.

Poor gentlewoman, my master wrongs her much.

SILVIA
Dost thou know her ?

JULIA
Almost as well as I do know myself.
To think upon her woes, I do protest
That I have wept a hundred several times.

SILVIA
Belike she thinks that Proteus hath forsook her.   144

JULIA
I think she doth, and that's her cause of sorrow.

SILVIA
Is she not passing fair ?   146

JULIA
She hath been fairer, madam, than she is.
When she did think my master loved her well,
She, in my judgment, was as fair as you ;
But since she did neglect her looking-glass
And threw her sun-expelling mask away,   151
The air hath starved the roses in her cheeks
And pinched the lily-tincture of her face,
That now she is become as black as I.   154

SILVIA
How tall was she ?

JULIA
About my stature ; for, at Pentecost,   156
When all our pageants of delight were played,   157
Our youth got me to play the woman's part,
And I was trimmed in Madam Julia's gown,   159
Which servèd me as fit, by all men's judgments,
As if the garment had been made for me.
Therefore I know she is about my height.
And at that time I made her weep agood,   163
For I did play a lamentable part.   164
Madam, 'twas Ariadne passioning   165
For Theseus' perjury and unjust flight,   166
Which I so lively acted with my tears
That my poor mistress, movèd therewithal,
Wept bitterly ; and would I might be dead,
If I in thought felt not her very sorrow !

SILVIA
She is beholding to thee, gentle youth.
Alas, poor lady, desolate and left !
I weep myself to think upon thy words.
Here, youth, there is my purse. I give thee this
For thy sweet mistress' sake, because thou lov'st her.
Farewell.   *[Exit Silvia, with Attendants.]*

JULIA
And she shall thank you for't, if e'er you know her.
A virtuous gentlewoman, mild and beautiful.
I hope my master's suit will be but cold,   179
Since she respects my mistress' love so much.
Alas, how love can trifle with itself !
Here is her picture. Let me see – I think,
If I had such a tire, this face of mine   183
Were full as lovely as is this of hers ;
And yet the painter flattered her a little,
Unless I flatter with myself too much.   186
Her hair is auburn, mine is perfect yellow –
If that be all the difference in his love,
I'll get me such a colored periwig.
Her eyes are grey as glass, and so are mine.
Ay, but her forehead's low, and mine's as high.
What should it be that he respects in her

105 *speed* succeed **107** *where to speak* where I may speak **118** *shadow* picture **120** *unadvised* inadvertently (there is no satisfactory explanation for this reference to a second letter) **138** *tender* feel sympathy for **144** *Belike* probably **146** *passing* surpassingly **151** *sun-expelling mask* complexion-guard **154** *black* swarthy **156** *Pentecost* Whitsuntide (early summer festival) **157** *pageants of delight* entertainments giving pleasure **159** *trimmed* dressed **163** *agood* in earnest **164** *lamentable* tragic **165** *Ariadne* Cretan princess deserted by Theseus after she had aided him in his exploit against the Minotaur **166** *unjust* unfaithful **179** *but cold* ineffective **183** *tire* headdress **186** *flatter with* flatter

193 But I can make respective in myself
194 If this fond Love were not a blinded god?
195 Come, shadow, come and take this shadow up,
For 'tis thy rival. O thou senseless form,
Thou shalt be worshipped, kissed, loved, and adored!
And, were there sense in his idolatry,
199 My substance should be statue in thy stead.
I'll use thee kindly for thy mistress' sake,
That used me so; or else, by Jove I vow
I should have scratched out your unseeing eyes
To make my master out of love with thee.   *Exit.*

*

V, i   *Enter Eglamour.*

EGLAMOUR
The sun begins to gild the western sky,
And now it is about the very hour
That Silvia at Friar Patrick's cell should meet me.
She will not fail, for lovers break not hours
Unless it be to come before their time,
6 So much they spur their expedition.
See where she comes.
       [Enter] Silvia.
                Lady, a happy evening!
SILVIA
Amen, amen! Go on, good Eglamour,
9 Out at the postern by the abbey wall.
10 I fear I am attended by some spies.
EGLAMOUR
Fear not; the forest is not three leagues off.
12 If we recover that, we are sure enough.   *Exeunt.*

*

V, ii   *Enter Thurio, Proteus, [and] Julia [disguised*
               as a boy].

THURIO
Sir Proteus, what says Silvia to my suit?
PROTEUS
O, sir, I find her milder than she was,
3 And yet she takes exceptions at your person.
THURIO What, that my leg is too long?
PROTEUS No, that it is too little.
THURIO
I'll wear a boot to make it somewhat rounder.
JULIA *[aside]*
But love will not be spurred to what it loathes.
THURIO
What says she to my face?
PROTEUS
She says it is a fair one.
THURIO
10 Nay then, the wanton lies; my face is black.
PROTEUS
But pearls are fair, and the old saying is,
Black men are pearls in beauteous ladies' eyes.
JULIA *[aside]*
13 'Tis true, such pearls as put out ladies' eyes;
14 For I had rather wink than look on them.
THURIO
How likes she my discourse?
PROTEUS
Ill, when you talk of war.
THURIO
But well, when I discourse of love and peace?

JULIA *[aside]*
But better, indeed, when you hold your peace.
THURIO
What says she to my valor?
PROTEUS
O, sir, she makes no doubt of that.
JULIA *[aside]*
She needs not, when she knows it cowardice.
THURIO
What says she to my birth?
PROTEUS
That you are well derived.   23
JULIA *[aside]*
True: from a gentleman to a fool.
THURIO
Considers she my possessions?
PROTEUS
O, ay, and pities them.
THURIO
Wherefore?
JULIA *[aside]*
That such an ass should owe them.   28
PROTEUS
That they are out by lease.   29
JULIA
Here comes the Duke.
       [Enter] Duke.
DUKE
How now, Sir Proteus? How now, Thurio?
Which of you saw Eglamour of late?
THURIO Not I.
PROTEUS Nor I.
DUKE Saw you my daughter?
PROTEUS Neither.
DUKE
Why then,
She's fled unto that peasant, Valentine,   38
And Eglamour is in her company.
'Tis true, for Friar Laurence met them both,
As he in penance wandered through the forest.
Him he knew well, and guessed that it was she,
But, being masked, he was not sure of it.
Besides, she did intend confession
At Patrick's cell this even, and there she was not.
These likelihoods confirm her flight from hence.
Therefore, I pray you, stand not to discourse,
But mount you presently and meet with me
Upon the rising of the mountain foot,
That leads toward Mantua, whither they are fled.
Dispatch, sweet gentlemen, and follow me.   *[Exit.]* 51
THURIO
Why, this it is to be a peevish girl,
That flies her fortune when it follows her.

---

193 *respective* i.e. equally worthy of respect   194 *fond* foolish   195 *shadow, shadow* (the same image was used by Proteus at IV, ii, 124–25); *take . . . up* (with a pun on the sense of 'oppose')   199 *My . . . stead* i.e. my substantial self, instead of this image, would be the idol (*statue*) he worships
V, i An abbey in Milan   6 *much . . . expedition* i.e. eagerly they speed   9 *postern* small door at back or side   10 *attended* followed   12 *recover* reach; *sure* safe
V, ii The palace of the Duke   3 *takes exceptions at* objects to   10 *black* swarthy   13 *pearls* i.e. cataracts   14 *wink* close (my) eyes   23 *derived* descended   28 *owe* own   29 *out by lease* rented out   38 *peasant* i.e. low fellow   51 *Dispatch* make haste

I'll after, more to be revenged on Eglamour
Than for the love of reckless Silvia.   *[Exit.]*

PROTEUS
And I will follow, more for Silvia's love
Than hate of Eglamour that goes with her.   *[Exit.]*

JULIA
And I will follow, more to cross that love
Than hate for Silvia that is gone for love.   *Exit.*

*

V, iii   *[Enter] Silvia, [led by] Outlaws.*

1. OUTLAW
Come, come,
Be patient; we must bring you to our captain.

SILVIA
A thousand more mischances than this one
4   Have learned me how to brook this patiently.

2. OUTLAW
Come, bring her away.

1. OUTLAW
Where is the gentleman that was with her?

3. OUTLAW
Being nimble-footed, he hath outrun us,
But Moyses and Valerius follow him.
Go thou with her to the west end of the wood;
There is our captain. We'll follow him that's fled.
11   The thicket is beset; he cannot 'scape.

1. OUTLAW
Come, I must bring you to our captain's cave.
Fear not; he bears an honorable mind,
And will not use a woman lawlessly.

SILVIA
O Valentine, this I endure for thee!   *Exeunt.*

*

V, iv   *Enter Valentine.*

VALENTINE
1   How use doth breed a habit in a man!
2   This shadowy desert, unfrequented woods,
3   I better brook than flourishing peopled towns.
    Here can I sit alone, unseen of any,
    And to the nightingale's complaining notes
6   Tune my distresses and record my woes.
    O thou that dost inhabit in my breast,
    Leave not the mansion so long tenantless,
    Lest, growing ruinous, the building fall
    And leave no memory of what it was.
11   Repair me with thy presence, Silvia.
    Thou gentle nymph, cherish thy forlorn swain.
                [Outlaws shout, near at hand.]
    What halloing and what stir is this to-day?
    These are my mates, that make their wills their law,
15   Have some unhappy passenger in chase.

They love me well, yet I have much to do
To keep them from uncivil outrages.
Withdraw thee, Valentine. Who's this comes here?
                     [Withdraws.]
    *[Enter] Proteus, Silvia, [and] Julia [disguised
    as a boy].*

PROTEUS
Madam, this service I have done for you –
Though you respect not aught your servant doth –   20
To hazard life and rescue you from him
That would have forced your honor and your love.
Vouchsafe me for my meed but one fair look;   23
A smaller boon than this I cannot beg,
And less than this, I am sure, you cannot give.

VALENTINE *[aside]*
How like a dream is this I see and hear!
Love, lend me patience to forbear awhile.

SILVIA
O, miserable, unhappy that I am!

PROTEUS
Unhappy were you, madam, ere I came;
But by my coming I have made you happy.

SILVIA
By thy approach thou mak'st me most unhappy.   31

JULIA *[aside]*
And me, when he approacheth to your presence.

SILVIA
Had I been seizèd by a hungry lion,
I would have been a breakfast to the beast,
Rather than have false Proteus rescue me.
O heaven, be judge how I love Valentine,
Whose life's as tender to me as my soul!   37
And full as much – for more there cannot be –
I do detest false perjured Proteus.
Therefore be gone, solicit me no more.

PROTEUS
What dangerous action, stood it next to death,
Would I not undergo for one calm look!   42
O, 'tis the curse in love, and still approved,   43
When women cannot love where they're beloved.

SILVIA
When Proteus cannot love where he's beloved!
Read over Julia's heart, thy first best love,
For whose dear sake thou didst then rend thy faith
Into a thousand oaths, and all those oaths
Descended into perjury, to love me.   49
Thou hast no faith left now, unless thou'dst two;   50
And that's far worse than none. Better have none
Than plural faith, which is too much by one.
Thou counterfeit to thy true friend!   53

PROTEUS   In love
Who respects friend?   54

SILVIA   All men but Proteus.

PROTEUS
Nay, if the gentle spirit of moving words
Can no way change you to a milder form,
I'll woo you like a soldier, at arm's end,   57
And love you 'gainst the nature of love – force ye.

SILVIA
O heaven!

PROTEUS   I'll force thee yield to my desire.

VALENTINE *[coming forward]*
Ruffian, let go that rude uncivil touch;
Thou friend of an ill fashion!   61

V, iii The forest at the border of Mantua   *4 learned* taught; *brook* endure
11 beset surrounded
V, iv Another part of the forest   *1 habit* i.e. settled way of looking at things
2 desert deserted place   *3 brook* tolerate   *6 record* sing   *11 Repair* restore
15 unhappy unlucky   *20 respect* heed   *23 meed* reward   *31 approach*
advances   *37 tender* dear   *42 calm* kind   *43 still approved* continually
demonstrated   *49 Descended into perjury* i.e. forsworn   *50 faith* constancy
in love   *53 counterfeit* i.e. traitor   *54 respects* considers   *57 arm's end* i.e.
sword's point   *61 friend ... fashion* false friend

PROTEUS   Valentine!

VALENTINE

62 Thou common friend, that's without faith or love,
For such is a friend now. Treacherous man,

64 Thou hast beguiled my hopes. Naught but mine eye
Could have persuaded me. Now I dare not say

66 I have one friend alive; thou wouldst disprove me.

67 Who should be trusted, when one's right hand
Is perjurèd to the bosom? Proteus,
I am sorry I must never trust thee more,

70 But count the world a stranger for thy sake.

71 The private wound is deepest. O time most accurst,
'Mongst all foes that a friend should be the worst!

PROTEUS

My shame and guilt confounds me.
Forgive me, Valentine. If hearty sorrow

75 Be a sufficient ransom for offense,
I tender 't here. I do as truly suffer

77 As e'er I did commit.

VALENTINE   Then I am paid,

78 And once again I do receive thee honest.
Who by repentance is not satisfied
Is nor of heaven nor earth, for these are pleased.
By penitence th' Eternal's wrath 's appeased;

82 And, that my love may appear plain and free,
All that was mine in Silvia I give thee.

JULIA O me unhappy!
        [Swoons.]

PROTEUS Look to the boy.

86 VALENTINE Why, boy! Why, wag! How now? What's
the matter? Look up; speak.

JULIA O good sir, my master charged me to deliver a ring
to Madam Silvia, which, out of my neglect, was never
done.

PROTEUS Where is that ring, boy?

JULIA Here 'tis. This is it.
        [Gives a ring.]

PROTEUS How? Let me see. Why, this is the ring I gave
to Julia!

JULIA

95 O, cry you mercy, sir. I have mistook.
This is the ring you sent to Silvia.
        [Shows another ring.]

PROTEUS But how cam'st thou by this ring? At my
depart I gave this unto Julia.

JULIA

And Julia herself did give it me;
And Julia herself hath brought it hither.

PROTEUS How? Julia!

JULIA

102 Behold her that gave aim to all thy oaths,

103 And entertained 'em deeply in her heart.

104 How oft hast thou with perjury cleft the root!

105 O Proteus, let this habit make thee blush;
Be thou ashamed that I have took upon me

107 Such an immodest raiment, if shame live
In a disguise of love.
It is the lesser blot, modesty finds,
Women to change their shapes than men their minds.

PROTEUS

Than men their minds! 'Tis true. O heaven, were man
But constant, he were perfect! That one error
Fills him with faults, makes him run through all th' sins;

114 Inconstancy falls off ere it begins.

What is in Silvia's face, but I may spy
More fresh in Julia's with a constant eye?   116

VALENTINE

Come, come, a hand from either –
Let me be blest to make this happy close;   118
'Twere pity two such friends should be long foes.

PROTEUS

Bear witness, heaven, I have my wish for ever.

JULIA

And I mine.
        [Enter] Duke, [and] Thurio, [led by] Outlaws.

OUTLAWS

A prize, a prize, a prize!

VALENTINE

Forbear, forbear I say. It is my lord the Duke.
Your Grace is welcome to a man disgraced,
Banishèd Valentine.

DUKE   Sir Valentine!

THURIO

Yonder is Silvia, and Silvia's mine.

VALENTINE

Thurio, give back, or else embrace thy death.   127
Come not within the measure of my wrath.   128
Do not name Silvia thine; if once again,
Verona shall not hold thee. Here she stands;   130
Take but possession of her with a touch –
I dare thee but to breathe upon my love.

THURIO

Sir Valentine, I care not for her, I.
I hold him but a fool that will endanger
His body for a girl that loves him not.
I claim her not, and therefore she is thine.

DUKE

The more degenerate and base art thou,
To make such means for her as thou hast done,
And leave her on such slight conditions.   139
Now, by the honor of my ancestry,
I do applaud thy spirit, Valentine,
And think thee worthy of an empress' love.
Know then, I here forget all former griefs,
Cancel all grudge, repeal thee home again,   144
Plead a new state in thy unrivalled merit,   145
To which I thus subscribe: Sir Valentine,
Thou art a gentleman and well derived;   147
Take thou thy Silvia, for thou hast deserved her.

VALENTINE

I thank your Grace; the gift hath made me happy.

62 *common* cheap   64 *beguiled* cheated   66 *disprove me* prove me wrong   67–68 *when . . . bosom* i.e. when one's closest friend proves false   70 *count . . . sake* i.e. remain an outlaw for what you have done (?), believe all men false because of your action (?)   71 *private* personal   75 *ransom* reparation   77 *commit* transgress; *paid* satisfied   78 *receive* acknowledge   82 *love* friendship; *plain and free* sincere and generous (?), plainly and freely (?)   86 *wag* (term of familiar friendship)   95 *cry you mercy* pardon me   102 *gave aim to* was the object of   103 *entertained* kept   104 *root* i.e. bottom of the heart   105 *habit* costume   107–08 *if shame . . . love* i.e. if something done for love can be shameful (?), if one who falsely pretends love can feel shame (?)   114 *Inconstancy . . . begins* i.e. the unfaithful lover is false even before he is fully in love   116 *with . . . eye* i.e. if I look with the eye of true love   118 *close* union (?), conclusion (?)   127 *give back* stand back   128 *measure* reach   130 *Verona* (again, probably a slip for Milan)   139 *on . . . conditions* with so little struggle   144 *repeal* recall (from exile)   145 *Plead . . . merit* (meaning obscure; the Duke may be asking to be forgiven; or, if a period is placed after *again*, the line can be read as inviting Valentine to sue for Silvia's hand)   147 *derived* descended

I now beseech you, for your daughter's sake,
To grant one boon that I shall ask of you.

DUKE

I grant it for thine own, what'er it be.

VALENTINE

153   These banished men, that I have kept withal,
Are men endued with worthy qualities.
Forgive them what they have committed here,
And let them be recalled from their exile.
They are reformèd, civil, full of good,
And fit for great employment, worthy lord.

DUKE

Thou hast prevailed; I pardon them, and thee.
Dispose of them as thou know'st their deserts.

Come, let us go; we will include all jars   161
With triumphs, mirth, and rare solemnity.   162

VALENTINE

And as we walk along, I dare be bold
With our discourse to make your Grace to smile.
What think you of this page, my lord?

DUKE

I think the boy hath grace in him; he blushes.

VALENTINE

I warrant you, my lord, more grace than boy.

DUKE

What mean you by that saying?

VALENTINE

Please you, I'll tell you as we pass along,
That you will wonder what hath fortunèd.   170
Come, Proteus, 'tis your penance but to hear   171
The story of your loves discoverèd;
That done, our day of marriage shall be yours:
One feast, one house, one mutual happiness.   *Exeunt.*

---

153 *kept withal* lived with   161 *include all jars* bring all dissension to an end
162 *triumphs* entertainments; *solemnity* festivity   170 *fortunèd* happened
171 *'tis ... but* your only penance shall be

A MIDSUMMER NIGHT'S DREAM

INTRODUCTION

A Midsummer Night's Dream is one of Shakespeare's happiest comedies. It is called a dream because the improbable events of the story seem to the participants when they are over like something dreamed, true yet not true – such a dream of crossed loves, futile quarrels, and frustrated searches, of fairy spells and strange transformations as belongs to Midsummer Eve, June 23, a night when men are proverbially subject to fairy tricks and queer fancies. "Methought I was, and methought I had – But man is but a patched fool if he will offer to say what methought I had." Yet the play is not just a fairy tale, for everyone knows that love is blind, and that mortals possessed with it readily make delightful fools of themselves. The characters in the play are only visited with the midsummer madness common to lovers in or out of fairy-haunted woods.

The absurd dream, however, is followed by a "solemnity," a happy but serious celebration of a multiple wedding. Marriage, of course, is the expected ending of a comedy of love; but the formality of these nuptials and the presence of the fairies to sing an epithalamium and to bless the bride-beds suggest that the play may have been written as an entertainment for a great wedding, just as Quince's play was written for the wedding festival of Theseus and Hippolyta. Attempts have been made to find such a wedding of a suitable date. Among the several noble weddings proposed, ranging from 1591 to 1598, the one most favored is that of William Stanley, Earl of Derby (whose father and whose brother had been patrons of Shakespeare's company of actors), to Elizabeth Vere, daughter of the Earl of Oxford, on January 26, 1595; it was performed at Greenwich Palace and Queen Elizabeth may have attended it. The manifest compliment to the Queen in Oberon's lines on "the imperial vot'ress" in Act II, scene i, would have been appropriate to an occasion when she was present. The few suspected topical allusions in the play appear to indicate a similar date. The most important one is the unseasonable weather described in II, i, 81–117, which would fit any one of the three years 1594–96 but especially the cold and sodden summer of 1594. The best indication of approximate date lies in the style. The blank verse shows the easy handling Shakespeare had attained after writing plays for six or seven years, without showing the bolder freedom and more complex rhythms of later years. Composition in 1594 or 1595 would make the play fall at the end of Shakespeare's first years of experiment with drama, during which time he learned to harness to the needs of a play his schoolboy training in rhetoric, his fondness for playing with words, metres, and rhymes, his delight in poetry for its own sake. Like *Richard II* and *Romeo and Juliet*, both probably to be dated about 1595, *A Midsummer Night's Dream* is full of lyricism, not subdued, yet fully controlled for a dramatic purpose. In *Richard II*, the hero's living in a world of poetic images is made the key to his psychological tragedy; in *Romeo and Juliet*, in which the intense and tragic love of two very young people is enacted against a background of family feud, setting and poetry are made to sustain and illuminate the action. So they are in *A Midsummer Night's Dream*. The poetry creates the wood, the moonlight, and the fairies, and it is in the wood, under fairy spells, that all the fantastic events of the night take place.

Whether or not there was a private occasion for the play, we know by the statement on the title page of the first edition, a quarto printed in 1600, that it was "sundry times publicly acted" by the Lord Chamberlain's servants, that is, by Shakespeare's company. Certain irregularities in the 1600 text and certain features of the play, notably inconsistencies in the time scheme (both in the duration of the action and in the state of the moon, which is dark when the play opens but most effectively shining the following night), suggest that the play may have undergone some rewriting, but when and how much we have no way of knowing. If Shakespeare revised the play, he did it skillfully enough not to destroy its unity. Inconsistencies in the calendar apart, the play is all of a piece, with its several actions, its fantasy and its low comedy, its variety of styles for different situations and characters, all contributing to the whole design.

That design falls into four component groups of characters and their actions: Theseus and Hippolyta, whose court in Athens furnishes a frame setting for the main plot and whose expected wedding makes an occasion for the play; the four young lovers, who run away from Athens and whose misadventures in the wood make up the principal action (on the eve of May Day, by the way, rather than on the eve of Midsummer Night, as we might expect); the fairies in the wood, who are having troubles of their own, but who, more or less by the way, intervene in the lovers' affairs to make them first worse, then better; and the "hempen homespuns," a group of Athenian craftsmen who come into the wood to rehearse a little play they hope to present at court for the wedding festivities, and who, in an unexpected way, also fall foul of the fairies. The fairies also come to court at the end to bring their blessings to the three newly wedded couples. And so each of the plots and groups of characters touches one of the others at some point.

The court, where the action begins and ends, is elegant, ceremonious, a scene "with pomp, with triumph, and with revelling." The blank verse generally spoken there helps to set off the courtly background, with its greater formality and decorum, from the comic adventures of the lovers. Duke Theseus is slightly, but adequately, sketched as a hero, a huntsman, and a sage prince. He is a strong, sensible, kind ruler, not particularly imaginative, and skeptical of fantasy, whether in lovers' brains or in poets'. To make him so, in this play of all others, is a nice touch of Shakespearean irony. The court, for all its gaiety, is the stable world of common sense and social order.

The desperate alternatives Theseus lays before Hermia – either to marry Demetrius, the man of her father's choice, or to betake herself to a cloister – drive her and Lysander into the woods, with Demetrius hot after them and Helena close behind. This device of taking his characters away from court and city into a freer, half fairy-tale world (a device he was to employ again in *As You Like It*, *The Winter's Tale*, and *The Tempest*) Shakespeare first fully discovered in *A Midsummer Night's Dream*. Credibility may be suspended for the sake of fun, of poetry, and of comic vision. By making the fairies responsible for the young men's change of heart, he plays lightly on his comic theme, that love is hardly a rational state; at the same time he saves his lovers from such harsh judgments of fickleness as readers are inclined to visit on Proteus in the earlier comedy of *The Two Gentlemen of Verona*. For one scarcely remembers, after such a night of errors, that Demetrius first altered his affections without the aid of the love-juice; his breach of faith seems like part of the dream. When the sick fancy is cured, the heart returns to its true-love. The plotting of the complications is neat. With Puck's applications of the juice and of its antidote, the young men's changes of heart follow a simple diagrammatic scheme: before the action of the play starts, each one loved his own girl; when it begins both love Hermia, then each loves the wrong girl, then both love Helena; finally, each loves the right girl again. As is fitting to such a state of things, neither lover can be much distinguished from the other, being both just infatuated young men, and as violently sure there was never anyone like Helena one minute as they had been sure the moment before there was never anyone like Hermia. The girls have more personality and individuality. Hermia is little and dark and a spitfire; Helena is tall and blonde and weepy, making much of her feminine woes and helplessness, yet quite as dogged in pursuit of her man as Hermia. The verse of the lovers varies between the blank verse they speak with the court group or when showing some elevation of feeling (as in Helena's lovely lines on her childhood friendship with Hermia) and the pentameter couplets and cross-rhymes they speak when they are quarrelling or making love. These rhyming passages, with their slight artificiality and lightness of touch, heighten the comedy.

The third element in the play, the fairy world, furnishes a slight secondary plot, as well as the machinery for the confusion of the main plot. The family quarrel of Titania and Oberon over the changeling boy is invented, perhaps, simply to bring the love-juice into the play. But, characteristically, Shakespeare gives this minor action depth and atmosphere, with glimpses of an Indian princess on a faraway shore and of Theseus' abandoned loves, hence endowing it with a vitality of its own. The primary purpose of the magic herbs – one to blind the sight with fancied love, the other to cure it – appears, of course, to be to further Oberon's revenge on Titania. But by his casual order to Puck to anoint the eyes of a disdainful youth in Athenian garments, the herbs are brought most naturally into the main plot, where Shakespeare uses them ingeniously both to tie and to untie the knot of his complication. The fairies appear to be very busy about mortal affairs, but their interventions are, on the whole, well intended. Though they are abroad at night, they are not powers of darkness. If their mischief or their spite sometimes brings vexations, their goodwill brings blessings. They are, in short, the minor powers of the unseen world that make the little things of daily life go right or wrong. Puck, besides, is the comic chorus of the play, its spirit of fun: "Lord, what fools these mortals be!" One would think he had had nothing to do with their foolishness.

Oberon and Titania, in their beauty, their rule over fairyland and a courtly train, their travelling of great distances, their powers of enchantment, and their limited influence over human affairs, are like "the Faery" of late medieval tales and ballads, known to everybody; sometimes, as well, of romances, which, extended and debased, had become the favorite popular reading of the sixteenth century. But Robin Goodfellow is a native country imp of folk superstition, a "puck," an ugly, merry, mischievous hobgoblin. His name "Goodfellow" is less a surname than a propitiatory epithet, for he has it in his power to annoy in the way that the modern gremlins have; but he is friendly enough if well treated. Left a bowl of milk on a tidy hearth, he will make the household chores go right; neglected, he will put everything at sixes and sevens. In associating "literary" with folk fairies Shakespeare was not doing anything novel or incongruous, for fairy lore in his day was already an inextricable mixture of literary tradition (both medieval and classical), folk belief, religious teaching (which associated the fairies with evil spirits), and poetic invention. Like other poets before him, Shakespeare enriched the blend, and added something unusual; that is, the miniature size of the fairies, who were commonly not smaller than children and were often the size of adults. But since the parts of Shakespeare's fairies must have been taken on the stage by boys old enough to play them, their diminutiveness is mainly for poetic effect (as in Mercutio's Queen Mab speech in *Romeo and Juliet*), an imaginative suggestion of elegance and daintiness. It is the poetry, after all, which creates the enchantment of the wood. Titania and Oberon, in keeping with decorum, generally speak in blank verse, like the characters in the human court; their verse, too, carries the weight of the imaginative description of the fairy world. But Oberon's description of Titania's bower and his instructions to Puck are given special emphasis by being rhymed; and his and Puck's spells are pronounced in verse of shorter metre, usually octosyllabic, or four-stress, lines rhyming alternately or in couplets. The little fairies sing in tripping measures with shorter lines.

The fourth element in the play, the group of "mechanicals," is brought into it for the salt of low comedy. But they, too, coming into the wood to rehearse their interlude, are led naturally into the action. Partly through the accident of their choosing a grassy plot near Titania's bower, partly through Puck's mischief, Bottom, with his "fair large ears," becomes the object of the dainty queen's deluded fancy. So the theme of love-blindness is played in another key, and given ludicrous emphasis. Bottom's part, probably performed by Will Kempe, the famous comedian of Shakespeare's company, is in the same line of clowns as Launce in *The Two Gentlemen* and Dogberry in *Much Ado about Nothing*. Like Dogberry, Bottom is wonderfully self-sufficient. His aplomb is quite undisturbed by the refinements of Titania's court and by the love of the Fairy Queen. Bottom and his friends speak in prose, not primarily because of their social class, but in order to set off the tone of their comedy from the rest of the play. The courtiers speak in prose, too, when they are joking at the performance of the interlude.

That little play, which Bottom and his friends so much admire, is written partly in pentameter couplets, partly in a variation of the common ballad stanza. The ballad metre, in a monotonous jog-trot line of fourteen syllables known as the "fourteener" (Quince's "eight and six"), had been common in stage-plays written before the development of blank verse. The language of the interlude is only a slightly exaggerated parody of the horrendous vocabulary and excessive alliteration to be found in early translations of Seneca's tragedies. The subject of the play, the story of Pyramus and Thisbe, was (like the story of Romeo and Juliet, its offshoot) a perennial tale of faithful and unfortunate love, and was well worn through centuries of retelling. The time and the scene of it, ancient Babylon, would seem fitting to the court of Theseus. For his version of the tale Shakespeare went directly to the first telling of it in his favorite classical book, the *Metamorphoses* of Ovid. But several versions, written in clumsy verse and in exaggerated rhetorical style, had been published during Shakespeare's youth in anthologies of verse; they give point to his outrageous parody. Narrative poems, too, on other famous legendary lovers (like Marlowe's *Hero and Leander*) were fashionable in the early nineties.

This admixture, in *A Midsummer Night's Dream*, of romantic adventure, sympathetic sentiment, fantasy, burlesque, and earthy comedy, and of characters of high and low degree, was agreeable to English taste and to Shakespeare's genius. It was his first masterpiece in this kind of comedy that we call romantic, a kind he continued to develop and to vary for the rest of his life. Compared with the greater comedies to follow, richer in portrayal of character and deeper in sympathy, and compared especially with his other fairy-tale play, *The Tempest*, which is the product of his ripest wisdom and of his maturest art, *A Midsummer Night's Dream* may seem a pretty toy. But the lesser thing it does it does to perfection. It is a little triumph – one of the earliest of Shakespeare's plays in which things so disparate and so various are gathered up into a single whole.

There is another kind of mixture in this play, also successfully achieved; that is the blending of material from different sources, classical, medieval, and contemporary, literary and popular. The lovers' plot appears to have no particular source (rather surprisingly, since there was no prejudice in Shakespeare's time against an author's taking a good story where he found it; what he did with it was what counted). But to enrich and complicate the core of his play, Shakespeare drew on a memory well stored with his varied reading and with the fairy lore he had absorbed in childhood. For the legend of Theseus he went to Chaucer's *Knight's Tale* and perhaps his *Legend of Good Women*, to Plutarch's *Lives* in Thomas North's translation (1579), and to Ovid's *Metamorphoses*; for the name of Oberon, probably to the French romance of *Huon of Bordeaux* (in English by about 1540), where Oberon is the

dwarf King of the Faery, or to *The Faerie Queene*, where he is an Elfin prince, father of Gloriana, Spenser's "Faerie Queene" (II, i, 8; II, x, 75, 76); for the name of Titania, to the *Metamorphoses*, where it is used as an epithet both of Diana (III, 173) and of Circe the enchantress (XIV, 14, 382, 438), descendants of the Titans; for Bottom's transformation, possibly, but not necessarily, to Apuleius' *Golden Ass* (translated by William Adlington, 1566); for the Pyramus and Thisbe story and much besides, to the *Metamorphoses* (IV, 55–166), both in a Latin edition and in Arthur Golding's many-times-printed English translation. Shakespeare fancied a metamorphosis of the pansy in playful Ovidian spirit, and allusions to other names and legends he wove delicately but persistently into the poetic texture of the play. He thus took some pains, it would appear, to give his comedy a "classical" flavor in keeping with the Athenian setting. But it is classical in the Renaissance manner. The ancient past is not, in Shakespeare and his contemporaries, a cold, reconstructed museum piece of archaeologically correct figures. Having been part of a continuous living tradition through intervening centuries, it is easily caught up into the present, for new meanings and purposes, when it is once again sought as a fresh source. In such art, anachronism is unobtrusive, because it has no absolute standard to falsify; it is, moreover, necessary. Shakespeare's Theseus has something in him of the legendary hero who rivalled Hercules in his exploits, of Plutarch's wise statesman, and of Chaucer's chivalric duke, who went a-hunting with horn and hounds in an English wood on a May morning, and who conquered and wedded "the queene Ipolita,"

> And broghte her hoom with him in his contree,
> With muchel glorie and greet solempnitee.

All this without jar, for he is a new character in his own right.

The play in one form or another has had a lively but not very satisfactory acting history. Some time before the printing of the folio in 1623 it may have been arranged for a newer style of performance, with act pauses; some slight changes were made in the assignment of minor parts. There are several references to performances in the early seventeenth century, but to only one, which Pepys found insipid and ridiculous, in the Restoration. Sufficient for performance as the play is, producers have seldom until recent times – and not always then – been willing to let it take care of itself. During the Restoration, the eighteenth century, and the early part of the nineteenth, it underwent two opposite kinds of mangling – one in the direction of burlesque, with action reduced to Bottom's transformation and to the craftsmen's rehearsal and performance of *Pyramus and Thisbe*; the other in the direction of opera, or pseudo-opera, with the low comedy drastically cut or omitted altogether, the lovers' and fairies' dialogue cut, but their parts expanded with songs, and the whole filled out with extraneous shows and dances. The earliest known example of the former kind of adaptation is a "droll" printed in 1661, *The Merry Conceited Humours of Bottom the Weaver*. (The title would have been appropriate to many later cut versions of the play.) The first and most famous of a long line of operatic adaptations was *The Fairy Queen* in 1692, for which Purcell wrote the music. (This has been successfully revived in our time, for the sake of the music.) Every act was supplied with ingenious and irrelevant shows; the one in Act V included a duet by a Chinese man and woman, a chorus of "Chineses," a dance of monkeys, and a "Grand Dance of 24 Chineses." Even the version of the play attributed to Garrick and performed in 1755, with a prologue spoken by him, was operatic. It was the mid-nineteenth century before the play was again seen on the English stage as a spoken play wholly in Shakespeare's words. Even during that century it was often severely cut and arranged. It has taken the great influence of William Poel and Harley Granville-Barker early in our own century to teach directors and producers that Shakespeare wrote his plays with the theatre in mind from the start and that to cut them up and pull them about is to lose the very things that make them most successful on the stage.

The style of the Victorian and Edwardian periods called for elaborate pictorial settings, even, in Herbert Beerbohm Tree's magnificent production in 1911, to the introduction of live rabbits in the wood. A return to Shakespeare's more fluid principles of staging, with nearly continuous action, with increased pace in the speaking, and with scenery and costume more symbolic and less literal, was made in Granville-Barker's production at the Savoy in 1914.

Among other productions notable for various reasons have been Ludwig Tieck's German version in Berlin in 1827, for which Mendelssohn wrote his still popular musical setting; Samuel Phelps's charming production at Sadler's Wells in 1853, with himself as Bottom; and Charles Kean's production in 1856, in which Ellen Terry at the age of eight played Puck. Contemporary productions are often boldly experimental. The play is a popular one among the various repertory and festival companies, and of course in any year it may be seen in school and college auditoriums – often very well played, too. Happily, its charm survives nearly any kind of treatment.

University of Wisconsin   MADELEINE DORAN

NOTE ON THE TEXT

The present edition follows the text of the first quarto (1600), which was probably printed from Shakespeare's own revised draft of the play. It is well printed as play quartos go, but it contains some troublesome misreadings of the manuscript as well as minor compositors' slips. This text was reprinted in 1619 in a second quarto falsely dated 1600, and the latter, altered by reference to theatrical manuscript, was used as copy by the printers of the folio of 1623. (Comment upon the interrelation of these early texts is provided in an appended note.) The text of the quartos is not divided into acts and scenes. That of the folio is divided into acts but not into scenes. The acts were divided into scenes by later editors, and this familiar division is provided marginally for reference in the present edition.

A MIDSUMMER NIGHT'S DREAM

[NAMES OF THE ACTORS

Theseus, Duke of Athens
Egeus, father to Hermia
Lysander, beloved of Hermia
Demetrius, suitor to Hermia, approved by Egeus
Philostrate, Master of the Revels to Theseus
Peter Quince, a carpenter ; Prologue in the interlude
Nick Bottom, a weaver ; Pyramus in the same
Francis Flute, a bellows-mender ; Thisby in the same
Tom Snout, a tinker ; Wall in the same
Snug, a joiner ; Lion in the same
Robin Starveling, a tailor ; Moonshine in the same
Hippolyta, Queen of the Amazons, betrothed to Theseus

Hermia, daughter to Egeus, in love with Lysander
Helena, in love with Demetrius
Oberon, King of the Fairies
Titania, Queen of the Fairies
Puck, or Robin Goodfellow
Peaseblossom
Cobweb
Moth } *fairies*
Mustardseed
Other Fairies attending Oberon and Titania.
Attendants on Theseus and Hippolyta.

Scene : *Athens, and a wood near by*]

*

I, i   *Enter Theseus, Hippolyta, [Philostrate,] with others.*

THESEUS
Now, fair Hippolyta, our nuptial hour
Draws on apace. Four happy days bring in
Another moon ; but O, methinks, how slow
This old moon wanes ! She lingers my desires,
Like to a stepdame or a dowager,
Long withering out a young man's revenue.

HIPPOLYTA
Four days will quickly steep themselves in night,
Four nights will quickly dream away the time ;
And then the moon, like to a silver bow
New-bent in heaven, shall behold the night
Of our solemnities.

THESEUS   Go, Philostrate,
Stir up the Athenian youth to merriments,
Awake the pert and nimble spirit of mirth,
Turn melancholy forth to funerals ;
15   The pale companion is not for our pomp.
                              [Exit Philostrate.]
16   Hippolyta, I wooed thee with my sword,
And won thy love doing thee injuries ;
But I will wed thee in another key,
19   With pomp, with triumph, and with revelling.
        *Enter Egeus and his daughter Hermia, and Lysander
        and Demetrius.*

EGEUS
Happy be Theseus, our renownèd Duke.

THESEUS
21   Thanks, good Egeus. What's the news with thee ?

EGEUS
Full of vexation come I, with complaint
Against my child, my daughter Hermia.
Stand forth, Demetrius. My noble lord,

This man hath my consent to marry her.
Stand forth, Lysander. And, my gracious Duke,
This man hath bewitched the bosom of my child.   27
Thou, thou, Lysander, thou hast given her rhymes
And interchanged love tokens with my child ;
Thou hast by moonlight at her window sung
With feigning voice verses of feigning love,
And stol'n the impression of her fantasy   32
With bracelets of thy hair, rings, gauds, conceits,   33
Knacks, trifles, nosegays, sweetmeats – messengers   34
Of strong prevailment in unhardened youth,
With cunning hast thou filched my daughter's heart,   36
Turned her obedience (which is due to me)
To stubborn harshness. And, my gracious Duke,
Be it so she will not here before your Grace
Consent to marry with Demetrius,
I beg the ancient privilege of Athens :
As she is mine, I may dispose of her,
Which shall be either to this gentleman
Or to her death, according to our law
Immediately provided in that case.   45

THESEUS
What say you, Hermia ? Be advised, fair maid.
To you your father should be as a god,

I, i The palace of the Duke   15 *companion* fellow ; *pomp* splendid ceremony, 'solemn sight' (Cawdrey's dictionary, 1604) 16 *Hippolyta . . . sword* (according to Chaucer and to one story in Plutarch, Theseus had taken Hippolyta captive when he conquered the Amazons) 19 *with triumph* (1) magnificently, with public festivities, (2) victoriously 21 *Egeus* (pronounced E-gè-us) 27 *bewitched* (with a literal as well as a metaphorical suggestion) 32 *stol'n . . . fantasy* i.e. stealthily imprinted thine image upon her fancy 33 *gauds* trinkets ; *conceits* fanciful trifles 34 *Knacks* knickknacks 36 *cunning* expert knowledge (cf. l. 27) 45 *Immediately* expressly

One that composed your beauties; yea, and one
To whom you are but as a form in wax,
By him imprinted, and within his power
51 To leave the figure, or disfigure it.
52 Demetrius is a worthy gentleman.

HERMIA
So is Lysander.

THESEUS   In himself he is;
54 But in this kind, wanting your father's voice,
The other must be held the worthier.

HERMIA
I would my father looked but with my eyes.

THESEUS
Rather your eyes must with his judgment look.

HERMIA
I do entreat your Grace to pardon me.
I know not by what power I am made bold,
Nor how it may concern my modesty
In such a presence here to plead my thoughts;
But I beseech your Grace that I may know
The worst that may befall me in this case
If I refuse to wed Demetrius.

THESEUS
Either to die the death, or to abjure
For ever the society of men.
Therefore, fair Hermia, question your desires,
68 Know of your youth, examine well your blood,
Whether, if you yield not to your father's choice,
70 You can endure the livery of a nun,
71 For aye to be in shady cloister mewed,
To live a barren sister all your life,
73 Chanting faint hymns to the cold fruitless moon.
Thrice blessèd they that master so their blood
To undergo such maiden pilgrimage;
76 But earthlier happy is the rose distilled
Than that which, withering on the virgin thorn,
Grows, lives, and dies in single blessedness.

HERMIA
So will I grow, so live, so die, my lord,
80 Ere I will yield my virgin patent up
Unto his lordship whose unwishèd yoke
My soul consents not to give sovereignty.

THESEUS
Take time to pause; and by the next new moon –
The sealing day betwixt my love and me
For everlasting bond of fellowship –
Upon that day either prepare to die
For disobedience to your father's will,
Or else to wed Demetrius, as he would,
Or on Diana's altar to protest

For aye austerity and single life.

DEMETRIUS
Relent, sweet Hermia; and, Lysander, yield
Thy crazèd title to my certain right.   92

LYSANDER
You have her father's love, Demetrius;
Let me have Hermia's: do you marry him.

EGEUS
Scornful Lysander, true, he hath my love,
And what is mine my love shall render him.
And she is mine, and all my right of her
I do estate unto Demetrius.   98

LYSANDER
I am, my lord, as well derived as he,   99
As well possessed; my love is more than his;   100
My fortunes every way as fairly ranked   101
(If not with vantage) as Demetrius';   102
And (which is more than all these boasts can be)
I am beloved of beauteous Hermia.
Why should not I then prosecute my right?
Demetrius, I'll avouch it to his head,   106
Made love to Nedar's daughter, Helena,
And won her soul; and she (sweet lady) dotes,
Devoutly dotes, dotes in idolatry,
Upon this spotted and inconstant man.   110

THESEUS
I must confess that I have heard so much,
And with Demetrius thought to have spoke thereof;
But, being over-full of self-affairs,
My mind did lose it. But Demetrius, come,
And come, Egeus. You shall go with me;
I have some private schooling for you both.
For you, fair Hermia, look you arm yourself   117
To fit your fancies to your father's will;   118
Or else the law of Athens yields you up
(Which by no means we may extenuate)   120
To death, or to a vow of single life.
Come, my Hippolyta. What cheer, my love?
Demetrius and Egeus, go along.
I must employ you in some business
Against our nuptial and confer with you   125
Of something nearly that concerns yourselves.   126

EGEUS
With duty and desire we follow you.
               Exeunt [all but Lysander and Hermia].

LYSANDER
How now, my love? Why is your cheek so pale?
How chance the roses there do fade so fast?

HERMIA
Belike for want of rain, which I could well   130
Beteem them from the tempest of my eyes.   131

LYSANDER
Ay me! for aught that I could ever read,
Could ever hear by tale or history,
The course of true love never did run smooth;
But either it was different in blood –

HERMIA
O cross! too high to be enthralled to low.

LYSANDER
Or else misgraffèd in respect of years –   137

HERMIA
O spite! too old to be engaged to young.

LYSANDER
Or else it stood upon the choice of friends –   139

51 *To leave . . . it* to leave the image as it is, or destroy it   52 *worthy* noble
54 *in this kind* in this respect (as a husband); *voice* consent   68 *blood*
passions   70 *livery* habit   71 *mewed* caged   73 *Chanting . . . moon* (Hermia
would be a votaress of Diana, the virgin goddess)   76 *earthlier happy*
(opposed to *blessèd*, l. 74); *distilled* i.e. made into perfume   80 *virgin
patent* patent or privilege of virginity   92 *crazèd* cracked, flawed   98
estate unto settle upon   99 *well derived* well born   100 *well possessed* rich
101 *fortunes . . . ranked* both wealth and position as good   102 *with vantage*
somewhat better   106 *head* face   110 *spotted* i.e. morally spotted, untrustworthy   117 *look . . . yourself* see that you get ready   118 *fancies*
love-thoughts ('fancy' means both imagination and love)   120 *extenuate*
mitigate   125 *Against* in preparation for   126 *nearly* closely (modifies
confer)   130 *Belike* perhaps   131 *Beteem* allow, afford   137 *misgraffèd*
ill-grafted   139 *friends* relatives, parents

HERMIA
O hell! to choose love by another's eyes.

LYSANDER
Or, if there were a sympathy in choice,
War, death, or sickness did lay siege to it,
143 Making it momentary as a sound,
Swift as a shadow, short as any dream,
145 Brief as the lightning in the collied night,
146 That, in a spleen, unfolds both heaven and earth,
And ere a man hath power to say 'Behold!'
The jaws of darkness do devour it up :
So quick bright things come to confusion.

HERMIA
If then true lovers have been ever crossed,
It stands as an edict in destiny :
152 Then let us teach our trial patience,
153 Because it is a customary cross,
As due to love as thoughts, and dreams, and sighs,
155 Wishes, and tears, poor Fancy's followers.

LYSANDER
A good persuasion. Therefore hear me, Hermia.
I have a widow aunt, a dowager,
158 Of great revenue, and she hath no child.
From Athens is her house remote seven leagues,
And she respects me as her only son.
There, gentle Hermia, may I marry thee,
And to that place the sharp Athenian law
Cannot pursue us. If thou lovest me then,
Steal forth thy father's house to-morrow night ;
And in the wood, a league without the town
(Where I did meet thee once with Helena
To do observance to a morn of May),
There will I stay for thee.

HERMIA   My good Lysander,
I swear to thee by Cupid's strongest bow,
170 By his best arrow, with the golden head,
171 By the simplicity of Venus' doves,
By that which knitteth souls and prospers loves,
173 And by that fire which burned the Carthage queen
When the false Troyan under sail was seen,
By all the vows that ever men have broke
(In number more than ever women spoke),
In that same place thou hast appointed me
To-morrow truly will I meet with thee.

LYSANDER
Keep promise, love. Look, here comes Helena.
Enter Helena.

HERMIA
180 God speed fair Helena. Whither away ?

HELENA
Call you me fair ? That fair again unsay.
182 Demetrius loves your fair. O happy fair !
183 Your eyes are lodestars, and your tongue's sweet air
More tuneable than lark to shepherd's ear
When wheat is green, when hawthorn buds appear.
186 Sickness is catching. O, were favor so,
Yours would I catch, fair Hermia, ere I go ;
My ear should catch your voice, my eye your eye,
My tongue should catch your tongue's sweet melody.
190 Were the world mine, Demetrius being bated,
191 The rest I'ld give to be to you translated.
192 O, teach me how you look, and with what art
193 You sway the motion of Demetrius' heart.

HERMIA
I frown upon him ; yet he loves me still.

HELENA
O that your frowns would teach my smiles such skill !

HERMIA
I give him curses ; yet he gives me love.

HELENA
O that my prayers could such affection move !

HERMIA
The more I hate, the more he follows me.

HELENA
The more I love, the more he hateth me.

HERMIA
His folly, Helena, is no fault of mine.

HELENA
None but your beauty. Would that fault were mine !

HERMIA
Take comfort. He no more shall see my face ;
Lysander and myself will fly this place.
Before the time I did Lysander see,
Seemed Athens as a paradise to me.
O, then, what graces in my love do dwell
That he hath turned a heaven unto a hell !

LYSANDER
Helen, to you our minds we will unfold.
To-morrow night, when Phoebe doth behold   209
Her silver visage in the wat'ry glass,
Decking with liquid pearl the bladed grass
(A time that lovers' flights doth still conceal),   212
Through Athens gates have we devised to steal.

HERMIA
And in the wood where often you and I
Upon faint primrose beds were wont to lie,   215
Emptying our bosoms of their counsel sweet,
There my Lysander and myself shall meet,
And thence from Athens turn away our eyes
To seek new friends and stranger companies.   219
Farewell, sweet playfellow. Pray thou for us ;
And good luck grant thee thy Demetrius.
Keep word, Lysander. We must starve our sight
From lovers' food till morrow deep midnight.

LYSANDER
I will, my Hermia.   *Exit Hermia.*
                Helena, adieu.
As you on him, Demetrius dote on you.   *Exit Lysander.*

HELENA
How happy some o'er other some can be !   226

143 *momentany* momentary (Latin '*momentaneus*') 145 *collied* murky (literally, blackened with coal-dust) 146 *in a spleen* (1) on a sudden impulse,
hence in a flash, (2) in a fit of violent temper 152 *teach . . . patience* i.e.
school ourselves to be patient in this trial 153 *cross* thwarting, vexation
155 *Fancy's* Love's 158 *revenue* (pronounced 'revènue') 170 *best . . .
head* (Cupid's sharp golden arrow causes love, his blunt leaden one dislike)
171 *simplicity* guilelessness, sincerity; *Venus' doves* (doves drew Venus'
chariot) 173–74 *fire . . . seen* (Dido Queen of Carthage immolated herself
on a funeral pyre when the Trojan Aeneas sailed away) 180 *fair* beautiful
(blonde only by implication, because a light complexion was the standard
of beauty) 182 *your fair* your type of beauty (Hermia is dark ; see II, ii, 114
and III, ii, 257); *happy fair* fortunate fair one ('lucky woman') 183
lodestars guiding stars (like the polestar) ; *air* music 186 *favor* looks,
especially good looks 190 *bated* excepted 191 *translated* transformed
192 *art* (carries suggestion of magic art ; cf. I, i, 27, 36) 193 *motion* impulses, affection 209 *Phoebe* the moon, or Diana 212 *still* always 215 *wont*
accustomed 219 *stranger companies* the company of strangers 226 *other
some* other persons

Through Athens I am thought as fair as she.
But what of that? Demetrius thinks not so;
He will not know what all but he do know.
And as he errs, doting on Hermia's eyes,
231   So I, admiring of his qualities.
232   Things base and vile, holding no quantity,
Love can transpose to form and dignity.
Love looks not with the eyes, but with the mind,
And therefore is winged Cupid painted blind.
236   Nor hath Love's mind of any judgment taste;
237   Wings, and no eyes, figure unheedy haste.
And therefore is Love said to be a child,
Because in choice he is so oft beguiled.
240   As waggish boys in game themselves forswear,
So the boy Love is perjured everywhere.
242   For ere Demetrius looked on Hermia's eyne,
He hailed down oaths that he was only mine;
And when this hail some heat from Hermia felt,
So he dissolved, and show'rs of oaths did melt.
I will go tell him of fair Hermia's flight.
Then to the wood will he to-morrow night
248   Pursue her; and for this intelligence
249   If I have thanks, it is a dear expense.
But herein mean I to enrich my pain,
To have his sight thither and back again.   *Exit.*

*

I, ii   *Enter Quince the Carpenter, and Snug the Joiner,*
and Bottom the Weaver, and Flute the Bellows-
mender, and Snout the Tinker, and Starveling the
Tailor.

QUINCE   Is all our company here?
2   BOTTOM   You were best to call them generally, man by
3   man, according to the scrip.
QUINCE   Here is the scroll of every man's name which is
5   thought fit, through all Athens, to play in our interlude
before the Duke and the Duchess on his wedding day at
night.
BOTTOM   First, good Peter Quince, say what the play
treats on, then read the names of the actors, and so grow
to a point.

---

231 *admiring of* marvelling at; *qualities* gifts, 'parts'   232 *holding no*
quantity i.e. without dimension, therefore shapeless, unlovely   236 *Nor*
... taste (since love resides in the imagination, not in the reason)   237
figure symbolize   240 *waggish* playful; *in game* in fun   242 *eyne* eyes (an
old plural)   248 *intelligence* piece of news   249 *a dear expense* i.e. an
expense very much worth incurring, a trouble worth taking
I, ii The house of Quince (?)   s.d. (J. D. Wilson points out that the craftsmen are all appropriately named: *Quince* probably for 'quoins' or 'quines,'
wedge-shaped pieces of wood used in building; *Snug* for the tightness of
the joints necessary in cabinet-making; *Bottom* for the reel on which
thread is wound; *Flute* perhaps for the fluted church-organs he would
have to mend; *Snout* for the spout of a kettle; *Starveling* for the proverbial
thinness of tailors)   2 *generally* (Bottom intends the reverse, i.e. individually)   3 *scrip* script   5 *interlude* short play, comedy   11 *Marry* (light
interjection; originally an oath by the Virgin Mary)   19 *lover . . . tyrant*
(typical roles in plays of the time)   23 *condole* lament   24 *humor* (1)
temperamental bent, (2) whim   25 *Ercles* Hercules (a stock ranting part;
cf. Seneca, *Hercules Furens*); *to tear . . . all split* (common expressions for
stage ranting)   30 *Phibbus' car* chariot of Phoebus Apollo the sun god
(the style parodies early translations of Seneca)   35 *condoling* sorrowing,
pathetic   39 *wand'ring knight* knight-errant (another typical role)   43
That's all one it makes no difference   45 *An* if   54-55, 57 *Thisby's mother,*
Pyramus' father, Thisby's father (the parents are mentioned in the source
story, but they do not appear in the interlude as acted)   59 *fitted* cast
64 *that* so that   68 *An* if

QUINCE   Marry, our play is 'The most lamentable 11
comedy and most cruel death of Pyramus and Thisby.'
BOTTOM   A very good piece of work, I assure you, and a
merry. Now, good Peter Quince, call forth your actors
by the scroll. Masters, spread yourselves.
QUINCE   Answer as I call you. Nick Bottom the weaver.
BOTTOM   Ready. Name what part I am for, and proceed.
QUINCE   You, Nick Bottom, are set down for Pyramus.
BOTTOM   What is Pyramus? a lover, or a tyrant?   19
QUINCE   A lover that kills himself, most gallant, for love.
BOTTOM   That will ask some tears in the true performing
of it. If I do it, let the audience look to their eyes. I will
move storms; I will condole in some measure. To the 23
rest. Yet my chief humor is for a tyrant. I could play 24
Ercles rarely, or a part to tear a cat in, to make all split. 25
               'The raging rocks
               And shivering shocks
               Shall break the locks
                 Of prison gates,
               And Phibbus' car   30
               Shall shine from far
               And make and mar
                 The foolish Fates.'
This was lofty. Now name the rest of the players. This
is Ercles' vein, a tyrant's vein. A lover is more condoling. 35
QUINCE   Francis Flute the bellows-mender.
FLUTE   Here, Peter Quince.
QUINCE   Flute, you must take Thisby on you.
FLUTE   What is Thisby? a wand'ring knight?   39
QUINCE   It is the lady that Pyramus must love.
FLUTE   Nay, faith, let not me play a woman. I have a beard
coming.
QUINCE   That's all one. You shall play it in a mask, and 43
you may speak as small as you will.
BOTTOM   An I may hide my face, let me play Thisby too. 45
I'll speak in a monstrous little voice:-'Thisne, Thisne!'
'Ah, Pyramus, my lover dear, thy Thisby dear, and lady
dear!'
QUINCE   No, no, you must play Pyramus; and Flute, you
Thisby.
BOTTOM   Well, proceed.
QUINCE   Robin Starveling the tailor.
STARVELING   Here, Peter Quince.
QUINCE   Robin Starveling, you must play Thisby's 54
mother. Tom Snout the tinker.
SNOUT   Here, Peter Quince.
QUINCE   You, Pyramus' father; myself, Thisby's father; 57
Snug, the joiner, you the lion's part. And I hope here is
a play fitted.   59
SNUG   Have you the lion's part written? Pray you, if it be,
give it me, for I am slow of study.
QUINCE   You may do it extempore, for it is nothing but
roaring.
BOTTOM   Let me play the lion too. I will roar that I will do 64
any man's heart good to hear me. I will roar that I will
make the Duke say, 'Let him roar again; let him roar
again.'
QUINCE   An you should do it too terribly, you would 68
fright the Duchess and the ladies, that they would
shriek; and that were enough to hang us all.
ALL   That would hang us, every mother's son.
BOTTOM   I grant you, friends, if you should fright the
ladies out of their wits, they would have no more dis-

74 cretion but to hang us; but I will aggravate my voice so
75 that I will roar you as gently as any sucking dove; I will
76 roar you an 'twere any nightingale.

QUINCE You can play no part but Pyramus; for Pyramus
78 is a sweet-faced man, a proper man as one shall see in a
summer's day, a most lovely gentlemanlike man. Therefore you must needs play Pyramus.

BOTTOM Well, I will undertake it. What beard were I
best to play it in?

QUINCE Why, what you will.

84 BOTTOM I will discharge it in either your straw-color
85 beard, your orange-tawny beard, your purple-in-grain
86 beard, or your French-crown-color beard, your perfit
yellow.

87 QUINCE Some of your French crowns have no hair at all,
and then you will play barefaced. But masters, here are
89 your parts; and I am to entreat you, request you, and
90 desire you to con them by to-morrow night; and meet
me in the palace wood, a mile without the town, by
moonlight. There will we rehearse; for if we meet in the
93 city, we shall be dogged with company, and our devices
94 known. In the meantime I will draw a bill of properties,
such as our play wants. I pray you fail me not.

BOTTOM We will meet, and there we may rehearse most
97 obscenely and courageously. Take pains, be perfit.
Adieu.

QUINCE At the Duke's Oak we meet.

99 BOTTOM Enough. Hold, or cut bowstrings.   *Exeunt.*

*

II, i   *Enter a Fairy at one door, and Robin Goodfellow*
        [Puck] at another.

PUCK
  How now, spirit, whither wander you?
FAIRY   Over hill, over dale,
3   Thorough bush, thorough brier,
4   Over park, over pale,
5   Thorough flood, thorough fire;
    I do wander everywhere,
7   Swifter than the moon's sphere;
    And I serve the Fairy Queen,
9   To dew her orbs upon the green.
10   The cowslips tall her pensioners be.
    In their gold coats spots you see:
    Those be rubies, fairy favors;
13   In those freckles live their savors.
    I must go seek some dewdrops here,
    And hang a pearl in every cowslip's ear.
16   Farewell, thou lob of spirits; I'll be gone.
    Our Queen and all her elves come here anon.
PUCK
  The King doth keep his revels here to-night.
  Take heed the Queen come not within his sight.
20 For Oberon is passing fell and wrath,
  Because that she, as her attendant, hath
  A lovely boy, stolen from an Indian king;
23 She never had so sweet a changeling.
24 And jealous Oberon would have the child
25 Knight of his train, to trace the forests wild.
26 But she perforce withholds the lovèd boy,
  Crowns him with flowers, and makes him all her joy.
  And now they never meet in grove or green,
29 By fountain clear or spangled starlight sheen,

But they do square, that all their elves, for fear,   30
Creep into acorn cups and hide them there.
FAIRY
Either I mistake your shape and making quite,
Or else you are that shrewd and knavish sprite   33
Called Robin Goodfellow. Are not you he   34
That frights the maidens of the villagery,   35
Skim milk, and sometimes labor in the quern,   36
And bootless make the breathless housewife churn,   37
And sometime make the drink to bear no barm,   38
Mislead night-wanderers, laughing at their harm?
Those that Hobgoblin call you, and sweet Puck,   40
You do their work, and they shall have good luck.
Are not you he?
PUCK   Thou speakest aright;
I am that merry wanderer of the night.
I jest to Oberon, and make him smile
When I a fat and bean-fed horse beguile,
Neighing in likeness of a filly foal;
And sometime lurk I in a gossip's bowl   47
In very likeness of a roasted crab,   48
And when she drinks, against her lips I bob
And on her withered dewlap pour the ale.
The wisest aunt, telling the saddest tale,   51
Sometime for three-foot stool mistaketh me;
Then slip I from her bum, down topples she,
And 'tailor' cries, and falls into a cough;   54
And then the whole quire hold their hips and laugh,   55
And waxen in their mirth, and neeze, and swear   56
A merrier hour was never wasted there.
But room, fairy: here comes Oberon.
FAIRY
And here my mistress. Would that he were gone!
    Enter [Oberon,] the King of Fairies, at one door, with
      his Train; and the Queen [Titania,] at another, with hers.
OBERON
Ill met by moonlight, proud Titania.

74 *aggravate* (Bottom means the opposite, i.e. diminish, soften)   75 *roar you* (a colloquialism, with vague sense of 'roar for you')   76 *an 'twere* as if it were   78 *proper* fine, handsome   84–85 *your . . . beard* i.e. one of those straw-color beards you know about (a colloquial use of 'your')   85 *orange-tawny* brownish orange or merely orange ('tawny' from '*tanné*,' tanned); *purple-in-grain* i.e. dyed with a fast purple or red (from 'grain,' name given the dried cochineal insects)   86 *French-crown-color* i.e. color of the gold coin; *perfit* perfect   87 *French crowns* heads bald from French disease (syphilis)   89 *am to* have to   90 *con* learn by heart   93 *devices* purposes, plans   94 *bill* list   97 *obscenely* (better leave the sense to Bottom!)   99 *Hold . . . bowstrings* i.e. keep your promise or be disgraced (probable sense; an archer's expression of uncertain meaning)
II, i A wood outside Athens   3 *Thorough* (common dissyllabic form of 'through')   4 *pale* enclosure (here, synonymous with *park*)   5 *flood* water   7 *moon's* (sometimes read as dissyllabic, as in the old genitive form 'moones')   9 *orbs* circles (here, fairy rings)   10 *pensioners* members of the royal bodyguard, in splendid uniforms   13 *savors* scent   16 *lob* lubber, lout   20 *passing fell and wrath* surpassingly fierce and wrathful   23 *changeling* (trisyllabic)   24 *jealous* envious   25 *trace* range through   26 *perforce* by force   29 *fountain* spring   30 *square* fall out, quarrel   33 *shrewd* naughty (literally, evil, 'cursed,' but generally used in weaker senses)   34 *Robin Goodfellow* (name for the household elf common in country folklore)   35 *villagery* villagers   36 *quern* handmill for grinding pepper, malt, etc.   37 *bootless* without reward (because the butter won't come); *housewife* (pronounced 'huz-if')   38 *barm* head on the ale   40 *Hobgoblin* Robin the goblin ('Hob' is a country form of Robert or Robin); *Puck* (a generic name, from Anglo-Saxon '*puca*,' for mischievous devils or imps)   47 *gossip's* old woman's, crony's   48 *crab* crab apple   51 *aunt* old dame; *saddest* most serious   54 *tailor* (proverbial exclamation, apparently because tailors sit on the floor to sew)   55 *quire* company, 'chorus'   56 *waxen* increase; *neeze* sneeze

TITANIA

61   What, jealous Oberon ? Fairy, skip hence.
      I have forsworn his bed and company.

OBERON

63   Tarry, rash wanton. Am not I thy lord ?

TITANIA

      Then I must be thy lady ; but I know
      When thou hast stolen away from fairyland,
66   And in the shape of Corin sat all day,
67   Playing on pipes of corn, and versing love
68   To amorous Phillida. Why art thou here,
      Come from the farthest steep of India,
      But that, forsooth, the bouncing Amazon,
71   Your buskined mistress and your warrior love,
      To Theseus must be wedded, and you come
      To give their bed joy and prosperity ?

OBERON

      How canst thou thus, for shame, Titania,
      Glance at my credit with Hippolyta,
      Knowing I know thy love to Theseus ?
      Didst thou not lead him through the glimmering night
78   From Perigenia, whom he ravishèd ?
79   And make him with fair Aegles break his faith,
80   With Ariadne, and Antiopa ?

TITANIA

      These are the forgeries of jealousy ;
82   And never, since the middle summer's spring,
      Met we on hill, in dale, forest, or mead,
84   By pavèd fountain or by rushy brook,
85   Or in the beachèd margent of the sea,
86   To dance our ringlets to the whistling wind,
      But with thy brawls thou hast disturbed our sport.
      Therefore the winds, piping to us in vain,

      As in revenge, have sucked up from the sea
      Contagious fogs ; which falling in the land   90
      Hath every pelting river made so proud   91
      That they have overborne their continents.   92
      The ox hath therefore stretched his yoke in vain,
      The ploughman lost his sweat, and the green corn   94
      Hath rotted ere his youth attained a beard ;
      The fold stands empty in the drownèd field,
      And crows are fatted with the murrion flock ;   97
      The nine men's morris is filled up with mud ;   98
      And the quaint mazes in the wanton green   99
      For lack of tread are undistinguishable.
      The human mortals want their winter here ;   101
      No night is now with hymn or carol blest.   102
      Therefore the moon, the governess of floods,   103
      Pale in her anger, washes all the air,
      That rheumatic diseases do abound.   105
      And thorough this distemperature we see   106
      The seasons alter : hoary-headed frosts
      Fall in the fresh lap of the crimson rose,
      And on old Hiems' thin and icy crown   109
      An odorous chaplet of sweet summer buds
      Is, as in mockery, set. The spring, the summer,
      The childing autumn, angry winter change   112
      Their wonted liveries ; and the mazèd world,   113
      By their increase, now knows not which is which.   114
      And this same progeny of evils comes
      From our debate, from our dissension ;   116
      We are their parents and original.

OBERON

      Do you amend it then ; it lies in you.
      Why should Titania cross her Oberon ?
      I do but beg a little changeling boy
      To be my henchman.   121

TITANIA   Set your heart at rest.
      The fairyland buys not the child of me.   122
      His mother was a vot'ress of my order,   123
      And in the spicèd Indian air, by night,
      Full often hath she gossiped by my side,
      And sat with me on Neptune's yellow sands,
      Marking th' embarkèd traders on the flood ;   127
      When we have laughed to see the sails conceive
      And grow big-bellied with the wanton wind ;   129
      Which she, with pretty and with swimming gait
      Following (her womb then rich with my young squire),
      Would imitate, and sail upon the land
      To fetch me trifles, and return again,
      As from a voyage, rich with merchandise.
      But she, being mortal, of that boy did die,
      And for her sake do I rear up her boy ;
      And for her sake I will not part with him.

OBERON

      How long within this wood intend you stay ?   138

TITANIA

      Perchance till after Theseus' wedding day.
      If you will patiently dance in our round   140
      And see our moonlight revels, go with us.
      If not, shun me, and I will spare your haunts.   142

OBERON

      Give me that boy, and I will go with thee.

TITANIA

      Not for thy fairy kingdom. Fairies, away !
      We shall chide downright if I longer stay.

           Exeunt [Titania and her Train].

---

61 *jealous* envious ; *Fairy* i.e. the fairy who has been talking with Robin (most editors follow Theobald's change to 'Fairies') **63** *rash wanton* willful creature ('wanton' means, literally, 'undisciplined') **66, 68** *Corin, Phillida* (typical names for a shepherd and shepherdess in pastoral poetry) **67** *pipes of corn* pipes made of grain stalks, usually oats **71** *buskined* in buskins, a kind of leather legging **78** *Perigenia* (in Plutarch *Perigouna*, one of Theseus' several mistresses) **79** *Aegles* (North's spelling, which Shakespeare evidently followed, for *Aegle*, another of Theseus' mistresses) **80** *Ariadne* daughter of Minos of Crete who helped Theseus thread the labyrinth to kill the Minotaur and was abandoned by him on an island on his return to Athens ; *Antiopa* a name given by some historians, instead of *Hippolyta*, to the Amazonian queen conquered by Theseus **82** *middle summer's spring* beginning of midsummer **84** *pavèd* i.e. with a pebbly bottom **85** *margent* margin **86** *ringlets* dances in a ring **90** *Contagious* pestilential **91** *pelting* paltry **92** *continents* containing banks **94** *corn* grain of any kind **97** *murrion flock* flock smitten with the murrain, a disease of sheep and cattle **98** *nine men's morris* square cut in the turf for a game played with counters **99** *quaint mazes* intricate paths laid out like a maze to be followed rapidly on foot ; *wanton* rank **101** *want . . . here* lack winter as well as other seasons (?), would like winter now as more tolerable than the present summer (?) (Most editors adopt Theobald's emendation, 'cheer' for 'here.') **102** *hymn or carol* i.e. of the Christmas season (probably not hymns to the moon) **103–05** *Therefore . . . abound* i.e. not because hymns to the moon are neglected, but because the fairies are quarrelling (cf. ll. 88, 93) **103** *floods* (1) tides, (2) inundations generally **105** *That* so that ; *rheumatic diseases* colds and grippe as well as rheumatism (accented here 'rheùmatic') **106** *distemperature* disorder in the natural constitution **109** *Hiems'* winter's **112** *childing* pregnant, fruitful **113** *wonted liveries* accustomed garments ; *mazèd* amazed, bewildered **114** *increase* products **116** *debate* contention **121** *henchman* page **122** *The fairyland* i.e. the whole of fairyland **123** *vot'ress* woman who had taken a vow in the order of which Titania was patroness **127** *traders* trading ships ; *flood* flood-tide **129** *wanton* sportive, amorous **138** *stay* (a noun, object of *intend*) **140** *round* round dance (cf. *ringlets*, II, i, 86) **142** *shun, spare* (synonyms)

OBERON

146 Well, go thy way. Thou shalt not from this grove
147 Till I torment thee for this injury.
My gentle Puck, come hither. Thou rememb'rest
149 Since once I sat upon a promontory
150 And heard a mermaid, on a dolphin's back,
151 Uttering such dulcet and harmonious breath
152 That the rude sea grew civil at her song,
And certain stars shot madly from their spheres
To hear the sea-maid's music.

PUCK   I remember.

OBERON

That very time I saw (but thou couldst not)
Flying between the cold moon and the earth
Cupid, all armed. A certain aim he took
158 At a fair vestal, thronèd by the west,
159 And loosed his love-shaft smartly from his bow,
160 As it should pierce a hundred thousand hearts.
But I might see young Cupid's fiery shaft
162 Quenched in the chaste beams of the wat'ry moon,
And the imperial vot'ress passèd on,
164 In maiden meditation, fancy-free.
Yet marked I where the bolt of Cupid fell.
It fell upon a little western flower,
Before milk-white, now purple with love's wound,
168 And maidens call it love-in-idleness.
Fetch me that flow'r; the herb I showed thee once.
The juice of it, on sleeping eyelids laid,
171 Will make or man or woman madly dote
Upon the next live creature that it sees.
Fetch me this herb, and be thou here again
174 Ere the Leviathan can swim a league.

PUCK

I'll put a girdle round about the earth
In forty minutes.   [Exit.]

OBERON   Having once this juice,
I'll watch Titania when she is asleep
178 And drop the liquor of it in her eyes.
The next thing then she, waking, looks upon
(Be it on lion, bear, or wolf, or bull,
181 On meddling monkey, or on busy ape)
She shall pursue it with the soul of love.
And ere I take this charm from off her sight
(As I can take it with another herb)
I'll make her render up her page to me.
But who comes here? I am invisible,
And I will overhear their conference.

Enter Demetrius, Helena following him.

DEMETRIUS

I love thee not; therefore pursue me not.
Where is Lysander and fair Hermia?
The one I'll slay, the other slayeth me.
Thou told'st me they were stol'n unto this wood;
192 And here am I, and wood within this wood
Because I cannot meet my Hermia.
Hence, get thee gone, and follow me no more!

HELENA

195 You draw me, you hard-hearted adamant!
196 But yet you draw not iron, for my heart
Is true as steel. Leave you your power to draw,
And I shall have no power to follow you.

DEMETRIUS

Do I entice you? Do I speak you fair?
Or rather do I not in plainest truth

Tell you I do not nor I cannot love you?

HELENA

And even for that do I love you the more.
I am your spaniel; and Demetrius,
The more you beat me, I will fawn on you.
Use me but as your spaniel – spurn me, strike me,
Neglect me, lose me; only give me leave
(Unworthy as I am) to follow you.
What worser place can I beg in your love
(And yet a place of high respect with me)
Than to be usèd as you use your dog?

DEMETRIUS

Tempt not too much the hatred of my spirit,
For I am sick when I do look on thee.

HELENA

And I am sick when I look not on you.

DEMETRIUS

You do impeach your modesty too much   214
To leave the city and commit yourself
Into the hands of one that loves you not,
To trust the opportunity of night
And the ill counsel of a desert place   218
With the rich worth of your virginity.

HELENA

Your virtue is my privilege. For that   220
It is not night when I do see your face,
Therefore I think I am not in the night;
Nor doth this wood lack worlds of company,
For you, in my respect, are all the world.   224
Then how can it be said I am alone
When all the world is here to look on me?

DEMETRIUS

I'll run from thee and hide me in the brakes   227
And leave thee to the mercy of wild beasts.

HELENA

The wildest hath not such a heart as you.
Run when you will. The story shall be changed:
Apollo flies and Daphne holds the chase,   231
The dove pursues the griffon, the mild hind   232
Makes speed to catch the tiger – bootless speed,
When cowardice pursues, and valor flies.

DEMETRIUS

I will not stay thy questions. Let me go!   235

---

146 *from* go from   147 *injury* insult   149 *Since* when   150 *mermaid* (equivalent to 'siren' in Renaissance dictionaries)   151 *dulcet* sweet; *breath* voice, song   152 *civil* mannerly, gentle   158 *vestal* virgin priestess (an allusion to Elizabeth, the Virgin Queen; she is fancied as a votaress of Diana, the virgin moon-goddess; cf. ll. 161–64); *by the west* i.e. in England   159 *love-shaft* i.e. the golden arrow (cf. I, i, 170)   160 *As* as if   162 *wat'ry moon* (cf. II, i, 103)   164 *fancy-free* free of love-thoughts   168 *love-in-idleness* the pansy (the fanciful metamorphosis in these lines may have been suggested by the change of the mulberries from white to purple by the blood of Pyramus, in Ovid, *Metamorphoses*, IV, 125–27)   171 *or . . . or* either . . . or   174 *Leviathan* Biblical sea-monster, usually identified with the whale   178 *liquor of it* juice of the flower (?), or essence of the juice (?)   181 *busy* meddlesome (cf. 'busybody')   192 *and wood* and mad   195 *adamant* (1) loadstone or magnet, (2) the hardest stone, diamond (often thought to be the same fabulous stone)   196–97 *But . . . steel* i.e. but in drawing me, you are attracting not base iron but refined steel, which will hold its temper   214 *impeach* call in question, discredit   218 *desert* deserted, wild   220 *Your . . . privilege* your power to attract is my warrant, gives me my special right to come (?), or your goodness is my guarantee of immunity from danger (?)   224 *respect* opinion   227 *brakes* thickets   231 *Apollo . . . chase* (Daphne fled from Apollo and was changed into a laurel tree)   232 *griffon* fabulous animal with the head of an eagle, the body of a lion; *hind* doe   235 *stay* wait for

Or if thou follow me, do not believe
But I shall do thee mischief in the wood.

HELENA
Ay, in the temple, in the town, the field
You do me mischief. Fie, Demetrius.
Your wrongs do set a scandal on my sex.
We cannot fight for love, as men may do;
We should be wooed, and were not made to woo.
[Exit Demetrius.]
I'll follow thee, and make a heaven of hell
To die upon the hand I love so well.   *[Exit.]*

OBERON
Fare thee well, nymph. Ere he do leave this grove,
Thou shalt fly him, and he shall seek thy love.
     Enter Puck.
Hast thou the flower there? Welcome, wanderer.

PUCK
Ay, there it is.

OBERON   I pray thee give it me.
I know a bank where the wild thyme blows,
250 Where oxlips and the nodding violet grows,
251 Quite over-canopied with luscious woodbine,
252 With sweet musk-roses, and with eglantine.
253 There sleeps Titania sometime of the night,
Lulled in these flowers with dances and delight;
And there the snake throws her enamelled skin,
Weed wide enough to wrap a fairy in.
And with the juice of this I'll streak her eyes
258 And make her full of hateful fantasies.
Take thou some of it and seek through this grove.
A sweet Athenian lady is in love
With a disdainful youth. Anoint his eyes;
But do it when the next thing he espies
May be the lady. Thou shalt know the man
By the Athenian garments he hath on.
Effect it with some care, that he may prove
266 More fond on her than she upon her love;
And look thou meet me ere the first cock crow.

PUCK
Fear not, my lord; your servant shall do so.   *Exeunt.*

*

II, ii   *Enter Titania, Queen of Fairies, with her Train.*
TITANIA
1 Come, now a roundel and a fairy song;
Then, for the third part of a minute, hence –
3 Some to kill cankers in the musk-rose buds,
4 Some war with reremice for their leathren wings,
To make my small elves coats, and some keep back
The clamorous owl, that nightly hoots and wonders

250 *oxlips* species of primrose similar to a cowslip   251 *over-canopied* (modifies *bank*); *woodbine* honeysuckle (but also applied to different vines; cf. IV, i, 41)   252 *musk-roses* single, sweet-scented, white garden roses; *eglantine* sweetbrier, a wild rose   253 *sometime of* at some time during   258 *fantasies* fancies   266 *fond* foolishly doting
II, ii The wood   1 *roundel* (cf. *ringlets, round,* II, ii, 86, 140)   3 *cankers* worms, caterpillars; *musk-rose* (cf. II, i, 252)   4 *reremice* bats   7 *quaint* fine, dainty (used of things skillfully made)   9 *double* forked   11 *blind-worms* slow-worms, small snakes   13 *Philomele* Philomela, the nightingale   30 *ounce* lynx   31 *Pard* leopard   36 *to speak troth* to speak truthfully, 'to tell the truth'   42 *troth* true love, pledged faith   45 *take . . . innocence* i.e. take my meaning in the light of my innocent intentions   46 *Love . . . conference* i.e. when lovers converse, love interprets the meaning   50 *troth* (cf. l. 42)

At our quaint spirits. Sing me now asleep.   7
Then to your offices, and let me rest.

Fairies sing.

[1. FAIRY] You spotted snakes with double tongue,   9
     Thorny hedgehogs, be not seen;
     Newts and blindworms, do no wrong,   11
     Come not near our Fairy Queen.

[Chorus.]

     Philomele, with melody   13
     Sing in our sweet lullaby,
   Lulla, lulla, lullaby; lulla, lulla, lullaby;
      Never harm
      Nor spell nor charm
   Come our lovely lady nigh.
   So good night, with lullaby.

1. FAIRY   Weaving spiders, come not here:
     Hence, you long-legged spinners, hence!
   Beetles black, approach not near;
     Worm nor snail, do no offense.

[Chorus.]

     Philomele, with melody, &c.
[She sleeps.]

2. FAIRY   Hence, away! Now all is well.
     One aloof stand sentinel.   *[Exeunt Fairies.]*

Enter Oberon [and squeezes the flower on Titania's eyelids].

OBERON   What thou seest when thou dost wake,
     Do it for thy true-love take;
     Love and languish for his sake.
     Be it ounce or cat or bear,   30
     Pard, or boar with bristled hair   31
     In thy eye that shall appear
     When thou wak'st, it is thy dear.
     Wake when some vile thing is near.   *[Exit.]*

Enter Lysander and Hermia.

LYSANDER
Fair love, you faint with wand'ring in the wood;
And to speak troth, I have forgot our way.   36
We'll rest us, Hermia, if you think it good,
And tarry for the comfort of the day.

HERMIA
Be't so, Lysander. Find you out a bed,
For I upon this bank will rest my head.

LYSANDER
One turf shall serve as pillow for us both,
One heart, one bed, two bosoms, and one troth.   42

HERMIA
Nay, good Lysander. For my sake, my dear,
Lie further off yet; do not lie so near.

LYSANDER
O, take the sense, sweet, of my innocence.   45
Love takes the meaning in love's conference.   46
I mean that my heart unto yours is knit,
So that but one heart we can make of it;
Two bosoms interchainèd with an oath –
So then two bosoms and a single troth.   50
Then by your side no bed-room me deny,
For lying so, Hermia, I do not lie.

HERMIA

Lysander riddles very prettily.

54   Now much beshrew my manners and my pride

If Hermia meant to say Lysander lied.

56   But, gentle friend, for love and courtesy

Lie further off, in human modesty.

Such separation as may well be said

Becomes a virtuous bachelor and a maid,

So far be distant; and good night, sweet friend.

Thy love ne'er alter till thy sweet life end.

LYSANDER

Amen, amen, to that fair prayer say I,

And then end life when I end loyalty.

Here is my bed. Sleep give thee all his rest!

HERMIA

65   With half that wish the wisher's eyes be pressed!

[They sleep.]

Enter Puck.

PUCK   Through the forest have I gone,

But Athenian found I none

68   On whose eyes I might approve

This flower's force in stirring love.

Night and silence! Who is here?

71   Weeds of Athens he doth wear.

This is he (my master said)

Despisèd the Athenian maid;

And here the maiden, sleeping sound

On the dank and dirty ground.

Pretty soul, she durst not lie

Near this lack-love, this kill-courtesy.

78   Churl, upon thy eyes I throw

79   All the power this charm doth owe:

When thou wak'st, let love forbid

Sleep his seat on thy eyelid.

So awake when I am gone,

For I must now to Oberon.   *Exit.*

Enter Demetrius and Helena, running.

HELENA

Stay, though thou kill me, sweet Demetrius.

DEMETRIUS

I charge thee, hence, and do not haunt me thus.

HELENA

86   O, wilt thou darkling leave me? Do not so.

DEMETRIUS

Stay, on thy peril! I alone will go.   *[Exit.]*

HELENA

88   O, I am out of breath in this fond chase.

89   The more my prayer, the lesser is my grace.

Happy is Hermia, wheresoe'er she lies,

For she hath blessèd and attractive eyes.

How came her eyes so bright? Not with salt tears.

If so, my eyes are oft'ner washed than hers.

No, no! I am as ugly as a bear,

For beasts that meet me run away for fear.

Therefore no marvel though Demetrius

Do, as a monster, fly my presence thus.

What wicked and dissembling glass of mine

99   Made me compare with Hermia's sphery eyne?

But who is here? Lysander, on the ground?

Dead, or asleep? I see no blood, no wound.

Lysander, if you live, good sir, awake.

LYSANDER *[starts up]*

And run through fire I will for thy sweet sake.

104   Transparent Helena, Nature shows art,

That through thy bosom makes me see thy heart.

Where is Demetrius? O, how fit a word

Is that vile name to perish on my sword!

HELENA

Do not say so, Lysander, say not so.

What though he love your Hermia? Lord! what though?

Yet Hermia still loves you. Then be content.

LYSANDER

Content with Hermia? No! I do repent

The tedious minutes I with her have spent.

Not Hermia, but Helena I love.

Who will not change a raven for a dove?

The will of man is by his reason swayed,   115

And reason says you are the worthier maid.

Things growing are not ripe until their season:

So I, being young, till now ripe not to reason.   118

And touching now the point of human skill,   119

Reason becomes the marshal to my will

And leads me to your eyes, where I o'erlook   121

Love's stories, written in Love's richest book.

HELENA

Wherefore was I to this keen mockery born?

When at your hands did I deserve this scorn?

Is't not enough, is't not enough, young man,

That I did never, no, nor never can,

Deserve a sweet look from Demetrius' eye,

But you must flout my insufficiency?

Good troth, you do me wrong! good sooth, you do,   129

In such disdainful manner me to woo.

But fare you well. Perforce I must confess

I thought you lord of more true gentleness.   132

O, that a lady, of one man refused,

Should of another therefore be abused!   *Exit.*

LYSANDER

She sees not Hermia. Hermia, sleep thou there,

And never mayst thou come Lysander near.

For, as a surfeit of the sweetest things

The deepest loathing to the stomach brings,

Or as the heresies that men do leave

Are hated most of those they did deceive,

So thou, my surfeit and my heresy,

Of all be hated, but the most of me!

And, all my powers, address your love and might   143

To honor Helen and to be her knight.   *Exit.* 144

HERMIA *[awakes]*

Help me, Lysander, help me! Do thy best

To pluck this crawling serpent from my breast.

Ay me, for pity. What a dream was here!

Lysander, look how I do quake with fear.

Methought a serpent eat my heart away,   149

And you sat smiling at his cruel prey.   150

---

54 *beshrew* curse (common in a very mild sense, as here)   **56–57** *gentle . . . modesty* (an appeal to Lysander as a civilized human being, who is not a beast or a savage; the implication is in *gentle, courtesy,* and *human*) **65** *pressed* closed in sleep   **68** *approve* test, put to the proof   **71** *Weeds* garments   **78** *Churl* boor, someone without manners (literally, a peasant) **79** *owe* own, possess   **86** *darkling* in the dark   **88** *fond* foolish   **89** *grace* answer to prayer, favor   **99** *sphery eyne* i.e. eyes as bright as stars in their spheres   **104** *Transparent* (1) ingenuous, able to be seen through, (2) bright, brilliant   **115** *will* desire   **118** *ripe not* not ripened   **119** *touching . . . skill* i.e. (reason,) now arriving at its maturity   **121** *o'erlook* look over, read   **129** *Good troth, good sooth* in truth (merely emphatic expletives – 'really,' 'indeed,' 'honestly')   **132** *gentleness* gentility, good breeding, courtesy   **143** *address* direct, apply   **144** *knight* true-love, true servant **149** *eat* ate (pronounced 'et')   **150** *prey* act of preying

Lysander! What, removed? Lysander! lord!
What, out of hearing? gone? No sound, no word?
153 Alack, where are you? Speak, an if you hear.
154 Speak, of all loves! I swoon almost with fear.
No? Then I well perceive you are not nigh.
Either death, or you, I'll find immediately.   *Exit.*

III, i   *Enter the Clowns [Quince, Snug, Bottom, Flute,*
       Snout, and Starveling].

BOTTOM Are we all met?

QUINCE Pat, pat; and here's a marvellous convenient
place for our rehearsal. This green plot shall be our
4   stage, this hawthorn brake our tiring house, and we will
do it in action as we will do it before the Duke.

BOTTOM Peter Quince?

7 QUINCE What sayest thou, bully Bottom?

BOTTOM There are things in this comedy of Pyramus and
Thisby that will never please. First, Pyramus must draw
a sword to kill himself; which the ladies cannot abide.
How answer you that?

12 SNOUT By'r lakin, a parlous fear.

STARVELING I believe we must leave the killing out,
when all is done.

15 BOTTOM. Not a whit. I have a device to make all well. Write
me a prologue, and let the prologue seem to say, we will
do no harm with our swords, and that Pyramus is not
killed indeed; and for the more better assurance, tell
them that I Pyramus am not Pyramus, but Bottom the
weaver. This will put them out of fear.

QUINCE Well, we will have such a prologue, and it shall
22   be written in eight and six.

BOTTOM No, make it two more; let it be written in eight
and eight.

SNOUT Will not the ladies be afeard of the lion?

STARVELING I fear it, I promise you.

BOTTOM Masters, you ought to consider with yourselves,
to bring in (God shield us) a lion among ladies is a most
dreadful thing. For there is not a more fearful wild-
fowl than your lion living; and we ought to look to't.

SNOUT Therefore another prologue must tell he is not a
lion.

BOTTOM Nay, you must name his name, and half his face
must be seen through the lion's neck, and he himself
must speak through, saying thus, or to the same defect:
'Ladies,' or 'Fair ladies, – I would wish you' or 'I would
request you' or 'I would entreat you – not to fear, not to

tremble. My life for yours! If you think I come hither as
a lion, it were pity of my life. No! I am no such thing. 38
I am a man as other men are.' And there, indeed, let him
name his name and tell them plainly he is Snug the
joiner.

QUINCE Well, it shall be so. But there is two hard things:
that is, to bring the moonlight into a chamber; for you
know, Pyramus and Thisby meet by moonlight.

SNOUT Doth the moon shine that night we play our play?

BOTTOM A calendar, a calendar! Look in the almanac.
Find out moonshine, find out moonshine.

QUINCE Yes, it doth shine that night.

BOTTOM Why, then may you leave a casement of the
great chamber window, where we play, open, and the
moon may shine in at the casement.

QUINCE Ay. Or else one must come in with a bush of 51
thorns and a lantern, and say he comes to disfigure, or 52
to present, the person of Moonshine. Then there is an- 53
other thing. We must have a wall in the great chamber;
for Pyramus and Thisby, says the story, did talk through
the chink of a wall.

SNOUT You can never bring in a wall. What say you,
Bottom?

BOTTOM Some man or other must present Wall; and let
him have some plaster, or some loam, or some roughcast
about him, to signify wall; and let him hold his fingers
thus; and through that cranny shall Pyramus and
Thisby whisper.

QUINCE If that may be, then all is well. Come, sit down
every mother's son, and rehearse your parts. Pyramus,
you begin. When you have spoken your speech, enter
into that brake; and so every one according to his cue.
      Enter Robin [Puck].

PUCK
What hempen homespuns have we swagg'ring here,
So near the cradle of the Fairy Queen?
What, a play toward? I'll be an auditor;   70
An actor too perhaps, if I see cause.

QUINCE Speak, Pyramus. Thisby, stand forth.

PYRAMUS
Thisby, the flowers of odious savors sweet –   73

QUINCE Odorous, odorous.

PYRAMUS —— odors savors sweet;
So hath thy breath, my dearest Thisby dear.
But hark, a voice! Stay thou but here awhile,
   And by and by I will to thee appear.   *Exit.* 78

PUCK
A stranger Pyramus than e'er played here!   *[Exit.]*

THISBY Must I speak now?

QUINCE Ay, marry, must you. For you must understand he
goes but to see a noise that he heard, and is to come again.

THISBY
Most radiant Pyramus, most lily-white of hue,
   Of color like the red rose on triumphant brier,
Most brisky juvenal, and eke most lovely Jew,   85
   As true as truest horse, that yet would never tire,
I'll meet thee, Pyramus, at Ninny's tomb.

QUINCE 'Ninus' tomb,' man. Why, you must not speak 88
that yet. That you answer to Pyramus. You speak all
your part at once, cues and all. Pyramus, enter. Your
cue is past; it is 'never tire.'

THISBY
O — As true as truest horse, that yet would never tire.   92
     [Enter Puck, and Pyramus with the ass-head.]

---

153 *an if* if   154 *of all loves* by all true love
III, i s.d. *Enter the Clowns* (the folio marks an act division here, but the
first quarto indicates that the action was originally continuous, with the
craftsmen rehearsing apart from where Titania lies sleeping) 4 *brake*
thicket or hedge; *tiring house* attiring house, dressing room 7 *bully*
worthy, 'jolly' 12 *By'r lakin* by our Lady; *parlous* 'terrible,' 'awful'
(literally, 'perilous') 15–16 *Write me* i.e. write (a colloquialism, like *roar
you,* I, ii, 75) 22 *eight and six* i.e. lines of eight and six syllables (or four
and three stresses) alternating: the common ballad metre 38 *it were . . .
life* my life would be in danger 51–52 *bush of thorns* bundle of faggots
(the man in the moon was traditionally supposed to have a bundle of
faggots and a dog; he had been transported to the moon, according to
one story, for gathering wood on a Friday) 52 *disfigure* (Quince means
'figure,' i.e. represent) 53 *present* represent (stage term) 70 *toward* on
the way 73 *of* (perhaps Pyramus' pronunciation of 'have') 78 *by and
by* shortly, presently 85 *juvenal* juvenile, youth; *eke* also (archaic in
Shakespeare's time); *Jew* (probably added merely to echo *juvenal* and rime
with *hue*) 88 *Ninus' tomb* (the lovers' rendezvous in Ovid. Ninus was the
mythical founder of Nineveh; his wife Semiramis was supposed to have
built the walls of Babylon, the city of Pyramus and Thisbe.) 92 s.d. (no
entrance marked in first quarto; folio adds at l. 101 'Enter Piramus with the
Asse head.' There was evidently only one ass-head in the property room.)

PYRAMUS

93 If I were fair, Thisby, I were only thine.

QUINCE O monstrous! O strange! We are haunted. Pray, masters! Fly, masters! Help!

[Exeunt all the Clowns but Bottom.]

PUCK

96 I'll follow you; I'll lead you about a round,
Through bog, through bush, through brake, through brier.
Sometime a horse I'll be, sometime a hound,

99 A hog, a headless bear, sometime a fire;
And neigh, and bark, and grunt, and roar, and burn,
Like horse, hound, hog, bear, fire, at every turn. *Exit.*

BOTTOM Why do they run away? This is a knavery of them to make me afeard.

Enter Snout.

SNOUT O Bottom, thou art changed. What do I see on thee?

BOTTOM What do you see? You see an ass-head of your own, do you? *[Exit Snout.]*

Enter Quince.

107 QUINCE Bless thee, Bottom, bless thee! Thou art translated. *Exit.*

BOTTOM I see their knavery. This is to make an ass of me, to fright me, if they could. But I will not stir from this place, do what they can. I will walk up and down here,

111 and I will sing, that they shall hear I am not afraid.

[Sings.]

112   The woosel cock so black of hue,
         With orange-tawny bill,
114   The throstle with his note so true,
115   The wren with little quill –

TITANIA

What angel wakes me from my flow'ry bed?

BOTTOM *[sings]*

     The finch, the sparrow, and the lark,
118   The plain-song cuckoo grey,
119   Whose note full many a man doth mark,
         And dares not answer nay.

For, indeed, who would set his wit to so foolish a bird?
Who would give a bird the lie, though he cry 'cuckoo'
never so?

TITANIA

I pray thee, gentle mortal, sing again.
Mine ear is much enamored of thy note;
So is mine eye enthrallèd to thy shape;

127 And thy fair virtue's force (perforce) doth move me,
On the first view, to say, to swear, I love thee.

BOTTOM Methinks, mistress, you should have little reason for that. And yet, to say the truth, reason and love keep little company together nowadays. The more the pity that some honest neighbors will not make them

133 friends. Nay, I can gleek, upon occasion.

TITANIA

Thou art as wise as thou art beautiful.

BOTTOM Not so, neither; but if I had wit enough to get out of this wood, I have enough to serve mine own turn.

TITANIA

Out of this wood do not desire to go.
Thou shalt remain here, whether thou wilt or no.

139 I am a spirit of no common rate,
140 The summer still doth tend upon my state;
And I do love thee. Therefore go with me.

I'll give thee fairies to attend on thee,
And they shall fetch thee jewels from the deep,
And sing while thou on pressèd flowers dost sleep;
And I will purge thy mortal grossness so
That thou shalt like an airy spirit go.

147 Peaseblossom, Cobweb, Moth, and Mustardseed!

Enter four Fairies [Peaseblossom, Cobweb, Moth, and Mustardseed].

PEASEBLOSSOM Ready.

COBWEB

And I.

MOTH And I.

MUSTARDSEED And I.

ALL   Where shall we go?

TITANIA

Be kind and courteous to this gentleman.
Hop in his walks and gambol in his eyes;
Feed him with apricocks and dewberries,
With purple grapes, green figs, and mulberries;

154 The honey-bags steal from the humblebees,
And for night tapers crop their waxen thighs,
And light them at the fiery glowworm's eyes,
To have my love to bed and to arise;
And pluck the wings from painted butterflies
To fan the moonbeams from his sleeping eyes.
Nod to him, elves, and do him courtesies.

PEASEBLOSSOM Hail, mortal!

COBWEB Hail!

MOTH Hail!

MUSTARDSEED Hail!

BOTTOM I cry your worships mercy, heartily. I beseech your worship's name.

COBWEB Cobweb.

169 BOTTOM I shall desire you of more acquaintance, good Master Cobweb. If I cut my finger, I shall make bold with you. Your name, honest gentleman?

PEASEBLOSSOM Peaseblossom.

172 BOTTOM I pray you, commend me to Mistress Squash,
173 your mother, and to Master Peascod, your father. Good Master Peaseblossom, I shall desire you of more acquaintance too. Your name, I beseech you, sir?

MUSTARDSEED Mustardseed.

BOTTOM Good Master Mustardseed, I know your patience well. That same cowardly, giantlike ox-beef hath devoured many a gentleman of your house. I promise you your kindred hath made my eyes water ere now. I desire you of more acquaintance, good Master Mustardseed.

TITANIA

Come wait upon him; lead him to my bower.
The moon, methinks, looks with a wat'ry eye;

---

93 *fair* handsome; *were only* would be only   96 *about a round* roundabout
99 *fire* will-o'-the-wisp   107 *translated* transformed   111 *that* so that
112 *woosel* ouzel (English blackbird or merle, of the thrush family)   114
throstle song thrush, mavis   115 *quill* pipe made of a reed or stalk (by
metonymy applied to the song)   118 *plain-song* i.e. with a song simple
and unvarying (as in the traditional chants of plain-song)   119 *Whose . . .
mark* (because in singing '*cuckoo*' the bird appears to be calling him
'cuckold')   127 *thy . . . force* the compelling attraction of thy manly charms
133 *gleek* make biting jests   139 *rate* rank   140 *still* always, continually;
doth tend upon waits upon, i.e. as one of my train   147 *Moth* i.e. probably
Mote, a speck (both words were usually spelled 'moth,' and both were
pronounced 'mote')   154 *humblebees* bumblebees   169-70 *If . . . you*
(cobweb was used to stanch blood)   172 *Squash* an unripe pea pod   173
Peascod a ripe pea pod

184   And when she weeps, weeps every little flower,
185   Lamenting some enforcèd chastity.
186   Tie up my lover's tongue, bring him silently.
          Exit [Titania with Bottom and Fairies].

            *

III, ii   *Enter [Oberon,] King of Fairies.*
    OBERON
        I wonder if Titania be awaked;
        Then, what it was that next came in her eye,
        Which she must dote on in extremity.
        [Enter Puck.]
        Here comes my messenger. How now, mad spirit?
5   What night-rule now about this haunted grove?
    PUCK
        My mistress with a monster is in love.
7   Near to her close and consecrated bower,
8   While she was in her dull and sleeping hour,
9   A crew of patches, rude mechanicals,
        That work for bread upon Athenian stalls,
        Were met together to rehearse a play,
        Intended for great Theseus' nuptial day.
13   The shallowest thickskin of that barren sort,
14   Who Pyramus presented in their sport,
15   Forsook his scene and entered in a brake.
        When I did him at this advantage take,
17   An ass's nole I fixèd on his head.
        Anon his Thisby must be answerèd,
19   And forth my mimic comes. When they him spy,
        As wild geese that the creeping fowler eye,
21   Or russet-pated choughs, many in sort,
        Rising and cawing at the gun's report,
        Sever themselves and madly sweep the sky;
        So at his sight away his fellows fly,
25   And at our stamp here o'er and o'er one falls;
        He murder cries and help from Athens calls.
        Their sense thus weak, lost with their fears thus strong,
        Made senseless things begin to do them wrong,
        For briers and thorns at their apparel snatch:
        Some, sleeves – some, hats; from yielders all things catch.
        I led them on in this distracted fear
32   And left sweet Pyramus translated there,
        When in that moment (so it came to pass)
        Titania waked, and straightway loved an ass.
    OBERON
        This falls out better than I could devise.

---

184 *she weeps* i.e. causes dew   185 *enforcèd* violated   186 *lover's* (many editors follow Pope's emendation, 'love's')
III, ii The wood   5 *night-rule* literally, order of conduct in the night – but perhaps with an overtone of 'misrule'   7 *close* private   8 *dull* drowsy   9 *patches* (1) 'tatterdemalions' (Dr Johnson), (2) clowns (cf. IV, i, 207); *rude mechanicals* unlettered craftsmen   13 *barren sort* stupid company   14 *presented* acted   15 *scene* stage   17 *nole* noddle, 'noodle'   19 *mimic* burlesque actor or mime   21 *russet-pated choughs* grey-headed jackdaws (russet was homespun cloth, reddish-brown or grey); *in sort* in a flock   25 *at our stamp* (Robin Goodfellow was known to stamp in a temper, and his stamp was frightening. Most editors follow Dr Johnson's conjecture, 'at a stump.')   32 *translated* transformed   36 *latched* moistened, dribbled on (from verb related to 'leak' and 'leach')   40 *That* so that; *of force* necessarily; *eyed* seen, looked at   53 *whole* intact, i.e. solid   55 *Her brother's* i.e. the sun's; *th' Antipodes* the people on the opposite side of the globe   57 *dead* deadly   61 *sphere* orbit (literally, the hollow sphere in which, according to Ptolemaic astronomy, a planet revolved about the earth)   70 *brave touch* noble stroke (ironical)   74 *misprised mood* mood based on a misunderstanding   78 *An if* if   84 *heaviness, heavier* (a quibble on 'heavy' in two senses of 'heavy-spirited' and 'drowsy')

        But hast thou yet latched the Athenian's eyes   36
        With the love-juice, as I did bid thee do?
    PUCK
        I took him sleeping (that is finished too)
        And the Athenian woman by his side,
        That, when he waked, of force she must be eyed.   40
        Enter Demetrius and Hermia.
    OBERON
        Stand close. This is the same Athenian.
    PUCK
        This is the woman, but not this the man.
    DEMETRIUS
        O, why rebuke you him that loves you so?
        Lay breath so bitter on your bitter foe.
    HERMIA
        Now I but chide; but I should use thee worse,
        For thou, I fear, hast given me cause to curse.
        If thou hast slain Lysander in his sleep,
        Being o'er shoes in blood, plunge in the deep,
        And kill me too.
        The sun was not so true unto the day
        As he to me. Would he have stolen away
        From sleeping Hermia? I'll believe as soon
        This whole earth may be bored, and that the moon   53
        May through the centre creep, and so displease
        Her brother's noontide with th' Antipodes.   55
        It cannot be but thou hast murd'red him.
        So should a murderer look – so dead, so grim.   57
    DEMETRIUS
        So should the murdered look, and so should I,
        Pierced through the heart with your stern cruelty.
        Yet you, the murderer, look as bright, as clear,
        As yonder Venus in her glimmering sphere.   61
    HERMIA
        What's this to my Lysander? Where is he?
        Ah, good Demetrius, wilt thou give him me?
    DEMETRIUS
        I had rather give his carcass to my hounds.
    HERMIA
        Out, dog! out, cur! Thou driv'st me past the bounds
        Of maiden's patience. Hast thou slain him then?
        Henceforth be never numb'red among men.
        O, once tell true: tell true, even for my sake.
        Durst thou have looked upon him, being awake?
        And hast thou killed him sleeping? O brave touch!   70
        Could not a worm, an adder, do so much?
        An adder did it; for with doubler tongue
        Than thine (thou serpent!) never adder stung.
    DEMETRIUS
        You spend your passion on a misprised mood.   74
        I am not guilty of Lysander's blood,
        Nor is he dead, for aught that I can tell.
    HERMIA
        I pray thee, tell me then that he is well.
    DEMETRIUS
        An if I could, what should I get therefore?   78
    HERMIA
        A privilege never to see me more;
        And from thy hated presence part I so.
        See me no more, whether he be dead or no.   *Exit.*
    DEMETRIUS
        There is no following her in this fierce vein.
        Here therefore for a while I will remain.
        So sorrow's heaviness doth heavier grow   84

85   For debt that bankrout sleep doth sorrow owe;
      Which now in some slight measure it will pay,
87   If for his tender here I make some stay.
         Lie down [and sleep].

OBERON
      What hast thou done? Thou hast mistaken quite
89   And laid the love-juice on some true-love's sight.
90   Of thy misprision must perforce ensue
      Some true-love turned, and not a false turned true.

PUCK
92   Then fate o'errules, that, one man holding troth,
93   A million fail, confounding oath on oath.

OBERON
      About the wood, go swifter than the wind,
      And Helena of Athens look thou find.
96   All fancy-sick she is, and pale of cheer
97   With sighs of love, that costs the fresh blood dear.
      By some illusion see thou bring her here.
99   I'll charm his eyes against she do appear.

PUCK
      I go, I go, look how I go,
      Swifter than arrow from the Tartar's bow.   *[Exit.]*

OBERON   Flower of this purple dye,
      Hit with Cupid's archery,
      Sink in apple of his eye!
      When his love he doth espy,
      Let her shine as gloriously
      As the Venus of the sky.
      When thou wak'st, if she be by,
      Beg of her for remedy.
      Enter Puck.

PUCK   Captain of our fairy band,
      Helena is here at hand,
      And the youth, mistook by me,
113   Pleading for a lover's fee.
114   Shall we their fond pageant see?
      Lord, what fools these mortals be!

OBERON   Stand aside. The noise they make
      Will cause Demetrius to awake.

PUCK   Then will two at once woo one:
119   That must needs be sport alone.
      And those things do best please me
      That befall prepost'rously.
      Enter Lysander and Helena.

LYSANDER
      Why should you think that I should woo in scorn?
      Scorn and derision never come in tears.
      Look, when I vow, I weep; and vows so born,
      In their nativity all truth appears.
      How can these things in me seem scorn to you,
127   Bearing the badge of faith to prove them true?

HELENA
128   You do advance your cunning more and more.
129   When truth kills truth, O devilish-holy fray!
      These vows are Hermia's. Will you give her o'er?
      Weigh oath with oath, and you will nothing weigh.
      Your vows to her and me, put in two scales,
      Will even weigh; and both as light as tales.

LYSANDER
      I had no judgment when to her I swore.

HELENA
      Nor none, in my mind, now you give her o'er.

LYSANDER
      Demetrius loves her; and he loves not you.

DEMETRIUS *[awakes]*
      O Helen, goddess, nymph, perfect, divine!
      To what, my love, shall I compare thine eyne?
      Crystal is muddy. O, how ripe in show
      Thy lips, those kissing cherries, tempting grow!
      That pure congealèd white, high Taurus' snow,   141
      Fanned with the eastern wind, turns to a crow   142
      When thou hold'st up thy hand. O, let me kiss
      This princess of pure white, this seal of bliss.   144

HELENA
      O spite! O hell! I see you all are bent
      To set against me for your merriment.
      If you were civil and knew courtesy,   147
      You would not do me thus much injury.   148
      Can you not hate me, as I know you do,
      But you must join in souls to mock me too?
      If you were men, as men you are in show,
      You would not use a gentle lady so;   152
      To vow, and swear, and superpraise my parts,   153
      When I am sure you hate me with your hearts.
      You both are rivals, and love Hermia;
      And now both rivals to mock Helena.
      A trim exploit, a manly enterprise,   157
      To conjure tears up in a poor maid's eyes
      With your derision! None of noble sort
      Would so offend a virgin and extort   160
      A poor soul's patience, all to make you sport.

LYSANDER
      You are unkind, Demetrius. Be not so!
      For you love Hermia: this you know I know.
      And here, with all good will, with all my heart,
      In Hermia's love I yield you up my part;
      And yours of Helena to me bequeath,
      Whom I do love, and will do till my death.

HELENA
      Never did mockers waste more idle breath.   168

DEMETRIUS
      Lysander, keep thy Hermia: I will none.
      If e'er I loved her, all that love is gone.
      My heart to her but as guestwise sojourned,
      And now to Helen is it home returned,
      There to remain.

LYSANDER   ·Helen, it is not so.

DEMETRIUS
      Disparage not the faith thou dost not know,
      Lest, to thy peril, thou aby it dear.   175
      Look where thy love comes. Yonder is thy dear.
      Enter Hermia.

85 *bankrout* bankrupt **87** *tender* offer; *make some stay* i.e. wait a while; s.d. *Lie . . . sleep* (imperative form of stage directions common in Elizabethan plays) **89** *true-love's* betrothed lover's **90** *misprision* mistake **92** *troth* faith **93** *confounding* destroying, breaking **96** *fancy-sick* love-sick; *cheer* face, look **97** *that . . . dear* (by drawing blood from the heart) **99** *against . . . appear* in preparation for her appearance **113** *lover's fee* right as a lover (proverbially three kisses) **114** *fond pageant* foolish spectacle **119** *alone* unique, unequalled **127** *badge of faith* (perhaps suggested by family crest worn on sleeves of servants) **128** *advance* put forward so that it can be seen **129** *truth kills truth* i.e. 'truth' to Helena implies falsehood to Hermia **141** *Taurus'* i.e. of the Taurus Mountains in Turkey **142** *Fanned with* (1) blown gently on by, (2) winnowed by **144** *This . . . white* i.e. her hand, 'of sovereign whiteness' (Wilson) **147** *civil* civilized **148** *injury* insult **152** *gentle* well-born **153** *parts* qualities **157** *trim* 'fine,' 'nice' (ironical; cf. *brave touch*, III, ii, 70) **160** *extort* wring, twist, torture **168** *idle* vain **175** *aby* pay for

HERMIA

177 Dark night, that from the eye his function takes,
The ear more quick of apprehension makes.
Wherein it doth impair the seeing sense,
It pays the hearing double recompense.
Thou art not by mine eye, Lysander, found;
Mine ear, I thank it, brought me to thy sound.
But why unkindly didst thou leave me so?

LYSANDER

Why should he stay whom love doth press to go?

HERMIA

What love could press Lysander from my side?

LYSANDER

Lysander's love, that would not let him bide —
Fair Helena; who more engilds the night
188 Than all yon fiery oes and eyes of light.
Why seek'st thou me? Could not this make thee know,
The hate I bare thee made me leave thee so?

HERMIA

You speak not as you think. It cannot be.

HELENA

Lo, she is one of this confederacy.
Now I perceive they have conjoined all three
194 To fashion this false sport in spite of me.
195 Injurious Hermia, most ungrateful maid,
196 Have you conspired, have you with these contrived
197 To bait me with this foul derision?
198 Is all the counsel that we two have shared,
The sister's vows, the hours that we have spent
When we have chid the hasty-footed time
For parting us — O, is all forgot?
All schooldays friendship, childhood innocence?
203 We, Hermia, like two artificial gods,
204 Have with our needles created both one flower,
Both on one sampler, sitting on one cushion,
Both warbling of one song, both in one key;
As if our hands, our sides, voices, and minds
208 Had been incorporate. So we grew together,
Like to a double cherry, seeming parted,
But yet an union in partition —
Two lovely berries moulded on one stem;
So, with two seeming bodies, but one heart;
213 Two of the first, like coats in heraldry,
Due but to one, and crownèd with one crest.
And will you rent our ancient love asunder,
To join with men in scorning your poor friend?
It is not friendly, 'tis not maidenly.

Our sex, as well as I, may chide you for it,
Though I alone do feel the injury.

HERMIA

I am amazèd at your passionate words.
I scorn you not. It seems that you scorn me.

HELENA

Have you not set Lysander, as in scorn,
To follow me and praise my eyes and face?
And made your other love, Demetrius
(Who even but now did spurn me with his foot),
To call me goddess, nymph, divine, and rare,
Precious, celestial? Wherefore speaks he this
To her he hates? And wherefore doth Lysander
Deny your love (so rich within his soul)
And tender me (forsooth) affection,   230
But by your setting on, by your consent?
What though I be not so in grace as you,   232
So hung upon with love, so fortunate;
But miserable most, to love unloved?
This you should pity rather than despise.

HERMIA

I understand not what you mean by this.

HELENA

Ay, do. Persever, counterfeit sad looks,   237
Make mouths upon me when I turn my back,
Wink each at other, hold the sweet jest up.
This sport, well carried, shall be chronicled.
If you have any pity, grace, or manners,
You would not make me such an argument.   242
But fare ye well. 'Tis partly my own fault,
Which death or absence soon shall remedy.

LYSANDER

Stay, gentle Helena; hear my excuse,
My love, my life, my soul, fair Helena!

HELENA

O excellent!

HERMIA   Sweet, do not scorn her so.

DEMETRIUS

If she cannot entreat, I can compel.

LYSANDER

Thou canst compel no more than she entreat.
Thy threats have no more strength than her weak
    prayers.
Helen, I love thee; by my life, I do!
I swear by that which I will lose for thee
To prove him false that says I love thee not.

DEMETRIUS

I say I love thee more than he can do.

LYSANDER

If thou say so, withdraw and prove it too.

DEMETRIUS

Quick, come!

HERMIA   Lysander, whereto tends all this?

LYSANDER

Away, you Ethiope!   257

DEMETRIUS   No, no, you'll
Seem to break loose, take on as you would follow,
But yet come not. You are a tame man, go!

LYSANDER

Hang off, thou cat, thou burr! Vile thing, let loose,
Or I will shake thee from me like a serpent.

HERMIA

Why are you grown so rude? What change is this,
Sweet love?

---

177 *his* its (the common neuter possessive in Shakespeare's day); *takes* takes away   188 *oes* round spangles (probably a pun in *oes and eyes*)   194 *in spite of me* to spite me   195 *Injurious* insulting   196 *contrived* plotted, conspired   197 *bait* torment (literally, to set on dogs to bite, as in bear-baiting)   198 *counsel* confidences   203 *artificial* i.e. skillful in artifice or creation   204 *needles* (pronounced 'neelds' or 'neeles'; often so spelled)   208 *incorporate* in one body   213 *the first* (heraldic term) the first color mentioned in a blazon or description of a shield, or the first quartering described   213–14 *Two . . . crest* (In the shield Helena has in mind, the coat-of-arms of the bearer evidently appears twice, and the shield is surmounted by his single crest; in the same way Hermia and Helena have two bodies, but one heart. Cf. the British royal standard, in which the three leopards of England appear both in the upper left and in the lower right quarters.)   230 *tender* offer   232 *grace* favor   237 *Persever* (accented 'persèver')   242 *argument* subject of jest   257 *No, no, you'll* (the present editor's emendation for 'No, no: heele' of quartos; folio reads 'No, no, Sir'; many editors follow Lettsom's emendation 'No, no, sir! You')

263 LYSANDER   Thy love? Out, tawny Tartar, out!
264   Out, loathèd med'cine! O hated potion, hence!
HERMIA
   Do you not jest?
265 HELENA   Yes, sooth! and so do you.
LYSANDER
   Demetrius, I will keep my word with thee.
DEMETRIUS
   I would I had your bond, for I perceive
   A weak bond holds you. I'll not trust your word.
LYSANDER
   What, should I hurt her, strike her, kill her dead?
   Although I hate her, I'll not harm her so.
HERMIA
   What, can you do me greater harm than hate?
   Hate me? Wherefore? O me, what news, my love?
   Am not I Hermia? Are not you Lysander?
   I am as fair now as I was erewhile.
   Since night you loved me; yet since night you left me.
   Why then, you left me (O, the gods forbid!)
   In earnest, shall I say?
LYSANDER   Ay, by my life!
   And never did desire to see thee more.
   Therefore be out of hope, of question, of doubt;
   Be certain. Nothing truer. 'Tis no jest
   That I do hate thee, and love Helena.
HERMIA
282   O me! you juggler, you canker blossom,
   You thief of love! What, have you come by night
   And stol'n my love's heart from him?
HELENA   Fine, i' faith.
   Have you no modesty, no maiden shame,
   No touch of bashfulness? What, will you tear
   Impatient answers from my gentle tongue?
288   Fie, fie, you counterfeit, you puppet you!
HERMIA
   Puppet? Why, so! Ay, that way goes the game.
   Now I perceive that she hath made compare
   Between our statures; she hath urged her height,
   And with her personage, her tall personage,
   Her height (forsooth), she hath prevailed with him.
   And are you grown so high in his esteem
295   Because I am so dwarfish and so low?
296   How low am I, thou painted maypole? Speak!
   How low am I? I am not yet so low
   But that my nails can reach unto thine eyes.
HELENA
   I pray you, though you mock me, gentlemen,
300   Let her not hurt me. I was never curst;
   I have no gift at all in shrewishness;
302   I am a right maid for my cowardice.
   Let her not strike me. You perhaps may think,
   Because she is something lower than myself,
305   That I can match her.
HERMIA   Lower? Hark again!
HELENA
   Good Hermia, do not be so bitter with me.
   I evermore did love you, Hermia,
   Did ever keep your counsels, never wronged you;
   Save that, in love unto Demetrius,
   I told him of your stealth unto this wood.
   He followed you; for love I followed him.
   But he hath chid me hence, and threat'ned me
   To strike me, spurn me, nay, to kill me too.

   And now, so you will let me quiet go,   314
   To Athens will I bear my folly back
   And follow you no further. Let me go.
   You see how simple and how fond I am.   317
HERMIA
   Why, get you gone. Who is't that hinders you?
HELENA
   A foolish heart, that I leave here behind.
HERMIA
   What, with Lysander?
HELENA   With Demetrius.
LYSANDER
   Be not afraid. She shall not harm thee, Helena.
DEMETRIUS
   No, sir, she shall not, though you take her part.
HELENA
   O, when she is angry, she is keen and shrewd.   323
   She was a vixen when she went to school;
   And though she be but little, she is fierce.
HERMIA
   'Little' again? nothing but 'low' and 'little'?
   Why will you suffer her to flout me thus?   327
   Let me come to her.
LYSANDER   Get you gone, you dwarf!
   You minimus, of hind'ring knotgrass made!   329
   You bead, you acorn!
DEMETRIUS   You are too officious
   In her behalf that scorns your services.
   Let her alone. Speak not of Helena;
   Take not her part. For if thou dost intend
   Never so little show of love to her,
   Thou shalt aby it.   335
LYSANDER   Now she holds me not.
   Now follow, if thou dar'st, to try whose right,   336
   Of thine or mine, is most in Helena.
DEMETRIUS
   Follow? Nay, I'll go with thee, cheek by jowl.
       [Exeunt Lysander and Demetrius.]
HERMIA
   You, mistress, all this coil is long of you.   339
   Nay, go not back.
HELENA   I will not trust you, I,
   Nor longer stay in your curst company.   341
   Your hands than mine are quicker for a fray;
   My legs are longer, though, to run away.
HERMIA
   I am amazed, and know not what to say.   344
       Exeunt [Helena and Hermia].
OBERON
   This is thy negligence. Still thou mistak'st,
   Or else committ'st thy knaveries willfully.

---

263 *tawny Tartar* (Hermia's brunette complexion exaggerated; cf. *Ethiope*, l. 257)   264 *med'cine, potion* (both often used synonymously with 'poison')   265 *sooth* truly, indeed   282 *canker blossom* wild rose or dog rose (?), or worm that cankers a blossom (?), or blossom cankered by a worm (?)   288 *puppet* (1) doll, mere counterfeit of a woman, (2) little person   295 *low* short   296 *painted maypole* i.e. tall, and with pink and white complexion (with a hint that her complexion isn't all her own?)   300 *curst* shrewish, quarrelsome   302 *right* downright, real   305 *match her* i.e. in a fight   314 *so* if only   317 *fond* foolish   323 *shrewd* shrewish   327 *flout* mock   329 *minimus* smallest thing; *knotgrass* a low-growing plant of the buckwheat family that hinders the plough and was thought to stunt the growth of children   335 *aby* pay for   336–37 *whose right . . . thine* whose right of the two   339 *coil* noisy disturbance, 'row'; *long of* because of   341 *curst* (cf. l. 300)   344 *amazed* bewildered, confused

PUCK

Believe me, king of shadows, I mistook.
Did not you tell me I should know the man
By the Athenian garments he had on?
And so far blameless proves my enterprise
352 That I have 'nointed an Athenian's eyes;
And so far am I glad it so did sort
As this their jangling I esteem a sport.

OBERON

Thou seest these lovers seek a place to fight.
Hie therefore, Robin, overcast the night.
356 The starry welkin cover thou anon
357 With drooping fog as black as Acheron,
And lead these testy rivals so astray
As one come not within another's way.
Like to Lysander sometime frame thy tongue,
361 Then stir Demetrius up with bitter wrong;
And sometime rail thou like Demetrius.
And from each other look thou lead them thus
Till o'er their brows death-counterfeiting sleep
365 With leaden legs and batty wings doth creep.
366 Then crush this herb into Lysander's eye,
367 Whose liquor hath this virtuous property,
368 To take from thence all error with his might
369 And make his eyeballs roll with wonted sight.
370 When they next wake, all this derision
371 Shall seem a dream and fruitless vision,
And back to Athens shall the lovers wend
373 With league whose date till death shall never end.
374 Whiles I in this affair do thee employ,
I'll to my queen and beg her Indian boy;
And then I will her charmèd eye release
From monster's view, and all things shall be peace.

PUCK

My fairy lord, this must be done with haste,
379 For night's swift dragons cut the clouds full fast,
380 And yonder shines Aurora's harbinger;
At whose approach ghosts, wand'ring here and there,
382 Troop home to churchyards; damnèd spirits all,
That in crossways and floods have burial,
Already to their wormy beds are gone.

For fear lest day should look their shames upon,
They willfully themselves exile from light,
And must for aye consort with black-browed night. 387

OBERON

But we are spirits of another sort.
I with the Morning's love have oft made sport, 389
And, like a forester, the groves may tread 390
Even till the eastern gate, all fiery red,
Opening on Neptune, with fair blessèd beams
Turns into yellow gold his salt green streams.
But notwithstanding, haste; make no delay.
We may effect this business yet ere day. [Exit.]

PUCK   Up and down, up and down,
I will lead them up and down.
I am feared in field and town.
Goblin, lead them up and down. 399
Here comes one.
Enter Lysander.

LYSANDER

Where art thou, proud Demetrius? Speak thou now.

PUCK

Here, villain, drawn and ready. Where art thou? 402

LYSANDER

I will be with thee straight.

PUCK   Follow me then
To plainer ground. [Exit Lysander.] 404
Enter Demetrius.

DEMETRIUS   Lysander, speak again!
Thou runaway, thou coward, art thou fled?
Speak! In some bush? Where dost thou hide thy head?

PUCK

Thou coward, art thou bragging to the stars,
Telling the bushes that thou look'st for wars,
And wilt not come? Come, recreant! come, thou child! 409
I'll whip thee with a rod. He is defiled 410
That draws a sword on thee.

DEMETRIUS   Yea, art thou there?

PUCK

Follow my voice. We'll try no manhood here. Exeunt. 412
[Enter Lysander.]

LYSANDER

He goes before me and still dares me on;
When I come where he calls, then he is gone.
The villain is much lighter-heeled than I.
I followed fast, but faster he did fly,
That fallen am I in dark uneven way, 417
And here will rest me.
[Lies down.]   Come, thou gentle day.
For if but once thou show me thy grey light,
I'll find Demetrius and revenge this spite.
[Sleeps.]
[Enter] Robin [Puck] and Demetrius.

PUCK

Ho, ho, ho! Coward, why com'st thou not? 421

DEMETRIUS

Abide me, if thou dar'st; for well I wot 422
Thou run'st before me, shifting every place,
And dar'st not stand nor look me in the face.
Where art thou now?

PUCK   Come hither. I am here.

DEMETRIUS

Nay then, thou mock'st me. Thou shalt buy this dear 426
If ever I thy face by daylight see.
Now go thy way. Faintness constraineth me

352 *sort* fall out, happen   356 *welkin* sky   357 *Acheron* hell (from the name of one of the rivers of Hades)   361 *wrong* insults   365 *batty* bat-like   366 *this herb* (not *love-in-idleness*, II, i, 166 ff., but another herb; cf. II, i, 184; IV, i, 72)   367 *liquor* juice; *virtuous* potent, efficacious   368 *his might* its power   369 *wonted* accustomed, usual   370 *derision* i.e. subject of derision or laughter   371 *fruitless* of no consequence in the world of reality   373 *date* term   374 *Whiles* whilst   379 *night's swift dragons* (probably suggested by Medea's team of dragons, which came down to her following her prayers to Hecate, in Ovid, *Metamorphoses*, VII, 218–21)   380 *Aurora's harbinger* i.e. the morning star   382–83 *damnèd spirits . . . burial* i.e. the ghosts of suicides, who have, according to custom, been buried at crossroads, or who have drowned themselves   387 *for aye* forever   389 *the Morning's love* Cephalus, beloved of Aurora, and a hunter (Ovid, *Metamorphoses*, VII, 700 ff.)   390 *forester* keeper of a royal forest   399 *Goblin* (Puck apparently addresses himself)   402 *drawn* i.e. with sword drawn   404 *plainer* more level and smooth   404, 412 s.d. *Exit Lysander, Enter Lysander* (added in all modern editions to clarify action. But Lysander may have stayed on stage and groped about to suggest the fog; cf. l. 357. The folio has a direction, 'shifting places,' though out of place at l. 416, suggesting a way of managing action with both Lysander and Demetrius on the stage part of the time.)   409 *recreant* coward (literally, one who breaks his faith)   410 *defiled* dishonored   417 *That* so that   421 *Ho, ho, ho* (meant as laughter; the traditional entrance cry of the devil in medieval religious drama)   422 *Abide me* wait for me; *wot* know   426 *buy this dear* pay dearly for this (probably a form of *aby*; cf. III, ii, 175)

To measure out my length on this cold bed.
By day's approach look to be visited.
    [Lies down and sleeps.]
    Enter Helena.

HELENA
O weary night, O long and tedious night,
    Abate thy hours. Shine comforts from the east,
That I may back to Athens by daylight
    From these that my poor company detest ;
And sleep, that sometimes shuts up sorrow's eye,
Steal me awhile from mine own company.
    Sleep.
PUCK   Yet but three ? Come one more.
    Two of both kinds makes up four.

439   Here she comes, curst and sad.
    Cupid is a knavish lad
    Thus to make poor females mad.
    [Enter Hermia.]

HERMIA
Never so weary, never so in woe,
    Bedabbled with the dew, and torn with briers,

444   I can no further crawl, no further go ;
    My legs can keep no pace with my desires.
Here will I rest me till the break of day.
Heavens shield Lysander, if they mean a fray !
    [Lies down and sleeps.]
PUCK   On the ground
        Sleep sound.
        I'll apply
        To your eye,
        Gentle lover, remedy.
    [Squeezes the herb on Lysander's eyelids.]
        When thou wak'st,
        Thou tak'st
        True delight
        In the sight
        Of thy former lady's eye ;
        And the country proverb known,
        That every man should take his own,
        In your waking shall be shown :
461   Jack shall have Jill,
        Naught shall go ill,
463 The man shall have his mare again, and all shall be well.
                   [Exit.]

IV, i   *Enter [Titania,] Queen of Fairies, and [Bottom the]*
       Clown and Fairies [Peaseblossom, Cobweb, Moth,
       Mustardseed, and others] ; and the King [Oberon]
       behind them.

TITANIA
Come, sit thee down upon this flow'ry bed,
2   While I thy amiable cheeks do coy,
3 And stick musk-roses in thy sleek smooth head,
    And kiss thy fair large ears, my gentle joy.
BOTTOM Where's Peaseblossom ?
PEASEBLOSSOM Ready.
BOTTOM Scratch my head, Peaseblossom. Where's Monsieur Cobweb ?
COBWEB Ready.
BOTTOM Monsieur Cobweb, good monsieur, get you your weapons in your hand, and kill me a red-hipped humblebee on the top of a thistle ; and, good monsieur, bring me the honey-bag. Do not fret yourself too much in the action, monsieur ; and, good monsieur, have a care the honey-bag break not. I would be loath to have

you overflowen with a honey-bag, signior. Where's Monsieur Mustardseed ?
MUSTARDSEED Ready.
BOTTOM Give me your neaf, Monsieur Mustardseed. 19
    Pray you, leave your curtsy, good monsieur.   20
MUSTARDSEED What's your will ?
BOTTOM Nothing, good monsieur, but to help Cavalery 22
Cobweb to scratch. I must to the barber's, monsieur ; 23
for methinks I am marvellous hairy about the face, and
I am such a tender ass, if my hair do but tickle me, I
must scratch.
TITANIA
What, wilt thou hear some music, my sweet love ?
BOTTOM I have a reasonable good ear in music. Let's
have the tongs and the bones.   29
TITANIA
Or say, sweet love, what thou desirest to eat.
BOTTOM Truly, a peck of provender. I could munch your
good dry oats. Methinks I have a great desire to a bottle 32
of hay. Good hay, sweet hay, hath no fellow.
TITANIA
I have a venturous fairy that shall seek
The squirrel's hoard, and fetch thee new nuts.   35
BOTTOM I had rather have a handful or two of dried
pease. But I pray you, let none of your people stir me. I
have an exposition of sleep come upon me.   38
TITANIA
Sleep thou, and I will wind thee in my arms.
Fairies, be gone, and be all ways away. *[Exeunt Fairies.]*
So doth the woodbine the sweet honeysuckle   41
Gently entwist ; the female ivy so
Enrings the barky fingers of the elm.
O, how I love thee ! how I dote on thee !
    [They sleep.]
    Enter Robin Goodfellow [Puck].
OBERON *[advances]*
Welcome, good Robin. Seest thou this sweet sight ?
Her dotage now I do begin to pity ;
For, meeting her of late behind the wood,
Seeking sweet favors for this hateful fool,   48
I did upbraid her and fall out with her.
For she his hairy temples then had rounded
With coronet of fresh and fragrant flowers ;
And that same dew which sometime on the buds   52

439 *curst* cross 444 *go* walk 461 *Jack, Jill* (common generic names for 'man' and 'woman') 463 *The man . . . well* (another proverb) s.d. (The folio adds the direction, 'They sleepe all the Act,' i.e. either through the act-interval or through l. 137 of the next act, as divided in the folio. The first quarto indicates that the action was originally continuous, with the lovers lying asleep on the stage.)
IV, i 2 *amiable* lovable, lovely ; *coy* caress 3 *musk-roses* (cf. II, i, 252) 19 *neaf* fist 20 *leave your curtsy* i.e. put on your hat (a curtsy was any customary gesture of respect) 22 *Cavalery* Cavalier (title of address for a gallant ; Bottom's form suggests the Italian '*cavaliere*') 23 *Cobweb* (most editors read *Peaseblossom*, because Cobweb has been sent on an errand ; but the alliteration shows that the slip is probably Shakespeare's) 29 *tongs and the bones* music made by tongs struck with a key, and by clappers of bone held between the fingers (folio adds direction : 'Musicke Tongs, Rurall Musicke') 32 *bottle* small bundle 35 *thee new nuts* (Hanmer read 'thee thence new nuts' to improve the metre, and most editors follow) 38 *exposition* (Bottom means 'disposition', i.e. inclination) 41 *woodbine* (applied to various climbing vines ; here probably a bindweed or convolvulus) 41–42 *So . . . entwist* i.e. in this way the morning-glory gently twists round the sweet honeysuckle 48 *favors* love tokens (here probably flowers) 52 *sometime* formerly

53 Was wont to swell like round and orient pearls,
54 Stood now within the pretty flouriets' eyes
Like tears that did their own disgrace bewail.
When I had at my pleasure taunted her,
And she in mild terms begged my patience,
I then did ask of her her changeling child ;
Which straight she gave me, and her fairy sent
To bear him to my bower in fairyland.
And now I have the boy, I will undo
This hateful imperfection of her eyes.
And, gentle Puck, take this transformèd scalp
From off the head of this Athenian swain ;
65 That, he awaking when the other do,
66 May all to Athens back again repair,
And think no more of this night's accidents
But as the fierce vexation of a dream.
But first I will release the Fairy Queen.
     Be as thou wast wont to be ;
     See as thou wast wont to see.
72   Dian's bud o'er Cupid's flower
     Hath such force and blessèd power.
Now, my Titania, wake you, my sweet queen.

TITANIA
My Oberon, what visions have I seen !
Methought I was enamored of an ass.

OBERON
There lies your love.

TITANIA   How came these things to pass ?
O, how mine eyes do loathe his visage now !

OBERON
Silence awhile. Robin, take off this head.
Titania, music call, and strike more dead
Than common sleep of all these five the sense.

TITANIA
Music, ho, music ! such as charmeth sleep.

PUCK
Now, when thou wak'st, with thine own fool's eyes peep.

OBERON
Sound, music !
     [Music.]
         Come, my queen, take hands with me.
And rock the ground whereon these sleepers be.
     [Dance.]

Now thou and I are new in amity,
And will to-morrow midnight solemnly 87
Dance in Duke Theseus' house triumphantly 88
And bless it to all fair prosperity.
There shall the pairs of faithful lovers be
Wedded, with Theseus, all in jollity.

PUCK   Fairy King, attend and mark :
     I do hear the morning lark.

OBERON   Then, my queen, in silence sad 94
     Trip we after night's shade.
     We the globe can compass soon,
     Swifter than the wand'ring moon.

TITANIA   Come, my lord, and in our flight
     Tell me how it came this night
     That I sleeping here was found
     With these mortals on the ground.   *Exeunt.*
Wind horn. Enter Theseus and all his Train [with Hippolyta and Egeus].

THESEUS
Go, one of you, find out the forester, 102
For now our observation is performed ; 103
And since we have the vaward of the day, 104
My love shall hear the music of my hounds.
Uncouple in the western valley ; let them go.
Dispatch, I say, and find the forester.
     [Exit an Attendant.]
We will, fair Queen, up to the mountain's top
And mark the musical confusion
Of hounds and echo in conjunction.

HIPPOLYTA
I was with Hercules and Cadmus once 111
When in a wood of Crete they bayed the bear 112
With hounds of Sparta. Never did I hear 113
Such gallant chiding ; for, besides the groves,
The skies, the fountains, every region near
Seemed all one mutual cry. I never heard
So musical a discord, such sweet thunder.

THESEUS
My hounds are bred out of the Spartan kind :
So flewed, so sanded, and their heads are hung 119
With ears that sweep away the morning dew ; ·
Crook-kneed, and dewlapped like Thessalian bulls ; 121
Slow in pursuit, but matched in mouth like bells, 122
Each under each. A cry more tuneable 123
Was never holloed to nor cheered with horn
In Crete, in Sparta, nor in Thessaly.
Judge when you hear. But soft ! What nymphs are these ? 126

EGEUS
My lord, this is my daughter here asleep ;
And this, Lysander ; this Demetrius is ;
This Helena, old Nedar's Helena.
I wonder of their being here together.

THESEUS
No doubt they rose up early to observe
The rite of May ; and, hearing our intent,
Came here in grace of our solemnity. 133
But speak, Egeus. Is not this the day
That Hermia should give answer of her choice ?

EGEUS
It is, my lord.

THESEUS
Go, bid the huntsmen wake them with their horns.
     [Exit an Attendant.]
Shout within. Wind horns. They all start up.

---

53 *Was wont to* used to ; *orient pearls* especially lustrous and precious pearls (from the fact that the best pearls came from the East) **54** *flouriets'* flowerets' **65** *other* others (common plural) **66** *May* they may **72** *Dian's bud* (the herb of II, i, 184 and III, ii, 366 – perhaps the '*agnus castus*,' said, in old herbals, to preserve chastity) ; *Cupid's flower* (the herb of II, i, 166 – the pansy) **87** *solemnly* with ceremony (cf. *solemnities*, I, i, 11) **88** *triumphantly* with festal ceremony (cf. I, i, 19) **94** *sad* sober **102** *forester* manager of the game and the cover in the royal forest (cf. III, ii, 390) **103** *observation* observance, i.e. of the rite of May (I, i, 167 ; IV, i, 132) **104** *vaward . . . day* forepart (literally, vanguard) of the day, morning **111-13** *I was . . . Sparta* (no corresponding episode in legend about Hippolyta, but in some accounts Theseus was a companion of Hercules in his Amazonian exploits, and hunted the Calydonian boar with other heroes) **112** *bayed* brought to bay **113** *hounds of Sparta* (a famous breed in antiquity) **119** *So* i.e. like the Spartan kind ; *flewed* with hanging chaps, or dewlaps ; *sanded* of sandy color **121** *Thessalian* (unexplained : Theseus killed the Marathonian bull, and did perform exploits in Thessaly) **122-23** *matched . . . each* i.e. with each voice of a different but harmonious pitch, like a chime of bells (a melodious pack was supposed to have in it 'bass,' 'countertenor,' and 'mean' voices) **123** *cry* noise of the pack, hence the pack itself ; *tuneable* in tune, musical **126** *soft* wait **133** *our solemnity* i.e. our observance of May Day

138   Good morrow, friends. Saint Valentine is past.
Begin these woodbirds but to couple now?

LYSANDER
Pardon my lord.
    [They kneel.]

THESEUS   I pray you all, stand up.
I know you two are rival enemies.
How comes this gentle concord in the world
143   That hatred is so far from jealousy
To sleep by hate and fear no enmity?

LYSANDER
145   My lord, I shall reply amazedly,
Half sleep, half waking; but as yet, I swear,
I cannot truly say how I came here.
But, as I think (for truly would I speak),
And now I do bethink me, so it is –
I came with Hermia hither. Our intent
151   Was to be gone from Athens, where we might,
152   Without the peril of the Athenian law –

EGEUS
Enough, enough, my lord! you have enough.
I beg the law, the law, upon his head.
They would have stol'n away; they would, Demetrius,
156   Thereby to have defeated you and me –
You of your wife, and me of my consent,
Of my consent that she should be your wife.

DEMETRIUS
My lord, fair Helen told me of their stealth,
Of this their purpose hither, to this wood,
And I in fury hither followed them,
162   Fair Helena in fancy following me.
But, my good lord, I wot not by what power
(But by some power it is) my love to Hermia,
Melted as the snow, seems to me now
166   As the remembrance of an idle gaud
Which in my childhood I did dote upon;
168   And all the faith, the virtue of my heart,
The object and the pleasure of mine eye,
Is only Helena. To her, my lord,
Was I betrothed ere I saw Hermia,
172   But, like a sickness, did I loathe this food;
But, as in health, come to my natural taste,
Now I do wish it, love it, long for it,
And will for evermore be true to it.

THESEUS
Fair lovers, you are fortunately met.
Of this discourse we more will hear anon.
Egeus, I will overbear your will,
179   For in the temple, by and by, with us,
These couples shall eternally be knit;
181   And, for the morning now is something worn,
Our purposed hunting shall be set aside.
Away, with us to Athens! Three and three,
We'll hold a feast in great solemnity.
Come, Hippolyta.
    [Exeunt Theseus, Hippolyta, Egeus, and Lords.]

DEMETRIUS
These things seem small and undistinguishable,
Like far-off mountains turnèd into clouds.

HERMIA
188   Methinks I see these things with parted eye,
When everything seems double.

HELENA   So methinks;
190   And I have found Demetrius like a jewel,

Mine own, and not mine own.

DEMETRIUS   Are you sure
That we are awake? It seems to me
That yet we sleep, we dream. Do not you think
The Duke was here, and bid us follow him?

HERMIA
Yea, and my father.

HELENA   And Hippolyta.

LYSANDER
And he did bid us follow to the temple.

DEMETRIUS
Why then, we are awake. Let's follow him,
And by the way let us recount our dreams.   *[Exeunt.]*

BOTTOM *[wakes]* When my cue comes, call me, and I will answer. My next is 'Most fair Pyramus.' Hey-ho. Peter Quince? Flute the bellows-mender? Snout the tinker? Starveling? God's my life! Stol'n hence, and left me 202 asleep? I have had a most rare vision. I have had a dream, past the wit of man to say what dream it was. Man is but an ass if he go about to expound this dream. Methought I was – there is no man can tell what. Methought I was, and methought I had – But man is but a patched fool if 207 he will offer to say what methought I had. The eye of man hath not heard, the ear of man hath not seen, man's hand is not able to taste, his tongue to conceive, nor his heart to report what my dream was. I will get Peter Quince to write a ballet of this dream. It shall be called 212 'Bottom's Dream,' because it hath no bottom; and I will sing it in the latter end of our play, before the Duke. Peradventure, to make it the more gracious, I shall sing it at her death.   *[Exit.]* 216

*

Enter Quince, Flute[, Snout, and Starveling].   IV, ii

QUINCE Have you sent to Bottom's house? Is he come home yet?

STARVELING He cannot be heard of. Out of doubt he is transported.   4

FLUTE If he come not, then the play is marred; it goes not forward, doth it?

QUINCE It is not possible. You have not a man in all Athens able to discharge Pyramus but he.

FLUTE No, he hath simply the best wit of any handicraft 9 man in Athens.

QUINCE Yea, and the best person too, and he is a very paramour for a sweet voice.

FLUTE You must say 'paragon.' A paramour is (God bless us!) a thing of naught.   14

Enter Snug the Joiner.

SNUG Masters, the Duke is coming from the temple, and

138–39 *Saint Valentine . . . now* (according to an old saying, birds begin to mate on Saint Valentine's Day)   143 *jealousy* suspicion   145 *amazedly* confusedly   151 *where* wherever   152 *Without* beyond   156 *defeated* (1) cheated, (2) deprived   162 *in fancy* in love   166 *idle gaud* worthless trinket   168 *virtue* power   172 *like a sickness* i.e. as in sickness   179 *by and by* shortly   181 *for* because   188 *with parted eye* i.e. with the two eyes not in focus   190–91 *And I . . . own* i.e. like a jewel found by accident, and therefore not certainly mine   202 *God's my life* (a common oath, perhaps contracted from 'God save my life')   207 *a patched fool* i.e. a fool in a motley or particolored suit   212 *ballet* ballad   216 *her death* (probably Thisby's)
IV, ii The house of Quince (?)   4 *transported* (1) carried away by spirits, (2) 'translated' (cf. III, i, 107)   9 *wit* intellect, 'brain'   14 *a thing of naught* (1) a wicked thing, (2) a thing of nothing, nought

there is two or three lords and ladies more married. If
our sport had gone forward, we had all been made
men.

18 FLUTE O sweet bully Bottom! Thus hath he lost sixpence
a day during his life. He could not have scaped sixpence
20 a day. An the Duke had not given him sixpence a day
for playing Pyramus, I'll be hanged! He would have
deserved it. Sixpence a day in Pyramus, or nothing!
Enter Bottom.

23 BOTTOM Where are these lads? Where are these hearts?

24 QUINCE Bottom! O most courageous day! O most happy
hour!

26 BOTTOM Masters, I am to discourse wonders; but ask me
not what. For if I tell you, I am not true Athenian. I
will tell you everything, right as it fell out.

QUINCE Let us hear, sweet Bottom.

30 BOTTOM Not a word of me. All that I will tell you is, that
the Duke hath dined. Get your apparel together, good
32 strings to your beards, new ribbands to your pumps;
33 meet presently at the palace; every man look o'er his
34 part; for the short and the long is, our play is preferred.
In any case, let Thisby have clean linen; and let not him
that plays the lion pare his nails, for they shall hang out
for the lion's claws. And, most dear actors, eat no onions
nor garlic, for we are to utter sweet breath; and I do not
doubt but to hear them say it is a sweet comedy. No
more words. Away, go, away!   *[Exeunt.]*

*

V, i   *Enter Theseus, Hippolyta, and Philostrate [with
Lords and Attendants].*

HIPPOLYTA

1   'Tis strange, my Theseus, that these lovers speak of.

THESEUS

  More strange than true. I never may believe
3   These antic fables nor these fairy toys.
  Lovers and madmen have such seething brains,
5   Such shaping fantasies, that apprehend

More than cool reason ever comprehends.
The lunatic, the lover, and the poet
Are of imagination all compact.   8
One sees more devils than vast hell can hold:
That is the madman. The lover, all as frantic,
Sees Helen's beauty in a brow of Egypt.   11
The poet's eye, in a fine frenzy rolling,
Doth glance from heaven to earth, from earth to heaven;
And as imagination bodies forth
The forms of things unknown, the poet's pen
Turns them to shapes, and gives to airy nothing
A local habitation and a name.
Such tricks hath strong imagination
That, if it would but apprehend some joy,
It comprehends some bringer of that joy;   20
Or in the night, imagining some fear,
How easy is a bush supposed a bear!

HIPPOLYTA

But all the story of the night told over,
And all their minds transfigured so together,   24
More witnesseth than fancy's images
And grows to something of great constancy;   26
But howsoever, strange and admirable.   27
    *Enter Lovers: Lysander, Demetrius, Hermia, and
    Helena.*

THESEUS

Here come the lovers, full of joy and mirth.
Joy, gentle friends, joy and fresh days of love
Accompany your hearts!

LYSANDER   More than to us
Wait in your royal walks, your board, your bed!

THESEUS

Come now, what masques, what dances shall we have,   32
To wear away this long age of three hours
Between our after-supper and bedtime?   34
Where is our usual manager of mirth?   35
What revels are in hand? Is there no play
To ease the anguish of a torturing hour?
Call Philostrate.   38

PHILOSTRATE   Here, mighty Theseus.

THESEUS

Say, what abridgment have you for this evening?   39
What masque? what music? How shall we beguile
The lazy time, if not with some delight?

PHILOSTRATE

There is a brief how many sports are ripe.   42
Make choice of which your Highness will see first.
    [Gives a paper.]

THESEUS

'The battle with the Centaurs, to be sung   44
By an Athenian eunuch to the harp.'
We'll none of that. That have I told my love
In glory of my kinsman Hercules.
'The riot of the tipsy Bacchanals,   48
Tearing the Thracian singer in their rage.'
That is an old device, and it was played   50
When I from Thebes came last a conqueror.
'The thrice three Muses mourning for the death   52
Of Learning, late deceased in beggary.'
That is some satire keen and critical,
Not sorting with a nuptial ceremony.   55
'A tedious brief scene of young Pyramus
And his love Thisby; very tragical mirth.'
Merry and tragical? tedious and brief?

18 *bully* (cf. III, i, 7)   18–19 *sixpence a day* i.e. a pension from the Duke of
this much   20 *An* if   23 *hearts* good fellows   24 *courageous* brave, fine (?),
or encouraging, auspicious (?); *happy* lucky, fortunate   26 *am to* have to
30 *word of* word out of   32 *ribbands* (common spelling of 'ribbons')   33
presently right away   34 *preferred* put forward, recommended
V, i The palace of the Duke   1 *that* that which, what   3 *antic* (1) grotesque, bizarre, (2) ancient, 'antique'; *fairy toys* i.e. silly tales about
fairies ('toys' are 'trifles')   5 *fantasies* imaginations   8 *compact* composed   11 *brow of Egypt* face of a gypsy, hence dark   20 *comprehends
. . . joy* i.e. includes as well the imaginary cause of the joy   24 *transfigured
so together* so changed at the same time   26 *constancy* certainty (because
the evidence is uniform or consistent and holds firm)   27 *howsoever* in
any case; *admirable* wonderful   32 *masques* courtly shows featuring a
dance of masked figures   34 *after-supper* last course, dessert (?), or light
evening repast (?)   35 *mirth* entertainment   38 *Philostrate* (who acts as
Master of the Revels; his part in this act is assigned in the folio to Egeus)
39 *abridgment* pastime, i.e. something to abridge or shorten the time
42 *brief* list, memorandum   44 *The battle . . . Centaurs* probably the
famous battle following the attempt of the Centaurs to carry off the bride
of Perithous, Theseus' friend (Shakespeare followed the medieval and
Renaissance versions of the legend in making Hercules present at the
battle)   48–49 *The riot . . . rage* the tearing apart of Orpheus by the Bac-
chantes (Ovid, XI, 1 ff.)   50 *device* show   52–53 *The thrice . . . beggary*
(perhaps suggested by the title of Spenser's poem, *The Teares of the Muses*,
1591; complaints of the neglect of learning and poetry were fashionable)
55 *sorting with* befitting

59 That is hot ice and wondrous strange snow.
How shall we find the concord of this discord?

PHILOSTRATE
A play there is, my lord, some ten words long,
Which is as brief as I have known a play;
But by ten words, my lord, it is too long,
Which makes it tedious. For in all the play
There is not one word apt, one player fitted.
And tragical, my noble lord, it is,
For Pyramus therein doth kill himself.
Which when I saw rehearsed, I must confess,
Made mine eyes water; but more merry tears
70 The passion of loud laughter never shed.

THESEUS
What are they that do play it?

PHILOSTRATE
Hard-handed men that work in Athens here,
Which never labored in their minds till now;
74 And now have toiled their unbreathed memories
75 With this same play, against your nuptial.

THESEUS
And we will hear it.

PHILOSTRATE   No, my noble lord,
It is not for you. I have heard it over,
And it is nothing, nothing in the world;
79 Unless you can find sport in their intents,
Extremely stretched and conned with cruel pain,
To do you service.

THESEUS   I will hear that play,
For never anything can be amiss
When simpleness and duty tender it.
Go bring them in; and take your places, ladies.
                     [Exit Philostrate.]

HIPPOLYTA
85 I love not to see wretchedness o'ercharged,
And duty in his service perishing.

THESEUS
Why, gentle sweet, you shall see no such thing.

HIPPOLYTA
88 He says they can do nothing in this kind.

THESEUS
The kinder we, to give them thanks for nothing.
Our sport shall be to take what they mistake;
91 And what poor duty cannot do, noble respect
92 Takes it in might, not merit.
93 Where I have come, great clerks have purposèd
To greet me with premeditated welcomes;
Where I have seen them shiver and look pale,
Make periods in the midst of sentences,
97 Throttle their practised accent in their fears,
And, in conclusion, dumbly have broke off,
Not paying me a welcome. Trust me, sweet,
Out of this silence yet I picked a welcome,
And in the modesty of fearful duty
I read as much as from the rattling tongue
Of saucy and audacious eloquence.
104 Love, therefore, and tongue-tied simplicity
105 In least speak most, to my capacity.
                     [Enter Philostrate.]

PHILOSTRATE
106 So please your Grace the Prologue is addressed.

THESEUS
107 Let him approach.
             [Flourish trumpets.] Enter the Prologue [Quince].

PROLOGUE
If we offend, it is with our good will.   108
     That you should think, we come not to offend,
But with good will. To show our simple skill,
     That is the true beginning of our end.
Consider then, we come but in despite.
     We do not come, as minding to content you,
Our true intent is. All for your delight,
     We are not here. That you should here repent you,
The actors are at hand: and, by their show,
You shall know all, that you are like to know.

THESEUS This fellow doth not stand upon points.   118

LYSANDER He hath rid his prologue like a rough colt; he 119
knows not the stop. A good moral, my lord: it is not 120
enough to speak, but to speak true.

HIPPOLYTA Indeed he hath played on this prologue like a
child on a recorder – a sound, but not in government.   123

THESEUS His speech was like a tangled chain; nothing
impaired, but all disordered. Who is next?
     Enter Pyramus and Thisby, and Wall and Moonshine
     and Lion.

PROLOGUE
Gentles, perchance you wonder at this show;
     But wonder on, till truth make all things plain.
This man is Pyramus, if you would know;
     This beauteous lady Thisby is certain.
This man, with lime and roughcast, doth present
     Wall, that vile Wall which did these lovers sunder;
And through Wall's chink, poor souls, they are content
     To whisper. At the which let no man wonder.
This man, with lantern, dog, and bush of thorn,   134
     Presenteth Moonshine. For, if you will know,
By moonshine did these lovers think no scorn
     To meet at Ninus' tomb, there, there to woo.
This grisly beast (which Lion hight by name)   138
The trusty Thisby, coming first by night,
Did scare away, or rather did affright;
And as she fled, her mantle she did fall,   141
     Which Lion vile with bloody mouth did stain.
Anon comes Pyramus, sweet youth and tall,   143
     And finds his trusty Thisby's mantle slain;
Whereat, with blade, with bloody blameful blade,
     He bravely broached his boiling bloody breast.
And Thisby, tarrying in mulberry shade,
     His dagger drew, and died. For all the rest,

---

59 *strange* (probably an error, since an oxymoron like *hot ice* is wanted; suggested emendations: scorching, scalding, seething, flaming, fiery, sable, sooty, swarthy) 70 *passion . . . laughter* (usually explained as 'passionate outburst,' but probably ironic, i.e. the 'grief' of loud laughter, in keeping with *tragical mirth*) 74 *unbreathed* unexercised 75 *against* in preparation for 79 *intents* (two different senses are required by the two participles in l. 80: both 'endeavors,' which are *stretched* or strained, and 'object of the endeavors,' i.e. the play, which has to be *conned* or learned) 85 *o'ercharged* overburdened 88 *this kind* this type of thing 91 *noble respect* generous consideration 92 *Takes . . . merit* i.e. takes the will for the deed 93 *clerks* scholars 97 *practised accent* rehearsed utterance or speech 104 *simplicity* artlessness, sincerity 105 *In least* i.e. in speaking least; *to my capacity* according to my understanding 106 *addressed* ready 107 s.d. (folio adds direction 'Flor. Trum.' and notes that Quince speaks the prologue) 108–17 (the mispunctuation in the prologue was a common form of humorous trick) 118 *stand upon points* (1) pay attention to marks of punctuation, (2) bother about niceties 119 *rough unbroken* 120 *stop* (1) sudden check in a horse's career, (2) punctuation mark 123 *recorder* wind instrument similar to a flute; *in government* controlled with skill 134–35 *This man . . . Moonshine* (cf. III, i, 51–52) 138 *hight* is named (archaic in Shakespeare's day) 141 *fall* let fall 143 *tall* valiant

       Let Lion, Moonshine, Wall, and lovers twain

150   At large discourse while here they do remain.

151 THESEUS I wonder if the lion be to speak.

DEMETRIUS No wonder, my lord. One lion may, when
    many asses do.

                 Exit [Prologue, with Pyramus,] Lion,
                        Thisby, and Moonshine.

WALL

154   In this same interlude it doth befall

       That I, one Snout by name, present a wall;

       And such a wall, as I would have you think,

       That had in it a crannied hole or chink,

       Through which the lovers, Pyramus and Thisby,

       Did whisper often, very secretly.

       This loam, this roughcast, and this stone doth show

       That I am that same wall: the truth is so.

162   And this the cranny is, right and sinister,

       Through which the fearful lovers are to whisper.

THESEUS Would you desire lime and hair to speak better?

165 DEMETRIUS It is the wittiest partition that ever I heard
    discourse, my lord.

       [Enter Pyramus.]

THESEUS Pyramus draws near the wall. Silence!

PYRAMUS

       O grim-looked night, O night with hue so black,

       O night, which ever art when day is not!

       O night, O night, alack, alack, alack,

       I fear my Thisby's promise is forgot.

       And thou, O wall, O sweet, O lovely wall,

       That stand'st between her father's ground and mine,

       Thou wall, O wall, O sweet and lovely wall,

       Show me thy chink, to blink through with mine eyne.

       [Wall holds up his fingers.]

       Thanks, courteous wall. Jove shield thee well for this.

       But what see I? No Thisby do I see.

       O wicked wall, through whom I see no bliss,

       Cursed be thy stones for thus deceiving me!

180 THESEUS The wall, methinks, being sensible, should
    curse again.

PYRAMUS No, in truth, sir, he should not. 'Deceiving me'
    is Thisby's cue. She is to enter now, and I am to spy her
    through the wall. You shall see it will fall pat as I told
    you. Yonder she comes.

       Enter Thisby.

THISBY

       O Wall, full often hast thou heard my moans

       For parting my fair Pyramus and me.

       My cherry lips have often kissed thy stones,

       Thy stones with lime and hair knit up in thee.

PYRAMUS

       I see a voice. Now will I to the chink,

       To spy an I can hear my Thisby's face.   191

       Thisby!

THISBY My love! thou art my love, I think.

PYRAMUS

       Think what thou wilt, I am thy lover's grace;   193

       And, like Limander, am I trusty still.   194

THISBY

       And I, like Helen, till the Fates me kill.

PYRAMUS

       Not Shafalus to Procrus was so true.   196

THISBY

       As Shafalus to Procrus, I to you.

PYRAMUS

       O, kiss me through the hole of this vile wall!

THISBY

       I kiss the wall's hole, not your lips at all.

PYRAMUS

       Wilt thou at Ninny's tomb meet me straightway?

THISBY

       Tide life, tide death, I come without delay.   201

                   [Exeunt Pyramus and Thisby.]

WALL

       Thus have I, Wall, my part dischargèd so;

       And, being done, thus Wall away doth go.   *[Exit.]*

THESEUS Now is the mural down between the two 204
neighbors.

DEMETRIUS No remedy, my lord, when walls are so
willful to hear without warning.   207

HIPPOLYTA This is the silliest stuff that ever I heard.

THESEUS The best in this kind are but shadows; and the 209
worst are no worse, if imagination amend them.

HIPPOLYTA It must be your imagination then, and not
theirs.

THESEUS If we imagine no worse of them than they of
themselves, they may pass for excellent men. Here
come two noble beasts in, a man and a lion.

       Enter Lion and Moonshine.

LION

       You, ladies, you, whose gentle hearts do fear   216

       The smallest monstrous mouse that creeps on floor,

       May now perchance both quake and tremble here,

       When lion rough in wildest rage doth roar.

       Then know that I as Snug the joiner am   220

       A lion fell, nor else no lion's dam;   221

       For if I should as lion come in strife

       Into this place, 'twere pity on my life.   223

THESEUS A very gentle beast, and of a good conscience. 224

DEMETRIUS The very best at a beast, my lord, that e'er I 225
saw.

LYSANDER This lion is a very fox for his valor.   227

THESEUS True; and a goose for his discretion.

DEMETRIUS Not so, my lord; for his valor cannot carry
his discretion, and the fox carries the goose.

THESEUS His discretion, I am sure, cannot carry his
valor; for the goose carries not the fox. It is well. Leave
it to his discretion, and let us listen to the moon.

---

150 *At large* at length   151 *be to* is going to   154 *interlude* (cf. I, ii, 5)
162 *right and sinister* i.e. running right and left, horizontal 165 *wittiest*
cleverest, most intelligent; *partition* (1) wall, (2) section of an oration
180 *sensible* capable of sensation and perception 191 *an* if 193 *thy
lover's grace* i.e. thy gracious lover 194-95 *Limander . . . Helen* (the
'author' of the interlude probably confused two pairs of famous lovers –
Leander and Hero, Alexander [Paris] and Helen) 196 *Shafalus . . .
Procrus* Cephalus and Procris, another pair of tragic lovers 201 *Tide . . .
death* come (betide) life, come death 204 *mural down* wall down (Pope's
famous conjecture; quartos read 'Moon vsed', folio 'morall downe'; other
emendations: 'mure all down,' 'wall down,' 'moon to see') 207 *to hear*
as to hear; *without warning* so unexpectedly (?), or without warning the
parents (?) 209 *in this kind* of this sort, i.e. players 216 *gentle* ladylike
220-21 *I . . . dam* i.e. only as Snug the joiner am I either a fierce lion or a
lioness (folio reads: 'I one Snug . . . am, A lion . . . dam,' and most editors
follow, or emend differently) 221 *lion fell* (probably a quibble on two
senses, 'fierce lion' and 'lion's skin') 223 *'twere . . . life* (cf. III, i, 38)
224 *gentle* well-bred, courteous 225 *best at a beast* (a quibble based on
similar pronunciation) 227 *This lion . . . valor* i.e. 'the better part of valor
is discretion'

MOON
234   This lanthorn doth the hornèd moon present –
235   DEMETRIUS He should have worn the horns on his head.

THESEUS He is no crescent, and his horns are invisible
within the circumference.

MOON
This lanthorn doth the hornèd moon present.
Myself the man i' th' moon do seem to be.

THESEUS This is the greatest error of all the rest. The
man should be put into the lanthorn. How is it else the
man i' th' moon?

243 DEMETRIUS He dares not come there, for the candle; for
244   you see it is already in snuff.

HIPPOLYTA I am aweary of this moon. Would he would
change!

THESEUS It appears, by his small light of discretion, that
he is in the wane; but yet, in courtesy, in all reason, we
must stay the time.

LYSANDER Proceed, Moon.

MOON All that I have to say is to tell you that the lanthorn
is the moon; I, the man i' th' moon; this thornbush,
my thornbush; and this dog, my dog.

DEMETRIUS Why, all these should be in the lanthorn, for
all these are in the moon. But silence: here comes Thisby.
Enter Thisby.

THISBY
This is old Ninny's tomb. Where is my love?
257 LION O!   *[The Lion roars. Thisby runs off.]*
DEMETRIUS Well roared, Lion.
THESEUS Well run, Thisby.
HIPPOLYTA Well shone, Moon. Truly, the moon shines
with a good grace.
        [The Lion tears Thisby's mantle, and exit.]
THESEUS Well moused, Lion.
DEMETRIUS And then came Pyramus.
LYSANDER And so the Lion vanished.
      Enter Pyramus.

PYRAMUS
Sweet moon, I thank thee for thy sunny beams;
I thank thee, moon, for shining now so bright;
For, by thy gracious, golden, glittering gleams,
I trust to take of truest Thisby sight.
269   But stay: O spite!
         But mark, poor knight,
271   What dreadful dole is here?
         Eyes, do you see?
         How can it be?
         O dainty duck, O dear!
         Thy mantle good,
         What, stained with blood?
277   Approach, ye Furies fell!
         O Fates, come, come,
279   Cut thread and thrum,
280   Quail, crush, conclude, and quell!
281 THESEUS This passion, and the death of a dear friend,
would go near to make a man look sad.

283 HIPPOLYTA Beshrew my heart but I pity the man.

PYRAMUS
O, wherefore, Nature, didst thou lions frame?
285   Since lion vile hath here deflow'red my dear;
       Which is – no, no! – which was the fairest dame
         That lived, that loved, that liked, that looked with cheer.
         Come, tears, confound,
         Out, sword, and wound

The pap of Pyramus:
       Ay, that left pap
       Where heart doth hop.
       [Stabs himself.]
       Thus die I, thus, thus, thus.
       Now am I dead,
       Now am I fled,
       My soul is in the sky.
       Tongue, lose thy light,
       Moon, take thy flight.   *[Exit Moonshine.]*
       Now die, die, die, die, die.
       [Dies.]
DEMETRIUS No die, but an ace, for him! for he is but one. 300
LYSANDER Less than an ace, man; for he is dead, he is
nothing.
THESEUS With the help of a surgeon he might yet
recover, and yet prove an ass.   304
HIPPOLYTA How chance Moonshine is gone before
Thisby comes back and finds her lover?
      [Enter Thisby.]
THESEUS She will find him by starlight. Here she comes;
and her passion ends the play.   308
HIPPOLYTA Methinks she should not use a long one for
such a Pyramus. I hope she will be brief.
DEMETRIUS A mote will turn the balance, which Pyra-
mus, which Thisby, is the better: he for a man, God
warr'nt us! – she for a woman, God bless us!   312
LYSANDER She has spied him already with those sweet
eyes.
DEMETRIUS And thus she means, videlicet: 315

THISBY   Asleep, my love?
         What, dead, my dove?
         O Pyramus, arise!
         Speak, speak. Quite dumb?
         Dead, dead? A tomb
       Must cover thy sweet eyes.
       These lily lips,
       This cherry nose,
       These yellow cowslip cheeks,
         Are gone, are gone.
       Lovers, make moan.
       His eyes were green as leeks.   327
         O Sisters Three,   328
         Come, come to me,
       With hands as pale as milk;
       Lay them in gore,
       Since you have shore
       With shears his thread of silk.
       Tongue, not a word.

234 *lanthorn* (pronounced 'lant-horn' or 'lantern'; spelling probably due to folk etymology, because lanterns were made of horn; note pun on *hornèd moon*) 235 *on his head* (as a cuckold) 243 *for the candle* for fear of the candle 244 *in snuff* (1) in need of snuffing, (2) in a passion 257 s.d. (from folio) 269 *spite* i.e. malice of fortune 271 *dole* cause of grief, piteous thing 277 *Furies* (invocations of the Furies were common in Senecan drama); *fell* fierce, terrible 279 *thrum* end of the warp thread left attached to the loom when the web is cut away (merely Bottom the weaver's way of saying, 'Do a complete job of it!') 280 *Quail* overpower, destroy; *quell* kill 281–82 *This . . . sad* i.e. this display of passion by itself wouldn't sadden anyone 283 *Beshrew* curse (but used lightly; cf. II, ii, 54) 285 *deflow'red* ravished 300 *ace* the one-spot on a die; *one* (quibble on 'one person' and 'unique') 304 *ass* (pun on *ace*) 308 *passion* speech of passion 312 *warr'nt* warrant, i.e. protect 315 *means* (1) laments (an Anglo-Saxon word), (2) lodges a complaint (in a legal sense) 327 *green* hazel 328 *Sisters Three* the Fates

Come, trusty sword,
336   Come, blade, my breast imbrue!
[Stabs herself.]
And farewell, friends.
Thus Thisby ends.
Adieu, adieu, adieu.
[Dies.]
[Enter Lion, Moonshine, and Wall.]
THESEUS Moonshine and Lion are left to bury the dead.
DEMETRIUS Ay, and Wall too.
342 LION No, I assure you; the wall is down that parted their
fathers. Will it please you to see the epilogue, or to hear
344   a Bergomask dance between two of our company?
THESEUS No epilogue, I pray you; for your play needs no
excuse. Never excuse, for when the players are all dead,
there need none to be blamed. Marry, if he that writ it
348 had played Pyramus and hanged himself in Thisby's garter, it would have been a fine tragedy; and so it is truly,
and very notably discharged. But, come, your Bergomask. Let your epilogue alone.
[A dance.]
352 The iron tongue of midnight hath told twelve.
Lovers, to bed; 'tis almost fairy time.
I fear we shall outsleep the coming morn
355 As much as we this night have overwatched.
This palpable gross play hath well beguiled
357 The heavy gait of night. Sweet friends, to bed.
A fortnight hold we this solemnity
In nightly revels and new jollity.   *Exeunt.*

Enter Puck [with a broom].
PUCK   Now the hungry lion roars,
And the wolf behowls the moon;
Whilst the heavy ploughman snores,
363   All with weary task fordone.
Now the wasted brands do glow,
Whilst the screech owl, screeching loud,
Puts the wretch that lies in woe
In remembrance of a shroud.
Now it is the time of night
That the graves, all gaping wide,
370   Every one lets forth his sprite,
In the churchway paths to glide.

And we fairies, that do run
By the triple Hecate's team   373
From the presence of the sun,
Following darkness like a dream,
Now are frolic. Not a mouse
Shall disturb this hallowed house.
I am sent, with broom, before,
To sweep the dust behind the door.   379
Enter King and Queen of Fairies, with all their Train.
OBERON Through the house give glimmering light,
By the dead and drowsy fire;
Every elf and fairy sprite
Hop as light as bird from brier;
And this ditty, after me,
Sing, and dance it trippingly.
TITANIA First rehearse your song by rote,
To each word a warbling note.
Hand in hand, with fairy grace,
Will we sing, and bless this place.   389

[Song and dance.]

OBERON Now, until the break of day,
Through this house each fairy stray.
To the best bride-bed will we,
Which by us shall blessèd be;
And the issue there create
Ever shall be fortunate.
So shall all the couples three
Ever true in loving be;
And the blots of Nature's hand
Shall not in their issue stand.
Never mole, harelip, nor scar,
Nor mark prodigious, such as are   401
Despisèd in nativity,
Shall upon their children be.
With this field-dew consecrate,   401
Every fairy take his gait,
And each several chamber bless,
Through this palace, with sweet peace.
And the owner of it blest
Ever shall in safety rest.
Trip away; make no stay;
Meet me all by break of day.
Exeunt [all but Puck].
PUCK   If we shadows have offended,
Think but this, and all is mended –
That you have but slumb'red here
While these visions did appear.
And this weak and idle theme,   416
No more yielding but a dream,   417
Gentles, do not reprehend.
If you pardon, we will mend.
And, as I am an honest Puck,
If we have unearnèd luck
Now to scape the serpent's tongue,   422
We will make amends ere long;
Else the Puck a liar call.
So, good night unto you all.
Give me your hands, if we be friends,   426
And Robin shall restore amends.   *[Exit.]*

336 *imbrue* stain with blood   342 *Lion* (the folio, followed by many editors, assigns this speech to Bottom)   344 *Bergomask dance* rustic or clownish dance named after the peasants of Bergamo, Italy   348–49 *hanged . . . garter* (a proverbial phrase)   352 *told* counted (perhaps with a quibble on 'tolled')   355 *overwatched* stayed awake too long   357 *heavy* drowsy   363 *fordone* worn out   370 *Every one* every grave; *his* its; *sprite* spirit, ghost (cf. III, ii, 381–83)   373 *triple Hecate* Ovid's '*dea triformis*' (*Metamorphoses*, vii, 94–5, 194), Hecate in her three aspects as Luna in the sky, Diana on earth, Proserpina in the underworld; here, both goddess of the moon and of night; *team* i.e. of dragons (cf. III, ii, 379)   379 *behind* from behind (Puck traditionally kept the house clean and was represented with a broom and a candle)   389 s.d. *Song and dance* (the song referred to in ll. 384–86 may be lost, or may survive in ll. 390–411, headed as 'The Song' in the folio)   401 *mark prodigious* ominous birthmark   404 *consecrate* consecrated   416 *idle* foolish   417 *No more yielding but* yielding no more than   422 *scape* escape; *serpent's tongue* i.e. hissing   426 *Give . . . hands* i.e. applaud

The first quarto, printed in 1600, is the authoritative text of the play, although it contains a number of errors difficult to emend. Judging from the sparse stage directions, the inconsistent speech-prefixes (such as both *Puck* and *Robin*, *Bottom* and *Clown*), the careless assignment of minor parts, many old-fashioned spellings, and other small signs, the text was very probably set up from Shakespeare's own working manuscript of the play rather than from a clean copy prepared for use in the theatre. Certain irregularities of the 1600 text, moreover, especially the mislining of passages of verse in the last scene (including Theseus' famous speech on the madman, the lover, and the poet), would seem to indicate that Shakespeare had made some marginal additions; and certain other features of the play, notably the inconsistencies in the time scheme, may have arisen from a more extensive revision. The duration of the action can be stretched, at most, to three days, not to the four days and four nights announced by Hippolyta as the interval until her wedding; and the moon, not expected to be new until that day, shines on the night the lovers elope and the actors rehearse, and is everywhere present in the poetry. But whether these and other anomalies all imply revision and whether, if they do, the revising was simply part of the process of composition or a more thorough job done after an interval for a particular occasion, there is no means of deciding. Professor J. Dover Wilson has suggested as such an occasion the wedding in 1598 of the Earl of Southampton to Elizabeth Vernon.

The first quarto was reprinted in 1619 in a second quarto falsely dated 1600; the reprint contained many minor corrections, but also many new errors, and many sophistications of spelling and punctuation. This second quarto was in turn reprinted, with a continuation of its errors and with the introduction of a number of "improved" readings carrying the text further away from Shakespeare, in the folio of 1623. The 1619 quarto used as copy for the folio printers, however, must have had transferred to it a number of stage directions, some corrected speech-prefixes, and some changed assignments of minor parts from a theatrical manuscript, presumably one in use by the company at that date. About half a dozen new readings for which a printer can hardly have been responsible must have come from the theatrical manuscript. Several of these are certainly wrong; the others (see list of emendations, III, ii, 19, 220; V, i, 189, 204) may or may not have been what Shakespeare wrote.

The division into acts introduced in the folio may have come from the theatrical manuscript, and if so reflects a change in the style of production; it may, however, have been only editorial, since it does great damage to the management of the scenes. In the original quarto text (which is undivided into acts and in which the scenes are not numbered) there are only seven scenes, counting a clear stage as a change of scene. Two scenes outside the wood begin the play (the first by implication of the text at the court of Theseus; the second, a meeting of the "mechanicals," not located by the text in any particular place), and two scenes outside (the same as the first two, in reverse order) end it. All the action in between (II, i through IV, i in the editorial numbering) is in the wood, and is nearly continuous, with the stage clear only twice (before II, ii and before III, ii). Titania remains asleep on the stage where the folio makes a break with Act III, and the lovers are so asleep where it makes a break with Act IV. The folio direction at the end of Act III, "They sleepe all the Act," is usually taken to mean "all the act-interval," but may mean "during the following act" (through IV, i, 137); in either case, it is consequent upon the

division into acts and tends to support, though it does not prove, the theory that the division had been made for presentation.

The following are the only readings in the present edition departing materially from the text of the first quarto. Corrections of simple literal errors, punctuation, and mislineation of verse are not noted unless they affect the sense. After each reading, in italics, the corresponding text actually appearing in the quartos and folio is given in roman. When the reading is from the second quarto or the folio, the fact is indicated; otherwise it is an emendation, usually one suggested quite early in the history of Shakespearean scholarship.

I, i, 4 *wanes* (Q2, F) waues (Q1)   10 *New-bent* Now bent (QQ, F)   19 s.d. *omitting 'Helena'* (F) including 'Helena' (QQ)   24 *Stand forth, Demetrius* printed as s.d. (QQ, F)   26 *Stand forth, Lysander* printed as s.d. (QQ, F)   136 *low* loue (QQ, F)   187 *Yours would* Your words (QQ, F)   191 *I'ld* ile (Q1) Ile (Q2, F)   216 *sweet* sweld (QQ, F)   219 *stranger companies* strange companions (QQ, F)

I, ii, 24 *rest. Yet* rest yet (QQ, F)   25–26 *split.* | *'The* split the (QQ, F)

II, i, 69 *steep* (Q2, F 'steepe') steppe (Q1)   79 *Aegles* Eagles (QQ, F)   109 *thin* chinne (QQ, F)   158 *by the* (F) by (QQ)   190 *slay . . . slayeth* stay . . . stayeth (QQ, F)   201 *nor I* (F) not I (QQ)

II, ii, 39 *Be't* Bet it (Q1) Be it (Q2, F)   43 *good* (Q2, F) god (Q1)   47 *is* (Q2, F) it (Q1)

III, i, 27 *yourselves* (F) your selfe (QQ)   49 *Bottom* (Q2, F 'Bot.') Cet. (Q1)   61 *and let* or let (QQ, F)   74 *Odorous, odorous* Odours, odorous (QQ) Odours, odours (F)   79 *Puck* (F) Quin. (QQ)   148–49 *Peaseblossom, etc.* Fairies. Readie: and I, and I, and I. Where shall we goe? (QQ, F)   161–64 *Peaseblossom, etc.* 1. Fai. Haile mortall, haile. | 2. Fai. Haile. | 3. Fai. Haile. (QQ, F)   181 *you of more* you more (QQ, F)

III, ii, 19 *mimic* (F 'Mimmick') minnick (Q1) Minnock (Q2)   80 *part I* so part I (QQ, F)   85 *sleep* slippe (Q1) slip (Q2, F)   213 *first, like* first life (QQ, F)   220 *passionate* (F) omitted (QQ)   237 *Ay, do. Persever* I doe. Perseuer (Q1) I, do, perseuer (Q2, F)   250 *prayers* praise (QQ, F)   257 *No, no, you'll* No, no: heele (Q1) No, no, he'l (Q2) No, no, Sir (F)   299 *gentlemen* (Q2, F) gentleman (Q1)   406 *Speak! In some bush?* Speake in some bush. (QQ, F)   451 *To your* your (QQ, F)

IV, i, 40 *all ways* alwaies (QQ, F)   41 *woodbine . . . honeysuckle* woodbine, . . . Honisuckle, (QQ, F)   65 *That, he* That hee, (Q1) That he (Q2, F)   72 *o'er* or (QQ, F)   81 *sleep of all these five sleep* : of all these, fine (QQ, F)   116 *Seemed* Seeme (QQ, F)   127 *this is* (Q2, F) this (Q1)   132 *rite* right (QQ, F)   171 *saw* see (QQ, F)   198 *let us* (Q2, F) lets (Q1)   205 *to expound* (Q2, F) expound (Q1)   207 *a patched* (F) patcht a (QQ)   214 *our play* a Play (QQ, F)

IV, ii, s.d. *Enter . . . Starveling* Enter Quince, Flute, Thisby and the rabble (QQ) Enter Quince, Flute, Thisbie, Snout, and Starueling (F)   3 *Starveling* (F 'Staru.') Flut. (QQ)   5, 9, 13, 18 *Flute* Thys. *or* This. (QQ, F)

V, i, 34 *our* (F) Or (Q1) or (Q2)   155 *Snout* (F) Flute (QQ)   189 *up in thee* (F) now againe (QQ)   192 *My love! thou art my love*, My loue thou art, my loue (QQ, F)   204 *mural down* Moon vsed (QQ) morall downe (F)   215 *beasts in, a* beasts, in a (QQ, F)   267 *gleams* beames (QQ, F)   305–06 *gone before Thisby* gone before? Thisby (QQ, F)   311 *mote* moth (QQ, F)   360 *lion* Lyons (QQ, F)   361 *behowls* beholds (Q, F)   408–09 these two lines transposed (QQ, F)

LOVE'S LABOR'S LOST

INTRODUCTION

To Tolstoy Shakespeare seemed a poet in motley, who was "only playing with words." If he felt this way about *Lear*, we can guess how he would have felt about *Love's Labor's Lost* had he been able to endure reading it. In a way Tolstoy was right. An irrepressible, almost irresponsible gaiety breaks through as verbal effervescence even in plays written when Shakespeare was allegedly in the depths, in scenes where other playwrights would have preserved a fitting decorum. Johnson noted the fact with temperate regret: word-play, the pun, the "clench," was the poet's "fatal Cleopatra." Since the Shakespeare of *Love's Labor's Lost* is visible in all his works, we can scarcely call the play uncharacteristic. It is quite characteristic of Shakespeare the virtuoso, the idea-juggler, the word-wright, who loved to play and, naturally, since it was his natural element, loved to play with language. The comedy is exceptional chiefly in this, that Tolstoy's word *only* is here almost applicable.

Before conceding its defects, we had better observe its merits, especially since they have languished in relative neglect until recent times. It is a mistake to suppose that the play is a kind of closet drama, offering its feast of language, "scraps" or otherwise, at the expense of effective action. On the contrary, it is excellent theatre and good – although delayed-action – drama. It has the tactical advantage of being built about a single acceptable idea, one that has become, if it was not so already, a situational cliché. Young men resolve to abstain from the society of young women until confronted with appealing young women, whereupon they break their resolution. What has to happen happens, to the gratification of the world which loves a lover. Shakespeare himself, here and in *Much Ado about Nothing*, may have been the first to exploit the "Benedick" theme, but an abundance of later literature demonstrates how eminently exploitable it was. Having grasped at once the basic idea, we watch its development in comfort. There are no teasing complications; each of the four young men falls patly in love with his opposite number. Interest is sustained less by the conjunction of episodes than by episodes in isolation, most of which could be played effectively as excerpts. Act IV, Scene iii, where each of the avowed celibates spies on the apostasy of his fellows, is a masterpiece of stage ingenuity, and the opening of Act V, Scene ii, where they break their temptresses wreck their "show of Muscovites," is full of irresistible business. The sketchy adventures of Armado, Moth, and the village eccentrics are just sufficient to float the interspersed series of comic dialogues, most of which could also be excerpted and played as vaudeville. Despite the absence of important action, the play is theatrically strong.

There is nothing reprehensible about word-play as

such, and that of *Love's Labor's Lost* has the virtue of whole-heartedness. The language is energetic even at its most frivolous. Nearly every long speech is a verbal tumbling act, and every short one a stroke in a game of wits. Two-ply, three-ply, and four-ply puns ricochet from line to line, and if badness is the test of a good pun, some of these are immortal. All kinds of language affectation are exploited – genteelism, pedanticism, obscurantism, even poeticism:

> Taffeta phrases, silken terms precise,
> Three-piled hyperboles, spruce affection,
> Figures pedantical. . . .

In his superior way Berowne is as much a linguistic fop as Armado, while Holofernes commits matchless assaults upon the Renaissance vocabulary. Even Jaquenetta's few lines perform a supplementary function, supplying a thumb-nail anthology of rustic comebacks of old, on the level of the modern "sez you." The conceits of the semi-serious passages are so complex and the comic puns so tenuous that one wonders how much the audience was able to catch. Probably a percentage only, although a larger one than we might suppose. Actually, almost every line is explicable, even those which at first seem gibberish, but instant and total comprehension was scarcely necessary. A listener could catch a share of the jokes and take the rest on faith, exulting meanwhile in the power of the characters and their creator to "keep it up."

The characterization is less impressive than the physical and verbal movement, partly because most of the types presented were improved upon by Shakespeare himself in other plays. The King of Navarre and the Princess of France show a trace, but a trace only, of the royal grace and *savoir-faire* of Theseus and Hippolyta. Rosaline has the pertness but lacks the charm of Rosalind. Even Berowne is a little disappointing: the role of giber-in-chief seems superimposed upon him, as during his excessive and pointless denigration of Boyet; he should have emerged more clearly as both the most intelligent person in the play and the most intoxicated by his own fluency. Perhaps when the play was written, Shakespeare himself was too much of a Berowne to see the character quite objectively. The other figures of the great world, Dumaine and Longaville, like Katharine and Maria, are so sketchy as to be scarcely distinguishable.

Among the low-comedy characters Dull is only a foreshadower of Dogberry, and Jaquenetta of Audrey. Costard is inferior to Shakespeare's later homespuns because he fails to stay in character. As the open-mouthed but dauntless simpleton he is fine, but he shifts sometimes into the smart-aleck and even the bawdy sophisticate. Armado and

Moth, at least at the beginning, are bores absolute, and one pities the recluses for whom they are to provide "quick recreation" for three years; but Armado becomes interesting when he becomes pathetic, then heroic, and Moth when he acts in the show of Nine Worthies and becomes truly a boy. Of course the true comic triumphs are Holofernes and Nathaniel: Shakespeare never did better with pompous asininity and limp obsequiousness.

All of the characters have a speech or two in which they seem to excel themselves, and this brings us to an odd feature of the play – its extreme unevenness. The opening scene and a number more are written in fine blank verse and rhyme. The poetry is rarely of the highest Shakespearean order, often recalling the logic-chopping and intricate prettiness of the lesser Sonnets, but it is true poetry and written by a master prosodist. It ill prepares us for the old-fashioned doggerel we find elsewhere, descending sometimes to jingling triteness. Or compare the first dialogue of Armado and Moth (I, ii) with the first dialogue of Holofernes and Nathaniel (IV, ii), which despite its comparable thicket of verbiage has the breath of life in it.

There is disparity of tone as well as quality. Conspicuously at the end, and intermittently elsewhere, the bright brittle surface of the play seems to crack and reveal a warmer, gentler, more human substance – such as we associate with a more familiar Shakespeare, the humorist rather than the wit, the amused and affectionate observer rather than the gleeful satirist. Sometimes the play seems almost to protest against itself – as when its speakers resolve to "lay these glozes [i.e. double-talk] by" and praise "honest plain words," "russet yeas and honest kersey noes." The concluding speech rejects the harsh words of Mercury (master-glozer) for the songs of Apollo. Though harmless in intent, the play has truly its strain of harshness. It is admirable in its pioneering of the mode of social comedy, and the themes of warfare between the sexes and between naturalness and affectation, but like other pioneers it is often more rugged than refined, the postures of its characters too muscular, their persiflage too aggressive, indeed at times even brutal. Rosaline's words condemning the gibing spirit –

> A jest's prosperity lies in the ear
> Of him that hears it, never in the tongue
> Of him that makes it –

might as well have been directed at herself and all the other ladies and gentlemen as at Berowne alone. The impression is inescapable that the play has not only been revised, but revised after the author had considerably matured both as artist and individual, and found the spirit of the original piece not wholly to his taste.

The mere fact of revision is generally conceded. The problem is when it took place and why. The first edition in 1598, evidently printed from the author's manuscript, contains several duplicate passages, where the printer mistakenly preserved lines which had been cancelled and rewritten. These are of small help in deciding the main point, since such revision may take place either during the original composition or the reworking of a play. Also of small help is the information on the title page that the play had been "newly corrected and augmented," since the legend may only mean, as in the case of a similar one on the title page of the 1599 quarto of *Romeo and Juliet*, that there had been an earlier edition, unauthorized and unreliable.

But the 1598 text of *Love's Labor's Lost*, the only authoritative one we have, shows signs of structural as well as stylistic revision, of shuffling about of speeches and speakers, and of an altered ending. It seems virtually certain that the play originally ended not with news of the death of the King of France, but with Boyet's production of the papers establishing the Princess's territorial claims. There is even a possibility that the suit of love succeeded as promptly as the suit of property, and that the original title was "Love's Labor's Won." A play with this title was attributed to Shakespeare by Francis Meres in 1598 along with *Love's Labor's Lost*, and a quarto so titled was extant in the early seventeenth century; however, the chances are somewhat in favor of its being a separate play rather than an earlier version of the one we have. There is no mention of either title before 1598, and the majority of present-day scholars believe that *Love's Labor's Lost* was originally written about 1594–95 in Shakespeare's "lyrical" period, and revised shortly before an event advertised on the title page, a performance at Elizabeth's court "this last Christmas" (probably that of 1596 or 1597).

It must be confessed that such a conclusion raises certain vexing questions: why was extensive revision necessary after so short a lapse of time? why does this particular play of the "lyrical" period contain patches of verse different from and inferior to anything else written by Shakespeare in the "lyrical" period? why should a play which seems to have been designed for a coterie audience have been performed by a popular troupe? The plays performed at Elizabeth's court in the nineties were all from the regular popular repertories, and the often repeated statement that *Love's Labor's Lost* was composed by a popular playwright for a private occasion rests on neither particular evidence nor general precedent but on strong and simple faith. One of the influences on the current dating has been the discussion of "topicalities" in the play. The earliest theory (1747) was Bishop Warburton's, that Holofernes was intended as a caricature of the busy translator and lexicographer John Florio. This theory has met with somewhat discriminatory disdain. The most prominent of more recent theories are that the Armado–Moth scenes make humorous capital of the personal quarrel between Thomas Nashe and Gabriel Harvey pursued in a series of notorious pamphlets in 1590–96, and that the fiction of a little "academe" with its courtly principals and orbiting eccentrics presents diffused satire of Royden, Raleigh, Harriot, Northumberland, Chapman, and other unorthodox thinkers who supposedly comprised an intellectual clique known as the "school of atheism," i.e. the "school of night" (cf. IV, iii, 250). A number of books and articles by reputable scholars have advanced these theories, which deserve the respectful attention they have received; however, none of them carries conviction except to those under the hypnosis induced by the shimmering nature of the evidence. A few suggestive phrases in the play there certainly are, but neither the characters nor the episodes resemble in the least the persons and events they are supposed to shadow forth.

There may be value in an alternative opinion on the date of original composition. Many generations of Shakespearean scholars believed *Love's Labor's Lost* to be Shakespeare's earliest play, and the more factual findings of modern scholarship have done nothing to discredit this belief. Although the plot is evidently original, a number of "sources" or ingredients have been discovered, and these are such as we would expect in a play of the late eighties rather than the middle nineties. The idea of a courtly philosophic retreat intruded upon by fetching ladies seems to have been suggested by an actual embassy to Henry of Navarre at Nerac by Marguerite de Valois, Catherine de Medici, and "l'escadron volant" of ladies-in-waiting in 1578. "Academies" were more in the news in the eighties than in the nineties; a suggestive one is described in de la Primaudaye's *Académie Française,* translated into English in 1586. The grouping and pairing of characters, as well as several episodes in the play, show the influence of comedies by John Lyly written between 1584 and 1587. The stock characters of Italian *commedia dell'arte* have helped to shape Armado (*capetano*), Moth (*zanni*), Holofernes (*dottore*), Nathaniel (*pantalone* and parasite), and it seems more plausible that this phenomenon would occur fresh upon the visit of Italian troupes to England rather than a decade later. The selection of the character names Navarre, Berowne (de Biron), Longaville, and Dumaine (du Maine or de Mayenne) would have been more feasible in the eighties than in the nineties, since the actual French owners of these family names became prominent in a war of blood rather than a war of words after 1589 and *personae non gratae* in England after 1593. An actual early Tudor mask of Muscovites with blackamoor torchbearers is described in Holinshed's *Chronicles,* 1587.

In the large number of parts for juvenile actors (four ladies and a boy), in its construction, spirit, and themes, *Love's Labor's Lost* is more suggestive of earlier chorister drama than of the drama of the Lord Chamberlain's Men. It is conceivable that Shakespeare wrote the play for Paul's theatre in 1588–89 and salvaged it as a novelty for his own company in 1596–97, so that it is unnecessary to postulate *abnormal* auspices of coterie production. Of course there is no proof that such is the case, but until current orthodoxy about the original date and auspices of production is more firmly based, this alternative should be kept in mind. What Shakespeare was doing at the age of twenty-four or twenty-five we do not know, and *Love's Labor's Lost* may provide a clue; speculation in this direction would prove at least as profitable as speculation on whether Armado represents Sir Walter Raleigh, Antonio Perez, or the King of Spain.

Whatever the date of the original version, and whether they first appeared in that version or in the revision, the play contains what Granville-Barker called "outcroppings of pure dramatic gold" – the more surprising and delightful for their sporadic appearance: for instance, the sudden deflation of the jesting Princess when Costard puns on her "thickness" – "What's your will, sir? What's your will?"; or Costard's modest pride in his own acting ability and patronage of Nathaniel's – "a marvellous good neighbor, faith, and a very good bowler; but for Alisander – alas, you see how 'tis – a little o'erparted"; or Holofernes' just reproof (without pedantry) of the merciless courtiers – "This is not generous, not gentle, not humble"; or Armado's defense of Hector – "Sweet chucks, beat not the bones of the buried. When he breathed, he was a man" – and his own manly recovery from humiliation. The ending, afterthought though it seems to be, is wonderfully effective – dissolving the play rather than concluding it, with sudden images of suffering and death, with gravity and tenderness. Here appears in full view the Shakespeare who was *not* only playing with words.

The only performances of *Love's Labor's Lost* of which we have certain knowledge are the court production mentioned on the title page of 1598 and a second court production, before Queen Anne, in 1605, but the late printing of a quarto in 1631 indicates a revival at Blackfriars. For centuries thereafter critics considered it not only Shakespeare's first but his worst play, and actors preferred to ignore it. It has the distinction of being the only Shakespearean play never performed in the Restoration and the eighteenth and early nineteenth centuries. One can understand why: it offered little opportunity for the increasingly egocentric acting of the great Shakespearean stars from Betterton to Kean, or for the increasing pomposity of Shakespearean staging from Kean to Irving. There were a few isolated productions as the nineteenth century progressed, by Madam Vestris (1839), Samuel Phelps (1857), and Augustin Daly (1874–91). Irving dismissed it as impossible, and even Granville-Barker was a little rueful in his commendations. The play has been rescued for the stage by the Shakespeare Festival companies, the Old Vic, and academic and experimental groups. Those who see it performed are delighted, and wonder why they have not had more frequent opportunities.

In a good performance the play even achieves a kind of homogeneity. Just as the final episode mitigates the frivolity which precedes, the closing songs mitigate the solemnity of the final episode. They are the songs of a very relaxed Apollo, so effortless as to seem to have grown like the "daisies pied and violets blue" rather than to have been composed, yet sharply focused upon realities and technically superb. They are nostalgic and gently ribald, like the closing song of *Twelfth Night,* but in some mysterious way they place our world in perspective.

Harvard University   ALFRED HARBAGE

Love's Labor's Lost was published in 1598 in a quarto almost certainly printed from the author's manuscript. If there was an earlier quarto, no copies have survived. The folio text was printed from the quarto, probably without independent authority. The text of the quarto contains numerous imperfections, owing in part to persisting confusion in the manuscript and to the compositor's difficulty in following word-play, especially that involving foreign languages. The act–scene division indicated marginally follows the divisions of the folio except that it splits the first act into two scenes. Below are listed all substantive departures from the quarto of 1598, with the adopted reading in italics followed by the quarto reading in roman.

I, i, 62 *feast* fast 104 *an* any 126–29 *A . . . devise* (joined in Q with Longaville's preceding speech) 129 *possibly* possible

I, ii, 13 *epitheton* apethaton 95 *blushing* blush-in 135 *Dull* (assigned in Q to Costard)

II, i, 32 *Importunes* Importuous 34 *visaged* visage 40 *Maria* 1 Lady 44 *parts* peerelsse 53 *Maria* Lady 56 *Katharine* 2 Lady 64 *Rosaline* 3 Lady 88 *unpeopled* unpeeled 99 *it ; will* it will 114–25 *Rosaline* Katharine 143 *On* One 193 *Katharine* Rosaline 208 *Rosaline* Katharine 211 *You* O you (The 'O' was probably a part of the speech-prefix. On this assumption an initial 'O' is also omitted at III, i, 134, 137, 139, 141, 145, 147, 162 ; IV, iii, 278, 284.) 252 *Rosaline* Lady 253 *Maria* Lady 2 254 *Katharine* Lady 3 255, 256 *Rosaline* Lady

III, i, 12 *as if* if 13 *through the* through : 16 *thin-belly* thin-bellies 21 *note – do you note – men that* note : do you note men that 24 *penny* penne 65–66 *the mail* thee male 169 *signor-junior* Signior Iunios 179 *clock* Cloake 193 *sue* shue

IV, i, 6 *On* Ore 69 *saw* see 70 *saw* See 75 *king's* king 107 *suitor . . . suitor* shooter . . . shooter 129 *hit it* hit 135 *pin is in* 143 *o' th' t'* one 'ath toothen

IV, ii, 35 *Dictynna . . . Dictynna* Dictisima . . . dictisima 36 *Dictynna* dictima 49 *call I* cald 51 *scurrility* squirilitie 58

sores – O sore l !* sores o sorell : 63 *Holofernes* Nathaniel 67 *pia mater* primater 68–69 *in whom* whom 70 *Nathaniel* Holofernes 74–89 *Holofernes* Nathaniel 76 *sapit* sapis 92–93 *Venechia . . . prechia* vemchie, vencha, que non te unde, que non te perreche 115 *apostrophus* apostraphas 116 *canzonet* cangenet 116–23 *Here . . . you* (assigned in Q to Nathaniel) 126–30 *I will . . . Berowne* (assigned in Q to Nathaniel) 129 *writing* written 131 *Sir Nathaniel* Sir Holofernes 151 *ben bien*

IV, iii, 44 *King* Longaville 48 *triumviry* triumphery 88 *I mine* mine 103 *Wished* wish 107 *thorn* throne 125 *o'erheard* orehard 175 *like you* like 243 *wood* word 254 *and usurping* usurping 354 *authors* author 378 *allons !* allons Alone, alone

V, i, 9 *hominem* hominum 25 *insane* infamie 26 *Deo bone* Deo, bene 27 *Bone . . . Priscian* Bome boon for boon prescian 55 *venew* vene we 62 *manu* unum 89 *importunate* importunt 98 *secrecy* secretie 106 *Sir Nathaniel* Sir Holofernes 108 *rendered* rended *assistance* assistants 138 *Allons* Alone

V, ii, 17 *ha' been a grandam* a bin Grandam 28 *cure . . . care care . . . cure* 43 *pencils, ho !* pensalls, How ? 53 *pearls* Pearle 65 *hests device* 74 *wantonness* wantons be 80 *stabbed* stable 89 *sycamore* siccamone 148 *her* his 152 *ne'er* ere 159 *Boyet* Berowne 161 *– backs –* backs 217 *The . . . it* (assigned in Q to Rosaline) 243–56 *Katharine* Maria 298 *vailing* varling 310 *run o'er* runnes ore 375 *wits* wits 464 *zany* saine 483 *manage* nuage 514 *least* best 528 *de la guerra* delaguar 562 *this* his 638 *gilt* gift 662 *The . . . gone* (printed as s.d. in Q) 679 *on !* stir or stir 720 *entreat,* entreat : 768 *the ambassadors* ambassadors 772 *this in our* this our 797 *instant* instance 802 *intitled* intiled 806 *hermit* herrite 808 *too,* to 814 *A wife* (included in following speech in Q) 884, 885 (these lines transposed in Q) 905 *foul* full 907, 916 *Tu-who* (omitted in Q) 919–20 *Armado . . . omnes* (The quarto text concludes with 'The words of Mercury are harsh after the songs of Apollo' printed in larger type below the song. The first folio adds the speech-prefix, together with 'You, that way : we, this way. Exeunt omnes.' Thus the words of the quarto are made, if they were not so already, an integral part of the play.)

LOVE'S LABOR'S LOST

[NAMES OF THE ACTORS

Ferdinand, King of Navarre
Berowne ⎫
Longaville ⎬ lords attending on the King in his retirement
Dumaine ⎭
Boyet ⎫
Marcade ⎬ lords attending on the Princess of France
Don Adriano de Armado, a fantastical Spaniard
Nathaniel, a curate
Dull, a constable
Holofernes, a schoolmaster

Costard, a clown
Moth, page to Don Adriano de Armado
A Forester
Princess of France
Rosaline ⎫
Maria ⎬ ladies attending on the Princess
Katharine ⎭
Jaquenetta, a country wench
Officers and other Attendants

Scene: Navarre]

*

I, i *Enter Ferdinand King of Navarre, Berowne,*
Longaville, and Dumaine.

KING
Let fame, that all hunt after in their lives,
Live regist'red upon our brazen tombs
3 And then grace us in the disgrace of death;
4 When, spite of cormorant devouring Time,
5 Th' endeavor of this present breath may buy
6 That honor which shall bate his scythe's keen edge
And make us heirs of all eternity.
Therefore, brave conquerors – for so you are
9 That war against your own affections
And the huge army of the world's desires –
Our late edict shall strongly stand in force:
Navarre shall be the wonder of the world;
13 Our court shall be a little academe,
14 Still and contemplative in living art.
You three, Berowne, Dumaine, and Longaville,
Have sworn for three years' term to live with me,
My fellow scholars, and to keep those statutes
That are recorded in this schedule here.
Your oaths are passed; and now subscribe your names,
20 That his own hand may strike his honor down
21 That violates the smallest branch herein.
If you are armed to do as sworn to do,
Subscribe to your deep oaths, and keep it too.
LONGAVILLE
I am resolved. 'Tis but a three years' fast.

The mind shall banquet though the body pine.
Fat paunches have lean pates, and dainty bits
Make rich the ribs, but bankrout quite the wits.   27
DUMAINE
My loving lord, Dumaine is mortified.   28
The grosser manner of these world's delights
He throws upon the gross world's baser slaves.
To love, to wealth, to pomp, I pine and die,
With all these living in philosophy.   32
BEROWNE
I can but say their protestation over;
So much, dear liege, I have already sworn,
That is, to live and study here three years.
But there are other strict observances:
As not to see a woman in that term,
Which I hope well is not enrollèd there;
And one day in a week to touch no food,
And but one meal on every day beside,
The which I hope is not enrollèd there;
And then to sleep but three hours in the night,
And not be seen to wink of all the day   43
(When I was wont to think no harm all night   44
And make a dark night too of half the day),
Which I hope well is not enrollèd there.
O, these are barren tasks, too hard to keep –
Not to see ladies, study, fast, not sleep.
KING
Your oath is passed to pass away from these.
BEROWNE
Let me say no, my liege, an if you please.   50
I only swore to study with your Grace
And stay here in your court for three years' space.
LONGAVILLE
You swore to that, Berowne, and to the rest.
BEROWNE
By yea and nay, sir, then I swore in jest.   54
What is the end of study, let me know?

I, i The action throughout takes place in or near the King of Navarre's park
3 *disgrace* deterioration   4 *cormorant* ravenous   5 *breath* breathing-time
6 *bate* blunt   9 *affections* passions   13 *academe* academy   14 *Still . . . art*
constantly contemplative of the art of living   20 *hand* i.e. testimony of
handwriting, signature   21 *branch* subdivision, by-law   27 *bankrout* bankrupt   28 *mortified* i.e. dead to desire   32 *all these* i.e. his companions (?),
or love, wealth, pomp, of which philosophy will prove the equivalent (?)
43 *wink* close the eyes, nap   44 *think no harm* i.e. sleep   50 *an if* if   54 *By
. . . nay* (1) irrevocably (derived in popular usage from Matthew v, 37),
(2) equivocally (in Berowne's play on the literal meaning)

KING
  Why, that to know which else we should not know.
BEROWNE
57 Things hid and barred, you mean, from common sense?
KING
  Ay, that is study's godlike recompense.
BEROWNE
  Come on then, I will swear to study so,
  To know the thing I am forbid to know:
  As thus – to study where I well may dine
  When I to feast expressly am forbid;
  Or study where to meet some mistress fine
  When mistresses from common sense are hid;
  Or having sworn too hard-a-keeping oath,
  Study to break it and not break my troth.
  If study's gain be thus, and this be so,
  Study knows that which yet it doth not know.
  Swear me to this, and I will ne'er say no.
  KING
70 These be the stops that hinder study quite,
71 And train our intellects to vain delight.
  BEROWNE
  Why, all delights are vain, but that most vain
73 Which, with pain purchased, doth inherit pain:
  As, painfully to pore upon a book,
  To seek the light of truth, while truth the while
76 Doth falsely blind the eyesight of his look.
77 Light seeking light doth light of light beguile;
  So, ere you find where light in darkness lies,
79 Your light grows dark by losing of your eyes.
80 Study me how to please the eye indeed,
  By fixing it upon a fairer eye,
82 Who dazzling so, that eye shall be his heed,
83 And give him light that it was blinded by.
  Study is like the heaven's glorious sun,
  That will not be deep-searched with saucy looks:
  Small have continual plodders ever won,
  Save base authority from others' books.
88 These earthly godfathers of heaven's lights,
  That give a name to every fixèd star,
90 Have no more profit of their shining nights
91 Than those that walk and wot not what they are.
92 Too much to know is to know nought but fame;
93 And every godfather can give a name.
  KING
94 How well he's read to reason against reading!
DUMAINE
95 Proceeded well, to stop all good proceeding!
LONGAVILLE
96 He weeds the corn, and still lets grow the weeding.
  BEROWNE
97 The spring is near, when green geese are a-breeding.
DUMAINE
  How follows that?
98 BEROWNE   Fit in his place and time.
  DUMAINE
  In reason nothing.
  BEROWNE   Something then in rime.
  KING
100 Berowne is like an envious sneaping frost
101 That bites the first-born infants of the spring.
  BEROWNE
102 Well, say I am; why should proud summer boast
  Before the birds have any cause to sing?

Why should I joy in an abortive birth?
At Christmas I no more desire a rose
Than wish a snow in May's new-fangled shows;
But like of each thing that in season grows.
So you, to study now it is too late,   108
Climb o'er the house to unlock the little gate.   109
KING
  Well, sit you out. Go home, Berowne. Adieu.
BEROWNE
  No, my good lord, I have sworn to stay with you;
  And though I have for barbarism spoke more   112
  Than for that angel knowledge you can say,
  Yet confident I'll keep what I have sworn,
  And bide the penance of each three years' day.   115
  Give me the paper, let me read the same,
  And to the strictest decrees I'll write my name.
KING
  How well this yielding rescues thee from shame!
BEROWNE [reads] 'Item. That no woman shall come
  within a mile of my court –' Hath this been proclaimed?
LONGAVILLE Four days ago.
BEROWNE Let's see the penalty. '– on pain of losing her
  tongue.' Who devised this penalty?
LONGAVILLE
  Marry, that did I.   124
BEROWNE   Sweet lord, and why?
LONGAVILLE
  To fright them hence with that dread penalty.
BEROWNE
  A dangerous law against gentility!   126
  [Reads] 'Item. If any man be seen to talk with a woman
  within the term of three years, he shall endure such
  public shame as the rest of the court can possibly devise.'
  This article, my liege, yourself must break;
  For well you know here comes in embassy
  The French king's daughter with yourself to speak,
  A maid of grace and complete majesty,
  About surrender up of Aquitaine
  To her decrepit, sick, and bed-rid father.
  Therefore this article is made in vain,
  Or vainly comes th' admirèd princess hither.
KING
  What say you, lords? why, this was quite forgot.
BEROWNE
  So study evermore is overshot.
  While it doth study to have what it would,
  It doth forget to do the thing it should;
  And when it hath the thing it hunteth most,
  'Tis won as towns with fire; so won, so lost.   143

57 *common sense* ordinary observation 70 *stops* impediments 71 *train* allure 73 *inherit* take possession of 76 *falsely* treacherously; *his look* its power to see 77 *Light . . . beguile* i.e. peering for truth deprives the eyes of their sight 79 *light* sight 80 *Study me* study for me 82 *dazzling so* thus bedazzled; *heed* guide 83 *it* i.e. his eye 88 *earthly godfathers* i.e. the astronomers 90 *shining* i.e. star-lit 91 *wot* know 92 *know nought* experience nothing 93 *every . . . name* i.e. anyone who serves as a godfather can do as much as astronomers do 94 *read . . . reading* studied . . . studying 95 *Proceeded* i.e. advanced through the academic curriculum 96 *weeds the corn* i.e. pulls up the wheat; *weeding* weeds 97 *green geese* young geese, fools 98 *Fit in his* precisely in its 100 *sneaping* nipping 101 *first-born infants* i.e. early buds 102–03 *why . . . sing* i.e. why should summer appear unseasonably 108 *too late* i.e. past his student days 109 *Climb . . . gate* i.e. act perversely (proverbial) 112 *barbarism* primitive ignorance 115 *bide . . . day* i.e. endure the deprivation each day of the three years 124 *Marry* by Mary (mild oath) 126 *gentility* civilized custom 143 *as . . . fire* i.e. like towns conquered by being burned down

KING

144 We must of force dispense with this decree;
145 She must lie here on mere necessity.

BEROWNE

    Necessity will make us all forsworn
    Three thousand times within this three years' space:
148 For every man with his affects is born,
149 Not by might mast'red, but by special grace.
    If I break faith, this word shall speak for me,
    I am forsworn 'on mere necessity.'
    So to the laws at large I write my name;
    [Signs.]
    And he that breaks them in the least degree
154 Stands in attainder of eternal shame.
155 Suggestions are to other as to me;
    But I believe, although I seem so loath,
    I am the last that will last keep his oath.
158 But is there no quick recreation granted?

KING

159 Ay, that there is. Our court you know is haunted
160 With a refinèd traveller of Spain,
161 A man in all the world's new fashion planted,
    That hath a mint of phrases in his brain;
    One who the music of his own vain tongue
    Doth ravish like enchanting harmony;
165 A man of complements, whom right and wrong
166 Have chose as umpire of their mutiny.
167 This child of fancy, that Armado hight,
168 For interim to our studies shall relate
169 In high-born words the worth of many a knight
170 From tawny Spain, lost in the world's debate.
    How you delight, my lords, I know not, I;
    But, I protest, I love to hear him lie,
173 And I will use him for my minstrelsy.

BEROWNE

    Armado is a most illustrious wight,
175 A man of fire-new words, fashion's own knight.

LONGAVILLE

176 Costard the swain and he shall be our sport;
    And so to study three years is but short.
    Enter [Dull,] a Constable, with Costard, with a letter.

CONSTABLE Which is the duke's own person?

BEROWNE This, fellow. What wouldst?

180 CONSTABLE I myself reprehend his own person, for I am
181 his Grace's farborough; but I would see his own person
    in flesh and blood.

BEROWNE This is he.

CONSTABLE Signior Arm – Arm – commends you.
    There's villainy abroad. This letter will tell you more.

COSTARD Sir, the contempts thereof are as touching me. 186
KING A letter from the magnificent Armado. 187
BEROWNE How low soever the matter, I hope in God for high words.
LONGAVILLE A high hope for a low heaven. God grant us 190 patience!
BEROWNE To hear, or forbear hearing? 192
LONGAVILLE To hear meekly, sir, and to laugh moderately, or to forbear both.
BEROWNE Well, sir, be it as the style shall give us cause to 195 climb in the merriness.
COSTARD The matter is to me, sir, as concerning Jaque- 197 netta. The manner of it is, I was taken with the manner. 198
BEROWNE In what manner?
COSTARD In manner and form following, sir; all those three: I was seen with her in the manor-house, sitting with her upon the form, and taken following her into 202 the park; which, put together, is, in manner and form following. Now, sir, for the manner – it is the manner of a man to speak to a woman. For the form – in some form.
BEROWNE For the following, sir?
COSTARD As it shall follow in my correction, and God 207 defend the right!
KING Will you hear this letter with attention?
BEROWNE As we would hear an oracle.
COSTARD Such is the simplicity of man to hearken after the flesh.
KING *[reads]* 'Great deputy, the welkin's vicegerent, and 213 sole dominator of Navarre, my soul's earth's God, and body's fostering patron –'
COSTARD Not a word of Costard yet.
KING 'So it is –'
COSTARD It may be so; but if he say it is so, he is, in telling true, but so. 219
KING Peace!
COSTARD Be to me and every man that dares not fight.
KING No words!
COSTARD Of other men's secrets, I beseech you.
KING 'So it is, besieged with sable-colored melancholy, I did commend the black-oppressing humor to the most wholesome physic of thy health-giving air; and, as I am 226 a gentleman, betook myself to walk. The time when? About the sixth hour; when beasts most graze, birds best peck, and men sit down to that nourishment which is called supper: so much for the time when. Now for the ground which; which, I mean, I walked upon: it is ycleped thy park. Then for the place where; where, I 232 mean, I did encounter that obscene and most preposterous event, that draweth from my snow-white pen the ebon-colored ink, which here thou viewest, beholdest, surveyest, or seest. But to the place where, it standeth north-north-east and by east from the west corner of thy curious-knotted garden. There did I see that low- 238 spirited swain, that base minnow of thy mirth –' 239
COSTARD Me?
KING 'that unlettered small-knowing soul –'
COSTARD Me?
KING 'that shallow vessel –'
COSTARD Still me.
KING 'which, as I remember, hight Costard –' 245
COSTARD O me!
KING 'sorted and consorted, contrary to thy established 247 proclaimed edict and continent canon, which with – O, 248 with – but with this I passion to say wherewith –' 249

144 *of force* perforce 145 *lie* lodge 148 *affects* passions 149 *might* i.e. his own strength; *special grace* heavenly intervention 154 *in attainder* under penalty 155 *Suggestions* temptations 158 *quick* lively 159–60 *haunted With* visited by 160 *refinèd* precious 161 *planted* rooted 165 *complements* affectations 166 *umpire . . . mutiny* rationalizer 167 *hight* is called 168 *interim* recess 169 *high-born* i.e. highfalutin 170 *tawny* sunburnt; *debate* warfare 173 *minstrelsy* i.e. diversion 175 *fire-new* brand-new 176 *swain* country youth 180 *reprehend* i.e. represent (malapropism) 181 *farborough* petty constable 186 *contempts* i.e. contents (malapropism) 187 *magnificent Armado* (play on magnificent or 'grand' Armada) 190 *low heaven* i.e. small blessing 192 *To hear . . . hearing* i.e. to take it or leave it 195 *be it so* be it 197 *is to* applies to 198 *with the manner* in the act (from legal term 'mainour') 202 *form* bench 207 *correction* punishment 213 *welkin's vicegerent* heaven's deputy 219 *but so* only in part 226 *physic* cure 232 *ycleped* called 238 *curious-knotted* intricately patterned 239 *minnow* i.e. small-fry 245 *hight* is called 247 *sorted* associated 248 *continent canon* law enjoining celibacy 249 *passion* grieve

COSTARD With a wench.

KING 'with a child of our grandmother Eve, a female; or, for thy more sweet understanding, a woman. Him I (as
253   my ever-esteemed duty pricks me on) have sent to thee, to receive the meed of punishment, by thy sweet Grace's officer, Anthony Dull, a man of good repute, carriage, bearing, and estimation.'

DULL Me, an't shall please you; I am Anthony Dull.

KING 'For Jaquenetta (so is the weaker vessel called), which I apprehended with the aforesaid swain, I keep
260   her as a vessel of thy law's fury; and shall, at the least of thy sweet notice, bring her to trial. Thine in all compliments of devoted and heart-burning heat of duty,
                 Don Adriano de Armado.'

BEROWNE This is not so well as I looked for, but the best that ever I heard.

266 KING Ay, the best for the worst. But, sirrah, what say you to this?

COSTARD Sir, I confess the wench.

KING Did you hear the proclamation?

COSTARD I do confess much of the hearing it, but little of the marking of it.

KING It was proclaimed a year's imprisonment to be taken with a wench.

COSTARD I was taken with none, sir; I was taken with a damsel.

KING Well, it was proclaimed 'damsel.'

COSTARD This was no damsel neither, sir; she was a virgin.

278 KING It is so varied too, for it was proclaimed 'virgin.'

COSTARD If it were, I deny her virginity; I was taken with a maid.

281 KING This maid will not serve your turn, sir.

COSTARD This maid will serve my turn, sir.

KING Sir, I will pronounce your sentence: you shall fast a week with bran and water.

285 COSTARD I had rather pray a month with mutton and porridge.

KING And Don Armado shall be your keeper.
My Lord Berowne, see him delivered o'er:
And go we, lords, to put in practice that
Which each to other hath so strongly sworn.
         [Exeunt King, Longaville, and Dumaine.]

BEROWNE
I'll lay my head to any good man's hat,
These oaths and laws will prove an idle scorn.
Sirrah, come on.

COSTARD I suffer for the truth, sir; for true it is I was taken with Jaquenetta, and Jaquenetta is a true girl; and
296 therefore welcome the sour cup of prosperity! Affliction
297 may one day smile again, and till then sit thee down, sorrow!   Exeunt.

*

I, ii   Enter Armado, [a Braggart,] and Moth, his Page.

ARMADO Boy, what sign is it when a man of great spirit grows melancholy?

MOTH A great sign, sir, that he will look sad.

ARMADO Why, sadness is one and the selfsame thing,
5   dear imp.

MOTH No, no. O Lord, sir, no!

7 ARMADO How canst thou part sadness and melancholy,
8   my tender juvenal?

MOTH By a familiar demonstration of the working, my 9
tough signor.   10

ARMADO Why tough signor? why tough signor?

MOTH Why tender juvenal? why tender juvenal?

ARMADO I spoke it, tender juvenal, as a congruent epi- 13
theton appertaining to thy young days, which we may
nominate tender.

MOTH And I, tough signor, as an appertinent title to your 16
old time, which we may name tough.

ARMADO Pretty, and apt.

MOTH How mean you, sir? I pretty, and my saying apt?
or I apt, and my saying pretty?

ARMADO Thou pretty, because little.

MOTH Little pretty, because little. Wherefore apt?

ARMADO And therefore apt, because quick.

MOTH Speak you this in my praise, master?

ARMADO In thy condign praise.   25

MOTH I will praise an eel with the same praise.

ARMADO What, that an eel is ingenious?

MOTH That an eel is quick.   28

ARMADO I do say thou art quick in answers. Thou heat'st 29
my blood.

MOTH I am answered, sir.

ARMADO I love not to be crossed.

MOTH [aside] He speaks the mere contrary – crosses love 33
not him.

ARMADO I have promised to study three years with the
duke.   35

MOTH You may do it in an hour, sir.

ARMADO Impossible.

MOTH How many is one thrice told?

ARMADO I am ill at reckoning; it fitteth the spirit of a
tapster.

MOTH You are a gentleman and a gamester, sir.

ARMADO I confess both. They are both the varnish of a 42
complete man.

MOTH Then, I am sure you know how much the gross
sum of deuce-ace amounts to.

ARMADO It doth amount to one more than two.

MOTH Which the base vulgar do call three.   47

ARMADO True.

MOTH Why, sir, is this such a piece of study? Now here is
three studied ere ye'll thrice wink; and how easy it is to
put 'years' to the word 'three,' and study three years in
two words, the dancing horse will tell you.   52

ARMADO A most fine figure.   53

MOTH [aside] To prove you a cipher.

ARMADO I will hereupon confess I am in love; and as it is
base for a soldier to love, so am I in love with a base

253 *pricks* spurs   260–61 *at . . . notice* i.e. at your first hint   266 *best . . . worst* i.e. prize example of the bad; *sirrah* (contemptuous or admonitory term of address)   278 *varied* (synonyms in the legal fashion were used in the proclamation)   281 *turn* purpose (with ribald pun following)   285–86 *mutton and porridge* mutton-broth   296 *prosperity! Affliction* (malapropisms)   297 *sit thee down* i.e. abide with me
I, ii   5 *imp* young shoot, child   7 *part* distinguish between   8 *juvenal* youth   9 *working* operation   10 *signor* sir (with pun on senior)   13 *congruent epitheton* appropriate epithet   16 *appertinent* belonging   25 *condign* well-merited   28 *quick* quick-bodied (whereas Armado had used the word to mean quick-witted or ingenious)   29–30 *heat'st my blood* anger me   33 *crosses* coins (which were commonly stamped with crosses)   35 *duke* i.e. the ruler, actually a king   42 *varnish* ornament, finish   47 *vulgar* common people   52 *dancing horse* (a performing horse, trained to 'count' in hoof-beats; the most famous of the time was Master Banks' horse Morocco)   53 *figure* metaphor (with play on numeral)

57 wench. If drawing my sword against the humor of affection would deliver me from the reprobate thought of
60 it, I would take Desire prisoner and ransom him to any
French courtier for a new devised curtsy. I think scorn
61 to sigh: methinks I should outswear Cupid. Comfort
me, boy. What great men have been in love?

MOTH Hercules, master.

ARMADO Most sweet Hercules! More authority, dear
boy, name more; and, sweet my child, let them be men
66 of good repute and carriage.

MOTH Samson, master – he was a man of good carriage,
68 great carriage, for he carried the town-gates on his back
like a porter, and he was in love.

ARMADO O well-knit Samson! strong-jointed Samson! I
do excel thee in my rapier as much as thou didst me in
carrying gates. I am in love too. Who was Samson's
love, my dear Moth?

MOTH A woman, master.

75 ARMADO Of what complexion?

76 MOTH Of all the four, or the three, or the two, or one of
the four.

ARMADO Tell me precisely of what complexion.

MOTH Of the sea-water green, sir.

ARMADO Is that one of the four complexions?

MOTH As I have read, sir, and the best of them too.

82 ARMADO Green indeed is the color of lovers; but to have a
love of that color, methinks Samson had small reason
84 for it. He surely affected her for her wit.

85 MOTH It was so, sir, for she had a green wit.

ARMADO My love is most immaculate white and red.

MOTH Most maculate thoughts, master, are masked
under such colors.

ARMADO Define, define, well-educated infant.

MOTH My father's wit, and my mother's tongue, assist me!

ARMADO Sweet invocation of a child, most pretty and
92 pathetical.

MOTH   If she be made of white and red,
        Her faults will ne'er be known,
      For blushing cheeks by faults are bred,
        And fears by pale white shown;
      Then if she fear, or be to blame,
        By this you shall not know,
      For still her cheeks possess the same
100   Which native she doth owe.

57–58 *humor of affection* inclination to passion   60 *new devised curtsy*
i.e. new-fangled French bow (abundant and worthless); *think scorn* disdain   61 *outswear* forswear   66 *carriage* bearing   68 *carried . . . back*
(cf. Judges xvi, 3)   75 *complexion* (1) skin-coloring, (2) disposition (deriving from the balance or imbalance of the four bodily 'humors' – blood,
choler, phlegm, melancholy)   76–77 *Of . . . four* (probably an allusion
to woman's changeableness)   82 *Green . . . lovers* i.e. lovers are prone
to 'green-sickness' (the melancholy of frustration; cf. *Twelfth Night*,
II, iv, 112)   82–83 *have a love of* i.e. love   84 *affected . . . wit* liked her
for her intelligence   85 *green wit* (1) immature mind, (2) a play on the
'green withes' with which Delilah bound Samson (cf. Judges xvi, 7–9)
92 *pathetical* moving   100 *native* naturally, by birth; *owe* own   101 *the
reason of* the case for   103 *ballet* ballad   103–04 *King . . . Beggar* (the
ballad of King Cophetua, who fell in love with a beggar-maid; cf. IV, i,
65–67)   107 *serve* be adequate   109 *example* justify; *digression* deviation,
lapse   111 *rational* i.e. rational for a yokel (patronizing rather than complimentary)   112 *love* partner in a love-affair   120 *penance* (a malapropism, possibly for 'pleasaunce'); *'a* he   121–22 *allowed . . . day-
woman* approved as the dairy-maid   130 *With that face* i.e. you don't say
so (slang; all of Jaquenetta's smart replies seem to be rustic cant)   138–39
on . . . stomach (1) courageously, (2) well-fed   146 *fast and loose* cheating
(deriving from a game involving cheating and associated with gypsies)
148 *desolation* (malapropism, possibly for 'consolation')   155 *affect*
love   157 *argument* proof

A dangerous rime, master, against the reason of white 101
and red.

ARMADO Is there not a ballet, boy, of the King and the 103
Beggar?

MOTH The world was very guilty of such a ballet some
three ages since; but I think now 'tis not to be found; or
if it were, it would neither serve for the writing nor the 107
tune.

ARMADO I will have that subject newly writ o'er, that I
may example my digression by some mighty precedent. 109
Boy, I do love that country girl that I took in the park
with the rational hind Costard. She deserves well. 111

MOTH [aside] To be whipped; and yet a better love than 112
my master.

ARMADO Sing, boy. My spirit grows heavy in love.

MOTH And that's great marvel, loving a light wench.

ARMADO I say, sing.

MOTH Forbear till this company be past.
     Enter [Costard, the] Clown, [Dull, the] Constable,
     and [Jaquenetta, a] Wench.

DULL Sir, the duke's pleasure is that you keep Costard
safe, and you must suffer him to take no delight nor no
penance, but 'a must fast three days a week. For this 120
damsel, I must keep her at the park; she is allowed for 121
the day-woman. Fare you well.

ARMADO I do betray myself with blushing. Maid!

JAQUENETTA Man?

ARMADO I will visit thee at the lodge.

JAQUENETTA That's hereby.

ARMADO I know where it is situate.

JAQUENETTA Lord, how wise you are!

ARMADO I will tell thee wonders.

JAQUENETTA With that face?   130

ARMADO I love thee.

JAQUENETTA So I heard you say.

ARMADO And so farewell.

JAQUENETTA Fair weather after you!

DULL Come, Jaquenetta, away!
        Exeunt [Dull and Jaquenetta].

ARMADO Villain, thou shalt fast for thy offenses ere thou
be pardoned.

COSTARD Well, sir, I hope when I do it I shall do it on a 138
full stomach.

ARMADO Thou shalt be heavily punished.

COSTARD I am more bound to you than your fellows, for
they are but lightly rewarded.

ARMADO Take away this villain. Shut him up.

MOTH Come, you transgressing slave, away!

COSTARD Let me not be pent up, sir. I will fast, being
loose.

MOTH No, sir; that were fast and loose. Thou shalt to 146
prison.

COSTARD Well, if ever I do see the merry days of desola- 148
tion that I have seen, some shall see –

MOTH What shall some see?

COSTARD Nay, nothing, Master Moth, but what they
look upon. It is not for prisoners to be too silent in their
words, and therefore I will say nothing. I thank God I
have as little patience as another man, and therefore I
can be quiet.   *Exit [with Moth].*

ARMADO I do affect the very ground (which is base) where 155
her shoe (which is baser) guided by her foot (which is
basest) doth tread. I shall be forsworn (which is a great ar- 157
gument of falsehood) if I love. And how can that be true

159 love which is falsely attempted? Love is a familiar; Love
is a devil. There is no evil angel but Love. Yet was Samson so tempted, and he had an excellent strength; yet
was Solomon so seduced, and he had a very good wit.
163 Cupid's butt-shaft is too hard for Hercules' club, and
164 therefore too much odds for a Spaniard's rapier. The first
165 and second cause will not serve my turn: the passado he
166 respects not, the duello he regards not. His disgrace is to
be called boy, but his glory is to subdue men. Adieu,
168 valor! rust, rapier! be still, drum! for your manager is
169 in love; yea, he loveth. Assist me some extemporal god
170 of rime, for I am sure I shall turn sonnet. Devise, wit!
write, pen! for I am for whole volumes in folio. *Exit.*

*

II, i   *Enter the Princess of France, with three attending*
Ladies, [Rosaline, Maria, Katharine,] and three
Lords [, one of whom is Boyet].

BOYET
1 Now, madam, summon up your dearest spirits.
Consider who the king your father sends,
3 To whom he sends, and what's his embassy:
Yourself, held precious in the world's esteem,
5 To parley with the sole inheritor
6 Of all perfections that a man may owe,
7 ·Matchless Navarre; the plea of no less weight
Than Aquitaine, a dowry for a queen.
Be now as prodigal of all dear grace
As Nature was in making graces dear,
When she did starve the general world beside,
And prodigally gave them all to you.

PRINCESS
Good Lord Boyet, my beauty, though but mean,
14 Needs not the painted flourish of your praise:
Beauty is bought by judgment of the eye,
16 Not uttered by base sale of chapmen's tongues.
17 I am less proud to hear you tell my worth
Than you much willing to be counted wise
In spending your wit in the praise of mine.
20 But now to task the tasker; good Boyet,
You are not ignorant, all-telling fame
Doth noise abroad Navarre hath made a vow
23 Till painful study shall outwear three years,
No woman may approach his silent court:
25 Therefore to's seemeth it a needful course,
Before we enter his forbidden gates,
To know his pleasure; and in that behalf,
28 Bold of your worthiness, we single you
29 As our best-moving fair solicitor.
Tell him, the daughter of the King of France,
On serious business, craving quick dispatch,
Importunes personal conference with his Grace.
Haste, signify so much; while we attend,
Like humble-visaged suitors, his high will.

BOYET
Proud of employment, willingly I go.   *Exit Boyet.*

PRINCESS
36 All pride is willing pride, and yours is so.
37 Who are the votaries, my loving lords,
That are vow-fellows with this virtuous duke?

LORD
Longaville is one.

PRINCESS   Know you the man?

MARIA
I know him, madam. At a marriage feast
Between Lord Perigort and the beauteous heir   41
Of Jacques Falconbridge solemnizèd   42
In Normandy saw I this Longaville.
A man of sovereign parts he is esteemed,
Well fitted in arts, glorious in arms;   45
Nothing becomes him ill that he would well.   46
The only soil of his fair virtue's gloss   47
(If virtue's gloss will stain with any soil)
Is a sharp wit matched with too blunt a will,   49
Whose edge hath power to cut, whose will still wills   50
It should none spare that come within his power.

PRINCESS
Some merry mocking lord, belike – is't so?

MARIA
They say so most that most his humors know.

PRINCESS
Such short-lived wits do wither as they grow.
Who are the rest?

KATHARINE
The young Dumaine, a well-accomplished youth,
Of all that virtue love for virtue loved;   57
Most power to do most harm, least knowing ill,   58
For he hath wit to make an ill shape good,
And shape to win grace though he had no wit.
I saw him at the Duke Alençon's once;
And much too little of that good I saw   62
Is my report to his great worthiness.   63

ROSALINE
Another of these students at that time
Was there with him, if I have heard a truth.
Berowne they call him; but a merrier man,
Within the limit of becoming mirth,
I never spent an hour's talk withal.   68
His eye begets occasion for his wit;
For every object that the one doth catch
The other turns to a mirth-moving jest,
Which his fair tongue, conceit's expositor,   72
Delivers in such apt and gracious words,
That agèd ears play truant at his tales,   74
And younger hearings are quite ravishèd,

159 *familiar* evil spirit 163 *butt-shaft* unbarbed target arrow **164–65**
first . . . cause (an allusion to certain procedures dictated by the punctilio
of the duelling code) 165 *passado* fencing thrust 166 *duello* duelling
code 168 *manager* skilled manipulator 169–70 *extemporal . . . rime* god of
fluent occasional verses 170 *turn sonnet* compose a sonnet (?), turn
sonneteer (?)
II, i 1 *dearest spirits* best wits 3 *what's* the nature of 5 *inheritor* possessor 6 *owe* own 7 *plea* suit 14 *flourish* adornment 16 *uttered*
vended; *chapmen's* retailers' 17 *tell* speak of (with play on 'count') 20
task assign tasks to 23 *painful* strenuous; *outwear* last out 25 *to's*
to us (royal plural) 28 *Bold* confident 29 *best-moving fair* most persuasive and just 36 *All . . . pride* i.e. all pride derives from man's rebellious will (?) 37 *votaries* those living under a vow, often including a
vow of celibacy 41, 42 *Lord Perigort, Jacques Falconbridge* (fictitious
persons) 45 *fitted in arts* equipped with learning 46 *Nothing . . . well*
i.e. lacking in no grace he values 47 *soil of* blot on 49 *blunt* ruthless
50 *Whose edge* i.e. the edge of his sharp wit 57 *Of . . . loved* loved for
his virtue by all who love virtue 58–60 *Most . . . wit* (the sense seems
to be that the most virtuous people, like Dumaine, can do the most harm,
because they induce in us a fallacious belief in perfection; in them even
vices look like virtues) 62 *little* short 63 *to* compared with, in view
of 68 *withal* with 72 *conceit's* fancy's 74 *play truant* i.e. neglect serious
matters

76 So sweet and voluble is his discourse.

PRINCESS
God bless my ladies! Are they all in love,
That every one her own hath garnishèd
With such bedecking ornaments of praise?

LORD
Here comes Boyet.
     Enter Boyet.

PRINCESS   Now, what admittance, lord?

BOYET
Navarre had notice of your fair approach;
82 And he and his competitors in oath
83 Were all addressed to meet you, gentle lady,
Before I came. Marry, thus much I have learnt;
He rather means to lodge you in the field,
Like one that comes here to besiege his court,
Than seek a dispensation for his oath
88 To let you enter his unpeopled house.
     Enter Navarre, Longaville, Dumaine, and Berowne.
Here comes Navarre.

KING Fair princess, welcome to the court of Navarre.

PRINCESS 'Fair' I give you back again; and 'welcome' I
92 have not yet. The roof of this court is too high to be yours,
and welcome to the wide fields too base to be mine.

KING
You shall be welcome, madam, to my court.

PRINCESS
I will be welcome, then. Conduct me thither.

KING
Hear me, dear lady – I have sworn an oath.

PRINCESS
Our Lady help my lord! he'll be forsworn.

KING
98 Not for the world, fair madam, by my will.

PRINCESS
Why, will shall break it; will, and nothing else.

KING
Your ladyship is ignorant what it is.

PRINCESS
Were my lord so, his ignorance were wise,
102 Where now his knowledge must prove ignorance.
103 I hear your Grace hath sworn out house-keeping:
'Tis deadly sin to keep that oath, my lord,
And sin to break it.
But pardon me, I am too sudden-bold:
To teach a teacher ill beseemeth me.
Vouchsafe to read the purpose of my coming,
109 And suddenly resolve me in my suit.
     [Gives a paper.]

KING
Madam, I will, if suddenly I may.

PRINCESS
111 You will the sooner that I were away,
For you'll prove perjured if you make me stay.

---

76 *voluble* fluent 82 *competitors* partners 83 *addressed* prepared 88 *unpeopled* without servants 92 *roof . . . court* i.e. the heavens 98 *by my will* willingly 102 *Where* whereas 103 *sworn out house-keeping* sworn away hospitality 109 *suddenly resolve* quickly dispatch 111 *that . . . away* to procure my absence 117 *'long* because 122 *fair befall* good luck to 123 *fall* befall 127 *doth intimate* goes into, canvasses 135 *valued* equal in value 142 *and not demands* i.e. instead of demanding 147 *gelded* maimed, stripped 150 *A . . . reason* i.e. a fairly reasonable yielding (as compared with the totally unreasonable one proposed by her father) 154 *unseeming* not seeming

BEROWNE
Did not I dance with you in Brabant once?

ROSALINE
Did not I dance with you in Brabant once?

BEROWNE
I know you did.

ROSALINE   How needless was it then
To ask the question!

BEROWNE   You must not be so quick.

ROSALINE
117 'Tis 'long of you that spur me with such questions.

BEROWNE
Your wit 's too hot, it speeds too fast, 'twill tire.

ROSALINE
Not till it leave the rider in the mire.

BEROWNE
What time o' day?

ROSALINE
The hour that fools should ask.

BEROWNE
122 Now fair befall your mask!

ROSALINE
123 Fair fall the face it covers!

BEROWNE
And send you many lovers!

ROSALINE
Amen, so you be none.

BEROWNE
Nay, then will I be gone.

KING
127 Madam, your father here doth intimate
The payment of a hundred thousand crowns;
Being but the one half of an entire sum
Disbursèd by my father in his wars.
But say that he, or we (as neither have),
Received that sum, yet there remains unpaid
A hundred thousand more; in surety of the which,
One part of Aquitaine is bound to us,
135 Although not valued to the money's worth.
If then the king your father will restore
But that one half which is unsatisfied,
We will give up our right in Aquitaine,
And hold fair friendship with his Majesty.
But that, it seems, he little purposeth,
For here he doth demand to have repaid
142 A hundred thousand crowns; and not demands,
On payment of a hundred thousand crowns,
To have his title live in Aquitaine;
Which we much rather had depart withal,
And have the money by our father lent,
147 Than Aquitaine, so gelded as it is.
Dear princess, were not his requests so far
From reason's yielding, your fair self should make
150 A yielding 'gainst some reason in my breast,
And go well satisfied to France again.

PRINCESS
You do the king my father too much wrong,
And wrong the reputation of your name,
154 In so unseeming to confess receipt
Of that which hath so faithfully been paid.

KING
I do protest I never heard of it;
And if you prove it, I'll repay it back
Or yield up Aquitaine.

158 PRINCESS   We arrest your word.
Boyet, you can produce acquittances
For such a sum from special officers
Of Charles his father.
KING   Satisfy me so.
BOYET
So please your Grace, the packet is not come
163 Where that and other specialties are bound.
To-morrow you shall have a sight of them.
KING
It shall suffice me – at which interview
All liberal reason I will yield unto.
Meantime, receive such welcome at my hand
As honor, without breach of honor, may
169 Make tender of to thy true worthiness.
You may not come, fair princess, within my gates;
But here without you shall be so received
172 As you shall deem yourself lodged in my heart,
Though so denied fair harbor in my house.
Your own good thoughts excuse me, and farewell.
To-morrow shall we visit you again.
PRINCESS
176 Sweet health and fair desires consort your Grace.
KING
Thy own wish wish I thee in every place.
              Exit [with Longaville and Dumaine].
BEROWNE Lady, I will commend you to mine own heart.
ROSALINE Pray you, do my commendations; I would be
glad to see it.
BEROWNE I would you heard it groan.
182 ROSALINE Is the fool sick?
BEROWNE Sick at the heart.
ROSALINE
184 Alack, let it blood.
BEROWNE
Would that do it good?
ROSALINE
My physic says 'ay.'
BEROWNE
Will you prick't with your eye?
ROSALINE
188 No point, with my knife.
BEROWNE
Now, God save thy life.
ROSALINE
And yours from long living.
BEROWNE
I cannot stay thanksgiving.   Exit.
              Enter Dumaine.
DUMAINE
Sir, I pray you a word: what lady is that same?
BOYET
The heir of Alençon, Katharine her name.
DUMAINE
A gallant lady. Monsieur, fare you well.   Exit.
              [Enter Longaville.]
LONGAVILLE
I beseech you a word: what is she in the white?
BOYET
196 A woman sometimes, an you saw her in the light.
LONGAVILLE
197 Perchance light in the light. I desire her name.
BOYET
She hath but one for herself; to desire that were a shame.

LONGAVILLE
Pray you, sir, whose daughter?
BOYET
Her mother's, I have heard.
LONGAVILLE
God's blessing on your beard!
BOYET
Good sir, be not offended.
She is an heir of Falconbridge.
LONGAVILLE
Nay, my choler is ended.
She is a most sweet lady.
BOYET
Not unlike, sir; that may be.   Exit Longaville.
              Enter Berowne.
BEROWNE
What's her name, in the cap?
BOYET
Rosaline, by good hap.
BEROWNE
Is she wedded or no?
BOYET
To her will, sir, or so.
BEROWNE
You are welcome, sir. Adieu.
BOYET
Farewell to me, sir, and welcome to you.   Exit Berowne. 212
MARIA
That last is Berowne, the merry madcap lord.
Not a word with him but a jest.
BOYET   And every jest but a word.
PRINCESS
It was well done of you to take him at his word.   215
BOYET
I was as willing to grapple, as he was to board.
KATHARINE
Two hot sheeps, marry!
BOYET   And wherefore not ships?
No sheep, sweet lamb, unless we feed on your lips.
KATHARINE
You sheep, and I pasture: shall that finish the jest?   219
BOYET
So you grant pasture for me.
KATHARINE   Not so, gentle beast.
My lips are no common, though several they be.   221
BOYET
Belonging to whom?
KATHARINE   To my fortunes and me.
PRINCESS
Good wits will be jangling; but, gentles, agree.
This civil war of wits were much better used
On Navarre and his book-men, for here 'tis abused.   225
BOYET
If my observation (which very seldom lies)

158 arrest seize as hostage 163 specialties documentary evidence 169
tender offer 172 As that 176 consort dwell with 182 fool (a common
term of affection or humorous abuse) 184 let it blood i.e. cure it by bleeding 188 No point no (adapted from French negative 'ne ... point' with a
pun on 'point') 196 an if 197 light ... light i.e. wanton, if clearly seen
212 Farewell ... you i.e. I welcome your farewell 215 take ... word i.e.
contend with him at word-play 219 pasture (a play on 'pastor,' meaning
shepherd) 221 common common grazing ground; though since; several
two lips (with play on 'several' in the legal sense of private lands as opposed
to common lands) 225 abused misused

227 By the heart's still rhetoric disclosèd with eyes
Deceive me not now, Navarre is infected.

PRINCESS With what?

BOYET

230 With that which we lovers entitle affected.

PRINCESS Your reason?

BOYET

232 Why, all his behaviors did make their retire
To the court of his eye, peeping thorough desire.

234 His heart, like an agate, with your print impressèd,
235 Proud with his form, in his eye pride expressèd.
236 His tongue, all impatient to speak and not see,
237 Did stumble with haste in his eyesight to be;
All senses to that sense did make their repair,
239 To feel only looking on fairest of fair.
Methought all his senses were locked in his eye,
As jewels in crystal for some prince to buy;
242 Who, tend'ring their own worth from where they were
glassed,
243 Did point you to buy them, along as you passed.
244 His face's own margent did quote such amazes,
That all eyes saw his eyes enchanted with gazes.
246 I'll give you Aquitaine, and all that is his,
247 An you give him for my sake but one loving kiss.

PRINCESS

248 Come to our pavilion. Boyet is disposed.

BOYET

But to speak that in words which his eye hath disclosed.
I only have made a mouth of his eye,
By adding a tongue which I know will not lie.

ROSALINE

Thou art an old love-monger, and speakest skilfully.

MARIA

He is Cupid's grandfather, and learns news of him.

KATHARINE

Then was Venus like her mother, for her father is but
grim.

BOYET

Do you hear, my mad wenches?

ROSALINE   No.

BOYET   What, then, do you see?

ROSALINE

Ay, our way to be gone.

BOYET   You are too hard for me.

Exeunt omnes.

*

227 *rhetoric* language   230 *affected* being moved by passion   232 *behaviors* attitudes   234 *agate* (initials and designs were commonly engraved
– *impressed* – on agates)   235 *with his* with its; *pride* i.e. the eye was proud
of the privilege of holding your image   236 *all . . . see* i.e. impatient at
being a speaking rather than a seeing organ   237 *in . . . be* i.e. to share
the sight of the eyes   239 *To feel only* i.e. to concentrate on   242 *Who,
tend'ring* which, offering; *glassed* encased in the crystal of his eyes   243
point indicate, invite   244 *His . . . amazes* i.e. his amazed expression was a
commentary on what his eyes beheld (commentaries or glosses were often
printed on the margin – *margent* – of books)   246 *I'll give you* i.e. you can
have   247 *An* if   248 *disposed* i.e. in the mood
III, i   1 *make passionate* render responsive   3 *Concolinel* (unidentified;
possibly the name or refrain of a song)   5 *festinately* quickly   7 *brawl*
(a figure dance)   10 *canary* dance with improvisations   14 *penthouse* (an
overhang, such as often sheltered shops)   15–16 *on . . . doublet* i.e. on
the doublet covering your thin belly   17 *old painting* (unidentified)   18
snip snippet, scrap   19 *complements* accomplishments; *humors* mannerisms; *nice coy*   22 *affected* drawn, given   25–26 *But O . . . forgot* (refrain
of a popular song)   27–29 *hobby-horse, colt, hackney* (cant terms for
prostitutes)   43 *me* for me   44 *sympathized* harmonized   53 *Minime* by
no means (Latin)

Enter [Armado, the] Braggart, and [Moth,] his Boy. III, i

ARMADO Warble, child; make passionate my sense of 1
hearing.

MOTH *[sings]* Concolinel. 3

ARMADO Sweet air! Go, tenderness of years, take this
key, give enlargement to the swain, bring him festinately 5
hither. I must employ him in a letter to my love.

MOTH Master, will you win your love with a French
brawl? 7

ARMADO How meanest thou? Brawling in French?

MOTH No, my complete master; but to jig off a tune at the
tongue's end, canary to it with your feet, humor it with 10
turning up your eyelids, sigh a note and sing a note, sometime through the throat as if you swallowed love with singing love, sometime through the nose as if you snuffed up
love by smelling love; with your hat penthouse-like o'er 14
the shop of your eyes; with your arms crossed on your 15
thin-belly doublet like a rabbit on a spit; or your hands
in your pocket like a man after the old painting; and 17
keep not too long in one tune, but a snip and away. These 18
are complements, these are humors, these betray nice 19
wenches (that would be betrayed without these), and
make them men of note – do you note – men that most are
affected to these. 22

ARMADO How hast thou purchased this experience?

MOTH By my penny of observation.

ARMADO But O – but O – 25

MOTH The hobby-horse is forgot.

ARMADO Call'st thou my love 'hobby-horse'? 27

MOTH No, master; the hobby-horse is but a colt, and
your love perhaps a hackney. But have you forgot your
love?

ARMADO Almost I had.

MOTH Negligent student! learn her by heart.

ARMADO By heart, and in heart, boy.

MOTH And out of heart, master. All those three I will
prove.

ARMADO What wilt thou prove?

MOTH A man, if I live; and this, by, in, and without, upon
the instant. By heart you love her, because your heart
cannot come by her; in heart you love her, because your
heart is in love with her; and out of heart you love her,
being out of heart that you cannot enjoy her.

ARMADO I am all these three.

MOTH *[aside]* And three times as much more, and yet
nothing at all.

ARMADO Fetch hither the swain. He must carry me a 43
letter.

MOTH *[aside]* A message well sympathized – a horse to be 44
ambassador for an ass.

ARMADO Ha, ha? what sayest thou?

MOTH Marry, sir, you must send the ass upon the horse,
for he is very slow-gaited. But I go.

ARMADO The way is but short. Away!

MOTH As swift as lead, sir.

ARMADO

The meaning, pretty ingenious?
Is not lead a metal heavy, dull, and slow?

MOTH

Minime, honest master; or rather, master, no. 53

ARMADO

I say, lead is slow.

MOTH   You are too swift, sir, to say so.
Is that lead slow which is fired from a gun?

ARMADO

56 Sweet smoke of rhetoric!
He reputes me a cannon; and the bullet, that's he:
I shoot thee at the swain.

58 MOTH   Thump, then, and I flee.
                         [Exit.]

ARMADO

59 A most acute juvenal; voluble and free of grace!
60 By thy favor, sweet welkin, I must sigh in thy face:
61 Most rude melancholy, valor gives thee place.
My herald is returned.
      Enter [Moth, the] Page, and [Costard, the] Clown.

MOTH

63 A wonder, master! Here's a costard broken in a shin.

ARMADO

64 Some enigma, some riddle. Come, thy l'envoy – begin.

65 COSTARD No egma, no riddle, no l'envoy; no salve in the
66 mail, sir. O, sir, plantain, a plain plantain. No l'envoy,
no l'envoy, no salve, sir, but a plantain.

ARMADO By virtue, thou enforcest laughter; thy silly
69 thought, my spleen; the heaving of my lungs provokes
me to ridiculous smiling. O, pardon me, my stars! Doth
71 the inconsiderate take salve for l'envoy, and the word
l'envoy for a salve?

MOTH

Do the wise think them other? Is not l'envoy a salve?

ARMADO

No, page; it is an epilogue, or discourse to make plain
75 Some obscure precedence that hath tofore been sain.
I will example it:
     The fox, the ape, and the humble-bee
     Were still at odds, being but three.
There's the moral. Now the l'envoy.

MOTH I will add the l'envoy. Say the moral again.

ARMADO The fox, the ape, and the humble-bee
     Were still at odds, being but three.

MOTH   Until the goose came out of door,
84   And stayed the odds by adding four.
Now will I begin your moral, and do you follow with
my l'envoy.
     The fox, the ape, and the humble-bee
     Were still at odds, being but three.

89 ARMADO Until the goose came out of door,
     Staying the odds by adding four.

MOTH A good l'envoy, ending in the goose. Would you
desire more?

COSTARD

93 The boy hath sold him a bargain, a goose – that's flat.
94 Sir, your pennyworth is good, an your goose be fat.
95 To sell a bargain well is as cunning as fast and loose.
Let me see – a fat l'envoy – ay, that's a fat goose.

ARMADO

97 Come hither, come hither. How did this argument
begin?

MOTH

By saying that a costard was broken in a shin.
Then called you for the l'envoy.

COSTARD

True, and I for a plantain; thus came your argument in;
Then the boy's fat l'envoy, the goose that you bought;
And he ended the market.

ARMADO But tell me, how was there a costard broken in a
shin?

105 MOTH I will tell you sensibly.

COSTARD Thou hast no feeling of it, Moth. I will speak
that l'envoy:
I, Costard, running out, that was safely within,
Fell over the threshold and broke my shin.

ARMADO We will talk no more of this matter.

COSTARD Till there be more matter in the shin.   111

ARMADO Sirrah Costard, I will enfranchise thee.   112

COSTARD O, marry me to one Frances! I smell some
l'envoy, some goose, in this.

ARMADO By my sweet soul, I mean setting thee at liberty,
enfreedoming thy person. Thou wert immured, restrained, captivated, bound.

COSTARD True, true, and now you will be my purgation
and let me loose.

ARMADO I give thee thy liberty, set thee from durance;
and in lieu thereof, impose on thee nothing but this.
[Gives a letter.] Bear this significant to the country   122
maid – Jaquenetta. *[Gives money.]* There is remuneration; for the best ward of mine honor is rewarding my   124
dependents. Moth, follow.   *[Exit.]*

MOTH

Like the sequel, I. Signor Costard, adieu.   *Exit.*

COSTARD

My sweet ounce of man's flesh, my incony Jew!   127
Now will I look to his remuneration. Remuneration?
O that's the Latin word for three farthings. Three far-
things – remuneration. 'What's the price of this inkle?'   130
'One penny,' 'No, I'll give you a remuneration.' Why, it
carries it! Remuneration! Why, it is a fairer name than   132
French crown. I will never buy and sell out of this word.   133
         Enter Berowne.

BEROWNE My good knave Costard, exceedingly well met.

COSTARD Pray you, sir, how much carnation ribbon may   135
a man buy for a remuneration?

BEROWNE What is a remuneration?

COSTARD Marry, sir, halfpenny farthing.

BEROWNE Why then, three-farthing-worth of silk.

COSTARD I thank your worship. God be wi' you.

BEROWNE Stay, slave; I must employ thee.
As thou wilt win my favor, good my knave,
Do one thing for me that I shall entreat.

COSTARD When would you have it done, sir?

BEROWNE This afternoon.

COSTARD Well, I will do it, sir. Fare you well.

BEROWNE Thou knowest not what it is.

COSTARD I shall know, sir, when I have done it.

BEROWNE Why, villain, thou must know first.

---

56 *smoke* product, essence   58 *Thump* (equivalent to 'bang')   59 *juvenal*
youth   60 *By thy favor* with your permission; *welkin* sky   61 *gives thee*
place gives place to you, i.e. to melancholy   63 *costard* apple or head
(and hence having no shin)   64 *l'envoy* (a commentary or injunction concluding a literary composition)   65 *salve* (the play seems to be on 'salve'
– salute – suggested by *l'envoy*)   66 *mail* pouch (such as might be carried
by a salve-vendor or quacksalver); *plantain* (a homely herbal remedy for
broken shins)   69 *spleen* risibility (laughter supposedly originated in
the spleen)   71 *inconsiderate* i.e. unthinking one   75 *precedence* preceding discourse; *sain* said   84 *stayed* wiped out; *four* a fourth   89
goose i.e. Armado (who has been tricked into the role)   93 *sold . . . bargain*
i.e. outwitted him   94 *your . . . good* i.e. you got your money's worth;
an if   95 *fast and loose* (cf. I, ii, 146)   97 *argument* topic, theme   105
sensibly feelingly   111 *matter* pus   112 *enfranchise* free   122 *significant*
communication   124 *ward* defense   127 *incony* darling; *Jew* (a term of
playful abuse, perhaps suggested by 'juvenile')   130 *inkle* tape   132 *carries*
it takes the prize   133 *French crown* (a coin, frequently associated with
jests about venereal disease); *out of* i.e. without using   135 *carnation* flesh-
colored

150 COSTARD I will come to your worship to-morrow morning.

BEROWNE

It must be done this afternoon. Hark, slave, it is but this:
The princess comes to hunt here in the park,
And in her train there is a gentle lady –
When tongues speak sweetly, then they name her name,
And Rosaline they call her. Ask for her,
And to her white hand see thou do commend

158 This sealed-up counsel. *[Gives letter and a shilling.]*
There's thy guerdon: go.

COSTARD Gardon, O sweet gardon! Better than remuneration – a 'leven-pence farthing better. Most sweet

161 gardon! I will do it, sir, in print. Gardon – remuneration.
Exit.

BEROWNE

And I, forsooth, in love!
I, that have been love's whip,

164 A very beadle to a humorous sigh,
A critic, nay, a night-watch constable,

166 A domineering pedant o'er the boy,
Than whom no mortal so magnificent.

168 This wimpled, whining, purblind, wayward boy,
169 This signor-junior, giant-dwarf, Dan Cupid,
170 Regent of love-rimes, lord of folded arms,
The anointed sovereign of sighs and groans,

172 Liege of all loiterers and malcontents,
173 Dread prince of plackets, king of codpieces,
Sole imperator and great general

175 Of trotting paritors – O my little heart!
And I to be a corporal of his field,

177 And wear his colors like a tumbler's hoop!
What? I love, I sue, I seek a wife!
A woman that is like a German clock,

180 Still a-repairing, ever out of frame,
And never going aright, being a watch,
But being watched that it may still go right!
Nay, to be perjured, which is worst of all;
And, among three, to love the worst of all;

185 A whitely wanton with a velvet brow,
With two pitch balls stuck in her face for eyes.
Ay, and, by heaven, one that will do the deed,

188 Though Argus were her eunuch and her guard.
189 And I to sigh for her, to watch for her,
To pray for her! Go to, it is a plague

158 *counsel* private message; *guerdon* reward 161 *in print* i.e. to the letter 164 *beadle . . . sigh* i.e. an officer of correction to symptoms of love 166 *pedant* schoolmaster 168 *wimpled* veiled; *purblind* wholly blind 169 *Dan* don, sir (from 'dominus') 170 *folded arms* (traditional posture of the melancholy lover) 172 *Liege* lord 173 *plackets* slits in petticoats; *codpieces* padded gussets at the crotch of breeches (like *plackets*, often used in ribald allusion) 175 *paritors* minor officers of ecclesiastical courts who profited by spying out sexual offenses 177 *tumbler's hoop* (an object conspicuously beribboned) 180 *frame* order 185 *whitely* pale-skinned 188 *Argus* (in mythology a monster with a thousand eyes); *eunuch* (guard in a seraglio) 189 *watch* stay awake 194 *Joan* (proverbial name for an ordinary woman)
IV, i 10 *stand* (concealed position toward which the game was driven) 16 *paint* flatter 17 *brow* i.e. face 18 *good my glass* my good mirror 20 *inherit* possess 21 *merit* i.e. good works, the 'alms' she has given the forester 22 *heresy* (in orthodox Anglican doctrine salvation came by faith rather than by good works) 24 *mercy . . . kill* i.e. to the merciful huntsman good shooting (which only wounded so that the kill might be left to the dogs) is ill doing 29 *That . . . kill* i.e. who shot well to win praise rather than from any desire to strike the deer 31 *Glory . . . of* i.e. desire for glory is responsible for 32 *an outward part* a superficial thing 33 *bend* adapt 36 *curst* shrewish; *self-sovereignty* self-rule (instead of rule by their husbands)

That Cupid will impose for my neglect
Of his almighty dreadful little might.
Well, I will love, write, sigh, pray, sue, groan:
Some men must love my lady, and some Joan. *[Exit.]* *194*

*

Enter the Princess, a Forester, her Ladies [Maria, IV, i
*Katharine, Rosaline], and her Lords [Boyet and
others].*

PRINCESS

Was that the king, that spurred his horse so hard
Against the steep uprising of the hill?

BOYET

I know not, but I think it was not he.

PRINCESS

Whoe'er 'a was, 'a showed a mounting mind.
Well, lords, to-day we shall have our dispatch;
On Saturday we will return to France.
Then, forester, my friend, where is the bush
That we must stand and play the murderer in?

FORESTER

Hereby, upon the edge of yonder coppice,
A stand where you may make the fairest shoot. 10

PRINCESS

I thank my beauty, I am fair that shoot,
And thereupon thou speak'st the fairest shoot.

FORESTER

Pardon me, madam, for I meant not so.

PRINCESS

What, what? First praise me, and again say no?
O short-lived pride! Not fair? Alack for woe!

FORESTER

Yes, madam, fair.

PRINCESS   Nay, never paint me now: 16
Where fair is not, praise cannot mend the brow. 17
Here, good my glass, take this for telling true – 18
[Gives money.]
Fair payment for foul words is more than due.

FORESTER

Nothing but fair is that which you inherit. 20

PRINCESS

See, see – my beauty will be saved by merit. 21
O heresy in fair, fit for these days, 22
A giving hand, though foul, shall have fair praise.
But come, the bow. Now mercy goes to kill, 24
And shooting well is then accounted ill.
Thus will I save my credit in the shoot:
Not wounding, pity would not let me do't;
If wounding, then it was to show my skill,
That more for praise than purpose meant to kill. 29
And out of question so it is sometimes,
Glory grows guilty of detested crimes, 31
When, for fame's sake, for praise, an outward part, 32
We bend to that the working of the heart; 33
As I for praise alone now seek to spill
The poor deer's blood, that my heart means no ill.

BOYET

Do not curst wives hold that self-sovereignty 36
Only for praise' sake, when they strive to be
Lords o'er their lords?

PRINCESS

Only for praise; and praise we may afford
To any lady that subdues a lord.
Enter [Costard, the] Clown.

BOYET
41 Here comes a member of the commonwealth.
42 COSTARD God dig-you-den all. Pray you, which is the
    head lady?
PRINCESS Thou shalt know her, fellow, by the rest that
    have no heads.
COSTARD Which is the greatest lady, the highest?
PRINCESS The thickest and the tallest.
COSTARD The thickest and the tallest – it is so. Truth is
    truth.
    An your waist, mistress, were as slender as my wit,
    One o' these maids' girdles for your waist should be fit.
    Are not you the chief woman? You are the thickest here.
PRINCESS What's your will, sir? What's your will?
COSTARD I have a letter from Monsieur Berowne to one
    Lady Rosaline.
PRINCESS
    O thy letter, thy letter! He's a good friend of mine.
    Stand aside, good bearer. Boyet, you can carve;
57 Break up this capon.
    BOYET   I am bound to serve.
58 This letter is mistook; it importeth none here.
    It is writ to Jaquenetta.
PRINCESS   We will read it, I swear.
60 Break the neck of the wax, and every one give ear.
    BOYET (reads) 'By heaven, that thou art fair is most infal-
    lible; true that thou art beauteous; truth itself that thou
    art lovely. More fairer than fair, beautiful than beaute-
    ous, truer than truth itself, have commiseration on thy
65 heroical vassal. The magnanimous and most illustrate
66 king Cophetua set eye upon the pernicious and indubit-
67 ate beggar Zenelophon, and he it was that might rightly
68 say veni, vidi, vici; which to anathomize in the vulgar
    (O base and obscure vulgar!) videlicet, he came, saw,
    and overcame. He came, one; saw, two; overcame,
    three. Who came? The king. Why did he come? To see.
    Why did he see? To overcome. To whom came he? To
    the beggar. What saw he? The beggar. Who overcame
    he? The beggar. The conclusion is victory. On whose
    side? The king's. The captive is enriched. On whose
76 side? The beggar's. The catastrophe is a nuptial. On
    whose side? The king's? No – on both in one, or one in
    both. I am the king (for so stands the comparison), thou
    the beggar (for so witnesseth thy lowliness). Shall I
    command thy love? I may. Shall I enforce thy love? I
    could. Shall I entreat thy love? I will. What shalt thou
82 exchange for rags? Robes. For tittles? Titles. For thy-
    self? Me. Thus, expecting thy reply, I profane my lips
    on thy foot, my eyes on thy picture, and my heart on thy
    every part.
85   Thine in the dearest design of industry,
                            Don Adriano de Armado.
87   Thus dost thou hear the Nemean lion roar
        'Gainst thee, thou lamb, that standest as his prey.
        Submissive fall his princely feet before,
90   And he from forage will incline to play.
        But if thou strive, poor soul, what art thou then?
92   Food for his rage, repasture for his den.'
    PRINCESS
93   What plume of feathers is he that indited this letter?
94   What vane? What weathercock? Did you ever hear
        better?
    BOYET
    I am much deceived but I remember the style.

PRINCESS
    Else your memory is bad, going o'er it erewhile.   96
BOYET
    This Armado is a Spaniard that keeps here in court;   97
    A phantasime, a Monarcho, and one that makes sport   98
    To the prince and his book-mates.
PRINCESS   Thou fellow, a word.
    Who gave thee this letter?
COSTARD   I told you – my lord.
PRINCESS
    To whom shouldst thou give it?
COSTARD   From my lord to my lady.
PRINCESS
    From which lord, to which lady?
COSTARD
    From my lord Berowne, a good master of mine,
    To a lady of France, that he called Rosaline.
PRINCESS
    Thou hast mistaken his letter. Come, lords, away.   105
    Here, sweet, put up this; 'twill be thine another day.   106
            Exeunt [Princess, Forester, and Attendants].
BOYET
    Who is the suitor? Who is the suitor?   107
ROSALINE   Shall I teach you to know?
BOYET
    Ay, my continent of beauty.   108
ROSALINE   Why, she that bears the bow.
    Finely put off!   109
BOYET
    My lady goes to kill horns, but, if thou marry,   110
    Hang me by the neck if horns that year miscarry.
    Finely put on!
ROSALINE
    Well then, I am the shooter.
BOYET   And who is your deer?
ROSALINE
    If we choose by the horns, yourself. Come not near.
    Finely put on, indeed!
MARIA
    You still wrangle with her, Boyet, and she strikes at the
    brow.
BOYET
    But she herself is hit lower. Have I hit her now?
ROSALINE Shall I come upon thee with an old saying that   118
    was a man when King Pepin of France was a little boy, 119
    as touching the hit it?
BOYET So I may answer thee with one as old – that was a

41 commonwealth citizenry 42 dig-you-den give you good evening 57
capon love-letter (from French slang – 'poulet') 58 importeth concerns
60 wax seal 65 illustrate illustrious 66 indubitate indubitable 67 Zenelophon (Penelophon, in the old ballad of 'King Cophetua and the Beggar-
maid') 68 anathomize anatomize, parse 76 catastrophe denouement
82 tittles jots, particles 85 dearest . . . industry i.e. best pattern of assiduous
courtship 87 Nemean lion (slain by Hercules as the first of his labors)
90 forage foraging, ravaging 92 repasture repast 93 plume of feathers
i.e. dandy, coxcomb 94 vane weather-vane (with play on 'vain') 96
erewhile just now 97 keeps dwells 98 phantasime one who indulges in
fantasies; Monarcho (the nickname of an Italian eccentric whose delusions
of grandeur entertained the English court for some years prior to 1580)
105 mistaken wrongly delivered 106 'twill be thine i.e. you will send
one like it 107 suitor (pronounced 'shooter') 108 continent of container
of all 109 put off turned aside 110 horns i.e. a deer (followed by an
allusion to the horns of cuckoldry) 118 come upon thee confront you
119 was a man i.e. was old; King Pepin (Carlovingian king who died in
768)

woman when Queen Guinever of Britain was a little
wench, as touching the hit it.

124 ROSALINE 'Thou canst not hit it, hit it, hit it,
       Thou canst not hit it, my good man.

BOYET   'An I cannot, cannot, cannot,
       An I cannot, another can.'   *Exit [Rosaline]*.

COSTARD
By my troth, most pleasant, how both did fit it!

MARIA
129 A mark marvellous well shot, for they both did hit it.

BOYET
A mark! (O mark but that mark!) A mark, says my lady!
131 Let the mark have a prick in't to mete at if it may be.

MARIA
132 Wide o' the bow hand! I' faith your hand is out.

COSTARD
133 Indeed 'a must shoot nearer, or he'll ne'er hit the clout.

BOYET
An if my hand be out, then belike your hand is in.

COSTARD
135 Then will she get the upshoot by cleaving the pin.

MARIA
136 Come, come, you talk greasily; your lips grow foul.

COSTARD
137 She's too hard for you at pricks. Sir, challenge her to
    bowl.

BOYET
138 I fear too much rubbing. Good night, my good owl.
                        [Exeunt Boyet and Maria.]

COSTARD
By my soul, a swain, a most simple clown!
Lord, lord, how the ladies and I have put him down!
141 O' my troth, most sweet jests, most incony vulgar wit!
142 When it comes so smoothly off, so obscenely as it were,
    so fit.
143 Armado o' th' t' one side – O, a most dainty man!
To see him walk before a lady, and to bear her fan,
To see him kiss his hand, and how most sweetly 'a will
    swear;

124–27 Thou . . . can (adapted from a ribald song and dance of the period)
129 mark target *131 prick* (center point or strip in the target); *mete
at* measure by *132 Wide . . . hand* too far left *133 clout* white-headed
pin in center of target *135 upshoot* leading shot in a contest *136 greasily*
grossly (referring to double-entendres preceding) *137 pricks* informal
or illegal archery *138 rubbing* grazing (a bowling term) *141 incony*
darling; *vulgar* popular (?) *142 obscenely* (unconsciously apt malapropism – for 'seemly'?) *143–47 Armado . . . nit* (unless Costard is
simply recalling something he has previously observed offstage, this unexpected reference to Armado and Moth may indicate a gap in the present
version of the scene) *147 pathetical nit* pleasing mite *148 Sola, sola* (a
hunting cry)
IV, ii *1 reverend* revered *1–2 in the testimony* with the warrant *3–4
in blood* in prime condition *4 pomewater* (a variety of apple) *6 crab*
crab-apple *9 at the least* to say the least *10 of . . . head* of the fifth
year (and therefore a *buck*; Holofernes has called it a *deer*) *11 Sir* dominus (term of address for a clergyman in minor orders); *haud credo* I do
not think so *12 not . . . credo* (Dull has mistaken the Latin 'credo' for a
reference to some kind of 'doe'); *pricket* (male deer of the second year)
13 intimation intrusion *14 insinuation* interpretation *15 facere . . .
replication* to give another explanation (Holofernes' words, exploiting
presumed literal meanings, may be called 'pedanticisms') *18 insert* put
in, interpret *21 sod* sodden; *bis coctus* twice-cooked, sodden *28 Which
we* we who; *fructify* grow fruitful; *he* in him *30 patch . . . learning* (1)
disfigurement of education, (2) clown put to school *31 omne bene* all's
well; *father's* sage's *32 brook* put up with (i.e. what can't be cured must
be endured) *35 Dictynna* Diana, the moon *39 raught* reached *40
allusion* dark saying, riddle; *exchange* substitution (of Adam's name for
Cain's)

And his page o' t' other side, that handful of wit,
Ah, heavens, it is a most pathetical nit!   147
     Shout within.
Sola, sola!   *[Exit.]* 148

*

    Enter Dull, Holofernes the Pedant, and Nathaniel.   IV, ii

NATHANIEL Very reverend sport, truly, and done in the 1
    testimony of a good conscience.

HOLOFERNES The deer was, as you know, sanguis, in 3
    blood; ripe as the pomewater, who now hangeth like a 4
    jewel in the ear of coelo, the sky, the welkin, the heaven;
    and anon falleth like a crab on the face of terra, the soil, 6
    the land, the earth.

NATHANIEL Truly, Master Holofernes, the epithets are
    sweetly varied, like a scholar at the least; but sir, I 9
    assure ye it was a buck of the first head.   10

HOLOFERNES Sir Nathaniel, haud credo.   11

DULL 'Twas not a haud credo; 'twas a pricket.   12

HOLOFERNES Most barbarous intimation! Yet a kind of 13
    insinuation, as it were, in via, in way, of explication; 14
    facere, as it were, replication, or rather, ostentare, to 15
    show, as it were, his inclination – after his undressed,
    unpolished, uneducated, unpruned, untrained, or,
    rather, unlettered, or, ratherest, unconfirmed fashion –
    to insert again my haud credo for a deer.   18

DULL I said the deer was not a haud credo – 'twas a
    pricket.

HOLOFERNES Twice sod simplicity, bis coctus!   21
    O thou monster Ignorance, how deformèd dost thou
    look!

NATHANIEL
Sir, he hath never fed of the dainties that are bred in a
    book.
He hath not eat paper, as it were; he hath not drunk ink.
His intellect is not replenished; he is only an animal,
    only sensible in the duller parts.
And such barren plants are set before us that we thank-
    ful should be,
Which we of taste and feeling are, for those parts that do 28
    fructify in us more than he;
For as it would ill become me to be vain, indiscreet, or a
    fool:
So were there a patch set on learning, to see him in a 30
    school.
But, omne bene, say I, being of an old father's mind,   31
Many can brook the weather that love not the wind.   32

DULL
You two are book-men. Can you tell me by your wit,
What was a month old at Cain's birth that's not five
    weeks old as yet?

HOLOFERNES
Dictynna, goodman Dull. Dictynna, goodman Dull.   35

DULL What is Dictynna?

NATHANIEL A title to Phoebe, to Luna, to the moon.

HOLOFERNES
The moon was a month old when Adam was no more,
And raught not to five weeks when he came to five-score. 39
Th' allusion holds in the exchange.   40

DULL 'Tis true indeed; the collusion holds in the ex-
    change.

HOLOFERNES God comfort thy capacity! I say th' allusion
    holds in the exchange.

DULL And I say the pollution holds in the exchange, for the moon is never but a month old; and I say beside that 'twas a pricket that the princess killed.

47 HOLOFERNES Sir Nathaniel, will you hear an extemporal epitaph on the death of the deer? And, to humor the ignorant, call I the deer the princess killed, a pricket.

50 NATHANIEL Perge, good Master Holofernes, perge, so it shall please you to abrogate scurrility.

52 HOLOFERNES I will something affect the letter, for it argues facility.

The preyful princess pierced and pricked a pretty pleasing pricket;

55 Some say a sore, but not a sore till now made sore with shooting.

56 The dogs did yell. Put l to sore, then sorel jumps from thicket;

57 Or pricket, sore, or else sorel. The people fall a hooting.

58 If sore be sore, then l to sore makes fifty sores – O sore l! Of one sore I an hundred make by adding but one more l.

NATHANIEL A rare talent!

61 DULL If a talent be a claw, look how he claws him with a talent.

HOLOFERNES This is a gift that I have, simple, simple; a foolish extravagant spirit, full of forms, figures, shapes, objects, ideas, apprehensions, motions, revolutions.

66 These are begot in the ventricle of memory, nourished

67 in the womb of pia mater, and delivered upon the mellowing of occasion. But the gift is good in those in whom it is acute, and I am thankful for it.

NATHANIEL Sir, I praise the Lord for you, and so may my parishioners; for their sons are well tutored by you, and their daughters profit very greatly under you. You are a good member of the commonwealth.

74 HOLOFERNES Mehercle, if their sons be ingenious, they

75 shall want no instruction; if their daughters be capable,

76 I will put it to them. But, vir sapit qui pauca, loquitur. A soul feminine saluteth us.

Enter Jaquenetta and [Costard,] the Clown.

78 JAQUENETTA God give you good morrow, Master Person.

79 HOLOFERNES Master Person, quasi pers-one? And if

80 one should be pierced, which is the one?

COSTARD Marry, Master Schoolmaster, he that is likest to a hogshead.

83 HOLOFERNES Of piercing a hogshead! A good lustre of conceit in a turf of earth, fire enough for a flint, pearl enough for a swine – 'tis pretty, it is well.

JAQUENETTA Good Master Person, be so good as read me this letter. It was given me by Costard, and sent me from Don Armado. I beseech you read it.

89 HOLOFERNES Facile precor gelida quando pecas omnia sub umbra ruminat, and so forth. Ah, good old Mantuan. I may speak of thee as the traveller doth of Venice:

92   Venechia, Venechia, Que non te vede, que non te prechia.

Old Mantuan, old Mantuan! Who understandeth thee

95 not, loves thee not. Ut, re, sol, la, mi, fa. Under pardon, sir, what are the contents? or, rather, as Horace says in his – What my soul! Verses?

NATHANIEL Ay, sir, and very learned.

99 HOLOFERNES Let me hear a staff, a stanze, a verse. Lege, domine.

NATHANIEL *[reads]*

'If love make me forsworn, how shall I swear to love?

Ah, never faith could hold if not to beauty vowed!

Though to myself forsworn, to thee I'll faithful prove;

104 Those thoughts to me were oaks, to thee like osiers bowed.

105 Study his bias leaves and makes his book thine eyes, Where all those pleasures live that art would comprehend.

If knowledge be the mark, to know thee shall suffice:

Well learnèd is that tongue that well can thee commend,

All ignorant that soul that sees thee without wonder;

110 Which is to me some praise, that I thy parts admire.

Thy eye Jove's lightning bears, thy voice his dreadful thunder,

Which, not to anger bent, is music and sweet fire.

Celestial as thou art, O pardon love this wrong,

That sings heaven's praise with such an earthly tongue!'

115 HOLOFERNES You find not the apostrophus, and so miss

116 the accent. Let me supervise the canzonet. Here are

117 only numbers ratified; but, for the elegancy, facility,

118 and golden cadence of poesy, caret. Ovidius Naso was the man; and why indeed 'Naso' but for smelling out

120 the odoriferous flowers of fancy, the jerks of invention?

121 Imitari is nothing. So doth the hound his master, the

122 ape his keeper, the tired horse his rider. But, damosella virgin, was this directed to you?

JAQUENETTA Ay, sir, from one Monsieur Berowne, one

125 of the strange queen's lords.

126 HOLOFERNES I will overglance the superscript. 'To the snow-white hand of the most beauteous Lady Rosaline.'

128 I will look again on the intellect of the letter, for the nomination of the party writing to the person written unto. 'Your ladyship's, in all desired employment, Berowne.' Sir Nathaniel, this Berowne is one of the votaries with

132 the king; and here he hath framed a letter to a sequent of

133 the stranger queen's, which accidentally, or by the way of progression, hath miscarried. Trip and go, my sweet; deliver this paper into the royal hand of the king; it may

---

47 *extemporal* extempory 50 *Perge* proceed 52 *affect the letter* i.e. lean to the use of alliteration 55 *sore* (deer of the fourth year) 56 *sorel* (deer of the third year) 57 *Or* either 58 *l* (roman numeral fifty) 61 *talent* i.e. talon; *claws* scratches, flatters 66 *ventricle* (of the three sections or 'ventricles' of the brain one was believed to contain the memory) 67 *womb of pia mater* center of the enclosing membrane or purse 74 *Mehercle* by Hercules 75 *capable* (1) able, (2) sexually mature (operating with other double-entendres of the passage) 76 *vir . . . loquitur* the man is wise who speaks little 78 *Person* (pronunciation of 'parson') 79 *quasi* that is 80 *pierced* (pronounced 'persed') 83–84 *lustre of conceit* gleam of fancy 89–90 *Facile . . . ruminat* (a misquotation of the opening of the first eclogue of Mantuanus – a common school tag: '*Fauste, precor gelida quando pecus omne sub umbra ruminat*': Faustus, I beg, while all the cattle ruminate beneath the cool shade) 92–93 *Venechia . . . prechia* (rugged form of an Italian proverb appearing in Florio's *First Fruits*, 1578: Venice, Venice, who loves you not sees you not) 95 *Ut* (since replaced by 'Do'; Holofernes is incorrectly singing the scale) 99–100 *Lege, domine* read, master 104 *thoughts . . . were* resolutions which seemed to me 105 *his bias leaves* i.e. abandons its previous inclinations 110 *praise* credit, honor 115 *find* regard; *apostrophus* apostrophe (disregarding contractions indicated by apostrophes can spoil the metre, but perhaps Holofernes is using learned terms at random) 116 *supervise* look over; *canzonet* ditty 117 *numbers ratified* i.e. mechanical versification 118 *caret* it is lacking; *Naso* (from 'nasus,' nose) 120 *jerks of invention* strokes of wit 121 *Imitari* to imitate 122 *tired* spiritless (Holofernes seems to be linking imitativeness and docility) 125 *strange* foreign (but Berowne, contrary to Jaquenetta's remark, is native) 126 *superscript* address 128 *intellect* final rhetorical flourish (?) 132 *sequent* follower 133–34 *by . . . progression* i.e. en route

136   concern much. Stay not thy compliment; I forgive thy
duty. Adieu.

JAQUENETTA Good Costard, go with me. Sir, God save
your life.

COSTARD Have with thee, my girl.

Exit [with Jaquenetta].

NATHANIEL Sir, you have done this in the fear of God
very religiously; and, as a certain father saith –

143 HOLOFERNES Sir, tell not me of the father; I do fear colorable colors. But to return to the verses – did they
please you, Sir Nathaniel?

146 NATHANIEL Marvellous well for the pen.

HOLOFERNES I do dine to-day at the father's of a certain
pupil of mine, where, if before repast it shall please you
to gratify the table with a grace, I will, on my privilege I
have with the parents of the foresaid child or pupil,
151   undertake your ben venuto; where I will prove those
verses to be very unlearned, neither savoring of poetry,
wit, nor invention. I beseech your society.

154 NATHANIEL And thank you too, for society (saith the text)
is the happiness of life.

HOLOFERNES And, certes, the text most infallibly concludes it. [to Dull] Sir, I do invite you too; you shall not
158   say me nay. Pauca verba. Away! The gentles are at their
game, and we will to our recreation.   *Exeunt.*

*

IV, iii   *Enter Berowne with a paper in his hand, alone.*

BEROWNE The king he is hunting the deer; I am coursing
2   myself. They have pitched a toil; I am toiling in a pitch
3   – pitch that defiles. Defile – a foul word! Well, set thee
down, sorrow, for so they say the fool said, and so say I,
and I the fool. Well proved, wit! By the Lord, this love is
6   as mad as Ajax: it kills sheep; it kills me – I a sheep. Well
proved again o' my side! I will not love; if I do, hang me.
I' faith, I will not. O but her eye! By this light, but for her
eye, I would not love her – yes, for her two eyes. Well, I
do nothing in the world but lie, and lie in my throat. By
heaven, I do love, and it hath taught me to rime, and to
12   be mallicholy; and here is part of my rime, and here my
mallicholy. Well, she hath one o' my sonnets already.
The clown bore it, the fool sent it, and the lady hath it –
sweet clown, sweeter fool, sweetest lady! By the world,
16   I would not care a pin if the other three were in. Here
comes one with a paper: God give him grace to groan!

He stands aside.

The King ent'reth [with a paper].

KING Ay me!

BEROWNE [aside] Shot, by heaven! Proceed, sweet Cu- 19
pid; thou hast thumped him with thy bird-bolt under 20
the left pap. In faith, secrets!   21

KING [reads]
'So sweet a kiss the golden sun gives not
   To those fresh morning drops upon the rose,
As thy eye-beams when their fresh rays have smote
   The night of dew that on my cheeks down flows.
Nor shines the silver moon one half so bright
   Through the transparent bosom of the deep
As doth thy face, through tears of mine, give light.
   Thou shin'st in every tear that I do weep;
No drop but as a coach doth carry thee;
   So ridest thou triumphing in my woe.
Do but behold the tears that swell in me,
   And they thy glory through my grief will show;
But do not love thyself – then thou will keep
My tears for glasses and still make me weep.   35
O queen of queens, how far dost thou excel
No thought can think, nor tongue of mortal tell!'
How shall she know my griefs? I'll drop the paper.
Sweet leaves, shade folly. Who is he comes here?   39
     *Enter Longaville [with a paper]. The King steps
     aside.*
What, Longaville? and reading? Listen, ear.

BEROWNE
Now, in thy likeness, one more fool appear!   41

LONGAVILLE
Ay me, I am forsworn.

BEROWNE
Why, he comes in like a perjure, wearing papers.   43

KING
In love, I hope – sweet fellowship in shame!

BEROWNE
One drunkard loves another of the name.

LONGAVILLE
Am I the first that have been perjured so?

BEROWNE
I could put thee in comfort – not by two that I know.
Thou mak'st the triumviry, the corner-cap of society,   48
The shape of love's Tyburn, that hangs up simplicity.

LONGAVILLE
I fear these stubborn lines lack power to move.   50
O sweet Maria, empress of my love!
These numbers will I tear, and write in prose.

BEROWNE
O, rimes are guards on wanton Cupid's hose;   53
Disfigure not his shop.   54

LONGAVILLE   This same shall go.
     He reads the sonnet.
'Did not the heavenly rhetoric of thine eye,
   'Gainst whom the world cannot hold argument,
Persuade my heart to this false perjury?
   Vows for thee broke deserve not punishment.
A woman I forswore, but I will prove,
   Thou being a goddess, I forswore not thee.
My vow was earthly, thou a heavenly love;
   Thy grace, being gained, cures all disgrace in me.   62
Vows are but breath, and breath a vapor is:
   Then thou, fair sun, which on my earth dost shine,
Exhal'st this vapor-vow; in thee it is.   65
   If broken then, it is no fault of mine;
If by me broke, what fool is not so wise
To lose an oath to win a paradise?'

---

136 *Stay . . . compliment* i.e. do not stand on ceremony   143–44 *colorable colors* plausible pretexts   146 *pen* style (as contrasted with content)   151 *ben venuto* welcome   154 *text* (unidentified)   158 *Pauca verba* few words   IV, iii   2 *pitched a toil* set a snare   3–4 *set . . . sorrow* (cf. I, i, 297)   6 *Ajax* (legendary Greek warrior who ran mad and mistook sheep for an army after he failed to be awarded the armor of Achilles)   12 *mallicholy* melancholy   16 *in* involved   19 *Proceed* i.e. rise in status   20 *bird-bolt* blunt arrow   21 *left pap* left breast (heart)   35 *glasses* mirrors   39 *shade* conceal   41 *in thy likeness* i.e. in the flesh   43 *perjure* perjurer; *wearing papers* i.e. exposed in the stocks and wearing the papers involved in his offense   48 *triumviry* triumvirate   48–49 *corner-cap . . . Tyburn* (an allusion to the three-cornered cap worn by Roman Catholic priests, such as Dr Story, who was hanged at Tyburn in 1571 on gallows shaped as a triangle, and thereafter called 'Dr Story's cap')   50 *stubborn* i.e. composed with difficulty   53 *guards* trimmings   54 *shop* (slang for 'codpiece')   62 *grace* favor   65 *Exhal'st* draws up, absorbs

BEROWNE

69   This is the liver-vein, which makes flesh a deity,
70   A green goose a goddess. Pure, pure idolatry.
       God amend us, God amend ! We are much out o' th'
       way.
         Enter Dumaine [with a paper].

LONGAVILLE
       By whom shall I send this ? – Company ? Stay.
       [Steps aside.]

BEROWNE

73   All hid, all hid – an old infant play.
74   Like a demi-god here sit I in the sky,
       And wretched fools' secrets heedfully o'er-eye.
76   More sacks to the mill – O heavens, I have my wish !
77   Dumaine transformed – four woodcocks in a dish !

DUMAINE
       O most divine Kate !

BEROWNE
       O most profane coxcomb !

DUMAINE
       By heaven, the wonder in a mortal eye !

BEROWNE

81   By earth, she is not, corporal ; there you lie.

DUMAINE

82   Her amber hairs for foul have amber quoted.

BEROWNE

83   An amber-colored raven was well noted.

DUMAINE
       As upright as the cedar.

84 BEROWNE   Stoop, I say –
85   Her shoulder is with child.

DUMAINE   As fair as day.

BEROWNE
       Ay, as some days, but then no sun must shine.

DUMAINE
       O that I had my wish !

LONGAVILLE   And I had mine !

KING
       And I mine too, good Lord !

BEROWNE
       Amen, so I had mine. Is not that a good word ?

DUMAINE
       I would forget her, but a fever she
       Reigns in my blood, and will rememb'red be.

BEROWNE

92   A fever in your blood ? Why, then incision
93   Would let her out in saucers. Sweet misprision !

DUMAINE
       Once more I'll read the ode that I have writ.

BEROWNE

95   Once more I'll mark how love can vary wit.
       Dumaine reads his sonnet.

DUMAINE   'On a day (alack the day !)
       Love, whose month is ever May,
       Spied a blossom passing fair
       Playing in the wanton air.
       Through the velvet leaves the wind,
       All unseen, can passage find ;
       That the lover, sick to death,
102   Wished himself the heaven's breath.
       Air, quoth he, thy cheeks may blow ;
       Air, would I might triumph so,
       But, alack, my hand is sworn
       Ne'er to pluck thee from thy thorn.

       Vow, alack, for youth unmeet,
       Youth so apt to pluck a sweet !
       Do not call it sin in me,
       That I am forsworn for thee ;
       Thou for whom Jove would swear
       Juno but an Ethiop were ;   113
       And deny himself for Jove,   114
       Turning mortal for thy love.'
This will I send, and something else more plain,
That shall express my true love's fasting pain.   117
O would the King, Berowne, and Longaville
Were lovers too ! Ill, to example ill,   119
Would from my forehead wipe a perjured note,   120
For none offend where all alike do dote.

LONGAVILLE *[advancing]*
Dumaine, thy love is far from charity,
That in love's grief desir'st society.
You may look pale, but I should blush, I know,
To be o'erheard and taken napping so.

KING *[advancing]*
Come, sir, you blush ! As his your case is such ;
You chide at him, offending twice as much.
You do not love Maria ! Longaville
Did never sonnet for her sake compile,
Nor never lay his wreathèd arms athwart
His loving bosom to keep down his heart.
I have been closely shrouded in this bush,
And marked you both, and for you both did blush.
I heard your guilty rimes, observed your fashion,
Saw sighs reek from you, noted well your passion.   135
Ay me ! says one ; O Jove ! the other cries ;
One, her hairs were gold ; crystal, the other's eyes.
       [To Longaville]
You would for paradise break faith and troth ;
       [To Dumaine]
And Jove, for your love, would infringe an oath.
What will Berowne say when that he shall hear
Faith infringèd, which such zeal did swear ?
How will he scorn ! How will he spend his wit !
How will he triumph, leap and laugh at it !
For all the wealth that ever I did see,
I would not have him know so much by me.   145

BEROWNE *[advancing]*
Now step I forth to whip hypocrisy.
Ah, good my liege, I pray thee pardon me.
Good heart, what grace hast thou, thus to reprove
These worms for loving, that art most in love ?
Your eyes do make no coaches ; in your tears
There is no certain princess that appears ;
You'll not be perjured, 'tis a hateful thing –
Tush, none but minstrels like of sonneting !
But are you not ashamed ? Nay, are you not,
All three of you, to be thus much o'ershot ?   155

---

69 *liver-vein* i.e. sentiment of the liver (organ of passion)   70 *green goose* i.e. gosling, young girl   73 *infant play* child's game   74 *in the sky* (Berowne is in an elevated position, perhaps in the rear stage gallery)   76 *More . . . mill* i.e. more work, more grain to be ground   77 *woodcocks* (birds notable for stupidity)   81 *corporal* (cf. III, i, 176)   82 *quoted* designated (i.e. her amber hair has made real amber appear foul in comparison)   83 *well noted* accurately observed (sarcasm)   84 *Stoop* stooped, misshapen   85 *is with child* i.e. has a hump   92 *incision* (for bleeding)   93 *misprision* error   95 *vary* variegate   102 *That* so that   113 *Ethiop* blackamoor (proverbially ugly)   114 *for* i.e. to be   117 *fasting* hungering   119 *example* serve as example for   120 *note* mark   135 *reek* breathe   145 *by* about   155 *o'ershot* worsted

156   You found his mote; the king your mote did see;
157   But I a beam do find in each of three.
    O what a scene of fool'ry have I seen,
159   Of sighs, of groans, of sorrow, and of teen!
    O me, with what strict patience have I sat,
161   To see a king transformèd to a gnat;
162   To see great Hercules whipping a gig,
163   And profound Solomon to tune a jig,
164   And Nestor play at push-pin with the boys,
165   And critic Timon laugh at idle toys!
    Where lies thy grief? O, tell me, good Dumaine.
    And, gentle Longaville, where lies thy pain?
    And where my liege's? All about the breast.
169   A caudle, ho!

KING   Too bitter is thy jest.
    Are we betrayed thus to thy over-view?

BEROWNE
    Not you by me, but I betrayed to you;
    I that am honest, I that hold it sin
    To break the vow I am engagèd in,
    I am betrayed by keeping company
    With men like you, men of inconstancy.
    When shall you see me write a thing in rime?
    Or groan for Joan or spend a minute's time
178   In pruning me? When shall you hear that I
    Will praise a hand, a foot, a face, an eye,
180   A gait, a state, a brow, a breast, a waist,
    A leg, a limb –

KING   Soft! Whither away so fast?
    A true man or a thief, that gallops so?

BEROWNE
    I post from love. Good lover, let me go.
    Enter Jaquenetta and [Costard, the] Clown.

JAQUENETTA
    God bless the king!

KING   What present hast thou there?

COSTARD
    Some certain treason.

185 KING   What makes treason here?

COSTARD
    Nay, it makes nothing, sir.

KING   If it mar nothing neither,
    The treason and you go in peace away together.

JAQUENETTA
    I beseech your Grace let this letter be read:
189   Our person misdoubts it; 'twas treason, he said.

KING Berowne, read it over.
    He [Berowne] reads the letter.
    Where hadst thou it?

JAQUENETTA Of Costard.

KING Where hadst thou it?

COSTARD Of Dun Adramadio, Dun Adramadio.
    [Berowne tears the letter.]

KING
    How now, what is in you? Why dost thou tear it?

BEROWNE
    A toy, my liege, a toy. Your Grace needs not fear it.   196

LONGAVILLE
    It did move him to passion, and therefore let's hear it.

DUMAINE *[picking up the pieces]*
    It is Berowne's writing, and here is his name.

BEROWNE *[to Costard]*
    Ah, you whoreson loggerhead, you were born to do me 199
    shame.
    Guilty, my lord, guilty. I confess, I confess.

KING What?

BEROWNE
    That you three fools lacked me fool to make up the
    mess.   202
    He, he, and you – and you my liege, and I,
    Are pick-purses in love, and we deserve to die.   204
    O dismiss this audience, and I shall tell you more.

DUMAINE
    Now the number is even.

BEROWNE   True, true; we are four.
    Will these turtles be gone?   207

KING   Hence, sirs, away.

COSTARD
    Walk aside the true folk, and let the traitors stay.
    [Exeunt Costard and Jaquenetta.]

BEROWNE
    Sweet lords, sweet lovers, O, let us embrace!
    As true we are as flesh and blood can be;
    The sea will ebb and flow, heaven show his face:
    Young blood doth not obey an old decree.
    We cannot cross the cause why we were born;   213
    Therefore, of all hands must we be forsworn.   214

KING
    What, did these rent lines show some love of thine?   215

BEROWNE
    Did they? quoth you. Who sees the heavenly Rosaline,
    That, like a rude and savage man of Inde,   217
    At the first opening of the gorgeous east,
    Bows not his vassal head and, strooken blind,
    Kisses the base ground with obedient breast?
    What peremptory eagle-sighted eye   221
    Dares look upon the heaven of her brow,
    That is not blinded by her majesty?

KING
    What zeal, what fury, hath inspired thee now?
    My love, her mistress, is a gracious moon;
    She, an attending star, scarce seen a light.

BEROWNE
    My eyes are then no eyes, nor I Berowne.
    O, but for my love, day would turn to night!
    Of all complexions the culled sovereignty   229
    Do meet, as at a fair, in her fair cheek,
    Where several worthies make one dignity,   231
    Where nothing wants that want itself doth seek.   232
    Lend me the flourish of all gentle tongues –   233
    Fie, painted rhetoric! O, she needs it not.   234
    To things of sale a seller's praise belongs;   235
    She passes praise; then praise too short doth blot.
    A withered hermit, five-score winters worn,
    Might shake off fifty, looking in her eye:

156, 157 *mote, beam* i.e. small defect, large defect (cf. Matthew vii, 3–5; Luke vi, 41–42)   159 *teen* grief   161 *gnat* i.e. a small buzzing creature   162 *gig* top   163 *tune a jig* sing a rime   164 *Nestor* (the oldest and most reverend of the Greek chieftains); *push-pin* (a child's game)   165 *critic* cynic; *Timon* (Greek misanthrope); *laugh . . . toys* i.e. delight in useless trifles   169 *caudle* (warm liquid nourishment for the ill)   178 *pruning* trimming, barbering   180 *state* bearing   185 *makes* does   189 *misdoubts* suspects   196 *toy* trifle   199 *loggerhead* blockhead   202 *mess* (a group of four at table)   204 *pick-purses* i.e. cheaters   207 *turtles* turtledoves, lovers   213 *cross . . . born* combat the cause of our birth (love between the sexes)   214 *of all hands* in all events, inevitably   215 *rent lines* torn verses   217 *Inde* India   221 *peremptory* bold   229 *the culled sovereignty* those selected as best   231 *several worthies* various excellences   232 *wants* lacks; *want* desire   233 *flourish* adornment   234 *painted* artificial   235 *of sale* for sale

Beauty doth varnish age as if new-born,
And gives the crutch the cradle's infancy.
O, 'tis the sun that maketh all things shine!

KING
By heaven, thy love is black as ebony.

BEROWNE
Is ebony like her? O wood divine!
A wife of such wood were felicity.
245 O, who can give an oath? Where is a book?
That I may swear beauty doth beauty lack,
247 If that she learn not of her eye to look.
No face is fair that is not full so black.

KING
O paradox! Black is the badge of hell,
250 The hue of dungeons, and the school of night;
251 And beauty's crest becomes the heavens well.

BEROWNE
252 Devils soonest tempt, resembling spirits of light.
O, if in black my lady's brows be decked,
254 It mourns that painting and usurping hair
Should ravish doters with a false aspect;
And therefore is she born to make black fair.
257 Her favor turns the fashion of the days,
258 For native blood is counted painting now;
And therefore red that would avoid dispraise
Paints itself black to imitate her brow.

DUMAINE
To look like her are chimney-sweepers black.

LONGAVILLE
And since her time are colliers counted bright.

KING
263 And Ethiops of their sweet complexion crack.

DUMAINE
Dark needs no candles now, for dark is light.

BEROWNE
Your mistresses dare never come in rain,
For fear their colors should be washed away.

KING
'Twere good yours did; for, sir, to tell you plain,
268 I'll find a fairer face not washed to-day.

BEROWNE
I'll prove her fair, or talk till doomsday here.

KING
270 No devil will fright thee then so much as she.

DUMAINE
I never knew man hold vile stuff so dear.

LONGAVILLE
Look, here's thy love –
[Shows his shoe.] my foot and her face see.

BEROWNE
O, if the streets were pavèd with thine eyes,
Her feet were much too dainty for such tread.

DUMAINE
O vile! Then, as she goes, what upward lies
The street should see as she walked overhead.

KING
But what of this? Are we not all in love?

BEROWNE
Nothing so sure, and thereby all forsworn.

KING
Then leave this chat; and, good Berowne, now prove
Our loving lawful and our faith not torn.

DUMAINE
281 Ay, marry, there; some flattery for this evil.

LONGAVILLE
O some authority how to proceed;
Some tricks, some quillets, how to cheat the devil.   283

DUMAINE
Some salve for perjury.

BEROWNE   'Tis more than need.
Have at you, then, affection's men-at-arms!   285
Consider what you first did swear unto:
To fast, to study, and to see no woman –
Flat treason 'gainst the kingly state of youth.
Say, can you fast? Your stomachs are too young,
And abstinence engenders maladies.
[And where that you have vowed to study, lords,   291
In that each of you have forsworn his book,   292
Can you still dream and pore and thereon look?
For when would you, my lord, or you, or you,
Have found the ground of study's excellence   295
Without the beauty of a woman's face?
From women's eyes this doctrine I derive:
They are the ground, the books, the academes,   298
From whence doth spring the true Promethean fire.   299
Why, universal plodding poisons up
The nimble spirits in the arteries,
As motion and long-during action tires   302
The sinewy vigor of the traveller.
Now, for not looking on a woman's face,
You have in that forsworn the use of eyes,
And study too, the causer of your vow;
For where is any author in the world
Teaches such beauty as a woman's eye?
Learning is but an adjunct to ourself,
And where we are our learning likewise is.
Then when ourselves we see in ladies' eyes,
Do we not likewise see our learning there?]
O, we have made a vow to study, lords,
And in that vow we have forsworn our books;
For when would you, my liege, or you, or you,
In leaden contemplation have found out
Such fiery numbers as the prompting eyes   317
Of beauty's tutors have enriched you with?
Other slow arts entirely keep the brain,   319
And therefore, finding barren practisers,
Scarce show a harvest of their heavy toil;
But love, first learnèd in a lady's eyes,
Lives not alone immurèd in the brain,
But, with the motion of all elements,   324
Courses as swift as thought in every power,
And gives to every power a double power,
Above their functions and their offices.   327

245 *book* i.e. Bible   247 *of . . . look* i.e. from her (dark) eyes how to appear   250 *school* i.e. training place for evil night-work (?)   251 *And* and yet; *beauty's crest* i.e. blackness (according to Berowne's paradoxical contention)   252 *resembling* simulating   254 *usurping* false   257 *favor* face   258 *native blood* i.e. naturally red cheeks; *counted* accounted   263 *crack* boast   268 *I'll . . . to-day* i.e. there are other unwashed faces fairer than hers   270 *then* i.e. on doomsday   281 *flattery* i.e. soothing lies   283 *quillets* quibbles   285 *affection's men-at-arms* passion's followers   291–312 *And where . . . learning there* (a passage probably marked for excision in the manuscript, since another version follows)   291 *where that* whereas   292 *In that* inasmuch as; *book* i.e. a woman's face   295 *ground* basis   298 *academes* academies   299 *Promethean* divine (the god Prometheus brought fire from heaven to earth)   302 *long-during* enduring   317 *numbers* verses, poems   319 *arts* branches of knowledge; *keep* remain in   324 *elements* (fire, air, water, earth, each of which had its own proper motion and proper seat in the body as elsewhere)   327 *Above their functions* i.e. beyond their ordinary functions

It adds a precious seeing to the eye :
A lover's eyes will gaze an eagle blind.
A lover's ear will hear the lowest sound,
331   When the suspicious head of theft is stopped.
332   Love's feeling is more soft and sensible
333   Than are the tender horns of cockled snails.
334   Love's tongue proves dainty Bacchus gross in taste.
For valor, is not Love a Hercules,
336   Still climbing trees in the Hesperides ?
Subtle as Sphinx ; as sweet and musical
As bright Apollo's lute, strung with his hair.
And when Love speaks, the voice of all the gods
Make heaven drowsy with the harmony.
Never durst poet touch a pen to write
342   Until his ink were temp'red with Love's sighs ;
O, then his lines would ravish savage ears
And plant in tyrants mild humility.
From women's eyes this doctrine I derive.
They sparkle still the right Promethean fire ;
They are the books, the arts, the academes,
That show, contain, and nourish all the world ;
Else none at all in aught proves excellent.
Then fools you were these women to forswear,
351   Or, keeping what is sworn, you will prove fools.
For wisdom's sake, a word that all men love,
353   Or for love's sake, a word that loves all men,
Or for men's sake, the authors of these women,
Or women's sake, by whom we men are men,
356   Let us once lose our oaths to find ourselves,
Or else we lose ourselves to keep our oaths.
It is religion to be thus forsworn,
359   For charity itself fulfils the law
And who can sever love from charity ?

KING

Saint Cupid then ! And, soldiers, to the field !

BEROWNE

Advance your standards, and upon them, lords !
Pell-mell, down with them ! But be first advised,
364   In conflict that you get the sun of them.

LONGAVILLE

365   Now to plain-dealing – lay these glozes by –
Shall we resolve to woo these girls of France ?

KING

And win them too ; therefore let us devise
Some entertainment for them in their tents.

BEROWNE

First from the park let us conduct them thither ;
Then homeward every man attach the hand
Of his fair mistress. In the afternoon
We will with some strange pastime solace them,
Such as the shortness of the time can shape ;
For revels, dances, masks, and merry hours
Forerun fair Love, strewing her way with flowers.

KING

Away, away ! No time shall be omitted
That will be time, and may by us be fitted.   377

BEROWNE

Allons ! allons ! Sowed cockle reaped no corn ;   378
And justice always whirls in equal measure.
Light wenches may prove plagues to men forsworn ;
If so, our copper buys no better treasure.   *[Exeunt.]* 381

                         *

Enter [Holofernes,] the Pedant, [Nathaniel,] the   V, i
Curate, and Dull [the Constable].

HOLOFERNES Satis quid sufficit.   1

NATHANIEL I praise God for you, sir. Your reasons at   2
dinner have been sharp and sententious, pleasant without scurrility, witty without affection, audacious with-   4
out impudency, learned without opinion, and strange   5
without heresy. I did converse this quondam day with a
companion of the king's, who is intituled, nominated, or
called, Don Adriano de Armado.

HOLOFERNES Novi hominem tanquam te. His humor is   9
lofty, his discourse peremptory, his tongue filed, his eye   10
ambitious, his gait majestical, and his general behavior
vain, ridiculous, and thrasonical. He is too picked, too   12
spruce, too affected, too odd, as it were, too peregrinate,   13
as I may call it.

NATHANIEL A most singular and choice epithet.   15

Draw out his table-book.

HOLOFERNES He draweth out the thread of his verbosity
finer than the staple of his argument. I abhor such fa-   17
natical phantasimes, such insociable and point-devise   18
companions ; such rackers of orthography as to speak
'dout' fine when he should say 'doubt' ; 'det,' when he   20
should pronounce 'debt' – d, e, b, t, not d, e, t. He
clepeth a calf 'cauf' ; half 'hauf' ; neighbor vocatur   22
'nebor,' neigh abbreviated 'ne.' This is abhominable,
which he would call 'abominable.' It insinuateth me of
insanie. Ne intelligis, domine ? To make frantic, lunatic.   25

NATHANIEL Laus Deo bone intelligo.   26

HOLOFERNES Bone ? Bone for bene ! Priscian a little   27
scratched – 'twill serve.   28

*Enter [Armado, the] Braggart, [Moth, the] Boy
[, and Costard, the Clown].*

NATHANIEL Videsne quis venit ?   29

HOLOFERNES Video, et gaudeo.   30

ARMADO *[to Moth]* Chirrah !

HOLOFERNES Quare 'chirrah,' not 'sirrah' ?   32

ARMADO Men of peace, well encountered.

HOLOFERNES Most military sir, salutation.

MOTH *[aside to Costard]* They have been at a great feast
of languages and stolen the scraps.

COSTARD O, they have lived long on the alms-basket of   37
words. I marvel thy master hath not eaten thee for a

---

331 *When . . . stopped* i.e. when even a timorously alert thief hears nothing
332 *sensible* sensitive   333 *cockled* in shells   334 *Bacchus* (god of wine
and feasting)   336 *Hesperides* (where the golden apples grew)   342
temp'red cooled and refined   351 *what is sworn* i.e. the oaths   353 *loves*
i.e. is lovable to   356 *once* for once (?), at once (?)   359 *For . . . law*
(Romans xiii, 8 : '. . . for he that loveth another hath fulfilled the law')
364 *get . . . them* i.e. maneuver them into facing the sun (with play on
'beget son')   365 *glozes* sophistries   377 *be time* betime, come to pass ;
fitted utilized   378 *Allons* come ; *cockle* a variety of weed ; *corn* wheat
381 *copper* base coin (i.e. as men forsworn, they have little of worth to
offer)
V, i   1 *Satis quid sufficit* (misquotation of '*satis est quod sufficit*' : enough
is as good as a feast)   2 *reasons* discourses   4 *affection* affectation   5
opinion self-conceit ; *strange* novel   9 *Novi . . . te* I know the man as well
as I know you   10 *filed* smooth   12 *thrasonical* boastful ; *picked* finick-
ing   13 *peregrinate* exotic   15 *singular* unique ; s.d. *table-book* tablet,
notebook   17 *staple* fibre ; *argument* subject matter   18 *phantasimes* (cf.
IV, i, 98) ; *insociable* incompatible ; *point-devise* precise   20 *fine* mincingly
22 *clepeth* calls ; *vocatur* is called   25 *insanie* madness ; *Ne . . . domine*
do you understand, sir   26 *Laus . . . intelligo* praise God, I understand
well   27 *Priscian* i.e. Latin grammar (after the fifth-century grammarian
whose textbooks were long standard)   28 *scratched* marred   29 *Videsne
quis venit* do you see who comes   30 *Video, et gaudeo* I see and rejoice
32 *Quare* why   37 *alms-basket* container in which scraps for the poor were
gathered

39 word ; for thou art not so long by the head as honorifica-
40 bilitudinitatibus. Thou art easier swallowed than a flap-
dragon.
42 MOTH Peace ! The peal begins.
43 ARMADO Monsieur, are you not lettered ?
44 MOTH Yes, yes ! He teaches boys the horn-hook. What is
a, b, spelled backward with the horn on his head ?
46 HOLOFERNES Ba, pueritia, with a horn added.
MOTH Ba, most silly sheep with a horn. You hear his
learning.
49 HOLOFERNES Quis, quis, thou consonant ?
MOTH The last of the five vowels, if you repeat them ; or
the fifth, if I.
HOLOFERNES I will repeat them : a, e, i –
53 MOTH The sheep. The other two concludes it – o, u.
ARMADO Now, by the salt wave of the Mediterranean, a
55 sweet touch, a quick venew of wit ! Snip, snap, quick
and home ! It rejoiceth my intellect. True wit !
57 MOTH Offered by a child to an old man – which is wit-old.
58 HOLOFERNES What is the figure ? What is the figure ?
MOTH Horns.
HOLOFERNES Thou disputes like an infant. Go whip thy
60 gig.
MOTH Lend me your horn to make one, and I will whip
62 about your infamy manu cita. A gig of a cuckold's horn.
COSTARD An I had but one penny in the world, thou
shouldst have it to buy gingerbread. Hold, there is the
65 very remuneration I had of thy master, thou halfpenny
purse of wit, thou pigeon-egg of discretion. O, an the
heavens were so pleased that thou wert but my bastard,
what a joyful father wouldest thou make me ! Go to,
69 thou hast it ad dunghill, at the fingers' ends, as they say.
HOLOFERNES O, I smell false Latin ! 'Dunghill' for
unguem.
71 ARMADO Arts-man, preambulate. We will be singled from
72 the barbarous. Do you not educate youth at the charge-
house on the top of the mountain ?
HOLOFERNES Or mons, the hill.
ARMADO At your sweet pleasure, for the mountain.
HOLOFERNES I do, sans question.
ARMADO Sir, it is the king's most sweet pleasure and
affection to congratulate the princess at her pavilion in
the posteriors of this day, which the rude multitude call
the afternoon.
81 HOLOFERNES The posterior of the day, most generous
82 sir, is liable, congruent, and measurable for the afternoon. The word is well culled, chose, sweet and apt, I do
assure you, sir, I do assure.
ARMADO Sir, the king is a noble gentleman, and my
86 familiar, I do assure ye, very good friend. For what is
87 inward between us, let it pass. I do beseech thee remem-
88 ber thy courtesy. I beseech thee apparel thy head. And
among other importunate and most serious designs,
and of great import indeed, too – but let that pass ; for I
must tell thee, it will please his Grace, by the world,
sometime to lean upon my poor shoulder, and with his
93 royal finger thus dally with my excrement, with my mustachio – but, sweet heart, let that pass. By the world, I
recount no fable : some certain special honors it pleaseth
his greatness to impart to Armado, a soldier, a man of
travel, that hath seen the world – but let that pass. The
very all of all is (but, sweet heart, I do implore secrecy)
that the king would have me present the princess, sweet
chuck, with some delightful ostentation, or show, or

pageant, or antic, or fire-work. Now, understanding 100
that the curate and your sweet self are good at such eruptions and sudden breaking out of mirth, as it were, I
have acquainted you withal, to the end to crave your
assistance.
HOLOFERNES Sir, you shall present before her the Nine 105
Worthies. Sir Nathaniel, as concerning some entertainment of time, some show in the posterior of this day, to
be rendered by our assistance, the king's command, and
this most gallant, illustrate, and learned gentleman,
before the princess – I say, none so fit as to present the
Nine Worthies.
NATHANIEL Where will you find men worthy enough to
present them ?
HOLOFERNES Joshua, yourself ; myself ; and this gallant 114
gentleman, Judas Maccabaeus ; this swain, because of
his great limb or joint, shall pass Pompey the Great ; the 116
page, Hercules –
ARMADO Pardon, sir – error. He is not quantity enough
for that Worthy's thumb ; he is not so big as the end of
his club.
HOLOFERNES Shall I have audience ? He shall present 121
Hercules in minority. His enter and exit shall be strang-
ling a snake ; and I will have an apology for that purpose. 123
MOTH An excellent device ! So if any of the audience hiss,
you may cry, 'Well done, Hercules ! Now thou crushest
the snake !' That is the way to make an offense gracious,
though few have the grace to do it.
ARMADO For the rest of the Worthies ?
HOLOFERNES I will play three myself.
MOTH Thrice-worthy gentleman !
ARMADO Shall I tell you a thing ?
HOLOFERNES We attend.
ARMADO We will have, if this fadge not, an antic. I be- 133
seech you, follow.
HOLOFERNES Via, goodman Dull ! Thou hast spoken no 135
word all this while.
DULL Nor understood none neither, sir.
HOLOFERNES Allons ! we will employ thee. 138

39 *honorificabilitudinitatibus* condition of being capable of honors (given
in the dative plural and often cited as the 'longest word' in existence)
40 *flap-dragon* a drink of brandy containing a burning raisin   42 *peal*
i.e. clatter of tongues   43 *lettered* i.e. a man of letters   44 *horn-book*
(printed sheets covered by transparent horn, for teaching the alphabet)
46 *pueritia* child   49 *Quis* what ; *consonant* i.e. nonentity (because in pronunciation the consonants require vowels)   53 *o, u* (oh you)   55 *venew*
venue, sally   57 *wit-old* i.e. wittol, tame cuckold   58 *figure* metaphor
60 *gig* top   62 *manu cita* with ready hand (the Latin is a conjectural emendation for the meaningless 'unum cita' of the quarto)   65–66 *halfpenny purse*
(a novelty purse, just large enough to hold a halfpenny)   69 *ad dunghill*
(malapropism for '*ad unguem*,' i.e. on the nail)   71 *Arts-man* scholar ;
preambulate come ; *singled* distinguished   72–73 *charge-house . . . mountain*
(an obscure allusion, possibly involving an academic joke about the kind
of school mentioned in Erasmus' *Familiaria Colloquia*, where the paying
pupils acquired more lice than Latin)   81 *generous* cultivated   82 *liable*
suitable ; *congruent* appropriate ; *measurable* meet   86 *familiar* intimate
87 *inward* private   88 *thy courtesy* i.e. that you have removed your hat
93 *excrement* excrescence, hair   100 *antic* (a pageant or pantomime in
whimsical costume ; 105–06 *Nine Worthies* (conquerors commonly featured
in folk-drama and pageants : Hector, Alexander, Caesar, Joshua, David,
Judas Maccabaeus, King Arthur, Charlemagne, and Godfrey of Bouillon
or Guy of Warwick ; in the present case Hercules and Pompey are substituted for more usual figures)   114 *myself* (Holofernes does not specify
his own part, perhaps by a printer's error)   116 *pass* perform   121 *audience*
a hearing   123 *snake* (the legendary Hercules strangled in his cradle two
snakes sent by Juno to destroy him) ; *apology* explanation, justification
133 *fadge not* does not succeed ; *antic* (cf. l. 100)   135 *Via* i.e. go on (a cry
of encouragement)   138 *Allons* come

DULL I'll make one in a dance, or so; or I will play on the
140   tabor to the Worthies, and let them dance the hay.
HOLOFERNES Most dull, honest Dull. To our sport,
     away!   *Exeunt.*

*

V, ii   *Enter the Ladies [Princess, Katharine, Rosaline, and*
          Maria].
PRINCESS
   Sweet hearts, we shall be rich ere we depart
2   If fairings come thus plentifully in.
   A lady walled about with diamonds!
   Look you what I have from the loving king.
ROSALINE
   Madam, came nothing else along with that?
PRINCESS
   Nothing but this? Yes, as much love in rime
   As would be crammed up in a sheet of paper,
8   Writ o' both sides the leaf, margent and all,
9   That he was fain to seal on Cupid's name.
ROSALINE
10   That was the way to make his godhead wax,
   For he hath been five thousand year a boy.
KATHARINE
12   Ay, and a shrewd unhappy gallows too.
ROSALINE
   You'll ne'er be friends with him: 'a killed your sister.
KATHARINE
   He made her melancholy, sad, and heavy;
   And so she died. Had she been light, like you,
   Of such a merry, nimble, stirring spirit,
   She might ha' been a grandam ere she died;
   And so may you, for a light heart lives long.
ROSALINE
   What's your dark meaning, mouse, of this light word?
KATHARINE
20   A light condition in a beauty dark.
ROSALINE
   We need more light to find your meaning out.
KATHARINE
22   You'll mar the light by taking it in snuff;
23   Therefore, I'll darkly end the argument.
ROSALINE
   Look, what you do, you do it still i' th' dark.

KATHARINE
   So do not you, for you are a light wench.
ROSALINE
   Indeed I weigh not you, and therefore light.   26
KATHARINE
   You weigh me not? O, that's you care not for me.
ROSALINE
   Great reason; for past cure is still past care.   28
PRINCESS
   Well bandied both, a set of wit well played.   29
   But, Rosaline, you have a favor too: 30
   Who sent it? and what is it?
ROSALINE   I would you knew.
   An if my face were but as fair as yours,
   My favor were as great. Be witness this.
   Nay, I have verses too, I thank Berowne:
   The numbers true; and, were the numb'ring too,   35
   I were the fairest goddess on the ground.
   I am compared to twenty thousand fairs.   37
   O, he hath drawn my picture in his letter!
PRINCESS Anything like?
ROSALINE Much in the letters, nothing in the praise.   40
PRINCESS Beauteous as ink – a good conclusion.
KATHARINE Fair as a text B in a copy-book.   42
ROSALINE
   'Ware pencils, ho! Let me not die your debtor,   43
   My red dominical, my golden letter.   44
   O, that your face were not so full of O's!
PRINCESS
   A pox of that jest, and I beshrew all shrows!   46
   But, Katharine, what was sent to you from fair
     Dumaine?
KATHARINE
   Madam, this glove.
PRINCESS   Did he not send you twain?
KATHARINE
   Yes, madam; and moreover,
   Some thousand verses of a faithful lover:
   A huge translation of hypocrisy,   51
   Vilely compiled, profound simplicity.   52
MARIA
   This, and these pearls, to me sent Longaville.
   The letter is too long by half a mile.
PRINCESS
   I think no less. Dost thou not wish in heart
   The chain were longer and the letter short?
MARIA
   Ay, or I would these hands might never part.
PRINCESS
   We are wise girls to mock our lovers so.
ROSALINE
   They are worse fools to purchase mocking so.   59
   That same Berowne I'll torture ere I go.
   O that I knew he were but in by th' week!   61
   How I would make him fawn, and beg, and seek,
   And wait the season, and observe the times,
   And spend his prodigal wits in bootless rimes,
   And shape his service wholly to my hests,   65
   And make him proud to make me proud that jests!   66
   So pertaunt-like would I o'ersway his state   67
   That he should be my fool, and I his fate.   68
PRINCESS
   None are so surely caught, when they are catched,
   As wit turned fool. Folly, in wisdom hatched,

---

140 *tabor* small drum; *the hay* (country dance resembling a reel)
V, ii   **2** *fairings* gifts, tokens bought at a fair   **8** *margent* margin   **9** *That . . . name* i.e. so that he was willing in the circumstances to include Cupid's name on an appended seal   **10** *wax* grow (with play on wax seal) **12** *shrewd unhappy gallows* vexing mischievous knave   **20** *light* wanton, wayward   **22** *taking . . . snuff* i.e. being offended by it (with play on snuffing a candle)   **23** *darkly* without clarifying (?)   **26** *weigh* (1) equal in weight, (2) regard   **28** *past cure* (Rosaline is calling Katharine 'incurable') **29** *bandied* volleyed   **30** *favor* gift   **35** *numbers* metre; *numb'ring* reckoning **37** *fairs* fair women   **40** *letters . . . praise* i.e. in the orthography rather than in the content (?)   **42** *a text B* (a capital printed in Gothic text or 'black-letter'; the allusion is to Rosaline's dark complexion)   **43** *'Ware pencils* i.e. have at you (with the metaphor still drawn from the arts of writing and portraiture)   **44** *red dominical* the red letters used to mark Sundays and holy days in almanacs, etc. (the allusion seems to be to Katharine's ruddy pock-marks)   **46** *beshrew all shrows* curse all scolds   **51** *translation* i.e. rendition   **52** *simplicity* stupidity   **59** *purchase* i.e. bid for, invite   **61** *in . . . week* permanently caught   **65** *hests* behests, commands **66** *proud to . . . jests* i.e. take pride in being the victim of my mockery (?) **67** *pertaunt* pair-taunt (winning hand in a card game called 'post and pair') **68** *fool* plaything

Hath wisdom's warrant and the help of school
And wit's own grace to grace a learnèd fool.

ROSALINE
The blood of youth burns not with such excess
As gravity's revolt to wantonness.

MARIA
Folly in fools bears not so strong a note
76 As fool'ry in the wise when wit doth dote;
Since all the power thereof it doth apply
To prove, by wit, worth in simplicity.
        Enter Boyet.

PRINCESS
Here comes Boyet, and mirth is in his face.

BOYET
O, I am stabbed with laughter! Where's her Grace?

PRINCESS
Thy news, Boyet?

BOYET   Prepare, madam, prepare!
Arm, wenches, arm! Encounters mounted are
Against your peace. Love doth approach disguised,
84 Armèd in arguments; you'll be surprised.
Muster your wits; stand in your own defense,
Or hide your heads like cowards, and fly hence.

PRINCESS
87 Saint Denis to Saint Cupid! What are they
That charge their breath against us? Say, scout, say.

BOYET
Under the cool shade of a sycamore
I thought to close mine eyes some half an hour,
When, lo, to interrupt my purposed rest,
92 Toward that shade I might behold address
The king and his companions! Warily
I stole into a neighbor thicket by,
And overheard what you shall overhear –
That, by and by, disguised they will be here.
Their herald is a pretty knavish page,
98 That well by heart hath conned his embassage.
99 Action and accent did they teach him there:
'Thus must thou speak, and thus thy body bear.'
101 And ever and anon they made a doubt
Presence majestical would put him out;
'For,' quoth the king, 'an angel shalt thou see;
104 Yet fear not thou, but speak audaciously.'
The boy replied, 'An angel is not evil;
I should have feared her had she been a devil.'
With that all laughed and clapped him on the shoulder,
Making the bold wag by their praises bolder.
109 One rubbed his elbows thus, and fleered, and swore
A better speech was never spoke before.
111 Another, with his finger and his thumb,
112 Cried 'Via, we will do't, come what will come!'
The third he capered and cried, 'All goes well!'
The fourth turned on the toe, and down he fell.
With that they all did tumble on the ground
116 With such a zealous laughter, so profound,
117 That in this spleen ridiculous appears,
To check their folly, passion's solemn tears.

PRINCESS
But what, but what? Come they to visit us?

BOYET
They do, they do; and are apparelled thus,
Like Muscovites or Russians, as I guess.
122 Their purpose is to parle, to court and dance;
123 And every one his love-feat will advance

Unto his several mistress, which they'll know   124
By favors several which they did bestow.

PRINCESS
And will they so? The gallants shall be tasked: 126
For, ladies, we will every one be masked,
And not a man of them shall have the grace,   128
Despite of suit, to see a lady's face.   129
Hold, Rosaline, this favor thou shalt wear,
And then the king will court thee for his dear:
Hold, take thou this, my sweet, and give me thine;
So shall Berowne take me for Rosaline.
And change you favors too; so shall your loves
Woo contrary, deceived by these removes.   135

ROSALINE
Come on, then – wear the favors most in sight.   136

KATHARINE
But in this changing what is your intent?

PRINCESS
The effect of my intent is to cross theirs.
They do it but in mockery merriment,   139
And mock for mock is only my intent.
Their several counsels they unbosom shall   141
To loves mistook and so be mocked withal
Upon the next occasion that we meet,
With visages displayed, to talk and greet.

ROSALINE
But shall we dance if they desire us to't?

PRINCESS
No, to the death we will not move a foot,   146
Nor to their penned speech render we no grace,
But while 'tis spoke each turn away her face.

BOYET
Why, that contempt will kill the speaker's heart,
And quite divorce his memory from his part.

PRINCESS
Therefore I do it, and I make no doubt
The rest will ne'er come in if he be out.
There's no such sport as sport by sport o'erthrown,
To make theirs ours, and ours none but our own.   154
So shall we stay, mocking intended game,   155
And they, well mocked, depart away with shame.
        Sound Trumpets.

BOYET
The trumpet sounds. Be masked. The maskers come.
        [The Ladies mask.]
        Enter Blackamoors with music; [Moth,] the Boy,
        with a speech, and the rest of the Lords disguised.

MOTH
All hail, the richest beauties on the earth!

BOYET
Beauties no richer than rich taffeta.   159

MOTH
A holy parcel of the fairest dames,

---

76 *dote* grow foolish 84 *surprised* i.e. overcome by surprise attack 87 *Saint Denis* (patron saint of France) 92 *addrest* marching 98 *embassage* message of state 99 *Action* gesture 101 *made a doubt* expressed a fear 104 *audaciously* boldly 109 *fleered* grinned 111 *with . . . thumb* i.e. with a snapping of the fingers 112 *Via* go on 116 *profound* deep 117 *spleen ridiculous* fit of laughing 122 *parle* parley 123 *love-feat* display of prowess in courtship 124 *which* whom 126 *tasked* hard put to it 128 *grace* favor 129 *Despite of suit* in spite of his plea 135 *removes* exchanges 136 *most in sight* conspicuously 139 *mockery* mocking 141 *several* individual; *unbosom* confide 146 *No . . . death* i.e. not on your life 154 *theirs* i.e. their sport 155 *game* i.e. mockery 159 *taffeta* i.e. the cloth of their masks

The Ladies turn their backs to him.
That ever turned their – backs – to mortal views !
BEROWNE 'Their eyes,' villain, 'their eyes.'
MOTH
  That ever turned their eyes to mortal views !
  Out –
165 BOYET True. 'Out' indeed.
MOTH
  Out of your favors, heavenly spirits, vouchsafe
  Not to behold –
BEROWNE 'Once to behold,' rogue.
MOTH
  Once to behold with your sun-beamèd eyes,
  – with your sun-beamèd eyes –
BOYET
  They will not answer to that epithet.
172 You were best call it 'daughter-beamèd eyes.'
MOTH
  They do not mark me, and that brings me out.
BEROWNE
  Is this your perfectness ? Be gone, you rogue !
                           [Exit Moth.]
ROSALINE
  What would these strangers ? Know their minds, Boyet.
  If they do speak our language, 'tis our will
  That some plain man recount their purposes.
  Know what they would.
BOYET
  What would you with the Princess ?
BEROWNE
  Nothing but peace and gentle visitation.
ROSALINE
  What would they, say they ?
BOYET
  Nothing but peace and gentle visitation.
ROSALINE
  Why, that they have, and bid them so be gone.
BOYET
  She says you have it and you may be gone.
KING
185 Say to her, we have measured many miles,
186 To tread a measure with her on this grass.
BOYET
  They say that they have measured many a mile,
  To tread a measure with you on this grass.
ROSALINE
  It is not so. Ask them how many inches
  Is in one mile. If they have measured many,
  The measure then of one is easily told.
BOYET
  If to come hither you have measured miles,
  And many miles, the princess bids you tell
  How many inches doth fill up one mile.
BEROWNE
  Tell her we measure them by weary steps.

BOYET
  She hears herself.
ROSALINE   How many weary steps,
  Of many weary miles you have o'ergone,
  Are numb'red in the travel of one mile ?
BEROWNE
  We number nothing that we spend for you.
  Our duty is so rich, so infinite,
  That we may do it still without accompt.   201
  Vouchsafe to show the sunshine of your face,
  That we, like savages, may worship it.
ROSALINE
  My face is but a moon, and clouded too.
KING
  Blessèd are clouds, to do as such clouds do.
  Vouchsafe, bright moon, and these thy stars, to shine
  (Those clouds removed) upon our watery eyne.   207
ROSALINE
  O vain petitioner, beg a greater matter !
  Thou now requests but moonshine in the water.   209
KING
  Then in our measure do but vouchsafe one change.   210
  Thou bid'st me beg ; this begging is not strange.   211
ROSALINE
  Play, music, then. Nay, you must do it soon.
              [Music plays.]
  Not yet – no dance ! Thus change I like the moon.   213
KING
  Will you not dance ? How come you thus estrangèd ?
ROSALINE
  You took the moon at full, but now she's changèd.
KING
  Yet still she is the moon, and I the man.   216
  The music plays ; vouchsafe some motion to it.   217
ROSALINE
  Our ears vouchsafe it.
KING   But your legs should do it.
ROSALINE
  Since you are strangers and come here by chance,
  We'll not be nice : take hands – we will not dance.   220
KING
  Why take we hands then ?
ROSALINE   Only to part friends.
  Curtsy, sweet hearts ; and so the measure ends.
KING
  More measure of this measure ! Be not nice.   223
ROSALINE
  We can afford no more at such a price.
KING
  Price you yourselves. What buys your company ?
ROSALINE
  Your absence only.
KING   That can never be.
ROSALINE
  Then cannot we be bought ; and so adieu –
  Twice to your visor, and half once to you.   228
KING
  If you deny to dance, let's hold more chat.
ROSALINE
  In private then.
KING   I am best pleased with that.
         [They converse apart.]
BEROWNE
  White-handed mistress, one sweet word with thee.

---

165 *Out* i.e. out of his part   **172** *daughter* (the inevitable play on 'sun-son')   **185** *measured* paced   **186** *measure* dance   **201** *accompt* accounting   **207** *eyne* eyes   **209** *moonshine . . . water* i.e. nothing at all   **210** *change* round in a dance (with play on 'change of the moon')   **211** *not strange* not foreign (even though begged by Muscovites)   **213** *Not . . . dance* (she abruptly revokes her consent)   **216** *man* i.e. man in the moon   **217** *motion* response   **220** *nice* coy   **223** *More measure* i.e. a greater quantity   **228** *visor* mask .

PRINCESS
Honey, and milk, and sugar – there is three.

BEROWNE
233 Nay then, two treys, an if you grow so nice,
234 Metheglin, wort, and malmsey – well run, dice!
There's half a dozen sweets.

PRINCESS   Seventh sweet, adieu.
236 Since you can cog, I'll play no more with you.

BEROWNE
One word in secret.

PRINCESS   Let it not be sweet.

BEROWNE
Thou grievest my gall.

PRINCESS   Gall! Bitter.

238 BEROWNE   Therefore meet.
[They converse apart.]

DUMAINE
Will you vouchsafe with me to change a word?

MARIA
Name it.

DUMAINE Fair lady –

MARIA   Say you so? Fair lord.
Take that for your 'fair lady.'

DUMAINE   Please it you,
As much in private, and I'll bid adieu.
[They converse apart.]

KATHARINE
243 What, was your vizard made without a tongue?

LONGAVILLE
I know the reason, lady, why you ask.

KATHARINE
O for your reason! Quickly, sir; I long.

LONGAVILLE
You have a double tongue within your mask
And would afford my speechless vizard half.

KATHARINE
248 'Veal,' quoth the Dutchman. Is not 'veal' a calf?

LONGAVILLE
A calf, fair lady?

KATHARINE   No, a fair lord calf.

LONGAVILLE
Let's part the word.

KATHARINE   No, I'll not be your half:
251 Take all and wean it – it may prove an ox.

LONGAVILLE
252 Look how you butt yourself in these sharp mocks.
253 Will you give horns, chaste lady? Do not so.

KATHARINE
Then die a calf before your horns do grow.

LONGAVILLE
One word in private with you ere I die.

KATHARINE
Bleat softly then. The butcher hears you cry.
[They converse apart.]

BOYET
The tongues of mocking wenches are as keen
As is the razor's edge invisible,
Cutting a smaller hair than may be seen;
260 Above the sense of sense, so sensible
261 Seemeth their conference, their conceits have wings
Fleeter than arrows, bullets, wind, thought, swifter
things.

ROSALINE
Not one word more, my maids! Break off, break off.

BEROWNE
By heaven, all dry-beaten with pure scoff!   264

KING
Farewell, mad wenches. You have simple wits.
Exeunt [King and Lords].

PRINCESS
Twenty adieus, my frozen Muscovits.
Are these the breed of wits so wondered at?

BOYET
Tapers they are, with your sweet breaths puffed out.

ROSALINE
Well-liking wits they have; gross, gross; fat, fat.   269

PRINCESS
O poverty in wit, kingly-poor flout!   270
Will they not, think you, hang themselves to-night?
Or ever but in vizards show their faces?
This pert Berowne was out of count'nance quite.

ROSALINE
They were all in lamentable cases.
The king was weeping-ripe for a good word.   275

PRINCESS
Berowne did swear himself out of all suit.   276

MARIA
Dumaine was at my service, and his sword:
'No point,' quoth I; my servant straight was mute.   278

KATHARINE
Lord Longaville said I came o'er his heart;
And trow you what he called me?   280

PRINCESS   Qualm, perhaps.

KATHARINE
Yes, in good faith.

PRINCESS   Go, sickness as thou art!   281

ROSALINE
Well, better wits have worn plain statute-caps.   282
But will you hear? The king is my love sworn.

PRINCESS
And quick Berowne hath plighted faith to me.

KATHARINE
And Longaville was for my service born.

MARIA
Dumaine is mine as sure as bark on tree.

BOYET
Madam, and pretty mistresses, give ear.
Immediately they will again be here
In their own shapes, for it can never be
They will digest this harsh indignity.

PRINCESS
Will they return?

BOYET   They will, they will, God knows,
And leap for joy though they are lame with blows.

---

233 *two treys* i.e. I'll double your 'trey' with three more words; *an if* if
234 *Metheglin* Welsh drink brewed from honey; *wort* unfermented or
'sweet' beer; *malmsey* sweet wine   236 *cog* cheat   238 *meet* appropriate
243 *vizard* mask   248 *Veal* i.e. 'well' in Dutch dialect (with play on 'veil'
– the vizard – as well as 'veal' – calf)   251 *wean* i.e. raise   252 *butt* i.e.
injure, cast aspersions upon   253 *give horns* i.e. prove an unfaithful wife
260 *sense of* i.e. reach of; *sensible* nimble-witted   261 *conference* conversation; *conceits* fancies   264 *dry-beaten* clubbed, bruised   269 *Well-liking*
ready for market, fat (as in 'fat-headed')   270 *kingly-poor* (a play on
preceding *liking* – i.e. like king, king-like, kingly)   275 *weeping-ripe* i.e.
ready to cry   276 *out . . . suit* (1) excessively, (2) unavailingly   278 *No
point* (cf. II, i, 188)   280 *trow you* would you believe   281 *Go, sickness* (a
play on *qualm* – pronounced 'come' – in the preceding line)   282 *Well
. . . statute-caps* i.e. there have been cleverer people among ordinary citizens
(whose head-dress was regulated by statute)

293 Therefore change favors, and when they repair,
Blow like sweet roses in this summer air.

PRINCESS
How blow? how blow? Speak to be understood.

BOYET
Fair ladies, masked, are roses in their bud;
297 Dismasked, their damask sweet commixture shown,
298 Are angels vailing clouds, or roses blown.

PRINCESS
299 Avaunt, perplexity! What shall we do
If they return in their own shapes to woo?

ROSALINE
Good madam, if by me you'll be advised,
Let's mock them still, as well known as disguised.
Let us complain to them what fools were here,
Disguised like Muscovites in shapeless gear;
And wonder what they were, and to what end
Their shallow shows and prologue vilely penned,
And their rough carriage so ridiculous,
Should be presented at our tent to us.

BOYET
Ladies, withdraw. The gallants are at hand.

PRINCESS
Whip to your tents, as roes run o'er the land.
Exeunt [Princess and Ladies].
Enter the King and the rest [the Lords].

KING
Fair sir, God save you. Where's the Princess?

BOYET
Gone to her tent. Please it your Majesty
Command me any service to her thither?

KING
That she vouchsafe me audience for one word.

BOYET
I will; and so will she, I know, my lord. *Exit.*

BEROWNE
This fellow pecks up wit, as pigeons pease,
317 And utters it again when God doth please.
He is wit's pedlar, and retails his wares
319 At wakes and wassails, meetings, markets, fairs;
320 And we that sell by gross, the Lord doth know,
Have not the grace to grace it with such show.
This gallant pins the wenches on his sleeve.
Had he been Adam, he had tempted Eve.
324 'A can carve too, and lisp. Why, this is he
That kissed his hand away in courtesy.
326 This is the ape of form, monsieur the nice,
327 That, when he plays at tables, chides the dice
In honorable terms. Nay, he can sing
329 A mean most meanly; and in ushering
Mend him who can. The ladies call him sweet.
The stairs, as he treads on them, kiss his feet.

293 *change favors* exchange tokens; *repair* i.e. repair hither, arrive   297 *damask* i.e. mingled red and white complexion   298 *vailing* shedding; *blown* i.e. full-blown   299 *Avaunt, perplexity* i.e. away with riddling   317 *utters* issues, vends   319 *wakes* night revels; *wassails* drinking sessions   320 *by gross* wholesale   324 *carve* i.e. woo by flattery   326 *nice* foppish   327 *tables* i.e. backgammon   329 *mean* (an 'in-between' vocal part); *ushering* i.e. playing the groom or gentleman-in-waiting   338 *Behavior* i.e. fine manners   339 *madman* wag, madcap   341 *all . . . foul* i.e. a fall of hail means foul weather   346 *so hold* so uphold   349 *virtue* power (with quibble following)   350 *nickname* miscall   356 *breaking cause* i.e. cause of breaking   362 *mess* group of four   366 *to* in   371 *happy* apt   374 *dry* tart   375 *Your wit* i.e. the greatness of your wit; *foolish* i.e. seem foolish in comparison   375–77 *When . . . lose light* i.e. the power of the sun dims even the keenest sight

This is the flow'r that smiles on every one,
To show his teeth as white as whalès-bone;
And consciences that will not die in debt
Pay him the due of 'honey-tongued Boyet.'

KING
A blister on his sweet tongue, with my heart,
That put Armado's page out of his part!
Enter the Ladies [with Boyet].

BEROWNE
338 See where it comes! Behavior, what wert thou,
339 Till this madman showed thee? and what art thou now?

KING
All hail, sweet madam, and fair time of day.

PRINCESS
341 'Fair' in 'all hail' is foul, as I conceive.

KING
Construe my speeches better, if you may.

PRINCESS
Then wish me better – I will give you leave.

KING
We came to visit you, and purpose now
To lead you to our court. Vouchsafe it then.

PRINCESS
346 This field shall hold me, and so hold your vow.
Nor God nor I delights in perjured men.

KING
Rebuke me not for that which you provoke.
349 The virtue of your eye must break my oath.

PRINCESS
350 You nickname virtue. 'Vice' you should have spoke;
For virtue's office never breaks men's troth.
Now, by my maiden honor, yet as pure
As the unsullied lily, I protest,
A world of torments though I should endure,
I would not yield to be your house's guest,
356 So much I hate a breaking cause to be
Of heavenly oaths, vowed with integrity.

KING
O, you have lived in desolation here,
Unseen, unvisited, much to our shame.

PRINCESS
Not so, my lord. It is not so, I swear.
We have had pastimes here and pleasant game.
362 A mess of Russians left us but of late.

KING
How, madam? Russians?

PRINCESS   Ay, in truth, my lord;
Trim gallants, full of courtship and of state.

ROSALINE
Madam, speak true. It is not so, my lord.
My lady, to the manner of the days,
366 In courtesy gives undeserving praise.
We four indeed confronted were with four
In Russian habit. Here they stayed an hour
And talked apace; and in that hour, my lord,
They did not bless us with one happy word.
371 I dare not call them fools; but this I think,
When they are thirsty, fools would fain have drink.

BEROWNE
This jest is dry to me. Gentle sweet,
374 Your wit makes wise things foolish. When we greet
375 With eyes best seeing heaven's fiery eye,
By light we lose light. Your capacity
Is of that nature that to your huge store

Wise things seem foolish and rich things but poor.

ROSALINE
This proves you wise and rich, for in my eye –

BEROWNE
I am a fool and full of poverty.

ROSALINE
But that you take what doth to you belong,
It were a fault to snatch words from my tongue.

BEROWNE
O, I am yours, and all that I possess.

ROSALINE
All the fool mine?

BEROWNE   I cannot give you less.

ROSALINE
Which of the vizards was it that you wore?

BEROWNE
Where? when? what vizard? Why demand you this?

ROSALINE
388   There, then, that vizard; that superfluous case
That hid the worse, and showed the better face.

KING
We were descried. They'll mock us now downright.

DUMAINE
Let us confess, and turn it to a jest.

PRINCESS
392   Amazed, my lord? Why looks your Highness sad?

ROSALINE
393   Help! Hold his brows! He'll sound. Why look you pale?
Seasick, I think, coming from Muscovy.

BROWNE
Thus pour the stars down plagues for perjury.
Can any face of brass hold longer out?
Here stand I, lady; dart thy skill at me.
Bruise me with scorn, confound me with a flout,
Thrust thy sharp wit quite through my ignorance,
400   Cut me to pieces with thy keen conceit;
401   And I will wish thee never more to dance,
402   Nor never more in Russian habit wait.
O, never will I trust to speeches penned,
Nor to the motion of a schoolboy's tongue,
405   Nor never come in vizard to my friend,
406   Nor woo in rime, like a blind harper's song.
407   Taffeta phrases, silken terms precise,
408   Three-piled hyperboles, spruce affection,
409   Figures pedantical – these summer flies
410   Have blown me full of maggot ostentation.
I do forswear them; and I here protest
By this white glove (how white the hand, God knows)
Henceforth my wooing mind shall be expressed
414   In russet yeas and honest kersey noes.
415   And to begin, wench – so God help me, law! –
416   My love to thee is sound, sans crack or flaw.

ROSALINE
Sans 'sans,' I pray you.

417 BEROWNE   Yet I have a trick
418   Of the old rage. Bear with me, I am sick.
I'll leave it by degrees. Soft, let us see –
420   Write 'Lord have mercy on us' on those three.
They are infected, in their hearts it lies;
They have the plague, and caught it of your eyes.
423   These lords are visited; you are not free,
424   For the Lord's tokens on you do I see.

PRINCESS
425   No, they are free that gave these tokens to us.

BEROWNE
Our states are forfeit. Seek not to undo us.   426

ROSALINE
It is not so, for how can this be true,
That you stand forfeit, being those that sue?   428

BEROWNE
Peace! for I will not have to do with you.

ROSALINE
Nor shall not if I do as I intend.

BEROWNE
Speak for yourselves. My wit is at an end.

KING
Teach us, sweet madam, for our rude transgression
Some fair excuse.

PRINCESS   The fairest is confession.
Were you not here but even now disguised?

KING
Madam, I was.

PRINCESS   And were you well advised?   435

KING
I was, fair madam.

PRINCESS   When you then were here,
What did you whisper in your lady's ear?

KING
That more than all the world I did respect her.

PRINCESS
When she shall challenge this, you will reject her.

KING
Upon mine honor, no.

PRINCESS   Peace, peace, forbear!
Your oath once broke, you force not to forswear.   441

KING
Despise me when I break this oath of mine.

PRINCESS
I will, and therefore keep it. Rosaline,
What did the Russian whisper in your ear?

ROSALINE
Madam, he swore that he did hold me dear
As precious eyesight, and did value me
Above this world; adding thereto, moreover,
That he would wed me or else die my lover.

PRINCESS
God give thee joy of him. The noble lord
Most honorably doth uphold his word.

KING
What mean you, madam? By my life, my troth,
I never swore this lady such an oath.

ROSALINE
By heaven you did, and to confirm it plain
You gave me this, but take it, sir, again.   454

388 *case* covering   392 *Amazed* confused   393 *sound* swoon   400 *conceit* fancy, ingenuity   401 *wish* invite   402 *wait* attend   405 *friend* sweetheart   406 *blind harper's* i.e. performing beggar's, street-singer's   407 *precise* i.e. finely discriminated, as in word-splitting   408 *Three-piled* deep-piled (as in richest velvet); *spruce affection* jaunty affectation   409 *Figures* figures of speech   410 *blown* laid eggs on   414 *russet* homespun; *kersey* woolen cloth   415 *law* (a 'homespun' expletive)   416 *sans* without   417 *Yet* still; *trick* trace   418 *rage* fever   420 *Lord . . . us* (the words posted on houses containing victims of the plague)   423 *visited* infected; *free* i.e. free of infection   424 *tokens* plague-spots   425 *free* i.e. liberal (with *tokens* taken up in the sense of 'gifts')   426 *states* estates; *forfeit* subject to confiscation; *undo* i.e. free, absolve (continuing the play on the word *free*)   428 *sue* (i.e. instead of the ones sued)   435 *well advised* rational   441 *force . . . forswear* i.e. forswear without effort   454 *this* i.e. the favor originally given the Princess

KING
My faith and this the Princess I did give.
I knew her by this jewel on her sleeve.

PRINCESS
Pardon me, sir, this jewel did she wear,
And Lord Berowne, I thank him, is my dear.
What, will you have me, or your pearl again?

BEROWNE
Neither of either; I remit both twain.
461 I see the trick on't. Here was a consent,
Knowing aforehand of our merriment,
463 To dash it like a Christmas comedy.
464 Some carry-tale, some please-man, some slight zany,
465 Some mumble-news, some trencher-knight, some Dick
466 That smiles his cheek in years, and knows the trick
To make my lady laugh when she's disposed,
Told our intents before; which once disclosed,
The ladies did change favors, and then we,
470 Following the signs, wooed but the sign of she.
Now, to our perjury to add more terror,
We are again forsworn, in will and error.
473 Much upon this 'tis. *[to Boyet]* And might not you
Forestall our sport, to make us thus untrue?
475 Do not you know my lady's foot by th' squier,
476 And laugh upon the apple of her eye?
And stand between her back, sir, and the fire,
478 Holding a trencher, jesting merrily?
479 You put our page out. Go, you are allowed.
480 Die when you will, a smock shall be your shroud.
You leer upon me, do you? There's an eye
Wounds like a leaden sword.

BOYET   Full merrily
483 Hath this brave manage, this career, been run.

BEROWNE
484 Lo, he is tilting straight. Peace! I have done.
Enter [Costard, the] Clown.
485 Welcome, pure wit! Thou part'st a fair fray.

COSTARD
O Lord, sir, they would know
Whether the three Worthies shall come in or no.

BEROWNE
What, are there but three?

COSTARD   No, sir; but it is vara fine,
For every one pursents three.

BEROWNE   And three times thrice is nine.

COSTARD
Not so, sir, under correction, sir, I hope, it is not so.
You cannot beg us, sir, I can assure you, sir; we know 491
what we know:
I hope, sir, three times thrice, sir –

BEROWNE   Is not nine?

COSTARD Under correction, sir, we know whereuntil it
doth amount.

BEROWNE By Jove, I always took three threes for nine.

COSTARD O Lord, sir, it were pity you should get your 496
living by reck'ning, sir.

BEROWNE How much is it?

COSTARD O Lord, sir, the parties themselves, the actors,
sir, will show whereuntil it doth amount. For mine own
part, I am, as they say, but to parfect one man in one 501
poor man – Pompion the Great, sir?   502

BEROWNE Art thou one of the Worthies?

COSTARD It pleased them to think me worthy of Pompey
the Great. For mine own part, I know not the degree of
the Worthy, but I am to stand for him.

BEROWNE Go, bid them prepare.

COSTARD
We will turn it finely off, sir; we will take some care. *Exit.*

KING
Berowne, they will shame us. Let them not approach.

BEROWNE
We are shame-proof, my lord; and 'tis some policy 510
To have one show worse than the king's and his company.

KING
I say they shall not come.

PRINCESS
Nay, my good lord, let me o'errule you now.
That sport best pleases that doth least know how;
Where zeal strives to content, and the contents 515
Dies in the zeal of that which it presents. 516
Their form confounded makes most form in mirth 517
When great things laboring perish in their birth.

BEROWNE
A right description of our sport, my lord. 519
Enter [Armado, the] Braggart.

ARMADO Anointed, I implore so much expense of thy
royal sweet breath as will utter a brace of words.
[Converses with the King, and delivers a paper to him.]

PRINCESS Doth this man serve God?

BEROWNE Why ask you?

PRINCESS 'A speaks not like a man of God his making.

ARMADO That is all one, my fair, sweet, honey monarch;
for, I protest, the schoolmaster is exceeding fantastical –
too-too vain, too-too vain – but we will put it, as they
say, to fortuna de la guerra. I wish you the peace of 528
mind, most royal couplement!   *Exit.* 529

KING Here is like to be a good presence of Worthies. He 530
presents Hector of Troy; the swain, Pompey the Great;
the parish curate, Alexander; Armado's page, Hercules;
the pedant, Judas Maccabaeus:
And if these four Worthies in their first show thrive,
These four will change habits and present the other five. 535

BEROWNE There is five in the first show.

KING You are deceivèd, 'tis not so.

BEROWNE
The pedant, the braggart, the hedge-priest, the fool, 538
and the boy –
Abate throw at novum, and the whole world again 540
Cannot pick out five such, take each one in his vein. 541

---

461 *consent* agreement   463 *like* i.e. as one does   464 *please-man* toady; *zany* stooge   465 *mumble-news* gossip; *trencher-knight* parasite   466 *in years* i.e. into the wrinkles of old age   470 *she* i.e. the mistress intended   473 *Much . . . 'tis* i.e. this is about the way of it   475 *squier* square (i.e. have her measure, know how to please her)   476 *apple* pupil (i.e. keep your pleasantries a center of her attention)   478 *trencher* plate   479 *out* out of his part; *allowed* i.e. a privileged fool or jester   480 *smock* petticoat   483 *manage* maneuver on horseback; *career* gallop   484 *tilting straight* i.e. at his word-play immediately   485 *pure wit* i.e. Costard (as compared to Boyet)   491 *beg us* prove us fools (derived from the practise of seeking administration of the property of mental defectives)   496 *pity* i.e. too bad if   501 *parfect* perform (malapropism)   502 *Pompion* pumpkin   510 *policy* good policy   515 *contents* substance   516 *of that . . . presents* i.e. of the performance which presents this substance   517 *form confounded* i.e. ruined artistry; *most form* i.e. superior artistry   519 *right* exact; *our sport* i.e. our show of Muscovites   528 *fortuna . . . guerra* fortunes of war   529 *couplement* couple   530 *presence* appearance, showing   535 *habits* costumes   538 *hedge-priest* (term of contempt for clergyman with no regular stipend)   540 *Abate* barring; *throw at novum* lucky throw (in the dice game of novum or nines)   541 *vein* i.e. characteristic manner

KING
The ship is under sail, and here she comes amain.
Enter [Costard armed, for] Pompey.

COSTARD
I Pompey am –

BOYET You lie, you are not he.

COSTARD
I Pompey am –

544 **BOYET** With libbard's head on knee.

BEROWNE
Well said, old mocker. I must needs be friends with
thee.

COSTARD
I Pompey am, Pompey surnamed the Big –

DUMAINE The 'Great.'

COSTARD It is 'Great,' sir –
Pompey surnamed the Great;
549 *That oft in field, with targe and shield, did make my foe to sweat.*
And travelling along this coast, I here am come by chance,
And lay my arms before the legs of this sweet lass of France.
If your ladyship would say, 'Thanks, Pompey,' I had
done.

PRINCESS Great thanks, great Pompey.

554 **COSTARD** 'Tis not so much worth; but I hope I was perfect. I made a little fault in 'Great.'

BEROWNE My hat to a halfpenny, Pompey proves the
best Worthy.
Enter [Nathaniel, the] Curate, for Alexander.

NATHANIEL
When in the world I lived, I was the world's commander;
By east, west, north, and south, I spread my conquering might;
My scutcheon plain declares that I am Alisander –

BOYET
561 Your nose says, no, you are not; for it stands too right.

BEROWNE
Your nose smells 'no' in this, most tender-smelling
knight.

PRINCESS
The conqueror is dismayed. Proceed, good Alexander.

NATHANIEL
When in the world I lived, I was the world's commander –
[He falters.]

BOYET Most true, 'tis right – you were so, Alisander.

BEROWNE Pompey the Great –

COSTARD Your servant, and Costard.

BEROWNE Take away the conqueror, take away Alisander.

COSTARD *[to Nathaniel]* O, sir, you have overthrown Alisander the conqueror! You will be scraped out of the
571 painted cloth for this. Your lion that holds his pollaxe
572 sitting on a close-stool will be given to Ajax. He will be
the ninth Worthy. A conqueror, and afeard to speak?
Run away for shame, Alisander. *[Nathaniel retires.]*
There, an't shall please you, a foolish mild man; an
honest man, look you, and soon dashed. He is a marvellous good neighbor, faith, and a very good bowler; but
578 for Alisander – alas, you see how 'tis – a little o'erparted.
But there are Worthies a-coming will speak their mind
in some other sort.

PRINCESS Stand aside, good Pompey.
Enter [Holofernes, the] Pedant, for Judas, and
[Moth,] the Boy, for Hercules.

HOLOFERNES
581 Great Hercules is presented by this imp,

Whose club killed Cerberus, that three-headed canus;   582
And when he was a babe, a child, a shrimp,
Thus did he strangle serpents in his manus.   584
Quoniam he seemeth in minority,   585
Ergo I come with this apology.   586
Keep some state in thy exit, and vanish.   *Exit Boy.* 587
Judas I am –

DUMAINE A Judas?   589

HOLOFERNES Not Iscariot, sir.
Judas I am, yclepèd Maccabaeus.   591

DUMAINE Judas Maccabaeus clipt is plain Judas.   592

BEROWNE A kissing traitor. How, art thou proved Judas?   593

HOLOFERNES
Judas I am –

DUMAINE The more shame for you, Judas.

HOLOFERNES What mean you, sir?

BOYET To make Judas hang himself.

HOLOFERNES Begin, sir; you are my elder.   598

BEROWNE Well followed: Judas was hanged on an elder.

HOLOFERNES I will not be put out of countenance.

BEROWNE Because thou hast no face.

HOLOFERNES What is this?

BOYET A cittern-head.   603

DUMAINE The head of a bodkin.   604

BEROWNE A death's face in a ring.   605

LONGAVILLE The face of an old Roman coin, scarce seen.

BOYET The pommel of Caesar's falchion.   607

DUMAINE The carved-bone face on a flask.   608

BEROWNE Saint George's half-cheek in a brooch.   609

DUMAINE Ay, and in a brooch of lead.   610

BEROWNE
Ay, and worn in the cap of a toothdrawer.
And now forward, for we have put thee in countenance.   612

HOLOFERNES You have put me out of countenance.

BEROWNE False. We have given thee faces.

HOLOFERNES But you have outfaced them all.   615

BEROWNE An thou wert a lion, we would do so.

BOYET
Therefore as he is (an ass), let him go.
And so adieu, sweet Jude. Nay, why dost thou stay?

DUMAINE For the latter end of his name.

BEROWNE
For the ass to the Jude? Give it him. Jud-as, away!

HOLOFERNES
This is not generous, not gentle, not humble.   621

BOYET
A light for Monsieur Judas! It grows dark, he may
stumble.   *[Holofernes retires.]*

---

544 *libbard's* leopard's (a reference to the insignia of Pompey, here presumably worn on the knee) 549 *targe* shield 554 *perfect* word-perfect
561 *right* (a reference to Alexander's wry neck which inclined his head
to the left) 571 *painted cloth* (wall hanging picturing the Nine Worthies)
571–72 *lion . . . close-stool* (Alexander's insignia pictured a lion seated in a
chair and holding a battleaxe) 572 *close-stool* seat in a privy; *Ajax* legendary Greek chieftain (with play on 'a jakes' – privy) 578 *o'erparted* i.e.
given too hard a role 581 *imp* shoot, boy 582 *canus* dog 584 *manus*
hands 585 *Quoniam* since 586 *Ergo* therefore 587 *state* dignity 589
A Judas i.e. a traitor 591 *yclepèd* called; *Maccabaeus* (Hebrew warrior)
592 *clipt* shortened 593 *How* how now 598 *you . . . elder* i.e. you are
so wise 603 *cittern* cithern, guitar 604 *bodkin* small dagger 605 *face
head; ring* (death's-head ring worn as a memento mori) 607 *falchion*
sword 608 *flask* i.e. engraved horn flask 609 *half-cheek* profile 610–11
brooch . . . toothdrawer (i.e. an inferior badge bearing insignia, possibly
jawbones, of an inferior occupation) 612 *put . . . countenance* i.e. portrayed you 615 *outfaced* abashed 621 *humble* i.e. considerate, the reverse
of arrogant

PRINCESS
Alas, poor Maccabaeus, how hath he been baited!
Enter [Armado, the] Braggart [for Hector].

624 BEROWNE Hide thy head, Achilles! Here comes Hector in arms.

626 DUMAINE Though my mocks come home by me, I will now be merry.

628 KING Hector was but a Troyan in respect of this.

BOYET But is this Hector?

630 KING I think Hector was not so clean-timbered.

LONGAVILLE His leg is too big for Hector's.

DUMAINE More calf, certain.

633 BOYET No; he is best indued in the small.

BEROWNE This cannot be Hector.

DUMAINE He's a god or a painter; for he makes faces.

ARMADO
636   The armipotent Mars, of lances the almighty,
      Gave Hector a gift –

638 DUMAINE A gilt nutmeg

BEROWNE A lemon.

LONGAVILLE Stuck with cloves.

DUMAINE No, cloven.

ARMADO Peace!
    The armipotent Mars, of lances the almighty,
644   Gave Hector a gift, the heir of Ilion;
645   A man so breathed that certain he would fight, yea
646   From morn till night, out of his pavilion.
      I am that flower –

DUMAINE   That mint.

LONGAVILLE   That columbine.

648 ARMADO Sweet Lord Longaville, rein thy tongue.

649 LONGAVILLE I must rather give it the rein, for it runs against Hector.

651 DUMAINE Ay, and Hector's a greyhound.

ARMADO The sweet war-man is dead and rotten. Sweet chucks, beat not the bones of the buried. When he breathed, he was a man. But I will forward with my device. *[to the Princess]* Sweet royalty, bestow on me the sense of hearing.
      Berowne steps forth [to prompt Costard].

PRINCESS Speak, brave Hector; we are much delighted.

ARMADO I do adore thy sweet Grace's slipper.

BOYET *[aside to Dumaine]* Loves her by the foot.

660 DUMAINE *[aside to Boyet]* He may not by the yard.

ARMADO
    This Hector far surmounted Hannibal –

---

624 *Hide . . . Achilles* i.e. beware, or skulk in your tent, Achilles (the Greek champion who defeated the Trojan Hector) **626** *by me* to me, to afflict me   **628** *Troyan* (1) roisterer, (2) Trojan; *respect of* comparison with **630** *clean-timbered* clean-limbed, well-built   **633** *indued . . . small* endowed in the ankle   **636** *armipotent* powerful in arms   **638–40** *gilt nutmeg . . . cloves* (nutmegs, sometimes gilded, were used to flavor ale and wine, as were lemons stuck with cloves; the latter were also valued for their scent: the joking is obscure but relates to Armado's artificiality)   **644** *Ilion* Troy **645** *so breathed* of such strong lungs, lasting power   **646** *pavilion* jousting-tent   **648** *rein* curb   **649–50** *runs against* (1) tilts against, (2) races   **651** *Hector's a greyhound* i.e. 'Hector' is a term for a greyhound   **660** *yard* (slang for penis)   **666** *quick* pregnant   **668** *infamonize* infamize, slander **678** *Ates* (underworld spirits of discord)   **681** *blood . . . belly* i.e. courage **684** *northern man* border ruffian   **690** *take . . . lower* (1) take you down to your underwear, (2) humiliate you (proverbial)   **691** *uncasing* undressing   **700** *woolward for penance* i.e. with wool next to the skin to discipline the flesh   **713–14** *I have . . . discretion* i.e. I have caught on to the fact that I am abused ('to see day through a little hole' was proverbial for 'to be no fool')

COSTARD The party is gone. Fellow Hector, she is gone. She is two months on her way.

ARMADO What meanest thou?

COSTARD Faith, unless you play the honest Troyan, the poor wench is cast away. She's quick; the child brags in 666 her belly already. 'Tis yours.

ARMADO Dost thou infamonize me among potentates? 668 Thou shalt die.

COSTARD Then shall Hector be whipped for Jaquenetta that is quick by him, and hanged for Pompey that is dead by him.

DUMAINE Most rare Pompey!

BOYET Renowned Pompey!

BEROWNE Greater than great. Great, great, great Pompey! Pompey the Huge!

DUMAINE Hector trembles.

BEROWNE Pompey is moved. More Ates, more Ates! 678 Stir them on! stir them on!

DUMAINE Hector will challenge him.

BEROWNE Ay, if 'a have no more man's blood in his belly 681 than will sup a flea.

ARMADO By the north pole, I do challenge thee.

COSTARD I will not fight with a pole, like a northern man. 684 I'll slash; I'll do it by the sword. I bepray you, let me borrow my arms again.

DUMAINE Room for the incensed Worthies!

COSTARD I'll do it in my shirt.

DUMAINE Most resolute Pompey!

MOTH Master, let me take you a button-hole lower. Do 690 you not see, Pompey is uncasing for the combat? What 691 mean you? You will lose your reputation.

ARMADO Gentlemen and soldiers, pardon me. I will not combat in my shirt.

DUMAINE You may not deny it. Pompey hath made the challenge.

ARMADO Sweet bloods, I both may and will.

BEROWNE What reason have you for't?

ARMADO The naked truth of it is, I have no shirt. I go woolward for penance.   700

BOYET True, and it was enjoined him in Rome for want of linen; since when, I'll be sworn he wore none but a dishclout of Jaquenetta's, and that 'a wears next his heart for a favor.
      Enter a Messenger, Monsieur Marcade.

MARCADE
God save you, madam.

PRINCESS
Welcome, Marcade;
But that thou interrupt'st our merriment.

MARCADE
I am sorry, madam, for the news I bring
Is heavy in my tongue. The king your father –

PRINCESS
Dead, for my life!

MARCADE
Even so. My tale is told.

BEROWNE
Worthies, away! The scene begins to cloud.

ARMADO For mine own part, I breathe free breath. I have 713 seen the day of wrong through the little hole of discretion, and I will right myself like a soldier.
                            Exeunt Worthies.

KING
How fares your Majesty?

PRINCESS
Boyet, prepare. I will away to-night.
KING
Madam, not so. I do beseech you, stay.
PRINCESS
Prepare, I say. I thank you, gracious lords,
For all your fair endeavors, and entreat,
Out of a new-sad soul, that you vouchsafe
722   In your rich wisdom to excuse or hide
723   The liberal opposition of our spirits,
If over-boldly we have borne ourselves
725   In the converse of breath : your gentleness
726   Was guilty of it. Farewell, worthy lord.
727   A heavy heart bears not a humble tongue ;
728   Excuse me so, coming too short of thanks
729   For my great suit so easily obtained.
KING
730   The extreme parts of time extremely forms
All causes to the purpose of his speed,
732   And often, at his very loose, decides
That which long process could not arbitrate.
734   And though the mourning brow of progeny
Forbid the smiling courtesy of love
736   The holy suit which fain it would convince,
Yet, since love's argument was first on foot,
Let not the cloud of sorrow justle it
From what it purposed ; since to wail friends lost
Is not by much so wholesome-profitable
As to rejoice at friends but newly found.
PRINCESS
742   I understand you not. My griefs are double.
BEROWNE
Honest plain words best pierce the ear of grief ;
744   And by these badges understand the king.
745   For your fair sakes have we neglected time,
Played foul play with our oaths. Your beauty, ladies,
Hath much deformed us, fashioning our humors
748   Even to the opposèd end of our intents ;
And what in us hath seemed ridiculous –
750   As love is full of unbefitting strains,
All wanton as a child, skipping and vain,
Formed by the eye and therefore, like the eye,
753   Full of straying shapes, of habits and of forms,
Varying in subjects as the eye doth roll
To every varied object in his glance ;
756   Which parti-coated presence of loose love
Put on by us, if, in your heavenly eyes,
758   Have misbecomed our oaths and gravities,
Those heavenly eyes that look into these faults
760   Suggested us to make. Therefore, ladies,
Our love being yours, the error that love makes
Is likewise yours. We to ourselves prove false,
By being once false for ever to be true
To those that make us both – fair ladies, you.
And even that falsehood, in itself a sin,
Thus purifies itself and turns to grace.
PRINCESS
We have received your letters, full of love ;
Your favors, the ambassadors of love ;
769   And in our maiden council rated them
770   At courtship, pleasant jest, and courtesy,
771   As bombast and as lining to the time.
772   But more devout than this in our respects
Have we not been, and therefore met your loves

In their own fashion, like a merriment.
DUMAINE
Our letters, madam, showed much more than jest.
LONGAVILLE
So did our looks.
ROSALINE   We did not quote them so.   776
KING
Now, at the latest minute of the hour,
Grant us your loves.
PRINCESS   A time, methinks, too short
To make a world-without-end bargain in.
No, no, my lord, your Grace is perjured much,
Full of dear guiltiness ; and therefore this –   781
If for my love (as there is no such cause)   782
You will do aught, this shall you do for me :   783
Your oath I will not trust, but go with speed
To some forlorn and naked hermitage,
Remote from all the pleasures of the world ;
There stay until the twelve celestial signs   787
Have brought about the annual reckoning.
If this austere insociable life
Change not your offer made in heat of blood ;
If frosts and fasts, hard lodging and thin weeds,   791
Nip not the gaudy blossoms of your love,
But that it bear this trial, and last love ;   793
Then, at the expiration of the year,
Come challenge me, challenge me by these deserts,   795
And, by this virgin palm now kissing thine,
I will be thine ; and till that instant, shut
My woeful self up in a mourning house,
Raining the tears of lamentation
For the remembrance of my father's death.
If this thou do deny, let our hands part ;
Neither intitled in the other's heart.
KING
If this, or more than this, I would deny,
To flatter up these powers of mine with rest,   804
The sudden hand of death close up mine eye !
Hence hermit then – my heart is in thy breast.   806
[BEROWNE
And what to me, my love ? and what to me ?   807
ROSALINE
You must be purgèd too ; your sins are racked,   808
You are attaint with faults and perjury ;
Therefore, if you my favor mean to get,

722 *hide* i.e. ignore   723 *liberal* too free   725 *converse of breath* exchange of conversation ; *gentleness* courtesy   726 *guilty of* responsible for   727 *humble* i.e. adapted to courtly civilities   728 *so* therefore   729 *suit* i.e. the property claims (which Navarre has evidently granted)   730–31 *The . . . speed* i.e. final moments enforce quick decisions   732 *his* i.e. time's ; *loose* slipping away, release (archery term)   734 *progeny* i.e. child of the deceased   736 *suit . . . convince* i.e. the case it would like to make   742 *double* i.e. her failure to understand is an additional grief (?)   744 *badges* tokens, testimony   745 *neglected time* i.e. disregarded proper occasion   748 *Even . . . intents* quite contrary to our intentions   750 *strains* impulses   753 *habits* demeanors   756 *parti-coated presence* i.e. jesting appearance   758 *misbecomed* been unbecoming to   760 *Suggested . . . make* tempted us to make them   769 *rated* evaluated   770 *At* at no more than   771 *bombast . . . time* i.e. way to fill in time ; *bombast, lining* padding   772 *devout* serious ; *respects* consideration   776 *quote* interpret   781 *dear* grievous   782 *such cause* i.e. reason why you should   783 *aught* anything (i.e. everything)   787 *signs* i.e. of the zodiac (the months)   791 *weeds* garments   793 *that* so long as ; *last* remain   795 *these deserts* i.e. demonstrated merit   804 *flatter up* pamper   806 *hermit* i.e. as a hermit   807–12 *Berowne . . . sick* (a passage probably marked for excision in the manuscript since another version appears below, ll. 827 ff.)   808 *racked* stretched out

A twelvemonth shall you spend, and never rest,
But seek the weary beds of people sick.]

DUMAINE
But what to me, my love ? but what to me ?
A wife ?

KATHARINE A beard, fair health, and honesty ;
With three-fold love I wish you all these three.

DUMAINE
O, shall I say 'I thank you, gentle wife' ?

KATHARINE
Not so, my lord. A twelvemonth and a day
I'll mark no words that smooth-faced wooers say.
Come when the kind doth to my lady come ;
Then, if I have much love, I'll give you some.

DUMAINE
I'll serve thee true and faithfully till then.

KATHARINE
Yet swear not, lest ye be forsworn again.

LONGAVILLE
What says Maria ?

MARIA   At the twelvemonth's end
I'll change my black gown for a faithful friend.

LONGAVILLE
825   I'll stay with patience, but the time is long.

MARIA
826   The liker you – few taller are so young.

BEROWNE
Studies my lady ? Mistress, look on me.
Behold the window of my heart, mine eye,
What humble suit attends thy answer there.
Impose some service on me for thy love.

ROSALINE
Oft have I heard of you, my Lord Berowne,
Before I saw you ; and the world's large tongue
Proclaims you for a man replete with mocks,
834   Full of comparisons and wounding flouts,
835   Which you on all estates will execute
That lie within the mercy of your wit.
837   To weed this wormwood from your fructful brain,
And therewithal to win me, if you please –
Without the which I am not to be won –
You shall this twelvemonth term from day to day
Visit the speechless sick, and still converse
With groaning wretches ; and your task shall be
With all the fierce endeavor of your wit
844   To enforce the painèd impotent to smile.

BEROWNE
To move wild laughter in the throat of death ?
It cannot be ; it is impossible :
Mirth cannot move a soul in agony.

ROSALINE
Why, that's the way to choke a gibing spirit,
849   Whose influence is begot of that loose grace
Which shallow laughing hearers give to fools.
A jest's prosperity lies in the ear

Of him that hears it, never in the tongue
Of him that makes it. Then, if sickly ears,
Deafed with the clamors of their own dear groans,   854
Will hear your idle scorns, continue then,
And I will have you and that fault withal ;   856
But if they will not, throw away that spirit,
And I shall find you empty of that fault,
Right joyful of your reformation.

BEROWNE
A twelvemonth ? Well, befall what will befall,
I'll jest a twelvemonth in an hospital.

PRINCESS [to the King]
Ay, sweet my lord ; and so I take my leave.

KING
No, madam ; we will bring you on your way.

BEROWNE
Our wooing doth not end like an old play ;
Jack hath not Jill. These ladies' courtesy   865
Might well have made our sport a comedy.

KING
Come, sir, it wants a twelvemonth and a day,
And then 'twill end.

BEROWNE   That's too long for a play.

Enter [Armado, the] Braggart.

ARMADO Sweet majesty, vouchsafe me –

PRINCESS Was not that Hector ?

DUMAINE The worthy knight of Troy.

ARMADO I will kiss thy royal finger, and take leave. I am a
votary ; I have vowed to Jaquenetta to hold the plough   873
for her sweet love three year. But, most esteemed greatness, will you hear the dialogue that the two learned   875
men have compiled in praise of the owl and the cuckoo ?
It should have followed in the end of our show.

KING Call them forth quickly ; we will do so.

ARMADO Holla ! approach.

Enter all.

This side is Hiems, Winter ; this Ver, the Spring ; the
one maintained by the owl, th' other by the cuckoo. Ver,
begin.

The Song.

[SPRING] When daisies pied and violets blue
     And lady-smocks all silver-white   884
     And cuckoo-buds of yellow hue   885
       Do paint the meadows with delight,
     The cuckoo then, on every tree,
     Mocks married men ; for thus sings he,
              Cuckoo ;
Cuckoo, cuckoo : O, word of fear,
Unpleasing to a married ear !

When shepherds pipe on oaten straws,   892
     And merry larks are ploughmen's clocks,   893
When turtles tread, and rooks, and daws,   894
     And maidens bleach their summer smocks,
     The cuckoo then, on every tree,
     Mocks married men ; for thus sings he,
              Cuckoo ;
Cuckoo, cuckoo : O, word of fear,
Unpleasing to a married ear !

WINTER   When icicles hang by the wall,
     And Dick the shepherd blows his nail,   902
     And Tom bears logs into the hall,
     And milk comes frozen home in pail,

825 *stay* wait   826 *liker* more like   834 *comparisons* i.e. similes of a derisive
sort ; *flouts* gibes   835 *estates* sorts of people   837 *fructful* fruitful   844
painèd impotent those prostrated by suffering   849 *loose grace* slack approval   854 *dear* grievous   856 *withal* in addition   865 *courtesy* polite
compliance   873 *hold the plough* i.e. toil at husbandry   875 *dialogue*
debate   884 *lady-smocks* cuckoo-flowers (cardamine pratensis)   885 *cuckoo-
buds* buttercups (ranunculus bulbosus)   892 *oaten straws* pipes made of oat
reeds   893 *ploughmen's clocks* (since ploughmen 'rise with the lark')   894
turtles tread turtledoves mate   902 *nail* fingernails

When blood is nipped, and ways be foul,
Then nightly sings the staring owl,
                    Tu-who;
Tu-whit, tu-who : a merry note,
909   While greasy Joan doth keel the pot.

When all aloud the wind doth blow,
911   And coughing drowns the parson's saw,
And birds sit brooding in the snow,
      And Marian's nose looks red and raw,
914   When roasted crabs hiss in the bowl,
Then nightly sings the staring owl,
                         Tu-who;

Tu-whit, tu-who : a merry note,
While greasy Joan doth keel the pot.

[ARMADO] The words of Mercury are harsh after the   919
songs of Apollo. [You, that way : we, this way.   920
                              Exeunt omnes.]

909 *keel* stir and skim (to prevent boiling over)   **911** *saw* moral maxim
914 *crabs* crab-apples   **919** *Mercury* messenger of the gods (but associated
with clever sophistry)   **920** *Apollo* Greek god (associated with song and
beauty)

THE MERCHANT OF VENICE

INTRODUCTION

The running title of the earliest edition describes *The Merchant of Venice* as a "comicall history" – in terms of the time, a play with a happy ending. The role of Shylock may have been comic also in the sense of being laughable, or even occasionally farcical. Public attitudes of the age suggest this. London playgoers of 1596–97 would have included many who jibed at Dr Roderigo Lopez, the Christianized Portuguese Jew and royal physician, who in 1594 was convicted on doubtful evidence of plotting to poison Queen Elizabeth. As Camden tells the story, just before Lopez was publicly hanged and quartered at Tyburn he protested from the scaffold that "he had loved the Queene as he loved Jesus Christ," an appeal, Camden adds, "which from a man of the Jewish profession was heard not without laughter" (*Annals*, 1635, p. 431). At the time of the Lopez affair Christopher Marlowe's older play, *The Jew of Malta*, was successfully revived by the Admiral's Men, the competitors of Shakespeare's company, and we may suppose that a year or two later *The Merchant* was written and staged. More than a hundred years afterward, in 1701, an adapted version of the play appeared with the comedian Thomas Dogget as Shylock. Of this production Nicholas Rowe, after referring to Shakespeare's Shylock as an "incomparable Character," wrote, " . . . tho' we have seen that Play Receiv'd and Acted as a Comedy and the Part of the *Jew* perform'd by an Excellent Comedian, yet I cannot but think it was design'd Tragically by the Author" (*Works of Shakespeare*, 1709, I, xix).

Such are a few of the well-known facts about *The Merchant*'s history and the tradition surrounding its earlier production. Facts, however, do not always speak clearly. What these tell us is that our ancestors could find entertainment in Jew-baiting; the question they do not answer is whether Shakespeare catered to that taste fully or with interesting modifications. If the question has an answer, only Shakespeare's play can give it.

Rowe's objection to a comic *Merchant of Venice* is sometimes called the beginning of sentimental interpretation, although he actually asked simply that tragic "fierceness and fellness" replace comedy as the mood and tone of the play. Much more than that ultimately happened. With a succession of eighteenth- and nineteenth-century actors the role of Shylock grew impressively, so that by Irving's day pride of race and noble scorn under persecution had replaced any motives of buffoonery there may have been in earlier tradition. Our own time, frequently one of contradictions, has seen Shylock sometimes cast as a pathetic victim of his environment, and recast in the name of historical accuracy as a comic butt and stock villain. For understandable reasons the historical interpretation has not dominated stage production.

At one extreme, then, is Shylock the scapegoat-clown, and at the other a broken figure who never meant harm with his "merry bond" until "warped" by betrayal and degradation. The reader or playgoer cannot avoid some kind of choice here, but if he respects Shakespeare's art he will see to it, so far as he can, that the play itself guides his judgment. He may, for example, desire a tragic Shylock but decide that the comically romantic fifth act makes this dramatically unworkable.

It is possible, of course, that the play by itself suggests no clear interpretation. One who adopts this view should be sure, however, that he is not transferring his own confusion to Shakespeare. Many critics have said that the Shylock role "ran away" with its creator, and thus remains at variance with the play. They add, correctly, that even with this contradiction *The Merchant* could have been a stage success. But in that case its success would have overlain an artistic failure. Before we assume such a failure, we owe to Shakespeare, and to ourselves, an examination of his play for any design which brings Shylock within a dominant theme and tone of the comedy. Such an inquiry may appear to overemphasize a single character, but its necessary purpose can be a consideration of something larger – the play and its meaning.

Two things at least become clear from Act IV: that Shakespeare's major ethical theme is Christian mercy versus pagan retaliation, and that in thoughtful comedy such moral issues can be the backbone of good entertainment. It is interesting, moreover, that Shakespeare prepares us from the beginning for the trial scene and its disposition of Shylock. Perhaps he realized that if mercy is to win effectively it must triumph over an adversary who is more than the butt of audience ridicule; but in addition he may have sensed that the adversary of mercy must not be allowed undue sympathy or stature, for then his dismissal and the final scene at Belmont would lack dramatic fitness. In any event, Shylock's first scene points to such matters of concern in Shakespeare's working plan. In I, iii, the pattern seems fully formed with a Shylock who is half impressive, half grotesque. Vividly introduced is his habit of phrasal repetition – "three thousand ducats," "three months," echoed and reechoed through the scene. He alternately grovels ("Ho no, no, no . . .") and stiffens ("I will be assured I may . . ."). His variety begins to be interesting; he can leave a formal soliloquy of hate to set forth informally and fondly on the story of Jacob and the lambs which is supposed to justify usury. Insulted for his pains, he briefly submits but then startles us with his first memorable passage of defiance, the "Jewish gaberdine" speech. And he surprises us again with a show of comic abasement and temporizing over the "merry bond."

After being depicted as spoil-sport and miser in his dealings with Jessica and Launcelot, and after being reported by Solanio and Salerio in the "passion so . . . strange, outrageous, and so variable" – "My daughter! O my ducats! O my daughter!" – Shylock encounters the Christians again in Act III. Once more his peculiar repetition, the speech habit one critic describes as "compulsive": "You knew, none so well, none so well as you . . . ," and later, "Go, Tubal, and meet me at our synagogue; go, good Tubal; at our synagogue, Tubal." Once again pathos and farce are combined, as laments for a lost daughter mingle with wails over lost money and treasure exchanged for monkeys. Within this odd complex the finest of Shylock's moments is now reached as Salerio, asking what human flesh is good for, brings on "Hath not a Jew eyes. . . ." Some historians tell us that this passage was meant to be as comic as the surrounding material, and their arguments can be persuasive until, perhaps, one re-experiences the quality of the passage, as well as a very different quality in the speech of Shakespearean characters (e.g., Polonius) when they are clearly meant to be rhetorically absurd. Such absurdity is wholly lacking in Shylock's better moments of retaliation and self-justification.

But if "Hath not a Jew eyes" is a splendid speech, it is not, as often read, a cry for tolerance. It expresses Shylock's just resentment and, at the same time, the vindictive fallacy which will undo him. If like Christians, Jews have eyes, are warmed and cooled by the same winter and summer, then like Christians they will exact revenge. "The villainy you teach me I will execute, and it shall go hard but I will better the instruction." The Elizabethan audience could have warmed to Shylock at this point – not "sympathetically" but with interest and a strange pause in the laughter. It knew as well as any audience has known that what Shylock says about Christian vengeance is true in too large a measure. Many of its members could have sensed, however, that Shylock is about to enter, understandably, the trap that awaits anyone, Jew *or* Christian, who reduces himself to the ethical level of his persecutors by meeting evil with evil. Those who did not perceive this could have caught it plainly as the fourth act unfolded, for it is the substance and point of the trial episode. Shylock's self-styled "Christian" course of revenge condemns him as it would condemn any Christian. Even so, there is much in the play and its age which condemns and ridicules him simply because he is a Jew, and we should not try to explain it away. But Shakespeare, like Marlowe before him, makes it very plain that Jews can learn bad habits from the large family of Christian hypocrites. An Elizabethan dramatist could not have gone much further in clear, unsentimental fair dealing without becoming, for his time, a prophetic visionary.

In a single long scene of Act IV the tables are turned. Again, as this time he moves not toward the trap but into it, Shylock insists that he is imitating Christians in all he does. Just as his persecutors cannot abide cats, pigs, or bagpipes, so he cannot abide Antonio. Once more the repetitive beat of phrase ("I'll not answer that" – "Is it answered?" – "Now for your answer" – "Are you answered?") as Shylock for the last time justifies himself to

Christians by citing Christian practise as an example: they own slaves; shall he say, "Let them be free"? They will answer that the slaves are theirs, that they bought them, and so does he answer:

> The pound of flesh which I demand of him
> Is dearly bought, is mine, and I will have it.

The point he makes is scarcely noble, but the passion and the eloquence and the scorn of hypocrisy are – for the moment – soon ended. The old cormorant is having his hour, but it is soon ended. If in tragedy the heavens may seem to collapse, in comedy the roof falls in, as it now does upon Shylock whetting his knife and chortling of Daniel: he is defeated on the bond and becomes a most uncomfortable recipient of mercy at the hands of Christians from whom he thought he had learned how to be legalistic and vengeful. Only Gratiano (in pointed contrast with the others) remains to cry revenge.

PORTIA What mercy can you render him, Antonio?
GRATIANO A halter gratis! Nothing else, for God's sake!

Gratiano, however, speaks alone. Shylock escapes with his life, his freedom, and half his wealth, all of which he had forfeited under his dedicated scheme for imitating the much too common behavior of Christians. These Christians – Portia, the Duke, and Antonio – have smothered him with mercy.

Modern readers often object to the mercy on two grounds; they say that Shylock is wrongfully compelled to forsake his religion and they complain that true mercy would "justify" him, since he resorted to evil because of persecution. To the first complaint only history can attempt an answer: our ancestors believed in eternal damnation and many of them considered it mercy to "enforce" Christianity which alone, they thought, could bring salvation. As for the second objection, Shakespeare is perhaps more clearheaded and less sentimental than many of us. He seems to understand that false Christians have made Shylock what he is; at least he allows Shylock to say so, strenuously and effectively. Yet Shakespeare dramatizes the homely but evasive truth that no matter how "understandable" hate and reprisal are, all who indulge them – even the persecuted – are equally guilty, and only the appearance of mercy can break the chain of evil returned for evil. Hence forgiveness and mercy redeem a discordant world in the fourth act and open the way for concord and a world of music in the fifth.

The Merchant of Venice is much more than Shylock and his bond. Shakespeare's plot skillfully joins several stories: the bond and the pound of flesh, the loyal friendship of Antonio and Bassanio, the suitors and the caskets, the Gratiano–Nerissa and Lorenzo–Jessica courtships, and the episode of the rings. *Il Pecorone* of Ser Giovanni Fiorentino, published at Milan in 1558, contained the pound-of-flesh story (complete with Jewish usurer and lady-as-lawyer), a wooing by "test" (although not the casket device), and the ring story. Marlowe's *The Jew of Malta* may have suggested the Shylock–Jessica relationship. The casket device was available in translation from the *Gesta Romanorum*. Possible minor sources are the ballad of *Gernutus* and Anthony Munday's *Zelauto* (1580). When one reads Shakespeare's sources it becomes clear, however, that the combination of diverse materials in the narrative originals gave him no real help in constructing his play. Those interested in the art of playwriting will enjoy following Shakespeare as he introduces and develops the various elements of *The Merchant* by an adroit sequence of scenes within the fluid Elizabethan staging, which this edition emphasizes. The process culminates in the scene of Bassanio's successful choice, where, as R. G. Moulton observed long ago, the several stories meet: Bassanio chooses, wins, and opens the way for Gratiano; Lorenzo and Jessica, newly eloped, bring in Salerio from Venice to reveal forfeiture of the bond, which raises the claims of friendship; and the lovers exchange the rings which will give such liveliness to the fifth act. An earlier play now lost may have contained some of the plot combinations, but if so, what we know of playwriting before Shakespeare makes it impossible to believe that it could have anticipated his structural plan.

The verse is Shakespeare at his early lyrical best, but its exuberance is controlled by dramatic purpose and fitness. Salerio's opening virtuosity ending in his image of the "wealthy Andrew docked in sand," and Gratiano's lines on men whose faces do "cream and mantle like a standing pond," nicely fit the speakers and the situation. So do Shylock's passages of self-justification in I, iii and III, i. Not only are they expertly set going but they are enhanced by dramatic context. "Hath not a Jew eyes" gains greatly from Salerio's taunting "What's that good for?" which launches it, and from Shylock's lines with Tubal which follow it and qualify its effect. Even the set pieces, the lyrical passages of Act V, are dramatically paced. At this relatively early date Shakespeare had mastered the art of poetry within the exacting medium of drama.

A unifying element of the verse is phrasal repetition in varying forms for varying purposes. As a rhythmic quality of Shylock's speech it runs steadily for four acts, but this important effect, already noted, has its counterparts. Begin, for example, with Shylock's words: "Two thousand ducats in that, and other precious, precious jewels. I would my daughter were dead at my foot, and the jewels in her ear! Would she were hearsed at my foot, and the ducats in her coffin!" (III, i, 77–80) Compare this echoing of phrase with Portia's:

> Though for myself alone
> I would not be ambitious in my wish
> To wish myself much better, yet for you
> I would be trebled twenty times myself,
> A thousand times more fair, ten thousand times more rich,
> That only to stand high in your account,
> I might in virtues, beauties, livings, friends,
> Exceed account.   (III, ii, 150–57)

Add another instance, Bassanio's speech at III, ii, 252–63, and observe finally how the unity in variety extends to the quite different but still analogous passages of V, i, 1–24 ("in such a night") and 192–208 ("the ring").

The Merchant of Venice fully represents Shakespeare's ability to generate "belief" in the fabulous. From the sparse account of one source he drew the wooing test and staged it as the cumulative fantasy of Morocco, Arragon, and Bassanio in their choosing of the caskets. Out of the simple double locale of his source material he built not just two cities, Venice and Belmont, but two symbolic worlds: one commercial, precarious, discordant; the other hospitable, gentle, filled with music. And starting with mere names and events he retold the ancient tale of the usurer and his pound of flesh; the result is Shylock, who in spite of his origin as a stock character is now one of the truly mythic figures of our literature. But these achievements can be misinterpreted. It may seem surprising that a romantic and fanciful play has excited so much moral judgment of its characters (as though they were real people), and so much argument about its law courts, its financial backgrounds, its Jews and its Gentiles (as though they were intendedly historical). In a broad, flexible sense, of course, even romantic fable is historically revealing; Shakespeare's usury theme, for instance, reflects actual economic problems of his time, and Bassanio's advantageous marriage suggests contemporary social customs. The difficulty, however, is that an interesting and frequently subtle relationship between romance and life is sometimes confused with a one-to-one correspondence between the details of fiction and the details of actuality. The literature-and-life relationship is thus mistaken for a kind of identity, and one reason for this is that the artist makes illusion more significant, and therefore more "real," than day-to-day experience. The more imaginatively meaningful he is, the more literally he may be taken. Those who confuse dramatic characters with real people are likely, for example, to consider Bassanio a materialist and opportunist; those who see that art creates its own world with its own emphasis will take him for what he is meant to be – a symbolic quester for love and the Golden Fleece who has the wit to find them in the leaden casket.

University of Washington   BRENTS STIRLING

NOTE ON THE TEXT

The Merchant of Venice was first published in 1600, in a good text which may have been printed from Shakespeare's own draft. From this (the "Heyes" quarto) were printed the "Roberts" quarto of 1619 (falsely dated 1600) and the folio text of 1623, the latter adding a few stage directions possibly derived from a prompt-copy. The present edition closely follows the text of the first quarto. As in other modern editions, the character-name "Salarino," which occurs in the quarto stage directions of I, i; II, iv, vi, viii; III, i, has been eliminated in favor of consistent use of the character-name "Salerio," which occurs elsewhere in the stage directions and in the speeches of the play. The quarto texts are not divided into acts and scenes; the folio text is divided only into acts. The act–scene division supplied marginally for reference in the present edition follows the act division of the folio and adds the subdivision into scenes provided by later editors. All substantive departures from the quarto text other than those noted above are here listed, with the adopted reading in italics followed by the quarto reading in roman. Many of the adopted readings are from the second quarto and the folio.

I, i, 27 *docked* docks   113 *Is that* It is that
II, i, s.d. *Morocco* Morochus   31 *thee*, the   35 *rogue* rage
II, ii, 3–8 *Gobbo* Iobbe
II, iii, 11 *did* do
II, vii, 69 *tombs* timber
II, viii, 39 *Slubber* Slumber
III, i, 95 *Heard* Heere
III, ii, 67 *eyes* eye   81 *vice* voyce   117 *whether* whither
III, iii s.d. *Solanio* Salerio
III, iv, 49 *Padua* Mantua   50 *cousin's* cosin   53 *traject* Tranect
III, v, 20 *e'en* in   70 *merit it* mean it, it   77 *a wife* wife
IV, i, 30 *his state* this states   31 *flint* flints   51 *Master* Maisters
   74 *bleat* bleake   75 *pines* of Pines   100 *is* as   208 *thrice* twice
   396 *Gratiano* Shylock
V, i, 41–42 *Master Lorenzo? Master Lorenzo!* M. Lorenzo, &
   M. Lorenzo   49 *Sweet soul* (appended to preceding speech)
   152 *give it you* give you

THE MERCHANT OF VENICE

[NAMES OF THE ACTORS

The Duke of Venice
The Prince of Morocco ⎫ suitors to Portia
The Prince of Arragon ⎭
Antonio, a merchant of Venice
Bassanio, his friend, suitor to Portia
Gratiano ⎫
Salerio ⎬ friends to Antonio and Bassanio
Solanio ⎭
Lorenzo, in love with Jessica
Shylock, a Jew
Tubal, a Jew, his friend

Launcelot Gobbo, a clown, servant to Shylock
Old Gobbo, father to Launcelot
Leonardo, servant to Bassanio
Balthasar ⎫ servants to Portia
Stephano ⎭
Portia, an heiress
Nerissa, her gentlewoman-in-waiting
Jessica, daughter to Shylock
Magnificoes of Venice, Court Officers,
  Jailer, Servants, and other Attendants

Scene: Venice and Belmont]

*

I, i　　*Enter Antonio, Salerio, and Solanio.*

ANTONIO

In sooth I know not why I am so sad.
It wearies me, you say it wearies you;
But how I caught it, found it, or came by it,
What stuff 'tis made of, whereof it is born,
5　I am to learn;
6　And such a want-wit sadness makes of me
That I have much ado to know myself.

SALERIO

Your mind is tossing on the ocean,
9　There where your argosies with portly sail –
Like signiors and rich burghers on the flood,
11　Or as it were, the pageants of the sea –
12　Do overpeer the petty traffickers
13　That cursy to them, do them reverence,
As they fly by them with their woven wings.

SOLANIO

Believe me, sir, had I such venture forth,
The better part of my affections would
Be with my hopes abroad. I should be still
Plucking the grass to know where sits the wind,
19　Peering in maps for ports and piers and roads;
And every object that might make me fear
Misfortune to my ventures, out of doubt
Would make me sad.

SALERIO　　　　　My wind cooling my broth
23　Would blow me to an ague when I thought

What harm a wind too great might do at sea.
I should not see the sandy hourglass run
But I should think of shallows and of flats,
And see my wealthy Andrew docked in sand, 　27
Vailing her high top lower than her ribs 　28
To kiss her burial. Should I go to church
And see the holy edifice of stone
And not bethink me straight of dangerous rocks,
Which touching but my gentle vessel's side
Would scatter all her spices on the stream,
Enrobe the roaring waters with my silks –
And in a word, but even now worth this,
And now worth nothing? Shall I have the thought
To think on this, and shall I lack the thought
That such a thing bechanced would make me sad? 　38
But tell not me! I know Antonio
Is sad to think upon his merchandise.

ANTONIO

Believe me, no. I thank my fortune for it
My ventures are not in one bottom trusted, 　42
Nor to one place; nor is my whole estate 　43
Upon the fortune of this present year.
Therefore my merchandise makes me not sad.

SOLANIO

Why then you are in love.

ANTONIO　　　　　Fie, fie!

SOLANIO

Not in love neither? Then let us say you are sad
Because you are not merry; and 'twere as easy
For you to laugh and leap, and say you are merry
Because you are not sad. Now by two-headed Janus, 　50
Nature hath framed strange fellows in her time:
Some that will evermore peep through their eyes
And laugh like parrots at a bagpiper,
And other of such vinegar aspect
That they'll not show their teeth in way of smile

I, i A street in Venice　5 *am to learn* have yet to learn　6 *want-wit* fool,
dullard　9 *argosies* large merchant ships; *portly* i.e. swelling, billowing
11 *pageants* i.e. like 'floats' in a procession　12 *overpeer* tower above
13 *cursy* bow　19 *roads* anchorages　23 *ague* fit of trembling　27 *Andrew*
name of a ship　28 *Vailing* bowing　38 *bechanced* having happened　42
bottom ship　43–44 *nor is . . . year* nor is all my wealth risked at this
one time　50 *Janus* Roman god with two faces, one smiling and the other
sad

56 Though Nestor swear the jest be laughable.

Enter Bassanio, Lorenzo, and Gratiano.

Here comes Bassanio your most noble kinsman,
Gratiano, and Lorenzo. Fare ye well ;
We leave you now with better company.

SALERIO
I would have stayed till I had made you merry,
If worthier friends had not prevented me.

ANTONIO
Your worth is very dear in my regard.
I take it your own business calls on you,
And you embrace th' occasion to depart.

SALERIO
Good morrow, my good lords.

BASSANIO
Good signiors both, when shall we laugh ? Say, when ?
67 You grow exceeding strange. Must it be so ?

SALERIO
68 We'll make our leisures to attend on yours.

Exeunt Salerio and Solanio.

LORENZO
My Lord Bassanio, since you have found Antonio,
We two will leave you ; but at dinner time
I pray you have in mind where we must meet.

BASSANIO
I will not fail you.

GRATIANO
You look not well, Signior Antonio.
74 You have too much respect upon the world ;
They lose it that do buy it with much care.
Believe me, you are marvellously changed.

ANTONIO
I hold the world but as the world, Gratiano –
A stage where every man must play a part,
And mine a sad one.

GRATIANO   Let me play the fool !
With mirth and laughter let old wrinkles come,
81 And let my liver rather heat with wine
82 Than my heart cool with mortifying groans.
Why should a man whose blood is warm within
84 Sit like his grandsire cut in alabaster ?
85 Sleep when he wakes ? and creep into the jaundice
By being peevish ? I tell thee what, Antonio,
I love thee, and 'tis my love that speaks :
There are a sort of men whose visages
89 Do cream and mantle like a standing pond,
90 And do a willful stillness entertain
91 With purpose to be dressed in an opinion
92 Of wisdom, gravity, profound conceit –
As who should say, 'I am Sir Oracle,
And when I ope my lips, let no dog bark !'
O my Antonio, I do know of these
That therefore only are reputed wise
For saying nothing, when I am very sure
98 If they should speak would almost damn those ears,
Which hearing them would call their brothers fools.
I'll tell thee more of this another time.
But fish not with this melancholy bait
102 For this fool gudgeon, this opinion.
Come, good Lorenzo. Fare ye well awhile ;
I'll end my exhortation after dinner.

LORENZO
Well, we will leave you then till dinner time.
I must be one of these same dumb wise men,

For Gratiano never lets me speak.

GRATIANO
Well, keep me company but two years moe,   108
Thou shalt not know the sound of thine own tongue.

ANTONIO
Fare you well ; I'll grow a talker for this gear.   110

GRATIANO
Thanks i' faith ; for silence is only commendable
In a neat's tongue dried and a maid not vendible.   112

Exeunt [Gratiano and Lorenzo].

ANTONIO   Is that anything now ?

BASSANIO   Gratiano speaks an infinite deal of nothing,
more than any man in all Venice. His reasons are as two
grains of wheat hid in two bushels of chaff : you shall
seek all day ere you find them, and when you have them
they are not worth the search.

ANTONIO
Well, tell me now what lady is the same
To whom you swore a secret pilgrimage,
That you to-day promised to tell me of.

BASSANIO
'Tis not unknown to you, Antonio,
How much I have disabled mine estate   123
By something showing a more swelling port   124
Than my faint means would grant continuance.   125
Nor do I now make moan to be abridged   126
From such a noble rate ; but my chief care   127
Is to come fairly off from the great debts
Wherein my time, something too prodigal,
Hath left me gaged. To you, Antonio,   130
I owe the most in money and in love,
And from your love I have a warranty
To unburden all my plots and purposes
How to get clear of all the debts I owe.

ANTONIO
I pray you, good Bassanio, let me know it,
And if it stand as you yourself still do,
Within the eye of honor, be assured
My purse, my person, my extremest means
Lie all unlocked to your occasions.

BASSANIO
In my schooldays, when I had lost one shaft   140
I shot his fellow of the selfsame flight   141
The selfsame way, with more advisèd watch,
To find the other forth ; and by adventuring both
I oft found both. I urge this childhood proof
Because what follows is pure innocence.   145

56 *Nestor* old and solemn character in the *Iliad*   67 *strange* like strangers
68 *attend on* wait on, i.e. fit   74 *respect upon* concern for   81 *liver* (to
Elizabethans, the seat of the emotions)   82 *mortifying* deadening, destructive of life and joy   84 *alabaster* stone used for monuments   85
jaundice condition of biliousness, depression   89 *cream and mantle* i.e.
become dull (with scum)   90 *entertain* take on, assume   91 *opinion* reputation (so also in l. 102)   92 *conceit* thought   98–99 *If they . . . fools* (see
Matthew v, 22 : '. . . but whosoever shall say, Thou fool, shall be in danger
of hell fire.')   102 *gudgeon* a fish   108 *moe* more   110 *for this gear* because
of this 'stuff' (what you have just said)   112 *neat's* ox's ; *vendible* marketable, i.e. marriageable   123 *disabled* impaired, reduced   124 *something
. . . port* somewhat exhibiting a more lavish behavior   125 *grant continuance* allow to continue   126 *abridged* cut down, reduced   127 *noble
rate* high scale   130 *gaged* pledged for, owing   140 *shaft* arrow   141
selfsame flight same size and kind   145 *innocence* childlike sincerity, with
perhaps a touch of folly

I owe you much, and like a willful youth
That which I owe is lost; but if you please
To shoot another arrow that self way
Which you did shoot the first, I do not doubt,
150 As I will watch the aim, or to find both
Or bring your latter hazard back again
And thankfully rest debtor for the first.

ANTONIO

153 You know me well, and herein spend but time
To wind about my love with circumstance;
And out of doubt you do me now more wrong
156 In making question of my uttermost
Than if you had made waste of all I have.
Then do but say to me what I should do
That in your knowledge may by me be done,
160 And I am prest unto it. Therefore speak.

BASSANIO

161 In Belmont is a lady richly left;
And she is fair, and fairer than that word,
Of wondrous virtues. Sometimes from her eyes
I did receive fair speechless messages.
165 Her name is Portia, nothing undervalued
To Cato's daughter, Brutus' Portia;
Nor is the wide world ignorant of her worth,
For the four winds blow in from every coast
Renownèd suitors, and her sunny locks
170 Hang on her temples like a golden fleece,
171 Which makes her seat of Belmont Colchos' strond,
And many Jasons come in quest of her.
O my Antonio, had I but the means
To hold a rival place with one of them,
175 I have a mind presages me such thrift
That I should questionless be fortunate!

ANTONIO

Thou know'st that all my fortunes are at sea;
178 Neither have I money, nor commodity
To raise a present sum. Therefore go forth.
Try what my credit can in Venice do;
181 That shall be racked even to the uttermost
To furnish thee to Belmont, to fair Portia.
Go presently inquire, and so will I,
Where money is; and I no question make
185 To have it of my trust or for my sake.   *Exeunt.*

*

---

150 *or* either   153–54 *spend . . . circumstance* i.e. needlessly persuade me
with elaborate talk   156 *making . . . uttermost* questioning that I will do
all I can   160 *prest unto* ready for   161 *richly left* rich by inheritance
165–66 *nothing undervalued To* of no less worth than   170–72 *golden . . .
of her* (reference to Jason's mythical quest for the Golden Fleece)   171
strond shore   175 *thrift* profit, thriving   178 *commodity* goods (?), business
connection (?)   181 *racked* stretched, as on the rack   185 *of my trust . . .
sake* on the basis of my credit or as a personal favor
I, ii The house of Portia in Belmont   1 *troth* faith   7 *seated . . . mean*
with neither too much nor too little   8 *comes sooner by* gets sooner; *competency* modest means   10 *sentences* maxims, proverbs   14 *divine* preacher
18 *temper* temperament   19 *meshes* net for catching hares   19–20 *good
counsel* wisdom   20 *not . . . fashion* not the way   23–24 *will of a dead father*
dead father's bequest (with pun)   25 *refuse none* refuse any a chance at the
lott'ry (l. 27)   34 *overname them* 'go over' their names   36 *level . . .
affection* try to decide, or to guess, how I feel toward them   39 *appropriation* addition   40 *parts* abilities   42 *County* count   44 *An* if; *choose*
choose whom you please (?), I defy you to choose anyone else (?)   56
throstle thrush

Enter Portia with her waiting woman, Nerissa.   I, ii

PORTIA By my troth, Nerissa, my little body is aweary of 1
this great world.

NERISSA You would be, sweet madam, if your miseries
were in the same abundance as your good fortunes are;
and yet for aught I see, they are as sick that surfeit with
too much as they that starve with nothing. It is no mean
happiness, therefore, to be seated in the mean; super- 7
fluity comes sooner by white hairs, but competency 8
lives longer.

PORTIA Good sentences, and well pronounced. 10

NERISSA They would be better if well followed.

PORTIA If to do were as easy as to know what were good
to do, chapels had been churches, and poor men's cottages princes' palaces. It is a good divine that follows his 14
own instructions; I can easier teach twenty what were
good to be done than to be one of the twenty to follow
mine own teaching. The brain may devise laws for the
blood, but a hot temper leaps o'er a cold decree; such a 18
hare is madness the youth to skip o'er the meshes of good 19
counsel the cripple. But this reasoning is not in the fash- 20
ion to choose me a husband. O me, the word 'choose'! I
may neither choose who I would nor refuse who I dislike, so is the will of a living daughter curbed by the will 23
of a dead father. Is it not hard, Nerissa, that I cannot
choose one, nor refuse none? 25

NERISSA Your father was ever virtuous, and holy men at
their death have good inspirations. Therefore the lott'ry
that he hath devised in these three chests of gold, silver,
and lead – whereof who chooses his meaning chooses
you – will no doubt never be chosen by any rightly but
one who you shall rightly love. But what warmth is
there in your affection towards any of these princely
suitors that are already come?

PORTIA I pray thee overname them; and as thou namest 34
them I will describe them, and according to my description level at my affection. 36

NERISSA First, there is the Neapolitan prince.

PORTIA Ay, that's a colt indeed, for he doth nothing but
talk of his horse, and he makes it a great appropriation 39
to his own good parts that he can shoe him himself. I am 40
much afeard my lady his mother played false with a smith.

NERISSA Then is there the County Palatine. 42

PORTIA He doth nothing but frown – as who should say,
'An you will not have me, choose!' He hears merry tales 44
and smiles not; I fear he will prove the weeping philosopher when he grows old, being so full of unmannerly
sadness in his youth. I had rather be married to a
death's-head with a bone in his mouth than to either of
these. God defend me from these two!

NERISSA How say you by the French lord, Monsieur Le
Bon?

PORTIA God made him, and therefore let him pass for a
man. In truth, I know it is a sin to be a mocker, but he –
why he hath a horse better than the Neapolitan's, a better bad habit of frowning than the Count Palatine; he is
every man in no man. If a throstle sing, he falls straight 56
a-cap'ring; he will fence with his own shadow. If I
should marry him, I should marry twenty husbands. If
he would despise me, I would forgive him; for if he
love me to madness, I shall never requite him.

NERISSA What say you then to Falconbridge, the young
baron of England?

PORTIA You know I say nothing to him, for he under-

stands not me, nor I him. He hath neither Latin, French,
nor Italian; and you will come into the court and swear
that I have a poor pennyworth in the English. He is a
67 proper man's picture, but alas! who can converse with a
68 dumb-show? How oddly he is suited! I think he bought
69 his doublet in Italy, his round hose in France, his
bonnet in Germany, and his behavior everywhere.

NERISSA What think you of the Scottish lord, his neighbor?

PORTIA That he hath a neighborly charity in him, for he
borrowed a box of the ear of the Englishman and swore
he would pay him again when he was able. I think the
75 Frenchman became his surety and sealed under for
another.

NERISSA How like you the young German, the Duke of
Saxony's nephew?

PORTIA Very vilely in the morning when he is sober, and
most vilely in the afternoon when he is drunk. When
he is best he is a little worse than a man, and when he is
worst he is little better than a beast. An the worst fall
83 that ever fell, I hope I shall make shift to go without him.

NERISSA If he should offer to choose, and choose the
right casket, you should refuse to perform your father's
will if you should refuse to accept him.

PORTIA Therefore, for fear of the worst, I pray thee set a
88 deep glass of Rhenish wine on the contrary casket, for if
the devil be within and that temptation without, I know
he will choose it. I will do anything, Nerissa, ere I will
be married to a sponge.

NERISSA You need not fear, lady, the having any of these
lords. They have acquainted me with their determina-
tions, which is indeed to return to their home and to
trouble you with no more suit, unless you may be won
96 by some other sort than your father's imposition, depending on the caskets.

98 PORTIA If I live to be as old as Sibylla, I will die as chaste
as Diana unless I be obtained by the manner of my
father's will. I am glad this parcel of wooers are so
reasonable, for there is not one among them but I dote
on his very absence; and I pray God grant them a fair
departure.

NERISSA Do you not remember, lady, in your father's
time, a Venetian, a scholar and a soldier, that came
hither in company of the Marquis of Montferrat?

PORTIA Yes, yes, it was Bassanio – as I think, so was he
called.

NERISSA True, madam. He, of all the men that ever my
foolish eyes looked upon, was the best deserving a fair
110 lady.

PORTIA I remember him well, and I remember him
worthy of thy praise.

Enter a Servingman.

How now? What news?

SERVINGMAN The four strangers seek for you, madam,
to take their leave; and there is a forerunner come from
a fifth, the Prince of Morocco, who brings word the
Prince his master will be here to-night.

PORTIA If I could bid the fifth welcome with so good
120 heart as I can bid the other four farewell, I should be
121 glad of his approach. If he have the condition of a saint
122 and the complexion of a devil, I had rather he should
shrive me than wive me. Come, Nerissa. Sirrah, go
before. Whiles we shut the gate upon one wooer, another knocks at the door.   *Exeunt.*

*

Enter Bassanio with Shylock the Jew.   I, iii

SHYLOCK Three thousand ducats – well.

BASSANIO Ay, sir, for three months.

SHYLOCK For three months – well.

BASSANIO For the which, as I told you, Antonio shall be
bound.   5

SHYLOCK Antonio shall become bound – well.

BASSANIO May you stead me? Will you pleasure me? 7
Shall I know your answer?

SHYLOCK Three thousand ducats for three months, and
Antonio bound.

BASSANIO Your answer to that.

SHYLOCK Antonio is a good man.   12

BASSANIO Have you heard any imputation to the contrary?

SHYLOCK Ho no, no, no, no! My meaning in saying he is a
good man is to have you understand me that he is suffi- 15
cient. Yet his means are in supposition. He hath an 16
argosy bound to Tripolis, another to the Indies; I
understand, moreover, upon the Rialto, he hath a third 18
at Mexico, a fourth for England – and other ventures he
hath squand'red abroad. But ships are but boards,
sailors but men; there be land rats and water rats,
water thieves and land thieves – I mean pirates; and 22
then there is the peril of waters, winds, and rocks. The
man is, notwithstanding, sufficient. Three thousand
ducats – I think I may take his bond.

BASSANIO Be assured you may.

SHYLOCK I will be assured I may; and that I may be
assured, I will bethink me. May I speak with Antonio?

BASSANIO If it please you to dine with us.

SHYLOCK Yes, to smell pork, to eat of the habitation
which your prophet the Nazarite conjured the devil into! 31
I will buy with you, sell with you, talk with you, walk
with you, and so following; but I will not eat with you,
drink with you, nor pray with you. What news on the
Rialto? Who is he comes here?

Enter Antonio.

BASSANIO
This is Signior Antonio.

SHYLOCK *[aside]*
How like a fawning publican he looks.   37
I hate him for he is a Christian;   38
But more, for that in low simplicity
He lends out money gratis and brings down
The rate of usance here with us in Venice.   41
If I can catch him once upon the hip,   42
I will feed fat the ancient grudge I bear him.

---

67 *proper* handsome 68 *dumb-show* pantomime; *suited* dressed 69
doublet coat; *hose* breeches 75 *became his surety* (reference to the alliance
of France and Scotland against England); *sealed under* put his seal under
the Scot's 83 *make shift* manage 88 *contrary* other, or 'wrong' 96
sort way 98 *Sibylla* prophetess to whom Apollo promised as many years
of life as there were grains in her handful of sand 120 *condition* character, nature 121 *complexion . . . devil* (refers to Morocco's blackness
which was also the devil's color) 122–24 *shrive . . . door* (note the
rhymes within the prose) 122 *shrive me* hear my confession; *Sirrah* form
of address to servants
I, iii A public place in Venice 5 *bound* responsible, as a surety 7 *stead*
accommodate 12 *good* reliable in business dealings 15 *sufficient* solvent 16 *in supposition* uncertain 18 *Rialto* Venetian Merchants' Exchange 22 *pirates* pi-rats (?) 31 *Nazarite . . . into* (reference to Christ's
casting of evil spirits into a herd of swine; see Luke viii, 26–33, Mark v,
1–13) 37 *publican* innkeeper 38 *for* because 41 *usance* interest 42
catch . . . hip (figure of speech from wrestling)

He hates our sacred nation, and he rails,
Even there where merchants most do congregate,
On me, my bargains, and my well-won thrift,
Which he calls interest. Cursèd be my tribe
If I forgive him.

BASSANIO   Shylock, do you hear?

SHYLOCK

49 I am debating of my present store,
And by the near guess of my memory
51 I cannot instantly raise up the gross
Of full three thousand ducats. What of that?
Tubal, a wealthy Hebrew of my tribe,
Will furnish me. But soft, how many months
Do you desire? *[to Antonio]* Rest you fair, good signior!
Your worship was the last man in our mouths.

ANTONIO

Shylock, albeit I neither lend nor borrow
58 By taking nor by giving of excess,
59 Yet to supply the ripe wants of my friend,
60 I'll break a custom. *[to Bassanio]* Is he yet possessed
How much ye would?

SHYLOCK   Ay, ay, three thousand ducats.

ANTONIO

And for three months.

SHYLOCK

I had forgot – three months, you told me so.
Well then, your bond. And let me see – but hear you,
65 Methoughts you said you neither lend nor borrow
Upon advantage.

ANTONIO   I do never use it.

SHYLOCK

67 When Jacob grazed his uncle Laban's sheep –
This Jacob from our holy Abram was,
As his wise mother wrought in his behalf,
The third possessor; ay, he was the third –

ANTONIO

And what of him? Did he take interest?

SHYLOCK

No, not take interest – not as you would say
Directly int'rest. Mark what Jacob did:
74 When Laban and himself were compromised
75 That all the eanlings which were streaked and pied
76 Should fall as Jacob's hire, the ewes being rank
In end of autumn turnèd to the rams;
And when the work of generation was
Between these woolly breeders in the act,
80 The skillful shepherd peeled me certain wands,
81 And in the doing of the deed of kind
He stuck them up before the fulsome ewes,
83 Who then conceiving, did in eaning time
Fall parti-colored lambs, and those were Jacob's.

This was a way to thrive, and he was blest;
And thrift is blessing if men steal it not.

ANTONIO

This was a venture, sir, that Jacob served for,   87
A thing not in his power to bring to pass,
But swayed and fashioned by the hand of heaven.
Was this inserted to make interest good?   90
Or is your gold and silver ewes and rams?

SHYLOCK

I cannot tell; I make it breed as fast.
But note me, signior –

ANTONIO   Mark you this, Bassanio,
The devil can cite Scripture for his purpose.
An evil soul producing holy witness
Is like a villain with a smiling cheek,
A goodly apple rotten at the heart.
O what a goodly outside falsehood hath!

SHYLOCK

Three thousand ducats – 'tis a good round sum.
Three months from twelve – then let me see, the rate –

ANTONIO

Well, Shylock, shall we be beholding to you?   101

SHYLOCK

Signior Antonio, many a time and oft
In the Rialto you have rated me   103
About my moneys and my usances.
Still have I borne it with a patient shrug,
For suff'rance is the badge of all our tribe.   106
You call me misbeliever, cutthroat dog,
And spit upon my Jewish gaberdine,   108
And all for use of that which is mine own.
Well then, it now appears you need my help.
Go to then. You come to me and you say,   111
'Shylock, we would have moneys' – you say so,
You that did void your rheum upon my beard   113
And foot me as you spurn a stranger cur
Over your threshold! Moneys is your suit.
What should I say to you? Should I not say,
'Hath a dog money? is it possible
A cur can lend three thousand ducats?' Or
Shall I bend low, and in a bondman's key,
With bated breath and whisp'ring humbleness,
Say this:
'Fair sir, you spit on me on Wednesday last,
You spurned me such a day, another time
You called me dog; and for these courtesies
I'll lend you thus much moneys'?

ANTONIO

I am as like to call thee so again,
To spit on thee again, to spurn thee too.
If thou wilt lend this money, lend it not
As to thy friends – for when did friendship take
A breed for barren metal of his friend? –   130
But lend it rather to thine enemy,
Who if he break, thou mayst with better face   132
Exact the penalty.

SHYLOCK   Why look you, how you storm!
I would be friends with you and have your love,
Forget the shames that you have stained me with,
Supply your present wants, and take no doit   136
Of usance for my moneys; and you'll not hear me.
This is kind I offer.   138

BASSANIO

This were kindness.

---

49 *store* wealth   51 *gross* full amount   58 *excess* interest   59 *ripe* immediate   60–61 *possessed . . . would* informed of how much you want   65 *Methoughts* it seemed to me   67 *Jacob* (see Genesis xxvii, xxx, 25–43)   74 *compromised* agreed   75 *eanlings* lambs; *pied* spotted   76 *hire* share, recompense; *rank* in heat   80 *peeled me* peeled (a colloquialism); *wands* branches, shoots   81 *kind* nature   83 *eaning* lambing   87–88 *venture . . . pass* i.e. a commercial venture of some uncertainty   90 *inserted . . . good* brought in to justify charging interest   101 *beholding* in debt   103 *rated* railed at, reviled   106 *suff'rance* patience, endurance   108 *gaberdine* cloak   111 *Go to* (exclamation of impatience, like 'Come, come!')   113 *rheum* spittle, mucous discharge   130 *breed . . . metal* offspring of barren metal, i.e. interest   132 *break* go bankrupt   136 *doit* coin of very small value   138 *kind I offer* i.e. a kindly offer (with a suggestion of 'natural' dealing; Antonio has called usury unnatural)

SHYLOCK   This kindness will I show :
Go with me to a notary ; seal me there
141 Your single bond, and – in a merry sport –
If you repay me not on such a day,
In such a place, such sum or sums as are
Expressed in the condition, let the forfeit
145 Be nominated for an equal pound
Of your fair flesh, to be cut off and taken
In what part of your body pleaseth me.

ANTONIO
Content, in faith. I'll seal to such a bond,
And say there is much kindness in the Jew.

BASSANIO
You shall not seal to such a bond for me !
151 I'll rather dwell in my necessity.

ANTONIO
Why fear not, man ; I will not forfeit it.
Within these two months – that's a month before
This bond expires – I do expect return
Of thrice three times the value of this bond.

SHYLOCK
O father Abram, what these Christians are,
Whose own hard dealings teaches them suspect
The thoughts of others ! Pray you tell me this :
159 If he should break his day, what should I gain
By the exaction of the forfeiture ?
A pound of man's flesh taken from a man
Is not so estimable, profitable neither,
As flesh of muttons, beefs, or goats. I say
To buy his favor I extend this friendship.
If he will take it, so ; if not, adieu.
166 And for my love I pray you wrong me not.

ANTONIO
Yes, Shylock, I will seal unto this bond.

SHYLOCK
Then meet me forthwith at the notary's ;
Give him direction for this merry bond,
170 And I will go and purse the ducats straight,
171 See to my house, left in the fearful guard
Of an unthrifty knave, and presently
I'll be with you.   *Exit.*
173 ANTONIO   Hie thee, gentle Jew.
The Hebrew will turn Christian ; he grows kind.

BASSANIO
I like not fair terms and a villain's mind.

ANTONIO
Come on. In this there can be no dismay ;
My ships come home a month before the day.   *Exeunt.*

*

II, i   *[Flourish of cornets.] Enter [the Prince of] Morocco,*
a tawny Moor all in white, and three or four Followers
accordingly, with Portia, Nerissa, and their Train.

MOROCCO
Mislike me not for my complexion,
2 The shadowed livery of the burnished sun,
To whom I am a neighbor and near bred.
Bring me the fairest creature northward born,
5 Where Phoebus' fire scarce thaws the icicles,
6 And let us make incision for your love
To prove whose blood is reddest, his or mine.
8 I tell thee, lady, this aspect of mine
9 Hath feared the valiant. By my love I swear

The best-regarded virgins of our clime
Have loved it too. I would not change this hue,
Except to steal your thoughts, my gentle queen.   12

PORTIA
In terms of choice I am not solely led   13
By nice direction of a maiden's eyes.   14
Besides, the lott'ry of my destiny
Bars me the right of voluntary choosing.
But if my father had not scanted me,   17
And hedged me by his wit to yield myself
His wife who wins me by that means I told you,
Yourself, renownèd Prince, then stood as fair
As any comer I have looked on yet
For my affection.

MOROCCO   Even for that I thank you.
Therefore I pray you lead me to the caskets
To try my fortune. By this scimitar,
That slew the Sophy and a Persian prince   25
That won three fields of Sultan Solyman,   26
I would o'erstare the sternest eyes that look,   27
Outbrave the heart most daring on the earth,
Pluck the young sucking cubs from the she-bear,
Yea, mock the lion when 'a roars for prey,   30
To win thee, lady. But alas the while,
If Hercules and Lichas play at dice   32
Which is the better man, the greater throw
May turn by fortune from the weaker hand.
So is Alcides beaten by his rogue,   35
And so may I, blind Fortune leading me,
Miss that which one unworthier may attain,
And die with grieving.

PORTIA   You must take your chance,
And either not attempt to choose at all
Or swear before you choose, if you choose wrong
Never to speak to lady afterward
In way of marriage. Therefore be advised.   42

MOROCCO
Nor will not. Come, bring me unto my chance.   43

PORTIA
First, forward to the temple ; after dinner   44
Your hazard shall be made.

MOROCCO   Good fortune then,
To make me blest or cursèd'st among men !
     [Flourish of cornets.] Exeunt.

*

Enter [Launcelot Gobbo,] the Clown, alone.   II, ii
LAUNCELOT Certainly my conscience will serve me to
run from this Jew my master. The fiend is at mine elbow

141 *single* without other security   145 *nominated* named, prescribed ;
equal exact   151 *dwell . . . necessity* i.e. remain in need   159 *break his day*
fail to pay on the due date   166 *wrong me not* think not unjustly of me
170 *purse* procure, gather   171 *fearful* precarious   173 *gentle* (with pun on
'gentile' ?)
II, i Within Portia's house in Belmont   2 *shadowed . . . sun* dark dress of
the sun's subjects or retainers, i.e. dark skin   5 *Phoebus'* the sun's   6 *make
incision* cut to draw blood   8 *aspect* countenance   9 *feared* frightened
12 *steal your thoughts* i.e. win your favor   13 *terms* matters   14 *nice* fastidious   17 *scanted* restricted   25 *Sophy* Shah of Persia   26 *Solyman* a
Turkish ruler   27 *o'erstare* outstare   30 *'a* he   32 *Lichas* servant of
Hercules   35 *Alcides* Hercules ; *rogue* menial servant   42 *be advised* take
care   43 *Nor will not* i.e. I agree to the conditions just imposed   44 *to the
temple* i.e. to swear the oath
II, ii A street in Venice

and tempts me, saying to me, 'Gobbo, Launcelot Gobbo, good Launcelot,' or 'good Gobbo,' or 'good Launcelot Gobbo – use your legs, take the start, run away.'
My conscience says, 'No. Take heed, honest Launcelot;
take heed, honest Gobbo,' or as aforesaid, 'honest Laun-
8 celot Gobbo – do not run; scorn running with thy heels.'
9 Well, the most courageous fiend bids me pack. 'Fia!'
10 says the fiend; 'away!' says the fiend. 'For the heavens,
rouse up a brave mind,' says the fiend, 'and run.' Well,
my conscience hanging about the neck of my heart says
very wisely to me, 'My honest friend Launcelot, being
an honest man's son' – or rather 'an honest woman's
15 son,' for indeed my father did something smack, something grow to; he had a kind of taste – Well, my conscience says, 'Launcelot, budge not.' 'Budge,' says the
fiend. 'Budge not,' says my conscience. 'Conscience,'
say I, 'you counsel well.' 'Fiend,' say I, 'you counsel
well.' To be ruled by my conscience, I should stay with
21 the Jew my master who, God bless the mark, is a kind of
devil; and to run away from the Jew, I should be ruled
23 by the fiend who, saving your reverence, is the devil
24 himself. Certainly the Jew is the very devil incarnation;
and in my conscience, my conscience is but a kind of
hard conscience to offer to counsel me to stay with the
Jew. The fiend gives the more friendly counsel. I will
run, fiend; my heels are at your commandment; I will
run.

Enter Old Gobbo with a basket.

GOBBO Master young man, you, I pray you, which is the
way to Master Jew's?
LAUNCELOT *[aside]* O heavens, this is my true-begotten
32 father who, being more than sand-blind, high-gravel-
blind, knows me not. I will try confusions with him.
GOBBO Master young gentleman, I pray you which is the
way to Master Jew's?
LAUNCELOT Turn up on your right hand at the next
turning, but at the next turning of all, on your left;
38 marry, at the very next turning turn of no hand, but
turn down indirectly to the Jew's house.
40 GOBBO Be God's sonties, 'twill be a hard way to hit! Can
you tell me whether one Launcelot that dwells with
him, dwell with him or no?
43 LAUNCELOT Talk you of young Master Launcelot?
44 *[aside]* Mark me now; now will I raise the waters. –
Talk you of young Master Launcelot?
GOBBO No master, sir, but a poor man's son. His father,
though I say't, is an honest exceeding poor man and,
48 God be thanked, well to live.
LAUNCELOT Well, let his father be what 'a will, we talk
of young Master Launcelot.

---

8 *scorn . . . heels* i.e. scorn running emphatically (by running from it? or
kicking at it?) 9 *pack* be off; *Fia* away (Italian 'via') 10 *For the heavens*
for heaven's sake 15–16 *did something . . . taste* i.e. was a bit promiscuous (?) 21, 23 *God . . . mark, saving . . . reverence* (conventional phrases
of apology for what one is about to say) 24 *incarnation* incarnate 32
sand-blind partly blind 32–33 *high-gravel-blind* blinder than sand-blind
(cf. 'stone-blind') 38 *marry* to be sure (an interjection) 40 *Be* by;
sonties saints (?), sanctities (?) 43 *Master* title applied to young gentlemen
44 *raise the waters* i.e. start something (raise tears?) 48 *well to live* lives
comfortably (?), with prospect of a long life (?) 52 *ergo* therefore 57–58
Sisters Three the three Fates 86 *beard* (perhaps the old man's hand is on
the back of Launcelot's head) 88 *fill-horse* cart horse 96 *set . . . rest*
i.e. determined 98 *halter* hangman's noose 99 *tell* count 101 *liveries*
costumes for servants 108 *anon* presently, at once 111 *Gramercy* many
thanks

GOBBO Your worship's friend, and Launcelot, sir.
LAUNCELOT But I pray you, ergo old man, ergo I be- 52
seech you, talk you of young Master Launcelot?
GOBBO Of Launcelot, an't please your mastership.
LAUNCELOT Ergo, Master Launcelot. Talk not of Master
Launcelot, father, for the young gentleman, according
to Fates and Destinies and such odd sayings, the Sisters 57
Three and such branches of learning, is indeed deceased,
or as you would say in plain terms, gone to heaven.
GOBBO Marry, God forbid! The boy was the very staff of
my age, my very prop.
LAUNCELOT Do I look like a cudgel or a hovel-post, a
staff or a prop? Do you know me, father?
GOBBO Alack the day, I know you not, young gentleman! but I pray you tell me, is my boy, God rest his
soul, alive or dead?
LAUNCELOT Do you not know me, father?
GOBBO Alack, sir, I am sand-blind! I know you not.
LAUNCELOT Nay, indeed if you had your eyes you might
fail of the knowing me; it is a wise father that knows his 70
own child. Well, old man, I will tell you news of your
son. *[Kneels.]* Give me your blessing. Truth will come
to light; murder cannot be hid long – a man's son may,
but in the end truth will out.
GOBBO Pray you, sir, stand up. I am sure you are not
Launcelot my boy.
LAUNCELOT Pray you let's have no more fooling about it,
but give me your blessing. I am Launcelot – your boy
that was, your son that is, your child that shall be.
GOBBO I cannot think you are my son.
LAUNCELOT I know not what I shall think of that; but I
am Launcelot, the Jew's man, and I am sure Margery
your wife is my mother.
GOBBO Her name is Margery indeed! I'll be sworn, if
thou be Launcelot thou art mine own flesh and blood.
Lord worshipped might he be, what a beard hast thou 86
got! Thou hast got more hair on thy chin than Dobbin
my fill-horse has on his tail. 88
LAUNCELOT *[rises]* It should seem then that Dobbin's
tail grows backward. I am sure he had more hair of his
tail than I have of my face when I last saw him.
GOBBO Lord, how art thou changed! How dost thou and
thy master agree? I have brought him a present. How
'gree you now?
LAUNCELOT Well, well; but for mine own part, as I have
set up my rest to run away, so I will not rest till I have 96
run some ground. My master's a very Jew. Give him a
present? Give him a halter! I am famished in his ser- 98
vice; you may tell every finger I have with my ribs. 99
Father, I am glad you are come. Give me your present to
one Master Bassanio, who indeed gives rare new liveries. 101
If I serve not him, I will run as far as God has any
ground. O rare fortune, here comes the man! To him,
father, for I am a Jew if I serve the Jew any longer.

*Enter Bassanio, with [Leonardo and] a Follower or
two.*

BASSANIO You may do so, but let it be so hasted that
supper be ready at the farthest by five of the clock. See
these letters delivered, put the liveries to making, and
desire Gratiano to come anon to my lodging. 108

[Exit one of his men.]

LAUNCELOT To him, father!
GOBBO God bless your worship!
BASSANIO Gramercy. Wouldst thou aught with me? 111

GOBBO Here's my son, sir, a poor boy –

LAUNCELOT Not a poor boy, sir, but the rich Jew's man that would, sir, as my father shall specify –

115 GOBBO He hath a great infection, sir, as one would say, to serve –

LAUNCELOT Indeed, the short and the long is, I serve the Jew, and have a desire, as my father shall specify –

GOBBO His master and he, saving your worship's rever-
120 ence, are scarce cater-cousins.

LAUNCELOT To be brief, the very truth is that the Jew having done me wrong doth cause me, as my father,
123 being I hope an old man, shall frutify unto you –

GOBBO I have here a dish of doves that I would bestow upon your worship, and my suit is –

126 LAUNCELOT In very brief, the suit is impertinent to my-self, as your worship shall know by this honest old man, and though I say it, though old man, yet poor man, my father.

BASSANIO One speak for both. What would you?

LAUNCELOT Serve you, sir.

131 GOBBO That is the very defect of the matter, sir.

BASSANIO
I know thee well; thou hast obtained thy suit.
Shylock thy master spoke with me this day,
134 And hath preferred thee, if it be preferment
To leave a rich Jew's service to become
The follower of so poor a gentleman.

137 LAUNCELOT The old proverb is very well parted be-tween my master Shylock and you, sir. You have the grace of God, sir, and he hath enough.

BASSANIO
Thou speak'st it well. Go, father, with thy son;
Take leave of thy old master and inquire
My lodging out. [to a Servant] Give him a livery
143 More guarded than his fellows'. See it done.

LAUNCELOT Father, in. I cannot get a service; no! I have ne'er a tongue in my head; well! [Looks at his palm.] If
146 any man in Italy have a fairer table which doth offer to swear upon a book – I shall have good fortune! Go to, here's a simple line of life. Here's a small trifle of wives! Alas, fifteen wives is nothing; eleven widows and nine maids is a simple coming-in for one man. And then to scape drowning thrice, and to be in peril of my life with
152 the edge of a feather-bed! Here are simple scapes. Well,
153 if Fortune be a woman, she's a good wench for this gear. Father, come. I'll take my leave of the Jew in the twinkling. *Exit Clown [Launcelot, with Old Gobbo].*

BASSANIO
I pray thee, good Leonardo, think on this:
These things being bought and orderly bestowed,
Return in haste, for I do feast to-night
My best-esteemed acquaintance. Hie thee, go.

LEONARDO
My best endeavors shall be done herein.
                    Enter Gratiano.

GRATIANO
Where's your master?

LEONARDO   Yonder, sir, he walks.   [Exit.]

GRATIANO
Signior Bassanio!

BASSANIO   Gratiano!

GRATIANO
I have suit to you.

BASSANIO   You have obtained it.

GRATIANO You must not deny me. I must go with you to Belmont.

BASSANIO
Why then you must. But hear thee, Gratiano:
Thou art too wild, too rude, and bold of voice –
Parts that become thee happily enough   168
And in such eyes as ours appear not faults;
But where thou art not known, why there they show
Something too liberal. Pray thee take pain   171
To allay with some cold drops of modesty
Thy skipping spirit, lest through thy wild behavior
I be misconst'red in the place I go to,   174
And lose my hopes.

GRATIANO   Signior Bassanio, hear me:
If I do not put on a sober habit,
Talk with respect, and swear but now and then,
Wear prayer books in my pocket, look demurely –
Nay more, while grace is saying hood mine eyes   179
Thus with my hat, and sigh and say amen,
Use all the observance of civility   181
Like one well studied in a sad ostent   182
To please his grandam – never trust me more.

BASSANIO
Well, we shall see your bearing.

GRATIANO
Nay, but I bar to-night. You shall not gauge me   185
By what we do to-night.

BASSANIO   No, that were pity.
I would entreat you rather to put on
Your boldest suit of mirth, for we have friends
That purpose merriment. But fare you well;
I have some business.

GRATIANO
And I must to Lorenzo and the rest,
But we will visit you at supper time.   *Exeunt.*

                    *

Enter Jessica and [Launcelot] the Clown.   II, iii

JESSICA
I am sorry thou wilt leave my father so;
Our house is hell, and thou a merry devil
Didst rob it of some taste of tediousness.
But fare thee well; there is a ducat for thee.
And, Launcelot, soon at supper shalt thou see
Lorenzo, who is thy new master's guest.
Give him this letter; do it secretly.
And so farewell; I would not have my father
See me in talk with thee.

LAUNCELOT Adieu! Tears exhibit my tongue. Most 10
beautiful pagan, most sweet Jew! if a Christian did not play the knave and get thee, I am much deceived. But 12

115 *infection* (blunder for 'affection') 120 *cater-cousins* close friends 123 *frutify* (blunder for some word such as 'certify') 126 *impertinent* (blunder for 'pertinent') 131 *defect* (blunder for 'effect') 134 *preferred* recommended for advancement 137–39 *proverb . . . enough* (play on the proverb 'He who has the grace of God has enough') 143 *guarded* decorated with braid 146 *table* palm of hand (Launcelot now 'reads' the lines of his palm) 152 *feather-bed* marriage bed (?); *scapes* escapes 153 *this gear* these matters 168 *Parts* qualities 171 *liberal* free 174 *misconst'red* mis-understood 179 *hood* cover 181 *civility* polite behavior 182 *sad ostent* solemn appearance 185 *gauge* measure, judge
II, iii Within Shylock's house 10 *exhibit* (blunder for 'inhibit') 12 *get* beget

adieu! These foolish drops do something drown my
manly spirit. Adieu!

JESSICA
  Farewell, good Launcelot.   *[Exit Launcelot.]*
  Alack, what heinous sin is it in me
  To be ashamed to be my father's child.
  But though I am a daughter to his blood,
  I am not to his manners. O Lorenzo,
  If thou keep promise, I shall end this strife,
  Become a Christian and thy loving wife!   *Exit.*

*

II, iv   *Enter Gratiano, Lorenzo, Salerio, and Solanio.*

LORENZO
  Nay, we will slink away in supper time,
  Disguise us at my lodging, and return
  All in an hour.

GRATIANO
  We have not made good preparation.

SALERIO
5 We have not spoke us yet of torchbearers.

SOLANIO
6 'Tis vile, unless it may be quaintly ordered,
  And better in my mind not undertook.

LORENZO
  'Tis now but four of clock. We have two hours
  To furnish us.
        Enter Launcelot [with a letter].
              Friend Launcelot, what's the news?

10 LAUNCELOT An it shall please you to break up this, it
  shall seem to signify.

LORENZO
  I know the hand. In faith, 'tis a fair hand,
  And whiter than the paper it writ on
  Is the fair hand that writ.

GRATIANO   Love-news, in faith!

LAUNCELOT By your leave, sir.

LORENZO Whither goest thou?

LAUNCELOT Marry, sir, to bid my old master the Jew to
  sup to-night with my new master the Christian.

LORENZO
  Hold here, take this. *[Gives money.]* Tell gentle Jessica
20 I will not fail her. Speak it privately.
              Exit Clown [Launcelot].
  Go, gentlemen;
  Will you prepare you for this masque to-night?
  I am provided of a torchbearer.

SALERIO
  Ay marry, I'll be gone about it straight.

SOLANIO
  And so will I.

LORENZO   Meet me and Gratiano

At Gratiano's lodging some hour hence.

SALERIO
  'Tis good we do so.   *Exit [with Solanio].*

GRATIANO
  Was not that letter from fair Jessica?

LORENZO
  I must needs tell thee all. She hath directed
  How I shall take her from her father's house,
  What gold and jewels she is furnished with,
  What page's suit she hath in readiness.
  If e'er the Jew her father come to heaven,
  It will be for his gentle daughter's sake;   34
  And never dare misfortune cross her foot,   35
  Unless she do it under this excuse,   36
  That she is issue to a faithless Jew.   37
  Come, go with me; peruse this as thou goest.
  Fair Jessica shall be my torchbearer.
                 Exit [with Gratiano].

*

Enter [Shylock the] Jew and [Launcelot,] his man   **II, v**
that was the Clown.

SHYLOCK
  Well, thou shalt see, thy eyes shall be thy judge,
  The difference of old Shylock and Bassanio –   2
  What, Jessica! – Thou shalt not gormandize
  As thou hast done with me – What, Jessica! –
  And sleep, and snore, and rend apparel out –
  Why, Jessica, I say!

LAUNCELOT   Why, Jessica!

SHYLOCK
  Who bids thee call? I do not bid thee call.

LAUNCELOT Your worship was wont to tell me I could
  do nothing without bidding.
        Enter Jessica.

JESSICA Call you? What is your will?

SHYLOCK
  I am bid forth to supper, Jessica.
  There are my keys. But wherefore should I go?   12
  I am not bid for love – they flatter me –
  But yet I'll go in hate to feed upon
  The prodigal Christian. Jessica my girl,
  Look to my house. I am right loath to go.
  There is some ill a-brewing towards my rest,
  For I did dream of money bags to-night.   18

LAUNCELOT I beseech you, sir, go. My young master
  doth expect your reproach.   20

SHYLOCK So do I his.

LAUNCELOT And they have conspired together. I will not
  say you shall see a masque, but if you do, then it was not
  for nothing that my nose fell a-bleeding on Black Mon- 24
  day last at six o' clock i' th' morning, falling out that year 25
  on Ash Wednesday was four year in th' afternoon.

SHYLOCK
  What, are there masques? Hear you me, Jessica:
  Lock up my doors; and when you hear the drum
  And the vile squealing of the wry-necked fife,   29
  Clamber not you up to the casements then,
  Nor thrust your head into the public street
  To gaze on Christian fools with varnished faces;   32
  But stop my house's ears – I mean my casements;
  Let not the sound of shallow fopp'ry enter   34
  My sober house. By Jacob's staff I swear
  I have no mind of feasting forth to-night;

II, iv A public place   **5** *spoke . . . torchbearers* ordered torchbearers **6** *quaintly ordered* nicely, or elaborately, arranged **10** *break up* break open **34** *gentle* (with pun on 'gentile'?) **35** *never dare misfortune* may misfortune never dare **36** *she* i.e. misfortune **37** *she* i.e. Jessica; *issue* offspring

II, v Before Shylock's house s.d. *his . . . Clown* (perhaps originally simply 'his man that was') **2** *of* between **12** *wherefore* why **18** *to-night* last night **20** *reproach* (blunder for 'approach') **24** *Black Monday* Easter Monday **25–26** *falling . . . afternoon* (Launcelot departs into a gibberish of omens and fortunetelling) **29** *wry-necked fife* i.e. played with the musician's head awry (?) **32** *varnished faces* painted masks **34** *fopp'ry* frivolity

But I will go. Go you before me, sirrah.
Say I will come.
LAUNCELOT   I will go before, sir.
Mistress, look out at window for all this :
    There will come a Christian by
    Will be worth a Jewess' eye.   [Exit.]
SHYLOCK
42   What says that fool of Hagar's offspring ? ha ?
JESSICA
His words were 'Farewell, mistress' – nothing else.
SHYLOCK
44   The patch is kind enough, but a huge feeder,
45   Snail-slow in profit, and he sleeps by day
More than the wildcat. Drones hive not with me ;
Therefore I part with him, and part with him
To one that I would have him help to waste
His borrowed purse. Well, Jessica, go in.
Perhaps I will return immediately.
Do as I bid you ; shut doors after you.
52   Fast bind, fast find –
A proverb never stale in thrifty mind.   Exit.
JESSICA
Farewell ; and if my fortune be not crost,
I have a father, you a daughter, lost.   Exit.
II, vi   Enter the Masquers, Gratiano and Salerio.
GRATIANO
1   This is the penthouse under which Lorenzo
Desired us to make stand.
SALERIO   His hour is almost past.
GRATIANO
And it is marvel he outdwells his hour,
For lovers ever run before the clock.
SALERIO
5   O ten times faster Venus' pigeons fly
To seal love's bonds new-made than they are wont
7   To keep obligèd faith unforfeited !
GRATIANO
That ever holds. Who riseth from a feast
With that keen appetite that he sits down ?
Where is the horse that doth untread again
His tedious measures with the unbated fire
That he did pace them first ? All things that are
Are with more spirit chasèd than enjoyed.
14   How like a younker or a prodigal
15   The scarfèd bark puts from her native bay,
Hugged and embracèd by the strumpet wind !
How like the prodigal doth she return,
With over-weathered ribs and ragged sails,
Lean, rent, and beggared by the strumpet wind !
    Enter Lorenzo.
SALERIO
Here comes Lorenzo ; more of this hereafter.
LORENZO
21   Sweet friends, your patience for my long abode.
Not I but my affairs have made you wait.
23   When you shall please to play the thieves for wives,
24   I'll watch as long for you then. Approach ;
Here dwells my father Jew. Ho ! who's within ?
    [Enter] Jessica above [in boy's clothes].
JESSICA
Who are you ? Tell me for more certainty,
Albeit I'll swear that I do know your tongue.
LORENZO
Lorenzo, and thy love.

JESSICA
Lorenzo certain, and my love indeed,
For who love I so much ? And now who knows
But you, Lorenzo, whether I am yours ?
LORENZO
Heaven and thy thoughts are witness that thou art.
JESSICA
Here, catch this casket ; it is worth the pains.
I am glad 'tis night – you do not look on me –
For I am much ashamed of my exchange.   35
But love is blind, and lovers cannot see
The pretty follies that themselves commit ;
For if they could, Cupid himself would blush
To see me thus transformèd to a boy.
LORENZO
Descend, for you must be my torchbearer.
JESSICA
What, must I hold a candle to my shames ?
They in themselves, good sooth, are too too light.   42
Why, 'tis an office of discovery, love –   43
And I should be obscured.
LORENZO   So are you, sweet,
Even in the lovely garnish of a boy.   45
But come at once,
For the close night doth play the runaway,   47
And we are stayed for at Bassanio's feast.   48
JESSICA
I will make fast the doors, and gild myself
With some moe ducats, and be with you straight.
    [Exit above.]
GRATIANO
Now by my hood, a gentle and no Jew !   51
LORENZO
Beshrow me but I love her heartily !   52
For she is wise, if I can judge of her,
And fair she is, if that mine eyes be true,
And true she is, as she hath proved herself ;
And therefore, like herself, wise, fair, and true,
Shall she be placèd in my constant soul.
    Enter Jessica [below].
What, art thou come ? On, gentlemen, away !
Our masquing mates by this time for us stay.
    Exit [with Jessica and Salerio].
    Enter Antonio.
ANTONIO Who's there ?
GRATIANO Signior Antonio ?
ANTONIO
Fie, fie, Gratiano ! where are all the rest ?
'Tis nine o'clock ; our friends all stay for you.
No masque to-night. The wind is come about ;
Bassanio presently will go aboard.   65
I have sent twenty out to seek for you.

---

42 *Hagar's offspring* i.e. a gentile and an outcast 44 *patch* fool 45 *profit* productive work 52 *Fast* secure
II, vi 1 *penthouse* slanting eaves or shelter 5 *Venus' pigeons* doves which draw Venus' chariot 7 *obligèd* bound by marriage or marriage contract ; *unforfeited* unbroken 14 *younker* youngster 15 *scarfèd* decked with flags or streamers 21 *abode* delay 23 *play the thieves for* steal 24 *watch* wait 35 *exchange* change of clothes 42 *light* frivolous, immodest (with pun) 43 *'tis . . . discovery* i.e. torchbearing is an act which reveals, sheds light upon 45 *garnish* dress, trimmings 47 *close* secret ; *doth . . . runaway* i.e. is passing rapidly 48 *stayed for* awaited 51 *gentle* gentile (with pun on 'gentle' ?) 52 *Beshrow me* evil come to me (used lightly) 65 *presently* immediately

GRATIANO
I am glad on't. I desire no more delight
Than to be under sail and gone to-night.   *Exeunt.*

*

II, vii   *[Flourish of cornets.] Enter Portia with Morocco and
both their Trains.*

PORTIA
1   Go, draw aside the curtains and discover
The several caskets to this noble Prince.
Now make your choice.
MOROCCO
This first, of gold, who this inscription bears,
'Who chooseth me shall gain what many men desire';
The second, silver, which this promise carries,
'Who chooseth me shall get as much as he deserves';
This third, dull lead, with warning all as blunt,
9   'Who chooseth me must give and hazard all he hath.'
How shall I know if I do choose the right?
PORTIA
The one of them contains my picture, Prince.
If you choose that, then I am yours withal.
MOROCCO
Some god direct my judgment! Let me see –
I will survey th' inscriptions back again.
What says this leaden casket?
'Who chooseth me must give and hazard all he hath.'
Must give – for what? for lead! hazard for lead?
This casket threatens; men that hazard all
Do it in hope of fair advantages.
A golden mind stoops not to shows of dross;
21   I'll then nor give nor hazard aught for lead.
What says the silver with her virgin hue?
'Who chooseth me shall get as much as he deserves.'
As much as he deserves? Pause there, Morocco,
And weigh thy value with an even hand:
26   If thou be'st rated by thy estimation,
Thou dost deserve enough; and yet enough
May not extend so far as to the lady;
And yet to be afeard of my deserving
30   Were but a weak disabling of myself.
As much as I deserve? Why that's the lady!
I do in birth deserve her, and in fortunes,
In graces, and in qualities of breeding;
But more than these, in love I do deserve.
What if I strayed no farther, but chose here?
Let's see once more this saying graved in gold:
'Who chooseth me shall gain what many men desire.'
Why that's the lady! All the world desires her;
From the four corners of the earth they come
40   To kiss this shrine, this mortal breathing saint.
The Hyrcanian deserts and the vasty wilds
Of wide Arabia are as throughfares now
For princes to come view fair Portia.
The watery kingdom, whose ambitious head

Spits in the face of heaven, is no bar
To stop the foreign spirits, but they come
As o'er a brook to see fair Portia.
One of these three contains her heavenly picture.
Is't like that lead contains her? 'Twere damnation
To think so base a thought; it were too gross   50
To rib her cerecloth in the obscure grave.   51
Or shall I think in silver she's immured,
Being ten times undervalued to tried gold?
O sinful thought! Never so rich a gem
Was set in worse than gold. They have in England
A coin that bears the figure of an angel
Stamped in gold – but that's insculped upon;   57
But here an angel in a golden bed
Lies all within. Deliver me the key.
Here do I choose, and thrive I as I may!
PORTIA
There, take it, Prince; and if my form lie there,
Then I am yours.
     [He opens the golden casket.]
MOROCCO   O hell! what have we here?
A carrion Death, within whose empty eye   63
There is a written scroll! I'll read the writing.
     'All that glisters is not gold;   65
     Often have you heard that told.
     Many a man his life hath sold
     But my outside to behold.   68
     Gilded tombs do worms infold.
     Had you been as wise as bold,
     Young in limbs, in judgment old,
     Your answer had not been inscrolled.   72
     Fare you well, your suit is cold.'
Cold indeed, and labor lost.
Then farewell heat, and welcome frost!
Portia, adieu. I have too grieved a heart
To take a tedious leave. Thus losers part.
     Exit [with his Train. Flourish of cornets].
PORTIA
A gentle riddance. Draw the curtains, go.
Let all of his complexion choose me so.   *Exeunt.*

*

Enter Salerio and Solanio.   II, viii
SALERIO
Why, man, I saw Bassanio under sail;
With him is Gratiano gone along,
And in their ship I am sure Lorenzo is not.
SOLANIO
The villain Jew with outcries raised the Duke,
Who went with him to search Bassanio's ship.
SALERIO
He came too late – the ship was under sail,
But there the Duke was given to understand
That in a gondola were seen together
Lorenzo and his amorous Jessica.
Besides, Antonio certified the Duke   10
They were not with Bassanio in his ship.
SOLANIO
I never heard a passion so confused,
So strange, outrageous, and so variable
As the dog Jew did utter in the streets:
'My daughter! O my ducats! O my daughter!
Fled with a Christian! O my Christian ducats!

THE MERCHANT OF VENICE

Justice! the law! my ducats and my daughter!
A sealèd bag, two sealèd bags of ducats,
Of double ducats, stol'n from me by my daughter!
And jewels – two stones, two rich and precious stones,
Stol'n by my daughter! Justice! Find the girl!
She hath the stones upon her, and the ducats!'

SALERIO
Why, all the boys in Venice follow him,
Crying his stones, his daughter, and his ducats.

SOLANIO
25 Let good Antonio look he keep his day,
Or he shall pay for this.

SALERIO   Marry, well rememb'red.
27 I reasoned with a Frenchman yesterday,
Who told me, in the narrow seas that part
The French and English there miscarrièd
30 A vessel of our country richly fraught.
I thought upon Antonio when he told me,
And wished in silence that it were not his.

SOLANIO
You were best to tell Antonio what you hear.
Yet do not suddenly, for it may grieve him.

SALERIO
A kinder gentleman treads not the earth.
I saw Bassanio and Antonio part:
Bassanio told him he would make some speed
Of his return; he answered, 'Do not so.
39 Slubber not business for my sake, Bassanio,
But stay the very riping of the time;
And for the Jew's bond which he hath of me,
42 Let it not enter in your mind of love.
Be merry, and employ your chiefest thoughts
44 To courtship and such fair ostents of love
As shall conveniently become you there.'
And even there, his eye being big with tears,
Turning his face, he put his hand behind him,
48 And with affection wondrous sensible
He wrung Bassanio's hand; and so they parted.

SOLANIO
I think he only loves the world for him.
I pray thee let us go and find him out,
52 And quicken his embracèd heaviness
With some delight or other.

SALERIO   Do we so.   Exeunt.

*

II, ix   Enter Nerissa and a Servitor.

NERISSA
1 Quick, quick I pray thee! draw the curtain straight.
The Prince of Arragon hath ta'en his oath,
3 And comes to his election presently.
          [Flourish of cornets.] Enter Arragon, his Train, and
          Portia.

PORTIA
Behold, there stand the caskets, noble Prince.
If you choose that wherein I am contained,
Straight shall our nuptial rites be solemnized;
But if you fail, without more speech, my lord,
You must be gone from hence immediately.

ARRAGON
I am enjoined by oath to observe three things:
First, never to unfold to any one
Which casket 'twas I chose; next, if I fail

Of the right casket, never in my life
To woo a maid in way of marriage;
Lastly, if I do fail in fortune of my choice,
Immediately to leave you and be gone.

PORTIA
To these injunctions every one doth swear
That comes to hazard for my worthless self.

ARRAGON
And so have I addressed me. Fortune now   18
To my heart's hope! Gold, silver, and base lead.
'Who chooseth me must give and hazard all he hath.'
You shall look fairer ere I give or hazard.   21
What says the golden chest? Ha, let me see!
'Who chooseth me shall gain what many men desire.'
What many men desire – that 'many' may be meant   24
By the fool multitude that choose by show,
Not learning more than the fond eye doth teach,   26
Which pries not to th' interior, but like the martlet   27
Builds in the weather on the outward wall,   28
Even in the force and road of casualty.   29
I will not choose what many men desire,
Because I will not jump with common spirits
And rank me with the barbarous multitudes.
Why then, to thee, thou silver treasure house!
Tell me once more what title thou dost bear.
'Who chooseth me shall get as much as he deserves.'
And well said too, for who shall go about
To cozen fortune, and be honorable   37
Without the stamp of merit? Let none presume
To wear an undeservèd dignity.
O that estates, degrees, and offices   40
Were not derived corruptly, and that clear honor
Were purchased by the merit of the wearer!
How many then should cover that stand bare,   43
How many be commanded that command;
How much low peasantry would then be gleaned   45
From the true seed of honor, and how much honor   46
Picked from the chaff and ruin of the times
To be new varnished. Well, but to my choice.   48
'Who chooseth me shall get as much as he deserves.'
I will assume desert. Give me a key for this,
And instantly unlock my fortunes here.
          [He opens the silver casket.]

PORTIA
Too long a pause for that which you find there.

ARRAGON
What's here? The portrait of a blinking idiot
Presenting me a schedule! I will read it.   54
How much unlike art thou to Portia!
How much unlike my hopes and my deservings!
'Who chooseth me shall have as much as he deserves.'
Did I deserve no more than a fool's head?
Is that my prize? Are my deserts no better?

25 *keep his day* repay his debt on the day agreed 27 *reasoned* talked 30
fraught laden 39 *Slubber* perform hastily, botch 42 *mind of love* thoughts
of wooing 44 *ostents* shows 48 *wondrous sensible* wonderfully strong in
feeling 52 *quicken ... heaviness* enliven the sadness he has embraced
II, ix Within Portia's house in Belmont 1 *straight* at once 3 *election*
choice; *presently* immediately 18 *addressed me* prepared myself, i.e. by
thus swearing 21 *You ... hazard* (addressed to the leaden casket) 24–25
meant By intended to mean, to suggest 26 *fond* foolish 27 *martlet* a bird
28 *in* exposed to 29 *force ... casualty* power and path of mishap 37
cozen cheat 40 *estates, degrees* social ranks 43 *cover ... bare* wear hats
who now stand bareheaded 45 *gleaned* culled 46 *honor* noble rank 48
new varnished refurbished 54 *schedule* scroll

PORTIA

60 To offend and judge are distinct offices,
And of opposèd natures.

ARRAGON   What is here?

62 'The fire seven times tried this;
Seven times tried that judgment is
That did never choose amiss.
Some there be that shadows kiss;
Such have but a shadow's bliss.

67 There be fools alive iwis,
Silvered o'er, and so was this.
Take what wife you will to bed,
I will ever be your head.

71 So be gone; you are sped.'
Still more fool I shall appear
By the time I linger here.
With one fool's head I came to woo,
But I go away with two.
Sweet, adieu. I'll keep my oath,

77 Patiently to bear my wroath.   *[Exit with his Train.]*

PORTIA

Thus hath the candle singed the moth.
O these deliberate fools! When they do choose,
They have the wisdom by their wit to lose.

NERISSA

The ancient saying is no heresy:
Hanging and wiving goes by destiny.

PORTIA

Come draw the curtain, Nerissa.
Enter Messenger.

MESSENGER

Where is my lady?

PORTIA   Here. What would my lord?

MESSENGER

Madam, there is alighted at your gate
A young Venetian, one that comes before
To signify th' approaching of his lord,

88 From whom he bringeth sensible regreets,
To wit, besides commends and courteous breath,
Gifts of rich value. Yet I have not seen
So likely an ambassador of love.
A day in April never came so sweet

93 To show how costly summer was at hand,

94 As this fore-spurrer comes before his lord.

PORTIA

No more, I pray thee. I am half afeard
Thou wilt say anon he is some kin to thee,

97 Thou spend'st such high-day wit in praising him.

Come, come, Nerissa, for I long to see
Quick Cupid's post that comes so mannerly.   99

NERISSA

Bassanio, Lord Love, if thy will it be!   *Exeunt.* 100

*

[Enter] Solanio and Salerio.   III, i

SOLANIO Now what news on the Rialto?

SALERIO Why, yet it lives there unchecked that Antonio 2
hath a ship of rich lading wracked on the narrow seas –
the Goodwins I think they call the place, a very danger- 4
ous flat, and fatal, where the carcasses of many a tall ship
lie buried as they say, if my gossip Report be an honest 6
woman of her word.

SOLANIO I would she were as lying a gossip in that as ever
knapped ginger or made her neighbors believe she wept 9
for the death of a third husband. But it is true, without
any slips of prolixity or crossing the plain highway of talk, 11
that the good Antonio, the honest Antonio – O that I
had a title good enough to keep his name company! –

SALERIO Come, the full stop! 14

SOLANIO Ha, what sayest thou? Why the end is, he hath
lost a ship.

SALERIO I would it might prove the end of his losses.

SOLANIO Let me say amen betimes lest the devil cross 18
my prayer, for here he comes in the likeness of a Jew.
Enter Shylock.
How now, Shylock? What news among the merchants?

SHYLOCK You knew, none so well, none so well as you, of
my daughter's flight.

SALERIO That's certain. I for my part knew the tailor
that made the wings she flew withal. 24

SOLANIO And Shylock for his own part knew the bird
was fledge, and then it is the complexion of them all to 26
leave the dam. 27

SHYLOCK She is damned for it.

SALERIO That's certain, if the devil may be her judge.

SHYLOCK My own flesh and blood to rebel!

SOLANIO Out upon it, old carrion! Rebels it at these 31
years?

SHYLOCK I say my daughter is my flesh and my blood.

SALERIO There is more difference between thy flesh and
hers than between jet and ivory, more between your
bloods than there is between red wine and Rhenish. But
tell us, do you hear whether Antonio have had any loss
at sea or no?

SHYLOCK There I have another bad match! A bankrout, 38
a prodigal, who dare scarce show his head on the Rialto,
a beggar that was used to come so smug upon the mart! 40
Let him look to his bond. He was wont to call me usurer.
Let him look to his bond. He was wont to lend money
for a Christian cursy. Let him look to his bond. 43

SALERIO Why, I am sure if he forfeit thou wilt not take
his flesh. What's that good for?

SHYLOCK To bait fish withal. If it will feed nothing else, it
will feed my revenge. He hath disgraced me and hind'red
me half a million, laughed at my losses, mocked at my
gains, scorned my nation, thwarted my bargains, cooled
my friends, heated mine enemies–and what's his reason?
I am a Jew. Hath not a Jew eyes? Hath not a Jew hands,
organs, dimensions, senses, affections, passions? – fed 52
with the same food, hurt with the same weapons, subject
to the same diseases, healed by the same means, warmed

60–61 *To offend . . . natures* i.e. those who are subject to judgment may not
be their own judges   62 *tried* tested (?), purified (?)   67 *iwis* certainly
71 *sped* done for   77 *wroath* disappointment (?), resentment (?)   88
sensible regreets tangible greetings, i.e. more than words   93 *costly* rich,
bountiful   94 *fore-spurrer* forerunner   97 *high-day* holiday, i.e. suitable
for a special occasion   99 *post* messenger   100 *Lord Love* god of love, i.e.
Cupid
III, i A street in Venice   2 *lives* i.e. circulates; *unchecked* without denial
(?), extensively (?)   4 *Goodwins* Goodwin Sands (off the English coast)
6 *gossip Report* i.e. Dame Rumor   9 *knapped* nibbled   11 *slips of prolixity* lapses into wordiness; *crossing . . . talk* i.e. deviation from plain
speech   14 *full stop* period, end of statement   18 *cross* thwart   24 *wings*
i.e. the boy's suit (with pun on *flight*)   26 *fledge* ready to fly; *complexion*
disposition   27 *dam* mother, i.e. parent   31 *carrion* dead, putrefied
flesh   31–32 *Rebels . . . years* i.e. do you have fleshly desires at your age
38 *match* bargain; *bankrout* bankrupt   40 *mart* market place, exchange
43 *for . . . cursy* as a Christian courtesy   52 *dimensions* bodily members,
form

and cooled by the same winter and summer as a Christian is? If you prick us, do we not bleed? If you tickle us, do we not laugh? If you poison us, do we not die? And if you wrong us, shall we not revenge? If we are like you in the rest, we will resemble you in that. If a Jew wrong
60 a Christian, what is his humility? Revenge. If a Christian
61 wrong a Jew, what should his sufferance be by Christian example? Why revenge! The villainy you teach me I will execute, and it shall go hard but I will better the instruction.

    Enter a Man from Antonio.

MAN Gentlemen, my master Antonio is at his house and desires to speak with you both.

SALERIO We have been up and down to seek him.

    Enter Tubal.

68 SOLANIO Here comes another of the tribe. A third cannot be matched, unless the devil himself turn Jew.

    Exeunt [Solanio, Salerio, and Man].

SHYLOCK How now, Tubal! What news from Genoa? Hast thou found my daughter?

TUBAL I often came where I did hear of her, but cannot find her.

SHYLOCK Why there, there, there, there! A diamond gone
75 cost me two thousand ducats in Frankford! The curse never fell upon our nation till now; I never felt it till now. Two thousand ducats in that, and other precious, precious jewels. I would my daughter were dead at my foot, and the jewels in her ear! Would she were hearsed at my foot, and the ducats in her coffin! No news of them, why so? – and I know not what's spent in the search. Why thou loss upon loss! the thief gone with so much, and so much to find the thief! – and no satisfaction, no revenge! nor no ill luck stirring but what lights o' my shoulders, no sighs but o' my breathing, no tears but o' my shedding.

TUBAL Yes, other men have ill luck too. Antonio, as I heard in Genoa –

SHYLOCK What, what, what? Ill luck, ill luck?

90 TUBAL Hath an argosy cast away coming from Tripolis.

SHYLOCK I thank God, I thank God! Is it true? is it true?

TUBAL I spoke with some of the sailors that escaped the wrack.

SHYLOCK I thank thee, good Tubal. Good news, good news! Ha, ha! Heard in Genoa?

TUBAL Your daughter spent in Genoa, as I heard, one night fourscore ducats.

SHYLOCK Thou stick'st a dagger in me. I shall never see my gold again. Fourscore ducats at a sitting, fourscore ducats!

100 TUBAL There came divers of Antonio's creditors in my company to Venice that swear he cannot choose but
102 break.

SHYLOCK I am very glad of it. I'll plague him; I'll torture him. I am glad of it.

TUBAL One of them showed me a ring that he had of your daughter for a monkey.

SHYLOCK Out upon her! Thou torturest me, Tubal. It
107 was my turquoise; I had it of Leah when I was a bachelor. I would not have given it for a wilderness of monkeys.

TUBAL But Antonio is certainly undone.

110 SHYLOCK Nay, that's true, that's very true. Go, Tubal, fee
111 me an officer; bespeak him a fortnight before. I will have the heart of him if he forfeit, for were he out of

Venice I can make what merchandise I will. Go, Tubal, 113 and meet me at our synagogue; go, good Tubal; at our synagogue, Tubal.   *Exeunt.*

    *

    Enter Bassanio, Portia, Gratiano, [Nerissa,] and all III, ii
    their Trains.

PORTIA
I pray you tarry; pause a day or two
Before you hazard, for in choosing wrong
I lose your company. Therefore forbear awhile.
There's something tells me, but it is not love,
I would not lose you; and you know yourself
Hate counsels not in such a quality.   6
But lest you should not understand me well –
And yet a maiden hath no tongue but thought –
I would detain you here some month or two
Before you venture for me. I could teach you
How to choose right, but then I am forsworn.   11
So will I never be. So may you miss me.
But if you do, you'll make me wish a sin –
That I had been forsworn. Beshrew your eyes!
They have o'erlooked me and divided me;   15
One half of me is yours, the other half yours –
Mine own I would say; but if mine then yours,
And so all yours! O these naughty times   18
Puts bars between the owners and their rights!
And so, though yours, not yours. Prove it so,   20
Let fortune go to hell for it, not I.
I speak too long, but 'tis to peize the time,   22
To eke it and to draw it out in length,   23
To stay you from election.
BASSANIO   Let me choose,
For as I am, I live upon the rack.   25
PORTIA
Upon the rack, Bassanio? Then confess
What treason there is mingled with your love.
BASSANIO
None but that ugly treason of mistrust
Which makes me fear th' enjoying of my love.
There may as well be amity and life
'Tween snow and fire, as treason and my love.
PORTIA
Ay, but I fear you speak upon the rack,
Where men enforcèd do speak anything.
BASSANIO
Promise me life and I'll confess the truth.
PORTIA
Well then, confess and live.
BASSANIO   Confess and love   35
Had been the very sum of my confession!
O happy torment, when my torturer

60 *his* i.e. the Christian's   61 *his* i.e. the Jew's   68–69 *cannot be matched* cannot be found to match them 75 *Frankford* Frankfort 100 *divers* various, several 102 *break* go bankrupt 107 *Leah* Shylock's wife 110 *fee* hire 111 *officer* arresting officer; *bespeak* engage 113 *make . . . will* drive what bargains I wish
III, ii Within Portia's house in Belmont 6 *quality* way 11 *forsworn* false to my oath 15 *o'erlooked* bewitched 18 *naughty* evil, worthless 20 *Prove it so* if it prove so 22 *peize* retard (?), augment, fill in (?) 23 *eke* increase 25–27 *upon the rack . . . treason* (refers to confessions of treason obtained by torture on the rack) 35–36 *Confess . . . confession* i.e. why, as for my confession, love would have been the gist of it (Bassanio leaps to this with a play on the words 'live' and 'love')

38   Doth teach me answers for deliverance.
    But let me to my fortune and the caskets.

PORTIA

    Away then! I am locked in one of them;
    If you do love me, you will find me out.
    Nerissa and the rest, stand all aloof.
    Let music sound while he doth make his choice;
44   Then if he lose he makes a swanlike end,
45   Fading in music. That the comparison
    May stand more proper, my eye shall be the stream
    And wat'ry deathbed for him. He may win,
    And what is music then? Then music is
49   Even as the flourish when true subjects bow
    To a new-crownèd monarch. Such it is
    As are those dulcet sounds in break of day
    That creep into the dreaming bridegroom's ear
    And summon him to marriage. Now he goes,
    With no less presence but with much more love
55   Than young Alcides when he did redeem
    The virgin tribute paid by howling Troy
57   To the sea monster. I stand for sacrifice;
58   The rest aloof are the Dardanian wives,
59   With blearèd visages come forth to view
60   The issue of th' exploit. Go, Hercules!
61   Live thou, I live. With much, much more dismay
    I view the fight than thou that mak'st the fray.

A song the whilst Bassanio comments on the caskets to himself.

63   Tell me where is fancy bred,
         Or in the heart, or in the head?
         How begot, how nourishèd?
          Reply, reply.
         It is engend'red in the eyes,
         With gazing fed, and fancy dies
         In the cradle where it lies.
          Let us all ring fancy's knell.
          I'll begin it – Ding, dong, bell.

ALL   Ding, dong, bell.

BASSANIO

73   So may the outward shows be least themselves;
    The world is still deceived with ornament.
    In law, what plea so tainted and corrupt
76   But being seasoned with a gracious voice,
    Obscures the show of evil? In religion,

What damnèd error but some sober brow
Will bless it and approve it with a text,
Hiding the grossness with fair ornament?
There is no vice so simple but assumes   81
Some mark of virtue on his outward parts.
How many cowards whose hearts are all as false
As stairs of sand, wear yet upon their chins
The beards of Hercules and frowning Mars,
Who inward searched, have livers white as milk!   86
And these assume but valor's excrement   87
To render them redoubted. Look on beauty,   88
And you shall see 'tis purchased by the weight,
Which therein works a miracle in nature,
Making them lightest that wear most of it: 91
So are those crispèd snaky golden locks,   92
Which maketh such wanton gambols with the wind
Upon supposèd fairness, often known   94
To be the dowry of a second head,   95
The skull that bred them in the sepulchre.
Thus ornament is but the guilèd shore   97
To a most dangerous sea, the beauteous scarf
Veiling an Indian beauty; in a word,   99
The seeming truth which cunning times put on
To entrap the wisest. Therefore then, thou gaudy gold,
Hard food for Midas, I will none of thee;   102
Nor none of thee, thou pale and common drudge   103
'Tween man and man. But thou, thou meagre lead
Which rather threaten'st than dost promise aught,
Thy paleness moves me more than eloquence;
And here choose I. Joy be the consequence!

PORTIA *[aside]*

How all the other passions fleet to air:
As doubtful thoughts, and rash-embraced despair,   109
And shudd'ring fear, and green-eyed jealousy.
O love, be moderate, allay thy ecstasy,
In measure rain thy joy, scant this excess!   112
I feel too much thy blessing. Make it less
For fear I surfeit.

BASSANIO *[opening the leaden casket]*
        What find I here?
Fair Portia's counterfeit! What demigod   115
Hath come so near creation? Move these eyes?
Or whether, riding on the balls of mine,   117
Seem they in motion? Here are severed lips
Parted with sugar breath; so sweet a bar
Should sunder such sweet friends. Here in her hairs   120
The painter plays the spider, and hath woven
A golden mesh t' entrap the hearts of men
Faster than gnats in cobwebs. But her eyes –   123
How could he see to do them? Having made one,
Methinks it should have power to steal both his
And leave itself unfurnished. Yet look, how far   126
The substance of my praise doth wrong this shadow   127
In underprizing it, so far this shadow
Doth limp behind the substance. Here's the scroll,   129
The continent and summary of my fortune.   130
    'You that choose not by the view
       Chance as fair, and choose as true.   132
    Since this fortune falls to you,
    Be content and seek no new.
    If you be well pleased with this
    And hold your fortune for your bliss,
    Turn you where your lady is,
    And claim her with a loving kiss.'

---

38 *answers for deliverance* answers that will obtain release   **44** *swanlike end* (the swan was thought to sing just before death)   **45** *comparison* figure, metaphor   **49** *flourish* sounding of trumpets   **55–57** *Alcides . . . monster* (Alcides, or Hercules, rescued the daughter of the Trojan king from sacrifice to a sea monster)   **57** *stand for sacrifice* represent the sacrificial victim   **58** *Dardanian* Trojan   **59** *blearèd* i.e. weeping   **60** *issue* outcome   **61** *Live thou* if you live   **63** *fancy* fond love, infatuation   **73** *be least themselves* i.e. belie the inner quality   **76** *seasoned* spiced   **81** *simple* unadulterated   **86** *livers . . . milk* (cowards were supposed to have white livers)   **87** *excrement* outer growth (as hair)   **88** *redoubted* feared   **91** *lightest* (with pun on 'light' in the sense of 'light woman')   **92** *crispèd* curled   **94** *Upon supposèd fairness* on the head of a supposed beauty   **95–96** *dowry . . . sepulchre* i.e. hair taken from a person now dead and buried   **97** *guilèd* beguiling   **99** *Indian* i.e. swarthy, not fair   **102** *Midas* (all that Midas touched, including food, turned to gold)   **103–04** *pale . . . and man* i.e. silver   **109** *As* such as   **112** *scant* lessen   **115** *counterfeit* image, portrait   **115–16** *What demigod . . . creation* i.e. only a demigod could have painted such a lifelike picture   **117** *Or whether* or   **120** *sweet friends* i.e. the two lips   **123** *Faster* more securely   **126** *unfurnished* i.e. without the other eye, since the painter could not see to paint it   **127** *shadow* picture   **129** *substance* i.e. the real Portia   **130** *continent* container   **132** *Chance as fair* hazard as fortunately

A gentle scroll. Fair lady, by your leave.
[Kisses her.]
140 I come by note, to give and to receive.
Like one of two contending in a prize,
That thinks he hath done well in people's eyes,
Hearing applause and universal shout,
Giddy in spirit, still gazing in a doubt
145 Whether those peals of praise be his or no –
So, thrice-fair lady, stand I even so,
As doubtful whether what I see be true,
Until confirmed, signed, ratified by you.

PORTIA
You see me, Lord Bassanio, where I stand,
Such as I am. Though for myself alone
I would not be ambitious in my wish
To wish myself much better, yet for you
I would be trebled twenty times myself,
A thousand times more fair, ten thousand times more
    rich,
155 That only to stand high in your account,
I might in virtues, beauties, livings, friends,
Exceed account. But the full sum of me
158 Is sum of something – which, to term in gross,
Is an unlessoned girl, unschooled, unpractised ;
Happy in this, she is not yet so old
But she may learn ; happier than this,
She is not bred so dull but she can learn ;
Happiest of all, is that her gentle spirit
Commits itself to yours to be directed,
165 As from her lord, her governor, her king.
Myself and what is mine to you and yours
167 Is now converted. But now I was the lord
Of this fair mansion, master of my servants,
Queen o'er myself ; and even now, but now,
This house, these servants, and this same myself
Are yours, my lord's. I give them with this ring,
Which when you part from, lose, or give away,
Let it presage the ruin of your love
174 And be my vantage to exclaim on you.

BASSANIO
Madam, you have bereft me of all words.
Only my blood speaks to you in my veins,
177 And there is such confusion in my powers
As, after some oration fairly spoke
By a belovèd prince, there doth appear
Among the buzzing pleasèd multitude,
Where every something being blent together
Turns to a wild of nothing, save of joy
Expressed and not expressed. But when this ring
Parts from this finger, then parts life from hence ;
O then be bold to say Bassanio's dead !

NERISSA
My lord and lady, it is now our time,
187 That have stood by and seen our wishes prosper,
To cry 'good joy.' Good joy, my lord and lady !

GRATIANO
My Lord Bassanio, and my gentle lady,
I wish you all the joy that you can wish –
For I am sure you can wish none from me ;
And when your honors mean to solemnize
The bargain of your faith, I do beseech you
Even at that time I may be married too.

BASSANIO
195 With all my heart, so thou canst get a wife.

GRATIANO
I thank your lordship ; you have got me one.
My eyes, my lord, can look as swift as yours :
You saw the mistress, I beheld the maid.
You loved, I loved ; for intermission   199
No more pertains to me, my lord, than you.
Your fortune stood upon the caskets there,
And so did mine too, as the matter falls ;
For wooing here until I sweat again,   203
And swearing till my very roof was dry   204
With oaths of love, at last – if promise last – 205
I got a promise of this fair one here
To have her love, provided that your fortune
Achieved her mistress.

PORTIA   Is this true, Nerissa ?

NERISSA
Madam, it is, so you stand pleased withal.   209

BASSANIO
And do you, Gratiano, mean good faith ?

GRATIANO Yes, faith, my lord.

BASSANIO
Our feast shall be much honored in your marriage.

GRATIANO We'll play with them the first boy for a thou- 213
sand ducats.

NERISSA What, and stake down ?   215

GRATIANO No, we shall ne'er win at that sport, and stake 216
down.
But who comes here ? Lorenzo and his infidel !   218
What, and my old Venetian friend Salerio !
    *Enter Lorenzo, Jessica, and Salerio, a Messenger
    from Venice.*

BASSANIO
Lorenzo and Salerio, welcome hither,
If that the youth of my new int'rest here   221
Have power to bid you welcome. By your leave,
I bid my very friends and countrymen,
Sweet Portia, welcome.

PORTIA   So do I, my lord.
They are entirely welcome.

LORENZO
I thank your honor. For my part, my lord,
My purpose was not to have seen you here,
But meeting with Salerio by the way,
He did entreat me past all saying nay
To come with him along.

SALERIO   I did, my lord,
And I have reason for it. Signior Antonio
Commends him to you.   232
    [Gives Bassanio a letter.]

BASSANIO   Ere I ope his letter,
I pray you tell me how my good friend doth.

SALERIO
Not sick, my lord, unless it be in mind,

---

140 *come by note* come according to directions of the scroll (?), present
my bill for payment (?) **145** *his* addressed to him **155** *That* so that ;
account estimation **158** *something* i.e. at least something ; *term in gross*
state in full **165** *from* by **167** *converted* transferred ; *But now* a moment
ago **174** *vantage . . . you* opportunity to reproach you **177** *powers*
faculties **187** *That* who **195** *so* if **199** *intermission* delay, inactivity
203 *again* repeatedly **204** *roof* (of the mouth) **205** *if promise last* i.e.
if Nerissa's promise is still good **209** *so . . . withal* if it pleases you **213–14**
play . . . ducats wager a thousand ducats, the couple having the first boy to
be the winner **215** *stake down* bets made with cash down **216–17** *stake
down* (with ribald pun) **218** *infidel* i.e. Jessica **221** *int'rest* position in the
household **232** *Commends him* sends his greetings

Nor well unless in mind. His letters there
236 Will show you his estate.
Open the letter.

GRATIANO
Nerissa, cheer yond stranger; bid her welcome.
Your hand, Salerio. What's the news from Venice?
239 How doth that royal merchant, good Antonio?
I know he will be glad of our success;
241 We are the Jasons, we have won the Fleece.

SALERIO
I would you had won the fleece that he hath lost!

PORTIA
243 There are some shrowd contents in yond same paper
That steals the color from Bassanio's cheek:
Some dear friend dead, else nothing in the world
Could turn so much the constitution
Of any constant man. What, worse and worse?
With leave, Bassanio – I am half yourself,
And I must freely have the half of anything
That this same paper brings you.

BASSANIO   O sweet Portia,
Here are a few of the unpleasant'st words
That ever blotted paper! Gentle lady,
When I did first impart my love to you,
I freely told you all the wealth I had
Ran in my veins – I was a gentleman –
And then I told you true; and yet, dear lady,
Rating myself at nothing, you shall see
How much I was a braggart. When I told you
259 My state was nothing, I should then have told you
That I was worse than nothing; for indeed
261 I have engaged myself to a dear friend,
262 Engaged my friend to his mere enemy
To feed my means. Here is a letter, lady,
The paper as the body of my friend,
And every word in it a gaping wound
Issuing lifeblood. But is it true, Salerio?
Hath all his ventures failed? What, not one hit?
From Tripolis, from Mexico and England,
From Lisbon, Barbary, and India,
And not one vessel scape the dreadful touch
271 Of merchant-marring rocks?

SALERIO   Not one, my lord.
Besides, it should appear that if he had
273 The present money to discharge the Jew,
274 He would not take it. Never did I know
A creature that did bear the shape of man
276 So keen and greedy to confound a man.
He plies the Duke at morning and at night,
278 And doth impeach the freedom of the state
If they deny him justice. Twenty merchants,
280 The Duke himself, and the magnificoes
281 Of greatest port have all persuaded with him,

But none can drive him from the envious plea   282
Of forfeiture, of justice, and his bond.

JESSICA
When I was with him, I have heard him swear
To Tubal and to Chus, his countrymen,
That he would rather have Antonio's flesh
Than twenty times the value of the sum
That he did owe him; and I know, my lord,
If law, authority, and power deny not,
It will go hard with poor Antonio.

PORTIA
Is it your dear friend that is thus in trouble?

BASSANIO
The dearest friend to me, the kindest man,
The best-conditioned and unwearied spirit   293
In doing courtesies, and one in whom
The ancient Roman honor more appears
Than any that draws breath in Italy.

PORTIA
What sum owes he the Jew?

BASSANIO
For me, three thousand ducats.

PORTIA   What, no more?
Pay him six thousand, and deface the bond.   299
Double six thousand and then treble that,
Before a friend of this description
Shall lose a hair through Bassanio's fault.
First go with me to church and call me wife,
And then away to Venice to your friend!
For never shall you lie by Portia's side
With an unquiet soul. You shall have gold
To pay the petty debt twenty times over;
When it is paid, bring your true friend along.
My maid Nerissa and myself meantime
Will live as maids and widows. Come away!
For you shall hence upon your wedding day.   311
Bid your friends welcome, show a merry cheer;   312
Since you are dear bought, I will love you dear.
But let me hear the letter of your friend.

[BASSANIO *(reads)*] 'Sweet Bassanio, my ships have all
miscarried, my creditors grow cruel, my estate is very
low, my bond to the Jew is forfeit. And since in paying
it, it is impossible I should live, all debts are cleared between you and I if I might but see you at my death.
Notwithstanding, use your pleasure. If your love do not
persuade you to come, let not my letter.'

PORTIA
O love, dispatch all business and be gone!

BASSANIO
Since I have your good leave to go away,
I will make haste, but till I come again
No bed shall e'er be guilty of my stay,
Nor rest be interposer 'twixt us twain.   *Exeunt.*

*

Enter [Shylock] the Jew and Solanio and Antonio   III, iii
and the Jailer.

SHYLOCK
Jailer, look to him. Tell not me of mercy.
This is the fool that lent out money gratis.
Jailer, look to him.

ANTONIO   Hear me yet, good Shylock.

SHYLOCK
I'll have my bond! Speak not against my bond!

---

236 *estate* condition, state of affairs   239 *royal merchant* merchant of great affluence ('merchant prince'); sometimes one engaged in royal employment   241 *Jasons . . . Fleece* (see I, i, 170–72)   243 *shrowd* cursed, bitter   259 *state* estate, property   261 *engaged myself* become indebted 262 *mere* unqualified, sheer   271 *merchant* merchant ship   273 *discharge* pay off   274 *He* i.e. the Jew   276 *confound* ruin   278 *freedom . . . state* freedom of commerce, of contract, in Venice   280 *magnificoes* Venetian magnates   281 *port* dignity   282 *envious* malicious   293 *best-conditioned* best natured   299 *deface* cancel   311 *hence* go hence   312 *cheer* counte-nance
III, iii A street in Venice

I have sworn an oath that I will have my bond.
Thou call'dst me dog before thou hadst a cause,
But since I am a dog, beware my fangs.
The Duke shall grant me justice. I do wonder,
9   Thou naughty jailer, that thou art so fond
To come abroad with him at his request.

ANTONIO
I pray thee hear me speak.

SHYLOCK
I'll have my bond. I will not hear thee speak.
I'll have my bond, and therefore speak no more.
I'll not be made a soft and dull-eyed fool,
To shake the head, relent, and sigh, and yield
To Christian intercessors. Follow not.
I'll have no speaking; I will have my bond.   *Exit.*

SOLANIO
It is the most impenetrable cur
19   That ever kept with men.

ANTONIO   Let him alone;
20   I'll follow him no more with bootless prayers.
He seeks my life. His reason well I know:
22   I oft delivered from his forfeitures
Many that have at times made moan to me.
Therefore he hates me.

SOLANIO   I am sure the Duke
Will never grant this forfeiture to hold.

ANTONIO
The Duke cannot deny the course of law;
27   For the commodity that strangers have
With us in Venice, if it be denied,
Will much impeach the justice of the state,
Since that the trade and profit of the city
Consisteth of all nations. Therefore go.
32   These griefs and losses have so bated me
That I shall hardly spare a pound of flesh
To-morrow to my bloody creditor.
Well, jailer, on. Pray God Bassanio come
To see me pay his debt, and then I care not!   *Exeunt.*

*

III, iv   *Enter Portia, Nerissa, Lorenzo, Jessica, and*
[Balthasar,] a Man of Portia's.

LORENZO
Madam, although I speak it in your presence,
2   You have a noble and a true conceit
Of godlike amity, which appears most strongly
In bearing thus the absence of your lord.
But if you knew to whom you show this honor,
How true a gentleman you send relief,
How dear a lover of my lord your husband,
I know you would be prouder of the work
9   Than customary bounty can enforce you.

PORTIA
I never did repent for doing good,
Nor shall not now; for in companions
12   That do converse and waste the time together,
Whose souls do bear an equal yoke of love,
There must be needs a like proportion
Of lineaments, of manners, and of spirit;
Which makes me think that this Antonio,
Being the bosom lover of my lord,
Must needs be like my lord. If it be so,
How little is the cost I have bestowed

In purchasing the semblance of my soul   20
From out the state of hellish cruelty!
This comes too near the praising of myself;
Therefore no more of it. Hear other things:
Lorenzo, I commit into your hands
The husbandry and manage of my house   25
Until my lord's return. For mine own part,
I have toward heaven breathed a secret vow
To live in prayer and contemplation,
Only attended by Nerissa here,
Until her husband and my lord's return.
There is a monastery two miles off,
And there we will abide. I do desire you
Not to deny this imposition,   33
The which my love and some necessity
Now lays upon you.

LORENZO   Madam, with all my heart;
I shall obey you in all fair commands.

PORTIA
My people do already know my mind
And will acknowledge you and Jessica
In place of Lord Bassanio and myself.
So fare you well till we shall meet again.

LORENZO
Fair thoughts and happy hours attend on you!

JESSICA
I wish your ladyship all heart's content.

PORTIA
I thank you for your wish, and am well pleased
To wish it back on you. Fare you well, Jessica.
          Exeunt [Jessica and Lorenzo].
Now, Balthasar,
As I have ever found thee honest-true,
So let me find thee still. Take this same letter,
And use thou all th' endeavor of a man
In speed to Padua. See thou render this
Into my cousin's hands, Doctor Bellario;
And look, what notes and garments he doth give thee
Bring them, I pray thee, with imagined speed   52
Unto the traject, to the common ferry   53
Which trades to Venice. Waste no time in words
But get thee gone. I shall be there before thee.

BALTHASAR
Madam, I go with all convenient speed.   *[Exit.]* 56

PORTIA
Come on, Nerissa; I have work in hand
That you yet know not of. We'll see our husbands
Before they think of us.

NERISSA   Shall they see us?

PORTIA
They shall, Nerissa, but in such a habit   60
That they shall think we are accomplishèd   61
With that we lack. I'll hold thee any wager,
When we are both accoutered like young men,

---

9 *naughty* wicked, corrupt; *fond* foolish   19 *kept* dwelt, associated   20
bootless fruitless   22 *delivered* saved   27 *commodity* trading rights or privileges; *strangers* non-Venetians, including Jews   32 *bated* reduced
III, iv Portia's house   2 *conceit* conception, attitude   9 *Than . . . you*
than ordinary kindness can make you   12 *waste* spend   20 *purchasing . . .*
soul i.e. redeeming Antonio, the likeness of Bassanio, 'my soul'   25
husbandry care   33 *imposition* duty, charge   52 *imagined speed* swiftness
of thought (?), all imaginable speed (?)   53 *traject* (from Italian '*traghetto*,'
a ferry)   56 *convenient* appropriate   60 *habit* costume   61 *accomplishèd*
equipped

I'll prove the prettier fellow of the two,
And wear my dagger with the braver grace,
And speak between the change of man and boy
67　With a reed voice, and turn two mincing steps
Into a manly stride, and speak of frays
69　Like a fine bragging youth, and tell quaint lies,
How honorable ladies sought my love,
Which I denying, they fell sick and died –
72　I could not do withal! Then I'll repent,
And wish, for all that, that I had not killed them.
And twenty of these puny lies I'll tell,
That men shall swear I have discontinued school
76　Above a twelvemonth. I have within my mind
A thousand raw tricks of these bragging Jacks,
Which I will practice.
78 NERISSA　　　　　　　Why, shall we turn to men?
PORTIA
　Fie, what a question 's that,
If thou wert near a lewd interpreter!
But come, I'll tell thee all my whole device
When I am in my coach, which stays for us
At the park gate; and therefore haste away,
For we must measure twenty miles to-day.　　　Exeunt.

*

III, v　　　Enter [Launcelot the] Clown and Jessica.
LAUNCELOT Yes truly; for look you, the sins of the father
　are to be laid upon the children. Therefore, I promise you
3　I fear you. I was always plain with you, and so now I
4　speak my agitation of the matter. Therefore be o' good
　cheer, for truly I think you are damned. There is but
　one hope in it that can do you any good, and that is but a
7　kind of bastard hope neither.
JESSICA And what hope is that, I pray thee?
LAUNCELOT Marry, you may partly hope that your father
　got you not – that you are not the Jew's daughter.
JESSICA That were a kind of bastard hope indeed! So the
　sins of my mother should be visited upon me.
LAUNCELOT Truly then, I fear you are damned both by
　father and mother. Thus when I shun Scylla your father,
15　I fall into Charybdis your mother. Well, you are gone
　both ways.
JESSICA I shall be saved by my husband. He hath made
　me a Christian.
LAUNCELOT Truly, the more to blame he! We were
20　Christians enow before, e'en as many as could well live
　one by another. This making of Christians will raise the

price of hogs; if we grow all to be pork-eaters, we shall
not shortly have a rasher on the coals for money.　　23
　　Enter Lorenzo.
JESSICA I'll tell my husband, Launcelot, what you say.
　Here he comes.
LORENZO I shall grow jealous of you shortly, Launcelot,
　if you thus get my wife into corners.
JESSICA Nay, you need not fear us, Lorenzo. Launcelot
　and I are out. He tells me flatly there's no mercy for me 29
　in heaven because I am a Jew's daughter; and he says
　you are no good member of the commonwealth, for in
　converting Jews to Christians you raise the price of
　pork.
LORENZO [to Launcelot] I shall answer that better to the 33
　commonwealth than you can the getting up of the
　Negro's belly. The Moor is with child by you, Launce-
　lot.
LAUNCELOT It is much that the Moor should be more 36
　than reason; but if she be less than an honest woman, 37
　she is indeed more than I took her for.
LORENZO How every fool can play upon the word!
　I think the best grace of wit will shortly turn into 40
　silence, and discourse grow commendable in none
　only but parrots. Go in, sirrah; bid them prepare for
　dinner.
LAUNCELOT That is done, sir. They have all stomachs.
LORENZO Goodly Lord, what a wit-snapper are you!
　Then bid them prepare dinner.
LAUNCELOT That is done too, sir. Only 'cover' is the 46
　word.
LORENZO Will you cover then, sir?
LAUNCELOT Not so, sir, neither! I know my duty.　　48
LORENZO Yet more quarrelling with occasion! Wilt thou 49
　show the whole wealth of thy wit in an instant? I pray
　thee understand a plain man in his plain meaning: go
　to thy fellows, bid them cover the table, serve in the
　meat, and we will come in to dinner.
LAUNCELOT For the table, sir, it shall be served in; for 54
　the meat, sir, it shall be covered; for your coming in to 55
　dinner, sir, why let it be as humors and conceits shall 56
　govern.　　　　　　　　　Exit Clown [Launcelot].
LORENZO
　O dear discretion, how his words are suited!　　　　58
　The fool hath planted in his memory
　An army of good words; and I do know
　A many fools that stand in better place,　　　　　61
　Garnished like him, that for a tricksy word　　　62
　Defy the matter. How cheer'st thou, Jessica?　　63
　And now, good sweet, say thy opinion –
　How dost thou like the Lord Bassanio's wife?
JESSICA
　Past all expressing. It is very meet
　The Lord Bassanio live an upright life
　For having such a blessing in his lady;
　He finds the joys of heaven here on earth,
　And if on earth he do not merit it,
　In reason he should never come to heaven.
　Why, if two gods should play some heavenly match
　And on the wager lay two earthly women,　　　　73
　And Portia one, there must be something else　　74
　Pawned with the other, for the poor rude world　75
　Hath not her fellow.
LORENZO　　　　　　　Even such a husband
　Hast thou of me as she is for a wife.

67 reed reedy, piping　69 quaint clever, contrived　72 I . . . withal I could
not help it　76 Above more than, i.e. at least　78 turn to turn into (with
pun; cf. I, iii, 77)
III, v The same　3 fear you fear for you　4 agitation (blunder for 'cogitation')　7 neither (simply emphasizes the statement)　15 gone done for
20 enow before i.e. numerous enough before Jessica became a Christian
23 rasher (of bacon)　29 are out have quarrelled　33 answer justify　36–37
more than reason larger than is reasonable (with pun on Moor)　37 honest
chaste　40 best grace highest quality　46 cover i.e. lay the table　48
Not so . . . duty (to Launcelot cover now means to put on his cap; cf. II,
ix, 43)　49 quarrelling with occasion i.e. quibbling　54 table (Launcelot
quibbles with the word so that it now means the food itself)　55 covered
served in a covered dish (?)　56 humors and conceits whims and ideas
58 dear discretion precious discrimination; suited dressed up (?), used to
suit the occasion (?)　61 A many many; stand . . . place have higher social
rank　62 Garnished like him i.e. resembling him　63 Defy the matter i.e.
refuse to talk sense; How cheer'st thou what cheer　73 lay stake　74 else
more　75 Pawned wagered

JESSICA
Nay, but ask my opinion too of that!

LORENZO
I will anon. First let us go to dinner.

JESSICA
80 Nay, let me praise you while I have a stomach.

LORENZO
No, pray thee, let it serve for table-talk;
82 Then howsome'er thou speak'st, 'mong other things
I shall digest it.
83 **JESSICA**   Well, I'll set you forth.

Exit [with Lorenzo].

∗

IV, i   *Enter the Duke, the Magnificoes, Antonio, Bassanio,*
[Salerio,] and Gratiano [with others].
DUKE What, is Antonio here?

ANTONIO Ready, so please your Grace.

DUKE
I am sorry for thee. Thou art come to answer
A stony adversary, an inhuman wretch,
Uncapable of pity, void and empty
6 From any dram of mercy.

ANTONIO   I have heard
7 Your Grace hath ta'en great pains to qualify
His rigorous course; but since he stands obdurate,
And that no lawful means can carry me
Out of his envy's reach, I do oppose
11 My patience to his fury, and am armed
To suffer with a quietness of spirit
The very tyranny and rage of his.

DUKE
Go one, and call the Jew into the court.

SALERIO
He is ready at the door; he comes, my lord.

Enter Shylock.

DUKE
16 Make room, and let him stand before our face.
Shylock, the world thinks, and I think so too,
18 That thou but leadest this fashion of thy malice
To the last hour of act; and then 'tis thought
20 Thou'lt show thy mercy and remorse more strange
Than is thy strange apparent cruelty;
And where thou now exacts the penalty,
Which is a pound of this poor merchant's flesh,
24 Thou wilt not only loose the forfeiture,
But touched with human gentleness and love,
26 Forgive a moiety of the principal,
Glancing an eye of pity on his losses,
That have of late so huddled on his back –
29 Enow to press a royal merchant down
And pluck commiseration of his state
From brassy bosoms and rough hearts of flint,
From stubborn Turks and Tartars never trained
33 To offices of tender courtesy.
We all expect a gentle answer, Jew.

SHYLOCK
35 I have possessed your Grace of what I purpose,
And by our holy Sabbath have I sworn
To have the due and forfeit of my bond.
If you deny it, let the danger light
39 Upon your charter and your city's freedom!

You'll ask me why I rather choose to have
A weight of carrion flesh than to receive
Three thousand ducats. I'll not answer that,
But say it is my humor. Is it answered?
What if my house be troubled with a rat,
And I be pleased to give ten thousand ducats
To have it baned? What, are you answered yet?   46
Some men there are love not a gaping pig,   47
Some that are mad if they behold a cat,
And others, when the bagpipe sings i' th' nose,
Cannot contain their urine; for affection,   50
Master of passion, sways it to the mood
Of what it likes or loathes. Now for your answer:
As there is no firm reason to be rend'red
Why he cannot abide a gaping pig,   54
Why he a harmless necessary cat,
Why he a woollen bagpipe, but of force   56
Must yield to such inevitable shame
As to offend, himself being offended;
So can I give no reason, nor I will not,
More than a lodged hate and a certain loathing   60
I bear Antonio, that I follow thus
A losing suit against him. Are you answered?   62

BASSANIO
This is no answer, thou unfeeling man,
To excuse the current of thy cruelty!

SHYLOCK
I am not bound to please thee with my answers.

BASSANIO
Do all men kill the things they do not love?

SHYLOCK
Hates any man the thing he would not kill?

BASSANIO
Every offense is not a hate at first.   68

SHYLOCK
What, wouldst thou have a serpent sting thee twice?

ANTONIO
I pray you think you question with the Jew.   70
You may as well go stand upon the beach
And bid the main flood bate his usual height;   72
You may as well use question with the wolf,
Why he hath made the ewe bleat for the lamb;
You may as well forbid the mountain pines
To wag their high tops and to make no noise
When they are fretten with the gusts of heaven;   77
You may as well do anything most hard
As seek to soften that – than which what's harder? –
His Jewish heart. Therefore I do beseech you
Make no moe offers, use no farther means,
But with all brief and plain conveniency   82
Let me have judgment, and the Jew his will.

80 *stomach* inclination, appetite   82 *howsome'er* however   83 *set you forth* serve you up, as at a feast; i.e. praise you ironically
IV, i A Venetian court of justice   6 *From* of   7 *qualify* moderate   11 *armed* prepared   16 *our* my (the 'royal' plural)   18–19 *thou . . . act* you but pursue this working of your malice to the last minute   20 *remorse* pity   24 *loose* waive   26 *moiety* portion   29 *Enow* enough; *royal merchant* (see III, ii, 239)   33 *offices* acts   35 *possessed* informed   39 *freedom* (see III, ii, 278)   46 *baned* poisoned   47 *gaping pig* i.e. served roasted with its mouth propped open   50 *affection* feeling, impulse   54–56 *he . . . he . . . he* i.e. one man . . . another . . . a third   56 *woollen bagpipe* (i.e. with flannel-covered bag); *of force* perforce   60 *lodged* deep-seated   62 *losing* unprofitable   68 *offense* injury, grievance   70 *think* keep in mind; *question* reason, argue   72 *main flood* sea at flood tide; *bate* reduce   77 *fretten* fretted   82 *conveniency* propriety

BASSANIO
For thy three thousand ducats here is six.

SHYLOCK
If every ducat in six thousand ducats
Were in six parts, and every part a ducat,
87   I would not draw them. I would have my bond.

DUKE
How shalt thou hope for mercy, rend'ring none?

SHYLOCK
What judgment shall I dread, doing no wrong?
You have among you many a purchased slave,
Which like your asses and your dogs and mules
92   You use in abject and in slavish parts,
Because you bought them. Shall I say to you,
'Let them be free! marry them to your heirs!
Why sweat they under burdens? Let their beds
Be made as soft as yours, and let their palates
Be seasoned with such viands'? You will answer,
'The slaves are ours.' So do I answer you.
The pound of flesh which I demand of him
Is dearly bought, is mine, and I will have it.
If you deny me, fie upon your law!
There is no force in the decrees of Venice.
I stand for judgment. Answer; shall I have it?

DUKE
104   Upon my power I may dismiss this court
Unless Bellario, a learned doctor
Whom I have sent for to determine this,
Come here to-day.

107   **SALERIO**   My lord, here stays without
A messenger with letters from the doctor,
New come from Padua.

DUKE
Bring us the letters. Call the messenger.

BASSANIO
Good cheer, Antonio! What, man, courage yet!
The Jew shall have my flesh, blood, bones, and all,
Ere thou shalt lose for me one drop of blood.

ANTONIO
114   I am a tainted wether of the flock,
115   Meetest for death. The weakest kind of fruit
Drops earliest to the ground, and so let me.
You cannot better be employed, Bassanio,
Than to live still, and write mine epitaph.

Enter Nerissa [dressed like a Lawyer's Clerk].

DUKE
Came you from Padua, from Bellario?

NERISSA
From both, my lord. Bellario greets your Grace.
[Presents a letter.]

BASSANIO
Why dost thou whet thy knife so earnestly?

SHYLOCK
To cut the forfeiture from that bankrout there.

GRATIANO
Not on thy sole, but on thy soul, harsh Jew,
Thou mak'st thy knife keen; but no metal can –
No, not the hangman's axe – bear half the keenness   125
Of thy sharp envy. Can no prayers pierce thee?

SHYLOCK
No, none that thou hast wit enough to make.

GRATIANO
O be thou damned, inexecrable dog,   128
And for thy life let justice be accused!   129
Thou almost mak'st me waver in my faith –
To hold opinion with Pythagoras   131
That souls of animals infuse themselves
Into the trunks of men. Thy currish spirit
Governed a wolf who, hanged for human slaughter,   134
Even from the gallows did his fell soul fleet,   135
And whilst thou layest in thy unhallowed dam,
Infused itself in thee; for thy desires
Are wolvish, bloody, starved, and ravenous.

SHYLOCK
Till thou canst rail the seal from off my bond,
Thou but offend'st thy lungs to speak so loud.
Repair thy wit, good youth, or it will fall
To cureless ruin. I stand here for law.

DUKE
This letter from Bellario doth commend
A young and learned doctor to our court.
Where is he?

NERISSA   He attendeth here hard by
To know your answer whether you'll admit him.

DUKE
With all my heart. Some three or four of you
Go give him courteous conduct to this place.
Meantime the court shall hear Bellario's letter.

[CLERK (reads)] 'Your Grace shall understand that at the   150
receipt of your letter I am very sick; but in the instant that
your messenger came, in loving visitation was with me a
young doctor of Rome. His name is Balthasar. I acquainted him with the cause in controversy between the Jew
and Antonio the merchant. We turned o'er many books
together. He is furnished with my opinion which, bettered with his own learning, the greatness whereof I cannot enough commend, comes with him at my importunity   158
to fill up your Grace's request in my stead. I beseech you   159
let his lack of years be no impediment to let him lack a   160
reverend estimation, for I never knew so young a body
with so old a head. I leave him to your gracious acceptance, whose trial shall better publish his commendation.'   163

*Enter Portia for Balthasar [dressed like a Doctor of
Laws].*

DUKE
You hear the learn'd Bellario, what he writes;
And here, I take it, is the doctor come.
Give me your hand. Come you from old Bellario?

PORTIA
I did, my lord.

DUKE   You are welcome; take your place.
Are you acquainted with the difference   169
That holds this present question in the court?

87 *draw* take   92 *parts* duties, functions   104 *Upon* in accordance with 107 *stays without* waits outside   114 *wether* sheep   115 *Meetest for death* most fit for slaughter   125 *hangman's* executioner's; *bear* have   128 *in-execrable dog* dog that cannot be execrated enough   129 *for thy life* i.e. because you are allowed to live   131 *Pythagoras* Greek philosopher who believed in transmigration of souls   134 *hanged* (animals were once hanged for 'crimes')   135 *fell* cruel   150 *Clerk* (no reader is designated in original texts, and it is possible that the letter is read by the Duke)   158 *comes with him* i.e. he brings my opinion   159 *to fill . . . stead* in my place in answer to your Grace's request   160 *to let him lack* i.e. which will cause him to lack   163 *trial* i.e. actual performance   169-70 *with . . . court* i.e. with the case being tried

PORTIA

171 I am informèd throughly of the cause.
Which is the merchant here? and which the Jew?

DUKE

Antonio and old Shylock, both stand forth.

PORTIA

Is your name Shylock?

SHYLOCK   Shylock is my name.

PORTIA

Of a strange nature is the suit you follow,
176 Yet in such rule that the Venetian law
Cannot impugn you as you do proceed.
    [To Antonio]
178 You stand within his danger, do you not?

ANTONIO

Ay, so he says.

PORTIA   Do you confess the bond?

ANTONIO

I do.

PORTIA Then must the Jew be merciful.

SHYLOCK

On what compulsion must I? Tell me that.

PORTIA

182 The quality of mercy is not strained;
It droppeth as the gentle rain from heaven
Upon the place beneath. It is twice blest;
It blesseth him that gives and him that takes.
'Tis mightiest in the mightiest; it becomes
The thronèd monarch better than his crown.
His sceptre shows the force of temporal power,
The attribute to awe and majesty,
Wherein doth sit the dread and fear of kings;
But mercy is above this scept'red sway;
It is enthronèd in the hearts of kings;
It is an attribute to God himself,
And earthly power doth then show likest God's
When mercy seasons justice. Therefore, Jew,
Though justice be thy plea, consider this:
197 That in the course of justice none of us
Should see salvation. We do pray for mercy,
And that same prayer doth teach us all to render
The deeds of mercy. I have spoke thus much
201 To mitigate the justice of thy plea,
Which if thou follow, this strict court of Venice
Must needs give sentence 'gainst the merchant there.

SHYLOCK

My deeds upon my head! I crave the law,
The penalty and forfeit of my bond.

PORTIA

Is he not able to discharge the money?

BASSANIO

Yes, here I tender it for him in the court,
Yea, thrice the sum. If that will not suffice,
I will be bound to pay it ten times o'er
On forfeit of my hands, my head, my heart.
If this will not suffice, it must appear
212 That malice bears down truth. And I beseech you,
213 Wrest once the law to your authority.
To do a great right, do a little wrong,
And curb this cruel devil of his will.

PORTIA

It must not be. There is no power in Venice
Can alter a decree establishèd.
'Twill be recorded for a precedent,

And many an error by the same example
Will rush into the state. It cannot be.

SHYLOCK

A Daniel come to judgment! yea, a Daniel!   221
O wise young judge, how I do honor thee!

PORTIA

I pray you let me look upon the bond.

SHYLOCK

Here 'tis, most reverend Doctor, here it is.

PORTIA

Shylock, there's thrice thy money off'red thee.

SHYLOCK

An oath, an oath! I have an oath in heaven;
Shall I lay perjury upon my soul?
No, not for Venice!

PORTIA   Why, this bond is forfeit;
And lawfully by this the Jew may claim
A pound of flesh, to be by him cut off
Nearest the merchant's heart. Be merciful.
Take thrice thy money; bid me tear the bond.

SHYLOCK

When it is paid, according to the tenor.   233
It doth appear you are a worthy judge;
You know the law, your exposition
Hath been most sound. I charge you by the law,
Whereof you are a well-deserving pillar,
Proceed to judgment. By my soul I swear
There is no power in the tongue of man
To alter me. I stay here on my bond.   240

ANTONIO

Most heartily I do beseech the court
To give the judgment.

PORTIA   Why then, thus it is:
You must prepare your bosom for his knife –

SHYLOCK

O noble judge! O excellent young man!

PORTIA

For the intent and purpose of the law
Hath full relation to the penalty,   246
Which here appeareth due upon the bond.

SHYLOCK

'Tis very true. O wise and upright judge!
How much more elder art thou than thy looks!

PORTIA

Therefore lay bare your bosom.

SHYLOCK   Ay, his breast –
So says the bond, doth it not, noble judge?
'Nearest his heart'; those are the very words.

PORTIA

It is so. Are there balance here to weigh   253
The flesh?

SHYLOCK   I have them ready.

PORTIA

Have by some surgeon, Shylock, on your charge,
To stop his wounds, lest he do bleed to death.

---

171 *throughly* thoroughly; *cause* case   176 *in such rule* so within the rules
178 *danger* power, control   182 *strained* constrained, forced   197 *in . . .
justice* i.e. if justice should actually run its course   201 *justice . . . plea*
your appeal to strict justice   212 *bears down* overwhelms   213 *Wrest . . .
law* i.e. for once, subject the law   221 *Daniel* the shrewd young man who
exposed the elders in their false charges against Susannah   233 *tenor*
substance of its terms   240 *stay* stand   246 *Hath full relation to* is completely in accord with   253 *balance* scales

SHYLOCK
Is it so nominated in the bond?
PORTIA
It is not so expressed, but what of that?
'Twere good you do so much for charity.
SHYLOCK
260 I cannot find it; 'tis not in the bond.
PORTIA
You, merchant, have you anything to say?
ANTONIO
But little. I am armed and well prepared.
Give me your hand, Bassanio; fare you well.
Grieve not that I am fall'n to this for you,
For herein Fortune shows herself more kind
Than is her custom: it is still her use
To let the wretched man outlive his wealth
To view with hollow eye and wrinkled brow
An age of poverty; from which ling'ring penance
Of such misery doth she cut me off.
Commend me to your honorable wife.
Tell her the process of Antonio's end,
273 Say how I loved you, speak me fair in death;
And when the tale is told, bid her be judge
275 Whether Bassanio had not once a love.
Repent but you that you shall lose your friend,
And he repents not that he pays your debt;
For if the Jew do cut but deep enough,
I'll pay it instantly with all my heart.
BASSANIO
Antonio, I am married to a wife
Which is as dear to me as life itself;
But life itself, my wife, and all the world
Are not with me esteemed above thy life.
I would lose all, ay sacrifice them all
Here to this devil, to deliver you.
PORTIA
Your wife would give you little thanks for that
If she were by to hear you make the offer.
GRATIANO
I have a wife who I protest I love.
I would she were in heaven, so she could
Entreat some power to change this currish Jew.
NERISSA
'Tis well you offer it behind her back;
The wish would make else an unquiet house.
SHYLOCK
These be the Christian husbands! I have a daughter;
294 Would any of the stock of Barabbas
Had been her husband, rather than a Christian!
We trifle time. I pray thee pursue sentence.
PORTIA
A pound of that same merchant's flesh is thine.
The court awards it, and the law doth give it –
SHYLOCK
Most rightful judge!
PORTIA
And you must cut this flesh from off his breast.
The law allows it, and the court awards it.

273 *speak me fair* speak well of me   275 *love* friend's love   294 *Barabbas* a
thief set free by Pontius Pilate when Christ was condemned; also the central
character's name in Marlowe's *Jew of Malta*   326–27 *substance . . . division*
quantity or a fraction   328 *scruple* a measure of very light weight   329
estimation of a hair a hair's breadth   332 *on the hip* (cf. I, iii, 42)   340 *barely*
even   344 *stay . . . question* press my case no further

SHYLOCK
Most learnèd judge! A sentence! Come, prepare!
PORTIA
Tarry a little; there is something else.
This bond doth give thee here no jot of blood;
The words expressly are 'a pound of flesh.'
Take then thy bond, take thou thy pound of flesh;
But in the cutting it if thou dost shed
One drop of Christian blood, thy lands and goods
Are by the laws of Venice confiscate
Unto the state of Venice.   310
GRATIANO
O upright judge! Mark, Jew. O learnèd judge!
SHYLOCK
Is that the law?
PORTIA   Thyself shalt see the act;
For, as thou urgest justice, be assured
Thou shalt have justice more than thou desir'st.
GRATIANO
O learnèd judge! Mark, Jew. A learnèd judge!
SHYLOCK
I take this offer then. Pay the bond thrice
And let the Christian go.
BASSANIO   Here is the money.
PORTIA
Soft!
The Jew shall have all justice. Soft, no haste;
He shall have nothing but the penalty.
GRATIANO
O Jew! an upright judge, a learnèd judge!
PORTIA
Therefore prepare thee to cut off the flesh.
Shed thou no blood, nor cut thou less nor more
But just a pound of flesh. If thou tak'st more
Or less than a just pound, be it but so much
As makes it light or heavy in the substance   326
Or the division of the twentieth part
Of one poor scruple – nay, if the scale do turn   328
But in the estimation of a hair –   329
Thou diest, and all thy goods are confiscate.
GRATIANO
A second Daniel! a Daniel, Jew!
Now, infidel, I have you on the hip!   332
PORTIA
Why doth the Jew pause? Take thy forfeiture.
SHYLOCK
Give me my principal, and let me go.
BASSANIO
I have it ready for thee; here it is.
PORTIA
He hath refused it in the open court.
He shall have merely justice and his bond.
GRATIANO
A Daniel still say I, a second Daniel!
I thank thee, Jew, for teaching me that word.
SHYLOCK
Shall I not have barely my principal?   340
PORTIA
Thou shalt have nothing but the forfeiture,
To be so taken at thy peril, Jew.
SHYLOCK
Why, then the devil give him good of it!
I'll stay no longer question.   344
PORTIA   Tarry, Jew!

The law hath yet another hold on you.
It is enacted in the laws of Venice,
If it be proved against an alien
That by direct or indirect attempts
He seek the life of any citizen,
The party 'gainst the which he doth contrive
Shall seize one half his goods ; the other half
352 Comes to the privy coffer of the state ;
353 And the offender's life lies in the mercy
Of the Duke only, 'gainst all other voice.
In which predicament I say thou stand'st,
For it appears by manifest proceeding
That indirectly, and directly too,
Thou hast contrived against the very life
Of the defendant, and thou hast incurred
360 The danger formerly by me rehearsed.
Down therefore, and beg mercy of the Duke.

GRATIANO
Beg that thou mayst have leave to hang thyself !
And yet, thy wealth being forfeit to the state,
Thou hast not left the value of a cord ;
365 Therefore thou must be hanged at the state's charge.

DUKE
That thou shalt see the difference of our spirit,
I pardon thee thy life before thou ask it.
368 For half thy wealth, it is Antonio's ;
The other half comes to the general state,
370 Which humbleness may drive unto a fine.

PORTIA
Ay, for the state, not for Antonio.

SHYLOCK
Nay, take my life and all ! Pardon not that !
You take my house when you do take the prop
That doth sustain my house. You take my life
When you do take the means whereby I live.

PORTIA
What mercy can you render him, Antonio ?

GRATIANO
377 A halter gratis ! Nothing else, for God's sake !

ANTONIO
So please my lord the Duke and all the court
379 To quit the fine for one half of his goods,
I am content ; so he will let me have
The other half in use, to render it
Upon his death unto the gentleman
That lately stole his daughter.
Two things provided more : that for this favor
385 He presently become a Christian ;
The other, that he do record a gift
Here in the court of all he dies possessed
Unto his son Lorenzo and his daughter.

DUKE
389 He shall do this, or else I do recant
The pardon that I late pronouncèd here.

PORTIA
391 Art thou contented, Jew ? What dost thou say ?

SHYLOCK
I am content.

PORTIA   Clerk, draw a deed of gift.

SHYLOCK
I pray you give me leave to go from hence.
I am not well. Send the deed after me,
And I will sign it.

DUKE   Get thee gone, but do it.

GRATIANO
In christ'ning shalt thou have two godfathers.
Had I been judge, thou shouldst have had ten more –   397
To bring thee to the gallows, not to the font. Exit [Shylock].

DUKE
Sir, I entreat you home with me to dinner.

PORTIA
I humbly do desire your Grace of pardon.
I must away this night toward Padua,
And it is meet I presently set forth.

DUKE
I am sorry that your leisure serves you not.   403
Antonio, gratify this gentleman,   404
For in my mind you are much bound to him.
                    Exit Duke and his Train.

BASSANIO
Most worthy gentleman, I and my friend
Have by your wisdom been this day acquitted
Of grievous penalties, in lieu whereof,   408
Three thousand ducats due unto the Jew
We freely cope your courteous pains withal.   410

ANTONIO
And stand indebted, over and above,
In love and service to you evermore.

PORTIA
He is well paid that is well satisfied,
And I delivering you am satisfied,
And therein do account myself well paid ;
My mind was never yet more mercenary.
I pray you know me when we meet again.
I wish you well, and so I take my leave.

BASSANIO
Dear sir, of force I must attempt you further.   419
Take some remembrance of us as a tribute,
Not as fee. Grant me two things, I pray you –
Not to deny me, and to pardon me.

PORTIA
You press me far, and therefore I will yield.
Give me your gloves ; I'll wear them for your sake.
          [Bassanio takes off his gloves.]
And for your love I'll take this ring from you.
Do not draw back your hand ; I'll take no more,
And you in love shall not deny me this.

BASSANIO
This ring, good sir, alas, it is a trifle !
I will not shame myself to give you this.

PORTIA
I will have nothing else but only this,
And now methinks I have a mind to it.

BASSANIO
There's more depends on this than on the value.   432
The dearest ring in Venice will I give you,
And find it out by proclamation.
Only for this, I pray you pardon me.   435

352 privy . . . state personal funds of the sovereign 353 lies in lies at
360 danger . . . rehearsed penalty I have cited 365 charge expense 368
For as for 370 Which . . . fine which humility on your part may reduce
to a fine 377 halter hangman's noose 379 quit remit (?), substitute (?)
385 presently immediately 389 recant withdraw 391 contented i.e. willing
to accept these terms 397 ten more i.e. a jury of twelve 403 your leisure
. . . not i.e. you do not have leisure 404 gratify reward 408 in lieu whereof in return for which 410 cope requite 419 attempt you i.e. try to
persuade you 432 more . . . value more than the ring's value involved in
this 435 for this as for this ring ; pardon me i.e. release me from my obligation

PORTIA
I see, sir, you are liberal in offers.
You taught me first to beg, and now methinks
You teach me how a beggar should be answered.

BASSANIO
Good sir, this ring was given me by my wife,
And when she put it on she made me vow
That I should neither sell nor give nor lose it.

PORTIA
That 'scuse serves many men to save their gifts.
And if your wife be not a madwoman,
And know how well I have deserved this ring,
She would not hold out enemy for ever
For giving it to me. Well, peace be with you!
         Exeunt [Portia and Nerissa].

ANTONIO
My Lord Bassanio, let him have the ring.
Let his deservings, and my love withal,
Be valued 'gainst your wife's commandèment.

BASSANIO
450   Go, Gratiano, run and overtake him;
Give him the ring and bring him if thou canst
Unto Antonio's house. Away, make haste!
         Exit Gratiano.
Come, you and I will thither presently,
And in the morning early will we both
Fly toward Belmont. Come, Antonio.   *Exeunt.*

*

IV, ii   *Enter [Portia and] Nerissa [disguised as before].*
PORTIA
1   Inquire the Jew's house out, give him this deed,
And let him sign it. We'll away to-night
And be a day before our husbands home.
This deed will be well welcome to Lorenzo.
     Enter Gratiano.

GRATIANO
5   Fair sir, you are well o'erta'en.
6   My Lord Bassanio upon more advice
Hath sent you here this ring, and doth entreat
Your company at dinner.

PORTIA   That cannot be.
His ring I do accept most thankfully,
And so I pray you tell him. Furthermore,
I pray you show my youth old Shylock's house.

GRATIANO
That will I do.

NERISSA   Sir, I would speak with you.
     [Aside to Portia]
I'll see if I can get my husband's ring,
Which I did make him swear to keep for ever.

PORTIA *[aside to Nerissa]*
15   Thou mayst, I warrant. We shall have old swearing

IV, ii A street in Venice   **1** *deed* deed of gift   **5** *o'erta'en* overtaken   **6** *advice* consideration   **15** *old* i.e. plenty of, continuous
V, i The park of Portia's house   **4** *Troilus* Trojan whose beloved but false Cressida was sent away to the Greek camp   **7** *Thisbe* beloved of Pyramus who fled from the lovers' meeting place when a lion approached   **8** *ere* before   **10** *Dido* queen of Carthage loved and then deserted by Aeneas; *willow* willow branch (symbol of forsaken love)   **11** *waft* beckoned   **13** *Medea* enchantress in the legend of Jason and the Golden Fleece   **14** *Aeson* Jason's father   **16** *unthrift love* unthrifty love (?), unthrifty lover, i.e. Lorenzo (?)   **21** *shrow* (form of the word 'shrew')   **31** *holy crosses* wayside shrines marked with crosses

That they did give the rings away to men;
But we'll outface them, and outswear them too. —
Away, make haste! Thou know'st where I will tarry.
NERISSA
Come, good sir, will you show me to this house?
            [Exeunt.]

*

     Enter Lorenzo and Jessica.   V, i
LORENZO
The moon shines bright. In such a night as this,
When the sweet wind did gently kiss the trees
And they did make no noise, in such a night
Troilus methinks mounted the Troyan walls,   4
And sighed his soul toward the Grecian tents
Where Cressid lay that night.
JESSICA   In such a night
Did Thisbe fearfully o'ertrip the dew,   7
And saw the lion's shadow ere himself,   8
And ran dismayed away.
LORENZO   In such a night
Stood Dido with a willow in her hand   10
Upon the wild sea banks, and waft her love   11
To come again to Carthage.
JESSICA   In such a night
Medea gathered the enchanted herbs   13
That did renew old Aeson.   14
LORENZO   In such a night
Did Jessica steal from the wealthy Jew,
And with an unthrift love did run from Venice   16
As far as Belmont.
JESSICA   In such a night
Did young Lorenzo swear he loved her well,
Stealing her soul with many vows of faith,
And ne'er a true one.
LORENZO   In such a night
Did pretty Jessica, like a little shrow,
Slander her love, and he forgave it her.   21
JESSICA
I would out-night you, did nobody come;
But hark, I hear the footing of a man.
     Enter [Stephano,] a Messenger.
LORENZO
Who comes so fast in silence of the night?
MESSENGER A friend.
LORENZO
A friend? What friend? Your name I pray you, friend.
MESSENGER
Stephano is my name, and I bring word
My mistress will before the break of day
Be here at Belmont. She doth stray about
By holy crosses where she kneels and prays   31
For happy wedlock hours.
LORENZO   Who comes with her?
MESSENGER
None but a holy hermit and her maid.
I pray you, is my master yet returned?
LORENZO
He is not, nor we have not heard from him.
But we go in, I pray thee, Jessica,
And ceremoniously let us prepare
Some welcome for the mistress of the house.
     Enter [Launcelot, the] Clown.

39 LAUNCELOT Sola, sola! wo ha! ho sola, sola!

LORENZO Who calls?

LAUNCELOT Sola! Did you see Master Lorenzo? Master Lorenzo! sola, sola!

LORENZO Leave holloaing, man! Here.

LAUNCELOT Sola! where? where?

LORENZO Here!

LAUNCELOT Tell him there's a post come from my master, with his horn full of good news. My master will be here ere morning.   *[Exit.]*

LORENZO
Sweet soul, let's in, and there expect their coming.
And yet no matter; why should we go in?
51 My friend Stephano, signify, I pray you,
Within the house, your mistress is at hand,
And bring your music forth into the air. *[Exit Stephano.]*
How sweet the moonlight sleeps upon this bank!
Here will we sit and let the sounds of music
Creep in our ears; soft stillness and the night
57 Become the touches of sweet harmony.
Sit, Jessica. Look how the floor of heaven
59 Is thick inlaid with patens of bright gold.
There's not the smallest orb which thou behold'st
61 But in his motion like an angel sings,
62 Still quiring to the young-eyed cherubins;
Such harmony is in immortal souls,
64 But whilst this muddy vesture of decay
Doth grossly close it in, we cannot hear it.
    [Enter Musicians.]
66 Come ho, and wake Diana with a hymn!
With sweetest touches pierce your mistress' ear
And draw her home with music.
    Play music.

JESSICA
I am never merry when I hear sweet music.

LORENZO
The reason is, your spirits are attentive.
For do but note a wild and wanton herd
Or race of youthful and unhandled colts
Fetching mad bounds, bellowing and neighing loud,
Which is the hot condition of their blood:
If they but hear perchance a trumpet sound,
Or any air of music touch their ears,
77 You shall perceive them make a mutual stand,
Their savage eyes turned to a modest gaze
By the sweet power of music. Therefore the poet
80 Did feign that Orpheus drew trees, stones, and floods;
81 Since naught so stockish, hard, and full of rage
But music for the time doth change his nature.
The man that hath no music in himself,
Nor is not moved with concord of sweet sounds,
85 Is fit for treasons, stratagems, and spoils;
The motions of his spirit are dull as night,
87 And his affections dark as Erebus.
Let no such man be trusted. Mark the music.
    Enter Portia and Nerissa.

PORTIA
That light we see is burning in my hall;
How far that little candle throws his beams!
91 So shines a good deed in a naughty world.

NERISSA
When the moon shone we did not see the candle.

PORTIA
So doth the greater glory dim the less.

A substitute shines brightly as a king   94
Until a king be by, and then his state
Empties itself, as doth an inland brook
Into the main of waters. Music! hark!

NERISSA
It is your music, madam, of the house.

PORTIA
Nothing is good, I see, without respect;   99
Methinks it sounds much sweeter than by day.

NERISSA
Silence bestows that virtue on it, madam.

PORTIA
The crow doth sing as sweetly as the lark
When neither is attended; and I think   103
The nightingale, if she should sing by day
When every goose is cackling, would be thought
No better a musician than the wren.
How many things by season seasoned are   107
To their right praise and true perfection!
Peace! *[Music ceases.]* How the moon sleeps with   109
    Endymion,
And would not be awaked.

LORENZO   That is the voice,
Or I am much deceived, of Portia.

PORTIA
He knows me as the blind man knows the cuckoo—
By the bad voice.

LORENZO   Dear lady, welcome home.

PORTIA
We have been praying for our husbands' welfare,
Which speed we hope the better for our words.
Are they returned?

LORENZO   Madam, they are not yet,
But there is come a messenger before
To signify their coming.

PORTIA   Go in, Nerissa.
Give order to my servants that they take
No note at all of our being absent hence—
Nor you, Lorenzo—Jessica, nor you.   121
    [A tucket sounds.]

LORENZO
Your husband is at hand; I hear his trumpet.
We are no telltales, madam; fear you not.

PORTIA
This night methinks is but the daylight sick;
It looks a little paler. 'Tis a day
Such as the day is when the sun is hid.
    Enter Bassanio, Antonio, Gratiano, and their Followers.

BASSANIO
We should hold day with the Antipodes   127

---

39 *Sola* imitation of a post horn (see ll. 46–47)   51 *signify* announce   57 *Become* befit; *touches* notes, strains (with reference to fingering of an instrument)   59 *patens* metal plates or tiling   61 *motion* (reference to the music of the spheres)   62 *quiring* singing   64 *muddy vesture* clay, i.e. flesh   66 *Diana* the moon goddess   77 *make . . . stand* all stand still together   80 *feign* imagine; *Orpheus* legendary musician; *drew* attracted, bent to his spell   81 *stockish* blockish, dull   85 *spoils* plundering   87 *Erebus* classical place of darkness in the region of hell   91 *naughty* wicked   94 *substitute* deputy (of the king)   99 *without respect* without reference to accompanying things; in itself   103 *attended* with the other   107–08 *by season . . . perfection* i.e. are made perfect by coming at the right time   109 *Endymion* shepherd loved by the moon goddess   121 s.d. *tucket* short flourish of trumpets   127 *hold . . . Antipodes* i.e. share daylight with the other side of the earth

If you would walk in absence of the sun.

PORTIA

129 Let me give light, but let me not be light,
130 For a light wife doth make a heavy husband,
And never be Bassanio so for me.
132 But God sort all! You are welcome home, my lord.

BASSANIO

I thank you, madam. Give welcome to my friend.
This is the man, this is Antonio,
To whom I am so infinitely bound.

PORTIA

You should in all sense be much bound to him,
For, as I hear, he was much bound for you.

ANTONIO

138 No more than I am well acquitted of.

PORTIA

Sir, you are very welcome to our house.
It must appear in other ways than words;
141 Therefore I scant this breathing courtesy.

GRATIANO [to Nerissa]

By yonder moon I swear you do me wrong!
In faith, I gave it to the judge's clerk.
144 Would he were gelt that had it, for my part,
Since you do take it, love, so much at heart.

PORTIA

A quarrel ho! already! What's the matter?

GRATIANO

About a hoop of gold, a paltry ring
148 That she did give me, whose posy was
For all the world like cutler's poetry
Upon a knife – 'Love me, and leave me not.'

NERISSA

151 What talk you of the posy or the value?
You swore to me when I did give it you
That you would wear it till your hour of death,
And that it should lie with you in your grave.
155 Though not for me, yet for your vehement oaths,
156 You should have been respective and have kept it.
Gave it a judge's clerk! No, God's my judge,
The clerk will ne'er wear hair on's face that had it!

GRATIANO

He will, an if he live to be a man.

NERISSA

Ay, if a woman live to be a man.

GRATIANO

Now by this hand, I gave it to a youth,
162 A kind of boy, a little scrubbèd boy
No higher than thyself, the judge's clerk,
A prating boy that begged it as a fee.
I could not for my heart deny it him.

PORTIA

You were to blame – I must be plain with you –
To part so slightly with your wife's first gift,

A thing stuck on with oaths upon your finger
And so riveted with faith unto your flesh.
I gave my love a ring, and made him swear
Never to part with it; and here he stands.
I dare be sworn for him he would not leave it   172
Nor pluck it from his finger for the wealth
That the world'masters. Now in faith, Gratiano,
You give your wife too unkind a cause of grief.
An 'twere to me, I should be mad at it.   176

BASSANIO [aside]

Why, I were best to cut my left hand off
And swear I lost the ring defending it.

GRATIANO

My Lord Bassanio gave his ring away
Unto the judge that begged it, and indeed
Deserved it too; and then the boy, his clerk
That took some pains in writing, he begged mine;
And neither man nor master would take aught
But the two rings.

PORTIA   What ring gave you, my lord?
Not that, I hope, which you received of me.

BASSANIO

If I could add a lie unto a fault,   186
I would deny it; but you see my finger
Hath not the ring upon it – it is gone.

PORTIA

Even so void is your false heart of truth.
By heaven, I will ne'er come in your bed
Until I see the ring!

NERISSA   Nor I in yours
Till I again see mine!

BASSANIO   Sweet Portia,
If you did know to whom I gave the ring,
If you did know for whom I gave the ring,
And would conceive for what I gave the ring,
And how unwillingly I left the ring
When naught would be accepted but the ring,
You would abate the strength of your displeasure.

PORTIA

If you had known the virtue of the ring,   199
Or half her worthiness that gave the ring,
Or your own honor to contain the ring,   201
You would not then have parted with the ring.
What man is there so much unreasonable,
If you had pleased to have defended it   204
With any terms of zeal, wanted the modesty
To urge the thing held as a ceremony?   206
Nerissa teaches me what to believe;
I'll die for't but some woman had the ring!   208

BASSANIO

No, by my honor, madam! By my soul
No woman had it, but a civil doctor,   210
Which did refuse three thousand ducats of me
And begged the ring, the which I did deny him,
And suffered him to go displeased away –   213
Even he that had held up the very life
Of my dear friend. What should I say, sweet lady?
I was enforced to send it after him.
I was beset with shame and courtesy.
My honor would not let ingratitude
So much besmear it. Pardon me, good lady!
For by these blessèd candles of the night,
Had you been there I think you would have begged
The ring of me to give the worthy doctor.

129 *be light* i.e. be unfaithful   130 *heavy* sad   132 *sort* dispose   138 *acquitted of* released from   141 *scant . . . courtesy* cut short this courtesy of breath, i.e. of words   144 *gelt* gelded; *for my part* so far as I am concerned   148 *posy* inscription (commonly in verse)   151 *What* why   155 *Though . . . yet for* even if not for my sake, still because of   156 *respective* careful   162 *scrubbèd* scrubby, short   172 *leave* part with   176 *mad* distracted   186 *fault* misdeed   199 *virtue* power   201 *honor to contain* solemn duty to keep   204 *defended it* i.e. resisted giving it away   206 *urge* demand as a gift; *ceremony* token, keepsake   208 *but . . . had* if some woman didn't get   210 *civil doctor* doctor of civil law   213 *suffered* allowed

PORTIA
Let not that doctor e'er come near my house.
Since he hath got the jewel that I loved,
And that which you did swear to keep for me.
I will become as liberal as you ;
I'll not deny him anything I have,
No, not my body nor my husband's bed.
Know him I shall, I am well sure of it.
230 Lie not a night from home ; watch me like Argus.
If you do not, if I be left alone –
Now by mine honor which is yet mine own,
I'll have that doctor for my bedfellow.
NERISSA
234 And his clerk. Therefore be well advised
How you do leave me to mine own protection.
GRATIANO
236 Well, do you so. Let not me take him then !
237 For if I do, I'll mar the young clerk's pen.
ANTONIO
I am th' unhappy subject of these quarrels.
PORTIA
Sir, grieve not you ; you are welcome notwithstanding.
BASSANIO
240 Portia, forgive me this enforcèd wrong,
And in the hearing of these many friends
I swear to thee, even by thine own fair eyes,
Wherein I see myself –
PORTIA   Mark you but that !
In both my eyes he doubly sees himself,
In each eye one. Swear by your double self,
246 And there's an oath of credit.
BASSANIO   Nay, but hear me.
Pardon this fault, and by my soul I swear
I never more will break an oath with thee.
ANTONIO
I once did lend my body for his wealth,
Which but for him that had your husband's ring
Had quite miscarried. I dare be bound again,
My soul upon the forfeit, that your lord
253 Will never more break faith advisedly.
PORTIA
Then you shall be his surety. Give him this,
And bid him keep it better than the other.
ANTONIO
Here, Lord Bassanio. Swear to keep this ring.
BASSANIO
By heaven, it is the same I gave the doctor !
PORTIA
258 I had it of him. Pardon me, Bassanio,
For by this ring the doctor lay with me.
NERISSA
And pardon me, my gentle Gratiano,
For that same scrubbèd boy, the doctor's clerk,
262 In lieu of this last night did lie with me.
GRATIANO
Why, this is like the mending of highways
In summer, where the ways are fair enough.
265 What, are we cuckolds ere we have deserved it ?
PORTIA
266 Speak not so grossly. You are all amazed.
Here is a letter ; read it at your leisure.

It comes from Padua from Bellario.
There you shall find that Portia was the doctor,
Nerissa there her clerk. Lorenzo here
Shall witness I set forth as soon as you,
And even but now returned – I have not yet
Entered my house. Antonio, you are welcome,
And I have better news in store for you
Than you expect. Unseal this letter soon ;
There you shall find three of your argosies
Are richly come to harbor suddenly.
You shall not know by what strange accident
I chancèd on this letter.
ANTONIO   I am dumb !
BASSANIO
Were you the doctor, and I knew you not ?   280
GRATIANO
Were you the clerk that is to make me cuckold ?
NERISSA
Ay, but the clerk that never means to do it,
Unless he live until he be a man.
BASSANIO
Sweet Doctor, you shall be my bedfellow.
When I am absent, then lie with my wife.
ANTONIO
Sweet lady, you have given me life and living !
For here I read for certain that my ships
Are safely come to road.   288
PORTIA   How now, Lorenzo ?
My clerk hath some good comforts too for you.
NERISSA
Ay, and I'll give them him without a fee.
There do I give to you and Jessica
From the rich Jew, a special deed of gift,
After his death, of all he dies possessed of.
LORENZO
Fair ladies, you drop manna in the way
Of starvèd people.
PORTIA   It is almost morning,
And yet I am sure you are not satisfied   296
Of these events at full. Let us go in,
And charge us there upon inter'gatories,   298
And we will answer all things faithfully.
GRATIANO
Let it be so. The first inter'gatory
That my Nerissa shall be sworn on is,
Whether till the next night she had rather stay,   302
Or go to bed now, being two hours to day.
But were the day come, I should wish it dark
Till I were couching with the doctor's clerk.   305
Well, while I live I'll fear no other thing
So sore as keeping safe Nerissa's ring.   *Exeunt.*

230 *Argus* mythological figure with a hundred eyes   234 *well advised* very careful   236 *take* catch   237 *pen* i.e. penis   240 *enforcèd* unavoidable   246 *oath of credit* oath that can be believed (said ironically)   253 *advisedly* intentionally   258 *of him* from him   262 *In lieu of* in return for   265 *cuckolds* deceived husbands   266 *amazed* lost in a maze, befuddled   288 *road* anchorage   296–97 *satisfied . . . full* fully satisfied with the explanation of these events   298 *charge . . . inter'gatories* require ourselves to answer interrogatories (legally framed questions answerable under oath)   302 *stay* wait   305 *clerk* (pronounced 'clark')

AS YOU LIKE IT

INTRODUCTION

As You Like It assembles a mixed cast of distinct individuals, insulates them temporarily in a pleasantly habitable woodland, and allows them to devote themselves to the pursuit of happiness. In the case of several characters the pursuit takes the form of ardent and successful courtship. To many readers, audiences, and producers, an escape into the Forest of Arden for a brief season with Rosalind and Orlando, Jaques and Touchstone, seems happiness enough.

Those who look to comedy for amusement, laughter, a play of the mind, here also find Shakespeare's plenty. His Arden contains people whose ideas on the pursuit and even the nature of happiness prove widely diverse. Vague as the boundaries of the forest may be, they are confining enough to produce frequent and intimate contacts between these people as they go about their separate pursuits. Sometimes their meetings provide amusement simply by the inherent incongruity of the situation, as when Touchstone, the born urbanite, becomes entangled with Audrey, the country wench, each impelled by different motives. At other times, the characters themselves take advantage of the situation to heighten the amusement, as when Rosalind in disguise draws out Orlando on the subject of his love, or seizes her unexpected opportunity to lecture Phebe and Silvius. Occasionally in these meetings, particularly those involving Touchstone, Rosalind, or Jaques, the dialogue becomes wittily brilliant. Shakespeare's light touch allows an audience or reader to skim over the intellectual edge of such passages. They are frequently capable, however, of producing a double-take.

In such juxtapositions the characters are led to sharpen up their individual ideas on the world and the way to happiness in it. These views not only reveal the character of the persons who express them, but illustrate widely different ways of seeing the world and conducting oneself in it. Each view springs from position in life, from character, and from personal experience, and is recognizable and viable (at least in the comedy); but when set beside a different reading of experience, each criticizes the other, each is seen to be partial. Yet they do not cancel each other out. The comic process, the civilizing procedure, requires the audience to hold all views in mind in the complicated overview that is the humane achievement of comedy.

The conflicting opinions in Arden tend to center around two aspects of the pursuit of happiness: the effect of surroundings, natural and social, and the nature and role of love and marriage. Since most of the characters are city dwellers, temporarily exiled to the country, they canvass pretty thoroughly the merits of a country atmosphere as an aid to happiness. The Duke Senior prefers a healthy country to a corrupt city; he admires the rugged features of country living as conducive to sane thinking; yet most of all he would like a healthy court-urban life. Touchstone, on the other hand, undisturbed by such moral discriminations, dislikes the country because it lacks creature comforts and sufficient cultural level to appreciate his wit. The Duke's retainers, scarcely noticing the lack of urban amenities, happily revert to the lives of their feudal forebears, and enjoy the forest life in hunting, eating, and singing. "I would not change it," says Amiens. Jaques, who seeks pleasure perversely in the achievement of melancholy, discovers in Arden ample occasion to exercise his sour talents, but he thinks it folly to live there. Finally, the genuine countryman finds the shepherd's life a source of happiness in its independence and security: "Sir, I am a true laborer; I earn that I eat, get that I wear, owe no man hate, envy no man's happiness."

Likewise the role of love and marriage provides a theme with variations. With worldly realism Touchstone views marriage as the answer to desire; his future wife sees it as a way to social improvement. Jaques regards love as a silly weakness. Silvius and Phebe take love as the whole of life, and make of it a painful frustration. Orlando and Rosalind are the romantic lovers, yet they know they have to live in a world busy with other occupations and preoccupations. Their problem is to domesticate love (a kind of madness) in marriage. In subjecting love to the corrosives of mundane attitudes, they do not destroy romantic love, but place it firmly in the real world.

Those who stay to look into the play a little longer may find another level to Shakespeare's vision. Perceptive readers and audiences become aware of the undertone of genuine melancholy which sounds through the major characters. The Duke and his fellow exiles have sufficient reason for this melancholy: they have faced a corrupt power, been victimized for their very virtues, and unjustly driven from public society. Shakespeare paints this corrupt authority with care. It forms, in fact, a major pole of contrasts to the life in Arden. Those who have faced corruption have been sickened by it; but given a forest island of temporary escape they have begun to reconstruct their lives and society. The natural woodland provides a morally restorative and regenerative stimulus (an idea which Shakespeare developed further in *The Winter's Tale*). Instead of sinking into despair Hamlet-like, here with the astringent qualities of forest life that "feelingly persuade me what I am," the Duke Senior has been able to "translate the stubbornness of fortune / Into so quiet and so sweet a style." In like manner, Orlando and Rosalind have achieved their happiness by being able to keep their spirits high and their minds alert to the realities of the world. The play thus presents the view that human beings, given a brief respite from corruption and placed in the healthy environment of nature, can and will build a good life. In entitling his play *As You Like It*, Shakespeare seems to express his confidence that we, his audience, share his vision.

It has been said that comedy makes the facts fit the dream. *As You Like It* presents a Shakespearean fusion of the visionary and the realistic. Shakespeare submits the dream to the facts; what happens is that the dream gives meaning to the facts – the stubborn actualities, infused with meaning, make the vision real.

Through the apparently casual flow of events in *As You Like It* may be seen some of Shakespeare's most skilled dramatic structure. In the first act he presents his sound characters as victims of a hostile world, and reveals the mutual love between Orlando and Rosalind. When in the second act he brings his characters to the salubrious environment of Arden he does not divert attention to a possible clash between the good forces and the bad; nor does he arouse any doubt as to the possible outcome of the principal love affair. In short, he eschews melodrama. Rather, Shakespeare concentrates on the present situation of the characters in the forest and their formation of a new community. In bringing these characters together in "encounters" he is not bothered by improbabilities: that two persons in love banished from different places on separate occasions should turn up at the same place, that the forest should contain both "literary" shepherds and genuine shepherds, that vengeful pursuers should be quickly converted to a new life on arrival in the forest. His care is directed to bringing the right persons together at the desired time. Thus, just before the first forest meeting between Orlando and Rosalind, Orlando confronts and overcomes Jaques; just before the second meeting, Rosalind encounters and defeats Jaques. Immediately after she has presented Orlando with false views of love in order to test him, Rosalind meets Phebe and gets a chance to express her genuine convictions. In the progress of the play the sequence of encounters forms a virtual permutation of character confrontations, a structural feature pleasing in itself. But through this sequence, with its cumulative revelation of characters, attitudes, relationships, and conflicts, Shakespeare presents that manifold view and acceptance of diversity within pattern which makes *As You Like It* a paradigm of civilized society.

Francis Meres does not include *As You Like It* in his list of Shakespeare's plays (*Palladis Tamia*, 1598). On August 4, 1600, the Lord Chamberlain's Men entered in the Stationers' Register "As you like yt, a booke" as one of four plays "to be staied" (i.e. to be held from publication). The play can thus be dated as of 1599 or early 1600.

Shakespeare's comedy is based on the prose romance *Rosalynde, Euphues' Golden Legacie* (1590) by Thomas Lodge, which had in its turn been suggested by the pseudo-Chaucerian *Tale of Gamelyn*. Shakespeare elaborates the role of Rosalind, somewhat curtails that of Orlando, and develops the character of the banished Duke from his slight role in *Rosalynde*. Jaques, Touchstone, and Audrey are wholly Shakespeare's creations. Although he presents most of the incidents in the story, he is careful to remove the bloody battle between the forces of the two dukes, and to substitute for it the conversion and retirement of the usurping duke.

Rosalynde exhibits the highly wrought style, with its balanced opposites and moral illustrations, made popular by John Lyly in *Euphues, The Anatomy of Wit* (1578). Thus Lodge writes: "Infortunate Rosalynde, whose misfortunes are more than thy years, and whose passions are greater than thy patience! The blossoms of thy youth are mixed with the frosts of envy, and the hope of thy ensuing fruits perish in the bud." In the midst of the colloquial prose which he uses for most of his drama, Shakespeare allows Touchstone to parody such Euphuism. Shakespeare's amusement at the expense of his source does not stop with a travesty of its style. Using the pastoral framework of *Rosalynde*, *As You Like It* ridicules the artificiality of the pastoral conceptions so popular in the poetry, fiction, and drama of his day. The introduction of genuine shepherds into Arden gives the literary figures, Silvius and Phebe, an anemic appearance. Further, Shakespeare makes Phebe something less than captivating in beauty, Silvius something less than manly in his abasement. Pastoral literature based its appeal on the fantasy that city people, by retiring to a shepherd's life, could escape the pressures of social responsibility, to concentrate on the fulfillment of personal desires. In Silvius and Phebe, Shakespeare shows that love, when divorced from the rest of life, becomes a tyrant in itself. By contrast, Rosalind and Orlando recognize that love must be taken as a part of social reality. *As You Like It*, while actively exploiting some of the appeal of pastoral escapism, contains within itself a critique of its conventions.

As You Like It also provides amusement at the expense of the elements of affectation in the current fashion for melancholy. The pretensions of the melancholy man to superiority are ridiculed when Jaques, impressed by Touchstone's cynicism and envious of his license, is moved to exclaim, in unconscious irony: "O that I were a fool!" Shakespeare even pinpoints his satire by making Jaques a melancholy traveller, a type of refined affectation. "A traveller!" declares Rosalind. "By my faith, you have great reason to be sad. I fear you have sold your own lands to see other men's. . . . And your experience makes you sad . . . and to travel for it too." As opposed to such loutish comic figures as Launce and Bottom in earlier plays, Touchstone represents the first of Shakespeare's witty professional court jesters. With his carnal eye and clever tongue, Touchstone provides amusement and a critical underview of human relations; yet he too, like Jaques, is revealed as the victim of his own folly.

To balance, as it were, the high proportion of prose in *As You Like It*, Shakespeare introduces the largest number of lyrics in any of his plays. They become an essential part of the atmosphere of Arden. The most famous of these, "It was a lover and his lass," sung by two page boys, was arranged as a two-part madrigal by Thomas Morley and published in his *First Booke of Ayres* (1600). The date suggests that Morley's may well have been the music for the original performance. Except for those sung by Hymen, the other songs are given to Amiens, evidently played by an adult actor-singer. (The earliest known surviving settings for "Blow, blow, thou winter wind" and "Under the greenwood tree" are those by Dr T. A. Arne, 1740.) It is now generally assumed that the part of Touchstone was originally played by Robert Armin, who replaced Will Kempe in the Lord Chamberlain's company some time about the turn of the century. In his *Notes* (1774) the scholar Edward Capell recorded, as a story current in Stratford, that a relative of Shakespeare remembered him as an actor in the part of an old man carried on the back of another. This story, amplified in other eighteenth-century accounts, forms the basis of the pleasant but tenuous tradition that Shakespeare was the original actor of the part of Adam.

The comedy was not revived in the Restoration period, but "improved" versions were acted in the eighteenth century. With the nineteenth century, and the Romantic approach to Shakespeare, *As You Like It* took on new popularity. To-day it holds a steady place in the active repertory of the Shakespearean theatre. Surveys regularly record at least half a dozen productions a year. With its many outdoor scenes the play has long been favored for open-air performances.

Among the many characters in *As You Like It*, two at least possess the depth and fullness to make them memorable : Jaques and Rosalind. Jaques, in his effort to establish himself as the superior person, stands outside life and merely observes it ; he refuses to become committed, engaged. From this vantage point he shoots his criticism. Thus he can sum up the Seven Ages of Man in a series of vignettes, sharp in visual and auditory imagery – but constituting a view which leaves human life without meaning. (Jaques, in fact, uses the same metaphor, representing the same attitude, as Macbeth's "a poor player / That struts and frets his hour upon the stage," spoken when life has lost its meaning for Macbeth.) Shakespeare immediately counters Jaques' view by introducing Orlando carrying old Adam ; these two reveal mutual devotion and love, the inward qualities which make all the difference in life. But they require commitment. Jaques, in the effort to avoid commitment, has become a traveller. In his role as outside observer, he never truly experiences life, either within himself or in relation to those around him. Dimly aware of his own emptiness, he cherishes his melancholy not only as a critical view of the world but as the sole achievement of his travels. His attitude, like that of Touchstone, presents a subtle inhibition to all meaningful action. The Duke Senior, Orlando, and Rosalind must all combat it, each in his own way. When Jaques reveals his single impulse to action, to scourge the world with satire, the Duke rises in anger. A man who sees only bad in the world, in fact has given himself up to it, cannot know the good : such a reformer will only destroy the good, by spreading corruption. At the end, Jaques, unsatisfied with the full life he has just witnessed in Arden, goes off once more looking for something to fill his own inner hollowness.

Rosalind, on the other hand, has had almost too much involvement with the world. She has encountered so many briers that she has to struggle with genuine melancholy. Rosalind has committed herself, engaged her heart ; in so doing she has increased her own vulnerability ; but she leads a full inner life, where she experiences silent pain – and also intense delight. Rosalind keeps herself alert to the world around her, to its snares and its opportunities. Outwardly she displays gaiety and wit with firmness and generosity. Inwardly she recognizes love as a kind of romantic madness, yet the very force that gives warmth and meaning to life. In her determination to maintain love in the midst of workaday pressures, she has the daring

to submit her lover, in advance, to the worst that can be said and thought of love domesticated in marriage. In the test, and its successful outcome, we know that she will continue to make life engaging and rich, for herself and those around her. It has often been suggested that women are the great civilizing force. Shakespeare in his portrait of Rosalind has come close to showing us why.

Although the play ends in the traditional battery of marriages, we may notice as evidence of Shakespeare's direction in comedy that all the exiled characters who have gone through their period of reformation in the forest will not stay in it but are now to return to court, there to play their renewed part in civilized life. As Jaques says to the restored Duke :

> You to your former honor I bequeath ;
> Your patience and your virtue well deserves it.

Haverford College   RALPH M. SARGENT

NOTE ON THE TEXT

As You Like It was first printed in the folio of 1623, from what textual scholars now believe to have been a theatrical prompt-book or a transcript of one. The act-scene division of the folio is supplied marginally in the present edition, and all material departures from the folio text are listed below except for extensive relineation. A number of prose passages, notably II, vi, 1–16 ; III, iv, 1–13 ; IV, iii, 1–5 ; V, ii, 13–18, are set as verse in the folio. The adopted readings in italics, most of which first appeared in the later folios or in eighteenth-century editions, are followed by the folio readings in roman.

I, i, 40 *Ay* I (thus throughout)   102 *she* hee
I, ii, 50 *and* (omitted in F)   54 *Touchstone* Clowne (thus throughout)   85 *Le Beau* the Beu   95 *decree* decrees   232 *lifeless* liuelesse
I, iii, 74 *her* per
II, i, 49 *much* must   59 *of the country* of country
II, iii, 10 *some* seeme   16 *Orlando* (omitted in F)   58 *meed* (some copies of F read 'neede')   73 *seventeen* seauentie
II, iv, 39 *O Phebe, Phebe, Phebe!* (separate line in F)   40 *thy wound* they would   64 *you,* your
II, v, 38–39 (F reads 'Here shall he see, &c.')   43 *Jaques* Amy (designation continues through l. 51)   50 *An* And (thus throughout)
II, vii, 38 *brain* braiue   55 *Within* (omitted in F)   64 *sin* fin   87 *comes* come   182 *Then* the   198 *master* masters
III, ii, 11 *Master* Mr (thus throughout)   25 *good* pood   139 *her* his   152 *How now? Back, friends.* How now backe friends :   226 *such* forth   232 *thy* the   234 *heart* hart   245 *b' mi'* buy   342 *deifying* defying
III, v, 104 *erewhile* yerewhile
IV, i, 1 *be* (omitted in F)   26 *travel* travaile   28 *b' mi'* buy   44 *heart-whole* heart hole   194 *in, it* in, in
IV, ii, 12 *(The rest shall bear this burden.)* (F prints as part of song)
IV, iii, 5 s.d. *Enter Silvius* (follows l. 3 in F)   143 *In* I
V, i, 36 *sir* sit   54 *policy* police
V, ii, 7 *her* (omitted in F)   30 *overcame* overcome   59 *heart* hart
V, iii, 18 *ringtime* rang time   29–32 *And . . . springtime, &c.* (follows l. 20 in F)   39 *b' mi'* buy
V, iv, 34 s.d. *Enter . . . Audrey* (follows l. 33 in F)   77 *to the* ro   108 *her* his   126 *heart . . . heart* hart . . . hart   158 *them* him   165 *were* vvete

AS YOU LIKE IT

[NAMES OF THE ACTORS

Duke Senior, *in banishment*	Touchstone, *a clown*
Duke Frederick, *his brother and usurper*	Sir Oliver Mar-text, *a country curate*
Amiens } *lords attending on Duke Senior*	Corin } *shepherds*
Jaques }	Silvius }
Oliver, *eldest son of Sir Rowland de Boys*	William, *a country fellow*
Jaques } *younger sons of Sir Rowland de Boys*	Hymen, *god of marriage*
Orlando }	Rosalind, *daughter of Duke Senior*
Le Beau, *a courtier attending on Duke Frederick*	Celia, *daughter of Duke Frederick*
Charles, *a wrestler at the court*	Phebe, *a shepherdess*
Adam, *an old servant to Sir Rowland de Boys*	Audrey, *a country wench*
Dennis, *a servant to Oliver*	*Lords, Pages, and Attendants*

Scene : *Oliver's orchard ; Duke Frederick's court ; the Forest of Arden*]

＊

I, i *Enter Orlando and Adam.*

ORLANDO As I remember, Adam, it was upon this fashion
2 bequeathed me by will but poor a thousand crowns, and,
as thou say'st, charged my brother on his blessing to
breed me well : and there begins my sadness. My brother
Jaques he keeps at school, and report speaks goldenly of
6 his profit. For my part, he keeps me rustically at home
7 or, to speak more properly, stays me here at home un-
kept : for call you that keeping for a gentleman of my
birth that differs not from the stalling of an ox ? His
horses are bred better, for, besides that they are fair with
11 their feeding, they are taught their manage, and to that
end riders dearly hired ; but I, his brother, gain nothing
under him but growth, for the which his animals on his
dunghills are as much bound to him as I. Besides this
nothing that he so plentifully gives me, the something
16 that nature gave me his countenance seems to take from
17 me : he lets me feed with his hinds, bars me the place of a
18 brother, and, as much as in him lies, mines my gentility
with my education. This is it, Adam, that grieves me ;
and the spirit of my father, which I think is within me,
begins to mutiny against this servitude. I will no longer
endure it, though yet I know no wise remedy how to
avoid it.

Enter Oliver.

ADAM Yonder comes my master, your brother.

ORLANDO Go apart, Adam, and thou shalt hear how he
will shake me up.

26 OLIVER Now, sir, what make you here ?

ORLANDO Nothing. I am not taught to make anything.

OLIVER What mar you then, sir ?

29 ORLANDO Marry, sir, I am helping you to mar that which
God made, a poor unworthy brother of yours, with
idleness.

32 OLIVER Marry, sir, be better employed, and be naught
awhile.

ORLANDO Shall I keep your hogs and eat husks with 34
them ? What prodigal portion have I spent that I
should come to such penury ?

OLIVER Know you where you are, sir ?

ORLANDO O, sir, very well : here in your orchard. 38

OLIVER Know you before whom, sir ?

ORLANDO Ay, better than him I am before knows me. I
know you are my eldest brother, and in the gentle con- 41
dition of blood you should so know me. The courtesy 42
of nations allows you my better in that you are the first
born, but the same tradition takes not away my blood
were there twenty brothers betwixt us. I have as much
of my father in me as you, albeit I confess your coming
before me is nearer to his reverence. 47

OLIVER What, boy !

[Strikes him.]

ORLANDO Come, come, elder brother, you are too young
in this.

[Seizes him.]

OLIVER Wilt thou lay hands on me, villain ?

ORLANDO I am no villain. I am the youngest son of Sir 52
Rowland de Boys ; he was my father, and he is thrice a
villain that says such a father begot villains. Wert thou
not my brother, I would not take this hand from thy
throat till this other had pulled out thy tongue for saying
so. Thou hast railed on thyself. 57

I, i The orchard of Oliver's manor house 2 *but poor* merely 6 *profit*
progress ; *keeps* maintains 7 *stays* detains 11 *manage* actions and paces
16 *countenance* attitude 17 *hinds* farm hands 18 *mines* undermines 26
make do (but Orlando pretends to take it in another sense) 29 *Marry* why,
indeed (originally an oath by the Virgin Mary) 32–33 *be naught awhile*
i.e. go to the devil 34–35 *eat husks . . . prodigal portion* (alluding to the
Prodigal Son, who wasted his patrimony and then had to eat with the
swine ; see Luke xv, 11–32) 38 *orchard* garden 41–42 *gentle . . . blood*
bond of family loyalty 42–43 *courtesy of nations* recognized custom (of
primogeniture) 47 *reverence* revered rank 52 *villain* serf (Orlando
quibbles on the two meanings of 'villain') 57 *railed on* reviled

246

ADAM Sweet masters, be patient : for your father's remembrance, be at accord.

OLIVER Let me go, I say.

ORLANDO I will not till I please. You shall hear me. My
father charged you in his will to give me good education :
you have trained me like a peasant, obscuring and hiding
64 from me all gentlemanlike qualities. The spirit of my
father grows strong in me, and I will no longer endure
it : therefore allow me such exercises as may become a
67 gentleman, or give me the poor allottery my father left
me by testament ; with that I will go buy my fortunes.
        [Releases him.]

OLIVER And what wilt thou do ? beg when that is spent ?
Well, sir, get you in. I will not long be troubled with
you. You shall have some part of your will. I pray you
leave me.

ORLANDO I will no further offend you than becomes me
for my good.

OLIVER Get you with him, you old dog.

ADAM Is 'old dog' my reward ? Most true, I have lost my
teeth in your service. God be with my old master ; he
would not have spoke such a word.
        Exeunt Orlando, Adam.

79 OLIVER Is it even so ? Begin you to grow upon me ? I will
80 physic your rankness and yet give no thousand crowns
neither. Holla, Dennis !
        Enter Dennis.

DENNIS Calls your worship ?

OLIVER Was not Charles the Duke's wrestler here to
speak with me ?

DENNIS So please you, he is here at the door and importunes access to you.

OLIVER Call him in. *[Exit Dennis.]* 'Twill be a good way ;
and to-morrow the wrestling is.
        Enter Charles.

CHARLES Good morrow to your worship.

90 OLIVER Good Monsieur Charles, what's the new news at
the new court ?

CHARLES There's no news at the court, sir, but the old
news : that is, the old Duke is banished by his younger
brother the new Duke, and three or four loving lords
have put themselves into voluntary exile with him,
whose lands and revenues enrich the new Duke ; therefore he gives them good leave to wander.

OLIVER Can you tell if Rosalind, the Duke's daughter,
be banished with her father ?

100 CHARLES O, no ; for the Duke's daughter her cousin so
loves her, being ever from their cradles bred together,
that she would have followed her exile, or have died to
stay behind her. She is at the court, and no less beloved
of her uncle than his own daughter, and never two
ladies loved as they do.

OLIVER Where will the old Duke live ?

CHARLES They say he is already in the Forest of Arden,
and a many merry men with him ; and there they live
like the old Robin Hood of England. They say many
young gentlemen flock to him every day, and fleet the 110
time carelessly as they did in the golden world.   111

OLIVER What, you wrestle to-morrow before the new
Duke ?

CHARLES Marry do I, sir ; and I came to acquaint you with
a matter. I am given, sir, secretly to understand that your
younger brother, Orlando, hath a disposition to come
in disguised against me to try a fall. To-morrow, sir, I 117
wrestle for my credit, and he that escapes me without 118
some broken limb shall acquit him well. Your brother is
but young and tender, and for your love I would be
loath to foil him, as I must for my own honor if he come 121
in : therefore, out of my love to you, I came hither to
acquaint you withal, that either you might stay him from
his intendment, or brook such disgrace well as he shall
run into, in that it is a thing of his own search and alto- 125
gether against my will.

OLIVER Charles, I thank thee for thy love to me, which
thou shalt find I will most kindly requite. I had myself
notice of my brother's purpose herein and have by under- 129
hand means labored to dissuade him from it ; but he is
resolute. I'll tell thee, Charles, it is the stubbornest young
fellow of France ; full of ambition, an envious emulator
of every man's good parts, a secret and villainous contriver against me his natural brother : therefore use thy
discretion. I had as lief thou didst break his neck as his
finger. And thou wert best look to't ; for if thou dost
him any slight disgrace, or if he do not mightily grace 137
himself on thee, he will practise against thee by poison, 138
entrap thee by some treacherous device, and never leave
thee till he hath ta'en thy life by some indirect means or
other ; for I assure thee, and almost with tears I speak it,
there is not one so young and so villainous this day living.
I speak but brotherly of him, but should I anatomize 143
him to thee as he is, I must blush and weep, and thou
must look pale and wonder.

CHARLES I am heartily glad I came hither to you. If he
come to-morrow, I'll give him his payment. If ever he go 147
alone again, I'll never wrestle for prize more. And so
God keep your worship.

OLIVER Farewell, good Charles. *Exit [Charles].* Now will
I stir this gamester. I hope I shall see an end of him ; for
my soul, yet I know not why, hates nothing more than
he. Yet he's gentle, never schooled and yet learned, full 153
of noble device, of all sorts enchantingly beloved ; and 154
indeed so much in the heart of the world, and especially
of my own people, who best know him, that I am altogether misprised. But it shall not be so long : this wrestler 157
shall clear all. Nothing remains but that I kindle the boy
thither, which now I'll go about.   *Exit.*

*

Enter Rosalind and Celia.   I, ii

CELIA I pray thee, Rosalind, sweet my coz, be merry.   1

ROSALIND Dear Celia, I show more mirth that I am mistress of, and would you yet I were merrier ? Unless you
could teach me to forget a banished father, you must not
learn me how to remember any extraordinary pleasure. 4

CELIA Herein I see thou lov'st me not with the full weight
that I love thee. If my uncle, thy banished father, had

64 *qualities* accomplishments 67 *allottery* portion 79 *grow upon me* i.e.
encroach on my place 80 *physic* cure ; *rankness* exuberant growth (cf. l. 79)
110 *fleet* pass 111 *the golden world* (described by Ovid in *Metamorphoses*,
Book I ; here men were innocent and food was plentiful) 117 *fall* bout
118 *credit* reputation 121 *foil* throw 125 *search* seeking 129 *underhand* indirect 137-38 *grace himself on thee* gain credit at your expense
138 *practise* plot 143 *anatomize* dissect, describe 147-48 *go alone* walk
without help 153 *gentle* possessed of the qualities of a gentleman 154
device designs ; *enchantingly* as by enchantment 157 *misprised* scorned
I, ii The grounds of Duke Frederick's palace 1 *coz* cousin 4 *learn* teach

banished thy uncle, the Duke my father, so thou hadst
been still with me, I could have taught my love to take
thy father for mine. So wouldst thou, if the truth of thy
11   love to me were so righteously tempered as mine is to
thee.

ROSALIND   Well, I will forget the condition of my estate
to rejoice in yours.

CELIA   You know my father hath no child but I, nor none
is like to have; and truly, when he dies, thou shalt be his
17   heir; for what he hath taken away from thy father perforce, I will render thee again in affection. By mine
honor, I will, and when I break that oath, let me turn
monster. Therefore, my sweet Rose, my dear Rose, be
merry.

ROSALIND   From henceforth I will, coz, and devise sports.
Let me see, what think you of falling in love?

CELIA   Marry, I prithee do, to make sport withal; but love
no man in good earnest, nor no further in sport neither
26   than with safety of a pure blush thou mayst in honor
27   come off again.

ROSALIND   What shall be our sport then?

29 CELIA   Let us sit and mock the good housewife Fortune
30   from her wheel, that her gifts may henceforth be bestowed equally.

ROSALIND   I would we could do so, for her benefits are
mightily misplaced, and the bountiful blind woman
doth most mistake in her gifts to women.

CELIA   'Tis true, for those that she makes fair she scarce
36   makes honest, and those that she makes honest she
makes very ill-favoredly.

ROSALIND   Nay, now thou goest from Fortune's office to
Nature's. Fortune reigns in gifts of the world, not in the
40   lineaments of Nature.

Enter [Touchstone, the] Clown.

CELIA   No; when Nature hath made a fair creature, may
she not by Fortune fall into the fire? Though Nature
hath given us wit to flout at Fortune, hath not Fortune
sent in this fool to cut off the argument?

ROSALIND   Indeed, there is Fortune too hard for Nature
46   when Fortune makes Nature's natural the cutter-off of
Nature's wit.

CELIA   Peradventure this is not Fortune's work neither,
but Nature's, who perceiveth our natural wits too dull to
reason of such goddesses and hath sent this natural for
our whetstone, for always the dullness of the fool is the
whetstone of the wits. How now, wit; whither wander
you?

TOUCHSTONE   Mistress, you must come away to your
father.

CELIA   Were you made the messenger?

TOUCHSTONE   No, by mine honor, but I was bid to come
for you.

ROSALIND   Where learned you that oath, fool?

TOUCHSTONE   Of a certain knight that swore by his honor
they were good pancakes, and swore by his honor the
mustard was naught. Now I'll stand to it, the pancakes
were naught, and the mustard was good, and yet was
63   not the knight forsworn.

CELIA   How prove you that in the great heap of your
knowledge?

ROSALIND   Ay, marry, now unmuzzle your wisdom.

TOUCHSTONE   Stand you both forth now. Stroke your
chins, and swear by your beards that I am a knave.

CELIA   By our beards, if we had them, thou art.

TOUCHSTONE   By my knavery, if I had it, then I were;
but if you swear by that that is not, you are not forsworn; no more was this knight, swearing by his honor,
for he never had any; or if he had, he had sworn it away
before ever he saw those pancakes or that mustard.

CELIA   Prithee, who is't that thou mean'st?

TOUCHSTONE   One that old Frederick, your father, loves.

CELIA   My father's love is enough to honor him enough:
speak no more of him; you'll be whipped for taxation 78
one of these days.

TOUCHSTONE   The more pity that fools may not speak
wisely what wise men do foolishly.

CELIA   By my troth, thou sayest true, for since the little
wit that fools have was silenced, the little foolery that
wise men have makes a great show. Here comes Monsieur Le Beau.

Enter Le Beau.

ROSALIND   With his mouth full of news.

CELIA   Which he will put on us as pigeons feed their 87
young.

ROSALIND   Then shall we be news-crammed.

CELIA   All the better; we shall be the more marketable.
Bon jour, Monsieur Le Beau, what's the news?

LE BEAU   Fair princess, you have lost much good sport.

CELIA   Sport; of what color?   92

LE BEAU   What color, madam? How shall I answer you?

ROSALIND   As wit and fortune will.

TOUCHSTONE   Or as the destinies decree.

CELIA   Well said; that was laid on with a trowel.   96

TOUCHSTONE   Nay, if I keep not my rank –   97

ROSALIND   Thou losest thy old smell.

LE BEAU   You amaze me, ladies. I would have told you of 99
good wrestling, which you have lost the sight of.

ROSALIND   Yet tell us the manner of the wrestling.

LE BEAU   I will tell you the beginning; and if it please your
ladyships, you may see the end, for the best is yet to do,
and here, where you are, they are coming to perform it.

CELIA   Well, the beginning that is dead and buried.

LE BEAU   There comes an old man and his three sons.

CELIA   I could match this beginning with an old tale.

LE BEAU   Three proper young men, of excellent growth
and presence.

ROSALIND   With bills on their necks, 'Be it known unto 110
all men by these presents.'

LE BEAU   The eldest of the three wrestled with Charles,
the Duke's wrestler; which Charles in a moment threw
him and broke three of his ribs, that there is little hope
of life in him. So he served the second, and so the third.
Yonder they lie, the poor old man, their father, making
such pitiful dole over them that all the beholders take 117
his part with weeping.

ROSALIND   Alas!

TOUCHSTONE   But what is the sport, monsieur, that the
ladies have lost?

LE BEAU   Why, this that I speak of.

---

11 *righteously tempered* properly composed   17 *perforce* forcibly   26
pure innocent   27 *come off* get away   29 *good housewife* i.e. one who spins
30 *her wheel* (which carried some up, others down)   36 *honest* chaste   40
s.d. *Touchstone* (his name means a kind of flint used to test for gold and
silver by the color of the streak made when rubbed across metal)   46
natural born fool   63 *forsworn* falsely sworn   78 *taxation* slander   87 *put
on* force upon   92 *color* sort   96 *with a trowel* i.e. slapped on thickly
97 *my rank* i.e. my rating as a witty person   99 *amaze* confuse   110 *bills*
notices   117 *dole* lament

TOUCHSTONE Thus men may grow wiser every day. It is the first time that ever I heard breaking of ribs was sport for ladies.

CELIA Or I, I promise thee.

127 ROSALIND But is there any else longs to see this broken music in his sides? Is there yet another dotes upon rib-breaking? Shall we see this wrestling, cousin?

LE BEAU You must, if you stay here, for here is the place appointed for the wrestling, and they are ready to perform it.

CELIA Yonder sure they are coming. Let us now stay and see it.

Flourish. Enter Duke [Frederick], Lords, Orlando, Charles, and Attendants.

DUKE FREDERICK Come on. Since the youth will not be
136 entreated, his own peril on his forwardness.

ROSALIND Is yonder the man?

LE BEAU Even he, madam.

139 CELIA Alas, he is too young; yet he looks successfully.

DUKE FREDERICK How now, daughter and cousin; are you crept hither to see the wrestling?

ROSALIND Ay, my liege, so please you give us leave.

DUKE FREDERICK You will take little delight in it, I can
144 tell you, there is such odds in the man. In pity of the challenger's youth I would fain dissuade him, but he will not be entreated. Speak to him, ladies; see if you can move him.

CELIA Call him hither, good Monsieur Le Beau.

DUKE FREDERICK Do so. I'll not be by.

[Steps aside.]

150 LE BEAU Monsieur the challenger, the princess calls for you.

ORLANDO I attend them with all respect and duty.

ROSALIND Young man, have you challenged Charles the wrestler?

ORLANDO No, fair princess. He is the general challenger; I come but in as others do, to try with him the strength of my youth.

CELIA Young gentleman, your spirits are too bold for your years. You have seen cruel proof of this man's strength; if you saw yourself with your eyes or knew yourself with your judgment, the fear of your adventure would counsel you to a more equal enterprise. We pray you for your own sake to embrace your own safety and give over this attempt.

ROSALIND Do, young sir. Your reputation shall not
165 therefore be misprised; we will make it our suit to the Duke that the wrestling might not go forward.

ORLANDO I beseech you, punish me not with your hard thoughts, wherein I confess me much guilty to deny so fair and excellent ladies anything. But let your fair eyes and gentle wishes go with me to my trial; wherein if I be
171 foiled, there is but one shamed that was never gracious; if killed, but one dead that is willing to be so. I shall do my friends no wrong, for I have none to lament me; the

world no injury, for in it I have nothing. Only in the world I fill up a place, which may be better supplied when I have made it empty.

ROSALIND The little strength that I have, I would it were with you.

CELIA And mine to eke out hers.

ROSALIND Fare you well. Pray heaven I be deceived in 180 you!

CELIA Your heart's desires be with you!

CHARLES Come, where is this young gallant that is so desirous to lie with his mother earth?

ORLANDO Ready, sir; but his will hath in it a more modest working. 185

DUKE FREDERICK You shall try but one fall.

CHARLES No, I warrant your Grace you shall not entreat him to a second that have so mightily persuaded him from a first.

ORLANDO You mean to mock me after. You should not have mocked me before. But come your ways. 191

ROSALIND Now Hercules be thy speed, young man! 192

CELIA I would I were invisible, to catch the strong fellow by the leg.

Wrestle.

ROSALIND O excellent young man!

CELIA If I had a thunderbolt in mine eye, I can tell who 196 should down.

[Charles is thrown.] Shout.

DUKE FREDERICK No more, no more.

ORLANDO Yes, I beseech your Grace; I am not yet well 199 breathed.

DUKE FREDERICK
How dost thou, Charles?

LE BEAU   He cannot speak, my lord.

DUKE FREDERICK
Bear him away.

[Charles is borne out.]
          What is thy name, young man?

ORLANDO Orlando, my liege, the youngest son of Sir Rowland de Boys.

DUKE FREDERICK
I would thou hadst been son to some man else.
The world esteemed thy father honorable,
But I did find him still mine enemy. 207
Thou shouldst have better pleased me with this deed
Hadst thou descended from another house.
But fare thee well; thou art a gallant youth;
I would thou hadst told me of another father.

Exit Duke [, with Train].

CELIA
Were I my father, coz, would I do this?

ORLANDO
I am more proud to be Sir Rowland's son,
His youngest son, and would not change that calling 214
To be adopted heir to Frederick.

ROSALIND
My father loved Sir Rowland as his soul,
And all the world was of my father's mind.
Had I before known this young man his son,
I should have given him tears unto entreaties
Ere he should thus have ventured.

CELIA   Gentle cousin,
Let us go thank him and encourage him.
My father's rough and envious disposition
Sticks me at heart. Sir, you have well deserved; 223

127–28 *broken music* wrong arrangement of parts   136 *forwardness* rashness   139 *successfully* likely to succeed   144 *odds* superiority   150 *princess* (taken as plural by Orlando)   165 *misprised* undervalued   171 *gracious* graced by fortune   180–81 *deceived in you* mistaken in my view of your abilities   185 *working* undertaking   191 *come your ways* come on   192 *Hercules* (symbol of strength); *be thy speed* favor you   196 *If ... eye* if I could cast a thunderbolt with my eyes   199–200 *well breathed* warmed up   207 *still* constantly   214 *calling* title   223 *Sticks* stabs

If you do keep your promises in love
But justly as you have exceeded all promise,
Your mistress shall be happy.
226 ROSALIND   Gentleman,
        [Gives chain.]
227 Wear this for me, one out of suits with fortune,
That could give more but that her hand lacks means.
Shall we go, coz?
    CELIA   Ay. Fare you well, fair gentleman.
    ORLANDO
230 Can I not say 'I thank you'? My better parts
Are all thrown down, and that which here stands up
232 Is but a quintain, a mere lifeless block.
    ROSALIND
He calls us back. My pride fell with my fortunes;
I'll ask him what he would. Did you call, sir?
Sir, you have wrestled well, and overthrown
More than your enemies.
    CELIA   Will you go, coz?
    ROSALIND
237 Have with you. Fare you well.   Exit [with Celia].
    ORLANDO
What passion hangs these weights upon my tongue?
239 I cannot speak to her, yet she urged conference.
        Enter Le Beau.
O poor Orlando, thou art overthrown!
Or Charles or something weaker masters thee.
    LE BEAU
Good sir, I do in friendship counsel you
To leave this place. Albeit you have deserved
High commendation, true applause, and love,
245 Yet such is now the Duke's condition
246 That he misconsters all that you have done.
247 The Duke is humorous. What he is, indeed,
More suits you to conceive than I to speak of.
    ORLANDO
I thank you, sir; and pray you tell me this:
Which of the two was daughter of the Duke,
That here was at the wrestling?
    LE BEAU
Neither his daughter, if we judge by manners,
253 But yet indeed the taller is his daughter,
The other is daughter to the banished Duke,
And here detained by her usurping uncle
To keep his daughter company, whose loves
Are dearer than the natural bond of sisters.
But I can tell you that of late this Duke
Hath ta'en displeasure 'gainst his gentle niece,
260 Grounded upon no other argument
But that the people praise her for her virtues
And pity her for her good father's sake;
And, on my life, his malice 'gainst the lady
Will suddenly break forth. Sir, fare you well.
265 Hereafter, in a better world than this,
I shall desire more love and knowledge of you.
    ORLANDO
I rest much bounden to you. Fare you well.
                    [Exit Le Beau.]
268 Thus must I from the smoke into the smother,
From tyrant Duke unto a tyrant brother.
But heavenly Rosalind!   Exit.

        Enter Celia and Rosalind.   I, iii
CELIA Why, cousin, why, Rosalind! Cupid have mercy,
    not a word?
ROSALIND Not one to throw at a dog.
CELIA No, thy words are too precious to be cast away
    upon curs; throw some of them at me; come, lame me 5
    with reasons.
ROSALIND Then there were two cousins laid up, when
    the one should be lamed with reasons and the other mad
    without any.
CELIA But is all this for your father?
ROSALIND No, some of it is for my child's father. O, how
    full of briers is this working-day world!
CELIA They are but burrs, cousin, thrown upon thee in
    holiday foolery; if we walk not in the trodden paths,
    our very petticoats will catch them.
ROSALIND I could shake them off my coat; these burrs
    are in my heart.
CELIA Hem them away.   18
ROSALIND I would try, if I could cry 'hem,' and have 19
    him.
CELIA Come, come, wrestle with thy affections.
ROSALIND O, they take the part of a better wrestler than
    myself!
CELIA O, a good wish upon you! You will try in time, in 23
    despite of a fall. But turning these jests out of service, 24
    let us talk in good earnest. Is it possible on such a sud-
    den you should fall into so strong a liking with old Sir
    Rowland's youngest son?
ROSALIND The Duke my father loved his father dearly.
CELIA Doth it therefore ensue that you should love his son
    dearly? By this kind of chase, I should hate him, for my 30
    father hated his father dearly; yet I hate not Orlando.
ROSALIND No, faith, hate him not, for my sake.
CELIA Why should I not? Doth he not deserve well?   33
        Enter Duke [Frederick], with Lords.
ROSALIND Let me love him for that, and do you love him
    because I do. Look, here comes the Duke.
CELIA With his eyes full of anger.
    DUKE FREDERICK
Mistress, dispatch you with your safest haste   37
And get you from our court.
    ROSALIND   Me, uncle?
    DUKE FREDERICK   You, cousin.
Within these ten days if that thou beest found
So near our public court as twenty miles,
Thou diest for it.
    ROSALIND   I do beseech your Grace
Let me the knowledge of my fault bear with me.
If with myself I hold intelligence   43
Or have acquaintance with mine own desires,

226 s.d. *chain* (see III, ii, 172) 227 *suits* favor 230 *better parts* i.e. composure and manners 232 *quintain* post with crossbars for tilting 237
Have with you come on 239 *urged conference* invited conversation 245
condition disposition 246 *misconsters* misconstrues 247 *humorous* subject
to emotional disturbances 253 *taller* (either Le Beau or Shakespeare is
here confused; Rosalind, not Celia, is later shown to be the taller) 260
argument reason 265 *world* state of affairs 268 *smother* suffocation
I, iii Duke Frederick's palace 5–6 *lame me with reasons* injure me with
explanations 18 *Hem* tuck 19 *cry 'hem'* clear the throat 23 *try* make
trial (as *wrestler*?) 24 *fall* (a quibble on this word) 30 *chase* argument
33 *deserve well* i.e. to be hated (but Rosalind ignores the implied conclusion)
37 *safest haste* i.e. the hastier the safer 43 *hold intelligence* am in communication

45 If that I do not dream or be not frantic,
    As I do trust I am not ; then, dear uncle,
    Never so much as in a thought unborn
    Did I offend your Highness.

DUKE FREDERICK   Thus do all traitors.
49 If their purgation did consist in words,
50 They are as innocent as grace itself.
    Let it suffice thee that I trust thee not.

ROSALIND
    Yet your mistrust cannot make me a traitor.
53 Tell me whereon the likelihoods depends.

DUKE FREDERICK
    Thou art thy father's daughter, there's enough.

ROSALIND
    So was I when your Highness took his dukedom ;
    So was I when your Highness banished him.
    Treason is not inherited, my lord,
58 Or if we did derive it from our friends,
    What's that to me ? My father was no traitor.
    Then, good my liege, mistake me not so much
    To think my poverty is treacherous.

CELIA
    Dear sovereign, hear me speak.

DUKE FREDERICK
    Ay, Celia. We stayed her for your sake,
    Else had she with her father ranged along.

CELIA
    I did not then entreat to have her stay ;
66 It was your pleasure and your own remorse.
    I was too young that time to value her,
    But now I know her. If she be a traitor,
    Why, so am I. We still have slept together,
    Rose at an instant, learned, played, eat together ;
71 And wheresoe'er we went, like Juno's swans,
    Still we went coupled and inseparable.

DUKE FREDERICK
73 She is too subtile for thee ; and her smoothness,
    Her very silence and her patience,
    Speak to the people, and they pity her.
    Thou art a fool. She robs thee of thy name,
77 And thou wilt show more bright and seem more virtuous
    When she is gone. Then open not thy lips.
    Firm and irrevocable is my doom
    Which I have passed upon her ; she is banished.

CELIA
    Pronounce that sentence then on me, my liege ;
    I cannot live out of her company.

DUKE FREDERICK
    You are a fool. You, niece, provide yourself ;
    If you outstay the time, upon mine honor,
85 And in the greatness of my word, you die.
                    Exit Duke, &c.

CELIA
    O my poor Rosalind, whither wilt thou go ?

Wilt thou change fathers ? I will give thee mine.
I charge thee be not thou more grieved than I am.

ROSALIND
    I have more cause.

CELIA   Thou hast not, cousin.
    Prithee be cheerful. Know'st thou not the Duke
    Hath banished me, his daughter ?

ROSALIND   That he hath not.

CELIA
    No ? hath not ? Rosalind lacks then the love
    Which teacheth thee that thou and I am one.
    Shall we be sund'red, shall we part, sweet girl ?
    No, let my father seek another heir.
    Therefore devise with me how we may fly,   96
    Whither to go, and what to bear with us ;
    And do not seek to take your change upon you, 98
    To bear your griefs yourself and leave me out ;
    For, by this heaven, now at our sorrows pale,
    Say what thou canst, I'll go along with thee.

ROSALIND
    Why, whither shall we go ?

CELIA
    To seek my uncle in the Forest of Arden.

ROSALIND
    Alas, what danger will it be to us,
    Maids as we are, to travel forth so far !
    Beauty provoketh thieves sooner than gold.

CELIA
    I'll put myself in poor and mean attire
    And with a kind of umber smirch my face ;   108
    The like do you ; so shall we pass along
    And never stir assailants.

ROSALIND   Were it not better,
    Because that I am more than common tall,
    That I did suit me all points like a man ?   112
    A gallant curtle-axe upon my thigh,   113
    A boar-spear in my hand ; and, in my heart
    Lie there what hidden woman's fear there will,
    We'll have a swashing and a martial outside, 116
    As many other mannish cowards have   117
    That do outface it with their semblances.   118

CELIA
    What shall I call thee when thou art a man ?

ROSALIND
    I'll have no worse a name than Jove's own page,
    And therefore look you call me Ganymede. 121
    But what will you be called ?

CELIA
    Something that hath a reference to my state :
    No longer Celia, but Aliena.   124

ROSALIND
    But, cousin, what if we assayed to steal 125
    The clownish fool out of your father's court ;
    Would he not be a comfort to our travel ?

CELIA
    He'll go along o'er the wide world with me ;
    Leave me alone to woo him. Let's away   129
    And get our jewels and our wealth together,
    Devise the fittest time and safest way
    To hide us from pursuit that will be made
    After my flight. Now go in we content
    To liberty, and not to banishment.   *Exeunt.*

---

45 *frantic* insane **49** *purgation* exoneration **50** *grace* virtue **53** *likeli-hoods* i.e. suspicion **58** *friends* kin **66** *remorse* compunction **71** *Juno's swans* (according to Ovid it was Venus who was drawn through the air by a pair of swans) **73** *subtile* crafty **77** *virtuous* possessed of good quali-ties **85** *greatness* authority **96** *devise* plan **98** *change* i.e. of fortunes **108** *umber* brown earth **112** *suit me all points* dress completely **113** *curtle-axe* curved sword **116** *swashing* blustering **117** *mannish* i.e. pre-tending manliness **118** *outface it* bluff **121** *Ganymede* (who for his beauty was made cupbearer to Jove) **124** *Aliena* i.e. estranged **125** *assayed* undertook **129** *woo* coax

*

II,i   *Enter Duke Senior, Amiens, and two or three Lords,*
like Foresters.

DUKE SENIOR

Now, my co-mates and brothers in exile,
Hath not old custom made this life more sweet
Than that of painted pomp ? Are not these woods
More free from peril than the envious court ?
5   Here feel we not the penalty of Adam ;
6   The seasons' difference, as the icy fang
7   And churlish chiding of the winter's wind,
Which, when it bites and blows upon my body
Even till I shrink with cold, I smile and say
'This is no flattery'; these are counsellors
That feelingly persuade me what I am.
Sweet are the uses of adversity,
13   Which, like the toad, ugly and venomous,
Wears yet a precious jewel in his head ;
15   And this our life, exempt from public haunt,
Finds tongues in trees, books in the running brooks,
Sermons in stones, and good in everything.

AMIENS

I would not change it ; happy is your Grace
19   That can translate the stubbornness of fortune
Into so quiet and so sweet a style.

DUKE SENIOR

Come, shall we go and kill us venison ?
22   And yet it irks me the poor dappled fools,
23   Being native burghers of this desert city,
24   Should, in their own confines, with forkèd heads
Have their round haunches gored.

1. LORD   Indeed, my lord,
The melancholy Jaques grieves at that,
27   And in that kind swears you do more usurp
Than doth your brother that hath banished you.
To-day my Lord of Amiens and myself
Did steal behind him as he lay along
Under an oak, whose antique root peeps out
32   Upon the brook that brawls along this wood,
33   To the which place a poor sequest'red stag
That from the hunter's aim had ta'en a hurt
Did come to languish ; and indeed, my lord,
The wretched animal heaved forth such groans
That their discharge did stretch his leathern coat
38   Almost to bursting, and the big round tears
Coursed one another down his innocent nose
In piteous chase ; and thus the hairy fool,
Much markèd of the melancholy Jaques,
Stood on th' extremest verge of the swift brook,
Augmenting it with tears.

DUKE SENIOR   But what said Jaques ?
44   Did he not moralize this spectacle ?

1. LORD

O, yes, into a thousand similes.
46   First, for his weeping into the needless stream :
'Poor deer,' quoth he, 'thou mak'st a testament
As worldlings do, giving thy sum of more
To that which had too much.' Then, being there alone,
50   Left and abandoned of his velvet friend :
' 'Tis right,' quoth he, 'thus misery doth part
52   The flux of company.' Anon a careless herd,
Full of the pasture, jumps along by him
And never stays to greet him ; 'Ay,' quoth Jaques,
'Sweep on, you fat and greasy citizens,
'Tis just the fashion ; wherefore do you look

Upon that poor and broken bankrupt there ?'
Thus most invectively he pierceth through
The body of the country, city, court,
Yea, and of this our life, swearing that we
Are mere usurpers, tyrants, and what's worse,
To fright the animals and to kill them up   62
In their assigned and native dwelling place.   63

DUKE SENIOR

And did you leave him in this contemplation ?

2. LORD

We did, my lord, weeping and commenting
Upon the sobbing deer.

DUKE SENIOR   Show me the place.
I love to cope him in these sullen fits,   67
For then he's full of matter.

1. LORD

I'll bring you to him straight.   *Exeunt.*

*

     Enter Duke [Frederick], with Lords.   II,ii

DUKE FREDERICK

Can it be possible that no man saw them ?
It cannot be ; some villains of my court
Are of consent and sufferance in this.   3

1. LORD

I cannot hear of any that did see her.
The ladies her attendants of her chamber
Saw her abed, and in the morning early
They found the bed untreasured of their mistress.

2. LORD

My lord, the roynish clown at whom so oft   8
Your Grace was wont to laugh is also missing.
Hisperia, the princess' gentlewoman,
Confesses that she secretly o'erheard
Your daughter and her cousin much commend
The parts and graces of the wrestler   13
That did but lately foil the sinewy Charles,
And she believes, wherever they are gone,
That youth is surely in their company.

DUKE FREDERICK

Send to his brother, fetch that gallant hither ;
If he be absent, bring his brother to me ;
I'll make him find him. Do this suddenly,   19
And let not search and inquisition quail   20
To bring again these foolish runaways.   *Exeunt.*

*

II, i The Forest of Arden   **5** *not* (frequently emended to 'but') ; *penalty of Adam* loss of innocence, expulsion from Garden of Eden (see Genesis iii) **6** *as* for example   **7** *churlish* rough   **13–14** *toad . . . head* ('The foul toad hath a fair stone in his head.' Lyly, *Euphues*)   **15** *haunt* society   **19** *stubbornness* hardness   **22** *fools* pitiable creatures   **23** *desert* uninhabited (rather than devoid of vegetation)   **24** *confines* territory ; *forkèd heads* barbed arrowheads   **27** *kind* way   **32** *brawls* makes noisy sounds   **33** *sequest'red* separated   **38** *tears* (wounded deer were commonly supposed to shed tears)   **44** *moralize* draw a moral from   **46** *needless* needing no more water   **50** *velvet* in the 'velvet' stage   **52** *flux* confluence   **62** *up* off **63** *assigned* i.e. in the natural order   **67** *cope* cope with
II, ii Duke Frederick's palace   **3** *of consent and sufferance* in connivance **8** *roynish* scurvy   **13** *parts* good qualities   **19** *suddenly* at once   **20** *inquisition quail* enquiry falter

Enter Orlando and Adam.

ORLANDO
Who's there?

ADAM
What, my young master, O my gentle master,
3 O my sweet master, O you memory
Of old Sir Rowland, why, what make you here?
Why are you virtuous? Why do people love you?
And wherefore are you gentle, strong, and valiant?
7 Why would you be so fond to overcome
8 The bonny prizer of the humorous Duke?
Your praise is come too swiftly home before you.
Know you not, master, to some kind of men
Their graces serve them but as enemies?
12 No more do yours. Your virtues, gentle master,
Are sanctified and holy traitors to you.
O, what a world is this, when what is comely
Envenoms him that bears it!

ORLANDO
Why, what's the matter?

ADAM   O unhappy youth,
Come not within these doors; within this roof
The enemy of all your graces lives.
Your brother, no, no brother, yet the son
(Yet not the son, I will not call him son)
Of him I was about to call his father,
Hath heard your praises, and this night he means
23 To burn the lodging where you use to lie
And you within it. If he fail of that,
He will have other means to cut you off.
26 I overheard him, and his practices;
This is no place, this house is but a butchery;
Abhor it, fear it, do not enter it!

ORLANDO
Why, whither, Adam, wouldst thou have me go?

ADAM
No matter whither, so you come not here.

ORLANDO
What, wouldst thou have me go and beg my food,
Or with a base and boist'rous sword enforce
A thievish living on the common road?
This I must do, or know not what to do;
Yet this I will not do, do how I can.
I rather will subject me to the malice
37 Of a diverted blood and bloody brother.

ADAM
But do not so. I have five hundred crowns,
39 The thrifty hire I saved under your father,
Which I did store to be my foster nurse
41 When service should in my old limbs lie lame

And unregarded age in corners thrown.
Take that, and he that doth the ravens feed,   43
Yea, providently caters for the sparrow,
Be comfort to my age. Here is the gold,
All this I give you. Let me be your servant;
Though I look old, yet I am strong and lusty,
For in my youth I never did apply
Hot and rebellious liquors in my blood,   49
Nor did not with unbashful forehead woo   50
The means of weakness and debility;
Therefore my age is as a lusty winter,
Frosty, but kindly. Let me go with you;
I'll do the service of a younger man
In all your business and necessities.

ORLANDO
O good old man, how well in thee appears
The constant service of the antique world,   57
When service sweat for duty, not for meed!   58
Thou art not for the fashion of these times,
Where none will sweat but for promotion,
And having that, do choke their service up   61
Even with the having; it is not so with thee.
But, poor old man, thou prun'st a rotten tree
That cannot so much as a blossom yield
In lieu of all thy pains and husbandry.   65
But come thy ways, we'll go along together,
And ere we have thy youthful wages spent,
We'll light upon some settled low content.   68

ADAM
Master, go on, and I will follow thee
To the last gasp with truth and loyalty.
From seventeen years till now almost fourscore
Here lived I, but now live here no more;
At seventeen years many their fortunes seek,
But at fourscore it is too late a week;   74
Yet fortune cannot recompense me better
Than to die well and not my master's debtor.   *Exeunt.*

*

Enter Rosalind for Ganymede, Celia for Aliena,   II, iv
and Clown, alias Touchstone.

ROSALIND O Jupiter, how merry are my spirits!   1
TOUCHSTONE I care not for my spirits if my legs were
not weary.
ROSALIND I could find in my heart to disgrace my man's
apparel and to cry like a woman; but I must comfort the
weaker vessel, as doublet and hose ought to show itself   6
courageous to petticoat. Therefore, courage, good
Aliena!
CELIA I pray you bear with me; I cannot go no further.
TOUCHSTONE For my part, I had rather bear with you
than bear you; yet I should bear no cross if I did bear   11
you; for I think you have no money in your purse.
ROSALIND Well, this is the Forest of Arden.
TOUCHSTONE Ay, now am I in Arden, the more fool I.
When I was at home, I was in a better place, but travel-
lers must be content.
Enter Corin and Silvius.
ROSALIND
Ay, be so, good Touchstone. Look you, who comes here,
A young man and an old in solemn talk.
CORIN
That is the way to make her scorn you still.

II, iii Before Oliver's house   **3** *memory* living memorial   **7** *fond* foolish
8 *bonny prizer* sturdy prize-fighter; *humorous* temperamental, capricious
12 *No more* no better   **12–13** *Your virtues . . . to you* i.e. Orlando's virtues,
although worthy of religious approval, have only worked against him in
the mind of his brother   **23** *use* are accustomed   **26** *practices* plots   **37**
diverted i.e. from natural affection   **39** *thrifty hire I saved* wages I thriftily
saved   **41** *service . . . lame* ability to serve should be weakened by old age
43–44 *ravens . . . sparrow* (see Psalms cxlvii, 9; Luke xii, 6)   **49** *rebellious*
causing rebellion against self-control   **50** *unbashful forehead* shameless
face   **57** *constant* faithful   **58** *meed* reward   **61–62** *do choke . . . having*
cease their service on gaining promotion   **65** *In lieu of* in return for   **68** *low
content* humble contentment   **74** *week* time
II, iv The Forest of Arden   **1** *merry* (presumably ironic; often emended
to 'weary')   **6** *doublet and hose* jacket and breeches   **11** *cross* (1) burden,
(2) penny, which had a cross stamped on it (a stock pun)

SILVIUS
O Corin, that thou knew'st how I do love her!
CORIN
I partly guess, for I have loved ere now.
SILVIUS
No, Corin, being old, thou canst not guess,
Though in thy youth thou wast as true a lover
As ever sighed upon a midnight pillow.
But if thy love were ever like to mine,
As sure I think did never man love so,
How many actions most ridiculous
28 Hast thou been drawn to by thy fantasy?
CORIN
Into a thousand that I have forgotten.
SILVIUS
O, thou didst then never love so heartily!
If thou rememb'rest not the slightest folly
That ever love did make thee run into,
Thou hast not loved.
Or if thou hast not sat as I do now,
35 Wearing thy hearer in thy mistress' praise,
Thou hast not loved.
Or if thou hast not broke from company
Abruptly, as my passion now makes me,
Thou hast not loved. O Phebe, Phebe, Phebe!   Exit.
ROSALIND
40 Alas, poor shepherd! Searching of thy wound,
I have by hard adventure found mine own.
TOUCHSTONE And I mine. I remember, when I was in
love I broke my sword upon a stone and bid him take
that for coming a-night to Jane Smile; and I remember
45 the kissing of her batler, and the cow's dugs that her
46 pretty chopt hands had milked; and I remember the
47 wooing of a peascod instead of her, from whom I took
two cods, and giving her them again, said with weeping
tears, 'Wear these for my sake.' We that are true lovers
run into strange capers; but as all is mortal in nature, so
51 is all nature in love mortal in folly.
52 ROSALIND Thou speak'st wiser than thou art ware of.
TOUCHSTONE Nay, I shall ne'er be ware of mine own
wit till I break my shins against it.
ROSALIND
Jove, Jove! this shepherd's passion
Is much upon my fashion.
TOUCHSTONE
And mine, but it grows something stale with me.
CELIA
I pray you, one of you question yond man
If he for gold will give us any food.
I faint almost to death.
61 TOUCHSTONE   Holla, you clown!
ROSALIND
Peace, fool! he's not thy kinsman.
CORIN
Who calls?
TOUCHSTONE Your betters, sir.
CORIN   Else are they very wretched.
ROSALIND
Peace, I say! Good even to you, friend.
CORIN
And to you, gentle sir, and to you all.
ROSALIND
I prithee, shepherd, if that love or gold
67 Can in this desert place buy entertainment,

Bring us where we may rest ourselves and feed.
Here's a young maid with travel much oppressed,
And faints for succor.
CORIN   Fair sir, I pity her
And wish, for her sake more than for mine own,
My fortunes were more able to relieve her;
But I am shepherd to another man
And do not shear the fleeces that I graze.
My master is of churlish disposition
And little recks to find the way to heaven   76
By doing deeds of hospitality.
Besides, his cote, his flocks, and bounds of feed   78
Are now on sale, and at our sheepcote now,
By reason of his absence, there is nothing
That you will feed on; but what is, come see,
And in my voice most welcome shall you be.   82
ROSALIND
What is he that shall buy his flock and pasture?
CORIN
That young swain that you saw here but erewhile,
That little cares for buying anything.
ROSALIND
I pray thee, if it stand with honesty,   86
Buy thou the cottage, pasture, and the flock,
And thou shalt have to pay for it of us.   88
CELIA
And we will mend thy wages. I like this place   89
And willingly could waste my time in it.   90
CORIN
Assuredly the thing is to be sold.
Go with me; if you like upon report   92
The soil, the profit, and this kind of life,
I will your very faithful feeder be   94
And buy it with your gold right suddenly.   Exeunt.

*

Enter Amiens, Jaques, and others.   II, v

Song.

[AMIENS]   Under the greenwood tree
      Who loves to lie with me,
    And turn his merry note   3
      Unto the sweet bird's throat,
  Come hither, come hither, come hither.
      Here shall he see no enemy
    But winter and rough weather.

JAQUES More, more, I prithee more!
AMIENS It will make you melancholy, Monsieur Jaques.
JAQUES I thank it. More, I prithee more! I can suck
melancholy out of a song as a weasel sucks eggs. More, I
prithee more!
AMIENS My voice is ragged. I know I cannot please you.

---

28 *fantasy* (Corin's love is likened to a mere fancy)   35 *Wearing* wearying
40 *Searching* probing   45 *batler* bat used in washing clothes   46 *chopt*
chapped   47 *peascod* pea pod (here used for whole plant)   51 *mortal in
folly* i.e. by its foolishness shows its human nature, which is subject to
mortality   52 *ware* aware   61 *clown* yokel   67 *desert* uninhabited; *entertainment* food and lodging   76 *recks* reckons   78 *cote* cottage; *bounds of
feed* pastures   82 *in my voice* as far as I have any influence   86 *if . . .
honesty* if it is consistent with honorable dealing   88 *have to pay* have the
money to pay   89 *mend* improve   90 *waste* spend   92 *report* further
information   94 *feeder* servant
II, v *The Forest*   3 *turn* attune

JAQUES I do not desire you to please me ; I do desire you to sing. Come, more, another stanzo ! Call you 'em stanzos ?

AMIENS What you will, Monsieur Jaques.

JAQUES Nay, I care not for their names ; they owe me nothing. Will you sing ?

AMIENS More at your request than to please myself.

JAQUES Well then, if ever I thank any man, I'll thank
21 you. But that they call compliment is like th' encounter
22 of two dog-apes, and when a man thanks me heartily, methinks I have given him a penny and he renders me
24 the beggarly thanks. Come, sing ; and you that will not, hold your tongues.
26 AMIENS Well, I'll end the song. Sirs, cover the while ; the Duke will drink under this tree. He hath been all this
28 day to look you.

JAQUES And I have been all this day to avoid him. He is too disputable for my company. I think of as many matters as he, but I give heaven thanks and make no boast of them. Come, warble, come.

Song.

All together here.

Who doth ambition shun
    And loves to live i' th' sun,
Seeking the food he eats,
    And pleased with what he gets,
Come hither, come hither, come hither.
    Here shall he see no enemy
    But winter and rough weather.

40 JAQUES I'll give you a verse to this note that I made
41 yesterday in despite of my invention.

AMIENS And I'll sing it.

JAQUES Thus it goes.
        [Gives paper.]
44 AMIENS   If it do come to pass
                That any man turn ass,
                Leaving his wealth and ease
                A stubborn will to please,
48   Ducdame, ducdame, ducdame.
                Here shall he see gross fools as he,
                An if he will come to me.

What's that 'ducdame' ?

JAQUES 'Tis a Greek invocation to call fools into a circle. I'll go sleep, if I can ; if I cannot, I'll rail against all the
54 first-born of Egypt.

---

21 *compliment* politeness 21–22 *th' encounter . . . dog apes* i.e. a mutual mockery 22 *dog-apes* baboons 24 *beggarly* effusive, like a beggar's 26 *cover the while* meanwhile set the cloth for a meal 28 *to look* looking for 40 *note* tune 41 *in . . . invention* although I lack imagination 44 *Amiens* (song sung by Jaques in second folio and many modern editions) 48 *Ducdame* (trisyllabic ; variously explained as deriving from gypsy 'dukrā mē,' a fortuneteller's cry to the gullible ; from Welsh 'dewch 'da mi,' meaning 'come with me' ; etc.) 54 *first-born of Egypt* (whose death finally resulted in sending the Israelites into the wilderness ; see Exodus xi, xii)
II, vi The Forest 6 *uncouth* uncivilized 7 *conceit* thought 8 *comfortable* cheerful
II, vii The Forest 5 *compact of jars* composed of discords 6 *spheres* (the harmonious crystal spheres in which the planets were supposedly set) 13 *motley* wearing a costume of mixed colors, the conventional dress of a professional jester 20 *dial* portable sundial ; *poke* pocket 26 *hour to hour* (perhaps a homonymic pun on 'whore') 29 *moral* moralize 30 *crow like chanticleer* exclaim triumphantly, like the crowing of the cock

---

AMIENS And I'll go seek the Duke. His banquet is prepared.
                                                    Exeunt.

                        *

ADAM Dear master, I can go no further. O, I die for food. Here lie I down and measure out my grave. Farewell, kind master.

ORLANDO Why, how now, Adam ? no greater heart in thee ? Live a little, comfort a little, cheer thyself a little. If this uncouth forest yield anything savage, I will either 6 be food for it or bring it for food to thee. Thy conceit is 7 nearer death than thy powers. For my sake be comfort- 8 able ; hold death awhile at the arm's end. I will here be with thee presently, and if I bring thee not something to eat, I will give thee leave to die ; but if thou diest before I come, thou art a mocker of my labor. Well said ; thou look'st cheerily, and I'll be with thee quickly. Yet thou liest in the bleak air. Come, I will bear thee to some shelter, and thou shalt not die for lack of a dinner if there live anything in this desert. Cheerily, good Adam.
                                                    Exeunt.

                        *

DUKE SENIOR
    I think he be transformed into a beast,
    For I can nowhere find him like a man.

1 . LORD
    My lord, he is but even now gone hence ;
    Here was he merry, hearing of a song.

DUKE SENIOR
    If he, compact of jars, grow musical,   5
    We shall have shortly discord in the spheres.   6
    Go seek him ; tell him I would speak with him.
        Enter Jaques.

1 . LORD
    He saves my labor by his own approach.

DUKE SENIOR
    Why, how now, monsieur, what a life is this,
    That your poor friends must woo your company ?
    What, you look merrily.

JAQUES
    A fool, a fool ! I met a fool i' th' forest,
    A motley fool ! a miserable world !   13
    As I do live by food, I met a fool
    Who laid him down and basked him in the sun
    And railed on Lady Fortune in good terms,
    In good set terms, and yet a motley fool.
    'Good morrow, fool,' quoth I. 'No, sir,' quoth he,
    'Call me not fool till heaven hath sent me fortune.'
    And then he drew a dial from his poke,   20
    And looking on it with lack-lustre eye,
    Says very wisely, 'It is ten o'clock.
    Thus we may see,' quoth he, 'how the world wags.
    'Tis but an hour ago since it was nine,
    And after one hour more 'twill be eleven ;
    And so, from hour to hour, we ripe and ripe,   26
    And then, from hour to hour, we rot and rot ;
    And thereby hangs a tale.' When I did hear
    The motley fool thus moral on the time,   29
    My lungs began to crow like chanticleer   30
    That fools should be so deep contemplative ;

32 And I did laugh sans intermission
    An hour by his dial. O noble fool,
34 A worthy fool! Motley 's the only wear.

DUKE SENIOR
    What fool is this?

JAQUES
    O worthy fool! One that hath been a courtier,
    And says, if ladies be but young and fair,
    They have the gift to know it. And in his brain,
39 Which is as dry as the remainder biscuit
    After a voyage, he hath strange places crammed
    With observation, the which he vents
    In mangled forms. O that I were a fool!
    I am ambitious for a motley coat.

DUKE SENIOR
    Thou shalt have one.

44 JAQUES   It is my only suit,
    Provided that you weed your better judgments
    Of all opinion that grows rank in them
    That I am wise. I must have liberty
48 Withal, as large a charter as the wind,
    To blow on whom I please, for so fools have.
50 And they that are most gallèd with my folly,
    They most must laugh. And why, sir, must they so?
    The why is plain as way to parish church:
    He that a fool doth very wisely hit
    Doth very foolishly, although he smart
55 Within, seem senseless of the bob. If not,
56 The wise man's folly is anatomized
57 Even by the squand'ring glances of the fool.
    Invest me in my motley, give me leave
    To speak my mind, and I will through and through
    Cleanse the foul body of th' infected world,
    If they will patiently receive my medicine.

DUKE SENIOR
    Fie on thee! I can tell what thou wouldst do.

JAQUES
63 What, for a counter, would I do but good?

DUKE SENIOR
    Most mischievous foul sin, in chiding sin.
    For thou thyself hast been a libertine,
66 As sensual as the brutish sting itself;
67 And all th' embossèd sores and headed evils
68 That thou with license of free foot hast caught,
    Wouldst thou disgorge into the general world.

JAQUES
    Why, who cries out on pride
71 That can therein tax any private party?
    Doth it not flow as hugely as the sea
73 Till that the weary very means do ebb?
    What woman in the city do I name
    When that I say the city woman bears
    The cost of princes on unworthy shoulders?
    Who can come in and say that I mean her,
    When such a one as she, such is her neighbor?
79 Or what is he of basest function
80 That says his bravery is not on my cost,
81 Thinking that I mean him, but therein suits
    His folly to the mettle of my speech?
    There then, how then, what then? Let me see wherein
    My tongue hath wronged him. If it do him right,
85 Then he hath wronged himself. If he be free,
    Why, then my taxing like a wild goose flies
    Unclaimed of any man. But who comes here?

Enter Orlando [with his sword drawn].

ORLANDO
    Forbear, and eat no more!

JAQUES   Why, I have eat none yet.

ORLANDO
    Nor shalt not, till necessity be served.

JAQUES
    Of what kind should this cock come of?

DUKE SENIOR
    Art thou thus boldened, man, by thy distress,
    Or else a rude despiser of good manners,
    That in civility thou seem'st so empty?

ORLANDO
    You touched my vein at first. The thorny point   94
    Of bare distress hath ta'en from me the show
    Of smooth civility; yet am I inland bred   96
    And know some nurture. But forbear, I say!   97
    He dies that touches any of this fruit
    Till I and my affairs are answerèd.   99

JAQUES
    An you will not be answered with reason, I must die. 100

DUKE SENIOR
    What would you have? Your gentleness shall force
    More than your force move us to gentleness.

ORLANDO
    I almost die for food, and let me have it!

DUKE SENIOR
    Sit down and feed, and welcome to our table.

ORLANDO
    Speak you so gently? Pardon me, I pray you.
    I thought that all things had been savage here,
    And therefore put I on the countenance   108
    Of stern commandment. But whate'er you are
    That in this desert inaccessible,
    Under the shade of melancholy boughs,
    Lose and neglect the creeping hours of time;
    If ever you have looked on better days,
    If ever been where bells have knolled to church,   114
    If ever sat at any good man's feast,
    If ever from your eyelids wiped a tear
    And know what 'tis to pity and be pitied,
    Let gentleness my strong enforcement be;   118
    In the which hope I blush, and hide my sword.   119

DUKE SENIOR
    True is it that we have seen better days,
    And have with holy bell been knolled to church,
    And sat at good men's feasts, and wiped our eyes
    Of drops that sacred pity hath engend'red;
    And therefore sit you down in gentleness,

32 *sans* without   34 *wear* costume   39 *dry* (a dry brain was supposedly
retentive)   44 *suit* (1) costume, (2) request   48 *large a charter* broad license
50 *gallèd* rubbed on a sore spot   55 *senseless of the bob* unaware of the taunt;
If not if he does not acknowledge the hit   56 *anatomized* revealed, as by
dissection   57 *squand'ring glances* random hits   63 *counter* worthless coin
66 *brutish sting* carnal appetite   67 *embossèd* swollen (the image here is from
venereal disease)   68 *license . . . foot* licentious freedom   71 *tax* censure
73 *weary . . . ebb* i.e. ostentation subsides from exhaustion   79 *function*
position in society   80 *says . . . cost* says his finery is not bought at my price,
i.e. denies my criticism   81–82 *therein . . . speech* thus matches his folly
with the substance of my remarks   85 *free* i.e. from blame   94 *vein* condition   96 *inland bred* raised in civilized society   97 *nurture* proper upbringing   99 *answerèd* given attention   100 *An* if; *reason* (perhaps a
homonymic pun on 'raisin,' i.e. grape, as Jaques takes fruit from the table)
108 *countenance* appearance   114 *knolled* called by chimes   118 *enforcement* inducement   119 *blush* (original sense 'glow')

125   And take upon command what help we have
     That to your wanting may be minist'red.

ORLANDO
     Then but forbear your food a little while,
     Whiles, like a doe, I go to find my fawn
     And give it food. There is an old poor man
     Who after me hath many a weary step
     Limped in pure love. Till he be first sufficed,
     Oppressed with two weak evils, age and hunger,
     I will not touch a bit.

DUKE SENIOR   Go find him out,
     And we will nothing waste till you return.

ORLANDO
     I thank ye, and be blest for your good comfort!   *[Exit.]*

DUKE SENIOR
     Thou seest we are not all alone unhappy :
     This wide and universal theatre
     Presents more woeful pageants than the scene
     Wherein we play in.

139 JAQUES   All the world's a stage,
     And all the men and women merely players ;
     They have their exits and their entrances,
     And one man in his time plays many parts,
     His acts being seven ages. At first, the infant,
144   Mewling and puking in the nurse's arms.
     Then the whining schoolboy, with his satchel
     And shining morning face, creeping like snail
     Unwillingly to school. And then the lover,
     Sighing like furnace, with a woeful ballad
     Made to his mistress' eyebrow. Then a soldier,
150   Full of strange oaths and bearded like the pard,
151   Jealous in honor, sudden and quick in quarrel,
     Seeking the bubble reputation
     Even in the cannon's mouth. And then the justice,
154   In fair round belly with good capon lined,
     With eyes severe and beard of formal cut,
156   Full of wise saws and modern instances ;
     And so he plays his part. The sixth age shifts
158   Into the lean and slippered pantaloon,
     With spectacles on nose and pouch on side ;
     His youthful hose, well saved, a world too wide
     For his shrunk shank, and his big manly voice,
     Turning again toward childish treble, pipes
163   And whistles in his sound. Last scene of all,
     That ends this strange eventful history,
     Is second childishness and mere oblivion,
166   Sans teeth, sans eyes, sans taste, sans everything.

Enter Orlando, with Adam.

DUKE SENIOR
     Welcome. Set down your venerable burden
     And let him feed.

ORLANDO
     I thank you most for him.

ADAM   So had you need.
     I scarce can speak to thank you for myself.

DUKE SENIOR
     Welcome, fall to. I will not trouble you
     As yet to question you about your fortunes.
     Give us some music ; and, good cousin, sing.

Song.

[AMIENS]   Blow, blow, thou winter wind,
       Thou art not so unkind
          As man's ingratitude :
       Thy tooth is not so keen,
       Because thou art not seen,   178
          Although thy breath be rude.
    Heigh-ho, sing heigh-ho, unto the green holly.
    Most friendship is faining, most loving mere folly :   181
          Then, heigh-ho, the holly.
          This life is most jolly.

       Freeze, freeze, thou bitter sky
       That dost not bite so nigh
          As benefits forgot :
       Though thou the waters warp,   187
       Thy sting is not so sharp
          As friend rememb'red not.
    Heigh-ho, sing, &c.

DUKE SENIOR
     If that you were the good Sir Rowland's son,
     As you have whispered faithfully you were,
     And as mine eye doth his effigies witness   193
     Most truly limned and living in your face,   194
     Be truly welcome hither. I am the Duke
     That loved your father. The residue of your fortune
     Go to my cave and tell me. Good old man,   197
     Thou art right welcome, as thy master is.
     Support him by the arm. Give me your hand,
     And let me all your fortunes understand.   *Exeunt.*

*

Enter Duke [Frederick], Lords, and Oliver.   III, i

DUKE FREDERICK
     Not see him since ? Sir, sir, that cannot be.
     But were I not the better part made mercy,
     I should not seek an absent argument   3
     Of my revenge, thou present. But look to it :   4
     Find out thy brother, wheresoe'er he is ;
     Seek him with candle ; bring him dead or living
     Within this twelvemonth, or turn thou no more   7
     To seek a living in our territory.
     Thy lands, and all things that thou dost call thine
     Worth seizure, do we seize into our hands
     Till thou canst quit thee by thy brother's mouth   11
     Of what we think against thee.

OLIVER
     O that your Highness knew my heart in this !
     I never loved my brother in my life.

DUKE FREDERICK
     More villain thou. Well, push him out of doors,
     And let my officers of such a nature
     Make an extent upon his house and lands.   17
     Do this expediently and turn him going.   *Exeunt.*

---

125 *upon command* for the asking   139 *All . . . stage* (a stock metaphor in classical and Renaissance literature, here given fresh vividness)   144 *Mewling* crying ; *puking* vomiting   150 *pard* leopard   151 *Jealous in* zealous in seeking ; *sudden* rash   154 *capon* (alluding to the well-known Elizabethan practice of offering a gift of a capon to a judge, in hope of gaining his favor)   156 *saws* maxims ; *modern instances* everyday examples   158 *pantaloon* ridiculous old man (a figure in Italian comedy)   163 *his* its   166 *s.d. Enter . . . Adam* (see Introduction)   178 *not seen* (hence, not personal) 181 *faining* longing, wishful thinking   187 *warp* freeze   193 *effigies* replica (accent on second syllable)   194 *limned* portrayed   197 *Go* walk III, i *Within* Duke Frederick's palace   3 *argument* subject, i.e. Orlando 4 *thou present* you being present   7 *turn* return   11 *quit* acquit   17 *Make . . . upon* seize by writ

*

III, ii   *Enter Orlando [, with a writing].*

ORLANDO

Hang there, my verse, in witness of my love;

2   And thou, thrice-crownèd Queen of Night, survey
With thy chaste eye, from thy pale sphere above,

4   Thy huntress' name that my full life doth sway.
O Rosalind! these trees shall be my books,

6   And in their barks my thoughts I'll character,
That every eye which in this forest looks

8   Shall see thy virtue witnessed everywhere.
Run, run, Orlando, carve on every tree

10   The fair, the chaste, and unexpressive she.   *Exit.*

Enter Corin and [Touchstone the] Clown.

CORIN   And how like you this shepherd's life, Master
Touchstone?

13   TOUCHSTONE   Truly, shepherd, in respect of itself, it is a
good life; but in respect that it is a shepherd's life, it is
naught. In respect that it is solitary, I like it very well;

16   but in respect that it is private, it is a very vile life. Now
in respect it is in the fields, it pleaseth me well; but in
respect it is not in the court, it is tedious. As it is a spare

19   life, look you, it fits my humor well; but as there is no
more plenty in it, it goes much against my stomach.
Hast any philosophy in thee, shepherd?

CORIN   No more but that I know the more one sickens the
worse at ease he is; and that he that wants money,
means, and content is without three good friends; that
the property of rain is to wet and fire to burn; that good
pasture makes fat sheep, and that a great cause of the
night is lack of the sun; that he that hath learned no wit

28   by nature nor art may complain of good breeding, or
comes of a very dull kindred.

TOUCHSTONE   Such a one is a natural philosopher. Wast
ever in court, shepherd?

CORIN   No, truly.

TOUCHSTONE   Then thou art damned.

CORIN   Nay, I hope.

TOUCHSTONE   Truly thou art damned, like an ill-
roasted egg, all on one side.

CORIN   For not being at court? Your reason.

TOUCHSTONE   Why, if thou never wast at court, thou
never saw'st good manners; if thou never saw'st good

39   manners, then thy manners must be wicked; and
wickedness is sin, and sin is damnation. Thou art in a

41   parlous state, shepherd.

CORIN   Not a whit, Touchstone. Those that are good
manners at the court are as ridiculous in the country as
the behavior of the country is most mockable at the

46   court. You told me you salute not at the court but you
kiss your hands. That courtesy would be uncleanly if
courtiers were shepherds.

49   TOUCHSTONE   Instance, briefly; come, instance.

50   CORIN   Why, we are still handling our ewes, and their

51   fells you know are greasy.

TOUCHSTONE   Why, do not your courtier's hands sweat?
and is not the grease of a mutton as wholesome as the
sweat of a man? Shallow, shallow. A better instance, I
say; come.

CORIN   Besides, our hands are hard.

TOUCHSTONE   Your lips will feel them the sooner. Shallow again. A more sounder instance, come.

59   CORIN   And they are often tarred over with the surgery of
our sheep, and would you have us kiss tar? The courtier's hands are perfumed with civet.

TOUCHSTONE   Most shallow man! Thou worms' meat in   62
respect of a good piece of flesh indeed! Learn of the wise,
and perpend. Civet is of a baser birth than tar, the very   64
uncleanly flux of a cat. Mend the instance, shepherd.   65

CORIN   You have too courtly a wit for me; I'll rest.

TOUCHSTONE   Wilt thou rest damned? God help thee,
shallow man! God make incision in thee! thou art raw.   68

CORIN   Sir, I am a true laborer; I earn that I eat, get that I
wear, owe no man hate, envy no man's happiness, glad
of other men's good, content with my harm; and the
greatest of my pride is to see my ewes graze and my
lambs suck.

TOUCHSTONE   That is another simple sin in you: to bring
the ewes and the rams together and to offer to get your
living by the copulation of cattle, to be bawd to a bellwether and to betray a she-lamb of a twelvemonth to a
crookèd-pated old cuckoldly ram, out of all reasonable   78
match. If thou beest not damned for this, the devil himself will have no shepherds; I cannot see else how thou
shouldst 'scape.

CORIN   Here comes young Master Ganymede, my new
mistress's brother.

Enter Rosalind [, with a writing].

ROSALIND   *[reads]*

'From the east to western Inde,
No jewel is like Rosalinde.
Her worth, being mounted on the wind,
Through all the world bears Rosalinde.
All the pictures fairest lined   87
Are but black to Rosalinde.
Let no face be kept in mind
But the fair of Rosalinde.'

TOUCHSTONE   I'll rhyme you so eight years together,
dinners and suppers and sleeping hours excepted. It is   92
the right butterwomen's rank to market.

ROSALIND   Out, fool!

TOUCHSTONE   For a taste:
If a hart do lack a hind,
Let him seek out Rosalinde.
If the cat will after kind,
So be sure will Rosalinde.
Wintred garments must be lined,   100
So must slender Rosalinde.
They that reap must sheaf and bind,
Then to cart with Rosalinde.   103
Sweetest nut hath sourest rind,
Such a nut is Rosalinde.
He that sweetest rose will find
Must find love's prick, and Rosalinde.

III, ii The Forest of Arden   2 *thrice-crownèd . . . Night* the moon (the triple crowning probably refers to the three goddesses associated with the moon: Cynthia, Diana, Proserpina)   4 *Thy huntress' name* (Rosalind is conceived as a chaste huntress waiting on Diana)   6 *character* inscribe   8 *virtue* excellence   10 *unexpressive* beyond expression   13 *in respect of* considering   16 *private* lonely   19 *humor* state of mind   28 *complain of* decry the lack of   39 *manners* (Touchstone plays on the meanings 'eti-quette' and 'morals')   41 *parlous* perilous   46 *but* unless   49 *Instance* proof   50 *still* continually   51 *fells* fleeces   59 *tarred . . . surgery* covered with the tar used as ointment for sores   62 *worms' meat* food for worms, moribund flesh   64 *perpend* consider   65 *flux* secretion   68 *make incision in* operate on; *raw* crude (with play on 'sore,' requiring operation)   78 *crookèd-pated* with crooked horns; *cuckoldly* i.e. because he has horns   87 *lined* outlined, drawn   92–93 *It is . . . market* i.e. the verses jog on monotonously like farm women riding to market   100 *Wintred* prepared for winter   103 *to cart* (female delinquents were publicly carted through the streets)

108 This is the very false gallop of verses. Why do you infect yourself with them?

ROSALIND Peace, you dull fool! I found them on a tree.

TOUCHSTONE Truly the tree yields bad fruit.

112 ROSALIND I'll graff it with you and then I shall graff it
113 with a medlar. Then it will be the earliest fruit i' th' country; for you'll be rotten ere you be half ripe, and that's the right virtue of the medlar.

TOUCHSTONE You have said; but whether wisely or no, let the forest judge.

Enter Celia, with a writing.

ROSALIND Peace! Here comes my sister reading; stand aside.

CELIA 'Why should this a desert be?
  For it is unpeopled? No.
  Tongues I'll hang on every tree
122 That shall civil sayings show:
  Some, how brief the life of man
  Runs his erring pilgrimage,
125 That the stretching of a span
126 Buckles in his sum of age;
  Some, of violated vows
  'Twixt the souls of friend and friend;
  But upon the fairest boughs,
  Or at every sentence end,
  Will I "Rosalinda" write,
  Teaching all that read to know
133 The quintessence of every sprite
134 Heaven would in little show.
  Therefore heaven Nature charged
  That one body should be filled
  With all graces wide-enlarged.
  Nature presently distilled
139 Helen's cheek, but not her heart,
  Cleopatra's majesty,
141 Atalanta's better part,
  Sad Lucretia's modesty.
  Thus Rosalinde of many parts
  By heavenly synod was devised,
  Of many faces, eyes, and hearts,
146 To have the touches dearest prized.
  Heaven would that she these gifts should have,
  And I to live and die her slave.'

149 ROSALIND O most gentle Jupiter, what tedious homily of love have you wearied your parishioners withal, and never cried, 'Have patience, good people'!

CELIA How now? Back, friends. Shepherd, go off a little. Go with him, sirrah.

TOUCHSTONE Come, shepherd, let us make an honorable retreat; though not with bag and baggage, yet with scrip and scrippage.   *Exit [with Corin].* 156

CELIA Didst thou hear these verses?

ROSALIND O, yes, I heard them all, and more too; for some of them had in them more feet than the verses would bear.

CELIA That's no matter. The feet might bear the verses.

ROSALIND Ay, but the feet were lame, and could not bear themselves without the verse, and therefore stood lamely in the verse.

CELIA But didst thou hear without wondering how thy name should be hanged and carved upon these trees?

ROSALIND I was seven of the nine days out of the wonder 166
before you came; for look here what I found on a palm 167
tree. I was never so berhymed since Pythagoras' time 168
that I was an Irish rat, which I can hardly remember. 169

CELIA Trow you who hath done this?   170

ROSALIND Is it a man?

CELIA And a chain that you once wore, about his neck. Change you color?

ROSALIND I prithee who?

CELIA O Lord, Lord, it is a hard matter for friends to meet; but mountains may be removed with earth- 176
quakes, and so encounter.   177

ROSALIND Nay, but who is it?

CELIA Is it possible?

ROSALIND Nay, I prithee now with most petitionary 180
vehemence, tell me who it is.

CELIA O wonderful, wonderful, and most wonderful wonderful, and yet again wonderful, and after that, out 183
of all hooping!

ROSALIND Good my complexion! Dost thou think, 185
though I am caparisoned like a man, I have a doublet 186
and hose in my disposition? One inch of delay more is a 187
South Sea of discovery. I prithee tell me who is it quickly, and speak apace. I would thou couldst stammer, that thou mightst pour this concealed man out of thy mouth as wine comes out of a narrow-mouthed bottle; either too much at once, or none at all. I prithee take the cork out of thy mouth, that I may drink thy tidings.

CELIA So you may put a man in your belly.

ROSALIND Is he of God's making? What manner of man? 195
Is his head worth a hat? or his chin worth a beard?

CELIA Nay, he hath but a little beard.

ROSALIND Why, God will send more, if the man will be thankful. Let me stay the growth of his beard, if thou delay me not the knowledge of his chin.

CELIA It is young Orlando, that tripped up the wrestler's heels and your heart both in an instant.

ROSALIND Nay, but the devil take mocking! Speak sad 203
brow and true maid.

CELIA I' faith, coz, 'tis he.

ROSALIND Orlando?

CELIA Orlando.

ROSALIND Alas the day! what shall I do with my doublet and hose? What did he when thou saw'st him? What said he? How looked he? Wherein went he? What 210
makes he here? Did he ask for me? Where remains he? 211

108 *false gallop* gallop starting on wrong foot   112 *graff* graft   113 *medlar* a kind of pear not ready to eat until it starts to decay (with pun on 'meddler')   122 *civil sayings* civilized comments   125 *stretching of a span* breadth of an open hand   126 *Buckles in* encompasses   133 *quintessence* pure essence (accent on first syllable); *sprite* spirit   134 *in little* i.e. in one person, the microcosm   139 *cheek* beauty; *heart* i.e. false heart   141 *Atalanta's better part* i.e. her beauty and swiftness, as opposed to her cruelty   146 *touches* features   149 *Jupiter* (frequently emended to 'pulpiter')   156 *scrip and scrippage* shepherd's pouch and its contents   166 *nine days* (a reference to the common expression 'a nine days' wonder')   167 *palm* (Lodge, in *Rosalynde*, mentions a palm tree in one of his euphuistic aphorisms)   168 *Pythagoras* (to whom was attributed the doctrine of transmigration of souls)   169 *Irish rat* (alluding to the belief that Irish sorcerers could kill animals by means of rhymed spells)   170 *Trow you* have you any idea   176 *removed with* moved by   177 *encounter* be brought together   180 *petitionary* suppliant   183–84 *out of all hooping* beyond all measure   185 *Good my complexion* O my (feminine) temperament   186 *caparisoned* bedecked (commonly used of horses)   187–88 *One . . . discovery* another minute of waiting will be as tedious as a journey to the South Seas for exploration   195 *of God's making* i.e. a real man, of flesh and blood   203–04 *sad . . . maid* seriously and truthfully   210 *Wherein went he* what did he wear   211 *makes* does

How parted he with thee? and when shalt thou see him again? Answer me in one word.

214 CELIA You must borrow me Gargantua's mouth first; 'tis a word too great for any mouth of this age's size. To say ay and no to these particulars is more than to answer in a catechism.

ROSALIND But doth he know that I am in this forest, and in man's apparel? Looks he as freshly as he did the day he wrestled?

221 CELIA It is as easy to count atomies as to resolve the propositions of a lover; but take a taste of my finding

223 him, and relish it with good observance. I found him under a tree, like a dropped acorn.

225 ROSALIND It may well be called Jove's tree when it drops such fruit.

CELIA Give me audience, good madam.

ROSALIND Proceed.

CELIA There lay he stretched along like a wounded knight.

ROSALIND Though it be pity to see such a sight, it well

231 becomes the ground.

232 CELIA Cry 'holla' to thy tongue, I prithee; it curvets unseasonably. He was furnished like a hunter.

234 ROSALIND O, ominous! he comes to kill my heart.

235 CELIA I would sing my song without a burden. Thou bring'st me out of tune.

ROSALIND Do you not know I am a woman? When I think, I must speak. Sweet, say on.

Enter Orlando and Jaques.

CELIA You bring me out. Soft. Comes he not here?

ROSALIND 'Tis he! Slink by, and note him.

JAQUES I thank you for your company; but, good faith, I had as lief have been myself alone.

ORLANDO And so had I; but yet for fashion sake I thank you too for your society.

JAQUES God b' wi' you; let's meet as little as we can.

ORLANDO I do desire we may be better strangers.

JAQUES I pray you mar no more trees with writing love songs in their barks.

249 ORLANDO I pray you mar no moe of my verses with
250 reading them ill-favoredly.

JAQUES Rosalind is your love's name?

ORLANDO Yes, just.

JAQUES I do not like her name.

ORLANDO There was no thought of pleasing you when she was christened.

JAQUES What stature is she of?

ORLANDO Just as high as my heart.

JAQUES You are full of pretty answers. Have you not
259 been acquainted with goldsmiths' wives, and conned them out of rings?

261 ORLANDO Not so; but I answer you right painted cloth, from whence you have studied your questions.

263 JAQUES You have a nimble wit; I think 'twas made of Atalanta's heels. Will you sit down with me? and we two will rail against our mistress the world and all our misery.

267 ORLANDO I will chide no breather in the world but myself, against whom I know most faults.

JAQUES The worst fault you have is to be in love.

ORLANDO 'Tis a fault I will not change for your best virtue. I am weary of you.

JAQUES By my troth, I was seeking for a fool when I found you.

ORLANDO He is drowned in the brook. Look but in and you shall see him.

JAQUES There I shall see mine own figure.

ORLANDO Which I take to be either a fool or a cipher.

JAQUES I'll tarry no longer with you. Farewell, good Signior Love.

ORLANDO I am glad of your departure. Adieu, good Monsieur Melancholy.   *[Exit Jaques.]*

ROSALIND I will speak to him like a saucy lackey, and under that habit play the knave with him. Do you hear, 283 forester?

ORLANDO Very well. What would you?

ROSALIND I pray you, what is't o'clock?

ORLANDO You should ask me, what time o' day. There's no clock in the forest.

ROSALIND Then there is no true lover in the forest, else sighing every minute and groaning every hour would detect the lazy foot of Time as well as a clock.   291

ORLANDO And why not the swift foot of Time? Had not that been as proper?

ROSALIND By no means, sir. Time travels in divers paces with divers persons. I'll tell you who Time ambles withal, who Time trots withal, who Time gallops 295 withal, and who he stands still withal.

ORLANDO I prithee, who doth he trot withal?

ROSALIND Marry, he trots hard with a young maid between the contract of her marriage and the day it is solemnized. If the interim be but a se'nnight, Time's 301 pace is so hard that it seems the length of seven year.

ORLANDO Who ambles Time withal?

ROSALIND With a priest that lacks Latin and a rich man that hath not the gout; for the one sleeps easily because he cannot study, and the other lives merrily because he feels no pain; the one lacking the burden of lean and wasteful learning, the other knowing no burden of 307 heavy tedious penury. These Time ambles withal.

ORLANDO Who doth he gallop withal?

ROSALIND With a thief to the gallows; for though he go as softly as foot can fall, he thinks himself too soon there. 312

ORLANDO Who stays it still withal?

ROSALIND With lawyers in the vacation; for they sleep between term and term, and then they perceive not how 315 time moves.

ORLANDO Where dwell you, pretty youth?

ROSALIND With this shepherdess, my sister; here in the skirts of the forest, like fringe upon a petticoat.

ORLANDO Are you native of this place?

ROSALIND As the cony that you see dwell where she is 321 kindled.   322

ORLANDO Your accent is something finer than you could purchase in so removed a dwelling.   324

ROSALIND I have been told so of many. But indeed an old

---

214 *Gargantua's mouth* (Rabelais' giant swallowed five pilgrims in a salad) 221 *atomies* motes   221–22 *resolve the propositions* answer the questions 223 *relish it* heighten it with sauce; *observance* attention   225 *Jove's tree* (the oak was sacred to Jupiter) 231 *becomes* adorns   232 *holla* halt; *curvets* prances   234 *heart* (quibble on 'hart')   235 *burden* undersong, refrain   249 *moe* more   250 *ill-favoredly* badly   259–60 *conned . . . rings* memorized them from the verses engraved in rings   261 *right painted cloth* cheap substitute tapestries, with painted pictures and mottoes   263–64 *Atalanta's heels* (Atalanta was speedy enough to outrun her suitors)   267 *breather* living creature   283 *habit* garb   291 *detect* call attention to   295 *withal* with you   301 *se'nnight* week   307 *wasteful* causing one to waste away   312 *softly* slowly   315 *term* court session   321 *cony* rabbit   322 *kindled* born   324 *purchase* acquire; *removed* remote

326 religious uncle of mine taught me to speak, who was in
327 his youth an inland man; one that knew courtship too
well, for there he fell in love. I have heard him read
many lectures against it; and I thank God I am not a
330 woman, to be touched with so many giddy offenses as he
hath generally taxed their whole sex withal.

ORLANDO Can you remember any of the principal evils
that he laid to the charge of women?

ROSALIND There were none principal. They were all like
one another as halfpence are, every one fault seeming
monstrous till his fellow-fault came to match it.

ORLANDO I prithee recount some of them.

ROSALIND No, I will not cast away my physic but on
those that are sick. There is a man haunts the forest that
abuses our young plants with carving 'Rosalind' on
their barks, hangs odes upon hawthorns, and elegies on
brambles; all, forsooth, deifying the name of Rosalind.
343 If I could meet that fancy-monger, I would give him
344 some good counsel, for he seems to have the quotidian
of love upon him.

ORLANDO I am he that is so love-shaked. I pray you tell
me your remedy.

ROSALIND There is none of my uncle's marks upon you.
349 He taught me how to know a man in love; in which cage
of rushes I am sure you are not a prisoner.

ORLANDO What were his marks?

352 ROSALIND A lean cheek, which you have not; a blue eye
353 and sunken, which you have not; an unquestionable
spirit, which you have not; a beard neglected, which you
355 have not: but I pardon you for that, for simply your
having in beard is a younger brother's revenue. Then
your hose should be ungartered, your bonnet unband-
ed, your sleeve unbuttoned, your shoe untied, and
everything about you demonstrating a careless desola-
360 tion. But you are no such man: you are rather point-
device in your accoutrements, as loving yourself than
seeming the lover of any other.

ORLANDO Fair youth, I would I could make thee believe
I love.

ROSALIND Me believe it? You may as soon make her that
you love believe it, which I warrant she is apter to do
than to confess she does; that is one of the points in the

which women still give the lie to their consciences. But
in good sooth, are you he that hangs the verses on the
trees wherein Rosalind is so admired?

ORLANDO I swear to thee, youth, by the white hand of
Rosalind, I am that he, that unfortunate he.

ROSALIND But are you so much in love as your rhymes
speak?

ORLANDO Neither rhyme nor reason can express how
much.

ROSALIND Love is merely a madness, and, I tell you,
deserves as well a dark house and a whip as madmen do; 377
and the reason why they are not so punished and cured
is that the lunacy is so ordinary that the whippers are in
love too. Yet I profess curing it by counsel.

ORLANDO Did you ever cure any so?

ROSALIND Yes, one, and in this manner. He was to imagine me his love, his mistress; and I set him every day to
woo me. At which time would I, being but a moonish 384
youth, grieve, be effeminate, changeable, longing and
liking, proud, fantastical, apish, shallow, inconstant,
full of tears, full of smiles; for every passion something
and for no passion truly anything, as boys and women
are for the most part cattle of this color; would now like
him, now loathe him; then entertain him, then forswear
him; now weep for him, then spit at him; that I drave
my suitor from his mad humor of love to a living humor 392
of madness, which was, to forswear the full stream of the
world and to live in a nook merely monastic. And thus I
cured him; and this way will I take upon me to wash
your liver as clean as a sound sheep's heart, that there 396
shall not be one spot of love in't.

ORLANDO I would not be cured, youth.

ROSALIND I would cure you, if you would but call me
Rosalind and come every day to my cote and woo me. 400

ORLANDO Now, by the faith of my love, I will. Tell me
where it is.

ROSALIND Go with me to it, and I'll show it you; and by
the way you shall tell me where in the forest you live.
Will you go?

ORLANDO With all my heart, good youth.

ROSALIND Nay, you must call me Rosalind. Come,
sister, will you go?   *Exeunt.*

*

---

326 *religious* in holy orders   327 *inland* (see II, vii, 96n.); *courtship* (quibble
on 'courtliness' and 'wooing')   330 *touched* tainted   343 *fancy-monger*
i.e. one who advertises his so-called love   344 *quotidian* daily fever   349–50
cage of rushes flimsy prison (with a glancing allusion to the 'rush rings'
used for mock marriages)   352 *blue eye* i.e. with dark circles   353 *unquestionable* unwilling to converse   355–56 *your having . . . revenue* you
have only a small portion of a beard   360–61 *point-device . . . accoutrements*
dressed with exactness   377 *a dark . . . whip* (the shock treatment by
which the Elizabethans attempted to cure insanity)   384 *moonish* fickle
392 *humor* state   396 *liver* (supposed to be the source of the passions,
especially love)   400 *cote* cottage
III, iii The Forest   3 *simple feature* plain appearance   4 *features* (Audrey
evidently misunderstands Touchstone, but the nature of the joke is
obscure)   5–7 *goats . . . Goths* (Ovid was exiled among the Goths, here
pronounced 'goats.' Touchstone quibbles on 'goats' and 'capricious,' the
latter deriving from Latin 'caper,' a male goat.)   7 *ill-inhabited* poorly
lodged   8 *Jove . . . house* (Jupiter, in human form, was once entertained
by two peasants in their thatched cottage)   9–11 *When . . . understanding*
i.e. Audrey has failed to appreciate Touchstone's wit, just as the Goths
failed to appreciate Ovid's poetry   11–12 *a great reckoning* in a large
bill for   16–18 *truest poetry . . . feign* (Touchstone apparently has in mind
here the first line of Sidney's *Astrophel and Stella*, 'Loving in truth,
and fain in verse my love to show.' But through his puns on 'fain' (desire)
and 'feign' (pretend) he is insinuating a carnal interpretation of 'poetic'
love.)

Enter [Touchstone the] Clown, Audrey; and Jaques   III, iii
[apart].

TOUCHSTONE Come apace, good Audrey. I will fetch up
your goats, Audrey. And how, Audrey, am I the man
yet? Doth my simple feature content you?   3

AUDREY Your features, Lord warrant us! What features? 4

TOUCHSTONE I am here with thee and thy goats, as the 5
most capricious poet, honest Ovid, was among the
Goths.

JAQUES [aside] O knowledge ill-inhabited, worse than 7
Jove in a thatched house!   8

TOUCHSTONE When a man's verses cannot be under-   9
stood, nor a man's good wit seconded with the forward
child, understanding, it strikes a man more dead than a 11
great reckoning in a little room. Truly, I would the gods
had made thee poetical.

AUDREY I do not know what poetical is. Is it honest in
deed and word? Is it a true thing?

TOUCHSTONE No, truly; for the truest poetry is the most 16

faining, and lovers are given to poetry, and what they swear in poetry may be said, as lovers, they do feign.

AUDREY Do you wish then that the gods had made me poetical?

TOUCHSTONE I do truly; for thou swear'st to me thou art honest. Now if thou wert a poet, I might have some hope thou didst feign.

AUDREY Would you not have me honest?

25 TOUCHSTONE No, truly, unless thou wert hard-favored;
26 for honesty coupled to beauty is to have honey a sauce to sugar.

28 JAQUES [aside] A material fool.

AUDREY Well, I am not fair, and therefore I pray the gods make me honest.

TOUCHSTONE Truly, and to cast away honesty upon a foul slut were to put good meat into an unclean dish.

33 AUDREY I am not a slut, though I thank the gods I am foul.

TOUCHSTONE Well, praised be the gods for thy foulness! Sluttishness may come hereafter. But be it as it may be,
36 I will marry thee; and to that end I have been with Sir Oliver Mar-text, the vicar of the next village, who hath promised to meet me in this place of the forest and to couple us.

JAQUES [aside] I would fain see this meeting.

AUDREY Well, the gods give us joy!

TOUCHSTONE Amen. A man may, if he were of a fearful heart, stagger in this attempt; for here we have no temple
44 but the wood, no assembly but horn-beasts. But what though? Courage! As horns are odious, they are necessary. It is said, 'Many a man knows no end of his goods.' Right! Many a man has good horns and knows no end of them. Well, that is the dowry of his wife; 'tis none of his own getting. Horns. Even so, poor men alone. No,
50 no; the noblest deer hath them as huge as the rascal. Is the single man therefore blessed? No; as a walled town is more worthier than a village, so is the forehead of a married man more honorable than the bare brow of a
54 bachelor; and by how much defense is better than no
55 skill, by so much is a horn more precious than to want.

Enter Sir Oliver Mar-text.

Here comes Sir Oliver. Sir Oliver Mar-text, you are
57 well met. Will you dispatch us here under this tree, or shall we go with you to your chapel?

OLIVER MAR-TEXT Is there none here to give the woman?

TOUCHSTONE I will not take her on gift of any man.

OLIVER MAR-TEXT Truly, she must be given, or the marriage is not lawful.

JAQUES [comes forward] Proceed, proceed; I'll give her.

64 TOUCHSTONE Good even, good Master What-ye-call't.
65 How do you, sir? You are very well met. Goddild you for your last company; I am very glad to see you. Even a
67 toy in hand here, sir. Nay, pray be covered.

JAQUES Will you be married, motley?

69 TOUCHSTONE As the ox hath his bow, sir, the horse his curb, and the falcon her bells, so man hath his desires; and as pigeons bill, so wedlock would be nibbling.

JAQUES And will you, being a man of your breeding, be
73 married under a bush like a beggar? Get you to church, and have a good priest that can tell you what marriage
75 is. This fellow will but join you together as they join wainscot; then one of you will prove a shrunk panel, and like green timber warp, warp.

TOUCHSTONE [aside] I am not in the mind but I were

better to be married of him than of another; for he is not like to marry me well; and not being well married, it will be a good excuse for me hereafter to leave my wife.

JAQUES Go thou with me and let me counsel thee.

TOUCHSTONE Come, sweet Audrey. We must be married, or we must live in bawdry. Fare well, good Master 84 Oliver: not

         O sweet Oliver,   86
         O brave Oliver,
         Leave me not behind thee;

but

         Wind away,
         Be gone, I say;
         I will not to wedding with thee.

       Exeunt [Jaques, Touchstone, and Audrey].

OLIVER MAR-TEXT 'Tis no matter. Ne'er a fantastical 93 knave of them all shall flout me out of my calling. [Exit.]

*

Enter Rosalind and Celia.   III, iv

ROSALIND Never talk to me; I will weep.

CELIA Do, I prithee; but yet have the grace to consider that tears do not become a man.

ROSALIND But have I not cause to weep?

CELIA As good cause as one would desire; therefore weep.

ROSALIND His very hair is of the dissembling color.   6

CELIA Something browner than Judas's. Marry, his kisses are Judas's own children.   8

ROSALIND I' faith, his hair is of a good color.

CELIA An excellent color. Your chestnut was ever the only color.

ROSALIND And his kissing is as full of sanctity as the touch of holy bread.

CELIA He hath bought a pair of cast lips of Diana. A nun 14 of winter's sisterhood kisses not more religiously; the 15 very ice of chastity is in them.

ROSALIND But why did he swear he would come this morning, and comes not?

CELIA Nay, certainly there is no truth in him.

ROSALIND Do you think so?

CELIA Yes; I think he is not a pickpurse nor a horse-stealer, but for his verity in love, I do think him as concave as a covered goblet or a worm-eaten nut.   23

ROSALIND Not true in love?

CELIA Yes, when he is in, but I think he is not in.

---

25 *hard-favored* ugly   26 *honesty* chastity (a meaning latent in Touchstone's earlier use of *honest*)   28 *material* making good sense   33 *foul* (Audrey interprets the word as 'ugly')   36 *Sir* (an old-fashioned designation for a clergyman)   44 *horn-beasts* (throughout this passage Touchstone plays on the old joke that cuckolds, i.e. men whose wives play them false, sprout horns)   50 *rascal* inferior deer   54 *defense* i.e. the art of defending oneself, probably fencing   55 *to want* i.e. to lack horns   57 *dispatch us* finish off our business   64 *Master What-ye-call't* (Touchstone calls attention to Jaques' name, which suggests the Elizabethan word for a privy, 'jakes')   65 *Goddild* God yield, i.e. reward   67 *toy* trifle   69 *bow* collar of the yoke   73 *married . . . bush* (Oliver is a 'hedge-priest,' i.e. uneducated, unable to expound the obligations of marriage)   75–76 *as . . . wainscot* i.e. as they set panelling together, without mortising or joining securely   84 *bawdry* immorality   86 ff. *O sweet Oliver . . .* (snatches from a current ballad)   93 *fantastical* affected

III, iv The Forest   6 *dissembling color* i.e. reddish, the traditional color of Judas' hair   8 *Judas's own children* i.e. offspring of a betrayer   14 *cast* (1) discarded, (2) statuary; perhaps with a play on 'chaste' (Diana was the goddess of chastity)   15 *of winter's sisterhood* i.e. sworn to coldness   23 *concave* hollow

ROSALIND You have heard him swear downright he was.

CELIA 'Was' is not 'is.' Besides, the oath of a lover is no stronger than the word of a tapster; they are both the confirmer of false reckonings. He attends here in the forest on the Duke your father.

ROSALIND I met the Duke yesterday and had much question with him. He asked me of what parentage I was. I told him, of as good as he; so he laughed and let me go. But what talk we of fathers when there is such a man as Orlando?

36 CELIA O, that's a brave man; he writes brave verses, speaks brave words, swears brave oaths, and breaks
38 them bravely, quite traverse, athwart the heart of his
39 lover, as a puisny tilter, that spurs his horse but on one
40 side, breaks his staff like a noble goose. But all's brave that youth mounts and folly guides. Who comes here?

Enter Corin.

CORIN
Mistress and master, you have oft enquired
After the shepherd that complained of love,
Who you saw sitting by me on the turf,
Praising the proud disdainful shepherdess
That was his mistress.

CELIA   Well, and what of him?

CORIN
47 If you will see a pageant truly played
Between the pale complexion of true love
And the red glow of scorn and proud disdain,
Go hence a little, and I shall conduct you,
If you will mark it.

ROSALIND   O, come, let us remove:
The sight of lovers feedeth those in love.
Bring us to this sight, and you shall say
I'll prove a busy actor in their play.   *Exeunt.*

*

III, v   *Enter Silvius and Phebe.*

SILVIUS
Sweet Phebe, do not scorn me; do not, Phebe!
Say that you love me not, but say not so
In bitterness. The common executioner,
Whose heart th'accustomed sight of death makes hard,
5 Falls not the axe upon the humbled neck
But first begs pardon. Will you sterner be
7 Than he that dies and lives by bloody drops?

Enter [apart] Rosalind, Celia, and Corin.

PHEBE
I would not be thy executioner.
I fly thee, for I would not injure thee.
Thou tell'st me there is murder in mine eye:
'Tis pretty, sure, and very probable

That eyes, that are the frail'st and softest things,
Who shut their coward gates on atomies,   13
Should be called tyrants, butchers, murderers.
Now I do frown on thee with all my heart,
And if mine eyes can wound, now let them kill thee.
Now counterfeit to swound; why, now fall down;   17
Or if thou canst not, O, for shame, for shame,
Lie not, to say mine eyes are murderers.
Now show the wound mine eye hath made in thee;
Scratch thee but with a pin, and there remains
Some scar of it; lean upon a rush,
The cicatrice and capable impressure   23
Thy palm some moment keeps; but now mine eyes,
Which I have darted at thee, hurt thee not,
Nor I am sure there is no force in eyes
That can do hurt.

SILVIUS   O dear Phebe,
If ever, as that ever may be near,
You meet in some fresh cheek the power of fancy,   29
Then shall you know the wounds invisible
That love's keen arrows make.

PHEBE   But till that time
Come thou not near me; and when that time comes,
Afflict me with thy mocks, pity me not,
As till that time I shall not pity thee.

ROSALIND
And why, I pray you? Who might be your mother,
That you insult, exult, and all at once,
Over the wretched? What though you have no beauty
(As, by my faith, I see no more in you
Than without candle may go dark to bed)   39
Must you be therefore proud and pitiless?
Why, what means this? Why do you look on me?
I see no more in you than in the ordinary   42
Of nature's sale-work. 'Od's my little life,   43
I think she means to tangle my eyes too!
No, faith, proud mistress, hope not after it;
'Tis not your inky brows, your black silk hair,
Your bugle eyeballs, nor your cheek of cream   47
That can entame my spirits to your worship.
You foolish shepherd, wherefore do you follow her,
Like foggy south, puffing with wind and rain?   50
You are a thousand times a properer man   51
Than she a woman. 'Tis such fools as you
That makes the world full of ill-favored children.
'Tis not her glass, but you, that flatters her,
And out of you she sees herself more proper
Than any of her lineaments can show her.
But mistress, know yourself. Down on your knees,
And thank heaven, fasting, for a good man's love;
For I must tell you friendly in your ear,
Sell when you can, you are not for all markets.
Cry the man mercy, love him, take his offer;   61
Foul is most foul, being foul to be a scoffer;   62
So take her to thee, shepherd. Fare you well.

PHEBE
Sweet youth, I pray you chide a year together;
I had rather hear you chide than this man woo.

ROSALIND *[aside]* He's fall'n in love with your foulness, and she'll fall in love with my anger. If it be so, as fast as she answers thee with frowning looks, I'll sauce her with bitter words. *[to Phebe]* Why look you so upon me?

PHEBE
For no ill will I bear you.

36 *brave* excellent   38 *traverse* (a term in tilting, for hitting an opponent sideways, awkwardly, instead of head-on)   39 *puisny* puny, i.e. inferior   40 *noble goose* grand fool   47 *pageant* performance   **III**, v The Forest   5 *Falls* lets fall   7 *dies and lives* makes his living   13 *atomies* motes   17 *counterfeit to swound* pretend to swoon   23 *cicatrice* mark (literally, scar); *capable impressure* i.e. impression capable of being seen   29 *fancy* love   39 *may . . . bed* i.e. she does not have the beauty which (metaphorically) illuminates the dark   42 *ordinary* common run   43 *sale-work* ready-made products, not distinctive   47 *bugle* glassy, with black center   50 *south* south wind   51 *properer* more handsome   61 *Cry . . . mercy* beg the man's pardon   62 *Foul is most foul* ugliness is most repulsive

263

ROSALIND
I pray you do not fall in love with me,
For I am falser than vows made in wine.
Besides, I like you not. If you will know my house,
'Tis at the tuft of olives, here hard by.
Will you go, sister? Shepherd, ply her hard.
Come, sister. Shepherdess, look on him better
And be not proud. Though all the world could see,
None could be so abused in sight as he.
Come, to our flock.   *Exit [with Celia and Corin].*

PHEBE
80   Dead shepherd, now I find thy saw of might,
81   'Who ever loved that loved not at first sight?'

SILVIUS
Sweet Phebe.

PHEBE   Ha! what say'st thou, Silvius?

SILVIUS
Sweet Phebe, pity me.

PHEBE
Why, I am sorry for thee, gentle Silvius.

SILVIUS
Wherever sorrow is, relief would be.
If you do sorrow at my grief in love,
By giving love your sorrow and my grief
88   Were both extermined.

PHEBE
89   Thou hast my love. Is not that neighborly?

SILVIUS
I would have you.

PHEBE   Why, that were covetousness.
Silvius, the time was that I hated thee;
92   And yet it is not that I bear thee love,
But since that thou canst talk of love so well,
Thy company, which erst was irksome to me,
I will endure; and I'll employ thee too;
But do not look for further recompense
Than thine own gladness that thou art employed.

SILVIUS
So holy and so perfect is my love,
And I in such a poverty of grace,
That I shall think it a most plenteous crop
To glean the broken ears after the man
That the main harvest reaps. Loose now and then
A scatt'red smile, and that I'll live upon.

PHEBE
Know'st thou the youth that spoke to me erewhile?

SILVIUS
Not very well, but I have met him oft,
And he hath bought the cottage and the bounds
107   That the old carlot once was master of.

PHEBE
Think not I love him, though I ask for him;
'Tis but a peevish boy; yet he talks well.
But what care I for words? Yet words do well
When he that speaks them pleases those that hear.
It is a pretty youth; not very pretty;
But sure he's proud; and yet his pride becomes him.
He'll make a proper man. The best thing in him
Is his complexion; and faster than his tongue
Did make offense, his eye did heal it up.
He is not very tall; yet for his years he's tall.
His leg is but so so; and yet 'tis well.
There was a pretty redness in his lip,
A little riper and more lusty red

Than that mixed in his cheek; 'twas just the difference
Betwixt the constant red and mingled damask.   122
There be some women, Silvius, had they marked him
In parcels as I did, would have gone near   124
To fall in love with him; but, for my part,
I love him not nor hate him not; and yet
I have more cause to hate him than to love him;
For what had he to do to chide at me?
He said mine eyes were black and my hair black;
And, now I am remember'd, scorned at me.   130
I marvel why I answered not again.
But that's all one: omittance is no quittance.   132
I'll write to him a very taunting letter,
And thou shalt bear it. Wilt thou, Silvius?

SILVIUS
Phebe, with all my heart.

PHEBE   I'll write it straight;   135
The matter's in my head and in my heart;
I will be bitter with him and passing short.   137
Go with me, Silvius.   *Exeunt.*

*

Enter Rosalind and Celia and Jaques.   IV, i

JAQUES I prithee, pretty youth, let me be better acquainted with thee.

ROSALIND They say you are a melancholy fellow.

JAQUES I am so; I do love it better than laughing.

ROSALIND Those that are in extremity of either are   5
abominable fellows, and betray themselves to every
modern censure worse than drunkards.   7

JAQUES Why, 'tis good to be sad and say nothing.

ROSALIND Why then, 'tis good to be a post.

JAQUES I have neither the scholar's melancholy, which is
emulation; nor the musician's, which is fantastical; nor   11
the courtier's, which is proud; nor the soldier's, which
is ambitious; nor the lawyer's, which is politic; nor the   13
lady's, which is nice; nor the lover's, which is all these: 14
but it is a melancholy of mine own, compounded of
many simples, extracted from many objects, and indeed   16
the sundry contemplation of my travels, which, by often   17
rumination, wraps me in a most humorous sadness.   18

ROSALIND A traveller! By my faith, you have great
reason to be sad. I fear you have sold your own lands to
see other men's. Then to have seen much and to have
nothing is to have rich eyes and poor hands.

JAQUES Yes, I have gained my experience.
Enter Orlando.

ROSALIND And your experience makes you sad. I had
rather have a fool to make me merry than experience
to make me sad: and to travel for it too.   26

---

80 *Dead shepherd* Christopher Marlowe (here referred to as a pastoral poet), who was killed in 1593; *saw* saying   81 *'Who . . . sight'* (Marlowe's *Hero and Leander* [pub. 1598], I, 175)   88 *extermined* expunged   89 *neighborly* (possibly a reference to the commandment 'Thou shalt love thy neighbor as thyself')   92 *it is not* the time has not come   107 *carlot* countryman 122 *mingled damask* pink and white, the colors of damask roses   124 *In parcels* part by part   130 *remember'd* reminded   132 *omittance is no quittance* i.e. failure to assert one's rights is not renunciation of them   135 *straight* straightway   137 *passing short* extremely curt
IV, i *The Forest*   5 *are in extremity* go to extremes   7 *modern* common 11 *emulation* envy; *fantastical* absurdly elaborate   13 *politic* a matter of policy (to appear learned)   14 *nice* over-refined   16 *simples* ingredients 17 *sundry* collected   18 *humorous* moody   26 *travel* (pun on 'travail,' i.e. labor)

ORLANDO Good day and happiness, dear Rosalind.

JAQUES Nay then, God b' wi' you, an you talk in blank
verse.

30 ROSALIND Farewell, Monsieur Traveller. Look you lisp
31 and wear strange suits, disable all the benefits of your
32 own country, be out of love with your nativity, and almost chide God for making you that countenance you
34 are; or I will scarce think you have swam in a gundello.
[Exit Jaques.]
Why, how now, Orlando, where have you been all this
while? You a lover? An you serve me such another
trick, never come in my sight more.

ORLANDO My fair Rosalind, I come within an hour of my
promise.

ROSALIND Break an hour's promise in love? He that will
divide a minute into a thousand parts and break but a
part of the thousand part of a minute in the affairs of
43 love, it may be said of him that Cupid hath clapped him
o' th' shoulder, but I'll warrant him heart-whole.

ORLANDO Pardon me, dear Rosalind.

ROSALIND Nay, an you be so tardy, come no more in my
sight. I had as lief be wooed of a snail.

ORLANDO Of a snail?

ROSALIND Ay, of a snail; for though he comes slowly, he
50 carries his house on his head; a better jointure, I think,
than you make a woman. Besides, he brings his destiny
with him.

ORLANDO What's that?

ROSALIND Why, horns; which such as you are fain to be
beholding to your wives for; but he comes armed in his
56 fortune and prevents the slander of his wife.

ORLANDO Virtue is no horn-maker, and my Rosalind is
virtuous.

ROSALIND And I am your Rosalind.

CELIA It pleases him to call you so; but he hath a Rosalind
61 of a better leer than you.

ROSALIND Come, woo me, woo me; for now I am in a
holiday humor and like enough to consent. What would
you say to me now, and I were your very very Rosalind?

ORLANDO I would kiss before I spoke.

ROSALIND Nay, you were better speak first, and when you
67 were gravelled for lack of matter, you might take occa-
68 sion to kiss. Very good orators, when they are out, they
69 will spit; and for lovers, lacking – God warn us! –
matter, the cleanliest shift is to kiss.

ORLANDO How if the kiss be denied?

ROSALIND Then she puts you to entreaty, and there
begins new matter.

ORLANDO Who could be out, being before his beloved
mistress?

ROSALIND Marry, that should you, if I were your mis-
tress, or I should think my honesty ranker than my wit. 77
ORLANDO What, of my suit? 78
ROSALIND Not out of your apparel, and yet out of your
suit. Am not I your Rosalind?
ORLANDO I take some joy to say you are, because I would
be talking of her.
ROSALIND Well, in her person, I say I will not have you.
ORLANDO Then, in mine own person, I die.
ROSALIND No, faith, die by attorney. The poor world is 85
almost six thousand years old, and in all this time there
was not any man died in his own person, videlicet, in a 87
love cause. Troilus had his brains dashed out with a 88
Grecian club; yet he did what he could to die before,
and he is one of the patterns of love. Leander, he would 90
have lived many a fair year though Hero had turned
nun, if it had not been for a hot midsummer night; for,
good youth, he went but forth to wash him in the
Hellespont, and being taken with the cramp, was
drowned; and the foolish chroniclers of that age found 95
it was 'Hero of Sestos.' But these are all lies. Men have
died from time to time, and worms have eaten them,
but not for love.
ORLANDO I would not have my right Rosalind of this
mind, for I protest her frown might kill me.
ROSALIND By this hand, it will not kill a fly. But come,
now I will be your Rosalind in a more coming-on 102
disposition; and ask me what you will, I will grant it.
ORLANDO Then love me, Rosalind.
ROSALIND Yes, faith, will I, Fridays and Saturdays and
all.
ORLANDO And wilt thou have me?
ROSALIND Ay, and twenty such.
ORLANDO What sayest thou?
ROSALIND Are you not good?
ORLANDO I hope so.
ROSALIND Why then, can one desire too much of a good
thing? Come, sister, you shall be the priest and marry
us. Give me your hand, Orlando. What do you say,
sister?
ORLANDO Pray thee marry us.
CELIA I cannot say the words.
ROSALIND You must begin, 'Will you, Orlando' –
CELIA Go to. Will you, Orlando, have to wife this Rosa- 117
lind?
ORLANDO I will.
ROSALIND Ay, but when?
ORLANDO Why now, as fast as she can marry us.
ROSALIND Then you must say, 'I take thee, Rosalind, for
wife.'
ORLANDO I take thee, Rosalind, for wife.
ROSALIND I might ask you for your commission; but I do 125
take thee, Orlando, for my husband. There's a girl goes 126
before the priest, and certainly a woman's thought runs
before her actions.
ORLANDO So do all thoughts; they are winged.
ROSALIND Now tell me how long you would have her
after you have possessed her.
ORLANDO For ever and a day.
ROSALIND Say 'a day,' without the 'ever.' No, no, Orlando; men are April when they woo, December when they
wed. Maids are May when they are maids, but the sky
changes when they are wives. I will be more jealous of
thee than a Barbary cock-pigeon over his hen, more 137

30 *lisp* i.e. use foreign sounds 31 *disable* disparage 32 *nativity* birthplace 34 *swam in a gundello* i.e. been to Venice, to ride in a gondola
43–44 *clapped him o' th' shoulder* accosted him 50 *jointure* marriage
settlement 56 *prevents* forestalls 61 *leer* look 67 *gravelled* stuck 68
out out of matter 69 *warn* save 77 *honesty* chastity; *ranker* less pure
78 *suit* plea (but Rosalind in reply puns on the word) 85 *by attorney* by
proxy 87 *videlicet* namely 88 *Troilus* the faithful lover of the faithless
Cressida in Chaucer's *Troilus and Criseyde* and earlier legends 88–89
brains . . . club (Rosalind's fiction is a travesty on Troilus) 90 *Leander*
the faithful lover in classical myth and Marlowe's *Hero and Leander*
(whose death Rosalind also travesties) 95–96 *foolish chroniclers . . . Sestos*
the dimwitted storytellers decided he died for love of Hero, the lady
of Sestos 102 *coming-on* yielding 117 *Go to* (equivalent to 'come now')
125 *commission* authority 126–27 *goes before* anticipates 137 *Barbary
cock-pigeon* the 'Barb' pigeon, which originally came from the north of
Africa

138 clamorous than a parrot against rain, more newfangled
than an ape, more giddy in my desires than a monkey.

140 I will weep for nothing, like Diana in the fountain, and
I will do that when you are disposed to be merry; I will
laugh like a hyen, and that when thou art inclined to sleep.

ORLANDO But will my Rosalind do so?

ROSALIND By my life, she will do as I do.

ORLANDO O, but she is wise.

ROSALIND Or else she could not have the wit to do this;
148 the wiser, the waywarder. Make the doors upon a
woman's wit, and it will out at the casement; shut that,
and 'twill out at the keyhole; stop that, 'twill fly with
the smoke out at the chimney.

ORLANDO A man that had a wife with such a wit, he
153 might say, 'Wit, whither wilt?'

154 ROSALIND Nay, you might keep that check for it till you
met your wife's wit going to your neighbor's bed.

ORLANDO And what wit could wit have to excuse that?

ROSALIND Marry, to say she came to seek you there. You
shall never take her without her answer unless you take
her without her tongue. O, that woman that cannot
160 make her fault her husband's occasion, let her never
161 nurse her child herself, for she will breed it like a fool.

ORLANDO For these two hours, Rosalind, I will leave thee.

ROSALIND Alas, dear love, I cannot lack thee two hours!

ORLANDO I must attend the Duke at dinner. By two
o'clock I will be with thee again.

ROSALIND Ay, go your ways, go your ways; I knew what
you would prove. My friends told me as much, and I
thought no less. That flattering tongue of yours won
me. 'Tis but one cast away, and so, come death! Two
o'clock is your hour?

ORLANDO Ay, sweet Rosalind.

ROSALIND By my troth, and in good earnest, and so God
mend me, and by all pretty oaths that are not dangerous,
if you break one jot of your promise or come one minute
176 behind your hour, I will think you the most pathetical
break-promise, and the most hollow lover, and the
most unworthy of her you call Rosalind, that may be
chosen out of the gross band of the unfaithful. Therefore beware my censure and keep your promise.

181 ORLANDO With no less religion than if thou wert indeed
my Rosalind. So adieu.

ROSALIND Well, Time is the old justice that examines all
such offenders, and let Time try. Adieu. *Exit [Orlando].*

CELIA You have simply misused our sex in your love-
prate. We must have your doublet and hose plucked
over your head, and show the world what the bird hath
done to her own nest.

ROSALIND O coz, coz, coz, my pretty little coz, that thou
didst know how many fathom deep I am in love! But
it cannot be sounded. My affection hath an unknown
192 bottom, like the Bay of Portugal.

CELIA Or rather, bottomless, that as fast as you pour
affection in, it runs out.

195 ROSALIND No, that same wicked bastard of Venus that
196 was begot of thought, conceived of spleen, and born of
madness, that blind rascally boy that abuses every one's
eyes because his own are out, let him be judge how deep
I am in love. I'll tell thee, Aliena, I cannot be out of the
sight of Orlando. I'll go find a shadow, and sigh till he
come.

CELIA And I'll sleep.   *Exeunt.*

*   *Enter Jaques; and Lords,[as] Foresters.*   IV, ii

JAQUES Which is he that killed the deer?

[1.] LORD Sir, it was I.

JAQUES Let's present him to the Duke like a Roman conqueror; and it would do well to set the deer's horns
upon his head for a branch of victory. Have you no
song, forester, for this purpose?

[2.] LORD Yes, sir.   7

JAQUES Sing it. 'Tis no matter how it be in tune, so it
make noise enough.

Music.

Song.

What shall he have that killed the deer?
His leather skin and horns to wear:
    Then sing him home. *(The rest shall bear this burden.)* 12
Take thou no scorn to wear the horn,
It was a crest ere thou wast born,
    Thy father's father wore it,
    And thy father bore it.
The horn, the horn, the lusty horn,
Is not a thing to laugh to scorn.   *Exeunt.*

*

Enter Rosalind and Celia.   IV, iii

ROSALIND How say you now, is it not past two o'clock?
And here much Orlando!

CELIA I warrant you, with pure love and troubled brain,
he hath ta'en his bow and arrows and is gone forth to
sleep.

Enter Silvius.

Look who comes here.

SILVIUS
My errand is to you, fair youth.
My gentle Phebe did bid me give you this.
    [Gives a letter.]
I know not the contents, but, as I guess
By the stern brow and waspish action
Which she did use as she was writing of it,
It bears an angry tenor. Pardon me;
I am but as a guiltless messenger.

ROSALIND
Patience herself would startle at this letter
And play the swaggerer. Bear this, bear all!
She says I am not fair, that I lack manners;
She calls me proud, and that she could not love me,
Were man as rare as phoenix. 'Od's my will!   18
Her love is not the hare that I do hunt.
Why writes she so to me? Well, shepherd, well,
This is a letter of your own device.

138 *against* in anticipation of   140 *Diana in the fountain* (Stow, in his
Survay of London, 1603, reported that in 1596 at 'the great Crosse in
West Cheape' was 'set up . . . an Alablaster Image of Diana, and water
convayed from the Thames, prilling from her naked brest.' Rosalind
changes the figure to weeping.)   148 *Make* make fast   153 *wilt* will you go
154 *check* retort   160 *make . . . occasion* make her husband the cause of her
fault   161 *breed* raise   176 *pathetical* pitiful   181 *With . . . religion* no
less religiously   192 *Bay of Portugal* (the sea off the coast of Portugal
was unplumbed)   195 *bastard of Venus* Cupid   196 *thought* i.e. fancy;
spleen impulse
IV, ii *The Forest*   7 *[2.] Lord* (speech sometimes assigned in modern
editions to Amiens the singer, who may have begun this song in which the
others join as they bear off the killer of the deer)   12 *burden* refrain
IV, iii *The Forest*   18 *phoenix* (there was supposed to be only one phoenix
in the world at a time)

SILVIUS

No, I protest, I know not the contents.
Phebe did write it.

ROSALIND   Come, come, you are a fool,
And turned into the extremity of love.
I saw her hand. She has a leathern hand,
26 A freestone-colored hand. I verily did think
That her old gloves were on, but 'twas her hands.
She has a housewife's hand; but that's no matter:
I say she never did invent this letter;
This is a man's invention and his hand.

SILVIUS

Sure it is hers.

ROSALIND

Why, 'tis a boisterous and a cruel style,
A style for challengers. Why, she defies me
Like Turk to Christian. Women's gentle brain
Could not drop forth such giant-rude invention,
Such Ethiop words, blacker in their effect
Than in their countenance. Will you hear the letter?

SILVIUS

So please you, for I never heard it yet;
Yet heard too much of Phebe's cruelty.

ROSALIND

40 She Phebes me. Mark how the tyrant writes.
(Read.) 'Art thou god, to shepherd turned,
That a maiden's heart hath burned?'
Can a woman rail thus?

SILVIUS   Call you this railing?

ROSALIND

45 *(Read.)* 'Why, thy godhead laid apart,
Warr'st thou with a woman's heart?'
Did you ever hear such railing?
'Whiles the eye of man did woo me,
49 That could do no vengeance to me.'
Meaning me a beast.
'If the scorn of your bright eyne
Have power to raise such love in mine,
Alack, in me what strange effect
54 Would they work in mild aspect!
Whiles you chid me, I did love;
How then might your prayers move!
He that brings this love to thee
Little knows this love in me;
59 And by him seal up thy mind,
60 Whether that thy youth and kind
Will the faithful offer take
Of me and all that I can make,
Or else by him my love deny,
And then I'll study how to die.'

SILVIUS

Call you this chiding?

CELIA   Alas, poor shepherd!

ROSALIND Do you pity him? No, he deserves no pity.

Wilt thou love such a woman? What, to make thee an 68
instrument, and play false strains upon thee? Not to be
endured! Well, go your way to her, for I see love hath
made thee a tame snake, and say this to her: that if she 71
love me, I charge her to love thee; if she will not, I will
never have her unless thou entreat for her. If you be a
true lover, hence, and not a word; for here comes more
company.   *Exit Silvius.*
Enter Oliver.

OLIVER

Good morrow, fair ones. Pray you, if you know,
Where in the purlieus of this forest stands
A sheepcote, fenced about with olive trees? 77

CELIA

West of this place, down in the neighbor bottom. 79
The rank of osiers by the murmuring stream 80
Left on your right hand brings you to the place.
But at this hour the house doth keep itself;
There's none within.

OLIVER

If that an eye may profit by a tongue,
Then should I know you by description,
Such garments and such years: 'The boy is fair,
Of female favor, and bestows himself 87
Like a ripe sister; the woman low, 88
And browner than her brother.' Are not you
The owner of the house I did enquire for?

CELIA

It is no boast, being asked, to say we are.

OLIVER

Orlando doth commend him to you both,
And to that youth he calls his Rosalind
He sends this bloody napkin. Are you he? 94

ROSALIND

I am. What must we understand by this?

OLIVER

Some of my shame, if you will know of me
What man I am, and how and why and where
This handkercher was stained.

CELIA   I pray you tell it.

OLIVER

When last the young Orlando parted from you,
He left a promise to return again
Within an hour; and pacing through the forest,
Chewing the food of sweet and bitter fancy,
Lo, what befell! He threw his eye aside,
And mark what object did present itself:
Under an old oak, whose boughs were mossed with age
And high top bald with dry antiquity,
A wretched ragged man, o'ergrown with hair,
Lay sleeping on his back; about his neck
A green and gilded snake had wreathed itself,
Who with her head, nimble in threats, approached
The opening of his mouth; but suddenly,
Seeing Orlando, it unlinked itself
And with indented glides did slip away 113
Into a bush, under which bush's shade
A lioness, with udders all drawn dry,
Lay couching, head on ground, with catlike watch 116
When that the sleeping man should stir; for 'tis
The royal disposition of that beast
To prey on nothing that doth seem as dead.
This seen, Orlando did approach the man
And found it was his brother, his elder brother.

26 *freestone* soft sandstone or limestone, yellowish brown 40 *Phebes me* addresses me with her characteristic cruelty 45 *thy . . . apart* i.e. as a god who has assumed human form 49 *vengeance* harm 54 *in mild aspect* i.e. if they looked on me pleasantly 59 *seal . . . mind* enclose your thoughts in a letter 60 *youth and kind* youthful nature 68–69 *make . . . upon thee* use you (with pun on *instrument*) and deceive you at the same time 71 *snake* i.e. base creature 77 *in the purlieus* within the borders 79 *neighbor bottom* nearby valley 80 *rank of osiers* row of willows 87 *favor* features; *bestows* conducts 88 *ripe* mature 94 *napkin* handkerchief 113 *indented* sinuous 116 *couching* crouched

CELIA
O, I have heard him speak of that same brother,
123 And he did render him the most unnatural
That lived amongst men.
OLIVER   And well he might so do,
For well I know he was unnatural.
ROSALIND
But, to Orlando : did he leave him there,
Food to the sucked and hungry lioness ?
OLIVER
Twice did he turn his back and purposed so ;
129 But kindness, nobler ever than revenge,
And nature, stronger than his just occasion,
Made him give battle to the lioness,
132 Who quickly fell before him ; in which hurtling
From miserable slumber I awaked.
CELIA
Are you his brother ?
ROSALIND   Was it you he rescued ?
CELIA
Was't you that did so oft contrive to kill him ?
OLIVER
'Twas I. But 'tis not I. I do not shame
To tell you what I was, since my conversion
So sweetly tastes, being the thing I am.
ROSALIND
But, for the bloody napkin ?
139 OLIVER   By and by.
When from the first to last, betwixt us two,
141 Tears our recountments had most kindly bathed,
As how I came into that desert place :
In brief, he led me to the gentle Duke,
Who gave me fresh array and entertainment,
Committing me unto my brother's love,
Who led me instantly unto his cave,
There stripped himself, and here upon his arm
The lioness had torn some flesh away,
Which all this while had bled ; and now he fainted,
And cried, in fainting, upon Rosalind.
151 Brief, I recovered him, bound up his wound ;
And after some small space, being strong at heart,
He sent me hither, stranger as I am,
To tell this story, that you might excuse
His broken promise, and to give this napkin,
Dyed in his blood, unto the shepherd youth
That he in sport doth call his Rosalind.
      [Rosalind swoons.]
CELIA
Why, how now, Ganymede, sweet Ganymede !
OLIVER
Many will swoon when they do look on blood.
CELIA
There is more in it. Cousin Ganymede !
OLIVER
Look, he recovers.
ROSALIND
I would I were at home.
CELIA   We'll lead you thither.
I pray you, will you take him by the arm ?
OLIVER Be of good cheer, youth. You a man ! You lack a
man's heart.
ROSALIND I do so, I confess it. Ah, sirrah, a body would
167 think this was well counterfeited. I pray you tell your
brother how well I counterfeited. Heigh-ho !

OLIVER This was not counterfeit. There is too great testi-
mony in your complexion that it was a passion of earnest. 170
ROSALIND Counterfeit, I assure you.
OLIVER Well then, take a good heart and counterfeit to be
a man.
ROSALIND So I do ; but, i' faith, I should have been a
woman by right.
CELIA Come, you look paler and paler. Pray you draw
homewards. Good sir, go with us.
OLIVER
That will I, for I must bear answer back
How you excuse my brother, Rosalind.
ROSALIND I shall devise something. But I pray you com-
mend my counterfeiting to him. Will you go ?   Exeunt.

                   *

     Enter [Touchstone the] Clown and Audrey.   V, i
TOUCHSTONE We shall find a time, Audrey. Patience,
gentle Audrey.
AUDREY Faith, the priest was good enough, for all the old
gentleman's saying.
TOUCHSTONE A most wicked Sir Oliver, Audrey, a most
vile Mar-text. But, Audrey, there is a youth here in the
forest lays claim to you.
AUDREY Ay, I know who 'tis. He hath no interest in me
in the world. Here comes the man you mean.
     Enter William.
TOUCHSTONE It is meat and drink to me to see a clown ; 10
by my troth, we that have good wits have much to
answer for. We shall be flouting ; we cannot hold.   12
WILLIAM Good ev'n, Audrey.
AUDREY God ye good ev'n, William.
WILLIAM And good ev'n to you, sir.
TOUCHSTONE Good ev'n, gentle friend. Cover thy head,
cover thy head. Nay, prithee be covered. How old are
you, friend ?
WILLIAM Five-and-twenty, sir.
TOUCHSTONE A ripe age. Is thy name William ?
WILLIAM William, sir.
TOUCHSTONE A fair name. Wast born i' th' forest here ?
WILLIAM Ay, sir, I thank God.
TOUCHSTONE 'Thank God.' A good answer. Art rich ?
WILLIAM Fair, sir, so so.
TOUCHSTONE 'So so' is good, very good, very excellent
good ; and yet it is not, it is but so so. Art thou wise ?
WILLIAM Ay, sir, I have a pretty wit.
TOUCHSTONE Why, thou say'st well. I do now remem- 29
ber a saying, 'The fool doth think he is wise, but the
wise man knows himself to be a fool.' The heathen
philosopher, when he had a desire to eat a grape, would
open his lips when he put it into his mouth, meaning
thereby that grapes were made to eat and lips to open.
You do love this maid ?
WILLIAM I do, sir.
TOUCHSTONE Give me your hand. Art thou learned ?

123 *render* describe   129 *kindness* affection in kinship   132 *hurtling* tumult
139 *By and by* presently   141 *recountments* accounts (of events since we
separated)   151 *Brief* in brief ; *recovered* revived   167 *counterfeited* acted,
pretended   170 *passion of earnest* display of genuine emotion
V, i The Forest   10 *clown* yokel (with a play on Touchstone's own profession)   12 *flouting* mocking ; *hold* i.e. hold our tongues   29–34 *I do . . .
to open* (in this and the following passages Touchstone is burlesquing the
style of Lyly's *Euphues* and Lodge's *Rosalynde*)

WILLIAM No, sir.

TOUCHSTONE Then learn this of me : to have is to have ; for it is a figure in rhetoric that drink, being poured out of a cup into a glass, by filling the one doth empty the other ; for all your writers do consent that *ipse* is he. Now, you are not *ipse*, for I am he.

WILLIAM Which he, sir ?

TOUCHSTONE He, sir, that must marry this woman. Therefore, you clown, abandon (which is in the vulgar, leave) the society (which in the boorish is, company) of this female (which in the common is, woman) ; which together is, abandon the society of this female, or, clown, thou perishest ; or, to thy better understanding, diest ; or, to wit, I kill thee, make thee away, translate thy life into death, thy liberty into bondage. I will deal in poison with thee, or in bastinado, or in steel ; I will bandy with thee in faction ; I will o'errun thee with policy ; I will kill thee a hundred and fifty ways. Therefore tremble and depart.

AUDREY Do, good William.

WILLIAM God rest you, merry sir.   *Exit.*

     Enter Corin.

CORIN Our master and mistress seeks you. Come away, away !

TOUCHSTONE Trip, Audrey, trip, Audrey. I attend, I attend.   *Exeunt.*

*

V, ii   *Enter Orlando and Oliver.*

ORLANDO Is't possible that on so little acquaintance you should like her ? that but seeing, you should love her ? and loving, woo ? and wooing, she should grant ? And will you persever to enjoy her ?

OLIVER Neither call the giddiness of it in question, the poverty of her, the small acquaintance, my sudden wooing, nor her sudden consenting ; but say with me, I love Aliena ; say with her that she loves me ; consent with both that we may enjoy each other. It shall be to your good ; for my father's house, and all the revenue that was old Sir Rowland's, will I estate upon you, and here live and die a shepherd.

     Enter Rosalind.

ORLANDO You have my consent. Let your wedding be to-morrow : thither will I invite the Duke and all 's contented followers. Go you and prepare Aliena ; for look you, here comes my Rosalind.

ROSALIND God save you, brother.

OLIVER And you, fair sister.   *[Exit.]*

ROSALIND O my dear Orlando, how it grieves me to see thee wear thy heart in a scarf !

ORLANDO It is my arm.

ROSALIND I thought thy heart had been wounded with the claws of a lion.

ORLANDO Wounded it is, but with the eyes of a lady.

ROSALIND Did your brother tell you how I counterfeited to sound when he showed me your handkercher ?

ORLANDO Ay, and greater wonders than that.

ROSALIND O, I know where you are ! Nay, 'tis true. There was never anything so sudden but the fight of two rams and Caesar's thrasonical brag of 'I came, saw, and over-came' ; for your brother and my sister no sooner met but they looked ; no sooner looked but they loved ; no sooner loved but they sighed ; no sooner sighed but they asked one another the reason ; no sooner knew the reason but they sought the remedy : and in these degrees have they made a pair of stairs to marriage, which they will climb incontinent, or else be incontinent before marriage : they are in the very wrath of love, and they will to-gether ; clubs cannot part them.

ORLANDO They shall be married to-morrow, and I will bid the Duke to the nuptial. But, O, how bitter a thing it is to look into happiness through another man's eyes ! By so much the more shall I to-morrow be at the height of heart-heaviness, by how much I shall think my brother happy in having what he wishes for.

ROSALIND Why then, to-morrow I cannot serve your turn for Rosalind ?

ORLANDO I can live no longer by thinking.

ROSALIND I will weary you then no longer with idle talking. Know of me then, for now I speak to some purpose, that I know you are a gentleman of good conceit. I speak not this that you should bear a good opinion of my knowledge, insomuch I say I know you are ; neither do I labor for a greater esteem than may in some little measure draw a belief from you, to do yourself good, and not to grace me. Believe then, if you please, that I can do strange things. I have, since I was three years old, conversed with a magician, most profound in his art and yet not damnable. If you do love Rosalind so near the heart as your gesture cries it out, when your brother marries Aliena shall you marry her. I know into what straits of fortune she is driven ; and it is not impossible to me, if it appear not inconvenient to you, to set her before your eyes to-morrow, human as she is, and without any danger.

ORLANDO Speak'st thou in sober meanings ?

ROSALIND By my life, I do, which I tender dearly, though I say I am a magician. Therefore put you in your best array, bid your friends ; for if you will be married to-morrow, you shall ; and to Rosalind, if you will.

     Enter Silvius and Phebe.

Look, here comes a lover of mine and a lover of hers.

PHEBE
Youth, you have done me much ungentleness
To show the letter that I writ to you.

ROSALIND
I care not if I have. It is my study
To seem despiteful and ungentle to you.
You are there followed by a faithful shepherd :
Look upon him, love him ; he worships you.

PHEBE
Good shepherd, tell this youth what 'tis to love.

---

42 *ipse is he* he is the man ('ipse' was a fashionable literary term ; Touchstone doubtless alludes to its use in *Euphues*)   53 *bastinado* beating with sticks   53–54 *bandy . . . faction* engage in controversy with you   54 *o'errun . . . policy* overwhelm you with political cunning

V, ii The Forest   5 *Neither . . . question* do not raise questions about the speed of it   11 *estate* settle   18 *fair sister* (although Rosalind is still dressed like a man, Oliver addresses her according to the manner in which she has been described to him by Orlando ; see IV, iii, 86–88)   26 *to sound* swooning   30 *thrasonical* boastful (like the braggart soldier, Thraso, in Terence's comedy *Eunuchus*)   35 *degrees* (Rosalind puns on the literal meaning 'steps')   37 *incontinent . . . incontinent* immediately . . . unrestrained sexually   38 *wrath* passion   39 *clubs* (commonly used to part combatants)   51 *conceit* intelligence   55 *belief* i.e. confidence in my ability   56 *grace me* bring favor on myself   57 *conversed* had dealings   59 *not damnable* not practicing black magic   60 *gesture . . . out* behavior proclaims   63 *inconvenient* inappropriate   67 *tender* value (the practice of magic was a capital offense. Rosalind is slyly admitting that she is not truly a magician.)   74 *study* conscious endeavor

SILVIUS
It is to be all made of sighs and tears;
And so am I for Phebe.
PHEBE And I for Ganymede.
ORLANDO And I for Rosalind.
ROSALIND And I for no woman.
SILVIUS
It is to be all made of faith and service;
And so am I for Phebe.
PHEBE And I for Ganymede.
ORLANDO And I for Rosalind.
ROSALIND And I for no woman.
SILVIUS
89   It is to be all made of fantasy,
All made of passion, and all made of wishes,
91   All adoration, duty, and observance,
All humbleness, all patience, and impatience,
93   All purity, all trial, all observance;
And so am I for Phebe.
PHEBE And so am I for Ganymede.
ORLANDO And so am I for Rosalind.
ROSALIND And so am I for no woman.
PHEBE [to Rosalind]
If this be so, why blame you me to love you?
SILVIUS [to Phebe]
If this be so, why blame you me to love you?
ORLANDO
If this be so, why blame you me to love you?
101 ROSALIND Why do you speak too, 'Why blame you me
to love you?'
ORLANDO
To her that is not here, nor doth not hear.
103 ROSALIND Pray you, no more of this; 'tis like the howling
of Irish wolves against the moon. [to Silvius] I will help
you if I can. [to Phebe] I would love you if I could.
To-morrow meet me all together. [to Phebe] I will
marry you if ever I marry woman, and I'll be married
to-morrow. [to Orlando] I will satisfy you if ever I satisfied man, and you shall be married to-morrow. [to
Silvius] I will content you if what pleases you contents
you, and you shall be married to-morrow. [to Orlando]
As you love Rosalind, meet. [to Silvius] As you love
Phebe, meet. And as I love no woman, I'll meet. So
fare you well. I have left you commands.
SILVIUS I'll not fail if I live.
PHEBE Nor I.
ORLANDO Nor I.   Exeunt.

*

V, iii   Enter [Touchstone the] Clown and Audrey.
TOUCHSTONE To-morrow is the joyful day, Audrey; to-
morrow will we be married.
AUDREY I do desire it with all my heart; and I hope it is
4   no dishonest desire to desire to be a woman of the world.
Here come two of the banished Duke's pages.
            Enter two Pages.
1. PAGE Well met, honest gentleman.
TOUCHSTONE By my troth, well met. Come, sit, sit, and
a song!
9 2. PAGE We are for you. Sit i' th' middle.
10 1. PAGE Shall we clap into't roundly, without hawking or
11   spitting or saying we are hoarse, which are the only
prologues to a bad voice?

2. PAGE I' faith, i' faith! and both in a tune, like two
gypsies on a horse.

Song.
It was a lover and his lass,
    With a hey, and a ho, and a hey nonino,
That o'er the green cornfield did pass   17
    In springtime, the only pretty ringtime,   18
When birds do sing, hey ding a ding, ding.
Sweet lovers love the spring.

Between the acres of the rye,
    With a hey, and a ho, and a hey nonino,
These pretty country folks would lie
    In springtime, &c.

This carol they began that hour,
    With a hey, and a ho, and a hey nonino,
How that a life was but a flower
    In springtime, &c.

And therefore take the present time,
    With a hey, and a ho, and a hey nonino,
For love is crownèd with the prime   31
    In springtime, &c.

TOUCHSTONE Truly, young gentlemen, though there
was no great matter in the ditty, yet the note was very un- 34
tuneable.
1. PAGE You are deceived, sir. We kept time, we lost not
our time.
TOUCHSTONE By my troth, yes; I count it but time lost
to hear such a foolish song. God b' wi' you, and God
mend your voices. Come, Audrey.   Exeunt.

*

Enter Duke Senior, Amiens, Jaques, Orlando,   V, iv
    Oliver, Celia.
DUKE SENIOR
Dost thou believe, Orlando, that the boy
Can do all this that he hath promisèd?
ORLANDO
I sometimes do believe, and sometimes do not,
As those that fear they hope, and know they fear.   4
    Enter Rosalind, Silvius, and Phebe.
ROSALIND
Patience once more, whiles our compact is urged.   5
You say, if I bring in your Rosalind,
You will bestow her on Orlando here?
DUKE SENIOR
That would I, had I kingdoms to give with her.
ROSALIND
And you say you will have her when I bring her?

89 *fantasy* fancy 91 *observance* devotion 93 *observance* (many editors,
assuming a compositor's error from two lines above, emend to 'obedience')
101 *Why . . . too* (often emended to 'Who . . . to') 103–04 *like . . . moon*
(corresponding simile in *Rosalynde* reads: 'thou barkest with the wolves of
Syria against the moon')
V, iii The Forest 4 *dishonest* immodest; *to be . . . world* to be married
(and also to go beyond her present rustic station in life) 9 *for you* ready
for you 10 *clap into't roundly* start right off 11 *only* common 17 *cornfield* wheatfield 18 *ringtime* wedding season 31 *prime* spring 34 *un-
tuneable* untuneful
V, iv The Forest 4 *fear they hope* i.e. fear they only hope 5 *urged*
stressed

ORLANDO
That would I, were I of all kingdoms king.

ROSALIND
You say you'll marry me, if I be willing?

PHEBE
That will I, should I die the hour after.

ROSALIND
But if you do refuse to marry me,
You'll give yourself to this most faithful shepherd?

PHEBE
So is the bargain.

ROSALIND
You say that you'll have Phebe, if she will?

SILVIUS
Though to have her and death were both one thing.

ROSALIND
18 I have promised to make all this matter even.
Keep you your word, O Duke, to give your daughter;
You yours, Orlando, to receive his daughter;
Keep you your word, Phebe, that you'll marry me,
Or else, refusing me, to wed this shepherd;
Keep your word, Silvius, that you'll marry her
If she refuse me; and from hence I go,
25 To make these doubts all even.
Exeunt Rosalind and Celia.

DUKE SENIOR
I do remember in this shepherd boy
27 Some lively touches of my daughter's favor.

ORLANDO
My lord, the first time that I ever saw him
Methought he was a brother to your daughter.
But, my good lord, this boy is forest-born,
And hath been tutored in the rudiments
32 Of many desperate studies by his uncle,
Whom he reports to be a great magician,
34 Obscurèd in the circle of this forest.
Enter [Touchstone the] Clown and Audrey.

35 JAQUES There is, sure, another flood toward, and these
couples are coming to the ark. Here comes a pair of very
strange beasts, which in all tongues are called fools.

TOUCHSTONE Salutation and greeting to you all!

JAQUES Good my lord, bid him welcome. This is the
motley-minded gentleman that I have so often met in
the forest. He hath been a courtier, he swears.

TOUCHSTONE If any man doubt that, let him put me to
43 my purgation. I have trod a measure; I have flattered a
44 lady; I have been politic with my friend, smooth with
45 mine enemy; I have undone three tailors; I have had
four quarrels, and like to have fought one.

JAQUES And how was that ta'en up?   47

TOUCHSTONE Faith, we met, and found the quarrel was
upon the seventh cause.

JAQUES How seventh cause? Good my lord, like this
fellow.

DUKE SENIOR I like him very well.

TOUCHSTONE God 'ild you, sir; I desire you of the like. I 52
press in here, sir, amongst the rest of the country copu- 53
latives, to swear and to forswear, according as marriage
binds and blood breaks. A poor virgin, sir, an ill-favored 55
thing, sir, but mine own; a poor humor of mine, sir, to 56
take that that no man else will. Rich honesty dwells like 57
a miser, sir, in a poor house, as your pearl in your foul
oyster.

DUKE SENIOR By my faith, he is very swift and senten- 60
tious.

TOUCHSTONE According to the fool's bolt, sir, and such 62
dulcet diseases.   63

JAQUES But, for the seventh cause. How did you find the
quarrel on the seventh cause?

TOUCHSTONE Upon a lie seven times removed (bear your
body more seeming, Audrey) as thus, sir. I did dislike 66
the cut of a certain courtier's beard. He sent me word,
if I said his beard was not cut well, he was in the mind
it was: this is called the Retort Courteous. If I sent him
word again it was not well cut, he would send me word
he cut it to please himself: this is called the Quip Modest. 71
If again, it was not well cut, he disabled my judgment: 72
this is called the Reply Churlish. If again, it was not well
cut, he would answer I spake not true: this is called the
Reproof Valiant. If again, it was not well cut, he would
say I lie: this is called the Countercheck Quarrelsome: 76
and so to the Lie Circumstantial and the Lie Direct.   77

JAQUES And how oft did you say his beard was not well
cut?

TOUCHSTONE I durst go no further than the Lie Circumstantial, nor he durst not give me the Lie Direct;
and so we measured swords and parted.

JAQUES Can you nominate in order now the degrees of
the lie?

TOUCHSTONE O sir, we quarrel in print, by the book, as 85
you have books for good manners. I will name you the
degrees. The first, the Retort Courteous; the second,
the Quip Modest; the third, the Reply Churlish; the
fourth, the Reproof Valiant; the fifth, the Countercheck
Quarrelsome; the sixth, the Lie with Circumstance; the 90
seventh, the Lie Direct. All these you may avoid but the
Lie Direct, and you may avoid that too, with an If. I
knew when seven justices could not take up a quarrel, 93
but when the parties were met themselves, one of them
thought but of an If: as, 'If you said so, then I said so';
and they shook hands and swore brothers. Your If is the
only peacemaker. Much virtue in If.

JAQUES Is not this a rare fellow, my lord? He's as good at
anything, and yet a fool.

DUKE SENIOR He uses his folly like a stalking horse, and 100
under the presentation of that he shoots his wit.   101
Enter Hymen, Rosalind, and Celia. Still music.

HYMEN
Then is there mirth in heaven
When earthly things made even
    Atone together.   104
Good Duke, receive thy daughter;
Hymen from heaven brought her,
    Yea, brought her hither,

That thou mightst join her hand with his
Whose heart within his bosom is.

ROSALIND [to Duke]
To you I give myself, for I am yours.
[To Orlando]
To you I give myself, for I am yours.

DUKE SENIOR
112   If there be truth in sight, you are my daughter.

ORLANDO
If there be truth in sight, you are my Rosalind.

PHEBE
If sight and shape be true,
Why then, my love adieu!

ROSALIND [to Duke]
I'll have no father, if you be not he.
[To Orlando]
I'll have no husband, if you be not he.
[To Phebe]
Nor ne'er wed woman, if you be not she.

HYMEN   Peace ho! I bar confusion:
'Tis I must make conclusion
Of these most strange events.
Here's eight that must take hands
To join in Hymen's bands,
124   If truth holds true contents.
[To Orlando and Rosalind]
125   You and you no cross shall part.
[To Oliver and Celia]
You and you are heart in heart.
[To Phebe]
127   You to his love must accord,
Or have a woman to your lord.
[To Touchstone and Audrey]
129   You and you are sure together
As the winter to foul weather.
[To all]
Whiles a wedlock hymn we sing,
132   Feed yourselves with questioning,
133   That reason wonder may diminish
How thus we met, and these things finish.

Song.

Wedding is great Juno's crown,
O blessed bond of board and bed!
'Tis Hymen peoples every town;
High wedlock then be honorèd.
Honor, high honor, and renown
To Hymen, god of every town!

DUKE SENIOR
O my dear niece, welcome thou art to me,
142   Even daughter, welcome, in no less degree!

PHEBE [to Silvius]
143   I will not eat my word, now thou art mine;
144   Thy faith my fancy to thee doth combine.
Enter Second Brother.

2. BROTHER
Let me have audience for a word or two.
I am the second son of old Sir Rowland
That bring these tidings to this fair assembly.
Duke Frederick, hearing how that every day
Men of great worth resorted to this forest,
150   Addressed a mighty power, which were on foot
151   In his own conduct, purposely to take

His brother here and put him to the sword;
And to the skirts of this wild wood he came,
Where, meeting with an old religious man,   154
After some question with him, was converted   155
Both from his enterprise and from the world,
His crown bequeathing to his banished brother,
And all their lands restored to them again
That were with him exiled. This to be true
I do engage my life.   160

DUKE SENIOR   Welcome, young man.
Thou offer'st fairly to thy brothers' wedding: 161
To one, his lands withheld; and to the other,
A land itself at large, a potent dukedom.
First, in this forest let us do those ends   164
That here were well begun and well begot;
And after, every of this happy number
That have endured shrewd days and nights with us   167
Shall share the good of our returnèd fortune,
According to the measure of their states.   169
Meantime forget this new-fall'n dignity
And fall into our rustic revelry.
Play, music, and you brides and bridegrooms all,
With measure heaped in joy, to th' measures fall.

JAQUES
Sir, by your patience. If I heard you rightly,
The Duke hath put on a religious life   175
And thrown into neglect the pompous court.

2. BROTHER   He hath.

JAQUES
To him will I. Out of these convertites   178
There is much matter to be heard and learned.
[To Duke]
You to your former honor I bequeath;
Your patience and your virtue well deserves it.
[To Orlando]
You to a love that your true faith doth merit;
[To Oliver]
You to your land and love and great allies;
[To Silvius]
You to a long and well-deservèd bed;
[To Touchstone]
And you to wrangling, for thy loving voyage
Is but for two months victualled. So, to your pleasures:
I am for other than for dancing measures.

DUKE SENIOR   Stay, Jaques, stay.

JAQUES
To see no pastime I. What you would have
I'll stay to know at your abandoned cave.   *Exit.*

DUKE SENIOR
Proceed, proceed. We'll begin these rites,
As we do trust they'll end, in true delights.
Exit [in the dance].

---

112 *If . . . sight* i.e. if he is not again deceived by appearances 124 *If
. . . contents* i.e. if the discoveries made by the couples reveal their genuine
affections 125 *cross* disagreement 127 *accord* assent 129 *sure together*
securely united 132 *Feed* satisfy 133 *reason* understanding 142 *Even
daughter* just as if you were my daughter 143 *eat* swallow, i.e. take back
144 *combine* unite s.d. *Second Brother* i.e. Jaques de Boys 150 *Addressed*
assembled; *power* force (of troops) 151 *conduct* command 154 *religious
man* (evidently an anchorite) 155 *question* discussion 160 *engage* pledge
161 *Thou . . . fairly* you bring handsome prospects 164 *do those ends*
complete those purposes 167 *shrewd* sharp, hard 169 *states* i.e. status
175 *put . . . life* adopted the life of a monk or hermit 178 *convertites*
converts

[EPILOGUE]

ROSALIND It is not the fashion to see the lady the epilogue,
2   but it is no more unhandsome than to see the lord the
3   prologue. If it be true that good wine needs no bush, 'tis
     true that a good play needs no epilogue; yet to good
     wine they do use good bushes, and good plays prove the
6   better by the help of good epilogues. What a case am I
     in then, that am neither a good epilogue, nor cannot
insinuate with you in the behalf of a good play! I am 8
not furnished like a beggar; therefore to beg will not 9
become me. My way is to conjure you, and I'll begin 10
with the women. I charge you, O women, for the love
you bear to men, to like as much of this play as please 12
you; and I charge you, O men, for the love you bear to
women (as I perceive by your simp'ring none of you
hates them), that between you and the women the play
may please. If I were a woman, I would kiss as many 16
of you as had beards that pleased me, complexions that
liked me, and breaths that I defied not; and I am sure, 18
as many as have good beards, or good faces, or sweet
breaths, will, for my kind offer, when I make curtsy, bid 20
me farewell.   *Exit.*

Epi. 2 *unhandsome* unbecoming 3 *bush* ivy bush (formerly the sign of a vintner) 6 *case* predicament 8 *insinuate* ingratiate myself 9 *furnished* equipped, i.e. with rags and cup 10 *conjure* adjure, i.e. charge, as if on oath 12 *like* (a reminder of the play's title); *please* may please 16 *If . . . woman* (a reminder that the actor was a boy) 18 *liked me* I liked; *defied* rejected 20–21 *bid me farewell* i.e. with applause

MUCH ADO ABOUT NOTHING

INTRODUCTION

Much Ado about Nothing is a feast of wit from the sententious rhetoric of Leonato's opening lines to Benedick's last pun. There is abundant variety from the delicious unconscious humor of Dogberry's anxiety to be "writ down an ass" to the delicate counterpoint of sentiment and semblance in Claudio's penance, when he is made to do obsequies to an empty tomb. Among the consciously witty characters Beatrice and Benedick easily carry off the prize, not so much because they have more wit than the others as because they are so sympathetically and so fully humanized. Shakespeare's acute observation of their kind of love-making has provided a pattern for the greatest English comedies from *The Way of the World* to *The Importance of Being Earnest*, yet Beatrice and Benedick have never been surpassed. It takes a very great actress, however, to convey the full womanly charm of Beatrice; to read her lines with spontaneity but without pertness, to make her Beatrice the warmhearted and not Katherine the shrew. As Ellen Terry has said, her lines "should be spoken with the lightest raillery, with mirth in voice and a charm in manner" which keeps her vivacious but never shrill.

The *Stationers' Register* confirms the internal evidence that this play was written when the poet was at the height of his skill in comedy. It was in the hands of the printer by August 4, 1600, along with *As You Like It, Henry V*, and Jonson's *Every Man in His Humor*, when all were "staied" from publication. But on August 23 the license for this play was granted, and it appeared before the end of the year. How long before August, 1600, it had been written is not clear; but it is not mentioned in the well-known list of Shakespeare's comedies in Francis Meres' *Palladis Tamia* (1598), and it is therefore usually dated 1598–1600, probably coming between *As You Like It* and *Twelfth Night*.

Unlike Rosalind and Viola, the heroines of these companion comedies, Beatrice does not protect herself by donning men's clothing. Her self-defense, we might say her disguise, is her wit; and her unmasking is not physical but psychological. She betrays in her very first words that self-conscious and intense interest in Benedick which is characteristic of young love. Modesty and propriety cannot keep her from breaking into the conversation of her elders to inquire whether "Signior Mountanto returned from the wars or no." She must be reassured that he is safe, yet she is too self-conscious to say his name. Her cousin understands her, however, and Beatrice plunges deeper into her self-betrayal in an effort to cover up her interest and yet to learn more about Benedick. "But how many hath he killed?" "Who is his companion now?" These are the questions that torment the woman in love: where is he? what is he doing? who is his companion? Beatrice's disparagement only emphasizes the fact that she can think

of nothing else. Yet her wit is her protection, the disguise which conceals her true feelings, even from herself.

It keeps Benedick at sparring distance, although he thinks that she exceeds Hero in beauty "as the first of May doth the last of December." His fear of her tongue and his habitual pose as a confirmed bachelor protect him doubly until the trick played upon him by the Prince, Claudio, and Leonato throws down both barriers at once. They were not very formidable barriers. His defiance of Cupid in the first scene is not only ominous, but it betrays a certain vulnerability. Claudio's defection from the fraternity of bachelors has its effect, and Benedick is already thinking what kind of woman he could love before he is persuaded that Beatrice loves him.

Even after each is convinced of the other's love, however, they cannot break through the barrier of persiflage until the emotion aroused by Hero's disgrace beats down their self-conscious reserve. Benedick blurts out his "I do love nothing in the world so well as you" almost involuntarily, and Beatrice is trembling on the verge of the same confession, though she keeps her guard up until she is sure that he is serious. She never for a moment forgets Hero, however. Her confession is prefaced by "I am sorry for my cousin," and when she has put Benedick on the defensive, so that he offers to prove his love, she responds instantly, "Kill Claudio." This is a very feminine seizing of an emotional advantage, but it does credit to her heart and head that she never wavers in her loyalty to her cousin, nor does she forget Hero's predicament in the excitement of her own confession of love. Her "O that I were a man" rings with womanly rage and frustration and forces Benedick to take up a responsible role in the vindication of Hero. In this scene we are shown the depth and honesty of Beatrice's character. Her earlier consternation when she overhears Hero and Ursula discussing her, and her quick decision to reform, expressed in joyful lyric, are no more than we might expect from the evidence of her interest in Benedick; but her steadfast loyalty to her cousin strikes a deeper note and a sweeter one. She will rule Benedick by her wit taking advantage of his love, but he has wit enough to be proud of her and do willing service. Once they have confessed, the revelation of the trick played upon them is, of course, something they can jest about and end with a kiss. They were not tricked into falling in love but only into the realization that they were in love.

The Hero–Claudio story must be regarded as the main plot because of its melodramatic and spectacular character, yet Shakespeare carefully keeps us from entering into the emotions of either Hero or Claudio. This he does by the title he gives the play, by the selection of a familiar story whose happy outcome was familiar to his audience, by his handling of the characters of Hero and Claudio, and finally by his manipulation of the plot so that we know even before Hero is denounced that the Watch have all the evidence necessary to clear her.

The title of the play is not, as is sometimes claimed, evidence of Shakespeare's indifference, but is his careful reassurance that the gravest events of the play will have no serious consequence. The story of the maiden falsely accused was a very old one, going back to post-classical romance. It was widely known because it had been retold by two very popular writers, Ariosto in the *Orlando Furioso* and Bandello in his *Novelle*. Ariosto's version was translated into English by Sir John Harington (1591), and it had been retold by Peter Beverley as the *Historie of Ariodanto and Ieneura* (1566) and by Spenser in the *Faerie Queene* (1590). Richard Mulcaster had presented a play before the Queen in 1583, *A Historie of Ariodante and Geneuora*. Bandello's version was known in England both in the original Italian and in the French of Belleforest's *Histoires Tragiques* (1576). The names and some elements in the plot indicate that Shakespeare knew both versions.

Considering the popularity of the story, and its theatrical qualities, it is not unreasonable to suppose that our poet knew some older dramatization, but a few mistakes in the stage directions and loose ends in the plot are insufficient to support the hypothesis that Shakespeare was making over an old play. The quarto and folio texts begin with the stage direction, "Enter Leonato Gouernour of Messina, Innogen his wife," etc., and at the opening of Act II they have, "Enter Leonato, his brother, his wife, Hero his daughter, and Beatrice his niece, and a kinsman." Yet Innogen (out of Bandello) has no part in the play. The "kinsman" also fails to appear and instead we have Margaret and Ursula. In I, ii we learn that Antonio has a son, and the son appears briefly to arrange the music, yet in V, i, 277 Claudio is told that Antonio's pretended daughter (Hero in disguise) "alone is heir to both of us." In the opening scene the messenger reports that he has already delivered letters to Claudio's uncle "here in Messina," yet the uncle is not mentioned again and is not used as explanation of Claudio's presence in Messina, as we might expect. However curious, these are all slight inconsistencies such as might very well survive from Shakespeare's own first draft.

In any case the Hero–Claudio story was a familiar one and the poet assumes his audience's familiarity with it. Modern critics have complained about the sketchy way in which he handles the deception of the Prince and Claudio and the evidence which exposed it. No less a scholar than Professor Boas objects to the omission of the "momentous episode outside Hero's chamber window." Instead we have the much more dramatic repudiation scene, the true crux of the plot. In Bandello's story the lover sends word to Leonato that he refuses to marry the girl because of her unchastity. The messenger denounces her to her father and mother, she faints and is pronounced dead, but revives, and her father, who is convinced of her innocence, conceals her in the country, etc. Shakespeare has economized on and heightened the climax by making the lover do his own accusing, and making the occasion the wedding scene. On the other hand he substitutes for the deception episode Borachio's boasting account of what actually happened. We are told beforehand of the plot against Hero's honor, and we hear Borachio boast of the sum he has been paid for deceiving the Prince and Claudio, and we see the Watch overhearing Borachio and arresting him. We have all the essentials of the deception without the scene itself. Such a scene could not be shown because it would either deceive and so confuse the audience, or it would fail to deceive the audience and so make the Prince and Claudio look too gullible.

The plot against Hero (and Claudio) is adequately presented but its melodramatic character is minimized not only by the title of the play and the management of the action so that Borachio is apprehended even before Hero is accused, but also by the characterization. Both Hero and Claudio are conventionalized so as to reduce our emotional involvement in their distresses. Hero is a very correct young lady and Claudio is a very proper wooer. Hero shows not a speck of interest in Claudio until Don Pedro hands her over to him. She is wooed by proxy and flaunts her permission to say "yes" before Don Pedro has had a chance to explain that it is Claudio who wants to marry her. The nearest we come to a love scene is the moment when Don Pedro announces the success of his proxy wooing. Claudio makes a pretty speech and Beatrice urges her cousin to speak, "or if you cannot, stop his mouth with a kiss." And she interprets Hero's pantomime, "My cousin tells him in his ear that he is in her heart." Hero herself says not a word to indicate that she is in love. She is too proper a young lady to make choice for herself or to do otherwise than acquiesce in the choice made for her. She is charming, with mischief enough in her to take part in the hoaxing of her cousin if it be "any modest office," but she has the docility expected, and often exacted (as in *The Taming of the Shrew*), of young women in Shakespeare's day.

Claudio too is conventionalized. Modern performers who romanticize the Hero–Claudio relationship by means of stage business not called for in the lines, end by making a perfect cad of him. He is no such thing. He is a proper young man of his age. He sees Hero, likes her looks, and when he has leisure he consults his superior about her. His first question is the correct one, "Hath Leonato any son, my lord?" Only a fool or a Romeo would rush into a marriage without inquiring about the dowry and fortune of the bride. Marriage was a young man's best opportunity to get ahead in the world. Claudio is enough in love to want to marry, but his reason is always in control of his emotions. He allows his Prince to woo for him, and Don Pedro's officiousness serves the double purpose of keeping Hero and Claudio apart and of showing us Claudio's character. He is neither furious nor jealous, as we might expect, at what appears to be Don Pedro's betrayal of his trust. He is only very sad and hurt. He blames himself and tries to be philosophical as a reasonable man should be.

This episode should prepare us for his behavior when he is made to believe that Hero is false and lewd. Nor is he too easily deceived, as some critics have said. He has seen a woman in Hero's clothes "talk with a ruffian at her chamber window"; he has heard her called "Hero"; he has heard Don John's story of her misbehavior, confirmed by Borachio. Don Pedro says that they have questioned Borachio,

> Who hath indeed, most like a liberal villain,
> Confessed the vile encounters they have had
> A thousand times in secret.

Don Pedro is perfectly convinced of Hero's guilt. How can we expect the reasonable Claudio to reject all this evidence of his eyes and ears? And being convinced, he has only one course open to him as an honorable man; he must reject her. That he does so dramatically, at the altar, indicates that he is deeply hurt and must strike back, must hurt her for having so hurt him. In this also he is seconded by the Prince.

After the altar scene, from which Claudio departs in tears, we do not see him again until the opening of the last act, where he and Don Pedro encounter Leonato and Antonio. In this tragicomic scene he speaks only three times. He reacts involuntarily to being called a "dissembler" but apologizes immediately for having laid his hand on his sword. And he asks two defensive questions, "Who wrongs him?" and "My villainy?" Not until the old men are gone and he sees Benedick can he recover his poise. His report of the encounter, "we had liked to have had our two noses snapped off with two old men without teeth," seems unfeeling; but the spectacle of two greybeards, one of them shaking with palsy, contending which shall challenge a young soldier to a duel, has its absurd as well as its pitiful side.

The management of the audience's emotions in this scene is very adroit. It opens with Leonato's eloquent refusal to be comforted. Yet the audience knows that the Sexton is already on his way to Leonato's with the evidence which will clear Hero of scandal and Claudio of seeming a heartless dissembler. We cannot, therefore, be too deeply moved by Leonato's grief, although we sympathize with him. But in his encounter with Don Pedro and Claudio he exaggerates his grief by claiming that Hero is dead, and so reduces our sympathy. And Antonio's officious blustering dissolves the situation into comedy. Then, when Benedick in turn challenges Claudio, the scene has lost all tragic potential, and the baiting of Benedick by the Prince and Claudio leaves him looking a little foolish. Don Pedro comments, "What a pretty thing is man when he goes in his doublet and hose and leaves off his wit," to which Claudio replies, "Then is an ape a doctor to such a man." Here, as in every situation in the play, Shakespeare by keeping the audience informed of the truth (while his characters deceive each other) flatters us into a mood for laughter and effectively insulates our emotions from the distresses of his deluded characters. Leonato's understandable indignation is toned down from a tragic to a comic level by carefully graduated stages. The scene is a clash of emotion with reason, in which if reason looks rather heartless, emotion is made to look rather childish. Both are put in the wrong, and therefore in a position to be reconciled as soon as Dogberry, with Borachio in tow, arrives.

Claudio behaves throughout as the Elizabethan moralists and physicians advised. Andrew Borde, in his *Breviarie of Health* (1547), gives the standard advice in early and brief form: "First I do advise every person not to set to the heart what another doth set at the heel, let no man set his love so far, but what he may withdraw it betime, and muse not, but use mirth and merry company, and be wise and not foolish" (ch. 174). But the correct young man whose reason is always in control of his emotions does not engage our sympathies very deeply. Nor is the wrong done to Hero the betrayal of love and trust, but only the sullying of her reputation and breaking off of a desirable marriage – wrongs which can be easily and thoroughly righted.

By using a familiar story with a happy ending, and by keeping our emotional involvement with Hero and Claudio to a minimum, Shakespeare has so lightened a melodramatic plot as to make it serve as background and occasion for the warmly human courtship of the witty Beatrice and the wayward Benedick. He has brought the two love affairs to contrasting climaxes in the same scene, using the rejection of Hero as emotional preparation for the breaking down of reserve, defended by wit, which has separated Beatrice and Benedick. And he has further reinforced the comic spirit of the play by bringing into romantically imagined Messina an English village constable and his Watch – and what a constable! We know that Will Kempe, the famous comedian of Shakespeare's company, acted the part of Dogberry, because in the quarto edition of the play the names "Kemp" and "Cowley" appear instead of "Dogberry" and "Verges" throughout most of Act IV, scene ii. These men, honest as the skin between their brows, manage to do their duty and comprehend all vagrom men. They are merciful men who will not meddle or make with a thief, nor will they let a child cry in the night if they can wake the nurse. But for all their ineptitude of purpose, speech, and action, they manage to overhear Borachio boasting of his villainy and to arrest him. The most suspense-charged moment of the play is the scene where Dogberry's tediousness and Leonato's impatience combine to prevent the disclosure of Don John's plot before Hero goes to church. But immediately after the rejection scene the Sexton manages, in spite of Dogberry's method of examining, to unravel the whole matter. One more brief appearance when Borachio confesses to the Prince is all we are allowed of Leonato's honest neighbor. Not the least of Shakespeare's comic art is his parsimony.

It is not an accident that Shakespeare's wittiest comedy is largely in prose. Here prose is the language of wit and reason, poetry the language of emotion, sentiment, and rhetoric. The wedding scene begins in prose but rises quickly into verse as feeling mounts. However, Beatrice keeps her wits about her and speaks to her cousin in prose. When the Friar takes the situation in hand, he begins in what is printed as prose in the quarto, and reads like prose, but in the fourth line emotion and poetry take over. Indeed, prose and poetry are so subtly mingled that what is spoken seems perfectly fitted to the speaker and the occasion. We are scarcely conscious of the medium used, but only of the tensions and relaxations of the emotions aroused by the simple, carefully ordered plot. Yet the cool rhythms of prose have much to do with preserving the balance between reason and emotion which gives this play much of its sparkling brilliance. Here we can see Shakespeare manipulating, not puppets on the stage, but the emotions of his audience. He knows their stops and how to sound them from the lowest note of their heart-strings to the top of their compass. He takes the old plot of the maiden falsely accused and transforms it into the burden or accompaniment, the foil for his most spirited lovers – and the occasion for the inimitable Dogberry.

Hunter College   JOSEPHINE WATERS BENNETT

The present edition follows closely the text of the only quarto of the play, that printed in 1600, evidently from Shakespeare's own draft. It is an excellent text despite irregularities in the speech and scene headings which are unusually numerous and may reflect indecisions and slight changes of plan during the process of composition. The names of the actors Will Kempe and Richard Cowley prefixing the speeches of Dogberry and Verges in IV, ii, indicate that the manuscript was closely related to the first stage production; however, the irregularities mentioned above would presumably have been eliminated if the manuscript had served as prompt-book. The quarto text is not divided into acts and scenes, and the text in the folio, which was printed from it, is divided into acts but not into scenes. The division supplied marginally for reference in the present edition is that of later editors, who divided the folio acts into scenes.

Below are listed all substantive departures from the quarto of 1600, with the adopted reading in italics followed by the quarto reading in roman. The need for emendation is remarkably slight, and most of the following instances involve mere normalization of stage directions and speech-prefixes. They are listed because of the theatrical interest of some of them. Most of the irregularities are repeated in the folio text of 1623, which was printed from the quarto and is of little value in forming the text. However, two of the folio stage directions have some slight theatrical interest. The folio adds to the stage direction at II, i, 74: "Maskers with a drum"; and gives as the stage direction at II, iii, 33: "Enter Prince, Leonato, Claudio, and Iacke Wilson," indicating that in some performance before 1623 the singer John Wilson played the part of Balthasar.

I, i, s.d. *Messina, Hero* Messina, Innogen his wife, Hero   8 *Pedro* Peter   180 s.d. *Enter Don Pedro* (Q adds: Iohn the Bastard)
I, ii, 3, 6, 16 *Antonio* Old   6 *event* euents   22 *Cousin* coosins   24 *skill* shill
I, iii, 29 *muzzle* mussel   42 *brother's* bothers
II, i, s.d. *brother* brother, his wife   *niece* neece, and a kinsman   2, 18, 43 *Antonio* brother   74 s.d. *Prince [Don] Pedro* prince, Pedro   *Don John* or dumb Iohn   88, 91, 93 *Bathasar* Bene   189 s.d. *Leonato* Leonato, Iohn and Borachio, and Conrade   292 *Pedro* Prince (thus throughout scene except l. 310: Pedro)

II, iii, 7 s.d. *Exit* (at l. 5 in Q)   23 *an* and   33 s.d. *Enter ... Music* (combines two stage directions in Q: 'Enter prince, Leonato, Claudio, Musicke' occurring here, and 'Enter Balthasar with musicke' occurring at l. 39)   34 *Pedro* Prince (thus throughout)   63–64 *Then ... go* (single line in Q)   86 s.d. *Exit Balthasar* (occurs after l. 85 in Q)   90 *ay!* I   107 *sit you* fit you   129 *us of* of us
III, i, 23 s.d. *Enter Beatrice* (occurs after l. 25 in Q)
III, ii, 1 *Pedro* Prince (thus throughout except at l. 48: Bene)   25 *can* cannot   70 *John* Bastard (thus throughout)   84–85 *brother, I ... heart hath* brother (I ... heart) hath   100 *her then* her, then
III, iii, 10 *1. Watch* Watch 1   15, 25 *2. Watch* Watch 2   35 *1. Watch* Watch   42 *2. Watch* Watch (thus thereafter until ll. 152ff; where 'Watch 1' and 'Watch 2' are resumed)   162–63 *Never ... us* (part of preceding speech by Conrade in Q)
III, iv, 17 *in* it
III, v, 2 *Dogberry* Const. Dog (thus throughout except ll. 52, 56)   7 *Verges* Headb (thus throughout except l. 55)   9 *off* of   47 *be suffigance* (Q adds Exit)
IV, i, 4 *Friar* Fran   27, 61, 85 *Pedro* Prince   48–49 *And ... Leonato* (single line in Q)   65, 109 *John* Bastard   153–56 *Hear ... marked* (printed as prose in Q, crowded at foot of page)
IV, ii, s.d. *Enter ... Watch* (Q reads 'Enter the Constables, Borachio, and the Towne clearke in gownes')   1 *Dogberry* Keeper   2, 5 *Verges* Cowley   4 *Dogberry* Andrew   9 *Dogberry* Kemp (thus throughout except l. 61: Constable)   35, 48 *1. Watch* Watch 1   43 *2. Watch* Watch 2   46 *Verges* Const   54 *Watchmen* Watch   62 *Verges* Couley   62–63 *hands – Conrade. Off, coxcomb* hands of Coxcombe   67 *Conrade* Couley
V, i, 1 *Antonio* Brother (thus throughout)   96 *anticly, show* antiquely and shew   97 *off* of   109 s.d. *Exeunt ambo* (occurs at l. 108 in Q)   134 *an* and   174 *on* one   198 *Dogberry* Const (thus throughout)   244 *Verges* Con. 2
V, ii, 24–27 *The ... deserve* (printed as prose in Q)   38 s.d. *Enter Beatrice* (occurs at l. 39 in Q)   43 *for* (omitted in Q)
V, iii, 3 *Claudio* (appears at l. 11 in Q)   10 *dumb* dead   22 *Claudio* Lo   22–23 *Now ... rite* (single line in Q)   24, 30 *Pedro* Prince
V, iv, 7, 17 *Antonio* old   34 *Pedro* Prince (thus throughout except at l. 40: P)   54 *Antonio* Leo   97 *Benedick* Leon

MUCH ADO ABOUT NOTHING

*

I, i   *Enter Leonato, Governor of Messina, Hero his
daughter, and Beatrice his niece, with a Messenger.*

LEONATO I learn in this letter that Don Pedro of Arragon comes this night to Messina.

MESSENGER He is very near by this. He was not three leagues off when I left him.

LEONATO How many gentlemen have you lost in this 5 action?

6 MESSENGER But few of any sort, and none of name.

LEONATO A victory is twice itself when the achiever brings home full numbers. I find here that Don Pedro hath bestowed much honor on a young Florentine called Claudio.

11 MESSENGER Much deserved on his part, and equally remembered by Don Pedro. He hath borne himself beyond the promise of his age, doing in the figure of a lamb the feats of a lion. He hath indeed bettered expectation than you must expect of me to tell you how.

LEONATO He hath an uncle here in Messina will be very much glad of it.

MESSENGER I have already delivered him letters, and there appears much joy in him ; even so much that joy 20 could not show itself modest enough without a badge of bitterness.

LEONATO Did he break out into tears?

MESSENGER In great measure.

24 LEONATO A kind overflow of kindness. There are no faces truer than those that are so washed. How much better is it to weep at joy than to joy at weeping !

27 BEATRICE I pray you, is Signior Mountanto returned from the wars or no?

MESSENGER I know none of that name, lady. There was none such in the army of any sort.

LEONATO What is he that you ask for, niece?

HERO My cousin means Signior Benedick of Padua.

MESSENGER O, he's returned, and as pleasant as ever he was.

BEATRICE He set up his bills here in Messina and chal- 34 lenged Cupid at the flight, and my uncle's fool, reading 35 the challenge, subscribed for Cupid and challenged him 36 at the burbolt. I pray you, how many hath he killed and 37 eaten in these wars? But how many hath he killed? For indeed I promised to eat all of his killing.

LEONATO Faith, niece, you tax Signior Benedick too 40 much ; but he'll be meet with you, I doubt it not. 41

MESSENGER He hath done good service, lady, in these wars.

BEATRICE You had musty victual, and he hath holp to eat it. He is a very valiant trencherman ; he hath an 44 excellent stomach. 45

MESSENGER And a good soldier too, lady.

BEATRICE And a good soldier to a lady ; but what is he to 47 a lord?

MESSENGER A lord to a lord, a man to a man ; stuffed with all honorable virtues.

BEATRICE It is so indeed. He is no less than a stuffed man ; 51 but for the stuffing – well, we are all mortal.

LEONATO You must not, sir, mistake my niece. There is a kind of merry war betwixt Signior Benedick and her. They never meet but there's a skirmish of wit between them.

I, i Before the house of Leonato **5** *action* battle **6** *name* importance **11** *remembered* rewarded **20** *modest* moderate **20–21** *badge of bitterness* i.e. tears **24** *kind* natural **27** *Mountanto* montanto, an upright blow in fencing **34** *set up his bills* posted notices **35** *at the flight* to an archery duel **36** *subscribed* signed (as Cupid's representative) **37** *burbolt* birdbolt, a small blunt arrow allowed to boys as harmless, but also Cupid's arrow **40** *tax* accuse **41** *meet* even **44** *trencherman* eater **45** *stomach* appetite **47** *to* in comparison with **51** *stuffed man* figure stuffed to look like a man

BEATRICE Alas, he gets nothing by that! In our last con-
58 flict four of his five wits went halting off, and now is the
whole man governed with one; so that if he have wit
60 enough to keep himself warm, let him bear it for a difference between himself and his horse; for it is all the
wealth that he hath left to be known a reasonable
creature. Who is his companion now? He hath every
month a new sworn brother.

MESSENGER Is't possible?

66 BEATRICE Very easily possible. He wears his faith but as
67 the fashion of his hat; it ever changes with the next block.

MESSENGER I see, lady, the gentleman is not in your
68 books.

69 BEATRICE No. An he were, I would burn my study. But I
pray you, who is his companion? Is there no young
71 squarer now that will make a voyage with him to the
devil?

MESSENGER He is most in the company of the right noble
Claudio.

75 BEATRICE O Lord, he will hang upon him like a disease!
He is sooner caught than the pestilence, and the taker
77 runs presently mad. God help the noble Claudio! If he
have caught the Benedick, it will cost him a thousand
pound ere 'a be cured.

80 MESSENGER I will hold friends with you, lady.

BEATRICE Do, good friend.

82 LEONATO You will never run mad, niece.

BEATRICE No, not till a hot January.

MESSENGER Don Pedro is approached.

*Enter Don Pedro, Claudio, Benedick, Balthasar, and
John the Bastard.*

85 PEDRO Good Signior Leonato, are you come to meet your
trouble? The fashion of the world is to avoid cost, and
you encounter it.

LEONATO Never came trouble to my house in the likeness of your grace; for trouble being gone, comfort
should remain; but when you depart from me, sorrow
abides and happiness takes his leave.

92 PEDRO You embrace your charge too willingly. I think
this is your daughter.

LEONATO Her mother hath many times told me so.

BENEDICK Were you in doubt, sir, that you asked her?

LEONATO Signior Benedick, no; for then were you a child.

97 PEDRO You have it full, Benedick. We may guess by this
98 what you are, being a man. Truly the lady fathers herself. Be happy, lady, for you are like an honorable father.

BENEDICK If Signior Leonato be her father, she would
not have his head on her shoulders for all Messina, as 101
like him as she is.

BEATRICE I wonder that you will still be talking, Signior
Benedick. Nobody marks you. 104

BENEDICK What, my dear Lady Disdain! are you yet
living?

BEATRICE Is it possible Disdain should die while she
hath such meet food to feed it as Signior Benedick? 107
Courtesy itself must convert to Disdain if you come in 108
her presence.

BENEDICK Then is courtesy a turncoat. But it is certain I
am loved of all ladies, only you excepted; and I would I
could find in my heart that I had not a hard heart, for
truly I love none.

BEATRICE A dear happiness to women! They would else 114
have been troubled with a pernicious suitor. I thank
God and my cold blood, I am of your humor for that. I 116
had rather hear my dog bark at a crow than a man swear
he loves me.

BENEDICK God keep your ladyship still in that mind! So
some gentleman or other shall scape a predestinate
scratched face.

BEATRICE Scratching could not make it worse an 'twere
such a face as yours were.

BENEDICK Well, you are a rare parrot-teacher. 124

BEATRICE A bird of my tongue is better than a beast of 125
yours.

BENEDICK I would my horse had the speed of your
tongue, and so good a continuer. But keep your way, a 127
God's name! I have done.

BEATRICE You always end with a jade's trick. I know you 129
of old.

PEDRO That is the sum of all, Leonato. Signior Claudio 131
and Signior Benedick, my dear friend Leonato hath invited you all. I tell him we shall stay here at the least a
month, and he heartily prays some occasion may detain
us longer. I dare swear he is no hypocrite, but prays
from his heart.

LEONATO If you swear, my lord, you shall not be forsworn. 136
[to Don John] Let me bid you welcome, my lord. Being 137
reconciled to the Prince your brother, I owe you all duty.

JOHN I thank you. I am not of many words, but I thank
you.

LEONATO Please it your grace lead on?

PEDRO Your hand, Leonato. We will go together. 142
Exeunt. Manent Benedick and Claudio.

CLAUDIO Benedick, didst thou note the daughter of Signior Leonato?

BENEDICK I noted her not, but I looked on her. 145

CLAUDIO Is she not a modest young lady?

BENEDICK Do you question me as an honest man should
do, for my simple true judgment? or would you have me
speak after my custom, as being a professed tyrant to 149
their sex?

CLAUDIO No, I pray thee speak in sober judgment.

BENEDICK Why, i' faith, methinks she's too low for a 152
high praise, too brown for a fair praise, and too little for
a great praise. Only this commendation I can afford her,
that were she other than she is, she were unhandsome,
and being no other but as she is, I do not like her.

CLAUDIO Thou thinkest I am in sport. I pray thee tell me
truly how thou lik'st her.

BENEDICK Would you buy her, that you enquire after 159
her?

---

58 *five wits* mental faculties; *halting* limping   60 *difference* distinguishing mark (heraldic term)   66 *faith* truth to his oath   67 *block* hat-block, i.e. style   68 *books* favor   69 *An* if   71 *squarer* squarer-off, quarreller   75 *he* i.e. Benedick   77 *presently* immediately   80 *hold* remain   82 *run mad* i.e. 'catch the Benedick'   85-86 *your trouble* the trouble of entertaining a noble guest   92 *charge* expense, but also responsibility   97 *have it full* are fully answered   98-99 *fathers herself* resembles and so indicates her father   101 *his head* (with its white hair and beard)   104 *marks* notices   107 *meet* suitable   108 *convert* change   114 *dear* great   116 *humor for that* opinion on that point   124 *rare* exceptional; *parrot-teacher* one who teaches a parrot by repeating monotonously   125 *A bird of my tongue* a bird that speaks   125-26 *a beast of yours* a dumb beast   127 *continuer* one having endurance   129 *a jade's trick* i.e. dropping out of a race just when the horse should be getting well started   131 *sum of all* whole account (of the recent campaign?)   136 *forsworn* proved a liar   137 *Being* since you are   142 *go together* (the Duke refuses to take precedence of his host)   145 *noted* noticed especially   149 *tyrant* to railer against, detractor of   152 *low* short   159 *buy* bid for, try to win

CLAUDIO Can the world buy such a jewel?

161 BENEDICK Yea, and a case to put it into. But speak you
162 this with a sad brow? or do you play the flouting Jack, to
163 tell us Cupid is a good hare-finder and Vulcan a rare
164 carpenter? Come, in what key shall a man take you to go
in the song?

CLAUDIO In mine eye she is the sweetest lady that ever I
looked on.

BENEDICK I can see yet without spectacles, and I see no
such matter. There's her cousin, an she were not possessed with a fury, exceeds her as much in beauty as the
first of May doth the last of December. But I hope you
have no intent to turn husband, have you?

CLAUDIO I would scarce trust myself, though I had
sworn the contrary, if Hero would be my wife.

BENEDICK Is't come to this? In faith, hath not the world
176 one man but he will wear his cap with suspicion? Shall I
never see a bachelor of threescore again? Go to, i' faith!
An thou wilt needs thrust thy neck into a yoke, wear the
179 print of it and sigh away Sundays. Look! Don Pedro
is returned to seek you.

Enter Don Pedro.

PEDRO What secret hath held you here, that you followed
not to Leonato's?

183 BENEDICK I would your grace would constrain me to tell.
184 PEDRO I charge thee on thy allegiance.

BENEDICK You hear, Count Claudio. I can be secret as a
dumb man, I would have you think so; but, on my
allegiance – mark you this – on my allegiance! he is in
188 love. With who? Now that is your grace's part. Mark
how short his answer is: With Hero, Leonato's short
daughter.

191 CLAUDIO If this were so, so were it uttered.
192 BENEDICK Like the old tale, my lord: 'It is not so, nor
'twas not so; but indeed, God forbid it should be so!'

CLAUDIO If my passion change not shortly, God forbid
it should be otherwise.

PEDRO Amen, if you love her, for the lady is very well
worthy.

198 CLAUDIO You speak this to fetch me in, my lord.
PEDRO By my troth, I speak my thought.
CLAUDIO And, in faith, my lord, I spoke mine.
201 BENEDICK And, by my two faiths and troths, my lord, I
spoke mine.
CLAUDIO That I love her, I feel.
PEDRO That she is worthy, I know.
BENEDICK That I neither feel how she should be loved,
nor know how she should be worthy, is the opinion that
207 fire cannot melt out of me. I will die in it at the stake.
208 PEDRO Thou wast ever an obstinate heretic in the despite
of beauty.
210 CLAUDIO And never could maintain his part but in the
force of his will.
BENEDICK That a woman conceived me, I thank her;
that she brought me up, I likewise give her most humble
214 thanks; but that I will have a rechate winded in my fore-
215 head, or hang my bugle in an invisible baldrick, all
women shall pardon me. Because I will not do them the
wrong to mistrust any, I will do myself the right to trust
218 none; and the fine is (for the which I may go the finer),
I will live a bachelor.
PEDRO I shall see thee, ere I die, look pale with love.
BENEDICK With anger, with sickness, or with hunger, my
222 lord, not with love. Prove that ever I lose more blood

with love than I will get again with drinking, pick out 223
mine eyes with a ballad-maker's pen and hang me up at
the door of a brothel house for the sign of blind Cupid.

PEDRO Well, if ever thou dost fall from this faith, thou
wilt prove a notable argument. 227

BENEDICK If I do, hang me in a bottle like a cat and shoot 228
at me; and he that hits me, let him be clapped on the
shoulder and called Adam. 230

PEDRO Well, as time shall try.
'In time the savage bull doth bear the yoke.' 232

BENEDICK The savage bull may, but if ever the sensible
Benedick bear it, pluck off the bull's horns and set them
in my forehead, and let me be vilely painted, and in such
great letters as they write 'Here is good horse to hire,'
let them signify under my sign 'Here you may see
Benedick the married man.'

CLAUDIO If this should ever happen, thou wouldst be
horn-mad. 240

PEDRO Nay, if Cupid have not spent all his quiver in
Venice, thou wilt quake for this shortly. 242

BENEDICK I look for an earthquake too then.

PEDRO Well, you will temporize with the hours. In the 244
meantime, good Signior Benedick, repair to Leonato's,
commend me to him and tell him I will not fail him at
supper; for indeed he hath made great preparation.

BENEDICK I have almost matter enough in me for such 248
an embassage, and so I commit you –

CLAUDIO To the tuition of God. From my house – if I 250
had it –

PEDRO The sixth of July. Your loving friend, Benedick.

BENEDICK Nay, mock not, mock not. The body of your
discourse is sometime guarded with fragments, and the 254
guards are but slightly basted on neither. Ere you flout 255
old ends any further, examine your conscience. And so
I leave you. *Exit.*

CLAUDIO
My liege, your highness now may do me good. 258

PEDRO
My love is thine to teach. Teach it but how,
And thou shalt see how apt it is to learn 260

---

161 *case* i.e. clothing   162 *sad brow* serious mind; *flouting Jack* mocking
fellow   163–64 *hare-finder . . . carpenter* (Cupid was blind, Vulcan a
blacksmith)   164–65 *go in the song* follow the tune   176 *with suspicion*
for fear he has grown horns, i.e. been made a cuckold by an unfaithful
wife   179 *sigh away Sundays* i.e. become a good 'Sunday-citizen,' a responsible and sober married man   183 *constrain* force   184 *allegiance*
loyalty to me as your prince   188 *part* speech, in the theatrical sense
191 *so were it uttered* so would he tell it   192 *old tale* (a version of the
Bluebeard story in which the heroine's report of her discoveries is punctuated by these words of protest from the murderer)   198 *fetch me in* get me
to confess   201 *two faiths and troths* one to each (but also double dealing
is implied)   207 *fire . . . me* i.e. he will die at the stake for his opinion   208
in the despite in showing scorn   210–11 *maintain . . . will* win the argument
except by stubborn refusal to give in   214 *rechate* recheat, series of notes
on a horn sounded to call the hounds together (with the usual reference
to the cuckold's horns)   215 *hang . . . baldrick* hang my horn on an invisible
belt, i.e. be unaware of my cuckoldry   218 *fine* finis, conclusion; *finer*
more richly dressed (because spared the expense of a wife)   222–23 *lose
. . . love* (lover's sighs were supposed to consume the blood)   223–24 *pick
out . . . pen* i.e. let me be blinded by weeping over love laments   227 *notable
argument* famous example   228 *bottle* basket or cage   230 *Adam* i.e.
Adam Bell, a famous archer   232 *In time . . . yoke* (proverbial)   240
horn-mad raving mad, also mad with jealousy   242 *Venice* (famous for
courtesans); *quake* i.e. with fear (with pun on *quiver*)   244 *temporize
with the hours* weaken with time   248 *matter* sense   250 *tuition* protection
(Claudio is imitating the formal close of a letter)   254 *guarded* trimmed
255 *basted* lightly sewed   255–56 *flout old ends* mock tag ends of wisdom
(or cloth)   258 *do me good* do me a favor   260 *apt* ready

Any hard lesson that may do thee good.

CLAUDIO
Hath Leonato any son, my lord?

PEDRO
No child but Hero; she's his only heir.
264 Dost thou affect her, Claudio?

CLAUDIO   O my lord,
265 When you went onward on this ended action,
I looked upon her with a soldier's eye,
That liked, but had a rougher task in hand
Than to drive liking to the name of love;
269 But now I am returned and that war-thoughts
Have left their places vacant, in their rooms
Come thronging soft and delicate desires,
272 All prompting me how fair young Hero is,
Saying I liked her ere I went to wars.

PEDRO
Thou wilt be like a lover presently
275 And tire the hearer with a book of words.
If thou dost love fair Hero, cherish it,
277 And I will break with her and with her father,
And thou shalt have her. Was't not to this end
279 That thou began'st to twist so fine a story?

CLAUDIO
How sweetly you do minister to love,
281 That know love's grief by his complexion!
But lest my liking might too sudden seem,
283 I would have salved it with a longer treatise.

PEDRO
What need the bridge much broader than the flood?
285 The fairest grant is the necessity.
286 Look, what will serve is fit. 'Tis once, thou lovest,
And I will fit thee with the remedy.
I know we shall have revelling to-night.
I will assume thy part in some disguise
And tell fair Hero I am Claudio,
291 And in her bosom I'll unclasp my heart
And take her hearing prisoner with the force
And strong encounter of my amorous tale.
Then after to her father will I break,
And the conclusion is, she shall be thine.
296 In practice let us put it presently.   Exeunt.

*

264 *affect* aim at, desire   265 *ended action* war just ended   269 *that* because
272 *prompting* reminding   275 *book of words* volume of pretty speeches
277 *break with* broach the subject to   279 *twist* (cf. 'spin a yarn')   281
complexion appearance (referring to the lover's pallor)   283 *salved* smoothed
over; *treatise* discourse   285 *The . . . necessity* the best gift is whatever is
needed   286 *'Tis once* it is beyond question   291 *in her bosom* in private
to her   296 *presently* immediately
I, ii The house of Leonato   1 *cousin* kinsman   6–7 *stamps . . . cover* (the
figure is of a printed book of news)   8 *thick-pleached alley* walk lined with
thickly interwoven boughs   9 *orchard* garden   10 *discovered* disclosed
12 *accordant* agreeable   13 *take . . . top* seize the moment   18 *appear* show
20 *peradventure* perhaps   23 *cry you mercy* beg your pardon
I, iii The house of Leonato   1 *What the goodyear* (mild expostulation)
2 *out of measure* immoderately   3 *breeds* causes it   7 *sufferance* endurance   10 *born under Saturn* saturnine, ill-disposed; *moral* philosophical
11 *mortifying mischief* deadly disease   13 *stomach* appetite   15 *claw* flatter
18 *controlment* restraint   19 *stood out* rebelled   24 *canker* wild dog-rose
(despised as a weed)   25 *blood* humor, temper   26 *fashion a carriage*
assume a manner; *rob love* gain love undeserved   29 *with a muzzle* but
muzzled (i.e. not fully trusted); *enfranchised with a clog* freed, but with a
ball and chain

Enter Leonato and an old man [Antonio], brother to   I, ii
Leonato [meeting].

LEONATO How now, brother? Where is my cousin your   1
son? Hath he provided this music?

ANTONIO He is very busy about it. But, brother, I can
tell you strange news that you yet dreamt not of.

LEONATO Are they good?

ANTONIO As the event stamps them; but they have a   6
good cover, they show well outward. The Prince and
Count Claudio, walking in a thick-pleached alley in   8
mine orchard, were thus much overheard by a man of   9
mine: the Prince discovered to Claudio that he loved   10
my niece your daughter and meant to acknowledge it
this night in a dance, and if he found her accordant, he   12
meant to take the present time by the top and instantly   13
break with you of it.

LEONATO Hath the fellow any wit that told you this?

ANTONIO A good sharp fellow. I will send for him, and
question him yourself.

LEONATO No, no. We will hold it as a dream till it appear   18
itself; but I will acquaint my daughter withal, that she
may be the better prepared for an answer, if peradventure   20
this be true. Go you and tell her of it.   *[Exit Antonio.]*
[Enter Antonio's son with a Musician.]
Cousin, you know what you have to do. – *[to the
Musician]* O, I cry you mercy, friend. Go you with me,   23
and I will use your skill. – Good cousin, have a care this
busy time.   *Exeunt.*

*

Enter Sir John the Bastard and Conrade, his   I, iii
companion.

CONRADE What the goodyear, my lord! Why are you   1
thus out of measure sad?   2

JOHN There is no measure in the occasion that breeds;   3
therefore the sadness is without limit.

CONRADE You should hear reason.

JOHN And when I have heard it, what blessing brings it?

CONRADE If not a present remedy, at least a patient suf-   7
ferance.

JOHN I wonder that thou (being, as thou say'st thou art,
born under Saturn) goest about to apply a moral medi-   10
cine to a mortifying mischief. I cannot hide what I am: 11
I must be sad when I have cause, and smile at no man's
jests; eat when I have stomach, and wait for no man's   13
leisure; sleep when I am drowsy, and tend on no man's
business; laugh when I am merry, and claw no man in   15
his humor.

CONRADE Yea, but you must not make the full show of
this till you may do it without controlment. You have of   18
late stood out against your brother, and he hath ta'en   19
you newly into his grace, where it is impossible you
should take true root but by the fair weather that you
make yourself. It is needful that you frame the season
for your own harvest.

JOHN I had rather be a canker in a hedge than a rose in his   24
grace, and it better fits my blood to be disdained of all   25
than to fashion a carriage to rob love from any. In this,   26
though I cannot be said to be a flattering honest man, it
must not be denied but I am a plain-dealing villain. I am
trusted with a muzzle and enfranchised with a clog;   29
therefore I have decreed not to sing in my cage. If I had
my mouth, I would bite; if I had my liberty, I would do

my liking. In the meantime let me be that I am, and seek
not to alter me.

CONRADE Can you make no use of your discontent?

JOHN I make all use of it, for I use it only. Who comes
here? What news, Borachio?

Enter Borachio.

BORACHIO I came yonder from a great supper. The
Prince your brother is royally entertained by Leonato,
and I can give you intelligence of an intended marriage.

JOHN Will it serve for any model to build mischief on?
41 What is he for a fool that betroths himself to unquietness?

42 BORACHIO Marry, it is your brother's right hand.

JOHN Who? the most exquisite Claudio?

BORACHIO Even he.

45 JOHN A proper squire! And who? and who? which way
looks he?

BORACHIO Marry, one Hero, the daughter and heir of
Leonato.

49 JOHN A very forward March-chick! How came you to
this?

51 BORACHIO Being entertained for a perfumer, as I was
52 smoking a musty room, comes me the Prince and
53 Claudio, hand in hand in sad conference. I whipt me
54 behind the arras and there heard it agreed upon that the
Prince should woo Hero for himself, and having obtained her, give her to Count Claudio.

JOHN Come, come, let us thither. This may prove food to
my displeasure. That young start-up hath all the glory
of my overthrow. If I can cross him any way, I bless my-
60 self every way. You are both sure, and will assist me?

CONRADE To the death, my lord.

JOHN Let us to the great supper. Their cheer is the greater
63 that I am subdued. Would the cook were o' my mind!
64 Shall we go prove what's to be done?

BORACHIO We'll wait upon your lordship.

Exit [with others].

*

II, i   *Enter Leonato, his brother [Antonio], Hero his
daughter, and Beatrice his niece [, also Margaret and
Ursula].*

LEONATO Was not Count John here at supper?

ANTONIO I saw him not.

3 BEATRICE How tartly that gentleman looks! I never can
4 see him but I am heart-burned an hour after.

HERO He is of a very melancholy disposition.

6 BEATRICE He were an excellent man that were made just
in the midway between him and Benedick. The one is
8 too like an image and says nothing, and the other too like
9 my lady's eldest son, evermore tattling.

LEONATO Then half Signior Benedick's tongue in Count
John's mouth, and half Count John's melancholy in
Signior Benedick's face –

BEATRICE With a good leg and a good foot, uncle, and
money enough in his purse, such a man would win any
woman in the world – if 'a could get her good will.

LEONATO By my troth, niece, thou wilt never get thee a
17 husband if thou be so shrewd of thy tongue.

18 ANTONIO In faith, she's too curst.

BEATRICE Too curst is more than curst. I shall lessen
20 God's sending that way, for it is said, 'God sends a curst
cow short horns,' but to a cow too curst he sends none.

LEONATO So, by being too curst, God will send you no
horns.

BEATRICE Just, if he send me no husband; for the which 24
blessing I am at him upon my knees every morning and
evening. Lord, I could not endure a husband with a
beard on his face. I had rather lie in the woollen! 27

LEONATO You may light on a husband that hath no beard. 28

BEATRICE What should I do with him? dress him in my
apparel and make him my waiting gentlewoman? He
that hath a beard is more than a youth, and he that hath
no beard is less than a man; and he that is more than a
youth is not for me; and he that is less than a man, I am
not for him. Therefore I will even take sixpence in 34
earnest of the berrord and lead his apes into hell. 35

LEONATO Well then, go you into hell?

BEATRICE No; but to the gate, and there will the devil
meet me like an old cuckold with horns on his head, and
say, 'Get you to heaven, Beatrice, get you to heaven.
Here's no place for you maids.' So deliver I up my apes,
and away to Saint Peter. For the heavens, he shows me 41
where the bachelors sit, and there live we as merry as the 42
day is long.

ANTONIO *[to Hero]* Well, niece, I trust you will be ruled
by your father.

BEATRICE Yes, faith. It is my cousin's duty to make cursy 45
and say, 'Father, as it please you.' But yet for all that,
cousin, let him be a handsome fellow, or else make another cursy, and say, 'Father, as it please me.'

LEONATO Well, niece, I hope to see you one day fitted
with a husband.

BEATRICE Not till God make men of some other metal 51
than earth. Would it not grieve a woman to be over-
mastered with a piece of valiant dust? to make an
account of her life to a clod of wayward marl? No, uncle, 54
I'll none. Adam's sons are my brethren, and truly I hold
it a sin to match in my kindred. 56

LEONATO Daughter, remember what I told you. If the
Prince do solicit you in that kind, you know your 58
answer.

BEATRICE The fault will be in the music, cousin, if you be
not wooed in good time. If the Prince be too important, 61
tell him there is measure in everything, and so dance out 62
the answer. For, hear me, Hero: wooing, wedding, and
repenting is as a Scotch jig, a measure, and a cinque- 64
pace: the first suit is hot and hasty like a Scotch jig (and
full as fantastical); the wedding, mannerly modest, as a
measure, full of state and ancientry; and then comes 67
Repentance and with his bad legs falls into the cinque-
pace faster and faster, till he sink into his grave.

41 *What is he for a fool* what fool is he   42 *Marry* why, to be sure (originally
an oath by the Virgin Mary)   45 *proper squire* fine fellow (contemptuous)
49 *forward March-chick* precocious youngster   51 *entertained for* hired as
52 *smoking* sweetening the odor with the smoke of burning juniper   53 *sad*
serious   54 *arras* tapestry wall-hanging   60 *sure* trustworthy   63 *o' my
mind* i.e. disposed to poison them   64 *prove* try
II, i The hall of Leonato's house   3 *tartly* sourly   4 *am heart-burned*
have indigestion   6 *He were* that man would be   8 *image* statue   9 *my
lady's eldest son* a spoiled child who talks too much   17 *shrewd* satirical
18 *curst* shrewish, ill-tempered   20 *that way* in that respect   24 *Just*
exactly   27 *in the woollen* between blankets without sheets   28 *light on*
find   34–35 *in earnest* as deposit   35 *berrord* bear-ward (who often also
kept trained apes); *lead his apes* (the proverbial punishment of women who
die virgins)   41 *For the heavens* bound for heaven   42 *bachelors* unmarried
men and women   45 *make cursy* curtsy, show respect   51 *metal* material
54 *marl* clay, earth   56 *match* i.e. wed a brother   58 *solicit
... kind* propose   61 *important* importunate   62 *measure* moderation (but
also a kind of dance)   64 *cinque-pace* lively dance   67 *state* dignity;
ancientry traditional formality

70 LEONATO Cousin, you apprehend passing shrewdly.

BEATRICE I have a good eye, uncle; I can see a church by daylight.

LEONATO The revellers are entering, brother. Make good room.

Enter [masked] Prince [Don] Pedro, Claudio, and Benedick, and Balthasar; [also, unmasked,] Don John [and Borachio, and musicians].

75 PEDRO Lady, will you walk about with your friend?

HERO So you walk softly and look sweetly and say nothing, I am yours for the walk; and especially when I walk away.

PEDRO With me in your company?

HERO I may say so when I please.

PEDRO And when please you to say so?

82 HERO When I like your favor, for God defend the lute should be like the case!

84 PEDRO My visor is Philemon's roof; within the house is Jove.

86 HERO Why then, your visor should be thatched.

PEDRO Speak low if you speak love.

[They step aside.]

BALTHASAR Well, I would you did like me.

MARGARET So would not I for your own sake, for I have

90 many ill qualities.

BALTHASAR Which is one?

MARGARET I say my prayers aloud.

BALTHASAR I love you the better. The hearers may cry amen.

MARGARET God match me with a good dancer!

BALTHASAR Amen.

MARGARET And God keep him out of my sight when the

97 dance is done! Answer, clerk.

BALTHASAR No more words. The clerk is answered.

[They step aside.]

URSULA I know you well enough. You are Signior Antonio.

ANTONIO At a word, I am not.

101 URSULA I know you by the waggling of your head.

ANTONIO To tell you true, I counterfeit him.

103 URSULA You could never do him so ill-well unless you

104 were the very man. Here's his dry hand up and down. You are he, you are he!

ANTONIO At a word, I am not.

URSULA Come, come, do you think I do not know you by your excellent wit? Can virtue hide itself? Go to, mum,

109 you are he. Graces will appear, and there's an end.

[They step aside.]

BEATRICE Will you not tell me who told you so?

BENEDICK No, you shall pardon me.

BEATRICE Nor will you not tell me who you are?

BENEDICK Not now.

BEATRICE That I was disdainful, and that I had my good wit out of the 'Hundred Merry Tales.' Well, this was 115 Signior Benedick that said so.

BENEDICK What's he?

BEATRICE I am sure you know him well enough.

BENEDICK Not I, believe me.

BEATRICE Did he never make you laugh?

BENEDICK I pray you, what is he?

BEATRICE Why, he is the Prince's jester, a very dull fool. Only his gift is in devising impossible slanders. None but 123 libertines delight in him; and the commendation is not 124 in his wit, but in his villainy; for he both pleases men and angers them, and then they laugh at him and beat him. I am sure he is in the fleet. I would he had boarded 127 me.

BENEDICK When I know the gentleman, I'll tell him what you say.

BEATRICE Do, do. He'll but break a comparison or two on 131 me; which peradventure, not marked or not laughed at, strikes him into melancholy; and then there's a partridge wing saved, for the fool will eat no supper 134 that night. *[Music.]* We must follow the leaders.

BENEDICK In every good thing.

BEATRICE Nay, if they lead to any ill, I will leave them at the next turning.

Dance. Exeunt [all but Don John, Borachio, and Claudio].

JOHN Sure my brother is amorous on Hero and hath withdrawn her father to break with him about it. The ladies follow her and but one visor remains.

BORACHIO And that is Claudio. I know him by his bearing.

JOHN Are not you Signior Benedick?

CLAUDIO You know me well. I am he.

JOHN Signior, you are very near my brother in his love. He is enamored on Hero. I pray you dissuade him from her; she is no equal for his birth. You may do the part of an honest man in it.

CLAUDIO How know you he loves her?

JOHN I heard him swear his affection.

BORACHIO So did I too, and he swore he would marry her to-night.

JOHN Come, let us to the banquet.   153

Exeunt. Manet Claudio.

CLAUDIO

Thus answer I in name of Benedick

But hear these ill news with the ears of Claudio.

'Tis certain so. The Prince woos for himself.

Friendship is constant in all other things

Save in the office and affairs of love.   158

Therefore all hearts in love use their own tongues;

Let every eye negotiate for itself

And trust no agent; for beauty is a witch

Against whose charms faith melteth into blood.   162

This is an accident of hourly proof,   163

Which I mistrusted not. Farewell therefore Hero!   164

Enter Benedick.

BENEDICK Count Claudio?

CLAUDIO Yea, the same.

BENEDICK Come, will you go with me?

CLAUDIO Whither?

---

70 *apprehend passing shrewdly* perceive with unusual sharpness   **75** *friend* a lover of either sex   **82** *favor* face; *defend* forbid, prevent   **82–83** *lute . . . case* i.e. your face should be like your mask   **84** *visor* mask; *Philemon* a peasant who entertained Jove and Mercury in his humble cottage   **86** *thatched* i.e. whiskered   **90** *qualities* traits of character   **97** *clerk* (the parish clerk read the responses in church services)   **101** *waggling* palsied motion   **103** *do him so ill-well* imitate his ills so well   **104** *dry hand* (a sign of age); *up and down* entirely   **109** *Graces* good qualities   **115** *Hundred Merry Tales* a popular jestbook   **123** *Only his gift* his only gift; *impossible* incredible   **124** *libertines* free thinkers, loose livers   **127** *fleet* company of maskers (with play on sea-fleet); *boarded* closed in on (nautical term)   **131** *break a comparison* tilt with words   **134** *partridge wing* (considered a great delicacy)   **153** *banquet* light repast of wine and sweets   **158** *office* business, employment   **162** *faith melteth* (as a witch melts the wax image of someone she wishes to destroy); *blood* passion   **163** *accident . . . proof* common occurrence   **164** *mistrusted* suspected

BENEDICK Even to the next willow, about your own busi-
170 ness, County. What fashion will you wear the garland
171 of? about your neck, like an usurer's chain? or under
your arm, like a lieutenant's scarf? You must wear it
one way, for the Prince hath got your Hero.

CLAUDIO I wish him joy of her.

175 BENEDICK Why, that's spoken like an honest drovier. So
they sell bullocks. But did you think the Prince would
have served you thus?

CLAUDIO I pray you leave me.

179 BENEDICK Ho! now you strike like the blind man! 'Twas
the boy that stole your meat, and you'll beat the post.

181 CLAUDIO If it will not be, I'll leave you.   Exit.

BENEDICK Alas, poor hurt fowl! now will he creep into
183 sedges. But, that my Lady Beatrice should know me,
and not know me! The Prince's fool! Ha! it may be I go
under that title because I am merry. Yea, but so I am
apt to do myself wrong. I am not so reputed. It is
187 the base (though bitter) disposition of Beatrice that
188 puts the world into her person and so gives me out.
Well, I'll be revenged as I may.

Enter the Prince [Don Pedro], Hero, Leonato.

PEDRO Now, signior, where's the Count? Did you see
him?

191 BENEDICK Troth, my lord, I have played the part of Lady
192 Fame. I found him here as melancholy as a lodge in a
warren. I told him, and I think I told him true, that your
grace had got the good will of this young lady, and I
offered him my company to a willow tree, either to make
him a garland, as being forsaken, or to bind him up a
rod, as being worthy to be whipt.

PEDRO To be whipt? What's his fault?

199 BENEDICK The flat transgression of a schoolboy who,
being overjoyed with finding a bird's nest, shows it his
companion, and he steals it.

PEDRO Wilt thou make a trust a transgression? The transgression is in the stealer.

BENEDICK Yet it had not been amiss the rod had been
made, and the garland too; for the garland he might
have worn himself, and the rod he might have bestowed
on you, who, as I take it, have stolen his bird's nest.

PEDRO I will but teach them to sing and restore them to
the owner.

210 BENEDICK If their singing answer your saying, by my
faith you say honestly.

PEDRO The Lady Beatrice hath a quarrel to you. The
gentleman that danced with her told her she is much
213 wronged by you.

BENEDICK O, she misused me past the endurance of a
block! An oak but with one green leaf on it would have
answered her; my very visor began to assume life and
scold with her. She told me, not thinking I had been myself, that I was the Prince's jester, that I was duller than
220 a great thaw; huddling jest upon jest with such impos-
221 sible conveyance upon me that I stood like a man at a
mark, with a whole army shooting at me. She speaks
poniards, and every word stabs. If her breath were as
224 terrible as her terminations, there were no living near
225 her; she would infect to the North Star. I would not
marry her though she were endowed with all that Adam
had left him before he transgressed. She would have
228 made Hercules have turned spit, yea, and have cleft his
club to make the fire too. Come, talk not of her. You
230 shall find her the infernal Ate in good apparel. I would

to God some scholar would conjure her, for certainly, 231
while she is here, a man may live as quiet in hell as in a
sanctuary; and people sin upon purpose, because they
would go thither; so indeed all disquiet, horror, and
perturbation follows her.

Enter Claudio and Beatrice.

PEDRO Look, here she comes.

BENEDICK Will your grace command me any service to
the world's end? I will go on the slightest errand now to
the Antipodes that you can devise to send me on; I will
fetch you a toothpicker now from the furthest inch of 239
Asia; bring you the length of Prester John's foot; fetch 240
you a hair off the great Cham's beard; do you any em- 241
bassage to the Pygmies – rather than hold three words'
conference with this harpy. You have no employment 243
for me?

PEDRO None, but to desire your good company.

BENEDICK O God, sir, here's a dish I love not! I cannot
endure my Lady Tongue.   Exit.

PEDRO Come, lady, come; you have lost the heart of
Signior Benedick.

BEATRICE Indeed, my lord, he lent it me awhile, and I
gave him use for it – a double heart for his single one. 250
Marry, once before he won it of me with false dice;
therefore your grace may well say I have lost it.

PEDRO You have put him down, lady; you have put him
down.

BEATRICE So I would not he should do me, my lord, lest
I should prove the mother of fools. I have brought
Count Claudio, whom you sent me to seek.

PEDRO Why, how now, Count? Wherefore are you sad?

CLAUDIO Not sad, my lord.

PEDRO How then? sick?

CLAUDIO Neither, my lord.

BEATRICE The Count is neither sad, nor sick, nor merry,
nor well; but civil Count – civil as an orange, and some- 263
thing of that jealous complexion.   264

PEDRO I' faith, lady, I think your blazon to be true; 265
though I'll be sworn, if he be so, his conceit is false. 266
Here, Claudio, I have wooed in thy name, and fair Hero
is won. I have broke with her father, and his good will
obtained. Name the day of marriage, and God give thee
joy!

170 *County* count; *garland* i.e. of willow, symbol of forsaken love 171
about your neck i.e. as a symbol of wealth 171–72 *under your arm* i.e. gaily,
as a symbol of honor 175 *drovier* drover, cattle trader 179 *the blind
man* (unidentified allusion to a proverb or familiar story) 181 *If . . . be* if
you will not go 183 *sedges* reeds 187 *bitter* biting 188 *puts . . . person*
attributes to the world her own personal feelings; *gives me out* reports me
191–92 *Lady Fame* bearer of tidings 192–93 *lodge . . . warren* hutch in a
rabbit warren (symbol of melancholy) 199 *flat* plain 210 *If . . . saying*
if it turns out as you say 213 *wronged* slandered 220 *thaw* (when roads
are impassable and one must stay at home) 220–21 *impossible conveyance*
incredible dexterity 221–22 *at a mark* beside a target 224 *terminations*
terms, i.e. name-calling 225 *infect* emit foul odors (supposed to carry
infection) 228 *Hercules . . . spit* (The Amazon Omphale enslaved Hercules
and set him to spinning. Turning a spit was an even more humble chore,
assigned to a boy or even a dog.) 230 *Ate* goddess of discord 231 *conjure
her* (scholars were supposed to have the power to call up or dismiss evil
spirits) 239 *toothpicker* toothpick 240 *Prester John* a fabulous monarch
of the Far East 241 *Cham* Khan of Tartary, ruler of the Mongols 243
harpy a bird-woman, predatory and befouling 250 *use* interest, usury
250–52 *double heart . . . lost it* (an obscure allusion; 'double' often meant
deceitful, and this may be a taunt that Benedick can only get his heart away
from her by trickery) 263 *civil* grave, sober (with a pun on oranges of
Seville) 264 *of . . . complexion* i.e. yellow (symbolic of jealousy) 265
blazon description (heraldic term) 266 *conceit* conception, idea (with the
additional suggestion here, after *blazon*, of the fanciful device painted on a
knight's shield)

LEONATO Count, take of me my daughter, and with her
271 my fortunes. His grace hath made the match, and all
grace say amen to it!

BEATRICE Speak, Count, 'tis your cue.

CLAUDIO Silence is the perfectest herald of joy. I were
but little happy if I could say how much. Lady, as you
are mine, I am yours. I give away myself for you and
dote upon the exchange.

BEATRICE Speak, cousin; or, if you cannot, stop his
mouth with a kiss and let not him speak neither.

PEDRO In faith, lady, you have a merry heart.

281 BEATRICE Yea, my lord; I thank it, poor fool, it keeps on
282 the windy side of care. My cousin tells him in his ear
that he is in her heart.

CLAUDIO And so she doth, cousin.

285 BEATRICE Good Lord, for alliance! Thus goes every one
286 to the world but I, and I am sunburnt. I may sit in a
287 corner and cry 'Heigh-ho for a husband!'

288 PEDRO Lady Beatrice, I will get you one.

289 BEATRICE I would rather have one of your father's getting.
Hath your grace ne'er a brother like you? Your father
got excellent husbands, if a maid could come by them.

PEDRO Will you have me, lady?

BEATRICE No, my lord, unless I might have another for
working days: your grace is too costly to wear every day.
But I beseech your grace pardon me. I was born to
296 speak all mirth and no matter.

PEDRO Your silence most offends me, and to be merry
best becomes you, for out o' question you were born in a
merry hour.

BEATRICE No, sure, my lord, my mother cried; but then
there was a star danced, and under that was I born.
Cousins, God give you joy!

LEONATO Niece, will you look to those things I told you
of?

304 BEATRICE I cry you mercy, uncle. By your grace's pardon.   *Exit Beatrice.*

PEDRO By my troth, a pleasant-spirited lady.

LEONATO There's little of the melancholy element in her,
my lord. She is never sad but when she sleeps, and not
ever sad then; for I have heard my daughter say she
hath often dreamt of unhappiness and waked herself
with laughing.

PEDRO She cannot endure to hear tell of a husband.

311 LEONATO O, by no means! She mocks all her wooers out
of suit.

PEDRO She were an excellent wife for Benedick.

LEONATO O Lord, my lord! if they were but a week
married, they would talk themselves mad.

PEDRO County Claudio, when mean you to go to church?

CLAUDIO To-morrow, my lord. Time goes on crutches
till Love have all his rites.

LEONATO Not till Monday, my dear son, which is hence
a just sevennight; and a time too brief too, to have all
things answer my mind.   321

PEDRO Come, you shake the head at so long a breathing;
but I warrant thee, Claudio, the time shall not go dully
by us. I will in the interim undertake one of Hercules'
labors, which is, to bring Signior Benedick and the Lady
Beatrice into a mountain of affection th' one with th'
other. I would fain have it a match, and I doubt not but 327
to fashion it if you three will but minister such assistance as I shall give you direction.

LEONATO My lord, I am for you, though it cost me ten
nights' watchings.

CLAUDIO And I, my lord.

PEDRO And you too, gentle Hero?

HERO I will do any modest office, my lord, to help my
cousin to a good husband.

PEDRO And Benedick is not the unhopefullest husband
that I know. Thus far can I praise him: he is of a noble
strain, of approved valor, and confirmed honesty. I will 337
teach you how to humor your cousin, that she shall fall
in love with Benedick; and I, *[to Leonato and Claudio]*
with your two helps, will so practice on Benedick that, in 341
despite of his quick wit and his queasy stomach, he shall 342
fall in love with Beatrice. If we can do this, Cupid is no
longer an archer; his glory shall be ours, for we are the
only love-gods. Go in with me, and I will tell you my
drift.   *Exit [with the others].* 345

*

Enter [Don] John and Borachio.   II, ii

JOHN It is so. The Count Claudio shall marry the daughter
of Leonato.

BORACHIO Yea, my lord; but I can cross it.

JOHN Any bar, any cross, any impediment will be medi- 4
cinable to me. I am sick in displeasure to him, and what- 5
soever comes athwart his affection ranges evenly with
mine. How canst thou cross this marriage?

BORACHIO Not honestly, my lord, but so covertly that no 8
dishonesty shall appear in me.

JOHN Show me briefly how.

BORACHIO I think I told your lordship, a year since, how
much I am in the favor of Margaret, the waiting gentlewoman to Hero.

JOHN I remember.

BORACHIO I can, at any unseasonable instant of the night,
appoint her to look out at her lady's chamber window.

JOHN What life is in that to be the death of this marriage?

BORACHIO The poison of that lies in you to temper. Go 18
you to the Prince your brother; spare not to tell him
that he hath wronged his honor in marrying the renowned Claudio (whose estimation do you mightily 21
hold up) to a contaminated stale, such a one as Hero. 22

JOHN What proof shall I make of that?

BORACHIO Proof enough to misuse the Prince, to vex
Claudio, to undo Hero, and kill Leonato. Look you for
any other issue?

JOHN Only to despite them I will endeavor anything. 27

BORACHIO Go then; find me a meet hour to draw Don 28
Pedro and the Count Claudio alone; tell them that you

271–72 *all grace* i.e. the Source of all grace 281 *fool* innocent creature
282 *windy* windward, safe 285 *for alliance* (Claudio has just called her
cousin in anticipation of becoming her cousin by marriage) 285–86 *goes
... world* everybody gets married 286 *sunburnt* i.e. no longer fair 287
Heigh-ho for a husband (from an old song) 288 *get* procure 289 *getting*
begetting 296 *matter* substance 304 *cry you mercy* beg your pardon (for
not having done his bidding already) 304–05 *By your grace's pardon*
excuse me (addressed to the Prince) 311–12 *mocks ... suit* makes fun of
them until they do not dare to woo her 321 *answer my mind* as I wish them
327 *fain* gladly 337 *strain* family 341–42 *in despite* in spite 342 *queasy*
delicate 345 *drift* plan
II, ii The house of Leonato 4 *medicinable* curative 5–7 *whatsoever ...
mine* whatever vexes him soothes me 8 *covertly* secretly 18 *temper* compound, mix 21 *estimation* reputation 22 *stale* prostitute 27 *despite*
spite 28 *meet hour* suitable time

30 know that Hero loves me; intend a kind of zeal both to
the Prince and Claudio, as – in love of your brother's
honor, who hath made this match, and his friend's repu-
33 tation, who is thus like to be cozened with the semblance
of a maid – that you have discovered thus. They will
35 scarcely believe this without trial. Offer them instances;
which shall bear no less likelihood than to see me at her
chamber window, hear me call Margaret Hero, hear
Margaret term me Claudio; and bring them to see this
the very night before the intended wedding (for in the
meantime I will so fashion the matter that Hero shall be
absent) and there shall appear such seeming truth of
42 Hero's disloyalty that jealousy shall be called assurance
and all the preparation overthrown.

JOHN Grow this to what adverse issue it can, I will put it
in practice. Be cunning in the working this, and thy fee
46 is a thousand ducats.

BORACHIO Be you constant in the accusation, and my
cunning shall not shame me.

49 JOHN I will presently go learn their day of marriage.

Exit [with Borachio].

*

II, iii   *Enter Benedick alone.*

BENEDICK Boy!

        [Enter Boy.]

BOY Signior?

BENEDICK In my chamber window lies a book. Bring it
hither to me in the orchard.

BOY I am here already, sir.

BENEDICK I know that, but I would have thee hence and
here again. *(Exit [Boy].)* I do much wonder that one
man, seeing how much another man is a fool when he
dedicates his behaviors to love, will, after he hath laughed
10 at such shallow follies in others, become the argument of
his own scorn by falling in love; and such a man is
Claudio. I have known when there was no music with
him but the drum and the fife; and now had he rather
hear the tabor and the pipe. I have known when he would
15 have walked ten mile afoot to see a good armor; and now
16 will he lie ten nights awake carving the fashion of a new
17 doublet. He was wont to speak plain and to the purpose,
like an honest man and a soldier; and now is he turned
19 orthography; his words are a very fantastical banquet –
20 just so many strange dishes. May I be so converted and
21 see with these eyes? I cannot tell; I think not. I will not be
sworn but love may transform me to an oyster; but I'll
take my oath on it, till he have made an oyster of me he
shall never make me such a fool. One woman is fair, yet
I am well; another is wise, yet I am well; another virtuous, yet I am well; but till all graces be in one woman,
one woman shall not come in my grace. Rich she shall
be, that's certain; wise, or I'll none; virtuous, or I'll
29 never cheapen her; fair, or I'll never look on her; mild,
30 or come not near me; noble, or not I for an angel; of
good discourse, an excellent musician, and her hair shall
be of what color it please God. Ha, the Prince and Mon-
33 sieur Love! *[retiring]* I will hide me in the arbor.

        *Enter Prince [Don Pedro], Leonato, Claudio,
        Balthasar, with Music.*

PEDRO

Come, shall we hear this music?

CLAUDIO

Yea, my good lord. How still the evening is,
As hushed on purpose to grace harmony!

PEDRO

See you where Benedick hath hid himself?

CLAUDIO

O, very well, my lord. The music ended,
We'll fit the kid-fox with a pennyworth.   39

PEDRO

Come, Balthasar, we'll hear that song again.

BALTHASAR

O, good my lord, tax not so bad a voice
To slander music any more than once.

PEDRO

It is the witness still of excellency   43
To put a strange face on his own perfection.   44
I pray thee sing, and let me woo no more.

BALTHASAR

Because you talk of wooing, I will sing,
Since many a wooer doth commence his suit
To her he thinks not worthy, yet he woos,
Yet will he swear he loves.

PEDRO   Nay, pray thee come;
Or if thou wilt hold longer argument,   50
Do it in notes.

BALTHASAR   Note this before my notes:
There's not a note of mine that's worth the noting.

PEDRO

Why, these are very crotchets that he speaks!   53
Note notes, forsooth, and nothing!   54

        [Music.]

BENEDICK *[aside]* Now divine air! Now is his soul
ravished! Is it not strange that sheep's guts should hale   56
souls out of men's bodies? Well, a horn for my money,
when all's done.

        [Balthasar sings.]

                    The Song.

Sigh no more, ladies, sigh no more!
    Men were deceivers ever,
One foot in sea, and one on shore;
    To one thing constant never.
        Then sigh not so,
        But let them go,
    And be you blithe and bonny,
Converting all your sounds of woe
    Into Hey nonny, nonny.

Sing no more ditties, sing no moe,
    Of dumps so dull and heavy!   69
The fraud of men was ever so,
    Since summer first was leavy.
        Then sigh not so, &c.

30 *intend* pretend 33 *cozened* deceived, cheated; *semblance* outward appearance 35 *instances* proofs 42 *jealousy* suspicion; *assurance* proof 46 *ducats* gold coins 49 *presently* immediately
II, iii Leonato's orchard 10 *argument* subject 15 *armor* suit of armor 16 *carving* designing 17 *doublet* jacket 19 *orthography* pedantic in his choice and pronunciation of words 20 *converted* changed 21 *these eyes* the eyes of a lover 29 *cheapen* bargain for 30 *noble . . . angel* (play on the names of gold coins. The noble was worth about a third less than the angel.) 33 s.d. *Music* accompanists 39 *fit . . . pennyworth* give the sly young fellow all he bargained for 43 *witness* evidence 44 *put . . . on* pretend not to know 50 *argument* talk 53 *crotchets* notes of half the value of a minim, very small notes 54 *nothing* (pronounced the same as *noting* above, and so punned on) 56 *hale* draw 69 *dumps* sad songs, usually love songs

PEDRO By my troth, a good song.

BALTHASAR And an ill singer, my lord.

PEDRO Ha, no, no, faith! Thou sing'st well enough for a
76 shift.

BENEDICK [aside] An he had been a dog that should have
howled thus, they would have hanged him; and I pray
79 God his bad voice bode no mischief. I had as live have
80 heard the night raven, come what plague could have
come after it.

PEDRO Yea, marry. Dost thou hear, Balthasar? I pray
thee get us some excellent music; for to-morrow night
we would have it at the Lady Hero's chamber window.

BALTHASAR The best I can, my lord.

PEDRO Do so. Farewell. Exit Balthasar [with Musicians].
Come hither, Leonato. What was it you told me of to-
day? that your niece Beatrice was in love with Signior
Benedick?

CLAUDIO O, ay! – [aside to Pedro] Stalk on, stalk on; the
fowl sits. – I did never think that lady would have loved
any man.

LEONATO No, nor I neither; but most wonderful that
she should so dote on Signior Benedick, whom she hath
in all outward behaviors seemed ever to abhor.

BENEDICK [aside] Is't possible? Sits the wind in that
corner?

LEONATO By my troth, my lord, I cannot tell what to
98 think of it, but that she loves him with an enraged
99 affection, it is past the infinite of thought.

PEDRO May be she doth but counterfeit.

CLAUDIO Faith, like enough.

LEONATO O God, counterfeit? There was never counterfeit of passion came so near the life of passion as she
104 discovers it.

PEDRO Why, what effects of passion shows she?

CLAUDIO [aside] Bait the hook well! This fish will bite.

LEONATO What effects, my lord? She will sit you – you
heard my daughter tell you how.

CLAUDIO She did indeed.

PEDRO How, how, I pray you? You amaze me. I would
have thought her spirit had been invincible against all
assaults of affection.

LEONATO I would have sworn it had, my lord – especially
against Benedick.

115 BENEDICK [aside] I should think this a gull but that the
white-bearded fellow speaks it. Knavery cannot, sure,
hide himself in such reverence.

118 CLAUDIO [aside] He hath ta'en th' infection. Hold it up.

PEDRO Hath she made her affection known to Benedick?

LEONATO No, and swears she never will. That's her torment.

CLAUDIO 'Tis true indeed. So your daughter says. 'Shall
I,' says she, 'that have so oft encountered him with
scorn, write to him that I love him?'

LEONATO This says she now when she is beginning to
write to him; for she'll be up twenty times a night, and
there will she sit in her smock till she have writ a sheet 126
of paper. My daughter tells us all.

CLAUDIO Now you talk of a sheet of paper, I remember a
pretty jest your daughter told us of.

LEONATO O, when she had writ it, and was reading it over,
she found 'Benedick' and 'Beatrice' between the sheet? 131

CLAUDIO That.

LEONATO O, she tore the letter into a thousand halfpence, 133
railed at herself that she should be so immodest to write
to one that she knew would flout her. 'I measure him,' 135
says she, 'by my own spirit; for I should flout him if he
writ to me. Yea, though I love him, I should.'

CLAUDIO Then down upon her knees she falls, weeps,
sobs, beats her heart, tears her hair, prays, curses – 'O
sweet Benedick! God give me patience!'

LEONATO She doth indeed; my daughter says so. And
the ecstasy hath so much overborne her that my 142
daughter is sometime afeard she will do a desperate outrage to herself. It is very true.

PEDRO It were good that Benedick knew of it by some
other, if she will not discover it.

CLAUDIO To what end? He would make but a sport of it
and torment the poor lady worse.

PEDRO An he should, it were an alms to hang him! She's 149
an excellent sweet lady, and (out of all suspicion) she is
virtuous.

CLAUDIO And she is exceeding wise.

PEDRO In everything but in loving Benedick.

LEONATO O, my lord, wisdom and blood combating in so 154
tender a body, we have ten proofs to one that blood hath
the victory. I am sorry for her, as I have just cause, being
her uncle and her guardian.

PEDRO I would she had bestowed this dotage on me. I 158
would have daffed all other respects and made her half 159
myself. I pray you tell Benedick of it and hear what 'a
will say.

LEONATO Were it good, think you?

CLAUDIO Hero thinks surely she will die; for she says she
will die if he love her not, and she will die ere she make
her love known, and she will die, if he woo her, rather
than she will bate one breath of her accustomed cross- 165
ness.

PEDRO She doth well. If she should make tender of her 166
love, 'tis very possible he'll scorn it; for the man (as you
know all) hath a contemptible spirit. 168

CLAUDIO He is a very proper man. 169

PEDRO He hath indeed a good outward happiness. 170

CLAUDIO Before God! and in my mind, very wise.

PEDRO He doth indeed show some sparks that are like wit. 172

CLAUDIO And I take him to be valiant.

PEDRO As Hector, I assure you; and in the managing of
quarrels you may say he is wise, for either he avoids
them with great discretion, or undertakes them with a
most Christianlike fear.

LEONATO If he do fear God, 'a must necessarily keep
peace. If he break the peace, he ought to enter into a
quarrel with fear and trembling.

PEDRO And so will he do; for the man doth fear God,
howsoever it seems not in him by some large jests he 182
will make. Well, I am sorry for your niece. Shall we go
seek Benedick and tell him of her love?

CLAUDIO Never tell him, my lord. Let her wear it out
with good counsel. 186

76 *shift* emergency   79 *live* lief, willingly   80 *night raven* (portent of
disaster)   98 *enraged* frenzied   99 *infinite* furthest reach   104 *discovers*
reveals   115 *gull* hoax, trick   118 *Hold* keep   126 *smock* garment which
served both as slip and nightdress   131 *between the sheet* in the folded
sheet of paper, with pun on bedsheets   133 *halfpence* i.e. small pieces
135 *flout* mock   142 *ecstasy* excess of passion   149 *an alms* a good deed
154 *blood* nature, natural feeling, passion   158 *dotage* doting affection
159 *daffed* doffed, put aside; *respects* considerations   165 *bate* abate, give
up   166 *tender* offer   168 *contemptible* contemptuous   169 *proper* handsome   170 *outward happiness* attractive exterior   172 *wit* intelligence
182 *by* to judge by   186 *counsel* reflection

LEONATO Nay, that's impossible; she may wear her heart out first.

PEDRO Well, we will hear further of it by your daughter. Let it cool the while. I love Benedick well, and I could wish he would modestly examine himself to see how much he is unworthy so good a lady.

LEONATO My lord, will you walk? Dinner is ready.

[They walk away.]

CLAUDIO If he do not dote on her upon this, I will never trust my expectation.

PEDRO Let there be the same net spread for her, and that
197 must your daughter and her gentlewomen carry. The
198 sport will be, when they hold one an opinion of another's dotage, and no such matter. That's the scene that I
200 would see, which will be merely a dumb show. Let us send her to call him in to dinner.

[Exeunt Don Pedro, Claudio, and Leonato.]

BENEDICK *[advancing]* This can be no trick. The confer-
203 ence was sadly borne; they have the truth of this from
204 Hero; they seem to pity the lady. It seems her affections have their full bent. Love me? Why, it must be requited. I hear how I am censured. They say I will bear myself proudly if I perceive the love come from her. They say too that she will rather die then give any sign of affection. I did never think to marry. I must not seem proud.
210 Happy are they that hear their detractions and can put them to mending. They say the lady is fair – 'tis a truth, I can bear them witness; and virtuous – 'tis so, I cannot
213 reprove it; and wise, but for loving me – by my troth, it is no addition to her wit, nor no great argument of her folly, for I will be horribly in love with her. I may chance
216 have some odd quirks and remnants of wit broken on me because I have railed so long against marriage. But doth not the appetite alter? A man loves the meat in his youth
219 that he cannot endure in his age. Shall quips and senten-
220 ces and these paper bullets of the brain awe a man from
221 the career of his humor? No, the world must be peopled. When I said I would die a bachelor, I did not think I should live till I were married. Here comes Beatrice. By this day, she's a fair lady! I do spy some marks of love in her.

Enter Beatrice.

BEATRICE Against my will I am sent to bid you come in to dinner.

BENEDICK Fair Beatrice, I thank you for your pains.

BEATRICE I took no more pains for those thanks than you take pains to thank me. If it had been painful, I would not have come.

BENEDICK You take pleasure then in the message?

BEATRICE Yea, just so much as you may take upon a
234 knive's point, and choke a daw withal. You have no
235 stomach, signior. Fare you well.   *Exit.*

BENEDICK Ha! 'Against my will I am sent to bid you come in to dinner.' There's a double meaning in that. 'I took no more pains for those thanks than you took pains to thank me.' That's as much as to say, 'Any pains that I take for you is as easy as thanks.' If I do not take pity of her, I am a villain; if I do not love her, I am a Jew. I will
241 go get her picture.   *Exit.*

*

Enter Hero and two Gentlewomen, Margaret and Ursula.   III, i

HERO
Good Margaret, run thee to the parlor.
There shalt thou find my cousin Beatrice
Proposing with the Prince and Claudio.   3
Whisper her ear and tell her, I and Ursley
Walk in the orchard, and our whole discourse
Is all of her. Say that thou overheard'st us;
And bid her steal into the pleachèd bower,   7
Where honeysuckles, ripened by the sun,   8
Forbid the sun to enter – like favorites,
Made proud by princes, that advance their pride
Against that power that bred it. There will she hide her
To listen our propose. This is thy office.   12
Bear thee well in it and leave us alone.   13

MARGARET
I'll make her come, I warrant you, presently.   *[Exit.]* 14

HERO
Now, Ursula, when Beatrice doth come,
As we do trace this alley up and down,   16
Our talk must only be of Benedick.
When I do name him, let it be thy part
To praise him more than ever man did merit.
My talk to thee must be how Benedick
Is sick in love with Beatrice. Of this matter
Is little Cupid's crafty arrow made,
That only wounds by hearsay.

Enter Beatrice [and hides].

                                Now begin;
For look where Beatrice like a lapwing runs   24
Close by the ground, to hear our conference.

URSULA
The pleasant'st angling is to see the fish
Cut with her golden oars the silver stream   27
And greedily devour the treacherous bait.
So angle we for Beatrice, who even now
Is couchèd in the woodbine coverture.   30
Fear you not my part of the dialogue.

HERO
Then go we near her, that her ear lose nothing
Of the false sweet bait that we lay for it.

[They move.]
No, truly, Ursula, she is too disdainful.
I know her spirits are as coy and wild
As haggards of the rock.   36

URSULA   But are you sure
That Benedick loves Beatrice so entirely?

HERO
So says the Prince, and my new-trothèd lord.

197 *carry* manage   198–99 *they . . . dotage* each thinks the other is in love
200 *dumb show* pantomime (because they can no longer carry on their usual banter)   203 *sadly borne* seriously carried on   204–05 *affections . . . bent* emotions are like a bow fully bent   210 *detractions* faults   213 *reprove* disprove   216 *quirks* quips, quibbles   219 *sentences* maxims, wise sayings
220 *paper bullets* words; *awe* frighten   221 *career of his humor* action he fancies   234 *withal* with   235 *stomach* appetite   241 *get her picture* i.e. so that he can 'feed his eyes' and fall in love
III, i Leonato's orchard   3 *Proposing* conversing   7 *pleachèd* hidden by thickly interwoven branches   8 *ripened* brought to full development   12 *propose* conversation   13 *leave us alone* leave the rest to us   14 *presently* immediately   16 *trace* walk along   24 *lapwing* kind of plover   27 *oars* i.e. fins   30 *woodbine* i.e. honeysuckle   36 *haggards* hawks captured full grown and hard to tame

URSULA
    And did they bid you tell her of it, madam?
HERO
    They did entreat me to acquaint her of it;
    But I persuaded them, if they loved Benedick,
    To wish him wrestle with affection
    And never to let Beatrice know of it.
URSULA
    Why did you so? Doth not the gentleman
45 Deserve as full as fortunate a bed
    As ever Beatrice shall couch upon?
HERO
    O god of love! I know he doth deserve
    As much as may be yielded to a man;
    But Nature never framed a woman's heart
    Of prouder stuff than that of Beatrice.
    Disdain and scorn ride sparkling in her eyes,
52 Misprizing what they look on; and her wit
    Values itself so highly that to her
    All matter else seems weak. She cannot love,
55 Nor take no shape nor project of affection,
    She is so self-endeared.
URSULA   Sure I think so;
    And therefore certainly it were not good
    She knew his love, lest she'll make sport at it.
HERO
    Why, you speak truth. I never yet saw man,
    How wise, how noble, young, how rarely featured,
61 But she would spell him backward. If fair-faced,
    She would swear the gentleman should be her sister;
63 If black, why, Nature, drawing of an antic,
    Made a foul blot; if tall, a lance ill-headed;
65 If low, an agate very vilely cut;
66 If speaking, why, a vane blown with all winds;
    If silent, why, a block movèd with none.
    So turns she every man the wrong side out
    And never gives to truth and virtue that
70 Which simpleness and merit purchaseth.
URSULA
71 Sure, sure, such carping is not commendable.
HERO
72 No, not to be so odd, and from all fashions,
    As Beatrice is, cannot be commendable.
    But who dare tell her so? If I should speak,
    She would mock me into air; O, she would laugh me
76 Out of myself, press me to death with wit!
    Therefore let Benedick, like covered fire,
    Consume away in sighs, waste inwardly.
    It were a better death than die with mocks,
    Which is as bad as die with tickling.

URSULA
    Yet tell her of it. Hear what she will say.
HERO
    No; rather I will go to Benedick
    And counsel him to fight against his passion.
    And truly, I'll devise some honest slanders   84
    To stain my cousin with. One doth not know
    How much an ill word may empoison liking.
URSULA
    O, do not do your cousin such a wrong!
    She cannot be so much without true judgment
    (Having so swift and excellent a wit
    As she is prized to have) as to refuse   90
    So rare a gentleman as Signior Benedick.
HERO
    He is the only man of Italy,
    Always excepted my dear Claudio.
URSULA
    I pray you be not angry with me, madam,
    Speaking my fancy: Signior Benedick,
    For shape, for bearing, argument, and valor,
    Goes foremost in report through Italy.   96
HERO
    Indeed he hath an excellent good name.
URSULA
    His excellence did earn it ere he had it.
    When are you married, madam?
HERO
    Why, every day to-morrow! Come, go in.   101
    I'll show thee some attires, and have thy counsel
    Which is the best to furnish me to-morrow.   103
                    [They walk away.]
URSULA
    She's limed, I warrant you! We have caught her, madam. 104
HERO
    If it prove so, then loving goes by haps;   105
    Some Cupid kills with arrows, some with traps.
                    [Exeunt Hero and Ursula.]
BEATRICE [coming forth from hiding]
    What fire is in mine ears? Can this be true?   107
        Stand I condemned for pride and scorn so much?
    Contempt, farewell! and maiden pride, adieu!
        No glory lives behind the back of such.   110
    And, Benedick, love on; I will requite thee,
        Taming my wild heart to thy loving hand.   112
    If thou dost love, my kindness shall incite thee
        To bind our loves up in a holy band;
    For others say thou dost deserve, and I
    Believe it better than reportingly.   Exit. 116

                        *

Enter Prince [Don Pedro], Claudio, Benedick, and   III, ii
    Leonato.
PEDRO I do but stay till your marriage be consummate,
    and then go I toward Arragon.
CLAUDIO I'll bring you thither, my lord, if you'll vouch- 3
    safe me.
PEDRO Nay, that would be as great a soil in the new gloss of
    your marriage as to show a child his new coat and forbid
    him to wear it. I will only be bold with Benedick for his 7
    company; for, from the crown of his head to the sole of
    his foot, he is all mirth. He hath twice or thrice cut

45 *as full* fully 52 *Misprizing* undervaluing, mistaking 55 *project* idea,
notion 61 *spell him backward* turn him inside out 63 *black* brunet;
antic grotesque figure, buffoon 65 *agate* figure carved on an agate and so
very small 66 *vane* weathervane; *with* by 70 *simpleness* plain sincerity
71 *carping* faultfinding 72 *from* contrary to 76 *press me to death* (the
usual penalty in England for refusing to plead guilty or not guilty. Weights
were piled on the victim's body until he either pleaded or died.) 84 *honest
slanders* adverse criticisms, but not of such a nature as to impugn her
honesty (i.e. her chastity) 90 *prized* esteemed 96 *bearing* deportment;
argument discourse 101 *every day to-morrow* to-morrow and for ever after
103 *furnish* dress 104 *limed* caught as with birdlime 105 *haps* chance
107 *What . . . ears* how my ears burn 110 *No . . . such* the proud and contemptuous are never praised except to their faces 112 *Taming . . . hand* (the
hawk figure again) 116 *better than reportingly* not merely as hearsay
III, ii The house of Leonato 3 *vouchsafe* permit 7 *be bold with* ask

10 Cupid's bowstring, and the little hangman dare not shoot at him. He hath a heart as sound as a bell; and his tongue is the clapper, for what his heart thinks, his tongue speaks.

BENEDICK Gallants, I am not as I have been.

14 LEONATO So say I. Methinks you are sadder.

CLAUDIO I hope he be in love.

16 PEDRO Hang him, truant! There's no true drop of blood in him to be truly touched with love. If he be sad, he wants money.

19 BENEDICK I have the toothache.

20 PEDRO Draw it.

BENEDICK Hang it!

CLAUDIO You must hang it first and draw it afterwards.

PEDRO What? sigh for the toothache?

24 LEONATO Where is but a humor or a worm.

25 BENEDICK Well, every one can master a grief but he that has it.

CLAUDIO Yet say I he is in love.

28 PEDRO There is no appearance of fancy in him, unless it
29 be a fancy that he hath to strange disguises; as to be a Dutchman to-day, a Frenchman to-morrow; or in the shape of two countries at once, as a German from the
32 waist downward, all slops, and a Spaniard from the hip upward, no doublet. Unless he have a fancy to this
34 foolery, as it appears he hath, he is no fool for fancy, as you would have it appear he is.

CLAUDIO If he be not in love with some woman, there is
37 no believing old signs. 'A brushes his hat o' mornings. What should that bode?

PEDRO Hath any man seen him at the barber's?

CLAUDIO No, but the barber's man hath been seen with
41 him, and the old ornament of his cheek hath already stuffed tennis balls.

LEONATO Indeed he looks younger than he did, by the loss of a beard.

45 PEDRO Nay, 'a rubs himself with civet. Can you smell him out by that?

CLAUDIO That's as much as to say, the sweet youth's in love.

PEDRO The greatest note of it is his melancholy.

49 CLAUDIO And when was he wont to wash his face?

PEDRO Yea, or to paint himself? for the which I hear what they say of him.

CLAUDIO Nay, but his jesting spirit, which is now crept
53 into a lutestring, and now governed by stops.

PEDRO Indeed that tells a heavy tale for him. Conclude, conclude, he is in love.

CLAUDIO Nay, but I know who loves him.

PEDRO That would I know too. I warrant, one that knows him not.

59 CLAUDIO Yes, and his ill conditions; and in despite of all, dies for him.

61 PEDRO She shall be buried with her face upwards.

62 BENEDICK Yet is this no charm for the toothache. Old signior, walk aside with me. I have studied eight or nine
64 wise words to speak to you, which these hobby-horses must not hear.   [Exeunt Benedick and Leonato.]

66 PEDRO For my life, to break with him about Beatrice!

CLAUDIO 'Tis even so. Hero and Margaret have by this played their parts with Beatrice, and then the two bears will not bite one another when they meet.

     Enter John the Bastard.

JOHN My lord and brother, God save you.

PEDRO Good den, brother.   71

JOHN If your leisure served, I would speak with you.

PEDRO In private?

JOHN If it please you. Yet Count Claudio may hear, for what I would speak of concerns him.

PEDRO What's the matter?

JOHN [to Claudio] Means your lordship to be married to-morrow?

PEDRO You know he does.

JOHN I know not that, when he knows what I know.

CLAUDIO If there be any impediment, I pray you discover 81 it.

JOHN You may think I love you not. Let that appear hereafter, and aim better at me by that I now will manifest. 83 For my brother, I think he holds you well and in dear- 84 ness of heart help to effect your ensuing marriage – 85 surely suit ill spent and labor ill bestowed!

PEDRO Why, what's the matter?

JOHN I came hither to tell you, and, circumstances short- 88 ened (for she has been too long a-talking of), the lady is 89 disloyal.   90

CLAUDIO Who? Hero?

JOHN Even she – Leonato's Hero, your Hero, every man's Hero.

CLAUDIO Disloyal?

JOHN The word is too good to paint out her wickedness. I 95 could say she were worse; think you of a worse title, and I will fit her to it. Wonder not till further warrant. Go 97 but with me to-night, you shall see her chamber window entered, even the night before her wedding day. If you love her then, to-morrow wed her. But it would better fit your honor to change your mind.

CLAUDIO May this be so?

PEDRO I will not think it.

JOHN If you dare not trust that you see, confess not that 104 you know. If you will follow me, I will show you enough; and when you have seen more and heard more, proceed accordingly.

CLAUDIO If I see anything to-night why I should not marry her to-morrow, in the congregation where I 109 should wed there will I shame her.

PEDRO And, as I wooed for thee to obtain her, I will join with thee to disgrace her.

JOHN I will disparage her no farther till you are my witnesses. Bear it coldly but till midnight, and let the issue 114 show itself.

10 *hangman* executioner, rogue   14 *sadder* more serious   16 *truant* tramp (especially in love)   19 *toothache* (supposed to be common among lovers) 20 *Draw* extract (but with punning reference below to the hanging, drawing, and quartering of traitors)   24 *humor* one of the four bodily fluids, in this case rheum; *worm* (supposed to cause toothache)   25 *grief* physical as well as mental pain   28–29 *fancy . . . fancy* love . . . whim   29 *strange disguises* (the Englishman's dress was a perennial joke)   32 *slops* loose breeches 34 *fool for fancy* i.e. lover   37 *'A* he   41–42 *ornament . . . balls* i.e. his beard has been shaved (tennis balls were stuffed with curled hair)   45 *civet* (a popular perfume)   49 *wash his face* apply cosmetics   53 *stops* fingerings, or positions marked for the fingers on the fingerboard of a lute, the lover's instrument   59 *ill conditions* bad qualities   61 *face upwards* like a Christian (?), but probably with a ribald double intention   62 *charm* i.e. cure; *Old* (a term of respect)   64 *hobby-horses* buffoons (originally an antic figure in a morris dance)   66 *For my life* upon my life   71 *Good den* good evening   81 *discover* disclose   83 *aim . . . me* judge better of me 84–85 *dearness of heart* friendship   85 *holp* helped   88–89 *circumstances shortened* circumstantial details omitted   89 *a-talking of* talked of   90 *disloyal* unfaithful   95 *paint out* portray   97 *till further warrant* till you are further assured by proof   104 *that* what   109 *congregation* company 114 *coldly* coolly

116 PEDRO O day untowardly turned!

CLAUDIO O mischief strangely thwarting!

118 JOHN O plague right well prevented!

So will you say when you have seen the sequel. *[Exeunt.]*

*

III, iii   *Enter Dogberry and his compartner [Verges], with the Watch.*

DOGBERRY Are you good men and true?

2 VERGES Yea, or else it were pity but they should suffer salvation, body and soul.

DOGBERRY Nay, that were a punishment too good for

5 them if they should have any allegiance in them, being

6 chosen for the Prince's watch.

7 VERGES Well, give them their charge, neighbor Dogberry.

8 DOGBERRY First, who think you the most desartless man

9 to be constable?

1. WATCH Hugh Oatcake, sir, or George Seacole, for they can write and read.

DOGBERRY Come hither, neighbor Seacole. God hath

13 blessed you with a good name. To be a well-favored man is the gift of fortune, but to write and read comes by nature.

2. WATCH Both which, master constable –

DOGBERRY You have. I knew it would be your answer.

17 Well, for your favor, sir, why, give God thanks and make no boast of it; and for your writing and reading, let that appear when there is no need of such vanity. You

20 are thought here to be the most senseless and fit man for the constable of the watch. Therefore bear you the lant-

22 horn. This is your charge: you shall comprehend all

23 vagrom men; you are to bid any man stand, in the Prince's name.

2. WATCH How if 'a will not stand?

DOGBERRY Why then, take no note of him, but let him go, and presently call the rest of the watch together and thank God you are rid of a knave.

VERGES If he will not stand when he is bidden, he is none of the Prince's subjects.

DOGBERRY True, and they are to meddle with none but the Prince's subjects. You shall also make no noise in the streets; for, for the watch to babble and to talk is most

34 tolerable, and not to be endured.

1. WATCH We will rather sleep than talk. We know what

36 belongs to a watch.

DOGBERRY Why, you speak like an ancient and most 37 quiet watchman, for I cannot see how sleeping should offend. Only have a care that your bills be not stolen. 39 Well, you are to call at all the alehouses and bid those that are drunk get them to bed.

2. WATCH How if they will not?

DOGBERRY Why then, let them alone till they are sober. If they make you not then the better answer, you may say they are not the men you took them for.

2. WATCH Well, sir.

DOGBERRY If you meet a thief, you may suspect him, by virtue of your office, to be no true man; and for such 48 kind of men, the less you meddle or make with them, 49 why, the more is for your honesty.

2. WATCH If we know him to be a thief, shall we not lay hands on him?

DOGBERRY Truly, by your office you may; but I think they that touch pitch will be defiled. The most peace- 53 able way for you, if you do take a thief, is to let him show himself what he is, and steal out of your company.

VERGES You have been always called a merciful man, partner.

DOGBERRY Truly, I would not hang a dog by my will, much more a man who hath any honesty in him.

VERGES If you hear a child cry in the night, you must call to the nurse and bid her still it.

2. WATCH How if the nurse be asleep and will not hear us?

DOGBERRY Why then, depart in peace and let the child wake her with crying; for the ewe that will not hear her lamb when it baes will never answer a calf when he 66 bleats.

VERGES 'Tis very true.

DOGBERRY This is the end of the charge: you, constable, are to present the Prince's own person. If you meet the 69 Prince in the night, you may stay him.

VERGES Nay, by'r lady, that I think 'a cannot. 71

DOGBERRY Five shillings to one on't with any man that knows the statutes, he may stay him! Marry, not without 73 the Prince be willing; for indeed the watch ought to offend no man, and it is an offense to stay a man against 75 his will.

VERGES By'r lady, I think it be so.

DOGBERRY Ha, ah, ha! Well, masters, good night. An 78 there be any matter of weight chances, call up me. Keep your fellows' counsels and your own, and good night. Come, neighbor.

2. WATCH Well, masters, we hear our charge. Let us go sit here upon the church bench till two, and then all to bed.

DOGBERRY One word more, honest neighbors. I pray you watch about Signior Leonato's door, for the wedding being there to-morrow, there is a great coil to-night. 86 Adieu. Be vigitant, I beseech you. 87

                             Exeunt [Dogberry and Verges].

               Enter Borachio and Conrade.

BORACHIO What, Conrade!

2. WATCH *[aside]* Peace! stir not!

BORACHIO Conrade, I say!

CONRADE Here, man. I am at thy elbow.

BORACHIO Mass, and my elbow itched! I thought there 92 would a scab follow. 93

CONRADE I will owe thee an answer for that; and now 94 forward with thy tale.

116 *untowardly* unfavorably, unluckily   118 *plague* misfortune; *prevented* forestalled

III, iii A street in Messina   2 *salvation* (his mistake for 'damnation') 5 *allegiance* (for 'treachery')   6 *watch* men chosen to police the streets at night   7 *charge* instructions   8 *desartless* (for 'deserving')   9 *constable* deputy leader of the watch (Dogberry is the *right master constable*) 13 *well-favored* handsome   17 *favor* appearance   20 *senseless* (for 'sensible')   22 *comprehend* (for 'apprehend')   23 *vagrom* vagrant   34 *tolerable* (for 'intolerable')   36 *belongs to* is the duty of   37 *ancient* elderly, staid   39 *bills* halberds, long poles with combination axe and spear heads carried chiefly as a badge of office   48 *true* honest   49 *meddle or make* associate   53 *they . . . defiled* (paraphrased from Ecclesiasticus xiii, 1) 66 *calf* (Dogberry's comparison has led him to call the watchman a calf, or dolt)   69 *present* represent   71 *by'r lady* by Our Lady (a mild oath) 73 *statutes* acts of Parliament (but the principle actually belongs to common law)   75 *offense* (in the legal sense)   78 *Ha, ah, ha* (a pompous clearing of the throat)   86 *coil* confusion, bustle   87 *vigitant* (for 'vigilant')   92 *Mass* a mild interjection (originally, by the Mass)   93 *scab* i.e. an itching scab, with play on slang term for a scurvy fellow   94 *owe thee an answer* answer that later

96 BORACHIO Stand thee close then under this penthouse,
97 　for it drizzles rain, and I will, like a true drunkard, utter
　　all to thee.

2. WATCH [aside] Some treason, masters. Yet stand close.

BORACHIO Therefore know I have earned of Don John a
　　thousand ducats.

CONRADE Is it possible that any villainy should be so
102 dear?

BORACHIO Thou shouldst rather ask if it were possible
　　any villainy should be so rich; for when rich villains
　　have need of poor ones, poor ones may make what price
　　they will.

CONRADE I wonder at it.

108 BORACHIO That shows thou art unconfirmed. Thou
　　knowest that the fashion of a doublet, or a hat, or a
　　cloak, is nothing to a man.

CONRADE Yes, it is apparel.

BORACHIO I mean the fashion.

CONRADE Yes, the fashion is the fashion.

BORACHIO Tush! I may as well say the fool's the fool.
115 But seest thou not what a deformed thief this fashion is?

1. WATCH [aside] I know that Deformed. 'A has been a
117 vile thief this seven year; 'a goes up and down like a
　　gentleman. I remember his name.

BORACHIO Didst thou not hear somebody?

120 CONRADE No; 'twas the vane on the house.

BORACHIO Seest thou not, I say, what a deformed thief
　　this fashion is? how giddily 'a turns about all the hot-
　　bloods between fourteen and five-and-thirty? some-
125 times fashioning them like Pharaoh's soldiers in the
126 reechy painting, sometime like god Bel's priests in the
127 old church window, sometime like the shaven Hercules
　　in the smirched worm-eaten tapestry, where his codpiece
　　seems as massy as his club?

CONRADE All this I see; and I see that the fashion wears
　　out more apparel than the man. But art not thou thyself
　　giddy with the fashion too, that thou hast shifted out of
　　thy tale into telling me of the fashion?

BORACHIO Not so neither. But know that I have to-night
　　wooed Margaret, the Lady Hero's gentlewoman, by the
　　name of Hero. She leans me out at her mistress' chamber
　　window, bids me a thousand times good night – I tell
　　this tale vilely; I should first tell thee how the Prince,
138 Claudio, and my master, planted and placed and pos-
　　sessed by my master Don John, saw afar off in the or-
140 chard this amiable encounter.

CONRADE And thought they Margaret was Hero?

BORACHIO Two of them did, the Prince and Claudio;
　　but the devil my master knew she was Margaret; and
144 partly by his oaths, which first possessed them, partly
　　by the dark night, which did deceive them, but chiefly
　　by my villainy, which did confirm any slander that Don
　　John had made, away went Claudio enraged; swore he
　　would meet her, as he was appointed, next morning at
　　the temple, and there, before the whole congregation,
　　shame her with what he saw o'ernight and send her
　　home again without a husband.

1. WATCH We charge you in the Prince's name stand!

2. WATCH Call up the right master constable. We have
154 here recovered the most dangerous piece of lechery that
　　ever was known in the commonwealth.

1. WATCH And one Deformed is one of them. I know
157 him; 'a wears a lock.

CONRADE Masters, masters –

2. WATCH You'll be made bring Deformed forth, I war-
　　rant you.

CONRADE Masters –

2. WATCH Never speak, we charge you. Let us obey you 162
　　to go with us.

BORACHIO We are like to prove a goodly commodity, 164
　　being taken up of these men's bills. 165

CONRADE A commodity in question, I warrant you. 166
　　Come, we'll obey you.　　　　　　　　　　　Exeunt.

*

Enter Hero, and Margaret and Ursula.　　　　　III, iv

HERO Good Ursula, wake my cousin Beatrice and desire
　　her to rise.

URSULA I will, lady.

HERO And bid her come hither.

URSULA Well.　　　　　　　　　　　　　　　　　[*Exit.*]

MARGARET Troth, I think your other rebato were better. 6

HERO No, pray thee, good Meg, I'll wear this.

MARGARET By my troth, 's not so good, and I warrant
　　your cousin will say so.

HERO My cousin's a fool, and thou art another. I'll wear
　　none but this.

MARGARET I like the new tire within excellently, if the 12
　　hair were a thought browner; and your gown's a most
　　rare fashion, i' faith. I saw the Duchess of Milan's gown
　　that they praise so.

HERO O, that exceeds, they say.

MARGARET By my troth, 's but a nightgown in respect of 17
　　yours – cloth a gold and cuts, and laced with silver, set 18
　　with pearls, down sleeves, side-sleeves, and skirts, round 19
　　underborne with a bluish tinsel. But for a fine, quaint, 20
　　graceful, and excellent fashion, yours is worth ten on't.

HERO God give me joy to wear it! for my heart is exceed-
　　ing heavy.

MARGARET 'Twill be heavier soon by the weight of a man.

HERO Fie upon thee! art not ashamed?

MARGARET Of what, lady? of speaking honorably? Is not
　　marriage honorable in a beggar? Is not your lord honor- 27
　　able without marriage? I think you would have me say,
　　'saving your reverence, a husband.' An bad thinking do 29
　　not wrest true speaking, I'll offend nobody. Is there any 30

96 *penthouse* open shed with a sloping roof　97 *true drunkard* (the word '*borracho*' is Spanish for 'drunkard,' and there was a proverb, 'The drunkard tells all')　102 *dear* expensive　108 *unconfirmed* inexperienced in villainy　115 *deformed thief* deforming rascal　117 *goes up and down* walks about　120 *vane* weathervane　125 *reechy* grimy, smoky; *Bel's priests* the priests of Baal (in the Apocryphal book of the Bible, 'Bel and the Dragon')　126 *shaven Hercules* (probably a confusion with Samson)　127 *codpiece* front part of breeches, often stuffed and ornamented　138 *possessed* deluded　140 *amiable encounter* lovers' meeting　144 *possessed* took possession of　154 *recovered* (for 'discovered'); *lechery* (for 'treachery')　157 *lock* lovelock, a wisp of hair worn beside the left ear, often down to the shoulder　162 *Let us obey you* (for 'we command you')　164 *commodity* merchandise　165 *taken up* (1) arrested, (2) accepted from a usurer; *bills* (1) halberds, (2) bills of goods　166 *in question* (1) subject to examination, (2) of doubtful quality
III, iv The house of Leonato　6 *rebato* stiff, flaring collar or ruff, usually of starched or wired lace　12 *tire* head-dress with elaborate ornaments attached; *within* in the next room　17 *nightgown* dressing gown　18 *cuts* slashes or notches to show the underbody; *laced with silver* with silver threads applied, usually in a diagonal pattern　19 *down sleeves* long sleeves; *side-sleeves* second, purely ornamental, sleeves hanging open from the armhole　19–20 *round underborne* held out, stiffened from underneath　20 *quaint* elegant　27 *in* even in　29 *saving your reverence* (conventional apology for mentioning a delicate subject)　30 *wrest* twist, misunderstand

harm in 'the heavier for a husband'? None, I think, an
it be the right husband and the right wife. Otherwise
33 'tis light, and not heavy. Ask my Lady Beatrice else.
Here she comes.

    Enter Beatrice.

35 HERO Good morrow, coz.

BEATRICE Good morrow, sweet Hero.

HERO Why, how now? Do you speak in the sick tune?

BEATRICE I am out of all other tune, methinks.

39 MARGARET Clap's into 'Light a love.' That goes without
40 a burden. Do you sing it, and I'll dance it.

41 BEATRICE Ye light a love with your heels! then, if your
husband have stables enough, you'll see he shall lack no
43 barnes.

MARGARET O illegitimate construction! I scorn that with
my heels.

BEATRICE 'Tis almost five o'clock, cousin; 'tis time you
were ready. By my troth, I am exceeding ill. Hey-ho!

MARGARET For a hawk, a horse, or a husband?

49 BEATRICE For the letter that begins them all, H.

50 MARGARET Well, an you be not turned Turk, there's no
51 more sailing by the star.

52 BEATRICE What means the fool, trow?

MARGARET Nothing I; but God send every one their
heart's desire!

HERO These gloves the Count sent me, they are an ex-
56 cellent perfume.

57 BEATRICE I am stuffed, cousin; I cannot smell.

58 MARGARET A maid, and stuffed! There's goodly catching of cold.

BEATRICE O, God help me! God help me! How long
61 have you professed apprehension?

MARGARET Ever since you left it. Doth not my wit become me rarely?

64 BEATRICE It is not seen enough. You should wear it in
your cap. By my troth, I am sick.

66 MARGARET Get you some of this distilled *carduus benedictus* and lay it to your heart. It is the only thing for a
68 qualm.

HERO There thou prick'st her with a thistle.

BEATRICE *Benedictus*? why *benedictus*? You have some
71 moral in this *benedictus*.

MARGARET Moral? No, by my troth, I have no moral
meaning; I meant plain holy thistle. You may think perchance that I think you are in love. Nay, by'r lady, I am
74 not such a fool to think what I list; nor I list not to think

what I can; nor indeed I cannot think, if I would think
my heart out of thinking, that you are in love, or that
you will be in love, or that you can be in love. Yet Benedick was such another, and now is he become a man. He 78
swore he would never marry, and yet now in despite of
his heart he eats his meat without grudging; and how 80
you may be converted I know not, but methinks you
look with your eyes as other women do.

BEATRICE What pace is this that thy tongue keeps?

MARGARET Not a false gallop.   84

    Enter Ursula.

URSULA Madam, withdraw. The Prince, the Count, Signior Benedick, Don John, and all the gallants of the
town are come to fetch you to church.

HERO Help to dress me, good coz, good Meg, good
Ursula.   *[Exeunt.]*

*

    Enter Leonato and the Constable [Dogberry] and the III, v
    Headborough [Verges].

LEONATO What would you with me, honest neighbor?

DOGBERRY Marry, sir, I would have some confidence 2
with you that decerns you nearly.   3

LEONATO Brief, I pray you, for you see it is a busy time
with me.

DOGBERRY Marry, this it is, sir.

VERGES Yes, in truth it is, sir.

LEONATO What is it, my good friends?

DOGBERRY Goodman Verges, sir, speaks a little off the
matter – an old man, sir, and his wits are not so blunt as, 10
God help, I would desire they were; but, in faith, honest 11
as the skin between his brows.

VERGES Yes, I thank God I am as honest as any man
living that is an old man and no honester than I.

DOGBERRY Comparisons are odorous. Palabras, neigh- 15
bor Verges.

LEONATO Neighbors, you are tedious.

DOGBERRY It pleases your worship to say so, but we are
the poor Duke's officers; but truly, for mine own part, if 19
I were as tedious as a king, I could find in my heart to
bestow it all of your worship.

LEONATO All thy tediousness on me, ah?

DOGBERRY Yea, an 'twere a thousand pound more than
'tis; for I hear as good exclamation on your worship as 24
of any man in the city, and though I be but a poor man, I
am glad to hear it.

VERGES And so am I.

LEONATO I would fain know what you have to say.

VERGES Marry, sir, our watch to-night, excepting your 29
worship's presence, ha' ta'en a couple of as arrant
knaves as any in Messina.

DOGBERRY A good old man, sir; he will be talking. As 32
they say, 'When the age is in, the wit is out.' God help
us! it is a world to see! Well said, i' faith, neighbor Verges. Well, God's a good man. An two men ride of a
horse, one must ride behind. An honest soul, i' faith, sir,
by my troth he is, as ever broke bread; but God is to be
worshipped; all men are not alike, alas, good neighbor!

LEONATO Indeed, neighbor, he comes too short of you.

DOGBERRY Gifts that God gives.

LEONATO I must leave you.

DOGBERRY One word, sir. Our watch, sir, have indeed
comprehended two aspicious persons, and we would 43

---

33 *light* (pun on 'wanton'); *else* if it be otherwise   35 *coz* cousin   39 *Clap's
into* let us begin briskly; *Light a love* (an old tune)   40 *burden* refrain (with a
punning reference to *heavier for a husband*)   41 *light . . . heels* i.e. grow
wanton   43 *barnes* children (with an obvious pun)   49 *H* (with a play on
'ache,' then pronounced 'aitch')   50 *turned Turk* i.e. turned pagan,
changed   51 *star* North Star   52 *trow* I wonder   56 *perfume* (gloves were
often perfumed)   57 *I am stuffed* i.e. my nose is stopped with a cold   58
stuffed pregnant   61 *professed apprehension* pretended to wit   64-65 *in
your cap* (like a feather, where it would show)   66-67 *carduus benedictus*
holy thistle, regarded as a universal remedy, with pun on 'Benedick'   68
qualm sudden faintness or pain   71 *moral* figurative meaning   74 *list* like,
please   78 *a man* i.e. a normal man   80 *eats . . . grudging* has a normal
appetite   84 *false gallop* canter, but the emphasis is on 'false'
III, v The house of Leonato   s.d. *Headborough* petty or local constable
2 *confidence* (for 'conference')   3 *decerns* (for 'concerns')   10 *blunt* (for
'sharp')   11-12 *honest . . . brows* (proverbial)   15 *odorous* (for 'odious');
Palabras from Spanish '*pocas palabras*,' (few words)   19 *poor Duke's* (for
'Duke's poor')   24 *exclamation* (for 'acclamation')   29 *excepting* (for
'respecting')   32 ff. *As they say*, etc. (what follows is a string of 'old ends'
or stock phrases)   43 *comprehended* (for 'apprehended'); *aspicious* (for
'suspicious')

have them this morning examined before your worship.

LEONATO Take their examination yourself and bring it
me. I am now in great haste, as it may appear unto you.

47 DOGBERRY It shall be suffigance.

LEONATO Drink some wine ere you go. Fare you well.
[Enter a Messenger.]

MESSENGER My lord, they stay for you to give your
daughter to her husband.

LEONATO I'll wait upon them. I am ready.
[Exeunt Leonato and Messenger.]

52 DOGBERRY Go, good partner, go get you to Francis
Seacole. Bid him bring his pen and inkhorn to the jail.

54 We are now to examination these men.

VERGES And we must do it wisely.

DOGBERRY We will spare for no wit, I warrant you. Here's
57 that shall drive some of them to a non-come. Only get
58 the learned writer to set down our excommunication,
and meet me at the jail.   [Exeunt.]

*

IV, i   Enter Prince [Don Pedro], [John the] Bastard,
Leonato, Friar [Francis], Claudio, Benedick, Hero,
and Beatrice [and Attendants].

LEONATO Come, Friar Francis, be brief. Only to the
2 plain form of marriage, and you shall recount their particular duties afterwards.

FRIAR You come hither, my lord, to marry this lady?

CLAUDIO No.

LEONATO To be married to her. Friar, you come to
marry her.

FRIAR Lady, you come hither to be married to this
count?

HERO I do.

10 FRIAR If either of you know any inward impediment why
you should not be conjoined, I charge you on your souls
to utter it.

CLAUDIO Know you any, Hero?

HERO None, my lord.

FRIAR Know you any, Count?

LEONATO I dare make his answer – none.

CLAUDIO O, what men dare do! what men may do! what
men daily do, not knowing what they do!

19 BENEDICK How now? interjections? Why then, some be
of laughing, as, ah, ha, he!

CLAUDIO
21 Stand thee by, friar. Father, by your leave,
Will you with free and unconstrainèd soul
Give me this maid your daughter?

LEONATO
As freely, son, as God did give her me.

CLAUDIO
And what have I to give you back whose worth
26 May counterpoise this rich and precious gift?

PEDRO
Nothing, unless you render her again.

CLAUDIO
28 Sweet Prince, you learn me noble thankfulness.
There, Leonato, take her back again.
Give not this rotten orange to your friend.
She's but the sign and semblance of her honor.
Behold how like a maid she blushes here!
33 O, what authority and show of truth
34 Can cunning sin cover itself withal!

Comes not that blood as modest evidence
To witness simple virtue? Would you not swear,   36
All you that see her, that she were a maid,
By these exterior shows? But she is none:
She knows the heat of a luxurious bed;   39
Her blush is guiltiness, not modesty.

LEONATO
What do you mean, my lord?

CLAUDIO   Not to be married,
Not to knit my soul to an approvèd wanton.   42

LEONATO
Dear my lord, if you, in your own proof,   43
Have vanquished the resistance of her youth
And made defeat of her virginity –

CLAUDIO
I know what you would say. If I have known her,
You will say she did embrace me as a husband,
And so extenuate the forehand sin.   48
No, Leonato,
I never tempted her with word too large,   50
But, as a brother to his sister, showed
Bashful sincerity and comely love.

HERO
And seemed I ever otherwise to you?

CLAUDIO
Out on thee seeming! I will write against it.   54
You seem to me as Dian in her orb,   55
As chaste as is the bud ere it be blown;   56
But you are more intemperate in your blood   57
Than Venus, or those pamp'red animals
That rage in savage sensuality.

HERO
Is my lord well that he doth speak so wide?   60

LEONATO
Sweet Prince, why speak not you?

PEDRO   What should I speak?
I stand dishonored that have gone about   62
To link my dear friend to a common stale.   63

LEONATO
Are these things spoken, or do I but dream?

JOHN
Sir, they are spoken, and these things are true.

BENEDICK
This looks not like a nuptial.

HERO   'True'! O God!

CLAUDIO
Leonato, stand I here?
Is this the Prince? Is this the Prince's brother?

47 *suffigance* (for 'sufficient')   52–53 *Francis Seacole* the Sexton or Town
Clerk of IV, ii, not the same as the George Seacole, constable of the watch,
in III, iii, who could read and write   54 *examination* (for 'examine')
57 *non-come* (abbreviation of '*non compos mentis*,' but he probably means
'nonplus')   58 *excommunication* (for 'examination')
IV, i Within a church in Messina   2 *plain form* simple prescribed formula
2–3 *particular duties* the usual preliminary sermon on the duties of husband
and wife   10 *inward impediment* secret, or mental reservation   19–20
some . . . ah, ha, he (he is quoting Lily's *Latin Grammar*, a standard textbook
of the day, which says of interjections, 'Some are of Laughing : as, Ha, ha,
he.')   21 *Stand thee by* stand aside; *by your leave* if I may call you so   26
counterpoise weigh as much as   28 *Sweet* dear; *learn* teach   33 *authority*
assurance   34 *withal* with   36 *witness* bear witness to   39 *luxurious* lustful
42 *approvèd* proved   43 *proof* experience   48 *extenuate . . . sin* excuse the
sin of anticipating the marriage state   50 *large* broad, immodest   54 *Out*
shame   55 *Dian* Diana, goddess of chastity; *orb* sphere, the moon   56
blown in blossom   57 *intemperate* ungoverned   60 *wide* far from the truth
62 *gone about* undertaken   63 *stale* harlot

Is this face Hero's? Are our eyes our own?

LEONATO

All this is so; but what of this, my lord?

CLAUDIO

Let me but move one question to your daughter,
72 And by that fatherly and kindly power
That you have in her, bid her answer truly.

LEONATO

I charge thee do so, as thou art my child.

HERO

O, God defend me! How am I beset!
What kind of catechising call you this?

CLAUDIO

To make you answer truly to your name.

HERO

Is it not Hero? Who can blot that name
With any just reproach?

CLAUDIO   Marry, that can Hero!
80 Hero itself can blot out Hero's virtue.
What man was he talked with you yesternight,
Out at your window betwixt twelve and one?
83 Now, if you are a maid, answer to this.

HERO

I talked with no man at that hour, my lord.

PEDRO

Why, then are you no maiden. Leonato,
I am sorry you must hear. Upon mine honor
87 Myself, my brother, and this grievèd Count
Did see her, hear her, at that hour last night
Talk with a ruffian at her chamber window,
90 Who hath indeed, most like a liberal villain,
Confessed the vile encounters they have had
A thousand times in secret.

JOHN

Fie, fie! they are not to be named, my lord –
Not to be spoke of;
There is not chastity enough in language
Without offense to utter them. Thus, pretty lady,
97 I am sorry for thy much misgovernment.

CLAUDIO

O Hero! what a Hero hadst thou been
If half thy outward graces had been placed
About thy thoughts and counsels of thy heart!
But fare thee well, most foul, most fair! Farewell,
Thou pure impiety and impious purity!
For thee I'll lock up all the gates of love,
104 And on my eyelids shall conjecture hang,
To turn all beauty into thoughts of harm,
And never shall it more be gracious.

LEONATO

Hath no man's dagger here a point for me?
[Hero swoons.]

BEATRICE

Why, how now, cousin? Wherefore sink you down?

JOHN

Come let us go. These things, come thus to light,
Smother her spirits up.   110
[Exeunt Don Pedro, Don John, and Claudio.]

BENEDICK

How doth the lady?

BEATRICE   Dead, I think. Help, uncle!
Hero! why, Hero! Uncle! Signior Benedick! Friar!

LEONATO

O Fate, take not away thy heavy hand!
Death is the fairest cover for her shame
That may be wished for.

BEATRICE   How now, cousin Hero?

FRIAR Have comfort, lady.

LEONATO Dost thou look up?   117

FRIAR Yea, wherefore should she not?

LEONATO

Wherefore? Why, doth not every earthly thing
Cry shame upon her? Could she here deny
The story that is printed in her blood?   120
Do not live, Hero; do not ope thine eyes;
For, did I think thou wouldst not quickly die,
Thought I thy spirits were stronger than thy shames,
Myself would on the rearward of reproaches   124
Strike at thy life. Grieved I, I had but one?
Chid I for that at frugal nature's frame?   126
O, one too much by thee! Why had I one?
Why ever wast thou lovely in my eyes?
Why had I not with charitable hand
Took up a beggar's issue at my gates,
Who smirchèd thus and mired with infamy,
I might have said, 'No part of it is mine;
This shame derives itself from unknown loins'?
But mine, and mine I loved, and mine I praised,
And mine that I was proud on – mine so much
That I myself was to myself not mine,   136
Valuing of her – why she, O, she is fall'n
Into a pit of ink, that the wide sea
Hath drops too few to wash her clean again,
And salt too little which may season give   140
To her foul tainted flesh!

BENEDICK Sir, sir, be patient. For my part, I am so
attired in wonder, I know not what to say.

BEATRICE

O, on my soul, my cousin is belied!

BENEDICK

Lady, were you her bedfellow last night?

BEATRICE

No, truly, not; although, until last night,
I have this twelvemonth been her bedfellow.

LEONATO

Confirmed, confirmed! O, that is stronger made
Which was before barred up with ribs of iron!
Would the two princes lie? and Claudio lie,
Who loved her so that, speaking of her foulness,
Washed it with tears? Hence from her! let her die.

FRIAR

Hear me a little;
For I have only been silent so long,
And given way unto this course of fortune,   155
By noting of the lady. I have marked
A thousand blushing apparitions   157
To start into her face, a thousand innocent shames
In angel whiteness beat away those blushes,

---

72 *kindly* natural   80 *Hero itself* i.e. the name by which he had heard
Borachio call Margaret   83 *answer to* explain   87 *grievèd* aggrieved,
wronged   90 *liberal* libertine   97 *much misgovernment* great misconduct
104 *conjecture* doubt, suspicion   110 *spirits* vital powers   117 *look up* (a
sign of innocence)   120 *printed in her blood* written in her blushes   124
on . . . reproaches after reproaching you   126 *frame* plan, design   136 *I
myself . . . mine* I lost or forgot myself   140 *season give* provide a preservative
155 *course of fortune* turn of events   157 *blushing apparitions* blushes
(personified)

And in her eye there hath appeared a fire
161 To burn the errors that these princes hold
Against her maiden truth. Call me a fool ;
Trust not my reading nor my observations,
164 Which with experimental seal doth warrant
The tenure of my book ; trust not my age,
My reverence, calling, nor divinity,
If this sweet lady lie not guiltless here
Under some biting error.

LEONATO   Friar, it cannot be.
Thou seest that all the grace that she hath left
Is that she will not add to her damnation
A sin of perjury : she not denies it.
Why seek'st thou then to cover with excuse
That which appears in proper nakedness ?

FRIAR
Lady, what man is he you are accused of ?

HERO
They know that do accuse me ; I know none.
If I know more of any man alive
Than that which maiden modesty doth warrant,
Let all my sins lack mercy ! O my father,
Prove you that any man with me conversed
180 At hours unmeet, or that I yesternight
181 Maintained the change of words with any creature,
182 Refuse me, hate me, torture me to death !

FRIAR
183 There is some strange misprision in the princes.

BENEDICK
184 Two of them have the very bent of honor ;
And if their wisdoms be misled in this,
186 The practice of it lives in John the bastard,
187 Whose spirits toil in frame of villainies.

LEONATO
I know not. If they speak but truth of her,
These hands shall tear her. If they wrong her honor,
The proudest of them shall well hear of it.
Time hath not yet so dried this blood of mine,
192 Nor age so eat up my invention,
Nor fortune made such havoc of my means,
Nor my bad life reft me so much of friends,
195 But they shall find awaked in such a kind
196 Both strength of limb and policy of mind,
Ability in means, and choice of friends,
198 To quit me of them throughly.

FRIAR   Pause awhile
And let my counsel sway you in this case.
200 Your daughter here the princess (left for dead),
201 Let her awhile be secretly kept in,
And publish it that she is dead indeed ;
203 Maintain a mourning ostentation,
And on your family's old monument
Hang mournful epitaphs, and do all rites
That appertain unto a burial.

LEONATO
What shall become of this ? What will this do ?

FRIAR
208 Marry, this well carried shall on her behalf
Change slander to remorse. That is some good.
But not for that dream I on this strange course,
211 But on this travail look for greater birth.
She dying, as it must be so maintained,
Upon the instant that she was accused,
Shall be lamented, pitied, and excused

Of every hearer ; for it so falls out
That what we have we prize not to the worth 216
Whiles we enjoy it, but being lacked and lost,
Why, then we rack the value, then we find 218
The virtue that possession would not show us
Whiles it was ours. So will it fare with Claudio.
When he shall hear she died upon his words,
Th' idea of her life shall sweetly creep 222
Into his study of imagination, 223
And every lovely organ of her life 224
Shall come apparelled in more precious habit, 225
More moving, delicate, and full of life,
Into the eye and prospect of his soul
Than when she lived indeed. Then shall he mourn
(If ever love had interest in his liver) 229
And wish he had not so accusèd her –
No, though he thought his accusation true.
Let this be so, and doubt not but success 232
Will fashion the event in better shape 233
Than I can lay it down in likelihood.
But if all aim but this be levelled false, 235
The supposition of the lady's death
Will quench the wonder of her infamy.
And if it sort not well, you may conceal her, 238
As best befits her wounded reputation,
In some reclusive and religious life, 240
Out of all eyes, tongues, minds, and injuries.

BENEDICK
Signior Leonato, let the friar advise you ;
And though you know my inwardness and love 243
Is very much unto the Prince and Claudio,
Yet, by mine honor, I will deal in this
As secretly and justly as your soul
Should with your body.

LEONATO   Being that I flow in grief, 247
The smallest twine may lead me.

FRIAR
'Tis well consented. Presently away ;
For to strange sores strangely they strain the cure. 250
Come, lady, die to live. This wedding day
Perhaps is but prolonged. Have patience and endure. 252
        Exit [with all but Beatrice and Benedick].

BENEDICK Lady Beatrice, have you wept all this while ?
BEATRICE Yea, and I will weep a while longer.
BENEDICK I will not desire that.

161 *errors* (personified as heretics)   164 *experimental seal* seal of experience 164–65 *warrant . . . book* confirm my interpretation of her expression (my book)   180 *unmeet* improper   181 *Maintained* carried on ; *change* exchange   182 *Refuse* disown   183 *misprision* mistake   184 *bent* shape, form   186 *practice* plotting   187 *in frame of* in framing   192 *invention* power to make plans   195 *kind* manner   196 *policy of mind* mental power 198 *quit me of* settle accounts with ; *throughly* thoroughly   200 *princess* (so in quarto and folio texts, although Hero is not, in this version of the story, a princess. Perhaps a courtesy title, or perhaps an author's inconsistency.)   201 *in* at home   203 *mourning ostentation* formal show of mourning   208 *carried* managed   211 *on this travail* as a result of this effort   216 *to the worth* for what it is worth   218 *rack* stretch as on a torture rack   222 *idea . . . life* i.e. memory of her   223 *his . . . imagination* the thoughts of his musing hours   224 *organ of her life* part of her when she was alive   225 *habit* apparel   229 *liver* (the presumed physiological seat of love, in contrast to the heart, the romantic seat)   232 *success* what succeeds or follows, i.e. the course of time   233 *event* outcome   235 *be levelled false* be directed falsely (and so miss the mark)   238 *sort* turn out 240 *reclusive* cloistered   243 *inwardness* intimacy   247 *flow* am afloat (and hence easily pulled)   250 *strain the cure* i.e. use desperate remedies   252 *prolonged* deferred

BEATRICE You have no reason. I do it freely.

BENEDICK Surely I do believe your fair cousin is wronged.

BEATRICE Ah, how much might the man deserve of me that would right her!

BENEDICK Is there any way to show such friendship?

261 BEATRICE A very even way, but no such friend.

BENEDICK May a man do it?

BEATRICE It is a man's office, but not yours.

BENEDICK I do love nothing in the world so well as you. Is not that strange?

BEATRICE As strange as the thing I know not. It were as possible for me to say I loved nothing so well as you. But believe me not; and yet I lie not. I confess nothing, nor I deny nothing. I am sorry for my cousin.

BENEDICK By my sword, Beatrice, thou lovest me.

271 BEATRICE Do not swear and eat it.

BENEDICK I will swear by it that you love me, and I will make him eat it that says I love not you.

BEATRICE Will you not eat your word?

BENEDICK With no sauce that can be devised to it. I
275   protest I love thee.

BEATRICE Why then, God forgive me!

BENEDICK What offense, sweet Beatrice?

279 BEATRICE You have stayed me in a happy hour. I was about to protest I loved you.

BENEDICK And do it with all thy heart.

BEATRICE I love you with so much of my heart that none is left to protest.

BENEDICK Come, bid me do anything for thee.

BEATRICE Kill Claudio.

BENEDICK Ha! not for the wide world!

BEATRICE You kill me to deny it. Farewell.

BENEDICK Tarry, sweet Beatrice.

BEATRICE I am gone, though I am here. There is no love in you. Nay, I pray you let me go.

BENEDICK Beatrice –

BEATRICE In faith, I will go.

BENEDICK We'll be friends first.

BEATRICE You dare easier be friends with me than fight with mine enemy.

BENEDICK Is Claudio thine enemy?

297 BEATRICE Is 'a not approved in the height a villain, that hath slandered, scorned, dishonored my kinswoman? O
299 that I were a man! What? bear her in hand until they
300 come to take hands, and then with public accusation,
301 uncovered slander, unmitigated rancor – O God, that I were a man! I would eat his heart in the market place.

BENEDICK Hear me, Beatrice –

BEATRICE Talk with a man out at a window! – a proper saying!

BENEDICK Nay, but Beatrice –

BEATRICE Sweet Hero! she is wronged, she is slandered,
308 she is undone.

BENEDICK Beat –

310 BEATRICE Princes and Counties! Surely a princely testi-

mony, a goodly count, Count Comfect, a sweet gallant 311 surely! O that I were a man for his sake! or that I had any friend would be a man for my sake! But manhood is melted into cursies, valor into compliment, and men are 314 only turned into tongue, and trim ones too. He is now as valiant as Hercules that only tells a lie, and swears it. I cannot be a man with wishing; therefore I will die a woman with grieving.

BENEDICK Tarry, good Beatrice. By this hand, I love thee.

BEATRICE Use it for my love some other way than swearing by it.

BENEDICK Think you in your soul the Count Claudio hath wronged Hero?

BEATRICE Yea, as sure as I have a thought or a soul.

BENEDICK Enough, I am engaged. I will challenge him. I will kiss your hand, and so I leave you. By this hand, Claudio shall render me a dear account. As you hear of me, so think of me. Go comfort your cousin. I must say she is dead – and so farewell.   *[Exeunt.]*

＊

Enter the Constables [Dogberry and Verges] and the IV, ii
Town Clerk [Sexton] in gowns, Borachio [, Conrade, and Watch].

DOGBERRY Is our whole dissembly appeared?

VERGES O, a stool and a cushion for the sexton.

SEXTON Which be the malefactors?

DOGBERRY Marry, that am I and my partner.

VERGES Nay, that's certain. We have the exhibition to 5 examine.

SEXTON But which are the offenders that are to be examined? let them come before master constable.

DOGBERRY Yea, marry, let them come before me. What is your name, friend?

BORACHIO Borachio.

DOGBERRY Pray write down Borachio. Yours, sirrah? 12

CONRADE I am a gentleman, sir, and my name is Conrade.

DOGBERRY Write down Master Gentleman Conrade. Masters, do you serve God?

BOTH Yea, sir, we hope.

DOGBERRY Write down that they hope they serve God; and write God first, for God defend but God should go 18 before such villains! Masters, it is proved already that you are little better than false knaves, and it will go near to be thought so shortly. How answer you for yourselves?

CONRADE Marry, sir, we say we are none.

DOGBERRY A marvellous witty fellow, I assure you; but I will go about with him. *[to Borachio]* Come you 24 hither, sirrah. A word in your ear. Sir, I say to you, it is thought you are false knaves.

BORACHIO Sir, I say to you we are none.

DOGBERRY Well, stand aside. Fore God, they are both in 28 a tale. Have you writ down that they are none?

SEXTON Master constable, you go not the way to examine. You must call forth the watch that are their accusers.

DOGBERRY Yea, marry, that's the eftest way. Let the 32 watch come forth. Masters, I charge you in the Prince's name accuse these men.

1. WATCH This man said, sir, that Don John the Prince's brother was a villain.

---

261 *even* direct   271 *swear and eat it* i.e. eat the words of this oath, go back on it   275 *protest* solemnly affirm   279 *stayed* stopped   297 *approved* proved; *height* highest degree   299 *bear her in hand* lead her on, delude her   300 *take hands* marry   301 *uncovered* undisguised   308 *undone* ruined   310 *Counties* counts   311 *count* legal indictment (with a pun on Claudio's title); *Comfect* comfit, sugar-candy   314 *cursies* curtsies
IV, ii A hearing-room in Messina   1 *dissembly* (for 'assembly')   5 *exhibition* (for 'commission')   12 *sirrah* sir (a derogatory form, resented by Conrade)   18 *defend* forbid   24 *go about with* undertake, deal with   28–29 *they . . . tale* both tell the same story   32 *eftest* easiest, quickest

DOGBERRY Write down Prince John a villain. Why, this is flat perjury, to call a prince's brother villain.

BORACHIO Master constable –

40 DOGBERRY Pray thee, fellow, peace. I do not like thy look, I promise thee.

SEXTON What heard you him say else?

2. WATCH Marry, that he had received a thousand ducats of Don John for accusing the Lady Hero wrongfully.

DOGBERRY Flat burglary as ever was committed.

VERGES Yea, by mass, that it is.

SEXTON What else, fellow?

1. WATCH And that Count Claudio did mean, upon his words, to disgrace Hero before the whole assembly, and not marry her.

DOGBERRY O villain! thou wilt be condemned into ever-
52 lasting redemption for this.

SEXTON What else?

WATCHMEN This is all.

SEXTON And this is more, masters, than you can deny. Prince John this morning secretly stolen away. Hero was in this manner accused, in this very manner refused, and upon the grief of this suddenly died. Master constable, let these men be bound and brought to Leonato's. I will go before and show him their examination. *[Exit.]*

61 DOGBERRY Come, let them be opinioned.

VERGES Let them be in the hands –

63 CONRADE Off, coxcomb!

DOGBERRY God's my life, where's the sexton? Let him write down the Prince's officer coxcomb. Come, bind
66 them. – Thou naughty varlet!

CONRADE Away! you are an ass, you are an ass.

68 DOGBERRY Dost thou not suspect my place? Dost thou not suspect my years? O that he were here to write me down an ass! But, masters, remember that I am an ass. Though it be not written down, yet forget not that I am
72 an ass. No, thou villain, thou art full of piety, as shall be proved upon thee by good witness. I am a wise fellow; and which is more, an officer; and which is more, a householder; and which is more, as pretty a piece of flesh as any is in Messina, and one that knows the law, go to! and a rich fellow enough, go to! and a fellow that
77 hath had losses; and one that hath two gowns and everything handsome about him. Bring him away. O that I had been writ down an ass! *Exit [with the others].*

*

V, i   *Enter Leonato and his brother [Antonio].*

ANTONIO
If you go on thus, you will kill yourself,
2 And 'tis not wisdom thus to second grief
Against yourself.

LEONATO   I pray thee cease thy counsel,
Which falls into mine ears as profitless
As water in a sieve. Give not me counsel,
Nor let no comforter delight mine ear
7 But such a one whose wrongs do suit with mine.
Bring me a father that so loved his child,
9 Whose joy of her is overwhelmed like mine,
And bid him speak of patience.
Measure his woe the length and breadth of mine,
12 And let it answer every strain for strain,
As thus for thus, and such a grief for such,
In every lineament, branch, shape, and form.

If such a one will smile and stroke his beard, 15
Bid sorrow wag, cry 'hem' when he should groan, 16
Patch grief with proverbs, make misfortune drunk
With candle-wasters – bring him yet to me, 18
And I of him will gather patience.
But there is no such man; for, brother, men
Can counsel and speak comfort to that grief
Which they themselves not feel; but, tasting it,
Their counsel turns to passion, which before
Would give preceptial medicine to rage, 24
Fetter strong madness in a silken thread,
Charm ache with air and agony with words. 26
No, no! 'Tis all men's office to speak patience
To those that wring under the load of sorrow, 28
But no man's virtue nor sufficiency
To be so moral when he shall endure
The like himself. Therefore give me no counsel.
My griefs cry louder than advertisement. 32

ANTONIO
Therein do men from children nothing differ.

LEONATO
I pray thee peace. I will be flesh and blood;
For there was never yet philosopher
That could endure the toothache patiently,
However they have writ the style of gods 37
And made a push at chance and sufferance. 38

ANTONIO
Yet bend not all the harm upon yourself.
Make those that do offend you suffer too.

LEONATO
There thou speak'st reason. Nay, I will do so.
My soul doth tell me Hero is belied;
And that shall Claudio know; so shall the Prince,
And all of them that thus dishonor her.
       Enter Prince [Don Pedro] and Claudio.

ANTONIO
Here comes the Prince and Claudio hastily.

PEDRO
Good den, good den. 46

CLAUDIO   Good day to both of you.

LEONATO
Hear you, my lords –

PEDRO   We have some haste, Leonato.

LEONATO
Some haste, my lord! well, fare you well, my lord.
Are you so hasty now? Well, all is one. 49

PEDRO
Nay, do not quarrel with us, good old man.

ANTONIO
If he could right himself with quarrelling,
Some of us would lie low.

CLAUDIO   Who wrongs him?

52 *redemption* (for 'damnation')   61 *opinioned* (for 'pinioned')   63 *coxcomb* fool (derived from the comb of red flannel worn on the head of a professional court jester)   66 *naughty* wicked; *varlet* scoundrel   68 *suspect* (for 'respect')   72 *piety* (for 'impiety')   77 *had losses* (implying that he has had possessions to lose)
V, i A street in Messina   2 *second* support, assist   7 *suit with* match   9 *overwhelmed* drowned, as with tears   12 *strain* trait   15 *stroke his beard* (a gesture of complacency)   16 *wag* go away   18 *candle-wasters* i.e. moral philosophers   24 *preceptial medicine* remedy in the form of precepts   26 *Charm . . . air* allay pain with talk   28 *wring* writhe   32 *advertisement* advice   37 *writ* written in   38 *made a push* said pish, scoffed; *chance* mischance; *sufferance* suffering   46 *Good den* good evening   49 *all is one* it does not matter

LEONATO

53 Marry, thou dost wrong me, thou dissembler, thou !
Nay, never lay thy hand upon thy sword ;
I fear thee not.

55 CLAUDIO   Marry, beshrew my hand
If it should give your age such cause of fear.
In faith, my hand meant nothing to my sword.

LEONATO

58 Tush, tush, man ! never fleer and jest at me.
I speak not like a dotard nor a fool,
As under privilege of age to brag
What I have done being young, or what would do,
Were I not old. Know, Claudio, to thy head,
64 Thou hast so wronged mine innocent child and me
65 That I am forced to lay my reverence by
66 And, with grey hairs and bruise of many days,
Do challenge thee to trial of a man.
I say thou hast belied mine innocent child.
Thy slander hath gone through and through her heart,
And she lies buried with her ancestors –
O, in a tomb where never scandal slept,
71 Save this of hers, framed by thy villainy !

CLAUDIO

My villainy ?

LEONATO   Thine, Claudio ; thine I say.

PEDRO

You say not right, old man.

LEONATO   My lord, my lord,
I'll prove it on his body if he dare,
75 Despite his nice fence and his active practice,
76 His May of youth and bloom of lustihood.

CLAUDIO

Away ! I will not have to do with you.

LEONATO

78 Canst thou so daff me ? Thou hast killed my child.
If thou kill'st me, boy, thou shalt kill a man.

ANTONIO

He shall kill two of us, and men indeed.
But that's no matter ; let him kill one first.
82 Win me and wear me ! Let him answer me.
Come, follow me, boy. Come, sir boy, come follow me.
84 Sir boy, I'll whip you from your foining fence !
Nay, as I am a gentleman, I will.

LEONATO

Brother –

ANTONIO

87 Content yourself. God knows I loved my niece,
And she is dead, slandered to death by villains,
That dare as well answer a man indeed

As I dare take a serpent by the tongue.
Boys, apes, braggarts, Jacks, milksops !

LEONATO   Brother Anthony –

ANTONIO

Hold you content. What, man ! I know them, yea,
And what they weigh, even to the utmost scruple,   93
Scambling, outfacing, fashion-monging boys,   94
That lie and cog and flout, deprave and slander,   95
Go anticly, show outward hideousness,   96
And speak off half a dozen dang'rous words,
How they might hurt their enemies, if they durst ;
And this is all.

LEONATO

But, brother Anthony –

ANTONIO   Come, 'tis no matter.
Do not you meddle ; let me deal in this.

PEDRO

Gentlemen both, we will not wake your patience.   102
My heart is sorry for your daughter's death ;
But, on my honor, she was charged with nothing
But what was true, and very full of proof.   105

LEONATO

My lord, my lord –

PEDRO

I will not hear you.

LEONATO

No ? Come, brother, away ! – I will be heard.

ANTONIO

And shall, or some of us will smart for it.   *Exeunt ambo.* 109
        Enter Benedick.

PEDRO See, see ! Here comes the man we went to seek.

CLAUDIO Now, signior, what news ?

BENEDICK Good day, my lord.

PEDRO Welcome, signior. You are almost come to part   113
almost a fray.

CLAUDIO We had liked to have had our two noses
snapped off with two old men without teeth.

PEDRO Leonato and his brother. What think'st thou ?
Had we fought, I doubt we should have been too young   118
for them.

BENEDICK In a false quarrel there is no true valor. I came
to seek you both.

CLAUDIO We have been up and down to seek thee ; for
we are high-proof melancholy, and would fain have it   123
beaten away. Wilt thou use thy wit ?

BENEDICK It is in my scabbard. Shall I draw it ?

PEDRO Dost thou wear thy wit by thy side ?

CLAUDIO Never any did so, though very many have been
beside their wit. I will bid thee draw, as we do the min-   128
strels – draw to pleasure us.

PEDRO As I am an honest man, he looks pale. Art thou
sick, or angry ?

CLAUDIO What, courage, man ! What though care killed
a cat, thou hast mettle enough in thee to kill care.   133

BENEDICK Sir, I shall meet your wit in the career an you   134
charge it against me. I pray you choose another subject.

CLAUDIO Nay then, give him another staff ; this last was
broke cross.   137

PEDRO By this light, he changes more and more. I think
he be angry indeed.

CLAUDIO If he be, he knows how to turn his girdle.   140

BENEDICK Shall I speak a word in your ear ?

CLAUDIO God bless me from a challenge !

BENEDICK *[aside to Claudio]* You are a villain. I jest not ;

---

53 *thou* (distinguished from the more respectful 'you' with which he addresses the Prince)   55 *beshrew* (mild curse)   58 *fleer* jeer   64 *lay . . . by* renounce the respect due to old age   65 *bruise* wear and tear   66 *trial of a man* manly trial, i.e. a duel   71 *framed* made   75 *nice fence* clever swordplay   76 *lustihood* vigor, strength   78 *daff* put aside   82 *Win . . . wear me* (a proverb, serving as a form of challenge)   84 *foining* thrusting   87 *Content* calm   93 *scruple* smallest measure of weight   94 *Scambling* quarrelsome ; *outfacing* impudent ; *monging* mongering   95 *cog* cheat ; *flout* jeer at ; *deprave* defame   96 *anticly* fantastically dressed ; *hideousness* frightening aspect   102 *wake your patience* cause you to need patience   105 *full of proof* fully proved   109 s.d. *ambo* both (Leonato and Antonio)   113 *almost come* come almost in time   118 *doubt* suspect   123 *high-proof* in a high degree of   128 *beside their wit* out of their minds ; *draw* (used of a sword, and of a minstrel's bow)   134 *in the career* while running at full speed   134–35 *an you charge it* if you charge with it (as with a lance in a tilt)   137 *broke cross* broken across (as by an unskillful tilter)   140 *turn his girdle* prepare for a bout, as in wrestling (?)

I will make it good how you dare, with what you dare,
145 and when you dare. Do me right, or I will protest your
cowardice. You have killed a sweet lady, and her death
shall fall heavy on you. Let me hear from you.

CLAUDIO Well, I will meet you, so I may have good cheer.

PEDRO What, a feast? a feast?

150 CLAUDIO I' faith, I thank him, he hath bid me to a calve's
151 head and a capon, the which if I do not carve most curi-
152 ously, say my knife's naught. Shall I not find a woodcock too?

BENEDICK Sir, your wit ambles well; it goes easily.

155 PEDRO I'll tell thee how Beatrice praised thy wit the other
156 day. I said thou hadst a fine wit: 'True,' said she, 'a fine
little one.' 'No,' said I, 'a great wit.' 'Right,' says she, 'a
great gross one.' 'Nay,' said I, 'a good wit.' 'Just,' said
she, 'it hurts nobody.' 'Nay,' said I, 'the gentleman is
160 wise.' 'Certain,' said she, 'a wise gentleman,' 'Nay,' said
161 I, 'he hath the tongues.' 'That I believe,' said she, 'for he
162 swore a thing to me on Monday night which he forswore
on Tuesday morning. There's a double tongue; there's
164 two tongues.' Thus did she an hour together transshape
thy particular virtues. Yet at last she concluded with a
166 sigh, thou wast the properest man in Italy.

CLAUDIO For the which she wept heartily and said she
cared not.

PEDRO Yea, that she did; but yet, for all that, an if she did
not hate him deadly, she would love him dearly. The
old man's daughter told us all.

172 CLAUDIO All, all! and moreover, God saw him when he
was hid in the garden.

174 PEDRO But when shall we set the savage bull's horns on
the sensible Benedick's head?

176 CLAUDIO Yea, and text underneath, 'Here dwells Benedick, the married man'?

BENEDICK Fare you well, boy; you know my mind. I will
leave you now to your gossip-like humor. You break
jests as braggards do their blades, which God be thanked
hurt not. [to the Prince] My lord, for your many courtesies I thank you. I must discontinue your company.
Your brother the bastard is fled from Messina. You have
among you killed a sweet and innocent lady. For my
Lord Lackbeard there, he and I shall meet; and till then
peace be with him.   [Exit.]

PEDRO He is in earnest.

CLAUDIO In most profound earnest; and, I'll warrant
you, for the love of Beatrice.

PEDRO And hath challenged thee?

CLAUDIO Most sincerely.

192 PEDRO What a pretty thing man is when he goes in his
doublet and hose and leaves off his wit!

*Enter Constables [Dogberry and Verges, with the
Watch, leading] Conrade and Borachio.*

194 CLAUDIO He is then a giant to an ape; but then is an ape a
doctor to such a man.

196 PEDRO But, soft you, let me be! Pluck up, my heart, and
be sad! Did he not say my brother was fled?

DOGBERRY Come you, sir. If justice cannot tame you, she
199 shall ne'er weigh more reasons in her balance. Nay, an
you be a cursing hypocrite once, you must be looked
to.

PEDRO How now? two of my brother's men bound?
Borachio one.

CLAUDIO Hearken after their offense, my lord.

PEDRO Officers, what offense have these men done?

DOGBERRY Marry, sir, they have committed false report;
moreover, they have spoken untruths; secondarily, they
are slanders; sixth and lastly, they have belied a lady;
thirdly, they have verified unjust things; and to con- 208
clude, they are lying knaves.

PEDRO First, I ask thee what they have done; thirdly, I
ask thee what's their offense; sixth and lastly, why they
are committed; and to conclude, what you lay to their 212
charge.

CLAUDIO Rightly reasoned, and in his own division; and
by my troth there's one meaning well suited. 215

PEDRO Who have you offended, masters, that you are
thus bound to your answer? This learned constable is 217
too cunning to be understood. What's your offense?

BORACHIO Sweet Prince, let me go no farther to mine answer. Do you hear me, and let this Count kill me. I have
deceived even your very eyes. What your wisdoms could
not discover, these shallow fools have brought to light,
who in the night overheard me confessing to this man,
how Don John your brother incensed me to slander the 224
Lady Hero; how you were brought into the orchard and
saw me court Margaret in Hero's garments; how you
disgraced her when you should marry her. My villainy
they have upon record, which I had rather seal with my
death than repeat over to my shame. The lady is dead
upon mine and my master's false accusation; and briefly,
I desire nothing but the reward of a villain.

PEDRO Runs not this speech like iron through your 232
blood?

CLAUDIO I have drunk poison whiles he uttered it.

PEDRO But did my brother set thee on to this?

BORACHIO Yea, and paid me richly for the practice of it. 235

PEDRO
He is composed and framed of treachery,
And fled he is upon this villainy.

CLAUDIO
Sweet Hero, now thy image doth appear
In the rare semblance that I loved it first.

DOGBERRY Come, bring away the plaintiffs. By this time 240
our sexton hath reformed Signior Leonato of the matter. 241
And, masters, do not forget to specify, when time and
place shall serve, that I am an ass.

VERGES Here, here comes Master Signior Leonato, and
the sexton too.

Enter Leonato, his brother [Antonio], and the Sexton.

LEONATO
Which is the villain? Let me see his eyes,
That, when I note another man like him,
I may avoid him. Which of these is he?

---

145 *Do me right* accept my challenge; *protest* report abroad 150 *bid* invited; *calve's* calf's, i.e. fool's 151 *capon* (another contemptuous allusion); *curiously* expertly 152 *naught* good for nothing; *woodcock* bird famous for its stupidity 155 *praised* appraised 156 *fine* excellent, also small 160 *wise gentleman* wiseacre 161 *hath the tongues* can speak several languages 162 *forswore* denied with an oath 164 *transshape* transform 166 *properest* handsomest 172 *God saw him* (alluding to Genesis iii, 8, but also to the hoaxing of Benedick) 174 *the savage bull's horns* (see I, i, 232 ff.) 176 *text* in capital letters 192–93 *in . . . hose* i.e. fully dressed 194–95 *a giant . . . a man* much bigger than an ape, but the ape is much wiser than he 196–97 *Pluck . . . sad* pull up a moment, my mind, and be serious 199 *balance* scales (symbol of justice) 208 *verified* sworn to 212 *committed* arrested and held for trial 215 *well suited* provided with several different suits, or modes of speech 217 *bound to your answer* bound over, indicted 224 *incensed* incited 232 *iron* a sword 235 *practice* accomplishment 240 *plaintiffs* (for 'defendants') 241 *reformed* (for 'informed')

BORACHIO
If you would know your wronger, look on me.

LEONATO
Art thou the slave that with thy breath hast killed
Mine innocent child?

BORACHIO   Yea, even I alone.

LEONATO
No, not so, villain! thou beliest thyself.
Here stand a pair of honorable men –
A third is fled – that had a hand in it.
I thank you princes for my daughter's death.
Record it with your high and worthy deeds.
257 'Twas bravely done, if you bethink you of it.

CLAUDIO
258 I know not how to pray your patience;
Yet I must speak. Choose your revenge yourself;
260 Impose me to what penance your invention
Can lay upon my sin. Yet sinned I not
But in mistaking.

PEDRO   By my soul, nor I!
And yet, to satisfy this good old man,
I would bend under any heavy weight
That he'll enjoin me to.

LEONATO
I cannot bid you bid my daughter live –
That were impossible; but I pray you both,
268 Possess the people in Messina here
How innocent she died; and if your love
Can labor aught in sad invention,
Hang her an epitaph upon her tomb,
And sing it to her bones – sing it to-night.
To-morrow morning come you to my house,
And since you could not be my son-in-law,
Be yet my nephew. My brother hath a daughter,
Almost the copy of my child that's dead,
And she alone is heir to both of us.
278 Give her the right you should have giv'n her cousin,
And so dies my revenge.

CLAUDIO   O noble sir!
Your over-kindness doth wring tears from me.
281 I do embrace your offer; and dispose
For henceforth of poor Claudio.

LEONATO
To-morrow then I will expect your coming;
To-night I take my leave. This naughty man
Shall face to face be brought to Margaret,
286 Who I believe was packed in all this wrong,
Hired to it by your brother.

BORACHIO   No, by my soul, she was not;
Nor knew not what she did when she spoke to me;

But always hath been just and virtuous
In anything that I do know by her.

DOGBERRY Moreover, sir, which indeed is not under 291
white and black, this plaintiff here, the offender, did call
me ass. I beseech you let it be remembered in his punishment. And also the watch heard them talk of one Deformed. They say he wears a key in his ear, and a lock 295
hanging by it, and borrows money in God's name, the
which he hath used so long and never paid that now
men grow hard-hearted and will lend nothing for God's
sake. Pray you examine him upon that point.

LEONATO I thank thee for thy care and honest pains.

DOGBERRY Your worship speaks like a most thankful
and reverent youth, and I praise God for you.

LEONATO There's for thy pains.
[Gives money.]

DOGBERRY God save the foundation!   304

LEONATO Go, I discharge thee of thy prisoner, and I 305
thank thee.

DOGBERRY I leave an arrant knave with your worship,
which I beseech your worship to correct yourself, for
the example of others. God keep your worship! I wish
your worship well. God restore you to health! I humbly
give you leave to depart; and if a merry meeting may be 311
wished, God prohibit it! Come, neighbor.   312
[Exeunt Dogberry and Verges.]

LEONATO
Until to-morrow morning, lords, farewell.

ANTONIO
Farewell, my lords. We look for you to-morrow.

PEDRO
We will not fail.

CLAUDIO   To-night I'll mourn with Hero.
[Exeunt Don Pedro and Claudio.]

LEONATO *[to the Watch]*
Bring you these fellows on. – We'll talk with Margaret,
How her acquaintance grew with this lewd fellow.   317
Exeunt.

＊

Enter Benedick and Margaret [meeting].   V, ii

BENEDICK Pray thee, sweet Mistress Margaret, deserve
well at my hands by helping me to the speech of Beatrice.

MARGARET Will you then write me a sonnet in praise of
my beauty?

BENEDICK In so high a style, Margaret, that no man 5
living shall come over it; for in most comely truth thou
deservest it.

MARGARET To have no man come over me? Why, shall I
always keep below stairs?   9

BENEDICK Thy wit is as quick as the greyhound's mouth
– it catches.

MARGARET And yours 's as blunt as the fencer's foils,
which hit but hurt not.

BENEDICK A most manly wit, Margaret: it will not hurt a
woman. And so I pray thee call Beatrice. I give thee the
bucklers.   16

MARGARET Give us the swords; we have bucklers of our
own.

BENEDICK If you use them, Margaret, you must put in
the pikes with a vice, and they are dangerous weapons 19
for maids.

257 *bethink you of* recall   258 *pray your patience* ask your forgiveness
260 *Impose me to* impose on me   268 *Possess* inform   278 *right* right of
becoming your wife (perhaps with pun on 'rite' of marriage)   281 *dispose*
you may dispose   286 *packed* in the pact, an accomplice   291–92 *under
. . . black* in writing   295 *key, lock* (his misunderstanding of the *lock* of
III, iii, 157)   304 *God . . . foundation* (conventional phrase used by beggars
receiving alms at the gates of religious or charitable foundations)   305
discharge relieve   311 *give you leave* (for 'ask your leave')   312 *prohibit*
(for 'grant')   317 *lewd* low, disreputable
V, ii Before Leonato's house   5 *style* i.e. of writing, but with a pun on
'stile,' a stairs over a fence   9 *keep below stairs* dwell in the servants'
quarters, i.e. never be mistress of a house   16 *bucklers* shields with spikes
in their centers (Margaret's retort is a ribald play on words)   19 *pikes*
spikes; *vice* screw

MARGARET Well, I will call Beatrice to you, who I think hath legs.   *Exit Margaret.*

BENEDICK And therefore will come.

[Sings]   The god of love,
                 That sits above
        And knows me, and knows me,
         How pitiful I deserve –

28 I mean in singing; but in loving, Leander the good
29 swimmer, Troilus the first employer of panders, and a
30 whole book full of these quondam carpet-mongers, whose names yet run smoothly in the even road of a
32 blank verse – why, they were never so truly turned over and over as my poor self in love. Marry, I cannot show it in rhyme. I have tried. I can find out no rhyme to 'lady'
35 but 'baby' – an innocent rhyme; for 'scorn,' 'horn' – a hard rhyme; for 'school,' 'fool' – a babbling rhyme. Very ominous endings! No, I was not born under a rhyming planet, nor I cannot woo in festival terms.

Enter Beatrice.

Sweet Beatrice, wouldst thou come when I called thee?

BEATRICE Yea, signior, and depart when you bid me.

BENEDICK O, stay but till then!

BEATRICE 'Then' is spoken. Fare you well now. And yet, ere I go, let me go with that I came for, which is, with knowing what hath passed between you and Claudio.

BENEDICK Only foul words; and thereupon I will kiss thee.

BEATRICE Foul words is but foul wind, and foul wind is
47 but foul breath, and foul breath is noisome. Therefore I will depart unkissed.

BENEDICK Thou hast frighted the word out of his right sense, so forcible is thy wit. But I must tell thee plainly,
51 Claudio undergoes my challenge; and either I must
52 shortly hear from him or I will subscribe him a coward. And I pray thee now tell me, for which of my bad parts didst thou first fall in love with me?

BEATRICE For them all together, which maintained so
56 politic a state of evil that they will not admit any good part to intermingle with them. But for which of my
58 good parts did you first suffer love for me?

BENEDICK Suffer love! – a good epithet. I do suffer love indeed, for I love thee against my will.

BEATRICE In spite of your heart, I think. Alas, poor heart! If you spite it for my sake, I will spite it for yours, for I will never love that which my friend hates.

BENEDICK Thou and I are too wise to woo peaceably.

BEATRICE It appears not in this confession. There's not one wise man among twenty that will praise himself.

BENEDICK An old, an old instance, Beatrice, that lived in
68 the time of good neighbors. If a man do not erect in this age his own tomb ere he dies, he shall live no longer in monument than the bell rings and the widow weeps.

BEATRICE And how long is that, think you?

BENEDICK Question: why, an hour in clamor and a quar-
73 ter in rheum. Therefore it is most expedient for the wise, if Don Worm (his conscience) find no impediment to the contrary, to be the trumpet of his own virtues, as I am to myself. So much for praising myself, who, I myself will bear witness, is praiseworthy. And now tell me, how doth your cousin?

BEATRICE Very ill.

BENEDICK And how do you?

BEATRICE Very ill too.

BENEDICK Serve God, love me, and mend. There will I leave you too, for here comes one in haste.

Enter Ursula.

URSULA Madam, you must come to your uncle. Yonder's old coil at home. It is proved my Lady Hero hath been 85 falsely accused, the Prince and Claudio mightily abused, 86 and Don John is the author of all, who is fled and gone. Will you come presently?

BEATRICE Will you go hear this news, signior?

BENEDICK I will live in thy heart, die in thy lap, and be buried in thy eyes; and moreover, I will go with thee to thy uncle's.   *Exit [with Beatrice and Ursula].*

*

Enter Claudio, Prince [Don Pedro, Lord], and three   V, iii
or four with tapers [followed by Musicians].

CLAUDIO Is this the monument of Leonato?

LORD It is, my lord.

CLAUDIO *[reads from a scroll]*

          Epitaph.

   Done to death by slanderous tongues
     Was the Hero that here lies.   4
   Death, in guerdon of her wrongs,   5
     Gives her fame which never dies.
   So the life that died with shame
   Lives in death with glorious fame.

[Hangs up the scroll.]
   Hang thou there upon the tomb,
   Praising her when I am dumb.
Now, music, sound, and sing your solemn hymn.

      Song [by one attending].

   Pardon, goddess of the night,   12
   Those that slew thy virgin knight;   13
   For the which, with songs of woe,
   Round about her tomb they go.
   Midnight, assist our moan,
   Help us to sigh and groan
     Heavily, heavily.
   Graves, yawn and yield your dead,
   Till death be utterèd   20
     Heavily, heavily.

CLAUDIO Now unto thy bones good night!
   Yearly will I do this rite.

PEDRO
Good morrow, masters. Put your torches out.
   The wolves have preyed, and look, the gentle day,
Before the wheels of Phoebus, round about   26
   Dapples the drowsy east with spots of grey.
Thanks to you all, and leave us. Fare you well.

28 *Leander* (who swam the Hellespont every night to see another Hero until he was drowned in a storm)   29 *Troilus* (who was helped to the love of Cressida by her uncle Pandarus)   30 *quondam carpet-mongers* ancient carpet knights (i.e. lovers rather than fighters)   32–33 *turned over and over* head over heels   35 *innocent* childish   47 *noisome* offensive, bad-smelling   51 *undergoes* bears   52 *subscribe him* write him down   56 *politic* well organized   58 *suffer* experience, but also feel the pain of   68 *time of good neighbors* i.e. Golden age   73 *rheum* tears   85 *old coil* confusion   86 *abused* deceived
V, iii A churchyard   4 *Hero* (pun intended)   5 *guerdon* reward   12 *goddess of the night* Diana, patroness of chastity   13 *virgin knight* (still punning on *Hero*)   20 *utterèd* fully expressed   26 *Phoebus* god who drives the chariot of the sun

CLAUDIO
Good morrow, masters. Each his several way.
PEDRO
30   Come, let us hence and put on other weeds,
And then to Leonato's we will go.
CLAUDIO
32   And Hymen now with luckier issue speeds
Than this for whom we rend'red up this woe.   *Exeunt.*

*

V, iv   *Enter Leonato, Benedick, [Beatrice,] Margaret,*
Ursula, Old Man [Antonio], Friar [Francis], Hero.
FRIAR
Did I not tell you she was innocent?
LEONATO
So are the Prince and Claudio, who accused her
3   Upon the error that you heard debated.
But Margaret was in some fault for this,
5   Although against her will, as it appears
6   In the true course of all the question.
ANTONIO
7   Well, I am glad that all things sort so well.
BENEDICK
8   And so am I, being else by faith enforced
To call young Claudio to a reckoning for it.
LEONATO
Well, daughter, and you gentlewomen all,
Withdraw into a chamber by yourselves,
And when I send for you, come hither masked.
The Prince and Claudio promised by this hour
To visit me. You know your office, brother:
You must be father to your brother's daughter,
And give her to young Claudio.   *Exeunt Ladies.*
ANTONIO
17   Which I will do with confirmed countenance.
BENEDICK
Friar, I must entreat your pains, I think.
FRIAR
To do what, signior?
BENEDICK
To bind me, or undo me – one of them.
Signior Leonato, truth it is, good signior,
Your niece regards me with an eye of favor.
LEONATO
That eye my daughter lent her. 'Tis most true.
BENEDICK
And I do with an eye of love requite her.
LEONATO
The sight whereof I think you had from me,
From Claudio, and the Prince; but what's your will?
BENEDICK
Your answer, sir, is enigmatical;
But, for my will, my will is, your good will
May stand with ours, this day to be conjoined

In the state of honorable marriage;
In which, good friar, I shall desire your help.
LEONATO
My heart is with your liking.
FRIAR   And my help.
Here comes the Prince and Claudio.
Enter Prince [Don Pedro] and Claudio and two or
three other.
PEDRO
Good morrow to this fair assembly.
LEONATO
Good morrow, Prince; good morrow, Claudio.
We here attend you. Are you yet determined   36
To-day to marry with my brother's daughter?
CLAUDIO
I'll hold my mind, were she an Ethiope.   38
LEONATO
Call her forth, brother. Here's the friar ready.
                     [Exit Antonio.]
PEDRO
Good morrow, Benedick. Why, what's the matter
That you have such a February face,
So full of frost, of storm, and cloudiness?
CLAUDIO
I think he thinks upon the savage bull.
Tush, fear not, man! We'll tip thy horns with gold,
And all Europa shall rejoice at thee,   45
As once Europa did at lusty Jove   46
When he would play the noble beast in love.
BENEDICK
Bull Jove, sir, had an amiable low,
And some such strange bull leaped your father's cow
And got a calf in that same noble feat
Much like to you, for you have just his bleat.
Enter [Leonato's] brother [Antonio], Hero, Beatrice,
Margaret, Ursula [the ladies wearing masks].
CLAUDIO
For this I owe you. Here comes other reck'nings.   52
Which is the lady I must seize upon?
ANTONIO
This same is she, and I do give you her.
CLAUDIO
Why then, she's mine. Sweet, let me see your face.
LEONATO
No, that you shall not till you take her hand
Before this friar and swear to marry her.
CLAUDIO
Give me your hand before this holy friar.
I am your husband if you like of me.
HERO
And when I lived I was your other wife;
    [Unmasks.]
And when you loved you were my other husband.
CLAUDIO
Another Hero!
HERO   Nothing certainer.
One Hero died defiled; but I do live,   63
And surely as I live, I am a maid.
PEDRO
The former Hero! Hero that is dead!
LEONATO
She died, my lord, but whiles her slander lived.
FRIAR
All this amazement can I qualify,   67

---

30 *weeds* clothes   32 *Hymen* god of marriage; *speeds* (perhaps for 'speed us')
V, iv The hall in Leonato's house   3 *Upon* because of   5 *against her will*
unintentionally   6 *question* investigation   7 *sort* turn out   8 *faith* fidelity
to my word   17 *confirmed countenance* straight face   36 *yet* still   38
Ethiope i.e. black, and hence ugly in an age which admired blondes   45
Europa Europe   46 *Europa* a girl who was wooed by Jove in the shape of a
bull   52 *I owe you* I will pay you later (Benedick has managed to call him
both a calf and a bastard); *reck'nings* bills to pay   63 *defiled* disgraced (by
the false charge)   67 *qualify* moderate, relieve

When, after that the holy rites are ended,

69 I'll tell you largely of fair Hero's death.

70 Meantime let wonder seem familiar,
And to the chapel let us presently.

BENEDICK
Soft and fair, friar. Which is Beatrice?

BEATRICE *[unmasks]*
I answer to that name. What is your will?

BENEDICK
Do not you love me?

BEATRICE   Why, no; no more than reason.

BENEDICK
Why, then your uncle, and the Prince, and Claudio
Have been deceived – they swore you did.

BEATRICE
Do not you love me?

BENEDICK   Troth, no; no more than reason.

BEATRICE
Why, then my cousin, Margaret, and Ursula
Are much deceived; for they did swear you did.

BENEDICK
They swore that you were almost sick for me.

BEATRICE
They swore that you were well-nigh dead for me.

BENEDICK
'Tis no such matter. Then you do not love me?

BEATRICE

83 No, truly, but in friendly recompense.

LEONATO
Come, cousin, I am sure you love the gentleman.

CLAUDIO
And I'll be sworn upon't that he loves her;
For here's a paper written in his hand,
A halting sonnet of his own pure brain,
Fashioned to Beatrice.

HERO   And here's another,
Writ in my cousin's hand, stol'n from her pocket,
Containing her affection unto Benedick.

91 BENEDICK A miracle! Here's our own hands against our
hearts. Come, I will have thee; but, by this light, I
take thee for pity.

BEATRICE I would not deny you; but, by this good day, I
yield upon great persuasion, and partly to save your life,
for I was told you were in a consumption.

BENEDICK Peace! I will stop your mouth.
[Kisses her.]

PEDRO How dost thou, Benedick, the married man?

BENEDICK I'll tell thee what, Prince: a college of wit- 99
crackers cannot flout me out of my humor. Dost thou
think I care for a satire or an epigram? No. If a man will
be beaten with brains, 'a shall wear nothing handsome 102
about him. In brief, since I do purpose to marry, I will
think nothing to any purpose that the world can say
against it; and therefore never flout at me for what I
have said against it; for man is a giddy thing, and this is
my conclusion. For thy part, Claudio, I did think to
have beaten thee; but in that thou art like to be my
kinsman, live unbruised, and love my cousin.

CLAUDIO I had well hoped thou wouldst have denied
Beatrice, that I might have cudgelled thee out of thy
single life, to make thee a double-dealer, which out of 112
question thou wilt be if my cousin do not look exceeding
narrowly to thee.

BENEDICK Come, come, we are friends. Let's have a
dance ere we are married, that we may lighten our own
hearts and our wives' heels.

LEONATO We'll have dancing afterward.

BENEDICK First, of my word! Therefore play, music. 119
Prince, thou art sad. Get thee a wife, get thee a wife!
There is no staff more reverent than one tipped with 121
horn.

Enter Messenger.

MESSENGER
My lord, your brother John is ta'en in flight,
And brought with armèd men back to Messina.

BENEDICK Think not on him till to-morrow. I'll devise
thee brave punishments for him. Strike up, pipers!
Dance. [Exeunt.]

---

69 *largely* in full   **70** *let . . . familiar* treat this marvel as if it were an
ordinary matter   **83** *friendly recompense* charitable repayment   **91** *hands*
written testimony   **99-100** *college of wit-crackers* assembly of jokers
102 *beaten with brains* defeated with witticisms (but with a play on the
literal sense of having brains flung at him which will spoil his clothes)
112 *double-dealer* married man, but also an unfaithful husband (a common
newly-wed joke)   **119** *of* upon   **121** *staff* rod of office, but also walking-
stick   **121-22** *tipped with horn* (the usual reference to horns and cuckoldry)

TWELFTH NIGHT, OR, WHAT YOU WILL

INTRODUCTION

On Candlemas Day, 1602, the Gentlemen of the Middle Temple, one of the Inns of Court, held their feast, and for their entertainment there was performed "... a play called 'Twelue Night, or What You Will' ...." John Manningham, a spectator on this occasion, continues his account with a description of the play, which was

... much like the Commedy of Errores, or Menechmi in Plautus, but most like and neere to that in Italian called *Inganni*. A good practise in it to make the Steward beleeve his Lady widdowe was in love with him, by counterfeyting a letter as from his Lady in generall termes, telling him what shee liked best in him, and prescribing his gesture in smiling, his apparaile, &c., and then when he came to practise making him beleeue they tooke him to be mad.

Since other evidence suggests that *Twelfth Night* may have been written as early as 1599, we may safely date it "about 1600." Whether it was written before *As You Like It* or *Much Ado about Nothing*, both certainly in existence by 1600, cannot be determined exactly. Actually all three of these "Joyous Comedies" are thematically of a piece, and any precise ordering of their composition can only be based on subjective judgments. In some ways it is tempting to accept Dr Leslie Hotson's recent theory that *Twelfth Night* was first performed on January 6, 1601, before the Queen at Whitehall with Don Virginio Orsino as an honored guest. There are, however, several objections to this theory and we must still rely on the approximate date of 1600. That the visiting Italian nobleman would have been flattered by the character of the Duke Orsino is somewhat difficult to understand.

In contrast to *As You Like It*, which has a single source, the sources or analogues of *Twelfth Night* are manifold. Manningham refers to two possible sources, Plautus' *Menaechmi* and the Italian *Inganni*. Modern scholarship has added to the list another Italian play *Gl'Ingannati* (which has characters named Fabio and Malevolti as well as a reference to Epiphany, or Twelfth Night), Italian novelle, French and English translations of the latter, Sidney's *Arcadia*, the play of *Sir Clyomon and Clamydes*, and Emanuel Forde's *Parismus* (which has the shipwreck as well as the names Olivia and Violetta). These deal in varying fashion with twins and the disguise of the girl as a page wooing in her master's behalf. As a matter of fact, Shakespeare had already used this latter device in *The Two Gentlemen of Verona* with the disguised Julia in the service of her false lover Proteus.

In all these varied materials there is no suggestion of the Malvolio plot, but a possible clue as to why Shakespeare added this to the traditional materials may be found in one of the English sources, the tale of Apolonius and Silla,

as related by Barnabe Riche in a collection entitled *Riche his Farewell to Militarie Profession*. The reason for this rather odd title is that Riche, abandoning the wars, now prepares to devote his labors "for the onely delight of the courteous Gentlewomen bothe of England and Irelande." The story itself is remote from Shakespeare's play in many respects. Duke Apolonius, returning from war against the Turks, is forced by a storm to take refuge in Cyprus. Silla, daughter of Pontus the governor of the island, promptly falls in love with the noble visitor. After his departure for Constantinople, she sets off in pursuit accompanied by a faithful servant. After a shipwreck, Silla disguises herself and gains service as a page to Apolonius, and must then woo, on his behalf, the Lady Julina. Silla's twin brother Silvio arrives in search of his sister and is mistaken for her by Julina. Complications ensue when the impetuous Julina becomes pregnant by Silvio without benefit of wedlock. Silvio has departed in further search for his sister, but fortunately returns in time to marry Julina, while Silla wins her Apolonius.

What is more interesting to us than the story itself is the prefatory comment of Riche on the subject of love and its particular manifestations in the tale. The conventions of love were of great concern to the young ladies and gentlemen of the Queen's Court and they were aped by those beneath them in the social scale. And it is these conventions, social and literary, that Shakespeare views with Puck's amused observation – Lord, what fools these mortals be! – in all three of the Joyous Comedies. Riche, however, sees no humor in his story, as his words witness:

There is no child that is borne into this wretched worlde, but before it doeth sucke the mother's milke, it taketh first a soope of the cupp of errour, which maketh us, when we come to riper yeres, not onely to enter into actions of injurie, but many tymes to straie from that is right and reason; but in all other thinges, wherein wee shewe our selves to bee moste dronken with this poisoned cuppe, it is in our actions of love; for the lover is so estranged from that is right, and wandereth so wide from the boundes of reason, that he is not able to deeme white from blacke, good from badde, vertue from vice; but onely led by the apetite of his owne affections, and groundyng them on the foolishnesse of his owne fancies, will so settle his likyng on such a one, as either by desert or unworthinesse will merite rather to be loathed then loved.

The unreasoning choice of lovers is exemplified in the story at hand, as Riche states:

Wherfore, right curteous gentilwomen, if it please you with pacience to persue this historie following, you shall see Dame Errour so plaie her parte with a leishe of lovers, a male and twoo femalles, as shall woorke a wonder to your wise judgement, in notyng the effecte of their amorous devises and conclusions of their actions : the firste neclectyng the love of a noble dame, yong, beautifull, and faire, who onely for his good will plaied the parte of a serving manne, contented to abide any maner of paine onely to behold him : he again setting his love of a dame, that despysing hym (beeyng a noble Duke) gave her self to a servyng manne (as she had thought) ; but it otherwise fell out, as the substance of this tale shall better discribe.

Just what group of "curteous gentilwomen" Riche was addressing is a question. In his attitude toward love and lovers he is not following the courtly or Petrarchan tradition with its glorification of love and its absorbed interest in the subtleties of the conventions. Instead Riche, in 1581, is speaking with the harsh moralistic voice of the emerging bourgeois Puritan. In 1567 Geoffrey Fenton had translated a number of tales from the French of Belleforest with the avowed object of praising virtuous love and excoriating vice, thus hoping that "the younglings of our countrey in reding my indevor, maye break the slepe of their longe follye, and retire at last to amendement of lyfe." For Fenton, as for his French source, and for Riche, love was a disease which deprived man or woman of reason. This idea was not original with these particular authors ; it had wide currency particularly in the middle class and may be traced to the classic past in Ovid's *De Remediis Amoris*, wherein that poet discusses remedies for the disease of love.

From this all-too-brief treatment of a large and complicated problem, it becomes clear that Riche and Shakespeare regard the story of the "leishe of lovers" from quite different points of view. Riche's use of "leishe" (leash), borrowed from the terminology of hunting and meaning a set of three hounds bound together, is sufficiently indicative of his moral scorn. For Riche the absolute folly and utter lack of rational conduct caused by love is demonstrated by the shifts which occur. Apolonius loves Julina ; Julina loves the disguised Silla, who in turn loves Apolonius. At the end Apolonius marries Silla, and Julina the twin brother Silvio. Love that changes so rapidly and with so little motivation is unreasoning and senseless.

But out of this very shift in the affections Shakespeare has created the gay and charming world of Illyria. His theme is love but there the similarity with Riche ends, for Shakespeare is not interested in moral judgments ; he accepts the conventions of love as they existed in the courtly world. Of course people fall in love at first sight ; they always do in the love poems and romances of the age. Orsino, Viola, and Olivia all behave in thoroughly traditional fashion. In his opening scene (I, i, 20–24) Orsino describes his fall :

> O, when mine eyes did see Olivia first,
> Methought she purged the air of pestilence.
> That instant was I turned into a hart,
> And my desires, like fell and cruel hounds,
> E'er since pursue me.

Whereas we have had some indication that the noble Duke suffers from love's torments, we are quite unprepared, at least by any dialogue, for Viola's sudden fall. Ordered by Orsino to woo Olivia on his behalf, Viola acquiesces (I, i, 39–41) :

> I'll do my best
> To woo your lady. [*aside*] Yet a barful strife !
> Whoe'er I woo, myself would be his wife.

Olivia requires a few more lines than Viola to announce her capitulation, but she is well aware of the rapidity of the fall (I, v, 278–84).

> Thy tongue, thy face, thy limbs, actions, and spirit
> Do give thee fivefold blazon. Not too fast ; soft, soft,
> Unless the master were the man. How now ?
> Even so quickly may one catch the plague ?
> Methinks I feel this youth's perfections
> With an invisible and subtle stealth
> To creep in at mine eyes. Well, let it be.

The nature of the love which afflicts our characters is not oversubtly revealed. The sophisticated Duke, well read in love's literature, needs but one cue to pun and learnedly compare. Concluding his apostrophe to the spirit of love, he is asked a simple question by Curio, "Will you go hunt, my lord ?" but his seemingly simple response is well pointed in the proper direction, "What, Curio ?" The answer is the one he wants, "The hart." Immediately Olivia becomes the hart (heart), "Why, so I do, the noblest that I have," which he pursues. At the next moment we are plunged into Ovid's *Metamorphoses* when the Duke now compares himself, after he has first seen Olivia, with Actaeon, who, having gazed on the nude Diana bathing, was punished by being transformed into a hart and pursued to death by his own hounds. Such mental agility, such appropriate references turned to the occasion of the moment were the very essence of the true courtly lover. Orsino knows the game, but Shakespeare has made him play it in seriousness.

In contrast, Olivia calmly accepts her infection with love's plague by the simple line, "Well, let it be." But this is deceptive simplicity, for properly read by a skilled actress this can be a most trenchant instance of high comedy travelling in an instant from all the conventional pretensions of her preceding lines to an amused reality.

Just such a tone distinguishes the difference in the various attitudes toward love found, for example, in I, v, where Viola goes a-wooing for Orsino. Here, particularly after the departure of Maria, when the two women are alone, we see that both are well skilled in the dialectic of love. Olivia opens with a well-known gambit, "Now, sir, what is your text ?" This is the familiar association of love as a religion with its holy books, and the two play through "what chapter" to "heresy." The point of this and the subsequent dialogue is that each knows that the other is playing the game, so that this knowledge on the part of the aware spectator develops the comic value, not so much of ridicule, as amused observation of the game itself. These two can see themselves objectively but Orsino cannot, nor can Malvolio.

In the source materials of the main plot, it would seem that Shakespeare saw the elements of high comedy. Here in a traditional story that had been told many times, always seriously, was an example of the absurdity of the literary conventions of love. As we have seen, it is with an amused eye that he views this story. At the first we have Orsino luxuriating in his own emotions ; he is more in love with love than with Olivia. His opening soliloquy is too much of a good thing and would have been so recognized by a cultivated Elizabethan. This delineation of Orsino is amplified as the play progresses : in II, iv, he describes himself as a true lover, ringing the changes on the clichés ; in Act V he epitomizes the eternal vacillations and improbabilities when at one moment he is prepared to kill Viola and in the next to marry her.

Similarly Olivia, having fallen in love with the disguised Viola, is perfectly willing to marry the twin brother Sebastian. If comment were needed on this sudden shift, we need only look back to Viola's analysis of the situation in II, ii. Olivia has sent Malvolio in pursuit of Viola-Cesario with a love ring, and the latter immediately recognizes what has happened:

> I left no ring with her. What means this lady?
> Fortune forbid my outside have not charmed her.

It is precisely with the outside, external aspects of the formalized love conventions that the main plot deals and therein lies another aspect of the humor. Nothing is serious, and after all the subtitle of the play is "What You Will."

On the other hand the subplot does approach the serious when Malvolio is imprisoned as a lunatic. Some critics have, in fact, said that Malvolio is dealt with much too harshly. It is precisely on this point that we may observe Shakespeare's probable reason for adding the characters and incidents of this original plot to a well-known story. Love is the controlling factor in both plots but here we have a quite different set of lovers. Aguecheek is urged on by Sir Toby to think that he may win Olivia. Malvolio, tricked by the letter, but led on by his own self-love, fancies himself as suitor and husband to Olivia. In the final resolution of Act V we hear from Fabian that Sir Toby has married Maria in recompense for her writing of the letter. Now the world in which these characters function is quite different from that of Orsino, Viola, and Olivia.

Sir Andrew is a mere caricature of the traditional lover, and this is pointed by the direct contrast between Sir Toby's description of him and the actuality which we see on his entrance a few lines later on. These are the attributes given him by Sir Toby: "as tall a man as any's in Illyria" ("tall" here means "brave," "outstanding"); "he plays o' th' viol-de-gamboys, and speaks three or four languages word for word without book, and hath all the good gifts of nature." If true, this description would well suit a gentleman seeking to follow the ideal of The Courtier. But Sir Andrew is, as Maria says, a "fool and a prodigal." Further he is stupid and vain, as his lines disclose when he completely misunderstands Sir Toby's injunction, "Accost, Sir Andrew, accost." He specifically points out his lack of knowledge of foreign languages, and though priding himself on his skill in dancing and in fencing he is last seen in I, iii, cutting a ludicrous caper, while subsequently both he and Sir Toby are given a sound beating in a fencing bout with Sebastian.

Equally apart from the tradition is Malvolio, who is early charged by Olivia with being "sick of self-love" and lacking a "free disposition." Through self-love he can naturally assume that the letter is meant for him and that it was written by the Lady Olivia. Even before he has found the letter in II, v, he is dreaming of such a marriage, but love for Malvolio has but one aspect: his own aggrandizement. He will become "Count Malvolio," will wear "some rich jewel," and Sir Toby will curtsy to him. To achieve such position and wealth he will, of course, wear yellow stockings and be ever cross-gartered. He will even attempt a free disposition and will smile.

Here then are two who have truly fallen into error, but it is not as a result of love. The fault lies rather in their own characters and attitudes toward love. Sir Andrew is fool enough to think himself a proper lover, and for his pains loses his money to Sir Toby and gets a good beating. Malvolio is presumptuous enough to think first of all that his lady would favor him and secondly that he could rise from his position as steward to that of lord of the household. Finally Sir Toby marries almost by inadvertence.

Thus the subplot may be seen as representing the obverse, the other side of the coin. In the main plot the characters move in the world of an established convention while in the other the characters are alien, if not antithetical, to the convention. We can smile with Olivia as she accepts love with "Well, let it be," or with Viola as she realizes that Olivia has fallen in love with her disguise:

> O Time, thou must untangle this, not I;
> It is too hard a knot for me t' untie.

In direct contrast with this spirit of high comedy we have the plots and trickery of low comedy where we laugh at Sir Andrew, Malvolio, and even Sir Toby, whose gulling of Sir Andrew into a duel has brought him "a bloody coxcomb." Two worlds of love and two worlds of comedy have been fused into Twelfth Night, or, What You Will.

The conventions and pretenses are not mocked in the satiric spirit, for here all is gaiety, and the lyricism which animates the play is found not only in the songs but in the characters themselves. When Viola describes how she would woo were she in love (I, v, 254–62), or tells Orsino of her concealed love (II, iv, 109–17), her lines sing with the ideal quality that is hers. So too both Orsino and Olivia reveal that they belong to the world of fancy or, in Sir Toby's words, a land of "cakes and ale" far removed from the mundane. Feste sums it all in his concluding stanza:

> A great while ago the world begun,
>   With hey, ho, the wind and the rain;
> But that's all one, our play is done,
>   And we'll strive to please you every day.

Yale University   CHARLES T. PROUTY

NOTE ON THE TEXT

The only text for *Twelfth Night* is that of the folio, which appears to have been printed from the prompt-copy or possibly a transcript of it. It is an excellent text, and it is here followed closely. There is some evidence that the text contains revisions of the copy originally designed for performance. In the second scene Viola says that she will enter Orsino's service as his eunuch (that is, his singer) and will "speak to him in many sorts of music," but in II, iv, when Viola-Cesario is asked by Orsino to sing, she does not do so; instead Feste is sent for. Evidently the boy playing the part of Viola was not deemed an adequate singer, so that additional dialogue was written to get Feste on the stage. (There is also a possibility that Malvolio's lines at II, v, 36–37, are an interpolation, since they may refer to an event of 1616.) The act–scene division supplied marginally is identical with that of the folio.

Following is a complete list of substantive departures from the folio text, with the adopted reading in italics followed by the folio reading in roman.

I, ii, 15 *Arion* Orion
I, iii, 48 *Andrew* Ma. 50 *Mary Accost* Mary, accost 55 *Fare* Far 82 *Pourquoi* Pur-quoy 83 *pourquoi* purquoy 89 *curl by* coole my 90 *me* we 92 *housewife* huswife 114 *Mall's* Mals 122 *dun* dam'd *set* sit 125 *That's* That

I, iv, 27 *nuncio's* Nuntio's
I, v, 109 *comes* – comes 141 *Has* Ha's 159 s.d. *Viola* Violenta 162 *beauty* – beautie. 199 *olive* Olyffe 241 *with fertile* fertill
II, ii, 11 *me.* me, 19 *as methought* methought 30 *our* O 31 *made of, such* made, if such
II, iii, 2 *diluculo* Deliculo 24 *leman* Lemon 31 *a–a* 124 *a nayword* an ayword
II, iv, 52 *Fly...fly* fye...fie 87 *I* It 98 *suffers* suffer
II, v, 57 *my – some* my some 106 *staniel* stallion 120 *sequel. That* sequell that 133 *born* become *achieve* atcheeues 146–47 *Unhappy.' Daylight* vnhappy daylight 163 *dear* deero
III, i, 8 *king lies* King s lyes 66 *wise men, folly-fall'n* wisemens folly falne 69 *vous garde* vou garde 70 *vous aussi; votre* vouz ousie vostre 88 *all ready* already
III, ii, 7 *thee* the the
III, iv, 22 *Olivia* Mal. 64 *tang* langer 82 *How...man* (joined to preceding speech by Fabian in F) 155 *Fare thee well* Far-theewell 161 *You* Yon 231 *competent* Computent 242 s.d. *Exit* Exit Toby 335 *babbling, drunkenness* babling drunken-nesse 374 s.d. *Exeunt* Exit
IV, ii, 5 *in* in in 37 *clerestories* cleere stores 69 *sport to* sport
V, i, 112 *thief* thief, 192 *pavin* panym 198 *help? An* help an 339 *mad. Thou cam'st* mad; then cam'st 383, 387, 391, 395 *the wind...rain* &c. 385, 389, 393 *it...day* &c. 395 *With hey* hey

TWELFTH NIGHT, OR, WHAT YOU WILL

*

I, i   *Enter Orsino Duke of Illyria, Curio, and other Lords*
         [with Musicians].

DUKE
  If music be the food of love, play on,
  Give me excess of it, that, surfeiting,
  The appetite may sicken, and so die.
4 That strain again. It had a dying fall ;
  O, it came o'er my ear like the sweet sound
  That breathes upon a bank of violets,
  Stealing and giving odor. Enough, no more.
  'Tis not so sweet now as it was before.
9 O spirit of love, how quick and fresh art thou,
  That, notwithstanding thy capacity,
  Receiveth as the sea. Nought enters there,
12 Of what validity and pitch soe'er,
14 But falls into abatement and low price
15 Even in a minute. So full of shapes is fancy
  That it alone is high fantastical.
CURIO
  Will you go hunt, my lord ?
DUKE
  What, Curio ?
CURIO
  The hart.
DUKE
  Why, so I do, the noblest that I have.
  O, when mine eyes did see Olivia first,
  Methought she purged the air of pestilence.
22 That instant was I turned into a hart,

  And my desires, like fell and cruel hounds,   23
  E'er since pursue me.
      Enter Valentine.
                      How now ? What news from her ?
VALENTINE
  So please my lord, I might not be admitted ;
  But from her handmaid do return this answer :
  The element itself, till seven years' heat,   27
  Shall not behold her face at ample view ;
  But like a cloistress she will veilèd walk,
  And water once a day her chamber round
  With eye-offending brine : all this to season   31
  A brother's dead love, which she would keep fresh
  And lasting in her sad remembrance.
DUKE
  O, she that hath a heart of that fine frame
  To pay this debt of love but to a brother,
  How will she love when the rich golden shaft   36
  Hath killed the flock of all affections else
  That live in her ; when liver, brain, and heart,
  These sovereign thrones, are all supplied and filled,
  Her sweet perfections, with one self king.
  Away before me to sweet beds of flow'rs ;
  Love-thoughts lie rich when canopied with bow'rs.
                                          Exeunt.

*

      Enter Viola, a Captain, and Sailors.   **I, ii**
VIOLA
  What country, friends, is this ?
CAPTAIN
  This is Illyria, lady.   2
VIOLA
  And what should I do in Illyria ?
  My brother he is in Elysium.   4
  Perchance he is not drowned. What think you, sailors ?
CAPTAIN
  It is perchance that you yourself were saved.

VIOLA
O my poor brother, and so perchance may he be.

CAPTAIN
8   True, madam; and, to comfort you with chance,
Assure yourself, after our ship did split,
When you, and those poor number saved with you,
11   Hung on our driving boat, I saw your brother,
Most provident in peril, bind himself
(Courage and hope both teaching him the practice)
14   To a strong mast that lived upon the sea;
15   Where, like Arion on the dolphin's back,
I saw him hold acquaintance with the waves
So long as I could see.

VIOLA
For saying so, there's gold.
19   Mine own escape unfoldeth to my hope,
Whereto thy speech serves for authority
The like of him. Know'st thou this country?

CAPTAIN
Ay, madam, well, for I was bred and born
Not three hours' travel from this very place.

VIOLA
Who governs here?

CAPTAIN
A noble duke, in nature as in name.

VIOLA
What is his name?

CAPTAIN
Orsino.

VIOLA
Orsino! I have heard my father name him.
He was a bachelor then.

CAPTAIN
And so is now, or was so very late;
For but a month ago I went from hence,
32   And then 'twas fresh in murmur (as you know
What great ones do, the less will prattle of)
That he did seek the love of fair Olivia.

VIOLA
What's she?

CAPTAIN
A virtuous maid, the daughter of a count
That died some twelvemonth since, then leaving her
In the protection of his son, her brother,
Who shortly also died; for whose dear love,
They say, she hath abjured the sight
And company of men.

VIOLA   O that I served that lady,
42   And might not be delivered to the world,
43   Till I had made mine own occasion mellow,
44   What my estate is.

CAPTAIN   That were hard to compass,
Because she will admit no kind of suit,
No, not the Duke's.

VIOLA
47   There is a fair behavior in thee, captain,
And though that nature with a beauteous wall
Doth oft close in pollution, yet of thee
I will believe thou hast a mind that suits
51   With this thy fair and outward character.
I prithee (and I'll pay thee bounteously)
Conceal me what I am, and be my aid
For such disguise as haply shall become
55   The form of my intent. I'll serve this duke.

Thou shalt present me as an eunuch to him;   56
It may be worth thy pains. For I can sing,
And speak to him in many sorts of music
That will allow me very worth his service.   59
What else may hap, to time I will commit;
Only shape thou thy silence to my wit.

CAPTAIN
Be you his eunuch, and your mute I'll be;
When my tongue blabs, then let mine eyes not see.

VIOLA
I thank thee. Lead me on.   *Exeunt.*

*

Enter Sir Toby and Maria.   I, iii

TOBY   What a plague means my niece to take the death of
her brother thus? I am sure care's an enemy to life.

MARIA   By my troth, Sir Toby, you must come in earlier
o' nights. Your cousin, my lady, takes great exceptions   4
to your ill hours.

TOBY   Why, let her except before excepted.   6

MARIA   Ay, but you must confine yourself within the
modest limits of order.

TOBY   Confine? I'll confine myself no finer than I am. 9
These clothes are good enough to drink in, and so be
these boots too. An they be not, let them hang them-   11
selves in their own straps.

MARIA   That quaffing and drinking will undo you. I heard
my lady talk of it yesterday; and of a foolish knight that
you brought in one night here to be her wooer.

TOBY   Who? Sir Andrew Aguecheek?

MARIA   Ay, he.

TOBY   He's as tall a man as any's in Illyria.   18

MARIA   What's that to th' purpose?

TOBY   Why, he has three thousand ducats a year.

MARIA   Ay, but he'll have but a year in all these ducats.
He's a very fool and a prodigal.

TOBY   Fie that you'll say so! He plays o' th' viol-de-gam- 23
boys, and speaks three or four languages word for word
without book, and hath all the good gifts of nature.   25

MARIA   He hath, indeed, almost natural; for, besides that 26
he's a fool, he's a great quarreller; and but that he hath
the gift of a coward to allay the gust he hath in quarrel- 28
ling, 'tis thought among the prudent he would quickly
have the gift of a grave.

TOBY   By this hand, they are scoundrels and substractors 31
that say so of him. Who are they?

MARIA   They that add, moreover, he's drunk nightly in
your company.

TOBY   With drinking healths to my niece. I'll drink to her
as long as there is a passage in my throat and drink in

---

8 *chance* what may have happened   11 *driving* drifting   14 *lived* floated
15 *Arion* a Greek bard who leapt overboard to escape murderous sailors,
and charmed dolphins with the music of his lyre so that they bore him to
land   19 *unfoldeth to my hope* gives me hope (for my brother)   32 *fresh in
murmur* a current rumor   42 *delivered* revealed   43 *mellow* ready to be
revealed   44 *estate* position in society   47 *behavior* both 'conduct' and
'appearance'   51 *character* personal appearance indicating moral qualities
55 *form of my intent* my outward purpose   56 *eunuch* i.e. singer (but she
enters his service simply as a page)   59 *allow me* cause me to be considered
I, iii   The house of Countess Olivia   4 *cousin* kinsman   6 *except before
excepted* (cant legal phrase)   9 *finer* both 'tighter' and 'better'   11 *An* if
18 *tall* both 'tall' and 'brave'   23 *viol-de-gamboys* 'leg-viola,' predecessor
of the violoncello   25 *without book* by memory   26 *natural* i.e. as a fool
28 *gust* taste   31 *substractors* detractors

37 Illyria. He's a coward and a coistrel that will not drink to
38 my niece till his brains turn o' th' toe like a parish top.
39 What, wench? Castiliano vulgo; for here comes Sir
40 Andrew Agueface.

Enter Sir Andrew.

ANDREW Sir Toby Belch. How now, Sir Toby Belch?

TOBY Sweet Sir Andrew.

ANDREW Bless you, fair shrew.

MARIA And you too, sir.

45 TOBY Accost, Sir Andrew, accost.

ANDREW What's that?

TOBY My niece's chambermaid.

ANDREW Good Mistress Accost, I desire better acquaintance.

MARIA My name is Mary, sir.

ANDREW Good Mistress Mary Accost.

51 TOBY You mistake, knight. 'Accost' is front her, board
her, woo her, assail her.

53 ANDREW By my troth, I would not undertake her in this
company. Is that the meaning of 'accost'?

MARIA Fare you well, gentlemen.

TOBY An thou let part so, Sir Andrew, would thou
mightst never draw sword again.

ANDREW An you part so, mistress, I would I might never
draw sword again! Fair lady, do you think you have
fools in hand?

MARIA Sir, I have not you by th' hand.

62 ANDREW Marry, but you shall have, and here's my hand.

MARIA Now, sir, thought is free. I pray you, bring your
64 hand to th' butt'ry bar and let it drink.

ANDREW Wherefore, sweetheart? What's your metaphor?

66 MARIA It's dry, sir.

ANDREW Why, I think so. I am not such an ass but I can
keep my hand dry. But what's your jest?

MARIA A dry jest, sir.

ANDREW Are you full of them?

MARIA Ay, sir, I have them at my fingers' ends. Marry,
72 now I let go your hand, I am barren.   *Exit.*

73 TOBY O knight, thou lack'st a cup of canary! When did I
74 see thee so put down?

ANDREW Never in your life, I think, unless you see
canary put me down. Methinks sometimes I have no
more wit than a Christian or an ordinary man has. But I

am a great eater of beef, and I believe that does harm to
my wit.

TOBY No question.

ANDREW An I thought that, I'd forswear it. I'll ride home
to-morrow, Sir Toby.

TOBY Pourquoi, my dear knight?   82

ANDREW What is 'pourquoi'? Do, or not do? I would I
had bestowed that time in the tongues that I have in   84
fencing, dancing, and bear-baiting. O, had I but followed the arts!   86

TOBY Then hadst thou had an excellent head of hair.

ANDREW Why, would that have mended my hair?   88

TOBY Past question, for thou seest it will not curl by
nature.

ANDREW But it becomes me well enough, does't not?

TOBY Excellent. It hangs like flax on a distaff; and I hope   91
to see a housewife take thee between her legs and spin it   92
off.

ANDREW Faith, I'll home to-morrow, Sir Toby. Your
niece will not be seen; or if she be, it's four to one she'll
none of me. The Count himself here hard by woos her.

TOBY She'll none o' th' Count. She'll not match above
her degree, neither in estate, years, nor wit; I have   98
heard her swear't. Tut, there's life in't, man.

ANDREW I'll stay a month longer. I am a fellow o' th'
strangest mind i' th' world. I delight in masques and
revels sometimes altogether.   102

TOBY Art thou good at these kickshawses, knight?   103

ANDREW As any man in Illyria, whatsoever he be, under
the degree of my betters, and yet I will not compare
with an old man.   106

TOBY What is thy excellence in a galliard, knight?   107

ANDREW Faith, I can cut a caper.   108

TOBY And I can cut the mutton to't.

ANDREW And I think I have the back-trick simply as   110
strong as any man in Illyria.

TOBY Wherefore are these things hid? Wherefore have
these gifts a curtain before 'em? Are they like to take   113
dust, like Mistress Mall's picture? Why dost thou not   114
go to church in a galliard and come home in a coranto?   115
My very walk should be a jig. I would not so much as
make water but in a sink-a-pace. What dost thou mean?   117
Is it a world to hide virtues in? I did think, by the excellent constitution of thy leg, it was formed under the star   119
of a galliard.

ANDREW Ay, 'tis strong, and it does indifferent well in a
dun-colored stock. Shall we set about some revels?   122

TOBY What shall we do else? Were we not born under
Taurus?   124

ANDREW Taurus? That's sides and heart.

TOBY No, sir; it is legs and thighs. Let me see thee caper.
Ha, higher; ha, ha, excellent!   *Exeunt.*

*

Enter Valentine, and Viola in man's attire.   I, iv

VALENTINE If the Duke continue these favors towards
you, Cesario, you are like to be much advanced. He hath
known you but three days and already you are no stranger.

VIOLA You either fear his humor or my negligence, that   4
you call in question the continuance of his love. Is he
inconstant, sir, in his favors?

VALENTINE No, believe me.

Enter Duke, Curio, and Attendants.

---

37 *coistrel* horsegroom, base fellow   38 *parish* kept by the parish (?)   39
Castiliano vulgo (of doubtful meaning. Castilians were noted for decorum,
and this may be a plea for 'common politeness.')   40 *Agueface* pale and
thin-faced, like a man suffering from the acute fever of ague   45 *Accost*
make up to (her)   51 *front* face; *board* greet (literally, go on board)   53
undertake (both literal and figurative senses intended)   62 *Marry* indeed,
to be sure (originally an oath by the Virgin Mary)   64 *butt'ry* ale-cellar; *it*
i.e. your hand   66 *dry* (a sign of age)   72 *barren* i.e. barren of jokes   73
canary a sweet wine from the Canary Islands   74 *put down* discomfited
82 *Pourquoi* why   84 *tongues* languages, perhaps with a pun on 'tongs,'
curling irons   86 *arts* liberal arts such as languages   88 *mended* improved
91 *flax on a distaff* straight strings of flax on a stick used in spinning   92-93
spin it off lose hair as a result of venereal disease   98 *degree* position in
society; *estate* fortune   102 *altogether* in all respects   103 *kickshawses*
trifles (French '*quelque chose*')   106 *old man* probably 'experienced person'
107 *galliard* quick dance in triple time   108 *caper* frolicsome leap; also a
spice used with mutton   110 *back-trick* backward step in a dance   113
take collect   114 *Mistress Mall's picture* any woman's portrait   115
coranto swift running dance   117 *sink-a-pace* rapid dance of five steps
(French '*cinque-pas*')   119-20 *under . . . galliard* i.e. under a dancing star
122 *stock* stocking   124 *Taurus* the Bull, one of the signs of the Zodiac
which governed the nose and throat
I, iv The palace of Duke Orsino   4 *humor* changeableness

VIOLA I thank you. Here comes the Count.

DUKE Who saw Cesario, ho?

VIOLA On your attendance, my lord, here.

DUKE

11 Stand you awhile aloof. Cesario,

12 Thou know'st no less but all. I have unclasped

To thee the book even of my secret soul.

14 Therefore, good youth, address thy gait unto her;

Be not denied access, stand at her doors,

And tell them there thy fixèd foot shall grow

Till thou have audience.

VIOLA   Sure, my noble lord,

If she be so abandoned to her sorrow

As it is spoke, she never will admit me.

DUKE

Be clamorous and leap all civil bounds

Rather than make unprofited return.

VIOLA

Say I do speak with her, my lord, what then?

DUKE

O, then unfold the passion of my love;

Surprise her with discourse of my dear faith;

It shall become thee well to act my woes.

She will attend it better in thy youth

27 Than in a nuncio's of more grave aspect.

VIOLA

I think not so, my lord.

DUKE   Dear lad, believe it;

For they shall yet belie thy happy years

That say thou art a man. Diana's lip

31 Is not more smooth and rubious; thy small pipe

32 Is as the maiden's organ, shrill and sound,

33 And all is semblative a woman's part.

34 I know thy constellation is right apt

For this affair. Some four or five attend him,

All, if you will; for I myself am best

When least in company. Prosper well in this,

And thou shalt live as freely as thy lord

To call his fortunes thine.

VIOLA   I'll do my best

40 To woo your lady. *[aside]* Yet a barful strife!

Whoe'er I woo, myself would be his wife.   *Exeunt.*

*

I, v   *Enter Maria and Clown.*

MARIA Nay, either tell me where thou hast been, or I will not open my lips so wide as a bristle may enter in way of thy excuse. My lady will hang thee for thy absence.

CLOWN Let her hang me. He that is well hanged in this

5 world needs to fear no colors.

MARIA Make that good.

CLOWN He shall see none to fear.

8 MARIA A good lenten answer. I can tell thee where that saying was born, of 'I fear no colors.'

CLOWN Where, good Mistress Mary?

MARIA In the wars; and that may you be bold to say in your foolery.

CLOWN Well, God give them wisdom that have it, and those that are fools, let them use their talents.

MARIA Yet you will be hanged for being so long absent, or to be turned away. Is not that as good as a hanging to you?

CLOWN Many a good hanging prevents a bad marriage,

19 and for turning away, let summer bear it out.

MARIA You are resolute then?

CLOWN Not so, neither; but I am resolved on two points. 21

MARIA That if one break, the other will hold; or if both 22 break, your gaskins fall. 23

CLOWN Apt, in good faith; very apt. Well, go thy way! If Sir Toby would leave drinking, thou wert as witty a piece of Eve's flesh as any in Illyria. 26

MARIA Peace, you rogue; no more o' that. Here comes my lady. Make your excuse wisely, you were best.   *[Exit.]* 28

Enter Lady Olivia with Malvolio.

CLOWN Wit, an't be thy will, put me into good fooling. Those wits that think they have thee do very oft prove fools, and I that am sure I lack thee may pass for a wise man. For what says Quinapalus? 'Better a witty fool 32 than a foolish wit.' God bless thee, lady.

OLIVIA Take the fool away.

CLOWN Do you not hear, fellows? Take away the lady.

OLIVIA Go to, y' are a dry fool! I'll no more of you. Be- 36 sides, you grow dishonest. 37

CLOWN Two faults, madonna, that drink and good coun- 38 sel will amend. For give the dry fool drink, then is the fool not dry. Bid the dishonest man mend himself: if he 40 mend, he is no longer dishonest; if he cannot, let the botcher mend him. Anything that's mended is but 42 patched; virtue that transgresses is but patched with sin, and sin that amends is but patched with virtue. If that this simple syllogism will serve, so; if it will not, what remedy? As there is no true cuckold but calamity, so beauty's a flower. The lady bade take away the fool; therefore, I say again, take her away.

OLIVIA Sir, I bade them take away you.

CLOWN Misprision in the highest degree. Lady, cucullus 50 non facit monachum. That's as much to say as, I wear not motley in my brain. Good madonna, give me leave 52 to prove you a fool.

OLIVIA Can you do it?

CLOWN Dexteriously, good madonna. 55

OLIVIA Make your proof.

CLOWN I must catechize you for it, madonna. Good my mouse of virtue, answer me. 58

OLIVIA Well, sir, for want of other idleness, I'll bide your proof.

CLOWN Good madonna, why mourn'st thou?

OLIVIA Good fool, for my brother's death.

CLOWN I think his soul is in hell, madonna.

OLIVIA I know his soul is in heaven, fool.

CLOWN The more fool, madonna, to mourn for your brother's soul, being in heaven. Take away the fool, gentlemen.

11 *you* i.e. all except Cesario   12 *no less but all* everything   14 *address thy gait* direct your steps   27 *nuncio's* messenger's   31 *rubious* ruby red; *pipe* throat, voice   32 *shrill and sound* high and clear   33 *semblative* like   34 *constellation* predestined nature   40 *barful strife* conflict full of hindrances

I, v Within the house of Olivia   5 *fear no colors* fear nothing (proverbial)   8 *lenten* thin, scanty   19 *let ... out* i.e. let mild weather make homelessness endurable   21 *points* laces fastening hose to doublet   22–23 *if one ... fall* (Maria puns on *points*, see l. 21)   23 *gaskins* loose breeches   26 *Eve's flesh* erring woman   28 *you were best* it would be best for you   32 *Quinapalus* (an invention of the Clown)   36 *Go to* enough, cease; *dry* dull   37 *dishonest* unreliable   38 *madonna* my lady   40 *dry* thirsty   42 *botcher* mender of clothes   50 *Misprision* error   50–51 *cucullus ... monachum* the cowl doesn't make the monk   52 *motley* clothing of a mixed color, worn by stage fools   55 *Dexteriously* (variant of 'dexterously')   58 *mouse* (term of endearment); *of virtue* virtuous

OLIVIA What think you of this fool, Malvolio? Doth he not mend?

70 **MALVOLIO** Yes, and shall do till the pangs of death shake him. Infirmity, that decays the wise, doth ever make the better fool.

CLOWN God send you, sir, a speedy infirmity, for the better increasing your folly. Sir Toby will be sworn that I am no fox, but he will not pass his word for twopence that you are no fool.

OLIVIA How say you to that, Malvolio?

MALVOLIO I marvel your ladyship takes delight in such a barren rascal. I saw him put down the other day with an ordinary fool that has no more brain than a stone. Look

81 you now, he's out of his guard already. Unless you laugh
82 and minister occasion to him, he is gagged. I protest I take these wise men that crow so at these set kind of
84 fools no better than the fools' zanies.

OLIVIA O, you are sick of self-love, Malvolio, and taste with a distempered appetite. To be generous, guiltless,
87 and of free disposition, is to take those things for bird-bolts that you deem cannon bullets. There is no slander
89 in an allowed fool, though he do nothing but rail; nor no railing in a known discreet man, though he do nothing but reprove.

92 **CLOWN** Now Mercury indue thee with leasing, for thou speak'st well of fools.

Enter Maria.

MARIA Madam, there is at the gate a young gentleman much desires to speak with you.

OLIVIA From the Count Orsino, is it?

MARIA I know not, madam. 'Tis a fair young man, and well attended.

OLIVIA Who of my people hold him in delay?

MARIA Sir Toby, madam, your kinsman.

OLIVIA Fetch him off, I pray you. He speaks nothing but madman. Fie on him! *[Exit Maria.]* Go you, Malvolio. If it be a suit from the Count, I am sick, or not at home. What you will, to dismiss it. *(Exit Malvolio.)* Now you
105 see, sir, how your fooling grows old, and people dislike it.

CLOWN Thou hast spoke for us, madonna, as if thy eldest son should be a fool; whose skull Jove cram with brains, for – here he comes – one of thy kin has a most weak
110 pia mater.

Enter Sir Toby.

OLIVIA By mine honor, half drunk. What is he at the gate, cousin?

TOBY A gentleman.

OLIVIA A gentleman? What gentleman?

TOBY 'Tis a gentleman here. A plague o' these pickle-herring! How now, sot?

CLOWN Good Sir Toby.

OLIVIA Cousin, cousin, how have you come so early by this lethargy?

TOBY Lechery? I defy lechery. There's one at the gate.

OLIVIA Ay, marry, what is he?

TOBY Let him be the devil an he will, I care not. Give me faith, say I. Well, it's all one.   *Exit.* 123

OLIVIA What's a drunken man like, fool?

CLOWN Like a drowned man, a fool, and a madman. One draught above heat makes him a fool, the second mads 126 him, and a third drowns him.

OLIVIA Go thou and seek the crowner, and let him sit o' 128 my coz; for he's in the third degree of drink – he's drowned. Go look after him.

CLOWN He is but mad yet, madonna, and the fool shall look to the madman.   *[Exit.]*

Enter Malvolio.

MALVOLIO Madam, yond young fellow swears he will speak with you. I told him you were sick; he takes on him to understand so much, and therefore comes to speak with you. I told him you were asleep; he seems to have a foreknowledge of that too, and therefore comes to speak with you. What is to be said to him, lady? He's fortified against any denial.

OLIVIA Tell him he shall not speak with me.

MALVOLIO Has been told so; and he says he'll stand at 141 your door like a sheriff's post, and be the supporter to a 142 bench, but he'll speak with you.

OLIVIA What kind o' man is he?

MALVOLIO Why, of mankind.

OLIVIA What manner of man?

MALVOLIO Of very ill manner. He'll speak with you, will you or no.

OLIVIA Of what personage and years is he?

MALVOLIO Not yet old enough for a man nor young enough for a boy; as a squash is before 'tis a peascod, or a 151 codling when 'tis almost an apple. 'Tis with him in 152 standing water, between boy and man. He is very well- 153 favored and he speaks very shrewishly. One would think his mother's milk were scarce out of him.

OLIVIA Let him approach. Call in my gentlewoman.

MALVOLIO Gentlewoman, my lady calls.   *Exit.*

Enter Maria.

OLIVIA Give me my veil; come, throw it o'er my face. We'll once more hear Orsino's embassy.

Enter Viola.

VIOLA The honorable lady of the house, which is she?

OLIVIA Speak to me; I shall answer for her. Your will?

VIOLA Most radiant, exquisite, and unmatchable beauty – I pray you tell me if this be the lady of the house, for I never saw her. I would be loath to cast away my speech; for, besides that it is excellently well penned, I have taken great pains to con it. Good beauties, let me sustain 166 no scorn. I am very comptible, even to the least sinister 167 usage.

OLIVIA Whence came you, sir?

VIOLA I can say little more than I have studied, and that question 's out of my part. Good gentle one, give me modest assurance if you be the lady of the house, that I may proceed in my speech.

OLIVIA Are you a comedian? 174

VIOLA No, my profound heart; and yet (by the very fangs of malice I swear) I am not that I play. Are you the lady of the house?

OLIVIA If I do not usurp myself, I am. 178

81 *out of his guard* without a defense (of wit)   82 *minister occasion* give an opportunity   84 *zanies* i.e. fools' assistants   87 *birdbolts* blunt-headed arrows for shooting birds   89 *allowed* licensed   92 *Mercury* god of guile and tricks; *indue . . . leasing* endow you with the art of casuistry   105 *old stale*   110 *pia mater* i.e. brain   123 *faith* i.e. to resist the devil   126 *above heat* above the amount to make him normally warm   128 *crowner* coroner   128–29 *sit o' my coz* hold an inquest on my kinsman (Sir Toby)   141 *Has* he has (from 'h' has)   142 *sheriff's post* post before a sheriff's house on which notices were posted   151 *squash* unripe pea pod; *peascod* ripe pea pod   152 *codling* unripe apple   153 *standing water* the tide at ebb or flood when it flows neither way   166 *con* memorize; *sustain* endure   167 *comptible* sensitive   174 *comedian* actor   178 *usurp* supplant

VIOLA Most certain, if you are she, you do usurp yourself; for what is yours to bestow is not yours to reserve.
181 But this is from my commission. I will on with my speech
in your praise and then show you the heart of my message.

183 OLIVIA Come to what is important in't. I forgive you the
praise.

VIOLA Alas, I took great pains to study it, and 'tis poetical.

OLIVIA It is the more like to be feigned; I pray you keep
it in. I heard you were saucy at my gates; and allowed
your approach rather to wonder at you than to hear you.
189 If you be not mad, be gone; if you have reason, be
190 brief. 'Tis not that time of moon with me to make one in
191 so skipping a dialogue.

MARIA Will you hoist sail, sir? Here lies your way.

193 VIOLA No, good swabber; I am to hull here a little longer.
194 Some mollification for your giant, sweet lady. Tell me
your mind. I am a messenger.

OLIVIA Sure you have some hideous matter to deliver,
197 when the courtesy of it is so fearful. Speak your office.

VIOLA It alone concerns your ear. I bring no overture of
199 war, no taxation of homage. I hold the olive in my hand.
My words are as full of peace as matter.

OLIVIA Yet you began rudely. What are you? What
would you?

VIOLA The rudeness that hath appeared in me have I
204 learned from my entertainment. What I am, and what I
205 would, are as secret as maidenhead: to your ears, divinity; to any other's, profanation.

OLIVIA Give us the place alone; we will hear this divinity.
[Exit Maria.] Now, sir, what is your text?

VIOLA Most sweet lady –

OLIVIA A comfortable doctrine, and much may be said of
it. Where lies your text?

VIOLA In Orsino's bosom.

OLIVIA In his bosom? In what chapter of his bosom?

214 VIOLA To answer by the method, in the first of his heart.

OLIVIA O, I have read it; it is heresy. Have you no more
to say?

VIOLA Good madam, let me see your face.

OLIVIA Have you any commission from your lord to negotiate with my face? You are now out of your text.
But we will draw the curtain and show you the picture.
221 [Unveils.] Look you, sir, such a one I was this present.
Is't not well done?

VIOLA Excellently done, if God did all.

224 OLIVIA 'Tis in grain, sir; 'twill endure wind and weather.

VIOLA
'Tis beauty truly blent, whose red and white
226 Nature's own sweet and cunning hand laid on.
Lady, you are the cruell'st she alive
If you will lead these graces to the grave,
And leave the world no copy.

OLIVIA O, sir, I will not be so hard-hearted. I will give out
231 divers schedules of my beauty. It shall be inventoried,
232 and every particle and utensil labelled to my will: as,
233 item, two lips, indifferent red; item, two grey eyes, with
lids to them; item, one neck, one chin, and so forth.
Were you sent hither to praise me?

VIOLA
I see you what you are; you are too proud;
237 But if you were the devil, you are fair.
My lord and master loves you. O, such love
239 Could be but recompensed though you were crowned
The nonpareil of beauty.

OLIVIA   How does he love me?

VIOLA
With adorations, with fertile tears,   241
With groans that thunder love, with sighs of fire.

OLIVIA
Your lord does know my mind; I cannot love him.
Yet I suppose him virtuous, know him noble,
Of great estate, of fresh and stainless youth;
In voices well divulged, free, learned, and valiant,   246
And in dimension and the shape of nature
A gracious person. But yet I cannot love him.
He might have took his answer long ago.

VIOLA
If I did love you in my master's flame,
With such a suff'ring, such a deadly life,   251
In your denial I would find no sense;
I would not understand it.

OLIVIA   Why, what would you?

VIOLA
Make me a willow cabin at your gate   254
And call upon my soul within the house;
Write loyal cantons of contemnèd love   256
And sing them loud even in the dead of night;
Hallo your name to the reverberate hills
And make the babbling gossip of the air   259
Cry out 'Olivia!' O, you should not rest
Between the elements of air and earth
But you should pity me.

OLIVIA
You might do much. What is your parentage?

VIOLA
Above my fortunes, yet my state is well.
I am a gentleman.

OLIVIA   Get you to your lord.
I cannot love him. Let him send no more,
Unless, perchance, you come to me again
To tell me how he takes it. Fare you well.
I thank you for your pains. Spend this for me.

VIOLA
I am no fee'd post, lady; keep your purse;   270
My master, not myself, lacks recompense.
Love make his heart of flint that you shall love;
And let your fervor, like my master's, be
Placed in contempt. Farewell, fair cruelty.   Exit.

OLIVIA
'What is your parentage?'
'Above my fortunes, yet my state is well.
I am a gentleman.' I'll be sworn thou art.
Thy tongue, thy face, thy limbs, actions, and spirit
Do give thee fivefold blazon. Not too fast; soft, soft,   279
Unless the master were the man. How now?   280

181 *from* outside   183 *forgive* excuse   189 *reason* sanity   190 *'Tis . . . me*
i.e. I am not in the mood   191 *skipping* sprightly   193 *swabber* one who
washes decks; *hull* float without sail   194 *giant* i.e. the small Maria
197 *courtesy* formality; *office* business   199 *taxation* demand   204 *entertainment* reception   205 *divinity* a holy message   214 *To . . . method* to
continue the figure   221 *this present* a minute ago   224 *in grain* fast
dyed   226 *cunning* skillful   231 *schedules* lists   232 *utensil* article;
labelled to added to   233 *item* namely; *indifferent* moderately   237 *if*
even if   239 *but recompensed* though no more than repaid even though
241 *fertile* abundant   246 *In voices well divulged* in public opinion well
reported   251 *deadly life* life which is like death   254 *willow* symbol of
grief for unrequited love   256 *cantons* songs; *contemnèd* rejected   259
babbling gossip echo   270 *fee'd post* messenger to be paid or tipped   279
blazon shield or coat of arms in heraldry   280 *Unless . . . man* i.e. unless
Orsino were Cesario

Even so quickly may one catch the plague?
Methinks I feel this youth's perfections
With an invisible and subtle stealth
To creep in at mine eyes. Well, let it be.
What ho, Malvolio!
    Enter Malvolio.

MALVOLIO   Here, madam, at your service.

OLIVIA
Run after that same peevish messenger,
287 The County's man. He left this ring behind him,
Would I or not. Tell him I'll none of it.
289 Desire him not to flatter with his lord
Nor hold him up with hopes. I am not for him.
If that the youth will come this way to-morrow,
I'll give him reasons for't. Hie thee, Malvolio.

MALVOLIO
Madam, I will.   *Exit.*

OLIVIA
I do I know not what, and fear to find
Mine eye too great a flatterer for my mind.
296 Fate, show thy force; ourselves we do not owe.
What is decreed must be – and be this so!   *[Exit.]*

*

II, i   *Enter Antonio and Sebastian.*

ANTONIO Will you stay no longer? Nor will you not that
I go with you?

3 SEBASTIAN By your patience, no. My stars shine darkly
over me; the malignancy of my fate might perhaps distemper yours. Therefore I shall crave of you your
leave, that I may bear my evils alone. It were a bad
recompense for your love to lay any of them on you.

ANTONIO Let me yet know of you whither you are bound.

9 SEBASTIAN No, sooth, sir. My determinate voyage is
10 mere extravagancy. But I perceive in you so excellent a
touch of modesty that you will not extort from me what I
12 am willing to keep in; therefore it charges me in manners
the rather to express myself. You must know of me then,
Antonio, my name is Sebastian, which I called Roderigo.
15 My father was that Sebastian of Messaline whom I know
you have heard of. He left behind him myself and a
17 sister, both born in an hour. If the heavens had been
pleased, would we had so ended! But you, sir, altered
19 that, for some hour before you took me from the breach
of the sea was my sister drowned.

ANTONIO Alas the day!

SEBASTIAN A lady, sir, though it was said she much resembled me, was yet of many accounted beautiful. But
24 though I could not with such estimable wonder overfar

believe that, yet thus far I will boldly publish her: she 25
bore a mind that envy could not but call fair. She is
drowned already, sir, with salt water, though I seem to
drown her remembrance again with more.

ANTONIO Pardon me, sir, your bad entertainment.   29

SEBASTIAN O good Antonio, forgive me your trouble.   30

ANTONIO If you will not murder me for my love, let me 31
be your servant.

SEBASTIAN If you will not undo what you have done,
that is, kill him whom you have recovered, desire it not. 34
Fare ye well at once. My bosom is full of kindness, and I
am yet so near the manners of my mother that, upon the 36
least occasion more, mine eyes will tell tales of me. I am
bound to the Count Orsino's court. Farewell.   *Exit.*

ANTONIO
The gentleness of all the gods go with thee.
I have many enemies in Orsino's court,
Else would I very shortly see thee there.
But come what may, I do adore thee so
That danger shall seem sport, and I will go.   *Exit.*

*

Enter Viola and Malvolio at several doors.   II, ii

MALVOLIO Were not you ev'n now with the Countess
Olivia?

VIOLA Even now, sir. On a moderate pace I have since
arrived but hither.

MALVOLIO She returns this ring to you, sir. You might
have saved me my pains, to have taken it away yourself.
She adds, moreover, that you should put your lord into
a desperate assurance she will none of him. And one 7
thing more, that you be never so hardy to come again in
his affairs, unless it be to report your lord's taking of
this. Receive it so.

VIOLA She took the ring of me. I'll none of it.

MALVOLIO Come, sir, you peevishly threw it to her, and
her will is, it should be so returned. If it be worth
stooping for, there it lies, in your eye; if not, be it his
that finds it.   *Exit.*

VIOLA
I left no ring with her. What means this lady?
Fortune forbid my outside have not charmed her.
She made good view of me; indeed, so much   18
That, as methought, her eyes had lost her tongue,   19
For she did speak in starts distractedly.
She loves me sure; the cunning of her passion   21
Invites me in this churlish messenger.
None of my lord's ring? Why, he sent her none.
I am the man. If it be so, as 'tis,
Poor lady, she were better love a dream.
Disguise, I see thou art a wickedness
Wherein the pregnant enemy does much.   27
How easy is it for the proper false   28
In women's waxen hearts to set their forms!   29
Alas, our frailty is the cause, not we,
For such as we are made of, such we be.
How will this fadge? My master loves her dearly;   32
And I (poor monster) fond as much on him;   33
And she (mistaken) seems to dote on me.
What will become of this? As I am man,
My state is desperate for my master's love.   36
As I am woman (now alas the day!),
What thriftless sighs shall poor Olivia breathe?   38

287 *County* count 289 *flatter with* encourage 296 *owe* own
II, i A lodging some distance from Orsino's court 3 *patience* leave 9
sooth truly; *determinate* determined upon 10 *extravagancy* wandering
12 *it . . . manners* I am compelled in good manners 15 *Messaline* Messina
in Sicily 17 *in an hour* in the same hour 19–20 *the breach of the sea* the
breaking waves 24 *estimable wonder* admiring judgment 25 *publish* describe publicly 29 *entertainment* treatment as my guest 30 *your trouble*
for causing you trouble 31 *murder me for* be my death in return for 34
recovered saved 36–37 *so near . . . tales of me* so effeminate I shall weep
II, ii A street near Olivia's house s.d. *several* different 7 *desperate*
without hope 18 *made good view of* looked intently at 19 *lost* caused her
to lose 21 *cunning* craftiness 27 *pregnant enemy* resourceful Satan 28
the proper false deceivers who are prepossessing in appearance 29 *forms*
impressions (as of a seal) 32 *fadge* turn out 33 *monster* (because both
man and woman); *fond* dote 36 *desperate* hopeless 38 *thriftless* unprofitable

O Time, thou must untangle this, not I;
It is too hard a knot for me t' untie.   *[Exit.]*

*

II, iii   *Enter Sir Toby and Sir Andrew.*

TOBY Approach, Sir Andrew. Not to be abed after mid-
2   night is to be up betimes; and 'diluculo surgere,' thou
       know'st.
ANDREW Nay, by my troth, I know not, but I know to be
       up late is to be up late.
6 TOBY A false conclusion; I hate it as an unfilled can. To
       be up after midnight, and to go to bed then, is early; so
       that to go to bed after midnight is to go to bed betimes.
       Does not our lives consist of the four elements?
ANDREW Faith, so they say; but I think it rather consists
       of eating and drinking.
TOBY Th' art a scholar! Let us therefore eat and drink.
13   Marian I say! a stoup of wine!
       Enter Clown.
ANDREW Here comes the fool, i' faith.
15 CLOWN How now, my hearts? Did you never see the pic-
       ture of We Three?
17 TOBY Welcome, ass. Now let's have a catch.
18 ANDREW By my troth, the fool has an excellent breast. I
       had rather than forty shillings I had such a leg, and so
       sweet a breath to sing, as the fool has. In sooth, thou
21   wast in very gracious fooling last night, when thou
22   spok'st of Pigrogromitus, of the Vapians passing the
       equinoctial of Queubus. 'Twas very good, i' faith. I
24   sent thee sixpence for thy leman. Hadst it?
25 CLOWN I did impeticos thy gratillity, for Malvolio's nose
26   is no whipstock. My lady has a white hand, and the Myr-
       midons are no bottle-ale houses.
ANDREW Excellent. Why, this is the best fooling, when
       all is done. Now a song!
TOBY Come on! there is sixpence for you. Let's have a
       song.
31 ANDREW There's a testril of me too. If one knight give a—
32 CLOWN Would you have a love song, or a song of good
       life?
TOBY A love song, a love song.
ANDREW Ay, ay, I care not for good life.

       Clown sings.

       O mistress mine, where are you roaming?
       O, stay and hear! your true-love's coming,
          That can sing both high and low.
       Trip no further, pretty sweeting;
40   Journeys end in lovers meeting,
          Every wise man's son doth know.

ANDREW Excellent good, i' faith.
TOBY Good, good.

       Clown [sings].

       What is love? 'Tis not hereafter;
       Present mirth hath present laughter;
          What's to come is still unsure:
       In delay there lies no plenty;
       Then come kiss me, sweet and twenty,
          Youth's a stuff will not endure.

ANDREW A mellifluous voice, as I am true knight.

TOBY A contagious breath.
ANDREW Very sweet and contagious, i' faith.
TOBY To hear by the nose, it is dulcet in contagion. But
       shall we make the welkin dance indeed? Shall we rouse   54
       the night owl in a catch that will draw three souls out of
       one weaver? Shall we do that?   56
ANDREW An you love me, let's do't. I am dog at a catch.
CLOWN By'r Lady, sir, and some dogs will catch well.
ANDREW Most certain. Let our catch be 'Thou knave.'
CLOWN 'Hold thy peace, thou knave,' knight? I shall be
       constrained in't to call thee knave, knight.
ANDREW 'Tis not the first time I have constrained one to
       call me knave. Begin, fool. It begins, 'Hold thy peace.'
CLOWN I shall never begin if I hold my peace.
ANDREW Good, i' faith! Come, begin.
       Catch sung. Enter Maria.
MARIA What a caterwauling do you keep here? If my
       lady have not called up her steward Malvolio and bid
       him turn you out of doors, never trust me.
TOBY My lady's a Cataian, we are politicians, Malvolio's   69
       a Peg-a-Ramsey, and *[sings]* 'Three merry men be we.' 70
       Am not I consanguineous? Am I not of her blood?   71
       Tilly-vally, lady. *[sings]* 'There dwelt a man in Babylon, 72
       lady, lady.'
CLOWN Beshrew me, the knight's in admirable fooling.
ANDREW Ay, he does well enough if he be disposed, and
       so do I too. He does it with a better grace, but I do it
       more natural.   77
TOBY *[sings]*
       'O the twelfth day of December.'
MARIA For the love o' God, peace!
       Enter Malvolio.
MALVOLIO My masters, are you mad? Or what are you?
       Have you no wit, manners, nor honesty, but to gabble
       like tinkers at this time of night? Do ye make an alehouse
       of my lady's house, that ye squeak out your coziers'   83
       catches without any mitigation or remorse of voice? Is 84
       there no respect of place, persons, nor time in you?
TOBY We did keep time, sir, in our catches. Sneck up.   86
MALVOLIO Sir Toby, I must be round with you. My lady   87
       bade me tell you that, though she harbors you as her
       kinsman, she's nothing allied to your disorders. If you
       can separate yourself and your misdemeanors, you are
       welcome to the house. If not, and it would please you to
       take leave of her, she is very willing to bid you farewell.
TOBY *[sings]*
       'Farewell, dear heart since I must needs be gone.'   93
MARIA Nay, good Sir Toby.

II, iii Within Olivia's house **2** *diluculo surgere [saluberrimum est]* to
get up at dawn is healthful (Lily's *Latin Grammar*) **6** *can* metal vessel
for holding liquor **13** *stoup* goblet **15** *hearts* (term of endearment)
15–16 *picture of We Three* picture showing two fools or asses inscribed
'We Three,' the onlooker making the third **17** *catch* round-song (such as
'Three Blind Mice') **18** *breast* voice **21** *gracious* elegant **22–23** *Pigrogromitus . . . Queubus* (meaningless mock-learning) **24** *leman* sweetheart
25 *impeticos* put in pocket of gown; *gratillity* gratuity **26** *Myrmidons*
Thessalian warriors (meaningless here) **31** *testril* tester, sixpence **32–33**
good life virtuous living **54** *welkin* sky **56** *weaver* (weavers were famous
for psalm-singing) **69** *Cataian* native of Cathay, trickster; *politicians*
intriguers **70** *Peg-a-Ramsey* characters in an old song, here used as a
term of contempt **71** *consanguineous* related **72** *Tilly-vally* nonsense
72–73 *There dwelt . . .* (from an old song, 'The Constancy of Susanna')
77 *natural* naturally (but the word also means 'like a fool') **83** *coziers'*
cobblers' **84** *mitigation or remorse* i.e. considerate lowering **86** *Sneck
up* go hang **87** *round* plain **93** *Farewell, dear heart . . .* (from an old song,
'Corydon's Farewell to Phyllis')

CLOWN *[sings]*
    'His eyes do show his days are almost done.'
MALVOLIO Is't even so?
TOBY *[sings]*
    'But I will never die.'
CLOWN *[sings]*
    Sir Toby, there you lie.
MALVOLIO This is much credit to you.
TOBY *[sings]*
    'Shall I bid him go?'
CLOWN *[sings]*
    'What an if you do?'
TOBY *[sings]*
    'Shall I bid him go, and spare not?'
CLOWN *[sings]*
    'O, no, no, no, no, you dare not!'
TOBY Out o' tune, sir? Ye lie. Art any more than a stew-
    ard? Dost thou think, because thou art virtuous, there
    shall be no more cakes and ale?
107 CLOWN Yes, by Saint Anne, and ginger shall be hot i' th'
    mouth too.
109 TOBY Th' art i' th' right. – Go, sir, rub your chain with
    crumbs. A stoup of wine, Maria!
MALVOLIO Mistress Mary, if you prized my lady's favor
112 at anything more than contempt, you would not give
    means for this uncivil rule. She shall know of it, by this
    hand.   *Exit.*
115 MARIA Go shake your ears.
ANDREW 'Twere as good a deed as to drink when a man's
    ahungry, to challenge him the field, and then to break
    promise with him and make a fool of him.
TOBY Do't, knight. I'll write thee a challenge; or I'll de-
    liver thy indignation to him by word of mouth.
MARIA Sweet Sir Toby, be patient for to-night. Since the
    youth of the Count's was to-day with my lady, she is
    much out of quiet. For Monsieur Malvolio, let me alone
124 with him. If I do not gull him into a nayword, and make
125 him a common recreation, do not think I have wit
    enough to lie straight in my bed. I know I can do it.
127 TOBY Possess us, possess us. Tell us something of him.
MARIA Marry, sir, sometimes he is a kind of Puritan.
ANDREW O, if I thought that, I'd beat him like a dog.
TOBY What, for being a Puritan? Thy exquisite reason,
    dear knight.
ANDREW I have no exquisite reason for't, but I have
    reason good enough.
MARIA The devil a Puritan that he is, or anything con-
135 stantly but a time-pleaser; an affectioned ass, that cons
136 state without book and utters it by great swarths; the
    best persuaded of himself; so crammed, as he thinks,
    with excellencies that it is his grounds of faith that all
    that look on him love him; and on that vice in him will
    my revenge find notable cause to work.

TOBY What wilt thou do?
MARIA I will drop in his way some obscure epistles of
    love, wherein by the color of his beard, the shape of his
    leg, the manner of his gait, the expressure of his eye, 144
    forehead, and complexion, he shall find himself most
    feelingly personated. I can write very like my lady your 146
    niece; on a forgotten matter we can hardly make dis-
    tinction of our hands.
TOBY Excellent. I smell a device.
ANDREW I have't in my nose too.
TOBY He shall think by the letters that thou wilt drop
    that they come from my niece, and that she's in love
    with him.
MARIA My purpose is indeed a horse of that color.
ANDREW And your horse now would make him an ass.
MARIA Ass, I doubt not.
ANDREW O, 'twill be admirable.
MARIA Sport royal, I warrant you. I know my physic will
    work with him. I will plant you two, and let the fool
    make a third, where he shall find the letter. Observe his
    construction of it. For this night, to bed, and dream on 161
    the event. Farewell.   *Exit.* 162
TOBY Good night, Penthesilea.   163
ANDREW Before me, she's a good wench.   164
TOBY She's a beagle true-bred, and one that adores me. 165
    What o' that?
ANDREW I was adored once too.
TOBY Let's to bed, knight. Thou hadst need send for
    more money.
ANDREW If I cannot recover your niece, I am a foul way 170
    out.   171
TOBY Send for money, knight. If thou hast her not i' th'
    end, call me Cut.   173
ANDREW If I do not, never trust me, take it how you will.
TOBY Come, come; I'll go burn some sack. 'Tis too late 175
    to go to bed now. Come, knight; come, knight. *Exeunt.*

*

    Enter Duke, Viola, Curio, and others.   II, iv
DUKE
    Give me some music. Now good morrow, friends.
    Now, good Cesario, but that piece of song,
    That old and antique song we heard last night.   3
    Methought it did relieve my passion much,
    More than light airs and recollected terms   5
    Of these most brisk and giddy-pacèd times.
    Come, but one verse.
CURIO He is not here, so please your lordship, that should
    sing it.
DUKE Who was it?
CURIO Feste the jester, my lord, a fool that the Lady
    Olivia's father took much delight in. He is about the
    house.
DUKE
    Seek him out, and play the tune the while. *[Exit Curio.]*
        Music plays.
    Come hither, boy. If ever thou shalt love,
    In the sweet pangs of it remember me;
    For such as I am all true lovers are,
    Unstaid and skittish in all motions else   17
    Save in the constant image of the creature
    That is beloved. How dost thou like this tune?

107 *ginger* (used to spice ale)   109–10 *rub . . . crumbs* (a contemptuous allusion to his steward's chain)   112–13 *give means* i.e. bring the wine   115 *your ears* i.e. your ass's ears   124 *gull* trick; *nayword* byword   125 *recreation* amusement   127 *Possess us* give us the facts   135 *time-pleaser* sycophant; *affectioned* affected   135–36 *cons . . . book* learns a stately manner by heart   136 *swarths* quantities   144 *expressure* expression   146 *personated* represented   161 *construction* interpretation   162 *event* outcome   163 *Penthesilea* queen of the Amazons   164 *Before me* I swear by myself   165 *beagle* small rabbit-hound   170 *recover* gain   171 *out* out of money   173 *Cut* horse with a docked tail   175 *burn some sack* warm some sherry   II, iv Within the palace of Orsino   3 *antique* quaint   5 *recollected* studied   17 *motions* emotions

VIOLA

20   It gives a very echo to the seat
Where Love is throned.

DUKE   Thou dost speak masterly.
My life upon't, young though thou art, thine eye
23   Hath stayed upon some favor that it loves.
Hath it not, boy?

VIOLA   A little, by your favor.

DUKE

What kind of woman is't?

VIOLA   Of your complexion.

DUKE

She is not worth thee then. What years, i' faith?

VIOLA

About your years, my lord.

DUKE

Too old, by heaven. Let still the woman take
29   An elder than herself: so wears she to him,
30   So sways she level in her husband's heart;
For, boy, however we do praise ourselves,
32   Our fancies are more giddy and unfirm,
More longing, wavering, sooner lost and worn,
Than women's are.

VIOLA   I think it well, my lord.

DUKE

Then let thy love be younger than thyself,
36   Or thy affection cannot hold the bent;
For women are as roses, whose fair flow'r,
Being once displayed, doth fall that very hour.

VIOLA

And so they are; alas, that they are so.
To die, even when they to perfection grow.

Enter Curio and Clown.

DUKE

O, fellow, come, the song we had last night.
Mark it, Cesario; it is old and plain.
43   The spinsters and the knitters in the sun,
44   And the free maids that weave their thread with bones,
45   Do use to chant it. It is silly sooth,
And dallies with the innocence of love,
47   Like the old age.

CLOWN Are you ready, sir?

DUKE I prithee sing.

Music.

The Song.

Come away, come away, death,
51   And in sad cypress let me be laid.
Fly away, fly away, breath;
     I am slain by a fair cruel maid.
54   My shroud of white, stuck all with yew,
     O, prepare it.
56   My part of death, no one so true
     Did share it.

Not a flower, not a flower sweet,
     On my black coffin let there be strown;
Not a friend, not a friend greet
     My poor corpse, where my bones shall be thrown.
A thousand thousand sighs to save,
     Lay me, O, where
Sad true lover never find my grave,
     To weep there.

DUKE There's for thy pains.

CLOWN No pains, sir. I take pleasure in singing, sir.

DUKE I'll pay thy pleasure then.

CLOWN Truly, sir, and pleasure will be paid one time or 69 another.

DUKE Give me now leave to leave thee.

CLOWN Now the melancholy god protect thee, and the tailor make thy doublet of changeable taffeta, for thy 73 mind is a very opal. I would have men of such constancy put to sea, that their business might be everything, and their intent everywhere; for that's it that always makes a good voyage of nothing. Farewell.   *Exit.* 77

DUKE

Let all the rest give place.   78

[Exeunt Curio and Attendants.]
         Once more, Cesario,
Get thee to yond same sovereign cruelty.   79
Tell her, my love, more noble than the world,
Prizes not quantity of dirty lands;
The parts that fortune hath bestowed upon her   82
Tell her I hold as giddily as fortune,
But 'tis that miracle and queen of gems
That nature pranks her in attracts my soul.   85

VIOLA

But if she cannot love you, sir?

DUKE

I cannot be so answered.

VIOLA   Sooth, but you must.
Say that some lady, as perhaps there is,
Hath for your love as great a pang of heart
As you have for Olivia. You cannot love her.
You tell her so. Must she not then be answered?

DUKE

There is no woman's sides
Can bide the beating of so strong a passion   93
As love doth give my heart; no woman's heart
So big to hold so much; they lack retention.   95
Alas, their love may be called appetite,
No motion of the liver but the palate,   97
That suffers surfeit, cloyment, and revolt;   98
But mine is all as hungry as the sea
And can digest as much. Make no compare
Between that love a woman can bear me
And that I owe Olivia.   102

VIOLA   Ay, but I know.

DUKE

What dost thou know?

VIOLA

Too well what love women to men may owe.
In faith, they are as true of heart as we.
My father had a daughter loved a man
As it might be perhaps, were I a woman,
I should your lordship.

DUKE   And what's her history?

20–21 *the seat . . . throned* i.e. the heart   23 *favor* face   29 *wears* adapts herself   30 *sways . . . heart* she keeps constant her husband's love   32 *fancies* loves   36 *bent* direction   43 *spinsters* spinners   44 *free* innocent; *bones* bone bobbins   45 *Do use* are accustomed; *silly sooth* simple truth   47 *old age* good old days   51 *cypress* coffin of cypress wood   54 *yew* yew sprigs, associated with mourning   56 *part* portion   69 *pleasure . . . paid* indulgence exacts its penalty   73 *changeable* i.e. opalescent in effect   77 *nothing* bringing back nothing   78 *give place* leave   79 *sovereign cruelty* supremely cruel person   82 *parts* possessions   85 *pranks* decks   93 *bide* withstand   95 *retention* capacity of retaining   97 *motion* emotion; *liver* seat of the emotion of love   98 *revolt* revulsion   102 *owe* have toward

VIOLA
A blank, my lord. She never told her love,
But let concealment, like a worm i' th' bud,
111 Feed on her damask cheek. She pined in thought;
And, with a green and yellow melancholy,
She sat like Patience on a monument,
Smiling at grief. Was not this love indeed?
We men may say more, swear more; but indeed
116 Our shows are more than will; for still we prove
Much in our vows but little in our love.

DUKE
But died thy sister of her love, my boy?

VIOLA
I am all the daughters of my father's house,
And all the brothers too, and yet I know not.
Sir, shall I to this lady?

DUKE   Ay, that's the theme.
To her in haste. Give her this jewel. Say
123 My love can give no place, bide no denay.   *Exeunt.*

*

II, v   *Enter Sir Toby, Sir Andrew, and Fabian.*
TOBY Come thy ways, Signior Fabian.
2 **FABIAN** Nay, I'll come. If I lose a scruple of this sport, let me be boiled to death with melancholy.
TOBY Wouldst thou not be glad to have the niggardly
5 rascally sheep-biter come by some notable shame?
FABIAN I would exult, man. You know he brought me out o' favor with my lady about a bear-baiting here.
TOBY To anger him we'll have the bear again, and we will fool him black and blue. Shall we not, Sir Andrew?
ANDREW An we do not, it is pity of our lives.
     Enter Maria.
11 **TOBY** Here comes the little villain. How now, my metal of India?
13 **MARIA** Get ye all three into the box tree. Malvolio 's coming down this walk. He has been yonder i' the sun
15 practicing behavior to his own shadow this half hour. Observe him, for the love of mockery; for I know this
17 letter will make a contemplative idiot of him. Close, in the name of jesting. *[The others hide.]* Lie thou there *[throws down a letter]*; for here comes the trout that
20 must be caught with tickling.   *Exit.*
     Enter Malvolio.
MALVOLIO 'Tis but fortune; all is fortune. Maria once
22 told me she did affect me; and I have heard herself come thus near, that, should she fancy, it should be one of my

complexion. Besides, she uses me with a more exalted 24
respect than any one else that follows her. What should 25
I think on't?
TOBY Here's an overweening rogue.
FABIAN O, peace! Contemplation makes a rare turkey cock of him. How he jets under his advanced plumes! 29
ANDREW 'Slight, I could so beat the rogue. 30
TOBY Peace, I say.
MALVOLIO To be Count Malvolio.
TOBY Ah, rogue!
ANDREW Pistol him, pistol him.
TOBY Peace, peace.
MALVOLIO There is example for't. The Lady of the 36
Strachy married the yeoman of the wardrobe.
ANDREW Fie on him, Jezebel. 38
FABIAN O, peace! Now he's deeply in. Look how imagination blows him. 40
MALVOLIO Having been three months married to her, sitting in my state – 42
TOBY O for a stone-bow, to hit him in the eye! 43
MALVOLIO Calling my officers about me, in my branched 44
velvet gown; having come from a day-bed, where I 45
have left Olivia sleeping –
TOBY Fire and brimstone!
FABIAN O, peace, peace!
MALVOLIO And then to have the humor of state; and 49
after a demure travel of regard, telling them I know my 50
place, as I would they should do theirs, to ask for my kinsman Toby –
TOBY Bolts and shackles!
FABIAN O peace, peace, peace, now, now.
MALVOLIO Seven of my people, with an obedient start, make out for him. I frown the while, and perchance wind up my watch, or play with my – some rich jewel. Toby approaches; curtsies there to me –
TOBY Shall this fellow live?
FABIAN Though our silence be drawn from us with cars, 60
yet peace.
MALVOLIO I extend my hand to him thus, quenching my familiar smile with an austere regard of control – 63
TOBY And does not Toby take you a blow o' the lips then? 64
MALVOLIO Saying, 'Cousin Toby, my fortunes having cast me on your niece, give me this prerogative of speech.'
TOBY What, what?
MALVOLIO 'You must amend your drunkenness.'
TOBY Out, scab!
FABIAN Nay, patience, or we break the sinews of our plot.
MALVOLIO 'Besides, you waste the treasure of your time with a foolish knight' –
ANDREW That's me, I warrant you.
MALVOLIO 'One Sir Andrew' –
ANDREW I knew 'twas I, for many do call me fool.
MALVOLIO What employment have we here?
     [Takes up the letter.]
FABIAN Now is the woodcock near the gin. 77
TOBY O, peace, and the spirit of humors intimate reading aloud to him!
MALVOLIO By my life, this is my lady's hand. These be her very C's, her U's, and her T's; and thus makes she her great P's. It is, in contempt of question, her hand. 82
ANDREW Her C's, her U's, and her T's? Why that?
MALVOLIO *[reads]* 'To the unknown beloved, this, and my good wishes.' Her very phrases! By your leave, wax. 85

---

111 *damask* pink and white, as of a damask rose 116 *will* our passions 123 *can give no place* cannot yield; *denay* denial
II, v The garden of Olivia's house 2 *scruple* bit 5 *sheep-biter* dog that bites sheep, sneaking fellow 11–12 *my metal of India* my golden one 13 *tree* i.e. hedge 15 *behavior* elegant conduct 17 *contemplative idiot* i.e. addled by his musings; *Close* hide 20 *tickling* stroking about the gills 22 *she did affect me* Olivia liked me 24 *complexion* personality 25 *that follows her* in her service 29 *jets* struts 30 *'Slight* an oath (by God's light) 36–37 *Lady of the Strachy* (unidentified allusion) 38 *Jezebel* wicked queen of Israel 40 *blows him* puffs him up 42 *state* chair of state 43 *stone-bow* stone-shooter 44 *branched* embroidered 45 *day-bed* sofa 49 *humor of state* manner and disposition of authority 50 *demure . . . regard* grave survey 60 *with cars* by force 63 *regard of control* look of authority 64 *take* give 77 *woodcock* (a stupid bird); *gin* snare, trap 82 *in contempt of* beyond 85 *By . . . wax* (a conventional apology for breaking a seal)

86   Soft, and the impressure her Lucrece, with which she uses to seal. 'Tis my lady. To whom should this be?

88   FABIAN   This wins him, liver and all.

MALVOLIO *[reads]*
     'Jove knows I love,
       But who?
     Lips, do not move;
       No man must know.'

93   'No man must know.' What follows? The numbers altered! 'No man must know.' If this should be thee, Malvolio?

96   TOBY   Marry, hang thee, brock!

MALVOLIO *[reads]*
     'I may command where I adore,
       But silence, like a Lucrece knife,
     With bloodless stroke my heart doth gore.
     M. O. A. I. doth sway my life.'

101   FABIAN   A fustian riddle.

102   TOBY   Excellent wench, say I.

MALVOLIO   'M. O. A. I. doth sway my life.' Nay, but first, let me see, let me see, let me see.

105   FABIAN   What dish o' poison has she dressed him!

106   TOBY   And with what wing the staniel checks at it!

MALVOLIO   'I may command where I adore.' Why, she may command me: I serve her; she is my lady. Why,

109   this is evident to any formal capacity. There is no obstruction in this. And the end; what should that alphabetical position portend? If I could make that resemble something in me! Softly, 'M. O. A. I.'

113   TOBY   O, ay, make up that. He is now at a cold scent.

114   FABIAN   Sowter will cry upon't for all this, though it be as rank as a fox.

MALVOLIO   M. – Malvolio. M. – Why, that begins my name.

FABIAN   Did not I say he would work it out? The cur is

118   excellent at faults.

119   MALVOLIO   M. – But then there is no consonancy in the

120   sequel. That suffers under probation. A should follow, but O does.

FABIAN   And O shall end, I hope.

TOBY   Ay, or I'll cudgel him, and make him cry O.

MALVOLIO   And then I comes behind.

FABIAN   Ay, an you had any eye behind you, you might see more detraction at your heels than fortunes before you.

127   MALVOLIO   M, O, A, I. This simulation is not as the for-

128   mer; and yet, to crush this a little, it would bow to me, for every one of these letters are in my name. Soft, here follows prose.

131   *[Reads]* 'If this fall into thy hand, revolve. In my stars I am above thee, but be not afraid of greatness. Some are born great, some achieve greatness, and some have greatness thrust upon 'em. Thy Fates open their hands; let

135   thy blood and spirit embrace them; and to inure thyself

136   to what thou art like to be, cast thy humble slough and appear fresh. Be opposite with a kinsman, surly with

138   servants. Let thy tongue tang arguments of state; put

139   thyself into the trick of singularity. She thus advises thee that sighs for thee. Remember who commended thy yel-

141   low stockings and wished to see thee ever cross-gartered. I say, remember. Go to, thou art made, if thou desir'st to be so. If not, let me see thee a steward still, the fellow of servants, and not worthy to touch Fortune's fingers. Farewell. She that would alter services with thee,

146   'The Fortunate Unhappy.'

Daylight and champian discovers not more. This is open. 147
I will be proud, I will read politic authors, I will baffle Sir 148
Toby, I will wash off gross acquaintance, I will be point- 149
devise, the very man. I do not now fool myself, to let
imagination jade me, for every reason excites to this, that 151
my lady loves me. She did commend my yellow stockings of late, she did praise my leg being cross-gartered;
and in this she manifests herself to my love, and with a
kind of injunction drives me to these habits of her liking. 155
I thank my stars, I am happy. I will be strange, stout, in 156
yellow stockings, and cross-gartered, even with the
swiftness of putting on. Jove and my stars be praised.
Here is yet a postscript.
[Reads] 'Thou canst not choose but know who I am. If
thou entertain'st my love, let it appear in thy smiling. 161
Thy smiles become thee well. Therefore in my presence
still smile, dear my sweet, I prithee.'
Jove, I thank thee. I will smile; I will do everything that
thou wilt have me.   *Exit.*

FABIAN   I will not give my part of this sport for a pension of thousands to be paid from the Sophy.   167

TOBY   I could marry this wench for this device.

ANDREW   So could I too.

TOBY   And ask no other dowry with her but such another jest.
    Enter Maria.

ANDREW   Nor I neither.

FABIAN   Here comes my noble gull-catcher.   173

TOBY   Wilt thou set thy foot o' my neck?

ANDREW   Or o' mine either?

TOBY   Shall I play my freedom at tray-trip and become 176 thy bondslave?

ANDREW   I' faith, or I either?

TOBY   Why, thou hast put him in such a dream that, when the image of it leaves him, he must run mad.

MARIA   Nay, but say true, does it work upon him?

TOBY   Like aqua-vitae with a midwife.   182

MARIA   If you will, then, see the fruits of the sport, mark his first approach before my lady. He will come to her in yellow stockings, and 'tis a color she abhors, and cross-gartered, a fashion she detests; and he will smile upon her, which will now be so unsuitable to her disposition, being addicted to a melancholy as she is, that it cannot but turn him into a notable contempt. If you will see it, follow me.

TOBY   To the gates of Tartar, thou most excellent devil of 190 wit.

ANDREW   I'll make one too.   *Exeunt.*

*

86 *Soft* careful, slow; *Lucrece* (her seal was a likeness of the chaste Lucrece) 88 *liver* the seat of passion   93 *numbers* metre   96 *brock* badger   101 *fustian* ridiculously lofty   102 *Excellent wench* clever girl (Maria)   105 *dressed* prepared   106 *staniel* an inferior hawk; *checks* turns to pursue the wrong prey   109 *formal* normal; *obstruction* difficulty   113 *cold scent* difficult trail   114 *Sowter . . . upon't* the hound will pick up the scent   118 *faults* gaps or breaks in the scent   119 *consonancy* agreement   120 *suffers* becomes strained; *probation* testing   127 *simulation* hidden meaning   128 *crush* force   131 *revolve* consider; *stars* fate   135 *inure* accustom   136 *slough* outer skin   138 *tang* sound with   139 *singularity* eccentricity   141 *cross-gartered* wearing hose-garters crossed above and below the knee   146 *Unhappy* unfortunate   147 *champian* open country; *discovers* reveals, discloses   148 *politic authors* writers on government; *baffle* subject to disgrace   149–50 *point-devise* perfectly correct   151 *jade* trick   155 *habits* attire   156 *strange* aloof; *stout* proud   161 *entertain'st* accept   167 *Sophy* shah of Persia   173 *gull-catcher* fool-catcher   176 *play* gamble; *tray-trip* a game of dice   182 *aqua-vitae* any distilled liquor   190 *Tartar* Tartarus, the section of hell reserved for the most evil

III, i   *Enter Viola and Clown [with a tabor].*

1 VIOLA Save thee, friend, and thy music. Dost thou live by
2   thy tabor?

CLOWN No, sir, I live by the church.

VIOLA Art thou a churchman?

CLOWN No such matter, sir. I do live by the church; for I
do live at my house, and my house doth stand by the
church.

8 VIOLA So thou mayst say, the king lies by a beggar, if a
beggar dwell near him; or, the church stands by thy
tabor, if thy tabor stand by the church.

CLOWN You have said, sir. To see this age! A sentence is
12   but a chev'ril glove to a good wit. How quickly the
wrong side may be turned outward!

14 VIOLA Nay, that's certain. They that dally nicely with
15   words may quickly make them wanton.

CLOWN I would therefore my sister had had no name, sir.

VIOLA Why, man?

CLOWN Why, sir, her name's a word, and to dally with
19   that word might make my sister wanton. But indeed
20   words are very rascals since bonds disgraced them.

VIOLA Thy reason, man?

CLOWN Troth, sir, I can yield you none without words,
and words are grown so false I am loath to prove reason
with them.

VIOLA I warrant thou art a merry fellow and car'st for
nothing.

CLOWN Not so, sir; I do care for something; but in my
conscience, sir, I do not care for you. If that be to care
for nothing, sir, I would it would make you invisible.

VIOLA Art not thou the Lady Olivia's fool?

CLOWN No, indeed, sir. The Lady Olivia has no folly.
She will keep no fool, sir, till she be married; and fools
33   are as like husbands as pilchers are to herrings, the
husband's the bigger. I am indeed not her fool, but her
corrupter of words.

VIOLA I saw thee late at the Count Orsino's.

CLOWN Foolery, sir, does walk about the orb like the sun;
it shines everywhere. I would be sorry, sir, but the fool
should be as oft with your master as with my mistress. I
think I saw your wisdom there.

41 VIOLA Nay, an thou pass upon me, I'll no more with thee.
Hold, there's expenses for thee.
   [Gives a coin.]

43 CLOWN Now Jove, in his next commodity of hair, send
thee a beard.

VIOLA By my troth, I'll tell thee, I am almost sick for one,

though I would not have it grow on my chin. Is thy lady
within?

CLOWN Would not a pair of these have bred, sir?

VIOLA Yes, being kept together and put to use.   49

CLOWN I would play Lord Pandarus of Phrygia, sir, to   50
bring a Cressida to this Troilus.

VIOLA I understand you, sir. 'Tis well begged.
   [Gives another coin.]

CLOWN The matter, I hope, is not great, sir, begging but
a beggar: Cressida was a beggar. My lady is within, sir. 54
I will conster to them whence you come. Who you are   55
and what you would are out of my welkin; I might say   56
'element,' but the word is over-worn.   *Exit.*

VIOLA
This fellow is wise enough to play the fool,
And to do that well craves a kind of wit.   59
He must observe their mood on whom he jests,
The quality of persons, and the time;
And like the haggard, check at every feather   62
That comes before his eye. This is a practice   63
As full of labor as a wise man's art;
For folly that he wisely shows, is fit;
But wise men, folly-fall'n, quite taint their wit.   66
   Enter Sir Toby and [Sir] Andrew.

TOBY Save you, gentleman.

VIOLA And you, sir.

ANDREW Dieu vous garde, monsieur.   69

VIOLA Et vous aussi; votre serviteur.

ANDREW I hope, sir, you are, and I am yours.

TOBY Will you encounter the house? My niece is desir-   72
ous you should enter, if your trade be to her.

VIOLA I am bound to your niece, sir; I mean, she is the list 74
of my voyage.

TOBY Taste your legs, sir; put them to motion.   76

VIOLA My legs do better understand me, sir, than I under- 77
stand what you mean by bidding me taste my legs.

TOBY I mean, to go, sir, to enter.

VIOLA I will answer you with gait and entrance. But we
are prevented.   81
   Enter Olivia and Gentlewoman [Maria].
Most excellent accomplished lady, the heavens rain
odors on you.

ANDREW That youth's a rare courtier. 'Rain odors' –
well!

VIOLA My matter hath no voice, lady, but to your own   85
most pregnant and vouchsafed ear.   86

ANDREW 'Odors,' 'pregnant,' and 'vouchsafed' – I'll get
'em all three all ready.

OLIVIA Let the garden door be shut, and leave me to my
hearing. *[Exeunt Sir Toby, Sir Andrew, and Maria.]*
Give me your hand, sir.

VIOLA
My duty, madam, and most humble service.

OLIVIA
What is your name?

VIOLA
Cesario is your servant's name, fair princess.

OLIVIA
My servant, sir? 'Twas never merry world
Since lowly feigning was called compliment.   96
Y' are servant to the Count Orsino, youth.

VIOLA
And he is yours, and his must needs be yours.
Your servant's servant is your servant, madam.

III, i Before the house of Olivia 1 *Save thee* God save thee; *live by* make
a living with 2 *tabor* drum 8 *lies* dwells 12 *chev'ril* kid 14 *dally
nicely* play subtly 15 *wanton* capricious 19 *wanton* abandoned 20 *since
. . . them* i.e. since bonds have been needed to guarantee them 33 *pilchers*
pilchards (small fish resembling herring) 41 *pass upon* jest at 43 *commodity* shipment 49 *put to use* put out at interest 50 *Pandarus* the go-
between in the tale told by Chaucer and others 54 *Cressida was a beggar*
(she became a leprous beggar in Henryson's continuation of Chaucer's
story) 55 *conster* construe, explain 56 *welkin* sky 59 *wit* intelligence
 62 *haggard* untrained hawk; *check . . . feather* forsake her quarry for other
game 63 *practice* skill 66 *folly-fall'n* fallen into folly; *taint their wit* ruin
their reputation for intelligence 69–70 *Dieu . . . serviteur* God protect
you, sir . . . And you also; your servant 72 *encounter* meet, i.e. go into
 74 *bound to* bound for; *list* limit, destination 76 *Taste* try 77 *understand*
both 'comprehend' and 'stand under' 81 *prevented* anticipated 85 *hath
no voice* can be told to no one 86 *pregnant* receptive 96 *lowly feigning*
false humility

OLIVIA

For him, I think not on him ; for his thoughts,
Would they were blanks, rather than filled with me.

VIOLA

Madam, I come to whet your gentle thoughts
On his behalf.

OLIVIA   O, by your leave, I pray you.

I bade you never speak again of him ;
But, would you undertake another suit,
I had rather hear you to solicit that

107   Than music from the spheres.

VIOLA   Dear lady –

OLIVIA

Give me leave, beseech you. I did send,
After the last enchantment you did here,

110   A ring in chase of you. So did I abuse
Myself, my servant, and, I fear me, you.

112   Under your hard construction must I sit,
To force that on you in a shameful cunning
Which you knew none of yours. What might you think ?
Have you not set mine honor at the stake

116   And baited it with all th' unmuzzled thoughts

117   That tyrannous heart can think ? To one of your
receiving

118   Enough is shown ; a cypress, not a bosom,
Hides my heart. So, let me hear you speak.

VIOLA

I pity you.

OLIVIA   That's a degree to love.

VIOLA

121   No, not a grize ; for 'tis a vulgar proof
That very oft we pity enemies.

OLIVIA

Why then, methinks 'tis time to smile again.
O world, how apt the poor are to be proud.
If one should be a prey, how much the better
To fall before the lion than the wolf.
                    Clock strikes.
The clock upbraids me with the waste of time.
Be not afraid, good youth, I will not have you,
And yet, when wit and youth is come to harvest,

130   Your wife is like to reap a proper man.
There lies your way, due west.

VIOLA   Then westward ho !

Grace and good disposition attend your ladyship.
You'll nothing, madam, to my lord by me ?

OLIVIA

Stay.
I prithee tell me what thou think'st of me.

VIOLA

That you do think you are not what you are.

OLIVIA

If I think so, I think the same of you.

VIOLA

Then think you right. I am not what I am.

OLIVIA

I would you were as I would have you be.

VIOLA

Would it be better, madam, than I am ?

141   I wish it might, for now I am your fool.

OLIVIA

O, what a deal of scorn looks beautiful
In the contempt and anger of his lip.
A murd'rous guilt shows not itself more soon

Than love that would seem hid : love's night is noon.
Cesario, by the roses of the spring,
By maidhood, honor, truth, and everything,
I love thee so that, maugre all thy pride,   148
Nor wit nor reason can my passion hide.
Do not extort thy reasons from this clause,
For that I woo, thou therefore hast no cause ;
But rather reason thus with reason fetter,
Love sought is good, but given unsought is better.

VIOLA

By innocence I swear, and by my youth,
I have one heart, one bosom, and one truth,
And that no woman has ; nor never none
Shall mistress be of it, save I alone.
And so adieu, good madam. Never more
Will I my master's tears to you deplore.

OLIVIA

Yet come again ; for thou perhaps mayst move
That heart which now abhors to like his love.   *Exeunt.*

*

ANDREW No, faith, I'll not stay a jot longer.

TOBY Thy reason, dear venom ; give thy reason.   2

FABIAN You must needs yield your reason, Sir Andrew.

ANDREW Marry, I saw your niece do more favors to the
Count's servingman than ever she bestowed upon me. I
saw't i' th' orchard.   6

TOBY Did she see thee the while, old boy ? Tell me that.

ANDREW As plain as I see you now.

FABIAN This was a great argument of love in her toward   9
you.

ANDREW 'Slight ! will you make an ass o' me ?

FABIAN I will prove it legitimate, sir, upon the oaths of 12
judgment and reason.

TOBY And they have been grand-jurymen since before
Noah was a sailor.

FABIAN She did show favor to the youth in your sight only
to exasperate you, to awake your dormouse valor, to put   17
fire in your heart and brimstone in your liver. You
should then have accosted her, and with some excellent
jests, fire-new from the mint, you should have banged
the youth into dumbness. This was looked for at your
hand, and this was balked. The double gilt of this op-   22
portunity you let time wash off, and you are now sailed
into the North of my lady's opinion, where you will hang 24
like an icicle on a Dutchman's beard unless you do redeem it by some laudable attempt either of valor or
policy.

---

107 *spheres* the several concentric revolving spheres in which the planets
and stars were thought to be placed   **110** *abuse* deceive   **112** *construction*
interpretation   **116** *baited* harassed, as a bear by dogs   **117** *receiving*
receptive capacity   **118** *cypress* transparent black cloth   **121** *grize* grece,
flight of steps ; *vulgar proof* common experience   **130** *proper* handsome
141 *fool* butt   **148** *maugre* despite
III, ii Within the house of Olivia   **2** *venom* (Sir Andrew is filled with
venom)   **6** *orchard* probably 'garden'   **9** *argument* proof   **12** *legitimate*
true ; *oaths* testimony   **17** *dormouse* i.e. sleepy   **22** *balked* missed ; *double
gilt* twice dipped in gold   **24** *into the North* i.e. out of the warmth

ANDREW An't be any way, it must be with valor; for
28   policy I hate. I had as lief be a Brownist as a politician.
TOBY Why then, build me thy fortunes upon the basis of
valor. Challenge me the Count's youth to fight with
him; hurt him in eleven places. My niece shall take note
of it, and assure thyself there is no love-broker in the
world can more prevail in man's commendation with
woman than report of valor.
FABIAN There is no way but this, Sir Andrew.
ANDREW Will either of you bear me a challenge to him?
37 TOBY Go, write it in a martial hand. Be curst and brief; it
is no matter how witty, so it be eloquent and full of in-
39   vention. Taunt him with the license of ink. If thou thou'st
him some thrice, it shall not be amiss; and as many lies as
will lie in thy sheet of paper, although the sheet were big
42   enough for the bed of Ware in England, set 'em down.
Go about it. Let there be gall enough in thy ink, though
thou write with a goose-pen, no matter. About it!
ANDREW Where shall I find you?
46 TOBY We'll call thee at the cubiculo. Go.

                             Exit Sir Andrew.

47 FABIAN This is a dear manikin to you, Sir Toby.
TOBY I have been dear to him, lad, some two thousand
strong or so.
FABIAN We shall have a rare letter from him, but you'll
not deliver't?
TOBY Never trust me then; and by all means stir on the
53   youth to an answer. I think oxen and wainropes cannot
54   hale them together. For Andrew, if he were opened, and
you find so much blood in his liver as will clog the foot of
a flea, I'll eat the rest of th' anatomy.
FABIAN And his opposite, the youth, bears in his visage
no great presage of cruelty.

              Enter Maria.

59 TOBY Look where the youngest wren of mine comes.
60 MARIA If you desire the spleen, and will laugh yourselves
61   into stitches, follow me. Yond gull Malvolio is turned
heathen, a very renegado; for there is no Christian that
means to be saved by believing rightly can ever believe
64   such impossible passages of grossness. He's in yellow
stockings.
TOBY And cross-gartered?
MARIA Most villainously; like a pedant that keeps a school
i' th' church. I have dogged him like his murderer. He
does obey every point of the letter that I dropped to betray him. He does smile his face into more lines than is
71   in the new map with the augmentation of the Indies.
You have not seen such a thing as 'tis. I can hardly forbear hurling things at him. I know my lady will strike

him. If she do, he'll smile, and take't for a great favor.
TOBY Come bring us, bring us where he is.

                            Exeunt omnes.

                           *

        Enter Sebastian and Antonio.   III, iii
SEBASTIAN
I would not by my will have troubled you;
But since you make your pleasure of your pains,
I will no further chide you.
ANTONIO
I could not stay behind you. My desire
(More sharp than filèd steel) did spur me forth;
And not all love to see you (though so much   6
As might have drawn one to a longer voyage)
But jealousy what might befall your travel,   8
Being skilless in these parts; which to a stranger,   9
Unguided and unfriended, often prove
Rough and unhospitable. My willing love,
The rather by these arguments of fear,
Set forth in your pursuit.
SEBASTIAN   My kind Antonio,
I can no other answer make but thanks,
And thanks, and ever oft good turns
Are shuffled off with such uncurrent pay.   16
But, were my worth as is my conscience firm,   17
You should find better dealing. What's to do?
Shall we go see the relics of this town?   19
ANTONIO
To-morrow, sir; best first go see your lodging.
SEBASTIAN
I am not weary, and 'tis long to night.
I pray you let us satisfy our eyes
With the memorials and the things of fame
That do renown this city.
ANTONIO   Would you'ld pardon me.
I do not without danger walk these streets.
Once in a sea-fight 'gainst the Count his galleys
I did some service; of such note indeed
That, were I ta'en here, it would scarce be answered.   28
SEBASTIAN
Belike you slew great number of his people?
ANTONIO
Th' offense is not of such a bloody nature,
Albeit the quality of the time and quarrel
Might well have given us bloody argument.
It might have since been answered in repaying
What we took from them, which for traffic's sake   34
Most of our city did. Only myself stood out;
For which, if I be lapsèd in this place,   36
I shall pay dear.
SEBASTIAN   Do not then walk too open.
ANTONIO
It doth not fit me. Hold, sir, here's my purse.
In the south suburbs at the Elephant   39
Is best to lodge. I will bespeak our diet,
Whiles you beguile the time and feed your knowledge
With viewing of the town. There shall you have me.
SEBASTIAN
Why I your purse?
ANTONIO
Haply your eye shall light upon some toy   44

---

28 *Brownist* early Congregationalist   37 *curst* perversely cross   39 *license
of ink* i.e. unrestrained writing   39–40 *thou'st him* call him 'thou' instead
of the polite 'you'   42 *bed of Ware* a famous bed, over ten feet wide   46
cubiculo little chamber   47 *manikin* puppet   53 *wainropes* wagon ropes
54 *hale* haul   59 *youngest wren* smallest of small birds   60 *spleen* a laughing
fit   61 *gull* dupe   64 *passages of grossness* statements of exaggerated
misinformation   71 *map . . . Indies* (Emerie Molyneux's map, ca. 1599,
which gave fuller details of the East Indies and North America, with
meridian lines, etc.)
III, iii A street in the Illyrian capital   6 *not all* not only, not entirely
8 *jealousy* solicitude   9 *skilless in* without knowledge of   16 *uncurrent*
valueless   17 *worth* wealth; *conscience* right inclination   19 *relics* monuments   28 *answered* atoned for   34 *traffic's* trade's   36 *lapsèd* surprised,
pounced upon   39 *the Elephant* an inn   44 *toy* trifle

45 You have desire to purchase, and your store
46 I think is not for idle markets, sir.

SEBASTIAN
I'll be your purse-bearer, and leave you for
An hour.

ANTONIO To th' Elephant.

SEBASTIAN   I do remember.   *Exeunt.*

*

III, iv   *Enter Olivia and Maria.*

OLIVIA
I have sent after him; he says he'll come.
2 How shall I feast him? What bestow of him?
For youth is bought more oft than begged or borrowed.
4 I speak too loud. Where's Malvolio? He is sad and civil,
And suits well for a servant with my fortunes.
Where is Malvolio?

MARIA He's coming, madam, but in very strange manner.
8 He is sure possessed, madam.

OLIVIA Why, what's the matter? Does he rave?

MARIA No, madam, he does nothing but smile. Your
ladyship were best to have some guard about you if he
come, for sure the man is tainted in 's wits.

OLIVIA
Go call him hither. I am as mad as he,
If sad and merry madness equal be.
Enter Malvolio.
How now, Malvolio?

MALVOLIO Sweet lady, ho, ho!

OLIVIA Smil'st thou? I sent for thee upon a sad occasion.

MALVOLIO Sad, lady? I could be sad. This does make
some obstruction in the blood, this cross-gartering; but
what of that? If it please the eye of one, it is with me as
21 the very true sonnet is, 'Please one, and please all.'

OLIVIA Why, how dost thou, man? What is the matter
with thee?

MALVOLIO Not black in my mind, though yellow in my
legs. It did come to his hands, and commands shall be
26 executed. I think we do know the sweet Roman hand.

OLIVIA Wilt thou go to bed, Malvolio?

MALVOLIO To bed? Ay, sweetheart, and I'll come to
thee.

OLIVIA God comfort thee. Why dost thou smile so, and
kiss thy hand so oft?

MARIA How do you, Malvolio?

MALVOLIO At your request? Yes, nightingales answer
32 daws!

MARIA Why appear you with this ridiculous boldness before my lady?

MALVOLIO 'Be not afraid of greatness.' 'Twas well writ.

OLIVIA What mean'st thou by that, Malvolio?

MALVOLIO 'Some are born great.'

OLIVIA Ha?

MALVOLIO 'Some achieve greatness.'

40 OLIVIA What say'st thou?

MALVOLIO 'And some have greatness thrust upon them.'

OLIVIA Heaven restore thee!

MALVOLIO 'Remember who commended thy yellow
stockings.'

OLIVIA Thy yellow stockings?

MALVOLIO 'And wished to see thee cross-gartered.'

OLIVIA Cross-gartered?

MALVOLIO 'Go to, thou art made, if thou desir'st to be
so.'

OLIVIA Am I made?

MALVOLIO 'If not, let me see thee a servant still.'

OLIVIA Why, this is very midsummer madness.
Enter Servant.

SERVANT Madam, the young gentleman of the Count
Orsino's is returned. I could hardly entreat him back.
He attends your ladyship's pleasure.

OLIVIA I'll come to him. *[Exit Servant.]* Good Maria, let
this fellow be looked to. Where's my cousin Toby? Let
some of my people have a special care of him. I would
not have him miscarry for the half of my dowry.   58
Exit [Olivia; then Maria].

MALVOLIO O ho, do you come near me now? No worse
man than Sir Toby to look to me. This concurs directly
with the letter. She sends him on purpose, that I may
appear stubborn to him; for she incites me to that in the   62
letter. 'Cast thy humble slough,' says she; 'be opposite
with a kinsman, surly with servants; let thy tongue tang
with arguments of state; put thyself into the trick of singularity.' And consequently sets down the manner how:
as, a sad face, a reverend carriage, a slow tongue, in the
habit of some sir of note, and so forth. I have limed her;   68
but it is Jove's doing, and Jove make me thankful. And
when she went away now, 'Let this fellow be looked to.'
'Fellow.' Not 'Malvolio,' nor after my degree, but 'fel-   71
low.' Why, everything adheres together, that no dram of   72
a scruple, no scruple of a scruple, no obstacle, no in-   73
credulous or unsafe circumstance – what can be said?
Nothing that can be can come between me and the full
prospect of my hopes. Well, Jove, not I, is the doer of
this, and he is to be thanked.
Enter [Sir] Toby, Fabian, and Maria.

TOBY Which way is he, in the name of sanctity? If all the
devils of hell be drawn in little, and Legion himself pos-   79
sessed him, yet I'll speak to him.

FABIAN Here he is, here he is! How is't with you, sir?

TOBY How is't with you, man?

MALVOLIO Go off; I discard you. Let me enjoy my
private. Go off.

MARIA Lo, how hollow the fiend speaks within him!
Did not I tell you? Sir Toby, my lady prays you to have
a care of him.

MALVOLIO Aha! does she so?

TOBY Go to, go to; peace, peace; we must deal gently
with him. Let me alone. How do you, Malvolio? How
is't with you? What, man, defy the devil? Consider,
he's an enemy to mankind.

MALVOLIO Do you know what you say?

MARIA La you, an you speak ill of the devil, how he takes
it at heart. Pray God he be not bewitched.

FABIAN Carry his water to th' wise woman.   96

MARIA Marry, and it shall be done to-morrow morning if

---

45 *store* store of money   46 *idle markets* useless purchasings
III, iv The garden of Olivia's house   2 *of* on   4 *sad and civil* serious and
sedate   8 *possessed* mad   21 *sonnet* any short poem   26 *Roman hand*
Italian style of handwriting   32 *daws* small crows   58 *miscarry* come to
harm   62 *stubborn* hard, stiff, rigid   68 *limed* caught   71 *Fellow* companion; *after my degree* according to my position   72 *dram* (1) small bit, (2)
one-eighth fluid ounce   73 *scruple* (1) doubt, (2) one-third of a dram;
incredulous incredible   79 *drawn in little* brought together in a small
space; *Legion* troop of fiends   96 *water* urine for medical analysis; *wise
woman* herb woman

I live. My lady would not lose him for more than I'll say.

MALVOLIO How now, mistress?

MARIA O Lord.

TOBY Prithee hold thy peace. This is not the way. Do you
102   not see you move him? Let me alone with him.

FABIAN No way but gentleness; gently, gently. The fiend
is rough and will not be roughly used.

105 TOBY Why, how now, my bawcock? How dost thou,
106   chuck?

MALVOLIO Sir.

108 TOBY Ay, biddy, come with me. What, man, 'tis not for
109   gravity to play at cherry-pit with Satan. Hang him, foul
110   collier!

MARIA Get him to say his prayers; good Sir Toby, get
him to pray.

MALVOLIO My prayers, minx?

MARIA No, I warrant you, he will not hear of godliness.

115 MALVOLIO Go hang yourselves all! You are idle shallow
things; I am not of your element. You shall know more
hereafter.   *Exit.*

TOBY Is't possible?

FABIAN If this were played upon a stage now, I could
condemn it as an improbable fiction.

121 TOBY His very genius hath taken the infection of the device, man.

123 MARIA Nay, pursue him now, lest the device take air and
taint.

FABIAN Why, we shall make him mad indeed.

MARIA The house will be the quieter.

TOBY Come, we'll have him in a dark room and bound.
My niece is already in the belief that he's mad. We may
129   carry it thus, for our pleasure and his penance, till our
very pastime, tired out of breath, prompt us to have
mercy on him; at which time we will bring the device to
the bar and crown thee for a finder of madmen. But see,
but see.

Enter Sir Andrew.

134 FABIAN More matter for a May morning.

ANDREW Here's the challenge; read it. I warrant there's
vinegar and pepper in't.

137 FABIAN Is't so saucy?

ANDREW Ay, is't, I warrant him. Do but read.

TOBY Give me. [*reads*] 'Youth, whatsoever thou art, thou
art but a scurvy fellow.'

FABIAN Good, and valiant.

142 TOBY [*reads*] 'Wonder not nor admire not in thy mind
why I do call thee so, for I will show thee no reason for't.'

FABIAN A good note that keeps you from the blow of the
law.

TOBY [*reads*] 'Thou com'st to the Lady Olivia, and in my
sight she uses thee kindly. But thou liest in thy throat;
that is not the matter I challenge thee for.'

FABIAN Very brief, and to exceeding good sense – less.

TOBY [*reads*] 'I will waylay thee going home; where if it
be thy chance to kill me' –

FABIAN Good.

TOBY [*reads*] 'Thou kill'st me like a rogue and a villain.'

FABIAN Still you keep o' th' windy side of the law. Good.   154

TOBY [*reads*] 'Fare thee well, and God have mercy upon
one of our souls. He may have mercy upon mine, but my
hope is better, and so look to thyself. Thy friend, as thou
usest him, and thy sworn enemy,

                              'Andrew Aguecheek.'
If this letter move him not, his legs cannot. I'll give't
him.

MARIA You may have very fit occasion for't. He is now in
some commerce with my lady and will by and by depart.

TOBY Go, Sir Andrew. Scout me for him at the corner of
the orchard like a bum-baily. So soon as ever thou seest   164
him, draw; and as thou draw'st, swear horrible; for it
comes to pass oft that a terrible oath, with a swaggering
accent sharply twanged off, gives manhood more appro-   167
bation than ever proof itself would have earned him.   168
Away!

ANDREW Nay, let me alone for swearing.   *Exit.* 170

TOBY Now will not I deliver his letter; for the behavior of
the young gentleman gives him out to be of good capacity and breeding; his employment between his lord and
my niece confirms no less. Therefore this letter, being so
excellently ignorant, will breed no terror in the youth.
He will find it comes from a clodpoll. But, sir, I will deliver his challenge by word of mouth, set upon Aguecheek a notable report of valor, and drive the gentleman
(as I know his youth will aptly receive it) into a most
hideous opinion of his rage, skill, fury, and impetuosity.
This will so fright them both that they will kill one
another by the look, like cockatrices.   184   182

Enter Olivia and Viola.

FABIAN Here he comes with your niece. Give them way
till he take leave, and presently after him.

TOBY I will meditate the while upon some horrid message for a challenge.

                    [*Exeunt Sir Toby, Fabian, and Maria.*]

OLIVIA
I have said too much unto a heart of stone
And laid mine honor too unchary on't.   188
There's something in me that reproves my fault;
But such a headstrong potent fault it is
That it but mocks reproof.

VIOLA
With the same havior that your passion bears   192
Goes on my master's griefs.

OLIVIA
Here, wear this jewel for me; 'tis my picture.   194
Refuse it not; it hath no tongue to vex you.
And I beseech you come again to-morrow.
What shall you ask of me that I'll deny,
That honor, saved, may upon asking give?

VIOLA
Nothing but this: your true love for my master.

OLIVIA
How with mine honor may I give him that
Which I have given to you?

VIOLA   I will acquit you.

OLIVIA
Well, come again to-morrow. Fare thee well.
A fiend like thee might bear my soul to hell.   [*Exit.*] 203

102 *move* rouse 105 *bawcock* fine fellow (French '*beau coq*') 106 *chuck*
chick 108 *biddy* chicken 109 *gravity* dignity; *cherry-pit* a child's game
110 *collier* coal peddler (Satan) 115 *idle* empty, trifling 121 *genius*
nature 123–4 *take air and taint* be exposed and thus contaminated 129
carry it carry the trick on 134 *matter . . . morning* material for a May-day
comedy 137 *saucy* (1) spicy, (2) impudent, sharp 142 *admire* be amazed
154 *windy* windward, safe 164 *bum-baily* an agent employed in making
arrests 167 *manhood more approbation* more reputation for courage
168 *proof* testing 170 *let . . . swearing* leave swearing to me 182 *cockatrices*
basilisks, reptiles able to kill with a glance 188 *unchary on't* carelessly on it
(the heart of stone) 192 *havior* behavior 194 *jewel* any ornament or
trinket; here perhaps 'locket' 203 *like thee* in your likeness

Enter [Sir] Toby and Fabian.

TOBY Gentleman, God save thee.

VIOLA And you, sir.

TOBY That defense thou hast, betake thee to't. Of what nature the wrongs are thou hast done him, I know not;
208 but thy intercepter, full of despite, bloody as the hunter,
209 attends thee at the orchard end. Dismount thy tuck, be
210 yare in thy preparation, for thy assailant is quick, skillful, and deadly.

VIOLA You mistake, sir. I am sure no man hath any quarrel to me. My remembrance is very free and clear from any image of offense done to any man.

TOBY You'll find it otherwise, I assure you. Therefore, if you hold your life at any price, betake you to your guard; for your opposite hath in him what youth, strength, skill, and wrath can furnish man withal.

VIOLA I pray you, sir, what is he?

220 TOBY He is knight, dubbed with unhatched rapier and on carpet consideration, but he is a devil in private brawl. Souls and bodies hath he divorced three; and his incensement at this moment is so implacable that satisfaction can be none but by pangs of death and sepulchre.
225 'Hob, nob' is his word; 'give't or take't.'

VIOLA I will return again into the house and desire some
227 conduct of the lady. I am no fighter. I have heard of some kind of men that put quarrels purposely on others
229 to taste their valor. Belike this is a man of that quirk.

TOBY Sir, no. His indignation derives itself out of a very
231 competent injury; therefore get you on and give him his desire. Back you shall not to the house, unless you undertake that with me which with as much safety you might answer him. Therefore on, or strip your sword stark
235 naked; for meddle you must, that's certain, or forswear to wear iron about you.

VIOLA This is as uncivil as strange. I beseech you do me this courteous office, as to know of the knight what my offense to him is. It is something of my negligence, nothing of my purpose.

TOBY I will do so. Signior Fabian, stay you by this gentleman till my return. *Exit.*

VIOLA Pray you, sir, do you know of this matter?

FABIAN I know the knight is incensed against you, even
245 to a mortal arbitrement; but nothing of the circumstance more.

VIOLA I beseech you, what manner of man is he?

FABIAN Nothing of that wonderful promise, to read him by his form, as you are like to find him in the proof of his valor. He is indeed, sir, the most skillful, bloody, and fatal opposite that you could possibly have found in any part of Illyria. Will you walk towards him? I will make your peace with him if I can.

VIOLA I shall be much bound to you for't. I am one that had rather go with sir priest than sir knight. I care not who knows so much of my mettle. *Exeunt.*

Enter [Sir] Toby and [Sir] Andrew.

TOBY Why, man, he's a very devil; I have not seen such a
258 firago. I had a pass with him, rapier, scabbard, and all,
259 and he gives me the stuck-in with such a mortal motion
260 that it is inevitable; and on the answer he pays you as surely as your feet hits the ground they step on. They say he has been fencer to the Sophy.

ANDREW Pox on't, I'll not meddle with him.

TOBY Ay, but he will not now be pacified. Fabian can scarce hold him yonder.

ANDREW Plague on't, an I thought he had been valiant, and so cunning in fence. I'd have seen him damned ere I'd have challenged him. Let him let the matter slip, and I'll give him my horse, grey Capilet.

TOBY I'll make the motion. Stand here; make a good 270 show on't. This shall end without the perdition of souls. 271 *[aside]* Marry, I'll ride your horse as well as I ride you.

Enter Fabian and Viola.

I have his horse to take up the quarrel. I have persuaded 273 him the youth's a devil.

FABIAN He is as horribly conceited of him, and pants and 275 looks pale, as if a bear were at his heels.

TOBY There's no remedy, sir; he will fight with you for's oath sake. Marry, he hath better bethought him of his quarrel, and he finds that now scarce to be worth talking of. Therefore draw for the supportance of his vow. He protests he will not hurt you.

VIOLA *[aside]* Pray God defend me! A little thing would make me tell them how much I lack of a man.

FABIAN Give ground if you see him furious.

TOBY Come, Sir Andrew, there's no remedy. The gentleman will for his honor's sake have one bout with you; he cannot by the duello avoid it; but he has promised me, 287 as he is a gentleman and a soldier, he will not hurt you. Come on, to't.

ANDREW Pray God he keep his oath!

[Draws.]

Enter Antonio.

VIOLA

I do assure you 'tis against my will.

[Draws.]

ANTONIO

Put up your sword. If this young gentleman

Have done offense, I take the fault on me;

If you offend him, I for him defy you.

TOBY You, sir? Why, what are you?

ANTONIO *[draws]*

One, sir, that for his love dares yet do more

Than you have heard him brag to you he will.

TOBY Nay, if you be an undertaker, I am for you. 298

[Draws.]

Enter Officers.

FABIAN O good Sir Toby, hold. Here come the officers.

TOBY *[to Antonio]* I'll be with you anon.

VIOLA *[to Sir Andrew]* Pray, sir, put your sword up, if you please.

ANDREW Marry, will I, sir; and for that I promised you, I'll be as good as my word. He will bear you easily, and reins well.

1. OFFICER This is the man; do thy office.

2. OFFICER

Antonio, I arrest thee at the suit

Of Count Orsino.

ANTONIO   You do mistake me, sir.

208 *despite* defiance   209 *Dismount thy tuck* take out your rapier   210 *yare* quick   220 *unhatched* unhacked   220–21 *on carpet consideration* through court favor   225 *Hob, nob* have or have not   227 *conduct* protective escort   229 *taste* test; *quirk* peculiarity   231 *competent* sufficient   235 *meddle* engage (in the fight)   235–36 *forswear . . . iron* repudiate on oath (your right) to wear a sword   245 *mortal arbitrement* deadly settlement   258 *firago* virago; *pass* bout   259 *stuck-in* thrust, lunge; *motion* action   260 *answer* return   270 *motion* offer   271 *the perdition of souls* i.e. killing   273 *take up* settle   275 *He . . . him* he (Cesario) has just as frightening a conception of him (Sir Andrew)   287 *duello* duelling code   298 *undertaker* one who takes up a challenge

1. OFFICER

309 No, sir, no jot. I know your favor well,
Though now you have no sea-cap on your head.
Take him away. He knows I know him well.

ANTONIO

I must obey. *[to Viola]* This comes with seeking you.
But there's no remedy; I shall answer it.
What will you do, now my necessity
Makes me to ask you for my purse? It grieves me
Much more for what I cannot do for you
Than what befalls myself. You stand amazed,
But be of comfort.

2. OFFICER Come, sir, away.

ANTONIO

I must entreat of you some of that money.

VIOLA

What money, sir?
For the fair kindness you have showed me here,
And part being prompted by your present trouble,
Out of my lean and low ability
I'll lend you something. My having is not much.
326 I'll make division of my present with you.
327 Hold, there's half my coffer.

ANTONIO   Will you deny me now?
Is't possible that my deserts to you
Can lack persuasion? Do not tempt my misery,
Lest that it make me so unsound a man
As to upbraid you with those kindnesses
That I have done for you.

VIOLA   I know of none,
Nor know I you by voice or any feature.
I hate ingratitude more in a man
Than lying, vainness, babbling, drunkenness,
Or any taint of vice whose strong corruption
Inhabits our frail blood.

ANTONIO   O heavens themselves!

2. OFFICER

Come, sir, I pray you go.

ANTONIO

Let me speak a little. This youth that you see here
I snatched one half out of the jaws of death;
Relieved him with such sanctity of love,
And to his image, which methought did promise
343 Most venerable worth, did I devotion.

1. OFFICER

What's that to us? The time goes by. Away.

ANTONIO

But, O, how vile an idol proves this god!
Thou hast, Sebastian, done good feature shame.
In nature there's no blemish but the mind;
348 None can be called deformed but the unkind.
349 Virtue is beauty; but the beauteous evil
350 Are empty trunks, o'erflourished by the devil.

1. OFFICER

The man grows mad; away with him! Come, come, sir.

ANTONIO Lead me on.   *Exit [with Officers].*

VIOLA

Methinks his words do from such passion fly
That he believes himself; so do not I.
Prove true, imagination, O, prove true,
That I, dear brother, be now ta'en for you!

TOBY Come hither, knight; come hither, Fabian. We'll
whisper o'er a couplet or two of most sage saws.   358

VIOLA

He named Sebastian. I my brother know
Yet living in my glass. Even such and so   360
In favor was my brother, and he went
Still in this fashion, color, ornament,
For him I imitate. O, if it prove,
Tempests are kind, and salt waves fresh in love! *[Exit.]*

TOBY A very dishonest paltry boy, and more a coward 365
than a hare. His dishonesty appears in leaving his friend
here in necessity and denying him; and for his coward-
ship, ask Fabian.

FABIAN A coward, a most devout coward; religious in it. 369

ANDREW 'Slid, I'll after him again and beat him.

TOBY Do; cuff him soundly, but never draw thy sword.

ANDREW An I do not –   *[Exit.]*

FABIAN Come, let's see the event.   373

TOBY I dare lay any money 'twill be nothing yet. *Exeunt.* 374

*

Enter Sebastian and Clown.   IV, i

CLOWN Will you make me believe that I am not sent for
you?

SEBASTIAN Go to, go to, thou art a foolish fellow. Let me
be clear of thee.

CLOWN Well held out, i' faith! No, I do not know you; 5
nor I am not sent to you by my lady, to bid you come
speak with her; nor your name is not Master Cesario;
nor this is not my nose neither. Nothing that is so is so.

SEBASTIAN I prithee vent thy folly somewhere else.
Thou know'st not me.

CLOWN Vent my folly! He has heard that word of some
great man, and now applies it to a fool. Vent my folly!
I am afraid this great lubber, the world, will prove a 13
cockney. I prithee now, ungird thy strangeness, and tell 14
me what I shall vent to my lady. Shall I vent to her that
thou art coming?

SEBASTIAN I prithee, foolish Greek, depart from me. 17
There's money for thee. If you tarry longer, I shall give
worse payment.

CLOWN By my troth, thou hast an open hand. These wise
men that give fools money get themselves a good report
– after fourteen years' purchase.   22

Enter [Sir] Andrew, [Sir] Toby, and Fabian.

ANDREW Now, sir, have I met you again? There's for
you!
    [Strikes Sebastian.]

SEBASTIAN Why, there's for thee, and there, and there!
    [Strikes Sir Andrew.]
Are all the people mad?

TOBY Hold, sir, or I'll throw your dagger o'er the house.
    [Seizes Sebastian.]

CLOWN This will I tell my lady straight. I would not be in
some of your coats for two-pence.   *Exit.*

TOBY Come on, sir; hold.

---

309 *favor* face   **326** *my present* what I have now   **327** *coffer* money   **343**
venerable worthy of veneration   **348** *unkind* unnatural   **349** *beauteous*
fair-seeming   **350** *trunks* chests; *o'erflourished* ornamented   **358** *sage*
saws wise sayings   **360** *Yet . . . glass* i.e. whenever I look in the mirror
365 *dishonest* dishonorable   **369** *religious* confirmed   **373** *event* result
374 *yet* nevertheless
IV, i Before Olivia's house   **5** *held out* kept up   **13** *lubber* lout   **14** *cockney*
affected person; *ungird thy strangeness* abandon your strange manner   **17**
Greek merry companion   **22** *after . . . purchase* i.e. at a high price

ANDREW Nay, let him alone. I'll go another way to work
31 with him. I'll have an action of battery against him, if
there be any law in Illyria. Though I struck him first,
yet it's no matter for that.

SEBASTIAN Let go thy hand.

TOBY Come, sir, I will not let you go. Come, my young
36 soldier, put up your iron. You are well fleshed. Come on.

SEBASTIAN
I will be free from thee.
    [Frees himself.]   What wouldst thou now?
If thou dar'st tempt me further, draw thy sword.
    [Draws.]

TOBY What, what? Nay then, I must have an ounce or
40 two of this malapert blood from you.
    [Draws.]
    Enter Olivia.

OLIVIA
Hold, Toby! On thy life I charge thee hold!

TOBY Madam.

OLIVIA
Will it be ever thus? Ungracious wretch,
Fit for the mountains and the barbarous caves,
Where manners ne'er were preached! Out of my sight!
Be not offended, dear Cesario.
47 Rudesby, be gone.
    [Exeunt Sir Toby, Sir Andrew, and Fabian.]
    I prithee, gentle friend,
Let thy fair wisdom, not thy passion, sway
49 In this uncivil and unjust extent
Against thy peace. Go with me to my house,
And hear thou there how many fruitless pranks
52 This ruffian hath botched up, that thou thereby
Mayst smile at this. Thou shalt not choose but go.
54 Do not deny. Beshrew his soul for me.
55 He started one poor heart of mine, in thee.

SEBASTIAN
56 What relish is in this? How runs the stream?
Or I am mad, or else this is a dream.
58 Let fancy still my sense in Lethe steep;
If it be thus to dream, still let me sleep!

OLIVIA
Nay, come, I prithee. Would thou'dst be ruled by me!

SEBASTIAN
Madam, I will.

OLIVIA   O, say so, and so be.   Exeunt.

         *

IV, ii   Enter Maria and Clown.

MARIA Nay, I prithee put on this gown and this beard;
2 make him believe thou art Sir Topas the curate; do it
quickly. I'll call Sir Toby the whilst.   [Exit.]

4 CLOWN Well, I'll put it on, and I will dissemble myself
in't, and I would I were the first that ever dissembled in
6 such a gown. I am not tall enough to become the function
well, nor lean enough to be thought a good student; but
8 to be said an honest man and a good housekeeper goes as
fairly as to say a careful man and a great scholar. The
10 competitors enter.
    Enter [Sir] Toby [and Maria].

TOBY Jove bless thee, Master Parson.

12 CLOWN Bonos dies, Sir Toby; for, as the old hermit of
Prague, that never saw pen and ink, very wittily said to a
14 niece of King Gorboduc, 'That that is is'; so, I, being

Master Parson, am Master Parson; for what is 'that'
but that, and 'is' but is?

TOBY To him, Sir Topas.

CLOWN What ho, I say. Peace in this prison!

TOBY The knave counterfeits well; a good knave.   19
    Malvolio within.

MALVOLIO Who calls there?

CLOWN Sir Topas the curate, who comes to visit Malvolio the lunatic.

MALVOLIO Sir Topas, Sir Topas, good Sir Topas, go to
my lady.

CLOWN Out, hyperbolical fiend! How vexest thou this 25
man! Talkest thou nothing but of ladies?

TOBY Well said, Master Parson.

MALVOLIO Sir Topas, never was man thus wronged.
Good Sir Topas, do not think I am mad. They have
laid me here in hideous darkness.

CLOWN Fie, thou dishonest Satan. I call thee by the 31
most modest terms, for I am one of those gentle ones
that will use the devil himself with courtesy. Say'st
thou that house is dark?   34

MALVOLIO As hell, Sir Topas.

CLOWN Why, it hath bay windows transparent as barri- 36
cadoes, and the clerestories toward the south north are 37
as lustrous as ebony; and yet complainest thou of
obstruction?

MALVOLIO I am not mad, Sir Topas. I say to you this
house is dark.

CLOWN Madman, thou errest. I say there is no darkness
but ignorance, in which thou art more puzzled than the
Egyptians in their fog.   44

MALVOLIO I say this house is as dark as ignorance,
though ignorance were as dark as hell; and I say there
was never man thus abused. I am no more mad than you
are. Make the trial of it in any constant question.   48

CLOWN What is the opinion of Pythagoras concerning 49
wild fowl?

MALVOLIO That the soul of our grandam might happily 51
inhabit a bird.

CLOWN What think'st thou of his opinion?

MALVOLIO I think nobly of the soul and no way approve
his opinion.

CLOWN Fare thee well. Remain thou still in darkness.
Thou shalt hold th' opinion of Pythagoras ere I will
allow of thy wits, and fear to kill a woodcock, lest thou 57
dispossess the soul of thy grandam. Fare thee well.

MALVOLIO Sir Topas, Sir Topas!

TOBY My most exquisite Sir Topas!

31 action of battery suit at law for beating (me)   36 well fleshed made
fierce by a taste of blood   40 malapert impudent   47 Rudesby unmannerly
fellow   49 uncivil uncivilized; extent probably 'display'   52 botched up
contrived   54 Beshrew curse   55 started startled; heart (with a pun on
'hart')   56 relish taste   58 Lethe the river of forgetfulness in the underworld
IV, ii Within Olivia's house   2 Sir (common title of address for the clergy);
Topas (comic knight in Chaucer; the topaz stone was thought to cure
insanity)   4 dissemble disguise   6 function function of a cleric   8 good
housekeeper householder, neighbor   10 competitors associates   12 Bonos
dies good day   12–13 the old hermit of Prague (probably the clown's invention)   14 King Gorboduc a legendary British king who appeared in an early
English tragedy   19 knave boy, fellow   25 hyperbolical enormous   31
dishonest dishonorable   34 house darkened room   36 barricadoes barri-
cades   37 clerestories upper windows   44 fog (Moses brought a three-day
fog on the Egyptians)   48 constant question consistent discussion   49
Pythagoras (who originated the doctrine of transmigration of souls)
51 happily haply, by chance   57 allow of acknowledge

62 CLOWN Nay, I am for all waters.

MARIA Thou mightest have done this without thy beard and gown. He sees thee not.

TOBY To him in thine own voice, and bring me word how thou find'st him. *[to Maria]* I would we were well rid of this knavery. If he may be conveniently delivered, I would he were; for I am now so far in offense with my niece that I cannot pursue with any safety this sport to
70 the upshot. *[to the Clown]* Come by and by to my chamber.   *Exit [with Maria]*.

71 CLOWN *[sings]*   'Hey, Robin, jolly Robin,
                 Tell me how thy lady does.'

MALVOLIO Fool.

74 CLOWN 'My lady is unkind, perdie!'

MALVOLIO Fool.

CLOWN 'Alas, why is she so?'

MALVOLIO Fool, I say.

CLOWN 'She loves another.' Who calls, ha?

MALVOLIO Good fool, as ever thou wilt deserve well at my hand, help me to a candle, and pen, ink, and paper. As I am a gentleman, I will live to be thankful to thee for't.

CLOWN Master Malvolio?

MALVOLIO Ay, good fool.

84 CLOWN Alas, sir, how fell you besides your five wits?

MALVOLIO Fool, there was never man so notoriously abused. I am as well in my wits, fool, as thou art.

CLOWN But as well? Then you are mad indeed, if you be no better in your wits than a fool.

89 MALVOLIO They have here propertied me; keep me in darkness, send ministers to me, asses, and do all they
91 can to face me out of my wits.

92 CLOWN Advise you what you say. The minister is here. – Malvolio, Malvolio, thy wits the heavens restore. Endeavor thyself to sleep and leave thy vain bibble babble.

MALVOLIO Sir Topas.

CLOWN Maintain no words with him, good fellow. – Who, I, sir? Not I, sir. God b' wi' you, good Sir Topas. – Marry, amen. – I will, sir, I will.

MALVOLIO Fool, fool, fool, I say!

100 CLOWN Alas, sir, be patient. What say you, sir? I am shent for speaking to you.

MALVOLIO Good fool, help me to some light and some paper. I tell thee, I am as well in my wits as any man in Illyria.

105 CLOWN Well-a-day that you were, sir.

MALVOLIO By this hand, I am. Good fool, some ink, paper, and light; and convey what I will set down to my lady. It shall advantage thee more than ever the bearing of letter did.

CLOWN I will help you to't. But tell me true, are you not mad indeed? or do you but counterfeit?

MALVOLIO Believe me, I am not. I tell thee true.

CLOWN Nay, I'll ne'er believe a madman till I see his brains. I will fetch you light and paper and ink.

MALVOLIO Fool, I'll requite it in the highest degree. I prithee be gone.

CLOWN *[sings]*   I am gone, sir,
                And anon, sir,
              I'll be with you again,
                 In a trice,
                 Like to the old Vice,   121
              Your need to sustain.
           Who with dagger of lath,
           In his rage and his wrath,
              Cries 'Ah ha' to the devil.
           Like a mad lad,
           'Pare thy nails, dad.'
              Adieu, goodman devil.   *Exit.*

*

Enter Sebastian.   IV, iii

SEBASTIAN
   This is the air; that is the glorious sun;
   This pearl she gave me, I do feel't and see't;
   And though 'tis wonder that enwraps me thus,
   Yet 'tis not madness. Where's Antonio then?
   I could not find him at the Elephant;
   Yet there he was, and there I found this credit,   6
   That he did range the town to seek me out.
   His counsel now might do me golden service;
   For though my soul disputes well with my sense
   That this may be some error, but no madness,
   Yet doth this accident and flood of fortune
   So far exceed all instance, all discourse,   12
   That I am ready to distrust mine eyes
   And wrangle with my reason that persuades me   14
   To any other trust but that I am mad,
   Or else the lady's mad. Yet, if 'twere so,
   She could not sway her house, command her followers,   17
   Take and give back affairs and their dispatch   18
   With such a smooth, discreet, and stable bearing
   As I perceive she does. There's something in't
   That is deceivable. But here the lady comes.   21
      Enter Olivia and Priest.

OLIVIA
   Blame not this haste of mine. If you mean well,
   Now go with me and with this holy man
   Into the chantry by. There, before him,
   And underneath that consecrated roof,   24
   Plight me the full assurance of your faith,
   That my most jealous and too doubtful soul
   May live at peace. He shall conceal it   27
   Whiles you are willing it shall come to note,   29
   What time we will our celebration keep
   According to my birth. What do you say?

SEBASTIAN
   I'll follow this good man and go with you
   And having sworn truth, ever will be true.

OLIVIA
   Then lead the way, good father, and heavens so shine
   That they may fairly note this act of mine.   *Exeunt.*

---

62 *for all waters* i.e. good for any trade   **70** *upshot* outcome   **71** *Hey, Robin* . . . (from an old song, sometimes attributed to Sir Thomas Wyatt) **74** *perdie* certainly   **84** *besides your five wits* out of your mind   **89** *propertied me* made me a property, a mere thing   **91** *face me* brazen me   **92** *Advise you* be careful   **100** *shent* reproved   **105** *Well-a-day* woe, alas   **121** *Vice* comic character of the morality plays
IV, iii The house of Olivia   **6** *was* had been; *credit* belief   **12** *instance* example; *discourse* logic   **14** *wrangle* dispute   **17** *sway* rule   **18** *dispatch* management   **21** *deceivable* deceptive   **24** *chantry by* chapel near by   **27** *jealous* anxious   **29** *Whiles* until

*

V, i   *Enter Clown and Fabian.*

FABIAN Now as thou lov'st me, let me see his letter.

CLOWN Good Master Fabian, grant me another request.

FABIAN Anything.

CLOWN Do not desire to see this letter.

FABIAN This is to give a dog, and in recompense desire
my dog again.

Enter Duke, Viola, Curio, and Lords.

7 DUKE Belong you to the Lady Olivia, friends?

CLOWN Ay, sir, we are some of her trappings.

DUKE I know thee well. How dost thou, my good fellow?

CLOWN Truly, sir, the better for my foes, and the worse
for my friends.

DUKE Just the contrary: the better for thy friends.

CLOWN No, sir, the worse.

DUKE How can that be?

CLOWN Marry, sir, they praise me and make an ass of me.
Now my foes tell me plainly I am an ass; so that by my
foes, sir, I profit in the knowledge of myself, and by my
18   friends I am abused; so that, conclusions to be as kisses,
if your four negatives make your two affirmatives, why
then, the worse for my friends, and the better for my
foes.

DUKE Why, this is excellent.

CLOWN By my troth, sir, no, though it please you to be
one of my friends.

DUKE Thou shalt not be the worse for me. There's gold.

25 CLOWN But that it would be double-dealing, sir, I would
you could make it another.

DUKE O, you give me ill counsel.

28 CLOWN Put your grace in your pocket, sir, for this once,
and let your flesh and blood obey it.

DUKE Well, I will be so much a sinner to be a double-
dealer. There's another.

32 CLOWN Primo, secundo, tertio is a good play; and the old
33   saying is 'The third pays for all.' The triplex, sir, is a
34   good tripping measure; or the bells of Saint Bennet, sir,
may put you in mind — one, two, three.

DUKE You can fool no more money out of me at this
37   throw. If you will let your lady know I am here to speak
with her, and bring her along with you, it may awake
my bounty further.

CLOWN Marry, sir, lullaby to your bounty till I come
again, I go, sir; but I would not have you to think that
my desire of having is the sin of covetousness. But, as
you say, sir, let your bounty take a nap; I will awake it
anon.   *Exit.*

Enter Antonio and Officers.

VIOLA
Here comes the man, sir, that did rescue me.

DUKE
That face of his I do remember well;
Yet when I saw it last, it was besmeared
47   As black as Vulcan in the smoke of war.
48   A baubling vessel was he captain of,
49   For shallow draught and bulk unprizable,
50   With which such scathful grapple did he make
51   With the most noble bottom of our fleet
52   That very envy and the tongue of loss
Cried fame and honor on him. What's the matter?

I. OFFICER
Orsino, this is that Antonio
55   That took the Phoenix and her fraught from Candy;
And this is he that did the Tiger board

When your young nephew Titus lost his leg.
Here in the streets, desperate of shame and state,   58
In private brabble did we apprehend him.   59

VIOLA
He did me kindness, sir; drew on my side;
But in conclusion put strange speech upon me.
I know not what 'twas but distraction.   62

DUKE
Notable pirate, thou salt-water thief,
What foolish boldness brought thee to their mercies
Whom thou in terms so bloody and so dear   65
Hast made thine enemies?

ANTONIO   Orsino, noble sir,
Be pleased that I shake off these names you give me.
Antonio never yet was thief or pirate,
Though I confess, on base and ground enough,   69
Orsino's enemy. A witchcraft drew me hither.
That most ingrateful boy there by your side
From the rude sea's enraged and foamy mouth
Did I redeem. A wrack past hope he was.
His life I gave him, and did thereto add
My love without retention or restraint,
All his in dedication. For his sake
Did I expose myself (pure for his love)   77
Into the danger of this adverse town;
Drew to defend him when he was beset;
Where being apprehended, his false cunning
(Not meaning to partake with me in danger)
Taught him to face me out of his acquaintance,   82
And grew a twenty years removèd thing   83
While one would wink; denied me mine own purse,
Which I had recommended to his use   85
Not half an hour before.

VIOLA   How can this be?

DUKE
When came he to this town?

ANTONIO
To-day, my lord; and for three months before,
No int'rim, not a minute's vacancy,
Both day and night did we keep company.

Enter Olivia and Attendants.

DUKE
Here comes the Countess; now heaven walks on earth.
But for thee, fellow: fellow, thy words are madness.
Three months this youth hath tended upon me;
But more of that anon. Take him aside.

OLIVIA
What would my lord, but that he may not have,   95
Wherein Olivia may seem serviceable?
Cesario, you do not keep promise with me.

VIOLA
Madam?

V, i Before Olivia's house 7 *Belong you* i.e. are you in the service of
18 *abused* deceived 25 *double-dealing* (1) double giving, (2) deceit 28
your grace (1) title of address, (2) your generosity 32 *play* (probably a
children's game) 33 *triplex* triple time in music 34 *Saint Bennet* St
Benedict's church 37 *throw* throw of the dice 47 *Vulcan* Roman god of
fire and patron of metal workers 48 *baubling* trifling 49 *unprizable* unworthy of being taken as a prize 50 *scathful* harmful 51 *bottom* ship
52 *very envy* even malice; *loss* the losers 55 *fraught* cargo; *Candy* Candia,
Crete 58 *desperate* reckless 59 *brabble* brawl 62 *distraction* madness
65 *dear* costly 69 *base and ground* solid grounds 77 *pure* purely 82 *face
... acquaintance* pretend not to know me 83 *removèd* estranged 85
recommended entrusted 95 *but that* except what

DUKE
Gracious Olivia –

OLIVIA
What do you say, Cesario ? – Good my lord –

VIOLA
My lord would speak ; my duty hushes me.

OLIVIA
If it be aught to the old tune, my lord,
103   It is as fat and fulsome to mine ear
As howling after music.

DUKE   Still so cruel ?

OLIVIA
Still so constant, lord.

DUKE
What, to perverseness ? You uncivil lady,
To whose ingrate and unauspicious altars
My soul the faithfull'st off'rings have breathed out
That e'er devotion tendered. What shall I do ?

OLIVIA
Even what it please my lord, that shall become him.

DUKE
Why should I not, had I the heart to do it,
112   Like to th' Egyptian thief at point of death,
Kill what I love ? (A savage jealousy
That sometime savors nobly.) But hear me this :
115   Since you to non-regardance cast my faith,
And that I partly know the instrument
117   That screws me from my true place in your favor,
Live you the marble-breasted tyrant still.
119   But this your minion, whom I know you love,
120   And whom, by heaven I swear, I tender dearly,
Him will I tear out of that cruel eye
122   Where he sits crownèd in his master's spite.
Come, boy, with me. My thoughts are ripe in mischief.
I'll sacrifice the lamb that I do love
To spite a raven's heart within a dove.   *[Going.]*

VIOLA
126   And I, most jocund, apt, and willingly,
127   To do you rest a thousand deaths would die. *[Following.]*

OLIVIA
Where goes Cesario ?

VIOLA   After him I love
More than I love these eyes, more than my life,
130   More, by all mores, than e'er I shall love wife.
If I do feign, you witnesses above
Punish my life for tainting of my love !

OLIVIA
Ay me detested ! how am I beguiled !

VIOLA
Who does beguile you ? Who does do you wrong ?

OLIVIA
Hast thou forgot thyself ? Is it so long ?
Call forth the holy father.   *[Exit an Attendant.]*

DUKE *[to Viola]*   Come, away !

---

103 *fat* superfluous ; *fulsome* offensive   112 *th' Egyptian thief* Thyamis in the *Aethiopica* by Heliodorus   115 *non-regardance* neglect   117 *screws* pries   119 *minion* favorite   120 *tender* hold   122 *in . . . spite* despite his master   126 *apt* properly   127 *do you rest* give you peace   130 *all mores* i.e. all conceivable comparisons   141 *propriety* identity   144 *that thou fear'st* i.e. the Duke   152 *close* meeting   159 *a grizzle* grey hair ; *case* sheath, i.e. skin   161 *trip* trickery   165 *little* a little   166 *presently* at once   169 *Has* he has   174 *incardinate* incarnate   176 *Od's lifelings* by God's little life   184 *halting* limping

OLIVIA
Whither, my lord ? Cesario, husband, stay.

DUKE
Husband ?

OLIVIA   Ay, husband. Can he that deny ?

DUKE
Her husband, sirrah ?

VIOLA   No, my lord, not I.

OLIVIA
Alas, it is the baseness of thy fear
That makes thee strangle thy propriety.   141
Fear not, Cesario ; take thy fortunes up ;
Be that thou know'st thou art, and then thou art
As great as that thou fear'st.   144
Enter Priest.
                O, welcome, father !
Father, I charge thee by thy reverence
Here to unfold – though lately we intended
To keep in darkness what occasion now
Reveals before 'tis ripe – what thou dost know
Hath newly passed between this youth and me.

PRIEST
A contract of eternal bond of love,
Confirmed by mutual joinder of your hands,
Attested by the holy close of lips,   152
Strength'ned by interchangement of your rings ;
And all the ceremony of this compact
Sealed in my function, by my testimony ;
Since when, my watch hath told me, toward my grave
I have travelled but two hours.

DUKE
O thou dissembling cub, what wilt thou be
When time hath sowed a grizzle on thy case ?   159
Or will not else thy craft so quickly grow
That thine own trip shall be thine overthrow ?   161
Farewell, and take her ; but direct thy feet
Where thou and I, henceforth, may never meet.

VIOLA
My lord, I do protest.

OLIVIA   O, do not swear.
Hold little faith, though thou hast too much fear.   165
Enter Sir Andrew.

ANDREW For the love of God, a surgeon ! Send one pres- 166
ently to Sir Toby.

OLIVIA What's the matter ?

ANDREW Has broke my head across, and has given Sir 169
Toby a bloody coxcomb too. For the love of God,
your help ! I had rather than forty pounds I were at
home.

OLIVIA Who has done this, Sir Andrew ?

ANDREW The Count's gentleman, one Cesario. We took
him for a coward, but he's the very devil incardinate. 174

DUKE My gentleman Cesario ?

ANDREW Od's lifelings, here he is ! You broke my head 176
for nothing ; and that that I did, I was set on to do't by
Sir Toby.

VIOLA
Why do you speak to me ? I never hurt you.
You drew your sword upon me without cause,
But I bespake you fair and hurt you not.
Enter [Sir] Toby and Clown.

ANDREW If a bloody coxcomb be a hurt, you have hurt
me. I think you set nothing by a bloody coxcomb. Here
comes Sir Toby halting ; you shall hear more. But if he 184

185 had not been in drink, he would have tickled you othergates than he did.

DUKE How now, gentleman? How is't with you?

TOBY That's all one! Has hurt me, and there's th' end
on't. Sot, didst see Dick Surgeon, sot?

CLOWN O, he's drunk, Sir Toby, an hour agone. His eyes
191 were set at eight i' th' morning.

192 TOBY Then he's a rogue and a passy measures pavin. I
hate a drunken rogue.

OLIVIA Away with him! Who hath made this havoc with
them?

ANDREW I'll help you, Sir Toby, because we'll be dressed
together.

TOBY Will you help? An ass-head and a coxcomb and a
knave, a thin-faced knave, a gull?

OLIVIA Get him to bed, and let his hurt be looked to.
    [Exeunt Clown, Fabian, Sir Toby, and Sir Andrew.]
    Enter Sebastian.

SEBASTIAN
I am sorry, madam, I have hurt your kinsman;
But had it been the brother of my blood,
203 I must have done no less with wit and safety.
204 You throw a strange regard upon me, and by that
I do perceive it hath offended you.
Pardon me, sweet one, even for the vows
We made each other but so late ago.

DUKE
208 One face, one voice, one habit, and two persons –
209 A natural perspective that is and is not.

SEBASTIAN
Antonio, O my dear Antonio,
How have the hours racked and tortured me
Since I have lost thee!

ANTONIO
Sebastian are you?

SEBASTIAN   Fear'st thou that, Antonio?

ANTONIO
How have you made division of yourself?
An apple cleft in two is not more twin
Than these two creatures. Which is Sebastian?

OLIVIA
Most wonderful.

SEBASTIAN
Do I stand there? I never had a brother;
Nor can there be that deity in my nature
Of here and everywhere. I had a sister,
Whom the blind waves and surges have devoured.
Of charity, what kin are you to me?
What countryman? What name? What parentage?

VIOLA
Of Messaline; Sebastian was my father;
Such a Sebastian was my brother too;
226 So went he suited to his watery tomb.
If spirits can assume both form and suit,
You come to fright us.

SEBASTIAN   A spirit I am indeed,
229 But am in that dimension grossly clad
230 Which from the womb I did participate.
231 Were you a woman, as the rest goes even,
I should my tears let fall upon your cheek
And say, 'Thrice welcome, drownèd Viola!'

VIOLA
My father had a mole upon his brow.

SEBASTIAN
And so had mine.

VIOLA
And died that day when Viola from her birth
Had numb'red thirteen years.

SEBASTIAN
O, that record is lively in my soul!   238
He finishèd indeed his mortal act
That day that made my sister thirteen years.

VIOLA
If nothing lets to make us happy both   241
But this my masculine usurped attire,
Do not embrace me till each circumstance
Of place, time, fortune do cohere and jump   244
That I am Viola; which to confirm,
I'll bring you to a captain in this town,
Where lie my maiden weeds; by whose gentle help   247
I was preserved to serve this noble Count.
All the occurrence of my fortune since
Hath been between this lady and this lord.

SEBASTIAN *[to Olivia]*
So comes it, lady, you have been mistook.
But nature to her bias drew in that.   252
You would have been contracted to a maid;
Nor are you therein, by my life, deceived:
You are betrothed both to a maid and man.

DUKE
Be not amazed; right noble is his blood.
If this be so, as yet the glass seems true,   257
I shall have share in this most happy wrack.
    [To Viola]
Boy, thou hast said to me a thousand times
Thou never shouldst love woman like to me.

VIOLA
And all those sayings will I over swear,   261
And all those swearings keep as true in soul
As doth that orbèd continent the fire   263
That severs day from night.

DUKE   Give me thy hand,
And let me see thee in thy woman's weeds.

VIOLA
The captain that did bring me first on shore
Hath my maid's garments. He upon some action   267
Is now in durance, at Malvolio's suit,
A gentleman, and follower of my lady's.

OLIVIA
He shall enlarge him. Fetch Malvolio hither.   270
And yet alas, now I remember me,
They say, poor gentleman, he's much distract.
    Enter Clown with a letter, and Fabian.
A most extracting frenzy of mine own   273
From my remembrance clearly banished his.
How does he, sirrah?

185 *othergates* otherwise   191 *set* fixed or gone down, i.e. closed   192
passy measures pavin an eight-bar double-slow dance   203 *wit and safety*
intelligent regard for my safety   204 *strange regard* estranged look   208
habit dress   209 *perspective* glass producing an optical illusion   226 *suited*
dressed   229 *dimension* form; *grossly* in the flesh   230 *participate* inherit
231 *rest goes even* other circumstances allow   238 *record* memory   241
lets hinders   244 *jump* agree completely   247 *weeds* clothes   252 *to her
bias drew* i.e. drew you into a natural course   257 *glass* perspective glass
261 *over swear* swear over again   263 *orbèd continent* sphere of the sun
267 *action* legal charge   270 *enlarge* free   273 *extracting* distracting

276 **CLOWN** Truly, madam, he holds Belzebub at the stave's
end as well as a man in his case may do. Has here writ a
letter to you ; I should have given't you to-day morning.
279 But as a madman's epistles are no gospels, so it skills not
much when they are delivered.
OLIVIA Open't and read it.
282 **CLOWN** Look then to be well edified, when the fool delivers the madman. *[Reads in a loud voice]* 'By the Lord,
madam' –
OLIVIA How now ? Art thou mad ?
CLOWN No, madam, I do but read madness. An your lady-
287 ship will have it as it ought to be, you must allow vox.
OLIVIA Prithee read i' thy right wits.
CLOWN So I do, madonna ; but to read his right wits is to
290 read thus. Therefore perpend, my princess, and give ear.
OLIVIA *[to Fabian]* Read it you, sirrah.
FABIAN *(reads)* 'By the Lord, madam, you wrong me,
and the world shall know it. Though you have put me
into darkness, and given your drunken cousin rule over
me, yet have I the benefit of my senses as well as your
ladyship. I have your own letter that induced me to the
semblance I put on ; with the which I doubt not but to
do myself much right, or you much shame. Think of me
as you please. I leave my duty a little unthought of,
and speak out of my injury.
'The madly used Malvolio.'
OLIVIA Did he write this ?
CLOWN Ay, madam.
DUKE This savors not much of distraction.
OLIVIA
See him delivered, Fabian ; bring him hither.
[Exit Fabian.]
My lord, so please you, these things further thought on,
To think me as well a sister as a wife,
One day shall crown th' alliance on't, so please you,
309 Here at my house and at my proper cost.
DUKE
310 Madam, I am most apt t' embrace your offer.
[To Viola]
311 Your master quits you ; and for your service done him,
So much against the mettle of your sex,
So far beneath your soft and tender breeding,
And since you called me master for so long,
Here is my hand ; you shall from this time be
Your master's mistress.
OLIVIA   A sister ; you are she.
Enter [Fabian, with] Malvolio.
DUKE
Is this the madman ?
OLIVIA   Ay, my lord; this same.
How now, Malvolio ?
MALVOLIO   Madam, you have done me wrong,
Notorious wrong.
OLIVIA   Have I, Malvolio ? No.

MALVOLIO
Lady, you have. Pray you peruse that letter.
You must not now deny it is your hand.
Write from it if you can, in hand or phrase,   322
Or say 'tis not your seal, not your invention.   323
You can say none of this. Well, grant it then,
And tell me, in the modesty of honor,   325
Why you have given me such clear lights of favor,
Bade me come smiling and cross-gartered to you,
To put on yellow stockings, and to frown
Upon Sir Toby and the lighter people ;   329
And, acting this in an obedient hope,
Why have you suffered me to be imprisoned,
Kept in a dark house, visited by the priest,
And made the most notorious geck and gull   333
That e'er invention played on ? Tell me why.
OLIVIA
Alas, Malvolio, this is not my writing,
Though I confess much like the character ;
But, out of question, 'tis Maria's hand.
And now I do bethink me, it was she
First told me thou wast mad. Thou cam'st in smiling,
And in such forms which here were presupposed   340
Upon thee in the letter. Prithee be content.
This practice hath most shrewdly passed upon thee ;   342
But when we know the grounds and authors of it,
Thou shalt be both the plaintiff and the judge
Of thine own cause.
FABIAN   Good madam, hear me speak,
And let no quarrel, nor no brawl to come,
Taint the condition of this present hour,
Which I have wond'red at. In hope it shall not,
Most freely I confess myself and Toby
Set this device against Malvolio here,
Upon some stubborn and uncourteous parts   351
We had conceived against him. Maria writ
The letter, at Sir Toby's great importance,   353
In recompense whereof he hath married her.
How with a sportful malice it was followed
May rather pluck on laughter than revenge,
If that the injuries be justly weighed
That have on both sides passed.
OLIVIA
Alas, poor fool, how have they baffled thee !   359
CLOWN Why, 'some are born great, some achieve great-
ness, and some have greatness thrown upon them.' I
was one, sir, in this interlude, one Sir Topas, sir ; but   362
that's all one. 'By the Lord, fool, I am not mad !' But do
you remember, 'Madam, why laugh you at such a
barren rascal ? An you smile not, he's gagged' ? And
thus the whirligig of time brings in his revenges.
MALVOLIO I'll be revenged on the whole pack of you !
[Exit.]
OLIVIA
He hath been most notoriously abused.
DUKE
Pursue him and entreat him to a peace.
He hath not told us of the captain yet.
When that is known, and golden time convents,   371
A solemn combination shall be made
Of our dear souls. Meantime, sweet sister,
We will not part from hence. Cesario, come –
For so you shall be while you are a man,

276–77 *holds . . . end* i.e. holds the devil off   279 *skills* matters   282
delivers speaks the words of   287 *vox* voice-volume   290 *perpend* consider
309 *proper* own   310 *apt* ready   311 *quits* releases   322 *from it* differently
323 *invention* composition   325 *in . . . honor* with honorable propriety
329 *lighter* lesser   333 *geck and gull* ludicrous dupe   340–41 *presupposed
Upon thee* put upon you beforehand   342 *shrewdly passed* maliciously been
put   351 *Upon* on account of   353 *importance* importunity   359 *baffled
thee* disgraced you publicly   362 *interlude* an early form of dramatic
entertainment   371 *convents* is convenient

But when in other habits you are seen,
377   Orsino's mistress and his fancy's queen.
                              Exeunt [all but the Clown].

                    Clown sings.

When that I was and a little tiny boy,
    With hey, ho, the wind and the rain,
A foolish thing was but a toy,
    For the rain it raineth every day.

But when I came to man's estate,
    With hey, ho, the wind and the rain,
'Gainst knaves and thieves men shut their gate,
    For the rain it raineth every day.

But when I came, alas, to wive,
    With hey, ho, the wind and the rain,
By swaggering could I never thrive,
    For the rain it raineth every day.

But when I came unto my beds,   390
    With hey, ho, the wind and the rain,
With tosspots still had drunken heads,
    For the rain it raineth every day.

A great while ago the world begun,
    With hey, ho, the wind and the rain ;
But that's all one, our play is done,
    And we'll strive to please you every day.   *[Exit.]*

377 *fancy's* love's

THE MERRY WIVES OF WINDSOR

INTRODUCTION

The Merry Wives of Windsor is a farce; a successful one, indeed, on the evidence of its being among the most frequently acted of all of Shakespeare's plays, as well as one of the most effectively adapted, as in Verdi's opera *Falstaff*. That it has proved less delightful to Shakespearean critics only goes to show that, with this kind of play at least, spectators in the theatre are better judges of values than readers in the study. To be a member of an audience, one must like plays as plays, and be capable of a "willing suspension of disbelief." The scholar-critic, on the other hand, may not be much of a playgoer; and in his concern with the enduring literary values of Shakespeare's art may forget that the drama of any age is a form of notable variety. Not all plays are to be taken with equal seriousness as illuminating the far reaches of human experience. Many serious dramatists have from time to time written for the moment, with no further intention than to supply simple entertainment. Shakespeare as a professional man of the theatre was not above doing so when the occasion warranted.

Perhaps fairer criteria would have been brought to bear, as in the case of his earlier farces, *The Comedy of Errors* and *The Taming of the Shrew*, if only Shakespeare had named certain of his characters differently. True, Ford's assumed name *Brook* has been altered in the folio received text to *Broom*, probably to avoid the appearance of some suspected personal reference, as Falstaff's own name had, in *Henry IV*, been altered from the original *Oldcastle*. But this is of no consequence; what has bothered critics, even more than various minor loosenesses in details of the plot, is the name of the principal character. If he had been called "Sir John Tunbelly," and his hangers-on by other names, the play would have been spared much adverse criticism, since few would have found him inadequate within the framework of the play. But he is called *Falstaff*, and the tendency has been to discuss him in an irrelevant context.

The Falstaff of the two parts of *Henry IV* is Shakespeare's supreme comic invention, and his admirers have often found it hard to reconcile themselves to what they regard as the debased version of the character who appears in the present play and only in flashes bears any resemblance to his former self. It may truly be said that the problem of *The Merry Wives* is the problem of Falstaff. In this context, "former self" is the key phrase, since even critics who should know better have felt that somehow *The Merry Wives* ought to form a sequence with the *Henry IV* plays and *Henry V*. For instance, it has been argued in all seriousness that because in *Henry V* Mistress Quickly is Pistol's wife, he would not have called her a "punk" (a coarse word for a prostitute) in *The Merry Wives* (II, ii, 123), and therefore the folio text is wrong and

the word should be emended to "pink" (a kind of ship). As Master Page would say, "This passes!"

If we are to read or see the play in the proper spirit, we should observe two caveats. First, *The Merry Wives* must not be thought of as dependent upon *1 & 2 Henry IV* and *Henry V*. This play (except for the pleasure of some of the characters' company) has nothing in common with those plays, and cannot be appreciated or illuminated in their terms. Second, *The Merry Wives* must not be thought of as a realistic comedy, least of all a comedy of manners, but as a farce. It operates under age-old rules for successful farce, and if we judge it by standards appropriate only to the more serious art of comedy, we are doing it a grave injustice and raising problems where none exist.

Had dramatic characters a life of their own apart from the plays in which we know them, we could place the action of *The Merry Wives* as occurring between the end of *2 Henry IV* and the beginning of *Henry V*, in which Pistol, Bardolph, and Nym are caught up in the French wars. However, the earliest probable date for the composition of the play is the closing months of 1599 (and 1600–1601 is rather better), whereas *Henry V*, the last of the relevant histories, was written and staged before September, 1599. Hence we cannot take the low-life characters in *The Merry Wives* as in any sense anticipating their roles in *Henry V*. They are, instead, in the nature of afterthoughts, along with Falstaff, whose death had been described in an early scene of *Henry V*.

It is clear that Falstaff and his crew were extremely popular on the Elizabethan stage. No doubt reluctantly, Shakespeare had nevertheless felt compelled to kill off Falstaff in *Henry V*, without his having made an appearance, in order to preserve certain patriotic emphases that would have been thrown out of balance by the counterweight of the anti-hero fat knight. If *The Merry Wives* were an attempt to revive Falstaff for his own sake, to squeeze one more popular play out of the character, we could understand that the drama would need to take some other form than that of a history play (for the events of the reigns of Henry IV and Henry V had been thoroughly exploited). But such a theory does not answer other questions. For instance, granting the necessity to exhibit Falstaff in what might be called private life, and apart from Prince Hal, we may well be puzzled by the almost deliberate neglect, in drawing the Falstaff of *The Merry Wives*, of certain of the established comic qualities that had insured the popularity of the Falstaff of the history plays. Moreover, there are more careless clashes within the time-scheme, and more unresolved loose ends, in this play than in any other play of Shakespeare, all arguing for some considerable haste in composition and very little attempt to straighten out anomalies, at least in the manuscript line from which the folio text derives.

In this circumstance a tradition of the sort that one usually distrusts may serve as at least a partial clue, provided that we do not take the story to be literally the truth in every detail. Over one hundred years after the time of the play, John Dennis in 1702 related that *The Merry Wives* was written at the command and by the direction of Queen Elizabeth, in fourteen days. In 1709 Nicholas Rowe, in his *Life of Shakespeare*, elaborated this story to include the Queen's direction that Falstaff should be shown in love, no doubt an original touch with him.

Whether or not Queen Elizabeth personally commanded Shakespeare to write another Falstaff play, and in such a hurry, the fifth act of *The Merry Wives* contains a personal compliment to Elizabeth, not customary in such a pointed fashion and under such circumstances in the drama of the day, as well as a concern with the royal palace of Windsor and the Garter ceremonies held there. These details have suggested to some that Shakespeare's company was commissioned at comparatively short notice by the court officials to produce an entertainment supplementing a Garter installation. They have suggested to others that the ending of a public-stage play has been altered on the occasion of a special performance before the Queen at Windsor, in which case the allusions to the Garter would be included incidentally because of the association of that order with the place. In either case there might reasonably attach to the play a tradition of dictation by the Queen and hasty composition. The remarks of Dennis and Rowe may contain some element of truth, and help to account for the somewhat inappropriate transfer of Falstaff from the realm of comedy, in London, to that of farce, at Windsor, in the country, where he is out of place.

By its very nature a farce has only one end in view: to entertain an audience not by engaging its deeper sympathies but instead by provoking its easy laughter at an amusing series of absurd actions, one following upon another rapidly and ingeniously, with artfully calculated surprise. The plot itself – usually of the intrigue variety – is the normal center of interest, and characters are necessarily subordinate. That is, when a playwright invites an audience to give its attention more to what characters do than what they are, subtlety of characterization becomes inappropriate, if not impossible. Type characters abound therefore – characters who are recognizable at first glance as familiar fictional persons whose reactions are always predictable and whose motivations need no searching enquiry. Correspondingly, the plot concerns itself with being a plot – with the rapidity, absurdity, and ingenuity of its twists and turns – and scarcely at all with holding a mirror up to life. The wounds of farce are easily healed, therefore, because the action cannot be taken seriously as a form of dramatized reality.

Hence Mistress Page, who has engaged our sympathy as a woman of most agreeable common sense and staunch virtue, one whose view of life is essentially sound, may suddenly for the purposes of the plot – and without losing our sympathy as a person – become in one respect a calculating social climber, willing to sacrifice her daughter in an obviously unnatural marriage. Likewise, her husband, whose friendly trust in his wife's virtue we are happy to share, and whose analysis of Ford's malady is certainly

acute, must welcome Master Slender with no second thoughts as a son-in-law.

Correspondingly, Falstaff, whose wit and effrontery on his first appearance enable him to beat down the threats of Shallow and Slender, becomes a dupe to a most barefaced gulling action, in which his ego and his greed quite submerge his realistic knowledge of the world. Yet, in fact, the gulf is not nearly so wide between his two aspects in this play as we are accustomed to imagine. The truth is, we cannot avoid associating this Falstaff with the character we have known in *Henry IV*, who under no circumstances could have been tricked by the merry wives (at least, more than once); and the temptation to bring him over intact is the stronger in that his initial scene seems to carry on the great comic tradition he had established in the history plays. The operative word here is "seems," however, for though his skill in manipulating appearances to show to his own advantage has lost nothing in this early scene, the action is in fact a dead end; it is not utilized as a factor in the plot and therefore cannot be developed naturally. At best it is only illustrative of Falstaff and his crew as unsavory intruders, and of Slender as a fool. In short, Shakespeare makes a calculated strong impact at the start of the play, although with a basically static situation, and then he shifts away from this picture of the old Falstaff when the fat knight enters the main stream of the plot. It is enough for dramatic purposes: the good will of the audience has been secured.

The Falstaff of *1 Henry IV* (and to a lesser degree of *2 Henry IV*) was a consummately shrewd realist, keenly observant of himself as well as of others, possessed of such an intelligence that he could rightly claim not only to be witty himself but, more important, the cause of wit in others. In *The Merry Wives* the exigencies of the plot reduce his flood of verbal humor to a relatively few scenes where he is forced to generate his own wit by belaboring his inferiors, like Pistol or Mistress Quickly. His verbal wit in *Henry IV* was accompanied by shrewd intelligence that fostered wit in others as a means of binding himself to his superiors. The process may have been one of intellectual dishonesty, when employed in cold blood and not merely as a virtuoso talent, but at least it was intellectual.

But in *The Merry Wives* his wit is merely exhibitionist after the opening scene. It reveals his love of words and their ways, but since he has no opponent worthy of his steel to react to the substance of his wit, we are the more willing to divorce his verbal fireworks from basic shrewdness and to permit this amusingly voluble old party to grow so overconfident that he falls a victim as much to self-deception as to the women's intrigue. If we feel that there are two Falstaffs in *The Merry Wives* we are mistaken; we have imposed on *The Merry Wives* a preconception about Falstaff improperly taken over from *Henry IV*. No actor in the part has the slightest difficulty in portraying a consistent character.

Shakespeare evidently relied on the audience's fond predilection for Falstaff to excuse some lack of effort. Not only does the effective opening lead nowhere, but Falstaff's menage take no effective part in the unfolding of the plot once they have fulfilled their function of warning Page and Ford of Falstaff's intended conquest of their wives. The play would be much the poorer without these humorists, but the attention given to them at the beginning is not warranted by their minor function in the plot.

Once the true action is under way and Falstaff's crew has dropped out of sight, another set of humorists order much of the subplot with its ramifications. The antagonists Slender, of matchless futility, and the excitable Caius are not well paired; but Evans takes over the conflict, even though his function in the story line is often peripheral. The Parson is a true Shakespeare creation, both pathetic and noble in his unquenchable humanity. The Host, another fat acting part, makes one forget that he is involved (like Evans) only in a subplot to the subplot.

These characters, with their parodies of the serious Jonsonian humors, wander in and out of the action and, indeed, through their bustle and inherent theatrical life, succeed in maintaining the play's interest at least as much as the central action. As Falstaff becomes more a creature of the wives' intrigue, acted upon both by the women and by Ford with no opportunity for independence of action himself, these other stalwarts provide the momentum for compensating action devoted to their own affairs. They exemplify the delight that Shakespeare always found in pure eccentricity or in invulnerable good will clothed in oddity. But they have a dramatic importance that goes far beyond the exhibition of their humors solely for its own sake. The powerful thrust of their humors gives them a theatrical vitality superior to that of the usual type characters who inhabit the world of farce. There is little question, then, that they represent Shakespeare's triumphant solution to the problem of the imbalance of character interest and plot interest in farce. We cannot help being as taken with these people for what they are (Shakespeare's expert manipulation of humors) as for what they do. This is the true English factor that counterbalances the Italianate action, however disguised, of the main plot.

From hints about the mishaps of a would-be seducer that he very likely found in versions of Italian novelle in Painter's *Palace of Pleasure*, 1566, and Tarlton's *News Out of Purgatory*, 1590, possibly with direct knowledge of the Italian in some form, Shakespeare constructed the framework of his central action, not a little aided by Jonson's portrait of the jealous husband Kitely in *Every Man in his Humour*, 1599. The gaps he filled with as striking an array of comic creations as he ever contrived. Parson Evans, the Host, Slender, and even Caius, Quickly, Shallow, and Robin, to say nothing of Pistol and Nym – these come to be of the very stuff of this play.

The Merry Wives of Windsor acts with all the ease of an expert theatrical creation, despite the fact that it is clear that Shakespeare is not engaging himself to a major effort. One of the striking features of the play is its abandonment of the central focus of a popular audience, the narrow streets of London, for the fields and woods of Windsor. The change in atmosphere is a deliberate one, away from the dog-eat-dog cheats of the city that Jonson and Middleton liked to explore, to the proverbial purity of the countryside where, in the best tradition, pastoral virtue triumphs over the city slicker. This retreat from the fiercely competitive life of court or city substituted good-natured country minor gentry for grasping city merchants, trulls, and impatient heirs. It enabled a charming portrait to be drawn of the sweet and wholesome Anne Page, that "pretty virginity." A self-respecting air of virtue permeates the drama. The merry wives are as much concerned with revenging an insult to their characters as they are with the jest of teaching a lesson to a lecherous old man, who never is in any danger of laying a hand on them. Adultery is not here a source of laughter. Necessarily, prose substitutes for poetry, and in the very little verse in the play Fenton and Anne speak in a low key appropriate for the milieu and not in the least "poetic."

Without Shakespeare's perhaps consciously intending it, *The Merry Wives* is firmly rooted in its Windsor background, even if this country life is less insisted upon than casually implied, with its open fields, its homely sports, its hospitality, its spooks, and its human warmth. The love affair of Anne Page is everybody's business, and an eye must be kept upon Master William's progress at school. A joke or a quarrel is a thing to be shared, like a gift of venison. When outside life intrudes on this peaceful setting, whether in the descent of the London cony-catcher Falstaff or in the topical humor of the cozening Germans (who seem to have some connection with a German duke who made a nuisance of himself in 1590 and again in 1597 in his pursuit of a Garter), the citizens are able to handle it in their own way and to win out. This is the sturdy middle-class self-respect and the admiration for unspoiled English virtue found in Greene, and pre-eminently in Dekker, but not elsewhere so prominent in Shakespeare, who usually depicts the aristocratic milieu and point of view.

The explanation may be that for once, whether in haste or in relaxation, he chose to write about his own people and a life that could not have been very different from that he knew at Stratford, one to which, indeed, he returned after he had made his fortune from the London stage. If this is the world as the world should be, the arcadianism has a basis in truth. *The Merry Wives of Windsor* may even be called a patriotic play. Despite its contrivances, it is a very English one. We should be thankful for it.

University of Virginia   FREDSON BOWERS

NOTE ON THE TEXT

A corrupt version of *The Merry Wives of Windsor* appeared in a quarto of 1602, an authorized version in the folio of 1623. The present edition follows the folio, on principles briefly explained in the Appendix. The quarto text is undivided into acts and scenes. The division here supplied marginally is identical with that of the folio.

THE MERRY WIVES OF WINDSOR

Sir John Falstaff	*Bardolph* ⎱
Fenton, a young gentleman	*Pistol* ⎬ *followers of Falstaff*
Shallow, a country justice	*Nym* ⎰
Slender, cousin to Shallow	*Robin, page to Falstaff*
Ford ⎱ *two gentlemen dwelling at Windsor*	*Simple, servant to Slender*
Page ⎰	*Rugby, servant to Doctor Caius*
William Page, a boy, son to Page	*Mistress Ford*
Sir Hugh Evans, a Welsh parson	*Mistress Page*
Doctor Caius, a French physician	*Anne Page, her daughter, in love with Fenton*
Host of the Garter Inn	*Mistress Quickly, servant to Doctor Caius*
	Servants to Page, Ford, &c.

Scene : *Windsor ; and the Neighborhood*]

*

I, i   *Enter Justice Shallow, Slender, [and] Sir Hugh Evans.*

1 SHALLOW Sir Hugh, persuade me not – I will make a Star-chamber matter of it. If he were twenty Sir John Falstaffs he shall not abuse Robert Shallow, Esquire.

SLENDER In the county of Gloucester, Justice of Peace,
5 and Coram.

6 SHALLOW Ay, cousin Slender, and Custalorum.

7 SLENDER Ay, and Ratolorum too ; and a gentleman born,
8 Master Parson, who writes himself Armigero, in any bill,
9 warrant, quittance, or obligation – Armigero !

SHALLOW Ay, that I do, and have done any time these three hundred years.

SLENDER All his successors gone before him hath done't ; and all his ancestors that come after him may. They may
14 give the dozen white luces in their coat.

SHALLOW It is an old coat.

EVANS The dozen white louses do become an old coat
17 well. It agrees well, passant ; it is a familiar peast to man, and signifies love.

19 SHALLOW The luce is the fresh fish. The salt fish is an old coat.

21 SLENDER I may quarter, coz ?

SHALLOW You may, by marrying.

EVANS It is marrying indeed, if he quarter it.

SHALLOW Not a whit.

EVANS Yes, py'r Lady. If he has a quarter of your coat,
25 there is but three skirts for yourself, in my simple conjectures. But that is all one. If Sir John Falstaff have committed disparagements unto you, I am of the Church, and will be glad to do my benevolence to make atonements and compromises between you.

30 SHALLOW The Council shall hear it. It is a riot.

EVANS It is not meet the Council hear a riot. There is no fear of Got in a riot. The Council, look you, shall desire to hear the fear of Got, and not to hear a riot. Take your vizaments in that.   34

SHALLOW Ha ! O' my life, if I were young again, the sword should end it.

EVANS It is petter that friends is the sword, and end it – and there is also another device in my prain, which peradventure prings goot discretions with it. There is Anne Page, which is daughter to Master George Page, which is pretty virginity.

SLENDER Mistress Anne Page ? She has brown hair, and speaks small like a woman ?   43

EVANS It is that fery person for all the 'orld, as just as you will desire. And seven hundred pounds of moneys, and gold and silver, is her grandsire, upon his death's-bed – Got deliver to a joyful resurrections – give, when she is able to overtake seventeen years old. It were a goot mo- 48
tion if we leave our pribbles and prabbles, and desire a 49
marriage between Master Abraham and Mistress Anne Page.

I, i Before Master Page's house in Windsor   1 *Sir* (courtesy title for a priest)   1–2 *Star-chamber* high court sitting in Westminster   5 *Coram* i.e. Quorum (common term for a justice)   6 *Custalorum* i.e. Custos Rotulorum, a principal justice of the peace   7 *Ratolorum* (Slender's mistake for 'Rotulorum')   8 *Armigero* i.e. Esquire, one entitled to bear heraldic arms ; *bill* bill for money credit by exchange (an early form of bank draft)   9 *quittance* discharge from debt ; *obligation* contract   14 *give* display (heraldic) : *luces* pikes, fish (in coat of arms ; perhaps a hit at Sir Thomas Lucy of Charlecote, Stratford, whose coat displayed three luces)   17 *passant* walking (heraldic) ; *familiar* domestic   19–20 *fresh fish . . . old coat* (a debated passage : perhaps a reference to the combined arms of the Fishmongers' Company, of which the Saltfishmongers' was the older coat ; there may be a play on *passant* vs another heraldic term, 'saltant' : rearing, leaping)   21 *quarter* combine arms of two families   25 *skirts* (French coats with skirts were in style)   30 *Council* Privy Council assembled in Star Chamber   34 *vizaments* i.e. advisements, deliberations   43 *small* shrill, in the treble   48 *motion* proposal   49 *pribbles and prabbles* small disputes (probably quibbles and brabbles, i.e. babblings)

338

SHALLOW Did her grandsire leave her seven hundred pound?

EVANS Ay, and her father is make her a petter penny.

SHALLOW I know the young gentlewoman. – She has
55 good gifts.

56 EVANS Seven hundred pounds and possibilities is goot gifts.

SHALLOW Well, let us see honest Master Page. Is Falstaff there?

EVANS Shall I tell you a lie? I do despise a liar as I do despise one that is false, or as I despise one that is not true. The knight Sir John is there; and, I beseech you, be ruled by your well-willers. I will peat the door for Master Page. *[Knocks.]* Who, ho! Got pless your house here.

PAGE *[within]* Who's there?

EVANS Here is Got's plessing, and your friend, and Justice Shallow; and here young Master Slender, that
68 peradventures shall tell you another tale, if matters grow to your likings.

[Enter] Master Page.

PAGE I am glad to see your worships well. I thank you for my venison, Master Shallow.

SHALLOW Master Page, I am glad to see you. Much good do it your good heart! I wished your venison better – it
74 was ill killed. How doth good Mistress Page? – and I thank you always with my heart, la; with my heart.

PAGE Sir, I thank you.

SHALLOW Sir, I thank you; by yea and no, I do.

PAGE I am glad to see you, good Master Slender.

79 SLENDER How does your fallow greyhound, sir? I heard
80 say he was outrun on Cotsall.

PAGE It could not be judged, sir.

SLENDER You'll not confess, you'll not confess.

83 SHALLOW That he will not – 'tis your fault, 'tis your fault. – 'Tis a good dog.

PAGE A cur, sir.

SHALLOW Sir, he's a good dog, and a fair dog. Can there be more said? He is good and fair. Is Sir John Falstaff here?

PAGE Sir, he is within. – And I would I could do a good office between you.

90 EVANS It is spoke as a Christians ought to speak.

SHALLOW He hath wronged me, Master Page.

PAGE Sir, he doth in some sort confess it.

SHALLOW If it be confessed, it is not redressed. Is not that so, Master Page? He hath wronged me; indeed, he hath. At a word, he hath, believe me. Robert Shallow, Esquire, saith he is wronged.

PAGE Here comes Sir John.

[Enter Sir John] Falstaff, Bardolph, Nym, [and] Pistol.

FALSTAFF Now, Master Shallow, you'll complain of me to the King?

SHALLOW Knight, you have beaten my men, killed my deer, and broke open my lodge.

FALSTAFF But not kissed your keeper's daughter?

SHALLOW Tut, a pin! This shall be answered. 103

FALSTAFF I will answer it straight – I have done all this. 104 That is now answered.

SHALLOW The Council shall know this.

FALSTAFF 'Twere better for you if it were known in 107 counsel – you'll be laughed at.

EVANS Pauca verba, Sir John; goot worts. 109

FALSTAFF Good worts? good cabbage! – Slender, I broke 110 your head. What matter have you against me? 111

SLENDER Marry, sir, I have matter in my head against 112 you, and against your cony-catching rascals, Bardolph, 113 Nym, and Pistol.

BARDOLPH You Banbury cheese! 115

SLENDER Ay, it is no matter.

PISTOL How now, Mephistophilus! 117

SLENDER Ay, it is no matter.

NYM Slice, I say! Pauca, pauca. Slice! that's my humor. 119

SLENDER Where's Simple, my man? Can you tell, cousin?

EVANS Peace, I pray you. Now let us understand. There is three umpires in this matter, as I understand; that is – Master Page, fidelicet, Master Page; and there is my- 123 self, fidelicet, myself; and the three party is, lastly and finally, mine Host of the Garter. 125

PAGE We three to hear it and end it between them.

EVANS Fery goot. I will make a prief of it in my notebook, and we will afterwards 'ork upon the cause with as great discreetly as we can.

FALSTAFF Pistol. –

PISTOL He hears with ears.

EVANS The tevil and his tam! What phrase is this, 'He hears with ear'? Why, it is affectations.

FALSTAFF Pistol, did you pick Master Slender's purse?

SLENDER Ay, by these gloves, did he – or I would I might never come in mine own great chamber again else – of 136 seven groats in mill-sixpences, and two Edward shovel- 137 boards, that cost me two shillings and two pence apiece of Yed Miller, by these gloves. 139

FALSTAFF Is this true, Pistol?

EVANS No, it is false, if it is a pick-purse.

PISTOL

Ha, thou mountain-foreigner! – Sir John and master 142 mine,

I combat challenge of this latten bilbo. 143

Word of denial in thy labras here! 144

Word of denial! Froth and scum, thou liest. 145

SLENDER By these gloves, then 'twas he.

NYM Be advised, sir, and pass good humors. I will say 'marry trap' with you, if you run the nuthook's humor 148 on me. That is the very note of it. 149

55 *gifts* i.e. qualities of mind and body 56 *possibilities* prospects 68 *tell . . . tale* i.e. have something else to say (proverbial) 74 *ill killed* not killed cleanly, with expedition (?), illegally killed by Falstaff (?) 79 *fallow* fawn-colored 80 *Cotsall* Cotswold Hills in Gloucestershire, famous for coursing 83 *fault* misfortune, loss 103 *pin* trifle; *answered* rendered account 104 *straight* straightway (with play on 'strait,' strictly) 107–08 *in counsel* privately, not publicly 109 *Pauca verba* few words 110 *worts* vegetable matter 110–11 *broke your head* drew blood by breaking skin 111 *matter* i.e. of importance 112 *matter* sense (as opposed to nonsense) 113 *cony-catching* i.e. rabbit-trapping, cheating 115 *Banbury cheese* (made in thin slices) 117 *Mephistophilus* (the name of the devil in Marlowe's *Doctor Faustus*; a term of abuse) 119 *Slice* (a punning threat: few words, keep the dispute thin like Banbury cheese; I will cut with my sword); *humor* mood, temperament 123 *fidelicet* i.e. videlicet, namely 125 *Garter* (actual inn in Windsor) 136 *great chamber* usually, main bedroom, but possibly reception room 137 *groats* fourpenny coins; *mill-sixpences* coins stamped, or milled 137–38 *Edward shovel-boards* Edward VI shillings used in game of shovel-board 139 *Yed* (like Ned, for Edward) 142 *mountain-foreigner* i.e. Welshman 143 *latten bilbo* brass sword 144 *labras* i.e. lips 145 *Froth and scum* base person, like a tapster 148 *marry trap* (contemptuous: either, disappear, as down a trap-door, or run off and play the children's game of trap; 'marry' is a mild oath) 148–49 *run . . . on me* i.e. threaten me with a constable 149 *very note* truthful observation (with pun on musical notation)

SLENDER By this hat, then he in the red face had it; for though I cannot remember what I did when you made me drunk, yet I am not altogether an ass.

153 FALSTAFF What say you, Scarlet and John?

BARDOLPH Why, sir, for my part, I say the gentleman had drunk himself out of his five sentences.

EVANS It is his 'five senses.' Fie, what the ignorance is.

157 BARDOLPH And being fap, sir, was, as they say, cash-
158 iered; and so conclusions passed the careers.

SLENDER Ay, you spake in Latin then too. – But 'tis no matter. I'll ne'er be drunk whilst I live again, but in honest, civil, godly company, for this trick. If I be drunk, I'll be drunk with those that have the fear of God, and not with drunken knaves.

164 EVANS So Got udge me, that is a firtuous mind.

FALSTAFF You hear all these matters denied, gentlemen. You hear it.

[Enter] Anne Page [with wine], Mistress Ford, [and] Mistress Page [following].

PAGE Nay, daughter, carry the wine in – we'll drink within.   *[Exit Anne Page.]*

SLENDER O heaven, this is Mistress Anne Page.

PAGE How now, Mistress Ford. –

FALSTAFF Mistress Ford, by my troth, you are very well
172 met. By your leave, good mistress.

[Kisses her.]

PAGE Wife, bid these gentlemen welcome. Come, we have a hot venison pasty to dinner. Come, gentlemen, I hope we shall drink down all unkindness.

[Exeunt all but Shallow, Slender, and Evans.]

SLENDER I had rather than forty shillings I had my Book
177 of Songs and Sonnets here.

[Enter] Simple.

How now, Simple; where have you been? I must wait on myself, must I? You have not the Book of Riddles about you, have you?

SIMPLE Book of Riddles? Why, did you not lend it to
182 Alice Shortcake upon Allhallowmas last, a fortnight
183 afore Michaelmas?

SHALLOW Come, coz, come, coz; we stay for you. A word
185 with you, coz. Marry, this, coz – there is as 'twere a ten-
186 der, a kind of tender, made afar off by Sir Hugh here. Do you understand me?

SLENDER Ay, sir, you shall find me reasonable. If it be so, I shall do that that is reason.

SHALLOW Nay, but understand me.

SLENDER So I do, sir.

EVANS Give ear to his motions – Master Slender, I will description the matter to you, if you be capacity of it.

SLENDER Nay, I will do as my cousin Shallow says – I pray you pardon me. He's a Justice of Peace in his
196 country, simple though I stand here.

EVANS But that is not the question. The question is concerning your marriage.

SHALLOW Ay, there's the point, sir.

EVANS Marry, is it, the fery point of it – to Mistress Anne Page.

SLENDER Why, if it be so, I will marry her upon any reasonable demands.

EVANS But can you affection the 'oman? Let us command to know that of your mouth, or of your lips – for
206 divers philosophers hold that the lips is parcel of the mouth. Therefore, precisely, can you marry your goot will to the maid?

SHALLOW Cousin Abraham Slender, can you love her?

SLENDER I hope, sir, I will do as it shall become one that would do reason.

EVANS Nay, Got's lords and his ladies! you must speak possitable, if you can carry her your desires towards her. 213

SHALLOW That you must. Will you, upon good dowry, marry her?

SLENDER I will do a greater thing than that upon your request, cousin, in any reason.

SHALLOW Nay, conceive me, conceive me, sweet coz – 218 what I do is to pleasure you, coz. Can you love the maid?

SLENDER I will marry her, sir, at your request; but if there be no great love in the beginning, yet heaven may decrease it upon better acquaintance when we are married and have more occasion to know one another. I hope upon familiarity will grow more contempt. But if you say, 'Marry her,' I will marry her; that I am freely dissolved, and dissolutely.

EVANS It is a fery discretion answer, save the faul' is in the 'ort 'dissolutely': the 'ort is, according to our meaning, 'resolutely.' His meaning is goot.

SHALLOW Ay, I think my cousin meant well.

SLENDER Ay, or else I would I might be hanged, la.

[Enter Anne Page.]

SHALLOW Here comes fair Mistress Anne. Would I were young for your sake, Mistress Anne.

ANNE The dinner is on the table. My father desires your worships' company.

SHALLOW I will wait on him, fair Mistress Anne. 236

EVANS Od's plessed will! I will not be absence at the 237 grace.   *[Exeunt Shallow and Evans.]*

ANNE Will't please your worship to come in, sir?

SLENDER No, I thank you, forsooth, heartily – I am very well.

ANNE The dinner attends you, sir.

SLENDER I am not a-hungry, I thank you forsooth. Go, sirrah, for all you are my man, go wait upon my cousin Shallow. *[Exit Simple.]* A Justice of Peace sometime may be beholding to his friend for a man. I keep but three men and a boy yet, till my mother be dead. But what though? Yet I live like a poor gentleman born. 247

ANNE I may not go in without your worship: they will not sit till you come.

SLENDER I'faith, I'll eat nothing. I thank you as much as though I did.

ANNE I pray you, sir, walk in.

SLENDER I had rather walk here, I thank you. I bruised my shin th' other day with playing at sword and dagger with a master of fence – three veneys for a dish of stewed 256 prunes – and, by my troth, I cannot abide the smell of hot meat since. Why do your dogs bark so? Be there 258 bears i' the town?

ANNE I think there are, sir; I heard them talked of.

153 *Scarlet and John* (Robin Hood's companions) 157 *fap* drunk; *cashiered* robbed 158 *conclusions . . . careers* i.e. the end was more serious than the sport (of drinking, equated with exhibition of horsemanship) 164 *udge* i.e. judge 172 *By your leave* (a kiss was an ordinary polite greeting; of course, advantage could be taken of the custom) 177 *Songs and Sonnets* (*Tottel's Miscellany*, 1557; old-fashioned love poetry) 182 *Allhallowmas* All Saints' Day, November 1 183 *Michaelmas* St Michael's Day, September 29 185 *tender* offer 186 *afar off* indirectly 196 *simple though* as sure as 206 *parcel* part 213 *possitable* i.e. positively 218 *conceive me* understand me, take my meaning 236 *wait on him* keep him company 237 *Od's* God's 247 *what though* what of it 256 *fence* fencing; *veneys* bouts 256–57 *stewed prunes* (a favorite dish with prostitutes) 258 *meat* any solid food

SLENDER I love the sport well, but I shall as soon quarrel 261
at it as any man in England. You are afraid if you see the
bear loose, are you not?

ANNE Ay indeed, sir.

SLENDER That's meat and drink to me, now. I have seen
Sackerson loose twenty times, and have taken him by 266
the chain; but, I warrant you, the women have so cried
and shrieked at it, that it passed. But women, indeed, 268
cannot abide 'em; they are very ill-favored rough things.
[Enter Page.]

PAGE Come, gentle Master Slender, come. We stay for
you.

SLENDER I'll eat nothing, I thank you, sir.

PAGE By cock and pie, you shall not choose, sir! Come, 272
come.

SLENDER Nay, pray you lead the way.

PAGE Come on, sir.

SLENDER Mistress Anne, yourself shall go first.

ANNE Not I, sir; pray you keep on.

SLENDER Truly, I will not go first; truly, la. I will not do
you that wrong.

ANNE I pray you, sir.

SLENDER I'll rather be unmannerly than troublesome.
You do yourself wrong, indeed, la.   *Exeunt.*

I, ii   *Enter Evans and Simple.*

EVANS Go your ways, and ask of Doctor Caius' house, 1
which is the way; and there dwells one Mistress Quickly, which is in the manner of his nurse, or his dry nurse, 3
or his cook, or his laundry, his washer, and his wringer.

SIMPLE Well, sir.

EVANS Nay, it is petter yet. Give her this letter, for it is a
'oman that altogether's acquaintance with Mistress
Anne Page; and the letter is to desire and require her to
solicit your master's desires to Mistress Anne Page. I
pray you be gone. I will make an end of my dinner –
there's pippins and seese to come.   *Exeunt.* 11

*

I, iii   *Enter Falstaff, Host, Bardolph, Nym, Pistol, [and*
Robin, Falstaff's] Page.

FALSTAFF Mine Host of the Garter. –

HOST What says my bully rook? Speak scholarly and 2
wisely.

FALSTAFF Truly, mine Host, I must turn away some of
my followers.

HOST Discard, bully Hercules, cashier. Let them wag; 6
trot, trot.

FALSTAFF I sit at ten pounds a week. 8

HOST Thou'rt an emperor – Caesar, Keisar, and Pheazar. 9
I will entertain Bardolph: he shall draw, he shall tap. 10
Said I well, bully Hector?

FALSTAFF Do so, good mine Host.

HOST I have spoke; let him follow. *[to Bardolph]* Let me
see thee froth and lime. I am at a word; follow.   *[Exit.]* 14

FALSTAFF Bardolph, follow him. A tapster is a good
trade. An old cloak makes a new jerkin; a withered 16
servingman, a fresh tapster. Go, adieu.

BARDOLPH It is a life that I have desired. I will thrive.

PISTOL O base Hungarian wight! Wilt thou the spigot 19
wield?   *[Exit Bardolph.]*

NYM He was gotten in drink. Is not the humor conceited? 21

FALSTAFF I am glad I am so acquit of this tinderbox. His 22
thefts were too open. His filching was like an unskilful
singer: he kept not time.

NYM The good humor is to steal at a minim-rest. 25

PISTOL 'Convey,' the wise it call. 'Steal?' foh, a fico for 26
the phrase!

FALSTAFF Well, sirs, I am almost out at heels. 28

PISTOL Why then, let kibes ensue. 29

FALSTAFF There is no remedy – I must cony-catch, I
must shift. 31

PISTOL Young ravens must have food.

FALSTAFF Which of you know Ford of this town?

PISTOL I ken the wight. He is of substance good.

FALSTAFF My honest lads, I will tell you what I am about.

PISTOL Two yards, and more.

FALSTAFF No quips now, Pistol. Indeed, I am in the
waist two yards about – but I am now about no waste; I
am about thrift. Briefly, I do mean to make love to 39
Ford's wife. I spy entertainment in her: she discourses, 40
she carves, she gives the leer of invitation. I can con- 41
strue the action of her familiar style; and the hardest
voice of her behavior, to be Englished rightly, is, 'I am
Sir John Falstaff's.'

PISTOL He hath studied her well, and translated her well,
out of honesty into English. 46

NYM The anchor is deep. Will that humor pass? 47

FALSTAFF Now, the report goes she has all the rule of her
husband's purse. He hath a legion of angels. 49

PISTOL As many devils entertain – and 'To her, boy,'
say I.

NYM The humor rises – it is good. Humor me the angels.

FALSTAFF I have writ me here a letter to her; and here
another to Page's wife, who even now gave me good eyes
too, examined my parts with most judicious oeillades. 54
Sometimes the beam of her view gilded my foot, sometimes my portly belly.

PISTOL *[aside]* Then did the sun on dunghill shine.

NYM *[aside]* I thank thee for that humor.

FALSTAFF O, she did so course o'er my exteriors with
such a greedy intention that the appetite of her eye did
seem to scorch me up like a burning-glass. – Here's another letter to her. She bears the purse too; she is a
region in Guiana, all gold and bounty. I will be 'cheator 63
to them both, and they shall be exchequers to me. They
shall be my East and West Indies, and I will trade to
them both. *[to Pistol]* Go, bear thou this letter to

---

261 *the sport* i.e. baiting bears with dogs **266** *Sackerson* (a famous bear)
268 *passed* i.e. surpassed belief **272** *cock and pie* i.e. God and his service
(petty oath)
I, ii 1 *Caius* (pronounced 'Ki-us') **3** *dry nurse* (as opposed to wet
nurse; a housekeeper to a mature person) **11** *pippins and seese* apples and
cheese (Welshmen were supposed to love cheese)
I, iii Within the Garter Inn **2** *bully rook* fine fellow **6** *wag* go their
way **8** *I sit* at my expenses are **9** *Keisar* Kaiser, emperor; *Pheazar* awesome person (invented word) **10** *entertain* employ; *draw . . . tap* draw
liquor . . . tap kegs **14** *froth and lime* give short measure and adulterate;
at a word in brief **16** *jerkin* jacket **19** *Hungarian wight* beggarly person
21 *gotten* begotten; *conceited* ingenious **22** *acquit* rid; *tinderbox* (alluding
to Bardolph's flaming nose) **25** *minim-rest* time taken to play the shortest
note in music **26** *fico* fig **28** *out at heels* i.e. without money **29** *kibes*
chilblains **31** *shift* devise a stratagem **39** *thrift* gain **40** *entertainment*
source of supply (with pun on receptiveness); *discourses* talks familiarly
41 *carves* i.e. shows courtesy; *leer* amorous side-glance **41–43** *construe
. . . voice* (extended grammatical pun: an analyst of her informal manner
must conclude that she loves me) **46** *honesty* chastity **47** *The anchor . . .
pass* i.e. his plan is a deep one; how do you like my phrase? **49** *angels*
(coins valued at about ten shillings) **54** *oeillades* amorous glances **63**
'cheator officer in charge of royal property by escheat (forfeit or fine), who
could readily defraud victims

Mistress Page ; *[to Nym]* and thou this to Mistress Ford. We will thrive, lads, we will thrive.

PISTOL

68 Shall I Sir Pandarus of Troy become,
And by my side wear steel ? Then Lucifer take all !

NYM I will run no base humor. Here, take the humor-letter. I will keep the havior of reputation.

FALSTAFF *[to Robin]*

72 Hold, sirrah, bear you these letters tightly :
Sail like my pinnace to these golden shores. *[Exit Robin.]*
Rogues, hence, avaunt ! Vanish like hailstones, go ;

75 Trudge, plod away o' the hoof ; seek shelter, pack !
Falstaff will learn the humor of the age :

77 French thrift, you rogues – myself and skirted page.
[Exit.]

PISTOL

78 Let vultures gripe thy guts ! for gourd and fullam holds,
79 And high and low beguiles the rich and poor.
80 Tester I'll have in pouch when thou shalt lack,
Base Phrygian Turk !

NYM I have operations which be humors of revenge.

PISTOL Wilt thou revenge ?

84 NYM By welkin and her star !

85 PISTOL With wit or steel ?

NYM

With both the humors, I.
87 I will discuss the humor of this love to Page.

PISTOL   And I to Ford shall eke unfold
How Falstaff, varlet vile,
His dove will prove, his gold will hold,
And his soft couch defile.

NYM My humor shall not cool. I will incense Page to deal
93 with poison. I will possess him with yellowness, for the
94 revolt of mine is dangerous. That is my true humor.

PISTOL Thou art the Mars of malcontents. I second thee ;
troop on.   *Exeunt.*

✳

I, iv   *Enter Mistress Quickly, Simple, [and] John Rugby.*

QUICKLY What, John Rugby. – I pray thee, go to the casement and see if you can see my master, Master Doctor Caius, coming. If he do, i' faith, and find any-
4 body in the house, here will be an old abusing of God's
5 patience and the King's English.

RUGBY I'll go watch.

7 QUICKLY Go, and we'll have a posset for't soon at night,
8 in faith, at the latter end of a sea-coal fire. *[Exit Rugby.]*
An honest, willing, kind fellow, as ever servant shall
10 come in house withal ; and, I warrant you, no telltale,
11 nor no breedbate. His worst fault is, that he is given to
12 prayer ; he is something peevish that way, but nobody but has his fault. But let that pass. – Peter Simple you say your name is ?

SIMPLE Ay, for fault of a better.

QUICKLY And Master Slender's your master ?

SIMPLE Ay, forsooth.

QUICKLY Does he not wear a great round beard like a glover's paring knife ?

20 SIMPLE No, forsooth. He hath but a little whey face, with
21 a little yellow beard – a Cain-colored beard.

22 QUICKLY A softly-sprighted man, is he not ?

23 SIMPLE Ay, forsooth. But he is as tall a man of his hands
24 as any is between this and his head : he hath fought with
25 a warrener.

QUICKLY How say you ? – O ! I should remember him. Does he not hold up his head, as it were, and strut in his gait ?

SIMPLE Yes indeed does he.

QUICKLY Well, heaven send Anne Page no worse for-tune. Tell Master Parson Evans I will do what I can for your master. Anne is a good girl, and I wish –
[Enter Rugby.]

RUGBY Out, alas, here comes my master !

QUICKLY We shall all be shent. Run in here, good young 33
man ; go into this closet. He will not stay long. *[Shuts* 34
Simple in the room.] What, John Rugby. – John, what,
John, I say ! Go, John, go inquire for my master. I doubt 36
he be not well, that he comes not home. *[Exit Rugby.]*
[Sings.] 'And down, down, adown-a,' &c.
[Enter] Doctor [Caius].

CAIUS Vat is you sing ? I do not like dese toys. Pray you go 39
and vetch me in my closset un boitier vert – a box, a
green-a box. Do intend vat I speak ? A green-a box.   41

QUICKLY Ay, forsooth, I'll fetch it you. *[aside]* I am glad
he went not in himself. If he had found the young man,
he would have been horn-mad.   44

CAIUS Fe, fe, fe, fe ! ma foi, il fait fort chaud. Je m'en 45
vais à la cour – la grande affaire.

QUICKLY Is it this, sir ?

CAIUS Oui ; mette le au mon pocket ; dépêche, quickly. 48
– Vere is dat knave Rugby ?

QUICKLY What, John Rugby ? John !
[Enter Rugby.]

RUGBY Here, sir.

CAIUS You are John Rugby, and you are Jack Rugby. Come, take-a your rapier and come after my heel to de court.

RUGBY 'Tis ready, sir, here in the porch.

CAIUS By my trot, I tarry too long. – Od's me ! Qu'ai 56
j'oublié ? Dere is some simples in my closset dat I vill 57
not vor de varld I shall leave behind.

QUICKLY *[aside]* Ay me, he'll find the young man there, and be mad.

CAIUS O diable ! diable ! Vat is in my closset ? – Villainy ! Larron ! *[Pulls Simple out.]* Rugby, my rapier !

QUICKLY Good master, be content.

CAIUS Verefore shall I be content-a ?

QUICKLY The young man is an honest man.

---

68 *Sir Pandarus* (character in Chaucer's *Troilus and Criseyde,* the archetype of bawd, or pander)   72 *tightly* deftly   75 *pack* be off   77 *French thrift* (a current economy in France of using a single page in place of a number of attendants) ; *skirted* (see I, i, 25n.)   78 *gourd and fullam* (two different kinds of false dice)   79 *high and low* (dice numbers)   80 *Tester* sixpence   84 *welkin* sky   85 *wit or steel* stratagem or force   87 *discuss* declare   93 *yellowness* i.e. jealousy   94 *revolt of mine* i.e. my revolt (with possible allusion to Falstaff, as being blown up by his own petard)
I, iv Within the house of Doctor Caius   4 *old* i.e. full-blown, plentiful   5 *patience* indulgence   7 *posset* hot milk curdled with ale or wine ; *soon at night* as soon as night falls   8 *sea-coal* coals brought by sea   10 *withal* with   11 *breedbate* mischief-maker   12 *peevish* foolish   20 *whey* i.e. pale   21 *Cain-colored* i.e. reddish (from traditional representation of Cain's beard in tapestries)   22 *softly-sprighted* gentle-spirited   23 *tall . . . hands* i.e. valiant in his actions   24 *this . . . head* (a common expression ; but 'this' could also mean neck and head in another expression, and a joke could be intended here meaning not very tall)   25 *warrener* gamekeeper   33 *shent* rebuked   34 *closet* private room   36 *doubt* fear   39 *toys* nonsen-sical actions   41 *intend* hear (Fr. *'entendre'*)   44 *horn-mad* enraged   45–46 *ma foi . . . affaire* on my faith, it is very hot ; I am going to court – an important matter   48 *Oui . . . pocket* yes ; put it in my pocket   56 *trot* i.e. troth   56–57 *Qu'ai j'oublié* what have I forgotten   57 *simples* medicinal herbs

CAIUS Vat shall de honest man do in my closset? Dere is no honest man dat shall come in my closset.

68 QUICKLY I beseech you, be not so phlegmatic. Hear the truth of it: he came of an errand to me from Parson Hugh.

CAIUS Vell?

SIMPLE Ay, forsooth, to desire her to –

QUICKLY Peace, I pray you.

CAIUS Peace-a your tongue. – Speak-a your tale.

SIMPLE To desire this honest gentlewoman, your maid, to speak a good word to Mistress Anne Page for my master in the way of marriage.

77 QUICKLY This is all, indeed, la; but I'll ne'er put my finger in the fire, and need not.

79 CAIUS Sir Hugh send-a you? – Rugby, baille me some paper. Tarry you a little-a while.   *[Writes.]*

QUICKLY *[aside to Simple]* I am glad he is so quiet: if he had been throughly moved, you should have heard him

83 so loud, and so melancholy. But notwithstanding, man, I'll do you your master what good I can; and the very yea and the no is, the French doctor, my master – I may call him my master, look you, for I keep his house; and I

87 wash, wring, brew, bake, scour, dress meat and drink, make the beds, and do all myself –

89 SIMPLE *[aside to Quickly]* 'Tis a great charge to come under one body's hand.

QUICKLY *[aside to Simple]* Are you avised o' that? You shall find it a great charge. And to be up early and down late; but notwithstanding – to tell you in your ear – I would have no words of it – my master himself is in love with Mistress Anne Page. But notwithstanding that, I know Anne's mind. That's neither here nor there.

97 CAIUS You jack'nape, give-a dis letter to Sir Hugh. By gar, it is a shallenge: I vill cut his troat in de Park; and I vill teach a scurvy jackanape priest to meddle or make. You may be gone; it is not good you tarry here. – By gar,

101 I vill cut all his two stones; by gar, he shall not have a stone to trow at his dog.   *[Exit Simple.]*

QUICKLY Alas, he speaks but for his friend.

CAIUS It is no matter-a vor dat. – Do not you tell-a me dat I shall have Anne Page for myself? By gar, I vill kill

106 de Jack priest; and I have appointed mine Host of de

107 Jarteer to measure our weapon. By gar, I vill myself have Anne Page.

QUICKLY Sir, the maid loves you, and all shall be well.

110 We must give folks leave to prate – what the good-year!

CAIUS Rugby, come to the court vit me. By gar, if I have not Anne Page, I shall turn your head out of my door. Follow my heels, Rugby.   *[Exeunt Caius and Rugby.]*

QUICKLY You shall have – An fool's-head of your own. 114 No, I know Anne's mind for that. Never a woman in Windsor knows more of Anne's mind than I do, nor can do more than I do with her, I thank heaven.

FENTON *[within]* Who's within there, ho?

QUICKLY Who's there, I trow? Come near the house, I 119 pray you.

[Enter] Fenton.

FENTON How now, good woman. – How dost thou?

QUICKLY The better that it pleases your good worship to ask.

FENTON What news? How does pretty Mistress Anne?

QUICKLY In truth, sir, and she is pretty, and honest, and 124 gentle; and one that is your friend, I can tell you that by 125 the way, I praise heaven for it.

FENTON Shall I do any good, thinkest thou? Shall I not lose my suit?

QUICKLY Troth, sir, all is in His hands above. But notwithstanding, Master Fenton, I'll be sworn on a book she loves you. Have not your worship a wart above your eye?

FENTON Yes, marry have I. What of that?

QUICKLY Well, thereby hangs a tale. Good faith, it is 133 such another Nan; but, I detest, an honest maid as ever 134 broke bread. We had an hour's talk of that wart. I shall never laugh but in that maid's company. – But, indeed, she is given too much to allicholy and musing. But for 137 you – well, go to. 138

FENTON Well, I shall see her to-day. Hold, there's money for thee: let me have thy voice in my behalf. If thou seest her before me, commend me. –

QUICKLY Will I? I' faith, that we will. And I will tell your worship more of the wart the next time we have confidence, and of other wooers.

FENTON Well, farewell. I am in great haste now.

QUICKLY Farewell to your worship. *[Exit Fenton.]* Truly, an honest gentleman. But Anne loves him not, for I know Anne's mind as well as another does. Out upon't, what have I forgot?   *Exit.*

*

Enter Mistress Page [with a letter].   II, i

MRS PAGE What, have I 'scaped love letters in the holiday 1 time of my beauty, and am I now a subject for them? Let me see. *[Reads.]*

'Ask me no reason why I love you; for though Love use Reason for his precisian, he admits him not for his coun- 5 sellor. You are not young, no more am I. Go to then, there's sympathy. You are merry, so am I. Ha, ha! then 7 there's more sympathy. You love sack, and so do I. 8 Would you desire better sympathy? Let it suffice thee, Mistress Page – at the least, if the love of soldier can suffice – that I love thee. I will not say, pity me – 'tis not a soldier-like phrase – but I say, love me. By me,

        Thine own true knight,
          By day or night,
        Or any kind of light,
         With all his might
          For thee to fight,
            John Falstaff.'

What a Herod of Jewry is this! O wicked, wicked world! 19 – One that is well-nigh worn to pieces with age, to show himself a young gallant? What an unweighed behavior 21

---

68 *phlegmatic* (a mistake for 'choleric')   77–78 *finger . . . fire* (i.e. as a trial of truth)   79 *baille* fetch   83 *melancholy* surly   87 *dress meat* prepare food   89 *charge* burden   97 *jack'nape* ape; hence, contemptible person   101 *cut . . . stones* i.e. emasculate him   106 *Jack* (nickname, meaning knave)   107 *measure* (as an umpire in a duel)   110 *what the good-year* (ejaculation of disgust)   114 *An fool's-head* ('An' is taken as a pun on Anne Page: i.e. you will get a fool's bauble representing Anne instead of the live girl)   119 *trow* i.e. wonder; *Come near* i.e. enter   124 *honest* chaste   125 *gentle* mild, but also well-born, hence well-mannered; *friend* i.e. one who favors you (not sweetheart, here)   133–34 *it is . . . Nan* i.e. Anne is a merry girl   134 *detest* i.e. protest   137 *allicholy* i.e. melancholy (fashionable)   138 *go to* that's enough

II, i Before Page's house   1 *holiday* sportive; hence, youthful   5 *precisian* i.e. rigidly punctilious adviser (like a Puritan preacher)   7 *sympathy* correspondence, agreement   8 *sack* Spanish white wine   19 *Herod of Jewry* i.e. ranter in high-flown language (as in miracle plays)   21 *unweighed* lacking in judgment

22 hath this Flemish drunkard picked – with the devil's
23 name! – out of my conversation that he dares in this
manner assay me? Why, he hath not been thrice in my
company. What should I say to him? I was then frugal
26 of my mirth – heaven forgive me! Why, I'll exhibit a bill
27 in the parliament for the putting down of men. How
shall I be revenged on him? for revenged I will be, as
29 sure as his guts are made of puddings.

    [Enter] Mistress Ford.

MRS FORD Mistress Page – trust me, I was going to your
house.

MRS PAGE And, trust me, I was coming to you. You look
very ill.

MRS FORD Nay, I'll ne'er believe that. I have to show to
the contrary.

MRS PAGE Faith, but you do, in my mind.

MRS FORD Well, I do then; yet I say I could show you to
the contrary. O Mistress Page, give me some counsel.

MRS PAGE What's the matter, woman?

MRS FORD O woman, if it were not for one trifling respect, I could come to such honor. –

MRS PAGE Hang the trifle, woman; take the honor. What
is it? – dispense with trifles – what is it?

44 MRS FORD If I would but go to hell for an eternal
moment or so, I could be knighted.

MRS PAGE What? thou liest. Sir Alice Ford? These
47 knights will hack; and so thou shouldst not alter the article of thy gentry.

49 MRS FORD We burn daylight. Here, read, read: perceive
how I might be knighted. I shall think the worse of fat
men as long as I have an eye to make difference of men's
52 liking. And yet he would not swear; praised women's
modesty; and gave such orderly and well-behaved re-
54 proof to all uncomeliness that I would have sworn his disposition would have gone to the truth of his words. But
they do no more adhere and keep place together than the
57 Hundredth Psalm to the tune of 'Greensleeves.' What
tempest, I trow, threw this whale, with so many tuns of
oil in his belly, ashore at Windsor? How shall I be re-
60 venged on him? I think the best way were to entertain
him with hope till the wicked fire of lust have melted
him in his own grease. Did you ever hear the like?

MRS PAGE Letter for letter, but that the name of Page and
Ford differs. – To thy great comfort in this mystery of ill
opinions, here's the twin brother of thy letter. But let
thine inherit first, for I protest mine never shall. I warrant he hath a thousand of these letters, writ with blank
space for different names – sure, more – and these are of
the second edition. He will print them, out of doubt; for
70 he cares not what he puts into the press, when he would
put us two. I had rather be a giantess and lie under
Mount Pelion. Well, I will find you twenty lascivious
73 turtles ere one chaste man.

MRS FORD Why, this is the very same: the very hand, the
very words. What doth he think of us?

MRS PAGE Nay, I know not. It makes me almost ready to
77 wrangle with mine own honesty. I'll entertain myself
like one that I am not acquainted withal; for sure, unless
79 he know some strain in me that I know not myself, he
would never have boarded me in this fury.

MRS FORD Boarding call you it? I'll be sure to keep him
above deck.

MRS PAGE So will I – if he come under my hatches, I'll
never to sea again. Let's be revenged on him. Let's

appoint him a meeting, give him a show of comfort in
his suit, and lead him on with a fine-baited delay till he 86
hath pawned his horses to mine Host of the Garter.

MRS FORD Nay, I will consent to act any villainy against
him that may not sully the chariness of our honesty. O 89
that my husband saw this letter! It would give eternal
food to his jealousy.

MRS PAGE Why, look where he comes, and my goodman 92
too. He's as far from jealousy as I am from giving him
cause; and that, I hope, is an unmeasurable distance.

MRS FORD You are the happier woman.

MRS PAGE Let's consult together against this greasy
knight. Come hither.   *[They retire.]*

    [Enter] Master Page, [with] Nym, [and] Master
    Ford, [with] Pistol.

FORD Well, I hope it be not so.

PISTOL

  Hope is a curtal dog in some affairs. 99
  Sir John affects thy wife. 100

FORD Why, sir, my wife is not young.

PISTOL

  He woos both high and low, both rich and poor,
  Both young and old, one with another, Ford.
  He loves the gallimaufry. Ford, perpend. 104

FORD Love my wife?

PISTOL

  With liver burning hot. Prevent, or go thou, 106
  Like Sir Actaeon he, with Ringwood at thy heels. – 107
  O, odious is the name!

FORD What name, sir?

PISTOL

  The horn, I say. Farewell. 110
  Take heed, have open eye, for thieves do foot by night.
  Take heed, ere summer comes or cuckoo birds do sing. 112
  Away, Sir Corporal Nym! –
  Believe it, Page; he speaks sense.   *[Exit.]*

FORD *[aside]* I will be patient; I will find out this.

NYM *[to Page]* And this is true; I like not the humor of lying. He hath wronged me in some humors. I should have
borne the humored letter to her, but I have a sword and it
shall bite upon my necessity. He loves your wife – there's
the short and the long. My name is Corporal Nym; I
speak, and I avouch 'tis true. My name is Nym, and Falstaff loves your wife. Adieu. I love not the humor of bread
and cheese – [and there's the humor of it.] Adieu. *[Exit.]*

---

22 *Flemish drunkard* (the Flemings, or Low-Country dwellers, were reputed
to be heavy drinkers) 23 *conversation* behavior 26 *exhibit* submit 27
putting down silencing or deposing from high office for lack of judgment
29 *puddings* stuffing, sausages 44 *go to hell* (the punishment for adultery)
47 *hack* i.e. fight with swords (with ribald connotations) 47–48 *article
. . . gentry* i.e. specifications of rank (and sex) that you were born with
49 *burn daylight* waste time 52 *liking* bodily condition (looks) 54 *uncomeliness* unseemly behavior 57 *Greensleeves* (a popular love song) 60
entertain treat 70 *press* (pun on printing-press, a crowd, a cupboard, and
carnal embraces) 73 *turtles* turtledoves (proverbially famous for constancy) 77 *wrangle* quarrel 79 *strain* natural quality 86 *fine-baited*
delicately wrought, alluring 89 *chariness* scrupulous integrity 92 *goodman* husband 99 *curtal* tail-docked 100 *affects* is inclined to, loves 104
gallimaufry a dish made of hashed-up odd ingredients; *perpend* take
thought 106 *liver* (supposed seat of love) 107 *Sir Actaeon . . . Ringwood*
(Actaeon, who saw Diana bathing, was hunted to death by her hounds;
the comparison here is to the coursing of a horned beast, i.e. a cuckold)
110 *horn* (signifying a cuckold, a deceived husband whose forehead sprouted
invisible horns) 112 *cuckoo birds* (who reminded cuckolds of their state
because they laid their eggs in the nests of other birds)

PAGE 'The humor of it,' quoth 'a! Here's a fellow frights
English out of his wits.

FORD [aside] I will seek out Falstaff.

PAGE [aside] I never heard such a drawling, affecting
rogue.

FORD [aside] If I do find it – well.

PAGE [aside] I will not believe such a Cataian, though the
priest o' the town commended him for a true man.

FORD [aside] 'Twas a good sensible fellow – well.
[Mistress Page and Mistress Ford come forward.]

PAGE How now, Meg. –

MRS PAGE Whither go you, George? – Hark you.
[Whispers.]

MRS FORD How now, sweet Frank. – Why art thou melancholy?

FORD I melancholy? I am not melancholy. Get you home,
go.

MRS FORD Faith, thou hast some crotchets in thy head
now. Will you go, Mistress Page?

MRS PAGE Have with you. – You'll come to dinner,
George?
[Enter Mistress Quickly.]
[Aside to Mistress Ford] Look who comes yonder. She
shall be our messenger to this paltry knight.

MRS FORD [aside to Mistress Page] Trust me, I thought
on her: she'll fit it.

MRS PAGE You are come to see my daughter Anne?

QUICKLY Ay, forsooth; and I pray, how does good Mistress Anne?

MRS PAGE Go in with us and see. We have an hour's talk
with you.
[Exeunt Mistress Page, Mistress Ford,
and Mistress Quickly.]

PAGE How now, Master Ford. –

FORD You heard what this knave told me, did you not?

PAGE Yes, and you heard what the other told me?

FORD Do you think there is truth in them?

PAGE Hang 'em, slaves! I do not think the knight would
offer it. But these that accuse him in his intent towards
our wives are a yoke of his discarded men – very rogues,
now they be out of service.

FORD Were they his men?

PAGE Marry were they.

FORD I like it never the better for that. Does he lie at the
Garter?

PAGE Ay, marry does he. If he should intend this voyage
toward my wife, I would turn her loose to him; and
what he gets more of her than sharp words, let it lie on
my head.

FORD I do not misdoubt my wife, but I would be loath to

turn them together. A man may be too confident. I
would have nothing lie on my head. I cannot be thus
satisfied.
[Enter] Host.

PAGE Look where my ranting Host of the Garter comes.
There is either liquor in his pate or money in his purse
when he looks so merrily. – How now, mine Host. –

HOST How now, bully rook, thou'rt a gentleman. – Cavaliero Justice, I say!
[Enter] Shallow.

SHALLOW I follow, mine Host, I follow. Good even and
twenty, good Master Page. Master Page, will you go
with us? We have sport in hand.

HOST Tell him, Cavaliero Justice; tell him, bully rook.

SHALLOW Sir, there is a fray to be fought between Sir
Hugh the Welsh priest and Caius the French doctor.

FORD Good mine Host o' the Garter, a word with you.

HOST What sayest thou, my bully rook? [They go aside.]

SHALLOW [to Page] Will you go with us to behold it?
My merry Host hath had the measuring of their
weapons, and, I think, hath appointed them contrary
places; for, believe me, I hear the Parson is no jester.
Hark, I will tell you what our sport shall be.
[They go aside.]

HOST Hast thou no suit against my knight, my Guest
Cavaliero?

FORD None, I protest. But I'll give you a pottle of burnt
sack to give me recourse to him and tell him my name is
Brook – only for a jest.

HOST My hand, bully. Thou shalt have egress and re-
gress – said I well? – and thy name shall be Brook. It is a
merry knight. Will you go, mynheers?

SHALLOW Have with you, mine Host.

PAGE I have heard the Frenchman hath good skill in his
rapier.

SHALLOW Tut, sir, I could have told you more. In these
times you stand on distance, your passes, stoccadoes,
and I know not what. 'Tis the heart, Master Page; 'tis
here, 'tis here. I have seen the time with my long sword
I would have made you four tall fellows skip like rats.

HOST Here, boys, here, here! Shall we wag?

PAGE Have with you. I had rather hear them scold than
fight.   Exeunt [Host, Shallow, and Page].

FORD Though Page be a secure fool and stands so firmly
on his wife's frailty, yet I cannot put off my opinion so
easily. She was in his company at Page's house, and what
they made there, I know not. Well, I will look further
into't; and I have a disguise to sound Falstaff. If I find
her honest, I lose not my labor. If she be otherwise, 'tis
labor well bestowed.   [Exit.]

*

125 his its 127 affecting affected 129 Cataian i.e. sharper (literally,
Chinese) 138 crotchets fancies 145 fit it be appropriate 156 offer venture, dare 157 yoke pair 165–66 lie on my head be my responsibility
(with a joke on the horns) 168 turn them put them out to pasture 173–74
Cavaliero Justice (a cavalier is a gallant, a man trained in arms) 175–76
Good . . . twenty good evening and twenty of them (a slip, for it is morning)
185 contrary wrong, opposite 190 pottle two-quart tankard 190–91 burnt
sack heated Spanish wine 191 recourse access 195 mynheers (Dutch for
'sirs'; equivalent of English 'my masters') 200 stand on depend upon;
distance space between fencers; passes lunges; stoccadoes thrusts 207
secure overconfident 209–10 what . . . there what they did (with a play on
making a monster, i.e. a cuckold) 211 sound measure the depth of
II, ii Within the Garter Inn 4 retort . . . equipage i.e. repay the total in
military stuff 6 lay . . . pawn i.e. borrow money on the strength of my
patronage; grated irritated 8 coach-fellow close companion (like a horse
yoked to another) 9 grate (i.e. of a prison window); geminy pair

Enter Falstaff, [and] Pistol.   II, ii

FALSTAFF I will not lend thee a penny.

PISTOL
Why, then the world's mine oyster,
Which I with sword will open.
[I will retort the sum in equipage.]

FALSTAFF Not a penny. I have been content, sir, you
should lay my countenance to pawn. I have grated
upon my good friends for three reprieves for you and
your coach-fellow Nym, or else you had looked through
the grate, like a geminy of baboons. I am damned in hell

for swearing to gentlemen my friends, you were good
soldiers and tall fellows; and when Mistress Bridget lost
12 the handle of her fan, I took't upon mine honor thou
hadst it not.

PISTOL

Didst thou not share? Hadst thou not fifteen pence?

FALSTAFF Reason, you rogue, reason: thinkest thou, I'll
endanger my soul gratis? At a word, hang no more about
17 me – I am no gibbet for you. Go! a short knife and a
18 throng! – to your manor of Pickt-hatch, go. You'll not
bear a letter for me, you rogue? You stand upon your
honor! Why, thou unconfinable baseness, it is as much
21 as I can do to keep the terms of mine honor precise. I, I, I
myself sometimes, leaving the fear of God on the left
23 hand and hiding mine honor in my necessity, am fain to
shuffle, to hedge, and to lurch; and yet you, rogue, will
25 ensconce your rags, your cat-a-mountain looks, your
26 red-lattice phrases, and your bold-beating oaths, under
the shelter of your honor! You will not do it, you!

PISTOL

I do relent. What wouldst thou more of man?
[Enter] Robin.

ROBIN Sir, here's a woman would speak with you.

FALSTAFF Let her approach.
[Enter Mistress] Quickly.

QUICKLY Give your worship good morrow.

FALSTAFF Good morrow, goodwife.

QUICKLY Not so, an't please your worship.

FALSTAFF Good maid then.

QUICKLY I'll be sworn, as my mother was, the first hour I
was born.

FALSTAFF I do believe the swearer. What with me?

QUICKLY Shall I vouchsafe your worship a word or two?

FALSTAFF Two thousand, fair woman, and I'll vouch-
40 safe thee the hearing.

QUICKLY There is one Mistress Ford, sir – I pray, come
a little nearer this ways. – I myself dwell with Master
Doctor Caius.

FALSTAFF Well, on; Mistress Ford, you say –

QUICKLY Your worship says very true – I pray your
worship, come a little nearer this ways.

FALSTAFF I warrant thee nobody hears – mine own
people, mine own people.

QUICKLY Are they so? God bless them and make them
his servants!   *[They go aside.]*

FALSTAFF Well, Mistress Ford – what of her?

QUICKLY Why, sir, she's a good creature. Lord, Lord,
53 your worship 's a wanton! Well, heaven forgive you,
and all of us, I pray. –

FALSTAFF Mistress Ford – come, Mistress Ford –

QUICKLY Marry, this is the short and the long of it. You
57 have brought her into such a canaries as 'tis wonderful.
The best courtier of them all, when the court lay at
Windsor, could never have brought her to such a canary.
Yet there has been knights, and lords, and gentlemen,
with their coaches. – I warrant you, coach after coach,
letter after letter, gift after gift; smelling so sweetly – all
63 musk – and so rushling, I warrant you, in silk and gold;
64 and in such alligant terms; and in such wine and sugar
of the best and the fairest that would have won any
woman's heart; and I warrant you they could never get
an eye-wink of her. I had myself twenty angels given me
68 this morning; but I defy all angels – in any such sort, as
they say – but in the way of honesty; and I warrant you

they could never get her so much as sip on a cup with
the proudest of them all; and yet there has been earls –
nay, which is more, pensioners; but, I warrant you, all 72
is one with her.

FALSTAFF But what says she to me? Be brief, my good
she-Mercury. 75

QUICKLY Marry, she hath received your letter; for the
which she thanks you a thousand times; and she gives
you to notify that her husband will be absence from his
house between ten and eleven.

FALSTAFF Ten and eleven.

QUICKLY Ay, forsooth; and then you may come and see
the picture, she says, that you wot of. Master Ford her
husband will be from home. Alas, the sweet woman
leads an ill life with him; he's a very jealousy man; she
leads a very frampold life with him, good heart. 84

FALSTAFF Ten and eleven. – Woman, commend me to
her; I will not fail her.

QUICKLY Why, you say well. But I have another messenger to your worship. Mistress Page hath her hearty commendations to you too; and let me tell you in your ear,
she's as fartuous a civil modest wife, and one, I tell you, 90
that will not miss you morning nor evening prayer, as
any is in Windsor, whoe'er be the other; and she bade
me tell your worship that her husband is seldom from
home, but she hopes there will come a time. I never
knew a woman so dote upon a man. Surely I think you
have charms, la; yes, in truth. 96

FALSTAFF Not I, I assure thee. Setting the attraction of
my good parts aside, I have no other charms. 98

QUICKLY Blessing on your heart for't!

FALSTAFF But, I pray thee, tell me this: has Ford's wife
and Page's wife acquainted each other how they love
me?

QUICKLY That were a jest indeed! They have not so little
grace, I hope; that were a trick indeed! But Mistress
Page would desire you to send her your little page, of all 104
loves; her husband has a marvellous infection to the little 105
page; and truly Master Page is an honest man. Never a
wife in Windsor leads a better life than she does. Do what
she will, say what she will, take all, pay all, go to bed
when she list, rise when she list, all is as she will. And
truly she deserves it; for if there be a kind woman in
Windsor, she is one. You must send her your page – no
remedy.

FALSTAFF Why, I will.

QUICKLY Nay, but do so then; and look you, he may come
and go between you both; and in any case have a nay- 114
word, that you may know one another's mind, and the
boy never need to understand anything; for 'tis not good
that children should know any wickedness. Old folks,
you know, have discretion, as they say, and know the
world.

12 *took't* took an oath   17 *short knife* (for cutting purses in a throng)   18
Pickt-hatch (a quarter of ill fame in London)   21 *terms* condition   23–24 *to
shuffle . . . lurch* to be tricky, to dodge, to rob (lurk)   25 *cat-a-mountain* wild
man (derived from leopard or panther)   26 *red-lattice* alehouse; *bold-beating*
blustering   53 *a wanton* roguish, sportive   57 *canaries* state of excitement
(possibly derived from the lively dance of the name)   63 *rushling* i.e. rustling
64 *alligant* *terms* elegant (?) or eloquent (?) language   68 *defy* reject, despise
72 *pensioners* gentlemen of the royal bodyguard   75 *she-Mercury* messenger
84 *frampold* disagreeable, quarrelsome   90 *fartuous* i.e. virtuous   96
charms spells, magic aids   98 *parts* i.e. talents, qualities, as well as physical
characteristics   104–05 *of all loves* (phrase of strong entreaty)   105 *infection* i.e. affection   114 *nayword* watchword

FALSTAFF Fare thee well, commend me to them both.
There's my purse; I am yet thy debtor. – Boy, go along
with this woman. – [Exeunt Mistress Quickly and Robin.]
This news distracts me.

PISTOL [aside]

123 This punk is one of Cupid's carriers.
124 Clap on more sails; pursue; up with your fights;
125 Give fire! She is my prize, or ocean whelm them all!
[Exit.]

FALSTAFF Sayest thou so, old Jack? Go thy ways; I'll
make more of thy old body than I have done. Will they
yet look after thee? Wilt thou, after the expense of so
much money, be now a gainer? Good body, I thank
130 thee. Let them say 'tis grossly done; so it be fairly done,
no matter.
[Enter] Bardolph.

BARDOLPH Sir John, there's one Master Brook below
would fain speak with you, and be acquainted with you;
and hath sent your worship a morning's draught of sack.

FALSTAFF Brook is his name?

BARDOLPH Ay, sir.

FALSTAFF Call him in. [Exit Bardolph.] Such Brooks are
welcome to me, that o'erflows such liquor. Aha! Mis-
138 tress Ford and Mistress Page, have I encompassed you?
139 Go to; via!
[Enter Bardolph, with] Ford [disguised].

FORD 'Bless you, sir. –

FALSTAFF And you, sir; would you speak with me?

FORD I make bold to press with so little preparation upon
you.

144 FALSTAFF You're welcome. What's your will? – Give us
leave, drawer.   [Exit Bardolph.]

FORD Sir, I am a gentleman that have spent much. My
name is Brook.

FALSTAFF Good Master Brook, I desire more acquaintance of you.

150 FORD Good Sir John, I sue for yours – not to charge you –
for I must let you understand I think myself in better
plight for a lender than you are, the which hath some-
153 thing emboldened me to this unseasoned intrusion; for
they say if money go before, all ways do lie open.

FALSTAFF Money is a good soldier, sir, and will on.

FORD Troth, and I have a bag of money here troubles me.
If you will help to bear it, Sir John, take all, or half, for
158 easing me of the carriage.

FALSTAFF Sir, I know not how I may deserve to be your
porter.

FORD I will tell you, sir, if you will give me the hearing.

FALSTAFF Speak, good Master Brook. I shall be glad to
be your servant.

FORD Sir, I hear you are a scholar – I will be brief with you
– and you have been a man long known to me, though I
had never so good means as desire to make myself acquainted with you. I shall discover a thing to you where- 167
in I must very much lay open mine own imperfection;
but, good Sir John, as you have one eye upon my follies,
as you hear them unfolded, turn another into the register 170
of your own, that I may pass with a reproof the easier,
sith you yourself know how easy it is to be such an
offender.

FALSTAFF Very well, sir – proceed.

FORD There is a gentlewoman in this town, her husband's name is Ford.

FALSTAFF Well, sir.

FORD I have long loved her, and, I protest to you, bestowed much on her, followed her with a doting observance, engrossed opportunities to meet her, fee'd 179
every slight occasion that could but niggardly give me
sight of her, not only bought many presents to give her
but have given largely to many to know what she would
have given. Briefly, I have pursued her as love hath pursued me, which hath been on the wing of all occasions.
But whatsoever I have merited – either in my mind or in
my means – meed, I am sure, I have received none, unless experience be a jewel. That I have purchased at
an infinite rate, and that hath taught me to say this,
'Love like a shadow flies when substance love pursues; 189
Pursuing that that flies, and flying what pursues.'

FALSTAFF Have you received no promise of satisfaction
at her hands?

FORD Never.

FALSTAFF Have you importuned her to such a purpose?

FORD Never.

FALSTAFF Of what quality was your love then?   196

FORD Like a fair house built on another man's ground, so
that I have lost my edifice by mistaking the place where
I erected it.

FALSTAFF To what purpose have you unfolded this to
me?

FORD When I have told you that, I have told you all. Some
say that though she appear honest to me, yet in other
places she enlargeth her mirth so far that there is shrewd 203
construction made of her. Now, Sir John, here is the
heart of my purpose. – You are a gentleman of excellent
breeding, admirable discourse, of great admittance, 206
authentic in your place and person, generally allowed for 207
your many warlike, courtlike, and learned prepara- 208
tions. –

FALSTAFF O sir!

FORD Believe it, for you know it. There is money. Spend
it, spend it; spend more; spend all I have. – Only give
me so much of your time in exchange of it as to lay an
amiable siege to the honesty of this Ford's wife. Use 212
your art of wooing, win her to consent to you; if any
man may, you may as soon as any.

FALSTAFF Would it apply well to the vehemency of your
affection that I should win what you would enjoy? Methinks you prescribe to yourself very preposterously.

FORD O, understand my drift. She dwells so securely on
the excellency of her honor that the folly of my soul dares
not present itself. She is too bright to be looked against. 221
Now, could I come to her with any detection in my hand,
my desires had instance and argument to commend 223
themselves. I could drive her then from the ward of her 224

123 punk strumpet; carriers messengers 124 fights protective screens for
the crew of a warship 125 prize merchant ship captured for booty 130
grossly (pun on clumsy and big-bodied) 138 encompassed got the better of
139 via go on 144–45 Give us leave leave us alone 150 charge be an
expense to 153 unseasoned unseasonable, ill-timed (with pun on 'without
savor or zest') 158 carriage burden 167 discover disclose 170 register
list 179 engrossed monopolized 179–80 fee'd . . . occasion used every
opportunity 189–90 Love . . . pursues (an adaptation of an Emblem verse
by G. Whitney or a Jonson song) 196 quality nature, character 203
enlargeth her mirth i.e. talks broadly, gives free scope to her jesting; shrewd
bad 206 great admittance high favor 207 authentic of authority; allowed
approved 208 preparations accomplishments 212 amiable i.e. amorous
221 against directly at (like the sun) 223 instance evidence; argument
proof 224 ward guard in fencing

purity, her reputation, her marriage vow, and a thousand other her defenses, which now are too too strongly embattled against me. What say you to't, Sir John?

FALSTAFF Master Brook, I will first make bold with your money; next, give me your hand; and last, as I am a gentleman, you shall, if you will, enjoy Ford's wife.

FORD O good sir!

FALSTAFF I say you shall.

233 FORD Want no money, Sir John; you shall want none.

FALSTAFF Want no Mistress Ford, Master Brook; you shall want none. I shall be with her, I may tell you, by her own appointment – even as you came in to me, her assistant or go-between parted from me. I say I shall be with her between ten and eleven, for at that time the jealous rascally knave her husband will be forth. Come you to me at night; you shall know how I speed.

FORD I am blest in your acquaintance. Do you know Ford, sir?

FALSTAFF Hang him, poor cuckoldly knave! I know him not. Yet I wrong him to call him poor: they say the
245 jealous wittolly knave hath masses of money; for the
246 which his wife seems to me well-favored. I will use her as the key of the cuckoldly rogue's coffer, and there's
248 my harvest-home.

FORD I would you knew Ford, sir, that you might avoid him if you saw him.

251 FALSTAFF Hang him, mechanical salt-butter rogue! I will stare him out of his wits. I will awe him with my cudgel; it shall hang like a meteor o'er the cuckold's horns.
254 Master Brook, thou shalt know I will predominate over the peasant, and thou shalt lie with his wife. Come to me
256 soon at night. Ford's a knave, and I will aggravate his style. Thou, Master Brook, shalt know him for knave and cuckold. Come to me soon at night. *[Exit.]*

259 FORD What a damned Epicurean rascal is this! My heart is ready to crack with impatience. Who says this is improvident jealousy? My wife hath sent to him, the hour is fixed, the match is made. Would any man have thought this? See the hell of having a false woman! My bed shall be abused, my coffers ransacked, my reputation gnawn at; and I shall not only receive this villainous wrong, but
266 stand under the adoption of abominable terms, and by
267 him that does me this wrong. Terms! names! Amaimon sounds well; Lucifer, well; Barbason, well; yet they are
269 devils' additions, the names of fiends. But Cuckold!
270 Wittol! – Cuckold! the devil himself hath not such a name. Page is an ass, a secure ass. He will trust his wife; he will not be jealous. – I will rather trust a Fleming with my butter, Parson Hugh the Welshman with my cheese,
274 an Irishman with my aqua vitae bottle, or a thief to walk my ambling gelding, than my wife with herself. Then she plots, then she ruminates, then she devises – and what they think in their hearts they may effect, they will break their hearts but they will effect. God be praised
279 for my jealousy. Eleven o'clock the hour. I will prevent this, detect my wife, be revenged on Falstaff, and laugh at Page. I will about it; better three hours too soon than
282 a minute too late. Fie, fie, fie! cuckold! cuckold! cuckold! *Exit.*

*

II, iii   *Enter [Doctor] Caius, [and] Rugby.*

CAIUS Jack Rugby. –

RUGBY Sir?

CAIUS Vat is de clock, Jack?

RUGBY 'Tis past the hour, sir, that Sir Hugh promised to meet.

CAIUS By gar, he has save his soul dat he is no come. He has pray his Pible vell dat he is no come. By gar, Jack Rugby, he is dead already if he be come.

RUGBY He is wise, sir. He knew your worship would kill him if he came.

CAIUS By gar, de herring is no dead so as I vill kill him. 11 Take your rapier, Jack; I vill tell you how I vill kill him.

RUGBY Alas, sir, I cannot fence.

CAIUS Villainy, take your rapier.

RUGBY Forbear; here's company.
     [Enter] Page, Shallow, Slender, [and] Host.

HOST 'Bless thee, bully Doctor.

SHALLOW 'Save you, Master Doctor Caius.

PAGE Now, good Master Doctor.

SLENDER 'Give you good morrow, sir.

CAIUS Vat be all you, one, two, tree, four, come for?

HOST To see thee fight, to see thee foin, to see thee tra- 21
verse; to see thee here, to see thee there; to see thee pass 22
thy punto, thy stock, thy reverse, thy distance, thy
montant. Is he dead, my Ethiopian? Is he dead, my
Francisco? Ha, bully? What says my Aesculapius? my 25
Galen? my heart of elder? Ha, is he dead, bully stale? is 26
he dead?

CAIUS By gar, he is de coward Jack-priest of de vorld. He is not show his face.

HOST Thou art a Castilian King-Urinal! Hector of 29
Greece, my boy!

CAIUS I pray you bear vitness dat me have stay six or seven, two, tree hours for him, and he is no come.

SHALLOW He is the wiser man, Master Doctor. He is a curer of souls, and you a curer of bodies. If you should fight, you go against the hair of your professions. Is it 35
not true, Master Page?

PAGE Master Shallow, you have yourself been a great fighter, though now a man of peace.

SHALLOW Bodykins, Master Page, though I now be old 39
and of the peace, if I see a sword out, my finger itches to
make one. Though we are justices and doctors and 41
churchmen, Master Page, we have some salt of our 42
youth in us. We are the sons of women, Master Page.

PAGE 'Tis true, Master Shallow.

SHALLOW It will be found so, Master Page. Master Doctor Caius, I am come to fetch you home. I am sworn of

233 *Want* lack   245 *wittolly* cuckoldly   246 *well-favored* good-looking
248 *harvest-home* i.e. occasion of profit   251 *mechanical* (contemptuous
term for one engaged in manual labour)   *salt-butter* i.e. smelly   254 *predominate* be in the ascendancy (like a planet)   256-57 *aggravate his style*
i.e. add to his title   259 *Epicurean* sensual   266 *stand . . . adoption* i.e. be
subject to christening by   267-68 *Amaimon, Lucifer, Barbason* (names of
devils)   269 *additions* titles   270 *Wittol* stupid or contented cuckold   274
aqua vitae (any ardent spirit like whisky or brandy)   279 *prevent* forestall
282 *Fie* (strong word of disapproval)
II, iii A field near Windsor   11 *herring* (cf. the proverbial simile 'dead as a
herring')   21 *foin* thrust; *traverse* march back and forth   22-24 *pass . . .
montant* i.e. thrust with the point, your stoccado (thrust), your backhanded stroke, keeping your correct distance apart, your upright thrust
25 *Francisco* i.e. Frenchman; *Aesculapius* Greek god of medicine   26
Galen ancient Greek physician; *heart of elder* (soft wood, and therefore
coward, unlike 'heart of oak'); *stale* horse's urine (a jocular reference to the
medical diagnosis remarked in *King-Urinal*, l. 29 and *Mock-water* ll. 50–51)
29–30 *Hector of Greece* (invented term for valiant fighting man)   35 *hair*
grain   39 *Bodykins* God's little body (mild oath)   41 *make one* join in
42 *salt* savor, vigor

the peace. You have showed yourself a wise physician,
and Sir Hugh hath shown himself a wise and patient
churchman. You must go with me, Master Doctor.

50 HOST Pardon, Guest-Justice. – A word, Monsieur Mock-
water.

CAIUS Mock-vater? vat is dat?

HOST Mock-water, in our English tongue, is valor, bully.

CAIUS By gar, den, I have as mush mock-vater as de
Englishman. – Scurvy jack-dog priest! By gar, me vill
cut his ears.

57 HOST He will clapperclaw thee tightly, bully.

CAIUS Clapper-de-claw? vat is dat?

HOST That is, he will make thee amends.

CAIUS By gar, me do look he shall clapper-de-claw me;
for, by gar, me vill have it.

HOST And I will provoke him to't, or let him wag.

CAIUS Me tank you vor dat.

HOST And moreover, bully – [aside] But first, Master
Guest, and Master Page, and eke Cavaliero Slender, go
66 you through the town to Frogmore.

PAGE Sir Hugh is there, is he?

HOST He is there; see what humor he is in. And I will
bring the doctor about by the fields. Will it do well?

SHALLOW We will do it.

PAGE, SHALLOW, AND SLENDER Adieu, good Master
Doctor.   [Exeunt Page, Shallow, and Slender.]

CAIUS By gar, me vill kill de priest, for he speak for a
jackanape to Anne Page.

HOST Let him die. Sheathe thy impatience; throw cold
water on thy choler. Go about the fields with me through
Frogmore. I will bring thee where Mistress Anne Page
is, at a farmhouse a-feasting; and thou shalt woo her.
78 Cried game; said I well?

CAIUS By gar, me tank you vor dat. By gar, I love you;
and I shall procure-a you de good guest – de earl, de
knight, de lords, de gentlemen, my patients.

HOST For the which I will be thy adversary toward Anne
Page. Said I well?

CAIUS By gar, 'tis good; vell said.

HOST Let us wag, then.

CAIUS Come at my heels, Jack Rugby.   Exeunt.

*

III, i   Enter Evans, [and] Simple.

EVANS I pray you now, good Master Slender's servingman, and friend Simple by your name, which way have
you looked for Master Caius, that calls himself Doctor
of Physic?

5 SIMPLE Marry, sir, the Pittie-ward, the Park-ward, every
way; old Windsor way, and every way but the town
way.

EVANS I most fehemently desire you, you will also look
that way.

SIMPLE I will, sir.   [Exit.]

EVANS 'Pless my soul, how full of cholers I am, and 11
trempling of mind. – I shall be glad if he have deceived
me. – How melancholies I am. – I will knog his urinals
about his knave's costard when I have goot opportuni- 14
ties for the 'ork. 'Pless my soul.

[Sings.] 'To shallow rivers, to whose falls   16
          Melodious pirds sing madrigals;
          There will we make our peds of roses,
          And a thousand fragrant posies.
          To shallow –'

Mercy on me, I have a great dispositions to cry.

[Sings.] 'Melodious pirds sing madrigals, –
          Whenas I sat in Pabylon, –   23
          And a thousand vagram posies.   24
          To shallow –'

          [Enter Simple.]

SIMPLE Yonder he is coming, this way, Sir Hugh.

EVANS He's welcome.

[Sings.] 'To shallow rivers, to whose falls –'

Heaven prosper the right! – What weapons is he?

SIMPLE No weapons, sir. There comes my master, Master Shallow, and another gentleman, from Frogmore,
over the stile, this way.

EVANS Pray you, give me my gown – or else keep it in
your arms.

          [Reads in a book.]
          [Enter] Page, Shallow, [and] Slender.

SHALLOW How now, Master Parson. Good morrow,
good Sir Hugh. Keep a gamester from the dice, and a
good student from his book, and it is wonderful.

SLENDER [aside] Ah sweet Anne Page!

PAGE 'Save you, good Sir Hugh.

EVANS 'Pless you from His mercy sake, all of you.

SHALLOW What, the sword and the word? Do you study
them both, Master Parson?

PAGE And youthful still – in your doublet and hose this 43
raw rheumatic day?

EVANS There is reasons and causes for it.

PAGE We are come to you to do a good office, Master
Parson.

EVANS Fery well; what is it?

PAGE Yonder is a most reverend gentleman who, belike
having received wrong by some person, is at most odds 50
with his own gravity and patience that ever you saw.

SHALLOW I have lived fourscore years and upward; I
never heard a man of his place, gravity, and learning so 53
wide of his own respect.   54

EVANS What is he?

PAGE I think you know him: Master Doctor Caius, the
renowned French physician.

EVANS Got's will, and his passion of my heart! I had as
lief you would tell me of a mess of porridge.

PAGE Why?

EVANS He has no more knowledge in Hibocrates and 61
Galen – and he is a knave besides, a cowardly knave as 62
you would desires to be acquainted withal.

PAGE I warrant you, he's the man should fight with him.

SLENDER [aside] O sweet Anne Page!

SHALLOW It appears so by his weapons.

50–51 Mock-water physician (see note on l. 26)   57 clapperclaw thrash
66 Frogmore (in Little Park, Windsor)   78 Cried game the sport is proclaimed (bear-baiting)
III, i A field near Frogmore   5 Pittie-ward towards Windsor Little Park;
Park-ward towards Windsor Great Park   11 cholers i.e. choler, angry
emotions   14 costard i.e. head (literally, a kind of apple)   16–20 To
shallow . . . (garbled version of Marlowe's 'The Passionate Shepherd to His
Love')   23 Whenas . . . Pabylon (an intrusion from Psalm cxxxvii)   24
vagram i.e. fragrant   43 in . . . hose i.e. without the warmth of a cloak (the
doublet was a close-fitting upper garment); hose breeches   50 odds strife
53 gravity dignity   54 wide . . . respect indifferent to his own reputation
61 Hibocrates i.e. Hippocrates, ancient Greek physician   62 Galen Greek
author of a standard medical treatise

[Enter] Host, Caius, [and] Rugby.
Keep them asunder; here comes Doctor Caius.
PAGE Nay, good Master Parson, keep in your weapon.
SHALLOW So do you, good Master Doctor.
70 HOST Disarm them, and let them question. Let them
keep their limbs whole and hack our English.
CAIUS I pray you let-a me speak a word vit your ear.
Verefore vill you not meet-a me?
EVANS *[aside to Caius]* Pray you use your patience.
75 *[aloud]* In good time.
CAIUS By gar, you are de coward, de Jack dog, John ape.
EVANS *[aside to Caius]* Pray you let us not be laughing-
stogs to other men's humors. I desire you in friendship,
and I will one way or other make you amends. *[aloud]* I
will knog your urinals about your knave's cogscomb
[for missing your meetings and appointments].
CAIUS Diable! – Jack Rugby – mine Host de Jarteer –
have I not stay for him to kill him? Have I not, at de
place I did appoint?
EVANS As I am a Christians soul, now, look you, this is
the place appointed. I'll be judgment by mine Host of
the Garter.
88 HOST Peace, I say, Gallia and Gaul, French and Welsh,
soul-curer and body-curer.
CAIUS Ay, dat is very good, excellent.
HOST Peace, I say. Hear mine Host of the Garter. – Am I
92 politic? am I subtle? am I a Machiavel? Shall I lose my
93 doctor? No; he gives me the potions and the motions.
Shall I lose my parson, my priest, my Sir Hugh? No; he
95 gives me the proverbs and the no-verbs. [Give me thy
hand, terrestrial; so.] Give me thy hand, celestial; so.
97 Boys of art, I have deceived you both; I have directed
you to wrong places. Your hearts are mighty, your skins
99 are whole, and let burnt sack be the issue. Come, lay
their swords to pawn. Follow me, lad of peace; follow,
follow, follow.
SHALLOW Trust me, a mad Host. – Follow, gentlemen,
follow.
SLENDER *[aside]* O sweet Anne Page!
[Exeunt Shallow, Slender, Page, and Host.]
105 CAIUS Ha, do I perceive dat? Have you make-a de sot of
us, ha, ha?
107 EVANS This is well – he has made us his vlouting-stog. I
desire you that we may be friends, and let us knog our
109 prains together to be revenge on this same scall, scurvy,
110 cogging companion, the Host of the Garter.
CAIUS By gar, vit all my heart. He promise to bring me
vere is Anne Page. By gar, he deceive me too.
EVANS Well, I will smite his noddles. Pray you follow.
[Exeunt.]

*

III, ii   *[Enter] Mistress Page, [and] Robin.*
MRS PAGE Nay, keep your way, little gallant – you were
2 wont to be a follower, but now you are a leader. Whether
had you rather lead mine eyes, or eye your master's
heels?
ROBIN I had rather, forsooth, go before you like a man
than follow him like a dwarf.
MRS PAGE O, you are a flattering boy. Now I see you'll
be a courtier.
[Enter] Ford.
FORD Well met, Mistress Page. Whither go you?

MRS PAGE Truly, sir, to see your wife. Is she at home?
FORD Ay, and as idle as she may hang together, for want 11
of company. I think if your husbands were dead, you
two would marry.
MRS PAGE Be sure of that – two other husbands.
FORD Where had you this pretty weathercock?   15
MRS PAGE I cannot tell what the dickens his name is my
husband had him of. What do you call your knight's
name, sirrah?
ROBIN Sir John Falstaff.
FORD Sir John Falstaff!
MRS PAGE He, he; I can never hit on's name. There is
such a league between my goodman and he. – Is your 22
wife at home indeed?
FORD Indeed she is.
MRS PAGE By your leave, sir. I am sick till I see her.
[Exeunt Mistress Page and Robin.]
FORD Has Page any brains? hath he any eyes? hath he any
thinking? Sure, they sleep; he hath no use of them. Why,
this boy will carry a letter twenty mile as easy as a cannon
will shoot pointblank twelve score. He pieces out his 29
wife's inclination; he gives her folly motion and ad- 30
vantage – and now she's going to my wife, and Falstaff's
boy with her. A man may hear this shower sing in the 32
wind. And Falstaff's boy with her. – Good plots! They
are laid, and our revolted wives share damnation together. Well, I will take him, then torture my wife, pluck
the borrowed veil of modesty from the so-seeming Mistress Page, divulge Page himself for a secure and wilful 37
Actaeon; and to these violent proceedings all my neighbors shall cry aim. *[Clock strikes.]* The clock gives me 39
my cue, and my assurance bids me search. There I shall
find Falstaff. I shall be rather praised for this than
mocked, for it is as positive as the earth is firm that
Falstaff is there. – I will go.
*[Enter] Page, Shallow, Slender, Host, [Sir Hugh]
Evans, Caius [, and Rugby].*
SHALLOW, PAGE, ETC. Well met, Master Ford.
FORD Trust me, a good knot. I have good cheer at home, 45
and I pray you all go with me.
SHALLOW I must excuse myself, Master Ford.
SLENDER And so must I, sir. We have appointed to dine
with Mistress Anne, and I would not break with her for
more money than I'll speak of.
SHALLOW We have lingered about a match between
Anne Page and my cousin Slender, and this day we
shall have our answer.
SLENDER I hope I have your good will, father Page.
PAGE You have, Master Slender – I stand wholly for you.
But my wife, Master Doctor, is for you altogether.
CAIUS Ay, by gar, and de maid is love-a me – my nursh-a
Quickly tell me so mush.

70 *question* debate 75 *In good time* at a suitable occasion 88 *Gallia*
Wales (Fr. '*Galles*') 92 *Machiavel* Florentine political writer, known as a
consummate intriguer 93 *motions* purges (with pun on 'motions': passions) 95 *no-verbs* (Host's coinage to describe Evans' diction) 97 *art*
learning 99 *burnt sack* mulled wine; *issue* outcome 105 *sot* fool 107
vlouting-stog flouting-stock, laughing-stock 109 *scall* i.e. scald, scurvy
110 *cogging* cheating
III, ii A street in Windsor 2 *Whether* I wonder whether 11 *as idle . . .*
together i.e. as bored as she can stand 15 *weathercock* i.e. spruce little
creature 22 *league* friendship, alliance 29 *pieces out* ekes out 30 *motion*
prompting 32–33 *hear . . . wind* trust to his senses (?), observe this storm
blowing up (?) 37–38 *secure . . . Actaeon* i.e. overconfident and stubborn
victim 39 *cry aim* encourage, applaud (archery) 45 *knot* company

HOST What say you to young Master Fenton? He capers,
he dances, he has eyes of youth, he writes verses, he
61 speaks holiday, he smells April and May. He will carry't,
62 he will carry't; 'tis in his buttons; he will carry't.
PAGE Not by my consent, I promise you. The gentleman is
64 of no having. He kept company with the wild Prince and
65 Poins; he is of too high a region; he knows too much.
No, he shall not knit a knot in his fortunes with the finger
67 of my substance. If he take her, let him take her simply.
The wealth I have waits on my consent, and my consent
goes not that way.
FORD I beseech you heartily, some of you go home with
me to dinner. Besides your cheer, you shall have sport –
72 I will show you a monster. Master Doctor, you shall go.
So shall you, Master Page, and you, Sir Hugh.
SHALLOW Well, fare you well. We shall have the freer
wooing at Master Page's. *[Exeunt Shallow and Slender.]*
CAIUS Go home, John Rugby. I come anon.
[Exit Rugby.]
HOST Farewell, my hearts. I will to my honest knight Fal-
78 staff, and drink canary with him. *[Exit.]*
79 FORD *[aside]* I think I shall drink in pipe-wine first with
him: I'll make him dance. – Will you go, gentles?
ALL Have with you to see this monster. *Exeunt.*

✻

III, iii   *Enter Mistress Ford, [and] Mistress Page.*
1 MRS FORD What, John; what, Robert. –
2 MRS PAGE Quickly, quickly. – Is the buck-basket –
MRS FORD I warrant. What, Robert, I say. –
[Enter] Servants [with a basket].
MRS PAGE Come, come, come.
MRS FORD Here, set it down.
MRS PAGE Give your men the charge. We must be brief.
MRS FORD Marry, as I told you before, John, and Robert,
be ready here hard by in the brewhouse; and when I suddenly call you, come forth, and without any pause or
staggering, take this basket on your shoulders. That
done, trudge with it in all haste, and carry it among the
12 whitsters in Datchet Mead, and there empty it in the
muddy ditch, close by the Thames side.
MRS PAGE You will do it?
MRS FORD I ha' told them over and over – they lack no
direction. Be gone, and come when you are called.
[Exeunt Servants.]

[Enter] Robin.
MRS PAGE Here comes little Robin.
MRS FORD How now, my eyas-musket, what news with 18
you?
ROBIN My master, Sir John, is come in at your back
door, Mistress Ford, and requests your company.
MRS PAGE You little Jack-a-Lent, have you been true 22
to us?
ROBIN Ay, I'll be sworn. My master knows not of your
being here, and hath threatened to put me into everlast-
ing liberty if I tell you of it; for he swears he'll turn me
away.
MRS PAGE Thou'rt a good boy. This secrecy of thine
shall be a tailor to thee and shall make thee a new
doublet and hose. I'll go hide me.
MRS FORD Do so. – Go tell thy master I am alone. *[Exit
Robin.]* Mistress Page, remember you your cue.
MRS PAGE I warrant thee. If I do not act it, hiss me.
[Exit.]
MRS FORD Go to, then. We'll use this unwholesome
humidity, this gross watery pumpion – we'll teach him 33
to know turtles from jays. 34
[Enter] Falstaff.
FALSTAFF 'Have I caught thee, my heavenly jewel?' 35
Why, now let me die, for I have lived long enough. This
is the period of my ambition. O this blessed hour! 37
MRS FORD O sweet Sir John!
FALSTAFF Mistress Ford, I cannot cog, I cannot prate, 39
Mistress Ford. Now shall I sin in my wish: I would thy
husband were dead. I'll speak it before the best lord, I
would make thee my lady.
MRS FORD I your lady, Sir John? Alas, I should be a
pitiful lady.
FALSTAFF Let the court of France show me such another.
I see how thine eye would emulate the diamond. Thou
hast the right arched beauty of the brow that becomes
the ship-tire, the tire-valiant, or any tire of Venetian ad- 48
mittance.
MRS FORD A plain kerchief, Sir John – my brows become nothing else, nor that well neither.
FALSTAFF *[By the Lord,]* thou art a tyrant to say so.
Thou wouldst make an absolute courtier, and the firm 53
fixture of thy foot would give an excellent motion to thy
gait in a semicircled farthingale. I see what thou wert if 55
Fortune thy foe were (not Nature) thy friend. Come,
thou canst not hide it.
MRS FORD Believe me, there's no such thing in me.
FALSTAFF What made me love thee? Let that persuade
thee there's something extraordinary in thee. Come, I
cannot cog and say thou art this and that, like a many of
these lisping hawthorn buds that come like women in 62
men's apparel and smell like Bucklersbury in simple- 63
time. I cannot. But I love thee, none but thee; and thou
deservest it.
MRS FORD Do not betray me, sir. I fear you love Mistress Page.
FALSTAFF Thou mightst as well say I love to walk by the
Counter-gate, which is as hateful to me as the reek of a 68
limekiln.
MRS FORD Well, heaven knows how I love you, and you
shall one day find it.
FALSTAFF Keep in that mind – I'll deserve it.
MRS FORD Nay, I must tell you, so you do, or else I
could not be in that mind.

61 *speaks holiday* uses choice language   62 *'tis . . . buttons* i.e. he is sure to
succeed   64 *having* property   64–65 *wild . . . Poins* (Prince Hal and his
companion Poins in *1 & 2 Henry IV*)   65 *region* status   67 *simply* by
herself   72 *monster* something wonderful (i.e. the horned cuckold Page)
78 *canary* light sweet wine from the Canary Islands   79 *pipe-wine* wine
from the cask (with pun on music for the canary as a lively dance)
III, iii Within the house of Master Ford   1 *What* i.e. get a move on
2 *buck-basket* dirty-linen basket   12 *whitsters* bleachers of linen; *Datchet
Mead* (two miles east of Windsor)   18 *eyas-musket* young male sparrow-
hawk   22 *Jack-a-Lent* puppet   33 *pumpion* pumpkin   34 *turtles from jays*
i.e. faithful wives from loose women   35 *Have I . . . jewel* (from Sidney's
Astrophel and Stella)   37 *period* end, goal   39 *cog* flatter, cheat   48 *ship-
tire* head-dress shaped like a ship; *tire-valiant* fanciful head-dress; *admittance* fashion   53 *absolute* perfect   55 *semicircled farthingale* petticoat with
hoops not joining in front   55–56 *I see . . . friend* i.e. I can imagine what you
would look like if Fortune should translate you to fashionable society
where you would not need to rely merely on your natural beauty, which
now befriends you ('Fortune My Foe' is the name of a popular tune)
62 *hawthorn buds* i.e. fops   63 *Bucklersbury* a street in London where
herbalists sold their wares   63–64 *simple-time* season for herbs   68 *Counter*
the debtors' prison

[Enter Robin.]

ROBIN Mistress Ford, Mistress Ford! Here's Mistress Page at the door, sweating and blowing and looking wildly, and would needs speak with you presently.

78 FALSTAFF She shall not see me; I will ensconce me be-
79 hind the arras.

MRS FORD Pray you, do so – she's a very tattling woman.

[Falstaff hides himself. Enter Mistress Page.]
What's the matter? how now. –

MRS PAGE O Mistress Ford, what have you done? You're shamed, you're overthrown, you're undone for ever!

MRS FORD What's the matter, good Mistress Page?

MRS PAGE O well-a-day, Mistress Ford – having an honest man to your husband, to give him such cause of suspicion!

MRS FORD What cause of suspicion?

MRS PAGE What cause of suspicion! Out upon you,
90 how am I mistook in you!

MRS FORD Why, alas, what's the matter?

MRS PAGE Your husband's coming hither, woman, with all the officers in Windsor, to search for a gentleman that he says is here now in the house by your consent, to take an ill advantage of his absence. You are undone.

MRS FORD 'Tis not so, I hope.

MRS PAGE Pray heaven it be not so, that you have such a man here! But 'tis most certain your husband's coming, with half Windsor at his heels, to search for such a one. I
100 come before to tell you. If you know yourself clear, why,
101 I am glad of it; but if you have a friend here, convey,
102 convey him out. Be not amazed, call all your senses to you, defend your reputation – or bid farewell to your good life for ever.

MRS FORD What shall I do? – There is a gentleman, my
106 dear friend; and I fear not mine own shame so much as his peril. I had rather than a thousand pound he were out of the house.

109 MRS PAGE For shame! Never stand 'you had rather' and 'you had rather.' Your husband's here at hand; bethink you of some conveyance. In the house you cannot hide him. – O, how have you deceived me! – Look, here is a basket. If he be of any reasonable stature, he may creep in here; and throw foul linen upon him, as if it
115 were going to bucking. Or – it is whiting-time – send him by your two men to Datchet Mead.

MRS FORD He's too big to go in there. What shall I do?

FALSTAFF *[coming forward]* Let me see't, let me see't, O let me see't! I'll in, I'll in. Follow your friend's counsel. – I'll in.

MRS PAGE What, Sir John Falstaff! *[aside]* Are these your letters, knight?

FALSTAFF *[aside]* I love thee. Help me away. – Let me creep in here. I'll never –

[Gets into the basket; they cover him with foul linen.]

MRS PAGE Help to cover your master, boy. Call your men, Mistress Ford. *[aside]* You dissembling knight!

MRS FORD What, John! Robert! John! *[Exit Robin.]*

[Enter Servants.]
128 Go take up these clothes here quickly. Where's the cowl-
129 staff? Look how you drumble! Carry them to the laundress in Datchet Mead – quickly, come!

[Enter] Ford, Page, Caius, [and] Evans.

FORD Pray you come near. If I suspect without cause, why then make sport at me; then let me be your jest; I deserve it. How now, whither bear you this?

SERVANTS To the laundress, forsooth.

MRS FORD Why, what have you to do whither they bear it? You were best meddle with buck-washing!

FORD Buck? I would I could wash myself of the buck! 137 Buck, buck, buck! Ay, buck; I warrant you, buck; and of the season too, it shall appear. *[Exeunt Servants with 139 the basket.]* Gentlemen, I have dreamed to-night; I'll 140 tell you my dream. Here, here, here be my keys. Ascend my chambers; search, seek, find out. I'll warrant we'll unkennel the fox. Let me stop this way first. *[Locks the 143 door.]* So, now uncope. 144

PAGE Good Master Ford, be contented. You wrong yourself too much.

FORD True, Master Page. – Up, gentlemen; you shall see sport anon. Follow me, gentlemen. *[Exit.]*

EVANS This is fery fantastical humors and jealousies.

CAIUS By gar, 'tis no de fashion of France; it is not jealous in France.

PAGE Nay, follow him, gentlemen – see the issue of his search. *[Exeunt Page, Caius, and Evans.]*

MRS PAGE Is there not a double excellency in this?

MRS FORD I know not which pleases me better: that my husband is deceived, or Sir John.

MRS PAGE What a taking was he in when your husband 157 asked who was in the basket!

MRS FORD I am half afraid he will have need of washing; so throwing him into the water will do him a benefit.

MRS PAGE Hang him, dishonest rascal! I would all of the same strain were in the same distress.

MRS FORD I think my husband hath some special suspicion of Falstaff's being here, for I never saw him so gross in his jealousy till now.

MRS PAGE I will lay a plot to try that, and we will yet 166 have more tricks with Falstaff – his dissolute disease will scarce obey this medicine.

MRS FORD Shall we send that foolish carrion Mistress 169 Quickly to him, and excuse his throwing into the water; and give him another hope, to betray him to another punishment?

MRS PAGE We will do it. Let him be sent for to-morrow eight o'clock, to have amends.

[Enter Ford, Page, Caius, and Evans.]

FORD I cannot find him – may be the knave bragged of that he could not compass.

MRS PAGE *[aside to Mistress Ford]* Heard you that?

MRS FORD You use me well, Master Ford, do you?

FORD Ay, I do so. –

MRS FORD Heaven make you better than your thoughts!

FORD Amen. –

MRS PAGE You do yourself mighty wrong, Master Ford.

FORD Ay, ay, I must bear it.

EVANS If there be any pody in the house, and in the chambers, and in the coffers, and in the presses, heaven 185 forgive my sins at the day of judgment.

---

78 *ensconce* conceal (military) 79 *arras* tapestry hanging 100 *clear* innocent 101 *friend* i.e. lover 102 *amazed* bewildered, as in a maze 106 *friend* (used here innocently) 109 *stand* lose time over 115 *bucking* washing; *whiting-time* bleaching-time 128–9 *cowl-staff* pole for carrying a basket between two men 129 *drumble* dawdle 137 *Buck* (Ford plays on the horned beast, the cuckold) 139 *of the season* in season 140 *to-night* last night 143 *unkennel* start, drive into the open 144 *uncope* unloose (as with the mouth of a ferret before setting it upon holed-up game) 157 *taking* fright 166 *try* test 169 *carrion* (contemptuous for aging rotten flesh; also for a loose woman or bawd) 185 *presses* cupboards

CAIUS By gar, nor I too, dere is nobodies.

PAGE Fie, fie, Master Ford, are you not ashamed? What spirit, what devil suggests this imagination? I would not ha' your distemper in this kind for the wealth of Windsor Castle. *190*

FORD 'Tis my fault, Master Page – I suffer for it.

EVANS You suffer for a pad conscience. Your wife is as honest a 'omans as I will desires among five thousand, and five hundred too.

CAIUS By gar, I see 'tis an honest woman.

FORD Well, I promised you a dinner. Come, come, walk in the Park. I pray you pardon me. I will hereafter make known to you why I have done this. – Come, wife; come, Mistress Page. – I pray you pardon me; pray heartily pardon me.

PAGE Let's go in, gentlemen; but, trust me, we'll mock him. I do invite you to-morrow morning to my house to breakfast. After, we'll a-birding together: I have a fine hawk for the bush. Shall it be so? *204* *205*

FORD Anything.

EVANS If there is one, I shall make two in the company.

CAIUS If dere be one, or two, I shall make-a de turd.

FORD Pray you go, Master Page.

EVANS I pray you now, remembrance to-morrow on the lousy knave, mine Host.

CAIUS Dat is good; by gar, vit all my heart.

EVANS A lousy knave, to have his gibes and his mockeries! *Exeunt.*

*

III, iv   *Enter Fenton, [and] Anne Page.*

FENTON
I see I cannot get thy father's love;
Therefore no more turn me to him, sweet Nan.

ANNE
         Alas, how then?

FENTON   Why, thou must be thyself.
He doth object I am too great of birth,
And that my state being galled with my expense, *5*
I seek to heal it only by his wealth.
Besides these, other bars he lays before me,
My riots past, my wild societies; *8*
And tells me 'tis a thing impossible
I should love thee but as a property. *10*

ANNE
May be he tells you true.

FENTON
No, heaven so speed me in my time to come!
Albeit I will confess thy father's wealth
Was the first motive that I wooed thee, Anne.
Yet, wooing thee, I found thee of more value
Than stamps in gold or sums in sealèd bags; *16*
And 'tis the very riches of thyself
That now I aim at.

ANNE   Gentle Master Fenton,
Yet seek my father's love; still seek it, sir.
If opportunity and humblest suit
Cannot attain it, why, then – hark you hither.
     [They talk apart.]
     [Enter] Shallow, Slender, [and Mistress] Quickly.

SHALLOW Break their talk, Mistress Quickly. My kinsman shall speak for himself.

SLENDER I'll make a shaft or a bolt on't. 'Slid, 'tis but venturing. *24*

SHALLOW Be not dismayed.

SLENDER No, she shall not dismay me. I care not for that, but that I am afeard.

QUICKLY Hark ye, Master Slender would speak a word with you.

ANNE
I come to him. *[aside]* This is my father's choice.
O, what a world of vile ill-favored faults
Looks handsome in three hundred pounds a year. –

QUICKLY And how does good Master Fenton? Pray you a word with you.

SHALLOW She's coming; to her, coz. O boy, thou hadst a father! *36*

SLENDER I had a father, Mistress Anne – my uncle can tell you good jests of him. Pray you, uncle, tell Mistress Anne the jest how my father stole two geese out of a pen, good uncle.

SHALLOW Mistress Anne, my cousin loves you. *42*

SLENDER Ay, that I do, as well as I love any woman in Gloucestershire.

SHALLOW He will maintain you like a gentlewoman.

SLENDER Ay, that I will, come cut and long-tail, under the degree of a squire. *46*

SHALLOW He will make you a hundred and fifty pounds jointure.

ANNE Good Master Shallow, let him woo for himself.

SHALLOW Marry, I thank you for it, I thank you for that good comfort. She calls you, coz. I'll leave you.

ANNE Now, Master Slender –

SLENDER Now, good Mistress Anne–

ANNE What is your will?

SLENDER My will? 'Od's heartlings, that's a pretty jest indeed! I ne'er made my will yet, I thank God. I am not such a sickly creature, I give heaven praise. *56*

ANNE I mean, Master Slender, what would you with me?

SLENDER Truly, for mine own part, I would little or nothing with you. Your father and my uncle have made motions. If it be my luck, so; if not, happy man be his dole. – They can tell you how things go better than I can. You may ask your father; here he comes. *62*
     [Enter] Page, [and] Mistress Page.

PAGE
Now, Master Slender. Love him, daughter Anne. –
Why, how now, what does Master Fenton here?
You wrong me, sir, thus still to haunt my house.
I told you, sir, my daughter is disposed of.

FENTON
Nay, Master Page, be not impatient.

MRS PAGE
Good Master Fenton, come not to my child.

PAGE
She is no match for you.

FENTON
Sir, will you hear me?

190 *distemper* deranged condition; *in this kind* of this species   **204** *a-birding* hawking   **205** *for the bush* i.e. for small birds in bushy fields where nets could not be used

III, iv Before the house of Master Page   **5** *state* estate; *galled . . . expense* hurt by my extravagance   **8** *societies* companionships   **10** *property* tool, mere means to an end   **16** *stamps* coins   **24** *a shaft or a bolt* a slender or a thick arrow   **36–37** *thou hadst a father* i.e. be resolute like your father, be a man   **42** *cousin* (used of any close relation; here, nephew)   **46** *come . . . long-tail* i.e. come what may (originally applied to short- or long-tailed horses)   **56** *'Od's heartlings* God's little heart (mild oath)   **62–63** *happy . . . dole* happiness be his portion

PAGE   No, good Master Fenton.
Come, Master Shallow; come, son Slender, in.
Knowing my mind, you wrong me, Master Fenton.
                    [Exeunt Page, Shallow, and Slender.]
QUICKLY Speak to Mistress Page.
FENTON
Good Mistress Page, for that I love your daughter
In such a righteous fashion as I do,
78 Perforce, against all checks, rebukes, and manners,
79 I must advance the colors of my love
And not retire. Let me have your good will.
ANNE Good mother, do not marry me to yond fool.
MRS PAGE I mean it not – I seek you a better husband.
QUICKLY *[aside]* That's my master, Master Doctor.
ANNE
84 Alas, I had rather be set quick i' th' earth,
And bowled to death with turnips.
MRS PAGE
Come, trouble not yourself. Good Master Fenton,
I will not be your friend, nor enemy.
My daughter will I question how she loves you,
And as I find her, so am I affected.
Till then, farewell, sir. She must needs go in;
Her father will be angry.
FENTON
Farewell, gentle mistress. – Farewell, Nan.
                    Exeunt [Mistress Page, and Anne].
QUICKLY This is my doing now. 'Nay,' said I, 'will you
cast away your child on a fool, and a physician? Look on
Master Fenton.' This is my doing.
FENTON
96 I thank thee, and I pray thee once to-night
Give my sweet Nan this ring. There's for thy pains.
QUICKLY Now heaven send thee good fortune! *[Exit Fen-
ton.]* A kind heart he hath. A woman would run through
fire and water for such a kind heart. But yet I would my
master had Mistress Anne; or I would Master Slender
had her; or, in sooth, I would Master Fenton had her. I
will do what I can for them all three, for so I have prom-
104 ised, and I'll be as good as my word; but speciously for
Master Fenton. Well, I must of another errand to Sir
John Falstaff from my two mistresses. What a beast am
I to slack it!   *[Exit.]*

                            *

III, v   *Enter Falstaff, [and] Bardolph.*
FALSTAFF Bardolph, I say. –
BARDOLPH Here, sir.
FALSTAFF Go fetch me a quart of sack – put a toast in't.
[Exit Bardolph.] Have I lived to be carried in a basket
like a barrow of butcher's offal? – And to be thrown in
the Thames! Well, if I be served such another trick, I'll
have my brains ta'en out, and buttered, and give them to
8   a dog for a New-Year's gift. The rogues slighted me into
the river with as little remorse as they would have
drowned a blind bitch's puppies, fifteen i' the litter –
and you may know by my size that I have a kind of alacrity in sinking; if the bottom were as deep as hell, I
should down. I had been drowned but that the shore
was shelvy and shallow – a death that I abhor, for the
water swells a man, and what a thing should I have been
when I had been swelled. – I should have been a moun-
16 tain of mummy.
                    [Enter Bardolph with wine.]

BARDOLPH Here's Mistress Quickly, sir, to speak with
you.
FALSTAFF Come, let me pour in some sack to the Thames
water, for my belly's as cold as if I had swallowed snow-
balls for pills to cool the reins. Call her in.   20
BARDOLPH Come in, woman.
                    [Enter Mistress] Quickly.
QUICKLY By your leave; I cry you mercy. Give your   22
worship good morrow.
FALSTAFF Take away these chalices. Go, brew me a
pottle of sack finely.
BARDOLPH With eggs, sir?
FALSTAFF Simple of itself – I'll no pullet-sperm in my
brewage. *[Exit Bardolph.]* How now. –
QUICKLY Marry, sir, I come to your worship from Mis-
tress Ford.
FALSTAFF Mistress Ford? I have had ford enough; I
was thrown into the ford; I have my belly full of ford.
QUICKLY Alas the day, good heart, that was not her fault.
She does so take on with her men – they mistook their
erection.   35
FALSTAFF So did I mine, to build upon a foolish woman's
promise.
QUICKLY Well, she laments, sir, for it that it would yearn 38
your heart to see it. Her husband goes this morning
a-birding. She desires you once more to come to her
between eight and nine. I must carry her word quickly.
She'll make you amends, I warrant you.
FALSTAFF Well, I will visit her, tell her so. And bid her
think what a man is – let her consider his frailty, and
then judge of my merit.
QUICKLY I will tell her.
FALSTAFF Do so. – Between nine and ten, sayest thou?
QUICKLY Eight and nine, sir.
FALSTAFF Well, begone. I will not miss her.
QUICKLY Peace be with you, sir.   *[Exit.]*   50
FALSTAFF I marvel I hear not of Master Brook – he sent
me word to stay within. I like his money well.
                    [Enter] Ford.
O, here he comes.
FORD 'Bless you, sir. –
FALSTAFF Now, Master Brook, you come to know what
hath passed between me and Ford's wife?
FORD That, indeed, Sir John, is my business.
FALSTAFF Master Brook, I will not lie to you. I was at
her house the hour she appointed me.
FORD And sped you, sir?
FALSTAFF Very ill-favoredly, Master Brook.   61
FORD How so, sir? Did she change her determination?
FALSTAFF No, Master Brook, but the peaking cornuto   63
her husband, Master Brook, dwelling in a continual
'larum of jealousy, comes me in the instant of our encounter, after we had embraced, kissed, protested, and,
as it were, spoke the prologue of our comedy; and at his
heels a rabble of his companions, thither provoked and
instigated by his distemper, and, forsooth, to search his
house for his wife's love.

---

78 *checks* reproofs 79 *colors* standards (military) 84 *quick* living 96 *once*
sometime 104 *speciously* i.e. especially
III, v Within the Garter Inn 8 *New-Year's* (traditional day for gifts);
slighted me i.e. tossed me slightingly 16 *mummy* cadaver 20 *reins* kidneys
22 *cry you mercy* beg your pardon 35 *erection* i.e. direction 38 *yearn*
grieve 61 *ill-favoredly* unpleasingly 63 *peaking cornuto* sneaking cuckold

FORD What, while you were there?

FALSTAFF While I was there.

FORD And did he search for you, and could not find you?

FALSTAFF You shall hear. As good luck would have it, comes in one Mistress Page, gives intelligence of Ford's approach, and in her invention, and Ford's wife's distraction, they conveyed me into a buck-basket.

FORD A buck-basket?

FALSTAFF By the Lord, a buck-basket! – Rammed me in
80   with foul shirts and smocks, socks, foul stockings, greasy napkins, that, Master Brook, there was the rankest compound of villainous smell that ever offended nostril.

FORD And how long lay you there?

FALSTAFF Nay, you shall hear, Master Brook, what I have suffered to bring this woman to evil for your good. Being thus crammed in the basket, a couple of Ford's knaves,
87   his hinds, were called forth by their mistress to carry me in the name of foul clothes to Datchet Lane. They took me on their shoulders, met the jealous knave their master in the door, who asked them once or twice what they had in their basket. I quaked for fear lest the lunatic knave would have searched it; but Fate, ordaining he should be a cuckold, held his hand. Well, on went he for a search, and away went I for foul clothes. – But mark the sequel, Master Brook. I suffered the pangs of three several
96   deaths: first, an intolerable fright to be detected with a
97   jealous rotten bellwether; next, to be compassed like a
98   good bilbo in the circumference of a peck, hilt to point, heel to head; and then, to be stopped in, like a strong
100   distillation, with stinking clothes that fretted in their own grease. Think of that, a man of my kidney – think of that – that am as subject to heat as butter; a man of con-
103   tinual dissolution and thaw. It was a miracle to 'scape suffocation. And in the height of this bath, when I was more than half stewed in grease like a Dutch dish, to be thrown into the Thames, and cooled, glowing hot, in that surge, like a horseshoe. – Think of that – hissing hot – think of that, Master Brook!

109 FORD In good sadness, sir, I am sorry that for my sake you have suffered all this. My suit then is desperate. You'll undertake her no more?

FALSTAFF Master Brook, I will be thrown into Aetna, as I have been into Thames, ere I will leave her thus. Her husband is this morning gone a-birding. I have received
115   from her another embassy of meeting – 'twixt eight and nine is the hour, Master Brook.

FORD 'Tis past eight already, sir.

118 FALSTAFF Is it? I will then address me to my appointment. Come to me at your convenient leisure, and you shall know how I speed; and the conclusion shall be crowned with your enjoying her. Adieu. You shall have her, Master Brook; Master Brook, you shall cuckold Ford.   *[Exit.]*

FORD Hum, ha! is this a vision? is this a dream? do I sleep? Master Ford, awake; awake, Master Ford! There's a hole made in your best coat, Master Ford. This 'tis to be married; this 'tis to have linen and buck-baskets! – Well, I will proclaim myself what I am. I will now take the lecher; he is at my house; he cannot 'scape me; 'tis impossible he should; he cannot creep into a halfpenny purse, nor into a pepperbox; but, lest the devil that guides him should aid him, I will search impossible places. Though what I am I cannot avoid, yet to be what I would not, shall not make me tame. If I have horns to make one mad, let the proverb go with me – I'll be horn-mad.   *[Exit.]*

*

Enter Mistresses Page, [Mistress] Quickly, [and]   IV, i
William.

MRS PAGE Is he at Master Ford's already, thinkest thou?

QUICKLY Sure he is by this, or will be presently. But truly, he is very courageous mad about his throwing into the water. Mistress Ford desires you to come suddenly.

MRS PAGE I'll be with her by and by – I'll but bring my 5 young man here to school. Look where his master comes; 'tis a playing-day, I see.

[Enter] Evans.

How now, Sir Hugh; no school to-day?

EVANS No. Master Slender is let the boys leave to play.

QUICKLY Blessing of his heart. –

MRS PAGE Sir Hugh, my husband says my son profits nothing in the world at his book. I pray you, ask him some questions in his accidence.   13

EVANS Come hither, William. Hold up your head; come.

MRS PAGE Come on, sirrah; hold up your head; answer your master, be not afraid.

EVANS William, how many numbers is in nouns?

WILLIAM Two.

QUICKLY Truly, I thought there had been one number more, because they say, 'Od's nouns.'   20

EVANS Peace your tattlings. What is 'fair,' William?

WILLIAM 'Pulcher.'

QUICKLY Polecats! There are fairer things than polecats, 23 sure.

EVANS You are a very simplicity 'oman. I pray you peace. What is 'lapis,' William?

WILLIAM A stone.

EVANS And what is 'a stone,' William?

WILLIAM A pebble.

EVANS No, it is 'lapis.' I pray you remember in your prain.

WILLIAM 'Lapis.'

EVANS That is a good William. What is he, William, that does lend articles?

WILLIAM Articles are borrowed of the pronoun, and be thus declined: 'Singulariter, nominativo, hic, haec, hoc.'

EVANS 'Nominativo, hig, hag, hog.' Pray you mark: 'genitivo, hujus.' Well, what is your accusative case?

WILLIAM 'Accusativo, hinc.'

EVANS I pray you, have your remembrance, child: 'accusativo, hung, hang, hog.'

QUICKLY 'Hang-hog' is Latin for bacon, I warrant you. 41

EVANS Leave your prabbles, 'oman. What is the focative case, William?

---

80 *smocks* linen undergarments something like slips   87 *hinds* country servants   96 *with* by   97 *bellwether* old ram (belled and leading a flock)   98 *bilbo* well-tempered sword   100 *fretted* decayed, fermented   103 *dissolution* liquefaction   109 *sadness* seriousness   115 *embassy* love message   118 *address* prepare

IV, i A street in Windsor   5 *by and by* very soon   13 *accidence* i.e. Latin grammar   20 *Od's nouns* God's wounds   23 *Polecats* panthers or leopards (but also slang for prostitutes)   41 *Hang-hog* (an old joke: hog is not bacon until it be hanged)

WILLIAM 'O, vocativo, O.'

45 EVANS Remember, William; focative is 'caret.'

QUICKLY And that's a good root.

EVANS 'Oman, forbear.

MRS PAGE Peace.

EVANS What is your genitive case plural, William?

WILLIAM Genitive case?

EVANS Ay.

WILLIAM 'Genitivo, horum, harum, horum.'

QUICKLY Vengeance of Jenny's case! fie on her! Never name her, child, if she be a whore.

EVANS For shame, 'oman.

QUICKLY You do ill to teach the child such words. He
57 teaches him to hick and to hack, which they'll do fast enough of themselves, and to call 'horum.' Fie upon you!

EVANS 'Oman, art thou lunatics? Hast thou no understandings for thy cases and the numbers of the genders? Thou art as foolish Christian creatures as I would desires.

MRS PAGE Prithee hold thy peace.

EVANS Show me now, William, some declensions of your pronouns.

WILLIAM Forsooth, I have forgot.

EVANS It is 'qui, quae, quod.' If you forget your 'qui's,'
67 your 'quae's,' and your 'quod's,' you must be preeches. Go your ways and play, go.

MRS PAGE He is a better scholar than I thought he was.

70 EVANS He is a good sprag memory. Farewell, Mistress Page.

MRS PAGE Adieu, good Sir Hugh. *[Exit Evans.]* Get you home, boy. – Come, we stay too long. *Exeunt.*

*

IV, ii   *Enter Falstaff, [and] Mistress Ford.*

FALSTAFF Mistress Ford, your sorrow hath eaten up my
2 sufferance. I see you are obsequious in your love, and I profess requital to a hair's breadth, not only, Mistress
4 Ford, in the simple office of love, but in all the accoutre-
5 ment, complement, and ceremony of it. But are you sure of your husband now?

MRS FORD He's a-birding, sweet Sir John.

8 MRS PAGE *[within]* What ho, gossip Ford. – What ho!

MRS FORD Step into the chamber, Sir John.
[Exit Falstaff.]
[Enter] Mistress Page.

MRS PAGE How now, sweetheart; who's at home besides yourself?

MRS FORD Why, none but mine own people.

MRS PAGE Indeed?

MRS FORD No, certainly. – *[aside to her]* Speak louder.

MRS PAGE Truly, I am so glad you have nobody here.

MRS FORD Why?

17 MRS PAGE Why, woman, your husband is in his old lunes again. He so takes on yonder with my husband; so rails against all married mankind; so curses all Eve's daugh-
20 ters, of what complexion soever; and so buffets himself
21 on the forehead, crying, 'Peer out, peer out!' that any madness I ever yet beheld seemed but tameness, civility, and patience to this his distemper he is in now. I am glad the fat knight is not here.

MRS FORD Why, does he talk of him?

MRS PAGE Of none but him; and swears he was carried out, the last time he searched for him, in a basket; protests to my husband he is now here, and hath drawn him and the rest of their company from their sport to
30 make another experiment of his suspicion. But I am glad the knight is not here. Now he shall see his own foolery.

MRS FORD How near is he, Mistress Page?

MRS PAGE Hard by, at street end; he will be here anon.

MRS FORD I am undone! – The knight is here.

MRS PAGE Why then you are utterly shamed, and he's but a dead man. What a woman are you! Away with him, away with him. – Better shame than murder.

MRS FORD Which way should he go? How should I bestow him? Shall I put him into the basket again?
[Enter] Falstaff.

FALSTAFF No. I'll come no more i' the basket. May I not go out ere he come?

MRS PAGE Alas, three of Master Ford's brothers watch the door with pistols that none shall issue out; otherwise you might slip away ere he came. But what make you here?

FALSTAFF What shall I do? I'll creep up into the chimney.

MRS FORD There they always use to discharge their birding pieces.

MRS PAGE Creep into the kiln-hole.   48

FALSTAFF Where is it?

MRS FORD He will seek there, on my word. Neither press, coffer, chest, trunk, well, vault, but he hath an abstract 51 for the remembrance of such places, and goes to them by his note. There is no hiding you in the house.

FALSTAFF I'll go out, then.

MRS PAGE If you go out in your own semblance, you die, Sir John. Unless you go out disguised –

MRS FORD How might we disguise him?

MRS PAGE Alas the day, I know not. There is no woman's gown big enough for him – otherwise, he might put on a hat, a muffler, and a kerchief, and so escape.

FALSTAFF Good hearts, devise something. Any extremity rather than a mischief.

MRS FORD My maid's aunt, the fat woman of Brainford, 63 has a gown above.

MRS PAGE On my word, it will serve him; she's as big as he is. And there's her thrummed hat and her muffler 66 too. Run up, Sir John.

MRS FORD Go, go, sweet Sir John. – Mistress Page and I will look some linen for your head.

MRS PAGE Quick, quick! We'll come dress you straight; put on the gown the while. *[Exit Falstaff.]*

MRS FORD I would my husband would meet him in this shape. He cannot abide the old woman of Brainford; he swears she's a witch, forbade her my house, and hath threatened to beat her.

---

45 *caret* it is lacking (Latin) 57 *to hick and to hack* to hiccup and cough (the results of debauchery) 67 *preeches* i.e. breeched, whipped 70 *sprag* i.e. sprack, alert
IV, ii Within Ford's house 2 *sufferance* suffering; *obsequious* ceremoniously dutiful 4 *accoutrement* furnishings 5 *complement* contributory elements 8 *gossip* friend, neighbor 17 *lunes* fits of lunacy 20 *complexion* temperament 21 *Peer out* (addressed to his supposed cuckold's horns) 48 *kiln-hole* oven 51 *abstract* list 63 *fat woman of Brainford* (a notorious person who kept a tavern in Brentford on the Thames twelve miles east of Windsor) 66 *thrummed* knit of coarse yarn

MRS PAGE Heaven guide him to thy husband's cudgel, and the devil guide his cudgel afterwards!

MRS FORD But is my husband coming?

MRS PAGE Ay, in good sadness, is he; and talks of the
80 basket too, howsoever he hath had intelligence.

MRS FORD We'll try that; for I'll appoint my men to carry the basket again, to meet him at the door with it, as they did last time.

MRS PAGE Nay, but he'll be here presently. – Let's go dress him like the witch of Brainford.

MRS FORD I'll first direct my men what they shall do with the basket. Go up; I'll bring linen for him straight. [Exit.]

88 MRS PAGE Hang him, dishonest varlet, we cannot misuse him enough.
We'll leave a proof, by that which we will do,
Wives may be merry, and yet honest too.
We do not act that often jest and laugh;
93 'Tis old but true, 'Still swine eats all the draff.'   [Exit.]
[Enter Mistress Ford, with two] Servants.

MRS FORD Go, sirs, take the basket again on your shoulders. Your master is hard at door; if he bid you set it
96 down, obey him. Quickly, dispatch.   [Exit.]

1. SERVANT Come, come, take it up.

2. SERVANT Pray heaven, it be not full of knight again.

1. SERVANT I hope not; I had as lief bear so much lead.
[Enter] Ford, Page, Caius, Evans, [and] Shallow.

FORD Ay, but if it prove true, Master Page, have you any way then to unfool me again? Set down the basket, villains. Somebody call my wife. Youth in a basket! O you
103 panderly rascals! There's a knot, a ging, a pack, a con-
104 spiracy against me. Now shall the devil be shamed. What, wife, I say! Come, come forth! Behold what honest clothes you send forth to bleaching.

PAGE Why, this passes! Master Ford, you are not to go loose any longer; you must be pinioned.

EVANS Why, this is lunatics, this is mad as a mad dog.

SHALLOW Indeed, Master Ford, this is not well, indeed.

FORD So say I too, sir. –
[Enter Mistress Ford.]
Come hither Mistress Ford; Mistress Ford, the honest woman, the modest wife; the virtuous creature that hath the jealous fool to her husband! I suspect without cause, mistress, do I?

MRS FORD Heaven be my witness, you do, if you suspect me in any dishonesty.

FORD Well said, brazen-face; hold it out. – Come forth, sirrah!
[Pulls clothes out of the basket.]
120 PAGE This passes!

MRS FORD Are you not ashamed? Let the clothes alone.

FORD I shall find you anon.

EVANS 'Tis unreasonable. Will you take up your wife's clothes? Come away.

FORD Empty the basket, I say!

MRS FORD Why, man, why?

FORD Master Page, as I am an honest man, there was one conveyed out of my house yesterday in this basket. Why may not he be there again? In my house I am sure he is – my intelligence is true; my jealousy is reasonable. Pluck 130 me out all the linen.

MRS FORD If you find a man there, he shall die a flea's death.

PAGE Here's no man.

SHALLOW By my fidelity, this is not well, Master Ford – this wrongs you.   135

EVANS Master Ford, you must pray, and not follow the imaginations of your own heart. This is jealousies.

FORD Well, he's not here I seek for.

PAGE No, nor nowhere else but in your brain.

FORD Help to search my house this one time. If I find not what I seek, show no color for my extremity – let me for 141 ever be your table-sport. Let them say of me, 'As jealous 142 as Ford, that searched a hollow walnut for his wife's leman.' Satisfy me once more; once more search with 144 me.

MRS FORD What ho, Mistress Page, come you and the old woman down. My husband will come into the chamber.

FORD Old woman! What old woman's that?

MRS FORD Why, it is my maid's aunt of Brainford.

FORD A witch, a quean, an old cozening quean! Have I not 149 forbid her my house? She comes of errands, does she? We are simple men; we do not know what's brought to pass under the profession of fortune-telling. She works by charms, by spells, by the figure, and such daubery as 153 this is, beyond our element – we know nothing. Come 154 down, you witch, you hag, you; come down, I say!

MRS FORD Nay, good, sweet husband! Good gentlemen, let him not strike the old woman.
[Enter Falstaff in woman's clothes, and Mistress Page.]

MRS PAGE Come, Mother Prat, come, give me your 158 hand.

FORD I'll 'prat' her. – [Beats him.] Out of my door, you 159 witch, you hag, you baggage, you polecat, you runnion! 160 Out, out! I'll conjure you. I'll fortune-tell you. –
[Falstaff runs out.]

MRS PAGE Are you not ashamed? I think you have killed the poor woman.

MRS FORD Nay, he will do it. 'Tis a goodly credit for you.

FORD Hang her, witch!

EVANS [aside] By Jeshu, I think the 'oman is a witch indeed. I like not when a 'oman has a great peard; I spy a great peard under his muffler.

FORD Will you follow, gentlemen? I beseech you, follow. See but the issue of my jealousy. If I cry out thus upon no trail, never trust me when I open again.

PAGE Let's obey his humor a little further. Come, gentle- 172 men.   [Exeunt Ford, Page, Shallow, Caius, and Evans.]

MRS PAGE Trust me, he beat him most pitifully.

MRS FORD Nay, by the mass, that he did not: he beat him most unpitifully, methought.

MRS PAGE I'll have the cudgel hallowed and hung o'er the altar – it hath done meritorious service.

MRS FORD What think you? May we, with the warrant of womanhood and the witness of a good conscience, pursue him with any further revenge?

---

88 *dishonest* unchaste   93 *draff* swill   96 *dispatch* hurry   103–04 *a knot . . . a conspiracy* a company, a gang, a group of confederates, a group of conspirators   104 *Now . . . shamed* i.e. now the truth will come out (from the proverbial 'Tell the truth and shame the devil')   130 *intelligence* information   135 *wrongs* i.e. disgraces   141 *show . . . extremity* suggest no excuse for my extravagance   142 *table-sport* laughingstock at table   144 *leman* lover   149 *quean* hussy   153 *by the figure* by making wax effigies to enchant; *daubery* false show   154 *element* sphere; hence, comprehension   158 *Mother Prat* (a popular name for the taverness of Brentford)   159 *'prat' her* strike her buttocks   160 *baggage* hussy; *polecat* prostitute; *runnion* bedraggled woman   172 *obey* defer to

MRS PAGE The spirit of wantonness is, sure, scared out
183 of him. If the devil have him not in fee simple, with fine
184 and recovery, he will never, I think, in the way of waste,
attempt us again.

MRS FORD Shall we tell our husbands how we have
served him?

MRS PAGE Yes, by all means, if it be but to scrape the
189 figures out of your husband's brains. If they can find in
their hearts the poor unvirtuous fat knight shall be any
191 further afflicted, we two will still be the ministers.

MRS FORD I'll warrant they'll have him publicly shamed,
and methinks there would be no period to the jest,
should he not be publicly shamed.

MRS PAGE Come, to the forge with it; then shape it. I
would not have things cool.   *Exeunt.*

*

IV, iii   *Enter Host and Bardolph.*

BARDOLPH Sir, the Germans desire to have three of your
horses. The Duke himself will be to-morrow at court,
and they are going to meet him.

HOST What duke should that be comes so secretly? I hear
not of him in the court. Let me speak with the gentlemen. They speak English?

BARDOLPH Ay, sir; I'll call them to you.

HOST They shall have my horses, but I'll make them pay;
9 I'll sauce them. They have had my house a week at
command. I have turned away my other guests. They
11 must come off; I'll sauce them. Come.   *Exeunt.*

*

IV, iv   *Enter Page, Ford, Mistress Page, Mistress Ford, and
Evans.*

1 **EVANS** 'Tis one of the pest discretions of a 'oman as ever I
did look upon.

PAGE And did he send you both these letters at an instant?

MRS PAGE Within a quarter of an hour.

FORD
Pardon me, wife. Henceforth do what thou wilt:
I rather will suspect the sun with cold
Than thee with wantonness. Now doth thy honor stand,
In him that was of late an heretic,
10 As firm as faith.

PAGE   'Tis well, 'tis well; no more.
Be not as extreme in submission as in offense. –
But let our plot go forward. Let our wives
Yet once again, to make us public sport,
Appoint a meeting with this old fat fellow,
Where we may take him and disgrace him for it.

FORD
There is no better way than that they spoke of.

PAGE How! to send him word they'll meet him in the
Park at midnight? Fie, fie, he'll never come.

EVANS You say he has been thrown in the rivers, and has
been grievously peaten as an old 'oman. Methinks there
should be terrors in him that he should not come. Methinks his flesh is punished; he shall have no desires.

PAGE So think I too.

MRS FORD
Devise but how you'll use him when he comes,
And let us two devise to bring him thither.

MRS PAGE
There is an old tale goes that Herne the Hunter,
Sometime a keeper here in Windsor Forest, 27
Doth all the wintertime, at still midnight,
Walk round about an oak, with great ragg'd horns; 29
And there he blasts the tree, and takes the cattle, 30
And makes milch kine yield blood, and shakes a chain
In a most hideous and dreadful manner.
You have heard of such a spirit, and well you know
The superstitious idle-headed eld 34
Received and did deliver to our age
This tale of Herne the Hunter for a truth.

PAGE
Why, yet there want not many that do fear
In deep of night to walk by this Herne's Oak.
But what of this?

MRS FORD   Marry, this is our device:
That Falstaff at that oak shall meet with us,
[Disguised like Herne, with huge horns on his head.]

PAGE
Well, let it not be doubted but he'll come,
And in this shape when you have brought him thither,
What shall be done with him? What is your plot?

MRS PAGE
That likewise have we thought upon, and thus:
Nan Page my daughter, and my little son,
And three or four more of their growth, we'll dress
Like urchins, ouphs, and fairies, green and white, 48
With rounds of waxen tapers on their heads,
And rattles in their hands. Upon a sudden,
As Falstaff, she, and I are newly met,
Let them from forth a sawpit rush at once
With some diffusèd song. Upon their sight, 53
We two in great amazedness will fly. 54
Then let them all encircle him about,
And, fairy-like, to pinch the unclean knight,
And ask him why, that hour of fairy revel,
In their so sacred paths he dares to tread
In shape profane.

MRS FORD   And till he tell the truth,
Let the supposèd fairies pinch him sound 60
And burn him with their tapers.

MRS PAGE   The truth being known,
We'll all present ourselves, dis-horn the spirit,
And mock him home to Windsor.

FORD   The children must
Be practised well to this, or they'll ne'er do't.

EVANS I will teach the children their behaviors; and I will
be like a jackanapes also, to burn the knight with my
taber.

FORD
That will be excellent. I'll go buy them vizards. 68

MRS PAGE
My Nan shall be the Queen of all the Fairies,
Finely attirèd in a robe of white.

183 *fee simple* absolute ownership   183–84 *fine and recovery* process by
which an entailed estate was transferred to fee simple   184 *waste* spoliation
189 *figures* phantasms   191 *ministers* agents
IV, iii The Garter Inn   9 *sauce them* make them pay dearly   11 *come off*
pay out
IV, iv Within Ford's house   1 *pest . . . 'oman* i.e. most discreet women
27 *Sometime* formerly   29 *ragg'd* pronged   30 *blasts* blights; *takes* bewitches   34 *eld* elders   48 *urchins, ouphs* (either word means goblins or
elves)   53 *diffusèd* wild, disorderly   54 *amazedness* bewilderment, fright
60 *sound* soundly   68 *vizards* masks

PAGE
That silk will I go buy. – *[aside]* And in that tire
Shall Master Slender steal my Nan away,

73 And marry her at Eton. – Go, send to Falstaff straight.

FORD
Nay, I'll to him again in name of Brook.
He'll tell me all his purpose. Sure, he'll come.

MRS PAGE

76 Fear not you that. Go, get us properties
77 And tricking for our fairies.

EVANS Let us about it. It is admirable pleasures and fery
honest knaveries.   *[Exeunt Page, Ford, and Evans.]*

MRS PAGE
Go, Mistress Ford,
Send Quickly to Sir John, to know his mind.
                     [Exit Mistress Ford.]
I'll to the Doctor : he hath my good will,
And none but he, to marry with Nan Page.
That Slender, though well landed, is an idiot ;

85 And him my husband best of all affects.
The Doctor is well moneyed, and his friends
Potent at court. He, none but he, shall have her,
Though twenty thousand worthier come to crave her.
                          [Exit.]

*

IV, v   *Enter Host, [and] Simple.*

HOST What wouldst thou have, boor ? What, thick-skin –
speak, breathe, discuss ; brief, short, quick, snap.

SIMPLE Marry, sir, I come to speak with Sir John Falstaff
from Master Slender.

HOST There's his chamber, his house, his castle, his

6 standing-bed and truckle-bed. 'Tis painted about with
the story of the Prodigal, fresh and new. Go, knock and

8 call. He'll speak like an Anthropophaginian unto thee.
Knock, I say.

SIMPLE There's an old woman, a fat woman, gone up
into his chamber. I'll be so bold as stay, sir, till she come
down – I come to speak with her, indeed.

HOST Ha, a fat woman ? The knight may be robbed : I'll
call. Bully knight, bully Sir John – speak from thy lungs

14 military : art thou there ? It is thine Host, thine Ephesian,
calls.

FALSTAFF *[within]* How now, mine Host ?

16 HOST Here's a Bohemian-Tartar tarries the coming down
of thy fat woman. Let her descend, bully, let her descend. My chambers are honorable. Fie, privacy, fie !
     [Enter] Falstaff.

FALSTAFF There was, mine Host, an old fat woman even
now with me, but she's gone.

SIMPLE Pray you, sir, was't not the wise woman of Brainford ?

23 FALSTAFF Ay, marry, was it, mussel-shell. What would
you with her ?

SIMPLE My master, sir, Master Slender, sent to her, seeing her go through the streets, to know, sir, whether one
Nym, sir, that beguiled him of a chain, had the chain or
no.

FALSTAFF I spake with the old woman about it.

SIMPLE And what says she, I pray, sir ?

FALSTAFF Marry, she says that the very same man that
beguiled Master Slender of his chain cozened him of it.

SIMPLE I would I could have spoken with the woman
herself. I had other things to have spoken with her too,
from him.

FALSTAFF What are they ? let us know.

HOST Ay, come ; quick.

SIMPLE I may not conceal them, sir.   37

HOST Conceal them, or thou diest.

SIMPLE Why, sir, they were nothing but about Mistress
Anne Page ; to know if it were my master's fortune to
have her, or no.

FALSTAFF 'Tis, 'tis his fortune.

SIMPLE What, sir ?

FALSTAFF To have her, or no. Go, say the woman told
me so.

SIMPLE May I be bold to say so, sir ?

FALSTAFF Ay, Sir Tyke ; who more bold ?   46

SIMPLE I thank your worship : I shall make my master
glad with these tidings.   *[Exit.]*

HOST Thou art clerkly, thou art clerkly, Sir John. Was 49
there a wise woman with thee ?

FALSTAFF Ay, that there was, mine Host : one that hath
taught me more wit than ever I learned before in my 52
life ; and I paid nothing for it neither, but was paid for
my learning.
     [Enter] Bardolph.

BARDOLPH Out, alas, sir, cozenage, mere cozenage !

HOST Where be my horses ? Speak well of them, varletto. 55

BARDOLPH Run away, with the cozeners ; for so soon as I
came beyond Eton, they threw me off, from behind one
of them, in a slough of mire ; and set spurs and away, like
three German devils, three Doctor Faustuses.   59

HOST They are gone but to meet the Duke, villain. Do 60
not say they be fled : Germans are honest men.
     [Enter] Evans.

EVANS Where is mine Host ?

HOST What is the matter, sir ?

EVANS Have a care of your entertainments. There is a
friend of mine come to town, tells me there is three
cozen-germans that has cozened all the hosts of Readins, 66
of Maidenhead, of Colebrook, of horses and money. I 67
tell you for good will, look you : you are wise and full of
gibes and vlouting-stogs, and 'tis not convenient you
should be cozened. Fare you well.   *[Exit.]*
     [Enter] Caius.

CAIUS Vere is mine Host de Jarteer ?

HOST Here, Master Doctor, in perplexity and doubtful
dilemma.

CAIUS I cannot tell vat is dat ; but it is tell-a me dat you
make grand preparation for a Duke de Jarmany. By my
trot, dere is no duke dat de court is know to come. I tell
you for good vill ; adieu.   *[Exit.]*

HOST Hue and cry, villain, go ! – Assist me, knight. – I am
undone. – Fly, run, hue and cry, villain ! – I am undone ! 79
     [Exeunt Host and Bardolph.]

FALSTAFF I would all the world might be cozened, for I
have been cozened and beaten too. If it should come to

73 *Eton* (across the Thames from Windsor) 76 *properties* i.e. stage
properties 77 *tricking* adornment, decoration 85 *affects* likes
IV, v Within the Garter Inn 6 *truckle-bed* trundle-bed (stored under the
standing-bed) 8 *Anthropophaginian* literally, a cannibal 14 *Ephesian*
boon companion 16 *Bohemian-Tartar* i.e. barbarian 23 *mussel-shell* i.e.
one who gapes 37 *conceal* i.e. reveal 46 *Sir Tyke* i.e. cur 49 *clerkly*
book-learned, wise 52 *wit* wisdom 55 *varletto* rascal 59 *Doctor Faustuses* (after the magician in Marlowe's play) 60 *villain* rascal 66 *cozen-
germans* (pun on cousin-germans, i.e. relatives, and cheating Germans) ;
Readins i.e. the town of Reading 67 *Colebrook* Colnbrook, near Windsor
79 *hue and cry* (the shout for pursuit of a felon)

the ear of the court how I have been transformed, and
how my transformation hath been washed and cudgelled, they would melt me out of my fat drop by drop,
85 and liquor fishermen's boots with me. I warrant they
86 would whip me with their fine wits till I were as crestfallen as a dried pear. I never prospered since I forswore
88 myself at primero. Well, if my wind were but long
enough [to say my prayers], I would repent.
    [Enter Mistress] Quickly.
Now, whence come you?

QUICKLY From the two parties forsooth.

FALSTAFF The devil take one party and his dam the
other! and so they shall be both bestowed. I have suffered more for their sakes, more than the villainous inconstancy of man's disposition is able to bear.

QUICKLY And have not they suffered? Yes, I warrant;
speciously one of them. Mistress Ford, good heart, is
beaten black and blue, that you cannot see a white spot
about her.

100 FALSTAFF What tellest thou me of black and blue? I was
beaten myself into all the colors of the rainbow; and I
was like to be apprehended for the witch of Brainford.
But that my admirable dexterity of wit, my counterfeiting the action of an old woman, delivered me, the knave
constable had set me i' the stocks, i'.the common stocks,
for a witch.

QUICKLY Sir, let me speak with you in your chamber.
You shall hear how things go, and, I warrant, to your
content. Here is a letter will say somewhat. Good hearts,
what ado here is to bring you together. – Sure, one of
111 you does not serve heaven well, that you are so crossed.

FALSTAFF Come up into my chamber.   *Exeunt.*

*

IV, vi   *Enter Fenton, [and] Host.*

HOST Master Fenton, talk not to me. My mind is heavy;
I will give over all.

FENTON
Yet hear me speak. Assist me in my purpose,
And, as I am a gentleman, I'll give thee
A hundred pound in gold more than your loss.

HOST I will hear you, Master Fenton, and I will, at the
least, keep your counsel.

FENTON
From time to time I have acquainted you
With the dear love I bear to fair Anne Page,
Who mutually hath answered my affection,
So far forth as herself might be her chooser,
Even to my wish. I have a letter from her
Of such contents as you will wonder at,
14   The mirth whereof so larded with my matter
That neither singly can be manifested
Without the show of both, wherein fat Falstaff
17   Hath a great scene. The image of the jest
18   I'll show you here at large.
        [Shows a letter.]   Hark, good mine Host:
To-night at Herne's Oak, just 'twixt twelve and one,
20   Must my sweet Nan present the Fairy Queen –
The purpose why, is here – in which disguise,
22   While other jests are something rank on foot,
Her father hath commanded her to slip
Away with Slender, and with him at Eton
Immediately to marry. She hath consented. –

Now, sir,
Her mother (even strong against that match   27
And firm for Doctor Caius) hath appointed
That he shall likewise shuffle her away,   29
While other sports are tasking of their minds,   30
And at the deanery, where a priest attends,
Straight marry her. To this her mother's plot
She, seemingly obedient, likewise hath
Made promise to the Doctor. – Now, thus it rests:
Her father means she shall be all in white,
And in that habit, when Slender sees his time
To take her by the hand and bid her go,
She shall go with him. Her mother hath intended,
The better to denote her to the Doctor
(For they must all be masked and vizarded),
That quaint in green she shall be loose enrobed,   41
With ribands pendent, flaring 'bout her head;
And when the Doctor spies his vantage ripe,
To pinch her by the hand, and on that token
The maid hath given consent to go with him.

HOST
Which means she to deceive, father or mother?

FENTON
Both, my good Host, to go along with me.
And here it rests, that you'll procure the Vicar
To stay for me at church 'twixt twelve and one,
And, in the lawful name of marrying,
To give our hearts united ceremony.   51

HOST
Well, husband your device; I'll to the Vicar.   52
Bring you the maid, you shall not lack a priest.

FENTON
So shall I evermore be bound to thee;
Besides, I'll make a present recompense.   *Exeunt.* 55

*

    Enter Falstaff, [and Mistress] Quickly.   V, i

FALSTAFF Prithee no more prattling. – Go: I'll hold. 1
This is the third time; I hope good luck lies in odd
numbers. Away; go. They say there is divinity in odd 3.
numbers, either in nativity, chance, or death. Away. – 4

QUICKLY I'll provide you a chain, and I'll do what I can
to get you a pair of horns.

FALSTAFF Away, I say; time wears. Hold up your head,
and mince.   *[Exit Mistress Quickly.]* 8
    [Enter] Ford.
How now, Master Brook. – Master Brook, the matter
will be known to-night, or never. Be you in the Park
about midnight, at Herne's Oak, and you shall see
wonders.

FORD Went you not to her yesterday, sir, as you told me 13
you had appointed?

FALSTAFF I went to her, Master Brook, as you see, like a
poor old man; but I came from her, Master Brook, like

85 *liquor* grease 86 *crestfallen* shrivelled up 88 *primero* a card game
111 *crossed* thwarted (as by malign influence of the stars)
IV, vi The same 14 *larded* intermixed; *my matter* what concerns me 17
image form 18 *at large* as a whole 20 *present* represent 22 *something
rank* very abundantly 27 *even* equally 29 *shuffle* trick 30 *tasking of*
fully occupying 41 *quaint* elaborately 51 *united ceremony* union in rite
of marriage 52 *husband* prudently manage 55 *present* immediate
V, i The same 1 *hold* be steadfast 3 *divinity* divination, oracular power
4 *nativity* birth 8 *mince* walk affectedly 13 *yesterday* (actually, the
beating had occurred in the morning of the present day)

a poor old woman. That same knave Ford, her husband, hath the finest mad devil of jealousy in him, Master Brook, that ever governed frenzy. I will tell you: he beat me grievously, in the shape of a woman; for in the shape of a man, Master Brook, I fear not Goliath with a weaver's beam, because I know also life is a shuttle. I am in haste. Go along with me; I'll tell you all, Master Brook. Since I plucked geese, played truant, and whipped top, I knew not what 'twas to be beaten till lately. Follow me. I'll tell you strange things of this knave Ford, on whom to-night I will be revenged, and I will deliver his wife into your hand. Follow. Strange things in hand, Master Brook! Follow.   *Exeunt.*

*

V, ii   *Enter Page, Shallow, [and] Slender.*

1 PAGE Come, come; we'll couch i' the Castle ditch till we see the light of our fairies. Remember, son Slender, my daughter.

SLENDER Ay, forsooth; I have spoke with her and we 6 have a nayword how to know one another. I come to her in white, and cry, 'mum'; she cries, 'budget'; and by that we know one another.

SHALLOW That's good too. But what needs either your 9 'mum,' or her 'budget'? The white will decipher her well enough. – It hath struck ten o'clock.

PAGE The night is dark; light and spirits will become it well. Heaven prosper our sport. No man means evil but the devil, and we shall know him by his horns. Let's away; follow me.   *Exeunt.*

*

V, iii   *Enter Mistress Page, Mistress Ford, [and Doctor] Caius.*

MRS PAGE Master Doctor, my daughter is in green. When you see your time, take her by the hand, away with her to the deanery, and dispatch it quickly. Go before into the Park. We two must go together.

CAIUS I know vat I have to do. Adieu.

MRS PAGE Fare you well, sir. *[Exit Caius.]* My husband will not rejoice so much at the abuse of Falstaff, as he will chafe at the Doctor's marrying my daughter. But 'tis no matter: better a little chiding than a great deal of heartbreak.

10 MRS FORD Where is Nan now and her troop of fairies, and the Welsh devil, Hugh?

MRS PAGE They are all couched in a pit hard by Herne's Oak, with obscured lights, which at the very instant of Falstaff's and our meeting they will at once display to the night.

MRS FORD That cannot choose but amaze him.

MRS PAGE If he be not amazed, he will be mocked; if he be amazed, he will every way be mocked.

MRS FORD We'll betray him finely.

MRS PAGE
Against such lewdsters and their lechery,   20
Those that betray them do no treachery.

MRS FORD The hour draws on. To the Oak, to the Oak!   *Exeunt.*

*

Enter Evans [as a Satyr] and [others as] Fairies.   V, iv

EVANS Trib, trib, fairies. Come, and remember your 1 parts. Be pold, I pray you. Follow me into the pit, and when I give the watch-'ords, do as I pid you. Come, come; trib, trib.   *Exeunt.*

Enter Falstaff [disguised as Herne, wearing a buck's V, v *head].*

FALSTAFF The Windsor bell hath struck twelve; the minute draws on. Now, the hot-blooded gods assist me! Remember, Jove, thou wast a bull for thy Europa: love 3 set on thy horns. O powerful love, that in some respects makes a beast a man; in some other, a man a beast. You were also, Jupiter, a swan for the love of Leda. O om- 6 nipotent love, how near the god drew to the complexion 7 of a goose! A fault done first in the form of a beast – O Jove, a beastly fault! – and then another fault in the semblance of a fowl. Think on't, Jove; a foul fault! When gods have hot backs, what shall poor men do? For me, I am here a Windsor stag; and the fattest, I think, i' the forest. Send me a cool rut-time, Jove, or who can blame me to piss my tallow? Who comes here? my doe?

[Enter] Mistress Page, [and] Mistress Ford.

MRS FORD Sir John? Art thou there, my deer, my male deer?

FALSTAFF My doe with the black scut! Let the sky rain 17 potatoes; let it thunder to the tune of 'Greensleeves,' 18 hail kissing-comfits, and snow eryngoes. Let there come 19 a tempest of provocation, I will shelter me here.   20
[Embraces her.]

MRS FORD Mistress Page is come with me, sweetheart.

FALSTAFF Divide me like a bribed buck, each a haunch. I 22 will keep my sides to myself, my shoulders for the fellow 23 of this walk, and my horns I bequeath your husbands. Am I a woodman, ha? Speak I like Herne the Hunter? 25 Why, now is Cupid a child of conscience; he makes 26 restitution. As I am a true spirit, welcome!
[Noise within.]

MRS PAGE Alas, what noise?

MRS FORD Heaven forgive our sins!

FALSTAFF What should this be?

MRS FORD, MRS PAGE Away, away!   *[They run off.]*

FALSTAFF I think the devil will not have me damned, lest the oil that's in me should set hell on fire. He would never else cross me thus.

Enter Evans, [as a Satyr, Mistress] Quickly, Anne Page, [and others as] Fairies, [with tapers, and] Pistol [as a Hobgoblin].

QUICKLY
Fairies, black, grey, green, and white,
You moonshine revellers, and shades of night,
You orphan heirs of fixèd destiny,   37
Attend your office and your quality.   38
Crier Hobgoblin, make the fairy oyes.   39

---

21 *weaver's beam* wooden roller in a loom (cf. 2 Samuel xxi, 19)
V, ii Windsor Park   1 *couch* lie hidden   6 *mum . . . budget* silence (mum-budget)   9 *decipher* distinguish
V, iii The same   20 *lewdsters* lechers
V, iv The same   1 *Trib* i.e. trip
V, v   3 *Europa* (abducted by Jove in the form of a bull)   6 *Leda* (ravished by Jove in the form of a swan)   7 *complexion* temperament   17 *scut* deer's tail   18 *potatoes* sweet potatoes (thought to be an aphrodisiac)   19 *kissing-comfits* perfumed sweetmeats; *eryngoes* candied root of a plant known as sea-holly (thought to be an aphrodisiac)   20 *provocation* erotic stimulation   22 *bribed* stolen   23 *fellow* keeper   25 *a woodman* i.e. skilled in woodcraft   26 *of conscience* conscientious   37 *orphan* (fairies did not have fathers)   38 *Attend . . . quality* i.e. heed your official position and rank   39 *oyes* hear ye (court crier's call)

PISTOL

Elves, list your names; silence, you airy toys!
Cricket, to Windsor chimneys shalt thou leap.
Where fires thou find'st unraked and hearths unswept,

43   There pinch the maids as blue as bilberry.
Our radiant Queen hates sluts and sluttery.

FALSTAFF

45   They are fairies; he that speaks to them shall die.
46   I'll wink and couch; no man their works must eye.

[Lies down upon his face.]

EVANS

Where's Bead? Go you, and where you find a maid
That ere she sleep has thrice her prayers said,

49   Raise up the organs of her fantasy,
Sleep she as sound as careless infancy.
But those as sleep and think not on their sins,
Pinch them, arms, legs, backs, shoulders, sides, and shins.

QUICKLY

About, about. –
Search Windsor Castle, elves, within and out.
Strew good luck, ouphs, on every sacred room,
That it may stand till the perpetual doom,
In state as wholesome as in state 'tis fit,
Worthy the owner, and the owner it.

59   The several chairs of order look you scour
With juice of balm and every precious flower.

61   Each fair instalment, coat, and several crest,
62   With loyal blazon, evermore be blest. –
And nightly, meadow-fairies, look you sing,

64   Like to the Garter's compass, in a ring.
65   Th' expressure that it bears, green let it be,
More fertile-fresh than all the field to see;

67   And 'Honi soit qui mal y pense' write
68   In emerald tufts, flowers purple, blue, and white,
Like sapphire, pearl, and rich embroidery,
Buckled below fair knighthood's bending knee.

71   (Fairies use flowers for their charactery.)
Away, disperse. – But till 'tis one o'clock,
Our dance of custom round about the Oak
Of Herne the Hunter, let us not forget.

EVANS

Pray you, lock hand in hand; yourselves in order set;
And twenty glowworms shall our lanterns be,
To guide our measure round about the tree.

78   But, stay – I smell a man of middle earth.

79 FALSTAFF Heavens defend me from that Welsh fairy,
80   lest he transform me to a piece of cheese!

PISTOL

81   Vile worm, thou wast o'erlooked even in thy birth.

QUICKLY

With trial-fire touch me his finger end.
If he be chaste, the flame will back descend
And turn him to no pain; but if he start,
It is the flesh of a corrupted heart.

PISTOL

A trial, come. –

EVANS   Come, will this wood take fire?

[They burn him with their tapers.]

FALSTAFF O, O, O!

QUICKLY

Corrupt, corrupt, and tainted in desire!
About him, fairies, sing a scornful rhyme;
And, as you trip, still pinch him to your time.

The Song.

Fie on sinful fantasy!
Fie on lust and luxury!   92
Lust is but a bloody fire,   93
   Kindled with unchaste desire,
   Fed in heart, whose flames aspire,
As thoughts do blow them, higher and higher.
Pinch him, fairies, mutually;   97
Pinch him for his villainy;
Pinch him, and burn him, and turn him about,
Till candles and starlight and moonshine be out.

*[During this song they pinch Falstaff. Doctor] Caius,
[comes one way and steals away a Fairy in green;]
Slender, [another way and takes off a Fairy in white;
and] Fenton [comes and steals away Anne Page.
A noise of hunting is heard within. All the Fairies run
away. Falstaff rises].
[Enter] Page, Ford [, Mistress Page, and
Mistress Ford].*

PAGE

Nay, do not fly: I think we have watched you now.   101
Will none but Herne the Hunter serve your turn?

MRS PAGE

I pray you, come, hold up the jest no higher.
Now, good Sir John, how like you Windsor wives?
See you these, husband? Do not these fair yokes   105
Become the forest better than the town?

FORD Now sir, who's a cuckold now? Master Brook, Falstaff 's a knave, a cuckoldly knave; here are his horns, Master Brook. And, Master Brook, he hath enjoyed nothing of Ford's but his buck-basket, his cudgel, and twenty pounds of money, which must be paid too, Master Brook; his horses are arrested for it, Master 112 Brook.

MRS FORD Sir John, we have had ill luck; we could never meet. I will never take you for my love again, but I will always count you my deer.

FALSTAFF I do begin to perceive that I am made an ass.

FORD Ay, and an ox too: both the proofs are extant.   118

FALSTAFF And these are not fairies? I was three or four times in the thought they were not fairies; and yet the guiltiness of my mind, the sudden surprise of my powers, 121 drove the grossness of the foppery into a received belief, 122 in despite of the teeth of all rhyme and reason, that they 123 were fairies. See now how wit may be made a Jack-a-Lent, when 'tis upon ill employment. –

EVANS Sir John Falstaff, serve Got and leave your desires, and fairies will not pinse you.

FORD Well said, fairy Hugh.

EVANS And leave you your jealousies too, I pray you.

FORD I will never mistrust my wife again, till thou art able to woo her in good English.

---

43 *bilberry* blueberry   45 *he . . . die* (an old superstition)   46 *wink* close eyes   49 *Raise . . . fantasy* give good dreams by elevating the organs that produce dreams   59 *chairs of order* stalls of the Garter knights   61 *instalment* stalls   62 *blazon* armorial bearings   64 *compass* circle   65 *expressure* picture, image   67 *Honi soit . . .* (motto of the Garter: Evil to him who evil thinks)   68 *tufts* bunches   71 *charactery* writing   78 *middle earth* (the habitation of men)   79 *defend* protect   80 *cheese* (the Welshman's favorite food)   81 *o'erlooked* bewitched   92 *luxury* sensuality   93 *bloody fire* fire in the blood   97 *mutually* jointly   101 *watched* caught in the act   105 *yokes* i.e. Falstaff's horns   112 *arrested* seized by warrant   118 *proofs* i.e. long ears and horns; *extant* present   121 *powers* faculties   122 *foppery* deceit   123 *in despite of the teeth* in the face

FALSTAFF Have I laid my brain in the sun and dried it,
133   that it wants matter to prevent so gross o'erreaching as
this? Am I ridden with a Welsh goat too? Shall I have a
135   coxcomb of frieze? 'Tis time I were choked with a
piece of toasted cheese.

EVANS Seese is not goot to give putter – your belly is all
putter.

FALSTAFF 'Seese' and 'putter'! Have I lived to stand at
140   the taunt of one that makes fritters of English? This is
enough to be the decay of lust and late-walking through
the realm.

MRS PAGE Why, Sir John, do you think, though we
would have thrust virtue out of our hearts by the head
and shoulders, and have given ourselves without scruple
to hell, that ever the devil could have made you our
delight?

147 FORD What, a hodge-pudding? a bag of flax?

MRS PAGE A puffed man?

PAGE Old, cold, withered, and of intolerable entrails?

FORD And one that is as slanderous as Satan?

PAGE And as poor as Job?

FORD And as wicked as his wife?

EVANS And given to fornications, and to taverns, and
154   sack and wine and metheglins, and to drinkings and
swearings and starings, pribbles and prabbles?

FALSTAFF Well, I am your theme. You have the start of
157   me; I am dejected; I am not able to answer the Welsh
158   flannel. Ignorance itself is a plummet o'er me – use me
as you will.

FORD Marry, sir, we'll bring you to Windsor, to one
Master Brook, that you have cozened of money, to
whom you should have been a pander. Over and above
that you have suffered, I think to repay that money will
be a biting affliction.

PAGE Yet be cheerful, knight. Thou shalt eat a posset to-
night at my house, where I will desire thee to laugh at
my wife that now laughs at thee. Tell her, Master
Slender hath married her daughter.

168 MRS PAGE [aside] Doctors doubt that. If Anne Page be
my daughter, she is, by this, Doctor Caius' wife.
[Enter Slender.]

SLENDER Whoa, ho, ho, father Page!

171 PAGE Son, how now; how now, son. – Have you dispatched?

SLENDER Dispatched? I'll make the best in Gloucestershire know on't; would I were hanged, la, else.

PAGE Of what, son?

SLENDER I came yonder at Eton to marry Mistress Anne
Page, and she's a great lubberly boy. If it had not been
178   i' the church, I would have swinged him, or he should
have swinged me. If I did not think it had been Anne
180   Page, would I might never stir – and 'tis a postmaster's
boy.

PAGE Upon my life, then, you took the wrong.

SLENDER What need you tell me that? I think so, when I
took a boy for a girl. If I had been married to him, for all 184
he was in woman's apparel, I would not have had him.

PAGE Why, this is your own folly. Did not I tell you how
you should know my daughter by her garments?

SLENDER I went to her in white, and cried, 'mum,' and
she cried 'budget,' as Anne and I had appointed; and
yet it was not Anne, but a postmaster's boy.

MRS PAGE Good George, be not angry. I knew of your
purpose; turned my daughter into green; and indeed
she is now with the Doctor at the deanery, and there
married.
[Enter Doctor Caius.]

CAIUS Vere is Mistress Page? By gar, I am cozened – I ha'
married un garçon, a boy; un paysan, by gar, a boy; it is 195
not Anne Page. By gar, I am cozened.

MRS PAGE Why, did you not take her in green?

CAIUS Ay, by gar, and 'tis a boy. By gar, I'll raise all
Windsor.   [Exit.]

FORD This is strange. Who hath got the right Anne?

PAGE My heart misgives me. Here comes Master Fenton.
[Enter Fenton and Anne Page.]
How now, Master Fenton?

ANNE
Pardon, good father; good my mother, pardon.

PAGE Now, mistress, how chance you went not with
Master Slender?

MRS PAGE
Why went you not with Master Doctor, maid?

FENTON
You do amaze her. Hear the truth of it. –   207
You would have married her most shamefully,
Where there was no proportion held in love.
The truth is, she and I, long since contracted,   210
Are now so sure that nothing can dissolve us.   211
Th' offense is holy that she hath committed,
And this deceit loses the name of craft,
Of disobedience, or unduteous title,
Since therein she doth evitate and shun   215
A thousand irreligious cursèd hours,
Which forcèd marriage would have brought upon her.

FORD
Stand not amazed. Here is no remedy.
In love the heavens themselves do guide the state;
Money buys lands, and wives are sold by fate.

FALSTAFF I am glad, though you have ta'en a special
stand to strike at me, that your arrow hath glanced.   221

PAGE
Well, what remedy? – Fenton, heaven give thee joy!
What cannot be eschewed must be embraced.

FALSTAFF
When night dogs run, all sorts of deer are chased.

MRS PAGE
Well, I will muse no further. Master Fenton,   226
Heaven give you many, many merry days!
Good husband, let us every one go home,
And laugh this sport o'er by a country fire;
Sir John and all.

FORD   Let it be so. Sir John,
To Master Brook you yet shall hold your word;
For he to-night shall lie with Mistress Ford.   *Exeunt.*

---

133 *matter* sense   135 *coxcomb* fool's cap; *frieze* coarse Welsh woolen cloth
140 *fritters* i.e. hash   147 *hodge-pudding* mixed sausage or stuffing; *bag of
flax* i.e. bulky and shapeless   154 *metheglins* spiced Welsh mead   157
dejected cast down   158 *flannel* Welsh cloth; *is . . . me* has sounded me
168 *Doctors doubt that* (proverbial phrase of disbelief)   171 *dispatched*
finished the business   178 *swinged* beaten   180 *postmaster* master of the
post horses   184 *took* mistook   195 *paysan* i.e. yokel   207 *amaze* bewilder
210 *contracted* betrothed   211 *sure* fast   215 *evitate* avoid   221 *stand*
place for shooting   226 *muse* grumble

APPENDIX: THE QUARTO AND FOLIO TEXTS

The only authoritative text of *The Merry Wives of Windsor* is that printed in the Shakespeare First Folio in 1623. However, in 1602 a debased version of the same, or of a closely related, text had been printed in quarto. It is customary to regard this corrupt 1602 version as an unauthorized memorial reconstruction (made perhaps by the actors who took the parts of the Host and Falstaff) which was then cut for performance in the provinces where Shakespeare's company could have no control over what was acted by travelling companies.

All editors have drawn on the 1602 quarto for phrases and lines assumed to be accidentally missing from the folio text. The present edition is more conservative than usual in admitting these borrowings from the quarto, and distinguishes them by square brackets. However, a limited number certainly represent Shakespeare's original that has suffered in the transmission of the text before the folio print. The quarto, also, gives us the original alias *Brook* adopted by Ford, instead of the expedient *Broom* substituted in the folio version presumably in deference to Lord Cobham, whose family name was Brook. Earlier, Cobham's sensibilities had apparently forced the change of name in *Henry IV* from *Oldcastle* (an ancestor) to *Falstaff*. Whether Falstaff in *The Merry Wives* had always been Falstaff, as seems possible, or was originally Oldcastle, is not known.

The folio text shares with the folio *The Two Gentlemen of Verona*, and in some part with *The Winter's Tale*, a peculiarity known as "massed entries." That is, in the initial stage direction to each scene are massed the names of all the characters, more or less in what is to be the order of their appearance but without regard for the actual point of entry in the scene, where no additional entrance directions are provided. Nor are exits or other stage directions found except for the entrance of the fairies in Act V. At one time it was conjectured that these massed entries were indications of the copying-out of the printer's manuscript from the actors' parts; but this theory is no longer taken seriously. Instead, the peculiarity (and other recognizable characteristics such as some features of the punctuation) is now ascertained as an occasional device of a scribe Ralph Crane, whose manuscript transcript in a similar style of Middleton's *A Game at Chess* has been preserved.

The evidence is sparse, but what there is suggests that the manuscript from which Crane copied was the theatrical company's prompt-book. If so, it would in turn have been copied from Shakespeare's papers, and in the double scribal transcription, complicated by the final stage of setting the text into type, we may find the origin of the several lacunae that need to be mended from the quarto. It may be that the prompt-book used by Crane was itself not entirely the original: it is very odd that in V, v Evans drops his Welsh dialect, although Falstaff is able to recognize his nationality from his speech; and there may have been cutting or alteration of some of the horse-stealing episodes with their personal application. However, the various carelessnesses in the play, such as the initial confusion about Page's first name, and the more complex confusion (in the original) about the colors of Anne Page's disguise in the abduction scene, may reflect hasty initial composition not subsequently normalized, instead of incomplete revision.

The present edition offers a text modernized from the first folio, including punctuation that attempts to reproduce the effect of the Elizabethan rhetorical pointing wedded to its characteristic syntax.

The dialect speeches have been thoroughly systematized for the first time according to what seem to have been Shakespeare's general intentions as determined by Dr Elizabeth Brock. As one instance, from many, an analysis of Evans' use of initial *p* for *b* discloses that this change takes place only in accented syllables and in words that would receive emphasis in the delivery of the lines. Thus he will say *peaten* for *beaten*, but *behaviors* and not *pehaviors*. For Doctor Caius the phonetic changes are less extensive than for Evans, and the humorous dialectal effects are secured largely by distortion of word order and by peculiarities of syntax. The Doctor's true French, phonetically spelled in the folio, has been modernized. In general, Shakespeare for these characters records most regularly those combinations of sounds that struck his ear as yielding the most amusing dialectal forms. For some details he was remarkably systematic, but for others he appears to have relied on the inspiration of the moment.

The following substantive departures have been made from the folio text. Some are readings from the quarto of 1602 (Q); some from the second (1632) and third (1663) folios; others are emendations made early in the history of Shakespearean scholarship and accepted by most modern editors. The adopted reading in italics represents an emendation and is followed in parentheses by its earliest source; then follows the reading of the folio copy-text. Both of these are in roman.

I, i, 40 *George* (Theobald) Thomas   52, 54 *Shallow.* (Capell) Slender.   224 *contempt* (Theobald) content
I, iii, 14 *lime* (Q) live   25 *minim-rest* (Singer + Wilson) minutes rest   45 *well . . . well* (Q + Pope) will . . . will   49 *legion* (Q + Rowe³) legend   54 *oeillades* (Hanmer) illiads   63 *'cheator* (Capell) Cheaters   75 *o'the* (Q) i'th'   76 *humor* (Theobald) honor   87 *Page* (Q) Ford   88 *Ford* (Q) Page   92 *Page* (Malone) Ford
I, iv, 20 *whey face* (Q + Capell) wee-face
II, i, 1 *I* (F2) omitted   52 *praised* (Theobald) praise   57 *Hundredth Psalm* (Rowe) hundred Psalms   190 *Ford* (Q3) Shallow   195 *mynheers* (Theobald) An-heires
II, ii, 22 *God* (Q) heaven   28 *wouldst* (Pope) would   49 *God* (Q) heaven   132 etc. *Brook* (Q) Broom   278 *God* (Q) heaven
II, iii, 50 *word* (Q) omitted
III, i, 80 *urinals* (Q) urinal
III, iii, 3 *Robert* (Bowers) Robin   144 *uncope* (Wilson) uncape
III, iv, 12 *Fenton* (F2) omitted   57 *God* (Q) Heaven
III, v, 79 *By the Lord* (Q) Yes
IV, ii, 17 *lunes* (Theobald) lines   48 *Mrs Page* (Malone) omitted   55 *Mrs Page* (Q) Mrs Ford   89 *him* (F2) omitted   127 *an honest man* (Q) a man   157 *not* (F2) omitted   160 *hag* (F3) Ragge   166 *Jeshu* (Q) yea, and no
IV, iii, 1 *Germans desire* (Capell) German desires   7 *them* (Q) him   9 *house* (Q) houses
IV, iv, 7 *cold* (Rowe) gold   59 *Mrs Ford* (Rowe) Ford   71 *tire* (Theobald) time
IV, v, 37 *Simple* (Rowe) Falstaff   46 *Sir Tyke* (Q) Sir: like
IV, vi, 16 *wherein* (Q) omitted
V, ii, 3 *daughter* (F2) omitted
V, iii, 11 *Hugh* (Capell) Herne
V, v, 188 *white* (Rowe³) green   192 *green* (Rowe³) white   197 *green* (Pope) white

ALL'S WELL THAT ENDS WELL

INTRODUCTION

All's Well That Ends Well has always been a stepchild among Shakespeare's plays. Eminent readers have sometimes responded warmly to the figure of Helena, but they have rarely spoken well of the play as a whole. Usually it has been viewed as self-evidently one of Shakespeare's worst, a thing of shreds and patches "scratched over by a master's hand upon a poor original," a repository of juvenile and even fatuous couplets alternating with passages of maturely wrought blank verse, a play in which the conduct of the narrative is undignified, the ethics of the plot, especially the bed trick, reprehensible, the clowning, such as it is, "uncouth," the part of Parolles irrelevant, Bertram irredeemably disagreeable, Helena – for all her virtue – too scheming, and the whole, despite incidental felicities, "a rather nasty play."

It is perhaps useless to answer such criticism by pointing out that it is proceeding largely by negatives, complaining of absences instead of responding to presences. Audiences who insist on ingratiating characters with whom to identify will always find Bertram repellent. Those who stipulate jocosity and high spirits in comic drama will always find the play "mirthless" and "unsmiling." Unquestionably it lacks the festival element of much other Shakespearean comedy: we hear no merry catches, no hunting songs, no amorous strains picked out on lutes; nor do we assist at dances, masques, or revels, at midnight frolics in the buttery, or sportive jesting among young wooers. But instead of lamenting the absence of these we might be prompted to suspect that Shakespeare's interest lay elsewhere on this occasion, that he was seeking effects different from the more usual ones of "happy" comedy. Spectators, again, who prescribe the orthodox procedures of courtship between lovers will never reconcile themselves to the wooing arrangements in this play – a young woman passionately in quest of a man who scorns her when she offers herself to him as a bride and abandons her brutally when she has become his wife. Even the clown, it may be agreed, is a "shrewd knave and an unhappy," skilled at deciphering the foolishness of the world but undelighted by its delights. And in the denouement, where Shakespeare would normally be working reconciliations and composing harmonies, here he seems deliberately to create fresh discords, to lead us into new irresolutions, so that we remain, at the end, somewhat doubting and wondering. But instead of dismissing these as failures of intention, we might more reasonably suppose that the unconventional wooing, the bleakness of the clown's humor, the ambiguous tone of the finale, together with the other unusual features of this play, form part of a conscious design, that they are meant to produce the effects of poignance and austerity that they do produce, and that these effects are as legitimate as the more customary ones of festive comedy.

All's Well That Ends Well was first printed in the folio of 1623. No external clues exist as to the date of writing or of first performance. Largely on stylistic grounds, and by virtue of resemblances to *Measure for Measure*, it is thought to have been written about the same time as that play (ca. 1602–04), and its links with it, and with *Troilus and Cressida*, have led to its being classified with them as a "problem play" or "problem comedy." By this the critics have sometimes meant that Shakespeare, in the plays in question, was investigating certain ethical issues, or "problems," and at other times that these plays share certain puzzling traits – a crabbedness of language, a preoccupation with disease and sexuality, an alleged "loathing" of spirit, a refusal to fit comfortably into the usual generic categories – that make them "problems" for critics.

Recent comment, more helpfully, has stressed the affinities of *All's Well* with the last plays, and seen it as belonging to the mainstream of Shakespearean comedy. Its "problematic" character would seem best described not by reference to some special state of revulsion, or disillusion, in Shakespeare at the time of writing, but, more prosaically, as a defect of artistic management, a relatively imperfect fusion of elements with which Shakespeare worked throughout his career. Like other Shakespearean comedy, *All's Well That Ends Well* moves between the two poles of romance and satire – between a vision of life as good and gracious, expressed in beneficent magic and marvellous coincidences, and a vision of it as absurd and degraded, expressed in scenes of folly and derision – and with these two modes of vision it merges a third, inherited from the English morality play, of life as a pilgrimage, a quest for salvation, in which men take wrong paths, stray into forests or labyrinths, but ultimately regain the road that leads to fulfillment.

The plot comes from a tale of Boccaccio, translated into English in Painter's *Palace of Pleasure*, one of the most familiar of sixteenth-century collections of Italian stories. Shakespeare reshapes the original narrative freely, but he is careful to preserve, and even insist on, the romance motif, the details suggestive of folklore such as Helena's magic cure of the king, her pilgrimage and mock death, and the lucky coincidences on which the successful working out of events depends.

At the same time he overlays the romance pattern with the morality pattern, making Bertram the central personage in the latter. Older morality drama had presented the hero's life, from birth to death, in a sequence of moral crises understood to be universal and exemplary. One common variant consisted in treating only a single phase of this life-history, usually the moment of young manhood, when the hero, setting forth into the world, fell into temptations peculiar to the young, and at length, after much suffering and wrongdoing, was reclaimed to happiness and virtue. This partial pattern, often consciously derived from the parable of the prodigal son, underlies the career of Bertram. Bertram is the raw youth whose impetuousness leads him swiftly, if not inevitably, into error when he enters the world. He places himself under the tutelage of a braggart, spurns wholesome advice, and behaves dishonorably toward those who love him. In rejecting Helena, he rejects a whole complex of traditional values embodied in the elders of his society – his dead father, his mother, and his king.

His rebellion, however, contains at least one positive element, his eagerness to win fame in battle. Soldiership is one traditional value he does honor, and it becomes the basis for his recovery of the rest. Italy, where he seeks his fortune in war, serves Bertram as the other country and place of exile in which Shakespearean characters often work out their destinies before returning, seasoned and in some measure purified, to resume their rightful posts at home. In Florence Bertram lays claim through his valor to some of the manhood impugned by his earlier acts. He wins the esteem of his seniors and differentiates himself from his cowardly hanger-on Parolles. His earlier acts, meantime, are breeding consequences that affect him in other ways. When he learns, in a rebuking letter from his mother, of the disappearance of Helena, his conscience awakens. He changes, we are told, "almost into another man." The two lords to whom Shakespeare entrusts this report go on to expound, in Shakespeare's gravest aphoristic prose, the ethical drift of the play : "The web of our life is of a mingled yarn, good and ill together ; our virtues would be proud if our faults whipped them not, and our crimes would despair if they were not cherished by our virtues." Bertram, viewed in this light, symbolizes errant humanity ; the texture of human life, radically multifold, intrinsically compounded of good and ill, makes it certain he will transgress, and the comments of the two lords seem partly designed to mitigate, on this score, the severity of the judgment we might otherwise be tempted to pass, by forcing us to recognize ourselves in Bertram.

While the two lords are discussing him, Bertram is keeping his assignation with Helena, whom he believes to be Diana. Shortly after, he participates in the unmasking of Parolles. The effect of these events is to transfer him decisively from the guardianship of his evil genius Parolles to that of his good genius Helena. But whereas the false glamour of Parolles, a thing of glitter and surface, can be dispelled in a moment, the true worth of Helena is more reticent ; it must work slowly and in the dark, its full impact deferred until the final moments of the play.

One aspect of Bertram's story is that it is worked out in terms of a distinction between inherited and achieved nobility. When the play opens, the Countess voices the hope that Bertram will be his father's heir in the true sense, by behaving nobly, by making his father's virtue his own in act. Her implied doubt on this point is confirmed by Bertram's rejection of Helena, where his harping on her low birth constitutes in itself a dereliction from his own nobility, from the nobility bequeathed him by a father who behaved with special punctiliousness toward those of humbler rank. Bertram in fact inherits from his father an acute class consciousness, but whereas in his father this manifested itself as courtesy, it turns in Bertram into vulgar snobbery. He misconceives his aristocratic heritage, at this moment, as a simple possession, rather than as a quality of spirit or an ideal to be realized. He thinks of it as a *thing*, totally *his*, to be guarded jealously (from upstarts like Helena) or expended carelessly as he pleases. He thinks of it, indeed, as an analogue to his ancestral ring, which he is ready to barter away to purchase a night's pleasure. The squandering of the ring, Bertram's patrimony embodied in the form most meaningful to him, a concrete emblem of family dignity and feudal worth, marks the low point in his falling away from his true heritage – the low point, and, hence, the turning point, since the fact that he bestows the ring on Helena means that it will return to him with value surcharged. The revelation of it on Diana's finger in the last scene makes public the extent of his offense, exposing the hollowness of the honor in behalf of which he has turned away Helena. Like previous morality heroes, Bertram plunges more deeply into shame with this repetition of his fault, and requires a correspondingly "deeper" intervention of beneficent forces in order to be rescued.

The weakness of this design, as so outlined, is that too much of it remains blueprint. Bertram's progress is diagrammed rather than fully realized poetically, assumed rather than demonstrated. Since we never hear him in soliloquy or meditation, we cannot assess the impact of events on him. From his interchanges with other characters we can draw only sketchy inferences. Even in the scene of Parolles' exposure, a crucial one for Bertram's development, Bertram can react only by calling Parolles a cat – three times. Such an inadequate response to an event of such magnitude robs the episode of much of its proper and legitimate weight. The trouble with Bertram is not, as commentators have complained, that he is "disagreeable," but that he is insufficiently interesting, too defective in nerve-tissue, too blunt in sensibility and wooden in his reactions, to command the attention that the plot would seem to be claiming for him. And this trouble, in turn, would seem to stem from his having been conceived to such an extent as a morality hero of the old-fashioned sort, as a passive creature, more acted on than acting, whose character consists largely of the sum of the pressures converging upon him.

Flanking Bertram stand the opposed forces of Helena and Parolles, the latter serving as evil tempter and agent of mischief. It is Parolles who foments Bertram's discontent at court, suggests flight to him, seconds him in his plan to abandon Helena, and acts as go-between in the attempt to seduce Diana. His name, of course, means "words," and he is above all a *word*-monger, claiming prowess he does not possess in an affected language designed to win admiration from foolish young courtiers. His duty as a soldier suggests his role in the plot : he is the drum, or drummer, the specialist in loud, hollow, booming sounds, the one who incites others to action but is incapable of it himself. That his fall from favor should hinge on a pretended exploit to recover the company drum, and that it should be carried out by means of such artful gibberish and calculated nonsense as he himself has traded in make for a peculiarly fitting poetic justice. Further, Parolles is a fop, much preoccupied with dress and fashion. As the noise of the drum symbolizes his emptiness, so his flashy appearance, and the repeated descriptions of him in terms of his scarves and plumes, signify his superficiality. Unlike Helena, whose worth is inner, Parolles is all outside; his soul, as Lafew warns Bertram, lies in his clothes.

His career forms the main satiric strand in the plot. Parolles is constructed after the model of certain comic characters in Ben Jonson, as an impostor, or poseur, whose mission it is to indulge his affectations for a time, impose them on others, and then, in a climactic scene, be stripped of them and revealed for what he is. In Jonsonian comedy, such characters usually collapse into non-existence and vanish at this point; once they have given themselves away, nothing remains. Shakespeare, characteristically, endows Parolles with a further layer of existence, the bedrock of the irreducible human, to which he reverts after his exposure. His pretenses unmasked, he survives henceforward as "the thing he is," coward and rascal, but a fellow creature, and as such able to enlist in the cause of his survival the caustic old counsellor Lafew.

In Helena, the chief romance character, George Bernard Shaw saw an early dramatic instance of the life force, the energy of the race manifesting itself in the feminine drive for procreation. Precisely the active element in Helena has sometimes repelled critics; they have found her "pushing" and "calculating." But it is clear that Shakespeare did not regard her as such. Nor did his source. Giletta of Narbona, in Painter, belongs to a familiar category of folk heroine, the girl who performs difficult or impossible tasks, and is rewarded with the hand of her high-born beloved. In the case of Bertram, Shakespeare underscores the coarseness of Count Beltramo's behavior, and so aggravates the indictment against him. In the case of Helena, he removes the faint traces of disapproval that clung to Giletta in the tale for her presumption in wishing to marry a count, and so mobilizes our sympathies more urgently in her behalf. In addition he chooses to make hers the most fully articulated consciousness in the play, the one whose feelings are projected with most intensity and explored with greatest complexity. Helena is at once Shakespeare's most ardent and most introspective heroine, and her presence in the centre of the design accounts for much of its mood of fervor and impassioned seriousness.

Shakespeare initiates, furthermore, from the outset a contrast between Helena and Bertram, with regard to their relations with their elders, their manner of claiming their birthrights, their notions of honor, and much else. Helena's father, like Bertram's, is dead before the play opens. But whereas the countess' exhortations stress the fact that Bertram is as yet – in the respects that matter – only potentially his father's son, Helena has already shown herself worthy of her stock; "she derives her honesty and achieves her goodness." She does not hold her heritage, as Bertram does his nobility, as an inert thing. She actualizes it, recreates it, *achieves* it in her daily existence.

Her skill as a physician, which borders on the magical, is the visible emblem of her patrimony, as Bertram's family ring is of his. But where Bertram spends his ring merely to buy an hour's pleasure, and regards himself as in no way committed by the transaction, Helena offers her remedy in a gesture of total engagement, ready to give herself to Bertram if she succeeds, ready to submit to death and torture if she fails. Such a gift, involving as it does her whole being, inevitably falls on stony ground, is

misunderstood, and perhaps feared, by one who at this moment is captivated by sounds and surfaces, and unacquainted with recesses in himself or others.

The sole error Helena makes is in supposing that love can be earned, that she can somehow *deserve* Bertram. And the only way in which her compact with the king resembles Bertram's bargain with Diana is that both are contracts. The one extenuation, hence, that may be allowed Bertram's otherwise inadmissible churlishness is that he is being asked, in effect, to render as a duty, to give as payment, what can only be bestowed freely and spontaneously. Love, like the mercy of which Portia speaks in *The Merchant of Venice*, cannot be wrung or "strained," but drops like rain from heaven. That Helena does not at first see this, or does not see it clearly, constitutes her sole flaw. But it is enough to make her feel she has sinned, offended through "ambitious love," and to prompt her to undertake a penitential pilgrimage. The central part of the play abounds in the ironies of juxtaposition in which Shakespearean drama is always fertile. As we pass back and forth from Florence to Rossillion, as the stage fills and clears, we move from the camp of war, where Bertram declares his hatred of love, to the home of love, where Helena confesses her terror of war. It is not until love and war can in some sense merge, through the agency of the bed trick, that Bertram's combativeness, which appears momentarily victorious, can in fact be subdued by love and turned to creative ends.

What is apt to bother modern readers about the bed trick that resolves the complications is not so much its indelicacy as its inappropriateness. It seems too mechanical an expedient, too remote from the nuances of the situation it is asked to catalyze. The folk tale premise, acceptable enough in folk tale – that two people otherwise wholly different can be indistinguishable in bed (because darkness constitutes a perfect disguise, and sexual intimacy involves recognition only on the bodily level) – seems unacceptable, even shocking, when applied to characters of the individuality of Bertram and Helena. A Bertram who really could not tell Helena from Diana in bed would not belong in a play by Shakespeare at all, nor would a Helena who thought such a deception possible.

Nevertheless the bed trick fosters our sense that events are moving darkly, that they drift on mysterious currents hidden from the eye of day and reason, that their outcome awaits the touch of forces beyond the characters' control. Such, too, would seem to be the sense of the curious series of "removes" through which Helena must pursue the court before catching up with it: even while actively engaged in her quest, she must await the propitious moment, the conjunction of other forces, to bring her plan to fruition. In her power to call into being the world of her desires, Helena forms a transitional figure between the heroines of earlier Shakespearean comedy – Portia and Rosalind and Viola – who transform their surroundings largely through natural means, and the explicit wielders of supernatural power, the Cerimons and Prosperos, who preside over the frankly miraculous worlds of the late romances.

Her power, however, so swift to take effect on the king's illness, must await, for its effect on Bertram, the final moment of the play, when Bertram's case, like the king's, seems hopeless. Dr Johnson very much to the contrary, Shakespeare does not during this last scene "contract his dialogue and precipitate his action." Rather, he constructs one of his most elaborate judicial finales, in which a ruler presides over a ceremonial unfolding of hidden truths, a public re-enactment of events that have already occurred. With Diana's arrival, Bertram finds himself caught in a net which he has helped to weave. As it tightens, he thrashes like a snared animal, managing, in his frenzy, to repeat and compound the errors of his past. Having rejected Helena for her low birth, he now spurns Diana for her supposed low morality, applying in this case as in that the coarsest measure of lowness, the one that blots out all ethical distinctions and most readily serves his own convenience. Having frivolously paid out his ancestral ring, he as lightly dismisses the binding claim of the ring accepted in return. The surrender of his own ring in the first place meant the breaking of a link with his patrician forebears; the refusal to honor its counterpart betokens an unsaying of the meaning of his own deeds, and a reducing of himself, thereby, to insignificance. All this as though to illustrate the stubbornness of "blood," the precariousness of virtue no matter how painfully purchased. What may chill us is that the Bertram who perpetrates this new offense remains the same Bertram as before – not one capable of feeling a deeper shame when his evasions are exposed, but the same self-willed, self-satisfied adolescent of the earlier scenes, ready to trivialize all of his experience. His behavior, indeed, would seem to contradict the claims made for him on various occasions, that he has "changed almost into another man," that he was "misled" by Parolles, that his "blames" were "high-repented." Shakespeare seems to go out of his way to insist that the conversion we thought we were witnessing was no conversion at all. Any trust in the metamorphosis fervently desired by the king, the countess, and Lafew, is blighted beyond repair by Bertram's lies when confronted with Diana, and his frantic attempts to make her pay for his own misdoings.

Why should he, then, in Dr Johnson's offended phrase, be "dismissed to happiness," upon the near-miraculous interposition of Helena? Because both life and art will have it so. Because the situation remains equivocal – "he's guilty, and he is not guilty" – his sinful intent having failed to produce hurtful consequences in the outer world. Because acts potentially tragic are capable, in the comic world, of leading to untragic fulfillment, just as trivial acts, in the tragic world, can forespell universal disaster. As tragedy gives us images of men suffering beyond their faults, so comedy shows us men rewarded beyond their deserts. On Bertram's success hangs the happy future of his whole community. Undoubtedly the impact of the play is diluted by the thinness of his reactions. Unquestionably we wish him more evolved, more alive and sentient, able to register the deeps and shallows of the situation more complexly. But there is no need for us to "like" Bertram to be moved by the ending of this play. *All's Well That Ends Well* is more, not less, of a comedy because of Bertram's unworthiness. His youth has led him to the crossroads of misery and happiness; his guardian angel, mysteriously conjoining with the good in himself, has guided him into the better path. If the finale contains its meed of bitterness, as the king's last line acknowledges, it also provides a measure of sweetness. If it does not leave us jubilant, it does not abandon us to dismal thinkings;

rather, it leaves us awed and clarified before the spectacle of a happy fatality working itself out through human agency. Few moments in drama are as highly charged as Diana's riddle, on which so much depends, with its triumphant cadence – "And now behold the meaning" – as Helena appears to irradiate the obscurities of the plot. And few are as affecting as the subsequent recognitions, which show us how our own goodness can join forces with the goodness outside, to rescue us from our own self-treachery.

University of California   J O N A S A . B A R I S H
at Berkeley

NOTE ON THE TEXT

All's Well That Ends Well was first published in the folio of 1623, with Shakespeare's own draft evidently serving as printer's copy. Although marred by certain misprints and minor irregularities, it is a reasonably good text and has been followed closely in the present edition. The folio text is divided into acts corresponding with those in modern editions, but not into scenes. The act–scene division here supplied marginally for reference purposes is the conventional one evolved by Shakespeare's editors. All material departures from the folio text are listed below, with the adopted reading in italics followed by the folio reading in roman.

I, i, 36 *promises. Her dispositions* promises her dispositions 48 *have.* have – 83 *above me.* above me 124 *got* goe 142 *ten, two,* 153 *wear* were
I, ii, 18 *Rossillion* Rosignoll
I, iii, 19 *and I will* and w will 82 *but or* but ore 108 *level;* *Dian no queen* leuell, Queene 164 *loneliness* louelinesse 170 *t' one to th' other* 'ton tooth to th' other 195 *intenible* intemible 242 *and* an
II, i, 3 *gain all*, gaine, all 43 *with his cicatrice, an emblem* his sicatrice, with an Embleme 62 *fee* see 109 *dear ; I have* dear I have 144 *fits* shifts 155 *impostor* Impostrue 173 *nay* ne 192 *heaven* helpe
II, ii, 57 *An* And
II, iii, 75 s.d. (appears after l. 61 in F) 93 *her* here 124 *when* whence 129 *it is* is is 140 *indeed. What* indeed, what 286 *detested* detected
II, iv, 16 *fortunes* fortune
II, v, 26 *End* And 88 *Where . . . Farewell* (assigned to Helena in F)
III, i, 23 *to th'* to'th the
III, ii, 9 *sold* hold 18 *E'en* In 64 *engrossest all* engrossest, all 108 *still-piecing* still-peering
III, iv, 7 *have* hane
III, v, 32 *le* la
III, vi, 32 *his* this 33 *ore* ours
III, vii, 19 *Resolved* Resolue
IV, i, 85 *art* are
IV, ii, 38 *may* make *snare* scarre
IV, iii, 77–79 *They . . . midnight* (assigned to Bertram in F) 85 *effected* affected 112 *Hush, hush* (assigned to Bertram in F) 131 *All's . . . him* (assigned to Parolles in F) 184 *lordship* Lord 225 *our* your 248 *him!* him
IV, iv, 3 *'fore* for 16 *you,* your
IV, v, 19 *grass* grace 36 *name* maine
V, i, 6 s.d. *a Gentleman* a gentle Astringer
V, ii, 24 *similes* smiles 32 *under her* vnder
V, iii, 58–59 *carried, . . . sender* carried . . . sender, 71–72 *Which . . . cesse* (assigned to the King in F) 122 *tax* taze 155 *sir, sith* sir, sir 183 *them. Fairer* them fairer: 207 *sickens but . . . truth.* sickens: but . . . truth, 216 *infinite cunning* insuite comming 310 *are* is

ALL'S WELL THAT ENDS WELL

*

I, i   *Enter young Bertram, Count of Rossillion, his*
       Mother [the Dowager Countess], and Helena ;
       Lord Lafew – all in black.

COUNTESS In delivering my son from me I bury a second
husband.

BERTRAM And I in going, madam, weep o'er my father's
death anew ; but I must attend his majesty's command,
5 to whom I am now in ward, evermore in subjection.

LAFEW You shall find of the king a husband, madam ; you,
7 sir, a father. He that so generally is at all times good
8 must of necessity hold his virtue to you, whose worthi-
9 ness would stir it up where it wanted, rather than lack it
where there is such abundance.

COUNTESS What hope is there of his majesty's amendment ?

LAFEW He hath abandoned his physicians, madam ;
13 under whose practices he hath persecuted time with
hope, and finds no other advantage in the process but
only the losing of hope by time.

COUNTESS This young gentlewoman had a father – O,
17 that 'had,' how sad a passage 'tis – whose skill was almost
as great as his honesty ; had it stretched so far, would
have made nature immortal, and death should have play
for lack of work. Would for the king's sake he were
living ! I think it would be the death of the king's disease.

LAFEW How called you the man you speak of, madam ?

COUNTESS He was famous, sir, in his profession, and it
was his great right to be so – Gerard de Narbon.

LAFEW He was excellent indeed, madam. The king very
lately spoke of him admiringly and mournfully. He was
skillful enough to have lived still, if knowledge could be 27
set up against mortality.

BERTRAM What is it, my good lord, the king languishes
of ?·

LAFEW A fistula, my lord.

BERTRAM I heard not of it before.

LAFEW I would it were not notorious. Was this gentlewoman the daughter of Gerard de Narbon ?

COUNTESS His sole child, my lord, and bequeathed to my
overlooking. I have those hopes of her good that her 35
education promises. Her dispositions she inherits, which
makes fair gifts fairer ; for where an unclean mind carries virtuous qualities, there commendations go with 38
pity – they are virtues and traitors too. In her they are
the better for their simpleness. She derives her honesty 40
and achieves her goodness. 41

LAFEW Your commendations, madam, get from her tears.

COUNTESS 'Tis the best brine a maiden can season her 43
praise in. The remembrance of her father never approaches her heart but the tyranny of her sorrows takes
all livelihood from her cheek. No more of this, Helena. 46
Go to, no more, lest it be rather thought you affect a
sorrow than to have.

HELENA *[aside]* I do affect a sorrow indeed, but I have it
too.

LAFEW Moderate lamentation is the right of the dead,
excessive grief the enemy to the living.

COUNTESS If the living be enemy to the grief, the excess 52
makes it soon mortal.

BERTRAM Madam, I desire your holy wishes.

LAFEW How understand we that ?

COUNTESS
Be thou blest, Bertram, and succeed thy father
In manners, as in shape. Thy blood and virtue 57
Contend for empire in thee, and thy goodness
Share with thy birthright. Love all, trust a few,

60   Do wrong to none. Be able for thine enemy
61   Rather in power than use, and keep thy friend
62   Under thy own life's key. Be checked for silence,
63   But never taxed for speech. What heaven more will,
      That thee may furnish, and my prayers pluck down,
      Fall on thy head ! – Farewell, my lord.
      'Tis an unseasoned courtier. Good my lord,
      Advise him.
    LAFEW   He cannot want the best
    That shall attend his love.
  COUNTESS Heaven bless him ! Farewell, Bertram.
                            [Exit.]
  BERTRAM The best wishes that can be forged in your
71   thoughts be servants to you ! [to Helena] Be comfortable
    to my mother, your mistress, and make much of her.
73 LAFEW Farewell, pretty lady. You must hold the credit
    of your father.   [Exeunt Bertram and Lafew.]
  HELENA
    O, were that all ! I think not on my father,
    And these great tears grace his remembrance more
77   Than those I shed for him. What was he like ?
    I have forgot him. My imagination
79   Carries no favor in't but Bertram's.
    I am undone ; there is no living, none,
    If Bertram be away. 'Twere all one
    That I should love a bright particular star
    And think to wed it, he is so above me.
84   In his bright radiance and collateral light
85   Must I be comforted, not in his sphere.
86   Th' ambition in my love thus plagues itself :
    The hind that would be mated by the lion
    Must die for love. 'Twas pretty, though a plague,
    To see him every hour, to sit and draw
90   His archèd brows, his hawking eye, his curls,
91   In our heart's table – heart too capable
92   Of every line and trick of his sweet favor.
    But now he's gone, and my idolatrous fancy
    Must sanctify his relics. Who comes here ?
      Enter Parolles.
95   One that goes with him ; I love him for his sake,
    And yet I know him a notorious liar,
    Think him a great way fool, solely a coward.
    Yet these fixed evils sit so fit in him
99   That they take place when virtue's steely bones
101   Looks bleak i' th' cold wind ; withal, full oft we see
    Cold wisdom waiting on superfluous folly.
  PAROLLES Save you, fair queen !
  HELENA And you, monarch !
  PAROLLES No.
  HELENA And no.
  PAROLLES Are you meditating on virginity ?
107 HELENA Ay. You have some stain of soldier in you ; let
    me ask you a question. Man is enemy to virginity ; how
    may we barricado it against him ?
  PAROLLES Keep him out.
  HELENA But he assails, and our virginity, though valiant,
    in the defense yet is weak. Unfold to us some warlike
    resistance.
114 PAROLLES There is none. Man setting down before you
115   will undermine you and blow you up.
  HELENA Bless our poor virginity from underminers and
    blowers-up ! Is there no military policy how virgins
    might blow up men ?
  PAROLLES Virginity being blown down, man will quick-

lier be blown up ; marry, in blowing him down again, 120
with the breach yourselves made you lose your city. It is
not politic in the commonwealth of nature to preserve 122
virginity. Loss of virginity is rational increase, and there 123
was never virgin got till virginity was first lost. That you 124
were made of is metal to make virgins. Virginity by
being once lost may be ten times found ; by being ever 126
kept it is ever lost. 'Tis too cold a companion. Away
with't !
HELENA I will stand for't a little, though therefore I die a 129
virgin.
PAROLLES There's little can be said in't ; 'tis against the 131
rule of nature. To speak on the part of virginity is to ac- 132
cuse your mothers, which is most infallible disobedience. 133
He that hangs himself is a virgin ; virginity murders itself, and should be buried in highways out of all sancti- 135
fied limit, as a desperate offendress against nature. Virginity breeds mites, much like a cheese, consumes itself 137
to the very paring, and so dies with feeding his own 138
stomach. Besides, virginity is peevish, proud, idle, made
of self-love, which is the most inhibited sin in the canon. 140
Keep it not ; you cannot choose but lose by't. Out 141
with't ! within ten year it will make itself ten, which is a
goodly increase, and the principal itself not much the 143
worse. Away with't !
HELENA How might one do, sir, to lose it to her own
liking ?
PAROLLES Let me see. Marry, ill, to like him that ne'er it 147
likes. 'Tis a commodity will lose the gloss with lying : 148
the longer kept, the less worth. Off with't while 'tis 149
vendible ; answer the time of request. Virginity, like an 150
old courtier, wears her cap out of fashion, richly suited, 151
but unsuitable, just like the brooch and the toothpick,
which wear not now. Your date is better in your pie and 153
your porridge than in your cheek ; and your virginity,
your old virginity, is like one of our French withered
pears : it looks ill, it eats drily. Marry, 'tis a withered 156
pear ; it was formerly better ; marry, yet 'tis a withered
pear ! Will you anything with it ?

60 *able* a match   61 *in power* potentially ; *use* as a matter of habit   61–62 *keep* . . . *key* defend your friend's life as you would your own   62 *checked* reproved   63 *taxed for speech* rebuked for chattering   71 *comfortable* comforting   73 *hold* uphold   77 *those . . . him* i.e. when he died   79 *favor* face   84 *collateral* i.e. shed from above, from a distance   85 *sphere* the orbit in which he himself moves   86 *plagues itself* becomes its own tormentor   90 *hawking* hawklike, sharpsighted   91 *table* drawing-board   91–92 *capable Of* readily impressed with   92 *trick* trait   95 *his* Bertram's   99 *take place* find welcome   99–100 *when . . . wind* when virtue looks puritanical and forbidding   101 *waiting on* dancing attendance on ; *superfluous* i.e. overdressed   107 *stain* tinge   114 *setting down before* besieging   115 *blow you up* (with pun on 'get you with child')   120 *blown up* i.e. 'reinflated'   120–21 *in . . . city* in quenching his ardor (by yielding to it) you lose the fortress of your virginity   122 *politic* statesmanlike   123 *rational increase* reasonable rate of population growth   124 *got* begotten ; *That* that which   126 *may . . . found* i.e. may engender ten more virgins   129 *stand for* defend   131 *in't* in its behalf   132 *on the part of* in defense of   133 *infallible* undoubted   135–36 *out . . . limit* in unsanctified ground   137 *breeds mites* i.e. breeds its own destruction   138–39 *feeding . . . stomach* maintaining its own pride   140 *inhibited* prohibited ; *canon* catalogue of sins   141 *Keep* hoard   141–42 *Out with't* lend it out at interest   143 *increase* rate of interest ; *principal* capital, i.e. the ex-virgin herself   147 *Marry* indeed   147–48 *ill . . . likes* one must do ill, and like the man who does not like virginity   148 *lying* lying idle   149 *Off with't* dispose of it   150 *answer . . . request* market it while it is still in demand   151 *out of fashion* unfashionably   151–52 *richly . . . unsuitable* dressed richly but inappropriately   153 *wear not* are not worn   153–54 *Your . . . cheek* dates (fruit) serve better to sweeten porridge than to show up (as years) in your face   156 *eats drily* tastes dry

HELENA

159 Not my virginity yet....

160 There shall your master have a thousand loves,
A mother, and a mistress, and a friend,
A phoenix, captain, and an enemy,
A guide, a goddess, and a sovereign,
A counsellor, a traitress, and a dear;
His humble ambition, proud humility,
His jarring concord, and his discord dulcet,
His faith, his sweet disaster; with a world

168 Of pretty, fond, adoptious christendoms

169 That blinking Cupid gossips. Now shall he –
I know not what he shall. God send him well!

171 The court's a learning place, and he is one –

PAROLLES

What one, i' faith?

HELENA   That I wish well. 'Tis pity –

PAROLLES

What's pity?

HELENA

175 That wishing well had not a body in't,
Which might be felt; that we, the poorer born,

177 Whose baser stars do shut us up in wishes,

178 Might with effects of them follow our friends,

179 And show what we alone must think, which never
Returns us thanks.

Enter Page.

PAGE Monsieur Parolles, my lord calls for you.   *[Exit.]*

PAROLLES Little Helen, farewell. If I can remember
thee, I will think of thee at court.

184 HELENA Monsieur Parolles, you were born under a charitable star.

PAROLLES Under Mars I.

HELENA I especially think, under Mars.

PAROLLES Why under Mars?

189 HELENA The wars hath so kept you under that you must
needs be born under Mars.

191 PAROLLES When he was predominant.

192 HELENA When he was retrograde, I think rather.

PAROLLES Why think you so?

HELENA You go so much backward when you fight.

PAROLLES That's for advantage.   195

HELENA So is running away when fear proposes the safety.
But the composition that your valor and fear makes in   197
you is a virtue of a good wing, and I like the wear well.   198

PAROLLES I am so full of businesses I cannot answer thee
acutely. I will return perfect courtier, in the which my   200
instruction shall serve to naturalize thee, so thou wilt be   201
capable of a courtier's counsel, and understand what ad-   202
vice shall thrust upon thee; else thou diest in thine unthankfulness, and thine ignorance makes thee away.   204
Farewell. When thou hast leisure, say thy prayers; when   205
thou hast none, remember thy friends. Get thee a good
husband, and use him as he uses thee. So, farewell.   207

                               [Exit.]

HELENA

Our remedies oft in ourselves do lie,
Which we ascribe to heaven. The fated sky   209
Gives us free scope; only doth backward pull
Our slow designs when we ourselves are dull.
What power is it which mounts my love so high?
That makes me see, and cannot feed mine eye?   213
The mightiest space in fortune nature brings   214
To join like likes, and kiss like native things.
Impossible be strange attempts to those
That weigh their pains in sense, and do suppose   217
What hath been cannot be. Who ever strove
To show her merit that did miss her love?
The king's disease – my project may deceive me,
But my intents are fixed, and will not leave me.   *[Exit.]*

                          *

Flourish cornets. Enter the King of France with   I, ii
letters, and divers Attendants.

KING

The Florentines and Senoys are by th' ears,   1
Have fought with equal fortune, and continue
A braving war.   3

1. LORD   So 'tis reported, sir.

KING

Nay, 'tis most credible. We here receive it
A certainty vouched from our cousin Austria,   5
With caution, that the Florentine will move us   6
For speedy aid; wherein our dearest friend
Prejudicates the business, and would seem   8
To have us make denial.

1. LORD   His love and wisdom,
Approved so to your majesty, may plead   10
For amplest credence.

KING   He hath armed our answer,
And Florence is denied before he comes.
Yet, for our gentlemen that mean to see
The Tuscan service, freely have they leave
To stand on either part.   15

2. LORD   It well may serve
A nursery to our gentry, who are sick   16
For breathing and exploit.   17

KING   What's he comes here?

Enter Bertram, Lafew, and Parolles.

1. LORD

It is the Count Rossillion, my good lord,
Young Bertram.

---

159 *Not . . . yet* the moment has not come for me to surrender my virginity (?)
(there may be an accidental omission in the text at this point) **160** *There*
at court (?) **160–67** *loves . . . disaster* (a series of epithets, similar to
those in much Elizabethan love poetry, used to characterize the beloved)
168 *fond . . . christendoms* foolish adopted nicknames **169** *That . . . gossips*
for which blind Cupid acts as godfather, i.e. inspired by love **171** *learning
place* place of learning, school **175–76** *That . . . felt* that good will were
not something substantial, and in itself effective **177** *Whose . . . wishes*
whose inferior fortunes confine us to mere wishing **178** *Might . . . follow*
might actively assist **179–80** *show . . . thanks* make manifest (in acts)
what we must otherwise conceal in our thoughts and so remain unthanked
for **184** *under* under the astrological influence of **189** *under* down
191 *predominant* in the ascendant **192** *retrograde* unfavorably disposed,
going *backward* (hence prompting those born under his influence to run
away) **195** *advantage* strategic benefit **197** *composition* mixture **198**
virtue property; *of . . . wing* useful for flight (especially from battle);
wear fashion **200** *acutely* aptly **201** *naturalize* familiarize and, in Parolles'
sense, deflower; *so if* **202** *capable of* able to profit from **204** *makes thee
away* destroys you **205–06** *when . . . friends* i.e. don't remember them at
all **207** *use* treat **209** *fated* fateful **213** *makes . . . eye* enables me to
envisage Bertram in my mind's eye without allowing me to see him in the
flesh **214–15** *The . . . things* nature causes things of the widest diversity in
station to unite and embrace as though born equals **217** *That . . . sense*
who count the cost and measure their discomforts
I, ii The palace of the King of France **1** *Senoys* Sienese; *by th' ears* at
war **3** *braving* defiant **5** *cousin* fellow monarch **6** *move* petition **8** *Prejudicates* prejudges **10** *Approved* proved **15** *stand* serve; *part* side
16 *nursery* training-ground **17** *breathing* exercise

KING   Youth, thou bear'st thy father's face.
20   Frank nature, rather curious than in haste,
21   Hath well composed thee. Thy father's moral parts
     Mayst thou inherit too! Welcome to Paris.

BERTRAM
     My thanks and duty are your majesty's.

KING
     I would I had that corporal soundness now
     As when thy father and myself in friendship
26   First tried our soldiership. He did look far
27   Into the service of the time, and was
     Discipled of the bravest. He lasted long,
     But on us both did haggish age steal on,
30   And wore us out of act. It much repairs me
     To talk of your good father; in his youth
     He had the wit which I can well observe
     To-day in our young lords; but they may jest
34   Till their own scorn return to them unnoted
35   Ere they can hide their levity in honor.
     So like a courtier, contempt nor bitterness
     Were in his pride, or sharpness. If they were,
     His equal had awaked them, and his honor,
39   Clock to itself, knew the true minute when
40   Exception bid him speak, and at this time
41   His tongue obeyed his hand. Who were below him
42   He used as creatures of another place,
     And bowed his eminent top to their low ranks,
     Making them proud of his humility,
45   In their poor praise he humbled. Such a man
     Might be a copy to these younger times,
     Which, followed well, would demonstrate them now
48   But goers backward.

BERTRAM   His good remembrance, sir,
     Lies richer in your thoughts than on his tomb.
50   So in approof lives not his epitaph
     As in your royal speech.

KING
     Would I were with him! He would always say –
53   Methinks I hear him now; his plausive words
54   He scattered not in ears, but grafted them
     To grow there, and to bear – 'Let me not live' –
     This his good melancholy oft began,
57   On the catastrophe and heel of pastime,
58   When it was out – 'Let me not live,' quoth he,
59   'After my flame lacks oil, to be the snuff
60   Of younger spirits, whose apprehensive senses
61   All but new things disdain; whose judgments are
     Mere fathers of their garments; whose constancies
     Expire before their fashions.' This he wished.
     I, after him, do after him wish too,
     Since I nor wax nor honey can bring home,
66   I quickly were dissolvèd from my hive,
     To give some laborers room.

2. LORD   You're loved, sir.
68   They that least lend it you shall lack you first.

KING
     I fill a place, I know't. How long is't, count,
     Since the physician at your father's died?
     He was much famed.

BERTRAM   Some six months since, my lord.

KING
     If he were living, I would try him yet.
     Lend me an arm. The rest have worn me out
74   With several applications; nature and sickness

     Debate it at their leisure. Welcome, count;
     My son's no dearer.

BERTRAM   Thank your majesty.

Exeunt. Flourish.

*

Enter Countess, Steward, and [Lavatch, a] Clown.   I, iii

COUNTESS I will now hear. What say you of this gentlewoman?

STEWARD Madam, the care I have had to even your con- 3
tent I wish might be found in the calendar of my past 4
endeavors; for then we wound our modesty, and make
foul the clearness of our deservings, when of ourselves 6
we publish them.   7

COUNTESS What does this knave here? Get you gone,
sirrah. The complaints I have heard of you I do not all
believe. 'Tis my slowness that I do not; for I know you
lack not folly to commit them, and have ability enough
to make such knaveries yours.

LAVATCH 'Tis not unknown to you, madam, I am a poor
fellow.

COUNTESS Well, sir.

LAVATCH No, madam, 'tis not so well that I am poor,
though many of the rich are damned; but if I may have
your ladyship's good will to go to the world, Isbel the 18
woman and I will do as we may.

COUNTESS Wilt thou needs be a beggar?

LAVATCH I do beg your good will in this case.

COUNTESS In what case?

LAVATCH In Isbel's case and mine own. Service is no
heritage, and I think I shall never have the blessing of
God till I have issue o' my body; for they say barnes are 25
blessings.

COUNTESS Tell me thy reason why thou wilt marry.

LAVATCH My poor body, madam, requires it; I am
driven on by the flesh; and he must needs go that the
devil drives.

COUNTESS Is this all your worship's reason?

LAVATCH Faith, madam, I have other holy reasons, such
as they are.

COUNTESS May the world know them?

LAVATCH I have been, madam, a wicked creature, as you
and all flesh and blood are, and indeed I do marry that
I may repent.

COUNTESS Thy marriage, sooner than thy wickedness.

---

20 *Frank* liberal; *curious* careful   21 *composed* constructed   26–27 *did
. . . time* deeply understood the business of war   27–28 *was . . . bravest*
numbered the bravest among his disciples   30 *wore . . . act* reduced us to
inaction   34 *unnoted* unnoticed   35 *hide . . . honor* cover their frivolity
with their dignity   39 *Clock to itself* 'self-regulating'; *true* exact   40
Exception disapproval   41 *obeyed his hand* said only what the hand (i.e. of
his clock of honor) prescribed; *Who* those who   42 *another place* i.e. a
higher rank   45 *In . . . humbled* he graciously condescended to the humble
by praising them (?)   48 *goers backward* laggards   50–51 *So . . . As* the
tribute on his tomb is nowhere better verified than   53 *plausive* plausible
54 *scattered . . . grafted* did not strew superficially among his hearers, but
planted deeply   57 *catastrophe and heel* end and completion   58 *it* i.e.
pastime; *out* over   59 *snuff* charred wicks impeding free burning, hence
hindrance, nuisance   60 *apprehensive* keen   61–62 *whose . . . garments*
whose minds are wholly taken up with devising new fashions   66 *dissolvèd*
separated   68 *lend it you* acknowledge it; *lack* miss   74 *several applications*
various treatments
I, iii The palace of the Count   3–4 *even your content* satisfy your wishes
4–5 *calendar . . . endeavors* record of my past service   6 *clearness* luster;
deservings deserts   7 *publish* make known   18 *go . . . world* get married
25 *barnes* children

37 LAVATCH I am out o' friends, madam, and I hope to have
friends for my wife's sake.

COUNTESS Such friends are thine enemies, knave.

40 LAVATCH Y' are shallow, madam, in great friends; for the
knaves come to do that for me which I am aweary of.
42 He that ears my land spares my team and gives me leave
43 to in the crop; if I be his cuckold, he's my drudge. He
that comforts my wife is the cherisher of my flesh and
blood; he that cherishes my flesh and blood loves my
flesh and blood; he that loves my flesh and blood is my
friend: ergo, he that kisses my wife is my friend. If men
48 could be contented to be what they are, there were no
49 fear in marriage; for young Charbon the puritan and
50 old Poysam the papist, howsome'er their hearts are sev-
51 ered in religion, their heads are both one – they may
52 jowl horns together like any deer i' th' herd.

COUNTESS Wilt thou ever be a foul-mouthed and calumnious knave?

LAVATCH A prophet I, madam, and I speak the truth the
56 next way:

For I the ballad will repeat,
Which men full true shall find:
Your marriage comes by destiny,
60 Your cuckoo sings by kind.

COUNTESS Get you gone, sir. I'll talk with you more anon.

STEWARD May it please you, madam, that he bid Helen
come to you. Of her I am to speak.

COUNTESS Sirrah, tell my gentlewoman I would speak
with her – Helen I mean.

66 LAVATCH 'Was this fair face the cause,' quoth she,
'Why the Grecians sackèd Troy?
68 Fond done, done fond,
69 Was this King Priam's joy?'
With that she sighèd as she stood,
With that she sighèd as she stood,
And gave this sentence then:
'Among nine bad if one be good,
Among nine bad if one be good,
There's yet one good in ten.'

76 COUNTESS What, one good in ten? You corrupt the song,
sirrah.

LAVATCH One good woman in ten, madam, which is a
purifying o' th' song. Would God would serve the world
80 so all the year! We'd find no fault with the tithe-woman,

if I were the parson. One in ten, quoth 'a? An we might 81
have a good woman born but or every blazing star, or 82
at an earthquake, 'twould mend the lottery well; a man 83
may draw his heart out ere 'a pluck one. 84

COUNTESS You'll be gone, sir knave, and do as I command you.

LAVATCH That man should be at woman's command,
and yet no hurt done! Though honesty be no puritan, 88
yet it will do no hurt; it will wear the surplice of humil- 89
ity over the black gown of a big heart. I am going, forsooth. The business is for Helen to come hither. *Exit.*

COUNTESS Well now.

STEWARD I know, madam, you love your gentlewoman
entirely.

COUNTESS Faith, I do. Her father bequeathed her to me,
and she herself, without other advantage, may lawfully 96
make title to as much love as she finds. There is more 97
owing her than is paid, and more shall be paid her than
she'll demand.

STEWARD Madam, I was very late more near her than I
think she wished me; alone she was, and did communicate to herself her own words to her own ears. She
thought, I dare vow for her, they touched not any 103
stranger sense. Her matter was, she loved your son.
Fortune, she said, was no goddess, that had put such
difference betwixt their two estates; Love no god, that
would not extend his might, only where qualities were 107
level; Dian no queen of virgins, that would suffer her
poor knight surprised without rescue in the first assault,
or ransom afterward. This she delivered in the most
bitter touch of sorrow that e'er I heard virgin exclaim in, 111
which I held my duty speedily to acquaint you withal,
sithence, in the loss that may happen, it concerns you 113
something to know it. 114

COUNTESS You have discharged this honestly; keep it to
yourself. Many likelihoods informed me of this before,
which hung so tottering in the balance that I could
neither believe nor misdoubt. Pray you leave me; stall 118
this in your bosom; and I thank you for your honest
care. I will speak with you further anon. *Exit Steward.*

Enter Helena.

Even so it was with me when I was young.
If ever we are nature's, these are ours. This thorn 122
Doth to our rose of youth rightly belong;
Our blood to us, this to our blood is born. 124
It is the show and seal of nature's truth, 125
Where love's strong passion is impressed in youth.
By our remembrances of days foregone,
Such were our faults, or then we thought them none. 128
Her eye is sick on't; I observe her now. 129

HELENA
What is your pleasure, madam?

COUNTESS   You know, Helen,
I am a mother to you.

HELENA
Mine honorable mistress.

COUNTESS   Nay, a mother.
Why not a mother? When I said 'a mother,'
Methought you saw a serpent. What's in 'mother'
That you start at it? I say I am your mother,
And put you in the catalogue of those
That were enwombèd mine. 'Tis often seen
Adoption strives with nature, and choice breeds 138
A native slip to us from foreign seeds.

---

37 *out o'* without   40 *shallow . . . in* superficial . . . in judging   42 *ears*
ploughs   43 *in* harvest   48 *what they are* i.e. cuckolds   49 *Charbon*
('chair bonne') i.e. meat-eater   50 *Poysam* ('poisson') i.e. fish-eater   50
severed divided   51 *both one* exactly alike   52 *jowl* knock; *deer . . . herd*
horned beasts, i.e. cuckolds   56 *next* nearest   60 *kind* nature   66 *she*
possibly Hecuba, widow of Priam   68 *Fond* foolishly (with pun on 'caress-
ingly')   69 *Priam* king of Troy   76 *corrupt the song* (the song presumably
found one *bad* in ten; the clown reverses the proportions)   80–81 *We'd
. . . parson* one good woman in ten (*tithe-woman*) ought to satisfy the
parson as well as one pig in ten   81 *An* if   82 *or . . . or* either . . . or; *blazing
star* new star, or comet   83 *mend the lottery* improve the existing odds
84 *pluck one* draw a good woman (in the lottery of marriage)   88 *honesty*
chastity   89–90 *wear . . . heart* conform to ecclesiastical rules by wearing
the surplice, but remain inwardly rebellious by wearing the puritan black
gown underneath   96 *without other advantage* other claims apart   97
make title to claim   103–04 *touched . . . sense* could not be overheard
107–08 *qualities were level* social rank was equal   111 *touch* note   113
sithence since   114 *something* somewhat   118 *stall* lodge   122 *these* i.e.
pangs of love   124 *blood* natural instincts   125 *show . . . truth* sign and
certificate of the genuineness of our human nature   128 *on't* with it   138
strives competes in strength of love   138–39 *choice . . . seeds* by adoption
we make wholly our own what was originally foreign

You ne'er oppressed me with a mother's groan,
Yet I express to you a mother's care.
God's mercy, maiden, does it curd thy blood
To say I am thy mother? What's the matter,

144   That this distemperèd messenger of wet,
145   The many-colored Iris, rounds thine eye?
     Why? that you are my daughter?

HELENA   That I am not.

COUNTESS
     I say I am your mother.

HELENA   Pardon, madam.
     The Count Rossillion cannot be my brother :
     I am from humble, he from honorèd name ;

150   No note upon my parents, his all noble.
     My master, my dear lord he is, and I
     His servant live and will his vassal die.
     He must not be my brother.

COUNTESS   Nor I your mother?

HELENA
     You are my mother, madam. Would you were –
     So that my lord your son were not my brother –

156   Indeed my mother ! or were you both our mothers,
     I care no more for than I do for heaven,
     So I were not his sister. Can 't no other,
     But I your daughter, he must be my brother ?

COUNTESS
     Yes, Helen, you might be my daughter-in-law.
     God shield you mean it not ! 'daughter' and 'mother'
     So strive upon your pulse. What, pale again ?

163   My fear hath catched your fondness. Now I see
     The myst'ry of your loneliness, and find

165   Your salt tears' head. Now to all sense 'tis gross :
166   You love my son. Invention is ashamed,
     Against the proclamation of thy passion,
     To say thou dost not. Therefore tell me true ;
     But tell me then, 'tis so ; for look, thy cheeks
     Confess it, t' one to th' other, and thine eyes

171   See it so grossly shown in thy behaviors
172   That in their kind they speak it. Only sin
     And hellish obstinacy tie thy tongue,
174   That truth should be suspected. Speak, is 't so ?
175   If it be so, you have wound a goodly clew ;
176   If it be not, forswear 't ; howe'er, I charge thee,
177   As heaven shall work in me for thine avail,
     To tell me truly.

HELENA   Good madam, pardon me.

COUNTESS
     Do you love my son ?

HELENA   Your pardon, noble mistress !

COUNTESS
     Love you my son ?

HELENA   Do not you love him, madam ?

COUNTESS
181   Go not about ; my love hath in 't a bond
     Whereof the world takes note. Come, come, disclose
     The state of your affection, for your passions
184   Have to the full appeached.

HELENA *[kneels]*   Then I confess
     Here on my knee before high heaven and you,
     That before you, and next unto high heaven,
     I love your son.
     My friends were poor but honest ; so 's my love.
     Be not offended, for it hurts not him
     That he is loved of me. I follow him not

     By any token of presumptuous suit,
     Nor would I have him till I do deserve him ;
     Yet never know how that desert should be.
     I know I love in vain, strive against hope ;

195   Yet in this captious and intenible sieve
196   I still pour in the waters of my love
197   And lack not to lose still. Thus, Indian-like,
     Religious in mine error, I adore
     The sun that looks upon his worshipper
     But knows of him no more. My dearest madam,

201   Let not your hate encounter with my love,
     For loving where you do ; but if yourself,
203   Whose agèd honor cites a virtuous youth,
     Did ever in so true a flame of liking,
205   Wish chastely and love dearly, that your Dian
206   Was both herself and Love, O, then give pity
     To her whose state is such that cannot choose
     But lend and give where she is sure to lose ;
209   That seeks not to find that her search implies,
210   But, riddle-like, lives sweetly where she dies.

COUNTESS
     Had you not lately an intent – speak truly –
     To go to Paris ?

HELENA   Madam, I had.

COUNTESS   Wherefore ? Tell true.

HELENA
     I will tell truth, by grace itself I swear :
     You know my father left me some prescriptions
     Of rare and proved effects, such as his reading
     And manifest experience had collected

217   For general sovereignty ; and that he willed me
218   In heedfull'st reservation to bestow them,
219   As notes whose faculties inclusive were
     More than they were in note. Amongst the rest
221   There is a remedy, approved, set down,
     To cure the desperate languishings whereof
223   The king is rendered lost.

COUNTESS   This was your motive
     For Paris, was it ? Speak.

HELENA
     My lord your son made me to think of this ;
     Else Paris, and the medicine, and the king
227   Had from the conversation of my thoughts
228   Happily been absent then.

COUNTESS   But think you, Helen,
229   If you should tender your supposèd aid,
     He would receive it ? He and his physicians

---

144 *distemperèd* disordered; *messenger of wet* tear 145 *Iris* rainbow; *rounds* encircles 150 *note* mark of distinction; *parents* kinsmen 156 *both our mothers* mother of us both 163 *fondness* sentimental weakness 165 *head* source; *gross* evident 166 *Invention* fabrication of excuses 171 *grossly* openly 172 *in their kind* after their nature, i.e. by weeping 174 *That . . . suspected* that the truth must be guessed at rather than plainly declared, as it ought to be 175 *wound . . . clew* snarled things up handsomely 176 *forswear't* deny it 177 *avail* benefit 181 *Go not about* don't beat about the bush 184 *appeached* informed against you 195 *captious* (1) capacious, (2) deceptive; *intenible* unretentive 196 *still* constantly 197 *lack . . . still* have enough to continue pouring out and losing indefinitely; *Indian-like* idolatrously 201 *encounter with* oppose itself to 203 *cites* betokens 205 *that* so that 206 *both . . . Love* i.e. both chaste and passionate 209 *that* what 210 *riddle-like* paradoxically 217 *For general sovereignty* as master remedies 218 *In . . . them* to reserve them carefully for special uses 219–20 *As . . . note* as prescriptions more potent than generally recognized 221 *approved* tested 223 *rendered lost* given up as incurable 227 *conversation* interchange 228 *Happily* haply, perchance 229 *tender* offer

Are of a mind : he, that they cannot help him ;
They, that they cannot help. How shall they credit

233 A poor unlearnèd virgin, when the schools,
234 Embowelled of their doctrine, have left off
The danger to itself ?

HELENA   There's something in't
More than my father's skill, which was the great'st

237 Of his profession, that his good receipt
Shall for my legacy be sanctified
By th' luckiest stars in heaven ; and would your honor
But give me leave to try success, I'd venture

241 The well-lost life of mine on his grace's cure
By such a day and hour.

COUNTESS   Dost thou believe't ?

HELENA

243 Ay, madam, knowingly.

COUNTESS

Why, Helen, thou shalt have my leave and love,
Means and attendants, and my loving greetings
To those of mine in court. I'll stay at home
And pray God's blessing into thy attempt.
Be gone to-morrow, and be sure of this,
What I can help thee to, thou shalt not miss.   *Exeunt.*

***

II, i   *Enter the King with divers young Lords taking leave*
        for the Florentine war ; [Bertram] Count Rossillion,
        and Parolles. Flourish cornets.

KING

Farewell, young lords ; these warlike principles
Do not throw from you. And you, my lords, farewell.

3 Share the advice betwixt you ; if both gain all,
The gift doth stretch itself as 'tis received,
And is enough for both.

1. LORD   'Tis our hope, sir,

6 After well-ent'red soldiers, to return
And find your grace in health.

KING

No, no, it cannot be. And yet my heart

9 Will not confess he owes the malady
That doth my life besiege. Farewell, young lords.
Whether I live or die, be you the sons
Of worthy Frenchmen. Let Higher Italy

13 (Those bated that inherit but the fall
Of the last monarchy) see that you come

Not to woo honor, but to wed it, when   15
The bravest questant shrinks : find what you seek,   16
That fame may cry you loud. I say, farewell.   17

2. LORD
Health at your bidding serve your majesty !

KING
Those girls of Italy, take heed of them.
They say our French lack language to deny
If they demand ; beware of being captives   21
Before you serve.

BOTH   Our hearts receive your warnings.

KING
Farewell. *[to Attendants]* Come hither to me.
                   [Exit, led by Attendants.]

1. LORD
O, my sweet lord, that you will stay behind us !

PAROLLES
'Tis not his fault, the spark.   25

2. LORD   O, 'tis brave wars !

PAROLLES
Most admirable. I have seen those wars.

BERTRAM I am commanded here and kept a coil with   27
'Too young,' and 'The next year,' and ''Tis too early.'

PAROLLES An thy mind stand to't, boy, steal away bravely.   29

BERTRAM
I shall stay here the forehorse to a smock,   30
Creaking my shoes on the plain masonry,   31
Till honor be bought up, and no sword worn   32
But one to dance with. By heaven, I'll steal away !

1. LORD
There's honor in the theft.

PAROLLES   Commit it, count.

2. LORD
I am your accessary ; and so farewell.

BERTRAM I grow to you, and our parting is a tortured   36
body.

1. LORD Farewell, captain.

2. LORD Sweet Monsieur Parolles !

PAROLLES Noble heroes, my sword and yours are kin.
Good sparks and lustrous, a word, good metals : you shall   41
find in the regiment of the Spinii one Captain Spurio,
with his cicatrice, an emblem of war, here on his sinister   43
cheek. It was this very sword entrenched it ; say to him I
live, and observe his reports for me.

1. LORD We shall, noble captain.

PAROLLES Mars dote on you for his novices !   47
                   [Exeunt Lords.]
What will ye do ?
    [Enter the King, led back to his chair by Attendants.]

BERTRAM Stay – the king.

PAROLLES Use a more spacious ceremony to the noble   50
lords, you have restrained yourself within the list of too   51
cold an adieu. Be more expressive to them ; for they wear   52
themselves in the cap of the time ; there do muster true   53
gait, eat, speak, and move under the influence of the   54
most received star ; and though the devil lead the mea-   55
sure, such are to be followed. After them, and take a   56
more dilated farewell.   57

BERTRAM And I will do so.

PAROLLES Worthy fellows, and like to prove most sinewy swordmen.   *Exeunt [Bertram and Parolles].*
     Enter Lafew.

LAFEW *[Kneels.]*
Pardon, my lord, for me and for my tidings.

---

233 *schools* medical faculties   234 *Embowelled . . . doctrine* depleted of
their knowledge   234–35 *left . . . itself* abandoned the disease to its course
237 *that* whereby ; *receipt* prescription   241 *well-lost* i.e. in such a cause
243 *knowingly* with full knowledge
II, i The palace of the King   3–5 *if . . . both* if both groups of you follow
all my advice, my gift will be that much ampler, and will serve for both
6 *After . . . soldiers* after making a worthy debut as soldiers   9 *owes* owns
13–14 *Those . . . monarchy* except those upstarts who have only won their
nobility in the most recent engagements (?)   15 *woo* i.e. flirt with ; *wed*
i.e. possess   16 *questant* seeker   17 *cry* proclaim   21 *captives* i.e. to love
25 *spark* elegant young man   27 *kept a coil* fussed over   29 *An* if   30
forehorse leading horse ; *smock* woman   31 *plain masonry* level palace
floors (instead of the rough battlefield)   32 *Till . . . up* till the supply of
honor is exhausted   36 *grow to* grow deeply attached to   36–37 *a tortured
body* like a body being torn apart   41 *metals* 'blades'   43 *sinister* left   47
Mars . . . novices may Mars favor you as his newest votaries   50 *spacious*
elaborate   51 *list* bounds   52 *expressive* unreserved   52–53 *wear . . . time*
shine in the fashionable world   53–54 *muster true gait* set the right pace
54–55 *move . . . star* conform to the reigning fashions   55 *measure* dance
56 *such* such leaders   57 *dilated* extended

KING
62   I'll fee thee to stand up.

LAFEW *[Rises.]*
Then here's a man stands that has brought his pardon.
I would you had kneeled, my lord, to ask me mercy,
And that at my bidding you could so stand up.

KING
I would I had, so I had broke thy pate
And asked thee mercy for't.

67 LAFEW   Good faith, across!
But, my good lord, 'tis thus: will you be cured
Of your infirmity?

KING   No.

LAFEW   O, will you eat
No grapes, my royal fox? Yes, but you will
71   My noble grapes, an if my royal fox
Could reach them. I have seen a medicine
That's able to breathe life into a stone,
74   Quicken a rock, and make you dance canary
With sprightly fire and motion; whose simple touch
76   Is powerful to araise King Pepin, nay,
To give great Charlemain a pen in 's hand,
And write to her a love-line.

KING   What 'her' is this?

LAFEW
Why, Doctor She! My lord, there's one arrived,
If you will see her. Now by my faith and honor,
If seriously I may convey my thoughts
82   In this my light deliverance, I have spoke
With one that in her sex, her years, profession,
84   Wisdom and constancy, hath amazed me more
Than I dare blame my weakness. Will you see her,
For that is her demand, and know her business?
That done, laugh well at me.

KING   Now, good Lafew,
88   Bring in the admiration, that we with thee
89   May spend our wonder too, or take off thine
90   By wond'ring how thou took'st it.

LAFEW   Nay, I'll fit you,
And not be all day neither.   *[Exit.]*

KING
92   Thus he his special nothing ever prologues.
     Enter [Lafew, with] Helena.

LAFEW
Nay, come your ways.

KING   This haste hath wings indeed.

LAFEW
Nay, come your ways;
This is his majesty; say your mind to him.
96   A traitor you do look like, but such traitors
97   His majesty seldom fears. I am Cressid's uncle,
That dare leave two together. Fare you well.   *Exit.*

KING
99   Now, fair one, does your business follow us?

HELENA
Ay, my good lord.
Gerard de Narbon was my father;
102   In what he did profess, well-found.

KING   I knew him.

HELENA
The rather will I spare my praises towards him;
Knowing him is enough. On's bed of death
105   Many receipts he gave me, chiefly one,

Which as the dearest issue of his practice   106
And of his old experience th' only darling,   107
He bade me store up as a triple eye,   108
Safer than mine own two, more dear; I have so;
And hearing your high majesty is touched
With that malignant cause wherein the honor   111
Of my dear father's gift stands chief in power,
I come to tender it and my appliance,   113
With all bound humbleness.   114

KING   We thank you, maiden;
But may not be so credulous of cure,
When our most learnèd doctors leave us, and   116
The congregated college have concluded   117
That laboring art can never ransom nature   118
From her inaidable estate. I say we must not   119
So stain our judgment, or corrupt our hope,   120
To prostitute our past-cure malady
To empirics, or to dissever so   122
Our great self and our credit, to esteem   123
A senseless help, when help past sense we deem.   124

HELENA
My duty then shall pay me for my pains.
I will no more enforce mine office on you,   126
Humbly entreating from your royal thoughts
A modest one, to bear me back again.   128

KING
I cannot give thee less, to be called grateful.
Thou thought'st to help me, and such thanks I give
As one near death to those that wish him live.
But what at full I know, thou know'st no part,
I knowing all my peril, thou no art.

HELENA
What I can do can do no hurt to try,
Since you set up your rest 'gainst remedy.   135
He that of greatest works is finisher
Oft does them by the weakest minister.
So holy writ in babes hath judgment shown
When judges have been babes; great floods have flown   139
From simple sources, and great seas have dried   140
When miracles have by the greatest been denied.
Oft expectation fails, and most oft there   142
Where most it promises; and oft it hits   143
Where hope is coldest and despair most fits.

---

62 *fee* pay   67 *across* wide of the mark (referring to the king's attempt at a jest in ll. 66–67)   71 *an if* if   74 *Quicken* bring to life; *canary* lively Spanish dance   76 *araise* raise up; *Pepin* eighth-century French king   82 *light deliverance* frivolous delivery   84–85 *more . . . weakness* more than I can account for by blaming my senility   88 *admiration* wonder   89 *spend* utter; *take off* dispel, remove   90 *took'st* came by   92 *special nothing* particular trifles   96 *traitor . . . like* (because Helena's eyes are cast down, out of modesty)   97 *Cressid's uncle* Pandarus, hence pander   99 *follow* concern   102 *In . . . well-found* found to be good at his profession, medicine   105 *receipts* prescriptions   106 *dearest issue* most treasured product   107 *of . . . darling* the most cherished treasure of his ripest professional skill   108 *triple* third   111 *cause* disease   111–12 *wherein . . . power* for which my father's remedy is most effective   113 *tender* offer; *appliance* treatment   114 *bound* dutiful   116 *leave* give up for dead   117 *congregated college* conclave of physicians   118 *art* medicine   119 *inaidable estate* condition of hopelessness   120 *corrupt our hope* hope foolishly   122 *empirics* quacks   122–23 *dissever . . . credit* divorce our greatness from our reputation, i.e. behave in an unkingly manner   123 *esteem* value   124 *senseless* irrational; *past sense* unreasonable   126 *office* function   128 *A modest one* a belief in my good intentions and natural modesty   135 *set . . . rest* are resolved at all cost   139 *babes* i.e. helpless, foolish   140 *simple* insignificant   142 *expectation* that which we most confidently anticipate   143 *hits* succeeds

KING

I must not hear thee ; fare thee well, kind maid.
Thy pains, not used, must by thyself be paid ;
Proffers not took reap thanks for their reward.

HELENA

148   Inspirèd merit so by breath is barred.
It is not so with Him that all things knows
150   As 'tis with us that square our guess by shows ;
But most it is presumption in us, when
The help of heaven we count the act of men.
Dear sir, to my endeavors give consent ;
Of heaven, not me, make an experiment.
155   I am not an impostor, that proclaim
Myself against the level of mine aim ;
But know I think, and think I know most sure,
My art is not past power, nor you past cure.

KING

Art thou so confident ? Within what space
Hop'st thou my cure ?

HELENA   The great'st grace lending grace,
Ere twice the horses of the sun shall bring
162   Their fiery torcher his diurnal ring,
163   Ere twice in murk and occidental damp
164   Moist Hesperus hath quenched her sleepy lamp,
165   Or four and twenty times the pilot's glass
Hath told the thievish minutes how they pass,
What is infirm from your sound parts shall fly,
Health shall live free, and sickness freely die.

KING

Upon thy certainty and confidence
What dar'st thou venture ?

170 HELENA   Tax of impudence,
171   A strumpet's boldness, a divulgèd shame
Traduced by odious ballads ; my maiden's name
173   Seared otherwise ; nay, worse of worst, extended
With vilest torture let my life be ended.

KING

Methinks in thee some blessèd spirit doth speak
His powerful sound within an organ weak ;
177   And what impossibility would slay
In common sense, sense saves another way.
Thy life is dear, for all that life can rate
180   Worth name of life in thee hath estimate :
Youth, beauty, wisdom, courage – all
182   That happiness and prime can happy call.

---

148 *Inspirèd* divinely inspired; *so* thus; *breath* words   150 *square . . . shows* rule our opinions by appearances   155–56 *that . . . aim* who boasts of what he knows he cannot do   162 *torcher* torchbearer; *diurnal ring* daily round   163 *occidental* of sunset   164 *Hesperus* evening star; *her* (since the evening star is in fact the planet Venus)   165 *glass* hourglass   170 *Tax* charge   171 *divulgèd* publicly proclaimed   173 *otherwise* in other ways as well; *extended* stretched out, racked   177–78 *what . . . may* what common sense would regard as impossible, a higher sense can believe   180 *estimate* value   182 *prime* youth   185 *practiser* practitioner; *physic* medicine   187 *break time* fail to perform in the stipulated time; *flinch in property* fall short in the particulars   191 *make it even* match it   204 *still* always
II, ii The palace of the Count   1 *put . . . height* test the extent   3 *highly . . . taught* i.e. like a rich man's son, overfed and underdisciplined   5 *make* consider   6 *put off* dismiss   10 *leg* respectful bow   17 *quatch* fat   20 *ten groats* (the attorney's usual fee)   21 *French crown* syphilis (with a pun on 'crown': a coin); *taffety punk* finely dressed strumpet   21–22 *Tib's rush* country wench's rush ring   22–23 *Shrove Tuesday* pre-Lenten holiday when quantities of pancakes were consumed   23 *morris* country dance

---

Thou this to hazard needs must intimate
Skill infinite, or monstrous desperate.
Sweet practiser, thy physic I will try,   185
That ministers thine own death if I die.

HELENA

If I break time or flinch in property   187
Of what I spoke, unpitied let me die,
And well deserved ; not helping, death 's my fee.
But if I help, what do you promise me ?

KING

Make thy demand.

HELENA   But will you make it even ?   191

KING

Ay, by my sceptre and my hopes of heaven.

HELENA

Then shalt thou give me with thy kingly hand
What husband in thy power I will command.
Exempted be from me the arrogance
To choose from forth the royal blood of France,
My low and humble name to propagate
With any branch or image of thy state ;
But such a one, thy vassal, whom I know
Is free for me to ask, thee to bestow.

KING

Here is my hand. The premises observed,
Thy will by my performance shall be served.
So make the choice of thy own time ; for I,
Thy resolved patient, on thee still rely.   204
More should I question thee, and more I must,
Though more to know could not be more to trust –
From whence thou cam'st, how tended on – but rest
Unquestioned welcome, and undoubted blest.
Give me some help here, ho ! – If thou proceed
As high as word, my deed shall match thy deed.

Flourish. Exeunt.

*

Enter Countess and [Lavatch, the] Clown.   II, ii

COUNTESS Come on, sir, I shall now put you to the height 1
of your breeding.

LAVATCH I will show myself highly fed and lowly taught. 3
I know my business is but to the court.

COUNTESS To the court ? Why, what place make you 5
special, when you put off that with such contempt ? But 6
to the court ?

LAVATCH Truly, madam, if God have lent a man any
manners, he may easily put it off at court : he that cannot
make a leg, put off's cap, kiss his hand, and say nothing, 10
has neither leg, hands, lip, nor cap ; and indeed such a
fellow, to say precisely, were not for the court. But for
me, I have an answer will serve all men.

COUNTESS Marry, that's a bountiful answer that fits all
questions.

LAVATCH It is like a barber's chair that fits all buttocks – the
pin-buttock, the quatch-buttock, the brawn-buttock, 17
or any buttock.

COUNTESS Will your answer serve fit to all questions ?

LAVATCH As fit as ten groats is for the hand of an attor- 20
ney, as your French crown for your taffety punk, as Tib's 21
rush for Tom's forefinger, as a pancake for Shrove 22
Tuesday, a morris for May-day, as the nail to his hole, 23

24   the cuckold to his horn, as a scolding quean to a wran-
       gling knave, as the nun's lip to the friar's mouth; nay, as
26   the pudding to his skin.

COUNTESS Have you, I say, an answer of such fitness for
all questions?

LAVATCH From below your duke to beneath your constable, it will fit any question.

COUNTESS It must be an answer of most monstrous size
that must fit all demands.

33 LAVATCH But a trifle neither, in good faith, if the learned
should speak truth of it. Here it is, and all that belongs
to't: ask me if I am a courtier; it shall do you no harm
to learn.

COUNTESS To be young again, if we could! I will be a
fool in question, hoping to be the wiser by your answer.
I pray you, sir, are you a courtier?

40 LAVATCH O Lord, sir! – There's a simple putting off.
More, more, a hundred of them.

COUNTESS Sir, I am a poor friend of yours, that loves you.

43 LAVATCH O Lord, sir! – Thick, thick, spare not me.

COUNTESS I think, sir, you can eat none of this homely
meat.

LAVATCH O Lord, sir! – Nay, put me to't, I warrant you.

COUNTESS You were lately whipped, sir, as I think.

LAVATCH O Lord, sir! – Spare not me.

COUNTESS Do you cry, 'O Lord, sir!' at your whipping,
49   and 'Spare not me'? Indeed, your 'O Lord, sir!' is very
50   sequent to your whipping; you would answer very well
51   to a whipping, if you were but bound to't.

LAVATCH I ne'er had worse luck in my life in my 'O
Lord, sir!' I see things may serve long, but not serve
ever.

COUNTESS
I play the noble housewife with the time,
To entertain it so merrily with a fool.

LAVATCH O Lord, sir! – Why, there't serves well again.

COUNTESS
An end, sir! To your business: give Helen this,
58   And urge her to a present answer back.
Commend me to my kinsmen and my son.
This is not much.

LAVATCH Not much commendation to them?

COUNTESS Not much employment for you. You understand me?

64 LAVATCH Most fruitfully. I am there before my legs.

65 COUNTESS Haste you again.   *Exeunt.*

*

II, iii   *Enter Count [Bertram], Lafew, and Parolles.*

LAFEW They say miracles are past, and we have our
2   philosophical persons, to make modern and familiar,
3   things supernatural and causeless. Hence is it that we
4   make trifles of terrors, ensconcing ourselves into seem-
      ing knowledge when we should submit ourselves to an
6   unknown fear.

7 PAROLLES Why, 'tis the rarest argument of wonder that
hath shot out in our latter times.

BERTRAM And so 'tis.

10 LAFEW To be relinquished of the artists –

11 PAROLLES So I say – both of Galen and Paracelsus –

12 LAFEW Of all the learned and authentic fellows –

PAROLLES Right! So I say.

LAFEW That gave him out incurable –

PAROLLES Why, there 'tis! so say I too.

LAFEW Not to be helped –

PAROLLES Right! as 'twere a man assured of a –

LAFEW Uncertain life, and sure death.

PAROLLES Just! you say well. So would I have said.

LAFEW I may truly say it is a novelty to the world.

PAROLLES It is indeed. If you will have it in showing, 21
you shall read it in What-do-ye-call there.

LAFEW *[reads]* 'A showing of a heavenly effect in an 23
earthly actor.'

PAROLLES That's it I would have said, the very same.

LAFEW Why, your dolphin is not lustier. Fore me, I speak 26
in respect –

PAROLLES Nay, 'tis strange, 'tis very strange! that is the
brief and the tedious of it; and he's of a most facinerious 29
spirit that will not acknowledge it to be the –

LAFEW Very hand of heaven –

PAROLLES Ay, so I say.

LAFEW In a most weak –

PAROLLES And debile minister; great power, great tran- 34
scendence, which should indeed give us a further use to
be made than alone the recovery of the king, as to be –

LAFEW Generally thankful.
       Enter King, Helena, and Attendants.

PAROLLES I would have said it! you say well. Here comes
the king.

LAFEW Lustick! as the Dutchman says. I'll like a maid 40
the better whilst I have a tooth in my head. Why, he's
able to lead her a coranto.   42

PAROLLES Mort du vinaigre! Is not this Helen?   43

LAFEW Fore God, I think so.

KING
Go, call before me all the lords in court.
                  [Exit an Attendant.]
Sit, my preserver, by thy patient's side,
And with this healthful hand whose banished sense
Thou hast repealed, a second time receive   48
The confirmation of my promised gift,
Which but attends thy naming.   50
       Enter three or four Lords.
Fair maid, send forth thine eye. This youthful parcel 51
Of noble bachelors stand at my bestowing,
O'er whom both sovereign power and father's voice
I have to use. Thy frank election make.   54
Thou hast power to choose, and they none to forsake.

---

24 *quean* wench   26 *pudding* sausage; *his* its   33 *neither* not at all   40 *simple putting off* rapid disposal of the question   43 *Thick* quick   49–50 *is . . . to* follows closely upon   50–51 *answer . . . to* repay (with pun on 'reply') 51 *bound* engaged (with pun on 'tied up')   58 *present* immediate   64 *fruitfully* abundantly   65 *again* back again

II, iii The palace of the King   2 *modern* commonplace   3 *causeless* of unknown cause   4–5 *ensconcing . . . knowledge* barricading ourselves within apparent knowledge   6 *unknown fear* fear of the unknown   7 *argument* theme   10 *relinquished . . . artists* abandoned by the learned physicians 11 *both . . . Paracelsus* of both schools of medical opinion   12 *authentic fellows* accredited physicians   21 *in showing* visibly, in print   23–24 *A . . . actor* (Lafew evidently reads from a printed ballad celebrating the king's recovery)   26 *dolphin* (proverbially sportive with pun on 'dauphin,' heir to the throne of France, hence a playful princeling)   26–27 *speak in respect* i.e. with no offence to the true dauphin   29 *tedious* long; *facinerious* wicked   34 *debile* feeble   40 *Lustick* lusty   42 *coranto* lively dance   43 *Mort du vinaigre* (expletive of obscure meaning)   48 *repealed* called back 50 *attends* awaits   51 *parcel* group   54 *frank election* unhindered choice

HELENA
To each of you one fair and virtuous mistress
Fall, when Love please ; marry, to each but one.

LAFEW *[aside]*
58 I'd give bay Curtal and his furniture
59 My mouth no more were broken than these boys',
60 And writ as little beard.

KING   Peruse them well :
Not one of those but had a noble father.

HELENA
Gentlemen,
Heaven hath through me restored the king to health.

ALL
We understand it, and thank heaven for you.

HELENA
I am a simple maid, and therein wealthiest
66 That I protest I simply am a maid.
Please it your majesty, I have done already.
The blushes in my cheeks thus whisper me,
'We blush that thou shouldst choose ; but be refused,
Let the white death sit on thy cheek forever,
We'll ne'er come there again.'

KING   Make choice and see ;
Who shuns thy love shuns all his love in me.

HELENA
Now, Dian, from thy altar do I fly,
And to imperial Love, that god most high,
Do my sighs stream.
                She addresses her to a Lord.
                              Sir, will you hear my suit ?

I. LORD
And grant it.

HELENA   Thanks, sir, all the rest is mute.

LAFEW *[aside]* I had rather be in this choice than throw
78   ames-ace for my life.

HELENA *[to another]*
The honor, sir, that flames in your fair eyes,
Before I speak, too threat'ningly replies.
Love make your fortunes twenty times above
Her that so wishes, and her humble love !

2. LORD
83 No better, if you please.

HELENA   My wish receive,
Which great Love grant ; and so I take my leave.

85 LAFEW *[aside]* Do all they deny her ? An they were sons
of mine, I'd have them whipped, or I would send them
to th' Turk to make eunuchs of.

HELENA *[to a third]*
Be not afraid that I your hand should take ;
I'll never do you wrong for your own sake.

Blessing upon your vows, and in your bed
Find fairer fortune, if you ever wed.

LAFEW *[aside]* These boys are boys of ice ; they'll none
have her. Sure they are bastards to the English ; the
French ne'er got 'em.

HELENA *[to a fourth]*
You are too young, too happy, and too good,
To make yourself a son out of my blood.

4. LORD
Fair one, I think not so.

LAFEW *[aside]* There's one grape yet ; I am sure thy 98
father drunk wine. But if thou be'st not an ass, I am a
youth of fourteen ; I have known thee already. 100

HELENA *[to Bertram]*
I dare not say I take you, but I give
Me and my service, ever whilst I live,
Into your guiding power. – This is the man.

KING
Why then, young Bertram, take her ; she's thy wife.

BERTRAM
My wife, my liege ? I shall beseech your highness,
In such a business give me leave to use
The help of mine own eyes.

KING   Know'st thou not, Bertram,
What she has done for me ?

BERTRAM   Yes, my good lord ;
But never hope to know why I should marry her.

KING
Thou know'st she has raised me from my sickly bed.

BERTRAM
But follows it, my lord, to bring me down
Must answer for your raising ? I know her well ;
She had her breeding at my father's charge.
A poor physician's daughter my wife ? Disdain
Rather corrupt me ever ! 115

KING
'Tis only title thou disdain'st in her, the which
I can build up. Strange is it that our bloods,
Of color, weight, and heat, poured all together, 118
Would quite confound distinction, yet stands off 119
In differences so mighty. If she be
All that is virtuous – save what thou dislik'st,
A poor physician's daughter – thou dislik'st
Of virtue for the name. But do not so.
From lowest place when virtuous things proceed,
The place is dignified by th' doer's deed.
Where great additions swell 's, and virtue none, 126
It is a dropsied honor. Good alone 127
Is good without a name ; vileness is so :
The property by what it is should go, 129
Not by the title. She is young, wise, fair ;
In these to nature she's immediate heir ; 131
And these breed honor. That is honor's scorn
Which challenges itself as honor's born 133
And is not like the sire. Honors thrive
When rather from our acts we them derive 135
Than our foregoers. The mere word 's a slave,
Deboshed on every tomb, on every grave 137
A lying trophy, and as oft is dumb, 138
Where dust and damned oblivion is the tomb
Of honored bones indeed. What should be said ?
If thou canst like this creature as a maid,
I can create the rest. Virtue and she

58 *bay Curtal* bay horse with docked tail ; *furniture* trappings 59 *My . . . boys* I still had all my teeth 60 *writ* claimed ; *Peruse* survey 66 *simply* truly 78 *ames-ace* a pair of aces, in a cast of dice 83 *No better* i.e. no better fortune than to be chosen by you ; *My wish receive* i.e. my wish, but not my love 85 *An* if 98 *one grape* one scion of good stock 98–99 *thy . . . wine* i.e. good blood flows in your veins 100 *known* seen through 115 *corrupt me ever* spoil my credit with you for as long as I live 118 *Of* in respect to 119 *confound distinction* merge indistinguishably 119–20 *stands . . . mighty* hold aloof as though totally different 126 *great additions swell 's* solemn titles puff us up 127 *dropsied* unhealthily swollen 129 *property* quality 131 *immediate* direct 133–34 *challenges . . . sire* claims descent from honorable stock but does not resemble it 135 *derive* inherit 137 *Deboshed* debauched, debased 138 *lying* both 'deceitful' and 'inertly recumbent' ; *dumb* silent

Is her own dower; honor and wealth from me.

BERTRAM
I cannot love her, nor will strive to do't.

KING
145 Thou wrong'st thyself if thou shouldst strive to choose.

HELENA
That you are well restored, my lord, I'm glad.
Let the rest go.

KING
148 My honor's at the stake, which to defeat,
I must produce my power. Here, take her hand,
Proud scornful boy, unworthy this good gift,
151 That dost in vile misprision shackle up
My love and her desert; that canst not dream,
153 We, poising us in her defective scale,
Shall weigh thee to the beam; that wilt not know,
It is in us to plant thine honor where
We please to have it grow. Check thy contempt.
157 Obey our will, which travails in thy good.
158 Believe not thy disdain, but presently
159 Do thine own fortunes that obedient right
Which both thy duty owes and our power claims;
Or I will throw thee from my care forever,
162 Into the staggers and the careless lapse
Of youth and ignorance, both my revenge and hate
Loosing upon thee, in the name of justice,
165 Without all terms of pity. Speak! thine answer!

BERTRAM
Pardon, my gracious lord; for I submit
My fancy to your eyes. When I consider
168 What great creation and what dole of honor
Flies where you bid it, I find that she, which late
Was in my nobler thoughts most base, is now
The praisèd of the king; who, so ennobled,
Is as 'twere born so.

KING   Take her by the hand,
And tell her she is thine; to whom I promise
174 A counterpoise, if not to thy estate,
A balance more replete.

BERTRAM   I take her hand.

KING
Good fortune and the favor of the king
177 Smile upon this contract, whose ceremony
Shall seem expedient on the now-born brief,
And be performed to-night. The solemn feast
180 Shall more attend upon the coming space,
181 Expecting absent friends. As thou lov'st her,
182 Thy love's to me religious; else, does err.

Exeunt. Parolles and Lafew stay behind,
commenting of this wedding.

LAFEW Do you hear, monsieur? A word with you.

PAROLLES Your pleasure, sir?

LAFEW Your lord and master did well to make his recantation.

PAROLLES Recantation? my lord? my master?

LAFEW Ay. Is it not a language I speak?

PAROLLES A most harsh one, and not to be understood
190 without bloody succeeding. My master?

191 LAFEW Are you companion to the Count Rossillion?

192 PAROLLES To any count; to all counts; to what is man.

193 LAFEW To what is count's man; count's master is of
another style.

195 PAROLLES You are too old, sir. Let it satisfy you, you are
too old.

LAFEW I must tell thee, sirrah, I write man, to which title 197
age cannot bring thee.

PAROLLES What I dare too well do, I dare not do. 199

LAFEW I did think thee, for two ordinaries, to be a pretty 200
wise fellow; thou didst make tolerable vent of thy travel; 201
it might pass. Yet the scarfs and the bannerets about 202
thee did manifoldly dissuade me from believing thee a
vessel of too great a burden. I have now found thee; 204
when I lose thee again, I care not. Yet art thou good for
nothing but taking up, and that thou'rt scarce worth. 206

PAROLLES Hadst thou not the privilege of antiquity
upon thee –

LAFEW Do not plunge thyself too far in anger, lest thou
hasten thy trial; which if – Lord have mercy on thee for
a hen! So, my good window of lattice, fare thee well; 211
thy casement I need not open, for I look through thee. 212
Give me thy hand.

PAROLLES My lord, you give me most egregious indignity.

LAFEW Ay, with all my heart; and thou art worthy of it.

PAROLLES I have not, my lord, deserved it.

LAFEW Yes, good faith, every dram of it, and I will not
bate thee a scruple. 218

PAROLLES Well, I shall be wiser.

LAFEW Ev'n as soon as thou canst, for thou hast to pull at 220
a smack o' th' contrary. If ever thou be'st bound in thy
scarf and beaten, thou shall find what it is to be proud of
thy bondage. I have a desire to hold my acquaintance 223
with thee, or rather my knowledge, that I may say, in 224
the default, 'He is a man I know.'

PAROLLES My lord, you do me most insupportable vexation.

LAFEW I would it were hell-pains for thy sake, and my
poor doing eternal; for doing I am past, as I will by 228
thee, in what motion age will give me leave.   *Exit.* 229

PAROLLES Well, thou hast a son shall take this disgrace
off me, scurvy, old, filthy, scurvy lord! Well, I must be
patient; there is no fettering of authority. I'll beat him,
by my life, if I can meet him with any convenience, an 233
he were double and double a lord. I'll have no more pity

---

145 *strive to choose* attempt to choose for yourself   148 *at the stake* (like
a bear being baited); *which* which challenge   151 *misprision* contempt
(with pun on 'false imprisonment'); *shackle up* i.e. paralyze, render
useless   153–54 *poising . . . beam* weighing our royal self on her side of
the balance, will outweigh your side and make it touch the crossbar   157
travails labors   158 *Believe not* do not trust to; *presently* instantly   159
obedient right right of obedience   162 *lapse* fall   165 *Without . . . pity*
without pity in any form   168 *dole* share   174–75 *A counterpoise . . .
replete* a counterweight (of wealth, by way of dowry), which if not equal
in value to your own estate, will exceed it   177–78 *whose . . . brief* the
consecration of which fittingly follows without delay on this fresh agreement   180 *more . . . space* be deferred a while longer   181 *Expecting*
while we await   182 *religious* scrupulous   190 *bloody succeeding* bloodshed following   191 *companion* fellow (used belittlingly)   192 *what is
man* any true man   193 *count's man* servant   195 *too old* i.e. for me to
thrash   197 *write man* claim manhood   199 *What . . . not do* what I can
do all too easily – beat you – the privilege of your age forbids me to do
200 *ordinaries* meals   201 *make tolerable vent of* discourse tolerably upon
202 *scarfs* (commonly worn by soldiers); *bannerets* scarfs, looking like a
ship's pennants   204 *burden* cargo; *found* seen through   206 *taking up*
purchasing at a discount, as surplus merchandise   211 *hen* i.e. a female of
your kind; *lattice* (the red-latticed window was the mark of an ale-house)
212 *casement* window; *look* see   218 *bate* deduct; *scruple* tiny part   220–21
pull . . . contrary take a swig from the large amount of foolishness in yourself   223 *bondage* what binds, i.e. the scarf   224–25 *in the default* when
you are weighed and found wanting   228 *for doing* for activity of any kind,
especially sexual   228–29 *by thee* i.e. pass by thee   229 *in what motion*
with what speed   233 *an* if

of his age than I would have of – I'll beat him, an if I could but meet him again.

Enter Lafew.

LAFEW Sirrah, your lord and master 's married; there's news for you. You have a new mistress.

PAROLLES I most unfeignedly beseech your lordship to 239 make some reservation of your wrongs. He is my good lord; whom I serve above is my master.

LAFEW Who? God?

PAROLLES Ay, sir.

LAFEW The devil it is that's thy master. Why dost thou garter up thy arms o' this fashion? Dost make hose of thy sleeves? Do other servants so? Thou wert best set thy lower part where thy nose stands. By mine honor, if I were but two hours younger, I'd beat thee. Methink'st 249 thou art a general offense, and every man should beat 250 thee. I think thou wast created for men to breathe themselves upon thee.

PAROLLES This is hard and undeserved measure, my lord.

253 LAFEW Go to, sir. You were beaten in Italy for picking a kernel out of a pomegranate. You are a vagabond, and no true traveller. You are more saucy with lords and honorable personages than the commission of your 257 birth and virtue gives you heraldry. You are not worth another word, else I'd call you knave. I leave you. *Exit.*

Enter [Bertram] Count Rossillion.

PAROLLES Good, very good! It is so then. Good, very good! Let it be concealed awhile.

BERTRAM
Undone, and forfeited to cares forever!

PAROLLES
What's the matter, sweetheart?

BERTRAM
Although before the solemn priest I have sworn,
I will not bed her.

PAROLLES
What? what, sweetheart?

BERTRAM
O my Parolles, they have married me!
I'll to the Tuscan wars, and never bed her.

PAROLLES
France is a dog-hole, and it no more merits
The tread of a man's foot. To th' wars!

BERTRAM
There's letters from my mother. What th' import is,
I know not yet.

PAROLLES
Ay, that would be known. To th' wars, my boy, to th'
wars!
He wears his honor in a box unseen
That hugs his kicky-wicky here at home,
Spending his manly marrow in her arms,
276 Which should sustain the bound and high curvet
Of Mars's fiery steed. To other regions!

France is a stable; we that dwell in't jades. 278
Therefore to th' war!

BERTRAM
It shall be so. I'll send her to my house,
Acquaint my mother with my hate to her,
And wherefore I am fled; write to the king
That which I durst not speak. His present gift
Shall furnish me to those Italian fields
Where noble fellows strike. Wars is no strife
To the dark house and the detested wife. 286

PAROLLES
Will this capriccio hold in thee? art sure? 287

BERTRAM
Go with me to my chamber, and advise me.
I'll send her straight away. To-morrow
I'll to the wars, she to her single sorrow.

PAROLLES
Why, these balls bound; there's noise in it! 'Tis hard: 291
A young man married is a man that's marred.
Therefore away, and leave her bravely; go. 293
The king has done you wrong; but hush, 'tis so. *Exeunt.*

*

Enter Helena and [Lavatch, the] Clown. II, iv

HELENA
My mother greets me kindly. Is she well?

LAVATCH She is not well, but yet she has her health; 2 she's very merry, but yet she is not well. But thanks be given, she's very well and wants nothing i' th' world. But yet she is not well.

HELENA If she be very well, what does she ail that she's not very well?

LAVATCH Truly she's very well indeed, but for two things.

HELENA What two things?

LAVATCH One, that she's not in heaven, whither God send her quickly; the other, that she's in earth, from whence God send her quickly.

Enter Parolles.

PAROLLES Bless you, my fortunate lady!

HELENA I hope, sir, I have your good will to have mine own good fortunes.

PAROLLES You had my prayers to lead them on, and to keep them on have them still. O, my knave, how does my old lady?

LAVATCH So that you had her wrinkles and I her money, I 19 would she did as you say.

PAROLLES Why, I say nothing.

LAVATCH Marry, you are the wiser man; for many a man's tongue shakes out his master's undoing. To say nothing, to do nothing, to know nothing, and to have nothing, is to be a great part of your title, which is 25 within a very little of nothing.

PAROLLES Away! th' art a knave.

LAVATCH You should have said, sir, 'Before a knave 28 th' art a knave'; that's 'Before me th' art a knave.' This 29 had been truth, sir.

PAROLLES Go to, thou art a witty fool; I have found thee. 31

LAVATCH Did you find me in yourself, sir, or were you 32 taught to find me?... The search, sir, was profitable; and much fool may you find in you, even to the world's 34 pleasure and the increase of laughter.

239 *make . . . wrongs* place some limits to your insults 249 *general offense* public nuisance 250 *breathe* exercise 253–54 *picking . . . pomegranate* i.e. some petty misdemeanor (?) 257 *heraldry* authority, warrant 276 *curvet* leap 278 *jades* nags 286 *To* in comparison with; *dark house* madhouse 287 *capriccio* whim 291 *balls* tennis balls 293 *bravely* boldly
II, iv The palace of the King 2 *not well* (evidently alluding to the pro-verbial belief that all is well with the dead; see l. 11) 19–20 *I . . . say* (meaning obscure) 25 *be . . . title* be very like you, in status and possessions 28 *Before* in presence of 29 *Before me* 'upon my word' (with pun on 'ahead of me') 31 *found thee* found thee out 32 *in yourself* unaided 34 *much . . . in you* much folly may you find in yourself

36 PAROLLES A good knave, i' faith, and well fed.
Madam, my lord will go away to-night;
A very serious business calls on him.
The great prerogative and rite of love,
Which, as your due, time claims, he does acknowledge;
41 But puts it off to a compelled restraint;
42 Whose want, and whose delay, is strewed with sweets,
43 Which they distil now in the curbèd time,
To make the coming hour o'erflow with joy
And pleasure drown the brim.
45 HELENA   What's his will else?
PAROLLES
That you will take your instant leave o' th' king,
And make this haste as your own good proceeding,
Strength'ned with what apology you think
49 May make it probable need.
HELENA   What more commands he?
PAROLLES
50 That, having this obtained, you presently
51 Attend his further pleasure.
HELENA
52 In everything I wait upon his will.
PAROLLES
I shall report it so.   *Exit Parolles.*
HELENA
I pray you. Come, sirrah.   *Exit [with Lavatch].*

                                 *

II, v   *Enter Lafew and Bertram.*
LAFEW But I hope your lordship thinks not him a soldier.
2 BERTRAM Yes, my lord, and of very valiant approof.
LAFEW You have it from his own deliverance.
BERTRAM And by other warranted testimony.
5 LAFEW Then my dial goes not true; I took this lark for a
6 bunting.
BERTRAM I do assure you, my lord, he is very great in
8 knowledge and accordingly valiant.
LAFEW I have then sinned against his experience and
10 transgressed against his valor; and my state that way is
dangerous, since I cannot yet find in my heart to repent.
     Enter Parolles.
Here he comes. I pray you make us friends; I will
pursue the amity.
PAROLLES [to Bertram] These things shall be done, sir.
15 LAFEW Pray you, sir, who's his tailor?
PAROLLES Sir?
LAFEW O, I know him well, I, sir. He, sir, 's a good work-
man, a very good tailor.
BERTRAM [aside to Parolles]
Is she gone to the king?
PAROLLES   She is.
BERTRAM
Will she away to-night?
PAROLLES   As you'll have her.
BERTRAM
I have writ my letters, casketed my treasure,
Given order for our horses; and to-night,
When I should take possession of the bride,
End ere I do begin.
27 LAFEW A good traveller is something at the latter end of a
dinner; but one that lies three thirds and uses a known
truth to pass a thousand nothings with, should be once
heard and thrice beaten. God save you, captain.

BERTRAM Is there any unkindness between my lord and
you, monsieur?
PAROLLES I know not how I have deserved to run into
my lord's displeasure.
LAFEW You have made shift to run into't, boots and
spurs and all, like him that leapt into the custard; and 36
out of it you'll run again rather than suffer question for 37
your residence.
BERTRAM It may be you have mistaken him, my lord.
LAFEW And shall do so ever, though I took him at's 40
prayers. Fare you well, my lord, and believe this of me:
there can be no kernel in this light nut; the soul of this
man is his clothes. Trust him not in matter of heavy
consequence. I have kept of them tame and know their 44
natures. – Farewell, monsieur. I have spoken better of
you than you have or will to deserve at my hand; but
we must do good against evil.   *[Exit.]*
PAROLLES An idle lord, I swear.   48
BERTRAM I think so.
PAROLLES Why, do you not know him?
BERTRAM
Yes, I do know him well, and common speech
Gives him a worthy pass.   52
     Enter Helena.
                     Here comes my clog.
HELENA
I have, sir, as I was commanded from you,
Spoke with the king, and have procured his leave
For present parting; only he desires   55
Some private speech with you.
BERTRAM   I shall obey his will.
You must not marvel, Helen, at my course,
Which holds not color with the time, nor does   58
The ministration and requirèd office
On my particular. Prepared I was not
For such a business; therefore am I found
So much unsettled. This drives me to entreat you
That presently you take your way for home,
And rather muse than ask why I entreat you;   64
For my respects are better than they seem,   65
And my appointments have in them a need   66
Greater than shows itself at the first view
To you that know them not. This to my mother.
     [Gives a letter.]
'Twill be two days ere I shall see you; so
I leave you to your wisdom.
HELENA   Sir, I can nothing say
But that I am your most obedient servant.
BERTRAM
Come, come; no more of that.

36 *well fed* i.e. and ill taught (see II, ii, 3) 41 *to* in consequence of 42
Whose (referring to the *rite of love*) 43 *they* i.e. people; *curbèd time* period
of distillation 45 *else* besides 49 *probable* plausible 50 *presently* immediately 51 *Attend* await 52 *wait upon* serve
II, v The palace of the King 2 *very valiant approof* proved valor 5 *dial*
'the compass of my judgment' 6 *bunting* common field bird 8 *accordingly*
correspondingly 10–11 *my . . . dangerous* my soul is in peril 15 *who's
his tailor* i.e. who made this manikin 27–28 *at . . . dinner* i.e. to relate
his travels 36 *him . . . custard* the clown that jumped into the custard at
the yearly Lord Mayor's feast 37–38 *suffer . . . residence* explain your
presence there, i.e. consider why you have displeased me 40 *do so* mistake, put an unfavorable interpretation on 44 *kept . . . tame* kept such
creatures as household pets 48 *idle* foolish 52 *pass* reputation 55
present immediate 58 *holds . . . time* seems inappropriate to the occasion
58–60 *nor . . . particular* nor fulfills my obligations as a husband 64 *muse*
remain in wonder 65 *respects* reasons 66 *appointments* arrangements

HELENA   And ever shall

73 With true observance seek to eke out that

74 Wherein toward me my homely stars have failed
To equal my great fortune.

BERTRAM   Let that go;
My haste is very great. Farewell. Hie home.

HELENA
Pray, sir, your pardon.

BERTRAM   Well, what would you say?

HELENA

78 I am not worthy of the wealth I owe,
Nor dare I say 'tis mine; and yet it is –

80 But, like a timorous thief, most fain would steal

81 What law does vouch mine own.

BERTRAM   What would you have?

HELENA
Something, and scarce so much; nothing, indeed.
I would not tell you what I would, my lord.
Faith, yes –
Strangers and foes do sunder, and not kiss.

BERTRAM
I pray you stay not, but in haste to horse.

HELENA
I shall not break your bidding, good my lord.

BERTRAM
Where are my other men, monsieur? Farewell.
Go thou toward home –   *Exit [Helena].*
            where I will never come
Whilst I can shake my sword or hear the drum.
Away, and for our flight!

91 PAROLLES   Bravely, coragio!   *[Exeunt.]*

*

III, i   *Flourish. Enter the Duke of Florence, the two*
Frenchmen, with a Troop of Soldiers.

DUKE
So that from point to point now have you heard
The fundamental reasons of this war,

3 Whose great decision hath much blood let forth,
And more thirsts after.

1. LORD   Holy seems the quarrel
Upon your grace's part; black and fearful
On the opposer.

DUKE

7 Therefore we marvel much our cousin France
Would in so just a business shut his bosom

9 Against our borrowing prayers.

2. LORD   Good my lord,

10 The reasons of our state I cannot yield

11 But like a common and an outward man
That the great figure of a council frames

By self-unable motion – therefore dare not
Say what I think of it, since I have found
Myself in my incertain grounds to fail
As often as I guessed.

DUKE   Be it his pleasure.

1. LORD
But I am sure the younger of our nature,   17
That surfeit on their ease, will day by day
Come here for physic.   19

DUKE   Welcome shall they be;
And all the honors that can fly from us
Shall on them settle. You know your places well;
When better fall, for your avails they fell.   22
To-morrow to th' field.   *Flourish. [Exeunt.]*

*

    Enter Countess and [Lavatch, the] Clown.   III, ii

COUNTESS It hath happened all as I would have had it,
save that he comes not along with her.

LAVATCH By my troth, I take my young lord to be a very
melancholy man.

COUNTESS By what observance, I pray you?   5

LAVATCH Why, he will look upon his boot, and sing;
mend the ruff, and sing; ask questions, and sing; pick
his teeth, and sing. I know a man that had this trick of 8
melancholy sold a goodly manor for a song.

COUNTESS Let me see what he writes, and when he
means to come.
   [Opens a letter.]

LAVATCH I have no mind to Isbel since I was at court.
Our old lings and our Isbels o' th' country are nothing 13
like your old ling and your Isbels o' th' court. The
brains of my Cupid's knocked out, and I begin to love,
as an old man loves money, with no stomach.   16

COUNTESS What have we here?

LAVATCH E'en that you have there.   *Exit.*

[COUNTESS *reads*] *a letter.* 'I have sent you a daughter-
in-law. She hath recovered the king, and undone me. I
have wedded her, not bedded her, and sworn to make
the "not" eternal. You shall hear I am run away; know 22
it before the report come. If there be breadth enough in
the world, I will hold a long distance. My duty to you.
            Your unfortunate son,
                    Bertram.'
This is not well, rash and unbridled boy,
To fly the favors of so good a king,
To pluck his indignation on thy head
By the misprizing of a maid too virtuous
For the contempt of empire.   31
    Enter [Lavatch, the] Clown.

LAVATCH O madam, yonder is heavy news within be- 32
tween two soldiers and my young lady!

COUNTESS What is the matter?

LAVATCH Nay, there is some comfort in the news, some
comfort – your son will not be killed so soon as I
thought he would.

COUNTESS Why should he be killed?

LAVATCH So say I, madam, if he run away, as I hear he
does. The danger is in standing to't; that's the loss of 40
men, though it be the getting of children. Here they 41
come will tell you more. For my part, I only hear your
son was run away.   *[Exit.]*
    Enter Helena and [the] two [French] Gentlemen.

---

73 *observance* dutiful service; *eke out* supplement 74 *homely stars* humble
origins 78 *owe* own 80 *fain* gladly 81 *vouch* confirm 91 *coragio* courage
III, i The palace of the Duke of Florence 3 *Whose great decision* the
deciding of which 7 *cousin* fellow ruler 9 *borrowing prayers* prayers for
aid 10 *yield* report 11–13 *a common . . . motion* an unskilled outsider
who imperfectly imagines to himself the great deliberations proceeding in
secret 17 *nature* disposition 19 *physic* medicine 22 *When . . . fell* when
better places fall vacant, they will become yours
III, ii The palace of the Count 5 *observance* observation 8 *trick* custom,
habit 13 *old lings* salted cods 16 *stomach* appetite, inclination 22 *not*
(with pun on 'knot') 31 *For . . . empire* for even an emperor to scorn
32 *heavy* sad 40 *standing to't* meeting danger head on (with sexual quibble)
41 *getting* begetting

2 . LORD Save you, good madam.

HELENA
Madam, my lord is gone, forever gone!

1 . LORD Do not say so.

COUNTESS
Think upon patience. Pray you, gentlemen –
48 I have felt so many quirks of joy and grief
That the first face of neither on the start
50 Can woman me unto't. Where is my son, I pray you?

1 . LORD
Madam, he's gone to serve the Duke of Florence.
We met him thitherward, for thence we came;
And after some dispatch in hand at court,
Thither we bend again.

55 HELENA Look on his letter, madam. Here's my passport.
[Reads.] 'When thou canst get the ring upon my finger,
which never shall come off, and show me a child begotten of thy body that I am father to, then call me husband; but in such a "then" I write a "never."'
This is a dreadful sentence.

COUNTESS
Brought you this letter, gentlemen?

1 . LORD   Ay, madam,
And for the contents' sake are sorry for our pains.

COUNTESS
I prithee, lady, have a better cheer.
64 If thou engrossest all the griefs are thine,
65 Thou robb'st me of a moiety. He was my son,
But I do wash his name out of my blood,
67 And thou art all my child. Towards Florence is he?

1 . LORD
Ay, madam.

COUNTESS   And to be a soldier?

1 . LORD
Such is his noble purpose, and believe't,
The duke will lay upon him all the honor
71 That good convenience claims.

COUNTESS   Return you thither?

2 . LORD
Ay, madam, with the swiftest wing of speed.

HELENA [reads]
'Till I have no wife, I have nothing in France.'
'Tis bitter.

COUNTESS   Find you that there?

HELENA   Ay, madam.

75 2 . LORD 'Tis but the boldness of his hand haply, which
his heart was not consenting to.

COUNTESS
Nothing in France until he have no wife!
There's nothing here that is too good for him
But only she, and she deserves a lord
That twenty such rude boys might tend upon
And call her hourly mistress. Who was with him?

2 . LORD
A servant only, and a gentleman
Which I have sometime known.

COUNTESS   Parolles, was it not?

2 . LORD
Ay, my good lady, he.

COUNTESS
85 A very tainted fellow, and full of wickedness.
86 My son corrupts a well-derivèd nature
87 With his inducement.

2 . LORD   Indeed, good lady,

The fellow has a deal of that too much   88
Which holds him much to have.

COUNTESS   Y' are welcome, gentlemen.
I will entreat you, when you see my son,
To tell him that his sword can never win
The honor that he loses. More I'll entreat you
Written to bear along.   93

1 . LORD   We serve you, madam,
In that and all your worthiest affairs.

COUNTESS
Not so, but as we change our courtesies.   95
Will you draw near?   Exit [with the Gentlemen].   96

HELENA
'Till I have no wife I have nothing in France.'
Nothing in France until he has no wife!
Thou shalt have none, Rossillion, none in France;
Then hast thou all again. Poor lord, is't I
That chase thee from thy country, and expose
Those tender limbs of thine to the event   102
Of the none-sparing war? And is it I
That drive thee from the sportive court, where thou
Wast shot at with fair eyes, to be the mark   105
Of smoky muskets? O you leaden messengers
That ride upon the violent speed of fire,
Fly with false aim; move the still-piecing air,   108
That sings with piercing; do not touch my lord!
Whoever shoots at him, I set him there.
Whoever charges on his forward breast,
I am the caitiff that do hold him to't.   112
And though I kill him not, I am the cause
His death was so effected. Better 'twere
I met the ravin lion when he roared   115
With sharp constraint of hunger; better 'twere
That all the miseries which nature owes   117
Were mine at once. No; come thou home, Rossillion,
Whence honor but of danger wins a scar,   119
As oft it loses all. I will be gone.
My being here it is that holds thee hence.
Shall I stay here to do't? No, no, although
The air of paradise did fan the house
And angels officed all. I will be gone,   124
That pitiful rumor may report my flight   125
To consolate thine ear. Come, night; end, day;   126
For with the dark, poor thief, I'll steal away.   Exit.

*

Flourish. Enter the Duke of Florence, [Bertram   III, iii
Count] Rossillion, Drum and Trumpets, Soldiers,
Parolles.

DUKE
The general of our horse thou art; and we,
Great in our hope, lay our best love and credence   2

48 *quirks* spells   50 *woman me* make me womanish, make me weep   55 *passport* license to beg   64 *engrossest* monopolize; *are* which are   65 *moiety* half   67 *all my child* my own child   71 *convenience* fitness   75 *haply* perhaps   85 *tainted* depraved   86 *well-derivèd nature* inherited goodness   87 *With his inducement* by his (Parolles') ill counsel   88–89 *has . . . have* possesses just the sort of superfluity that endears him to Bertram   93 *Written* in writing   95 *Not so . . . courtesies* you serve me only in the sense that we mutually serve each other   96 *draw near* come in   102 *event* outcome   105 *mark* target   108 *still-piecing* always closing again   112 *caitiff* wretch   115 *ravin* ravenous   117 *owes* owns   119–20 *Whence . . . all* from where honor wins nothing from danger but scars, and sometimes pays with its life   124 *officed all* did all the household chores   125 *pitiful* i.e. full of pity for Bertram   126 *consolate* console
III, iii The palace of the Duke of Florence   2 *Great* pregnant

Upon thy promising fortune.

BERTRAM   Sir, it is
A charge too heavy for my strength, but yet
We'll strive to bear it for your worthy sake
6   To th' extreme edge of hazard.

DUKE   Then go thou forth,
And Fortune play upon thy prosperous helm
As thy auspicious mistress!

BERTRAM   This very day,
9   Great Mars, I put myself into thy file.
10   Make me but like my thoughts, and I shall prove
A lover of thy drum, hater of love.   *Exeunt omnes.*

*

III, iv   *Enter Countess and Steward.*

COUNTESS
Alas! and would you take the letter of her?
Might you not know she would do as she has done,
By sending me a letter? Read it again.

[STEWARD *reads the*] *letter.*

4   'I am Saint Jaques' pilgrim, thither gone.
Ambitious love hath so in me offended
That barefoot plod I the cold ground upon,
With sainted vow my faults to have amended.
Write, write, that from the bloody course of war
My dearest master, your dear son, may hie.
Bless him at home in peace, whilst I from far
His name with zealous fervor sanctify.
12   His taken labors bid him me forgive.
13   I, his despiteful Juno, sent him forth
From courtly friends, with camping foes to live,
Where death and danger dogs the heels of worth.
He is too good and fair for death and me;
17   Whom I myself embrace to set him free.'

COUNTESS
Ah, what sharp stings are in her mildest words!
19   Rinaldo, you did never lack advice so much
As letting her pass so. Had I spoke with her,
I could have well diverted her intents,
22   Which thus she hath prevented.

STEWARD   Pardon me, madam.
23   If I had given you this at overnight,
She might have been o'erta'en; and yet she writes
Pursuit would be but vain.

COUNTESS   What angel shall
Bless this unworthy husband? He cannot thrive,
Unless her prayers, whom heaven delights to hear
And loves to grant, reprieve him from the wrath
Of greatest justice. Write, write, Rinaldo,

To this unworthy husband of his wife.
Let every word weigh heavy of her worth
That he does weigh too light. My greatest grief,   32
Though little he do feel it, set down sharply.
Dispatch the most convenient messenger.
When haply he shall hear that she is gone,   35
He will return; and hope I may that she,
Hearing so much, will speed her foot again,
Led hither by pure love. Which of them both
Is dearest to me, I have no skill in sense   39
To make distinction. Provide this messenger.
My heart is heavy, and mine age is weak.
Grief would have tears, and sorrow bids me speak.
                     Exeunt.

*

III, v   *A tucket afar off. Enter old Widow of Florence, her
Daughter [Diana], Violenta, and Mariana, with
other Citizens.*

WIDOW Nay, come; for if they do approach the city, we
shall lose all the sight.

DIANA They say the French count has done most honorable service.

WIDOW It is reported that he has taken their great'st commander, and that with his own hand he slew the duke's
brother. [*Tucket.*] We have lost our labor; they are gone
a contrary way. Hark! You may know by their trumpets.

MARIANA Come, let's return again, and suffice ourselves 9
with the report of it. Well, Diana, take heed of this
French earl. The honor of a maid is her name, and no
legacy is so rich as honesty.   12

WIDOW I have told my neighbor how you have been 13
solicited by a gentleman his companion.

MARIANA I know that knave, hang him! one Parolles, a
filthy officer he is in those suggestions for the young earl. 16
Beware of them, Diana; their promises, enticements,
oaths, tokens, and all these engines of lust, are not the 18
things they go under. Many a maid hath been seduced 19
by them; and the misery is, example, that so terrible 20
shows in the wrack of maidenhood, cannot for all that
dissuade succession but that they are limed with the 22
twigs that threatens them. I hope I need not to advise
you further, but I hope your own grace will keep you
where you are, though there were no further danger 25
known but the modesty which is so lost.

DIANA You shall not need to fear me.   27

Enter Helena [like a pilgrim].

WIDOW I hope so. Look, here comes a pilgrim. I know
she will lie at my house; thither they send one another. 29
I'll question her.
God save you, pilgrim! Whither are you bound?

HELENA
To Saint Jaques le Grand.
Where do the palmers lodge, I do beseech you?

WIDOW
At the Saint Francis here, beside the port.   34

HELENA
Is this the way?

WIDOW
Ay, marry, is't.   36
     A march afar.
                Hark you! they come this way.
If you will tarry, holy pilgrim,

---

6 *edge of hazard* limit of danger   9 *file* ranks   10 *like my thoughts* i.e.
valiant

III, iv The palace of the Count   4 *thither* i.e. to the shrine of St Jaques,
at Compostella   12 *taken* undertaken   13 *despiteful* cruel   17 *Whom
death; him* Bertram   19 *advice* judgment   22 *prevented* forestalled   23 *at
overnight* last night   32 *weigh* value   35 *haply* perchance   39 *skill* ability;
sense feeling

III, v The highway approaching Florence   s.d. *tucket* trumpet fanfare
9 *suffice* satisfy   12 *honesty* chastity   13 *my neighbor* i.e. Mariana   16
officer agent; *suggestions* enticements   18 *engines* artifices   19 *go under*
pretend to be   20 *example* past precedent   20–21 *so . . . maidenhood* is so
filled with terrifying instances of wrecked maidenheads   22 *dissuade
succession* discourage others from following the same course; *they* i.e.
other maidens   22–23 *limed . . . twigs* caught in the snares   25 *further
danger* i.e. pregnancy   27 *fear* mistrust   29 *lie* lodge   34 *the Saint
Francis* (an inn); *port* city gate   36 *marry* indeed

But till the troops come by,
I will conduct you where you shall be lodged,
The rather for I think I know your hostess
41 As ample as myself.
HELENA   Is it yourself?
WIDOW
If you shall please so, pilgrim.
HELENA
43 I thank you, and will stay upon your leisure.
WIDOW
You came, I think, from France?
HELENA   I did so.
WIDOW
Here you shall see a countryman of yours
That has done worthy service.
HELENA   His name, I pray you?
DIANA
The Count Rossillion. Know you such a one?
HELENA
But by the ear, that hears most nobly of him;
His face I know not.
DIANA   Whatsome'er he is,
50 He's bravely taken here. He stole from France,
As 'tis reported, for the king had married him
Against his liking. Think you it is so?
HELENA
53 Ay, surely, mere the truth; I know his lady.
DIANA
There is a gentleman that serves the count
Reports but coarsely of her.
HELENA   What's his name?
DIANA
Monsieur Parolles.
HELENA   O, I believe with him,
57 In argument of praise or to the worth
Of the great count himself, she is too mean
59 To have her name repeated. All her deserving
60 Is a reservèd honesty, and that
61 I have not heard examined.
DIANA   Alas, poor lady!
'Tis a hard bondage to become the wife
Of a detesting lord.
WIDOW
64 I write, good creature, whereso'er she is,
Her heart weighs sadly. This young maid might do her
66 A shrewd turn, if she pleased.
HELENA   How do you mean?
May be the amorous count solicits her
In the unlawful purpose.
WIDOW   He does indeed,
69 And brokes with all that can in such a suit
Corrupt the tender honor of a maid;
But she is armed for him, and keeps her guard
In honestest defense.
Drum and Colors. Enter [Bertram] Count Rossillion,
Parolles, and the whole Army.
MARIANA   The gods forbid else!
WIDOW
So, now they come.
That is Antonio, the duke's eldest son;
That, Escalus.
HELENA   Which is the Frenchman?
DIANA   He –
That with the plume. 'Tis a most gallant fellow;

I would he loved his wife. If he were honester, 77
He were much goodlier. Is't not a handsome gentleman?
HELENA
I like him well.
DIANA
'Tis pity he is not honest. Yond's that same knave
That leads him to these places. Were I his lady, 81
I would poison that vile rascal.
HELENA   Which is he?
DIANA
That jackanapes with scarfs. Why is he melancholy?
HELENA
Perchance he's hurt i' th' battle.
PAROLLES Lose our drum? Well!
MARIANA He's shrewdly vexed at something. Look, he 86
has spied us.
WIDOW Mary, hang you!
MARIANA And your curtsy, for a ring-carrier! 88
Exeunt [Bertram, Parolles, and Army].
WIDOW
The troop is past. Come, pilgrim, I will bring you
Where you shall host. Of enjoined penitents 90
There's four or five, to great Saint Jaques bound,
Already at my house.
HELENA   I humbly thank you.
Please it this matron and this gentle maid
To eat with us to-night, the charge and thanking 94
Shall be for me; and, to requite you further,
I will bestow some precepts of this virgin, 96
Worthy the note.
BOTH   We'll take your offer kindly. *Exeunt.*

*

Enter [Bertram] Count Rossillion and the III, vi
Frenchmen, as at first.
2. LORD Nay, good my lord, put him to't; let him have
his way.
1. LORD If your lordship finds him not a hilding, hold me 3
no more in your respect.
2. LORD On my life, my lord, a bubble. 5
BERTRAM Do you think I am so far deceived in him?
2. LORD Believe it, my lord, in mine own direct knowledge, without any malice, but to speak of him as my 8
kinsman, he's a most notable coward, an infinite and
endless liar, an hourly promise-breaker, the owner of no
one good quality worthy your lordship's entertainment. 11
1. LORD It were fit you knew him, lest reposing too far in
his virtue, which he hath not, he might at some great
and trusty business in a main danger fail you.
BERTRAM I would I knew in what particular action to try
him.
1. LORD None better than to let him fetch off his drum,
which you hear him so confidently undertake to do.

41 *ample* well 43 *stay upon* await 50 *bravely taken* made a splendid impression 53 *mere the truth* the absolute truth 57 *In argument of* as a subject of; *to* compared to 59 *All her deserving* her only merit 60 *reservèd honesty* preserved chastity 61 *examined* called into question 64 *write* certify, declare 66 *shrewd* ill-natured 69 *brokes* bargains 77 *honester* more honorable 81 *places* infamous actions (?) 86 *shrewdly* sorely 88 *curtsy* ceremony; *ring-carrier* go-between 90 *host* lodge; *enjoined penitents* pilgrims bound by oath to their pilgrimage 94 *charge and thanking* i.e. both expense and gratitude 96 *of* on
III, vi A camp outside Florence 3 *hilding* base fellow 5 *bubble* impostor 8 *as* as if he were 11 *entertainment* maintenance

2. LORD I with a troop of Florentines will suddenly surprise him; such I will have whom I am sure he knows
21 not from the enemy. We will bind and hoodwink him so, that he shall suppose no other but that he is carried into
23 the leaguer of the adversaries when we bring him to our own tents. Be but your lordship present at his examination. If he do not, for the promise of his life and in the highest compulsion of base fear, offer to betray you and deliver all the intelligence in his power against you, and that with the divine forfeit of his soul upon oath, never trust my judgment in anything.

1. LORD O, for the love of laughter, let him fetch his drum! He says he has a stratagem for't. When your
32 lordship sees the bottom of his success in't, and to what metal this counterfeit lump of ore will be melted, if you
34 give him our John Drum's entertainment, your inclining cannot be removed. Here he comes.

Enter Parolles.

2. LORD O, for the love of laughter, hinder not the honor
37 of his design; let him fetch off his drum in any hand.

BERTRAM How now, monsieur? This drum sticks sorely in your disposition.

1. LORD A pox on't, let it go! 'tis but a drum.

PAROLLES But a drum? Is't but a drum? A drum so lost! There was excellent command: to charge in with our horse upon our own wings and to rend our own soldiers!

1. LORD That was not to be blamed in the command of the service; it was a disaster of war that Caesar himself could not have prevented if he had been there to command.

48 BERTRAM Well, we cannot greatly condemn our success. Some dishonor we had in the loss of that drum, but it is not to be recovered.

PAROLLES It might have been recovered.

BERTRAM It might, but it is not now.

PAROLLES It is to be recovered. But that the merit of service is seldom attributed to the true and exact performer,
55 I would have that drum or another, or *hic jacet*!

BERTRAM Why, if you have a stomach, to't, monsieur! If
57 you think your mystery in stratagem can bring this
58 instrument of honor again into his native quarter, be
59 magnanimous in the enterprise and go on; I will grace
60 the attempt for a worthy exploit. If you speed well in it, the duke shall both speak of it and extend to you what further becomes his greatness, even to the utmost syllable of your worthiness.

PAROLLES By the hand of a soldier, I will undertake it.

BERTRAM But you must not now slumber in it.

66 PAROLLES I'll about it this evening, and I will presently
67 pen down my dilemmas, encourage myself in my cer-

tainty, put myself into my mortal preparation; and by 68 midnight look to hear further from me.

BERTRAM May I be bold to acquaint his grace you are gone about it?

PAROLLES I know not what the success will be, my lord, but the attempt I vow.

BERTRAM I know th'art valiant, and to the possibility of 74 thy soldiership will subscribe for thee. Farewell. 75

PAROLLES I love not many words. *Exit.*

2. LORD No more than a fish loves water. Is not this a strange fellow, my lord, that so confidently seems to undertake this business, which he knows is not to be done; damns himself to do, and dares better be damned 80 than to do't?

1. LORD You do not know him, my lord, as we do. Certain it is that he will steal himself into a man's favor, and for a week escape a great deal of discoveries; but when you find him out, you have him ever after. 85

BERTRAM Why, do you think he will make no deed at all of this that so seriously he does address himself unto?

2. LORD None in the world; but return with an invention, and clap upon you two or three probable lies. But 89 we have almost embossed him. You shall see his fall to- 90 night; for indeed he is not for your lordship's respect.

1. LORD We'll make you some sport with the fox ere we case him. He was first smoked by the old Lord Lafew. 93 When his disguise and he is parted, tell me what a sprat 94 you shall find him, which you shall see this very night.

2. LORD
I must go look my twigs; he shall be caught. 96

BERTRAM
Your brother, he shall go along with me.

2. LORD
As't please your lordship. I'll leave you. *[Exit.]*

BERTRAM
Now will I lead you to the house, and show you
The lass I spoke of.

1. LORD But you say she's honest. 100

BERTRAM
That's all the fault. I spoke with her but once
And found her wondrous cold, but I sent to her,
By this same coxcomb that we have i' th' wind, 103
Tokens and letters, which she did resend, 104
And this is all I have done. She's a fair creature;
Will you go see her?

1. LORD With all my heart, my lord. *Exeunt.*

*

Enter Helena and Widow. III, vii

HELENA
If you misdoubt me that I am not she, 1
I know not how I shall assure you further
But I shall lose the grounds I work upon. 3

WIDOW
Though my estate be fallen, I was well born, 4
Nothing acquainted with these businesses,
And would not put my reputation now
In any staining act.

HELENA Nor would I wish you.
First give me trust the count he is my husband,
And what to your sworn counsel I have spoken
Is so from word to word; and then you cannot, 10
By the good aid that I of you shall borrow, 11

21 *hoodwink* blindfold 23 *leaguer* camp 32 *bottom* extent 34 *John Drum's entertainment* unceremonious dismissal; *inclining* partiality 37 *in any hand* in any case 48 *success* fortune 55 *hic jacet* 'here lies'; i.e. 'die in the attempt' 57 *mystery* skill 58 *again . . . quarter* back home 59 *grace* honor 60 *speed* succeed 66 *presently* immediately 67 *pen . . . dilemmas* repress my doubts (?) 68 *mortal* death-dealing 74 *possibility* capacity 75 *subscribe for* answer for 80 *better* sooner 85 *have him* have his number 89 *probable* plausible 90 *embossed* driven to extremity 93 *case* uncase, unmask; *smoked* smoked out 94 *sprat* contemptible creature 96 *look my twigs* look after my traps 100 *honest* chaste 103 *coxcomb* fool; *that . . . wind* whom we're hunting 104 *resend* send back

III, vii The house of a Florentine widow 1 *misdoubt* doubt 3 *But . . . upon* unless I wreck my plans by disclosing my identity to Bertram 4 *estate* condition 10 *from . . . word* in every particular 11 *By* in respect to

Err in bestowing it.

WIDOW   I should believe you,
For you have showed me that which well approves
Y'are great in fortune.

HELENA   Take this purse of gold,
And let me buy your friendly help thus far,
Which I will overpay, and pay again
When I have found it. The count he woos your daughter,
Lays down his wanton siege before her beauty,
19   Resolved to carry her. Let her in fine consent,
As we'll direct her how 'tis best to bear it.
21   Now his important blood will naught deny
22   That she'll demand. A ring the county wears
That downward hath succeeded in his house
From son to son some four or five descents
Since the first father wore it. This ring he holds
26   In most rich choice; yet in his idle fire,
27   To buy his will, it would not seem too dear,
Howe'er repented after.

WIDOW   Now I see
The bottom of your purpose.

HELENA
You see it lawful then; it is no more
But that your daughter, ere she seems as won,
Desires this ring; appoints him an encounter;
33   In fine, delivers me to fill the time,
Herself most chastely absent. After,
35   To marry her, I'll add three thousand crowns
To what is passed already.

WIDOW   I have yielded.
Instruct my daughter how she shall persever,
That time and place with this deceit so lawful
39   May prove coherent. Every night he comes
With musics of all sorts, and songs composed
41   To her unworthiness. It nothing steads us
To chide him from our eaves, for he persists
As if his life lay on't.

HELENA   Why then to-night
44   Let us assay our plot, which if it speed,
45   Is wicked meaning in a lawful deed,
And lawful meaning in a lawful act,
47   Where both not sin, and yet a sinful fact.
But let's about it.   *[Exeunt.]*

*

IV, i   *Enter one of the Frenchmen, [the Second Lord,]*
        with five or six other Soldiers, in ambush.

2 . LORD He can come no other way but by this hedge
corner. When you sally upon him, speak what terrible
language you will; though you understand it not yourselves, no matter; for we must not seem to understand
5   him, unless some one among us whom we must produce
for an interpreter.

1 . SOLDIER Good captain, let me be th' interpreter.

2 . LORD Art not acquainted with him? Knows he not thy
voice?

1 . SOLDIER No, sir, I warrant you.

11 2 . LORD But what linsey-woolsey hast thou to speak to us
again?

1 . SOLDIER E'en such as you speak to me.

14 2 . LORD He must think us some band of strangers i' th'
15   adversary's entertainment. Now he hath a smack of all
neighboring languages; therefore we must every one be

a man of his own fancy, not to know what we speak 17
one to another; so we seem to know, is to know straight 18
our purpose. Choughs' language – gabble enough, and 19
good enough. As for you, interpreter, you must seem
very politic. But couch, ho! Here he comes, to beguile 21
two hours in a sleep, and then to return and swear the 22
lies he forges.   *[They hide.]*
     Enter Parolles.

PAROLLES Ten o'clock. Within these three hours 'twill be
time enough to go home. What shall I say I have done?
It must be a very plausive invention that carries it. They 26
begin to smoke me, and disgraces have of late knocked 27
too often at my door. I find my tongue is too foolhardy;
but my heart hath the fear of Mars before it, and of his 29
creatures, not daring the reports of my tongue.   30

2 . LORD This is the first truth that e'er thine own tongue
was guilty of.

PAROLLES What the devil should move me to undertake
the recovery of this drum, being not ignorant of the impossibility, and knowing I had no such purpose? I must
give myself some hurts and say I got them in exploit;
yet slight ones will not carry it. They will say, 'Came
you off with so little?' And great ones I dare not give.
Wherefore, what's the instance? Tongue, I must put 39
you into a butter-woman's mouth, and buy myself an- 40
other of Bajazet's mule, if you prattle me into these 41
perils.

2 . LORD Is it possible he should know what he is, and be
that he is?

PAROLLES I would the cutting of my garments would
serve the turn, or the breaking of my Spanish sword.

2 . LORD We cannot afford you so.   46

PAROLLES Or the baring of my beard, and to say it was in 47
stratagem.

2 . LORD 'Twould not do.

PAROLLES Or to drown my clothes, and say I was stripped.

2 . LORD Hardly serve.

PAROLLES Though I swore I leapt from the window of
the citadel –

2 . LORD How deep?

PAROLLES Thirty fathom.

2 . LORD Three great oaths would scarce make that be
believed.

PAROLLES I would I had any drum of the enemy's; I
would swear I recovered it.

2 . LORD You shall hear one anon.   60

PAROLLES A drum now of the enemy's –
     Alarum within.

2 . LORD Throca movousus, cargo, cargo, cargo.

ALL Cargo, cargo, cargo, villianda par corbo, cargo.

---

19 *in fine* at length   21 *important* importunate   22 *county* count   26 *most rich choice* highest esteem; *idle* careless   27 *will* pleasure   33 *to fill the time* to keep the assignation   35 *To marry her* i.e. by way of dowry   39 *coherent* in accord   41 *steads* avails   44 *speed* succeed   45 *meaning* intention   47 *fact* deed, crime
IV, i A field near the camp   5 *unless* except for   11 *linsey-woolsey* gibberish   14 *strangers* foreigners   15 *entertainment* employment   17 *of . . . fancy* with a fancied language of his own   18–19 *so . . . purpose* it will suffice if we merely seem to understand each other   19 *Choughs'* jackdaws'   21 *politic* cunning; *couch, ho* to our hiding-places   22 *swear* swear to   26 *plausive* plausible   27 *smoke* detect   29–30 *his creatures* soldiers   30 *not . . . tongue* not daring to execute my boasts   39 *what's the instance* what is to be the evidence   40 *butter-woman* (a proverbial scold)   41 *Bajazet's mule* (unexplained)   46 *afford you so* let you off so easily   47 *baring* shaving

PAROLLES

O, ransom, ransom! Do not hide mine eyes.

[*They blindfold him.*]

[1. SOLDIER AS] INTERPRETER Boskos thromuldo boskos.

PAROLLES

I know you are the Muskos' regiment,

67 And I shall lose my life for want of language.
If there be here German, or Dane, Low Dutch,
Italian, or French, let him speak to me,

70 I'll discover that which shall undo the Florentine.

INTERPRETER Boskos vauvado. I understand thee, and can speak thy tongue. Kerelybonto. Sir, betake thee to thy faith, for seventeen poniards are at thy bosom.

PAROLLES O!

INTERPRETER O, pray, pray, pray! Manka revania dulche.

2. LORD Oscorbidulchos volivorco.

INTERPRETER

The general is content to spare thee yet,

78 And, hoodwinked as thou art, will lead thee on
79 To gather from thee. Haply thou mayst inform
Something to save thy life.

PAROLLES   O, let me live,
And all the secrets of our camp I'll show,
Their force, their purposes; nay, I'll speak that
Which you will wonder at.

83 INTERPRETER   But wilt thou faithfully?

PAROLLES

If I do not, damn me.

INTERPRETER

85 Acordo linta. Come on; thou art granted space.

         Exit [with Parolles].

A short alarum within.

2. LORD

Go tell the Count Rossillion and my brother,

87 We have caught the woodcock, and will keep him muffled
Till we do hear from them.

2. SOLDIER   Captain, I will.

2. LORD

'A will betray us all unto ourselves;
Inform on that.

2. SOLDIER   So I will, sir.

2. LORD

Till then I'll keep him dark and safely locked.   *Exeunt.*

*

IV, ii   *Enter Bertram and the Maid called Diana.*

BERTRAM

They told me that your name was Fontybell.

DIANA

No, my good lord, Diana.

BERTRAM   Titled goddess,

3 And worth it, with addition! But, fair soul,

---

67 *want of language* ignorance of your language   70 *discover* reveal   78 *hoodwinked* blindfolded   79 *gather* acquire information; *Haply* perhaps   83 *faithfully* in good faith   85 *space* time   87 *woodcock* (proverbially foolish bird)

IV, ii The house of a Florentine widow   3 *worth . . . addition* deserving of that title, and more   4 *quality* position   5 *quick* vital   10 *got* begotten   11 *honest* chaste   14 *vows* i.e. those sworn against Helena   19 *our bareness* i.e. the loss of our virginity   27 *ill* poorly, or not at all; *holding* consistency   28 *protest* promise   30 *poor . . . unsealed* unworthy provisos without binding force (?)   42 *'longing* belonging   45 *honor* chastity   49 *proper* with regard to yourself   53 *bid* commanded

---

In your fine frame hath love no quality?   4
If the quick fire of youth light not your mind,   5
You are no maiden, but a monument.
When you are dead you should be such a one
As you are now, for you are cold and stern;
And now you should be as your mother was
When your sweet self was got.   10

DIANA

She then was honest.   11

BERTRAM   So should you be.

DIANA   No.

My mother did but duty – such, my lord,
As you owe to your wife.

BERTRAM   No more o' that;

I prithee do not strive against my vows.   14
I was compelled to her, but I love thee
By love's own sweet constraint, and will forever
Do thee all rights of service.

DIANA   Ay, so you serve us

Till we serve you; but when you have our roses,
You barely leave our thorns to prick ourselves,
And mock us with our bareness.   19

BERTRAM   How have I sworn!

DIANA

'Tis not the many oaths that makes the truth,
But the plain single vow that is vowed true.
What is not holy, that we swear not by,
But take the High'st to witness; then pray you tell me,
If I should swear by Jove's great attributes
I loved you dearly, would you believe my oaths
When I did love you ill? This has no holding,   27
To swear by Him whom I protest to love,   28
That I will work against Him. Therefore your oaths
Are words, and poor conditions but unsealed –   30
At least in my opinion.

BERTRAM   Change it, change it;

Be not so holy-cruel; love is holy,
And my integrity ne'er knew the crafts
That you do charge men with. Stand no more off,
But give thyself unto my sick desires,
Who then recovers. Say thou art mine, and ever
My love, as it begins, shall so persever.

DIANA

I see that men may rope 's in such a snare
That we'll forsake ourselves. Give me that ring.

BERTRAM

I'll lend it thee, my dear, but have no power
To give it from me.

DIANA   Will you not, my lord?

BERTRAM

It is an honor 'longing to our house,   42
Bequeathèd down from many ancestors,
Which were the greatest obloquy i' th' world
In me to lose.

DIANA   Mine honor 's such a ring;   45

My chastity 's the jewel of our house,
Bequeathèd down from many ancestors,
Which were the greatest obloquy i' th' world
In me to lose. Thus your own proper wisdom   49
Brings in the champion Honor on my part
Against your vain assault.

BERTRAM   Here, take my ring!

My house, mine honor, yea, my life be thine,
And I'll be bid by thee.   53

DIANA

When midnight comes, knock at my chamber window;
I'll order take my mother shall not hear.
56 Now will I charge you in the band of truth,
When you have conquered my yet maiden bed,
Remain there but an hour, nor speak to me;
My reasons are most strong, and you shall know them
When back again this ring shall be delivered.
And on your finger in the night I'll put
Another ring, that what in time proceeds
May token to the future our past deeds.
Adieu till then; then, fail not; you have won
65 A wife of me, though there my hope be done.

BERTRAM

A heaven on earth I have won by wooing thee. *[Exit.]*

DIANA

For which live long to thank both heaven and me!
You may so in the end.
My mother told me just how he would woo,
As if she sat in's heart. She says all men
Have the like oaths. He had sworn to marry me
When his wife's dead; therefore I'll lie with him
73 When I am buried. Since Frenchmen are so braid,
74 Marry that will, I live and die a maid.
Only, in this disguise I think't no sin
76 To cozen him that would unjustly win.   *Exit.*

*

IV, iii   *Enter the two French Captains and some two or*
    three Soldiers.

2. LORD You have not given him his mother's letter?
1. LORD I have delivered it an hour since. There is something in't that stings his nature, for on the reading it he changed almost into another man.
5 2. LORD He has much worthy blame laid upon him for shaking off so good a wife and so sweet a lady.
1. LORD Especially he hath incurred the everlasting displeasure of the king, who had even tuned his bounty to sing happiness to him. I will tell you a thing, but you shall let it dwell darkly with you.
2. LORD When you have spoken it, 'tis dead, and I am the grave of it.
1. LORD He hath perverted a young gentlewoman here in Florence, of a most chaste renown, and this night he
15 fleshes his will in the spoil of her honor. He hath given
16 her his monumental ring, and thinks himself made in
17 the unchaste composition.
18 2. LORD Now God delay our rebellion! As we are ourselves, what things are we!
20 1. LORD Merely our own traitors. And as in the common
21 course of all treasons, we still see them reveal themselves
22 till they attain to their abhorred ends, so he that in this
23. action contrives against his own nobility, in his proper stream o'erflows himself.
25 2. LORD Is it not meant damnable in us to be trumpeters of our unlawful intents? We shall not then have his company to-night?
28 1. LORD Not till after midnight, for he is dieted to his hour.
2. LORD That approaches apace. I would gladly have him
30 see his company anatomized, that he might take a meas-
31 ure of his own judgments, wherein so curiously he had set this counterfeit.

1. LORD We will not meddle with him till he come, for his 33 presence must be the whip of the other. 34
2. LORD In the meantime, what hear you of these wars?
1. LORD I hear there is an overture of peace.
2. LORD Nay, I assure you, a peace concluded.
1. LORD What will Count Rossillion do then? Will he travel higher, or return again into France? 39
2. LORD I perceive by this demand you are not altogether of his council. 41
1. LORD Let it be forbid, sir! So should I be a great deal of 42 his act.
2. LORD Sir, his wife some two months since fled from his house. Her pretense is a pilgrimage to Saint Jaques le 45 Grand; which holy undertaking with most austere sanctimony she accomplished; and there residing, the tenderness of her nature became as a prey to her grief; in 48 fine, made a groan of her last breath, and now she sings in heaven.
1. LORD How is this justified? 51
2. LORD The stronger part of it by her own letters, which 52 makes her story true, even to the point of her death. Her 53 death itself, which could not be her office to say is come, 54 was faithfully confirmed by the rector of the place.
1. LORD Hath the count all this intelligence?
2. LORD Ay, and the particular confirmations, point from point, to the full arming of the verity. 58
1. LORD I am heartily sorry that he'll be glad of this.
2. LORD How mightily sometimes we make us comforts of our losses!
1. LORD And how mightily some other times we drown our gain in tears! The great dignity that his valor hath 63 here acquired for him shall at home be encountered with a shame as ample.
2. LORD The web of our life is of a mingled yarn, good and ill together; our virtues would be proud if our faults whipped them not, and our crimes would despair if they were not cherished by our virtues.

Enter a Messenger.

How now? Where's your master?

MESSENGER He met the duke in the street, sir, of whom he hath taken a solemn leave; his lordship will next morning for France. The duke hath offered him letters of commendations to the king.   *[Exit.]*
2. LORD They shall be no more than needful there, if 75 they were more than they can commend.

Enter [Bertram] Count Rossillion.

---

56 *band* bond 65 *though . . . done* though I thereby forfeit all hope of becoming your wife myself; *done* lost 73 *braid* deceitful 74 *that* who 76 *cozen* cheat
IV, iii The camp 5 *worthy* deserved 15 *fleshes his will* gratifies his lust; *spoil* ruin; *honor* chastity 16 *monumental* serving as a token of identity; *made* i.e. a made man 17 *unchaste composition* dishonorable bargain 18 *delay* mitigate; *rebellion* outbreaks of lust; *ourselves* unaided by heaven 20 *Merely* entirely 21 *still* always; *reveal themselves* i.e. for what they are 22 *attain . . . ends* reach their abhorrent conclusions, i.e. self-destruction 23 *contrives* plots 23–24 *in . . . himself* undoes his own nobility with his own plots 25 *meant damnable* a sign of damnation 28 *dieted* restricted 30 *company* companion, i.e. Parolles; *anatomized* laid bare, exposed 30–31 *take . . . judgments* appreciate his own misjudgment 31–32 *so . . . counterfeit* so elaborately he had set this false jewel 33 *him* Parolles; *he* Bertram; *his* Bertram's 34 *the other* Parolles 39 *higher* farther 41 *of his council* in his confidence 42–43 *of his act* answerable for his actions 45 *pretense* intent 48–49 *in fine* at last 51 *justified* verified 52 *stronger* larger 53 *point* moment 54 *which . . . come* which she could not herself report 58 *arming* corroboration 63 *gain* profits 75 *no . . . needful* i.e. of the utmost necessity 75–76 *if . . . commend* even if they outdid all possible commendation

1. LORD They cannot be too sweet for the king's tartness. Here's his lordship now. How now, my lord, is't not after midnight?

BERTRAM I have to-night dispatched sixteen businesses, a
81 month's length apiece. By an abstract of success: I have
82 congied with the duke, done my adieu with his nearest, buried a wife, mourned for her, writ to my lady mother
84 I am returning, entertained my convoy, and between
85 these main parcels of dispatch effected many nicer needs.
86 The last was the greatest, but that I have not ended yet.

2. LORD If the business be of any difficulty, and this morning your departure hence, it requires haste of your lordship.

90 BERTRAM I mean the business is not ended, as fearing to hear of it hereafter. But shall we have this dialogue between the Fool and the Soldier? Come, bring forth this
93 counterfeit module has deceived me like a double-meaning prophesier.

2. LORD Bring him forth. *[Exeunt Soldiers.]* Has sat i' th'
96 stocks all night, poor gallant knave.

BERTRAM No matter, his heels have deserved it, in usurping his spurs so long. How does he carry himself?

2. LORD I have told your lordship already: the stocks carry him. But to answer you as you would be understood, he
101 weeps like a wench that had shed her milk; he hath confessed himself to Morgan, whom he supposes to be a
103 friar, from the time of his remembrance to this very
104 instant disaster of his setting i' th' stocks. And what think you he hath confessed?

BERTRAM Nothing of me, has 'a?

2. LORD His confession is taken, and it shall be read to his face. If your lordship be in't, as I believe you are, you must have the patience to hear it.

Enter Parolles [guarded,] with [First Soldier as] his Interpreter.

110 BERTRAM A plague upon him! muffled! He can say nothing of me.

1. LORD Hush, hush! Hoodman comes! Portotartarossa.

INTERPRETER He calls for the tortures; what will you say without 'em?

PAROLLES I will confess what I know without constraint.
116 If ye pinch me like a pasty, I can say no more.

INTERPRETER Bosko chimurcho.

1. LORD Boblibindo chicurmurco.

INTERPRETER You are a merciful general. Our general
120 bids you answer to what I shall ask you out of a note.

PAROLLES And truly, as I hope to live.

INTERPRETER *[reads]* 'First demand of him how many horse the duke is strong.' What say you to that?

PAROLLES Five or six thousand, but very weak and unserviceable. The troops are all scattered, and the commanders very poor rogues, upon my reputation and credit, and as I hope to live.

INTERPRETER Shall I set down your answer so?

PAROLLES Do. I'll take the sacrament on't, how and which way you will.

BERTRAM All's one to him. What a past-saving slave is 131 this!

1. LORD Y'are deceived, my lord. This is Monsieur Parolles, the gallant militarist – that was his own phrase – that had the whole theoric of war in the knot of his 134 scarf, and the practice in the chape of his dagger. 135

2. LORD I will never trust a man again for keeping his sword clean, nor believe he can have everything in him by wearing his apparel neatly. 138

INTERPRETER Well, that's set down.

PAROLLES 'Five or six thousand horse,' I said – I will say true – 'or thereabouts' set down, for I'll speak truth.

1. LORD He's very near the truth in this.

BERTRAM But I con him no thanks for't, in the nature he 143 delivers it.

PAROLLES 'Poor rogues,' I pray you say.

INTERPRETER Well, that's set down.

PAROLLES I humbly thank you, sir; a truth 's a truth – the rogues are marvellous poor. 148

INTERPRETER *[reads]* 'Demand of him of what strength they are afoot.' What say you to that?

PAROLLES By my troth, sir, if I were to live this present 151 hour, I will tell true. Let me see: Spurio, a hundred and fifty; Sebastian, so many; Corambus, so many; Jaques, so many; Guiltian, Cosmo, Lodowick, and Gratii, two hundred fifty each; mine own company, Chitopher, Vaumond, Bentii, two hundred fifty each; so that the muster file, rotten and sound, upon my life amounts not 157 to fifteen thousand poll, half of which dare not shake 158 the snow from off their cassocks, lest they shake them- 159 selves to pieces.

BERTRAM What shall be done to him?

1. LORD Nothing, but let him have thanks. Demand of him my condition, and what credit I have with the duke.

INTERPRETER Well, that's set down. *[Reads]* 'You shall demand of him whether one Captain Dumain be i' th' camp, a Frenchman; what his reputation is with the duke; what his valor, honesty, and expertness in wars; or whether he thinks it were not possible, with well- 168 weighing sums of gold, to corrupt him to a revolt.' What say you to this? What do you know of it?

PAROLLES I beseech you let me answer to the particular of the inter'gatories. Demand them singly. 172

INTERPRETER Do you know this Captain Dumain?

PAROLLES I know him. 'A was a botcher's prentice in 174 Paris, from whence he was whipped for getting the shrieve's fool with child – a dumb innocent, that could 176 not say him nay.

[First Lord makes as if to strike him.]

BERTRAM Nay, by your leave, hold your hands, though I know his brains are forfeit to the next tile that falls. 179

INTERPRETER Well, is this captain in the Duke of Florence's camp?

PAROLLES Upon my knowledge he is, and lousy.

1. LORD Nay, look not so upon me; we shall hear of your lordship anon.

INTERPRETER What is his reputation with the duke?

---

81 *By . . . success* to enumerate my successes   82 *congied with* taken leave of   84 *entertained my convoy* arranged my transportation   85 *parcels of dispatch* items of business; *nicer* more delicate   86 *The last* i.e. the assignation with Diana   90–91 *as . . . hear* since I fear I may hear   93 *module* mere image   93–94 *double-meaning* equivocating   96 *gallant* overdressed   101 *shed* spilled   103 *time . . . remembrance* as far back as he can remember   104 *instant* present   110 *muffled* blindfolded   116 *pasty* meat-pie   120 *note* memorandum   131 *past-saving* damned   134 *theoric* theory   135 *chape* tip of the scabbard   138 *neatly* elegantly   143 *con* offer; *in the nature* considering the manner   148 *marvellous* remarkably   151–52 *if . . . hour* if I had but this one hour to live   157 *file* roll   158 *poll* heads   159 *cassocks* cloaks   168–69 *well-weighing* (1) heavy, (2) apt to influence   172 *inter'gatories* questions   174 *botcher's* cobbler, tailor   176 *shrieve's fool* feeble-minded person in the custody of the sheriff; *innocent* mental defective   179 *his . . . falls* he's in danger of death at any moment

PAROLLES The duke knows him for no other but a poor officer of mine, and writ to me this other day to turn him out o' th' band. I think I have his letter in my pocket.

INTERPRETER Marry, we'll search.

190 PAROLLES In good sadness, I do not know; either it is
191 there, or it is upon a file with the duke's other letters in my tent.

INTERPRETER Here 'tis; here's a paper; shall I read it to you?

PAROLLES I do not know if it be it or no.

BERTRAM Our interpreter does it well.

1. LORD Excellently.

INTERPRETER [reads]
'Dian, the count 's a fool, and full of gold.'

198 PAROLLES That is not the duke's letter, sir; that is an ad-
199 vertisement to a proper maid in Florence, one Diana, to take heed of the allurement of one Count Rossillion, a
201 foolish idle boy, but for all that very ruttish. I pray you, sir, put it up again.

INTERPRETER Nay, I'll read it first, by your favor.

PAROLLES My meaning in't, I protest, was very honest in the behalf of the maid; for I knew the young count to be a dangerous and lascivious boy, who is a whale to vir-
207 ginity, and devours up all the fry it finds.

BERTRAM Damnable both-sides rogue!

INTERPRETER [reads]
'When he swears oaths, bid him drop gold, and take it;
210 After he scores, he never pays the score.
211 Half-won is match well made; match, and well make it;
212 He ne'er pays after-debts, take it before.
And say a soldier, Dian, told thee this:
214 Men are to mell with, boys are not to kiss.
215 For count of this, the count 's a fool, I know it,
216 Who pays before, but not when he does owe it.
Thine, as he vowed to thee in thine ear,
Parolles.'

BERTRAM He shall be whipped through the army with this rhyme in's forehead.

221 2. LORD This is your devoted friend, sir, the manifold
222 linguist and the armipotent soldier.

BERTRAM I could endure anything before but a cat, and now he's a cat to me.

INTERPRETER I perceive, sir, by our general's looks, we
226 shall be fain to hang you.

PAROLLES My life, sir, in any case! Not that I am afraid to die, but that my offenses being many, I would repent
229 out the remainder of nature. Let me live, sir, in a dungeon, i' th' stocks, or anywhere, so I may live.

INTERPRETER We'll see what may be done, so you confess freely. Therefore, once more to this Captain Dumain: you have answered to his reputation with the duke and to his valor. What is his honesty?

PAROLLES He will steal, sir, an egg out of a cloister. For
236 rapes and ravishments he parallels Nessus. He professes not keeping of oaths; in breaking 'em he is stronger than Hercules. He will lie, sir, with such volubility that you would think truth were a fool; drunkenness is his best virtue, for he will be swine-drunk, and in his sleep he does little harm, save to his bedclothes about him; but
242 they know his conditions and lay him in straw. I have but little more to say, sir, of his honesty: he has everything that an honest man should not have; what an honest man should have, he has nothing.

1. LORD I begin to love him for this.

BERTRAM For this description of thine honesty? A pox upon him! For me, he's more and more a cat.

INTERPRETER What say you to his expertness in war?

PAROLLES Faith, sir, has led the drum before the English 250 tragedians – to belie him I will not – and more of his soldiership I know not, except in that country he had the honor to be the officer at a place there called Mile-end, 253 to instruct for the doubling of files. I would do the man 254 what honor I can, but of this I am not certain. 255

1. LORD He hath out-villained villainy so far that the rarity redeems him.

BERTRAM A pox on him! He's a cat still.

INTERPRETER His qualities being at this poor price, I 259 need not to ask you if gold will corrupt him to revolt.

PAROLLES Sir, for a cardecue he will sell the fee simple of 261 his salvation, the inheritance of it, and cut th' entail 262 from all remainders, and a perpetual succession for it 263 perpetually.

INTERPRETER What's his brother, the other Captain Dumain?

2. LORD Why does he ask him of me?

INTERPRETER What's he?

PAROLLES E'en a crow o' th' same nest; not altogether so great as the first in goodness, but greater a great deal in evil. He excels his brother for a coward, yet his brother is reputed one of the best that is. In a retreat he outruns any lackey; marry, in coming on he has the cramp. 271

INTERPRETER If your life be saved, will you undertake to betray the Florentine?

PAROLLES Ay, and the captain of his horse, Count Rossillion.

INTERPRETER I'll whisper with the general, and know his pleasure.

PAROLLES [aside] I'll no more drumming; a plague of all drums! Only to seem to deserve well, and to beguile the 278 supposition of that lascivious young boy, the count, have I run into this danger; yet who would have suspected an ambush where I was taken?

INTERPRETER There is no remedy, sir, but you must die. The general says, you that have so traitorously dis- 283 covered the secrets of your army, and made such pes- 284 tiferous reports of men very nobly held, can serve the 285 world for no honest use; therefore you must die. Come, headsman, off with his head!

PAROLLES
O Lord, sir, let me live, or let me see my death!

190 *sadness* earnest   191 *upon* in   198 *advertisement* warning   199 *proper* respectable   201 *ruttish* lecherous   207 *fry* i.e. unsuspecting victims 210 *scores* buys on credit; *score* reckoning   211 *match well made* bargain well concluded   212 *after-debts* debts payable after the transaction is completed; *it* i.e. Bertram's gold   214 *mell* have sexual intercourse   215 *count of* attend to   216 *before* in advance   221 *manifold* multiple   222 *armipotent* mighty in arms   226 *fain* obliged   229 *remainder of nature* rest of my natural life   236 *Nessus* centaur who tried to rape Hercules' wife   236–37 *professes not* does not make a practise of   242 *they* i.e. other people; *conditions* disposition   250–51 *led . . . tragedians* banged the drum to help advertise plays   253 *Mile-end* field in London where citizen recruits were drilled   254 *doubling of files* simple drill maneuvers   255 *this* i.e. his service at Mile-end   259 *qualities* virtues, abilities   261 *cardecue* quart d'ecu, a small French coin; *fee simple* absolute and perpetual ownership   262 *entail* succession   263 *remainders* possible future heirs 271 *lackey* running footman; *marry* indeed; *coming on* advancing, attacking 278–79 *beguile the supposition* deceive the judgment   283 *discovered* disclosed   284 *pestiferous* mischievous   285 *held* esteemed

INTERPRETER
That shall you, and take your leave of all your friends.
        [Unmuffles him.]
So, look about you. Know you any here?
BERTRAM Good morrow, noble captain.
2. LORD God bless you, Captain Parolles.
1. LORD God save you, noble captain.
2. LORD Captain, what greeting will you to my Lord
    Lafew? I am for France.
1. LORD Good captain, will you give me a copy of the
    sonnet you writ to Diana in behalf of the Count Rossil-
298   lion? An I were not a very coward, I'd compel it of you;
    but fare you well.   *Exeunt [Bertram and Lords].*
INTERPRETER You are undone, captain – all but your
    scarf; that has a knot on't yet.
PAROLLES Who cannot be crushed with a plot?
INTERPRETER If you could find out a country where but
    women were that had received so much shame, you
    might begin an impudent nation. Fare ye well, sir; I am
    for France too; we shall speak of you there.
                            Exit [with Soldiers].
PAROLLES
Yet am I thankful. If my heart were great,
'Twould burst at this. Captain I'll be no more,
But I will eat and drink and sleep as soft
As captain shall. Simply the thing I am
Shall make me live. Who knows himself a braggart,
Let him fear this; for it will come to pass
That every braggart shall be found an ass.
Rust, sword! cool, blushes! and, Parolles, live
315 Safest in shame; being fooled, by foolery thrive.
There's place and means for every man alive.
I'll after them.   *Exit.*

                    *

IV, iv   *Enter Helena, Widow, and Diana.*
HELENA
That you may well perceive I have not wronged you,
One of the greatest in the Christian world
3   Shall be my surety; 'fore whose throne 'tis needful,
Ere I can perfect mine intents, to kneel.
Time was I did him a desirèd office,
6   Dear almost as his life; which gratitude
Through flinty Tartar's bosom would peep forth
And answer thanks. I duly am informed
9   His grace is at Marseilles, to which place
We have convenient convoy. You must know
11   I am supposèd dead; the army breaking,

My husband hies him home, where, heaven aiding,
And by the leave of my good lord the king,
We'll be before our welcome.   14
WIDOW   Gentle madam,
You never had a servant to whose trust
Your business was more welcome.
HELENA   Nor you, mistress,
Ever a friend whose thoughts more truly labor
To recompense your love. Doubt not but heaven
Hath brought me up to be your daughter's dower,
As it hath fated her to be my motive   20
And helper to a husband. But, O strange men!
That can such sweet use make of what they hate,
When saucy trusting of the cozened thoughts   23
Defiles the pitchy night; so lust doth play
With what it loathes, for that which is away.   25
But more of this hereafter. You, Diana,
Under my poor instructions yet must suffer
Something in my behalf.
DIANA   Let death and honesty   28
Go with your impositions, I am yours
Upon your will to suffer.
HELENA   Yet, I pray you.   30
But with the word the time will bring on summer, 31
When briars shall have leaves as well as thorns,
And be as sweet as sharp. We must away;
Our wagon is prepared, and time revives us.   34
All's well that ends well; still the fine 's the crown. 35
Whate'er the course, the end is the renown.   *Exeunt.*

                    *

Enter [Lavatch, the] Clown, Old Lady [Countess],   IV, v
and Lafew.
LAFEW No, no, no, your son was misled with a snipped- 1
taffeta fellow there, whose villainous saffron would have 2
made all the unbaked and doughy youth of a nation in 3
his color. Your daughter-in-law had been alive at this
hour, and your son here at home, more advanced by the
king than by that red-tailed humblebee I speak of.   6
COUNTESS I would I had not known him; it was the
death of the most virtuous gentlewoman that ever
nature had praise for creating. If she had partaken of
my flesh and cost me the dearest groans of a mother, I 10
could not have owed her a more rooted love.
LAFEW 'Twas a good lady, 'twas a good lady. We may
pick a thousand sallets ere we light on such another herb. 13
LAVATCH Indeed, sir, she was the sweet marjoram of the
sallet, or rather, the herb of grace.   15
LAFEW They are not herbs, you knave; they are nose   16
herbs.
LAVATCH I am no great Nebuchadnezzar, sir; I have not 18
much skill in grass.   19
LAFEW Whether dost thou profess thyself, a knave or a 20
fool?
LAVATCH A fool, sir, at a woman's service, and a knave at
a man's.
LAFEW Your distinction?
LAVATCH I would cozen the man of his wife, and do his 24
service.
LAFEW So you were a knave at his service indeed.
LAVATCH And I would give his wife my bauble, sir, to do 27
her service.

---

298 *An* if; *very* perfect   315 *fooled* proved a fool; *foolery* folly
IV, iv The house of the Florentine widow   3 *surety* guarantee   6 *which
gratitude* gratitude for which   9 *Marseilles* (a trisyllable, spelled 'Marcellus' in the folio)   14 *be before* arrive ahead of
20 *motive* means, agent (?)   23–24 *When . . . night* when wanton yielding
to the deceptions of lust makes black night even blacker   25 *for* in place
of   28–30 *Let . . . suffer* so long as your instructions allow me to preserve
my honor, I am ready to die at your command   30 *Yet* a while longer
31 *with the word* only with the saying of it (?)   34 *wagon* carriage   35 *fine*
end
IV, v The palace of the Count   1–2 *snipped-taffeta* slashed silk, both gaudy
and flimsy   2 *saffron* yellow dye   3 *unbaked* i.e. half-baked; *doughy* raw
6 *red-tailed humblebee* brightly colored bumblebee   10 *dearest* direst   13
sallets salads   15 *herb of grace* rue   16 *not herbs* not edible plants   16–17
nose herbs aromatic plants   18 *Nebuchadnezzar* (who went mad and ate
grass)   19 *grass* (with pun on 'grace')   20 *Whether* which   24–25 *do his service*
take his place sexually   27 *bauble* coxcomb (with sexual double-entendre)

29 LAFEW I will subscribe for thee, thou art both knave and fool.

LAVATCH At your service.

32 LAFEW No, no, no!

LAVATCH Why, sir, if I cannot serve you, I can serve as great a prince as you are.

LAFEW Who's that? a Frenchman?

36 LAVATCH Faith, sir, 'a has an English name, but his fisnomy is more hotter in France than there.

LAFEW What prince is that?

39 LAVATCH The Black Prince, sir, alias the prince of darkness, alias the devil.

LAFEW Hold thee, there's my purse. I give thee not this
42 to suggest thee from thy master thou talk'st of; serve
43 him still.

44 LAVATCH I am a woodland fellow, sir, that always loved a great fire, and the master I speak of ever keeps a good fire. But sure he is the prince of the world; let his nobility remain in's court; I am for the house with the narrow gate, which I take to be too little for pomp to enter.
49 Some that humble themselves may, but the many will
50 be too chill and tender, and they'll be for the flowery way that leads to the broad gate and the great fire.

LAFEW Go thy ways; I begin to be aweary of thee; and I
53 tell thee so before, because I would not fall out with thee. Go thy ways; let my horses be well looked to, without any tricks.

LAVATCH If I put any tricks upon 'em, sir, they shall be
57 jades' tricks, which are their own right by the law of nature.   *Exit.*

59 LAFEW A shrewd knave and an unhappy.

COUNTESS So 'a is. My lord that's gone made himself much sport out of him. By his authority he remains here, which he thinks is a patent for his sauciness; and
63 indeed he has no pace, but runs where he will.

LAFEW I like him well; 'tis not amiss. And I was about to tell you, since I heard of the good lady's death, and that my lord your son was upon his return home, I moved the king my master to speak in the behalf of my daughter; which, in the minority of them both, his majesty out
69 of a self-gracious remembrance did first propose. His
70 highness hath promised me to do it; and to stop up the displeasure he hath conceived against your son there is no fitter matter. How does your ladyship like it?

COUNTESS With very much content, my lord, and I wish it happily effected.

LAFEW His highness comes post from Marseilles, of as
76 able body as when he numbered thirty; 'a will be here to-morrow, or I am deceived by him that in such intelligence hath seldom failed.

COUNTESS It rejoices me that I hope I shall see him ere I die. I have letters that my son will be here to-night. I shall beseech your lordship to remain with me till they meet together.

LAFEW Madam, I was thinking with what manners I might safely be admitted.

85 COUNTESS You need but plead your honorable privilege.

86 LAFEW Lady, of that I have made a bold charter, but I thank my God it holds yet.

Enter [Lavatch, the] Clown.

LAVATCH O madam, yonder's my lord your son with a patch of velvet on's face. Whether there be a scar under't or no, the velvet knows, but 'tis a goodly patch

of velvet; his left cheek is a cheek of two pile and a half, 91
but his right cheek is worn bare. 92

LAFEW A scar nobly got, or a noble scar, is a good livery of honor; so belike is that.

LAVATCH But it is your carbonadoed face. 95

LAFEW Let us go see your son, I pray you. I long to talk with the young noble soldier.

LAVATCH Faith, there's a dozen of 'em, with delicate fine hats, and most courteous feathers which bow the head and nod at every man.   *Exeunt.*

*

Enter Helena, Widow, and Diana, with two   V, i
Attendants.

HELENA
But this exceeding posting day and night 1
Must wear your spirits low. We cannot help it;
But since you have made the days and nights as one,
To wear your gentle limbs in my affairs, 4
Be bold you do so grow in my requital 5
As nothing can unroot you.
      Enter a Gentleman.
           In happy time –
This man may help me to his majesty's ear,
If he would spend his power. God save you, sir!

GENTLEMAN
And you.

HELENA
Sir, I have seen you in the court of France.

GENTLEMAN
I have been sometimes there.

HELENA
I do presume, sir, that you are not fall'n
From the report that goes upon your goodness;
And therefore, goaded with most sharp occasions,
Which lay nice manners by, I put you to 15
The use of your own virtues, for the which
I shall continue thankful.

GENTLEMAN   What's your will?

HELENA
That it will please you
To give this poor petition to the king,
And aid me with that store of power you have 20
To come into his presence.

GENTLEMAN
The king's not here.

HELENA   Not here, sir?

GENTLEMAN   Not indeed;
He hence removed last night, and with more haste
Than is his use.

WIDOW   Lord, how we lose our pains!

29 *subscribe* vouch   32 *No, no, no!* (Lafew has no intention of accepting Lavatch's *service* as either knave or fool)   36 *fisnomy* physiognomy   39 *Black Prince* nickname of the eldest son of Edward III, hence the *English name* of l. 36   42 *suggest* lure   43 *still* ever   44 *woodland* rustic   49 *many* multitude   50 *chill and tender* susceptible to cold   53 *before* beforehand   57 *jades' tricks* mischievous tricks   59 *shrewd* sharp-tongued   63 *has no pace* is unrestrained   69 *self-gracious remembrance* unprompted generosity   70 *stop up* plug (like a pipeline)   76 *numbered thirty* was thirty years old   85 *honorable privilege* privilege due your honor   86 *charter* license   91 *two . . . half* especially thick velvet   92 *worn bare* unpatched   95 *carbonadoed* slashed (to drain venereal ulcers)
V, i A street in Marseilles   1 *posting* riding   4 *wear* wear out, tire   5 *bold assured; requital* thankfulness   15 *nice* scrupulous   15–16 *I . . . virtues* I help you put your goodness into action

HELENA
All's well that ends well yet,
Though time seem so adverse and means unfit.
I do beseech you, whither is he gone?

GENTLEMAN
Marry, as I take it, to Rossillion,
Whither I am going.

HELENA   I do beseech you, sir,
Since you are like to see the king before me,
Commend the paper to his gracious hand,
Which I presume shall render you no blame,
But rather make you thank your pains for it.
I will come after you with what good speed

35   Our means will make us means.

GENTLEMAN   This I'll do for you.

HELENA
And you shall find yourself to be well thanked,
Whate'er falls more. – We must to horse again.
Go, go, provide.   [Exeunt.]

          *

V, ii   Enter [Lavatch, the] Clown, and Parolles.

PAROLLES Good Master Lavatch, give my Lord Lafew
this letter. I have ere now, sir, been better known to
you, when I have held familiarity with fresher clothes;
4   but I am now, sir, muddied in Fortune's mood, and
smell somewhat strong of her strong displeasure.

LAVATCH Truly, Fortune's displeasure is but sluttish if it
smell so strongly as thou speak'st of; I will henceforth
8   eat no fish of Fortune's buttering. Prithee, allow the
wind!

PAROLLES Nay, you need not to stop your nose, sir; I
spake but by a metaphor.

LAVATCH Indeed, sir, if your metaphor stink, I will stop
my nose, or against any man's metaphor. Prithee, get
thee further.

PAROLLES Pray you, sir, deliver me this paper.

LAVATCH Foh! prithee, stand away! A paper from For-
17   tune's close-stool, to give to a nobleman! Look, here he
comes himself.

       Enter Lafew.

19   Here is a pur of Fortune's, sir, or of Fortune's cat – but
20   not a musk-cat – that has fallen into the unclean fishpond of her displeasure, and, as he says, is muddied
22   withal. Pray you, sir, use the carp as you may, for he
23   looks like a poor decayed, ingenious, foolish, rascally
knave. I do pity his distress in my similes of comfort,
and leave him to your lordship.   [Exit.]

PAROLLES My lord, I am a man whom Fortune hath
cruelly scratched.

LAFEW And what would you have me to do? 'Tis too late
to pare her nails now. Wherein have you played the
knave with Fortune that she should scratch you, who of
herself is a good lady, and would not have knaves thrive
long under her? There's a cardecue for you. Let the
justices make you and Fortune friends; I am for other 33
business.

PAROLLES I beseech your honor to hear me one single
word.

LAFEW You beg a single penny more. Come, you shall
ha't; save your word.

PAROLLES My name, my good lord, is Parolles.

LAFEW You beg more than word then. Cox my passion! 39
Give me your hand. How does your drum?

PAROLLES O my good lord, you were the first that found
me.

LAFEW Was I, in sooth? And I was the first that lost thee.

PAROLLES It lies in you, my lord, to bring me in some
grace, for you did bring me out.

LAFEW Out upon thee, knave! Dost thou put upon me at
once both the office of God and the devil? One brings
thee in grace, and the other brings thee out. [Trumpets
sound.] The king's coming; I know by his trumpets.
Sirrah, inquire further after me; I had talk of you last
night; though you are a fool and a knave, you shall eat.
Go to; follow.

PAROLLES I praise God for you.   [Exeunt.]

          *

     Flourish. Enter King, Old Lady [Countess], Lafew,   V, iii
     the two French Lords, with Attendants.

KING
We lost a jewel of her, and our esteem   1
Was made much poorer by it; but your son,
As mad in folly, lacked the sense to know   3
Her estimation home.

COUNTESS   'Tis past, my liege,
And I beseech your majesty to make it
Natural rebellion, done i' th' blade of youth,   6
When oil and fire, too strong for reason's force,
O'erbears it and burns on.

KING   My honored lady,
I have forgiven and forgotten all,
Though my revenges were high bent upon him,   10
And watched the time to shoot.   11

LAFEW   This I must say –
But first I beg my pardon – the young lord
Did to his majesty, his mother, and his lady,
Offense of mighty note, but to himself
The greatest wrong of all. He lost a wife
Whose beauty did astonish the survey
Of richest eyes, whose words all ears took captive,   17
Whose dear perfection hearts that scorned to serve
Humbly called mistress.

KING   Praising what is lost
Makes the remembrance dear. Well, call him hither;
We are reconciled, and the first view shall kill
All repetition. Let him not ask our pardon;   22
The nature of his great offense is dead,   23
And deeper than oblivion we do bury
Th' incensing relics of it. Let him approach,   25
A stranger, no offender; and inform him

---

35 *Our means ... means* our resources will permit
V, ii The palace of the Count   4 *mood* anger   8 *of Fortune's buttering*
served up by Fortune   8–9 *allow the wind* stand aside   17 *close-stool*
privy   19 *pur* knave (in cards, with pun on 'purr')   20 *musk-cat* (prized
for its scent)   22 *carp* inhabitant of *unclean fishpond*, and a proverbial
chatterer   23 *ingenious* inept (?)   33 *justices* (under Elizabethan law,
responsible for beggars)   39 *more than word* i.e. many words, 'Parolles';
Cox God's
V, iii The palace of the Count   1 *our esteem* our own value   3–4 *know ...
home* appreciate her worth to the full   6 *blade* i.e. greenness, callowness
10 *high bent* grimly aimed   11 *watched the time* waited for the right moment
17 *richest* more experienced   22 *repetition* rehearsing of past grievances
23 *The ... dead* the particular wrongs he committed are forgotten   25 *relics*
reminders

So 'tis our will he should.

GENTLEMAN   I shall, my liege.   [*Exit.*]

KING
What says he to your daughter? Have you spoke?

LAFEW
29   All that he is hath reference to your highness.

KING
Then shall we have a match. I have letters sent me
That sets him high in fame.
                    Enter Count Bertram.

LAFEW   He looks well on't.

KING
32   I am not a day of season,
For thou mayst see a sunshine and a hail
In me at once. But to the brightest beams
Distracted clouds give way; so stand thou forth,
The time is fair again.

BERTRAM   My high-repented blames,
Dear sovereign, pardon to me.

KING   All is whole;
Not one word more of the consumèd time.
39   Let's take the instant by the forward top;
For we are old, and on our quick'st decrees
Th' inaudible and noiseless foot of time
Steals ere we can effect them. You remember
The daughter of this lord?

BERTRAM
Admiringly, my liege. At first
I stuck my choice upon her, ere my heart
Durst make too bold a herald of my tongue;
47   Where the impression of mine eye infixing,
48   Contempt his scornful perspective did lend me,
49   Which warped the line of every other favor,
50   Scorned a fair color or expressed it stol'n,
51   Extended or contracted all proportions
To a most hideous object. Thence it came
53   That she whom all men praised, and whom myself,
Since I have lost, have loved, was in mine eye
The dust that did offend it.

KING   Well excused;
That thou didst love her strikes some scores away
57   From the great compt. But love that comes too late,
Like a remorseful pardon slowly carried,
59   To the great sender turns a sour offense,
Crying, 'That's good that's gone.' Our rash faults
Make trivial price of serious things we have,
62   Not knowing them until we know their grave.
63   Oft our displeasures, to ourselves unjust,
64   Destroy our friends, and after weep their dust;
65   Our own love, waking, cries to see what's done,
66   While shameful hate sleeps out the afternoon.
Be this sweet Helen's knell, and now forget her.
Send forth your amorous token for fair Maudlin.
The main consents are had, and here we'll stay
To see our widower's second marriage day.

COUNTESS
Which better than the first, O dear heaven, bless,
72   Or, ere they meet, in me, O nature, cesse!

LAFEW
Come on, my son, in whom my house's name
74   Must be digested, give a favor from you
To sparkle in the spirits of my daughter,
That she may quickly come.
                    [*Bertram gives him a ring.*]

By my old beard
And every hair that's on't, Helen that's dead
Was a sweet creature; such a ring as this,
The last that e'er I took her leave at court,   79
I saw upon her finger.

BERTRAM   Hers it was not.

KING
Now pray you let me see it; for mine eye,
While I was speaking, oft was fastened to't.
                    [*Takes the ring.*]
This ring was mine, and when I gave it Helen
I bade her, if her fortunes ever stood
Necessitied to help, that by this token   85
I would relieve her. Had you that craft to reave her   86
Of what should stead her most?   87

BERTRAM   My gracious sovereign,
Howe'er it pleases you to take it so,
The ring was never hers.

COUNTESS   Son, on my life,
I have seen her wear it, and she reckoned it
At her life's rate.

LAFEW   I am sure I saw her wear it.

BERTRAM
You are deceived, my lord; she never saw it.
In Florence was it from a casement thrown me,
Wrapped in a paper, which contained the name
Of her that threw it. Noble she was, and thought
I stood engaged; but when I had subscribed   96
To mine own fortune, and informed her fully
I could not answer in that course of honor   98
As she had made the overture, she ceased
In heavy satisfaction, and would never   100
Receive the ring again.

KING   Plutus himself,   101
That knows the tinct and multiplying med'cine,   102
Hath not in nature's mystery more science   103
Than I have in this ring. 'Twas mine, 'twas Helen's,
Whoever gave it you. Then if you know   105
That you are well acquainted with yourself,
Confess 'twas hers, and by what rough enforcement
You got it from her. She called the saints to surety
That she would never put it from her finger
Unless she gave it to yourself in bed –
Where you have never come – or sent it us
Upon her great disaster.   112

BERTRAM   She never saw it.

29 *hath reference to* submits himself to   32 *of season* of any one season, i.e. of steady weather   39 *forward top* forelock   47 *Where* i.e. upon Lafew's daughter   48 *perspective* distorting optical glass   49 *warped . . . favor* made the features of all other faces seem ugly   50 *color* complexion; *expressed it stol'n* declared it artificial   51–52 *Extended . . . object* stretched out or cramped together all other forms till they appeared hideous   53 *she* Helena   57 *compt* account   59 *turns . . . offense* goes sour on him   62 *Not . . . grave* not appreciating them till we've lost them for good   63 *displeasures* offenses   64 *weep their dust* mourn over their ashes   65 *waking* belatedly coming to its senses   66 *hate sleeps* i.e. having sated itself by destroying the friend, while love slept   72 *they* the two marriages; *meet* resemble each other; *cesse* cease   74 *digested* assimilated; *favor* love-token   79 *last . . . leave* last time I took leave of her   85 *Necessitied to* in need of   86 *reave* despoil   87 *stead* aid   96 *stood engaged* was interested (in her)   96–97 *subscribed . . . fortune* explained my situation   98 *answer . . . honor* commit myself to the same degree   100 *In heavy satisfaction* disappointed but convinced   101 *Plutus* god of riches   102 *tinct . . . med'cine* elixir for converting base metals to gold   103 *science* knowledge   105–06 *if . . . yourself* if you know what's good for you (?)   112 *Upon . . . disaster* in time of direst peril

KING
Thou speak'st it falsely, as I love mine honor,
And mak'st conjectural fears to come into me
Which I would fain shut out. If it should prove
That thou art so inhuman – 'twill not prove so,
And yet I know not – thou didst hate her deadly,
And she is dead ; which nothing but to close
Her eyes myself could win me to believe,
More than to see this ring. Take him away.
                    [Attendants arrest Bertram.]
121   My forepast proofs, howe'er the matter fall,
122   Shall tax my fears of little vanity,
123   Having vainly feared too little. Away with him ;
We'll sift this matter further.
BERTRAM   If you shall prove
This ring was ever hers, you shall as easy
Prove that I husbanded her bed in Florence,
Where yet she never was.   *[Exit, guarded.]*
KING
I am wrapped in dismal thinkings.
          Enter a Gentleman.
GENTLEMAN   Gracious sovereign,
Whether I have been to blame or no, I know not :
Here's a petition from a Florentine,
131   Who hath for four or five removes come short
132   To tender it herself. I undertook it,
Vanquished thereto by the fair grace and speech
Of the poor suppliant, who by this, I know,
135   Is here attending. Her business looks in her
136   With an importing visage, and she told me,
137   In a sweet verbal brief, it did concern
Your highness with herself.
[KING *reads*] *a letter.* 'Upon his many protestations to
marry me when his wife was dead, I blush to say it, he
won me. Now is the Count Rossillion a widower, his
vows are forfeited to me, and my honor 's paid to him.
He stole from Florence, taking no leave, and I follow
him to his country for justice : grant it me, O king ! In
you it best lies ; otherwise a seducer flourishes, and a
poor maid is undone.
                              Diana Capilet.'
148   LAFEW I will buy me a son-in-law in a fair, and toll for
this. I'll none of him.
KING
The heavens have thought well on thee, Lafew,
To bring forth this discov'ry. Seek these suitors.
Go speedily, and bring again the count.
          [Exeunt Gentleman and an Attendant.]
I am afeard the life of Helen, lady,
Was foully snatched.
COUNTESS   Now justice on the doers !
          Enter Bertram [guarded].
KING
155   I wonder, sir, sith wives are monsters to you,

And that you fly them as you swear them lordship,   156
Yet you desire to marry.
          Enter Widow, [and] Diana.
                    What woman 's that ?
DIANA
I am, my lord, a wretched Florentine,
Derivèd from the ancient Capilet.   159
My suit, as I do understand, you know,
And therefore know how far I may be pitied.
WIDOW
I am her mother, sir, whose age and honor
Both suffer under this complaint we bring,
And both shall cease, without your remedy.
KING
Come hither, count ; do you know these women ?
BERTRAM
My lord, I neither can nor will deny
But that I know them. Do they charge me further ?
DIANA
Why do you look so strange upon your wife ?
BERTRAM
She's none of mine, my lord.
DIANA   If you shall marry,
You give away this hand, and that is mine ;   170
You give away heaven's vows, and those are mine ;
You give away myself, which is known mine ;
For I by vow am so embodied yours   173
That she which marries you must marry me –
Either both or none.
LAFEW Your reputation comes too short for my daugh-
ter ; you are no husband for her.
BERTRAM
My lord, this is a fond and desp'rate creature,   178
Whom sometime I have laughed with ; let your highness   179
Lay a more noble thought upon mine honor
Than for to think that I would sink it here.
KING
Sir, for my thoughts, you have them ill to friend
Till your deeds gain them. Fairer prove your honor
Than in my thought it lies !
DIANA   Good my lord,
Ask him upon his oath if he does think
He had not my virginity.
KING
What say'st thou to her ?
BERTRAM   She's impudent, my lord,   187
And was a common gamester to the camp.   188
DIANA
He does me wrong, my lord. If I were so,
He might have bought me at a common price.
Do not believe him. O, behold this ring,
Whose high respect and rich validity   192
Did lack a parallel ; yet for all that
He gave it to a commoner o' th' camp,
If I be one.
COUNTESS   He blushes, and 'tis hit.   195
Of six preceding ancestors, that gem,
Conferred by testament to th' sequent issue,   197
Hath it been owed and worn. This is his wife ;   198
That ring 's a thousand proofs.
KING   Methought you said
You saw one here in court could witness it.
DIANA
I did, my lord, but loath am to produce

---

121 *forepast proofs* ills already undergone   122 *tax . . . vanity* suffice to
establish the legitimacy of my fears   123 *vainly* foolishly   131 *removes*
changes of residence of the court   132 *tender* offer   135 *looks* manifests
itself   136 *importing* urgent   137 *verbal brief* oral message   148 *in a fair*
(where cheap and stolen goods are sold); *toll for* get rid of   155 *sith* since
156 *smear them lordship* promise them marriage   159 *Derivèd* descended
170 *this hand* Bertram's   173 *embodied yours* united to you   178 *fond*
foolish   179 *sometime* formerly   187 *impudent* immodest, wanton   188
gamester lewd person   192 *respect* worth ; *validity* value   195 *'tis hit* the
charge is proved   197 *sequent issue* next generation   198 *owed* owned

So bad an instrument; his name 's Parolles.

LAFEW
I saw the man to-day, if man he be.

KING
Find him and bring him hither.   *[Exit an Attendant.]*

BERTRAM   What of him?
205   He's quoted for a most perfidious slave,
206   With all the spots o' th' world taxed and deboshed,
Whose nature sickens but to speak a truth.
Am I or that or this for what he'll utter,
That will speak anything?

KING   She hath that ring of yours.

BERTRAM
I think she has. Certain it is I liked her,
211   And boarded her i' th' wanton way of youth.
She knew her distance and did angle for me,
213   Madding my eagerness with her restraint –
214   As all impediments in fancy's course
215   Are motives of more fancy – and in fine
216   Her infinite cunning with her modern grace
217   Subdued me to her rate. She got the ring,
And I had that which any inferior might
At market price have bought.

DIANA   I must be patient.
You that have turned off a first so noble wife
221   May justly diet me. I pray you yet –
Since you lack virtue, I will lose a husband –
Send for your ring, I will return it home,
And give me mine again.

BERTRAM   I have it not.

KING
What ring was yours, I pray you?

DIANA   Sir, much like
The same upon your finger.

KING
Know you this ring? This ring was his of late.

DIANA
And this was it I gave him, being abed.

KING
The story then goes false, you threw it him
Out of a casement?

DIANA   I have spoke the truth.
          Enter Parolles.

BERTRAM
My lord, I do confess the ring was hers.

KING
232   You boggle shrewdly; every feather starts you.
Is this the man you speak of?

DIANA   Ay, my lord.

KING
Tell me, sirrah – but tell me true, I charge you,
Not fearing the displeasure of your master,
236   Which, on your just proceeding, I'll keep off –
237   By him and by this woman here what know you?

PAROLLES So please your majesty, my master hath been
an honorable gentleman. Tricks he hath had in him,
which gentlemen have.

KING Come, come, to th' purpose. Did he love this
woman?

PAROLLES Faith, sir, he did love her; but how?

KING How, I pray you?

PAROLLES He did love her, sir, as a gentleman loves a
woman.

KING How is that?

PAROLLES He loved her, sir, and loved her not.   248

KING As thou art a knave, and no knave. What an equivocal companion is this!   250

PAROLLES I am a poor man, and at your majesty's command.

LAFEW He's a good drum, my lord, but a naughty orator. 253

DIANA Do you know he promised me marriage?

PAROLLES Faith, I know more than I'll speak.

KING But wilt thou not speak all thou know'st?

PAROLLES Yes, so please your majesty. I did go between
them as I said; but more than that, he loved her – for
indeed he was mad for her, and talked of Satan and of
Limbo and of Furies and I know not what. Yet I was
in that credit with them at that time that I knew of their
going to bed, and of other motions, as promising her   261
marriage, and things which would derive me ill will to   262
speak of; therefore I will not speak what I know.

KING Thou hast spoken all already, unless thou canst say
they are married; but thou art too fine in thy evidence; 265
therefore stand aside.
This ring you say was yours?

DIANA   Ay, my good lord.

KING
Where did you buy it? or who gave it you?

DIANA
It was not given me, nor I did not buy it.

KING
Who lent it you?

DIANA   It was not lent me neither.

KING
Where did you find it then?

DIANA   I found it not.

KING
If it were yours by none of all these ways,
How could you give it him?

DIANA   I never gave it him.

LAFEW This woman 's an easy glove, my lord; she goes
off and on at pleasure.

KING
This ring was mine; I gave it his first wife.

DIANA
It might be yours or hers for aught I know.

KING
Take her away, I do not like her now;
To prison with her, and away with him.
Unless thou tell'st me where thou hadst this ring,
Thou diest within this hour.

DIANA   I'll never tell you.

KING
Take her away.

DIANA   I'll put in bail, my liege.

KING
I think thee now some common customer.   283

DIANA
By Jove, if ever I knew man, 'twas you.

205 *quoted* noted   206 *taxed and deboshed* charged with debauchery   211
boarded accosted   213 *Madding* spurring   214 *in fancy's course* in amorous
pursuit   215 *fancy* erotic fantasies; *in fine* at length   216 *modern* commonplace   217 *Subdued . . . rate* made me accept her terms   221 *diet me* i.e. pay
me my wages and send me packing   232 *boggle shrewdly* shy nervously;
starts startles   236 *on . . . proceeding* if you tell the truth   237 *By* concerning
248 *loved . . . not* pursued her sexually but had no other interest in her
250 *companion* rascal   253 *drum* drummer; *naughty* worthless   261 *motions*
proposals   262 *derive* gain   265 *fine* subtle   283 *customer* prostitute

KING
Wherefore hast thou accused him all this while?
DIANA
Because he's guilty, and he is not guilty.
He knows I am no maid, and he'll swear to't;
I'll swear I am a maid and he knows not.
Great king, I am no strumpet, by my life;
I am either maid, or else this old man's wife.
      [Points to Lafew.]
KING
She does abuse our ears; to prison with her!
DIANA
Good mother, fetch my bail. Stay, royal sir,
                              [Exit Widow.]
293   The jeweller that owes the ring is sent for,
294   And he shall surety me. But for this lord,
       Who hath abused me, as he knows himself,
296   Though yet he never harmed me, here I quit him.
       He knows himself my bed he hath defiled,
       And at that time he got his wife with child.
       Dead though she be, she feels her young one kick.
300   So there's my riddle: one that's dead is quick –
       And now behold the meaning.
            Enter Helena and Widow.
301   KING   Is there no exorcist
302   Beguiles the truer office of mine eyes?
       Is't real that I see?
       HELENA   No, my good lord,
       'Tis but the shadow of a wife you see,
       The name and not the thing.
       BERTRAM   Both, both; O, pardon!
       HELENA
       O my good lord, when I was like this maid

I found you wondrous kind. There is your ring,
And look you, here's your letter. This it says:
'When from my finger you can get this ring,
And are by me with child,' etc. This is done.
Will you be mine, now you are doubly won?
BERTRAM
If she, my liege, can make me know this clearly,
I'll love her dearly – ever, ever dearly.
HELENA
If it appear not plain, and prove untrue,
Deadly divorce step between me and you.
O my dear mother, do I see you living?
LAFEW
Mine eyes smell onions; I shall weep anon.
      [To Parolles]
Good Tom Drum, lend me a handkercher. So, I thank
thee. Wait on me home; I'll make sport with thee. Let
thy curtsies alone; they are scurvy ones.   320
KING
Let us from point to point this story know,
To make the even truth in pleasure flow.   322
      [To Diana]
If thou beest yet a fresh uncroppèd flower,
Choose thou thy husband, and I'll pay thy dower;
For I can guess that by thy honest aid
Thou kept'st a wife herself, thyself a maid.
Of that and all the progress more and less
Resolvedly more leisure shall express.   328
All yet seems well, and if it end so meet,   329
The bitter past, more welcome is the sweet.   *Flourish.*

[EPILOGUE]

The king's a beggar, now the play is done.
All is well ended if this suit be won,
That you express content; which we will pay   333
With strife to please you, day exceeding day.   334
Ours be your patience then, and yours our parts;   335
Your gentle hands lend us, and take our hearts.
                              Exeunt omnes.

293 *owes* owns 294 *surety me* be my security 296 *quit* acquit, release
300 *quick* alive (with pun on *with child*) 301 *exorcist* magician 302
Beguiles . . . office deceives the true vision 320 *curtsies* reverences 322 *even*
exact 328 *Resolvedly* with full explanation 329 *meet* fittingly 333 *ex-press content* i.e. by applause 334 *strife* effort 335 *Ours . . . parts* we will
become the audience (to your applause) while you become the actors (by
applauding)

MEASURE FOR MEASURE

INTRODUCTION

Measure for Measure did not fare well at the hands of the nineteenth-century critics, who, not unnaturally, were inclined to look askance at its outspoken treatment of sex. Not only were they made uncomfortable by certain parts of the plot, especially the trick by which Mariana is substituted for Isabella in the assignation with Angelo, but they found the comic scenes offensive. Even so intelligent a critic as Dowden thought that the purpose of parts of the play was "to present without disguise or extenuation a world of moral licence and corruption." The twentieth century, however, has been more receptive to the play. We are no longer shocked by its theme, and we can approach the plot with a fuller understanding of the feelings of Shakespeare and his contemporaries towards the situations which it portrays. Above all, those who have been fortunate enough to see the play performed by a good cast have learnt that it is a brilliant piece of stagecraft.

"A play Caled Mesur for Mesur" by "Shaxberd" was performed "by his Majesties plaiers" before King James I and his court on December 26, during the Christmastide festivities, in the year 1604, although it remained in manuscript until 1623, when it was included in the collected edition of Shakespeare's plays (the first folio). The play had almost certainly been but recently written and acted when it was given at court in 1604, and it was thus composed at about the same time as *Othello*. It was therefore later than *Hamlet* by three or four years, and a year or so earlier than *Lear* and *Macbeth*, but it was written when Shakespeare's powers were at their full maturity and during the period which also produced his great tragic masterpieces.

The story on which Shakespeare based his plot had been told in Italian by Giraldi Cinthio in his *Hecatommithi* (or Hundred Tales), among which Shakespeare also found the story of Othello. The same tale had been the basis for George Whetstone's *Promos and Cassandra* (1578), a play in two parts, and for one of the novels in the same author's *Heptameron of Civil Discourses* (1582), both of which were known to Shakespeare. Whether he knew any of the other versions of the same story is doubtful. In all of them, however, the character corresponding to Isabella yields up her chastity in a vain attempt to save the condemned man, so Mariana and her substitution are Shakespeare's addition to the traditional pattern of the tale. Shakespeare had recently made use of a similar substitution in the plot of *All's Well That Ends Well*, and he availed himself of the device a second time in order to keep Isabella's chastity inviolate. The comic scenes may have been suggested to Shakespeare by certain episodes in *Promos and Cassandra*, but in the main they are of his own invention.

Shakespeare thus based his play, as he so often did, on a story compounded of situations which were in some degree already familiar to many of his audience, and he could count on this very familiarity to determine some of their responses to those situations. The substitution, or "bed trick" as it has been called, would not have been regarded as a mean and rather offensive piece of deception; it was a time-honored ruse by which the injured heroine had won her rights against the man who had wronged her. And Mariana had been formally betrothed to Angelo; as the Duke tells her,

> He is your husband on a pre-contract;
> To bring you thus together, 'tis no sin.

Such a contract was binding in Shakespeare's day; neither party could contract a legal marriage with anyone else while it remained in force, and in some circumstances it was regarded as constituting marriage, without the church ceremony which normally followed after a brief interval. But if this was true of Angelo and Mariana, what of Claudio and Juliet? Claudio declares:

> ... upon a true contract
> I got possession of Julietta's bed.
> You know the lady, she is fast my wife
> Save that we do the denunciation lack
> Of outward order. This we came not to,
> Only for propagation of a dower
> Remaining in the coffer of her friends,
> From whom we thought it meet to hide our love
> Till time had made them for us.

There is a distinction here which Shakespeare's audience would not have been slow to observe. Though the lovers had plighted their troth in secret to one another, they were not formally betrothed; they had postponed the open declaration of intention that would make the contract binding, in the hope that Juliet's family would in time come to favor the match and provide a dowry. Hence the conduct of Claudio and Juliet had brought them within the scope of the law against fornication which Angelo was striving to put into effect. Still, even though they are guilty in the eyes of the law, we cannot help feeling that their offense was a comparatively light one, and the fact that Claudio has been condemned to death for his offense is presented to the audience as an example of Angelo's extreme rigor in the administration of justice.

Some present-day readers may grant readily enough the changes in manners and habits of thought that demand such explanations as the foregoing, but still feel that, when all is said, Isabella shows a quite unnecessary excess of horror in the face of Angelo's proposal. It may be true that, as a character remarks in one of Aldous Huxley's novels, "Contraception has rendered chastity superfluous," and that, in the last resort, sexual purity is a matter of personal fastidiousness, but we are not yet so far removed from the past that we cannot recognize an insistence on chastity as the expression not only of a long-enduring concept of social order but of the ideals of self-abnegation and devotion inculcated by centuries of Christian teaching. Besides, Isabella is on the eve of entering her novitiate; she longs for a life of self-denial and religious discipline; and even to the worldly Lucio she is "as a thing enskied and sainted." Angelo, too, is acutely conscious of her purity when, with feelings akin to horror, he exclaims:

> O cunning enemy that, to catch a saint,
> With saints dost bait thy hook: most dangerous
> Is that temptation that doth goad us on
> To sin in loving virtue. Never could the strumpet
> With all her double vigor, art and nature,
> Once stir my temper; but this virtuous maid
> Subdues me quite;

and, indeed, Isabella's unsullied innocence is nowhere more effectively revealed than in her complete inability to respond to or even perceive Angelo's innuendoes. Even if there is a hint of shrillness in her outbursts against Angelo and her wavering brother, it must not be forgotten that she is under severe emotional stress, faced with a horrible dilemma from which there seems to be no escape. Any momentary criticism of her is stilled by her words near the end of the play when, still believing Claudio to be dead, she kneels beside Mariana to plead for Angelo:

> I partly think
> A due sincerity governed his deeds
> Till he did look on me. Since it is so,
> Let him not die; my brother had but justice,
> In that he did the thing for which he died.
> For Angelo,
> His act did not o'ertake his bad intent,
> And must be buried but as an intent
> That perished by the way.

Angelo, too, is presented with penetrating insight. He is not a villain by nature, and Shakespeare shows him as having earned his reputation for firmness and probity. But he is too sure of himself, too self-confident of his character and position, and hence, when temptation comes, his weakness is revealed. His soliloquies betray full consciousness of the moral obloquy of his intentions, and one has the feeling in the first half of the play of watching the moral disintegration of a resolute and upright man. Yet Angelo is never wholly lost, entangled as he becomes in the consequences of his fall from grace; he never becomes so hardened that to him, as to Macbeth, "Returning were as tedious as go o'er." When his guilt is revealed he attempts no defense or extenuation, but admits his shame almost with a sense of relief:

> O my dread lord,
> I should be guiltier than my guiltiness
> To think I can be undiscernible,
> When I perceive your grace, like power divine,
> Hath looked upon my passes. Then, good prince,
> No longer session hold upon my shame,
> But let my trial be mine own confession.
> Immediate sentence, then, and sequent death
> Is all the grace I beg.

But, though Angelo is saved, he is saved only by good fortune, not by his character or his intentions, and tragedy has been averted.

In no other comedy of Shakespeare is there quite the same sense of tragedy averted, and to this fact are closely related the peculiar tone and technique of the play. *Measure for Measure* falls into two parts, and the division comes in III, i when the Duke steps forward at line 152. Up to this point the action and characterization have been developed with a full awareness of all the moral and tragic issues implicit in them, so that an *impasse* has been reached where it seems that any further change in the situation must inevitably produce immediate tragic consequences. At this moment, however, the Duke intervenes and for the rest of the play he manipulates every phase of the action in order to bring it to a happy conclusion. "Craft against vice I must apply," he proclaims, and his method is that of the comedy of intrigue. Shakespeare uses all his art to cover up this sudden change of technique, so that in performance it is barely noticed. He shows us as little as possible of the characters who have thus far been the center of interest; Claudio speaks not another word after III, i, 151; until the last scene just enough is shown of Angelo to suggest his uneasiness and stifled remorse; during the same interval Isabella is little more than the Duke's assistant in bringing Mariana into the plot. Instead we are distracted by the lively humor of the prison scenes and the impertinences of Lucio, by the glimpse of Mariana's "moated grange," by one of the loveliest songs in all Shakespeare, and by the sense of approaching climax in the Duke's decision to "return." Finally, the long last scene (V, i) is carefully and ingeniously organized for the maximum of theatrical effect, and builds up step by step to the reappearance of Claudio and the final forgiveness. All this is in marked contrast to the weightier, more meditative movement of the earlier part of the play.

In the first half of the play Shakespeare shows a full awareness of the human issues involved: Angelo's shock at the discovery of something in himself that he is powerless to resist, Isabella's distress in the dilemma in which she finds herself, and, above all, Claudio's sudden discovery of the horror of death and his pitiful wish to cling to life. What is perhaps the most disturbing feature of the play, however, is the disregard of similar human feelings throughout the greater part of the final scene. For a while it seems as if Isabella and Mariana have merely been brought on to the stage to be played with as a cat plays with a mouse; the structure of the scene, in its dependence on mere dramatic contrivance and manipulation, is such that until near the end normal human reactions in these characters would have been out of place. Yet, though human feelings have been temporarily ignored, moral issues have not; it is essential to the conception of the play that not only should Angelo be forced to make full acknowledgment of his guilt, but that before he can be saved Isabella, against whom he had most offended, should kneel to plead for his life in ignorance of her brother's safety.

Moral issues, indeed, dominate the play. Its title, *Measure for Measure*, recalls Matthew vii, 1–2, a part of the Sermon on the Mount: "Judge not that ye be not judged. For with what judgment ye judge, ye shall be judged; and with what measure ye mete, it shall be measured to you again." These words were a plea for the mitigation of the old Mosaic law, yet in the one place in the text of the play where the title phrase occurs it is interpreted as "an eye for an eye, and a tooth for a tooth":

> "An Angelo for Claudio, death for death!"
> Haste still pays haste, and leisure answers leisure,
> Like doth quit like, and Measure still for Measure.

But this rigid interpretation, which seemingly condemns Angelo to the block, actually saves him from it; the wider application of Christ's words was uppermost in Shakespeare's mind. Isabella's plea for Claudio earlier in the play was based on the old antithesis of justice and mercy, on which Shakespeare had already based the trial scene in *The Merchant of Venice* (so that, almost inevitably, echoes of Portia's famous speech fall from Isabella's lips), and the conclusion of the play exalts the Christian ideal of forgiveness at the expense of justice.

Nevertheless, *Measure for Measure* is rich in ironies which complicate the dramatic as well as the verbal texture, and add to the fascination of the play. It is not the gay comic irony of *As You Like It* and *Twelfth Night*, but something far closer to that of the great tragedies. Angelo's words,

> 'Tis one thing to be tempted, Escalus,
> Another thing to fall....
> You may not so extenuate his offense
> For I have had such faults; but rather tell me,
> When I that censure him do so offend,
> Let mine own judgment pattern out my death
> And nothing come in partial,

echo in our minds through many subsequent scenes. The sinister double meanings of Angelo's first suggestions to Isabella and her innocent misrepresentation of them are highly ironical, and there is even a certain grim logic, barely hinted at, in Angelo's demand that if Isabella would have him ignore her brother's offense she should be prepared to condone it by committing it herself. The sense of irony in the later part of the play is less oppressive, but it is still there, especially in the contrast between the words in which the Duke addresses Angelo and his real feelings toward him. Yet the final impression left by the play is not one of a clouded or warped attitude toward life. Even though the Duke may allege that he has seen "corruption boil and bubble/Till it o'errun the stew," the picture the play presents is far from being one of mere corruption and disorder. Dark and light are constantly set over against one another. Even Claudio's terror in the face of death is counterbalanced by the nonchalance of Barnardine, which, however horrifying to a strict churchman, symbolizes an enduring human trait. Laws against sexual offenses, too, may by their very stringency defeat their aims; the last word is with Pompey: "Does your worship mean to geld and splay all the youth of the city?" Nor is Angelo, who has sinned most of all, beyond redemption:

> They say best men are moulded out of faults,
> And, for the most, become much more the better
> For being a little bad....

Shakespeare's final judgment in this play is sane and sure; he may be aware, sometimes terribly aware, of human vice and folly, but there is no hint that he despairs of mankind.

University of Chicago   R. C. BALD

NOTE ON THE TEXT

Measure for Measure was first printed in the folio of 1623 from copy which appears to have been a transcript of Shakespeare's draft made by the scrivener Ralph Crane. The act–scene division supplied marginally for reference in the present edition is that given currency by later editors, and differs from the folio division at several points: I, ii combines two scenes in the folio (correctly), and III, i and ii divide one scene in the folio (incorrectly). Below are listed all material departures from the folio text, with the adopted reading in italics followed by the ·folio reading in roman.

The names of all the Actors ... The Scene : Vienna (printed at the end of the play in F)
I, ii, 12 *Why, Why?* 130 *morality* mortality
I, iii, 20 *jades* weedes 27 *Becomes* (not in F) 42 *sight* fight 43 *it* in
I, iv, 54 *givings-out* giving-out 77 *doubt–* doubt. 78 *make* makes
II, i, 12 *your* our 39 *breaks* brakes 67 *honor–* honour. 70 *woman–* woman.
II, ii, 58 *back* (not in F) 96 *new* now 99 *ere* here 149 *sicles* Sickles 150 *rates* rate
II, iv, 9 *sere* feard 53 *or* and 76 *me* (not in F) 94 *all-binding* all-building 127 *Women, help heaven!* Women? Helpe heaven;
III, i, 29 *sire* fire 52 *me to hear them* them to heare me 69 *Though* Through 91 *enew* emmew 96 *damnedest* damnest 130 *penury* periury 210 *by* to
III, ii, 7 *law* Law; 23 *array* away 37 *Free from* From 45 *it* (not in F) 70 *bondage: if* bondage if 142 *dearer* deare 211 *and* and as
IV, i, 3 *day,* day 25 *welcome* well come 58 s.d. *Exeunt* Exit
IV, ii, 39 *thief. If* Theefe. / Clo. If 53 *yare* Y'are 55 s.d. *Exeunt* Exit 96 *lordship's* Lords 139 *reckless* wreaklesse
IV, iii, 7 *marry, then* marrie then, 15 *Forthright* Forthlight 22 *What . . . Barnardine!* (followed in F by s.d. 'Barnardine within.') 86 *th' under* yond 102 *I'll . . . speed* (followed in F by s.d. 'Isabell within.')
IV, iv, 2 *manner.* manner, 5 *redeliver* reliver 13–16 *Well, I . . . you well* (prose in F) 24 *off* of 30 *lived* livèd
IV, v, 6 *Flavius'* Flavia's
V, i, 13 *our* your 116 *ripened* ripenèd 168 *her face* your face 181–82 *Silence . . . himself* (prose in F) 225 *affianced* affiancèd 258 *My . . . throughly* (prose in F) 303 *unhallowed* unhallowèd 419 *confiscation* confutation 442 *governed* governèd 473 s.d. *Juliet* Iulietta 534 *that's* that

MEASURE FOR MEASURE

Vincentio, the Duke
Angelo, the deputy
Escalus, an ancient lord
Claudio, a young gentleman
Lucio, a fantastic
Two other like Gentlemen
[Varrius, a gentleman attending on the Duke]
Provost
[A Justice]
Thomas ⎫
Peter ⎭ two friars

Elbow, a simple constable
Froth, a foolish gentleman
Clown [Pompey, tapster to Mistress Overdone]
Abhorson, an executioner
Barnardine, a dissolute prisoner
Isabella, sister to Claudio
Mariana, betrothed to Angelo
Juliet, beloved of Claudio
Francisca, a nun
Mistress Overdone, a bawd
[Lords, Officers, Citizens, Boy, and Attendants]

The Scene : Vienna

*

I, i   *Enter Duke, Escalus, Lords [, and Attendants].*
DUKE Escalus.
ESCALUS My lord.
DUKE
    Of government the properties to unfold,
    Would seem in me t'affect speech and discourse,
5   Since I am put to know that your own science
6   Exceeds, in that, the lists of all advice
    My strength can give you. Then no more remains
8   But that, to your sufficiency, as your worth is able,
    And let them work. The nature of our people,
    Our city's institutions, and the terms
    For common justice, y'are as pregnant in
    As art and practice hath enrichèd any
    That we remember. There is our commission,
14 From which we would not have you warp. Call hither,
    I say, bid come before us Angelo.   *[Exit an Attendant.]*
16 What figure of us think you he will bear ?
    For you must know, we have with special soul
    Elected him our absence to supply,
    Lent him our terror, dressed him with our love,
20 And given his deputation all the organs
    Of our own power. What think you of it ?
ESCALUS
    If any in Vienna be of worth

To undergo such ample grace and honor,
It is Lord Angelo.
        Enter Angelo.
DUKE   Look where he comes.
ANGELO
    Always obedient to your grace's will,
    I come to know your pleasure.
DUKE   Angelo,
    There is a kind of character in thy life,   27
    That to th' observer doth thy history
    Fully unfold. Thyself and thy belongings   29
    Are not thine own so proper, as to waste   30
    Thyself upon thy virtues, they on thee.
    Heaven doth with us as we with torches do,
    Not light them for themselves ; for if our virtues
    Did not go forth of us, 'twere all alike
    As if we had them not. Spirits are not finely touched 35
    But to fine issues, nor Nature never lends   36
    The smallest scruple of her excellence
    But like a thrifty goddess she determines
    Herself the glory of a creditor,
    Both thanks and use. But I do bend my speech   40
    To one that can my part in him advertise.   41
    Hold therefore, Angelo :
    In our remove be thou at full ourself.   43
    Mortality and mercy in Vienna
    Live in thy tongue and heart. Old Escalus,
    Though first in question, is thy secondary.   46
    Take thy commission.
ANGELO   Now, good my lord,
    Let there be some more test made of my mettle   48
    Before so noble and so great a figure
    Be stamped upon it.
DUKE   No more evasion.
    We have with a leavened and preparèd choice   51

I, i The palace of Duke Vincentio **5** *science* knowledge **6** *lists* limits
8 (one or more lines probably missing after this line) **14** *warp* swerve **16**
What . . . bear i.e. how will he represent me **20** *deputation* office as deputy ;
organs instruments, authority **27** *character* charactry (legible sign) **29**
belongings endowments **30** *proper* exclusively **35** *touched* i.e. endowed
36 *But . . . issues* i.e. except to the extent that something fine comes of them
('. . . the tree is known by his fruit' Matthew xii, 33) **40** *use* interest **41** *my
part . . . advertise* instruct that part of me now vested in him **43** *remove*
absence **46** *first in question* the first to be considered **48** *mettle* (Angelo
converts ll. 35–36 into a coining image ; and a suggestion of counterfeiting
is conveyed) **51** *leavened* slowly rising (in the mind)

Proceeded to you ; therefore take your honors.
Our haste from hence is of so quick condition
54 That it prefers itself, and leaves unquestioned
Matters of needful value. We shall write to you,
As time and our concernings shall importune,
How it goes with us, and do look to know
What doth befall you here. So fare you well :
To th' hopeful execution do I leave you
Of your commissions.

ANGELO   Yet give leave, my lord,
61 That we may bring you something on the way.

DUKE
My haste may not admit it ;
Nor need you, on mine honor, have to do
With any scruple. Your scope is as mine own,
So to enforce or qualify the laws
As to your soul seems good. Give me your hand.
I'll privily away ; I love the people,
But do not like to stage me to their eyes ;
Though it do well, I do not relish well
70 Their loud applause and aves vehement,
Nor do I think the man of safe discretion
That does affect it. Once more, fare you well.

ANGELO
The heavens give safety to your purposes.

ESCALUS
Lead forth and bring you back in happiness !

DUKE
I thank you ; fare you well.   *Exit.*

ESCALUS
I shall desire you, sir, to give me leave
To have free speech with you ; and it concerns me
78 To look into the bottom of my place.
A power I have, but of what strength and nature
I am not yet instructed.

ANGELO
'Tis so with me. Let us withdraw together,
And we may soon our satisfaction have
Touching that point.

ESCALUS   I'll wait upon your honor. *Exeunt.*

*

I, ii   *Enter Lucio and two other Gentlemen.*
1 LUCIO If the Duke, with the other dukes, come not to composition with the king of Hungary, why then all the
dukes fall upon the king.
1. GENTLEMAN Heaven grant us its peace, but not the
king of Hungary's !
2. GENTLEMAN Amen.
LUCIO Thou conclud'st like the sanctimonious pirate,
that went to sea with the Ten Commandments, but
scraped one out of the table.
2. GENTLEMAN 'Thou shalt not steal' ?
11 LUCIO Ay, that he razed.
1. GENTLEMAN Why, 'twas a commandment to command the captain and all the rest from their functions ;
they put forth to steal. There's not a soldier of us all that,
in the thanksgiving before meat, do relish the petition
well that prays for peace.
2. GENTLEMAN I never heard any soldier dislike it.
LUCIO I believe thee, for I think thou never wast where
grace was said.

2. GENTLEMAN No ? A dozen times at least.
1. GENTLEMAN What ? In meter ?
LUCIO In any proportion or in any language.   22
1. GENTLEMAN I think, or in any religion.
LUCIO Ay, why not ? Grace is grace, despite of all controversy : as, for example, thou thyself art a wicked
villain, despite of all grace.
2. GENTLEMAN Well, there went but a pair of shears be- 27
tween us.
LUCIO I grant : as there may between the lists and the 29
velvet. Thou art the list.
1. GENTLEMAN And thou the velvet. Thou art good
velvet ; thou'rt a three-piled piece, I warrant thee. I had 32
as lief be a list of an English kersey as be piled, as thou 33
art piled, for a French velvet. Do I speak feelingly now ? 34
LUCIO I think thou dost ; and indeed with most painful
feeling of thy speech. I will, out of thine own confession,
learn to begin thy health ; but, whilst I live, forget to 37
drink after thee.
1. GENTLEMAN I think I have done myself wrong, have 39
I not ?
2. GENTLEMAN Yes, that thou hast, whether thou art
tainted or free.
        Enter Bawd [Mistress Overdone].
LUCIO Behold, behold, where Madam Mitigation comes ! 42
[1. GENTLEMAN] I have purchased as many diseases
under her roof as come to –
2. GENTLEMAN To what, I pray ?
LUCIO Judge.
2. GENTLEMAN To three thousand dolors a year.   47
1. GENTLEMAN Ay, and more.
LUCIO A French crown more.
1. GENTLEMAN Thou art always figuring diseases in
me ; but thou art full of error. I am sound.
LUCIO Nay, not – as one would say – healthy, but so
sound as things that are hollow. Thy bones are hollow ; 53
impiety has made a feast of thee.
1. GENTLEMAN How now, which of your hips has the
most profound sciatica ?
MISTRESS OVERDONE Well, well ; there's one yonder
arrested and carried to prison was worth five thousand
of you all.
2. GENTLEMAN Who's that, I pray thee ?
MISTRESS OVERDONE Marry, sir, that's Claudio, Signior Claudio.
1. GENTLEMAN Claudio to prison ? 'Tis not so.
MISTRESS OVERDONE Nay, but I know 'tis so. I saw him
arrested, saw him carried away, and, which is more,
within these three days his head to be chopped off.
LUCIO But, after all this fooling, I would not have it so.
Art thou sure of this ?
MISTRESS OVERDONE I am too sure of it ; and it is for
getting Madam Julietta with child.

54 *prefers* presents ; *unquestioned* uninvestigated **61** *bring . . . way* escort
you part of the way **70** *aves* salutations **78** *bottom . . . place* scope of my
power
I, ii A street in Vienna **1** *composition* agreement **11** *razed* erased **22**
proportion form **27–28** *there went . . . us* i.e. we are cut from the same cloth
29 *lists* selvage **32** *three-piled* with triple nap **33** *kersey* homespun ;
be piled (1) having a nap, (2) be afflicted with piles **34** *French* (syphilis was
known as 'the French disease') **37–38** *learn . . . after thee* drink a health
to you but not drink out of the same cup after you (to avoid infection)
39 *done . . . wrong* i.e. laid myself open to the jest (?) **42** *Mitigation* (so
called because her profession is to relieve desire) **47** *dolors* painful ill-
nesses (with pun on 'dollars') **53** *sound* resounding

LUCIO Believe me, this may be. He promised to meet me
71 two hours since, and he was ever precise in promise-
keeping.

2. GENTLEMAN Besides, you know, it draws something
near to the speech we had to such a purpose.

1. GENTLEMAN But most of all agreeing with the proclamation.

LUCIO Away; let's go learn the truth of it.

Exit [Lucio with the Gentlemen].

MISTRESS OVERDONE Thus, what with the war, what
79 with the sweat, what with the gallows, and what with
poverty, I am custom-shrunk.

Enter Clown [Pompey].

How now? What's the news with you?

POMPEY Yonder man is carried to prison.

MISTRESS OVERDONE Well, what has he done?

POMPEY A woman.

MISTRESS OVERDONE But what's his offense?

86 POMPEY Groping for trouts in a peculiar river.

MISTRESS OVERDONE What? Is there a maid with child
by him?

POMPEY No, but there's a woman with maid by him.
You have not heard of the proclamation, have you?

MISTRESS OVERDONE What proclamation, man?

92 POMPEY All houses in the suburbs of Vienna must be
plucked down.

MISTRESS OVERDONE And what shall become of those
in the city?

96 POMPEY They shall stand for seed: they had gone down
97 too, but that a wise burgher put in for them.

MISTRESS OVERDONE But shall all our houses of resort
in the suburbs be pulled down?

POMPEY To the ground, mistress.

MISTRESS OVERDONE Why, here's a change indeed in
the commonwealth; what shall become of me?

POMPEY Come, fear not you; good counsellors lack no
clients. Though you change your place, you need not
change your trade; I'll be your tapster still. Courage,
106 there will be pity taken on you; you that have worn your
eyes almost out in the service, you will be considered.

MISTRESS OVERDONE What's to do here, Thomas Tapster? Let's withdraw.

POMPEY Here comes Signior Claudio, led by the provost
to prison; and there's Madam Juliet.   *Exeunt.*

*Enter Provost, Claudio, Juliet, Officers, Lucio, and
two Gentlemen.*

CLAUDIO
Fellow, why dost thou show me thus to th' world?
Bear me to prison, where I am committed.

PROVOST
I do it not in evil disposition,
But from Lord Angelo by special charge.

CLAUDIO
Thus can the demigod Authority
Make us pay down for our offense by weight   117
The words of heaven; on whom it will, it will;   118
On whom it will not, so: yet still 'tis just.

LUCIO
Why, how now, Claudio? Whence comes this restraint?

CLAUDIO
From too much liberty, my Lucio, liberty.
As surfeit is the father of much fast,
So every scope by the immoderate use   123
Turns to restraint. Our natures do pursue,
Like rats that ravin down their proper bane,   125
A thirsty evil, and when we drink we die.

LUCIO If I could speak so wisely under an arrest, I would
send for certain of my creditors. And yet, to say the
truth, I had as lief have the foppery of freedom as the 129
morality of imprisonment. What's thy offense, Claudio?

CLAUDIO
What but to speak of would offend again.

LUCIO What, is't murder?

CLAUDIO No.

LUCIO Lechery?

CLAUDIO Call it so.

PROVOST Away, sir, you must go.

CLAUDIO
One word, good friend. Lucio, a word with you.

LUCIO A hundred, if they'll do you any good. Is lechery
so looked after?   139

CLAUDIO
Thus stands it with me: upon a true contract
I got possession of Julietta's bed.
You know the lady, she is fast my wife
Save that we do the denunciation lack   143
Of outward order. This we came not to,
Only for propagation of a dower   145
Remaining in the coffer of her friends,   146
From whom we thought it meet to hide our love
Till time had made them for us. But it chances   148
The stealth of our most mutual entertainment
With character too gross is writ on Juliet.

LUCIO
With child, perhaps?

CLAUDIO   Unhappily, even so.
And the new deputy now for the Duke –
Whether it be the fault and glimpse of newness,
Or whether that the body public be
A horse whereon the governor doth ride,
Who, newly in the seat, that it may know
He can command, lets it straight feel the spur;
Whether the tyranny be in his place,   158
Or in his eminence that fills it up,
I stagger in – but this new governor   160
Awakes me all the enrollèd penalties   161
Which have, like unscoured armor, hung by th' wall
So long that nineteen zodiacs have gone round   163
And none of them been worn; and for a name
Now puts the drowsy and neglected act
Freshly on me: 'tis surely for a name.

LUCIO I warrant it is, and thy head stands so tickle on thy 167
shoulders that a milkmaid, if she be in love, may sigh it
off. Send after the Duke and appeal to him.

CLAUDIO
I have done so, but he's not to be found.

---

71 *precise* punctilious 79 *sweat* sweating sickness, plague 86 *peculiar*
private 92 *suburbs* (in London, the area of the brothels) 96 *shall . . .
seed* i.e. be kept to preserve the species (with pun) 97 *burgher . . . in*
i.e. business man interceded 106–07 *worn . . . service* i.e. become almost
as blind as Cupid in the service of Venus 117 (one or more lines probably
missing after this line) 118 *words of heaven* (probably Romans ix, 18)
123 *scope* freedom 125 *ravin . . . bane* gulp down what is poisonous to
them 129 *foppery* foolishness 139 *looked after* i.e. taken so seriously
143 *denunciation* declaration 145 *propagation* begetting 146 *friends*
relatives 148 *for us* i.e. cease opposing the match 158 *in . . . place* i.e.
obligatory 160 *stagger in* am uncertain 161 *enrolled* written out in
full on a parchment roll 163 *zodiacs* i.e. years 167 *tickle* unsteady

I prithee, Lucio, do me this kind service :
This day my sister should the cloister enter,
173 And there receive her approbation.
Acquaint her with the danger of my state ;
Implore her, in my voice, that she make friends
To the strict deputy ; bid herself assay him.
I have great hope in that ; for in her youth
178 There is a prone and speechless dialect,
Such as move men ; beside, she hath prosperous art
180 When she will play with reason and discourse,
And well she can persuade.

LUCIO I pray she may, as well for the encouragement of
the like, which else would stand under grievous imposition, as for the enjoying of thy life, who I would be
185 sorry should be thus foolishly lost at a game of tick-tack.
I'll to her.

CLAUDIO
I thank you, good friend Lucio.

LUCIO
Within two hours.

CLAUDIO   Come, officer, away.   *Exeunt.*

*

I, iii   *Enter Duke and Friar Thomas.*

DUKE
No, holy father, throw away that thought ;
2 Believe not that the dribbling dart of love
3 Can pierce a complete bosom ; why I desire thee
To give me secret harbor hath a purpose
More grave and wrinkled than the aims and ends
Of burning youth.

FRIAR   May your grace speak of it ?

DUKE
My holy sir, none better knows than you
How I have ever loved the life removèd
And held in idle price to haunt assemblies
10 Where youth and cost witless bravery keeps.
I have delivered to Lord Angelo,
12 A man of stricture and firm abstinence,
My absolute power and place here in Vienna,
And he supposes me travelled to Poland ;
For so I have strewed it in the common ear,
And so it is received. Now, pious sir,
You will demand of me why I do this ?

FRIAR
Gladly, my lord.

DUKE
We have strict statutes and most biting laws,
The needful bits and curbs to headstrong jades,
21 Which for this fourteen years we have let slip ;
Even like an o'ergrown lion in a cave,
That goes not out to prey. Now, as fond fathers,
Having bound up the threat'ning twigs of birch,
Only to stick it in their children's sight
For terror, not to use, in time the rod
Becomes more mocked than feared ; so our decrees,
28 Dead to infliction, to themselves are dead,
29 And Liberty plucks Justice by the nose ;
30 The baby beats the nurse, and quite athwart
Goes all decorum.

FRIAR   It rested in your grace
To unloose this tied-up justice when you pleased ;
And it in you more dreadful would have seemed

Than in Lord Angelo.

DUKE   I do fear, too dreadful ;
Sith 'twas my fault to give the people scope,
'Twould be my tyranny to strike and gall them
For what I bid them do : for we bid this be done
When evil deeds have their permissive pass
And not the punishment. Therefore, indeed, my father,
I have on Angelo imposed the office,
Who may, in th' ambush of my name, strike home,   41
And yet my nature never in the sight
To do it slander. And to behold his sway
I will, as 'twere a brother of your order,
Visit both prince and people. Therefore, I prithee,
Supply me with the habit, and instruct me
How I may formally in person bear
Like a true friar. Moe reasons for this action   48
At our more leisure shall I render you ;
Only this one : Lord Angelo is precise,   50
Stands at a guard with envy ; scarce confesses   51
That his blood flows, or that his appetite
Is more to bread than stone. Hence shall we see,
If power change purpose, what our seemers be.
                              Exit [with Friar].

*

                    Enter Isabella and Francisca, a Nun.   I, iv
ISABELLA
And have you nuns no farther privileges ?

NUN
Are not these large enough ?

ISABELLA
Yes, truly. I speak not as desiring more,
But rather wishing a more strict restraint
Upon the sisterhood, the votarists of Saint Clare.   5
          Lucio within.

LUCIO
Ho ! Peace be in this place.

ISABELLA   Who's that which calls ?

NUN
It is a man's voice. Gentle Isabella,
Turn you the key, and know his business of him.
You may, I may not ; you are yet unsworn.
When you have vowed, you must not speak with men
But in the presence of the prioress ;
Then, if you speak, you must not show your face,
Or, if you show your face, you must not speak.
He calls again ; I pray you, answer him.   [*Exit.*]

ISABELLA
Peace and prosperity ; who is't that calls ?
          [*Enter Lucio.*]

LUCIO
Hail, virgin, if you be, as those cheek-roses
Proclaim you are no less. Can you so stead me   17
As bring me to the sight of Isabella,

173 *approbation* novitiate 178 *prone* apt ; *dialect* language 180 *play with*
employ 185 *tick-tack* (a variety of backgammon)
I, iii A friar's cell 2 *dribbling* feeble 3 *complete* strong, mature 10 *witless bravery* senseless display 12 *stricture* strictness 21 *fourteen* (Claudio,
I, ii, 163 has said *nineteen* ; xiv or xix has probably been misread by compositor) 28 *Dead to infliction* completely unenforced 29 *Liberty . . .
nose* lack of restraint flouts justice 30 *athwart* awry 41 *in th'ambush*
under the cover 48 *Moe* more 50 *precise* morally strict 51 *at a guard* on
defense
I, iv Within the gate of a nunnery 5 *votarists . . . Clare* (an order of white-
habited nuns) 17 *stead* help

A novice of this place, and the fair sister
To her unhappy brother, Claudio ? ·

ISABELLA

Why 'her unhappy brother' ? let me ask,
The rather for I now must make you know
I am that Isabella, and his sister.

LUCIO

Gentle and fair, your brother kindly greets you.
25 Not to be weary with you, he's in prison.

ISABELLA

Woe me, for what ?

LUCIO

For that which, if myself might be his judge,
He should receive his punishment in thanks.
He hath got his friend with child.

ISABELLA

30   Sir, make me not your story.

LUCIO   'Tis true.
I would not, though 'tis my familiar sin
32 With maids to seem the lapwing and to jest,
Tongue far from heart, play with all virgins so.
I hold you as a thing enskied and sainted,
By your renouncement an immortal spirit,
And to be talked with in sincerity,
As with a saint.

ISABELLA

You do blaspheme the good in mocking me.

LUCIO

39 Do not believe it. Fewness and truth, 'tis thus :
Your brother and his lover have embraced ;
As those that feed grow full, as blossoming time
42 That from the seedness the bare fallow brings
43 To teeming foison, even so her plenteous womb
Expresseth his full tilth and husbandry.

ISABELLA

Someone with child by him ? My cousin Juliet ?

LUCIO

Is she your cousin ?

ISABELLA

Adoptedly, as schoolmaids change their names
48 By vain though apt affection.

LUCIO   She it is.

ISABELLA

O, let him marry her.

LUCIO   This is the point.
The Duke is very strangely gone from hence ;
51 Bore many gentlemen – myself being one –
In hand and hope of action ; but we do learn
By those that know the very nerves of state,
His givings-out were of an infinite distance
From his true-meant design. Upon his place,
And with full line of his authority,
Governs Lord Angelo, a man whose blood
Is very snow-broth ; one who never feels
59 The wanton stings and motions of the sense,

But doth rebate and blunt his natural edge   60
With profits of the mind, study and fast.
He – to give fear to use and liberty,   62
Which have for long run by the hideous law,
As mice by lions – hath picked out an act,
Under whose heavy sense your brother's life   65
Falls into forfeit ; he arrests him on it,
And follows close the rigor of the statute
To make him an example. All hope is gone,
Unless you have the grace by your fair prayer
To soften Angelo. And that's my pith of business
'Twixt you and your poor brother.

ISABELLA

Doth he so seek his life ?

LUCIO   Has censured him   72
Already and, as I hear, the provost hath
A warrant for's execution.

ISABELLA

Alas, what poor ability 's in me
To do him good ?

LUCIO   Assay the power you have.   76

ISABELLA

My power ? Alas, I doubt –

LUCIO   Our doubts are traitors
And make us lose the good we oft might win,
By fearing to attempt. Go to Lord Angelo
And let him learn to know, when maidens sue,
Men give like gods ; but when they weep and kneel,
All their petitions are as freely theirs
As they themselves would owe them.   83

ISABELLA

I'll see what I can do.

LUCIO   But speedily.

ISABELLA

I will about it straight,
No longer staying but to give the Mother
Notice of my affair. I humbly thank you ;
Commend me to my brother ; soon at night
I'll send him certain word of my success.   89

LUCIO

I take my leave of you.

ISABELLA   Good sir, adieu.   *Exeunt.*

*

Enter Angelo, Escalus, and Servants, Justice.   II, i

ANGELO

We must not make a scarecrow of the law,
Setting it up to fear the birds of prey,   2
And let it keep one shape, till custom make it
Their perch and not their terror.

ESCALUS   Ay, but yet
Let us be keen and rather cut a little,
Than fall and bruise to death. Alas, this gentleman   6
Whom I would save had a most noble father.
Let but your honor know,
Whom I believe to be most strait in virtue,
That, in the working of your own affections,   10
Had time cohered with place or place with wishing,
Or that the resolute acting of your blood
Could have attained th' effect of your own purpose,
Whether you had not sometime in your life
Erred in this point which now you censure him,
And pulled the law upon you.

---

25 *weary* tedious   30 *story* joke   32 *lapwing* bird which runs to and fro to divert attention from its nest   39 *Fewness and truth* briefly and truly   42 *seedness* sowing   43 *foison* harvest   48 *vain . . . apt* foolish but natural   51–52 *Bore . . . In hand and hope* deluded . . . with the hope   59 *motions . . . sense* promptings of the senses   60 *rebate* dull   62 *use and liberty* habitual license   65 *heavy sense* onerous meaning   72 *censured* passed judgment on   76 *Assay* make trial of   83 *owe* possess   89 *success* fortune   II, i *A courtroom*   2 *fear* frighten   6 *fall* let fall   10 *affections* passions

ANGELO
  'Tis one thing to be tempted, Escalus,
  Another thing to fall. I not deny,
  The jury passing on the prisoner's life
  May in the sworn twelve have a thief or two
  Guiltier than him they try; what's open made to justice,
  That justice seizes; what knows the laws
23 That thieves do pass on thieves? 'Tis very pregnant
  The jewel that we find, we stoop and take't
  Because we see it; but what we do not see
  We tread upon, and never think of it.
  You may not so extenuate his offense
28 For I have had such faults; but rather tell me,
  When I that censure him do so offend,
  Let mine own judgment pattern out my death
31 And nothing come in partial. Sir, he must die.
      Enter Provost.

ESCALUS
  Be it as your wisdom will.
ANGELO   Where is the provost?
PROVOST
33 Here, if it like your honor.
ANGELO   See that Claudio
  Be executed by nine to-morrow morning;
  Bring him his confessor, let him be prepared;
  For that's the utmost of his pilgrimage.   *[Exit Provost.]*
ESCALUS
  Well, heaven forgive him, and forgive us all.
  Some rise by sin, and some by virtue fall:
39 Some run from breaks of ice, and answer none,
  And some condemnèd for a fault alone.
      Enter Elbow, Froth, Clown [Pompey], Officers.
ELBOW Come, bring them away. If these be good people
  in a commonweal that do nothing but use their abuses
43 in common houses, I know no law. Bring them away.
ANGELO How now, sir, what's your name? And what's
  the matter?
ELBOW If it please your honor, I am the poor Duke's
  constable, and my name is Elbow. I do lean upon justice, sir, and do bring in here before your good honor
  two notorious benefactors.
ANGELO Benefactors? Well, what benefactors are they?
  Are they not malefactors?
ELBOW If it please your honor, I know not well what they
  are; but precise villains they are, that I am sure of, and
  void of all profanation in the world that good Christians
  ought to have.
ESCALUS This comes off well; here's a wise officer.
ANGELO Go to: what quality are they of? Elbow is your
  name? Why dost thou not speak, Elbow?
59 POMPEY He cannot, sir; he's out at elbow.
ANGELO What are you, sir?
61 ELBOW He, sir, a tapster, sir, parcel-bawd; one that
  serves a bad woman, whose house, sir, was, as they say,
  plucked down in the suburbs, and now she professes a
64 hot-house, which I think is a very ill house too.
ESCALUS How know you that?
ELBOW My wife, sir, whom I detest before heaven and
  your honor –
ESCALUS How? Thy wife?
ELBOW Ay, sir, whom I thank heaven is an honest
  woman –
ESCALUS Dost thou detest her therefore?
ELBOW I say, sir, I will detest myself also, as well as she,

that this house, if it be not a bawd's house, it is pity of 72
  her life, for it is a naughty house.
ESCALUS How dost thou know that, constable?
ELBOW Marry, sir, by my wife, who, if she had been a
  woman cardinally given, might have been accused in 76
  fornication, adultery, and all uncleanliness there.
ESCALUS By the woman's means?
ELBOW Ay, sir, by Mistress Overdone's means; but as
  she spit in his face, so she defied him.
POMPEY Sir, if it please your honor, this is not so.
ELBOW Prove it before these varlets here, thou honorable
  man, prove it.
ESCALUS Do you hear how he misplaces?   84
POMPEY Sir, she came in great with child, and longing –
  saving your honor's reverence – for stewed prunes. Sir,
  we had but two in the house, which at that very distant
  time stood, as it were, in a fruit dish, a dish of some
  threepence; your honors have seen such dishes; they
  are not china dishes, but very good dishes –
ESCALUS Go to, go to; no matter for the dish, sir.
POMPEY No, indeed, sir, not of a pin; you are therein in 92
  the right: but to the point. As I say, this Mistress Elbow, being, as I say, with child, and being great-bellied,
  and longing, as I said, for prunes, and having but two in
  the dish, as I said, Master Froth here, this very man,
  having eaten the rest, as I said, and, as I say, paying for
  them very honestly, for, as you know, Master Froth, I
  could not give you threepence again –
FROTH No, indeed.
POMPEY Very well: you being then, if you be remembered, cracking the stones of the foresaid prunes –
FROTH Ay, so I did, indeed.
POMPEY Why, very well: I telling you then, if you be re-
  membered, that such a one and such a one were past
  cure of the thing you wot of, unless they kept very good 106
  diet, as I told you –
FROTH All this is true.
POMPEY Why, very well then –
ESCALUS Come, you are a tedious fool; to the purpose.
  What was done to Elbow's wife, that he hath cause to
  complain of? Come me to what was done to her.   112
POMPEY Sir, your honor cannot come to that yet.
ESCALUS No, sir, nor I mean it not.
POMPEY Sir, but you shall come to it, by your honor's
  leave. And I beseech you look into Master Froth here,
  sir; a man of fourscore pound a year, whose father died
  at Hallowmas. Was't not at Hallowmas, Master Froth? 118
FROTH Allhallond-Eve.   119
POMPEY Why, very well; I hope here be truths. He, sir,
  sitting, as I say, in a lower chair, sir – 'twas in the Bunch 121
  of Grapes, where indeed you have a delight to sit, have
  you not?
FROTH I have so, because it is an open room and good for
  winter.
POMPEY Why, very well then; I hope here be truths.

---

23 *pass on* pass judgment on; *pregnant* apparent 28 *For* because 31 *partial* in my favor 33 *like* please 39 *answer none* do not have to account for their acts 43 *common houses* brothels 59 *out at elbow* (a pun on missing his cue) 61 *parcel-bawd* partly a bawd 64 *hot-house* bath-house, bagnio 72–73 *pity . . . life* i.e. a sad state of affairs 76 *cardinally* i.e. carnally 84 *misplaces* i.e. reverses meanings 92 *not . . . pin* i.e. not a bit 106 *wot* know 112 *Come me* come 118 *Hallowmas* All Saints' Day, November 1 119 *Allhallond-Eve* Hallowe'en, October 31 121–22 *Bunch of Grapes* (name of the room at the inn)

ANGELO
This will last out a night in Russia
When nights are longest there. I'll take my leave,
129 And leave you to the hearing of the cause,
Hoping you'll find good cause to whip them all.

ESCALUS
131 I think no less. Good morrow to your lordship.

Exit [Angelo].

Now, sir, come on ; what was done to Elbow's wife, once
more ?

POMPEY Once, sir ? There was nothing done to her once.

ELBOW I beseech you, sir, ask him what this man did to
my wife.

POMPEY I beseech your honor, ask me.

ESCALUS Well, sir, what did this gentleman to her ?

POMPEY I beseech you, sir, look in this gentleman's face.
Good Master Froth, look upon his honor ; 'tis for a good
purpose. Doth your honor mark his face ?

ESCALUS Ay, sir, very well.

POMPEY Nay, I beseech you, mark it well.

ESCALUS Well, I do so.

POMPEY Doth your honor see any harm in his face ?

ESCALUS Why, no.

147 POMPEY I'll be supposed upon a book, his face is the
worst thing about him. Good, then ; if his face be the
worst thing about him, how could Master Froth do the
constable's wife any harm ? I would know that of your
honor.

ESCALUS He's in the right. Constable, what say you to it ?

153 ELBOW First, an it like you, the house is a respected
house ; next, this is a respected fellow ; and his mistress
is a respected woman.

POMPEY By this hand, sir, his wife is a more respected
person than any of us all.

ELBOW Varlet, thou liest ; thou liest, wicked varlet. The
time is yet to come that she was ever respected with
man, woman, or child.

POMPEY Sir, she was respected with him before he
married with her.

163 ESCALUS Which is the wiser here, Justice or Iniquity ? Is
this true ?

ELBOW O thou caitiff, O thou varlet, O thou wicked Hannibal ! I respected with her before I was married to her ?
If ever I was respected with her, or she with me, let not
your worship think me the poor Duke's officer. Prove
this, thou wicked Hannibal, or I'll have mine action of
batt'ry on thee.

ESCALUS If he took you a box o' th' ear, you might have
your action of slander, too.

ELBOW Marry, I thank your good worship for it ; what
is't your worship's pleasure I shall do with this wicked
caitiff ?

ESCALUS Truly, officer, because he hath some offenses in
177 him that thou wouldst discover if thou couldst, let him
continue in his courses till thou know'st what they are.

ELBOW Marry, I thank your worship for it. Thou seest,
thou wicked varlet, now, what's come upon thee ; thou
art to continue now, thou varlet, thou art to continue.

ESCALUS Where were you born, friend ?

FROTH Here in Vienna, sir.

ESCALUS Are you of fourscore pounds a year ? 184

FROTH Yes, an't please you, sir.

ESCALUS So. *[to Pompey]* What trade are you of, sir ?

POMPEY A tapster, a poor widow's tapster.

ESCALUS Your mistress' name ?

POMPEY Mistress Overdone.

ESCALUS Hath she had any more than one husband ?

POMPEY Nine, sir ; Overdone by the last.

ESCALUS Nine ! Come hither to me, Master Froth. Master Froth, I would not have you acquainted with tapsters ; they will draw you, Master Froth, and you will 194
hang them. Get you gone, and let me hear no more of
you.

FROTH I thank your worship. For mine own part, I never
come into any room in a taphouse but I am drawn
in.

ESCALUS Well, no more of it, Master Froth ; farewell.

[Exit Froth.]

Come you hither to me, master tapster. What's your
name, master tapster ?

POMPEY Pompey.

ESCALUS What else ?

POMPEY Bum, sir.

ESCALUS Troth, and your bum is the greatest thing about
you, so that, in the beastliest sense, you are Pompey the
Great. Pompey, you are partly a bawd, Pompey, howsoever you color it in being a tapster, are you not ? 208
Come, tell me true ; it shall be the better for you.

POMPEY Truly, sir, I am a poor fellow that would live.

ESCALUS How would you live, Pompey ? By being a
bawd ? What do you think of the trade, Pompey ? Is it a
lawful trade ?

POMPEY If the law would allow it, sir.

ESCALUS But the law will not allow it, Pompey ; nor it
shall not be allowed in Vienna.

POMPEY Does your worship mean to geld and splay all
the youth of the city ?

ESCALUS No, Pompey.

POMPEY Truly, sir, in my poor opinion, they will to't
then. If your worship will take order for the drabs and 221
the knaves, you need not to fear the bawds.

ESCALUS There is pretty orders beginning, I can tell
you ; it is but heading and hanging. 224

POMPEY If you head and hang all that offend that way
but for ten year together, you'll be glad to give out a
commission for more heads. If this law hold in Vienna
ten year, I'll rent the fairest house in it after threepence
a bay ; if you live to see this come to pass, say Pompey 228
told you so.

ESCALUS Thank you, good Pompey ; and, in requital of
your prophecy, hark you : I advise you, let me not find
you before me again upon any complaint whatsoever ;
no, not for dwelling where you do. If I do, Pompey, I
shall beat you to your tent, and prove a shrewd Caesar 235
to you. In plain dealing, Pompey, I shall have you
whipped ; so, for this time, Pompey, fare you well.

POMPEY I thank your worship for your good counsel ;
[aside] but I shall follow it as the flesh and fortune shall
better determine.

Whip me ! No, no, let carman whip his jade. 241
The valiant heart 's not whipped out of his trade. *Exit.*

129 *cause* case   131 *I . . . less* i.e. I probably shall   147 *supposed* i.e. deposed
153 *respected* i.e. suspected   163 *Justice or Iniquity* i.e. Elbow or Pompey
(compared as stock characters in morality plays)   177 *discover* uncover,
disclose   184 *of* possessed of   194 *draw you* empty you   208 *color*
camouflage   221 *take . . . for* attend to   224 *heading* beheading   228
bay part of a house, viz. that part beneath a single gable   235 *beat . . . tent* i.e.
drive from the field (as Julius Caesar drove Pompey)   241 *carman* carter

ESCALUS Come hither to me, Master Elbow; come
  hither, master constable. How long have you been in
  this place of constable?

ELBOW Seven year and a half, sir.

ESCALUS I thought, by the readiness in the office, you had
  continued in it some time; you say, seven years together?

ELBOW And a half, sir.

ESCALUS Alas, it hath been great pains to you; they do
  you wrong to put you so oft upon't. Are there not men
  in your ward sufficient to serve it?

254 ELBOW Faith, sir, few of any wit in such matters. As they
  are chosen, they are glad to choose me for them; I do it
  for some piece of money, and go through with all.

ESCALUS Look you bring me in the names of some six or
257   seven, the most sufficient of your parish.

ELBOW To your worship's house, sir?

ESCALUS To my house. Fare you well.   *[Exit Elbow.]*
  What's o'clock, think you?

JUSTICE Eleven, sir.

ESCALUS I pray you home to dinner with me.

JUSTICE I humbly thank you.

ESCALUS
  It grieves me for the death of Claudio,
  But there's no remedy.

JUSTICE
  Lord Angelo is severe.

ESCALUS   It is but needful.
  Mercy is not itself, that oft looks so;
  Pardon is still the nurse of second woe.
  But yet poor Claudio; there is no remedy.
  Come, sir.   *Exeunt.*

                *

II, ii   *Enter Provost, [and a] Servant.*

SERVANT
  He's hearing of a cause; he will come straight;
  I'll tell him of you.

PROVOST   Pray you, do. *[Exit Servant.]* I'll know
  His pleasure; may be he will relent. Alas,
  He hath but as offended in a dream.
5   All sects, all ages smack of this vice – and he
  To die for't!
          Enter Angelo.

ANGELO   Now, what's the matter, provost?

PROVOST
  Is it your will Claudio shall die to-morrow?

ANGELO
  Did not I tell thee, yea? Hadst thou not order?
  Why dost thou ask again?

PROVOST   Lest I might be too rash.
  Under your good correction, I have seen
  When, after execution, judgment hath
  Repented o'er his doom.

12 ANGELO   Go to; let that be mine.
  Do you your office, or give up your place,
  And you shall well be spared.

PROVOST   I crave your honor's pardon.
15   What shall be done, sir, with the groaning Juliet?
  She's very near her hour.

ANGELO   Dispose of her
  To some more fitter place, and that with speed.
        [Enter Servant.]

SERVANT
  Here is the sister of the man condemned

Desires access to you.

ANGELO   Hath he a sister?

PROVOST
  Ay, my good lord, a very virtuous maid,
  And to be shortly of a sisterhood,
  If not already.

ANGELO   Well, let her be admitted. *[Exit Servant.]*
  See you the fornicatress be removed;
  Let her have needful, but not lavish, means;
  There shall be order for't.   25
       Enter Lucio and Isabella.

PROVOST   'Save your honor.

ANGELO
  Stay a little while.
     [To Isabella] Y'are welcome: what's your will?

ISABELLA
  I am a woeful suitor to your honor,
  Please but your honor hear me.

ANGELO   Well: what's your suit?

ISABELLA
  There is a vice that most I do abhor,
  And most desire should meet the blow of justice,
  For which I would not plead, but that I must,
  For which I must not plead, but that I am
  At war 'twixt will and will not.

ANGELO   Well: the matter?

ISABELLA
  I have a brother is condemned to die.
  I do beseech you, let it be his fault,   35
  And not my brother.

PROVOST *[aside]*   Heaven give thee moving graces.

ANGELO
  Condemn the fault, and not the actor of it?
  Why, every fault's condemned ere it be done:
  Mine were the very cipher of a function,
  To fine the faults whose fine stands in record,   40
  And let go by the actor.

ISABELLA   O just, but severe law!
  I had a brother then; heaven keep your honor.

LUCIO *[aside to Isabella]*
  Give't not o'er so: to him again, entreat him,
  Kneel down before him, hang upon his gown;
  You are too cold. If you should need a pin,
  You could not with more tame a tongue desire it;
  To him, I say.

ISABELLA
  Must he needs die?

ANGELO   Maiden, no remedy.

ISABELLA
  Yes, I do think that you might pardon him,
  And neither heaven nor man grieve at the mercy.

ANGELO
  I will not do't.

ISABELLA   But can you if you would?

ANGELO
  Look what I will not, that I cannot do.   52

ISABELLA
  But might you do't, and do the world no wrong,

---

254 *for them* i.e. as their deputy   257 *sufficient* substantial
II, ii Within the house of Angelo   5 *sects* kinds   12 *mine* my concern
15 *groaning* i.e. in labor   25 *order* a requisition   35 *fault* i.e. fault that is
condemned   40 *To fine . . . record* i.e. to do what has already been done,
condemn faults as faults   52 *Look what* whatever

54   If so your heart were touched with that remorse
       As mine is to him ?

ANGELO
       He's sentenced ; 'tis too late.

LUCIO *[aside to Isabella]*   You are too cold.

ISABELLA
       Too late ? Why, no : I that do speak a word
       May call it back again. Well believe this,
       No ceremony that to great ones 'longs,
60   Not the king's crown, nor the deputed sword,
       The marshal's truncheon, nor the judge's robe,
       Become them with one half so good a grace
       As mercy does ;
       If he had been as you, and you as he,
       You would have slipped like him ; but he, like you,
       Would not have been so stern.

ANGELO   Pray you, be gone.

ISABELLA
       I would to heaven I had your potency,
       And you were Isabel ; should it then be thus ?
       No, I would tell what 'twere to be a judge,
       And what a prisoner.
70 LUCIO *[aside to Isabella]* Ay, touch him ; there's the vein.

ANGELO
       Your brother is a forfeit of the law,
       And you but waste your words.

ISABELLA   Alas, alas ;
       Why, all the souls that were were forfeit once,
       And He that might the vantage best have took,
       Found out the remedy. How would you be,
76   If He, which is the top of judgment, should
       But judge you as you are ? O think on that,
       And mercy then will breathe within your lips,
79   Like man new made.

ANGELO   Be you content, fair maid,
       It is the law, not I, condemn your brother ;
       Were he my kinsman, brother, or my son,
       It should be thus with him : he must die to-morrow.

ISABELLA
       To-morrow ? O, that's sudden ; spare him, spare him ;
       He's not prepared for death. Even for our kitchens
85   We kill the fowl of season ; shall we serve heaven
       With less respect than we do minister
       To our gross selves ? Good, good my lord, bethink you :
       Who is it that hath died for this offense ?
       There's many have committed it.

LUCIO *[aside to Isabella]*   Ay, well said.

ANGELO
       The law hath not been dead, though it hath slept.
       Those many had not dared to do that evil
       If the first that did th' edict infringe
       Had answered for his deed. Now 'tis awake,
       Takes note of what is done, and like a prophet
95   Looks in a glass that shows what future evils,
       Either new, or by remissness new-conceived,

And so in progress to be hatched and born,   97
Are now to have no successive degrees,   98
But, ere they live, to end.

ISABELLA   Yet show some pity.

ANGELO
       I show it most of all when I show justice,
       For then I pity those I do not know,
       Which a dismissed offense would after gall,   102
       And do him right that, answering one foul wrong,   103
       Lives not to act another. Be satisfied ;
       Your brother dies to-morrow ; be content.

ISABELLA
       So you must be the first that gives this sentence,
       And he, that suffers. O, it is excellent
       To have a giant's strength, but it is tyrannous
       To use it like a giant.

LUCIO *[aside to Isabella]* That's well said.

ISABELLA
       Could great men thunder
       As Jove himself does, Jove would ne'er be quiet,
       For every pelting, petty officer   112
       Would use his heaven for thunder,
       Nothing but thunder. Merciful heaven,
       Thou rather with thy sharp and sulphurous bolt
       Splits the unwedgeable and gnarlèd oak   116
       Than the soft myrtle ; but man, proud man,
       Dressed in a little brief authority,
       Most ignorant of what he's most assured –   119
       His glassy essence – like an angry ape   120
       Plays such fantastic tricks before high heaven
       As makes the angels weep ; who, with our spleens,
       Would all themselves laugh mortal.

LUCIO *[aside to Isabella]*
       O, to him, to him, wench ; he will relent.
       He's coming, I perceive't.

PROVOST *[aside]*   Pray heaven she win him.

ISABELLA
       We cannot weigh our brother with ourself :
       Great men may jest with saints : 'tis wit in them,
       But in the less foul profanation.

LUCIO *[aside to Isabella]*
       Thou'rt i'th'right, girl, more o'that.

ISABELLA
       That in the captain's but a choleric word,
       Which in the soldier is flat blasphemy.

LUCIO *[aside to Isabella]*
       Art avised o' that ? More on't.   132

ANGELO
       Why do you put these sayings upon me ?

ISABELLA
       Because authority, though it err like others,
       Hath yet a kind of medicine in itself
       That skins the vice o' th' top ; go to your bosom,   136
       Knock there, and ask your heart what it doth know
       That's like my brother's fault ; if it confess
       A natural guiltiness such as is his,
       Let it not sound a thought upon your tongue
       Against my brother's life.

ANGELO *[aside]*   She speaks, and 'tis
       Such sense that my sense breeds with it. – Fare you well.   142

ISABELLA
       Gentle my lord, turn back.

ANGELO
       I will bethink me ; come again to-morrow.

---

54 *remorse* pity **60** *deputed sword* emblematic sword of justice held by an official **70** *vein* proper theme **76** *which . . . judgment* who is supreme judge **79** *new made* redeemed, restored to innocence **85** *of season* in season **95** *glass* crystal **97** *in progress* in due course **98** *degrees* stages **102** *dismissed* forgiven ; *gall* hurt **103** *do him right* do right by him (Claudio) **112** *pelting* paltry **116** *unwedgeable* unsplittable **119** *Most . . . assured* i.e. trusting most in what he knows least about **120** *glassy* fragile (?), mirrored (?) **132** *avised* informed **136** *That . . . top* that skims off the upper, and visible, layer of vice **142** *Such sense . . . with it* i.e. of such import that it arouses my sensuality

ISABELLA
Hark how I'll bribe you ; good my lord, turn back.
ANGELO
How ! Bribe me ?
ISABELLA
Ay, with such gifts that heaven shall share with you.
LUCIO [aside to Isabella]
You had marred all else.
ISABELLA
149 Not with fond sicles of the tested gold,
150 Or stones whose rates are either rich or poor
As fancy values them ; but with true prayers
That shall be up at heaven and enter there
153 Ere sunrise : prayers from preservèd souls,
From fasting maids whose minds are dedicate
To nothing temporal.
ANGELO   Well, come to me to-morrow
LUCIO [aside to Isabella]
Go to, 'tis well ; away.
ISABELLA
Heaven keep your honor safe.
ANGELO [aside]   Amen.
For I am that way going to temptation,
159 Where prayers cross.
ISABELLA   At what hour to-morrow
Shall I attend your lordship ?
ANGELO   At any time 'fore-noon.
ISABELLA
'Save your honor. [Exeunt Isabella, Lucio, and Provost.]
ANGELO   From thee : even from thy virtue.
What's this ? what's this ? is this her fault or mine ?
The tempter, or the tempted, who sins most ?
Ha !
Not she, nor doth she tempt ; but it is I
That, lying by the violet in the sun,
Do as the carrion does, not as the flower,
168 Corrupt with virtuous season. Can it be
That modesty may more betray our sense
Than woman's lightness ? Having waste ground enough,
Shall we desire to raze the sanctuary
172 And pitch our evils there ? O fie, fie, fie !
What dost thou ? or what are thou, Angelo ?
Dost thou desire her foully for those things
That make her good ? O, let her brother live :
Thieves for their robbery have authority
When judges steal themselves. What, do I love her,
That I desire to hear her speak again,
And feast upon her eyes ? what is't I dream on ?
180 O cunning enemy that, to catch a saint,
With saints dost bait thy hook : most dangerous
Is that temptation that doth goad us on
To sin in loving virtue. Never could the strumpet
With all her double vigor, art and nature,
185 Once stir my temper ; but this virtuous maid
Subdues me quite. Ever till now,
187 When men were fond, I smiled and wondered how. *Exit.*

*

II, iii   *Enter Duke [disguised as a friar] and Provost.*
DUKE
Hail to you, provost – so I think you are.
PROVOST
I am the provost. What's your will, good friar ?

DUKE
Bound by my charity and my blest order,
I come to visit the afflicted spirits
Here in the prison ; do me the common right
To let me see them and to make me know
The nature of their crimes, that I may minister
To them accordingly.
PROVOST
I would do more than that, if more were needful.
            Enter Juliet.
Look, here comes one : a gentlewoman of mine,
Who, falling in the flaws of her own youth,   11
Hath blistered her report. She is with child,   12
And he that got it, sentenced : a young man
More fit to do another such offense
Than die for this.
DUKE
When must he die ?
PROVOST   As I do think, to-morrow.
            [To Juliet]
I have provided for you ; stay a while
And you shall be conducted.
DUKE
Repent you, fair one, of the sin you carry ?
JULIET
I do, and bear the shame most patiently.
DUKE
I'll teach you how you shall arraign your conscience
And try your penitence, if it be sound,
Or hollowly put on.   23
JULIET   I'll gladly learn.
DUKE
Love you the man that wronged you ?
JULIET
Yes, as I love the woman that wronged him.
DUKE
So then it seems your most offenseful act
Was mutually committed ?
JULIET   Mutually.
DUKE
Then was your sin of heavier kind than his.
JULIET
I do confess it, and repent it, father.
DUKE
'Tis meet so, daughter : but lest you do repent
As that the sin hath brought you to this shame,
Which sorrow is always toward ourselves, not heaven,
Showing we would not spare heaven as we love it,   33
But as we stand in fear –
JULIET
I do repent me as it is an evil,
And take the shame with joy.
DUKE   There rest.
Your partner, as I hear, must die to-morrow,
And I am going with instruction to him.   38
Grace go with you, Benedicite.   *Exit.*

149 *sicles* shekels   150 *rates* worths   153 *preservèd* protected (from the sinful world)   159 *cross* are at cross purposes   168 *Corrupt . . . season* go bad in the season that matures the flower   172 *pitch our evils* erect our evil structures   180 *cunning enemy* i.e. Satan   185 *temper* passion   187 *fond* infatuated
II, iii A prison   11 *flaws* gusts of passion   12 *report* reputation   23 *hollowly* falsely   33 *spare* i.e. refrain from offending   38 *instruction* religious counsel

JULIET
Must die to-morrow! O injurious love,
That respites me a life whose very comfort
Is still a dying horror.
PROVOST   'Tis pity of him.   *Exeunt.*

*

II, iv   *Enter Angelo.*
ANGELO
When I would pray and think, I think and pray
2   To several subjects: heaven hath my empty words,
3   Whilst my invention, hearing not my tongue,
Anchors on Isabel: heaven in my mouth,
As if I did but only chew his name,
And in my heart the strong and swelling evil
7   Of my conception. The state, whereon I studied,
Is like a good thing, being often read,
Grown sere and tedious; yea, my gravity,
Wherein, let no man hear me, I take pride,
11   Could I, with boot, change for an idle plume
Which the air beats for vain. O place, O form,
How often dost thou with thy case, thy habit,
Wrench awe from fools, and tie the wiser souls
To thy false seeming! Blood, thou art blood;
16   Let's write 'good Angel' on the devil's horn,
17   'Tis not the devil's crest. How now, who's there?
        Enter Servant.
SERVANT
One Isabel, a sister, desires access to you.
ANGELO
Teach her the way. *[Exit Servant.]* O heavens,
Why does my blood thus muster to my heart,
Making both it unable for itself,
And dispossessing all my other parts
Of necessary fitness?
So play the foolish throngs with one that swounds,
Come all to help him, and so stop the air
By which he should revive; and even so
The general, subject to a well-wished king,
28   Quit their own part, and in obsequious fondness
Crowd to his presence, where their untaught love
Must needs appear offense.
        Enter Isabella.
             How now, fair maid!
ISABELLA
I am come to know your pleasure.
ANGELO
That you might know it, would much better please me
Than to demand what 'tis. Your brother cannot live.
ISABELLA
Even so: heaven keep your honor.
ANGELO
Yet may he live a while; and it may be

As long as you or I: yet he must die.
ISABELLA
Under your sentence?
ANGELO   Yea.
ISABELLA
When, I beseech you? that in his reprieve,   39
Longer or shorter, he may be so fitted
That his soul sicken not.
ANGELO
Ha! fie, these filthy vices! It were as good
To pardon him that hath from nature stol'n
A man already made, as to remit   44
Their saucy sweetness that do coin heaven's image   45
In stamps that are forbid: 'tis all as easy
Falsely to take away a life true made,
As to put mettle in restrainèd means   48
To make a false one.
ISABELLA
'Tis set down so in heaven, but not in earth.
ANGELO
Say you so? then I shall pose you quickly.   51
Which had you rather, that the most just law
Now took your brother's life, or to redeem him
Give up your body to such sweet uncleanness
As she that he hath stained?
ISABELLA   Sir, believe this,
I had rather give my body than my soul.
ANGELO
I talk not of your soul: our compelled sins   57
Stand more for number than for accompt.   58
ISABELLA   How say you?
ANGELO
Nay, I'll not warrant that; for I can speak
Against the thing I say. Answer to this:
I, now the voice of the recorded law,
Pronounce a sentence on your brother's life;
Might there not be a charity in sin
To save this brother's life?
ISABELLA   Please you to do't,
I'll take it as a peril to my soul;
It is no sin at all, but charity.
ANGELO
Pleased you to do't, at peril of your soul,
Were equal poise of sin and charity.   68
ISABELLA
That I do beg his life, if it be sin,
Heaven let me bear it: you granting of my suit,
If that be sin, I'll make it my morn prayer
To have it added to the faults of mine
And nothing of your answer.   73
ANGELO   Nay, but hear me;
Your sense pursues not mine: either you are ignorant,   74
Or seem so, crafty; and that's not good.
ISABELLA
Let me be ignorant, and in nothing good
But graciously to know I am no better.
ANGELO
Thus wisdom wishes to appear most bright
When it doth tax itself, as these black masks   79
Proclaim an enshield beauty ten times louder   80
Than beauty could, displayed. But mark me;
To be receivèd plain, I'll speak more gross:
Your brother is to die.
ISABELLA So.

II, iv Within the house of Angelo **2** *several* separate **3** *invention* imagination **7** *conception* thought; *The state* i.e. statecraft **11** *with boot* profitably **16** *Angel* (Angelo is punning on his own name) **17** *crest* i.e. proper designation **28** *part* places **39** *reprieve* delay of execution **44** *remit* pardon **45** *saucy sweetness* wanton enjoyments **48** *restrainèd* forbidden **51** *pose* put a question to **57** *compelled* involuntary **58** *Stand . . . accompt* are recorded but not added up against us **68** *poise* balance **73** *of . . . answer* to which you need answer **74** *ignorant* i.e. lacking in understanding **79** *tax* accuse **80** *enshield* screened, hidden

ANGELO
And his offense is so, as it appears,
86 Accountant to the law upon that pain.

ISABELLA True.

ANGELO
Admit no other way to save his life –
89 As I subscribe not that, nor any other,
90 But in the loss of question – that you, his sister,
Finding yourself desired of such a person
Whose credit with the judge, or own great place,
Could fetch your brother from the manacles
Of the all-binding law ; and that there were
No earthly mean to save him, but that either
You must lay down the treasures of your body
97 To this supposèd, or else to let him suffer,
What would you do ?

   ISABELLA
As much for my poor brother as myself :
That is, were I under the terms of death,
Th' impression of keen whips I'ld wear as rubies,
And strip myself to death as to a bed
103 That longing have been sick for, ere I'ld yield
My body up to shame.

ANGELO   Then must your brother die.

   ISABELLA
And 'twere the cheaper way :
Better it were a brother died at once
Than that a sister, by redeeming him,
Should die for ever.

ANGELO
Were not you then as cruel as the sentence
That you have slandered so ?

   ISABELLA
111 Ignomy in ransom and free pardon
112 Are of two houses : lawful mercy
Is nothing kin to foul redemption.

ANGELO
You seemed of late to make the law a tyrant,
And rather proved the sliding of your brother
116 A merriment than a vice.

   ISABELLA
O pardon me, my lord ; it oft falls out
To have what we would have, we speak not what we
   mean.
I something do excuse the thing I hate
For his advantage that I dearly love.

ANGELO
We are all frail.

   ISABELLA   Else let my brother die,
122 If not a fedary, but only he
Owe and succeed thy weakness.

ANGELO
Nay, women are frail too.

   ISABELLA
Ay, as the glasses where they view themselves,
126 Which are as easy broke as they make forms.
Women, help heaven ! Men their creation mar
In profiting by them. Nay, call us ten times frail,
For we are soft as our complexions are,
130 And credulous to false prints.

   ANGELO   I think it well :
And from this testimony of your own sex –
Since I suppose we are made to be no stronger
Than faults may shake our frames – let me be bold.

I do arrest your words. Be that you are,   134
That is, a woman ; if you be more, you're none.
If you be one, as you are well expressed   136
By all external warrants, show it now,
By putting on the destined livery.   138

ISABELLA
I have no tongue but one. Gentle my lord,
Let me entreat you speak the former language.   140

ANGELO
Plainly conceive, I love you.

ISABELLA
My brother did love Juliet,
And you tell me that he shall die for't.

ANGELO
He shall not, Isabel, if you give me love.

ISABELLA
I know your virtue hath a license in't,
Which seems a little fouler than it is,
To pluck on others.   147

ANGELO   Believe me, on mine honor,
My words express my purpose.

ISABELLA
Ha ! little honor to be much believed,
And most pernicious purpose. Seeming, seeming !
I will proclaim thee, Angelo, look for't !
Sign me a present pardon for my brother,
Or with an outstretched throat I'll tell the world aloud
What man thou art.

ANGELO   Who will believe thee, Isabel ?
My unsoiled name, th' austereness of my life,
My vouch against you, and my place i' th' state,   156
Will so your accusation overweigh
That you shall stifle in your own report
And smell of calumny. I have begun,
And now I give my sensual race the rein.   160
Fit thy consent to my sharp appetite,
Lay by all nicety and prolixious blushes,   162
That banish what they sue for : redeem thy brother
By yielding up thy body to my will,
Or else he must not only die the death,
But thy unkindness shall his death draw out
To ling'ring sufferance. Answer me to-morrow,   167
Or, by the affection that now guides me most,   168
I'll prove a tyrant to him. As for you,
Say what you can, my false o'erweighs your true.   *Exit.*

ISABELLA
To whom should I complain ? Did I tell this,
Who would believe me ? O perilous mouths,
That bear in them one and the selfsame tongue,
Either of condemnation or approof,   174
Bidding the law make curtsy to their will,   175
Hooking both right and wrong to th' appetite,
To follow as it draws. I'll to my brother.   177

---

86 *Accountant* accountable ; *pain* penalty   89 *subscribe* assent to   90 *But
. . . question* except that discussion would flag   97 *supposèd* imaginary person   103 *longing . . . for* i.e. sick with longing for   111 *Ignomy* ignominy
112 *of two houses* i.e. completely different   116 *merriment* light matter
122 *fedary* accomplice   122–23 (meaning uncertain ; a line has probably
dropped out)   126 *forms* images   130 *credulous* susceptible   134 *I . . .
words* I take you at your word   136 *expressed* shown to be   138 *destined
livery* behavior which properly belongs to you   140 *former* i.e. customary
147 *pluck* lure   156 *vouch* testimony   160 *race* (implies both 'course' and
'courser')   162 *prolixious* long-drawn-out   167 *sufferance* torture   168
affection passion   174 *approof* approval   175 *make curtsy to* i.e. bow down
before   177 *as* in whatever direction

178   Though he hath fall'n by prompture of the blood,
Yet hath he in him such a mind of honor
That, had he twenty heads to tender down
On twenty bloody blocks, he'ld yield them up,
Before his sister should her body stoop
To such abhorred pollution.
Then, Isabel, live chaste, and, brother, die :
More than our brother is our chastity.
I'll tell him yet of Angelo's request,
And fit his mind to death, for his soul's rest.   *Exit.*

*

III, i   *Enter Duke [as a friar], Claudio, and Provost.*

DUKE
So then you hope of pardon from Lord Angelo ?
CLAUDIO
The miserable have no other medicine
But only hope :
I have hope to live, and am prepared to die.
DUKE
Be absolute for death : either death or life
Shall thereby be the sweeter. Reason thus with life :
If I do lose thee, I do lose a thing
That none but fools would keep ; a breath thou art,
9   Servile to all the skyey influences
10   That dost this habitation where thou keep'st
Hourly afflict ; merely, thou art death's fool,
For him thou labor'st by thy flight to shun,
And yet run'st toward him still. Thou art not noble,
14   For all th'accommodations that thou bear'st
Are nursed by baseness. Thou'rt by no means valiant,
For thou dost fear the soft and tender fork
Of a poor worm ; thy best of rest is sleep,
And that thou oft provok'st, yet grossly fear'st
Thy death, which is no more. Thou art not thyself,
For thou exists on many a thousand grains
That issue out of dust. Happy thou art not,
For what thou hast not, still thou striv'st to get,
23   And what thou hast, forget'st. Thou art not certain,
24   For thy complexion shifts to strange effects,
After the moon. If thou art rich, thou'rt poor,
For, like an ass whose back with ingots bows,
Thou bear'st thy heavy riches but a journey,
And death unloads thee. Friend hast thou none,
29   For thine own bowels, which do call thee sire,
30   The mere effusion of thy proper loins,
31   Do curse the gout, serpigo, and the rheum
For ending thee no sooner. Thou hast nor youth nor age,
But as it were an after-dinner's sleep,
Dreaming on both, for all thy blessèd youth
Becomes as agèd, and doth beg the alms
36   Of palsied eld : and when thou art old and rich,
37   Thou hast neither heat, affection, limb, nor beauty,

To make thy riches pleasant. What's yet in this
That bears the name of life ? Yet in this life
Lie hid moe thousand deaths ; yet death we fear,   40
That makes these odds all even.
CLAUDIO   I humbly thank you.
To sue to live, I find I seek to die,   42
And, seeking death, find life : let it come on.
     Enter Isabella.
ISABELLA
What, ho ! Peace here ; grace and good company.
PROVOST
Who's there ? Come in, the wish deserves a welcome.
DUKE
Dear sir, ere long I'll visit you again.
CLAUDIO
Most holy sir, I thank you.
ISABELLA
My business is a word or two with Claudio.
PROVOST
And very welcome. Look, signior, here's your sister.
DUKE
Provost, a word with you.
PROVOST
As many as you please.
DUKE
Bring me to hear them speak, where I may be concealed.
     [Duke and Provost withdraw.]
CLAUDIO
Now, sister, what's the comfort ?
ISABELLA
Why,
As all comforts are : most good, most good indeed.
Lord Angelo, having affairs to heaven,
Intends you for his swift ambassador,
Where you shall be an everlasting leiger ;   59
Therefore your best appointment make with speed ;   60
To-morrow you set on.
CLAUDIO   Is there no remedy ?
ISABELLA
None but such remedy as, to save a head,
To cleave a heart in twain.
CLAUDIO   But is there any ?
ISABELLA
Yes, brother, you may live ;
There is a devilish mercy in the judge,
If you'll implore it, that will free your life,
But fetter you till death.
CLAUDIO   Perpetual durance ?   67
ISABELLA
Ay, just – perpetual durance, a restraint,
Though all the world's vastidity you had,   69
To a determined scope.
CLAUDIO   But in what nature ?
ISABELLA
In such a one as, you consenting to't,
Would bark your honor from that trunk you bear,
And leave you naked.
CLAUDIO   Let me know the point.
ISABELLA
O, I do fear thee, Claudio, and I quake,
Lest thou a feverous life shouldst entertain,
And six or seven winters more respect
Than a perpetual honor. Dar'st thou die ?
The sense of death is most in apprehension,   78

---

178 *prompture* prompting
III, i The prison   **9** *skyey influences* influences of the stars   **10** *keep'st live*   **14** *accommodations* comforts   **23** *certain* constant   **24–25** *thy . . . moon* i.e. your nature is changeable in its desires   **29** *bowels* offspring   **30** *mere* very ; *proper* own   **31** *serpigo* skin eruption ; *rheum* catarrh   **36** *eld* old age   **37** *heat, affection, limb* warmth of blood, strength of feeling, vigor of limb   **40** *moe* more   **42** *To sue* i.e. in suing   **59** *leiger* resident ambassador   **60** *appointment* preparation   **67** *durance* imprisonment   **69–70** *Though . . . scope* though you had the whole extent of the world set out to move about in   **78** *sense* feeling

And the poor beetle that we tread upon
In corporal sufferance finds a pang as great
As when a giant dies.

CLAUDIO   Why give you me this shame ?
Think you I can a resolution fetch
83   From flow'ry tenderness ? If I must die,
I will encounter darkness as a bride,
And hug it in mine arms.

ISABELLA
There spake my brother : there my father's grave
Did utter forth a voice. Yes, thou must die :
Thou art too noble to conserve a life
89   In base appliances. This outward-sainted deputy,
Whose settled visage and deliberate word
91   Nips youth i' th' head, and follies doth enew
As falcon doth the fowl, is yet a devil :
93   His filth within being cast, he would appear
A pond as deep as hell.

94 CLAUDIO   The prenzie Angelo !

ISABELLA
O, 'tis the cunning livery of hell,
The damnedest body to invest and cover
97   In prenzie guards ; dost thou think, Claudio,
If I would yield him my virginity,
Thou mightst be freed !

CLAUDIO   O heavens, it cannot be.

ISABELLA
Yes, he would give't thee, from this rank offense,
So to offend him still. This night's the time
That I should do what I abhor to name,
Or else thou diest tomorrow.

CLAUDIO   Thou shalt not do't.

ISABELLA
O, were it but my life,
I'd throw it down for your deliverance
106   As frankly as a pin.

CLAUDIO   Thanks, dear Isabel.

ISABELLA
Be ready, Claudio, for your death to-morrow.

CLAUDIO
108   Yes. Has he affections in him,
109   That thus can make him bite the law by th' nose,
When he would force it ? Sure it is no sin,
Or of the deadly seven it is the least.

ISABELLA
Which is the least ?

CLAUDIO
If it were damnable, he being so wise,
114   Why would he for the momentary trick
115   Be perdurably fined ? O Isabel !

ISABELLA
What says my brother ?

CLAUDIO   Death is a fearful thing.

ISABELLA
And shamèd life a hateful.

CLAUDIO
Ay, but to die, and go we know not where,
119   To lie in cold obstruction and to rot,
120   This sensible warm motion to become
121   A kneaded clod ; and the delighted spirit
To bathe in fiery floods, or to reside
123   In thrilling region of thick-ribbèd ice,
124   To be imprisoned in the viewless winds
And blown with restless violence round about

The pendent world ; or to be worse than worst   126
Of those that lawless and incertain thought   127
Imagine howling, 'tis too horrible.
The weariest and most loathèd worldly life
That age, ache, penury, and imprisonment
Can lay on nature is a paradise
To what we fear of death.

ISABELLA
Alas, alas.

CLAUDIO   Sweet sister, let me live.
What sin you do to save a brother's life,
Nature dispenses with the deed so far   135
That it becomes a virtue.

ISABELLA   O you beast,
O faithless coward, O dishonest wretch !
Wilt thou be made a man out of my vice ?
Is't not a kind of incest, to take life
From thine own sister's shame ? What should I think ?
Heaven shield my mother played my father fair,
For such a warpèd slip of wilderness   142
Ne'er issued from his blood. Take my defiance,
Die, perish. Might but my bending down
Reprieve thee from thy fate, it should proceed.
I'll pray a thousand prayers for thy death,
No word to save thee.

CLAUDIO
Nay, hear me, Isabel.

ISABELLA   O, fie, fie, fie !
Thy sin's not accidental, but a trade ;
Mercy to thee would prove itself a bawd,
'Tis best that thou diest quickly.   [Going.]

CLAUDIO   O hear me, Isabella.

[Duke comes forward.]

DUKE
Vouchsafe a word, young sister, but one word.

ISABELLA What is your will ?

DUKE Might you dispense with your leisure, I would by
and by have some speech with you : the satisfaction I
would require is likewise your own benefit.

ISABELLA I have no superfluous leisure ; my stay must
be stolen out of other affairs, but I will attend you a   158
while.

DUKE [aside to Claudio] Son, I have overheard what hath
passed between you and your sister. Angelo had never
the purpose to corrupt her ; only he hath made an assay   162
of her virtue to practice his judgment with the disposi-   163
tion of natures. She, having the truth of honor in her,
hath made him that gracious denial which he is most
glad to receive. I am confessor to Angelo, and I know
this to be true ; therefore prepare yourself to death. Do

83 *flow'ry tenderness* i.e. comforting figures of speech 89 *appliances*
remedies, means 91 *Nips . . . head* checks youth from above ; *enew* drive
down into water 93 *cast* vomited up 94, 97 *prenzie* (word of uncertain
meaning sometimes read as 'precise,' sometimes as an Italianate title
equivalent to 'prince' or 'princely') 97 *guards* trimmings 106 *frankly*
freely 108 *affections* feelings, desires 109–10 *bite . . . force it* assail the
law when he would enforce it 114 *trick* trifle 115 *perdurably fined*
eternally damned 119 *obstruction* stagnation 120 *sensible* sentient ; *motion*
organism 121 *delighted* capable of delight (?), deprived of light (?) 123
thrilling piercingly cold 124 *viewless* invisible 126 *pendent* suspended in
space 127 *lawless . . . thought* i.e. wild conjecture 135 *dispenses with*
grants a dispensation, or permit, for 142 *wilderness* wildness 158 *attend*
wait for 162 *assay* trial 163–64 *practice . . . natures* test his judgment of
character

not satisfy your resolution with hopes that are fallible : tomorrow you must die ; go to your knees and make ready.

CLAUDIO Let me ask my sister pardon. I am so out of love with life that I will sue to be rid of it.

DUKE Hold you there : farewell.   [Exit Claudio.]
[Enter Provost.]

Provost, a word with you.

PROVOST What's your will, father?

DUKE That now you are come, you will be gone. Leave
176   me a while with the maid ; my mind promises with my habit no loss shall touch her by my company.

PROVOST In good time.   Exit.

DUKE The hand that hath made you fair hath made you good. The goodness that is cheap in beauty makes beauty
181   brief in goodness ; but grace, being the soul of your complexion, shall keep the body of it ever fair. The assault that Angelo hath made to you, fortune hath conveyed to my understanding ; and, but that frailty hath examples for his falling, I should wonder at Angelo. How will you do to content this substitute, and to save your brother?

187 ISABELLA I am now going to resolve him. I had rather my brother die by the law than my son should be unlawfully born. But O, how much is the good Duke deceived in Angelo ! If ever he return and I can speak to him, I will
191   open my lips in vain, or discover his government.

DUKE That shall not be much amiss : yet, as the matter now stands, he will avoid your accusation ; he made trial of you only. Therefore fasten your ear on my advisings : to the love I have in doing good a remedy presents itself. I do make myself believe that you may most uprightously do a poor wronged lady a merited benefit, redeem your brother from the angry law, do no stain to your own gracious person, and much please the
200   absent Duke, if peradventure he shall ever return to have hearing of this business.

ISABELLA Let me hear you speak farther ; I have spirit to do anything that appears not foul in the truth of my spirit.

DUKE Virtue is bold, and goodness never fearful. Have you not heard speak of Mariana, the sister of Frederick, the great soldier who miscarried at sea?

ISABELLA I have heard of the lady, and good words went with her name.

DUKE She should this Angelo have married, was affianced by her oath, and the nuptial appointed : between which
211   time of the contract and limit of the solemnity, her brother Frederick was wracked at sea, having in that perished vessel the dowry of his sister. But mark how heavily this befell to the poor gentlewoman : there she lost a noble and renowned brother, in his love toward her ever most kind and natural ; with him the portion and sinew of her fortune, her marriage dowry ; with
218   both, her combinate husband, this well-seeming Angelo.

ISABELLA Can this be so? Did Angelo so leave her?

DUKE Left her in her tears, and dried not one of them with his comfort ; swallowed his vows whole, pretending in her discoveries of dishonor ; in few, bestowed her on her own lamentation, which she yet wears for his sake ; and he, a marble to her tears, is washed with them, but relents not.

ISABELLA What a merit were it in death to take this poor maid from the world ! What corruption in this life, that
it will let this man live ! But how out of this can she avail? 228

DUKE It is a rupture that you may easily heal ; and the cure of it not only saves your brother, but keeps you from dishonor in doing it.

ISABELLA Show me how, good father.

DUKE This forenamed maid hath yet in her the continuance of her first affection ; his unjust unkindness, that in all reason should have quenched her love, hath, like an impediment in the current, made it more violent and unruly. Go you to Angelo, answer his requiring with a plausible obedience, agree with his demands to the point. 238 Only refer yourself to this advantage : first, that your stay with him may not be long, that the time may have
all shadow and silence in it, and the place answer to con- 241 venience. This being granted in course – and now follows all – we shall advise this wronged maid to stead up 243 your appointment, go in your place. If the encounter acknowledge itself hereafter, it may compel him to her recompense ; and here, by this is your brother saved, your honor untainted, the poor Mariana advantaged,
and the corrupt deputy scaled. The maid will I frame 248 and make fit for his attempt. If you think well to carry this, as you may, the doubleness of the benefit defends the deceit from reproof. What think you of it?

ISABELLA The image of it gives me content already, and I trust it will grow to a most prosperous perfection.

DUKE It lies much in your holding up. Haste you speedily 254 to Angelo ; if for this night he entreat you to his bed,
give him promise of satisfaction. I will presently to St 256
Luke's ; there at the moated grange resides this dejec- 257 ted Mariana. At that place call upon me, and dispatch with Angelo, that it may be quickly.

ISABELLA I thank you for this comfort ; fare you well, good father.   Exit.

ELBOW Nay, if there be no remedy for it but that you will needs buy and sell men and women like beasts, we shall
have all the world drink brown and white bastard.   3

DUKE O heavens, what stuff is here?

POMPEY 'Twas never merry world since, of two usuries, the merriest was put down, and the worser allowed by order of law a furred gown to keep him warm ; and furred with fox and lamb skins too, to signify that craft,
being richer than innocency, stands for the facing.   9

ELBOW Come your way, sir. Bless you, good father friar.

DUKE And you, good brother father. What offense hath this man made you, sir?

ELBOW Marry, sir, he hath offended the law ; and, sir, we take him to be a thief too, sir, for we have found upon him, sir, a strange picklock, which we have sent to the deputy.

DUKE
Fie, sirrah, a bawd, a wicked bawd !
The evil that thou causest to be done,
That is thy means to live. Do thou but think
What 'tis to cram a maw or clothe a back   20

176–77 *with my habit* i.e. as well as my priestly robes 181 *complexion* character 187 *resolve* answer 191 *discover his government* expose his conduct 200 *peradventure* perchance 211 *limit of the solemnity* date set for the marriage ceremony 218 *combinate* affianced 228 *avail* benefit 238 *to the point* precisely 241 *shadow* secrecy 243–44 *stead up your appointment* keep your appointment for you 248 *scaled* weighed ; *frame* prepare 254 *It . . . up* it depends much on your support 256 *presently* at once 257 *moated grange* country house surrounded by a moat
III, ii 3 *bastard* a sweet Spanish wine (with pun) 9 *stands . . . facing* supports the trimming 20 *cram a maw* fill a mouth

From such a filthy vice; say to thyself,
From their abominable and beastly touches
I drink, I eat, array myself, and live.
Canst thou believe thy living is a life,
25 So stinkingly depending? Go mend, go mend.

POMPEY Indeed, it does stink in some sort, sir; but yet,
sir, I would prove –

DUKE
Nay, if the devil have given thee proofs for sin,
Thou wilt prove his. Take him to prison, officer.
Correction and instruction must both work
Ere this rude beast will profit.

ELBOW He must before the deputy, sir; he has given him
warning. The deputy cannot abide a whoremaster; if he
34 be a whoremonger, and comes before him, he were as
good go a mile on his errand.

DUKE
That we were all, as some would seem to be,
Free from our faults, as faults from seeming free.

Enter Lucio.

38 ELBOW His neck will come to your waist – a cord, sir.

POMPEY I spy comfort, I cry bail. Here's a gentleman
and a friend of mine.

LUCIO How now, noble Pompey? What, at the wheels of
Caesar? Art thou led in triumph? What, is there none
43 of Pygmalion's images newly made woman to be had
now, for putting the hand in the pocket and extracting
it clutched? What reply? ha? What say'st thou to this
tune, matter and method? Is't not drowned i' th' last
47 rain, ha? What say'st thou, trot? Is the world as it was,
man? Which is the way? Is it sad, and few words, or
how? The trick of it?

DUKE Still thus, and thus, still worse.

LUCIO How doth my dear morsel, thy mistress? Procures she still, ha?

POMPEY Troth, sir, she hath eaten up all her beef, and
54 she is herself in the tub.

LUCIO Why, 'tis good. It is the right of it; it must be so.
56 Ever your fresh whore and your powdered bawd; an
unshunned consequence, it must be so. Art going to
prison, Pompey?

POMPEY Yes, faith, sir.

LUCIO Why, 'tis not amiss, Pompey; farewell. Go, say I
sent thee thither. For debt, Pompey? or how?

ELBOW For being a bawd, for being a bawd.

LUCIO Well, then, imprison him. If imprisonment be the
due of a bawd, why, 'tis his right. Bawd is he doubtless,
and of antiquity too; bawd-born. Farewell, good Pompey; commend me to the prison, Pompey. You will turn
67 good husband now, Pompey, you will keep the house.

POMPEY I hope, sir, your good worship will be my bail.

69 LUCIO No, indeed will I not, Pompey; it is not the wear. I
will pray, Pompey, to increase your bondage: if you
71 take it not patiently, why, your mettle is the more.
Adieu, trusty Pompey. 'Bless you, friar.

DUKE And you.

LUCIO Does Bridget paint still, Pompey, ha?

ELBOW Come your ways, sir, come.

POMPEY You will not bail me then, sir?

LUCIO Then, Pompey, nor now. What news abroad,
friar, what news?

79 ELBOW Come your ways, sir, come.

LUCIO Go to kennel, Pompey, go.

[Exeunt Elbow, Pompey, and Officers.]

What news, friar, of the Duke?

DUKE I know none. Can you tell me of any?

LUCIO Some say he is with the emperor of Russia; other
some, he is in Rome. But where is he, think you?

DUKE I know not where; but wheresoever, I wish him
well.

LUCIO It was a mad fantastical trick of him to steal from
the state, and usurp the beggary he was never born to.
Lord Angelo dukes it well in his absence; he puts 89
transgression to't.

DUKE He does well in't.

LUCIO A little more lenity to lechery would do no harm
in him. Something too crabbed that way, friar.

DUKE It is too general a vice, and severity must cure it.

LUCIO Yes, in good sooth, the vice is of a great kindred; it
is well allied, but it is impossible to extirp it quite, friar, 96
till eating and drinking be put down. They say this
Angelo was not made by man and woman after this
downright way of creation. Is it true, think you?

DUKE How should he be made then?

LUCIO Some report a sea-maid spawned him; some that
he was begot between two stock-fishes. But it is certain 102
that when he makes water his urine is congealed ice,
that I know to be true. And he is a motion generative, 104
that's infallible.

DUKE You are pleasant, sir, and speak apace. 106

LUCIO Why, what a ruthless thing is this in him, for the
rebellion of a cod-piece to take away the life of a man!
Would the Duke that is absent have done this? Ere he
would have hanged a man for the getting a hundred
bastards, he would have paid for the nursing a thousand.
He had some feeling of the sport, he knew the service,
and that instructed him to mercy.

DUKE I never heard the absent Duke much detected for 114
women; he was not inclined that way.

LUCIO O, sir, you are deceived.

DUKE 'Tis not possible.

LUCIO Who? Not the Duke? Yes, your beggar of fifty,
and his use was to put a ducat in her clack-dish; the 119
Duke had crotchets in him. He would be drunk, too; 120
that let me inform you.

DUKE You do him wrong, surely.

LUCIO Sir, I was an inward of his. A shy fellow was 123
the Duke, and I believe I know the cause of his with-
drawing.

DUKE What, I prithee, might be the cause?

LUCIO No, pardon. 'Tis a secret must be locked within
the teeth and the lips. But this I can let you understand,
the greater file of the subject held the Duke to be wise. 129

DUKE Wise? Why, no question but he was.

LUCIO A very superficial, ignorant, unweighing fellow.

DUKE Either this is envy in you, folly, or mistaking. The
very stream of his life and the business he hath helmed 133

---

25 *depending* dependant   34–35 *he . . . errand* i.e. he has a hard road ahead
38 *cord* (worn with the friar's habit)   43 *Pygmalion's images* i.e. prostitutes
(in classical myth Pygmalion's work of sculpture came to life in response to
his passion for it)   47 *trot* midwife   54 *in the tub* taking the cure for
venereal disease   56 *powdered* pickled   67 *husband* manager; *keep the
house* stay indoors (pun)   69 *wear* fashion   71 *mettle* impatience (with pun
on the 'metal' of shackles)   79 *your ways* along   89–90 *puts . . . to't* i.e. puts
transgression at hazard   96 *extirp* eradicate   102 *stock-fishes* dried cod
104 *motion generative* masculine puppet   106 *pleasant* jovial   114 *detected* open to accusation   119 *clack-dish* wooden dish   120 *crotchets* whims
123 *inward* intimate   129 *file of the subject* rank and file   133 *helmed*
steered

134 must, upon a warranted need, give him a better pro-
135 clamation. Let him be but testimonied in his own bring-
ings-forth, and he shall appear to the envious a scholar,
a statesman, and a soldier. Therefore you speak unskillfully; or, if your knowledge be more, it is much
darkened in your malice.

LUCIO Sir, I know him, and I love him.

DUKE Love talks with better knowledge, and knowledge with dearer love.

LUCIO Come, sir, I know what I know.

DUKE I can hardly believe that, since you know not what
you speak. But if ever the Duke return, as our prayers
146 are he may, let me desire you to make your answer
before him. If it be honest you have spoke, you have
courage to maintain it. I am bound to call upon you;
and, I pray you, your name?

LUCIO Sir, my name is Lucio, well known to the Duke.

DUKE He shall know you better, sir, if I may live to report
you.

LUCIO I fear you not.

DUKE O, you hope the Duke will return no more, or you
155 imagine me too unhurtful an opposite, but indeed I can
do you little harm; you'll forswear this again.

LUCIO I'll be hanged first; thou art deceived in me, friar.
But no more of this; canst thou tell if Claudio die to-
morrow or no?

DUKE Why should he die, sir?

161 LUCIO Why? For filling a bottle with a tun-dish. I would
162 the Duke we talk of were returned again; this ungenitured agent will unpeople the province with continency.
Sparrows must not build in his house-eaves because
they are lecherous. The Duke yet would have dark
deeds darkly answered; he would never bring them to
light; would he were returned. Marry, this Claudio is
168 condemned for untrussing. Farewell, good friar; I
prithee, pray for me. The Duke, I say to thee again,
170 would eat mutton on Fridays. He's now past it; yet and I
say to thee, he could mouth with a beggar, though she
smelt brown bread and garlic. Say that I said so;
farewell.   *Exit.*

DUKE
No might nor greatness in mortality
Can censure 'scape; back-wounding calumny
The whitest virtue strikes. What king so strong
Can tie the gall up in the slanderous tongue?
But who comes here?

*Enter Escalus, Provost, and [Officers with] Bawd
[Mistress Overdone].*

ESCALUS Go, away with her to prison.

MISTRESS OVERDONE Good my lord, be good to me.
Your honor is accounted a merciful man, good my lord.

181 ESCALUS Double and treble admonition, and still forfeit
in the same kind! This would make mercy swear, and
play the tyrant.

134 *must . . . proclamation* must, if he should really need it, proclaim
that he is better than you allege   135–36 *testimonied . . . brings-forth*
tested by his own actions   146 *make . . . answer* i.e. defend your allegations
155 *opposite* opponent   161 *tun-dish* funnel   162 *ungenitured* sexless
168 *untrussing* undressing   170 *mutton* harlot (pun)   181–82 *forfeit . . .
kind* guilty of the same offense   189 *Philip and Jacob* May 1   200 *advised*
. . . *entertainment* counseled him for the reception   211–12 *it is . . . undertaking* to be constant is as dangerous as it is virtuous   214 *security* . . .
accursed i.e. endorsing bonds has become the curse of friendship   224
events affairs   228 *sinister measure* left-handed judgment   236–37 *extremest
. . . modesty* furthest limits of propriety   239 *straitness* strictness

PROVOST A bawd of eleven years' continuance, may it
please your honor.

MISTRESS OVERDONE My lord, this is one Lucio's information against me. Mistress Kate Keepdown was
with child by him in the Duke's time; he promised her
marriage. His child is a year and a quarter old, come
Philip and Jacob; I have kept it myself, and see how he   189
goes about to abuse me.

ESCALUS That fellow is a fellow of much license; let him
be called before us. Away with her to prison; go to, no
more words. *[Exeunt Officers with Mistress Overdone.]*
Provost, my brother Angelo will not be altered; Claudio
must die tomorrow. Let him be furnished with divines,
and have all charitable preparation. If my brother
wrought by my pity, it should not be so with him.

PROVOST So please you, this friar hath been with him,
and advised him for th' entertainment of death.   200

ESCALUS Good even, good father.

DUKE Bliss and goodness on you!

ESCALUS Of whence are you?

DUKE
Not of this country, though my chance is now
To use it for my time. I am a brother
Of gracious order, late come from the See,
In special business from his Holiness.

ESCALUS What news abroad i' th' world?

DUKE None, but that there is so great a fever on goodness
that the dissolution of it must cure it. Novelty is only in
request, and it is as dangerous to be aged in any kind of   211
course as it is virtuous to be constant in any undertaking.
There is scarce truth enough alive to make societies
secure, but security enough to make fellowships accur-   214
sed. Much upon this riddle runs the wisdom of the
world. This news is old enough, yet it is every day's
news. I pray you, sir, of what disposition was the Duke?

ESCALUS One that, above all other strifes, contended
especially to know himself.

DUKE What pleasure was he given to?

ESCALUS Rather rejoicing to see another merry, than
merry at anything which professed to make him rejoice:
a gentleman of all temperance. But leave we him to his
events, with a prayer they may prove prosperous, and   224
let me desire to know how you find Claudio prepared.
I am made to understand that you have lent him visitation.

DUKE He professes to have received no sinister measure   228
from his judge, but most willingly humbles himself to
the determination of justice; yet had he framed to himself, by the instruction of his frailty, many deceiving
promises of life, which I, by my good leisure, have discredited to him, and now is he resolved to die.

ESCALUS You have paid the heavens your function, and
the prisoner the very debt of your calling. I have labored
for the poor gentleman to the extremest shore of my   236
modesty, but my brother-justice have I found so severe
that he hath forced me to tell him he is indeed Justice.

DUKE If his own life answer the straitness of his proceed-   239
ing, it shall become him well; wherein if he chance to
fail, he hath sentenced himself.

ESCALUS I am going to visit the prisoner. Fare you well.
      [Exeunt Escalus and Provost.]

DUKE Peace be with you!
He who the sword of heaven will bear
Should be as holy as severe;

Pattern in himself to know,
Grace to stand, and virtue go ;
More nor less to others paying
Than by self-offenses weighing.
Shame to him whose cruel striking
Kills for faults of his own liking.
Twice treble shame on Angelo,
To weed my vice and let his grow.
O, what may man within him hide,
Though angel on the outward side !
256   How may likeness made in crimes,
Making practice on the times,
To draw with idle spider's strings
Most ponderous and substantial things ?
Craft against vice I must apply ;
With Angelo tonight shall lie
His old betrothèd, but despisèd :
So disguise shall be th' disguisèd
Pay with falsehood, false exacting,
And perform an old contracting.   *Exit.*

               *

IV, i   *Enter Mariana, and Boy singing.*
             Song.
Take, O take those lips away,
    That so sweetly were forsworn ;
And those eyes, the break of day,
    Lights that do mislead the morn ;
But my kisses bring again, bring again,
Seals of love, but sealed in vain, sealed in vain.

    Enter Duke [disguised as before].
MARIANA
Break off thy song, and haste thee quick away.
Here comes a man of comfort, whose advice
9   Hath often stilled my brawling discontent.   *[Exit Boy.]*
I cry you mercy, sir, and well could wish
You had not found me here so musical.
Let me excuse me, and believe me so,
My mirth it much displeased, but pleased my woe.
DUKE
'Tis good ; though music oft hath such a charm
To make bad good, and good provoke to harm.
I pray you tell me, hath anybody inquired for me here
to-day ? Much upon this time have I promised here to
meet.
MARIANA You have not been inquired after ; I have sat
here all day.
    Enter Isabella.
21 DUKE I do constantly believe you ; the time is come even
now. I shall crave your forbearance a little ; may be I will
call upon you anon, for some advantage to yourself.
MARIANA I am always bound to you.   *Exit.*
DUKE
Very well met, and welcome.
What is the news from this good deputy ?
ISABELLA
27   He hath a garden circummured with brick,
Whose western side is with a vineyard backed ;
29   And to that vineyard is a planchèd gate,
30   That makes his opening with this bigger key.
This other doth command a little door
Which from the vineyard to the garden leads.

There have I made my promise,
Upon the heavy middle of the night,
To call upon him.
DUKE
But shall you on your knowledge find this way ?
ISABELLA
I have ta'en a due and wary note upon't.
With whispering and most guilty diligence,
In action all of precept, he did show me   39
The way twice o'er.
DUKE   Are there no other tokens
Between you 'greed concerning her observance ?   41
ISABELLA
No, none, but only a repair i' th' dark,
And that I have possessed him my most stay   43
Can be but brief ; for I have made him know
I have a servant comes with me along,
That stays upon me, whose persuasion is   46
I come about my brother.
DUKE   'Tis well borne up.
I have not yet made known to Mariana
A word of this. What ho, within ; come forth.
    Enter Mariana.
I pray you, be acquainted with this maid ;
She comes to do you good.
ISABELLA   I do desire the like.   51
DUKE
Do you persuade yourself that I respect you ?
MARIANA
Good friar, I know you do, and have found it.
DUKE
Take then this your companion by the hand,
Who hath a story ready for your ear.
I shall attend your leisure, but make haste ;
The vaporous night approaches.
MARIANA
Will't please you walk aside ?
        Exeunt [Mariana and Isabella].
DUKE
O place and greatness, millions of false eyes
Are stuck upon thee ; volumes of report
Run with these false, and most contrarious quest   61
Upon thy doings ; thousand escapes of wit   62
Make thee the father of their idle dream,
And rack thee in their fancies.   64
    Enter Mariana and Isabella.
             Welcome, how agreed ?
ISABELLA
She'll take the enterprise upon her, father,
If you advise it.
DUKE   It is not my consent,
But my entreaty too.
ISABELLA   Little have you to say
When you depart from him but, soft and low,
'Remember now my brother.'

---

256 *likeness . . . crimes* (obscure passage, possibly corrupt, suggesting 'hypocrisy')
IV, i The moated grange   9 *brawling* clamorous   21 *constantly* assuredly
27 *circummured* walled about   29 *planchèd* boarded   30 *makes his opening* may be opened   39 *In . . . precept* teaching by demonstration   41 *observance* prescribed conduct   43 *possessed* informed   46 *stays upon* waits for   51 *the like* i.e. that very thing   61 *false* i.e. false eyes ; *contrarious quest* i.e. perversely track (like hunters)   62 *escapes* sallies   64 *rack thee* twist thee about

MARIANA   Fear me not.

DUKE

Nor, gentle daughter, fear you not at all ;

71   He is your husband on a pre-contract ;

To bring you thus together, 'tis no sin,

Sith that the justice of your title to him

Doth flourish the deceit. Come, let us go ;

75   Our corn 's to reap, for yet our tithe 's to sow.   *Exeunt.*

＊

IV, ii   *Enter Provost and Clown [Pompey].*

PROVOST Come hither, sirrah ; can you cut off a man's head ?

POMPEY If the man be a bachelor, sir, I can ; but if he be a married man, he's his wife's head, and I can never cut off a woman's head.

5 PROVOST Come, sir, leave me your snatches, and yield me a direct answer. To-morrow morning are to die Claudio and Barnardine. Here is in our prison a common executioner, who in his office lacks a helper ; if you will take it on you to assist him, it shall redeem you from

9   your gyves ; if not, you shall have your full time of imprisonment, and your deliverance with an unpitied whipping, for you have been a notorious bawd.

POMPEY Sir, I have been an unlawful bawd time out of mind, but yet I will be content to be a lawful hangman. I would be glad to receive some instruction from my fellow partner.

PROVOST What ho, Abhorson ; where's Abhorson there ?

Enter Abhorson.

ABHORSON Do you call, sir ?

PROVOST Sirrah, here's a fellow will help you to-morrow

20   in your execution. If you think it meet, compound with him by the year, and let him abide here with you ; if not, use him for the present and dismiss him. He cannot

23   plead his estimation with you ; he hath been a bawd.

ABHORSON A bawd, sir ? Fie upon him, he will discredit

25   our mystery.

PROVOST Go to, sir, you weigh equally ; a feather will turn the scale.   *Exit.*

POMPEY Pray, sir, by your good favor – for surely, sir, a

29   good favor you have, but that you have a hanging look – do you call, sir, your occupation a mystery ?

ABHORSON Ay, sir, a mystery.

POMPEY Painting, sir, I have heard say, is a mystery, and your whores, sir, being members of my occupation, using painting, do prove my occupation a mystery ; but what mystery there should be in hanging, if I should be hanged, I cannot imagine.

ABHORSON Sir, it is a mystery.

POMPEY Proof ?

39 ABHORSON Every true man's apparel fits your thief. If it be too little for your thief, your true man thinks it big enough. If it be too big for your thief, your thief thinks it little enough ; so every true man's apparel fits your thief.

---

71 *pre-contract* legally binding proposal   75 *tithe* seed-corn (?)
IV, ii The prison   5 *snatches* quips   9 *gyves* fetters   20 *compound* make an agreement   23 *estimation* reputation   25 *mystery* profession   29 *favor* face (pun)   39 *true* honest   46 *ask forgiveness* (the executioner always asked forgiveness of the condemned man)   52 *turn* execution (pun)   53 *yare* ready   62 *starkly* stiffly   70 *curfew* i.e. the prison's evening bell   78 *qualify* mitigate ; *mealed* stained   82 *steelèd* hardened   84 *unsisting* unassisting (?) unresisting (?) ; *postern* small door

---

Enter Provost.

PROVOST Are you agreed ?

POMPEY Sir, I will serve him, for I do find your hangman is a more penitent trade than your bawd ; he doth oftener ask forgiveness.   46

PROVOST You, sirrah, provide your block and your axe to-morrow four o'clock.

ABHORSON Come on, bawd. I will instruct thee in my trade ; follow.

POMPEY I do desire to learn, sir ; and I hope, if you have occasion to use me for your own turn, you shall find me 52 yare. For truly, sir, for your kindness I owe you a good 53 turn.

PROVOST

Call hither Barnardine and Claudio.

           Exeunt [Pompey and Abhorson].

Th' one has my pity, not a jot the other,

Being a murderer, though he were my brother.

    Enter Claudio.

Look, here's the warrant, Claudio, for thy death.

'Tis now dead midnight, and by eight to-morrow

Thou must be made immortal. Where's Barnardine ?

CLAUDIO

As fast locked up in sleep as guiltless labor

When it lies starkly in the traveller's bones ;   62

He will not wake.

PROVOST   Who can do good on him ?

Well, go, prepare yourself.

    [Knocking within.]   But hark, what noise ?

Heaven give your spirits comfort.   *[Exit Claudio.]*

                       By and by.

I hope it is some pardon or reprieve

For the most gentle Claudio.

    Enter Duke [disguised as before].

               Welcome, father.

DUKE

The best and wholesom'st spirits of the night

Envelop you, good provost. Who called here of late ?

PROVOST

None since the curfew rung.   70

DUKE

Not Isabel ?

PROVOST   No.

DUKE   They will then, ere't be long.

PROVOST

What comfort is for Claudio ?

DUKE

There's some in hope.

PROVOST   It is a bitter deputy.

DUKE

Not so, not so ; his life is paralleled

Even with the stroke and line of his great justice.

He doth with holy abstinence subdue

That in himself which he spurs on his power

To qualify in others. Were he mealed with that   78

Which he corrects, then were he tyrannous,

But this being so, he's just.

    [Knocking within.]   Now are they come.

                     [Exit Provost.]

This is a gentle provost ; seldom when

The steelèd gaoler is the friend of men.   82

    [Knocking.]

How now, what noise ? That spirit's possessed with haste

That wounds th'unsisting postern with these strokes.   84

[Enter Provost.]

PROVOST
There he must stay until the officer
Arise to let him in ; he is called up.

DUKE
Have you no countermand for Claudio yet,
But he must die to-morrow ?

PROVOST   None, sir, none.

DUKE
As near the dawning, provost, as it is,
You shall hear more ere morning.

PROVOST   Happily
You something know, yet I believe there comes
No countermand ; no such example have we.
93 Besides, upon the very siege of justice,
Lord Angelo hath to the public ear
Professed the contrary.

Enter a Messenger.

DUKE
This is his lordship's man.

PROVOST
And here comes Claudio's pardon.

MESSENGER My lord hath sent you this note, and by me
this further charge ; that you swerve not from the
100 smallest article of it, neither in time, matter, or other
circumstance. Good morrow ; for, as I take it, it is
almost day.

PROVOST I shall obey him.   *[Exit Messenger.]*

DUKE *[aside]*
This is his pardon, purchased by such sin
For which the pardoner himself is in :
106 Hence hath offense his quick celerity,
When it is borne in high authority.
When vice makes mercy, mercy 's so extended
That for the fault's love is th' offender friended.
Now, sir, what news ?

111 PROVOST I told you. Lord Angelo, belike thinking me remiss in mine office, awakens me with this unwonted
113 putting on – methinks strangely, for he hath not used it
before.

DUKE Pray you, let's hear.

[PROVOST *reads*] *the letter.* 'Whatsoever you may hear to
the contrary, let Claudio be executed by four of the
clock ; and, in the afternoon, Barnardine. For my better
satisfaction, let me have Claudio's head sent me by five.
Let this be duly performed, with a thought that more
depends on it than we must yet deliver. Thus fail not to
do your office, as you will answer it at your peril.'
What say you to this, sir ?

124 DUKE What is that Barnardine who is to be executed in
th'afternoon ?

PROVOST A Bohemian born, but here nursed up and
bred ; one that is a prisoner nine years old.

DUKE How came it that the absent Duke had not either
delivered him to his liberty or executed him ? I have
heard it was ever his manner to do so.

PROVOST His friends still wrought reprieves for him ;
132 and, indeed, his fact, till now in the government of Lord
Angelo, came not to an undoubtful proof.

DUKE It is now apparent ?

PROVOST Most manifest, and not denied by himself.

DUKE Hath he borne himself penitently in prison ? How
seems he to be touched ?

PROVOST A man that apprehends death no more dread-

fully but as a drunken sleep : careless, reckless, and fearless of what's past, present, or to come ; insensible of
mortality, and desperately mortal.

DUKE He wants advice.   142

PROVOST He will hear none. He hath evermore had the
liberty of the prison ; give him leave to escape hence, he
would not. Drunk many times a day, if not many days
entirely drunk. We have very oft awaked him, as if to
carry him to execution, and showed him a seeming
warrant for it ; it hath not moved him at all.

DUKE More of him anon. There is written in your brow,
provost, honesty and constancy ; if I read it not truly,
my ancient skill beguiles me ; but in the boldness of my   151
cunning I will lay myself in hazard. Claudio, whom   152
here you have warrant to execute, is no greater forfeit to
the law than Angelo who hath sentenced him. To make
you understand this in a manifested effect, I crave but   155
four days' respite, for the which you are to do me both a
present and a dangerous courtesy.

PROVOST Pray, sir, in what ?

DUKE In the delaying death.

PROVOST Alack, how may I do it, having the hour limi-   160
ted, and an express command, under penalty, to deliver
his head in the view of Angelo ? I may make my case as
Claudio's, to cross this in the smallest.

DUKE By the vow of mine order I warrant you, if my instructions may be your guide. Let this Barnardine be
this morning executed, and his head borne to Angelo.

PROVOST Angelo hath seen them both, and will discover   167
the favor.

DUKE O, death 's a great disguiser, and you may add to it.
Shave the head, and tie the beard ; and say it was the de-   170
sire of the penitent to be so bared before his death ; you
know the course is common. If anything fall to you upon
this, more than thanks and good fortune, by the saint   173
whom I profess, I will plead against it with my life.

PROVOST Pardon me, good father, it is against my oath.

DUKE Were you sworn to the Duke or to the deputy ?

PROVOST To him, and to his substitutes.

DUKE You will think you have made no offense, if the
Duke avouch the justice of your dealing ?

PROVOST But what likelihood is in that ?

DUKE Not a resemblance, but a certainty ; yet since I see
you fearful, that neither my coat, integrity, nor persuasion can with ease attempt you, I will go further than
I meant, to pluck all fears out of you. Look you, sir ;
here is the hand and seal of the Duke ; you know the
character, I doubt not, and the signet is not strange to   185
you.

PROVOST I know them both.

DUKE The contents of this is the return of the Duke. You
shall anon over-read it at your pleasure, where you shall
find within these two days he will be here. This is a thing
that Angelo knows not, for he this very day receives
letters of strange tenor, perchance of the Duke's death,
perchance entering into some monastery, but by chance

---

93 *siege* seat 100 *matter* i.e. manner 106 *quick celerity* living means of acceleration 111 *belike* perhaps 113 *putting on* urging 124 *What* i.e. who 132 *fact* deed, crime 142 *wants* needs 151–52 *boldness of my cunning* assurance of my knowledge 152 *lay myself in hazard* take a risk 155 *in a manifested effect* by direct evidence 160 *limited* determined 167–68 *discover the favor* recognize the face 170 *tie* dress, trim (?) 173–74 *saint ...profess* i.e. patron saint of my order 185 *character* handwriting

194 nothing of what is writ. Look, th' unfolding star calls up the shepherd. Put not yourself into amazement how these things should be; all difficulties are but easy when they are known. Call your executioner, and off with

198 Barnardine's head; I will give him a present shrift and advise him for a better place. Yet you are amazed, but this shall absolutely resolve you. Come away; it is almost clear dawn.   *Exit [with Provost].*

IV, iii   *Enter Clown [Pompey].*

POMPEY I am as well acquainted here as I was in our house of profession: one would think it were Mistress Overdone's own house, for here be many of her old customers. First, here's young Master Rash; he's in for a

5 commodity of brown paper and old ginger, nine-score

6 and seventeen pounds, of which he made five marks ready money; marry, then ginger was not much in request, for the old women were all dead. Then is there here one Master Caper, at the suit of Master Three-pile the mercer, for some four suits of peach-colored satin,

11 which now peaches him a beggar. Then have we here young Dizzy, and young Master Deep-vow, and Master Copper-spur, and Master Starve-lackey, the rapier and dagger man, and young Drop-heir that killed lusty

15 Pudding, and Master Forthright the tilter, and brave Master Shoe-tie the great traveller, and wild Half-can that stabbed Pots, and I think forty more, all great doers

18 in our trade, and are now 'for the Lord's sake.'
     Enter Abhorson.

ABHORSON Sirrah, bring Barnardine hither.

POMPEY Master Barnardine, you must rise and be hanged, Master Barnardine.

ABHORSON What ho, Barnardine!

BARNARDINE *[within]* A pox o' your throats, who makes that noise there? What are you?

POMPEY Your friends, sir, the hangman. You must be so good, sir, to rise and be put to death.

BARNARDINE *[within]* Away, you rogue, away! I am sleepy.

ABHORSON Tell him he must awake, and that quickly too.

POMPEY Pray, Master Barnardine, awake till you are executed, and sleep afterwards.

ABHORSON Go in to him, and fetch him out.

32 POMPEY He is coming, sir, he is coming; I hear his straw rustle.
     Enter Barnardine.

ABHORSON Is the axe upon the block, sirrah?

POMPEY Very ready, sir.

BARNARDINE How now, Abhorson, what's the news with you?

ABHORSON Truly, sir, I would desire you to clap into your prayers: for look you, the warrant's come.

BARNARDINE You rogue, I have been drinking all night; I am not fitted for't.

POMPEY O, the better, sir: for he that drinks all night,

and is hanged betimes in the morning, may sleep the 43 sounder all the next day.
     Enter Duke [disguised as before].

ABHORSON Look you, sir, here comes your ghostly father; do we jest now, think you?

DUKE Sir, induced by my charity, and hearing how hastily you are to depart, I am come to advise you, comfort you, and pray with you.

BARNARDINE Friar, not I: I have been drinking hard all night and I will have more time to prepare me, or they shall beat out my brains with billets. I will not consent 52 to die this day, that's certain.

DUKE O, sir, you must; and therefore I beseech you look forward on the journey you shall go.

BARNARDINE I swear I will not die to-day for any man's persuasion.

DUKE But hear you –

BARNARDINE Not a word; if you have anything to say to me, come to my ward, for thence will not I to-day. *Exit.* 60
     Enter Provost.

DUKE
Unfit to live or die. O gravel heart!
After him, fellows: bring him to the block.
       [Exeunt Abhorson and Pompey.]

PROVOST
Now, sir, how do you find the prisoner?

DUKE
A creature unprepared, unmeet for death,
And to transport him in the mind he is   65
Were damnable.

PROVOST   Here in the prison, father,
There died this morning of a cruel fever
One Ragozine, a most notorious pirate,
A man of Claudio's years, his beard and head
Just of his color. What if we do omit
This reprobate till he were well inclined,
And satisfy the deputy with the visage
Of Ragozine, more like to Claudio?

DUKE
O, 'tis an accident that heaven provides;
Dispatch it presently; the hour draws on   75
Prefixed by Angelo. See this be done,   76
And sent according to command, whiles I
Persuade this rude wretch willingly to die.

PROVOST
This shall be done, good father, presently;
But Barnardine must die this afternoon,
And how shall we continue Claudio,
To save me from the danger that might come
If he were known alive?

DUKE   Let this be done.
Put them in secret holds, both Barnardine and Claudio. 84
Ere twice the sun hath made his journal greeting 85
To th' under generation, you shall find
Your safety manifested.

PROVOST
I am your free dependant.   88

DUKE
Quick, dispatch, and send the head to Angelo.
       Exit [Provost].
Now will I write letters to Angelo –
The provost, he shall bear them – whose contents
Shall witness to him I am near at home,
And that by great injunctions I am bound

---

194 *th' unfolding star* morning star, signal for leading the sheep from the fold
198 *shrift* absolution after confession
IV, iii 5 *commodity* goods bought on credit for resale   6 *marks* (a mark was two-thirds of a pound)   11 *peaches* betrays   15 *tilter* fighter   18 *for the Lord's sake* (the cry of poor prisoners who begged of passers-by through the grating)   32 *straw* (i.e. of his pallet)   43 *betimes* early   52 *billets* cudgels   60 *ward* cell   65 *transport* dispatch   75 *presently* at once   76 *Prefixed* determined in advance   84 *holds* cells   85 *journal* daily   88 *your free dependant* freely at your service

To enter publicly. Him I'll desire
To meet me at the consecrated fount
A league below the city ; and from thence,
97   By cold gradation and well-balanced form,
We shall proceed with Angelo.
     Enter Provost.

PROVOST
Here is the head ; I'll carry it myself.

DUKE
Convenient is it ; make a swift return,
For I would commune with you of such things
102   That want no ear but yours.

PROVOST   I'll make all speed.   *Exit.*

ISABELLA [*within*]
Peace, ho, be here.

DUKE
The tongue of Isabel. She's come to know
If yet her brother's pardon be come hither,
106   But I will keep her ignorant of her good,
107   To make her heavenly comforts of despair
When it is least expected.
     Enter Isabella.

ISABELLA   Ho, by your leave !

DUKE
Good morning to you, fair and gracious daughter.

ISABELLA
The better, given me by so holy a man.
Hath yet the deputy sent my brother's pardon ?

DUKE
He hath released him, Isabel, from the world ;
His head is off and sent to Angelo.

ISABELLA
Nay, but it is not so.

DUKE
It is no other. Show your wisdom, daughter,
116   In your close patience.

ISABELLA
O, I will to him and pluck out his eyes !

DUKE
You shall not be admitted to his sight.

ISABELLA
Unhappy Claudio, wretched Isabel,
Injurious world, most damnèd Angelo !

DUKE
This nor hurts him nor profits you a jot ;
Forbear it therefore, give your cause to heaven.
Mark what I say, which you shall find
By every syllable a faithful verity.
The Duke comes home to-morrow – nay, dry your eyes –
126   One of our covent, and his confessor,
127   Gives me this instance ; already he hath carried
Notice to Escalus and Angelo,
Who do prepare to meet him at the gates,
There to give up their power. If you can, pace your
      wisdom
In that good path that I would wish it go,
132   And you shall have your bosom on this wretch,
Grace of the Duke, revenges to your heart,
And general honor.

ISABELLA   I am directed by you.

DUKE
This letter then to Friar Peter give –
'Tis that he sent me of the Duke's return –
Say, by this token, I desire his company

At Mariana's house to-night. Her cause and yours
I'll perfect him withal, and he shall bring you
Before the Duke ; and to the head of Angelo
Accuse him home and home. For my poor self,
I am combinèd by a sacred vow   142
And shall be absent. Wend you with this letter ;
Command these fretting waters from your eyes
With a light heart ; trust not my holy order
If I pervert your course. Who's here ?
     Enter Lucio.

LUCIO   Good even. Friar, where's the provost ?

DUKE   Not within, sir.

LUCIO   O pretty Isabella, I am pale at mine heart to see
thine eyes so red ; thou must be patient. I am fain to dine
and sup with water and bran ; I dare not for my head fill   151
my belly ; one fruitful meal would set me to't. But they
say the Duke will be here to-morrow. By my troth,
Isabel, I loved thy brother ; if the old fantastical Duke of
dark corners had been at home, he had lived.
     [*Exit Isabella.*]

DUKE   Sir, the Duke is marvellous little beholding to your
reports ; but the best is, he lives not in them.

LUCIO   Friar, thou knowest not the Duke so well as I do ;
he's a better woodman than thou tak'st him for.   159

DUKE   Well, you'll answer this one day. Fare ye well.

LUCIO   Nay, tarry, I'll go along with thee ; I can tell thee
pretty tales of the Duke.

DUKE   You have told me too many of him already, sir, if
they be true ; if not true, none were enough.

LUCIO   I was once before him for getting a wench with
child.

DUKE   Did you such a thing ?

LUCIO   Yes, marry, did I ; but I was fain to forswear it.
They would else have married me to the rotten medlar.   169

DUKE   Sir, your company is fairer than honest. Rest you
well.

LUCIO   By my troth, I'll go with thee to the lane's end. If
bawdy talk offend you, we'll have very little of it. Nay,
friar, I am a kind of burr ; I shall stick.   *Exeunt.*

*

     Enter Angelo and Escalus.   IV, iv

ESCALUS   Every letter he hath writ hath disvouched other.   1

ANGELO   In most uneven and distracted manner. His
actions show much like to madness ; pray heaven his
wisdom be not tainted. And why meet him at the gates,
and redeliver our authorities there ?

ESCALUS   I guess not.

ANGELO   And why should we proclaim it in an hour
before his entering, that if any crave redress of injustice,
they should exhibit their petitions in the street ?

ESCALUS   He shows his reason for that : to have a dispatch
of complaints, and to deliver us from devices hereafter,   11
which shall then have no power to stand against us.

ANGELO
Well, I beseech you let it be proclaimed.

---

97 *cold gradation* deliberate steps   102 *want* need   106 *good* i.e. good
fortune   107 *comforts* alleviation   116 *close* silent   126 *covent* convent
127 *instance* proof   132 *bosom* desire   142 *combinèd* bound   151 *for my
head* i.e. lest I lose my head   159 *woodman* hunter (here, of women)   169
medlar a pear that rotted as it ripened (here, a prostitute)
IV, iv The house of Angelo   1 *disvouched* disavowed   11 *devices* contrived
complaints

14 Betimes i' th' morn I'll call you at your house;
15 Give notice to such men of sort and suit
As are to meet him.
ESCALUS   I shall, sir : fare you well.
ANGELO Good night.   *Exit [Escalus].*
This deed unshapes me quite, makes me unpregnant
And dull to all proceedings. A deflowered maid,
And by an eminent body that enforced
The law against it ! But that her tender shame
Will not proclaim against her maiden loss,
How might she tongue me ! Yet reason dares her no,
24 For my authority bears off a credent bulk,
That no particular scandal once can touch
26 But it confounds the breather. He should have lived,
27 Save that his riotous youth with dangerous sense
Might in the times to come have ta'en revenge,
By so receiving a dishonored life
With ransom of such shame. Would yet he had lived.
Alack, when once our grace we have forgot,
Nothing goes right ; we would, and we would not. *Exit.*

*

IV, v   *Enter Duke [in his own habit] and Friar Peter.*
DUKE
These letters at fit time deliver me.
The provost knows our purpose and our plot ;
The matter being afoot, keep your instruction,
4 And hold you ever to our special drift,
5 Though sometimes you do blench from this to that,
As cause doth minister. Go call at Flavius' house,
And tell him where I stay ; give the like notice
To Valencius, Rowland, and to Crassus,
And bid them bring the trumpets to the gate,
But send me Flavius first.
FRIAR PETER   It shall be speeded well. *[Exit.]*
       Enter Varrius.
DUKE
I thank thee, Varrius ; thou hast made good haste.
Come, we will walk ; there's other of our friends
Will greet us here anon, my gentle Varrius.   *Exeunt.*

*

IV, vi   *Enter Isabella and Mariana.*
ISABELLA
1 To speak so indirectly I am loath ;
I would say the truth ; but to accuse him so,
That is your part. Yet I am advised to do it,
He says, to veil full purpose.
MARIANA   Be ruled by him.
ISABELLA
Besides, he tells me that if peradventure
He speak against me on the adverse side,

I should not think it strange, for 'tis a physic
That's bitter to sweet end.
MARIANA
I would Friar Peter –
       Enter [Friar] Peter.
ISABELLA   O, peace, the friar is come.
FRIAR PETER
Come, I have found you out a stand most fit,
Where you may have such vantage on the Duke
He shall not pass you. Twice have the trumpets sounded.
The generous and gravest citizens   13
Have hent the gates, and very near upon   14
The Duke is ent'ring ; therefore hence, away.   *Exeunt.*

*

      Enter Duke, Varrius, Lords, Angelo, Escalus, Lucio,   V, i
      [Provost, Officers, and] Citizens at several doors.
DUKE
My very worthy cousin, fairly met.   1
Our old and faithful friend, we are glad to see you.
ANGELO, ESCALUS
Happy return be to your royal grace.
DUKE
Many and hearty thankings to you both ;
We have made inquiry of you, and we hear
Such goodness of your justice, that our soul
Cannot but yield you forth to public thanks,
Forerunning more requital.   8
ANGELO   You make my bonds still greater.
DUKE
O, your desert speaks loud, and I should wrong it
To lock it in the wards of covert bosom,   10
When it deserves with characters of brass
A forted residence 'gainst the tooth of time
And razure of oblivion. Give we our hand,   13
And let the subject see, to make them know
That outward courtesies would fain proclaim
Favors that keep within. Come, Escalus,   16
You must walk by us on our other hand ;
And good supporters are you.
       Enter [Friar] Peter and Isabella.
FRIAR PETER
Now is your time. Speak loud and kneel before him.
ISABELLA
Justice, O royal Duke ; vail your regard   20
Upon a wronged – I would fain have said, a maid.
O worthy prince, dishonor not your eye
By throwing it on any other object
Till you have heard me in my true complaint
And given me justice, justice, justice, justice !
DUKE
Relate your wrongs. In what ? By whom ? Be brief.
Here is Lord Angelo shall give you justice ;
Reveal yourself to him.   28
ISABELLA   O worthy Duke,
You bid me seek redemption of the devil ;
Hear me yourself ; for that which I must speak
Must either punish me, not being believed,   31
Or wring redress from you. Hear me, O hear me, here.
ANGELO
My lord, her wits, I fear me, are not firm.
She hath been a suitor to me for her brother,
Cut off by course of justice –

---

14 *Betimes* early   15 *men of sort and suit* courtiers of rank   24 *bears . . . bulk* keeps away a great deal otherwise credible   26 *But it confounds* without confounding   27 *sense* reason
IV, v A meeting place near Vienna   4 *drift* aim   5 *blench* turn aside
IV, vi A street in Vienna   1 *indirectly* unstraightforwardly   13 *generous* well-born   14 *hent* taken up positions on   *very near upon* almost at once
V, i The city gates   1 *cousin* (a sovereign formally addresses a nobleman as 'cousin')   8 *more requital* further reward   10 *lock . . . bosom* confine it in the secret cell of the heart   13 *razure* erasure   16 *keep* dwell   20 *vail* let fall   28 *Reveal yourself* explain   31 *punish me* bring punishment to me

ISABELLA   By course of justice!
ANGELO
And she will speak most bitterly and strange.
ISABELLA
Most strange, but yet most truly, will I speak.
That Angelo's forsworn, is it not strange?
That Angelo's a murderer, is't not strange?
40 That Angelo is an adulterous thief,
An hypocrite, a virgin-violator,
Is it not strange, and strange?
DUKE   Nay, it is ten times strange.
ISABELLA
It is not truer he is Angelo
Than this is all as true as it is strange.
Nay, it is ten times true, for truth is truth
To th'end of reck'ning.
DUKE   Away with her; poor soul,
She speaks this in th' infirmity of sense.
ISABELLA
O prince, I conjure thee, as thou believ'st
There is another comfort than this world,
50 That thou neglect me not with that opinion
That I am touched with madness. Make not impossible
That which but seems unlike. 'Tis not impossible
But one, the wicked'st caitiff on the ground,
May seem as shy, as grave, as just, as absolute
As Angelo; even so may Angelo,
56 In all his dressings, caracts, titles, forms,
Be an arch-villain; believe it, royal prince.
If he be less, he's nothing; but he's more,
Had I more name for badness.
DUKE   By mine honesty,
If she be mad, as I believe no other,
Her madness hath the oddest frame of sense,
Such a dependency of thing on thing,
As e'er I heard in madness.
ISABELLA   O gracious Duke,
Harp not on that; nor do not banish reason
65 For inequality, but let your reason serve
To make the truth appear where it seems hid,
67 And hide the false seems true.
DUKE   Many that are not mad
Have sure more lack of reason; what would you say?
ISABELLA
I am the sister of one Claudio,
Condemned upon the act of fornication
To lose his head, condemned by Angelo.
72 I, in probation of a sisterhood,
Was sent to by my brother, one Lucio
As then the messenger –
LUCIO   That's I, an't like your grace.
I came to her from Claudio, and desired her
To try her gracious fortune with Lord Angelo
For her poor brother's pardon.
ISABELLA   That's he indeed.
DUKE
You were not bid to speak
LUCIO   No, my good lord,
Nor wished to hold my peace.
DUKE   I wish you now, then;
Pray you, take note of it, and when you have
A business for yourself, pray heaven you then
82 Be perfect.
LUCIO   I warrant your honor.

DUKE
The warrant's for yourself: take heed to't.
ISABELLA
This gentleman told somewhat of my tale –
LUCIO Right.
DUKE
It may be right, but you are i' the wrong
To speak before your time; proceed.
ISABELLA   I went
To this pernicious caitiff deputy –
DUKE
That's somewhat madly spoken.
ISABELLA   Pardon it,
The phrase is to the matter.   90
DUKE
Mended again. The matter: proceed.
ISABELLA
In brief, to set the needless process by,
How I persuaded, how I prayed, and kneeled,
How he refelled me, and how I replied –   94
For this was of much length – the vile conclusion
I now begin with grief and shame to utter.
He would not, but by gift of my chaste body
To his concupiscible intemperate lust,
Release my brother; and after much debatement
My sisterly remorse confutes mine honor,   100
And I did yield to him; but the next morn betimes,
His purpose surfeiting, he sends a warrant
For my poor brother's head.
DUKE   This is most likely!
ISABELLA
O, that it were as like as it is true.
DUKE
By heaven, fond wretch, thou know'st not what thou
   speak'st,
Or else thou art suborned against his honor
In hateful practice. First, his integrity   107
Stands without blemish; next, it imports no reason
That with such vehemency he should pursue
Faults proper to himself. If he had so offended,   110
He would have weighed thy brother by himself,
And not have cut him off. Someone hath set you on;
Confess the truth, and say by whose advice
Thou cam'st here to complain.
ISABELLA   And is this all?
Then, O you blessèd ministers above,
Keep me in patience, and with ripened time
Unfold the evil which is here wrapped up
In countenance. Heaven shield your grace from woe,   118
As I thus wronged hence unbelievèd go.
DUKE
I know you'ld fain be gone. An officer!
To prison with her. Shall we thus permit
A blasting and a scandalous breath to fall
On him so near us? This needs must be a practice;   123
Who knew of your intent and coming hither?
ISABELLA
One that I would were here, Friar Lodowick.

40 *adulterous thief* i.e. stealthy adulterer   50 *neglect me not with* ignore me not because of   56 *dressings* ceremonial attire; *caracts* insignia of office   65 *inequality* injustice   67 *seems* which seems   72 *in probation* i.e. a novice   82 *perfect* well prepared   90 *matter* purpose   94 *refelled* refuted   100 *remorse* pity   107 *practice* conspiracy   110 *proper to* adhering to   118 *countenance* authority   123 *practice* plot

DUKE
A ghostly father, belike; who knows that Lodowick?
LUCIO
My lord, I know him; 'tis a meddling friar,
128 I do not like the man. Had he been lay, my lord,
For certain words he spake against your grace
In your retirement I had swinged him soundly.
DUKE
Words against me? This' a good friar, belike,
And to set on this wretched woman here
Against our substitute! Let this friar be found.
LUCIO
But yesternight, my lord, she and that friar,
135 I saw them at the prison; a saucy friar,
A very scurvy fellow.
FRIAR PETER
Blessèd be your royal grace,
I have stood by, my lord, and I have heard
Your royal ear abused. First, hath this woman
Most wrongfully accused your substitute,
Who is as free from touch or soil with her
As she from one ungot.
DUKE   We did believe no less.
Know you that Friar Lodowick that she speaks of?
FRIAR PETER
I know him for a man divine and holy,
145 Not scurvy, nor a temporary meddler,
As he's reported by this gentleman;
And, on my trust, a man that never yet
Did, as he vouches, misreport your grace.
LUCIO
My lord, most villainously, believe it.
FRIAR PETER
Well, he in time may come to clear himself,
But at this instant he is sick, my lord,
Of a strange fever. Upon his mere request,
Being come to knowledge that there was complaint
Intended 'gainst Lord Angelo, came I hither,
To speak, as from his mouth, what he doth know
Is true and false; and what he with his oath
157 And all probation will make up full clear,
158 Whensoever he's convented. First, for this woman,
To justify this worthy nobleman,
160 So vulgarly and personally accused,
Her shall you hear disprovèd to her eyes,
Till she herself confess it.
DUKE   Good friar, let's hear it.
[Isabella withdraws, guarded.]
Enter Mariana.
Do you not smile at this, Lord Angelo?
O heaven, the vanity of wretched fools!
Give us some seats. Come, cousin Angelo,
In this I'll be impartial; be you judge
Of your own cause. Is this the witness, friar?
First, let her show her face, and after speak.
MARIANA
Pardon, my lord, I will not show my face
Until my husband bid me.

DUKE What, are you married?
MARIANA No, my lord.
DUKE Are you a maid?
MARIANA No, my lord.
DUKE A widow, then?
MARIANA Neither, my lord.
DUKE Why, you are nothing then; neither maid, widow,
nor wife?
LUCIO My lord, she may be a punk; for many of them are 179
neither maid, widow, nor wife.
DUKE
Silence that fellow. I would he had some cause
To prattle for himself.
LUCIO Well, my lord.
MARIANA
My lord, I do confess I ne'er was married,
And I confess besides I am no maid;
I have known my husband, yet my husband 186
Knows not that ever he knew me.
LUCIO He was drunk, then, my lord; it can be no better.
DUKE For the benefit of silence, would thou wert so too.
LUCIO Well, my lord.
DUKE
This is no witness for Lord Angelo.
MARIANA
Now I come to't, my lord:
She that accuses him of fornication,
In selfsame manner doth accuse my husband;
And charges him, my lord, with such a time
When, I'll depose, I had him in mine arms,
With all th' effect of love. 197
ANGELO
Charges she moe than me?
MARIANA   Not that I know.
DUKE
No? You say your husband?
MARIANA
Why, just, my lord, and that is Angelo,
Who thinks he knows that he ne'er knew my body,
But knows he thinks that he knows Isabel's.
ANGELO
This is a strange abuse; let's see thy face. 203
MARIANA
My husband bids me; now I will unmask.
[Unveiling.]
This is that face, thou cruel Angelo,
Which once thou swor'st was worth the looking on;
This is the hand which, with a vowed contract,
Was fast belocked in thine; this is the body
That took away the match from Isabel,
And did supply thee at thy garden-house
In her imagined person.
DUKE   Know you this woman?
LUCIO
Carnally, she says.
DUKE   Sirrah, no more!
LUCIO
Enough, my lord.
ANGELO
My lord, I must confess I know this woman,
And five years since there was some speech of marriage
Betwixt myself and her, which was broke off,
Partly for that her promisèd proportions 217
Came short of composition, but in chief 218

128 lay i.e. not a cleric 135 saucy foul-mouthed 145 temporary meddler
meddler in temporal affairs 157 probation proof 158 convented summoned 160 vulgarly publicly 179 punk harlot 186 known cohabited
with 197 th' effect the manifestations 203 abuse deception 217 proportions portion, dowry 218 composition agreement

427

219 For that her reputation was disvalued
220 In levity; since which time of five years
I never spake with her, saw her, nor heard from her,
Upon my faith and honor.

MARIANA   Noble prince,
As there comes light from heaven and words from breath,
As there is sense in truth and truth in virtue,
I am affianced this man's wife as strongly
As words could make up vows; and, my good lord,
But Tuesday night last gone in's garden-house
He knew me as a wife. As this is true,
Let me in safety raise me from my knees
230 Or else forever be confixèd here
A marble monument.

ANGELO   I did but smile till now;
Now, good my lord, give me the scope of justice;
My patience here is touched. I do perceive
234 These poor informal women are no more
But instruments of some more mightier member
That sets them on. Let me have way, my lord,
To find this practice out.

DUKE   Ay, with my heart,
And punish them to your height of pleasure.
Thou foolish friar, and thou pernicious woman,
240 Compact with her that's gone, think'st thou thy oaths,
Though they would swear down each particular saint,
Were testimonies against his worth and credit
243 That's sealed in approbation? You, Lord Escalus,
Sit with my cousin; lend him your kind pains
To find out this abuse, whence 'tis derived.
There is another friar that set them on;
Let him be sent for.

FRIAR PETER
Would he were here, my lord, for he indeed
Hath set the women on to this complaint.
Your provost knows the place where he abides
And he may fetch him.

DUKE   Go do it instantly; [Exit Provost.]
252 And you, my noble and well-warranted cousin,
Whom it concerns to hear this matter forth,
Do with your injuries as seems you best,
In any chastisement; I for a while
Will leave you, but stir not you till you have
Well determined upon these slanderers.

ESCALUS
My lord, we'll do it throughly.   Exit [Duke].
Signior Lucio, did not you say you knew that Friar
Lodowick to be a dishonest person?
261 LUCIO 'Cucullus non facit monachum'; honest in noth-
ing but in his clothes, and one that hath spoke most
villainous speeches of the Duke.
ESCALUS We shall entreat you to abide here till he come
and enforce them against him; we shall find this friar a
notable fellow.
LUCIO As any in Vienna, on my word.
ESCALUS Call that same Isabel here once again; I would
speak with her. [Exit an Attendant.] Pray you, my lord,
give me leave to question; you shall see how I'll handle
her.
LUCIO Not better than he, by her own report.
ESCALUS Say you?
LUCIO Marry, sir, I think, if you handled her privately,
she would sooner confess; perchance publicly she'll be
ashamed.

Enter Duke [in his friar's habit], Provost, Isabella
[, and Officers].

ESCALUS I will go darkly to work with her.   277
LUCIO That's the way, for women are light at midnight.
ESCALUS Come on, mistress, here's a gentlewoman de-
nies all that you have said.
LUCIO My lord, here comes the rascal I spoke of – here
with the provost.
ESCALUS In very good time. Speak not you to him, till
we call upon you.
LUCIO Mum.
ESCALUS Come, sir, did you set these women on to slan-
der Lord Angelo? They have confessed you did.
DUKE 'Tis false.
ESCALUS How! know you where you are?
DUKE
Respect to your great place; and let the devil
Be sometime honored for his burning throne.   291
Where is the Duke? 'Tis he should hear me speak.
ESCALUS
The Duke's in us, and we will hear you speak;
Look you speak justly.
DUKE
Boldly at least. But O, poor souls,
Come you to seek the lamb here of the fox?
Good night to your redress! Is the Duke gone?
Then is your cause gone too. The Duke's unjust,
Thus to retort your manifest appeal   299
And put your trial in the villain's mouth
Which here you come to accuse.
LUCIO
This is the rascal; this is he I spoke of.
ESCALUS
Why, thou unreverend and unhallowed friar,
Is't not enough thou hast suborned these women
To accuse this worthy man but, in foul mouth,
And in the witness of his proper ear,   306
To call him villain? And then to glance from him
To th' Duke himself, to tax him with injustice?
Take him hence; to th' rack with him. We'll touse you   309
Joint by joint, but we will know his purpose.
What, unjust?
DUKE   Be not so hot. The Duke
Dare no more stretch this finger of mine than he
Dare rack his own: his subject am I not,
Nor here provincial. My business in this state   314
Made me a looker-on here in Vienna,
Where I have seen corruption boil and bubble
Till it o'errun the stew. Laws for all faults,
But faults so countenanced that the strong statutes
Stand like the forfeits in a barber's shop,   319
As much in mock as mark.   320
ESCALUS
Slander to th' state. Away with him to prison.
ANGELO
What can you vouch against him, Signior Lucio?
Is this the man that you did tell us of?

219 *disvalued* discredited   220 *In levity* for lightness   230 *confixèd* fastened   234 *informal* rash, turbulent   240 *Compact* leagued   243 *approbation* proof   252 *well-warranted* i.e. trustworthy   261 *Cucullus non facit mona-chum* a cowl does not make a monk   277 *darkly* slyly   291 *sometime* on occasion   299 *retort* turn back   306 *proper* very   309 *touse* tear   314 *provincial* subject to the laws of this province, or state   319 *forfeits* extracted teeth (since barbers acted as dentists)   320 *mock as mark* jest as earnest

LUCIO 'Tis he, my lord. Come hither, goodman bald-
pate; do you know me?

DUKE I remember you, sir, by the sound of your voice. I
met you at the prison in the absence of the Duke.

LUCIO O, did you so? And do you remember what you
said of the Duke?

330 DUKE Most notedly, sir.

LUCIO Do you so, sir? And was the Duke a fleshmonger,
a fool, and a coward, as you then reported him to be?

DUKE You must, sir, change persons with me, ere you
make that my report. You, indeed, spoke so of him, and
much more, much worse.

LUCIO O thou damnable fellow, did not I pluck thee by
the nose for thy speeches?

DUKE I protest I love the Duke as I love myself.

339 ANGELO Hark how the villain would close now, after his
treasonable abuses.

341 ESCALUS Such a fellow is not to be talked withal; away
with him to prison. Where is the provost? Away with

343 him to prison, lay bolts enough upon him, let him speak

344 no more. Away with those giglets too, and with the
other confederate companion.
[The Provost lays hands on the Duke.]

DUKE Stay, sir, stay a while.

ANGELO What, resists he? Help him, Lucio.

LUCIO Come, sir, come, sir, come, sir. Foh, sir, why, you
bald-pated, lying rascal, you must be hooded, must
you? Show your knave's visage, with a pox to you; show

351 your sheep-biting face, and be hanged an hour. Will't
not off?
[Pulls off the friar's hood, and discovers the Duke.]

DUKE
Thou art the first knave that e'er mad'st a duke.
First, provost, let me bail these gentle three;
[To Lucio]
Sneak not away, sir, for the friar and you
Must have a word anon. Lay hold on him.

LUCIO
This may prove worse than hanging.

DUKE [to Escalus]
What you have spoke I pardon. Sit you down,
We'll borrow place of him. [to Angelo] Sir, by your leave.
Hast thou or word, or wit, or impudence

360 That yet can do thee office? If thou hast,
Rely upon it till my tale be heard,
And hold no longer out.

ANGELO   O my dread lord,
I should be guiltier than my guiltiness
To think I can be undiscernible,
When I perceive your grace, like power divine,

366 Hath looked upon my passes. Then, good prince,
No longer session hold upon my shame,
But let my trial be mine own confession.
Immediate sentence, then, and sequent death
Is all the grace I beg.

DUKE   Come hither, Mariana.
Say, wast thou ere contracted to this woman?

ANGELO
I was, my lord.

DUKE
Go take her hence, and marry her instantly.
Do you the office, friar; which consummate,   374
Return him here again. Go with him, provost.
        Exit [Angelo, with Mariana, Friar Peter, and Provost].

ESCALUS
My lord, I am more amazed at his dishonor
Than at the strangeness of it.

DUKE   Come hither, Isabel;
Your friar is now your prince. As I was then
Advertising and holy to your business,   379
Not changing heart with habit, I am still
Attorneyed at your service.   381

ISABELLA   O, give me pardon,
That I, your vassal, have employed and pained
Your unknown sovereignty.

DUKE   You are pardoned, Isabel;
And now, dear maid, be you as free to us.
Your brother's death, I know, sits at your heart,
And you may marvel why I obscured myself,
Laboring to save his life, and would not rather
Make rash remonstrance of my hidden power   388
Than let him so be lost. O most kind maid,
It was the swift celerity of his death,
Which I did think with slower foot came on,
That brained my purpose; but peace be with him.
That life is better life past fearing death,
Than that which lives to fear. Make it your comfort,
So happy is your brother.
        Enter Angelo, Mariana, [Friar] Peter, Provost.

ISABELLA   I do, my lord.

DUKE
For this new-married man approaching here,
Whose salt imagination yet hath wronged   397
Your well-defended honor, you must pardon
For Mariana's sake. But as he adjudged your brother,
Being criminal, in double violation
Of sacred chastity, and of promise-breach,
Thereon dependent, for your brother's life,
The very mercy of the law cries out   403
Most audible, even from his proper tongue,
'An Angelo for Claudio, death for death!'
Haste still pays haste, and leisure answers leisure,
Like doth quit like, and Measure still for Measure.
Then, Angelo, thy fault's thus manifested,
Which though thou wouldst deny, denies thee vantage.   409
We do condemn thee to the very block
Where Claudio stooped to death, and with like haste.
Away with him.

MARIANA   O, my most gracious lord,
I hope you will not mock me with a husband.

DUKE
It is your husband mocked you with a husband.
Consenting to the safeguard of your honor,
I thought your marriage fit; else imputation,
For that he knew you, might reproach your life
And choke your good to come. For his possessions,
Although by confiscation they are ours,
We do instate and widow you with all,
To buy you a better husband.   421

MARIANA   O my dear lord,
I crave no other, nor no better man.

330 *notedly* literally   339 *close* come to terms   341 *withal* with   343 *bolts* fetters   344 *giglets* lewd women   351 *sheep-biting* currish   360 *office* service
366 *passes* trespasses   374 *consummate* concluded   379 *Advertising* attentive
381 *Attorneyed* acting as attorney   388 *remonstrance* demonstration   397
salt salacious   403 *mercy* justice (the law's mercy; see II, ii, 100)   409
vantage way of escape   421 *buy* (i.e. obtain by providing a dowry)

DUKE

423   Never crave him ; we are definitive.

MARIANA

Gentle my liege –

DUKE   You do but lose your labor.

Away with him to death. *[to Lucio]* Now, sir, to you.

MARIANA

O my good lord ! Sweet Isabel, take my part,

Lend me your knees, and, all my life to come,

I'll lend you all my life to do you service.

DUKE

Against all sense you do importune her ;

Should she kneel down in mercy of this fact,

431   Her brother's ghost his pavèd bed would break,

And take her hence in horror.

MARIANA   Isabel,

Sweet Isabel, do yet but kneel by me,

Hold up your hands, say nothing, I'll speak all.

They say best men are moulded out of faults,

And, for the most, become much more the better

For being a little bad ; so may my husband.

O Isabel, will you not lend a knee ?

DUKE

He dies for Claudio's death.

ISABELLA *[kneeling]*   Most bounteous sir,

Look, if it please you, on this man condemned

As if my brother lived. I partly think

A due sincerity governed his deeds

Till he did look on me. Since it is so,

Let him not die ; my brother had but justice,

In that he did the thing for which he died.

For Angelo,

His act did not o'ertake his bad intent,

And must be buried but as an intent

449   That perished by the way. Thoughts are no subjects,

Intents but merely thoughts.

MARIANA   Merely, my lord.

DUKE

Your suit 's unprofitable ; stand up, I say.

I have bethought me of another fault.

Provost, how came it Claudio was beheaded

At an unusual hour ?

PROVOST   It was commanded so.

DUKE

Had you a special warrant for the deed ?

PROVOST

No, my good lord, it was by private message.

DUKE

For which I do discharge you of your office ;

Give up your keys.

PROVOST   Pardon me, noble lord ;

459   I thought it was a fault, but knew it not,

460   Yet did repent me after more advice ;

For testimony whereof, one in the prison

That should by private order else have died

I have reserved alive.

DUKE   What's he ?

PROVOST   His name is Barnardine.

DUKE

I would thou hadst done so by Claudio.

Go, fetch him hither ; let me look upon him.

                 [Exit Provost.]

ESCALUS

I am sorry, one so learned and so wise

As you, Lord Angelo, have still appeared,   467

Should slip so grossly, both in the heat of blood

And lack of tempered judgment afterward.

ANGELO

I am sorry that such sorrow I procure,

And so deep sticks it in my penitent heart

That I crave death more willingly than mercy ;

'Tis my deserving, and I do entreat it.

     Enter Barnardine and Provost, Claudio [muffled],

     Juliet.

DUKE

Which is that Barnardine ?

PROVOST   This, my lord.

DUKE

There was a friar told me of this man.

Sirrah, thou art said to have a stubborn soul,

That apprehends no further than this world,

And squar'st thy life according. Thou'rt condemned ;   478

But, for those earthly faults, I quit them all,   479

And pray thee take this mercy to provide

For better times to come. Friar, advise him :

I leave him to your hand. What muffled fellow's that ?

PROVOST

This is another prisoner that I saved,

Who should have died when Claudio lost his head –

As like almost to Claudio as himself.

     [Unmuffles Claudio.]

DUKE *[to Isabella]*

If he be like your brother, for his sake

Is he pardoned, and for your lovely sake –

Give me your hand and say you will be mine –

He is my brother too. But fitter time for that.

By this Lord Angelo perceives he's safe ;

Methinks I see a quick'ning in his eye.

Well, Angelo, your evil quits you well.   492

Look that you love your wife ; her worth, worth yours.

I find an apt remission in myself,   494

And yet here's one in place I cannot pardon.

     [To Lucio]

You, sirrah, that knew me for a fool, a coward,

One all of luxury, an ass, a madman,   497

Wherein have I so deserved of you,

That you extol me thus ?

LUCIO 'Faith, my lord, I spoke it but according to the

trick. If you will hang me for it, you may ; but I had   500

rather it would please you, I might be whipped.

DUKE

Whipped first, sir, and hanged after.

Proclaim it, provost, round about the city,

If any woman wronged by this lewd fellow –

As I have heard him swear himself there's one

Whom he begot with child – let her appear,

And he shall marry her. The nuptial finished,

Let him be whipped and hanged.

LUCIO I beseech your highness, do not marry me to a

whore. Your highness said even now, I made you a

duke ; good my lord, do not recompense me in making

me a cuckold.

---

423 *definitive* determined   431 *pavèd bed* slab-covered grave   449 *no subjects* not answerable to authority   459 *knew it not* was not sure   460 *advice* consideration   467 *still* always   478 *squar'st* regulate   479 *quit* pardon   492 *quits* requites   494 *remission* wish to remit, or pardon   497 *luxury* lust   500 *trick* fashion

DUKE
  Upon mine honor, thou shalt marry her.
  Thy slanders I forgive, and therewithal
515 Remit thy other forfeits. Take him to prison,
  And see our pleasure herein executed.
LUCIO Marrying a punk, my lord, is pressing to death,
  whipping, and hanging.
DUKE
  Slandering a prince deserves it.
                    [Exeunt Officers with Lucio.]
  She, Claudio, that you wronged, look you restore.

515 *forfeits* penalties   524 *behind* in store ; *gratulate* gratifying   530 *motion*
proposal   534 *What's yet behind* what remains to be told

  Joy to you, Mariana ; love her, Angelo ;
  I have confessed her and I know her virtue.
  Thanks, good friend Escalus, for thy much goodness ;
  There's more behind that is more gratulate.   524
  Thanks, provost, for thy care and secrecy ;
  We shall employ thee in a worthier place.
  Forgive him, Angelo, that brought you home
  The head of Ragozine for Claudio's ;
  Th' offense pardons itself. Dear Isabel,
  I have a motion much imports your good,   530
  Whereto if you'll a willing ear incline,
  What's mine is yours, and what is yours is mine.
  So, bring us to our palace, where we'll show
  What's yet behind, that's meet you all should know.   534
                              [Exeunt.]

THE HISTORIES

FOREWORD

Although history has been dramatized at many times, the history play as a distinctive genre is uniquely Elizabethan. It was a purely popular type, never appearing in the select "private" theatres as distinct from the large arenas, and its life span was little more than fifteen years: only isolated examples fall outside the period 1589–1604. Entries in the *Stationers' Register* and the titles of plays issued in quarto let us trace the increasing awareness of its separate identity. At first the term "history" was most often applied to some comic or romantic stage fiction, while plays treating actual past events were issued under a variety of labels such as "Reign of," "Contention of," "Life and Death of," and, especially, "Tragedy of." Shakespeare's *3 Henry VI, Richard III,* and *Richard II* were all originally published as "tragedies." However, a few years later, his *1 Henry IV* and *Henry V* were published as "histories," and the term began to appear in the classifications mentioned above in the foreword to the comedies. Shakespeare not only excelled in this genre; he, more than anyone else, created it. Although there had been earlier intimations of its appearance, the only actual examples that can be plausibly dated before Shakespeare's *Henry VI* plays are *The Troublesome Reign of King John* and *The Famous Victories of Henry V,* and there is some doubt even about these. It used to be thought that Marlowe's *Edward II* pointed Shakespeare the way, but it now appears likely that the indebtedness was the other way round.

The type emerged ca. 1587–90 amidst a theatrical brood which may be described in general as "documentaries." Biblical history had been dramatized for centuries, and when the commercial theatre burgeoned in London it was natural that the playwrights should exploit historical and biographical accounts, Roman, Persian, Turkish, ancient British, and so on. Why it was that only plays about native kings, and those since the Norman Conquest, should have come to be thought of as "histories" is an interesting question. The stories of Lear, Macbeth, and Cymbeline, as well as those of John, the Richards, and the Henrys appear in Holinshed's *Chronicles*. The stories of Caesar, Antony, and Coriolanus are just as "historical" as those of the English kings. Externally there is little distinction between Shakespeare's treatment of English and Roman history. There are the same broad canvases teeming with national figures, the same telescoping of actual events, the same interplay of personal and political forces, the same arbitrariness upon the field of battle, and, at least in some of the plays on English history, the same tragic end for the titular characters. Nevertheless the editors of the folio made the separation as a matter of course. Plays previously published as "tragedies" like *Richard III* and *Richard II* were grouped with the histories while plays previously published as "histories" such as *Titus Andronicus, King Lear,* and *Troilus and Cressida* were grouped with the Roman plays and others as tragedies.

The critical consensus is that the distinction made was not a superficial one based merely upon subject matter. The history play is distinct because the inescapable relevance of its subject matter exerted a shaping influence. Nashe praised *1 Henry VI* as a "reproofe to these degenerate effeminate dayes of ours," and Heywood exclaimed, "What English blood, seeing the person of any bold Englishman presented, and doth not hugge his fame and hunnye at his valor . . . !" Authors and audience had a personal stake in such drama, which was bound to arouse emotions of pride and solicitude, and which inevitably attached to itself the function of providing inspiration and admonition. The characters alter from play to play but the protagonist remains the same: England. No corresponding entity appears in the Roman, Turkish, and other "historical" plays. This does not mean that, in the histories, Shakespeare sacrificed art to propaganda. There is more objectivity, subtlety, and suspension of issues than we have any right to expect, not to mention the rich vein of pure entertainment, but it does mean that he expressed in these plays certain attitudes and ideals born of the past national experience and the present national situation. What these attitudes and ideals were is explained elsewhere in this volume, in the General Introduction and in the introductions to the plays themselves.

In the folio the histories are arranged in the order of the reigns they treat. The eight from *Richard II* to *Richard III* provide a synoptic view of the crucial period from 1398 to 1485 when modern England was being born. We witness the dynastic struggle between the houses of York and Lancaster (the "Wars of the Roses"), stemming from the deposition of Richard Plantagenet by Henry Bolingbroke, and ending on Bosworth Field with the ascendance of the first Tudor monarch, Henry VII. The two additional plays have been called "prologue" and "epilogue" to the series, *King John* because it provides an early thirteenth-century preview of the evils of civil war, and *Henry VIII* because it provides an early sixteenth-century demonstration of the Tudor success in establishing national unity, symbolized in the birth of Princess Elizabeth. (A genealogical chart appended to *3 Henry VI* traces the lines of the leaders in the eight central plays.)

Although something is to be said for the folio arrangement, it has not been followed in the present edition. We are interested in the plays as literature rather than history, and an arrangement in order of composition suggests something about Shakespeare's development as a literary artist. The histories offer an especially good opportunity, because it so happens that we are pretty certain of their order and of the fact that each play as we have it represents the author's abilities in the year to which it is assigned. It is possible that *1 Henry VI* was written or revised a little later than *2 & 3 Henry VI,* but the possibility scarcely affects the above generalization. The Jack Cade scenes in *2 Henry VI* prove that Shakespeare's comic talents ripened early and that he was able to burlesque rebellion as well in 1592 as he was in 1611 (in *The Tempest*). As we proceed from *Richard III* to *Richard II,* both good but good in strikingly different ways, we see the poet-dramatist come into his own. It should be added that neither a chronological arrangement, nor our interest in the history play as a type, should mislead us into viewing the plays merely in terms of each other. Except possibly for the *Henry VI* group, each is radically different from the rest. As with the comedies, a variety of elements is successfully fused in a variety of ways. If we focus our attention upon Henry, Hal, and Falstaff in *1 Henry IV,* "historical-comical" seems an apt label, but Hotspur is in it too – and a strand of the "tragical." Most conspicuously absent from the histories is romantic love-interest, the "pastoral," but in *Henry V* there is even a trace of that.

A. H.

BIBLIOGRAPHY

For anthologies of criticism, see *Shakespeare : The Histories,* ed. E. W. Waith (1965); *Discussions of Shakespeare's Histories,* ed. R. J. Dorius (1964). A pioneer work on the type is Felix E. Schelling, *The English Chronicle Play* (1902) and a recent one is Irving Ribner, *The English History Play in the Age of Shakespeare* (1957, rev. ed. 1965). For general criticism and interpretation see J. Marriott, *English History in Shakespeare* (1918); Alfred Hart, *Shakespeare and the Homilies* (1934); R. W. Chambers, *Man's Unconquerable Mind* (1939); E. M. W. Tillyard, *Shakespeare's History Plays* (1944); Lily B. Campbell, *Shakespeare's 'Histories' : Mirrors of Elizabethan Policy* (1947); Derek Traversi, *Shakespeare from Richard II to Henry V* (1957); M. M. Reese, *The Cease of Majesty* (1961); S. C. Sen Gupta, *Shakespeare's Historical Plays* (1964). For related topics see Brents Stirling, *The Populace in Shakespeare* (1949); Paul Jorgensen, *Shakespeare's Military World* (1956); Ernest W. Talbert, *The Problem of Order* (1962). For books on individual histories, see P. M. Kendall, *Richard the Third* (1955); W. H. Clemen, *Commentary on Shakespeare's Richard III* (1968); A. P. Rossiter, *Angel with Horns [Richard III]* (1961); J. Dover Wilson, *The Fortunes of Falstaff [1 & 2 Henry IV]* (1943); Harold Jenkins, *The Structural Problem in Shakespeare's Henry the Fourth* (1956). Shakespeare's possible priority among originators of the type is discussed in F. P. Wilson, *Marlowe and the Early Shakespeare* (1953). A number of the books listed in the bibliography on the intellectual and political background in the General Introduction are especially relevant in a study of the histories. For a survey of twentieth-century criticism of the histories see Harold Jenkins in *Shakespeare Survey,* ed. A. Nicoll, VI (1953).

THE FIRST PART OF
KING HENRY THE SIXTH

INTRODUCTION

The First Part of King Henry the Sixth is a play about the outbreak of civil war. As the first in a four-play series depicting the Wars of the Roses, it is naturally concerned with causes of that conflict. Its dominant note is helpless anxiety. The prevailing metaphors are of disharmony, in the cosmos, the kingdom, the family, and the individual. Foreboding comets and "bad revolting stars" signify the death of Henry V and the misrule of his son. Planetary omens threaten the English, seem to favor the French. Other pervasive metaphors of discord are drawn from fire, disease, and grim personifications of Death. The kingdom is portrayed as a rebellious family wherein uncle turns against nephew, wife against husband, cousin against cousin.

As the Duke of Exeter informs us in choral soliloquy, the meaning of the play is plain, didactic, and sobering:

> no simple man that sees
> This jarring discord of nobility,
> This shouldering of each other in the court,
> This factious bandying of their favorites,
> But that it doth presage some ill event.
> 'Tis much when sceptres are in children's hands,
> But more when envy breeds unkind division.
> There comes the ruin, there begins confusion.
>
> IV, i, 187–94

Shakespeare's theme, as in his later tetralogy from *Richard II* to *Henry V*, stresses the need for orthodox succession to the throne. The idea was a commonplace, readily apparent in Shakespeare's chief sources, the chronicles of Hall, Fabyan, and Holinshed. Nevertheless the dramatic treatment is characteristically Shakespearean even in this early play. Henry VI, like his predecessor Richard II, is presented as an immature king surrounded by ambitious kinsmen. Worse still in view of the Elizabethan concern for secure dynasty, Henry's claim to the throne is uncertain because of the usurpation of power by his grandfather, Henry IV (Bolingbroke). From this genealogical uncertainty arise the factions of Lancaster and York. The confrontation of these two houses gives unity and balance to a portrait of political chaos.

Scenes of confrontation abound, and characters usually appear in contrasting pairs. One such grouping pits the Bishop of Winchester against Humphrey, Duke of Gloucester. Winchester is the illegitimate great-uncle of the king, a man of thwarted ambition plotting against his legitimately born relatives who rule. As a priest he is wholly corrupt and hypocritical, neglecting pastoral duties, flaunting elegant robes, and buying political power with his exorbitant income derived in part from houses of prostitution. Humphrey is uncle to the king and Protector during Henry's minority, doing his best to uphold civil order. Shakespeare's sympathies are undisguised. The power of the Catholic Church opposes that of the state; the priest's tawny coats openly defy the authority of the Protector's blue coats. The good Humphrey is powerless in time of civil unrest to prevent continual ecclesiastical scheming.

The parallel confrontation of the Duke of Somerset and Richard Plantagenet gives rise to the dynastic names of Lancaster and York. Somerset, an ally of Winchester and the wily Earl of Suffolk, is head of the "Lancastrian" party not out of loyalty to King Henry VI (who inherited the title of Lancaster from his great-grandfather, John of Gaunt) but out of factious envy of Richard and a desire to rule the king and realm for his own benefit. Shakespeare does not wish to give the impression, however, that the Lancastrians alone are in the wrong. Richard Plantagenet is also an opportunist, albeit with an understandable motive. He claims a right of succession from Edward III superior to the claim of his kinsman Henry VI. He is a man of political sagacity, tact, bravery, and honor. His dying uncle Mortimer and his father the Earl of Cambridge appear to have been persecuted by the Lancastrian kings because of the Yorkist claim. The virtuous Humphrey supports Richard against the taunts of Somerset. Richard deserves at least to be restored to his lost title of York, like the wronged Bolingbroke in the first act of *Richard II*. But, again like Bolingbroke, how much greater power will Richard seek once his ambition is aroused? Shakespeare's fascination with this question produces the most subtle characterization in this early play. Richard has learned the art of silence while still seeking support, but he confides that his silences are deliberately deceptive. He almost flares into speech when King Henry chooses to wear the red rose of Lancaster, but mutters instead: "An if I wist he did – But let it rest. / Other affairs must now be managèd." The choric Exeter in soliloquy interprets the ominously unfinished sentence:

> Well didst thou, Richard, to suppress thy voice;
> For, had the passions of thy heart burst out,
> I fear we should have seen deciphered there
> More rancorous spite, more furious raging broils,
> Than yet can be imagined or supposed.
>
> IV, i, 182–86

Shakespeare gives us a vivid premonition of his first fully developed villain: Richard Plantagenet's son and namesake, who was to become Richard III.

Civil conflict is imminent because unscrupulous men of both parties are taking advantage of a weak child king. The play does not, however, portray the wars at home. The actual military encounters take place in France rather than in England. The subject is not civil butchery, but the loss of England's greatness abroad owing to division at home:

Amongst the soldiers this is mutterèd,
That here you maintain several factions,
And whilst a field should be dispatched and fought
You are disputing of your generals.

I, i, 70–73

Throughout the play the action alternates between the English court and the French campaign. Scenes in France are often comic, especially in portraying Joan of Arc and her lover the Dauphin. The depraved portrait of Joan, founded upon English conceptions current in Shakespeare's time, may be distasteful to modern sensibilities but it is dramatically useful. It suggests that France triumphs in England's weakness, not in her own strength. Shakespeare is able to have it both ways: to affirm the natural superiority of Englishmen to the effete and unprincipled French, and at the same time to explain the downfall of the English armies.

Moreover, Joan's devil-worship, profligacy, and brazen falsehood echo similar corruptions among the factious English at home. Even Humphrey's wife, Eleanor, is guilty of trafficking with evil spirits in the next play of the sequence, 2 Henry VI. Suffolk's machinations with Margaret of Anjou or Winchester's exploitation of houses of prostitution are scarcely more defensible than Joan's wantonness. And even Joan cannot outface Winchester in hypocrisy. In any case Joan is captured and led to execution; Winchester prospers as a disloyal ambassador, concluding a peace with France at the very moment the English are winning and could take all. The infection at home is more disastrous than the exterior threat of French force.

Most significant is the parallel of the great leaders who are victimized on these two fronts: Humphrey the Protector, and Lord Talbot the English general. They are both in the right, urging political stability, an end to quarrelling, united action against the French. Such voices of moderation and national purpose are destined to be silenced by hysteria, self-serving, and vacillation. Other well-intentioned men join Talbot and Humphrey: the Duke of Bedford, the Earl of Salisbury, Lucy, Glansdale, Gargrave. They die bravely but for a lost cause, while Sir John Falstaff saves his life with dishonor and loss of a battle. Like his more famous namesake, this Falstaff counsels discretion as the better part of valor. In this early play, however, such advice lacks humorous awareness of the ironic complexities of "honor." This Falstaff is a simple coward and traitor. War against the French is sanctioned by divine right and national destiny as in Henry V. Talbot is a national hero betrayed, not a Hotspur or Troilus entrapped by an outmoded and idealistic code of chivalry. If this French war is absurd, it is so not for ambiguity of cause but for inadequacy of political leadership.

The victim who must bear the weight of political betrayal is Lord Talbot – "bought and sold Lord Talbot," "ringed about with bold adversity," who "Drops bloody sweat from his war-wearied limbs." He is indeed a soldier of Christ, radiant and cheerful in death, forgiving toward his enemies, more concerned for his son than for himself. He is above all triumphant over Death – not merely his own, but the personified figure who would reap a harvest of misery from man's fallen condition:

Thou antic Death, which laugh'st us here to scorn,
Anon, from thy insulting tyranny,
Coupled in bonds of perpetuity,
Two Talbots, wingèd through the lither sky,
In thy despite shall scape mortality.

IV, vii, 18–22

The image of Daedalus and Icarus escaping the Cretan labyrinth, and the explicitly Christian image of resurrection, combine to produce triumph at the moment of ultimate meaninglessness. Father and son are rejoined in everlasting harmony. The right relation of the family has been preserved.

Shakespeare may be forgiven if, in his effort to counterbalance his stark theme, he overstates the character of Talbot. The general is superhuman in life as in death. In his first appearance he tells Salisbury how he had held off a troop of armed French with his bare hands, "And with my nails digged stones out of the ground / To hurl at the beholders of my shame." He would like to take vengeance on Falstaff with "bare fists." He is reputed to twist bars of steel. He is Samson among the Philistines but without Samson's earlier weakness for women. In fact the light-hearted episode with the Countess of Auvergne reveals the temperate ideal in the relation of the sexes. Talbot is as Mars should be with Venus: witty, debonair, courteous yet wary, supremely masculine and rational, fair-minded in victory. As such he is implicitly contrasted with the frail, uxorious King Henry.

Indeed, Talbot is the standard of patriotic right reason by which Shakespeare measures the decline in other characters. Talbot is the embodiment of firmness and yet fair play toward the French. By his wit and friendly courtesy he wins the allegiance of the Countess of Auvergne, who had hoped to destroy him as an enemy. Anticipating Shakespeare's later portrait of Henry V, Talbot forbids his men to pillage the French countryside. His methods of siege are just though rigorous, publicized and infallible so that his enemies know what they can expect and how they can avoid it by timely surrender. Talbot demonstrates also the temperate ideal of man's quest for earthly fame – an underlying theme of major consequence in this didactic play. Neither unscrupulous in personal ambition like Winchester and York, nor timorous in commitment to the right cause like Henry VI, Talbot and his virtuous son are concerned that their name be remembered forever as a synonym for valor. This fame, along with their achieving heaven, compensates for the seeming injustice of their deaths. Yet Talbot is denied the sort of tragic experience in which a man discovers a causal relationship between his character and his fate. No flaw exists in Talbot to produce his fate. He is victimized rather than self-destroyed. The First Part of King Henry the Sixth is not even his play; it ends not tragically but anticlimactically.

The contrast between Talbot and Henry is instructive. Henry is in part a victim, too. He has been forced to accept leadership in a world he did not make, a leadership for which he is woefully unprepared. He starts with the finest intentions. He occupies the impartial ground of regal authority, aided by the wise Protector Humphrey. He attempts not to choose sides in the squabbles of Lancaster and York. Yet in his vacillation he becomes an appeaser rather than a moderator. Presumably in the interest of being "fair" to both sides, he gives Somerset and York equal but divided authority in France. This decision costs the life of Talbot. Henry lacks insight to fathom the motives of his peers, and so commissions the untrustworthy Winchester to make peace with France when the English could in fact have won.

Such a pathetic figure has no claim to tragic stature. Yet in many ways the play, as its title suggests, is his. He is the pivot of all the antagonisms, the pawn of destiny, the weakling Everyman unable to distinguish Good Counsel from Evil Counsel. He takes on broadly representative characteristics in England's secular soul struggle, becoming the human symbol of England divided against herself. The uninterrupted decline of such a generic figure is intentionally distressing. Inclined at first to follow the counsel of Humphrey, Henry is at last the tool of Somerset and Suffolk. His decisions are no longer ignorantly misdirected, but willful. Ultimately we see him afflicted with unreal passion for a domineering woman he has never seen (Margaret of Anjou), surrendering control of himself in a trite simile of mocking epic grandeur:

> And like as rigor of tempestuous gusts
> Provokes the mightiest hulk against the tide,
> So am I driven by breath of her renown
> Either to suffer shipwreck or arrive
> Where I may have fruition of her love.
>
> V, v, 5–9

Only such a tyranny of will over reason can explain Henry's refusal of a far more prudent match already contracted by Humphrey's means. Henry voids his solemn oath, refuses a dowry and a political alliance of great advantage, turns loose two of the best territories in France, and authorizes Suffolk to levy a ruinous tax on the English – all to satisfy a whim of the flesh.

Structural, thematic, and metaphoric unity argue for Shakespeare's authorship of the whole play. Until recently, however, scholars have been reluctant to accord the play firm status in the canon. Theories of multiple authorship have assigned portions of the text to Greene, Marlowe, Nashe, Peele, or Lodge, and have recognized Shakespeare's hand only in such scenes as the Temple garden quarrel (II, iv), the death of Mortimer (II, v), the death of Talbot (IV, ii–vii), and Suffolk's wooing of Margaret (V, iii). The unreliable criteria for such disintegration are chiefly those of "taste" and style. Nineteenth-century critics in particular found repellent the treatment of Joan of Arc and declared it unworthy of Shakespeare's genius. Although unable to concur as to which parts belong to whom, the disintegrators have pointed out verbal similarities to writings of Shakespeare's contemporaries as evidence of multiple authorship. Numerous irregularities of verse and contradictions in fact (e.g., in I, iii the Bishop of Winchester wears a "broad cardinal's hat" whereas in V, i he has just been "called unto a cardinal's degree") have been offered as signs of revision. The hypothesis alleges that young Shakespeare was employed as a journeyman mender of an old play, and that Heminge and Condell included it in the first folio because Shakespeare had made a slight contribution or because they needed it to fill out the Lancastrian cycle of plays. The theory is by no means dead but is now largely discredited. Shakespeare himself may have committed some errors in this early play; other errors may be due to his reliance on chronicle sources or to transcription.

Equally vexed is the question of order of composition among the three parts of *Henry VI*. Part One was regis-tered for printing in the first folio as "The thirde parte of Henry ye Sixt." This odd numbering seems to imply later composition, but may simply reflect the fact that Parts Two and Three had appeared in print years before (as pirated quartos) and so were already registered. Nevertheless, scholars have argued from internal evidence that Part One was adapted to conform with Parts Two and Three, and that the Suffolk–Margaret episode in particular is an afterthought intended as a transition to Part Two. Against this hypothesis evidence has been offered that the bad quartos of Parts Two and Three recollect important portions of Part One, including alleged alterations like the Margaret–Suffolk scenes. Furthermore, in theme the ending of the play is not an unconnected new episode but a melancholy fulfillment of Exeter's prophecies. It now seems possible that Shakespeare wrote all parts of *Henry VI* in normal chronological order. If this view prevails, scholarship will have returned full circle to the position of Dr Johnson in 1765, who gave all of *Henry VI* to Shakespeare and observed of Part Two, "It is apparent that this play begins where the former ends, and continues the series of transactions, of which it presupposes the first part already known. This is sufficient proof that the second and third parts were not written without dependence on the first."

If *The First Part of King Henry the Sixth* was written before Parts Two and Three, it was early indeed and of momentous importance in the history of the Elizabethan chronicle play. Unless there was a rival play on Talbot of which we know nothing – and this seems unlikely – Shakespeare's play was in existence by August, 1592, when Nashe's *Pierce Penilesse* eloquently praised the spectacle of Lord Talbot:

How would it have joyed brave Talbot (the terror of the French) to think that after he had lain two hundred years in his tomb he should triumph again on the stage, and have his bones new embalmed with the tears of ten thousand spectators at least (at several times) who, in the tragedian that represents his person, imagine they behold him fresh bleeding.

As a tremendous stage success capitalizing on feelings of national pride in the aftermath of the Armada (July, 1588), the play must have done much to set the vogue in a new genre only clumsily explored by the earlier anonymous *Famous Victories of Henry V*. Shakespeare was evidently a pioneer as well as perfector of the English chronicle play. His *Henry VI* plays almost certainly preceded and influenced Marlowe's *Edward II*.

The play, to be sure, is a work more of promise than perfection. Aside from Richard Plantagenet and Henry, its characters are simplified heroes or villains. The language is declamatory, the examination of character external and public, the political commentary overtly didactic. Patterns of structural balancing reveal the young artist questing for the certainties of controlling form. Verbal ingenuity, and such staging gymnastics as sieges or scaling operations, suggest intoxication with a new medium. Nevertheless, these extravagances are part of the play's appeal, like the vigor, the dramatic variety, the full panoply, the moral zeal investing Talbot's triumph and death. As Nashe testifies, Shakespeare's audience responded instinctively to a new genius of the stage.

University of Chicago   DAVID BEVINGTON

NOTE ON THE TEXT

The play was first printed in the folio of 1623 as *The first Part of Henry the Sixt*. The nature of the copy used by the printers is still in dispute, but recent opinion favors the position that it was a manuscript in Shakespeare's own hand. The folio text is divided, erratically, into acts and scenes; the act–scene division employed marginally for reference in the present edition is the somewhat more rational one of later editors. Otherwise the folio text is followed closely except for the usual modernization of spelling and punctuation, and the normalization of the speech-prefixes. Proper names have been regularized: *Reignier* (for the common Reigneir and occasional Reynold or Reignard), *Dauphin* (for Dolphin), *Pucelle* (for Puzel), *Woodville* (for Wooduile), *Auvergne* (for Ouergne), *Pole* (for Poole), *Beaufort* (for Beauford), *Coeur-de-lion* (for Cordelion), *Burgundy* (for Burgonie), *Basset* (for Bassit), *Armagnac* (for Arminack). The only other substantive departures from the folio text (F) are listed below, with the adopted reading in italics followed by the folio reading in roman.

I, i, 176 *steal* (Mason conjecture; adopted by Singer) send (F)

I, ii, 30 *bred* (Rowe) breed (F)   76 *whilst* (Eds) whilest (F)   99 *five* (Steevens) fine (F)   113 *rites* (Pope) rights (F)   131 *halcyon* (F3) Halcyons (F)

I, iii, 29 *Humphrey* (Theobald) Vmpheir (F)

I, iv, 10 *Wont* (Tyrwhitt conj.; Steevens) Went (F)   27 *Duke* (Theobald) Earle (F)   69 s.d. *shoot* (Rowe) shot (F)

I, vi, 22 *of* (Capell conj.; Dyce) or (F)

II, i, 7 s.d. *Enter . . . ladders* (Cairncross) Enter . . . ladders : Their Drummes beating a Dead March (F)   29 *all together* (Rowe) altogether (F)   77 *them* (Capell) them. Exeunt (F)

II, ii, s.d. *their . . . dead march* (This ed.; placed at II, i, 7 s.d. in F)   20 *Arc* (Rowe) Acre (F)   59 s.d. *Whispers* (Johnson; placed at end of line in F)

II, iv, 117 *wiped* (F2) whipt (F)   132 *sir* (F2; omitted in F)

II, v, 3 *rack* (Pope) Wrack (F)   121 s.d. *Exeunt* (Eds) Exit (F)

III, i, 52 *Somerset* (Theobald; the line is part of preceding speech by Warwick in F)   53 *Warwick* (Theobald) Som. (F)   162 *that alone* (F2) that all alone (F)   198 *should lose* (F2) loose (F)

III, iv, 27 s.d. *Manent* (Eds) Manet (F)

IV, i, s.d. *Exeter, and Governor* (Pope) and Gouernor Exeter (F)   151 *umpire* (Eds) Vmper (F)   173 s.d. *Manent* (Eds) Manet (F)   180 *wist* (Capell) wish (F)

IV, ii, 3 *calls* (Eds) call (F)   15 *General* (Eds) Cap. (F)   34 *due* (Theobald) dew (F)   50 *moody-mad and* (Capell) moodie mad : And (F)

IV, iii, 5 *Talbot. As* (F2 : Talbot; as) Talbot as (F)   17, 30, 34, 47 *Lucy* (Theobald) 2. Mes. (F)   20 *waist* (Eds) waste (F)

IV, iv, 16 *legions* (Rowe) Regions (F)

IV, vii, 89, 94 *'em* (Theobald) him (F)   96 s.d. *Exeunt* (Eds) Exit (F)

V, iii, 11 *legions* (Warburton conj.; Singer) Regions (F)   47 *reverent* (Eds) reuerend (F)   57 *her* (F3) his (F)   179 *modestly* (Eds) modestie (F)   192 *And* (Capell) Mad (F)

V, iv, 28 *suck'dst* (Eds) suck'st (F)   37 *one* (Malone) me (F)   49 *Arc* (Rowe) Aire (F)   93 s.d. *Enter Cardinal* (Capell; placed at line 91 in F)

V, v, 60 *It most* (Rowe) Most (F)   82 *love* (F2) Ioue (F)

THE FIRST PART OF
KING HENRY THE SIXTH

*

I, i   *Dead march. Enter the Funeral of King Henry the*
Fifth, attended on by the Duke of Bedford, Regent of
France ; the Duke of Gloucester, Protector ; the
Duke of Exeter, [the Earl of] Warwick, the Bishop of
Winchester, and the Duke of Somerset [with
Heralds, etc.].

BEDFORD
Hung be the heavens with black, yield day to night !
Comets, importing change of times and states,
Brandish your crystal tresses in the sky
And with them scourge the bad revolting stars
That have consented unto Henry's death –
King Henry the Fifth, too famous to live long !
England ne'er lost a king of so much worth.

GLOUCESTER
England ne'er had a king until his time.
9   Virtue he had, deserving to command ;
10   His brandished sword did blind men with his beams ;

His arms spread wider than a dragon's wings ;
His sparkling eyes, replete with wrathful fire,
More dazzled and drove back his enemies
Than midday sun fierce bent against their faces.
What should I say ? His deeds exceed all speech.
He ne'er lift up his hand but conquerèd.   16

EXETER
We mourn in black. Why mourn we not in blood ?
Henry is dead and never shall revive.
Upon a wooden coffin we attend,
And death's dishonorable victory
We with our stately presence glorify,
Like captives bound to a triumphant car.
What ? Shall we curse the planets of mishap
That plotted thus our glory's overthrow ?
Or shall we think the subtile-witted French
Conjurers and sorcerers, that, afraid of him,
By magic verses have contrived his end ?

WINCHESTER
He was a king blessed of the King of Kings.
Unto the French the dreadful judgment day
So dreadful will not be as was his sight.

I, i Westminster Abbey   **9** *Virtue* excellence in culture   **10** *his* its   **16** *lift*
lifted ; *but conquerèd* without conquering

The battles of the Lord of Hosts he fought ;
The church's prayers made him so prosperous.

GLOUCESTER

33   The church ? Where is it ? Had not churchmen prayed,
His thread of life had not so soon decayed.
None do you like but an effeminate prince
Whom like a schoolboy you may overawe.

WINCHESTER

Gloucester, whate'er we like, thou art Protector
And lookest to command the prince and realm.

39   Thy wife is proud. She holdeth thee in awe
More than God or religious churchmen may.

GLOUCESTER

Name not religion, for thou lov'st the flesh,
And ne'er throughout the year to church thou go'st,
Except it be to pray against thy foes.

BEDFORD

44   Cease, cease these jars, and rest your minds in peace !
Let's to the altar. Heralds, wait on us.

46   Instead of gold we'll offer up our arms,
Since arms avail not, now that Henry's dead.

48   Posterity, await for wretched years,
When at their mothers' moist'ned eyes babes shall suck,

50   Our isle be made a nourish of salt tears,
And none but women left to wail the dead.
Henry the Fifth, thy ghost I invocate :
Prosper this realm, keep it from civil broils !
Combat with adverse planets in the heavens !
A far more glorious star thy soul will make
Than Julius Caesar or bright –
        Enter a Messenger.

MESSENGER

My honorable lords, health to you all.
Sad tidings bring I to you out of France,
Of loss, of slaughter, and discomfiture.
Guyenne, Champagne, Rheims, Orleans,
Paris, Guysors, Poictiers, are all quite lost.

BEDFORD

What say'st thou, man, before dead Henry's corse ?
Speak softly, or the loss of those great towns

64   Will make him burst his lead and rise from death.

GLOUCESTER

65   Is Paris lost ? Is Roan yielded up ?
If Henry were recalled to life again,
These news would cause him once more yield the ghost.

EXETER

How were they lost ? What treachery was used ?

MESSENGER

No treachery, but want of men and money.
Amongst the soldiers this is mutterèd,
That here you maintain several factions,

72   And whilst a field should be dispatched and fought

73   You are disputing of your generals.
One would have ling'ring wars, with little cost ;

75   Another would fly swift, but wanteth wings ;
A third thinks, without expense at all,
By guileful fair words peace may be obtained.
Awake, awake, English nobility !
Let not sloth dim your honors new begot.

80   Cropped are the flower-de-luces in your arms ;
Of England's coat one half is cut away.   *[Exit.]*

EXETER

82   Were our tears wanting to this funeral,
These tidings would call forth her flowing tides.

BEDFORD

Me they concern ; regent I am of France.
Give me my steelèd coat, I'll fight for France.
Away with these disgraceful wailing robes !
Wounds will I lend the French, instead of eyes,   87
To weep their intermissive miseries.   88
        Enter to them another Messenger.

MESSENGER

Lords, view these letters, full of bad mischance.
France is revolted from the English quite,
Except some petty towns of no import.
The Dauphin Charles is crownèd king in Rheims ;
The Bastard of Orleans with him is joined ;
Reignier, Duke of Anjou, doth take his part ;
The Duke of Alençon flieth to his side.   *Exit.*

EXETER

The Dauphin crownèd king ? All fly to him ?
O, whither shall we fly from this reproach ?

GLOUCESTER

We will not fly, but to our enemies' throats !
Bedford, if thou be slack, I'll fight it out.

BEDFORD

Gloucester, why doubt'st thou of my forwardness ?
An army have I mustered in my thoughts,
Wherewith already France is overrun.
        Enter another Messenger.

MESSENGER

My gracious lords, to add to your laments,
Wherewith you now bedew King Henry's hearse,
I must inform you of a dismal fight   105
Betwixt the stout Lord Talbot and the French.

WINCHESTER

What ? Wherein Talbot overcame, is't so ?

MESSENGER

O, no ! wherein Lord Talbot was o'erthrown.
The circumstance I'll tell you more at large.   109
The tenth of August last this dreadful lord,   110
Retiring from the siege of Orleans,
Having full scarce six thousand in his troop,   112
By three and twenty thousand of the French
Was round encompassèd and set upon.
No leisure had he to enrank his men ;
He wanted pikes to set before his archers ;   116
Instead whereof, sharp stakes plucked out of hedges
They pitchèd in the ground confusedly
To keep the horsemen off from breaking in.
More than three hours the fight continuèd,
Where valiant Talbot above human thought
Enacted wonders with his sword and lance.

33 *prayed* (with pun on 'preyed') 39 *Thy wife* (Eleanor, guilty of ambition and witchcraft in 2 *Henry VI*); *holdeth . . . awe* i.e. keeps you in subjection 44 *jars* discords 46 *arms* weapons 48–50 *Posterity . . . tears* i.e. later generations, look for evil times, when mothers shall feed their children with their tears, and Britain shall also nurse her children (i.e. inhabitants) with tears only 50 *nourish* nurse 64 *lead* leaden wrappings for corpse 65 *Roan* Rouen 72 *field* battle ; *dispatched* settled 73 *of* about 75 *wanteth* lacks 80 *Cropped* plucked ; *arms* coat of arms (Henry VI was supposed to be 'Heir of France,' since the French had yielded to his victorious father. Instead, Charles Dauphin was proclaimed king. Henry VI thus faced the loss of his right to wear the '*fleurs-de-lis*,' national emblem of France, in his coat of arms.) 82 *wanting* lacking 87 *Wounds . . . eyes* i.e. he will cause them to shed blood instead of tears 88 *intermissive* temporarily interrupted, now to be resumed 105 *dismal* unlucky 109 *at large* in detail 110 *dreadful* inspiring dread 112 *full scarce* i.e. scarce full, barely 116 *wanted pikes* lacked ironbound stakes (for defense against cavalry)

Hundreds he sent to hell, and none durst stand him;
Here, there, and everywhere enraged he slew.
The French exclaimed the devil was in arms;
126 All the whole army stood agazed on him.
His soldiers, spying his undaunted spirit,
128 'A Talbot! a Talbot!' cried out amain
And rushed into the bowels of the battle.
Here had the conquest fully been sealed up
131 If Sir John Falstaff had not played the coward.
132 He, being in the vaward, placed behind
With purpose to relieve and follow them,
Cowardly fled, not having struck one stroke.
Hence grew the general wrack and massacre.
136 Enclosèd were they with their enemies.
137 A base Walloon, to win the Dauphin's grace,
Thrust Talbot with a spear into the back,
Whom all France with their chief assembled strength
Durst not presume to look once in the face.

BEDFORD
Is Talbot slain? Then I will slay myself
For living idly here in pomp and ease
Whilst such a worthy leader, wanting aid,
Unto his dastard foemen is betrayed.

MESSENGER
O, no, he lives, but is took prisoner,
And Lord Scales with him, and Lord Hungerford;
Most of the rest slaughtered or took likewise.

BEDFORD
148 His ransom there is none but I shall pay.
I'll hale the Dauphin headlong from his throne;
His crown shall be the ransom of my friend.
151 Four of their lords I'll change for one of ours.
Farewell, my masters; to my task will I.
Bonfires in France forthwith I am to make
154 To keep our great Saint George's feast withal.
Ten thousand soldiers with me I will take,
Whose bloody deeds shall make all Europe quake.

MESSENGER
So you had need, for Orleans is besieged;
The English army is grown weak and faint;
159 The Earl of Salisbury craveth supply
And hardly keeps his men from mutiny,
Since they, so few, watch such a multitude.   [Exit.]

EXETER
Remember, lords, your oaths to Henry sworn,

Either to quell the Dauphin utterly
Or bring him in obedience to your yoke.

BEDFORD
I do remember it, and here take my leave
To go about my preparation.   Exit Bedford.

GLOUCESTER
I'll to the Tower with all the haste I can   167
To view th' artillery and munition,
And then I will proclaim young Henry king.
                                        Exit Gloucester.

EXETER
To Eltham will I, where the young king is,   170
Being ordained his special governor,
And for his safety there I'll best devise.   Exit.

WINCHESTER
Each hath his place and function to attend.
I am left out; for me nothing remains.
But long I will not be Jack out of office.
The king from Eltham I intend to steal
And sit at chiefest stern of public weal.   Exit. 177

*

Sound a flourish. Enter Charles [the Dauphin],   I, ii
Alençon, and Reignier, marching with Drum and
Soldiers.

CHARLES
Mars his true moving, even as in the heavens   1
So in the earth, to this day is not known.
Late did he shine upon the English side;   3
Now we are victors, upon us he smiles.
What towns of any moment but we have?   5
At pleasure here we lie, near Orleans;
Otherwhiles the famished English, like pale ghosts,   7
Faintly besiege us one hour in a month.

ALENÇON
They want their porridge and their fat bull-beeves.
Either they must be dieted like mules   10
And have their provender tied to their mouths,
Or piteous they will look, like drownèd mice.

REIGNIER
Let's raise the siege. Why live we idly here?   13
Talbot is taken, whom we wont to fear.   14
Remaineth none but mad-brained Salisbury,
And he may well in fretting spend his gall.   16
Nor men nor money hath he to make war.   17

CHARLES
Sound, sound alarum! We will rush on them.   18
Now for the honor of the forlorn French!
Him I forgive my death that killeth me
When he sees me go back one foot or fly.   Exeunt.
Here alarum. They are beaten back by the English with
great loss. Enter Charles, Alençon, and Reignier.

CHARLES
Who ever saw the like? What men have I!
Dogs! cowards! dastards! I would ne'er have fled
But that they left me 'midst my enemies.

REIGNIER
Salisbury is a desperate homicide;
He fighteth as one weary of his life.
The other lords, like lions wanting food,
Do rush upon us as their hungry prey.   28

ALENÇON
Froissart, a countryman of ours, records   29

126 *agazed on* astounded at   128 *amain* vehemently   131 *Falstaff* ('Fastolfe' in the chronicles; but Shakespeare wrote 'Falstaff' and later gave the same name, replacing 'Oldcastle' in the chronicles, to the more famous coward knight of *1 & 2 Henry IV* and *Merry Wives*)   132 *being ... behind* bringing up the rear of the vanguard   136 *with* by   137 *Walloon* citizen of a province now in southern Belgium   148 *His ... pay* i.e. my deeds of vengeance and rescue are all the ransom the French can expect from us   151 *change* exchange, i.e. kill in retaliation (since four Frenchmen are worth but one Englishman)   154 *Saint George's feast* (traditionally April 23; but England's patron saint might be celebrated with bonfires after any military victory)   159 *supply* reinforcements   167 *Tower* Tower of London   170 *Eltham* a royal residence, south of London   177 *at chiefest stern* supremely at the helm
I, ii *Before Orleans in France*   1 *Mars ... moving* Mars' precise movement (the planet's seemingly eccentric orbit was a source of astronomical controversy)   3 *Late* lately   5 *of ... have* i.e. of any importance that we do not possess   7 *Otherwhiles* at times   10 *dieted* fed   13 *raise* i.e. end by driving off the besieging armies   14 *wont* were accustomed   16 *spend his gall* expend his irritation   17 *Nor* neither   18 *alarum* call to arms   28 *hungry* arousing hunger   29 *Froissart* a fourteenth-century French chronicler

30 England all Olivers and Rowlands bred
   During the time Edward the Third did reign.
   More truly now may this be verified,
33 For none but Samsons and Goliases
   It sendeth forth to skirmish. One to ten?
35 Lean raw-boned rascals, who would e'er suppose
   They had such courage and audacity?

CHARLES
   Let's leave this town; for they are harebrained slaves,
38 And hunger will enforce them to be more eager.
   Of old I know them. Rather with their teeth
   The walls they'll tear down than forsake the siege.

REIGNIER
41 I think by some odd gimmors or device
42 Their arms are set, like clocks, still to strike on.
   Else ne'er could they hold out so as they do.
   By my consent, we'll even let them alone.

ALENÇON
   Be it so.
        Enter the Bastard of Orleans.

BASTARD
   Where's the Prince Dauphin? I have news for him.

CHARLES
   Bastard of Orleans, thrice welcome to us.

BASTARD
48 Methinks your looks are sad, your cheer appalled.
   Hath the late overthrow wrought this offense?
   Be not dismayed, for succor is at hand.
   A holy maid hither with me I bring
   Which by a vision sent to her from heaven
   Ordainèd is to raise this tedious siege
   And drive the English forth the bounds of France.
   The spirit of deep prophecy she hath,
56 Exceeding the nine sibyls of old Rome.
   What's past and what's to come she can descry.
   Speak, shall I call her in? Believe my words,
   For they are certain and unfallible.

CHARLES
   Go, call her in. *[Exit Bastard.]* But first, to try her skill,
   Reignier, stand thou as Dauphin in my place.
   Question her proudly, let thy looks be stern.
63 By this means shall we sound what skill she hath.
        Enter Joan Pucelle [and Bastard].

REIGNIER
   Fair maid, is't thou wilt do these wondrous feats?

PUCELLE
   Reignier, is't thou that thinkest to beguile me?
   Where is the Dauphin? Come, come from behind.
   I know thee well, though never seen before.
   Be not amazed, there's nothing hid from me.
   In private will I talk with thee apart.
   Stand back, you lords, and give us leave awhile.

REIGNIER
71 She takes upon her bravely at first dash.

PUCELLE
   Dauphin, I am by birth a shepherd's daughter,
   My wit untrained in any kind of art.
   Heaven and our Lady gracious hath it pleased
   To shine on my contemptible estate.
   Lo, whilst I waited on my tender lambs
   And to sun's parching heat displayed my cheeks,
   God's Mother deignèd to appear to me,
   And in a vision full of majesty
   Willed me to leave my base vocation

And free my country from calamity.
   Her aid she promised and assured success.
   In complete glory she revealed herself;
   And whereas I was black and swart before,
   With those clear rays which she infused on me   85
   That beauty am I blessed with, which you may see.
   Ask me what question thou canst possible,
   And I will answer unpremeditated.
   My courage try by combat, if thou dar'st,
   And thou shalt find that I exceed my sex.
   Resolve on this: thou shalt be fortunate   91
   If thou receive me for thy warlike mate.   92

CHARLES
   Thou hast astonished me with thy high terms.   93
   Only this proof I'll of thy valor make: 94
   In single combat thou shalt buckle with me,   95
   And if thou vanquishest, thy words are true.
   Otherwise I renounce all confidence.   97

PUCELLE
   I am prepared. Here is my keen-edged sword,
   Decked with five flower-de-luces on each side,
   The which at Touraine in Saint Katherine's churchyard
   Out of a great deal of old iron I chose forth.

CHARLES
   Then come, a God's name! I fear no woman.

PUCELLE
   And while I live, I'll ne'er fly from a man.
        Here they fight, and Joan de Pucelle overcomes.

CHARLES
   Stay, stay thy hands! Thou art an Amazon
   And fightest with the sword of Deborah.   105

PUCELLE
   Christ's Mother helps me, else I were too weak.

CHARLES
   Whoe'er helps thee, 'tis thou that must help me!
   Impatiently I burn with thy desire;   108
   My heart and hands thou hast at once subdued.
   Excellent Pucelle, if thy name be so,
   Let me thy servant and not sovereign be.
   'Tis the French Dauphin sueth to thee thus.

PUCELLE
   I must not yield to any rites of love,
   For my profession's sacred from above.
   When I have chasèd all thy foes from hence,
   Then will I think upon a recompense.

CHARLES
   Meantime, look gracious on thy prostrate thrall.

REIGNIER
   My lord, methinks, is very long in talk.

ALENÇON
   Doubtless he shrives this woman to her smock;   119
   Else ne'er could he so long protract his speech.

---

30 *England . . . bred* i.e. England's knights were all as chivalrous as the best who followed Charlemagne   33 *Goliases* Goliaths   35 *rascals* wretches   38 *eager* (1) fierce, (2) hungry   41 *gimmors* gimmals, mechanical joints for transmitting motion as in clockwork   42 *still* continually   48 *cheer appalled* countenance made pale and downcast   56 *sibyls* prophetesses in the ancient world   63 s.d. *Pucelle* virgin   71 *takes . . . bravely* plays her part well   85 *With* by virtue of   91 *Resolve on* be sure of   92 *warlike mate* (throughout this scene the military terms have ribald double meanings)   93 *high terms* lofty language   94 *proof* trial   95 *buckle* join in close struggle (with erotic suggestion)   97 *confidence* (1) firm trust, (2) intimacy   105 *Deborah* Hebrew prophetess, judge over Israel, and successful commander of the army against Sisera (Judges iv)   108 *thy desire* i.e. desire for thee   119 *shrives* examines; *to her smock* i.e. completely (with double meaning)

REIGNIER

121　Shall we disturb him, since he keeps no mean?

ALENÇON

He may mean more than we poor men do know.
These women are shrewd tempters with their tongues.

REIGNIER

My lord, where are you? What devise you on?
Shall we give o'er Orleans, or no?

PUCELLE

Why, no, I say, distrustful recreants,
Fight till the last gasp. I'll be your guard.

CHARLES

What she says, I'll confirm. We'll fight it out.

PUCELLE

Assigned am I to be the English scourge.
This night the siege assuredly I'll raise.

131　Expect Saint Martin's summer, halcyon days,
Since I have enterèd into these wars.
Glory is like a circle in the water,
Which never ceaseth to enlarge itself
Till by broad spreading it disperse to naught.
With Henry's death the English circle ends;
Dispersèd are the glories it included.

138　Now am I like that proud insulting ship
Which Caesar and his fortune bare at once.

CHARLES

140　Was Mahomet inspirèd with a dove?
Thou with an eagle art inspirèd then!

142　Helen, the mother of great Constantine,

143　Nor yet Saint Philip's daughters, were like thee.
Bright star of Venus, fall'n down on the earth,
How may I reverently worship thee enough?

ALENÇON

Leave off delays and let us raise the siege.

REIGNIER

Woman, do what thou canst to save our honors.
Drive them from Orleans and be immortalized.

CHARLES

149　Presently we'll try. Come, let's away about it.
No prophet will I trust if she prove false.　　　　*Exeunt.*

*

Enter Gloucester, with his Servingmen　　　　I, iii
[in blue coats].

GLOUCESTER

I am come to survey the Tower this day.　　　　1
Since Henry's death I fear there is conveyance.　　　　2
Where be these warders that they wait not here?
Open the gates! 'Tis Gloucester that calls.
[Servingmen knock.]

1. WARDER *[within]*

Who's there that knocks so imperiously?

GLOUCESTER'S 1. MAN

It is the noble Duke of Gloucester.

2. WARDER *[within]*

Whoe'er he be, you may not be let in.

1. MAN

Villains, answer you so the Lord Protector?

1. WARDER *[within]*

The Lord protect him! So we answer him.
We do no otherwise than we are willed.　　　　10

GLOUCESTER

Who willèd you? or whose will stands but mine?
There's none Protector of the realm but I.
Break up the gates, I'll be your warrantize.　　　　13
Shall I be flouted thus by dunghill grooms?　　　　14
*Gloucester's men rush at the Tower gates, and
Woodville the Lieutenant speaks within.*

WOODVILLE

What noise is this? What traitors have we here?

GLOUCESTER

Lieutenant, is it you whose voice I hear?
Open the gates. Here's Gloucester that would enter.

WOODVILLE

Have patience, noble Duke. I may not open;
The Cardinal of Winchester forbids.
From him I have express commandement
That thou nor none of thine shall be let in.

GLOUCESTER

Faint-hearted Woodville, prizest him 'fore me?
Arrogant Winchester, that haughty prelate,
Whom Henry our late sovereign ne'er could brook?　　　　24
Thou art no friend to God or to the king.
Open the gates, or I'll shut thee out shortly.

SERVINGMEN

Open the gates unto the Lord Protector,
Or we'll burst them open if that you come not quickly.　　　　28
*Enter to the Protector at the Tower gates Winchester
and his men in tawny coats.*

WINCHESTER

How now, ambitious Humphrey, what means this?

GLOUCESTER

Peeled priest, dost thou command me to be shut out?　　　　30

WINCHESTER

I do, thou most usurping proditor,　　　　31
And not Protector of the king or realm.

GLOUCESTER

Stand back, thou manifest conspirator,
Thou that contrivedst to murder our dead lord,　　　　34
Thou that giv'st whores indulgences to sin.　　　　35
I'll canvass thee in thy broad cardinal's hat　　　　36
If thou proceed in this thy insolence.

WINCHESTER

Nay, stand thou back. I will not budge a foot.
This be Damascus, be thou cursèd Cain,　　　　39
To slay thy brother Abel, if thou wilt.　　　　40

121 *keeps no mean* is immoderate　131 *Saint Martin's summer* i.e. Indian summer (since St Martin's day is November 11), hence, success after a period of stormy fortune; *halcyon days* a period of calm around December when the kingfisher (halcyon) supposedly breeds in a nest on the sea 138–39 *Now . . . once* (according to Plutarch, Caesar, aboard a small vessel in a storm, calmed the mariners with the thought that Caesar and his fortune were proof against drowning) 140 *Mahomet . . . dove* (Mohammed reputedly taught a dove to take feed at his ears; he claimed that the dove was the Holy Ghost and that it brought him divine revelation) 142 *Helen* St Helena, purported discoverer of the true cross 143 *Saint Philip's daughters* i.e. prophesying virgins (Acts xxi, 9) 149 *Presently* immediately I, iii Before the Tower of London s.d. *blue coats* (customarily worn by servingmen) 1 *survey* inspect 2 *conveyance* sharp dealings, theft 10 *willed* commanded 13 *warrantize* authorization 14 s.d. *within* i.e. from the tiring house or actors' dressing area (the stage backdrop or façade is envisaged in this scene as the Tower, with occupants of the Tower behind the gates backstage) 24 *brook* endure 28 s.d. *tawny coats* (worn by summoners of an ecclesiastical court) 30 *Peeled* i.e. tonsured 31 *proditor* traitor 34 *dead lord* i.e. Henry V 35 *giv'st . . . sin* (Winchester historically received revenue from houses of prostitution in the London suburb of Southwark) 36 *canvass* buffet (literally, toss in a blanket) 39 *Damascus* (popular belief held that Cain slew Abel on the site of this later city) 40 *brother* (Winchester is actually Gloucester's half-uncle)

GLOUCESTER
I will not slay thee, but I'll drive thee back.
42 Thy scarlet robes as a child's bearing cloth
I'll use to carry thee out of this place.
WINCHESTER
44 Do what thou dar'st! I beard thee to thy face.
GLOUCESTER
What? Am I dared and bearded to my face?
46 Draw, men, for all this privilegèd place,
Blue coats to tawny coats. Priest, beware your beard.
I mean to tug it and to cuff you soundly.
Under my feet I stamp thy cardinal's hat.
50 In spite of pope or dignities of church,
Here by the cheeks I'll drag thee up and down.
WINCHESTER
52 Gloucester, thou wilt answer this before the pope.
GLOUCESTER
53 Winchester goose! I cry a rope, a rope!
Now beat them hence. Why do you let them stay?
Thee I'll chase hence, thou wolf in sheep's array.
Out, tawny coats! Out, scarlet hypocrite!
Here Gloucester's men beat out the Cardinal's men,
and enter in the hurly-burly the Mayor of London
and his Officers.
MAYOR
Fie, lords, that you, being supreme magistrates,
Thus contumeliously should break the peace!
GLOUCESTER
Peace, mayor, thou know'st little of my wrongs.
Here's Beaufort, that regards nor God nor king,
61 Hath here distrained the Tower to his use.
WINCHESTER
Here's Gloucester, a foe to citizens;
63 One that still motions war and never peace,
O'ercharging your free purses with large fines,
That seeks to overthrow religion
Because he is Protector of the realm,
And would have armor here out of the Tower
68 To crown himself king and suppress the prince.
GLOUCESTER
I will not answer thee with words, but blows.
Here they skirmish again.
MAYOR
Naught rests for me in this tumultuous strife
But to make open proclamation.
Come, officer, as loud as e'er thou canst,
Cry.
[OFFICER] All manner of men assembled here in arms this
day against God's peace and the king's, we charge and
command you, in his highness' name, to repair to your
several dwelling places, and not to wear, handle, or use
any sword, weapon, or dagger henceforward, upon pain
of death.
GLOUCESTER
Cardinal, I'll be no breaker of the law;
81 But we shall meet and break our minds at large.
WINCHESTER
Gloucester, we'll meet to thy cost, be sure.
Thy heart-blood I will have for this day's work.
MAYOR
84 I'll call for clubs if you will not away.
This cardinal's more haughty than the devil.
GLOUCESTER
Mayor, farewell. Thou dost but what thou mayst.

WINCHESTER
Abominable Gloucester, guard thy head;
For I intend to have it ere long.
Exeunt [severally, Gloucester and Winchester
with their Servingmen].
MAYOR
See the coast cleared, and then we will depart.
Good God, these nobles should such stomachs bear!   90
I myself fight not once in forty year.   *Exeunt.*

*

Enter the Master Gunner of Orleans and his Boy.   I, iv
MASTER GUNNER
Sirrah, thou know'st how Orleans is besieged   1
And how the English have the suburbs won.
BOY
Father, I know, and oft have shot at them,
Howe'er unfortunate I missed my aim.   4
MASTER GUNNER
But now thou shalt not. Be thou ruled by me.
Chief master gunner am I of this town;
Something I must do to procure me grace.   7
The Prince's espials have informèd me   8
How the English, in the suburbs close intrenched,
Wont through a secret grate of iron bars
In yonder tower to overpeer the city,
And thence discover how with most advantage
They may vex us with shot or with assault.
To intercept this inconvenience   14
A piece of ordnance 'gainst it I have placed,   15
And even these three days have I watched,
If I could see them. Now do thou watch,
For I can stay no longer.
If thou spy'st any, run and bring me word,
And thou shalt find me at the governor's.   *Exit.*
BOY
Father, I warrant you; take you no care.
I'll never trouble you if I may spy them.   *Exit.* 22
Enter Salisbury and Talbot on the turrets with
[Sir William Glansdale, Sir Thomas Gargrave, and]
others.
SALISBURY
Talbot, my life, my joy, again returned?
How wert thou handled being prisoner,
Or by what means gots thou to be released?   25
Discourse, I prithee, on this turret's top.
TALBOT
The Duke of Bedford had a prisoner
Called the brave Lord Ponton de Santrailles;
For him was I exchanged and ransomèd.
But with a baser man-of-arms by far   30

42 *bearing cloth* christening robe   44 *beard* defy   46 *for . . . place* i.e.
despite ordinances forbidding drawing of weapons near a royal residence
50 *dignities* dignitaries   52 *answer* pay for   53 *Winchester goose* a venereal
disorder   61 *distrained* confiscated   63 *still motions* always advocates   68
prince king, i.e. Henry VI   81 *break our minds* (1) express our views, (2)
crack heads; *at large* at length   84 *call for clubs* rallying cry for London
apprentices with their clubs   90 *stomachs* tempers
I, iv The fortifications of Orleans   1 *Sirrah* (form of address used to
inferiors)   4 *Howe'er* although   7 *grace* honor   8 *espials* spies   14 *in-*
convenience mischief   15 *'gainst* directed toward   22 s.d. *turrets* i.e. rear
stage gallery or some higher vantage point in the theatre   25 *gots* gottest
30 *baser man-of-arms* soldier of lower birth or rank

Once in contempt they would have bartered me;
Which I disdaining scorned, and cravèd death
33 Rather than I would be so pilled esteemed.
34 In fine, redeemed I was as I desired.
But, O, the treacherous Falstaff wounds my heart,
Whom with my bare fists I would execute
If I now had him brought into my power.

SALISBURY

38 Yet tell'st thou not how thou wert entertained.

TALBOT

With scoffs and scorns and contumelious taunts
In open market place produced they me
To be a public spectacle to all.
'Here,' said they, 'is the terror of the French,
The scarecrow that affrights our children so.'
Then broke I from the officers that led me
And with my nails digged stones out of the ground
To hurl at the beholders of my shame.
My grisly countenance made others fly;
None durst come near for fear of sudden death.
In iron walls they deemed me not secure;
So great fear of my name 'mongst them were spread
That they supposed I could rend bars of steel
52 And spurn in pieces posts of adamant.
53 Wherefore a guard of chosen shot I had
54 That walked about me every minute while;
And if I did but stir out of my bed,
56 Ready they were to shoot me to the heart.

Enter the Boy with a linstock.

SALISBURY

I grieve to hear what torments you endured.
But we will be revenged sufficiently.
Now it is supper time in Orleans.
Here, through this grate, I count each one
And view the Frenchmen how they fortify.
Let us look in; the sight will much delight thee.
Sir Thomas Gargrave and Sir William Glansdale,
64 Let me have your express opinions
65 Where is best place to make our batt'ry next.

GARGRAVE

I think at the north gate, for there stands lords.

GLANSDALE

67 And I here, at the bulwark of the bridge.

TALBOT

68 For aught I see, this city must be famished
69 Or with light skirmishes enfeeblèd.

*Here they shoot, and Salisbury falls down [together
with Gargrave].*

SALISBURY

O Lord have mercy on us, wretched sinners!

GARGRAVE

O Lord have mercy on me, woeful man!

TALBOT

What chance is this that suddenly hath crossed us?   72
Speak, Salisbury; at least if thou canst speak.
How far'st thou, mirror of all martial men?   74
One of thy eyes and thy cheek's side struck off?
Accursèd tower! Accursèd fatal hand
That hath contrived this woeful tragedy!
In thirteen battles Salisbury o'ercame;
Henry the Fifth he first trained to the wars.
Whilst any trump did sound or drum struck up
His sword did ne'er leave striking in the field.   81
Yet liv'st thou, Salisbury? Though thy speech doth fail,
One eye thou hast to look to heaven for grace.
The sun with one eye vieweth all the world.
Heaven, be thou gracious to none alive
If Salisbury wants mercy at thy hands!
Bear hence his body; I will help to bury it.
Sir Thomas Gargrave, hast thou any life?
Speak unto Talbot. Nay, look up to him.
Salisbury, cheer thy spirit with this comfort,
Thou shalt not die whiles –
He beckons with his hand and smiles on me,
As who should say, 'When I am dead and gone,
Remember to avenge me on the French.'
Plantagenet, I will, and like thee,   95
Play on the lute, beholding the towns burn.   96
Wretched shall France be only in my name.   97

Here an alarum, and it thunders and lightens.

What stir is this? What tumult's in the heavens?
Whence cometh this alarum and the noise?

Enter a Messenger.

MESSENGER

My lord, my lord, the French have gathered head!   100
The Dauphin, with one Joan de Pucelle joined,
A holy prophetess new risen up,
Is come with a great power to raise the siege.   103

Here Salisbury lifteth himself up and groans.

TALBOT

Hear, hear, how dying Salisbury doth groan!
It irks his heart he cannot be revenged.
Frenchmen, I'll be a Salisbury to you.
Pucelle or pussel, Dolphin or dogfish,   107
Your hearts I'll stamp out with my horse's heels
And make a quagmire of your mingled brains.
Convey me Salisbury into his tent,   110
And then we'll try what these dastard Frenchmen dare.

Alarum. Exeunt [with the bodies].

Here an alarum again, and Talbot pursueth the   I, v
*Dauphin and driveth him. Then enter Joan de Pucelle
driving Englishmen before her [and exit]. Then
enter Talbot.*

TALBOT

Where is my strength, my valor, and my force?
Our English troops retire, I cannot stay them;
A woman clad in armor chaseth them.

Enter Pucelle.

Here, here she comes. I'll have a bout with thee.   4
Devil or devil's dam, I'll conjure thee.   5

33 *pilled* peeled, i.e. stripped of dignity   34 *In fine* in short; *redeemed* ransomed   38 *entertained* treated   52 *spurn* kick   53 *chosen shot* outstanding marksmen   54 *minute while* minute's space   56 s.d. *linstock* forked stick holding gunner's match   64 *express* definite   65 *batt'ry* artillery platform   67 *bulwark* fortification   68 *must be* will have to be   69 s.d. *they* i.e. the French (implies that the cannon, not visible to the audience, is fired behind the scenes)   72 *chance* mischance   74 *mirror* example   81 *leave* cease from   95 *Plantagenet* (Salisbury's family name was Montacute, but he was descended from Edward I)   96 *Play . . . burn* (Salisbury is likened to Nero as a type of heartless destroyer of cities; Talbot vows to emulate them both)   97 *only in* at the mere sound of   100 *gathered head* drawn their forces together   103 *power* army   107 *Pucelle* maid; *pussel* slut; *Dolphin* (near homonym for *Dauphin* – the dolphin was often thought to be highest in the chain of being among fish); *dogfish* a small shark (contemptibly low order of fish)   110 *me* at my request (ethical dative)
I, v   4 *bout* a round at fighting (cf. Charles' 'buckling' with Joan in I, ii)   5 *conjure* constrain by sacred oath (a supernatural good, similar in method but opposite in intent to her supernatural evil)

6   Blood will I draw on thee, thou art a witch,
7   And straightway give thy soul to him thou serv'st.

PUCELLE

Come, come 'tis only I that must disgrace thee.

Here they fight.

TALBOT

Heavens, can you suffer hell so to prevail?
My breast I'll burst with straining of my courage
And from my shoulders crack my arms asunder
12   But I will chastise this high-minded strumpet.

They fight again.

PUCELLE

Talbot, farewell; thy hour is not yet come.
I must go victual Orleans forthwith.

A short alarum. Then enter the town with Soldiers.

O'ertake me if thou canst! I scorn thy strength.
Go, go, cheer up thy hungry-starvèd men.
Help Salisbury to make his testament.
This day is ours, as many more shall be.   *Exit.*

TALBOT

My thoughts are whirlèd like a potter's wheel;
I know not where I am nor what I do.
21   A witch by fear, not force, like Hannibal,
22   Drives back our troops and conquers as she lists.
So bees with smoke and doves with noisome stench
Are from their hives and houses driven away.
They called us, for our fierceness, English dogs;
Now, like to whelps, we crying run away.

A short alarum.

Hark, countrymen! Either renew the fight
28   Or tear the lions out of England's coat,
29   Renounce your soil, give sheep in lions' stead.
30   Sheep run not half so treacherous from the wolf,
Or horse or oxen from the leopard,
As you fly from your oft-subduèd slaves.

Alarum. Here another skirmish.

It will not be. Retire into your trenches.
You all consented unto Salisbury's death,
35   For none would strike a stroke in his revenge.
Pucelle is ent'red into Orleans
In spite of us or aught that we could do.
O, would I were to die with Salisbury!
The shame hereof will make me hide my head.

            Exit Talbot. Alarum. Retreat.

I, vi   *Flourish. Enter, on the walls, Pucelle, Dauphin,*
       Reignier, Alençon, and Soldiers.

PUCELLE

1   Advance our waving colors on the walls;
Rescued is Orleans from the English.
Thus Joan de Pucelle hath performed her word.

CHARLES

4   Divinest creature, Astraea's daughter,
How shall I honor thee for this success?
6   Thy promises are like Adonis' garden,
That one day bloomed and fruitful were the next.
France, triumph in thy glorious prophetess!
Recovered is the town of Orleans.
More blessèd hap did ne'er befall our state.

REIGNIER

Why ring not out the bells aloud throughout the town?
Dauphin, command the citizens make bonfires
And feast and banquet in the open streets
To celebrate the joy that God hath given us.

ALENÇON

All France will be replete with mirth and joy
When they shall hear how we have played the men.

CHARLES

'Tis Joan, not we, by whom the day is won;
For which I will divide my crown with her,
And all the priests and friars in my realm
Shall in procession sing her endless praise.
A statelier pyramis to her I'll rear
22   Than Rhodope's of Memphis ever was.
In memory of her, when she is dead,
Her ashes, in an urn more precious
25   Than the rich-jewelled coffer of Darius,
Transported shall be at high festivals
Before the kings and queens of France.
28   No longer on Saint Denis will we cry,
But Joan de Pucelle shall be France's saint.
Come in, and let us banquet royally
After this golden day of victory.   *Flourish. Exeunt.*

*

     Enter a [French] Sergeant of a Band, with two   II, i
     Sentinels.

SERGEANT

Sirs, take your places and be vigilant.
If any noise or soldier you perceive
3   Near to the walls, by some apparent sign
4   Let us have knowledge at the court of guard.

SENTINEL

Sergeant, you shall.   *[Exit Sergeant.]*
5   Thus are poor servitors,
When others sleep upon their quiet beds,
Constrained to watch in darkness, rain, and cold.

Enter Talbot, Bedford, and Burgundy, [and Forces,]
with scaling ladders.

TALBOT

8   Lord regent, and redoubted Burgundy,
By whose approach the regions of Artois,
Wallon, and Picardy are friends to us,

6 *Blood . . . witch* (Talbot again proposes to fight black magic by virtuous magic, gaining power over her by obtaining a sample of her blood in honest combat)   7 *him* i.e. the Devil   12 *But I* if I do not; *high-minded* presumptuous   21 *Hannibal* Carthaginian general (who once rescued his army from encirclement by tying firebrands to the horns of 2,000 oxen and driving the oxen into the terrified Roman ranks)   22 *lists* pleases   28 *lions* (the English coat of arms displayed three lions passant)   29 *soil* country; *give . . . stead* i.e. display sheep on your coat of arms as symbols of cowardice   30 *treacherous* i.e. cowardly and treasonous   35 *his revenge* i.e. revenge of him

I, vi s.d. *on the walls* (in scenes I, v through II, i the tiring-house façade becomes the defended walls of Orleans; the city is within the tiring house; the rear stage gallery is a walkway on the walls)   1 *Advance* raise aloft   4 *Astraea* goddess of Justice, who lived among men during the Golden Age but was forced to reascend to the heavens in the Iron Age; her return to earth would signal a new age of justice   6 *Adonis' garden* mythical garden of eternal profusion   22 *Rhodope* a Greek courtesan who became queen of Memphis and reputedly built the third pyramid   25 *coffer of Darius* (Alexander, vanquishing Darius in battle, took from him a priceless jewelled chest, in which Alexander is said to have placed the works of Homer as his worthiest possession deserving such a container)   28 *Saint Denis* patron saint of Paris

II, i The fortifications of Orleans   3 *apparent* plain   4 *court of guard* guard house   5 *servitors* common soldiers   8–10 *Burgundy . . . us* (Burgundy's alliance with the English in the time of Henry V had brought support not only from the important Duchy of Burgundy, southeast of Paris, but from territories friendly to him in the Low Countries)

11   This happy night the Frenchmen are secure,
Having all day caroused and banqueted.
Embrace we then this opportunity,
14   As fitting best to quittance their deceit,
15   Contrived by art and baleful sorcery.

BEDFORD
16   Coward of France! How much he wrongs his fame,
Despairing of his own arm's fortitude,
To join with witches and the help of hell!

BURGUNDY
Traitors have never other company.
But what's that Pucelle whom they term so pure?

TALBOT
A maid, they say.

BEDFORD   A maid? and be so martial?

BURGUNDY
22   Pray God she prove not masculine ere long,
If underneath the standard of the French
She carry armor as she hath begun.

TALBOT
Well, let them practice and converse with spirits.
God is our fortress, in whose conquering name
Let us resolve to scale their flinty bulwarks.

BEDFORD
28   Ascend, brave Talbot. We will follow thee.

TALBOT
Not all together. Better far, I guess,
That we do make our entrance several ways;
That, if it chance the one of us do fail,
The other yet may rise against their force.

BEDFORD
Agreed. I'll to yond corner.

BURGUNDY   And I to this.

TALBOT
And here will Talbot mount, or make his grave.
Now, Salisbury, for thee, and for the right
Of English Henry, shall this night appear
How much in duty I am bound to both.

SENTINEL
38   Arm, arm! the enemy doth make assault!
[The English scale the walls.] Cry: 'Saint George!
a Talbot!'
*The French leap o'er the walls in their shirts. Enter,
several ways, Bastard [of Orleans], Alençon,
Reignier, half ready and half unready.*

ALENÇON
How now, my lords? What, all unready so?

BASTARD
Unready? Ay, and glad we scaped so well.

REIGNIER
41   'Twas time, I trow, to wake and leave our beds,
Hearing alarums at our chamber doors.

ALENÇON
Of all exploits since first I followed arms
Ne'er heard I of a warlike enterprise
More venturous or desperate than this.

BASTARD
I think this Talbot be a fiend of hell.

REIGNIER
If not of hell, the heavens sure favor him.

ALENÇON
Here cometh Charles. I marvel how he sped.   48
Enter Charles and Joan.

BASTARD
Tut, holy Joan was his defensive guard.

CHARLES
Is this thy cunning, thou deceitful dame?   50
Didst thou at first, to flatter us withal,   51
Make us partakers of a little gain
That now our loss might be ten times so much?

PUCELLE
Wherefore is Charles impatient with his friend?
At all times will you have my power alike?
Sleeping or waking must I still prevail,
Or will you blame and lay the fault on me?
Improvident soldiers, had your watch been good,
This sudden mischief never could have fall'n!   59

CHARLES
Duke of Alençon, this was your default
That, being captain of the watch to-night,   61
Did look no better to that weighty charge.

ALENÇON
Had all your quarters been as safely kept   63
As that whereof I had the government,
We had not been thus shamefully surprised.

BASTARD
Mine was secure.

REIGNIER   And so was mine, my lord.

CHARLES
And for myself, most part of all this night
Within her quarter and mine own precinct
I was employed in passing to and fro
About relieving of the sentinels.
Then how or which way should they first break in?

PUCELLE
Question, my lords, no further of the case,
How or which way. 'Tis sure they found some place
But weakly guarded, where the breach was made.   74
And now there rests no other shift but this –   75
To gather our soldiers, scattered and dispersed,
And lay new platforms to endamage them.   77
Alarum. Enter a Soldier, crying 'A Talbot!
a Talbot!' *They fly, leaving their clothes behind.*

SOLDIER
I'll be so bold to take what they have left.
The cry of 'Talbot' serves me for a sword;
For I have loaden me with many spoils,
Using no other weapon but his name.   *Exit.*
Enter Talbot, Bedford, Burgundy, [a Captain, and   II, ii
others,] their drums beating a dead march.

BEDFORD
The day begins to break and night is fled,
Whose pitchy mantle overveiled the earth.
Here sound retreat and cease our hot pursuit.
Retreat [sounded].

---

11 *secure* unsuspecting   14 *quittance* requite   15 *art* black magic   16 *Coward* i.e. Dauphin; *fame* reputation   22–25 *masculine, standard, carry armor, practice, converse* (ribald double entendres)   28–34 *Ascend ... grave* (the three leaders actually ascend to the rear stage gallery on separate scaling ladders brought on stage, Talbot in the center and one companion at each side)   38 s.d. *o'er the walls* (some of the routed French, emerging from the tiring house, leap from the rear stage gallery down to the main stage; some use other entrances)   41 *trow* believe   48 *sped* fared   50 *cunning* skill   51 *flatter* encourage with false hopes   59 *mischief* calamity   61 *to-night* last night   63 *kept* guarded   74 *But* only   75 *rests* remains; *shift* device   77 *platforms* schemes

TALBOT

Bring forth the body of old Salisbury

5   And here advance it in the market place,

6   The middle center of this cursèd town.

Now have I paid my vow unto his soul :

8   For every drop of blood was drawn from him

There hath at least five Frenchmen died to-night.

And that hereafter ages may behold

What ruin happened in revenge of him,

Within their chiefest temple I'll erect

A tomb, wherein his corpse shall be interred ;

Upon the which, that every one may read,

Shall be engraved the sack of Orleans,

16   The treacherous manner of his mournful death,

And what a terror he had been to France.

But, lords, in all our bloody massacre,

19   I muse we met not with the Dauphin's grace,

20   His new-come champion, virtuous Joan of Arc,

Nor any of his false confederates.

BEDFORD

'Tis thought, Lord Talbot, when the fight began,

Roused on the sudden from their drowsy beds,

They did amongst the troops of armèd men

Leap o'er the walls for refuge in the field.

BURGUNDY

Myself, as far as I could well discern

For smoke and dusky vapors of the night,

28   Am sure I scared the Dauphin and his trull,

When arm in arm they both came swiftly running,

Like to a pair of loving turtledoves

That could not live asunder day or night.

After that things are set in order here,

We'll follow them with all the power we have.

Enter a Messenger.

MESSENGER

All hail, my lords ! Which of this princely train

Call ye the warlike Talbot, for his acts

So much applauded through the realm of France ?

TALBOT

Here is the Talbot. Who would speak with him ?

MESSENGER

The virtuous lady, Countess of Auvergne,

With modesty admiring thy renown,

By me entreats, great lord, thou wouldst vouchsafe

41   To visit her poor castle where she lies,

That she may boast she hath beheld the man

43   Whose glory fills the world with loud report.

BURGUNDY

Is it even so ? Nay, then I see our wars

Will turn unto a peaceful comic sport,

46   When ladies crave to be encount'red with.

47   You may not, my lord, despise her gentle suit.

TALBOT

Ne'er trust me then ; for when a world of men

Could not prevail with all their oratory,

Yet hath a woman's kindness overruled ;

And therefore tell her I return great thanks

And in submission will attend on her.

Will not your honors bear me company ?

BEDFORD

54   No, truly, 'tis more than manners will ;

And I have heard it said, unbidden guests

Are often welcomest when they are gone.

TALBOT

Well, then, alone (since there's no remedy)

I mean to prove this lady's courtesy.   58

Come hither, captain. *(Whispers).* You perceive my

mind.   59

CAPTAIN

I do, my lord, and mean accordingly.   *Exeunt.* 60

*

Enter Countess [and her Porter].   II, iii

COUNTESS

Porter, remember what I gave in charge,   1

And when you have done so, bring the keys to me.

PORTER

Madam, I will.   *Exit.*

COUNTESS

The plot is laid. If all things fall out right,

I shall as famous be by this exploit

As Scythian Tomyris by Cyrus' death.   6

Great is the rumor of this dreadful knight,   7

And his achievements of no less account.

Fain would mine eyes be witness with mine ears,

To give their censure of these rare reports.   10

Enter Messenger and Talbot.

MESSENGER

Madam,

According as your ladyship desired,

By message craved, so is Lord Talbot come.

COUNTESS

And he is welcome. What ? Is this the man ?

MESSENGER

Madam, it is.

COUNTESS   Is this the scourge of France ?

Is this the Talbot, so much feared abroad   16

That with his name the mothers still their babes ?   17

I see report is fabulous and false.

I thought I should have seen some Hercules,   19

A second Hector, for his grim aspect   20

And large proportion of his strong-knit limbs.   21

Alas, this is a child, a silly dwarf.   22

It cannot be this weak and writhled shrimp   23

Should strike such terror to his enemies.

TALBOT

Madam, I have been bold to trouble you ;

But since your ladyship is not at leisure,

I'll sort some other time to visit you.   *[Going.]* 27

COUNTESS

What means he now ? Go ask him whither he goes.

MESSENGER

Stay, my Lord Talbot ; for my lady craves

II, ii   5 *advance* raise aloft on bier   6 *middle . . . town* (the stage is now the center of Orleans by a simple imaginative transfer of outside to inside) 8 *was* i.e. that was   16 *mournful* causing sorrow   19 *muse* wonder   20 *virtuous* (ironic)   28 *trull* strumpet   41 *lies* dwells   43 *report* (1) acclaim, (2) noise   46 *encount'red* (1) met, (2) wooed   47 *gentle* well-bred   54 *will* require   58 *prove* test   59 *mind* intent   60 *mean* intent to act
II, iii   The castle of the Countess of Auvergne   1 *gave in charge* ordered 6 *Tomyris* queen of Scythia who overcame Cyrus in battle, and in revenge for her son's death had Cyrus' head thrown into a wineskin of human blood 7 *dreadful* causing dread   10 *censure* judgment (echoing the story of Solomon and the Queen of Sheba; see II Chronicles ix, 6)   16 *abroad* everywhere   17 *still* quiet   19, 20 *Hercules, Hector* (types of manly strength) 20 *for* on account of   21 *proportion* size   22 *silly* frail   23 *writhled* shrivelled 27 *sort* choose

To know the cause of your abrupt departure.

TALBOT

31 Marry, for that she's in a wrong belief,
32 I go to certify her Talbot's here.

Enter Porter with keys.

COUNTESS

If thou be he, then art thou prisoner.

TALBOT

Prisoner? to whom?

COUNTESS   To me, bloodthirsty lord.

35 And for that cause I trained thee to my house.
36 Long time thy shadow hath been thrall to me,
For in my gallery thy picture hangs;
But now the substance shall endure the like,
And I will chain these legs and arms of thine
40 That hast by tyranny these many years
Wasted our country, slain our citizens,
42 And sent our sons and husbands captivate.

TALBOT Ha, ha, ha!

COUNTESS

44 Laughest thou, wretch? Thy mirth shall turn to moan.

TALBOT

45 I laugh to see your ladyship so fond
To think that you have aught but Talbot's shadow
Whereon to practice your severity.

COUNTESS

Why, art not thou the man?

TALBOT   I am indeed.

COUNTESS

Then have I substance too.

TALBOT

No, no, I am but shadow of myself.
You are deceived, my substance is not here;
52 For what you see is but the smallest part
And least proportion of humanity.
54 I tell you, madam, were the whole frame here,
55 It is of such a spacious lofty pitch
Your roof were not sufficient to contain't.

COUNTESS

57 This is a riddling merchant for the nonce!
He will be here, and yet he is not here.
How can these contrarieties agree?

TALBOT

60 That will I show you presently.

*Winds his horn. Drums strike up. A peal of ordnance.
Enter Soldiers.*

How say you, madam? Are you now persuaded

That Talbot is but a shadow of himself?
These are his substance, sinews, arms, and strength,
With which he yoketh your rebellious necks,
Razeth your cities, and subverts your towns   65
And in a moment makes them desolate.

COUNTESS

Victorious Talbot, pardon my abuse.   67
I find thou art no less than fame hath bruited,   68
And more than may be gathered by thy shape.
Let my presumption not provoke thy wrath,
For I am sorry that with reverence
I did not entertain thee as thou art.   72

TALBOT

Be not dismayed, fair lady, nor misconster   73
The mind of Talbot as you did mistake
The outward composition of his body.
What you have done hath not offended me;
Nor other satisfaction do I crave
But only, with your patience, that we may   78
Taste of your wine and see what cates you have;   79
For soldiers' stomachs always serve them well.   80

COUNTESS

With all my heart, and think me honorèd
To feast so great a warrior in my house.   *Exeunt.*

*

Enter Richard Plantagenet, Warwick, Somerset,   II, iv
Pole [Earl of Suffolk, Vernon], and others.

RICHARD

Great lords and gentlemen, what means this silence?
Dare no man answer in a case of truth?

SUFFOLK

Within the Temple hall we were too loud.   3
The garden here is more convenient.   4

RICHARD

Then say at once if I maintained the truth;   5
Or else was wrangling Somerset in th' error?

SUFFOLK

Faith, I have been a truant in the law   7
And never yet could frame my will to it,   8
And therefore frame the law unto my will.

SOMERSET

Judge you, my Lord of Warwick, then between us.

WARWICK

Between two hawks, which flies the higher pitch,   11
Between two dogs, which hath the deeper mouth,   12
Between two blades, which bears the better temper,
Between two horses, which doth bear him best,   14
Between two girls, which hath the merriest eye,
I have perhaps some shallow spirit of judgment;
But in these nice sharp quillets of the law,   17
Good faith, I am no wiser than a daw.   18

RICHARD

Tut, tut, here is a mannerly forbearance.
The truth appears so naked on my side
That any purblind eye may find it out.   21

SOMERSET

And on my side it is so well apparelled,
So clear, so shining, and so evident,
That it will glimmer through a blind man's eye.

RICHARD

Since you are tongue-tied and so loath to speak,

31 *Marry* (a mild interjection); *for that* because   32 *certify* inform   35 *trained* lured   36 *shadow* image, portrait; *thrall* slave   40 *tyranny* cruelty   42 *captivate* made prisoner   44 *moan* lamentation   45 *fond* foolish   52–53 *what . . . humanity* (1) the body is the least significant part of the whole of man, (2) I am a mere fraction of my army   54 *frame* (1) structure of man, (2) engine (i.e. his army)   55 *pitch* height   57 *riddling merchant* riddle-monger; *nonce* occasion   60 *presently* immediately; s.d. *Winds* blows   65 *subverts* overthrows   67 *abuse* (1) deceiving of you, (2) self-delusion   68 *fame* report; *bruited* announced   72 *entertain* receive   73 *misconster* misconstrue   78 *patience* permission   79 *cates* delicacies   80 *stomachs* (1) appetites, (2) courage
II, iv The Temple garden, London   3, 4 *Temple hall, garden* (the Wars of the Roses are imagined as beginning in a quarrel among young aristocrats studying law at the London Inns of Court)   3 *mere* should have been   5–6 *Then . . . error* i.e. heads I win, tails you lose   7 *a truant* neglectful of study   8 *frame* adapt   11 *pitch* elevation   12 *mouth* bark   14 *bear him* carry himself   17 *nice sharp quillets* fine subtle distinctions   18 *daw* jackdaw (proverbially a stupid bird)   21 *purblind* partially blind

26 In dumb significants proclaim your thoughts.
Let him that is a true-born gentleman
28 And stands upon the honor of his birth,
29 If he suppose that I have pleaded truth,
From off this brier pluck a white rose with me.

SOMERSET
Let him that is no coward nor no flatterer,
32 But dare maintain the party of the truth,
Pluck a red rose from off this thorn with me.

WARWICK
34 I love no colors, and without all color
Of base insinuating flattery
I pluck this white rose with Plantagenet.

SUFFOLK
I pluck this red rose with young Somerset,
38 And say withal I think he held the right.

VERNON
Stay, lords and gentlemen, and pluck no more
Till you conclude that he upon whose side
The fewest roses are cropped from the tree
42 Shall yield the other in the right opinion.

SOMERSET
43 Good Master Vernon, it is well objected.
44 If I have fewest, I subscribe in silence.

RICHARD
And I.

VERNON
Then for the truth and plainness of the case
I pluck this pale and maiden blossom here,
Giving my verdict on the white rose side.

SOMERSET
Prick not your finger as you pluck it off,
Lest, bleeding, you do paint the white rose red
And fall on my side so against your will.

VERNON
If I, my lord, for my opinion bleed,
53 Opinion shall be surgeon to my hurt
And keep me on the side where still I am.

SOMERSET
Well, well, come on! Who else?

LAWYER [to Somerset]
Unless my study and my books be false,
The argument you held was wrong in you;
In sign whereof I pluck a white rose too.

RICHARD
Now, Somerset, where is your argument?

SOMERSET
60 Here in my scabbard, meditating that
Shall dye your white rose in a bloody red.

RICHARD
62 Meantime your cheeks do counterfeit our roses;
For pale they look with fear, as witnessing
The truth on our side.

SOMERSET   No, Plantagenet,
'Tis not for fear, but anger, that thy cheeks
Blush for pure shame to counterfeit our roses,
And yet thy tongue will not confess thy error.

RICHARD
68 Hath not thy rose a canker, Somerset?

SOMERSET
Hath not thy rose a thorn, Plantagenet?

RICHARD
70 Ay, sharp and piercing, to maintain his truth,
Whiles thy consuming canker eats his falsehood.

SOMERSET
Well, I'll find friends to wear my bleeding roses,
That shall maintain what I have said is true
Where false Plantagenet dare not be seen.

RICHARD
Now by this maiden blossom in my hand,
I scorn thee and thy fashion, peevish boy.   76

SUFFOLK
Turn not thy scorns this way, Plantagenet.

RICHARD
Proud Pole, I will, and scorn both him and thee.   78

SUFFOLK
I'll turn my part thereof into thy throat.

SOMERSET
Away, away, good William de la Pole.
We grace the yeoman by conversing with him.   81

WARWICK
Now, by God's will, thou wrong'st him, Somerset.
His grandfather was Lionel Duke of Clarence,   83
Third son to the third Edward, King of England.
Spring crestless yeoman from so deep a root?   85

RICHARD
He bears him on the place's privilege,   86
Or durst not for his craven heart say thus.

SOMERSET
By him that made me, I'll maintain my words
On any plot of ground in Christendom.
Was not thy father, Richard Earl of Cambridge,
For treason executed in our late king's days?
And by his treason stand'st not thou attainted,   92
Corrupted, and exempt from ancient gentry?   93
His trespass yet lives guilty in thy blood,
And till thou be restored thou art a yeoman.   95

RICHARD
My father was attachèd, not attainted,   96
Condemned to die for treason, but no traitor;
And that I'll prove on better men than Somerset,
Were growing time once ripened to my will.
For your partaker Pole, and you yourself,   100
I'll note you in my book of memory
To scourge you for this apprehension.   102
Look to it well and say you are well warned.

SOMERSET
Ah, thou shalt find us ready for thee still;
And know us by these colors for thy foes,
For these my friends in spite of thee shall wear.

26 *dumb significants* silent symbols   28 *stands upon* insists on   29 *pleaded* argued (one of many legal terms in this scene)   32 *party* side in a legal case   34 *color* semblance   38 *withal* besides   42 *yield* concede (at law)   43 *objected* urged, brought forward (at law)   44 *subscribe* concur (literally, sign at bottom of a document)   53 *Opinion* reputation (punning on the sense of 'belief' in the line above)   60 *that* i.e. that which   62 *counterfeit* imitate   68 *canker* i.e. cankerworm, a caterpillar that feeds on buds and leaves   70 *his* its   76 *fashion* i.e. of wearing red roses   78 *Pole* Suffolk's family name (as in l. 80)   81 *grace* honor; *yeoman* freeholder below rank of gentleman (Plantagenet lost his lands and titles when his father was executed for treason by Henry V)   83 *grandfather* (actually great-great-grandfather)   85 *crestless* (1) lacking heraldic crest, (2) cowardly   86 *bears . . . privilege* i.e. presumes upon the legal asylum of the Inns of Court (granted them as ancient religious houses and as courts of law)   92–93 *attainted, Corrupted* (the legal effects of a bill of attainder were to deprive the culprit's descendants of title)   93 *exempt* excluded; *gentry* rank of gentlemen   95 *restored* given back lands and titles   96 *attachèd, not attainted* (as Plantagenet insists, his father was actually arrested and executed summarily for treason by order of Henry V, not by a full bill of attainder in Parliament; he implies that perfect justice was not done)   100 *partaker* part-taker, ally   102 *apprehension* notion

RICHARD

108 And, by my soul, this pale and angry rose,
As cognizance of my blood-drinking hate,
Will I for ever, and my faction, wear
Until it wither with me to my grave

111 Or flourish to the height of my degree.

SUFFOLK

Go forward, and be choked with thy ambition!
And so farewell until I meet thee next.   *Exit.*

SOMERSET

114 Have with thee, Pole. Farewell, ambitious Richard. *Exit.*

RICHARD

115 How I am braved and must perforce endure it!

WARWICK

116 This blot that they object against your house
Shall be wiped out in the next parliament,
Called for the truce of Winchester and Gloucester;
And if thou be not then created York,
I will not live to be accounted Warwick.

121 Meantime, in signal of my love to thee,
Against proud Somerset and William Pole
Will I upon thy party wear this rose;
And here I prophesy: this brawl to-day
Grown to this faction in the Temple garden
Shall send, between the red rose and the white,
A thousand souls to death and deadly night.

RICHARD

Good Master Vernon, I am bound to you
That you on my behalf would pluck a flower.

VERNON

In your behalf still will I wear the same.

LAWYER

And so will I.

RICHARD

Thanks, gentle sir.
Come, let us four to dinner. I dare say
This quarrel will drink blood another day.   *Exeunt.*

*

II, v   *Enter Mortimer, brought in a chair, and Jailers.*

MORTIMER

Kind keepers of my weak decaying age,
Let dying Mortimer here rest himself.
Even like a man new halèd from the rack,
So fare my limbs with long imprisonment;

5 And these grey locks, the pursuivants of death,
6 Nestor-like agèd in an age of care,
7 Argue the end of Edmund Mortimer.
These eyes, like lamps whose wasting oil is spent,
9 Wax dim, as drawing to their exigent;

Weak shoulders, overborne with burdening grief,
And pithless arms, like to a withered vine
That droops his sapless branches to the ground.

13 Yet are these feet (whose strengthless stay is numb,
Unable to support this lump of clay)
Swift-wingèd with desire to get a grave,

16 As witting I no other comfort have.
But tell me, keeper, will my nephew come?

KEEPER

Richard Plantagenet, my lord, will come.
We sent unto the Temple, unto his chamber,
And answer was returned that he will come.

MORTIMER

Enough. My soul shall then be satisfied.
22 Poor gentleman, his wrong doth equal mine.
23 Since Henry Monmouth first began to reign
Before whose glory I was great in arms,
25 This loathsome sequestration have I had;
And even since then hath Richard been obscured,
Deprived of honor and inheritance.
But now the arbitrator of despairs,
Just Death, kind umpire of men's miseries,
30 With sweet enlargement doth dismiss me hence.
31 I would his troubles likewise were expired,
That so he might recover what was lost.

Enter Richard.

KEEPER

My lord, your loving nephew now is come.

MORTIMER

Richard Plantagenet, my friend, is he come?

RICHARD

Ay, noble uncle, thus ignobly used,
36 Your nephew, late despisèd Richard, comes.

MORTIMER

Direct mine arms I may embrace his neck
38 And in his bosom spend my latter gasp.
O, tell me when my lips do touch his cheeks,
40 That I may kindly give one fainting kiss!
41 And now declare, sweet stem from York's great stock,
Why didst thou say of late thou wert despised?

RICHARD

First lean thine agèd back against mine arm,
44 And in that ease I'll tell thee my disease.
45 This day in argument upon a case
Some words there grew 'twixt Somerset and me;
Among which terms he used his lavish tongue
And did upbraid me with my father's death;
Which obloquy set bars before my tongue,
Else with the like I had requited him.
Therefore, good uncle, for my father's sake,
In honor of a true Plantagenet,
53 And for alliance sake, declare the cause
My father, Earl of Cambridge, lost his head.

MORTIMER

That cause, fair nephew, that imprisoned me
And hath detained me all my flow'ring youth
Within a loathsome dungeon, there to pine,
Was cursèd instrument of his decease.

RICHARD

59 Discover more at large what cause that was,
For I am ignorant and cannot guess.

MORTIMER

I will, if that my fading breath permit
And death approach not ere my tale be done.

108 *cognizance* badge   111 *degree* noble rank   114 *Have with thee* let us go
115 *braved* defied   116 *object* urge   121 *signal* token
II, v The Tower of London   5 *pursuivants* heralds   6 *Nestor* aged leader
in the Trojan wars   7 *Argue* portend   9 *exigent* end   13 *stay is numb*
support is powerless   16 *As witting* as if they knew   22 *his wrong* i.e. the
wrong done him   23 *Henry Monmouth* Henry V   25 *sequestration* isolation, loss of property and freedom (Shakespeare apparently confuses
Edmund Mortimer with his cousin Sir John, who was imprisoned)   30
enlargement freedom   31 *expired* ended   36 *late* lately   38 *latter* final
40 *kindly* (1) affectionately, (2) to a kinsman   41 *stem* (from the metaphor of
the genealogical tree)   44 *disease* grievance   45 *This day* (Plantagenet has
come to the Tower prison directly after his argument in Temple garden, to
find out more about his father's disgrace)   53 *alliance* kinship's   59
Discover expound; *at large* fully

Henry the Fourth, grandfather to this king,
64　Deposed his nephew Richard, Edward's son,
The first-begotten and the lawful heir
Of Edward king, the third of that descent;
67　During whose reign, the Percies of the north,
Finding his usurpation most unjust,
Endeavored my advancement to the throne.
The reason moved these warlike lords to this
Was for that (young Richard thus removed,
Leaving no heir begotten of his body)
I was the next by birth and parentage;
74　For by my mother I derivèd am
From Lionel Duke of Clarence, third son
To King Edward the Third; whereas he
From John of Gaunt doth bring his pedigree,
Being but fourth of that heroic line.
79　But mark. As in this haughty great attempt
They laborèd to plant the rightful heir,
I lost my liberty, and they their lives.
Long after this, when Henry the Fifth
(Succeeding his father Bolingbroke) did reign,
Thy father, Earl of Cambridge, then derived
From famous Edmund Langley, Duke of York,
Marrying my sister that thy mother was,
Again, in pity of my hard distress,
Levied an army, weening to redeem
And have installed me in the diadem;
90　But, as the rest, so fell that noble earl,
And was beheaded. Thus the Mortimers,
In whom the title rested, were suppressed.

RICHARD
Of which, my lord, your honor is the last.

MORTIMER
True, and thou seest that I no issue have,
95　And that my fainting words do warrant death.
96　Thou art my heir. The rest I wish thee gather;
But yet be wary in thy studious care.

RICHARD
Thy grave admonishments prevail with me.
But yet methinks my father's execution
Was nothing less than bloody tyranny.

MORTIMER
With silence, nephew, be thou politic.
Strong fixèd is the house of Lancaster
And like a mountain, not to be removed.
But now thy uncle is removing hence,
As princes do their courts when they are cloyed
With long continuance in a settled place.

RICHARD
O uncle, would some part of my young years
108　Might but redeem the passage of your age!

MORTIMER
Thou dost then wrong me, as that slaughterer doth
Which giveth many wounds when one will kill.
Mourn not, except thou sorrow for my good;
112　Only give order for my funeral.
And so farewell, and fair be all thy hopes,
And prosperous be thy life in peace and war!
　　Dies.

RICHARD
And peace, no war, befall thy parting soul!
In prison hast thou spent a pilgrimage
And like a hermit overpassed thy days.
Well, I will lock his counsel in my breast,

And what I do imagine, let that rest.　　119
Keepers, convey him hence, and I myself
Will see his burial better than his life.
　　　　Exeunt [Jailers, with Mortimer's body].
Here dies the dusky torch of Mortimer,
Choked with ambition of the meaner sort.　　123
And for those wrongs, those bitter injuries,
Which Somerset hath offered to my house
I doubt not but with honor to redress;
And therefore haste I to the parliament,
Either to be restorèd to my blood　　128
Or make my will th' advantage of my good.　　Exit.　129

＊

　　Flourish. Enter King, Exeter, Gloucester,　　III, i
　　Winchester, Warwick, Somerset, Suffolk, Richard
　　Plantagenet [and others]. Gloucester offers to put up
　　a bill. Winchester snatches it, tears it.

WINCHESTER
Com'st thou with deep premeditated lines,
With written pamphlets studiously devised,
Humphrey of Gloucester? If thou canst accuse
Or aught intend'st to lay unto my charge,
Do it without invention, suddenly,　　5
As I with sudden and extemporal speech
Purpose to answer what thou canst object.　　7

GLOUCESTER
Presumptuous priest, this place commands my patience,
Or thou shouldst find thou hast dishonored me.
Think not, although in writing I preferred　　10
The manner of thy vile outrageous crimes,
That therefore I have forged, or am not able
Verbatim to rehearse the method of my pen.　　13
No, prelate, such is thy audacious wickedness,
Thy lewd, pestiferous, and dissentious pranks,　　15
As very infants prattle of thy pride.
Thou art a most pernicious usurer;
Froward by nature, enemy to peace,　　18
Lascivious, wanton, more than well beseems
A man of thy profession and degree.
And for thy treachery, what's more manifest,
In that thou laids't a trap to take my life
As well at London Bridge as at the Tower?
Beside, I fear me, if thy thoughts were sifted,
The King thy sovereign is not quite exempt
From envious malice of thy swelling heart.

WINCHESTER
Gloucester, I do defy thee. Lords, vouchsafe
To give me hearing what I shall reply.
If I were covetous, ambitious, or perverse,
As he will have me, how am I so poor?

64 nephew blood relative (here, first cousin)　67 whose i.e. Henry IV's
74 mother (Shakespeare here confuses Edmund with his uncle Edmund)
79 haughty high-pitched　90 noble earl (treated unsympathetically in
Henry V)　95 warrant assure　96 gather (1) infer, (2) collect　108 redeem
buy back　112 give order make arrangements　119 let that rest leave that
alone　123 the meaner sort people of inferior rank (i.e. Bolingbroke and his
family)　128 blood hereditary rights　129 make . . . good make some
opportunity for advancement out of my sheer determination
III, i The Parliament house　s.d. put up a bill present an indictment　5
invention premeditation; suddenly extempore　7 object urge, argue　10 preferred set out　13 rehearse . . . pen recount the sum of what I have written
15 lewd wicked　18 Froward perverse

Or how haps it I seek not to advance
Or raise myself, but keep my wonted calling?
And for dissension, who preferreth peace
34 More than I do, except I be provoked?
35 No, my good lords, it is not that offends;
It is not that that hath incensed the duke.
It is because no one should sway but he,
No one but he should be about the king;
And that engenders thunder in his breast
And makes him roar these accusations forth.
But he shall know I am as good –

GLOUCESTER
42 As good? Thou bastard of my grandfather!

WINCHESTER
Ay, lordly sir! For what are you, I pray,
But one imperious in another's throne?

GLOUCESTER
Am I not Protector, saucy priest?

WINCHESTER
And am not I a prelate of the church?

GLOUCESTER
47 Yes, as an outlaw in a castle keeps
48 And useth it to patronage his theft.

WINCHESTER
Unreverent Gloucester.

GLOUCESTER   Thou art reverent
50 Touching thy spiritual function, not thy life.

WINCHESTER
Rome shall remedy this.

WARWICK   Roam thither then.

SOMERSET
My lord, it were your duty to forbear.

WARWICK
Ay, see the bishop be not overborne.

SOMERSET
Methinks my lord should be religious
And know the office that belongs to such.

WARWICK
Methinks his lordship should be humbler.
If fitteth not a prelate so to plead.

SOMERSET
58 Yes, when his holy state is touched so near.

WARWICK
State holy, or unhallowed, what of that?
Is not his grace Protector to the king?

RICHARD [aside]
Plantagenet, I see, must hold his tongue,
Lest it be said, 'Speak, sirrah, when you should;
Must your bold verdict enter talk with lords?'
Else would I have a fling at Winchester.

KING
Uncles of Gloucester and of Winchester,
The special watchmen of our English weal,
I would prevail, if prayers might prevail,
To join your hearts in love and amity.

O, what a scandal is it to our crown
That two such noble peers as ye should jar!   70
Believe me, lords, my tender years can tell
Civil dissension is a viperous worm
That gnaws the bowels of the commonwealth.
A noise within, 'Down with the tawny coats!'
What tumult's this?

WARWICK   An uproar, I dare warrant,
Begun through malice of the bishop's men.
A noise again, 'Stones! stones!'
Enter Mayor.

MAYOR
O my good lords, and virtuous Henry,
Pity the city of London, pity us!
The bishop and the Duke of Gloucester's men,   78
Forbidden late to carry any weapon,   79
Have filled their pockets full of pebble stones
And, banding themselves in contrary parts,   81
Do pelt so fast at one another's pate
That many have their giddy brains knocked out.
Our windows are broke down in every street
And we, for fear, compelled to shut our shops.
Enter in skirmish [Servingmen of Gloucester and
Winchester] with bloody pates.

KING
We charge you, on allegiance to ourself,
To hold your slaught'ring hands and keep the peace.
Pray, uncle Gloucester, mitigate this strife.

1. SERVINGMAN Nay, if we be forbidden stones, we'll
fall to it with our teeth.

2. SERVINGMAN
Do what ye dare, we are as resolute.
Skirmish again.

GLOUCESTER
You of my household, leave this peevish broil   92
And set this unaccustomed fight aside.   93

3. SERVINGMAN
My lord, we know your grace to be a man
Just and upright, and for your royal birth
Inferior to none but to his majesty;
And ere that we will suffer such a prince,
So kind a father of the commonweal,
To be disgracèd by an inkhorn mate,   99
We and our wives and children all will fight
And have our bodies slaught'red by thy foes.

1. SERVINGMAN
Ay, and the very parings of our nails
Shall pitch a field when we are dead.   103
Begin again.

GLOUCESTER   Stay, stay, I say!
And if you love me, as you say you do,
Let me persuade you to forbear awhile.

KING
O, how this discord doth afflict my soul!
Can you, my Lord of Winchester, behold
My sighs and tears and will not once relent?
Who should be pitiful if you be not?
Or who should study to prefer a peace   110
If holy churchmen take delight in broils?

WARWICK
Yield, my Lord Protector, yield, Winchester,
Except you mean with obstinate repulse   113
To slay your sovereign and destroy the realm.
You see what mischief, and what murder too,

34 _except_ unless   35 _that_ i.e. that which   42 _grandfather_ John of Gaunt (who fathered the illegitimate Beauforts by his mistress, Catherine Swynford)   47 _keeps_ dwells   48 _patronage_ maintain   50 _Touching . . . function_ i.e. in title only   58 _holy . . . near_ high ecclesiastical status is so closely attacked   78 _bishop_ i.e. bishop's   79 _late_ lately   81 _contrary parts_ opposing factions   92 _peevish_ senseless   93 _unaccustomed_ (1) unusual, (2) contrary to good custom   99 _inkhorn mate_ low pedant   103 _pitch a field_ drive in sharp stakes to protect against cavalry   110 _prefer_ assist in bringing about   113 _Except_ unless; _repulse_ refusal

Hath been enacted through your enmity.
Then be at peace, except ye thirst for blood.

WINCHESTER
He shall submit, or I will never yield.

GLOUCESTER
Compassion on the king commands me stoop,
Or I would see his heart out ere the priest
121   Should ever get that privilege of me.

WARWICK
Behold, my Lord of Winchester, the duke
123   Hath banished moody discontented fury,
As by his smoothèd brows it doth appear.
Why look you still so stern and tragical?

GLOUCESTER
Here, Winchester, I offer thee my hand.

KING
Fie, uncle Beaufort, I have heard you preach
That malice was a great and grievous sin;
And will not you maintain the thing you teach,
But prove a chief offender in the same?

WARWICK
131   Sweet king! The bishop hath a kindly gird.
For shame, my Lord of Winchester, relent.
What, shall a child instruct you what to do?

WINCHESTER
Well, Duke of Gloucester, I will yield to thee.
Love for thy love and hand for hand I give.

GLOUCESTER [aside]
Ay, but I fear me with a hollow heart. –
See here, my friends and loving countrymen:
This token serveth for a flag of truce
Betwixt ourselves and all our followers.
So help me God as I dissemble not.

WINCHESTER [aside]
So help me God as I intend it not.

KING
O loving uncle, kind Duke of Gloucester,
How joyful am I made by this contract!
144   Away, my masters. Trouble us no more,
But join in friendship, as your lords have done.

1. SERVINGMAN
Content. I'll to the surgeon's.

2. SERVINGMAN   And so will I.

3. SERVINGMAN
147   And I will see what physic the tavern affords.
Exeunt [Servingmen, Mayor, etc.].

WARWICK
Accept this scroll, most gracious sovereign,
Which in the right of Richard Plantagenet
We do exhibit to your majesty.

GLOUCESTER
Well urged, my Lord of Warwick; for, sweet prince,
152   An if your grace mark every circumstance,
You have great reason to do Richard right,
154   Especially for those occasions
At Eltham Place I told your majesty.

KING
And those occasions, uncle, were of force.
Therefore, my loving lords, our pleasure is
158   That Richard be restorèd to his blood.

WARWICK
Let Richard be restorèd to his blood.
160   So shall his father's wrongs be recompensed.

WINCHESTER
As will the rest, so willeth Winchester.

KING
If Richard will be true, not that alone
But all the whole inheritance I give
That doth belong unto the house of York,
From whence you spring by lineal descent.

RICHARD
Thy humble servant vows obedience
And humble service till the point of death.

KING
Stoop then and set your knee against my foot,
And in reguerdon of that duty done   169
I girt thee with the valiant sword of York.
Rise, Richard, like a true Plantagenet,
And rise created princely Duke of York.

RICHARD
And so thrive Richard as thy foes may fall;
And as my duty springs, so perish they
That grudge one thought against your majesty.

ALL
Welcome, high prince, the mighty Duke of York!

SOMERSET [aside]
Perish, base prince, ignoble Duke of York!

GLOUCESTER
Now will it best avail your majesty
To cross the seas and to be crowned in France.
The presence of a king engenders love
Amongst his subjects and his loyal friends,
As it disanimates his enemies.   182

KING
When Gloucester says the word, King Henry goes,
For friendly counsel cuts off many foes.

GLOUCESTER
Your ships already are in readiness.
Sennet. Flourish. Exeunt. Manet Exeter.

EXETER
Ay, we may march in England or in France,
Not seeing what is likely to ensue.
This late dissension grown betwixt the peers
Burns under feignèd ashes of forged love
And will at last break out into a flame.
As fest'red members rot but by degree
Till bones and flesh and sinews fall away,
So will this base and envious discord breed.
And now I fear that fatal prophecy
Which in the time of Henry named the Fifth
Was in the mouth of every sucking babe:
That Henry born at Monmouth should win all
And Henry born at Windsor should lose all;
Which is so plain that Exeter doth wish
His days may finish ere that hapless time.   *Exit.*

*

121 *privilege of* advantage yielded by   123 *moody* haughty   131 *kindly gird* proper rebuke   144 *masters* (condescending term for servants)   147 *physic* remedy   152 *An if* if   154 *occasions* circumstances   158 *restorèd . . . blood* i.e. reinstated in the inherited titles forfeited by his father   160 *recompensed* compensated   169 *reguerdon* requital   182 *disanimates* dispirits

III, ii

Enter Pucelle disguised, with four Soldiers [dressed like countrymen] with sacks upon their backs.

PUCELLE

1   These are the city gates, the gates of Roan,
2   Through which our policy must make a breach.
3   Take heed, be wary how you place your words ;
4   · Talk like the vulgar sort of marketmen
5   That come to gather money for their corn.
    If we have entrance, as I hope we shall,
7   And that we find the slothful watch but weak,
    I'll by a sign give notice to our friends,
    That Charles the Dauphin may encounter them.

SOLDIER

    Our sacks shall be a mean to sack the city,
    And we be lords and rulers over Roan.
    Therefore we'll knock.
                                        Knock.

13 WATCH *[within]* Che la ?

PUCELLE

    Peasauns, la pouvre gens de Fraunce,
    Poor market folks that come to sell their corn.

WATCH *[opening the gates]*
    Enter, go in ; the market bell is rung.

PUCELLE

    Now, Roan, I'll shake thy bulwarks to the ground.
                              Exeunt [into the city].
    *Enter Charles, Bastard, Alençon [, Reignier, and
    Soldiers].*

CHARLES

    Saint Denis bless this happy stratagem,
    And once again we'll sleep secure in Roan.

BASTARD

20 Here ent'red Pucelle and her practisants.
    Now she is there, how will she specify
    Here is the best and safest passage in ?

REIGNIER

    By thrusting out a torch from yonder tower,
    Which, once discerned, shows that her meaning is,
25 No way to that, for weakness, which she ent'red.
    *Enter Pucelle on the top, thrusting out a torch
    burning.*

PUCELLE

    Behold, this is the happy wedding torch
    That joineth Roan unto her countrymen,
    But burning fatal to the Talbonites.   *[Exit.]*

BASTARD

    See, noble Charles, the beacon of our friend.
    The burning torch in yonder turret stands.

CHARLES

31 Now shine it like a comet of revenge,
32 A prophet to the fall of all our foes !

REIGNIER

    Defer no time ; delays have dangerous ends.
    Enter and cry 'The Dauphin !' presently,   34
    And then do execution on the watch.
        Alarum. [They storm the gates.]
        An alarum. Talbot in an excursion [from within].

TALBOT

    France, thou shalt rue this treason with thy tears
    If Talbot but survive thy treachery.
    Pucelle, that witch, that damnèd sorceress,
    Hath wrought this hellish mischief unawares,   39
    That hardly we escaped the pride of France.   *Exit.* 40
        *An alarum. Excursions. Bedford brought in sick in a
        chair. Enter Talbot and Burgundy without ; within,
        Pucelle, Charles, Bastard, [Alençon,] and Reignier
        on the walls.*

PUCELLE

    Good morrow, gallants, want ye corn for bread ?
    I think the Duke of Burgundy will fast
    Before he'll buy again at such a rate.
    'Twas full of darnel. Do you like the taste ?   44

BURGUNDY

    Scoff on, vile fiend and shameless courtesan !
    I trust ere long to choke thee with thine own
    And make thee curse the harvest of that corn.

CHARLES

    Your grace may starve, perhaps, before that time.

BEDFORD

    O, let no words, but deeds, revenge this treason !

PUCELLE

    What will you do, good greybeard, break a lance
    And run a-tilt at death within a chair ?

TALBOT

    Foul fiend of France and hag of all despite,
    Encompassed with thy lustful paramours,
    Becomes it thee to taunt his valiant age
    And twit with cowardice a man half dead ?
    Damsel, I'll have a bout with you again,   56
    Or else let Talbot perish with this shame.

PUCELLE

    Are ye so hot, sir ? Yet, Pucelle, hold thy peace.   58
    If Talbot do but thunder, rain will follow.
        They [the English] whisper together in counsel.
    God speed the parliament ; who shall be the Speaker ?

TALBOT

    Dare ye come forth and meet us in the field ?

PUCELLE

    Belike your lordship takes us then for fools,
    To try if that our own be ours or no.

TALBOT

    I speak not to that railing Hecate,   64
    But unto thee, Alençon, and the rest.
    Will ye, like soldiers, come and fight it out ?

ALENÇON

    Signior, no.

TALBOT

    Signior, hang ! Base muleters of France !   68
    Like peasant footboys do they keep the walls
    And dare not take up arms like gentlemen.

PUCELLE

    Away, captains. Let's get us from the walls,
    For Talbot means no goodness by his looks.
    God b'uy, my lord. We came but to tell you   73

III, ii Before Rouen in France **1** *These . . . Roan* (the gates lead into the
tiring house, representing Rouen in this scene ; appearances 'on the walls'
are from the rear stage gallery as in I, vi) **2** *policy* stratagem **3** *place*
arrange **4** *vulgar* common (not disparaging) **5** *corn* wheat **7** *that* if
13 *Che la ?* who is there ? (argot French) **20** *practisants* conspirators **25**
No . . . weakness i.e. no way compares in weakness with that ; s.d. *on the
top* (an upper vantage point in the tiring-house façade ?) **31** *shine it* may
it shine **32** *prophet* omen **34** *presently* immediately **39** *mischief unawares* harm unexpectedly **40** *hardly* with difficulty ; *pride* power **44**
darnel weed **56, 58** *bout, hot* (sexual double entendres) **64** *Hecate* goddess
identified with the moon and the underworld (hence guardian of witches)
68 *Base muleters* mule drivers of low birth **73** *b'uy* be with you

That we are here.   *Exeunt from the walls.*

TALBOT

And there will we be too ere it be long,
Or else reproach be Talbot's greatest fame!
Vow, Burgundy, by honor of thy house,
78 Pricked on by public wrongs sustained in France,
Either to get the town again or die;
And I, as sure as English Henry lives
81 And as his father here was conqueror,
As sure as in this late betrayèd town
83 Great Coeur-de-lion's heart was buried,
So sure I swear to get the town or die.

BURGUNDY

My vows are equal partners with thy vows.

TALBOT

86 But, ere we go, regard this dying prince,
The valiant Duke of Bedford. Come, my lord,
We will bestow you in some better place,
89 Fitter for sickness and for crazy age.

BEDFORD

Lord Talbot, do not so dishonor me.
Here will I sit, before the walls of Roan,
And will be partner of your weal or woe.

BURGUNDY

Courageous Bedford, let us now persuade you.

BEDFORD

Not to be gone from hence; for once I read
95 That stout Pendragon in his litter sick
Came to the field and vanquishèd his foes.
97 Methinks I should revive the soldiers' hearts,
Because I ever found them as myself.

TALBOT

Undaunted spirit in a dying breast!
Then be it so. Heavens keep old Bedford safe!
And now no more ado, brave Burgundy,
102 But gather we our forces out of hand
And set upon our boasting enemy.
          Exit [Talbot with others to the assault.
          Manent Bedford and Attendants].
An alarum. Excursions. Enter Sir John Falstaff
and a Captain.

CAPTAIN

Whither away, Sir John Falstaff, in such haste?

FALSTAFF

Whither away? To save myself by flight.
We are like to have the overthrow again.

CAPTAIN

What? will you fly and leave Lord Talbot?

FALSTAFF   Ay,
All the Talbots in the world, to save my life.   *Exit.*

CAPTAIN

Cowardly knight, ill fortune follow thee!   *Exit.*
          Retreat. Excursions. Pucelle, Alençon and Charles
          fly.

BEDFORD

110 Now, quiet soul, depart when heaven please,
For I have seen our enemies' overthrow.
What is the trust or strength of foolish man?
They that of late were daring with their scoffs
114 Are glad and fain by flight to save themselves.
          Bedford dies and is carried in by two in his chair.
          An alarum. Enter Talbot, Burgundy, and the rest.

TALBOT

Lost and recovered in a day again!

This is a double honor, Burgundy.
Yet heavens have glory for this victory!

BURGUNDY

Warlike and martial Talbot, Burgundy
Enshrines thee in his heart and there erects
Thy noble deeds as valor's monuments.

TALBOT

Thanks, gentle duke. But where is Pucelle now?   121
I think her old familiar is asleep.   122
Now where's the Bastard's braves and Charles his 123
    glikes?
What, all amort? Roan hangs her head for grief   124
That such a valiant company are fled.
Now will we take some order in the town,   126
Placing therein some expert officers,
And then depart to Paris to the king,
For there young Henry with his nobles lie.

BURGUNDY

What wills Lord Talbot pleaseth Burgundy.

TALBOT

But yet, before we go, let's not forget
The noble Duke of Bedford, late deceased,
But see his exequies fulfilled in Roan.   133
A braver soldier never couchèd lance,
A gentler heart did never sway in court.
But kings and mightiest potentates must die,
For that's the end of human misery.   *Exeunt.*

*

Enter Charles, Bastard, Alençon, Pucelle [and   III, iii
Soldiers].

PUCELLE

Dismay not, princes, at this accident,   1
Nor grieve that Roan is so recoverèd.
Care is no cure, but rather corrosive,   3
For things that are not to be remedied.
Let frantic Talbot triumph for a while
And like a peacock sweep along his tail;
We'll pull his plumes and take away his train,   7
If Dauphin and the rest will be but ruled.   8

CHARLES

We have been guided by thee hitherto
And of thy cunning had no diffidence.   10
One sudden foil shall never breed distrust.   11

BASTARD

Search out thy wit for secret policies,
And we will make thee famous through the world.

ALENÇON

We'll set thy statue in some holy place
And have thee reverenced like a blessèd saint.
Employ thee then, sweet virgin, for our good.   16

78 *Pricked on* goaded   81 *father . . . conqueror* (Henry V captured Rouen in
1418)   83 *Great . . . burièd* (Richard I willed his heart to be buried in Rouen
as an expression of esteem for that city)   86 *regard* attend to   89 *crazy*
decrepit   95–96 *Pendragon . . . foes* (told of Uther Pendragon's brother in
his victory against the Saxons)   97 *Methinks* it seems to me   102 *out of
hand* at once   110–11 *Now . . . overthrow* (an echo of the *Nunc Dimittis*;
see Luke ii, 29–32)   114 *fain* well pleased   121 *gentle* noble   122 *old
familiar* customary attendant spirit (i.e. the Devil)   123 *braves* bravado;
Charles his glikes Charles' scoffs   124 *amort* sick to death   126 *take some
order* make arrangements   133 *exequies* funeral rites
III, iii Fields near Rouen   1 *accident* unforeseen event   3 *corrosive*
aggravating   7 *train* (1) army, (2) peacock's tail   8 *be but ruled* follow
instructions   10 *cunning* skill in magic; *diffidence* distrust   11 *foil* repulse
16 *Employ thee* exert thyself

PUCELLE
Then thus it must be ; this doth Joan devise :
By fair persuasions, mixed with sug'red words,
We will entice the Duke of Burgundy
To leave the Talbot and to follow us.

CHARLES
Ay, marry, sweeting, if we could do that,
France were no place for Henry's warriors,
Nor should that nation boast it so with us,
24   But be extirpèd from our provinces.

ALENÇON
25   For ever should they be expulsed from France
And not have title of an earldom here.

PUCELLE
Your honors shall perceive how I will work
To bring this matter to the wishèd end.
    Drum sounds afar off.
Hark, by the sound of drum you may perceive
Their powers are marching unto Paris-ward.
    Here sound an English march.
There goes the Talbot, with his colors spread,
And all the troops of English after him.
    [Here sound a] French march.
Now in the rearward comes the duke and his.
34   Fortune in favor makes him lag behind.
Summon a parley ; we will talk with him.
    Trumpets sound a parley.

CHARLES
A parley with the Duke of Burgundy !
    [Enter Burgundy and Troops.]

BURGUNDY
Who craves a parley with the Burgundy ?

PUCELLE
The princely Charles of France, thy countryman.

BURGUNDY
What say'st thou, Charles ? for I am marching hence.

CHARLES
Speak, Pucelle, and enchant him with thy words.

PUCELLE
41   Brave Burgundy, undoubted hope of France,
Stay, let thy humble handmaid speak to thee.

BURGUNDY
Speak on ; but be not over-tedious.

PUCELLE
Look on thy country, look on fertile France,
And see the cities and the towns defaced
By wasting ruin of the cruel foe,
As looks the mother on her lowly babe
48   When death doth close his tender-dying eyes.
50   Behold the wounds, the most unnatural wounds,
Which thou thyself hast given her woeful breast.
O, turn thy edgèd sword another way ;
Strike those that hurt, and hurt not those that help !
One drop of blood drawn from thy country's bosom
Should grieve thee more than streams of foreign gore.
Return thee therefore with a flood of tears
And wash away thy country's stainèd spots.

BURGUNDY
Either she hath bewitched me with her words,
Or nature makes me suddenly relent.

PUCELLE
Besides, all French and France exclaims on thee,   60
Doubting thy birth and lawful progeny.   61
Who join'st thou with but with a lordly nation
That will not trust thee but for profit's sake ?
When Talbot hath set footing once in France
And fashioned thee that instrument of ill,
Who then but English Henry will be lord,
And thou be thrust out like a fugitive ?
Call we to mind, and mark but this for proof :
Was not the Duke of Orleans thy foe ?
And was he not in England prisoner ?
But when they heard he was thine enemy,
They set him free without his ransom paid,
In spite of Burgundy and all his friends.
See then, thou fight'st against thy countrymen
And join'st with them will be thy slaughtermen.
Come, come, return. Return, thou wandering lord.   76
Charles and the rest will take thee in their arms.

BURGUNDY
I am vanquishèd. These haughty words of hers   78
Have batt'red me like roaring cannon-shot
And made me almost yield upon my knees. –
Forgive me, country, and sweet countrymen !
And, lords, accept this hearty kind embrace.
My forces and my power of men are yours.
So farewell, Talbot. I'll no longer trust thee.

PUCELLE
Done like a Frenchman – *[aside]* turn and turn again.

CHARLES
Welcome, brave duke. Thy friendship makes us fresh.

BASTARD
And doth beget new courage in our breasts.

ALENÇON
Pucelle hath bravely played her part in this   88
And doth deserve a coronet of gold.

CHARLES
Now let us on, my lords, and join our powers,
And seek how we may prejudice the foe.   *Exeunt.* 91

*

Duke of] York, Suffolk, Somerset, Warwick,
Exeter [, Vernon, Basset, and others]. To them, with
his Soldiers, Talbot.

TALBOT
My gracious prince, and honorable peers,
Hearing of your arrival in this realm,
I have awhile given truce unto my wars
To do my duty to my sovereign ;   4
In sign whereof this arm that hath reclaimed
To your obedience fifty fortresses,
Twelve cities, and seven wallèd towns of strength,
Beside five hundred prisoners of esteem,
Lets fall his sword before your highness' feet
    [Kneels.]
And with submissive loyalty of heart
Ascribes the glory of his conquest got
First to my God and next unto your grace.

24 *extirpèd* rooted out   25 *expulsed* expelled   34 *in favor* benevolently
41 *undoubted* fearless   48 *tender-dying* dying at a tender age   50 *unnatural*
against law of kinship   60 *exclaims on* accuses loudly   61 *progeny* ancestry
76 *wandering* erring   78 *haughty* lofty   88 *bravely* (1) courageously, (2)
splendidly   91 *prejudice* harm
III, iv The royal palace in Paris   4 *duty* feudal obeisance

KING
Is this the Lord Talbot, uncle Gloucester,
That hath so long been resident in France?
GLOUCESTER
Yes, if it please your majesty, my liege.
KING
Welcome, brave captain and victorious lord!
When I was young (as yet I am not old)
I do remember how my father said
A stouter champion never handled sword.
20 Long since we were resolvèd of your truth,
Your faithful service, and your toil in war;
Yet never have you tasted our reward
23 Or been reguerdoned with so much as thanks,
Because till now we never saw your face.
Therefore stand up, and for these good deserts
We here create you Earl of Shrewsbury,
And in our coronation take your place.
     Sennet. Flourish. Exeunt. Manent Vernon and Basset.
VERNON
28 Now, sir, to you, that were so hot at sea,
Disgracing of these colors that I wear
In honor of my noble Lord of York –
Dar'st thou maintain the former words thou spak'st?
BASSET
32 Yes, sir, as well as you dare patronage
The envious barking of your saucy tongue
Against my lord the Duke of Somerset.
VERNON
Sirrah, thy lord I honor as he is.
BASSET
Why, what is he? As good a man as York.
VERNON
Hark ye, not so. In witness take ye that.
     Strikes him.
BASSET
Villain, thou knowest the law of arms is such
39 That whoso draws a sword, 'tis present death,
Or else this blow should broach thy dearest blood.
But I'll unto his majesty and crave
I may have liberty to venge this wrong,
When thou shalt see I'll meet thee to thy cost.
VERNON
Well, miscreant, I'll be there as soon as you,
And after meet you, sooner than you would.   *Exeunt.*
IV, i   *Enter King, Gloucester, Winchester, [Richard*
Duke of] York, Suffolk, Somerset, Warwick,
Talbot, Exeter, and Governor [of Paris].
GLOUCESTER
Lord Bishop, set the crown upon his head.
WINCHESTER
God save King Henry, of that name the sixth!
GLOUCESTER
Now, governor of Paris, take your oath,
     [Governor kneels.]
4 That you elect no other king but him,
Esteem none friends but such as are his friends,
6 And none your foes but such as shall pretend
Malicious practices against his state.
This shall ye do, so help you righteous God.
     [Governor retires.]
     Enter Falstaff.
FALSTAFF
My gracious sovereign, as I rode from Calais

To haste unto your coronation,
A letter was delivered to my hands,
Writ to your grace from th' Duke of Burgundy.
TALBOT
Shame to the Duke of Burgundy and thee!
I vowed, base knight, when I did meet thee next
To tear the Garter from thy craven's leg,   15
     [Plucks it off.]
Which I have done, because unworthily
Thou wast installèd in that high degree.
Pardon me, princely Henry, and the rest.
This dastard, at the battle of Poictiers,   19
When, but in all, I was six thousand strong
And that the French were almost ten to one,
Before we met or that a stroke was given,
Like to a trusty squire did run away;   23
In which assault we lost twelve hundred men.
Myself and divers gentlemen beside
Were there surprised and taken prisoners.
Then judge, great lords, if I have done amiss,
Or whether that such cowards ought to wear
This ornament of knighthood, yea or no?
GLOUCESTER
To say the truth, this fact was infamous,   30
And ill beseeming any common man;   31
Much more a knight, a captain, and a leader.
TALBOT
When first this order was ordained, my lords,
Knights of the Garter were of noble birth,
Valiant and virtuous, full of haughty courage,   35
Such as were grown to credit by the wars;   36
Not fearing death nor shrinking for distress,   37
But always resolute in most extremes.   38
He then that is not furnished in this sort   39
Doth but usurp the sacred name of knight,
Profaning this most honorable order,
And should (if I were worthy to be judge)
Be quite degraded, like a hedge-born swain   43
That doth presume to boast of gentle blood.
KING
Stain to thy countrymen, thou hear'st thy doom.
Be packing therefore, thou that wast a knight.   46
Henceforth we banish thee on pain of death.
     [Exit Falstaff.]
And now, Lord Protector, view the letter
Sent from our uncle Duke of Burgundy.
GLOUCESTER
What means his grace that he hath changed his style?   50
No more but plain and bluntly 'To the king'?
Hath he forgot he is his sovereign?
Or doth this churlish superscription
Pretend some alteration in good will?   54
What's here? *[Reads]* 'I have, upon especial cause,
Moved with compassion of my country's wrack

---

20 *we* (the royal plural); *resolvèd* convinced   23 *reguerdoned* rewarded
28 *hot* angry   32 *patronage* defend   39 *present* immediate (since duelling at
court was punishable by death)
IV, i   4 *elect* acknowledge   6 *pretend* intend   15 *Garter* badge of the
Order of the Garter   19 *Poictiers* (perhaps confused with Patay)   23
trusty squire (contemptuous)   30 *fact* misdeed   31 *common* lacking noble
rank   35 *haughty* lofty   36 *were . . . credit* had risen to renown   37 *for
distress* in face of hardship   38 *most* greatest   39 *furnished . . . sort* so
endowed   43 *hedge-born swain* low-born rustic   46 *Be packing* be off   50
style form of address   54 *Pretend* import

Together with the pitiful complaints
Of such as your oppression feeds upon,
Forsaken your pernicious faction
And joined with Charles, the rightful King of France.'
O monstrous treachery! Can this be so?
That in alliance, amity, and oaths
There should be found such false dissembling guile?

KING

64   What? Doth my uncle Burgundy revolt?

GLOUCESTER

He doth, my lord, and is become your foe.

KING

Is that the worst this letter doth contain?

GLOUCESTER

It is the worst, and all, my lord, he writes.

KING

Why, then Lord Talbot there shall talk with him
And give him chastisement for this abuse.
How say you, my lord? Are you not content?

TALBOT

71   Content, my liege? Yes. But that I am prevented,
I should have begged I might have been employed.

KING

73   Then gather strength and march unto him straight.
74   Let him perceive how ill we brook his treason
And what offense it is to flout his friends.

TALBOT

76   I go, my lord, in heart desiring still
You may behold confusion of your foes.   *[Exit.]*
    Enter Vernon and Basset.

VERNON

78   Grant me the combat, gracious sovereign.

BASSET

And me, my lord, grant me the combat too.

RICHARD

80   This is my servant. Hear him, noble prince.

SOMERSET

And this is mine. Sweet Henry, favor him.

KING

Be patient, lords, and give them leave to speak.
Say, gentlemen, what makes you thus exclaim?
And wherefore crave you combat? or with whom?

VERNON

With him, my lord, for he hath done me wrong.

BASSET

And I with him, for he hath done me wrong.

KING

What is that wrong whereof you both complain?
First let me know, and then I'll answer you.

BASSET

Crossing the sea from England into France,
This fellow here with envious carping tongue
Upbraided me about the rose I wear,
92   Saying the sanguine color of the leaves
Did represent my master's blushing cheeks

When stubbornly he did repugn the truth   94
About a certain question in the law
Argued betwixt the Duke of York and him;
With other vile and ignominious terms.
In confutation of which rude reproach,
And in defense of my lord's worthiness,
I crave the benefit of law of arms.   100

VERNON

And that is my petition, noble lord.
For though he seem with forgèd quaint conceit   102
To set a gloss upon his bold intent,   103
Yet know, my lord, I was provoked by him,
And he first took exceptions at this badge,
Pronouncing that the paleness of this flower
Bewrayed the faintness of my master's heart.   107

RICHARD

Will not this malice, Somerset, be left?

SOMERSET

Your private grudge, my Lord of York, will out,
Though ne'er so cunningly you smother it.

KING

Good Lord, what madness rules in brainsick men
When for so slight and frivolous a cause
Such factious emulations shall arise!   113
Good cousins both, of York and Somerset,
Quiet yourselves, I pray, and be at peace.

RICHARD

Let his dissension first be tried by fight,
And then your highness shall command a peace.

SOMERSET

The quarrel toucheth none but us alone.   118
Betwixt ourselves let us decide it then.

RICHARD

There is my pledge. Accept it, Somerset.   120

VERNON

Nay, let it rest where it began at first.

BASSET

Confirm it so, mine honorable lord.

GLOUCESTER

Confirm it so? Confounded be your strife,
And perish ye with your audacious prate!
Presumptuous vassals, are you not ashamed
With this immodest clamorous outrage
To trouble and disturb the king and us?
And you, my lords, methinks you do not well
To bear with their perverse objections: 129
Much less to take occasion from their mouths
To raise a mutiny betwixt yourselves.
Let me persuade you take a better course.

EXETER

It grieves his highness. Good my lords, be friends.

KING

Come hither you that would be combatants.
Henceforth I charge you, as you love our favor,
Quite to forget this quarrel and the cause.
And you, my lords: remember where we are,
In France, amongst a fickle wavering nation.
If they perceive dissension in our looks
And that within ourselves we disagree,
How will their grudging stomachs be provoked   141
To willfull disobedience, and rebel!
Beside, what infamy will there arise
When foreign princes shall be certified   144
That for a toy, a thing of no regard,   145

---

64 *uncle* (Henry's uncle the Duke of Bedford married Burgundy's sister Anne)   71 *am prevented* have been anticipated   73 *strength* forces; *straight* immediately   74 *brook* endure   76 *still* always   78 *the combat* a duel   80 *servant* retainer (not menial)   92 *sanguine* blood-red; *leaves* petals   94 *repugn* oppose   100 *benefit* legal privilege   102 *quaint conceit* ingenious fancy   103 *set . . . upon* give fair outward appearance to   107 *Bewrayed* revealed   113 *emulations* rivalries   118 *toucheth* involves   120 *pledge* gage in a duel (usually a glove)   129 *objections* mutual accusations   141 *grudging stomachs* resentful tempers   144 *certified* informed   145 *toy* trifle; *regard* consequence

King Henry's peers and chief nobility
Destroyed themselves and lost the realm of France !
O, think upon the conquest of my father,
My tender years, and let us not forgo
150   That for a trifle that was bought with blood !
Let me be umpire in this doubtful strife.
I see no reason, if I wear this rose,
[Puts on a red rose.]
That any one should therefore be suspicious
I more incline to Somerset than York.
Both are my kinsmen, and I love them both.
As well they may upbraid me with my crown
Because forsooth the King of Scots is crowned.
But your discretions better can persuade
Than I am able to instruct or teach ;
And therefore, as we hither came in peace,
So let us still continue peace and love.
Cousin of York, we institute your grace
To be our regent in these parts of France ;
And, good my Lord of Somerset, unite
Your troops of horsemen with his bands of foot ;
And like true subjects, sons of your progenitors,
167   Go cheerfully together and digest
Your angry choler on your enemies.
Ourself, my Lord Protector, and the rest,
After some respite will return to Calais ;
From thence to England, where I hope ere long
To be presented, by your victories,
173   With Charles, Alençon, and that traitorous rout.
Exeunt. Manent [Richard Duke of] York,
Warwick, Exeter, Vernon.

WARWICK
My Lord of York, I promise you, the king
Prettily, methought, did play the orator.

RICHARD
And so he did ; but yet I like it not,
In that he wears the badge of Somerset.

WARWICK
Tush, that was but his fancy. Blame him not.
I dare presume, sweet prince, he thought no harm.

RICHARD
180   An if I wist he did – But let it rest.
Other affairs must now be managèd.
Exeunt. Flourish. Manet Exeter.

EXETER
Well didst thou, Richard, to suppress thy voice ;
For, had the passions of thy heart burst out,
I fear we should have seen deciphered there
More rancorous spite, more furious raging broils,
Than yet can be imagined or supposed.
187   But howsoe'er, no simple man that sees
This jarring discord of nobility,
This shouldering of each other in the court,
190   This factious bandying of their favorites,
But that it doth presage some ill event.
192   'Tis much when sceptres are in children's hands,
193   But more when envy breeds unkind division.
There comes the ruin, there begins confusion.   *Exit.*

Enter Talbot, with Trump and Drum before   IV, ii
Bordeaux.

TALBOT
Go to the gates of Bordeaux, trumpeter.
Summon their general unto the wall.
[Trumpet] sounds. Enter General, aloft [with his men].
English John Talbot, captains, calls you forth,
Servant in arms to Harry King of England ;
And thus he would : Open your city gates,   5
Be humble to us, call my sovereign yours
And do him homage as obedient subjects,
And I'll withdraw me and my bloody power ;
But if you frown upon this proffered peace,
You tempt the fury of my three attendants,
Lean famine, quartering steel, and climbing fire,   11
Who in a moment even with the earth
Shall lay your stately and air-braving towers,
If you forsake the offer of their love.

GENERAL
Thou ominous and fearful owl of death,
Our nation's terror and their bloody scourge,
The period of thy tyranny approacheth.   17
On us thou canst not enter but by death ;
For I protest we are well fortified
And strong enough to issue out and fight.
If thou retire, the Dauphin, well appointed,   21
Stands with the snares of war to tangle thee.
On either hand thee there are squadrons pitched   23
To wall thee from the liberty of flight ;   24
And no way canst thou turn thee for redress
But death doth front thee with apparent spoil   26
And pale destruction meets thee in the face.
Ten thousand French have ta'en the sacrament   28
To rive their dangerous artillery   29
Upon no Christian soul but English Talbot.
Lo, there thou stand'st, a breathing valiant man
Of an invincible unconquered spirit.
This is the latest glory of thy praise
That I thy enemy due thee withal ;   34
For ere the glass that now begins to run
Finish the process of his sandy hour,
These eyes that see thee now well-colored
Shall see thee withered, bloody, pale, and dead.
Drum afar off.
Hark, hark ! The Dauphin's drum, a warning bell,
Sings heavy music to thy timorous soul ;
And mine shall ring thy dire departure out.
Exit [with his men].

TALBOT
He fables not ; I hear the enemy.
Out, some light horsemen, and peruse their wings.   43
O, negligent and heedless discipline !
How are we parked and bounded in a pale,   45
A little herd of England's timorous deer,

150 *That . . . that* for a trifle that which   167 *digest* dissipate   173 *rout*
rabble   180 *An . . . wist* if I knew for certain   187 *simple* common   190
bandying verbal contending ; *favorites* followers   192 *much* serious   193
unkind intra-family
IV, ii Before the walls of Bordeaux   5 *would* wishes   11 *quartering* dis-
membering the slain enemy   17 *period* end   21 *appointed* equipped   23
thee of thee ; *pitched* set in battle order   24 *wall* hem in   26 *front* face ;
spoil slaughter (hunting metaphor, continued from *snares* in l. 22)   28 *ta'en
the sacrament* i.e. sworn a solemn oath   29 *rive* fire   34 *due* endue   43
peruse reconnoitre   45 *parked* enclosed ; *pale* fenced-in area

47 Mazed with a yelping kennel of French curs!
48 If we be English deer, be then in blood:
49 Not rascal-like, to fall down with a pinch,
But rather, moody-mad and desperate stags,
51 Turn on the bloody hounds with heads of steel
And make the cowards stand aloof at bay.
Sell every man his life as dear as mine,
And they shall find dear deer of us, my friends.
God and Saint George, Talbot and England's right,
Prosper our colors in this dangerous fight!   [Exeunt.]

*

IV, iii   *Enter a Messenger that meets [Richard Duke of] York.*
Enter York, with Trumpet and many Soldiers.

RICHARD
Are not the speedy scouts returned again
That dogged the mighty army of the Dauphin?

MESSENGER
3 They are returned, my lord, and give it out
That he is marched to Bordeaux with his power
To fight with Talbot. As he marched along,
By your espials were discoverèd
Two mightier troops than that the Dauphin led,
Which joined with him and made their march for
Bordeaux.

RICHARD
A plague upon that villain Somerset
That thus delays my promisèd supply
Of horsemen that were levied for this siege!
Renownèd Talbot doth expect my aid,
13 And I am louted by a traitor villain
And cannot help the noble chevalier.
God comfort him in this necessity!
16 If he miscarry, farewell wars in France.
Enter another Messenger [Sir William Lucy].

LUCY
Thou princely leader of our English strength,
Never so needful on the earth of France,
Spur to the rescue of the noble Talbot,
Who now is girdled with a waist of iron
And hemmed about with grim destruction.
To Bordeaux, warlike duke! to Bordeaux, York!
Else farewell Talbot, France, and England's honor.

RICHARD
O God, that Somerset, who in proud heart
25 Doth stop my cornets, were in Talbot's place!
So should we save a valiant gentleman
By forfeiting a traitor and a coward.
Mad ire and wrathful fury makes me weep
That thus we die while remiss traitors sleep.

LUCY
30 O, send some succor to the distressed lord!

RICHARD
He dies, we lose; I break my warlike word;
We mourn, France smiles; we lose, they daily get;
All long of this vile traitor Somerset.   33

LUCY
Then God take mercy on brave Talbot's soul
And on his son, young John, who two hours since
I met in travel toward his warlike father.
This seven years did not Talbot see his son,
And now they meet where both their lives are done.

RICHARD
Alas, what joy shall noble Talbot have
To bid his young son welcome to his grave?
Away! Vexation almost stops my breath
That sund'red friends greet in the hour of death.
Lucy, farewell. No more my fortune can   43
But curse the cause I cannot aid the man.
Maine, Blois, Poictiers, and Tours are won away,
Long all of Somerset and his delay.
                Exit [with Soldiers].

LUCY
Thus, while the vulture of sedition
Feeds in the bosom of such great commanders,
Sleeping neglection doth betray to loss
The conquest of our scarce-cold conqueror,
That ever-living man of memory,   51
Henry the Fifth. Whiles they each other cross,
Lives, honors, lands, and all hurry to loss.
     Enter Somerset, with his Army [, a Captain of   IV, iv
     Talbot's with him].

SOMERSET
It is too late; I cannot send them now.
This expedition was by York and Talbot
Too rashly plotted. All our general force   3
Might with a sally of the very town
Be buckled with. The over-daring Talbot
Hath sullied all his gloss of former honor
By this unheedful, desperate, wild adventure.
York set him on to fight, and die in shame,
That, Talbot dead, great York might bear the name.

CAPTAIN
Here is Sir William Lucy, who with me
Set from our o'ermatched forces forth for aid.

SOMERSET
How now, Sir William, whither were you sent?

LUCY
Whither, my lord? From bought and sold Lord Talbot,   13
Who, ringed about with bold adversity,
Cries out for noble York and Somerset
To beat assailing death from his weak legions;
And whiles the honorable captain there
Drops bloody sweat from his war-wearied limbs,
And, in advantage ling'ring, looks for rescue,   19
You, his false hopes, the trust of England's honor,   20
Keep off aloof with worthless emulation.   21
Let not your private discord keep away
The levied succors that should lend him aid,
While he, renownèd noble gentleman,
Yields up his life unto a world of odds.
Orleans the Bastard, Charles, Burgundy,
Alençon, Reignier compass him about,
And Talbot perisheth by your default.

SOMERSET
York set him on; York should have sent him aid.

47 *Mazed* bewildered   48 *in blood* in prime vigor   49 *rascal* (1) lean or inferior deer, (2) rabble; *pinch* nip of the hounds   51 *heads of steel* horns like swords
IV, iii Fields in Gascony   3 *give it out* report   13 *louted* made a fool of   16 *miscarry* come to harm   25 *cornets* companies of cavalry   30 *distressed* in difficulties (not 'upset')   33 *long of* on account of   43 *can* is able to do   51 *ever-living . . . memory* man of ever-living memory
IV, iv   3–5 *All . . . with* the mere town garrison, without other aid, might safely come forth to engage our whole army   13 *bought and sold* i.e. betrayed as by Judas   19 *in advantage ling'ring* finding his best hope in delaying action   20 *trust* trustee   21 *worthless emulation* senseless rivalry

LUCY

30 And York as fast upon your grace exclaims,
Swearing that you withhold his levied host,
Collected for this expedition.

SOMERSET

33 York lies. He might have sent and had the horse.
I owe him little duty, and less love,
And take foul scorn to fawn on him by sending.

LUCY

The fraud of England, not the force of France,
Hath now entrapped the noble-minded Talbot.
Never to England shall he bear his life,
But dies betrayed to fortune by your strife.

SOMERSET

Come, go. I will dispatch the horsemen straight;
Within six hours they will be at his aid.

LUCY

Too late comes rescue. He is ta'en or slain;
For fly he could not, if he would have fled;
And fly would Talbot never, though he might.

SOMERSET

If he be dead, brave Talbot, then adieu!

LUCY

His fame lives in the world, his shame in you.   *Exeunt.*

*

IV, v   *Enter Talbot and his Son.*

TALBOT

O young John Talbot, I did send for thee
To tutor thee in stratagems of war,
That Talbot's name might be in thee revived
When sapless age and weak unable limbs
Should bring thy father to his drooping chair.
But O malignant and ill-boding stars!
Now thou art come unto a feast of death,
8 A terrible and unavoided danger.
Therefore, dear boy, mount on my swiftest horse,
And I'll direct thee how thou shalt escape
By sudden flight. Come, dally not, be gone.

JOHN

Is my name Talbot? and am I your son?
And shall I fly? O, if you love my mother,
Dishonor not her honorable name
To make a bastard and a slave of me.
The world will say he is not Talbot's blood
That basely fled when noble Talbot stood.

TALBOT

Fly, to revenge my death if I be slain.

JOHN

He that flies so will ne'er return again.

TALBOT

If we both stay, we both are sure to die.

JOHN

Then let me stay, and father, do you fly.
22 Your loss is great, so your regard should be:
My worth unknown, no loss is known in me.
Upon my death the French can little boast;
In yours they will, in you all hopes are lost.
Flight cannot stain the honor you have won;
But mine it will, that no exploit have done.
28 You fled for vantage, every one will swear;
But if I bow, they'll say it was for fear.
There is no hope that ever I will stay

If the first hour I shrink and run away.
Here on my knee I beg mortality   32
Rather than life preserved with infamy.

TALBOT

Shall all thy mother's hopes lie in one tomb?

JOHN

Ay, rather than I'll shame my mother's womb.

TALBOT

Upon my blessing I command thee go.

JOHN

To fight I will, but not to fly the foe.

TALBOT

Part of thy father may be saved in thee.

JOHN

No part of him but will be shame in me.

TALBOT

Thou never hadst renown, nor canst not lose it.

JOHN

Yes, your renownèd name. Shall flight abuse it?

TALBOT

Thy father's charge shall clear thee from that stain.

JOHN

You cannot witness for me, being slain.   43
If death be so apparent, then both fly.   44

TALBOT

And leave my followers here to fight and die?
My age was never tainted with such shame.   46

JOHN

And shall my youth be guilty of such blame?
No more can I be severed from your side
Than can yourself yourself in twain divide.
Stay, go, do what you will – the like do I;
For live I will not if my father die.

TALBOT

Then here I take my leave of thee, fair son,
Born to eclipse thy life this afternoon.
Come, side by side together live and die,
And soul with soul from France to heaven fly.
                         Exit [with Son].
   Alarum. Excursions, wherein Talbot's Son is hemmed IV, vi
   about and Talbot rescues him.

TALBOT

Saint George and victory! Fight, soldiers, fight!
The regent hath with Talbot broke his word
And left us to the rage of France his sword.   3
Where is John Talbot? Pause, and take thy breath.
I gave thee life and rescued thee from death.

JOHN

O twice my father, twice am I thy son!
The life thou gav'st me first was lost and done
Till with thy warlike sword, despite of fate,
To my determined time thou gav'st new date.   9

TALBOT

When from the Dauphin's crest thy sword struck fire,
It warmed thy father's heart with proud desire
Of bold-faced victory. Then leaden age,
Quickened with youthful spleen and warlike rage,   13

---

30 *upon . . . exclaims* accuses your grace   33 *might . . . had* i.e. had and might
have sent
IV, v *Fields near Bordeaux*   8 *unavoided* unavoidable   22 *regard* heed for
your safety   28 *vantage* military advantage   32 *mortality* death   43 *being
slain* if you are slain   44 *apparent* certain   46 *age* lifetime
IV, vi   3 *France his* France's   9 *determined* to which a limit has been set;
date limit   13 *Quickened* revived; *spleen* ardor

Beat down Alençon, Orleans, Burgundy,
And from the pride of Gallia rescued thee.
The ireful Bastard Orleans, that drew blood
From thee, my boy, and had the maidenhood
Of thy first fight, I soon encounterèd
And interchanging blows, I quickly shed
20 Some of his bastard blood ; and in disgrace
Bespoke him thus : 'Contaminated, base,
And misbegotten blood I spill of thine,
23 Mean and right poor, for that pure blood of mine
Which thou didst force from Talbot, my brave boy.'
25 Here, purposing the Bastard to destroy,
Came in strong rescue. Speak, thy father's care.
Art thou not weary, John ? How dost thou fare ?
Wilt thou yet leave the battle, boy, and fly,
29 Now thou art sealed the son of chivalry ?
Fly, to revenge my death when I am dead.
The help of one stands me in little stead.
32 O, too much folly is it, well I wot,
To hazard all our lives in one small boat.
If I to-day die not with Frenchmen's rage,
35 To-morrow I shall die with mickle age.
By me they nothing gain an if I stay ;
'Tis but the short'ning of my life one day.
In thee thy mother dies, our household's name,
My death's revenge, thy youth, and England's fame.
All these, and more, we hazard by thy stay ;
All these are saved if thou wilt fly away.

JOHN
42 The sword of Orleans hath not made me smart ;
These words of yours draw lifeblood from my heart.
44 On that advantage, bought with such a shame,
To save a paltry life and slay bright fame,
Before young Talbot from old Talbot fly,
The coward horse that bears me fall and die !
48 And like me to the peasant boys of France,
To be shame's scorn and subject of mischance !
Surely, by all the glory you have won,
An if I fly, I am not Talbot's son.
52 Then talk no more of flight. It is no boot.
If son to Talbot, die at Talbot's foot.

TALBOT
54 Then follow thou thy desp'rate sire of Crete,
Thou Icarus. Thy life to me is sweet.
If thou wilt fight, fight by thy father's side ;
And, commendable proved, let's die in pride.
        Exit [with Son].

IV, vii   *Alarum. Excursions. Enter old Talbot, led [by a*
       Servant].

TALBOT
Where is my other life ? Mine own is gone.
O, where's young Talbot ? Where is valiant John ?
Triumphant Death, smeared with captivity,

Young Talbot's valor makes me smile at thee.
When he perceived me shrink and on my knee,   5
His bloody sword he brandished over me
And like a hungry lion did commence
Rough deeds of rage and stern impatience ;
But when my angry guardant stood alone,   9
Tend'ring my ruin and assailed of none,   10
Dizzy-eyed fury and great rage of heart
Suddenly made him from my side to start
Into the clust'ring battle of the French ;   13
And in that sea of blood my boy did drench
His over-mounting spirit ; and there died
My Icarus, my blossom, in his pride.
   Enter [Soldiers] with John Talbot, borne.
SERVANT
O my dear lord, lo where your son is borne !
TALBOT
Thou antic Death, which laugh'st us here to scorn,
Anon, from thy insulting tyranny,
Coupled in bonds of perpetuity,
Two Talbots, wingèd through the lither sky,   21
In thy despite shall scape mortality.
O thou whose wounds become hard-favored Death,   23
Speak to thy father ere thou yield thy breath !
Brave Death by speaking, whether he will or no.   25
Imagine him a Frenchman, and thy foe.
Poor boy ! he smiles, methinks, as who should say,   27
'Had Death been French, then Death had died to-day.'
Come, come, and lay him in his father's arms.
My spirit can no longer bear these harms.
Soldiers, adieu. I have what I would have,
Now my old arms are young John Talbot's grave.   *Dies.*
   Enter Charles, Alençon, Burgundy, Bastard, and
    Pucelle.
CHARLES
Had York and Somerset brought rescue in,
We should have found a bloody day of this.
BASTARD
How the young whelp of Talbot's, raging wood,   35
Did flesh his puny sword in Frenchmen's blood !   36
PUCELLE
Once I encount'red him and thus I said,
'Thou maiden youth, be vanquished by a maid.'   38
But with a proud majestical high scorn
He answered thus, 'Young Talbot was not born
To be the pillage of a giglot wench.'   41
So, rushing in the bowels of the French,
He left me proudly, as unworthy fight.
BURGUNDY
Doubtless he would have made a noble knight.
See where he lies inhearsèd in the arms   45
Of the most bloody nurser of his harms.   46
BASTARD
Hew them to pieces, hack their bones asunder
Whose life was England's glory, Gallia's wonder.
CHARLES
O, no, forbear ! For that which we have fled
During the life, let us not wrong it dead.
   Enter Lucy [attended, a French Herald preceding].
LUCY
Herald, conduct me to the Dauphin's tent,
To know who hath obtained the glory of the day.
CHARLES
On what submissive message art thou sent ?

---

20 *in disgrace* as an insult   23 *Mean* inferior   25 *purposing* as I purposed   29 *sealed* certified   32 *wot* know   35 *mickle* great   42 *smart* suffer   44 *On that advantage* to gain these benefits (i.e. safety, revenge)   48 *like* liken   52 *boot* use   54 *Crete* (site of labyrinth from which Daedalus and his son Icarus attempted to escape on wings)
IV, vii   5 *shrink* give way in battle   9 *guardant* protector   10 *Tend'ring* being concerned for   13 *clust'ring battle* swarming army   21 *lither* yielding   23 *become . . . Death* make beautiful even the hideous visage of death   25 *Brave* defy   27 *as who* as if one   35 *wood* mad   36 *puny* used for the first time in battle   38 *maiden* untried in battle   41 *giglot* wanton   45 *inhearsèd* as in a coffin   46 *nurser . . . harms* one who fostered his injurious power (toward the French)

LUCY
Submission, Dauphin? 'Tis a mere French word.
We English warriors wot not what it means.
I come to know what prisoners thou hast ta'en
And to survey the bodies of the dead.
CHARLES
58 For prisoners ask'st thou? Hell our prison is.
But tell me whom thou seek'st.
LUCY
60 But where's the great Alcides of the field,
Valiant Lord Talbot, Earl of Shrewsbury,
Created for his rare success in arms
Great Earl of Washford, Waterford, and Valence,
Lord Talbot of Goodrig and Urchinfield,
Lord Strange of Blackmere, Lord Verdun of Alton,
Lord Cromwell of Wingfield, Lord Furnival of Shef-
field,
The thrice-victorious Lord of Falconbridge,
Knight of the noble order of Saint George,
Worthy Saint Michael, and the Golden Fleece,
70 Great Marshal to Henry the Sixth
Of all his wars within the realm of France?
PUCELLE
Here's a silly stately style indeed!
The Turk, that two and fifty kingdoms hath,
Writes not so tedious a style as this.
Him that thou magnifi'st with all these titles,
Stinking and flyblown lies here at our feet.
LUCY
Is Talbot slain, the Frenchmen's only scourge,
Your kingdom's terror and black Nemesis?
O, were mine eyeballs into bullets turned,
80 That I in rage might shoot them at your faces!
O that I could but call these dead to life!
It were enough to fright the realm of France.
Were but his picture left amongst you here,
It would amaze the proudest of you all.
Give me their bodies, that I may bear them hence
And give them burial as beseems their worth.
PUCELLE
I think this upstart is old Talbot's ghost,
He speaks with such a proud commanding spirit.
For God's sake, let him have 'em! To keep them here,
They would but stink and putrefy the air.
CHARLES
Go take their bodies hence.
LUCY
I'll bear them hence; but from their ashes shall be
reared
93 A phoenix that shall make all France afeard.
CHARLES
So we be rid of them, do with 'em what thou wilt.
And now to Paris in this conquering vein.
All will be ours, now bloody Talbot's slain.   *Exeunt.*

*

V, i   *Sennet. Enter King, Gloucester, and Exeter.*
KING
Have you perused the letters from the pope,
The emperor, and the Earl of Armagnac?
GLOUCESTER
I have, my lord, and their intent is this:
They humbly sue unto your excellence

To have a godly peace concluded of
Between the realms of England and of France.
KING
How doth your grace affect their motion?   7
GLOUCESTER
Well, my good lord, and as the only means
To stop effusion of our Christian blood
And stablish quietness on every side.
KING
Ay, marry, uncle; for I always thought
It was both impious and unnatural
That such immanity and bloody strife   13
Should reign among professors of one faith.
GLOUCESTER
Beside, my lord, the sooner to effect
And surer bind this knot of amity,
The Earl of Armagnac, near knit to Charles,   17
A man of great authority in France,
Proffers his only daughter to your grace
In marriage, with a large and sumptuous dowry.
KING
Marriage, uncle? Alas, my years are young,
And fitter is my study and my books
Than wanton dalliance with a paramour.
Yet, call th' ambassadors; and as you please,
So let them have their answers every one.
I shall be well content with any choice
Tends to God's glory and my country's weal.   27
Enter Winchester [in cardinal's habit] and three
Ambassadors [one a Papal Legate].
EXETER *[aside]*
What, is my Lord of Winchester installed,
And called unto a cardinal's degree?
Then I perceive that will be verified
Henry the Fifth did sometime prophesy:
'If once he come to be a cardinal,
He'll make his cap coequal with the crown.'
KING
My lords ambassadors, your several suits
Have been considered and debated on.
Your purpose is both good and reasonable,
And therefore are we certainly resolved
To draw conditions of a friendly peace,
Which by my Lord of Winchester we mean
Shall be transported presently to France.   40
GLOUCESTER
And for the proffer of my lord your master,
I have informed his highness so at large   42
As, liking of the lady's virtuous gifts,
Her beauty, and the value of her dower,
He doth intend she shall be England's queen.
KING
In argument and proof of which contract
Bear her this jewel, pledge of my affection.
And so, my Lord Protector, see them guarded
And safely brought to Dover, wherein shipped
Commit them to the fortune of the sea.
Exeunt [all but Winchester and the Legate].

---

58 *Hell . . . is* i.e. we dispatch our victims straight to hell **60** *Alcides*
Hercules, son of Alcaeus **93** *phoenix* mythical bird that arises regenerated
from its own ashes
V, i The royal palace in London **7** *affect* incline toward; *motion* proposal
13 *immanity* monstrous cruelty **17** *knit* related **27** *Tends* which tends
40 *presently* immediately **42** *at large* fully

WINCHESTER
Stay, my lord legate. You shall first receive
The sum of money which I promisèd
Should be delivered to his holiness
54   For clothing me in these grave ornaments.
LEGATE
I will attend upon your lordship's leisure.
[Steps aside.]
WINCHESTER
Now Winchester will not submit, I trow,
Or be inferior to the proudest peer.
Humphrey of Gloucester, thou shalt well perceive
That neither in birth or for authority
The bishop will be overborne by thee.
I'll either make thee stoop and bend thy knee
Or sack this country with a mutiny.   *Exeunt.*

*

V, ii   *Enter Charles, Burgundy, Alençon, Bastard,*
         Reignier, and Joan.
CHARLES
These news, my lords, may cheer our drooping spirits:
2   'Tis said the stout Parisians do revolt
And turn again unto the warlike French.
ALENÇON
Then march to Paris, royal Charles of France,
And keep not back your powers in dalliance.
PUCELLE
Peace be amongst them if they turn to us;
7   Else ruin combat with their palaces!
     Enter Scout.
SCOUT
Success unto our valiant general
9   And happiness to his accomplices!
CHARLES
What tidings send our scouts? I prithee speak.
SCOUT
The English army, that divided was
Into two parties, is now conjoined in one
And means to give you battle presently.
CHARLES
Somewhat too sudden, sirs, the warning is,
But we will presently provide for them.
BURGUNDY
I trust the ghost of Talbot is not there.
Now he is gone, my lord, you need not fear.
PUCELLE
Of all base passions fear is most accursed.
Command the conquest, Charles, it shall be thine,
Let Henry fret and all the world repine.
CHARLES
Then on, my lords; and France be fortunate!   *Exeunt.*

     Alarum. Excursions. Enter Joan de Pucelle.   V, iii
PUCELLE
The regent conquers and the Frenchmen fly.
Now help, ye charming spells and periapts;   2
And ye choice spirits that admonish me,   3
And give me signs of future accidents.   4
     Thunder.
You speedy helpers that are substitutes   5
Under the lordly monarch of the north,
Appear and aid me in this enterprise!
     Enter Fiends.
This speedy and quick appearance argues proof
Of your accustomed diligence to me.
Now, ye familiar spirits that are culled
Out of the powerful legions under earth,
Help me this once, that France may get the field.   12
     They walk, and speak not.
O, hold me not with silence over-long!
Where I was wont to feed you with my blood,
I'll lop a member off and give it you
In earnest of a further benefit,
So you do condescend to help me now.
     They hang their heads.
No hope to have redress? My body shall
Pay recompense if you will grant my suit.
     They shake their heads.
Cannot my body nor blood-sacrifice
Entreat you to your wonted furtherance?
Then take my soul – my body, soul, and all,
Before that England give the French the foil. *They depart.*
See, they forsake me! Now the time is come
That France must vail her lofty-plumèd crest   25
And let her head fall into England's lap.
My ancient incantations are too weak,   27
And hell too strong for me to buckle with.
Now, France, thy glory droopeth to the dust.   *Exit.*
     Excursions. Burgundy and [Richard Duke of] York
     fight hand to hand. French fly. [Pucelle is taken.]
RICHARD
Damsel of France, I think I have you fast.
Unchain your spirits now with spelling charms   31
And try if they can gain your liberty.
A goodly prize, fit for the devil's grace!   33
See how the ugly witch doth bend her brows
As if, with Circe, she would change my shape.   35
PUCELLE
Changed to a worser shape thou canst not be.
RICHARD
O, Charles the Dauphin is a proper man!   37
No shape but his can please your dainty eye.   38
PUCELLE
A plaguing mischief light on Charles and thee.
And may ye both be suddenly surprised   40
By bloody hands in sleeping on your beds!
RICHARD
Fell banning hag, enchantress, hold thy tongue.   42
PUCELLE
I prithee give me leave to curse awhile.
RICHARD
Curse, miscreant, when thou com'st to the stake. *Exeunt.*
     Alarum. Enter Suffolk, with Margaret in his hand.
SUFFOLK
Be what thou wilt, thou art my prisoner.
     Gazes on her.

---

54 *grave ornaments* robes of official dignity
V, ii Fields before Angiers   2 *stout* brave   7 *Else . . . palaces* otherwise let
ruin destroy their palaces   9 *accomplices* associates
V, iii   2 *charming* working by incantation; *periapts* amulets   3 *admonish*
forewarn   4 *accidents* occurrences   5 *substitutes* deputies   12 *get the
field* win the battle   25 *vail* lower   27 *ancient* former   31 *spelling charms*
charms that cast spells   33 *devil's grace* his grace the devil (a mocking
title)   35 *Circe* a fabled sorceress who turned men into swine   37 *proper*
handsome   38 *dainty* fastidious   40 *surprised* captured   42 *Fell banning*
fierce cursing

O fairest beauty, do not fear nor fly!
For I will touch thee but with reverent hands;
48 I kiss these fingers for eternal peace
And lay them gently on thy tender side.
Who art thou? Say, that I may honor thee.
MARGARET
Margaret my name, and daughter to a king,
The King of Naples, whosoe'er thou art.
SUFFOLK
An earl I am and Suffolk am I called.
Be not offended, nature's miracle,
Thou art allotted to be ta'en by me.
So doth the swan her downy cygnets save,
Keeping them prisoner underneath her wings.
Yet, if this servile usage once offend,
Go and be free again as Suffolk's friend.
    She is going.
O, stay! [*Aside*] I have no power to let her pass.
My hand would free her, but my heart says no.
62 As plays the sun upon the glassy streams,
Twinkling another counterfeited beam,
So seems this gorgeous beauty to mine eyes.
Fain would I woo her, yet I dare not speak.
I'll call for pen and ink and write my mind.
Fie, de la Pole, disable not thyself.
Hast not a tongue? Is she not here?
Wilt thou be daunted at a woman's sight?
Ay, beauty's princely majesty is such
71 Confounds the tongue and makes the senses rough.
MARGARET
Say, Earl of Suffolk, if thy name be so,
What ransom must I pay before I pass?
For I perceive I am thy prisoner.
SUFFOLK
How canst thou tell she will deny thy suit
Before thou make a trial of her love?
MARGARET
Why speak'st thou not? What ransom must I pay?
SUFFOLK
She's beautiful, and therefore to be wooed;
She is a woman, therefore to be won.
MARGARET
Will thou accept of ransom, yea or no?
SUFFOLK
81 Fond man, remember that thou hast a wife.
Then how can Margaret be thy paramour?
MARGARET
I were best to leave him, for he will not hear.
SUFFOLK
84 There all is marred; there lies a cooling card.
MARGARET
85 He talks at randon. Sure the man is mad.
SUFFOLK
And yet a dispensation may be had.
MARGARET
And yet I would that you would answer me.
SUFFOLK
I'll win this Lady Margaret. For whom?
89 Why, for my king. Tush, that's a wooden thing!
MARGARET
He talks of wood. It is some carpenter.
SUFFOLK
Yet so my fancy may be satisfied
And peace establishèd between these realms.

But there remains a scruple in that too;
For though her father be the King of Naples,
Duke of Anjou and Maine, yet is he poor,
And our nobility will scorn the match.
MARGARET
Hear ye, captain? Are you not at leisure?
SUFFOLK
It shall be so, disdain they ne'er so much.
Henry is youthful and will quickly yield. –
Madam, I have a secret to reveal.
MARGARET
What though I be enthralled? He seems a knight   101
And will not any way dishonor me.
SUFFOLK
Lady, vouchsafe to listen what I say.
MARGARET
Perhaps I shall be rescued by the French,
And then I need not crave his courtesy.
SUFFOLK
Sweet madam, give me hearing in a cause –
MARGARET
Tush, women have been captive ere now.
SUFFOLK
Lady, wherefore talk you so?
MARGARET
I cry you mercy, 'tis but quid for quo.   109
SUFFOLK
Say, gentle princess, would you not suppose
Your bondage happy, to be made a queen?
MARGARET
To be a queen in bondage is more vile
Than is a slave in base servility;
For princes should be free.
SUFFOLK   And so shall you,
If happy England's royal king be free.
MARGARET
Why, what concerns his freedom unto me?
SUFFOLK
I'll undertake to make thee Henry's queen,
To put a golden sceptre in thy hand
And set a precious crown upon thy head,
If thou wilt condescend to be my –
MARGARET   What?
SUFFOLK
His love.
MARGARET
I am unworthy to be Henry's wife.
SUFFOLK
No, gentle madam. I unworthy am
To woo so fair a dame to be his wife
And have no portion in the choice myself.   125
How say you, madam? Are ye so content?
MARGARET
An if my father please, I am content.
SUFFOLK
Then call our captains and our colors forth.
And, madam, at your father's castle walls

48 *for* in token of   62–64 *As plays . . . eyes* i.e. she seems as gorgeous as the sun's reflection twinkling upon the water's surface   71 *Confounds* that it confounds   81 *Fond* foolish   84 *cooling card* opponent's card which dashes one's hopes   85 *randon* random   89 *wooden* stupid (either the king, or the plan itself)   101 *enthralled* captive   109 *cry you mercy* beg your pardon; *quid for quo* tit for tat   125 *the choice* (1) the choosing, (2) the thing chosen

We'll crave a parley to confer with him.
>   *Sound [a parley]. Enter Reignier on the walls.*
See, Reignier, see, thy daughter prisoner.

REIGNIER
To whom?

SUFFOLK   To me.

REIGNIER   Suffolk, what remedy?
I am a soldier, and unapt to weep
Or to exclaim on fortune's fickleness.

SUFFOLK
Yes, there is remedy enough, my lord.
Consent, and for thy honor give consent,
Thy daughter shall be wedded to my king,
Whom I with pain have wooed and won thereto;
And this her easy-held imprisonment
Hath gained thy daughter princely liberty.

REIGNIER
Speaks Suffolk as he thinks?

SUFFOLK   Fair Margaret knows
142   That Suffolk doth not flatter, face, or feign.

REIGNIER
Upon thy princely warrant I descend
To give thee answer of thy just demand.
>   *[Exit from the walls.]*

SUFFOLK
And here I will expect thy coming.
>   *Trumpets sound. Enter Reignier [below].*

REIGNIER
Welcome, brave earl, into our territories.
Command in Anjou what your honor pleases.

SUFFOLK
Thanks, Reignier, happy for so sweet a child,
Fit to be made companion with a king.
What answer makes your grace unto my suit?

REIGNIER
Since thou dost deign to woo her little worth
To be the princely bride of such a lord,
Upon condition I may quietly
Enjoy mine own, the country Maine and Anjou,
Free from oppression or the stroke of war,
My daughter shall be Henry's, if he please.

SUFFOLK
That is her ransom. I deliver her,
And those two counties I will undertake
Your grace shall well and quietly enjoy.

REIGNIER
160   And I again, in Henry's royal name,
161   As deputy unto that gracious king,
Give thee her hand for sign of plighted faith.

SUFFOLK
Reignier of France, I give thee kingly thanks,
164   Because this is in traffic of a king.
>   *[Aside]*
And yet methinks I could be well content
To be mine own attorney in this case. –

I'll over then to England with this news
And make this marriage to be solemnized.
So, farewell, Reignier. Set this diamond safe
In golden palaces, as it becomes.   170

REIGNIER
I do embrace thee as I would embrace
The Christian prince King Henry, were he here.

MARGARET
Farewell, my lord. Good wishes, praise and prayers
Shall Suffolk ever have of Margaret.
>   *She is going.*

SUFFOLK
Farewell, sweet madam. But hark you, Margaret –
No princely commendations to my king?

MARGARET
Such commendations as becomes a maid,
A virgin, and his servant, say to him.

SUFFOLK
Words sweetly placed and modestly directed.
But, madam, I must trouble you again –
No loving token to his majesty?

MARGARET
Yes, my good lord: a pure unspotted heart,
Never yet taint with love, I send the king.   183

SUFFOLK
And this withal.   184
>   *Kiss her.*

MARGARET
That for thyself. I will not so presume
To send such peevish tokens to a king.   186
>   *[Exeunt Reignier and Margaret.]*

SUFFOLK
O wert thou for myself! But, Suffolk, stay.
Thou mayst not wander in that labyrinth;
There Minotaurs and ugly treasons lurk.   189
Solicit Henry with her wondrous praise.   190
Bethink thee on her virtues that surmount,
And natural graces that extinguish art;   192
Repeat their semblance often on the seas,   193
That, when thou com'st to kneel at Henry's feet,
Thou mayst bereave him of his wits with wonder. *Exit.*

>   *

>   *Enter [Richard, Duke of] York, Warwick,*   V, iv
>   *Shepherd, Pucelle [guarded].*

RICHARD
Bring forth that sorceress condemned to burn.

SHEPHERD
Ah, Joan, this kills thy father's heart outright.
Have I sought every country far and near,
And, now it is my chance to find thee out,
Must I behold thy timeless cruel death?   5
Ah, Joan, sweet daughter Joan, I'll die with thee!

PUCELLE
Decrepit miser! base ignoble wretch!   7
I am descended of a gentler blood.
Thou art no father nor no friend of mine.   9

SHEPHERD
Out, out! My lords, an please you, 'tis not so.
I did beget her, all the parish knows.
Her mother liveth yet, can testify
She was the first fruit of my bach'lorship.

WARWICK
Graceless, wilt thou deny thy parentage?

142 *face* deceive   160 *again* in return   161 *deputy* (refers to Suffolk)
164 *traffic* business   170 *as it becomes* as befits such a jewel   183 *taint*
tainted   184 *withal* moreover   186 *peevish* trifling   189 *Minotaurs* (there
was but one Minotaur, a monster part bull and part man, at the center of
the Cretan labyrinth built by Daedalus)   190 *her wondrous praise* praise of
this wondrous woman   192 *extinguish* eclipse   193 *Repeat their semblance*
rehearse the description of her virtues
V, iv The English camp in Anjou   5 *timeless* premature   7 *miser* wretch
9 *friend* kinsman

RICHARD
This argues what her kind of life hath been,
16   Wicked and vile ; and so her death concludes.
SHEPHERD
17   Fie, Joan, that thou wilt be so obstacle !
18   God knows thou art a collop of my flesh,
And for thy sake have I shed many a tear.
Deny me not, I prithee, gentle Joan.
PUCELLE
Peasant, avaunt ! You have suborned this man,
Of purpose to obscure my noble birth.
SHEPHERD
23   'Tis true, I gave a noble to the priest
The morn that I was wedded to her mother.
Kneel down and take my blessing, good my girl.
Wilt thou not stoop ? Now cursèd be the time
Of thy nativity ! I would the milk
Thy mother gave thee when thou suck'dst her breast
Had been a little ratsbane for thy sake.
Or else, when thou didst keep my lambs afield,
I wish some ravenous wolf had eaten thee.
32   Dost thou deny thy father, cursèd drab ?
O, burn her, burn her ! Hanging is too good.   *Exit.*
RICHARD
Take her away ; for she hath lived too long,
To fill the world with vicious qualities.
PUCELLE
First let me tell you whom you have condemned :
Not one begotten of a shepherd swain,
But issued from the progeny of kings,
Virtuous and holy, chosen from above
By inspiration of celestial grace
To work exceeding miracles on earth.
I never had to do with wicked spirits.
But you, that are polluted with your lusts,
Stained with the guiltless blood of innocents,
Corrupt and tainted with a thousand vices –
Because you want the grace that others have,
You judge it straight a thing impossible
To compass wonders but by help of devils.
No, misconceivèd, Joan of Arc hath been
50   A virgin from her tender infancy,
Chaste and immaculate in very thought,
Whose maiden blood, thus rigorously effused,
Will cry for vengeance at the gates of heaven.
RICHARD
Ay, ay. Away with her to execution.
WARWICK
And hark ye, sirs. Because she is a maid,
Spare for no fagots, let there be enow.
Place barrels of pitch upon the fatal stake,
That so her torture may be shortenèd.
PUCELLE
Will nothing turn your unrelenting hearts ?
60   Then, Joan, discover thine infirmity,
That warranteth by law to be thy privilege.
I am with child, ye bloody homicides.
Murder not then the fruit within my womb,
Although ye hale me to a violent death.
RICHARD
65   Now heaven forfend ! The holy maid with child ?
WARWICK
The greatest miracle that e'er ye wrought.
Is all your strict preciseness come to this ?

RICHARD
She and the Dauphin have been juggling.
I did imagine what would be her refuge.
WARWICK
Well, go to. We'll have no bastards live,
Especially since Charles must father it.
PUCELLE
You are deceived. My child is none of his.
It was Alençon that enjoyed my love.
RICHARD
Alençon, that notorious Machiavel ?   74
It dies, an if it had a thousand lives.
PUCELLE
O, give me leave, I have deluded you.
'Twas neither Charles nor yet the duke I named,
But Reignier, King of Naples, that prevailed.
WARWICK
A married man ! That's most intolerable.
RICHARD
Why, here's a girl ! I think she knows not well,
There were so many, whom she may accuse.
WARWICK
It's sign she hath been liberal and free.
RICHARD
And yet, forsooth, she is a virgin pure !
Strumpet, thy words condemn thy brat and thee.
Use no entreaty, for it is in vain.
PUCELLE
Then lead me hence ; with whom I leave my curse.
May never glorious sun reflex his beams
Upon the country where you make abode ;
But darkness and the gloomy shade of death
Environ you, till mischief and despair   90
Drive you to break your necks or hang yourselves !
     Exit [guarded].
RICHARD
Break thou in pieces and consume to ashes,
Thou foul accursèd minister of hell !
     Enter [Winchester, now] Cardinal [, attended].
WINCHESTER
Lord regent, I do greet your excellence
With letters of commission from the king.
For know, my lords, the states of Christendom,
Moved with remorse of these outrageous broils,
Have earnestly implored a general peace
Betwixt our nation and the aspiring French ;
And here at hand the Dauphin and his train
Approacheth, to confer about some matter.
RICHARD
Is all our travail turned to this effect ?   102
After the slaughter of so many peers,
So many captains, gentlemen, and soldiers,
That in this quarrel have been overthrown
And sold their bodies for their country's benefit,
Shall we at last conclude effeminate peace ?
Have we not lost most part of all the towns
By treason, falsehood, and by treachery
Our great progenitors had conquerèd ?

---

16 *concludes* (1) verifies, (2) ends   17 *obstacle* (he means to say 'obstinate')
18 *collop* slice   23 *noble* coin worth 6s. 8d.   32 *drab* whore   60 *discover*
reveal   65 *forfend* forbid   74 *Machiavel* Italian whose doctrines Elizabethans regarded as the epitome of intrigue and immoral expediency
102 *travail* toil

O, Warwick, Warwick! I foresee with grief
The utter loss of all the realm of France.

WARWICK
Be patient, York. If we conclude a peace,
114 It shall be with such strict and severe covenants
115 As little shall the Frenchmen gain thereby.
      Enter Charles, Alençon, Bastard, Reignier [and
      others].

CHARLES
Since, lords of England, it is thus agreed
That peaceful truce shall be proclaimed in France,
We come to be informèd by yourselves
What the conditions of that league must be.

RICHARD
120 Speak, Winchester; for boiling choler chokes
The hollow passage of my poisoned voice
By sight of these our baleful enemies.

WINCHESTER
Charles, and the rest, it is enacted thus:
124 That, in regard King Henry gives consent,
125 Of mere compassion and of lenity,
To ease your country of distressful war
And suffer you to breathe in fruitful peace,
You shall become true liegemen to his crown;
And, Charles, upon condition thou wilt swear
To pay him tribute and submit thyself,
Thou shalt be placed as viceroy under him
And still enjoy thy regal dignity.

ALENÇON
Must he be then as shadow of himself?
Adorn his temples with a coronet,
And yet, in substance and authority,
Retain but privilege of a private man?
This proffer is absurd and reasonless.

CHARLES
'Tis known already that I am possessed
With more than half the Gallian territories
140 And therein reverenced for their lawful king.
Shall I, for lucre of the rest unvanquished,
Detract so much from that prerogative
As to be called but viceroy of the whole?
No, lord ambassador. I'll rather keep
That which I have than, coveting for more,
146 Be cast from possibility of all.

RICHARD
Insulting Charles, hast thou by secret means
Used intercession to obtain a league,
149 And, now the matter grows to compromise,
150 Stand'st thou aloof upon comparison?
Either accept the title thou usurp'st,
152 Of benefit proceeding from our king
153 And not of any challenge of desert,
Or we will plague thee with incessant wars.

REIGNIER *[aside to Charles]*
My lord, you do not well in obstinacy
To cavil in the course of this contract.
If once it be neglected, ten to one
We shall not find like opportunity.

ALENÇON *[aside to Charles]*
To say the truth, it is your policy   159
To save your subjects from such massacre
And ruthless slaughters as are daily seen
By our proceeding in hostility;
And therefore take this compact of a truce,
Although you break it when your pleasure serves.

WARWICK
How say'st thou, Charles? Shall our condition stand?   165

CHARLES
It shall;
Only reserved, you claim no interest
In any of our towns of garrison.

RICHARD
Then swear allegiance to his majesty:
As thou art knight, never to disobey
Nor be rebellious to the crown of England,
Thou, nor thy nobles, to the crown of England.
      [Charles and the rest give tokens of fealty.]
So, now dismiss your army when ye please,
Hang up your ensigns, let your drums be still,
For here we entertain a solemn peace.   *Exeunt.*

                         *

      Enter Suffolk, in conference with the King,   V, v
      Gloucester, and Exeter.

KING
Your wondrous rare description, noble earl,
Of beauteous Margaret hath astonished me.
Her virtues, graced with external gifts,
Do breed love's settled passions in my heart;   4
And like as rigor of tempestuous gusts
Provokes the mightiest hulk against the tide,   6
So am I driven by breath of her renown
Either to suffer shipwrack or arrive
Where I may have fruition of her love.

SUFFOLK
Tush, my good lord, this superficial tale   10
Is but a preface of her worthy praise.   11
The chief perfections of that lovely dame,
Had I sufficient skill to utter them,
Would make a volume of enticing lines
Able to ravish any dull conceit;   15
And, which is more, she is not so divine,
So full replete with choice of all delights,
But with as humble lowliness of mind
She is content to be at your command –
Command, I mean, of virtuous chaste intents,
To love and honor Henry as her lord.

KING
And otherwise will Henry ne'er presume.
Therefore, my Lord Protector, give consent
That Marg'ret may be England's royal queen.

GLOUCESTER
So should I give consent to flatter sin.   25
You know, my lord, your highness is betrothed
Unto another lady of esteem.
How shall we then dispense with that contract

114 *covenants* articles of agreement   115 *As* that   120 *choler* anger   124
in regard inasmuch as   125 *mere* pure; *lenity* mercifulness   146 *cast*
excluded   149 *grows to compromise* approaches a peaceful solution   150
comparison rhetorical quibbling   152 *Of benefit* as feudal beneficiary
153 *challenge of desert* claim of right to the title   159 *policy* politic course
165 *condition* treaty terms
V, v The royal palace in London   4 *settled* rooted   6 *Provokes* impels;
hulk ship   10 *superficial* dealing merely with her most obvious virtues
11 *her worthy praise* praise of her full worth   15 *conceit* imagination
25 *flatter* extenuate

And not deface your honor with reproach?

SUFFOLK
As doth a ruler with unlawful oaths,
31   Or one that at a triumph, having vowed
32   To try his strength, forsaketh yet the lists
By reason of his adversary's odds.
A poor earl's daughter is unequal odds,
And therefore may be broke without offense.

GLOUCESTER
Why, what, I pray, is Margaret more than that?
Her father is no better than an earl,
Although in glorious titles he excel.

SUFFOLK
Yes, my lord, her father is a king,
The King of Naples and Jerusalem,
And of such great authority in France
As his alliance will confirm our peace
And keep the Frenchmen in allegiance.

GLOUCESTER
And so the Earl of Armagnac may do,
Because he is near kinsman unto Charles.

EXETER
46   Beside, his wealth doth warrant a liberal dower,
Where Reignier sooner will receive than give.

SUFFOLK
A dow'r, my lords? Disgrace not so your king
That he should be so abject, base, and poor
To choose for wealth and not for perfect love.
Henry is able to enrich his queen,
And not to seek a queen to make him rich.
So worthless peasants bargain for their wives,
As market men for oxen, sheep, or horse.
Marriage is a matter of more worth
Than to be dealt in by attorneyship.
57   Not whom we will, but whom his grace affects,
Must be companion of his nuptial bed.
And therefore, lords, since he affects her most,
It most of all these reasons bindeth us
In our opinions she should be preferred.
For what is wedlock forcèd but a hell,
An age of discord and continual strife?
Whereas the contrary bringeth bliss
And is a pattern of celestial peace.
Whom should we match with Henry, being a king,
But Margaret, that is daughter to a king?
Her peerless feature, joinèd with her birth,
Approves her fit for none but for a king.
70   Her valiant courage and undaunted spirit
(More than in women commonly is seen)

Will answer our hope in issue of a king.
For Henry, son unto a conqueror,
Is likely to beget more conquerors
If with a lady of so high resolve
As is fair Margaret he be linked in love.
Then yield, my lords, and here conclude with me
That Margaret shall be queen, and none but she.

KING
Whether it be through force of your report,
My noble Lord of Suffolk, or for that   80
My tender youth was never yet attaint   81
With any passion of inflaming love,
I cannot tell; but this I am assured,
I feel such sharp dissension in my breast,
Such fierce alarums both of hope and fear,
As I am sick with working of my thoughts.
Take therefore shipping; post, my lord, to France;   87
Agree to any covenants, and procure
That Lady Margaret do vouchsafe to come
To cross the seas to England and be crowned
King Henry's faithful and anointed queen.
For your expenses and sufficient charge,   92
Among the people gather up a tenth.   93
Be gone, I say; for till you do return
I rest perplexèd with a thousand cares.   95
And you, good uncle, banish all offense.
If you censure me by what you were,   97
Not what you are, I know it will excuse
This sudden execution of my will.
And so conduct me where, from company,   100
I may revolve and ruminate my grief.   *Exit.*

GLOUCESTER
Ay, grief, I fear me, both at first and last.
          Exit Gloucester [with Exeter].

SUFFOLK
Thus Suffolk hath prevailed; and thus he goes,
As did the youthful Paris once to Greece,
With hope to find the like event in love   105
But prosper better than the Trojan did.
Margaret shall now be queen, and rule the king;
But I will rule both her, the king, and realm.   *Exit.*

---

31 *triumph* tournament   32 *lists* tilting area at a tournament   46 *warrant* guarantee   57 *affects* desires   80 *for that* because   81 *attaint* diseased   87 *post* hurry   92 *charge* money to spend   93 *tenth* percentage of value of personal property appropriated as tax   95 *rest* remain   97-98 *censure . . . are* i.e. measure my proposed extravagances by the libertinism of your own youth, not by the gravity of your present age   100 *from company* alone   105 *event* outcome (i.e. Paris' winning of Helen)

THE SECOND AND THIRD PARTS OF
KING HENRY THE SIXTH

INTRODUCTION

During the fifteenth century the English won and lost France, fought a disastrous civil war at home, and brought Henry VII, the first of the Tudor monarchs, to the throne. This period had a special fascination for the Elizabethans. The times were near enough to be influential and well remembered, yet far enough away to be safely idealized. Readily available were extensive historical and legendary accounts devoted wholly or partially to fifteenth-century personages and happenings, among them John Foxe's *Acts and Monuments of Martyrs*, the *Mirror for Magistrates*, Fabyan's, Stowe's, Grafton's, and Holinshed's chronicles, and Edward Hall's *Union of the Two Noble and Illustre Families of Lancaster and York*. Very early in his career, Shakespeare sensed the poetic, dramatic, and patriotic possibilities in these materials and began to shape from them historical dramas designed to edify and delight. He thus became one of the first of the popular dramatists to turn to English history for source material, and it is just possible that he was the first to do so. He may, then, have been the originator, at least as far as the commercial theatre is concerned, of a kind of play that was to figure prominently in the development of the Elizabethan drama.

From Edward Hall particularly, Shakespeare derived not only information about the men, manners, and events of the preceding era but also a theory of history which imposed a unity on diverse and seemingly inexplicable phenomena, for it was Hall (and from him, Holinshed) who expressed most clearly for Renaissance England the doctrine that God's hand is present in human history, that events, while subject to the free will of the participants, are nonetheless overseen ultimately by a Providence through which order will eventually be restored to a world rendered chaotic by sin. In addition, the focus of Shakespeare's history plays was determined by the view taken by Hall and earlier writers of what was historically significant; history for them was chiefly political history, an account of the rise and fall of great men or those who aspired to be great, of statecraft and public affairs, of faction, sedition, rebellion, war and battle – in short, an account of the vicissitudes and triumphs of the state and its prince. In his sources, then, Shakespeare found a great wealth of detail pertaining to character and event preselected according to a well-defined concept of significance, and, underlying all the detail, a philosophy of history which allowed the actions of men to stand in the foreground but which saw behind these actions a logic proceeding from the irrevocable, although sometimes obscure, development of God's plan for England's good.

In the works of these chroniclers Shakespeare saw also an interpretation of fifteenth-century history which has been called the "Tudor myth"; he seems not only to have found this interpretation compatible with his own personal beliefs but also to have recognized in it a strong dramatic potential, particularly suited for didactic purposes. The Tudor myth sprang from the Elizabethans' strong sense of cosmic order, of which political order was a part, and their acute discomfort upon the emergence of symptoms construed to indicate a dislocation of order. The political disasters of the fifteenth century were obviously a kind of disorder, which, according to the concept of sin and retribution, could best be understood as a punishment visited by God upon the people of England for some grave wrong. Logic and a sense of justice required that a sin deserving this punishment be identified, and the chroniclers, looking back to 1399 and 1400, settled upon the deposition and murder of Richard II by Henry Bolingbroke as the crucial event. Richard had been a weak and irresponsible ruler but he had been a king, God's anointed, and the theory was developed that to rebel against a king, however bad a monarch he was, was to violate God's will and thus to commit the cardinal political crime. The troubles that attended Bolingbroke's reign as Henry IV were seen as ample proof of God's displeasure with him and with the realm. During the time of the hero-king Henry V there was a temporary respite, but, as justice remained unsatisfied, the subjects of his son Henry VI had to suffer the lawlessness and confusion that marked the Wars of the Roses and a culminating horror in the tyranny of the monstrous Richard III. But as suffering leads to penitence and finally to forgiveness, God at last relented, and in the person of Henry VII, the founder of the Tudor dynasty, He again blessed England with a strong and able leader who brought peace to the land and instituted an enlightened statecraft which was to lead eventually to the glorious reign of his granddaughter, Elizabeth I. So went the myth. It was fostered by the Tudors because in a general way it strengthened the position of the monarch at the same time that it specifically provided a divine sanction for the somewhat questionable legitimacy of Henry VII's claim to the crown. It was accepted by most Elizabethans because, as they looked at the cycle from the vantage point of their own time, it had a fitness and an appealing optimism. That it did not fully accord with historical data was a matter of no very great concern, for historical truth, while comprehending facts, was not regarded as being precisely correspondent to them but correspondent as well to doctrines acceptable to and significant for the present. This view permitted the chroniclers a certain latitude in their accounts of the past, and it also gave Shakespeare the license necessary for the transformation of history into drama.

Although Shakespeare tightened the narrative fabric somewhat by condensing, altering the chronology of events, and changing the age of some of the characters, the span of time covered by *2* and *3 Henry VI* is so large and so crowded with great affairs that the structure of the plays was almost bound to be loose. Such episodic structure had an authority derived from the medieval mystery cycles, and it had been given fresh sanction by Marlowe's *Tamburlaine*; it permitted the inclusion within a single dramatic framework of highly diversified materials which contributed to the effect of copiousness greatly admired in Elizabethan literature. Yet, evidently in an attempt to achieve some unity and to increase the significance of the episodes, Shakespeare also made use of a theme inherited from the morality play and previously employed in the morality-like interlude *Respublica* and in such courtly historical dramas as *King Johan* and *Gorboduc*. This theme worked allegorically to make the realm itself the center of the dramatic action; the plays, then, are not ultimately about Henry VI or York or Edward or the others but about England itself as it suffers through a retributive civil war immediately caused by the weakness of the king and the corruption of the nobility. They are, in addition, part of a series of essays in definition, as Shakespeare explores the attributes of kingship. What makes a strong and happy state? A good king. What makes a good king? This for Shakespeare seems to have been a complicated question to the many branches of which he gave no easy or final answers.

That it was Shakespeare's intention to convey this complex theme is suggested by certain parts of the action which he developed either entirely on his own or from meagre suggestions in his sources and which he rendered in the stylized, ritualistic manner of the morality play, such as the formal alignment of characters in the opening scene of *2 Henry VI*, the representation of the flatly virtuous Iden (*2 Henry VI*, IV, x), the scene depicting the king on the molehill (*3 Henry VI*, II, v), the abuse of Clifford's corpse by the Yorkists (*3 Henry VI*, II, vi), and Edward's wooing of Lady Grey to the accompaniment of Clarence's and Gloucester's mocking commentary (*3 Henry VI*, III, ii). Dramatic action of this kind serves as an articulation of theme rather than as a rendition of events supposed to be true; it directs our understanding toward the internal significance of the entire action rather than to its depiction alone. But his sense of theatre was too keen for Shakespeare to rest content with a rigidly allegorical representation of a doctrinaire political ideology. He entered imaginatively into the life of many of his characters; moreover, he seized whatever opportunity he could to create effects which would be striking in performance at the same time that they contributed to the general ideas upon which the plays were based. A good example is his handling in *2 Henry VI* of the conflict between Queen Margaret and the Duchess of Gloucester. According to history, Queen Margaret did not arrive in England until several years after the Duchess' fall, but Shakespeare departed from his sources to bring the two together, evidently because he thought that dramatic capital could thus be gained. Not only is the clash between the two ambitious and overbearing women intrinsically interesting, but it helps to define the divided loyalties of the nobility, to create the atmosphere of jealous strife which pervades the court, and to foreshadow the

ruin of the good Duke Humphrey. An equally good example of Shakespeare's manipulation of his sources for dramatic effect is his treatment of Jack Cade, whose thematic importance is discussed more fully below. We may note here, however, that many of the incidents represented as occurring during Cade's Rebellion Shakespeare found in the chronicle accounts of the Peasants' Revolt of 1381 and that he completely ignored certain favorable traits in Cade's character as it was described by Holinshed because they obviously ran counter to his purposes.

In spite of these efforts to achieve coherence, *2* and *3 Henry VI* remain rather sprawling plays which lack a strongly represented central character, either good or evil, about whom incidents within their complicated plots could have been arranged. The king, to be sure, is present throughout, but he, far from being a dynamic figure, is nearly the perfect symbol of inaction. That he has many private virtues is clear, but they express themselves publicly only as impotence, irresolution, and for all his conscientiousness, an extraordinary indifference to the preservation of England's power and dignity among nations. Duke Humphrey, whose fall from power provides the focal point of the first two acts and part of the third of *2 Henry VI*, has many of the public virtues wanting in the king – particularly a practical shrewdness combined with a vigorous and self-sacrificing dedication to an ideal of service to the realm – but his confidence in the power of his own innocence and good faith makes him a rather easy victim of the queen and the wolvish nobles, who see him as an obstacle to their own acquisition of power. As Duke Humphrey descends, York rises. His claim to the throne is better than Henry's, and, as he has courage, patriotism (self-interested though it may be), and force of character, he would undoubtedly make a better ruler, but his ambition is flagrant and his method of satisfying it Machiavellian. He is further guilty in ignoring the principle that all kings, regardless of the manner in which their crowns were obtained, are inviolate. As a part of his program, he has stimulated Jack Cade's Rebellion, the development and suppression of which occupies the fourth act. By the beginning of the fifth, York has an army in the field and, with the support of his sons and the Nevils, declares for the crown by open rebellion, against the opposition of Queen Margaret and the Cliffords. York's victory at the Battle of St Albans ensues, yet, as Henry still lives, *2 Henry VI* ends with York still short of achieving the crown.

The action of *3 Henry VI*, which begins immediately after the Battle of St Albans, is set in motion by Henry's proposal that he be allowed to reign during his lifetime at the price of disinheriting his son in favor of York, a compromise which York swears to respect but which causes Queen Margaret to seek military support from the northern barons. During the first act Margaret's army forces the surrender of the city of York; the act closes with York dead, his head impaled upon the battlements of the city. The Lancastrians are temporarily triumphant, but a Yorkist army under Edward and Richard has yet to be encountered. The second act is devoted chiefly to the Yorkists' defeat of Margaret's powers, with Warwick's help, and Edward's subsequent claiming of the crown; and the third to the capture of King Henry, Edward's proposal to Lady Grey and the consequent destruction of a possible French alliance, Margaret's appeal to Lewis of France for aid, and Warwick's shift of allegiance to the

Lancastrian cause. In the long and busy fourth act, Edward is overthrown and then regains his power. The fifth is given over to the campaign, replete with alarms and excursions, which culminates in the final Yorkist victory at Tewkesbury and the murder of the Prince of Wales and King Henry. At the end of the play it would seem that the Yorkist cause should be won and that King Edward should be secure upon the throne, but by this time a new contender has appeared in Richard of Gloucester, who vows to wade to majesty through the blood of his brothers and nephews. The plays, then, are of epic scope, and the tentative emergence of York as the central figure of the Second Part and of Edward as the central figure of the Third is obstructed by a shifting emphasis upon a bewildering number of minor characters who strut and fret for a scene or two, sell one another out, and then die their gory deaths at the base of Fortune's relentless wheel. The implication of the historical accounts becomes, in fact, something of an embarrassment to the plays themselves; the tragedy of the times was that no one man was both strong enough and good enough to lead the country, the king being deficient in public virtue and the house of York in private. As yet not even such a villain as Richard of Gloucester was later to prove had come forward with sufficient force to be dominant. Thus no well-defined protagonist was at hand, and the allegorical figure of England was too vague to serve as an agent of dramatic concentration.

Certain episodes, however, are brilliantly rendered and skillfully fitted into the framework of the whole drama. For example, Shakespeare apparently wanted to show that corruption at the top of the state was certain to penetrate to the bottom, that if the nobles were so criminally foolish as to abandon the ideal of loyalty to the king and commonwealth to serve themselves it was only to be expected that the people would behave in a similar way. His vehicle for conveying this important aspect of his theme was the sinister farce of Cade's Rebellion, which not only shows political chaos manifesting itself on a lower social level than that occupied by the nobles but also, in pointing toward the Wars of the Roses, characterizes them as a kind of universal folly that would be ridiculous were its consequences not so grave. In the world of Cade and his followers, ordinary values are completely inverted, manifest impossibility replaces fact, and right reason becomes a series of puns, defective syllogisms, and contradictions in terms. In Cade's England all is in order when most out of order – seven halfpenny loaves will be sold for a penny, the three-hooped pot will have ten hoops, the pissing conduit will run nothing but claret for a year; it is a capital crime to read and write English and high treason to speak Latin. The massive confusion of such a world is shown not only by the brutality of Cade's actions but also by the havoc wrought upon the arts of language when the rebels speak. The dialogue succeeds in being very funny while simultaneously serving sternly serious purposes, among them the reflection of such cruelty as Clifford's murder of Rutland and such false logic as Warwick's legalistic argument in support of York's claim to the throne (2 Henry VI, II, ii, 53–62).

What emerges most strongly from such scenes is a powerful irony. The characters in the plays are living, all unaware, within a web of significance which connects individual actions. The law of cause and effect is always operating, but the individual, having lost his hold upon

moral realities because of pride, selfishness, or weakness, cannot see beyond the moment. With morality gone, the old values which make for goodness in men and stability in the state become perverted. The keeping of oaths becomes a matter of expediency. Family loyalty breeds only revenge, which breeds only counter-revenge. Caught up in circumstances which are very imperfectly understood, fathers kill their sons and sons their fathers. Desire for the sweet fruition of an earthly crown leads only to a molehill like that upon which an actual king is to sit and wish that he were anything but a king. Justice becomes confused with self-interest, piety becomes cowardice, and good reasons replace right reason. The ultimate origin of this anarchy lies behind, in history; its ultimate outcome lies ahead, and no character can perceive it except dimly in very occasional moments of foreboding or prophesy. Within the plays certain incidents provide ironical commentaries on others (as, for instance, the mock-heroic combat of the drunken Horner and the frightened Peter casts an ironic light on the hollow chivalry of the nobles), but throughout both our perspective is modified by the discrepancy between our historical knowledge of the outcome of it all and the characters' more limited vision.

It is no doubt impossible to read or to see 2 and 3 Henry VI without thinking of the Shakespeare that was to come, for in them many things are attempted that were later to be better done. Their language is sometimes stilted and inflexible, adorned with elaborate conceits which are more ornamental than integral; their psychology does not often inquire very far beyond the self-love to which Renaissance moralists conventionally attributed man's corruption. It is a mistake, however, to underrate them. When they were written, there was only one other playwright, Marlowe, who just might have done the job more expertly, and there is no real assurance that he could have managed so well. The mature Shakespeare is noted, among many other things, for unsurpassed skill in dramatic design, for language so pregnant and beautiful that one can only wonder at it, for characters so admirably conceived that they never release their holds upon the imagination, and for as deep an insight into the mystery of things as any writer ever achieved. All these virtues are present, at least in embryonic form, in 2 and 3 Henry VI.

University of Wisconsin ROBERT K. TURNER, JR
Milwaukee

Duke University GEORGE WALTON WILLIAMS

NOTE ON THE TEXTS

The Second and Third Parts of King Henry the Sixth were printed in the folio of 1623, evidently from a manuscript in Shakespeare's hand except for a few brief passages, and the folio text has been closely followed in the present edition. The version of Part Two printed in quarto in 1594 and the version of Part Three printed in octavo in 1595 are discussed in Appendix B, with an explanation of the use made of them in this edition. A list of all substantive departures from the folio text is included in this Appendix. Neither the quarto–octavo nor the folio versions are divided into acts and scenes. The act–scene division here supplied marginally is that of earlier editors. (The present editors have collaborated closely on all portions of this edition, with Professor Turner drafting the Introduction, Professor Williams collating the text, and both writing the glosses.)

THE SECOND PART OF
KING HENRY THE SIXTH

*

I, i   *Flourish of trumpets, then hautboys. Enter King,*
        Duke Humphrey [of Gloucester], Salisbury,
        Warwick, and [Cardinal] Beaufort [of Winchester],
        on the one side ; the Queen, Suffolk, York,
        Somerset, and Buckingham on the other.

SUFFOLK
As by your high imperial majesty
I had in charge at my depart for France,
3   As procurator to your excellence,
To marry Princess Margaret for your grace,
So, in the famous ancient city Tours,
6   In presence of the Kings of France and Sicil,
The Dukes of Orleans, Calaber, Bretagne, and Alençon,
Seven earls, twelve barons, and twenty reverend bishops,
I have performed my task and was espoused ;
And humbly now upon my bended knee
In sight of England and her lordly peers
Deliver up my title in the queen
To your most gracious hands, that are the substance
Of that great shadow I did represent :
The happiest gift that ever marquess gave,
The fairest queen that ever king received.

KING
Suffolk, arise. Welcome, Queen Margaret.
18 I can express no kinder sign of love

Than this kind kiss. O Lord, that lends me life,
Lend me a heart replete with thankfulness.
For thou hast given me in this beauteous face
A world of earthly blessings to my soul,
If sympathy of love unite our thoughts.

QUEEN
Great King of England and my gracious lord,
The mutual conference that my mind hath had,   25
By day, by night, waking and in my dreams,
In courtly company or at my beads,
With you, mine alderliefest sovereign,   28
Makes me the bolder to salute my king   29
With ruder terms, such as my wit affords
And over-joy of heart doth minister.   31

KING
Her sight did ravish, but her grace in speech,
Her words yclad with wisdom's majesty,   33
Makes me from wond'ring fall to weeping joys,
Such is the fullness of my heart's content.
Lords, with one cheerful voice welcome my love.

I, i The royal palace in London s.d. *Flourish* fanfare, more elaborate than
a sennet (see I, iii, 98 s.d., n.) **3** *procurator* legal agent, proxy **6** *Sicil* i.e.
Sicily ; Queen Margaret's father, Reignier **18–19** *kinder . . . kind* more
natural . . . loving **25** *mutual conference* intimate intercourse **28** *alder-*
liefest most dear **29** *salute* greet **31** *minister* suggest **33** *yclad* clad

ALL *(kneel)*
Long live Queen Margaret, England's happiness!

QUEEN
We thank you all.
    Flourish.

SUFFOLK
My Lord Protector, so it please your grace,
Here are the articles of contracted peace
Between our sovereign and the French king Charles,
For eighteen months concluded by consent.

43 GLOUCESTER *(reads)* 'Inprimis, It is agreed between the
French king Charles and William de la Pole, Marquess
of Suffolk, ambassador for Henry King of England, that
the said Henry shall espouse the Lady Margaret,
daughter unto Reignier King of Naples, Sicilia, and
Jerusalem, and crown her Queen of England ere the
thirtieth of May next ensuing.
'*Item*, that the duchy of Anjou and the county of Maine
shall be released and delivered to the king her father' –
    [Gloucester lets it fall.]

KING
Uncle, how now?

GLOUCESTER   Pardon me, gracious lord,
Some sudden qualm hath struck me at the heart,
And dimmed mine eyes that I can read no further.

KING
55 Uncle of Winchester, I pray read on.

CARDINAL *[reads]* '*Item*, It is further agreed between
them that the duchies of Anjou and Maine shall be
released and delivered over to the king her father, and
she sent over of the King of England's own proper cost
and charges, without having any dowry.'

KING
They please us well. Lord marquess, kneel down.
We here create thee the first Duke of Suffolk
And girt thee with the sword. Cousin of York,
We here discharge your grace from being regent
I' th' parts of France till term of eighteen months
Be full expired. Thanks, uncle Winchester,
Gloucester, York, Buckingham, Somerset,
Salisbury, and Warwick.
We thank you all for this great favor done
70 In entertainment to my princely queen.
Come, let us in, and with all speed provide
To see her coronation be performed.
    Exit King, [with] Queen, and Suffolk.
    Manet [Gloucester, staying all] the rest.

GLOUCESTER
Brave peers of England, pillars of the state,
To you Duke Humphrey must unload his grief –
Your grief, the common grief of all the land.
76 What? Did my brother Henry spend his youth,
His valor, coin, and people in the wars?
78 Did he so often lodge in open field,

In winter's cold and summer's parching heat,
To conquer France, his true inheritance?   80
And did my brother Bedford toil his wits
To keep by policy what Henry got?
Have you yourselves, Somerset, Buckingham,
Brave York, Salisbury, and victorious Warwick,
Received deep scars in France and Normandy?
Or hath mine uncle Beaufort and myself,
With all the learned council of the realm,
Studied so long, sat in the Council House
Early and late, debating to and fro
How France and Frenchmen might be kept in awe,   90
And hath his highness in his infancy
Crownèd in Paris in despite of foes?
And shall these labors and these honors die?
Shall Henry's conquest, Bedford's vigilance,
Your deeds of war, and all our counsel die?
O peers of England, shameful is this league.
Fatal this marriage, cancelling your fame,
Blotting your names from books of memory.
Rasing the characters of your renown,   99
Defacing monuments of conquered France,   100
Undoing all as all had never been!

CARDINAL
Nephew, what means this passionate discourse,
This peroration with such circumstance?   103
For France, 'tis ours; and we will keep it still.

GLOUCESTER
Ay, uncle, we will keep it if we can,
But now it is impossible we should.
Suffolk, the new-made duke that rules the roast,   107
Hath given the duchy of Anjou and Maine
Unto the poor King Reignier, whose large style   109
Agrees not with the leanness of his purse.

SALISBURY
Now, by the death of Him that died for all,
These counties were the keys of Normandy.
But wherefore weeps Warwick, my valiant son?

WARWICK
For grief that they are past recovery;
For were there hope to conquer them again,
My sword should shed hot blood, mine eyes no tears.
Anjou and Maine? Myself did win them both;
Those provinces these arms of mine did conquer;
And are the cities that I got with wounds
Delivered up again with peaceful words?
Mort Dieu!   121

YORK
For Suffolk's duke, may he be suffocate,
That dims the honor of this warlike isle.
France should have torn and rent my very heart
Before I would have yielded to this league.
I never read but England's kings have had
Large sums of gold and dowries with their wives,
And our King Henry gives away his own
To match with her that brings no vantages.

GLOUCESTER
A proper jest, and never heard before,
That Suffolk should demand a whole fifteenth   131
For costs and charges in transporting her.
She should have stayed in France, and starved in France,
Before –

CARDINAL
My Lord of Gloucester, now ye grow too hot.

---

43 *Inprimis* imprimis, first (marks the first point agreed upon in a contract; subsequent points are signalled by *item*, 'similarly,' as at l. 50) 55 *Uncle* i.e. great-uncle (the cardinal was the half-brother of Henry VI's grandfather, Henry IV) 76 *brother Henry* i.e. Henry V 78 *lodge* lie 80 *true inheritance* (through Henry V's ancestor Isabella of France, wife of Edward II of England; see *Henry V*, I, i, 87–89) 90 *awe* reverential obedience 99 *Rasing . . . of* erasing the letters which record 100 *monuments* (1) stones, (2) documents (preservers of memory) 103 *circumstance* detail 107 *rules the roast* domineers 109 *large style* pompous title 121 *Mort Dieu* (an oath; literally, by God's death) 131 *fifteenth* i.e. the proceeds from a tax of this amount on subjects' real property

It was the pleasure of my lord the king.

GLOUCESTER

My Lord of Winchester, I know your mind.
'Tis not my speeches that you do mislike,
But 'tis my presence that doth trouble ye.
Rancor will out. Proud prelate, in thy face
I see thy fury. If I longer stay,
We shall begin our ancient bickerings.
143   Lordings, farewell; and say, when I am gone,
I prophesied, France will be lost ere long.

Exit Humphrey [Duke of Gloucester].

CARDINAL

So, there goes our Protector in a rage.
'Tis known to you he is mine enemy;
Nay more, an enemy unto you all,
And no great friend, I fear me, to the king.
149   Consider, lords, he is the next of blood
And heir apparent to the English crown.
Had Henry got an empire by his marriage
And all the wealthy kingdoms of the west,
There's reason he should be displeased at it.
Look to it, lords. Let not his smoothing words
Bewitch your hearts; be wise and circumspect.
What though the common people favor him,
Calling him 'Humphrey, the good Duke of Gloucester,'
Clapping their hands and crying with loud voice
'Jesu maintain your royal Excellence!'
With 'God preserve the good Duke Humphrey!'
161   I fear me, lords, for all this flattering gloss,
He will be found a dangerous Protector.

BUCKINGHAM

Why should he then protect our sovereign,
He being of age to govern of himself?
Cousin of Somerset, join you with me,
And all together with the Duke of Suffolk,
167   We'll quickly hoise Duke Humphrey from his seat.

CARDINAL

168   This weighty business will not brook delay;
169   I'll to the Duke of Suffolk presently.   *Exit Cardinal.*

SOMERSET

Cousin of Buckingham, though Humphrey's pride
And greatness of his place be grief to us,
Yet let us watch the haughty cardinal;
His insolence is more intolerable
Than all the princes' in the land beside.
If Gloucester be displaced, he'll be Protector.

BUCKINGHAM

Or thou or I, Somerset, will be Protector
Despite Duke Humphrey or the cardinal.

Exeunt Buckingham and Somerset.

SALISBURY

178   Pride went before, ambition follows him.
While these do labor for their own preferment,
Behooves it us to labor for the realm.
I never saw but Humphrey Duke of Gloucester
Did bear him like a noble gentleman.
Oft have I seen the haughty cardinal,
More like a soldier than a man o' th' church,
As stout and proud as he were lord of all,
Swear like a ruffian and demean himself
Unlike the ruler of a commonweal.
Warwick my son, the comfort of my age,
189   Thy deeds, thy plainness, and thy housekeeping
Hath won the greatest favor of the commons,

Excepting none but good Duke Humphrey.
And, brother York, thy acts in Ireland   192
In bringing them to civil discipline,
Thy late exploits done in the heart of France
When thou wert regent for our sovereign,
Have made thee feared and honored of the people.
Join we together for the public good,
In what we can to bridle and suppress
The pride of Suffolk and the cardinal
With Somerset's and Buckingham's ambition;
And, as we may, cherish Duke Humphrey's deeds
While they do tend the profit of the land.

WARWICK

So God help Warwick, as he loves the land
And common profit of his country.

YORK

And so says York – *[aside]* for he hath greatest cause.

SALISBURY

Then let's make haste away, and look unto the main.   206

WARWICK

Unto the main? O father, Maine is lost.
That Maine which by main force Warwick did win,   208
And would have kept so long as breath did last.
Main chance, father, you meant, but I meant Maine,
Which I will win from France or else be slain.

Exeunt Warwick and Salisbury. Manet York.

YORK

Anjou and Maine are given to the French,
Paris is lost; the state of Normandy
Stands on a tickle point now they are gone.   214
Suffolk concluded on the articles,
The peers agreed, and Henry was well pleased
To change two dukedoms for a duke's fair daughter.
I cannot blame them all. What is't to them?
'Tis thine they give away, and not their own.   219
Pirates may make cheap pennyworths of their pillage,   220
And purchase friends, and give to courtesans,
Still revelling like lords till all be gone,   222
While as the silly owner of the goods   223
Weeps over them and wrings his hapless hands   224
And shakes his head and trembling stands aloof
While all is shared and all is borne away,
Ready to starve and dare not touch his own.
So York must sit and fret and bite his tongue   228
While his own lands are bargained for and sold.
Methinks the realms of England, France, and Ireland
Bear that proportion to my flesh and blood
As did the fatal brand Althaea burnt   232
Unto the prince's heart of Calydon.
Anjou and Maine both given unto the French?
Cold news for me! for I had hope of France,

143 *Lordings* my lords   149 *next of blood* (since Henry VI has no child as yet, the crown would pass, in the event of his death, to Gloucester, his uncle and nearest blood relative)   161 *flattering gloss* specious praise 167 *hoise* hoist   168 *brook* endure   169 *presently* immediately   178 *Pride . . . ambition* i.e. the cardinal . . . Buckingham and Somerset   189 *housekeeping* hospitality, management of personal affairs   192 *brother* i.e. brother-in-law   206 *main* most important stake (a term in hazard, a dice game, to which Warwick alludes further at l. 210)   208 *main* overpowering 214 *tickle* unstable   219 *thine* (York addresses himself in the second person)   220 *pennyworths* bargains   222 *Still* continually   223 *silly* helpless   224 *hapless* unlucky   228 *bite his tongue* hold his tongue   232 *fatal brand* (the prince of Calydon, Meleager, died when his mother, Althaea, in a rage burned a piece of wood [brand] upon which the Fates had said his life depended)

Even as I have of fertile England's soil.
A day will come when York shall claim his own ;
238 And therefore I will take the Nevils' parts,
And make a show of love to proud Duke Humphrey,
And when I spy advantage, claim the crown,
For that's the golden mark I seek to hit.
242 Nor shall proud Lancaster usurp my right,
Nor hold the sceptre in his childish fist,
Nor wear the diadem upon his head,
Whose churchlike humors fits not for a crown.
Then, York, be still awhile, till time do serve.
Watch thou and wake when others be asleep,
To pry into the secrets of the state,
Till Henry, surfeiting in joys of love,
With his new bride and England's dear-bought queen,
251 And Humphrey with the peers be fallen at jars,
252 Then will I raise aloft the milk-white rose,
With whose sweet smell the air shall be perfumed,
And in my standard bear the arms of York
To grapple with the house of Lancaster ;
256 And force perforce I'll make him yield the crown
Whose bookish rule hath pulled fair England down.
Exit York.

*

I, ii   *Enter Duke Humphrey [of Gloucester] and his wife*
     Eleanor.

ELEANOR
Why droops my lord like over-ripened corn
2 Hanging the head at Ceres' plenteous load ?
Why doth the great Duke Humphrey knit his brows,
As frowning at the favors of the world ?
Why are thine eyes fixed to the sullen earth,
Gazing on that which seems to dim thy sight ?
What seest thou there ? King Henry's diadem,
8 Enchased with all the honors of the world ?
9 If so, gaze on and grovel on thy face
Until thy head be circled with the same.
Put forth thy hand, reach at the glorious gold.
What, is't too short ? I'll lengthen it with mine ;
And having both together heaved it up,
We'll both together lift our heads to heaven
And never more abase our sight so low
As to vouchsafe one glance unto the ground.

GLOUCESTER
O Nell, sweet Nell, if thou dost love thy lord,
18 Banish the canker of ambitious thoughts.
And may that thought, when I imagine ill
Against my king and nephew, virtuous Henry,
Be my last breathing in this mortal world.
My troublous dreams this night doth make me sad.

ELEANOR
What dreamed my lord ? Tell me, and I'll requite it
With sweet rehearsal of my morning's dream.

GLOUCESTER
Methought this staff, mine office-badge in court,

Was broke in twain, by whom I have forgot,
But as I think, it was by th' cardinal ;
And on the pieces of the broken wand
Were placed the heads of Edmund Duke of Somerset
And William de la Pole, first Duke of Suffolk.
This was my dream ; what it doth bode, God knows.

ELEANOR
Tut, this was nothing but an argument   32
That he that breaks a stick of Gloucester's grove
Shall lose his head for his presumption.
But list to me, my Humphrey, my sweet duke.
Methought I sat in seat of majesty
In the cathedral church of Westminster ;
And in that chair where kings and queens were crowned,
Where Henry and Dame Margaret kneeled to me
And on my head did set the diadem –

GLOUCESTER
Nay, Eleanor, then must I chide outright.
Presumptuous dame, ill-nurtured Eleanor,   42
Art thou not second woman in the realm,
And the Protector's wife, beloved of him ?
Hast thou not worldly pleasure at command
Above the reach or compass of thy thought ?
And wilt thou still be hammering treachery   47
To tumble down thy husband and thyself
From top of honor to disgrace's feet ?
Away from me, and let me hear no more.

ELEANOR
What, what, my lord ? Are you so choleric
With Eleanor for telling but her dream ?
Next time I'll keep my dreams unto myself
And not be checked.   54

GLOUCESTER
Nay, be not angry. I am pleased again.
Enter Messenger.

MESSENGER
My Lord Protector, 'tis his highness' pleasure
You do prepare to ride unto Saint Albans,
Where as the king and queen do mean to hawk.

GLOUCESTER
I go. Come, Nell, thou wilt ride with us ?

ELEANOR
Yes, my good lord, I'll follow presently.
Exit Humphrey [with Messenger].
Follow I must ; I cannot go before
While Gloucester bears this base and humble mind.
Were I a man, a duke, and next of blood,
I would remove these tedious stumbling blocks
And smooth my way upon their headless necks ;
And being a woman, I will not be slack
To play my part in Fortune's pageant.
Where are you there ? Sir John ! Nay, fear not, man.   68
We are alone ; here's none but thee, and I.
Enter Hume.

HUME
Jesus preserve your royal majesty.

ELEANOR
What say'st thou ? Majesty ? I am but grace.   71

HUME
But by the grace of God and Hume's advice
Your grace's title shall be multiplied.

ELEANOR
What say'st thou, man ? Hast thou as yet conferred
With Margery Jourdain, the cunning witch,

---

238 *Nevils'* i.e. Salisbury's and Warwick's   242 *Lancaster* (Henry VI was also Duke of Lancaster)   251 *be . . . jars* quarrel   252 *milk-white rose* (the symbol of the house of York)   256 *force perforce* by violent force
I, ii The Duke of Gloucester's house   2 *Ceres* goddess of agriculture   8 *Enchased* adorned   9 *grovel . . . face* i.e. in adoration   18 *canker* ulcer   32 *argument* proof   42 *ill-nurtured* ill-bred   47 *hammering* hammering out, devising   54 *checked* rebuked   68 *Sir* (the title of respect given priests as well as knights)   71 *grace* (only monarchs could be addressed as 'majesty' ; 'grace' was the proper appellation for a duke or duchess)

With Roger Bolingbroke, the conjurer?
And will they undertake to do me good?

HUME
This they have promisèd, to show your highness
A spirit raised from depth of under ground
That shall make answer to such questions
As by your grace shall be propounded him.

ELEANOR
It is enough. I'll think upon the questions.
When from Saint Albans we do make return
We'll see these things effected to the full.
Here, Hume, take this reward; make merry, man,
With thy confederates in this weighty cause.
                                    Exit Eleanor.

HUME
Hume must make merry with the duchess' gold.
88   Marry and shall! But how now, Sir John Hume?
Seal up your lips and give no words but mum;
The business asketh silent secrecy.
Dame Eleanor gives gold to bring the witch;
Gold cannot come amiss, were she a devil.
Yet have I gold flies from another coast:
I dare not say, from the rich cardinal
And from the great and new-made Duke of Suffolk;
Yet I do find it so; for, to be plain,
97   They (knowing Dame Eleanor's aspiring humor)
Have hirèd me to undermine the duchess
99   And buzz these conjurations in her brain.
100 They say, 'A crafty knave does need no broker';
Yet am I Suffolk and the cardinal's broker.
Hume, if you take not heed, you shall go near
To call them both a pair of crafty knaves.
Well, so it stands; and thus, I fear, at last
105 Hume's knavery will be the duchess' wrack
106 And her attainture will be Humphrey's fall.
107 Sort how it will, I shall have gold for all.   *Exit.*

*

I, iii   *Enter three or four Petitioners, the Armorer's Man
          [Peter] being one.*
1. PETITIONER My masters, let's stand close. My Lord
Protector will come this way by and by, and then we
3   may deliver our supplications in the quill.
2. PETITIONER Marry, the Lord protect him, for he's a
good man, Jesu bless him!
          Enter Suffolk and Queen.
1. PETITIONER Here 'a comes, methinks, and the queen
with him. I'll be the first, sure.
2. PETITIONER Come back, fool. This is the Duke of
Suffolk and not my Lord Protector.
SUFFOLK How now, fellow? Wouldst anything with me?
1. PETITIONER I pray, my lord, pardon me. I took ye
for my Lord Protector.
QUEEN For my Lord Protector? Are your supplications
to his lordship? Let me see them. What is thine?
1. PETITIONER Mine is, an't please your grace, against
John Goodman, my Lord Cardinal's man, for keeping
my house, and lands, and wife and all, from me.
SUFFOLK Thy wife too? That's some wrong indeed.
What's yours? What's here? *[reads]* 'Against the Duke
20   of Suffolk, for enclosing the commons of Melford.'
How now, sir knave?

2. PETITIONER Alas, sir, I am but a poor petitioner of
our whole township.
PETER *[presents his petition]* Against my master, Thomas
Horner, for saying that the Duke of York was rightful
heir to the crown.
QUEEN What say'st thou? Did the Duke of York say he
was rightful heir to the crown?
PETER That my master was? No, forsooth! My master
said that he was, and that the king was an usurper.
SUFFOLK Who is there?
          Enter Servant.
Take this fellow in and send for his master with a pur- 32
suivant presently. We'll hear more of your matter before
the king.   *Exit [Servant with Peter].*
QUEEN
And as for you that love to be protected
Under the wings of our Protector's grace,
Begin your suits anew and sue to him.
          Tear the supplication.
Away, base cullions! Suffolk, let them go.   38
ALL Come, let's be gone.   *Exeunt.*
QUEEN
My Lord of Suffolk, say, is this the guise,   40
Is this the fashions in the court of England?
Is this the government of Britain's isle,
And this the royalty of Albion's king?   43
What, shall King Henry be a pupil still,
Under the surly Gloucester's governance?
Am I a queen in title and in style
And must be made a subject to a duke?
I tell thee, Pole, when in the city Tours
Thou ran'st a-tilt in honor of my love   49
And stol'st away the ladies' hearts of France,
I thought King Henry had resembled thee
In courage, courtship, and proportion;   52
But all his mind is bent to holiness,
To number Ave-Maries on his beads;   54
His champions are the prophets and apostles,   55
His weapons holy saws of sacred writ;   56
His study is his tiltyard, and his loves
Are brazen images of canonized saints.
I would the college of the cardinals   59
Would choose him pope and carry him to Rome
And set the triple crown upon his head.   61
That were a state fit for his holiness.
SUFFOLK
Madam, be patient. As I was cause
Your highness came to England, so will I
In England work your grace's full content.
QUEEN
Beside the haughty Protector, have we Beaufort
The imperious churchman, Somerset, Buckingham,
And grumbling York; and not the least of these

88 *Marry and shall* indeed he will   97 *humor* inclination   99 *buzz* whisper
100 *broker* agent   105 *wrack* ruin   106 *attainture* conviction   107 *Sort ...
will* no matter how it turns out
I, iii The palace   3 *in the quill* (1) in a body, (2) illiterate error for 'in
sequel' (?)   20 *enclosing the commons* fencing public ground for private
use   32 *pursuivant* officer   38 *cullions* rascals, scum   40 *guise* manner
43 *Albion's* England's   49 *ran'st a-tilt* jousted   52 *courtship* courtliness;
proportion physique   54 *Ave-Maries* Hail Maries (prayers to the Blessed
Virgin)   55 *champions* defenders (with reference to valiant fighting men
who defend the honor and title of the king)   56 *saws* sayings   59 *college ...
cardinals* the pope's council   61 *triple crown* papal crown

But can do more in England than the king.

SUFFOLK
70 And he of these that can do most of all
Cannot do more in England than the Nevils;
Salisbury and Warwick are no simple peers.

QUEEN
Not all these lords do vex me half so much
As that proud dame, the Lord Protector's wife.
She sweeps it through the court with troops of ladies,
More like an empress than Duke Humphrey's wife.
Strangers in court do take her for the queen.
She bears a duke's revenues on her back,
And in her heart she scorns our poverty.
Shall I not live to be avenged on her?
81 Contemptuous base-born callet as she is,
She vaunted 'mongst her minions t' other day,
The very train of her worst wearing gown
Was better worth than all my father's lands
Till Suffolk gave two dukedoms for his daughter.

SUFFOLK
86 Madam, myself have limed a bush for her,
87 And placed a choir of such enticing birds
And she will light to listen to the lays
That never mount to trouble you again.
So let her rest. And, madam, list to me,
For I am bold to counsel you in this:
Although we fancy not the cardinal,
Yet must we join with him and with the lords
Till we have brought Duke Humphrey in disgrace.
As for the Duke of York, this late complaint
Will make but little for his benefit.
So one by one we'll weed them all at last.
98 And you yourself shall steer the happy helm.
Sound a sennet. Enter the King, [York and
Somerset on both sides of the King, whispering with
him,] Duke Humphrey [of Gloucester], Cardinal
[Beaufort], Buckingham, Salisbury, Warwick,
and [Eleanor] the Duchess [of Gloucester].

KING
For my part, noble lords, I care not which:
Or Somerset or York, all's one to me.

YORK
If York have ill demeaned himself in France,
102 Then let him be denayed the regentship.

SOMERSET
If Somerset be unworthy of the place,
Let York be regent; I will yield to him.

WARWICK
Whether your grace be worthy, yea or no,
Dispute not that. York is the worthier.

CARDINAL
Ambitious Warwick, let thy betters speak!

WARWICK
The cardinal's not my better in the field.

BUCKINGHAM
All in this presence are thy betters, Warwick.

WARWICK
Warwick may live to be the best of all.

SALISBURY
Peace, son! and show some reason, Buckingham,
Why Somerset should be preferred in this.

QUEEN
Because the king forsooth will have it so.

GLOUCESTER
Madam, the king is old enough himself
To give his censure. These are no women's matters.   115

QUEEN
If he be old enough, what needs your grace
To be Protector of his excellence?

GLOUCESTER
Madam, I am Protector of the realm,
And at his pleasure will resign my place.

SUFFOLK
Resign it then and leave thine insolence.
Since thou wert king (as who is king but thou?)
The commonwealth hath daily run to wrack,
The Dauphin hath prevailed beyond the seas,   123
And all the peers and nobles of the realm
Have been as bondmen to thy sovereignty.

CARDINAL
The commons hast thou racked; the clergy's bags   126
Are lank and lean with thy extortions.

SOMERSET
Thy sumptuous buildings and thy wife's attire   128
Have cost a mass of public treasury.

BUCKINGHAM
Thy cruelty in execution
Upon offenders hath exceeded law,
And left thee to the mercy of the law.

QUEEN
Thy sale of offices and towns in France –
If they were known, as the suspect is great –   134
Would make thee quickly hop without thy head.
Exit Humphrey.
[The Queen drops her fan.]
Give me my fan. What, minion, can ye not?
She gives the Duchess a box on the ear.
I cry you mercy, madam. Was it you?   137

ELEANOR
Was't I? Yea, I it was, proud Frenchwoman.
Could I come near your beauty with my nails,
I would set my ten commandments in your face.   140

KING
Sweet aunt, be quiet. 'Twas against her will.   141

ELEANOR
Against her will, good king? Look to't in time.
She'll hamper thee and dandle thee like a baby.   143
Though in this place most master wear no breeches,   144
She shall not strike Dame Eleanor unrevenged.
Exit Eleanor.

BUCKINGHAM
Lord Cardinal, I will follow Eleanor,
And listen after Humphrey, how he proceeds.
She's tickled now; her fume needs no spurs,   148
She'll gallop far enough to her destruction.
Exit Buckingham.

---

81 *callet* strumpet   86 *limed a bush* put lime on twigs of a bush to catch birds, i.e. set a trap   87 *enticing birds* i.e. decoys   98 s.d. *sennet* trumpet call signalling a ceremonial entrance or exit   102 *denayed* denied   115 *censure* decision   123 *Dauphin* eldest son of the King of France; here, Charles VII (so called by the English because they consider Henry VI the true King of France)   126 *racked* taxed exorbitantly (literally, tortured on the rack)   128 *sumptuous buildings* (Somerset refers specifically to Greenwich Palace)   137 *cry you mercy* beg your pardon   140 *ten commandments* i.e. fingernails   141 *against her will* i.e. an accident   143 *hamper* (1) obstruct, (2) cradle   144 *most master* the greatest master (i.e. the queen, who wears no breeches)   148 *tickled* irritated; *fume* rage

Enter [Duke] Humphrey.

GLOUCESTER
Now, lords, my choler being overblown
With walking once about the quadrangle,
I come to talk of commonwealth affairs.
As for your spiteful false objections,
Prove them, and I lie open to the law;
But God in mercy so deal with my soul
As I in duty love my king and country.
But to the matter that we have in hand:
158 I say, my sovereign, York is meetest man
To be your regent in the realm of France.

SUFFOLK
Before we make election, give me leave
To show some reason, of no little force,
That York is most unmeet of any man.

YORK
I'll tell thee, Suffolk, why I am unmeet:
First, for I cannot flatter thee in pride;
Next, if I be appointed for the place,
My Lord of Somerset will keep me here
167 Without discharge, money, or furniture
Till France be won into the Dauphin's hands.
169 Last time I danced attendance on his will
Till Paris was besieged, famished, and lost.

WARWICK
171 That can I witness; and a fouler fact
Did never traitor in the land commit.

SUFFOLK
Peace, headstrong Warwick!

WARWICK
Image of pride, why should I hold my peace?
*Enter [Horner the] Armorer, and his Man
[Peter, guarded].*

SUFFOLK
Because here is a man accused of treason.
Pray God the Duke of York excuse himself.

YORK
Doth any one accuse York for a traitor?

KING
What mean'st thou, Suffolk? Tell me, what are these?

SUFFOLK
Please it your majesty, this is the man
That doth accuse his master of high treason.
His words were these: that Richard Duke of York
Was rightful heir unto the English crown
And that your majesty was an usurper.

KING
Say, man, were these thy words?

ARMORER An't shall please your majesty, I never said
nor thought any such matter. God is my witness, I am
falsely accused by the villain.

188 PETER By these ten bones, my lords, he did speak them
to me in the garret one night, as we were scouring my
Lord of York's armor.

YORK
191 Base dunghill villain and mechanical,
I'll have thy head for this thy traitor's speech.
I do beseech your royal majesty,
Let him have all the rigor of the law.

ARMORER Alas, my lord, hang me if ever I spake the
words! My accuser is my prentice; and when I did correct him for his fault the other day, he did vow upon his
knees he would be even with me. I have good witness of

this. Therefore I beseech your majesty, do not cast
away an honest man for a villain's accusation.

KING
Uncle, what shall we say to this in law?

GLOUCESTER
This doom, my lord, if I may judge: 202
Let Somerset be regent o'er the French,
Because in York this breeds suspicion;
And let these have a day appointed them
For single combat in convenient place,
For he hath witness of his servant's malice.
This is the law, and this Duke Humphrey's doom.

SOMERSET
I humbly thank your royal majesty.

ARMORER
And I accept the combat willingly.

PETER Alas, my lord, I cannot fight; for God's sake pity
my case. The spite of man prevaileth against me. O
Lord have mercy upon me; I shall never be able to fight
a blow. O Lord, my heart!

GLOUCESTER
Sirrah, or you must fight or else be hanged.

KING
Away with them to prison! and the day
Of combat shall be the last of the next month.
Come, Somerset, we'll see thee sent away.
Flourish. Exeunt.

*

Enter [Margery Jourdain] the Witch, the two Priests I, iv
[Hume and Southwell], and Bolingbroke.

HUME Come, my masters. The duchess, I tell you, expects performance of your promises.

BOLINGBROKE Master Hume, we are therefore provided. Will her ladyship behold and hear our exorcisms? 4

HUME Ay, what else? Fear you not her courage.

BOLINGBROKE I have heard her reported to be a woman
of an invincible spirit. But it shall be convenient, Master
Hume, that you be by her aloft while we be busy below;
and so I pray you go in God's name and leave us. (*Exit
Hume.*) Mother Jourdain, be you prostrate and grovel
on the earth. John Southwell, read you, and let us to our
work.
Enter [Duchess] Eleanor aloft [, followed by Hume].

ELEANOR Well said, my masters, and welcome all. To
this gear, the sooner the better. 13

BOLINGBROKE
Patience, good lady; wizards know their times.
Deep night, dark night, the silence of the night,
The time of night when Troy was set on fire,
The time when screech owls cry and bandogs howl 17
And spirits walk and ghosts break up their graves –
That time best fits the work we have in hand.
Madam, sit you and fear not. Whom we raise
We will make fast within a hallowed verge. 21
*Here do the ceremonies belonging [to conjuring],
and make the circle. Bolingbroke or Southwell reads:*

---

158 *meetest* fittest   167 *furniture* furnishings   169 *Last time* (cf. 1 *Henry VI*,
IV, iii, 9–11)   171 *fact* deed   188 *ten bones* i.e. fingers   191 *mechanical*
manual laborer, i.e. low person   202 *doom* judgment
I, iv *Gloucester's house*   4 *exorcisms* conjurations   13 *gear* business   17
bandogs leashed watch-dogs   21 *verge* circle; s.d. *Conjuro te* I conjure you
(the beginning of a typical conjuration; it would perhaps continue 'by the
infernal powers' and, after these were named, 'to appear')

'Conjuro te,' *etc. It thunders and lightens terribly;*
then the Spirit riseth.

22 SPIRIT Adsum.

23 WITCH Asnath,
By the eternal God, whose name and power
Thou tremblest at, answer that I shall ask;
For till thou speak thou shalt not pass from hence.

SPIRIT

27 Ask what thou wilt. That I had said and done!

BOLINGBROKE [*reads*]
'First of the king; what shall of him become?'

SPIRIT

29 The duke yet lives that Henry shall depose;
But him outlive, and die a violent death.
[*As the Spirit speaks, Southwell writes the answer.*]

BOLINGBROKE
'What fates await the Duke of Suffolk?'

SPIRIT
By water shall he die and take his end.

BOLINGBROKE
'What shall befall the Duke of Somerset?'

SPIRIT
Let him shun castles.
Safer shall he be upon the sandy plains
Than where castles mounted stand.

37 Have done, for more I hardly can endure.

BOLINGBROKE
Descend to darkness and the burning lake.

39 False fiend, avoid!
Thunder and lightning. Exit Spirit
[*sinking down again*].
Enter the Duke of York and the Duke of Buckingham,
with their Guard, and break in.

YORK
Lay hands upon these traitors and their trash.

41 Beldam, I think we watched you at an inch.
What, madam, are you there? The king and common-
weal
Are deeply indebted for this piece of pains.
My Lord Protector will, I doubt it not,

45 See you well guerdoned for these good deserts.

ELEANOR
Not half so bad as thine to England's king,

47 Injurious duke, that threatest where's no cause.

BUCKINGHAM
True, madam, none at all. What call you this?
[*Shows her the papers.*]
Away with them! Let them be clapped up close   49
And kept asunder. You, madam, shall with us.
Stafford, take her to thee.   51
We'll see your trinkets here all forthcoming.   52
All away!   *Exit* [*Stafford, those above and those below*
following, guarded].

YORK
Lord Buckingham, methinks you watched her well.
A pretty plot, well chosen to build upon.
Now pray, my lord, let's see the devil's writ.   56
What have we here?
Reads.
'The duke yet lives that Henry shall depose;
But him outlive, and die a violent death.'
Why, this is just 'Aio te, Aeacida,   60
Romanos vincere posse.' Well, to the rest:
'Tell me, what fate awaits the Duke of Suffolk?'
'By water shall he die and take his end.'
'What shall betide the Duke of Somerset?'
'Let him shun castles.
Safer shall he be upon the sandy plains
Than where castles mounted stand.'
Come, come, my lords; these oracles
Are hardly attained and hardly understood.   69
The king is now in progress towards Saint Albans,
With him the husband of this lovely lady.
Thither goes these news as fast as horse can carry them –
A sorry breakfast for my Lord Protector.

BUCKINGHAM
Your grace shall give me leave, my Lord of York,
To be the post, in hope of his reward.

YORK
At your pleasure, my good lord.   [*Exit Buckingham.*]
Who's within there, ho?
Enter a Servingman.
Invite my lords of Salisbury and Warwick
To sup with me to-morrow night. Away!   *Exeunt.*

*

Enter the King, Queen, [*with her hawk on her fist,*]   II, i
Protector [*Gloucester*], *Cardinal, and Suffolk,* [*as if*
they came from hawking;] *with Falconers halloaing.*

QUEEN
Believe me, lords, for flying at the brook   1
I saw not better sport these seven years' day.   2
Yet, by your leave, the wind was very high,
And ten to one old Joan had not gone out.   4

KING [*to Gloucester*]
But what a point, my lord, your falcon made   5
And what a pitch she flew above the rest.   6
To see how God in all his creatures works:
Yea, man and birds are fain of climbing high.

SUFFOLK
No marvel, an it like your majesty,
My Lord Protector's hawks do tower so well;   10
They know their master loves to be aloft
And bears his thoughts above his falcon's pitch.

GLOUCESTER
My lord, 'tis but a base ignoble mind
That mounts no higher than a bird can soar.

---

22 *Adsum* I am here   23 *Asnath* (anagram of 'Sat[h]an'; evil spirits were
frequently addressed in anagrams)   27 *That* would that   29–30 *The . . .*
death (deliberately ambiguous; cf. ll. 60–61)   37 *Have done* finish quickly
39 *False* treacherous (without reference to the information he has given);
avoid begone   41 *Beldam* witch; *at an inch* closely   45 *guerdoned . . .*
deserts rewarded for these worthy actions (ironically)   47 *Injurious* insulting   49 *clapped up* imprisoned   51 *Stafford* (presumably the captain of
the guard and one of Buckingham's kinsmen)   52 *We'll . . . forthcoming*
we'll take charge of your magic gear until it is produced as evidence against
you   56 *devil's writ* devil's writing (as opposed to Holy Writ)   60 *just*
precisely   60–61 *Aio . . . posse* (1) I say that you, descendant of Aeacus,
can overcome the Romans, (2) I say that the Romans can overcome you,
descendant of Aeacus (the ambiguous answer given by the oracle to Pyrrhus,
king of Epirus, when he asked whether he could conquer Rome)   69 *hardly . . . hardly* with difficulty . . . barely
II, i St Albans   1 *at the brook* beside the brook, i.e. for water-fowl   2
these . . . day for the last seven years   4 *had . . . out* would not have flown
at the game (because of the wind)   5 *point* position of vantage to windward about which the hawk flies as she awaits her prey   6 *pitch* altitude;
the peak of the hawk's flight, from which she swoops down   10 *hawks*
(Suffolk and later the cardinal allude not only to the hawks just flown
by Gloucester but also to his heraldic badge, a hawk with a maiden's
head)

CARDINAL
I thought as much. He would be above the clouds.

GLOUCESTER
Ay, my Lord Cardinal, how think you by that?
Were it not good your grace could fly to heaven?

KING
The treasury of everlasting joy.

CARDINAL
Thy heaven is on earth, thine eyes and thoughts
Beat on a crown, the treasure of thy heart;
Pernicious Protector, dangerous peer,
22   That smooth'st it so with king and commonweal.

GLOUCESTER
What, cardinal, is your priesthood grown peremptory?
24   'Tantaene animis coelestibus irae?'
Churchmen so hot? Good uncle, hide such malice;
26   With such holiness can you do it.

SUFFOLK
No malice, sir, no more than well becomes
So good a quarrel and so bad a peer.

GLOUCESTER
As who, my lord?

SUFFOLK   Why, as you, my lord,
An't like your lordly Lord's Protectorship.

GLOUCESTER
Why, Suffolk, England knows thine insolence.

QUEEN
And thy ambition, Gloucester.

KING   I prithee, peace,
Good queen, and whet not on these furious peers,
For blessed are the peacemakers on earth.

CARDINAL
Let me be blessed for the peace I make
Against this proud Protector with my sword.

GLOUCESTER *[aside to Cardinal]*
Faith, holy uncle, would 'twere come to that.

CARDINAL *[aside to Gloucester]*
Marry, when thou dar'st.

GLOUCESTER *[aside to Cardinal]*
39   Make up no factious numbers for the matter;
In thine own person answer thy abuse.

CARDINAL *[aside to Gloucester]*
Ay, where thou dar'st not peep; and if thou dar'st,
This evening on the east side of the grove.

KING
How now, my lords?

CARDINAL   Believe me, cousin Gloucester,
44   Had not your man put up the fowl so suddenly,
We had had more sport. – *[Aside to Gloucester]* Come
with thy two-hand sword.

GLOUCESTER
True uncle –
    [Aside to Cardinal]
47   Are ye advised? The east side of the grove.

CARDINAL *[aside to Gloucester]*
I am with you.

KING   Why, how now, uncle Gloucester?

GLOUCESTER
Talking of hawking; nothing else, my lord.
    [Aside to Cardinal]
Now, by God's Mother, priest, I'll shave your crown for
this,
51   Or all my fence shall fail.

CARDINAL *[aside to Gloucester]*
'Medice, teipsum.'   52
Protector, see to't well; protect yourself.

KING
The winds grow high; so do your stomachs, lords.   54
How irksome is this music to my heart!
When such strings jar, what hope of harmony?
I pray, my lords, let me compound this strife.   57
    Enter one [Townsman] crying 'A miracle!'

GLOUCESTER
What means this noise?
Fellow, what miracle dost thou proclaim?

TOWNSMAN
A miracle! a miracle!

SUFFOLK
Come to the king and tell him what miracle.

TOWNSMAN
Forsooth, a blind man at Saint Alban's shrine
Within this half hour hath received his sight –
A man that ne'er saw in his life before.

KING
Now God be praised, that to believing souls
Gives light in darkness, comfort in despair.
    Enter the Mayor of Saint Albans and his Brethren,
    [with music,] bearing the man [Simpcox] between
    two in a chair [, Simpcox's Wife and a crowd of
    Townsmen following].

CARDINAL
Here comes the townsmen on procession   67
To present your highness with the man.

KING
Great is his comfort in this earthly vale,
Although by his sight his sin be multiplied.

GLOUCESTER
Stand by, my masters. Bring him near the king;
His highness' pleasure is to talk with him.

KING
Good fellow, tell us here the circumstance,
That we for thee may glorify the Lord.
What, hast thou been long blind, and now restored?

SIMPCOX
Born blind, an't please your grace.

WIFE Ay indeed was he.

SUFFOLK What woman is this?

WIFE His wife, an't like your worship.

GLOUCESTER
Hadst thou been his mother, thou couldst have better   80
told.

KING
Where wert thou born?

SIMPCOX
At Berwick in the North, an't like your grace.

KING
Poor soul, God's goodness hath been great to thee.
Let never day nor night unhallowed pass
But still remember what the Lord hath done.

---

22 *smooth'st it* flatters   24 *Tantaene . . . irae?* do heavenly minds nourish such great wrath? (*Aeneid*, I, 11)   26 *can you* i.e. you can (but defective metre suggests that the line is corrupt)   39 *Make . . . numbers* do not make up a war-party   44 *put . . . fowl* startled the game into flight   47 *advised* agreed   51 *fence* skill in swordsmanship   52 *Medice, teipsum* physician, [cure] thyself   54 *stomachs* passions   57 *compound* compose   67 *on* in

QUEEN
Tell me, good fellow, cam'st thou here by chance
Or of devotion to this holy shrine?
SIMPCOX
God knows, of pure devotion, being called
A hundred times and oft'ner in my sleep
90 By good Saint Alban, who said, 'Simon, come;
Come offer at my shrine and I will help thee.'
WIFE
Most true, forsooth, and many time and oft
Myself have heard a voice to call him so.
CARDINAL
What, art thou lame?
SIMPCOX   Ay, God Almighty help me.
SUFFOLK
How cam'st thou so?
SIMPCOX   A fall off of a tree.
WIFE
A plum tree, master.
GLOUCESTER   How long hast thou been blind?
SIMPCOX
O, born so, master.
GLOUCESTER   What, and wouldst climb a tree?
SIMPCOX
98 But that in all my life, when I was a youth.
WIFE
Too true, and bought his climbing very dear.
GLOUCESTER
Mass, thou lovedst plums well, that wouldst venture so.
SIMPCOX
101 Alas, good master, my wife desired some damsons
And made me climb, with danger of my life.
GLOUCESTER
A subtle knave. But yet it shall not serve.
Let me see thine eyes. Wink now. Now open them.
In my opinion yet thou seest not well.
SIMPCOX Yes, master, clear as day, I thank God and Saint
Alban.
GLOUCESTER
Say'st thou me so? What color is this cloak of?
SIMPCOX
Red, master; red as blood.
GLOUCESTER
110 Why, that's well said. What color is my gown of?
SIMPCOX
Black, forsooth; coal-black, as jet.
KING
Why then, thou know'st what color jet is of?
SUFFOLK
And yet, I think, jet did he never see.
GLOUCESTER
But cloaks and gowns before this day a many.
WIFE
Never before this day in all his life.
GLOUCESTER Tell me, sirrah, what's my name?
SIMPCOX Alas, master, I know not.

GLOUCESTER What's his name?
SIMPCOX I know not.
GLOUCESTER Nor his?
SIMPCOX No indeed, master.
GLOUCESTER What's thine own name?
SIMPCOX Saunder Simpcox, an if it please you, master.
GLOUCESTER Then, Saunder, sit there, the lying'st
knave in Christendom. If thou hadst been born blind,
thou mightst as well have known all our names as thus to
name the several colors we do wear. Sight may dis-
tinguish of colors; but suddenly to nominate them all, it 128
is impossible. My lords, Saint Alban here hath done a
miracle; and would ye not think his cunning to be great
that could restore this cripple to his legs again?
SIMPCOX O master, that you could!
GLOUCESTER My masters of Saint Albans, have you not
beadles in your town, and things called whips?   134
MAYOR Yes, my lord, if it please your grace.
GLOUCESTER Then send for one presently.
MAYOR Sirrah, go fetch the beadle hither straight.
                             Exit [a Townsman].
GLOUCESTER Now fetch me a stool hither by and by. *[A
stool brought.]* Now, sirrah, if you mean to save yourself
from whipping, leap me over this stool and run away. 140
SIMPCOX
Alas, master, I am not able to stand alone;
You go about to torture me in vain.
          Enter a Beadle with whips.
GLOUCESTER Well, sir, we must have you find your legs.
Sirrah beadle, whip him till he leap over that same stool.
BEADLE I will, my lord. Come on, sirrah, off with your
doublet quickly.
SIMPCOX Alas, master, what shall I do? I am not able to
stand.
         *After the Beadle hath hit him once, he leaps over the
         stool and runs away; and they follow and cry
         'A miracle!'*
KING
O God, seest thou this, and bearest so long?
QUEEN
It made me laugh to see the villain run.
GLOUCESTER
Follow the knave, and take this drab away.   151
WIFE
Alas, sir, we did it for pure need.
GLOUCESTER Let them be whipped through every mar-
ket town till they come to Berwick, from whence they
came.   *Exit [Mayor with the Townsmen].*
CARDINAL
Duke Humphrey has done a miracle to-day.
SUFFOLK
True; made the lame to leap and fly away.
GLOUCESTER
But you have done more miracles than I;
You made in a day, my lord, whole towns to fly.   158
         Enter Buckingham.
KING
What tidings with our cousin Buckingham?
BUCKINGHAM
Such as my heart doth tremble to unfold.
A sort of naughty persons, lewdly bent,   161
Under the countenance and confederacy
Of Lady Eleanor, the Protector's wife,

90 *Simon* (the name of which Simpcox [Simon-boy] is an informal variant)
98 *But . . . life* never in all my life except   101 *damsons* a kind of plum
128 *nominate* name   134 *beadles* constables   140 *me* for me (ethical dative)
151 *drab* low woman   158 *made . . . fly* i.e. by giving the French provinces
away in exchange for the queen   161 *sort* gang; *naughty* worthless (with
implications of wickedness); *lewdly* wickedly

164 The ringleader and head of all this rout,
Have practiced dangerously against your state,
Dealing with witches and with conjurers,
Whom we have apprehended in the fact,
Raising up wicked spirits from under ground,
169 Demanding of King Henry's life and death
And other of your highness' privy council,
171 As more at large your grace shall understand.

CARDINAL [aside to Gloucester]
And so, my Lord Protector, by this means
173 Your lady is forthcoming yet at London.
This news, I think, hath turned your weapon's edge.
'Tis like, my lord, you will not keep your hour.

GLOUCESTER [aside to Cardinal]
Ambitious churchman, leave to afflict my heart.
Sorrow and grief have vanquished all my powers;
And, vanquished as I am, I yield to thee
Or to the meanest groom.

KING
O God, what mischiefs work the wicked ones,
Heaping confusion on their own heads thereby!

QUEEN
182 Gloucester, see here the taincture of thy nest,
And look thyself be faultless, thou wert best.

GLOUCESTER
Madam, for myself, to heaven I do appeal,
How I have loved my king and commonweal;
And for my wife, I know not how it stands.
Sorry I am to hear what I have heard.
Noble she is; but if she have forgot
Honor and virtue and conversed with such
As, like to pitch, defile nobility,
I banish her my bed and company
And give her as a prey to law and shame
That hath dishonored Gloucester's honest name.

KING
Well, for this night we will repose us here.
To-morrow toward London back again
To look into this business thoroughly
And call these foul offenders to their answers
198 And poise the cause in justice' equal scales,
199 Whose beam stands sure, whose rightful cause prevails.
Flourish. Exeunt.

*

II, ii   *Enter York, Salisbury, and Warwick.*

YORK
Now, my good Lords of Salisbury and Warwick,
Our simple supper ended, give me leave
3 In this close walk to satisfy myself
In craving your opinion of my title,
Which is infallible, to England's crown.

SALISBURY
My lord, I long to hear it at full.

WARWICK
Sweet York, begin; and if thy claim be good,
The Nevils are thy subjects to command.

YORK
Then thus:
10 Edward the Third, my lords, had seven sons:
The first, Edward the Black Prince, Prince of Wales;
The second, William of Hatfield; and the third,
Lionel Duke of Clarence; next to whom
Was John of Gaunt, the Duke of Lancaster;

The fifth was Edmund Langley, Duke of York;
The sixth was Thomas of Woodstock, Duke of Gloucester;
William of Windsor was the seventh and last.
Edward the Black Prince died before his father
And left behind him Richard, his only son,
Who after Edward the Third's death reigned as king   20
Till Henry Bolingbroke, Duke of Lancaster,
The eldest son and heir of John of Gaunt,
Crowned by the name of Henry the Fourth,
Seized on the realm, deposed the rightful king,
Sent his poor queen to France from whence she came,
And him to Pomfret, where, as all you know,
Harmless Richard was murdered traitorously.

WARWICK
Father, the duke hath told the truth.
Thus got the house of Lancaster the crown.

YORK
Which now they hold by force, and not by right;   30
For Richard, the first son's heir, being dead,
The issue of the next son should have reigned.

SALISBURY
But William of Hatfield died without an heir.

YORK
The third son, Duke of Clarence, from whose line
I claim the crown, had issue, Philippe, a daughter,
Who married Edmund Mortimer, Earl of March.
Edmund had issue, Roger Earl of March;
Roger had issue, Edmund, Anne, and Eleanor.

SALISBURY
This Edmund in the reign of Bolingbroke,   39
As I have read, laid claim unto the crown;
And, but for Owen Glendower, had been king,
Who kept him in captivity till he died.
But to the rest.

YORK   His eldest sister, Anne,
My mother, being heir unto the crown,
Married Richard Earl of Cambridge, who was son
To Edmund Langley, Edward the Third's fifth son.
By her I claim the kingdom. She was heir
To Roger Earl of March, who was the son
Of Edmund Mortimer, who married Philippe,
Sole daughter unto Lionel Duke of Clarence.
So, if the issue of the elder son
Succeed before the younger, I am king.

WARWICK
What plain proceedings is more plain than this?   53
Henry doth claim the crown from John of Gaunt,
The fourth son; York claims it from the third.

---

164 *rout* disorderly crowd   **169** *Demanding* inquiring   **171** *at large* in full
173 *forthcoming* to be tried (see I, iv, 52)   **182** *taincture* fouling (with
overtones of 'treason')   **198** *poise* weigh   **199** *stands sure* is perfectly level
(indicating no bias)
II, ii The Duke of York's garden   **3** *close* private, secluded   **39** *Edmund*
(Shakespeare here follows the chroniclers in an error and adds some
confusion of his own. Edmund Mortimer, 3rd Earl of March, and son-in-
law of Lionel, Duke of Clarence, actually had two sons, Roger, 4th Earl of
March, and Sir Edmund. Sir Edmund was captured by Glendower and
married his daughter [see *1 Henry IV*]. It was Roger Mortimer's son
Edmund, 5th Earl of March and nephew of Sir Edmund, who was York's
mother's brother and had been named heir to the throne by Richard II.
These two are confused in *1 Henry IV* and *1 Henry VI* as well as here. But
the further detail, that Edmund was kept by Glendower captive until his
death [l. 42], seems to have been derived by Shakespeare incorrectly from
Hall, who mentions, in conjunction with his account of Edmund, that
Glendower kept Lord Grey of Ruthvin, another son-in-law, 'in captivitee
till he died.')   **53** *proceedings* line of descent

56 Till Lionel's issue fails, his should not reign.
It fails not yet, but flourishes in thee
58 And in thy son, fair slips of such a stock.
Then, father Salisbury, kneel we together,
And in this private plot be we the first
That shall salute our rightful sovereign
With honor of his birthright to the crown.

BOTH
Long live our sovereign Richard, England's king.

YORK
We thank you, lords. But I am not your king
Till I be crowned and that my sword be stained
With heart-blood of the house of Lancaster.
And that's not suddenly to be performed,
68 But with advice and silent secrecy.
Do you as I do in these dangerous days :
70 Wink at the Duke of Suffolk's insolence,
At Beaufort's pride, at Somerset's ambition,
At Buckingham and all the crew of them,
Till they have snared the shepherd of the flock,
That virtuous prince, the good Duke Humphrey.
'Tis that they seek ; and they in seeking that
Shall find their deaths, if York can prophesy.

SALISBURY
My lord, break we off. We know your mind at full.

WARWICK
My heart assures me that the Earl of Warwick
Shall one day make the Duke of York a king.

YORK
And, Nevil, this I do assure myself,
Richard shall live to make the Earl of Warwick
The greatest man in England but the king.   *Exeunt.*

*

II, iii   *Sound trumpets. Enter the King and State, [i.e. the*
Queen, Gloucester, Suffolk, Buckingham, and the
Cardinal,] with Guard, to banish the Duchess.
[Enter, guarded, the Duchess of Gloucester, Margery
Jourdain, Hume, Southwell, and Bolingbroke. And
then enter to them York, Salisbury, and Warwick.]

KING
Stand forth, Dame Eleanor Cobham, Gloucester's wife.
In sight of God and us your guilt is great.
Receive the sentence of the law for sins
Such as by God's book are adjudged to death.
    [To Jourdain and the others]
You four, from hence to prison back again ;
From thence unto the place of execution.
The witch in Smithfield shall be burned to ashes,
And you three shall be strangled on the gallows.
    [To the Duchess]
You, madam, for you are more nobly born,
10 Despoilèd of your honor in your life,
Shall, after three days' open penance done,
Live in your country here in banishment
With Sir John Stanley in the Isle of Man.

ELEANOR
Welcome is banishment. Welcome were my death.

GLOUCESTER
Eleanor, the law, thou seest, hath judgèd thee.
I cannot justify whom the law condemns.
    [Exeunt the Duchess and the
    other prisoners, guarded.]
Mine eyes are full of tears, my heart of grief.
Ah, Humphrey, this dishonor in thine age
Will bring thy head with sorrow to the ground.
I beseech your majesty give me leave to go ;
Sorrow would solace, and mine age would ease.   21

KING
Stay, Humphrey Duke of Gloucester, ere thou go,
Give up thy staff. Henry will to himself
Protector be ; and God shall be my hope,
My stay, my guide, and lantern to my feet.
And go in peace, Humphrey, no less beloved
Than when thou wert Protector to thy king.

QUEEN
I see no reason why a king of years
Should be to be protected like a child.
God and King Henry govern England's helm.   30
Give up your staff, sir, and the king his realm.   31

GLOUCESTER
My staff ? Here, noble Henry, is my staff.
As willingly do I the same resign
As e'er thy father Henry made it mine ;
And even as willingly at thy feet I leave it
As others would ambitiously receive it.
Farewell, good king. When I am dead and gone,
May honorable peace attend thy throne. *Exit Gloucester.*

QUEEN
Why, now is Henry king, and Margaret queen,
And Humphrey Duke of Gloucester scarce himself,
That bears so shrewd a maim ; two pulls at once –   41
His lady banished, and a limb lopped off.
This staff of honor raught, there let it stand   43
Where it best fits to be, in Henry's hand.

SUFFOLK
Thus droops this lofty pine and hangs his sprays ;
Thus Eleanor's pride dies in her youngest days.   46

YORK
Lords, let him go. Please it your majesty,
This is the day appointed for the combat,
And ready are the appellant and defendant,
The armorer and his man, to enter the lists ;   50
So please your highness to behold the fight.

QUEEN
Ay, good my lord ; for purposely therefore
Left I the court, to see this quarrel tried.

KING
A God's name see the lists and all things fit.   54
Here let them end it, and God defend the right.

YORK
I never saw a fellow worse bestead   56
Or more afraid to fight than is the appellant,
The servant of this armorer, my lords.
    Enter, at one door, the Armorer [Horner] and his
    Neighbors, drinking to him so much that he is drunk ;
    and he enters with a Drum before him, and his staff
    with a sandbag fastened to it ; and, at the other door,
    his Man [Peter], with a Drum and sandbag, and
    Prentices drinking to him.

56 *his* i.e. Gaunt's   58 *slips* cuttings   68 *advice* mature reflection   70 *Wink at* ignore
II, iii The palace in London   21 *would* would have   30 *govern* (with the Latin sense of 'steer')   31 *king his* king's   41 *bears . . . maim* suffers so severe a loss ; *pulls* pluckings   43 *raught* reached (by us)   46 *in . . . days* at last (?)   50 *lists* the barriers defining an arena for fighting or tilting ; hence, the arena itself   54 *A* in   56 *bestead* prepared

1. NEIGHBOR Here, neighbor Horner, I drink to you in a
60   cup of sack ; and fear not, neighbor, you shall do well
enough.
62 2. NEIGHBOR And here, neighbor, here's a cup of charneco.
64 3. NEIGHBOR And here's a pot of good double-beer,
neighbor. Drink, and fear not your man.
ARMORER Let it come, i' faith, and I'll pledge you all ;
67   and a fig for Peter.
1. PRENTICE Here, Peter, I drink to thee ; and be not
afraid.
2. PRENTICE Be merry, Peter, and fear not thy master.
Fight for credit of the prentices.
PETER I thank you all. Drink, and pray for me, I pray
you ; for I think I have taken my last draught in this
world. Here, Robin, an if I die, I give thee my apron ;
and, Will, thou shalt have my hammer ; and here, Tom,
take all the money that I have. O Lord bless me, I pray
God, for I am never able to deal with my master, he
hath learnt so much fence already.
SALISBURY Come, leave your drinking and fall to blows.
Sirrah, what's thy name ?
PETER Peter, forsooth.
SALISBURY Peter ? What more ?
PETER Thump.
SALISBURY Thump ? Then see thou thump thy master
well.
ARMORER Masters, I am come hither, as it were, upon my
man's instigation, to prove him a knave and myself an
honest man ; and touching the Duke of York, I will take
my death I never meant him any ill, nor the king, nor the
86   queen ; and therefore, Peter, have at thee with a down-
right blow.
YORK Dispatch. This knave's tongue begins to double.
Sound, trumpets, alarum to the combatants !
     [Alarum.] They fight, and Peter strikes him down.
ARMORER Hold, Peter, hold ! I confess, I confess treason.
     [Dies.]
YORK Take away his weapon. Fellow, thank God, and the
good wine in thy master's way.
PETER O God, have I overcome mine enemies in this
presence ? O Peter, thou hast prevailed in right.
KING
Go, take hence that traitor from our sight,
For by his death we do perceive his guilt,
And God in justice hath revealed to us
The truth and innocence of this poor fellow,
Which he had thought to have murdered wrongfully.
Come, fellow, follow us for thy reward.
                 Sound a flourish. Exeunt.
                 *

II, iv   *Enter Duke Humphrey [of Gloucester] and his*
          Men in mourning cloaks.
GLOUCESTER
Thus sometimes hath the brightest day a cloud,
And after summer evermore succeeds
Barren winter with his wrathful nipping cold ;
So cares and joys abound, as seasons fleet.
Sirs, what's o'clock ?
SERVANT   Ten, my lord.
GLOUCESTER
Ten is the hour that was appointed me
To watch the coming of my punished duchess.

Uneath may she endure the flinty streets   8
To tread them with her tender-feeling feet.
Sweet Nell, ill can thy noble mind abrook
The abject people gazing on thy face,   11
With envious looks laughing at thy shame,
That erst did follow thy proud chariot wheels   13
When thou didst ride in triumph through the streets.
But, soft, I think she comes, and I'll prepare
My tear-stained eyes to see her miseries.
     Enter the Duchess [barefoot] in a white sheet, [with
     verses pinned upon her back] and a taper burning in
     her hand, with the Sheriff and Officers [and Sir John
     Stanley. A crowd following].
SERVANT
So please your grace, we'll take her from the sheriff.
GLOUCESTER
No, stir not for your lives. Let her pass by.
ELEANOR
Come you, my lord, to see my open shame ?
Now thou dost penance too. Look how they gaze.
See how the giddy multitude do point
And nod their heads and throw their eyes on thee.
Ah, Gloucester, hide thee from their hateful looks,
And in thy closet pent up, rue my shame,   24
And ban thine enemies, both mine and thine.   25
GLOUCESTER
Be patient, gentle Nell ; forget this grief.
ELEANOR
Ah, Gloucester, teach me to forget myself.
For, whilst I think I am thy married wife
And thou a prince, Protector of this land,
Methinks I should not thus be led along,
Mailed up in shame, with papers on my back,   31
And followed with a rabble that rejoice
To see my tears and hear my deep-fet groans.   33
The ruthless flint doth cut my tender feet ;
And when I start, the envious people laugh
And bid me be advisèd how I tread.
Ah, Humphrey, can I bear this shameful yoke ?
Trowest thou that e'er I'll look upon the world   38
Or count them happy that enjoys the sun ?
No ; dark shall be my light, and night my day ;
To think upon my pomp shall be my hell.
Sometime I'll say, I am Duke Humphrey's wife,
And he a prince, and ruler of the land ;
Yet so he ruled, and such a prince he was,
As he stood by whilst I, his forlorn duchess,
Was made a wonder and a pointing-stock   46
To every idle rascal follower.
But be thou mild and blush not at my shame,
Nor stir at nothing till the axe of death
Hang over thee, as sure it shortly will.
For Suffolk – he that can do all in all
With her that hateth thee and hates us all –
And York and impious Beaufort, that false priest,

60 *sack* a stong, dry wine   62 *charneco* a sweet wine   64 *double-beer* strong
beer   67 *a fig for Peter* I hold Peter in the utmost contempt (usually
accompanied with a gesture made by putting the thumb between the first
and second fingers)   86 *downright* straight down
II, iv *a street*   8 *Uneath* with difficulty, scarcely   11 *abject* common, low-
born   13 *erst* formerly   24 *closet* private room   25 *ban* curse   31 *Mailed
up* wrapped up (as a hawk is wrapped up to prevent her struggling)   33
deep-fet deeply fetched   38 *Trowest thou* do you believe   46 *pointing-stock*
a person pointed at in scorn

Have all limed bushes to betray thy wings,
And fly thou how thou canst, they'll tangle thee.
But fear not thou until thy foot be snared,
57   Nor never seek prevention of thy foes.

GLOUCESTER
Ah, Nell, forbear; thou aimest all awry.
59   I must offend before I be attainted;
And had I twenty times so many foes,
And each of them had twenty times their power,
62   All these could not procure me any scathe
So long as I am loyal, true, and crimeless.
Wouldst have me rescue thee from this reproach?
Why, yet thy scandal were not wiped away,
But I in danger for the breach of law.
Thy greatest help is quiet, gentle Nell.
68   I pray thee sort thy heart to patience;
These few days' wonder will be quickly worn.
Enter a Herald.

HERALD
I summon your grace to his majesty's parliament,
71   Holden at Bury the first of this next month.

GLOUCESTER
And my consent ne'er asked herein before?
73   This is close dealing. Well, I will be there.
[Exit Herald.]
My Nell, I take my leave. And, master sheriff,
Let not her penance exceed the king's commission.

SHERIFF
76   An't please your grace, here my commission stays,
And Sir John Stanley is appointed now
To take her with him to the Isle of Man.

GLOUCESTER
Must you, Sir John, protect my lady here?

STANLEY
So am I given in charge, may't please your grace.

GLOUCESTER
81   Entreat her not the worse in that I pray
You use her well. The world may laugh again,
And I may live to do you kindness if
You do it her; and so, Sir John, farewell.

ELEANOR
What, gone, my lord, and bid me not farewell?

GLOUCESTER
Witness my tears, I cannot stay to speak.
Exit Gloucester [with his Men].

ELEANOR
Art thou gone too? All comfort go with thee!
For none abides with me. My joy is death –
Death, at whose name I oft have been afeard,
90   Because I wished this world's eternity.
Stanley, I prithee go, and take me hence;
I care not whither, for I beg no favor.
Only convey me where thou art commanded.

STANLEY
Why, madam, that is to the Isle of Man,
There to be used according to your state.   95

ELEANOR
That's bad enough, for I am but reproach;   96
And shall I then be used reproachfully?

STANLEY
Like to a duchess and Duke Humphrey's lady –
According to that state you shall be used.

ELEANOR
Sheriff, farewell, and better than I fare,
Although thou hast been conduct of my shame.   101

SHERIFF
It is my office; and, madam, pardon me.

ELEANOR
Ay, ay, farewell; thy office is discharged.
Come, Stanley, shall we go?

STANLEY
Madam, your penance done, throw off this sheet,
And go we to attire you for our journey.

ELEANOR
My shame will not be shifted with my sheet.   107
No, it will hang upon my richest robes
And show itself, attire me how I can.
Go, lead the way; I long to see my prison.   *Exeunt.*

*

*Sound a sennet. Enter [two Heralds before, then]
Buckingham [and] Suffolk, [then] York [and the]
Cardinal, [then the] King [and the] Queen, [then]
Salisbury and Warwick [with their attendants]
to the Parliament.*

KING
I muse my Lord of Gloucester is not come.   1
'Tis not his wont to be the hindmost man,
Whate'er occasion keeps him from us now.

QUEEN
Can you not see? or will ye not observe
The strangeness of his altered countenance?
With what a majesty he bears himself,
How insolent of late he is become,
How proud, how peremptory, and unlike himself?
We know the time since he was mild and affable,   9
And if we did but glance a far-off look,
Immediately he was upon his knee,
That all the court admired him for submission;
But meet him now, and, be it in the morn,
When every one will give the time of day,   14
He knits his brow and shows an angry eye
And passeth by with stiff unbowèd knee,
Disdaining duty that to us belongs.
Small curs are not regarded when they grin,   18
But great men tremble when the lion roars,   19
And Humphrey is no little man in England.
First note that he is near you in descent,
And should you fall, he is the next will mount.
Me seemeth then it is no policy,   23
Respecting what a rancorous mind he bears   24
And his advantage following your decease,
That he should come about your royal person
Or be admitted to your highness' council.
By flattery hath he won the commons' hearts;
And when he please to make commotion,

57 *prevention of* prior safeguards against   59 *attainted* condemned for
treason   62 *scathe* harm   68 *sort* adapt   71 *Holden* to be held; *Bury* i.e.
Bury St Edmunds   73 *close* secret   76 *commission stays* authority stops
81 *Entreat* treat   90 *this world's eternity* endless worldly pleasures   95
state social rank (but Eleanor at l. 96 shifts the meaning to 'condition')
96 *but reproach* entirely a thing to be reproached   101 *conduct* conductor
107 *shifted* changed (with a pun on 'shift,' a chemise)
III, i A hall for the session of Parliament (at Bury St Edmunds)   1 *muse*
wonder   9 *We . . . since* we remember that once   14 *give . . . day* say good
morning   18 *grin* show their teeth   19 *lion* i.e. Gloucester (who, as the
prince, is symbolized by the kingly lion)   23 *Me . . . policy* it seems to me
that it is not wise   24 *Respecting* considering

'Tis to be feared they all will follow him.
Now 'tis the spring, and weeds are shallow-rooted.
Suffer them now, and they'll o'ergrow the garden

33 And choke the herbs for want of husbandry.
The reverent care I bear unto my lord

35 Made me collect these dangers in the duke.

36 If it be fond, call it a woman's fear ;
Which fear if better reasons can supplant,

38 I will subscribe and say I wronged the duke.
My Lord of Suffolk, Buckingham, and York,
Reprove my allegation if you can,
Or else conclude my words effectual.

SUFFOLK
Well hath your highness seen into this duke,
And had I first been put to speak my mind,
I think I should have told your grace's tale.

45 The duchess by his subornation,

46 Upon my life, began her devilish practices ;
Or if he were not privy to those faults,

48 Yet by reputing of his high descent –
As next the king he was successive heir,
And such high vaunts of his nobility –

51 Did instigate the bedlam brainsick duchess
By wicked means to frame our sovereign's fall.
Smooth runs the water where the brook is deep,
And in his simple show he harbors treason.
The fox barks not when he would steal the lamb.
No, no, my sovereign ; Gloucester is a man

57 Unsounded yet and full of deep deceit.

CARDINAL
Did he not, contrary to form of law,

59 Devise strange deaths for small offenses done ?

YORK
And did he not in his protectorship
Levy great sums of money through the realm
For soldiers' pay in France, and never sent it ?
By means whereof the towns each day revolted.

BUCKINGHAM
Tut, these are petty faults to faults unknown
Which time will bring to light in smooth Duke
  Humphrey.

KING

66 My lords at once, the care you have of us,
To mow down thorns that would annoy our foot,
Is worthy praise ; but, shall I speak my conscience,
Our kinsman Gloucester is as innocent
From meaning treason to our royal person
As is the sucking lamb or harmless dove.

72 The duke is virtuous, mild, and too well-given
To dream on evil or to work my downfall.

QUEEN

74 Ah, what's more dangerous than this fond affiance ?
Seems he a dove ? His feathers are but borrowed,
For he's disposèd as the hateful raven.
Is he a lamb ? His skin is surely lent him,
For he's inclined as is the ravenous wolves.

79 Who cannot steal a shape that means deceit ?
Take heed, my lord. The welfare of us all
Hangs on the cutting short that fraudful man.
  Enter Somerset.

SOMERSET
All health unto my gracious sovereign.

KING
Welcome, Lord Somerset. What news from France ?

SOMERSET
That all your interest in those territories
Is utterly bereft you ; all is lost.

KING
Cold news, Lord Somerset ; but God's will be done.

YORK *[aside]*
Cold news for me, for I had hope of France
As firmly as I hope for fertile England.
Thus are my blossoms blasted in the bud,
And caterpillars eat my leaves away ;
But I will remedy this gear ere long   91
Or sell my title for a glorious grave.
  Enter Gloucester.

GLOUCESTER
All happiness unto my lord the king.
Pardon, my liege, that I have stayed so long.   94

SUFFOLK
Nay, Gloucester, know that thou art come too soon
Unless thou wert more loyal than thou art.
I do arrest thee of high treason here.

GLOUCESTER
Well, Suffolk, thou shalt not see me blush
Nor change my countenance for this arrest.
A heart unspotted is not easily daunted.
The purest spring is not so free from mud
As I am clear from treason to my sovereign.
Who can accuse me ? Wherein am I guilty ?

YORK
'Tis thought, my lord, that you took bribes of France
And, being Protector, stayed the soldiers' pay,   105
By means whereof his highness hath lost France.

GLOUCESTER
Is it but thought so ? What are they that think it ?
I never robbed the soldiers of their pay
Nor ever had one penny bribe from France.
So help me God as I have watched the night –   110
Ay, night by night – in studying good for England !
That doit that e'er I wrested from the king,   112
Or any groat I hoarded to my use,   113
Be brought against me at my trial day !
No ! Many a pound of mine own proper store,   115
Because I would not tax the needy commons,
Have I dispursèd to the garrisons   117
And never asked for restitution.

CARDINAL
It serves you well, my lord, to say so much.

GLOUCESTER
I say no more than truth, so help me God.

YORK
In your protectorship you did devise
Strange tortures for offenders, never heard of,
That England was defamed by tyranny.

GLOUCESTER
Why, 'tis well known that, whiles I was Protector,

---

33 *husbandry* cultivation   35 *collect* infer   36 *fond* foolish   38 *subscribe* acknowledge in writing   45 *subornation* instigation to crime   46 *Upon my life* (an oath : Eleanor was accused of practicing upon the king's life, not Suffolk's)   48 *reputing* thinking repeatedly   51 *bedlam* crazy   57 *Unsounded* unrevealed   59 *strange* exceptionally cruel, illegal   66 *at once* going to the heart of the matter (?), collectively (?)   72 *well-given* well-disposed   74 *fond affiance* foolish confidence   79 *Who . . . deceit* i.e. who that intends to deceive cannot assume a role   91 *gear* business   94 *stayed* delayed   105 *stayed* withheld   110 *watched* remained awake throughout   112, 113 *doit, groat* coins of little value   115 *proper* personal   117 *dispursèd* paid from the purse

Pity was all the fault that was in me;
For I should melt at an offender's tears
And lowly words were ransom for their fault.
Unless it were a bloody murderer,
Or foul felonious thief that fleeced poor passengers,
130 I never gave them condign punishment.
Murder indeed, that bloody sin, I tortured
132 Above the felon or what trespass else.

SUFFOLK
133 My lord, these faults are easy, quickly answered;
But mightier crimes are laid unto your charge,
Whereof you cannot easily purge yourself.
I do arrest you in his highness' name
And here commit you to my Lord Cardinal
To keep until your further time of trial.

KING
My Lord of Gloucester, 'tis my special hope
140 That you will clear yourself from all suspense.
My conscience tells me you are innocent.

GLOUCESTER
Ah, gracious lord, these days are dangerous.
Virtue is choked with foul ambition
And charity chased hence by rancor's hand;
Foul subornation is predominant
And equity exiled your highness' land.
147 I know their complot is to have my life,
And if my death might make this island happy
149 And prove the period of their tyranny,
I would expend it with all willingness.
But mine is made the prologue to their play,
For thousands more, that yet suspect no peril,
Will not conclude their plotted tragedy.
Beaufort's red sparkling eyes blab his heart's malice
And Suffolk's cloudy brow his stormy hate;
Sharp Buckingham unburdens with his tongue
The envious load that lies upon his heart;
And dogged York, that reaches at the moon,
Whose overweening arm I have plucked back,
160 By false accuse doth level at my life;
And you, my sovereign lady, with the rest,
Causeless have laid disgraces on my head
And with your best endeavor have stirred up
164 My liefest liege to be mine enemy.
Ay, all of you have laid your heads together –
166 Myself had notice of your conventicles –
And all to make away my guiltless life.
I shall not want false witness to condemn me
Nor store of treasons to augment my guilt.
The ancient proverb will be well effected:
'A staff is quickly found to beat a dog.'

CARDINAL
My liege, his railing is intolerable.
If those that care to keep your royal person
From treason's secret knife and traitor's rage
175 Be thus upbraided, chid, and rated at,
And the offender granted scope of speech,

'Twill make them cool in zeal unto your grace.

SUFFOLK
Hath he not twit our sovereign lady here   178
With ignominious words, though clerkly couched,   179
As if she had suborned some to swear
False allegations to o'erthrow his state?

QUEEN
But I can give the loser leave to chide.

GLOUCESTER
Far truer spoke than meant; I lose indeed.
Beshrew the winners, for they played me false;   184
And well such losers may have leave to speak.

BUCKINGHAM
He'll wrest the sense and hold us here all day.   186
Lord Cardinal, he is your prisoner.

CARDINAL
Sirs, take away the duke and guard him sure.

GLOUCESTER
Ah, thus King Henry throws away his crutch
Before his legs be firm to bear his body.
Thus is the shepherd beaten from thy side,
And wolves are gnarling who shall gnaw thee first. 192
Ah that my fear were false, ah that it were!
For, good King Henry, thy decay I fear.
      Exit Gloucester [with the Cardinal's men].

KING
My lords, what to your wisdoms seemeth best
Do or undo, as if ourself were here.

QUEEN
What, will your highness leave the parliament?

KING
Ay, Margaret. My heart is drowned with grief,
Whose flood begins to flow within mine eyes:
My body round engirt with misery –   200
For what's more miserable than discontent?
Ah, uncle Humphrey, in thy face I see
The map of honor, truth, and loyalty;
And yet, good Humphrey, is the hour to come
That e'er I proved thee false or feared thy faith.
What low'ring star now envies thy estate
That these great lords and Margaret our queen
Do seek subversion of thy harmless life?
Thou never didst them wrong nor no man wrong.
And as the butcher takes away the calf
And binds the wretch and beats it when it strains,
Bearing it to the bloody slaughterhouse,
Even so remorseless have they borne him hence;
And as the dam runs lowing up and down,   214
Looking the way her harmless young one went,
And can do naught but wail her darling's loss,
Even so myself bewails good Gloucester's case
With sad unhelpful tears, and with dimmed eyes
Look after him and cannot do him good,
So mighty are his vowèd enemies.
His fortunes I will weep, and 'twixt each groan
Say 'Who's a traitor? Gloucester he is none.'
      [*Exit King with Buckingham, Salisbury,*
                    and Warwick.]

QUEEN
Free lords, cold snow melts with the sun's hot beams. 223
Henry my lord is cold in great affairs,
Too full of foolish pity; and Gloucester's show
Beguiles him as the mournful crocodile
With sorrow snares relenting passengers,

---

130 *condign* well-deserved 132 *Above . . . else* beyond felony or any other crime 133 *easy* unimportant 140 *suspense* doubt as to your character 147 *complot* conspiracy 149 *period* end 160 *accuse* accusation; *level* aim 164 *liefest liege* dearest sovereign 166 *conventicles* secret gatherings 175 *rated at* complained against 178 *twit* twitted 179 *clerkly couched* artfully, learnedly phrased 184 *Beshrew* bad luck to 186 *wrest the sense* distort the meaning 192 *gnarling* snarling 214 *dam* mother 223 *Free* noble, generous

Or as the snake, rolled in a flow'ring bank,
229 With shining checkered slough, doth sting a child
That for the beauty thinks it excellent.
Believe me, lords, were none more wise than I –
And yet herein I judge mine own wit good –
This Gloucester should be quickly rid the world,
To rid us from the fear we have of him.

CARDINAL
That he should die is worthy policy;
236 But yet we want a color for his death.
'Tis meet he be condemned by course of law.

SUFFOLK
But, in my mind, that were no policy.
The king will labor still to save his life,
240 The commons haply rise to save his life;
241 And yet we have but trivial argument,
More than mistrust, that shows him worthy death.

YORK
243 So that, by this, you would not have him die.

SUFFOLK
244 Ah, York, no man alive so fain as I.

YORK [aside]
'Tis York that hath more reason for his death. –
But, my Lord Cardinal, and you, my Lord of Suffolk,
Say as you think and speak it from your souls:
248 Were't not all one an empty eagle were set
To guard the chicken from a hungry kite
As place Duke Humphrey for the king's Protector?

QUEEN
So the poor chicken should be sure of death.

SUFFOLK
Madam, 'tis true; and were't not madness then
253 To make the fox surveyor of the fold?
Who being accused a crafty murderer,
255 His guilt should be but idly posted over
Because his purpose is not executed.
No, let him die in that he is a fox,
By nature proved an enemy to the flock,
259 Before his chaps be stained with crimson blood,
As Humphrey, proved by treasons, to my liege.
261 And do not stand on quillets how to slay him;
262 Be it by gins, by snares, by subtlety,
Sleeping or waking, 'tis no matter how,
So he be dead; for that is good deceit
265 Which mates him first that first intends deceit.

QUEEN
Thrice-noble Suffolk, 'tis resolutely spoke.

SUFFOLK
Not resolute, except so much were done,
For things are often spoke and seldom meant;
But that my heart accordeth with my tongue,
Seeing the deed is meritorious,
And to preserve my sovereign from his foe,
272 Say but the word, and I will be his priest.

CARDINAL
But I would have him dead, my Lord of Suffolk,
274 Ere you can take due orders for a priest.
275 Say you consent and censure well the deed,
And I'll provide his executioner,
I tender so the safety of my liege.

SUFFOLK
Here is my hand, the deed is worthy doing.

QUEEN
And so say I.

YORK
And I. And now we three have spoke it,
It skills not greatly who impugns our doom.   281
    Enter a Post.

POST
Great lords, from Ireland am I come amain   282
To signify that rebels there are up   283
And put the Englishmen unto the sword.
Send succors, lords, and stop the rage betime,   285
Before the wound do grow uncurable;
For, being green, there is great hope of help.   287

CARDINAL
A breach that craves a quick expedient stop.
What counsel give you in this weighty cause?

YORK
That Somerset be sent as regent thither.
'Tis meet that lucky ruler be employed;   291
Witness the fortune he hath had in France.

SOMERSET
If York with all his far-fet policy   293
Had been the regent there instead of me,
He never would have stayed in France so long.

YORK
No, not to lose it all, as thou hast done.
I rather would have lost my life betimes   297
Than bring a burden of dishonor home
By staying there so long till all were lost.
Show me one scar charactered on thy skin.   300
Men's flesh preserved so whole do seldom win.

QUEEN
Nay then, this spark will prove a raging fire
If wind and fuel be brought to feed it with.
No more, good York; sweet Somerset, be still.
Thy fortune, York, hadst thou been regent there,
Might happily have proved far worse than his.   306

YORK
What, worse than naught? Nay, then a shame take all!

SOMERSET
And, in the number, thee that wishest shame!

CARDINAL
My Lord of York, try what your fortune is.
Th' uncivil kerns of Ireland are in arms   310
And temper clay with blood of Englishmen.   311
To Ireland will you lead a band of men,
Collected choicely, from each county some,
And try your hap against the Irishmen?

YORK
I will, my lord, so please his majesty.

SUFFOLK
Why, our authority is his consent,
And what we do establish he confirms.
Then, noble York, take thou this task in hand.

229 *slough* skin   236 *color* legal pretext (with a quibble arising from *die* / *dye* in l. 235)   240 *haply* perhaps   241 *argument* proof   243 *by this* i.e. by your reasoning   244 *fain* eager   248 *empty* i.e. hungry   253 *surveyor* overseer   255 *posted over* disregarded   259 *chaps* i.e. chops, jaws   261 *stand on quillets* be scrupulous about details   262 *gins* engines, i.e. traps   265 *mates* checkmates   272 *be his priest* i.e. give him the last rites (with obvious irony)   274 *take . . . priest* prepare yourself for the priesthood   275 *censure well* approve   281 *doom* judgment   282 *amain* hastily   283 *signify* announce   285 *betime* soon   287 *green* fresh   291 *meet* fitting   293 *far-fet* far-fetched, artfully contrived   297 *betimes* forthwith   300 *charactered* inscribed   306 *happily* haply, perhaps   310 *uncivil kerns* wild and irregular foot-soldiers   311 *temper* soften

YORK

I am content. Provide me soldiers, lords,

320 Whiles I take order for mine own affairs.

SUFFOLK

A charge, Lord York, that I will see performed.

But now return we to the false Duke Humphrey.

CARDINAL

No more of him ; for I will deal with him

That henceforth he shall trouble us no more.

325 And so break off ; the day is almost spent.

326 Lord Suffolk, you and I must talk of that event.

YORK

My Lord of Suffolk, within fourteen days

328 At Bristow I expect my soldiers,

For there I'll ship them all for Ireland.

SUFFOLK

I'll see it truly done, my Lord of York.

Exeunt. Manet York.

YORK

Now, York, or never, steel thy fearful thoughts

332 And change misdoubt to resolution.

Be that thou hop'st to be ; or what thou art

Resign to death : it is not worth th' enjoying.

335 Let pale-faced fear keep with the mean-born man

And find no harbor in a royal heart.

Faster than springtime show'rs comes thought on

thought,

338 And not a thought but thinks on dignity.

My brain, more busy than the laboring spider,

340 Weaves tedious snares to trap mine enemies.

Well, nobles, well, 'tis politicly done

To send me packing with an host of men.

343 I fear me you but warm the starvèd snake,

Who, cherished in your breasts, will sting your hearts.

'Twas men I lacked, and you will give them me ;

I take it kindly. Yet be well assured

You put sharp weapons in a madman's hands.

Whiles I in Ireland nourish a mighty band,

I will stir up in England some black storm

Shall blow ten thousand souls to heaven – or hell ;

And this fell tempest shall not cease to rage

Until the golden circuit on my head,

Like to the glorious sun's transparent beams,

354 Do calm the fury of this mad-bred flaw.

355 And for a minister of my intent

I have seduced a headstrong Kentishman,

John Cade of Ashford,

To make commotion, as full well he can,

359 Under the title of John Mortimer.

In Ireland have I seen this stubborn Cade

Oppose himself against a troop of kerns,

362 And fought so long till that his thighs with darts

Were almost like a sharp-quilled porpentine ;   363

And in the end being rescued, I have seen

Him caper upright like a wild Morisco,   365

Shaking the bloody darts as he his bells.

Full often, like a shag-haired crafty kern,

Hath he conversèd with the enemy

And undiscovered come to me again

And given me notice of their villainies.

This devil here shall be my substitute ;

For that John Mortimer which now is dead

In face, in gait, in speech, he doth resemble.

By this I shall perceive the commons' mind,

How they affect the house and claim of York.   375

Say he be taken, racked, and torturèd ;

I know no pain they can inflict upon him

Will make him say I moved him to those arms.

Say that he thrive, as 'tis great like he will ;   379

Why, then from Ireland come I with my strength

And reap the harvest which that rascal sowed ;

For, Humphrey being dead, as he shall be,

And Henry put apart, the next for me.   *Exit.*

*

Enter two or three running over the stage, from the   III, ii
murder of Duke Humphrey.

1. MURDERER

Run to my Lord of Suffolk ; let him know

We have dispatched the duke, as he commanded.

2. MURDERER

O that it were to do ! What have we done ?   3

Didst ever hear a man so penitent ?

Enter Suffolk.

1. MURDERER

Here comes my lord.

SUFFOLK

Now, sirs, have you dispatched this thing ?

1. MURDERER

Ay, my good lord ; he's dead.

SUFFOLK

Why, that's well said. Go, get you to my house ;

I will reward you for this venturous deed.

The king and all the peers are here at hand.

Have you laid fair the bed ? Is all things well,

According as I gave directions ?

1. MURDERER

'Tis, my good lord.

SUFFOLK

Away ! be gone !   *Exeunt [Murderers].*

Sound trumpets. Enter the King, the Queen,
Cardinal, Somerset, with Attendants.

KING

Go call our uncle to our presence straight.

Say we intend to try his grace to-day,

If he be guilty, as 'tis publishèd.   17

SUFFOLK

I'll call him presently, my noble lord.   *Exit.*

KING

Lords, take your places ; and I pray you all

Proceed no straiter 'gainst our uncle Gloucester   20

Than from true evidence, of good esteem,

He be approved in practice culpable.   22

QUEEN

God forbid any malice should prevail

That faultless may condemn a nobleman ;   24

---

320 *take order for* arrange   325 *break off* talk no more   326 *event* outcome
328 *Bristow* Bristol   332 *misdoubt* fear   335 *keep* live   338 *dignity* high
position   340 *tedious* complicated   343 *starvèd* frozen   354 *flaw* squall
355 *minister* agent   359 *Mortimer* (the family name of the descendants of
Philippe, daughter of Lionel, Duke of Clarence, third son of Edward III.
Cade would thus claim the crown through the same line as York himself,
cf. II, ii, 10 ff.)   362 *darts* light spears (with which kerns were usually
armed)   363 *porpentine* porcupine   365 *Morisco* morris-dancer   375 *affect*
like   379 *great like* very likely
III, ii A room adjoining Gloucester's bedchamber   3 *O . . . do* i.e. would
that it had not been done yet   17 *If* whether   20 *straiter* stricter   22
approved proved   24 *That . . . nobleman* i.e. that may condemn a nobleman
who is faultless

Pray God he may acquit him of suspicion.

KING
I thank thee, Meg. These words content me much.
    Enter Suffolk.
How now? Why look'st thou pale? Why tremblest thou?
Where is our uncle? What's the matter, Suffolk?

SUFFOLK
Dead in his bed, my lord; Gloucester is dead.

QUEEN
30   Marry, God forfend!

CARDINAL
God's secret judgment. I did dream to-night
32   The duke was dumb and could not speak a word.
    King sounds.

QUEEN
How fares my lord? Help, lords! The king is dead.

SOMERSET
34   Rear up his body; wring him by the nose.

QUEEN
Run, go! help, help! O Henry, ope thine eyes.

SUFFOLK
He doth revive again. Madam, be patient.

KING
O heavenly God.

QUEEN   How fares my gracious lord?

SUFFOLK
Comfort, my sovereign. Gracious Henry, comfort.

KING
What, doth my Lord of Suffolk comfort me?
40   Came he right now to sing a raven's note
Whose dismal tune bereft my vital pow'rs,
And thinks he that the chirping of a wren
By crying comfort from a hollow breast
Can chase away the first-conceivèd sound?
Hide not thy poison with such sugared words.
Lay not thy hands on me. Forbear, I say!
Their touch affrights me as a serpent's sting.
Thou baleful messenger, out of my sight!
Upon thy eyeballs murderous tyranny
Sits in grim majesty to fright the world.
Look not upon me, for thine eyes are wounding.
52   Yet do not go away. Come, basilisk,
And kill the innocent gazer with thy sight;
For in the shade of death I shall find joy –
In life but double death, now Gloucester's dead.

QUEEN
56   Why do you rate my Lord of Suffolk thus?
Although the duke was enemy to him,
Yet he most Christianlike laments his death;
And for myself, foe as he was to me,
Might liquid tears or heart-offending groans
61   Or blood-consuming sighs recall his life,
I would be blind with weeping, sick with groans,
Look pale as primrose with blood-drinking sighs,
And all to have the noble duke alive.
What know I how the world may deem of me?
66   For it is known we were but hollow friends.
It may be judged I made the duke away;
So shall my name with slander's tongue be wounded
And princes' courts be filled with my reproach.
This get I by his death. Ay me unhappy,
To be a queen, and crowned with infamy!

KING
Ah, woe is me for Gloucester, wretched man.

QUEEN
Be woe for me, more wretched than he is.
What, dost thou turn away, and hide thy face?
I am no loathsome leper. Look on me.
What? Art thou like the adder waxen deaf?   76
Be poisonous too, and kill thy forlorn queen.
Is all thy comfort shut in Gloucester's tomb?
Why, then Dame Margaret was ne'er thy joy.
Erect his statue and worship it,   80
And make my image but an alehouse sign.
Was I for this nigh wracked upon the sea
And twice by awkward wind from England's bank   83
Drove back again unto my native clime?
What boded this but well-forewarning wind
Did seem to say, 'Seek not a scorpion's nest
Nor set no footing on this unkind shore'?
What did I then but cursed the gentle gusts
And he that loosed them forth their brazen caves,   89
And bid them blow toward England's blessèd shore
Or turn our stern upon a dreadful rock?
Yet Aeolus would not be a murderer,
But left that hateful office unto thee.
The pretty vaulting sea refused to drown me,
Knowing that thou wouldst have me drowned on shore
With tears as salt as sea through thy unkindness.
The splitting rocks cowered in the sinking sands
And would not dash me with their ragged sides,
Because thy flinty heart, more hard than they,   99
Might in thy palace perish Margaret.
As far as I could ken thy chalky cliffs,   101
When from thy shore the tempest beat us back,
I stood upon the hatches in the storm,
And when the dusky sky began to rob
My earnest-gaping sight of thy land's view,
I took a costly jewel from my neck,
A heart it was, bound in with diamonds,
And threw it toward thy land. The sea received it,
And so I wished thy body might my heart;
And even with this I lost fair England's view,
And bid mine eyes be packing with my heart,   111
And called them blind and dusky spectacles   112
For losing ken of Albion's wishèd coast.   113
How often have I tempted Suffolk's tongue
(The agent of thy foul inconstancy)
To sit and witch me as Ascanius did   116
When he to madding Dido would unfold   117
His father's acts commencèd in burning Troy!
Am I not witched like her? or thou not false like him?
Ay me, I can no more. Die, Margaret!
For Henry weeps that thou dost live so long.
    Noise within. Enter Warwick, [Salisbury,] and
    many Commons.

---

30 *forfend* forbid   **32 s.d.** *sounds* swoons   **34** *Rear up* raise; *wring . . . nose* (supposed to aid in restoring consciousness)   **40** *raven's note* (a bad omen)   **52** *basilisk* a fabulous serpent, said to kill by its look   **56** *rate* complain against, berate   **61** *blood-consuming* (because each sigh was thought to cost the heart a drop of blood)   **66** *hollow friends* i.e. enemies   **76** *waxen* grown   **80** *statue* (trisyllabic: 'statuë')   **83** *awkward* adverse   **89** *he* i.e. Aeolus, god of the winds   **99** *Because* so that   **101** *ken* discern   **111** *be packing* be gone   **112** *spectacles* viewers (specifically telescopes)   **113** *Albion's* England's   **116** *witch* bewitch; *Ascanius* son of the Trojan hero Aeneas (in the *Aeneid* it is Cupid disguised as Ascanius who is on hand when Aeneas himself tells Dido, queen of Carthage, of his adventures)   **117** *madding* going mad (in this case, with love)

WARWICK

It is reported, mighty sovereign,
That good Duke Humphrey traitorously is murdered
By Suffolk and the Cardinal Beaufort's means.
The commons, like an angry hive of bees
That want their leader, scatter up and down
And care not who they sting in his revenge.
128 Myself have calmed their spleenful mutiny
129 Until they hear the order of his death.

KING

That he is dead, good Warwick, 'tis too true;
But how he died God knows, not Henry.
Enter his chamber, view his breathless corpse,
133 And comment then upon his sudden death.

WARWICK

That shall I do, my liege. Stay, Salisbury,
With the rude multitude till I return.   *[Exit.]*
               [Exit Salisbury with the Commons.]

KING

O thou that judgest all things, stay my thoughts –
My thoughts, that labor to persuade my soul
Some violent hands were laid on Humphrey's life.
139 If my suspect be false, forgive me, God;
For judgment only doth belong to thee.
141 Fain would I go to chafe his paly lips
With twenty thousand kisses and to drain
Upon his face an ocean of salt tears,
To tell my love unto his dumb deaf trunk,
And with my fingers feel his hand unfeeling.
146 But all in vain are these mean obsequies;
      Bed put forth [with the body. Enter Warwick].
And to survey his dead and earthy image,
What were it but to make my sorrow greater?

WARWICK

Come hither, gracious sovereign, view this body.

KING

That is to see how deep my grave is made;
For with his soul fled all my worldly solace,
For seeing him, I see my life in death.

WARWICK

As surely as my soul intends to live
With that dread King that took our state upon him
To free us from his Father's wrathful curse,
I do believe that violent hands were laid
Upon the life of this thrice-famèd duke.

SUFFOLK

A dreadful oath, sworn with a solemn tongue.
159 What instance gives Lord Warwick for his vow?

WARWICK

See how the blood is settled in his face.
161 Oft have I seen a timely-parted ghost,
Of ashy semblance, meagre, pale, and bloodless,
Being all descended to the laboring heart,
Who, in the conflict that it holds with death,
Attracts the same for aidance 'gainst the enemy,
Which with the heart there cools, and ne'er returneth
To blush and beautify the cheek again.

But see, his face is black and full of blood;
His eyeballs further out than when he lived,
Staring full ghastly, like a strangled man;
His hair upreared, his nostrils stretched with struggling;
His hands abroad displayed, as one that grasped
And tugged for life and was by strength subdued.
Look, on the sheets his hair, you see, is sticking;
His well-proportioned beard made rough and rugged,
Like to the summer's corn by tempest lodged.   176
It cannot be but he was murdered here.
The least of all these signs were probable.

SUFFOLK

Why, Warwick, who should do the duke to death?
Myself and Beaufort had him in protection,
And we, I hope, sir, are no murderers.

WARWICK

But both of you were vowed Duke Humphrey's foes,
And you (forsooth) had the good duke to keep.
'Tis like you would not feast him like a friend,
And 'tis well seen he found an enemy.

QUEEN

Then you belike suspect these noblemen
As guilty of Duke Humphrey's timeless death.   187

WARWICK

Who finds the heifer dead and bleeding fresh
And sees fast-by a butcher with an axe,
But will suspect 'twas he that made the slaughter?
Who finds the partridge in the puttock's nest   191
But may imagine how the bird was dead,
Although the kite soar with unbloodied beak?
Even so suspicious is this tragedy.

QUEEN

Are you the butcher, Suffolk? Where's your knife?
Is Beaufort termed a kite? Where are his talons?

SUFFOLK

I wear no knife to slaughter sleeping men;
But here's a vengeful sword, rusted with ease,
That shall be scourèd in his rancorous heart
That slanders me with murder's crimson badge.
Say, if thou dar'st, proud Lord of Warwickshire,
That I am faulty in Duke Humphrey's death.
     [Exeunt Cardinal, Somerset, and Attendants.
               Bed drawn in.]

WARWICK

What dares not Warwick, if false Suffolk dare him?

QUEEN

He dares not calm his contumelious spirit,   204
Nor cease to be an arrogant controller,   205
Though Suffolk dare him twenty thousand times.

WARWICK

Madam, be still – with reverence may I say,
For every word you speak in his behalf
Is slander to your royal dignity.

SUFFOLK

Blunt-witted lord, ignoble in demeanor!
If ever lady wronged her lord so much,
Thy mother took into her blameful bed
Some stern untutored churl, and noble stock
Was graft with crab-tree slip, whose fruit thou art,   214
And never of the Nevils' noble race.

WARWICK

But that the guilt of murder bucklers thee,   216
And I should rob the deathsman of his fee,
Quitting thee thereby of ten thousand shames,   218

---

128 *spleenful* angry   129 *order* manner   133 *comment . . . upon* explain
139 *suspect* suspicion   141 *chafe* warm; *paly* pale   146 *obsequies* funeral
rites   159 *instance* proof   161 *timely-parted* departed at a fitting time
176 *lodged* levelled   187 *timeless* untimely   191 *puttock's* kite's (cf. l. 196)
204 *contumelious* contentious   205 *controller* critic   214 *slip* cutting
(probably with punning reference to the sense 'moral lapse')   216 *bucklers*
shields   218 *Quitting* ridding

And that my sovereign's presence makes me mild,
I would, false murd'rous coward, on thy knee
221   Make thee beg pardon for thy passèd speech
And say it was thy mother that thou meant'st,
That thou thyself wast born in bastardy ;
224   And after all this fearful homage done,
Give thee thy hire, and send thy soul to hell,
Pernicious bloodsucker of sleeping men !

SUFFOLK
Thou shalt be waking while I shed thy blood,
If from this presence thou dar'st go with me.

WARWICK
Away even now, or I will drag thee hence !
Unworthy though thou art, I'll cope with thee
And do some service to Duke Humphrey's ghost.
        Exeunt [Suffolk and Warwick, pulling him out].

KING
What stronger breastplate than a heart untainted ?
Thrice is he armed that hath his quarrel just,
And he but naked, though locked up in steel,
Whose conscience with injustice is corrupted.
        *A noise within [of Commons crying 'Down with
        Suffolk'].*

QUEEN
What noise is this ?
        *Enter Suffolk and Warwick, with their weapons
        drawn.*

KING
Why, how now, lords ? your wrathful weapons drawn
Here in our presence ? Dare you be so bold ?
Why, what tumultuous clamor have we here ?

SUFFOLK
The trait'rous Warwick, with the men of Bury,
Set all upon me, mighty sovereign.
        *Enter Salisbury [from the Commons within, again
        crying 'Down with Suffolk'].*

SALISBURY *[to the Commons within]*
242   Sirs, stand apart. The king shall know your mind. –
Dread lord, the commons send you word by me,
Unless Lord Suffolk straight be done to death
Or banishèd fair England's territories,
They will by violence tear him from your palace
And torture him with grievous ling'ring death.
They say, by him the good Duke Humphrey died ;
They say, in him they fear your highness' death ;
And mere instinct of love and loyalty –
251   Free from a stubborn opposite intent,
As being thought to contradict your liking –
253   Makes them thus forward in his banishment.
They say, in care of your most royal person,
That if your highness should intend to sleep
And charge that no man should disturb your rest
In pain of your dislike or pain of death,
Yet, notwithstanding such a strait edict,
Were there a serpent seen with forkèd tongue
That slily glided towards your majesty,
It were but necessary you were waked,
Lest, being suffered in that harmful slumber,
263   The mortal worm might make the sleep eternal.
And therefore do they cry, though you forbid,
That they will guard you, whe'r you will or no,
266   From such fell serpents as false Suffolk is ;
With whose envenomèd and fatal sting
Your loving uncle, twenty times his worth,

They say is shamefully bereft of life.

COMMONS *[within]*
An answer from the king, my Lord of Salisbury !

SUFFOLK
'Tis like the commons, rude unpolished hinds,   271
Could send such message to their sovereign !
But you, my lord, were glad to be employed,
To show how quaint an orator you are.   274
But all the honor Salisbury hath won
Is that he was the lord ambassador
Sent from a sort of tinkers to the king.   277

COMMONS *[within]*
An answer from the king, or we will all break in !

KING
Go, Salisbury, and tell them all from me
I thank them for their tender loving care ;
And had I not been cited so by them,   281
Yet did I purpose as they do entreat.
For sure my thoughts do hourly prophesy
Mischance unto my state by Suffolk's means ;
And therefore by His Majesty I swear
Whose far unworthy deputy I am,
He shall not breathe infection in this air   287
But three days longer, on the pain of death.
        [Exit Salisbury.]

QUEEN
O Henry, let me plead for gentle Suffolk.

KING
Ungentle queen, to call him gentle Suffolk.
No more, I say. If thou dost plead for him,
Thou wilt but add increase unto my wrath.
Had I but said, I would have kept my word ;
But when I swear, it is irrevocable. –
If after three days' space thou here be'st found
On any ground that I am ruler of,
The world shall not be ransom for thy life. –
Come, Warwick, come, good Warwick, go with me ;
I have great matters to impart to thee.
        Exit [King with Warwick].

QUEEN
Mischance and sorrow go along with you ;
Heart's discontent and sour affliction
Be playfellows to keep you company.
There's two of you ; the devil make a third,
And threefold vengeance tend upon your steps.

SUFFOLK
Cease, gentle queen, these execrations
And let thy Suffolk take his heavy leave.   306

QUEEN
Fie, coward woman and soft-hearted wretch.
Hast thou not spirit to curse thine enemy ?

SUFFOLK
A plague upon them ! Wherefore should I curse them ?
Would curses kill as doth the mandrake's groan,   310

---

221 *passèd* just spoken 224 *fearful homage* cowardly submission 242
stand apart separate, fall back 251–52 *Free . . . liking* i.e. innocent of any
stubbornness in crossing your desire 253 *forward* in insistent upon
263 *mortal worm* deadly snake 266 *fell* savage, cruel 271 *'Tis like* it is
likely (ironic) ; *hinds* boors 274 *quaint* clever 277 *sort* gang 281 *cited*
incited 287 *breathe infection in* infect by breathing into 306 *heavy*
mournful 310 *mandrake's groan* (the mandrake, a poisonous plant with a
forked root that gave it a vague similarity to the human form, was supposed, when pulled from the ground, to utter a cry or groan which could
kill the hearer or drive him mad)

I would invent as bitter searching terms,
312 As curst, as harsh, and horrible to hear,
Delivered strongly through my fixèd teeth,
With full as many signs of deadly hate,
As lean-faced Envy in her loathsome cave.
My tongue should stumble in mine earnest words,
Mine eyes should sparkle like the beaten flint,
318 Mine hair be fixed an end, as one distract;
319 Ay, every joint should seem to curse and ban;
And even now my burdened heart would break
Should I not curse them. Poison be their drink!
Gall, worse than gall, the daintiest that they taste;
323 Their sweetest shade a grove of cypress trees;
324 Their chiefest prospect murd'ring basilisks;
325 Their softest touch as smart as lizards' stings;
Their music frightful as the serpent's hiss,
327 And boding screech owls make the consort full!
All the foul terrors in dark-seated hell –

QUEEN
Enough, sweet Suffolk. Thou torment'st thyself;
And these dread curses, like the sun 'gainst glass,
Or like an overchargèd gun, recoil
And turn the force of them upon thyself.

SUFFOLK
333 You bade me ban, and will you bid me leave?
Now by the ground that I am banished from,
Well could I curse away a winter's night,
Though standing naked on a mountain top
Where biting cold would never let grass grow,
And think it but a minute spent in sport.

QUEEN
O, let me entreat thee cease! Give me thy hand,
That I may dew it with my mournful tears;
Nor let the rain of heaven wet this place
342 To wash away my woeful monuments.
O, could this kiss be printed in thy hand,
[Kisses his hand.]
344 That thou mightst think upon these by the seal
Through whom a thousand sighs are breathed for thee!
346 So get thee gone, that I may know my grief.
347 'Tis but surmised whiles thou art standing by,
As one that surfeits, thinking on a want.
349 I will repeal thee or, be well assured,
350 Adventure to be banishèd myself;
And banishèd I am, if but from thee.
Go, speak not to me. Even now be gone.
O, go not yet! Even thus two friends condemned
Embrace, and kiss, and take ten thousand leaves,
Loather a hundred times to part than die.
Yet now farewell, and farewell life with thee.

SUFFOLK
Thus is poor Suffolk ten times banishèd,
Once by the king and three times thrice by thee.
'Tis not the land I care for, wert thou thence.
A wilderness is populous enough,
So Suffolk had thy heavenly company;
For where thou art, there is the world itself
With every several pleasure in the world; 363
And where thou art not, desolation.
I can no more. Live thou to joy thy life;
Myself no joy in naught, but that thou liv'st.
Enter Vaux.

QUEEN
Whither goes Vaux so fast? What news, I prithee?

VAUX
To signify unto his majesty
That Cardinal Beaufort is at point of death,
For suddenly a grievous sickness took him
That makes him gasp and stare and catch the air,
Blaspheming God and cursing men on earth.
Sometime he talks as if Duke Humphrey's ghost
Were by his side; sometime he calls the king
And whispers to his pillow, as to him,
The secrets of his overchargèd soul;
And I am sent to tell his majesty
That even now he cries aloud for him.

QUEEN
Go tell this heavy message to the king.   Exit [Vaux]. 379
Ay me! What is this world? What news are these?
But wherefore grieve I at an hour's poor loss, 381
Omitting Suffolk's exile, my soul's treasure?
Why only, Suffolk, mourn I not for thee,
And with the southern clouds contend in tears – 384
Theirs for the earth's increase, mine for my sorrow's?
Now get thee hence. The king thou know'st is coming.
If thou be found by me, thou art but dead.

SUFFOLK
If I depart from thee, I cannot live;
And in thy sight to die, what were it else
But like a pleasant slumber in thy lap?
Here could I breathe my soul into the air,
As mild and gentle as the cradle-babe
Dying with mother's dug between its lips;
Where, from thy sight, I should be raging mad
And cry out for thee to close up mine eyes,
To have thee with thy lips to stop my mouth.
So shouldst thou either turn my flying soul,
Or I should breathe it so into thy body,
And then it lived in sweet Elysium. 399
To die by thee were but to die in jest;
From thee to die were torture more than death.
O, let me stay, befall what may befall!

QUEEN
Away! Though parting be a fretful corrosive, 403
It is applièd to a deathful wound. 404
To France, sweet Suffolk. Let me hear from thee;
For wheresoe'er thou art in this world's globe,
I'll have an Iris that shall find thee out. 407

SUFFOLK
I go.

QUEEN   And take my heart with thee.
[She kisses him.]

SUFFOLK
A jewel, locked into the woefull'st cask 409

312 *curst* full of damnation   318 *an* on; *distract* distracted   319 *ban* chide bitterly   323 *cypress trees* (because often planted near cemeteries)   324 *basilisks* (see III, ii, 52n.)   325 *lizards'*, serpents'   327 *consort* band of musicians   333 *leave* stop   342 *monuments* remembrances (i.e. the marks of my tears)   344 *That . . . seal* i.e. that by the impression (seal) my lips make upon your hand, you may think of them (*these* [lips] is the antecedent of *whom*)   346 *know* fully realize   347–48 *'Tis . . . want* i.e. while you remain here, I can only guess at the experience of hunger   349 *repeal thee* have your banishment repealed   350 *Adventure* risk   363 *several* different, distinct   379 *heavy* serious, sad   381 *hour's poor loss* (the cardinal, an old man, had only a short time to live; the loss of this 'hour' is not worth great grief)   384 *southern clouds* (conventional source of rain)   399 *Elysium* classical Paradise   403 *corrosive* painful medicine   404 *deathful* deadly   407 *Iris* messenger of Juno, queen of the gods   409 *cask* casket

That ever did contain a thing of worth.
Even as a splitted bark, so sunder we.
This way fall I to death.

QUEEN   This way for me.
                                    Exeunt [severally].

*

III, iii   *Enter the King, Salisbury, and Warwick, to the*
          Cardinal in bed [raving and staring as if mad].

KING
    How fares my lord? Speak, Beaufort, to thy sovereign.
CARDINAL
    If thou be'st Death, I'll give thee England's treasure,
    Enough to purchase such another island,
    So thou wilt let me live and feel no pain.
KING
    Ah, what a sign it is of evil life
    Where death's approach is seen so terrible.
WARWICK
    Beaufort, it is thy sovereign speaks to thee.
CARDINAL
    Bring me unto my trial when you will.
9   Died he not in his bed? Where should he die?
    Can I make men live, whe'r they will or no?
    O, torture me no more! I will confess.
    Alive again? Then show me where he is.
    I'll give a thousand pound to look upon him.
    He hath no eyes; the dust hath blinded them.
    Comb down his hair. Look, look! it stands upright,
16 Like lime-twigs set to catch my wingèd soul.
    Give me some drink, and bid the apothecary
    Bring the strong poison that I bought of him.
KING
    O thou eternal Mover of the heavens,
    Look with a gentle eye upon this wretch.
    O, beat away the busy meddling fiend
    That lays strong siege unto this wretch's soul,
    And from his bosom purge this black despair.
WARWICK
    See how the pangs of death do make him grin.
SALISBURY
    Disturb him not; let him pass peaceably.
KING
    Peace to his soul, if God's good pleasure be.
    Lord Cardinal, if thou think'st on heaven's bliss,
    Hold up thy hand, make signal of thy hope.
    He dies and makes no sign. O God, forgive him.
WARWICK
30 So bad a death argues a monstrous life.
KING
    Forbear to judge, for we are sinners all.
32 Close up his eyes and draw the curtain close,
    And let us all to meditation.   *Exeunt.*

*

IV, i   *Alarum. Fight at sea. Ordnance goes off. Enter*
        Lieutenant, [Master, Mate, Walter Whitmore, and
        Soldiers, guarding] Suffolk [disguised, and
        Gentlemen].

LIEUTENANT
1   The gaudy, blabbing, and remorseful day
    Is crept into the bosom of the sea,

And now loud-howling wolves arouse the jades   3
That drag the tragic melancholy night,
Who with their drowsy, slow, and flagging wings
Clip dead men's graves, and from their misty jaws   6
Breathe foul contagious darkness in the air.
Therefore bring forth the soldiers of our prize;   8
For, whilst our pinnace anchors in the Downs,   9
Here shall they make their ransom on the sand
Or with their blood stain this discolored shore.
Master, this prisoner freely give I thee;
And thou that art his Mate, make boot of this;   13
The other, Walter Whitmore, is thy share.
1. GENTLEMAN
    What is my ransom, Master? Let me know.
MASTER
    A thousand crowns, or else lay down your head.
MATE
    And so much shall you give, or off goes yours.
LIEUTENANT
    What, think you much to pay two thousand crowns,
    And bear the name and port of gentlemen?   19
    Cut both the villains' throats, for die you shall.
    The lives of those which we have lost in fight
    Be counterpoised with such a petty sum?
1. GENTLEMAN
    I'll give it, sir, and therefore spare my life.
2. GENTLEMAN
    And so will I, and write home for it straight.
WHITMORE
    I lost mine eye in laying the prize aboard,   25
        [To Suffolk]
    And therefore to revenge it shalt thou die;
    And so should these, if I might have my will.
LIEUTENANT
    Be not so rash; take ransom, let him live.
SUFFOLK
    Look on my George; I am a gentleman.   29
    Rate me at what thou wilt, thou shalt be paid. 30
WHITMORE
    And so am I. My name is Walter Whitmore.
    How now? Why starts thou? What, doth death affright?
SUFFOLK
    Thy name affrights me, in whose sound is death. 33
    A cunning man did calculate my birth   34
    And told me that by water I should die.
    Yet let not this make thee be bloody-minded;
    Thy name is Gaultier, being rightly sounded.   37
WHITMORE
    Gaultier or Walter, which it is I care not.
    Never yet did base dishonor blur our name
    But with our sword we wiped away the blot;
    Therefore, when merchantlike I sell revenge,

III, iii The Cardinal's bedchamber   9 *he* i.e. Duke Humphrey   16 *lime-twigs* (see I, iii, 86n.)   30 *argues* gives proof of   32 *curtain* i.e. of the bed
IV, i The coast of Kent, near the Downs   1 *gaudy* bright; *blabbing* garrulous, telltale; *remorseful* full of pitiable events   3 *jades* horses, i.e. the dragons of Hecate, which draw the night across the sky   6 *Clip* embrace   8 *soldiers . . . prize* i.e. the soldiers we have captured   9 *Downs* anchorage off Kent   13 *boot* profit   19 *port* demeanor   25 *laying . . . aboard* boarding the captured ship   29 *George* badge representing Saint George and the dragon, an insigne of the Order of the Garter   30 *Rate* value   33 *sound* (*Walter* was pronounced 'Wa'ter')   34 *cunning man* fortune-teller; *calculate my birth* (astrologers required the moment of one's birth in order to cast a horoscope)   37 *Gaultier* (*Walter* in French)

42 Broke be my sword, my arms torn and defaced,
And I proclaimed a coward through the world.

SUFFOLK
Stay, Whitmore, for thy prisoner is a prince,
The Duke of Suffolk, William de la Pole.

WHITMORE
The Duke of Suffolk muffled up in rags?

SUFFOLK
Ay, but these rags are no part of the duke.
[Jove sometime went disguised, and why not I?]

LIEUTENANT
But Jove was never slain, as thou shalt be.

SUFFOLK
50 Obscure and lousy swain, King Henry's blood,
The honorable blood of Lancaster,
52 Must not be shed by such a jaded groom.
Hast thou not kissed thy hand and held my stirrup?
54 Bare-headed plodded by my footcloth mule,
And thought thee happy when I shook my head?
How often hast thou waited at my cup,
57 Fed from my trencher, kneeled down at the board,
When I have feasted with Queen Margaret?
59 Remember it, and let it make thee crestfall'n,
60 Ay, and allay this thy abortive pride.
61 How in our voiding lobby hast thou stood
And duly waited for my coming forth!
This hand of mine hath writ in thy behalf,
And therefore shall it charm thy riotous tongue.

WHITMORE
65 Speak, captain, shall I stab the forlorn swain?

LIEUTENANT
First let my words stab him, as he hath me.

SUFFOLK
Base slave, thy words are blunt, and so art thou.

LIEUTENANT
Convey him hence, and on our long-boat's side
Strike off his head.

SUFFOLK   Thou dar'st not, for thy own.

70 LIEUTENANT Pole –
SUFFOLK Pole?

LIEUTENANT
72 Ay, kennel, puddle, sink! whose filth and dirt
Troubles the silver spring where England drinks.
Now will I dam up this thy yawning mouth
For swallowing the treasure of the realm.
Thy lips that kissed the queen shall sweep the ground,
And thou that smiledst at good Duke Humphrey's death

Against the senseless winds shall grin in vain, 78
Who in contempt shall hiss at thee again.
And wedded be thou to the hags of hell
For daring to affy a mighty lord 81
Unto the daughter of a worthless king,
Having neither subject, wealth, nor diadem.
By devilish policy art thou grown great,
And, like ambitious Sulla, overgorged 85
With gobbets of thy mother's bleeding heart. 86
By thee Anjou and Maine were sold to France;
The false revolting Normans thorough thee 88
Disdain to call us lord, and Picardy
Hath slain their governors, surprised our forts,
And sent the ragged soldiers wounded home.
The princely Warwick and the Nevils all,
Whose dreadful swords were never drawn in vain,
As hating thee, are rising up in arms;
And now the house of York, thrust from the crown
By shameful murder of a guiltless king
And lofty, proud, encroaching tyranny,
Burns with revenging fire, whose hopeful colors
Advance our half-faced sun, striving to shine, 99
Under the which is writ 'Invitis nubibus.' 100
The commons here in Kent are up in arms,
And to conclude, reproach and beggary
Is crept into the palace of our king,
And all by thee. Away! convey him hence.

SUFFOLK
O that I were a god, to shoot forth thunder
Upon these paltry, servile, abject drudges.
Small things make base men proud. This villain here,
Being captain of a pinnace, threatens more
Than Bargulus, the strong Illyrian pirate. 109
Drones suck not eagles' blood but rob beehives.
It is impossible that I should die
By such a lowly vassal as thyself.
Thy words move rage and not remorse in me.
I go of message from the queen to France.
I charge thee waft me safely 'cross the Channel. 115

LIEUTENANT Walter!

WHITMORE
Come, Suffolk, I must waft thee to thy death.

SUFFOLK Paene gelidus timor occupat artus. It is thee 118
I fear.

WHITMORE
Thou shalt have cause to fear before I leave thee.
What, are ye daunted now? Now will ye stoop?

I. GENTLEMAN
My gracious lord, entreat him, speak him fair.

SUFFOLK
Suffolk's imperial tongue is stern and rough,
Used to command, untaught to plead for favor.
Far be it we should honor such as these
With humble suit. No, rather let my head
Stoop to the block than these knees bow to any
Save to the God of heaven and to my king;
And sooner dance upon a bloody pole
Than stand uncovered to the vulgar groom. 129
True nobility is exempt from fear.
More can I bear than you dare execute.

LIEUTENANT
Hale him away and let him talk no more.

SUFFOLK
Come, soldiers, show what cruelty ye can,

42 *arms* coat of arms   50 *King Henry's blood* (Suffolk falsely claimed that his mother was a distant cousin of Henry VI)   52 *jaded* (1) lowly-bred, (2) having to do with horses   54 *footcloth mule* mule covered with an ornamented caparison   57 *trencher* platter   59 *crestfall'n* humble (with punning allusion to Whitmore's claim to gentility, the 'crest' being a part of the armorial bearings)   60 *abortive* monstrous   61 *voiding lobby* waiting room   65 *captain* (a courtesy title given – as customarily – to the lieutenant because he is the commander of a ship)   70–72 *Pole . . . kennel* (word-play on 'poll' [head], 'Pole' [Suffolk's family name, pronounced 'pool'], and 'pool' [of water]; a kennel is an open gutter)   72 *sink* cesspool   78 *senseless* unfeeling   81 *affy* affiance   85 *Sulla* Lucius Cornelius Sulla (138–78 B.C.), the first Roman dictator to issue proscriptions   86 *gobbets* chunks of flesh   88 *thorough* through   99 *half-faced sun* (a sun bursting through clouds was the device of Edward III and Richard II, the *guiltless king* of l. 96)   100 *Invitis nubibus* in spite of clouds (source unidentified)   109 *Bargulus* i.e. Bardylis (fl. 383 B.C.) a Balkan chieftain (Shakespeare's 'Bargulus' comes from Cicero, *De Officiis*, II, 11)   115 *waft* transport by water   118 *Paene . . . artus* cold fear seizes my limbs almost entirely   129 *uncovered* bareheaded

That this my death may never be forgot.
135 Great men oft die by vile bezonians.
A Roman sworder and banditto slave
137 Murdered sweet Tully; Brutus' bastard hand
138 Stabbed Julius Caesar; savage islanders
Pompey the Great; and Suffolk dies by pirates.
Exit Walter [Whitmore] with Suffolk.

LIEUTENANT
And as for these whose ransom we have set,
It is our pleasure one of them depart.
Therefore come you with us, and let him go.
Exeunt Lieutenant and the rest.
Manet the First Gentleman.
Enter Walter [Whitmore] with the body [of Suffolk].

WHITMORE
There let his head and lifeless body lie
Until the queen his mistress bury it.   *Exit Walter.*

1. GENTLEMAN
O barbarous and bloody spectacle!
His body will I bear unto the king.
If he revenge it not, yet will his friends;
148 So will the queen, that living held him dear.
[Exit with the body.]

*

IV, ii   *Enter two Rebels [with long staves].*
1. REBEL Come and get thee a sword, though made of a
2   lath. They have been up these two days.
2. REBEL They have the more need to sleep now then.
1. REBEL I tell thee Jack Cade the clothier means to dress
5   the commonwealth and turn it and set a new nap upon it.
2. REBEL So he had need, for 'tis threadbare. Well, I say
it was never merry world in England since gentlemen
8   came up.
1. REBEL O miserable age! Virtue is not regarded in
handicraftsmen.
11 2. REBEL The nobility think scorn to go in leather aprons.
1. REBEL Nay, more, the king's council are no good
workmen.
2. REBEL True; and yet it is said, 'Labor in thy vocation'; which is as much to say as 'Let the magistrates be
laboring men'; and therefore should we be magistrates.
1. REBEL Thou hast hit it; for there's no better sign of a
brave mind than a hard hand.
2. REBEL I see them, I see them! There's Best's son, the
20   tanner of Wingham –
1. REBEL He shall have the skins of our enemies to make
22   dog's leather of.
2. REBEL And Dick the butcher –
1. REBEL Then is sin struck down like an ox and iniquity's throat cut like a calf.
2. REBEL And Smith the weaver.
27 1. REBEL Argo, their thread of life is spun.
2. REBEL Come, come, let's fall in with them.
Drum. Enter Cade, Dick [the] Butcher, Smith the
Weaver, and a Sawyer, with infinite numbers
[bearing long staves].
CADE We, John Cade, so termed of our supposed father –
30 BUTCHER *[aside]* Or rather, of stealing a cade of herrings.
31 CADE For our enemies shall fall before us, inspired with
the spirit of putting down kings and princes – Command silence!
BUTCHER Silence!
35 CADE My father was a Mortimer –

BUTCHER *[aside]* He was an honest man and a good brick- 36
layer.
CADE My mother a Plantagenet –
BUTCHER *[aside]* I knew her well. She was a midwife.
CADE My wife descended of the Lacies. 39
BUTCHER *[aside]* She was indeed a pedlar's daughter and
sold many laces.
WEAVER *[aside]* But now of late, not able to travel with
her furred pack, she washes bucks here at home. 43
CADE Therefore am I of an honorable house.
BUTCHER *[aside]* Ay, by my faith, the field is honorable 45
and there was he born, under a hedge; for his father had
never a house but the cage. 47
CADE Valiant I am.
WEAVER *[aside]* 'A must needs, for beggary is valiant. 49
CADE I am able to endure much.
BUTCHER *[aside]* No question of that, for I have seen him
whipped three market days together.
CADE I fear neither sword nor fire.
WEAVER *[aside]* He need not fear the sword, for his coat
is of proof. 55
BUTCHER *[aside]* But methinks he should stand in fear of
fire, being burnt i' th' hand for stealing of sheep. 57
CADE Be brave then, for your captain is brave and vows
reformation. There shall be in England seven halfpenny
loaves sold for a penny; the three-hooped pot shall have 60
ten hoops, and I will make it felony to drink small beer. 61
All the realm shall be in common, and in Cheapside 62
shall my palfrey go to grass; and when I am king, as 63
king I will be –
ALL God save your majesty!
CADE I thank you, good people – there shall be no money;
all shall eat and drink on my score; and I will apparel 67
them all in one livery, that they may agree like brothers
and worship me their lord.
BUTCHER The first thing we do, let's kill all the lawyers.
CADE Nay, that I mean to do. Is not this a lamentable
thing, that of the skin of an innocent lamb should be
made parchment? that parchment, being scribbled o'er,

135 *bezonians* beggars   137 *Tully* i.e. Marcus Tullius Cicero; *Brutus'*
bastard hand (Brutus was reputed to be the bastard son of Julius Caesar)
138 *savage islanders* i.e. of Lesbos (according to one version of the story;
according to Plutarch, Pompey was killed in Egypt by his former officers
in Ptolemy's hire)   148 s.d. *body* (and the head, with which the queen
enters at IV, iv)
IV, ii A heath in Kent near London (Blackheath)   2 *lath* slight piece of
wood   5 *nap* the fuzz or down on the surface of a piece of cloth (with
allusion to Cade's occupation of shearman, mentioned at l. 121)   8 *came*
up rose into fashion   11 *leather aprons* (worn by workmen)   20 *Wingham* a
village near Canterbury   22 *dog's leather* (used for gloves)   27 *Argo* ergo,
therefore (mispronounced)   30 *cade* barrel   31 *fall* (punning on 'cado,' I
fall)   35 *Mortimer* (who could, like York, claim the crown through Lionel,
Duke of Clarence; see III, i, 359n.)   36 *bricklayer* (invited by a pun on
'Mortimer' / 'mortarer')   39 *Lacies* (Lacy was the surname of the Earls of
Lincoln)   43 *furred pack* pedlar's pack, made of skin with the hair outward;
washes bucks does laundry ('buck' is lye; 'bucks' are the clothes treated with
it. There is also a punning reference to 'furred pack' as a herd of deer.)   45
field (with punning allusion to a heraldic 'field,' the surface of an escutcheon)   47 *cage* a small portable prison for the exposure of minor criminals
in public places   49 *valiant* sturdy (the giving of alms to 'valiant beggars,'
those able to work, was illegal)   55 *proof* (1) of good quality, reliable (of a
coat of mail), (2) well-worn   57 *burnt i' th' hand* branded   60 *three-*
hooped pot (Wooden drinking pots were banded with metal, a quart pot
having three bands or hoops. Cade means that for the price of a quart
one will be able to buy more than three quarts.)   61 *small beer* weak beer
(everyone will drink stronger double-beer)   62 *Cheapside* the location
of many of the London markets   63 *palfrey* saddle horse   67 *score*
account

should undo a man? Some say the bee stings, but I say 'tis the bee's wax; for I did but seal once to a thing, and I was never mine own man since. How now? Who's there?

Enter a Clerk [as prisoner].

77 WEAVER The clerk of Chartham. He can write and read
78 and cast account.

CADE O monstrous!

80 WEAVER We took him setting of boys' copies.

CADE Here's a villain.

82 WEAVER Has a book in his pocket with red letters in't.

CADE Nay, then he is a conjurer.

84 BUTCHER Nay, he can make obligations and write court-hand.

85 CADE I am sorry for't. The man is a proper man, of mine honor. Unless I find him guilty, he shall not die. Come hither, sirrah, I must examine thee. What is thy name?

CLERK Emmanuel.

89 BUTCHER They use to write it on the top of letters. 'Twill go hard with you.

CADE Let me alone. Dost thou use to write thy name? or hast thou a mark to thyself, like an honest plain-dealing man?

CLERK Sir, I thank God, I have been so well brought up that I can write my name.

ALL He hath confessed. Away with him! He's a villain and a traitor.

CADE Away with him, I say. Hang him with his pen and inkhorn about his neck.   *Exit one with the Clerk.*

Enter Messenger.

MESSENGER Where's our general?

100 CADE Here I am, thou particular fellow.

MESSENGER Fly, fly, fly! Sir Humphrey Stafford and his brother are hard by, with the king's forces.

CADE Stand, villain, stand, or I'll fell thee down. He shall be encount'red with a man as good as himself. He is but a knight, is 'a?

106 MESSENGER No.

CADE To equal him, I will make myself a knight presently. *[Kneels.]* Rise up Sir John Mortimer. *[Rises.]* Now have at him!

Enter Sir Humphrey Stafford and his brother [William], with Drum and Soldiers.

STAFFORD
110 Rebellious hinds, the filth and scum of Kent,
Marked for the gallows, lay your weapons down;
Home to your cottages, forsake this groom.
113 The king is merciful, if you revolt.

WILLIAM
But angry, wrathful, and inclined to blood,
If you go forward. Therefore yield or die.

CADE
As for these silken-coated slaves, I pass not. 116
It is to you, good people, that I speak,
Over whom (in time to come) I hope to reign,
For I am rightful heir unto the crown.

STAFFORD
Villain, thy father was a plasterer,
And thou thyself a shearman, art thou not? 121

CADE
And Adam was a gardener.

WILLIAM And what of that?

CADE
Marry, this: Edmund Mortimer, Earl of March,
Married the Duke of Clarence' daughter, did he not?

STAFFORD Ay, sir.

CADE
By her he had two children at one birth.

WILLIAM That's false.

CADE
Ay, there's the question. But I say 'tis true.
The elder of them, being put to nurse,
Was by a beggar woman stol'n away
And, ignorant of his birth and parentage,
Became a bricklayer when he came to age.
His son am I. Deny it if you can.

BUTCHER
Nay, 'tis too true. Therefore he shall be king. 135

WEAVER Sir, he made a chimney in my father's house,
and the bricks are alive at this day to testify it. Therefore
deny it not.

STAFFORD
And will you credit this base drudge's words 139
That speaks he knows not what?

ALL
Ay, marry, will we. Therefore get ye gone.

WILLIAM
Jack Cade, the Duke of York hath taught you this.

CADE *[aside]*
He lies, for I invented it myself. –
Go to, sirrah, tell the king from me that, for his father's
sake, Henry the Fifth (in whose time boys went to span- 145
counter for French crowns), I am content he shall reign, 146
but I'll be Protector over him.

BUTCHER And furthermore we'll have the Lord Say's 148
head for selling the dukedom of Maine.

CADE And good reason; for thereby is England mained 150
and fain to go with a staff, but that my puissance holds it
up. Fellow kings, I tell you that that Lord Say hath
gelded the commonwealth and made it an eunuch; and
more than that, he can speak French, and therefore he is
a traitor.

STAFFORD
O gross and miserable ignorance.

CADE Nay, answer, if you can. The Frenchmen are our
enemies. Go to then, I ask but this: Can he that speaks
with the tongue of an enemy be a good counsellor, or
no?

ALL No, no! and therefore we'll have his head.

WILLIAM
Well, seeing gentle words will not prevail, 160
Assail them with the army of the king.

STAFFORD
Herald, away; and throughout every town
Proclaim them traitors that are up with Cade,

That those which fly before the battle ends
May, even in their wives' and children's sight,
Be hanged up for example at their doors;
And you that be the king's friends, follow me.
Exit [Stafford with his men].

CADE
And you that love the commons, follow me.
Now show yourself men; 'tis for liberty!
We will not leave one lord, one gentleman;
171   Spare none but such as go in clouted shoon,
For they are thrifty honest men and such
As would (but that they dare not) take our parts.

BUTCHER They are all in order and march toward us.

CADE But then are we in order when we are most out of
order. Come, march forward!   *Exeunt.*

IV, iii   *Alarums to the fight, wherein both the Staffords are
slain. Enter Cade and the rest.*

CADE Where's Dick, the butcher of Ashford?

BUTCHER Here, sir.

CADE They fell before thee like sheep and oxen, and thou
behavedst thyself as if thou hadst been in thine own
slaughterhouse. Therefore thus will I reward thee: the
6   Lent shall be as long again as it is, and thou shalt have a
license to kill for a hundred lacking one.

BUTCHER I desire no more.

CADE And, to speak truth, thou deserv'st no less. This
monument of the victory will I bear *[puts on Sir Humphrey's helmet]*; and the bodies shall be dragged at my
horse heels till I do come to London, where we will have
the mayor's sword borne before us.

BUTCHER If we mean to thrive and do good, break open
the jails and let out the prisoners.

16 CADE Fear not that, I warrant thee. Come, let's march towards London.   *Exeunt.*

*

IV, iv   *Enter the King, with a supplication, and the Queen
with Suffolk's head; the Duke of Buckingham and
the Lord Say.*

QUEEN *[apart]*
Oft have I heard that grief softens the mind
And makes it fearful and degenerate.
Think therefore on revenge and cease to weep.
But who can cease to weep, and look on this?
Here may his head lie on my throbbing breast,
But where's the body that I should embrace?

BUCKINGHAM What answer makes your grace to the
rebels' supplication?

KING
I'll send some holy bishop to entreat,
10   For God forbid so many simple souls
Should perish by the sword. And I myself,
Rather than bloody war shall cut them short,
Will parley with Jack Cade their general.
But stay, I'll read it over once again.

QUEEN *[apart]*
Ah, barbarous villains; hath this lovely face
Ruled like a wandering planet over me,
And could it not enforce them to relent
That were unworthy to behold the same?

KING
Lord Say, Jack Cade hath sworn to have thy head.

SAY
20   Ay, but I hope your highness shall have his.

KING
How now, madam?
Still lamenting and mourning for Suffolk's death?
I fear me, love, if that I had been dead,
Thou wouldest not have mourned so much for me.

QUEEN
No, my love, I should not mourn, but die for thee.
Enter a Messenger.

KING
How now, what news? Why com'st thou in such haste?

MESSENGER
The rebels are in Southwark. Fly, my lord!   27
Jack Cade proclaims himself Lord Mortimer,
Descended from the Duke of Clarence' house,
And calls your grace usurper openly
And vows to crown himself in Westminster.
His army is a ragged multitude
Of hinds and peasants, rude and merciless.   33
Sir Humphrey Stafford and his brother's death
Hath given them heart and courage to proceed.
All scholars, lawyers, courtiers, gentlemen,
They call false caterpillars and intend their death.

KING
O graceless men! they know not what they do.

BUCKINGHAM
My gracious lord, retire to Killingworth   39
Until a power be raised to put them down.

QUEEN
Ah, were the Duke of Suffolk now alive,
These Kentish rebels would be soon appeased.

KING
Lord Say, the traitors hate thee;
Therefore away with us to Killingworth.

SAY
So might your grace's person be in danger.
The sight of me is odious in their eyes;
And therefore in this city will I stay
And live alone as secret as I may.
Enter another Messenger.

MESSENGER
Jack Cade hath gotten London Bridge;
The citizens fly and forsake their houses;
The rascal people, thirsting after prey,
Join with the traitor, and they jointly swear
To spoil the city and your royal court.   53

BUCKINGHAM
Then linger not, my lord. Away, take horse!

KING
Come, Margaret. God, our hope, will succor us.

QUEEN *[aside]*
My hope is gone now Suffolk is deceased.

KING *[to Lord Say]*
Farewell, my lord. Trust not the Kentish rebels.

BUCKINGHAM
Trust nobody, for fear you be betrayed.

171 *clouted shoon* hobnailed shoes
IV, iii 6–7 *Lent . . . one* (In Queen Elizabeth's reign the slaughtering
of meat was forbidden during Lent except for the provision of the sick.
For Dick's benefit Cade will double the length of Lent and allow him to
supply meat to ninety-nine people a week or, possibly, to slaughter ninety-
nine animals a week.)   16 *Fear* doubt
IV, iv The royal palace in London   s.d. *Lord Say* (see IV, ii, 148n.)   27
Southwark a suburb south of London, in Surrey   33 *hinds* workers, peasants
39 *Killingworth* i.e. Kenilworth Castle in Warwickshire   53 *spoil* despoil

SAY
> The trust I have is in mine innocence,
> And therefore am I bold and resolute.   *Exeunt.*

*

IV, v   *Enter [aloft] Lord Scales upon the Tower, walking.*
            Then enters two or three Citizens below.

SCALES
> How now? Is Jack Cade slain?

1. CITIZEN No, my lord, nor likely to be slain; for they
have won the Bridge, killing all those that withstand
them. The Lord Mayor craves aid of your honor from
the Tower to defend the city from the rebels.

SCALES
> Such aid as I can spare you shall command,
> But I am troubled here with them myself;
> The rebels have assayed to win the Tower.
9   But get you to Smithfield and gather head,
> And thither I will send you Matthew Goffe.
> Fight for your king, your country, and your lives;
> And so farewell, for I must hence again.   *Exeunt.*

*

IV, vi   *Enter Jack Cade and the rest, and strikes his staff on*
            London Stone.

CADE Now is Mortimer lord of this city. And here, sitting
upon London Stone, I charge and command that, of the
3   city's cost, the pissing conduit run nothing but claret
wine this first year of our reign. And now henceforward
it shall be treason for any that calls me other than Lord
Mortimer.
         Enter a Soldier, running.
SOLDIER Jack Cade! Jack Cade!
CADE Knock him down there.
         They kill him.
BUTCHER If this fellow be wise, he'll never call ye Jack
Cade more. I think he hath a very fair warning.
         [Enter Messenger.]
MESSENGER My lord, there's an army gathered together
in Smithfield.
CADE Come then, let's go fight with them. But first go and
set London Bridge on fire, and, if you can, burn down
the Tower too. Come, let's away.   *Exeunt omnes.*

IV, v *Before the Tower of London*   s.d. *Lord Scales* (Lord Thomas Scales,
who had fought with Talbot in France, was charged by the king with the
defense of the Tower)   9 *Smithfield* a section of London, in which there
were open fields
IV, vi *The streets of London*   s.d. *London Stone* an ancient landmark, in
Cannon Street   3 *pissing conduit* a fountain from which the poor drew water
IV, vii   1 *Savoy* the London residence of the Duke of Lancaster (an
anachronism, as the building was burned during Wat Tyler's rebellion and
not rebuilt until 1505)   2 *Inns of Court* the centre of legal training and
practice   7 *sore* (1) poor, (2) painful   19–20 *one-and-twenty . . . pound*
i.e. very high personal property taxes ('fifteens' were a levy of one-fifteenth
the value; 'one-and-twenty fifteens' is a deliberate exaggeration)   20 *the
last subsidy* at the time of the last general tax   22 *serge* (from 'say,' a silk
resembling serge); *buckram* a stiff, coarse linen (used in making props and
artificial figures for the stage; thus, 'false')   23 *within point-blank of*
i.e. directly before   25 *Basimecu* i.e. '*baise-mon-cul*,' kiss-my-arse   27
besom broom   31 *score . . . tally* (To furnish a record of a debt, a stick
would be scored or marked transversely and then split lengthwise, one
half being retained by the debtor and one by the creditor. The two halves
were called tallies.)   32 *king his* king's   39–40 *could not read* i.e. could not
read Latin and thus claim exemption from civil trial through 'benefit of
clergy'   42 *footcloth* (see IV, i, 54n.)   51 *bona . . . gens* a good country, a
wicked people

     Alarums. Matthew Goffe is slain, and all the rest   IV, vii
     [of the loyal forces]. Then enter Jack Cade with his
     company.

CADE So, sirs. Now go some and pull down the Savoy; 1
others to th' Inns of Court. Down with them all!   2
BUTCHER I have a suit unto your lordship.
CADE Be it a lordship, thou shalt have it for that word.
BUTCHER Only that the laws of England may come out of
your mouth.
2. REBEL *[aside]* Mass, 'twill be sore law then, for he was 7
thrust in the mouth with a spear, and 'tis not whole yet.
WEAVER *[aside]* Nay, John, it will be stinking law, for his
breath stinks with eating toasted cheese.
CADE I have thought upon it; it shall be so. Away, burn
all the records of the realm! My mouth shall be the
parliament of England.
2. REBEL *[aside]* Then we are like to have biting statutes,
unless his teeth be pulled out.
CADE And henceforward all things shall be in common.
         Enter a Messenger.
MESSENGER My lord, a prize, a prize! Here's the Lord
Say, which sold the towns in France; he that made us
pay one-and-twenty fifteens, and one shilling to the 19
pound, the last subsidy.   20
         Enter First Rebel, with the Lord Say.
CADE Well, he shall be beheaded for it ten times. Ah, thou
say, thou serge, nay, thou buckram lord: now art thou 22
within point-blank of our jurisdiction regal. What canst 23
thou answer to my majesty for giving up of Normandy
unto Mounsieur Basimecu, the Dauphin of France? Be 25
it known unto thee by these presence, even the presence
of Lord Mortimer, that I am the besom that must sweep 27
the court clean of such filth as thou art. Thou hast most
traitorously corrupted the youth of the realm in erecting
a grammar school; and whereas, before, our forefathers
had no other books but the score and the tally, thou hast 31
caused printing to be used, and, contrary to the king his 32
crown and dignity, thou hast built a paper mill. It will be
proved to thy face that thou hast men about thee that usually talk of a noun and a verb and such abominable words
as no Christian ear can endure to hear. Thou hast appointed justices of peace, to call poor men before them
about matters they were not able to answer. Moreover,
thou hast put them in prison, and because they could 39
not read, thou hast hanged them, when, indeed, only for
that cause they have been most worthy to live. Thou
dost ride in a footcloth, dost thou not?   42
SAY What of that?
CADE Marry, thou ought'st not to let thy horse wear a
cloak when honester men than thou go in their hose and
doublets.
BUTCHER And work in their shirt too; as myself, for
example, that am a butcher.
SAY You men of Kent –
BUTCHER What say you of Kent?
SAY Nothing but this – 'tis 'bona terra, mala gens.'   51
CADE Away with him, away with him! He speaks Latin.
SAY
> Hear me but speak, and bear me where'er you will.
> Kent, in the Commentaries Caesar writ,
> Is termed the civil'st place of all this isle.
> Sweet is the country, because full of riches;
> The people liberal, valiant, active, wealthy,
> Which makes me hope you are not void of pity.

I sold not Maine, I lost not Normandy ;
Yet to recover them would lose my life.

61 Justice with favor have I always done ;
Prayers and tears have moved me, gifts could never.
When have I aught exacted at your hands,
But to maintain the king, the realm, and you ?
Large gifts have I bestowed on learnèd clerks,

66 Because my book preferred me to the king.
And, seeing ignorance is the curse of God,
Knowledge the wing wherewith we fly to heaven,
Unless you be possessed with devilish spirits,
You cannot but forbear to murder me.
This tongue hath parleyed unto foreign kings

72 For your behoof.

CADE Tut ! when struck'st thou one blow in the field ?

SAY
Great men have reaching hands. Oft have I struck
Those that I never saw, and struck them dead.

1. REBEL O monstrous coward ! What, to come behind
folks ?

SAY
These cheeks are pale for watching for your good.

CADE Give him a box o' th' ear, and that will make 'em
red again.

SAY
80 Long sitting to determine poor men's causes
82 Hath made me full of sickness and diseases.

CADE Ye shall have a hempen caudle then and pap with a
hatchet.

BUTCHER Why dost thou quiver, man ?

SAY
The palsy, and not fear, provokes me.

CADE Nay, he nods at us, as who should say, 'I'll be even
with you.' I'll see if his head will stand steadier on a pole
or no. Take him away and behead him.

SAY
Tell me : wherein have I offended most ?
Have I affected wealth or honor ? Speak.
Are my chests filled up with extorted gold ?
Is my apparel sumptuous to behold ?
Whom have I injured, that ye seek my death ?
These hands are free from guiltless blood-shedding,
This breast from harboring foul deceitful thoughts.
O, let me live !

CADE [aside] I feel remorse in myself with his words, but
I'll bridle it. He shall die, an it be but for pleading so
99 well for his life. – Away with him ! he has a familiar under
100 his tongue ; he speaks not a God's name. Go, take him
away, I say, and strike off his head presently ; and then
102 break into his son-in-law's house, Sir James Cromer,
and strike off his head, and bring them both upon two
poles hither.

ALL It shall be done.

SAY
Ah, countrymen ! If when you make your prayers,
God should be so obdurate as yourselves,
How would it fare with your departed souls ?
And therefore yet relent, and save my life.

CADE Away with him, and do as I command ye.
[Exeunt some with the Lord Say.]
The proudest peer in the realm shall not wear a head on
his shoulders unless he pay me tribute. There shall not a
maid be married but she shall pay to me her maidenhead
113 ere they have it. Men shall hold of me in capite ; and we

charge and command that their wives be as free as heart
can wish or tongue can tell.

BUTCHER My lord, when shall we go to Cheapside and
take up commodities upon our bills ?   117

CADE Marry, presently.   118

ALL O brave !   119

*Enter two with the heads [of the Lord Say and
Sir James Cromer upon two poles].*

CADE But is not this braver ? Let them kiss one another, 120
for they loved well when they were alive. Now part them
again, lest they consult about the giving up of some
more towns in France. Soldiers, defer the spoil of the
city until night ; for with these borne before us instead
of maces will we ride through the streets, and at every 125
corner have them kiss. Away !

Exit [Cade with his Company].
Alarum and retreat. Enter again Cade and all his   IV, viii
rabblement.

CADE Up Fish Street ! down Saint Magnus Corner ! Kill 1
and knock down ! Throw them into Thames !   2
Sound a parley.
What noise is this I hear ? Dare any be so bold to sound
retreat or parley when I command them kill ?
Enter Buckingham and Old Clifford.

BUCKINGHAM
Ay, here they be that dare and will disturb thee.
Know, Cade, we come ambassadors from the king
Unto the commons, whom thou hast misled,
And here pronounce free pardon to them all
That will forsake thee and go home in peace.

CLIFFORD
What say ye, countrymen ? Will ye relent
And yield to mercy whilst 'tis offered you,
Or let a rebel lead you to your deaths ?
Who loves the king, and will embrace his pardon,
Fling up his cap and say 'God save his majesty !'
Who hateth him and honors not his father,
Henry the Fifth, that made all France to quake,
Shake he his weapon at us and pass by.

ALL God save the king ! God save the king !

CADE What, Buckingham and Clifford, are ye so brave ?
And you, base peasants, do ye believe him ? Will you
needs be hanged with your pardons about your necks ? 21
Hath my sword therefore broke through London gates,
that you should leave me at the White Hart in South- 23
wark ? I thought ye would never have given out these 24
arms till you had recovered your ancient freedom. But
you are all recreants and dastards and delight to live in
slavery to the nobility. Let them break your backs with

61 *favor* lenience   66 *book* learning   72 *behoof* behalf   80 *sitting* i.e. as a
judge   82 *caudle* warm gruel ('hempen caudle' was a euphemism for the
hangman's rope)   82–83 *pap . . . hatchet* (proverbial, meaning to punish –
children, usually – under the guise of kindness)   99 *familiar* attendant evil
spirit, for whose services one sold his soul to the Devil   100 *a* in   102 *Sir
James Cromer* (actually Sir William Cromer, who was sheriff of Kent in
1445 and perhaps in 1450. His widow, Lord Say's daughter, was later to
marry Sir Alexander Iden, who killed Cade).   113 *in capite* by grant
directly from the king ('*capite*': head, permitting a punning allusion to
maidenhead l. 112)   117 *take . . . bills* buy goods on credit (with pun on
'bills': halberds)   118 *presently* immediately   119 *brave* splendid   120
braver worthier, better   125 *maces* staffs of office
IV, viii   1 *Fish Street* (just across London Bridge from Southwark);
Saint Magnus Corner (St Magnus' Church was at the end of Fish Street,
near London Bridge)   2 s.d. *parley* trumpet call indicating a temporary
truce   21 *hanged . . . necks* i.e. pardons will be worthless   23 *White Hart*
an inn, next to Chaucer's Tabard   24 *given out* abandoned

burdens, take your houses over your heads, ravish your wives and daughters before your faces. For me, I will make shift for one ; and so God's curse light upon you all !

ALL We'll follow Cade ! We'll follow Cade !

CLIFFORD
Is Cade the son of Henry the Fifth
That thus you do exclaim you'll go with him ?
Will he conduct you through the heart of France
And make the meanest of you earls and dukes ?
Alas, he hath no home, no place to fly to ;
Nor knows he how to live but by the spoil,
Unless by robbing of your friends and us.
39   Were't not a shame that whilst you live at jar
The fearful French, whom you late vanquishèd,
41   Should make a start o'er seas and vanquish you ?
Methinks already in this civil broil
I see them lording it in London streets,
44   Crying 'Villiago !' unto all they meet.
Better ten thousand base-born Cades miscarry
Than you should stoop unto a Frenchman's mercy.
To France, to France, and get what you have lost ;
Spare England, for it is your native coast.
Henry hath money, you are strong and manly ;
God on our side, doubt not of victory.

ALL A Clifford ! a Clifford ! We'll follow the king and Clifford.

CADE [aside] Was ever feather so lightly blown to and fro as this multitude ? The name of Henry the Fifth hales them to an hundred mischiefs and makes them leave me
56   desolate. I see them lay their heads together to surprise
57   me. My sword make way for me, for here is no staying. In despite of the devils and hell, have through the very middest of you ! and heavens and honor be witness that no want of resolution in me, but only my followers' base and ignominious treason, makes me betake me to my heels.   Exit [Cade, running through them with his sword, and flies away].

BUCKINGHAM
What, is he fled ? Go some, and follow him ;
And he that brings his head unto the king
Shall have a thousand crowns for his reward.
    Exeunt some of them.
Follow me, soldiers. We'll devise a mean
To reconcile you all unto the king.   Exeunt omnes.

*

IV, ix   Sound trumpets. Enter King, Queen, and [Edmund, Duke of] Somerset, on the terrace [aloft].

KING
1   Was ever king that joyed an earthly throne
And could command no more content than I ?
No sooner was I crept out of my cradle
But I was made a king, at nine months old.

Was never subject longed to be a king
As I do long and wish to be a subject.
    Enter [below] Buckingham and [Old] Clifford.

BUCKINGHAM
Health and glad tidings to your majesty !

KING
Why, Buckingham, is the traitor Cade surprised ?   8
Or is he but retired to make him strong ?
    Enter [below] Multitudes with halters about their necks.

CLIFFORD
He is fled, my lord, and all his powers do yield,
And humbly thus, with halters on their necks,
Expect your highness' doom of life or death.   12

KING
Then, heaven, set ope thy everlasting gates
To entertain my vows of thanks and praise.   14
Soldiers, this day have you redeemed your lives
And showed how well you love your prince and country.
Continue still in this so good a mind,
And Henry, though he be infortunate,
Assure yourselves, will never be unkind.
And so, with thanks, and pardon to you all,
I do dismiss you to your several countries.   21

ALL
God save the king ! God save the king !
    Enter a Messenger.

MESSENGER
Please it your grace to be advertisèd   23
The Duke of York is newly come from Ireland
And with a puissant and a mighty power
Of gallowglasses and stout kerns   26
Is marching hitherward in proud array,
And still proclaimeth, as he comes along,
His arms are only to remove from thee
The Duke of Somerset, whom he terms a traitor.

KING
Thus stands my state, 'twixt Cade and York distressed ;
Like to a ship that, having 'scaped a tempest,
Is straightway calmed, and boarded with a pirate.   33
But now is Cade driven back, his men dispersed,   34
And now is York in arms to second him.   35
I pray thee, Buckingham, go and meet him,
And ask him what's the reason of these arms ;
Tell him I'll send Duke Edmund to the Tower.
And, Somerset, we will commit thee thither
Until his army be dismissed from him.

SOMERSET
My lord,
I'll yield myself to prison willingly,
Or unto death, to do my country good.

KING
In any case, be not too rough in terms,
For he is fierce and cannot brook hard language.   45

BUCKINGHAM
I will, my lord, and doubt not so to deal
As all things shall redound unto your good.

KING
Come, wife, let's in, and learn to govern better ;
For yet may England curse my wretched reign.   49
    Flourish. Exeunt.

---

39 *jar* discord 41 *start* sudden attack 44 *Villiago* villain 56 *surprise* capture 57 *staying* hesitating
IV, ix A royal palace (Kenilworth) 1 *joyed* enjoyed 8 *surprised* taken
12 *Expect* await ; *doom* judgment 14 *entertain* receive 21 *countries* regions 23 *advertisèd* informed 26 *gallowglasses . . . kerns* Irish clans-men, foot soldiers usually armed with axe and sword or darts respectively
33 *calmed* becalmed 34 *But now* just now 35 *second* follow 45 *brook* endure 49 *yet* up to now

IV, x   *Enter Cade.*

CADE Fie on ambitions! Fie on myself, that have a sword
and yet am ready to famish. These five days have I hid me
in these woods and durst not peep out, for all the country
4 is laid for me; but now am I so hungry that, if I might
5 have a lease of my life for a thousand years, I could stay
no longer. Wherefore, on a brick wall have I climbed
7 into this garden, to see if I can eat grass, or pick a sallet
8 another while, which is not amiss to cool a man's stomach this hot weather. And I think this word 'sallet' was
10 born to do me good; for many a time, but for a sallet, my
11 brainpan had been cleft with a brown bill; and many a
time, when I have been dry, and bravely marching, it
hath served me instead of a quart pot to drink in; and
now the word 'sallet' must serve me to feed on.

   Enter Iden [and his men].

IDEN
Lord, who would live turmoilèd in the court
And may enjoy such quiet walks as these?
This small inheritance my father left me
Contenteth me, and worth a monarchy.
I seek not to wax great by others' waning,
Or gather wealth, I care not with what envy.
21 Sufficeth that I have maintains my state
And send the poor well pleasèd from my gate.

CADE Here's the lord of the soil come to seize me for a
24 stray, for entering his fee simple without leave. – Ah,
villain, thou wilt betray me and get a thousand crowns of
the king by carrying my head to him; but I'll make thee
27 eat iron like an ostrich and swallow my sword like a
great pin ere thou and I part.

IDEN
29 Why, rude companion, whatsoe'er thou be,
I know thee not. Why then should I betray thee?
Is't not enough to break into my garden
And like a thief to come to rob my grounds,
Climbing my walls in spite of me the owner,
34 But thou wilt brave me with these saucy terms?

CADE Brave thee? Ay, by the best blood that ever was
36 broached, and beard thee too. Look on me well. I have
37 eat no meat these five days; yet, come thou and thy five
men, and if I do not leave you all as dead as a doornail, I
pray God I may never eat grass more.

IDEN
Nay, it shall ne'er be said, while England stands,
That Alexander Iden, an esquire of Kent,
42 Took odds to combat a poor famished man.
Oppose thy steadfast-gazing eyes to mine;
See if thou canst outface me with thy looks.
Set limb to limb, and thou art far the lesser;
Thy hand is but a finger to my fist,
47 Thy leg a stick comparèd with this truncheon;
My foot shall fight with all the strength thou hast;
And if mine arm be heavèd in the air,
Thy grave is digged already in the earth.
As for words, whose greatness answers words,
Let this my sword report what speech forbears.

CADE By my valor, the most complete champion that ever
I heard. Steel, if thou turn the edge, or cut not out the
burly-boned clown in chines of beef ere thou sleep in
thy sheath, I beseech God on my knees thou mayst
be turned to hobnails.

   Here they fight. [Cade falls.]

O, I am slain! Famine and no other hath slain me. Let

ten thousand devils come against me, and give me but
the ten meals I have lost, and I'd defy them all. Wither, 60
garden, and be henceforth a burying place to all that do
dwell in this house, because the unconquered soul of
Cade is fled.

IDEN
Is't Cade that I have slain, that monstrous traitor?
Sword, I will hallow thee for this thy deed
And hang thee o'er my tomb when I am dead.
Ne'er shall this blood be wipèd from thy point,
But thou shalt wear it as a herald's coat,
To emblaze the honor that thy master got. 69

CADE Iden, farewell, and be proud of thy victory. Tell
Kent from me, she hath lost her best man, and exhort
all the world to be cowards; for I, that never feared any,
am vanquished by famine, not by valor.

   Dies.

IDEN
How much thou wrong'st me, heaven be my judge.
Die, damnèd wretch, the curse of her that bare thee!
And as I thrust thy body in with my sword, 76
So wish I, I might thrust thy soul to hell!
Hence will I drag thee headlong by the heels 78
Unto a dunghill, which shall be thy grave,
And there cut off thy most ungracious head,
Which I will bear in triumph to the king,
Leaving thy trunk for crows to feed upon.

   Exit [with his men and Cade's body].

*

   Enter York and his army of Irish, with Drum and   V, i
   Colors.

YORK
From Ireland thus comes York to claim his right
And pluck the crown from feeble Henry's head.
Ring bells aloud, burn bonfires clear and bright,
To entertain great England's lawful king.
Ah, Sancta Majestas! who would not buy thee dear; 5
Let them obey that knows not how to rule.
This hand was made to handle naught but gold;
I cannot give due action to my words
Except a sword or sceptre balance it.
A sceptre shall it have, have I a soul, 10
On which I'll toss the fleur-de-luce of France. 11

   Enter Buckingham.

   [Aside]

Whom have we here? Buckingham, to disturb me?
The king hath sent him sure. I must dissemble.

BUCKINGHAM
York, if thou meanest well, I greet thee well.

IV, x Iden's garden (Kent) 4 *is laid for* is watching for (cf. 'They are
laying for him') 5 *stay* wait 7 *a sallet* salad greens 8 *while* time 10
sallet helmet (cf. IV, iii, 9–11) 11 *brown bill* halberd, varnished to prevent
rust 21 *that* that which 24 *fee simple* land held in unencumbered legal
possession (the holder of which had the right to seize stray animals found
on his property) 27 *eat . . . ostrich* (according to Elizabethan natural
history, the ostrich ate iron for his health) 29 *rude companion* base fellow
34 *brave* confront boldly; *saucy* insolent 36 *beard* defy 37 *eat* (pronounced 'et') 42 *odds* advantage 47 *truncheon* stout staff (i.e. Iden's
leg) 69 *emblaze* signify, set forth publicly 76 *thrust . . . sword* thrust my
sword into thy body 78 *headlong* at full length
V, i Fields (between London and St Albans) s.d. *Drum* i.e. drummer;
Colors flags 5 *Sancta Majestas* sacred majesty 10 *have I* as sure as I have
11 *toss* impale, as on a pike; *fleur-de-luce* (device on the arms of France)

YORK
Humphrey of Buckingham, I accept thy greeting.
Art thou a messenger or come of pleasure ?

BUCKINGHAM
A messenger from Henry, our dread liege,
To know the reason of these arms in peace ;
Or why thou, being a subject as I am,
Against thy oath and true allegiance sworn
Should raise so great a power without his leave,
Or dare to bring thy force so near the court.

YORK *[aside]*
Scarce can I speak, my choler is so great.
O, I could hew up rocks and fight with flint,
I am so angry at these abject terms ;
26 And now, like Ajax Telamonius,
On sheep or oxen could I spend my fury.
I am far better born than is the king,
More like a king, more kingly in my thoughts.
30 But I must make fair weather yet a while,
Till Henry be more weak, and I more strong. –
Buckingham, I prithee pardon me
That I have given no answer all this while.
My mind was troubled with deep melancholy.
The cause why I have brought this army hither
Is to remove proud Somerset from the king,
Seditious to his grace and to the state.

BUCKINGHAM
That is too much presumption on thy part.
But if thy arms be to no other end,
The king hath yielded unto thy demand,
The Duke of Somerset is in the Tower.

YORK
Upon thine honor, is he prisoner ?

BUCKINGHAM
Upon mine honor, he is prisoner.

YORK
Then, Buckingham, I do dismiss my powers.
Soldiers, I thank you all. Disperse yourselves ;
46 Meet me to-morrow in Saint George's Field,
You shall have pay and everything you wish.
                [Exeunt Soldiers.]
And let my sovereign, virtuous Henry,
49 Command my eldest son, nay, all my sons,
As pledges of my fealty and love.
I'll send them all as willing as I live.
Land, goods, horse, armor, anything I have
Is his to use, so Somerset may die.

BUCKINGHAM
York, I commend this kind submission.
We twain will go into his highness' tent.
        Enter King and Attendants.

KING
Buckingham, doth York intend no harm to us
That thus he marcheth with thee arm in arm ?

YORK
In all submission and humility
York doth present himself unto your highness.

KING
Then what intends these forces thou dost bring ?

YORK
To heave the traitor Somerset from hence
And fight against that monstrous rebel Cade,
Who since I heard to be discomfited.   63
        Enter Iden, with Cade's head.

IDEN
If one so rude and of so mean condition   64
May pass into the presence of a king,
Lo, I present your grace a traitor's head,
The head of Cade, whom I in combat slew.

KING
The head of Cade ? Great God, how just art thou !
O, let me view his visage, being dead,
That living wrought me such exceeding trouble.
Tell me my friend, art thou the man that slew him ?

IDEN
I was, an't like your majesty.

KING
How art thou called, and what is thy degree ?   73

IDEN
Alexander Iden, that's my name ;
A poor esquire of Kent that loves his king.

BUCKINGHAM
So please it you, my lord, 'twere not amiss
He were created knight for his good service.

KING
Iden, kneel down. *[He kneels.]* Rise up a knight.
    [He rises.]
We give thee for reward a thousand marks,
And will that thou henceforth attend on us.

IDEN
May Iden live to merit such a bounty,
And never live but true unto his liege.
        Enter Queen and Somerset.

KING
See, Buckingham, Somerset comes with th' queen.
Go bid her hide him quickly from the duke.

QUEEN
For thousand Yorks he shall not hide his head,
But boldly stand and front him to his face.   86

YORK
How now ? Is Somerset at liberty ?
Then, York, unloose thy long-imprisoned thoughts
And let thy tongue be equal with thy heart.
Shall I endure the sight of Somerset ?
False king, why hast thou broken faith with me,
Knowing how hardly I can brook abuse ?   92
King did I call thee ? No ! thou art not king,
Not fit to govern and rule multitudes,
Which dar'st not, no, nor canst not rule a traitor.
That head of thine doth not become a crown ;
Thy hand is made to grasp a palmer's staff   97
And not to grace an awful princely sceptre.
That gold must round engirt these brows of mine,
Whose smile and frown, like to Achilles' spear,   100
Is able with the change to kill and cure.
Here is a hand to hold a sceptre up
And with the same to act controlling laws.   103
Give place. By heaven, thou shalt rule no more
O'er him whom heaven created for thy ruler.

SOMERSET
O monstrous traitor ! I arrest thee, York,

---

26 *Ajax Telamonius* (Ajax, son of Telamon, in a mad rage attacked a flock
of sheep, believing them to be his enemies)   30 *make fair weather* dissemble
46 *Saint George's Field* an open field between Southwark and Lambeth,
used as a parade ground   49 *Command* demand   63 *discomfited* routed
64 *rude* simple, uncultivated   73 *degree* social rank   86 *front* confront   92
brook endure (with pun on *broken*, l. 91)   97 *palmer's* pilgrim's   100
Achilles' spear (Telephus was cured by rust from the spear of Achilles, by
which he had been wounded)   103 *act* enact

Of capital treason 'gainst the king and crown.
Obey, audacious traitor ; kneel for grace.

YORK
Wouldst have me kneel ? First let me ask of these
110   If they can brook I bow a knee to man.
Sirrah, call in my sons to be my bail. *[Exit an Attendant.]*
112   I know, ere they will have me go to ward,
113   They'll pawn their swords for my enfranchisement.

QUEEN
114   Call hither Clifford. Bid him come amain
To say if that the bastard boys of York
Shall be the surety for their traitor father.
             [Exit an Attendant.]

YORK
117   O blood-bespotted Neapolitan,
Outcast of Naples, England's bloody scourge,
The sons of York, thy betters in their birth,
120   Shall be their father's bail ; and bane to those
That for my surety will refuse the boys !
     Enter Edward and Richard [with Drum and Soldiers
     at one door].
See where they come. I'll warrant they'll make it good.
     Enter Clifford [and his Son with Drum and Soldiers
     at the other door. Clifford kneels to King Henry].

QUEEN
And here comes Clifford to deny their bail.

CLIFFORD
Health and all happiness to my lord the king.

YORK
I thank thee, Clifford. Say, what news with thee ?
Nay, do not fright us with an angry look.
We are thy sovereign, Clifford ; kneel again.
For thy mistaking so, we pardon thee.

CLIFFORD
This is my king, York, I do not mistake ;
But thou mistakes me much to think I do.
131   To Bedlam with him ! Is the man grown mad ?

KING
132   Ay, Clifford. A bedlam and ambitious humor
Makes him oppose himself against his king.

CLIFFORD
He is a traitor ; let him to the Tower,
And chop away that factious pate of his.

QUEEN
He is arrested, but will not obey.
His sons, he says, shall give their words for him.

YORK
Will you not, sons ?

EDWARD
Ay, noble father, if our words will serve.

RICHARD
And if words will not, then our weapons shall.

CLIFFORD
Why, what a brood of traitors have we here.

YORK
Look in a glass and call thy image so.
I am thy king, and thou a false-heart traitor.
144   Call hither to the stake my two brave bears,
That with the very shaking of their chains
146   They may astonish these fell-lurking curs.
Bid Salisbury and Warwick come to me.
             [Exit an Attendant.]
     Enter the Earls of Warwick and Salisbury [with
     Drum and Soldiers].

CLIFFORD
Are these thy bears ? We'll bait thy bears to death
And manacle the berard in their chains   149
If thou dar'st bring them to the baiting place.

RICHARD
Oft have I seen a hot o'erweening cur
Run back and bite because he was withheld,
Who, being suffered with the bear's fell paw,   153
Hath clapped his tail between his legs and cried ;
And such a piece of service will you do
If you oppose yourselves to match Lord Warwick.

CLIFFORD
Hence, heap of wrath, foul indigested lump,   157
As crooked in thy manners as thy shape.

YORK
Nay, we shall heat you thoroughly anon.

CLIFFORD
Take heed lest by your heat you burn yourselves.

KING
Why Warwick, hath thy knee forgot to bow ?
Old Salisbury, shame to thy silver hair,
Thou mad misleader of thy brainsick son.
What, wilt thou on thy deathbed play the ruffian
And seek for sorrow with thy spectacles ?   165
O, where is faith ? O, where is loyalty ?
If it be banished from the frosty head,
Where shall it find a harbor in the earth ?
Wilt thou go dig a grave to find our war,
And shame thine honorable age with blood ?
Why art thou old, and want'st experience ?
Or wherefore dost abuse it if thou hast it ?
For shame ! In duty bend thy knee to me,
That bows unto the grave with mickle age.   174

SALISBURY
My lord, I have considered with myself
The title of this most renownèd duke
And, in my conscience, do repute his grace   177
The rightful heir to England's royal seat.

KING
Hast thou not sworn allegiance unto me ?

SALISBURY   I have.

KING
Canst thou dispense with heaven for such an oath ?   181

SALISBURY
It is great sin to swear unto a sin,
But greater sin to keep a sinful oath.
Who can be bound by any solemn vow
To do a murd'rous deed, to rob a man,
To force a spotless virgin's chastity,
To reave the orphan of his patrimony,   187
To wring the widow from her customed right,   188

110 *they* i.e. his hands (cf. l. 102) (?), his weapons (?) (perhaps a line has been lost)   112 *to ward* into custody   113 *pawn . . . enfranchisement* pledge (used ironically) their swords for my freedom   114 *amain* speedily   117 *Neapolitan* (because Margaret's father claimed the kingdom of Naples)   120 *bane* destruction   131 *Bedlam* Bethlehem Hospital, for the insane   132 *bedlam . . . humor* mad . . . disposition   144–46 *stake, bears, chains, curs* (allusions to bearbaiting, at which chained bears were attacked by dogs. Warwick's badge was a bear and a ragged staff.)   146 *fell-lurking* treacherous   149 *berard* i.e. bear-herd, keeper of the bears   153 *suffered* hurt; *fell* ruthless, dangerous   157–58 *heap . . . shape* (in reference to Richard's premature birth and his deformities. Bear cubs too were supposed to be born as lumps of matter which were licked into shape by their dam.)   165 *spectacles* eyes   174 *mickle* much   177 *repute* consider   181 *dispense* make terms   187 *reave* bereave   188 *customed right* traditional right to a portion of her husband's estate

And have no other reason for this wrong
But that he was bound by a solemn oath?

QUEEN

191   A subtle traitor needs no sophister.

KING

Call Buckingham and bid him arm himself.

YORK

Call Buckingham and all the friends thou hast,
I am resolved for death or dignity.

CLIFFORD

The first I warrant thee, if dreams prove true.

WARWICK

Thou were best to go to bed and dream again
To keep thee from the tempest of the field.

CLIFFORD

I am resolved to bear a greater storm
Than any thou canst conjure up to-day;
200   And that I'll write upon thy burgonet,
Might I but know thee by thy house's badge.

WARWICK

202   Now, by my father's badge, old Nevil's crest,
The rampant bear chained to the ragged staff,
This day I'll wear aloft my burgonet,
205   As on a mountain top the cedar shows,
That keeps his leaves in spite of any storm,
Even to affright thee with the view thereof.

CLIFFORD

And from thy burgonet I'll rend thy bear
And tread it under foot with all contempt,
Despite the berard that protects the bear.

YOUNG CLIFFORD

And so to arms, victorious father,
To quell the rebels and their complices.

RICHARD

Fie! charity, for shame! Speak not in spite,
For you shall sup with Jesu Christ to-night.

YOUNG CLIFFORD

215   Foul stigmatic, that's more than thou canst tell.

RICHARD

If not in heaven, you'll surely sup in hell.

Exeunt [severally].

V, ii   *[Alarums to the battle.] Enter Warwick.*

WARWICK

Clifford of Cumberland, 'tis Warwick calls!
And if thou dost not hide thee from the bear,
Now, when the angry trumpet sounds alarum
And dead men's cries do fill the empty air,
Clifford, I say, come forth and fight with me!
Proud Northern lord, Clifford of Cumberland,
Warwick is hoarse with calling thee to arms.

Enter York.

How now, my noble lord? What, all afoot?

YORK

The deadly-handed Clifford slew my steed;
But match to match I have encount'red him
And made a prey for carrion kites and crows
Even of the bonny beast he loved so well.

Enter Clifford.

WARWICK

Of one or both of us the time is come.

YORK

Hold, Warwick, seek thee out some other chase,   14
For I myself must hunt this deer to death.

WARWICK

Then nobly, York! 'Tis for a crown thou fight'st.
As I intend, Clifford, to thrive to-day,
It grieves my soul to leave thee unassailed.

Exit Warwick.

CLIFFORD

What seest thou in me, York? Why dost thou pause?

YORK

With thy brave bearing should I be in love   20
But that thou art so fast mine enemy.   21

CLIFFORD

Nor should thy prowess want praise and esteem
But that 'tis shown ignobly and in treason.

YORK

So let it help me now against thy sword
As I in justice and true right express it.

CLIFFORD

My soul and body on the action both.

YORK

A dreadful lay! Address thee instantly.   27

[Alarums. They fight, and York kills Clifford.]

CLIFFORD   La fin couronne les oeuvres.   28

[Dies.]

YORK

Thus war hath given thee peace, for thou art still.
Peace with his soul, heaven, if it be thy will.   *[Exit.]*

Enter Young Clifford.

YOUNG CLIFFORD

Shame and confusion! All is on the rout.
Fear frames disorder, and disorder wounds   32
Where it should guard. O war, thou son of hell,
Whom angry heavens do make their minister,
Throw in the frozen bosoms of our part   35
Hot coals of vengeance. Let no soldier fly.
He that is truly dedicate to war   37
Hath no self-love; nor he that loves himself   38
Hath not essentially, but by circumstance,
The name of valor. *[Sees his father's body.]* O, let the vile world end
And the premisèd flames of the last day   41
Knit earth and heaven together.
Now let the general trumpet blow his blast,
Particularities and petty sounds   44
To cease. Wast thou ordained, dear father,
To lose thy youth in peace and to achieve
The silver livery of advisèd age,
And in thy reverence and thy chair-days thus   48
To die in ruffian battle? Even at this sight
My heart is turned to stone; and while 'tis mine,
It shall be stony. York not our old men spares;
No more will I their babes. Tears virginal
Shall be to me even as the dew to fire;   53

191 *sophister* clever disputer   200 *burgonet* light helmet, upon which the wearer's device was usually mounted   202 *old Nevil's crest* (Warwick actually inherited his earldom and the bear device from his wife's family, the Beauchamps; the Nevils' device was a bull)   205 *cedar* (symbol of royalty)   215 *stigmatic* a criminal branded with the mark of his crime (as Richard is 'branded' by his deformities)
V, ii   14 *chase* game   20 *bearing* demeanor   21 *fast* firmly   27 *lay* wager; *Address thee* prepare yourself   28 *La fin . . . oeuvres* the end crowns every work   32 *frames* fashions   35 *part* party   37 *dedicate* dedicated   38–40 *nor he . . . valor* i.e. the man who loves himself may have the outward trappings of valor (*circumstance* : accident), but he lacks the essence of valor   41 *premisèd* foretold (?), being sent before their time (?)   44 *Particularities* details   48 *chair-days* days of comfort and ease enjoyed in old age   53 *dew to fire* (there was a common notion that fine droplets of water sprayed on fire would make it burn hotter by reducing the flames to coals)

And beauty, that the tyrant oft reclaims,
Shall to my flaming wrath be oil and flax.
Henceforth I will not have to do with pity.
Meet I an infant of the house of York,
58 Into as many gobbets will I cut it
59 As wild Medea young Absyrtus did.
In cruelty will I seek out my fame.
61 Come, thou new ruin of old Clifford's house:
62 As did Aeneas old Anchises bear,
So bear I thee upon my manly shoulders;
But then Aeneas bare a living load,
65 Nothing so heavy as these woes of mine.
                              [Exit with the body.]
[Alarums.] Enter Richard and Somerset to fight.
[Somerset is killed.]

RICHARD
So lie thou there.
For underneath an alehouse' paltry sign,
The Castle in Saint Albans, Somerset
69 Hath made the wizard famous in his death.
Sword, hold thy temper; heart, be wrathful still.
71 Priests pray for enemies, but princes kill.   [Exit.]
[Alarums again.] Fight. Excursions. [And then
enter some bearing the Duke of Buckingham wounded
to his tent; they pass over and go off.] Enter King,
Queen, and others.

QUEEN
Away, my lord! You are slow. For shame, away!
KING
73 Can we outrun the heavens? Good Margaret, stay.
QUEEN
74 What are you made of? You'll nor fight nor fly.
Now is it manhood, wisdom, and defense
76 To give the enemy way, and to secure us
By what we can, which can no more but fly.
                    Alarum afar off.
If you be ta'en, we then should see the bottom
79 Of all our fortunes; but if we haply 'scape
(As well we may, if not through your neglect),
We shall to London get, where you are loved,
And where this breach now in our fortunes made
May readily be stopped.
                    Enter [Young] Clifford.
YOUNG CLIFFORD
But that my heart's on future mischief set,
I would speak blasphemy ere bid you fly,
86 But fly you must. Uncurable discomfit
Reigns in the hearts of all our present parts.
Away, for your relief! and we will live
89 To see their day and then our fortune give.
Away, my lord, away!   Exeunt.
V, iii   Alarum. Retreat. [Flourish.] Enter York, Richard,
Warwick, and Soldiers, with Drum and Colors.
YORK
Old Salisbury, who can report of him,
2 That winter lion, who in rage forgets

Agèd contusions and all brush of time   3
And, like a gallant in the brow of youth,   4
Repairs him with occasion? This happy day   5
Is not itself, nor have we won one foot,
If Salisbury be lost.
RICHARD   My noble father,
Three times to-day I holp him to his horse,   8
Three times bestrid him; thrice I led him off, 9
Persuaded him from any further act;
But still where danger was, still there I met him; 11
And like rich hangings in a homely house,   12
So was his will in his old feeble body.
But, noble as he is, look where he comes.
                    Enter Salisbury.
SALISBURY
Now, by my sword, well hast thou fought to-day.
By th' mass, so did we all. I thank you, Richard;
God knows how long it is I have to live,
And it hath pleased Him that three times to-day
You have defended me from imminent death.
Well, lords, we have not got that which we have.   20
'Tis not enough our foes are this time fled,
Being opposites of such repairing nature.   22
YORK
I know our safety is to follow them;
For, as I hear, the king is fled to London
To call a present court of parliament.
Let us pursue him ere the writs go forth.   26
What says Lord Warwick? Shall we after them?
WARWICK
After them? Nay, before them, if we can.
Now, by my faith, lords, 'twas a glorious day.
Saint Albans battle, won by famous York,
Shall be eternized in all age to come.   31
Sound drum and trumpets, and to London all;
And more such days as these to us befall!   Exeunt.

58 *gobbets* lumps of flesh 59 *Medea . . . Absyrtus* (as she fled by ship with Jason, Medea murdered her brother Absyrtus and threw pieces of his body into the sea, so that her father, stopping to collect them, would be delayed in his pursuit) 61 *new . . . house* i.e. old Clifford's body 62 *Aeneas . . . Anchises* (as they escaped from fallen Troy, Aeneas carried his aged father, Anchises, on his shoulders) 65 *heavy* (1) weighty, (2) sorrowful 69 *Hath . . . death* (the spirit raised by Margery Jourdain had said that Somerset should shun castles; see I, iv, 34) 71 s.d. *Excursions* attacks and counter-attacks 73 *outrun the heavens* escape the decision of God 74 *nor . . . nor* neither . . . nor 76 *secure us* make us safe 79 *haply* perhaps 86 *Uncurable discomfit* hopeless defeat 89 *To see . . . give* i.e. to see their day of defeat and give them the bad luck we now suffer
V, iii s.d. *Drum* i.e. drummer 2 *winter* i.e. ancient 3 *brush* collision 4 *gallant* young lover; *brow* front, top 5 *Repairs . . . occasion* revives himself with action 8 *holp* helped 9 *bestrid him* stood over him to protect him 11 *still . . . still* always . . . always 12 *homely* modest 20 *got . . . have* i.e. secured what we have won 22 *opposites . . . nature* enemies who can so quickly recover 26 *writs* (calling the parliament) 31 *eternized* immortalized

THE THIRD PART OF
KING HENRY THE SIXTH

*

I, i   *Alarum. Enter [wearing white roses in their hats,*
      Richard] Plantagenet, [Duke of York,] Edward,
      Richard, Norfolk, Montague, Warwick, [with
      Drum] and Soldiers.

WARWICK
   I wonder how the king escaped our hands ?
YORK
   While we pursued the horsemen of the North,
   He slily stole away and left his men ;
   Whereat the great Lord of Northumberland,
5 Whose warlike ears could never brook retreat,
   Cheered up the drooping army ; and himself,
   Lord Clifford, and Lord Stafford, all abreast,
   Charged our main battle's front and, breaking in,
9 Were by the swords of common soldiers slain.
EDWARD
   Lord Stafford's father, Duke of Buckingham,

Is either slain or wounded dangerous ;
I cleft his beaver with a downright blow.   12
That this is true, father, behold his blood.
     [Shows his bloody sword.]
MONTAGUE
   And, cousin, here's the Earl of Wiltshire's blood,
   Whom I encount'red as the battles joined.
RICHARD
   Speak thou for me and tell them what I did.
     [Throws down Somerset's head.]
YORK
   Richard hath best deserved of all my sons.
   But is your grace dead, my Lord of Somerset ?
NORFOLK
   Such hope have all the line of John of Gaunt.   19
RICHARD
   Thus do I hope to shake King Henry's head.
WARWICK
   And so do I. Victorious Prince of York,
   Before I see thee seated in that throne
   Which now the house of Lancaster usurps,
   I vow by heaven these eyes shall never close.
   This is the palace of the fearful king
   And this the regal seat. Possess it, York ;
   For this is thine, and not King Henry's heirs'.

I, i Parliament House in London **s.d.** *Alarum* a trumpet call **5** *brook* endure ; *retreat* i.e. the trumpet call signalling retreat **9** *Were . . . slain* (in *2 Henry VI*, V, ii, Clifford is killed by York) **12** *beaver* helmet (actually the face-piece) **19** *Such . . . Gaunt* i.e. may all the descendants of John of Gaunt look for the same fate (Edmund, 2nd Duke of Somerset, was a grandson of John of Gaunt, Duke of Lancaster ; Henry VI was a great-grandson)

YORK
Assist me then, sweet Warwick, and I will;
For hither we have broken in by force.

NORFOLK
We'll all assist you. He that flies shall die.

YORK
Thanks, gentle Norfolk. Stay by me, my lords;
32   And, soldiers, stay, and lodge by me this night.
       They go up.

WARWICK
And when the king comes, offer him no violence
34   Unless he seek to thrust you out perforce.
       [The Soldiers conceal themselves.]

YORK
The queen this day here holds her parliament,
But little thinks we shall be of her council.
By words or blows here let us win our right.

RICHARD
Armed as we are, let's stay within this house.

WARWICK
The bloody parliament shall this be called
Unless Plantagenet, Duke of York, be king
And bashful Henry deposed, whose cowardice
Hath made us bywords to our enemies.

YORK
Then leave me not, my lords. Be resolute.
I mean to take possession of my right.

WARWICK
Neither the king, nor he that loves him best,
The proudest he that holds up Lancaster,
47   Dares stir a wing if Warwick shake his bells.
I'll plant Plantagenet, root him up who dares.
49   Resolve thee, Richard; claim the English crown.
       [York sits in the throne.]
       Flourish. Enter King Henry, Clifford, Northumber-
       land, Westmoreland, Exeter, and the rest [with red
       roses in their hats].

KING HENRY
My lords, look where the sturdy rebel sits,
51   Even in the chair of state! Belike he means,
Backed by the power of Warwick, that false peer,
To aspire unto the crown and reign as king.
Earl of Northumberland, he slew thy father,
And thine, Lord Clifford, and you both have vowed
     revenge
On him, his sons, his favorites, and his friends.

NORTHUMBERLAND
If I be not, heavens be revenged on me.

CLIFFORD
The hope thereof makes Clifford mourn in steel.

WESTMORELAND
What, shall we suffer this? Let's pluck him down.
My heart for anger burns. I cannot brook it.

KING HENRY
Be patient, gentle Earl of Westmoreland.

CLIFFORD
62   Patience is for poltroons, such as he.
He durst not sit there, had your father lived.
My gracious lord, here in the parliament
Let us assail the family of York.

NORTHUMBERLAND
Well hast thou spoken, cousin. Be it so.

KING HENRY
67   Ah, know you not the city favors them

And they have troops of soldiers at their beck?

EXETER
But when the duke is slain, they'll quickly fly.

KING HENRY
Far be the thought of this from Henry's heart,
To make a shambles of the parliament house.   71
Cousin of Exeter, frowns, words, and threats
Shall be the war that Henry means to use.
Thou factious Duke of York, descend my throne
And kneel for grace and mercy at my feet.
I am thy sovereign.

YORK   I am thine.

EXETER
For shame, come down. He made thee Duke of York.

YORK
It was my inheritance, as the earldom was.   78

EXETER
Thy father was a traitor to the crown.   79

WARWICK
Exeter, thou art a traitor to the crown
In following this usurping Henry.

CLIFFORD
Whom should he follow but his natural king?

WARWICK
True, Clifford; and that's Richard Duke of York.

KING HENRY
And shall I stand, and thou sit in my throne?

YORK
It must and shall be so. Content thyself.

WARWICK
Be Duke of Lancaster; let him be king.

WESTMORELAND
He is both king and Duke of Lancaster,
And that the Lord of Westmoreland shall maintain.

WARWICK
And Warwick shall disprove it. You forget
That we are those which chased you from the field
And slew your fathers and with colors spread   91
Marched through the city to the palace gates.

NORTHUMBERLAND
Yes, Warwick, I remember it to my grief;
And, by his soul, thou and thy house shall rue it.

WESTMORELAND
Plantagenet, of thee and these thy sons,
Thy kinsmen, and thy friends, I'll have more lives
Than drops of blood were in my father's veins.

CLIFFORD
Urge it no more; lest that instead of words
I send thee, Warwick, such a messenger
As shall revenge his death before I stir.

WARWICK
Poor Clifford, how I scorn his worthless threats.

YORK
Will you we show our title to the crown?

32 s.d. *They go up* (the chair of state, which York occupies, is probably placed on a raised platform)   34 *perforce* by force   47 *if . . . bells* i.e. when his blood is up (bells were fastened to the legs of hawks; their ringing supposedly increased the falcons' ferocity in attacking their prey)   49 *Resolve thee* decide firmly   51 *Belike* it is likely that   62 *poltroons* cowards   67 *the city* i.e. London (as distinct from the court)   71 *shambles* slaughterhouse   78 *earldom* i.e. the Earldom of March (a title inherited by York from his mother, Anne Mortimer; it was through the Mortimers that he also claimed the crown – cf. II, i, 179)   79 *Thy father . . . crown* (York's father, Richard, Earl of Cambridge, was executed during the reign of Henry V)   91 *colors* flags

If not, our swords shall plead it in the field.

KING HENRY
What title hast thou, traitor, to the crown?

105 Thy father was, as thou art, Duke of York;
Thy grandfather, Roger Mortimer, Earl of March.
I am the son of Henry the Fifth,
Who made the Dauphin and the French to stoop
And seized upon their towns and provinces.

WARWICK
110 Talk not of France, sith thou hast lost it all.

KING HENRY
111 The Lord Protector lost it, and not I.
When I was crowned I was but nine months old.

RICHARD
You are old enough now, and yet methinks you lose.
Father, tear the crown from the usurper's head.

EDWARD
Sweet father, do so. Set it on your head.

MONTAGUE [to York]
Good brother, as thou lov'st and honorest arms,
Let's fight it out and not stand cavilling thus.

RICHARD
Sound drums and trumpets, and the king will fly.

YORK
Sons, peace!

KING HENRY
Peace thou! and give King Henry leave to speak.

WARWICK
Plantagenet shall speak first. Hear him, lords,
And be you silent and attentive too,
For he that interrupts him shall not live.

KING HENRY
Think'st thou that I will leave my kingly throne,
Wherein my grandsire and my father sat?
No! First shall war unpeople this my realm;
Ay, and their colors, often borne in France,
And now in England to our heart's great sorrow,
129 Shall be my winding sheet. Why faint you, lords?
My title's good, and better far than his.

WARWICK
Prove it, Henry, and thou shalt be king.

KING HENRY
Henry the Fourth by conquest got the crown.

YORK
'Twas by rebellion against his king.

KING HENRY [aside]
I know not what to say; my title's weak. —
Tell me, may not a king adopt an heir?

YORK
What then?

KING HENRY
137 An if he may, then am I lawful king,
For Richard, in the view of many lords,
Resigned the crown to Henry the Fourth,
Whose heir my father was, and I am his.

YORK
He rose against him, being his sovereign,
And make him to resign his crown perforce.

WARWICK
Suppose, my lords, he did it unconstrained,
Think you 'twere prejudicial to his crown?

EXETER
No; for he could not so resign his crown
But that the next heir should succeed and reign.

KING HENRY
Art thou against us, Duke of Exeter?

EXETER
His is the right, and therefore pardon me.

YORK
Why whisper you, my lords, and answer not?

EXETER
My conscience tells me he is lawful king.   150

KING HENRY [aside]
All will revolt from me and turn to him.

NORTHUMBERLAND
Plantagenet, for all the claim thou lay'st,
Think not that Henry shall be so deposed.

WARWICK
Deposed he shall be, in despite of all.

NORTHUMBERLAND
Thou art deceived. 'Tis not thy Southern power
Of Essex, Norfolk, Suffolk, nor of Kent,
Which makes thee thus presumptuous and proud,
Can set the Duke up in despite of me.

CLIFFORD
King Henry, be thy title right or wrong,
Lord Clifford vows to fight in thy defense.   160
May that ground gape and swallow me alive
Where I shall kneel to him that slew my father.

KING HENRY
O Clifford, how thy words revive my heart.

YORK
Henry of Lancaster, resign thy crown.
What mutter you or what conspire you, lords?

WARWICK
Do right unto this princely Duke of York,
Or I will fill the house with armèd men
And over the chair of state, where now he sits,
Write up his title with usurping blood.   169
He stamps with his foot, and the Soldiers show
themselves.

KING HENRY
My Lord of Warwick, hear but one word.
Let me for this my lifetime reign as king.

YORK
Confirm the crown to me and to mine heirs
And thou shalt reign in quiet while thou liv'st.

KING HENRY
I am content. Richard Plantagenet,
Enjoy the kingdom after my decease.

CLIFFORD
What wrong is this unto the prince your son!

WARWICK
What good is this to England and himself!

WESTMORELAND
Base, fearful, and despairing Henry.

CLIFFORD
How hast thou injured both thyself and us!

WESTMORELAND
I cannot stay to hear these articles.   180

NORTHUMBERLAND
Nor I.

---

105 *Thy father . . . York* (York actually inherited his title from his uncle; cf. ll. 77–79) 110 *sith* since 111 *Lord Protector* i.e. Humphrey, Duke of Gloucester 129 *winding sheet* shroud; *faint* lose heart 137 *An if* if 169 *usurping blood* i.e. King Henry's 180 *articles* clauses in a legal document (i.e. further details of the agreement)

CLIFFORD
Come, cousin, let us tell the queen these news.

WESTMORELAND
Farewell, faint-hearted and degenerate king,
In whose cold blood no spark of honor bides.
[Exit Westmoreland with his men.]

NORTHUMBERLAND
Be thou a prey unto the house of York
186   And die in bands for this unmanly deed.
[Exit Northumberland with his men.]

CLIFFORD
In dreadful war mayst thou be overcome
Or live in peace abandoned and despised!
[Exit Clifford with his men.]

WARWICK
Turn this way, Henry, and regard them not.

EXETER
They seek revenge and therefore will not yield.

KING HENRY
Ah, Exeter.

WARWICK   Why should you sigh, my lord?

KING HENRY
Not for myself, Lord Warwick, but my son,
Whom I unnaturally shall disinherit.
194   But be it as it may. *[To York.]* I here entail
The crown to thee and to thine heirs forever,
Conditionally that here thou take an oath
To cease this civil war, and whilst I live
To honor me as thy king and sovereign,
And neither by treason nor hostility
To seek to put me down and reign thyself.

YORK
This oath I willingly take, and will perform.
Here they come down.

WARWICK
Long live King Henry! Plantagenet, embrace him.

KING HENRY
203   And long live thou, and these thy forward sons.

YORK
Now York and Lancaster are reconciled.

EXETER
205   Accursed be he that seeks to make them foes!   *Sennet.*

YORK
206   Farewell, my gracious lord. I'll to my castle.
[Exit York with his sons.]

WARWICK
And I'll keep London with my soldiers.
[Exit Warwick with his men.]

NORFOLK
And I to Norfolk with my followers.
[Exit Norfolk with his men.]

MONTAGUE
209   And I unto the sea, from whence I came.
[Exit Montague with his men.]

KING HENRY
And I with grief and sorrow to the court.
Enter the Queen [Margaret and Edward, Prince of Wales].

EXETER
211   Here comes the queen, whose looks bewray her anger.
I'll steal away.

KING HENRY   Exeter, so will I.

QUEEN MARGARET
Nay, go not from me. I will follow thee.

KING HENRY
Be patient, gentle queen, and I will stay.

QUEEN MARGARET
Who can be patient in such extremes?
Ah, wretched man! Would I had died a maid
And never seen thee, never borne thee son,
Seeing thou hast proved so unnatural a father.
Hath he deserved to lose his birthright thus?
Hadst thou but loved him half so well as I,   220
Or felt that pain which I did for him once,
Or nourished him as I did with my blood,
Thou wouldst have left thy dearest heart-blood there
Rather than have made that savage duke thine heir
And disinherited thine only son.

PRINCE
Father, you cannot disinherit me.
If you be king, why should not I succeed?

KING HENRY
Pardon me, Margaret. Pardon me, sweet son.
The Earl of Warwick and the duke enforced me.

QUEEN MARGARET
Enforced thee? Art thou king, and wilt be forced?
I shame to hear thee speak. Ah, timorous wretch,
Thou hast undone thyself, thy son, and me,
And giv'n unto the house of York such head   233
As thou shalt reign but by their sufferance.
To entail him and his heirs unto the crown,
What is it but to make thy sepulchre
And creep into it far before thy time?
Warwick is chancellor and the lord of Calais;
Stern Falconbridge commands the narrow seas;   239
The duke is made Protector of the realm;
And yet shalt thou be safe? Such safety finds
The trembling lamb environèd with wolves.   242
Had I been there, which am a silly woman,   243
The soldiers should have tossed me on their pikes   244
Before I would have granted to that act.   245
But thou preferr'st thy life before thine honor;
And seeing thou dost, I here divorce myself
Both from thy table, Henry, and thy bed
Until that act of parliament be repealed
Whereby my son is disinherited.
The Northern lords, that have forsworn thy colors,
Will follow mine, if once they see them spread;
And spread they shall be, to thy foul disgrace
And utter ruin of the house of York.
Thus do I leave thee. Come, son, let's away.
Our army is ready. Come, we'll after them.

KING HENRY
Stay, gentle Margaret, and hear me speak.

QUEEN MARGARET
Thou hast spoke too much already. Get thee gone.

186 *bands* bonds 194 *entail* bequeath inalienably 203 *forward* spirited
205 s.d. *Sennet* a trumpet call indicating a ceremonial entrance or exit
206 *castle* i.e. Sandal, near Wakefield, Yorkshire 209 *I . . . came* (John
Nevil, Marquess of Montague, did not come from the sea, and in I, ii at
Sandal Castle. It is possible that he has been confused with his uncle,
William Nevil. See l. 239n.) 211 *bewray* expose 233 *giv'n . . . head* i.e.
slackened the horse's reins so as to allow him to move his head more freely
and, hence, to run more rapidly 239 *Stern . . . seas* (William Nevil, Baron
Fauconberg and Warwick's uncle, served as Warwick's deputy at Calais
in 1459–60, whence he would have commanded the Straits of Dover – the
'narrow seas') 242 *environèd* surrounded 243 *silly* helpless 244 *pikes*
halberds 245 *granted* conceded

KING HENRY
Gentle son Edward, thou wilt stay with me?

QUEEN MARGARET
260 Ay, to be murdered by his enemies!

PRINCE
When I return with victory from the field
I'll see your grace. Till then I'll follow her.

QUEEN MARGARET
Come, son, away. We may not linger thus.
[Exeunt Queen Margaret and the Prince.]

KING HENRY
Poor queen! How love to me and to her son
Hath made her break out into terms of rage.
Revengèd may she be on that hateful duke,
Whose haughty spirit, wingèd with desire,
268 Will cost my crown and like an empty eagle
269 Tire on the flesh of me and of my son.
The loss of those three lords torments my heart.
I'll write unto them and entreat them fair.
Come, cousin, you shall be the messenger.

EXETER
273 And I hope, shall reconcile them all.
Exit [King Henry with Exeter]. Flourish.

*

I, ii   *Enter Richard, Edward, and Montague.*

RICHARD
1 Brother, though I be youngest, give me leave.

EDWARD
No, I can better play the orator.

MONTAGUE
But I have reasons strong and forcible.
Enter the Duke of York.

YORK
Why, how now, sons and cousin? at a strife?
What is your quarrel? How began it first?

EDWARD
No quarrel, but a slight contention.

YORK
About what?

RICHARD
About that which concerns your grace and us –
The crown of England, father, which is yours.

YORK
Mine, boy? Not till King Henry be dead.

RICHARD
Your right depends not on his life or death.

EDWARD
Now you are heir; therefore enjoy it now.
13 By giving the house of Lancaster leave to breathe,
It will outrun you, father, in the end.

YORK
I took an oath that he should quietly reign.

EDWARD
But for a kingdom any oath may be broken.
I would break a thousand oaths to reign one year.

---

268 *cost* accost, assail 269 *Tire* feed greedily 273 s.d. *Flourish* a trumpet fanfare
I, ii The Duke of York's castle, Sandal (Wakefield) 1 *give me leave* allow me (to speak) 13 *leave to breathe* i.e. a respite 22 *moment* importance
26 *depose* swear 30 *Elysium* classical Paradise 36 *presently* immediately
39 *privily* secretly 44 *what resteth more* what else remains 46 *privy to* aware of 48 *post* haste 52 *hold* stronghold 58 *policy* stratagem

RICHARD
No. God forbid your grace should be forsworn.

YORK
I shall be, if I claim by open war.

RICHARD
I'll prove the contrary if you'll hear me speak.

YORK
Thou canst not, son. It is impossible.

RICHARD
An oath is of no moment, being not took
Before a true and lawful magistrate
That hath authority over him that swears.
Henry had none, but did usurp the place.
Then, seeing 'twas he that made you to depose,
Your oath, my lord, is vain and frivolous.
Therefore, to arms! And, father, do but think
How sweet a thing it is to wear a crown,
Within whose circuit is Elysium
And all that poets feign of bliss and joy.
Why do we linger thus? I cannot rest
Until the white rose that I wear be dyed
Even in the lukewarm blood of Henry's heart.

YORK
Richard, enough. I will be king or die.
Cousin, thou shalt to London presently
And whet on Warwick to this enterprise.
Thou, Richard, shalt to the Duke of Norfolk
And tell him privily of our intent.
You, Edward, shall unto my Lord Cobham,
With whom the Kentishmen will willingly rise.
In them I trust; for they are soldiers,
Witty, courteous, liberal, full of spirit.
While you are thus employed, what resteth more
But that I seek occasion how to rise,
And yet the king not privy to my drift,
Nor any of the house of Lancaster?
Enter a Messenger.
But stay, what news? Why com'st thou in such post?

MESSENGER
The queen with all the Northern earls and lords
Intend here to besiege you in your castle.
She is hard by with twenty thousand men;
And therefore fortify your hold, my lord.

YORK
Ay, with my sword. What, think'st thou that we fear them?
Edward and Richard, you shall stay with me;
My cousin Montague shall post to London.
Let noble Warwick, Cobham, and the rest,
Whom we have left protectors of the king,
With pow'rful policy strengthen themselves
And trust not simple Henry nor his oaths.

MONTAGUE
Cousin, I go. I'll win them; fear it not.
And thus most humbly I do take my leave.
Exit Montague.
Enter [Sir John] Mortimer, and [Sir Hugh,] his brother.

YORK
Sir John and Sir Hugh Mortimer, mine uncles,
You are come to Sandal in a happy hour.
The army of the queen mean to besiege us.

JOHN
She shall not need; we'll meet her in the field.

Line numbers right column: 22, 26, 30, 36, 39, 44, 46, 48, 52, 58

YORK
What, with five thousand men?
RICHARD
Ay, with five hundred, father, for a need.
68 A woman's general. What should we fear?
A march afar off.
EDWARD
I hear their drums. Let's set our men in order
70 And issue forth and bid them battle straight.
YORK
Five men to twenty! Though the odds be great,
I doubt not, uncle, of our victory.
Many a battle have I won in France
74 When as the enemy hath been ten to one.
Why should I not now have the like success?
Alarum. Exit [York with the rest].

*

I, iii   *Enter Rutland and his Tutor.*
RUTLAND
Ah, whither shall I fly to scape their hands?
Ah, tutor, look where bloody Clifford comes.
Enter Clifford [and Soldiers].
CLIFFORD
Chaplain, away! Thy priesthood saves thy life.
As for the brat of this accursèd duke,
Whose father slew my father, he shall die.
TUTOR
And I, my lord, will bear him company.
CLIFFORD
Soldiers, away with him!
TUTOR
Ah, Clifford, murder not this innocent child,
Lest thou be hated both of God and man.
Exit [dragged off by Soldiers].
CLIFFORD
How now? Is he dead already? Or is it fear
That makes him close his eyes? I'll open them.
RUTLAND
12 So looks the pent-up lion o'er the wretch
That trembles under his devouring paws;
14 And so he walks, insulting o'er his prey,
And so he comes, to rend his limbs asunder.
Ah, gentle Clifford, kill me with thy sword
And not with such a cruel threat'ning look.
Sweet Clifford, hear me speak before I die.
I am too mean a subject for thy wrath.
20 Be thou revenged on men and let me live.
CLIFFORD
In vain thou speak'st, poor boy. My father's blood
Hath stopped the passage where thy words should enter.
RUTLAND
Then let my father's blood open it again.
He is a man, and, Clifford, cope with him.
CLIFFORD
Had I thy brethren here, their lives and thine
Were not revenge sufficient for me.
No, if I digged up thy forefathers' graves
And hung their rotten coffins up in chains,
It could not slake mine ire nor ease my heart.
30 The sight of any of the house of York
Is as a Fury to torment my soul;
And till I root out their accursèd line

And leave not one alive, I live in hell.
Therefore –
RUTLAND
O, let me pray before I take my death!
To thee I pray. Sweet Clifford, pity me.
CLIFFORD
Such pity as my rapier's point affords.
RUTLAND
I never did thee harm. Why wilt thou slay me?
CLIFFORD
Thy father hath.
RUTLAND   But 'twas ere I was born.
Thou hast one son. For his sake pity me.
Lest in revenge thereof, sith God is just,   41
He be as miserably slain as I.
Ah, let me live in prison all my days;
And when I give occasion of offense,
Then let me die, for now thou hast no cause.
CLIFFORD
No cause?
Thy father slew my father. Therefore die.
[Stabs him.]
RUTLAND
Di faciant laudis summa sit ista tuae!   48
[Dies.]
CLIFFORD
Plantagenet, I come, Plantagenet!
And this thy son's blood cleaving to my blade
Shall rust upon my weapon till thy blood,
Congealed with this, do make me wipe off both.   *Exit.*
Alarum. Enter Richard Duke of York.   I, iv
YORK
The army of the queen hath got the field.
My uncles both are slain in rescuing me,
And all my followers to the eager foe
Turn back and fly, like ships before the wind   4
Or lambs pursued by hunger-starvèd wolves.
My sons – God knows what hath bechancèd them;
But this I know, they have demeaned themselves   7
Like men born to renown by life or death.
Three times did Richard make a lane to me
And thrice cried 'Courage, father! fight it out!'
And full as oft came Edward to my side
With purple falchion, painted to the hilt   12
In blood of those that had encount'red him.
And when the hardiest warriors did retire,
Richard cried 'Charge! and give no foot of ground!'
And cried 'A crown, or else a glorious tomb!
A sceptre, or an earthly sepulchre!'
With this we charged again; but out alas!
We bodged again, as I have seen a swan   19
With bootless labor swim against the tide   20
And spend her strength with overmatching waves.   21
A short alarum within.
Ah, hark! The fatal followers do pursue,
And I am faint and cannot fly their fury;
And were I strong, I would not shun their fury.

68 s.d. *A march* drum-beats 70 *straight* immediately 74 *When as* when
I, iii Fields near York's castle 12 *pent-up* caged, hence fierce 14 *insulting*
exulting 41 *sith* since 48 *Di . . . tuae* may the gods grant that this be the
height of your fame (Ovid, *Heroides*, II, 66)
I, iv 4 *Turn back* i.e. turn their backs 7 *demeaned* behaved 12 *falchion*
curved broadsword 19 *bodged* botched 20 *bootless* fruitless 21 *with*
against

25 The sands are numb'red that makes up my life.
    Here must I stay and here my life must end.
    Enter the Queen [Margaret], Clifford, Northumber-
    land, the young Prince, and Soldiers.
    Come, bloody Clifford, rough Northumberland,
    I dare your quenchless fury to more rage.
29 I am your butt and I abide your shot.

NORTHUMBERLAND
    Yield to our mercy, proud Plantagenet.

CLIFFFORD
    Ay, to such mercy as his ruthless arm
    With downright payment showed unto my father.
33 Now Phaeton hath tumbled from his car
34 And made an evening at the noontide prick.

YORK
35 My ashes, as the phoenix, may bring forth
    A bird that will revenge upon you all ;
    And in that hope I throw mine eyes to heaven,
    Scorning whate'er you can afflict me with.
    Why come you not ? What ? multitudes, and fear ?

CLIFFORD
    So cowards fight when they can fly no further ;
    So doves do peck the falcon's piercing talons ;
    So desperate thieves, all hopeless of their lives,
    Breathe out invectives 'gainst the officers.

YORK
    O Clifford, but bethink thee once again,
45 And in thy thought o'errun my former time ;
    And, if thou canst for blushing, view this face,
    And bite thy tongue that slanders him with cowardice
    Whose frown hath made thee faint and fly ere this.

CLIFFORD
49 I will not bandy with thee word for word,
50 But buckle with thee blows, twice two for one.

QUEEN MARGARET
    Hold, valiant Clifford ! For a thousand causes
    I would prolong awhile the traitor's life.
    Wrath makes him deaf. Speak thou, Northumberland.

NORTHUMBERLAND
    Hold, Clifford ! Do not honor him so much
    To prick thy finger, though to wound his heart.
56 What valor were it, when a cur doth grin,
    For one to thrust his hand between his teeth
    When he might spurn him with his foot away ?
59 It is war's prize to take all vantages ;
60 And ten to one is no impeach of valor.
    [Fight and take him.]

CLIFFORD
61 Ay, ay, so strives the woodcock with the gin.

NORTHUMBERLAND
    So doth the cony struggle in the net.   62

YORK
    So triumph thieves upon their conquered booty ;
    So true men yield, with robbers so o'ermatched.   64

NORTHUMBERLAND
    What would your grace have done unto him now ?

QUEEN MARGARET
    Brave warriors, Clifford and Northumberland,
    Come, make him stand upon this molehill here   67
    That raught at mountains with outstretchèd arms,   68
    Yet parted but the shadow with his hand.   69
    What, was it you that would be England's king ?
    Was't you that revelled in our parliament   71
    And made a preachment of your high descent ?
    Where are your mess of sons to back you now ?   73
    The wanton Edward, and the lusty George ?
    And where's that valiant crookback prodigy,   75
    Dicky your boy, that with his grumbling voice
    Was wont to cheer his dad in mutinies ?   77
    Or, with the rest, where is your darling Rutland ?
    Look, York ! I stained this napkin with the blood   79
    That valiant Clifford with his rapier's point
    Made issue from the bosom of the boy ;
    And if thine eyes can water for his death,
    I give thee this to dry thy cheeks withal.
    Alas, poor York ! but that I hate thee deadly,
    I should lament thy miserable state.
    I prithee grieve, to make me merry, York.
    What ? hath thy fiery heart so parched thine entrails
    That not a tear can fall for Rutland's death ?
    Why art thou patient, man ? Thou shouldst be mad ;
    And I to make thee mad do mock thee thus.
    Stamp, rave, and fret, that I may sing and dance.
    Thou wouldst be fee'd, I see, to make me sport.   92
    York cannot speak unless he wear a crown.
    A crown for York ! and, lords, bow low to him.
    Hold you his hands whilst I do set it on.
    [Puts a paper crown on his head.]
    Ay, marry, sir, now looks he like a king.   96
    Ay, this is he that took King Henry's chair
    And this is he was his adopted heir.
    But how is it that great Plantagenet
    Is crowned so soon, and broke his solemn oath ?
    As I bethink me, you should not be king
    Till our King Henry had shook hands with death.
    And will you pale your head in Henry's glory   103
    And rob his temples of the diadem
    Now in his life, against your holy oath ?
    O, 'tis a fault too too unpardonable.
    Off with the crown, and with the crown his head.
    And whilst we breathe, take time to do him dead.   108

CLIFFORD
    That is my office, for my father's sake.

QUEEN MARGARET
    Nay, stay. Let's hear the orisons he makes.   110

YORK
    She-wolf of France, but worse than wolves of France,
    Whose tongue more poisons than the adder's tooth,
    How ill-beseeming is it in thy sex
    To triumph like an Amazonian trull   114
    Upon their woes whom fortune captivates.
    But that thy face is vizard-like, unchanging,   116
    Made impudent with use of evil deeds,

---

25 *sands* i.e. in the hourglass **29** *butt* target for archery **33** *Phaeton* the son of Apollo, who took his father's sun-chariot and, unable to manage it, was dashed to pieces (a conventional symbol of presumption, appropriate here because the sun was a Yorkist device) **34** *noontide prick* mark on sundial indicating noon **35** *phoenix* a miraculous bird that died through spontaneous combustion and rose again from its own ashes **45** *o'errun* review **49** *bandy* exchange **50** *buckle* grapple, engage **56** *grin* show his teeth **59** *prize* reward **60** *impeach* calling in question **61** *woodcock* (proverbially stupid, as was the *cony*, l. 62) ; *gin* engine, trap **62** *cony* rabbit **64** *true* honest **67** *stand . . . here* (with allusion to the 'king of the molehill,' a term of contempt) **68** *raught* reached **69** *but* only **71** *revelled* enjoyed yourself **73** *mess* a group of four **75** *prodigy* monster **77** *mutinies* rebellions **79** *napkin* handkerchief **92** *fee'd* paid **96** *marry* by the Virgin Mary (with weakened force) **103** *pale* encircle **108** *breathe* rest **110** *orisons* prayers **114** *Amazonian* (the Amazons, who figure in classical story, were a legendary race of female warriors) **116** *vizard-like* mask-like

118 I would assay, proud queen, to make thee blush.
To tell thee whence thou cam'st, of whom derived,
Were shame enough to shame thee, wert thou not shame-
    less.
121 Thy father bears the type of King of Naples,
122 Of both the Sicils and Jerusalem,
123 Yet not so wealthy as an English yeoman.
Hath that poor monarch taught thee to insult?
125 It needs not nor it boots thee not, proud queen,
126 Unless the adage must be verified,
That beggars mounted run their horse to death.
'Tis beauty that doth oft make women proud;
But God he knows thy share thereof is small.
'Tis virtue that doth make them most admired;
The contrary doth make thee wond'red at.
132 'Tis government that makes them seem divine;
The want thereof makes thee abominable.
Thou art as opposite to every good
135 As the Antipodes are unto us
136 Or as the South to the Septentrion.
O tiger's heart wrapped in a woman's hide!
How couldst thou drain the lifeblood of the child,
To bid the father wipe his eyes withal,
And yet be seen to bear a woman's face?
Women are soft, mild, pitiful, and flexible;
Thou stern, obdurate, flinty, rough, remorseless.
Bid'st thou me rage? Why, now thou hast thy wish.
Wouldst have me weep? Why, now thou hast thy will.
For raging wind blows up incessant showers,
And when the rage allays the rain begins.
147 These tears are my sweet Rutland's obsequies,
And every drop cries vengeance for his death
149 'Gainst thee, fell Clifford, and thee, false Frenchwoman.

NORTHUMBERLAND
150 Beshrew me but his passions moves me so
That hardly can I check my eyes from tears.

YORK
That face of his the hungry cannibals
Would not have touched, would not have stained with
    blood;
But you are more inhuman, more inexorable –
155 O, ten times more! – than tigers of Hyrcania.
156 See, ruthless queen, a hapless father's tears.
This cloth thou dipp'dst in blood of my sweet boy,
And I with tears do wash the blood away.
Keep thou the napkin and go boast of this;
160 And if thou tell'st the heavy story right,
Upon my soul, the hearers will shed tears.
Yea, even my foes will shed fast-falling tears
And say, 'Alas, it was a piteous deed!'
There, take the crown, and with the crown my curse;
And in thy need such comfort come to thee
As now I reap at thy too cruel hand.
Hard-hearted Clifford, take me from the world.
My soul to heaven, my blood upon your heads.

NORTHUMBERLAND
Had he been slaughterman to all my kin,
I should not for my life but weep with him
171 To see how inly sorrow gripes his soul.

QUEEN MARGARET
172 What, weeping-ripe, my Lord Northumberland?
Think but upon the wrong he did us all
174 And that will quickly dry thy melting tears.

CLIFFORD
Here's for my oath, here's for my father's death.
    [Stabs him.]

QUEEN MARGARET
And here's to right our gentle-hearted king.
    [Stabs him.]

YORK
Open thy gate of mercy, gracious God,
My soul flies through these wounds to seek out thee.
    [Dies.]

QUEEN MARGARET
Off with his head and set it on York gates,
So York may overlook the town of York.
    Flourish. Exit [Queen Margaret with her followers].

*

    A march. Enter Edward, Richard, and their Power.   II, i

EDWARD
I wonder how our princely father scaped,
Or whether he be 'scaped away or no
From Clifford's and Northumberland's pursuit.
Had he been ta'en, we should have heard the news;
Had he been slain, we should have heard the news;
Or had he scaped, methinks we should have heard
The happy tidings of his good escape.
How fares my brother? Why is he so sad?

RICHARD
I cannot joy until I be resolved
Where our right valiant father is become.   10
I saw him in the battle range about
And watched him how he singled Clifford forth.   12
Methought he bore him in the thickest troop
As doth a lion in a herd of neat,   14
Or as a bear encompassed round with dogs,
Who having pinched a few and made them cry,   16
The rest stand all aloof and bark at him.
So fared our father with his enemies;
So fled his enemies my warlike father.
Methinks 'tis prize enough to be his son.   20
See how the morning opes her golden gates
And takes her farewell of the glorious sun.
How well resembles it the prime of youth
Trimmed like a younker prancing to his love.   24

EDWARD
Dazzle mine eyes, or do I see three suns?   25

RICHARD
Three glorious suns, each one a perfect sun,
Not separated with the racking clouds,   27
But severed in a pale clear-shining sky.
See, see! They join, embrace, and seem to kiss,

118 *assay* try 121 *type* title 122 *both the Sicils* i.e. Sicily and Naples
123 *yeoman* landowner (below the rank of gentleman) 125 *boots* profits
126 *adage* proverb 132 *government* self-control 135 *Antipodes* the other
side of the world 136 *Septentrion* the Big Dipper, i.e. the North 147
obsequies funeral rites 149 *fell* cruel 150 *Beshrew* curse 155 *Hyrcania* a
region of ancient Persia (the reference to the fierceness of Hyrcanian tigers
is ultimately from the *Aeneid*, IV, 366–67) 156 *hapless* luckless 160
heavy sorrowful 171 *inly* heartfelt 172 *weeping-ripe* ready for weeping
174 *melting tears* tears arising from a softened heart
II, i Fields near the Welsh border (Marches) 10 *Where ... is become* what
has happened to . . . 12 *forth* out 14 *neat* cattle 16 *pinched* bitten
20 *prize* privilege 24 *Trimmed* dressed up; *younker* young man 25
Dazzle mine eyes do my eyes blur 27 *racking* passing

As if they vowed some league inviolable.
Now are they but one lamp, one light, one sun.
32 In this the heaven figures some event.

EDWARD
'Tis wondrous strange, the like yet never heard of.
34 I think it cites us, brother, to the field,
That we, the sons of brave Plantagenet,
36 Each one already blazing by our meeds,
Should notwithstanding join our lights together
38 And overshine the earth, as this the world.
Whate'er it bodes, henceforward will I bear
Upon my target three fair-shining suns.

RICHARD
41 Nay, bear three daughters. By your leave I speak it,
42 You love the breeder better than the male.
    Enter one [Messenger] blowing [a horn].
But what art thou whose heavy looks foretell
Some dreadful story hanging on thy tongue?

MESSENGER
Ah, one that was a woeful looker-on
46 When as the noble Duke of York was slain,
Your princely father and my loving lord.

EDWARD
O speak no more, for I have heard too much.

RICHARD
Say how he died, for I will hear it all.

MESSENGER
50 Environèd he was with many foes,
51 And stood against them as the hope of Troy
Against the Greeks that would have ent'red Troy.
But Hercules himself must yield to odds;
And many strokes, though with a little axe,
Hews down and fells the hardest-timbered oak.
By many hands your father was subdued,
But only slaught'red by the ireful arm
Of unrelenting Clifford and the queen,
59 Who crowned the gracious duke in high despite,
Laughed in his face, and when with grief he wept,
The ruthless queen gave him, to dry his cheeks,
A napkin steepèd in the harmless blood
Of sweet young Rutland, by rough Clifford slain;
And after many scorns, many foul taunts,
They took his head and on the gates of York
They set the same; and there it doth remain,
The saddest spectacle that e'er I viewed.

EDWARD
Sweet Duke of York, our prop to lean upon,
Now thou art gone, we have no staff, no stay.
70 O Clifford, boist'rous Clifford, thou hast slain
The flow'r of Europe for his chivalry;
And treacherously hast thou vanquished him,
For hand to hand he would have vanquished thee.

Now my soul's palace is become a prison.   74
Ah, would she break from hence, that this my body
Might in the ground be closèd up in rest.
For never henceforth shall I joy again;
Never, O never, shall I see more joy.

RICHARD
I cannot weep, for all my body's moisture
Scarce serves to quench my furnace-burning heart;
Nor can my tongue unload my heart's great burden,
For selfsame wind that I should speak withal
Is kindling coals that fires all my breast
And burns me up with flames that tears would quench.
To weep is to make less the depth of grief.
Tears, then, for babes; blows and revenge for me!
Richard, I bear thy name; I'll venge thy death
Or die renownèd by attempting it.

EDWARD
His name that valiant duke hath left with thee;
His dukedom and his chair with me is left.

RICHARD
Nay, if thou be that princely eagle's bird,   91
Show thy descent by gazing 'gainst the sun;   92
For chair and dukedom, throne and kingdom say,   93
Either that is thine, or else thou wert not his.
    *March. Enter Warwick, Marquess Montague, and
    their Army.*

WARWICK
How now, fair lords, what fare? What news abroad?

RICHARD
Great Lord of Warwick, if we should recompt
Our baleful news and at each word's deliverance   97
Stab poniards in our flesh till all were told,
The words would add more anguish than the wounds.
O valiant lord, the Duke of York is slain.

EDWARD
O Warwick, Warwick, that Plantagenet
Which held thee dearly as his soul's redemption
Is by the stern Lord Clifford done to death.

WARWICK
Ten days ago I drowned these news in tears;
And now, to add more measure to your woes,
I come to tell you things sith then befallen.   106
After the bloody fray at Wakefield fought,
Where your brave father breathed his latest gasp,   108
Tidings, as swiftly as the posts could run,
Were brought me of your loss and his depart.   110
I, then in London, keeper of the king,
Mustered my soldiers, gathered flocks of friends,
[And very well appointed, as I thought,]   113
Marched toward Saint Albans to intercept the queen,
Bearing the king in my behalf along;
For by my scouts I was advertisèd   116
That she was coming with a full intent
To dash our late decree in parliament
Touching King Henry's oath and your succession.
Short tale to make, we at Saint Albans met,
Our battles joined, and both sides fiercely fought;
But whether 'twas the coldness of the king,
Who looked full gently on his warlike queen,
That robbed my soldiers of their heated spleen,   124
Or whether 'twas report of her success,
Or more than common fear of Clifford's rigor,
Who thunders to his captives blood and death,

---

32 *figures* prefigures, foretells   34 *cites* incites   36 *meeds* merits   38 *overshine* light up; *this* i.e. this phenomenon   41 *daughters* (with obvious pun on *suns*, l. 40)   42 *breeder* female; **s.d.** *blowing [a horn]* (indicating that the Messenger is a post-rider)   46 *When as* when   50 *Environèd* surrounded   51 *hope of Troy* i.e. Hector   59 *in high despite* with great contempt   70 *boist'rous* savage   74 *soul's palace* i.e. body   91 *bird* young   92 *gazing 'gainst the sun* (Eagles, according to Pliny and many later writers, could gaze at the sun without blinking. The sun here may symbolize the king; the eagle may be an allusion to a Yorkist badge.)   93 *chair* (symbol of a duke's authority, as *throne* is of a king's)   97 *baleful* deadly   106 *sith* since   108 *latest* last   110 *depart* death   113 *appointed* equipped   116 *advertisèd* informed   124 *spleen* spirit

I cannot judge ; but to conclude with truth,
Their weapons like to lightning came and went ;
Our soldiers', like the night owl's lazy flight
131 Or like an idle thresher with a flail,
Fell gently down, as if they struck their friends.
I cheered them up with justice of our cause,
With promise of high pay and great rewards ;
But all in vain ; they had no heart to fight,
And we (in them) no hope to win the day ;
So that we fled : the king unto the queen ;
Lord George your brother, Norfolk, and myself,
139 In haste, post-haste, are come to join with you ;
140 For in the Marches here we heard you were,
141 Making another head to fight again.

EDWARD
Where is the Duke of Norfolk, gentle Warwick ?
And when came George from Burgundy to England ?

WARWICK
Some six miles off the duke is with the soldiers,
And for your brother, he was lately sent
146 From your kind aunt, Duchess of Burgundy,
With aid of soldiers to this needful war.

RICHARD
148 'Twas odds belike when valiant Warwick fled.
Oft have I heard his praises in pursuit,
150 But ne'er till now his scandal of retire.

WARWICK
Nor now my scandal, Richard, dost thou hear ;
For thou shalt know this strong right hand of mine
Can pluck the diadem from faint Henry's head
154 And wring the awful sceptre from his fist,
Were he as famous and as bold in war
As he is famed for mildness, peace, and prayer.

RICHARD
I know it well, Lord Warwick. Blame me not.
'Tis love I bear thy glories make me speak.
But in this troublous time what's to be done ?
Shall we go throw away our coats of steel
And wrap our bodies in black mourning gowns,
162 Numb'ring our Ave-Maries with our beads ?
Or shall we on the helmets of our foes
164 Tell our devotion with revengeful arms ?
If for the last, say 'Ay,' and to it, lords.

WARWICK
Why, therefore Warwick came to seek you out,
And therefore comes my brother Montague.
Attend me, lords. The proud insulting queen,
169 With Clifford and the haught Northumberland,
170 And of their feather many moe proud birds,
171 Have wrought the easy-melting king like wax.
He swore consent to your succession,
His oath enrollèd in the parliament ;
And now to London all the crew are gone,
To frustrate both his oath, and what beside
May make against the house of Lancaster.
Their power, I think, is thirty thousand strong.
Now if the help of Norfolk and myself
179 With all the friends that thou, brave Earl of March,
Amongst the loving Welshmen canst procure,
Will but amount to five-and-twenty thousand,
182 Why, via ! to London will we march
And once again bestride our foaming steeds,
And once again cry 'Charge !' upon our foes,
But never once again turn back and fly.

RICHARD
Ay, now methinks I hear great Warwick speak.
Ne'er may he live to see a sunshine day   187
That cries 'Retire !' if Warwick bid him stay.

EDWARD
Lord Warwick, on thy shoulder will I lean,
And when thou fail'st (as God forbid the hour)
Must Edward fall, which peril heaven forfend.   191

WARWICK
No longer Earl of March, but Duke of York,
The next degree is England's royal throne ;   193
For King of England shalt thou be proclaimed
In every borough as we pass along ;
And he that throws not up his cap for joy
Shall for the fault make forfeit of his head.
King Edward, valiant Richard, Montague,
Stay we no longer, dreaming of renown,
But sound the trumpets and about our task.

RICHARD
Then, Clifford, were thy heart as hard as steel,
As thou hast shown it flinty by thy deeds,
I come to pierce it or to give thee mine.

EDWARD
Then strike up drums. God and Saint George for us !
Enter a Messenger.

WARWICK
How now ? What news ?

MESSENGER
The Duke of Norfolk sends you word by me
The queen is coming with a puissant host,   207
And craves your company for speedy counsel.

WARWICK
Why, then it sorts. Brave warriors, let's away.   209
Exeunt omnes.

*

Flourish. Enter the King [Henry], the Queen   II, ii
[Margaret], Clifford, Northumberland, and young
Prince, with Drum and Trumpets.

QUEEN MARGARET
Welcome, my lord, to this brave town of York.
Yonder's the head of that arch-enemy
That sought to be encompassed with your crown.
Doth not the object cheer your heart, my lord ?

KING HENRY
Ay, as the rocks cheer them that fear their wrack.   5
To see this sight it irks my very soul.
Withhold revenge, dear God ! 'Tis not my fault,
Nor wittingly have I infringed my vow.   8

131 *flail* an instrument for threshing, a stout stick joined to a longer handle by a leather thong   139 *post-haste* as speedily as post-riders   140 *Marches* borders (here, of Wales)   141 *Making another head* gathering another force   146 *aunt . . . Burgundy* (Isabel, Duchess of Burgundy, was a grand-daughter of John of Gaunt and a distant cousin to Edward. Holinshed says that George and Richard were sent for protection to the Duke of Burgundy after York's death and remained with him until Edward was crowned.)   148 *'Twas odds belike* no doubt the odds were heavily against him   150 *scandal of retire* disgrace because of retreating   154 *awful* awe-inspiring   162 *Ave-Maries* Hail Maries (prayers to the Blessed Virgin)   164 *Tell our devotion* (1) count off our prayers, as on a rosary, (2) declare our love (ironically)   169 *haught* haughty   170 *moe* more   171 *wrought* worked on, persuaded ; *easy-melting* soft-hearted, easily swayed   179 *Earl of March* i.e. Edward (his title before York's death ; see l. 192)   182 *via* forward   187 *he* i.e. anyone   191 *forfend* forbid   193 *degree* rank   207 *puissant* powerful   209 *sorts* works out well
II, ii Before the walls of York   5 *wrack* ruin   8 *wittingly* knowingly

CLIFFORD

9 My gracious liege, this too much lenity
And harmful pity must be laid aside.
To whom do lions cast their gentle looks?
Not to the beast that would usurp their den.
Whose hand is that the forest bear doth lick?
14 Not his that spoils her young before her face.
Who scapes the lurking serpent's mortal sting?
Not he that sets his foot upon her back.
The smallest worm will turn, being trodden on,
And doves will peck in safeguard of their brood.
19 Ambitious York did level at thy crown,
Thou smiling while he knit his angry brows.
He, but a duke, would have his son a king
22 And raise his issue like a loving sire;
Thou, being a king, blest with a goodly son,
Didst yield consent to disinherit him,
Which argued thee a most unloving father.
Unreasonable creatures feed their young;
And though man's face be fearful to their eyes,
Yet, in protection of their tender ones,
Who hath not seen them, even with those wings
Which sometime they have used with fearful flight,
Make war with him that climbed unto their nest,
Offering their own lives in their young's defense?
For shame, my liege. Make them your precedent.
Were it not pity that this goodly boy
Should lose his birthright by his father's fault
And long hereafter say unto his child,
'What my great-grandfather and grandsire got
38 My careless father fondly gave away'?
Ah, what a shame were this. Look on the boy,
And let his manly face, which promiseth
Successful fortune, steel thy melting heart
To hold thine own and leave thine own with him.

KING HENRY

Full well hath Clifford played the orator,
44 Inferring arguments of mighty force.
But, Clifford, tell me, didst thou never hear
That things ill got had ever bad success?
47 And happy always was it for that son
48 Whose father for his hoarding went to hell?
I'll leave my son my virtuous deeds behind,
And would my father had left me no more.
51 For all the rest is held at such a rate
As brings a thousandfold more care to keep
Than in possession any jot of pleasure.
Ah, cousin York, would thy best friends did know
How it doth grieve me that thy head is here.

QUEEN MARGARET

My lord, cheer up your spirits. Our foes are nigh,
57 And this soft courage makes your followers faint.
58 You promised knighthood to our forward son.
Unsheathe your sword and dub him presently.

Edward, kneel down.

KING HENRY

Edward Plantagenet, arise a knight,
And learn this lesson: Draw thy sword in right.

PRINCE

My gracious father, by your kingly leave,
I'll draw it as apparent to the crown   64
And in that quarrel use it to the death.

CLIFFORD

Why, that is spoken like a toward prince.   66
Enter a Messenger.

MESSENGER

Royal commanders, be in readiness;
For with a band of thirty thousand men
Comes Warwick, backing of the Duke of York,   69
And in the towns, as they do march along,
Proclaims him king, and many fly to him.
Darraign your battle, for they are at hand.   72

CLIFFORD

I would your highness would depart the field.
The queen hath best success when you are absent.

QUEEN MARGARET

Ay, good my lord, and leave us to our fortune.

KING HENRY

Why, that's my fortune too. Therefore I'll stay.

NORTHUMBERLAND

Be it with resolution, then, to fight.

PRINCE

My royal father, cheer these noble lords
And hearten those that fight in your defense.
Unsheathe your sword, good father. Cry 'Saint George!' 80
March. Enter Edward, Warwick, Richard, Clarence,
Norfolk, Montague, and Soldiers.

EDWARD

Now, perjured Henry, wilt thou kneel for grace
And set thy diadem upon my head,
Or bide the mortal fortune of the field?   83

QUEEN MARGARET

Go rate thy minions, proud insulting boy   84
Becomes it thee to be thus bold in terms
Before thy sovereign and thy lawful king?

EDWARD

I am his king, and he should bow his knee.
I was adopted heir by his consent;
Since when, his oath is broke; for, as I hear,
You that are king, though he do wear the crown,
Have caused him by new act of parliament
To blot out me and put his own son in.

CLIFFORD

And reason too;
Who should succeed the father but the son?

RICHARD

Are you there, butcher? O, I cannot speak.

CLIFFORD

Ay, Crookback, here I stand to answer thee,
Or any he, the proudest of thy sort.   97

RICHARD

'Twas you that killed young Rutland, was it not?

CLIFFORD

Ay, and old York, and yet not satisfied.

RICHARD

For God's sake, lords, give signal to the fight.

WARWICK

What say'st thou, Henry? Wilt thou yield the crown?

---

9 *lenity* gentleness 14 *spoils* destroys 19 *level* aim 22 *raise* promote
38 *fondly* foolishly 44 *Inferring* adducing 47 *happy . . . it* were things
always good 48 *for* because of 51 *rate* cost 57 *faint* faint-hearted
58 *forward* high-spirited, precocious 64 *apparent* heir apparent 66 *toward* promising 69 *backing of* in support of; *Duke of York* i.e. Edward
72 *Darraign your battle* deploy your forces 80 s.d. *Clarence* i.e. George
(though George is not created Duke of Clarence until II, vi, 104, he is
consistently termed Clarence in stage directions and speech-prefixes
before then) 83 *bide* await 84 *rate thy minions* berate your favorites
97 *sort* gang

QUEEN MARGARET
Why, how now, long-tongued Warwick?
Dare you speak?
When you and I met at Saint Albans last,
Your legs did better service than your hands.

WARWICK
Then 'twas my turn to fly, and now 'tis thine.

CLIFFORD
You said so much before, and yet you fled.

WARWICK
'Twas not your valor, Clifford, drove me thence.

NORTHUMBERLAND
No, nor your manhood that durst make you stay.

RICHARD
109   Northumberland, I hold thee reverently.
Break off the parley, for scarce I can refrain
The execution of my big-swol'n heart
Upon that Clifford, that cruel child-killer.

CLIFFORD
I slew thy father. Call'st thou him a child?

RICHARD
Ay, like a dastard and a treacherous coward,
As thou didst kill our tender brother Rutland.
But ere sun set I'll make thee curse the deed.

KING HENRY
Have done with words, my lords, and hear me speak.

QUEEN MARGARET
Defy them then, or else hold close thy lips.

KING HENRY
I prithee give no limits to my tongue.
I am a king, and privileged to speak.

CLIFFORD
My liege, the wound that bred this meeting here
Cannot be cured by words. Therefore be still.

RICHARD
Then, executioner, unsheathe thy sword.
124   By Him that made us all, I am resolved
125   That Clifford's manhood lies upon his tongue.

EDWARD
Say, Henry, shall I have my right, or no?
A thousand men have broke their fasts to-day
That ne'er shall dine unless thou yield the crown.

WARWICK
129   If thou deny, their blood upon thy head.
For York in justice puts his armor on.

PRINCE
If that be right which Warwick says is right,
There is no wrong, but everything is right.

RICHARD
133   Whoever got thee, there thy mother stands;
134   For well I wot thou hast thy mother's tongue.

QUEEN MARGARET
But thou art neither like thy sire nor dam,
136   But like a foul misshapen stigmatic,
Marked by the Destinies to be avoided,
138   As venom toads or lizards' dreadful stings.

RICHARD
139   Iron of Naples, hid with English gilt,
Whose father bears the title of a king
141   (As if a channel should be called the sea),
142   Sham'st thou not, knowing whence thou art extraught,
To let thy tongue detect thy base-born heart?

EDWARD
144   A wisp of straw were worth a thousand crowns,

To make this shameless callet know herself.   145
Helen of Greece was fairer far than thou,   146
Although thy husband may be Menelaus;
And ne'er was Agamemnon's brother wronged
By that false woman as this king by thee.
His father revelled in the heart of France,   150
And tamed the king, and made the Dauphin stoop;
And had he matched according to his state,   152
He might have kept that glory to this day;
But when he took a beggar to his bed
And graced thy poor sire with his bridal day,   155
Even then that sunshine brewed a show'r for him
That washed his father's fortunes forth of France   157
And heaped sedition on his crown at home.
For what hath broached this tumult but thy pride?   159
Hadst thou been meek, our title still had slept,   160
And we, in pity of the gentle king,
Had slipped our claim until another age.   162

CLARENCE
But when we saw our sunshine made thy spring
And that thy summer bred us no increase,   164
We set the axe to thy usurping root;   165
And though the edge hath something hit ourselves,   166
Yet know thou, since we have begun to strike,
We'll never leave till we have hewn thee down
Or bathed thy growing with our heated bloods.   169

EDWARD
And in this resolution I defy thee,
Not willing any longer conference,
Since thou denied'st the gentle king to speak.   172
Sound trumpets! Let our bloody colors wave,
And either victory, or else a grave!

QUEEN MARGARET
Stay, Edward.

EDWARD
No, wrangling woman, we'll no longer stay.
These words will cost ten thousand lives this day.
                                                Exeunt omnes.

*

Alarum. Excursions. Enter Warwick.   II, iii

WARWICK
Forspent with toil, as runners with a race,   1
I lay me down a little while to breathe;   2
For strokes received and many blows repaid

109 *reverently* in respect   124 *resolved* convinced   125 *Clifford's . . . tongue* i.e. he talks better than he fights   129 *deny* refuse   133 *got* begot   134 *wot* know   136 *stigmatic* one branded (stigmatized) by deformity   138 *venom* venomous   139 *Iron . . . gilt* i.e. you cheap Neapolitan, whose worthlessness is concealed by English gold (probably with punning allusion to Suffolk's 'guilt' in paying so high a price for her)   141 *channel* gutter   142 *Sham'st thou not* are you not ashamed; *extraught* extracted   144 *wisp of straw* (traditional mark of a scold)   145 *callet* lewd woman   146–48 *Helen . . . Menelaus . . . Agamemnon* (Paris of Troy abducted Helen, wife of Menelaus, King of Sparta, who was brother to Agamemnon, King of Mycenae; here Helen is the typical false woman and Menelaus the typical cuckold. There is an allusion to the belief that Prince Edward was not the son of Henry VI.)   150 *His father* i.e. Henry V   152 *he* i.e. Henry VI; *matched* wedded; *state* worth, dignity   155 *graced . . . day* i.e. did honor (grace) to him by marrying his daughter   157 *of* from   159 *broached* started (literally, set flowing)   160 *title* claim to the throne   162 *slipped* forgone   164 *increase* harvest   165 *usurping* (because she is wife to Henry, regarded by the Yorkists as a usurper)   166 *something* somewhat   169 *bathed* watered   172 *denied'st* forbade
II, iii Fields near York (Towton)   s.d. *Alarum* trumpet call – 'to arms'; *Excursions* attacks and counter-attacks   1 *Forspent* utterly wearied   2 *breathe* rest

Have robbed my strong-knit sinews of their strength,

5 And spite of spite needs must I rest awhile.
Enter Edward, running.

EDWARD

Smile, gentle heaven, or strike, ungentle death,

7 For this world frowns, and Edward's sun is clouded.

WARWICK

8 How now, my lord ? What hap ? What hope of good ?
Enter Clarence.

CLARENCE

Our hap is loss, our hope but sad despair,

Our ranks are broke and ruin follows us.

What counsel give you ? Whither shall we fly ?

EDWARD

12 Bootless is flight. They follow us with wings,

13 And weak we are and cannot shun pursuit.
Enter Richard.

RICHARD

Ah, Warwick, why hast thou withdrawn thyself ?

15 Thy brother's blood the thirsty earth hath drunk,

16 Broached with the steely point of Clifford's lance ;

And in the very pangs of death he cried,

Like to a dismal clangor heard from far,

'Warwick, revenge ! Brother, revenge my death !'

So, underneath the belly of their steeds,

That stained their fetlocks in his smoking blood,

The noble gentleman gave up the ghost.

WARWICK

Then let the earth be drunken with our blood !

I'll kill my horse, because I will not fly.

Why stand we like soft-hearted women here,

26 Wailing our losses, whiles the foe doth rage,

27 And look upon, as if the tragedy

Were played in jest by counterfeiting actors ?

Here on my knee I vow to God above

I'll never pause again, never stand still,

Till either death hath closed these eyes of mine

Or fortune given me measure of revenge.

EDWARD

O Warwick, I do bend my knee with thine

And in this vow do chain my soul to thine.

And ere my knee rise from the earth's cold face,

I throw my hands, mine eyes, my heart to thee,

Thou setter up and plucker down of kings,

38 Beseeching thee (if with thy will it stands)

That to my foes this body must be prey,

Yet that thy brazen gates of heaven may ope

And give sweet passage to my sinful soul.

Now, lords, take leave until we meet again,

Where'er it be, in heaven or in earth.

RICHARD

Brother, give me thy hand ; and, gentle Warwick,

Let me embrace thee in my weary arms.

I, that did never weep, now melt with woe

That winter should cut off our springtime so.

WARWICK

Away, away ! Once more, sweet lords, farewell.

CLARENCE

Yet let us all together to our troops,

And give them leave to fly that will not stay,

And call them pillars that will stand to us ;

And, if we thrive, promise them such rewards

As victors wear at the Olympian games.

This may plant courage in their quailing breasts ;

For yet is hope of life and victory.

Forslow no longer ! Make we hence amain !   56
Exeunt.

*Excursions. Enter Richard [at one door] and   II, iv
Clifford [at the other].*

RICHARD

Now, Clifford, I have singled thee alone.   1

Suppose this arm is for the Duke of York,

And this for Rutland – both bound to revenge,

Wert thou environed with a brazen wall.   4

CLIFFORD

Now, Richard, I am with thee here alone.

This is the hand that stabbed thy father York,

And this the hand that slew thy brother Rutland !

And here's the heart that triumphs in their death

And cheers these hands that slew thy sire and brother

To execute the like upon thyself.

And so have at thee !
They fight. Warwick comes. Clifford flies.

RICHARD

Nay, Warwick, single out some other chase,   12

For I myself will hunt this wolf to death.   *Exeunt.*
Alarum. Enter King Henry alone.   II, v

KING HENRY

This battle fares like to the morning's war,

When dying clouds contend with growing light,

What time the shepherd, blowing of his nails,   3

Can neither call it perfect day nor night.

Now sways it this way, like a mighty sea

Forced by the tide to combat with the wind ;

Now sways it that way, like the selfsame sea

Forced to retire by fury of the wind.

Sometime the flood prevails, and then the wind ;

Now one the better, then another best ;

Both tugging to be victors, breast to breast,

Yet neither conqueror nor conquerèd.

So is the equal poise of this fell war.   13

Here on this molehill will I sit me down.   14

To whom God will, there be the victory.

For Margaret my queen, and Clifford too,

Have chid me from the battle, swearing both

They prosper best of all when I am thence.

Would I were dead, if God's good will were so,

For what is in this world but grief and woe ?

O God ! methinks it were a happy life

To be no better than a homely swain ;   22

To sit upon a hill, as I do now,

To carve out dials quaintly, point by point,   24

Thereby to see the minutes how they run –

How many makes the hour full complete,

How many hours brings about the day,

How many days will finish up the year,

How many years a mortal man may live ;

When this is known, then to divide the times –

5 *spite of spite* come what may 7 *sun* i.e. good fortune (with allusion to the Yorkist sun device) 8 *hap* fortune 12 *Bootless* worthless, hopeless 13 *shun* avoid 15 *Thy brother's blood* (a reference to the 'Bastard of Salisbury,' Warwick's half-brother, killed at Ferrybridge) 16 *Broached* set flowing 26 *whiles* while 27 *upon* on 38 *stands* agrees 56 *Forslow* delay II, iv 1 *singled* chosen one from the herd (a hunting term) 4 *environed* surrounded 12 *chase* prey
II, v 3 *of* on (for warmth) 13 *fell* cruel 14 *on this molehill* (see I, iv, 67n.) 22 *swain* countryman 24 *dials quaintly* sundials artfully (perhaps alluding to the shepherds' practise of cutting sundials in the turf of hillsides)

So many hours must I tend my flock,
So many hours must I take my rest,
33 So many hours must I contemplate,
34 So many hours must I sport myself;
So many days my ewes have been with young,
36 So many weeks ere the poor fools will ean,
So many months ere I shall shear the fleece.
So minutes, hours, days, weeks, months, and years,
39 Passed over to the end they were created,
Would bring white hairs unto a quiet grave.
Ah, what a life were this! how sweet, how lovely!
Gives not the hawthorn bush a sweeter shade
43 To shepherds looking on their silly sheep
Than doth a rich embroidered canopy
To kings that fear their subjects' treachery?
O yes, it doth, a thousandfold it doth.
And to conclude, the shepherd's homely curds,
His cold thin drink out of his leather bottle,
49 His wonted sleep under a fresh tree's shade,
All which secure and sweetly he enjoys,
51 Is far beyond a prince's delicates,
His viands sparkling in a golden cup,
53 His body couchèd in a curious bed,
When care, mistrust, and treason waits on him.

*Alarum. Enter a Son that hath killed his father,
at one door [bearing the body in his arms].*

SON
Ill blows the wind that profits nobody.
This man whom hand to hand I slew in fight
57 May be possessèd with some store of crowns;
58 And I that, haply, take them from him now
May yet, ere night, yield both my life and them
To some man else, as this dead man doth me.
Who's this? O God! It is my father's face,
62 Whom in this conflict I, unwares, have killed.
63 O heavy times, begetting such events.
64 From London by the king was I pressed forth;
My father, being the Earl of Warwick's man,
Came on the part of York, pressed by his master;
And I, who at his hands received my life,
Have by my hands of life bereavèd him.
Pardon me, God, I knew not what I did.
And pardon, father, for I knew not thee.
My tears shall wipe away these bloody marks;
And no more words till they have flowed their fill.

KING HENRY
O piteous spectacle, O bloody times!
Whiles lions war and battle for their dens,
75 Poor harmless lambs abide their enmity.
Weep, wretched man, I'll aid thee tear for tear;
And let our hearts and eyes, like civil war,
78 Be blind with tears and break o'ercharged with grief.

*Enter, at another door, a Father that hath killed
his son, bearing of his son.*

FATHER
Thou that so stoutly hast resisted me,
Give me thy gold, if thou hast any gold;
For I have bought it with an hundred blows.
But let me see. Is this our foeman's face?
Ah, no, no, no! It is mine only son!
Ah, boy, if any life be left in thee,
Throw up thine eye. See, see what show'rs arise,
Blown with the windy tempest of my heart
Upon thy wounds, that kills mine eye and heart.

O, pity, God, this miserable age.
What stratagems, how fell, how butcherly,   89
Erroneous, mutinous, and unnatural,   90
This deadly quarrel daily doth beget.
O boy! thy father gave thee life too soon,
And hath bereft thee of thy life too late.   93
KING HENRY
Woe above woe, grief more than common grief;
O that my death would stay these ruthful deeds!   95
O, pity, pity, gentle heaven, pity!
The red rose and the white are on his face,
The fatal colors of our striving houses.
The one his purple blood right well resembles;
The other his pale cheeks, methinks, presenteth.   100
Wither one rose, and let the other flourish.
If you contend, a thousand lives must wither.
SON
How will my mother for a father's death
Take on with me, and ne'er be satisfied.   104
FATHER
How will my wife for slaughter of my son
Shed seas of tears, and ne'er be satisfied.
KING HENRY
How will the country for these woeful chances
Misthink the king, and not be satisfied.   108
SON
Was ever son so rued a father's death?
FATHER
Was ever father so bemoaned his son?
KING HENRY
Was ever king so grieved for subject's woe?
Much is your sorrow; mine ten times so much.
SON
I'll bear thee hence, where I may weep my fill.
[Exit with the body.]
FATHER
These arms of mine shall be thy winding sheet;
My heart, sweet boy, shall be thy sepulchre,
For from my heart thine image ne'er shall go.
My sighing breast shall be thy funeral bell;
And so obsequious will thy father be,   118
Even for the loss of thee, having no more,
As Priam was for all his valiant sons.   120
I'll bear thee hence, and let them fight that will,
For I have murdered where I should not kill.
Exit [with the body].
KING HENRY
Sad-hearted men, much overgone with care,   123
Here sits a king more woeful than you are.
*Alarums. Excursions. Enter the Queen [Margaret],
the Prince, and Exeter.*
PRINCE
Fly, father, fly! for all your friends are fled
And Warwick rages like a chafèd bull.   126

33 *contemplate* meditate, pray 34 *sport* amuse 36 *ean* give birth 39 *end they* end for which they 43 *silly* innocent 49 *wonted* accustomed 51 *delicates* dainty foods 53 *curious* (1) elaborately wrought, (2) full of cares 57 *crowns* money 58 *haply* by chance 62 *unwares* unknowingly 63 *heavy* miserable 64 *pressed* impressed, drafted 75 *abide* endure 78 *o'ercharged* overfilled 89 *stratagems* bloody acts; *fell* cruel 90 *Erroneous* criminal 93 *late* recently 95 *ruthful* pitiful 100 *presenteth* symbolizes 104 *Take on* be profoundly distressed; *satisfied* comforted 108 *Misthink* misunderstand, blame 118 *obsequious* dutiful in mourning 120 *Priam* king of Troy (whose fifty sons were killed defending the city) 123 *overgone* overcome 126 *chafèd* angry

Away! for death doth hold us in pursuit.

QUEEN MARGARET

128   Mount you, my lord. Toward Berwick post amain.
Edward and Richard, like a brace of greyhounds
Having the fearful flying hare in sight,
With fiery eyes, sparkling for very wrath,
And bloody steel grasped in their ireful hands,
Are at our backs; and therefore hence amain.

EXETER

Away! for vengeance comes along with them.
Nay, stay not to expostulate; make speed!
Or else come after. I'll away before.

KING HENRY

Nay, take me with thee, good sweet Exeter.
Not that I fear to stay, but love to go
Whither the queen intends. Forward, away!   *Exeunt.*

II, vi   *A loud alarum. Enter Clifford, wounded [with an*
     arrow in his neck].

CLIFFORD

Here burns my candle out; ay, here it dies,
2   Which, whiles it lasted, gave King Henry light.
3   O Lancaster! I fear thy overthrow
More than my body's parting with my soul.
5   My love and fear glued many friends to thee,
6   And now I fall, thy tough commixture melts,
7   Impairing Henry, strength'ning misproud York.
[The common people swarm like summer flies;]
9   And whither fly the gnats but to the sun?
And who shines now but Henry's enemies?
11   O Phoebus, hadst thou never given consent
12   That Phaeton should check thy fiery steeds,
13   Thy burning car never had scorched the earth!
14   And, Henry, hadst thou swayed as kings should do,
Or as thy father and his father did,
Giving no ground unto the house of York,
17   They never then had sprung like summer flies;
I and ten thousand in this luckless realm
Had left no mourning widows for our death,
20   And thou this day hadst kept thy chair in peace.
21   For what doth cherish weeds but gentle air?
And what makes robbers bold but too much lenity?
23   Bootless are plaints and cureless are my wounds;
No way to fly, nor strength to hold out flight;
The foe is merciless and will not pity,
For at their hands I have deserved no pity.
The air hath got into my deadly wounds
And much effuse of blood doth make me faint.
Come, York and Richard, Warwick and the rest.
30   I stabbed your fathers' bosoms; split my breast.
    [Faints.]
    Alarum and retreat. Enter Edward, Warwick,
    Richard, and Soldiers, Montague, and Clarence.

128 *Berwick* Berwick-on-Tweed, Northumberland; *post amain* ride speedily
II, vi   2 *whiles* while   3 *Lancaster* i.e. the house of Lancaster   5 *My . . .
fear* the love and respect I commanded   6 *commixture* compound   7 *Impairing* weakening; *misproud* unjustly proud   9 *sun* (another allusion to the
Yorkist sun device)   11 *Phoebus* Phoebus Apollo, the sun   12 *Phaeton* (see
I, iv, 33n.); *check* manage   13 *car* chariot   14 *swayed* ruled   17 *sprung*
multiplied   20 *chair* i.e. of state, throne   21 *cherish* foster   23 *Bootless*
useless   30 s.d. *retreat* a trumpet call – 'recall'   35 *fretting* (1) blowing in
gusts, (2) nagging   36 *argosy* large merchant ship   46 *doom* judgment   54
this i.e. Clifford's head; *supply the room* take the place   56 *screech owl* (a
bird of ill omen)   59 *ill-boding* foretelling ill   60 *understanding* consciousness   63 *nor . . . nor* neither . . . nor   65 *policy* stratagem   68 *eager* biting,
bitter   72 *fell* cruel   75 *fence* protect

EDWARD

Now breathe we, lords. Good fortune bids us pause
And smooth the frowns of war with peaceful looks.
Some troops pursue the bloody-minded queen
That led calm Henry, though he were a king,
As doth a sail, filled with a fretting gust,   35
Command an argosy to stem the waves.   36
But thinks you, lords, the Clifford fled with them?

WARWICK

No, 'tis impossible he should escape;
For, though before his face I speak the words,
Your brother Richard marked him for the grave;
And wheresoe'er he is, he's surely dead.
    Clifford groans [and dies].

EDWARD

Whose soul is that which takes her heavy leave?

RICHARD

A deadly groan, like life and death's departing.

EDWARD

See who it is, and now the battle's ended,
If friend or foe, let him be gently used.

RICHARD

Revoke that doom of mercy, for 'tis Clifford,   46
Who not contented that he lopped the branch
In hewing Rutland when his leaves put forth,
But set his murd'ring knife unto the root
From whence that tender spray did sweetly spring:
I mean our princely father, Duke of York.

WARWICK

From off the gates of York fetch down the head,
Your father's head, which Clifford placed there;
Instead whereof let this supply the room.   54
Measure for measure must be answerèd.

EDWARD

Bring forth that fatal screech owl to our house,   56
That nothing sung but death to us and ours.
Now death shall stop his dismal threat'ning sound
And his ill-boding tongue no more shall speak.   59

WARWICK

I think his understanding is bereft.   60
Speak, Clifford, dost thou know who speaks to thee?
Dark cloudy death o'ershades his beams of life,
And he nor sees, nor hears us what we say.   63

RICHARD

O, would he did! and so, perhaps, he doth.
'Tis but his policy to counterfeit,   65
Because he would avoid such bitter taunts
Which in the time of death he gave our father.

CLARENCE

If so thou think'st, vex him with eager words.   68

RICHARD

Clifford, ask mercy, and obtain no grace.

EDWARD

Clifford, repent in bootless penitence.

WARWICK

Clifford, devise excuses for thy faults.

CLARENCE

While we devise fell tortures for thy faults.   72

RICHARD

Thou didst love York, and I am son to York.

EDWARD

Thou pitied'st Rutland; I will pity thee.

CLARENCE

Where's Captain Margaret, to fence you now?   75

WARWICK

76 They mock thee, Clifford. Swear as thou wast wont.

RICHARD

What, not an oath ? Nay, then the world goes hard
When Clifford cannot spare his friends an oath.
I know by that he's dead ; and, by my soul,
If this right hand would buy two hours' life,
That I (in all despite) might rail at him,
This hand should chop it off, and with the issuing blood
83 Stifle the villain whose unstanchèd thirst
York and young Rutland could not satisfy.

WARWICK

Ay, but he's dead. Off with the traitor's head
And rear it in the place your father's stands.
And now to London with triumphant march,
There to be crownèd England's royal king ;
From whence shall Warwick cut the sea to France
And ask the Lady Bona for thy queen.
91 So shalt thou sinew both these lands together ;
And, having France thy friend, thou shalt not dread
The scattered foe that hopes to rise again ;
For though they cannot greatly sting to hurt,
95 Yet look to have them buzz to offend thine ears.
First will I see the coronation,
And then to Brittany I'll cross the sea
To effect this marriage, so it please my lord.

EDWARD

Even as thou wilt, sweet Warwick, let it be ;
For in thy shoulder do I build my seat,
And never will I undertake the thing
Wherein thy counsel and consent is wanting.
Richard, I will create thee Duke of Gloucester ;
And George, of Clarence. Warwick, as ourself,
Shall do and undo as him pleaseth best.

RICHARD

Let me be Duke of Clarence, George of Gloucester ;
107 For Gloucester's dukedom is too ominous.

WARWICK

108 Tut, that's a foolish observation ;
Richard, be Duke of Gloucester. Now to London
To see these honors in possession.   *Exeunt.*

*

III, i   *Enter two Keepers with crossbows in their hands.*

I. KEEPER

1 Under this thick-grown brake we'll shroud ourselves,
2 For through this laund anon the deer will come,
And in this covert will we make our stand,
4 Culling the principal of all the deer.

2. KEEPER

I'll stay above the hill, so both may shoot.

I. KEEPER

That cannot be ; the noise of thy crossbow
Will scare the herd, and so my shoot is lost.
8 Here stand we both and aim we at the best ;
9 And, for the time shall not seem tedious,
I'll tell thee what befell me on a day
11 In this self-place where now we mean to stand.

2. KEEPER

Here comes a man. Let's stay till he be past.
Enter the King [Henry, disguised,] with a prayer book.

KING HENRY

From Scotland am I stol'n, even of pure love,   13
To greet mine own land with my wishful sight.   14
No, Harry, Harry, 'tis no land of thine ;
Thy place is filled, thy sceptre wrung from thee,
Thy balm washed off wherewith thou was anointed.
No bending knee will call thee Caesar now,
No humble suitors press to speak for right :   19
No, not a man comes for redress of thee ;   20
For how can I help them, and not myself ?

I. KEEPER

Ay, here's a deer whose skin 's a keeper's fee.   22
This is the quondam king. Let's seize upon him.   23

KING HENRY

Let me embrace thee, sour adversity,
For wise men say it is the wisest course.   25

2. KEEPER

Why linger we ? Let us lay hands upon him.

I. KEEPER

Forbear awhile. We'll hear a little more.

KING HENRY

My queen and son are gone to France for aid ;
And, as I hear, the great commanding Warwick
Is thither gone to crave the French king's sister
To wife for Edward. If this news be true,
Poor queen and son, your labor is but lost ;
For Warwick is a subtle orator
And Lewis a prince soon won with moving words.
By this account, then, Margaret may win him ;
For she's a woman to be pitied much.
Her sighs will make a batt'ry in his breast ;   37
Her tears will pierce into a marble heart ;
The tiger will be mild whiles she doth mourn,
And Nero will be tainted with remorse   40
To hear and see her plaints, her brinish tears.   41
Ay, but she's come to beg ; Warwick, to give ;
She on his left side, craving aid for Henry ;
He on his right, asking a wife for Edward.
She weeps, and says her Henry is deposed ;
He smiles, and says his Edward is installed ;
That she, poor wretch, for grief can speak no more,   47
While Warwick tells his title, smooths the wrong,   48
Inferreth arguments of mighty strength,   49
And in conclusion wins the king from her
With promise of his sister, and what else,   51
To strengthen and support King Edward's place.
O Margaret, thus 'twill be ; and thou, poor soul,
Art then forsaken, as thou went'st forlorn.

2. KEEPER

Say, what art thou that talk'st of kings and queens ?

---

76 *wont* accustomed   83 *unstanchèd* unquenchable   91 *sinew* join (as if tied with sinew)   95 *buzz* circulate scandal   107 *too ominous* (because the three immediately preceding Dukes of Gloucester had died violent deaths. These were Humphrey, in *2 Henry VI*; Thomas of Woodstock, often referred to in *Richard II*; and Hugh Spenser, a favorite of Edward II.) 108 *observation* comment

III, i A forest glade near Scottish border *s.d. Keepers* gamekeepers 1 *brake* thicket   2 *laund* glade   4 *Culling* selecting   8 *at the best* as well as we can 9 *for* so that   11 *self-place* same place   13 *even of* precisely because of   14 *wishful* longing   19 *speak for right* beg for justice   20 *of* from   22 *fee* perquisite   23 *quondam* former   25 i.e. accepting adversity   37 *batt'ry* breach   40 *Nero* (traditionally hard-hearted and cruel); *tainted* affected 41 *brinish* salty   47 *That* so that   48 *tells his title* explains Edward's claim to the throne; *smooths* glosses over   49 *Inferreth* adduces   51 *and what else* i.e. and who knows what other promises

KING HENRY
More than I seem, and less than I was born to :
A man at least, for less I should not be ;
And men may talk of kings, and why not I ?

2. KEEPER
Ay, but thou talk'st as if thou wert a king.

KING HENRY
Why, so I am in mind, and that's enough.

2. KEEPER
But if thou be a king, where is thy crown ?

KING HENRY
My crown is in my heart, not on my head ;
63   Not decked with diamonds and Indian stones,
Nor to be seen. My crown is called content ;
A crown it is that seldom kings enjoy.

2. KEEPER
Well, if you be a king crowned with content,
Your crown content and you must be contented
To go along with us ; for, as we think,
You are the king King Edward hath deposed ;
And we his subjects, sworn in all allegiance,
Will apprehend you as his enemy.

KING HENRY
But did you never swear, and break an oath ?

2. KEEPER
No, never such an oath ; nor will not now.

KING HENRY
Where did you dwell when I was King of England ?

2. KEEPER
Here in this country where we now remain.

KING HENRY
I was anointed king at nine months old ;
My father and my grandfather were kings ;
And you were sworn true subjects unto me ;
And tell me then, have you not broke your oaths ?

1. KEEPER
No ;
81   For we were subjects but while you were king.

KING HENRY
Why, am I dead ? Do I not breathe a man ?
Ah, simple men, you know not what you swear.
Look, as I blow this feather from my face
And as the air blows it to me again,
Obeying with my wind when I do blow
And yielding to another when it blows,
Commanded always by the greater gust –
Such is the lightness of you common men.
90   But do not break your oaths ; for of that sin
My mild entreaty shall not make you guilty.
Go where you will, the king shall be commanded ;
And be you kings. Command, and I'll obey.

1. KEEPER
We are true subjects to the king, King Edward.

KING HENRY
So would you be again to Henry
If he were seated as King Edward is.

1. KEEPER
We charge you, in God's name and the king's,
To go with us unto the officers.

KING HENRY
In God's name, lead. Your king's name be obeyed ;
And what God will, that let your king perform ;
And what he will, I humbly yield unto.   100   *Exeunt.*

*

Enter King Edward, [Richard of] Gloucester,   III, ii
Clarence, Lady Grey [a widow].

KING EDWARD
Brother of Gloucester, at Saint Albans field
This lady's husband, Sir Richard Grey, was slain,   2
His lands then seized on by the conqueror.
Her suit is now to repossess those lands ;
Which we in justice cannot well deny,
Because in quarrel of the house of York
The worthy gentleman did lose his life.

RICHARD
Your highness shall do well to grant her suit.
It were dishonor to deny it her.

KING EDWARD
It were no less ; but yet I'll make a pause.

RICHARD *[aside to Clarence]*
Yea, is it so ?
I see the lady hath a thing to grant
Before the king will grant her humble suit.

CLARENCE *[aside to Richard]*
He knows the game. How true he keeps the wind.   14

RICHARD *[aside to Clarence]*
Silence.

KING EDWARD
Widow, we will consider of your suit ;
And come some other time to know our mind.

WIDOW
Right gracious lord, I cannot brook delay.   18
May it please your highness to resolve me now,   19
And what your pleasure is shall satisfy me.

RICHARD *[aside]*
Ay, widow ? Then I'll warrant you all your lands   21
An if what pleases him shall pleasure you.
Fight closer or, good faith, you'll catch a blow.   23

CLARENCE *[aside to Richard]*
I fear her not, unless she chance to fall.

RICHARD *[aside to Clarence]*
God forbid that, for he'll take vantages.

KING EDWARD
How many children hast thou, widow ? Tell me.

CLARENCE *[aside to Richard]*
I think he means to beg a child of her.   27

RICHARD *[aside to Clarence]*
Nay, then, whip me ; he'll rather give her two.   28

WIDOW
Three, my most gracious lord.

RICHARD *[aside]*
You shall have four if you'll be ruled by him.

KING EDWARD
'Twere pity they should lose their father's lands.

---

63 *Indian stones* gems (probably pearls)   **81** *but* only
III, ii The royal palace in London   **2** *Sir Richard Grey* (Lady Grey's husband, actually Sir John, was killed at the second battle of St Albans, where he fought for the Lancastrians. The facts are given correctly in *Richard III*, I, iii, 126–29.)   **14** *keeps the wind* hunts downwind, so as not to alarm the game   **18** *brook* endure   **19** *resolve me* free me from uncertainty
21 *warrant* guarantee   **23–25** *Fight closer . . . catch a blow . . . fall . . . vantages* (all duelling terms, here used with obvious double meaning)   **27** *beg . . . her* apply to her for a wardship, a source of profit if the child were high-born (with bawdy overtones)   **28** *whip me* (a mild imprecation ; or perhaps, literally, for being so childish as to think so)

WIDOW
Be pitiful, dread lord, and grant it then.
KING EDWARD
33   Lords, give us leave. I'll try this widow's wit.
RICHARD [aside]
34   Ay, good leave have you; for you will have leave
Till youth take leave and leave you to the crutch.
[Retires with Clarence.]
KING EDWARD
Now tell me, madam, do you love your children?
WIDOW
Ay, full as dearly as I love myself.
KING EDWARD
And would you not do much to do them good?
WIDOW
To do them good I would sustain some harm.
KING EDWARD
Then get your husband's lands, to do them good.
WIDOW
Therefore I came unto your majesty.
KING EDWARD
I'll tell you how these lands are to be got.
WIDOW
So shall you bind me to your highness' service.
KING EDWARD
44   What service wilt thou do me if I give them?
WIDOW
What you command that rests in me to do.
KING EDWARD
46   But you will take exceptions to my boon.
WIDOW
47   No, gracious lord, except I cannot do it.
KING EDWARD
Ay, but thou canst do what I mean to ask.
WIDOW
Why, then I will do what your grace commands.
RICHARD [aside to Clarence]
50   He plies her hard, and much rain wears the marble.
CLARENCE [aside to Richard]
As red as fire? Nay then, her wax must melt.
WIDOW
Why stops my lord? Shall I not hear my task?
KING EDWARD
An easy task. 'Tis but to love a king.
WIDOW
That's soon performed, because I am a subject.
KING EDWARD
Why then, thy husband's lands I freely give thee.
WIDOW
I take my leave with many thousand thanks.
RICHARD [aside to Clarence]
The match is made. She seals it with a curtsy.
KING EDWARD
But stay thee. 'Tis the fruits of love I mean.
WIDOW
The fruits of love I mean, my loving liege.
KING EDWARD
Ay, but, I fear me, in another sense.
What love, think'st thou, I sue so much to get?
WIDOW
My love till death, my humble thanks, my prayers;
That love which virtue begs and virtue grants.
KING EDWARD
No, by my troth, I did not mean such love.

WIDOW
Why, then you mean not as I thought you did.
KING EDWARD
But now you partly may perceive my mind.
WIDOW
My mind will never grant what I perceive
Your highness aims at, if I aim aright.   68
KING EDWARD
To tell thee plain, I aim to lie with thee.
WIDOW
To tell you plain, I had rather lie in prison.
KING EDWARD
Why, then thou shalt not have thy husband's lands.
WIDOW
Why, then mine honesty shall be my dower;   72
For by that loss I will not purchase them.
KING EDWARD
Therein thou wrong'st thy children mightily.
WIDOW
Herein your highness wrongs both them and me.
But, mighty lord, this merry inclination
Accords not with the sadness of my suit.   77
Please you dismiss me, either with ay or no.
KING EDWARD
Ay, if thou wilt say ay to my request;
No, if thou dost say no to my demand.
WIDOW
Then, no, my lord. My suit is at an end.
RICHARD [aside to Clarence]
The widow likes him not; she knits her brows.
CLARENCE [aside to Richard]
He is the bluntest wooer in Christendom.
KING EDWARD [aside]
Her looks doth argue her replete with modesty;
Her words doth show her wit incomparable;
All her perfections challenge sovereignty.
One way or other, she is for a king;
And she shall be my love, or else my queen. –
Say that King Edward take thee for his queen?
WIDOW
'Tis better said than done, my gracious lord.
I am a subject fit to jest withal,
But far unfit to be a sovereign.
KING EDWARD
Sweet widow, by my state I swear to thee   93
I speak no more than what my soul intends;
And that is, to enjoy thee for my love.
WIDOW
And that is more than I will yield unto.
I know I am too mean to be your queen,
And yet too good to be your concubine.
KING EDWARD
You cavil, widow. I did mean my queen.   99
WIDOW
'Twill grieve your grace my sons should call you father.
KING EDWARD
No more than when my daughters call thee mother.

33 *give us leave* pardon us (i.e. please go away)   34–35 *good leave . . . have leave . . . take leave . . . leave you to* willing pardon . . . take liberties . . . bid farewell . . . pass you on to (because you will be too old to be amorous)   44 *service* (1) duty, (2) sexual attention   46 *boon* request   47 *except* unless   50 *plies* urges   68 *aim* guess   72 *honesty* virtue   77 *sadness* seriousness   93 *state* kingship   99 *cavil* make frivolous objections

Thou art a widow, and thou hast some children;
And, by God's Mother, I, being but a bachelor,
104   Have other some. Why, 'tis a happy thing
To be the father unto many sons.
Answer no more, for thou shalt be my queen.

RICHARD *[aside to Clarence]*
107   The ghostly father now hath done his shrift.

CLARENCE *[aside to Richard]*
108   When he was made a shriver, 'twas for shift.

KING EDWARD
109   Brothers, you muse what chat we two have had.

RICHARD
110   The widow likes it not, for she looks very sad.

KING EDWARD
You'ld think it strange if I should marry her.

CLARENCE
To who, my lord?

KING EDWARD   Why, Clarence, to myself.

RICHARD
113   That would be ten days' wonder at the least.

CLARENCE
That's a day longer than a wonder lasts.

RICHARD
By so much is the wonder in extremes.

KING EDWARD
Well, jest on, brothers. I can tell you both
Her suit is granted for her husband's lands.
       Enter a Nobleman.

NOBLEMAN
My gracious lord, Henry your foe is taken
And brought your prisoner to your palace gate.

KING EDWARD
See that he be conveyed unto the Tower.
And go we, brothers, to the man that took him
122   To question of his apprehension.
Widow, go you along. Lords, use her honorably.
       Exeunt. Manet Richard.

RICHARD
Ay, Edward will use women honorably.
Would he were wasted, marrow, bones, and all,
That from his loins no hopeful branch may spring
127   To cross me from the golden time I look for.
And yet, between my soul's desire and me –
The lustful Edward's title burièd –

Is Clarence, Henry, and his son young Edward,
And all the unlooked-for issue of their bodies,   131
To take their rooms ere I can place myself.   132
A cold premeditation for my purpose.   133
Why, then I do but dream on sovereignty,
Like one that stands upon a promontory
And spies a far-off shore where he would tread,
Wishing his foot were equal with his eye,   137
And chides the sea that sunders him from thence,
Saying he'll lade it dry to have his way: 139
So do I wish the crown, being so far off;
And so I chide the means that keeps me from it,   141
And so, I say, I'll cut the causes off,
Flattering me with impossibilities.   143
My eye's too quick, my heart o'erweens too much,   144
Unless my hand and strength could equal them.
Well, say there is no kingdom then for Richard:
What other pleasure can the world afford?
I'll make my heaven in a lady's lap
And deck my body in gay ornaments
And witch sweet ladies with my words and looks.   150
O miserable thought, and more unlikely
Than to accomplish twenty golden crowns.
Why, love forswore me in my mother's womb;
And, for I should not deal in her soft laws,   154
She did corrupt frail nature with some bribe
To shrink mine arm up like a withered shrub;
To make an envious mountain on my back,   157
Where sits deformity to mock my body;
To shape my legs of an unequal size;
To disproportion me in every part,
Like to a chaos, or an unlicked bear-whelp,   161
That carries no impression like the dam.   162
And am I then a man to be beloved?
O monstrous fault to harbor such a thought.
Then, since this earth affords no joy to me
But to command, to check, to o'erbear such   166
As are of better person than myself,   167
I'll make my heaven to dream upon the crown
And, whiles I live, t'account this world but hell
Until my misshaped trunk that bears this head
Be round impalèd with a glorious crown.   171
And yet I know not how to get the crown,
For many lives stand between me and home;   173
And I – like one lost in a thorny wood,
That rents the thorns and is rent with the thorns,
Seeking a way and straying from the way,
Not knowing how to find the open air
But toiling desperately to find it out –
Torment myself to catch the English crown;
And from that torment I will free myself
Or hew my way out with a bloody axe.
Why, I can smile, and murder whiles I smile,
And cry 'Content!' to that which grieves my heart,
And wet my cheeks with artificial tears,
And frame my face to all occasions.
I'll drown more sailors than the mermaid shall;   186
I'll slay more gazers than the basilisk;   187
I'll play the orator as well as Nestor,   188
Deceive more slily than Ulysses could   189
And, like a Sinon, take another Troy.   190
I can add colors to the chameleon,
Change shapes with Proteus for advantages,   192
And set the murderous Machiavel to school.   193

---

104 *other some* some others   107 *ghostly father* i.e. confessor ('ghostly': spiritual); *done his shrift* finished hearing confession   108 *for shift* (1) as a trick to serve some purpose, (2) for the sake of a chemise (to say that a woman was 'shriven to her shift' was a common off-color joke meaning that she had been seduced)   109 *muse* wonder   110 *sad* serious   113 *ten days' wonder* i.e. a most marvellous thing (proverbially, a novelty attracts for only nine days)   122 *question . . . apprehension* inquire about his capture   127 *cross me from* interfere with my attaining   131 *unlooked-for* unanticipated   132 *rooms* places   133 *cold premeditation* discouraging forecast   137 *equal with* as capable as   139 *lade* ladle, scoop   141 *means* obstacles   143 *me* myself   144 *o'erweens* presumes   150 *witch* bewitch   154 *for* so that   157 *envious* detested   161 *chaos* unformed mass; *unlicked bear-whelp* (bear cubs were supposedly born as lumps of matter and licked into shape by their dams)   162 *impression* shape   166 *check* rebuke; *o'erbear* dominate   167 *of better person* more personable   171 *impalèd* encircled   173 *home* i.e. my goal   186 *mermaid* siren   187 *basilisk* a fabulous serpent whose look killed   188 *Nestor* aged Greek warrior at the siege of Troy, noted for his wisdom   189 *Ulysses* Greek warrior, subject of the *Odyssey*, noted for his craft   190 *Sinon* the Greek who persuaded the Trojans to bring the Wooden Horse into the city   192 *Proteus* a sea-deity who, when captured, changed his shape; *for advantages* as my purpose dictates   193 *Machiavel* Machiavelli, Italian political philosopher, known in England as an advocate of guile and ruthlessness in the attainment of political objectives

      Can I do this, and cannot get a crown?
      Tut, were it farther off, I'll pluck it down.   *Exit.*

          *

III, iii   *Flourish. Enter Lewis the French King, his sister*
         Bona, his Admiral, called Bourbon; Prince Edward,
         Queen Margaret, and the Earl of Oxford. Lewis
         sits, and riseth up again.

LEWIS
     Fair Queen of England, worthy Margaret,
2   Sit down with us. It ill befits thy state
     And birth that thou shouldst stand while Lewis doth sit.

QUEEN MARGARET
     No, mighty King of France. Now Margaret
5   Must strike her sail, and learn awhile to serve
     Where kings command. I was, I must confess,
7   Great Albion's queen in former golden days;
     But now mischance hath trod my title down
     And with dishonor laid me on the ground,
     Where I must take like seat unto my fortune
     And to my humble seat conform myself.

LEWIS
     Why, say, fair queen, whence springs this deep despair?

QUEEN MARGARET
     From such a cause as fills mine eyes with tears
     And stops my tongue, while heart is drowned in cares.

LEWIS
15 Whate'er it be, be thou still like thyself,
     And sit thee by our side. *Seats her by him.* Yield not thy
       neck
     To fortune's yoke – but let thy dauntless mind
     Still ride in triumph over all mischance.
     Be plain, Queen Margaret, and tell thy grief.
20 It shall be eased if France can yield relief.

QUEEN MARGARET
     Those gracious words revive my drooping thoughts
     And give my tongue-tied sorrows leave to speak.
     Now therefore be it known to noble Lewis
     That Henry, sole possessor of my love,
25 Is, of a king, become a banished man
26 And forced to live in Scotland a forlorn;
     While proud ambitious Edward Duke of York
     Usurps the regal title and the seat
     Of England's true anointed lawful king.
     This is the cause that I, poor Margaret,
     With this my son, Prince Edward, Henry's heir,
     Am come to crave thy just and lawful aid;
     And if thou fail us, all our hope is done.
     Scotland hath will to help, but cannot help;
     Our people and our peers are both misled,
     Our treasure seized, our soldiers put to flight,
     And (as thou seest) ourselves in heavy plight.

LEWIS
     Renowned queen, with patience calm the storm
39 While we bethink a means to break it off.

QUEEN MARGARET
40 The more we stay, the stronger grows our foe.

LEWIS
     The more I stay, the more I'll succor thee.

QUEEN MARGARET
42 O, but impatience waiteth on true sorrow.
     And see where comes the breeder of my sorrow.
     Enter Warwick.

LEWIS
     What's he approacheth boldly to our presence?

QUEEN MARGARET
     Our Earl of Warwick, Edward's greatest friend.

LEWIS
     Welcome, brave Warwick, what brings thee to France?
       He descends. She ariseth.

QUEEN MARGARET *[aside]*
     Ay, now begins a second storm to rise;
     For this is he that moves both wind and tide.

WARWICK
     From worthy Edward, King of Albion,
     My lord and sovereign and thy vowèd friend,
     I come, in kindness and unfeignèd love,
     First to do greetings to thy royal person,
     And then to crave a league of amity,
     And lastly to confirm that amity
     With nuptial knot, if thou vouchsafe to grant
     That virtuous Lady Bona, thy fair sister,   56
     To England's king in lawful marriage.

QUEEN MARGARET *[aside]*
     If that go forward, Henry's hope is done.

WARWICK *[speaking to Bona]*
     And, gracious madam, in our king's behalf,
     I am commanded, with your leave and favor,
     Humbly to kiss your hand, and with my tongue
     To tell the passion of my sovereign's heart;
     Where fame, late ent'ring at his heedful ears,
     Hath placed thy beauty's image and thy virtue.

QUEEN MARGARET
     King Lewis, and Lady Bona, hear me speak
     Before you answer Warwick. His demand
     Springs not from Edward's well-meant honest love,
     But from deceit, bred by necessity;
     For how can tyrants safely govern home
     Unless abroad they purchase great alliance?   70
     To prove him tyrant this reason may suffice,
     That Henry liveth still; but were he dead,
     Yet here Prince Edward stands, King Henry's son.
     Look, therefore, Lewis, that by this league and marriage
     Thou draw not on thy danger and dishonor;
     For though usurpers sway the rule awhile,   76
     Yet heav'ns are just and time suppresseth wrongs.

WARWICK
     Injurious Margaret!   78

PRINCE   And why not queen?

WARWICK
     Because thy father Henry did usurp,
     And thou no more art prince than she is queen.

OXFORD
     Then Warwick disannuls great John of Gaunt,   81
     Which did subdue the greatest part of Spain;   82
     And after John of Gaunt, Henry the Fourth,
     Whose wisdom was a mirror to the wisest;
     And after that wise prince, Henry the Fifth,
     Who by his prowess conquerèd all France.

III, iii The royal palace in France **2** *state* status **5** *strike her sail* lower her sail (a mark of deference rendered at sea to a senior) **7** *Albion's* England's **15** *be thou . . . thyself* i.e. behave always in a way appropriate to your greatness **20** *France* the King of France **25** *of* instead of **26** *forlorn* outcast **39** *break it off* stop it **40** *stay* delay **42** *waiteth on* attends **56** *sister* i.e. sister-in-law **76** *sway* exercise **78** *Injurious* insulting **81** *disannuls* cancels out **82** *Which . . . Spain* (Gaunt did campaign in Spain, but his successes were minor)

From these our Henry lineally descends.

WARWICK
Oxford, how haps it in this smooth discourse
You told not how Henry the Sixth hath lost
All that which Henry the Fifth had gotten?
Methinks these peers of France should smile at that.
92 But for the rest: you tell a pedigree
Of threescore and two years – a silly time
To make prescription for a kingdom's worth.

OXFORD
Why, Warwick, canst thou speak against thy liege,
Whom thou obeyèd'st thirty and six years,
And not bewray thy treason with a blush?

WARWICK
Can Oxford, that did ever fence the right,
99 Now buckler falsehood with a pedigree?
For shame! Leave Henry and call Edward king.

OXFORD
101 Call him my king by whose injurious doom
102 My elder brother, the Lord Aubrey Vere,
103 Was done to death? and more than so, my father,
Even in the downfall of his mellowed years,
When nature brought him to the door of death?
No, Warwick, no! While life upholds this arm,
This arm upholds the house of Lancaster.

WARWICK
And I the house of York.

LEWIS
Queen Margaret, Prince Edward, and Oxford,
Vouchsafe at our request to stand aside
While I use further conference with Warwick.
They stand aloof.

QUEEN MARGARET
Heavens grant that Warwick's words bewitch him not.

LEWIS
Now, Warwick, tell me, even upon thy conscience,
Is Edward your true king? For I were loath
To link with him that were not lawful chosen.

WARWICK
Thereon I pawn my credit and mine honor.

LEWIS
But is he gracious in the people's eye?

WARWICK
The more that Henry was unfortunate.

LEWIS
Then further: all dissembling set aside,
Tell me for truth the measure of his love
Unto our sister Bona.

WARWICK   Such it seems
122 As may beseem a monarch like himself.
Myself have often heard him say and swear
124 That this his love was an eternal plant,

Whereof the root was fixed in virtue's ground,
The leaves and fruit maintained with beauty's sun,
Exempt from envy, but not from disdain,   127
Unless the Lady Bona quit his pain.

LEWIS
Now, sister, let us hear your firm resolve.

BONA
Your grant, or your denial, shall be mine.   130
    (Speaks to Warwick)
Yet I confess that often ere this day,
When I have heard your king's desert recounted,   132
Mine ear hath tempted judgment to desire.

LEWIS
Then, Warwick, thus: our sister shall be Edward's,
And now forthwith shall articles be drawn
Touching the jointure that your king must make,   136
Which with her dowry shall be counterpoised.   137
Draw near, Queen Margaret, and be a witness
That Bona shall be wife to the English king.

PRINCE
To Edward, but not to the English king.

QUEEN MARGARET
Deceitful Warwick, it was thy device
By this alliance to make void my suit.
Before thy coming Lewis was Henry's friend.

LEWIS
And still is friend to him, and Margaret.
But if your title to the crown be weak,
As may appear by Edward's good success,
Then 'tis but reason that I be released
From giving aid which late I promisèd.
Yet shall you have all kindness at my hand
That your estate requires and mine can yield.

WARWICK
Henry now lives in Scotland at his ease,
Where having nothing, nothing can he lose.
And as for you yourself, our quondam queen,   153
You have a father able to maintain you,
And better 'twere you troubled him than France.

QUEEN MARGARET
Peace, impudent and shameless Warwick, peace,
Proud setter up and puller down of kings,
I will not hence till with my talk and tears
(Both full of truth) I make King Lewis behold
Thy sly conveyance and thy lord's false love;   160
For both of you are birds of selfsame feather.   161
Post blowing a horn within.

LEWIS
Warwick, this is some post to us or thee.
Enter the Post.

POST *[speaks to Warwick]*
My lord ambassador, these letters are for you,
Sent from your brother, Marquess Montague;
    [To Lewis]
These from our king unto your majesty;
    [To Margaret]
And, madam, these for you: from whom I know not.
They all read their letters.

OXFORD
I like it well that our fair queen and mistress
Smiles at her news, while Warwick frowns at his.

PRINCE
Nay, mark how Lewis stamps as he were nettled.
I hope all's for the best.

92–94 *you . . . worth* i.e. the line you describe runs for sixty-two years, a ridiculously short time upon which to base a claim sanctioned by custom (*prescription*) to the wealth and honor of kingship 99 *buckler* shield 101 *injurious doom* unjust judgment 102 *Lord Aubrey Vere* (Holinshed reports that in 1462 the 12th Earl of Oxford and Lord Aubrey Vere, his eldest son, were accused of treason and executed) 103 *more than so* yet more 122 *beseem* befit 124 *eternal* i.e. heavenly 127–28 *Exempt . . . pain* i.e. Edward's love will be free from the effects of sharp criticism (*envy*) of Lady Bona (because of her coldness to his suit), but it will suffer from rejection (*disdain*) unless she reward his passion for her (*quit his pain*) 130 *grant* concurrence 132 *desert* merit 136 *jointure* marriage settlement 137 *counterpoised* matched 153 *quondam* former 160 *conveyance* trickery 161 s.d. *Post* dispatch-rider

LEWIS
Warwick, what are thy news ? and yours, fair queen ?

QUEEN MARGARET
Mine such as fill my heart with unhoped joys.

WARWICK
Mine full of sorrow and heart's discontent.

LEWIS
What ? Has your king married the Lady Grey ?
175   And now, to soothe your forgery and his,
Sends me a paper to persuade me patience ?
Is this th' alliance that he seeks with France ?
Dare he presume to scorn us in this manner ?

QUEEN MARGARET
I told your majesty as much before.
This proveth Edward's love and Warwick's honesty.

WARWICK
King Lewis, I here protest in sight of heaven
And by the hope I have of heavenly bliss
That I am clear from this misdeed of Edward's –
No more my king, for he dishonors me,
But most himself, if he could see his shame.
Did I forget that by the House of York
187   My father came untimely to his death ?
188   Did I let pass th' abuse done to my niece ?
189   Did I impale him with the regal crown ?
Did I put Henry from his native right ?
191   And am I guerdoned at the last with shame ?
Shame on himself, for my desert is honor ;
And to repair my honor, lost for him,
I here renounce him and return to Henry.
My noble queen, let former grudges pass,
And henceforth I am thy true servitor.
I will revenge his wrong to Lady Bona
And replant Henry in his former state.

QUEEN MARGARET
Warwick, these words have turned my hate to love,
And I forgive and quite forget old faults
And joy that thou becom'st King Henry's friend.

WARWICK
So much his friend, ay, his unfeignèd friend,
That, if King Lewis vouchsafe to furnish us
With some few bands of chosen soldiers,
I'll undertake to land them on our coast
And force the tyrant from his seat by war.
'Tis not his new-made bride shall succor him.
And as for Clarence, as my letters tell me,
He's very likely now to fall from him
210   For matching more for wanton lust than honor
Or than for strength and safety of our country.

BONA
Dear brother, how shall Bona be revenged
But by thy help to this distressèd queen ?

QUEEN MARGARET
Renownèd prince, how shall poor Henry live
Unless thou rescue him from foul despair ?

BONA
My quarrel and this English queen's are one.

WARWICK
And mine, fair Lady Bona, joins with yours.

LEWIS
And mine with hers and thine and Margaret's.
Therefore, at last, I firmly am resolved
You shall have aid.

QUEEN MARGARET
Let me give humble thanks for all at once.

LEWIS
Then, England's messenger, return in post
And tell false Edward, thy supposèd king,
That Lewis of France is sending over masquers   224
To revel it with him and his new bride.
Thou seest what's passed. Go fear thy king withal.   226

BONA
Tell him, in hope he'll prove a widower shortly,
I'll wear the willow garland for his sake.   228

QUEEN MARGARET
Tell him my mourning weeds are laid aside
And I am ready to put armor on.

WARWICK
Tell him from me that he hath done me wrong
And therefore I'll uncrown him ere't be long.
There's thy reward. Be gone.   *Exit Post.*

LEWIS   But, Warwick,
Thou and Oxford, with five thousand men,
Shall cross the seas and bid false Edward battle ;
And as occasion serves, this noble queen
And prince shall follow with a fresh supply.
Yet, ere thou go, but answer me one doubt :
What pledge have we of thy firm loyalty ?

WARWICK
This shall assure my constant loyalty,
That if our queen and this young prince agree,
I'll join mine eldest daughter, and my joy,   242
To him forthwith in holy wedlock bands.

QUEEN MARGARET
Yes, I agree, and thank you for your motion.   244
Son Edward, she is fair and virtuous.
Therefore delay not ; give thy hand to Warwick
And, with thy hand, thy faith irrevocable
That only Warwick's daughter shall be thine.

PRINCE
Yes, I accept her, for she well deserves it,
And here to pledge my vow I give my hand.
     He gives his hand to Warwick.

LEWIS
Why stay we now ? Those soldiers shall be levied,
And thou, Lord Bourbon, our High Admiral,
Shall waft them over with our royal fleet.   253
I long till Edward fall by war's mischance
For mocking marriage with a dame of France.
     Exeunt. Manet Warwick.

WARWICK
I came from Edward as ambassador,
But I return his sworn and mortal foe.
Matter of marriage was the charge he gave me,
But dreadful war shall answer his demand.
Had he none else to make a stale but me ?   260

175 *forgery* deceit   187 *My ... death* (according to the chronicles, Salisbury, Warwick's father, was captured by the Lancastrians at Wakefield and beheaded, as was York)   188 *Did ... niece* (Holinshed reports that Edward 'would have defloured' Warwick's 'daughter or his neece')   189 *impale him* encircle his brow   191 *guerdoned* rewarded   210 *matching* marrying   224 *masquers* participants in a courtly dramatic performance or revel (ironically)   226 *fear* frighten ; *withal* with it   228 *willow garland* (symbol of rejected love)   242 *eldest daughter* (actually his younger daughter, Anne, as his elder daughter, Isabella, is to marry Clarence. In the chronicles, Isabella and Clarence are already married at this time.)   244 *motion* offer   253 *waft* transport by water   260 *stale* dupe

Then none but I shall turn his jest to sorrow.
I was the chief that raised him to the crown
And I'll be chief to bring him down again;
Not that I pity Henry's misery,
But seek revenge on Edward's mockery.   *Exit.*

*

IV, i   *Enter Richard, Clarence, Somerset, and Montague.*

RICHARD
Now tell me, brother Clarence, what think you
Of this new marriage with the Lady Grey?
Hath not our brother made a worthy choice?

CLARENCE
Alas, you know 'tis far from hence to France,
5   How could he stay till Warwick made return?

SOMERSET
My lords, forbear this talk. Here comes the king.
*Flourish. Enter King Edward, Lady Grey [as
Queen Elizabeth], Pembroke, Stafford, Hastings.
Four stand on one side and four on the other.*

RICHARD
And his well-chosen bride.

CLARENCE
8   I mind to tell him plainly what I think.

KING EDWARD
Now, brother of Clarence, how like you our choice,
10   That you stand pensive, as half malcontent?

CLARENCE
As well as Lewis of France or the Earl of Warwick,
Which are so weak of courage and in judgment
13   That they'll take no offense at our abuse.

KING EDWARD
Suppose they take offense without a cause:
They are but Lewis and Warwick; I am Edward,
Your king and Warwick's, and must have my will.

RICHARD
And shall have your will, because our king.
Yet hasty marriage seldom proveth well.

KING EDWARD
Yea, brother Richard, are you offended too?

RICHARD
Not I.
No, God forbid that I should wish them severed
Whom God hath joined together. Ay, and 'twere pity
To sunder them that yoke so well together.

KING EDWARD
24   Setting your scorns and your mislike aside,
Tell me some reason why the Lady Grey
Should not become my wife and England's queen.
And you too, Somerset, and Montague,
Speak freely what you think.

CLARENCE
Then this is mine opinion, that King Lewis
Becomes your enemy for mocking him
About the marriage of the Lady Bona.

RICHARD
And Warwick, doing what you gave in charge,
Is now dishonorèd by this new marriage.

KING EDWARD
What if both Lewis and Warwick be appeased
By such invention as I can devise?   35

MONTAGUE
Yet, to have joined with France in such alliance
Would more have strengthened this our commonwealth
'Gainst foreign storms than any home-bred marriage.

HASTINGS
Why, knows not Montague that of itself
England is safe, if true within itself?

MONTAGUE
But the safer when 'tis backed with France.

HASTINGS
'Tis better using France than trusting France.
Let us be backed with God, and with the seas,
Which he hath giv'n for fence impregnable,
And with their helps only defend ourselves.
In them and in ourselves our safety lies.

CLARENCE
For this one speech Lord Hastings well deserves
To have the heir of the Lord Hungerford.

KING EDWARD
Ay, what of that? It was my will and grant.
And for this once my will shall stand for law.

RICHARD
And yet methinks your grace hath not done well
To give the heir and daughter of Lord Scales
Unto the brother of your loving bride.   53
She better would have fitted me or Clarence;
But in your bride you bury brotherhood.

CLARENCE
Or else you would not have bestowed the heir
Of the Lord Bonville on your new wife's son   57
And leave your brothers to go speed elsewhere.   58

KING EDWARD
Alas, poor Clarence! Is it for a wife
That thou art malcontent? I will provide thee.

CLARENCE
In choosing for yourself you showed your judgment,
Which being shallow, you shall give me leave
To play the broker in mine own behalf;   63
And to that end I shortly mind to leave you.

KING EDWARD
Leave me or tarry, Edward will be king
And not be tied unto his brother's will.

QUEEN ELIZABETH
My lords, before it pleased his majesty
To raise my state to title of a queen,
Do me but right, and you must all confess
That I was not ignoble of descent,
And meaner than myself have had like fortune.
But as this title honors me and mine,
So your dislikes, to whom I would be pleasing,   73
Doth cloud my joys with danger and with sorrow.   74

KING EDWARD
My love, forbear to fawn upon their frowns.
What danger or what sorrow can befall thee
So long as Edward is thy constant friend
And their true sovereign, whom they must obey?
Nay, whom they shall obey, and love thee too,

IV, i The royal palace in London   **5** *stay* wait   **8** *mind* intend   **10** *malcontent* one disgusted with the world   **13** *abuse* insult   **24** *mislike* displeasure   **35** *invention* plan   **53** *brother . . . bride* i.e. Lord Rivers   **57** *son* i.e. Sir Thomas Grey, Marquess Dorset   **58** *go speed* prosper (for themselves)   **63** *broker* agent   **73** *dislikes* disapproval   **74** *danger* apprehension

Unless they seek for hatred at my hands;
Which if they do, yet will I keep thee safe,
And they shall feel the vengeance of my wrath.

RICHARD *[aside]*
I hear; yet say not much, but think the more.
Enter a Post.

KING EDWARD
Now, messenger, what letters or what news
From France?

POST
My sovereign liege, no letters, and few words,
But such as I, without your special pardon,
Dare not relate.

KING EDWARD
89 Go to, we pardon thee. Therefore, in brief,
90 Tell me their words as near as thou canst guess them.
What answer makes King Lewis unto our letters?

POST
92 At my depart these were his very words:
'Go tell false Edward, thy supposèd king,
That Lewis of France is sending over masquers
To revel it with him and his new bride.'

KING EDWARD
96 Is Lewis so brave? Belike he thinks me Henry.
But what said Lady Bona to my marriage?

POST
These were her words, uttered with mild disdain:
'Tell him, in hope he'll prove a widower shortly,
I'll wear the willow garland for his sake.'

KING EDWARD
I blame not her. She could say little less.
She had the wrong. But what said Henry's queen?
103 For I have heard that she was there in place.

POST
'Tell him,' quoth she, 'my mourning weeds are done
And I am ready to put armor on.'

KING EDWARD
Belike she minds to play the Amazon.
But what said Warwick to these injuries?

POST
He, more incensed against your majesty
Than all the rest, discharged me with these words:
'Tell him from me that he hath done me wrong,
And therefore I'll uncrown him ere't be long.'

KING EDWARD
Ha! durst the traitor breathe out so proud words?
Well, I will arm me, being thus forewarned.
They shall have wars and pay for their presumption.
But say, is Warwick friends with Margaret?

POST
Ay, gracious sovereign. They are so linked in friendship
That young Prince Edward marries Warwick's daughter.

CLARENCE *[aside]*
118 Belike the elder; Clarence will have the younger. –
Now, brother king, farewell, and sit you fast;
For I will hence to Warwick's other daughter,
121 That, though I want a kingdom, yet in marriage
I may not prove inferior to yourself.
You that love me and Warwick, follow me.
Exit Clarence, and Somerset follows.

RICHARD *[aside]*
Not I.
My thoughts aim at a further matter. I
Stay not for the love of Edward but the crown.

KING EDWARD
Clarence and Somerset both gone to Warwick?
Yet am I armed against the worst can happen;
And haste is needful in this desp'rate case.
Pembroke and Stafford, you in our behalf
Go levy men and make prepare for war.   131
They are already, or quickly will be landed.
Myself in person will straight follow you.
Exeunt Pembroke and Stafford.
But ere I go, Hastings and Montague,
Resolve my doubt. You twain, of all the rest,
Are near to Warwick by blood and by alliance.
Tell me if you love Warwick more than me.
If it be so, then both depart to him;
I rather wish you foes than hollow friends.   139
But if you mind to hold your true obedience,
Give me assurance with some friendly vow,
That I may never have you in suspect.   142

MONTAGUE
So God help Montague as he proves true.

HASTINGS
And Hastings as he favors Edward's cause.

KING EDWARD
Now, brother Richard, will you stand by us?

RICHARD
Ay, in despite of all that shall withstand you.

KING EDWARD
Why, so! then am I sure of victory.
Now therefore let us hence, and lose no hour
Till we meet Warwick with his foreign power. *Exeunt.*

*

Enter Warwick and Oxford in England with French   IV, ii
Soldiers.

WARWICK
Trust me, my lord, all hitherto goes well.
The common people by numbers swarm to us.
Enter Clarence and Somerset.
But see where Somerset and Clarence comes.
Speak suddenly, my lords, are we all friends?

CLARENCE
Fear not that, my lord.

WARWICK
Then, gentle Clarence, welcome unto Warwick;
And welcome, Somerset. I hold it cowardice
To rest mistrustful where a noble heart
Hath pawned an open hand in sign of love.   9
Else might I think that Clarence, Edward's brother,
Were but a feignèd friend to our proceedings.
But welcome, sweet Clarence. My daughter shall be
  thine.
And now what rests but, in night's coverture,   13
Thy brother being carelessly encamped,
His soldiers lurking in the towns about,   15
And but attended by a simple guard,
We may surprise and take him at our pleasure?

89 *Go to* all right, don't worry   90 *guess* approximate   92 *depart* departure
96 *Belike* perhaps   103 *in place* present   118 *Belike . . . younger* (see III,
iii, 242n.)   121 *want* lack   131 *prepare* preparation   139 *hollow* empty,
i.e. untrustworthy   142 *suspect* suspicion
IV, ii *Fields near Warwick*   9 *pawned* pledged   13 *rests* remains; *in night's
coverture* under cover of night   15 *lurking* idling

Our scouts have found the adventure very easy;
19   That as Ulysses and stout Diomede
With sleight and manhood stole to Rhesus' tents
And brought from thence the Thracian fatal steeds,
So we, well covered with the night's black mantle,
At unawares may beat down Edward's guard
25   And seize himself. I say not, slaughter him,
For I intend but only to surprise him.
You that will follow me to this attempt,
Applaud the name of Henry with your leader.
     They all cry 'Henry!'
28   Why then, let's on our way in silent sort.
For Warwick and his friends, God and Saint George!
                 Exeunt.

*

IV, iii   *Enter three Watchmen, to guard King Edward's tent.*
1. WATCHMAN
Come on, my masters. Each man take his stand.
2   The king by this is set him down to sleep.
2. WATCHMAN
What, will he not to bed?
1. WATCHMAN
Why, no; for he hath made a solemn vow
Never to lie and take his natural rest
Till Warwick or himself be quite suppressed.
2. WATCHMAN
To-morrow then belike shall be the day,
If Warwick be so near as men report.
3. WATCHMAN
But say, I pray, what nobleman is that
That with the king here resteth in his tent?
1. WATCHMAN
'Tis the Lord Hastings, the king's chiefest friend.
3. WATCHMAN
O, is it so? But why commands the king
That his chief followers lodge in towns about him,
While he himself keeps in the cold field?
2. WATCHMAN
'Tis the more honor, because more dangerous.
3. WATCHMAN
16   Ay, but give me worship and quietness.
I like it better than a dangerous honor.
18   If Warwick knew in what estate he stands,
19   'Tis to be doubted he would waken him.
1. WATCHMAN
Unless our halberds did shut up his passage.
2. WATCHMAN
Ay! wherefore else guard we his royal tent
But to defend his person from night-foes?
     Enter Warwick, Clarence, Oxford, Somerset, and
     French Soldiers, silent all.

WARWICK
This is his tent; and see where stand his guard.
Courage, my masters, honor now or never!
But follow me, and Edward shall be ours.
1. WATCHMAN Who goes there?
2. WATCHMAN Stay, or thou diest!
     Warwick and the rest cry all 'Warwick! Warwick!'
     and set upon the Guard, who fly, crying 'Arm! arm!',
     Warwick and the rest following them.
     The Drum playing and Trumpet sounding, enter
     Warwick, Somerset, and the rest, bringing [Edward]
     the King out in his gown, sitting in a chair.
     Richard and Hastings flies over the stage.
SOMERSET
What are they that fly there?
WARWICK
Richard and Hastings. Let them go. Here is the duke.
KING EDWARD
The duke? Why, Warwick, when we parted
Thou called'st me king.
WARWICK   Ay, but the case is altered.   31
When you disgraced me in my embassade,   32
Then I degraded you from being king,
And come now to create you Duke of York.
Alas, how should you govern any kingdom
That know not how to use ambassadors,
Nor how to be contented with one wife,
Nor how to use your brothers brotherly,
Nor how to study for the people's welfare,
Nor how to shroud yourself from enemies?   40
KING EDWARD
Yea, brother of Clarence, art thou here too?
Nay, then I see that Edward needs must down.   42
Yet, Warwick, in despite of all mischance,
Of thee thyself, and all thy complices,   44
Edward will always bear himself as king.
Though Fortune's malice overthrow my state,
My mind exceeds the compass of her wheel.   47
WARWICK
Then, for his mind, be Edward England's king,
     Takes off his crown.
But Henry now shall wear the English crown
And be true king indeed, thou but the shadow.
My Lord of Somerset, at my request
See that forthwith Duke Edward be conveyed
Unto my brother, Archbishop of York.   53
When I have fought with Pembroke and his fellows,
I'll follow you and tell what answer
Lewis and the Lady Bona send to him.
Now for a while farewell, good Duke of York.
KING EDWARD
What fates impose, that men must needs abide;
It boots not to resist both wind and tide.   59
     They lead him out forcibly. Exeunt.
OXFORD
What now remains, my lords, for us to do
But march to London with our soldiers?
WARWICK
Ay, that's the first thing that we have to do,
To free King Henry from imprisonment
And see him seated in the regal throne.
     Exit [Warwick with the rest].

19–21 *That . . . steeds* (The oracle predicted that Troy would not fall if the horses of Rhesus, king of Thrace, grazed on the Trojan plain. To prevent their doing so, Ulysses and Diomedes captured them on a night raid.) **25** *surprise* capture **28** *sort* manner
IV, iii Edward's camp near Warwick **2** *this* i.e. this time **16** *worship* a place of dignity **18** *estate* condition **19** *doubted* feared **31** *the case is altered* things have changed (a proverbial expression) **32** *embassade* embassy **40** *shroud* conceal, protect **42** *needs must down* must necessarily be put down **44** *complices* accomplices **47** *compass* circumference **53** *Archbishop of York* i.e. George Nevil **59** *boots not* is no use

IV, iv   *Enter Rivers and Lady Grey [as Queen Elizabeth].*

RIVERS
Madam, what makes you in this sudden change?

QUEEN ELIZABETH
Why, brother Rivers, are you yet to learn
What late misfortune is befall'n King Edward?

RIVERS
What? Loss of some pitched battle against Warwick?

QUEEN ELIZABETH
No, but the loss of his own royal person.

RIVERS
Then is my sovereign slain?

QUEEN ELIZABETH
Ay, almost slain, for he is taken prisoner,
Either betrayed by falsehood of his guard
Or by his foe surprised at unawares;
And, as I further have to understand,
11   Is new committed to the Bishop of York,
12   Fell Warwick's brother, and by that our foe.

RIVERS
These news, I must confess, are full of grief.
Yet, gracious madam, bear it as you may;
Warwick may lose, that now hath won the day.

QUEEN ELIZABETH
Till then fair hope must hinder life's decay.
And I the rather wean me from despair
For love of Edward's offspring in my womb.
This is it that makes me bridle passion
And bear with mildness my misfortune's cross.
Ay, ay, for this I draw in many a tear
22   And stop the rising of bloodsucking sighs,
Lest with my sighs or tears I blast or drown
King Edward's fruit, true heir to th' English crown.

RIVERS
25   But, madam, where is Warwick then become?

QUEEN ELIZABETH
I am informèd that he comes toward London
To set the crown once more on Henry's head.
Guess thou the rest. King Edward's friends must down.
29   But, to prevent the tyrant's violence
(For trust not him that hath once broken faith),
I'll hence forthwith unto the sanctuary,
To save, at least, the heir of Edward's right.
There shall I rest secure from force and fraud.
Come, therefore, let us fly while we may fly.
If Warwick take us, we are sure to die.   *Exeunt.*

*

IV, v   *Enter Richard, Lord Hastings, and Sir William
Stanley.*

RICHARD
Now, my Lord Hastings and Sir William Stanley,
Leave off to wonder why I drew you hither
3   Into this chiefest thicket of the park.
Thus stands the case: you know our king, my brother,
Is prisoner to the bishop here, at whose hands
He hath good usage and great liberty;
And often, but attended with weak guard,
8   Comes hunting this way to disport himself.
9   I have advertised him by secret means
That if about this hour he make this way
11   Under the color of his usual game,
He shall here find his friends with horse and men
To set him free from his captivity.

Enter King Edward and a Huntsman with him.

HUNTSMAN
This way, my lord, for this way lies the game.

KING EDWARD
Nay, this way, man, see where the huntsmen stand.
Now, brother of Gloucester, Lord Hastings, and the rest,
Stand you thus close to steal the bishop's deer?   17

RICHARD
Brother, the time and case requireth haste.
Your horse stands ready at the park corner.

KING EDWARD
But whither shall we then?

HASTINGS
To Lynn, my lord.   21

KING EDWARD   And ship from thence to Flanders?

RICHARD
Well guessed, believe me; for that was my meaning.

KING EDWARD
Stanley, I will requite thy forwardness.   23

RICHARD
But wherefore stay we? 'Tis no time to talk.

KING EDWARD
Huntsman, what say'st thou? Wilt thou go along?

HUNTSMAN
Better do so than tarry and be hanged.

RICHARD
Come then, away. Let's ha' no more ado.

KING EDWARD
Bishop, farewell. Shield thee from Warwick's frown
And pray that I may repossess the crown.   *Exeunt.*

*

IV, vi   *Flourish. Enter King Henry the Sixth, Clarence,
Warwick, Somerset, young Henry [Earl of
Richmond], Oxford, Montague, and Lieutenant
[of the Tower].*

KING HENRY
Master lieutenant, now that God and friends
Have shaken Edward from the regal seat
And turned my captive state to liberty,
My fear to hope, my sorrows unto joys,
At our enlargement what are thy due fees?   5

LIEUTENANT
Subjects may challenge nothing of their sovereigns;
But if an humble prayer may prevail,
I then crave pardon of your majesty.

KING HENRY
For what, lieutenant? for well using me?
Nay, be thou sure I'll well requite thy kindness
For that it made my imprisonment a pleasure;
Ay, such a pleasure as incagèd birds
Conceive when, after many moody thoughts,
At last by notes of household harmony

IV, iv The royal palace in London   11 *new* recently; *Bishop* i.e. archbishop   12 *Fell* cruel; *by that* i.e. because of that relationship   22 *bloodsucking sighs* (sighing was supposed to waste the heart's blood, which
explains why *hope* can *hinder life's decay* [l. 16])   25 *become* gone   29
prevent forestall
IV, v The Archbishop of York's park   3 *chiefest* largest   8 *disport* amuse
9 *advertised* notified   11 *Under . . . game* i.e. as though he were merely
hunting   17 *close* hidden   21 *Lynn* i.e. King's Lynn, on the Norfolk coast
23 *forwardness* zeal
IV, vi The Tower of London   s.d. *Lieutenant* Deputy Warden   5 *enlargement* release; *fees* (due because prisoners who could afford it were
charged for special quarters and food)

They quite forget their loss of liberty.
But, Warwick, after God, thou set'st me free,
And chiefly therefore I thank God and thee;
He was the author, thou the instrument.
Therefore, that I may conquer fortune's spite
By living low, where fortune cannot hurt me,
And that the people of this blessèd land
22   May not be punished with my thwarting stars,
Warwick, although my head still wear the crown,
I here resign my government to thee,
For thou art fortunate in all thy deeds.

WARWICK
26   Your grace hath still been famed for virtuous,
And now may seem as wise as virtuous
By spying and avoiding fortune's malice,
29   For few men rightly temper with the stars.
Yet in this one thing let me blame your grace,
31   For choosing me when Clarence is in place.

CLARENCE
32   No, Warwick, thou art worthy of the sway,
To whom the heavens in thy nativity
Adjudged an olive branch and laurel crown,
As likely to be blest in peace and war;
And therefore I yield thee my free consent.

WARWICK
37   And I choose Clarence only for Protector.

KING HENRY
Warwick and Clarence, give me both your hands.
Now join your hands, and with your hands your hearts,
That no dissension hinder government.
I make you both Protectors of this land,
While I myself will lead a private life
And in devotion spend my latter days,
To sin's rebuke and my Creator's praise.

WARWICK
What answers Clarence to his sovereign's will?

CLARENCE
That he consents, if Warwick yield consent,
For on thy fortune I repose myself.

WARWICK
Why then, though loath, yet must I be content.
We'll yoke together, like a double shadow
50   To Henry's body, and supply his place;
I mean, in bearing weight of government,
While he enjoys the honor and his ease.
And, Clarence, now then it is more than needful
Forthwith that Edward be pronounced a traitor
And all his lands and goods be confiscate.

CLARENCE
What else? And that succession be determined.

WARWICK
Ay, therein Clarence shall not want his part.

KING HENRY
But with the first of all your chief affairs,
Let me entreat (for I command no more)
60   That Margaret your queen and my son Edward

Be sent for, to return from France with speed;
For till I see them here, by doubtful fear
My joy of liberty is half eclipsed.

CLARENCE
It shall be done, my sovereign, with all speed.

KING HENRY
My Lord of Somerset, what youth is that
Of whom you seem to have so tender care?

SOMERSET
My liege, it is young Henry, Earl of Richmond.   67

KING HENRY
Come hither, England's hope. *Lays his hand on his head.*
   If secret powers
Suggest but truth to my divining thoughts,   69
This pretty lad will prove our country's bliss.
His looks are full of peaceful majesty,
His head by nature framed to wear a crown,
His hand to wield a sceptre, and himself
Likely in time to bless a regal throne.
Make much of him, my lords; for this is he
Must help you more than you are hurt by me.
     Enter a Post.

WARWICK
What news, my friend?

POST
That Edward is escapèd from your brother
And fled, as he hears since, to Burgundy.   79

WARWICK
Unsavory news! But how made he escape?

POST
He was conveyed by Richard Duke of Gloucester   81
And the Lord Hastings, who attended him   82
In secret ambush on the forest side
And from the bishop's huntsmen rescued him;
For hunting was his daily exercise.

WARWICK
My brother was too careless of his charge.
But let us hence, my sovereign, to provide
A salve for any sore that may betide.   88
     Exeunt. Manent Somerset, Richmond, and Oxford.

SOMERSET
My lord, I like not of this flight of Edward's,
For doubtless Burgundy will yield him help
And we shall have more wars before't be long.
As Henry's late presaging prophecy
Did glad my heart with hope of this young Richmond,
So doth my heart misgive me, in these conflicts
What may befall him, to his harm and ours.
Therefore, Lord Oxford, to prevent the worst,
Forthwith we'll send him hence to Brittany
Till storms be past of civil enmity.

OXFORD
Ay, for if Edward repossess the crown,
'Tis like that Richmond with the rest shall down.

SOMERSET
It shall be so; he shall to Brittany.
Come therefore, let's about it speedily.   *Exeunt.*

              *

22 *thwarting stars* stars (instruments of fortune) whose influence impedes happiness and success   26 *still* always   29 *temper . . . stars* i.e. come to terms with their fate   31 *in place* here   32 *sway* rule   37 *only* alone   67 *Henry* (the future Henry VII; at his accession to the throne the Wars of the Roses finally ceased)   69 *divining* foretelling the future   79 *he* i.e. your brother, the Archbishop of York   81 *conveyed* secretly carried away   82 *attended* waited for   88 *betide* develop
IV, vii Before the walls of York

Flourish. Enter [King] Edward, Richard, Hastings,   IV, vii
and Soldiers [a troop of Hollanders].

KING EDWARD
Now, brother Richard, Lord Hastings, and the rest,
Yet thus far Fortune maketh us amends

And says that once more I shall interchange
4 My wanèd state for Henry's regal crown.
Well have we passed and now repassed the seas
And brought desirèd help from Burgundy.
What then remains, we being thus arrived
8 From Ravenspurgh haven before the gates of York,
But that we enter, as into our dukedom?

RICHARD
The gates made fast! Brother, I like not this.
11 For many men that stumble at the threshold
Are well foretold that danger lurks within.

KING EDWARD
13 Tush, man, abodements must not now affright us;
By fair or foul means we must enter in,
For hither will our friends repair to us.

HASTINGS
My liege, I'll knock once more to summon them.
Enter [aloft], on the walls, the Mayor of York and his
Brethren [the Aldermen].

MAYOR
My lords, we were forewarnèd of your coming
And shut the gates for safety of ourselves;
For now we owe allegiance unto Henry.

KING EDWARD
But, Master Mayor, if Henry be your king,
Yet Edward at the least is Duke of York.

MAYOR
True, my good lord. I know you for no less.

KING EDWARD
23 Why, and I challenge nothing but my dukedom,
As being well content with that alone.

RICHARD [aside]
But when the fox hath once got in his nose,
He'll soon find means to make the body follow.

HASTINGS
Why, Master Mayor, why stand you in a doubt?
Open the gates. We are King Henry's friends.

MAYOR
Ay, say you so? The gates shall then be opened.
He descends [with the Aldermen].

RICHARD
A wise stout captain, and soon persuaded.

HASTINGS
31 The good old man would fain that all were well,
32 So 'twere not long of him; but being entered,
I doubt not, I, but we shall soon persuade
Both him and all his brothers unto reason.
Enter [below] the Mayor, [bringing the keys in
his hand,] and two Aldermen.

KING EDWARD
So, Master Mayor. These gates must not be shut
But in the night or in the time of war.
What, fear not, man, but yield me up the keys;
Takes his keys.
For Edward will defend the town and thee
39 And all those friends that deign to follow me.
March. Enter Montgomery with Drum and Soldiers.

RICHARD
40 Brother, this is Sir John Montgomery,
Our trusty friend, unless I be deceived.

KING EDWARD
Welcome, Sir John; but why come you in arms?

MONTGOMERY
To help King Edward in his time of storm,
As every loyal subject ought to do.

KING EDWARD
Thanks, good Montgomery. But we now forget
Our title to the crown and only claim
Our dukedom till God please to send the rest.

MONTGOMERY
Then fare you well, for I will hence again.
I came to serve a king and not a duke.
Drummer, strike up, and let us march away. 50
The Drum begins to march.

KING EDWARD
Nay, stay, Sir John, awhile, and we'll debate
By what safe means the crown may be recovered.

MONTGOMERY
What talk you of debating? In few words,
If you'll not here proclaim yourself our king,
I'll leave you to your fortune and be gone
To keep them back that come to succor you.
Why shall we fight, if you pretend no title? 57

RICHARD
Why, brother, wherefore stand you on nice points? 58

KING EDWARD
When we grow stronger, then we'll make our claim;
Till then 'tis wisdom to conceal our meaning.

HASTINGS
Away with scrupulous wit! Now arms must rule. 61

RICHARD
And fearless minds climb soonest unto crowns.
Brother, we will proclaim you out of hand; 63
The bruit thereof will bring you many friends. 64

KING EDWARD
Then be it as you will; for 'tis my right,
And Henry but usurps the diadem.

MONTGOMERY
Ay, now my sovereign speaketh like himself
And now will I be Edward's champion. 68

HASTINGS
Sound trumpet. Edward shall be here proclaimed.
Come, fellow soldier, make thou proclamation.
Flourish. Sound.

SOLDIER 'Edward the Fourth, by the grace of God, King
of England and France, and Lord of Ireland, etc.' 72

MONTGOMERY
And whosoe'er gainsays King Edward's right,
By this I challenge him to single fight.
Throws down his gauntlet.

ALL Long live Edward the Fourth!

KING EDWARD
Thanks, brave Montgomery, and thanks unto you all.
If fortune serve me I'll requite this kindness.
Now for this night let's harbor here in York,
And when the morning sun shall raise his car 79
Above the border of this horizon,
We'll forward towards Warwick and his mates;

---

4 *wanèd* faded, declined   8 *Ravenspurgh* (on the Yorkshire coast, at the mouth of the River Humber)   11 *stumble at the threshold* (a sign of bad luck)   13 *abodements* omens   23 *challenge* claim   31 *would fain* desires   32 *So . . . him* as long as he bears no responsibility   39 *deign* are willing   40 *Sir John Montgomery* (called Sir Thomas in the Chronicles, which report that he met Edward at Nottingham after the securing of York)   50 s.d. *march* i.e. commence beating a march   57 *pretend* claim   58 *nice points* minor details   61 *wit* reasoning   63 *out of hand* immediately   64 *bruit* news   68 *champion* defender   72 *etc.* (the soldier adds the conventional titles of the monarch)   79 *car* chariot

82 For well I wot that Henry is no soldier.
83 Ah, froward Clarence, how evil it beseems thee
To flatter Henry and forsake thy brother.
Yet, as we may, we'll meet both thee and Warwick.
Come on, brave soldiers. Doubt not of the day,
And that once gotten, doubt not of large pay.
       Exeunt [as into the city].

*

IV, viii   *Flourish. Enter the King [Henry], Warwick,*
              Montague, Clarence, Oxford, and Exeter.
WARWICK
1 What counsel, lords? Edward from Belgia,
2 With hasty Germans and blunt Hollanders,
Hath passed in safety through the narrow seas
4 And with his troops doth march amain to London,
And many giddy people flock to him.
OXFORD
Let's levy men and beat him back again.
CLARENCE
A little fire is quickly trodden out,
8 Which, being suffered, rivers cannot quench.
WARWICK
In Warwickshire I have true-hearted friends,
Not mutinous in peace, yet bold in war.
11 Those will I muster up; and thou, son Clarence,
Shalt stir up in Suffolk, Norfolk, and in Kent
The knights and gentlemen to come with thee.
Thou, brother Montague, in Buckingham,
Northampton, and in Leicestershire shalt find
Men well inclined to hear what thou command'st.
And thou, brave Oxford, wondrous well beloved,
In Oxfordshire shalt muster up thy friends.
My sovereign, with the loving citizens,
Like to his island girt in with the ocean
Or modest Dian circled with her nymphs,
Shall rest in London till we come to him.
Fair lords, take leave and stand not to reply.
Farewell, my sovereign.
KING HENRY
25 Farewell, my Hector and my Troy's true hope.
CLARENCE
In sign of truth I kiss your highness' hand.
KING HENRY
Well-minded Clarence, be thou fortunate.
MONTAGUE
Comfort, my lord, and so I take my leave.
OXFORD *[kisses Henry's hand]*
And thus I seal my truth and bid adieu.
KING HENRY
Sweet Oxford, and my loving Montague,
31 And all at once, once more a happy farewell.

WARWICK
Farewell, sweet lords. Let's meet at Coventry.
       Exeunt [all but King Henry and Exeter].
KING HENRY
Here at the palace will I rest awhile.
Cousin of Exeter, what thinks your lordship?
Methinks the power that Edward hath in field
Should not be able to encounter mine.
EXETER
The doubt is that he will seduce the rest.   37
KING HENRY
That's not my fear. My meed hath got me fame.   38
I have not stopped mine ears to their demands
Nor posted off their suits with slow delays.   40
My pity hath been balm to heal their wounds,
My mildness hath allayed their swelling griefs,
My mercy dried their water-flowing tears.
I have not been desirous of their wealth
Nor much oppressed them with great subsidies,   45
Nor forward of revenge, though they much erred.   46
Then why should they love Edward more than me?
No, Exeter, these graces challenge grace;
And when the lion fawns upon the lamb,
The lamb will never cease to follow him.
      Shout within, 'A Lancaster! A Lancaster!'
EXETER
Hark, hark, my lord! what shouts are these?
      Enter [King] Edward and his Soldiers [, with
          Richard].
KING EDWARD
Seize on the shamefaced Henry, bear him hence,   52
And once again proclaim us King of England.
You are the fount that makes small brooks to flow.
Now stops thy spring; my sea shall suck them dry
And swell so much the higher by their ebb.
Hence with him to the Tower. Let him not speak.
      Exit [Guard] with King Henry [and Exeter].
And, lords, toward Coventry bend we our course,
Where peremptory Warwick now remains.   59
The sun shines hot, and if we use delay,   60
Cold biting winter mars our hoped-for hay.
RICHARD
Away betimes, before his forces join,   62
And take the great-grown traitor unawares.
Brave warriors, march amain toward Coventry. *Exeunt.*

*

      Enter [aloft] Warwick, the Mayor of Coventry,   V, i
       two Messengers, and others, upon the walls.
WARWICK
Where is the post that came from valiant Oxford?
How far hence is thy lord, mine honest fellow?
1. MESSENGER
By this at Dunsmore, marching hitherward.   3
WARWICK
How far off is our brother Montague?
Where is the post that came from Montague?
2. MESSENGER
By this at Daintry, with a puissant troop.   6
      Enter Somervile [aloft].
WARWICK
Say, Somervile, what says my loving son?
And by thy guess how nigh is Clarence now?

SOMERVILE

9   At Southam I did leave him with his forces
And do expect him here some two hours hence.

WARWICK

Then Clarence is at hand. I hear his drum.

SOMERVILE

12   It is not his, my lord. Here Southam lies.
The drum your honor hears marcheth from Warwick.

WARWICK

14   Who should that be ? Belike unlooked-for friends.

SOMERVILE

They are at hand, and you shall quickly know.
March. Flourish. Enter [below, King] Edward,
Richard, and Soldiers.

KING EDWARD

16   Go, trumpet, to the walls, and sound a parle.

RICHARD

See how the surly Warwick mans the wall.

WARWICK

18   O unbid spite ! Is sportful Edward come ?
Where slept our scouts or how are they seduced
20   That we could hear no news of his repair ?

KING EDWARD

Now, Warwick, wilt thou ope the city gates,
Speak gentle words, and humbly bend thy knee.
Call Edward king and at his hands beg mercy,
And he shall pardon thee these outrages.

WARWICK

Nay, rather, wilt thou draw thy forces hence,
Confess who set thee up and plucked thee down,
Call Warwick patron, and be penitent ?
And thou shalt still remain the Duke of York.

RICHARD

I thought at least he would have said 'the king' ;
Or did he make the jest against his will ?

WARWICK

Is not a dukedom, sir, a goodly gift ?

RICHARD

Ay, by my faith, for a poor earl to give ;
33   I'll do thee service for so good a gift.

WARWICK

'Twas I that gave the kingdom to thy brother.

KING EDWARD

Why, then 'tis mine, if but by Warwick's gift.

WARWICK

36   Thou art no Atlas for so great a weight ;
And, weakling, Warwick takes his gift again,
And Henry is my king, Warwick his subject.

KING EDWARD

But Warwick's king is Edward's prisoner ;
And, gallant Warwick, do but answer this :
What is the body when the head is off ?

RICHARD

42   Alas that Warwick had no more forecast,
43   But, whiles he thought to steal the single ten,
The king was slily fingered from the deck.
You left poor Henry at the bishop's palace
And ten to one you'll meet him in the Tower.

KING EDWARD

'Tis even so. Yet you are Warwick still.

RICHARD

48   Come, Warwick, take the time. Kneel down, kneel
down.

49   Nay, when ? Strike now, or else the iron cools.

WARWICK

I had rather chop this hand off at a blow
And with the other fling it at thy face
Than bear so low a sail to strike to thee.   52

KING EDWARD

Sail how thou canst, have wind and tide thy friend,
This hand, fast wound about thy coal-black hair,
Shall, whiles thy head is warm and new cut off,
Write in the dust this sentence with thy blood :
'Wind-changing Warwick now can change no more.'   57
Enter Oxford, with Drum and Colors.

WARWICK

O cheerful colors, see where Oxford comes.

OXFORD

Oxford, Oxford, for Lancaster !
[Exeunt Oxford and his men as into the city.]

RICHARD

The gates are open ; let us enter too.

KING EDWARD

So other foes may set upon our backs.   61
Stand we in good array, for they no doubt
Will issue out again and bid us battle.   63
If not, the city being but of small defense,
We'll quickly rouse the traitors in the same.   65
[Enter Oxford aloft.]

WARWICK

O, welcome, Oxford, for we want thy help.
Enter Montague, with Drum and Colors.

MONTAGUE

Montague, Montague, for Lancaster !
[Exeunt Montague and his men as into the city.]

RICHARD

Thou and thy brother both shall buy this treason
Even with the dearest blood your bodies bear.

KING EDWARD

The harder matched, the greater victory.
My mind presageth happy gain and conquest.
Enter Somerset, with Drum and Colors.

SOMERSET

Somerset, Somerset, for Lancaster !
[Exeunt Somerset and his men as into the city.]

RICHARD

Two of thy name, both Dukes of Somerset,   73
Have sold their lives unto the house of York ;
And thou shalt be the third, if this sword hold.
Enter Clarence, with Drum and Colors.

WARWICK

And lo where George of Clarence sweeps along,

---

9 *Southam* (about ten miles southeast of Coventry)   12–13 *It . . . Warwick* (the city of Warwick lies southwest of Coventry ; the earl has slightly mistaken his directions, as Somervile points out)   14 *Belike* no doubt   16 *parle* parley, a trumpet call requesting a truce for conference   18 *unbid* uninvited, unwelcome ; *sportful* lascivious   20 *repair* approach   33 *do thee service* accept you as my feudal overlord (ironically)   36 *Thou . . . Atlas* i.e. you cannot bear (Atlas, a Titan, supported the world on his shoulders)   42 *forecast* forethought   43 *single ten* mere ten (the ten, highest of the plain cards, is worth having, but not in comparison with the king)   48 *take the time* seize the opportunity   49 *Nay, when* (an exclamation indicating impatience)   52 *bear . . . thee* (see III, iii, 5n.)   57 *Wind-changing* i.e. fickle, inconstant   61 *So* if so   63 *bid* offer   65 *rouse . . . in* drive . . . from (a hunting term)   73 *Two . . . name* (The Somerset being addressed is Edmund, the 4th duke. His elder brother, Henry Beaufort, 3rd duke, was executed after the Battle of Hexham, 1464, though his defection from Edward is described in IV, i and ii as taking place in 1470. Their father, Edmund, 2nd duke, was killed at St Albans, 1445 ; it is his head that Richard flings down at I, i, 16.)

Of force enough to bid his brother battle ;
With whom an upright zeal to right prevails
More than the nature of a brother's love.
Come, Clarence, come ; thou wilt, if Warwick call.
   [Sound a parle and Richard and Clarence whisper
   together.]

CLARENCE
Father of Warwick, know you what this means ?
   [Takes his red rose out of his hat.]
Look here, I throw my infamy at thee.
I will not ruinate my father's house,
84 Who gave his blood to lime the stones together,
85 And set up Lancaster. Why, trowest thou, Warwick,
86 That Clarence is so harsh, so blunt, unnatural,
To bend the fatal instruments of war
Against his brother and his lawful king ?
89 Perhaps thou wilt object my holy oath.
To keep that oath were more impiety
91 Than Jephtha when he sacrificed his daughter.
I am so sorry for my trespass made
That, to deserve well at my brother's hands,
I here proclaim myself thy mortal foe,
With resolution, wheresoe'er I meet thee
(As I will meet thee if thou stir abroad),
To plague thee for thy foul misleading me.
And so, proud-hearted Warwick, I defy thee
And to my brother turn my blushing cheeks.
Pardon me, Edward, I will make amends ;
And, Richard, do not frown upon my faults,
102 For I will henceforth be no more unconstant.

KING EDWARD
Now welcome more, and ten times more beloved,
Than if thou never hadst deserved our hate.

RICHARD
Welcome, good Clarence. This is brotherlike.

WARWICK
106 O passing traitor, perjured and unjust.

KING EDWARD
What, Warwick, wilt thou leave the town and fight ?
Or shall we beat the stones about thine ears ?

WARWICK
Alas, I am not cooped here for defense.
110 I will away towards Barnet presently
And bid thee battle, Edward, if thou dar'st.

---

84 *lime* cement   85 *trowest thou* do you believe   86 *blunt* unfeeling   89 *object* raise as an objection   91 *Jephtha* (see Judges xi, 30–40)   102 *unconstant* fickle, disloyal   106 *passing* surpassing   110 *Barnet* (about ten miles north of London and seventy-five miles southeast of Coventry. At IV, viii the dramatist had departed from the historical order of events: in mid-March, 1471, from York [IV, vii] Edward had moved south to Coventry, to which Warwick had withdrawn. Here the Yorkist army invited battle. When Warwick declined, Edward continued south, occupying the town of Warwick, whence he doubled back to Coventry to challenge the Lancastrian forces once more. When Warwick again refused, Edward marched south, capturing London and Henry VI on April 11, this time with the Lancastrians following. By April 13 Warwick had reached Barnet, where early the next day he encountered the Yorkist army, which had marched north from London. Because he put Henry's capture [IV, viii] out of its historical sequence, the dramatist is here forced to treat Barnet as though it lay adjacent to Coventry.)
V, ii Fields near Coventry (Barnet)   2 *bug* goblin ; *feared* frightened   11 *cedar* (symbol of pre-eminence)   12–13 *eagle . . . lion* (the allusion may be general, i.e. 'royal creatures'; or it may be intended specifically, through the identification of the men with their emblems: i.e. 'eagle': Richard of York, as perhaps at II, i, 92, and 'lion': Henry VI, three rampant lions being represented on his royal arms)   13 *ramping* rampant   14 *overpeered* overlooked; *Jove's . . . tree* i.e. the oak   31 *puissant* strong   41 *latest* final   45 *mought* might

KING EDWARD
Yes, Warwick, Edward dares and leads the way.
Lords, to the field. Saint George and victory !
   Exeunt [King Edward and his company below,
   Warwick and his company aloft]. March.
   [Enter below as out of the city] Warwick and
   his company [and] follows [King Edward].

*

   Alarum and excursions. Enter [King] Edward,   V, ii
   bringing forth Warwick wounded.

KING EDWARD
So, lie thou there ! Die thou, and die our fear !
For Warwick was a bug that feared us all.   2
Now, Montague, sit fast. I seek for thee,
That Warwick's bones may keep thine company.   *Exit.*

WARWICK
Ah, who is nigh ? Come to me, friend or foe,
And tell me who is victor, York or Warwick.
Why ask I that ? My mangled body shows,
My blood, my want of strength, my sick heart shows,
That I must yield my body to the earth
And, by my fall, the conquest to my foe.
Thus yields the cedar to the axe's edge,   11
Whose arms gave shelter to the princely eagle,   12
Under whose shade the ramping lion slept,   13
Whose top-branch overpeered Jove's spreading tree   14
And kept low shrubs from winter's powerful wind.
These eyes, that now are dimmed with death's black veil,
Have been as piercing as the midday sun
To search the secret treasons of the world.
The wrinkles in my brows, now filled with blood,
Were likened oft to kingly sepulchres ;
For who lived king but I could dig his grave ?
And who durst smile when Warwick bent his brow ?
Lo now my glory smeared in dust and blood ;
My parks, my walks, my manors that I had,
Even now forsake me ; and of all my lands
Is nothing left me but my body's length.
Why, what is pomp, rule, reign, but earth and dust ?
And, live we how we can, yet die we must.
   Enter Oxford and Somerset.

SOMERSET
Ah, Warwick, Warwick, wert thou as we are,
We might recover all our loss again.
The queen from France hath brought a puissant power.   31
Even now we heard the news. Ah, couldst thou fly !

WARWICK
Why, then I would not fly. Ah, Montague,
If thou be there, sweet brother, take my hand
And with thy lips keep in my soul awhile.
Thou lov'st me not ; for, brother, if thou didst,
Thy tears would wash this cold congealèd blood
That glues my lips and will not let me speak.
Come quickly, Montague, or I am dead.

SOMERSET
Ah, Warwick, Montague hath breathed his last,
And to the latest gasp cried out for Warwick   41
And said, 'Commend me to my valiant brother.'
And more he would have said, and more he spoke,
Which sounded like a cannon in a vault,
That mought not be distinguished ; but at last   45
I well might hear, delivered with a groan,
'O, farewell, Warwick !'

WARWICK

Sweet rest his soul. Fly, lords, and save yourselves ;
For Warwick bids you all farewell, to meet in heaven.
    [Dies.]

OXFORD

Away, away, to meet the queen's great power.
    Here they bear away his body. Exeunt.

V, iii   *Flourish. Enter King Edward in triumph ;*
       with Richard, Clarence, and the rest.

KING EDWARD

Thus far our fortune keeps an upward course
And we are graced with wreaths of victory ;
But in the midst of this bright-shining day
I spy a black, suspicious, threat'ning cloud
That will encounter with our glorious sun
Ere he attain his easeful western bed.
I mean, my lords, those powers that the queen
8   Hath raised in Gallia have arrived our coast
And, as we hear, march on to fight with us.

CLARENCE

A little gale will soon disperse that cloud
And blow it to the source from whence it came.
Thy very beams will dry those vapors up,
13   For every cloud engenders not a storm.

RICHARD

The queen is valued thirty thousand strong,
And Somerset, with Oxford, fled to her.
16   If she have time to breathe, be well assured
Her faction will be full as strong as ours.

KING EDWARD

18   We are advertised by our loving friends
That they do hold their course toward Tewkesbury.
20   We, having now the best at Barnet field,
21   Will thither straight, for willingness rids way ;
And as we march our strength will be augmented
In every county as we go along.
Strike up the drum. Cry 'Courage !' and away.   *Exeunt.*

*

V, iv   *Flourish. March. Enter the Queen [Margaret],*
       young [Prince] Edward, Somerset, Oxford, and
       Soldiers.

QUEEN MARGARET

Great lords, wise men ne'er sit and wail their loss
2   But cheerly seek how to redress their harms.
What though the mast be now blown overboard,
The cable broke, the holding anchor lost,
And half our sailors swallowed in the flood ?
Yet lives our pilot still. Is't meet that he
Should leave the helm and, like a fearful lad,
With tearful eyes add water to the sea
And give more strength to that which hath too much,
10   Whiles, in his moan, the ship splits on the rock,
Which industry and courage might have saved ?
Ah, what a shame, ah, what a fault were this.
Say Warwick was our anchor. What of that ?
And Montague our topmast. What of him ?
15   Our slaught'red friends the tackles. What of these ?
Why, is not Oxford here, another anchor ?
And Somerset, another goodly mast ?
18   The friends of France our shrouds and tacklings ?
And, though unskillful, why not Ned and I
20   For once allowed the skillful pilot's charge ?
We will not from the helm, to sit and weep,

But keep our course (though the rough wind say no)
From shelves and rocks that threaten us with wrack.   23
As good to chide the waves as speak them fair.
And what is Edward but a ruthless sea ?
What Clarence but a quicksand of deceit ?
And Richard but a ragged fatal rock ?
All these the enemies to our poor bark.
Say you can swim – alas, 'tis but a while,
Tread on the sand – why there you quickly sink,
Bestride the rock – the tide will wash you off
Or else you famish : that's a threefold death.
This speak I, lords, to let you understand,
If case some one of you would fly from us,   34
That there's no hoped-for mercy with the brothers
More than with ruthless waves, with sands and rocks.
Why, courage then, what cannot be avoided
'Twere childish weakness to lament or fear.

PRINCE

Methinks a woman of this valiant spirit
Should, if a coward heard her speak these words,
Infuse his breast with magnanimity
And make him, naked, foil a man-at-arms.   42
I speak not this as doubting any here ;
For did I but suspect a fearful man,
He should have leave to go away betimes,   45
Lest in our need he might infect another
And make him of like spirit to himself.
If any such be here (as God forbid !)
Let him depart before we need his help.

OXFORD

Women and children of so high a courage,
And warriors faint ? Why, 'twere perpetual shame.
O brave young prince, thy famous grandfather   52
Doth live again in thee. Long mayst thou live
To bear his image and renew his glories.

SOMERSET

And he that will not fight for such a hope,
Go home to bed, and, like the owl by day,
If he arise, be mocked and wondered at.

QUEEN MARGARET

Thanks, gentle Somerset ; sweet Oxford, thanks.

PRINCE

And take his thanks that yet hath nothing else.
    Enter a Messenger.

MESSENGER

Prepare you, lords ; for Edward is at hand,
Ready to fight. Therefore be resolute.

OXFORD

I thought no less. It is his policy
To haste thus fast, to find us unprovided.   63

SOMERSET

But he's deceived ; we are in readiness.

QUEEN MARGARET

This cheers my heart, to see your forwardness.   65

V, iii   **8** *Gallia* France   **13** *engenders* begets   **16** *breathe* i.e. gather her
strength   **18** *advertised* notified   **20** *having . . . best* having now overcome
21 *rids way* i.e. decreases the distance
V, iv   Fields near Tewkesbury   **2** *cheerly* cheerfully   **10** *in* at   **15** *tackles*
lines and pulleys for raising sail (running rigging)   **18** *shrouds* lines bracing
the mast (standing rigging); *tacklings* fittings and similar equipment
20 *charge* responsibility (i.e. to guide the ship)   **23** *shelves* sandbanks ;
wrack wreck, ruin   **34** *If* in   **42** *foil a man-at-arms* defeat an armed man
45 *betimes* immediately   **52** *grandfather* i.e. Henry V   **63** *unprovided* unprepared   **65** *forwardness* zeal

OXFORD

66 Here pitch our battle ; hence we will not budge.
      Flourish and march. Enter [King] Edward, Richard,
      Clarence, and Soldiers.

KING EDWARD

Brave followers, yonder stands the thorny wood
Which, by the heavens' assistance and your strength,
Must by the roots be hewn up yet ere night.
I need not add more fuel to your fire,
71 For well I wot ye blaze to burn them out.
Give signal to the fight, and to it, lords !

QUEEN MARGARET

Lords, knights and gentlemen, what I should say
74 My tears gainsay ; for every word I speak,
Ye see I drink the water of my eye.
Therefore, no more but this : Henry, your sovereign,
Is prisoner to the foe, his state usurped,
His realm a slaughterhouse, his subjects slain,
His statutes cancelled, and his treasure spent ;
And yonder is the wolf that makes this spoil.
You fight in justice. Then, in God's name, lords,
82 Be valiant and give signal to the fight.
      Alarum [to the battle : they fight] ; retreat [and King
      Edward and his company fly, driven out by Queen
      Margaret and her company]. Excursions [and the
      chambers be discharged, and re-enter King Edward
      and his company, making a great shout and cry
      'A York, a York' ; and then the Queen Margaret,
      Prince, Oxford, and Somerset are taken].   Exeunt.

V, v   *Flourish. Enter [King] Edward, Richard, [with*
        Soldiers guarding] Queen [Margaret as prisoner],
        Clarence, [with Soldiers guarding] Oxford,
        Somerset [as prisoners].

KING EDWARD

1 Now here a period of tumultuous broils.
2 Away with Oxford to Hames Castle straight.
   For Somerset, off with his guilty head !
   Go bear them hence. I will not hear them speak.

OXFORD

For my part, I'll not trouble thee with words.

SOMERSET

Nor I, but stoop with patience to my fortune.
      Exeunt [Oxford and Somerset, guarded].

QUEEN MARGARET

So part we sadly in this troublous world
8 To meet with joy in sweet Jerusalem.

KING EDWARD

Is proclamation made that who finds Edward
Shall have a high reward, and he his life ?

RICHARD

It is. And lo where youthful Edward comes.
      Enter [Soldiers, with] the Prince.

KING EDWARD

Bring forth the gallant ; let us hear him speak.
What ? Can so young a thorn begin to prick ?
Edward, what satisfaction canst thou make   14
For bearing arms, for stirring up my subjects,
And all the trouble thou hast turned me too ?

PRINCE

Speak like a subject, proud ambitious York !
Suppose that I am now my father's mouth ;
Resign thy chair, and where I stand kneel thou,
Whilst I propose the selfsame words to thee
Which, traitor, thou wouldst have me answer to.

QUEEN MARGARET

Ah, that thy father had been so resolved.

RICHARD

That you might still have worn the petticoat   23
And ne'er have stol'n the breech from Lancaster.   24

PRINCE

Let Aesop fable in a winter's night.   25
His currish riddles sorts not with this place.   26

RICHARD

By heaven, brat, I'll plague ye for that word.

QUEEN MARGARET

Ay, thou wast born to be a plague to men.

RICHARD

For God's sake take away this captive scold.

PRINCE

Nay, take away this scolding crook-back rather.

KING EDWARD

Peace, willful boy, or I will charm your tongue.   31

CLARENCE

Untutored lad, thou art too malapert.   32

PRINCE

I know my duty ; you are all undutiful.
Lascivious Edward, and thou perjured George,
And thou misshapen Dick, I tell ye all
I am your better, traitors as ye are,
And thou usurp'st my father's right and mine.

KING EDWARD

Take that, the likeness of this railer here.   38
      Stabs him.

RICHARD

Sprawl'st thou ? Take that, to end thy agony.   39
      Richard stabs him.

CLARENCE

And there's for twitting me with perjury.
      Clarence stabs him.

QUEEN MARGARET

O, kill me too !

RICHARD

Marry, and shall.   42
      Offers to kill her.

KING EDWARD

Hold, Richard, hold ; for we have done too much.

RICHARD

Why should she live to fill the world with words ?

KING EDWARD

What ? Doth she swoon ? Use means for her recovery.

RICHARD

Clarence, excuse me to the king my brother.
I'll hence to London on a serious matter ;
Ere ye come there, be sure to hear some news.   48

CLARENCE What ? what ?

RICHARD The Tower, the Tower.   *Exit.*

66 *pitch our battle* deploy our forces 71 *wot* know 74 *gainsay* forbid
82 s.d. *chambers* saluting cannon (to simulate ordnance)
V, v 1 *period* full stop 2 *Hames Castle* i.e. Hanmes Castle, near Calais
(where Oxford was confined after his capture in 1474, three years later than
Tewkesbury) 8 *Jerusalem* i.e. Heaven, the New Jerusalem 14 *satisfaction* recompense 23 *still* always 24 *breech* breeches 25–26 *Let . . . place*
i.e. you lie about the relationship between my mother and father (with a
gibe at Richard, for Aesop was supposedly stunted and deformed) 26
currish mean, cynical ; *sorts not* are not appropriate 31 *charm your tongue*
i.e. silence you ('charm' : cast a spell upon) 32 *malapert* impertinent
38 *this railer* i.e. Queen Margaret 39 *Sprawl'st thou* do you struggle in
your death-throes 42 *Marry, and shall* I will indeed ('marry' : by the
Virgin Mary) 48 *be sure to* be confident that you will

QUEEN MARGARET
O Ned, sweet Ned, speak to thy mother, boy.
Canst thou not speak ? O traitors ! murderers !
They that stabbed Caesar shed no blood at all,
Did not offend, nor were not worthy blame,
55 If this foul deed were by, to equal it.
56 He was a man ; this (in respect) a child,
And men ne'er spend their fury on a child.
What's worse than murderer, that I may name it ?
No, no, my heart will burst an if I speak.
And I will speak, that so my heart may burst.
Butchers and villains, bloody cannibals,
How sweet a plant have you untimely cropped.
You have no children, butchers ; if you had,
The thought of them would have stirred up remorse ;
But if you ever chance to have a child,
Look in his youth to have him so cut off
67 As, deathsmen, you have rid this sweet young prince.
KING EDWARD
Away with her ! Go bear her hence perforce !
QUEEN MARGARET
Nay, never bear me hence, dispatch me here.
Here sheathe thy sword, I'll pardon thee my death.
What, wilt thou not ? Then, Clarence, do it thou.
CLARENCE
By heaven, I will not do thee so much ease.
QUEEN MARGARET
Good Clarence, do ! Sweet Clarence, do thou do it !
CLARENCE
Didst thou not hear me swear I would not do it ?
QUEEN MARGARET
75 Ay, but thou usest to forswear thyself.
'Twas sin before, but now 'tis charity.
What, wilt thou not ? Where is that devil's butcher,
78 Hard-favored Richard ? Richard, where art thou ?
79 Thou art not here. Murder is thy almsdeed.
80 Petitioners for blood thou ne'er put'st back.
KING EDWARD
Away, I say. I charge ye bear her hence.
QUEEN MARGARET
So come to you and yours as to this prince.
Exit Queen [Margaret, guarded].
KING EDWARD
Where's Richard gone ?
CLARENCE
84 To London, all in post ; and, as I guess,
To make a bloody supper in the Tower.
KING EDWARD
He's sudden if a thing comes in his head.
87 Now march we hence, discharge the common sort
With pay and thanks, and let's away to London
And see our gentle queen how well she fares.
90 By this, I hope, she hath a son for me.
Exit [King Edward with his company].

*

V, vi *Enter [King] Henry the Sixth and Richard, with the*
Lieutenant in the Tower.
RICHARD
1 Good day, my lord. What, at your book so hard ?
KING HENRY
Ay, my good lord – 'my lord' I should say rather.
'Tis sin to flatter. 'Good' was little better.
'Good Gloucester' and 'good devil' were alike,

And both preposterous. Therefore, not 'good lord.' 5
RICHARD
Sirrah, leave us to ourselves ; we must confer.
[Exit Lieutenant.]
KING HENRY
So flies the reckless shepherd from the wolf ; 7
So first the harmless sheep doth yield his fleece,
And next his throat unto the butcher's knife.
What scene of death hath Roscius now to act ? 10
RICHARD
Suspicion always haunts the guilty mind ;
The thief doth fear each bush an officer.
KING HENRY
The bird that hath been limèd in a bush 13
With trembling wings misdoubteth every bush ; 14
And I, the hapless male to one sweet bird, 15
Have now the fatal object in my eye
Where my poor young was limed, was caught, and killed.
RICHARD
Why, what a peevish fool was that of Crete 18
That taught his son the office of a fowl.
And yet, for all his wings, the fool was drowned.
KING HENRY
I, Daedalus ; my poor boy, Icarus ;
Thy father, Minos, that denied our course ;
The sun that seared the wings of my sweet boy,
Thy brother Edward ; and thyself, the sea
Whose envious gulf did swallow up his life. 25
Ah, kill me with thy weapon, not with words.
My breast can better brook thy dagger's point 27
Than can my ears that tragic history.
But wherefore dost thou come ? Is't for my life ?
RICHARD
Think'st thou I am an executioner ?
KING HENRY
A persecutor I am sure thou art.
If murdering innocents be executing,
Why, then thou art an executioner.
RICHARD
Thy son I killed for his presumption.
KING HENRY
Hadst thou been killed when first thou didst presume,
Thou hadst not lived to kill a son of mine.
And thus I prophesy, that many a thousand
Which now mistrust no parcel of my fear, 38
And many an old man's sigh and many a widow's,
And many an orphan's water-standing eye – 40
Men for their sons, wives for their husbands,
Orphans for their parents' timeless death – 42
Shall rue the hour that ever thou wast born.
The owl shrieked at thy birth, an evil sign ;

---

55 *equal* compare with 56 *in respect* by comparison 67 *rid* killed 75 *thou . . . to forswear* you have the habit of forswearing 78 *Hard-favored* grim in appearance 79 *almsdeed* charity 80 *Petitioners . . . back* you never turn away those who ask for blood 84 *post* haste 87 *common sort* ordinary soldiers 90 *this* this time
V, vi The Tower of London 1 *book* (of devotions) 5 *preposterous* unnatural 7 *reckless* heedless 10 *Roscius* famous Roman actor (died 62 B.C.), supposed by the Elizabethans to be a tragedian 13 *limèd* caught with birdlime 14 *misdoubteth* suspects 15 *male* father ; *bird* chick 18–25 *fool . . . life* (Daedalus wished to escape from Crete, having been imprisoned there by King Minos. He devised wings for himself and his son Icarus, fastening them on with wax. The father flew to safety, but Icarus rose too near the sun ; the heat melted the wax, and Icarus fell into the sea and drowned.) 25 *envious gulf* hateful gullet 27 *brook* tolerate 38 *mistrust no parcel* do not suspect any part 40 *water-standing* full of tears 42 *timeless* untimely

45 The night crow cried, aboding luckless time;
Dogs howled and hideous tempest shook down trees;
47 The raven rooked her on the chimney's top,
48 And chattering pies in dismal discords sung.
Thy mother felt more than a mother's pain,
And yet brought forth less than a mother's hope,
To wit, an indigested and deformèd lump,
Not like the fruit of such a goodly tree.
Teeth hadst thou in thy head when thou wast born,
To signify thou cam'st to bite the world;
And, if the rest be true which I have heard,
Thou cam'st –

RICHARD
I'll hear no more. Die, prophet, in thy speech.
          Stabs him.
For this (amongst the rest) was I ordained.

KING HENRY
Ay, and for much more slaughter after this.
O, God forgive my sins and pardon thee.
          Dies.

RICHARD
What? Will the aspiring blood of Lancaster
Sink in the ground? I thought it would have mounted.
See how my sword weeps for the poor king's death.
64 O may such purple tears be always shed
From those that wish the downfall of our house.
If any spark of life be yet remaining,
Down, down to hell, and say I sent thee thither,
          Stabs him again.
I, that have neither pity, love, nor fear.
Indeed 'tis true that Henry told me of;
For I have often heard my mother say
I came into the world with my legs forward.
Had I not reason, think ye, to make haste
And seek their ruin that usurped our right?
The midwife wondered, and the women cried,
'O, Jesus bless us! He is born with teeth!'
And so I was; which plainly signified
That I should snarl and bite and play the dog.
Then, since the heavens have shaped my body so,
79 Let hell make crook'd my mind to answer it.
I have no brother, I am like no brother;
And this word 'love,' which greybeards call divine,
Be resident in men like one another,
And not in me. I am myself alone.
Clarence, beware. Thou keep'st me from the light;
85 But I will sort a pitchy day for thee;
86 For I will buzz abroad such prophecies
That Edward shall be fearful of his life;
And then, to purge his fear, I'll be thy death.
King Henry and the prince his son are gone.
Clarence, thy turn is next, and then the rest,
Counting myself but bad till I be best.
I'll throw thy body in another room

And triumph, Henry, in thy day of doom.
          Exit [with the body].
                    *

Flourish. Enter King [Edward], Queen [Elizabeth],   V, vii
*Clarence, Richard, Hastings, Nurse [with the young
Prince], and Attendants.*

KING EDWARD
Once more we sit in England's royal throne,
Repurchased with the blood of enemies.
What valiant foemen, like to autumn's corn,   3
Have we mowed down in tops of all their pride.
Three Dukes of Somerset, threefold renowned
For hardy and undoubted champions;   6
Two Cliffords, as the father and the son;   7
And two Northumberlands – two braver men
Ne'er spurred their coursers at the trumpet's sound;   9
With them, the two brave bears, Warwick and   10
  Montague,
That in their chains fettered the kingly lion
And made the forest tremble when they roared.
Thus have we swept suspicion from our seat   13
And made our footstool of security.
Come hither, Bess, and let me kiss my boy.
Young Ned, for thee thine uncles and myself
Have in our armors watched the winter's night,   17
Went all afoot in summer's scalding heat,
That thou mightst repossess the crown in peace;
And of our labors thou shalt reap the gain.

RICHARD *[aside]*
I'll blast his harvest, if your head were laid;   21
For yet I am not looked on in the world.   22
This shoulder was ordained so thick to heave,
And heave it shall some weight or break my back.
Work thou the way, and thou shalt execute.   25

KING EDWARD
Clarence and Gloucester, love my lovely queen,
And kiss your princely nephew, brothers both.

CLARENCE
The duty that I owe unto your majesty
I seal upon the lips of this sweet babe.   29

QUEEN ELIZABETH
Thanks, noble Clarence; worthy brother, thanks.

RICHARD
And that I love the tree from whence thou sprang'st
Witness the loving kiss I give the fruit.
          [Aside]
To say the truth, so Judas kissed his master
And cried 'All hail!' when as he meant all harm.

KING EDWARD
Now am I seated as my soul delights,
Having my country's peace and brothers' loves.

CLARENCE
What will your grace have done with Margaret?
Reignier, her father, to the King of France
Hath pawned the Sicils and Jerusalem,
And hither have they sent it for her ransom.

KING EDWARD
Away with her, and waft her hence to France.   41
And now what rests but that we spend the time
With stately triumphs, mirthful comic shows,   43
Such as befits the pleasure of the court?
Sound drums and trumpets! Farewell sour annoy!
For here I hope begins our lasting joy.   *Exeunt omnes.*

---

45 *night crow* nightjar or owl; *aboding* foreboding 47 *rooked her* squatted
48 *pies* magpies 64 *purple* i.e. bloody 79 *answer* accord with 85 *sort*
seek out (as being befitting); *pitchy* black 86 *buzz* whisper (scandal)
V, vii The royal palace in London 3 *corn* wheat 6 *undoubted* fearless
7 *as* to wit 9 *coursers* war horses 10 *bears* (the bear was the emblem of
the Nevils) 13 *suspicion* apprehension 17 *watched* stayed awake during
21 *laid* laid down (dead) 22 *looked on* respected 25 *thou . . . thou* (he
indicates his head and his arm or shoulder) 29 *seal* pledge 41 *waft* convoy
43 *triumphs* festivities

These charts do not attempt to be complete records of the families included, but they cite all the descendants of Edward III who are of consequence (by presence or parenthood) in these two plays and they mention every person of quality in the two lists of dramatis personae with the exception of the following:

PART TWO

William de la Pole, Duke of Suffolk. Not of royal blood, despite his claim in Part II, IV, i, 50–51.
Lord Say. Sir James Fiennes, Lord Say and Sele, Treasurer of England (d. 1450).
Sir Humphrey Stafford and *William Stafford.* These brothers appear to have been kinsmen of the Earls of Stafford.
Vaux. Presumably Sir William Vaux (d. 1471).
Sir Matthew Gough. A military man, friend of the Lord Scales.

PART THREE

Earl of Pembroke. Sir William Herbert (d. 1469).
Lord Stafford. Sir Humphrey Stafford, Earl of Devon (d. 1469).
Sir John and *Sir Hugh Mortimer.* These brothers are thought to be illegitimate sons of an unidentified Mortimer.
Sir John Montgomery. Called Sir Thomas in Holinshed (d. 1495).
Somervile. Not identified.

In the charts the names of persons in the plays of the two tetralogies are printed in italics. The order of the names does not necessarily indicate the order of birth.

THE LINE OF EDWARD III

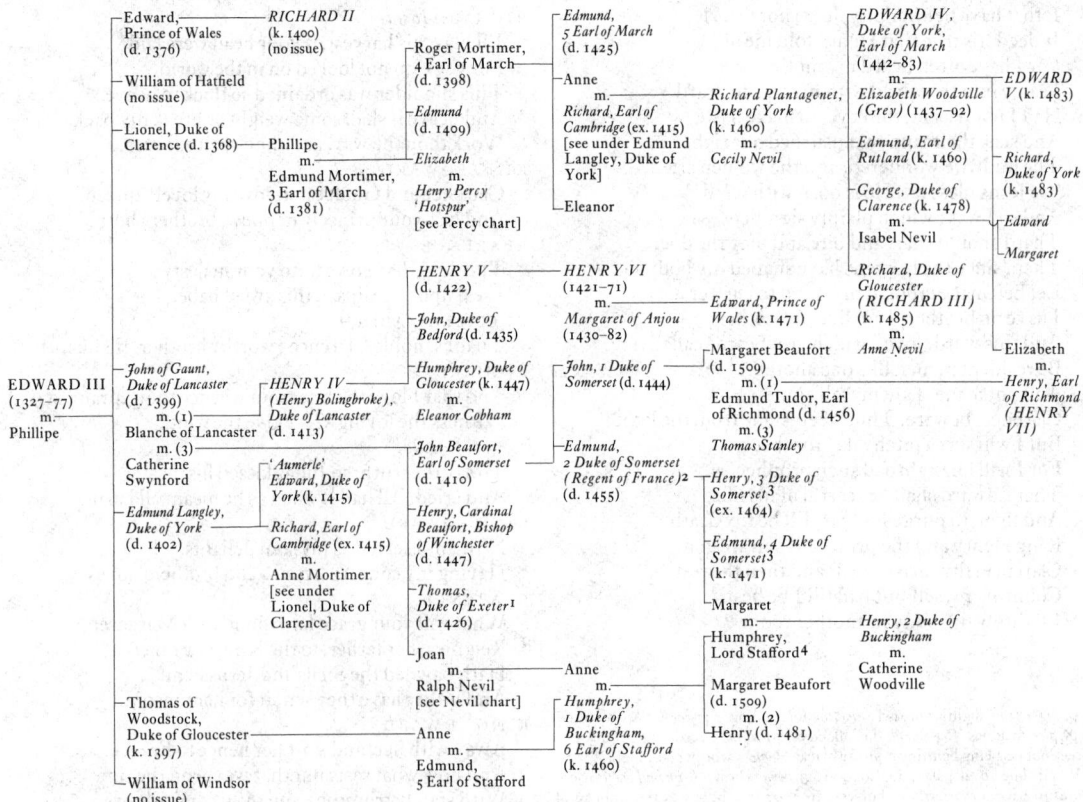

1. Though Thomas died in 1426, Shakespeare has evidently retained him for Part Three.
2. Part Two; Part Three, I, i, 16.
3. Part Three; these have been combined: Henry is in Act IV, Edmund in Act V.
4. Part Three, I, i, 7.

PERCY-NEVIL

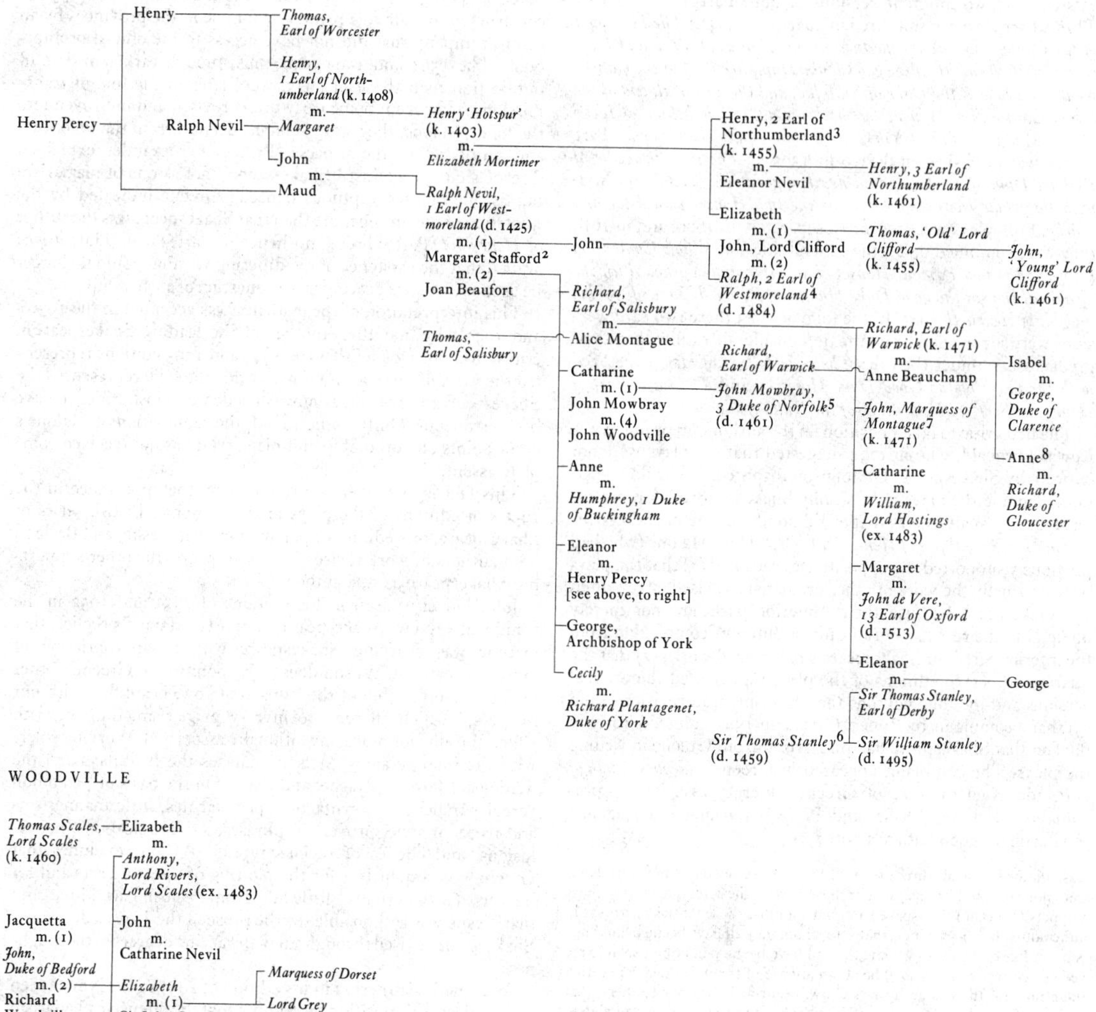

Henry Percy
- Henry
  - Thomas, *Earl of Worcester*
  - *Henry, 1 Earl of Northumberland* (k. 1408)
    m. *Margaret* — Henry 'Hotspur' (k. 1403) m. *Elizabeth Mortimer*
    - Henry, 2 Earl of Northumberland[3] (k. 1455) m. Eleanor Nevil
      - *Henry, 3 Earl of Northumberland* (k. 1461)
    - Elizabeth m. (1) John, Lord Clifford — *Thomas, 'Old' Lord Clifford* (k. 1455) — *John, 'Young' Lord Clifford* (k. 1461)
      m. (2) *Ralph, 2 Earl of Westmoreland*[4] (d. 1484)
- Ralph Nevil
  - John
    m. Maud
  - *Ralph Nevil, 1 Earl of Westmoreland* (d. 1425)
    m. (1) Margaret Stafford[2]
    m. (2) Joan Beaufort
    - *Thomas, Earl of Salisbury*
    - John
    - Richard, *Earl of Salisbury* m. Alice Montague
      - *Richard, Earl of Warwick* — Richard, *Earl of Warwick* (k. 1471) m. Anne Beauchamp
        - Isabel m. *George, Duke of Clarence*
        - Anne[8] m. *Richard, Duke of Gloucester*
      - *John, Marquess of Montague*[7] (k. 1471)
      - Catharine m. *William, Lord Hastings* (ex. 1483)
      - Margaret m. *John de Vere, 13 Earl of Oxford* (d. 1513)
      - Eleanor m. George — *Sir Thomas Stanley, Earl of Derby*
    - Catharine
      m. (1) *John Mowbray, 3 Duke of Norfolk*[5] (d. 1461)
      m. (4) John Woodville
    - Anne
      m. *Humphrey, 1 Duke of Buckingham*
    - Eleanor
      m. Henry Percy [see above, to right]
    - George, Archbishop of York
    - Cecily
      m. *Richard Plantagenet, Duke of York*

Sir Thomas Stanley[6] (d. 1459) — *Sir Thomas Stanley, Earl of Derby* — *Sir William Stanley* (d. 1495)

WOODVILLE

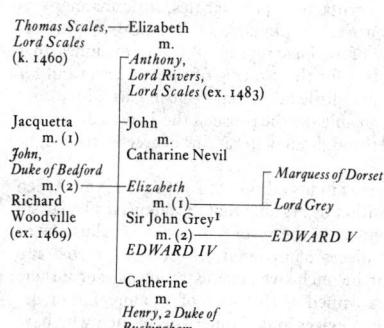

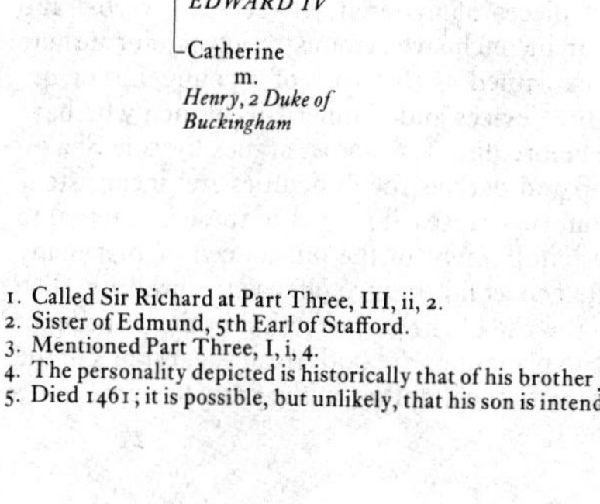

Thomas Scales, Lord Scales (k. 1460) — Elizabeth m. *Anthony, Lord Rivers, Lord Scales* (ex. 1483)

Jacquetta m. (1) *John, Duke of Bedford* m. (2) Richard Woodville (ex. 1469)
- John m. Catharine Nevil
- *Elizabeth* m. (1) Sir John Grey[1] — *Marquess of Dorset* — *Lord Grey* — m. (2) *EDWARD V*
  EDWARD IV
- Catherine m. *Henry, 2 Duke of Buckingham*

---

1. Called Sir Richard at Part Three, III, ii, 2.
2. Sister of Edmund, 5th Earl of Stafford.
3. Mentioned Part Three, I, i, 4.
4. The personality depicted is historically that of his brother John.
5. Died 1461; it is possible, but unlikely, that his son is intended.

6. The guardian of Eleanor Cobham, called John in Part Two.
7. And from 1464 to 1470, Earl of Northumberland.
8. Betrothed to Edward, son of Henry VI, but not married. Shakespeare has reversed the ages of Isabel and Anne.

Among scholars the question of the authorship of *2* and *3 Henry VI* has long been a vexing one. The inclusion of the plays in the folio of 1623 indicates that Heminge and Condell, Shakespeare's friends and fellow-actors who compiled the volume, considered him to have been their author. However, as these same compilers also included at least one play, *Henry VIII*, which is generally admitted to have been written jointly by Shakespeare and John Fletcher, the degree of Shakespeare's involvement in the Henry VI plays is left open. The problem is further complicated by the existence of two different versions of both Part Two and Part Three. Part Two first appeared in quarto in 1594 as *The First part of the Contention betwixt the two famous Houses of York and Lancaster, with the death of the good Duke Humphrey: And the banishment and death of the Duke of Suffolke, and the Tragicall end of the proud Cardinall of Winchester, with the notable Rebellion of Iacke Cade: And the Duke of Yorkes first claime unto the Crowne*; Part Three was published in octavo in 1595 as *The true Tragedie of Richard Duke of Yorke, and the death of good King Henrie the Sixt, with the whole contention betweene the two Houses Lancaster and Yorke*. Both plays were reprinted separately in 1600, and in 1619 they were combined under the general title *The Whole Contention betweene the two Famous Houses, Lancaster and Yorke. With the Tragicall ends of the good Duke Humfrey, Richard Duke of Yorke, and King Henrie the sixt*. In the folio of 1623 these two early versions were superseded by new texts, considerably fuller than their predecessors, under the titles *The second Part of Henry the Sixt, with the death of the Good Duke Humfrey* and *The third Part of Henry the Sixt, with the death of the Duke of Yorke*.

The first critic to take a position on the authorship problem was Lewis Theobald, who in 1734 suggested that the plays were not entirely by Shakespeare. Dr Johnson disputed Theobald's position, claiming the plays to be wholly Shakespearean. A more extensive early analysis was that of Edmond Malone in *A Dissertation on the Three Parts of Henry VI* (1787). Here Malone (who had previously supported the opposite view) argued (1) that the plays were originally the work of other dramatists, revised or rewritten by Shakespeare because their "inferior parts are not merely unequal to the rest ... but of quite a different complexion from the inferior parts" of Shakespeare's recognized work; (2) that the quarto and octavo editions of the plays represented the original versions and the folio editions the Shakespearean revisions; and (3) that a complaint by Robert Greene in 1592 pointed clearly to the fact that Shakespeare had plagiarized from Greene in writing the plays. The complaint appeared in Greene's *Groats-worth of Wit*, addressed to three of Greene's literary associates – presumably Marlowe, Nashe, and Peele – warning them against relying on the good faith of actors:

Base minded men, all three of you, if by my miserie you be not warnd: for unto none of you (like mee) sought those burres [the actors] to cleave: those Puppets (I meane) that spake from our mouths, those Anticks garnisht in our colours. Is it not strange, that I, to whom they all have beene beholding: is it not like that you, to whome they all have beene beholding, shall (were yee in that case as I am now) bee both at once of them forsaken? Yes trust them not: for there is an upstart Crow, beautified with our feathers, that with his *Tygers hart wrapt in a Players hyde*, supposes he is as well able to bombast out a blanke verse as the best of you: and beeing an absolute *Johannes fac totum*, is in his owne conceit the onely Shake-scene in a countrey ... whilest you may, seeke you better Maisters.

Malone interpreted this complaint as Greene's retaliation for the hard treatment that he – an educated man – had received from ignorant and callous players who had made their fortunes by parroting his lines while he lay dying in penury. Greene singled out one player who was so presumptuous as to attempt to write plays and, specifically, to rewrite a play on Henry VI written by Greene himself. This "Shake-scene" was Shakespeare: the "Tygers hart wrapt in a Players hyde" was Greene's parody of Shakespeare's "tiger's heart wrapped in a woman's hide" (*3 Henry VI*, I, iv, 137), a phrase, according to Malone, stolen from Greene.

Malone's view of the evidence, though often questioned, was not supplanted until in 1929 Professor Peter Alexander and in 1930 Miss Madeleine Doran, working independently in Great Britain and America, reached the conclusion that the quarto and octavo editions were not early plays by Greene or others but were versions of the folio texts which had been derived chiefly by actors writing down (or dictating to a scribe) what they could remember of parts they had learned for performances of Shakespeare's plays. The two scholars demonstrated that the 1594 and 1595 editions bore marks regularly accepted as denoting texts memorially reconstructed for sale to a printer or for use in the provinces by an acting company that did not have access to the official promptbook. The 1594 and 1595 texts thus, though earlier in date of publication than those of 1623, were later in the line of transmission; so far from being early drafts revised and improved into the folio versions, they were versions derived from the folio texts and mutilated in the process. Professor Alexander explained Greene's charge against "Shake-scene" not as one of plagiarism but as one of presumptuous conceit; Greene indicated by the quotation of the line no more than that Shakespeare was the author of *Henry VI*, Part Three (and hence of Part Two). Thus it was argued that the existence of the differing versions could no longer be used as evidence bearing on the question of authorship.

This interpretation of the evidence was accepted in the 1930's and 1940's by one after another of the leading Shakespearean critics. Malone's belief that the 1594 and 1595 editions represented the work of Greene and others while the folio represented the Shakespearean revisions is now conceded by most critics to have been erroneous. On the other hand, the repudiation of Malone's other points on authorship and plagiarism has not received complete assent.

This fact is effectively represented by the appearance in the 1950's of editions of the plays in the two chief British series of Shakespeare, one editor supporting Greene, Nashe, and Peele as joint authors of work revised by Shakespeare, the other supporting Shakespeare as sole author.

John Dover Wilson in his editions of 1951 and 1952 in the Cambridge New Shakespeare supports Malone's belief that Greene was charging Shakespeare with misappropriation of Greene's material. Wilson does so by pointing to Greene's other uses of Aesop's fable of the "upstart Crow, beautified with our feathers," which all refer to literary plagiarism, the vice with which the allusion was conventionally associated. Working solely with the folio versions, Wilson analyzes the two plays and the writings of Greene, Nashe, and Peele. On the basis of "common verbal parallels, . . . syntactical peculiarities, little mannerisms and tricks of style, proverbial phrases, . . . classical or other allusions, and clichés of various types," Wilson concludes that Greene was responsible for the plotting of the two Parts and for the verse (with perhaps a little help from Peele in Part Three) and that Nashe was responsible for the prose of the Jack Cade scenes. Shakespeare revised throughout with varying degrees of thoroughness.

Andrew S. Cairncross in his edition of 1957 in the New Arden series rejects this position by arguing that the offensive plagiarism was not wholesale but only the re-use of particular allusions or occasional bits and pieces of material. He sees the verbal and stylistic parallels as an inconclusive demonstration of joint authorship; they can be explained as the work of a young author deliberately copying the devices and mannerisms of men who have practiced the craft before him. Cairncross argues for sole Shakespearean authorship and derives the difficulties and inconsistencies in the plays from two causes. The first of these is external to transmission – the requirement of the official censor that many passages be rewritten so as not to give offense to authority. The second is textual – the use of the early version in the printing of the late. These two explanations are both fresh suggestions in the argument; their evaluation will follow in the years to come.

Both Wilson and Cairncross took for granted Alexander's and Miss Doran's demonstrations of memorial reconstruction as the method of origin of *The Contention* and *The True Tragedy*, but this matter has been recently re-opened by C. T. Prouty, who, in a study of *The Contention and Shakespeare's 2 Henry VI* (1954), argues for a return to Malone's theory of revision. While Prouty's thesis has received little support from other scholars, its very existence proves the continuing uncertainty over the textual history of the plays. And, as if the authorship question were not sufficiently troublesome, there is also disagreement about the date of composition of the two Parts, a matter linked not only with authorship but also with the date of composition of the plays which adjoin them, *1 Henry VI* and *Richard III*.

The Diary of Philip Henslowe, who had financial interests in the Elizabethan theatre, records that in March, 1592, Lord Strange's Men performed a play called *Harey the vj*, and beside the entry is the notation "ne," which presumably means that the play was new and being presented for the first time. Because in the same year Thomas Nashe in *Pierce Pennilesse* referred to a current play featuring the exploits of Talbot, the hero of the wars in France, and because Talbot has a significant role in Shakespeare's *1 Henry VI*, it is tempting to identify *1 Henry VI* with the play mentioned by Nashe as well as with *Harey the vj*. One difficulty with this interpretation of the evidence is that *Harey the vj* definitely belonged to Strange's Men while the other plays in the series belonged to Pembroke's Men, at least at some period in their history. *Harey the vj* may thus have no direct bearing on the problems related to Shakespeare's Henry VI plays, and Nashe's allusion may have been either to a lost *Harey the vj* or to *1 Henry VI*.

The anterior date of the Henry VI plays, it has recently been argued, can be fixed by the registering for publication in December, 1589, of Books I–III of Spenser's *The Faerie Queene*, for *1 Henry VI* shows the influence of this work in several places, and their posterior date by the publication in 1591 of a play called *The Troublesome Raigne of King John*, which seems to draw some of its language from other dramatic works, including *Richard III*, generally agreed to be the last in Shakespeare's series to be written. As Greene died on September 3, 1592, his parody of the line from *3 Henry VI* proves the existence of the play by that date. Within these limits, 1590 has been assigned as the approximate date of composition of both *2* and *3 Henry VI*. There are some, however, who, while willing to accept a date of 1589, 1590, or 1591 for *2* and *3 Henry VI*, feel that *Harey the vj* was probably *1 Henry VI*; if Henslowe's "ne" means "new" in 1592, then it would follow that the plays were not written sequentially but *1 Henry VI* after *2* and *3 Henry VI*, although it may later have been revised to make it fit into the first place in the series. Supporting this line of reasoning is the fact that Talbot, who looms large in *1 Henry VI*, is ignored in *2* and *3*, even being omitted from Gloucester's list of those who suffered in France (*2 Henry VI*, I, i, 78–87).

Although scholars cannot as yet agree on precise dates for *2* and *3 Henry VI*, there is no question of the fact that Shakespeare had a hand in them very early in his career, about the same time as his writing of *Titus Andronicus* and *The Comedy of Errors* and possibly before. There is, moreover, general agreement that even if he was not the sole author of the two history plays, Shakespeare exercised the dominant force in shaping them into their present form, and that he worked on them sequentially and meant them to be considered as related, even though both plays are sufficiently self-contained to be performed separately. Thus we are probably not far off the mark in speaking of them as though their conception and execution were altogether his while silently acknowledging the possibility that he worked from earlier plays.

The present edition is based on the assumption that *The First Part of the Contention* and *The True Tragedie* are versions of the two Parts memorially reconstructed by actors. Hence they possess little authority for the text of the dialogue, but in disclosing details of performance they solve some theatrical problems which seem to have been left by Shakespeare to the discretion of the dramatic

company. Their stage directions have therefore been generously incorporated in square brackets into this text, but where these directions offer a staging clearly not intended by the folio text, they have been ignored.

The folio versions give indications of having been printed from authorial manuscript, and on them the present editions are based. Two brief passages in the folio (Part Two, IV, v, 1 – IV, vi, 6; Part Three, IV, ii, 1–18) would seem to have been printed directly from the quarto versions of 1619, perhaps because the manuscript was illegible. For the present editions, the folio versions have been corrected and emended by reference to the quarto and octavo, and the following lines have been admitted to supply omissions in the folio: Part Two, IV, i, 48; Part Three, II, i, 113; II, vi, 8. The collation of the folio by Mr Charlton Hinman has disclosed three substantive press variants, all in Part Three, V, vii, 25–42; these have been printed in the corrected readings.

The folio preserves in stage directions and speech-prefixes the names of five or six "bit" actors: Part Two, IV, ii, 1–28, the two Rebels are named Bevis and John Holland; IV, vii, 7, 14, the Rebel is named John (see l. 9); IV, vii, 20, the Rebel with the Lord Say is named George (presumably Bevis' Christian name); IV, ii, 99–106, the Messenger is named Michael (possibly an actor's name); Part Three, I, ii, 47 s.d. and 49, the Messenger is named Gabriel (Gabriel Spencer); III, i, the two Keepers are named Sinklo and Humfrey (John Sinklo and Humfrey Jeffes). The present edition substitutes dramatic designations for each of the above in both stage directions and speech-prefixes as indicated in the following list of emendations, which includes all substantive departures from the copy text. The adopted reading in italics is followed by the folio reading in roman.

2 HENRY VI

I, i, 176 *Protector* (Q) Protectors   177, 211 s.d. *Exeunt* (Eds) Exit   254 *in* (F2) in in

I, ii, 37 *Westminster*; (This ed.) Westminster,   40 *diadem* – (This ed.) Diadem.

I, iii, 6 *1. Petitioner* (F4) Peter   13 *For* (Wordsworth) To   29 *master was* (Warburton) Mistresse was   39 s.d. *Exeunt* (Eds) Exit   98 *helm.* (Eds) Helme. Exit.   140 *would* (Q) could

I, iv, 15 *silence* (Q) silent   23 *Asnath* (Cairncross) Asmath   60 *te* (Warburton) Omitted   61 *posse* (Eds) posso

II, i, 48 *Cardinal* (Theobald) Cardinall,   106 *Alban* (F3) Albones   130 *his* (Q) it,

II, ii, 45 *son* (Rowe) Omitted   46 *son* (Theobald) Sonnes Sonne

II, iii, 3 *sins* (Theobald) sinne   30 *helm* (Steevens) Realme

III, i, s.d. (order of entrance in procession is from Q; the order in F is King, Queen, Cardinal, Suffolk, York, Buckingham, Salisbury, Warwick)   211 *strains* (Vaughan) strayes   260 *treasons* (Hudson) Reasons

III, ii, 14 s.d. *Somerset* (Eds) Suffolke, Somerset   26 *Meg* (Capell) Nell   79, 100, 120 *Margaret* (Rowe) Elianor   116 *witch* (Theobald) watch   332 *turn* (Rowe) turnes   385 *sorrow's* (This ed.) sorrowes

IV, i, s.d. (characters other than Lieutenant and Suffolk listed from Q; F reads 'and others')   48 *Jove . . . I?* (Q) Omitted   50 *Suffolk* (before l. 51 in F)   71 *Suffolk* (Alexander) Sir   72 *Lieutenant* (Alexander) Lord   86 mother's bleeding (Rowe) Mother-bleeding   94 *are* (Rowe) and   118 *Paene* (Malone) Pine   133 *Suffolk* (before l. 134 in F)   142 s.d. *Exeunt* (Eds) Exit

IV, ii, s.d. *two Rebels* (This ed.) Bevis, and Iohn Holland   1–28 *1. Rebel, 2. Rebel* (This ed.) Bevis, Hol.   31 *fall* (F4) faile   92 *an* (F2) a   98 s.d., 99, 101, 106 *Messenger* (This ed.) Michael   124 *this :* (Eds) this

IV, iv, 43 *hate* (F2) hateth   58 *be* (F2) Omitted   59 *Say* (Q) Omitted

IV, vi, 11 *Messenger* (This ed.) Dicke

IV, vii, 7, 14 *2. Rebel* (This ed.) Iohn   9 *Weaver* (Cairncross) Smith   20 s.d. *First Rebel* (This ed.) George   63–64 *hands, / But* (Johnson conj.; Rann) hands? / Kent   76 *1. Rebel* (This

ed.) George   82 *caudle* (F4) Candle   *pap with a* (Farmer conj.;
Cairncross) the help of   119 s.d. *two* (Q) one
IV, viii, 12 *rebel* (Singer) rabble
IV, ix, 33 *calmed* (F4) calme
IV, x, 19 *waning* (Rowe) warning   56 *God* (Q) Iove
V, i, 109 *these* (Theobald) thee   111 *sons* (Q) sonne   113 *for* (F2)
of   194 *or* (Rowe) and   196 *Thou* (Cairncross) You   201
house's (F2) housed
V, ii, 28 *oeuvres* (Eds) eumenes
V, iii, 1 *Old* (Q) Of   29 *faith* (Q) hand

3 HENRY VI

I, i, 14 *cousin* (as in O at I, ii, 1, 36, 55) Brother   69 *Exeter* (O)
Westm   83 *and* (F2) Omitted   105 *Thy* (O) My   201 s.d.
(after l. 205 in F)   205 s.d. *Sennet* (followed by 'Here they come
down' in F)   259 *with* (F2) Omitted   261 *from* (O) to
I, ii, 4 *cousin* (as in O at I, ii, 1, 36, 55) Brother   36 *Cousin* (O)
Brother   47 s.d. *a Messenger* (O) Gabriel   49 *Messenger* (O)
Gabriel   55 *cousin* (O) Brother   60 *Cousin* (O) Brother
I, iv, 50 *buckle* (O) buckler
II, i, 113 *And . . . thought* (O) Omitted   131 *an idle* (O) a lazie
II, ii, 89 *Since* (Eds) Cla. Since   116 *sun set* (O) Sunset   133
Richard (O) War
II, iii, 49 *all together* (Rowe) altogether
II, v, 37 *months* (Rowe) yeares   54 s.d. *door* (followed by 'and a
Father that hath kill'd his Sonne at another doore' in F)   78 s.d.
Enter . . . son (replaces 'Enter Father, bearing of his Sonne' in
F)   79 *hast* (F3) hath   119 *Even* (Capell) Men
II, vi, 1 *commixture* (O) Commixtures   8 *The . . . flies* (O) Omitted
42 *Edward* (O) Rich   43 *Richard* (O) Omitted   44 *Edward. See
who it is, and* (Capell) See who it is. / Ed. And   60 *his* (F2) is

III, i, s.d. *two Keepers* (O) Sinklo, and Humfrey   1–97 *1. Keeper,
2. Keeper* (Malone) Sink., Hum.   24 *thee . . . adversity* (Dyce)
the . . . Adversaries   55 *that* (O) Omitted
III, ii, 3 *lands* (O) Land   123 *honorably* (O) honourable
III, iii, 124 *eternal* (O) externall   156 *peace* (F2) Omitted   161 s.d.
(after l. 160 in F)   228 *I'll* (O) I
IV, i, 93 *thy* (O) the
IV, ii, 15 *towns* (Theobald) Towne
IV, iii, s.d. *King Edward's* (Eds) the Kings   59 s.d. (after l. 57 in F)
IV, v, 4 *stands* (F2) stand   8 *Comes* (F2) Come   21 *King Edward*
(Wilson) Omitted   *ship* (F2) shipt
IV, vi, 55 *be* (Malone) Omitted   88 s.d. *Manent* (Eds) Manet
IV, viii, s.d. *Exeter* (Capell) Somerset   6 *Oxford* (O) King
V, i, 78 *an* (Rowe) in
V, iv, 27 *ragged* (Rowe) raged
V, v, 50 *The* (O) Omitted   77 *butcher* (O) butcher Richard
V, vi, s.d. *in the Tower* (O) on the Walles*
V, vii, 5 *renowned* (Rowe) Renowne   25 *and* (corrected F) add
(uncorrected F)   *and thou* (O) and that   27 *kiss* (corrected F)
'tis (uncorrected F)   30 *Queen Elizabeth* (O) Cla   *Thanks* (F3)
Thanke   38 *Reignier* (Rowe) Reynard   42 *rests* (corrected F)
tests (uncorrected F)

---

* Stage directions throughout have indicated the use of the usual facilities
of an Elizabethan stage with the exception of a "discovery" recess. The rear
stage gallery has several times been used to represent the walls of a city, or an
elevated gallery. Only in the present instance does the folio direction locate
the action "on the Walles" when there is no simultaneous and related action
on the stage proper. The location given in the octavo "in the Tower" suggests that this scene, too, was played on the stage proper, with the locale
given in the author's script regarded as literary and not theatrical.

THE TRAGEDY OF
KING RICHARD THE THIRD

INTRODUCTION

From the earliest times *The Tragedy of King Richard the Third* has proved one of Shakespeare's most successful plays in the theatre, but the enthusiasms it arouses are of a different order from, let us say, the enthusiasms we feel for a *Macbeth*. It is in fact Shakespeare's most whole-hearted excursion into melodrama, and a brief comparison with a tragedy like *Macbeth*, in certain surface appearances so similar, in so many vital respects so different, can be revealing. Both Richard and Macbeth fascinate us, but our concern for Richard moves only (with the exception of one brief moment in Act V) on the level of admiration for a kind of virtuoso in evil who satisfies us by being so utterly competent, a creation which wins us, partly in spite of ourselves, by his sheer audacity and enormity. Macbeth, however, wins us simply because he is first of all a man, with the glories, failures, and complexities which that proud title carries with it – "What a piece of work is a man!" Of this feeling there is essentially nothing in *Richard III*. Where then lies the secret of the perennial popularity of the play, next to *Hamlet* the most frequently produced of Shakespeare's plays?

In part the answer lies in the uncomplicated, even obvious nature of the play and its principal characters. They wear their hearts upon their sleeves, and no mystery of the unresolved teases an audience into taking thought. An easy virtue perhaps, but one to be reckoned with, especially when it is combined with immense energy, an energy which pervades not only the central character but the play as a whole. From the Marlowe-like opening soliloquy in which Richard with engaging frankness invites us to watch him play the villain to the famous closing cry – "A horse! a horse! my kingdom for a horse!" – Shakespeare rarely allows the pace to slacken or tensions to relax. In one way this effect of pace is achieved through the ruthless handling of historical time, creating always a sense of the pressure both of the moment and of the threatening future. The pattern or formal structure of the play also furthers the effect of pace. As a structural device, Shakespeare, in defiance of history, has introduced the commanding and ominous old Queen Margaret, who, in her choric role (she is nothing but a voice), evokes the past, lashes the present, and forebodes the future, setting up in her memorable curse scene (I, iii) the pattern through which we watch, with a growing sense of the inevitable, the seemingly inexorable march of events. Other devices, similar in effect to the curse pattern – foreshadowing dreams, oaths sworn only to be broken, continual flashes of rather obvious dramatic irony – serve to give form to the play, as, at the same time, they accelerate and regulate its pace. In this connection, Shakespeare's use of the "dramatic moment" deserves particular attention. Little

episodes or sudden turns are skillfully exploited to bring out the full theatrical potentiality of the larger and dominating pattern of the scene. For example: the brilliant trick by which Richard turns Margaret's curse upon herself (I, iii); the clever device for announcing Clarence's death (II, i); the strawberry scene heralding the fall of Hastings (III, iv); the clock scene (IV, ii); Richard's abortive attempt to drown out the curses of his mother and Queen Elizabeth with trumpet and drum (IV, iv).

As the center of energy in the play stands Richard himself. Professor E. M. W. Tillyard has well remarked that he is Shakespeare's first character to impress himself upon us as being "larger than life." Shakespeare spares him and us nothing, even heightening the already "monstrous" portrait left for us by his political enemies, and leaving us in no doubt about Richard's ultimate responsibility for all the evil in the play. Such focussing and concentration justifies itself in terms of sheer theatrical effectiveness, and Richard pursues evil with a whole-souled quality which almost achieves a kind of inverted moral significance – he works so hard at being the very best kind of villain. In projecting this character Shakespeare was influenced, of course, by the extreme Elizabethan conception of Machiavellian policy. Already in *3 Henry VI* Richard had promised to "set the murderous Machiavel to school" (III, ii, 193) and had flaunted his rejection of all such human weaknesses as "pity, love, nor fear" – "I am myself alone" (V, vi, 68, 83):

> Why, I can smile, and murder whiles I smile,
> And cry 'Content!' to that which grieves my heart,
> And wet my cheeks with artificial tears,
> And frame my face to all occasions....
> I'll play the orator as well as Nestor,
> Deceive more slily than Ulysses could
> And, like a Sinon, take another Troy.
> I can add colors to the chameleon.... (III, ii, 182–91)

Here already is the essential Richard whom Shakespeare presents in the opening lines of *Richard III*: his hypocrisy, his play-acting (cf. *Richard III*, III, v, 1–11), his powers of persuasion, his fox-like slyness (a special attribute of the Machiavellian), above all his virtuosity as a villain. Richard's only virtue is his courage (also granted to him by Shakespeare's sources), though one is tempted to admit his gruesome sense of humor as another. Once only does the audience suffer any real emotional involvement with Richard. When he awakes after the ghostly visitation of his eleven victims, he momentarily exposes himself as a mere man; in place of the brilliant artifact we see a terrified human creature unable to find pity or love in himself even for himself – nothing but fear. It is a moving moment, but to speak of development in Richard's character would be, I think, to set the emphasis in the wrong place and to confuse this play with Shakespearean tragedy. Richard is a static character; he emerges complete at the very beginning and never undergoes any basic change. "I am determinèd to prove a villain," he says, and the play consists largely in our watching breathlessly as he moves from crime to crime keeping his promise to us. Such singleness and simplicity of purpose has, of course, both structural and dramatic value, but we never really allow ourselves to be blinded to the limitations which, like other aspects of this play, it imposes ultimately on the kind of play Shakespeare is writing.

The Tragedy of King Richard the Third, or, as it is perhaps better described in the running titles of the first folio, *The Life and Death of Richard the Third*, may safely be dated between 1591 and 1594. For historical materials Shakespeare turned, as in his other English history plays, to the second edition of Holinshed's *Chronicles* (1587), a compilation drawing heavily, through Hall's *Chronicle* (1550), on the celebrated *Life of Richard the Third* usually attributed to Sir Thomas More and on Polydore Vergil's *Historia Anglica* (1534). A few details may be traced directly to Hall. Both More's *Life* (if indeed More and not Cardinal Morton was the author) and Polydore Vergil's account are savagely anti-Yorkist, and the portrait of Richard which emerges is darkly colored and almost wholly unfavorable. Curiously different is the verdict of many modern historians who tend to equal extremes in rehabilitating Richard. For the average reader, however, Shakespeare has once and for all settled Richard's character – as well try, in the words of a favorite Elizabethan proverb, to wash the Ethiop! In addition to his use of the chronicles, Shakespeare probably owes a few suggestions to an anonymous play, *The True Tragedie of Richard the Third* (printed 1594), and possibly even to the early three-part Latin play *Richardus Tertius* (1579) by Thomas Legge.

An extreme, but not uncharacteristic, example of Shakespeare's dramatic treatment of history may be found in the two opening scenes. In the first, Shakespeare combines events of 1477 (the arrest of Clarence), of 1483 (the reported final sickness of Edward IV), and of 1471 (the projected marriage of Richard with Lady Anne), the last date being underscored by Richard's opening soliloquy which implies the beginning of Edward's reign. This preparation leads directly into the second scene: the funeral procession of the recently dead Henry VI (1471), a situation which is made to serve for the occasion of Richard's triumphantly outrageous wooing of Lady Anne, daughter-in-law of Henry VI and widow of his son, Edward, Prince of Wales, both his victims. Thus with a few bold strokes Shakespeare highhandedly telescopes and confuses the events of thirteen years, reducing them, as it were, to a single moment. With what justification, we may ask. The answer: art and the theatre. With Richard as the center of his play, Shakespeare is most vitally concerned to concentrate on him any situation which can be made to exploit the immediate dramatic potentialities of his character; for this he needs the Clarence affair and the Anne wooing, both nicely calculated to play up different facets of Richard's personality. For the same reason, Edward IV must be relegated to a subordinate role and dismissed from the play with a quick hand. Even as he recognizes all

this and arranges for it, Shakespeare also senses the dramatic advantage of preserving an immediate continuity with *3 Henry VI* by picking up the story where that play had left it – with Richard's murder of Henry VI and the accession of Edward IV. In the place of history, time, and logic Shakespeare gives us a dramatic fiction, a play.

Paradoxically, however, *Richard III* remains very much a "history" play, for Shakespeare is here deeply concerned with political themes: the role of the king, good (Henry) and bad (Richard), with an intermediate type in Edward IV; Richard both as the type of the Scourge of God, working out England's crime in the deposition and murder of Richard II, and as the "unsuccessive" tyrant whom, even under Tudor doctrine, it was righteous to depose; the emergence of the great Tudor dynasty under the newly crowned Lancastrian Henry VII, who by his marriage to the Yorkist Princess Elizabeth was to heal the long-festering wounds of the Wars of the Roses. One must always remember, too, that *Richard III* is the last in a series of eight closely interrelated plays (though at this time only the three parts of *Henry VI* had been written) and that throughout it Shakespeare is careful by reference and allusion (particularly through the figure of old Queen Margaret) to preserve a sense of a larger historical continuity – of the flow of events seen in terms of cause and effect, of a past and a future, as well as of a bare present.

In style and diction *Richard III* belongs markedly to Shakespeare's early serious manner, a manner much influenced by the University playwrights, Marlowe and Greene, sometimes to such a degree that it is difficult to recognize Shakespeare's special idiom. In general the style is more rhetorical than poetic, depending for its effect upon a variety of artificial and cleverly manipulated figures or "flowers of rhetoric." In many ways, of course, it is the perfect instrument for a Richard – witty, hard, and brilliantly efficient, always glancing, parrying, thrusting. This effect comes out most obviously in the rapier-like exchanges (a development of Senecan stichomythia, one of a great many Senecan traces in the play) between Richard and Lady Anne (I, ii) or Richard and Queen Elizabeth (IV, iv). Like so many of the other rhetorical devices in the play, this device depends for its effect on some variety of verbal or structural "repetition": of words within the line to give a turn of thought or play on words, of words or phrases linking line to line, of phrase balanced against phrase, of line against line, of speech against speech. But it must be noticed that although this wrought and overwrought kind of verse sets the dominant stylistic tone and is admirably effective in realizing for us the peculiarly hard-edged, amoral world on the surface of which the characters move, it does not exclude a great deal of stylistic variety even within itself. Moreover, in contrast are the moments of sudden racy colloquialism – like a breath of fresh air – most of which occur in Richard's speeches and lend him a personal turn of speech which we quickly come to recognize as peculiarly a part of him. In this respect, as critics have noticed, he is Shakespeare's first character to possess a "voice" of his own. To this may be added some occasional touches of effective pathos in lines like those at IV, i, 97–103 and the grimly humorous prose of the First and Second Murderers, an early example of Shakespeare's use of comedy to intensify the horror of the moment, here set against a background of what are almost the only imaginatively poetic speeches in the whole play – those in which Clarence relates his dream (I, iv). These and some later speeches of Clarence in the same scene look forward to the kind of poetry with which, a year or two later, Shakespeare endows Richard II and which, in its turn, becomes the perfect medium for expressing the weak, indeterminate, word-drunk king – one, so unlike Richard III, with no capacity for a "world . . . to bustle in."

The Restoration and earlier eighteenth century were temperamentally given to "improving" Shakespeare's plays, and in 1700 Colley Cibber produced his version of *Richard III*. Briefly, Cibber omits Edward IV, Clarence, and Queen Margaret and begins the play just before Richard's murder of Henry VI. The result is a generally tightened-up play which is even more theatrical than Shakespeare's. For roughly a hundred and fifty years Cibber's version, with slight changes, held the stage un-challenged, and Cibber's lines "Off with his head – so much for Buckingham!" and "Conscience avaunt! Richard's himself again!" are often understandably attri-buted to Shakespeare. Even today Cibber is still very much alive. Witness Sir Lawrence Olivier's motion pic-ture version which drew heavily not only on Cibber but on Cibber's "improver," David Garrick! There is perhaps a moral worth pondering here, for Cibber's longevity is unique among the many "improvers" of Shakespearean plays, and *Richard III* is the only Shakespearean play in which we can still tolerate an alien hand.

Harvard University   G. BLAKEMORE EVANS

NOTE ON THE TEXT

Richard III was first printed in quarto form in 1597 from copy evidently representing the communal effort of the acting company to reconstruct the play when deprived of their regular prompt-book. There were seven additional quarto editions, Quarto 6 (1622), after correction against an independent manuscript, pre-sumably serving as copy for the first folio text (1623), except for two sections (III, i, 1–158, and V, iii, 48 to end) which appear to have been set up from an uncorrected copy of Quarto 3 (1602). The textual problem involved is one of the most complex in Shakespeare, and is further discussed in the appendix. The present edition is based on the folio text, with the addition, in square brackets, of about thirty-three lines from the first quarto, the most important group being IV, ii, 97–115. The quartos are undivided into acts and scenes. The folio text is divided, and this division received editorial elaboration: III, iv became III, iv, v, vi, vii; IV, ii became IV, ii, iii; and V, ii became V, ii, iii, iv, v. In the present edition the editorial divisions are indicated margin-ally, but the points where the action is continuous are treated as explained in the general foreword. Stage directions not in the folio are bracketed even though they may appear in the quartos.

THE TRAGEDY OF
KING RICHARD THE THIRD

*

I, i   *Enter Richard, Duke of Gloucester, solus.*

RICHARD
    Now is the winter of our discontent
2 Made glorious summer by this son of York;
    And all the clouds that lowered upon our house
    In the deep bosom of the ocean buried.
    Now are our brows bound with victorious wreaths,
6 Our bruisèd arms hung up for monuments,
7 Our stern alarums changed to merry meetings,
8 Our dreadful marches to delightful measures.
9 Grim-visaged war hath smoothed his wrinklèd front,
10 And now, instead of mounting barbèd steeds
11 To fright the souls of fearful adversaries,
    He capers nimbly in a lady's chamber
13 To the lascivious pleasing of a lute.
    But I, that am not shaped for sportive tricks
    Nor made to court an amorous looking-glass;
    I, that am rudely stamped, and want love's majesty
17 To strut before a wanton ambling nymph;
    I, that am curtailed of this fair proportion,
19 Cheated of feature by dissembling Nature,

Deformed, unfinished, sent before my time
Into this breathing world, scarce half made up,   21
And that so lamely and unfashionable   22
That dogs bark at me as I halt by them –
Why I, in this weak piping time of peace,   24
Have no delight to pass away the time,
Unless to see my shadow in the sun
And descant on mine own deformity.   27
And therefore, since I cannot prove a lover
To entertain these fair well-spoken days,
I am determinèd to prove a villain
And hate the idle pleasures of these days.

I, i A London street 2 *son* (with play on 'sun') 6 *arms* armor; *monuments* memorials 7 *alarums* calls to arms 8 *measures* stately dances 9 *front* forehead 10 *barbèd* armed with protective covering, studded or spiked, on breast and flanks 11 *fearful* timid 13 *lascivious pleasing* seductive charm 17 *ambling* walking affectedly 19 *feature* form of body; *dissembling* deceiving (because my greatness is cloaked by a false appearance) 21 *breathing* living 22 *unfashionable* misshapen (cf. I, ii, 250) 24 *piping* the pipe or recorder was associated with peace, as the fife with war) 27 *descant* compose variations on a simple theme (the speech illustrates this line: the theme, Richard's deformity)

32 Plots have I laid, inductions dangerous,
33 By drunken prophecies, libels, and dreams,
To set my brother Clarence and the king
In deadly hate the one against the other ;
And if King Edward be as true and just
As I am subtle, false, and treacherous,
38 This day should Clarence closely be mewed up
About a prophecy which says that G
Of Edward's heirs the murderer shall be.
Dive, thoughts, down to my soul – here Clarence comes !
Enter Clarence guarded, and Brakenbury
[Lieutenant of the Tower].
Brother, good day. What means this armèd guard
That waits upon your grace ?

CLARENCE   His majesty,
44 Tend'ring my person's safety, hath appointed
45 This conduct to convey me to the Tower.

RICHARD
Upon what cause ?

CLARENCE   Because my name is George.

RICHARD
Alack, my lord, that fault is none of yours :
He should for that commit your godfathers.
49 O, belike his majesty hath some intent
50 That you should be new christ'ned in the Tower.
But what's the matter, Clarence, may I know ?

CLARENCE
Yea, Richard, when I know ; for I protest
As yet I do not. But, as I can learn,
He hearkens after prophecies and dreams,
55 And from the cross-row plucks the letter G,
56 And says a wizard told him that by G
His issue disinherited should be.
And, for my name of George begins with G,
It follows in his thought that I am he.
60 These (as I learn) and suchlike toys as these
Hath moved his highness to commit me now.

RICHARD
Why this it is, when men are ruled by women :
'Tis not the king that sends you to the Tower ;
My Lady Grey his wife, Clarence, 'tis she
65 That tempers him to this extremity.
Was it not she, and that good man of worship,
67 Anthony Woodeville, her brother there,
That made him send Lord Hastings to the Tower,
From whence this present day he is deliverèd ?
We are not safe, Clarence – we are not safe.

CLARENCE
By heaven, I think there is no man is secure
But the queen's kindred, and night-walking heralds   72
That trudge betwixt the king and Mistress Shore.   73
Heard you not what an humble suppliant
Lord Hastings was for his delivery ?

RICHARD
Humbly complaining to her deity
Got my Lord Chamberlain his liberty.
I'll tell you what, I think it is our way,
If we will keep in favor with the king,
To be her men and wear her livery.
The jealous o'erworn widow and herself,   81
Since that our brother dubbed them gentlewomen,   82
Are mighty gossips in our monarchy.   83

BRAKENBURY
I beseech your graces both to pardon me :
His majesty hath straitly given in charge   85
That no man shall have private conference
(Of what degree soever) with your brother.

RICHARD
Even so ? An please your worship, Brakenbury,   88
You may partake of anything we say.
We speak no treason, man. We say the king
Is wise and virtuous, and his noble queen
Well struck in years, fair, and not jealous.   92
We say that Shore's wife hath a pretty foot,
A cherry lip, a bonny eye, a passing pleasing tongue ;
And that the queen's kindred are made gentlefolks.
How say you, sir ? Can you deny all this ?

BRAKENBURY
With this, my lord, myself have nought to do.   97

RICHARD
Naught to do with Mistress Shore ? I tell thee, fellow,
He that doth naught with her (excepting one)   99
Were best to do it secretly alone.

BRAKENBURY
What one, my lord ?

RICHARD
Her husband, knave. Wouldst thou betray me ?

BRAKENBURY
I do beseech your grace to pardon me, and withal   103
Forbear your conference with the noble duke.

CLARENCE
We know thy charge, Brakenbury, and will obey.

RICHARD
We are the queen's abjects, and must obey.   106
Brother, farewell. I will unto the king ;
And whatsoe'er you will employ me in,
Were it to call King Edward's widow sister,
I will perform it to enfranchise you.   110
Meantime, this deep disgrace in brotherhood   111
Touches me deeper than you can imagine.

CLARENCE
I know it pleaseth neither of us well.

RICHARD
Well, your imprisonment shall not be long :
I will deliver you, or else lie for you.   115
Meantime, have patience.

CLARENCE   I must perforce. Farewell.   116
Exit Clarence [with Brakenbury and Guard].

RICHARD
Go, tread the path that thou shalt ne'er return :
Simple plain Clarence, I do love thee so

32 *inductions* initial plans   33 *drunken prophecies* prophecies uttered under the influence of drink   38 *mewed up* imprisoned (cf. l. 132)   44 *Tend'ring* being concerned for (irony)   45 *conduct* escort; *convey* conduct (with play on 'steal'); *Tower* the Tower of London (frequently used as a prison)   49 *belike* probably   50 *new christ'ned* (anticipates, ironically, Clarence's drowning in I, iv)   55 *cross-row* alphabet   56 *wizard* wise man or male witch   60 *toys* trifles, fancies   65 *tempers* moulds   67 *Woodeville* i.e. Earl Rivers (trisyllabic)   72 *night-walking heralds* i.e. secret messengers (agents of assignation)   73 *Mistress Shore* i.e. Jane Shore, mistress of Edward IV ('mistress,' however, was regularly applied to any woman, married or unmarried, as a title of respect)   81 *widow* i.e. Queen Elizabeth (cf. l. 109)   82 *dubbed* knighted (a malicious pairing of Queen Elizabeth and Mistress Shore entirely without basis)   83 *gossips* (people, traditionally, with a lot to say)   85 *straitly* strictly   88 *An* if   92 *Well struck in years* (a politic way of saying 'old')   97 *nought* nothing   99 *naught* i.e. the sexual act   103 *withal* at the same time   106 *abjects* most servile subjects (with play on 'outcasts')   110 *enfranchise* release from confinement   111–12 *disgrace . . . imagine* (with an obvious double meaning)   115 *lie for* go to prison in place of (with play on 'tell lies about')   116 *perforce* of necessity

That I will shortly send thy soul to heaven,
If heaven will take the present at our hands.
But who comes here? The new-deliverèd Hastings?
    Enter Lord Hastings.

HASTINGS
Good time of day unto my gracious lord.

RICHARD
As much unto my good Lord Chamberlain.
Well are you welcome to the open air.
125 How hath your lordship brooked imprisonment?

HASTINGS
With patience, noble lord, as prisoners must;
But I shall live, my lord, to give them thanks
That were the cause of my imprisonment.

RICHARD
No doubt, no doubt; and so shall Clarence too,
For they that were your enemies are his
And have prevailed as much on him as you.

HASTINGS
More pity that the eagles should be mewed,
Whiles kites and buzzards prey at liberty.

RICHARD
What news abroad?

HASTINGS
No news so bad abroad as this at home:
The king is sickly, weak, and melancholy,
And his physicians fear him mightily.

RICHARD
Now, by Saint John, that news is bad indeed!
O, he hath kept an evil diet long
140 And overmuch consumed his royal person:
'Tis very grievous to be thought upon.
Where is he? In his bed?

HASTINGS He is.

RICHARD
Go you before, and I will follow you.   *Exit Hastings.*
He cannot live, I hope, and must not die
146 Till George be packed with posthorse up to heaven.
147 I'll in, to urge his hatred more to Clarence
148 With lies well steeled with weighty arguments;
And, if I fail not in my deep intent,
Clarence hath not another day to live:
Which done, God take King Edward to his mercy
And leave the world for me to bustle in!
153 For then I'll marry Warwick's youngest daughter.
What though I killed her husband and her father?
The readiest way to make the wench amends
Is to become her husband and her father:
The which will I – not all so much for love
158 As for another secret close intent
By marrying her which I must reach unto.
But yet I run before my horse to market:
Clarence still breathes; Edward still lives and reigns;
When they are gone, then must I count my gains.   *Exit.*

*

I, ii   *Enter the corse of Henry the Sixth, with Halberds to*
    guard it; Lady Anne being the mourner [attended
    by Tressel and Berkeley].

ANNE
Set down, set down your honorable load –
If honor may be shrouded in a hearse –
3 Whilst I awhile obsequiously lament

Th' untimely fall of virtuous Lancaster.
    [The Bearers set down the hearse.]
Poor key-cold figure of a holy king,   5
Pale ashes of the house of Lancaster,
Thou bloodless remnant of that royal blood,
Be it lawful that I invocate thy ghost
To hear the lamentations of poor Anne,
Wife to thy Edward, to thy slaught'red son
Stabbed by the selfsame hand that made these wounds!
Lo, in these windows that let forth thy life
I pour the helpless balm of my poor eyes.   13
O, cursèd be the hand that made these holes!
Cursèd the heart that had the heart to do it!
Cursèd the blood that let this blood from hence!
More direful hap betide that hated wretch   17
That makes us wretched by the death of thee
Than I can wish to wolves – to spiders, toads,
Or any creeping venomed thing that lives!
If ever he have child, abortive be it,
Prodigious, and untimely brought to light,   22
Whose ugly and unnatural aspect
May fright the hopeful mother at the view,
And that be heir to his unhappiness!   25
If ever he have wife, let her be made
More miserable by the life of him
Than I am made by my young lord and thee!
Come, now towards Chertsey with your holy load,   29
Taken from Paul's to be interrèd there.   30
    [The Bearers take up the hearse.]
And still, as you are weary of this weight,   31
Rest you, whiles I lament King Henry's corse.   32
    Enter Richard, Duke of Gloucester.

RICHARD
Stay, you that bear the corse, and set it down.

ANNE
What black magician conjures up this fiend
To stop devoted charitable deeds?   35

RICHARD
Villains, set down the corse, or, by Saint Paul,
I'll make a corse of him that disobeys!

GENTLEMAN
My lord, stand back, and let the coffin pass.

RICHARD
Unmannered dog! Stand thou, when I command!   39
Advance thy halberd higher than my breast,   40
Or, by Saint Paul, I'll strike thee to my foot
And spurn upon thee, beggar, for thy boldness.   42
    [The Bearers set down the hearse.]

ANNE
What, do you tremble? Are you all afraid?
Alas, I blame you not, for you are mortal,

---

125 *brooked* tolerated   146 *with posthorse* (figuratively, the quickest way) 147 *urge . . . to* incite his anger more against   148 *steeled* strengthened as with iron   153 *Warwick's youngest daughter* i.e. Lady Anne, widow of Prince Edward   158 *secret close intent* (Richard, aiming at the throne, schemes to ally himself with the line of Lancaster as a useful preliminary move)
I, ii The same   s.d. *corse* corpse; *Halberds* halberdiers (guards, carrying halberds; see l. 40 below)   3 *obsequiously* in a manner fitting a funeral   5 *key-cold* very cold (as a metal key)   13 *helpless* affording no help   17 *hap betide* fortune befall   22 *Prodigious* unnatural, monstrous   25 *unhappiness* innate evil   29 *Chertsey* the monastery of Chertsey near London   30 *Paul's* St Paul's Cathedral, London   31 *still, as* whenever   32 *whiles I lament* during which time I will lament   35 *devoted* sacred   39 *Stand* halt 40 *Advance . . . breast* raise your halberd (a long-handled poleaxe with a pike attached) to upright position   42 *spurn upon* stamp under foot

And mortal eyes cannot endure the devil.
Avaunt, thou dreadful minister of hell!
Thou hadst but power over his mortal body;
His soul thou canst not have. Therefore, be gone.

RICHARD

49   Sweet saint, for charity, be not so curst.

ANNE

Foul devil, for God's sake hence, and trouble us not,
51   For thou hast made the happy earth thy hell,
Filled it with cursing cries and deep exclaims.
If thou delight to view thy heinous deeds,
54   Behold this pattern of thy butcheries.
O gentlemen, see! See dead Henry's wounds
56   Open their congealed mouths and bleed afresh!
Blush, blush, thou lump of foul deformity;
58   For 'tis thy presence that exhales this blood
From cold and empty veins where no blood dwells.
Thy deeds inhuman and unnatural
Provokes this deluge most unnatural.
O God, which this blood mad'st, revenge his death!
O earth, which this blood drink'st, revenge his death!
Either heav'n with lightning strike the murd'rer dead;
65   Or earth gape open wide and eat him quick,
As thou dost swallow up this good king's blood
Which his hell-governed arm hath butcherèd!

RICHARD

Lady, you know no rules of charity,
Which renders good for bad, blessings for curses.

ANNE

Villain, thou know'st nor law of God nor man:
No beast so fierce but knows some touch of pity.

RICHARD

But I know none, and therefore am no beast.

ANNE

O wonderful, when devils tell the truth!

RICHARD

More wonderful, when angels are so angry.
Vouchsafe, divine perfection of a woman,
Of these supposèd crimes to give me leave
By circumstance but to acquit myself.

ANNE

78   Vouchsafe, diffused infection of a man,
Of these known evils, but to give me leave
By circumstance t' accuse thy cursèd self.

RICHARD

Fairer than tongue can name thee, let me have
Some patient leisure to excuse myself.

ANNE

Fouler than heart can think thee, thou canst make
84   No excuse current but to hang thyself.

RICHARD

By such despair I should accuse myself.

ANNE

And by despairing shalt thou stand excusèd
For doing worthy vengeance on thyself
That didst unworthy slaughter upon others.

RICHARD

Say that I slew them not?

ANNE   Then say they were not slain.
But dead they are, and, devilish slave, by thee.

RICHARD

I did not kill your husband.

ANNE   Why, then he is alive.

RICHARD

Nay, he is dead, and slain by Edward's hands.

ANNE

In thy foul throat thou li'st! Queen Margaret saw
Thy murd'rous falchion smoking in his blood;
The which thou once didst bend against her breast,   94
But that thy brothers beat aside the point.

RICHARD

I was provokèd by her sland'rous tongue
That laid their guilt upon my guiltless shoulders.

ANNE

Thou wast provokèd by thy bloody mind
That never dream'st on aught but butcheries.
Didst thou not kill this king?

RICHARD   I grant ye.

ANNE

Dost grant me, hedgehog? Then God grant me too
Thou mayst be damnèd for that wicked deed!
O, he was gentle, mild, and virtuous!

RICHARD

The better for the King of Heaven that hath him.

ANNE

He is in heaven, where thou shalt never come.

RICHARD

Let him thank me that holp to send him thither;   107
For he was fitter for that place than earth.

ANNE

And thou unfit for any place, but hell.

RICHARD

Yes, one place else, if you will hear me name it.

ANNE

Some dungeon.

RICHARD   Your bedchamber.

ANNE

Ill rest betide the chamber where thou liest!

RICHARD

So will it, madam, till I lie with you.

ANNE

I hope so.

RICHARD   I know so. But, gentle Lady Anne,
To leave this keen encounter of our wits
And fall something into a slower method –
Is not the causer of the timeless deaths
Of these Plantagenets, Henry and Edward,   117
As blameful as the executioner?

ANNE

Thou wast the cause and most accursed effect.   120

RICHARD

Your beauty was the cause of that effect –
Your beauty, that did haunt me in my sleep
To undertake the death of all the world,
So I might live one hour in your sweet bosom.

ANNE

If I thought that, I tell thee, homicide,   125
These nails should rent that beauty from my cheeks.

RICHARD

These eyes could not endure that beauty's wrack;   127

---

49 *curst* shrewish   51 *happy* naturally pleasant   54 *pattern* example   56
bleed afresh (in popular belief the wounds of a murdered man bled in the
presence of the murderer)   58 *exhales* draws out   65 *quick* alive   78
diffused infection shapeless plague (more for sound than sense; cf. l. 75)   84
current authentic or acceptable   94 *falchion* slightly hooked sword   107 *holp*
helped   117 *timeless* untimely   120 *effect* i.e. executioner (l. 119) or efficient
agent   125 *homicide* murderer   127 *wrack* ruin

You should not blemish it, if I stood by :
As all the world is cheerèd by the sun,
So I by that. It is my day, my life.

ANNE
Black night o'ershade thy day, and death thy life !

RICHARD
Curse not thyself, fair creature – thou art both.

ANNE
I would I were, to be revenged on thee.

RICHARD
It is a quarrel most unnatural,
To be revenged on him that loveth thee.

ANNE
It is a quarrel just and reasonable,
To be revenged on him that killed my husband.

RICHARD
He that bereft thee, lady, of thy husband,
Did it to help thee to a better husband.

ANNE
140   His better doth not breathe upon the earth.

RICHARD
He lives, that loves thee better than he could.

ANNE
Name him.

RICHARD   Plantagenet.

ANNE   Why that was he.

RICHARD
The selfsame name, but one of better nature.

ANNE
Where is he ?

RICHARD   Here.
          [She] spits at him. Why dost thou spit at me ?

ANNE
Would it were mortal poison for thy sake !

RICHARD
Never came poison from so sweet a place.

ANNE
147   Never hung poison on a fouler toad.
Out of my sight ! Thou dost infect mine eyes.

RICHARD
149   Thine eyes, sweet lady, have infected mine.

ANNE
150   Would they were basilisks to strike thee dead !

RICHARD
151   I would they were, that I might die at once ;
For now they kill me with a living death.
Those eyes of thine from mine have drawn salt tears,
154   Shamed their aspects with store of childish drops :
These eyes, which never shed remorseful tear –
No, when my father York and Edward wept
To hear the piteous moan that Rutland made
158   When black-faced Clifford shook his sword at him ;
159   Nor when thy warlike father, like a child,
Told the sad story of my father's death
And twenty times made pause to sob and weep,
That all the standers-by had wet their cheeks
Like trees bedashed with rain – in that sad time
My manly eyes did scorn an humble tear ;
And what these sorrows could not thence exhale,
Thy beauty hath, and made them blind with weeping.
I never sued to friend nor enemy ;
168   My tongue could never learn sweet smoothing word ;
But, now thy beauty is proposed my fee,
My proud heart sues, and prompts my tongue to speak.

She looks scornfully at him.
Teach not thy lip such scorn ; for it was made
For kissing, lady, not for such contempt.
If thy revengeful heart cannot forgive,
Lo, here I lend thee this sharp-pointed sword,
Which if thou please to hide in this true breast
And let the soul forth that adoreth thee,
I lay it naked to the deadly stroke   177
And humbly beg the death upon my knee.
     He lays his breast open. She offers at [it] with his
     sword.
Nay, do not pause : for I did kill King Henry –
But 'twas thy beauty that provokèd me.
Nay, now dispatch : 'twas I that stabbed young Edward –
But 'twas thy heavenly face that set me on.   182
     She falls the sword.
Take up the sword again, or take up me.

ANNE
Arise, dissembler : though I wish thy death,
I will not be thy executioner.

RICHARD
Then bid me kill myself, and I will do it.

ANNE
I have already.

RICHARD   That was in thy rage :
Speak it again, and even with the word
This hand, which for thy love did kill thy love,
Shall for thy love kill a far truer love ;
To both their deaths shalt thou be accessary.   191

ANNE
I would I knew thy heart.

RICHARD
'Tis figured in my tongue.

ANNE
I fear me both are false.

RICHARD
Then never was man true.

ANNE
Well, well, put up your sword.

RICHARD
Say then my peace is made.

ANNE
That shalt thou know hereafter.

RICHARD
But shall I live in hope ?

ANNE
All men, I hope, live so.

[RICHARD]
Vouchsafe to wear this ring.

[ANNE]
To take is not to give.]
     [Richard slips the ring on her finger.]

RICHARD
Look how my ring encompasseth thy finger,
Even so thy breast encloseth my poor heart :
Wear both of them, for both of them are thine.

---

147 *poison . . . toad* (toads were considered venomous)   149 *eyes . . . mine*
(the eyes were believed to be the entry-ports of love)   150 *basilisks* fabulous
reptiles capable of killing with a look   151 *at once* once and for all   154
aspects glances   158 *black-faced* gloomy, evilly portentous   159 *thy . . . father*
i.e. Richard Nevil, Earl of Warwick, known as the 'King-maker'   168
smoothing flattering   177 *naked* (1) bare, (2) unarmed   182 **s.d.** *falls* drops
191 *accessary* acceding

206 And if thy poor devoted servant may
But beg one favor at thy gracious hand,
Thou dost confirm his happiness for ever.

ANNE What is it?

RICHARD
That it may please you leave these sad designs
To him that hath most cause to be a mourner,
212 And presently repair to Crosby House;
Where – after I have solemnly interred
At Chertsey monast'ry this noble king
And wet his grave with my repentant tears –
216 I will with all expedient duty see you.
217 For divers unknown reasons I beseech you,
Grant me this boon.

ANNE
With all my heart; and much it joys me too
To see you are become so penitent.
Tressel and Berkeley, go along with me.

RICHARD
Bid me farewell.

222 ANNE 'Tis more than you deserve;
But since you teach me how to flatter you,
Imagine I have said farewell already.
Exeunt two [Tressel and Berkeley], with Anne.

[RICHARD
Sirs, take up the corse.]

GENTLEMAN Towards Chertsey, noble lord?

RICHARD
226 No, to Whitefriars – there attend my coming.
Exit [Guard with Bearers and] corse.
Was ever woman in this humor wooed?
Was ever woman in this humor won?
I'll have her, but I will not keep her long.
What? I that killed her husband and his father
To take her in her heart's extremest hate,
With curses in her mouth, tears in her eyes,
The bleeding witness of my hatred by,
Having God, her conscience, and these bars against me,
And I no friends to back my suit at all
But the plain devil and dissembling looks?
237 And yet to win her! All the world to nothing!
Ha!
Hath she forgot already that brave prince,
Edward, her lord, whom I, some three months since,
241 Stabbed in my angry mood at Tewkesbury?
A sweeter and a lovelier gentleman,
243 Framed in the prodigality of nature –
Young, valiant, wise, and (no doubt) right royal –
The spacious world cannot again afford;
246 And will she yet abase her eyes on me,

That cropped the golden prime of this sweet prince 247
And made her widow to a woeful bed?
On me, whose all not equals Edward's moi'ty? 249
On me, that halts and am misshapen thus?
My dukedom to a beggarly denier, 251
I do mistake my person all this while!
Upon my life, she finds (although I cannot)
Myself to be a marv'llous proper man. 254
I'll be at charges for a looking-glass 255
And entertain a score or two of tailors
To study fashions to adorn my body:
Since I am crept in favor with myself,
I will maintain it with some little cost.
But first I'll turn yon fellow in his grave, 260
And then return lamenting to my love.
Shine out, fair sun, till I have bought a glass,
That I may see my shadow as I pass. *Exit.*

*

Enter the Queen Mother [Elizabeth], Lord Rivers, I, iii
[Marquess of Dorset,] and Lord Grey.

RIVERS
Have patience, madam; there's no doubt his majesty
Will soon recover his accustomed health.

GREY
In that you brook it ill, it makes him worse: 3
Therefore for God's sake entertain good comfort
And cheer his grace with quick and merry eyes.

QUEEN ELIZABETH
If he were dead, what would betide on me? 6

GREY
No other harm but loss of such a lord.

QUEEN ELIZABETH
The loss of such a lord includes all harms.

GREY
The heavens have blessed you with a goodly son
To be your comforter when he is gone.

QUEEN ELIZABETH
Ah, he is young; and his minority
Is put unto the trust of Richard Gloucester,
A man that loves not me, nor none of you.

RIVERS
Is it concluded he shall be Protector?

QUEEN ELIZABETH
It is determined, not concluded yet: 15
But so it must be, if the king miscarry.
Enter Buckingham and [Stanley, Earl of] Derby.

GREY
Here come the lords of Buckingham and Derby.

BUCKINGHAM
Good time of day unto your royal grace!

DERBY
God make your majesty joyful, as you have been!

QUEEN ELIZABETH
The Countess Richmond, good my Lord of Derby, 20
To your good prayer will scarcely say 'Amen.'
Yet, Derby, notwithstanding she's your wife
And loves not me, be you, good lord, assured
I hate not you for her proud arrogance.

DERBY
I do beseech you, either not believe
The envious slanders of her false accusers;

---

206 *servant* (1) one in subjection, (2) lover 212 *presently* at once; *Crosby House* (Richard's center of operations) 216 *expedient* speedy 217 *unknown* secret 222 *'Tis . . . deserve* i.e. to fare well is more than you deserve 226 *Whitefriars* a Carmelite priory, south of Fleet Street, London 237 *All . . . nothing* all odds against me 241 *Tewkesbury* (scene of the battle in which the Lancastrians were finally defeated and Prince Edward killed) 243 *prodigality* profuseness 246 *abase* cast down or make base 247 *cropped . . . prince* i.e. cut him off in the flower of youth 249 *moi'ty* half 251 *denier* copper coin, twelfth of a sou (dissyllabic) 254 *marv'llous proper* wonderfully handsome 255 *at charges for* at the expense of 260 *in* into
I, iii The royal palace 3 *brook* endure 6 *betide* on happen to 15 *determined, not concluded* resolved, not officially decreed 20 *Countess Richmond* mother of the Earl of Richmond (later Henry VII), now wife of Lord Stanley, Earl of Derby

Or, if she be accused on true report,
Bear with her weakness, which I think proceeds
29   From wayward sickness, and no grounded malice.

QUEEN ELIZABETH
Saw you the king to-day, my Lord of Derby?

DERBY
31   But now the Duke of Buckingham and I
Are come from visiting his majesty.

QUEEN ELIZABETH
What likelihood of his amendment, lords?

BUCKINGHAM
Madam, good hope; his grace speaks cheerfully.

QUEEN ELIZABETH
God grant him health! Did you confer with him?

BUCKINGHAM
36   Ay, madam: he desires to make atonement
Between the Duke of Gloucester and your brothers,
And between them and my Lord Chamberlain,
And sent to warn them to his royal presence.

QUEEN ELIZABETH
Would all were well! but that will never be:
41   I fear our happiness is at the height.
Enter Richard [and Lord Hastings].

RICHARD
They do me wrong, and I will not endure it!
Who is it that complains unto the king
That I (forsooth) am stern, and love them not?
By holy Paul, they love his grace but lightly
That fill his ears with such dissentious rumors.
Because I cannot flatter and look fair,
48   Smile in men's faces, smooth, deceive, and cog,
49   Duck with French nods and apish courtesy,
I must be held a rancorous enemy.
Cannot a plain man live and think no harm,
But thus his simple truth must be abused
53   With silken, sly, insinuating Jacks?

GREY
To who in all this presence speaks your grace?

RICHARD
55   To thee, that hast nor honesty nor grace:
When have I injured thee? when done thee wrong?
Or thee? or thee? or any of your faction?
A plague upon you all! His royal grace
(Whom God preserve better than you would wish!)
60   Cannot be quiet scarce a breathing while
61   But you must trouble him with lewd complaints.

QUEEN ELIZABETH
Brother of Gloucester, you mistake the matter:
63   The king, on his own royal disposition,
And not provoked by any suitor else,
Aiming (belike) at your interior hatred,
That in your outward action shows itself
Against my children, brothers, and myself,
Makes him to send, that he may learn the ground.

RICHARD
I cannot tell: the world is grown so bad
That wrens make prey where eagles dare not perch.
Since every Jack became a gentleman,
There's many a gentle person made a Jack.

QUEEN ELIZABETH
Come, come, we know your meaning, brother
    Gloucester:
You envy my advancement and my friends'.
God grant we never may have need of you!

RICHARD
Meantime, God grants that I have need of you.
Our brother is imprisoned by your means,
Myself disgraced, and the nobility
Held in contempt, while great promotions
Are daily given to ennoble those
That scarce, some two days since, were worth a noble.   81

QUEEN ELIZABETH
By Him that raised me to this careful height   82
From that contented hap which I enjoyed,   83
I never did incense his majesty
Against the Duke of Clarence, but have been
An earnest advocate to plead for him.
My lord, you do me shameful injury
Falsely to draw me in these vile suspects.   88

RICHARD
You may deny that you were not the mean
Of my Lord Hastings' late imprisonment.

RIVERS
She may, my lord, for –

RICHARD
She may, Lord Rivers! why, who knows not so?
She may do more, sir, than denying that:
She may help you to many fair preferments,
And then deny her aiding hand therein
And lay those honors on your high desert.
What may she not? She may – ay, marry, may she –   97

RIVERS
What, marry, may she?

RICHARD
What, marry, may she? Marry with a king,
A bachelor and a handsome stripling too:
Iwis your grandam had a worser match.   101

QUEEN ELIZABETH
My Lord of Gloucester, I have too long borne
Your blunt upbraidings and your bitter scoffs:
By heaven, I will acquaint his majesty
Of those gross taunts that oft I have endured.
I had rather be a country servant maid
Than a great queen with this condition,
To be so baited, scorned, and stormèd at: 108
Enter old Queen Margaret [behind].
Small joy have I in being England's queen.

QUEEN MARGARET *[aside]*
And less'ned be that small, God I beseech him!
Thy honor, state, and seat is due to me.   111

RICHARD
What? Threat you me with telling of the king?
[Tell him, and spare not. Look, what I have said]
I will avouch't in presence of the king:
I dare adventure to be sent to th' Tow'r.
'Tis time to speak: my pains are quite forgot.   116

---

29 *wayward sickness* illness not yielding readily to treatment   31 *But now* just now   36 *atonement* reconciliation   41 *happiness . . . height* good fortune has reached its peak (any further movement of the wheel of fortune will be down)   48 *smooth* flatter; *cog* cheat   49 *French nods* affected salutations   53 *Jacks* low-bred, worthless fellows (with play on French *Jacques*)   55 *grace* sense of duty or virtue (with play on the title *your grace*, l. 54)   60 *breathing while* i.e. long enough to catch his breath   61 *lewd* wicked   63–68 *The king . . . send* (syntax confused; for 'Makes him to send' understand 'sends')   63 *disposition* inclination   81 *noble* (1) gold coin, worth 6s. 8d., (2) nobleman   82 *careful* full of anxiety   83 *hap* fortune   88 *in* into; *suspects* suspicions   97 *marry* indeed (with play on 'wed')   101 *Iwis* certainly   108 *baited* harassed   111 *state* high rank (as queen); *seat* throne   116 *pains* efforts on his behalf

QUEEN MARGARET [aside]
    Out, devil! I do remember them too well:
    Thou kill'dst my husband Henry in the Tower,
    And Edward, my poor son, at Tewkesbury.

RICHARD
    Ere you were queen, ay, or your husband king,
121 I was a packhorse in his great affairs;
    A weeder-out of his proud adversaries,
    A liberal rewarder of his friends:
    To royalize his blood I spent mine own.

QUEEN MARGARET [aside]
    Ay, and much better blood than his or thine.

RICHARD
126 In all which time you and your husband Grey
    Were factious for the house of Lancaster;
    And, Rivers, so were you. Was not your husband
    In Margaret's battle at Saint Albans slain?
    Let me put in your minds, if you forget,
    What you have been ere this, and what you are;
    Withal, what I have been, and what I am.

QUEEN MARGARET [aside]
    A murd'rous villain, and so still thou art.

RICHARD
134 Poor Clarence did forsake his father, Warwick;
    Ay, and forswore himself (which Jesu pardon!) –

QUEEN MARGARET [aside]
    Which God revenge!

RICHARD
    To fight on Edward's party for the crown;
138 And for his meed, poor lord, he is mewèd up.
    I would to God my heart were flint like Edward's,
    Or Edward's soft and pitiful like mine:
    I am too childish-foolish for this world.

QUEEN MARGARET [aside]
    Hie thee to hell for shame, and leave this world,
143 Thou cacodemon! there thy kingdom is.

RIVERS
    My Lord of Gloucester, in those busy days
    Which here you urge to prove us enemies,
    We followed then our lord, our sovereign king.
    So should we you, if you should be our king.

RICHARD
    If I should be? I had rather be a pedlar:
    Far be it from my heart, the thought thereof!

QUEEN ELIZABETH
    As little joy, my lord, as you suppose
    You should enjoy, were you this country's king –
    As little joy you may suppose in me
    That I enjoy, being the queen thereof.

QUEEN MARGARET [aside]
    A little joy enjoys the queen thereof;
    For I am she, and altogether joyless.
    I can no longer hold me patient.
       [Comes forward.]

Hear me, you wrangling pirates, that fall out
In sharing that which you have pilled from me! 158
Which of you trembles not that looks on me?
If not, that I am queen, you bow like subjects, 160
Yet that, by you deposed, you quake like rebels?
Ah, gentle villain, do not turn away!

RICHARD
Foul wrinklèd witch, what mak'st thou in my sight? 163

QUEEN MARGARET
But repetition of what thou hast marred:
That will I make before I let thee go.

RICHARD
Wert thou not banishèd on pain of death?

QUEEN MARGARET
I was; but I do find more pain in banishment
Than death can yield me here by my abode.
A husband and a son thou ow'st to me –
And thou a kingdom – all of you allegiance.
This sorrow that I have, by right is yours,
And all the pleasures you usurp are mine.

RICHARD
The curse my noble father laid on thee 173
When thou didst crown his warlike brows with paper
And with thy scorns drew'st rivers from his eyes
And then, to dry them, gav'st the duke a clout 176
Steeped in the faultless blood of pretty Rutland –
His curses then, from bitterness of soul
Denounced against thee, are all fall'n upon thee;
And God, not we, hath plagued thy bloody deed.

QUEEN ELIZABETH
So just is God, to right the innocent.

HASTINGS
O, 'twas the foulest deed to slay that babe,
And the most merciless, that e'er was heard of!

RIVERS
Tyrants themselves wept when it was reported.

DORSET
No man but prophesied revenge for it.

BUCKINGHAM
Northumberland, then present, wept to see it.

QUEEN MARGARET
What? were you snarling all before I came,
Ready to catch each other by the throat,
And turn you all your hatred now on me?
Did York's dread curse prevail so much with heaven
That Henry's death, my lovely Edward's death,
Their kingdom's loss, my woeful banishment,
Should all but answer for that peevish brat? 193
Can curses pierce the clouds and enter heaven?
Why then, give way, dull clouds, to my quick curses! 195
Though not by war, by surfeit die your king,
As ours by murder, to make him a king!
Edward thy son, that now is Prince of Wales,
For Edward our son, that was Prince of Wales,
Die in his youth by like untimely violence!
Thyself a queen, for me that was a queen,
Outlive thy glory, like my wretched self!
Long mayst thou live to wail thy children's death
And see another, as I see thee now,
Decked in thy rights as thou art stalled in mine! 205
Long die thy happy days before thy death,
And, after many length'ned hours of grief,
Die neither mother, wife, nor England's queen!
Rivers and Dorset, you were standers-by, 209

121 *packhorse* beast of burden, drudge   126–9 *husband . . . Saint Albans* (the queen's first husband, Sir John Grey, was killed at the battle of Saint Albans fighting against the Yorkists)   134 *father, Warwick* (Clarence temporarily went over to the Lancastrians to marry Warwick's daughter, Isabel Nevil)   138 *meed* reward; *mewèd up* imprisoned   143 *cacodemon* evil spirit   158 *pilled* plundered   160–61 *that . . . that* because . . . because   163 *mak'st thou* are you doing (but Margaret replies as if Richard had meant 'What are you making?')   173–80 *The curse . . . deed* (see *3 Henry VI*, I, iv)   176 *clout* handkerchief   193 *but answer for* merely be equal to   195 *quick* full of life   205 *stalled* installed   209–11 *Rivers . . . daggers* (none of them was present in the scene as shown in *3 Henry VI*, V, v)

And so wast thou, Lord Hastings, when my son
Was stabbed with bloody daggers : God, I pray him
That none of you may live his natural age,
But by some unlooked accident cut off !

RICHARD

214   Have done thy charm, thou hateful with'red hag !

QUEEN MARGARET

And leave out thee ? stay, dog, for thou shalt hear me.
If heaven have any grievous plague in store
Exceeding those that I can wish upon thee,
O, let them keep it till thy sins be ripe,
And then hurl down their indignation
On thee, the troubler of the poor world's peace !
The worm of conscience still begnaw thy soul !
Thy friends suspect for traitors while thou liv'st,
And take deep traitors for thy dearest friends !

224   No sleep close up that deadly eye of thine,
Unless it be while some tormenting dream
Affrights thee with a hell of ugly devils !

227   Thou elvish-marked, abortive, rooting hog !
Thou that wast sealed in thy nativity

229   The slave of nature and the son of hell !

230   Thou slander of thy heavy mother's womb !
Thou loathèd issue of thy father's loins !
Thou rag of honor ! thou detested –

RICHARD

Margaret.

QUEEN MARGARET   Richard !

RICHARD   Ha !

QUEEN MARGARET   I call thee not.

RICHARD

234   I cry thee mercy then ; for I did think
That thou hadst called me all these bitter names.

QUEEN MARGARET

Why, so I did, but looked for no reply.

237   O, let me make the period to my curse !

RICHARD

'Tis done by me, and ends in 'Margaret.'

QUEEN ELIZABETH

Thus have you breathed your curse against yourself.

QUEEN MARGARET

240   Poor painted queen, vain flourish of my fortune !
Why strew'st thou sugar on that bottled spider
Whose deadly web ensnareth thee about ?
Fool, fool ! thou whet'st a knife to kill thyself.
The day will come that thou shalt wish for me
To help thee curse this poisonous bunch-backed toad.

HASTINGS

246   False-boding woman, end thy frantic curse,
247   Lest to thy harm thou move our patience.

QUEEN MARGARET

Foul shame upon you ! you have all moved mine.

RIVERS

Were you well served, you would be taught your duty.

QUEEN MARGARET

To serve me well, you all should do me duty,
Teach me to be your queen, and you my subjects :
O, serve me well, and teach yourselves that duty !

DORSET

Dispute not with her ; she is lunatic.

QUEEN MARGARET

254   Peace, Master Marquess, you are malapert :
255   Your fire-new stamp of honor is scarce current.
256   O, that your young nobility could judge

What 'twere to lose it and be miserable !
They that stand high have many blasts to shake them,
And if they fall, they dash themselves to pieces.

RICHARD

Good counsel, marry ! Learn it, learn it, Marquess.

DORSET

It touches you, my lord, as much as me.

RICHARD

Ay, and much more ; but I was born so high :
Our aery buildeth in the cedar's top   263
And dallies with the wind and scorns the sun.   264

QUEEN MARGARET

And turns the sun to shade – alas ! alas !
Witness my son, now in the shade of death,
Whose bright outshining beams thy cloudy wrath
Hath in eternal darkness folded up.
Your aery buildeth in our aery's nest :
O God, that seest it, do not suffer it !
As it is won with blood, lost be it so !

BUCKINGHAM

Peace, peace, for shame ! if not, for charity.

QUEEN MARGARET

Urge neither charity nor shame to me :
     [Turning to the others]
Uncharitably with me have you dealt,
And shamefully my hopes by you are butchered.
My charity is outrage, life my shame,
And in that shame still live my sorrow's rage !

BUCKINGHAM

Have done, have done.

QUEEN MARGARET

O princely Buckingham, I'll kiss thy hand
In sign of league and amity with thee :   280
Now fair befall thee and thy noble house !
Thy garments are not spotted with our blood,
Nor thou within the compass of my curse.

BUCKINGHAM

Nor no one here ; for curses never pass
The lips of those that breathe them in the air.

QUEEN MARGARET

I will not think but they ascend the sky   286
And there awake God's gentle-sleeping peace.
O Buckingham, take heed of yonder dog !
Look when he fawns he bites ; and when he bites,   289
His venom tooth will rankle to the death.
Have not to do with him, beware of him :
Sin, death, and hell have set their marks on him,
And all their ministers attend on him.

RICHARD

What doth she say, my Lord of Buckingham ?

BUCKINGHAM

Nothing that I respect, my gracious lord.

---

214 *charm* magic spell (Richard addresses Margaret as a witch ; cf. l. 163 above)   224 *deadly* killing (like the eye of a basilisk ; cf. I, ii, 150)   227 *elvish-marked* marked at birth by evil fairies ; *hog* (Richard's badge was a white boar)   229 *slave of nature* naturally slavish or base-minded   230 *heavy mother's* mother's heavy womb, or sad mother's womb   234 *cry thee mercy* beg your pardon (sarcasm)   237 *period* end (as of a sentence ; cf. II, i, 44)   240 *painted queen* queen in outward show ; *flourish* meaningless decoration   246 *False-boding* prophesying falsely   247 *patience* (trisyllabic)   254 *malapert* impudent   255 *Your . . . current* your title is so new-coined that it is scarcely legal tender   256 *young nobility* new state of honor   263 *aery* brood of young eagles   264–65 *sun . . . sun* (double play on 'sun,' (1) as king symbol and (2) as son)   286 *not think but* believe   289 *Look when* whenever

QUEEN MARGARET
What, dost thou scorn me for my gentle counsel?
And soothe the devil that I warn thee from?
O, but remember this another day,
When he shall split thy very heart with sorrow,
300 And say poor Margaret was a prophetess!
Live each of you the subjects to his hate,
And he to yours, and all of you to God's!   *Exit.*

BUCKINGHAM
My hair doth stand an end to hear her curses.

RIVERS
And so doth mine. I muse why she's at liberty.

RICHARD
I cannot blame her. By God's holy Mother,
She hath had too much wrong, and I repent
My part thereof that I have done to her.

QUEEN ELIZABETH
I never did her any to my knowledge.

RICHARD
Yet you have all the vantage of her wrong:
310 I was too hot to do somebody good
That is too cold in thinking of it now.
Marry, as for Clarence, he is well repaid;
313 He is franked up to fatting for his pains –
God pardon them that are the cause thereof!

RIVERS
316 A virtuous and a Christianlike conclusion –
To pray for them that have done scathe to us.

RICHARD
So do I ever – *(speaks to himself)* being well advised;
For had I cursed now, I had cursed myself.
         Enter Catesby.

CATESBY
Madam, his majesty doth call for you;
And for your grace; and yours, my gracious lord.

QUEEN ELIZABETH
Catesby, I come. Lords, will you go with me?

RIVERS
We wait upon your grace.
       Exeunt all but [Richard of] Gloucester.

RICHARD
I do the wrong, and first begin to brawl.
The secret mischiefs that I set abroach
325 I lay unto the grievous charge of others.
Clarence, who I indeed have cast in darkness,
327 I do beweep to many simple gulls –
Namely, to Derby, Hastings, Buckingham –
And tell them 'tis the queen and her allies
That stir the king against the duke my brother.
Now they believe it, and withal whet me
To be revenged on Rivers, Dorset, Grey.
But then I sigh, and, with a piece of Scripture,
Tell them that God bids us do good for evil:
And thus I clothe my naked villainy
With odd old ends stol'n forth of holy writ,
And seem a saint, when most I play the devil.

Enter two Murderers.
But soft! Here come my executioners.
How now, my hardy, stout, resolvèd mates!
Are you now going to dispatch this thing?   340

1. MURDERER
We are, my lord, and come to have the warrant,
That we may be admitted where he is.

RICHARD
Well thought upon; I have it here about me:
     [Gives the warrant.]
When you have done, repair to Crosby Place.
But, sirs, be sudden in the execution,
Withal obdurate, do not hear him plead;
For Clarence is well-spoken, and perhaps
May move your hearts to pity if you mark him.

1. MURDERER
Tut, tut, my lord! we will not stand to prate;   349
Talkers are no good doers. Be assured:
We go to use our hands, and not our tongues.

RICHARD
Your eyes drop millstones when fools' eyes fall tears.   352
I like you, lads: about your business straight.
Go, go, dispatch.

1. MURDERER   We will, my noble lord.   *[Exeunt.]*

             *

       Enter Clarence and Keeper.   I, iv

KEEPER
Why looks your grace so heavily to-day?

CLARENCE
O, I have passed a miserable night,
So full of fearful dreams, of ugly sights,
That, as I am a Christian faithful man,   4
I would not spend another such a night
Though 'twere to buy a world of happy days –
So full of dismal terror was the time.

KEEPER
What was your dream, my lord? I pray you tell me.

CLARENCE
Methoughts that I had broken from the Tower
And was embarked to cross to Burgundy,
And in my company my brother Gloucester,
Who from my cabin tempted me to walk
Upon the hatches: thence we looked toward England   13
And cited up a thousand heavy times,
During the wars of York and Lancaster,
That had befall'n us. As we paced along
Upon the giddy footing of the hatches,   17
Methought that Gloucester stumblèd, and in falling
Struck me (that thought to stay him) overboard
Into the tumbling billows of the main.
O Lord! methought what pain it was to drown!
What dreadful noise of waters in mine ears!
What sights of ugly death within mine eyes!
Methoughts I saw a thousand fearful wracks;
A thousand men that fishes gnawed upon;
Wedges of gold, great anchors, heaps of pearl,
Inestimable stones, unvaluèd jewels,   27
All scatt'red in the bottom of the sea:
Some lay in dead men's skulls, and in the holes
Where eyes did once inhabit, there were crept
(As 'twere in scorn of eyes) reflecting gems,

---

310 *too hot . . . good* i.e. too eager in helping Edward to the crown   313
franked . . . fatting shut in a sty for fattening (i.e. slaughter)   316 *scathe*
injury   325 *lay . . . of* impute as a severe accusation against   327 *gulls* fools
349 *prate* talk idly, chatter   352 *fall* let fall
I, iv The Tower of London   4 *faithful* believing in religion   13 *hatches*
moveable planks forming a kind of deck   17 *giddy footing* foothold producing dizziness   27 *Inestimable . . . jewels* i.e. precious stones without
number and costly ornaments (jewels) beyond price

That wooed the slimy bottom of the deep
And mocked the dead bones that lay scatt'red by.

KEEPER
Had you such leisure in the time of death
To gaze upon these secrets of the deep?

CLARENCE
Methought I had; and often did I strive
37 To yield the ghost; but still the envious flood
Stopped in my soul, and would not let it forth
To find the empty, vast, and wand'ring air,
40 But smothered it within my panting bulk,
Who almost burst to belch it in the sea.

KEEPER
Awaked you not in this sore agony?

CLARENCE
No, no, my dream was lengthened after life.
O, then, began the tempest to my soul!
I passed (methought) the melancholy flood,
46 With that sour ferryman which poets write of,
Unto the kingdom of perpetual night.
48 The first that there did greet my stranger soul
Was my great father-in-law, renownèd Warwick,
Who spake aloud, 'What scourge for perjury
Can this dark monarchy afford false Clarence?'
And so he vanished. Then came wand'ring by
53 A shadow like an angel, with bright hair
Dabbled in blood, and he shrieked out aloud,
55 'Clarence is come – false, fleeting, perjured Clarence,
That stabbed me in the field by Tewkesbury:
Seize on him, Furies, take him unto torment!'
With that (methoughts) a legion of foul fiends
Environed me, and howlèd in mine ears
Such hideous cries that with the very noise
I, trembling, waked, and for a season after
Could not believe but that I was in hell,
Such terrible impression made my dream.

KEEPER
No marvel, lord, though it affrighted you;
I am afraid (methinks) to hear you tell it.

CLARENCE
Ah, keeper, keeper, I have done these things
(That now give evidence against my soul)
For Edward's sake, and see how he requites me!
O God! if my deep pray'rs cannot appease thee,
But thou wilt be avenged on my misdeeds,
Yet execute thy wrath in me alone:
O, spare my guiltless wife and my poor children!
Keeper, I prithee sit by me awhile.
74 My soul is heavy, and I fain would sleep.

KEEPER
I will, my lord. God give your grace good rest!
[Clarence sleeps.]
Enter Brakenbury, the Lieutenant.

BRAKENBURY
76 Sorrow breaks seasons and reposing hours,
Makes the night morning and the noontide night:
Princes have but their titles for their glories,
An outward honor for an inward toil;
80 And for unfelt imaginations
They often feel a world of restless cares;
So that between their titles and low name
There's nothing differs but the outward fame.
Enter two Murderers.

1. MURDERER Ho! who's here?

BRAKENBURY
What wouldst thou, fellow? and how cam'st thou hither?

1. MURDERER I would speak with Clarence, and I came
hither on my legs.

BRAKENBURY What, so brief?

2. MURDERER 'Tis better, sir, than to be tedious. Let
him see our commission, and talk no more.
[Brakenbury] reads [it].

BRAKENBURY
I am, in this, commanded to deliver
The noble Duke of Clarence to your hands.
I will not reason what is meant hereby,
Because I will be guiltless from the meaning. 94
There lies the duke asleep, and there the keys.
I'll to the king and signify to him
That thus I have resigned to you my charge.

1. MURDERER You may, sir; 'tis a point of wisdom. Fare
you well. *Exit [Brakenbury with Keeper].*

2. MURDERER What? Shall I stab him as he sleeps?

1. MURDERER No. He'll say 'twas done cowardly when
he wakes.

2. MURDERER Why, he shall never wake until the great
Judgment Day.

1. MURDERER Why, then he'll say we stabbed him sleeping.

2. MURDERER The urging of that word 'judgment' hath
bred a kind of remorse in me.

1. MURDERER What? Art thou afraid?

2. MURDERER Not to kill him, having a warrant; but to
be damned for killing him, from the which no warrant 110
can defend me.

1. MURDERER I thought thou hadst been resolute.

2. MURDERER So I am – to let him live.

1. MURDERER I'll back to the Duke of Gloucester and
tell him so.

2. MURDERER Nay, I prithee stay a little. I hope this pas- 116
sionate humor of mine will change. It was wont to hold
me but while one tells twenty.

1. MURDERER How dost thou feel thyself now?

2. MURDERER Faith, some certain dregs of conscience
are yet within me.

1. MURDERER Remember our reward when the deed 's
done.

2. MURDERER Zounds, he dies! I had forgot the reward.

1. MURDERER Where's thy conscience now?

2. MURDERER O, in the Duke of Gloucester's purse.

1. MURDERER When he opens his purse to give us our
reward, thy conscience flies out.

2. MURDERER 'Tis no matter; let it go. There's few or
none will entertain it.

1. MURDERER What if it come to thee again? 130

2. MURDERER I'll not meddle with it; it makes a man a
coward. A man cannot steal, but it accuseth him; a man
cannot swear, but it checks him; a man cannot lie with
his neighbor's wife, but it detects him. 'Tis a blushing
shame-faced spirit that mutinies in a man's bosom. It
fills a man full of obstacles. It made me once restore a

37 *yield the ghost* i.e. die; *still* always 40 *bulk* body 46 *ferryman* Charon
48 *stranger* newly arrived 53 *A shadow* i.e. Edward, Prince of Wales, son
of Henry VI 55 *fleeting* unstable 74 *My soul . . . sleep* (an omen of
disaster) 76 *reposing hours* i.e. hours proper to sleep 80 *for unfelt imaginations* for the sake of imaginary and unreal gratifications (Dr Johnson) 94
will be wish to be 116 *passionate* compassionate

purse of gold that (by chance) I found. It beggars any man that keeps it. It is turned out of towns and cities for a dangerous thing, and every man that means to live well endeavors to trust to himself and live without it.

1 . MURDERER Zounds, 'tis even now at my elbow, persuading me not to kill the duke.

143 2 . MURDERER Take the devil in thy mind, and believe
144 him not. He would insinuate with thee but to make thee sigh.

1 . MURDERER I am strong-framed; he cannot prevail with me.

147 2 . MURDERER Spoke like a tall man that respects thy reputation. Come, shall we fall to work?

149 1 . MURDERER Take him on the costard with the hilts of thy sword, and then throw him into the malmsey butt in the next room.

152 2 . MURDERER O excellent device! and make a sop of him.

1 . MURDERER Soft! he wakes.

2 . MURDERER Strike!

1 . MURDERER No, we'll reason with him.

CLARENCE
Where art thou, keeper? Give me a cup of wine.

2 . MURDERER
You shall have wine enough, my lord, anon.

CLARENCE
In God's name, what art thou?

1 . MURDERER
A man, as you are.

CLARENCE
But not as I am, royal.

1 . MURDERER
Nor you as we are, loyal.

CLARENCE
Thy voice is thunder, but thy looks are humble.

1 . MURDERER
My voice is now the king's, my looks mine own.

CLARENCE
164 How darkly and how deadly dost thou speak!
Your eyes do menace me. Why look you pale?
Who sent you hither? Wherefore do you come?

BOTH To, to, to –

CLARENCE
To murder me?

BOTH Ay, ay.

CLARENCE
You scarcely have the hearts to tell me so,
And therefore cannot have the hearts to do it.
Wherein, my friends, have I offended you?

1 . MURDERER
Offended us you have not, but the king.

CLARENCE
I shall be reconciled to him again.

2 . MURDERER
Never, my lord; therefore prepare to die.

CLARENCE
176 Are you drawn forth among a world of men

To slay the innocent? What is my offense?
Where is the evidence that doth accuse me?
What lawful quest have given their verdict up   179
Unto the frowning judge? or who pronounced
The bitter sentence of poor Clarence' death
Before I be convict by course of law?
To threaten me with death is most unlawful:
I charge you, as you hope [to have redemption
By Christ's dear blood shed for our grievous sins,]
That you depart, and lay no hands on me.
The deed you undertake is damnable.   187

1 . MURDERER
What we will do, we do upon command.

2 . MURDERER
And he that hath commanded is our king.

CLARENCE
Erroneous vassals! the great King of Kings
Hath in the table of his law commanded
That thou shalt do no murder. Will you then
Spurn at his edict, and fulfil a man's?
Take heed; for he holds vengeance in his hand
To hurl upon their heads that break his law.

2 . MURDERER
And that same vengeance doth he hurl on thee
For false forswearing and for murder too:
Thou didst receive the sacrament to fight
In quarrel of the house of Lancaster.

1 . MURDERER
And like a traitor to the name of God
Didst break that vow, and with thy treacherous blade
Unrip'st the bowels of thy sov'reign's son.

2 . MURDERER
Whom thou wast sworn to cherish and defend.

1 . MURDERER
How canst thou urge God's dreadful law to us
When thou hast broke it in such dear degree?   205

CLARENCE
Alas! for whose sake did I that ill deed?
For Edward, for my brother, for his sake.
He sends you not to murder me for this,
For in that sin he is as deep as I.
If God will be avengèd for the deed,
O, know you yet he doth it publicly!
Take not the quarrel from his pow'rful arm.
He needs no indirect or lawless course
To cut off those that have offended him.

1 . MURDERER
Who made thee then a bloody minister
When gallant-springing brave Plantagenet,
That princely novice, was struck dead by thee?   217

CLARENCE
My brother's love, the devil, and my rage.

1 . MURDERER
Thy brother's love, our duty, and thy faults
Provoke us hither now to slaughter thee.

CLARENCE
O, if you love my brother, hate not me:
I am his brother, and I love him well.
If you are hired for meed, go back again,
And I will send you to my brother Gloucester,   223
Who shall reward you better for my life
Than Edward will for tidings of my death.

2 . MURDERER
You are deceived. Your brother Gloucester hates you.

143–44 *Take . . . not* call on the devil's aid and pay no heed to conscience (?) or, trap the devil conscience in your reason and pay no heed to him (?)   144 *insinuate* ingratiate himself   147 *tall* valiant   149 *costard* head   152 *sop* wafer floated in a cup of wine   164 *deadly* threatening death   176 *drawn . . . men* i.e. specially chosen among all mankind   179 *quest* jury   187 *damnable* leading to damnation (for you)   205 *dear degree* serious measure   217 *novice* one just beginning his duties   223 *meed* reward

CLARENCE
O, no, he loves me and he holds me dear :
Go you to him from me.
1 . MURDERER   Ay, so we will.
CLARENCE
Tell him, when that our princely father York
Blessed his three sons with his victorious arm
[And charged us from his soul to love each other,]
He little thought of this divided friendship :
Bid Gloucester think of this, and he will weep.
1 . MURDERER
Ay, millstones, as he lessoned us to weep.
CLARENCE
236   O, do not slander him, for he is kind.
1 . MURDERER
237   Right as snow in harvest. Come, you deceive yourself ;
'Tis he that sends us to destroy you here.
CLARENCE
It cannot be, for he bewept my fortune,
And hugged me in his arms, and swore with sobs
That he would labor my delivery.
1 . MURDERER
Why so he doth, when he delivers you
From this earth's thraldom to the joys of heaven.
2 . MURDERER
Make peace with God, for you must die, my lord.
CLARENCE
Have you that holy feeling in your souls
To counsel me to make my peace with God,
And are you yet to your own souls so blind
That you will war with God by murd'ring me ?
O, sirs, consider, they that set you on
250   To do this deed will hate you for the deed.
2 . MURDERER
What shall we do ?
CLARENCE   Relent, and save your souls.
Which of you, if you were a prince's son,
Being pent from liberty, as I am now,
If two such murderers as yourselves came to you,
Would not entreat for life ?
1 . MURDERER
Relent ? No : 'tis cowardly and womanish.
CLARENCE
Not to relent is beastly, savage, devilish.
My friend [to Second Murderer], I spy some pity in thy
looks.
O, if thine eye be not a flatterer,
260   Come thou on my side, and entreat for me
As you would beg, were you in my distress.
A begging prince what beggar pities not ?
2 . MURDERER
Look behind you, my lord !
1 . MURDERER
Take that ! and that ! (Stabs him.) If all this will not do,
I'll drown you in the malmsey butt within.
                              Exit [with the body].
2 . MURDERER
A bloody deed, and desperately dispatched !
How fain (like Pilate) would I wash my hands
Of this most grievous murder !
        Enter First Murderer.
1 . MURDERER
How now ? What mean'st thou that thou help'st me not ?
270   By heavens, the duke shall know how slack you have been.

2 . MURDERER
I would he knew that I had saved his brother !
Take thou the fee and tell him what I say,
For I repent me that the duke is slain.   Exit.
1 . MURDERER
So do not I. Go, coward as thou art.
Well, I'll go hide the body in some hole
Till that the duke give order for his burial ;
And when I have my meed, I will away,
For this will out, and then I must not stay.   Exit. 278

*

Flourish. Enter the King [Edward], sick, the   II, i
Queen, Lord Marquess Dorset, [Grey,] Rivers,
Hastings, Catesby, [and] Buckingham.
KING EDWARD
Why, so : now have I done a good day's work.
You peers, continue this united league.
I every day expect an embassage
From my Redeemer to redeem me hence ;
And more in peace my soul shall part to heaven,
Since I have made my friends at peace on earth.
Hastings and Rivers, take each other's hand ;
Dissemble not your hatred, swear your love.   8
RIVERS
By heaven, my soul is purged from grudging hate,
And with my hand I seal my true heart's love.
HASTINGS
So thrive I as I truly swear the like !
KING EDWARD
Take heed you dally not before your king,   12
Lest he that is the supreme King of Kings
Confound your hidden falsehood and award
Either of you to be the other's end.
HASTINGS
So prosper I as I swear perfect love !
RIVERS
And I as I love Hastings with my heart !
KING EDWARD
Madam, yourself is not exempt from this ;
Nor you, son Dorset ; Buckingham, nor you :
You have been factious one against the other.   20
Wife, love Lord Hastings, let him kiss your hand,
And what you do, do it unfeignedly.
QUEEN ELIZABETH
There, Hastings. I will never more remember
Our former hatred, so thrive I and mine !
KING EDWARD
Dorset, embrace him ; Hastings, love Lord Marquess.
DORSET
This interchange of love, I here protest,
Upon my part shall be inviolable.
HASTINGS
And so swear I.
KING EDWARD
Now, princely Buckingham, seal thou this league
With thy embracements to my wife's allies,
And make me happy in your unity.

236 *kind* (1) with feelings natural to a brother, (2) good   237 *Right as* just as
much as   278 *this will out* i.e. murder will out (proverbial)
II, i The royal palace   8 *Dissemble . . . hatred* do not hide hatred under a
false appearance (of love)   12 *dally* trifle

BUCKINGHAM [to the Queen]

32 Whenever Buckingham doth turn his hate
Upon your grace, but with all duteous love
Doth cherish you and yours, God punish me
With hate in those where I expect most love!
When I have most need to employ a friend,
And most assurèd that he is a friend,
Deep, hollow, treacherous, and full of guile
Be he unto me! This do I beg of God,
When I am cold in love to you or yours.
    Embrace.

KING EDWARD

A pleasing cordial, princely Buckingham,
Is this thy vow unto my sickly heart.
There wanteth now our brother Gloucester here
44 To make the blessèd period of this peace.

BUCKINGHAM

And in good time,
Here comes Sir Richard Ratcliffe and the duke.
    Enter [Sir Richard] Ratcliffe and [Richard, Duke of]
    Gloucester.

RICHARD

Good morrow to my sovereign king and queen;
And, princely peers, a happy time of day!

KING EDWARD

Happy indeed, as we have spent the day:
Gloucester, we have done deeds of charity,
Made peace of enmity, fair love of hate,
Between these swelling wrong-incensèd peers.

RICHARD

A blessèd labor, my most sovereign lord:
Among this princely heap, if any here
By false intelligence or wrong surmise
Hold me a foe –
If I unwittingly, or in my rage,
Have aught committed that is hardly borne
By any in this presence, I desire
60 To reconcile me to his friendly peace.
'Tis death to me to be at enmity:
I hate it, and desire all good men's love.
First, madam, I entreat true peace of you,
Which I will purchase with my duteous service;
Of you, my noble cousin Buckingham,
If ever any grudge were lodged between us;
67 Of you, and you, Lord Rivers, and of Dorset,
68 That, all without desert, have frowned on me;
Dukes, earls, lords, gentlemen – indeed, of all.
I do not know that Englishman alive
With whom my soul is any jot at odds
72 More than the infant that is born to-night.
I thank my God for my humility.

QUEEN ELIZABETH

A holy day shall this be kept hereafter:

I would to God all strifes were well compounded.
My sovereign lord, I do beseech your highness
To take our brother Clarence to your grace.

RICHARD

Why, madam, have I off'red love for this,
To be so flouted in this royal presence?   79
Who knows not that the gentle duke is dead?
    They all start.
You do him injury to scorn his corse.   81

KING EDWARD

Who knows not he is dead? Who knows he is?

QUEEN ELIZABETH

All-seeing heaven, what a world is this!

BUCKINGHAM

Look I so pale, Lord Dorset, as the rest?

DORSET

Ay, my good lord; and no man in the presence   85
But his red color hath forsook his cheeks.

KING EDWARD

Is Clarence dead? The order was reversed.

RICHARD

But he (poor man) by your first order died,
And that a wingèd Mercury did bear:
Some tardy cripple bare the countermand,
That came too lag to see him burièd.   91
God grant that some, less noble and less loyal,
Nearer in bloody thoughts, but not in blood,
Deserve not worse than wretched Clarence did,
And yet go current from suspicion!   95
    Enter [Lord Stanley,] Earl of Derby.

DERBY

A boon, my sovereign, for my service done!   96

KING EDWARD

I prithee peace. My soul is full of sorrow.

DERBY

I will not rise unless your highness hear me.

KING EDWARD

Then say at once what is it thou requests.

DERBY

The forfeit, sovereign, of my servant's life,   100
Who slew to-day a riotous gentleman
Lately attendant on the Duke of Norfolk.

KING EDWARD

Have I a tongue to doom my brother's death,
And shall that tongue give pardon to a slave?
My brother killed no man – his fault was thought –
And yet his punishment was bitter death.
Who sued to me for him? Who (in my wrath)
Kneeled at my feet and bid me be advised?
Who spoke of brotherhood? Who spoke of love?
Who told me how the poor soul did forsake
The mighty Warwick and did fight for me?   111
Who told me, in the field at Tewkesbury,
When Oxford had me down, he rescuèd me   113
And said, 'Dear brother, live, and be a king'?
Who told me, when we both lay in the field
Frozen (almost) to death, how he did lap me
Even in his garments, and did give himself
(All thin and naked) to the numb-cold night?
All this from my remembrance brutish wrath
Sinfully plucked, and not a man of you   120
Had so much grace to put it in my mind.
But when your carters or your waiting vassals
Have done a drunken slaughter and defaced

32–35 *Whenever . . . love* (construction incoherent; for 'but,' l. 33, understand 'nor')   44 *period* conclusion (cf. I, iii, 237)   60 *reconcile . . . peace* i.e. bring myself into friendly relations with him   67 *of Dorset* ('Lord' understood)   68 *all without desert* entirely without my having deserved it   72 *More . . . infant* i.e. more than that infant's soul is   79 *flouted* mocked at   81 *scorn his corse* i.e. joke about the dead   85 *presence* i.e. king's presence   91 *lag* late   95 *go . . . suspicion* are accepted (as legal tender at face value) without question   96 *boon* favor   100 *forfeit . . . life* (the remission of the forfeit is the boon)   111 *Warwick* (Clarence returned to the Yorkist side after marrying Warwick's daughter, thus perjuring himself)   113 *Oxford* (an incident neither historical nor in *3 Henry VI*)

The precious image of our dear Redeemer,
You straight are on your knees for pardon, pardon ;
And I (unjustly too) must grant it you.
    [Derby rises.]
But for my brother not a man would speak,
Nor I (ungracious) speak unto myself
For him, poor soul ! The proudest of you all
130   Have been beholding to him in his life ;
Yet none of you would once beg for his life.
O God ! I fear thy justice will take hold
On me and you, and mine and yours, for this.
Come, Hastings, help me to my closet. Ah, poor Clar-
ence !   *Exeunt some with King and Queen.*

RICHARD
This is the fruits of rashness ! Marked you not
How that the guilty kindred of the queen
Looked pale when they did hear of Clarence' death ?
O, they did urge it still unto the king !
God will revenge it. Come, lords, will you go
140   To comfort Edward with our company ?

BUCKINGHAM
We wait upon your grace.   *Exeunt.*

                *

II, ii   *Enter the old Duchess of York, with the two*
          Children of Clarence [Edward and Margaret
          Plantagenet].

BOY
Good grandam, tell us, is our father dead ?

DUCHESS OF YORK   No, boy.

GIRL
Why do you weep so oft, and beat your breast,
And cry 'O Clarence, my unhappy son' ?

BOY
Why do you look on us, and shake your head,
And call us orphans, wretches, castaways,
If that our noble father were alive ?

DUCHESS OF YORK
8   My pretty cousins, you mistake me both.
I do lament the sickness of the king,
As loath to lose him, not your father's death :
It were lost sorrow to wail one that's lost.

BOY
Then you conclude, my grandam, he is dead.
13   The king mine uncle is too blame for it :
God will revenge it, whom I will importune
With earnest prayers all to that effect.

GIRL
And so will I.

DUCHESS OF YORK
Peace, children, peace ! The king doth love you well.
18   Incapable and shallow innocents,
You cannot guess who caused your father's death.

BOY
Grandam, we can ; for my good uncle Gloucester
Told me the king, provoked to it by the queen,
22   Devised impeachments to imprison him ;
And when my uncle told me so, he wept,
And pitied me, and kindly kissed my cheek ;
Bade me rely on him as on my father,
And he would love me dearly as a child.

DUCHESS OF YORK
27   Ah, that deceit should steal such gentle shape

And with a virtuous visor hide deep vice !   28
He is my son – ay, and therein my shame ;
Yet from my dugs he drew not this deceit.

BOY
Think you my uncle did dissemble, grandam ?

DUCHESS OF YORK   Ay, boy.

BOY
I cannot think it. Hark ! What noise is this ?
     Enter the Queen [Elizabeth], with her hair about
     her ears, Rivers and Dorset after her.

QUEEN ELIZABETH
Ah, who shall hinder me to wail and weep,
To chide my fortune, and torment myself ?
I'll join with black despair against my soul
And to myself become an enemy.

DUCHESS OF YORK
What means this scene of rude impatience ?   38

QUEEN ELIZABETH
To make an act of tragic violence.
Edward, my lord, thy son, our king, is dead !
Why grow the branches when the root is gone ?
Why wither not the leaves that want their sap ?
If you will live, lament ; if die, be brief,
That our swift-wingèd souls may catch the king's,
Or like obedient subjects follow him
To his new kingdom of ne'er-changing night.

DUCHESS OF YORK
Ah, so much interest have I in thy sorrow
As I had title in thy noble husband.   48
I have bewept a worthy husband's death,
And lived with looking on his images ;   50
But now two mirrors of his princely semblance   51
Are cracked in pieces by malignant death,
And I for comfort have but one false glass
That grieves me when I see my shame in him.
Thou art a widow ; yet thou art a mother,
And hast the comfort of thy children left ;
But death hath snatched my husband from mine arms
And plucked two crutches from my feeble hands,
Clarence and Edward. O, what cause have I   59
(Thine being but a moi'ty of my moan)   60
To overgo thy woes and drown thy cries !

BOY
Ah, aunt ! you wept not for our father's death.
How can we aid you with our kindred tears ?   63

GIRL
Our fatherless distress was left unmoaned :
Your widow-dolor likewise be unwept !

QUEEN ELIZABETH
Give me no help in lamentation ;
I am not barren to bring forth complaints.   67
All springs reduce their currents to mine eyes,   68
That I, being governed by the watery moon,

II, ii The same   **8** *you . . . both* you both misunderstand me   **13** *too blame* blameworthy ('blame' felt as adjectival)   **18** *Incapable* without power of understanding   **22** *impeachments* accusations   **27** *shape* disguise   **28** *visor* mask   **38–9** *scene . . . violence* (note the playhouse imagery ; cf. ll. 27–28 and III, v, 1–11)   **48** *title* legal right   **50** *lived with* i.e. kept myself alive by ; *images* i.e. children   **51** *mirrors* i.e. Clarence and King Edward   **59** *what . . . I* what a cause have I   **60** *moi'ty of my moan* half (the cause) of my grief   **63** *kindred tears* i.e. tears belonging to relatives   **67** *I . . . complaints* I have a full capacity for uttering complaints   **68** *reduce* bring (as to a reservoir)

May send forth plenteous tears to drown the world.
Ah for my husband, for my dear lord Edward!

CHILDREN

Ah for our father, for our dear lord Clarence!

DUCHESS OF YORK

Alas for both, both mine, Edward and Clarence!

QUEEN ELIZABETH

What stay had I but Edward? and he's gone.

CHILDREN

What stay had we but Clarence? and he's gone.

DUCHESS OF YORK

What stays had I but they? and they are gone.

QUEEN ELIZABETH

Was never widow had so dear a loss.

CHILDREN

Were never orphans had so dear a loss.

DUCHESS OF YORK

Was never mother had so dear a loss.
Alas! I am the mother of these griefs:

81   Their woes are parcelled, mine is general.
She for an Edward weeps, and so do I;
I for a Clarence weep, so doth not she:
These babes for Clarence weep, [and so do I;
I for an Edward weep,] so do not they.
Alas, you three on me, threefold distressed,
Pour all your tears! I am your sorrow's nurse,

88   And I will pamper it with lamentation.

DORSET

Comfort, dear mother; God is much displeased
That you take with unthankfulness his doing.
In common worldly things 'tis called ungrateful
With dull unwillingness to repay a debt
Which with a bounteous hand was kindly lent;

94   Much more to be thus opposite with heaven
95   For it requires the royal debt it lent you.

RIVERS

Madam, bethink you like a careful mother
Of the young prince your son. Send straight for him;
Let him be crowned; in him your comfort lives.
Drown desperate sorrow in dead Edward's grave
And plant your joys in living Edward's throne.

    Enter Richard, Buckingham, [Stanley Earl of]
    Derby, Hastings, and Ratcliffe.

RICHARD

Sister, have comfort. All of us have cause
To wail the dimming of our shining star;
But none can help our harms by wailing them.
Madam, my mother, I do cry you mercy;
I did not see your grace. Humbly on my knee
I crave your blessing.

DUCHESS OF YORK

God bless thee, and put meekness in thy breast,
Love, charity, obedience, and true duty!

RICHARD

Amen! – *[aside]* and make me die a good old man!

That is the butt-end of a mother's blessing;
I marvel that her grace did leave it out.

BUCKINGHAM

You cloudy princes and heart-sorrowing peers
That bear this heavy mutual load of moan,   113
Now cheer each other in each other's love.
Though we have spent our harvest of this king,
We are to reap the harvest of his son.
The broken rancor of your high-swol'n hates,   117
But lately splintered, knit, and joined together,   118
Must gently be preserved, cherished, and kept.
Me seemeth good that with some little train   120
Forthwith from Ludlow the young prince be fet   121
Hither to London, to be crowned our king.

RIVERS

Why with some little train, my Lord of Buckingham?

BUCKINGHAM

Marry, my lord, lest by a multitude   124
The new-healed wound of malice should break out,
Which would be so much the more dangerous
By how much the estate is green and yet ungoverned.   127
Where every horse bears his commanding rein
And may direct his course as please himself,
As well the fear of harm as harm apparent,
In my opinion, ought to be prevented.

RICHARD

I hope the king made peace with all of us;
And the compact is firm and true in me.

RIVERS

And so in me; and so (I think) in all.
Yet, since it is but green, it should be put
To no apparent likelihood of breach,
Which haply by much company might be urged.
Therefore I say with noble Buckingham
That it is meet so few should fetch the prince.

HASTINGS

And so say I.

RICHARD

Then be it so; and go we to determine
Who they shall be that straight shall post to Ludlow.
Madam, and you, my sister, will you go
To give your censures in this business?   144

[**BOTH**

With all our hearts.]

    Exeunt. Manent Buckingham and Richard.

BUCKINGHAM

My lord, whoever journeys to the prince,
For God sake let not us two stay at home;
For by the way I'll sort occasion,   148
As index to the story we late talked of,   149
To part the queen's proud kindred from the prince.

RICHARD

My other self, my counsel's consistory,   151
My oracle, my prophet, my dear cousin,
I, as a child, will go by thy direction.
Toward Ludlow then, for we'll not stay behind. *Exeunt.*

*

    Enter one Citizen at one door and another at the other. II, iii

1. CITIZEN

Good morrow, neighbor. Whither away so fast?

2. CITIZEN

I promise you, I scarcely know myself.

---

81 *parcelled* particular to each one   88 *pamper . . . lamentation* i.e. feed sorrow with sorrow   94 *opposite with* opposed to   95 *For* because   113 *load of moan* i.e. weight or cause of lamentation   117–19 *The broken . . . kept* (meaning confused; understand 'broken rancor' as implying 'new-found amity')   118 *splintered* set in splints   120 *Me seemeth* it seems to me   121 *Ludlow* town in south Shropshire; *fet* fetched   124 *multitude* large train or following   127 *estate is green* administration of government is untried   144 *censures* judgments   148 *sort occasion* make an opportunity   149 *index* prologue   151 *consistory* council chamber
II, iii A London street

Hear you the news abroad ?

1 . CITIZEN   Yes, that the king is dead.

2 . CITIZEN

4 Ill news, by'r Lady – seldom comes the better :
5 I fear, I fear 'twill prove a giddy world.

Enter another Citizen.

3 . CITIZEN
Neighbors, God speed !

1 . CITIZEN   Give you good morrow, sir.

3 . CITIZEN
Doth the news hold of good King Edward's death ?

2 . CITIZEN
Ay, sir, it is too true. God help the while !

3 . CITIZEN
Then, masters, look to see a troublous world.

1 . CITIZEN
No, no ! By God's good grace his son shall reign.

3 . CITIZEN
Woe to that land that's governed by a child !

2 . CITIZEN

12 In him there is a hope of government,
Which, in his nonage, council under him,
And, in his full and ripenèd years, himself,
No doubt shall then, and till then, govern well.

1 . CITIZEN
So stood the state when Henry the Sixth
Was crowned in Paris but at nine months old.

3 . CITIZEN

18 Stood the state so ? No, no, good friends, God wot !
For then this land was famously enriched
20 With politic grave counsel ; then the king
Had virtuous uncles to protect his grace.

1 . CITIZEN
Why, so hath this, both by his father and mother.

3 . CITIZEN
Better it were they all came by his father,
Or by his father there were none at all ;
For emulation who shall now be nearest
Will touch us all too near, if God prevent not.
O, full of danger is the Duke of Gloucester,
28 And the queen's sons and brothers haught and proud ;
And were they to be ruled, and not to rule,
30 This sickly land might solace as before.

1 . CITIZEN
Come, come, we fear the worst. All will be well.

3 . CITIZEN

32 When clouds are seen, wise men put on their cloaks ;
When great leaves fall, then winter is at hand ;
When the sun sets, who doth not look for night ?
Untimely storms makes men expect a dearth.
36 All may be well ; but if God sort it so,
'Tis more than we deserve or I expect.

2 . CITIZEN
Truly, the hearts of men are full of fear :
39 You cannot reason (almost) with a man
That looks not heavily and full of dread.

3 . CITIZEN
Before the days of change, still is it so.
By a divine instinct men's minds mistrust
Ensuing danger ; as by proof we see
The water swell before a boist'rous storm.
But leave it all to God. Whither away ?

2 . CITIZEN
Marry, we were sent for to the justices.

3 . CITIZEN
And so was I. I'll bear you company.   *Exeunt.*

*

Enter [the] Archbishop [of York], [the] young   II, iv
[Duke of] York, the Queen [Elizabeth], and the
Duchess [of York].

ARCHBISHOP
Last night, I hear, they lay at Stony Stratford ;   1
And at Northampton they do rest to-night ;   2
To-morrow, or next day, they will be here.

DUCHESS OF YORK
I long with all my heart to see the prince :
I hope he is much grown since last I saw him.

QUEEN ELIZABETH
But I hear no. They say my son of York
Has almost overta'en him in his growth.

YORK
Ay, mother ; but I would not have it so.

DUCHESS OF YORK
Why, my good cousin ? it is good to grow.

YORK
Grandam, one night as we did sit at supper,
My uncle Rivers talked how I did grow
More than my brother. 'Ay,' quoth my uncle
    Gloucester,
'Small herbs have grace ; great weeds do grow apace.'   13
And since, methinks, I would not grow so fast,
Because sweet flow'rs are slow and weeds make haste.

DUCHESS OF YORK
Good faith, good faith, the saying did not hold
In him that did object the same to thee :   17
He was the wretched'st thing when he was young,
So long a-growing and so leisurely
That, if his rule were true, he should be gracious.   20

ARCHBISHOP
And so no doubt he is, my gracious madam.

DUCHESS OF YORK
I hope he is ; but yet let mothers doubt.

YORK
Now, by my troth, if I had been rememb'red,   23
I could have given my uncle's grace a flout   24
To touch his growth nearer than he touched mine.

DUCHESS OF YORK
How, my young York ? I prithee let me hear it.

YORK
Marry (they say) my uncle grew so fast
That he could gnaw a crust at two hours old :
'Twas full two years ere I could get a tooth.

4 *seldom . . . better* (times are bad) but are likely to be worse (proverbial)
5 *giddy* inconstant or mad   12–15 *In him . . . well* (confused construction :
there is hope for the land ; for one who in his minority governs wisely with
the aid of counsel will in his maturity govern well in his own person)   18
wot knows   20 *counsel* professional advisers   28 *haught* haughty   30
solace be happy   32–35 *When . . . dearth* (a series of 'moral sentences' in
the manner of Senecan tragedy)   36 *sort* dispose   39 *You . . . man* i.e. there
is almost no man with whom you can reason
II, iv The royal palace   1 *Stony Stratford* town in Buckinghamshire   2
Northampton town in Northamptonshire (Historically the order of these
two towns is correct, though dramatically the order is difficult since Stony
Stratford is closer to London than Northampton is – see l. 3. The quartos
reverse the order.)   13 *grace* beneficent virtue   17 *object* urge   20 *gracious*
(playing on *grace*, l. 13)   23 *troth* faith ; *been rememb'red* considered   24
flout scoff

30 Grandam, this would have been a biting jest.

DUCHESS OF YORK
I prithee, pretty York, who told thee this?

YORK
Grandam, his nurse.

DUCHESS OF YORK
His nurse? Why, she was dead ere thou wast born.

YORK
If 'twere not she, I cannot tell who told me.

QUEEN ELIZABETH
35 A parlous boy! Go to, you are too shrewd.

DUCHESS OF YORK
Good madam, be not angry with the child.

QUEEN ELIZABETH
37 Pitchers have ears.
            Enter a Messenger.

ARCHBISHOP
Here comes a messenger. What news?

MESSENGER
Such news, my lord, as grieves me to report.

QUEEN ELIZABETH
How doth the prince?

MESSENGER   Well, madam, and in health.

DUCHESS OF YORK
What is thy news?

MESSENGER   The mighty dukes,

42 Lord Rivers and Lord Grey are sent to Pomfret,
43 And with them Sir Thomas Vaughan, prisoners.

DUCHESS OF YORK
Who hath committed them?

MESSENGER   The mighty dukes,
Gloucester and Buckingham.

ARCHBISHOP   For what offense?

MESSENGER
46 The sum of all I can I have disclosed.
Why or for what the nobles were committed
Is all unknown to me, my gracious lord.

QUEEN ELIZABETH
Ay me! I see the ruin of my house.
The tiger now hath seized the gentle hind;
51 Insulting tyranny begins to jut
52 Upon the innocent and aweless throne:
Welcome destruction, blood, and massacre!
54 I see (as in a map) the end of all.

DUCHESS OF YORK
Accursèd and unquiet wrangling days,
How many of you have mine eyes beheld!
57 My husband lost his life to get the crown,
And often up and down my sons were tossed
For me to joy and weep their gain and loss;
And being seated, and domestic broils
Clean overblown, themselves the conquerors

Make war upon themselves, brother to brother,
Blood to blood, self against self. O preposterous   63
And frantic outrage, end thy damnèd spleen,   64
Or let me die, to look on death no more!

QUEEN ELIZABETH
Come, come, my boy; we will to sanctuary.   66
Madam, farewell.

DUCHESS OF YORK Stay, I will go with you.

QUEEN ELIZABETH
You have no cause.

ARCHBISHOP *[to the Queen]* My gracious lady, go,
And thither bear your treasure and your goods.
For my part, I'll resign unto your grace
The seal I keep; and so betide to me
As well I tender you and all of yours!   72
Go, I'll conduct you to the sanctuary.   *Exeunt.*

*

The trumpets sound. Enter young Prince   III, i
[Edward of Wales], the Dukes of Gloucester and
Buckingham, Lord Cardinal [Bourchier, Catesby,]
with others.

BUCKINGHAM
Welcome, sweet prince, to London, to your chamber.   1

RICHARD
Welcome, dear cousin, my thoughts' sovereign:
The weary way hath made you melancholy.

PRINCE EDWARD
No, uncle; but our crosses on the way   4
Have made it tedious, wearisome, and heavy.
I want more uncles here to welcome me.   6

RICHARD
Sweet prince, the untainted virtue of your years
Hath not yet dived into the world's deceit:
Nor more can you distinguish of a man
Than of his outward show, which, God he knows,
Seldom or never jumpeth with the heart.   11
Those uncles which you want were dangerous;
Your grace attended to their sug'red words
But looked not on the poison of their hearts:
God keep you from them, and from such false friends!

PRINCE EDWARD
God keep me from false friends! – but they were none.

RICHARD
My lord, the Mayor of London comes to greet you.
        Enter Lord Mayor [and his Train].

LORD MAYOR
God bless your grace with health and happy days!

PRINCE EDWARD
I thank you, good my lord, and thank you all.
        [Mayor and his Train stand aside.]
I thought my mother and my brother York
Would long ere this have met us on the way.
Fie, what a slug is Hastings that he comes not   22
To tell us whether they will come or no!
        Enter Lord Hastings.

BUCKINGHAM
And, in good time, here comes the sweating lord.

PRINCE EDWARD
Welcome, my lord. What, will our mother come?

HASTINGS
On what occasion God he knows, not I,   26
The queen your mother and your brother York

---

30 *biting* (note play on 'teeth' in ll. 28–29) 35 *parlous* cunning 37
Pitchers have ears (proverbial: little pitchers have wide ears – said of
children) 42 *Pomfret* castle in Yorkshire 43 *Vaughan* (dissyllabic throughout) 46 *can* know 51 *jut* encroach upon 52 *aweless* inspiring no awe
54 *map* (figuratively) something representing (future) events in epitome
57–63 *My husband . . . self* (note the 'wheel of fortune' theme underlying
these lines) 63 *preposterous* inverting the natural order 64 *spleen* malice
66 *sanctuary* the cathedral precincts in which civil law was powerless 72
tender care for
III, i A London street 1 *chamber* (London was known as *camera regis* or
king's chamber) 4 *crosses* annoyances (play on *melancholy*, l. 3) 6 *want*
(1) am lacking in, (2) desire (cf. l. 12) 11 *jumpeth* accords 22 *slug* lazy
fellow (sluggard) 26 *On what occasion* for what reason

Have taken sanctuary. The tender prince
Would fain have come with me to meet your grace,
30 But by his mother was perforce withheld.
BUCKINGHAM
31 Fie, what an indirect and peevish course
Is this of hers! Lord Cardinal, will your grace
Persuade the queen to send the Duke of York
34 Unto his princely brother presently?
If she deny, Lord Hastings, go with him
And from her jealous arms pluck him perforce.
CARDINAL BOURCHIER
My Lord of Buckingham, if my weak oratory
Can from his mother win the Duke of York,
Anon expect him here; but if she be obdurate
To mild entreaties, God in heaven forbid
We should infringe the holy privilege
Of blessèd sanctuary! Not for all this land
Would I be guilty of so deep a sin.
BUCKINGHAM
You are too senseless-obstinate, my lord,
45 Too ceremonious and traditional.
46 Weigh it but with the grossness of this age,
You break not sanctuary in seizing him:
The benefit thereof is always granted
To those whose dealings have deserved the place
And those who have the wit to claim the place.
This prince hath neither claimed it nor deserved it,
And therefore, in mine opinion, cannot have it.
Then, taking him from thence that is not there,
You break no privilege nor charter there.
Oft have I heard of sanctuary men,
But sanctuary children never till now.
CARDINAL BOURCHIER
My lord, you shall overrule my mind for once.
Come on, Lord Hastings, will you go with me?
HASTINGS
I go, my lord.
PRINCE EDWARD
Good lords, make all the speedy haste you may.
                    Exeunt Cardinal and Hastings.
Say, uncle Gloucester, if our brother come,
Where shall we sojourn till our coronation?
RICHARD
Where it seems best unto your royal self.
If I may counsel you, some day or two
65 Your highness shall repose you at the Tower;
Then where you please, and shall be thought most fit
For your best health and recreation.
PRINCE EDWARD
68 I do not like the Tower, of any place.
Did Julius Caesar build that place, my lord?
BUCKINGHAM
He did, my gracious lord, begin that place,
Which, since, succeeding ages have re-edified.
PRINCE EDWARD
Is it upon record, or else reported
Successively from age to age, he built it?
BUCKINGHAM
Upon record, my gracious lord.
PRINCE EDWARD
But say, my lord, it were not regist'red,
Methinks the truth should live from age to age,
As 'twere retailed to all posterity,

Even to the general all-ending day.
RICHARD _[aside]_
So wise so young, they say, do never live long.
PRINCE EDWARD
What say you, uncle?
RICHARD
I say, without characters fame lives long.   81
    [Aside]
Thus, like the formal Vice, Iniquity,   82
I moralize two meanings in one word.   83
PRINCE EDWARD
That Julius Caesar was a famous man:
With what his valor did enrich his wit,   85
His wit set down to make his valor live.
Death makes no conquest of this conqueror,
For now he lives in fame, though not in life.
I'll tell you what, my cousin Buckingham –
BUCKINGHAM
What, my gracious lord?
PRINCE EDWARD
An if I live until I be a man,   91
I'll win our ancient right in France again
Or die a soldier as I lived a king.
RICHARD _[aside]_
Short summers lightly have a forward spring.   94
    _Enter [the] young [Duke of] York, Hastings, and
    Cardinal [Bourchier]._
BUCKINGHAM
Now in good time, here comes the Duke of York.
PRINCE EDWARD
Richard of York, how fares our loving brother?
YORK
Well, my dread lord – so must I call you now.   97
PRINCE EDWARD
Ay, brother – to our grief, as it is yours:
Too late he died that might have kept that title,   99
Which by his death hath lost much majesty.
RICHARD
How fares our cousin, noble Lord of York?
YORK
I thank you, gentle uncle. O, my lord,
You said that idle weeds are fast in growth:
The prince my brother hath outgrown me far.
RICHARD
He hath, my lord.
YORK   And therefore is he idle?
RICHARD
O my fair cousin, I must not say so.
YORK
Then he is more beholding to you than I.   107
RICHARD
He may command me as my sovereign,

30 _perforce_ forcibly 31 _indirect and peevish_ devious and perverse 34 _presently_ at once 45 _ceremonious_ tied by formalities 46 _grossness_ coarseness or lack of refinement (in a moral sense) 65 _Tower_ the Tower of London (associated in the prince's mind with imprisonment; cf. I, i, 45) 68 _of any place_ of all places 81 _characters_ written records 82 _formal Vice, Iniquity_ i.e. the conventional Vice figure called Iniquity (the Vice in sixteenth-century morality plays symbolized in one character all the vices) 83 _moralize . . . word_ play on a double meaning (as the Vice did) in a single phrase (i.e. _live long_, l. 79) 85 _what_ that with which 91 _An if_ if 94 _Short . . . spring_ i.e. those who die young are usually (_lightly_) precocious (proverbial; cf. l. 79) 97 _dread_ to be feared (as king) 99 _late_ recently 107 _beholding_ indebted

But you have power in me as in a kinsman.

YORK
I pray you, uncle, give me this dagger.

RICHARD
111   My dagger, little cousin ? With all my heart.

PRINCE EDWARD
A beggar, brother ?

YORK
Of my kind uncle, that I know will give,
And being but a toy, which is no grief to give.

RICHARD
A greater gift than that I'll give my cousin.

YORK
A greater gift ? O, that's the sword to it.

RICHARD
Ay, gentle cousin, were it light enough.

YORK
118   O, then I see you will part but with light gifts !
In weightier things you'll say a beggar nay.

RICHARD
It is too heavy for your grace to wear.

YORK
121   I weigh it lightly, were it heavier.

RICHARD
What, would you have my weapon, little lord ?

YORK
I would, that I might thank you as you call me.

RICHARD How ?

YORK Little.

PRINCE EDWARD
126   My Lord of York will still be cross in talk.
Uncle, your grace knows how to bear with him.

YORK
You mean, to bear me, not to bear with me.
Uncle, my brother mocks both you and me :
Because that I am little, like an ape,
He thinks that you should bear me on your shoulders.

BUCKINGHAM [aside to Hastings]
132   With what a sharp-provided wit he reasons !
To mitigate the scorn he gives his uncle,
He prettily and aptly taunts himself :
So cunning, and so young, is wonderful.

RICHARD
My lord, will't please you pass along ?
Myself and my good cousin Buckingham
Will to your mother, to entreat of her
To meet you at the Tower and welcome you.

YORK
What, will you go unto the Tower, my lord ?

PRINCE EDWARD
My Lord Protector needs will have it so.

YORK
I shall not sleep in quiet at the Tower.

RICHARD
Why, what should you fear ?

YORK
Marry, my uncle Clarence' angry ghost :
My grandam told me he was murd'red there.

PRINCE EDWARD
I fear no uncles dead.

RICHARD
Nor none that live, I hope.

PRINCE EDWARD
An if they live, I hope I need not fear.   148
But come, my lord ; with a heavy heart,
Thinking on them, go I unto the Tower.
*A sennet. Exeunt Prince [Edward], York, Hastings
[, Cardinal Bourchier, and others]. Manent Richard,
Buckingham, and Catesby.*

BUCKINGHAM
Think you, my lord, this little prating York   151
Was not incensèd by his subtle mother   152
To taunt and scorn you thus opprobriously ?

RICHARD
No doubt, no doubt. O, 'tis a perilous boy,   154
Bold, quick, ingenious, forward, capable :
He is all the mother's, from the top to toe.   156

BUCKINGHAM
Well, let them rest. Come hither, Catesby.   157
Thou art sworn as deeply to effect what we intend
As closely to conceal what we impart.
Thou know'st our reasons urged upon the way.
What think'st thou ? Is it not an easy matter
To make William Lord Hastings of our mind
For the instalment of this noble duke   163
In the seat royal of this famous isle ?

CATESBY
He for his father's sake so loves the prince
That he will not be won to aught against him.

BUCKINGHAM
What think'st thou then of Stanley ? Will not he ?   167

CATESBY
He will do all in all as Hastings doth.

BUCKINGHAM
Well then, no more but this : go, gentle Catesby,
And, as it were far off, sound thou Lord Hastings
How he doth stand affected to our purpose,   171
And summon him to-morrow to the Tower
To sit about the coronation.   173
If thou dost find him tractable to us,   174
Encourage him, and tell him all our reasons :
If he be leaden, icy, cold, unwilling,
Be thou so too, and so break off the talk,
And give us notice of his inclination ;
For we to-morrow hold divided councils,   179
Wherein thyself shalt highly be employed.

RICHARD
Commend me to Lord William. Tell him, Catesby,   181
His ancient knot of dangerous adversaries
To-morrow are let blood at Pomfret Castle,
And bid my lord, for joy of this good news,
Give Mistress Shore one gentle kiss the more.

111 *My . . . heart* (Richard would, with all his heart, like to give York his dagger in his heart)   118 *light* slight or trivial   121 *weigh it lightly* consider it of little value   126 *still be cross* i.e. always be twisting words   132 *sharp-provided* keenly thought out   148 *they* i.e. Rivers and Grey (Grey was actually Prince Edward's stepbrother)   151 *prating* overtalkative   152 *incensèd* incited   154 *perilous* shrewd or dangerously cunning (cf. *parlous*, II, iv, 35, the more usual form, but Richard's use of the stronger form may here be intentional)   156 *He . . . mother's* i.e. he takes after his mother   157 *let them rest* i.e. leave them (for the moment)   163 *instalment* formal installation   167 *Stanley* i.e. the Earl of Derby, Lord Stanley   171 *How . . . affected* how he is disposed   173 *sit* i.e. hold consultation   174 *tractable* compliant   179 *divided councils* i.e. two separate council meetings (cf. III, ii, 12–14), one a private consultation unknown to the public council   181 *Lord William* i.e. Hastings

BUCKINGHAM
Good Catesby, go effect this business soundly.

CATESBY
My good lords both, with all the heed I can.

RICHARD
Shall we hear from you, Catesby, ere we sleep?

CATESBY
You shall, my lord.

RICHARD
At Crosby House, there shall you find us both.
                       Exit Catesby.

BUCKINGHAM
Now, my lord, what shall we do if we perceive
192 Lord Hastings will not yield to our complots?

RICHARD
Chop off his head! Something we will determine.
194 And look when I am king, claim thou of me
195 The earldom of Hereford and all the moveables
Whereof the king my brother was possessed.

BUCKINGHAM
I'll claim that promise at your grace's hand.

RICHARD
And look to have it yielded with all kindness.
199 Come, let us sup betimes, that afterwards
We may digest our complots in some form.   *Exeunt.*

                       *

III, ii   *Enter a Messenger to the door of Hastings.*

MESSENGER
My lord! my lord!

HASTINGS [*within*]
Who knocks?

MESSENGER
One from the Lord Stanley.
        Enter Lord Hastings.

HASTINGS
What is't a clock?

MESSENGER
Upon the stroke of four.

HASTINGS
6 Cannot my Lord Stanley sleep these tedious nights?

MESSENGER
So it appears by that I have to say:
First, he commends him to your noble self.

HASTINGS
What then?

MESSENGER
Then certifies your lordship that this night
11 He dreamt the boar had rasèd off his helm:
Besides, he says there are two councils kept;
And that may be determined at the one
14 Which may make you and him to rue at th' other.
Therefore he sends to know your lordship's pleasure,
16 If you will presently take horse with him
And with all speed post with him toward the North
To shun the danger that his soul divines.

HASTINGS
Go, fellow, go, return unto thy lord;
Bid him not fear the separated council.
His honor and myself are at the one,
And at the other is my good friend Catesby;
Where nothing can proceed that toucheth us
Whereof I shall not have intelligence.

Tell him his fears are shallow, without instance;   25
And for his dreams, I wonder he's so simple
To trust the mock'ry of unquiet slumbers.
To fly the boar before the boar pursues
Were to incense the boar to follow us,
And make pursuit where he did mean no chase.
Go, bid thy master rise and come to me,
And we will both together to the Tower,
Where he shall see the boar will use us kindly.

MESSENGER
I'll go, my lord, and tell him what you say.   *Exit.*
     Enter Catesby.

CATESBY
Many good morrows to my noble lord!

HASTINGS
Good morrow, Catesby; you are early stirring.
What news, what news, in this our tott'ring state?

CATESBY
It is a reeling world indeed, my lord,   38
And I believe will never stand upright
Till Richard wear the garland of the realm.

HASTINGS
How! wear the garland! Dost thou mean the crown?

CATESBY
Ay, my good lord.

HASTINGS
I'll have this crown of mine cut from my shoulders   43
Before I'll see the crown so foul misplaced.
But canst thou guess that he doth aim at it?

CATESBY
Ay, on my life, and hopes to find you forward   46
Upon his party for the gain thereof;
And thereupon he sends you this good news,
That this same very day your enemies,
The kindred of the queen, must die at Pomfret.

HASTINGS
Indeed I am no mourner for that news,
Because they have been still my adversaries;   52
But that I'll give my voice on Richard's side
To bar my master's heirs in true descent –
God knows I will not do it, to the death!

CATESBY
God keep your lordship in that gracious mind!

HASTINGS
But I shall laugh at this a twelvemonth hence,   57
That they which brought me in my master's hate,
I live to look upon their tragedy.
Well, Catesby, ere a fortnight make me older,
I'll send some packing that yet think not on't.

CATESBY
'Tis a vile thing to die, my gracious lord,
When men are unprepared and look not for it.

HASTINGS
O monstrous, monstrous! and so falls it out

---

192 *complots* conspiracies   194 *look when* as soon as   195 *moveables* (cf. Holinshed: 'a great quantitie of the kings treasure, and of his household stuffe')   199 *betimes* soon

III, ii Before Lord Hastings' house   6 *tedious* (this word seems to suggest that Hastings cannot sleep either)   11 *boar* (see I, iii, 227); *rasèd . . . helm* figuratively, cut off his head   14 *rue* grieve (at what was decided)   16 *presently* at once   25 *instance* evidence   38 *reeling* (cf. II, iii, 5)   43 *crown . . . shoulders* (foreshadows Hastings' death and looks back to l. 11)   46–47 *forward Upon* lending strong support to   52 *still* always   57–59 *But . . . tragedy* (construction difficult; for the sense, omit *they* in l. 58 and insert l. 59 after *That* in l. 58)

With Rivers, Vaughan, Grey ; and so 'twill do
With some men else, that think themselves as safe
As thou and I, who (as thou know'st) are dear
To princely Richard and to Buckingham.

CATESBY
The princes both make high account of you –
    [Aside]
70 For they account his head upon the Bridge.

HASTINGS
I know they do, and I have well deserved it.
    Enter Lord Stanley [Earl of Derby].
Come on, come on ! Where is your boar-spear, man ?
Fear you the boar, and go so unprovided ?

DERBY
My lord, good morrow. Good morrow, Catesby.
75 You may jest on, but, by the Holy Rood,
I do not like these several councils, I.

HASTINGS
My lord,
I hold my life as dear as you do yours,
And never in my days, I do protest,
Was it so precious to me as 'tis now.
Think you, but that I know our state secure,
82 I would be so triumphant as I am ?

DERBY
The lords at Pomfret, when they rode from London,
84 Were jocund and supposed their states were sure,
And they indeed had no cause to mistrust ;
But yet you see how soon the day o'ercast.
87 This sudden stab of rancor I misdoubt :
Pray God, I say, I prove a needless coward !
89 What, shall we toward the Tower ? The day is spent.

HASTINGS
Come, come, have with you. Wot you what, my lord ?
To-day the lords you talked of are beheaded.

DERBY
They, for their truth, might better wear their heads
93 Than some that have accused them wear their hats.
94 But come, my lord, let's away.
    Enter a Pursuivant [also named Hastings].

HASTINGS
Go on before. I'll talk with this good fellow.
    Exeunt Lord Stanley [Earl of Derby],
    and Catesby.
How now, sirrah ? How goes the world with thee ?

PURSUIVANT
The better that your lordship please to ask.

HASTINGS
I tell thee, man, 'tis better with me now
Than when thou met'st me last where now we meet.

Then was I going prisoner to the Tower
By the suggestion of the queen's allies ;
But now I tell thee (keep it to thyself)
This day those enemies are put to death,
And I in better state than e'er I was.

PURSUIVANT
God hold it, to your honor's good content !   105

HASTINGS
Gramercy, fellow. There, drink that for me.   106
    Throws him his purse.

PURSUIVANT I thank your honor.   *Exit Pursuivant.*
    Enter a Priest.

PRIEST
Well met, my lord. I am glad to see your honor.

HASTINGS
I thank thee, good Sir John, with all my heart.   109
I am in your debt for your last exercise ;   110
Come the next Sabbath, and I will content you.
    [He whispers in his ear.]

PRIEST
I'll wait upon your lordship.
    Enter Buckingham.

BUCKINGHAM
What, talking with a priest, Lord Chamberlain ?
Your friends at Pomfret, they do need the priest ;
Your honor hath no shriving work in hand.   115

HASTINGS
Good faith, and when I met this holy man,
The men you talk of came into my mind.
What, go you toward the Tower ?

BUCKINGHAM
I do, my lord, but long I cannot stay there.
I shall return before your lordship thence.

HASTINGS
Nay, like enough, for I stay dinner there.

BUCKINGHAM *[aside]*
And supper too, although thou know'st it not. –
Come, will you go ?

HASTINGS   I'll wait upon your lordship. *Exeunt.*

        *

    Enter Sir Richard Ratcliffe, with Halberds, carrying III, iii
    the Nobles [Rivers, Grey, and Vaughan] to death at
    Pomfret.
[RATCLIFFE Come, bring forth the prisoners.]

RIVERS
Sir Richard Ratcliffe, let me tell thee this :
To-day shalt thou behold a subject die
For truth, for duty, and for loyalty.

GREY
God bless the prince from all the pack of you !
A knot you are of damnèd bloodsuckers.

VAUGHAN
You live that shall cry woe for this hereafter.

RATCLIFFE
Dispatch ! The limit of your lives is out.

RIVERS
O Pomfret, Pomfret ! O thou bloody prison,
Fatal and ominous to noble peers !
Within the guilty closure of thy walls
Richard the Second here was hacked to death ;
And, for more slander to thy dismal seat,   13
We give to thee our guiltless blood to drink.

---

70 *Bridge* London Bridge (traitors' heads were displayed on poles on the gateway entrances to it) 75 *Holy Rood* Christ's cross 82 *triumphant* exultant 84 *jocund* merry 87 *This . . . misdoubt* i.e. I fear this sudden blow (the capture of Rivers, Vaughan, and Grey) arising out of hatred 89 *day is spent* (the folio reading is questionable since it is just after 4 a.m. ; the quartos omit the time reference) 93 *some . . . hats* (probably a veiled reference to Richard and Buckingham, whose rank as dukes gave them the privilege of wearing the so-called ducal cap in the royal presence, no head-covering resembling a hat being allowed below the rank of duke) 94 s.d. *Pursuivant* state messenger with authority to execute warrants 105 *God hold it* i.e. may God continue this state of affairs 106 *Gramercy* much thanks 109 *Sir John* ('sir' was a title of respect applied to the clergy ; no reference here to knighthood) 110 *exercise* sermon 115 *shriving work* i.e. 'deathbed' confessions

III, iii *Pomfret* Castle 13 *for . . . seat* i.e. in order to bring greater shame upon Pomfret, a place which already bodes disaster

GREY

Now Margaret's curse is fall'n upon our heads,
When she exclaimed on Hastings, you, and I,
For standing by when Richard stabbed her son.

RIVERS

Then cursed she Richard, then cursed she Buckingham,
Then cursed she Hastings. O, remember, God,
To hear her prayer for them, as now for us!
And for my sister and her princely sons,
Be satisfied, dear God, with our true blood,
Which, as thou know'st, unjustly must be spilt.

RATCLIFFE

24   Make haste. The hour of death is expiate.

RIVERS

Come, Grey; come, Vaughan; let us here embrace.
Farewell, until we meet again in heaven.   *Exeunt.*

*

III, iv   *Enter Buckingham, [Lord Stanley Earl of] Derby,*
Hastings, Bishop of Ely, Norfolk, Ratcliffe, Lovel,
with others, at a table.

HASTINGS

Now, noble peers, the cause why we are met
2   Is to determine of the coronation.
In God's name, speak. When is the royal day?

BUCKINGHAM

Is all things ready for the royal time?

DERBY

5   It is, and wants but nomination.

BISHOP OF ELY

To-morrow then I judge a happy day.

BUCKINGHAM

Who knows the Lord Protector's mind herein?
8   Who is most inward with the noble duke?

BISHOP OF ELY

Your grace, we think, should soonest know his mind.

BUCKINGHAM

We know each other's faces; for our hearts,
He knows no more of mine than I of yours;
Or I of his, my lord, than you of mine.
Lord Hastings, you and he are near in love.

HASTINGS

I thank his grace, I know he loves me well;
But, for his purpose in the coronation,
16   I have not sounded him, nor he delivered
His gracious pleasure any way therein;
But you, my honorable lords, may name the time,
And in the duke's behalf I'll give my voice,
Which, I presume, he'll take in gentle part.
    Enter [Richard, Duke of] Gloucester.

BISHOP OF ELY

In happy time, here comes the duke himself.

RICHARD

My noble lords and cousins all, good morrow.
I have been long a sleeper; but I trust
24   My absence doth neglect no great design
Which by my presence might have been concluded.

BUCKINGHAM

Had you not come upon your cue, my lord,
William Lord Hastings had pronounced your part –
I mean, your voice for crowning of the king.

RICHARD

Than my Lord Hastings no man might be bolder.

His lordship knows me well, and loves me well.
My Lord of Ely, when I was last in Holborn
I saw good strawberries in your garden there.
I do beseech you send for some of them.

BISHOP OF ELY

Marry and will, my lord, with all my heart.   *Exit Bishop.*

RICHARD

Cousin of Buckingham, a word with you.
    [Takes him aside.]
Catesby hath sounded Hastings in our business
And finds the testy gentleman so hot   37
That he will lose his head ere give consent
His master's child, as worshipfully he terms it,   39
Shall lose the royalty of England's throne.   40

BUCKINGHAM

Withdraw yourself awhile. I'll go with you.
    Exeunt [Richard and Buckingham].

DERBY

We have not yet set down this day of triumph:
To-morrow, in my judgment, is too sudden;
For I myself am not so well provided
As else I would be, were the day prolonged.   45
    Enter the Bishop of Ely.

BISHOP OF ELY

Where is my lord the Duke of Gloucester?
I have sent for these strawberries.

HASTINGS

His grace looks cheerfully and smooth this morning;
There's some conceit or other likes him well   49
When that he bids good morrow with such spirit.
I think there's never a man in Christendom
Can lesser hide his love or hate than he,
For by his face straight shall you know his heart.

DERBY

What of his heart perceive you in his face
By any livelihood he showed to-day?   55

HASTINGS

Marry, that with no man here he is offended;
For were he, he had shown it in his looks.

[DERBY

I pray God he be not, I say.]
    Enter Richard and Buckingham.

RICHARD

I pray you all, tell me what they deserve
That do conspire my death with devilish plots
Of damnèd witchcraft, and that have prevailed   61
Upon my body with their hellish charms.

HASTINGS

The tender love I bear your grace, my lord,
Makes me most forward in this princely presence
To doom th' offenders, whosoe'er they be:
I say, my lord, they have deservèd death.

RICHARD

Then be your eyes the witness of their evil.
Look how I am bewitched. Behold, mine arm

---

24 *expiate* fully come (cf. l. 8)
III, iv *Within the Tower of London*   2 *determine of* come to a decision concerning   5 *nomination* the fixing   8 *inward* intimate   16 *I . . . him* (but Richard had in fact sounded Hastings; cf. l. 36)   24 *neglect . . . design* i.e. cause no great design to be neglected   37 *testy* quick-tempered; *hot* burning (with his resolve)   39 *worshipfully* i.e. using words expressing honor or regard   40 *royalty* sovereignty   45 *the day prolonged* i.e. a later day set   49 *conceit* (happy) idea or device   55 *livelihood* vivacity   61–62 *prevailed Upon* got the better of

Is like a blasted sapling, withered up;
And this is Edward's wife, that monstrous witch,
71   Consorted with that harlot, strumpet Shore,
That by their witchcraft thus have markèd me.

HASTINGS
If they have done this deed, my noble lord –

RICHARD
If? Thou protector of this damnèd strumpet,
Talk'st thou to me of ifs? Thou art a traitor.
Off with his head! Now by Saint Paul I swear
I will not dine until I see the same.
Lovel and Ratcliffe, look that it be done:
The rest that love me, rise and follow me.

*Exeunt. Manent Lovel and Ratcliffe,
with the Lord Hastings.*

HASTINGS
80   Woe, woe for England, not a whit for me!
81   For I, too fond, might have prevented this.
Stanley did dream the boar did rase our helms;
But I did scorn it and disdain to fly.
84   Three times to-day my footcloth horse did stumble,
And started when he looked upon the Tower,
As loath to bear me to the slaughterhouse.
O, now I need the priest that spake to me!
I now repent I told the pursuivant,
89   As too triumphing, how mine enemies
To-day at Pomfret bloodily were butchered,
91   And I myself secure, in grace and favor.
O Margaret, Margaret, now thy heavy curse
Is lighted on poor Hastings' wretched head!

RATCLIFFE
Come, come, dispatch! The duke would be at dinner.
Make a short shrift; he longs to see your head.

HASTINGS
96   O momentary grace of mortal men,
Which we more hunt for than the grace of God!
98   Who builds his hope in air of your good looks
Lives like a drunken sailor on a mast,
Ready with every nod to tumble down
Into the fatal bowels of the deep.

LOVEL
102   Come, come, dispatch! 'Tis bootless to exclaim.

HASTINGS
O bloody Richard! Miserable England!
I prophesy the fearfull'st time to thee
That ever wretched age hath looked upon.
Come, lead me to the block; bear him my head.
They smile at me who shortly shall be dead.   *Exeunt.*

*

71 *Consorted* associated   80 *whit* bit   81 *fond* foolish   84 *footcloth horse* horse caparisoned with a richly wrought covering reaching almost to the ground   89 *triumphing* exulting   91 *secure* (1) safe, (2) careless   96 *grace* favor   98 *of . . . looks* out of your kind glances (suggesting approval)   102 *bootless* useless
III, v The walls of the Tower   s.d. *rotten* rusty; *ill-favored* ugly   8 *Intending* pretending   10 *offices* particular functions   17 *o'erlook* inspect   25 *harmless* (supply 'most'; cf. l. 33)   27 *book* i.e. table book or 'diary'   31 *conversation* sexual intimacy   32 *attainder of suspects* stain of suspicions   33 *shelt'red* hidden (supply 'most')   36 *great preservation* i.e. the fortunate forestalling of an evil that might have happened

*Enter Richard [Duke of Gloucester], and
Buckingham, in rotten armor, marvellous ill-favored.*

RICHARD
Come, cousin, canst thou quake and change thy color,
Murder thy breath in middle of a word,
And then again begin, and stop again,
As if thou were distraught and mad with terror?

BUCKINGHAM
Tut, I can counterfeit the deep tragedian,
Speak and look back, and pry on every side,
Tremble and start at wagging of a straw:
Intending deep suspicion, ghastly looks   8
Are at my service, like enforcèd smiles;
And both are ready in their offices,   10
At any time to grace my stratagems.
But what, is Catesby gone?

RICHARD
He is; and see, he brings the Mayor along.

Enter the Mayor and Catesby.

BUCKINGHAM
Lord Mayor –

RICHARD
Look to the drawbridge there!

BUCKINGHAM
Hark! a drum.

RICHARD
Catesby, o'erlook the walls.   17

BUCKINGHAM
Lord Mayor, the reason we have sent –

RICHARD
Look back! defend thee! Here are enemies!

BUCKINGHAM
God and our innocence defend and guard us!

Enter Lovel and Ratcliffe, with Hastings' head.

RICHARD
Be patient, they are friends – Ratcliffe and Lovel.

LOVEL
Here is the head of that ignoble traitor,
The dangerous and unsuspected Hastings.

RICHARD
So dear I loved the man that I must weep:
I took him for the plainest harmless creature   25
That breathed upon the earth a Christian;
Made him my book, wherein my soul recorded   27
The history of all her secret thoughts.
So smooth he daubed his vice with show of virtue
That, his apparent open guilt omitted –
I mean, his conversation with Shore's wife –   31
He lived from all attainder of suspects.   32

BUCKINGHAM
Well, well, he was the covert'st shelt'red traitor   33
That ever lived. [Look ye, my Lord Mayor.]
Would you imagine, or almost believe,
Were't not that by great preservation   36
We live to tell it, that the subtle traitor
This day had plotted, in the Council House,
To murder me and my good Lord of Gloucester?

MAYOR
Had he done so?

RICHARD
What? Think you we are Turks or infidels?
Or that we would, against the form of law,
Proceed thus rashly in the villain's death
But that the extreme peril of the case,

The peace of England, and our persons' safety
Enforced us to this execution?

MAYOR

Now fair befall you! He deserved his death,
48 And your good graces both have well proceeded
To warn false traitors from the like attempts.

BUCKINGHAM

I never looked for better at his hands
After he once fell in with Mistress Shore:
Yet had we not determined he should die
Until your lordship came to see his end,
Which now the loving haste of these our friends,
55 Something against our meanings, have prevented;
Because, my lord, I would have had you heard
57 The traitor speak, and timorously confess
The manner and the purpose of his treasons,
That you might well have signified the same
60 Unto the citizens, who haply may
61 Misconster us in him and wail his death.

MAYOR

But, my good lord, your grace's words shall serve,
As well as I had seen, and heard him speak;
And do not doubt, right noble princes both,
But I'll acquaint our duteous citizens
66 With all your just proceedings in this cause.

RICHARD

And to that end we wished your lordship here,
68 T' avoid the censures of the carping world.

BUCKINGHAM

69 But since you come too late of our intent,
70 Yet witness what you hear we did intend:
And so, my good Lord Mayor, we bid farewell.
Exit Mayor.

RICHARD

Go after, after, cousin Buckingham.
73 The Mayor towards Guildhall hies him in all post:
74 There, at your meet'st advantage of the time,
Infer the bastardy of Edward's children.
Tell them how Edward put to death a citizen
Only for saying he would make his son
78 Heir to the Crown, meaning indeed his house,
Which by the sign thereof was termèd so.
80 Moreover, urge his hateful luxury
81 And bestial appetite in change of lust,
Which stretched unto their servants, daughters, wives,
Even where his raging eye or savage heart,
Without control, lusted to make a prey.
Nay, for a need, thus far come near my person:
Tell them, when that my mother went with child
Of that insatiate Edward, noble York,
My princely father, then had wars in France,
And by true computation of the time
Found that the issue was not his begot;
Which well appearèd in his lineaments,
Being nothing like the noble duke my father.
Yet touch this sparingly, as 'twere far off,
Because, my lord, you know my mother lives.

BUCKINGHAM

Doubt not, my lord, I'll play the orator
96 As if the golden fee for which I plead
Were for myself – and so, my lord, adieu.

RICHARD

98 If you thrive well, bring them to Baynard's Castle,
Where you shall find me well accompanied

With reverend fathers and well-learnèd bishops.

BUCKINGHAM

I go; and towards three or four a clock
Look for the news that the Guildhall affords.
Exit Buckingham.

RICHARD

Go, Lovel, with all speed to Doctor Shaw – 103
[*To Catesby*]
Go thou to Friar Penker. – Bid them both 104
Meet me within this hour at Baynard's Castle.
Exeunt [Lovel, Catesby, and Ratcliffe].
Now will I go to take some privy order 106
To draw the brats of Clarence out of sight,
And to give order that no manner person 108
Have any time recourse unto the princes. *Exit.*

       *

Enter a Scrivener [with a paper in his hand].   III, vi

SCRIVENER

Here is the indictment of the good Lord Hastings,
Which in a set hand fairly is engrossed 2
That it may be to-day read o'er in Paul's. 3
And mark how well the sequel hangs together:
Eleven hours I have spent to write it over,
For yesternight by Catesby was it sent me;
The precedent was full as long a-doing; 7
And yet within these five hours Hastings lived,
Untainted, unexamined, free, at liberty.
Here's a good world the while! Who is so gross 10
That cannot see this palpable device?
Yet who's so bold but says he sees it not?
Bad is the world, and all will come to nought
When such ill dealing must be seen in thought. 14
Exit.

Enter Richard [Duke of Gloucester] and   III, vii
Buckingham at several doors.

RICHARD

How now, how now? What say the citizens?

BUCKINGHAM

Now, by the holy Mother of our Lord,
The citizens are mum, say not a word.

RICHARD

Touched you the bastardy of Edward's children?

BUCKINGHAM

I did, with his contract with Lady Lucy 5
And his contract by deputy in France; 6
Th' unsatiate greediness of his desire

48 *proceeded* done   55 *prevented* anticipated   57 *timorously* full of fear
60 *haply* perhaps   61 *Misconster . . . him* i.e. misunderstand our manner of
dealing with him   66 *cause* affair or action (perhaps with legal overtones)
68 *carping* overcritical   69 *of* i.e. in terms of   70 *witness* i.e. bear witness to
73 *Guildhall* the 'town hall' of London; *post* haste   74 *meet'st . . . time* i.e.
the psychological moment   78 *Crown . . . house* i.e. a tavern called 'The
Crown'   80 *luxury* lasciviousness   81 *change of lust* i.e. alteration in the
object of his lust   96 *golden fee* i.e. the crown (play on 'lawyer's fee')   98
Baynard's Castle Richard's stronghold between Blackfriars and London
Bridge   103, 104 *Shaw, Penker* well-known preachers   106 *take . . . order*
make some secret arrangement   108–09 *no . . . unto* i.e. no person of any sort
should have, at any time, admittance to
III, vi Before Baynard's Castle   2 *in . . . engrossed* is written neatly in a
formal legal hand   3 *Paul's* i.e. St Paul's Cathedral   7 *precedent* exemplar
(i.e. the prepared indictment)   10 *the while* just now; *gross* stupid   14 *seen
in thought* expressed only in thinking
III, vii   5 *Lady Lucy* Elizabeth Lucy (to whom Edward IV was not actually
contracted, although she bore him a child)   6 *contract . . . France* (reference
to Edward IV's overtures for marriage with Bona, sister-in-law of Lewis IX
of France; cf. *3 Henry VI*, III, iii, and below, ll. 181–82)

And his enforcement of the city wives ;
His tyranny for trifles ; his own bastardy,
As being got, your father then in France,
And his resemblance, being not like the duke.
Withal I did infer your lineaments,
13   Being the right idea of your father
Both in your form and nobleness of mind ;
Laid open all your victories in Scotland,
Your discipline in war, wisdom in peace,
Your bounty, virtue, fair humility ;
Indeed, left nothing fitting for your purpose
Untouched, or slightly handlèd in discourse ;
And when mine oratory drew to an end,
I bid them that did love their country's good
Cry, 'God save Richard, England's royal king !'

RICHARD
And did they so ?

BUCKINGHAM
No, so God help me, they spake not a word,
But, like dumb statuës or breathing stones,
Stared each on other, and looked deadly pale.
Which when I saw, I reprehended them
And asked the Mayor what meant this wilful silence.
His answer was, the people were not usèd
30   To be spoke to but by the Recorder.
Then he was urged to tell my tale again :
'Thus saith the duke, thus hath the duke inferred,' –
But nothing spake in warrant from himself.
When he had done, some followers of mine own,
At lower end of the hall, hurled up their caps,
And some ten voices cried, 'God save King Richard !'
And thus I took the vantage of those few :
'Thanks, gentle citizens and friends,' quoth I.
'This general applause and cheerful shout
Argues your wisdoms and your love to Richard' –
And even here brake off and came away.

RICHARD
What tongueless blocks were they ! Would they not
   speak ?

[BUCKINGHAM
No, by my troth, my lord.]

RICHARD
Will not the Mayor then and his brethren come ?

BUCKINGHAM
45   The Mayor is here at hand. Intend some fear ;
46   Be not you spoke with but by mighty suit ;
And look you get a prayer book in your hand
And stand between two churchmen, good my lord,
49   For on that ground I'll make a holy descant ;
And be not easily won to our requests.
51   Play the maid's part : still answer nay, and take it.

RICHARD
I go ; and if you plead as well for them

As I can say nay to thee for myself,
No doubt we bring it to a happy issue.

BUCKINGHAM
Go, go, up to the leads ! The Lord Mayor knocks.   55
                              [Exit Richard.]
   Enter the Mayor [, Aldermen,] and Citizens.
Welcome, my lord. I dance attendance here ;
I think the duke will not be spoke withal.   57
   Enter Catesby.
Now, Catesby, what says your lord to my request ?

CATESBY
He doth entreat your grace, my noble lord,
To visit him to-morrow or next day :
He is within, with two right reverend fathers,
Divinely bent to meditation,   62
And in no worldly suits would he be moved
To draw him from his holy exercise.

BUCKINGHAM
Return, good Catesby, to the gracious duke :
Tell him, myself, the Mayor and Aldermen,
In deep designs, in matter of great moment,
No less importing than our general good,   68
Are come to have some conference with his grace.

CATESBY
I'll signify so much unto him straight.   Exit.

BUCKINGHAM
Ah ha, my lord ! this prince is not an Edward.
He is not lulling on a lewd love-bed,
But on his knees at meditation ;   72
Not dallying with a brace of courtesans,
But meditating with two deep divines ;   75
Not sleeping, to engross his idle body,   76
But praying, to enrich his watchful soul.
Happy were England, would this virtuous prince
Take on his grace the sovereignty thereof ;
But sure I fear we shall not win him to it.

MAYOR
Marry, God defend his grace should say us nay !   81

BUCKINGHAM
I fear he will. Here Catesby comes again.
   Enter Catesby.
Now, Catesby, what says his grace ?

CATESBY   My lord,
He wonders to what end you have assemblèd
Such troops of citizens to come to him,
His grace not being warned thereof before :
He fears, my lord, you mean no good to him.

BUCKINGHAM
Sorry I am my noble cousin should
Suspect me that I mean no good to him :
By heaven, we come to him in perfit love ;   90
And so once more return and tell his grace.
                              Exit [Catesby].
When holy and devout religious men
Are at their beads, 'tis much to draw them thence, 93
So sweet is zealous contemplation.
   Enter Richard aloft, between two Bishops. [Catesby
   returns.]

MAYOR
See where his grace stands, 'tween two clergymen.

BUCKINGHAM
Two props of virtue for a Christian prince,
To stay him from the fall of vanity ;   97
And see, a book of prayer in his hand –

13 *right idea* true image   30 *Recorder* (a magistrate appointed by the mayor and aldermen to serve as an 'oral record' of proceedings in city law courts and government)   45 *Intend* pretend   46 *by mighty suit* by great solicitation   49 *descant* (see I, i, 27)   51 *maid's* girl's ; *answer . . . it* i.e. keep saying no, but at the same time accept whatever is being offered (proverbial)   55 *leads* sheets of metal used to cover a (flat) roof   57 *withal* with   62 *Divinely bent* (1) spiritually inclined, (2) kneeling like a divine (cf. l. 73)   68 *No . . . than* i.e. of no less significance than one concerned with   72 *lulling* lolling, lounging   75 *deep* i.e. spiritually and academically learned   76 *engross* fatten   81 *defend* forbid   90 *perfit* perfect   93 *'tis much* i.e. it takes a great deal   97 *fall of vanity* downfall caused by vanity

99   True ornaments to know a holy man.
Famous Plantagenet, most gracious prince,
Lend favorable ear to our requests,
And pardon us the interruption
Of thy devotion and right Christian zeal.

RICHARD
My lord, there needs no such apology :
I do beseech your grace to pardon me,
Who, earnest in the service of my God,
Deferred the visitation of my friends.
But, leaving this, what is your grace's pleasure ?

BUCKINGHAM
Even that (I hope) which pleaseth God above
And all good men of this ungoverned isle.

RICHARD
I do suspect I have done some offense
112   That seems disgracious in the city's eye,
And that you come to reprehend my ignorance.

BUCKINGHAM
You have, my lord. Would it might please your grace,
On our entreaties, to amend your fault !

RICHARD
Else wherefore breathe I in a Christian land ?

BUCKINGHAM
Know then it is your fault that you resign
The supreme seat, the throne majestical,
The scept'red office of your ancestors,
120   Your state of fortune and your due of birth,
The lineal glory of your royal house,
To the corruption of a blemished stock ;
123   Whiles, in the mildness of your sleepy thoughts,
Which here we waken to our country's good,
125   The noble isle doth want her proper limbs ;
Her face defaced with scars of infamy,
Her royal stock graft with ignoble plants,
128   And almost should'red in the swallowing gulf
Of dark forgetfulness and deep oblivion.
130   Which to recure, we heartily solicit
Your gracious self to take on you the charge
And kingly government of this your land ;
Not as Protector, steward, substitute,
134   Or lowly factor for another's gain ;
135   But as successively, from blood to blood,
136   Your right of birth, your empery, your own.
For this, consorted with the citizens,
Your very worshipful and loving friends,
And by their vehement instigation,
In this just cause come I to move your grace.

RICHARD
I cannot tell if to depart in silence,
Or bitterly to speak in your reproof,
143   Best fitteth my degree or your condition.
If not to answer, you might haply think
145   Tongue-tied ambition, not replying, yielded
To bear the golden yoke of sovereignty
147   Which fondly you would here impose on me.
If to reprove you for this suit of yours,
149   So seasoned with your faithful love to me,
Then, on the other side, I checked my friends.
Therefore – to speak, and to avoid the first,
And then, in speaking, not to incur the last –
153   Definitively thus I answer you.
Your love deserves my thanks, but my desert
Unmeritable shuns your high request.

First, if all obstacles were cut away,
And that my path were even to the crown,   157
As the ripe revenue and due of birth,
Yet so much is my poverty of spirit,   159
So mighty and so many my defects,
That I would rather hide me from my greatness,
Being a bark to brook no mighty sea,   162
Than in my greatness covet to be hid   163
And in the vapor of my glory smothered.
But, God be thanked, there is no need of me,
And much I need to help you, were there need :
The royal tree hath left us royal fruit,
Which, mellowed by the stealing hours of time,
Will well become the seat of majesty
And make (no doubt) us happy by his reign.
On him I lay that you would lay on me,
The right and fortune of his happy stars,   172
Which God defend that I should wring from him !

BUCKINGHAM
My lord, this argues conscience in your grace,
But the respects thereof are nice and trivial,   175
All circumstances well considerèd.
You say that Edward is your brother's son :
So say we too, but not by Edward's wife ;
For first was he contract to Lady Lucy –
Your mother lives a witness to his vow –
And afterward by substitute betrothed   181
To Bona, sister to the King of France.
These both put off, a poor petitioner,
A care-crazed mother to a many sons,
A beauty-waning and distressèd widow,
Even in the afternoon of her best days,
Made prize and purchase of his wanton eye,   187
Seduced the pitch and height of his degree   188
To base declension and loathed bigamy.   189
By her, in his unlawful bed, he got
This Edward, whom our manners call the prince.
More bitterly could I expostulate,
Save that, for reverence to some alive,
I give a sparing limit to my tongue.
Then, good my lord, take to your royal self   195
This proffered benefit of dignity ;
If not to bless us and the land withal,
Yet to draw forth your noble ancestry
From the corruption of abusing times
Unto a lineal true-derivèd course.

MAYOR
Do, good my lord ; your citizens entreat you.

99 *ornaments* (referring to the clergymen and prayer book) 112 *disgracious* disliked 120 *state of fortune* position of greatness 123 *sleepy* reposeful 125 *proper* own 128 *should'red in* violently jostled into 130 *recure* restore to health 134 *factor* agent 135 *successively* in order of succession 136 *empery* empire or sole rule 143 *fitteth . . . condition* accords with my rank (as duke) or your social position (as commoners) 145 *Tongue-tied . . . yielded* i.e. silence yields consent (proverbial) 147 *fondly* foolishly 149 *seasoned* made agreeable (given a pleasant taste) 153 *Definitively* once and for all 157 *even* without impediment 159 *poverty of spirit* lack of self-assertion (perhaps meant also as an indirect compliment to himself, since 'Blessed are the poor in spirit' [Matthew v, 3]) 162 *bark* small sailing vessel 163 *Than . . . hid* than desire to be enveloped by my greatness 172 *happy* auspicious 175 *respects . . . nice* i.e. the considerations on which you argue are overscrupulous 181 *substitute* proxy 187 *purchase* booty 188 *Seduced . . . degree* i.e. led away (or down from) the eminence and greatness associated with his noble rank 189 *declension* falling away from a high standard 195 *good my lord* my good lord

BUCKINGHAM
Refuse not, mighty lord, this proffered love.
CATESBY
O, make them joyful, grant their lawful suit!
RICHARD
Alas, why would you heap this care on me?
I am unfit for state and majesty:
I do beseech you take it not amiss,
I cannot nor I will not yield to you.
BUCKINGHAM
208   If you refuse it – as, in love and zeal,
Loath to depose the child, your brother's son;
As well we know your tenderness of heart
211   And gentle, kind, effeminate remorse,
Which we have noted in you to your kindred
213   And egally indeed to all estates –
214   Yet know, whe'er you accept our suit or no,
Your brother's son shall never reign our king,
But we will plant some other in the throne
To the disgrace and downfall of your house;
And in this resolution here we leave you.
Come, citizens. Zounds, I'll entreat no more!
[RICHARD
O, do not swear, my lord of Buckingham.]
     Exeunt [Buckingham, Mayor, Aldermen,
         and Citizens].
CATESBY
Call him again, sweet prince, accept their suit:
222   If you deny them, all the land will rue it.
RICHARD
Will you enforce me to a world of cares?
Call them again. I am not made of stones,
But penetrable to your kind entreaties,
Albeit against my conscience and my soul.
     Enter Buckingham and the rest.
Cousin of Buckingham, and sage grave men,
Since you will buckle fortune on my back,
229   To bear her burden, whe'er I will or no,
I must have patience to endure the load;
But if black scandal or foul-faced reproach
232   Attend the sequel of your imposition,
233   Your mere enforcement shall acquittance me
From all the impure blots and stains thereof;
For God doth know, and you may partly see,
How far I am from the desire of this.
MAYOR
God bless your grace! We see it and will say it.
RICHARD
In saying so you shall but say the truth.
BUCKINGHAM
Then I salute you with this royal title –
Long live King Richard, England's worthy king!
ALL
Amen.

BUCKINGHAM
To-morrow may it please you to be crowned?
RICHARD
Even when you please, for you will have it so.
BUCKINGHAM
To-morrow then we will attend your grace,
And so most joyfully we take our leave.
RICHARD *[to the Bishops]*
Come, let us to our holy work again. –
Farewell, my cousin; farewell, gentle friends.   *Exeunt.*

         *

   Enter the Queen [Elizabeth], the Duchess of   IV, i
   York, and Marquess [of] Dorset [at one door];
   Anne Duchess of Gloucester [, Lady Margaret
   Plantagenet, Clarence's young daughter, at
   another door].
DUCHESS OF YORK
Who meets us here? My niece Plantagenet,
Led in the hand of her kind aunt of Gloucester?
Now, for my life, she's wand'ring to the Tower   3
On pure heart's love, to greet the tender prince.
Daughter, well met.
ANNE   God give your graces both
A happy and a joyful time of day!
QUEEN ELIZABETH
As much to you, good sister. Whither away?
ANNE
No farther than the Tower, and, as I guess,
Upon the like devotion as yourselves,
To gratulate the gentle princes there.   10
QUEEN ELIZABETH
Kind sister, thanks. We'll enter all together.
     Enter the Lieutenant [Brakenbury].
And in good time, here the Lieutenant comes.
Master Lieutenant, pray you, by your leave,
How doth the prince, and my young son of York?
LIEUTENANT
Right well, dear madam. By your patience,
I may not suffer you to visit them;
The king hath strictly charged the contrary.
QUEEN ELIZABETH
The king? Who's that?
LIEUTENANT   I mean the Lord Protector.
QUEEN ELIZABETH
The Lord protect him from that kingly title!   19
Hath he set bounds between their love and me?   20
I am their mother; who shall bar me from them?
DUCHESS OF YORK
I am their father's mother; I will see them.
ANNE
Their aunt I am in law, in love their mother;
Then bring me to their sights. I'll bear thy blame
And take thy office from thee on my peril.   25
LIEUTENANT
No, madam, no! I may not leave it so: 26
I am bound by oath, and therefore pardon me.
         Exit Lieutenant.
     Enter Stanley [Earl of Derby].
DERBY
Let me but meet you, ladies, an hour hence,
And I'll salute your grace of York as mother
And reverend looker-on of two fair queens.   30

208 *as* i.e. as the result of being   211 *kind, effeminate remorse* natural, tender pity   213 *egally* equally   214 *whe'er* whether   222 *rue* suffer for   229 *To* i.e. in order to make me   232 *your imposition* i.e. the fortune (kingship) which you lay upon me   233 *mere* absolute; *acquittance* acquit
IV, i *Before the Tower*   3 *for my life* i.e. staking my life upon it   10 *gratulate* congratulate   19 *The Lord . . . title* i.e. may God in his capacity as Richard's legal guardian exercise his authority to prevent Richard from getting the title of king   20 *bounds* barriers   25 *take . . . thee* i.e. take your office upon myself   26 *leave it* i.e. give up my office   30 *looker-on* beholder (or here perhaps 'guardian')

[To Anne]
Come, madam, you must straight to Westminster,
There to be crownèd Richard's royal queen.

QUEEN ELIZABETH

33 Ah, cut my lace asunder,
That my pent heart may have some scope to beat,
Or else I swoon with this dead-killing news!

ANNE

Despiteful tidings! O unpleasing news!

DORSET

Be of good cheer. Mother, how fares your grace?

QUEEN ELIZABETH

O Dorset, speak not to me, get thee gone!
Death and destruction dogs thee at thy heels;
40 Thy mother's name is ominous to children.
If thou wilt outstrip death, go cross the seas,
And live with Richmond, from the reach of hell.
Go hie thee, hie thee from this slaughterhouse,
Lest thou increase the number of the dead
And make me die the thrall of Margaret's curse,
46 Nor mother, wife, nor England's counted queen.

DERBY

Full of wise care is this your counsel, madam:
48 Take all the swift advantage of the hours.
49 You shall have letters from me to my son
50 In your behalf, to meet you on the way:
51 Be not ta'en tardy by unwise delay.

DUCHESS OF YORK

52 O ill-dispersing wind of misery!
O my accursèd womb, the bed of death!
54 A cockatrice hast thou hatched to the world,
Whose unavoided eye is murderous.

DERBY

Come, madam, come! I in all haste was sent.

ANNE

And I with all unwillingness will go.
58 O, would to God that the inclusive verge
Of golden metal that must round my brow
Were red-hot steel, to sear me to the brains!
61 Anointed let me be with deadly venom
And die ere men can say, 'God save the queen!'

QUEEN ELIZABETH

Go, go, poor soul! I envy not thy glory.
To feed my humor wish thyself no harm.

ANNE

No? Why! when he that is my husband now
Came to me as I followed Henry's corse,
When scarce the blood was well washed from his hands
Which issuèd from my other angel husband
And that dear saint which then I weeping followed –
O, when, I say, I looked on Richard's face,
This was my wish: 'Be thou,' quoth I, 'accursed
72 For making me, so young, so old a widow!
And when thou wed'st, let sorrow haunt thy bed;
And be thy wife, if any be so mad,
More miserable by the life of thee
Than thou hast made me by my dear lord's death!'
Lo, ere I can repeat this curse again,
Within so small a time, my woman's heart
Grossly grew captive to his honey words
And proved the subject of mine own soul's curse,
Which hitherto hath held mine eyes from rest;
For never yet one hour in his bed
83 Did I enjoy the golden dew of sleep,

But with his timorous dreams was still awaked.   84
Besides, he hates me for my father Warwick.
And will (no doubt) shortly be rid of me.

QUEEN ELIZABETH

Poor heart, adieu! I pity thy complaining.   87

ANNE

No more than with my soul I mourn for yours.

DORSET

Farewell, thou woeful welcomer of glory.

ANNE

Adieu, poor soul, that tak'st thy leave of it.

DUCHESS OF YORK *[to Dorset]*

Go thou to Richmond, and good fortune guide thee!
[To Anne]
Go thou to Richard, and good angels tend thee!
[To Queen Elizabeth]
Go thou to sanctuary, and good thoughts possess thee!
I to my grave, where peace and rest lie with me!
Eighty odd years of sorrow have I seen,
And each hour's joy wracked with a week of teen.   96

QUEEN ELIZABETH

Stay, yet look back with me unto the Tower.
Pity, you ancient stones, those tender babes
Whom envy hath immured within your walls –
Rough cradle for such little pretty ones!
Rude ragged nurse, old sullen playfellow
For tender princes – use my babies well!
So foolish sorrows bids your stones farewell.   *Exeunt.*

*

Sound a sennet. Enter Richard [as King], in pomp,   IV, ii
Buckingham, Catesby, Ratcliffe, Lovel [, a Page,
and others].

KING RICHARD

Stand all apart. Cousin of Buckingham –

BUCKINGHAM

My gracious sovereign?

KING RICHARD

Give me thy hand.
Sound. [Here he ascendeth the throne.]
Thus high, by thy advice
And thy assistance, is King Richard seated:
But shall we wear these glories for a day?
Or shall they last, and we rejoice in them?

BUCKINGHAM

Still live they, and for ever let them last!

KING RICHARD

Ah, Buckingham, now do I play the touch,   8
To try if thou be current gold indeed:
Young Edward lives. Think now what I would speak.

33 *cut my lace* (Elizabethan women wore tightly laced bodices) 40 *ominous*
portending evil 46 *counted* esteemed 48 *Take* . . . *hours* i.e. make full use
of your head start 49 *You* . . . *me* i.e. I will have letters written 50 *to*
. . . *way* (supply 'telling him' before 'to') 51 *ta'en* taken, caught 52 *ill-*
dispersing misfortune-scattering 54 *cockatrice* basilisk (see I, ii, 150)
58 *inclusive verge* surrounding circle (i.e. the crown, with reference to the
band of red-hot steel sometimes placed as punishment on the heads of
traitors) 61 *Anointed* (anointing with holy oil was part of the ceremony
of coronation) 72 *so young* . . . *widow* (being so young she will be a widow
for a long time before she too dies) 83 *golden dew* i.e. precious refreshment
84 *timorous* full of fear; *still* continuously 87 *complaining* cause for complaint 96 *wracked* destroyed; *teen* grief
IV, ii The royal palace s.d. *sennet* a special set of notes on the trumpet
used for entrance and exit of processions 8 *touch* touchstone (a means of
testing gold)

BUCKINGHAM
Say on, my loving lord.
KING RICHARD
Why, Buckingham, I say I would be king.
BUCKINGHAM
Why, so you are, my thrice-renownèd liege.
KING RICHARD
Ha ! Am I king ? 'Tis so. But Edward lives.
BUCKINGHAM
True, noble prince.
15 KING RICHARD   O bitter consequence,
That Edward still should live true noble prince !
Cousin, thou wast not wont to be so dull.
Shall I be plain ? I wish the bastards dead,
And I would have it suddenly performed.
What say'st thou now ? Speak suddenly, be brief.
BUCKINGHAM
Your grace may do your pleasure.
KING RICHARD
Tut, tut, thou art all ice ; thy kindness freezes.
Say, have I thy consent that they shall die ?
BUCKINGHAM
Give me some little breath, some pause, dear lord,
Before I positively speak in this :
26 I will resolve you herein presently. *Exit Buck[ingham].*
CATESBY *[aside to another]*
The king is angry. See, he gnaws his lip.
KING RICHARD
28 I will converse with iron-witted fools
And unrespective boys. None are for me
30 That look into me with considerate eyes.
High-reaching Buckingham grows circumspect.
Boy !
PAGE
My lord ?
KING RICHARD
Know'st thou not any whom corrupting gold
Will tempt unto a close exploit of death ?
PAGE
I know a discontented gentleman
Whose humble means match not his haughty spirit :
Gold were as good as twenty orators,
And will, no doubt, tempt him to anything.
KING RICHARD
What is his name ?
PAGE   His name, my lord, is Tyrrel.
KING RICHARD
I partly know the man. Go call him hither, boy.
                                        Exit [Page].
42 The deep-revolving witty Buckingham
No more shall be the neighbor to my counsels.
44 Hath he so long held out with me, untired,
And stops he now for breath ? Well, be it so.
        Enter Stanley [Earl of Derby].
How now, Lord Stanley ? What's the news ?
DERBY   Know, my loving lord,

The Marquess Dorset, as I hear, is fled
To Richmond in the parts where he abides.
        [Stands aside.]
KING RICHARD
Come hither, Catesby. Rumor it abroad
That Anne my wife is very grievous sick :
I will take order for her keeping close.   51
Inquire me out some mean poor gentleman,
Whom I will marry straight to Clarence' daughter.
The boy is foolish, and I fear not him.   54
Look how thou dream'st ! I say again, give out
That Anne, my queen, is sick and like to die.
About it ! for it stands me much upon   57
To stop all hopes whose growth may damage me.
                            [Exit Catesby.]
I must be married to my brother's daughter,
Or else my kingdom stands on brittle glass :
Murder her brothers, and then marry her –
Uncertain way of gain ! But I am in
So far in blood that sin will pluck on sin.
Tear-falling pity dwells not in this eye.   64
        Enter [Page, with] Tyrrel.
Is thy name Tyrrel ?
TYRREL
James Tyrrel, and your most obedient subject.
KING RICHARD
Art thou indeed ?
TYRREL   Prove me, my gracious lord.
KING RICHARD
Dar'st thou resolve to kill a friend of mine ?
TYRREL
Please you ;   69
But I had rather kill two enemies.
KING RICHARD
Why, there thou hast it ! Two deep enemies,
Foes to my rest and my sweet sleep's disturbers,
Are they that I would have thee deal upon :
Tyrrel, I mean those bastards in the Tower.
TYRREL
Let me have open means to come to them,   75
And soon I'll rid you from the fear of them.
KING RICHARD
Thou sing'st sweet music. Hark, come hither, Tyrrel.
Go, by this token. Rise, and lend thine ear.
        Whispers.
There is no more but so : say it is done,
And I will love thee and prefer thee for it.
TYRREL
I will dispatch it straight.   *Exit.*
        Enter Buckingham.
BUCKINGHAM
My lord, I have considered in my mind
The late request that you did sound me in.
KING RICHARD
Well, let that rest. Dorset is fled to Richmond.
BUCKINGHAM
I hear the news, my lord.
KING RICHARD
Stanley, he is your wife's son. Well, look unto it.
BUCKINGHAM
My lord, I claim the gift, my due by promise,
For which your honor and your faith is pawned :
Th' earldom of Hereford and the moveables
Which you have promisèd I shall possess.   90

---

15 *consequence* conclusion 26 *presently* at once 28-29 *iron-witted . . . unrespective* unfeeling . . . thoughtless 30 *considerate* (eyes) which weigh my motives, thoughtful 42 *deep-revolving* profoundly politic 44 *held out* i.e. lasted the course 51 *take . . . close* make arrangements for her imprisonment 54 *foolish* i.e. an idiot 57 *stands . . . upon* is of great importance to me 64 *Tear-falling* i.e. weeping 69 *Please you* if it pleases you 75 *open* free

KING RICHARD
Stanley, look to your wife : if she convey
Letters to Richmond, you shall answer it.
BUCKINGHAM
What says your highness to my just request?
KING RICHARD
I do remember me Henry the Sixth
Did prophesy that Richmond should be king
96   When Richmond was a little peevish boy.
A king ! – perhaps – [perhaps –
BUCKINGHAM
My lord –
KING RICHARD
How chance the prophet could not at that time
Have told me, I being by, that I should kill him?
BUCKINGHAM
My lord, your promise for the earldom !
KING RICHARD
Richmond ! When last I was at Exeter,
The Mayor in courtesy showed me the castle,
104   And called it Rouge-mount ; at which name I started,
105   Because a bard of Ireland told me once
I should not live long after I saw Richmond.
BUCKINGHAM
My lord –
KING RICHARD
Ay, what's a clock ?
BUCKINGHAM
I am thus bold to put your grace in mind
Of what you promised me.
KING RICHARD   Well, but what's a clock ?
BUCKINGHAM
Upon the stroke of ten.
KING RICHARD   Well, let it strike.
BUCKINGHAM
Why let it strike ?
KING RICHARD
113   Because that like a Jack thou keep'st the stroke
Betwixt thy begging and my meditation.
I am not in the giving vein to-day.]
BUCKINGHAM
116   May it please you to resolve me in my suit.
KING RICHARD
Thou troublest me ; I am not in the vein.
               Exeunt [all but Buckingham].
BUCKINGHAM
And is it thus ? Repays he my deep service
With such contempt ? Made I him king for this ?
O, let me think on Hastings, and be gone
121   To Brecknock while my fearful head is on !   *Exit.*

            *

IV, iii   *Enter Tyrrel.*
TYRREL
The tyrannous and bloody act is done,
2   The most arch deed of piteous massacre
That ever yet this land was guilty of.
Dighton and Forrest, who I did suborn
To do this piece of ruthless butchery,
Albeit they were fleshed villains, bloody dogs,
7   Melted with tenderness and kind compassion,
Wept like to children in their death's sad story.
'O, thus,' quoth Dighton, 'lay the gentle babes.'
'Thus, thus,' quoth Forrest, 'girdling one another

Within their alablaster innocent arms.   11
Their lips were four red roses on a stalk,
Which in their summer beauty kissed each other.
A book of prayers on their pillow lay,
Which once,' quoth Forrest, 'almost changed my mind ;
But O ! the devil' – there the villain stopped ;
When Dighton thus told on – 'We smotherèd
The most replenishèd sweet work of nature   18
That from the prime creation e'er she framèd.'   19
Hence both are gone with conscience and remorse :
They could not speak ; and so I left them both,
To bear this tidings to the bloody king.
           Enter [King] Richard.
And here he comes. All health, my sovereign lord !
KING RICHARD
Kind Tyrrel, am I happy in thy news ?
TYRREL
If to have done the thing you gave in charge   25
Beget your happiness, be happy then,
For it is done.
KING RICHARD   But didst thou see them dead ?
TYRREL
I did, my lord.
KING RICHARD   And buried, gentle Tyrrel ?
TYRREL
The chaplain of the Tower hath buried them ;
But where (to say the truth) I do not know.
KING RICHARD
Come to me, Tyrrel, soon at after supper,
When thou shalt tell the process of their death.   32
Meantime, but think how I may do thee good,
And be inheritor of thy desire.
Farewell till then.
TYRREL   I humbly take my leave.   *[Exit.]*
KING RICHARD
The son of Clarence have I pent up close,
His daughter meanly have I matched in marriage,
The sons of Edward sleep in Abraham's bosom,
And Anne my wife hath bid this world good night.
Now, for I know the Britain Richmond aims   40
At young Elizabeth, my brother's daughter,
And by that knot looks proudly on the crown,   42
To her go I, a jolly thriving wooer.
           Enter Ratcliffe.
RATCLIFFE
My lord –
KING RICHARD
Good or bad news, that thou com'st in so bluntly ?
RATCLIFFE
Bad news, my lord. Morton is fled to Richmond,
And Buckingham, backed with the hardy Welshmen,
Is in the field, and still his power increaseth.

96 *peevish* foolish   104 *Rouge-mount* i.e. Redhill (the incident is historical, but the play on 'Richmond' is forced)   105 *bard* (the Celtic bards or poets were also considered prophets)   113 *Jack* a metal figure of a man which appeared to strike the hours in early clocks (play on 'lowbred fellow'; cf. *begging*, l. 114)   113–14 *keep'st . . . meditation* (like a Jack you) suspend the moment of striking (i.e. coming to the point in your begging suit) and thus disturb my train of thought (so *let it strike*, l. 111)   116 *resolve* i.e. give a final answer   121 *Brecknock* a manor house in Wales ; *fearful* full of fears

IV, iii The same   2 *most arch* chiefest   7 *kind* natural   11 *alablaster* white (same as 'alabaster')   18 *replenishèd* complete (in the sense of being full of virtues and beauty)   19 *prime* first   25 *done* i.e. had done   32 *process* story   40 *for* because ; *Britain* Breton   42 *knot* i.e. marriage

KING RICHARD

Ely with Richmond troubles me more near
Than Buckingham and his rash-levied strength.
51 Come ! I have learned that fearful commenting
Is leaden servitor to dull delay ;
53 Delay leads impotent and snail-paced beggary.
54 Then fiery expedition be my wing,
55 Jove's Mercury, and herald for a king !
Go, muster men. My counsel is my shield ;
We must be brief when traitors brave the field.   *Exeunt.*

*

IV, iv   *Enter old Queen Margaret.*

QUEEN MARGARET

1 So now prosperity begins to mellow
And drop into the rotten mouth of death.
Here in these confines slily have I lurked
To watch the waning of mine enemies.
5 A dire induction am I witness to,
6 And will to France, hoping the consequence
Will prove as bitter, black, and tragical.
Withdraw thee, wretched Margaret ! Who comes here ?
          [Retires.]
    Enter Duchess [of York] and Queen [Elizabeth].

QUEEN ELIZABETH

Ah, my poor princes ! ah, my tender babes !
10 My unblown flowers, new-appearing sweets !
If yet your gentle souls fly in the air
12 And be not fixed in doom perpetual,
Hover about me with your airy wings
And hear your mother's lamentation !

QUEEN MARGARET *[aside]*

Hover about her. Say that right for right
Hath dimmed your infant morn to agèd night.

DUCHESS OF YORK

17 So many miseries have crazed my voice
That my woe-wearied tongue is still and mute.
Edward Plantagenet, why art thou dead ?

QUEEN MARGARET *[aside]*

20 Plantagenet doth quit Plantagenet ;
21 Edward for Edward pays a dying debt.

QUEEN ELIZABETH

Wilt thou, O God, fly from such gentle lambs
And throw them in the entrails of the wolf ?
24 When didst thou sleep when such a deed was done ?

QUEEN MARGARET *[aside]*

When holy Harry died, and my sweet son.

DUCHESS OF YORK

Dead life, blind sight, poor mortal-living ghost,   26
Woe's scene, world's shame, grave's due by life usurped,   27
Brief abstract and record of tedious days,   28
Rest thy unrest on England's lawful earth,
        [Sits down.]
Unlawfully made drunk with innocent blood !

QUEEN ELIZABETH

Ah that thou wouldst as soon afford a grave
As thou canst yield a melancholy seat !
Then would I hide my bones, not rest them here.
Ah, who hath any cause to mourn but we ?
        [Sits down by her.]

QUEEN MARGARET *[comes forward]*

If ancient sorrow be most reverent,
Give mine the benefit of seniory   36
And let my griefs frown on the upper hand.   37
If sorrow can admit society,
        [Sits down with them.]
[Tell over your woes again by viewing mine].   39
I had an Edward, till a Richard killed him ;
I had a Harry, till a Richard killed him :
Thou hadst an Edward, till a Richard killed him ;
Thou hadst a Richard, till a Richard killed him.

DUCHESS OF YORK

I had a Richard too, and thou didst kill him ;
I had a Rutland too, thou holp'st to kill him.   45

QUEEN MARGARET

Thou hadst a Clarence too, and Richard killed him.
From forth the kennel of thy womb hath crept
A hellhound that doth hunt us all to death :
That dog, that had his teeth before his eyes,
To worry lambs and lap their gentle blood,
That foul defacer of God's handiwork,
That excellent grand tyrant of the earth   52
That reigns in gallèd eyes of weeping souls,   53
Thy womb let loose to chase us to our graves.
O upright, just, and true-disposing God,
How do I thank thee that this carnal cur   56
Preys on the issue of his mother's body
And makes her pew-fellow with others' moan !   58

DUCHESS OF YORK

O Harry's wife, triumph not in my woes !
God witness with me, I have wept for thine.

QUEEN MARGARET

Bear with me ! I am hungry for revenge,
And now I cloy me with beholding it.
Thy Edward he is dead, that killed my Edward ;
Thy other Edward dead, to quit my Edward ;   64
Young York he is but boot, because both they   65
Matched not the high perfection of my loss.
Thy Clarence he is dead that stabbed my Edward,
And the beholders of this frantic play,
Th'adulterate Hastings, Rivers, Vaughan, Grey,   69
Untimely smoth'red in their dusky graves.
Richard yet lives, hell's black intelligencer ;   71
Only reserved their factor to buy souls   72
And send them thither. But at hand, at hand,
Ensues his piteous and unpitied end.
Earth gapes, hell burns, fiends roar, saints pray,   75
To have him suddenly conveyed from hence.
Cancel his bond of life, dear God, I pray,

51–52 *fearful . . . servitor* timorous talk is the sluggish attendant   53 *beggary* ruin   54 *expedition* speed   55 *Mercury* messenger of the gods (note Richard's neat equation of himself with Jove, king of the gods)
IV, iv Before the royal palace   1–2 *So . . . death* (image taken from ripe fruit falling and rotting on the ground)   5 *induction* beginning (as of a play)   6 *consequence* conclusion (as the catastrophe of a play)   10 *sweets* fragrant flowers   12 *fixed . . . perpetual* i.e. assigned by God's judgment to their final place of punishment or reward   17 *crazed* cracked   20 *quit* make up for   21 *dying debt* i.e. a debt for which the payment is death   24 *When* when ever (before this time)   26 *mortal-living* dead-alive   27 *grave's . . . usurped* i.e. a dead body tyrannized over by life   28 *Brief abstract* epitome ('brief' may also be intended to limit 'record')   36 *seniory* seniority   37 *frown . . . hand* i.e. have the mastery in looking grim or dismal   39 *Tell over* count   45 *holp'st* helpedest   52 *excellent* pre-eminently   53 *reigns . . . souls* i.e. flourishes (as a ruler) upon the tears wept from sore eyes of those individuals (whom he has injured)   56 *carnal* carnivorous   58 *pew-fellow* companion   64 *quit* redeem   65 *but boot* i.e. thrown in as an extra   69 *adulterate* guilty of adultery   71 *intelligencer* secret agent   72 *Only . . . factor* above all others chosen as their agent   75–77 *Earth . . . pray* (Shakespeare seems to be thinking of the conclusion of Marlowe's *Doctor Faustus*)

That I may live and say, 'The dog is dead.'

QUEEN ELIZABETH

O, thou didst prophesy the time would come
That I should wish for thee to help me curse
That bottled spider, that foul bunch-backed toad!

QUEEN MARGARET

I called thee then vain flourish of my fortune;
I called thee then poor shadow, painted queen,
The presentation of but what I was,

85 The flattering index of a direful pageant,
One heaved a-high to be hurled down below,
A mother only mocked with two fair babes,

88 A dream of what thou wast, a garish flag,
To be the aim of every dangerous shot;
A sign of dignity, a breath, a bubble,

91 A queen in jest, only to fill the scene.
Where is thy husband now? Where be thy brothers?
Where be thy two sons? Wherein dost thou joy?
Who sues and kneels and says, 'God save the queen'?
Where be the bending peers that flattered thee?
Where be the thronging troops that followed thee?

97 Decline all this, and see what now thou art:
For happy wife, a most distressèd widow;
For joyful mother, one that wails the name;
For one being sued to, one that humbly sues;

101 For queen, a very caitiff crowned with care;
For she that scorned at me, now scorned of me;
For she being feared of all, now fearing one;
For she commanding all, obeyed of none.
Thus hath the course of justice whirled about
And left thee but a very prey to time,
Having no more but thought of what thou wast,
To torture thee the more, being what thou art.
Thou didst usurp my place, and dost thou not
Usurp the just proportion of my sorrow?

111 Now thy proud neck bears half my burdened yoke,
From which even here I slip my weary head
And leave the burden of it all on thee.
Farewell, York's wife, and queen of sad mischance!
These English woes shall make me smile in France.

QUEEN ELIZABETH

O thou well skilled in curses, stay awhile
And teach me how to curse mine enemies!

QUEEN MARGARET

Forbear to sleep the nights, and fast the days;
Compare dead happiness with living woe;
Think that thy babes were sweeter than they were
And he that slew them fouler than he is:

122 Bett'ring thy loss makes the bad causer worse;
Revolving this will teach thee how to curse.

QUEEN ELIZABETH

124 My words are dull. O, quicken them with thine!

QUEEN MARGARET

Thy woes will make them sharp and pierce like mine.
                              Exit [Queen] Margaret.

DUCHESS OF YORK

Why should calamity be full of words?

QUEEN ELIZABETH

127 Windy attorneys to their client's woes,
128 Airy succeeders of intestate joys,
Poor breathing orators of miseries,
Let them have scope! Though what they will impart
Help nothing else, yet do they ease the heart.

DUCHESS OF YORK

If so, then be not tongue-tied: go with me,
And in the breath of bitter words let's smother
My damnèd son that thy two sweet sons smothered.
The trumpet sounds. Be copious in exclaims.
        *Enter King Richard and his Train [marching, with
        Drums and Trumpets].*

KING RICHARD

Who intercepts me in my expedition?   136

DUCHESS OF YORK

O, she that might have intercepted thee,
By strangling thee in her accursèd womb,
From all the slaughters (wretch!) that thou hast done!

QUEEN ELIZABETH

Hid'st thou that forehead with a golden crown
Where should be branded, if that right were right,
The slaughter of the prince that owed that crown   142
And the dire death of my poor sons and brothers?
Tell me, thou villain-slave, where are my children?   144

DUCHESS OF YORK

Thou toad, thou toad, where is thy brother Clarence?
And little Ned Plantagenet, his son?

QUEEN ELIZABETH

Where is the gentle Rivers, Vaughan, Grey?

DUCHESS OF YORK

Where is kind Hastings?

KING RICHARD

A flourish, trumpets! Strike alarum, drums!
Let not the heavens hear these telltale women
Rail on the Lord's anointed. Strike, I say!
        Flourish. Alarums.
Either be patient and entreat me fair,
Or with the clamorous report of war
Thus will I drown your exclamations.

DUCHESS OF YORK

Art thou my son?

KING RICHARD

Ay, I thank God, my father, and yourself.

DUCHESS OF YORK

Then patiently hear my impatience.

KING RICHARD

Madam, I have a touch of your condition   158
That cannot brook the accent of reproof.   159

DUCHESS OF YORK

O, let me speak!

KING RICHARD Do then, but I'll not hear.

DUCHESS OF YORK

I will be mild and gentle in my words.

KING RICHARD

And brief, good mother, for I am in haste.

---

85 *index* prologue; *pageant* play or show   88–89 *garish . . . shot* brightly
colored standard-bearer (an appearance only, thus picking up *painted
queen*, l. 83) who draws the fire of all enemies   91 *queen . . . scene* i.e. a
mute player-queen   97 *Decline* run through in order (as in a paradigm)
101 *caitiff* wretch   111 *burdened* burdensome   122 *Bett'ring . . . worse*
i.e. magnifying thy loss makes the perpetrator of the evil appear even
worse than he is   124 *quicken* put life into   127 *Windy . . . woes* (words
are) airy pleaders for the woes of their client (i.e. the one suffering)   128
succeeders . . . joys heirs of joys which died without issue (folio reading
'intestine' [inward] may possibly be right; 'intestate' from quartos)
136 *expedition* (1) military undertaking, (2) haste   142 *owed* possessed by
right   144 *villain-slave* lowest criminal (with suggestions of 'lowbred'
in 'villain' [serf] and 'slave')   158 *condition* temperament   159 *accent*
language

DUCHESS OF YORK

163   Art thou so hasty ? I have stayed for thee
(God knows) in torment and in agony.

KING RICHARD

And came I not at last to comfort you ?

DUCHESS OF YORK

166   No, by the Holy Rood, thou know'st it well,
Thou cam'st on earth to make the earth my hell.
A grievous burden was thy birth to me ;
169   Tetchy and wayward was thy infancy ;
170   Thy schooldays frightful, desp'rate, wild, and furious ;
Thy prime of manhood daring, bold, and venturous ;
172   Thy age confirmed, proud, subtle, sly, and bloody,
More mild, but yet more harmful – kind in hatred.
What comfortable hour canst thou name
That ever graced me with thy company ?

KING RICHARD

176   Faith, none, but Humphrey Hour, that called your grace
To breakfast once, forth of my company.
178   If I be so disgracious in your eye,
Let me march on and not offend you, madam.
Strike up the drum.

DUCHESS OF YORK   I prithee hear me speak.

KING RICHARD

You speak too bitterly.

DUCHESS OF YORK   Hear me a word ;
For I shall never speak to thee again.

KING RICHARD

So.

DUCHESS OF YORK

Either thou wilt die by God's just ordinance
Ere from this war thou turn a conqueror,
Or I with grief and extreme age shall perish
And never more behold thy face again.
Therefore take with thee my most grievous curse,
Which in the day of battle tire thee more
190   Than all the complete armor that thou wear'st !
My prayers on the adverse party fight,
And there the little souls of Edward's children
Whisper the spirits of thine enemies
And promise them success and victory !
Bloody thou art, bloody will be thy end ;
Shame serves thy life and doth thy death attend.   *Exit.*

QUEEN ELIZABETH

Though far more cause, yet much less spirit to curse
Abides in me. I say amen to her.

KING RICHARD

Stay, madam ; I must talk a word with you.

QUEEN ELIZABETH

I have no moe sons of the royal blood   200
For thee to slaughter. For my daughters, Richard,
They shall be praying nuns, not weeping queens ;
And therefore level not to hit their lives.   203

KING RICHARD

You have a daughter called Elizabeth,
Virtuous and fair, royal and gracious.

QUEEN ELIZABETH

And must she die for this ? O, let her live,
And I'll corrupt her manners, stain her beauty,   207
Slander myself as false to Edward's bed,
Throw over her the veil of infamy :
So she may live unscarred of bleeding slaughter, ·
I will confess she was not Edward's daughter.

KING RICHARD

Wrong not her birth ; she is a royal princess.

QUEEN ELIZABETH

To save her life, I'll say she is not so.

KING RICHARD

Her life is safest only in her birth.   214

QUEEN ELIZABETH

And only in that safety died her brothers.

KING RICHARD

Lo, at their birth good stars were opposite.

QUEEN ELIZABETH

No, to their lives ill friends were contrary.   217

KING RICHARD

All unavoided is the doom of destiny.   218

QUEEN ELIZABETH

True, when avoided grace makes destiny :   219
My babes were destined to a fairer death
If grace had blessed thee with a fairer life.

KING RICHARD

You speak as if that I had slain my cousins !

QUEEN ELIZABETH

Cousins indeed, and by their uncle cozened   223
Of comfort, kingdom, kindred, freedom, life :
Whose hand soever lanched their tender hearts,   225
Thy head (all indirectly) gave direction.   226
No doubt the murd'rous knife was dull and blunt
Till it was whetted on thy stone-hard heart
To revel in the entrails of my lambs.
But that still use of grief makes wild grief tame,   230
My tongue should to thy ears not name my boys
Till that my nails were anchored in thine eyes ;
And I, in such a desp'rate bay of death,   233
Like a poor bark of sails and tackling reft,
Rush all to pieces on thy rocky bosom.

KING RICHARD

Madam, so thrive I in my enterprise
And dangerous success of bloody wars
As I intend more good to you and yours
Than ever you or yours by me were harmed !

QUEEN ELIZABETH

What good is covered with the face of heaven,   240
To be discovered, that can do me good ?

KING RICHARD

Th' advancement of your children, gentle lady.

QUEEN ELIZABETH

Up to some scaffold, there to lose their heads !

KING RICHARD

Unto the dignity and height of fortune,

163 *stayed* waited   166 *Holy Rood* Christ's cross   169 *Tetchy and wayward* fretful and willful   170 *frightful* full of fears   172 *age confirmed*
i.e. having reached full maturity   176 *Humphrey Hour* (meaning uncertain ; perhaps 'that hour when you were paradoxically without food'
[cf. 'dining with Duke Humphrey' : going hungry])   178 *disgracious* unpleasing   190 *complete armor* i.e. a full suit of armor, from head to foot
200 *moe* more (in number)   203 *level . . . lives* i.e. do not take aim to kill
them   207 *manners* moral character   214 *only* above all else   217 *contrary* opposed   218 *unavoided* unavoidable ; *doom* lot   219 *avoided grace*
one who has rejected God's prevenient grace (i.e. Richard)   223 *cozened*
cheated or betrayed   225 *lanched* pierced   226 *all indirectly* i.e. even if
not in express terms   230 *But that still* except that continual   233 *bay*
inlet (with play on the hunting term 'at bay' : driven to a last stand)   240
What . . . heaven i.e. what good is yet to be found in this world (not already
discovered)

245   The high imperial type of this earth's glory.

QUEEN ELIZABETH
Flatter my sorrow with report of it :
Tell me, what state, what dignity, what honor
248   Canst thou demise to any child of mine ?

KING RICHARD
Even all I have – ay, and myself and all –
250   Will I withal endow a child of thine,
251   So in the Lethe of thy angry soul
Thou drown the sad remembrance of those wrongs
Which thou supposest I have done to thee.

QUEEN ELIZABETH
Be brief, lest that the process of thy kindness
Last longer telling than thy kindness' date.

KING RICHARD
256   Then know that from my soul I love thy daughter.

QUEEN ELIZABETH
My daughter's mother thinks it with her soul.

KING RICHARD
What do you think ?

QUEEN ELIZABETH
That thou dost love my daughter from thy soul.
So from thy soul's love didst thou love her brothers,
And from my heart's love I do thank thee for it.

KING RICHARD
Be not so hasty to confound my meaning :
I mean that with my soul I love thy daughter
And do intend to make her Queen of England.

QUEEN ELIZABETH
Well then, who dost thou mean shall be her king ?

KING RICHARD
Even he that makes her queen. Who should be else ?

QUEEN ELIZABETH
What, thou ?

KING RICHARD   Even so. How think you of it ?

QUEEN ELIZABETH
How canst thou woo her ?

KING RICHARD   That would I learn of you,
269   As one being best acquainted with her humor.

QUEEN ELIZABETH
And wilt thou learn of me ?

KING RICHARD   Madam, with all my heart.

QUEEN ELIZABETH
Send to her by the man that slew her brothers
A pair of bleeding hearts ; thereon engrave
'Edward' and 'York' ; then haply will she weep :
Therefore present to her – as sometimes Margaret
Did to thy father, steeped in Rutland's blood –
A handkercher, which say to her did drain
The purple sap from her sweet brother's body,
278   And bid her wipe her weeping eyes withal.
If this inducement move her not to love,
Send her a letter of thy noble deeds :
Tell her thou mad'st away her uncle Clarence,
Her uncle Rivers ; ay (and for her sake !),
283   Mad'st quick conveyance with her good aunt Anne.

KING RICHARD
You mock me, madam ; this is not the way
To win your daughter.

QUEEN ELIZABETH   There is no other way,
Unless thou couldst put on some other shape,
And not be Richard that hath done all this.

KING RICHARD
Say that I did all this for love of her.

QUEEN ELIZABETH
Nay, then indeed she cannot choose but hate thee,
Having bought love with such a bloody spoil.   290

KING RICHARD
Look what is done cannot be now amended :   291
Men shall deal unadvisedly sometimes,
Which after-hours gives leisure to repent.
If I did take the kingdom from your sons,
To make amends I'll give it to your daughter ;
If I have killed the issue of your womb,
To quicken your increase I will beget   297
Mine issue of your blood upon your daughter.
A grandam's name is little less in love
Than is the doting title of a mother ;
They are as children but one step below,
Even of your metal, of your very blood,   302
Of all one pain, save for a night of groans
Endured of her for whom you bid like sorrow :   304
Your children were vexation to your youth,
But mine shall be a comfort to your age.
The loss you have is but a son being king,
And by that loss your daughter is made queen.
I cannot make you what amends I would ;
Therefore accept such kindness as I can.   310
Dorset your son, that with a fearful soul   311
Leads discontented steps in foreign soil,
This fair alliance quickly shall call home
To high promotions and great dignity.
The king, that calls your beauteous daughter wife,
Familiarly shall call thy Dorset brother :
Again shall you be mother to a king,
And all the ruins of distressful times
Repaired with double riches of content.
What ! we have many goodly days to see :
The liquid drops of tears that you have shed
Shall come again, transformed to orient pearl,   322
Advantaging their love with interest   323
Of ten times double gain of happiness.
Go then, my mother ; to thy daughter go ;
Make bold her bashful years with your experience ;
Prepare her ears to hear a wooer's tale ;
Put in her tender heart th' aspiring flame
Of golden sovereignty ; acquaint the princess
With the sweet silent hours of marriage joys ;
And when this arm of mine hath chastisèd
The petty rebel, dull-brained Buckingham,
Bound with triumphant garlands will I come   333
And lead thy daughter to a conqueror's bed ;
To whom I will retail my conquest won,   335
And she shall be sole victoress, Caesar's Caesar.

QUEEN ELIZABETH
What were I best to say ? Her father's brother

245 *imperial type* symbol of rule   248 *demise* transmit   250 *withal* with
251 *Lethe* a river in Hell (to drink of which induced forgetfulness)   256
from my soul with my very soul (but Queen Elizabeth takes Richard to
mean that his love is 'from' [i.e. separated from] his inmost feelings)   269
humor temperament   278 *withal* with (it)   283 *quick conveyance with*
speedy removal of   290 *spoil* slaughter (hunting term : the breaking up of
the quarry after the kill)   291 *Look what* whatever   297 *quicken your
increase* i.e. give new life to your (dead) offspring   302 *metal* substance
304 *of* by ; *bid* underwent, suffered   310 *can* i.e. am able to give   311 *fearful* full of fears   322 *orient* shining   323 *love* i.e. the love which gave rise
to the tears   333 *triumphant garlands* i.e. garlands befitting a military
triumph (in the Roman sense)   335 *retail* recount (though Shakespeare
would seem to mean 'transmit')

    Would be her lord? Or shall I say her uncle?
    Or he that slew her brothers and her uncles?
    Under what title shall I woo for thee
    That God, the law, my honor, and her love
    Can make seem pleasing to her tender years?

KING RICHARD
343   Infer fair England's peace by this alliance.

QUEEN ELIZABETH
    Which she shall purchase with still-lasting war.

KING RICHARD
    Tell her the king, that may command, entreats.

QUEEN ELIZABETH
    That at her hands which the king's King forbids.

KING RICHARD
    Say she shall be a high and mighty queen.

QUEEN ELIZABETH
348   To vail the title, as her mother doth.

KING RICHARD
    Say I will love her everlastingly.

QUEEN ELIZABETH
    But how long shall that title 'ever' last?

KING RICHARD
    Sweetly in force unto her fair life's end.

QUEEN ELIZABETH
    But how long fairly shall her sweet life last?

KING RICHARD
    As long as heaven and nature lengthens it.

QUEEN ELIZABETH
    As long as hell and Richard likes of it.

KING RICHARD
    Say I, her sovereign, am her subject low.

QUEEN ELIZABETH
356   But she, your subject, loathes such sovereignty.

KING RICHARD
    Be eloquent in my behalf to her.

QUEEN ELIZABETH
    An honest tale speeds best being plainly told.

KING RICHARD
    Then plainly to her tell my loving tale.

QUEEN ELIZABETH
360   Plain and not honest is too harsh a style.

KING RICHARD
    Your reasons are too shallow and too quick.

QUEEN ELIZABETH
    O no, my reasons are too deep and dead –
    Too deep and dead (poor infants) in their graves.

KING RICHARD
    Harp not on that string, madam; that is past.

QUEEN ELIZABETH
    Harp on it still shall I till heartstrings break.

KING RICHARD
366   Now, by my George, my garter, and my crown –

QUEEN ELIZABETH
    Profaned, dishonored, and the third usurped.

KING RICHARD
    I swear –

QUEEN ELIZABETH By nothing, for this is no oath:
    Thy George, profaned, hath lost his lordly honor;
    Thy garter, blemished, pawned his knightly virtue;
    Thy crown, usurped, disgraced his kingly glory.
    If something thou wouldst swear to be believed,
    Swear then by something that thou hast not wronged.

KING RICHARD
    Then by myself –

QUEEN ELIZABETH Thyself is self-misused.

KING RICHARD
    Now by the world –

QUEEN ELIZABETH 'Tis full of thy foul wrongs.

KING RICHARD
    My father's death –

QUEEN ELIZABETH Thy life hath it dishonored.

KING RICHARD
    Why then, by God –

QUEEN ELIZABETH God's wrong is most of all:
    If thou didst fear to break an oath with him,
    The unity the king my husband made   379
    Thou hadst not broken, nor my brothers died.
    If thou hadst feared to break an oath by him,
    Th' imperial metal, circling now thy head,   382
    Had graced the tender temples of my child,
    And both the princes had been breathing here,
    Which now, two tender bedfellows for dust,
    Thy broken faith hath made the prey for worms.
    What canst thou swear by now?

KING RICHARD   The time to come.

QUEEN ELIZABETH
    That thou hast wrongèd in the time o'erpast;
    For I myself have many tears to wash
    Hereafter time, for time past wronged by thee.   390
    The children live whose fathers thou hast slaughtered,
    Ungoverned youth, to wail it in their age;   392
    The parents live whose children thou hast butchered,
    Old barren plants, to wail it with their age.
    Swear not by time to come, for that thou hast
    Misused ere used, by times ill-used o'erpast.

KING RICHARD
    As I intend to prosper and repent,   397
    So thrive I in my dangerous affairs
    Of hostile arms! Myself myself confound!
    Heaven and fortune bar me happy hours!
    Day, yield me not thy light, nor, night, thy rest!
    Be opposite all planets of good luck
    To my proceeding if, with dear heart's love,
    Immaculate devotion, holy thoughts,
    I tender not thy beauteous princely daughter!
    In her consists my happiness and thine;
    Without her, follows to myself and thee,
    Herself, the land, and many a Christian soul,
    Death, desolation, ruin, and decay.
    It cannot be avoided but by this;   410
    It will not be avoided but by this.
    Therefore, dear mother (I must call you so),
    Be the attorney of my love to her:
    Plead what I will be, not what I have been –
    Not my deserts, but what I will deserve;
    Urge the necessity and state of times,

---

343 *Infer* imply   348 *vail* abase, lower (quarto reading 'wail' is perhaps preferable)   356 *sovereignty* (1) rule, (2) ruler (i.e. Richard)   360 *Plain . . . style* i.e. plain style (cf. the proverb 'Truth is plain') unless it is sincere will be too harsh; lies (i.e. things not honest) need the decorated style   366 *George . . . garter* (a jewelled pendant with the figure of St George and the gold collar from which it hung were parts of the insignia of the Order of the Garter)   379 *unity* (the 'reconciliation' in II, i)   382 *imperial metal* i.e. royal crown   390 *Hereafter* future   392 *Ungoverned* i.e. without parents   397–98 *As . . . So* to the degree I mean to do well and repent, to such a degree   397–405 *As . . . daughter* (note that Richard here in effect curses himself, bringing the curses in this scene to a final focus)

417 And be not peevish-fond in great designs.

QUEEN ELIZABETH
Shall I be tempted of the devil thus?

KING RICHARD
Ay, if the devil tempt you to do good.

QUEEN ELIZABETH
420 Shall I forget myself to be myself?

KING RICHARD
Ay, if yourself's remembrance wrong yourself.

QUEEN ELIZABETH
Yet thou didst kill my children.

KING RICHARD
But in your daughter's womb I bury them,
Where, in that nest of spicery, they will breed
425 Selves of themselves, to your recomforture.

QUEEN ELIZABETH
Shall I go win my daughter to thy will?

KING RICHARD
And be a happy mother by the deed.

QUEEN ELIZABETH
I go. Write to me very shortly,
And you shall understand from me her mind.

KING RICHARD
Bear her my true love's kiss; and so farewell –
                 Exit Q[ueen Elizabeth].
431 Relenting fool, and shallow, changing woman!
    Enter Ratcliffe [, Catesby following].
How now? What news?

RATCLIFFE
Most mighty sovereign, on the western coast
Rideth a puissant navy; to our shores
Throng many doubtful hollow-hearted friends,
436 Unarmed, and unresolved to beat them back.
437 'Tis thought that Richmond is their admiral;
438 And there they hull, expecting but the aid
Of Buckingham to welcome them ashore.

KING RICHARD
Some light-foot friend post to the Duke of Norfolk:
Ratcliffe, thyself – or Catesby – where is he?

CATESBY
Here, my good lord.

KING RICHARD   Catesby, fly to the duke.

CATESBY
I will, my lord, with all convenient haste.

KING RICHARD
Ratcliffe, come hither. Post to Salisbury.
When thou com'st thither –
     [To Catesby]   Dull unmindful villain,
Why stay'st thou here and go'st not to the duke?

CATESBY
First, mighty liege, tell me your highness' pleasure,
What from your grace I shall deliver to him.

KING RICHARD
O, true, good Catesby: bid him levy straight
The greatest strength and power that he can make
And meet me suddenly at Salisbury.

CATESBY
I go.   *Exit.*

RATCLIFFE
What, may it please you, shall I do at Salisbury?

KING RICHARD
Why, what wouldst thou do there before I go?

RATCLIFFE
455 Your highness told me I should post before.

KING RICHARD
My mind is changed.
     Enter Lord Stanley [Earl of Derby].
             Stanley, what news with you?

DERBY
None good, my liege, to please you with the hearing,
Nor none so bad but well may be reported.

KING RICHARD
Hoyday, a riddle! Neither good nor bad!
What need'st thou run so many miles about,
When thou mayest tell thy tale the nearest way?
Once more, what news?

DERBY   Richmond is on the seas.

KING RICHARD
There let him sink, and be the seas on him!
White-livered runagate, what doth he there?   464

DERBY
I know not, mighty sovereign, but by guess.

KING RICHARD
Well, as you guess?

DERBY
Stirred up by Dorset, Buckingham, and Morton,
He makes for England, here to claim the crown.

KING RICHARD
Is the chair empty? is the sword unswayed?   469
Is the king dead? the empire unpossessed?   470
What heir of York is there alive but we?
And who is England's king but great York's heir?
Then tell me, what makes he upon the seas?   473

DERBY
Unless for that, my liege, I cannot guess.

KING RICHARD
Unless for that he comes to be your liege,
You cannot guess wherefore the Welshman comes.
Thou wilt revolt and fly to him, I fear.

DERBY
No, my good lord; therefore mistrust me not.

KING RICHARD
Where is thy power then to beat him back?
Where be thy tenants and thy followers?
Are they not now upon the western shore,
Safe-conducting the rebels from their ships?

DERBY
No, my good lord, my friends are in the North.

KING RICHARD
Cold friends to me! What do they in the North   484
When they should serve their sovereign in the West?

DERBY
They have not been commanded, mighty king:
Pleaseth your majesty to give me leave,
I'll muster up my friends and meet your grace
Where and what time your majesty shall please.

KING RICHARD
Ay, thou wouldst be gone to join with Richmond:

417 *peevish-fond* foolishly self-willed (folio reading 'peevish found' may possibly be correct; Q1 reads 'peevish, fond') 420 *Shall . . . be myself* i.e. shall I forget who I am 425 *recomforture* consolation 431 *shallow* superficial 436 *unresolved* undetermined how to act 437 *their admiral* i.e. of the *navy* of l. 434 438 *hull* drift with the winds 455 *post* hasten 464 *runagate* vagabond or, perhaps, deserter (cf. V, iii, 317) 469 *sword* i.e. the sword of state, part of the king's regalia symbolic of power 470 *empire* kingdom (i.e. the thing requiring rule) 473 *makes he* is he doing 484 *Cold* chilling (with play on Derby's friends being in the North)

But I'll not trust thee.
DERBY   Most mighty sovereign,
  You have no cause to hold my friendship doubtful.
  I never was nor never will be false.
KING RICHARD
  Go then and muster men. But leave behind
  Your son, George Stanley. Look your heart be firm,
496 Or else his head's assurance is but frail.
DERBY
  So deal with him as I prove true to you.   Exit.
    Enter a Messenger.
1. MESSENGER
  My gracious sovereign, now in Devonshire,
499 As I by friends am well advertisèd,
500 Sir Edward Courtney and the haughty prelate,
  Bishop of Exeter, his elder brother,
502 With many moe confederates, are in arms.
    Enter another Messenger.
2. MESSENGER
503 In Kent, my liege, the Guildfords are in arms,
  And every hour more competitors
  Flock to the rebels, and their power grows strong.
    Enter another Messenger.
3. MESSENGER
  My lord, the army of great Buckingham –
KING RICHARD
507 Out on you, owls! Nothing but songs of death?
    He striketh him.
  There, take thou that, till thou bring better news.
3. MESSENGER
  The news I have to tell your majesty
  Is that by sudden floods and fall of waters
  Buckingham's army is dispersed and scattered,
  And he himself wand'red away alone,
  No man knows whither.
513 KING RICHARD   I cry thee mercy:
  There is my purse to cure that blow of thine.
515 Hath any well-advisèd friend proclaimed
  Reward to him that brings the traitor in?
3. MESSENGER
  Such proclamation hath been made, my lord.
    Enter another Messenger.
4. MESSENGER
518 Sir Thomas Lovel and Lord Marquess Dorset,
  'Tis said, my liege, in Yorkshire are in arms.
  But this good comfort bring I to your highness:
521 The Britain navy is dispersed by tempest;
  Richmond in Dorsetshire sent out a boat
  Unto the shore to ask those on the banks
  If they were his assistants, yea or no;

Who answered him they came from Buckingham
Upon his party. He, mistrusting them,
Hoised sail, and made his course again for Britain.   527
KING RICHARD
  March on, march on, since we are up in arms;
  If not to fight with foreign enemies,
  Yet to beat down these rebels here at home.
    Enter Catesby.
CATESBY
  My liege, the Duke of Buckingham is taken.
  That is the best news. That the Earl of Richmond
  Is with a mighty power landed at Milford
  Is colder tidings, but yet they must be told.
KING RICHARD
  Away towards Salisbury! While we reason here,
  A royal battle might be won and lost.
  Some one take order Buckingham be brought
  To Salisbury; the rest march on with me.
    Flourish. Exeunt.

*

    Enter [Lord Stanley Earl of] Derby, and   IV, v
      Sir Christopher [Urswick, a priest].
DERBY
  Sir Christopher, tell Richmond this from me:
  That in the sty of the most deadly boar
  My son George Stanley is franked up in hold;   3
  If I revolt, off goes young George's head;
  The fear of that holds off my present aid.
  So get thee gone; commend me to thy lord.
  Withal say that the queen hath heartily consented
  He should espouse Elizabeth her daughter.   8
  But tell me, where is princely Richmond now?
CHRISTOPHER
  At Pembroke, or at Ha'rford-West in Wales.   10
DERBY
  What men of name resort to him?
CHRISTOPHER
  Sir Walter Herbert, a renownèd soldier,
  Sir Gilbert Talbot, Sir William Stanley,
  Oxford, redoubted Pembroke, Sir James Blunt,   14
  And Rice ap Thomas, with a valiant crew,
  And many other of great name and worth;
  And towards London do they bend their power,
  If by the way they be not fought withal.
DERBY
  Well, hie thee to thy lord. I kiss his hand:
  My letter will resolve him of my mind.
    [Gives letter.]
  Farewell.   Exeunt.

*

    Enter Buckingham with Halberds [and the Sheriff], V, i
      led to execution.
BUCKINGHAM
  Will not King Richard let me speak with him?
SHERIFF
  No, my good lord; therefore be patient.
BUCKINGHAM
  Hastings, and Edward's children, Grey and Rivers,
  Holy King Henry and thy fair son Edward,
  Vaughan and all that have miscarrièd
  By underhand corrupted foul injustice,

496 head's assurance i.e. that his head will not be cut off 499 advertisèd informed 500, 503 Courtney, Guildfords (supporters of Buckingham) 502 moe more (in number) 507 owls (the hoot or song of the owl was frequently believed to portend evil) 513 cry thee mercy beg your pardon 515 well-advisèd foresighted 518 Lovel (supporter of Buckingham) 521 Britain Breton 527 Hoised hoisted; Britain Brittany IV, v Lord Stanley's house s.d. Sir (see III, ii, 109) 3 franked up in hold shut up (as in a sty, l. 2) in custody (the boar in l. 2 being, of course, Richard) 8 He . . . daughter (Shakespeare's reference here to Richmond's projected marriage with Princess Elizabeth makes it fairly certain that we should interpret Queen Elizabeth's apparent capitulation to Richard in IV, iv, 426–29 as a ruse to trick him) 10 Pembroke county in southwestern Wales (see reference to the Pembroke family, l. 14); Ha'rford-West town in Pembroke 14 redoubted dreaded; Pembroke i.e. Jasper Tudor, Richmond's uncle V, i An open place in Salisbury

7 If that your moody discontented souls
Do through the clouds behold this present hour,
9 Even for revenge mock my destruction!
10 This is All Souls' day, fellow, is it not?

SHERIFF

It is, my lord.

BUCKINGHAM

12 Why, then All Souls' day is my body's doomsday.
This is the day which in King Edward's time
I wished might fall on me when I was found
False to his children and his wife's allies;
This is the day wherein I wished to fall
By the false faith of him whom most I trusted;
18 This, this All Souls' day to my fearful soul
19 Is the determined respite of my wrongs:
That high All-seer which I dallied with
Hath turned my feignèd prayer on my head
And given in earnest what I begged in jest.
Thus doth He force the swords of wicked men
To turn their own points in their masters' bosoms;
Thus Margaret's curse falls heavy on my neck:
'When he,' quoth she, 'shall split thy heart with sorrow,
Remember Margaret was a prophetess.' –
Come lead me, officers, to the block of shame.
Wrong hath but wrong, and blame the due of blame.

Exeunt Buckingham with Officers.

*

V, ii   *Enter Richmond, Oxford, [Sir James] Blunt, [Sir
Walter] Herbert, and others, with Drum and Colors.*

RICHMOND

Fellows in arms, and my most loving friends,
Bruised underneath the yoke of tyranny,
3 Thus far into the bowels of the land
Have we marched on without impediment;
5 And here receive we from our father Stanley
Lines of fair comfort and encouragement.
The wretched, bloody, and usurping boar,
That spoiled your summer fields and fruitful vines,
Swills your warm blood like wash, and makes his trough
10 In your embowelled bosoms – this foul swine
11 Is now even in the centry of this isle,
Near to the town of Leicester, as we learn:
From Tamworth thither is but one day's march.
In God's name cheerly on, courageous friends,
To reap the harvest of perpetual peace
By this one bloody trial of sharp war.

OXFORD

17 Every man's conscience is a thousand men,
To fight against this guilty homicide.

HERBERT

I doubt not but his friends will turn to us.

BLUNT

He hath no friends but what are friends for fear,
Which in his dearest need will fly from him.

RICHMOND

All for our vantage. Then in God's name march!
True hope is swift and flies with swallow's wings;
Kings it makes gods, and meaner creatures kings.

Exeunt omnes.

*

Enter King Richard in arms, with Norfolk, Ratcliffe,   V, iii
and the Earl of Surrey [, and Soldiers].

KING RICHARD

Here pitch our tent, even here in Bosworth field.
My Lord of Surrey, why look you so sad?   2

SURREY

My heart is ten times lighter than my looks.

KING RICHARD

My Lord of Norfolk –

NORFOLK   Here, most gracious liege.

KING RICHARD

Norfolk, we must have knocks. Ha! must we not?

NORFOLK

We must both give and take, my loving lord.

KING RICHARD

Up with my tent! Here will I lie to-night;
[Soldiers begin to set up the King's tent.]
But where to-morrow? Well, all's one for that.   8
Who hath descried the number of the traitors?

NORFOLK

Six or seven thousand is their utmost power.

KING RICHARD

Why, our battalia trebles that account: 11
Besides, the king's name is a tower of strength,
Which they upon the adverse faction want.   13
Up with the tent! Come, noble gentlemen,
Let us survey the vantage of the ground.   15
Call for some men of sound direction: 16
Let's lack no discipline, make no delay,
For, lords, to-morrow is a busy day.   *Exeunt.*

*Enter Richmond, Sir William Brandon, Oxford, and
Dorset [, Herbert, and Blunt. Some of the Soldiers
pitch Richmond's tent].*

RICHMOND

The weary sun hath made a golden set
And by the bright tract of his fiery car   20
Gives token of a goodly day to-morrow.
Sir William Brandon, you shall bear my standard.
Give me some ink and paper in my tent:
I'll draw the form and model of our battle,
Limit each leader to his several charge,
And part in just proportion our small power.
My Lord of Oxford, – you, Sir William Brandon, –
And you, Sir Walter Herbert – stay with me.
The Earl of Pembroke keeps his regiment;
Good Captain Blunt, bear my good-night to him,   30

7 *discontented souls* i.e. souls which could not rest in peace until their violent deaths had been revenged   9 *Even for* i.e. impelled by   10 *All Souls' day* November 2, the day on which the Roman Catholic Church intercedes for all Christian souls   12 *doomsday* day of final judgment (death being the sentence)   18 *fearful* terrified   19 *determined . . . wrongs* i.e. the foreordained moment past which no cessation (of punishment) will be granted for all the wrongs I have committed
V, ii A camp near Tamworth   3 *bowels* heart or center (Richmond's army is at Tamworth, Staffordshire, on its way to the scene of the final battle with Richard at Bosworth Field, Leicestershire; cf. ll. 12–13)   5 *our* (royal plural); *father Stanley* (Richmond was the son of Edmund Tudor and Margaret Beaufort; Lord Stanley, Earl of Derby, was his mother's third husband)   10 *embowelled* disembowelled   11 *centry* center   17 *conscience* i.e. his conscience tells him that he is on the 'right' side
V, iii Bosworth Field   2 *sad* heavy-spirited   8 *all's . . . that* i.e. it makes no difference   11 *battalia* armed forces   13 *want* lack   15 *the vantage . . . ground* i.e. the military advantages offered by the spot chosen for the battle   16 *of sound direction* capable of giving sound orders   20 *tract* track; *car* chariot (with reference to the chariot of Phoebus, god of the sun)

And by the second hour in the morning
Desire the earl to see me in my tent:
Yet one thing more, good captain, do for me –
Where is Lord Stanley quartered, do you know?

BLUNT
Unless I have mista'en his colors much
(Which well I am assured I have not done),
His regiment lies half a mile at least
South from the mighty power of the king.

RICHMOND
If without peril it be possible,
40 Sweet Blunt, make some good means to speak with him
And give him from me this most needful note.

BLUNT
Upon my life, my lord, I'll undertake it;
And so God give you quiet rest to-night!

RICHMOND
Good night, good Captain Blunt. [Exit Blunt.]
Come, gentlemen,
Let us consult upon to-morrow's business.
In to my tent; the dew is raw and cold.
They withdraw into the tent.
Enter [, to his tent, King] Richard, Ratcliffe,
Norfolk, and Catesby.

KING RICHARD
What is't a clock?

CATESBY It's supper time, my lord;
48 It's nine a clock.

KING RICHARD I will not sup to-night.
Give me some ink and paper.
50 What? is my beaver easier than it was?
And all my armor laid into my tent?

CATESBY
It is, my liege; and all things are in readiness.

KING RICHARD
Good Norfolk, hie thee to thy charge;
54 Use careful watch, choose trusty sentinels.

NORFOLK
I go, my lord.

KING RICHARD
Stir with the lark to-morrow, gentle Norfolk.

NORFOLK
I warrant you, my lord. Exit.

KING RICHARD
Catesby!

CATESBY
My lord?

59 KING RICHARD Send out a pursuivant-at-arms
To Stanley's regiment; bid him bring his power
Before sunrising, lest his son George fall

Into the blind cave of eternal night. [Exit Catesby.]
Fill me a bowl of wine. Give me a watch. 63
Saddle white Surrey for the field to-morrow. 64
Look that my staves be sound and not too heavy. 65
Ratcliffe!

RATCLIFFE
My lord?

KING RICHARD
Saw'st thou the melancholy Lord Northumberland?

RATCLIFFE
Thomas the Earl of Surrey and himself,
Much about cockshut time, from troop to troop 70
Went through the army, cheering up the soldiers.

KING RICHARD
So, I am satisfied. Give me a bowl of wine.
I have not that alacrity of spirit
Nor cheer of mind that I was wont to have.
[Wine brought.]
Set it down. Is ink and paper ready?

RATCLIFFE
It is, my lord.

KING RICHARD
Bid my guard watch. Leave me. Ratcliffe,
About the mid of night come to my tent
And help to arm me. Leave me, I say. Exit Ratcliffe.
[King Richard withdraws
into his tent, and sleeps.]
Enter [Lord Stanley Earl of] Derby, to Richmond
in his tent [, Lords and others attending].

DERBY
Fortune and victory sit on thy helm!

RICHMOND
All comfort that the dark night can afford
Be to thy person, noble father-in-law!
Tell me, how fares our loving mother?

DERBY
I, by attorney, bless thee from thy mother, 84
Who prays continually for Richmond's good:
So much for that. The silent hours steal on
And flaky darkness breaks within the east. 87
In brief, for so the season bids us be,
Prepare thy battle early in the morning 89
And put thy fortune to the arbitrement
Of bloody strokes and mortal-staring war. 91
I, as I may – that which I would I cannot –
With best advantage will deceive the time 93
And aid thee in this doubtful shock of arms.
But on thy side I may not be too forward,
Lest, being seen, thy brother, tender George,
Be executed in his father's sight.
Farewell. The leisure and the fearful time 98
Cuts off the ceremonious vows of love
And ample interchange of sweet discourse
Which so long sund'red friends should dwell upon.
God give us leisure for these rites of love!
Once more adieu: be valiant, and speed well!

RICHMOND
Good lords, conduct him to his regiment.
I'll strive with troubled thoughts, to take a nap, 105
Lest leaden slumber peise me down to-morrow, 106
When I should mount with wings of victory:
Once more, good night, kind lords and gentlemen.
Exeunt. Manet Richmond.
O Thou, whose captain I account myself,

48 nine a clock (too late for an Elizabethan supper; the 'six of clocke'
of Quarto 1 fits this context better, but is obviously too early for the time
indications in scene ii and later) 50 beaver face-guard of a helmet 54
Use careful watch i.e. see that a thorough alert is observed 59 pursuivant-
at-arms junior officer, attending on a herald 63 a watch a special guard
(cf. l. 77) or a timepiece 64 white Surrey (Richard entered Leicester on a
'great white courser' [Holinshed], but the name is Shakespeare's and
must not be confused with Surrey in l. 69) 65 staves lance shafts 70
cockshut time evening twilight 84 attorney proxy 87 flaky darkness
i.e. darkness still flaked with light 89 battle armed forces (see battalia,
l. 11 above) 91 mortal-staring killing (like the basilisk) with a glance of
the eye 93 With . . . time i.e. will make the greatest profit of the moment
without giving the appearance of doing so 98 leisure . . . time (lack of)
time and the threat of the moment 105 with troublèd thoughts i.e. in spite
of my disturbing thoughts 106 peise weigh

Look on my forces with a gracious eye;
111 Put in their hands thy bruising irons of wrath,
That they may crush down with a heavy fall
The usurping helmets of our adversaries;
Make us thy ministers of chastisement,
That we may praise thee in the victory.
To thee I do commend my watchful soul
117 Ere I let fall the windows of mine eyes:
Sleeping and waking. O, defend me still!
Sleeps.
Enter the Ghost of Prince Edward, son to Henry the Sixth.

GHOST *(to Richard)*
Let me sit heavy on thy soul to-morrow!
Think how thou stab'st me in my prime of youth
At Tewkesbury: despair therefore, and die!
(To Richmond)
122 Be cheerful, Richmond; for the wrongèd souls
Of butcherèd princes fight in thy behalf.
King Henry's issue, Richmond, comforts thee.
Enter the Ghost of Henry the Sixth.

GHOST *(to Richard)*
125 When I was mortal, my anointed body
By thee was punchèd full of deadly holes.
Think on the Tower, and me: despair, and die!
Harry the Sixth bids thee despair, and die!
(To Richmond)
Virtuous and holy, be thou conqueror!
Harry, that prophesied thou shouldst be king,
Doth comfort thee in thy sleep: live, and flourish!
Enter the Ghost of Clarence.

GHOST *[to Richard]*
Let me sit heavy in thy soul to-morrow –
133 I that was washed to death with fulsome wine,
Poor Clarence by thy guile betrayed to death!
To-morrow in the battle think on me,
136 And fall thy edgeless sword: despair, and die!
(To Richmond)
137 Thou offspring of the house of Lancaster,
The wrongèd heirs of York do pray for thee;
Good angels guard thy battle! live, and flourish!
Enter the Ghosts of Rivers, Grey, and Vaughan.

RIVERS *[to Richard]*
Let me sit heavy in thy soul to-morrow,
Rivers, that died at Pomfret! despair, and die!

GREY
Think upon Grey, and let thy soul despair!

VAUGHAN
Think upon Vaughan, and with guilty fear
Let fall thy lance: despair, and die!

ALL *(to Richmond)*
Awake, and think our wrongs in Richard's bosom
Will conquer him! Awake, and win the day!
Enter the Ghost of Lord Hastings.

GHOST *[to Richard]*
Bloody and guilty, guiltily awake
And in a bloody battle end thy days!
Think on Lord Hastings: despair, and die!
(To Richmond)
150 Quiet untroublèd soul, awake, awake!
Arm, fight, and conquer, for fair England's sake!
Enter the Ghosts of the two young Princes.

GHOSTS *[to Richard]*
Dream on thy cousins smotherèd in the Tower.

Let us be lead within thy bosom, Richard,
And weigh thee down to ruin, shame, and death!
Thy nephews' souls bid thee despair, and die!
(To Richmond)
Sleep, Richmond, sleep in peace and wake in joy.
Good angels guard thee from the boar's annoy! 157
Live, and beget a happy race of kings!
Edward's unhappy sons do bid thee flourish.
Enter the Ghost of Anne, his wife.

GHOST *(to Richard)*
Richard, thy wife, that wretched Anne thy wife,
That never slept a quiet hour with thee,
Now fills thy sleep with perturbations:
To-morrow in the battle think on me,
And fall thy edgeless sword: despair, and die!
(To Richmond)
Thou quiet soul, sleep thou a quiet sleep.
Dream of success and happy victory!
Thy adversary's wife doth pray for thee.
Enter the Ghost of Buckingham.

GHOST *(to Richard)*
The first was I that helped thee to the crown;
The last was I that felt thy tyranny.
O, in the battle think on Buckingham,
And die in terror of thy guiltiness!
Dream on, dream on, of bloody deeds and death:
Fainting, despair; despairing, yield thy breath!
(To Richmond)
I died for hope ere I could lend thee aid; 174
But cheer thy heart and be thou not dismayed:
God and good angels fight on Richmond's side,
And Richard falls in height of all his pride!
[The Ghosts vanish.] Richard starts out of his dream.

KING RICHARD
Give me another horse! Bind up my wounds!
Have mercy, Jesu! Soft! I did but dream.
O coward conscience, how dost thou afflict me!
The lights burn blue. It is now dead midnight.
Cold fearful drops stand on my trembling flesh.
What do I fear? Myself? There's none else by.
Richard loves Richard: that is, I am I. 184
Is there a murderer here? No. Yes, I am:
Then fly. What, from myself? Great reason why –
Lest I revenge. What, myself upon myself?
Alack, I love myself. Wherefore? For any good
That I myself have done unto myself?
O no! Alas, I rather hate myself
For hateful deeds committed by myself.
I am a villain. Yet I lie, I am not.
Fool, of thyself speak well. Fool, do not flatter.
My conscience hath a thousand several tongues, 194
And every tongue brings in a several tale,
And every tale condemns me for a villain.

111 *irons* swords 117 *windows* eyelids 122 *cheerful* full of joy 125 *anointed* (see IV, i, 61n.) 133 *fulsome* sickening or satiating 136 *fall* . . . *sword* i.e. let thy sword, figuratively blunted by thinking about Clarence's murder, drop (1) out of your hand, or (2) down, so that it is no longer a means of defense 137 *offspring . . . Lancaster* (Richmond's mother was a Beaufort and the Beaufort line traced back to John of Gaunt, Duke of Lancaster, the father of Bolingbroke, who became Henry IV) 157 *annoy* molestation 174 *for hope* for the intent (of helping) (?) 184 *I am I* (this reading, that of all texts except Quarto 1, has the sanction of all later editors, but the reading 'I and I' of Quarto 1, here admittedly the basic text, makes equally good sense) 194 *several* separate

Perjury, perjury, in the highest degree,
Murder, stern murder, in the direst degree,
199   All several sins, all used in each degree,
Throng to the bar, crying all, 'Guilty! guilty!'
I shall despair. There is no creature loves me ;
And if I die, no soul will pity me.
And, wherefore should they, since that I myself
Find in myself no pity to myself ?
Methought the souls of all that I had murdered
Came to my tent, and every one did threat
To-morrow's vengeance on the head of Richard.
     Enter Ratcliffe.

RATCLIFFE
My lord !

KING RICHARD
Zounds, who is there ?

RATCLIFFE
210   Ratcliffe, my lord, 'tis I. The early village cock
Hath twice done salutation to the morn :
Your friends are up and buckle on their armor.

[KING RICHARD
O Ratcliffe, I have dreamed a fearful dream !
What think'st thou ? Will our friends prove all true ?

RATCLIFFE
No doubt, my lord.]

KING RICHARD   O Ratcliffe, I fear, I fear !

RATCLIFFE
Nay, good my lord, be not afraid of shadows.

KING RICHARD
By the apostle Paul, shadows to-night
Have struck more terror to the soul of Richard
Than can the substance of ten thousand soldiers
Armèd in proof and led by shallow Richmond.
'Tis not yet near day. Come, go with me.
222   Under our tents I'll play the easedropper,
To see if any mean to shrink from me.
     Exeunt Richard and Ratcliffe.
     Enter the Lords to Richmond sitting in his tent.

LORDS
Good morrow, Richmond.

RICHMOND
225   Cry mercy, lords and watchful gentlemen,
That you have ta'en a tardy sluggard here.

LORDS
How have you slept, my lord ?

RICHMOND
228   The sweetest sleep, and fairest-boding dreams
That ever ent'red in a drowsy head
Have I since your departure had, my lords.
Methought their souls whose bodies Richard murdered
232   Came to my tent and cried on victory.
233   I promise you my soul is very jocund

In the remembrance of so fair a dream.
How far into the morning is it, lords ?

LORDS
Upon the stroke of four.

RICHMOND
Why, then 'tis time to arm and give direction.
     His Oration to his Soldiers.
More than I have said, loving countrymen,
The leisure and enforcement of the time   239
Forbids to dwell upon. Yet remember this :
God and our good cause fight upon our side ;
The prayers of holy saints and wrongèd souls,
Like high-reared bulwarks, stand before our faces.   243
Richard except, those whom we fight against
Had rather have us win than him they follow.
For what is he they follow ? Truly, gentlemen,
A bloody tyrant and a homicide ;
One raised in blood and one in blood established ;   248
One that made means to come by what he hath,   249
And slaughterèd those that were the means to help him ;
A base foul stone, made precious by the foil   251
Of England's chair, where he is falsely set ;
One that hath ever been God's enemy.
Then if you fight against God's enemy,
God will in justice ward you as his soldiers ;   255
If you do sweat to put a tyrant down,
You sleep in peace, the tyrant being slain ;
If you do fight against your country's foes,
Your country's fat shall pay your pains the hire ;   259
If you do fight in safeguard of your wives,
Your wives shall welcome home the conquerors ;
If you do free your children from the sword,
Your children's children quits it in your age :   263
Then in the name of God and all these rights,
Advance your standards, draw your willing swords.
For me, the ransom of my bold attempt   266
Shall be this cold corpse on the earth's cold face ;
But if I thrive, the gain of my attempt
The least of you shall share his part thereof.
Sound drums and trumpets boldly and cheerfully :
God and Saint George ! Richmond and victory !
     [Exeunt.]
     Enter King Richard, Ratcliffe [and Soldiers].

KING RICHARD
What said Northumberland as touching Richmond ?

RATCLIFFE
That he was never trainèd up in arms.

KING RICHARD
He said the truth. And what said Surrey then ?

RATCLIFFE
He smiled and said, 'The better for our purpose.'

KING RICHARD
He was in the right, and so indeed it is.
     Clock strikes.
Tell the clock there. Give me a calendar.   277
Who saw the sun to-day ?

RATCLIFFE   Not I, my lord.

KING RICHARD
Then he disdains to shine ; for by the book
He should have braved the East an hour ago.
A black day will it be to somebody.
Ratcliffe !

RATCLIFFE
My lord ?

---

199 *All . . . degree* all kinds of sins, each one practised in all its comparative stages (e.g. bad, worse, worst; cf. ll. 197–98)   222 *easedropper* eavesdropper   225 *Cry mercy* beg pardon   228 *fairest-boding* most propitious   232 *cried on* urged (me) on to   233 *jocund* joyful   239 *leisure* (see l. 98)   243 *bulwarks* defensive ramparts   248 *One . . . established* i.e. one who came to the throne through bloodshed and has held it through further bloodshed (this is the theme of Richmond's justification for deposing Richard)   249 *One . . . means* i.e. one who did not let events take their natural course but engineered them to his advantage   251 *foil* metal leaf (*England's chair* or throne) placed under a jewel (Richard) to make it appear more brilliant than it is   255 *ward* protect   259 *fat* abundant fertility   263 *quits* requites   266–67 *the ransom . . . face* i.e. (if we fail) my only ransom (freeing from captivity) will be by death   277 *calendar* almanac

KING RICHARD   The sun will not be seen to-day;
The sky doth frown and low'r upon our army.
285   I would these dewy tears were from the ground.
Not shine to-day? Why, what is that to me
More than to Richmond? For the selfsame heaven
That frowns on me looks sadly upon him.
Enter Norfolk.
NORFOLK
Arm, arm, my lord; the foe vaunts in the field.
KING RICHARD
290   Come, bustle, bustle! Caparison my horse!
Call up Lord Stanley, bid him bring his power.
I will lead forth my soldiers to the plain,
And thus my battle shall be orderèd:
My foreward shall be drawn out all in length,
Consisting equally of horse and foot;
Our archers shall be placèd in the midst;
John Duke of Norfolk, Thomas Earl of Surrey,
Shall have the leading of this foot and horse.
299   They thus directed, we will follow
300   In the main battle, whose puissance on either side
301   Shall be well wingèd with our chiefest horse.
302   This, and Saint George to boot! What think'st thou,
Norfolk?
NORFOLK
A good direction, warlike sovereign.
This found I on my tent this morning.
[He showeth him a paper.]
305   'Jockey of Norfolk, be not so bold,
306   For Dickon thy master is bought and sold.'
KING RICHARD
A thing devisèd by the enemy.
308   Go, gentlemen, every man unto his charge.
Let not our babbling dreams affright our souls;
Conscience is but a word that cowards use,
Devised at first to keep the strong in awe:
312   Our strong arms be our conscience, swords our law!
March on, join bravely, let us to it pell-mell,
If not to heaven, then hand in hand to hell.
[His Oration to his Army.]
315   What shall I say more than I have inferred?
316   Remember whom you are to cope withal –
317   A sort of vagabonds, rascals, and runaways,
318   A scum of Britains and base lackey peasants,
Whom their o'ercloyèd country vomits forth
To desperate adventures and assured destruction.
You sleeping safe, they bring to you unrest;
You having lands, and blessed with beauteous wives,
323   They would restrain the one, distain the other.
And who doth lead them but a paltry fellow,
325   Long kept in Britain at our mother's cost,
A milksop, one that never in his life
327   Felt so much cold as over shoes in snow?
Let's whip these stragglers o'er the seas again,
Lash hence these overweening rags of France,
These famished beggars, weary of their lives,
331   Who (but for dreaming on this fond exploit)
332   For want of means (poor rats) had hanged themselves.
If we be conquerèd, let men conquer us,
And not these bastard Britains, whom our fathers
Have in their own land beaten, bobbed, and thumped,
And, in record, left them the heirs of shame.
Shall these enjoy our lands? lie with our wives?
Ravish our daughters?

Drum afar off.   Hark! I hear their drum.
Fight, gentlemen of England! Fight, bold yeomen!
Draw, archers, draw your arrows to the head!
Spur your proud horses hard, and ride in blood!   341
Amaze the welkin with your broken staves!   342
Enter a Messenger.
What says Lord Stanley? Will he bring his power?
MESSENGER
My lord, he doth deny to come.
KING RICHARD
Off with his son George's head!
NORFOLK
My lord, the enemy is past the marsh:
After the battle let George Stanley die.
KING RICHARD
A thousand hearts are great within my bosom!
Advance our standards, set upon our foes.
Our ancient word of courage, fair Saint George,   350
Inspire us with the spleen of fiery dragons!   351
Upon them! Victory sits on our helms.   *[Exeunt.]*

*

Alarum; excursions. Enter [Norfolk and Forces;   V, iv
to him] Catesby.
CATESBY
Rescue, my Lord of Norfolk, rescue, rescue!
The king enacts more wonders than a man,
Daring an opposite to every danger: 3
His horse is slain, and all on foot he fights,
Seeking for Richmond in the throat of death.
Rescue, fair lord, or else the day is lost!
Alarums. Enter [King] Richard.
KING RICHARD
A horse! a horse! my kingdom for a horse!   7
CATESBY
Withdraw, my lord; I'll help you to a horse.
KING RICHARD
Slave, I have set my life upon a cast,   9
And I will stand the hazard of the die.   10
I think there be six Richmonds in the field;   11
Five have I slain to-day instead of him.
A horse! a horse! my kingdom for a horse!   *[Exeunt.]*

285 *dewy tears* i.e. morning dew ('tears' because the sky frowns, l. 284)
290 *Caparison* cover with a rich horse-cloth   299 *directed* placed tactically
300 *puissance* force or power   301 *well wingèd . . . horse* i.e. the best horsemen will be well deployed as wings (on either side of the main body of
troops; cf. *main battle*, l. 300)   302 *to boot* as a helper   305 *Jockey* i.e.
John or Jack (familiar form)   306 *Dickon* i.e. Richard or Dick (familiar
form)   308–42 *Go . . . staves* (note how Shakespeare is moved imaginatively by Richard in these lines; cf. the comparative flatness of Richmond's
oration, ll. 238–71)   312 *strong . . . conscience* i.e. might makes right   315
inferred reported   316 *cope withal* meet with   317 *sort* band   318 *Britains*
Bretons; *lackey* camp-following   323 *restrain* deprive you of; *distain*
dishonor, sully   325 *Britain* Brittany   327 *over . . . snow* i.e. snow deeper
than shoe level   331 *but for* if it were not for; *fond* foolish   332 *means* the
wherewithal to live   341 *in blood* (1) in full vigor (a hunting term), (2)
smeared with blood from spurring   342 *welkin* sky; *staves* lance shafts
350 *word* battle cry   351 *spleen* fiery temper
V, iv The same   3 *Daring an opposite* offering himself as an opponent
7 *A horse . . . horse* (cf. *The True Tragedie of Richard III:* 'A horse, a
horse, a fresh horse.' It seems likely that Shakespeare derived his famous
line from this rather flat hint.)   9 *cast* throw (of the dice)   10 *die* (singular
of dice)   11 *six Richmonds* i.e. in addition to Richmond, five other men
dressed and armed to resemble Richmond (a common safety measure)

V, v   *Alarum. Enter [King] Richard and Richmond; they*
fight; Richard is slain. Retreat and flourish.
Enter Richmond, [Lord Stanley Earl of] Derby,
bearing the crown, with divers other Lords.

RICHMOND
God and your arms be praised, victorious friends!
The day is ours; the bloody dog is dead.
DERBY
Courageous Richmond, well hast thou acquit thee.
Lo, here this long usurpèd royalty
From the dead temples of this bloody wretch
Have I plucked off, to grace thy brows withal.
Wear it, enjoy it, and make much of it.
RICHMOND
Great God of heaven, say amen to all!
But tell me, is young George Stanley living?
DERBY
He is, my lord, and safe in Leicester town,
Whither, if it please you, we may now withdraw us.
RICHMOND
What men of name are slain on either side?

DERBY
John Duke of Norfolk, Walter Lord Ferrers,
Sir Robert Brakenbury, and Sir William Brandon.
RICHMOND
Inter their bodies as become their births.
Proclaim a pardon to the soldiers fled
That in submission will return to us;
And then, as we have ta'en the sacrament,   18
We will unite the White Rose and the Red.   19
Smile heaven upon this fair conjunction,   20
That long have frowned upon their enmity!
What traitor hears me, and says not amen?
England hath long been mad and scarred herself;
The brother blindly shed the brother's blood;
The father rashly slaughtered his own son;   25
The son, compelled, been butcher to the sire:
All this divided York and Lancaster,
Divided in their dire division,
O, now let Richmond and Elizabeth,
The true succeeders of each royal house,
By God's fair ordinance conjoin together!
And let their heirs (God, if thy will be so)
Enrich the time to come with smooth-faced peace,
With smiling plenty, and fair prosperous days!
Abate the edge of traitors, gracious Lord,   35
That would reduce these bloody days again   36
And make poor England weep in streams of blood!
Let them not live to taste this land's increase
That would with treason wound this fair land's peace!
Now civil wounds are stopped, peace lives again:
That she may long live here, God say amen!
                                               Exeunt.

V, v   s.d. *Retreat* a trumpet signal for Richard's men to retire   18 *as
. . . sacrament* (referring to the oath, taken by Richmond in the cathedral
at Rheims, that he would marry Princess Elizabeth as soon as he was
possessed of the crown)   19 *White Rose . . . Red* i.e. the badges of the
Yorkist and Lancastrian factions respectively; the marriage of Richmond
(Lancastrian) and Princess Elizabeth (Yorkist) will bring an end to the
so-called Wars of the Roses (see ll. 27–31)   20 *conjunction* marriage union
(with play on the astrological meaning: the Sun [the king symbol: Rich-
mond] and Venus [Elizabeth] will be 'in conjunction,' i.e. in the same sign of
the zodiac at the same time)   25–26 *The father . . . sire* (Shakespeare
seems to be recalling *3 Henry VI*, II, v)   35 *Abate the edge* i.e. blunt the
sharpness (of traitors' swords)   36 *reduce* bring back

APPENDIX: THE QUARTO AND FOLIO TEXTS

As pointed out in the "Note on the text," the textual problems
involved in *Richard III* are extremely complex and no completely
satisfactory agreement among textual critics has yet been reached.
The fact that the greater part of the first folio (1623) text is probably printed from a copy of Quarto 6 (1622) which had been corrected against a manuscript (possibly Shakespeare's autograph or
a "fair copy" of Shakespeare's autograph) opens the way to many
possibilities of corruption. First, the person (or persons) responsible for collating the manuscript with Quarto 6 seems to have
been erratic in the care with which he executed his task. Second,
two substantial stretches of text (III, i, 1–158, and V, iii, 48 to
end), in all about 500 lines, appear to have been printed directly
from an uncorrected copy of Quarto 3 (1602). Third, Quarto 1
(1597), from which the succeeding seven quartos derive in a
mounting spiral of compositorial error and unauthoritative emendation, is generally accepted as a memorially reported text and
hence of uncertain authority in all its readings. It will thus be seen
that the first folio text may be considered open to question at
almost every point; nevertheless, because it shows evidence of
authoritative correction from a manuscript source and because it
contains a substantial number of unique lines, it remains the best
extant text of the play and has been used as the basis of the present
edition.

In the passages unique to the first folio we come closer perhaps
to Shakespeare's original and unadulterated text than in any other
parts of the play. They have, therefore, a special interest. The
following is a complete list of these passages (single words and
phrases not included):

I, ii, 16, 25, 155–66   I, iii, 115, 166–68, 353–54 ('straight . . .

lord')   I, iv, 28, 36–37 ('and . . . ghost'), 69–72, 84, 98–99
('Fare you well'), 112–13, 129 ("'Tis no matter"), 165, 211,
252–55, 261, 263
II, i, 25, 141   II, ii, 16, 89–100, 123–40   II, iii, 6 ('Give . . . sir')
II, iv, 67
III, i, 172–73   III, ii, 112, 123 ('I'll . . . lordship')   III, iii, 7–8,
16   III, iv, 102–05   III, v, 7, 97 ('and . . . adieu'), 103–05
III, vii, 5–6, 8, 11, 24 ('they . . . word'), 37, 82 ('Here . . .
again'), 98–99, 120, 127, 144–53, 202, 245
IV, i, 2–6, 14 ('and . . . York'), 36, 97–103   IV, ii, 2, 41 ('I . . .
man'), 45 ('Well, be it so')   IV, iii, 35 ('I . . . leave')   IV, iv,
20–21, 28, 52–53, 103, 160, 173, 180 ('Strike . . . drum'),
222–35, 276–77 ('which . . . body'), 288–342, 387 ('What . . .
now'), 400, 429, 432, 443–44 ('I will . . . hither'), 452
V, iii, 27–28, 43

Stated generally, the theory on which the present text has been
constructed is as follows. Taking the first folio text as a basis,
the readings of the folio text have been preferred to those of the
quarto texts (in most cases only Quarto 1 is concerned) except
(1) where the folio text follows readings of Quartos 2–6 in prefer-
ence to the reading of Quarto 1 (the inference is that, since the
readings of the later quartos are without authority, the corrector
of the copy for the first folio, working probably for the most part
with a copy of Quarto 6, has failed to correct his text at these
points and that we, therefore, approach more nearly to Shakespeare's original by reverting to Quarto 1); (2) where the folio
text (at III, i, 1–158, and V, iii, 48 to end) is apparently printed
directly from an uncorrected copy of Quarto 3, since in these passages Quarto 1, equivocal though it may be, must be considered

APPENDIX

as the basic text (the folio readings for these two sections of the text are recorded in the textual notes); (3) where the folio text omits passages or words in Quarto 1 which are so excellent that they stand on their own merits (e.g. IV, ii, 97–115) or are necessary for the meaning (the additional passages supplied from Quarto 1 have been placed in square brackets and are not otherwise recorded in the textual notes, whereas additions of one or two words are unbracketed but are recorded); (4) where the folio text is manifestly in error (e.g. see the textual note at II, i, 68). This is the theory, but in practice some editorial judgment in the choice of readings has still to be admitted.

In the following textual notes all significant variations from the first folio text (1623) have been recorded, but no attempt has been made to set up a complete textual apparatus in terms of the eight quarto and four folio editions. The student will find such an apparatus in either the "Cambridge Shakespeare" (1892) or the New Variorum *Richard III* (1909). The abbreviations here used are : F = the folios of 1623, 1632, 1664, 1685. Where the folios do not agree among themselves the reading of F1 (= the first folio) has been given; the readings of the later folios, whether one or more may agree with F1, have not been recorded. Q = the six quartos of 1597, 1598, 1602, 1605, 1612, 1622 (the last two quartos of 1629 and 1634 are of no concern here). Where there is disagreement among the quartos the reading of Q1 (= Quarto 1) has been given, but this distinction is not intended to exclude the possible agreement of some of the remaining five quartos with Q1. In a majority of cases where a Q1 reading has been preferred to a F1 reading, the F1 reading represents a reading inherited from Quartos 2–6. QF = agreement of the first six quartos and the four folios. Eds = emendation by editors of Shakespeare from Nicholas Rowe (1709) to the present day. Significant readings in the quartos for which there is no general equivalent in the folio text and which have not otherwise been included as part of the present edition are also recorded in the textual notes.

Stage directions or parts of stage directions enclosed in square brackets have been added either from Q1 or from Rowe and later editors and are not recorded in the textual notes. In III, i, 1–158, and V, iii, 48 to end, where the copy-text is basically Q1, the stage directions of F1 have still been preferred to those of Q1, and Q1 stage directions bracketed as elsewhere. The usage of *u* and *v* has been modernized in the QF readings, and a grave accent has been added in some QF readings to clarify the pronunciation of the final -*èd*. Throughout the adopted reading is in italics.

I, i, 38 *up* (Q subs.) up : (F) 41 s.d. *Clarence guarded* (Eds) Clarence with a gard of men (Q) Clarence, and Brakenbury, guarded (F) 45 *the* (Q) th' (F) 52 *for* (Q) but (F) 64 *she* (Q subs.) shee. (F1) 65 *tempers . . . extremity* (Q1) tempts him to this harsh Extremity (F) 71 *is secure* (Eds) is securde (Q1) secure (F) 75 *Lord . . . delivery* (Q adds 'to her' after *was*) *his* (Q) her (F1) 88 *so?* (Eds) so (Q) so, (F) 95 *gentlefolks* (Q1) gentle Folkes (F1) 101–02 *Brakenbury. What . . . betray me?* (first appears in Q2, 1598) 124 *the* (Q1) this (F) 133 *prey* (Q) play (F)

I, ii, 27 *life* (Eds; cf. IV, i, 75) death (QF) 39 *Stand* (Q) Stand'st (F1) 78 *a* (Q) Omitted (F) 80 *t'accuse* (Eds) to curse (QF) 102 *hedgehog?* (Eds) hedgehogge (Q1) Hedgehogge, (F) 138 *thee* (Q) the (F1) 141 *He lives . . . could* (Q adds 'Go to,' before *He*) 195 *was man* (Q1) man was (F) 201 *Vouchsafe . . . ring* (given to Anne in F; here assigned as in Q) 235 *at all* (Q1) withall (F)

I, iii, 17 *come the lords* (Q1) comes the Lord (F) 68 *he . . . ground* (F) thereby he may gather / The ground of your ill will and to remove it (Q1) 101 *Iwis* (Q1) I wis (F) 141 *childish-foolish* (Eds) childish, foolish (Q1) childish foolish (F) 159 *of* (Q) off (F1) 214 *with'red* (Q1) wither'd (F) 246 False-boding (Eds) false boading (QF) 287 *gentle-sleeping* (Eds) gentle sleeping (QF) 303 *Buckingham* (F) Hast. (Q) 308 *Queen Elizabeth* (Eds) Qu. (Q1) Hast. (Q6) Mar. (F1) 341, 349 *1. Murderer* (Eds) Execu. (Q) Vil. (F) 343 *Well . . . about me* (Q precedes *Well* with 'It was') 350 *doers. Be* (F4) doers be (Q1) dooers, be (F1) 354 *1. Murderer* (Eds) Vil. (F) Speech omitted (Q)

I, iv, s.d. *Keeper* (Keeper's role is given to Brakenbury in Q) 13 *thence* (Q1) there (F) 22 *waters* (Q1) water (F) 48 *stranger soul* (Q) Stranger-soule (F) 58 *methoughts* (Q1) me thought (F) 68 *requites* (Q) requits (F1) 86 *1. Murderer* (Eds) Execu. (Q) 2. Mur. (F) 89 *2. Murderer* (Eds) 2 Exe. (F) 100 *I* (Q1) we (F) 103 *Why, he* (Q reads 'When he wakes, / Why foole he') 110–11 *warrant can* (Q adds 'for it' after *warrant*) 120 *Faith* (Q) Omitted (F) 124 *Zounds* (Q) Come (F) 131 *I'll not . . . with it* (Q adds 'it is a dangerous thing' after *it*) 138 *It is turned . . . towns* (Q adds 'all' before *towns*) 141 *Zounds* (Q) Omitted (F) 146 *I am strong-framed* (Q adds 'Tut' before *I am*) *strong-framed* (Eds) strong in fraud (Q) strong fram'd (F) 146 *he cannot prevail . . . me* (Q adds 'I warrant thee' after *me*) 153–54 *Soft! . . . Strike!* (Q reads '1 Harke he stirs, shall I strike.') 166 *Who . . . come* (Q reads 'Tell me who are you, wherefore come you thither') 167 *Both* (Eds) Am. (Q) 2 (F) 184–85 *to have . . . sins* (Q) for any goodnesse (F) 208 *He sends . . . this* (Q adds 'Why sirs' before *He*) 216 *gallant-springing* (Eds) gallant springing (QF) 221 *O, if you* (Q) If you do (F) 234 *of* (Q) on (F) 235 *lessoned* (Q1) lessonèd (F) 261 *As . . . distress* (after l. 255 in F; omitted in Q) 265 *drown . . . within* (Q reads 'chop thee in the malmesey But, in the next roome') 270 *heavens* (Q1) Heaven (F)

II, i, s.d. (F adds 'Woodvill' in repetition of *Rivers*) 5 *in* (Q) to (F) 7 *Hastings and Rivers* (Q) Rivers and Hastings (Q) Dorset and Rivers (F) 28 *And so swear I* (Q adds 'my Lord' after *I*) 39 *God* (Q) heaven (F) 46 *comes . . . duke* (Q reads 'comes the noble Duke') 52 *wrong-incensèd* (Eds) wrong insencèd (QF) 57 *unwittingly* (Q) unwillingly (F; i.e. unintentionally, possibly the true reading) 59 *By* (Q) To (F) 68 *That, all . . . frowned on me* (F follows this line with 'Of you Lord Woodvill, and Lord Scales of you'; both names are titles of Rivers, already referred to in l. 67) 82 *King Edward* (F) Ryv. (Q) 93 *but* (Q) and (F) 108 *at* (Q) and (F1) 117 *Even . . . give himself* (Q1 adds 'owne' before *garments*)

II, ii, 1 *Boy* (Q) Edw. (F) 3 *Girl* (Eds) Daugh. (F; throughout) Boy (Q) 47 *I* (Q) Omitted (F) 83 *weep* (Q) weepes (F1) 86 *distressed,* (Q1) distrest: (F1) 112 *cloudy princes* (Q) clowdy-Princes (F) *heart-sorrowing peers* (Q1) hart-sorrowing-Peeres (F) 142, 154 *Ludlow* (Q) London (F) 144 *To give . . . business* (Q adds 'waighty' before *business*) 145 *Both* (Eds) Ans. (Q; speech omitted in F)

II, iii, 8 *Ay, sir . . . true* (Q reads '1 It doth.') 32 *wise men* (Q) wisemen (F1) 43 *Ensuing* (Eds) Pursuing (F; catchword 'Ensuing' in F1)

II, iv, 1 *hear* (Q1) heard (F) 21 *Archbishop* (Eds) Car. (Q) Yor. (F) 38 *Here . . . news?* (Q reads 'Here comes your sonne, Lo: M. Dorset. / What newes Lo: Marques?) 65 *death* (Q) earth (F)

III, i, 8 *dived* (F) divèd (Q) 9 *Nor* (Q) No (F) 40 *God in heaven* (Q1) God (F) 43 *deep* (Q1) great (F) 44 *senseless-obstinate* (Eds) sencelesse obstinate (QF) 51 *claimed . . . deserved* (Eds) claimèd . . . deservèd (Q) 56 *never* (Q) ne're (F) 57 *overrule* (Q) o're-rule (F) 60 s.d. *Exeunt* (Eds) Exit (Q3, F) 63 *seems* (Q1) thinkst (F) 71 *since, succeeding* (F) since succeeding (Q) 78 *all-ending* (Q1) ending (F) 82 *Vice, Iniquity* (F) vice iniquity (Q1) 86 *valor* (F) valure (Q1) 87 *this* (Q1) his (F) 96 *loving* (Q1) noble (F) 97 *dread* (Q1) deare (F) 98 *brother – to* (Eds) brother to (Q1) brother, to (F) 111 *With all* (F) withall (Q1) 120 *heavy* (Q1) weightie (F) 123 *as* (Q1) as, as (F1) 132 *sharp-provided* (Eds) sharpe provided (QF) 133–34 *uncle, . . . himself :* (F) Unckle: . . . himselfe, (Q1) 141 *needs* (Q1) Omitted (F) 145 *grandam* (F1) Granam (Q) *murd'red* (Q) murther'd (F) 149 *with* (Q) and with (F) 150 s.d. *Hastings* (Eds) Hast. Dors. (Q) Hastings, and Dorset (F; Dorset has not been present in the scene) s.d. *Manent* (F2) manet (Q, F1) 171–74 *purpose . . . us* (Q reads 'purpose, if he be willing')

III, ii, 2 *Who knocks* (Q adds 'at the dore' after *knocks*) 3 s.d. *Enter Lord Hastings* (after l. 5 in F) 41 *How! . . . garland!* (Eds) Howe? . . . garland? (Q1) How . . . Garland? (F) *Dost* (F3) Doest (Q, F1) 60 *Well . . . older* (Q reads 'I tell thee Catesby. Cat. What my Lord? / Hast. Ere a fortnight make me elder') 78 *you do* (Q) Omitted (F) 89–91 *What . . . lords* (Q reads 'But come my Lo: shall we to the tower? *Hast.* I go: but stay, heare you not the newes, / This day those men') 91 *talked* (Q1) talke (F) 95 *Go . . . fellow* (Q reads 'Go you before, Ile follow presently') s.d. *Exeunt* (Eds) Exit (Q3, F) 96 *How now, sirrah* (Q reads 'Well met Hastings') 108–09 *Priest. Well . . . heart* (Q reads '*Hast.* What Sir Iohn, you are wel met')

III, iv, 10 *We know . . . hearts* (In Q Buckingham precedes this line with 'Who I my Lo?') 31 *My . . . when* (Q reads '*Hast.* I thanke your Grace. / *Glo.* My Lo: of Elie, *Bish.* My Lo: / *Glo.* When) 34 *Marry . . . heart* (Q reads 'I go my Lord') 79 s.d. *Manent* (F2) manet (Q, F1) 82 *rase* (Q) rowse (F) *our helms* (F) his helme (Q; perhaps correctly) 83 *But* (Q) And (F)

III, v, 5 *Tut . . . tragedian* (Q adds 'feare not me' after *Tut*) 12–14 *But . . . Mayor* – (Q reads '*Glo.* Here comes the Maior. / *Buc.* Let me alone to entertaine him. Lo: Maior,') 20 *innocence* (Q1) Innocencie (F) 21 *Be . . . Lovel.* (Q reads 'O, O, be quiet, it is Catesby.' with Lovel's following speech given to Catesby) 34 *Look . . . Mayor* (from Q, where it follows l. 26) 50–51 *I never . . . Shore* (assigned to Mayor in Q) 66 *cause* (Q1) case (F) 74 *meet's advantage* (Q1) meetest vantage (F) 102 *Look for . . . affords* (Q adds 'and so my Lord farewell' after *affords*) 104 *Penker* (Eds) Peuker (F1) Omitted (Q) 105 s.d. *Exeunt* (Eds) Exit (F, Omitted Q) 109 s.d. *Exit* (Q) Exeunt (F1)

III, vi, 12 *who's* (Q1) who (F)

III, vii, 20 *mine* (Q1) my (F) *to an* (Q1) toward (F) 33 *spake* (Q1) spoke (F) 40 *wisdoms* (Q1) wisdome (F) 52 *I . . . plead* (Q reads 'Feare not me, if thou canst pleade') 55–56 *Go . . . lord* (Q reads 'You shal see what I can do, get you up to the leads. Exit. / Now my L. Maior,') 58 *Now . . . request?* (Q reads 'Here coms his servant: how now Catesby what saies he.') 83 *My lord* (Q) Omitted (F) 125 *her* (Q1) his (F) 126 *Her* (F) His (F) 127 *Her* (Eds) His (F; line omitted in Q) 131–32 *charge . . . land* (Q reads 'soveraingtie thereof') 219 *Zounds, I'll* (Q) we will (F) 222 *If . . . it* (Q reads '*Ano.* Doe, good my lord, least all the land do rew it) 247 *cousin* (Q) Cousins (F)

IV, i, 2–7 *Led . . . away* (Q reads 'Sister well met, whether awaie so fast') 14 *How . . . York* (Q reads 'How fares the Prince') 16 *them* (F) him (Q) 18 *The king . . . Protector* (Q adds 'I crie you mercie' before *mean*) 28 *an* (Q1) one (F) 30 *looker-on* (Eds) looker on (QF)

IV, ii, 13 *liege* (Q) Lord (F) 36 *I know . . . gentleman* (Q precedes this line with 'My lord') 42 *deep-revolving* (Eds) deepe revolving (QF) 48 *To Richmond . . . abides* (Q adds 'beyond the seas' after *parts*) 49 *Come hither, Catesby.* (Q reads 'Catesby. *Cat.* My lord.') 71 *there* (Q) then (F) 81 *I . . . straight* (Q1 reads 'Tis done my gracious lord. / *King* Shal we heare from thee Tirrel ere we sleep? / *Tir.* Ye shall my lord' – apparently a memorial slip repeating III, i, 188–89) 89 *Hereford* (F2) Herford (Q) Hertford (F1) 104 *called* (Eds) callèd (Q) 116–17 *May . . . Thou* (Q reads 'Whie then resolve me whether you wil or no? / *King.* Tut, tut, thou') 117 s.d. *Exeunt* (Eds) Exit (QF)

IV, iii, 5 *ruthless* (Q1) ruthfull (F) 7 *kind* (Q1) milde (F) 8 *to* (F) two (Q) 13 *Which* (Q1) And (F) 15 *once* (Q) one (F) 27 *For it is done* (Q adds 'my Lord' after *done*) 31 *at* (Q) and (F) 33 *thee* (Q) the (F1) 50 *rash-levied* (Eds) rash levied (QF) 53 *leads* (Q) leds (F1)

IV, iv, 10 *unblown* (Q) unblowed (F1) *new-appearing* (Eds) new appearing (QF) 17–19 *Duchess of York. So . . . dead?* (after l. 34 in Q) 26 *mortal-living* (Eds) mortal living (QF) 41 *Harry* (Eds) Richard (Q) Husband (F) 45 *holp'st* (Q3) hopst (Q1, F1) 52 *That excellent . . . earth* (follows l. 53 in F; both lines omitted in Q) 64 *Thy* (Q) The (F) 70 *smoth'red* (Q1) smother'd (F) 86 *a-high* (Eds) a high (QF) 100–01 *For one . . . with care* (Q reverses order of lines) 103 *feared* (Eds) fearèd (F) 112 *weary* (Q1) wearied (F) 118 *nights . . . days* (Q1) night . . . day (F) 128 *intestate* (Q) intestine (F) 132 *so, then* (Q) so then, (F1) 141 *Where* (Q) Where't (F) 147–48 *Where . . . Hastings* (Q reads 'Where is kind Hastings, Rivers, Vaughan, Gray') 180–81 *I prithee . . . bitterly* (Q reads 'O heare me speake for I shal never see thee more. / *King.* Come, come, you are too

bitter') 200 *moe* (Q1) more (F) 239 *or* (Q1) and (F) 241 *discovered* (Q1) discoverèd (F) 266 *should be else* (Q1) else should bee (F) 268 *would I* (Q1) I would (F) 274 *sometimes* (Q1) sometime (F) 276 *handkercher* (Q1) hand-kercheefe (F) 284 *is* (Q) Omitted (F1) 324 *Of ten times* (Eds) Of ten-times (F1) Often-times (F2) 344 *still-lasting* (Eds) still lasting (QF) 365 *Harp . . . break* (follows l. 363 in F; order here from Q1) 368 *swear* – (Eds) sweare by nothing. (Q) sweare. (F) 377 *God* – / *God's* (Q) Heaven. / Heanens (F) 392 *in* (Q1) with (F) 396 *o'erpast* (Q) repast (F) 417 *peevish-fond* (Eds) peevish, fond (Q1) peevish found (F) 431 *shallow, changing* (Eds) shallow changing (Q) shallow-changing (F) s.d. *Enter Ratcliffe* (as in Q, which omits l. 432; comes after l. 432 in F) 444 *Ratcliffe* (Eds) Catesby (F) Omitted (Q) 457 *None good,* (F4) None good (Q) None, good (F1) 494 *Go then . . . behind* (Q adds 'heare you' after *But*) 507 *you* (Q1) ye (F) 509–10 *The news . . . waters* (Q reads 'Your grace mistakes, the newes I bring is good, / My newes is that by sudden floud, and fall of water') 513–14 *I cry . . . thine* (Q reads 'O I crie you mercie, I did mistake, / Ratcliffe reward him, for the blow I gave him') 534 *tidings* (Q1) Newes (F)

IV, v, 10 *Ha'rford-West* (Q) Hertford West (F)

V, i, 11 *my lord* (Q) Omitted (F)

V, iii, 2 *My Lord of Surrey* (Q reads 'Whie, how now Catesbie' with next speech-prefix '*Cat*,') 4 *My . . . liege* (Q reads 'Norffolke, come hether') 28 *you* (Q1) your (F) 46 *In to* (Q1) Into (F) 48 *nine* (F) sixe (Q) 54 *sentinels* (F) centinell (Q) 58 *Catesby* (Q) Ratcliffe (F) 59 *Catesby* (Eds) Rat. (QF) 61 *sun-rising* (F) sun rising (Q1) 65–66 *heavy. / Ratcliffe* (F) heavy Ratcliffe (Q1) 68 *thou* (Q) Omitted (F) 80 *sit* (F) set (Q1) 83 *loving* (Q1) Noble (F)· 86 *that. The* (F) that the (Q1) 90 *the* (Q) th' (F) 91 *mortal-staring* (Eds) mortal staring (QF) 101 *sund'red* (F) sundried (Q1) 102 *rites* (F) rights (Q) 105 *thoughts* (Q) noise (F) 113 *The* (Q) Th' (F) 115 *the* (Q1) thy (F) 123 *butchered* (Q1) butcher'd (F) 126 *deadly* (Q1) Omitted (F) 127 *me: despair* (F) me despaire (Q1) 131 *thy* (Q) Omitted (F) *sleep: live* (Eds) sleepe live (Q1) 132 *sit* (F) set (Q1) 146 *Will* (F) Wel (Q1) 151 s.d. *Enter . . . young Princes* (in Q1 the ghosts of the two young princes precede the ghost of Hastings; the F order is that of the time of their deaths, as in Q3) 155 *souls bid* (Q) soule bids (F1) 162 *perturbations* (F) preturbations (Q1) 177 *falls* (Q) fall (F) 181 *now* (Q1) not (F) 183 *What . . . fear? Myself?* (Q1) What? . . . feare my Selfe? (F) 184 *am* (F) and (Q1) 186 *reason why* – (Eds) reason whie (Q1) reason: why? (F) 197 *perjury* (Q1) Omitted (F) *highest* (Q) high'st (F) 198 *direst* (Q) dyr'st (F) 200 *Throng* (Q1) Throng all (F) *the* (Q) th' (F) 202 *will* (Q1) shall (F) 203 *And* (Q) Nay (F) 209 *Zounds, who is* (Q) Who's (F) 223 *see* (Q1) heare (F) 228 *fairest-boding* (Eds) fairest boding (QF) 233 *soul* (Q) Heart (F) 243 *high-reared* (Eds) high reard (QF) 244 *Richard except,* (Q3) Richard, except (Q1) (Richard except) (F) 248 *established* (F) establishèd (Q) 250 *slaughtered* (Q) slaughter'd (F) 251 *foil* (Q1) soile (F) 266 *sweat* (Q1) sweare (F) 271 s.d. *Ratcliffe [and Soldiers]* (Eds) Rat, &c. (Q) Ratcliffe, and Catesby (F) 275 *smiled* (F) smilèd (Q) 281–82 *somebody. / Ratcliffe!* (F1) some bodie Rat. (Q) 293 *ordered* (Q) ordred (F1) 294 *out all* (Q) Omitted (F) 298 *this* (Q1) the (F) 301 *well winged* (Q) well-wingèd (F1) 302 *boot* (F) bootes (Q1) 308 *unto* (Q) to (F) 310 *Conscience is but* (Q1) For Conscience is (F) 312 *conscience, swords* (F) conscience swords, (Q1) 313 *to it* (Q) too't (F) 321 *to you* (Q1) you to (F) 322 *wives* (Q1) wifes (Q1) 326 *milksop* (F) milkesopt (Q1) 336 *in* (Q1) on (F) 339 *Fight* (Q1) Right (F) *bold* (Q1) boldly (F) 352 *them! Victory* (Eds) them victorie (Q1) them, Victorie (F) *helms* (Q1) helpes (F1)

V, v, 4 *this . . . royalty* (Q1) these long usurped Royalties (F) 7 *enjoy it* (Q1) Omitted (F) 11 *if it please . . . now* (Q) (if you please) we may (F) 13 *Derby* (F); speech printed as s.d. in Q *Walter Lord Ferrers* (Eds) Water Lord Ferris (Q1) Walter Lord Ferris (F) 25 *slaughtered* (Q) slaughterèd (F1) 28 *division,* (Eds) devision. (QF) 32 *their* (Q1) thy (F) 33 *smooth-faced* (F1) smooth-faste (Q1)

THE LIFE AND DEATH OF KING JOHN

INTRODUCTION

King John is not only a powerful and moving drama in its own right, but it is particularly interesting for the insight it affords into Shakespeare's development as a dramatic artist, since it occupies a pivotal position in relation to his history plays as well as his tragedies. As a history play, it reveals Shakespeare's mastery of techniques he had employed in the looser, more episodic *Henry VI* plays and *Richard III*, and his experimentation with techniques he was to master in *Richard II* and the *Henry IV* plays. As a tragedy, it is interesting for its conception of a hero frustrated by a sin which he repents but cannot cancel, doomed to destruction by his commitment to evil means in striving for great ends. With such a view of man Shakespeare had dealt in the earlier *Titus Andronicus*, and he was to return to it with greater power in such plays as *Julius Caesar* and *Coriolanus*. As Shakespeare's revision of *The Troublesome Reign of John*, an anonymous two-part play printed in 1591, *King John* enables us to see how Shakespeare could shape the crude matter of an unpalatable source play into a sophisticated and original work of art.

History and tragedy are closely fused in *King John*, for the hero is destroyed by complicity in the death of Arthur, son of his elder brother Geoffrey, and thus with a better claim to the throne than his own. The king's sin is dictated by political necessity, for Arthur's claim can lead only to perpetual civil war; and Arthur stands, moreover, for the power of Rome, supported by France and Austria. The opposing political forces are clearly aligned at the beginning of the play: John and the Bastard stand for English nationalism and royal supremacy, while Arthur stands for a divided England, prey to invading foreign forces and subject to the power of the papacy. John represents principles dear to Tudor Englishmen, and his cause must triumph, but Shakespeare, in his usual manner, tempers the emotional commitment of his audience to the Tudor political position by his portrait of the cruel Queen Elinor and by causing this position to demand the death of a child, as he similarly heightens sympathy for Arthur by his portrait of the pathetic Constance. The tragedy of King John is that to attain political victory he must sacrifice his own humanity. He is destroyed by a cleavage between his public and private morality, just as a similar division in a somewhat later play is to destroy the noble Brutus of *Julius Caesar*.

Unfortunately there is no external evidence of any kind as to the date of *King John*, but its stylistic relation to the plays which clearly preceded it and to those which seem to have followed it would suggest that it was written sometime between 1592 and 1596, with 1594 perhaps most likely. It follows *The Troublesome Reign* closely, although

it tempers the virulent anti-Catholicism of the source, omitting the most offensive scenes, perhaps – as has been suggested – out of deference to the Catholic Earl of Southampton whose patronage Shakespeare was seeking. It has been suggested in recent years that the play may have been written as early as 1590, based directly on Holinshed's *Chronicles*, Foxe's *Book of Martyrs*, the *Historia Maior* of Matthew Paris, and several Latin chronicles which could have been available to Shakespeare only in manuscript. This theory would hold further that *The Troublesome Reign*, printed in 1591, is not Shakespeare's source, but rather a corrupt version (bad quarto) of a play written in imitation of Shakespeare's some months later in the same year of 1590. Were this theory sustained, we would have to reconsider many of our views of *King John*, but it has won little acceptance among scholars, since it is based upon very tenuous "evidence" involving hypotheses more difficult to entertain than the simpler one that *The Troublesome Reign* was the earlier of the two plays and Shakespeare's source.

King John would have been "timely" whatever its date, since it deals with political issues which had come to be associated by Tudor historians with the reign of its titular character; we must remember that a very important value of history in Shakespeare's day was its power to teach political lessons, and that Shakespeare was, to some extent, bound in this play by the view of King John which had been shaped before him by Protestant chroniclers and by the political issues which they had found inherent in his story. We must note that a central issue of the play (as of its source) – the relation of England to the church of Rome – was also the most pressing political problem of Shakespeare's England, and that many Elizabethan writers were particularly interested in King John because they saw his reign as parallel in many respects to that of their own queen.

Although the early British historians, right through the humanist Polydore Vergil, had been fairly harsh in their treatment of King John, with the Reformation we note a change. William Tyndale in 1528 accused the chronicles of distortion and praised John for his opposition to the papacy. Tyndale was followed in this by John Bale, a fiery Reformation polemicist, who in the following decade wrote a two-part morality play called *Kynge Johan* in which he used John's career to champion the cause of the Reformation. King John was similarly eulogized by the reformer John Foxe in his *Book of Martyrs*, and this Protestant view was adopted by chroniclers such as Richard Grafton and Raphael Holinshed, upon whose works *The Troublesome Reign* was based; and they were works Shakespeare undoubtedly read also before revising the old play. These writers, with little regard for historical fact, had made King John into a pre-Reformation hero, a king before Henry VIII who had dared oppose the papacy. He was not the tyrannical signer of *Magna Carta* whom we know. Indeed, *Magna Carta* receives no mention in this play, for it was regarded by Shakespeare's contemporaries not as a triumph for liberty, but rather as a shameful attempt to weaken the central monarchy in which most Elizabethans firmly believed, and whose virtues they saw reflected in the absolute rule of Queen Elizabeth. John to them was rather the symbol of English nationalism who had rallied the dissident barons against France and Austria, as well as the champion of royal supremacy who had defied the papal legate and died a martyr, poisoned by a treacherous monk, although historically King John appears to have died of overeating.

Shakespeare's play is informed by this view of King John, and like its source it asserts the doctrines which John's career commonly was called upon to illustrate: nationalism, royal supremacy, the evils of rebellion, and the right of a king to be answerable for his sins to God alone. But more than anything else – and here Shakespeare goes beyond his sources and reveals his own particular bent – the play affirms the inseparability of public and private virtue, that only a good man can be a good king. It asserts also that a nation can be united only when a king has learned to subordinate his personal desires to the good of his country. These themes are carried in the parallel progressions of King John and the Bastard, Faulconbridge, two characters created as foils to one another: the Bastard strong where John is weak, and learning to rise and re-establish the glory of England as John declines and lets it fall. By their relation to one another the play is unified. When the Bastard surrenders his power to the new king in the final act, the audience sees that the goal of national unity which John had vainly sought has in fact been realized. John the man has been destroyed, but England, through the Bastard, is nevertheless triumphant.

Shakespeare makes clear that John is a usurper, but he establishes also that until the death of Arthur, John is a good, even a great, king, and that as the *de facto* ruler he merits the support of the nobility, a political point to be made again in the *Henry IV* plays. Arthur's inadequacy is emphasized by his own weakness and by the forces with whom he is associated. He stands also for the kind of child king which Tudor Englishmen conventionally mirrored in the unfortunate Henry VI, and such as they feared most among the possible successors to the now old and ailing Queen Elizabeth. John's greatness appears in his defiance of the French ambassador and the papal legate, in his victory before Angiers, and in the love and loyalty with which he is served by Faulconbridge, one of the most remarkable creations of Shakespeare's early career, a character so dear to audiences that some critics have been tempted to see him as the hero of the play, although to do so is to distort *King John* and destroy its unity.

John is the hero, and his greatness is emphasized up to the middle of the third act. He begins to degenerate both as man and as king when in III, iii he calls for the murder of Arthur. The Bastard, conversely, wins little triumph until the beginning of John's decline. At the beginning of the play he is fairly low on Fortune's wheel, a landless bastard, albeit the son of Coeur-de-lion, bearing the moral stigma of his illegitimacy, which he affirms proudly in spite of his mother's shame. He has a straightforward heartiness and charm which immediately win us to him, but he has little initial claim to virtue. Only as John declines does the Bastard's moral stature begin to be evident, becoming more and more clear until he is ready to assume the leadership of England which John, because of his own sin, can no longer bear.

The role of Constance is relatively brief, but historically it has been prized by actresses and has been performed by some of the greatest, although her savage interchange with Queen Elinor usually has been omitted on the stage. She is the last of Shakespeare's wailing women, bridging the gap between the weeping queens of *Richard III* and the queen of *Richard II*, with her gentle, more controlled, and finally more moving sorrow. The lamentations of Constance may disturb modern audiences by their excess, but they are Shakespeare's dramatic means of swaying the sympathies of his audience away from King John in the third act, and when this has been accomplished Constance drops out of the play. The alienation of the audience from John is completed in the scene, almost too painful to be staged, in which Arthur pleads with Hubert for his eyes. We now behold the fall of John and the collapse of his power as Hubert shows his inability to execute his commission and as England's enemies prepare their forces for a new onslaught. The fourth act shows us not a triumphant King John but a fearful one, vainly trusting in a new coronation to consolidate the power which the audience knows he has lost already. He is now struck repeated blows: he learns that his mother is dead, that his nobles have deserted him, and that the French army is prepared to invade England. He sees at once that his troubles all stem from his order to Hubert. He is torn by remorse – there is no pretense in his joy when he hears that Arthur has not been killed after all – but his remorse is of no avail, and even though he has had no hand in the actual death of Arthur he must bear the guilt for it. How abject and powerless he has now become appears in his ignominious capitulation to the papal legate he had once so proudly defied.

When the Bastard castigates Hubert for the death of Arthur, Shakespeare is placing Faulconbridge in opposition to what John has become, aligning him clearly on the side of virtue. He has every reason to desert John, but in spite of Arthur's death he decides to remain with his king rather than join the rebelling nobles, and in this decision he attains his full stature, for he masters his own personal passion and places the good of England above all other considerations. He now becomes the symbol of English strength and unity, and it is only fitting that John should relinquish his power to him. Before this symbol the French army is powerless; John's capitulation to Pandulph is undone, the rebellious lords are won back to the crown, and the Bastard closes the play with his great apostrophe to England. He might at the end become king himself, but he recognizes the primacy of legitimate succession, and in surrendering his power to the young Henry III he sets the welfare of England above his personal glory, assuring to his country a continuance of orderly government, with a lawful king upon the throne. Under the new regime England will enjoy a greater degree of felicity than it had ever known under King John, and in assuring this the triumph of Faulconbridge is both an ethical and a political one, for while serving his country he has learned also to master himself.

In Shakespeare's English history plays the kingdom itself is conceived of as a kind of dramatic entity, for in its welfare dramatic interest is always centered. In this play England is finally victorious in spite of the sins of her king, and she is able to achieve victory through the rise of Faulconbridge, who comes to occupy John's forfeited role and to stand for the political and ethical ideals which John was incapable of attaining. The king himself dies ignobly, but Shakespeare suggests (V, vii, 70–73) that he is able at last to save his soul. His sincere remorse for the death of Arthur, and the victory of England in spite of all, win for him the possibility of expiation. Faulconbridge and Prince Henry indicate Shakespeare's final judgment as they sing the dead king's praises. King John dies not a treacherous villain but the royal martyr he had been made into before Shakespeare approached the subject.

Although there is no evidence of a specific performance of *King John* earlier than the revival at Covent Garden by John Rich in 1737, the play has been fairly popular ever since. In early performances the part of Arthur was played usually by a girl, and even more unfortunate, during the eighteenth and nineteenth centuries the play was often adapted and distorted for purposes of political propaganda, the most notable instance being Colley Cibber's *Papal Tyranny in the Reign of King John*, produced at Covent Garden in 1745, after many years of preparation, with Cibber making his final stage appearance as Pandulph. Five days after this opening David Garrick launched a rival version – presumably going back to Shakespeare – at Drury Lane, playing the part of John himself. In later years he played the Bastard as well, but he always preferred the titular role. The play had its first American production in Philadelphia in 1768.

King John owes much of its stage popularity to the appeal for actors of three great roles: King John, the Bastard, and Constance. These parts have been played by the greatest figures in both the British and American theatre. The play was a favorite in the repertory of John Philip Kemble and Sarah Siddons from 1783 until their retirement, Mrs Siddons playing Constance for the last time in 1812 and Kemble appearing as John just a few days before he left the stage in 1817. Edmund and Charles Kean, William Macready, and Sir Herbert Beerbohm Tree were all responsible for memorable productions, as were Edwin Booth and Robert Mantell in the United States. In more recent years the play has had a new burst of popularity, and scarcely a year goes by without at least one important production. *King John* has all the ingredients of great drama: action, character, poetry, and a presiding moral vision.

State University of New York IRVING RIBNER
at Stony Brook

NOTE ON THE TEXT

This edition follows closely the only substantive text of *King John*, that of the first folio (1623). The folio text seems to have been set up from Shakespeare's own draft, possibly corrected before printing, particularly in the two final acts, by reference to the theatre prompt-copy. It is a fairly good text, but it shows some confusion and inconsistency in the names of characters in speech headings and stage directions. These have been corrected and regularized in the present edition, and a few additional emendations have been made, as listed below. The folio text is divided, somewhat haphazardly, into acts and scenes. In the act–scene division here supplied marginally II, i corresponds to folio I, ii ; III, i to folio II and III, i ; III, ii and iii to folio III, ii ; III, iv to folio III, iii.

The following substantive departures in italics have been made from the folio text. Some are readings from the second (1632), third (1663), or fourth (1683) folios; others are emendations made early in the history of Shakespearean scholarship and accepted by most modern editors. The authority for each is indicated parenthetically, followed by the first folio reading in roman.

I, i, 147 *I would* (F2) It would 237 *Could he get me* (Vaughan) Could get me 257 *Thou art* (F4) That art
II, i, 1 *King Philip* (Theobald) Lewis 63 *Ate* (Rowe) Ace 113 *breast* (F2) beast 144 *shows* (Theobald) shooes 149 *King Philip* (Theobald) King Lewis 150 *King Philip* (Theobald) Lewis 215 *Confront* (Rowe) Comfort 259 *roundure* (Capell) rounder 325 *Citizen* (Rowe) Hubert 335 *run* (F2) room 368 *Citizen* (Rowe) Fra. 371 *Kinged* (Tyrwhitt) Kings 416 *Citizen* (Rowe) Hubert
III, i, 110 *day* (Theobald) daies 148 *task* (Theobald) tast
III, iii, 39 *ear* (Collier) race
III, iv, 44 *not holy* (F4) holy 64 *friends* (Rowe) fiends 110 *world's* (Pope) words
IV, i, 92 *mote* (Wilson) moth
IV, ii, 1 *again* (F3) against 42 *when* (Tyrwhitt) then 73 *Does* (F4) Do
IV, iii, 33 *man* (F2) mans 41 *Have you* (F3) you have 155 *ceinture* (Moore Smith) center
V, ii, 26 *Were* (F2) Was 36 *grapple* (Pope) cripple 43 *hast thou* (F4) hast 135 *these* (Rowe) this
V, vi, 12 *eyeless* (Theobald) endless
V, vii, 17 *mind* (Rowe) winde 21 *cygnet* (Rowe) Symet 42 *strait* (Pope) straight 108 *give you thanks* (Rowe) giue thankes

THE LIFE AND DEATH OF KING JOHN

King John
Prince Henry, son to the King
Arthur, Duke of Britain, nephew to the King
The Earl of Pembroke
The Earl of Essex
The Earl of Salisbury
The Lord Bigot
Hubert de Burgh
Robert Faulconbridge, son to Sir Robert Faulconbridge
Philip the Bastard, his half-brother
James Gurney, servant to Lady Faulconbridge
Peter of Pomfret, a prophet

Philip, King of France
Lewis, the Dauphin
Lymoges, Duke of Austria
Cardinal Pandulph, the Pope's legate
Melun, a French lord
Chatillion, ambassador from France
Queen Elinor, mother to King John
Constance, mother to Arthur
Blanch of Spain, niece to King John
Lady Faulconbridge
Lords, Ladies, Citizens of Angiers, Sheriff, Heralds, Officers,
Soldiers, Executioners, Messengers, and other Attendants

Scene : *England and France*]

*

I, i   *Enter King John, Queen Elinor, Pembroke, Essex,*
and Salisbury, with the Chatillion of France.

KING JOHN
Now, say, Chatillion, what would France with us ?

CHATILLION
Thus, after greeting, speaks the King of France
3   In my behavior to the majesty,
4   The borrowed majesty, of England here.

ELINOR
A strange beginning : 'borrowed majesty' !

KING JOHN
6   Silence, good mother ; hear the embassy.

CHATILLION
7   Philip of France, in right and true behalf
Of thy deceasèd brother Geoffrey's son,
Arthur Plantagenet, lays most lawful claim
To this fair island and the territories,
To Ireland, Poitiers, Anjou, Touraine, Maine,
Desiring thee to lay aside the sword
Which sways usurpingly these several titles,
And put the same into young Arthur's hand,
Thy nephew and right royal sovereign.

KING JOHN
16   What follows if we disallow of this ?

CHATILLION
17   The proud control of fierce and bloody war,

To enforce these rights so forcibly withheld.

KING JOHN
Here have we war for war and blood for blood,
Controlment for controlment ; so answer France.   20

CHATILLION
Then take my king's defiance from my mouth,
The farthest limit of my embassy.

KING JOHN
Bear mine to him, and so depart in peace.
Be thou as lightning in the eyes of France,
For, ere thou canst report, I will be there.   25
The thunder of my cannon shall be heard.   26
So, hence ! Be thou the trumpet of our wrath   27
And sullen presage of your own decay.   28
An honorable conduct let him have ;   29
Pembroke, look to't. Farewell, Chatillion.
Exit Chatillion and Pembroke.

ELINOR
What now, my son ! Have I not ever said
How that ambitious Constance would not cease
Till she had kindled France and all the world
Upon the right and party of her son ?
This might have been prevented and made whole
With very easy arguments of love,   36
Which now the manage of two kingdoms must   37
With fearful bloody issue arbitrate.

KING JOHN
Our strong possession and our right for us.

ELINOR
Your strong possession much more than your right,
Or else it must go wrong with you and me –
So much my conscience whispers in your ear,
Which none but heaven, and you, and I, shall hear.
Enter a Sheriff [who speaks aside to Essex].

I, i The court of King John   3 *In my behavior* through my person   4
borrowed stolen   6 *embassy* message   7 *in right and true behalf* in support
of the lawful claim   16 *disallow of* refuse   17 *proud control* overbearing
compulsion   20 *Controlment* compulsion   25 *report* deliver your message
(with secondary meaning of thunder)   26 *cannon* (an anachronism, since
gunpowder had not yet been invented)   27 *trumpet* (as a herald)   28 *decay*
destruction   29 *conduct* escort   36 *arguments of love* (1) expressions of
affection, (2) friendly discussions   37 *manage* government

ESSEX
My liege, here is the strangest controversy,
Come from the country to be judged by you,
That e'er I heard. Shall I produce the men?

KING JOHN
Let them approach.
Our abbeys and our priories shall pay
49 This expeditious charge.
Enter Robert Faulconbridge, and Philip [his bastard brother].
                What men are you?

BASTARD
Your faithful subject, I, a gentleman,
Born in Northamptonshire, and eldest son,
As I suppose, to Robert Faulconbridge,
A soldier, by the honor-giving hand
54 Of Cordelion knighted in the field.

KING JOHN
What art thou?

ROBERT
The son and heir to that same Faulconbridge.

KING JOHN
Is that the elder, and art thou the heir?
You came not of one mother then, it seems.

BASTARD
Most certain of one mother, mighty king;
That is well known; and, as I think, one father.
But for the certain knowledge of that truth
62 I put you o'er to heaven and to my mother.
Of that I doubt, as all men's children may.

ELINOR
Out on thee, rude man! Thou dost shame thy mother
65 And wound her honor with this diffidence.

BASTARD
I, madam? No, I have no reason for it;
That is my brother's plea and none of mine;
68 The which if he can prove, 'a pops me out
At least from fair five hundred pound a year.
Heaven guard my mother's honor and my land!

KING JOHN
A good blunt fellow. Why, being younger born,
Doth he lay claim to thine inheritance?

BASTARD
I know not why, except to get the land.
74 But once he slandered me with bastardy.
75 But whe'r I be as true begot or no,
76 That still I lay upon my mother's head;
But that I am as well begot, my liege –
78 Fair fall the bones that took the pains for me –
Compare our faces and be judge yourself.
If old Sir Robert did beget us both,
And were our father, and this son like him,
O old Sir Robert, father, on my knee
I give heaven thanks I was not like to thee!

KING JOHN
Why, what a madcap hath heaven lent us here!

ELINOR
85 He hath a trick of Cordelion's face;
86 The accent of his tongue affecteth him.
Do you not read some tokens of my son
In the large composition of this man?

KING JOHN
Mine eye hath well examinèd his parts,
And finds them perfect Richard. Sirrah, speak.

What doth move you to claim your brother's land?

BASTARD
Because he hath a half-face like my father. 92
With half that face would he have all my land –
A half-faced groat five hundred pound a year! 94

ROBERT
My gracious liege, when that my father lived,
Your brother did employ my father much –

BASTARD
Well sir, by this you cannot get my land.
Your tale must be how he employed my mother.

ROBERT
And once dispatched him in an embassy 99
To Germany, there with the emperor
To treat of high affairs touching that time.
Th' advantage of his absence took the king,
And in the mean time sojourned at my father's;
Where how he did prevail I shame to speak, 104
But truth is truth; large lengths of seas and shores
Between my father and my mother lay,
As I have heard my father speak himself,
When this same lusty gentleman was got. 108
Upon his death-bed he by will bequeathed
His lands to me, and took it on his death 110
That this my mother's son was none of his;
And if he were, he came into the world
Full fourteen weeks before the course of time.
Then, good my liege, let me have what is mine,
My father's land, as was my father's will.

KING JOHN
Sirrah, your brother is legitimate.
Your father's wife did after wedlock bear him,
And if she did play false, the fault was hers,
Which fault lies on the hazards of all husbands 119
That marry wives. Tell me, how if my brother,
Who, as you say, took pains to get this son,
Had of your father claimed this son for his?
In sooth, good friend, your father might have kept
This calf, bred from his cow, from all the world.
In sooth he might; then, if he were my brother's,
My brother might not claim him, nor your father,
Being none of his, refuse him. This concludes; 127
My mother's son did get your father's heir;
Your father's heir must have your father's land.

ROBERT
Shall then my father's will be of no force
To dispossess that child which is not his?

BASTARD
Of no more force to dispossess me, sir,
Than was his will to get me, as I think.

ELINOR
Whether hadst thou rather be a Faulconbridge,
And like thy brother, to enjoy thy land, 135

---

49 *expeditious* speedy, sudden 54 *Cordelion* Coeur-de-lion, i.e. King Richard I 62 *put you o'er* refer you 65 *diffidence* distrust 68 *'a* he 74 *once* on a single occasion which he dare not repeat 75 *whe'r* whether 76 *lay . . . head* let my mother account for 78 *fall* befall 85 *trick* characteristic expression 86 *affecteth* resembles 92 *half-face* profile (with secondary meaning of imperfect) 94 *half-faced groat* a thin silver coin with a profile stamped upon it, also an imperfect or inferior coin 99 *dispatched* sent 104 *shame* am ashamed 108 *lusty* merry; *got* conceived 110 *took it on his death* swore on his deathbed (the most solemn kind of oath) 119 *lies on the hazards* is one of the risks 127 *refuse* disclaim; *concludes* settles the question decisively 135 *like thy brother* i.e. in physical appearance (being of the same father), and therefore not a bastard, and entitled to his land

Or the reputed son of Cordelion,
137 Lord of thy presence and no land beside?
BASTARD
Madam, and if my brother had my shape
And I had his, Sir Robert's his, like him,
140 And if my legs were two such riding-rods,
My arms such eel-skins stuffed, my face so thin
142 That in mine ear I durst not stick a rose
Lest men should say, 'Look where three-farthings
goes!'
And, to his shape, were heir to all this land,
Would I might never stir from off this place,
I would give it every foot to have this face;
I would not be Sir Nob in any case.
ELINOR
I like thee well. Wilt thou forsake thy fortune,
Bequeath thy land to him, and follow me?
I am a soldier and now bound to France.
BASTARD
Brother, take you my land, I'll take my chance.
Your face hath got five hundred pound a year,
Yet sell your face for five pence and 'tis dear.
Madam, I'll follow you unto the death.
ELINOR
Nay, I would have you go before me thither.
BASTARD
Our country manners give our betters way.
KING JOHN
What is thy name?
BASTARD
Philip, my liege, so is my name begun;
Philip, good old Sir Robert's wife's eldest son.
KING JOHN
160 From henceforth bear his name whose form thou
bearest.
Kneel thou down Philip, but rise more great;
Arise Sir Richard, and Plantagenet.
BASTARD
Brother by th' mother's side, give me your hand.
My father gave me honor, yours gave land.
165 Now blessèd be the hour, by night or day,
When I was got, Sir Robert was away!
ELINOR
The very spirit of Plantagenet!

137 *presence* person 140 *riding-rods* switches used by riders 142–43 *ear . . . goes* (certain coins were distinguished from others by a rose behind Queen Elizabeth's head; he is saying that his brother dare not place a rose behind his ear, as a lover might, lest he be taken for a three-farthing piece, his face being so thin) 160 *form* physical characteristics 165 *hour* (with a possible pun on 'whore,' since both words were pronounced identically) 169 *truth* honesty, chaste conduct 171 *In . . . hatch* (proverbial expressions referring to illegitimate birth) 177 *landless knight* i.e. the Bastard (who has just renounced his land in favor of his brother) 184 *Joan* (name used for any girl of lowly station) 185 *Good den* God give you good even; *God-a-mercy* God reward you 188 *respective* respectful, courteous 189 *conversion* change of status 190 *toothpick* (a sign of affectation, associated particularly with the foreign traveller); *mess* dinner table 193 *pickèd* (1) refined, rarefied, (2) whose teeth have been picked 196 *Absey-book* ABC book, primer for instruction of children (the Bastard is mimicking the kind of question-and-answer exercise found in such books) 201 *dialogue of compliment* formal, elegant address 207 *but a bastard to the time* no true son of the age 208 *observation* obsequiousness 210 *habit* dress 212 *motion* impulse 213 *Sweet . . . poison* flattery 215 *deceit* being deceived 216 *it . . . rising* i.e. flattery will accompany his rise to greatness as rushes are strewn upon a great man's floor 218 *woman-post* female courier 219 *blow a horn* i.e. announce his cuckoldry and her infidelity 223 *holds in chase* pursues to destroy

I am thy grandam, Richard; call me so.
BASTARD
Madam, by chance but not by truth; what though? 169
Something about, a little from the right,
In at the window, or else o'er the hatch: 171
Who dares not stir by day must walk by night,
And have is have, however men do catch.
Near or far off, well won is still well shot,
And I am I, howe'er I was begot.
KING JOHN
Go, Faulconbridge. Now hast thou thy desire;
A landless knight makes thee a landed squire. 177
Come, madam, and come, Richard, we must speed
For France, for France, for it is more than need.
BASTARD
Brother, adieu; good fortune come to thee!
For thou wast got i' th' way of honesty.
Exeunt all but Bastard.
A foot of honor better than I was,
But many a many foot of land the worse.
Well, now can I make any Joan a lady. 184
'Good den, Sir Richard!' – 'God-a-mercy, fellow' – 185
And if his name be George, I'll call him Peter,
For new-made honor doth forget men's names;
'Tis too respective and too sociable 188
For your conversion. Now your traveller, 189
He and his toothpick at my worship's mess, 190
And when my knightly stomach is sufficed,
Why then I suck my teeth and catechize
My pickèd man of countries: 'My dear sir' – 193
Thus, leaning on mine elbow, I begin –
'I shall beseech you' – that is question now;
And then comes answer like an Absey-book; 196
'O, sir,' says answer, 'at your best command,
At your employment, at your service, sir';
'No, sir,' says question, 'I, sweet sir, at yours';
And so, ere answer knows what question would,
Saving in dialogue of compliment, 201
And talking of the Alps and Apennines,
The Pyrenean and the river Po,
It draws toward supper in conclusion so.
But this is worshipful society,
And fits the mounting spirit like myself,
For he is but a bastard to the time 207
That doth not smack of observation. 208
And so am I, whether I smack or no,
And not alone in habit and device, 210
Exterior form, outward accoutrement,
But from the inward motion to deliver 212
Sweet, sweet, sweet poison for the age's tooth, 213
Which, though I will not practise to deceive,
Yet, to avoid deceit, I mean to learn; 215
For it shall strew the footsteps of my rising. 216
But who comes in such haste in riding-robes?
What woman-post is this? Hath she no husband 218
That will take pains to blow a horn before her? 219
Enter Lady Faulconbridge and James Gurney.
O me! 'Tis my mother. How now, good lady!
What brings you here to court so hastily?
LADY FAULCONBRIDGE
Where is that slave, thy brother? Where is he,
That holds in chase mine honor up and down? 223
BASTARD
My brother Robert? Old Sir Robert's son?

225 Colbrand the giant, that same mighty man?
Is it Sir Robert's son that you seek so?

LADY FAULCONBRIDGE
Sir Robert's son! Ay, thou unreverend boy,
Sir Robert's son! Why scorn'st thou at Sir Robert?
He is Sir Robert's son, and so art thou.

BASTARD
James Gurney, wilt thou give us leave awhile?

GURNEY
Good leave, good Philip.

231 BASTARD   Philip sparrow! James,
232 There's toys abroad; anon I'll tell thee more. *Exit James.*
Madam, I was not old Sir Robert's son.
Sir Robert might have eat his part in me
Upon Good Friday and ne'er broke his fast.
236 Sir Robert could do well – marry, to confess –
Could he get me! Sir Robert could not do it.
We know his handiwork. Therefore, good mother,
239 To whom am I beholding for these limbs?
240 Sir Robert never holp to make this leg.

LADY FAULCONBRIDGE
Hast thou conspirèd with thy brother too,
That for thine own gain shouldst defend mine honor?
243 What means this scorn, thou most untoward knave?

BASTARD
244 Knight, knight, good mother, Basilisco-like.
245 What! I am dubbed; I have it on my shoulder.
But, mother, I am not Sir Robert's son;
I have disclaimed Sir Robert and my land;
Legitimation, name, and all is gone.
Then, good my mother, let me know my father;
250 Some proper man I hope; who was it, mother?

LADY FAULCONBRIDGE
Hast thou denied thyself a Faulconbridge?

BASTARD
As faithfully as I deny the devil.

LADY FAULCONBRIDGE
King Richard Cordelion was thy father.
By long and vehement suit I was seduced
To make room for him in my husband's bed.
Heaven lay not my transgression to my charge!
Thou art the issue of my dear offense,
258 Which was so strongly urged past my defense.

BASTARD
259 Now, by this light, were I to get again,
Madam, I would not wish a better father.
261 Some sins do bear their privilege on earth,
And so doth yours; your fault was not your folly.
263 Needs must you lay your heart at his dispose,
Subjected tribute to commanding love,
Against whose fury and unmatchèd force
266 The aweless lion could not wage the fight,
Nor keep his princely heart from Richard's hand.
He that perforce robs lions of their hearts
May easily win a woman's. Ay, my mother,
With all my heart I thank thee for my father!
Who lives and dares but say thou didst not well
When I was got, I'll send his soul to hell.
Come, lady, I will show thee to my kin,
And they shall say, when Richard me begot,
If thou hadst said him nay, it had been sin.
Who says it was, he lies; I say 'twas not.   *Exeunt.*

*

Enter before Angiers, Philip, King of France, Lewis,   II, i
[the] Dauphin, Austria, Constance, Arthur
[and Attendants].

KING PHILIP
Before Angiers well met, brave Austria.
Arthur, that great forerunner of thy blood,   2
Richard, that robbed the lion of his heart
And fought the holy wars in Palestine,
By this brave duke came early to his grave;   5
And for amends to his posterity,
At our importance hither is he come   7
To spread his colors, boy, in thy behalf,
And to rebuke the usurpation
Of thy unnatural uncle, English John.
Embrace him, love him, give him welcome hither.

ARTHUR
God shall forgive you Cordelion's death
The rather that you give his offspring life,
Shadowing their right under your wings of war.   14
I give you welcome with a powerless hand,
But with a heart full of unstainèd love.
Welcome before the gates of Angiers, duke.

LEWIS
A noble boy! Who would not do thee right?

AUSTRIA
Upon thy cheek lay I this zealous kiss,
As seal to this indenture of my love,   20
That to my home I will no more return
Till Angiers and the right thou hast in France,
Together with that pale, that white-faced shore,
Whose foot spurns back the ocean's roaring tides
And coops from other lands her islanders,   25
Even till that England, hedged in with the main,
That water-wallèd bulwark, still secure   27
And confident from foreign purposes,
Even till that utmost corner of the west
Salute thee for her king. Till then, fair boy,
Will I not think of home, but follow arms.

CONSTANCE
O, take his mother's thanks, a widow's thanks,
Till your strong hand shall help to give him strength
To make a more requital to your love.   34

AUSTRIA
The peace of heaven is theirs that lift their swords
In such a just and charitable war.

225 *Colbrand* a Danish giant killed by Guy of Warwick in the old romance
231 *Philip sparrow* (since he has just been knighted, he objects to being
called merely Philip, the common name for a sparrow) 232 *toys* rumors
236–37 *Sir Robert . . . get me* (he is incredulous at the suggestion that one
like Sir Robert might be his father) 239 *beholding* indebted 240 *holp*
helped 243 *untoward* ill-mannered 244 *Basilisco-like* (the Bastard mocks
himself by comparing himself to Basilisco, the cowardly, braggart knight
in *Soliman and Perseda*, an old play probably by Thomas Kyd) 245
dubbed made a knight 250 *proper* handsome 258 *urged . . . defense* forced
in spite of my protests 259 *get* be conceived 261 *do bear . . . earth* are
allowed on earth but not in heaven 263 *dispose* disposal 266 *aweless
lion* (King Richard, according to legend, had slain a lion by thrusting his
hand down its throat and tearing out its heart, which he then ate; hence his
nickname)
II, i Before the gates of Angiers 2 *forerunner of thy blood* ancestor (Arthur
was actually the nephew of Richard, son of his brother Geoffrey) 5 *brave
duke* Austria (although Richard actually was killed before the castle of
the Viscount Limoges; Shakespeare, following his source, combines the
two characters) 7 *importance* request 14 *Shadowing* sheltering 20 *indenture* sealed contract 25 *coops* encloses for protection 27 *still* forever
34 *more* greater

KING PHILIP

37 Well then, to work; our cannon shall be bent
Against the brows of this resisting town.
39 Call for our chiefest men of discipline,
40 To cull the plots of best advantages.
We'll lay before this town our royal bones,
Wade to the market-place in Frenchmen's blood,
But we will make it subject to this boy.

CONSTANCE

Stay for an answer to your embassy,
45 Lest unadvised you stain your swords with blood.
My Lord Chatillion may from England bring
That right in peace which here we urge in war,
And then we shall repent each drop of blood
49 That hot rash haste so indirectly shed.
Enter Chatillion.

KING PHILIP

A wonder, lady! Lo, upon thy wish,
Our messenger, Chatillion, is arrived!
What England says, say briefly, gentle lord;
53 We coldly pause for thee; Chatillion, speak.

CHATILLION

Then turn your forces from this paltry siege
And stir them up against a mightier task.
England, impatient of your just demands,
Hath put himself in arms. The adverse winds,
58 Whose leisure I have stayed, have given him time
To land his legions all as soon as I.
60 His marches are expedient to this town,
His forces strong, his soldiers confident.
With him along is come the mother-queen,
63 An Ate; stirring him to blood and strife;
With her her niece, the Lady Blanch of Spain;
With them a bastard of the king's deceased;
66 And all th' unsettled humors of the land,
67 Rash, inconsiderate, fiery voluntaries,
68 With ladies' faces and fierce dragons' spleens,
Have sold their fortunes at their native homes,
70 Bearing their birthrights proudly on their backs,
To make a hazard of new fortunes here.
In brief, a braver choice of dauntless spirits
73 Than now the English bottoms have waft o'er
Did never float upon the swelling tide,
75 To do offense and scathe in Christendom.

The interruption of their churlish drums   76
Cuts off more circumstance; they are at hand.   77
Drum beats.
To parley or to fight, therefore prepare.

KING PHILIP

How much unlooked for is this expedition!   79

AUSTRIA

By how much unexpected, by so much
We must awake endeavor for defense,
For courage mounteth with occasion.   82
Let them be welcome then; we are prepared.
*Enter King [John] of England, Bastard,
Queen [Elinor], Blanch, Pembroke, and others.*

KING JOHN

Peace be to France, if France in peace permit
Our just and lineal entrance to our own.   85
If not, bleed France, and peace ascend to heaven,
Whiles we, God's wrathful agent, do correct   87
Their proud contempt that beats His peace to heaven.

KING PHILIP

Peace be to England, if that war return
From France to England, there to live in peace.
England we love, and for that England's sake   91
With burden of our armor here we sweat.
This toil of ours should be a work of thine,   93
But thou from loving England art so far
That thou hast under-wrought his lawful king,   95
Cut off the sequence of posterity,   96
Outfacèd infant state, and done a rape   97
Upon the maiden virtue of the crown.
Look here upon thy brother Geoffrey's face.
These eyes, these brows, were molded out of his;
This little abstract doth contain that large   101
Which died in Geoffrey, and the hand of time
Shall draw this brief into as huge a volume.
That Geoffrey was thy elder brother born,
And this his son. England was Geoffrey's right
And this is Geoffrey's in the name of God.   106
How comes it then that thou art called a king,
When living blood doth in these temples beat,
Which owe the crown that thou o'ermasterest?   109

KING JOHN

From whom hast thou this great commission, France,
To draw my answer from thy articles?   111

KING PHILIP

From that supernal judge that stirs good thoughts   112
In any breast of strong authority,
To look into the blots and stains of right.
That judge hath made me guardian to this boy,
Under whose warrant I impeach thy wrong   116
And by whose help I mean to chastise it.

KING JOHN

Alack, thou dost usurp authority.

KING PHILIP

Excuse it is to beat usurping down.

ELINOR

Who is it thou dost call usurper, France?

CONSTANCE

Let me make answer: thy usurping son.

ELINOR

Out, insolent! Thy bastard shall be king
That thou mayst be a queen and check the world!   123

CONSTANCE

My bed was ever to thy son as true

---

37 *bent* directed   39 *discipline* military training or experience   40 *cull . . . advantages* select the most suitable locations for placing cannons 45 *unadvised* unwisely, without adequate consideration   49 *indirectly* unjustly   53 *coldly* calmly   58 *stayed* waited for   60 *expedient* to hastening towards   63 *Ate* the Greek goddess of mischief and vengeance   66 *unsettled humors* restless disgruntled men   67 *voluntaries* volunteers   68 *dragons' spleens* hot tempers (since the spleen was regarded as the seat of the passions)   70 *Bearing . . . backs* having sold their estates to purchase armor   73 *bottoms* ships   75 *scathe* harm   76 *churlish* lowly, inferior   77 *circumstance* details   79 *expedition* haste   82 *occasion* emergency 85 *lineal* due by right of descent   87 *correct* punish   91 *England's* i.e. Arthur's (since Philip takes him to be the lawful king of England)   93 *This toil . . . thine* i.e. John should be fighting for Arthur's cause rather than against him   95 *under-wrought* undermined   96 *sequence of posterity* hereditary succession to the throne   97 *Outfacèd infant state* intimidated a child king   101–03 *little abstract . . . volume* i.e. Arthur as a child is like a shortened edition of his father, Geoffrey, but in time he will grow to be as complete a volume (of virtues) as his father was   106 *this* (a famous crux; may refer to Arthur, John's crown, or the city of Angiers, depending upon what the actor indicates by his arm)   109 *owe* own; *o'ermasterest* usurpest   111 *draw . . . articles* demand that I answer your charges   112 *supernal* heavenly   116 *impeach* accuse   123 *queen* (with play on 'quean,' whore); *check* control (with possible allusion to game of chess)

As thine was to thy husband, and this boy
Liker in feature to his father Geoffrey
Than thou and John in manners, being as like
128 As rain to water, or devil to his dam.
My boy a bastard! By my soul I think
His father never was so true begot.
It cannot be and if thou wert his mother.

ELINOR
132 There's a good mother, boy, that blots thy father.

CONSTANCE
133 There's a good grandam, boy, that would blot thee.

AUSTRIA
Peace!

134 BASTARD Hear the crier.

AUSTRIA   What the devil art thou?

BASTARD
One that will play the devil, sir, with you,
136 An 'a may catch your hide and you alone.
137 You are the hare of whom the proverb goes,
Whose valor plucks dead lions by the beard.
139 I'll smoke your skin-coat, an I catch you right.
Sirrah, look to't; i' faith, I will, i' faith.

BLANCH
O well did he become that lion's robe,
That did disrobe the lion of that robe!

BASTARD
143 It lies as sightly on the back of him
144 As great Alcides' shows upon an ass.
But, ass, I'll take that burden from your back,
Or lay on that shall make your shoulders crack.

AUSTRIA
147 What cracker is this same that deafs our ears
With this abundance of superfluous breath?
149 King Philip, determine what we shall do straight.

KING PHILIP
150 Women and fools, break off your conference.
King John, this is the very sum of all:
152 England and Ireland, Angiers, Touraine, Maine,
In right of Arthur do I claim of thee.
Wilt thou resign them and lay down thy arms?

KING JOHN
My life as soon! I do defy thee, France.
Arthur of Britain, yield thee to my hand,
And out of my dear love I'll give thee more
Than e'er the coward hand of France can win.
Submit thee, boy.

ELINOR   Come to thy grandam, child.

CONSTANCE
160 Do, child, go to it grandam, child;
Give grandam kingdom, and it grandam will
Give it a plum, a cherry, and a fig.
There's a good grandam.

ARTHUR   Good my mother, peace!
I would that I were low laid in my grave.
165 I am not worth this coil that's made for me.

ELINOR
His mother shames him so, poor boy, he weeps.

CONSTANCE
167 Now shame upon you, whe'r she does or no!
His grandam's wrongs, and not his mother's shames,
169 Draws those heaven-moving pearls from his poor eyes,
Which heaven shall take in nature of a fee.
Ay, with these crystal beads heaven shall be bribed
To do him justice and revenge on you.

ELINOR
Thou monstrous slanderer of heaven and earth!

CONSTANCE
Thou monstrous injurer of heaven and earth!
Call not me slanderer; thou and thine usurp
The dominations, royalties, and rights   176
Of this oppressèd boy. This is thy eldest son's son,   177
Infortunate in nothing but in thee.   178
Thy sins are visited in this poor child;   179
The canon of the law is laid on him,   180
Being but the second generation
Removèd from thy sin-conceiving womb.

KING JOHN
Bedlam, have done.   183

CONSTANCE   I have but this to say,
That he is not only plaguèd for her sin,   184
But God hath made her sin and her the plague
On this removèd issue, plagued for her   186
And with her plague; her sin his injury,
Her injury the beadle to her sin,   188
All punished in the person of this child,
And all for her; a plague upon her.

ELINOR
Thou unadvisèd scold, I can produce   191
A will that bars the title of thy son.   192

CONSTANCE
Ay, who doubts that? A will! A wicked will;
A woman's will; a cankered grandam's will!   194

KING PHILIP
Peace, lady! Pause, or be more temperate.
It ill beseems this presence to cry aim   196
To these ill-tunèd repetitions.
Some trumpet summon hither to the walls   198
These men of Angiers. Let us hear them speak
Whose title they admit, Arthur's or John's.
Trumpet sounds. Enter a Citizen upon the walls.

CITIZEN
Who is it that hath warned us to the walls?   201

KING PHILIP
'Tis France, for England.

KING JOHN   England for itself.
You men of Angiers, and my loving subjects –

128 *dam* mother   132 *blots* slanders   133 *grandam* grandmother   134 *Hear the crier* (the Bastard mocks Austria by likening him to the town crier who called for silence in the courts)   136 *An 'a* if he   137 *the proverb* i.e. 'hares may pull dead lions by the beard' (it occurs in the *Adagia* of Erasmus)   139 *smoke your skin-coat* thrash you (alluding also to King Richard's lion skin, which Austria is wearing)   143 *sightly* appropriately   144 *Alcides* Hercules, who wore the skin of the Nemean lion he had slain   147 *cracker* boaster   149 *straight* immediately   150 *fools* children   152 *Angiers* (here confused with Anjou)   160–63 *Do . . . grandam* (Constance uses baby talk to ridicule Elinor's invitation)   165 *coil* fuss   167 *whe'r* whether   169 *Draws* draw; *pearls* tears · 176 *dominations* sovereignties   177 *eldest son's son* oldest grandson, a biblical form (not son of your oldest son, which Arthur was not)   178 *Infortunate* unfortunate   179 *visited* punished   180 *canon of the law* i.e. that the sins of parents be visited upon their children to the third and fourth generation   183 *Bedlam* lunatic   184–90 *That . . . upon her* (a perhaps intentionally obscure passage, the sense being that Arthur is being punished for the sin of Elinor – her giving birth to John, whom Constance is calling a bastard – by the very presence of Elinor and John, that they are laying the scourge upon him which should be laid upon Elinor)   186 *removed issue* distant descendant   188 *beadle* a parish official who meted out corporal punishment, to prostitutes in particular   191 *unadvised* rash   192 *A will* (the last testament of King Richard I, which named his brother John heir to the throne)   194 *cankered* malignant   196 *cry aim* give encouragement   198 *trumpet* trumpeter   201 *warned* summoned

KING PHILIP

You loving men of Angiers, Arthur's subjects,
205 Our trumpet called you to this gentle parle –

KING JOHN

For our advantage; therefore hear us first.
207 These flags of France, that are advancèd here
208 Before the eye and prospect of your town,
209 Have hither marched to your endamagement.
The cannons have their bowels full of wrath,
And ready mounted are they to spit forth
Their iron indignation 'gainst your walls.
All preparation for a bloody seige
And merciless proceeding by these French
215 Confront your city's eyes, your winking gates,
And but for our approach those sleeping stones,
217 That as a waist doth girdle you about,
218 By the compulsion of their ordinance
By this time from their fixèd beds of lime
220 Had been dishabited, and wide havoc made
For bloody power to rush upon your peace.
But on the sight of us your lawful king,
223 Who painfully with much expedient march
Have brought a countercheck before your gates,
To save unscratched your city's threat'ned cheeks,
Behold, the French amazed vouchsafe a parle;
And now, instead of bullets wrapped in fire,
To make a shaking fever in your walls,
They shoot but calm words folded up in smoke,
230 To make a faithless error in your ears.
Which trust accordingly, kind citizens,
232 And let us in, your king, whose labored spirits,
233 Forwearied in this action of swift speed,
234 Craves harborage within your city walls.

KING PHILIP

When I have said, make answer to us both.
236 Lo! In this right hand, whose protection
Is most divinely vowed upon the right
238 Of him it holds, stands young Plantagenet,
Son to the elder brother of this man,
240 And king o'er him and all that he enjoys.
For this downtrodden equity we tread
242 In warlike march these greens before your town,
Being no further enemy to you
Than the constraint of hospitable zeal,
In the relief of this oppressèd child,
Religiously provokes. Be pleasèd then
To pay that duty which you truly owe
248 To him that owes it, namely this young prince;
And then our arms, like to a muzzled bear,
250 Save in aspect, hath all offense sealed up.

Our cannons' malice vainly shall be spent
Against th' invulnerable clouds of heaven,
And with a blessèd and unvexed retire, 253
With unhacked swords and helmets all unbruised,
We will bear home that lusty blood again
Which here we came to spout against your town,
And leave your children, wives, and you, in peace.
But if you fondly pass our proffered offer, 258
'Tis not the roundure of your old-faced walls 259
Can hide you from our messengers of war. 260
Though all these English and their discipline 261
Were harbored in their rude circumference.
Then tell us, shall your city call us lord,
In that behalf which we have challenged it? 264
Or shall we give the signal to our rage
And stalk in blood to our possession?

CITIZEN

In brief, we are the King of England's subjects.
For him, and in his right, we hold this town.

KING JOHN

Acknowledge then the king, and let me in.

CITIZEN

That can we not; but he that proves the king, 270
To him will we prove loyal. Till that time
Have we rammed up our gates against the world.

KING JOHN

Doth not the crown of England prove the king?
And if not that, I bring you witnesses,
Twice fifteen thousand hearts of England's breed –

BASTARD

Bastards, and else. 276

KING JOHN

To verify our title with their lives.

KING PHILIP

As many and as well-born bloods as those – 278

BASTARD

Some bastards, too.

KING PHILIP

Stand in his face to contradict his claim. 280

CITIZEN

Till you compound whose right is worthiest, 281
We for the worthiest hold the right from both.

KING JOHN

Then God forgive the sins of all those souls
That to their everlasting residence,
Before the dew of evening fall, shall fleet, 285
In dreadful trial of our kingdom's king!

KING PHILIP

Amen, amen! Mount, chevaliers! To arms!

BASTARD

Saint George, that swinged the dragon, and e'er since 288
Sits on's horseback at mine hostess' door,
Teach us some fence! [to Austria] Sirrah, were I at home 290
At your den, sirrah, with your lioness, 291
I would set an ox head to your lion's hide, 292
And make a monster of you.

AUSTRIA   Peace! No more.

BASTARD

O tremble, for you hear the lion roar.

KING JOHN

Up higher to the plain, where we'll set forth
In best appointment all our regiments.

BASTARD

Speed then, to take advantage of the field.

205 *parle* conference 207 *advancèd* raised 208 *prospect* view 209 *endamagement* injury 215 *winking* closed as in sleep 217 *waist* belt; *doth* do 218 *ordinance* artillery 220 *dishabited* dislodged 223 *painfully* laboriously; *expedient* speedy 230 *faithless* perfidious, disloyal; *error* falsehood 232 *labored* oppressed by labor 233 *Forwearied* tired out; *action* campaign 234 *harborage* shelter, acceptance 236 *In this right hand* led by my right hand 238 *holds* supports 240 *enjoys* possesses 242 *greens* grassy ground outside the city gates 248 *owes* owns 250 *Save in aspect* except for appearance 253 *retire* withdrawal 258 *fondly pass* foolishly ignore 259 *roundure* circumference 260 *messengers of war* cannon balls 261 *discipline* military skill 264 *which* in which 270 *proves* is proved 276 *and else* and otherwise 278 *bloods* men of mettle, and of good family 280 *in his face* opposing him 281 *compound* agree 285 *fleet* pass away 288 *swinged* thrashed 290 *fence* swordsmanship, defense 291 *lioness* (a slang expression for whore) 292–93 *set . . . you* cause you to grow the horns of a cuckold (a common joke of the time)

KING PHILIP
It shall be so ; and at the other hill
Command the rest to stand. God, and our right ! *Exeunt.*
Here after excursions, enter the Herald of France
with Trumpets, to the gates.

FRENCH HERALD
You men of Angiers, open wide your gates,
And let young Arthur, Duke of Britain, in,
Who by the hand of France this day hath made
Much work for tears in many an English mother,
Whose sons lie scattered on the bleeding ground.
305 Many a widow's husband grovelling lies,
Coldly embracing the discolored earth,
And victory with little loss doth play
Upon the dancing banners of the French,
309 Who are at hand, triumphantly displayed,
To enter conquerors and to proclaim
Arthur of Britain England's king and yours.
Enter English Herald, with Trumpet.

ENGLISH HERALD
Rejoice, you men of Angiers, ring your bells.
King John, your king and England's, doth approach,
314 Commander of this hot malicious day.
Their armors, that marched hence so silver-bright,
316 Hither return all gilt with Frenchmen's blood.
There stuck no plume in any English crest
318 That is removèd by a staff of France.
Our colors do return in those same hands
That did display them when we first marched forth,
And like a jolly troop of huntsmen come
322 Our lusty English, all with purpled hands
323 Dyed in the dying slaughter of their foes.
Open your gates and give the victors way.

CITIZEN
325 Heralds, from off our towers we might behold,
326 From first to last, the onset and retire
Of both your armies, whose equality
328 By our best eyes cannot be censurèd.
Blood hath bought blood, and blows have answered
    blows,
Strength matched with strength, and power confronted
    power.
Both are alike, and both alike we like..
One must prove greatest. While they weigh so even,
We hold our town for neither, yet for both.
Enter the two Kings, with their powers, at several
doors.

KING JOHN
France, hast thou yet more blood to cast away ?
Say, shall the current of our right run on ?
Whose passage, vexed with thy impediment,
Shall leave his native channel and o'erswell
With course disturbed even thy confining shores,
Unless thou let his silver water keep
A peaceful progress to the ocean.

KING PHILIP
England, thou hast not saved one drop of blood
In this hot trial more than we of France ;
Rather, lost more. And by this hand I swear,
344 That sways the earth this climate overlooks,
Before we will lay down our just-borne arms,
We'll put thee down, 'gainst whom these arms we bear,
347 Or add a royal number to the dead,
Gracing the scroll that tells of this war's loss

With slaughter couplèd to the name of kings.

BASTARD
Ha, majesty ! How high thy glory towers
When the rich blood of kings is set on fire !
352 O now doth death line his dead chaps with steel !
The swords of soldiers are his teeth, his fangs ;
354 And now he feasts, mousing the flesh of men
355 In undetermined differences of kings.
356 Why stand these royal fronts amazèd thus ?
357 Cry 'havoc !', kings ; back to the stainèd field,
358 You equal potents, fiery kindled spirits !
359 Then let confusion of one part confirm
The other's peace ; till then, blows, blood, and death !

KING JOHN
Whose party do the townsmen yet admit ?   361

KING PHILIP
Speak, citizens, for England ; who's your king ?

CITIZEN
The King of England, when we know the king.

KING PHILIP
Know him in us, that here hold up his right.

KING JOHN
In us, that are our own great deputy,
And bear possession of our person here,
Lord of our presence, Angiers, and of you.

CITIZEN
A greater power than we denies all this,
And till it be undoubted, we do lock
Our former scruple in our strong-barred gates,
Kinged of our fear, until our fears, resolved,   371
Be by some certain king purged and deposed.

BASTARD
By heaven, these scroyles of Angiers flout you, kings,   373
And stand securely on their battlements
As in a theatre, whence they gape and point
At your industrious scenes and acts of death.
Your royal presences be ruled by me.
Do like the mutines of Jerusalem,   378
Be friends awhile and both conjointly bend   379
Your sharpest deeds of malice on this town.
By east and west let France and England mount
Their battering cannon chargèd to the mouths,
Till their soul-fearing clamors have brawled down   383
The flinty ribs of this contemptuous city.
I'd play incessantly upon these jades,   385
Even till unfencèd desolation   386
Leave them as naked as the vulgar air.   387
That done, dissever your united strengths,

---

305 *grovelling* prone, on his belly   309 *displayed* deployed, spread out
314 *hot malicious* hotly and violently fought   316 *gilt* made red   318
staff shaft of a spear   322 *purpled* bloody   323 *Dyed . . . foes* (it was a
custom for hunters to dip their hands in the blood of the slain deer)   325
Citizen (in the folio this speech is given to Hubert, identifying him with
the citizen of Angiers)   326 *retire* retreat   328 *censured* estimated   344
climate portion of the sky   347 *royal number* a royal item (on the scroll
bearing the official list of the dead)   352 *chaps* jaws   354 *mousing* tearing
355 *undetermined differences* unsettled quarrels   356 *fronts* faces (literally,
foreheads)   357 *havoc* (this cry was a traditional signal for indiscriminate
slaughter with no taking of prisoners)   358 *potents* powers   359 *confusion*
defeat; *part* party   361 *yet* now   371 *Kinged of* ruled by   373 *scroyles*
scoundrels   378 *mutines of Jerusalem* (when Jerusalem was besieged by
the Emperor Titus, warring factions within the city united in common
struggle against the Romans)   379 *bend* direct   383 *brawled down* beaten
down with noise   385 *play . . . jades* fire repeatedly upon these wretches
386 *unfenced* defenseless   387 *naked* unarmed ; *vulgar* common to all

And part your mingled colors once again;
Turn face to face and bloody point to point.
391 Then in a moment fortune shall cull forth
392 Out of one side her happy minion,
To whom in favor she shall give the day,
And kiss him with a glorious victory.
395 How like you this wild counsel, mighty states?
396 Smacks it not something of the policy?

KING JOHN
Now, by the sky that hangs above our heads,
I like it well. France, shall we knit our powers
And lay this Angiers even with the ground,
Then after fight who shall be king of it?

BASTARD
And if thou hast the mettle of a king,
402 Being wronged as we are by this peevish town,
Turn thou the mouth of thy artillery,
As we will ours, against these saucy walls;
And when that we have dashed them to the ground,
406 Why then defy each other, and pell-mell
Make work upon ourselves, for heaven or hell.

KING PHILIP
Let it be so. Say, where will you assault?

KING JOHN
We from the west will send destruction
Into this city's bosom.

AUSTRIA
I from the north.
411 KING PHILIP   Our thunder from the south
412 Shall rain their drift of bullets on this town.

BASTARD [aside]
413 O prudent discipline! From north to south
Austria and France shoot in each other's mouth.
I'll stir them to it. Come, away, away!

CITIZEN
Hear us, great kings; vouchsafe a while to stay,
And I shall show you peace and fair-faced league,
Win you this city without stroke or wound,
Rescue those breathing lives to die in beds,
That here come sacrifices for the field.
Persever not, but hear me, mighty kings.

KING JOHN
422 Speak on with favor; we are bent to hear.

CITIZEN
That daughter there of Spain, the Lady Blanch,

Is near to England. Look upon the years 424
Of Lewis the Dauphin and that lovely maid.
If lusty love should go in quest of beauty,
Where should he find it fairer than in Blanch?
If zealous love should go in search of virtue, 428
Where should he find it purer than in Blanch?
If love ambitious sought a match of birth,
Whose veins bound richer blood than Lady Blanch? 431
Such as she is, in beauty, virtue, birth,
Is the young Dauphin every way complete. 433
If not complete of, say he is not she, 434
And she again wants nothing, to name want,
If want it be not that she is not he.
He is the half part of a blessèd man,
Left to be finishèd by such as she,
And she a fair divided excellence,
Whose fulness of perfection lies in him.
O, two such silver currents when they join 441
Do glorify the banks that bound them in;
And two such shores to two such streams made one,
Two such controlling bounds shall you be, kings,
To these two princes, if you marry them.
This union shall do more than battery can
To our fast-closèd gates; for at this match, 447
With swifter spleen than powder can enforce, 448
The mouth of passage shall we fling wide ope,
And give you entrance; but without this match,
The sea enragèd is not half so deaf,
Lions more confident, mountains and rocks
More free from motion, no, not death himself
In mortal fury half so peremptory, 454
As we to keep this city.

BASTARD   Here's a stay, 455
That shakes the rotten carcass of old death
Out of his rags! Here's a large mouth, indeed, 457
That spits forth death and mountains, rocks and seas,
Talks as familiarly of roaring lions
As maids of thirteen do of puppy-dogs.
What cannoneer begot this lusty blood?
He speaks plain cannon fire and smoke and bounce. 462
He gives the bastinado with his tongue. 463
Our ears are cudgelled; not a word of his
But buffets better than a fist of France.
Zounds! I was never so bethumped with words 466
Since I first called my brother's father dad.

ELINOR
Son, list to this conjunction, make this match. 468
Give with our niece a dowry large enough,
For by this knot thou shalt so surely tie
Thy now unsured assurance to the crown 471
That yon green boy shall have no sun to ripe
The bloom that promiseth a mighty fruit.
I see a yielding in the looks of France.
Mark how they whisper. Urge them while their souls
Are capable of this ambition, 476
Lest zeal, now melted by the windy breath 477
Of soft petitions, pity, and remorse, 478
Cool and congeal again to what it was.

CITIZEN
Why answer not the double majesties
This friendly treaty of our threat'ned town? 481

KING PHILIP
Speak England first, that hath been forward first
To speak unto this city. What say you?

391 *fortune* chance (commonly personified in medieval and Renaissance literature as a fickle goddess)   392 *minion* sweetheart, favorite   395 *states* kings   396 *policy* art of politics in pejorative sense, involving trickery and deceit (the Bastard is rather naively boasting of his ability as a politician)   402 *peevish* obstinate   406 *pell-mell* in confusion   411 *thunder* cannon   412 *drift* rain   413 *discipline* military skill   422 *favor* permission; *bent* inclined   424 *near to England* a close relative of King John   428 *zealous love* holy love, as opposed to lust   431 *bound* contain   433 *complete* perfect   434–36 *If . . . not he* (a type of word play in which Elizabethans delighted, the sense being that each requires the other to make his own perfection even more perfect)   441 *silver currents* (marriage was often celebrated in Elizabethan love poetry as a joining of two streams of water)   447 *match* (1) marriage, (2) the match which fires the cannon   448 *spleen* violent energy   454 *peremptory* determined   455 *stay* obstacle   457 *rags* (death was often portrayed in medieval art as a skeleton clad in rags)   462 *bounce* bang   463 *bastinado* a beating with a stick   466 *Zounds* by God's wounds   468 *list* pay close heed   471 *unsured* insecure   476 *capable of* susceptible to; *ambition* desire to come to terms   477–79 *Lest . . . what it was* lest the French king's desire to help Arthur, now melted by the pleas of the citizen of Angiers, become as firm as it was before   478 *remorse* compassion   481 *treaty* proposal

KING JOHN
If that the Dauphin there, thy princely son,
Can in this book of beauty read 'I love,'
Her dowry shall weigh equal with a queen ;
487 For Angiers and fair Touraine, Maine, Poitiers,
And all that we upon this side the sea,
490 Except this city now by us besieged.
Find liable to our crown and dignity,
Shall gild her bridal bed and make her rich
In titles, honors, and promotions,
As she in beauty, education, blood,
494 Holds hand with any princess of the world.

KING PHILIP
What sayst thou, boy ? Look in the lady's face.

LEWIS
I do, my lord, and in her eye I find
A wonder or a wondrous miracle,
498 The shadow of myself formed in her eye,
Which, being but the shadow of your son,
Becomes a sun, and makes your son a shadow.
I do protest I never loved myself
Till now infixèd I beheld myself,
503 Drawn in the flattering table of her eye.
Whispers with Blanch.

BASTARD
504 Drawn in the flattering table of her eye !
Hanged in the frowning wrinkle of her brow !
506 And quartered in her heart ! He doth espy
Himself love's traitor ; this is pity now,
That hanged and drawn and quartered, there should be
In such a love so vile a lout as he.

BLANCH
My uncle's will in this respect is mine.
If he see aught in you that makes him like,
That anything he sees which moves his liking,
513 I can with ease translate it to my will ;
Or if you will, to speak more properly,
I will enforce it easily to my love.
Further I will not flatter you, my lord,
That all I see in you is worthy love,
Than this : that nothing do I see in you,
519 Though churlish thoughts themselves should be your judge,
That I can find should merit any hate.

KING JOHN
What say these young ones ? What say you, my niece ?

BLANCH
522 That she is bound in honor still to do
523 What you in wisdom still vouchsafe to say.

KING JOHN
Speak then, Prince Dauphin. Can you love this lady ?

LEWIS
Nay, ask me if I can refrain from love,
For I do love her most unfeignèdly.

KING JOHN
Then do I give Volquessen, Touraine, Maine,
Poitiers, and Anjou, these five provinces,
With her to thee ; and this addition more,
Full thirty thousand marks of English coin.
Philip of France, if thou be pleased withal,
Command thy son and daughter to join hands.

KING PHILIP
533 It likes us well. Young princes, close your hands.

AUSTRIA
And your lips too, for I am well assured
That I did so when I was first assured. 535

KING PHILIP
Now, citizens of Angiers, ope your gates,
Let in that amity which you have made, 537
For at Saint Mary's chapel presently
The rites of marriage shall be solemnized.
Is not the Lady Constance in this troop ?
I know she is not, for this match made up
Her presence would have interrupted much.
Where is she and her son ? Tell me, who knows.

LEWIS
She is sad and passionate at your highness' tent. 544

KING PHILIP
And, by my faith, this league that we have made
Will give her sadness very little cure.
Brother of England, how may we content
This widow lady ? In her right we came,
Which we, God knows, have turned another way,
To our own vantage.

KING JOHN   We will heal up all,
For we'll create young Arthur Duke of Britain
And Earl of Richmond, and this rich fair town
We make him lord of. Call the Lady Constance.
Some speedy messenger bid her repair
To our solemnity. I trust we shall, 555
If not fill up the measure of her will,
Yet in some measure satisfy her so,
That we shall stop her exclamation. 558
Go we, as well as haste will suffer us, 559
To this unlooked for, unpreparèd pomp.
Exeunt [all but the Bastard].

BASTARD
Mad world ! Mad kings ! Mad composition ! 561
John, to stop Arthur's title in the whole,
Hath willingly departed with a part, 563
And France, whose armor conscience buckled on,
Whom zeal and charity brought to the field
As God's own soldier, rounded in the ear 566
With that same purpose-changer, that sly devil, 567
That broker, that still breaks the pate of faith, 568
That daily break-vow, he that wins of all,
Of kings, of beggars, old men, young men, maids,
Who, having no external thing to lose 571
But the word 'maid,' cheats the poor maid of that,
That smooth-faced gentleman, tickling commodity, 573
Commodity, the bias of the world ; 574
The world, who of itself is peisèd well, 575

487 *Angiers* i.e. Anjou   490 *liable* subject   494 *Holds hand with* equals 498 *shadow* reflection (the elaborate sun-mistress conceit, very common in Shakespeare's day, emphasizes the artificiality of the wooing)   503 *Drawn* pictured ; *table* flat surface on which a picture is painted   504 *Drawn* (with a quibble on the sense of disembowelled)   506 *quartered* lodged (with quibble ; Elizabethan traitors were hanged, drawn, and quartered)   513 *translate it to my will* cause it to suit my own desires 519 *churlish* miserly (of praise)   522, 523 *still* always   533 *likes* pleases 535 *assured* betrothed   537 *that amity* those friends   544 *passionate* angry   555 *our solemnity* the wedding ceremony   558 *stop her exclamation* silence her loud complaints   559 *suffer* permit   561 *composition* agreement   563 *departed with* relinquished   566 *rounded* whispered   567 *With* by   568 *broker* go-between (in a pejorative sense, as a pander)   571 *Who* i.e. the maids   573 *tickling* flattering ; *commodity* self-interest   574 *bias* the weight in a bowling ball which causes it to curve   575 *peisèd* balanced, weighted

Made to run even upon even ground,
577 Till this advantage, this vile-drawing bias,
This sway of motion, this commodity,
579 Makes it take head from all indifferency,
From all direction, purpose, course, intent.
And this same bias, this commodity,
This bawd, this broker, this all-changing word,
583 Clapped on the outward eye of fickle France,
Hath drawn him from his own determined aid,
585 From a resolved and honorable war,
To a most base and vile-concluded peace.
And why rail I on this commodity?
588 But for because he hath not wooed me yet.
Not that I have the power to clutch my hand
590 When his fair angels would salute my palm,
591 But for my hand, as unattempted yet,
Like a poor beggar, raileth on the rich.
Well, whiles I am a beggar, I will rail
And say there is no sin but to be rich;
And being rich, my virtue then shall be
To say there is no vice but beggary.
597 Since kings break faith upon commodity,
Gain, be my lord, for I will worship thee!   *Exit.*

*

III, i   *Enter Constance, Arthur, and Salisbury.*
CONSTANCE
Gone to be married! Gone to swear a peace!
False blood to false blood joined! Gone to be friends!
Shall Lewis have Blanch, and Blanch those provinces?
It is not so; thou hast misspoke, misheard.
Be well advised, tell o'er thy tale again.
It cannot be; thou dost but say 'tis so.
I trust I may not trust thee, for thy word
Is but the vain breath of a common man.
Believe me, I do not believe thee, man;
I have a king's oath to the contrary.
Thou shalt be punished for thus frighting me,
For I am sick and capable of fears,
Oppressed with wrongs, and therefore full of fears,
A widow, husbandless, subject to fears,
A woman, naturally born to fears;
And though thou now confess thou didst but jest,
17 With my vexed spirits I cannot take a truce,
But they will quake and tremble all this day.
What dost thou mean by shaking of thy head?
Why dost thou look so sadly on my son?

What means that hand upon that breast of thine?
Why holds thine eye that lamentable rheum,   22
Like a proud river peering o'er his bounds?   23
Be these sad signs confirmers of thy words?
Then speak again, not all thy former tale,
But this one word, whether thy tale be true.
SALISBURY
As true as I believe you think them false   27
That give you cause to prove my saying true.
CONSTANCE
O if thou teach me to believe this sorrow,
Teach thou this sorrow how to make me die!
And let belief and life encounter so
As doth the fury of two desperate men
Which in the very meeting fall and die.
Lewis marry Blanch! O boy, then where art thou?
France friend with England, what becomes of me?
Fellow, be gone! I cannot brook thy sight.
This news hath made thee a most ugly man.
SALISBURY
What other harm have I, good lady, done,
But spoke the harm that is by others done?
CONSTANCE
Which harm within itself so heinous is
As it makes harmful all that speak of it.
ARTHUR
I do beseech you, madam, be content.   42
CONSTANCE
If thou that bid'st me be content wert grim,
Ugly and slanderous to thy mother's womb,   44
Full of unpleasing blots and sightless stains,   45
Lame, foolish, crooked, swart, prodigious,   46
Patched with foul moles and eye-offending marks,
I would not care, I then would be content,
For then I should not love thee; no, nor thou
Become thy great birth, nor deserve a crown.
But thou art fair, and at thy birth, dear boy,
Nature and fortune joined to make thee great.
Of nature's gifts thou mayst with lilies boast
And with the half-blown rose. But fortune, O!
She is corrupted, changed, and won from thee.
Sh' adulterates hourly with thine uncle John,   56
And with her golden hand hath plucked on France   57
To tread down fair respect of sovereignty,
And made his majesty the bawd to theirs.
France is a bawd to fortune and King John,
That strumpet fortune, that usurping John!
Tell me, thou fellow, is not France forsworn?
Envenom him with words, or get thee gone   63
And leave those woes alone which I alone
Am bound to underbear.   65
SALISBURY   Pardon me, madam,
I may not go without you to the kings.
CONSTANCE
Thou mayst, thou shalt; I will not go with thee.
I will instruct my sorrows to be proud,
For grief is proud and makes his owner stoop.   69
To me and to the state of my great grief   70
Let kings assemble, for my grief 's so great
That no supporter but the huge firm earth
Can hold it up. Here I and sorrows sit.
Here is my throne; bid kings come bow to it.
[Seats herself on the ground.]

577 *vile-drawing* leading into evil   579 *take . . . indifferency* rush away
from all moderation   583 *eye* (1) vision, (2) that part of the bowl where the
bias was placed; *France* (Philip is now the bowl drawn aside by the bias in
his eye; the outward eye is distinguished from the inner, or conscience)
585 *resolved* already decided upon   588 *But for because* merely because
590 *angels* Elizabethan coins bearing the relief of an angel   591 *unattempted*
untempted   597 *upon* because of
III, i The quarters of the French King   17 *take a truce* make peace   22
rheum moisture, tears   23 *peering o'er* overflowing   27 *them* i.e. the French
king and his advisers   42 *content* calm, quiet   44 *slanderous* a disgrace
45 *blots* blemishes; *sightless* unsightly   46 *swart* of dark complexion;
prodigious deformed, bearing the mark of the Devil   56 *adulterates* (1)
commits adultery, (2) changes, shows her fickleness   57 *with her golden
hand* by bribery; *plucked on* incited   63 *Envenom* vituperate   65 *underbear* endure   69 *grief . . . stoop* (Constance sees herself as the slave of the
grief which she possesses but which masters her)   70 *state* royal court

Enter King John, [King Philip of] France,
[Lewis, the] Dauphin, Blanch, Elinor, Philip [the
Bastard], Austria, Constance [and Attendants].

KING PHILIP

'Tis true, fair daughter, and this blessèd day
76 Ever in France shall be kept festival.
To solemnize this day the glorious sun
Stays in his course and plays the alchemist,
Turning with splendor of his precious eye
80 The meagre cloddy earth to glittering gold.
The yearly course that brings this day about
Shall never see it but a holy day.

CONSTANCE *[rising]*

A wicked day, and not a holy day!
What hath this day deserved? What hath it done
That it in golden letters should be set
86 Among the high tides in the calendar?
Nay, rather turn this day out of the week,
This day of shame, oppression, perjury.
89 Or, if it must stand still, let wives with child
Pray that their burdens may not fall this day,
91 Lest that their hopes prodigiously be crossed.
92 But on this day let seamen fear no wrack;
No bargains break that are not this day made;
This day all things begun come to ill end;
Yea, faith itself to hollow falsehood change!

KING PHILIP

By heaven, lady, you shall have no cause
To curse the fair proceedings of this day.
98 Have I not pawned to you my majesty?

CONSTANCE

99 You have beguiled me with a counterfeit
100 Resembling majesty, which, being touched and tried,
Proves valueless. You are forsworn, forsworn.
102 You came in arms to spill mine enemies' blood,
103 But now in arms you strengthen it with yours.
The grappling vigor and rough frown of war
105 Is cold in amity and painted peace,
106 And our oppression hath made up this league.
Arm, arm, you heavens, against these perjured kings!
A widow cries; be husband to me, heavens!
Let not the hours of this ungodly day
Wear out the day in peace; but, ere sunset,
Set armèd discord 'twixt these perjured kings!
Hear me! O, hear me!

AUSTRIA   Lady Constance, peace!

CONSTANCE

War! War! No peace! Peace is to me a war.
O, Lymoges! O, Austria! Thou dost shame
115 That bloody spoil. Thou slave, thou wretch, thou
coward!
Thou little valiant, great in villainy!
Thou ever strong upon the stronger side!
Thou fortune's champion, that dost never fight
119 But when her humorous ladyship is by
To teach thee safety! Thou art perjured too,
121 And sooth'st up greatness. What a fool art thou,
122 A ramping fool, to brag and stamp and swear
123 Upon my party! Thou cold-blooded slave,
Hast thou not spoke like thunder on my side,
Been sworn my soldier, bidding me depend
Upon thy stars, thy fortune, and thy strength,
127 And dost thou now fall over to my foes?
Thou wear a lion's hide! Doff it for shame,

And hang a calfskin on those recreant limbs.   129

AUSTRIA

O that a man should speak those words to me!

BASTARD

And hang a calfskin on those recreant limbs.

AUSTRIA

Thou dar'st not say so, villain, for thy life.

BASTARD

And hang a calfskin on those recreant limbs.

KING JOHN

We like not this; thou dost forget thyself.
Enter Pandulph.

KING PHILIP

Here comes the holy legate of the Pope.

PANDULPH

Hail, you anointed deputies of heaven!
To thee, King John, my holy errand is.
I Pandulph, of fair Milan cardinal,
And from Pope Innocent the legate here,
Do in his name religiously demand
Why thou against the church, our holy mother,
So wilfully dost spurn; and force perforce   142
Keep Stephen Langton, chosen Archbishop
Of Canterbury, from that holy see.
This, in our foresaid holy father's name,
Pope Innocent, I do demand of thee.

KING JOHN

What earthy name to interrogatories   147
Can task the free breath of a sacred king?
Thou canst not, cardinal, devise a name
So slight, unworthy and ridiculous,
To charge me to an answer, as the Pope.   151
Tell him this tale, and from the mouth of England
Add thus much more, that no Italian priest
Shall tithe or toll in our dominions,   154
But as we under heaven are supreme head,
So under Him that great supremacy,
Where we do reign, we will alone uphold,
Without th' assistance of a mortal hand.
So tell the Pope, all reverence set apart   159
To him and his usurped authority.

KING PHILIP

Brother of England, you blaspheme in this.

KING JOHN

Though you and all the kings of Christendom
Are led so grossly by this meddling priest,   163
Dreading the curse that money may buy out,
And by the merit of vile gold, dross, dust,
Purchase corrupted pardon of a man,

---

76 *festival* as a holiday 80 *meagre* barren 86 *high tides* great festivals
89 *stand still* remain 91 *prodigiously be crossed* be disappointed by the
birth of a monster 92 *But* except; *wrack* shipwreck 98 *pawned* pledged
99 *counterfeit* false coin 100 *touched and tried* tested by being rubbed on
a touchstone 102 *in arms* wearing armor 103 *in arms* embracing one
another; *yours* your blood relative, Lewis 105 *Is . . . peace* lies dead in a
new friendship and pretended peace 106 *oppression* distress 115 *bloody
spoil* i.e. the lion skin he wears 119 *humorous* fickle, capricious 121
sooth'st up flatterest 122 *ramping* rushing wildly about like a lion 123
Upon my party on my side 127 *fall over* desert 129 *calfskin* (material
of which coats for household fools traditionally were made; alluding also
to the cowardice of Austria); *recreant* cowardly 142 *spurn* oppose with
contempt; *force perforce* by forcible means 147-48 *What . . . king* what
mortal man can compel a king to answer questions 147 *interrogatories*
formal questions put to a witness in a court of law 151 *charge* command
154 *tithe or toll* collect church revenues 159 *set apart* discarded 163
grossly stupidly

167 Who in that sale sells pardon from himself,
Though you and all the rest, so grossly led,
This juggling witchcraft with revenue cherish,
Yet I alone, alone do me oppose
Against the Pope, and count his friends my foes.

PANDULPH
Then, by the lawful power that I have,
Thou shalt stand cursed and excommunicate;
And blessèd shall he be that doth revolt
From his allegiance to an heretic;
And meritorious shall that hand be called,
Canonized and worshipped as a saint,
That takes away by any secret course
Thy hateful life.

CONSTANCE   O lawful let it be
That I have room with Rome to curse awhile!
Good father cardinal, cry thou amen
182 To my keen curses, for without my wrong
There is no tongue hath power to curse him right.

PANDULPH
There's law and warrant, lady, for my curse.

CONSTANCE
And for mine too. When law can do no right,
Let it be lawful that law bar no wrong.
Law cannot give my child his kingdom here,
For he that holds his kingdom holds the law;
Therefore, since law itself is perfect wrong,
How can the law forbid my tongue to curse?

PANDULPH
Philip of France, on peril of a curse,
Let go the hand of that arch-heretic,
193 And raise the power of France upon his head,
Unless he do submit himself to Rome.

ELINOR
Look'st thou pale, France? Do not let go thy hand.

CONSTANCE
196 Look to that, devil, lest that France repent,
And by disjoining hands, hell lose a soul.

AUSTRIA
King Philip, listen to the cardinal.

BASTARD
And hang a calfskin on his recreant limbs.

AUSTRIA
200 Well, ruffian, I must pocket up these wrongs,
Because –

BASTARD   Your breeches best may carry them.

KING JOHN
Philip, what sayst thou to the cardinal?

CONSTANCE
What should he say, but as the cardinal?

LEWIS
Bethink you, father, for the difference
Is purchase of a heavy curse from Rome,
Or the light loss of England for a friend.

Forgo the easier.
207

BLANCH   That's the curse of Rome.

CONSTANCE
O Lewis, stand fast! The devil tempts thee here
In likeness of a new untrimmèd bride.
209

BLANCH
The Lady Constance speaks not from her faith,
But from her need.

CONSTANCE   O, if thou grant my need,
Which only lives but by the death of faith,
That need must needs infer this principle,
213
That faith would live again by death of need.
O then, tread down my need, and faith mounts up;
Keep my need up, and faith is trodden down!

KING JOHN
The king is moved and answers not to this.

CONSTANCE
O be removed from him, and answer well!

AUSTRIA
Do so, King Philip; hang no more in doubt.

BASTARD
Hang nothing but a calfskin, most sweet lout.

KING PHILIP
I am perplexed, and know not what to say.

PANDULPH
What canst thou say but will perplex thee more,
If thou stand excommunicate and cursed?

KING PHILIP
Good reverend father, make my person yours,
224
And tell me how you would bestow yourself.
225
This royal hand and mine are newly knit,
And the conjunction of our inward souls
Married in league, coupled and linked together
With all religious strength of sacred vows.
The latest breath that gave the sound of words
230
Was deep-sworn faith, peace, amity, true love
Between our kingdoms and our royal selves,
And even before this truce, but new before,
No longer than we well could wash our hands
To clap this royal bargain up of peace,
235
Heaven knows, they were besmeared and overstained
With slaughter's pencil, where revenge did paint
The fearful difference of incensèd kings.
238
And shall these hands, so lately purged of blood,
So newly joined in love, so strong in both,
Unyoke this seizure and this kind regreet?
241
Play fast and loose with faith? So jest with heaven,
242
Make such unconstant children of ourselves,
243
As now again to snatch our palm from palm,
Unswear faith sworn, and on the marriage-bed
Of smiling peace to march a bloody host,
And make a riot on the gentle brow
Of true sincerity? O holy sir,
My reverend father, let it not be so!
Out of your grace, devise, ordain, impose
Some gentle order, and then we shall be blessed
To do your pleasure and continue friends.

PANDULPH
All form is formless, order orderless,
Save what is opposite to England's love.
Therefore to arms! Be champion of our church,
Or let the church, our mother, breathe her curse,
A mother's curse, on her revolting son.
France, thou mayst hold a serpent by the tongue,

---

167 *Who . . . himself* i.e. the seller of indulgences damns his own soul
182–83 *without . . . right* he cannot be adequately cursed without recognition of his wrong against me   193 *upon* against   196 *devil* i.e. Elinor
200 *pocket up* put up with   207 *Forgo the easier* relinquish the less important
209 *new untrimmèd* having just removed her bridal gown, still a virgin
213 *needs* of necessity   224 *make my person yours* put yourself in my position   225 *bestow yourself* behave   230 *latest breath* most recent speech
235 *clap* strike hands together to seal a bargain   238 *difference* quarrel
241 *Unyoke this seizure* separate the hands clasped in friendship; *regreet*
return of the salutation of friendship   242 *Play fast and loose* cheat   243
unconstant fickle

259 A casèd lion by the mortal paw,
A fasting tiger safer by the tooth,
Than keep in peace that hand which thou dost hold.

KING PHILIP
I may disjoin my hand, but not my faith.

PANDULPH
263 So mak'st thou faith an enemy to faith,
And like a civil war set'st oath to oath,
Thy tongue against thy tongue. O, let thy vow
First made to heaven, first be to heaven performed,
That is, to be the champion of our church.
What since thou swor'st is sworn against thyself
And may not be performèd by thyself,
270 For that which thou hast sworn to do amiss
Is not amiss when it is truly done ;
And being not done, where doing tends to ill,
The truth is then most done not doing it.
The better act of purposes mistook
Is to mistake again ; though indirect,
Yet indirection thereby grows direct,
And falsehood falsehood cures, as fire cools fire
Within the scorchèd veins of one new burned.
It is religion that doth make vows kept,
280 But thou hast sworn against religion,
By what thou swear'st, against the thing thou swear'st,
And mak'st an oath the surety for thy truth
Against an oath ; the truth thou art unsure
To swear swears only not to be forsworn ;
Else what a mockery should it be to swear !
But thou dost swear only to be forsworn ;
And most forsworn to keep what thou dost swear.
Therefore thy later vows against thy first
Is in thyself rebellion to thyself,
And better conquest never canst thou make
291 Than arm thy constant and thy nobler parts
292 Against these giddy loose suggestions ;
Upon which better part our prayers come in,
If thou vouchsafe them. But, if not, then know
The peril of our curses light on thee
296 So heavy as thou shalt not shake them off,
But in despair die under their black weight.

AUSTRIA
Rebellion, flat rebellion !

298 BASTARD   Will't not be ?
Will not a calfskin stop that mouth of thine ?

LEWIS
Father, to arms !

BLANCH   Upon thy wedding-day ?
301 Against the blood that thou hast married ?
What, shall our feast be kept with slaughtered men ?
303 Shall braying trumpets and loud churlish drums,
304 Clamors of hell, be measures to our pomp ?
O husband, hear me ! Ay, alack, how new
Is 'husband' in my mouth ! Even for that name,
Which till this time my tongue did ne'er pronounce,
Upon my knee I beg, go not to arms
Against mine uncle.

CONSTANCE   O, upon my knee,
Made hard with kneeling, I do pray to thee,
311 Thou virtuous Dauphin, alter not the doom
312 Forethought by heaven.

BLANCH
Now shall I see thy love. What motive may
Be stronger with thee than the name of wife ?

CONSTANCE
That which upholdeth him that thee upholds,
His honor. O thine honor, Lewis, thine honor !

LEWIS
I muse your majesty doth seem so cold,
When such profound respects do pull you on.   318

PANDULPH
I will denounce a curse upon his head.   319

KING PHILIP
Thou shalt not need. England, I will fall from thee.   320

CONSTANCE
O fair return of banished majesty !

ELINOR
O foul revolt of French inconstancy !

KING JOHN
France, thou shalt rue this hour within this hour.

BASTARD
Old time the clock-setter, that bald sexton time,   324
Is it as he will ? Well then, France shall rue.

BLANCH
The sun 's o'ercast with blood. Fair day, adieu !
Which is the side that I must go withal ?
I am with both. Each army hath a hand,
And in their rage, I having hold of both,
They whirl asunder and dismember me.
Husband, I cannot pray that thou mayst win.
Uncle, I needs must pray that thou mayst lose.
Father, I may not wish the fortune thine.
Grandam, I will not wish thy wishes thrive.
Whoever wins, on that side shall I lose ;
Assurèd loss before the match be played.

LEWIS
Lady, with me, with me thy fortune lies.

BLANCH
There where my fortune lives, there my life dies.

KING JOHN
Cousin, go draw our puissance together. *[Exit Bastard.]* 339
France, I am burned up with inflaming wrath,
A rage whose heat hath this condition,   341
That nothing can allay, nothing but blood,
The blood, and dearest-valued blood, of France.

KING PHILIP
Thy rage shall burn thee up, and thou shalt turn
To ashes, ere our blood shall quench that fire.
Look to thyself, thou art in jeopardy.

KING JOHN
No more than he that threats. To arms let's hie ! *Exeunt.*

*

259 *casèd* caged; *mortal* deadly   263–65 *So . . . tongue* you are swearing against the religious faith to which you already are pledged   270–78 *For . . . burned* i.e. Philip by not performing what he has just vowed may turn his wrong to right; when one has done wrong it is often easier to return to the true path by another wrong than to retrace one's steps (this doctrine of equivocation was particularly hated by Elizabethan Protestants)   280–87 *But . . . swear* since you have sworn by your faith against your faith (true religion), you make a mockery of swearing; you commit the greatest breach of faith by keeping the oath you have just sworn   291 *arm* by arming   292 *giddy* unsafe, insecure; *suggestions* temptations   296 *as* that   298 *Will't not be* is nothing of any use   301 *blood* blood-relationship   303 *churlish* rude   304 *measures* melodies   311 *doom* decision   312 *Forethought* predestined   318 *profound respects* weighty considerations   319 *denounce* proclaim   320 *fall from* forsake   324 *Old time the clock-setter* (the sexton's job included setting the church clock as well as digging graves; he is thus easily identified with time, the destroyer of life)   339 *Cousin* kinsman; *draw our puissance* muster our army   341 *condition* quality

III, ii   *Alarums, excursions. Enter Bastard, with Austria's head.*

BASTARD

Now, by my life, this day grows wondrous hot.

2   Some airy devil hovers in the sky

And pours down mischief. Austria's head lie there,

4   While Philip breathes.

    Enter [King] John, Arthur, Hubert.

KING JOHN

5   Hubert, keep this boy. Philip, make up ;

My mother is assailèd in our tent,

And ta'en, I fear.

BASTARD   My lord, I rescued her ;

Her highness is in safety, fear you not.

But on, my liege, for very little pains

Will bring this labor to a happy end.

          Exit [with the others].

III, iii   *Alarums, excursions, retreat. Enter [King] John, Elinor, Arthur, Bastard, Hubert, Lords.*

KING JOHN *[to Elinor]*

So shall it be ; your grace shall stay behind

So strongly guarded. *[to Arthur]* Cousin, look not sad.

Thy grandam loves thee, and thy uncle will

As dear be to thee as thy father was.

ARTHUR

O this will make my mother die with grief !

KING JOHN *[to the Bastard]*

6   Cousin, away for England ! Haste before,

And ere our coming see thou shake the bags

8   Of hoarding abbots ; imprisoned angels

Set at liberty. The fat ribs of peace

Must by the hungry now be fed upon.

Use our commission in his utmost force.

BASTARD

12   Bell, book, and candle shall not drive me back

13   When gold and silver becks me to come on.

I leave your highness. Grandam, I will pray –

If ever I remember to be holy –

For your fair safety ; so I kiss your hand.

ELINOR

Farewell, gentle cousin.

17 KING JOHN   Coz, farewell.   *[Exit Bastard.]*

ELINOR

Come hither, little kinsman. Hark, a word.

    [She takes Arthur aside.]

KING JOHN

Come hither, Hubert. O my gentle Hubert,

We owe thee much ! Within this wall of flesh

There is a soul counts thee her creditor,

22   And with advantage means to pay thy love ;

And, my good friend, thy voluntary oath

Lives in this bosom, dearly cherishèd.

Give me thy hand. I had a thing to say,

But I will fit it with some better tune.

By heaven, Hubert, I am almost ashamed

28   To say what good respect I have of thee.

HUBERT

I am much bounden to your majesty.   29

KING JOHN

Good friend, thou hast no cause to say so yet,

But thou shalt have ; and creep time ne'er so slow,

Yet it shall come for me to do thee good.

I had a thing to say, but let it go.

The sun is in the heaven, and the proud day,

Attended with the pleasures of the world,

Is all too wanton and too full of gawds   36

To give me audience. If the midnight bell

Did with his iron tongue and brazen mouth

Sound on into the drowsy ear of night ;

If this same were a churchyard where we stand,

And thou possessèd with a thousand wrongs ;

Or if that surly spirit, melancholy,

Had baked thy blood and made it heavy, thick,

Which else runs tickling up and down the veins,

Making that idiot, laughter, keep men's eyes

And strain their cheeks to idle merriment,

A passion hateful to my purposes ;

Or if that thou couldst see me without eyes,

Hear me without thine ears, and make reply

Without a tongue, using conceit alone,   50

Without eyes, ears, and harmful sound of words ;

Then, in despite of brooded watchful day,   52

I would into thy bosom pour my thoughts.

But ah, I will not. Yet I love thee well,

And, by my troth, I think thou lov'st me well.

HUBERT

So well, that what you bid me undertake,

Though that my death were adjunct to my act,   57

By heaven, I would do it.

KING JOHN   Do not I know thou wouldst ?

Good Hubert ! Hubert, Hubert, throw thine eye

On yon young boy. I'll tell thee what, my friend,

He is a very serpent in my way,

And wheresoe'er this foot of mine doth tread

He lies before me. Dost thou understand me ?

Thou art his keeper.

HUBERT   And I'll keep him so

That he shall not offend your majesty.

KING JOHN

Death.

HUBERT My lord ?

KING JOHN   A grave.

HUBERT   He shall not live.

KING JOHN   Enough.

I could be merry now. Hubert, I love thee.

Well, I'll not say what I intend for thee.

Remember. Madam, fare you well.

I'll send those powers o'er to your majesty.   70

ELINOR

My blessing go with thee !

KING JOHN   For England, cousin, go.

Hubert shall be your man, attend on you   72

With all true duty. On toward Calais, ho !   *Exeunt.*

III, ii A field of battle near Angiers   2 *Some . . . sky* a thunderstorm threatens   4 *breathes* rests   5 *make up* advance to the front line
III, iii   6 *before* ahead of us   8 *angels* coins (with the usual pun)   12 *Bell, book, and candle* (instruments used in the ritual of excommunication)   13 *becks* beckons   17 *Coz* kinsman   22 *advantage* interest ; *pay* repay   28 *respect* opinion   29 *bounden* obliged   36 *gawds* showy ornaments, such as the flowers in springtime   50 *conceit* understanding   52 *brooded* brooding   57 *adjunct to* the result of   70 *powers* troops   72 *man* servant

*

III, iv   *Enter [King Philip of] France, [Lewis, the]*
    Dauphin, Pandulph, Attendants.

KING PHILIP

1 So, by a roaring tempest on the flood,
2 A whole armado of convicted sail
  Is scattered and disjoined from fellowship.

PANDULPH

  Courage and comfort ! All shall yet go well.

KING PHILIP

  What can go well when we have run so ill ?
  Are we not beaten ? Is not Angiers lost ?
  Arthur ta'en prisoner ? Divers dear friends slain ?
  And bloody England into England gone,
9 O'erbearing interruption, spite of France ?

LEWIS

  What he hath won, that hath he fortified.
11 So hot a speed with such advice disposed,
  Such temperate order in so fierce a cause,
13 Doth want example. Who hath read or heard
  Of any kindred action like to this ?

KING PHILIP

  Well could I bear that England had this praise,
16 So we could find some pattern of our shame.
    Enter Constance.
  Look, who comes here ! A grave unto a soul,
  Holding th' eternal spirit, against her will,
19 In the vile prison of afflicted breath.
  I prithee, lady, go away with me.

CONSTANCE

  Lo, now ! Now see the issue of your peace !

KING PHILIP

  Patience, good lady ! Comfort, gentle Constance !

CONSTANCE

23 No, I defy all counsel, all redress,
  But that which ends all counsel, true redress,
  Death, death. O, amiable, lovely death !
  Thou odoriferous stench ! Sound rottenness !
27 Arise forth from the couch of lasting night,
  Thou hate and terror to prosperity,
  And I will kiss thy detestable bones,
30 And put my eyeballs in thy vaulty brows,
  And ring these fingers with thy household worms,
32 And stop this gap of breath with fulsome dust,
  And be a carrion monster like thyself.
  Come, grin on me, and I will think thou smil'st
35 And buss thee as thy wife ! Misery's love,
  O, come to me !

KING PHILIP   O fair affliction, peace !

CONSTANCE

  No, no, I will not, having breath to cry.
  O that my tongue were in the thunder's mouth !
  Then with a passion would I shake the world,
40 And rouse from sleep that fell anatomy
  Which cannot hear a lady's feeble voice,
42 Which scorns a modern invocation.

PANDULPH

  Lady, you utter madness and not sorrow.

CONSTANCE

  Thou art not holy to belie me so.
  I am not mad ; this hair I tear is mine.
  My name is Constance ; I was Geoffrey's wife.
  Young Arthur is my son, and he is lost !
  I am not mad. I would to heaven I were,
49 For then 'tis like I should forget myself.

O, if I could, what grief should I forget !
Preach some philosophy to make me mad,
And thou shalt be canonized, cardinal.
For, being not mad but sensible of grief,   53
My reasonable part produces reason
How I may be delivered of these woes,   55
And teaches me to kill or hang myself.
If I were mad, I should forget my son,
Or madly think a babe of clouts were he.   58
I am not mad. Too well, too well I feel
The different plague of each calamity.

KING PHILIP

Bind up those tresses. O, what love I note
In the fair multitude of those her hairs !
Where but by chance a silver drop hath fallen,   63
Even to that drop ten thousand wiry friends   64
Do glue themselves in sociable grief,   65
Like true, inseparable, faithful loves,
Sticking together in calamity.

CONSTANCE

To England, if you will.   68

KING PHILIP   Bind up your hairs.

CONSTANCE

Yes, that I will ; and wherefore will I do it ?
I tore them from their bonds and cried aloud :
'O that these hands could so redeem my son,
As they have given these hairs their liberty !'
But now I envy at their liberty,
And will again commit them to their bonds,
Because my poor child is a prisoner.
And, Father Cardinal, I have heard you say
That we shall see and know our friends in heaven.
If that be true, I shall see my boy again,
For since the birth of Cain, the first male child,
To him that did but yesterday suspire,
There was not such a gracious creature born.   81
But now will canker sorrow eat my bud   82
And chase the native beauty from his cheek,
And he will look as hollow as a ghost,
As dim and meagre as an ague's fit,   85
And so he'll die ; and rising so again,
When I shall meet him in the court of heaven
I shall not know him. Therefore never, never
Must I behold my pretty Arthur more.

PANDULPH

You hold too heinous a respect of grief.   90

CONSTANCE

He talks to me that never had a son.

III, iv The quarters of the French King 1 *flood* ocean 2 *armado* fleet of warships ; *convicted* doomed to destruction 9 *interruption* resistance ; *spite of* despite 11 *with such advice disposed* controlled with such good judgment 13 *Doth want example* is without precedent 16 *So* if ; *pattern* example in the past 19 *breath* life 23 *defy* reject 27 *lasting* everlasting 30 *vaulty* arched 32 *stop . . . breath* stop up this mouth ; *fulsome* physically disgusting 35 *buss* kiss 40 *fell anatomy* cruel skeleton (as death traditionally was personified) 42 *modern invocation* ordinary supplication 49 *like* probable 53 *sensible* capable 55 *be delivered of* give birth to, separate myself from (Constance sees death as her lover, grief as her child) 58 *babe of clouts* rag doll 63 *silver drop* tear 64 *wiry friends* hairs (wire was a common metaphor for hair) 65 *sociable* sympathetic 68 *To England . . . will* (a line which is usually taken as evidence of some revision in this scene, since it bears no relation to its immediate context, but which may be an answer to King Philip's invitation at l. 20) 81 *gracious* meriting divine grace, destined for heaven 82 *canker* like a canker worm (which destroys plants) 85 *dim* pale 90 *heinous a respect* terrible an opinion

KING PHILIP

92   You are as fond of grief as of your child.

CONSTANCE

Grief fills the room up of my absent child,
Lies in his bed, walks up and down with me,
Puts on his pretty looks, repeats his words,
96   Remembers me of all his gracious parts,
Stuffs out his vacant garments with his form.
Then have I reason to be fond of grief.
Fare you well. Had you such a loss as I,
I could give better comfort than you do.
101   I will not keep this form upon my head,
102   When there is such disorder in my wit.
O Lord! My boy, my Arthur, my fair son!
My life, my joy, my food, my all the world!
My widow-comfort, and my sorrows' cure!   *Exit.*

KING PHILIP

I fear some outrage, and I'll follow her.   *Exit.*

LEWIS

There's nothing in this world can make me joy.
Life is as tedious as a twice-told tale,
Vexing the dull ear of a drowsy man,
And bitter shame hath spoiled the sweet world's taste,
That it yields nought but shame and bitterness.

PANDULPH

Before the curing of a strong disease,
113   Even in the instant of repair and health,
The fit is strongest. Evils that take leave,
On their departure most of all show evil.
116   What have you lost by losing of this day?

LEWIS

All days of glory, joy, and happiness.

PANDULPH

If you had won it, certainly you had.
No, no; when fortune means to men most good,
She looks upon them with a threat'ning eye.
'Tis strange to think how much King John hath lost
In this which he accounts so clearly won.
Are not you grieved that Arthur is his prisoner?

LEWIS

As heartily as he is glad he hath him.

PANDULPH

Your mind is all as youthful as your blood.
Now hear me speak with a prophetic spirit,
For even the breath of what I mean to speak
128   Shall blow each dust, each straw, each little rub,
Out of the path which shall directly lead

Thy foot to England's throne. And therefore mark:
John hath seized Arthur, and it cannot be
That, whiles warm life plays in that infant's veins,
The misplaced John should entertain an hour,   133
One minute, nay, one quiet breath of rest.
A sceptre snatched with an unruly hand
Must be as boisterously maintained as gained,   136
And he that stands upon a slippery place
Makes nice of no vile hold to stay him up.   138
That John may stand, then Arthur needs must fall;
So be it, for it cannot be but so.

LEWIS

But what shall I gain by young Arthur's fall?

PANDULPH

You, in the right of Lady Blanch your wife,
May then make all the claim that Arthur did.

LEWIS

And lose it, life and all, as Arthur did.

PANDULPH

How green you are and fresh in this old world!   145
John lays you plots; the times conspire with you,   146
For he that steeps his safety in true blood   147
Shall find but bloody safety and untrue.
This act so evilly borne shall cool the hearts   149
Of all his people and freeze up their zeal,
That none so small advantage shall step forth   151
To check his reign, but they will cherish it;
No natural exhalation in the sky,   153
No scope of nature, no distempered day,   154
No common wind, no customèd event,   155
But they will pluck away his natural cause   156
And call them meteors, prodigies, and signs,
Abortives, presages, and tongues of heaven,   158
Plainly denouncing vengeance upon John.

LEWIS

May be he will not touch young Arthur's life,
But hold himself safe in his prisonment.

PANDULPH

O, sir, when he shall hear of your approach,
If that young Arthur be not gone already,
Even at that news he dies; and then the hearts
Of all his people shall revolt from him
And kiss the lips of unacquainted change,   166
And pick strong matter of revolt and wrath   167
Out of the bloody fingers' ends of John.
Methinks I see this hurly all on foot;   169
And, O, what better matter breeds for you   170
Than I have named! The bastard Faulconbridge
Is now in England ransacking the church,
Offending charity. If but a dozen French   173
Were there in arms, they would be as a call   174
To train ten thousand English to their side,   175
Or as a little snow, tumbled about,
Anon becomes a mountain. O noble Dauphin,   177
Go with me to the king. 'Tis wonderful
What may be wrought out of their discontent,
Now that their souls are topful of offense.   180
For England go; I will whet on the king.   181

LEWIS

Strong reasons make strange actions. Let us go.
If you say ay, the king will not say no.   *Exeunt.*

---

92 *fond of* foolishly infatuated with   **96** *Remembers* reminds   **101** *form* orderly arrangement of hair   **102** *wit* mind   **113** *repair* recovery   **116** *day* day of battle   **128** *dust* grain of dust; *rub* obstacle (in the game of bowls)   **133** *misplaced* usurping   **136** *boisterously* violently   **138** *Makes . . . up* is not scrupulous about what evil means he uses to support himself   **145** *green* inexperienced   **146** *lays you plots* makes plans for your advantage   **147–48** *he . . . untrue* he who bases his safety on his killing of the true king (Arthur) will find his safety bloody and false   **149** *so evilly borne* carried out so wickedly   **151** *advantage* opportunity   **153** *exhalation* meteor   **154** *scope of nature* a seemingly impossible event which is nevertheless within the possibility of nature; *distempered* full of bad weather   **155** *customèd* ordinary   **156** *his* its   **158** *Abortives* corruptions of nature by untimely birth   **166** *kiss . . . change* be enamored of any new change   **167–68** *pick . . . John* find cause for revolt and anger in John's bloody deeds   **169** *hurly* commotion; *on foot* started   **170** *breeds* is ripening   **173** *charity* good will   **174** *call* decoy (as a bird call)   **175** *train* attract   **177** *Anon* soon   **180** *topful of offense* filled to the brim with grievances   **181** *whet on* incite

IV, i   *Enter Hubert and Executioners.*

HUBERT

Heat me these irons hot, and look thou stand
2 Within the arras. When I strike my foot
3 Upon the bosom of the ground, rush forth
And bind the boy which you shall find with me
Fast to the chair. Be heedful. Hence, and watch.

[1.] EXECUTIONER

6 I hope your warrant will bear out the deed.

HUBERT

7 Uncleanly scruples ! Fear not you. Look to 't.
                              [Exeunt Executioners.]
8 Young lad, come forth ; I have to say with you.
         Enter Arthur.

ARTHUR

Good morrow, Hubert.

HUBERT   Good morrow, little prince.

ARTHUR

10 As little prince, having so great a title
To be more prince, as may be. You are sad.

HUBERT

Indeed, I have been merrier.

ARTHUR   Mercy on me !

Methinks nobody should be sad but I.
Yet I remember, when I was in France
15 Young gentlemen would be as sad as night,
16 Only for wantonness. By my christendom,
17 So I were out of prison and kept sheep,
I should be as merry as the day is long ;
19 And so I would be here, but that I doubt
20 My uncle practises more harm to me.
He is afraid of me and I of him.
Is it my fault that I was Geoffrey's son ?
No, indeed, is 't not, and I would to heaven
I were your son, so you would love me, Hubert.

HUBERT *[aside]*

25 If I talk to him, with his innocent prate
He will awake my mercy which lies dead ;
27 Therefore I will be sudden and dispatch.

ARTHUR

Are you sick, Hubert ? You look pale to-day.
29 In sooth, I would you were a little sick,
That I might sit all night and watch with you.
I warrant I love you more than you do me.

HUBERT *[aside]*

His words do take possession of my bosom.
Read here, young Arthur. *[Shows a paper.]*
         [Aside]   How now, foolish rheum,
34 Turning dispiteous torture out of door !
I must be brief, lest resolution drop
Out at mine eyes in tender womanish tears.
37 Can you not read it ? Is it not fair writ ?

ARTHUR

38 Too fairly, Hubert, for so foul effect.
Must you with hot irons burn out both mine eyes ?

HUBERT

Young boy, I must.

ARTHUR   And will you ?

HUBERT   And I will.

ARTHUR

Have you the heart ? When your head did but ache,
I knit my handkercher about your brows –
43 The best I had, a princess wrought it me –
And I did never ask it you again ;

And with my hand at midnight held your head,
And like the watchful minutes to the hour,   46
Still and anon cheered up the heavy time,   47
Saying, 'What lack you ?' and 'Where lies your grief ?'
Or 'What good love may I perform for you ?'   49
Many a poor man's son would have lien still,   50
And ne'er have spoke a loving word to you,
But you at your sick service had a prince.   52
Nay, you may think my love was crafty love,   53
And call it cunning ; do and if you will.
If heaven be pleased that you must use me ill,
Why then you must. Will you put out mine eyes ?
These eyes that never did nor never shall
So much as frown on you ?

HUBERT   I have sworn to do it,
And with hot irons must I burn them out.

ARTHUR

Ah, none but in this iron age would do it !   60
The iron of itself, though heat red-hot,   61
Approaching near these eyes, would drink my tears
And quench this fiery indignation
Even in the matter of mine innocence,   64
Nay, after that, consume away in rust,
But for containing fire to harm mine eye.   66
Are you more stubborn-hard than hammered iron ?
And if an angel should have come to me
And told me Hubert should put out mine eyes,
I would not have believed him – no tongue but Hubert's.

HUBERT *[stamps]*

Come forth.
         [Enter Executioners, with a cord, irons, etc.]
Do as I bid you do.

ARTHUR

O ! save me, Hubert, save me ! My eyes are out
Even with the fierce looks of these bloody men.

HUBERT

Give me the iron, I say, and bind him here.

ARTHUR

Alas, what need you be so boist'rous rough ?   76
I will not struggle, I will stand stone still.
For heaven sake, Hubert, let me not be bound !
Nay, hear me, Hubert ! Drive these men away,
And I will sit as quiet as a lamb.
I will not stir, nor wince, nor speak a word,
Nor look upon the iron angerly.   82
Thrust but these men away, and I'll forgive you,
Whatever torment you do put me to.

IV, i Within an English castle 2 *Within the arras* behind the curtains
3 *bosom* surface 6 *bear out* be sufficient to justify 7 *Uncleanly* improper,
unbecoming ; *Fear not you* don't you worry 8 *to say with* something to say
to 10–11 *As . . . may be* as little of a prince (since I am in captivity) as one
with my great title possibly could be 15–16 *as sad . . . wantonness* melancholy merely as a whimsical affectation (a common pose among gentlemen
of Shakespeare's day) 16 *christendom* baptism, hence faith as a Christian
17 *So* if 19 *doubt* fear 20 *practises* plots 25 *prate* prattle 27 *dispatch*
do the job quickly 29 *sooth* truth 34 *dispiteous* merciless 37 *fair writ*
clearly written 38 *effect* purpose 43 *wrought it me* embroidered it for me
46 *watchful . . . hour* minutes which mark the progress of the hour 47 *Still
and anon* continually from time to time (Arthur compares his questions to
the ticking of the minutes, which makes the hour go by more quickly) ;
heavy dreary 49 *love* loving deed 50 *lien* lain (an archaic form preserved
for the metre) 52 *at your sick service* at your service (as a nurse) when you
were sick 53 *crafty* pretended 60 *iron age* cruel, degenerate present (as
opposed to the heroic golden age of antiquity) 61 *heat* heated 64 *matter
of mine innocence* tears, the signs of innocence 66 *But* merely 76 *what*
why 82 *angerly* angrily

HUBERT

85   Go, stand within. Let me alone with him.

[1.] EXECUTIONER

86   I am best pleased to be from such a deed.

                  [Exeunt Executioners.]

ARTHUR

87   Alas! I then have chid away my friend!
     He hath a stern look but a gentle heart.
     Let him come back, that his compassion may
     Give life to yours.

HUBERT   Come, boy, prepare yourself.

ARTHUR

     Is there no remedy?

HUBERT   None, but to lose your eyes.

ARTHUR

92   O heaven, that there were but a mote in yours,
     A grain, a dust, a gnat, a wandering hair,
     Any annoyance in that precious sense.
95   Then feeling what small things are boisterous there,
     Your vile intent must needs seem horrible.

HUBERT

     Is this your promise? Go to, hold your tongue.

ARTHUR

98   Hubert, the utterance of a brace of tongues
     Must needs want pleading for a pair of eyes.
     Let me not hold my tongue, let me not, Hubert;
     Or, Hubert, if you will, cut out my tongue,
     So I may keep mine eyes. O, spare mine eyes,
     Though to no use but still to look on you!
104   Lo, by my troth, the instrument is cold
     And would not harm me.

HUBERT   I can heat it, boy.

ARTHUR

     No, in good sooth. The fire is dead with grief,
107   Being create for comfort, to be used
108   In undeserved extremes. See else yourself.
     There is no malice in this burning coal.
     The breath of heaven hath blown his spirit out
     And strewed repentant ashes on his head.

HUBERT

     But with my breath I can revive it, boy.

ARTHUR

     And if you do, you will but make it blush
     And glow with shame of your proceedings, Hubert.
115   Nay, it perchance will sparkle in your eyes,

And like a dog that is compelled to fight,
Snatch at his master that doth tarre him on.   117
All things that you should use to do me wrong
Deny their office. Only you do lack   119
That mercy which fierce fire and iron extends,   120
Creatures of note for mercy-lacking uses.   121

HUBERT

Well, see to live; I will not touch thine eye
For all the treasure that thine uncle owes.   123
Yet am I sworn and I did purpose, boy,
With this same very iron to burn them out.

ARTHUR

O, now you look like Hubert! All this while
You were disguisèd.

HUBERT   Peace! No more. Adieu.
Your uncle must not know but you are dead.   128
I'll fill these doggèd spies with false reports.   129
And, pretty child, sleep doubtless and secure   130
That Hubert for the wealth of all the world
Will not offend thee.

ARTHUR   O heaven! I thank you, Hubert.

HUBERT

Silence! No more! Go closely in with me.   133
Much danger do I undergo for thee.   *Exeunt.*

                  *

Enter [King] John, Pembroke, Salisbury, and other   IV, ii
Lords.

KING JOHN

Here once again we sit, once again crowned,   1
And looked upon, I hope, with cheerful eyes.

PEMBROKE

This 'once again,' but that your highness pleased,
Was once superfluous. You were crowned before,
And that high royalty was ne'er plucked off,
The faiths of men ne'er stainèd with revolt.   6
Fresh expectation troubled not the land   7
With any longed for change or better state.   8

SALISBURY

Therefore, to be possessed with double pomp,   9
To guard a title that was rich before,   10
To gild refinèd gold, to paint the lily,
To throw a perfume on the violet,
To smooth the ice, or add another hue
Unto the rainbow, or with taper-light   14
To seek the beauteous eye of heaven to garnish,
Is wasteful and ridiculous excess.

PEMBROKE

But that your royal pleasure must be done,
This act is as an ancient tale new told,
And in the last repeating troublesome,
Being urgèd at a time unseasonable.

SALISBURY

In this the antique and well noted face
Of plain old form is much disfigurèd,
And like a shifted wind unto a sail,   22
It makes the course of thoughts to fetch about,   23
Startles and frights consideration,   24
Makes sound opinion sick and truth suspected,   25
For putting on so new a fashioned robe.

PEMBROKE

When workmen strive to do better than well,
They do confound their skill in covetousness,   29

85 *Let ... him* leave me to deal with him alone   **86** *from* away from   **87** *my friend* i.e. the executioner   **92** *mote* speck of dust   **95** *boisterous* irritating   **98–99** *the utterance ... pleading* even two tongues could not plead adequately   **104** *troth* faith   **107** *create* created   **108** *In undeserved extremes* to inflict acts of cruelty which have not been deserved   **115** *sparkle* throw out sparks   **117** *tarre* provoke to fight   **119** *Deny their office* refuse to perform their proper function   **120** *extends* exhibit   **121** *Creatures* i.e. fire and iron; *of note ... uses* noted for their customary use in cruel affairs   **123** *owes* owns   **128** *but* other than that   **129** *doggèd* malicious   **130** *doubtless* without fear; *secure* assured   **133** *closely* secretly

IV, ii The court of King John   **1** *once again* (John has just had himself recrowned to mark the end of his domination by the church of Rome)   **6** *stainèd* corrupted   **7** *expectation* excited anticipation of change   **8** *state* government   **9** *pomp* solemn ceremony (coronation)   **10** *guard* ornament a garment with trimmings   **14–15** *with taper-light ... garnish* to try to add to the sun's beauty by means of candlelight   **22** *plain old form* simple customary behavior   **23** *shifted wind* change of wind   **24** *fetch about* change their direction   **25** *consideration* thought (about the succession; by a second coronation John is causing others to question the validity of his title)   **29** *confound ... covetousness* destroy what they have done well by their desire to do even better

And oftentimes excusing of a fault
Doth make the fault the worse by the excuse,
32 As patches set upon a little breach
33 Discredit more in hiding of the fault
Than did the fault before it was so patched.

SALISBURY
To this effect, before you were new crowned,
36 We breathed our counsel, but it pleased your highness
37 To overbear it, and we are all well pleased,
38 Since all and every part of what we would
Doth make a stand at what your highness will.

KING JOHN
Some reasons of this double coronation
41 I have possessed you with and think them strong ;
And more, more strong, when lesser is my fear,
43 I shall indue you with. Meantime but ask
What you would have reformed that is not well,
And well shall you perceive how willingly
I will both hear and grant you your requests.

PEMBROKE
Then I, as one that am the tongue of these
48 To sound the purposes of all their hearts,
Both for myself and them – but, chief of all,
50 Your safety, for the which myself and them
51 Bend their best studies – heartily request
52 Th' enfranchisement of Arthur, whose restraint
Doth move the murmuring lips of discontent
To break into this dangerous argument :
55 If what in rest you have in right you hold,
Why then your fears, which, as they say, attend
57 The steps of wrong, should move you to mew up
Your tender kinsman, and to choke his days
With barbarous ignorance and deny his youth
60 The rich advantage of good exercise.
61 That the time's enemies may not have this
62 To grace occasions, let it be our suit
That you have bid us ask, his liberty,
64 Which for our goods we do no further ask
65 Than whereupon our weal, on you depending,
Counts it your weal he have his liberty.
    Enter Hubert.

KING JOHN
Let it be so. I do commit his youth
To your direction. Hubert, what news with you ?
    [Takes him apart.]

PEMBROKE
This is the man should do the bloody deed ;
He showed his warrant to a friend of mine.
71 The image of a wicked heinous fault
72 Lives in his eye. That close aspect of his
Does show the mood of a much troubled breast,
And I do fearfully believe 'tis done,
75 What we so feared he had a charge to do.

SALISBURY
The color of the king doth come and go
Between his purpose and his conscience,
78 Like heralds 'twixt two dreadful battles set.
79 His passion is so ripe it needs must break.

PEMBROKE
And when it breaks, I fear will issue thence
81 The foul corruption of a sweet child's death.

KING JOHN
We cannot hold mortality's strong hand.
Good lords, although my will to give is living,

The suit which you demand is gone and dead.
He tells us Arthur is deceased to-night.

SALISBURY
Indeed we feared his sickness was past cure.

PEMBROKE
Indeed we heard how near his death he was,
Before the child himself felt he was sick.
This must be answered either here or hence.   89

KING JOHN
Why do you bend such solemn brows on me ?   90
Think you I bear the shears of destiny ?   91
Have I commandment on the pulse of life ?

SALISBURY
It is apparent foul play, and 'tis shame
That greatness should so grossly offer it.   94
So thrive it in your game ! And so, farewell.   95

PEMBROKE
Stay yet, Lord Salisbury. I'll go with thee
And find th' inheritance of this poor child,
His little kingdom of a forcèd grave.   98
That blood which owed the breadth of all this isle,   99
Three foot of it doth hold – bad world the while !   100
This must not be thus borne. This will break out   101
To all our sorrows, and ere long, I doubt.   102
    Exeunt [Lords].

KING JOHN
They burn in indignation. I repent.
    Enter Messenger.
There is no sure foundation set on blood,
No certain life achieved by others' death.
A fearful eye thou hast. Where is that blood   106
That I have seen inhabit in those cheeks ?
So foul a sky clears not without a storm.
Pour down thy weather. How goes all in France ?   109

MESSENGER
From France to England. Never such a power
For any foreign preparation   111
Was levied in the body of a land.
The copy of your speed is learned by them,   113
For when you should be told they do prepare,
The tidings comes that they are all arrived.   115

KING JOHN
O, where hath our intelligence been drunk ?   116
Where hath it slept ? Where is my mother's care,
That such an army could be drawn in France,   118

32 *breach* hole in a garment   33 *fault* defect   36 *breathed* spoke   37 *overbear* veto by superior power   38–39 *Since . . . will* since our wishes can never run counter to your desires   41 *possessed you with* informed you of   43 *indue* furnish   48 *sound the purposes* express the proposals   50 *them* they   51 *Bend their best studies* direct their most diligent efforts   52 *enfranchisement* release from prison   55 *If . . . hold* if you hold rightfully what you possess peaceably   57 *mew up* shut up   60 *exercise* education of a gentleman   61 *time's enemies* those opposed to the present state of affairs   62 *grace occasions* make proper and acceptable their opportunities to attack   64 *our goods* our own good   65 *whereupon* to the extent that ; *weal* welfare   71 *image* reflection   72 *close aspect* secret expression   75 *charge* order   78 *battles* armies arranged for battle ; *set* assigned to perform duties   79 *break* burst open (like a boil)   81 *corruption* pus   89 *answered* accounted or atoned for ; *here or hence* in this world or the next   90 *bend . . . brows* frown   91 *shears of destiny* instrument with which Atropos, one of the three Fates, cuts the thread of life   94 *That . . . offer it* that a king should act so outrageously   95 *So . . . game* may you suffer accordingly   98 *forcèd* imposed by violence   99 *blood* life ; *owed* owned   100 *the while* where such things can happen   101 *borne* tolerated   102 *doubt* fear   106 *fearful* full of fear   109 *weather* tempest   111 *preparation* expedition   113 *copy* example ; *learned* imitated   115 *arrived* landed   116 *intelligence* spy system   118 *drawn* mustered

And she not hear of it?

119 MESSENGER   My liege, her ear
Is stopped with dust. The first of April died
Your noble mother; and, as I hear, my lord,
The Lady Constance in a frenzy died
Three days before. But this from rumor's tongue
124 I idly heard; if true or false I know not.

KING JOHN
125 Withhold thy speed, dreadful occasion!
O, make a league with me, till I have pleased
My discontented peers. What! Mother dead!
128 How wildly then walks my estate in France!
129 Under whose conduct came those powers of France
That thou for truth giv'st out are landed here?

MESSENGER
Under the Dauphin.

KING JOHN   Thou hast made me giddy
With these ill tidings.
Enter Bastard and Peter of Pomfret.
       Now, what says the world
To your proceedings? Do not seek to stuff
My head with more ill news, for it is full.

BASTARD
But if you be afeard to hear the worst,
Then let the worst unheard fall on your head.

KING JOHN
137 Bear with me, cousin, for I was amazed
Under the tide; but now I breathe again
139 Aloft the flood and can give audience
To any tongue, speak it of what it will.

BASTARD
141 How I have sped among the clergymen
The sums I have collected shall express.
But as I travelled hither through the land,
144 I find the people strangely fantasied,
Possessed with rumors, full of idle dreams,
Not knowing what they fear, but full of fear.
And here's a prophet that I brought with me
148 From forth the streets of Pomfret, whom I found
With many hundreds treading on his heels,
To whom he sung, in rude harsh-sounding rimes,
That ere the next Ascension-day at noon,
Your highness should deliver up your crown.

KING JOHN
153 Thou idle dreamer, wherefore didst thou so?

PETER
Foreknowing that the truth will fall out so.

KING JOHN
Hubert, away with him; imprison him,
And on that day at noon, whereon he says

I shall yield up my crown, let him be hanged.
Deliver him to safety and return,   158
For I must use the.   *[Exit Hubert, with Peter.]*
       O my gentle cousin,   159
Hear'st thou the news abroad, who are arrived?

BASTARD
The French, my lord. Men's mouths are full of it.
Besides, I met Lord Bigot and Lord Salisbury,
With eyes as red as new-enkindled fire,
And others more, going to seek the grave
Of Arthur, whom they say is killed to-night
On your suggèstion.

KING JOHN   Gentle kinsman, go,
And thrust thyself into their companies.   167
I have a way to win their loves again.
Bring them before me.

BASTARD   I will seek them out.

KING JOHN
Nay, but make haste, the better foot before.
O, let me have no subject enemies,
When adverse foreigners affright my towns   172
With dreadful pomp of stout invasion.   173
Be Mercury, set feathers to thy heels,   174
And fly like thought from them to me again.

BASTARD
The spirit of the time shall teach me speed.   *Exit.*

KING JOHN
Spoke like a sprightful noble gentleman.   177
Go after him, for he perhaps shall need
Some messenger betwixt me and the peers;
And be thou he.

MESSENGER   With all my heart, my liege.   *[Exit.]*

KING JOHN
My mother dead!
Enter Hubert.

HUBERT
My lord, they say five moons were seen to-night –   182
Four fixèd, and the fifth did whirl about
The other four in wondrous motion.

KING JOHN
Five moons!

HUBERT   Old men and beldams in the streets   185
Do prophesy upon it dangerously.   186
Young Arthur's death is common in their mouths,
And when they talk of him, they shake their heads
And whisper one another in the ear;
And he that speaks doth gripe the hearer's wrist,
Whilst he that hears makes fearful action,   191
With wrinkled brows, with nods, with rolling eyes.
I saw a smith stand with his hammer, thus,
The whilst his iron did on the anvil cool,
With open mouth swallowing a tailor's news;
Who, with his shears and measure in his hand,
Standing on slippers, which his nimble haste
Had falsely thrust upon contrary feet,   198
Told of a many thousand warlike French,
That were embattailèd and ranked in Kent.   200
Another lean unwashed artificer
Cuts off his tale and talks of Arthur's death.

KING JOHN
Why seek'st thou to possess me with these fears?
Why urgest thou so oft young Arthur's death?
Thy hand hath murdered him. I had a mighty cause
To wish him dead, but thou hadst none to kill him.

119–23 *her ear . . . before* (Queen Elinor actually died on April 1, 1204, but how Shakespeare could have gotten the day and month exactly right remains a mystery, for this was not recorded in any Elizabethan chronicle. Constance had died three years before, in 1201. Shakespeare compresses time.)   124 *idly* without paying full attention   125 *occasion* course of events   128 *walks* proceeds; *estate* power   129 *conduct* leadership   137 *amazed* bewildered   139 *Aloft* above   141 *sped* succeeded   144 *strangely fantasied* full of strange notions   148 *Pomfret* Pontefract in Yorkshire   153 *idle* foolish   158 *safety* safekeeping   159 *gentle* noble   167 *thrust . . . companies* associate with them   172 *adverse* hostile   173 *stout* bold   174 *Mercury* the messenger of the gods, who wore winged sandals   177 *sprightful* full of spirit   182 *five moons* (a type of unnatural phenomenon believed to herald disaster to a kingdom)   185 *beldams* hags   186 *prophesy upon it* attempt to explain the unnatural phenomenon   191 *action* gesticulation   198 *contrary* wrong   200 *embattailèd and ranked* ready for battle and arrayed in proper order

HUBERT

207 No had, my lord ? Why, did you not provoke me ?

KING JOHN

208 It is the curse of kings to be attended
209 By slaves that take their humors for a warrant
210 To break within the bloody house of life,
211 And on the winking of authority
212 To understand a law, to know the meaning
     Of dangerous majesty, when, perchance, it frowns
214 More upon humor than advised respect.

HUBERT

     Here is your hand and seal for what I did.

KING JOHN

216 O, when the last accompt 'twixt heaven and earth
     Is to be made, then shall this hand and seal
     Witness against us to damnation !
     How oft the sight of means to do ill deeds
     Makes deeds ill done ! Hadst not thou been by,
     A fellow by the hand of nature marked,
222 Quoted and signed to do a deed of shame,
     This murder had not come into my mind ;
224 But taking note of thy abhorred aspect,
     Finding thee fit for bloody villainy,
226 Apt, liable to be employed in danger,
227 I faintly broke with thee of Arthur's death ;
     And thou, to be endearèd to a king,
229 Made it no conscience to destroy a prince.

HUBERT

     My lord –

KING JOHN

     Hadst thou but shook thy head or made a pause
232 When I spake darkly what I purposèd,
     Or turned an eye of doubt upon my face,
234 As bid me tell my tale in express words,
     Deep shame had struck me dumb, made me break off,
     And those thy fears might have wrought fears in me.
     But thou didst understand me by my signs
     And didst in signs again parley with sin ;
     Yea, without stop, didst let thy heart consent,
     And consequently thy rude hand to act
     The deed which both our tongues held vile to name.
     Out of my sight, and never see me more !
243 My nobles leave me, and my state is braved,
     Even at my gates, with ranks of foreign powers.
245 Nay, in the body of this fleshly land,
246 This kingdom, this confine of blood and breath,
247 Hostility and civil tumult reigns
     Between my conscience and my cousin's death.

HUBERT

     Arm you against your other enemies ;
     I'll make a peace between your soul and you.
     Young Arthur is alive. This hand of mine
252 Is yet a maiden and an innocent hand,
     Not painted with the crimson spots of blood.
     Within this bosom never entered yet
255 The dreadful motion of a murderous thought,
256 And you have slandered nature in my form,
     Which, howsoever rude exteriorly,
     Is yet the cover of a fairer mind
     Than to be butcher of an innocent child.

KING JOHN

     Doth Arthur live ? O, haste thee to the peers !
261 Throw this report on their incensèd rage,
     And make them tame to their obedience.

     Forgive the comment that my passion made
     Upon thy feature, for my rage was blind, 264
     And foul imaginary eyes of blood 265
     Presented thee more hideous than thou art.
     O, answer not, but to my closet bring 267
     The angry lords with all expedient haste.
     I conjure thee but slowly ; run more fast.   *Exeunt.* 269

*

     Enter Arthur, on the walls.   IV, iii

ARTHUR

     The wall is high, and yet will I leap down.
     Good ground, be pitiful and hurt me not !
     There's few or none do know me ; if they did,
     This ship-boy's semblance hath disguised me quite. 4
     I am afraid, and yet I'll venture it.
     If I get down, and do not break my limbs,
     I'll find a thousand shifts to get away. 7
     As good to die and go, as die and stay.
     [Leaps down.]
     O me ! My uncle's spirit is in these stones !
     Heaven take my soul, and England keep my bones ! *Dies.*
     Enter Pembroke, Salisbury, and Bigot.

SALISBURY

     Lords, I will meet him at Saint Edmundsbury. 11
     It is our safety, and we must embrace 12
     This gentle offer of the perilous time.

PEMBROKE

     Who brought that letter from the cardinal ?

SALISBURY

     The Count Melun, a noble lord of France,
     Whose private with me of the Dauphin's love 16
     Is much more general than these lines import. 17

BIGOT

     To-morrow morning let us meet him then.

SALISBURY

     Or rather then set forward, for 'twill be
     Two long days' journey, lords, or ere we meet. 20
     Enter Bastard.

BASTARD

     Once more to-day well met, distempered lords ! 21
     The king by me requests your presence straight. 22

SALISBURY

     The king hath dispossessed himself of us.
     We will not line his thin bestainèd cloak

---

207 *No had* had I not; *provoke* incite **208** *attended* served **209** *humors* whims **210** *bloody house of life* human body, containing blood **211** *winking of authority* failure of the king to enforce the law **212** *understand* infer **214** *upon humor* because of a whim; *advised respect* carefully considered decision **216** *accompt* account, judgment **222** *Quoted and signed* especially noted and marked out **224** *abhorred aspect* horrible appearance **226** *liable* suitable **227** *faintly broke with* hesitatingly confided in **229** *conscience* matter of conscience **232** *darkly* vaguely **234** *As* as if to; *in express words* clearly **243** *braved* defied **245** *fleshly land* his human body (conceived of as a little world paralleling the physical universe in its composition) **246** *confine* territory bound by frontiers **247** *civil tumult* internal war **252** *maiden* bloodless **255** *motion* impulse **256** *form* outward appearance **261** *Throw* i.e. as water, to quench the fire of rage **264** *feature* appearance **265** *imaginary eyes of blood* i.e. Hubert's eyes, which in John's imagination seemed full of blood **267** *closet* private room **269** *conjure* solemnly urge

IV, iii Outside the wall of an English castle **4** *semblance* disguise **7** *shifts* stratagems **11** *him* i.e. the Dauphin **12** *embrace* welcome **16** *private* private communication; *love* friendship **17** *general* comprehensive **20** *or ere* before **21** *distempered* disgruntled **22** *straight* at once

With our pure honors, nor attend the foot
That leaves the print of blood where'er it walks.
Return and tell him so. We know the worst.

BASTARD
Whate'er you think, good words, I think, were best.

SALISBURY
29 Our griefs, and not our manners, reason now.

BASTARD
But there is little reason in your grief;
Therefore 'twere reason you had manners now.

PEMBROKE
Sir, sir, impatience hath his privilege.

BASTARD
'Tis true, to hurt his master, no man else.

SALISBURY
This is the prison. [Sees Arthur.] What is he lies here?

PEMBROKE
O death, made proud with pure and princely beauty!
The earth had not a hole to hide this deed.

SALISBURY
Murder, as hating what himself hath done,
Doth lay it open to urge on revenge.

BIGOT
Or when he doomed this beauty to a grave,
40 Found it too precious princely for a grave.

SALISBURY
Sir Richard, what think you? Have you beheld,
Or have you read or heard, or could you think,
Or do you almost think, although you see,
44 That you do see? Could thought, without this object,
Form such another? This is the very top,
The height, the crest, or crest unto the crest,
Of murder's arms. This is the bloodiest shame,
The wildest savagery, the vilest stroke,
49 That ever wall-eyed wrath or staring rage
50 Presented to the tears of soft remorse.

PEMBROKE
All murders past do stand excused in this.
52 And this, so sole and so unmatchable,
Shall give a holiness, a purity,
54 To the yet unbegotten sin of times,
And prove a deadly bloodshed but a jest,
56 Exampled by this heinous spectacle.

BASTARD
It is a damnèd and a bloody work,
58 The graceless action of a heavy hand,
If that it be the work of any hand.

SALISBURY
If that it be the work of any hand!
61 We had a kind of light what would ensue.
It is the shameful work of Hubert's hand,
63 The practice and the purpose of the king,

From whose obedience I forbid my soul,
Kneeling before this ruin of sweet life,
And breathing to his breathless excellence
The incense of a vow, a holy vow,
Never to taste the pleasures of the world,
Never to be infected with delight,   69
Nor conversant with ease and idleness,
Till I have set a glory to this hand,   71
By giving it the worship of revenge.   72

PEMBROKE, BIGOT
Our souls religiously confirm thy words.
          Enter Hubert.

HUBERT
Lords, I am hot with haste in seeking you.
Arthur doth live; the king hath sent for you.

SALISBURY
O, he is bold and blushes not at death.
Avaunt, thou hateful villain! Get thee gone!   77

HUBERT
I am no villain.

SALISBURY [drawing his sword] Must I rob the law?

BASTARD
Your sword is bright, sir; put it up again.

SALISBURY
Not till I sheathe it in a murderer's skin.

HUBERT
Stand back, Lord Salisbury, stand back, I say!
By heaven, I think my sword's as sharp as yours.
I would not have you, lord, forget yourself,
Nor tempt the danger of my true defense,   84
Lest I, by marking of your rage, forget   85
Your worth, your greatness, and nobility.

BIGOT
Out, dunghill! Dar'st thou brave a nobleman?   87

HUBERT
Not for my life, but yet I dare defend
My innocent life against an emperor.

SALISBURY
Thou art a murderer.

HUBERT   Do not prove me so.   90
Yet I am none. Whose tongue soe'er speaks false,
Not truly speaks; who speaks not truly, lies.

PEMBROKE
Cut him to pieces.

BASTARD   Keep the peace, I say.

SALISBURY
Stand by, or I shall gall you, Faulconbridge.   94

BASTARD
Thou wert better gall the devil, Salisbury.
If thou but frown on me, or stir thy foot,
Or teach thy hasty spleen to do me shame,   97
I'll strike thee dead. Put up thy sword betime,   98
Or I'll so maul you and your toasting-iron   99
That you shall think the devil is come from hell.

BIGOT
What wilt thou do, renownèd Faulconbridge?
Second a villain and a murderer?   102

HUBERT
Lord Bigot, I am none.

BIGOT   Who killed this prince?

HUBERT
'Tis not an hour since I left him well.
I honored him, I loved him, and will weep
My date of life out for his sweet life's loss.   106

29 *griefs* grievances; *reason* talk 40 *too . . . grave* (bodies of princes were entombed above ground) 44 *That* that which 49 *wall-eyed* with glaring eyes; *rage* madness 50 *remorse* pity 52 *sole* unique 54 *times* future ages 56 *Exampled by* compared with 58 *graceless* unholy; *heavy* wicked 61 *light* inkling 63 *practice* machination 69 *infected* diseased (delight under such circumstances is conceived of as a disease) 71 *this hand* i.e. either the dead Arthur's hand which Salisbury kisses, or his own hand raised in celebration of his vow 72 *worship* honor, dignity 77 *Avaunt* be gone 84 *true defense* (1) honest defense of my cause, (2) skilful use of my sword 85 *marking of* (1) observing, (2) striking a blow at 87 *brave* insult 90 *Do . . . so* i.e. by compelling me to kill you 94 *by* aside; *gall* injure 97 *spleen* wrath 98 *betime* at once 99 *toasting-iron* sword (a term of contempt) 102 *Second* support 106 *date* duration

SALISBURY
Trust not those cunning waters of his eyes,
For villainy is not without such rheum,
109   And he, long traded in it, makes it seem
Like rivers of remorse and innocency.
Away with me, all you whose souls abhor
112   Th' uncleanly savors of a slaughter-house,
For I am stifled with this smell of sin.

BIGOT
Away toward Bury, to the Dauphin there!

PEMBROKE
There tell the king he may inquire us out.   *Exeunt Lords.*

BASTARD
Here's a good world! Knew you of this fair work?
Beyond the infinite and boundless reach
Of mercy, if thou didst this deed of death,
Art thou damned, Hubert.

HUBERT   Do but hear me, sir.

BASTARD
Ha! I'll tell thee what.
121   Thou'rt damned as black – nay, nothing is so black.
Thou art more deep damned than Prince Lucifer.
There is not yet so ugly a fiend of hell
As thou shalt be, if thou didst kill this child.

HUBERT
Upon my soul –

BASTARD   If thou didst but consent
To this most cruel act, do but despair,
And if thou want'st a cord, the smallest thread
That ever spider twisted from her womb
129   Will serve to strangle thee; a rush will be a beam
To hang thee on. Or wouldst thou drown thyself,
Put but a little water in a spoon,
And it shall be as all the ocean,
Enough to stifle such a villain up.
I do suspect thee very grievously.

HUBERT
If I in act, consent, or sin of thought,
Be guilty of the stealing that sweet breath
137   Which was embounded in this beauteous clay,
Let hell want pains enough to torture me.
I left him well.

BASTARD   Go, bear him in thine arms.
140   I am amazed, methinks, and lose my way
Among the thorns and dangers of this world.
How easy dost thou take all England up!
From forth this morsel of dead royalty
The life, the right and truth of all this realm
Is fled to heaven, and England now is left
146   To tug and scamble and to part by th' teeth
147   The unowed interest of proud swelling state.
Now for the bare-picked bone of majesty
149   Doth doggèd war bristle his angry crest
And snarleth in the gentle eyes of peace.
151   Now powers from home and discontents at home
152   Meet in one line, and vast confusion waits,
As doth a raven on a sick-fallen beast,
154   The imminent decay of wrested pomp.
155   Now happy he whose cloak and ceinture can
Hold out this tempest. Bear away that child,
And follow me with speed. I'll to the king.
158   A thousand businesses are brief in hand,
And heaven itself doth frown upon the land.   *Exit.*

*

Enter King John and Pandulph, [with] Attendants.   V, i

KING JOHN
Thus have I yielded up into your hand
The circle of my glory.   2

PANDULPH *[giving King John the crown]* Take again
From this my hand, as holding of the Pope,
Your sovereign greatness and authority.

KING JOHN
Now keep your holy word. Go meet the French,
And from his holiness use all your power
To stop their marches 'fore we are enflamed.
Our discontented counties do revolt.   8
Our people quarrel with obedience,
Swearing allegiance and the love of soul   10
To stranger blood, to foreign royalty.
This inundation of mistempered humor   12
Rests by you only to be qualified.   13
Then pause not, for the present time's so sick,
That present med'cine must be ministered,   15
Or overthrow incurable ensues.   16

PANDULPH
It was my breath that blew this tempest up,
Upon your stubborn usage of the Pope,   18
But since you are a gentle convertite,   19
My tongue shall hush again this storm of war
And make fair weather in your blust'ring land.
On this Ascension-day, remember well,
Upon your oath of service to the Pope,
Go I to make the French lay down their arms.   *Exit.*

KING JOHN
Is this Ascension-day? Did not the prophet
Say that before Ascension-day at noon
My crown I should give off? Even so I have.   27
I did suppose it should be on constraint,
But, heaven be thanked, it is but voluntary.

Enter Bastard.

BASTARD
All Kent hath yielded; nothing there holds out
But Dover Castle. London hath received,
Like a kind host, the Dauphin and his powers.
Your nobles will not hear you, but are gone
To offer service to your enemy,
And wild amazement hurries up and down   35
The little number of your doubtful friends.   36

KING JOHN
Would not my lords return to me again
After they heard young Arthur was alive?

BASTARD
They found him dead and cast into the streets,
An empty casket, where the jewel of life
By some damned hand was robbed and ta'en away.

109 *long traded* experienced 112 *savors* odors 121 *black* (the traditional
color of the devil and of all damned souls) 129 *rush* slender reed 137
embounded . . . clay enclosed within this beautiful body 140 *amazed*
bewildered 146 *scamble* scramble 147 *unowed interest* disputed ownership 149 *dogged* (1) fierce, (2) like a dog 151 *from home* foreign; *discontents* rebels 152 *in one line* together 154 *wrested pomp* usurped kingship 155 *ceinture* belt 158 *brief in hand* calling for immediate attention
V, i The court of King John 2 *circle* crown 8 *counties* shires, or noblemen 10 *love of soul* deepest love, loyalty 12 *inundation . . . humor* overgrowth, because of disorder, of one of the four elements of the body (John
is drawing his metaphor from current medical terminology) 13 *Rests . . .
qualified* can be reduced to proper proportions only by you 15 *ministered*
administered 16 *overthrow* destruction 18 *Upon* because of 19 *convertite* convert 27 *give off* relinquish 35 *amazement* bewilderment 36
doubtful (1) frightened, (2) of questionable loyalty

KING JOHN
That villain Hubert told me he did live.

BASTARD
So, on my soul, he did, for aught he knew.
But wherefore do you droop? Why look you sad?
Be great in act, as you have been in thought.
Let not the world see fear and sad distrust
Govern the motion of a kingly eye.
48   Be stirring as the time; be fire with fire.
49   Threaten the threat'ner, and outface the brow
Of bragging horror. So shall inferior eyes,
That borrow their behaviors from the great,
Grow great by your example and put on
The dauntless spirit of resolution.
54   Away, and glister like the god of war
55   When he intendeth to become the field.
Show boldness and aspiring confidence.
What, shall they seek the lion in his den
And fright him there? And make him tremble there?
59   O, let it not be said! Forage, and run
To meet displeasure farther from the doors,
And grapple with him ere he come so nigh.

KING JOHN
The legate of the Pope hath been with me,
63   And I have made a happy peace with him,
And he hath promised to dismiss the powers
Led by the Dauphin.

BASTARD   O inglorious league!
66   Shall we, upon the footing of our land,
67   Send fair-play orders and make compromise,
68   Insinuation, parley, and base truce
69   To arms invasive? Shall a beardless boy,
70   A cockered silken wanton, brave our fields
71   And flesh his spirit in a warlike soil,
72   Mocking the air with colors idly spread,
73   And find no check? Let us, my liege, to arms!
Perchance the cardinal cannot make your peace;
Or if he do, let it at least be said
They saw we had a purpose of defense.

KING JOHN
Have thou the ordering of this present time.

BASTARD
Away then, with good courage! Yet, I know,
79   Our party may well meet a prouder foe.   *Exeunt.*

*

48 *stirring* energetic   49 *outface* stare down   54 *glister* shine in armor   55 *become* adorn   59 *Forage* seek out the enemy   63 *happy* favorable   66 *upon . . . land* standing on our native ground   67 *fair-play orders* chivalric stipulations   68 *Insinuation* self-ingratiation   69 *invasive* invading   70 *cockered* pampered; *wanton* spoilt child; *brave* (1) insult, (2) display his finery in   71 *flesh* initiate in bloodshed   72 *idly* carelessly   73 *check* resistance   79 *prouder* more powerful
V, ii The Dauphin's quarters at St Edmundsbury   3 *precedent* first draft of the treaty   4 *fair order* equitable conditions   10 *unurged* uncompelled   13 *plaster* dressing for a wound; *contemned* despised   14 *inveterate canker* chronic sore   16 *metal* sword   19 *Cries out upon* appeals to   21 *physic* cure   22 *deal* act   30 *spot* disgrace; *enforced* forced upon us   31 *grace* pay homage to   32 *unacquainted colors* foreign banners   33 *remove* move yourself, depart   34 *clippeth* embraces   35 *knowledge* awareness   38 *vein* (1) blood vessel, (2) mood   40 *temper* state of mind   41 *affections* emotions   44 *compulsion* what you were forced to do; *brave respect* courageous consideration of your true duty   45 *dew* i.e. tears   46 *progress* move slowly (like a king or queen in state; the metaphor emphasizes the nobility of Salisbury's tears)   53 *Figured* decorated   56 *Commend* leave   59 *Full . . . blood* full of human feeling

Enter (in arms) [Lewis, the] Dauphin, Salisbury,   V, ii
Melun, Pembroke, Bigot, Soldiers.

LEWIS
My Lord Melun, let this be copied out,
And keep it safe for our remembrance.
Return the precedent to those lords again,   3
That, having our fair order written down,   4
Both they and we, perusing o'er these notes,
May know wherefore we took the sacrament,
And keep our faiths firm and inviolable.

SALISBURY
Upon our sides it never shall be broken.
And, noble Dauphin, albeit we swear
A voluntary zeal and an unurged faith   10
To your proceedings, yet believe me, prince,
I am not glad that such a sore of time
Should seek a plaster by contemned revolt,   13
And heal the inveterate canker of one wound   14
By making many. O, it grieves my soul
That I must draw this metal from my side   16
To be a widow-maker! O, and there
Where honorable rescue and defense
Cries out upon the name of Salisbury.   19
But such is the infection of the time
That, for the health and physic of our right,   21
We cannot deal but with the very hand   22
Of stern injustice and confusèd wrong.
And is't not pity, O my grievèd friends,
That we, the sons and children of this isle,
Were born to see so sad an hour as this,
Wherein we step after a stranger, march
Upon her gentle bosom, and fill up
Her enemies' ranks – I must withdraw and weep
Upon the spot of this enforcèd cause –   30
To grace the gentry of a land remote,   31
And follow unacquainted colors here?   32
What, here? O nation, that thou couldst remove!   33
That Neptune's arms, who clippeth thee about,   34
Would bear thee from the knowledge of thyself,   35
And grapple thee unto a pagan shore,
Where these two Christian armies might combine
The blood of malice in a vein of league,   38
And not to spend it so unneighborly!

LEWIS
A noble temper dost thou show in this,   40
And great affections wrestling in thy bosom   41
Doth make an earthquake of nobility.
O, what a noble combat hast thou fought
Between compulsion and a brave respect!   44
Let me wipe off this honorable dew,   45
That silverly doth progress on thy cheeks.   46
My heart hath melted at a lady's tears,
Being an ordinary inundation,
But this effusion of such manly drops,
This shower, blown up by tempest of the soul,
Startles mine eyes, and makes me more amazed
Than had I seen the vaulty top of heaven
Figured quite o'er with burning meteors.   53
Lift up thy brow, renownèd Salisbury,
And with a great heart heave away this storm.
Commend these waters to those baby eyes   56
That never saw the giant world enraged,
Nor met with fortune other than at feasts,
Full warm of blood, of mirth, of gossiping.   59

Come, come ; for thou shalt thrust thy hand as deep
Into the purse of rich prosperity
As Lewis himself. So, nobles, shall you all,
That knit your sinews to the strength of mine.
    Enter Pandulph.
64 And even there, methinks, an angel spake.
Look, where the holy legate comes apace,
To give us warrant from the hand of heaven,
67 And on our actions set the name of right
With holy breath.

PANDULPH   Hail, noble prince of France !
The next is this : King John hath reconciled
70 Himself to Rome ; his spirit is come in
That so stood out against the holy church,
The great metropolis and see of Rome.
Therefore thy threat'ning colors now wind up,
And tame the savage spirit of wild war,
That, like a lion fostered up at hand,
It may lie gently at the foot of peace,
And be no further harmful than in show.

LEWIS
78 Your grace shall pardon me ; I will not back.
79 I am too high-born to be propertied,
80 To be a secondary at control,
Or useful serving-man and instrument
To any sovereign state throughout the world.
Your breath first kindled the dead coal of wars
Between this chastised kingdom and myself,
85 And brought in matter that should feed this fire ;
And now 'tis far too huge to be blown out
With that same weak wind which enkindled it.
You taught me how to know the face of right,
89 Acquainted me with interest to this land,
Yea, thrust this enterprise into my heart ;
And come ye now to tell me John hath made
His peace with Rome ? What is that peace to me ?
I, by the honor of my marriage-bed,
After young Arthur, claim this land for mine,
And, now it is half-conquered, must I back
Because that John hath made his peace with Rome ?
Am I Rome's slave ? What penny hath Rome borne,
What men provided, what munition sent,
99 To underprop this action ? Is't not I
100 That undergo this charge ? Who else but I,
101 And such as to my claim are liable,
Sweat in this business and maintain this war ?
Have I not heard these islanders shout out,
104 *Vive le roi !* as I have banked their towns ?
Have I not here the best cards for the game
To win this easy match played for a crown ?
107 And shall I now give o'er the yielded set ?
No, no, on my soul, it never shall be said.

PANDULPH
You look but on the outside of this work.

LEWIS
Outside or inside, I will not return
Till my attempt so much be glorified
As to my ample hope was promisèd
113 Before I drew this gallant head of war,
114 And culled these fiery spirits from the world,
115 To outlook conquest and to win renown
Even in the jaws of danger and of death.
    [Trumpet sounds.]
117 What lusty trumpet thus doth summon us ?

Enter Bastard.
BASTARD
According to the fair play of the world,   118
Let me have audience ; I am sent to speak.   119
My holy Lord of Milan, from the king
I come, to learn how you have dealt for him,
And, as you answer, I do know the scope   122
And warrant limited unto my tongue.   123
PANDULPH
The Dauphin is too wilful-opposite,   124
And will not temporize with my entreaties.   125
He flatly says he'll not lay down his arms.
BASTARD
By all the blood that ever fury breathed,
The youth says well. Now hear our English king,
For thus his royalty doth speak in me.
He is prepared, and reason too he should.
This apish and unmannerly approach,   131
This harnessed masque and unadvisèd revel,   132
This unhaired sauciness and boyish troops,   133
The king doth smile at, and is well prepared
To whip this dwarfish war, these pigmy arms,
From out the circle of his territories.   136
That hand which had the strength, even at your door,
To cudgel you and make you take the hatch,   138
To dive, like buckets, in concealèd wells,
To crouch in litter of your stable planks,   140
To lie like pawns locked up in chests and trunks,   141
To hug with swine, to seek sweet safety out
In vaults and prisons, and to thrill and shake
Even at the crying of your nation's crow,   144
Thinking this voice an armèd Englishman –
Shall that victorious hand be feebled here
That in your chambers gave you chastisement ?
No ! Know the gallant monarch is in arms,
And like an eagle o'er his aery towers,   149
To souse annoyance that comes near his nest.   150
And you degenerate, you ingrate revolts,   151
You bloody Neroes, ripping up the womb   152
Of your dear mother England, blush for shame ;
For your own ladies and pale-visaged maids
Like Amazons come tripping after drums,   155
Their thimbles into armèd gauntlets change,

---

64 *an angel spake* (has been variously explained : (1) a trumpet, like that of the angel announcing the last judgment, has just sounded, (2) Pandulph, the angel since he bears heaven's warrant, has just entered, (3) a pun on angel, a coin, with contemptuous reference to the Dauphin's mercenary motives)   67 *set* i.e. like a seal upon a warrant   70 *is come in* has submitted   78 *shall* must ; *back* retreat   79 *propertied* treated like property, made a tool of   80 *secondary at control* agent controlled by another   85 *matter* fuel   89 *interest to* claim in   99 *underprop* support   100 *charge* expense   101 *liable* subject   104 *banked* sailed by   107 *give o'er* abandon ; *yielded set* game already forfeited to me   113 *head* army   114 *culled* carefully selected   115 *outlook* stare down   117 *lusty* vigorous   118 *fair play* rules of chivalry   119 *to speak* i.e. rather than to fight   122 *as* according as ; *scope* latitude   123 *limited* appointed   124 *wilful-opposite* stubbornly hostile   125 *temporize* come to terms   131 *apish* fantastic   132 *harnessed* in armor ; *unadvised revel* thoughtless entertainment   133 *unhaired* beardless   136 *circle* compass   138 *take the hatch* leap over a half door or stile (like beaten dogs fleeing their masters)   140 *litter* bedding (for animals) ; *planks* floors   141 *pawns* articles in pawn   144 *your nation's crow* sound of the rooster, traditional symbol of France   149 *aery* eagle's nest ; *towers* soars   150 *souse* swoop down on (like a bird of prey) ; *annoyance* threat of danger   151 *ingrate revolts* ungrateful rebels   152 *Neroes* (the Roman emperor Nero was said to have ripped open his mother's womb after murdering her)   155 *Amazons* female warriors of Greek mythology

157   Their needles to lances, and their gentle hearts
158   To fierce and bloody inclination.
      LEWIS
159   There end thy brave, and turn thy face in peace.
      We grant thou canst outscold us. Fare thee well.
      We hold our time too precious to be spent
162   With such a brabbler.
      PANDULPH   Give me leave to speak.
      BASTARD
      No, I will speak.
163 LEWIS   We will attend to neither.
      Strike up the drums, and let the tongue of war
      Plead for our interest and our being here.
      BASTARD
      Indeed, your drums, being beaten, will cry out,
      And so shall you, being beaten. Do but start
      An echo with the clamor of thy drum,
169   And even at hand a drum is ready braced
      That shall reverberate all as loud as thine.
      Sound but another, and another shall
172   As loud as thine rattle the welkin's ear
      And mock the deep-mouthed thunder. For at hand –
174   Not trusting to this halting legate here,
      Whom he hath used rather for sport than need –
      Is warlike John; and in his forehead sits
177   A bare-ribbed death, whose office is this day
      To feast upon whole thousands of the French.
      LEWIS
      Strike up our drums to find this danger out.
      BASTARD
      And thou shalt find it, Dauphin, do not doubt.   *Exeunt.*

*

V, iii   *Alarums. Enter [King] John and Hubert.*
      KING JOHN
      How goes the day with us? O, tell me, Hubert.
      HUBERT
      Badly, I fear. How fares your majesty?
      KING JOHN
      This fever that hath troubled me so long
      Lies heavy on me. O, my heart is sick!
      Enter a Messenger.
      MESSENGER
      My lord, your valiant kinsman, Faulconbridge,
      Desires your majesty to leave the field
      And send him word by me which way you go.

KING JOHN
      Tell him, toward Swinstead, to the abbey there.
      MESSENGER
      Be of good comfort, for the great supply   9
      That was expected by the Dauphin here,
      Are wracked three nights ago on Goodwin sands.   11
      This news was brought to Richard but even now.
      The French fight coldly and retire themselves.   13
KING JOHN
      Ay me! This tyrant fever burns me up,   14
      And will not let me welcome this good news.
      Set on toward Swinstead. To my litter straight;
      Weakness possesseth me, and I am faint.   *Exeunt.*

*

      Enter Salisbury, Pembroke, and Bigot.   V, iv
      SALISBURY
      I did not think the king so stored with friends.   1
      PEMBROKE
      Up once again; put spirit in the French.
      If they miscarry we miscarry too.
      SALISBURY
      That misbegotten devil, Faulconbridge,
      In spite of spite, alone upholds the day.   5
      PEMBROKE
      They say King John, sore sick, hath left the field.
      Enter Melun wounded.
      MELUN
      Lead me to the revolts of England here.   7
      SALISBURY
      When we were happy we had other names.
      PEMBROKE
      It is the Count Melun.
      SALISBURY   Wounded to death.
      MELUN
      Fly, noble English; you are bought and sold.   10
      Unthread the rude eye of rebellion,   11
      And welcome home again discarded faith.
      Seek out King John and fall before his feet,
      For if the French be lords of this loud day,
      He means to recompense the pains you take   15
      By cutting off your heads. Thus hath he sworn,
      And I with him, and many moe with me,   17
      Upon the altar at Saint Edmundsbury,
      Even on that altar where we swore to you
      Dear amity and everlasting love.
      SALISBURY
      May this be possible? May this be true?
      MELUN
      Have I not hideous death within my view,
      Retaining but a quantity of life,   23
      Which bleeds away, even as a form of wax   24
      Resolveth from his figure 'gainst the fire?   25
      What in the world should make me now deceive,
      Since I must lose the use of all deceit?   27
      Why should I then be false, since it is true
      That I must die here and live hence by truth?   29
      I say again, if Lewis do win the day,
      He is forsworn if e'er those eyes of yours   31
      Behold another day break in the east.
      But even this night, whose black contagious breath   33
      Already smokes about the burning crest   34
      Of the old, feeble, and day-wearied sun,

---

157 *needles* (monosyllable; in folio, 'Needl's')   158 *inclination* (1) disposition, (2) the slanting position of a knight charging with a lance (a quibble)   159 *brave* defiant boast   162 *brabbler* braggart   163 *attend* listen   169 *braced* with tightened skin (ready for playing)   172 *welkin's* sky's   174 *halting* wavering, ineffectual   177 *bare-ribbed death* i.e. death conceived of as a skeleton; *office* function
V, iii The field of battle   9 *supply* reinforcements   11 *wracked* shipwrecked   13 *coldly* without enthusiasm   14 *tyrant* merciless
V, iv Open place near the field of battle   1 *stored* provided   5 *In spite of spite* despite anything we can do   7 *revolts* rebels   10 *bought and sold* betrayed   11 *Unthread . . . eye* retrace your steps (as a thread is withdrawn from the needle's eye)   15 *He* i.e. the Dauphin   17 *moe* more   23 *quantity* small amount   24–25 *as a form . . . fire* (witches were said to destroy their enemies by melting waxen images of them before a fire)   25 *Resolveth* dissolves; *his* figure its shape   27 *use* profit, advantage   29 *live hence by truth* i.e. he will live in heaven to the extent that he has been truthful on earth   31 *forsworn* perjured   33 *contagious* bearing disease   34 *smokes* grows misty (as evening approaches)

Even this ill night, your breathing shall expire,
37 Paying the fine of rated treachery
38 Even with a treacherous fine of all your lives,
If Lewis by your assistance win the day.
Commend me to one Hubert with your king.
41 The love of him, and this respect besides,
42 For that my grandsire was an Englishman,
Awakes my conscience to confess all this.
44 In lieu whereof, I pray you, bear me hence
45 From forth the noise and rumor of the field,
Where I may think the remnant of my thoughts
In peace, and part this body and my soul
With contemplation and devout desires.

SALISBURY
49 We do believe thee, and beshrew my soul
50 But I do love the favor and the form
Of this most fair occasion, by the which
52 We will untread the steps of damnèd flight,
53 And like a bated and retirèd flood,
54 Leaving our rankness and irregular course,
55 Stoop low within those bounds we have o'erlooked,
And calmly run on in obedience
Even to our ocean, to our great King John.
My arm shall give thee help to bear thee hence,
For I do see the cruel pangs of death
60 Right in thine eye. Away, my friends! New flight,
61 And happy newness, that intends old right.

Exeunt [leading off Melun].

*

V, v   *Enter [Lewis, the] Dauphin, and his train.*
LEWIS
The sun of heaven methought was loath to set,
2 But stayed and made the western welkin blush,
When English measure backward their own ground
4 In faint retire. O, bravely came we off,
When with a volley of our needless shot,
After such bloody toil, we bid good night
7 And wound our tott'ring colors clearly up,
Last in the field, and almost lords of it!

Enter a Messenger.
MESSENGER
Where is my prince, the Dauphin?
LEWIS   Here. What news?
MESSENGER
The Count Melun is slain. The English lords,
11 By his persuasion, are again fall'n off,
12 And your supply, which you have wished so long,
Are cast away and sunk on Goodwin sands.
LEWIS
14 Ah, foul, shrewd news! Beshrew thy very heart!
I did not think to be so sad to-night
As this hath made me. Who was he that said
King John did fly an hour or two before
18 The stumbling night did part our weary powers?
MESSENGER
Whoever spoke it, it is true, my lord.
LEWIS
20 Well, keep good quarter and good care to-night.
The day shall not be up so soon as I
22 To try the fair adventure of to-morrow.   *Exeunt.*

*

Enter Bastard and Hubert, severally.   V, vi
HUBERT
Who's there? Speak, ho! Speak quickly, or I shoot.
BASTARD
A friend. What art thou?
HUBERT   Of the part of England.   2
BASTARD
Whither dost thou go?
HUBERT
What's that to thee? Why may not I demand
Of thine affairs as well as thou of mine?
BASTARD
Hubert, I think?
HUBERT   Thou hast a perfect thought.   6
I will upon all hazards well believe
Thou art my friend, that know'st my tongue so well.
Who art thou?
BASTARD   Who thou wilt; and if thou please,
Thou mayst befriend me so much as to think
I come one way of the Plantagenets.
HUBERT
Unkind remembrance! Thou and eyeless night   12
Have done me shame. Brave soldier, pardon me,   13
That any accent breaking from thy tongue   14
Should scape the true acquaintance of mine ear.
BASTARD
Come, come! Sans compliment, what news abroad?   16
HUBERT
Why, here walk I in the black brow of night
To find you out.
BASTARD   Brief, then; and what's the news?
HUBERT
O, my sweet sir, news fitting to the night,
Black, fearful, comfortless, and horrible.
BASTARD
Show me the very wound of this ill news.
I am no woman; I'll not swound at it.   22
HUBERT
The king, I fear, is poisoned by a monk.
I left him almost speechless and broke out   24
To acquaint you with this evil, that you might
The better arm you to the sudden time   26
Than if you had at leisure known of this.   27
BASTARD
How did he take it? Who did taste to him?   28
HUBERT
A monk, I tell you, a resolvèd villain,   29

37 *fine* penalty; *rated* (1) exposed at its true value, (2) rebuked, punished 38 *fine* end (note quibble) 41 *respect* consideration 42 *For that* because 44 *In lieu whereof* in payment for which 45 *rumor* noise 49 *beshrew* a curse upon 50 *favor and the form* outward appearance 52 *untread* retrace 53 *bated* abated 54 *rankness* overgrowth 55 *o'erlooked* overflowed 60 *Right* clearly 61 *happy newness* propitious change
V, v The Dauphin's quarters 2 *welkin* sky 4 *faint retire* timid retreat; *bravely* excellently; *came we off* we retired from battle 7 *tott'ring* (1) wavering, (2) in tatters (rags); *colors* banners; *clearly* neatly, without interference from the enemy 11 *are again fall'n off* have again broken faith 12 *supply* reinforcements 14 *shrewd* grievous, bitter; *Beshrew* curse 18 *stumbling* causing to stumble 20 *quarter* watch 22 *fair adventure* good fortune
V, vi An open place near Swinstead Abbey 2 *Of the part* on the side 6 *perfect* correct 12 *remembrance* memory; *eyeless* i.e. black 13 *done me shame* disgraced me (by causing my discourteous failure to recognize a friend) 14 *accent* speech 16 *Sans compliment* without formal speech 22 *swound* faint 24 *broke out* rushed away 26 *arm . . . time* prepare yourself for the emergency 27 *at leisure* after delay 28 *taste to* serve as food taster for 29 *resolvèd* determined

Whose bowels suddenly burst out. The king
31   Yet speaks and peradventure may recover.

BASTARD
Whom didst thou leave to tend his majesty?

HUBERT
Why, know you not? The lords are all come back,
And brought Prince Henry in their company,
At whose request the king hath pardoned them,
And they are all about his majesty.

BASTARD
Withhold thine indignation, mighty heaven,
38   And tempt us not to bear above our power!
39   I'll tell thee, Hubert, half my power this night,
40   Passing these flats, are taken by the tide.
These Lincoln Washes have devourèd them.
42   Myself, well mounted, hardly have escaped.
Away before! Conduct me to the king;
44   I doubt he will be dead or ere I come.   *Exeunt.*

*

V, vii   *Enter Prince Henry, Salisbury, and Bigot.*
PRINCE HENRY
It is too late. The life of all his blood
2   Is touched corruptibly, and his pure brain,
Which some suppose the soul's frail dwelling-house,
4   Doth, by the idle comments that it makes,
5   Foretell the ending of mortality.
          Enter Pembroke.
PEMBROKE
6   His highness yet doth speak, and holds belief
That, being brought into the open air,
It would allay the burning quality
9   Of that fell poison which assaileth him.
PRINCE HENRY
Let him be brought into the orchard here.
11   Doth he still rage?   *[Exit Bigot.]*
PEMBROKE   He is more patient
Than when you left him; even now he sung.
PRINCE HENRY
13   O, vanity of sickness! Fierce extremes
14   In their continuance will not feel themselves.
Death, having preyed upon the outward parts,
16   Leaves them invisible, and his siege is now

Against the mind, the which he pricks and wounds
With many legions of strange fantasies,   18
Which, in their throng and press to that last hold,   19
Confound themselves. 'Tis strange that death should   20
     sing.
I am the cygnet to this pale faint swan,   21
Who chants a doleful hymn to his own death,
And from the organ-pipe of frailty sings
His soul and body to their lasting rest.
SALISBURY
Be of good comfort, prince, for you are born
To set a form upon that indigest   26
Which he hath left so shapeless and so rude.
          [King] John brought in.
KING JOHN
Ay, marry, now my soul hath elbow-room.
It would not out at windows, nor at doors.
There is so hot a summer in my bosom
That all my bowels crumble up to dust.
I am a scribbled form, drawn with a pen
Upon a parchment, and against this fire
Do I shrink up.
PRINCE HENRY How fares your majesty?
KING JOHN
Poisoned – ill fare! Dead, forsook, cast off,   35
And none of you will bid the winter come
To thrust his icy fingers in my maw,   37
Nor let my kingdom's rivers take their course
Through my burned bosom, nor entreat the north
To make his bleak winds kiss my parchèd lips
And comfort me with cold. I do not ask you much.
I beg cold comfort; and you are so strait   42
And so ingrateful, you deny me that.
PRINCE HENRY
O, that there were some virtue in my tears   44
That might relieve you.
KING JOHN   The salt in them is hot.
Within me is a hell, and there the poison
Is as a fiend confined to tyrannize
On unreprievable condemnèd blood.   48
          Enter Bastard.
BASTARD
O, I am scalded with my violent motion   49
And spleen of speed to see your majesty.   50
KING JOHN
O cousin, thou art come to set mine eye!   51
The tackle of my heart is cracked and burnt,   52
And all the shrouds wherewith my life should sail   53
Are turnèd to one thread, one little hair.
My heart hath one poor string to stay it by,
Which holds but till thy news be utterèd,
And then all this thou seest is but a clod
And module of confounded royalty.   58
BASTARD
The Dauphin is preparing hitherward,
Where heaven he knows how we shall answer him,   60
For in a night the best part of my power,
As I upon advantage did remove,   62
Were in the Washes all unwarily   63
Devourèd by the unexpected flood.   64
          [The King dies.]
SALISBURY
You breathe these dead news in as dead an ear.   65
My liege! My lord! But now a king, now thus!

31 *peradventure* perhaps   38 *tempt . . . power* do not test us by making us
endure more than we are able to   39 *power* army   40 *flats* low lands near
the sea   42 *hardly* barely   44 *doubt* fear
V, vii The orchard of Swinstead Abbey   2 *touched corruptibly* infected so
as to cause corruption   4 *idle* foolish   5 *mortality* life   6 *yet* still   9
fell cruel   11 *rage* rave   13 *extremes* extremities   14 *In . . . themselves*
as they continue cease to be felt   16 *invisible* (modifies *Death*)   18 *fantasies* hallucinations   19 *throng and press* disordered rush; *hold* stronghold
(the mind)   20 *Confound themselves* destroy one another (i.e. his delirious
thoughts negate one another so that he is totally incoherent)   21 *cygnet*
young swan (the swan was said to sing only one song during his life, just
before his death)   26 *indigest* shapeless mass, state of confusion   35 *ill
fare* (1) ill lot, (2) bad food   37 *maw* throat   42 *strait* niggardly   44
virtue healing power   48 *unreprievable* beyond reprieve   49 *scalded*
heated   50 *spleen* eagerness   51 *set mine eye* i.e. close my eyes in death
52 *tackle* rigging of a ship   53 *shrouds* ropes supporting the mast of a ship
58 *module* mere image; *confounded* destroyed   60 *heaven he knows* only
God knows   62 *upon advantage* to take advantage of a favorable opportunity; *remove* change position   63 *unwarily* unexpectedly   64 *unexpected
flood* sudden flowing in of the tide   65 *dead news* (1) deadly news, (2) news
of death

PRINCE HENRY

Even so must I run on, and even so stop.

68 What surety of the world, what hope, what stay,

When this was now a king, and now is clay?

BASTARD

Art thou gone so? I do but stay behind

To do the office for thee of revenge,

And then my soul shall wait on thee to heaven,

73 As it on earth hath been thy servant still.

74 Now, now, you stars that move in your right spheres,

75 Where be your powers? Show now your mended faiths,

And instantly return with me again,

To push destruction and perpetual shame

Out of the weak door of our fainting land.

79 Straight let us seek, or straight we shall be sought.

The Dauphin rages at our very heels.

SALISBURY

It seems you know not, then, so much as we.

The Cardinal Pandulph is within at rest,

Who half an hour since came from the Dauphin,

And brings from him such offers of our peace

85 As we with honor and respect may take,

With purpose presently to leave this war.

BASTARD

He will the rather do it when he sees

88 Ourselves well sinewèd to our defense.

SALISBURY

Nay, 'tis in a manner done already;

90 For many carriages he hath dispatched

To the seaside, and put his cause and quarrel

To the disposing of the cardinal;

With whom yourself, myself, and other lords,

If you think meet, this afternoon will post

To consummate this business happily.

BASTARD

Let it be so. And you, my noble prince,

With other princes that may best be spared,

Shall wait upon your father's funeral.

PRINCE HENRY

At Worcester must his body be interred,

For so he willed it.

BASTARD   Thither shall it then.

And happily may your sweet self put on   101

The lineal state and glory of the land!   102

To whom, with all submission, on my knee,

I do bequeath my faithful services

And true subjection everlastingly.

SALISBURY

And the like tender of our love we make,   106

To rest without a spot for evermore.   107

PRINCE HENRY

I have a kind soul that would give you thanks,

And knows not how to do it but with tears.

BASTARD

O, let us pay the time but needful woe,   110

Since it hath been beforehand with our griefs.

This England never did, nor never shall,

Lie at the proud foot of a conqueror

But when it first did help to wound itself.

Now these her princes are come home again,

Come the three corners of the world in arms,   116

And we shall shock them. Nought shall make us rue   117

If England to itself do rest but true.   *Exeunt.*

---

68 *surety* certainty; *stay* support   73 *still* always   74 *stars . . . spheres* i.e. noblemen who have returned to their proper allegiance (revolving around the throne, as stars were believed in a harmonious cosmos to revolve around the earth)   75 *powers* armies; *mended faiths* restored loyalties   79 *Straight* immediately   85 *respect* self-respect   88 *sinewèd* strengthened   90 *carriages* vehicles   101 *happily* propitiously   102 *lineal state* kingship by right of birth   106 *tender* offer   107 *spot* blemish (of disloyalty)   110–11 *let . . . griefs* i.e. let us not weep more than necessary, since we have already paid the sad occasion enough of the grief due to it   116 *three corners* i.e. the rest of the world, England being the fourth corner   117 *shock* meet them with force

THE TRAGEDY OF
KING RICHARD THE SECOND

INTRODUCTION

The increasing interest of thoughtful modern readers in *The Tragedy of King Richard the Second* is probably due in part to its unique position in Shakespeare's artistic development. Symbolic of this position is the fact that it is the only one of his better plays to be written entirely in verse. It would, perhaps, be fanciful to conclude that this is because poetry here plays a more functional role than in any of his other dramas. Yet the coincidence is striking, for *Richard II* is the first play in which Shakespeare makes his central figure an introspective, imaginative, and eloquent man – in short, a poet. This is the first of his characters into which he could freely have poured certain aspects of his own character and experience.

Richard is a lover of music, of pageantry, of luxurious hospitality; he is mercurial; he is highly self-conscious; he has the feeling for situations, the instinct for self-dramatization, of a born actor. It has indeed been supposed that Shakespeare the actor wrote the part for himself. We can at least agree that Richard is a person with whom Shakespeare as fact and tradition reveal him could eagerly have identified in these respects. If so, this may account for the unusual length of the part, and for the impression recorded by critics as diverse in temper as Coleridge and Sir Edmund Chambers that Richard is drawn with a skill unequalled except perhaps in *King Lear*, "a work of art and of love." It is worth remembering also that when some five years later Shakespeare next turned to a story in which the central figure was a self-conscious, sensitive, imaginative, and eloquent young prince, the result was the longest of all Shakespearean roles and the most popular, Hamlet.

At all events, the king's poetic nature is all-important in the total effect of *Richard II*. The story is that of a youthful, thoughtless, extravagant, and willfully unjust king who is responsible for the murder of his good uncle, Thomas, Duke of Gloucester, and the confiscation of his cousin Bolingbroke's estates, but whose dethronement leads eventually to the long and bloody Wars of the Roses,* and who in his fall becomes a sympathetic figure – in the eyes of his French biographers, indeed, a martyr. This seemingly impossible transformation is effected by exhibiting in the first two acts Richard's weakness as a king, and progressively thereafter his charm as a man. And the essence of that charm is that he is a poet, a minor poet, to be sure, a self-conscious, artificial poet, overfond of words and of rhetorical devices, but enough of a poet to win our hearts and make us forget how richly he deserves to be deposed.

But Richard's is one of the kinds of poetry with which

* The subject of Shakespeare's earlier tetralogy, *1, 2,* and *3 Henry VI* and *Richard III*.

his creator was experimenting toward the end of 1595, when *Richard II* was written, and therein lies the significance of the play in Shakespeare's progress as an artist. No thoughtful reader of Shakespeare's early work can resist the impression that his natural bent was toward poetry, and that he learned the dramatist's trade, the constructing of a theatrically effective plot, slowly and with conscious effort. Pegasus was never allowed to run away with the team, for that would have courted failure in the theatre, but his irresponsibility is evident in the unconvincing lyricism of Tyrrel's report of the murderers in *Richard III*, IV, iii, or of Mercutio's speech about Queen Mab in *Romeo and Juliet*, I, iv, some forty lines of delightful fantasy which merely retard the plot. In the other plays of the so-called "lyrical group" written between 1593 and 1596, Shakespeare finds other important and legitimate uses for poetry in drama. But only *Richard II*, both protagonist and poet, allows his creator's winged horse full rein.

Thus with the economy of genius Shakespeare here solves two problems, one professional and the other personal, with a single stroke. Some of the satisfaction he must have felt is apparent in the profusion and splendor of the imagery in the play, in the intricate interweaving of image-patterns, and in the symmetry with which the images point up every stage in what Holinshed called God's "advancing" of Bolingbroke and "dejecting" of Richard. A good example is the emblematic transference of the sun from Richard (II, iv, 21; III, ii, 36 ff.; III, iii, 62 ff., 178 ff.) to Bolingbroke (IV, i, 260–62). Many other skeins of imagery may be traced through the play, such as the rise and fall of Fortune's buckets, the "theatre-like state," and the neglected or well-tended garden. But nothing is more delusory than the supposition that the poet deliberately planned these patterns; they illustrate the instinctive workings of his poetic imagination.

As implied above, *Richard II* is artistically akin to a cluster of plays which can be assigned with some confidence to the years 1593–96. It has much in common also (though less than the other plays of the "lyrical group" because of its paucity of love scenes) with his sonnets, many of which presumably belong to the same period, since we hear of them circulating "among his private friends" as early as 1598. These relationships, together with an admittedly equivocal reference to the private presentation of a "King Richard" in 1595, impel the majority of recent editors to assign the composition of the piece to the latter year. It came at a time when the aged Elizabeth I and her councillors were extremely sensitive to the possible political repercussions of stage plays. Consequently when it appeared in print in 1597 the actual dethronement (IV, i, 154–318) had been excised. It had almost certainly been included in the stage performances and may well have been banned by the censor of books for that very reason. It was not printed until 1608, when Elizabeth's successor, James I, was firmly seated on the English throne.

As for the queen's anxiety, the perspective of three and a half centuries makes clear that while, like every re-enactment of history, the play had political meaning, it can have had no political purpose, and that, in supposing it could be useful as propaganda, both her majesty's government and the opposition were deceived. It is a vivid, impartial re-creation of a political impasse which brought death to a tyrant, but to a usurper a troublesome reign, and to the realm eventually some thirty years of civil war. It *is* full of conflicting political ideas: the divine right of kings, the subject's duty of passive obedience, the dangers of irresponsible despotism, the complex qualities of an ideal ruler. But which of these ideas were Shakespeare's own is impossible to discern. On politics as on religion he preserves as always "the taciturnity of nature." What can be said of this aspect of *Richard II* is that here, as in all the histories, Shakespeare wrote as a true patriot and that England was the heroine. The continuing power of the play to interest audiences in England and elsewhere can come only from its universal human appeal as drama.

That *Richard II* was also planned as the first part of a great tetralogy completed in *1* and *2 Henry IV* and *Henry V*, is far from certain, although this view has been brilliantly maintained by recent scholars. Carlisle's prophecy (IV, i, 114–49, 322–23) does indeed foretell the woes to come in Henry VI and Richard III's time, while Richard himself (V, i, 57–65) predicts to one of the actual rebels the treacherous rebellion of the Percies in *1 Henry IV*:

> The time shall not be many hours of age
> More than it is, ere foul sin gathering head
> Shall break into corruption. Thou shalt think,
> Though he divide the realm and give thee half,
> It is too little, helping him to all.
> And he shall think that thou, which knowest the way
> To plant unrightful kings, wilt know again,
> Being ne'er so little urged another way,
> To pluck him headlong from the usurped throne.

Henry at the beginning of V, iii does foreshadow the character of Prince Hal in the next two histories as well as his transformation into the hero of *Henry V*. Many passages in the later three "parts" link them *retrospectively* with *Richard II*. But in the Hotspur of *Richard II* there is hardly any trace of the "gunpowder Percy" of *1 Henry IV*, and there is no hint anywhere of Falstaff. Highly qualified critics of the consecutive performance of the four pieces at Stratford in 1951 have commented that when played as a prologue to the tetralogy, *Richard II* becomes rather the rise of Bolingbroke than the tragedy of Richard, and such a reading is difficult to reconcile with the impression of Richard dwelt upon above. Perhaps the safest guess is that before writing *Richard II* the dramatist had in mind the whole framework of events as it was presented to him in his chronicle sources, but not the details of his characters and scenes. The four plays, though intricately and strongly connected, fall short of complete artistic unity.

The principal source of *Richard II* is the second edition (1587) of a popular compilation called *The Chronicles of England* by Raphael Holinshed, which provides the outlines of the events and characters. But there is evidence in both the plot and the dialogue that Shakespeare knew, and remembered striking details from, practically all the different versions of Richard's story available to him: the chronicles of Froissart and of Edward Hall; two or three French accounts of the deposition, favorable to Richard; the *Mirror for Magistrates*; the first four books of Samuel Daniel's poetical history of *The Civil Wars*; an earlier play, *Woodstock*, which deals with the murder of the Duke of Gloucester; and just possibly another earlier play on Richard II, of which however no record remains. It would be an obvious exaggeration to say that Shakespeare "did the research" on his subject with the thoroughness of a historian. He may, for example, have known *Woodstock* simply through having acted in it. But it is no less misleading to suppose that he was content with Holinshed's rather pedestrian narrative.

As usual, too, he altered history for dramatic effect, though in this instance without damage to the enduring truth of his picture. He also added brilliant improvisations not found in any of his sources: the conversation between Gaunt and the widowed Duchess of Gloucester (I, ii); Gaunt's deathbed speech and the conference of Northumberland, Ross, and Willoughby (II, i); the several appearances of the queen, especially in the Duke of York's garden at Langley (III, iv); the conception of Isabella as having the maturity and vitality of Richard's first queen, Anne of Bohemia, whereas she was in fact a child of eight when he married her; the deposition scene; the appearance of the Duchess of York to plead for her "son," Aumerle (he was actually her stepson); the presentation of Richard's coffin to Henry in the final scene. Unless the "old play" on Richard II should somewhere miraculously turn up, and prove to contain hints for all these alterations and additions, we must describe at least a quarter of the play as Shakespeare's invention.

The early stage history of *Richard II* is of unusual interest. Elizabeth herself exclaimed against it: "I am Richard II, know ye not that? . . . This tragedy was played forty times in open streets and houses." Even if we discount "forty" as a common round number, an angry exaggeration, or both, Dover Wilson's statement that the play "took London by storm" seems amply justified. Two new editions came out in a single year, 1598. In a poetical miscellany of 1600, more excerpts were included from *Richard II* than from any other drama. On Saturday, February 7, 1601, a performance by Shakespeare's company at the Globe was paid for by supporters of the Earl of Essex to stir up popular feeling in favor of his ill-starred attempt to seize the throne, and although the gentlemen who bespoke the performance were tried and punished, Shakespeare and his company apparently were not. On September 30, 1607, the piece was played by the crew of a ship en route to the West Indies. New editions were printed in 1608, 1615, 1623 (in the first folio), and 1634. In the summer of 1631 the Master of the Revels had £5 6s. 6d. from a benefit production at the Globe.

During the Restoration, the eighteenth, and the early nineteenth century at least six different stage adaptations of it were put on with some success in England and America. The chief Shakespearean actors of their respective centuries, Garrick (whose friend Dr Johnson disliked the play) and Irving (who planned a production but never put it on), are absent from the list of stars who have essayed the title role since 1700. But it has attracted such famous names as Macready, Edmund Kean, Wallack, Charles Kean, Junius Brutus Booth the elder, Edwin Booth, Benson, Granville-Barker, Beerbohm Tree, John Gielgud, Maurice Evans, Alec Guinness, and Michael Redgrave. In the twentieth-century American revival of 1937–38, directed by Miss Margaret Webster, Evans played it over three hundred times, and seemingly won for it some measure of continuing popularity on the stage and in television.

Curiously enough, considering its earlier and later success, until the third decade of the present century *Richard II* ranked well below several of Shakespeare's other histories – notably *1 Henry IV*, *Henry V*, and *Richard III* – in popularity on the stage. Critics have found it wanting in dramatic action, arresting characters (except Richard himself), and comic relief. But producers have been able to counterbalance these defects by spectacular staging of the pageantry of the tournament (I, iii) and – in an interpolated "episode" – of Richard's entry into London (V, ii); by expert playing of such scenes as the tearful interview of Gaunt and the Duchess of Gloucester (I, ii), the garden scene (III, iv), and Richard's farewell to his queen (V, i), which certainly lend variety of effect; and sometimes – though with questionable propriety – by portraying York throughout, and his duchess in V, ii, iii, as mildly humorous.

But on the stage, and even more surely for the reader, the play has its great moments. It is, in the words of Henry Morley, "full of passages that have floated out of their place in the drama to live in the minds of the people." Chief among these is John of Gaunt's apostrophe to England (II, i, 40 ff.), which even in American performances usually evokes a solid round of applause. And there are others: Saintsbury calls York's description of "our two cousins coming into London" (especially V, ii, 23–36) the most famous passage in the play; the pathos of Richard's soliloquy in prison (V, v, 1–66) has been highly praised, as have his monody on the divine right of kings (III, ii, 36–62) and that on the irony of kingship (III, ii, 144–70), the Bishop of Carlisle's prophecy (IV, i, 114–49), and Bolingbroke's forthright, vividly human rejection of the consolations of philosophy (I, iii, 294–303).

It would be a feeble actor who could not hold his audience, and an unimaginative reader who felt no thrill in the great moments of Richard's story: his passionate outbursts of hope and despair when he returns from Ireland, as Salisbury and then Scroop reluctantly tell of the disbanding of his Welsh army, the flocking of his subjects to Bolingbroke, and the deaths of his favorites; his cry as he descends to parley with the usurper, "Down, down I come, like glist'ring Phaethon"; above all, his tragic eloquence as he dramatizes his abdication before the Parliament which had so recently been his, and under the inscrutable eye of the "silent king."

University of Pennsylvania   MATTHEW W. BLACK

The present edition follows the text of the first quarto, 1597, which appears to have been printed from the author's draft. The abdication speeches, IV, i, 154–318, have been added from the text in the folio, 1623, which, though printed in the main from one of the later quartos of the play, was evidently corrected – especially in these speeches – by means of a playhouse prompt-copy. The speeches had first been printed in the fourth quarto, 1608, but with mislinings and omissions indicative of faulty copy. Nonetheless, many modern editions, including the present one, prefer some thirteen fourth-quarto readings. The quartos are not divided into acts and scenes. The act–scene division here supplied marginally follows the division in the folio except that V, iii is split into V, iii and iv, thus giving six scenes for this act instead of the five in the folio.

Below is a list of the substantive departures from the copy-texts, i.e. the folio of 1623 (F) for IV, i, 154–318, and the quarto of 1597 as press-corrected in all extant copies (Q). The adopted reading in italics with an indication of its source – usually the quartos of 1598 (Q2) and (Q3), of 1608 (Q4), of 1615 (Q5), and of 1634 (Q6), or the folios and early editors – is followed by the reading of the copy-texts in roman. Expansions of unmistakable abbreviations and corrections of obvious printing errors are not listed.

I, i, 118 *by my* (F) by (Q) 162 *Harry, when?* (Pope) Harry? when (Q) 178 *reputation. That* (F) Reputation that (Q)

I, ii, 47 *sit* (F) set (Q) 58 *it* (Q2) is (Q) 60 *begun* (Q2) begone (Q)

I, iii, 15 *thee* (Q2) the (Q) 33 *comest* (Q5) comes (Q) 43 *daring-hardy* (Theobald) daring, hardy, (Q) 58 *thee* (Q3) the (Q) 172 *then but* (F) but (Q) 180 *you owe* (F) y'owe (Q) 193 *far* (F2) fare (Q) 222 *night* (Q4) nightes (Q) 239 *had it* (Theobald) had't (Q) 289 *strewed* (Malone) strowd (Q) 308 *Where'er* (Q2) Where care (Q)

I, iv, 20 *cousin,* (F) Coosens (Q) 52 s.d. *Enter Bushy* (F) Enter Bushy with newes (Q) 53 *Bushy, what news* (F) omitted (Q)

II, i, 15 *life's* (Rowe) liues (Q) 18 *fond* (Collier conj.; Camb.) found (Q) 19 *metres* (Steevens conj.; Malone) meeters (Q) 48 *a moat* (Q4) moat (Q) 85 *No, misery* (Q3) No misery (Q) 102 *incagèd* (Dyce) inraged (Q) 113 *now, not* (Theobald) now not, not (Q) 124 *brother* (Q2) brothers (Q) 130 *precedent* (Pope) president (Q) 168 *my own* (all but Petworth copy of Q) his own (Petworth copy) 177 *the* (F) a (Q) 229 *Ere't* (F) Eart (Q) 257 *king's* (Q3) King (Q) 277 *Blanc* (Camb. ii) Blan (Q) 280 *The son and heir of the Earl of Arundel* (supplied by Halliwell; not in early texts) 284 *Coint* (Halliwell) Coines (Q) 294 *gilt* (F) guilt (Q)

II, ii, 16 *eye* (F) eyes (Q) 25 *More's* (F) more is (Q) 31 *though in* (Collier) though on (Q2) thought on (Q) 39 *known – what* (Capell) knowen what (Q) 53 *Henry* (Var. 1821) H. (Q) 112 *Th' one* (F) T one (Q) 129 *that's* (F) that is (Q) 148 *Bagot* (White) omitted (Q)

II, iii, 9 *Cotswold* (Hanmer) Cotshall (Q) 25 *Why,* (Q3) Why (Q) 30 *lordship* (Q2) Lo: (Q) 36 *Hereford, boy?* (Q3) Herefords boy. (Q)

II, iv, 8 *all are* (Q2) are al (Q)

III, ii, 31 *offer* (Pope) offer, (Q) 32 *succor* (Pope) succors (Q) 40 *boldly* (Collier conj.; Hudson) bouldy (Q) 72 *O'erthrows* (F) Ouerthrowes (Q) 130 *won* (Q3) woon (Q) 134 *this offense* (F) this (Q) 170 *through* (Q2) thorough (Q)

III, iii, 13 *brief with you to* (F) brief to (Q) 59 *rain* (F) raigne (Q) 119 *a prince and just* (Sisson) princesse iust (Q) 202 *hand* (F) handes (Q)

III, iv, 11 *joy?* (Var. 1773) griefe (Q) 26 *pins* (F) pines (Q) 28 *change:* (F) change (Q) 29 *yon* (Q2) yong (Q) 55 *seized* (Q3) ceasde (Q) 57 *garden! We at* (Capell) garden at (Q) 80 *Cam'st* (Q2) Canst (Q) 85 *lord's* (F) Lo: (Q)

IV, i, 22 *him* (Q3) them (Q) 43 *Fitzwater* (F) Fitzwaters (Q) 54 *As* (Johnson) As it (Q) 55 *sun . . . sun* (Capell) sinne . . . sinne (Q) *is my* (Q3) is (Q) 109 *thee* (Q2) the (Q) 114 *Marry* (F3) Mary (Q) 145 *you* (Q2) yon (Q) 165 *limbs* (Q4) knee (F) 183 *and on* (Q4) on (F) 199 *tend* (Q4) 'tend (F) 210 *duty's* (Var. 1821) duties (Q4) dutious (F) *rites* (Q4) Oathes (F) 215 *that swear* (Q4) are made (F) 229 *folly* (Q4) follyes (F) 237 *upon* (Q4) upon me (F) 250 *To undeck* (Q4) T'vndeck (F) 251 *and* (Q4) a (F) 255 *Nor* (Q4) No, nor (F) 260 *mockery king* (Q4) Mockerie, King (F) 267 *bankrout* (Q4) Bankrupt (F) 276 *the* (Q4) that (F) 285 *Was* (Q4) Is (F) *that* (Q4) which (F) 286 *And* (Q4) That (F) 289 *a* (Q4) an (F) 296 *manners* (Q4) manner (F) 319 *On Wednesday next* (Q4) Let it be so, and loe on Wednesday next (Q) 333 *I will lay* (Pope) Ile lay (Q)

V, i, 32 *correction mildly* (Neilson) correction, mildly (Q) 41 *thee* (Q2) the (Q) 62 *And he* (Keightly conj.; Wilson) He (Q)

V, ii, 2 *off* (F) of (Q) 11 *thee* (F) the (Q) 17 *thee! Welcome* (Theobald) the Welcome (Q) 65 *bond* (F) band (Q) 94 *thee* (Q2) the (Q) 116 *And* (Q2) An (Q)

V, iii, 36 *that I may* (Q2) that May (Q) 43 *foolhardy* (Rolfe) foole, hardie (Q) 51 *passed* (Dyce) past (Q) 68 *And* (Q2) An (Q) 75 *voiced* (Q3) voice (Q) 111 *King Henry* (Q2) Yorke (Q) 135–36 *With all my heart I pardon him* (Pope) I pardon him with all my heart (Q)

V, v, 20 *through* (F) thorow (Q) 27 *sit* (Q3) set (Q) 79 *bestrid* (F) bestride (Q)

V, vi, 12 s.d. *Fitzwater* (Q6) Fitzwaters (Q) 25 *reverend* (Q3) reuerent (Q) 43 *thorough* (Camb.) through (Q)

THE TRAGEDY OF
KING RICHARD THE SECOND

*

I, i   *Enter King Richard, John of Gaunt, with other*
        Nobles and Attendants.

KING
1   Old John of Gaunt, time-honored Lancaster,
2   Hast thou, according to thy oath and band,
     Brought hither Henry Hereford, thy bold son,
4   Here to make good the boist'rous late appeal,
5   Which then our leisure would not let us hear,
     Against the Duke of Norfolk, Thomas Mowbray ?
GAUNT
     I have, my liege.
KING
     Tell me, moreover, hast thou sounded him
9   If he appeal the duke on ancient malice,
10   Or worthily, as a good subject should,
     On some known ground of treachery in him ?
GAUNT
     As near as I could sift him on that argument,
13   On some apparent danger seen in him

Aimed at your highness, no inveterate malice.
KING
     Then call them to our presence.   [*Exit Attendant.*]
                                        Face to face,
     And frowning brow to brow, ourselves will hear
     The accuser and the accusèd freely speak.
     High-stomached are they both and full of ire,   18
     In rage deaf as the sea, hasty as fire.
          Enter Bolingbroke and Mowbray.
BOLINGBROKE
     Many years of happy days befall
     My gracious sovereign, my most loving liege !
MOWBRAY
     Each day still better other's happiness
     Until the heavens, envying earth's good hap,   23
     Add an immortal title to your crown !   24
KING
     We thank you both. Yet one but flatters us,
     As well appeareth by the cause you come –   26
     Namely, to appeal each other of high treason.
     Cousin of Hereford, what dost thou object   28
     Against the Duke of Norfolk, Thomas Mowbray ?
BOLINGBROKE
     First – heaven be the record to my speech ! –
     In the devotion of a subject's love,
     Tend'ring the precious safety of my prince   32
     And free from other, misbegotten hate,   33
     Come I appellant to this princely presence.   34
     Now, Thomas Mowbray, do I turn to thee,
     And mark my greeting well ; for what I speak
     My body shall make good upon this earth

I, i A room of state (Holinshed's *Chronicles*, Shakespeare's principal source
for *Richard II*, locates this scene 'within the castle of Windsor,' where the
king and his nobles sat on 'a great scaffold,' and gives the time as the latter
part of April, 1398) **s.d.** *Gaunt* Ghent (his birthplace) 1 *time-honored*
venerable (he was actually fifty-eight) 2 *band* bond (Gaunt was a pledge
for Bolingbroke's appearance) 4 *appeal* accusation (here of treason) made
by one who undertook under penalty to prove it 5 *our . . . us* (the royal
plural) ; *leisure* i.e. lack of leisure 9 *appeal* accuse ; *malice* enmity 10
worthily justly 13 *apparent* obvious 18 *High-stomached* haughty 23
hap luck 24 *immortal title* i.e. angel or saint 26 *cause you come* matter you
come about 28 *what . . . object* what accusation do you make 32 *Tend'ring*
being lovingly mindful of 33 *misbegotten* of any other kind than that
begotten of love for the king 34 *appellant* as accuser

Or my divine soul answer it in heaven.

39 Thou art a traitor and a miscreant,
Too good to be so, and too bad to live,
Since the more fair and crystal is the sky,
The uglier seem the clouds that in it fly.

43 Once more, the more to aggravate the note,
With a foul traitor's name stuff I thy throat
And wish, so please my sovereign, ere I move,

46 What my tongue speaks my right-drawn sword may
prove.

MOWBRAY

47 Let not my cold words here accuse my zeal.

48 'Tis not the trial of a woman's war,

49 The bitter clamor of two eager tongues,
Can arbitrate this cause betwixt us twain;
The blood is hot that must be cooled for this.
Yet can I not of such tame patience boast
As to be hushed and naught at all to say.
First, the fair reverence of your highness curbs me
From giving reins and spurs to my free speech,

56 Which else would post until it had returned
These terms of treason doubled down his throat.
Setting aside his high blood's royalty,
And let him be no kinsman to my liege,
I do defy him and I spit at him,
Call him a slanderous coward and a villain;
Which to maintain, I would allow him odds

63 And meet him, were I tied to run afoot
Even to the frozen ridges of the Alps,

65 Or any other ground inhabitable
Where ever Englishman durst set his foot.
Meantime let this defend my loyalty:
By all my hopes, most falsely doth he lie.

BOLINGBROKE

69 Pale trembling coward, there I throw my gage,

70 Disclaiming here the kinred of the king,
And lay aside my high blood's royalty,

72 Which fear, not reverence, makes thee to except.
If guilty dread have left thee so much strength

74 As to take up mine honor's pawn, then stoop.
By that and all the rites of knighthood else,
Will I make good against thee, arm to arm,

77 What I have spoke or thou canst worse devise.

MOWBRAY

I take it up; and by that sword I swear
Which gently laid my knighthood on my shoulder,
I'll answer thee in any fair degree
Or chivalrous design of knightly trial;

82 And when I mount, alive may I not light
If I be traitor or unjustly fight!

KING

What doth our cousin lay to Mowbray's charge?

85 It must be great that can inherit us
So much as of a thought of ill in him.

BOLINGBROKE

87 Look what I speak, my life shall prove it true –

88 That Mowbray hath received eight thousand nobles

89 In name of lendings for your highness' soldiers,

90 The which he hath detained for lewd employments,
Like a false traitor and injurious villain.
Besides I say, and will in battle prove –

93 Or here, or elsewhere to the furthest verge
That ever was surveyed by English eye –

95 That all the treasons for these eighteen years

Complotted and contrived in this land
Fetch from false Mowbray their first head and spring. 97
Further I say, and further will maintain, 98
Upon his bad life to make all this good,
That he did plot the Duke of Gloucester's death, 100
Suggest his soon-believing adversaries, 101
And consequently, like a traitor coward, 102
Sluiced out his innocent soul through streams of blood;
Which blood, like sacrificing Abel's, cries,
Even from the tongueless caverns of the earth,
To me for justice and rough chastisement; 106
And, by the glorious worth of my descent,
This arm shall do it, or this life be spent.

KING

How high a pitch his resolution soars! 109
Thomas of Norfolk, what say'st thou to this?

MOWBRAY

O, let my sovereign turn away his face
And bid his ears a little while be deaf,
Till I have told this slander of his blood 113
How God and good men hate so foul a liar!

KING

Mowbray, impartial are our eyes and ears.
Were he my brother, nay, my kingdom's heir,
As he is but my father's brother's son,
Now by my sceptre's awe I make a vow, 118
Such neighbor nearness to our sacred blood
Should nothing privilege him nor partialize 120
The unstooping firmness of my upright soul.
He is our subject, Mowbray; so art thou:
Free speech and fearless I to thee allow.

MOWBRAY

Then, Bolingbroke, as low as to thy heart
Through the false passage of thy throat, thou liest!
Three parts of that receipt I had for Calais 126
Disbursed I duly to his highness' soldiers.
The other part reserved I by consent,
For that my sovereign liege was in my debt 129
Upon remainder of a dear account 130
Since last I went to France to fetch his queen. 131
Now swallow down that lie! For Gloucester's death,
I slew him not, but, to my own disgrace, 133
Neglected my sworn duty in that case.

---

39 *miscreant* un-Christian villain   43 *note* charge (of treason)   46 *right-drawn* drawn in a just cause   47 *accuse my zeal* cast doubt upon my ardor or loyalty   48 *woman's war* war of words   49 *eager* sharp   56 *post* ride at high speed   63 *tied* under bond   65 *inhabitable* uninhabitable   69 *gage* glove in token of defiance   70 *kinred* kinship   72 *except* use as an exception   74 *mine honor's pawn* i.e. the gage   77 *or . . . devise* or anything worse you can imagine I have said   82 *light* dismount   85–86 *inherit us . . . of* make us have   87 *Look what* whatever   88 *nobles* gold coins worth 6s. 8d. each   89 *lendings* pay advanced when regular pay cannot be given   90 *lewd* base   93 *Or* either   95 *eighteen years* (since the commons' revolt of 1381)   97 *head* source   98–99 *maintain . . . good* undertake to prove, by ending his wicked life   100 *Duke of Gloucester's death* (at Calais, while Mowbray was in command there; Gloucester was Richard's uncle and severest critic, and it is probable that the king ordered his execution)   101 *Suggest . . . adversaries* put his easily persuaded enemies up to it   102 *consequently* subsequently and as a result   106 *To me* (spoken with menacing emphasis, aimed at Richard)   109 *pitch* peak of a falcon's flight   113 *slander of* disgrace to   118 *my . . . awe* the reverence due my sceptre   120 *partialize* make partial, bias   126 *that receipt I had* the money I received   129 *For that* because   130 *dear account* heavy debt   131 *Since . . . queen* since my latest voyage in furtherance of Richard's marriage to Isabella of France   133–34 *I . . . case* (Mowbray speaks ambiguously; there is some evidence that he postponed the execution, and he probably did not actually perform it)

For you, my noble Lord of Lancaster,
The honorable father to my foe,
Once did I lay an ambush for your life –
A trespass that doth vex my grievèd soul;
140 But ere I last received the sacrament,
I did confess it and exactly begged
Your grace's pardon, and I hope I had it.
142 This is my fault. As for the rest appealed,
It issues from the rancor of a villain,
144 A recreant and most degenerate traitor;
145 Which in myself I boldly will defend,
146 And interchangeably hurl down my gage
Upon this overweening traitor's foot
To prove myself a loyal gentleman
Even in the best blood chambered in his bosom.
150 In haste whereof most heartily I pray
Your highness to assign our trial day.

KING
Wrath-kindled gentlemen, be ruled by me;
153 Let's purge this choler without letting blood.
This we prescribe, though no physician;
Deep malice makes too deep incision.
156 Forget, forgive; conclude and be agreed;
157 Our doctors say this is no month to bleed.
Good uncle, let this end where it begun;
We'll calm the Duke of Norfolk, you your son.

GAUNT
160 To be a make-peace shall become my age.
Throw down, my son, the Duke of Norfolk's gage.

KING
And, Norfolk, throw down his.

GAUNT   When, Harry, when?
Obedience bids I should not bid again.

KING
164 Norfolk, throw down, we bid. There is no boot.

MOWBRAY
Myself I throw, dread sovereign, at thy foot.
My life thou shalt command, but not my shame.
The one my duty owes; but my fair name,
168 Despite of death that lives upon my grave,
To dark dishonor's use thou shalt not have.
170 I am disgraced, impeached, and baffled here;
Pierced to the soul with slander's venomed spear,
172 The which no balm can cure but his heart-blood
173 Which breathed this poison.

KING   Rage must be withstood.

Give me his gage. Lions make leopards tame.   174

MOWBRAY
Yea, but not change his spots! Take but my shame,
And I resign my gage. My dear dear lord,
The purest treasure mortal times afford
Is spotless reputation. That away,
Men are but gilded loam or painted clay.
A jewel in a ten-times-barred-up chest
Is a bold spirit in a loyal breast.
Mine honor is my life, both grow in one;
Take honor from me, and my life is done.
Then, dear my liege, mine honor let me try;   184
In that I live, and for that will I die.

KING
Cousin, throw up your gage. Do you begin.   186

BOLINGBROKE
O, God defend my soul from such deep sin!
Shall I seem crestfallen in my father's sight?
Or with pale beggar-fear impeach my height   189
Before this outdared dastard? Ere my tongue   190
Shall wound my honor with such feeble wrong   191
Or sound so base a parle, my teeth shall tear   192
The slavish motive of recanting fear   193
And spit it bleeding in his high disgrace,   194
Where shame doth harbor, even in Mowbray's face.
[Exit Gaunt.]

KING
We were not born to sue, but to command;
Which since we cannot do to make you friends,
Be ready, as your lives shall answer it,
At Coventry upon Saint Lambert's day.   199
There shall your swords and lances arbitrate
The swelling difference of your settled hate.
Since we cannot atone you, we shall see   202
Justice design the victor's chivalry.   203
Lord Marshal, command our officers-at-arms
Be ready to direct these home alarms.   205
Exit [with others].

*

Enter John of Gaunt with the Duchess of Gloucester.   I, ii

GAUNT
Alas, the part I had in Woodstock's blood   1
Doth more solicit me than your exclaims
To stir against the butchers of his life!
But since correction lieth in those hands   4
Which made the fault that we cannot correct,
Put we our quarrel to the will of heaven,
Who, when they see the hours ripe on earth,
Will rain hot vengeance on offenders' heads.

DUCHESS
Finds brotherhood in thee no sharper spur?
Hath love in thy old blood no living fire?
Edward's seven sons, whereof thyself art one,   11
Were as seven vials of his sacred blood,
Or seven fair branches springing from one root,
Some of those seven are dried by nature's course,
Some of those branches by the Destinies cut;
But Thomas, my dear lord, my life, my Gloucester,
One vial full of Edward's sacred blood,
One flourishing branch of his most royal root,
Is cracked, and all the precious liquor spilt,
Is hacked down, and his summer leaves all faded,

140 *exactly* completely and expressly   142 *rest appealed* remainder of the charge   144 *recreant* cowardly   145 *Which* which assertion   146 *interchangeably* in turn   150 *In haste whereof* to speed which proof   153 *choler* anger; *letting blood* bleeding medicinally, with a quibble on bloodshed in combat   156 *conclude* make terms   157 *no month to bleed* (the almanacs prescribed certain seasons as favorable for bleeding)   160 *shall* will certainly   164 *boot* help for it   168 *Despite . . . lives* that will live, in spite of death   170 *impeached* accused; *baffled* publicly disgraced   172–73 *his heart-blood Which* the heart-blood of that man who   173 *breathed* uttered   174 *Lions . . . leopards* i.e. kings . . . nobles   184 *try* put to trial   186 *throw up* (possibly to the king on his high seat)   189 *impeach my height* dishonor my high rank   190 *outdared* intimidated; *dastard* coward   191 *feeble wrong* injury only a weak man would submit to   192 *parle* parley, truce   193 *motive* moving part, here his tongue   194 *in* to   199 *Saint Lambert's day* September 17   202 *atone* reconcile   203 *Justice . . . chivalry* justice point out the true knight by giving him the victory   205 *home alarms* troubles in England as distinct from the Irish war
I, ii *Within a residence of the Duke of Lancaster*   1 *the part . . . blood* my being his brother; *Woodstock* (the Duke of Gloucester's name was Thomas of Woodstock)   4 *those hands* i.e. Richard's   11 *Edward* Edward III

21 By envy's hand and murder's bloody axe.
Ah, Gaunt, his blood was thine! That bed, that womb,
23 That metal, that self mould that fashioned thee,
Made him a man; and though thou livest and breathest,
Yet art thou slain in him. Thou dost consent
In some large measure to thy father's death
In that thou seest thy wretched brother die,
28 Who was the model of thy father's life.
Call it not patience, Gaunt; it is despair.
30 In suff'ring thus thy brother to be slaught'red
31 Thou showest the naked pathway to thy life,
Teaching stern murder how to butcher thee.
That which in mean men we entitle patience
Is pale cold cowardice in noble breasts.
What shall I say? To safeguard thine own life
The best way is to venge my Gloucester's death.

GAUNT
37 God's is the quarrel; for God's substitute,
His deputy anointed in his sight,
Hath caused his death; the which if wrongfully,
Let heaven revenge; for I may never lift
An angry arm against his minister.

DUCHESS
Where then, alas, may I complain myself?

GAUNT
To God, the widow's champion and defense.

DUCHESS
Why then, I will. Farewell, old Gaunt.
Thou goest to Coventry, there to behold
46 Our cousin Hereford and fell Mowbray fight.
O, sit my husband's wrongs on Hereford's spear,
That it may enter butcher Mowbray's breast!
49 Or, if misfortune miss the first career,
Be Mowbray's sins so heavy in his bosom
That they may break his foaming courser's back
And throw the rider headlong in the lists,
53 A caitiff recreant to my cousin Hereford!
54 Farewell, old Gaunt. Thy sometimes brother's wife
With her companion, Grief, must end her life.

GAUNT
Sister, farewell; I must to Coventry.
As much good stay with thee as go with me!

DUCHESS
Yet one word more! Grief boundeth where it falls,
Not with the empty hollowness, but weight.
I take my leave before I have begun,
For sorrow ends not when it seemeth done.
Commend me to thy brother, Edmund York.
Lo, this is all. Nay, yet depart not so!
Though this be all, do not so quickly go.
I shall remember more. Bid him – ah, what? –
66 With all good speed at Plashy visit me.
Alack, and what shall good old York there see
68 But empty lodgings and unfurnished walls,
69 Unpeopled offices, untrodden stones?
And what hear there for welcome but my groans?
Therefore commend me – let him not come there
To seek out sorrow that dwells everywhere.
Desolate, desolate will I hence and die!
The last leave of thee takes my weeping eye. *Exeunt.*

*

Enter Lord Marshal and the Duke Aumerle.   I, iii

MARSHAL
My Lord Aumerle, is Harry Hereford armed?

AUMERLE
Yea, at all points, and longs to enter in.

MARSHAL
The Duke of Norfolk, sprightfully and bold,   3
Stays but the summons of the appellant's trumpet.

AUMERLE
Why, then the champions are prepared, and stay
For nothing but his majesty's approach.   6
*The trumpets sound and the King enters with his
Nobles [, Gaunt, Bushy, Bagot, Green, and others].
When they are set, enter [Mowbray,] the Duke of
Norfolk, in arms, defendant [, and Herald].*

KING
Marshal, demand of yonder champion
The cause of his arrival here in arms.
Ask him his name and orderly proceed
To swear him in the justice of his cause.

MARSHAL
In God's name and the king's, say who thou art,
And why thou comest thus knightly clad in arms;
Against what man thou com'st, and what thy quarrel.
Speak truly on thy knighthood and thy oath,
As so defend thee heaven and thy valor!

MOWBRAY
My name is Thomas Mowbray, Duke of Norfolk,
Who hither come engagèd by my oath
(Which God defend a knight should violate!)   18
Both to defend my loyalty and truth
To God, my king, and my succeeding issue
Against the Duke of Hereford that appeals me;
And, by the grace of God and this mine arm,
To prove him, in defending of myself,
A traitor to my God, my king, and me;
And as I truly fight, defend me heaven!
*The trumpets sound. Enter [Bolingbroke,] Duke of
Hereford, appellant, in armor [and Herald].*

KING
Marshal, ask yonder knight in arms
Both who he is and why he cometh hither
Thus plated in habiliments of war;   28
And formally, according to our law,
Depose him in the justice of his cause.   30

MARSHAL
What is thy name? and wherefore com'st thou hither,
Before King Richard in his royal lists?
Against whom comest thou? and what's thy quarrel?
Speak like a true knight, so defend thee heaven!

BOLINGBROKE
Harry of Hereford, Lancaster, and Derby
Am I, who ready here do stand in arms
To prove, by God's grace and my body's valor
In lists on Thomas Mowbray, Duke of Norfolk,

---

21 *envy* malicious enmity   **23** *self* selfsame   **28** *model* image   **30** *suff'ring* permitting   **31** *the naked pathway* the path to be open   **37** *God's substitute* the king by divine right   **46** *cousin* kinsman   **49** *career* charge   **53** *caitiff* captive   **54** *sometimes* 'late'   **66** *Plashy* Gloucester's country seat, in Essex   **68** *unfurnished walls* rooms bare of furniture and hangings   **69** *offices* workrooms
I, iii The lists at Coventry   **s.d.** *Aumerle* (as High Constable of England)   **3** *sprightfully and bold* with spirit and boldly   **6 s.d.** *defendant* the challenged   **18** *defend* forbid   **28** *plated* armored   **30** *Depose him* take his sworn deposition

That he is a traitor foul and dangerous
To God of heaven, King Richard, and to me;
And as I truly fight, defend me heaven!
MARSHAL
On pain of death, no person be so bold
Or daring-hardy as to touch the lists,
Except the Marshal and such officers
45 Appointed to direct these fair designs.
BOLINGBROKE
Lord Marshal, let me kiss my sovereign's hand
And bow my knee before his majesty;
For Mowbray and myself are like two men
That vow a long and weary pilgrimage.
Then let us take a ceremonious leave
And loving farewell of our several friends.
MARSHAL
The appellant in all duty greets your highness
And craves to kiss your hand and take his leave.
KING
We will descend and fold him in our arms.
Cousin of Hereford, as thy cause is right,
So be thy fortune in this royal fight!
Farewell, my blood; which if to-day thou shed,
Lament we may, but not revenge thee dead.
BOLINGBROKE
59 O, let no noble eye profane a tear
For me, if I be gored with Mowbray's spear.
As confident as is the falcon's flight
Against a bird, do I with Mowbray fight.
My loving lord, I take my leave of you;
Of you, my noble cousin, Lord Aumerle;
Not sick, although I have to do with death,
66 But lusty, young, and cheerly drawing breath.
67 Lo, as at English feasts, so I regreet
The daintiest last, to make the end most sweet.
O thou, the earthly author of my blood,
Whose youthful spirit, in me regenerate,
Doth with a twofold vigor lift me up
To reach at victory above my head,
73 Add proof unto mine armor with thy prayers,
And with thy blessings steel my lance's point,
75 That it may enter Mowbray's waxen coat
76 And furbish new the name of John a Gaunt
Even in the lusty havior of his son.
GAUNT
God in thy good cause make thee prosperous!
Be swift like lightning in the execution
And let thy blows, doubly redoublèd,
81 Fall like amazing thunder on the casque
Of thy adverse pernicious enemy.
Rouse up thy youthful blood; be valiant and live.
BOLINGBROKE
84 Mine innocence and Saint George to thrive!
MOWBRAY
However God or fortune cast my lot,

There lives or dies, true to King Richard's throne,
A loyal, just, and upright gentleman.
Never did captive with a freer heart   88
Cast off his chains of bondage and embrace
His golden uncontrolled enfranchisement,
More than my dancing soul doth celebrate
This feast of battle with mine adversary.
Most mighty liege, and my companion peers,
Take from my mouth the wish of happy years.
As gentle and as jocund as to jest   95
Go I to fight. Truth hath a quiet breast.
KING
Farewell, my lord. Securely I espy   97
Virtue with valor couchèd in thine eye.   98
Order the trial, Marshal, and begin.
MARSHAL
Harry of Hereford, Lancaster, and Derby,
Receive thy lance, and God defend the right!
BOLINGBROKE
Strong as a tower in hope, I cry amen.
MARSHAL [to an Officer]
Go bear this lance to Thomas, Duke of Norfolk.
[1.] HERALD
Harry of Hereford, Lancaster, and Derby
Stands here for God, his sovereign, and himself,
On pain to be found false and recreant,
To prove the Duke of Norfolk, Thomas Mowbray,
A traitor to his God, his king, and him,
And dares him to set forward to the fight.
2. HERALD
Here standeth Thomas Mowbray, Duke of Norfolk,
On pain to be found false and recreant,
Both to defend himself and to approve   112
Henry of Hereford, Lancaster, and Derby
To God, his sovereign, and to him disloyal,
Courageously and with a free desire
Attending but the signal to begin.   116
MARSHAL
Sound trumpets, and set forward combatants.
        [A charge sounded.]
Stay! The king hath thrown his warder down.   118
KING
Let them lay by their helmets and their spears
And both return back to their chairs again.
Withdraw with us; and let the trumpets sound
While we return these dukes what we decree.   122
        [A long flourish.]
Draw near,
And list what with our council we have done.   124
For that our kingdom's earth should not be soiled
With that dear blood which it hath fosterèd;
And for our eyes do hate the dire aspect
Of civil wounds ploughed up with neighbors' sword;
And for we think the eagle-wingèd pride
Of sky-aspiring and ambitious thoughts
With rival-hating envy set on you   131
To wake our peace, which in our country's cradle
Draws the sweet infant breath of gentle sleep;
Which so roused up with boist'rous untuned drums,
With harsh-resounding trumpets' dreadful bray
And grating shock of wrathful iron arms,
Might from our quiet confines fright fair peace
And make us wade even in our kinred's blood:
Therefore we banish you our territories.

45 direct . . . designs conduct this combat fairly   59 profane (because
Bolingbroke's defeat would mean that he was a traitor)   66 cheerly cheerily
67 regreet greet   73 proof invulnerability   75 enter . . . coat pierce his
armor as though it were wax   76 a of   81 amazing stupefying; casque
helmet   84 to thrive I rely for success on   88 freer more willing   95
gentle tranquil; jest mock-fight   97 Securely I espy I am confident that I
see   98 couchèd expressed   112 approve prove   116 Attending awaiting
118 warder gilded wand (held by Richard as commander of the trial)
122 While until; s.d. flourish trumpet-call   124 list listen to   131 set on
you set you on

You, cousin Hereford, upon pain of life,
Till twice five summers have enriched our fields
142 Shall not regreet our fair dominions
143 But tread the stranger paths of banishment.

BOLINGBROKE
Your will be done. This must my comfort be –
That sun that warms you here shall shine on me,
And those his golden beams to you here lent
Shall point on me and gild my banishment.

KING
Norfolk, for thee remains a heavier doom,
Which I with some unwillingness pronounce :
150 The sly slow hours shall not determinate
151 The dateless limit of thy dear exile.
The hopeless word of 'never to return'
Breathe I against thee, upon pain of life.

MOWBRAY
A heavy sentence, my most sovereign liege,
And all unlooked for from your highness' mouth.
156 A dearer merit, not so deep a maim
As to be cast forth in the common air,
Have I deservèd at your highness' hands.
The language I have learnt these forty years,
My native English, now I must forgo ;
And now my tongue's use is to me no more
Than an unstringèd viol or a harp,
163 Or like a cunning instrument cased up
164 Or, being open, put into his hands
That knows no touch to tune the harmony.
Within my mouth you have enjailed my tongue,
167 Doubly portcullised with my teeth and lips ;
And dull, unfeeling, barren ignorance
Is made my jailer to attend on me.
I am too old to fawn upon a nurse,
Too far in years to be a pupil now.
What is thy sentence then but speechless death,
173 Which robs my tongue from breathing native breath ?

KING
174 It boots thee not to be compassionate.
175 After our sentence plaining comes too late.

MOWBRAY
Then thus I turn me from my country's light
To dwell in solemn shades of endless night.

KING
Return again and take an oath with thee.
179 Lay on our royal sword your banished hands ;
Swear by the duty that you owe to God
(Our part therein we banish with yourselves)
To keep the oath that we administer :
You never shall, so help you truth and God,
Embrace each other's love in banishment ;
Nor never look upon each other's face ;
Nor never write, regreet, nor reconcile
187 This low'ring tempest of your home-bred hate ;
188 Nor never by advisèd purpose meet
To plot, contrive, or complot any ill
'Gainst us, our state, our subjects, or our land.

BOLINGBROKE
I swear.

MOWBRAY
And I, to keep all this.

BOLINGBROKE
193 Norfolk, so far as to mine enemy :
By this time, had the king permitted us,

One of our souls had wand'red in the air,
Banished this frail sepulchre of our flesh,
As now our flesh is banished from this land.
Confess thy treasons ere thou fly the realm.
Since thou hast far to go, bear not along
The clogging burden of a guilty soul.

MOWBRAY
No, Bolingbroke. If ever I were traitor,
My name be blotted from the book of life
And I from heaven banished as from hence !
But what thou art, God, thou, and I do know ;
And all too soon, I fear, the king shall rue.
Farewell, my liege. Now no way can I stray.
Save back to England, all the world's my way.   Exit.

KING
Uncle, even in the glasses of thine eyes   208
I see thy grievèd heart. Thy sad aspect
Hath from the number of his banished years
Plucked four away.
      [To Bolingbroke]
           Six frozen winters spent,
Return with welcome home from banishment.

BOLINGBROKE
How long a time lies in one little word !
Four lagging winters and four wanton springs   214
End in a word, such is the breath of kings.

GAUNT
I thank my liege that in regard of me
He shortens four years of my son's exile.
But little vantage shall I reap thereby ;
For ere the six years that he hath to spend
Can change their moons and bring their times about,
My oil-dried lamp and time-bewasted light
Shall be extinct with age and endless night,
My inch of taper will be burnt and done,
And blindfold death not let me see my son.   224

KING
Why, uncle, thou hast many years to live.

GAUNT
But not a minute, king, that thou canst give.
Shorten my days thou canst with sullen sorrow
And pluck nights from me, but not lend a morrow.
Thou canst help time to furrow me with age,
But stop no wrinkle in his pilgrimage.   230
Thy word is current with him for my death,   231
But dead, thy kingdom cannot buy my breath.

KING
Thy son is banished upon good advice,
Whereto thy tongue a party-verdict gave.   234
Why at our justice seem'st thou then to low'r ?

GAUNT
Things sweet to taste prove in digestion sour.
You urged me as a judge ; but I had rather

142 *regreet* greet again   143 *stranger* alien   150 *determinate* end   151 *dateless* unlimited ; *limit* term ; *dear* bitter   156 *dearer* more welcome ; *merit* reward ; *maim* crippling injury   163 *cunning* skillfully made   164 *open* out of its case   167 *portcullised* enclosed by a movable grating   173 *Which* thy sentence, which ; *breath* speech   174 *boots* helps ; *compassionate* sorrowfully lamenting   175 *plaining* complaining   179 *Lay . . . hands* (he addresses both combatants)   187 *low'ring* threatening   188 *advisèd* concerted   193 *so . . . enemy* so far as I may speak to my sworn enemy   208 *glasses . . . eyes* your eyes as mirrors   214 *wanton* luxuriant   224 *blindfold death* death, like a blindfold   230 *stop . . . pilgrimage* prevent no wrinkle that time's course brings   231 *current* valid   234 *party-verdict* part of the verdict

You would have bid me argue like a father.
O, had it been a stranger, not my child,
240 To smooth his fault I should have been more mild.
241 A partial slander sought I to avoid,
And in the sentence my own life destroyed.
Alas, I looked when some of you should say
I was too strict to make mine own away;
But you gave leave to my unwilling tongue
246 Against my will to do myself this wrong.

KING
Cousin, farewell; and, uncle, bid him so.
Six years we banish him, and he shall go.

[Flourish.] Exit [King with his Train].

AUMERLE
249 Cousin, farewell. What presence must not know,
From where you do remain let paper show.

MARSHAL
My lord, no leave take I; for I will ride,
As far as land will let me, by your side.

GAUNT
O, to what purpose dost thou hoard thy words
That thou returnest no greeting to thy friends?

BOLINGBROKE
I have too few to take my leave of you,
When the tongue's office should be prodigal
To breathe the abundant dolor of the heart.

GAUNT
Thy grief is but thy absence for a time.

BOLINGBROKE
Joy absent, grief is present for that time.

GAUNT
What is six winters? They are quickly gone.

BOLINGBROKE
To men in joy; but grief makes one hour ten.

GAUNT
Call it a travel that thou tak'st for pleasure.

BOLINGBROKE
My heart will sigh when I miscall it so,
Which finds it an enforcèd pilgrimage.

GAUNT
The sullen passage of thy weary steps
266 Esteem as foil wherein thou art to set
The precious jewel of thy home return.

BOLINGBROKE
Nay, rather every tedious stride I make
269 Will but remember me what a deal of world
I wander from the jewels that I love.
Must I not serve a long apprenticehood
272 To foreign passages and, in the end,
Having my freedom, boast of nothing else
274 But that I was a journeyman to grief?

GAUNT
All places that the eye of heaven visits
Are to a wise man ports and happy havens.
Teach thy necessity to reason thus:
There is no virtue like necessity. 278
Think not the king did banish thee,
But thou the king. Woe doth the heavier sit
Where it perceives it is but faintly borne. 281
Go, say I sent thee forth to purchase honor,
And not, the king exiled thee; or suppose
Devouring pestilence hangs in our air
And thou art flying to a fresher clime.
Look what thy soul holds dear, imagine it 286
To lie that way thou goest, not whence thou com'st.
Suppose the singing birds musicians,
The grass whereon thou tread'st the presence strewed, 289
The flowers fair ladies, and thy steps no more
Than a delightful measure or a dance; 291
For gnarling sorrow hath less power to bite 292
The man that mocks at it and sets it light.

BOLINGBROKE
O, who can hold a fire in his hand
By thinking on the frosty Caucasus?
Or cloy the hungry edge of appetite
By bare imagination of a feast?
Or wallow naked in December snow
By thinking on fantastic summer's heat? 299
O, no! The apprehension of the good
Gives but the greater feeling to the worse.
Fell sorrow's tooth doth never rankle more 302
Than when he bites, but lanceth not the sore.

GAUNT
Come, come, my son, I'll bring thee on thy way.
Had I thy youth and cause, I would not stay.

BOLINGBROKE
Then, England's ground, farewell; sweet soil, adieu,
My mother, and my nurse, that bears me yet!
Where'er I wander, boast of this I can,
Though banished, yet a true-born English man.

Exeunt.

*

Enter the King, with Green, &c. [Bagot], at one   I, iv
door, and the Lord Aumerle at another.

KING
We did observe. Cousin Aumerle,
How far brought you high Hereford on his way?

AUMERLE
I brought high Hereford, if you call him so,
But to the next high way, and there I left him.

KING
And say, what store of parting tears were shed?

AUMERLE
Faith, none for me; except the northeast wind, 6
Which then blew bitterly against our faces,
Awaked the sleeping rheum, and so by chance 8
Did grace our hollow parting with a tear. 9

KING
What said our cousin when you parted with him?

AUMERLE
'Farewell!'
And, for my heart disdainèd that my tongue
Should so profane the word, that taught me craft
To counterfeit oppression of such grief
That words seemed buried in my sorrow's grave.
Marry, would the word 'farewell' have length'ned hours 16

240 *smooth* gloss over   241 *partial slander* slander of partiality to my own son   246 *wrong* injury   249 *What . . . know* what you can't say here 266 *foil* thin, bright metal leaf placed under a gem to give it additional brilliance   269 *remember* remind   272 *foreign passages* experiences abroad 274 *journeyman* worker for a daily wage, often itinerant   278 *necessity* patiently enduring the inevitable   281 *faintly* faint-heartedly   286 *Look what* whatever   289 *presence* royal audience chamber; *strewed* i.e. the floor covered with rushes   291 *measure* slow, formal dance   292 *gnarling* snarling   299 *fantastic* imaginary   302 *rankle* inflict a painful, festering wound

I, iv The court of King Richard   6 *for me* for my part   8 *rheum* moisture, tears   9 *hollow* insincere   16 *Marry* indeed

And added years to his short banishment,
He should have had a volume of farewells;
But since it would not, he had none of me.

KING

20 He is our cousin, cousin; but 'tis doubt,
When time shall call him home from banishment,
22 Whether our kinsman come to see his friends.
Ourself and Bushy, Bagot here, and Green
Observed his courtship to the common people;
How he did seem to dive into their hearts
With humble and familiar courtesy;
What reverence he did throw away on slaves,
Wooing poor craftsmen with the craft of smiles
29 And patient underbearing of his fortune,
30 As 'twere to banish their affects with him.
Off goes his bonnet to an oyster-wench;
A brace of draymen bid God speed him well
And had the tribute of his supple knee,
With 'Thanks, my countrymen, my loving friends';
35 As were our England in reversion his,
And he our subjects' next degree in hope.

GREEN

Well, he is gone, and with him go these thoughts!
38 Now for the rebels which stand out in Ireland,
39 Expedient manage must be made, my liege,
Ere further leisure yield them further means
For their advantage and your highness' loss.

KING

We will ourself in person to this war;
43 And, for our coffers, with too great a court
44 And liberal largess, are grown somewhat light,
45 We are enforced to farm our royal realm,
The revenue whereof shall furnish us
For our affairs in hand. If that come short,
48 Our substitutes at home shall have blank charters,
Whereto, when they shall know what men are rich,
50 They shall subscribe them for large sums of gold
And send them after to supply our wants,
52 For we will make for Ireland presently.

Enter Bushy.

Bushy, what news?

BUSHY

Old John of Gaunt is grievous sick, my lord,
Suddenly taken, and hath sent posthaste
To entreat your majesty to visit him.

KING

Where lies he?

BUSHY

58 At Ely House.

KING

Now put it, God, in the physician's mind
To help him to his grave immediately!
61 The lining of his coffers shall make coats
To deck our soldiers for these Irish wars.
Come, gentlemen, let's all go visit him.
Pray God we may make haste, and come too late!

[ALL]

Amen.   *Exeunt.*

II, i   *Enter John of Gaunt, sick, with the Duke of York, &c.*

GAUNT

Will the king come, that I may breathe my last
In wholesome counsel to his unstaid youth?

YORK

Vex not yourself nor strive not with your breath,
For all in vain comes counsel to his ear.

GAUNT

O, but they say the tongues of dying men
Enforce attention like deep harmony.
Where words are scarce, they are seldom spent in vain,
For they breathe truth that breathe their words in pain.
He that no more must say is listened more
    Than they whom youth and ease have taught to glose. 10
More are men's ends marked than their lives before. 11
    The setting sun, and music at the close,
As the last taste of sweets, is sweetest last, 13
Writ in remembrance more than things long past.
Though Richard my life's counsel would not hear, 15
My death's sad tale may yet undeaf his ear. 16

YORK

No; it is stopped with other, flattering sounds,
As praises, of whose taste the wise are fond, 18
Lascivious metres, to whose venom sound 19
The open ear of youth doth always listen;
Report of fashions in proud Italy,
Whose manners still our tardy apish nation 22
Limps after in base imitation.
Where doth the world thrust forth a vanity
(So it be new, there's no respect how vile) 25
That is not quickly buzzed into his ears?
Then all too late comes counsel to be heard
Where will doth mutiny with wit's regard. 28
Direct not him whose way himself will choose.
'Tis breath thou lack'st, and that breath wilt thou lose.

GAUNT

Methinks I am a prophet new inspired
And thus, expiring, do foretell of him:
His rash fierce blaze of riot cannot last,
For violent fires soon burn out themselves;
Small show'rs last long, but sudden storms are short;
He tires betimes that spurs too fast betimes; 36
With eager feeding food doth choke the feeder;
Light vanity, insatiate cormorant, 38
Consuming means, soon preys upon itself.
This royal throne of kings, this scept'red isle,
This earth of majesty, this seat of Mars,
This other Eden, demi-paradise,
This fortress built by Nature for herself
Against infection and the hand of war, 44
This happy breed of men, this little world,
This precious stone set in the silver sea,

20 *'tis* there is   22 *his friends* us of his own rank   29 *underbearing* enduring   30 *affects* affections   35 *in reversion* by right of legal succession   38 *stand out* resist   39 *Expedient* speedy; *manage* plans for controlling   43 *for* because; *too . . . court* too many courtiers (Richard's extravagance was notorious)   44 *largess* gifts   45 *farm* lease (the authority to collect taxes was deputed in exchange for cash in hand)   48 *blank charters* in effect, loans to the crown on which the amount was filled in by the king's agents   50 *subscribe* put them down   52 *presently* at once   58 *Ely House* the Bishop of Ely's palace in London   61 *coats* coats of mail   II, i *Within Ely House*   10 *glose* speak empty words in flattery   11 *marked* heeded   13 *is sweetest last* lingers longest in memory   15 *life's* lifelong   16 *My . . . tale* my serious dying words   18 *of . . . fond* which even the wise are too fond of   19 *venom* poisonous   22 *still* always; *tardy apish* aping foreign fashions after they have become stale   25 *there's no respect* no one considers   28 *will* natural inclination; *wit's regard* what reason esteems   36 *betimes* early   38 *cormorant* glutton   44 *infection* plague and moral contamination

Which serves it in the office of a wall,
Or as a moat defensive to a house,
Against the envy of less happier lands;
This blessed plot, this earth, this realm, this England,
This nurse, this teeming womb of royal kings,
52   Feared by their breed and famous by their birth,
Renownèd for their deeds as far from home,
For Christian service and true chivalry,
55   As is the sepulchre in stubborn Jewry
Of the world's ransom, blessed Mary's son;
This land of such dear souls, this dear dear land,
Dear for her reputation through the world,
Is now leased out (I die pronouncing it)
60   Like to a tenement or pelting farm.
England, bound in with the triumphant sea,
Whose rocky shore beats back the envious siege
Of wat'ry Neptune, is now bound in with shame,
64   With inky blots and rotten parchment bonds.
That England that was wont to conquer others
Hath made a shameful conquest of itself.
Ah, would the scandal vanish with my life,
How happy then were my ensuing death!

YORK
The king is come. Deal mildly with his youth;
70   For young hot colts, being raged, do rage the more.
    Enter King and Queen, &c. [Aumerle, Bushy, Green,
    Bagot, Ross, and Willoughby].

QUEEN
How fares our noble uncle Lancaster?

KING
What comfort, man? How is't with aged Gaunt?

GAUNT
73   O, how that name befits my composition!
Old Gaunt indeed, and gaunt in being old.
Within me grief hath kept a tedious fast;
And who abstains from meat that is not gaunt?
77   For sleeping England long time have I watched;
Watching breeds leanness, leanness is all gaunt.
The pleasure that some fathers feed upon
Is my strict fast – I mean my children's looks –
And therein fasting hast thou made me gaunt.
Gaunt am I for the grave, gaunt as a grave,
83   Whose hollow womb inherits naught but bones.

KING
84   Can sick men play so nicely with their names?

GAUNT
85   No, misery makes sport to mock itself.
Since thou dost seek to kill my name in me,
I mock my name, great king, to flatter thee.

KING
88   Should dying men flatter with those that live?

GAUNT
No, no! men living flatter those that die.

KING
Thou, now a-dying, sayest thou flatterest me.

GAUNT
O, no! thou diest, though I the sicker be.

KING
I am in health, I breathe, and see thee ill.

GAUNT
Now, he that made me knows I see thee ill;
Ill in myself to see, and in thee seeing ill.
Thy deathbed is no lesser than thy land,
Wherein thou liest in reputation sick;
And thou, too careless patient as thou art,
Committ'st thy anointed body to the cure
Of those physicians that first wounded thee.
A thousand flatterers sit within thy crown,
Whose compass is no bigger than thy head;
And yet, incagèd in so small a verge,   102
The waste is no whit lesser than thy land.
O, had thy grandsire, with a prophet's eye,
Seen how his son's son should destroy his sons,
From forth thy reach he would have laid thy shame,
Deposing thee before thou wert possessed,   107
Which art possessed now to depose thyself.
Why, cousin, wert thou regent of the world,
It were a shame to let this land by lease;
But, for thy world enjoying but this land,
Is it not more than shame to shame it so?
Landlord of England art thou now, not king.   113
Thy state of law is bondslave to the law,   114
And thou –

KING   A lunatic lean-witted fool,
Presuming on an ague's privilege,   116
Darest with thy frozen admonition   117
Make pale our cheek, chasing the royal blood
With fury from his native residence.   119
Now, by my seat's right royal majesty,
Wert thou not brother to great Edward's son,
This tongue that runs so roundly in thy head   122
Should run thy head from thy unreverent shoulders.

GAUNT
O, spare me not, my brother Edward's son,
For that I was his father Edward's son!
That blood already, like the pelican,   126
Hast thou tapped out and drunkenly caroused.
My brother Gloucester, plain well-meaning soul –
Whom fair befall in heaven 'mongst happy souls! –   129
May be a precedent and witness good   130
That thou respect'st not spilling Edward's blood.
Join with the present sickness that I have,
And thy unkindness be like crooked age,   133
To crop at once a too-long-withered flower.
Live in thy shame, but die not shame with thee!
These words hereafter thy tormenters be!
Convey me to my bed, then to my grave.
Love they to live that love and honor have.
    Exit [borne off by Attendants].

KING
And let them die that age and sullens have;   139
For both hast thou, and both become the grave.

YORK
I do beseech your majesty impute his words
To wayward sickliness and age in him.

---

52 *breed* ancestral reputation for valor   55 *stubborn* obstinate in rejecting Christ and resisting the Crusaders   60 *tenement* rented land or building; *pelting* paltry   70 *raged* enraged   73 *composition* body and mind   77 *watched* stayed awake at night   83 *inherits* will get   84 *so nicely* making such fine puns (Richard is ironical)   85 *to mock* of mocking   88 *flatter with* seek to please   102 *verge* compass   107–08 *possessed . . . possessed* put in possession . . . possessed of a devil   113 *Landlord* one who leases out a property   114 *Thy . . . to the law* your legal status is that of subject, not king   116 *ague's privilege* a not-too-ill man's privilege to be cross   117 *frozen* chilly – cold and caused by a chill   119 *his* its   122 *roundly* freely and bluntly   126 *pelican* (believed to feed its young with its own blood)   129 *fair befall* may good befall   130 *precedent* token   133 *crooked* bent like a sickle   139 *sullens* sulks

He loves you, on my life, and holds you dear
As Harry Duke of Hereford, were he here.

KING

145   Right, you say true ! As Hereford's love, so his ;
As theirs, so mine ; and all be as it is !

[Enter Northumberland.]

NORTHUMBERLAND

My liege, old Gaunt commends him to your majesty.

KING

What says he ?

NORTHUMBERLAND   Nay, nothing ; all is said.
His tongue is now a stringless instrument ;
Words, life, and all, old Lancaster hath spent.

YORK

151   Be York the next that must be bankrout so !
Though death be poor, it ends a mortal woe.

KING

The ripest fruit first falls, and so doth he ;
154   His time is spent, our pilgrimage must be.
So much for that. Now for our Irish wars.
156   We must supplant those rough rug-headed kerns,
157   Which live like venom where no venom else
But only they have privilege to live.
159   And, for these great affairs do ask some charge,
Towards our assistance we do seize to us
The plate, coin, revenues, and moveables
Whereof our uncle Gaunt did stand possessed.

YORK

How long shall I be patient ? Ah, how long
Shall tender duty make me suffer wrong ?
Not Gloucester's death, nor Hereford's banishment,
166   Nor Gaunt's rebukes, nor England's private wrongs,
167   Nor the prevention of poor Bolingbroke
About his marriage, nor my own disgrace,
Have ever made me sour my patient cheek
Or bend one wrinkle on my sovereign's face.
I am the last of noble Edward's sons,
Of whom thy father, Prince of Wales, was first.
In war was never lion raged more fierce,
In peace was never gentle lamb more mild,
Than was that young and princely gentleman.
His face thou hast, for even so looked he,
177   Accomplished with the number of thy hours ;
But when he frowned, it was against the French
And not against his friends. His noble hand
Did win what he did spend, and spent not that
Which his triumphant father's hand had won.
His hands were guilty of no kinred blood,
But bloody with the enemies of his kin.
O Richard ! York is too far gone with grief,
185   Or else he never would compare between.

KING

Why, uncle, what's the matter ?

YORK   O my liege,
Pardon me, if you please ; if not, I, pleased
188   Not to be pardoned, am content withal.
Seek you to seize and gripe into your hands
190   The royalties and rights of banished Hereford ?
Is not Gaunt dead ? and doth not Hereford live ?
Was not Gaunt just ? and is not Harry true ?
Did not the one deserve to have an heir ?
Is not his heir a well-deserving son ?
Take Hereford's rights away, and take from Time
196   His charters and his customary rights ;

Let not to-morrow then ensue to-day ;   197
Be not thyself – for how art thou a king
But by fair sequence and succession ?
Now, afore God (God forbid I say true !)
If you do wrongfully seize Hereford's rights,
Call in the letters patents that he hath   202
By his attorneys general to sue
His livery, and deny his off'red homage,   204
You pluck a thousand dangers on your head,
You lose a thousand well-disposèd hearts,
And prick my tender patience to those thoughts
Which honor and allegiance cannot think.

KING

Think what you will, we seize into our hands
His plate, his goods, his money, and his lands.

YORK

I'll not be by the while. My liege, farewell.
What will ensue hereof there's none can tell ;
But by bad courses may be understood   213
That their events can never fall out good.   Exit.   214

KING

Go, Bushy, to the Earl of Wiltshire straight.   215
Bid him repair to us to Ely House
To see this business. To-morrow next   217
We will for Ireland ; and 'tis time, I trow.   218
And we create, in absence of ourself,
Our uncle York Lord Governor of England ;
For he is just and always loved us well.
Come on, our queen. To-morrow must we part.
Be merry, for our time of stay is short.

[Flourish.] Exeunt King and Queen.
Manet Northumberland [with Willoughby and Ross].

NORTHUMBERLAND

Well, lords, the Duke of Lancaster is dead.

ROSS

And living too ; for now his son is duke.

WILLOUGHBY

Barely in title, not in revenues.

NORTHUMBERLAND

Richly in both, if justice had her right.

ROSS

My heart is great ; but it must break with silence,   228
Ere't be disburdened with a liberal tongue.

NORTHUMBERLAND

Nay, speak thy mind ; and let him ne'er speak more
That speaks thy words again to do thee harm !

WILLOUGHBY

Tends that thou wouldst speak to the Duke of   232
    Hereford ?
If it be so, out with it boldly, man !
Quick is mine ear to hear of good towards him.

145 *Right . . . his* (the king purposely takes the opposite of York's meaning) 151 *bankrout* bankrupt   154 *must be* is yet to be finished   156 *rug-headed* shaggy-haired ; *kerns* light-armed footsoldiers 157 *venom* poisonous snakes 159 *charge* outlay   166 *Gaunt's rebukes* reprimands to Gaunt 167–68 *prevention . . . marriage* (Richard forestalled Bolingbroke's match with the Duc du Berri's daughter) 177 *Accomplished . . . hours* at your age   185 *compare between* make comparisons   188 *withal* nonetheless 190 *royalties* rights as a member of the royal family   196 *his customary rights* (one of Time's rights was to bring the heir his inheritance) 197 *ensue* follow   202–04 *letters patents . . . livery* royal grants through legal representatives to sue for possession of his inheritance 204 *homage* avowal of allegiance   213 *by* with respect to   214 *events* outcomes   215 *Earl of Wiltshire* Richard's Lord Treasurer ; *straight* at once   217 *see* see to ; *To-morrow next* to-morrow   218 *trow* believe   228 *great* swollen, heavy   232 *Tends . . . to* does . . . concern

ROSS
No good at all that I can do for him;
Unless you call it good to pity him,
Bereft and gelded of his patrimony.

NORTHUMBERLAND
Now, afore God, 'tis shame such wrongs are borne
239 In him a royal prince and many moe
Of noble blood in this declining land.
The king is not himself, but basely led
By flatterers; and what they will inform,
243 Merely in hate, 'gainst any of us all,
244 That will the king severely prosecute
'Gainst us, our lives, our children, and our heirs.

ROSS
246 The commons hath he pilled with grievous taxes
And quite lost their hearts; the nobles hath he fined
For ancient quarrels and quite lost their hearts.

WILLOUGHBY
And daily new exactions are devised,
250 As blanks, benevolences, and I wot not what;
251 But what, a God's name, doth become of this?

NORTHUMBERLAND
Wars hath not wasted it, for warred he hath not,
But basely yielded upon compromise
That which his noble ancestors achieved with blows.
More hath he spent in peace than they in wars.

ROSS
The Earl of Wiltshire hath the realm in farm.

WILLOUGHBY
The king's grown bankrout, like a broken man.

NORTHUMBERLAND
Reproach and dissolution hangeth over him.

ROSS
He hath not money for these Irish wars,
His burdenous taxations notwithstanding,
But by the robbing of the banished duke.

NORTHUMBERLAND
His noble kinsman. Most degenerate king!
But, lords, we hear this fearful tempest sing,
Yet seek no shelter to avoid the storm.
265 We see the wind sit sore upon our sails,
266 And yet we strike not, but securely perish.

ROSS
We see the very wrack that we must suffer,
268 And unavoided is the danger now
For suffering so the causes of our wrack.

NORTHUMBERLAND
Not so. Even through the hollow eyes of death
I spy life peering; but I dare not say

How near the tidings of our comfort is.

WILLOUGHBY
Nay, let us share thy thoughts as thou dost ours.

ROSS
Be confident to speak, Northumberland.
We three are but thyself, and speaking so,
Thy words are but as thoughts. Therefore be bold.

NORTHUMBERLAND
Then thus: I have from Le Port Blanc, a bay
In Brittaine, received intelligence   278
That Harry Duke of Hereford, Rainold Lord Cobham,
[The son and heir of the Earl of Arundel,]   280
That late broke from the Duke of Exeter,   281
His brother, Archbishop late of Canterbury,   282
Sir Thomas Erpingham, Sir John Ramston,
Sir John Norbery, Sir Robert Waterton, and Francis
    Coint,
All these well furnished by the Duke of Brittaine
With eight tall ships, three thousand men of war,   286
Are making hither with all due expedience   287
And shortly mean to touch our northern shore.
Perhaps they had ere this, but that they stay
The first departing of the king for Ireland.   290
If then we shall shake off our slavish yoke,
Imp out our drooping country's broken wing,   292
Redeem from broking pawn the blemished crown,   293
Wipe off the dust that hides our sceptre's gilt,   294
And make high majesty look like itself,
Away with me in post to Ravenspurgh;   296
But if you faint, as fearing to do so,   297
Stay and be secret, and myself will go.

ROSS
To horse, to horse! Urge doubts to them that fear.

WILLOUGHBY
Hold out my horse, and I will first be there. *Exeunt.* 300

*

Enter the Queen, Bushy, Bagot.   II, ii
BUSHY
Madam, your majesty is too much sad.
You promised, when you parted with the king,
To lay aside life-harming heaviness
And entertain a cheerful disposition.

QUEEN
To please the king, I did; to please myself,
I cannot do it. Yet I know no cause
Why I should welcome such a guest as grief
Save bidding farewell to so sweet a guest
As my sweet Richard. Yet again, methinks,
Some unborn sorrow, ripe in fortune's womb,
Is coming towards me, and my inward soul
With nothing trembles. At something it grieves   12
More than with parting from my lord the king.

BUSHY
Each substance of a grief hath twenty shadows,
Which shows like grief itself, but is not so;
For sorrow's eye, glazèd with blinding tears,
Divides one thing entire to many objects,
Like perspectives, which rightly gazed upon,   18
Show nothing but confusion – eyed awry,
Distinguish form. So your sweet majesty,
Looking awry upon your lord's departure,
Find shapes of grief more than himself to wail,

239 *moe* more   243 *Merely* purely   244 *prosecute* follow up   246 *pilled* skinned   250 *blanks* blank charters (see I, iv, 48n.); *benevolences* 'voluntary' loans to the crown; *wot* know   251 *a* in   265 *sit sore* press grievously   266 *strike* lower sail or strike back; *securely* overconfidently   268 *unavoided* unavoidable   278 *Brittaine* Brittany; *intelligence* information   280 (this line or a similarly worded one was deleted for political reasons; Elizabeth had imprisoned the son of the then Earl of Arundel)   281 *broke* escaped   282 *late* until recently (he had been deprived of the office by the Pope at Richard's request)   286 *tall* fine; *men of war* fighting men   287 *expedience* speed   290 *The first departing* until after the departure   292 *Imp out* graft new feathers on   293 *broking pawn* the possession of the king's moneylenders   294 *gilt* golden lustre   296 *post* haste; *Ravenspurgh* a port on the River Humber, now submerged by the sea   297 *faint* are faint-hearted   300 *Hold . . . and* if my horse holds out
II, ii Within Windsor Castle   12 *With* at   18 *perspectives* raised pictures or designs which appear only when looked at from the side (*awry*)

Which, looked on as it is, is naught but shadows
Of what it is not. Then, thrice-gracious queen,
More than your lord's departure weep not. More's not
    seen;
Or if it be, 'tis with false sorrow's eye,
Which for things true weeps things imaginary.
QUEEN
It may be so; but yet my inward soul
Persuades me it is otherwise. Howe'er it be,
I cannot but be sad – so heavy sad
As, though in thinking on no thought I think,
Makes me with heavy nothing faint and shrink.
BUSHY
33   'Tis nothing but conceit, my gracious lady.
QUEEN
34   'Tis nothing less. Conceit is still derived
From some forefather grief. Mine is not so,
For nothing hath begot my something grief,
37   Or something hath the nothing that I grieve.
38   'Tis in reversion that I do possess;
But what it is, that is not yet known – what,
I cannot name. 'Tis nameless woe, I wot.
        [Enter Green.]
GREEN
God save your majesty! and well met, gentlemen.
I hope the king is not yet shipped for Ireland.
QUEEN
Why hopest thou so? 'Tis better hope he is;
For his designs crave haste, his haste good hope.
Then wherefore dost thou hope he is not shipped?
GREEN
46   That he, our hope, might have retired his power
And driven into despair an enemy's hope
48   Who strongly hath set footing in this land.
49   The banished Bolingbroke repeals himself
50   And with uplifted arms is safe arrived
At Ravenspurgh.
QUEEN   Now God in heaven forbid!
GREEN
52   Ah, madam, 'tis too true; and that is worse,
The Lord Northumberland, his son young Henry Percy,
The Lords of Ross, Beaumond, and Willoughby,
With all their powerful friends, are fled to him.
BUSHY
Why have you not proclaimed Northumberland
57   And all the rest revolted faction traitors?
GREEN
We have; whereupon the Earl of Worcester
59   Hath broken his staff, resigned his stewardship,
And all the household servants fled with him
To Bolingbroke.
QUEEN
So, Green, thou art the midwife to my woe,
63   And Bolingbroke my sorrow's dismal heir.
64   Now hath my soul brought forth her prodigy;
And I, a gasping new-delivered mother,
Have woe to woe, sorrow to sorrow joined.
BUSHY
Despair not, madam.
QUEEN   Who shall hinder me?
I will despair, and be at enmity
69   With cozening Hope. He is a flatterer,
A parasite, a keeper-back of Death,
71   Who gently would dissolve the bands of life,

Which false Hope lingers in extremity.   72
        [Enter York.]
GREEN
Here comes the Duke of York.
QUEEN
With signs of war about his aged neck.   74
O, full of careful business are his looks.   75
Uncle, for God's sake, speak comfortable words!
YORK
Should I do so, I should belie my thoughts.
Comfort's in heaven, and we are on the earth,
Where nothing lives but crosses, cares, and grief.   79
Your husband, he is gone to save far off,
Whilst others come to make him lose at home.
Here am I left to underprop his land,
Who, weak with age, cannot support myself.
Now comes the sick hour that his surfeit made;   84
Now shall he try his friends that flattered him.
        [Enter a Servingman.]
SERVINGMAN
My lord, your son was gone before I came.
YORK
He was? Why, so! Go all which way it will!
The nobles they are fled, the commons they are cold
And will, I fear, revolt on Hereford's side.
Sirrah, get thee to Plashy to my sister Gloucester;
Bid her send me presently a thousand pound.
Hold, take my ring.
SERVINGMAN
My lord, I had forgot to tell your lordship
To-day, as I came by, I callèd there –
But I shall grieve you to report the rest.
YORK
What is't, knave?
SERVINGMAN
An hour before I came the duchess died.
YORK
God for his mercy! what a tide of woes
Comes rushing on this woeful land at once!
I know not what to do. I would to God
(So my untruth had not provoked him to it)   101
The king had cut off my head with my brother's.
What, are there no posts dispatched for Ireland?
How shall we do for money for these wars?
Come, sister – cousin I would say – pray pardon me.
Go, fellow, get thee home, provide some carts
And bring away the armor that is there.
                        [Exit Servingman.]
Gentlemen, will you go muster men?
If I know how or which way to order these affairs,
Thus disorderly thrust into my hands,
Never believe me. Both are my kinsmen.
Th' one is my sovereign, whom both my oath
And duty bids defend; t' other again

33 *conceit* fancy 34 *nothing less* anything but that 37 *something . . . grieve*
my causeless grief has something in it 38 *'Tis . . . possess* what I feel is
like a property which will devolve upon me later; I can't describe it yet
(see I, iv, 35n.) 46 *retired* drawn back 48 *strongly* with strong support
49 *repeals* recalls 50 *uplifted arms* brandished weapons 52 *that* what
57 *revolted . . . traitors* a rebellious clique of traitors 59 *staff* (the sign
of his office) 63 *dismal* ill-omened 64 *prodigy* monster 69 *cozening*
deceitful 71 *bands* bonds 72 *lingers* causes to linger 74 *With . . . neck*
in armor 75 *careful business* anxious preoccupation 79 *crosses* thwartings
84 *surfeit* excess 101 *untruth* disloyalty

Is my kinsman, whom the king hath wronged,
Whom conscience and my kinred bids to right.
Well, somewhat we must do. Come, cousin, I'll
117 Dispose of you.
Gentlemen, go muster up your men,
And meet me presently at Berkeley.
I should to Plashy too,
But time will not permit. All is uneven,
122 And everything is left at six and seven.

Exeunt Duke, Queen.
Manent Bushy, [Bagot,] Green.

BUSHY
The wind sits fair for news to go for Ireland,
But none returns. For us to levy power
Proportionable to the enemy
Is all unpossible.

GREEN
Besides, our nearness to the king in love
128 Is near the hate of those love not the king.

BAGOT
And that's the wavering commons; for their love
Lies in their purses, and whoso empties them,
By so much fills their hearts with deadly hate.

BUSHY
132 Wherein the king stands generally condemned.

BAGOT
133 If judgment lie in them, then so do we,
Because we ever have been near the king.

GREEN
Well, I will for refuge straight to Bristol Castle.
The Earl of Wiltshire is already there.

BUSHY
137 Thither will I with you; for little office
138 Will the hateful commons perform for us,
Except like curs to tear us all to pieces.
Will you go along with us?

BAGOT
No; I will to Ireland to his majesty.
Farewell. If heart's presages be not vain,
We three here part that ne'er shall meet again.

BUSHY
That's as York thrives to beat back Bolingbroke.

GREEN
Alas, poor duke! The task he undertakes
Is numb'ring sands and drinking oceans dry.
Where one on his side fights, thousands will fly.

BAGOT
Farewell at once – for once, for all, and ever.

BUSHY
Well, we may meet again.

BAGOT   I fear me, never.   *[Exeunt.]*

*

II, iii   *Enter [Bolingbroke the Duke of] Hereford, [and]*
        Northumberland.

BOLINGBROKE
How far is it, my lord, to Berkeley now?

117 *Dispose of* make arrangements for 122 *at six and seven* in confusion
128 *those love* those who love 132 *Wherein* on which grounds 133 *If . . .*
them if our doom depends on them 137 *office* service 138 *hateful* angry
II, iii An open place in Gloucestershire 10 *In* by 12 *tediousness and*
process tedious process 16 *this* this expectation 22 *whencesoever* wherever
he may be 42 *raw* inexperienced 44 *approvèd* demonstrated

NORTHUMBERLAND
Believe me, noble lord,
I am a stranger here in Gloucestershire.
These high wild hills and rough uneven ways
Draws out our miles and makes them wearisome;
And yet your fair discourse hath been as sugar,
Making the hard way sweet and delectable.
But I bethink me what a weary way
From Ravenspurgh to Cotswold will be found
In Ross and Willoughby, wanting your company,   10
Which, I protest, hath very much beguiled
The tediousness and process of my travel;   12
But theirs is sweet'ned with the hope to have
The present benefit which I possess;
And hope to joy is little less in joy
Than hope enjoyed. By this the weary lords   16
Shall make their way seem short, as mine hath done
By sight of what I have, your noble company.

BOLINGBROKE
Of much less value is my company
Than your good words. But who comes here?

Enter Harry Percy.

NORTHUMBERLAND
It is my son, young Harry Percy,
Sent from my brother Worcester, whencesoever.   22
Harry, how fares your uncle?

PERCY
I had thought, my lord, to have learned his health of
you.

NORTHUMBERLAND
Why, is he not with the queen?

PERCY
No, my good lord; he hath forsook the court,
Broken his staff of office, and dispersed
The household of the king.

NORTHUMBERLAND   What was his reason?
He was not so resolved when last we spake together.

PERCY
Because your lordship was proclaimèd traitor.   30
But he, my lord, is gone to Ravenspurgh
To offer service to the Duke of Hereford;
And sent me over by Berkeley to discover
What power the Duke of York had levied there;
Then with directions to repair to Ravenspurgh.

NORTHUMBERLAND
Have you forgot the Duke of Hereford, boy?

PERCY
No, my good lord, for that is not forgot
Which ne'er I did remember. To my knowledge,
I never in my life did look on him.

NORTHUMBERLAND
Then learn to know him now. This is the duke.

PERCY
My gracious lord, I tender you my service,
Such as it is, being tender, raw, and young;   42
Which elder days shall ripen and confirm
To more approvèd service and desert.   44

BOLINGBROKE
I thank thee, gentle Percy; and be sure
I count myself in nothing else so happy
As in a soul rememb'ring my good friends;
And, as my fortune ripens with thy love,
It shall be still thy true love's recompense.
My heart this covenant makes, my hand thus seals it.

NORTHUMBERLAND
How far is it to Berkeley? and what stir
Keeps good old York there with his men of war?
PERCY
There stands the castle by yon tuft of trees,
Manned with three hundred men, as I have heard;
And in it are the Lords of York, Berkeley, and Seymour,
None else of name and noble estimate.
[Enter Ross and Willoughby.]
NORTHUMBERLAND
Here come the Lords of Ross and Willoughby,
Bloody with spurring, fiery red with haste.
BOLINGBROKE
Welcome, my lords. I wot your love pursues
A banished traitor. All my treasury
61   Is yet but unfelt thanks, which, more enriched,
Shall be your love and labor's recompense.
ROSS
Your presence makes us rich, most noble lord.
WILLOUGHBY
And far surmounts our labor to attain it.
BOLINGBROKE
Evermore thanks, the exchequer of the poor,
Which, till my infant fortune comes to years,
Stands for my bounty. But who comes here?
[Enter Berkeley.]
NORTHUMBERLAND
It is my Lord of Berkeley, as I guess.
BERKELEY
My Lord of Hereford, my message is to you.
BOLINGBROKE
My lord, my answer is – 'to Lancaster';
And I am come to seek that name in England;
And I must find that title in your tongue
Before I make reply to aught you say.
BERKELEY
Mistake me not, my lord. 'Tis not my meaning
75   To rase one title of your honor out.
To you, my lord, I come (what lord you will)
From the most gracious regent of this land,
The Duke of York, to know what pricks you on
79   To take advantage of the absent time
80   And fright our native peace with self-borne arms.
[Enter York attended.]
BOLINGBROKE
I shall not need transport my words by you;
Here comes his grace in person. My noble uncle!
[Kneels.]
YORK
Show me thy humble heart, and not thy knee,
84   Whose duty is deceivable and false.
BOLINGBROKE
My gracious uncle!
YORK
Tut, tut!
Grace me no grace, nor uncle me no uncle.
I am no traitor's uncle, and that word 'grace'
In an ungracious mouth is but profane.
Why have those banished and forbidden legs
91   Dared once to touch a dust of England's ground?
But then more why? – why have they dared to march
So many miles upon her peaceful bosom,
Frighting her pale-faced villages with war
95   And ostentation of despisèd arms?

Com'st thou because the anointed king is hence?
Why, foolish boy, the king is left behind,
And in my loyal bosom lies his power.
Were I but now lord of such hot youth
As when brave Gaunt thy father and myself
Rescued the Black Prince, that young Mars of men,
From forth the ranks of many thousand French,
O, then how quickly should this arm of mine,
Now prisoner to the palsy, chastise thee
And minister correction to thy fault!
BOLINGBROKE
My gracious uncle, let me know my fault;
On what condition stands it and wherein?   107
YORK
Even in condition of the worst degree,
In gross rebellion and detested treason,
Thou art a banished man; and here art come,
Before the expiration of thy time,
In braving arms against thy sovereign.   112
BOLINGBROKE
As I was banished, I was banished Hereford;
But as I come, I come for Lancaster.   114
And, noble uncle, I beseech your grace
Look on my wrongs with an indifferent eye.   116
You are my father, for methinks in you
I see old Gaunt alive. O, then, my father,
Will you permit that I shall stand condemned
A wandering vagabond, my rights and royalties
Plucked from my arms perforce, and given away
To upstart unthrifts? Wherefore was I born?   122
If that my cousin king be King in England,
It must be granted I am Duke of Lancaster.
You have a son, Aumerle, my noble cousin.
Had you first died, and he been thus trod down,   126
He should have found his uncle Gaunt a father
To rouse his wrongs and chase them to the bay.   128
I am denied to sue my livery here,
And yet my letters patents give me leave.
My father's goods are all distrained and sold;   131
And these, and all, are all amiss employed.
What would you have me do? I am a subject,
And I challenge law. Attorneys are denied me,   134
And therefore personally I lay my claim
To my inheritance of free descent.   136
NORTHUMBERLAND
The noble duke hath been too much abused.
ROSS
It stands your grace upon to do him right.   138
WILLOUGHBY
Base men by his endowments are made great.   139
YORK
My lords of England, let me tell you this:
I have had feeling of my cousin's wrongs,
And labored all I could to do him right;
But in this kind to come, in braving arms,   143

61 *unfelt* intangible   75 *rase* erase   79 *absent time* time of the king's absence   80 *self-borne* begotten and carried by you   84 *duty* i.e. act of kneeling; *deceivable* deceitful   91 *dust* speck   95 *ostentation* display; *despisèd* despicable   107 *On . . . it* on what defect in me is it based; *wherein* of what does it consist   112 *braving* defiant   114 *for* as   116 *indifferent* impartial   122 *unthrifts* spendthrifts   126 *first* i.e. before Gaunt   128 *rouse* rout from cover; *chase . . . bay* hunt them to the death   131 *distrained* seized   134 *challenge law* demand my rights   136 *my inheritance of* that which I inherit by   138 *It . . . upon* it's up to you   139 *his endowments* what they got from him   143 *kind* fashion

Be his own carver and cut out his way,
To find out right with wrong – it may not be ;
And you that do abet him in this kind
Cherish rebellion and are rebels all.

NORTHUMBERLAND

The noble duke hath sworn his coming is
But for his own ; and for the right of that
We all have strongly sworn to give him aid ;
And let him never see joy that breaks that oath !

YORK

Well, well, I see the issue of these arms.
I cannot mend it, I must needs confess,
154   Because my power is weak and all ill left ;
But if I could, by him that gave me life,
156   I would attach you all and make you stoop
Unto the sovereign mercy of the king ;
But since I cannot, be it known unto you
159   I do remain as neuter. So fare you well –
Unless you please to enter in the castle
And there repose you for this night.

BOLINGBROKE

An offer, uncle, that we will accept ;
But we must win your grace to go with us
To Bristol Castle, which they say is held
By Bushy, Bagot, and their complices,
166   The caterpillars of the commonwealth,
167   Which I have sworn to weed and pluck away.

YORK

It may be I will go with you ; but yet I'll pause,
For I am loath to break our country's laws.
170   Nor friends nor foes, to me welcome you are.
Things past redress are now with me past care.   *Exeunt.*

*

II, iv   *Enter Earl of Salisbury and a Welsh Captain.*

WELSH CAPTAIN

My Lord of Salisbury, we have stayed ten days
2   And hardly kept our countrymen together,
And yet we hear no tidings from the king.
Therefore we will disperse ourselves. Farewell.

SALISBURY

Stay yet another day, thou trusty Welshman.
The king reposeth all his confidence in thee.

WELSH CAPTAIN

'Tis thought the king is dead. We will not stay.
8   The bay trees in our country all are withered,
And meteors fright the fixèd stars of heaven ;
The pale-faced moon looks bloody on the earth,
11   And lean-looked prophets whisper fearful change ;
Rich men look sad, and ruffians dance and leap –
The one in fear to lose what they enjoy,

The other to enjoy by rage and war.   14
These signs forerun the death or fall of kings.
Farewell. Our countrymen are gone and fled,
As well assured Richard their king is dead.   *[Exit.]* 17

SALISBURY

Ah, Richard ! with the eyes of heavy mind,
I see thy glory, like a shooting star,
Fall to the base earth from the firmament.
Thy sun sets weeping in the lowly west,
Witnessing storms to come, woe, and unrest ;   22
Thy friends are fled to wait upon thy foes,   23
And crossly to thy good all fortune goes.   *[Exit.]* 24

*

Enter [Bolingbroke] Duke of Hereford, York,   III, i
Northumberland, [Ross, Percy, Willoughby, with]
Bushy and Green prisoners.

BOLINGBROKE

Bring forth these men.
Bushy and Green, I will not vex your souls
(Since presently your souls must part your bodies)   3
With too much urging your pernicious lives,   4
For 'twere no charity ; yet, to wash your blood
From off my hands, here in the view of men
I will unfold some causes of your deaths.
You have misled a prince, a royal king,
A happy gentleman in blood and lineaments,
By you unhappied and disfigured clean.   10
You have in manner with your sinful hours   11
Made a divorce betwixt his queen and him,
Broke the possession of a royal bed,
And stained the beauty of a fair queen's cheeks
With tears drawn from her eyes by your foul wrongs.
Myself – a prince by fortune of my birth,
Near to the king in blood, and near in love
Till you did make him misinterpret me –
Have stooped my neck under your injuries
And sighed my English breath in foreign clouds,   20
Eating the bitter bread of banishment,
Whilst you have fed upon my signories,   22
Disparked my parks and felled my forest woods,   23
From my own windows torn my household coat,   24
Rased out my imprese, leaving me no sign,   25
Save men's opinions and my living blood,
To show the world I am a gentleman.
This and much more, much more than twice all this,
Condemns you to the death. See them delivered over
To execution and the hand of death.

BUSHY

More welcome is the stroke of death to me
Than Bolingbroke to England. Lords, farewell.

GREEN

My comfort is that heaven will take our souls
And plague injustice with the pains of hell.

BOLINGBROKE

My Lord Northumberland, see them dispatched.
     [Exeunt Northumberland and others,
                 with the prisoners.]
Uncle, you say the queen is at your house.
For God's sake, fairly let her be entreated.   37
Tell her I send to her my kind commends ;   38
Take special care my greetings be delivered.

YORK

A gentleman of mine I have dispatched

---

154 *all ill left* everything left in disorder   156 *attach* arrest   159 *neuter*
neutral   166 *caterpillars* i.e. devourers   167 *weed* get rid of   170 *Nor . . .*
are as a neutral I welcome you
II, iv A Welsh camp   s.d. *Welsh Captain* (perhaps the famous Owen
Glendower who is mentioned in III, i, 43 and appears in *1 Henry IV*)   2
hardly with difficulty   8–10 *The . . . earth* i.e. earth and the heavens show
omens of disaster   11 *change* political upheaval   14 *to enjoy* in hope to
enjoy ; *rage* violence   17 *As* as being   22 *Witnessing* betokening   23 *wait*
upon offer allegiance to   24 *crossly* adversely
III, i Before Bristol Castle   3 *part* leave   4 *urging* stressing   10 *clean*
completely   11–12 *You have in manner . . . Made a divorce* you have . . .
made a kind of divorce   20 *foreign clouds* clouds of breath exhaled in a
foreign land   22 *signories* domains   23 *Disparked* thrown open to other
uses   24 *torn* broken ; *coat* coat of arms   25 *Rased out* erased ; *imprese*
heraldic emblem   37 *entreated* treated   38 *commends* remembrances

41   With letters of your love to her at large.
BOLINGBROKE
     Thanks, gentle uncle. Come, lords, away,
43   To fight with Glendower and his complices.
44   A while to work, and after holiday.   Exeunt.

                              *

III, ii   [Drums. Flourish and Colors.] Enter the King,
           Aumerle, [the Bishop of] Carlisle, &c. [Soldiers and
           Attendants].
KING
     Barkloughly Castle call they this at hand?
AUMERLE
2   Yea, my lord. How brooks your grace the air
     After your late tossing on the breaking seas?
KING
     Needs must I like it well. I weep for joy
     To stand upon my kingdom once again.
     Dear earth, I do salute thee with my hand,
     Though rebels wound thee with their horses' hoofs.
8   As a long-parted mother with her child
9   Plays fondly with her tears and smiles in meeting,
     So weeping, smiling, greet I thee, my earth,
11   And do thee favors with my royal hands.
     Feed not thy sovereign's foe, my gentle earth,
     Nor with thy sweets comfort his ravenous sense;
     But let thy spiders that suck up thy venom,
     And heavy-gaited toads, lie in their way,
     Doing annoyance to the treacherous feet
     Which with usurping steps do trample thee.
     Yield stinging nettles to mine enemies;
     And when they from thy bosom pluck a flower,
     Guard it, I pray thee, with a lurking adder
21   Whose double tongue may with a mortal touch
     Throw death upon thy sovereign's enemies.
23   Mock not my senseless conjuration, lords.
     This earth shall have a feeling, and these stones
25   Prove armèd soldiers ere her native king
     Shall falter under foul rebellion's arms.
CARLISLE
     Fear not, my lord. That Power that made you king
     Hath power to keep you king in spite of all.
     The means that heavens yield must be embraced
     And not neglected. Else heaven would,
     And we will not. Heaven's offer we refuse,
     The proffered means of succor and redress.
AUMERLE
     He means, my lord, that we are too remiss,
34   Whilst Bolingbroke, through our security,
     Grows strong and great in substance and in power.
KING
36   Discomfortable cousin! know'st thou not
37   That when the searching eye of heaven is hid
     Behind the globe, that lights the lower world,
     Then thieves and robbers range abroad unseen
     In murders and in outrage boldly here;
     But when from under this terrestrial ball
     He fires the proud tops of the eastern pines
     And darts his light through every guilty hole,
     Then murders, treasons, and detested sins,
     The cloak of night being plucked from off their backs,
     Stand bare and naked, trembling at themselves?

     So when this thief, this traitor Bolingbroke,
     Who all this while hath revelled in the night
     Whilst we were wand'ring with the Antipodes,   49
     Shall see us rising in our throne, the east,
     His treasons will sit blushing in his face,
     Not able to endure the sight of day,
     But self-affrighted tremble at his sin.
     Not all the water in the rough rude sea
     Can wash the balm off from an anointed king.   55
     The breath of worldly men cannot depose   56
     The deputy elected by the Lord.
     For every man that Bolingbroke hath pressed   58
     To lift shrewd steel against our golden crown,   59
     God for his Richard hath in heavenly pay
     A glorious angel. Then, if angels fight,
     Weak men must fall; for heaven still guards the right.
          Enter Salisbury.
     Welcome, my lord. How far off lies your power?   63
SALISBURY
     Nor near nor farther off, my gracious lord,   64
     Than this weak arm. Discomfort guides my tongue
     And bids me speak of nothing but despair.
     One day too late, I fear me, noble lord,
     Hath clouded all thy happy days on earth.
     O, call back yesterday, bid time return,
     And thou shalt have twelve thousand fighting men!
     To-day, to-day, unhappy day too late,
     O'erthrows thy joys, friends, fortune, and thy state;
     For all the Welshmen, hearing thou wert dead,
     Are gone to Bolingbroke, dispersed, and fled.
AUMERLE
     Comfort, my liege. Why looks your grace so pale?
KING
     But now the blood of twenty thousand men   76
       Did triumph in my face, and they are fled;
     And, till so much blood thither come again,
       Have I not reason to look pale and dead?
     All souls that will be safe, fly from my side;
     For time hath set a blot upon my pride.
AUMERLE
     Comfort, my liege. Remember who you are.
KING
     I had forgot myself. Am I not king?
     Awake, thou coward majesty! thou sleepest.
     Is not the king's name twenty thousand names?
     Arm, arm, my name! A puny subject strikes
     At thy great glory. Look not to the ground,
     Ye favorites of a king. Are we not high?
     High be our thoughts. I know my uncle York
     Hath power enough to serve our turn. But who comes
       here?

41 *at large* conveyed in full   43 *Glendower* (see II, iv, s.d.n.)   44 *after*
afterwards
III, ii Before Barkloughly Castle (Harlech in Wales)   2 *brooks* enjoys
8 *long-parted mother with* mother long parted from   9 *fondly* dotingly
11 *do . . . hands* salute thee by touching   21 *double* forked; *touch* wound
23 *senseless conjuration* solemn entreaty to things which cannot understand
it   25 *native* legitimate (Richard was born at Bordeaux)   34 *security*
overconfidence   36 *Discomfortable* discouraging   37–38 *when . . . world*
when the sun, lighting the other side of the world, is hidden from view
49 *Antipodes* the people on the other side of the world   55 *balm* consecrated
oil used in the coronation   56 *worldly* earthly   58 *pressed* drafted   59
shrewd keen   63 *power* army   64 *near* nearer   76 *twenty* (Richard exaggerates Salisbury's *twelve*)

Enter Scroop.

SCROOP

More health and happiness betide my liege
Than can my care-tuned tongue deliver him!

KING

Mine ear is open and my heart prepared.
94　The worst is worldly loss thou canst unfold.
Say, is my kingdom lost? Why, 'twas my care;
And what loss is it to be rid of care?
Strives Bolingbroke to be as great as we?
Greater he shall not be; if he serve God,
We'll serve him too, and be his fellow so.
Revolt our subjects? That we cannot mend;
They break their faith to God as well as us.
Cry woe, destruction, ruin, and decay:
The worst is death, and death will have his day.

SCROOP

Glad am I that your highness is so armed
To bear the tidings of calamity.
Like an unseasonable stormy day
Which makes the silver rivers drown their shores
As if the world were all dissolved to tears,
109　So high above his limits swells the rage
Of Bolingbroke, covering your fearful land
With hard bright steel, and hearts harder than steel.
112　White-beards have armed their thin and hairless scalps
Against thy majesty. Boys with women's voices
114　Strive to speak big, and clap their female joints
In stiff unwieldy arms against thy crown.
116　Thy very beadsmen learn to bend their bows
117　Of double-fatal yew against thy state.
118　Yea, distaff-women manage rusty bills
119　Against thy seat. Both young and old rebel,
And all goes worse than I have power to tell.

KING

Too well, too well thou tell'st a tale so ill.
Where is the Earl of Wiltshire? Where is Bagot?
What is become of Bushy? Where is Green?
That they have let the dangerous enemy
125　Measure our confines with such peaceful steps?
If we prevail, their heads shall pay for it.
I warrant they have made peace with Bolingbroke.

SCROOP

Peace have they made with him indeed, my lord.

KING

O villains, vipers, damned without redemption!
Dogs easily won to fawn on any man!
Snakes in my heart-blood warmed that sting my heart!
Three Judases, each one thrice worse than Judas!
Would they make peace? Terrible hell make war

Upon their spotted souls for this offense!　134

SCROOP

Sweet love, I see, changing his property,　135
Turns to the sourest and most deadly hate.
Again uncurse their souls. Their peace is made
With heads, and not with hands. Those whom you curse　138
Have felt the worst of death's destroying wound
And lie full low, graved in the hollow ground.

AUMERLE

Is Bushy, Green, and the Earl of Wiltshire dead?

SCROOP

Ay, all of them at Bristol lost their heads.

AUMERLE

Where is the duke my father with his power?

KING

No matter where. Of comfort no man speak!
Let's talk of graves, of worms, and epitaphs,
Make dust our paper, and with rainy eyes
Write sorrow on the bosom of the earth.
Let's choose executors and talk of wills.
And yet not so – for what can we bequeath,
Save our deposèd bodies to the ground?
Our lands, our lives, and all are Bolingbroke's,
And nothing can we call our own but death
And that small model of the barren earth　153
Which serves as paste and cover to our bones.
For God's sake let us sit upon the ground
And tell sad stories of the death of kings!
How some have been deposed, some slain in war,
Some haunted by the ghosts they have deposed,　158
Some poisoned by their wives, some sleeping killed –
All murdered; for within the hollow crown
That rounds the mortal temples of a king
Keeps Death his court; and there the antic sits,　162
Scoffing his state and grinning at his pomp;
Allowing him a breath, a little scene,　164
To monarchize, be feared, and kill with looks;
Infusing him with self and vain conceit,　166
As if this flesh which walls about our life
Were brass impregnable; and humored thus,　168
Comes at the last, and with a little pin　169
Bores through his castle wall, and farewell king!
Cover your heads, and mock not flesh and blood
With solemn reverence. Throw away respect,
Tradition, form, and ceremonious duty;
For you have but mistook me all this while.
I live with bread like you, feel want, taste grief,
Need friends. Subjected thus,　176
How can you say to me I am a king?

CARLISLE

My lord, wise men ne'er sit and wail their woes,
But presently prevent the ways to wail.　179
To fear the foe, since fear oppresseth strength,
Gives, in your weakness, strength unto your foe,
And so your follies fight against yourself.
Fear, and be slain – no worse can come to fight;　183
And fight and die is death destroying death,
Where fearing dying pays death servile breath.　185

AUMERLE

My father hath a power. Inquire of him,　186
And learn to make a body of a limb.

KING

Thou chid'st me well. Proud Bolingbroke, I come

---

94 *The worst . . . unfold* the worst thou canst unfold is worldly loss　109 *his limits* its banks　112 *thin* sparsely haired　114 *clap* thrust; *female* i.e. weak　116 *beadsmen* old pensioners who pray for their benefactor　117 *double-fatal* poisonous and used to make war-bows　118 *distaff-women* spinning women; *manage* wield; *bills* halberds　119 *seat* throne　125 *Measure* travel over　134 *spotted* stained with treason　135 *property* distinctive quality　138 *with hands* by lifting their hands in surrender　153–54 *that . . . bones* that mould of earth that covers our bones – the body　158 *the ghosts . . . deposed* the ghosts of the kings they have murdered　162 *antic* clown　164–65 *scene, To monarchize* time on life's stage to play the monarch　166 *self . . . conceit* vain conceit of himself　168 *humored thus* while the king is thus puffed up　169 *Comes* Death comes　176 *Subjected thus* subject as I am – to these universal human needs　179 *prevent . . . wail* block the paths to grief　183 *to fight* by fighting　185 *Where* whereas; *fearing dying* to be afraid to die　186 *of* about

To change blows with thee for our day of doom.
This ague fit of fear is overblown.
An easy task it is to win our own.
Say, Scroop, where lies our uncle with his power?
Speak sweetly, man, although thy looks be sour.

SCROOP
Men judge by the complexion of the sky
195   The state and inclination of the day;
So may you by my dull and heavy eye:
    My tongue hath but a heavier tale to say.
198 I play the torturer, by small and small
To lengthen out the worst that must be spoken.
Your uncle York is joined with Bolingbroke,
And all your northern castles yielded up,
And all your southern gentlemen in arms
Upon his party.

KING   Thou hast said enough.
    [To Aumerle]
204 Beshrew thee, cousin, which didst lead me forth
Of that sweet way I was in to despair!
What say you now? What comfort have we now?
By heaven, I'll hate him everlastingly
That bids me be of comfort any more.
Go to Flint Castle. There I'll pine away;
A king, woe's slave, shall kingly woe obey.
That power I have, discharge; and let them go
212 To ear the land that hath some hope to grow,
For I have none. Let no man speak again
To alter this, for counsel is but vain.

AUMERLE
My liege, one word.

KING   He does me double wrong
That wounds me with the flatteries of his tongue.
Discharge my followers. Let them hence away,
From Richard's night to Bolingbroke's fair day.
                   [Exeunt.]

*

III,iii   *Enter [with Drum and Colors] Bolingbroke, York,*
        Northumberland [, Attendants, and Soldiers].

BOLINGBROKE
1 So that by this intelligence we learn
The Welshmen are dispersed, and Salisbury
Is gone to meet the king, who lately landed
With some few private friends upon this coast.

NORTHUMBERLAND
5 The news is very fair and good, my lord,
Richard not far from hence hath hid his head.

YORK
It would beseem the Lord Northumberland
To say 'King Richard.' Alack the heavy day
When such a sacred king should hide his head!

NORTHUMBERLAND
Your grace mistakes. Only to be brief,
Left I his title out.

YORK   The time hath been,
Would you have been so brief with him, he would
13 Have been so brief with you, to shorten you,
14 For taking so the head, your whole head's length.

BOLINGBROKE
Mistake not, uncle, further than you should.

YORK
Take not, good cousin, further than you should,
17 Lest you mistake the heavens are over our heads.

BOLINGBROKE
I know it, uncle, and oppose not myself
Against their will. But who comes here?
    Enter Percy.
Welcome, Harry. What, will not this castle yield?

PERCY
The castle royally is manned, my lord,
Against thy entrance.

BOLINGBROKE
Royally?
Why, it contains no king?

PERCY   Yes, my good lord,
It doth contain a king. King Richard lies
Within the limits of yon lime and stone;
And with him are the Lord Aumerle, Lord Salisbury,
Sir Stephen Scroop, besides a clergyman
Of holy reverence – who, I cannot learn.

NORTHUMBERLAND
O, belike it is the Bishop of Carlisle.   30

BOLINGBROKE
Noble lords,
Go to the rude ribs of that ancient castle;
Through brazen trumpet send the breath of parley
Into his ruined ears, and thus deliver:
Henry Bolingbroke
On both his knees doth kiss King Richard's hand
And sends allegiance and true faith of heart
To his most royal person; hither come
Even at his feet to lay my arms and power,
Provided that my banishment repealed   40
And lands restored again be freely granted.
If not, I'll use the advantage of my power,
And lay the summer's dust with show'rs of blood
Rained from the wounds of slaughtered Englishmen;
The which, how far off from the mind of Bolingbroke
It is, such crimson tempest should bedrench
The fresh green lap of fair King Richard's land,
My stooping duty tenderly shall show.   48
Go signify as much, while here we march
Upon the grassy carpet of this plain.
Let's march without the noise of threat'ning drum,
That from this castle's tottered battlements   52
Our fair appointments may be well perused.   53
Methinks King Richard and myself should meet
With no less terror than the elements
Of fire and water when their thund'ring shock   56
At meeting tears the cloudy cheeks of heaven.
Be he the fire, I'll be the yielding water;
The rage be his, whilst on the earth I rain.   59
My water's on the earth, and not on him.   60
March on, and mark King Richard how he looks.
    The trumpets sound [a parle without and within, then
    a flourish. King] Richard appeareth on the walls
    [with the Bishop of Carlisle, Aumerle, Scroop, and
    Salisbury].

195 *inclination . . . day* trend of the weather   198–99 *by . . . spoken* in breaking the worst news little by little   204 *Beshrew thee* confound you; *forth* out   212 *ear* plough
III, iii Before Flint Castle in Wales   1 *intelligence* news   5–6 *The . . . head* the news that Richard is in hiding not far away is auspicious and good   13 *to* as to   14 *taking . . . head* thus omitting his title   17 *mistake* ignore the fact that   40 *repealed* revoked   48 *stooping duty* submissive kneeling; *tenderly* considerately   52 *tottered* tattered, saw-toothed, crenellated   53 *appointments* equipment   56 *fire and water* lightning and clouds   59 *rain* 'reign'   60 *My . . . him* I fall upon the land, not upon him

See, see, King Richard doth himself appear,
As doth the blushing discontented sun
From out the fiery portal of the east
65 When he perceives the envious clouds are bent
To dim his glory and to stain the track
Of his bright passage to the occident.

YORK
68 Yet looks he like a king. Behold, his eye,
69 As bright as is the eagle's, lightens forth
Controlling majesty. Alack, alack, for woe,
That any harm should stain so fair a show!

KING [to Northumberland]
72 We are amazed; and thus long have we stood
To watch the fearful bending of thy knee,
Because we thought ourself thy lawful king.
And if we be, how dare thy joints forget
76 To pay their awful duty to our presence?
If we be not, show us the hand of God
That hath dismissed us from our stewardship;
For well we know no hand of blood and bone
Can gripe the sacred handle of our sceptre,
Unless he do profane, steal, or usurp.
And though you think that all, as you have done,
83 Have torn their souls by turning them from us
And we are barren and bereft of friends,
Yet know, my master, God omnipotent,
Is mustering in his clouds on our behalf
Armies of pestilence, and they shall strike
88 Your children yet unborn and unbegot
89 That lift your vassal hands against my head
And threat the glory of my precious crown.
Tell Bolingbroke, for yon methinks he stands,
That every stride he makes upon my land
93 Is dangerous treason. He is come to open
The purple testament of bleeding war.
But ere the crown he looks for live in peace,
Ten thousand bloody crowns of mothers' sons
97 Shall ill become the flower of England's face,
Change the complexion of her maid-pale peace
To scarlet indignation, and bedew
100 Her pastor's grass with faithful English blood.

NORTHUMBERLAND
The King of Heaven forbid our lord the king
102 Should with civil and uncivil arms
Be rushed upon! Thy thrice-noble cousin
Harry Bolingbroke doth humbly kiss thy hand;
And by the honorable tomb he swears
That stands upon your royal grandsire's bones,
And by the royalties of both your bloods
(Currents that spring from one most gracious head),
And by the buried hand of warlike Gaunt,

And by the worth and honor of himself,
Comprising all that may be sworn or said,
His coming hither hath no further scope
113 Than for his lineal royalties, and to beg
114 Enfranchisement immediate on his knees;
115 Which on thy royal party granted once,
116 His glittering arms he will commend to rust,
117 His barbèd steeds to stables, and his heart
To faithful service of your majesty.
This swears he, as he is a prince and just;
And as I am a gentleman, I credit him.

KING
121 Northumberland, say thus. The king returns:
His noble cousin is right welcome hither;
And all the number of his fair demands
Shall be accomplished without contradiction.
With all the gracious utterance thou hast
126 Speak to his gentle hearing kind commends.
[To Aumerle]
We do debase ourselves, cousin, do we not,
To look so poorly and to speak so fair?
Shall we call back Northumberland and send
Defiance to the traitor, and so die?

AUMERLE
No, good my lord. Let's fight with gentle words
Till time lend friends, and friends their helpful swords.

KING
O God, O God! that e'er this tongue of mine
That laid the sentence of dread banishment
On yon proud man, should take it off again
136 With words of sooth! O that I were as great
137 As is my grief, or lesser than my name!
Or that I could forget what I have been!
Or not remember what I must be now!
140 Swell'st thou, proud heart? I'll give thee scope to beat,
141 Since foes have scope to beat both thee and me.

AUMERLE
Northumberland comes back from Bolingbroke.

KING
What must the king do now? Must he submit?
The king shall do it. Must he be deposed?
The king shall be contented. Must he lose
146 The name of king? A God's name, let it go!
147 I'll give my jewels for a set of beads,
My gorgeous palace for a hermitage,
149 My gay apparel for an almsman's gown,
150 My figured goblets for a dish of wood,
151 My sceptre for a palmer's walking staff,
My subjects for a pair of carvèd saints,
And my large kingdom for a little grave,
A little little grave, an obscure grave;
Or I'll be buried in the king's high way,
156 Some way of common trade, where subjects' feet
May hourly trample on their sovereign's head;
For on my heart they tread now whilst I live,
And buried once, why not upon my head?
Aumerle, thou weep'st, my tender-hearted cousin!
We'll make foul weather with despisèd tears;
162 Our sighs and they shall lodge the summer corn
163 And make a dearth in this revolting land.
164 Or shall we play the wantons with our woes
And make some pretty match with shedding tears?
As thus – to drop them still upon one place
167 Till they have fretted us a pair of graves

65 he the sun   68 he King Richard   69 *lightens forth* flashes out   72 *amazed* in a maze, utterly confused   76 *awful duty* awed obeisance   83 *torn* torn asunder   88–89 *Your . . . That* of you . . . who   89 *vassal* subject 93–94 *open . . . war* carry out the terms of war's bloody will   97 *flower . . . face* blooming surface of the land   100 *Her pastor's* her shepherd's, i.e. Richard's   102 *civil* borne by Englishmen against Englishmen; *uncivil* rude   113 *lineal royalties* royal birthrights   114 *Enfranchisement* freedom from banishment   115 *on . . . party* on your majesty's part   116 *commend* hand over   117 *barbèd* armored   121 *returns* replies as follows   126 *commends* regards   136 *sooth* flattery   137 *name* title of king   140 *scope* room, permission   141 *have scope* aim   146 *A* in   147 *set of beads* rosary   149 *almsman* one living on charity   150 *figured* embossed   151 *palmer* pilgrim 156 *trade* passage   162 *lodge* beat down   163 *revolting* rebelling   164 *play the wantons* sport   167 *fretted us* washed out for us

Within the earth ; and therein laid – there lies
Two kinsmen digged their graves with weeping eyes.
Would not this ill do well ? Well, well, I see
I talk but idly, and you laugh at me.
Most mighty prince, my Lord Northumberland,
What says King Bolingbroke ? Will his majesty
Give Richard leave to live till Richard die ?
175 You make a leg, and Bolingbroke says ay.

NORTHUMBERLAND
176 My lord, in the base court he doth attend
To speak with you, may it please you to come down.

KING
178 Down, down I come, like glist'ring Phaeton,
179 Wanting the manage of unruly jades.
In the base court ? Base court, where kings grow base,
To come at traitors' calls and do them grace !
In the base court come down ? Down court ! down king !
For night owls shriek where mounting larks should sing.
        [Exeunt from above.]

BOLINGBROKE
What says his majesty ?

NORTHUMBERLAND Sorrow and grief of heart
185 Makes him speak fondly, like a frantic man.
Yet he is come.
   [Enter King Richard attended, below.]

BOLINGBROKE
Stand all apart
And show fair duty to his majesty.
   He kneels down.
My gracious lord –

KING
Fair cousin, you debase your princely knee
To make the base earth proud with kissing it.
192 Me rather had my heart might feel your love
Than my unpleased eye see your courtesy.
Up, cousin, up ! Your heart is up, I know,
Thus high at least *[touches his own head]*, although your
  knee be low.

BOLINGBROKE *[rises]*
My gracious lord, I come but for mine own.

KING
Your own is yours, and I am yours, and all.

BOLINGBROKE
198 So far be mine, my most redoubted lord,
As my true service shall deserve your love.

KING
Well you deserve. They well deserve to have
That know the strong'st and surest way to get.
Uncle, give me your hand. Nay, dry your eyes.
203 Tears show their love, but want their remedies.
Cousin, I am too young to be your father,
Though you are old enough to be my heir.
What you will have, I'll give, and willing too ;
For do we must what force will have us do.
Set on towards London. Cousin, is it so ?

BOLINGBROKE
Yea, my good lord.

KING   Then I must not say no. *[Flourish. Exeunt.]*

      *

III, iv *Enter the Queen with [two Ladies,] her Attendants.*

QUEEN
What sport shall we devise here in this garden
To drive away the heavy thought of care ?

LADY
Madam, we'll play at bowls.

QUEEN
'Twill make me think the world is full of rubs 4
And that my fortune runs against the bias. 5

LADY
Madam, we'll dance.

QUEEN
My legs can keep no measure in delight 7
When my poor heart no measure keeps in grief.
Therefore no dancing, girl ; some other sport.

LADY
Madam, we'll tell tales.

QUEEN
Of sorrow or of joy ?

LADY   Of either, madam.

QUEEN
Of neither, girl ;
For if of joy, being altogether wanting,
It doth remember me the more of sorrow ;
Or if of grief, being altogether had, 15
It adds more sorrow to my want of joy ;
For what I have I need not to repeat,
And what I want it boots not to complain. 18

LADY
Madam, I'll sing.

QUEEN   'Tis well that thou hast cause ;
But thou shouldst please me better, wouldst thou weep.

LADY
I could weep, madam, would it do you good.

QUEEN
And I could sing, would weeping do me good,
And never borrow any tear of thee.
   Enter Gardeners [one the Master, the other two his
    Men].
But stay, here come the gardeners.
Let's step into the shadow of these trees.
My wretchedness unto a row of pins, 26
They will talk of state, for every one doth so 27
Against a change : woe is forerun with woe. 28
   [Queen and Ladies step aside.]

GARDENER
Go bind thou up yon dangling apricocks, 29
Which, like unruly children, make their sire
Stoop with oppression of their prodigal weight. 31
Give some supportance to the bending twigs.
Go thou and, like an executioner,
Cut off the heads of too-fast-growing sprays
That look too lofty in our commonwealth.
All must be even in our government. 36
You thus employed, I will go root away
The noisome weeds which without profit suck
The soil's fertility from wholesome flowers.

175 *You . . . ay* if you curtsy to him, Bolingbroke will say yes 176 *base court* lower or outer courtyard ; *attend* wait 178 *Phaeton* (he borrowed the chariot of his father, the sun god, drove it unskillfully, nearly set the world on fire) 179 *Wanting . . . of* lacking control over ; *jades* poor horses 185 *fondly* foolishly ; *frantic* mad 192 *Me rather had* I would rather 198 *redoubted* dread 203 *want their remedies* cannot cure what causes them
III, iv The garden of the Duke of York's seat at Langley 4 *rubs* impediments (in the game of bowls) 5 *bias* curving course (of a bowl) 7–8 *measure . . . measure* stately dance . . . moderation 15 *had* had by me 18 *boots* helps 26 *My . . . pins* my grief against a trifle 27 *state* politics 28 *Against* expecting 29 *apricocks* apricots 31 *prodigal* excessive 36 *even* equal

[1.] MAN

40 Why should we, in the compass of a pale,
Keep law and form and due proportion,
Showing, as in a model, our firm estate,
When our sea-wallèd garden, the whole land,
Is full of weeds, her fairest flowers choked up,
Her fruit trees all unpruned, her hedges ruined,
46 Her knots disordered, and her wholesome herbs
Swarming with caterpillars?

GARDENER   Hold thy peace.
He that hath suffered this disordered spring
Hath now himself met with the fall of leaf.
The weeds which his broad-spreading leaves did
     shelter,
51 That seemed in eating him to hold him up,
Are plucked up root and all by Bolingbroke –
I mean the Earl of Wiltshire, Bushy, Green.

[2.] MAN
What, are they dead?

GARDENER   They are; and Bolingbroke
Hath seized the wasteful king. O, what pity is it
That he had not so trimmed and dressed his land
57 As we this garden! We at time of year
Do wound the bark, the skin of our fruit trees,
59 Lest, being overproud in sap and blood,
60 With too much riches it confound itself.
Had he done so to great and growing men,
They might have lived to bear, and he to taste
Their fruits of duty. Superfluous branches
We lop away, that bearing boughs may live.
Had he done so, himself had borne the crown,
Which waste of idle hours hath quite thrown down.

[2.] MAN
What, think you the king shall be deposed?

GARDENER
68 Depressed he is already, and deposed
69 'Tis doubt he will be. Letters came last night
To a dear friend of the good Duke of York's
That tell black tidings.

QUEEN
72 O, I am pressed to death through want of speaking!
     [Comes forward.]
73 Thou old Adam's likeness, set to dress this garden,
How dares thy harsh rude tongue sound this unpleasing
     news?
75 What Eve, what serpent, hath suggested thee
To make a second fall of cursèd man?
Why dost thou say King Richard is deposed?
Dar'st thou, thou little better thing than earth,
79 Divine his downfall? Say, where, when, and how
Cam'st thou by this ill tidings? Speak, thou wretch!

GARDENER
Pardon me, madam. Little joy have I
To breathe this news; yet what I say is true.   82
King Richard, he is in the mighty hold
Of Bolingbroke. Their fortunes both are weighed.
In your lord's scale is nothing but himself,
And some few vanities that make him light;
But in the balance of great Bolingbroke,
Besides himself, are all the English peers,
And with that odds he weighs King Richard down.
Post you to London, and you will find it so.
I speak no more than every one doth know.

QUEEN
Nimble mischance, that art so light of foot,
Doth not thy embassage belong to me,   93
And am I last that knows it? O, thou thinkest
To serve me last, that I may longest keep
Thy sorrow in my breast. Come, ladies, go   96
To meet at London London's king in woe.
What, was I born to this, that my sad look
Should grace the triumph of great Bolingbroke?   99
Gard'ner, for telling me these news of woe,
Pray God the plants thou graft'st may never grow.
                    Exit [with Ladies].

GARDNER
Poor queen, so that thy state might be no worse,
I would my skill were subject to thy curse!
Here did she fall a tear; here in this place   104
I'll set a bank of rue, sour herb of grace.   105
Rue, even for ruth, here shortly shall be seen,   106
In the remembrance of a weeping queen.   *Exeunt.*

                         *

Enter Bolingbroke, with the Lords [Aumerle,   IV, i
Northumberland, Percy, Fitzwater, Surrey, and
another, with Bishop of Carlisle, Abbot of
Westminster, Attendants, and Herald] to
Parliament.

BOLINGBROKE
Call forth Bagot.
     Enter [Officers with] Bagot.
Now, Bagot, freely speak thy mind,
What thou dost know of noble Gloucester's death;
Who wrought it with the king, and who performed   4
The bloody office of his timeless end.   5

BAGOT
Then set before my face the Lord Aumerle.

BOLINGBROKE
Cousin, stand forth, and look upon that man.

BAGOT
My Lord Aumerle, I know your daring tongue
Scorns to unsay what once it hath delivered.
In that dead time when Gloucester's death was plotted,   10
I heard you say, 'Is not my arm of length,   11
That reacheth from the restful English court   12
As far as Calais to mine uncle's head?'
Amongst much other talk that very time
I heard you say that you had rather refuse
The offer of an hundred thousand crowns
Than Bolingbroke's return to England;   17
Adding withal, how blest this land would be   18
In this your cousin's death.

AUMERLE   Princes and noble lords,
What answer shall I make to this base man?

---

40 *pale* enclosed garden   46 *knots* flower-beds laid out in patterns   51
in while   57 *at . . . year* in season   59 *overproud in* swollen with   60
confound destroy   68 *Depressed* brought low   69 *'Tis doubt* there is fear
72 *pressed to death* tortured as by a heavy weight crushing me   73 *old*
Adam the first gardener   75 *suggested* tempted   79 *Divine* prophesy by
occult means   82 *To breathe* in speaking   93 *embassage* message   96 *Thy*
sorrow the sorrow you report   99 *triumph* triumphal procession; *Boling-*
broke (in the original spelling, 'Bullingbrooke,' the name rimes with *look*
in l. 98)   104 *fall* drop   105 *grace* repentance   106 *ruth* pity
IV, i Westminster Hall (September–October, 1399)   4 *wrought . . . king*
worked on the king's mind to bring it about   5 *timeless* untimely   10 *dead*
dark, silent   11 *of length* long   12 *restful* calm, untroubled by Gloucester
17 *Than . . . return* than have Bolingbroke return   18 *withal* besides

21 Shall I so much dishonor my fair stars
22 On equal terms to give him chastisement?
Either I must, or have mine honor soiled
24 With the attainder of his slanderous lips.
25 There is my gage, the manual seal of death
That marks thee out for hell. I say thou liest,
And will maintain what thou hast said is false
28 In thy heart-blood, though being all too base
29 To stain the temper of my knightly sword.

BOLINGBROKE
Bagot, forbear; thou shalt not take it up.

AUMERLE
31 Excepting one, I would he were the best
32 In all this presence that hath moved me so.

FITZWATER
33 If that thy valor stand on sympathy,
There is my gage, Aumerle, in gage to thine.
By that fair sun which shows me where thou stand'st,
I heard thee say, and vauntingly thou spak'st it,
That thou wert cause of noble Gloucester's death.
If thou deniest it twenty times, thou liest,
And I will turn thy falsehood to thy heart,
Where it was forgèd, with my rapier's point.

AUMERLE
Thou dar'st not, coward, live to see that day.

FITZWATER
Now, by my soul, I would it were this hour.

AUMERLE
Fitzwater, thou art damned to hell for this.

PERCY
Aumerle, thou liest. His honor is as true
45 In this appeal as thou art all unjust;
And that thou art so, there I throw my gage
To prove it on thee to the extremest point
Of mortal breathing. Seize it if thou dar'st.

AUMERLE
And if I do not, may my hands rot off
And never brandish more revengeful steel
Over the glittering helmet of my foe!

ANOTHER LORD
52 I task the earth to the like, forsworn Aumerle;
53 And spur thee on with full as many lies
As may be holloed in thy treacherous ear
55 From sun to sun. There is my honor's pawn.
56 Engage it to the trial, if thou darest.

AUMERLE
57 Who sets me else? By heaven, I'll throw at all!
I have a thousand spirits in one breast
To answer twenty thousand such as you.

SURREY
My Lord Fitzwater, I do remember well
The very time Aumerle and you did talk.

FITZWATER
62 'Tis very true. You were in presence then,
And you can witness with me this is true.

SURREY
As false, by heaven, as heaven itself is true!

FITZWATER
Surrey, thou liest.

SURREY   Dishonorable boy!
That lie shall lie so heavy on my sword
That it shall render vengeance and revenge
Till thou the lie-giver and that lie do lie
In earth as quiet as thy father's skull.

In proof whereof there is my honor's pawn.
Engage it to the trial if thou dar'st.

FITZWATER
How fondly dost thou spur a forward horse!   72
If I dare eat, or drink, or breathe, or live,
I dare meet Surrey in a wilderness,   74
And spit upon him whilst I say he lies,
And lies, and lies. There is my bond of faith
To tie thee to my strong correction.
As I intend to thrive in this new world,   78
Aumerle is guilty of my true appeal.
Besides, I heard the banished Norfolk say
That thou, Aumerle, didst send two of thy men
To execute the noble duke at Calais.

AUMERLE
Some honest Christian trust me with a gage
That Norfolk lies. Here do I throw down this,
If he may be repealed to try his honor.   85

BOLINGBROKE
These differences shall all rest under gage   86
Till Norfolk be repealed. Repealed he shall be
And, though mine enemy, restored again
To all his lands and signories. When he is returned,
Against Aumerle we will enforce his trial.

CARLISLE
That honorable day shall never be seen.
Many a time hath banished Norfolk fought
For Jesu Christ in glorious Christian field,
Streaming the ensign of the Christian cross   94
Against black pagans, Turks, and Saracens;
And, toiled with works of war, retired himself   96
To Italy; and there, at Venice, gave
His body to that pleasant country's earth
And his pure soul unto his captain, Christ,
Under whose colors he had fought so long.

BOLINGBROKE
Why, Bishop, is Norfolk dead?

CARLISLE
As surely as I live, my lord.

BOLINGBROKE
Sweet peace conduct his sweet soul to the bosom   103
Of good old Abraham! Lords appellants,
Your differences shall all rest under gage
Till we assign you to your days of trial.
       Enter York [attended].

YORK
Great Duke of Lancaster, I come to thee
From plume-plucked Richard, who with willing soul   108
Adopts thee heir and his high sceptre yields
To the possession of thy royal hand.
Ascend his throne, descending now from him,
And long live Henry, fourth of that name!

21 *fair stars* high rank and fortune   22 *On . . . chastisement* as to fight him as my equal in rank   24 *attainder* disgraceful accusation   25 *manual . . . death* your death warrant sealed by my hand   28 *being* it is   29 *temper* honorable quality   31 *one* i.e. Bolingbroke   32 *moved* angered   33 *If . . . sympathy* if your valor can show itself only on those who are your equals in blood   45 *all unjust* completely false   52 *task . . . like* burden the ground with another gage   53 *lies* accusations of lying   55 *pawn* pledge   56 *Engage . . . trial* take it as a challenge to fight   57 *sets me* puts up stakes against me; *throw at all* throw down gloves, like wagers at dice, against you all   62 *in presence* present at court   72 *forward* willing   74 *in a wilderness* i.e. where there would be no help and no escape   78 *in . . . world* under the new king   85 *repealed* called back   86 *under gage* as challenges   94 *Streaming* flying   96 *toiled* worn out   103–04 *bosom . . . Abraham* heavenly rest   108 *plume-plucked* sorry-looking, denuded

BOLINGBROKE
In God's name I'll ascend the regal throne.

CARLISLE

114 Marry, God forbid!
115 Worst in this royal presence may I speak,
116 Yet, best beseeming me to speak the truth:
Would God that any in this noble presence
Were enough noble to be upright judge
Of noble Richard! then true noblesse would
Learn him forbearance from so foul a wrong.
What subject can give sentence on his king?
And who sits here that is not Richard's subject?
Thieves are not judged but they are by to hear,
Although apparent guilt be seen in them;
And shall the figure of God's majesty,
His captain, steward, deputy elect,
Anointed, crownèd, planted many years,
Be judged by subject and inferior breath,
129 And he himself not present? O, forfend it God
130 That, in a Christian climate, souls refined
131 Should show so heinous, black, obscene a deed!
I speak to subjects, and a subject speaks,
Stirred up by God, thus boldly for his king.
My Lord of Hereford here, whom you call king,
Is a foul traitor to proud Hereford's king;
And if you crown him, let me prophesy,
The blood of English shall manure the ground
And future ages groan for this foul act;
Peace shall go sleep with Turks and infidels,
And in this seat of peace tumultuous wars
141 Shall kin with kin and kind with kind confound;
Disorder, horror, fear, and mutiny
Shall here inhabit, and this land be called
144 The field of Golgotha and dead men's skulls.
O, if you raise this house against this house,
It will the woefullest division prove
That ever fell upon this cursèd earth.
Prevent it, resist it, let it not be so,
Lest child, child's children cry against you woe.

NORTHUMBERLAND
Well have you argued, sir; and for your pains
151 Of capital treason we arrest you here.
My Lord of Westminster, be it your charge
To keep him safely till his day of trial.
154 [May it please you, lords, to grant the commons' suit.

BOLINGBROKE
Fetch hither Richard, that in common view
He may surrender. So we shall proceed
Without suspicion.
157 YORK   I will be his conduct.   *Exit.*

BOLINGBROKE
Lords, you that here are under our arrest,
Procure your sureties for your days of answer.   159
Little are we beholding to your love,
And little looked for at your helping hands.
     *Enter Richard and York [with Officers bearing the
     crown, &c.].*

RICHARD
Alack, why am I sent for to a king
Before I have shook off the regal thoughts
Wherewith I reigned? I hardly yet have learned
To insinuate, flatter, bow, and bend my limbs.
Give sorrow leave a while to tutor me
To this submission. Yet I well remember
The favors of these men. Were they not mine?   168
Did they not sometime cry 'All hail!' to me?
So Judas did to Christ; but he, in twelve,
Found truth in all but one; I, in twelve thousand none.
God save the king! Will no man say amen?
Am I both priest and clerk? Well then, amen!   173
God save the king! although I be not he;
And yet amen, if heaven do think him me.
To do what service am I sent for hither?

YORK
To do that office of thine own good will
Which tired majesty did make thee offer –   178
The resignation of thy state and crown
To Henry Bolingbroke.

RICHARD
Give me the crown. Here, cousin, seize the crown.
Here, cousin,
On this side my hand, and on that side yours.
Now is this golden crown like a deep well
That owes two buckets, filling one another,   185
The emptier ever dancing in the air,
The other down, unseen, and full of water.
That bucket down and full of tears am I,
Drinking my griefs whilst you mount up on high.

BOLINGBROKE
I thought you had been willing to resign.

RICHARD
My crown I am, but still my griefs are mine.
You may my glories and my state depose,
But not my griefs. Still am I king of those.

BOLINGBROKE
Part of your cares you give me with your crown.

RICHARD
Your cares set up do not pluck my cares down.
My care is loss of care, by old care done;   196
Your care is gain of care, by new care won.   197
The cares I give I have, though given away;
They tend the crown, yet still with me they stay.   199

BOLINGBROKE
Are you contented to resign the crown?

RICHARD
Ay, no; no, ay; for I must nothing be;   201
Therefore no no, for I resign to thee.
Now mark me how I will undo myself.   203
I give this heavy weight from off my head
And this unwieldy sceptre from my hand,
The pride of kingly sway from out my heart.
With mine own tears I wash away my balm,
With mine own hands I give away my crown,
With mine own tongue deny my sacred state,

114 *Marry* by the Virgin Mary   115 *Worst . . . speak* I may be by birth and position the most unfit to speak   116 *best . . . truth* since it best beseems me, a clergyman, to speak the truth, I say   129 *forfend* forbid   130 *souls refined* civilized people   131 *obscene* ill-omened   141 *kin . . . kind* kinsmen . . . fellow-countrymen   144 *Golgotha* 'the place of a skull,' Calvary   151 *Of* on the charge of; *capital* carrying the death penalty   154–318 *May . . . fall* (see 'Note on the Text,' p. 636)   154 *suit* request that the causes of Richard's deposition be published   157 *conduct* escort   159 *sureties* men who will be responsible for your appearance   168 *favors* faces and friendly acts   173 *Am . . . clerk* must I pray like the priest and say amen like the clerk   178 *tired majesty* weariness of kingship   185 *owes* owns, has   196 *care . . . care . . . old care* grief . . . responsibility . . . failing diligence   197 *care . . . care . . . new care* anxiety . . . responsibility . . . fresh zeal   199 *tend* go with   201 *Ay . . . ay* 'yes, no; no, yes,' but also 'I, no; no I'   203 *undo* strip and ruin

210 With mine own breath release all duty's rites.
    All pomp and majesty I do forswear;
    My manors, rents, revenues I forgo;
    My acts, decrees, and statutes I deny.
    God pardon all oaths that are broke to me!
215 God keep all vows unbroke that swear to thee!
    Make me, that nothing have, with nothing grieved,
    And thou with all pleased, that hast all achieved!
    Long mayst thou live in Richard's seat to sit,
    And soon lie Richard in an earthy pit!
    God save King Harry, unkinged Richard says,
    And send him many years of sunshine days!
    What more remains?

      NORTHUMBERLAND No more, but that you read
    These accusations and these grievous crimes
    Committed by your person and your followers
225 Against the state and profit of this land,
    That, by confessing them, the souls of men
227 May deem that you are worthily deposed.

      RICHARD
228 Must I do so? and must I ravel out
    My weaved-up folly? Gentle Northumberland,
    If thy offenses were upon record,
    Would it not shame thee in so fair a troop
232 To read a lecture of them? If thou wouldst,
    There shouldst thou find one heinous article,
    Containing the deposing of a king
235 And cracking the strong warrant of an oath,
    Marked with a blot, damned in the book of heaven.
    Nay, all of you that stand and look upon
238 Whilst that my wretchedness doth bait myself,
    Though some of you, with Pilate, wash your hands,
    Showing an outward pity, yet you Pilates
241 Have here delivered me to my sour cross,
    And water cannot wash away your sin.

      NORTHUMBERLAND
243 My lord, dispatch. Read o'er these articles.

      RICHARD
    Mine eyes are full of tears; I cannot see.
    And yet salt water blinds them not so much
246 But they can see a sort of traitors here.
    Nay, if I turn mine eyes upon myself,
    I find myself a traitor with the rest;
    For I have given here my soul's consent
250 To undeck the pompous body of a king;
    Made glory base, and sovereignty a slave,
    Proud majesty a subject, state a peasant.

      NORTHUMBERLAND
    My lord –

      RICHARD
254 No lord of thine, thou haught, insulting man,
    Nor no man's lord. I have no name, no title –
256 No, not that name was given me at the font –
    But 'tis usurped. Alack the heavy day,
    That I have worn so many winters out
    And know not now what name to call myself!
    O that I were a mockery king of snow,
    Standing before the sun of Bolingbroke
    To melt myself away in water drops!
    Good king, great king, and yet not greatly good,
264 An if my word be sterling yet in England,
    Let it command a mirror hither straight,
    That it may show me what a face I have
    Since it is bankrout of his majesty.

      BOLINGBROKE
    Go some of you and fetch a looking glass.
                              [Exit an Attendant.]

      NORTHUMBERLAND
    Read o'er this paper while the glass doth come.

      RICHARD
    Fiend, thou torments me ere I come to hell!   270

      BOLINGBROKE
    Urge it no more, my Lord Northumberland.

      NORTHUMBERLAND
    The commons will not then be satisfied.

      RICHARD
    They shall be satisfied. I'll read enough
    When I do see the very book indeed
    Where all my sins are writ, and that's myself.
        Enter one with a glass.
    Give me the glass, and therein will I read.
    No deeper wrinkles yet? Hath sorrow struck
    So many blows upon this face of mine
    And made no deeper wounds? O flattering glass,
    Like to my followers in prosperity,
    Thou dost beguile me! Was this face the face
    That every day under his household roof
    Did keep ten thousand men? Was this the face
    That like the sun did make beholders wink?   284
    Was this the face that faced so many follies   285
    And was at last outfaced by Bolingbroke?
    A brittle glory shineth in this face.
    As brittle as the glory is the face,
        [Dashes the glass to the floor.]
    For there it is, cracked in a hundred shivers.
    Mark, silent king, the moral of this sport –
    How soon my sorrow hath destroyed my face.

      BOLINGBROKE
    The shadow of your sorrow hath destroyed   292
    The shadow of your face.

      RICHARD   Say that again.
    The shadow of my sorrow? Ha! let's see!
    'Tis very true: my grief lies all within;
    And these external manners of laments
    Are merely shadows to the unseen grief
    That swells with silence in the tortured soul.
    There lies the substance; and I thank thee, king,
    For thy great bounty that not only giv'st   300
    Me cause to wail, but teachest me the way
    How to lament the cause. I'll beg one boon,   302
    And then be gone and trouble you no more.
    Shall I obtain it?

      BOLINGBROKE   Name it, fair cousin.

      RICHARD
    Fair cousin? I am greater than a king;
    For when I was a king, my flatterers
    Were then but subjects; being now a subject,
    I have a king here to my flatterer.   308
    Being so great, I have no need to beg.

210 *duty's rites* ceremonies of respect 215 *swear* are sworn 225 *state and profit* ordered prosperity 227 *worthily* justly 228 *ravel out* unravel 232 *read . . . them* read them out like the lesson in church 235 *oath* i.e. your oath of allegiance to me 238 *bait* torment 241 *sour* bitter 243 *dispatch* make haste 246 *sort* gang 250 *pompous* stately 254 *haught* arrogant 256–57 *No . . . usurped* (Richard's enemies spread a rumor that he was illegitimate) 264 *An if* if; *sterling* valid currency 284 *wink* close their eyes 285 *faced* countenanced 292–93 *shadow . . . shadow* outward show . . . reflection 300 *that* who 302 *boon* favor 308 *to* as

BOLINGBROKE
Yet ask.

RICHARD
And shall I have?

BOLINGBROKE
You shall.

RICHARD
Then give me leave to go.

BOLINGBROKE
Whither?

RICHARD
Whither you will, so I were from your sights.

BOLINGBROKE
316 Go some of you, convey him to the Tower.

RICHARD
317 O, good! Convey? Conveyers are you all,
That rise thus nimbly by a true king's fall.]
[Exit Richard, with some Lords and a Guard.]

BOLINGBROKE
On Wednesday next we solemnly proclaim
Our coronation. Lords, be ready all.
*Exeunt. Manent [the Abbot of] Westminster,
[the Bishop of] Carlisle, Aumerle.*

ABBOT
A woeful pageant have we here beheld.

CARLISLE
The woe's to come. The children yet unborn
Shall feel this day as sharp to them as thorn.

AUMERLE
You holy clergymen, is there no plot
To rid the realm of this pernicious blot?

ABBOT
My lord,
Before I freely speak my mind herein,
You shall not only take the sacrament
329 To bury mine intents, but also to effect
Whatever I shall happen to devise.
I see your brows are full of discontent,
Your hearts of sorrow, and your eyes of tears.
Come home with me to supper. I will lay
A plot shall show us all a merry day.   *Exeunt.*

*

V, i   *Enter the Queen with [Ladies,] her Attendants.*

QUEEN
This way the king will come. This is the way
2 To Julius Caesar's ill-erected tower,
To whose flint bosom my condemnèd lord
Is doomed a prisoner by proud Bolingbroke.
Here let us rest, if this rebellious earth
Have any resting for her true king's queen.
Enter Richard [and Guard].
But soft, but see, or rather do not see,

My fair rose wither. Yet look up, behold,
That you in pity may dissolve to dew
And wash him fresh again with true-love tears.
Ah, thou the model where old Troy did stand,   11
Thou map of honor, thou King Richard's tomb,   12
And not King Richard! Thou most beauteous inn,   13
Why should hard-favored grief be lodged in thee
When triumph is become an alehouse guest?

RICHARD
Join not with grief, fair woman, do not so,
To make my end too sudden. Learn, good soul,
To think our former state a happy dream;
From which awaked, the truth of what we are
Shows us but this. I am sworn brother, sweet,
To grim Necessity, and he and I
Will keep a league till death. Hie thee to France
And cloister thee in some religious house.
Our holy lives must win a new world's crown,   24
Which our profane hours here have thrown down.   25

QUEEN
What, is my Richard both in shape and mind
Transformed and weak'ned? Hath Bolingbroke deposed
Thine intellect? Hath he been in thy heart?
The lion dying thrusteth forth his paw
And wounds the earth, if nothing else, with rage
To be o'erpow'red; and wilt thou pupil-like   31
Take the correction mildly, kiss the rod,
And fawn on rage with base humility,
Which art a lion and the king of beasts?

RICHARD
A king of beasts indeed! If aught but beasts,
I had been still a happy king of men.
Good sometimes queen, prepare thee hence for France.
Think I am dead, and that even here thou takest,
As from my deathbed, thy last living leave.
In winter's tedious nights sit by the fire
With good old folks, and let them tell thee tales   41
Of woeful ages long ago betid;
And ere thou bid good night, to quite their griefs   43
Tell thou the lamentable tale of me,
And send the hearers weeping to their beds.
For why, the senseless brands will sympathize   46
The heavy accent of thy moving tongue
And in compassion weep the fire out;
And some will mourn in ashes, some coal-black,
For the deposing of a rightful king.
Enter Northumberland [attended].

NORTHUMBERLAND
My lord, the mind of Bolingbroke is changed.
You must to Pomfret, not unto the Tower.   52
And, madam, there is order ta'en for you:
With all swift speed you must away to France.

RICHARD
Northumberland, thou ladder wherewithal   55
The mounting Bolingbroke ascends my throne,
The time shall not be many hours of age
More than it is, ere foul sin gathering head   58
Shall break into corruption. Thou shalt think,
Though he divide the realm and give thee half,
It is too little, helping him to all.
And he shall think that thou, which knowest the way
To plant unrightful kings, wilt know again,
Being ne'er so little urged another way,
To pluck him headlong from the usurped throne.   65

316 *convey* escort   317 *Convey* slang for 'steal'   329 *bury mine intents* hide what I intend
V, i A London street   2 *ill-erected* erected with evil results   11 *model . . . stand* ground plan of ruin, like that of Troy after its fall   12 *map* pattern   13–15 *inn . . . alehouse* mansion (Richard) . . . tavern (Bolingbroke)   24 *new world's* heavenly   25 *thrown* (two syllables)   31 *To be* at being   41–42 *tales . . . betid* tales of woe which happened in ages long past   43 *quite* requite; *griefs* tales of woe   46 *For why* because; *sympathize* respond to   52 *Pomfret* Pontefract, or Pomfret, Castle in Yorkshire (the scene of V, v)   55 *wherewithal* by means of which   58 *gathering head* coming to a head, like a boil   65 *To* how to

66 The love of wicked men converts to fear ;
That fear to hate, and hate turns one or both
68 To worthy danger and deservèd death.

NORTHUMBERLAND
My guilt be on my head, and there an end !
70 Take leave and part, for you must part forthwith.

RICHARD
Doubly divorced ! Bad men, you violate
A twofold marriage – 'twixt my crown and me,
And then betwixt me and my married wife.
Let me unkiss the oath 'twixt thee and me ;
And yet not so, for with a kiss 'twas made.
Part us, Northumberland – I towards the north,
77 Where shivering cold and sickness pines the clime ;
My wife to France, from whence, set forth in pomp,
She came adornèd hither like sweet May,
80 Sent back like Hallowmas or short'st of day.

QUEEN
And must we be divided ? Must we part ?

RICHARD
Ay, hand from hand, my love, and heart from heart.

QUEEN
Banish us both, and send the king with me.

NORTHUMBERLAND
84 That were some love, but little policy.

QUEEN
Then whither he goes, thither let me go.

RICHARD
86 So two, together weeping, make one woe.
Weep thou for me in France, I for thee here.
88 Better far off than near, be ne'er the near.
Go, count thy way with sighs ; I mine with groans.

QUEEN
So longest way shall have the longest moans.

RICHARD
Twice for one step I'll groan, the way being short,
And piece the way out with a heavy heart.
Come, come, in wooing sorrow let's be brief,
Since, wedding it, there is such length in grief.
One kiss shall stop our mouths, and dumbly part.
Thus give I mine, and thus take I thy heart.

QUEEN
Give me mine own again. 'Twere no good part
To take on me to keep and kill thy heart.
So, now I have mine own again, be gone,
That I may strive to kill it with a groan.

RICHARD
101 We make woe wanton with this fond delay.
Once more adieu ! The rest let sorrow say.   Exeunt.

*

V, ii   Enter Duke of York and the Duchess.

DUCHESS
My lord, you told me you would tell the rest,
When weeping made you break the story off
Of our two cousins coming into London.

YORK
4 Where did I leave ?

DUCHESS   At that sad stop, my lord,
5 Where rude misgoverned hands from windows' tops
Threw dust and rubbish on King Richard's head.

YORK
Then, as I said, the duke, great Bolingbroke,

Mounted upon a hot and fiery steed
Which his aspiring rider seemed to know,   9
With slow but stately pace kept on his course,
Whilst all tongues cried, 'God save thee, Bolingbroke !'
You would have thought the very windows spake,
So many greedy looks of young and old
Through casements darted their desiring eyes
Upon his visage ; and that all the walls
With painted imagery had said at once,   16
'Jesu preserve thee ! Welcome, Bolingbroke !'
Whilst he, from the one side to the other turning,
Bareheaded, lower than his proud steed's neck,
Bespake them thus, 'I thank you, countrymen.'
And thus still doing, thus he passed along.

DUCHESS
Alack, poor Richard ! Where rode he the whilst ?

YORK
As in a theatre the eyes of men,
After a well-graced actor leaves the stage,   24
Are idly bent on him that enters next,   25
Thinking his prattle to be tedious,
Even so, or with much more contempt, men's eyes
Did scowl on gentle Richard. No man cried, 'God save
    him !'
No joyful tongue gave him his welcome home,
But dust was thrown upon his sacred head ;
Which with such gentle sorrow he shook off,
His face still combating with tears and smiles,
The badges of his grief and patience,   33
That, had not God for some strong purpose steeled
The hearts of men, they must perforce have melted
And barbarism itself have pitied him.   36
But heaven hath a hand in these events,
To whose high will we bound our calm contents.   38
To Bolingbroke are we sworn subjects now,
Whose state and honor I for aye allow.   40
    [Enter Aumerle.]

DUCHESS
Here comes my son Aumerle.

YORK   Aumerle that was ;
But that is lost for being Richard's friend,   42
And, madam, you must call him Rutland now.
I am in parliament pledge for his truth
And lasting fealty to the new-made king.   45

DUCHESS
Welcome, my son. Who are the violets now   46
That strew the green lap of the new-come spring ?

AUMERLE
Madam, I know not, nor I greatly care not.
God knows I had as lief be none as one.

YORK
Well, bear you well in this new spring of time,

66 *converts* changes 68 *worthy* merited 70 *part . . . part* separate . . .
depart 77 *pines the clime* make the climate an enfeebling one 80 *Hallowmas* All Saint's Day, November 1 ; *short'st of day* the winter solstice 84
policy political wisdom 86 *So* no, for thus 88 *near . . . near* being near,
never be nearer 101 *We . . . wanton* we play with our grief ; *fond* foolishly
affectionate
V, ii The palace of the Duke of York 4 *leave* leave off 5 *misgoverned*
unruly ; *windows' tops* upper windows 9 *Which . . . know* that seemed to
know its ambitious rider 16 *With . . . imagery* painted with figures like
a tapestry 24 *well-graced* graceful and well received 25 *idly* listlessly
33 *badges* tokens 36 *barbarism itself* even savages 38 *To . . . contents* we
limit our wishes to calm content with heaven's high will 40 *state* high
rank 42 *that* that title 45 *fealty* loyalty 46-47 *Who . . . spring* who are
the new king's favorites

Lest you be cropped before you come to prime.
52 What news from Oxford? Do these justs and triumphs
     hold?

AUMERLE
For aught I know, my lord, they do.

YORK
You will be there, I know.

AUMERLE
If God prevent not, I purpose so.

YORK
What seal is that that hangs without thy bosom?
Yea, look'st thou pale? Let me see the writing.

AUMERLE
My lord, 'tis nothing.

YORK   No matter then who see it.
I will be satisfied; let me see the writing.

AUMERLE
I do beseech your grace to pardon me.
It is a matter of small consequence
Which for some reasons I would not have seen.

YORK
Which for some reasons, sir, I mean to see.
I fear, I fear –

DUCHESS   What should you fear?
65 'Tis nothing but some bond that he is ent'red into
66 For gay apparel 'gainst the triumph day.

YORK
Bound to himself? What doth he with a bond
That he is bound to? Wife, thou art a fool.
Boy, let me see the writing.

AUMERLE
I do beseech you pardon me. I may not show it.

YORK
I will be satisfied. Let me see it, I say.
     He plucks it out of his bosom and reads it.
Treason, foul treason! Villain! traitor! slave!

DUCHESS
What is the matter, my lord?

YORK
Ho! who is within there?
     [Enter a Servant.]   Saddle my horse.
75 God for his mercy, what treachery is here!

DUCHESS
Why, what is it, my lord?

YORK
Give me my boots, I say. Saddle my horse.
                            [Exit Servant.]
Now, by mine honor, by my life, by my troth,
79 I will appeach the villain.

DUCHESS   What is the matter?

YORK
Peace, foolish woman.

DUCHESS
I will not peace. What is the matter, Aumerle?

AUMERLE
Good mother, be content. It is no more
Than my poor life must answer.

DUCHESS   Thy life answer?

YORK
Bring me my boots! I will unto the king.
     His Man enters with his boots.

DUCHESS
Strike him, Aumerle. Poor boy, thou art amazed. –   85
     [To York's Man]
Hence, villain! Never more come in my sight.

YORK
Give me my boots, I say!   *[Servant does so and exit.]*

DUCHESS
Why, York, what wilt thou do?
Wilt thou not hide the trespass of thine own?
Have we more sons? or are we like to have?
Is not my teeming date drunk up with time?   91
And wilt thou pluck my fair son from mine age
And rob me of a happy mother's name?
Is he not like thee? Is he not thine own?

YORK
Thou fond mad woman,
Wilt thou conceal this dark conspiracy?
A dozen of them here have ta'en the sacrament,
And interchangeably set down their hands,   98
To kill the king at Oxford.

DUCHESS   He shall be none;
We'll keep him here. Then what is that to him?   100

YORK
Away, fond woman! Were he twenty times
My son, I would appeach him.

DUCHESS   Hadst thou groaned for him
As I have done, thou wouldst be more pitiful.   103
But now I know thy mind. Thou dost suspect
That I have been disloyal to thy bed
And that he is a bastard, not thy son.
Sweet York, sweet husband, be not of that mind!
He is as like thee as a man may be,
Not like to me, or any of my kin,
And yet I love him.

YORK   Make way, unruly woman!   *Exit.*

DUCHESS
After, Aumerle! Mount thee upon his horse,   111
Spur post and get before him to the king,   112
And beg thy pardon ere he do accuse thee.
I'll not be long behind. Though I be old,
I doubt not but to ride as fast as York;
And never will I rise up from the ground
Till Bolingbroke have pardoned thee. Away, be gone!
                             [Exeunt.]

                *

     Enter the King [Henry IV] with his Nobles [Percy   V, iii
     and others].

KING HENRY
Can no man tell me of my unthrifty son?   1
'Tis full three months since I did see him last.
If any plague hang over us, 'tis he.   3
I would to God, my lords, he might be found.
Inquire at London, 'mongst the taverns there,
For there, they say, he daily doth frequent,
With unrestrainèd loose companions,   7
Even such, they say, as stand in narrow lanes

---

52 *Do . . . hold* will these tourneys and victory celebrations be held   65 *is ent'red into* has signed   66 *'gainst* in anticipation of   75 *God . . . mercy* I pray God for his mercy   79 *appeach* accuse publicly   85 *him* i.e. the servant   91 *teeming date* period of childbearing   98 *interchangeably . . . hands* signed reciprocally, so that each had an indenture signed by all   100 *that* what they do   103 *pitiful* full of pity   111 *his horse* one of his horses   112 *Spur post* ride fast
V, iii Windsor Castle   1 *unthrifty* prodigal   3 *plague* calamity (as prophesied by Carlisle)   7 *loose* wild

9 And beat our watch and rob our passengers,
10 Which he, young wanton and effeminate boy,
11 Takes on the point of honor to support
    So dissolute a crew.
PERCY
    My lord, some two days since I saw the prince
    And told him of those triumphs held at Oxford.
KING HENRY
    And what said the gallant?
PERCY
16 His answer was, he would unto the stews,
    And from the common'st creature pluck a glove
    And wear it as a favor, and with that
    He would unhorse the lustiest challenger.
KING HENRY
    As dissolute as desperate! Yet through both
    I see some sparks of better hope, which elder years
    May happily bring forth. But who comes here?
    Enter Aumerle, amazed.
AUMERLE
    Where is the king?
KING HENRY
    What means our cousin, that he stares and looks
    So wildly?
AUMERLE
    God save your grace! I do beseech your majesty
    To have some conference with your grace alone.
KING HENRY
    Withdraw yourselves and leave us here alone.
                 [Exeunt Percy and Lords.]
    What is the matter with our cousin now?
AUMERLE
    For ever may my knees grow to the earth,
       [Kneels.]
    My tongue cleave to my roof within my mouth,
    Unless a pardon ere I rise or speak.
KING HENRY
    Intended, or committed, was this fault?
34 If on the first, how heinous e'er it be,
    To win thy after-love I pardon thee.
AUMERLE
    Then give me leave that I may turn the key,
    That no man enter till my tale be done.
KING HENRY
    Have thy desire.
    [Aumerle locks the door.] The Duke of York knocks
    at the door and crieth.
YORK *[within]*
    My liege, beware! look to thyself!
    Thou hast a traitor in thy presence there.
KING HENRY
    Villain, I'll make thee safe.
       [Draws.]
AUMERLE
    Stay thy revengeful hand; thou hast no cause to fear.
YORK *[within]*
43 Open the door, secure foolhardy king!
44 Shall I for love speak treason to thy face?
    Open the door, or I will break it open!
    [Enter York.]
KING HENRY
    What is the matter, uncle? Speak.
    Recover breath; tell us how near is danger,
    That we may arm us to encounter it.

YORK
    Peruse this writing here, and thou shalt know
    The treason that my haste forbids me show.   50
AUMERLE
    Remember, as thou read'st, thy promise passed.
    I do repent me. Read not my name there.
    My heart is not confederate with my hand.
YORK
    It was, villain, ere thy hand did set it down.
    I tore it from the traitor's bosom, king.
    Fear, and not love, begets his penitence.
57 Forget to pity him, lest thy pity prove   57
    A serpent that will sting thee to the heart.
KING HENRY
    O heinous, strong, and bold conspiracy!   59
    O loyal father of a treacherous son!
    Thou sheer, immaculate, and silver fountain,   61
    From whence this stream through muddy passages
    Hath held his current and defiled himself!
    Thy overflow of good converts to bad,   64
    And thy abundant goodness shall excuse
    This deadly blot in thy digressing son.   66
YORK
    So shall my virtue be his vice's bawd,
    And he shall spend mine honor with his shame,
    As thriftless sons their scraping fathers' gold.
    Mine honor lives when his dishonor dies,
    Or my shamed life in his dishonor lies.
    Thou kill'st me in his life; giving him breath,
    The traitor lives, the true man's put to death.
DUCHESS *[within]*
    What ho, my liege! For God's sake let me in!
KING HENRY
    What shrill-voiced suppliant makes this eager cry?
DUCHESS *[within]*
    A woman, and thy aunt, great king. 'Tis I.
    Speak with me, pity me, open the door!
    A beggar begs that never begged before.
KING HENRY
    Our scene is alt'red from a serious thing,
    And now changed to 'The Beggar and the King.'   80
    My dangerous cousin, let your mother in.
    I know she is come to pray for your foul sin.
YORK
    If thou do pardon, whosoever pray,
    More sins for this forgiveness prosper may.
    This fest'red joint cut off, the rest rest sound;
    This let alone will all the rest confound.
    [Enter Duchess.]
DUCHESS
    O king, believe not this hardhearted man!
    Love loving not itself, none other can.   88
YORK
    Thou frantic woman, what dost thou make here?   89
    Shall thy old dugs once more a traitor rear?

9 *watch* night patrolmen; *passengers* wayfarers 10 *Which* as to which; *wanton* 'sport'; *effeminate* self-indulgent 11 *Takes on the* takes it as a 16 *stews* brothels 34 *on the first* in the first category, intended 43 *secure* overconfident 44 *speak treason* call you a fool 50 *haste* breathlessness from hurrying 57 *Forget* forget your promise 59 *strong* flagrant 61 *sheer* pure 64 *converts* changes 66 *digressing* transgressing 80 'The . . . King' acting out the ballad of King Cophetua and the beggar-maid 88 *Love . . . can* if he does not love his own son, he cannot love anyone else 89 *make* do

DUCHESS
Sweet York, be patient. Hear me, gentle liege.
  [Kneels.]
KING HENRY
Rise up, good aunt.
DUCHESS   Not yet, I thee beseech.
For ever will I walk upon my knees,
And never see day that the happy sees,
Till thou give joy, until thou bid me joy
By pardoning Rutland, my transgressing boy.
AUMERLE
Unto my mother's prayers I bend my knee.
  [Kneels.]
YORK
Against them both my true joints bended be.
  [Kneels.]
Ill mayst thou thrive if thou grant any grace !
DUCHESS
Pleads he in earnest ? Look upon his face.
His eyes do drop no tears, his prayers are in jest ;
His words come from his mouth, ours from our breast.
He prays but faintly and would be denied ;
We pray with heart and soul and all beside.
His weary joints would gladly rise, I know ;
106   Our knees still kneel till to the ground they grow.
His prayers are full of false hypocrisy ;
Ours of true zeal and deep integrity.
Our prayers do outpray his ; then let them have
That mercy which true prayer ought to have.
KING HENRY
Good aunt, stand up.
DUCHESS   Nay, do not say 'stand up.'
Say 'pardon' first, and afterwards 'stand up.'
An if I were thy nurse, thy tongue to teach,
'Pardon' should be the first word of thy speech.
I never longed to hear a word till now.
Say 'pardon' king ; let pity teach thee how.
The word is short, but not so short as sweet ;
No word like 'pardon' for kings' mouths so meet.
YORK
119   Speak it in French, king. Say 'Pardonne moi.'
DUCHESS
Dost thou teach pardon pardon to destroy ?
Ah, my sour husband, my hardhearted lord,
That sets the word itself against the word !
123   Speak 'pardon' as 'tis current in our land ;
124   The chopping French we do not understand.
Thine eye begins to speak, set thy tongue there ;
Or in thy piteous heart plant thou thine ear,
127   That hearing how our plaints and prayers do pierce,
128   Pity may move thee 'pardon' to rehearse.
KING HENRY
Good aunt, stand up.

DUCHESS   I do not sue to stand.
Pardon is all the suit I have in hand.
KING HENRY
I pardon him as God shall pardon me.
DUCHESS
O happy vantage of a kneeling knee !
Yet am I sick for fear. Speak it again.
Twice saying 'pardon' doth not pardon twain,
But makes one pardon strong.
KING HENRY   With all my heart
I pardon him.
DUCHESS   A god on earth thou art.
  [Rises.]
KING HENRY
But for our trusty brother-in-law and the abbot,   137
With all the rest of that consorted crew,   138
Destruction straight shall dog them at the heels.
Good uncle, help to order several powers,
To Oxford, or where'er these traitors are.
They shall not live within this world, I swear,
But I will have them, if I once know where.
Uncle, farewell ; and, cousin, adieu.
Your mother well hath prayed, and prove you true.
DUCHESS
Come, my old son. I pray God make thee new.
  Exeunt [as Exton and Servant enter].
  Manet Sir Pierce Exton, & c. [Servant].   V, iv
EXTON
Didst thou not mark the king, what words he spake ?
'Have I no friend will rid me of this living fear ?'
Was it not so ?
MAN   These were his very words.
EXTON
'Have I no friend ?' quoth he. He spake it twice
And urged it twice together, did he not ?   5
MAN
He did.
EXTON
And speaking it, he wishtly looked on me,   7
As who should say, 'I would thou wert the man
That would divorce this terror from my heart !'
Meaning the king at Pomfret. Come, let's go.
I am the king's friend, and will rid his foe.   *[Exeunt.]*   11

               *

        Enter Richard, alone.   V, v
RICHARD
I have been studying how I may compare
This prison where I live unto the world ;
And, for because the world is populous,
And here is not a creature but myself,
I cannot do it. Yet I'll hammer it out.
My brain I'll prove the female to my soul,
My soul the father ; and these two beget
A generation of still-breeding thoughts ;   8
And these same thoughts people this little world,
In humors like the people of this world,   10
For no thought is contented. The better sort,
As thoughts of things divine, are intermixed
With scruples, and do set the word itself   13
Against the word :
As thus, 'Come, little ones,' and then again,
'It is as hard to come as for a camel
To thread the postern of a small needle's eye.'   17

106 *still kneel* (will) kneel continually   119 '*Pardonne moi*' 'excuse me' – a polite 'no'   123 *as . . . land* as customarily used in English   124 *The chopping French* the French phrase, in which the words change their meaning   127 *pierce* (then pronounced to rhyme with *rehearse*)   128 *rehearse* repeat   137 *brother-in-law* the Duke of Exeter ; *the abbot* of Westminster   138 *consorted crew* conniving gang
V, iv   5 *urged . . . together* emphasized it by repeating it   7 *wishtly* intently   11 *rid* get rid of
V, v   The keep in Pomfret Castle   8 *still-breeding* constantly breeding   10 *In . . . world* the creatures of fancy have their peculiar dispositions as real people do   13 *scruples* doubts   13–14 *set . . . word* find one passage of Scripture which contradicts another   17 *postern* narrow gate

Thoughts tending to ambition, they do plot
Unlikely wonders – how these vain weak nails
May tear a passage through the flinty ribs
21 Of this hard world, my ragged prison walls;
22 And, for they cannot, die in their own pride.
Thoughts tending to content flatter themselves
That they are not the first of fortune's slaves,
25 Nor shall not be the last; like seely beggars
26 Who, sitting in the stocks, refuge their shame,
That many have, and others must sit there.
And in this thought they find a kind of ease,
Bearing their own misfortunes on the back
Of such as have before endured the like.
Thus play I in one person many people,
And none contented. Sometimes am I king:
Then treasons make me wish myself a beggar,
And so I am. Then crushing penury
Persuades me I was better when a king;
Then am I kinged again; and by and by
Think that I am unkinged by Bolingbroke,
And straight am nothing. But whate'er I be,
Nor I, nor any man that but man is,
With nothing shall be pleased till he be eased
41 With being nothing. *(The music plays.)* Music do I hear?
Ha – ha – keep time! How sour sweet music is
When time is broke and no proportion kept!
So is it in the music of men's lives.
And here have I the daintiness of ear
46 To check time broke in a disordered string;
But, for the concord of my state and time,
Had not an ear to hear my true time broke.
I wasted time, and now doth time waste me;
50 For now hath time made me his numb'ring clock:
51 My thoughts are minutes; and with sighs they jar
52 Their watches on unto mine eyes, the outward watch,
53 Whereto my finger, like a dial's point,
Is pointing still, in cleansing them from tears.
Now, sir, the sound that tells what hour it is
Are clamorous groans, which strike upon my heart,
Which is the bell. So sighs and tears and groans
58 Show minutes, times, and hours. But my time
Runs posting on in Bolingbroke's proud joy,
60 While I stand fooling here, his Jack of the clock.
This music mads me. Let it sound no more;
62 For though it have holp madmen to their wits,
63 In me it seems it will make wise men mad.
Yet blessing on his heart that gives it me!
For 'tis a sign of love, and love to Richard
66 Is a strange brooch in this all-hating world.
Enter a Groom of the stable.
GROOM
67 Hail, royal prince!
RICHARD   Thanks, noble peer.
The cheapest of us is ten groats too dear.
What art thou? and how comest thou hither,
70 Where no man never comes but that sad dog
That brings me food to make misfortune live?
GROOM
I was a poor groom of thy stable, king,
When thou wert king; who, travelling towards York,
With much ado, at length, have gotten leave
To look upon my sometimes royal master's face.
76 O, how it erned my heart when I beheld,
In London streets, that coronation day,

When Bolingbroke rode on roan Barbary,
That horse that thou so often hast bestrid,
That horse that I so carefully have dressed! 80
RICHARD
Rode he on Barbary? Tell me, gentle friend,
How went he under him?
GROOM
So proudly as if he disdained the ground.
RICHARD
So proud that Bolingbroke was on his back!
That jade hath eat bread from my royal hand; 85
This hand hath made him proud with clapping him. 86
Would he not stumble? would he not fall down,
Since pride must have a fall, and break the neck
Of that proud man that did usurp his back?
Forgiveness, horse! Why do I rail on thee,
Since thou, created to be awed by man,
Wast born to bear? I was not made a horse;
And yet I bear a burden like an ass,
Spurred, galled, and tired by jauncing Bolingbroke. 94
Enter one [Keeper] to Richard with meat.
KEEPER
Fellow, give place. Here is no longer stay.
RICHARD
If thou love me, 'tis time thou wert away.
GROOM
What my tongue dares not, that my heart shall say.
Exit Groom.
KEEPER
My lord, will't please you to fall to?
RICHARD
Taste of it first, as thou art wont to do. 99
KEEPER
My lord, I dare not. Sir Pierce of Exton,
Who lately came from the king, commands the contrary.
RICHARD
The devil take Henry of Lancaster, and thee!
Patience is stale, and I am weary of it.
[Beats the Keeper.]
KEEPER
Help, help, help!
The Murderers [Exton and Servants] rush in.
RICHARD
How now! What means Death in this rude assault?
Villain, thy own hand yields thy death's instrument.
[Snatches a weapon from a Servant and kills him.]
Go thou and fill another room in hell. 107
[Kills another.] Here Exton strikes him down.
That hand shall burn in never-quenching fire
That staggers thus my person. Exton, thy fierce hand
Hath with the king's blood stained the king's own land.

21 *ragged* rugged   22 *pride* prime   25 *seely* simple-minded   26–27 *refuge ... That* find refuge for their shame in the thought that   41 *being nothing* death   46 *check* rebuke; *disordered* playing ahead of or behind the beat   50 *numb'ring clock* clock showing hours and minutes (not an hourglass)   51 *jar* tick   52 *watches* periods; *outward watch* clock face, with a play on Richard's eyes, sleepless, peering outward   53 *dial's point* clock hand   58 *times* quarters and halves   60 *Jack of the clock* mannikin which strikes the hours   62 *holp* helped   63 *wise* sane   66 *strange brooch* rare jewel; *all-hating world* world where I am universally hated   67–68 *royal ... dear* (a royal was a coin worth 10s., a noble 6s. 8d.; the difference was ten groats, a groat being fourpence)   70 *no ... never* (an emphatic double negative); *sad dog* dismal fellow   76 *erned my heart* caused my heart to mourn   80 *dressed* groomed   85 *eat* eaten   86 *with clapping* by petting   94 *jauncing* making the horse prance, riding showily   99 *Taste ... first* (a taster to insure that food was not poisoned was a royal prerogative)   107 *room* place

Mount, mount, my soul! thy seat is up on high;
Whilst my gross flesh sinks downward, here to die.
[Dies.]

EXTON
As full of valor as of royal blood!
Both have I spilled. O, would the deed were good!
For now the devil, that told me I did well,
Says that this deed is chronicled in hell.
This dead king to the living king I'll bear.
Take hence the rest, and give them burial here.
[Exeunt.]

*

V, vi   [Flourish.] Enter Bolingbroke [as King], with the
Duke of York [, other Lords, and Attendants].

KING
Kind uncle York, the latest news we hear
Is that the rebels have consumed with fire
3   Our town of Ciceter in Gloucestershire;
But whether they be ta'en or slain we hear not.
Enter Northumberland.
Welcome, my lord. What is the news?

NORTHUMBERLAND
First, to thy sacred state wish I all happiness.
The next news is, I have to London sent
The heads of Oxford, Salisbury, Blunt, and Kent.
9   The manner of their taking may appear
At large discoursèd in this paper here.

KING
We thank thee, gentle Percy, for thy pains
And to thy worth will add right worthy gains.
Enter Lord Fitzwater.

FITZWATER
My lord, I have from Oxford sent to London
The heads of Brocas and Sir Bennet Seely,
Two of the dangerous consorted traitors
That sought at Oxford thy dire overthrow.

KING
Thy pains, Fitzwater, shall not be forgot.
Right noble is thy merit, well I wot.
Enter Henry Percy [and the Bishop of Carlisle].

PERCY
The grand conspirator, Abbot of Westminster,
With clog of conscience and sour melancholy   20
Hath yielded up his body to the grave;
But here is Carlisle living, to abide   22
Thy kingly doom and sentence of his pride.

KING
Carlisle, this is your doom:
Choose out some secret place, some reverend room, 25
More than thou hast, and with it joy thy life.   26
So, as thou liv'st in peace, die free from strife;
For though mine enemy thou hast ever been,
High sparks of honor in thee have I seen.
Enter Exton, with [Attendants bearing] the coffin.

EXTON
Great king, within this coffin I present
Thy buried fear. Herein all breathless lies
The mightiest of thy greatest enemies,
Richard of Bordeaux, by me hither brought.

KING
Exton, I thank thee not; for thou hast wrought
A deed of slander, with thy fatal hand,   35
Upon my head and all this famous land.

EXTON
From your own mouth, my lord, did I this deed.

KING
They love not poison that do poison need,
Nor do I thee. Though I did wish him dead,
I hate the murderer, love him murderèd.
The guilt of conscience take thou for thy labor,
But neither my good word nor princely favor.
With Cain go wander thorough shades of night,   43
And never show thy head by day nor light.
Lords, I protest my soul is full of woe
That blood should sprinkle me to make me grow.
Come, mourn with me for what I do lament,
And put on sullen black incontinent.   48
I'll make a voyage to the Holy Land
To wash this blood off from my guilty hand.
March sadly after. Grace my mournings here   51
In weeping after this untimely bier.   [Exeunt.]

V, vi Windsor Castle   3 Ciceter i.e. Cirencester   9 taking capture   20 With
clog under the crippling weight   22 abide await   25 reverend room place of
religious retirement   26 joy gladden   35 deed of slander deed to rouse
slanderous talk against the crown   43 thorough through   48 incontinent
immediately   51 Grace dignify with your presence

THE FIRST PART OF
KING HENRY THE FOURTH

INTRODUCTION

Shakespeare wrote *1 Henry IV* soon after *Richard II*. The plays are closely linked: *1 Henry IV* begins very soon after the end of *Richard II* and often refers to the events of that play; anticipations of *1 Henry IV* are planted in *Richard II*. As *Richard II* was written by 1596, the likely date for *1 Henry IV* is 1597.

Although the play was called *The History of Henry IV* in all the early printings beginning with the quarto of 1598 (it was differentiated from the second part only when the two were first printed together in the folio of 1623), it is not chiefly concerned with King Henry IV, and when he wrote it Shakespeare evidently had other interests in mind. As he followed it up with *2 Henry IV* and *Henry V*, it may seem that his idea was to write a series of plays on the ultimate origins of the Wars of the Roses similar to the series on these wars – the three parts of *Henry VI* and *Richard III* – which he had written more than five years earlier. But though the ultimate origins of the rivalry of Lancaster and York are to be found in the deposition of Richard II, the dire effects prophesied by the Bishop of Carlisle (*Richard II*, IV, i) were long postponed and fighting did not break out for almost half a century. Over this interval loomed the heroic figure of Henry of Monmouth, the savior of his country (or at least his father's reign) as Prince of Wales, the conqueror of France as King Henry V, who while he lived averted the consequences of disaffection. He is the theme of the two *Henry IV* plays and of *Henry V*. Moreover, it is a story with a triumphant, not a tragic, outcome, and it required a different mode of treatment from *Richard II*.

The real center of *1 Henry IV*, the only character active in all the elements of the plot, is Prince Hal. Shakespeare's decision to present him in two plays* rather than one must have grown out of the curious legend of the prince's wild youth that he found in the histories. These credited the victor of Agincourt, the most Christian of the medieval kings of England, with an unruly and profligate youth, spent in dissolute company, which, however, he shed like a coat the moment he was called upon to rule. The first phase of this astonishing development is the subject of this play; it is the prelude to the revelation of Henry V in all his glory.

Though the contrast between the truant prince and the glorious king is kept before us in this play, just as it is in *Henry V*, it is a contrast of appearances rather than realities. To Shakespeare the prince is the same man potentially as the king. The discrepancy is not between a bad prince and a good king but between the prince's true nature and his reputation, between what he will be when called upon to assert himself and what he seems to be while idly, even basely, biding his time. There is no real reformation: the prince always knows what is right and prefers it; only appearances are against him. To reconcile this discrepancy Shakespeare resorted to a most unpsychological explanation, that the prince was deliberately waiting for the best opportunity to show the stuff he was made of, but evidently he thought it sufficient. Actually the play, by implication, gives a much better reason – that the prince was enjoying Falstaff – and this reason spectators at the play cordially accept.

The play, then, is a true story expanded and given additional dramatic force by the playwright's art. Much of it is based on the chronicler Holinshed's account of the reigns of Henry IV and Henry V. Shakespeare had also read the earlier chronicle of Hall (with whose story Holinshed's for the most part coincides) and Samuel Daniel's poem, *The Civil Wars* (1595), which magnifies the part of the prince in the battle of Shrewsbury and suggests his combat with Hotspur. An old play called *The Famous Victories of Henry V* had already covered the ground, beginning with the robbery on Gad's Hill and ending with the French marriage. As it is known to us only from an abbreviated and garbled version printed in 1598, it is hard to say how much Shakespeare, who presumably knew the authentic version of it, drew from it. But Shakespeare was not a historian but a playwright and his task was not to reproduce history but to transform it into drama. When good drama and history happened to coincide, he would give a faithful enough account of history as his informants had recorded it; when history proved recalcitrant to dramatization, he would ignore it or remold it to serve his purpose. As a result the play combines details perfectly true with others wholly imaginary. In a manner of speaking, the former warrant the latter. Shakespeare remembers that Bolingbroke landed at Ravenspurgh, swore an oath at Doncaster, and met Hotspur at Berkeley Castle; when he makes the king older than he really was and Hotspur younger it is not out of ignorance but out of a sense of what will make his play more effective. With the playwright's instinct for compressed and continuous action, he suppresses all indications of intervals of time between the successive episodes of the story, so that everything seems to happen in a few weeks, though actually a year elapsed between the defeat of Mortimer (June 22, 1402) and the battle of Shrewsbury (July 21, 1403). When history is silent, failing to explain why the prince played the madcap, what form his pranks took, what kind of man Hotspur really was, Shakespeare falls back on his invention. Occasionally history misled him: Holinshed confused the Sir Edmund

---

* *1 Henry IV* and *Henry V*: to the present editor it seems more likely than not that *2 Henry IV* is an unpremeditated sequel to the first part, supplying the demand for more Falstaff.

Mortimer who married Glendower's daughter with his nephew Edmund Mortimer, fifth earl of March, who was proclaimed heir to the throne by Richard II in 1398, and Shakespeare followed.

The structure of the play is simple and the plot moves somewhat slowly. In the early scenes three oppositions are lined up: that of the rebels and the king and the loyal party, that of Hotspur and the prince, that of the prince's bad reputation and truant disposition and his actual sterling worth. All these are to be resolved on the battlefield of Shrewsbury and the play has little to do but march undeviatingly toward that final arbitrement. Successive scenes showing one or another of these opposed forces advancing towards the day of decision sharpen the oppositions. As the battle approaches, the alternating scenes become shorter and the various oppositions tend to merge. The events of the battle answer all questions: loyalty triumphs over disaffection, Hal over Hotspur, and the prince's valor and fidelity over all suspicions.

This simple plot (lacking the fresh complications and changes of alignment which make the plot of *Richard III* more exciting) is, however, greatly enlivened by the skill with which individual scenes are developed. The story of the robbery on Gad's Hill, a series of scenes which might be called a subplot if it did not come to an end before the play is half over, obviously gathers momentum as it develops and reaches its own peculiar climax. Some scenes are planned like miniature dramas. A good example is the scene at Glendower's house. It is useful to the plot only so far as it shows the rebels forging ahead with their preparations and wickedly planning to divide England. Shakespeare imposes dramatic form upon it by working up a temperamental antagonism between Hotspur and Glendower which reaches a high pitch a moment before Glendower backs down. The advantage which Hotspur gains thereby – it is not very great, for it lets him in for a dressing-down by Mortimer and Worcester – is short-lived, for presently Glendower takes the wind out of his sails by producing the supernatural music he had promised. The occasion of this music is brought about by the development of a contrast between the sentimental Mortimers, those odd victims of the barrier of language, and the unsentimental Percies. The scene is full of dramatic tension peculiar to itself and attains something like a dramatic resolution before it is over. The second tavern scene and the scene between the king and the prince also contain complete reversals of the situation presented at the outset.

The opposition of the Percies to the king, the historical backbone of the play, is no doubt a simple struggle for power, but dramatically at least it is a little more than that, for the whole is tinged with irony because of the king's equivocal claim to the throne and his consciousness of the instability of his position. The picture of him – old, shaken, and wan with care – is dramatic, not historical; he was actually a vigorous man in his middle thirties. He hankers after going on a crusade to expiate the wrong he did King Richard; he looks upon the prince's recalcitrance as a "rod of heaven" to punish his "mistreadings." The ambiguousness of his conduct – his determination to hold on to the prize he has gained and his twinges of conscience – is never resolved; he is more impressive and sounds deeper notes because he is never unequivocally presented as either the "vile politician" that Hotspur thinks he is or as something else.

The rivalry of the prince and Hotspur is the dramatic mainspring of the play: the stroke that kills the latter awards the palm of supremacy to the prince, checks rebellion, and confirms the prince's loyalty to his father. This antagonism is announced in the first scene of the play and kept alive, in one way or another, in almost every other. It is pure invention. Far from being a "northern youth," Hotspur was older than the prince's father, and, though he was certainly killed at Shrewsbury, nobody knows who killed him. Shakespeare undoubtedly strove to make the prince seem the better man. Hotspur's uncertain temper is emphasized in every scene in which he appears. His intractability is deplored by his father and his uncle (I, iii) and by his wife (II, iii); the prince's travesty of his daily routine of killing some six or seven dozen of Scots at a breakfast is a shrewd stroke. Worcester and Vernon question his leadership (IV, iii). His impatience of any praise of his adversary is twice underscored. His valedictory on the eve of the battle is a curious combination of bravado and fatalism. The crowning touch is added to his infatuation in the scene in which he partitions England and cavils at the details of the partition: obviously there is no sympathy for one who would dismember his native country. On the other hand, the prince is justified at every point. We are assured of his essential sobriety and dependability in the soliloquy he speaks at the end of the first scene in which he appears. The odium of his wild oats is transferred to Falstaff and dissolves in laughter. At the midpoint of the play he assures his father that he is true blue in spite of appearances, and though promise is not performance, performance follows in due course. He does full justice to Hotspur's prowess and reputation. His enemies testify to his valor and modesty (IV, i, 97 ff.; V, ii, 51 ff.). And on the day of decision he redeems his lost opinion triumphantly.

Yet all this careful weighting of the scales has often gone for nothing. Readers and spectators in the theatre become partisans of Hotspur and wish to reverse the verdict. Hotspur's disloyalty to the country he would divide out of selfish ambition is overlooked: we have a sneaking sympathy for rebels, especially in fiction. The prince is put down as a hypocrite because his cloaking of his right royal nature is the result of calculation – as if calculation were not the duty of a reasonable man and impulsive conduct a form of disorder. His later offenses, his rejection of Falstaff in *2 Henry IV* and his sanctimoniousness in *Henry V*, are made retroactive and added to the indictment. The real cause of this reversal of the verdict is, however, dramatic: Hotspur's part is aggressive and dynamic throughout while the prince must be kept under wraps till almost the end. The advantage to the actor who plays Hotspur, and the disadvantage to the actor who plays the prince, is enormous. Hotspur is by far the best acting part in the historical action of the play; he dazzles us so thoroughly as to disarm criticism. Since this is so, Shakespeare cannot escape responsibility, but in his defense it may be said that he has put up plenty of signposts to show which way our sympathies should take.

But even Hotspur is overshadowed by Falstaff, who is indeed the great triumph of this play. Otherwise a superior battle-piece, it is transfigured by his presence into something unique and transcendent. Falstaff was made out of whole cloth. There is a character corresponding to him in

The Famous Victories, but even if his part in that play as Shakespeare knew it was much more amusing than it is in the version we know, it hardly seems likely that he afforded Shakespeare more than a start. Nothing that history tells about either the Lollard martyr Sir John Oldcastle (as Falstaff was called in the earliest performances, before the name was changed out of deference to the displeasure of his living descendants) or Sir John Fastolfe (*1 Henry VI,* III, ii; IV, i) accounts for the immortal character that Shakespeare made. Falstaff is fitted to the role designed for him with the greatest adroitness. He becomes the embodiment of the prince's wild oats. The prince really does little or nothing reprehensible: he takes part in the robbery, but his character is carefully safeguarded from the start and he restores the money with advantage; otherwise he only gets a little tipsy, plays a poor practical joke on the drawer, and exchanges vituperation with Falstaff. It is Falstaff who creates the atmosphere of depravity, the prince sharing in it but not responsible for it and always standing somewhat apart from it. Falstaff is a kind of scapegoat: he takes upon him the vices which legend imputed to the prince. Further to exculpate the prince, the sting is extracted from these vices by presenting them only in the element of laughter, the infallible solvent of morality. Only the sternest self-control enables us to remember, as we laugh at Falstaff's drollery, that he is really a liar, a sponger, a glutton, a drunkard, a thief, and much more that we must disapprove of. As insulation for the prince's character, Falstaff is a superb dramatic invention.

Traditionally a comic character is the butt of ridicule, a simpleton, a monomaniac, or an impostor who, like that other Falstaff who swaggers through *The Merry Wives of Windsor,* overreaches himself in the end and is exposed to the derisive laughter of men of better judgment. But the Falstaff of this play, for all the verbal derision hurled at him by the prince and others, which he always parries skillfully enough, is never completely exposed, discomfited, or humiliated by the turn of events; he always manages to earn at least a draw and often something like a triumph. At the end of the play he is even left in dubious possession of the claim of victory over Hotspur. For success like this we have no derision; indeed, at least in fiction, it excites something much more like sympathy, and Falstaff carries away our admiration, or at least our astonishment, by his overwhelming effrontery. When we laugh with him we forfeit all chance of sitting in judgment upon him. The utter disabling of our normal censoriousness, the assigning to Falstaff of a role that is sympathetic as well as depraved, is indeed a triumph of the comic imagination.

Moreover, the equivocal Falstaff is the essential Falstaff. He is never twice quite the same; he is a series of impersonations. He is an inveterate comic actor and every man is a stooge who must play up to him. His parts are without number and every one is followed by its opposite: the old man and the frisky youth, the fat man and the active man (or at least a simulacrum thereof), the sponger and the lordly patron (of Bardolph and the likes of him), the libertine and the critic of manners (whose ruminations on the ways of the world are heavily flavored with biblical phraseology), the soldier and the coward – or at least the propounder of the axiom that the better part of valor is discretion. Of all his parts the most famous is that of the artful dodger: at least three times he is backed into a corner, only to wriggle out by a triumphant equivocation (he was a coward on instinct, the prince owes him his love and his love is worth a million, he gave Hotspur a wound in the thigh). Of all his parts the most surprising is that of debunker of honor: the soliloquy in which he proves it only a word might seem to undermine the whole basis of the serious parts of the play, but by that time we are so used to Falstaff's "wrenching the true cause the false way" that we take it as another piece of pseudo-logic like his argument that robbery is no sin if it is a man's vocation. His protean character makes the wrangle over his cowardice, which literary critics have been carrying on for a hundred and fifty years now, seem irrelevant. Of course Falstaff is a coward when he runs away or shams death; a brave man running away or playing dead would not be funny. But at the same time the complete aplomb with which he carries off these pieces of "discretion," utterly different from the teeth-chattering and knee-knocking of the craven coward, makes him a coward different from all others and much funnier. The laughter that greets Falstaff's sallies, so far as it is more than merely a tribute to his wit, is a delighted recognition of the adroitness with which he is always pretending to be something that we know he is not or at least was not a minute, an hour, or a day ago. His bright eye, his rum-soaked voice, and his unwieldy bulk dominate every situation in which he finds himself and he turns them all into mirth by assuming whatever part one would least expect of him. He blows through the play like a great gust of laughter and comes within an ace of turning Shakespeare's history of Henry IV into the comedy of Falstaff.

University of Pennsylvania   M. A. SHAABER

NOTE ON THE TEXT

The present text follows, with only a few emendations, that of the first quarto (1598), which is believed to have been printed from the author's draft. In the folio text of 1623, printed from the fifth quarto (1613), the play was first divided into acts and scenes. The act–scene division supplied marginally in the present text is that of the folio except that V, ii of the folio is divided into two scenes. Below are listed all substantive departures from the quarto text, with the adopted reading in italics followed by the quarto reading in roman. The letters Q0 represent a quarto of which only four leaves survive. It was probably published in 1598 and served as copy for Q1.

I, i, 30 *Therefor* (ed.) Therefore 62 *a dear* (Q5) deere 69 *blood* (Q5) bloud.

I, ii, 30–31 *moon. . . . proof now :* (Rowe) moone, . . . proofe. Now 74 *similes* (Q5) smiles 106 *Sugar? Jack,* (Capell) Sugar Iacke? 117 *Gad's Hill* (Wilson) Gadshill 148 *thou* (Pope) the 152 *Bardolph* (Theobald) Haruey *Peto* (Dering) Rossill

I, iii, 96 *tongue* (Hanmer) tongue: 139 *struck* (Malone) strooke 201 *Hotspur* (Q5) Omitted (Q1) 254 *for I* (F) I 262 *granted. . . . lord,* (Thirlby) granted . . . Lord. 290 *course.* (Johnson) course

II, i, 32 *1. Carrier* (Hanmer) Car. 71 *foot land-rakers* (Hanmer) footlande rakers

II, ii, 16 *two-and-twenty* (F) xxii 20 (and throughout the play) *Bardolph* (F) Bardoll (or Bardol) 40 *Go hang* (Q3) Hang 48 *Bardolph. What* (Johnson) Bardoll, what 49 *Gadshill* (Johnson) Bar. 78 *Ah* (Rowe) a 102 *fat rogue* (Q0) rogue

II, iii, 4 *In respect* (Q6) in the respect 45 *thee* (Q2) the 66 *A roan* (Q3) Roane

II, iv, 31 *precedent* (President F) present 114 *(pitiful-hearted Titan !)* (Warburton) pittiful harted titan 164 *Prince* (Dering) Gads. 165, 167, 171 *Gadshill* (F) Ross. 232 *eel-skin* (Hanmer) elsskin 288 *Tell* (F) Faith tell 324 *Owen* (Dering) O 375 *tristful* (Dering) trustfull 431 *reverend* (F) reverent 450 *lean* (Q2) lane 468 *mad* (F3) made 510 *Peto* (F) Omitted (Q) 514 *Prince* (F) Omitted (Q)

III, i, 100 *cantle* (F) scantle 116 *I will* (Pope) I'le 128 *metre* (F) miter 131 *on* (Q3) an 261 *hot* (F) Hot.

III, ii, 110 *capital* (Q2) capitall.

III, iii, 32 *that's* (Q3) that 35 *Gad's Hill* (Wilson) Gadshill 54 *tithe* (Theobald) tight 71 *four-and-twenty* (F) xxiiii. 113 *no thing* (Q3) nothing 165 *guests* (Q2) ghesse 168 *court.* (Keightley) court 181 *two-and-twenty* (F) xxii. 191 *o'clock* (Q2) of clocke

IV, i, 20 *lord* (Capell) mind 55 *Is* (F) tis 108 *dropped* (Q2) drop 116 *altar* (Q4) altars 126 *cannot* (Q5) can 127 *yet* (Q5) it

IV, ii, 3 *Sutton Co'fil'* (Cambridge eds) Sutton cophill

IV, iii, 21 *horse* (Q5) horses 28 *ours* (Q6) our 72 *heirs as pages,* (Singer) heires, as Pages 82 *country's* (Q5) Countrey

V, i, 25 *I do* (F) I 131 *then?* (Q2) then 137 *will it* (Q2) wil

V, ii, 3 *undone* (Q5) vnder one 10 *ne'er* (F) neuer 70 *Upon* (Pope) On

V, iii, 22 *A* (Capell) Ah 39 *stand'st* (Q2) stands 50 *get'st* (Q2) gets

V, iv, 33 *So* (F) and 67 *Nor* (F) Now 91 *thee* (Q7) the 155 *ours* (Q2) our 156 *let's* (Q4) let us

V, v, 36 *bend you* (Q4) bend, you

THE FIRST PART OF
KING HENRY THE FOURTH

[NAMES OF THE ACTORS

King Henry the Fourth	*Gadshill*
Henry, Prince of Wales } *the King's sons*	*Peto*
Prince John of Lancaster }	*Bardolph*
Earl of Westmoreland	*Vintner of an Eastcheap Tavern*
Sir Walter Blunt	*Francis, a waiter*
Thomas Percy, Earl of Worcester	*Chamberlain of an inn at Rochester*
Henry Percy, Earl of Northumberland	*Ostler*
Henry Percy ('Hotspur'), his son	*Mugs and another Carrier*
Edmund Mortimer, Earl of March	*Travellers on the road from Rochester to London*
Richard Scroop, Archbishop of York	*Sheriff*
Archibald, Earl of Douglas	*Hotspur's Servant*
Owen Glendower	*Messenger from Northumberland*
Sir Richard Vernon	*Two Messengers (soldiers in Hotspur's army)*
Sir John Falstaff	*Lady Percy, Hotspur's wife and Mortimer's sister*
Sir Michael, a friend of the Archbishop of York	*Lady Mortimer, Glendower's daughter*
Poins	*Mistress Quickly, hostess of an Eastcheap Tavern*

Scene : *England and Wales*]

*

I, i *Enter the King, Lord John of Lancaster, Earl of*
Westmoreland, [Sir Walter Blunt,] with others.

KING

So shaken as we are, so wan with care,
2   Find we a time for frighted peace to pant
3   And breathe short-winded accents of new broils
4   To be commenced in stronds afar remote.
5   No more the thirsty entrance of this soil
Shall daub her lips with her own children's blood :
7   No more shall trenching war channel her fields,
Nor bruise her flow'rets with the armèd hoofs
Of hostile paces. Those opposèd eyes
10 Which, like the meteors of a troubled heaven,
All of one nature, of one substance bred,
Did lately meet in the intestine shock
13 And furious close of civil butchery,
Shall now in mutual well-beseeming ranks
March all one way and be no more opposed
Against acquaintance, kindred, and allies.
The edge of war, like an ill-sheathèd knife,
18 No more shall cut his master. Therefore, friends,
As far as to the sepulchre of Christ –
Whose soldier now, under whose blessèd cross
We are impressèd and engaged to fight –
22 Forthwith a power of English shall we levy,
Whose arms were moulded in their mother's womb
To chase these pagans in those holy fields
Over whose acres walked those blessèd feet
Which fourteen hundred years ago were nailed
For our advantage on the bitter cross.

But this our purpose now is twelve month old,
And bootless 'tis to tell you we will go.   29
Therefor we meet not now. Then let me hear
Of you, my gentle cousin Westmoreland,   31
What yesternight our council did decree
In forwarding this dear expedience.   33

WESTMORELAND

My liege, this haste was hot in question   34
And many limits of the charge set down   35
But yesternight; when all athwart there came   36
A post from Wales, loaden with heavy news,   37
Whose worst was that the noble Mortimer,
Leading the men of Herefordshire to fight
Against the irregular and wild Glendower,
Was by the rude hands of that Welshman taken,
A thousand of his people butcherèd;
Upon whose dead corpse there was such misuse,   43
Such beastly shameless transformation,   44
By those Welshwomen done as may not be
Without much shame retold or spoken of.

I, i The Court of King Henry IV **2** *Find we* let us find **3** *accents* words
4 *stronds* strands, shores **5** *entrance* fissures (through which moisture
is absorbed) **7** *trenching* cutting; *channel* cut furrows in **10** *meteors*
atmospheric disturbances (perhaps a thunderstorm) **13** *close* hand-to-
hand fighting **18** *his* its **22** *power* army **29** *bootless* useless **31** *cousin*
form of address (no kinship implied) **33** *dear expedience* important expedition **34** *liege* feudal superior; *hot in question* warmly debated **35**
limits . . . charge assignments of responsibility **36** *athwart* contrarily **37**
post messenger; *heavy* depressing **43** *corpse* corpses **44** *transformation*
i.e. mutilation

KING

It seems then that the tidings of this broil
Brake off our business for the Holy Land.

WESTMORELAND

49 This, matched with other, did, my gracious lord;
50 For more uneven and unwelcome news
Came from the north, and thus it did import:
On Holy-rood Day the gallant Hotspur there,
Young Harry Percy, and brave Archibald,
54 That ever-valiant and approvèd Scot,
55 At Holmedon met,
Where they did spend a sad and bloody hour;
57 As by discharge of their artillery
And shape of likelihood the news was told;
59 For he that brought them, in the very heat
60 And pride of their contention did take horse,
Uncertain of the issue any way.

KING

Here is a dear, a true-industrious friend,
Sir Walter Blunt, new lighted from his horse,
Stained with the variation of each soil
Betwixt that Holmedon and this seat of ours,
And he hath brought us smooth and welcome news.
The Earl of Douglas is discomfited;
Ten thousand bold Scots, two-and-twenty knights,
69 Balked in their own blood did Sir Walter see
On Holmedon's plains. Of prisoners, Hotspur took
71 Mordake Earl of Fife and eldest son
To beaten Douglas, and the Earl of Athol,
Of Murray, Angus, and Menteith.
And is not this an honourable spoil?
A gallant prize? Ha, cousin, is it not?

WESTMORELAND

In faith,
It is a conquest for a prince to boast of.

KING

Yea, there thou mak'st me sad, and mak'st me sin
In envy that my Lord Northumberland
Should be the father to so blest a son –
A son who is the theme of honor's tongue,
Amongst a grove the very straightest plant;
83 Who is sweet fortune's minion and her pride;
Whilst I, by looking on the praise of him,
See riot and dishonor stain the brow

Of my young Harry. O that it could be proved
That some night-tripping fairy had exchanged
In cradle clothes our children where they lay,
And called mine Percy, his Plantagenet! 89
Then would I have his Harry, and he mine. 90
But let him from my thoughts. What think you, coz, 91
Of this young Percy's pride? The prisoners
Which he in this adventure hath surprised
To his own use he keeps, and sends me word
I shall have none but Mordake Earl of Fife. 94

WESTMORELAND

This is his uncle's teaching, this is Worcester,
Malevolent to you in all aspects, 97
Which makes him prune himself and bristle up 98
The crest of youth against your dignity.

KING

But I have sent for him to answer this;
And for this cause awhile we must neglect
Our holy purpose to Jerusalem.
Cousin, on Wednesday next our council we
Will hold at Windsor. So inform the lords;
But come yourself with speed to us again;
For more is to be said and to be done
Than out of anger can be utterèd.

WESTMORELAND

I will, my liege.   *Exeunt.*

                              *

Enter Prince of Wales and Sir John Falstaff. I, ii

FALSTAFF Now, Hal, what time of day is it, lad? 1
PRINCE Thou art so fat-witted with drinking of old sack, 2
and unbuttoning thee after supper, and sleeping upon
benches after noon, that thou hast forgotten to demand 4
that truly which thou wouldest truly know. What a devil 5
hast thou to do with the time of the day? Unless hours
were cups of sack, and minutes capons, and clocks the
tongues of bawds, and dials the signs of leaping houses, 8
and the blessed sun himself a fair hot wench in flame-
colored taffeta, I see no reason why thou shouldst be so 10
superfluous to demand the time of the day.

FALSTAFF Indeed you come near me now, Hal; for we that 12
take purses go by the moon and the seven stars, and not by 13
Phoebus, he, that wand'ring knight so fair. And I 14
prithee, sweet wag, when thou art a king, as, God save
thy grace – majesty I should say, for grace thou wilt 16
have none –

PRINCE What, none?

FALSTAFF No, by my troth; not so much as will serve to 18
be prologue to an egg and butter. 19

PRINCE Well, how then? Come, roundly, roundly. 20

FALSTAFF Marry, then, sweet wag, when thou art a king, 21
let not us that are squires of the night's body be called 22
thieves of the day's beauty. Let us be Diana's foresters, 23
gentlemen of the shade, minions of the moon; and let
men say we be men of good government, being 25
governed as the sea is, by our noble and chaste mistress
the moon, under whose countenance we steal. 27

PRINCE Thou sayest well, and it holds well too; for the 28
fortune of us that are the moon's men doth ebb and flow
like the sea, being governed, as the sea is, by the moon.
As, for proof now: a purse of gold most resolutely
snatched on Monday night and most dissolutely spent
on Tuesday morning; got with swearing 'Lay by,' and 33
spent with crying 'Bring in'; now in as low an ebb as the

49 *other* others, other tidings 50 *uneven* disconcerting 54 *approvèd* of
proved valor 55 *Holmedon* Humbleton in Northumberland 57–58 *by . . .
shape of likelihood* according to . . . probability 59 *them* news 60 *pride*
height 69 *Balked* (1) heaped up, (2) defeated 71 *Mordake* i.e. Murdoch
(actually son of the Duke of Albany) 83 *minion* favorite 89 *Plantagenet*
family name of the kings descended from Henry II 90 *would I have* I would
demand 91 *let him* let him go; *coz* cousin 94 *To . . . use* i.e. to collect their
ransoms 97 *aspects* (literally) positions of a star 98 *prune* preen
I, ii An apartment of the Prince? 1 *what . . . it* (implies doubt that the
person addressed is bright enough to know what time it is) 2 *sack* Spanish
white wine 4 *benches* privy-seats 5 *truly* correctly 8 *dials* clocks 10–11
be . . . demand allow yourself the luxury of demanding 12 *you . . . now* i.e.
you have me there 13 *go* (1) count time, (2) walk; *seven stars* Big Dipper
14 *Phoebus* the sun; *wand'ring knight* knight errant (suggested by the Knight
of the Sun, the hero of a romance called *The Mirror of Knighthood*) 16 *thy
grace* used, like 'your majesty,' in addressing royalty; *grace* virtuous
motives 18 *troth* faith 19 *egg and butter* a mere snack, requiring only a
short grace 20 *roundly* without beating about the bush 21 *Marry* well,
indeed 22 *squires* body-servants 23 *thieves . . . beauty* idlers by day;
Diana's foresters i.e. a better-sounding name than 'thieves' 25 *government*
conduct 27 *countenance* (1) face, (2) patronage; *steal* (1) rob, (2) walk
stealthily 28 *it holds well* the comparison is appropriate 33 *Lay by* put
down your weapons

35 foot of the ladder, and by-and-by in as high a flow as the ridge of the gallows.

FALSTAFF By the Lord, thou say'st true, lad – and is not my hostess of the tavern a most sweet wench?

39 PRINCE As the honey of Hybla, my old lad of the castle –
40 and is not a buff jerkin a most sweet robe of durance?

FALSTAFF How now, how now, mad wag? What, in thy
42 quips and thy quiddities? What a plague have I to do with a buff jerkin?

44 PRINCE Why, what a pox have I to do with my hostess of the tavern?

46 FALSTAFF Well, thou hast called her to a reckoning many a time and oft.

PRINCE Did I ever call for thee to pay thy part?

FALSTAFF No; I'll give thee thy due, thou hast paid all there.

PRINCE Yea, and elsewhere, so far as my coin would stretch; and where it would not, I have used my credit.

FALSTAFF Yea, and so used it that, were it not here apparent that thou art heir apparent – But I prithee, sweet wag, shall there be gallows standing in England
55 when thou art king? and resolution thus fubbed as it is
56 with the rusty curb of old father antic the law? Do not thou, when thou art king, hang a thief.

PRINCE No; thou shalt.

59 FALSTAFF Shall I? O rare! By the Lord, I'll be a brave judge.

PRINCE Thou judgest false already. I mean, thou shalt have the hanging of the thieves and so become a rare hangman.

64 FALSTAFF Well, Hal, well; and in some sort it jumps with
65 my humor as well as waiting in the court, I can tell you.

66 PRINCE For obtaining of suits?

FALSTAFF Yea, for obtaining of suits, whereof the hang-
68 man hath no lean wardrobe. 'Sblood, I am as melan-
69 choly as a gib-cat or a lugged bear.

PRINCE Or an old lion, or a lover's lute.

71 FALSTAFF Yea, or the drone of a Lincolnshire bagpipe.

72 PRINCE What sayest thou to a hare, or the melancholy of
73 Moor Ditch?

FALSTAFF Thou hast the most unsavory similes, and art
75 indeed the most comparative, rascalliest, sweet young prince. But, Hal, I prithee trouble me no more with
77 vanity. I would to God thou and I knew where a
78 commodity of good names were to be bought. An old
79 lord of the council rated me the other day in the street about you, sir, but I marked him not; and yet he talked very wisely, but I regarded him not; and yet he talked wisely, and in the street too.

83 PRINCE Thou didst well, for wisdom cries out in the streets, and no man regards it.

85 FALSTAF O, thou hast damnable iteration, and art indeed able to corrupt a saint. Thou hast done much harm upon me, Hal – God forgive thee for it! Before I knew
88 thee, Hal, I knew nothing; and now am I, if a man should speak truly, little better than one of the wicked. I must give over this life, and I will give it over! By the
91 Lord, an I do not, I am a villain! I'll be damned for never a king's son in Christendom.

PRINCE Where shall we take a purse to-morrow, Jack?

94 FALSTAFF Zounds, where thou wilt, lad! I'll make one.
95 An I do not, call me villain and baffle me.

PRINCE I see a good amendment of life in thee – from praying to purse-taking.

FALSTAFF Why, Hal, 'tis my vocation, Hal. 'Tis no sin for a man to labor in his vocation.

Enter Poins.

Poins! Now shall we know if Gadshill have set a match. 100
O, if men were to be saved by merit, what hole in hell 101
were hot enough for him? This is the most omnipotent 102
villain that ever cried 'stand!' to a true man. 103

PRINCE Good morrow, Ned. 104

POINS Good morrow, sweet Hal. What says Monsieur Remorse? What says Sir John Sack and Sugar? Jack, how agrees the devil and thee about thy soul, that thou soldest him on Good Friday last for a cup of Madeira and a cold capon's leg?

PRINCE Sir John stands to his word, the devil shall have 110 his bargain; for he was never yet a breaker of proverbs. He will give the devil his due. 112

POINS Then art thou damned for keeping thy word with the devil.

PRINCE Else he had been damned for cozening the devil. 115

POINS But, my lads, my lads, to-morrow morning, by four o'clock early, at Gad's Hill! There are pilgrims 117 going to Canterbury with rich offerings, and traders riding to London with fat purses. I have vizards for you 119 all; you have horses for yourselves. Gadshill lies to- 120 night in Rochester. I have bespoke supper to-morrow night in Eastcheap. We may do it as secure as sleep. If you will go, I will stuff your purses full of crowns; if you will not, tarry at home and be hanged!

FALSTAFF Hear ye, Yedward: if I tarry at home and go not, I'll hang you for going.

POINS You will, chops? 127

FALSTAFF Hal, wilt thou make one?

PRINCE Who, I rob? I a thief? Not I, by my faith.

FALSTAFF There's neither honesty, manhood, nor good fellowship in thee, nor thou cam'st not of the blood royal if thou darest not stand for ten shillings. 132

PRINCE Well then, once in my days I'll be a madcap.

FALSTAFF Why, that's well said.

PRINCE Well, come what will, I'll tarry at home.

FALSTAFF By the Lord, I'll be a traitor then, when thou art king.

PRINCE I care not.

POINS Sir John, I prithee, leave the prince and me alone.

35 *ladder* that from the platform to the ridge of the gallows, climbed by the culprit 39 *Hybla* place in Sicily famous for honey; *old . . . castle* (1) roisterer, (2) Oldcastle 40 *buff jerkin* leather jacket; *durance* (1) kind of durable cloth, (2) imprisonment 42 *quiddities* hair-splittings 44 *pox* syphilis 46 *reckoning* settlement (of the bill) 55 *resolution* courage; *fubbed* thwarted 56 *antic* buffoon 59 *brave* splendid 64 *jumps with* suits 65 *waiting* being in attendance; *court* i.e. the royal court 66 *suits* petitions 68 *wardrobe* the clothes of those he hangs are the hangman's perquisite; *'Sblood* by God's blood 69 *gib-cat* tomcat; *lugged* baited 71 *drone* bass pipe 72 *hare* proverbially melancholy 73 *Moor Ditch* an open sewer 75 *comparative* abusive 77 *vanity* worldliness 78 *commodity* lot 79 *rated* rebuked 83–84 *wisdom . . . regards it* 'Wisdom crieth without; she uttereth her voice in the streets. She crieth . . . saying, " . . . I have stretched out my hand, and no man regarded"' (Proverbs i, 20–24) 85 *iteration* repetition (of scriptural texts) 88 *knew nothing* was innocent 91 *an* if; *villain* the opposite of a gentleman 94 *Zounds* by God's wounds; *make one* be one of the party 95 *baffle* degrade 100 *set a match* made arrangements (for a holdup) 101 *saved by merit* i.e. as they are not: they are saved by grace 102 *omnipotent* complete 103 *stand* i.e. hands up; *true* honest 104 *morrow* morning 110 *stands to* i.e. is as good as 112 *his due* i.e. Falstaff's soul 115 *cozening* cheating 117 *Gad's Hill* on the road from Canterbury to London 119 *vizards* masks 120 *lies* lodges 126 *chops* fat-cheeks 132 *stand* (1) make a fight, (2) pass current (*royal*: 10-shilling piece)

I will lay him down such reasons for this adventure that
he shall go.

FALSTAFF Well, God give thee the spirit of persuasion
and him the ears of profiting, that what thou speakest
may move and what he hears may be believed, that the
true prince may (for recreation sake) prove a false thief;
146 for the poor abuses of the time want countenance. Farewell; you shall find me in Eastcheap.

148 PRINCE Farewell, thou latter spring! farewell, All-
hallown summer!   *[Exit Falstaff.]*

POINS Now, my good sweet honey lord, ride with us to-
morrow. I have a jest to execute that I cannot manage
alone. Falstaff, Bardolph, Peto, and Gadshill shall rob
153 those men that we have already waylaid; yourself and I
will not be there; and when they have the booty, if you
and I do not rob them, cut this head off from my
shoulders.

PRINCE How shall we part with them in setting forth?

POINS Why, we will set forth before or after them and appoint them a place of meeting, wherein it is at our
pleasure to fail; and then will they adventure upon the
exploit themselves, which they shall have no sooner
achieved, but we'll set upon them.

PRINCE Yea, but 'tis like that they will know us by our
164 horses, by our habits, and by every other appointment,
to be ourselves.

POINS Tut! our horses they shall not see – I'll tie them in
the wood; our vizards we will change after we leave
168 them; and, sirrah, I have cases of buckram for the
169 nonce, to immask our noted outward garments.

170 PRINCE Yea, but I doubt they will be too hard for us.

POINS Well, for two of them, I know them to be as true-
bred cowards as ever turned back; and for the third, if
he fight longer than he sees reason, I'll forswear arms.
174 The virtue of this jest will be the incomprehensible lies
that this same fat rogue will tell us when we meet at
176 supper: how thirty, at least, he fought with; what wards,
177 what blows, what extremities he endured; and in the reproof of this lives the jest.

PRINCE Well, I'll go with thee. Provide us all things
necessary and meet me to-morrow night in Eastcheap.
There I'll sup. Farewell.

POINS Farewell, my lord.   *Exit.*

PRINCE
I know you all, and will awhile uphold
184 The unyoked humor of your idleness.
Yet herein will I imitate the sun,
186 Who doth permit the base contagious clouds
To smother up his beauty from the world,
188 That, when he please again to be himself,
Being wanted, he may be more wond'red at

By breaking through the foul and ugly mists
Of vapors that did seem to strangle him.
If all the year were playing holidays,
To sport would be as tedious as to work;
But when they seldom come, they wished-for come,
And nothing pleaseth but rare accidents.   195
So, when this loose behavior I throw off
And pay the debt I never promisèd,
By how much better than my word I am,
By so much shall I falsify men's hopes;   199
And, like bright metal on a sullen ground,
My reformation, glitt'ring o'er my fault,
Shall show more goodly and attract more eyes
Than that which hath no foil to set it off.   203
I'll so offend to make offense a skill,   204
Redeeming time when men think least I will.   *Exit.*   205

*

Enter the King, Northumberland, Worcester,   I, iii
Hotspur, Sir Walter Blunt, with others.

KING
My blood hath been too cold and temperate,
Unapt to stir at these indignities,
And you have found me, for accordingly   3
You tread upon my patience; but be sure
I will from henceforth rather be myself,   5
Mighty and to be feared, than my condition,   6
Which hath been smooth as oil, soft as young down,
And therefore lost that title of respect
Which the proud soul ne'er pays but to the proud.

WORCESTER
Our house, my sovereign liege, little deserves
The scourge of greatness to be used on it –
And that same greatness too which our own hands
Have holp to make so portly.   13

NORTHUMBERLAND
My lord –

KING
Worcester, get thee gone, for I do see
Danger and disobedience in thine eye.   16
O, sir, your presence is too bold and peremptory,
And majesty might never yet endure
The moody frontier of a servant brow.   19
You have good leave to leave us: when we need
Your use and counsel, we shall send for you.
    Exit Worcester.
You were about to speak.

NORTHUMBERLAND   Yea, my good lord.
Those prisoners in your highness' name demanded
Which Harry Percy here at Holmedon took,
Were, as he says, not with such strength denied
As is deliverèd to your majesty.   26
Either envy, therefore, or misprision   27
Is guilty of this fault, and not my son.

HOTSPUR
My liege, I did deny no prisoners.
But I remember, when the fight was done,
When I was dry with rage and extreme toil,
Breathless and faint, leaning upon my sword,
Came there a certain lord, neat and trimly dressed,
Fresh as a bridegroom, and his chin new reaped
Showed like a stubble land at harvest home.
He was perfumèd like a milliner,   36

---

146 *countenance* encouragement   148–49 *All-hallown summer* Indian summer   153 *waylaid* set an ambush for   164 *appointment* accoutrement   168
sirrah sir (as a rule addressed to inferiors; here it implies familiarity); *cases*
suits   168–69 *for the nonce* for this purpose   169 *noted* well-known   170
doubt fear; *too hard* too much   174 *incomprehensible* unlimited   176 *wards*
parries   177 *extremities* extreme hazards; *reproof* disproof   184 *idleness*
frivolity   186 *contagious* noxious   188 *That* so that   195 *accidents* events
199 *hopes* expectations   203 *foil* contrast   204 *to* as to; *skill* piece of good
policy   205 *Redeeming time* saving time from being lost
I, iii The Court of King Henry IV   3 *found me* found me out   5 *myself*
i.e. every inch a king   6 *condition* (mild) natural disposition   13 *holp*
helped; *portly* majestic   16 *Danger* defiance   19 *frontier* (literally) earth-
works (alluding to 'front': forehead)   26 *deliverèd* reported   27 *envy* ill
will; *misprision* misunderstanding   36 *milliner* (who sells scented gloves
and other haberdashery)

       And 'twixt his finger and his thumb he held

38   A pouncet box, which ever and anon

       He gave his nose, and took 't away again;

40   Who therewith angry, when it next came there,

41   Took it in snuff; and still he smiled and talked;

       And as the soldiers bore dead bodies by,

       He called them untaught knaves, unmannerly,

44   To bring a slovenly unhandsome corse

       Betwixt the wind and his nobility.

46   With many holiday and lady terms

47   He questioned me, amongst the rest demanded

       My prisoners in your majesty's behalf.

       I then, all smarting with my wounds being cold,

       To be so pestered with a popingay,

51   Out of my grief and my impatience

       Answered neglectingly, I know not what –

       He should, or he should not; for he made me mad

       To see him shine so brisk, and smell so sweet,

       And talk so like a waiting gentlewoman

56   Of guns and drums and wounds – God save the mark! –

57   And telling me the sovereignest thing on earth

58   Was parmacity for an inward bruise,

       And that it was great pity, so it was,

       This villainous saltpetre should be digged

       Out of the bowels of the harmless earth,

62   Which many a good tall fellow had destroyed

       So cowardly, and but for these vile guns,

       He would himself have been a soldier.

65   This bald unjointed chat of his, my lord,

66   I answered indirectly, as I said,

       And I beseech you, let not his report

68   Come current for an accusation

       Betwixt my love and your high majesty.

BLUNT

       The circumstance considered, good my lord,

       Whate'er Lord Harry Percy then had said

       To such a person, and in such a place,

       At such a time, with all the rest retold,

       May reasonably die, and never rise

75   To do him wrong, or any way impeach

       What then he said, so he unsay it now.

KING

       Why, yet he doth deny his prisoners,

       But with proviso and exception,

79   That we at our own charge shall ransom straight

       His brother-in-law, the foolish Mortimer;

       Who, on my soul, hath willfully betrayed

       The lives of those that he did lead to fight

       Against that great magician, damned Glendower,

       Whose daughter, as we hear, that Earl of March

       Hath lately married. Shall our coffers, then,

       Be emptied to redeem a traitor home?

87   Shall we buy treason? and indent with fears

       When they have lost and forfeited themselves?

       No, on the barren mountains let him starve!

       For I shall never hold that man my friend

       Whose tongue shall ask me for one penny cost

       To ransom home revolted Mortimer.

HOTSPUR

       Revolted Mortimer?

94   He never did fall off, my sovereign liege,

       But by the chance of war. To prove that true

       Needs no more but one tongue for all those wounds,

97   Those mouthèd wounds, which valiantly he took

       When on the gentle Severn's sedgy bank,

       In single opposition hand to hand,

       He did confound the best part of an hour   100

       In changing hardiment with great Glendower.   101

       Three times they breathed, and three times did they 102

         drink,

       Upon agreement, of swift Severn's flood;

       Who then, affrighted with their bloody looks,

       Ran fearfully among the trembling reeds

       And hid his crisp head in the hollow bank,   106

       Bloodstainèd with these valiant combatants.

       Never did bare and rotten policy   108

       Color her working with such deadly wounds;   109

       Nor never could the noble Mortimer

       Receive so many, and all willingly.

       Then let not him be slandered with revolt.

KING

       Thou dost belie him, Percy, thou dost belie him!   113

       He never did encounter with Glendower.

       I tell thee

       He durst as well have met the devil alone

       As Owen Glendower for an enemy.

       Art thou not ashamed? But, sirrah, henceforth

       Let me not hear you speak of Mortimer.

       Send me your prisoners with the speediest means,

       Or you shall hear in such a kind from me

       As will displease you. My Lord Northumberland,

       We license your departure with your son. –

       Send us your prisoners, or you will hear of it.

           Exeunt King [, Blunt, and train].

HOTSPUR

       An if the devil come and roar for them,

       I will not send them. I will after straight   126

       And tell him so; for I will ease my heart,

       Albeit I make a hazard of my head.

NORTHUMBERLAND

       What, drunk with choler? Stay, and pause awhile.   129

       Here comes your uncle.

       Enter Worcester.

HOTSPUR   Speak of Mortimer?

       Zounds, I will speak of him, and let my soul

       Want mercy if I do not join with him!

       Yea, on his part I'll empty all these veins,

       And shed my dear blood drop by drop in the dust,

       But I will lift the downtrod Mortimer

       As high in the air as this unthankful king,

       As this ingrate and cankered Bolingbroke.   137

NORTHUMBERLAND

       Brother, the king hath made your nephew mad.

WORCESTER

       Who struck this heat up after I was gone?

---

38 *pouncet box* perfume-box; *ever and anon* now and then 40 *Who* i.e. his nose 41 *Took . . . snuff* (1) inhaled it, (2) resented (its being taken away); *still* continually 44 *slovenly* nasty 46 *holiday and lady* affected and effeminate 47 *questioned* kept on talking to 51 *grief* pain (from wounds) 56 *save the mark* avert anything so ridiculous 57 *sovereignst* most powerful (to cure) 58 *parmacity* spermaceti ointment 62 *tall* stout 65 *bald* trivial 66 *indirectly* offhand 68 *Come current* be accepted 75 *do him wrong* put him in the wrong; *impeach* discredit 79 *straight* at once 87 *indent* make terms; *fears* what we fear 94 *fall off* break his allegiance 97 *mouthèd* gaping 100 *confound* spend 101 *changing hardiment* trading blows 102 *breathed* stopped to catch their breath 106 *crisp* curly 108 *policy* craft 109 *Color* disguise 113 *belie* tell lies about 126 *will after* will go after 129 *choler* anger 137 *cankered* corrupt

HOTSPUR

140 He will (forsooth) have all my prisoners;
And when I urged the ransom once again
Of my wive's brother, then his cheek looked pale,
143 And on my face he turned an eye of death,
Trembling even at the name of Mortimer.

WORCESTER

I cannot blame him. Was not he proclaimed
By Richard that dead is, the next of blood?

NORTHUMBERLAND

He was; I heard the proclamation.
And then it was when the unhappy king
149 (Whose wrongs in us God pardon!) did set forth
Upon his Irish expedition;
From whence he intercepted did return
To be deposed, and shortly murderèd.

WORCESTER

And for whose death we in the world's wide mouth
Live scandalized and foully spoken of.

HOTSPUR

155 But soft, I pray you. Did King Richard then
156 Proclaim my brother Edmund Mortimer
Heir to the crown?

NORTHUMBERLAND He did; myself did hear it.

HOTSPUR

Nay, then I cannot blame his cousin king,
That wished him on the barren mountains starve.
But shall it be that you, that set the crown
Upon the head of this forgetful man,
And for his sake wear the detested blot
163 Of murderous subornation – shall it be
That you a world of curses undergo,
Being the agents or base second means,
The cords, the ladder, or the hangman rather?
O, pardon me that I descend so low
168 To show the line and the predicament
Wherein you range under this subtle king!
Shall it for shame be spoken in these days,
Or fill up chronicles in time to come,
That men of your nobility and power
173 Did gage them both in an unjust behalf
(As both of you, God pardon it! have done)
To put down Richard, that sweet lovely rose,
176 And plant this thorn, this canker, Bolingbroke?
And shall it in more shame be further spoken
That you are fooled, discarded, and shook off
By him for whom these shames ye underwent?
No! yet time serves wherein you may redeem
181 Your banished honors and restore yourselves
Into the good thoughts of the world again;
183 Revenge the jeering and disdained contempt

Of this proud king, who studies day and night
To answer all the debt he owes to you
185 Even with the bloody payment of your deaths.
Therefore I say –

WORCESTER Peace, cousin, say no more;
187 And now I will unclasp a secret book,
And to your quick-conceiving discontents
189 I'll read you matter deep and dangerous,
As full of peril and adventurous spirit
As to o'erwalk a current roaring loud
On the unsteadfast footing of a spear.

HOTSPUR

If he fall in, good night, or sink or swim!
194 Send danger from the east unto the west,
So honor cross it from the north to south,
196 And let them grapple. O, the blood more stirs
To rouse a lion than to start a hare!

NORTHUMBERLAND

Imagination of some great exploit
Drives him beyond the bounds of patience.
200

HOTSPUR

By heaven, methinks it were an easy leap
To pluck bright honor from the pale-faced moon,
Or dive into the bottom of the deep,
Where fathom line could never touch the ground,
And pluck up drownèd honor by the locks,
So he that doth redeem her thence might wear
206 Without corrival all her dignities;
207 But out upon this half-faced fellowship!
208

WORCESTER

He apprehends a world of figures here,
209 But not the form of what he should attend.
210 Good cousin, give me audience for a while.

HOTSPUR

I cry you mercy.
212

WORCESTER Those same noble Scots
That are your prisoners –

HOTSPUR I'll keep them all.
By God, he shall not have a Scot of them!
No, if a Scot would save his soul, he shall not.
I'll keep them, by this hand!

WORCESTER You start away
And lend no ear unto my purposes.
Those prisoners you shall keep.

HOTSPUR Nay, I will! That's flat!
He said he would not ransom Mortimer,
Forbade my tongue to speak of Mortimer,
But I will find him when he lies asleep,
And in his ear I'll hollo 'Mortimer.'
Nay, I'll have a starling shall be taught to speak
Nothing but 'Mortimer,' and give it him
To keep his anger still in motion.
225

WORCESTER

Hear you, cousin, a word.

HOTSPUR

All studies here I solemnly defy
227 Save how to gall and pinch this Bolingbroke;
And that same sword-and-buckler Prince of Wales:
229 But that I think his father loves him not
And would be glad he met with some mischance,
I would have him poisoned with a pot of ale.

WORCESTER

Farewell, kinsman. I will talk to you
When you are better tempered to attend.

---

140 *forsooth* indeed, in truth **143** *death* deadly fear **149** *wrongs in us* wrongs suffered because of us **155** *soft* hold on, wait a minute **156** *brother* i.e. brother-in-law **163** *murderous subornation* prompting of murder **168** *line* station; *predicament* category **173** *gage* bind; *in . . . behalf* for the benefit of injustice **176** *canker* (1) wild rose, (2) ulcer **181** *banished* forfeited **183** *disdained* disdainful **185** *answer* satisfy **187** *Peace* be quiet, hold your tongue **189** *quick-conceiving* understanding quickly **194** *he* i.e. the man on the spear; *or . . . swim* whether he sinks or swims **196** *So* so that **200** *patience* self-control **206** *So* provided that **207** *corrival* partner **208** *out upon* away with; *half-faced fellowship* sharing honor fifty-fifty **209** *figures* figments of the imagination **210** *form* essence; *attend* give his attention to **212** *cry you mercy* beg your pardon **225** *still* ever **227** *studies* interests; *defy* renounce **229** *sword-and-buckler* ruffianly

NORTHUMBERLAND
Why, what a wasp-stung and impatient fool
Art thou to break into this woman's mood,
Tying thine ear to no tongue but thine own!

HOTSPUR
Why, look you, I am whipped and scourged with rods,
239   Nettled, and stung with pismires when I hear
240   Of this vile politician, Bolingbroke.
In Richard's time – what do you call the place?
A plague upon it! it is in Gloucestershire;
243   'Twas where the madcap duke his uncle kept,
244   His uncle York – where I first bowed my knee
Unto this king of smiles, this Bolingbroke –
'Sblood! – when you and he came back from Ravenspurgh –

NORTHUMBERLAND
At Berkeley Castle.

HOTSPUR
You say true.
249   Why, what a candy deal of courtesy
This fawning greyhound then did proffer me!
'Look when his infant fortune came to age,'
252   And 'gentle Harry Percy,' and 'kind cousin' –
253   O, the devil take such cozeners! – God forgive me!
Good uncle, tell your tale, for I have done.

WORCESTER
Nay, if you have not, to it again.
256   We will stay your leisure.

HOTSPUR   I have done, i' faith.

WORCESTER
Then once more to your Scottish prisoners.
Deliver them up without their ransom straight,
And make the Douglas' son your only mean
For powers in Scotland – which, for divers reasons
Which I shall send you written, be assured
Will easily be granted.
[To Northumberland] You, my lord,
Your son in Scotland being thus employed,
Shall secretly into the bosom creep
Of that same noble prelate well-beloved,
The archbishop.

HOTSPUR   Of York, is it not?

WORCESTER
267   True; who bears hard
268   His brother's death at Bristow, the Lord Scroop.
269   I speak not this in estimation,
As what I think might be, but what I know
Is ruminated, plotted, and set down,
And only stays but to behold the face
Of that occasion that shall bring it on.

HOTSPUR
I smell it. Upon my life, it will do well.

NORTHUMBERLAND
275   Before the game is afoot thou still let'st slip.

HOTSPUR
Why, it cannot choose but be a noble plot.
And then the power of Scotland and of York
To join with Mortimer, ha?

WORCESTER   And so they shall.

HOTSPUR
In faith, it is exceedingly well aimed.

WORCESTER
And 'tis no little reason bids us speed
281   To save our heads by raising of a head;

For, bear ourselves as even as we can,   282
The king will always think him in our debt,
And think we think ourselves unsatisfied,
Till he hath found a time to pay us home.   285
And see already how he doth begin
To make us strangers to his looks of love.

HOTSPUR
He does, he does! We'll be revenged on him.

WORCESTER
Cousin, farewell. No further go in this
Than I by letters shall direct your course.
When time is ripe, which will be suddenly,   291
I'll steal to Glendower and Lord Mortimer,
Where you and Douglas, and our pow'rs at once,
As I will fashion it, shall happily meet,
To bear our fortunes in our own strong arms,
Which now we hold at much uncertainty.

NORTHUMBERLAND
Farewell, good brother. We shall thrive, I trust.

HOTSPUR
Uncle, adieu. O, let the hours be short
Till fields and blows and groans applaud our sport!
                             Exeunt.

                 *

Enter a Carrier with a lantern in his hand.   II, i

1. CARRIER   Heigh-ho! an it be not four by the day, I'll be   1
hanged. Charles' wain is over the new chimney, and yet   2
our horse not packed. – What, ostler!   3

OSTLER [*within*]   Anon, anon.   4

1. CARRIER   I prithee, Tom, beat Cut's saddle, put a few
flocks in the point. Poor jade is wrung in the withers out   6
of all cess.
Enter another Carrier.

2. CARRIER   Peas and beans are as dank here as a dog, and   8
that is the next way to give poor jades the bots. This   9
house is turned upside down since Robin Ostler died.

1. CARRIER   Poor fellow never joyed since the price of oats
rose. It was the death of him.

2. CARRIER   I think this be the most villainous house in all
London road for fleas. I am stung like a tench.   14

1. CARRIER   Like a tench? By the mass, there is ne'er a
king christen could be better bit than I have been since   16
the first cock.   17

2. CARRIER   Why, they will allow us ne'er a jordan, and   18
then we leak in your chimney, and your chamber-lye   19
breeds fleas like a loach.   20

1. CARRIER   What, ostler! come away and be hanged!   21
come away!

---

239 *pismires* ants   240 *politician* ignoble schemer   243 *kept* dwelt   244 *bowed* (see *Richard II*, II, iii)   249 *candy* sugary   252 *gentle* of gentle birth   253 *cozeners* cheaters   256 *stay* await   267 *bears hard* resents   268 *Scroop* Earl of Wiltshire (*Richard II*, III, ii)   269 *in estimation* conjecturally   275 *still* always; *slip* loose the dogs   281 *head* army   282 *even* carefully   285 *home* fully   291 *suddenly* at once
II, i   An inn yard at Rochester   1 *four . . . day* four in the morning   2 *Charles' wain* the Great Bear   3 *horse* horses   4 *Anon* right away   6 *flocks* tufts of wool; *point* pommel; *jade* (contemptuous name for) horse; *wrung* chafed   6-7 *out . . . cess* beyond estimation   8 *Peas and beans* fodder for horses; *as dank . . . dog* i.e. very soggy   9 *next* quickest; *bots* maggots in the intestines   14 *tench* a fish whose red spots may be likened to flea-bites   16 *king christen* Christian king   17 *first cock* i.e. midnight   18 *jordan* chamberpot   19 *chimney* fireplace; *chamber-lye* urine   20 *like a loach* as a loach (a prolific fish) breeds loaches   21 *come away* come here

23 2. CARRIER I have a gammon of bacon and two razes of
ginger, to be delivered as far as Charing Cross.

1. CARRIER God's body! the turkeys in my pannier are
quite starved. What, ostler! A plague on thee! hast thou
never an eye in thy head? Canst not hear? An 'twere not
28 as good deed as drink to break the pate on thee, I am a
29 very villain. Come, and be hanged! Hast no faith in
thee?

Enter Gadshill.

GADSHILL Good morrow, carriers. What's o'clock?

1. CARRIER I think it be two o'clock.

GADSHILL I prithee lend me thy lantern to see my gelding in the stable.

1. CARRIER Nay, by God, soft! I know a trick worth two
of that, i' faith.

GADSHILL I pray thee lend me thine.

37 2. CARRIER Ay, when? canst tell? Lend me thy lantern,
quoth he? Marry, I'll see thee hanged first!

GADSHILL Sirrah carrier, what time do you mean to
come to London?

2. CARRIER Time enough to go to bed with a candle, I
warrant thee. Come, neighbor Mugs, we'll call up the
43 gentlemen. They will along with company, for they
44 have great charge. *Exeunt [Carriers].*

45 GADSHILL What, ho! chamberlain!

Enter Chamberlain.

46 CHAMBERLAIN At hand, quoth pickpurse.

47 GADSHILL That's even as fair as 'at hand, quoth the
chamberlain'; for thou variest no more from picking of
purses than giving direction doth from laboring: thou
layest the plot how.

51 CHAMBERLAIN Good morrow, Master Gadshill. It holds
52 current that I told you yesternight. There's a franklin in
53 the Wild of Kent hath brought three hundred marks
with him in gold. I heard him tell it to one of his company last night at supper – a kind of auditor, one that
hath abundance of charge, God knows what. They
are up already and call for eggs and butter. They will
58 away presently.

59 GADSHILL Sirrah, if they meet not with Saint Nicholas'
clerks, I'll give thee this neck.

61 CHAMBERLAIN No, I'll none of it. I pray thee keep that
for the hangman; for I know thou worshippest Saint
Nicholas as truly as a man of falsehood may.

GADSHILL What talkest thou to me of the hangman? If I
hang, I'll make a fat pair of gallows; for if I hang, old Sir

John hangs with me, and thou knowest he is no starveling. Tut! there are other Troyans that thou dream'st 67
not of, the which for sport sake are content to do the
profession some grace; that would (if matters should be 69
looked into) for their own credit sake make all whole. I
am joined with no foot land-rakers, no long-staff six- 71
penny strikers, none of these mad mustachio purple- 72
hued maltworms; but with nobility and tranquillity, 73
burgomasters and great oneyers, such as can hold in, 74
such as will strike sooner than speak, and speak sooner 75
than drink, and drink sooner than pray; and yet,
zounds, I lie; for they pray continually to their saint,
the commonwealth, or rather, not pray to her, but prey
on her, for they ride up and down on her and make her
their boots. 79

CHAMBERLAIN What, the commonwealth their boots?
Will she hold out water in foul way? 81

GADSHILL She will, she will! Justice hath liquored her. 82
We steal as in a castle, cocksure. We have the receipt of 83
fernseed, we walk invisible. 84

CHAMBERLAIN Nay, by my faith, I think you are more
beholding to the night than to fernseed for your walking
invisible.

GADSHILL Give me thy hand. Thou shalt have a share in
our purchase, as I am a true man. 89

CHAMBERLAIN Nay, rather let me have it, as you are a
false thief.

GADSHILL Go to; 'homo' is a common name to all men. 92
Bid the ostler bring my gelding out of the stable.
Farewell, you muddy knave. *[Exeunt.]* 94

*

Enter Prince, Poins, Peto [and Bardolph].   II, ii

POINS Come, shelter, shelter! I have removed Falstaff's
horse, and he frets like a gummed velvet. 2

PRINCE Stand close. *[They step aside.]* 3

Enter Falstaff.

FALSTAFF Poins! Poins, and be hanged! Poins!

PRINCE *[comes forward]* Peace, ye fat-kidneyed rascal! 5
What a brawling dost thou keep! 6

FALSTAFF Where's Poins, Hal?

PRINCE He is walked up to the top of the hill; I'll go seek
him. *[Steps aside.]*

FALSTAFF I am accursed to rob in that thieve's company.
The rascal hath removed my horse and tied him I know
not where. If I travel but four foot by the squire further 12
afoot, I shall break my wind. Well, I doubt not but to
die a fair death for all this, if I scape hanging for killing
that rogue. I have forsworn his company hourly any
time this two-and-twenty years, and yet I am bewitched
with the rogue's company. If the rascal have not given
me medicines to make me love him, I'll be hanged. It 18
could not be else: I have drunk medicines. Poins! Hal!
A plague upon you both! Bardolph! Peto! I'll starve ere
I'll rob a foot further. An 'twere not as good a deed as
drink to turn true man and to leave these rogues, I am 22
the veriest varlet that ever chewed with a tooth. Eight 23
yards of uneven ground is threescore and ten miles afoot
with me, and the stony-hearted villains know it well
enough. A plague upon it when thieves cannot be true
one to another! *(They whistle.)* Whew! A plague upon
you all! Give me my horse, you rogues! give me my
horse and be hanged!

23 *gammon of bacon* ham; *razes* roots   28 *the pate on thee* your head   29
faith trustworthiness   37 *Ay . . . tell* i.e. never   43 *will along* wish to go
along   44 *charge* baggage   45 *chamberlain* male servant corresponding to
chambermaid   46 *At . . . pickpurse* (proverbial)   47 *fair* apt   51–52
holds current is still true   52 *franklin* small landowner   53 *Wild* forest;
three hundred marks £200   58 *presently* at once   59–60 *Saint Nicholas'
clerks* highwaymen   61 *I'll none* I want none   67 *Troyans* sports   69
profession i.e. robbery; *grace* credit   71 *foot land-rakers* footpads   72
strikers holdup men   72–73 *mustachio . . . maltworms* topers with mus-
taches stained with beer   73 *tranquillity* those who live an easy life   74
oneyers officers; *hold in* keep their mouths shut   75 *speak* i.e. say 'hands
up'   79 *boots* booty   81 *foul way* muddy road, i.e. tight place   82 *liquored*
(1) greased, (2) bribed   83 *as . . . castle* with impunity   84 *fernseed* reputed
to be invisible and to confer invisibility   89 *purchase* loot; *true* honest
92 *Go to* 'nuts'; '*homo' . . . men* i.e. they're all the same   94 *muddy* stupid
II, ii The highway at Gad's Hill   2 *frets* (1) fumes, (2) wears away; *gummed
velvet* velvet stiffened with gum (and therefore liable to wear)   3 *close*
where you won't be seen   5 *rascal* (literally) lean deer   6 *keep* keep up
12 *squire* foot-rule   18 *medicines* love potions   22 *true* honest   23 *varlet*
scamp

PRINCE *[comes forward]* Peace, ye fat-guts! Lie down, lay thine ear close to the ground, and list if thou canst hear the tread of travellers.

FALSTAFF Have you any levers to lift me up again, being down? 'Sblood, I'll not bear mine own flesh so far afoot again for all the coin in thy father's exchequer. What a
35 plague mean ye to colt me thus?

PRINCE Thou liest; thou art not colted, thou art un-colted.

FALSTAFF I prithee, good Prince Hal, help me to my horse, good king's son.

39 PRINCE Out, ye rogue! Shall I be your ostler?

FALSTAFF Go hang thyself in thine own heir-apparent
41 garters! If I be ta'en, I'll peach for this. An I have not
42 ballads made on you all, and sung to filthy tunes, let a cup of sack be my poison. When a jest is so forward – and afoot too – I hate it.

Enter Gadshill.

GADSHILL Stand!

FALSTAFF So I do, against my will.

47 POINS *[comes forward]* O, 'tis our setter; I know his voice.

BARDOLPH What news?

49 GADSHILL Case ye, case ye! On with your vizards! There's money of the king's coming down the hill; 'tis going to the king's exchequer.

FALSTAFF You lie, ye rogue! 'Tis going to the king's tavern.

53 GADSHILL There's enough to make us all.

FALSTAFF To be hanged.

PRINCE Sirs, you four shall front them in the narrow lane; Ned Poins and I will walk lower. If they scape from your encounter, then they light on us.

PETO How many be there of them?

GADSHILL Some eight or ten.

FALSTAFF Zounds, will they not rob us?

PRINCE What, a coward, Sir John Paunch?

FALSTAFF Indeed, I am not John of Gaunt, your grand-father, but yet no coward, Hal.

64 PRINCE Well, we leave that to the proof.

POINS Sirrah Jack, thy horse stands behind the hedge. When thou need'st him, there thou shalt find him. Fare-well and stand fast.

FALSTAFF Now cannot I strike him, if I should be hanged.

PRINCE *[aside to Poins]* Ned, where are our disguises?

POINS *[aside to Prince]* Here, hard by. Stand close.

[Exeunt Prince and Poins.]

71 FALSTAFF Now, my masters, happy man be his dole, say I. Every man to his business.

Enter the Travellers.

TRAVELLER Come, neighbor. The boy shall lead our horses down the hill; we'll walk afoot awhile and ease our legs.

THIEVES Stand!

TRAVELLER Jesus bless us!

FALSTAFF Strike! down with them! cut the villains'
78 throats! Ah, whoreson caterpillars! bacon-fed knaves! they hate us youth. Down with them! fleece them!

80 TRAVELLER O, we are undone, both we and ours for ever!

81 FALSTAFF Hang ye, gorbellied knaves, are ye undone?
82 No, ye fat chuffs; I would your store were here! On,
83 bacons, on! What, ye knaves! young men must live.
84 You are grandjurors, are ye? We'll jure ye, faith!

Here they rob them and bind them. Exeunt.

Enter the Prince and Poins [in buckram suits].

PRINCE The thieves have bound the true men. Now 85 could thou and I rob the thieves and go merrily to London, it would be argument for a week, laughter for a 87 month, and a good jest for ever.

POINS Stand close! I hear them coming.

[They stand aside.]

Enter the Thieves again.

FALSTAFF Come, my masters, let us share, and then to horse before day. An the prince and Poins be not two arrant cowards, there's no equity stirring. There's no 92 more valor in that Poins than in a wild duck. 93

PRINCE   ⎧ *As they are sharing, the prince and Poins*
Your money! ⎨ *set upon them. They all run away, and*
POINS   ⎪ *Falstaff, after a blow or two, runs away*
Villains!   ⎩ *too, leaving the booty behind them.*

PRINCE Got with much ease. Now merrily to horse. The thieves are all scattered, and possessed with fear so strongly that they dare not meet each other: each takes his fellow for an officer. Anyway, good Ned. Falstaff sweats to death and lards the lean earth as he walks along. Were't not for laughing, I should pity him.

POINS How the fat rogue roared!   *Exeunt.*

*

Enter Hotspur solus, reading a letter.   II, iii

HOTSPUR 'But, for mine own part, my lord, I could be well contented to be there, in respect of the love I bear 2 your house.' He could be contented – why is he not 3 then? In respect of the love he bears our house! He shows in this he loves his own barn better than he loves our house. Let me see some more. 'The purpose you undertake is dangerous' – why, that's certain! 'Tis dangerous to take a cold, to sleep, to drink; but I tell you, my lord fool, out of this nettle, danger, we pluck this flower, safety. 'The purpose you undertake is dangerous, the friends you have named uncertain, the time itself unsorted, and your whole plot too light for 12 the counterpoise of so great an opposition.' Say you so, say you so? I say unto you again, you are a shallow, cowardly hind, and you lie. What a lackbrain is this! By 14 the Lord, our plot is a good plot as ever was laid; our friends true and constant: a good plot, good friends, and full of expectation; an excellent plot, very good friends. 17 What a frosty-spirited rogue is this! Why, my Lord of York commends the plot and the general course of the action. Zounds, an I were now by this rascal, I could brain him with his lady's fan. Is there not my father, my uncle, and myself; Lord Edmund Mortimer, my Lord of York, and Owen Glendower? Is there not, besides, the Douglas? Have I not all their letters to meet me in arms by the ninth of the next month, and are they not

35 *colt* befool   39 *Out* get out   41 *ta'en* arrested   42 *ballads* (scurrilous) songs   47 *setter* one who sets a match (I, ii, 100)   49 *Case ye* put on your masks   53 *make us all* make our fortunes   64 *proof* test   71 *dole* lot 78 *caterpillars* parasites   80 *ours* our families   81 *gorbellied* fat-paunched 82 *chuffs* misers; *your store* all your possessions   83 *bacons* fat men   84 *grandjurors* i.e. well-to-do citizens   85 *true* honest   87 *argument* something to talk about   92 *arrant* out-and-out; *equity* judicial discernment   93 *wild duck* notoriously timid
II, iii Hotspur's castle (at Warkworth)   2 *in respect of* on account of   3 *house* family   12 *unsorted* ill-chosen   12–13 *for the counterpoise of* to counterbalance   14 *hind* peasant   17 *expectation* promise

26 some of them set forward already? What a pagan rascal
27 is this! an infidel! Ha! you shall see now, in very sincerity of fear and cold heart will he to the king and lay
open all our proceedings. O, I could divide myself and
30 go to buffets for moving such a dish of skim milk with so
honorable an action! Hang him, let him tell the king!
we are prepared. I will set forward to-night.

    Enter his Lady.

How now, Kate? I must leave you within these two
hours.

LADY
O my good lord, why are you thus alone?
For what offense have I this fortnight been
A banished woman from my Harry's bed?
Tell me, sweet lord, what is't that takes from thee
38 Thy stomach, pleasure, and thy golden sleep?
Why dost thou bend thine eyes upon the earth,
And start so often when thou sit'st alone?
Why hast thou lost the fresh blood in thy cheeks
And given my treasures and my rights of thee
43 To thick-eyed musing and cursed melancholy?
In thy faint slumbers I by thee have watched,
And heard thee murmur tales of iron wars,
46 Speak terms of manage to thy bounding steed,
Cry 'Courage! to the field!' And thou hast talked
Of sallies and retires, of trenches, tents,
49 Of palisadoes, frontiers, parapets,
50 Of basilisks, of cannon, culverin,
Of prisoners' ransom, and of soldiers slain,
52 And all the currents of a heady fight.
Thy spirit within thee hath been so at war,
And thus hath so bestirred thee in thy sleep,
That beads of sweat have stood upon thy brow
Like bubbles in a late-disturbèd stream,
And in thy face strange motions have appeared,
Such as we see when men restrain their breath
59 On some great sudden hest. O, what portents are these?
60 Some heavy business hath my lord in hand,
And I must know it, else he loves me not.

HOTSPUR
What, ho!

    [Enter a Servant.]
               Is Gilliams with the packet gone?

SERVANT
He is, my lord, an hour ago.

HOTSPUR
Hath Butler brought those horses from the sheriff?

SERVANT
One horse, my lord, he brought even now.

HOTSPUR
What horse? A roan, a crop-ear, is it not?

SERVANT
It is, my lord.

HOTSPUR   That roan shall be my throne.
Well, I will back him straight. O esperancè!   68
Bid Butler lead him forth into the park.   *[Exit Servant.]*

LADY
But hear you, my lord.

HOTSPUR
What say'st thou, my lady?

LADY
What is it carries you away?

HOTSPUR
Why, my horse, my love – my horse!

LADY
Out, you mad-headed ape!
A weasel hath not such a deal of spleen   75
As you are tossed with. In faith,
I'll know your business, Harry; that I will!
I fear my brother Mortimer doth stir
About his title and hath sent for you   79
To line his enterprise; but if you go –   80

HOTSPUR
So far afoot, I shall be weary, love.

LADY
Come, come, you paraquito, answer me   82
Directly unto this question that I ask.
In faith, I'll break thy little finger, Harry,
An if thou wilt not tell me all things true.

HOTSPUR
Away, away, you trifler! Love? I love thee not;
I care not for thee, Kate. This is no world
To play with mammets and to tilt with lips.   88
We must have bloody noses and cracked crowns,
And pass them current too. Gods me, my horse!   90
What say'st thou, Kate? What wouldst thou have
    with me?

LADY
Do you not love me? do you not indeed?
Well, do not then; for since you love me not,
I will not love myself. Do you not love me?
Nay, tell me if you speak in jest or no.

HOTSPUR
Come, wilt thou see me ride?
And when I am a-horseback, I will swear
I love thee infinitely. But hark you, Kate:
I must not have you henceforth question me
Whither I go, nor reason whereabout.   100
Whither I must, I must, and to conclude,
This evening must I leave you, gentle Kate.
I know you wise, but yet no farther wise
Than Harry Percy's wife; constant you are,
But yet a woman; and for secrecy,
No lady closer, for I well believe
Thou wilt not utter what thou dost not know,
And so far will I trust thee, gentle Kate.

LADY
How? so far?

HOTSPUR
Not an inch further. But hark you, Kate:
Whither I go, thither shall you go too;
To-day will I set forth, to-morrow you.
Will this content you, Kate?

LADY   It must of force.   *Exeunt.* 113

26 *pagan* unbelieving 27 *very* veritable 30 *go to buffets* fall to blows 38 *stomach* appetite 43 *thick-eyed* dim-sighted 46 *manage* horsemanship 49 *palisadoes* stakes set in the ground to stop a charge; *frontiers* outworks 50 *basilisks, culverin* kinds of cannon 52 *heady* headlong 59 *hest* command, i.e. when making a special effort 60 *heavy* (1) weighty, (2) woeful 68 *esperancè* hope (the Percy battle-cry) 75 *weasel* proverbially quarrelsome; *spleen* irascibility 79 *title* claim to the throne 80 *line* reinforce 82 *paraquito* parrot 88 *mammets* dolls 90 *pass them current* (1) deal them out, (2) circulate (*crowns*: 5-shilling pieces); *Gods me* God save me 100 *reason whereabout* discuss what for 113 *of force* of necessity

II, iv   *Enter Prince and Poins.*

1 PRINCE Ned, prithee come out of that fat room and lend
me thy hand to laugh a little.

POINS Where hast been, Hal?

4 PRINCE With three or four loggerheads amongst three or
fourscore hogsheads. I have sounded the very bass-
6 string of humility. Sirrah, I am sworn brother to a leash
7 of drawers and can call them all by their christen names,
as Tom, Dick, and Francis. They take it already upon
their salvation that, though I be but Prince of Wales,
yet I am the king of courtesy, and tell me flatly I am no
11 proud Jack like Falstaff, but a Corinthian, a lad of
12 mettle, a good boy (by the Lord, so they call me!), and
when I am king of England I shall command all the
good lads in Eastcheap. They call drinking deep, dye-
15 ing scarlet; and when you breathe in your watering,
16 they cry 'hem!' and bid you play it off. To conclude, I
am so good a proficient in one quarter of an hour that I
can drink with any tinker in his own language during
19 my life. I tell thee, Ned, thou hast lost much honor that
thou wert not with me in this action. But, sweet Ned –
21 to sweeten which name of Ned, I give thee this penny-
22 worth of sugar, clapped even now into my hand by an
under-skinker, one that never spake other English in his
life than 'Eight shillings and sixpence,' and 'You are
24 welcome,' with this shrill addition, 'Anon, anon, sir!
25 Score a pint of bastard in the Half-moon,' or so – but,
Ned, to drive away the time till Falstaff come, I prithee
do thou stand in some by-room while I question my
puny drawer to what end he gave me the sugar; and do
thou never leave calling 'Francis!' that his tale to me
may be nothing but 'Anon!' Step aside, and I'll show
31 thee a precedent.

POINS Francis!

33 PRINCE Thou art perfect.

POINS Francis!   *[Exit Poins.]*
Enter [Francis, a] Drawer.

35 FRANCIS Anon, anon, sir. – Look down into the Pomgarnet, Ralph.

PRINCE Come hither, Francis.

FRANCIS My lord?

39 PRINCE How long hast thou to serve, Francis?

FRANCIS Forsooth, five years, and as much as to –

POINS *[within]* Francis!

FRANCIS Anon, anon, sir.

PRINCE Five year! by'r Lady, a long lease for the clinking
of pewter. But, Francis, darest thou be so valiant as to
play the coward with thy indenture and show it a fair
pair of heels and run from it?

47 FRANCIS O Lord, sir, I'll be sworn upon all the books in
England I could find in my heart –

POINS *[within]* Francis!

FRANCIS Anon, sir.

PRINCE How old art thou, Francis?

52 FRANCIS Let me see: about Michaelmas next I shall be –

POINS *[within]* Francis!

FRANCIS Anon, sir. Pray stay a little, my lord.

PRINCE Nay, but hark you, Francis. For the sugar thou
gavest me – 'twas a pennyworth, was't not?

FRANCIS O Lord! I would it had been two!

PRINCE I will give thee for it a thousand pound. Ask me
when thou wilt, and thou shalt have it.

POINS *[within]* Francis!

FRANCIS Anon, anon.

PRINCE Anon, Francis? No, Francis; but to-morrow,
Francis; or, Francis, a Thursday; or indeed, Francis, 63
when thou wilt. But, Francis –

FRANCIS My lord?

PRINCE Wilt thou rob this leathern-jerkin, crystal- 66
button, not-pated, agate-ring, puke-stocking, caddis- 67
garter, smooth-tongue, Spanish-pouch –

FRANCIS O Lord, sir, who do you mean?

PRINCE Why then, your brown bastard is your only
drink; for look you, Francis, your white canvas doublet 71
will sully. In Barbary, sir, it cannot come to so much. 72

FRANCIS What, sir?

POINS *[within]* Francis!

PRINCE Away, you rogue! Dost thou not hear them
call?   76
*Here they both call him. The Drawer stands amazed,
not knowing which way to go.
Enter Vintner.*

VINTNER What, stand'st thou still, and hear'st such a
calling? Look to the guests within. *[Exit Francis.]* My
lord, old Sir John, with half-a-dozen more, are at the
door. Shall I let them in?

PRINCE Let them alone awhile, and then open the door.
[Exit Vintner.] Poins!

POINS *[within]* Anon, anon, sir.
Enter Poins.

PRINCE Sirrah, Falstaff and the rest of the thieves are at
the door. Shall we be merry?

POINS As merry as crickets, my lad. But hark ye; what
cunning match have you made with this jest of the 87
drawer? Come, what's the issue? 88

PRINCE I am now of all humors that have showed themselves humors since the old days of goodman Adam to
the pupil age of this present twelve o'clock at midnight. 91
[Enter Francis.]
What's o'clock, Francis?

FRANCIS Anon, anon, sir.   *[Exit.]*

PRINCE That ever this fellow should have fewer words
than a parrot, and yet the son of a woman! His industry
is upstairs and downstairs, his eloquence the parcel of a 96
reckoning. I am not yet of Percy's mind, the Hotspur of
the North; he that kills me some six or seven dozen of 98
Scots at a breakfast, washes his hands, and says to his
wife, 'Fie upon this quiet life! I want work.' 'O my
sweet Harry,' says she, 'how many hast thou killed to-
day?' 'Give my roan horse a drench,' says he, and 102
answers 'Some fourteen,' an hour after, 'a trifle, a
trifle.' I prithee call in Falstaff. I'll play Percy, and that
damned brawn shall play Dame Mortimer his wife. 105

II, iv Within an Eastcheap tavern   1 *fat* stuffy   4 *loggerheads* blockheads
6 *leash* i.e. three   7 *drawers* waiters   11 *Corinthian* good sport   12 *a good
boy* one of the boys   15 *scarlet* the best scarlet dyes were made with
topers' urine; *breathe* pause; *watering* drinking   16 *play* i.e. toss   19
action encounter, (literally) battle   21 *sugar* used to sweeten wine   22
under-skinker bartender's assistant   24 *Anon* i.e. coming   25 *bastard* sweet
Spanish wine; *Half-moon* a room in the tavern   31 *precedent* something
worth following   33 *Thou art perfect* you have learned your part   35
Pomgarnet Pomegranate (a room in the tavern)   39 *serve* i.e. as an apprentice   47 *books* i.e. Bibles   52 *Michaelmas* September 29   63 *a* on   66
rob i.e. by running away   67 *not-pated* short-haired; *agate-ring* seal ring;
puke-stocking woolen-stocking; *caddis-garter* garter of worsted tape   71–72
your . . . sully i.e. you'll have to put up with a drawer's life   72 *it* i.e. sugar,
imported from Barbary   76 s.d. *amazed* dumbfounded   87 *cunning match*
sly game   88 *issue* outcome   91 *pupil age* youth   96 *parcel* details   98
me (redundant: ethical dative)   102 *drench* dose of medicine; *says he* (i.e.
to a servant)   105 *brawn* fat pig

106   'Rivo!' says the drunkard. Call in ribs, call in tallow.

Enter Falstaff [, Gadshill, Bardolph, and Peto ;
Francis follows with wine].

POINS Welcome, Jack. Where hast thou been?

108 FALSTAFF A plague of all cowards, I say, and a vengeance too! Marry and amen! Give me a cup of sack,
110 boy. Ere I lead this life long, I'll sew netherstocks, and
mend them and foot them too. A plague of all cowards!
112 Give me a cup of sack, rogue. Is there no virtue extant?
He drinketh.

113 PRINCE Didst thou never see Titan kiss a dish of butter
(pitiful-hearted Titan!) that melted at the sweet tale of
115 the sun's? If thou didst, then behold that compound.

116 FALSTAFF You rogue, here's lime in this sack too! There
is nothing but roguery to be found in villainous man.
Yet a coward is worse than a cup of sack with lime in it –
a villainous coward! Go thy ways, old Jack, die when
120 thou wilt; if manhood, good manhood, be not forgot
121 upon the face of the earth, then am I a shotten herring.
There lives not three good men unhanged in England;
and one of them is fat, and grows old. God help the
124 while! A bad world, I say. I would I were a weaver; I
125 could sing psalms or anything. A plague of all cowards, I
say still!

PRINCE How now, woolsack? What mutter you?

FALSTAFF A king's son! If I do not beat thee out of thy
kingdom with a dagger of lath and drive all thy subjects
afore thee like a flock of wild geese, I'll never wear hair
on my face more. You Prince of Wales?

PRINCE Why, you whoreson round man, what's the
matter?

FALSTAFF Are not you a coward? Answer me to that –
and Poins there?

POINS Zounds, ye fat paunch, an ye call me coward, by
the Lord, I'll stab thee.

FALSTAFF I call thee coward? I'll see thee damned ere I
call thee coward, but I would give a thousand pound I
could run as fast as thou canst. You are straight enough
140 in the shoulders; you care not who sees your back. Call
you that backing of your friends? A plague upon such
backing! Give me them that will face me. Give me a
cup of sack. I am a rogue if I drunk to-day.

PRINCE O villain! thy lips are scarce wiped since thou
drunk'st last.

146 FALSTAFF All is one for that. *(He drinketh.)* A plague of
all cowards, still say I.

PRINCE What's the matter?

FALSTAFF What's the matter? There be four of us here
have ta'en a thousand pound this day morning.

PRINCE Where is it, Jack? where is it?

FALSTAFF Where is it? Taken from us it is. A hundred
upon poor four of us!

---

106 *Rivo* (perhaps) bottoms up 108 *of* on 110 *sew netherstocks* a menial
occupation 112 *virtue* valor 113 *Titan* the sun 115 *compound* (sweating)
lump of butter 116 *lime* added surreptitiously to wine to make it sparkle
120 *manhood* valor 121 *shotten herring* a herring that has deposited its roe
124 *while* present time 125 *sing psalms* a habit for which the weavers
were notorious 146 *All . . . that* it makes no difference 155 *at half-
sword* at close quarters 159 *ecce signum* look at the evidence 160 *dealt*
dealt blows 173 *other* others 177 *three and fifty* the number of Spanish
ships engaged by Sir Richard Grenville in the *Revenge* (1591) 180 *peppered* made it hot for 181 *paid* i.e. killed 184 *ward* defensive stance; *lay*
stood 189 *afront* abreast; *mainly* violently 190 *me* (ethical dative) 191
target shield 195 *villain* no gentleman 203 *points* (1) sword-points, (2)
laces which hold up the clothes 206 *came in* advanced; *with a thought* as
quick as thought 208 *monstrous* astounding

PRINCE What, a hundred, man?

FALSTAFF I am a rogue if I were not at half-sword with a 155
dozen of them two hours together. I have scaped by
miracle. I am eight times thrust through the doublet,
four through the hose; my buckler cut through and
through; my sword hacked like a handsaw – ecce sig- 159
num! I never dealt better since I was a man. All would 160
not do. A plague of all cowards! Let them speak. If they
speak more or less than truth, they are villains and the
sons of darkness.

PRINCE Speak, sirs. How was it?

GADSHILL We four set upon some dozen –

FALSTAFF Sixteen at least, my lord.

GADSHILL And bound them.

PETO No, no, they were not bound.

FALSTAFF You rogue, they were bound, every man of
them, or I am a Jew else – an Ebrew Jew.

GADSHILL As we were sharing, some six or seven fresh
men set upon us –

FALSTAFF And unbound the rest, and then come in the
other. 173

PRINCE What, fought you with them all?

FALSTAFF All? I know not what you call all, but if I
fought not with fifty of them, I am a bunch of radish! If
there were not two or three and fifty upon poor old 177
Jack, then am I no two-legged creature.

PRINCE Pray God you have not murd'red some of
them.

FALSTAFF Nay, that's past praying for. I have peppered 180
two of them. Two I am sure I have paid, two rogues in 181
buckram suits. I tell thee what, Hal – if I tell thee a lie,
spit in my face, call me horse. Thou knowest my old
ward. Here I lay, and thus I bore my point. Four 184
rogues in buckram let drive at me.

PRINCE What, four? Thou saidst but two even now.

FALSTAFF Four, Hal. I told thee four.

POINS Ay, ay, he said four.

FALSTAFF These four came all afront and mainly thrust 189
at me. I made me no more ado but took all their seven 190
points in my target, thus. 191

PRINCE Seven? Why, there were but four even now.

FALSTAFF In buckram?

POINS Ay, four, in buckram suits.

FALSTAFF Seven, by these hilts, or I am a villain else. 195

PRINCE *[aside to Poins]* Prithee let him alone. We shall
have more anon.

FALSTAFF Dost thou hear me, Hal?

PRINCE Ay, and mark thee too, Jack.

FALSTAFF Do so, for it is worth the list'ning to. These
nine in buckram that I told thee of –

PRINCE So, two more already.

FALSTAFF Their points being broken – 203

POINS Down fell their hose.

FALSTAFF Began to give me ground; but I followed me
close, came in, foot and hand, and with a thought seven 206
of the eleven I paid.

PRINCE O monstrous! Eleven buckram men grown out of 208
two!

FALSTAFF But, as the devil would have it, three misbegotten knaves in Kendal green came at my back and
let drive at me; for it was so dark, Hal, that thou couldst
not see thy hand.

PRINCE These lies are like their father that begets them –
gross as a mountain, open, palpable. Why, thou clay-

216 brained guts, thou knotty-pated fool, thou whoreson
217 obscene greasy tallow-catch –

FALSTAFF What, art thou mad? art thou mad? Is not the truth the truth?

PRINCE Why, how couldst thou know these men in Kendal green when it was so dark thou couldst not see thy hand? Come, tell us your reason. What sayest thou to this?

POINS Come, your reason, Jack, your reason.

FALSTAFF What, upon compulsion? Zounds, an I were
225 at the strappado or all the racks in the world, I would not tell you on compulsion. Give you a reason on compul-
227 sion? If reasons were as plentiful as blackberries, I would give no man a reason upon compulsion, I.

229 PRINCE I'll be no longer guilty of this sin; this sanguine coward, this bed-presser, this horseback-breaker, this huge hill of flesh –

FALSTAFF 'Sblood, you starveling, you eel-skin, you
233 dried neat's-tongue, you bull's pizzle, you stockfish – O for breath to utter what is like thee! – you tailor's yard,
235 you sheath, you bowcase, you vile standing tuck!

236 PRINCE Well, breathe awhile, and then to it again; and when thou hast tired thyself in base comparisons, hear me speak but this.

POINS Mark, Jack.

PRINCE We two saw you four set on four, and bound them and were masters of their wealth. Mark now how a plain tale shall put you down. Then did we two set on
243 you four and, with a word, outfaced you from your prize, and have it; yea, and can show it you here in the house. And, Falstaff, you carried your guts away as nimbly, with as quick dexterity, and roared for mercy, and still run and roared, as ever I heard bullcalf. What a slave art thou to hack thy sword as thou hast done, and then say it was in fight! What trick, what device, what
250 starting hole canst thou now find out to hide thee from this open and apparent shame?

POINS Come, let's hear, Jack. What trick hast thou now?

FALSTAFF By the Lord, I knew ye as well as he that made ye. Why, hear you, my masters. Was it for me to kill the heir apparent? Should I turn upon the true prince? Why, thou knowest I am as valiant as Hercules, but
257 beware instinct. The lion will not touch the true prince. Instinct is a great matter. I was now a coward on instinct. I shall think the better of myself, and thee, during my life – I for a valiant lion, and thou for a true prince. But, by the Lord, lads, I am glad you have the money. Host-
262 ess, clap to the doors. Watch to-night, pray to-morrow. Gallants, lads, boys, hearts of gold, all the titles of good fellowship come to you! What, shall we be merry? Shall we have a play extempore?

266 PRINCE Content – and the argument shall be thy running away.

FALSTAFF Ah, no more of that, Hal, an thou lovest me!

Enter Hostess.

HOSTESS O Jesu, my lord the Prince!

PRINCE How now, my lady the hostess? What say'st thou to me?

HOSTESS Marry, my lord, there is a noble man of the court at door would speak with you. He says he comes from your father.

275 PRINCE Give him as much as will make him a royal man, and send him back again to my mother.

FALSTAFF What manner of man is he?

HOSTESS An old man.

FALSTAFF What doth gravity out of his bed at midnight? Shall I give him his answer?

PRINCE Prithee do, Jack.

FALSTAFF Faith, and I'll send him packing.   *Exit.*

PRINCE Now, sirs. By'r Lady, you fought fair; so did you, 283 Peto; so did you, Bardolph. You are lions too, you ran away upon instinct, you will not touch the true prince; no – fie!

BARDOLPH Faith, I ran when I saw others run.

PRINCE Tell me now in earnest, how came Falstaff's sword so hacked?

PETO Why, he hacked it with his dagger, and said he would swear truth out of England but he would make 291 you believe it was done in fight, and persuaded us to do the like.

BARDOLPH Yea, and to tickle our noses with speargrass to make them bleed, and then to beslubber our garments with it and swear it was the blood of true men. I did that 295 I did not this seven year before – I blushed to hear his monstrous devices.

PRINCE O villain! thou stolest a cup of sack eighteen years ago and wert taken with the manner, and ever since thou 299 hast blushed extempore. Thou hadst fire and sword on 300 thy side, and yet thou ran'st away. What instinct hadst thou for it?

BARDOLPH My lord, do you see these meteors? Do you 303 behold these exhalations?

PRINCE I do.

BARDOLPH What think you they portend?

PRINCE Hot livers and cold purses.   307

BARDOLPH Choler, my lord, if rightly taken.   308

PRINCE No, if rightly taken, halter.   309

Enter Falstaff.

Here comes lean Jack; here comes bare-bone. How now, my sweet creature of bombast? How long is't ago, Jack, 311 since thou sawest thine own knee?

FALSTAFF My own knee? When I was about thy years, Hal, I was not an eagle's talent in the waist; I could have 314 crept into any alderman's thumb-ring. A plague of sighing and grief! It blows a man up like a bladder. 316 There's villainous news abroad. Here was Sir John Bracy from your father. You must to the court in the morning. That same mad fellow of the north, Percy, and he of Wales that gave Amamon the bastinado, and 320 made Lucifer cuckold, and swore the devil his true 321

216 *knotty-pated* thick-headed 217 *tallow-catch* tub or lump of tallow 225 *strappado* kind of torture 227 *reasons* (pronounced like 'raisins') 229 *sanguine* daring 233 *stockfish* dried cod 235 *standing tuck* unpliant rapier 236 *breathe* catch your breath; *to it* go to it 243 *with a word* in short; *outfaced* frightened away 250 *starting hole* subterfuge, (literally) refuge for hunted animals 257 *beware* take heed of 262 *Watch . . . to-morrow* cf. 'Watch and pray, that ye enter not into temptation' (Matthew xxvi, 41) 266 *argument* subject 275 *a royal man* i.e. worth 10 shillings (3s. 4d. more than a noble) 283 *fair* well 291 *but he would* if he did not 295 *true* law-abiding; *that* what 299 *taken . . . manner* caught with the goods 300 *fire* i.e. red nose and cheeks 303 *meteors* i.e. the red blotches on his face 307 *Hot livers* the effect of drinking 308 *Choler* a choleric (aggressive) disposition; *rightly taken* rightly understood 309 *rightly taken* well captured; *halter* i.e. collar 311 *bombast* cotton padding 314 *talent* talon 316 *blows . . . up* (actually it was supposed to make him waste away) 320 *Amamon* a devil; *bastinado* beating on the soles of the feet 321 *made . . . cuckold* i.e. gave him his horns

liegeman upon the cross of a Welsh hook – what a plague call you him?

POINS Owen Glendower.

FALSTAFF Owen, Owen – the same; and his son-in-law Mortimer, and old Northumberland, and that sprightly Scot of Scots, Douglas, that runs a-horseback up a hill perpendicular –

PRINCE He that rides at high speed and with his pistol kills a sparrow flying.

FALSTAFF You have hit it.

PRINCE So did he never the sparrow.

332 FALSTAFF Well, that rascal hath good metal in him; he
333 will not run.

PRINCE Why, what a rascal art thou then, to praise him so for running!

FALSTAFF A-horseback, ye cuckoo! but afoot he will not budge a foot.

PRINCE Yes, Jack, upon instinct.

FALSTAFF I grant ye, upon instinct. Well, he is there too,
340 and one Mordake, and a thousand bluecaps more. Worcester is stol'n away to-night; thy father's beard is turned white with the news; you may buy land now as cheap as stinking mack'rel.

PRINCE Why then, it is like, if there come a hot June, and this civil buffeting hold, we shall buy maidenheads as they buy hobnails, by the hundreds.

FALSTAFF By the mass, lad, thou sayest true; it is like we shall have good trading that way. But tell me, Hal, art not thou horrible afeard? Thou being heir apparent, could the world pick thee out three such enemies again
351 as that fiend Douglas, that spirit Percy, and that devil Glendower? Art thou not horribly afraid? Doth not thy
353 blood thrill at it?

PRINCE Not a whit, i' faith. I lack some of thy instinct.

FALSTAFF Well, thou wilt be horribly chid to-morrow when thou comest to thy father. If thou love me, practise an answer.

PRINCE Do thou stand for my father and examine me upon the particulars of my life.

360 FALSTAFF Shall I? Content. This chair shall be my state, this dagger my sceptre, and this cushion my crown.

362 PRINCE Thy state is taken for a joined-stool, thy golden sceptre for a leaden dagger, and thy precious rich crown for a pitiful bald crown.

FALSTAFF Well, an the fire of grace be not quite out of thee, now shalt thou be moved. Give me a cup of sack to make my eyes look red, that it may be thought I have wept; for I must speak in passion, and I will do it in
369 King Cambyses' vein.

370 PRINCE Well, here is my leg.

FALSTAFF And here is my speech. Stand aside, nobility.

HOSTESS O Jesu, this is excellent sport, i' faith!

FALSTAFF

Weep not, sweet queen, for trickling tears are vain.

HOSTESS O, the Father, how he holds his countenance! 374

FALSTAFF

For God's sake, lords, convey my tristful queen! 375
For tears do stop the floodgates of her eyes.

HOSTESS O Jesu, he doth it as like one of these harlotry 377 players as ever I see!

FALSTAFF Peace, good pintpot. Peace, good ticklebrain. – Harry, I do not only marvel where thou spendest thy time, but also how thou art accompanied. For though the camomile, the more it is trodden on, the faster it grows, yet youth, the more it is wasted, the sooner it wears. That thou art my son I have partly thy mother's word, partly my own opinion, but chiefly a villainous trick of thine eye and a foolish hanging of thy 386 nether lip that doth warrant me. If then thou be son to 387 me, here lies the point: why, being son to me, art thou so pointed at? Shall the blessed sun of heaven prove a micher and eat blackberries? A question not to be 390 asked. Shall the son of England prove a thief and take purses? A question to be asked. There is a thing, Harry, which thou hast often heard of, and it is known to many in our land by the name of pitch. This pitch, as ancient 394 writers do report, doth defile; so doth the company thou keepest. For, Harry, now I do not speak to thee in drink, but in tears; not in pleasure, but in passion; not in words only, but in woes also: and yet there is a virtuous man whom I have often noted in thy company, but I know not his name.

PRINCE What manner of man, an it like your majesty?

FALSTAFF A goodly portly man, i' faith, and a corpulent; 401 of a cheerful look, a pleasing eye, and a most noble carriage; and, as I think, his age some fifty, or, by'r Lady, inclining to threescore; and now I remember me, his name is Falstaff. If that man should be lewdly given, 405 he deceiveth me; for, Harry, I see virtue in his looks. If then the tree may be known by the fruit, as the fruit by 407 the tree, then, peremptorily I speak it, there is virtue in 408 that Falstaff. Him keep with, the rest banish. And tell me now, thou naughty varlet, tell me where hast thou 410 been this month?

PRINCE Dost thou speak like a king? Do thou stand for me, and I'll play my father.

FALSTAFF Depose me? If thou dost it half so gravely, so majestically, both in word and matter, hang me up by the heels for a rabbit-sucker or a poulter's hare. 415

PRINCE Well, here I am set.

FALSTAFF And here I stand. Judge, my masters.

PRINCE Now, Harry, whence come you?

FALSTAFF My noble lord, from Eastcheap.

PRINCE The complaints I hear of thee are grievous.

FALSTAFF 'Sblood, my lord, they are false! Nay, I'll tickle ye for a young prince, i' faith. 422

PRINCE Swearest thou, ungracious boy? Henceforth 423 ne'er look on me. Thou art violently carried away from grace. There is a devil haunts thee in the likeness of an old fat man; a tun of man is thy companion. Why dost thou converse with that trunk of humors, that bolting 427 hutch of beastliness, that swoll'n parcel of dropsies, that huge bombard of sack, that stuffed cloakbag of guts, 429 that roasted Manningtree ox with the pudding in his 430

---

332 *metal* material   333 *run* (1) run away, (2) melt   340 *bluecaps* Scots
351 *spirit* evil spirit   353 *thrill* run cold   360 *state* chair of state   362 *taken for* understood to be   369 *King Cambyses' vein* that of an early ranting tragedy   370 *leg* bow   374 *holds his countenance* keeps a straight face   375 *convey* escort hence; *tristful* sorrowful   377 *harlotry* scurvy   386 *trick* peculiarity   387 *warrant* assure   390 *micher* truant   394-95 *ancient writers* i.e. Ecclesiasticus xiii, 1   401 *goodly* handsome; *portly* dignified   405 *lewdly* wickedly   407 *tree* . . . *by the fruit* cf. Matthew xii, 33   408 *peremptorily* positively   410 *varlet* rascal   415 *rabbit-sucker* very young rabbit   422 *tickle* . . . *prince* divert you in the role of a young prince   423 *ungracious* graceless   427 *converse* associate; *humors* fluids of the body 427-28 *bolting hutch* large flour bin   429 *bombard* leather vessel   430 *Manningtree ox* famous for size; *pudding* stuffing

431 belly, that reverend vice, that grey iniquity, that father
432 ruffian, that vanity in years? Wherein is he good, but to
433 taste sack and drink it? wherein neat and cleanly, but to
434 carve a capon and eat it? wherein cunning, but in craft?
wherein crafty, but in villainy? wherein villainous, but
in all things? wherein worthy, but in nothing?
437 FALSTAFF I would your grace would take me with you.
Whom means your grace?
PRINCE That villainous abominable misleader of youth,
Falstaff, that old white-bearded Satan.
FALSTAFF My lord, the man I know.
PRINCE I know thou dost.
FALSTAFF But to say I know more harm in him than in
myself were to say more than I know. That he is old (the
more the pity), his white hairs do witness it; but that he
446 is (saving your reverence) a whoremaster, that I utterly
deny. If sack and sugar be a fault, God help the wicked!
If to be old and merry be a sin, then many an old host
that I know is damned. If to be fat be to be hated, then
450 Pharaoh's lean kine are to be loved. No, my good lord:
banish Peto, banish Bardolph, banish Poins; but for
sweet Jack Falstaff, kind Jack Falstaff, true Jack Falstaff,
valiant Jack Falstaff, and therefore more valiant being,
as he is, old Jack Falstaff, banish not him thy Harry's
company, banish not him thy Harry's company. Banish
plump Jack, and banish all the world!
PRINCE I do, I will.
    [A knocking heard.]
    [Exeunt Hostess, Francis, and Bardolph.]
    Enter Bardolph, running.
BARDOLPH O, my lord, my lord! the sheriff with a most
459 monstrous watch is at the door.
FALSTAFF Out, ye rogue! Play out the play. I have much
to say in the behalf of that Falstaff.
    Enter the Hostess.
HOSTESS O Jesu, my lord, my lord!
463 PRINCE Heigh, heigh, the devil rides upon a fiddlestick!
What's the matter?
HOSTESS The sheriff and all the watch are at the door.
They are come to search the house. Shall I let them in?
467 FALSTAFF Dost thou hear, Hal? Never call a true piece of
gold a counterfeit. Thou art essentially mad without
seeming so.
PRINCE And thou a natural coward without instinct.
471 FALSTAFF I deny your major. If you will deny the sheriff,
472 so; if not, let him enter. If I become not a cart as well as
another man, a plague on my bringing up! I hope I shall
474 as soon be strangled with a halter as another.
475 PRINCE Go hide thee behind the arras. The rest walk up
476 above. Now, my masters, for a true face and good conscience.
478 FALSTAFF Both which I have had; but their date is out,
and therefore I'll hide me.   *Exit.*
PRINCE Call in the sheriff.
    [Exeunt. Manent the Prince and Peto.]
    Enter Sheriff and the Carrier.
Now, master sheriff, what is your will with me?
SHERIFF
First, pardon me, my lord. A hue and cry
Hath followed certain men unto this house.
PRINCE
What men?
SHERIFF
One of them is well known, my gracious lord –

A gross fat man.
CARRIER   As fat as butter.
PRINCE
The man, I do assure you, is not here,
For I myself at this time have employed him.
And, sheriff, I will engage my word to thee   489
That I will by to-morrow dinner time
Send him to answer thee, or any man,
For anything he shall be charged withal;
And so let me entreat you leave the house.
SHERIFF
I will, my lord. There are two gentlemen
Have in this robbery lost three hundred marks.
PRINCE
It may be so. If he have robbed these men,
He shall be answerable; and so farewell.
SHERIFF
Good night, my noble lord.
PRINCE
I think it is good morrow, is it not?   499
SHERIFF
Indeed, my lord, I think it be two o'clock.
    Exit [with Carrier].
PRINCE This oily rascal is known as well as Paul's. Go 501
call him forth.
PETO Falstaff! Fast asleep behind the arras, and snorting
like a horse.
PRINCE Hark how hard he fetches breath. Search his
pockets.
    He searcheth his pockets and findeth certain papers.
What hast thou found?
PETO Nothing but papers, my lord.
PRINCE Let's see what they be. Read them.
PETO *[reads]* 'Item, A capon   .   .   .   ii s. ii d.
    Item, Sauce .   .   .   .   iiii d.
    Item, Sack two gallons   .   .   v s. viii d.
    Item, Anchovies and sack after
        supper   .   .   .   ii s. vi d.
    Item, Bread   .   .   .   ob.' 513
PRINCE O monstrous! but one halfpennyworth of bread 514
to this intolerable deal of sack! What there is else, keep
close; we'll read it at more advantage. There let him 516
sleep till day. I'll to the court in the morning. We must
all to the wars, and thy place shall be honorable. I'll
procure this fat rogue a charge of foot, and I know his 519
death will be a march of twelve score. The money shall be 520
paid back again with advantage. Be with me betimes in 521
the morning, and so good morrow, Peto.
PETO Good morrow, good my lord.   *Exeunt.*

*

431 *vice* chief comic character and mischief-maker of the moral plays   432 *vanity* (incarnation of) worldliness   433 *cleanly* deft   434 *cunning* skillful   437 *take . . . you* make yourself clear   446 *saving your reverence* excuse my speaking plainly   450 *kine* cf. Genesis xli, 18–21   459 *watch* posse of watchmen (constables)   463 *the devil . . . fiddlestick* much ado about nothing   467–69 *Never . . . so* (perhaps) you are crazy to banish such a sterling fellow as plump Jack   471 *major* (1) major premise, (2) mayor   472 *cart* (in which criminals were carried to execution)   474 *soon* quickly   475 *arras* tapestry which screened the walls   476 *true* honest   478 *date is out* term has expired   489 *engage* pledge   499 *morrow* morning   501 *Paul's* St Paul's Cathedral, the center of London life   513 *ob.* obolus, halfpenny   514 *monstrous* astounding   516 *close* to yourself; *advantage* favorable opportunity   519 *a charge of foot* command of a company of infantry   520 *twelve score* i.e. yards   521 *advantage* interest

Enter Hotspur, Worcester, Lord Mortimer, Owen
Glendower.

MORTIMER
These promises are fair, the parties sure,
2   And our induction full of prosperous hope.
HOTSPUR Lord Mortimer, and cousin Glendower, will
you sit down? And uncle Worcester. A plague upon it! I
have forgot the map.
GLENDOWER
No, here it is. Sit, cousin Percy;
Sit, good cousin Hotspur, for by that name
8   As oft as Lancaster doth speak of you,
His cheek looks pale, and with a rising sigh
He wisheth you in heaven.
HOTSPUR And you in hell, as oft as he hears Owen
Glendower spoke of.
GLENDOWER
I cannot blame him. At my nativity
14 The front of heaven was full of fiery shapes
15 Of burning cressets, and at my birth
The frame and huge foundation of the earth
Shaked like a coward.
HOTSPUR Why, so it would have done at the same season
if your mother's cat had but kittened, though yourself
had never been born.
GLENDOWER
I say the earth did shake when I was born.
HOTSPUR
And I say the earth was not of my mind,
If you suppose as fearing you it shook.
GLENDOWER
The heavens were all on fire, the earth did tremble.
HOTSPUR
O, then the earth shook to see the heavens on fire,
And not in fear of your nativity.
Diseasèd nature oftentimes breaks forth
In strange eruptions; oft the teeming earth
Is with a kind of colic pinched and vexed
By the imprisoning of unruly wind
31 Within her womb, which, for enlargement striving,
32 Shakes the old beldame earth and topples down
Steeples and mossgrown towers. At your birth
34 Our grandam earth, having this distemp'rature,
35 In passion shook.
GLENDOWER   Cousin, of many men
36 I do not bear these crossings. Give me leave
To tell you once again that at my birth
The front of heaven was full of fiery shapes,
The goats ran from the mountains, and the herds
Were strangely clamorous to the frighted fields.
These signs have marked me extraordinary,
And all the courses of my life do show

III, i Within Glendower's castle in Wales (Holinshed names as the meeting-place the Archdeacon's house at Bangor, but in the play Glendower is acting as host) **2** *induction* first step; *prosperous hope* hope of prospering **8** *Lancaster* i.e. the king **14** *front* forehead **15** *cressets* lights burning in baskets mounted on poles **31** *enlargement* release **32** *beldame* grand-mother **34** *distemp'rature* ailment **35** *passion* pain **36** *crossings* con-tradictions **44** *clipped in with* enclosed by **45** *chides* lashes **46** *read to* instructed **48** *trace* follow; *tedious* laborious; *art* i.e. magic **49** *hold me pace* keep pace with me; *deep* occult **50** *Welsh* i.e. bragging **53** *vasty deep* abyss of the lower world **64** *made head* raised troops **67** *Booteless* without advantage **69** *agues* malaria **70** *right* rightful possessions **71** *order* arrangement **73** *limits* territories **74** *hitherto* to this spot **79** *lying off* starting **80** *tripartite* i.e. in triplicate; *drawn* drawn up **87** *father* i.e. father-in-law **89** *may* will be able to

I am not in the roll of common men.
Where is he living, clipped in with the sea   44
That chides the banks of England, Scotland, Wales,   45
Which calls me pupil or hath read to me?   46
And bring him out that is but woman's son
Can trace me in the tedious ways of art   48
And hold me pace in deep experiments.   49
HOTSPUR I think there's no man speaks better Welsh.   50
I'll to dinner.
MORTIMER
Peace, cousin Percy; you will make him mad.
GLENDOWER
I can call spirits from the vasty deep.   53
HOTSPUR
Why, so can I, or so can any man;
But will they come when you do call for them?
GLENDOWER Why, I can teach you, cousin, to command
the devil.
HOTSPUR
And I can teach thee, coz, to shame the devil –
By telling truth. Tell truth and shame the devil.
If thou have power to raise him, bring him hither,
And I'll be sworn I have power to shame him hence.
O, while you live, tell truth and shame the devil!
MORTIMER
Come, come, no more of this unprofitable chat.
GLENDOWER
Three times hath Henry Bolingbroke made head   64
Against my power; thrice from the banks of Wye
And sandy-bottomed Severn have I sent him
Bootless home and weather-beaten back.   67
HOTSPUR
Home without boots, and in foul weather too?
How scapes he agues, in the devil's name?   69
GLENDOWER
Come, here is the map. Shall we divide our right   70
According to our threefold order ta'en?   71
MORTIMER
The archdeacon hath divided it
Into three limits very equally.   73
England, from Trent and Severn hitherto,   74
By south and east is to my part assigned;
All westward, Wales beyond the Severn shore,
And all the fertile land within that bound,
To Owen Glendower; and, dear coz, to you
The remnant northward lying off from Trent.   79
And our indentures tripartite are drawn,   80
Which being sealèd interchangeably
(A business that this night may execute),
To-morrow, cousin Percy, you and I
And my good Lord of Worcester will set forth
To meet your father and the Scottish power,
As is appointed us, at Shrewsbury.
My father Glendower is not ready yet,   87
Nor shall we need his help these fourteen days.
     [To Glendower]
Within that space you may have drawn together   89
Your tenants, friends, and neighboring gentlemen.
GLENDOWER
A shorter time shall send me to you, lords;
And in my conduct shall your ladies come,
From whom you now must steal and take no leave,
For there will be a world of water shed
Upon the parting of your wives and you.

HOTSPUR

96   Methinks my moiety, north from Burton here,
In quantity equals not one of yours.
98   See how this river comes me cranking in
And cuts me from the best of all my land
100   A huge half-moon, a monstrous cantle out.
I'll have the current in this place dammed up,
102   And here the smug and silver Trent shall run
103   In a new channel fair and evenly.
It shall not wind with such a deep indent
105   To rob me of so rich a bottom here.

GLENDOWER

Not wind? It shall, it must! You see it doth.

MORTIMER

Yea, but
Mark how he bears his course, and runs me up
With like advantage on the other side,
110   Gelding the opposèd continent as much
As on the other side it takes from you.

WORCESTER

112   Yea, but a little charge will trench him here
And on this north side win this cape of land;
And then he runs straight and even.

HOTSPUR

I'll have it so. A little charge will do it.

GLENDOWER

I will not have it alt'red.

HOTSPUR   Will not you?

GLENDOWER

No, nor you shall not.

HOTSPUR   Who shall say me nay?

GLENDOWER

Why, that will I.

HOTSPUR

Let me not understand you then; speak it in Welsh.

GLENDOWER

I can speak English, lord, as well as you;
For I was trained up in the English court,
Where, being but young, I framèd to the harp
Many an English ditty lovely well,
124   And gave the tongue a helpful ornament –
125   A virtue that was never seen in you.

HOTSPUR

Marry, and I am glad of it with all my heart!
I had rather be a kitten and cry mew
128   Than one of these same metre ballet-mongers.
129   I had rather hear a brazen canstick turned
Or a dry wheel grate on the axletree,
And that would set my teeth nothing on edge,
Nothing so much as mincing poetry.
133   'Tis like the forced gait of a shuffling nag.

GLENDOWER

Come, you shall have Trent turned.

HOTSPUR

I do not care. I'll give thrice so much land
To any well-deserving friend;
But in the way of bargain, mark ye me,
I'll cavil on the ninth part of a hair.
Are the indentures drawn? Shall we be gone?

GLENDOWER

The moon shines fair; you may away by night.
I'll haste the writer, and withal
142   Break with your wives of your departure hence.
I am afraid my daughter will run mad,

So much she doteth on her Mortimer.   *Exit.*

MORTIMER

Fie, cousin Percy! how you cross my father!

HOTSPUR

I cannot choose. Sometimes he angers me
With telling me of the moldwarp and the ant,   147
Of the dreamer Merlin and his prophecies,
And of a dragon and a finless fish,
A clip-winged griffin and a moulten raven,   150
A couching lion and a ramping cat,   151
And such a deal of skimble-skamble stuff   152
As puts me from my faith. I tell you what –   153
He held me last night at least nine hours
In reckoning up the several devils' names   155
That were his lackeys. I cried 'hum,' and 'well, go to!'   156
But marked him not a word. O, he is as tedious
As a tired horse, a railing wife;
Worse than a smoky house. I had rather live
With cheese and garlic in a windmill far
Than feed on cates and have him talk to me   161
In any summer house in Christendom.

MORTIMER

In faith, he is a worthy gentleman,
Exceedingly well read, and profited   164
In strange concealments, valiant as a lion,   165
And wondrous affable, and as bountiful
As mines of India. Shall I tell you, cousin?
He holds your temper in a high respect
And curbs himself even of his natural scope   169
When you come 'cross his humor. Faith, he does.
I warrant you that man is not alive
Might so have tempted him as you have done   172
Without the taste of danger and reproof.
But do not use it oft, let me entreat you.   174

WORCESTER

In faith, my lord, you are too willful-blame,   175
And since your coming hither have done enough
To put him quite besides his patience.   177
You must needs learn, lord, to amend this fault.
Though sometimes it show greatness, courage, blood –   179
And that's the dearest grace it renders you –   180
Yet oftentimes it doth present harsh rage,   181
Defect of manners, want of government,
Pride, haughtiness, opinion, and disdain;   183
The least of which haunting a nobleman
Loseth men's hearts, and leaves behind a stain
Upon the beauty of all parts besides,   186
Beguiling them of commendation.   187

HOTSPUR

Well, I am schooled. Good manners be your speed!   188
Here come our wives, and let us take our leave.

---

96 *moiety* share   98 *cranking* winding   100 *cantle* hunk   102 *smug* smooth
103 *fair* gently   105 *bottom* valley   110 *continent* land which it bounds
112 *charge* expenditure; *trench* dig a new channel   124 *tongue* i.e. words;
ornament i.e. music   125 *virtue* accomplishment   128 *ballet-mongers* ballad-
makers   129 *canstick* candlestick   133 *shuffling* hobbled   142 *Break with*
inform   147 *moldwarp* mole   150 *griffin* half lion, half eagle   151 *couching* crouching; *ramping* rearing on hind legs   152 *skimble-skamble* non-
sensical   153 *puts* forces   155 *several* different   156 *go to* 'you don't
say'   161 *cates* delicacies   164 *profited* proficient   165 *concealments*
secrets   169 *scope* freedom of speech   172 *tempted* provoked   174 *use* do
175 *willful-blame* willfully blamable   177 *besides* out of   179 *blood* spirit
180 *dearest grace* best credit   181 *present* represent   183 *opinion* arrogance
186 *parts* abilities   187 *Beguiling* robbing   188 *be your speed* give you good
fortune

Enter Glendower with the Ladies.

MORTIMER

190 This is the deadly spite that angers me –
    My wife can speak no English, I no Welsh.

GLENDOWER

    My daughter weeps; she will not part with you;
    She'll be a soldier too, she'll to the wars.

MORTIMER

194 Good father, tell her that she and my aunt Percy
    Shall follow in your conduct speedily.
    Glendower speaks to her in Welsh, and she answers
    him in the same.

GLENDOWER

196 She is desperate here. A peevish self-willed harlotry,
    One that no persuasion can do good upon.
    The Lady speaks in Welsh.

MORTIMER

    I understand thy looks. That pretty Welsh
199 Which thou pourest down from these swelling heavens
200 I am too perfect in; and, but for shame,
201 In such a parley should I answer thee.
    The Lady again in Welsh.
    I understand thy kisses, and thou mine,
203 And that's a feeling disputation.
    But I will never be a truant, love,
    Till I have learnt thy language; for thy tongue
206 Makes Welsh as sweet as ditties highly penned,
    Sung by a fair queen in a summer's bow'r,
208 With ravishing division, to her lute.

GLENDOWER

    Nay, if you melt, then will she run mad.
    The Lady speaks again in Welsh.

MORTIMER

    O, I am ignorance itself in this!

GLENDOWER

211 She bids you on the wanton rushes lay you down
    And rest your gentle head upon her lap,
    And she will sing the song that pleaseth you
    And on your eyelids crown the god of sleep,
215 Charming your blood with pleasing heaviness,
    Making such difference 'twixt wake and sleep
    As is the difference betwixt day and night
    The hour before the heavenly-harnessed team
    Begins his golden progress in the east.

MORTIMER

    With all my heart I'll sit and hear her sing.
221 By that time will our book, I think, be drawn.

GLENDOWER

    Do so, and those musicians that shall play to you
    Hang in the air a thousand leagues from hence,
    And straight they shall be here. Sit, and attend.

HOTSPUR Come, Kate, thou art perfect in lying down. 225
    Come, quick, quick, that I may lay my head in thy lap.

LADY PERCY Go, ye giddy goose.
    The music plays.

HOTSPUR

    Now I perceive the devil understands Welsh.
    And 'tis no marvel he is so humorous, 229
    By'r Lady, he is a good musician.

LADY PERCY Then should you be nothing but musical,
    for you are altogether governed by humors. Lie still, ye 232
    thief, and hear the lady sing in Welsh.

HOTSPUR I had rather hear Lady, my brach, howl in 234
    Irish.

LADY PERCY Wouldst thou have thy head broken?

HOTSPUR No.

LADY PERCY Then be still.

HOTSPUR Neither! 'Tis a woman's fault.

LADY PERCY Now God help thee!

HOTSPUR To the Welsh lady's bed.

LADY PERCY What's that?

HOTSPUR Peace! she sings.
    Here the Lady sings a Welsh song.
    Come, Kate, I'll have your song too.

LADY PERCY Not mine, in good sooth. 244

HOTSPUR Not yours, in good sooth? Heart! you swear
    like a comfit-maker's wife. 'Not you, in good sooth!' and 246
    'as true as I live!' and 'as God shall mend me!' and 'as
    sure as day!'
    And givest such sarcenet surety for thy oaths 249
    As if thou never walk'st further than Finsbury. 250
    Swear me, Kate, like a lady as thou art, 251
    A good mouth-filling oath, and leave 'in sooth'
    And such protest of pepper gingerbread 253
    To velvet guards and Sunday citizens. 254
    Come, sing.

LADY PERCY I will not sing.

HOTSPUR 'Tis the next way to turn tailor or be red- 257
    breast-teacher. An the indentures be drawn, I'll away
    within these two hours; and so come in when ye will.
                                         Exit.

GLENDOWER

    Come, come, Lord Mortimer. You are as slow
    As hot Lord Percy is on fire to go.
    By this our book is drawn; we'll but seal,
    And then to horse immediately.

MORTIMER   With all my heart. *Exeunt.*

*

Enter the King, Prince of Wales, and others.   III, ii

KING

    Lords, give us leave: the Prince of Wales and I
    Must have some private conference; but be near at
    hand,
    For we shall presently have need of you. *Exeunt Lords.*
    I know not whether God will have it so
    For some displeasing service I have done,
    That, in his secret doom, out of my blood 6
    He'll breed revengement and a scourge for me;
    But thou dost in thy passages of life 8
    Make me believe that thou art only marked 9
    For the hot vengeance and the rod of heaven
    To punish my mistreadings. Tell me else,

---

190 *spite* vexation   194 *aunt* (to Edmund Mortimer, Earl of March, but sister-in-law to Glendower's son-in-law)   196 *here* on this point; *peevish* childish; *harlotry* silly wench   199 *heavens* i.e. eyes   200 *perfect* proficient 201 *such a parley* the same language   203 *disputation* conversation   206 *highly* nobly   208 *division* melody   211 *wanton* luxurious   215 *blood* mood   221 *book* the indenture   225 *perfect* well-trained   229 *humorous* emotional   232 *humors* whims   234 *brach* bitch-hound   244 *sooth* truth 246 *comfit-maker's* confectioner's   249 *sarcenet surety* flimsy confirmation 250 *Finsbury* field near London frequented by citizens on Sundays   251 *me* (ethical dative)   253 *protest . . . gingerbread* mealy-mouthed swearing 254 *velvet guards* (middle-class women dressed up in clothes with) velvet trimmings   257 *next* easiest; *tailor* proverbially a singer   257–58 *be redbreast-teacher* teach birds to sing
III, ii Within the palace of King Henry IV   6 *doom* judgment   8 *thy . . . life* the actions of your life   9–10 *marked For* destined to be

12 Could such inordinate and low desires,
13 Such poor, such bare, such lewd, such mean attempts,
Such barren pleasures, rude society,
As thou art matched withal and grafted to,
Accompany the greatness of thy blood
17 And hold their level with thy princely heart?

PRINCE
So please your majesty, I would I could
19 Quit all offenses with as clear excuse
20 As well as I am doubtless I can purge
Myself of many I am charged withal.
22 Yet such extenuation let me beg
23 As, in reproof of many tales devised,
Which oft the ear of greatness needs must hear
25 By smiling pickthanks and base newsmongers,
I may, for some things true wherein my youth
Hath faulty wand'red and irregular,
28 Find pardon on my true submission.

KING
God pardon thee! Yet let me wonder, Harry,
30 At thy affections, which do hold a wing
31 Quite from the flight of all thy ancestors.
32 Thy place in council thou hast rudely lost,
Which by thy younger brother is supplied,
And art almost an alien to the hearts
Of all the court and princes of my blood.
36 The hope and expectation of thy time
Is ruined, and the soul of every man
Prophetically do forethink thy fall.
Had I so lavish of my presence been,
40 So common-hackneyed in the eyes of men,
So stale and cheap to vulgar company,
42 Opinion, that did help me to the crown,
43 Had still kept loyal to possession
And left me in reputeless banishment,
A fellow of no mark nor likelihood.
By being seldom seen, I could not stir
But, like a comet, I was wond'red at;
That men would tell their children, 'This is he!'
Others would say, 'Where? Which is Bolingbroke?'
50 And then I stole all courtesy from heaven,
And dressed myself in such humility
That I did pluck allegiance from men's hearts,
Loud shouts and salutations from their mouths
Even in the presence of the crownèd king.
Thus did I keep my person fresh and new,
My presence, like a robe pontifical,
57 Ne'er seen but wond'red at; and so my state,
Seldom but sumptuous, showed like a feast
59 And wan by rareness such solemnity.
60 The skipping king, he ambled up and down
61 With shallow jesters and rash bavin wits,
62 Soon kindled and soon burnt; carded his state;
Mingled his royalty with cap'ring fools;
64 Had his great name profanèd with their scorns
65 And gave his countenance, against his name,
66 To laugh at gibing boys and stand the push
67 Of every beardless vain comparative;
Grew a companion to the common streets,
69 Enfeoffed himself to popularity;
That, being daily swallowed by men's eyes,
They surfeited with honey and began
To loathe the taste of sweetness, whereof a little
More than a little is by much too much.

So, when he had occasion to be seen,
He was but as the cuckoo is in June,
Heard, not regarded – seen, but with such eyes
As, sick and blunted with community, 77
Afford no extraordinary gaze,
Such as is bent on sunlike majesty
When it shines seldom in admiring eyes;
But rather drowsed and hung their eyelids down,
Slept in his face, and rend'red such aspect 82
As cloudy men use to their adversaries, 83
Being with his presence glutted, gorged, and full.
And in that very line, Harry, standest thou; 85
For thou hast lost thy princely privilege
With vile participation. Not an eye 87
But is aweary of thy common sight,
Save mine, which hath desired to see thee more;
Which now doth that I would not have it do –
Make blind itself with foolish tenderness.

PRINCE
I shall hereafter, my thrice-gracious lord,
Be more myself.

KING   For all the world,
As thou art to this hour was Richard then
When I from France set foot at Ravenspurgh;
And even as I was then is Percy now.
Now, by my sceptre, and my soul to boot,
He hath more worthy interest to the state 98
Than thou, the shadow of succession; 99
For of no right, nor color like to right, 100
He doth fill fields with harness in the realm, 101
Turns head against the lion's armèd jaws, 102
And, being no more in debt to years than thou,
Leads ancient lords and reverend bishops on
To bloody battles and to bruising arms.
What never-dying honor hath he got
Against renownèd Douglas! whose high deeds,
Whose hot incursions and great name in arms
Holds from all soldiers chief majority 109
And military title capital 110
Through all the kingdoms that acknowledge Christ.
Thrice hath this Hotspur, Mars in swathling clothes,
This infant warrior, in his enterprises
Discomfited great Douglas; ta'en him once,
Enlargèd him, and made a friend of him, 115
To fill the mouth of deep defiance up 116
And shake the peace and safety of our throne.

12 *inordinate* beneath your position   13 *lewd* low; *attempts* undertakings
17 *hold . . . with* be on an equality with   19 *Quit* acquit myself of   20 *am
doubtless* have no doubt; *purge* acquit   22 *extenuation* mitigation   23 *in
reproof* upon disproof   25 *pickthanks* flatterers; *newsmongers* talebearers
28 *submission* admission of fault   30 *affections* inclinations; *hold a wing*
take a course   31 *from* contrary to   32 *rudely* by violence   36 *time* i.e.
youth   40 *common-hackneyed* vulgarized   42 *Opinion* i.e. public opinion
43 *Had* would have; *possession* i.e. the possessor   50 *courtesy* humility
57 *state* i.e. appearances in state   59 *wan* won; *such solemnity* i.e. that of a
festival   60 *skipping* flighty   61 *rash* quick to burn; *bavin* (literally)
brushwood   62 *carded* mixed with baseness   64 *their scorns* the scorn
felt for them   65 *name* reputation   66 *stand the push* serve as the butt
67 *comparative* wise-cracker   69 *Enfeoffed* surrendered; *popularity* the
populace   77 *community* commonness   82 *Slept in* disregarded; *aspect*
look   83 *cloudy* sullen   85 *line* station   87 *vile participation* association
with the mean   98 *interest* title   99 *the shadow of succession* a successor
with a poor claim   100 *color* pretext   101 *harness* (men in) armor   102
Turns head marches with an army; *lion's* i.e. king's   109 *majority* pre-
eminence   110 *capital* principal   115 *Enlargèd* set free   116 *fill . . . up*
make defiance roar all the more loudly

And what say you to this? Percy, Northumberland,
The Archbishop's grace of York, Douglas, Mortimer
120 Capitulate against us and are up.
But wherefore do I tell these news to thee?
Why, Harry, do I tell thee of my foes,
Which art my nearest and dearest enemy?
124 Thou that art like enough, through vassal fear,
125 Base inclination, and the start of spleen,
To fight against me under Percy's pay,
To dog his heels and curtsy at his frowns,
To show how much thou art degenerate.

PRINCE
Do not think so. You shall not find it so.
And God forgive them that so much have swayed
Your majesty's good thoughts away from me.
132 I will redeem all this on Percy's head
And, in the closing of some glorious day,
Be bold to tell you that I am your son,
When I will wear a garment all of blood,
136 And stain my favors in a bloody mask,
137 Which, washed away, shall scour my shame with it.
138 And that shall be the day, whene'er it lights,
That this same child of honor and renown,
This gallant Hotspur, this all-praisèd knight,
And your unthought-of Harry chance to meet.
For every honor sitting on his helm,
Would they were multitudes, and on my head
My shames redoubled! For the time will come
That I shall make this northern youth exchange
146 His glorious deeds for my indignities.
147 Percy is but my factor, good my lord,
148 To engross up glorious deeds on my behalf;
And I will call him to so strict account
That he shall render every glory up,
151 Yea, even the slightest worship of his time,
Or I will tear the reckoning from his heart.
This in the name of God I promise here;
The which if he be pleased I shall perform,
I do beseech your majesty may salve
156 The long-grown wounds of my intemperance.
157 If not, the end of life cancels all bands,
And I will die a hundred thousand deaths
Ere break the smallest parcel of this vow.

KING
A hundred thousand rebels die in this!

Thou shalt have charge and sovereign trust herein. 161
Enter Blunt.
How now, good Blunt? Thy looks are full of speed.
BLUNT
So hath the business that I come to speak of. 163
Lord Mortimer of Scotland hath sent word 164
That Douglas and the English rebels met
The eleventh of this month at Shrewsbury.
A mighty and a fearful head they are, 167
If promises be kept on every hand,
As ever off'red foul play in a state.
KING
The Earl of Westmoreland set forth to-day;
With him my son, Lord John of Lancaster;
For this advertisement is five days old. 172
On Wednesday next, Harry, you shall set forward;
On Thursday we ourselves will march. Our meeting 174
Is Bridgenorth; and, Harry, you shall march
Through Gloucestershire; by which account,
Our business valuèd, some twelve days hence 177
Our general forces at Bridgenorth shall meet.
Our hands are full of business. Let's away:
Advantage feeds him fat while men delay. *Exeunt.* 180

*

Enter Falstaff and Bardolph.   III, iii
FALSTAFF Bardolph, am I not fall'n away vilely since
this last action? Do I not bate? Do I not dwindle? Why, 2
my skin hangs about me like an old lady's loose gown! I
am withered like an old apple-john. Well, I'll repent, 4
and that suddenly, while I am in some liking. I shall be 5
out of heart shortly, and then I shall have no strength to 6
repent. An I have not forgotten what the inside of a
church is made of, I am a peppercorn, a brewer's horse. 8
The inside of a church! Company, villainous company,
hath been the spoil of me.
BARDOLPH Sir John, you are so fretful you cannot live
long.
FALSTAFF Why, there is it! Come, sing me a bawdy song;
make me merry. I was as virtuously given as a gentleman need to be, virtuous enough: swore little, diced not
above seven times a week, went to a bawdy house not
above once in a quarter of an hour, paid money that I
borrowed three or four times, lived well, and in good
compass; and now I live out of all order, out of all 17
compass.
BARDOLPH Why, you are so fat, Sir John, that you must
needs be out of all compass – out of all reasonable compass, Sir John.
FALSTAFF Do thou amend thy face, and I'll amend my 22
life. Thou art our admiral, thou bearest the lantern in 23
the poop – but 'tis in the nose of thee. Thou art the
Knight of the Burning Lamp. 25
BARDOLPH Why, Sir John, my face does you no harm.
FALSTAFF No, I'll be sworn. I make as good use of it as
many a man doth of a death's-head or a memento mori. 28
I never see thy face but I think upon hellfire and Dives 29
that lived in purple; for there he is in his robes, burning,
burning. If thou wert any way given to virtue, I would
swear by thy face; my oath should be 'By this fire, that's 32
God's angel.' But thou art altogether given over, and 33
wert indeed, but for the light in thy face, the son of utter
darkness. When thou ran'st up Gad's Hill in the night

120 *Capitulate* draw up articles of agreement; *up* in arms 124 *vassal* slavish 125 *Base inclination* inclination towards baseness; *start of spleen* perversity 132 *redeem* make up for 136 *favors* features 137 *shame* disgrace 138 *lights* dawns 146 *indignities* unworthy traits 147 *factor* agent 148 *engross up* buy up 151 *worship* honor; *time* lifetime 156 *intemperance* dissolute behavior 157 *bands* bonds 161 *charge* command 163 *hath* i.e. hath speed, is urgent 164 *Lord Mortimer of Scotland* a Scottish nobleman, no relative of Edmund Mortimer 167 *head* force 172 *advertisement* information 174 *meeting* meeting-place 177 *Our business valuèd* considering how long our business will take 180 *Advantage* opportunity; *fat* i.e. lazy

III, iii Within an Eastcheap tavern 2 *action* battle, i.e. the robbery; *bate* grow thin 4 *apple-john* an apple eaten when the skin has shrivelled 5 *suddenly* immediately; *liking* (1) inclination, (2) good fettle 6 *out of heart* depressed 8 *peppercorn* berry of pepper; *brewer's horse* i.e. lean and worn out 17 *compass* (1) limit, (2) girth 22 *face* (which is violently inflamed and pimpled) 23 *admiral* flagship; *lantern* (which the fleet follows) 25 *Knight . . . Lamp* i.e. if you were a knight the lamp would be your emblem 28 *death's-head* skull and crossbones (a pious reminder of mortality) 29 *Dives* the rich man of the parable in Luke xvi, 19–31 32–33 *By . . . angel* cf. 'Who [God] maketh his angels spirits, his ministers a flaming fire' (Psalms civ, 4) 33 *given over* abandoned as a reprobate

to catch my horse, if I did not think thou hadst been an

37 ignis fatuus or a ball of wildfire, there's no purchase in
38 money. O, thou art a perpetual triumph, an everlasting
bonfire-light! Thou hast saved me a thousand marks in
40 links and torches, walking with thee in the night betwixt
tavern and tavern; but the sack that thou hast drunk me
42 would have bought me lights as good cheap at the
dearest chandler's in Europe. I have maintained that
44 salamander of yours with fire any time this two-and-
thirty years. God reward me for it!

46 BARDOLPH 'Sblood, I would my face were in your belly!

FALSTAFF God-a-mercy! so should I be sure to be heart-
burnt.

Enter Hostess.

49 How now, Dame Partlet the hen? Have you enquired
yet who picked my pocket?

HOSTESS Why, Sir John, what do you think, Sir John?
Do you think I keep thieves in my house? I have
searched, I have enquired, so has my husband, man by
54 man, boy by boy, servant by servant. The tithe of a hair
was never lost in my house before.

FALSTAFF Ye lie, hostess. Bardolph was shaved and lost
many a hair, and I'll be sworn my pocket was picked.
58 Go to, you are a woman, go!

HOSTESS Who, I? No; I defy thee! God's light, I was
never called so in mine own house before!

FALSTAFF Go to, I know you well enough.

HOSTESS No, Sir John; you do not know me, Sir John. I
know you, Sir John. You owe me money, Sir John, and
now you pick a quarrel to beguile me of it. I bought you
a dozen of shirts to your back.

66 FALSTAFF Dowlas, filthy dowlas! I have given them away
67 to bakers' wives; they have made bolters of them.

68 HOSTESS Now, as I am a true woman, holland of eight
69 shillings an ell. You owe money here besides, Sir John,
for your diet and by-drinkings, and money lent you,
four-and-twenty pound.

FALSTAFF He had his part of it; let him pay.

HOSTESS He? Alas, he is poor; he hath nothing.

FALSTAFF How? Poor? Look upon his face. What call
you rich? Let them coin his nose, let them coin his
76 cheeks. I'll not pay a denier. What, will you make a
77 younker of me? Shall I not take mine ease in mine inn
but I shall have my pocket picked? I have lost a seal-
ring of my grandfather's worth forty mark.

HOSTESS O Jesu, I have heard the prince tell him, I know
not how oft, that that ring was copper!

82 FALSTAFF How? the prince is a Jack, a sneak-up.
'Sblood, an he were here, I would cudgel him like a dog
84 if he would say so.

*Enter the Prince [and Peto], marching, and Falstaff
meets them, playing upon his truncheon like a fife.*

85 How now, lad? Is the wind in that door, i' faith? Must
we all march?

87 BARDOLPH Yea, two and two, Newgate fashion.

HOSTESS My lord, I pray you hear me.

PRINCE What say'st thou, Mistress Quickly? How doth
thy husband? I love him well; he is an honest man.

HOSTESS Good my lord, hear me.

FALSTAFF Prithee let her alone and list to me.

PRINCE What say'st thou, Jack?

FALSTAFF The other night I fell asleep here behind the
arras and had my pocket picked. This house is turned
bawdy house; they pick pockets.

PRINCE What didst thou lose, Jack?

FALSTAFF Wilt thou believe me, Hal, three or four bonds
of forty pound apiece and a seal-ring of my grandfather's.

PRINCE A trifle, some eightpenny matter.   100

HOSTESS So I told him, my lord, and I said I heard your
grace say so; and, my lord, he speaks most vilely of you,
like a foulmouthed man as he is, and said he would
cudgel you.

PRINCE What! he did not?

HOSTESS There's neither faith, truth, nor womanhood
in me else.

FALSTAFF There's no more faith in thee than in a
stewed prune, nor no more truth in thee than in a drawn 108
fox; and for womanhood, Maid Marian may be the 109
deputy's wife of the ward to thee. Go, you thing, go!   110

HOSTESS Say, what thing? what thing?

FALSTAFF What thing? Why, a thing to thank God on.

HOSTESS I am no thing to thank God on, I would thou
shouldst know it! I am an honest man's wife, and,
setting thy knighthood aside, thou art a knave to call me
so.

FALSTAFF Setting thy womanhood aside, thou art a
beast to say otherwise.

HOSTESS Say, what beast, thou knave, thou?

FALSTAFF What beast? Why, an otter.

PRINCE An otter, Sir John? Why an otter?

FALSTAFF Why? She's neither fish nor flesh; a man
knows not where to have her.   122

HOSTESS Thou art an unjust man in saying so. Thou or
any man knows where to have me, thou knave, thou!

PRINCE Thou say'st true, hostess, and he slanders thee
most grossly.

HOSTESS So he doth you, my lord, and said this other
day you ought him a thousand pound.   128

PRINCE Sirrah, do I owe you a thousand pound?

FALSTAFF A thousand pound, Hal? A million! Thy love
is worth a million; thou owest me thy love.

HOSTESS Nay, my lord, he called you Jack and said he
would cudgel you.

FALSTAFF Did I, Bardolph?

BARDOLPH Indeed, Sir John, you said so.

FALSTAFF Yea, if he said my ring was copper.

PRINCE I say 'tis copper. Darest thou be as good as thy
word now?

FALSTAFF Why, Hal, thou knowest, as thou art but man,
I dare; but as thou art prince, I fear thee as I fear the 140
roaring of the lion's whelp.

PRINCE And why not as the lion?

FALSTAFF The king himself is to be feared as the lion.
Dost thou think I'll fear thee as I fear thy father? Nay,
an I do, I pray God my girdle break.

---

37 *ignis fatuus* will-o'-the-wisp; *wildfire* fireworks   38 *triumph* torchlight
parade   40 *links* torches   42 *as good cheap* as cheap   44 *salamander* lizard
reputed to live in fire   46 *in your belly* i.e. rather than on your tongue   49
Dame Partlet hen in animal stories   54 *tithe* tenth part   58 *Go to* go on
66 *Dowlas* coarse linen   67 *bolters* flour-sifters   68 *holland* fine linen   69
ell measure of forty-five inches   76 *denier* one-twelfth of a sou   77 *younker*
greenhorn, victim   82 *Jack* knave; *sneak-up* sneak   84 **s.d.** *truncheon*
officer's stick   85 *in that door* in that quarter   87 *Newgate fashion* chained
together (like inmates of Newgate prison)   108–09 *drawn fox* driven from
cover (therefore tricky)   109 *womanhood* womanly respectability   *Maid
Marian* (disreputable) woman in morris dances   110 *deputy's wife* i.e.
eminently respectable woman; *to* compared to   122 *where . . . her* what to
make of her   128 *ought* owed

PRINCE O, if it should, how would thy guts fall about thy
knees! But, sirrah, there's no room for faith, truth, nor
honesty in this bosom of thine. It is all filled up with
guts and midriff. Charge an honest woman with picking
150 thy pocket? Why, thou whoreson, impudent, embossed
151 rascal, if there were anything in thy pocket but tavern
reckonings, memorandums of bawdy houses, and one
poor pennyworth of sugar candy to make thee long-
winded – if thy pocket were enriched with any other
155 injuries but these, I am a villain. And yet you will
156 stand to it; you will not pocket up wrong. Art thou not
ashamed?

FALSTAFF Dost thou hear, Hal? Thou knowest in the
state of innocency Adam fell, and what should poor
Jack Falstaff do in the days of villainy? Thou seest I
have more flesh than another man, and therefore more
frailty. You confess then, you picked my pocket?

PRINCE It appears so by the story.

FALSTAFF Hostess, I forgive thee. Go make ready breakfast. Love thy husband, look to thy servants, cherish
thy guests. Thou shalt find me tractable to any honest
166 reason. Thou seest I am pacified still. Nay, prithee be
gone.   *Exit Hostess.*
Now, Hal, to the news at court. For the robbery, lad –
how is that answered?

PRINCE O my sweet beef, I must still be good angel to
thee. The money is paid back again.

FALSTAFF O, I do not like that paying back! 'Tis a
double labor.

PRINCE I am good friends with my father, and may do
anything.

FALSTAFF Rob me the exchequer the first thing thou
176 doest, and do it with unwashed hands too.

BARDOLPH Do, my lord.

178 PRINCE I have procured thee, Jack, a charge of foot.

FALSTAFF I would it had been of horse. Where shall I
find one that can steal well? O for a fine thief of the age
181 of two-and-twenty or thereabouts! I am heinously unprovided. Well, God be thanked for these rebels. They
offend none but the virtuous. I laud them, I praise them.

PRINCE Bardolph!

BARDOLPH My lord?

PRINCE
Go bear this letter to Lord John of Lancaster,
To my brother John; this to my Lord of Westmoreland.
                                        [Exit Bardolph.]
Go, Peto, to horse, to horse; for thou and I
Have thirty miles to ride yet ere dinner time.
                                        [Exit Peto.]
Jack, meet me to-morrow in the Temple Hall
At two o'clock in the afternoon.
There shalt thou know thy charge, and there receive

Money and order for their furniture.   193
The land is burning; Percy stands on high;
And either we or they must lower lie.   *[Exit.]*

FALSTAFF
Rare words! brave world! Hostess, my breakfast, come. 196
O, I could wish this tavern were my drum!   *Exit.* 197

*

[Enter Hotspur, Worcester, and Douglas.]   IV, i

HOTSPUR
Well said, my noble Scot. If speaking truth
In this fine age were not thought flattery,
Such attribution should the Douglas have   3
As not a soldier of this season's stamp
Should go so general current through the world.   5
By God, I cannot flatter, I do defy   6
The tongues of soothers! but a braver place   7
In my heart's love hath no man than yourself.
Nay, task me to my word; approve me, lord.   9

DOUGLAS
Thou art the king of honor.
No man so potent breathes upon the ground
But I will beard him.   12
        Enter one with letters.

HOTSPUR   Do so, and 'tis well. –
What letters hast thou there? – I can but thank you.

MESSENGER
These letters come from your father.

HOTSPUR
Letters from him? Why comes he not himself?

MESSENGER
He cannot come, my lord; he is grievous sick.

HOTSPUR
Zounds! how has he the leisure to be sick
In such a justling time? Who leads his power?   18
Under whose government come they along?

MESSENGER
His letters bears his mind, not I, my lord.

WORCESTER
I prithee tell me, doth he keep his bed?

MESSENGER
He did, my lord, four days ere I set forth,
And at the time of my departure thence
He was much feared by his physicians.   24

WORCESTER
I would the state of time had first been whole   25
Ere he by sickness had been visited.
His health was never better worth than now.

HOTSPUR
Sick now? droop now? This sickness doth infect
The very lifeblood of our enterprise.
'Tis catching hither, even to our camp.
He writes me here that inward sickness –
And that his friends by deputation could not   32
So soon be drawn; nor did he think it meet   33
To lay so dangerous and dear a trust
On any soul removed but on his own.   35
Yet doth he give us bold advertisement,   36
That with our small conjunction we should on,   37
To see how fortune is disposed to us;
For, as he writes, there is no quailing now,
Because the king is certainly possessed   40
Of all our purposes. What say you to it?

---

150 *embossed* swollen   151 *rascal* (literally) lean deer   155 *injuries* things
the loss of which would injure you   156 *stand to it* make a stand; *pocket up*
endure   166 *still* always   176 *with unwashed hands* i.e. without delay
178 *charge of foot* infantry command   181 *unprovided* unprepared   193
furniture equipment   196 *brave* splendid   197 *tavern* (1) inn, (2) drum
called 'tabor' or 'taborn'; *drum* (which leads soldiers into battle)
IV, i The rebel camp at Shrewsbury   3 *attribution* tribute   5 *go . . . current*
be so universally honored   6 *defy* despise   7 *soothers* flatterers; *braver*
better   9 *task* challenge; *approve* put to the test   12 *But* but that; *beard*
defy   18 *justling* turbulent   24 *feared* feared for   25 *time* the times   32
deputation deputies   33 *drawn* assembled   35 *removed* but i.e. other than
36 *advertisement* advice   37 *conjunction* united force; *on* go on   40 *possessed*
informed

WORCESTER
Your father's sickness is a maim to us.
HOTSPUR
A perilous gash, a very limb lopped off.
And yet, in faith, it is not! His present want
Seems more than we shall find it. Were it good
46 To set the exact wealth of all our states
47 All at one cast? to set so rich a main
48 On the one nice hazard of one doubtful hour?
49 It were not good; for therein should we read
50 The very bottom and the soul of hope,
51 The very list, the very utmost bound
Of all our fortunes.
DOUGLAS Faith, and so we should.
53 Where now remains a sweet reversion,
We may boldly spend upon the hope of what
Is to come in.
A comfort of retirement lives in this.
HOTSPUR
A rendezvous, a home to fly unto,
58 If that the devil and mischance look big
59 Upon the maidenhead of our affairs.
WORCESTER
But yet I would your father had been here.
61 The quality and hair of our attempt
62 Brooks no division. It will be thought
By some that know not why he is away,
64 That wisdom, loyalty, and mere dislike
Of our proceedings kept the earl from hence.
And think how such an apprehension
67 May turn the tide of fearful faction
And breed a kind of question in our cause.
For well you know we of the off'ring side
70 Must keep aloof from strict arbitrement,
71 And stop all sight-holes, every loop from whence
The eye of reason may pry in upon us.
73 This absence of your father's draws a curtain
That shows the ignorant a kind of fear
Before not dreamt of.
75 HOTSPUR You strain too far.
I rather of his absence make this use:
77 It lends a lustre and more great opinion,
A larger dare to our great enterprise,
Than if the earl were here; for men must think,
80 If we, without his help, can make a head
To push against a kingdom, with his help
We shall o'erturn it topsy-turvy down.
Yet all goes well; yet all our joints are whole.
DOUGLAS
As heart can think. There is not such a word
Spoke of in Scotland as this term of fear.
Enter Sir Richard Vernon.
HOTSPUR
My cousin Vernon! welcome, by my soul.
VERNON
Pray God my news be worth a welcome, lord.
The Earl of Westmoreland, seven thousand strong,
Is marching hitherwards; with him Prince John.
HOTSPUR
No harm. What more?
VERNON And further, I have learned
The king himself in person is set forth,
92 Or hitherwards intended speedily,
With strong and mighty preparation.

HOTSPUR
He shall be welcome too. Where is his son,
The nimble-footed madcap Prince of Wales,
And his comrades, that daffed the world aside 96
And bid it pass? 97
VERNON All furnished, all in arms;
All plumed like estridges that with the wind 98
Bated like eagles having lately bathed; 99
Glittering in golden coats like images;
As full of spirit as the month of May
And gorgeous as the sun at midsummer;
Wanton as youthful goats, wild as young bulls. 103
I saw young Harry with his beaver on, 104
His cushes on his thighs, gallantly armed, 105
Rise from the ground like feathered Mercury,
And vaulted with such ease into his seat
As if an angel dropped down from the clouds
To turn and wind a fiery Pegasus 109
And witch the world with noble horsemanship. 110
HOTSPUR
No more, no more! Worse than the sun in March,
This praise doth nourish agues. Let them come. 112
They come like sacrifices in their trim, 113
And to the fire-eyed maid of smoky war 114
All hot and bleeding will we offer them.
The mailèd Mars shall on his altar sit
Up to the ears in blood. I am on fire
To hear this rich reprisal is so nigh, 118
And yet not ours. Come, let me taste my horse, 119
Who is to bear me like a thunderbolt
Against the bosom of the Prince of Wales.
Harry to Harry shall, hot horse to horse,
Meet, and ne'er part till one drop down a corse.
O that Glendower were come!
VERNON There is more news.
I learned in Worcester, as I rode along,
He cannot draw his power this fourteen days. 126
DOUGLAS
That's the worst tidings that I hear of yet.
WORCESTER
Ay, by my faith, that bears a frosty sound.
HOTSPUR
What may the king's whole battle reach unto? 129
VERNON
To thirty thousand.
HOTSPUR Forty let it be.
My father and Glendower being both away,
The powers of us may serve so great a day.
Come, let us take a muster speedily.
Doomsday is near. Die all, die merrily.

46 *states* estates 47 *main* stake 48 *hazard* (1) peril, (2) dice game 49 *read* learn 50 *soul* (1) essence, (2) sole 51 *list* limit 53 *reversion* future prospects 58 *big* threatening 59 *maidenhead* early phase 61 *hair* nature 62 *Brooks* tolerates 64 *mere* utter 67 *fearful* timid; *faction* conspiracy 70 *arbitrement* scrutiny 71 *loop* loophole 73 *draws* opens 75 *strain* exaggerate 77 *opinion* prestige 80 *make a head* raise a force 92 *intended* intended to come 96 *daffed* thrust 97 *bid it pass* refused to take it seriously; *furnished* fitted out 98 *estridges* ostriches 99 *Bated* fluttered their wings 103 *Wanton* sportive 104 *beaver* i.e. helmet 105 *cushes* armor for the thighs 109 *wind* wheel; *Pegasus* i.e. mettlesome horse (literally, the winged horse of Greek mythology) 110 *witch* charm 112 *agues* (attributed to vapors drawn up by the sun) 113 *trim* decorations 114 *maid* the goddess Bellona 118 *reprisal* prize 119 *taste* feel 126 *draw* muster 129 *battle* army

DOUGLAS
135 Talk not of dying. I am out of fear
     Of death or death's hand for this one half-year.   *Exeunt.*

*

IV, ii   *Enter Falstaff and Bardolph.*

FALSTAFF Bardolph, get thee before to Coventry; fill me
a bottle of sack. Our soldiers shall march through. We'll
to Sutton Co'fil' to-night.

BARDOLPH Will you give me money, captain?

5 FALSTAFF Lay out, lay out.

6 BARDOLPH This bottle makes an angel.

7 FALSTAFF An if it do, take it for thy labor; an if it make
8 twenty, take them all; I'll answer the coinage. Bid my
lieutenant Peto meet me at town's end.

BARDOLPH I will, captain. Farewell.   *Exit.*

FALSTAFF If I be not ashamed of my soldiers, I am a
12 soused gurnet. I have misused the king's press dam-
13 nably. I have got, in exchange of a hundred and fifty
14 soldiers, three hundred and odd pounds. I press me
none but good householders, yeomen's sons; inquire
me out contracted bachelors, such as had been asked
17 twice on the banes – such a commodity of warm slaves
as had as lieve hear the devil as a drum, such as fear the
19 report of a caliver worse than a struck fowl or a hurt
wild duck. I pressed me none but such toasts-and-
butter, with hearts in their bellies no bigger than pins'
22 heads, and they have bought out their services; and
23 now my whole charge consists of ancients, corporals,
24 lieutenants, gentlemen of companies – slaves as ragged
25 as Lazarus in the painted cloth, where the glutton's
dogs licked his sores; and such as indeed were never
27 soldiers, but discarded unjust servingmen, younger
28 sons to younger brothers, revolted tapsters, and
29 ostlers trade-fall'n; the cankers of a calm world and a
long peace; ten times more dishonorable ragged than an
30 old fazed ancient; and such have I to fill up the rooms of
them as have bought out their services that you would
think that I had a hundred and fifty tattered prodigals
33 lately come from swine-keeping, from eating draff and
husks. A mad fellow met me on the way, and told me I
had unloaded all the gibbets and pressed the dead
bodies. No eye hath seen such scarecrows. I'll not
march through Coventry with them, that's flat. Nay,
and the villains march wide betwixt the legs, as if they
had gyves on, for indeed I had the most of them out of
prison. There's not a shirt and a half in all my company,

and the half-shirt is two napkins tacked together and
thrown over the shoulders like a herald's coat without
sleeves; and the shirt, to say the truth, stol'n from my
host at Saint Alban's, or the red-nose innkeeper of
Daventry. But that's all one; they'll find linen enough
on every hedge.

Enter the Prince and the Lord of Westmoreland.

PRINCE How now, blown Jack? How now, quilt?

FALSTAFF What, Hal? How now, mad wag? What a devil
dost thou in Warwickshire? My good Lord of Westmoreland, I cry you mercy. I thought your honor had 49
already been at Shrewsbury.

WESTMORELAND Faith, Sir John, 'tis more than time
that I were there, and you too, but my powers are there
already. The king, I can tell you, looks for us all. We
must away all night.   54

FALSTAFF Tut, never fear me: I am as vigilant as a cat to 55
steal cream.

PRINCE I think, to steal cream indeed, for thy theft hath
already made thee butter. But tell me, Jack, whose
fellows are these that come after?

FALSTAFF Mine, Hal, mine.

PRINCE I did never see such pitiful rascals.

FALSTAFF Tut, tut! good enough to toss; food for 62
powder, food for powder. They'll fill a pit as well as
better. Tush, man, mortal men, mortal men.

WESTMORELAND Ay, but, Sir John, methinks they are
exceeding poor and bare – too beggarly.

FALSTAFF Faith, for their poverty, I know not where
they had that, and for their bareness, I am sure they
never learned that of me.

PRINCE No, I'll be sworn, unless you call three fingers in
the ribs bare. But, sirrah, make haste. Percy is already
in the field.   *Exit.*

FALSTAFF What, is the king encamped?

WESTMORELAND He is, Sir John. I fear we shall stay
too long.   *[Exit.]*

FALSTAFF Well, to the latter end of a fray and the beginning of a feast fits a dull fighter and a keen guest.
                                                      Exit.

*

Enter Hotspur, Worcester, Douglas, Vernon.   IV, iii

HOTSPUR
We'll fight with him to-night.

WORCESTER   It may not be.

DOUGLAS
You give him then advantage.

VERNON   Not a whit.

HOTSPUR
Why say you so? Looks he not for supply?   3

VERNON
So do we.

HOTSPUR His is certain, ours is doubtful.

WORCESTER
Good cousin, be advised; stir not to-night.   5

VERNON
Do not, my lord.

DOUGLAS   You do not counsel well.
You speak it out of fear and cold heart.

VERNON
Do me no slander, Douglas. By my life –
And I dare well maintain it with my life –
If well-respected honor bid me on,   10

135 *out of* free from
IV, ii The road to Coventry   5 *Lay out* put up the money yourself 6
angel 10 shillings   7 *An . . . do* (Falstaff pretends that Bardolph speaks of
coining angels)   8 *answer* be responsible for   12 *soused gurnet* pickled fish;
press right of conscription   13 *in exchange of* i.e. for letting off (150 con-
scripts)   14 *press* draft   17 *banes* banns (public announcement of intent
to marry, made three times); *warm* well-to-do   19 *caliver* musket   22
bought . . . services i.e. bribed me to let them stay at home   23 *charge* company; *ancients* ensigns (Falstaff has signed on a disproportionate number of
his recruits as officers in order to collect, and appropriate, their higher pay)
24 *gentlemen of companies* gentlemen volunteers   25 *Lazarus* the beggar in
the parable (Luke xvi, 19–31); *painted cloth* wall-hangings   27 *unjust*
dishonest   28 *revolted* runaway   29 *trade-fall'n* out of work; *cankers*
cankerworms   30 *fazed ancient* frayed flag   33 *draff* garbage   49 *cry you
mercy* beg your pardon   54 *must away* must march   55 *fear* worry about;
vigilant wakeful   62 *toss* i.e. on a pike
IV, iii The rebel camp   3 *supply* reinforcements   5 *be advised* listen to
reason   10 *well-respected* well-considered

I hold as little counsel with weak fear
As you, my lord, or any Scot that this day lives.
Let it be seen to-morrow in the battle
Which of us fears.

DOUGLAS   Yea, or to-night.

VERNON   Content.

HOTSPUR
To-night, say I.

VERNON
Come, come, it may not be. I wonder much,
17   Being men of such great leading as you are,
That you foresee not what impediments
19   Drag back our expedition. Certain horse
Of my cousin Vernon's are not yet come up.
Your uncle Worcester's horse came but to-day;
22   And now their pride and mettle is asleep,
Their courage with hard labor tame and dull,
That not a horse is half the half of himself.

HOTSPUR
So are the horses of the enemy
26   In general journey-bated and brought low.
The better part of ours are full of rest.

WORCESTER
The number of the king exceedeth ours.
For God's sake, cousin, stay till all come in.
The trumpet sounds a parley.
Enter Sir Walter Blunt.

BLUNT
I come with gracious offers from the king,
31   If you vouchsafe me hearing and respect.

HOTSPUR
Welcome, Sir Walter Blunt, and would to God
33   You were of our determination.
Some of us love you well; and even those some
Envy your great deservings and good name,
36   Because you are not of our quality,
But stand against us like an enemy.

BLUNT
38   And God defend but still I should stand so,
39   So long as out of limit and true rule
You stand against anointed majesty.
But to my charge. The king hath sent to know
The nature of your griefs, and whereupon
43   You conjure from the breast of civil peace
Such bold hostility, teaching his duteous land
Audacious cruelty. If that the king
Have any way your good deserts forgot,
Which he confesseth to be manifold,
He bids you name your griefs, and with all speed
You shall have your desires with interest,
And pardon absolute for yourself and these
51   Herein misled by your suggestion.

HOTSPUR
The king is kind, and well we know the king
Knows at what time to promise, when to pay.
My father and my uncle and myself
Did give him that same royalty he wears;
And when he was not six-and-twenty strong,
Sick in the world's regard, wretched and low,
A poor unminded outlaw sneaking home,
My father gave him welcome to the shore;
And when he heard him swear and vow to God
He came but to be Duke of Lancaster,
62   To sue his livery and beg his peace,

With tears of innocency and terms of zeal,
My father, in kind heart and pity moved,
Swore him assistance, and performed it too.
Now when the lords and barons of the realm
Perceived Northumberland did lean to him,
The more and less came in with cap and knee;   68
Met him in boroughs, cities, villages,
Attended him on bridges, stood in lanes,   70
Laid gifts before him, proffered him their oaths,
Gave him their heirs as pages, followed him
Even at the heels in golden multitudes.   73
He presently, as greatness knows itself,   74
Steps me a little higher than his vow
Made to my father, while his blood was poor,   76
Upon the naked shore at Ravenspurgh;
And now, forsooth, takes on him to reform   78
Some certain edicts and some strait decrees   79
That lie too heavy on the commonwealth;
Cries out upon abuses, seems to weep   81
Over his country's wrongs; and by this face,   82
This seeming brow of justice, did he win
The hearts of all that he did angle for;
Proceeded further – cut me off the heads   85
Of all the favorites that the absent king
In deputation left behind him here   87
When he was personal in the Irish war.

BLUNT
Tut! I came not to hear this.

HOTSPUR   Then to the point.
In short time after, he deposed the king;
Soon after that deprived him of his life;
And in the neck of that tasked the whole state;   92
To make that worse, suff'red his kinsman March
(Who is, if every owner were well placed,
Indeed his king) to be engaged in Wales,   95
There without ransom to lie forfeited;
Disgraced me in my happy victories,   97
Sought to entrap me by intelligence;   98
Rated mine uncle from the council board;   99
In rage dismissed my father from the court;
Broke oath on oath, committed wrong on wrong;
And in conclusion drove us to seek out
This head of safety, and withal to pry   103
Into his title, the which we find
Too indirect for long continuance.

BLUNT
Shall I return this answer to the king?

HOTSPUR
Not so, Sir Walter. We'll withdraw awhile.
Go to the king; and let there be impawned   108
Some surety for a safe return again,
And in the morning early shall mine uncle
Bring him our purposes; and so farewell.

---

17 *leading* leadership   19 *expedition* progress   22 *pride* mettle   26 *journey-bated* wearied   31 *respect* attention   33 *determination* mind   36 *quality* party   38 *defend* forbid   39 *rule* conduct   43 *civil* orderly   51 *suggestion* instigation   62 *sue his livery* sue as heir for his inheritance   68 *more and less* great and small   70 *stood in lanes* lined the roads   73 *golden* richly dressed   74 *knows itself* feels its own strength   76 *blood* spirit   78 *forsooth* (ironical)   79 *strait* strict   81 *Cries out upon* denounces   82 *face* pretext   85 *cut . . . heads* (see *Richard II*, III, i); *me* (ethical dative)   87 *In deputation* as deputies   92 *in the neck of* immediately after; *tasked* taxed   95 *engaged* held as hostage   97 *happy* fortunate   98 *intelligence* espionage   99 *Rated* scolded   103 *head* army; *withal* at the same time   108 *impawned* pledged

BLUNT

I would you would accept of grace and love.

HOTSPUR

And may be so we shall.

BLUNT　　　　　　　　　Pray God you do.　　　*Exeunt.*

*

IV, iv　　　*Enter the Archbishop of York and Sir Michael.*

ARCHBISHOP

1　Hie, good Sir Michael; bear this sealèd brief
2　With wingèd haste to the lord marshal;
3　This to my cousin Scroop; and all the rest
　　To whom they are directed. If you knew
　　How much they do import, you would make haste.

SIR MICHAEL

　　My good lord,
　　I guess their tenor.

ARCHBISHOP　　　　　Like enough you do.
　　To-morrow, good Sir Michael, is a day
　　Wherein the fortune of ten thousand men
10　Must bide the touch; for, sir, at Shrewsbury,
　　As I am truly given to understand,
　　The king with mighty and quick-raisèd power
　　Meets with Lord Harry; and I fear, Sir Michael,
　　What with the sickness of Northumberland,
15　Whose power was in the first proportion,
　　And what with Owen Glendower's absence thence,
17　Who with them was a rated sinew too
　　And comes not in, overruled by prophecies –
　　I fear the power of Percy is too weak
20　To wage an instant trial with the king.

SIR MICHAEL

　　Why, my good lord, you need not fear;
　　There is Douglas and Lord Mortimer.

ARCHBISHOP

　　No, Mortimer is not there.

SIR MICHAEL

　　But there is Mordake, Vernon, Lord Harry Percy,
25　And there is my Lord of Worcester, and a head
　　Of gallant warriors, noble gentlemen.

ARCHBISHOP

　　And so there is; but yet the king hath drawn
　　The special head of all the land together –
　　The Prince of Wales, Lord John of Lancaster,
　　The noble Westmoreland and warlike Blunt,
31　And many moe corrivals and dear men
　　Of estimation and command in arms.

SIR MICHAEL

　　Doubt not, my lord, they shall be well opposed.

ARCHBISHOP

　　I hope no less, yet needful 'tis to fear;

IV, iv The palace of the Archbishop of York　1 *brief* letter　2 *lord marshal*
Thomas Mowbray, son of the Duke of Norfolk (*Richard II*, I, i, iii), an
inveterate enemy of the king　3 *Scroop* possibly Lord Scroop of Masham,
the archbishop's nephew, later executed for treason (*Henry V*, II, ii)　10
bide the touch withstand the test (touchstone)　15 *proportion* magnitude
17 *rated sinew* mainstay they counted on　20 *wage* risk; *instant* immediate
25 *head* force　31 *moe* more; *corrivals* partners, allies　36 *thrive* succeed
38 *confederacy* conspiracy
V, i The royal camp at Shrewsbury　3 *distemp'rature* unhealthy appearance
4 *trumpet* trumpeter　7 *sympathize* accord　8 *foul* i.e. foul weather　17
obedient orb orb of obedience　19 *exhaled meteor* vapor drawn up by the
sun (visible as streaks of light), regarded as an omen (*prodigy*)　24 *entertain* occupy, while away　26 *dislike* discord　29 *chewet* chatterer　32
remember remind　35 *posted* rode at top speed　40 *outdare* defy

And, to prevent the worst, Sir Michael, speed.
For if Lord Percy thrive not, ere the king　　　36
Dismiss his power, he means to visit us,
For he hath heard of our confederacy,　　　　　38
And 'tis but wisdom to make strong against him.
Therefore make haste. I must go write again
To other friends; and so farewell, Sir Michael.　*Exeunt.*

*

Enter the King, Prince of Wales, Lord John of　　V, i
Lancaster, Sir Walter Blunt, Falstaff.

KING

How bloodily the sun begins to peer
Above yon bulky hill! The day looks pale
At his distemp'rature.　　　　　　　　　　　3

PRINCE　　　　　　　The southern wind
Doth play the trumpet to his purposes　　　　4
And by his hollow whistling in the leaves
Foretells a tempest and a blust'ring day.

KING

Then with the losers let it sympathize,　　　　7
For nothing can seem foul to those that win.　　8

　　The trumpet sounds. Enter Worcester [and Vernon].

How now, my Lord of Worcester? 'Tis not well
That you and I should meet upon such terms
As now we meet. You have deceived our trust
And made us doff our easy robes of peace
To crush our old limbs in ungentle steel.
This is not well, my lord; this is not well.
What say you to it? Will you again unknit
This churlish knot of all-abhorrèd war,
And move in that obedient orb again　　　　　17
Where you did give a fair and natural light,
And be no more an exhaled meteor,　　　　　19
A prodigy of fear, and a portent
Of broachèd mischief to the unborn times?

WORCESTER

Hear me, my liege.
For mine own part, I could be well content
To entertain the lag-end of my life　　　　　24
With quiet hours, for I do protest
I have not sought the day of this dislike.　　　26

KING

You have not sought it! How comes it then?

FALSTAFF

Rebellion lay in his way, and he found it.

PRINCE

Peace, chewet, peace!　　　　　　　　　　29

WORCESTER

It pleased your majesty to turn your looks
Of favor from myself and all our house;
And yet I must remember you, my lord,　　　　32
We were the first and dearest of your friends.
For you my staff of office did I break
In Richard's time, and posted day and night　　35
To meet you on the way and kiss your hand
When yet you were in place and in account
Nothing so strong and fortunate as I.
It was myself, my brother, and his son
That brought you home and boldly did outdare　40
The dangers of the time. You swore to us,
And you did swear that oath at Doncaster,
That you did nothing purpose 'gainst the state,

44 Nor claim no further than your new-fall'n right,
     The seat of Gaunt, dukedom of Lancaster.
     To this we swore our aid. But in short space
     It rained down fortune show'ring on your head,
     And such a flood of greatness fell on you –
     What with our help, what with the absent king,
50 What with the injuries of a wanton time,
51 The seeming sufferances that you had borne,
     And the contrarious winds that held the king
     So long in his unlucky Irish wars
     That all in England did repute him dead –
     And from this swarm of fair advantages
     You took occasion to be quickly wooed
57 To gripe the general sway into your hand;
     Forgot your oath to us at Doncaster;
     And, being fed by us, you used us so
60 As that ungentle gull, the cuckoo's bird,
     Useth the sparrow – did oppress our nest;
     Grew by our feeding to so great a bulk
     That even our love durst not come near your sight
     For fear of swallowing; but with nimble wing
     We were enforced for safety sake to fly
66 Out of your sight and raise this present head;
     Whereby we stand opposèd by such means
     As you yourself have forged against yourself
69 By unkind usage, dangerous countenance,
70 And violation of all faith and troth
     Sworn to us in your younger enterprise.
     KING
72 These things, indeed, you have articulate,
     Proclaimed at market crosses, read in churches,
74 To face the garment of rebellion
75 With some fine color that may please the eye
76 Of fickle changelings and poor discontents,
     Which gape and rub the elbow at the news
     Of hurlyburly innovation.
     And never yet did insurrection want
80 Such water colors to impaint his cause,
     Nor moody beggars, starving for a time
     Of pell-mell havoc and confusion.
     PRINCE
     In both your armies there is many a soul
     Shall pay full dearly for this encounter,
     If once they join in trial. Tell your nephew
     The Prince of Wales doth join with all the world
87 In praise of Henry Percy. By my hopes,
88 This present enterprise set off his head,
     I do not think a braver gentleman,
     More active-valiant or more valiant-young,
     More daring or more bold, is now alive
     To grace this latter age with noble deeds.
     For my part, I may speak it to my shame,
     I have a truant been to chivalry;
     And so I hear he doth account me too.
     Yet this before my father's majesty –
     I am content that he shall take the odds
98 Of his great name and estimation,
     And will, to save the blood on either side,
     Try fortune with him in a single fight.
     KING
101 And, Prince of Wales, so dare we venture thee,
102 Albeit considerations infinite
     Do make against it. No, good Worcester, no!
     We love our people well; even those we love

That are misled upon your cousin's part;
And, will they take the offer of our grace,
Both he, and they, and you, yea, every man
Shall be my friend again, and I'll be his.
So tell your cousin, and bring me word
What he will do. But if he will not yield,
Rebuke and dread correction wait on us,   111
And they shall do their office. So be gone.
We will not now be troubled with reply.
We offer fair; take it advisedly.
            Exit Worcester [with Vernon].
PRINCE
It will not be accepted, on my life.
The Douglas and the Hotspur both together
Are confident against the world in arms.
KING
Hence, therefore, every leader to his charge;
For, on their answer, will we set on them,
And God befriend us as our cause is just!
            Exeunt. Manent Prince, Falstaff.
FALSTAFF Hal, if thou see me down in the battle and
     bestride me, so! 'Tis a point of friendship.   122
PRINCE Nothing but a colossus can do thee that friend-
     ship. Say thy prayers, and farewell.   124
FALSTAFF I would 'twere bedtime, Hal, and all well.
PRINCE Why, thou owest God a death.   *[Exit.]*
FALSTAFF 'Tis not due yet: I would be loath to pay him
     before his day. What need I be so forward with him that
     calls not on me? Well, 'tis no matter; honor pricks me   129
     on. Yea, but how if honor prick me off when I come on?   130
     How then? Can honor set to a leg? No. Or an arm? No.   131
     Or take away the grief of a wound? No. Honor hath no
     skill in surgery then? No. What is honor? A word. What
     is that word honor? Air – a trim reckoning! Who hath
     it? He that died a Wednesday. Doth he feel it? No. Doth
     he hear it? No. 'Tis insensible then? Yea, to the dead.   136
     But will it not live with the living? No. Why? Detrac-
     tion will not suffer it. Therefore I'll none of it. Honor is
     a mere scutcheon – and so ends my catechism.   *Exit.*   139

                      *

       Enter Worcester and Sir Richard Vernon.   V, ii
WORCESTER
O no, my nephew must not know, Sir Richard,
The liberal and kind offer of the king.
VERNON
'Twere best he did.
WORCESTER   Then are we all undone.
It is not possible, it cannot be,
The king should keep his word in loving us.
He will suspect us still and find a time   6

---

44 *new-fall'n* lately inherited   50 *injuries* evils; *wanton* disordered   51 *sufferances* sufferings   57 *gripe* seize   60 *ungentle* rude; *gull* unfledged bird   66 *head* armed force   69 *dangerous* threatening   70 *troth* truth   72 *articulate* specified   74 *face* trim   75 *color* i.e. excuse   76 *changelings* turncoats   80 *water colors* i.e. thin pretexts   87 *hopes* i.e. of salvation   88 *set . . . head* not charged to his account   98 *estimation* reputation   101 *dare* would dare   102 *Albeit* were it not that   111 *wait* attend   122 *so good*   124 *Say thy prayers* prepare for death   129 *calls . . . me* doesn't demand payment   130 *prick me off* check me off   131 *set to* graft on   136 *insensible* imperceptible to the senses   139 *scutcheon* coat of arms borne at a funeral
V, ii The battlefield at Shrewsbury   6 *still* constantly

To punish this offense in other faults.

8   Supposition all our lives shall be stuck full of eyes;
For treason is but trusted like the fox,
Who, ne'er so tame, so cherished and locked up,

11   Will have a wild trick of his ancestors.
Look how we can, or sad or merrily,
Interpretation will misquote our looks,
And we shall feed like oxen at a stall,

15   The better cherished still the nearer death.
My nephew's trespass may be well forgot;
It hath the excuse of youth and heat of blood,
And an adopted name of privilege –

19   A hare-brained Hotspur, governed by a spleen.
All his offenses live upon my head

21   And on his father's. We did train him on;

22   And, his corruption being ta'en from us,
We, as the spring of all, shall pay for all.
Therefore, good cousin, let not Harry know,
In any case, the offer of the king.

Enter Hotspur [and Douglas].

VERNON

26   Deliver what you will, I'll say 'tis so.
Here comes your cousin.

HOTSPUR   My uncle is returned.
Deliver up my Lord of Westmoreland.
Uncle, what news?

WORCESTER

The king will bid you battle presently.

DOUGLAS

Defy him by the Lord of Westmoreland.

HOTSPUR

Lord Douglas, go you and tell him so.

DOUGLAS

Marry, and shall, and very willingly.   *Exit.*

WORCESTER

There is no seeming mercy in the king.

HOTSPUR

Did you beg any? God forbid!

WORCESTER

I told him gently of our grievances,

37   Of his oath-breaking, which he mended thus,

38   By now forswearing that he is forsworn.
He calls us rebels, traitors, and will scourge
With haughty arms this hateful name in us.

Enter Douglas.

DOUGLAS

Arm, gentlemen! to arms! for I have thrown

42   A brave defiance in King Henry's teeth,

43   And Westmoreland, that was engaged, did bear it;
Which cannot choose but bring him quickly on.

WORCESTER

The Prince of Wales stepped forth before the king
And, nephew, challenged you to single fight.

HOTSPUR

O, would the quarrel lay upon our heads,
And that no man might draw short breath to-day
But I and Harry Monmouth! Tell me, tell me,
How showed his tasking? Seemed it in contempt?   50

VERNON

No, by my soul. I never in my life
Did hear a challenge urged more modestly,
Unless a brother should a brother dare
To gentle exercise and proof of arms.
He gave you all the duties of a man;   55
Trimmed up your praises with a princely tongue;   56
Spoke your deservings like a chronicle;
Making you ever better than his praise
By still dispraising praise valued with you;   59
And, which became him like a prince indeed,
He made a blushing cital of himself,   61
And chid his truant youth with such a grace
As if he mast'red there a double spirit
Of teaching and of learning instantly.   64
There did he pause; but let me tell the world,
If he outlive the envy of this day,   66
England did never owe so sweet a hope,   67
So much misconstrued in his wantonness.   68

HOTSPUR

Cousin, I think thou art enamorèd
Upon his follies. Never did I hear
Of any prince so wild a liberty.   71
But be he as he will, yet once ere night
I will embrace him with a soldier's arm,
That he shall shrink under my courtesy.
Arm, arm with speed! and, fellows, soldiers, friends,
Better consider what you have to do
Than I, that have not well the gift of tongue,
Can lift your blood up with persuasion.

Enter a Messenger.

MESSENGER

My lord, here are letters for you.

HOTSPUR

I cannot read them now. –
O gentlemen, the time of life is short!
To spend that shortness basely were too long
If life did ride upon a dial's point,   83
Still ending at the arrival of an hour.   84
An if we live, we live to tread on kings;
If die, brave death, when princes die with us!   86
Now for our consciences, the arms are fair,
When the intent of bearing them is just.

Enter another Messenger.

MESSENGER

My lord, prepare. The king comes on apace.

HOTSPUR

I thank him that he cuts me from my tale,
For I profess not talking. Only this –
Let each man do his best; and here draw I
A sword whose temper I intend to stain
With the best blood that I can meet withal
In the adventure of this perilous day.   95
Now, Esperance! Percy! and set on.   96
Sound all the lofty instruments of war,
And by that music let us all embrace;
For, heaven to earth, some of us never shall
A second time do such a courtesy.

Here they embrace. The trumpets sound.   *[Exeunt.]*

---

8 *Supposition* suspicious conjecture 11 *wild trick* trait of wildness 15 *cherished* fed 19 *spleen* fiery temper 21 *train* lure 22 *corruption* guilt; *ta'en* contracted 26 *Deliver* report 37 *mended* made up for 38 *forswearing* denying; *is forsworn* has repudiated (his oath) 42 *brave* haughty 43 *engaged* held as hostage 50 *tasking* challenge 55 *duties* due merits 56 *Trimmed up* adorned 59 *valued* compared 61 *cital* (1) citation, (2) impeachment 64 *instantly* simultaneously 66 *envy* malice 67 *owe* own 68 *wantonness* sportiveness 71 *liberty* licentiousness 83 *If* even if; *dial's* clock's 84 *Still . . . hour* i.e. if life were only an hour long; *Still* inevitably 86 *brave* glorious 95 *adventure* hazard 96 *Esperance* hope (the Percy battle-cry)

V, iii   *The King enters with his power. Alarum to the battle.*
         [Exeunt.] Then enter Douglas and Sir Walter Blunt.

BLUNT
What is thy name, that in battle thus
Thou crossest me? What honor dost thou seek
Upon my head?
DOUGLAS   Know then my name is Douglas,
And I do haunt thee in the battle thus
Because some tell me that thou art a king.
BLUNT
They tell thee true.
DOUGLAS
The Lord of Stafford dear to-day hath bought
Thy likeness, for instead of thee, King Harry,
This sword hath ended him. So shall it thee,
10   Unless thou yield thee as my prisoner.
BLUNT
I was not born a yielder, thou proud Scot;
And thou shalt find a king that will revenge
Lord Stafford's death.
         They fight. Douglas kills Blunt. Then enter Hotspur.
HOTSPUR O Douglas, hadst thou fought at Holmedon
thus, I never had triumphed upon a Scot.
DOUGLAS
All's done, all's won. Here breathless lies the king.
HOTSPUR Where?
DOUGLAS Here.
HOTSPUR
This, Douglas? No. I know this face full well.
A gallant knight he was, his name was Blunt;
21   Semblably furnished like the king himself.
DOUGLAS
22   A fool go with thy soul, whither it goes!
A borrowed title hast thou bought too dear:
Why didst thou tell me that thou wert a king?
HOTSPUR
The king hath many marching in his coats.
DOUGLAS
Now, by my sword, I will kill all his coats;
I'll murder all his wardrobe, piece by piece,
Until I meet the king.
HOTSPUR   Up and away!
29   Our soldiers stand full fairly for the day.   *Exeunt.*
         Alarum. Enter Falstaff solus.
30 FALSTAFF Though I could scape shot-free at London, I
31   fear the shot here. Here's no scoring but upon the pate.
Soft! who are you? Sir Walter Blunt. There's honor for
33   you! Here's no vanity! I am as hot as molten lead, and as
heavy too. God keep lead out of me. I need no more
weight than mine own bowels. I have led my rag-of-
36   muffins where they are peppered. There's not three of
my hundred and fifty left alive, and they are for the
town's end, to beg during life. But who comes here?
         Enter the Prince.
PRINCE
What, stand'st thou idle here? Lend me thy sword.
Many a nobleman lies stark and stiff
Under the hoofs of vaunting enemies,
Whose deaths are yet unrevenged. I prithee
Lend me thy sword.
FALSTAFF O Hal, I prithee give me leave to breathe
45   awhile. Turk Gregory never did such deeds in arms as I
46   have done this day. I have paid Percy; I have made him
sure.

PRINCE
He is indeed, and living to kill thee.   47
I prithee lend me thy sword.
FALSTAFF Nay, before God, Hal, if Percy be alive, thou
get'st not my sword; but take my pistol, if thou wilt.
PRINCE Give it me. What, is it in the case?
FALSTAFF Ay, Hal. 'Tis hot, 'tis hot. There's that will
sack a city.
         The Prince draws it out and finds it to be a bottle of
         sack.
PRINCE
What, is it a time to jest and dally now?
         He throws the bottle at him.   *Exit.*
FALSTAFF Well, if Percy be alive, I'll pierce him. If he do 55
come in my way, so; if he do not, if I come in his will-
ingly, let him make a carbonado of me. I like not such 57
grinning honor as Sir Walter hath. Give me life; which
if I can save, so; if not, honor comes unlooked for, and
there's an end.   *Exit.*
         Alarum. Excursions. Enter the King, the Prince, Lord V, iv
         John of Lancaster, Earl of Westmoreland.
KING
I prithee, Harry, withdraw thyself; thou bleedest too
much.
Lord John of Lancaster, go you with him.
JOHN
Not I, my lord, unless I did bleed too.
PRINCE
I do beseech your majesty make up,   4
Lest your retirement do amaze your friends.   5
KING
I will do so.
My Lord of Westmoreland, lead him to his tent.
WESTMORELAND
Come, my lord, I'll lead you to your tent.
PRINCE
Lead me, my lord? I do not need your help;
And God forbid a shallow scratch should drive
The Prince of Wales from such a field as this,
Where stained nobility lies trodden on,
And rebels' arms triumph in massacres!
JOHN
We breathe too long. Come, cousin Westmoreland,
Our duty this way lies. For God's sake, come.
         [Exeunt Prince John and Westmoreland.]
PRINCE
By God, thou hast deceived me, Lancaster!
I did not think thee lord of such a spirit.
Before, I loved thee as a brother, John;
But now, I do respect thee as my soul.   19
KING
I saw him hold Lord Percy at the point
With lustier maintenance than I did look for   21
Of such an ungrown warrior.
PRINCE   O, this boy
Lends mettle to us all!   *Exit.*

V, iii s.d. *Alarum* signal to advance 21 *Semblably furnished* similarly
equipped 22 *A . . . soul* i.e. you are a fool 29 *fairly* auspiciously; *day*
victory 30 *shot-free* without paying bills 31 *scoring* (1) cutting, (2)
chalking up a debt 33 *Here's no vanity* (ironical) here's no empty honor
36 *peppered* done for 45 *Turk Gregory* a ferocious tyrant (invented by
Falstaff) 46 *made him sure* destroyed him 47 *indeed* i.e. sure (safe) 55
pierce pronounced 'perce' 57 *carbonado* broiled steak
V, iv s.d. *Excursions* sorties 4 *make up* advance 5 *amaze* bewilder 19
respect regard 21 *lustier maintenance* more vigorous bearing

[Enter Douglas.]

DOUGLAS

24 Another king? They grow like Hydra's heads.
I am the Douglas, fatal to all those
That wear those colors on them. What art thou
That counterfeit'st the person of a king?

KING

The king himself, who, Douglas, grieves at heart

29 So many of his shadows thou hast met,
And not the very king. I have two boys
Seek Percy and thyself about the field;
But, seeing thou fall'st on me so luckily,

33 I will assay thee. So defend thyself.

DOUGLAS

I fear thou art another counterfeit;
And yet, in faith, thou bearest thee like a king.
But mine I am sure thou art, whoe'er thou be,
And thus I win thee.
     They fight. The King being in danger, enter Prince of
     Wales.

PRINCE

Hold up thy head, vile Scot, or thou art like
Never to hold it up again. The spirits
Of valiant Shirley, Stafford, Blunt are in my arms.
It is the Prince of Wales that threatens thee,
Who never promiseth but he means to pay.
     They fight. Douglas flieth.

43 Cheerly, my lord. How fares your grace?
Sir Nicholas Gawsey hath for succor sent,
And so hath Clifton. I'll to Clifton straight.

KING

Stay and breathe awhile.

47 Thou hast redeemed thy lost opinion,

48 And showed thou mak'st some tender of my life,
In this fair rescue thou hast brought to me.

PRINCE

O God, they did me too much injury

51 That ever said I heark'ned for your death.
If it were so, I might have let alone

53 The insulting hand of Douglas over you,
Which would have been as speedy in your end
As all the poisonous potions in the world,
And saved the treacherous labor of your son.

KING

Make up to Clifton; I'll to Sir Nicholas Gawsey.   *Exit.*
     Enter Hotspur.

HOTSPUR

If I mistake not, thou art Harry Monmouth.

PRINCE

Thou speak'st as if I would deny my name.

HOTSPUR

My name is Harry Percy.

PRINCE   Why, then I see
A very valiant rebel of the name.

I am the Prince of Wales, and think not, Percy,
To share with me in glory any more.
Two stars keep not their motion in one sphere,   64
Nor can one England brook a double reign   65
Of Harry Percy and the Prince of Wales.

HOTSPUR

Nor shall it, Harry, for the hour is come
To end the one of us; and would to God
Thy name in arms were now as great as mine!

PRINCE

I'll make it greater ere I part from thee,
And all the budding honors on thy crest   71
I'll crop to make a garland for my head.

HOTSPUR

I can no longer brook thy vanities.   73
     They fight. Enter Falstaff.

FALSTAFF Well said, Hal! to it, Hal! Nay, you shall find 74
no boy's play here, I can tell you.
     Enter Douglas. He fighteth with Falstaff, who falls
     down as if he were dead. [Exit Douglas.] The Prince
     killeth Percy.

HOTSPUR

O Harry, thou hast robbed me of my youth!
I better brook the loss of brittle life
Than those proud titles thou hast won of me.
They wound my thoughts worse than thy sword my
flesh.
But thoughts the slaves of life, and life time's fool,   80
And time, that takes survey of all the world,   81
Must have a stop. O, I could prophesy,
But that the earthy and cold hand of death
Lies on my tongue. No, Percy, thou art dust,
And food for –
     [Dies.]

PRINCE

For worms, brave Percy. Fare thee well, great heart.
Ill-weaved ambition, how much art thou shrunk!
When that this body did contain a spirit,
A kingdom for it was too small a bound;
But now two paces of the vilest earth
Is room enough. This earth that bears thee dead
Bears not alive so stout a gentleman.
If thou wert sensible of courtesy,   93
I should not make so dear a show of zeal.   94
But let my favors hide thy mangled face;   95
And, even in thy behalf, I'll thank myself
For doing these fair rites of tenderness.
Adieu, and take thy praise with thee to heaven.
Thy ignominy sleep with thee in the grave,
But not rememb'red in thy epitaph.
     He spieth Falstaff on the ground.
What, old acquaintance? Could not all this flesh
Keep in a little life? Poor Jack, farewell!
I could have better spared a better man.
O, I should have a heavy miss of thee   104
If I were much in love with vanity.   105
Death hath not struck so fat a deer to-day,
Though many dearer, in this bloody fray.
Embowelled will I see thee by-and-by;   108
Till then in blood by noble Percy lie.   *Exit.*
     Falstaff riseth up.

FALSTAFF Embowelled? If thou embowel me to-day, I'll
give you leave to powder me and eat me too to-morrow. 111
'Sblood, 'twas time to counterfeit, or that hot termagant 112

24 *Hydra's heads* (as soon as one was cut off, two others grew in its place)
29 *shadows* likenesses 33 *assay* challenge to trial 43 *Cheerly* cheer up
47 *redeemed* regained; *opinion* good name 48 *mak'st some tender of* have
some regard for 51 *heark'ned* waited 53 *insulting* exulting 64 *sphere*
orbit 65 *brook* endure 71 *crest* helmet 73 *vanities* boasts 74 *Well said*
well done 80 *fool* dupe, plaything 81 *takes survey of* oversees 93
sensible able to feel 94 *dear* heartfelt; *zeal* admiration 95 *favors* plumes
(of his helmet) 104 *have . . . thee* (1) miss you sadly, (2) miss something
heavy 105 *vanity* frivolity 108 *Embowelled* eviscerated (the first step in
embalming) 111 *powder* pickle in brine 112 *termagant* violent

113 Scot had paid me scot and lot too. Counterfeit? I lie; I
am no counterfeit. To die is to be a counterfeit, for he is
but the counterfeit of a man who hath not the life of a
man; but to counterfeit dying when a man thereby
liveth, is to be no counterfeit, but the true and perfect
118 image of life indeed. The better part of valor is discretion, in the which better part I have saved my life.
Zounds, I am afraid of this gunpowder Percy, though he
be dead. How if he should counterfeit too, and rise? By
my faith, I am afraid he would prove the better counterfeit. Therefore I'll make him sure; yea, and I'll swear I
killed him. Why may not he rise as well as I? Nothing
confutes me but eyes, and nobody sees me. Therefore,
sirrah *[stabs him]*, with a new wound in your thigh,
come you along with me.

    *He takes up Hotspur on his back. Enter Prince, and
    John of Lancaster.*

PRINCE
128 Come, brother John; full bravely hast thou fleshed
Thy maiden sword.

    JOHN   But, soft! whom have we here?
Did you not tell me this fat man was dead?

PRINCE
I did; I saw him dead,
Breathless and bleeding on the ground. Art thou alive,
133 Or is it fantasy that plays upon our eyesight?
I prithee speak. We will not trust our eyes
Without our ears. Thou art not what thou seem'st.

136 FALSTAFF No, that's certain, I am not a double man; but
137 if I be not Jack Falstaff, then am I a Jack. There is
Percy. If your father will do me any honor, so; if not, let
him kill the next Percy himself. I look to be either earl
or duke, I can assure you.

PRINCE Why, Percy I killed myself, and saw thee dead!

FALSTAFF Didst thou? Lord, Lord, how this world is
given to lying. I grant you I was down, and out of breath,
and so was he; but we rose both at an instant and fought
a long hour by Shrewsbury clock. If I may be believed,
so; if not, let them that should reward valor bear the sin
upon their own heads. I'll take it upon my death, I gave
him this wound in the thigh. If the man were alive and
would deny it, zounds! I would make him eat a piece of
my sword.

JOHN
This is the strangest tale that ever I heard.

PRINCE
This is the strangest fellow, brother John.
Come, bring your luggage nobly on your back.
153 For my part, if a lie may do thee grace,
I'll gild it with the happiest terms I have.

    A retreat is sounded.

The trumpet sounds retreat; the day is ours.
Come, brother, let's to the highest of the field,
To see what friends are living, who are dead.

    Exeunt [Prince Henry and Prince John].

FALSTAFF I'll follow, as they say, for reward. He that rewards me, God reward him. If I do grow great, I'll grow
160 less; for I'll purge, and leave sack, and live cleanly, as a
nobleman should do.   *Exit [bearing off the body].*

*

The trumpets sound. Enter the King, Prince of Wales, V, v
*Lord John of Lancaster, Earl of Westmoreland, with
Worcester and Vernon prisoners.*

KING
Thus ever did rebellion find rebuke.
Ill-spirited Worcester, did not we send grace,   2
Pardon, and terms of love to all of you?
And wouldst thou turn our offers contrary?
Misuse the tenor of thy kinsman's trust?
Three knights upon our party slain to-day,
A noble earl, and many a creature else
Had been alive this hour,
If like a Christian thou hadst truly borne
Betwixt our armies true intelligence.

WORCESTER
What I have done my safety urged me to;
And I embrace this fortune patiently,   12
Since not to be avoided it falls on me.

KING
Bear Worcester to the death, and Vernon too;
Other offenders we will pause upon.
    [Exeunt Worcester and Vernon, guarded.]
How goes the field?

PRINCE
The noble Scot, Lord Douglas, when he saw
The fortune of the day quite turned from him,
The noble Percy slain, and all his men
Upon the foot of fear, fled with the rest;   20
And falling from a hill, he was so bruised
That the pursuers took him. At my tent
The Douglas is, and I beseech your grace
I may dispose of him.

KING   With all my heart.

PRINCE
Then, brother John of Lancaster, to you
This honorable bounty shall belong.   26
Go to the Douglas and deliver him
Up to his pleasure, ransomless and free.
His valors shown upon our crests to-day
Have taught us how to cherish such high deeds,
Even in the bosom of our adversaries.

JOHN
I thank your grace for this high courtesy,
Which I shall give away immediately.

KING
Then this remains, that we divide our power.
You, son John, and my cousin Westmoreland,
Towards York shall bend you with your dearest speed   36
To meet Northumberland and the prelate Scroop,
Who, as we hear, are busily in arms.
Myself and you, son Harry, will towards Wales
To fight with Glendower and the Earl of March.
Rebellion in this land shall lose his sway,
Meeting the check of such another day;
And since this business so fair is done,
Let us not leave till all our own be won.   *Exeunt.* 44

---

113 *scot and lot* i.e. thoroughly   118 *part* quality   128 *fleshed* initiated
133 *fantasy* hallucination   136 *double man* (1) spectre, (2) two men   137
Jack knave   153 *grace* credit   160 *purge* (1) repent, (2) 'grow less'
V, v The command post of the King   2 *grace* mercy   12 *patiently* with
fortitude   20 *Upon . . . fear* in flight for fear   26 *bounty* benevolence   36
bend you direct yourselves   44 *leave* cease

THE SECOND PART OF
KING HENRY THE FOURTH

INTRODUCTION

To Shakespeare and his contemporaries, the history of their country between the accession of Richard II in 1377 and the Battle of Bosworth Field in 1485 provided a double fascination. It was a period of stirring events – of rebellion and counter-rebellion, and of victories over enemies abroad. Shrewsbury and Agincourt were names as familiar and evocative to Shakespeare's audience as are Antietam and Gettysburg to Americans of our own day. Owen Glendower and Harry Hotspur and Henry Bolingbroke were as well-remembered as John Brown and Stonewall Jackson and Ulysses Grant. As with us, the events and the men had been misted over with the passage of time, and the facts of history had been transmuted into tradition and even legend. But to the Elizabethans this period meant something more than romantic history. It served also as a "mirror," as they themselves put it, wherein Elizabeth's England might perceive important truths having to do with theories of government, the responsibility of the monarch, the duty of the subject, and the evil consequences of rebellion.

In the light of this interest, and of the consequent vogue for dramatized history which flourished in the theatres of the 1590's, it is not surprising that Shakespeare wrote no fewer than eight plays dealing with this period of English history. Four of these – the three Henry VI plays and *Richard III* – were written early in his career, but the other four – *Richard II,* the two parts of *Henry IV,* and *Henry V* – belong to the period when his craft as a dramatist and his lordship of language were approaching their full powers. *Richard II* portrayed the weakness and folly of Richard, his forced abdication, the succession of his cousin Henry Bolingbroke as King Henry IV, and finally the murder of Richard at Pomfret Castle. *1 Henry IV* told of the rebellion of those who had aided Henry to the throne and subsequently repented having done so, and of the defeat of the rebels at Shrewsbury; *2 Henry IV* told of the later rebellions, of the death of Henry IV, and of the succession of his son, Prince Hal, as Henry V. *Henry V,* treating of the English victories in France, brought the tetralogy to a close.

The present play, third in the tetralogy, was probably written in the spring of 1598 and produced on the stage immediately thereafter. It was printed in quarto in 1600, with a title page reading as follows: *The Second part of Henrie the fourth, continuing to his death, and coronation of Henrie the fift. With the humours of sir Iohn Falstaffe, and swaggering Pistoll. As it hath been sundrie times publikely acted by the right honourable, the Lord Chamberlaine his seruants. Written by William Shakespeare. London. Printed by V. S. for Andrew Wise, and William Aspley. 1600.* Unlike *1 Henry IV,* which went through six quarto

editions between 1598 and 1622, *2 Henry IV* was not reprinted until it appeared in the First Folio of 1623. Whether it was originally conceived as an afterthought, designed to capitalize upon the great success of its predecessor, or whether Shakespeare had planned from the start two plays on the reign of Henry IV is a point on which authorities differ. In either case the two plays constitute a dramatic entity. When read consecutively, they tell a unified and dramatically satisfying story.

For the principal events and the broad character outlines of the historical personages in the Henry IV plays, Shakespeare drew chiefly upon one of his favorite books – Raphael Holinshed's *Chronicles of the History of England.* He also levied to a certain extent upon other sources. He may have taken a hint or two from the chronicles of Edward Hall and John Stow. Some details of the exploits of the unregenerate Prince Hal he derived from Sir Thomas Elyot's *The Book Named the Governor* and from the old play called *The Famous Victories of Henry V.* In dealing with his source material, Shakespeare worked, here as always in his chronicle plays, as an artist, not as an historian. He telescoped chronology in the interest of compression – the historical period covered in *2 Henry IV* was ten years (1403–13), but the play conveys no impression of this lapse of time. He discarded historical details which were dramatically irrelevant, altered the ages of some of his characters, expanded or suppressed character traits. The result is imperfect history; the modern reader or playgoer derives from the plays only a vague or confused notion of chronology and the order of events. But Shakespeare was not exclusively concerned with what John Drinkwater has called "that vast mutability which is event"; he was concerned also with the wonder of personality and the dramatic interplay of one character with another. And of course with poetry.

In dramatizing the reign of Henry IV, Shakespeare was confronted with the difficulty that the character of the monarch himself was neither winsome nor essentially dramatic. In Richard II, the poet discovered a pathetic, perhaps a tragic figure; Henry IV, despite his grief for the conduct of a wayward son, was neither pathetic nor tragic. Henry V was a military hero; Bolingbroke, despite the victories which won and kept his throne, was not. Moreover, the historical Henry IV did not participate directly in some of the most significant events of the reign. Hence Shakespeare did not attempt to make the king the pivotal figure of the action. He wisely chose to focus much of our attention upon other characters. In *1 Henry IV* his problem was the less by reason of the presence in his sources of certain historical personages of indubitable dramatic value. Prince Hal, the rhapsodic Glendower, the madcap

Harry Percy and his charming wife Kate – these could be developed on the stage as vital figures. Especially Hotspur, whose reckless dedication to his cause made him an admirable foil to the apparently dissolute Hal. The contrast and conflict between the two Harry's becomes the most dramatic element in the play, overshadowing the father-son situation between king and prince, and the audience feels that the play has reached a suitable climax with the death of Hotspur at Shrewsbury Field.

Even so, however, Shakespeare chose not to rely solely upon the historical personages supplied him by the chroniclers. He invented the character of Falstaff, perhaps the most memorable comic character in the whole range of English fiction. The literary historians have taught us that Shakespeare's Falstaff is the culmination of a long tradition of the braggart soldier in Renaissance drama. No doubt Shakespeare was in some measure indebted to the tradition. But into this *miles gloriosus* he breathed the breath of individual life, and with a stroke of dramatic genius made him the center of a rowdy crew which included the Prince of Wales. Falstaff is a braggart, a liar, a lecher, a drunkard, a scrounger, a thief. But he is more – much more. His triumphant gift for extricating himself from the consequences of his misdoings has understandably endeared him to generations of theatre-goers. It is not surprising that a statue of the gargantuan knight stands among the figures in the grounds of the Memorial Theatre at Stratford, the symbol of Shakespeare's genius for comedy.

In *2 Henry IV*, dealing with events of the last years of Henry's reign, Shakespeare found the historical material less tractable than in *1 Henry IV*. Hotspur and Glendower were gone, the former slain by Prince Hal at Shrewsbury, the latter historically unavailable for the central action. Kate Percy indeed survives to make a fine speech lamenting her mate that's lost and denouncing the pusillanimity of her father-in-law Northumberland. Among the historical personages there remained the king, Prince Hal, the three other sons of the king, and the principal noblemen of the rival factions. With these Shakespeare does the best that he can. He also builds up, with moderate success, the characters of Richard Scroop, Archbishop of York, and the Lord Chief Justice. The former, who played but a minor role in *1 Henry IV*, is here the central figure in the rebellion in the north. He becomes the symbol of one of the political ideas of the play, the dilemma of the subject who, though acknowledging the principle of the divine right of kings, is yet galled by the abuse of power and feels compelled to take action against it. The Chief Justice, too, emerges as a lively personality, wise, humorous, realistic, who serves also as the voice of private decency and public authority to denounce the excesses of Falstaff and the profligacy of the Prince of Wales.

As with the characters, so with the principal dramatic narrative. In *1 Henry IV* there was the heroic action at Shrewsbury, where Prince Hal could speak a valedictory for the dead Hotspur:

> Fare thee well, great heart.
> Ill-weaved ambition, how much art thou shrunk!
> When that this body did contain a spirit,
> A kingdom for it was too small a bound;
> But now two paces of the vilest earth
> Is room enough. This earth that bears thee dead
> Bears not alive so stout a gentleman.

The later years of Henry's reign saw no such gallantry as this. Instead there was the bloodless, treacherous betrayal of the rebels at Gaultree Forest, which can end with nothing more heroic than Prince John of Lancaster's

> Strike up our drums, pursue the scattered stray.
> God, and not we, hath safely fought to-day.
> Some guard these traitors to the block of death,
> Treason's true bed and yielder up of breath.

Apart from this, Shakespeare's historical sources provided him with little material more dramatic than reports on the progress of the wars, debates concerning policy and strategy, and the like. On the historical side, the high moments of the play come at the end of Act IV and in Act V, with the portrayal of the old king on his deathbed, his final unscrupulous advice to the Prince of Wales concerning foreign wars, his death, and the coronation and transformation of the new king.

It is not surprising that Shakespeare, thus confronted with a paucity of truly dramatic history, develops his non-historical personages and situations to the extent that they dominate the play. It has often been pointed out that in *1 Henry IV* the proportion of the historical plot to the Falstaff story is 1649 lines to 1305, or roughly 5 to 4. In *2 Henry IV* the proportion has become 1422 lines to 1760, almost the precise reverse. Even without such statistics to guide him, the reader or playgoer is well aware that in this play Falstaff is the central figure. He overshadows the king and Hal, and his cronies overshadow the noble personages in the play. The Falstaff of most of the action of *2 Henry IV* is quite the equal of the Falstaff of *1 Henry IV*. We may say of him, as he says of himself, "The brain of this foolish compounded clay-man is not able to invent anything that intends to laughter more than I invent or is invented on me. I am not only witty in myself, but the cause that wit is in other men."

But Shakespeare has here done more than sustain and enlarge the Falstaff of the earlier play. He has also developed and individualized the characters of Falstaff's boon companions, and from a mere sketch in one scene in *1 Henry IV* he has created the memorable comic figure of Mistress Quickly, hostess of a tavern which tradition (but not Shakespeare, save for the merest hint – "Doth the old boar feed in the old frank?") identifies with the Boar's Head, which in Shakespeare's time (but not in Henry's) stood hard by the parish church of St Michael in Eastcheap. Mistress Quickly, a forebear of Mrs Malaprop, has been guilty of most of the amiable sins, but she is redeemed by simplicity and kindness of heart.

Apart from these, Shakespeare in this play invents four comic personages who had no existence in the earlier play – swaggering Pistol, Doll Tearsheet, a lady of joy, and the country justices Shallow and Silence. Modern audiences may find the rantings of Pistol tiresome and the love passages between Doll and Falstaff tasteless. But the two justices remain as entertaining to-day as they were on Shakespeare's stage – Shallow garrulous and gullible, Silence with his weakness for wine and his snatches of old songs. Generations of scholars have seen in the comic figure of Shallow a lampoon on some justice of the peace of Shakespeare's acquaintance. Identifications have ranged from Sir Thomas Lucy of Charlecote, near Stratford, on whose preserves, according to unsupported tradition, the youthful Shakespeare was involved in a poaching escapade, to William Gardiner, justice of the peace in the county of Surrey, with whom Shakespeare quarrelled in 1596. None of the identifications convinces a judicious mind. But the richness of the Gloucestershire local color against which Shallow is portrayed and the particularity of his fictitious recollections of his student days at Clement's Inn go far to explain the persistent belief that Shakespeare drew Shallow from the life.

In assigning to Falstaff a dominant role in the Henry IV plays and bringing him into close association with Prince Hal, Shakespeare created for himself the problem of disposing of Falstaff after the prince had become king. In the end, Shakespeare causes the new king to reject Falstaff summarily:

> I know thee not, old man. Fall to thy prayers.
> How ill white hairs become a fool and jester!
> I have long dreamed of such a kind of man,
> So surfeit-swelled, so old, and so profane,
> But, being awaked, I do despise my dream.

Our sympathy goes out to Falstaff; his "Master Shallow, I owe you a thousand pound" has for us a poignancy which Shakespeare did not intend. Yet we cannot deny the necessity for the rejection. A play portraying the victories of Henry V was in the offing. Obviously the hero of Agincourt could not continue to consort with Falstaff and his crew. As a concession to Fat Jack's popularity with the audience, the Epilogue to the present play promises that Sir John will appear in the sequel. But he does not appear. We hear only the Hostess's account of his passage to "Arthur's bosom," and Pistol's muted epitaph, "Falstaff he is dead, / And we must earn [grieve] therefore."

No element in *2 Henry IV* has provoked more critical comment than the rejection of Falstaff. Most commentators have found it in their hearts to wish that the playwright had been able to dispose of old Jack in some way which would have permitted us to feel a greater admiration for the regenerate Hal. But an attentive reading will disclose the fact that Shakespeare has prepared us for the rejection. Nowhere in this play do we see Falstaff and the prince in the same kind of intimacy which marked their relationship in *1 Henry IV*. Indeed, except for the rejection scene they are together just once, in the tavern scene in which Falstaff, as in the famous Gad's Hill episode of *1 Henry IV*, is the victim of a princely joke. But the Gad's Hill episode ended on a note of friendly banter; here there is no banter. The prince's last words are

> By heaven, Poins, I feel me much to blame,
> So idly to profane the precious time....
> Give me my sword and cloak. Falstaff, good night.

We have been warned of what is to follow. We need not condemn Hal too severely. Good judgment would have taught Falstaff that the laws of England would *not* be at his commandment after the death of the old king, and delicacy would have forbidden him to obtrude himself so abruptly into Hal's new situation. But good judgment and delicacy were not among Falstaff's qualities. It is Falstaff, not the prince, who compels the rejection.

Falstaff has provoked roars of laughter from the theatregoers of almost four centuries. Usually it is the Falstaff of *1 Henry IV* who is presented on the stage. Occasionally, from Betterton's time to our own, actors and producers have ventured to condense both parts into a single play of manageable proportions. *2 Henry IV* is less frequently presented as a separate play and in its entirety. However, on those occasions when it is, audiences find the experience delightful, and critics are impressed anew with Shakespeare's skill in mounting history upon the stage.

University of Pennsylvania   ALLAN G. CHESTER

NOTE ON THE TEXT

The present edition is based on the quarto of 1600, which is believed to have been printed from Shakespeare's own manuscript and to supply a better text than the folio, although that of the latter is fuller. The list of characters has been added from the folio text, as well as certain passages evidently omitted from the quarto because they dwell at length upon the censorable subject of civil rebellion. (These are the bracketed lines, I, i, 166–79, 189–209; I, iii, 21–24, 36–55, 85–108; II, iii, 23–45; IV, i, 55–79, 103–39.) The quarto is not divided into acts and scenes, and the division here indicated marginally is that of the folio text, except that in the latter the first act contains five scenes owing to the Induction's being counted as a separate scene, and the fourth act contains only two scenes. The wording of the stage directions of the quarto has been retained, but the names of four characters who neither speak nor are referred to in the dialogue have been eliminated: "Fauconbridge" in the opening stage direction at I, iii; "Sir John Russell" in that at II, ii; "Bardolph" in that at IV, i; and "Kent" in that at IV, iv. In V, iv, "Sincklo" (presumably the actor taking the part) has been emended to "Beadle." Listed below are substantive departures from the quarto text, including additions from the folio other than those mentioned above. The adopted reading is given in italics followed by the quarto reading in roman.

The Actors' Names (printed at the end of the play in F)
Ind. *Induction* (i.e. the heading, F; omitted in Q) 35 *hold* (Theobald) hole (F; passage not in Q)
I, i, 126 *Too* (F) so 161 *Travers* (Capell) Umfr. 164 *Lean on your* (F) leaue on you 178 *brought* (F2) bring (F; passage not in Q) 183 *ventured,...proposed* (Capell) ventured...proposde,
I, ii, 19 *fledged* (F) fledge 35 *rascally* (F) rascal! 46 *Where's Bardolph?* (F; follows 'through it' in line above in Q) 47 *into* (F) in 92 *age* (F) an ague 114 *Falstaff* (F) Old. 161 *bear-herd* (F) Berod 165 *them, are* (F) the one 192–93 *and Prince Harry* (F; omitted in Q)
I, iii, 28 *on* (F) and 66 *a* (F) so, 79 *He...Welsh* (F) French and Welch he leaues his back vnarmde, they 109 *Mowbray* (F) Bish.
II, i, 14 *and that* (F; omitted in Q) 21 *vice* (F) view 25 *continuantly* (F) continually 76 *Fie!* (F; omitted in Q) 158 s.d. (follows line 155 in Q) 162 *Basingstoke* (F) Billingsgate

II, ii, 15 *viz.* (F) with 21 *thy* (F) the *made a shift to* (F; omitted in Q) 77 *new* (F; omitted in Q) 80 *rabbit* (F) rabble 107 *borrower's* (Warburton) borrowed 122 *familiars* (F) family
II, iii, 11 *endeared* (F) endeere
II, iv, 12–13 *Dispatch...straight* (F; assigned to 'Dra.' in Q) 13 s.d. (follows line 17 in Q) 14 *3. Drawer* (Alexander) 2 Drawer (F) Francis (Q) 20 *2. Drawer* (F) Francis 106 *shall* (F) shall not 159 *Die* (F; omitted in Q) 202 *Ah* (F) a 205 *Ah,* (F) a 300 *him* (F) thee
III, ii, 25 *This...cousin* (F) Coosin, this sir Iohn 53 *[Shallow]...gentlemen* (F; assigned to 'Silence' in Q) 107 *Falstaff. Prick him* (F; printed as s.d. 'Iohn prickes him' after line 106 in Q) 131 *to* (F; omitted in Q) 186–87 *no more of that* (F; omitted in Q) 198 *Clement's Inn* (F) Clemham 216 *old* (F; omitted in Q) 277 *Master Shallow* (F; omitted in Q)
IV, i, 30 *Then, my lord,* (F; omitted in Q) 34 *rags* (F) rage 139 *indeed* (Theobald) and did (F; passage not in Q)
IV, ii, s.d. (follows IV, i, 226 in Q) 8 *man* (F) man talking 24 *Employ* (F) Imply 97 s.d. (follows line 96 in Q) 117 *and...yours* (F; omitted in Q) 122 *these traitors* (F) this traitour
IV, iii, 2 *I pray* (F; omitted in Q) 40 *their* (Q catchword) there 41 *Caesar* (Theobald) cosin 77–82 (printed as prose in Q) 80 *pray,* (F; omitted in Q)
IV, iv, 32 *meting* (F) meeting 52 *Canst...that?* (F; omitted in Q) 94 *heaven* (F) heavens 104 *write* (F) wet *letters* (F) termes 132 *Softly, pray* (F; omitted in Q)
IV, v, 13 *altered* (F) uttred 49 *How...grace?* (F; omitted in Q) 75 *The virtuous sweets* (F; omitted in Q) 81 *hath* (F) hands 107 *Which* (F) Whom 160 *worst of* (F) worse then 177 *O my son,* (F; omitted in Q)
V, i, 21 *the other day* (F; omitted in Q) *Hinckley* (F) Hunkley 43 *but a very* (F; omitted in Q)
V, ii, s.d. ('duke Humphrey, Thomas Clarence, Prince John, Westmerland' also listed in Q)
V, iii, 17–22, 32–36, 44–46, 51–52, 71–73, 90–94, 97–104, 113–17, 124–25, 137–38 (printed as prose in Q)
V, iv, 5 *enough* (F; omitted in Q) 6 *lately* (F; omitted in Q) 11 *He* (F) I
V, v, 5 *Robert* (F; omitted in Q) 15 *Shallow* (F) Pist. 17, 19 *Shallow* (Hanmer) Pist. 29 *all* (F; omitted in Q) 31–38 (printed as prose in Q)
Epi. 29–30 *and...queen* (F; follows line 14 in Q)

THE SECOND PART OF
KING HENRY THE FOURTH

THE ACTORS' NAMES

Rumor, the Presenter
King Henry the Fourth
Prince Henry, afterwards crowned King Henry the Fifth
Prince John of Lancaster ⎤
Humphrey of Gloucester ⎬ sons to Henry IV and
Thomas of Clarence ⎦ brethren to Henry V
[Earl of] Northumberland
[Richard Scroop] the Archbishop of York
[Lord] Mowbray
[Lord] Hastings ⎱ opposites
Lord Bardolph ⎰ against King
Travers ⎱ Henry IV
Morton
[Sir John] Coleville
[Earl of] Warwick
[Earl of] Westmoreland
[Earl of] Surrey
[Sir John Blunt]
Gower ⎬ of the King's party
Harcourt
Lord Chief Justice
[His Servant]

[Robert] Shallow ⎱ both country justices
Silence ⎰
Davy, servant to Shallow
Fang and Snare, two sergeants
[Ralph] Mouldy ⎤
[Simon] Shadow ⎥
[Thomas] Wart ⎬ country soldiers
[Francis] Feeble ⎥
[Peter] Bullcalf ⎦
Poins
[Sir John] Falstaff ⎤
Bardolph ⎥
Pistol ⎬ irregular humorists
Peto ⎥
[Falstaff's] Page ⎦
Northumberland's Wife
Percy's Widow [Lady Percy]
Hostess Quickly
Doll Tearsheet
[A Dancer as] Epilogue
[Francis and other] Drawers, Beadle [and other Officers],
    Grooms [, Porter, Messenger, Soldiers, Lords, Attendants]

[Scene: England]

*

Ind.   INDUCTION

Enter Rumor, painted full of tongues.

RUMOR
Open your ears, for which of you will stop
The vent of hearing when loud Rumor speaks?
I, from the orient to the drooping west,
4   Making the wind my post-horse, still unfold
The acts commencèd on this ball of earth.
Upon my tongues continual slanders ride,
The which in every language I pronounce,
Stuffing the ears of men with false reports.
I speak of peace while covert enmity
Under the smile of safety wounds the world.
And who but Rumor, who but only I,
Make fearful musters and prepared defense

Whiles the big year, swoln with some other grief,
Is thought with child by the stern tyrant war,
And no such matter? Rumor is a pipe   15
Blown by surmises, jealousies, conjectures,   16
And of so easy and so plain a stop   17
That the blunt monster with uncounted heads, 18
The still-discordant wavering multitude,
Can play upon it. But what need I thus
My well-known body to anatomize
Among my household? Why is Rumor here?   22
I run before King Harry's victory,
Who in a bloody field by Shrewsbury
Hath beaten down young Hotspur and his troops, 25
Quenching the flame of bold rebellion
Even with the rebels' blood. But what mean I
To speak so true at first? My office is   28
To noise about that Harry Monmouth fell   29
Under the wrath of noble Hotspur's sword,
And that the king before the Douglas' rage
Stooped his anointed head as low as death.   32
This have I rumored through the peasant towns 33
Between that royal field of Shrewsbury
And this worm-eaten hold of ragged stone,   35
Where Hotspur's father, old Northumberland,

Ind. 4 *still* ever 15 *pipe* wind instrument 16 *jealousies* suspicions 17
of . . . stop whose stops are so easily played upon 18 *blunt* stupid 22 *my
household* i.e. the audience 25 *Hotspur* Harry Percy, killed by the Prince
of Wales at Shrewsbury 28 *office* function 29 *Harry Monmouth* the
Prince of Wales (Prince Hal) 32 *Stooped . . . death* was mortally wounded
33 *peasant towns* villages 35 *hold* stronghold (Warkworth Castle, seat of
the Earl of Northumberland, where the action of the next scene occurs)

37 Lies crafty-sick. The posts come tiring on,
And not a man of them brings other news
Than they have learned of me. From Rumor's tongues
They bring smooth comforts false, worse than true
wrongs.   *Exit Rumor.*

I, i   *Enter the Lord Bardolph at one door.*

LORD BARDOLPH
Who keeps the gate here, ho?
   [Enter the Porter.]   Where is the earl?

PORTER
What shall I say you are?

LORD BARDOLPH   Tell thou the earl
That the Lord Bardolph doth attend him here.

PORTER
His lordship is walked forth into the orchard.
Please it your honor, knock but at the gate,
And he himself will answer.
   Enter the Earl of Northumberland.

LORD BARDOLPH   Here comes the earl.
                         [Exit Porter.]

NORTHUMBERLAND
What news, Lord Bardolph? Every minute now
Should be the father of some stratagem.
The times are wild. Contention, like a horse
Full of high feeding, madly hath broke loose
And bears down all before him.

LORD BARDOLPH   Noble earl,
I bring you certain news from Shrewsbury.

NORTHUMBERLAND
13 Good, an God will!

LORD BARDOLPH   As good as heart can wish.
The king is almost wounded to the death;
And, in the fortune of my lord your son,
Prince Harry slain outright; and both the Blunts
Killed by the hand of Douglas. Young Prince John
And Westmoreland and Stafford fled the field;
19 And Harry Monmouth's brawn, the hulk Sir John,
Is prisoner to your son. O, such a day,
So fought, so followed, and so fairly won,
Came not till now to dignify the times
23 Since Caesar's fortunes!

NORTHUMBERLAND   How is this derived?
Saw you the field? Came you from Shrewsbury?

LORD BARDOLPH
I spake with one, my lord, that came from thence,
A gentleman well bred and of good name,
That freely rendered me these news for true.

NORTHUMBERLAND
Here comes my servant Travers, whom I sent
On Tuesday last to listen after news.
   Enter Travers.

LORD BARDOLPH
30 My lord, I overrode him on the way,
And he is furnished with no certainties
32 More than he haply may retail from me.

NORTHUMBERLAND
Now, Travers, what good tidings comes with you?

TRAVERS
My lord, Sir John Umfrevile turned me back
With joyful tidings, and, being better horsed,
Outrode me. After him came spurring hard
37 A gentleman, almost forspent with speed,

That stopped by me to breathe his bloodied horse.
He asked the way to Chester, and of him
I did demand what news from Shrewsbury.
He told me that rebellion had bad luck
And that young Harry Percy's spur was cold.
With that, he gave his able horse the head,
And bending forward struck his armèd heels
Against the panting sides of his poor jade
Up to the rowel-head, and starting so
He seemed in running to devour the way,
Staying no longer question.   48

NORTHUMBERLAND   Ha! Again.
Said he young Harry Percy's spur was cold?
Of Hotspur Coldspur? That rebellion
Had met ill luck?

LORD BARDOLPH   My lord, I'll tell you what.
If my young lord your son have not the day,
Upon mine honor, for a silken point   53
I'll give my barony. Never talk of it.

NORTHUMBERLAND
Why should that gentleman that rode by Travers
Give then such instances of loss?

LORD BARDOLPH   Who, he?
He was some hilding fellow that had stolen   57
The horse he rode on, and, upon my life,
Spoke at a venture. Look, here comes more news.
   Enter Morton.

NORTHUMBERLAND
Yea, this man's brow, like to a title-leaf,   60
Foretells the nature of a tragic volume.
So looks the strand whereon the imperious flood
Hath left a witnessed usurpation.   63
Say, Morton, didst thou come from Shrewsbury?

MORTON
I ran from Shrewsbury, my noble lord,
Where hateful death put on his ugliest mask
To fright our party.

NORTHUMBERLAND   How doth my son and brother?
Thou tremblest, and the whiteness in thy cheek
Is apter than thy tongue to tell thy errand.
Even such a man, so faint, so spiritless,
So dull, so dead in look, so woebegone,
Drew Priam's curtain in the dead of night,   72
And would have told him half his Troy was burnt.
But Priam found the fire ere he his tongue,
And I my Percy's death ere thou report'st it.
This thou wouldst say, 'Your son did thus and thus;
Your brother thus. So fought the noble Douglas' –
Stopping my greedy ear with their bold deeds.   78
But in the end, to stop my ear indeed,
Thou hast a sigh to blow away this praise,
Ending with 'Brother, son, and all are dead.'

MORTON
Douglas is living, and your brother, yet;
But, for my lord your son –

NORTHUMBERLAND   Why, he is dead.
See what a ready tongue suspicion hath!

37 *crafty-sick* feigning sickness; *tiring on* riding until exhausted
I, i Before Northumberland's castle (at Warkworth) 13 *an if* 19 *brawn*
swine (referring to Falstaff's size and habits) 23 *fortunes* successes 30
overrode overtook 32 *haply* perhaps 37 *forspent* exhausted 48 *Staying*
waiting for 53 *point* lace for tying the breeches 57 *hilding* worthless
60 *title-leaf* title page 63 *a witnessed usurpation* evidences of its destruction
72 *Priam* king of Troy 78 *Stopping* filling

He that but fears the thing he would not know
Hath by instinct knowledge from others' eyes
That what he feared is chancèd. Yet speak, Morton.
Tell thou an earl his divination lies,
And I will take it as a sweet disgrace
And make thee rich for doing me such wrong.

MORTON
You are too great to be by me gainsaid.
Your spirit is too true, your fears too certain.

NORTHUMBERLAND
93 Yet, for all this, say not that Percy 's dead.
I see a strange confession in thine eye.
Thou shakest thy head and hold'st it fear or sin
To speak a truth. If he be slain, say so.
The tongue offends not that reports his death;
And he doth sin that doth belie the dead,
Not he which says the dead is not alive.
Yet the first bringer of unwelcome news
101 Hath but a losing office, and his tongue
Sounds ever after as a sullen bell,
Remem'red tolling a departing friend.

LORD BARDOLPH
I cannot think, my lord, your son is dead.

MORTON
I am sorry I should force you to believe
That which I would to God I had not seen.
But these mine eyes saw him in bloody state,
108 Rendering faint quittance, wearied and outbreathed,
To Harry Monmouth, whose swift wrath beat down
The never-daunted Percy to the earth,
From whence with life he never more sprung up.
112 In few, his death, whose spirit lent a fire
Even to the dullest peasant in his camp,
114 Being bruited once, took fire and heat away
From the best-tempered courage in his troops.
For from his metal was his party steeled,
Which once in him abated, all the rest
Turned on themselves, like dull and heavy lead.
And as the thing that's heavy in itself,
Upon enforcement flies with greatest speed,
So did our men, heavy in Hotspur's loss,
Lend to this weight such lightness with their fear
That arrows fled not swifter toward their aim
Than did our soldiers, aiming at their safety,
Fly from the field. Then was that noble Worcester
Too soon ta'en prisoner; and that furious Scot,
The bloody Douglas, whose well-laboring sword
128 Had three times slain the appearance of the king,
129 'Gan vail his stomach and did grace the shame
Of those that turned their backs, and in his flight,
Stumbling in fear, was took. The sum of all
Is that the king hath won, and hath sent out
A speedy power to encounter you, my lord,

Under the conduct of young Lancaster
And Westmoreland. This is the news at full.

NORTHUMBERLAND
For this I shall have time enough to mourn.
In poison there is physic; and these news,
Having been well, that would have made me sick,
Being sick, have in some measure made me well.
And as the wretch whose fever-weakened joints,
Like strengthless hinges, buckle under life,
Impatient of his fit, breaks like a fire
Out of his keeper's arms, even so my limbs,
Weakened with grief, being now enraged with grief, 144
Are thrice themselves. Hence, therefore, thou nice 145
   crutch!
A scaly gauntlet now with joints of steel
Must glove this hand. And hence, thou sickly quoif! 147
Thou art a guard too wanton for the head 148
Which princes, fleshed with conquest, aim to hit. 149
Now bind my brows with iron, and approach
The ragged'st hour that time and spite dare bring 151
To frown upon the enraged Northumberland!
Let heaven kiss earth! Now let not Nature's hand
Keep the wild flood confined! Let order die!
And let this world no longer be a stage
To feed contention in a lingering act.
But let one spirit of the first-born Cain 157
Reign in all bosoms, that, each heart being set
On bloody courses, the rude scene may end,
And darkness be the burier of the dead!

[TRAVERS]
This strainèd passion doth you wrong, my lord. 161

LORD BARDOLPH
Sweet earl, divorce not wisdom from your honor.

MORTON
The lives of all your loving complices
Lean on your health, the which, if you give o'er
To stormy passion, must perforce decay.
[You cast the event of war, my noble lord, 166
And summed the account of chance, before you said,
'Let us make head.' It was your presurmise 168
That, in the dole of blows, your son might drop. 169
You knew he walked o'er perils, on an edge,
More likely to fall in than to get o'er.
You were advised his flesh was capable 172
Of wounds and scars and that his forward spirit
Would lift him where most trade of danger ranged.
Yet did you say, 'Go forth.' And none of this,
Though strongly apprehended, could restrain
The stiff-borne action. What hath then befallen, 177
Or what hath this bold enterprise brought forth,
More than that being which was like to be?] 179

LORD BARDOLPH
We all that are engagèd to this loss 180
Knew that we ventured on such dangerous seas
That if we wrought out life 'twas ten to one.
And yet we ventured, for the gain proposed
Choked the respect of likely peril feared. 184
And since we are o'erset, venture again.
Come, we will all put forth, body and goods.

MORTON
'Tis more than time. And, my most noble lord,
I hear for certain, and dare speak the truth,
[The gentle Archbishop of York is up 189
With well-appointed powers. He is a man

93 for in spite of   **101** losing office thankless task   **108** faint quittance weak
return of blows   **112** In few in few words   **114** bruited reported   **128** the
appearance . . . king noblemen disguised as the king   **129** 'Gan . . . stomach
began to let his courage fail; grace excuse   **144** grief . . . grief pain . . . sorrow
145 nice effeminate   **147** quoif nightcap (or bandage)   **148** wanton trifling
149 fleshed aroused, as a dog is aroused from feeding on raw meat   **151**
ragged'st roughest   **157** spirit . . . Cain i.e. spirit of murder   **161** strainèd
passion outburst of feeling   **166** cast the event calculated the consequences
168 make head raise an army   **169** dole chance distribution   **172** advised
aware   **177** stiff-borne obstinately carried out   **179** More . . . be more than
the event which you knew was a possibility   **180** engaged to involved in
184 respect consideration   **189–90** is up . . . powers has taken the field with a
well-equipped army

Who with a double surety binds his followers.
192 My lord your son had only but the corpse,
But shadows and the shows of men, to fight.
For that same word 'rebellion' did divide
The action of their bodies from their souls,
And they did fight with queasiness, constrained,
As men drink potions, that their weapons only
Seemed on our side. But for their spirits and souls,
This word 'rebellion,' it had froze them up,
As fish are in a pond. But now the bishop
Turns insurrection to religion.
Supposed sincere and holy in his thoughts,
He's followed both with body and with mind,
204 And doth enlarge his rising with the blood
205 Of fair King Richard, scraped from Pomfret stones;
206 Derives from heaven his quarrel and his cause;
Tells them he doth bestride a bleeding land,
208 Gasping for life under great Bolingbroke;
209 And more and less do flock to follow him.]
NORTHUMBERLAND
I knew of this before; but, to speak truth,
This present grief had wiped it from my mind.
Go in with me, and counsel every man
The aptest way for safety and revenge.
214 Get posts and letters, and make friends with speed.
Never so few, and never yet more need.   *Exeunt.*

*

I, ii   *Enter Sir John [Falstaff] alone, with his Page*
        bearing his sword and buckler.
FALSTAFF Sirrah, you giant, what says the doctor to my
2 water?
PAGE He said, sir, the water itself was a good healthy
4 water; but, for the party that owed it, he might have
5 moe diseases than he knew for.
6 FALSTAFF Men of all sorts take a pride to gird at me. The
brain of this foolish compounded clay-man is not able
to invent anything that intends to laughter more than I
invent or is invented on me. I am not only witty in myself, but the cause that wit is in other men. I do here walk
before thee like a sow that hath overwhelmed all her
litter but one. If the prince put thee into my service for
any other reason than to set me off, why then I have no
14 judgment. Thou whoreson mandrake, thou art fitter to
be worn in my cap than to wait at my heels. I was never
16 manned with an agate till now. But I will inset you
neither in gold nor silver, but in vile apparel, and send
18 you back again to your master, for a jewel – the juvenal,
19 the prince your master, whose chin is not yet fledged. I
will sooner have a beard grow in the palm of my hand
than he shall get one off his cheek, and yet he will not
22 stick to say his face is a face-royal. God may finish it
when he will, 'tis not a hair amiss yet. He may keep it
24 still at a face-royal, for a barber shall never earn sixpence
25 out of it; and yet he'll be crowing as if he had writ man
ever since his father was a bachelor. He may keep his
27 own grace, but he's almost out of mine, I can assure
him. What said Master Dombledon about the satin for
29 my short cloak and my slops?
PAGE He said, sir, you should procure him better as-
31 surance than Bardolph. He would not take his band and
yours; he liked not the security.
33 FALSTAFF Let him be damned, like the glutton! Pray

God his tongue be hotter! A whoreson Achitophel! A 34
rascally yea-forsooth knave! To bear a gentleman in 35
hand, and then stand upon security! The whoreson
smooth-pates do now wear nothing but high shoes, and 37
bunches of keys at their girdles; and if a man is through 38
with them in honest taking up, then they must stand
upon security. I had as lief they would put ratsbane in
my mouth as offer to stop it with security. I looked 'a 41
should have sent me two-and-twenty yards of satin, as I
am a true knight, and he sends me security. Well, he
may sleep in security, for he hath the horn of abundance, 44
and the lightness of his wife shines through it. And yet
cannot he see, though he have his own lanthorn to light 46
him. Where's Bardolph?
PAGE He's gone into Smithfield to buy your worship a 47
horse.
FALSTAFF I bought him in Paul's, and he'll buy me a 49
horse in Smithfield. An I could get me but a wife in the
stews, I were manned, horsed, and wived. 51
        Enter Lord Chief Justice [and Servant].
PAGE Sir, here comes the nobleman that committed the 52
prince for striking him about Bardolph.
FALSTAFF Wait close; I will not see him. 54
CHIEF JUSTICE What's he that goes there?
SERVANT Falstaff, an't please your lordship.
CHIEF JUSTICE He that was in question for the robbery? 57
SERVANT He, my lord. But he hath since done good ser-
vice at Shrewsbury, and, as I hear, is now going with
some charge to the Lord John of Lancaster.
CHIEF JUSTICE What, to York? Call him back again.
SERVANT Sir John Falstaff!
FALSTAFF Boy, tell him I am deaf.
PAGE You must speak louder; my master is deaf.
CHIEF JUSTICE I am sure he is, to the hearing of any-
thing good. Go, pluck him by the elbow; I must speak
with him.
SERVANT Sir John!
FALSTAFF What! A young knave, and begging! Is there 69
not wars? Is there not employment? Doth not the king
lack subjects? Do not the rebels need soldiers? Though
it be a shame to be on any side but one, it is worse shame

192 *only . . . corpse* only the bodies of men whose hearts were not in the
fight 204 *enlarge his rising* extend the significance of his revolt 205
Pomfret Pomfret Castle, where Richard II was murdered 206 *Derives
from heaven* gives a religious significance to 208 *Bolingbroke* Henry IV
209 *more and less* high and low 214 *make* collect
I, ii A London street 2 *water* urine 4 *owed* owned 5 *moe* more 6 *gird*
jeer 14 *mandrake* a root popularly supposed to resemble a man 16
manned . . . agate served by a man as small as a carved agate stone 18
juvenal young man 19 *fledged* covered with down 22, 24 *face-royal* a pun
centering around a coin, the royal (worth 10s.), with the king's face stamped
on it 25 *writ man* attained manhood 27 *grace* (1) title of address ('your
grace'), (2) favor 29 *slops* wide breeches 31 *Bardolph* one of Falstaff's
cronies, not to be confused with Lord Bardolph; *band* bond 33 *glutton*
i.e. Dives, referred to in Luke xvi, 24 34 *Achitophel* the adviser of Absalom
(2 Samuel xv-xvii) 35-36 *bear . . . in hand* encourage 37 *smooth-pates*
city tradesmen, who wore their hair short 37-38 *high shoes . . . keys*
(tokens of prosperity and rank) 38-40 *if . . . security* if a man has ordered a
suit of clothes on promise of future payment, they demand security before
making delivery 41 *'a* he 44 *horn of abundance* the horn of the cuckold
46 *lanthorn* lantern (the pun is that the wife's lightness shines in the
cuckold's horn) 47 *Smithfield* a famous market 49 *Paul's* St Paul's
Cathedral (the nave of which was often used as a labor exchange) 51 *stews*
brothels; *manned . . . wived* (the sense is that a man who gets his horse at
Smithfield, his servant at Paul's, and his wife in the stews will get a poor
bargain in each case) 52 *committed* committed to prison (see V, ii, 70n.)
54 *close* close by 57 *in question* under judicial examination 69 *knave*
boy

to beg than to be on the worst side, were it worse than the name of rebellion can tell how to make it.

75 SERVANT You mistake me, sir.

FALSTAFF Why, sir, did I say you were an honest man? Setting my knighthood and my soldiership aside, I had lied in my throat if I had said so.

SERVANT I pray you, sir, then set your knighthood and your soldiership aside and give me leave to tell you you lie in your throat if you say I am any other than an honest man.

82 FALSTAFF I give thee leave to tell me so! I lay aside that which grows to me! If thou get'st any leave of me, hang me; if thou tak'st leave, thou wert better be hanged. You 85 hunt counter. Hence! Avaunt!

SERVANT Sir, my lord would speak with you.

CHIEF JUSTICE Sir John Falstaff, a word with you.

FALSTAFF My good lord! God give your lordship good time of day. I am glad to see your lordship abroad. I heard say your lordship was sick. I hope your lordship 91 goes abroad by advice. Your lordship, though not clean past your youth, have yet some smack of age in you, some relish of the saltness of time in you; and I most humbly beseech your lordship to have a reverent care of your health.

CHIEF JUSTICE Sir John, I sent for you before your expedition to Shrewsbury.

FALSTAFF An't please your lordship, I hear his majesty is returned with some discomfort from Wales.

CHIEF JUSTICE I talk not of his majesty. You would not come when I sent for you.

FALSTAFF And I hear, moreover, his highness is fallen into this same whoreson apoplexy.

CHIEF JUSTICE Well, God mend him! I pray you, let me speak with you.

FALSTAFF This apoplexy, as I take it, is a kind of lethargy, an't please your lordship, a kind of sleeping in the blood, a whoreson tingling.

CHIEF JUSTICE What tell you me of it? Be it as it is.

109 FALSTAFF It hath it original from much grief, from study and perturbation of the brain. I have read the cause of 111 his effects in Galen. It is a kind of deafness.

CHIEF JUSTICE I think you are fallen into the disease, for you hear not what I say to you.

FALSTAFF Very well, my lord, very well. Rather, an't please you, it is the disease of not listening, the malady of not marking, that I am troubled withal.

117 CHIEF JUSTICE To punish you by the heels would

amend the attention of your ears, and I care not if I do become your physician.

FALSTAFF I am as poor as Job, my lord, but not so patient. Your lordship may minister the potion of im- prisonment to me in respect of poverty; but how I 122 should be your patient to follow your prescriptions, the wise may make some dram of a scruple, or indeed a 124 scruple itself.

CHIEF JUSTICE I sent for you, when there were matters against you for your life, to come speak with me.   126

FALSTAFF As I was then advised by my learned counsel in the laws of this land-service, I did not come.   128

CHIEF JUSTICE Well, the truth is, Sir John, you live in great infamy.

FALSTAFF He that buckles himself in my belt cannot live in less.

CHIEF JUSTICE Your means are very slender and your waste is great.

FALSTAFF I would it were otherwise. I would my means were greater and my waist slenderer.

CHIEF JUSTICE You have misled the youthful prince.

FALSTAFF The young prince hath misled me. I am the fellow with the great belly, and he my dog.

CHIEF JUSTICE Well, I am loath to gall a new-healed 140 wound. Your day's service at Shrewsbury hath a little gilded over your night's exploit on Gad's Hill. You may 142 thank the unquiet time for your quiet o'erposting that 143 action.

FALSTAFF My lord?

CHIEF JUSTICE But since all is well, keep it so. Wake not a sleeping wolf.

FALSTAFF To wake a wolf is as bad as smell a fox.   147

CHIEF JUSTICE What! You are as a candle, the better part burnt out.

FALSTAFF A wassail candle, my lord, all tallow. If I did 150 say of wax, my growth would approve the truth.   151

CHIEF JUSTICE There is not a white hair in your face but should have his effect of gravity.   153

FALSTAFF His effect of gravy, gravy, gravy.

CHIEF JUSTICE You follow the young prince up and down like his ill angel.

FALSTAFF Not so, my lord. Your ill angel is light, but I 157 hope he that looks upon me will take me without weighing. And yet, in some respects, I grant, I cannot 159 go. I cannot tell. Virtue is of so little regard in these costermongers' times that true valor is turned bear- 161 herd. Pregnancy is made a tapster, and hath his quick 162 wit wasted in giving reckonings. All the other gifts 163 appertinent to man, as the malice of this age shapes them, are not worth a gooseberry. You that are old consider not the capacities of us that are young; you do measure the heat of our livers with the bitterness of your galls. And we that are in the vaward of our youth, I 168 must confess, are wags too.

CHIEF JUSTICE Do you set down your name in the scroll of youth, that are written down old with all the charac- 170 ters of age? Have you not a moist eye? A dry hand? A yellow cheek? A white beard? A decreasing leg? An increasing belly? Is not your voice broken? Your wind short? Your chin double? Your wit single? And every 174 part about you blasted with antiquity? And will you yet call yourself young? Fie, fie, fie, Sir John!

FALSTAFF My lord, I was born about three of the clock in the afternoon, with a white head and something a

---

75 *mistake* misunderstand 82–83 *that . . . to me* i.e. my knighthood, which is an integral part of myself 85 *counter* in the wrong direction (with play upon 'the Counter,' a debtors' prison) 91 *by advice* i.e. with your physi- cian's approval 109 *it original* its origin 111 *Galen* Greek medical writer of the second century A.D. 117 *by the heels* in the stocks (or in prison) 122 *in respect* by reason 124 *make . . . scruple* hesitate to admit ('dram' and 'scruple' are small weights used by apothecaries) 126 *for your life* for which your life might have been forfeit 128 *land-service* military service 140 *gall* irritate 142 *your . . . on Gad's Hill* (a robbing escapade of Falstaff and the prince; see *I Henry IV*, II) 143 *o'erposting* escape from the con- sequences of 147 *smell a fox* be suspicious 150 *wassail candle* large candle used at feasts 151 *wax* a pun on (1) beeswax, (2) grow 153 *effect* outward sign 157 *ill angel* a clipped coin 159–60 *cannot go* cannot pass for currency 161 *costermongers' times* i.e. materialistic times (a coster- monger is a huckster of apples and other fruits) 162 *Pregnancy* in- tellectual attainment 163 *reckonings* tavern bills 168 *vaward* van- guard 170 *characters* (1) characteristics, (2) letters 174 *single* poor, trivial

179 round belly. For my voice, I have lost it with halloing and singing of anthems. To approve my youth further, I will not. The truth is, I am only old in judgment and
182 understanding; and he that will caper with me for a
183 thousand marks, let him lend me the money, and have at him! For the box of the ear that the prince gave you, he gave it like a rude prince, and you took it like a sensible lord. I have checked him for it, and the young lion repents; marry, not in ashes and sackcloth, but in new
187 silk and old sack.

CHIEF JUSTICE Well, God send the prince a better companion!

FALSTAFF God send the companion a better prince! I cannot rid my hands of him.

CHIEF JUSTICE Well, the king hath severed you and Prince Harry. I hear you are going with Lord John of Lancaster against the archbishop and the Earl of Northumberland.

194 FALSTAFF Yea, I thank your pretty sweet wit for it. But
195 look you pray, all you that kiss my lady Peace at home, that our armies join not in a hot day, for, by the Lord, I take but two shirts out with me, and I mean not to sweat extraordinarily. If it be a hot day, and I brandish any-
199 thing but a bottle, I would I might never spit white again. There is not a dangerous action can peep out his head but I am thrust upon it. Well, I cannot last ever. But it was alway yet the trick of our English nation, if they have a good thing, to make it too common. If ye will needs say I am an old man, you should give me rest. I would to God my name were not so terrible to the enemy as it is. I were better to be eaten to death with a rust than to be scoured to nothing with perpetual motion.

CHIEF JUSTICE Well, be honest, be honest, and God bless your expedition!

FALSTAFF Will your lordship lend me a thousand pound to furnish me forth?

CHIEF JUSTICE Not a penny, not a penny. You are too
213 impatient to bear crosses. Fare you well. Commend me to my cousin Westmoreland.

[Exeunt Chief Justice and Servant.]

215 FALSTAFF If I do, fillip me with a three-man beetle. A man can no more separate age and covetousness than 'a can part young limbs and lechery. But the gout galls the one and the pox pinches the other, and so both the
219 degrees prevent my curses. Boy!

PAGE Sir?

FALSTAFF What money is in my purse?

222 PAGE Seven groats and two pence.

FALSTAFF I can get no remedy against this consumption of the purse. Borrowing only lingers and lingers it out, but the disease is incurable. Go bear this letter to my Lord of Lancaster, this to the prince, this to the Earl of Westmoreland, and this to old Mistress Ursula, whom I have weekly sworn to marry since I perceived the first white hair of my chin. About it. You know where to find me. *[Exit Page.]* A pox of this gout! Or a gout of this pox! For the one or the other plays the rogue with my
232 great toe. 'Tis no matter if I do halt; I have the wars for
233 my color, and my pension shall seem the more reason- able. A good wit will make use of anything. I will turn
235 diseases to commodity. *[Exit.]*

*

Enter the Archbishop, Thomas Mowbray [Earl   I, iii
Marshal], the Lords Hastings and Bardolph.

ARCHBISHOP
Thus have you heard our cause and known our means;
And, my most noble friends, I pray you all,
Speak plainly your opinions of our hopes.
And first, lord marshal, what say you to it?

MOWBRAY
I well allow the occasion of our arms,   5
But gladly would be better satisfied
How in our means we should advance ourselves   7
To look with forehead bold and big enough
Upon the power and puissance of the king.   9

HASTINGS
Our present musters grow upon the file   10
To five-and-twenty thousand men of choice;
And our supplies live largely in the hope   12
Of great Northumberland, whose bosom burns
With an incensèd fire of injuries.

LORD BARDOLPH
The question then, Lord Hastings, standeth thus:
Whether our present five-and-twenty thousand
May hold up head without Northumberland?

HASTINGS
With him, we may.

LORD BARDOLPH   Yea, marry, there's the point.
But if without him we be thought too feeble,
My judgment is, we should not step too far
[Till we had his assistance by the hand.
For in a theme so bloody-faced as this,   22
Conjecture, expectation, and surmise
Of aids incertain should not be admitted.]

ARCHBISHOP
'Tis very true, Lord Bardolph, for indeed
It was young Hotspur's case at Shrewsbury.   26

LORD BARDOLPH
It was, my lord, who lined himself with hope,   27
Eating the air on promise of supply,
Flattering himself in project of a power   29
Much smaller than the smallest of his thoughts,
And so, with great imagination
Proper to madmen, led his powers to death
And winking leaped into destruction.   33

HASTINGS
But, by your leave, it never yet did hurt
To lay down likelihoods and forms of hope.

LORD BARDOLPH
[Yes, if this present quality of war,   36
Indeed the instant action, a cause on foot,
Lives so in hope as in an early spring

179 *halloing* shouting to hounds   182 *caper* compete in a dance   183 *marks* coins worth 13s. 6d. apiece   187 *sack* a Spanish wine   194 *wit* intellect 195 *look you pray* be sure to pray   199 *spit white* (meaning uncertain; in the light of Falstaff's character, the general sense is probably: May I never take another drink)   213 *crosses* (1) afflictions, (2) coins stamped with a cross 215 *fillip* strike; *three-man beetle* ram or pile driver requiring three men to lift it   219 *prevent* anticipate   222 *groats* coins worth 4d. apiece   232 *halt* limp   233 *color* excuse   235 *commodity* profit

I, iii The palace of the Archbishop of York   5 *allow the occasion* admit the justification   7 *in* with   9 *puissance* power   10 *file* roll   12 *supplies* reinforcements   22 *theme* matter   26 *case* situation   27 *lined* reinforced 29–30 *in ... thoughts* in the foolish notion that his army was much larger than it was in fact   33 *winking* shutting his eyes   36–41 (an obscure passage; the sense is: Yes, but in this instance there is harm in over-optimism, just as there is harm in being overhopeful about the buds of early spring and forgetting the possibility of a killing frost)

We see the appearing buds, which to prove fruit,
Hope gives not so much warrant as despair
That frosts will bite them. When we mean to build,
42 We first survey the plot, then draw the model.
43 And when we see the figure of the house,
Then must we rate the cost of the erection,
Which if we find outweighs ability,
What do we then but draw anew the model
47 In fewer offices, or at least desist
To build at all? Much more, in this great work,
Which is almost to pluck a kingdom down
And set another up, should we survey
The plot of situation and the model,
52 Consent upon a sure foundation,
53 Question surveyors, know our own estate,
How able such a work to undergo,
55 To weigh against his opposite. Or else]
56 We fortify in paper and in figures,
Using the names of men instead of men,
Like one that draws the model of a house
Beyond his power to build it, who, half through,
60 Gives o'er and leaves his part-created cost
A naked subject to the weeping clouds
62 And waste for churlish winter's tyranny.

HASTINGS
Grant that our hopes, yet likely of fair birth,
Should be still-born, and that we now possessed
The utmost man of expectation,
I think we are a body strong enough,
Even as we are, to equal with the king.

LORD BARDOLPH
What, is the king but five-and-twenty thousand?

HASTINGS
To us no more, nay, not so much, Lord Bardolph.
For his divisions, as the times do brawl,
Are in three heads: one power against the French,
And one against Glendower, perforce a third
Must take up us. So is the unfirm king
74 In three divided, and his coffers sound
With hollow poverty and emptiness.

ARCHBISHOP
76 That he should draw his several strengths together
And come against us in full puissance
Need not be dreaded.

HASTINGS   If he should do so,
[He leaves his back unarmed, the French and Welsh]
Baying him at the heels. Never fear that.

LORD BARDOLPH
81 Who is it like should lead his forces hither?

HASTINGS
The Duke of Lancaster and Westmoreland.
Against the Welsh, himself and Harry Monmouth.
But who is substituted 'gainst the French,   84
I have no certain notice.

[ARCHBISHOP   Let us on,
And publish the occasion of our arms.
The commonwealth is sick of their own choice;
Their overgreedy love hath surfeited.   88
An habitation giddy and unsure
Hath he that buildeth on the vulgar heart.
O thou fond many, with what loud applause   91
Didst thou beat heaven with blessing Bolingbroke,   92
Before he was what thou wouldst have him be!
And being now trimmed in thine own desires,   94
Thou, beastly feeder, art so full of him
That thou provok'st thyself to cast him up.
So, so, thou common dog, didst thou disgorge
Thy glutton bosom of the royal Richard;
And now thou wouldst eat thy dead vomit up,
And howl'st to find it. What trust is in these times?
They that when Richard lived would have him die
Are now become enamored on his grave.
Thou that threw'st dust upon his goodly head   103
When through proud London he came sighing on
After the admired heels of Bolingbroke
Criest now, 'O earth, yield us that king again,
And take thou this!' O thoughts of men accursed!
Past and to come seems best, things present worst.]

[MOWBRAY]
Shall we go draw our numbers and set on?   109

HASTINGS
We are time's subjects, and time bids be gone. *[Exeunt.]*

               *

Enter Hostess of the Tavern and an Officer or two   II, i
[Fang and another, followed by Snare].

HOSTESS Master Fang, have you entered the action?   1
FANG It is entered.
HOSTESS Where's your yeoman? Is't a lusty yeoman?   3
Will 'a stand to't?
FANG *[to Officer]* Sirrah, where's Snare?
HOSTESS O Lord, ay! Good Master Snare.
SNARE Here, here.
FANG Snare, we must arrest Sir John Falstaff.
HOSTESS Yea, good Master Snare, I have entered him
and all.
SNARE It may chance cost some of us our lives, for he will
stab.
HOSTESS Alas the day! Take heed of him. He stabbed me
in mine own house, and that most beastly. In good
faith, he cares not what mischief he does, if his weapon
be out. He will foin like any devil; he will spare neither   16
man, woman, nor child.
FANG If I can close with him, I care not for his thrust.   18
HOSTESS No, nor I neither. I'll be at your elbow.
FANG An I but fist him once, an 'a come but within my   20
vice—   21
HOSTESS I am undone by his going. I warrant you, he's
an infinitive thing upon my score. Good Master Fang,   23
hold him sure. Good Master Snare, let him not 'scape.
'A comes continuantly to Pie Corner – saving your
manhoods – to buy a saddle; and he is indited to dinner   26
to the Lubber's Head in Lumbert Street, to Master   27

42 *model* plan   43 *figure* design   47 *offices* supplementary rooms for services   52 *Consent* agree   53 *surveyors* architects   55 *his opposite* the opposition   56 *We fortify in paper* our strength is all on paper   60 *part-created cost* building unfinished because there was insufficient money to complete it   62 *churlish* violent   74 *sound* echo   76 *several* separate   81 *Who . . . should* who is likely to   84 *substituted* delegated   88 *surfeited* overeaten   91 *fond many* foolish multitude   92 *beat heaven* assail heaven with prayers   94 *trimmed* dressed   103 *Thou* i.e. the multitude   109 *draw our numbers* assemble our troops
II, i   Before an Eastcheap tavern   1 *Master Fang* the sheriff's sergeant; *entered the action* begun the lawsuit   3 *yeoman* the sergeant's man   16 *foin* thrust (with an indecent double meaning)   18 *close* grapple   20 *fist* punch   21 *vice* grip   23 *infinitive* infinite (Mistress Quickly's spectacular misuse of words will be obvious throughout); *score* tavern account   26 *indited* i.e. invited   27 *Lubber's Head* Libbard's (Leopard's) Head (a shop sign); *Lumbert* Lombard

28 Smooth's the silkman. I pray you, since my exion is entered and my case so openly known to the world, let him be brought in to his answer. A hundred mark is a long one for a poor lone woman to bear, and I have
32 borne, and borne, and borne, and have been fubbed off, and fubbed off, and fubbed off, from this day to that day, that it is a shame to be thought on. There is no honesty in such dealing, unless a woman should be made an ass and a beast, to bear every knave's wrong.
37 Yonder he comes, and that arrant malmsey-nose knave, Bardolph, with him. Do your offices, do your offices. Master Fang and Master Snare, do me, do me, do me your offices.

Enter Sir John [Falstaff] and Bardolph, and the Boy [Page].

FALSTAFF How now! Whose mare 's dead? What's the matter?

FANG Sir John, I arrest you at the suit of Mistress Quickly.

FALSTAFF Away, varlets! Draw, Bardolph. Cut me off
44 the villain's head. Throw the quean in the channel.

HOSTESS Throw me in the channel! I'll throw thee in the channel. Wilt thou? Wilt thou? Thou bastardly rogue!
47 Murder, murder! Ah, thou honeysuckle villain! Wilt
48 thou kill God's officers and the king's? Ah, thou honey-
49 seed rogue! Thou art a honeyseed, a man-queller, and a woman-queller.

FALSTAFF Keep them off, Bardolph.

FANG A rescue! A rescue!

HOSTESS Good people, bring a rescue or two. Thou wo't, wo't thou? Thou wo't, wo't ta? Do, do, thou rogue!
55 Do, thou hempseed!
56 PAGE Away, you scullion! You rampallian! You fustilar-
57 ian! I'll tickle your catastrophe.

Enter Lord Chief Justice and his Men.

CHIEF JUSTICE
What is the matter? Keep the peace here, ho!

HOSTESS Good my lord, be good to me. I beseech you,
60 stand to me.

CHIEF JUSTICE
How now, Sir John! What are you brawling here?
Doth this become your place, your time and business?
You should have been well on your way to York.
Stand from him, fellow. Wherefore hang'st upon him?

HOSTESS O my most worshipful lord, an't please your grace, I am a poor widow of Eastcheap, and he is arrested at my suit.

CHIEF JUSTICE For what sum?

HOSTESS It is more than for some, my lord; it is for all, all I have. He hath eaten me out of house and home; he hath put all my substance into that fat belly of his. But I will have some of it out again, or I will ride thee o' nights
73 like the mare.

FALSTAFF I think I am as like to ride the mare, if I have any vantage of ground to get up.

CHIEF JUSTICE How comes this, Sir John? Fie! what man of good temper would endure this tempest of exclamation? Are you not ashamed to enforce a poor widow to so rough a course to come by her own?

FALSTAFF What is the gross sum that I owe thee?

HOSTESS Marry, if thou wert an honest man, thyself and
82 the money too. Thou didst swear to me upon a parcel-
83 gilt goblet, sitting in my Dolphin chamber, at the round
84 table, by a sea-coal fire, upon Wednesday in Wheeson

week, when the prince broke thy head for liking his 85 father to a singing-man of Windsor, thou didst swear to me then, as I was washing thy wound, to marry me and make me my lady thy wife. Canst thou deny it? Did not goodwife Keech, the butcher's wife, come in then and call me gossip Quickly? Coming in to borrow a mess of 90 vinegar, telling us she had a good dish of prawns, where- 91 by thou didst desire to eat some, whereby I told thee they were ill for a green wound? And didst thou not, 93 when she was gone down stairs, desire me to be no more so familiarity with such poor people, saying that ere long they should call me madam? And didst thou not kiss me and bid me fetch thee thirty shillings? I put thee now to thy book-oath. Deny it, if thou canst.

FALSTAFF My lord, this is a poor mad soul, and she says up and down the town that her eldest son is like you. She hath been in good case, and the truth is, poverty hath 101 distracted her. But for these foolish officers, I beseech 102 you I may have redress against them.

CHIEF JUSTICE Sir John, Sir John, I am well acquainted with your manner of wrenching the true cause the false way. It is not a confident brow, nor the throng of words that come with such more than impudent sauciness from you, can thrust me from a level consideration. You 108 have, as it appears to me, practiced upon the easy-yielding spirit of this woman, and made her serve your uses both in purse and in person.

HOSTESS Yea, in truth, my lord.

CHIEF JUSTICE Pray thee, peace. Pay her the debt you owe her and unpay the villainy you have done with her. The one you may do with sterling money, and the other with current repentance. 116

FALSTAFF My lord, I will not undergo this sneap with- 117 out reply. You call honorable boldness impudent sauciness. If a man will make curtsy and say nothing, he is virtuous. No, my lord, my humble duty remembered, I will not be your suitor. I say to you, I do desire deliverance from these officers, being upon hasty employment in the king's affairs.

CHIEF JUSTICE You speak as having power to do wrong. But answer in the effect of your reputation, and satisfy 125 the poor woman.

FALSTAFF Come hither, hostess.

Enter a Messenger [Gower].

CHIEF JUSTICE Now, Master Gower, what news?

GOWER
The king, my lord, and Harry Prince of Wales
Are near at hand. The rest the paper tells.

FALSTAFF As I am a gentleman.

HOSTESS Faith, you said so before.

FALSTAFF As I am a gentleman. Come, no more words of it.

HOSTESS By this heavenly ground I tread on, I must be

---

28 *exion* action 32 *fubbed off* put off 37 *malmsey-nose* red-nosed from drinking wine 44 *quean* slut; *channel* gutter 47 *honeysuckle* i.e. homicidal 48 *honeyseed* i.e. homicide 49 *man-queller* i.e. man-killer 55 *hempseed* gallows-bird 56 *scullion* kitchen wench; *rampallian* scoundrel; *fustilarian* frowsy fat woman 57 *catastrophe* backside 60 *stand to* help 73 *mare* nightmare 82 *parcel-gilt* partly gilded 83 *Dolphin chamber* (a room in her tavern) 84 *sea-coal* coal mined from sea-coast veins; *Wheeson* Whitsun (Pentecost) 85 *liking* comparing 90 *gossip* (a familiar term of address) 91 *prawns* shrimps 93 *green* raw 101 *in good case* prosperous 102 *distracted her* driven her mad 108 *level* unbiased 116 *current* genuine 117 *sneap* rebuke 125 *in . . . reputation* suitably for a man of your reputation

fain to pawn both my plate and the tapestry of my dining-chambers.

137 FALSTAFF Glasses, glasses, is the only drinking. And for
138 thy walls, a pretty slight drollery, or the story of the
139 Prodigal, or the German hunting in water-work, is worth a thousand of these bed-hangings and these fly-bitten tapestries. Let it be ten pound, if thou canst.
142 Come, an 'twere not for thy humors, there's not a better
143 wench in England. Go, wash thy face, and draw the action. Come, thou must not be in this humor with me. Dost not know me? Come, come, I know thou wast set on to this.

146 HOSTESS Pray thee, Sir John, let it be but twenty nobles. I' faith, I am loath to pawn my plate, so God save me, la!

FALSTAFF Let it alone; I'll make other shift. You'll be a fool still.

HOSTESS Well, you shall have it, though I pawn my gown. I hope you'll come to supper. You'll pay me all together?

FALSTAFF Will I live? [to Bardolph] Go, with her, with
155 her. Hook on, hook on.

HOSTESS Will you have Doll Tearsheet meet you at supper?

FALSTAFF No more words. Let's have her.
Exeunt Hostess and Sergeant [Fang, Bardolph, and others].

CHIEF JUSTICE I have heard better news.

FALSTAFF What's the news, my lord?

CHIEF JUSTICE Where lay the king last night?

GOWER At Basingstoke, my lord.

FALSTAFF I hope, my lord, all's well. What is the news, my lord?

CHIEF JUSTICE Come all his forces back?

GOWER
No. Fifteen hundred foot, five hundred horse,
Are marched up to my lord of Lancaster,
Against Northumberland and the archbishop.

FALSTAFF
Comes the king back from Wales, my noble lord?

CHIEF JUSTICE
You shall have letters of me presently.
170 Come, go along with me, good Master Gower.

FALSTAFF My lord!

CHIEF JUSTICE What's the matter?

FALSTAFF Master Gower, shall I entreat you with me to dinner?

GOWER I must wait upon my good lord here, I thank you, good Sir John.

CHIEF JUSTICE Sir John, you loiter here too long, being
you are to take soldiers up in counties as you go. 178

FALSTAFF Will you sup with me, Master Gower?

CHIEF JUSTICE What foolish master taught you these manners, Sir John?

FALSTAFF Master Gower, if they become me not, he was a fool that taught them me. This is the right fencing 183
grace, my lord – tap for tap, and so part fair.

CHIEF JUSTICE Now the Lord lighten thee! Thou art a 185
great fool. *[Exeunt.]*

*

Enter the Prince [Henry], and Poins, with others. II, ii

PRINCE Before God, I am exceeding weary.

POINS Is't come to that? I had thought weariness durst
not have attached one of so high blood. 3

PRINCE Faith, it does me, though it discolors the com- 4
plexion of my greatness to acknowledge it. Doth it not
show vilely in me to desire small beer?

POINS Why, a prince should not be so loosely studied as 7
to remember so weak a composition. 8

PRINCE Belike, then, my appetite was not princely got, 9
for, by my troth, I do now remember the poor creature,
small beer. But indeed these humble considerations
make me out of love with my greatness. What a disgrace
is it to me to remember thy name! Or to know thy face
to-morrow! Or to take note how many pair of silk
stockings thou hast, viz. these, and those that were thy
peach-colored ones! Or to bear the inventory of thy
shirts, as, one for superfluity, and another for use! But 17
that the tennis-court-keeper knows better than I; for it
is a low ebb of linen with thee when thou keepest not
racket there, as thou hast not done a great while, because the rest of thy low countries have made a shift to 21
eat up thy holland. And God knows whether those that 22
bawl out the ruins of thy linen shall inherit his kingdom.
But the midwives say the children are not in the fault,
whereupon the world increases, and kindreds are
mightily strengthened.

POINS How ill it follows, after you have labored so hard,
you should talk so idly! Tell me, how many good young
princes would do so, their fathers being so sick as yours
at this time is?

PRINCE Shall I tell thee one thing, Poins?

POINS Yes, faith, and let it be an excellent good thing.

PRINCE It shall serve among wits of no higher breeding
than thine.

POINS Go to. I stand the push of your one thing that you 34
will tell.

PRINCE Marry, I tell thee, it is not meet that I should be
sad, now my father is sick. Albeit I could tell to thee, as
to one it pleases me, for fault of a better, to call my
friend, I could be sad, and sad indeed too.

POINS Very hardly upon such a subject. 40

PRINCE By this hand, thou thinkest me as far in the
devil's book as thou and Falstaff for obduracy and 42
persistency. Let the end try the man. But I tell thee, my
heart bleeds inwardly that my father is so sick. And
keeping such vile company as thou art hath in reason
taken from me all ostentation of sorrow. 46

POINS The reason?

PRINCE What wouldst thou think of me if I should weep?

---

137 *Glasses . . . drinking* glasses, not metal tankards, are now fashionable
138 *drollery* comic picture 139 *water-work* water color 142 *humors*
vagaries 143 *draw* withdraw 146 *nobles* coins worth 6s. 8d. each 155
Hook on stay with her and don't let her change 178 *take soldiers up*
recruit soldiers 183–84 *right fencing grace* correct form in fencing 185
lighten enlighten
II, ii The London dwelling of Prince Henry 3 *attached* seized 4 *discolors the complexion* makes me blush 7 *so loosely studied* such a careless
student 8 *so weak a composition* such small beer, i.e. trifles 9 *got* begotten
17 *one for superfluity* an extra one 17–20 *But . . . while* (the sense of the
passage is that a courtier needs to change his shirt after playing tennis;
Poins, with only one shirt, has not been seen recently on the tennis-courts)
21 *thy low countries* i.e. the brothels frequented by Poins; *made a shift*
contrived, with a play upon 'shift' meaning shirt 22 *holland* best linen
22–23 *those . . . linen* i.e. your bastards, who wear your shirts 34 *push*
thrust 40 *Very hardly* with great difficulty 42 *obduracy* unregeneracy
46 *ostentation* outward display

POINS I would think thee a most princely hypocrite.

PRINCE It would be every man's thought, and thou art a blessed fellow to think as every man thinks. Never a man's thought in the world keeps the roadway better than thine. Every man would think me an hypocrite
55 indeed. And what accites your most worshipful thought to think so?

57 POINS Why, because you have been so lewd and so much
58 engraffed to Falstaff.

PRINCE And to thee.

POINS By this light, I am well spoke on; I can hear it with mine own ears. The worst that they can say of me is that
62 I am a second brother and that I am a proper fellow of my hands, and those two things I confess I cannot help. By the mass, here comes Bardolph.

Enter Bardolph and Boy [Page].

PRINCE And the boy that I gave Falstaff. 'A had him from me Christian, and look if the fat villain have not transformed him ape.

BARDOLPH God save your grace!

PRINCE And yours, most noble Bardolph!

POINS Come, you virtuous ass, you bashful fool, must
71 you be blushing? Wherefore blush you now? What a maidenly man-at-arms are you become! Is't such a
73 matter to get a pottle-pot's maidenhead?

74 PAGE 'A calls me e'en now, my lord, through a red lattice, and I could discern no part of his face from the window. At last I spied his eyes, and methought he had made two holes in the ale-wife's new petticoat and so peeped through.

79 PRINCE Has not the boy profited?

BARDOLPH Away, you whoreson upright rabbit, away!

81 PAGE Away, you rascally Althaea's dream, away!

PRINCE Instruct us, boy. What dream, boy?

83 PAGE Marry, my lord, Althaea dreamed she was delivered of a firebrand, and therefore I call him her dream.

PRINCE A crown's worth of good interpretation. There 'tis, boy.

POINS O, that this good blossom could be kept from
88 cankers! Well, there is sixpence to preserve thee.

BARDOLPH An you do not make him hanged among you, the gallows shall have wrong.

PRINCE And how doth thy master, Bardolph?

BARDOLPH Well, my lord. He heard of your grace's coming to town. There's a letter for you.

94 POINS Delivered with good respect. And how doth the
95 martlemas, your master?

BARDOLPH In bodily health, sir.

POINS Marry, the immortal part needs a physician, but that moves not him. Though that be sick, it dies not.

99 PRINCE I do allow this wen to be as familiar with me as my dog, and he holds his place, for look you how he writes.

POINS *[reads]* 'John Falstaff, knight' – every man must know that, as oft as he has occasion to name himself. Even like those that are kin to the king, for they never prick their finger but they say, 'There's some of the king's blood spilt.' 'How comes that?' says he that takes upon him not to conceive. The answer is as ready as a borrower's cap, 'I am the king's poor cousin, sir.'

108 PRINCE Nay, they will be kin to us, or they will fetch it from Japhet. But to the letter. *[reads]* 'Sir John Falstaff,

knight, to the son of the king, nearest his father, Harry Prince of Wales, greeting.'

POINS Why, this is a certificate.   112

PRINCE Peace! *[reads]* 'I will imitate the honorable Romans in brevity.'

POINS He sure means brevity in breath, short-winded.

[PRINCE reads] 'I commend me to thee, I commend thee, and I leave thee. Be not too familiar with Poins, for he misuses thy favors so much that he swears thou art to marry his sister Nell. Repent at idle times as thou mayest, and so farewell.

'Thine, by yea and no, which is as much as to say, as 121 thou usest him, JACK FALSTAFF with my familiars, JOHN with my brothers and sisters, and SIR JOHN with all Europe.'

POINS My lord, I'll steep this letter in sack and make him eat it.

PRINCE That's to make him eat twenty of his words. But 127 do you use me thus, Ned? Must I marry your sister?

POINS God send the wench no worse fortune! But I never said so.

PRINCE Well, thus we play the fools with the time, and the spirits of the wise sit in the clouds and mock us. Is your master here in London?

BARDOLPH Yea, my lord.

PRINCE Where sups he? Doth the old boar feed in the old frank?   136

BARDOLPH At the old place, my lord, in Eastcheap.

PRINCE What company?

PAGE Ephesians, my lord, of the old church.   139

PRINCE Sup any women with him?

PAGE None, my lord, but old Mistress Quickly and Mistress Doll Tearsheet.

PRINCE What pagan may that be?   143

PAGE A proper gentlewoman, sir, and a kinswoman of my master's.

PRINCE Even such kin as the parish heifers are to the town bull. Shall we steal upon them, Ned, at supper?

POINS I am your shadow, my lord; I'll follow you.

PRINCE Sirrah, you boy, and Bardolph, no word to your master that I am yet come to town. There's for your 150 silence.

BARDOLPH I have no tongue, sir.

PAGE And for mine, sir, I will govern it.

PRINCE Fare you well; go. *[Exeunt Bardolph and Page.]* This Doll Tearsheet should be some road.   155

POINS I warrant you, as common as the way between Saint Alban's and London.

---

55 *accites* arouses   57 *lewd* base   58 *engraffed* attached   62 *second brother* younger son, without inheritance   62–63 *proper . . . hands* good fighter   71 *blushing* (Bardolph's red face calls forth this jibe and what follows)   73 *get . . . maidenhead* drink up a two-quart tankard of ale   74 *red lattice* (the lattices of the tavern windows were painted red)   79 *profited* become proficient   81 *Althaea's dream* (Althaea dreamed that her son would live only so long as a brand burned in the fire)   83–85 (the page, suffering from a little learning, describes Hecuba's dream, not Althaea's)   88 *cankers* canker worms   94 *good respect* proper ceremony (spoken ironically)   95 *martlemas* martlemas beef, i.e. beef fattened for slaughter on Martinmas Day (November 11)   99 *wen* tumor   108–09 *fetch . . . Japhet* trace their ancestry back to Noah's son Japhet (traditionally regarded as the progenitor of the peoples of Europe)   112 *certificate* legal document   121 *by yea and no* (a Puritan oath)   127 *twenty* (used loosely to mean a large number)   136 *frank* sty   139 *Ephesians . . . church* i.e. boon companions   143 *pagan* strumpet   150 *There's* there's money   155 *road* i.e. whore (who, like a highway, is common to all)

158 PRINCE How might we see Falstaff bestow himself to-
night in his true colors, and not ourselves be seen?
160 POINS Put on two leathern jerkins and aprons, and wait
161 upon him at his table as drawers.
PRINCE From a God to a bull? A heavy descension! It
163 was Jove's case. From a prince to a prentice? A low
transformation! That shall be mine, for in everything
165 the purpose must weigh with the folly. Follow me, Ned.
Exeunt.

*

II, iii   *Enter Northumberland, his Wife [Lady*
Northumberland], and the Wife to Harry Percy
[Lady Percy].

NORTHUMBERLAND
1   I pray thee, loving wife, and gentle daughter,
2   Give even way unto my rough affairs.
Put not you on the visage of the times
And be like them to Percy troublesome.

LADY NORTHUMBERLAND
I have given over, I will speak no more.
Do what you will, your wisdom be your guide.

NORTHUMBERLAND
Alas, sweet wife, my honor is at pawn,
8   And, but my going, nothing can redeem it.

LADY PERCY
O yet, for God's sake, go not to these wars!
The time was, father, that you broke your word,
11   When you were more endeared to it than now,
12   When your own Percy, when my heart's dear Harry,
Threw many a northward look to see his father
Bring up his powers, but he did long in vain.
Who then persuaded you to stay at home?
There were two honors lost, yours and your son's.
17   For yours, the God of heaven brighten it!
For his, it stuck upon him as the sun
19   In the grey vault of heaven, and by his light
Did all the chivalry of England move
21   To do brave acts. He was indeed the glass
Wherein the noble youth did dress themselves.
[He had no legs that practiced not his gait;
24   And speaking thick, which nature made his blemish,
Became the accents of the valiant,
For those that could speak low and tardily
Would turn their own perfection to abuse,
To seem like him. So that in speech, in gait,
29   In diet, in affections of delight,
30   In military rules, humors of blood,
He was the mark and glass, copy and book,
That fashioned others. And him – O wondrous him!
O miracle of men! – him did you leave,

Second to none, unseconded by you,
To look upon the hideous god of war
In disadvantage, to abide a field   36
Where nothing but the sound of Hotspur's name
Did seem defensible. So you left him.   38
Never, O never, do his ghost the wrong
To hold your honor more precise and nice
With others than with him! Let them alone.
The marshal and the archbishop are strong.
Had my sweet Harry had but half their numbers,
To-day might I, hanging on Hotspur's neck,
Have talked of Monmouth's grave.]   45

NORTHUMBERLAND   Beshrew your heart,
Fair daughter, you do draw my spirits from me
With new lamenting ancient oversights.
But I must go and meet with danger there,
Or it will seek me in another place
And find me worse provided.

LADY NORTHUMBERLAND   O, fly to Scotland,
Till that the nobles and the armèd commons
Have of their puissance made a little taste.

LADY PERCY
If they get ground and vantage of the king,
Then join you with them, like a rib of steel,
To make strength stronger. But, for all our loves,
First let them try themselves. So did your son;
He was so suffered. So came I a widow,   57
And never shall have length of life enough
To rain upon remembrance with mine eyes,   59
That it may grow and sprout as high as heaven,
For recordation to my noble husband.   61

NORTHUMBERLAND
Come, come, go in with me. 'Tis with my mind
As with the tide swelled up unto his height,
That makes a still-stand, running neither way.
Fain would I go to meet the archbishop,
But many thousand reasons hold me back.
I will resolve for Scotland. There am I,
Till time and vantage crave my company.   *Exeunt.* 68

*

Enter a Drawer or two [Francis and a second].   II, iv

FRANCIS What the devil hast thou brought there? Apple-   1
johns? Thou knowest Sir John cannot endure an apple-
john.
2. DRAWER Mass, thou sayest true. The prince once set a
dish of apple-johns before him, and told him there were
five more Sir Johns, and, putting off his hat, said, 'I will
now take my leave of these six dry, round, old, withered
knights.' It angered him to the heart. But he hath forgot
that.
FRANCIS Why, then, cover, and set them down. And see   10
if thou canst find out Sneak's noise; Mistress Tear-   11
sheet would fain hear some music. Dispatch. The room
where they supped is too hot; they'll come in straight.
Enter Will [a third Drawer].
3. DRAWER Sirrah, here will be the prince and Master
Poins anon, and they will put on two of our jerkins and
aprons, and Sir John must not know of it. Bardolph
hath brought word.   *[Exit.]*
FRANCIS By the mass, here will be old Utis. It will be an   18
excellent stratagem.
2. DRAWER I'll see if I can find out Sneak.   *Exit.*

---

158 *bestow* behave   160 *jerkins* jackets   161 *drawers* servers of liquor   163
Jove's case (for love of Europa, Jove transformed himself into a bull)
165 *weigh with* be equal to
II, iii Northumberland's castle   1 *daughter* i.e. daughter-in-law   2 *even
way* free scope   8 *but* except for   11 *endeared* bound by duty   12–14 *When
. . . vain* (a reference to Northumberland's failure to come to his son's
support at Shrewsbury)   17 *For* as for   19 *grey* sky-blue   21 *glass* mirror
24 *thick* fast   29 *affections of delight* pleasures   30 *humors of blood* temperament   36 *abide a field* fight a battle   38 *defensible* able to defend   45
Monmouth's Prince Hal's; *Beshrew* plague on   57 *suffered* allowed to have his
own way   59 *rain* weep   61 *recordation* memorial   68 *vantage* superiority
II, iv Within an Eastcheap tavern   1–2 *Apple-johns* kind of apple that
looks withered when ripe   10 *cover* lay the cloth   11 *noise* band of
musicians   18 *old Utis* a noisy row

Enter Mistress Quickly [the Hostess] and Doll Tearsheet.

HOSTESS I' faith, sweetheart, methinks now you are in an
22 excellent good temperality. Your pulsidge beats as
23 extraordinarily as heart would desire, and your color, I
warrant you, is as red as any rose, in good truth, la! But,
25 i' faith, you have drunk too much canaries, and that's a
26 marvellous searching wine, and it perfumes the blood
ere one can say, 'What's this?' How do you now?

DOLL Better than I was. Hem!

HOSTESS Why, that's well said. A good heart 's worth
gold. Lo, here comes Sir John.

Enter Sir John [Falstaff].

31 FALSTAFF [sings] 'When Arthur first in court' – Empty
32 the jordan. [Exit Francis.] – [sings] 'And was a worthy
king.' – How now, Mistress Doll!

34 HOSTESS Sick of a calm, yea, good faith.

35 FALSTAFF So is all her sect. An they be once in a calm,
they are sick.

37 DOLL A pox damn you, you muddy rascal, is that all the
comfort you give me?

39 FALSTAFF You make fat rascals, Mistress Doll.

DOLL I make them! Gluttony and diseases make them; I
make them not.

FALSTAFF If the cook help to make the gluttony, you
help to make the diseases, Doll. We catch of you, Doll,
we catch of you. Grant that, my poor virtue, grant that.

DOLL Yea, joy, our chains and our jewels.

46 FALSTAFF 'Your brooches, pearls, and ouches.' For to
serve bravely is to come halting off, you know. To come
off the breach with his pike bent bravely, and to surgery
49 bravely; to venture upon the charged chambers
bravely –

50 DOLL Hang yourself, you muddy conger, hang yourself!

HOSTESS By my troth, this is the old fashion. You two
never meet but you fall to some discord. You are both, i'
53 good truth, as rheumatic as two dry toasts; you cannot
54 one bear with another's confirmities. What the good-
year! One must bear, and that must be you [to Doll].
You are the weaker vessel, as they say, the emptier
vessel.

DOLL Can a weak empty vessel bear such a huge full hogs-
58 head? There's a whole merchant's venture of Bordeaux
stuff in him; you have not seen a hulk better stuffed in
the hold. Come, I'll be friends with thee, Jack. Thou art
going to the wars, and whether I shall ever see thee
again or no, there is nobody cares.

Enter Drawer [Francis].

63 FRANCIS Sir, Ancient Pistol 's below and would speak
with you.

DOLL Hang him, swaggering rascal! Let him not come
hither. It is the foul-mouthed'st rogue in England.

HOSTESS If he swagger, let him not come here. No, by my
faith. I must live among my neighbors, I'll no swaggerers. I am in good name and fame with the very best.
Shut the door, there comes no swaggerers here. I have
not lived all this while to have swaggering now. Shut the
door, I pray you.

FALSTAFF Dost thou hear, hostess?

HOSTESS Pray ye, pacify yourself, Sir John. There comes
no swaggerers here.

FALSTAFF Dost thou hear? It is mine ancient.

77 HOSTESS Tilly-fally, Sir John, ne'er tell me. Your ancient
swaggerer comes not in my doors. I was before Master

Tisick, the debuty, t' other day, and, as he said to me, 79
'twas no longer ago than Wednesday last, 'I' good faith,
neighbor Quickly,' says he – Master Dumbe, our minister, was by then – 'neighbor Quickly,' says he, 'receive
those that are civil, for,' said he, 'you are in an ill name.'
Now 'a said so, I can tell whereupon. 'For,' says he, 'you
are an honest woman, and well thought on; therefore
take heed what guests you receive. Receive,' says he,
'no swaggering companions.' There comes none here. 87
You would bless you to hear what he said. No, I'll no
swaggerers.

FALSTAFF He's no swaggerer, hostess; a tame cheater, i' 90
faith; you may stroke him as gently as a puppy greyhound. He'll not swagger with a Barbary hen, if her 92
feathers turn back in any show of resistance. Call him
up, drawer.   [Exit Francis.]

HOSTESS Cheater, call you him? I will bar no honest man
my house, nor no cheater. But I do not love swaggering,
by my troth; I am the worse when one says swagger.
Feel, masters, how I shake, look you, I warrant you.

DOLL So you do, hostess.

HOSTESS Do I? Yea, in very truth, do I, an 'twere an
aspen leaf. I cannot abide swaggerers.

*Enter Ancient Pistol, [Bardolph,] and Bardolph's
Boy [Page].*

PISTOL God save you, Sir John!

FALSTAFF Welcome, Ancient Pistol. Here, Pistol, I
charge you with a cup of sack. Do you discharge upon 102
mine hostess.

PISTOL I will discharge upon her, Sir John, with two
bullets. 105

FALSTAFF She is pistol-proof, sir; you shall hardly offend 106
her.

HOSTESS Come, I'll drink no proofs nor no bullets. I'll
drink no more than will do me good, for no man's
pleasure, I.

PISTOL Then to you, Mistress Dorothy; I will charge you.

DOLL Charge me! I scorn you, scurvy companion. What!
You poor, base, rascally, cheating, lack-linen mate! 111
Away, you mouldy rogue, away! I am meat for your
master.

PISTOL I know you, Mistress Dorothy.

DOLL Away, you cut-purse rascal! You filthy bung, 115
away! By this wine, I'll thrust my knife in your mouldy
chaps, an you play the saucy cuttle with me. Away, you 117
bottle-ale rascal! You basket-hilt stale juggler, you! 118
Since when, I pray you, sir? God's light, with two
points on your shoulder? Much! 120

22 *temperality* i.e. temper; *pulsidge* i.e. pulse   23 *extraordinarily* i.e. ordinarily   25 *canaries* a sweet wine   26 *searching* potent   31 *When . . . court*
(a snatch from the ballad *Sir Launcelot du Lake*)   32 *jordan* chamber-pot
34 *calm* i.e. qualm   35 *sect* sex   37 *muddy* dirty   39 *rascals* (a pun on
'rascal' meaning lean deer)   46 *Your . . . ouches* (a snatch from another
ballad); *ouches* gems   49 *charged chambers* small cannon   50 *conger*
conger eel   53 *rheumatic* (perhaps she means 'splenetic'); *dry toasts* (which
grate upon each other)   54 *confirmities* i.e. infirmities   54–55 *What the
good-year* what the devil   58–59 *merchant's . . . stuff* shipload of Bordeaux
wine   63 *Ancient* ensign, lieutenant   77 *Tilly-fally* nonsense   79 *debuty*
deputy   87 *companions* ruffians   90 *cheater* come-on man in a team of
confidence men   92 *Barbary hen* guinea hen   102 *charge* toast (with a play
on the name Pistol)   102–03 *discharge . . . hostess* toast the hostess   105
bullets (an indecency which the hostess fails to understand)   106 *offend*
wound   111 *mate* (a term of contempt)   115 *bung* pickpocket   117 *chaps*
cheeks; *cuttle* cut-throat   118 *basket-hilt stale juggler* an impostor who
pretends to be a soldier by carrying a sword with a basketlike hand-guard
120 *points* laces by which pieces of armor were tied to the shoulders

PISTOL God let me not live but I will murder your ruff for this.

FALSTAFF No more, Pistol; I would not have you go off here. Discharge yourself of our company, Pistol.

HOSTESS No, good Captain Pistol, not here, sweet captain.

DOLL Captain! Thou abominable damned cheater, art thou not ashamed to be called captain? An captains were
128 of my mind, they would truncheon you out for taking their names upon you before you have earned them. You a captain! You slave, for what? For tearing a poor whore's ruff in a bawdy-house? He a captain! Hang him, rogue! He lives upon mouldy stewed prunes and dried cakes. A captain! God's light, these villains will
134 make the word as odious as the word 'occupy,' which
135 was an excellent good word before it was ill sorted. Therefore captains had need look to 't.

BARDOLPH Pray thee, go down, good ancient.

FALSTAFF Hark thee hither, Mistress Doll.

PISTOL Not I. I tell thee what, Corporal Bardolph, I could tear her. I'll be revenged of her.

PAGE Pray thee, go down.

142 PISTOL I'll see her damned first, to Pluto's damned lake,
143 by this hand, to the infernal deep, with Erebus and tortures vile also. Hold hook and line, say I. Down,
145 down, dogs! Down, faitors! Have we not Hiren here?

HOSTESS Good Captain Peesel, be quiet; 'tis very late, i'
147 faith. I beseek you now, aggravate your choler.

PISTOL
These be good humors, indeed! Shall pack-horses
149 And hollow pampered jades of Asia,
Which cannot go but thirty mile a-day,
151 Compare with Caesars, and with Cannibals,
152 And Trojan Greeks? Nay, rather damn them with
153 King Cerberus, and let the welkin roar.
Shall we fall foul for toys?

HOSTESS By my troth, captain, these are very bitter words.

BARDOLPH Be gone, good ancient. This will grow to a brawl anon.

PISTOL Die men like dogs! Give crowns like pins! Have we not Hiren here?

HOSTESS O' my word, captain, there's none such here. What the good-year! Do you think I would deny her? For God's sake, be quiet.

PISTOL
Then feed, and be fat, my fair Calipolis. 163
Come, give 's some sack.
'Si fortune me tormente, sperato me contento.' 165
Fear we broadsides? No, let the fiend give fire.
Give me some sack. And, sweetheart, lie thou there.
[Lays down his sword.]
Come we to full points here, and are etceteras nothing? 168

FALSTAFF Pistol, I would be quiet.

PISTOL Sweet knight, I kiss thy neif. What! We have 170 seen the seven stars. 171

DOLL For God's sake, thrust him down stairs. I cannot endure such a fustian rascal. 173

PISTOL Thrust him down stairs! Know we not Galloway 174 nags?

FALSTAFF Quoit him down, Bardolph, like a shove- 176 groat shilling. Nay, an 'a do nothing but speak nothing, 'a shall be nothing here.

BARDOLPH Come, get you down stairs.

PISTOL
What! shall we have incision? Shall we imbrue? 180
[Snatches up his sword.]
Then death rock me asleep, abridge my doleful days!
Why, then, let grievous, ghastly, gaping wounds
Untwine the Sisters Three! Come, Atropos, I say! 183

HOSTESS Here's a goodly stuff toward!

FALSTAFF Give me my rapier, boy.

DOLL I pray thee, Jack, I pray thee, do not draw.

FALSTAFF Get you down stairs.
[Draws, and drives Pistol out.]

HOSTESS Here's a goodly tumult! I'll forswear keeping house afore I'll be in these tirrits and frights. So, 189 murder, I warrant now. Alas, alas! Put up your naked weapons, put up your naked weapons.
[Exeunt Pistol and Bardolph.]

DOLL I pray thee, Jack, be quiet; the rascal 's gone. Ah, you whoreson little valiant villain, you!

HOSTESS Are you not hurt i' the groin? Methought 'a made a shrewd thrust at your belly.
[Enter Bardolph.]

FALSTAFF Have you turned him out o' doors?

BARDOLPH Yea, sir. The rascal 's drunk. You have hurt him, sir, i' the shoulder.

FALSTAFF A rascal! to brave me!

DOLL Ah, you sweet little rogue, you! Alas, poor ape, how thou sweatest! Come, let me wipe thy face; come on, you whoreson chops. Ah, rogue! i' faith, I love thee. 202 Thou art as valorous as Hector of Troy, worth five of Agamemnon, and ten times better than the Nine Wor- 204 thies. Ah, villain!

FALSTAFF A rascally slave! I will toss the rogue in a blanket.

DOLL Do, an thou darest for thy heart. An thou dost, I'll canvass thee between a pair of sheets. 208
Enter Music.

PAGE The music is come, sir.

FALSTAFF Let them play. Play, sirs. Sit on my knee, Doll. A rascal bragging slave! The rogue fled from me like quicksilver.

DOLL I' faith, and thou followedst him like a church. Thou whoreson little tidy Bartholomew boar-pig, when 214 wilt thou leave fighting o' days and foining o' nights, 215 and begin to patch up thine old body for heaven?
Enter [behind] Prince [Henry] and Poins [disguised].

128 *truncheon* beat with a truncheon or staff   134 *occupy* fornicate   135 *ill sorted* misused   142 *Pluto's . . . lake* (Pistol confuses the river Styx with a lake)   143 *Erebus* the underworld   145 *faitors* impostors; *Have . . . here* (a quotation from a play by George Peele)   147 *aggravate* i.e. moderate   149–50 *And . . . day* (a garbled quotation from Marlowe's *Tamburlaine*, Part II)   151 *Cannibals* i.e. Hannibals   152 *Trojan Greeks* (Trojans and Greeks are all one to the excited Pistol)   153 *Cerberus* the three-headed dog who guarded the entrance to Hades   163 *Then . . . Calipolis* (a burlesque of a line in another play by Peele)   165 *Si . . . contento* (a multilingual mis-quotation of a proverb meaning 'If fortune torments me, hope contents me')   168 *full points* full stops, periods   170 *neif* fist   171 *seven stars* the Pleiades (the idea is that Falstaff and Pistol have often made a night of it)   173 *fustian* worthless   174–75 *Galloway nags* Irish horses of inferior breed   176 *Quoit* throw   176–77 *shove-groat shilling* a coin used in a game somewhat like shuffleboard played on a smooth table   180 *incision* bloodshed; *imbrue* shed blood   183 *Sisters Three* the Fates, of whom Atropos was one   189 *tirrits* fits of temper   202 *chops* fat-cheeked fellow   204 *Nine Worthies* Hector, Alexander, Julius Caesar, Joshua, David, Judas Macca-baeus, Arthur, Charlemagne, Godfrey of Bouillon   208 *canvass* toss in a canvas sheet (but Doll gives her own special meaning to the expression); s.d. *Music* musicians   214 *Bartholomew boar-pig* (roast pig was a favorite delicacy at Bartholomew Fair, held annually on August 24 at Smithfield)   215 *foining* thrusting

217 FALSTAFF Peace, good Doll! Do not speak like a death's-head. Do not bid me remember mine end.

DOLL Sirrah, what humor 's the prince of?

FALSTAFF A good shallow young fellow. 'A would have
221 made a good pantler, 'a would ha' chipped bread well.

DOLL They say Poins has a good wit.

FALSTAFF He a good wit? Hang him, baboon! His wit 's
224 as thick as Tewkesbury mustard. There's no more
225 conceit in him than is in a mallet.

DOLL Why does the prince love him so, then?

FALSTAFF Because their legs are both of a bigness, and 'a
228 plays at quoits well, and eats conger and fennel, and
229 drinks off candles' ends for flap-dragons, and rides the
230 wild-mare with the boys, and jumps upon joined-stools,
and swears with a good grace, and wears his boots very
232 smooth, like unto the sign of the leg, and breeds no bate
with telling of discreet stories; and such other gambol
faculties 'a has, that show a weak mind and an able body,
for the which the prince admits him. For the prince
himself is such another; the weight of a hair will turn
the scales between their avoirdupois.

238 PRINCE Would not this nave of a wheel have his ears cut
off?

POINS Let's beat him before his whore.

240 PRINCE Look, whether the withered elder hath not his
poll clawed like a parrot.

POINS Is it not strange that desire should so many years
outlive performance?

FALSTAFF Kiss me, Doll.

245 PRINCE Saturn and Venus this year in conjunction!
What says the almanac to that?

247 POINS And look whether the fiery Trigon, his man, be
248 not lisping to his master's old tables, his note-book, his
counsel-keeper.

250 FALSTAFF Thou dost give me flattering busses.

DOLL By my troth, I kiss thee with a most constant
heart.

FALSTAFF I am old, I am old.

DOLL I love thee better than I love e'er a scurvy young
boy of them all.

255 FALSTAFF What stuff wilt have a kirtle of? I shall receive
money o' Thursday. Shalt have a cap to-morrow. A
merry song, come. It grows late; we'll to bed. Thou'lt
forget me when I am gone.

DOLL By my troth, thou'lt set me a-weeping, an thou
sayest so. Prove that ever I dress myself handsome till
261 thy return. Well, hearken a' th' end.

FALSTAFF Some sack, Francis.

PRINCE, POINS Anon, anon, sir.

[Come forward.]

FALSTAFF Ha! a bastard son of the king's? And art not
thou Poins his brother?

266 PRINCE Why, thou globe of sinful continents, what a life
dost thou lead!

FALSTAFF A better than thou. I am a gentleman, thou
art a drawer.

PRINCE Very true, sir, and I come to draw you out by the
ears.

HOSTESS O, the Lord preserve thy good grace! By my
troth, welcome to London. Now, the Lord bless that
sweet face of thine! O Jesu, are you come from Wales?

275 FALSTAFF Thou whoreson mad compound of majesty,
276 by this light flesh and corrupt blood, thou art welcome.

DOLL How, you fat fool! I scorn you.

POINS My lord, he will drive you out of your revenge and
turn all to a merriment, if you take not the heat. 279

PRINCE You whoreson candle-mine you, how vilely did 280
you speak of me even now before this honest, virtuous,
civil gentlewoman!

HOSTESS God's blessing of your good heart! And so she
is, by my troth.

FALSTAFF Didst thou hear me?

PRINCE Yea, and you knew me, as you did when you ran 286
away by Gad's Hill. You knew I was at your back, and
spoke it on purpose to try my patience.

FALSTAFF No, no, no; not so. I did not think thou wast
within hearing.

PRINCE I shall drive you then to confess the willful
abuse, and then I know how to handle you.

FALSTAFF No abuse, Hal, o' mine honor, no abuse.

PRINCE Not to dispraise me and call me pantler and
bread-chipper and I know not what?

FALSTAFF No abuse, Hal.

POINS No abuse?

FALSTAFF No abuse, Ned, i' the world. Honest Ned,
none. I dispraised him before the wicked, that the
wicked might not fall in love with him. In which doing, 300
I have done the part of a careful friend and a true subject, and thy father is to give me thanks for it. No abuse,
Hal. None, Ned, none. No, faith, boys, none.

PRINCE See now, whether pure fear and entire cowardice
doth not make thee wrong this virtuous gentlewoman to
close with us. Is she of the wicked? Is thine hostess here 306
of the wicked? Or is thy boy of the wicked? Or honest
Bardolph, whose zeal burns in his nose, of the wicked?

POINS Answer, thou dead elm, answer.

FALSTAFF The fiend hath pricked down Bardolph irre- 310
coverable, and his face is Lucifer's privy-kitchen,
where he doth nothing but roast malt-worms. For the 312
boy, there is a good angel about him, but the devil
blinds him too.

PRINCE For the women?

FALSTAFF For one of them, she is in hell already, and
burns poor souls. For the other, I owe her money, and 316
whether she be damned for that, I know not.

HOSTESS No, I warrant you.

FALSTAFF No, I think thou art not. I think thou art quit 319
for that. Marry, there is another indictment upon thee,

217–18 death's-head (the figure of a skull was used traditionally as a reminder of mortality)   221 pantler pantryman; chipped bread cut off the
crusts   224 Tewkesbury mustard (Tewkesbury mustard balls were famous)
225 conceit wit   228 conger and fennel the meat of conger eel highly seasoned
with fennel   229 drinks . . . flap-dragons (lighted candles were floated in a
glass of liquor, and the trick was either to drink the liquor without disturbing the candle, or, more daringly, to take the candle in the mouth and
extinguish the flame by closing the mouth)   230 wild-mare seesaw;
joined-stools stools expertly made by a joiner   232 sign . . . leg sign over the
door of a bootmaker's shop; bate quarrel   238 nave large hub of the wheel
of a country cart (with a play upon 'knave')   240–41 elder . . . parrot (Doll is
rumpling Falstaff's hair)   245 Saturn the planet believed to be especially
influential upon the aged   247 fiery Trigon the three fiery signs of the
Zodiac – Aries, Leo, and Sagittarius (alluding to Bardolph's red face)
248 lisping . . . tables making love to his master's old note-book, i.e. Mistress
Quickly   250 busses kisses   255 kirtle skirt   261 hearken a' th' end i.e. in
the end you will have proof of my fidelity   266 continents (with a play upon
'continence')   275 compound lump   276 light . . . blood i.e. Doll   279
if . . . heat if you do not strike while the iron is hot   280 candle-mine mine
of tallow   286–87 as . . . Gad's Hill (see 1 Henry IV, II, ii; iv)   306
close come to terms   310 pricked down chosen   312 malt-worms topers
316 burns infects with venereal disease   319–20 quit for that acquitted of
that charge

321 for suffering flesh to be eaten in thy house, contrary to the law, for the which I think thou wilt howl.

HOSTESS All victuallers do so. What's a joint of mutton or two in a whole Lent?

PRINCE You, gentlewoman –

DOLL What says your grace?

FALSTAFF His grace says that which his flesh rebels against.

Peto knocks at door.

HOSTESS Who knocks so loud at door? Look to the door there, Francis.

[Enter Peto.]

PRINCE

Peto, how now! What news?

PETO

The king your father is at Westminster,
332 And there are twenty weak and wearied posts
Come from the north. And as I came along
I met and overtook a dozen captains,
Bareheaded, sweating, knocking at the taverns,
And asking every one for Sir John Falstaff.

PRINCE

By heaven, Poins, I feel me much to blame,
So idly to profane the precious time,
339 When tempest of commotion, like the south
340 Borne with black vapor, doth begin to melt
And drop upon our bare unarmèd heads.
Give me my sword and cloak. Falstaff, good night.

Exeunt Prince Henry, Poins [, Peto, and Bardolph].

FALSTAFF Now comes in the sweetest morsel of the night, and we must hence and leave it unpicked. *[Knocking within.]* More knocking at the door!

[Enter Bardolph.]

How now! What's the matter?

BARDOLPH

347 You must away to court, sir, presently.
A dozen captains stay at door for you.

FALSTAFF *[to the Page]* Pay the musicians, sirrah. Farewell, hostess. Farewell, Doll. You see, my good wenches, how men of merit are sought after. The undeserver may sleep when the man of action is called on.
353 Farewell, good wenches. If I be not sent away post, I will see you again ere I go.

DOLL I cannot speak. If my heart be not ready to burst – well, sweet Jack, have a care of thyself.

FALSTAFF Farewell, farewell.

[Exeunt Falstaff and Bardolph.]

HOSTESS Well, fare thee well. I have known thee these
359 twenty-nine years, come peascod-time, but an honester and truer-hearted man – well, fare thee well.

BARDOLPH *[within]* Mistress Tearsheet!

HOSTESS What's the matter?

BARDOLPH *[within]* Bid Mistress Tearsheet come to my master.

HOSTESS O, run, Doll, run. Run, good Doll. Come. *[to Bardolph within]* She comes blubbered. Yea, will you 366 come, Doll? *Exeunt.*

*

Enter the King in his nightgown, alone [with a Page]. III, i

KING

Go call the Earls of Surrey and of Warwick.
But, ere they come, bid them o'erread these letters
And well consider of them. Make good speed.

[Exit Page.]

How many thousand of my poorest subjects
Are at this hour asleep! O sleep, O gentle sleep,
Nature's soft nurse, how have I frighted thee,
That thou no more wilt weigh my eyelids down
And steep my senses in forgetfulness? 8
Why rather, sleep, liest thou in smoky cribs, 9
Upon uneasy pallets stretching thee 10
And hushed with buzzing night-flies to thy slumber,
Than in the perfumed chambers of the great,
Under the canopies of costly state, 13
And lulled with sound of sweetest melody?
O thou dull god, why liest thou with the vile 15
In loathsome beds, and leavest the kingly couch
A watch-case or a common 'larum-bell? 17
Wilt thou upon the high and giddy mast
Seal up the ship-boy's eyes, and rock his brains
In cradle of the rude imperious surge
And in the visitation of the winds,
Who take the ruffian billows by the top,
Curling their monstrous heads and hanging them
With deafening clamor in the slippery clouds,
That, with the hurly, death itself awakes? 25
Canst thou, O partial sleep, give thy repose
To the wet sea-son in an hour so rude,
And in the calmest and most stillest night,
With all appliances and means to boot, 29
Deny it to a king? Then happy low, lie down! 30
Uneasy lies the head that wears a crown.

Enter Warwick, Surrey, and Sir John Blunt.

WARWICK

Many good morrows to your majesty!

KING

Is it good morrow, lords?

WARWICK

'Tis one o'clock, and past.

KING

Why, then, good morrow to you all, my lords.
Have you read o'er the letters that I sent you?

WARWICK

We have, my liege.

KING

Then you perceive the body of our kingdom
How foul it is, what rank diseases grow, 39
And with what danger, near the heart of it.

WARWICK

It is but as a body yet distempered, 41
Which to his former strength may be restored
With good advice and little medicine.
My Lord Northumberland will soon be cooled.

KING

O God! that one might read the book of fate,
And see the revolution of the times

321–22 *suffering . . . law* permitting meat to be served at your inn during Lent in defiance of the ordinance which forbade such sale 332 *posts* messengers 339 *commotion* insurrection; *south* south wind 340 *Borne* laden 347 *presently* immediately 353 *post* posthaste 359 *peascod-time* early summer, when the peas are in blossom 366 *blubbered* weeping III, i King Henry's palace (Westminster) s.d. *nightgown* dressing gown 8 *steep* saturate 9 *cribs* hovels 10 *uneasy pallets* uncomfortable beds 13 *canopies . . . state* elaborate canopies over the beds of the wealthy 15 *dull god* Morpheus 17 *watch-case* sentry-box; *'larum-bell* alarm bell 25 *hurly* tumult 29 *to boot* in addition 30 *low* lowly folk 39 *rank* festering 41 *distempered* sick

47 Make mountains level, and the continent,
Weary of solid firmness, melt itself
Into the sea! And other times to see
The beachy girdle of the ocean
Too wide for Neptune's hips, how chances mock,
And changes fill the cup of alteration
With divers liquors! O, if this were seen,
The happiest youth, viewing his progress through,
55 What perils past, what crosses to ensue,
Would shut the book, and sit him down and die.
'Tis not ten years gone
Since Richard and Northumberland, great friends,
Did feast together, and in two years after
Were they at wars. It is but eight years since
This Percy was the man nearest my soul,
Who like a brother toiled in my affairs
63 And laid his love and life under my foot,
Yea, for my sake, even to the eyes of Richard
Gave him defiance. But which of you was by –
[To Warwick]
66 You, cousin Nevil, as I may remember –
When Richard, with his eye brimful of tears,
68 Then checked and rated by Northumberland,
Did speak these words, now proved a prophecy?
70 'Northumberland, thou ladder by the which
My cousin Bolingbroke ascends my throne' –
Though then, God knows, I had no such intent,
But that necessity so bowed the state
That I and greatness were compelled to kiss –
'The time shall come,' thus did he follow it,
76 'The time will come that foul sin, gathering head,
Shall break into corruption.' So went on,
Foretelling this same time's condition
And the division of our amity.
  WARWICK   There is a history in all men's lives,
81 Figuring the nature of the times deceased,
The which observed, a man may prophesy,
83 With a near aim, of the main chance of things
As yet not come to life, which in their seeds
85 And weak beginnings lie intreasurèd.
Such things become the hatch and brood of time,
87 And by the necessary form of this
King Richard might create a perfect guess
That great Northumberland, then false to him,
Would of that seed grow to a greater falseness,
Which should not find a ground to root upon,
Unless on you.
  KING   Are these things then necessities?
Then let us meet them like necessities.
And that same word even now cries out on us.
They say the bishop and Northumberland
Are fifty thousand strong.
  WARWICK   It cannot be, my lord.
Rumor doth double, like the voice and echo,
The numbers of the feared. Please it your grace
To go to bed. Upon my soul, my lord,
The powers that you already have sent forth
Shall bring this prize in very easily.
To comfort you the more, I have received
103 A certain instance that Glendower is dead.
Your majesty hath been this fortnight ill,
105 And these unseasoned hours perforce must add
Unto your sickness.

KING   I will take your counsel.
And were these inward wars once out of hand,   107
We would, dear lords, unto the Holy Land.   *Exeunt.*

*

Enter Justice Shallow and Justice Silence [with   III, ii
Mouldy, Shadow, Wart, Feeble, Bullcalf].

SHALLOW Come on, come on, come on, sir. Give me your
hand, sir, give me your hand, sir; an early stirrer, by the
rood! And how doth my good cousin Silence?   3
SILENCE Good morrow, good cousin Shallow.
SHALLOW And how doth my cousin, your bedfellow?
And your fairest daughter and mine, my god-daughter
Ellen?
SILENCE Alas, a black ousel, cousin Shallow!   7
SHALLOW By yea and no, sir, I dare say my cousin
William is become a good scholar. He is at Oxford still,
is he not?
SILENCE Indeed, sir, to my cost.
SHALLOW 'A must, then, to the Inns o' Court shortly. I   11
was once of Clement's Inn, where I think they will talk   12
of mad Shallow yet.
SILENCE You were called 'lusty Shallow' then, cousin.
SHALLOW By the mass, I was called anything. And I
would have done anything indeed too, and roundly too.   16
There was I, and little John Doit of Staffordshire, and
black George Barnes, and Francis Pickbone, and Will
Squele, a Cotswold man; you had not four such swinge-   19
bucklers in all the Inns o' Court again. And I may say to
you we knew where the bona-robas were and had the   21
best of them all at commandment. Then was Jack Fal-   22
staff, now Sir John, a boy, and page to Thomas Mowbray, Duke of Norfolk.
SILENCE This Sir John, cousin, that comes hither anon
about soldiers?
SHALLOW The same Sir John, the very same. I see him
break Skogan's head at the court-gate, when 'a was a
crack not thus high. And the very same day did I fight   29
with one Sampson Stockfish, a fruiterer, behind Gray's   30
Inn. Jesu, Jesu, the mad days that I have spent! And to
see how many of my old acquaintance are dead!
SILENCE We shall all follow, cousin.
SHALLOW Certain, 'tis certain, very sure, very sure.
Death, as the Psalmist saith, is certain to all, all shall die.
How a good yoke of bullocks at Stamford fair?   36
SILENCE By my troth, I was not there.
SHALLOW Death is certain. Is old Double of your town
living yet?
SILENCE Dead, sir.

47 *continent* dry land   55 *crosses* troubles   63 *under my foot* at my disposal   66 *Nevil* (actually the family name of the Earl of Warwick at this
period was not Nevil but Beauchamps)   68 *rated* berated   70–77 (the
lines in quotation marks are paraphrased from *Richard II*, V, i, 55–68)
76 *gathering head* coming to a head   81 *Figuring* revealing   83 *main
chance* general probability   85 *intreasurèd* stored up   87 *necessary . . . this*
logical application of this principle   103 *instance* proof   105 *unseasoned*
unseasonable   107 *inward* civil; *out of hand* done with
III, ii Before Shallow's house in Gloucestershire   3 *rood* cross   7 *ousel*
blackbird   11 *Inns o' Court* the law schools   12 *Clement's Inn* one of the
Inns of Chancery, which in Shallow's time were preparatory to the Inns
of Court   16 *roundly* thoroughly   19 *Cotswold* (the Cotswolds are a range
of hills in Gloucestershire); *swinge-bucklers* swashbucklers   21 *bona-
robas* wenches   22 *at commandment* at will   29 *crack* lively boy   30–31
Gray's Inn one of the Inns of Court   36 *How* how much

SHALLOW Jesu, Jesu, dead! 'A drew a good bow, and
42 dead! 'A shot a fine shoot. John a Gaunt loved him well
    and betted much money on his head. Dead! 'A would
44 have clapped i' the clout at twelve score, and carried
    you a forehand shaft a fourteen and fourteen and a half,
    that it would have done a man's heart good to see. How
    a score of ewes now?
48 SILENCE Thereafter as they be. A score of good ewes
    may be worth ten pounds.
SHALLOW And is old Double dead?
SILENCE Here come two of Sir John Falstaff's men, as I
    think.
        Enter Bardolph and one with him.
[SHALLOW] Good morrow, honest gentlemen.
BARDOLPH I beseech you, which is Justice Shallow?
54 SHALLOW I am Robert Shallow, sir, a poor esquire of
    this county, and one of the king's justices of the peace.
    What is your good pleasure with me?
BARDOLPH My captain, sir, commends him to you, my
58 captain, Sir John Falstaff, a tall gentleman, by heaven,
    and a most gallant leader.
SHALLOW He greets me well, sir. I knew him a good
61 backsword man. How doth the good knight? May I ask
    how my lady his wife doth?
63 BARDOLPH Sir, pardon, a soldier is better accommo-
    dated than with a wife.
SHALLOW It is well said, in faith, sir, and it is well said
    indeed too. Better accommodated! It is good, yea, in-
    deed, is it. Good phrases are surely, and ever were, very
    commendable. Accommodated! It comes of 'accom-
    modo.' Very good, a good phrase.
BARDOLPH Pardon me, sir. I have heard the word.
    Phrase call you it? By this good day, I know not the
    phrase, but I will maintain the word with my sword to
    be a soldierlike word, and a word of exceeding good
    command, by heaven. Accommodated, that is, when a
    man is, as they say, accommodated; or when a man is,
    being, whereby 'a may be thought to be accommodated,
    which is an excellent thing.
        Enter Sir John Falstaff.
78 SHALLOW It is very just. Look, here comes good Sir
    John. Give me your good hand, give me your worship's
80 good hand. By my troth, you like well and bear your
    years very well. Welcome, good Sir John.
FALSTAFF I am glad to see you well, good Master Robert
    Shallow. Master Surecard, as I think?
84 SHALLOW No, Sir John, it is my cousin Silence, in com-
    mission with me.
FALSTAFF Good Master Silence, it well befits you should
    be of the peace.

---

42 *shot . . . shoot* (referring to archery); *John a Gaunt* father of Henry IV
44 *clapped . . . score* hit the mark at 240 yards   44–45 *carried . . . half* could
shoot a heavy arrow point blank (rather than in a curved trajectory) so that
it carried 280 or 290 yards   48 *Thereafter . . . be* the price varies according
to the quality   54 *esquire* gentleman, just below the rank of knight   58
tall valiant   61 *backsword* stick with a basket hilt used instead of a sword
in fencing   63 *accommodated* provided (in Shakespeare's time the word
was considered 'precious')   78 *It . . . just* that's very true   80 *like* thrive
84–85 *in . . . me* we both hold commissions as justices of the peace   90
sufficient able   94–95 *So . . . so* (Shallow goes through the business of
checking the men against the names on the muster roll)   100 *friends*
family   107 *Prick* choose   109 *dame* mother   110 *husbandry* farm work
131 *shadows* names of non-existent men for whom the commanding officer
received pay   140 *stands* depends   142 *you . . . it* you know how to do it
149 *pricked* attired   150 *battle* army

SILENCE Your good worship is welcome.
FALSTAFF Fie! This is hot weather, gentlemen. Have
    you provided me here half a dozen sufficient men?   90
SHALLOW Marry, have we, sir. Will you sit?
FALSTAFF Let me see them, I beseech you.
SHALLOW Where's the roll? Where's the roll? Where's
    the roll? Let me see, let me see, let me see. So, so, so, so, 94
    so, so, so. Yea, marry, sir. Ralph Mouldy! Let them
    appear as I call, let them do so, let them do so. Let me
    see, where is Mouldy?
MOULDY Here, an't please you.
SHALLOW What think you, Sir John? A good-limbed
    fellow, young, strong, and of good friends.   100
FALSTAFF Is thy name Mouldy?
MOULDY Yea, an't please you.
FALSTAFF 'Tis the more time thou wert used.
SHALLOW Ha, ha, ha! most excellent, i' faith! Things
    that are mouldy lack use. Very singular good! In faith,
    well said, Sir John, very well said.
[FALSTAFF Prick him.]   107
MOULDY I was pricked well enough before, an you could 109
    have let me alone. My old dame will be undone now for 110
    one to do her husbandry and her drudgery. You need not
    to have pricked me. There are other men fitter to go out
    than I.
FALSTAFF Go to. Peace, Mouldy, you shall go. Mouldy,
    it is time you were spent.
MOULDY Spent!
SHALLOW Peace, fellow, peace. Stand aside. Know you
    where you are? For the other, Sir John, let me see.
    Simon Shadow!
FALSTAFF Yea, marry, let me have him to sit under. He's
    like to be a cold soldier.   120
SHALLOW Where's Shadow?
SHADOW Here, sir.
FALSTAFF Shadow, whose son art thou?
SHADOW My mother's son, sir.
FALSTAFF Thy mother's son! Like enough, and thy
    father's shadow. So the son of the female is the shadow
    of the male. It is often so, indeed, but much of the
    father's substance!
SHALLOW Do you like him, Sir John?
FALSTAFF Shadow will serve for summer. Prick him, for
    we have a number of shadows to fill up the muster-book. 131
SHALLOW Thomas Wart!
FALSTAFF Where's he?
WART Here, sir.
FALSTAFF Is thy name Wart?
WART Yea, sir.
FALSTAFF Thou art a very ragged wart.
SHALLOW Shall I prick him down, Sir John?
FALSTAFF It were superfluous, for his apparel is built
    upon his back and the whole frame stands upon pins. 140
    Prick him no more.
SHALLOW Ha, ha, ha! you can do it, sir, you can do it. I 142
    commend you well. Francis Feeble!
FEEBLE Here, sir.
SHALLOW What trade art thou, Feeble?
FEEBLE A woman's tailor, sir.
SHALLOW Shall I prick him, sir?
FALSTAFF You may. But if he had been a man's tailor,
    he'd a' pricked you. Wilt thou make as many holes in an 149
    enemy's battle as thou hast done in a woman's petticoat? 150
FEEBLE I will do my good will, sir. You can have no more.

FALSTAFF Well said, good woman's tailor! Well said, courageous Feeble! Thou wilt be as valiant as the
154 wrathful dove or most magnanimous mouse. Prick the woman's tailor well, Master Shallow, deep, Master Shallow.

FEEBLE I would Wart might have gone, sir.

FALSTAFF I would thou wert a man's tailor, that thou mightst mend him and make him fit to go. I cannot put him to a private soldier that is the leader of so many
159 thousands. Let that suffice, most forcible Feeble.

FEEBLE It shall suffice, sir.

FALSTAFF I am bound to thee, reverend Feeble. Who is next?

SHALLOW Peter Bullcalf o' the green!

FALSTAFF Yea, marry, let's see Bullcalf.

BULLCALF Here, sir.

FALSTAFF 'Fore God, a likely fellow! Come, prick Bullcalf till he roar again.

BULLCALF O Lord! good my lord captain –

FALSTAFF What, dost thou roar before thou art pricked?

BULLCALF O Lord, sir! I am a diseased man.

FALSTAFF What disease hast thou?

BULLCALF A whoreson cold, sir, a cough, sir, which I
173 caught with ringing in the king's affairs upon his coronation day, sir.

175 FALSTAFF Come, thou shalt go to the wars in a gown. We will have away thy cold, and I will take such order that thy friends shall ring for thee. Is here all?

SHALLOW Here is two more called than your number. You must have but four here, sir. And so, I pray you, go in with me to dinner.

FALSTAFF Come, I will go drink with you, but I cannot
182 tarry dinner. I am glad to see you, by my troth, Master Shallow.

184 SHALLOW O, Sir John, do you remember since we lay all
185 night in the Windmill in Saint George's Field?

FALSTAFF No more of that, good Master Shallow, no more of that.

SHALLOW Ha! 'Twas a merry night. And is Jane Nightwork alive?

FALSTAFF She lives, Master Shallow.

190 SHALLOW She never could away with me.

FALSTAFF Never, never, she would always say she could not abide Master Shallow.

SHALLOW By the mass, I could anger her to the heart. She was then a bona-roba. Doth she hold her own well?

FALSTAFF Old, old, Master Shallow.

SHALLOW Nay, she must be old. She cannot choose but be old. Certain she's old, and had Robin Nightwork by old Nightwork before I came to Clement's Inn.

SILENCE That's fifty-five year ago.

SHALLOW Ha, cousin Silence, that thou hadst seen that that this knight and I have seen! Ha, Sir John, said I well?

FALSTAFF We have heard the chimes at midnight, Master Shallow.

SHALLOW That we have, that we have, that we have, in
205 faith, Sir John, we have. Our watchword was 'Hem, boys!' Come, let's to dinner, come, let's to dinner. Jesus, the days that we have seen! Come, come.

Exeunt [Falstaff and the Justices].

208 BULLCALF Good Master Corporate Bardolph, stand my
209 friend, and here's four Harry ten shillings in French crowns for you. In very truth, sir, I had as lief be hanged,

sir, as go. And yet for mine own part, sir, I do not care, but rather, because I am unwilling, and, for mine own part, have a desire to stay with my friends. Else, sir, I did not care, for mine own part, so much.

BARDOLPH Go to, stand aside.

MOULDY And, good master corporal captain, for my old dame's sake, stand my friend. She has nobody to do anything about her when I am gone, and she is old, and can-
219 not help herself. You shall have forty, sir.

BARDOLPH Go to, stand aside.

FEEBLE By my troth, I care not. A man can die but once. We owe God a death. I'll ne'er bear a base mind. An't be
222 my destiny, so. An't be not, so. No man is too good to serve's prince. And let it go which way it will, he that
225 dies this year is quit for the next.

BARDOLPH Well said. Th' art a good fellow.

FEEBLE Faith, I'll bear no base mind.

Enter Falstaff and the Justices.

FALSTAFF Come, sir, which men shall I have?

SHALLOW Four of which you please.

BARDOLPH Sir, a word with you. I have three pound to free Mouldy and Bullcalf.

FALSTAFF Go to, well.

SHALLOW Come, Sir John, which four will you have?

FALSTAFF Do you choose for me.

SHALLOW Marry, then, Mouldy, Bullcalf, Feeble, and Shadow.

FALSTAFF Mouldy and Bullcalf. For you, Mouldy, stay at home till you are past service. And for your part, Bullcalf, grow till you come unto it. I will none of you.

SHALLOW Sir John, Sir John, do not yourself wrong. They are your likeliest men, and I would have you served with the best.

FALSTAFF Will you tell me, Master Shallow, how to choose
244 a man? Care I for the limb, the thews, the stature, bulk,
245 and big assemblance of a man! Give me the spirit, Master Shallow. Here's Wart. You see what a ragged appear-
247 ance it is. 'A shall charge you and discharge you with the
248 motion of a pewterer's hammer, come off and on swifter
249 than he that gibbets on the brewer's bucket. And this same half-faced fellow, Shadow. Give me this man. He presents no mark to the enemy; the foeman may with as great aim level at the edge of a penknife. And for a retreat, how swiftly will this Feeble the woman's tailor run off! O, give me the spare men, and spare me the great
255 ones. Put me a caliver into Wart's hand, Bardolph.

256 BARDOLPH Hold, Wart, traverse. Thus, thus, thus.

FALSTAFF Come, manage me your caliver. So. Very well. Go to. Very good, exceeding good. O, give me always a little, lean, old, chopped, bald shot. Well said, i' faith,
259

154 *magnanimous* stout-hearted 159 *thousands* i.e. of lice 173–74 *ringing . . . day* ringing church bells in celebration of the anniversary of the king's coronation 175 *gown* dressing gown 182 *tarry* stay for 184 *since* when 185 *Windmill* a brothel; *Saint George's Field* a favorite Sunday resort of Londoners, on the Surrey side of the Thames 190 *away with* tolerate 205–06 *Hem, boys!* here's how! down the hatch! 208 *Corporate* i.e. corporal 209–10 *four . . . crowns* (an anachronism; the 'Harry ten shilling' piece was first coined in the reign of Henry VII. In Shakespeare's time one of these pieces was worth 5s.; a French crown was worth 4s. Bullcalf's 'present' was five French crowns, the equivalent of one pound.) 219 *forty* probably forty shillings, or two pounds 222 *bear* harbor 225 *quit* free 244 *thews* strength 245 *assemblance* appearance 247 *charge . . . discharge you* load and fire 248 *motion . . . hammer* i.e. swift, regular beat 249 *gibbets . . . bucket* hangs the pails of brew on the yoke of the carrier 255 *caliver* light musket 256 *traverse* take aim 259 *chopped* chapped; *shot* armed soldier

260 Wart. Th' art a good scab. Hold, there's a tester for thee.
SHALLOW He is not his craft's master, he doth not do it
262 right. I remember at Mile-end Green, when I lay at
263 Clement's Inn – I was then Sir Dagonet in Arthur's show
264 – there was a little quiver fellow, and 'a would manage
you his piece thus, and 'a would about and about, and
come you in and come you in. 'Rah, tah, tah,' would 'a
say, 'Bounce,' would 'a say, and away again would 'a go,
and again would 'a come. I shall ne'er see such a fellow.
FALSTAFF These fellows will do well, Master Shallow.
God keep you, Master Silence. I will not use many
words with you. Fare you well, gentlemen both. I thank
you. I must a dozen mile to-night. Bardolph, give the
soldiers coats.
SHALLOW Sir John, the Lord bless you! God prosper
your affairs! God send us peace! At your return visit our
house, let our old acquaintance be renewed. Peradventure I will with ye to the court.
FALSTAFF 'Fore God, would you would, Master Shallow.
278 SHALLOW Go to, I have spoke at a word. God keep you.
FALSTAFF Fare you well, gentle gentlemen. *Exeunt [Jus-
tices]. On, Bardolph, lead the men away. [Exeunt all but*
281 *Falstaff.]* As I return, I will fetch off these justices. I do
see the bottom of Justice Shallow. Lord, Lord, how subject we old men are to this vice of lying! This same starved
285 justice hath done nothing but prate to me of the wildness
286 of his youth and the feats he hath done about Turnbull
287 Street, and every third word a lie, duer paid to the hearer
than the Turk's tribute. I do remember him at Clement's
Inn like a man made after supper of a cheese-paring.
When 'a was naked, he was, for all the world, like a forked
radish, with a head fantastically carved upon it with a
291 knife. 'A was so forlorn that his dimensions to any thick
292 sight were invincible. 'A was the very genius of famine,
yet lecherous as a monkey, and the whores called him
294 mandrake. 'A came ever in the rearward of the fashion,
295 and sung those tunes to the overscutched huswives that
296 he heard the carmen whistle, and sware they were his
297 fancies or his good-nights. And now is this Vice's dagger
become a squire, and talks as familiarly of John a Gaunt
as if he had been sworn brother to him, and I'll be sworn
'a ne'er saw him but once in the Tilt-yard, and then he
burst his head for crowding among the marshal's men. I
saw it, and told John a Gaunt he beat his own name, for

you might have thrust him and all his apparel into an
eel-skin, the case of a treble hautboy was a mansion for 304
him, a court. And now has he land and beefs. Well, I'll
be acquainted with him, if I return, and 't shall go hard
but I will make him a philosopher's two stones to me. If 307
the young dace be a bait for the old pike, I see no reason 308
in the law of nature but I may snap at him. Let time
shape, and there an end.   *Exit.*

*

Enter the Archbishop [of York], Mowbray, Hastings IV, i
[and others], within the Forest of Gaultree.
ARCHBISHOP
What is this forest called?
HASTINGS
'Tis Gaultree Forest, an't shall please your grace.
ARCHBISHOP
Here stand, my lords, and send discoverers forth   3
To know the numbers of our enemies.
HASTINGS
We have sent forth already.
ARCHBISHOP   'Tis well done.
My friends and brethren in these great affairs,
I must acquaint you that I have received
New-dated letters from Northumberland,
Their cold intent, tenor, and substance, thus:
Here doth he wish his person, with such powers   10
As might hold sortance with his quality,   11
The which he could not levy. Whereupon
He is retired, to ripe his growing fortunes,   13
To Scotland, and concludes in hearty prayers
That your attempts may overlive the hazard   15
And fearful meeting of their opposite.   16
MOWBRAY
Thus do the hopes we have in him touch ground
And dash themselves to pieces.
Enter a Messenger.
HASTINGS   Now, what news?
MESSENGER
West of this forest, scarcely off a mile,
In goodly form comes on the enemy,   20
And, by the ground they hide, I judge their number
Upon or near the rate of thirty thousand.   22
MOWBRAY
The just proportion that we gave them out.   23
Let us sway on and face them in the field.   24
ARCHBISHOP
What well-appointed leader fronts us here?   25
Enter Westmoreland.
MOWBRAY
I think it is my Lord of Westmoreland.
WESTMORELAND
Health and fair greeting from our general,
The prince, Lord John and Duke of Lancaster.
ARCHBISHOP
Say on, my Lord of Westmoreland, in peace.
What doth concern your coming?
WESTMORELAND   Then, my lord,
Unto your grace do I in chief address   31
The substance of my speech. If that rebellion
Came like itself, in base and abject routs,   33
Led on by bloody youth, guarded with rags,   34
And countenanced by boys and beggary,   35

260 *scab* a pun on the name 'Wart'; *tester* sixpence 262 *Mile-end Green* a training ground for citizen soldiers 263 *Sir Dagonet* King Arthur's fool; *Arthur's show* a group who staged an annual archery exhibition, each member taking the name of a character from Arthurian legend 264 *quiver* nimble 278 *at a word* hastily 281 *fetch off* get the better of 285–86 *Turnbull Street* a resort of prostitutes 286 *duer* more promptly 287 *Turk's tribute* tribute-money exacted by the Turk 291 *thick* dull 292 *invincible* i.e. invisible 294 *mandrake* (the mandrake root resembles the figure of a man) 295 *overscutched huswives* worn-out hussies 296 *carmen* wagoners 297 *fancies* musical compositions; *good-nights* good-night songs; *Vice's dagger* thin wooden dagger carried by Vice, the comic character in the old morality plays 304 *hautboy* oboe 307 *philosopher's two stones* i.e. the elixir of life (which was believed to preserve health) and the philosopher's stone (which, it was believed, could transmute base metal into gold). Both were referred to as stones, although the *'elixir vitae'* was also regarded as a liquid 308 *dace* small fish used as live bait
IV, i *Within the forest of Gaultree* s.d. *Forest of Gaultree* a royal forest in Yorkshire 3 *discoverers* scouts 10 *powers* forces 11 *hold sortance* accord; *quality* rank 13 *ripe* make ripe 15 *overlive* outlive 16 *opposite* adversary 20 *form* formation 22 *rate* estimated number 23 *just . . . out* exact number we estimated 24 *sway* move 25 *well-appointed* well-armed; *fronts* faces 31 *in chief* principally 33 *routs* mobs 34 *guarded* trimmed 35 *countenanced* supported; *beggary* beggars

36 I say, if damned commotion so appeared,
In his true, native and most proper shape,
You, reverend father, and these noble lords
Had not been here, to dress the ugly form
Of base and bloody insurrection
With your fair honors. You, lord archbishop,
42 Whose see is by a civil peace maintained,
Whose beard the silver hand of peace hath touched,
44 Whose learning and good letters peace hath tutored,
45 Whose white investments figure innocence,
The dove and very blessèd spirit of peace,
47 Wherefore do you so ill translate yourself
Out of the speech of peace that bears such grace,
Into the harsh and boisterous tongue of war,
Turning your books to graves, your ink to blood,
Your pens to lances, and your tongue divine
52 To a loud trumpet and a point of war?

ARCHBISHOP
Wherefore do I this? So the question stands.
Briefly to this end: we are all diseased,
55 [And with our surfeiting and wanton hours
Have brought ourselves into a burning fever,
57 And we must bleed for it. Of which disease
Our late king, Richard, being infected, died.
But, my most noble Lord of Westmoreland,
60 I take not on me here as a physician,
Nor do I as an enemy to peace
Troop in the throngs of military men,
But rather show awhile like fearful war,
64 To diet rank minds sick of happiness
And purge the obstructions which begin to stop
Our very veins of life. Hear me more plainly.
67 I have in equal balance justly weighed
What wrongs our arms may do, what wrongs we suffer,
69 And find our griefs heavier than our offenses.
We see which way the stream of time doth run,
And are enforced from our most quiet there
72 By the rough torrent of occasion,
And have the summary of all our griefs,
74 When time shall serve, to show in articles;
Which long ere this we offered to the king,
And might by no suit gain our audience.
When we are wronged and would unfold our griefs,
We are denied access unto his person
Even by those men that most have done us wrong.]
The dangers of the days but newly gone,
Whose memory is written on the earth
With yet appearing blood, and the examples
83 Of every minute's instance, present now,
Hath put us in these ill-beseeming arms,
Not to break peace or any branch of it,
But to establish here a peace indeed,
87 Concurring both in name and quality.

WESTMORELAND
When ever yet was your appeal denied?
89 Wherein have you been gallèd by the king?
90 What peer hath been suborned to grate on you,
That you should seal this lawless bloody book
Of forged rebellion with a seal divine
And consecrate commotion's bitter edge?

ARCHBISHOP
94 My brother general, the commonwealth,
95 To brother born an household cruelty,
I make my quarrel in particular.

WESTMORELAND
There is no need of any such redress,
Or if there were, it not belongs to you.

MOWBRAY
Why not to him in part, and to us all
That feel the bruises of the days before,
And suffer the condition of these times
To lay a heavy and unequal hand   102
Upon our honors?

WESTMORELAND [O, my good Lord Mowbray,
Construe the times to their necessities,   104
And you shall say indeed, it is the time,
And not the king, that doth you injuries.
Yet for your part, it not appears to me
Either from the king or in the present time
That you should have an inch of any ground
To build a grief on. Were you not restored
To all the Duke of Norfolk's signories,   111
Your noble and right well remembered father's?

MOWBRAY
What thing, in honor, had my father lost,   113
That need to be revived and breathed in me?
The king that loved him, as the state stood then,
Was force perforce compelled to banish him.   116
And then that Henry Bolingbroke and he,
Being mounted and both rousèd in their seats,
Their neighing coursers daring of the spur,
Their armèd staves in charge, their beavers down,   120
Their eyes of fire sparkling through sights of steel,
And the loud trumpet blowing them together,
Then, then, when there was nothing could have stayed
My father from the breast of Bolingbroke,
O, when the king did throw his warder down,   125
His own life hung upon the staff he threw.
Then threw he down himself and all their lives
That by indictment and by dint of sword
Have since miscarried under Bolingbroke.   129

WESTMORELAND
You speak, Lord Mowbray, now you know not what.
The Earl of Hereford was reputed then   131
In England the most valiant gentleman.
Who knows on whom fortune would then have smiled?
But if your father had been victor there,
He ne'er had borne it out of Coventry.   135
For all the country in a general voice
Cried hate upon him, and all their prayers and love
Were set on Hereford, whom they doted on
And blessed and graced indeed, more than the king.]

---

36 *commotion* rebellion 42 *see* diocese 44 *good letters* study of correct
authors 45 *investments* vestments 47 *translate* transform 52 *point of
war* signal on the trumpet 55 *surfeiting* gluttony; *wanton* self-indulgent
57 *bleed* be bled, as a therapeutic measure 60 *take . . . as* do not assume the
character of 64 *rank* obese 67 *equal* exact 69 *griefs* grievances 72
occasion circumstances 74 *articles* an itemized list 83 *Of . . . instance*
occurring every minute 87 *Concurring . . . quality* which shall be peace in
both name and fact 89 *gallèd* made sore 90 *suborned* bribed; *grate on*
vex 94 *brother general* my brothers the people at large 95 (This line has
never been explained satisfactorily. It was dropped from the folio, and,
along with line 93, from some copies of the quarto. Without it, the archbishop's words are perfectly intelligible.) 102 *unequal* unjust 104 *to*
according to 111 *signories* properties 113–29 (for the quarrel between
Mowbray and Bolingbroke see *Richard II*, I, i; iii) 116 *force perforce*
whether he wished it or not 120 *staves in charge* lances ready for action;
beavers visors of their helmets 125 *warder* staff 129 *miscarried* perished
131 *Hereford* i.e. Bolingbroke 135 *borne it* carried the prize; *Coventry*
(where the combat took place)

But this is mere digression from my purpose.
Here come I from our princely general
To know your griefs, to tell you from his grace
That he will give you audience, and wherein
It shall appear that your demands are just,
145 You shall enjoy them, everything set off
That might so much as think you enemies.

MOWBRAY
But he hath forced us to compel this offer,
And it proceeds from policy, not love.

WESTMORELAND
149 Mowbray, you overween to take it so.
This offer comes from mercy, not from fear.
151 For, lo! within a ken our army lies,
Upon mine honor, all too confident
To give admittance to a thought of fear.
154 Our battle is more full of names than yours,
Our men more perfect in the use of arms,
Our armor all as strong, our cause the best.
157 Then reason will our hearts should be as good.
Say you not then our offer is compelled.

MOWBRAY
Well, by my will we shall admit no parley.

WESTMORELAND
That argues but the shame of your offense.
161 A rotten case abides no handling.

HASTINGS
Hath the Prince John a full commission,
163 In very ample virtue of his father,
To hear and absolutely to determine
Of what conditions we shall stand upon?

WESTMORELAND
That is intended in the general's name.
167 I muse you make so slight a question.

ARCHBISHOP
Then take, my Lord of Westmoreland, this schedule,
For this contains our general grievances.
170 Each several article herein redressed,
All members of our cause, both here and hence,
172 That are insinewed to this action,
173 Acquitted by a true substantial form
And present execution of our wills
To us and to our purposes confined,
176 We come within our awful banks again
And knit our powers to the arm of peace.

WESTMORELAND
This will I show the general. Please you, lords,
In sight of both our battles we may meet,
180 And either end in peace – which God so frame –
181 Or to the place of difference call the swords

Which must decide it.

ARCHBISHOP   My lord, we will do so.
Exit Westmoreland.

MOWBRAY
There is a thing within my bosom tells me
That no conditions of our peace can stand.

HASTINGS
Fear you not that. If we can make our peace
Upon such large terms and so absolute
As our conditions shall consist upon,
Our peace shall stand as firm as rocky mountains.

MOWBRAY
189 Yea, but our valuation shall be such
That every slight and false-derivèd cause,
191 Yea, every idle, nice, and wanton reason
Shall to the king taste of this action,
193 That, were our royal faiths martyrs in love,
We shall be winnowed with so rough a wind
That even our corn shall seem as light as chaff
196 And good from bad find no partition.

ARCHBISHOP
No, no, my lord. Note this. The king is weary
198 Of dainty and such picking grievances.
199 For he hath found to end one doubt by death
Revives two greater in the heirs of life,
201 And therefore will he wipe his tables clean
And keep no tell-tale to his memory
That may repeat and history his loss
To new remembrance. For full well he knows
205 He cannot so precisely weed this land
206 As his misdoubts present occasion.
His foes are so enrooted with his friends
That, plucking to unfix an enemy,
He doth unfasten so and shake a friend.
So that this land, like an offensive wife
That hath enraged him on to offer strokes,
As he is striking, holds his infant up
213 And hangs resolved correction in the arm
That was upreared to execution.

HASTINGS
Besides, the king hath wasted all his rods
On late offenders, that he now doth lack
The very instruments of chastisement.
So that his power, like to a fangless lion,
219 May offer, but not hold.

ARCHBISHOP   'Tis very true.
And therefore be assured, my good lord marshal,
221 If we do now make our atonement well,
Our peace will, like a broken limb united,
Grow stronger for the breaking.

MOWBRAY   Be it so.
Here is returned my Lord of Westmoreland.
Enter Westmoreland.

WESTMORELAND
The prince is here at hand. Pleaseth your lordship
226 To meet his grace just distance 'tween our armies.

MOWBRAY
Your grace of York, in God's name then, set forward.

ARCHBISHOP
Before, and greet his grace, my lord; we come.
228

---

145 *set off* removed   149 *overween* are presumptuous   151 *ken* range of vision   154 *battle . . . names* army has more leaders with distinguished reputations   157 *reason will* it is reasonable that   161 *rotten* weak   163 *In . . . virtue* by full authority   167 *muse* am surprised   170 *several* separate 172 *insinewed* joined by strong sinews   173 *substantial form* formal agreement   176 *banks* i.e. as a stream which has been in flood subsides to the confines of its banks   180 *frame* bring to pass   181 *difference* battle   189 *our valuation* the king's valuation of us   191 *nice* petty; *wanton* frivolous 193 *That . . . love* so that even if we suffered martyrdom for our love of the king   196 *partition* distinction   198 *dainty* precise; *picking* trifling 199 *doubt* danger   201 *tables* note-book   205 *precisely* thoroughly   206 *misdoubts* suspicions   213-14 *hangs . . . execution* causes him to stay his arm and resolve upon correction rather than execution   219 *offer* threaten   221 *atonement* reconciliation   226 *just* exact   228 *Before* go before

IV, ii   *Enter Prince John [of Lancaster] and his army.*

LANCASTER
You are well encountered here, my cousin Mowbray.
Good day to you, gentle lord archbishop.
And so to you, Lord Hastings, and to all.
My Lord of York, it better showed with you
When that your flock, assembled by the bell,
Encircled you to hear with reverence
Your exposition on the holy text
8   Than now to see you here an iron man,
Cheering a rout of rebels with your drum,
10   Turning the word to sword and life to death.
That man that sits within a monarch's heart
And ripens in the sunshine of his favor,
Would he abuse the countenance of the king,
14   Alack, what mischiefs might he set abroach
In shadow of such greatness. With you, lord bishop,
It is even so. Who hath not heard it spoken
How deep you were within the books of God?
To us the speaker in His parliament,
To us the imagined voice of God himself,
20   The very opener and intelligencer
Between the grace, the sanctities of heaven
22   And our dull workings. O, who shall believe
But you misuse the reverence of your place,
Employ the countenance and grace of heaven,
As a false favorite doth his prince's name,
26   In deeds dishonorable? You have ta'en up,
Under the counterfeited zeal of God,
28   The subjects of His substitute, my father,
And both against the peace of heaven and him
Have here upswarmed them.

ARCHBISHOP   Good my Lord of Lancaster,
I am not here against your father's peace,
But, as I told my Lord of Westmoreland,
33   The time misordered doth, in common sense,
34   Crowd us and crush us to this monstrous form,
To hold our safety up. I sent your grace
36   The parcels and particulars of our grief,
The which hath been with scorn shoved from the court,
38   Whereon this Hydra son of war is born,
Whose dangerous eyes may well be charmed asleep
With grant of our most just and right desires,
And true obedience, of this madness cured,
Stoop tamely to the foot of majesty.

MOWBRAY
If not, we ready are to try our fortunes
To the last man.

HASTINGS   And though we here fall down,
45   We have supplies to second our attempt.
If they miscarry, theirs shall second them,
47   And so success of mischief shall be born
And heir from heir shall hold this quarrel up
49   Whiles England shall have generation.

LANCASTER
You are too shallow, Hastings, much too shallow,
To sound the bottom of the after-times.

WESTMORELAND
Pleaseth your grace to answer them directly
How far forth you do like their articles.

LANCASTER
I like them all, and do allow them well,
And swear here, by the honor of my blood,
My father's purposes have been mistook,

And some about him have too lavishly   57
Wrested his meaning and authority.   58
My lord, these griefs shall be with speed redressed,
Upon my soul, they shall. If this may please you,
Discharge your powers unto their several counties,
As we will ours. And here between the armies
Let's drink together friendly and embrace,
That all their eyes may bear those tokens home
Of our restorèd love and amity.

ARCHBISHOP
I take your princely word for these redresses.

[LANCASTER]
I give it you, and will maintain my word.
And thereupon I drink unto your grace.

[HASTINGS]
Go, captain, and deliver to the army
This news of peace. Let them have pay, and part.   70
I know it will well please them. Hie thee, captain.
                              Exit [Officer].

ARCHBISHOP
To you, my noble Lord of Westmoreland.

WESTMORELAND
I pledge your grace, and, if you knew what pains
I have bestowed to breed this present peace,
You would drink freely. But my love to ye
Shall show itself more openly hereafter.

ARCHBISHOP
I do not doubt you.

WESTMORELAND   I am glad of it.
Health to my lord and gentle cousin, Mowbray.

MOWBRAY
You wish me health in very happy season,
For I am, on the sudden, something ill.   80

ARCHBISHOP
Against ill chances men are ever merry,   81
But heaviness foreruns the good event.

WESTMORELAND
Therefore be merry, coz, since sudden sorrow
Serves to say thus, 'Some good thing comes to-morrow.'

ARCHBISHOP
Believe me, I am passing light in spirit.   85

MOWBRAY
So much the worse, if your own rule be true.
                    Shouts [within].

LANCASTER
The word of peace is rendered. Hark, how they shout!   87

MOWBRAY
This had been cheerful after victory.

ARCHBISHOP
A peace is of the nature of a conquest,
For then both parties nobly are subdued,
And neither party loser.

IV, ii (It is not certain that any change of scene was intended here. In the quarto the stage direction follows l. 226. The folio has instead 'Enter Prince John' following l. 228, which seems a better position. Neither stage direction indicates a change of scene; but the dialogue of ll. 227–28 seems to indicate that the stage was cleared after l. 228.)   8 *an iron man* clad in armor   10 *the word* the Scripture   14 *abroach* afoot   20 *opener* interpreter; *intelligencer* messenger   22 *workings* operations of the mind   26 *ta'en up* enlisted   28 *substitute* deputy   33 *common sense* the judgment of all the people   34 *monstrous* unnatural   36 *parcels* details   38 *Hydra* many-headed   45 *supplies* reinforcements; *second* take the place of   47 *success* succession   49 *generation* offspring   57 *lavishly* loosely   58 *Wrested* twisted   70 *part* depart   80 *something* somewhat   81 *Against* in expectation of   85 *passing* exceedingly   87 *rendered* declared

LANCASTER   Go, my lord,
And let our army be dischargèd too.
> *[Exit Westmoreland.]*

93   And, good my lord, so please you, let our trains
March by us, that we may peruse the men
95   We should have coped withal.

ARCHBISHOP   Go, good Lord Hastings,
And, ere they be dismissed, let them march by.
> *[Exit Hastings.]*

LANCASTER
I trust, lords, we shall lie to-night together.
> *Enter Westmoreland.*

Now cousin, wherefore stands our army still?

WESTMORELAND
The leaders, having charge from you to stand,
Will not go off until they hear you speak.

LANCASTER
They know their duties.
> *Enter Hastings.*

HASTINGS
My lord, our army is dispersed already.
Like youthful steers unyoked, they take their courses
East, west, north, south, or, like a school broke up,
105   Each hurries toward his home and sporting-place.

WESTMORELAND
Good tidings, my Lord Hastings, for the which
I do arrest thee, traitor, of high treason.
And you, lord archbishop, and you, Lord Mowbray,
109   Of capital treason I attach you both.

MOWBRAY
Is this proceeding just and honorable?

WESTMORELAND
Is your assembly so?

ARCHBISHOP
Will you thus break your faith?

112 LANCASTER   I pawned thee none.
I promised you redress of these same grievances
Whereof you did complain, which, by mine honor,
I will perform with a most Christian care.
But for you, rebels, look to taste the due
Meet for rebellion and such acts as yours.
Most shallowly did you these arms commence,
119   Fondly brought here and foolishly sent hence.
120   Strike up our drums, pursue the scattered stray.
God, and not we, hath safely fought to-day.
Some guard these traitors to the block of death,
Treason's true bed and yielder up of breath.   *[Exeunt.]*

IV, iii   *Alarum. Excursions. Enter Falstaff [and Coleville, meeting].*

1 FALSTAFF   What's your name, sir? Of what condition are
you, and of what place, I pray?

COLEVILLE   I am a knight, sir, and my name is Coleville
of the dale.

FALSTAFF   Well, then, Coleville is your name, a knight is
your degree, and your place the dale. Coleville shall be

still your name, a traitor your degree, and the dungeon
your place, a place deep enough. So shall you be still
Coleville of the dale.

COLEVILLE   Are not you Sir John Falstaff?

FALSTAFF   As good a man as he, sir, whoe'er I am. Do ye
yield, sir, or shall I sweat for you? If I do sweat, they are
the drops of thy lovers, and they weep for thy death. 13
Therefore rouse up fear and trembling, and do observance to my mercy.

COLEVILLE   I think you are Sir John Falstaff, and in that
thought yield me.

FALSTAFF   I have a whole school of tongues in this belly of 18
mine, and not a tongue of them all speaks any other word
but my name. An I had but a belly of any indifferency, I 20
were simply the most active fellow in Europe. My
womb, my womb, my womb undoes me. Here comes 22
our general.
> *Enter [Prince] John [of Lancaster], Westmoreland,*
> *[Blunt,] and the rest. Retreat [sounded].*

LANCASTER
The heat is past, follow no further now.   24
Call in the powers, good cousin Westmoreland.
> *[Exit Westmoreland.]*

Now, Falstaff, where have you been all this while?
When everything is ended, then you come.
These tardy tricks of yours will, on my life,
One time or other break some gallows' back.

FALSTAFF   I would be sorry, my lord, but it should be
thus. I never knew yet but rebuke and check was the
reward of valor. Do you think me a swallow, an arrow, or
a bullet? Have I, in my poor and old motion, the expedition of thought? I have speeded hither with the very extremest inch of possibility. I have foundered nine score 35
and odd posts, and here, travel-tainted as I am, have, in 36
my pure and immaculate valor, taken Sir John Coleville
of the dale, a most furious knight and valorous enemy.
But what of that? He saw me, and yielded, that I may
justly say, with the hook-nosed fellow of Rome, their
Caesar, 'I came, saw, and overcame.'

LANCASTER   It was more of his courtesy than your deserving.

FALSTAFF   I know not. Here he is, and here I yield him.
And I beseech your grace, let it be booked with the rest
of this day's deeds, or, by the Lord, I will have it in a par- 45
ticular ballad else, with mine own picture on the top on't,
Coleville kissing my foot. To the which course if I be
enforced, if you do not all show like gilt twopences to 48
me, and I in the clear sky of fame o'ershine you as much
as the full moon doth the cinders of the element, which 50
show like pins' heads to her, believe not the word of the
noble. Therefore let me have right, and let desert
mount.

LANCASTER   Thine's too heavy to mount.

FALSTAFF   Let it shine, then.

LANCASTER   Thine's too thick to shine.

FALSTAFF   Let it do something, my good lord, that may
do me good, and call it what you will.

LANCASTER   Is thy name Coleville?

COLEVILLE   It is, my lord.

LANCASTER   A famous rebel art thou, Coleville.

FALSTAFF   And a famous true subject took him.

COLEVILLE
I am, my lord, but as my betters are
That led me hither. Had they been ruled by me,

---

93 *trains* armies   95 *coped withal* been matched with   105 *sporting-place*
playground   109 *capital* punishable by death   112 *pawned* pledged   119
Fondly foolishly   120 *stray* stragglers
IV, iii   1 *condition* rank   13 *drops* tear-drops; *lovers* friends   18–20 *I . . .
name* i.e. my corpulency makes my identity unmistakable   18 *school*
crowd   20 *indifferency* moderate size   22 *womb* belly   24 *heat* height of
the action   35 *foundered* lamed   36 *posts* post-horses   45–46 *particular
ballad* broadside ballad celebrating my own exploits   48 *show* appear; *to*
in comparison with   50 *cinders . . . element* stars

You should have won them dearer than you have.

FALSTAFF I know not how they sold themselves. But
thou, like a kind fellow, gavest thyself away gratis, and I
thank thee for thee.

Enter Westmoreland.

LANCASTER
Now, have you left pursuit?

WESTMORELAND
69 Retreat is made and execution stayed.

LANCASTER
Send Coleville with his confederates
71 To York, to present execution.
Blunt, lead him hence, and see you guard him sure.

[Exeunt Blunt and others with Coleville.]

73 And now dispatch we toward the court, my lords.
I hear the king my father is sore sick.
Our news shall go before us to his majesty,
Which, cousin, you shall bear to comfort him,
And we with sober speed will follow you.

FALSTAFF
My lord, I beseech you give me leave to go
Through Gloucestershire. And when you come to court,
80 Stand my good lord, pray, in your good report.

LANCASTER
81 Fare you well, Falstaff. I, in my condition,
Shall better speak of you than you deserve.

[Exeunt all but Falstaff.]

FALSTAFF I would you had but the wit. 'Twere better than
your dukedom. Good faith, this same young sober-
blooded boy doth not love me, nor a man cannot make
him laugh. But that's no marvel, he drinks no wine.
87 There's never none of these demure boys come to any
88 proof, for thin drink doth so overcool their blood, and
making many fish-meals, that they fall into a kind of
90 male green-sickness, and then, when they marry, they get
wenches. They are generally fools and cowards, which
92 some of us should be too, but for inflammation. A good
93 sherris-sack hath a twofold operation in it. It ascends me
into the brain, dries me there all the foolish and dull and
95 crudy vapors which environ it, makes it apprehensive,
96 quick, forgetive, full of nimble, fiery, and delectable
shapes, which, delivered o'er to the voice, the tongue,
98 which is the birth, becomes excellent wit. The second
property of your excellent sherris is the warming of the
100 blood, which, before cold and settled, left the liver white
and pale, which is the badge of pusillanimity and cowardice. But the sherris warms it and makes it course from
the inwards to the parts extremes. It illumineth the face,
which as a beacon gives warning to all the rest of this
105 little kingdom, man, to arm, and then the vital commoners and inland petty spirits muster me all to their
captain, the heart, who, great and puffed up with this
retinue, doth any deed of courage, and this valor comes
of sherris. So that skill in the weapon is nothing without
sack, for that sets it a-work, and learning a mere hoard of
111 gold kept by a devil, till sack commences it and sets it in
act and use. Hereof comes it that Prince Harry is valiant,
for the cold blood he did naturally inherit of his father,
114 he hath, like lean, sterile, and bare land, manured, husbanded, and tilled with excellent endeavor of drinking
good and good store of fertile sherris, that he is become
very hot and valiant. If I had a thousand sons, the first
humane principle I would teach them should be to forswear thin potations and to addict themselves to sack.

Enter Bardolph.

How now, Bardolph?

BARDOLPH The army is discharged all and gone.

FALSTAFF Let them go. I'll through Gloucestershire, and
there will I visit Master Robert Shallow, esquire. I have 123
him already tempering between my finger and my
thumb, and shortly will I seal with him. Come away. 125

[Exeunt.]

*

Enter the King, Warwick, Thomas Duke of Clarence, IV, iv
Humphrey [Duke] of Gloucester [, and others].

KING
Now, lords, if God doth give successful end
To this debate that bleedeth at our doors, 2
We will our youth lead on to higher fields 3
And draw no swords but what are sanctified.
Our navy is addressed, our power collected, 5
Our substitutes in absence well invested, 6
And everything lies level to our wish. 7
Only, we want a little personal strength,
And pause us, till these rebels, now afoot,
Come underneath the yoke of government.

WARWICK
Both which we doubt not but your majesty
Shall soon enjoy.

KING   Humphrey, my son of Gloucester,
Where is the prince your brother?

GLOUCESTER
I think he's gone to hunt, my lord, at Windsor.

KING
And how accompanied?

GLOUCESTER   I do not know, my lord.

KING
Is not his brother, Thomas of Clarence, with him?

GLOUCESTER
No, my good lord, he is in presence here. 17

CLARENCE
What would my lord and father?

KING
Nothing but well to thee, Thomas of Clarence.
How chance thou art not with the prince thy brother?
He loves thee, and thou dost neglect him, Thomas;
Thou hast a better place in his affection
Than all thy brothers. Cherish it, my boy,
And noble offices thou mayst effect
Of mediation, after I am dead,
Between his greatness and thy other brethren.
Therefore omit him not, blunt not his love, 27

69 *Retreat is made* the order for retreat has been given; *stayed* stopped
71 *present* immediate   73 *dispatch we* let us hurry   80 *Stand . . . lord* be
my patron   81 *in my condition* i.e. as commanding officer   87–88 *come
. . . proof* stand up under testing   88 *thin drink* beer   90 *green-sickness* a
form of anemia, usually associated with young girls; *get* beget   92 *inflammation* i.e. inflaming the mind with liquor   93 *sherris-sack* sherry
95 *crudy* curded;   *apprehensive* discerning   96 *forgetive* inventive   98
wit understanding   100 *liver* (regarded as the seat of courage)   105–06
vital . . . spirits vital spirits which inhabit man's inward parts   111 *commences it* gives it license to act (as a university commencement gives the
graduate authority to put his knowledge to use)   114 *manured* cultivated
123–25 *I . . . thumb* I am warming him, as sealing-wax is warmed between
the fingers   125 *seal with* i.e. make use of
IV, iv *Within King Henry's palace, Westminster   2 debate* quarrel   3–4
(for the king's intention to go on crusade to the Holy Land, see *1 Henry IV*,
I, i, 18–29)   5 *addressed* ready   6 *substitutes* deputies   7 *level to* in accordance with   17 *in presence* present at court   27 *omit* neglect

Nor lose the good advantage of his grace
By seeming cold or careless of his will.
30 For he is gracious, if he be observed.
He hath a tear for pity and a hand
32 Open as day for meting charity.
Yet notwithstanding, being incensed, he's flint,
34 As humorous as winter and as sudden
35 As flaws congealèd in the spring of day.
His temper, therefore, must be well observed.
Chide him for faults, and do it reverently,
When you perceive his blood inclined to mirth,
But, being moody, give him time and scope,
Till that his passions, like a whale on ground,
41 Confound themselves with working. Learn this, Thomas,
And thou shalt prove a shelter to thy friends,
A hoop of gold to bind thy brothers in,
That the united vessel of their blood,
45 Mingled with venom of suggestion –
As, force perforce, the age will pour it in –
Shall never leak, though it do work as strong
48 As aconitum or rash gunpowder.

CLARENCE
I shall observe him with all care and love.

KING
Why art thou not at Windsor with him, Thomas?

CLARENCE
He is not there to-day; he dines in London.

KING
And how accompanied? Canst thou tell that?

CLARENCE
With Poins and other his continual followers.

KING
54 Most subject is the fattest soil to weeds,
And he, the noble image of my youth,
Is overspread with them. Therefore my grief
Stretches itself beyond the hour of death.
The blood weeps from my heart when I do shape
In forms imaginary the unguided days
And rotten times that you shall look upon
When I am sleeping with my ancestors.
For when his headstrong riot hath no curb,
When rage and hot blood are his counsellors,
64 When means and lavish manners meet together,
O, with what wings shall his affections fly
66 Towards fronting peril and opposed decay!

WARWICK
67 My gracious lord, you look beyond him quite.
The prince but studies his companions
Like a strange tongue, wherein, to gain the language,
'Tis needful that the most immodest word
Be looked upon and learned, which once attained,
Your highness knows, comes to no further use

But to be known and hated. So, like gross terms, 73
The prince will in the perfectness of time 74
Cast off his followers, and their memory
Shall as a pattern or a measure live,
By which his grace must mete the lives of others, 77
Turning past evils to advantages.

KING
'Tis seldom when the bee doth leave her comb 79
In the dead carrion.
  Enter Westmoreland.
                          Who's here? Westmoreland?

WESTMORELAND
Health to my sovereign, and new happiness
Added to that that I am to deliver.
Prince John your son doth kiss your grace's hand.
Mowbray, the Bishop Scroop, Hastings and all
Are brought to the correction of your law.
There is not now a rebel's sword unsheathed,
But Peace puts forth her olive everywhere.
The manner how this action hath been borne
Here at more leisure may your highness read,
With every course in his particular. 90

KING
O Westmoreland, thou art a summer bird,
Which ever in the haunch of winter sings 92
The lifting up of day.
  Enter Harcourt.
                    Look, here's more news.

HARCOURT
From enemies heaven keep your majesty,
And, when they stand against you, may they fall
As those that I am come to tell you of!
The Earl Northumberland and the Lord Bardolph,
With a great power of English and of Scots,
Are by the shrieve of Yorkshire overthrown. 99
The manner and true order of the fight
This packet, please it you, contains at large.

KING
And wherefore should these good news make me sick?
Will Fortune never come with both hands full,
But write her fair words still in foulest letters? 104
She either gives a stomach and no food –
Such are the poor, in health – or else a feast
And takes away the stomach – such are the rich,
That have abundance and enjoy it not.
I should rejoice now at this happy news,
And now my sight fails, and my brain is giddy.
O me! Come near me. Now I am much ill.

GLOUCESTER
Comfort, your majesty!

CLARENCE   O my royal father!

WESTMORELAND
My sovereign lord, cheer up yourself, look up.

WARWICK
Be patient, princes. You do know these fits
Are with his highness very ordinary.
Stand from him, give him air, he'll straight be well. 116

CLARENCE
No, no, he cannot long hold out these pangs. 117
The incessant care and labor of his mind
Hath wrought the mure that should confine it in 119
So thin that life looks through and will break out.

GLOUCESTER
The people fear me, for they do observe 121

30 *observed* respected 32 *meting* distributing 34 *humorous* capricious 35 *flaws congealèd* snowflakes 41 *Confound* consume; *working* struggling 45 *suggestion* false insinuation 48 *aconitum* monkshood, a violent poison; *rash* quick and strong 54 *fattest* richest 64 *lavish* licentious 66 *fronting* opposing; *decay* ruin 67 *look beyond* misunderstand 73 *terms* expressions 74 *perfectness* perfection 77 *mete* appraise 79–80 '*Tis . . . carrion* the bee which has placed her comb in a carcass seldom leaves her honey 90 *every . . . particular* every phase of the action set forth in detail 92 *haunch* hinder part, end 99 *shrieve* sheriff 104 *still* ever 116 *straight* straightway 117 *hold out* endure 119 *wrought the mure* made the wall 121 *fear* frighten

122 Unfathered heirs and loathly births of nature.
The seasons change their manners, as the year
Had found some months asleep and leaped them over.

CLARENCE

125 The river hath thrice flowed, no ebb between,
And the old folk, time's doting chronicles,
Say it did so a little time before

128 That our great-grandsire, Edward, sicked and died.

WARWICK

Speak lower, princes, for the king recovers.

GLOUCESTER

This apoplexy will certain be his end.

KING

I pray you, take me up, and bear me hence

132 Into some other chamber. Softly, pray.
[They bear him to another place.]

IV, v Let there be no noise made, my gentle friends,

2 Unless some dull and favorable hand
Will whisper music to my weary spirit.

WARWICK

Call for the music in the other room.

KING

Set me the crown upon my pillow here.

CLARENCE

6 His eye is hollow, and he changes much.

WARWICK

Less noise, less noise!
Enter Prince Henry.

PRINCE   Who saw the Duke of Clarence?

CLARENCE

I am here, brother, full of heaviness.

PRINCE

9 How now! Rain within doors, and none abroad!
How doth the king?

GLOUCESTER

Exceeding ill.

PRINCE   Heard he the good news yet?
Tell it him.

GLOUCESTER

He altered much upon the hearing it.

PRINCE

If he be sick with joy, he'll recover without physic.

WARWICK

Not so much noise, my lords. Sweet prince, speak low.
The king your father is disposed to sleep.

CLARENCE

Let us withdraw into the other room.

WARWICK

Will't please your grace to go along with us?

PRINCE

No, I will sit and watch here by the king.
[Exeunt all but the Prince.]

Why doth the crown lie there upon his pillow,
Being so troublesome a bedfellow?

22 O polished perturbation! Golden care!

23 That keep'st the ports of slumber open wide
To many a watchful night! Sleep with it now!
Yet not so sound and half so deeply sweet

26 As he whose brow with homely biggen bound
Snores out the watch of night. O majesty!
When thou dost pinch thy bearer, thou dost sit
Like a rich armor worn in heat of day,

30 That scald'st with safety. By his gates of breath
There lies a downy feather which stirs not.

Did he suspire, that light and weightless down   32
Perforce must move. My gracious lord! my father!
This sleep is sound indeed. This is a sleep

35 That from this golden rigol hath divorced
So many English kings. Thy due from me
Is tears and heavy sorrows of the blood,
Which nature, love, and filial tenderness
Shall, O dear father, pay thee plenteously.
My due from thee is this imperial crown,
Which, as immediate from thy place and blood,   41
Derives itself to me. *[Puts on the crown.]* Lo, where it sits,   42
Which God shall guard. And put the world's whole
strength
Into one giant arm, it shall not force
This lineal honor from me. This from thee   45
Will I to mine leave, as 'tis left to me.   *[Exit.]*

KING

Warwick! Gloucester! Clarence!
Enter Warwick, Gloucester, Clarence.

CLARENCE

Doth the king call?

WARWICK

What would your majesty? How fares your grace?

KING

Why did you leave me here alone, my lords?

CLARENCE

We left the prince my brother here, my liege,
Who undertook to sit and watch by you.

KING

The Prince of Wales! Where is he? Let me see him.
He is not here.

WARWICK

The door is open; he is gone this way.

GLOUCESTER

He came not through the chamber where we stayed.

KING

Where is the crown? Who took it from my pillow?

WARWICK

When we withdrew, my liege, we left it here.

KING

The prince hath ta'en it hence. Go, seek him out.
Is he so hasty that he doth suppose
My sleep my death?
Find him, my Lord of Warwick, chide him hither.
         [Exit Warwick.]
This part of his conjoins with my disease   63
And helps to end me. See, sons, what things you are!
How quickly nature falls into revolt
When gold becomes her object!
For this the foolish overcareful fathers
Have broke their sleep with thoughts, their brains with   68
care,
Their bones with industry.
For this they have engrossed and pilèd up   70

122 *Unfathered heirs* persons thought to be supernaturally conceived;
loathly births monstrous infants   125 *river* Thames   128 *Edward* Edward
III   132 *Into some other chamber* (the king remains in view, and so was
perhaps borne to a bed placed at some other point on the stage)
IV, v   2 *dull* soothing; *favorable* kindly   6 *changes* grows pale   9 *Rain*
i.e. tears   22 *perturbation* cause of perturbation   23 *ports* gates   26
biggen nightcap   30 *scald'st with safety* burns while it protects; *gates of
breath* lips   32 *suspire* breathe   35 *rigol* circle   41 *immediate from* nearest
to   42 *Derives* descends   45 *lineal* inherited   63 *part* conduct   68
thoughts anxieties   70 *engrossed* accumulated

71 The cankered heaps of strange-achievèd gold;
72 For this they have been thoughtful to invest
73 Their sons with arts and martial exercises.
74 When, like the bee, tolling from every flower
[The virtuous sweets],
Our thighs packed with wax, our mouths with honey,
We bring it to the hive, and, like the bees,
78 Are murdered for our pains. This bitter taste
79 Yields his engrossments to the ending father.
Enter Warwick.
Now, where is he that will not stay so long
81 Till his friend sickness hath determined me?

WARWICK
My lord, I found the prince in the next room,
83 Washing with kindly tears his gentle cheeks,
84 With such a deep demeanor in great sorrow
That tyranny, which never quaffed but blood,
Would, by beholding him, have washed his knife
With gentle eye-drops. He is coming hither.

KING
But wherefore did he take away the crown?
Enter [Prince] Henry.
Lo, where he comes. Come hither to me, Harry.
Depart the chamber, leave us here alone.
Exeunt [Warwick and the rest].

PRINCE
I never thought to hear you speak again.

KING
Thy wish was father, Harry, to that thought.
I stay too long by thee, I weary thee.
Dost thou so hunger for mine empty chair
That thou wilt needs invest thee with my honors
Before thy hour be ripe? O foolish youth!
Thou seek'st the greatness that will overwhelm thee.
Stay but a little, for my cloud of dignity
Is held from falling with so weak a wind
That it will quickly drop. My day is dim.
Thou hast stolen that which after some few hours
Were thine without offense, and at my death
103 Thou hast sealed up my expectation.
Thy life did manifest thou lovedst me not,
And thou wilt have me die assured of it.
Thou hidest a thousand daggers in thy thoughts,
Which thou hast whetted on thy stony heart,
To stab at half an hour of my life.
What! Canst thou not forbear me half an hour?
Then get thee gone and dig my grave thyself,
And bid the merry bells ring to thine ear
That thou art crownèd, not that I am dead.
Let all the tears that should bedew my hearse
114 Be drops of balm to sanctify thy head.
115 Only compound me with forgotten dust;
Give that which gave thee life unto the worms.
Pluck down my officers, break my decrees,
118 For now a time is come to mock at form.

Harry the Fifth is crowned. Up, vanity! *119*
Down, royal state! All you sage counsellors, hence!
And to the English court assemble now,
From every region, apes of idleness!
Now, neighbor confines, purge you of your scum. *123*
Have you a ruffian that will swear, drink, dance,
Revel the night, rob, murder, and commit
The oldest sins the newest kind of ways?
Be happy, he will trouble you no more.
England shall double gild his treble guilt,
England shall give him office, honor, might,
For the fifth Harry from curbed license plucks
The muzzle of restraint, and the wild dog
Shall flesh his tooth on every innocent. *132*
O my poor kingdom, sick with civil blows!
When that my care could not withhold thy riots, *134*
What wilt thou do when riot is thy care? *135*
O, thou wilt be a wilderness again,
Peopled with wolves, thy old inhabitants.

PRINCE
O, pardon me, my liege! But for my tears,
The moist impediments unto my speech,
I had forestalled this dear and deep rebuke *140*
Ere you with grief had spoke and I had heard
The course of it so far. There is your crown,
And He that wears the crown immortally
Long guard it yours. If I affect it more *144*
Than as your honor and as your renown,
Let me no more from this obedience rise, *146*
Which my most inward true and duteous spirit
Teacheth, this prostrate and exterior bending.
God witness with me, when I here came in,
And found no course of breath within your majesty,
How cold it struck my heart. If I do feign,
O, let me in my present wildness die
And never live to show the incredulous world
The noble change that I have purposèd.
Coming to look on you, thinking you dead,
And dead almost, my liege, to think you were,
I spake unto this crown as having sense,
And thus upbraided it: 'The care on thee depending
Hath fed upon the body of my father.
Therefore, thou best of gold art worst of gold.
Other, less fine in carat, is more precious,
Preserving life in medicine potable, *162*
But thou, most fine, most honored, most renowned,
Hast eat thy bearer up.' Thus, my most royal liege,
Accusing it, I put it on my head,
To try with it, as with an enemy
That had before my face murdered my father,
The quarrel of a true inheritor.
But if it did infect my blood with joy,
Or swell my thoughts to any strain of pride, *170*
If any rebel or vain spirit of mine
Did with the least affection of a welcome
Give entertainment to the might of it,
Let God for ever keep it from my head
And make me as the poorest vassal is
That doth with awe and terror kneel to it.

KING
[O my son,]
God put it in thy mind to take it hence,
That thou mightst win the more thy father's love,
Pleading so wisely in excuse of it!

71 *cankered* tarnished 72 *thoughtful* careful 73 *arts* learning 74 *tolling* gathering 78–79 *This . . . engrossments* his accumulations leave this bitter taste 79 *ending* dying 81 *determined* put an end to 83 *kindly* natural 84 *deep* intense 103 *sealed up* confirmed 114 *balm* oil of consecration 115 *compound* mix 118 *form* ceremony 119 *vanity* folly 123 *confines* regions 132 *flesh* plunge into flesh 134 *care* carefulness 135 *care* occupation 140 *dear* severe 144 *affect* desire 146 *obedience* obeisance, low curtsy 162 *medicine potable* (gold in solution was often prescribed as a medicine) 170 *strain* feeling

Come hither, Harry, sit thou by my bed,
182 And hear, I think, the very latest counsel
That ever I shall breathe. God knows, my son,
By what bypaths and indirect crooked ways
I met this crown, and I myself know well
How troublesome it sat upon my head.
To thee it shall descend with better quiet,
188 Better opinion, better confirmation,
189 For all the soil of the achievement goes
With me into the earth. It seemed in me
But as an honor snatched with boisterous hand,
And I had many living to upbraid
My gain of it by their assistances,
Which daily grew to quarrel and to bloodshed
195 Wounding supposèd peace. All these bold fears
Thou seest with peril I have answerèd,
For all my reign hath been but as a scene
198 Acting that argument. And now my death
199 Changes the mode, for what in me was purchased
Falls upon thee in a more fairer sort,
201 So thou the garland wear'st successively.
Yet, though thou stand'st more sure than I could do,
203 Thou art not firm enough, since griefs are green.
And all my friends, which thou must make thy friends,
Have but their stings and teeth newly ta'en out,
206 By whose fell working I was first advanced
207 And by whose power I well might lodge a fear
To be again displaced. Which to avoid,
I cut them off, and had a purpose now
To lead out many to the Holy Land,
211 Lest rest and lying still might make them look
Too near unto my state. Therefore, my Harry,
Be it thy course to busy giddy minds
214 With foreign quarrels, that action, hence borne out,
May waste the memory of the former days.
More would I, but my lungs are wasted so
That strength of speech is utterly denied me.
How I came by the crown, O God forgive,
And grant it may with thee in true peace live!

PRINCE
[My gracious liege,]
You won it, wore it, kept it, gave it me.
Then plain and right must my possession be,
223 Which I with more than with a common pain
'Gainst all the world will rightfully maintain.

Enter [Prince John of] Lancaster [and Warwick].

KING
Look, look, here comes my John of Lancaster.

LANCASTER
Health, peace, and happiness to my royal father!

KING
Thou bring'st me happiness and peace, son John,
But health, alack, with youthful wings is flown
From this bare withered trunk. Upon thy sight
My worldly business makes a period.
Where is my Lord of Warwick?

PRINCE   My Lord of Warwick!

KING
Doth any name particular belong
Unto the lodging where I first did swoon?

WARWICK
234 'Tis called Jerusalem, my noble lord.

KING
Laud be to God! Even there my life must end.

It hath been prophesied to me many years
I should not die but in Jerusalem,
Which vainly I supposed the Holy Land.
But bear me to that chamber; there I'll lie.
In that Jerusalem shall Harry die.   *[Exeunt.]*

*

Enter Shallow, Falstaff, and Bardolph [and Page].   V, i

SHALLOW By cock and pie, sir, you shall not away to- 1
night. What, Davy, I say!

FALSTAFF You must excuse me, Master Robert Shallow.

SHALLOW I will not excuse you, you shall not be excused,
excuses shall not be admitted, there is no excuse shall
serve, you shall not be excused. Why, Davy!

Enter Davy.

DAVY Here, sir.

SHALLOW Davy, Davy, Davy, Davy, let me see, Davy.
Let me see, Davy, let me see. Yea, marry, William cook,
bid him come hither. Sir John, you shall not be excused.

DAVY Marry, sir, thus, those precepts cannot be served. 11
And, again, sir, shall we sow the headland with wheat? 12

SHALLOW With red wheat, Davy. But for William cook –
are there no young pigeons?

DAVY Yes, sir. Here is now the smith's note for shoeing 15
and plough-irons.

SHALLOW Let it be cast and paid. Sir John, you shall not 17
be excused.

DAVY Now, sir, a new link to the bucket must needs be 19
had. And, sir, do you mean to stop any of William's
wages, about the sack he lost the other day at Hinckley
fair?

SHALLOW 'A shall answer it. Some pigeons, Davy, a 23
couple of short-legged hens, a joint of mutton, and any
pretty little tiny kickshaws, tell William cook. 25

DAVY Doth the man of war stay all night, sir?

SHALLOW Yea, Davy. I will use him well. A friend i' th'
court is better than a penny in purse. Use his men well,
Davy, for they are arrant knaves and will backbite.

DAVY No worse than they are backbitten, sir, for they 30
have marvellous foul linen.

SHALLOW Well conceited, Davy. About thy business, 32
Davy.

DAVY I beseech you, sir, to countenance William Visor of 34
Woncot against Clement Perkes o' th' hill. 35

SHALLOW There is many complaints, Davy, against that
Visor. That Visor is an arrant knave, on my knowledge.

DAVY I grant your worship that he is a knave, sir, but yet,
God forbid, sir, but a knave should have some countenance at his friend's request. An honest man, sir, is able
to speak for himself, when a knave is not. I have served
your worship truly, sir, this eight years, and if I cannot

---

182 *latest* last   188 *opinion* reputation   189 *soil* stain   195 *bold fears*
grave dangers   198 *argument* theme   199 *mode* musical key, mood;
purchased acquired by my own act   201 *garland* crown; *successively* by
hereditary right   203 *griefs are green* grievances are fresh   206 *fell* fierce
207 *lodge* harbor   211–12 *look . . . near* examine too closely   214 *action . . .
out* military action waged abroad   223 *pain* effort   234 *Jerusalem* (actually
in Westminster Abbey rather than in the palace)
V, i Shallow's house in Gloucestershire   1 *By cock and pie* (a mild oath)
11 *precepts* orders   12 *headland* unploughed strip between two ploughed
fields   15 *note* bill   17 *cast* verified   19 *bucket* yoke   23 *answer* pay for
25 *kickshaws* delicacies   30 *backbitten* i.e. by vermin   32 *Well conceited*
wittily said   34 *countenance* favor   34, 35 *Visor, Perkes* familiar Gloucestershire names in Shakespeare's day

42 once or twice in a quarter bear out a knave against an
honest man, I have but a very little credit with your worship. The knave is mine honest friend, sir. Therefore, I
beseech you, let him be countenanced.

46 SHALLOW Go to, I say he shall have no wrong. Look
about, Davy. *[Exit Davy.]* Where are you, Sir John?
Come, come, come, off with your boots. Give me your
hand, Master Bardolph.

BARDOLPH I am glad to see your worship.

SHALLOW I thank thee with all my heart, kind Master
Bardolph. *[to the Page]* And welcome, my tall fellow.
Come, Sir John.

FALSTAFF I'll follow you, good Master Robert Shallow.
[Exit Shallow.] Bardolph, look to our horses. *[Exeunt*
56 *Bardolph and Page.]* If I were sawed into quantities, I
should make four dozen of such bearded hermits' staves
58 as Master Shallow. It is a wonderful thing to see the semblable coherence of his men's spirits and his. They, by
observing him, do bear themselves like foolish justices;
he, by conversing with them, is turned into a justice-like
serving-man. Their spirits are so married in conjunction
63 with the participation of society that they flock together
64 in consent, like so many wild geese. If I had a suit to
Master Shallow, I would humor his men with the imputation of being near their master. If to his men, I would
curry with Master Shallow that no man could better
command his servants. It is certain that either wise bearing or ignorant carriage is caught, as men take diseases,
one of another. Therefore let men take heed of their company. I will devise matter enough out of this Shallow to
keep Prince Harry in continual laughter the wearing out
73 of six fashions, which is four terms, or two actions, and
74 'a shall laugh without intervallums. O, it is much that a lie
75 with a slight oath and a jest with a sad brow will do with
a fellow that never had the ache in his shoulders! O, you
77 shall see him laugh till his face be like a wet cloak ill laid
up!

SHALLOW *[within]* Sir John!

FALSTAFF I come, Master Shallow, I come, Master
Shallow.   *[Exit.]*

           *

V, ii   *Enter Warwick, [meeting the] Lord Chief Justice.*

WARWICK
How now, my lord chief justice! whither away?

CHIEF JUSTICE
How doth the king?

WARWICK
Exceeding well. His cares are now all ended.

CHIEF JUSTICE
I hope, not dead.

42 *quarter* i.e. of a year; *bear out* support   **46–47** *Look about* on your toes!
56 *quantities* small pieces   **58–59** *semblable coherence* similarity   **63** *the
participation of society* close association   **64** *consent* unanimity   **73** *four
terms* i.e. a year, since there are four 'terms' in the legal year; *actions* suits
for the recovery of debt   **74** *intervallums* interruptions (literally, intervals
between legal 'terms')   **75** *sad* serious   **77–78** *ill laid up* i.e. full of
wrinkles
V, ii Within King Henry's palace   **7** *truly* faithfully   **13** *fantasy* fancy
14 *heavy issue* sorrowing sons   **18** *strike sail* i.e. submit themselves   **23**
argument situation   **30** *grace to find* favor he will find   **31** *coldest* gloomiest
34 *swims . . . stream of* goes against the grain of your   **37–38** *beg . . . remission* ask pardon, like a ragged beggar, for an offense I have not committed

WARWICK
He's walked the way of nature,
And to our purposes he lives no more.

CHIEF JUSTICE
I would his majesty had called me with him.
The service that I truly did his life   7
Hath left me open to all injuries.

WARWICK
Indeed I think the young king loves you not.

CHIEF JUSTICE
I know he doth not, and do arm myself
To welcome the condition of the time,
Which cannot look more hideously upon me
Than I have drawn it in my fantasy.   13

     *Enter [Prince] John [of Lancaster], Thomas
     [of Clarence], and Humphrey [of Gloucester,
     with Westmoreland].*

WARWICK
Here come the heavy issue of dead Harry.   14
O that the living Harry had the temper
Of him, the worst of these three gentlemen!
How many nobles then should hold their places
That must strike sail to spirits of vile sort!   18

CHIEF JUSTICE
O God, I fear all will be overturned!

LANCASTER
Good morrow, cousin Warwick, good morrow.

GLOUCESTER, CLARENCE
Good morrow, cousin.

LANCASTER
We meet like men that had forgot to speak.

WARWICK
We do remember, but our argument   23
Is all too heavy to admit much talk.

LANCASTER
Well, peace be with him that hath made us heavy.

CHIEF JUSTICE
Peace be with us, lest we be heavier.

GLOUCESTER
O, good my lord, you have lost a friend indeed,
And I dare swear you borrow not that face
Of seeming sorrow, it is sure your own.

LANCASTER
Though no man be assured what grace to find,   30
You stand in coldest expectation.   31
I am the sorrier. Would 'twere otherwise.

CLARENCE
Well, you must now speak Sir John Falstaff fair,
Which swims against your stream of quality.   34

CHIEF JUSTICE
Sweet princes, what I did, I did in honor,
Led by the impartial conduct of my soul,
And never shall you see that I will beg   37
A ragged and forestalled remission.
If truth and upright innocency fail me,
I'll to the king my master that is dead,
And tell him who hath sent me after him.

WARWICK
Here comes the prince.

     Enter the Prince [as King Henry the Fifth] and Blunt.

CHIEF JUSTICE
Good morrow, and God save your majesty!

KING
This new and gorgeous garment, majesty,
Sits not so easy on me as you think.

Brothers, you mix your sadness with some fear.
This is the English, not the Turkish court.
48 Not Amurath an Amurath succeeds,
But Harry Harry. Yet be sad, good brothers,
For, by my faith, it very well becomes you.
Sorrow so royally in you appears
52 That I will deeply put the fashion on
And wear it in my heart. Why then, be sad,
But entertain no more of it, good brothers,
Than a joint burden laid upon us all.
For me, by heaven, I bid you be assured,
I'll be your father and your brother too.
Let me but bear your love, I'll bear your cares.
Yet weep that Harry 's dead, and so will I,
But Harry lives, that shall convert those tears
By number into hours of happiness.

PRINCES
We hope no other from your majesty.

KING
63 You all look strangely on me.
      [To the Chief Justice]   And you most.
You are, I think, assured I love you not.

CHIEF JUSTICE
65 I am assured, if I be measured rightly,
Your majesty hath no just cause to hate me.

KING
No?
How might a prince of my great hopes forget
So great indignities you laid upon me?
70 What! Rate, rebuke, and roughly send to prison
71 The immediate heir of England! Was this easy?
May this be washed in Lethe, and forgotten?

CHIEF JUSTICE
73 I then did use the person of your father.
74 The image of his power lay then in me.
And, in the administration of his law,
Whiles I was busy for the commonwealth,
Your highness pleasèd to forget my place,
The majesty and power of law and justice,
79 The image of the king whom I presented,
And struck me in my very seat of judgement.
Whereon, as an offender to your father,
I gave bold way to my authority
83 And did commit you. If the deed were ill,
Be you contented, wearing now the garland,
To have a son set your decrees at nought,
86 To pluck down justice from your awful bench,
To trip the course of law and blunt the sword
That guards the peace and safety of your person,
Nay, more, to spurn at your most royal image
90 And mock your workings in a second body.
Question your royal thoughts, make the case yours.
92 Be now the father and propose a son,
Hear your own dignity so much profaned,
See your most dreadful laws so loosely slighted,
Behold yourself so by a son disdained,
And then imagine me taking your part
And in your power soft silencing your son.
98 After this cold considerance, sentence me,
99 And, as you are a king, speak in your state
What I have done that misbecame my place,
My person, or my liege's sovereignty.

KING
You are right, justice, and you weigh this well.

Therefore still bear the balance and the sword.
And I do wish your honors may increase,
Till you do live to see a son of mine
Offend you and obey you, as I did.
So shall I live to speak my father's words:
'Happy am I, that have a man so bold
That dares do justice on my proper son,
And not less happy, having such a son
That would deliver up his greatness so
Into the hands of justice.' You did commit me.
For which, I do commit into your hand
The unstained sword that you have used to bear,
With this remembrance, that you use the same   115
With the like bold, just, and impartial spirit
As you have done 'gainst me. There is my hand.
You shall be as a father to my youth.
My voice shall sound as you do prompt mine ear,   119
And I will stoop and humble my intents
To your well-practiced wise directions.
And, princes all, believe me, I beseech you,
My father is gone wild into his grave,   123
For in his tomb lie my affections,   124
And with his spirit sadly I survive,
To mock the expectation of the world,
To frustrate prophecies and to raze out
Rotten opinion, who hath writ me down
After my seeming. The tide of blood in me   129
Hath proudly flowed in vanity till now.
Now doth it turn and ebb back to the sea,
Where it shall mingle with the state of floods   132
And flow henceforth in formal majesty.
Now call we our high court of parliament.
And let us choose such limbs of noble counsel
That the great body of our state may go
In equal rank with the best-governed nation;
That war, or peace, or both at once, may be
As things acquainted and familiar to us,
In which you, father, shall have foremost hand.
Our coronation done, we will accite,   141
As I before remembered, all our state.   142
And, God consigning to my good intents,   143
No prince nor peer shall have just cause to say,
God shorten Harry's happy life one day!   Exeunt.

*

Enter Sir John [Falstaff], Shallow, Silence, Davy,   V, iii
Bardolph, Page.

SHALLOW Nay, you shall see my orchard, where, in an
arbor, we will eat a last year's pippin of my own graffing,   2

48 _Amurath_ a Turkish sultan who, upon his accession, caused all his brothers to be strangled 52 _deeply_ solemnly 63 _strangely_ suspiciously 65 _measured_ judged 70 _Rate_ chide; _send to prison_ (the story of Prince Hal's imprisonment for striking the Chief Justice was first told in Sir Thomas Elyot's _The Book Named the Governor_, 1531) 71 _easy_ insignificant 73 _use the person_ perform the function 74 _image_ symbol 79 _presented_ represented 83 _commit_ commit to prison 86 _awful_ awesome 90 _your . . . body_ the actions of your deputy 92 _propose_ imagine 98 _cold considerance_ cool consideration 99 _state_ royal capacity 115 _remembrance_ reminder 119 _sound_ speak 123 _My . . . grave_ i.e. my wildness is buried with my father 124 _affections_ wayward propensities 129 _seeming_ outward appearance 132 _state of floods_ majesty of the sea 141 _accite_ summon 142 _remembered_ mentioned; _state_ nobles and great men of the realm 143 _consigning_ agreeing
V, iii Within Shallow's orchard 2 _pippin_ a variety of apple; _graffing_ grafting

3 with a dish of caraways, and so forth. Come, cousin
Silence. And then to bed.

FALSTAFF 'Fore God, you have here a goodly dwelling
and a rich.

SHALLOW Barren, barren, barren. Beggars all, beggars
8 all, Sir John. Marry, good air. Spread, Davy, spread,
9 Davy. Well said, Davy.

FALSTAFF This Davy serves you for good uses. He is
11 your serving-man and your husband.

12 SHALLOW A good varlet, a good varlet, a very good varlet, Sir John. By the mass, I have drunk too much sack
at supper. A good varlet. Now sit down, now sit down.
Come, cousin.

16 SILENCE Ah, sirrah! quoth-a, we shall
[Sings]
    Do nothing but eat, and make good cheer,
    And praise God for the merry year,
19   When flesh is cheap and females dear,
    And lusty lads roam here and there
        So merrily,
    And ever among so merrily.

FALSTAFF There's a merry heart! Good Master Silence,
I'll give you a health for that anon.

SHALLOW Give Master Bardolph some wine, Davy.

DAVY Sweet sir, sit, I'll be with you anon. Most sweet sir,
27 sit. Master page, good master page, sit. Proface! What
28 you want in meat, we'll have in drink. But you must
29 bear, the heart's all.   [Exit.]

SHALLOW Be merry, Master Bardolph, and, my little
soldier there, be merry.

SILENCE [sings]
    Be merry, be merry, my wife has all,
    For women are shrews, both short and tall.
    'Tis merry in hall when beards wag all,
35   And welcome merry Shrove-tide.
    Be merry, be merry.

FALSTAFF I did not think Master Silence had been a man
of this mettle.

SILENCE Who, I? I have been merry twice and once ere
now.

    Enter Davy.

40 DAVY [to Bardolph] There's a dish of leather-coats for you.

SHALLOW Davy!

DAVY Your worship! [to Bardolph] I'll be with you
straight. – A cup of wine, sir?

SILENCE [sings]
    A cup of wine that's brisk and fine,
45   And drink unto the leman mine,
        And a merry heart lives long-a.

FALSTAFF Well said, Master Silence.

SILENCE An we shall be merry, now comes in the sweet o'
the night.

FALSTAFF Health and long life to you, Master Silence.

SILENCE [sings]
    Fill the cup, and let it come,
    I'll pledge you a mile to the bottom.

SHALLOW Honest Bardolph, welcome. If thou want'st
anything, and wilt not call, beshrew thy heart. [to the 54
Page] Welcome, my little tiny thief, and welcome indeed too. I'll drink to Master Bardolph, and to all the
cabileros about London.   57

DAVY I hope to see London once ere I die.

BARDOLPH An I might see you there, Davy –

SHALLOW By the mass, you'll crack a quart together, ha!
Will you not, Master Bardolph?

BARDOLPH Yea, sir, in a pottle-pot.   62

SHALLOW By God's liggens, I thank thee. The knave will 63
stick by thee, I can assure thee that. 'A will not out, he is 64
true bred.

BARDOLPH And I'll stick by him, sir.
    One knocks at door.

SHALLOW Why, there spoke a king. Lack nothing. Be
merry. Look who's at door there, ho! Who knocks?
                    [Exit Davy.]

FALSTAFF [to Silence, seeing him drinking] Why, now you
have done me right.   70

SILENCE [sings]
    Do me right,
    And dub me knight.
        Samingo.
Is't not so?   73

FALSTAFF 'Tis so.

SILENCE Is't so? Why then, say an old man can do somewhat.

    [Enter Davy.]

DAVY An't please your worship, there's one Pistol come
from the court with news.

FALSTAFF From the court! Let him come in.
    Enter Pistol.
How now, Pistol!

PISTOL Sir John, God save you!

FALSTAFF What wind blew you hither, Pistol?

PISTOL Not the ill wind which blows no man to good.
Sweet knight, thou art now one of the greatest men in
this realm.

SILENCE By'r lady, I think 'a be, but goodman Puff of 87
Barson.

PISTOL Puff!
Puff i' thy teeth, most recreant coward base!
Sir John, I am thy Pistol and thy friend,
And helter-skelter have I rode to thee,
And tidings do I bring and lucky joys
And golden times and happy news of price.

FALSTAFF I pray thee now, deliver them like a man of this
world.

PISTOL
A foutra for the world and worldlings base!   97
I speak of Africa and golden joys.

FALSTAFF
O base Assyrian knight, what is thy news?   99
Let King Cophetua know the truth thereof.   100

SILENCE [sings]
    And Robin Hood, Scarlet, and John.

PISTOL
Shall dunghill curs confront the Helicons?   102
And shall good news be baffled?   103
Then, Pistol, lay thy head in Furies' lap.

---

3 *caraways* caraway seeds 8 *Spread* lay the table 9 *said* done 11
husband steward 12 *varlet* servant 16 *quoth-a* said he 19 *flesh* meat
27 *Proface* a form of welcome at dinner 28 *want* lack 29 *bear* be patient
35 *Shrove-tide* season of feasting before Lent 40 *leather-coats* russet
apples 45 *leman* sweetheart 54 *beshrew* the devil take 57 *cabileros*
gallants 62 *pottle-pot* two quart tankard 63 *By God's liggens* (this oath
has not been satisfactorily explained) 64 *'A . . . out* he won't pass out
70 *done me right* drunk even with me 73 *Samingo* Sir Mingo, the hero of
the song 87 *but* except; *goodman* yeoman 97 *foutra* an indecent term of
contempt 99 *Assyrian* i.e. heathen 100 *Cophetua* (an allusion to the
ballad of the king who married a beggar-maid) 102 *Helicons* poets 103
baffled disgraced

SHALLOW Honest gentleman, I know not your breeding.

106 PISTOL Why then, lament therefore.

SHALLOW Give me pardon, sir. If, sir, you come with news from the court, I take it there's but two ways, either to utter them, or to conceal them. I am, sir, under the king, in some authority.

PISTOL

111 Under which king, Besonian? Speak, or die.

SHALLOW

Under King Harry.

PISTOL   Harry the Fourth? or Fifth?

SHALLOW

Harry the Fourth.

PISTOL   A foutra for thine office!

Sir John, thy tender lambkin now is king.

Harry the Fifth's the man. I speak the truth.

116 When Pistol lies, do this, and fig me, like

The bragging Spaniard.

FALSTAFF

What, is the old king dead?

PISTOL

As nail in door. The things I speak are just.

FALSTAFF Away, Bardolph! Saddle my horse. Master Robert Shallow, choose what office thou wilt in the

122 land, 'tis thine. Pistol, I will double-charge thee with dignities.

BARDOLPH

O joyful day!

I would not take a knighthood for my fortune.

PISTOL

What! I do bring good news.

FALSTAFF Carry Master Silence to bed. Master Shallow, my Lord Shallow – be what thou wilt, I am fortune's steward – get on thy boots. We'll ride all night. O sweet Pistol! Away, Bardolph! [Exit Bardolph.] Come, Pistol, utter more to me, and withal devise something to do thyself good. Boot, boot, Master Shallow. I know the young king is sick for me. Let us take any man's horses; the laws of England are at my commandment. Blessed are they that have been my friends, and woe to my lord chief justice!

PISTOL

Let vultures vile seize on his lungs also!

137 'Where is the life that late I led?' say they.

Why, here it is. Welcome these pleasant days!   Exeunt.

*

   Enter Beadle and three or four Officers [with Hostess Quickly and Doll Tearsheet].

HOSTESS No, thou arrant knave, I would to God that I might die, that I might have thee hanged. Thou hast drawn my shoulder out of joint.

BEADLE The constables have delivered her over to me,

5 and she shall have whipping-cheer enough, I warrant

6 her. There hath been a man or two lately killed about her.

7 DOLL Nut-hook, nut-hook, you lie. Come on, I'll tell thee

8 what, thou damned tripe-visaged rascal, an the child I now go with do miscarry, thou wert better thou hadst struck thy mother, thou paper-faced villain.

HOSTESS O the Lord, that Sir John were come! He would make this a bloody day to somebody. But I pray God the fruit of her womb miscarry!

BEADLE If it do, you shall have a dozen of cushions again. You have but eleven now. Come, I charge you both go 15 with me, for the man is dead that you and Pistol beat amongst you. 17

DOLL I'll tell you what, you thin man in a censer, I will 18 have you as soundly swinged for this – you blue-bottle 19 rogue, you filthy famished correctioner, if you be not swinged, I'll forswear half-kirtles. 21

BEADLE Come, come, you she knight-errant, come.

HOSTESS O God, that right should thus overcome might! Well, of sufferance comes ease. 24

DOLL Come, you rogue, come, bring me to a justice.

HOSTESS Ay, come, you starved bloodhound.

DOLL Goodman death, goodman bones!

HOSTESS Thou atomy, thou! 28

DOLL Come, you thin thing, come, you rascal.

BEADLE Very well.   [Exeunt.]

*

Enter [Grooms as] strewers of rushes.

1. GROOM More rushes, more rushes. 1

2. GROOM The trumpets have sounded twice.

3. GROOM 'Twill be two o'clock ere they come from the coronation. Dispatch, dispatch.   [Exeunt.]

Trumpets sound, and the King and his Train pass over the stage. After them enter Falstaff, Shallow, Pistol, Bardolph, and the Boy [Page].

FALSTAFF Stand here by me, Master Robert Shallow, I will make the king do you grace. I will leer upon him as 6 'a comes by, and do but mark the countenance that he will give me.

PISTOL God bless thy lungs, good knight.

FALSTAFF Come here, Pistol, stand behind me. O, if I had had time to have made new liveries, I would have be- 11 stowed the thousand pound I borrowed of you. But 'tis no matter; this poor show doth better. This doth infer the zeal I had to see him.

SHALLOW It doth so.

FALSTAFF It shows my earnestness of affection –

SHALLOW It doth so.

FALSTAFF My devotion –

SHALLOW It doth, it doth, it doth.

FALSTAFF As it were, to ride day and night, and not to de- liberate, not to remember, not to have patience to shift 21 me –

SHALLOW It is best, certain.

FALSTAFF But to stand stained with travel, and sweating with desire to see him, thinking of nothing else, putting all affairs else in oblivion, as if there were nothing else to be done but to see him.

106 *therefore* on that account   111 *Besonian* knave   116 *fig* insult by putting the thumb between the index and third fingers   122 *double-charge* (another play on Pistol's name)   137 *'Where . . . led'* (a snatch from an old song)

V, iv A London street   5 *whipping-cheer* a whipping for supper   6 *about her* on her account   7 *Nut-hook* a hooked stick used in nutting   8 *tripe-visaged* flabby-faced   15 *eleven now* (Doll has used one of the cushions to simulate pregnancy)   17 *amongst you* the two of you together   18 *thin . . . censer* embossed figure on the lid of a censer, a pot for burning incense   19 *swinged* thrashed; *blue-bottle* (the beadles wore blue coats)   21 *half-kirtles* skirts   24 *sufferance* suffering   28 *atomy* anatomy, skeleton

V, v Before Westminster Abbey   1 *rushes* (floors were strewn with rushes on ceremonial occasions; in this case the streets seem to have been lined with them)   6 *grace* honor; *leer* glance sidewise   11 *bestowed* spent   21–22 *shift me* change my clothes

28 PISTOL 'Tis 'semper idem,' for 'obsque hoc nihil est.'
'Tis all in every part.

SHALLOW 'Tis so, indeed.

PISTOL
My knight, I will inflame thy noble liver,
And make thee rage.
Thy Doll, and Helen of thy noble thoughts,
34 Is in base durance and contagious prison,
Haled thither
36 By most mechanical and dirty hand.
37 Rouse up revenge from ebon den with fell Alecto's
snake,
For Doll is in. Pistol speaks nought but truth.

FALSTAFF
I will deliver her.

PISTOL
There roared the sea, and trumpet-clangor sounds.
 *[The trumpets sound.] Enter the King and his Train
 [, the Lord Chief Justice among them].*

FALSTAFF
God save thy grace, King Hal, my royal Hal!

PISTOL
42 The heavens thee guard and keep, most royal imp of
fame!

FALSTAFF
God save thee, my sweet boy!

KING
My lord chief justice, speak to that vain man.

CHIEF JUSTICE
Have you your wits? Know you what 'tis you speak?

FALSTAFF
My king! My Jove! I speak to thee, my heart!

KING
I know thee not, old man. Fall to thy prayers.
How ill white hairs become a fool and jester!
I have long dreamed of such a kind of man,
So surfeit-swelled, so old, and so profane,
But, being awaked, I do despise my dream.
53 Make less thy body hence, and more thy grace.
Leave gormandizing. Know the grave doth gape
For thee thrice wider than for other men.
Reply not to me with a fool-born jest.
Presume not that I am the thing I was,
For God doth know, so shall the world perceive,
That I have turned away my former self.
So will I those that kept me company.
When thou dost hear I am as I have been,
Approach me, and thou shalt be as thou wast,
The tutor and the feeder of my riots.
Till then, I banish thee, on pain of death,
As I have done the rest of my misleaders,
Not to come near our person by ten mile.
67 For competence of life I will allow you,
That lack of means enforce you not to evils.
And, as we hear you do reform yourselves,

We will, according to your strengths and qualities,
Give you advancement. Be it your charge, my lord,
To see performed the tenor of our word.
72 Set on.   *[Exeunt the King and his Train.]*

FALSTAFF Master Shallow, I owe you a thousand pound.

SHALLOW Yea, marry, Sir John, which I beseech you to
let me have home with me.

FALSTAFF That can hardly be, Master Shallow. Do not
you grieve at this. I shall be sent for in private to him.
Look you, he must seem thus to the world. Fear not
your advancements; I will be the man yet that shall
make you great.

SHALLOW I cannot well perceive how, unless you should
give me your doublet and stuff me out with straw. I
beseech you, good Sir John, let me have five hundred of
my thousand.

FALSTAFF Sir, I will be as good as my word. This that
you heard was but a color.   87

SHALLOW A color that I fear you will die in, Sir John.

FALSTAFF Fear no colors. Go with me to dinner. Come,   89
Lieutenant Pistol, come, Bardolph. I shall be sent for
soon at night.   91
 *Enter [the Lord Chief] Justice and Prince John [of
 Lancaster, with Officers].*

CHIEF JUSTICE
Go, carry Sir John Falstaff to the Fleet.   92
Take all his company along with him.

FALSTAFF
My lord, my lord –

CHIEF JUSTICE
I cannot now speak. I will hear you soon.
Take them away.

PISTOL
'Si fortuna me tormenta, spero contenta.'   97
 *Exeunt [all but Prince John and the
 Chief Justice].*

LANCASTER
I like this fair proceeding of the king's.
He hath intent his wonted followers   99
Shall all be very well provided for,
But all are banished till their conversations
Appear more wise and modest to the world.

CHIEF JUSTICE
And so they are.

LANCASTER
The king hath called his parliament, my lord.

CHIEF JUSTICE
He hath.

LANCASTER
I will lay odds that, ere this year expire,
We bear our civil swords and native fire   107
As far as France. I heard a bird so sing,
Whose music, to my thinking, pleased the king.
Come, will you hence?   *[Exeunt.]*

---

28 *semper idem* always the same; *obsque . . . est* without this, nothing 34
contagious noxious 36 *mechanical* workman's, base 37 *ebon* black;
Alecto one of the Furies 42 *royal imp* young son of the royal house
53 *hence* henceforth 67 *competence of life* allowance for support 72
tenor intention 87 *color* pretense 89 *colors* enemy 91 *soon at night*
early in the evening 92 *Fleet* a famous London prison 97 *Si . . . contenta* if fortune torments me, hope contents me 99 *wonted* accustomed
107 *civil swords* swords used in civil wars
Epi. 4 *undo* ruin 5 *doubt* fear

EPILOGUE   Epi.
[Spoken by a Dancer]

First my fear, then my curtsy, last my speech. My fear is,
your displeasure; my curtsy, my duty; and my speech,
to beg your pardons. If you look for a good speech now, you
undo me, for what I have to say is of mine own making,   4
and what indeed I should say will, I doubt, prove mine own   5

marring. But to the purpose, and so to the venture. Be it known to you, as it is very well, I was lately here in the end of a displeasing play, to pray your patience for it and to promise you a better. I meant indeed to pay you with this, which, if like an ill venture it come unluckily home, I break, and you, my gentle creditors, lose. Here I promised you I would be and here I commit my body to your mercies. Bate me some and I will pay you some and, as most debtors do, promise you infinitely.

If my tongue cannot entreat you to acquit me, will you command me to use my legs? And yet that were but light payment, to dance out of your debt. But a good conscience will make any possible satisfaction, and so would I. All the gentlewomen here have forgiven me. If the gentlemen will not, then the gentlemen do not agree with the gentle-women, which was never seen before in such an assembly.

One word more, I beseech you. If you be not too much cloyed with fat meat, our humble author will continue the story, with Sir John in it, and make you merry with fair Katherine of France. Where, for anything I know, Falstaff shall die of a sweat, unless already 'a be killed with your hard opinions, for Oldcastle died a martyr, and this is not the man. My tongue is weary. When my legs are too, I will bid you good night, and so kneel down before you, but, in-deed, to pray for the queen.

---

8 *displeasing play* (this play has never been identified) 10 *break* am bankrupt 13 *Bate me some* relieve me of some of my debts 27-28 *Oldcastle . . . man* (In the Henry IV plays Falstaff was originally called Oldcastle. Objection was made to the use of this name since the historical Sir John Oldcastle, who was executed for treason in 1417, was in the sixteenth century honored as a martyr in the cause of Protestantism. Here Shakespeare is saying 'My character was not intended as the historical Oldcastle.')

THE LIFE OF KING HENRY THE FIFTH

INTRODUCTION

The Epilogue to *2 Henry IV* promises that "our humble author will continue the story, with Sir John in it, and make you merry with fair Katherine of France" – will provide, in other words, more light entertainment spun out of Harry of Monmouth's famous victories and rollicking pastimes. This jovial preview little prepares us for the opening of *Henry V*:

> O for a Muse of fire, that would ascend
> The brightest heaven of invention;
> A kingdom for a stage, princes to act
> And monarchs to behold the swelling scene!

Still, the original promise is substantially kept. No other play of the Lancastrian trilogy so persistently bids for laughter, even though Sir John is *not* "in it." If this play were referred to Polonius, he might accurately classify it as "comical heroical."

There are various reasons why *Henry V* assumed its present curious form – in part dramatic epic, in part comic pastiche. The dramatic adventures of Prince and King Hal had in a measure been pre-selected, with Shakespeare bound by a theatrical tradition. *The Famous Victories of Henry V*, an anonymous play registered for publication in 1594 and printed in 1598, is a visible token of this tradition, presenting in crude outline most of the episodes, historical and fictitious, which reappear in *1 & 2 Henry IV* and, even more conspicuously, in *Henry V*. There had been stage treatments of Henry's career at least since 1588, and although the precise relation to them of the extant *Famous Victories* and Shakespeare's trilogy must remain conjectural, it is clear that audiences had come to expect fun as well as fireworks whenever Hal appeared. After 1598 these audiences preferred Sir John Falstaff as the funster in chief, and if he were denied them, the playwright must be liberal in providing substitutes. It has been argued that Falstaff was at first included in *Henry V* according to plan, in the role assigned in the present version to Pistol, but was deleted by death in order to placate the Brooke family, which still resented the fact that he had originally been named for its revered Lollard ancestor Sir John Oldcastle. This may be so, but to most readers the explosive ensign sounds Pistol-pure, and it is hard to imagine him as Sir John transmogrified.

A reason at least equally plausible for the exclusion of Falstaff is that he was a character to whom Henry could scarcely have remained aloof, and aloofness, at least to scalawag knights, would seem to be the order of the day for the pious and patriotic hero of Agincourt. Shakespeare had special reasons for sounding the high heroic note when *Henry V* was written. Not only would it be the capstone of his series of histories ascending through *Richard II* and

1 & 2 Henry IV and descending through *1, 2, & 3 Henry VI* and *Richard III*, but the audiences of the moment were athirst for glory. Within the memory of most living men, the English had been ruled by a woman, and although loyal at heart to their Elizabeth, they had come to find something slightly dispiriting about an elderly woman and pacifist as the available royal image. Henry's image was that of a man and a warrior, endowed with eternal youth by virtue of his early death; and to intensify the emotions which his memory stirred there was the figure of the Earl of Essex leading, during the summer and fall of 1599, an English army in Ireland to put down Tyrone's rebellion. Henry's triumphant return from Agincourt evokes a reference to Essex in the fifth chorus of Shakespeare's play:

> Were now the general of our gracious empress,
> As in good time he may, from Ireland coming,
> Bringing rebellion broachèd on his sword,
> How many would the peaceful city quit
> To welcome him!

These lines provide us with the date of composition of *Henry V*, and a hint of the warlike spirit in London just before Essex proceeded to demonstrate how inglorious an English expedition could sometimes be.

Although Shakespeare may have worked hastily upon his play, and resorted to considerable patching (cf. II, Cho., 41–42 and note), he took its serious portions seriously, and went beyond the existing theatrical versions of Henry's career for his materials. He read with more than usual attentiveness the account of the reign in Holinshed, and turned for details to Hall and perhaps older chroniclers as well as to non-dramatic poets.

Before considering the portrait of Henry which Shakespeare produced, we had best come to what terms we can with the comic interludes. An inventory proves revealing: we have the preparation of Sir John's "staff" to follow and exploit the French wars, with a quarrel between Pistol and Nym (II, i); Hostess Quickly's report of Falstaff's death before his survivors shog off to the port of embarkation (II, iii); their reluctant participation in the assault on Harfleur, followed by a dispute in assorted dialects between Fluellen, Macmorris, and Jamy (III, ii); the English lesson of Princess Katherine (III, iv); Fluellen's quarrel with Pistol (first episode of III, vi); the Dauphin's infatuation with his horse, and the contest in proverb-capping between Orleans and the Constable of France (III, vii); Pistol's threat against Fluellen made to Henry incognito (middle episode of IV, i); further display of the Dauphin's fatuousness (IV, ii); Pistol's conquest of a cowardly Frenchman (IV, iv); Fluellen's groping comparison of

Henry and King Alexander (first episode in IV, vii); Fluellen's expression of devotion to the leek and to Henry, and the latter's ruse in making him wear in his cap the glove offered by Williams as a gage (final episode in IV, vii); the averted conflict between Williams and Fluellen (first episode in IV, viii); Fluellen's forcing of Pistol to eat the leek worn in his cap, and Pistol's final deflation (V, i); Henry's bluff courtship of Katherine (middle episode, and bulk, of V, ii).

This implacably regular insertion of the comic episodes in alternate scenes would seem mechanical were it not for their diversity. Their diversity, on the other hand, and their fragmentary character, make the episodes seem gratuitous as compared with the comic matter in *1 & 2 Henry IV*. We may even mildly complain that either leeks or gloves, but not both, may be fittingly "worn" in the caps of a single play. Abundant enough already, the comedy of the play is often augmented in modern productions by making the Bishops of Ely and Canterbury senile (which they are not), the King of France a mental defective (which he may have been in fact, but is not in Shakespeare's portrayal), and the French lords ludicrously foppish as well as over-confident, although Shakespeare confers upon all except the Dauphin a fair degree of dignity. Although introduced adroitly enough, considering the unlikely setting in wartime courts and camps, the comic episodes cannot be considered neatly "thematic." The presence of the English, Welsh, Irish, and Scots captains in Henry's army has been taken as expressing an aspiration for British unity, but the portrait of Macmorris would scarcely propitiate the Irish, and that of Jamy is not favorable enough to offset the animadversions upon Scotland expressed by Henry and his counsellors early in the play. Gower and Fluellen, to be sure, are good and companionable men, but the union of the English and Welsh was more than an aspiration in 1599.

The contest for comic honors is between Pistol and Fluellen. We can understand why the former won the palm in contemporary esteem, as suggested by the title page of the first (and bad) quarto of 1600: *The Cronicle History of Henry the Fift. With his battel fought at Agin Court in France. Togither with Auntient Pistol*. While Bardolph's carbuncular face fails to project its pristine glow when there is only the Boy and not Falstaff to crack jests on it, and Nym's sullen "humors" lack variety, the dauntless fakery of Pistol and his on-beat rodomontade retains the true touch of Cheapside magic. Pistol's final passing drew a sigh from Dr Johnson. The Fluellen-funniness does not quite come off, at least in the reading, but it follows an interesting formula. Fluellen is an anti-Falstaff, not only in his unmasking of Pistol, who is serving as Falstaff's surrogate, but in his very character and personality. Fluellen is a ponderously dutiful non-wit, master of "the disciplines of the wars" but not of the English language, which issues from him like cold whey, whereas Falstaff had been a nimbly non-dutiful wit, master of nothing but brisk prose. Although Henry can safely associate with Fluellen, and we must give our moral approval to the substitution of good comic angel for bad comic angel, we cannot pretend that solemn respectability is as amusing as its reverse.

By common critical consent, the high moment in the comedy comes early and involves neither Pistol nor Fluellen, but the passing of Sir John Falstaff as reported by Hostess Nell. The wonder of the speech is that it hovers just this side of sacrilege (that side ribaldry) and yet is truly pathetic, with a touch of rough poetry. When this deplorable woman, who confuses Arthur and Abraham, and fails even to recognize the 23rd Psalm, speaks of having told the dying old sinner that he "should not think of God; I hoped there was no need to trouble himself with any such thoughts yet," we should recoil at the grim irony, but, strangely, we do not. She told him so "to comfort him." With every conceivable defect, moral as well as mental – except bad nature – the Hostess is still godly after her fashion.

No doubt Shakespeare considered fun its own excuse for being, and his dissatisfaction with *Henry V*, expressed in prologue, epilogue, and choruses, had nothing to do with its motley. He felt, or professed to feel, that the resources of his theatre, indeed the dramatic form itself, were inadequate for the presentation of an epic theme. In epic fashion his "plot" concentrates on one great action – the victory at Agincourt – and all else in Henry's three actual invasions of France, spread over a period of five years, is ignored or made to serve merely as prelude and postlude to that victory. The choral speeches do not really, as they purport to do, fill in the historical record, but merely link together the chosen episodes so as to contribute to the epic sweep of the play. The size of the action is made the measure of the size of Henry, the epic hero, with everything contributing to his aggrandizement.

It is noteworthy, under the circumstances, that Henry has failed to win from readers anything like uniform approval, in fact has provoked occasional cold hostility. Certainly Shakespeare did not intentionally "undercut" his hero, any more than he intentionally "undercut" the glory of the English feat of arms by displaying the martial failings of Pistol, Bardolph, and Nym. Bardolph's exhortation (from a stationary position) "On, on, on, on, on! to the breach, to the breach!" follows like travesty immediately upon Henry's famous battle speech at Harfleur; and Pistol's mulcting of his captive is the only military exploit on the glorious field of Agincourt which we actually *see*. The intention is not parodic. If the effect is so, it is a consequence of the comical-heroical blend to which the playwright had committed himself. So far as the character of his hero is concerned, he had committed himself to something even more dangerous, a kind of religio-comical-heroical blend.

Henry V is a hard play to analyze in respect to intentional and unintentional effects. Ely and Canterbury provoke Henry to war in order to sidetrack a movement to expropriate church lands. In the course of their private discussion, they mention what may appeal to us (and may have appealed to sixteenth-century Englishmen) as some very good economic and charitable results of such expropriation, and yet if we approve of Henry's conquest, we must presumably approve of their ruse. Why did Shakespeare choose to include this matter from his sources when there was so much else which he excluded? Was Henry to be shown as now so pious that he took suggestion from holy men without reflecting that they might act from somewhat less than holy motives? He sternly adjures them to speak the truth, so far as the legality of his claim to France is concerned, but he displays no curiosity about their present interest in it. Perhaps we are intended to conclude that if high churchmen approve of war, it would be too much to expect their royal parishioner to do otherwise.

The "faults" which critics have found in Henry are really the side-effects of Shakespeare's having tried to do too much for him – by conferring upon him incompatible virtues. He is the religious convert, the pattern of a Christian Prince – morally impeccable, careful of his subjects by whom he is beloved, and highly competent in his judicial and administrative capacity. But at the same time that he exemplifies Christian virtue, he also exemplifies non-Christian *virtu* – that of pagan conquerors like Alexander and Caesar, or medieval champions like Hotspur, by whose light "Did all the chivalry of England move / To do brave acts." As blatantly as Hotspur he confesses that he is as covetous of "honor" as the "most offending soul alive." He proclaims that

> In peace there's nothing so becomes a man
> As modest stillness and humility,
> But when the blast of war blows in our ears,
> Then imitate the action of the tiger.

Presumably the opposite types of virtue are adaptable to the opposite conditions of peace and war, but the fact stands that Henry chooses war. A man of peace cannot be a man of war unless his own nation is under attack. Henry is not the attacked but the attacker. It is the King of France who shows a disposition to negotiate, with the offer of his daughter's hand and, in Henry's view, some "petty and unprofitable dukedoms." Now it is quite true that the historical Henry and his nation considered his cause just, but it is difficult for us to grow excited about the illegality of the Salic law, or the eagerness of a litigant to recover family property. It is impossible for us to consider his cause religious. But Henry, the religious man and humane ruler, is obliged to think of his war as a crusade, and his assumption taints the air.

At the same time that he loves this war, he loathes war in general. The expression of loathing takes the form of listing its horrors and holding others responsible for them – the Archbishop of Canterbury if he wrongly "incites" him, the Dauphin for sending him a "mock," the citizens of Harfleur if they resist, and so on. It is impossible for the religious wielder of a secular sword to do anything quite to our satisfaction. Even Henry's modesty comes under question. He attributes the victory at Agincourt to God, but we might prefer a claim of personal prowess to a claim of special influence with God. Henry's incompatible virtues sometimes produce the effect of duplicity since his actions and words contend with each other, as when he preaches at the Dauphin and the French in general about provocations which are not the true cause of the war, or when he orders the slaying of the French prisoners (as a justifiable military measure) and then, retroactively (unless this is a defect in the text of the play), speaks of it as retaliation for the French attack on the camp-boys – "I was not angry since I came to France / Until this instant." The killing of the prisoners, though an historical fact, has caused Henry's admirers more concern than anything else. The true fault is that Henry is not permitted by the over-zealous playwright to wear his religio-moral and military haloes turn and turn about, but is forced to wear them both at once.

Finally, Henry is given a quality, intermittently displayed, which is compatible neither with the "modest stillness and humility" proper to peace, nor the "action of the tiger" proper to war. He must be shown as an informal, humorous "regular guy" – a self-styled "king of good

fellows." He interrupts his reflections upon God's grace in visiting carnage upon the French in order to play a friendly practical joke on Fluellen, and he courts Princess Katherine with a manly bluntness which is ultimately a trial to our nerves. It contains amusing matter, but it does go on and on; never has anyone advertised his inarticulateness with such loquacity.

Henry is, in fact, the victim of Shakespeare's good will. It is somewhat naive to mistake defects in the playwright's conception for defects in Henry's personal character. More in the true spirit of the play is another kind of naiveté – the fervor of the patriotic Englishman as he contemplates Agincourt and Shakespeare's tribute to its hero. The nineteenth-century American was little inclined to grow analytical about the portrait of George Washington produced by Parson Weems, and Weems was something less than a literary genius. In its fine moments *Henry V* expresses perfectly the spirit (including perhaps the sense of divine call) of a little nation with a great history:

> O England! model to thy inward greatness,
> Like little body with a mighty heart....

The play is also able to achieve a foreign conquest of its own, and to stir non-English hearts. If Henry is the aggressor, he is also the underdog, and his devotion to his purpose confers a kind of purity upon him and his tattered host. The choruses, which show that Shakespeare might have succeeded where other Elizabethans failed – in writing an epic poem – dazzle with their descriptions of the youth of England selling "the pasture now to buy the horse," the brave fleet "on th' inconstant billows dancing," the remnant army with "lank-lean cheeks and war-worn coats" as "by their watchful fires" they "Sit patiently and inly ruminate."

The chorus and early scenes of Act IV are admirable. As Henry in disguise shares the watch of Bates, Court, and Williams, and utters his troubled defense of kingship, we are expected to reflect upon what a fine monarch he is. We must try to do so. But it requires no effort for us to reflect upon what fine subjects he has. There is something amazingly modern about Bates, Court, and Williams. Unique in their day as straight portraits of common soldiers, they have become the prototypes of such in a host of British war dramas and motion pictures. Grumpy, undemonstrative, unillusioned, they are still men of tenacious faith – resolved to trust their leaders and to do their duty well. Their character more than Henry's explains the victory at Agincourt. Henry himself grows in appeal as he accepts the loneliness of leadership and kneels in solitary prayer. For once he escapes self-righteousness.

Henry's address at Agincourt is in a class by itself as inspirational poetry. It is a different kind of thing from the battle oration before Harfleur, because it defines the moral value, perhaps the only moral value, which battle can develop. The *comitatus* is restored, and for a moment the high and the low, the leaders and the led, come together as a unit in mutual interdependence, trust, and admiration. The great day is seen prophetically as a point in history –

> Old men forget; yet all shall be forgot,
> But he'll remember, with advantages,
> What feats he did that day.

No one, English or non-English, can read the lines and fail to "rouse him at the name of Crispian" or escape a momentary pang of regret that he could not have been one of that "happy few" who on that day were able (Pistol excepted) to "gentle" their condition. The late John Kennedy was neither English nor recognizably kin to Macmorris, but when Shakespeare entered the White House in the brave new days of 1961, Henry's speech at Agincourt was the Shakespearean passage which this young leader was most eager once more to hear.

Harvard University   ALFRED HARBAGE

NOTE ON THE TEXT

King Henry the Fifth was first printed in a quarto of 1600 in "cut" and corrupted form, and this version was twice reprinted. A much-improved version was printed in the folio of 1623, evidently from pages of the later quartos corrected by reference to the author's draft. The present edition is based on the folio text on principles explained in the Appendix. The quarto text is not divided into acts and scenes. The folio text is divided, imperfectly, into acts; the relation of this division to the one supplied marginally in the present edition is indicated in the Appendix.

THE LIFE OF KING HENRY THE FIFTH

[NAMES OF THE ACTORS

Chorus
King Henry the Fifth
Dukes of Gloucester and Bedford, brothers of the King
Duke of Exeter, uncle of the King
Duke of York, cousin of the King
Earls of Salisbury, Westmoreland, Warwick,
*   and Cambridge*
Archbishop of Canterbury
Bishop of Ely
Lord Scroop
Sir Thomas Grey
Sir Thomas Erpingham
Gower, Fluellen, Macmorris, Jamy, officers in the
*   English army*
John Bates, Alexander Court, Michael Williams,
*   soldiers in the English army*
Pistol, Nym, Bardolph

Boy
An English Herald
Charles the Sixth, King of France
Lewis, the Dauphin
Dukes of Burgundy, Orleans, Bourbon, and Britaine
The Constable of France
Rambures, Grandpré, French lords
Governor of Harfleur
Montjoy, a French herald
Ambassadors to King Henry
Isabel, Queen of France
Katherine, daughter of the French King and Queen
Alice, an attendant to Katherine
Hostess Quickly of an Eastcheap tavern,
*   wedded to Pistol*
Lords, Ladies, Officers, Soldiers, Citizens,
*   Messengers, and Attendants*

Scene : *England and France*]

*

Pro.	*Enter Prologue.*	
1	O for a Muse of fire, that would ascend	
2	The brightest heaven of invention ;	

A kingdom for a stage, princes to act
4 And monarchs to behold the swelling scene !
5 Then should the warlike Harry, like himself,
6 Assume the port of Mars, and at his heels,
Leashed in like hounds, should famine, sword, and fire
Crouch for employment. But pardon, gentles all,
9 The flat unraisèd spirits that hath dared
10 On this unworthy scaffold to bring forth
So great an object. Can this cockpit hold
The vasty fields of France ? Or may we cram
13 Within this wooden O the very casques
That did affright the air at Agincourt ?
15 O, pardon ! since a crooked figure may
Attest in little place a million ;

And let us, ciphers to this great accompt,   17
On your imaginary forces work.
Suppose within the girdle of these walls
Are now confined two mighty monarchies,
Whose high-uprearèd and abutting fronts   21
The perilous narrow ocean parts asunder.   22
Piece out our imperfections with your thoughts :
Into a thousand parts divide one man
And make imaginary puissance.   25
Think, when we talk of horses, that you see them
Printing their proud hoofs i' th' receiving earth ;
For 'tis your thoughts that now must deck our kings,   28
Carry them here and there, jumping o'er times,
Turning th' accomplishment of many years
Into an hourglass – for the which supply,   31
Admit me Chorus to this history,
Who, Prologue-like, your humble patience pray,
Gently to hear, kindly to judge, our play.   *Exit.*

Pro.   **1** *fire* (most buoyant of the four elements : earth, water, air, fire ; the one which ascended to the empyrean)   **2** *invention* creative imagination   **4** *swelling* increasing in grandeur   **5** *like* in a manner worthy of   **6** *port* bearing   **9** *unraised* unleavened   **10** *scaffold* stage   **13** *wooden O* circular theatre (depreciatory, like *cockpit* at l. 11) ; *the very casques* i.e. even the helmets   **15** *crooked figure* cipher (which can raise 100,000 to 1,000,000)   **17** *accompt* (1) story, (2) reckoning (continuing the word-play on 'cipher' initiated by *wooden O*)   **21** *abutting fronts* frontiers   **22** *perilous . . . ocean* i.e. English Channel   **25** *puissance* armed forces   **28** *deck* array   **31** *hourglass* i.e. short measure of time ; *for . . . supply* in aid whereof

I, i Within the palace of the King of England   **1** *self* selfsame   **4** *scambling* snatching, predatory   **5** *question* discussion

Enter the two Bishops, [the Archbishop] of   I, i
Canterbury and [the Bishop of] Ely.

CANTERBURY

My lord, I'll tell you, that self bill is urged   1
Which in th' eleventh year of the last king's reign
Was like, and had indeed against us passed
But that the scambling and unquiet time   4
Did push it out of farther question.   5

ELY
But how, my lord, shall we resist it now?
CANTERBURY
It must be thought on. If it pass against us,
We lose the better half of our possession;
9 For all the temporal lands which men devout
By testament have given to the Church
Would they strip from us; being valued thus –
As much as would maintain, to the king's honor,
Full fifteen earls and fifteen hundred knights,
Six thousand and two hundred good esquires,
15 And to relief of lazars, and weak age
Of indigent faint souls past corporal toil,
A hundred almshouses right well supplied;
And to the coffers of the king beside
A thousand pounds by th' year. Thus runs the bill.
ELY
This would drink deep.
CANTERBURY   'Twould drink the cup and all.
ELY
But what prevention?
CANTERBURY
The king is full of grace and fair regard.
ELY
And a true lover of the holy Church.
CANTERBURY
The courses of his youth promised it not.
The breath no sooner left his father's body
26 But that his wildness, mortified in him,
Seemed to die too. Yea, at that very moment
28 Consideration like an angel came
And whipped th' offending Adam out of him,
Leaving his body as a paradise
T' envelop and contain celestial spirits.
32 Never was such a sudden scholar made;
Never came reformation in a flood
34 With such a heady currance scouring faults;
35 Nor never Hydra-headed willfulness
36 So soon did lose his seat – and all at once –
As in this king.
ELY   We are blessèd in the change.
CANTERBURY
Hear him but reason in divinity,
And, all-admiring, with an inward wish
You would desire the king were made a prelate;
Hear him debate of commonwealth affairs,
You would say it hath been all in all his study;
List his discourse of war, and you shall hear
A fearful battle rend'red you in music;
45 Turn him to any cause of policy,
46 The Gordian knot of it he will unloose,
47 Familiar as his garter; that when he speaks,
48 The air, a chartered libertine, is still,
49 And the mute wonder lurketh in men's ears
To steal his sweet and honeyed sentences;
51 So that the art and practic part of life
Must be the mistress to this theoric;
Which is a wonder how his grace should glean it,
Since his addiction was to courses vain,
His companies unlettered, rude, and shallow,
His hours filled up with riots, banquets, sports;
And never noted in him any study,
Any retirement, any sequestration
59 From open haunts and popularity.

ELY
The strawberry grows underneath the nettle,
And wholesome berries thrive and ripen best
Neighbored by fruit of baser quality;
And so the prince obscured his contemplation
Under the veil of wildness, which, no doubt,
Grew like the summer grass, fastest by night,
Unseen, yet crescive in his faculty.   66
CANTERBURY
It must be so, for miracles are ceased
And therefore we must needs admit the means   68
How things are perfected.
ELY   But, my good lord,
How now for mitigation of this bill
Urged by the commons? Doth his majesty
Incline to it or no?
CANTERBURY   He seems indifferent,
Or rather swaying more upon our part
Than cherishing th' exhibiters against us;   74
For I have made an offer to his majesty,
Upon our spiritual Convocation   76
And in regard of causes now in hand
Which I have opened to his grace at large
As touching France, to give a greater sum
Than ever at one time the clergy yet
Did to his predecessors part withal.
ELY
How did this offer seem received, my lord?
CANTERBURY
With good acceptance of his majesty,
Save that there was not time enough to hear,
As I perceived his grace would fain have done,
The severals and unhidden passages   86
Of his true titles to some certain dukedoms,
And generally to the crown and seat of France
Derived from Edward his great-grandfather.   89
ELY
What was th' impediment that broke this off?
CANTERBURY
The French ambassador upon that instant
Craved audience; and the hour I think is come
To give him hearing. Is it four o'clock?
ELY
It is.
CANTERBURY
Then go we in to know his embassy,
Which I could with a ready guess declare
Before the Frenchman speak a word of it.
ELY
I'll wait upon you, and I long to hear it.   *Exeunt.*

*

9 *temporal* in secular use 15 *lazars* lepers 26 *mortified* struck dead 28 *Consideration* penitent reflection 32 *scholar* i.e. man of disciplined mind 34 *heady currance* headlong current 35 *Hydra* the monster with proliferating heads slain by Hercules at Lerna 36 *his seat* its throne 45 *cause of policy* political issue 46 *Gordian knot* intricate knot cut by Alexander in asserting his destiny to rule over Asia 47 *Familiar* offhandedly, mechanically 48 *chartered* licensed; *libertine* one free from bondage or restraint 49 *mute wonder* silent wonderer 51–52 *the art . . . theoric* i.e. study and practise must be the teacher of this mastery of theory 59 *open haunts* places of public resort; *popularity* low company 66 *crescive . . . faculty* i.e. given to growth 68 *means* i.e. natural means 74 *exhibiters* introducers of the bill 76 *Upon* on behalf of 86 *severals* particulars; *unhidden passages* open transmission 89 *Edward* i.e. King Edward III

I, ii   *Enter the King, Humphrey [Duke of Gloucester],*
Bedford, Clarence, Warwick, Westmoreland, and
Exeter [with Attendants].

KING

  Where is my gracious Lord of Canterbury ?

EXETER

  Not here in presence.

KING   Send for him, good uncle.

WESTMORELAND

  Shall we call in th' ambassador, my liege ?

KING

4 Not yet, my cousin. We would be resolved,
  Before we hear him, of some things of weight
6 That task our thoughts concerning us and France.

    Enter two Bishops [the Archbishop of Canterbury
    and the Bishop of Ely].

CANTERBURY

  God and his angels guard your sacred throne
  And make you long become it !

KING   Sure we thank you.

  My learnèd lord, we pray you to proceed
  And justly and religiously unfold
  Why the Law Salic, that they have in France,
12 Or should or should not bar us in our claim.
  And God forbid, my dear and faithful lord,
  That you should fashion, wrest, or bow your reading,
15 Or nicely charge your understanding soul
16 With opening titles miscreate, whose right
  Suits not in native colors with the truth ;
  For God doth know how many now in health
19 Shall drop their blood in approbation
  Of what your reverence shall incite us to.
21 Therefore take heed how you impawn our person,
  How you awake our sleeping sword of war.
  We charge you in the name of God take heed ;
  For never two such kingdoms did contend
  Without much fall of blood, whose guiltless drops
26 Are every one a woe, a sore complaint
27 'Gainst him whose wrongs gives edge unto the swords
  That makes such waste in brief mortality.
  Under this conjuration speak, my lord ;
  For we will hear, note, and believe in heart
  That what you speak is in your conscience washed
32 As pure as sin with baptism.

CANTERBURY

  Then hear me, gracious sovereign, and you peers,
  That owe yourselves, your lives, and services
  To this imperial throne. There is no bar
  To make against your highness' claim to France
37 But this which they produce from Pharamond :
  'In terram Salicam mulieres ne succedant' ;
  'No woman shall succeed in Salic land.'
  Which Salic land the French unjustly gloze

To be the realm of France, and Pharamond
The founder of this law and female bar.
Yet their own authors faithfully affirm
That the land Salic is in Germany,
Between the floods of Sala and of Elbe ;
Where Charles the Great, having subdued the Saxons, 46
There left behind and settled certain French ;
Who, holding in disdain the German women
For some dishonest manners of their life, 49
Established then this law : to wit, no female
Should be inheritrix in Salic land ;
Which Salic, as I said, 'twixt Elbe and Sala
Is at this day in Germany called Meisen.
Then doth it well appear the Salic Law
Was not devisèd for the realm of France ;
Nor did the French possess the Salic land
Until four hundred one and twenty years
After defunction of King Pharamond, 58
Idly supposed the founder of this law,
Who died within the year of our redemption
Four hundred twenty-six ; and Charles the Great
Subdued the Saxons, and did seat the French
Beyond the river Sala, in the year
Eight hundred five. Besides, their writers say,
King Pepin, which deposèd Childeric,
Did, as heir general, being descended
Of Blithild, which was daughter to King Clothair,
Make claim and title to the crown of France.
Hugh Capet also, who usurped the crown
Of Charles the Duke of Lorraine, sole heir male
Of the true line and stock of Charles the Great,
To find his title with some shows of truth, 72
Though in pure truth it was corrupt and naught,
Conveyed himself as th' heir to th' Lady Lingard,
Daughter to Charlemain, who was the son 75
To Lewis the Emperor, and Lewis the son
Of Charles the Great. Also King Lewis the Tenth, 77
Who was sole heir to the usurper Capet,
Could not keep quiet in his conscience,
Wearing the crown of France, till satisfied
That fair Queen Isabel, his grandmother,
Was lineal of the Lady Ermengard,
Daughter to Charles the foresaid Duke of Lorraine ;
By the which marriage the line of Charles the Great
Was reunited to the crown of France.
So that, as clear as is the summer's sun,
King Pepin's title and Hugh Capet's claim,
King Lewis his satisfaction, all appear 88
To hold in right and title of the female :
So do the kings of France unto this day.
Howbeit they would hold up this Salic Law
To bar your highness claiming from the female,
And rather choose to hide them in a net 93
Than amply to imbar their crooked titles 94
Usurped from you and your progenitors.

KING

  May I with right and conscience make this claim ?

CANTERBURY

  The sin upon my head, dread sovereign !
  For in the Book of Numbers is it writ : 98
  When the man dies, let the inheritance
  Descend unto the daughter. Gracious lord,
  Stand for your own, unwind your bloody flag,
  Look back into your mighty ancestors ;

I, ii The presence chamber of the palace **s.d.** *Clarence* (a 'ghost' character, mute and appearing only in this single stage direction) **4** *resolved* freed from doubt **6** *task* burden **12** *Or* either **15** *nicely . . . soul* subtly impugn your rational faculty ; i.e. rationalize **16–17** *opening . . . colors* advancing illegitimate claims, the validity of which fails to harmonize **19** *approbation* support **21** *impawn* engage **26** *woe* grievance **27** *wrongs* wrongdoing **32** *sin* original sin **37** *Pharamond* legendary Frankish king **46** *Charles the Great* Charlemagne **49** *dishonest* unchaste **58** *defunction* death **72** *find* furnish **75, 77** *Charlemain, Lewis the Tenth* (actually Charles the Bald and Louis IX ; errors repeated from the chronicles) **88** *his satisfaction* i.e. King Lewis's conviction **93** *net* i.e. web of sophistry **94** *imbar* bar claim to, impeach **98** *Numbers* (see Numbers xxvii, 8)

Go, my dread lord, to your great-grandsire's tomb,
From whom you claim; invoke his warlike spirit,
And your great-uncle's, Edward the Black Prince,
106 Who on the French ground played a tragedy,
Making defeat on the full power of France,
Whiles his most mighty father on a hill
Stood smiling to behold his lion's whelp
110 Forage in blood of French nobility.
111 O noble English, that could entertain
With half their forces the full pride of France
And let another half stand laughing by,
114 All out of work and cold for action!

ELY
Awake remembrance of these valiant dead,
116 And with your puissant arm renew their feats.
You are their heir; you sit upon their throne;
118 The blood and courage that renownèd them
Runs in your veins; and my thrice-puissant liege
Is in the very May-morn of his youth,
Ripe for exploits and mighty enterprises.

EXETER
Your brother kings and monarchs of the earth
Do all expect that you should rouse yourself
As did the former lions of your blood.

WESTMORELAND
They know your grace hath cause, and means, and
  might –
126 So hath your highness! Never king of England
Had nobles richer and more loyal subjects,
Whose hearts have left their bodies here in England
129 And lie pavilioned in the fields of France.

CANTERBURY
O, let their bodies follow, my dear liege,
With blood, and sword, and fire to win your right!
132 In aid whereof we of the spiritualty
Will raise your highness such a mighty sum
As never did the clergy at one time
Bring in to any of your ancestors.

KING
We must not only arm t' invade the French,
137 But lay down our proportions to defend
138 Against the Scot, who will make road upon us
139 With all advantages.

CANTERBURY
140 They of those marches, gracious sovereign,
Shall be a wall sufficient to defend
Our inland from the pilfering borderers.

KING
143 We do not mean the coursing snatchers only,
144 But fear the main intendment of the Scot,
145 Who hath been still a giddy neighbor to us;
For you shall read that my great-grandfather
Never went with his forces into France
148 But that the Scot on his unfurnished kingdom
Came pouring like the tide into a breach,
With ample and brim fullness of his force,
151 Galling the gleanèd land with hot assays,
Girding with grievous siege castles and towns;
That England, being empty of defense,
154 Hath shook and trembled at th' ill neighborhood.

CANTERBURY
155 She hath been then more feared than harmed, my liege;
For hear her but exampled by herself;
When all her chivalry hath been in France

And she a mourning widow of her nobles,
She hath herself not only well defended
But taken and impounded as a stray   160
The King of Scots; whom she did send to France
To fill King Edward's fame with prisoner kings,
And make her chronicle as rich with praise
As is the ooze and bottom of the sea   164
With sunken wrack and sumless treasuries.   165

ELY
But there's a saying very old and true:
  'If that you will France win,
    Then with Scotland first begin.'
For once the eagle England being in prey,
To her unguarded nest the weasel Scot
Comes sneaking, and so sucks her princely eggs,
Playing the mouse in absence of the cat,
To 'tame and havoc more than she can eat.   173

EXETER
It follows then, the cat must stay at home;
Yet that is but a crushed necessity,   175
Since we have locks to safeguard necessaries
And pretty traps to catch the petty thieves.   177
While that the armèd hand doth fight abroad,
Th' advisèd head defends itself at home;   179
For government, though high, and low, and lower,   180
Put into parts, doth keep in one consent,   181
Congreeing in a full and natural close   182
Like music.

CANTERBURY Therefore doth heaven divide
The state of man in divers functions,
Setting endeavor in continual motion;
To which is fixèd as an aim or butt   186
Obedience; for so work the honeybees,
Creatures that by a rule in nature teach
The act of order to a peopled kingdom.
They have a king, and officers of sorts,
Where some like magistrates correct at home,   191
Others like merchants venture trade abroad,
Others like soldiers armèd in their stings
Make boot upon the summer's velvet buds,   194
Which pillage they with merry march bring home
To the tent-royal of their emperor,
Who, busied in his majesties, surveys   197
The singing masons building roofs of gold,
The civil citizens kneading up the honey,
The poor mechanic porters crowding in
Their heavy burdens at his narrow gate,
The sad-eyed justice with his surly hum   202
Delivering o'er to executors pale   203

106 *tragedy* i.e. Battle of Crécy, 1346   110 *Forage in* prey on   111 *entertain* engage   114 *action* i.e. inaction   116 *puissant* powerful   118 *renownèd* brought renown to   126 *So* so indeed   129 *pavilioned* in tents of war   132 *spiritualty* clergy   137 *lay . . . proportions* estimate our forces   138 *road* inroads   139 *all advantages* every opportunity   140 *marches* i.e. northern borderlands   143 *coursing snatchers* mounted raiders   144 *intendment* intent, design   145 *still* always; *giddy* unstable   148 *unfurnished* unprepared   151 *gleanèd* stripped (of manpower)   154 *neighborhood* neighborliness   155 *feared* frightened   160 *as a stray* like a stray beast   164 *ooze and bottom* oozy bottom   165 *sumless* inestimable   173 *'tame* attame, broach   175 *crushed* voided   177 *pretty* neat   179 *advisèd* prudent   180–81 *though . . . parts* i.e. though made up of three estates   181 *one* mutual   182 *Congreeing* agreeing; *close* cadence   186 *fixèd* as attached like; *aim or butt* i.e. target   191 *correct* maintain discipline   194 *Make boot* prey   197 *majesties* royal functions   202 *sad-eyed* solemn-eyed   203 *executors* executioners

The lazy yawning drone. I this infer,
205 That many things having full reference
206 To one consent may work contrariously,
207 As many arrows loosèd several ways
Come to one mark;
As many several ways meet in one town,
As many fresh streams meet in one salt sea,
As many lines close in the dial's centre;
So may a thousand actions, once afoot,
End in one purpose, and be all well borne
Without defeat. Therefore to France, my liege!
Divide your happy England into four,
Whereof take you one quarter into France,
217 And you withal shall make all Gallia shake.
If we, with thrice such powers left at home,
Cannot defend our own doors from the dog,
Let us be worried, and our nation lose
221 The name of hardiness and policy.

KING
Call in the messengers sent from the Dauphin.
            [Exeunt some Attendants.]
Now are we well resolved, and by God's help
And yours, the noble sinews of our power,
225 France being ours, we'll bend it to our awe
Or break it all to pieces. Or there we'll sit,
227 Ruling in large and ample empery
O'er France and all her almost kingly dukedoms,
Or lay these bones in an unworthy urn,
Tombless, with no remembrance over them.
Either our history shall with full mouth
Speak freely of our acts, or else our grave,
Like Turkish mute, shall have a tongueless mouth,
234 Not worshipped with a waxen epitaph.
            Enter Ambassadors of France [attended].
Now are we well prepared to know the pleasure
Of our fair cousin Dauphin; for we hear
Your greeting is from him, not from the king.

AMBASSADOR
May't please your majesty to give us leave
Freely to render what we have in charge,
Or shall we sparingly show you far off
The Dauphin's meaning and our embassy?

KING
We are no tyrant, but a Christian king,
Unto whose grace our passion is as subject
As is our wretches fett'rèd in our prisons.
Therefore with frank and with uncurbèd plainness
Tell us the Dauphin's mind.

AMBASSADOR   Thus then, in few:
Your highness, lately sending into France,
Did claim some certain dukedoms in the right
Of your great predecessor, King Edward the Third.

In answer of which claim, the prince our master
Says that you savor too much of your youth,
And bids you be advised: There's naught in France   252
That can be with a nimble galliard won;   253
You cannot revel into dukedoms there.
He therefore sends you, meeter for your spirit,
This tun of treasure; and in lieu of this,
Desires you let the dukedoms that you claim
Hear no more of you. This the Dauphin speaks.

KING
What treasure, uncle?

EXETER   Tennis balls, my liege.

KING
We are glad the Dauphin is so pleasant with us.
His present and your pains we thank you for.
When we have matched our rackets to these balls,
We will in France, by God's grace, play a set
Shall strike his father's crown into the hazard.   264
Tell him he hath made a match with such a wrangler   265
That all the courts of France will be disturbed   266
With chases. And we understand him well,   267
How he comes o'er us with our wilder days,   268
Not measuring what use we made of them.
We never valued this poor seat of England,
And therefore, living hence, did give ourself   271
To barbarous license; as 'tis ever common
That men are merriest when they are from home.
But tell the Dauphin I will keep my state,   274
Be like a king, and show my sail of greatness
When I do rouse me in my throne of France.   276
For that I have laid by my majesty
And plodded like a man for working days,
But I will rise there with so full a glory
That I will dazzle all the eyes of France,
Yea, strike the Dauphin blind to look on us.
And tell the pleasant prince this mock of his
Hath turned his balls to gunstones, and his soul   283
Shall stand sore chargèd for the wasteful vengeance   284
That shall fly with them; for many a thousand widows
Shall this his mock mock out of their dear husbands,
Mock mothers from their sons, mock castles down;
And some are yet ungotten and unborn
That shall have cause to curse the Dauphin's scorn.
But this lies all within the will of God,   290
To whom I do appeal, and in whose name,
Tell you the Dauphin, I am coming on
To venge me as I may, and to put forth
My rightful hand in a well-hallowed cause.
So get you hence in peace. And tell the Dauphin
His jest will savor but of shallow wit
When thousands weep more than did laugh at it.
Convey them with safe conduct. Fare you well.
            Exeunt Ambassadors.

EXETER
This was a merry message.

KING
We hope to make the sender blush at it.
Therefore, my lords, omit no happy hour
That may give furth'rance to our expedition;
For we have now no thought in us but France,
Save those to God, that run before our business.
Therefore let our proportions for these wars   305
Be soon collected, and all things thought upon
That may with reasonable swiftness add

205–06 *reference . . . consent* i.e. relationship to a single agreement   206 *contrariously* diversely   207 *loosèd . . . ways* i.e. shot from different angles   217 *Gallia* France   221 *policy* statesmanship   225 *our awe* awe of us   227 *empery* sovereignty   234 *with . . . epitaph* i.e. with even so much as a wax (as opposed to durable bronze) epitaph   252 *be advised* take counsel   253 *galliard* merry dance   264 *crown* (1) symbol of majesty, (2) wager-money; *hazard* (1) an aperture functioning like a goal in an Elizabethan type of tennis court, (2) jeopardy   265 *wrangler* opponent   266 *courts* (1) tennis courts, (2) royal courts   267 *chases* (1) unsuccessful attempts to return tennis ball on first bounce, (2) pursuits   268 *comes o'er* taunts   271 *hence* i.e. out of our proper realm (France)   274 *state* kingly decorum   276 *rouse me in* mount   283 *gunstones* cannon balls   284 *sore chargèd* grievously accused   305 *proportions* required forces

308 More feathers to our wings; for, God before,
We'll chide this Dauphin at his father's door.
310 Therefore let every man now task his thought
That this fair action may on foot be brought.   *Exeunt.*

*

II, Cho.   *Flourish. Enter Chorus.*
Now all the youth of England are on fire,
2 And silken dalliance in the wardrobe lies.
Now thrive the armorers, and honor's thought
Reigns solely in the breast of every man.
They sell the pasture now to buy the horse,
6 Following the mirror of all Christian kings
7 With wingèd heels, as English Mercuries.
For now sits Expectation in the air
9 And hides a sword, from hilts unto the point,
With crowns imperial, crowns, and coronets
Promised to Harry and his followers.
The French, advised by good intelligence
Of this most dreadful preparation,
14 Shake in their fear, and with pale policy
Seek to divert the English purposes.
16 O England! model to thy inward greatness,
Like little body with a mighty heart,
What mightst thou do that honor would thee do,
19 Were all thy children kind and natural!
But see, thy fault France hath in thee found out,
21 A nest of hollow bosoms, which he fills
With treacherous crowns; and three corrupted men –
One, Richard Earl of Cambridge, and the second,
Henry Lord Scroop of Masham, and the third,
Sir Thomas Grey, knight, of Northumberland –
26 Have, for the gilt of France (O guilt indeed!),
Confirmed conspiracy with fearful France,
And by their hands this grace of kings must die,
If hell and treason hold their promises,
Ere he take ship for France, and in Southampton.
31 Linger your patience on, and we'll digest
Th' abuse of distance, force a play.
The sum is paid, the traitors are agreed,
The king is set from London, and the scene
Is now transported, gentles, to Southampton.
There is the playhouse now, there must you sit,
And thence to France shall we convey you safe
And bring you back, charming the narrow seas
39 To give you gentle pass; for, if we may,
40 We'll not offend one stomach with our play.
41 But, till the king come forth, and not till then,
Unto Southampton do we shift our scene.   *Exit.*

II, i   *Enter Corporal Nym and Lieutenant Bardolph.*
BARDOLPH Well met, Corporal Nym.
NYM Good morrow, Lieutenant Bardolph.
3 BARDOLPH What, are Ancient Pistol and you friends yet?
NYM For my part, I care not. I say little; but when time
shall serve, there shall be smiles – but that shall be as it
may. I dare not fight, but I will wink and hold out mine
iron. It is a simple one, but what though? It will toast
cheese, and it will endure cold as another man's sword
will – and there's an end.

BARDOLPH I will bestow a breakfast to make you friends,
and we'll be all three sworn brothers to France. Let 't be
so, good Corporal Nym.
NYM Faith, I will live so long as I may, that's the certain
of it; and when I cannot live any longer, I will do as I
may. That is my rest, that is the rendezvous of it.   15
BARDOLPH It is certain, corporal, that he is married to
Nell Quickly, and certainly she did you wrong, for you
were troth-plight to her.   18
NYM I cannot tell. Things must be as they may. Men may
sleep, and they may have their throats about them at
that time, and some say knives have edges. It must be as
it may. Though patience be a tired mare, yet she will
plod. There must be conclusions. Well, I cannot tell.   23
   Enter Pistol and [Hostess] Quickly.
BARDOLPH Here comes Ancient Pistol and his wife.
Good corporal, be patient here.
NYM How now, mine host Pistol?
PISTOL
Base tyke, call'st thou me host?
Now by this hand I swear I scorn the term;
Nor shall my Nell keep lodgers!
HOSTESS No, by my troth, not long; for we cannot lodge
and board a dozen or fourteen gentlewomen that live
honestly by the prick of their needles but it will be
thought we keep a bawdy house straight. *[Nym and Pistol*
draw.] O well-a-day, Lady, if he be not hewn now, we   34
shall see willful adultery and murder committed.   35
BARDOLPH Good lieutenant – good corporal – offer   36
nothing here.
NYM Pish!
PISTOL Pish for thee, Iceland dog, thou prick-eared cur   39
of Iceland!
HOSTESS Good Corporal Nym, show thy valor, and put
up your sword.
NYM Will you shog off? I would have you solus.   43
PISTOL
'Solus,' egregious dog? O viper vile!
The 'solus' in thy most mervailous face!   45
The 'solus' in thy teeth, and in thy throat,
And in thy hateful lungs, yea, in thy maw, perdy!   47
And, which is worse, within thy nasty mouth!   48
I do retort the 'solus' in thy bowels;
For I can take, and Pistol's cock is up.   50
And flashing fire will follow.

---

308 *God before* i.e. God leading   310 *task* exercise
II, Cho. 2 *silken dalliance* pleasure garments of silk   6 *mirror* image,
pattern   7 *Mercuries* (Mercury, messenger of the gods, was usually
pictured wearing winged sandals)   9 *hides a sword* i.e. completely impaled
with captured crowns   14 *pale policy* timorous intrigue   16 *model to* i.e.
small visible replica of   19 *kind* loyal to kindred   21 *hollow bosoms* (1)
hypocrites, (2) empty receptacles for money   26 *gilt* i.e. gold crowns
31–32 *digest . . . play* i.e. render intelligible the shifting scene and compress
the action   39 *pass* passage   40 *offend . . . stomach* (1) make seasick, (2)
displease   41 *But, till* i.e. only when (ll. 41–42 were apparently added to
the original speech – cf. ll. 35–36 – when the following comic episode, still
set in London, was interpolated)
II, i A London street   3 *Ancient* ensign, standardbearer   15 *rest* last
stake (in the game of primero); *rendezvous* resort   18 *troth-plight* betrothed   23 *conclusions* i.e. an end to everything   34 *if . . . hewn* i.e. if
Nym is not cut down (?)   35 *adultery* (malapropism, for 'battery'?)
36–37 *offer nothing* i.e. do not offer to fight   39 *Iceland dog* (a breed with
long hair and pointed ears)   43 *shog off* move along; *solus* alone (taken by
Pistol as an insult)   45 *mervailous* marvellous (?)   47 *maw* belly; *perdy*
(mild oath, from 'par dieu')   48 *nasty* foul-speaking   50 *take* strike;
cock is up i.e. anger is aroused (with play on 'cocked Pistol')

52 NYM I am not Barbason ; you cannot conjure me. I have an
53   humor to knock you indifferently well. If you grow foul
54   with me, Pistol, I will scour you with my rapier, as I may,
     in fair terms. If you would walk off, I would prick your
56   guts a little in good terms, as I may, and that's the humor
     of it.
     PISTOL
     O braggard vile, and damnèd furious wight,
     The grave doth gape, and doting death is near.
60   Therefore exhale !
     BARDOLPH Hear me, hear me what I say ! He that strikes
     the first stroke, I'll run him up to the hilts, as I am a
     soldier.   *[Draws.]*
     PISTOL
     An oath of mickle might, and fury shall abate.
     [Pistol and Nym sheathe their swords.]
     Give me thy fist, thy forefoot to me give.
     Thy spirits are most tall.
     NYM I will cut thy throat one time or other in fair terms.
     That is the humor of it.
     PISTOL
68   Coupe la gorge !
     That is the word. I thee defy again.
70   O hound of Crete, think'st thou my spouse to get ?
71   No ; to the spital go,
72   And from the powd'ring tub of infamy
73   Fetch forth the lazar kite of Cressid's kind,
     Doll Tearsheet, she by name, and her espouse.
     I have, and I will hold, the quondam Quickly
76   For the only she ; and, pauca ! there's enough.
     Go to !
     Enter the Boy.
     BOY Mine host Pistol, you must come to my master – and
     you, hostess. He is very sick and would to bed. Good
     Bardolph, put thy face between his sheets and do the
     office of a warming pan. Faith, he's very ill.
     BARDOLPH Away, you rogue !
83 HOSTESS By my troth, he'll yield the crow a pudding one
     of these days. The king has killed his heart. Good hus-
85   band, come home presently.   *Exit.*
     BARDOLPH Come, shall I make you two friends ? We
     must to France together : why the devil should we keep
     knives to cut one another's throats ?
     PISTOL
     Let floods o'erswell and fiends for food howl on !
     NYM You'll pay me the eight shillings I won of you at
     betting ?

PISTOL
     Base is the slave that pays.
NYM That now I will have. That's the humor of it.
PISTOL
     As manhood shall compound. Push home.   94
     [They] draw.
BARDOLPH By this sword, he that makes the first thrust,
     I'll kill him ! By this sword, I will.
     [Draws.]
PISTOL
     'Sword' is an oath, and oaths must have their course.
     [Sheathes his sword.]
BARDOLPH Corporal Nym, an thou wilt be friends, be
     friends ; an thou wilt not, why then be enemies with me
     too. Prithee put up.
[NYM I shall have my eight shillings I won of you at bet-
     ting ?]
PISTOL
     A noble shalt thou have, and present pay ;   103
     And liquor likewise will I give to thee,
     And friendship shall combine, and brotherhood.
     I'll live by Nym, and Nym shall live by me.
     Is not this just ? For I shall sutler be
     Unto the camp, and profits will accrue.
     Give me thy hand.
     [Nym sheathes his sword.]
NYM I shall have my noble ?
PISTOL
     In cash, most justly paid.
NYM Well then, that's the humor of't.
     Enter Hostess.
HOSTESS As ever you come of women, come in quickly to   113
     Sir John. Ah, poor heart ! he is so shaked of a burning
     quotidian tertian that it is most lamentable to behold.   115
     Sweet men, come to him.
NYM The king hath run bad humors on the knight ; that's
     the even of it.   118
PISTOL
     Nym, thou hast spoke the right.
     His heart is fracted and corroborate.   120
NYM The king is a good king, but it must be as it may :
     he passes some humors and careers.   122
PISTOL
     Let us condole the knight ; for, lambkins, we will live.
     [Exeunt.]

*

     Enter Exeter, Bedford, and Westmoreland.   II, ii
BEDFORD
     'Fore God, his grace is bold to trust these traitors.
EXETER
     They shall be apprehended by and by.
WESTMORELAND
     How smooth and even they do bear themselves,
     As if allegiance in their bosoms sat
     Crownèd with faith and constant loyalty !
BEDFORD
     The king hath note of all that they intend
     By interception which they dream not of.
EXETER
     Nay, but the man that was his bedfellow,   8
     Whom he hath dulled and cloyed with gracious favors –   9
     That he should, for a foreign purse, so sell
     His sovereign's life to death and treachery !

---

52 *Barbason* (name of a devil, Pistol's preceding speech having resembled a formula for exorcising devils) **53** *foul* (from firing) **54** *rapier* (serving as a scouring-rod) **56–57** *that's . . . it* i.e. that's my mood (an all-purpose tag, glancing at popular abuse of the terms of 'humoral' psychology) **60** *exhale* expire **68** *Coupe la gorge* cut the throat **70** *hound of Crete* (a shaggy breed) **71** *spital* hospital **72** *powd'ring tub* sweating tub (used as cure for venereal disease) **73** *lazar kite* leprous bird of prey; *Cressid's kind* i.e. prostitute (a popular epithet, derived from Cressida's fate in Henryson's *Testament*) **76** *pauca* i.e. in few words **83** *yield . . . pudding* i.e. become carrion food **85** *presently* at once **94** *compound* settle it **103** *noble* 6s. 8d. (in cash) **113** *come* are born **115** *quotidian tertian* (a confusion of the 'tertian' fever, which occurs on alternate days, and the 'quotidian,' which occurs daily) **118** *the even of it* i.e. on the level **120** *fracted* broken; *corroborate* pieced together by grace, reconciled (probably a malapropism) **122** *passes* indulges in ; *careers* capers
II, ii The King's quarters at Southampton **8** *bedfellow* favorite (Scroop) **9** *cloyed* surfeited

Sound trumpets. Enter the King, Scroop, Cambridge,
and Grey [, Lords, and Attendants].

KING

Now sits the wind fair, and we will aboard.
My Lord of Cambridge, and my kind Lord of Masham,
And you, my gentle knight, give me your thoughts.
Think you not that the pow'rs we bear with us
Will cut their passage through the force of France,
Doing the execution and the act
18 For which we have in head assembled them?

SCROOP

No doubt, my liege, if each man do his best.

KING

I doubt not that, since we are well persuaded
We carry not a heart with us from hence
That grows not in a fair consent with ours,
Nor leave not one behind that doth not wish
Success and conquest to attend on us.

CAMBRIDGE

Never was monarch better feared and loved
Than is your majesty. There's not, I think, a subject
That sits in heart-grief and uneasiness
Under the sweet shade of your government.

GREY

True. Those that were your father's enemies
30 Have steeped their galls in honey and do serve you
With hearts create of duty and of zeal.

KING

We therefore have great cause of thankfulness,
33 And shall forget the office of our hand
34 Sooner than quittance of desert and merit
According to the weight and worthiness.

SCROOP

So service shall with steelèd sinews toil,
And labor shall refresh itself with hope,
To do your grace incessant services.

KING

We judge no less. Uncle of Exeter,
40 Enlarge the man committed yesterday
That railed against our person. We consider
It was excess of wine that set him on,
43 And on his more advice, we pardon him.

SCROOP

44 That's mercy, but too much security:
Let him be punished, sovereign, lest example
46 Breed by his sufferance more of such a kind.

KING

O, let us yet be merciful.

CAMBRIDGE

So may your highness, and yet punish too.

GREY

Sir,
You show great mercy if you give him life
After the taste of much correction.

KING

Alas, your too much love and care of me
53 Are heavy orisons 'gainst this poor wretch.
54 If little faults proceeding on distemper
Shall not be winked at, how shall we stretch our eye
56 When capital crimes, chewed, swallowed, and digested,
Appear before us? We'll yet enlarge that man,
Though Cambridge, Scroop, and Grey, in their dear care
And tender preservation of our person,

Would have him punished. And now to our French
causes.
Who are the late commissioners? 61

CAMBRIDGE

I one, my lord.
Your highness bade me ask for it to-day. 63

SCROOP

So did you me, my liege.

GREY

And I, my royal sovereign.

KING

Then, Richard Earl of Cambridge, there is yours;
There yours, Lord Scroop of Masham; and, sir knight,
Grey of Northumberland, this same is yours.
Read them, and know I know your worthiness.
My Lord of Westmoreland, and uncle Exeter,
We will aboard to-night. – Why, how now, gentlemen?
What see you in those papers that you lose
So much complexion? – Look ye, how they change!
Their cheeks are paper. – Why, what read you there
That hath so cowarded and chased your blood 75
Out of appearance? 76

CAMBRIDGE   I do confess my fault,
And do submit me to your highness' mercy.

GREY, SCROOP

To which we all appeal.

KING

The mercy that was quick in us but late, 79
By your own counsel is suppressed and killed.
You must not dare for shame to talk of mercy;
For your own reasons turn into your bosoms 82
As dogs upon their masters, worrying you.
See you, my princes and my noble peers,
These English monsters! My Lord of Cambridge here – 85
You know how apt our love was to accord 86
To furnish him with all appertinents 87
Belonging to his honor; and this man
Hath, for a few light crowns, lightly conspired
And sworn unto the practices of France 90
To kill us here in Hampton; to the which
This knight, no less for bounty bound to us
Than Cambridge is, hath likewise sworn. But O,
What shall I say to thee, Lord Scroop, thou cruel,
Ingrateful, savage, and inhuman creature?
Thou that didst bear the key of all my counsels,
That knew'st the very bottom of my soul,
That almost mightst have coined me into gold,
Wouldst thou have practiced on me for thy use?
May it be possible that foreign hire
Could out of thee extract one spark of evil
That might annoy my finger? 'Tis so strange 102
That, though the truth of it stands off as gross
As black and white, my eye will scarcely see it.
Treason and murder ever kept together,

18 *head* an army 30 *galls* sources of bitterness 33 *office* use 34 *quittance* requital 40 *Enlarge* set free 43 *more advice* i.e. recovered judgment 44 *security* overconfidence 46 *his sufferance* toleration of him 53 *Are heavy orisons* i.e. beget weighty pleas 54 *proceeding on distemper* following drunkenness 56 *chewed . . . digested* i.e. premeditated 61 *late* lately appointed 63 *it* i.e. the commission 75 *cowarded* frightened 76 *appearance* sight 79 *quick* living 82 *turn* return 85 *English monsters* (as distinct from exotic freaks imported for exhibition) 86 *accord* consent 87 *appertinents* appurtenances 90 *practices* plots 102 *annoy* injure

As two yoke-devils sworn to either's purpose,
107 Working so grossly in a natural cause
That admiration did not whoop at them;
109 But thou, 'gainst all proportion, didst bring in
110 Wonder to wait on treason and on murder;
And whatsoever cunning fiend it was
112 That wrought upon thee so preposterously
113 Hath got the voice in hell for excellence.
114 All other devils that suggest by treasons
115 Do botch and bungle up damnation
With patches, colors, and with forms being fetched
From glist'ring semblances of piety;
118 But he that tempered thee bade thee stand up,
Gave thee no instance why thou shouldst do treason,
120 Unless to dub thee with the name of traitor.
If that same demon that hath gulled thee thus
Should with his lion gait walk the whole world,
123 He might return to vasty Tartar back
And tell the legions, 'I can never win
A soul so easy as that Englishman's.'
126 O, how hast thou with jealousy infected
127 The sweetness of affiance! Show men dutiful?
Why, so didst thou. Seem they grave and learnèd?
Why, so didst thou. Come they of noble family?
Why, so didst thou. Seem they religious?
Why, so didst thou. Or are they spare in diet,
Free from gross passion or of mirth or anger,
133 Constant in spirit, not swerving with the blood,
134 Garnished and decked in modest complement,
135 Not working with the eye without the ear,
And but in purgèd judgment trusting neither?
137 Such and so finely bolted didst thou seem;
And thus thy fall hath left a kind of blot
139 To mark the full-fraught man and best indued
With some suspicion. I will weep for thee;
For this revolt of thine, methinks, is like
Another fall of man. Their faults are open.
Arrest them to the answer of the law;
And God acquit them of their practices!

EXETER I arrest thee of high treason by the name of
Richard Earl of Cambridge.
     I arrest thee of high treason by the name of Henry
Lord Scroop of Masham.
     I arrest thee of high treason by the name of Thomas
Grey, knight, of Northumberland.

SCROOP
     Our purposes God justly hath discovered,

And I repent my faults more than my death,
Which I beseech your highness to forgive,
Although my body pay the price of it.
CAMBRIDGE
For me, the gold of France did not seduce,
Although I did admit it as a motive   156
The sooner to effect what I intended.
But God be thankèd for prevention,
Which I in sufferance heartily will rejoice,   159
Beseeching God, and you, to pardon me.
GREY
Never did faithful subject more rejoice
At the discovery of most dangerous treason
Than I do at this hour joy o'er myself,
Prevented from a damnèd enterprise.
My fault, but not my body, pardon, sovereign.
KING
God quit you in his mercy! Hear your sentence.   166
You have conspired against our royal person,
Joined with an enemy proclaimed, and from his coffers
Received the golden earnest of our death;   169
Wherein you would have sold your king to slaughter,
His princes and his peers to servitude,
His subjects to oppression and contempt,
And his whole kingdom into desolation.
Touching our person, seek we no revenge;
But we our kingdom's safety must so tender,   175
Whose ruin you have sought, that to her laws
We do deliver you. Get you therefore hence,
Poor miserable wretches, to your death;
The taste whereof God of his mercy give
You patience to endure and true repentance
Of all your dear offenses! Bear them hence.   181
      Exit [Guard, with Cambridge, Scroop, and Grey].
Now, lords, for France; the enterprise whereof
Shall be to you as us, like glorious.   183
We doubt not of a fair and lucky war,
Since God so graciously hath brought to light
This dangerous treason, lurking in our way
To hinder our beginnings. We doubt not now
But every rub is smoothèd on our way.   188
Then forth, dear countrymen. Let us deliver
Our puissance into the hand of God,
Putting it straight in expedition.   191
Cheerly to sea the signs of war advance.   192
No king of England, if not King of France!
      Flourish. [Exeunt.]

*

107–08 *Working . . . them* i.e. cooperating with such obvious fitness as to provoke no cry of wonder   109 *proportion* fitness   110 *wait on* attend   112 *preposterously* abnormally   113 *voice* vote; *excellence* supreme achievement   114 *suggest* tempt   115–17 *Do botch . . . piety* i.e. trick out sin with disguises of shining virtue   118 *tempered* moulded; *stand up* volunteer   120 *dub . . . name* acquire the title   123 *Tartar* Tartarus (deepest Hades)   126 *jealousy* suspicion   127 *affiance* trust   133 *blood* passions   134 *decked . . . complement* i.e. wearing the look of modesty   135–36 *Not . . . neither* i.e. judiciously trusting neither eye nor ear alone   137 *bolted* sifted, refined   139 *full-fraught* most richly endowed   156 *did admit* allowed to stand (the actual 'motive' of Cambridge, here scarcely glanced at, was to further Mortimer's claim to the crown)   159 *sufferance* suffering   166 *quit* acquit, forgive   169 *earnest* advance payment   175 *tender* hold dear   181 *dear* rare   183 *like* alike   188 *But* but that; *rub* obstacle (bowling term)   191 *expedition* motion   192 *signs* ensigns
II, iii A London street   2 *Staines* place on the road to Southampton   3, 6 *earn* grieve   9 *Arthur* (confused with Abraham)   11 *christom* newly baptized

Enter Pistol, Nym, Bardolph, Boy, and Hostess.   **II, iii**
HOSTESS Prithee, honey-sweet husband, let me bring
thee to Staines.   2
PISTOL
No; for my manly heart doth earn.   3
Bardolph, be blithe; Nym, rouse thy vaunting veins;
Boy, bristle thy courage up; for Falstaff he is dead,
And we must earn therefore.   6
BARDOLPH Would I were with him, wheresome'er he is,
either in heaven or in hell!
HOSTESS Nay sure, he's not in hell! He's in Arthur's   9
bosom, if ever man went to Arthur's bosom. 'A made a
finer end, and went away an it had been any christom   11

child. 'A parted ev'n just between twelve and one, ev'n
at the turning o' th' tide. For after I saw him fumble with
the sheets, and play with flowers, and smile upon his
finger's end, I knew there was but one way ; for his nose
16   was as sharp as a pen, and 'a babbled of green fields.
'How now, Sir John ?' quoth I. 'What, man ? be o' good
cheer.' So 'a cried out 'God, God, God !' three or four
times. Now I, to comfort him, bid him 'a should not
think of God ; I hoped there was no need to trouble himself with any such thoughts yet. So 'a bade me lay more
clothes on his feet. I put my hand into the bed and felt
them, and they were as cold as any stone. Then I felt to
his knees, and so upward and upward, and all was as
cold as any stone.

25   NYM   They say he cried out of sack.

HOSTESS   Ay, that 'a did.

BARDOLPH   And of women.

HOSTESS   Nay, that 'a did not.

BOY   Yes, that 'a did, and said they were devils incarnate.

HOSTESS   'A could never abide carnation ; 'twas a color he
never liked.

BOY   'A said once the devil would have him about women.

HOSTESS   'A did in some sort, indeed, handle women ; but
34   then he was rheumatic, and talked of the Whore of
Babylon.

BOY   Do you not remember 'a saw a flea stick upon Bardolph's nose, and 'a said it was a black soul burning in
hell ?

38   BARDOLPH   Well, the fuel is gone that maintained that
fire. That's all the riches I got in his service.

40   NYM   Shall we shog ? The king will be gone from Southampton.

PISTOL
Come, let's away. My love, give me thy lips.
Look to my chattels and my moveables.
44   Let senses rule. The word is 'Pitch and pay.'
Trust none ;
46   For oaths are straws, men's faiths are wafer-cakes,
47   And Hold-fast is the only dog, my duck.
48   Therefore Caveto be thy counsellor.
49   Go, clear thy crystals. Yoke-fellows in arms,
Let us to France, like horse-leeches, my boys,
To suck, to suck, the very blood to suck !

BOY   And that's but unwholesome food, they say.

PISTOL
Touch her soft mouth, and march.

BARDOLPH   Farewell, hostess.
     [Kisses her.]

NYM   I cannot kiss, that is the humor of it ; but adieu !

PISTOL
56   Let housewifery appear. Keep close, I thee command.

HOSTESS   Farewell, adieu !   Exeunt.

            *

II, iv   *Flourish. Enter the French King, the Dauphin,
the Dukes of Berri and Britaine [, the Constable,
and others].*

KING
Thus comes the English with full power upon us,
And more than carefully it us concerns
To answer royally in our defenses.
Therefore the Dukes of Berri and Britaine,
Of Brabant and of Orleans, shall make forth,

And you, Prince Dauphin, with all swift dispatch,
To line and new repair our towns of war   7
With men of courage and with means defendant ;
For England his approaches makes as fierce
As waters to the sucking of a gulf.   10
It fits us then to be as provident
As fear may teach us out of late examples   12
Left by the fatal and neglected English   13
Upon our fields.

DAUPHIN   My most redoubted father,
It is most meet we arm us 'gainst the foe ;   15
For peace itself should not so dull a kingdom
Though war nor no known quarrel were in question
But that defenses, musters, preparations
Should be maintained, assembled, and collected,
As were a war in expectation.
Therefore I say 'tis meet we all go forth
To view the sick and feeble parts of France ;
And let us do it with no show of fear –
No, with no more than if we heard that England
Were busied with a Whitsun morris dance ;   25
For, my good liege, she is so idly kinged,   26
Her sceptre so fantastically borne,
By a vain, giddy, shallow, humorous youth,
That fear attends her not.   29

CONSTABLE   O peace, Prince Dauphin !
You are too much mistaken in this king.
Question your grace the late ambassadors,
With what great state he heard their embassy,
How well supplied with noble counsellors,
How modest in exception, and withal   34
How terrible in constant resolution,
And you shall find his vanities forespent   36
Were but the outside of the Roman Brutus,   37
Covering discretion with a coat of folly ;
As gardeners do with ordure hide those roots
That shall first spring and be most delicate.

DAUPHIN
Well, 'tis not so, my Lord High Constable !
But though we think it so, it is no matter.
In cases of defense 'tis best to weigh
The enemy more mighty than he seems.
So the proportions of defense are filled ;   45
Which of a weak and niggardly projection   46
Doth, like a miser, spoil his coat with scanting
A little cloth.

16 *'a . . . fields* (authenticating this famous emendation is the likelihood that
the Hostess, whose religious education is defective – cf. *Arthur's bosom* –
has been puzzled by 'green pastures' as Falstaff repeated the 23rd Psalm)
25 *cried . . . sack* exclaimed against wine   34 *rheumatic* i.e. feverish (with
pronunciation 'rom-atic' triggering the allusion to 'Whore of Babylon,'
i.e the Roman Church)   38 *fuel* i.e. liquor supplied by Falstaff   40 *shog*
move along   44 *Let . . . rule* i.e. use your eyes and ears ; *Pitch and pay*
i.e. cash down   46 *wafer-cakes* i.e. easily broken (proverbial)   47 *Hold-
fast . . . dog* (from proverb, 'Brag is a good dog, but Hold-fast is a better')
48 *Caveto* beware   49 *clear thy crystals* i.e. wipe your eyes   56 *Let . . .
appear* i.e. be a good housekeeper ; *close* i.e. indoors
II, iv Within the palace of the French King   7 *line* reinforce   10 *sucking*
i.e. whirlpool   12 *examples* i.e. of military defeats   13 *fatal and neglected*
fatally disregarded   15 *meet* fitting   25 *Whitsun* festal week beginning
the seventh Sunday after Easter ; *morris dance* folk dance in antic costumes
26 *idly* worthlessly   29 *attends* accompanies   34 *exception* taking issue
36 *forespent* now done with   37 *Brutus* Lucius Junius Brutus, who disguised his acumen from the tyrant Tarquin Superbus until ready to join
in revolt   45 *proportions* adequate forces   46-47 *Which . . . Doth* (grammatically incoherent, possibly owing to a missing line, but clear in sense)
46 *weak . . . projection* small and miserly scale

KING   Think we King Harry strong;
And, princes, look you strongly arm to meet him.
50   The kindred of him hath been fleshed upon us;
And he is bred out of that bloody strain
That haunted us in our familiar paths.
Witness our too much memorable shame
54   When Crécy battle fatally was struck,
And all our princes captived, by the hand
Of that black name, Edward, Black Prince of Wales;
57   Whiles that his mountain sire – on mountain standing,
Up in the air, crowned with the golden sun –
Saw his heroical seed, and smiled to see him
Mangle the work of nature, and deface
The patterns that by God and by French fathers
Had twenty years been made. This is a stem
Of that victorious stock; and let us fear
64   The native mightiness and fate of him.
      Enter a Messenger.
MESSENGER
Ambassadors from Harry King of England
Do crave admittance to your majesty.
KING
We'll give them present audience. Go, and bring them.
      [Exeunt Messenger and certain Lords.]
You see this chase is hotly followed, friends.
DAUPHIN
69   Turn head, and stop pursuit; for coward dogs
Most spend their mouths when what they seem to
     threaten
Runs far before them. Good my sovereign,
Take up the English short and let them know
Of what a monarchy you are the head.
Self-love, my liege, is not so vile a sin
As self-neglecting.
      Enter [Lords, with] Exeter [and Train].
KING   From our brother of England?
EXETER
From him, and thus he greets your majesty:
He wills you, in the name of God Almighty,
That you divest yourself, and lay apart
The borrowed glories that by gift of heaven,
80   By law of nature and of nations, 'longs
To him and to his heirs – namely, the crown
82   And all wide-stretchèd honors that pertain
83   By custom, and the ordinance of times,
Unto the crown of France. That you may know
85   'Tis no sinister nor no awkward claim,
Picked from the wormholes of long-vanished days,
Nor from the dust of old oblivion raked,
88   He sends you this most memorable line,
      [Gives a paper.]
In every branch truly demonstrative;

Willing you overlook this pedigree;
And when you find him evenly derived   91
From his most famed of famous ancestors,
Edward the Third, he bids you then resign
Your crown and kingdom, indirectly held   94
From him, the native and true challenger.   95
KING
Or else what follows?
EXETER
Bloody constraint; for if you hide the crown   97
Even in your hearts, there will he rake for it.
Therefore in fierce tempest is he coming,
In thunder and in earthquake, like a Jove;
That if requiring fail, he will compel;   101
And bids you, in the bowels of the Lord,   102
Deliver up the crown, and to take mercy
On the poor souls for whom this hungry war
Opens his vasty jaws; and on your head
Turning the widows' tears, the orphans' cries,   106
The dead men's blood, the privèd maidens' groans,   107
For husbands, fathers, and betrothèd lovers
That shall be swallowed in this controversy.
This is his claim, his threat'ning, and my message;
Unless the Dauphin be in presence here,
To whom expressly I bring greeting too.
KING
For us, we will consider of this further.
To-morrow shall you bear our full intent
Back to our brother of England.
DAUPHIN   For the Dauphin,
I stand here for him. What to him from England?
EXETER
Scorn and defiance, slight regard, contempt,
And anything that may not misbecome
The mighty sender, doth he prize you at.
Thus says my king: and if your father's highness
Do not, in grant of all demands at large,
Sweeten the bitter mock you sent his majesty,
He'll call you to so hot an answer of it
That caves and womby vaultages of France   124
Shall chide your trespass, and return your mock
In second accent of his ordinance.   126
DAUPHIN
Say, if my father render fair return,
It is against my will; for I desire
Nothing but odds with England. To that end,
As matching to his youth and vanity,
I did present him with the Paris balls.   131
EXETER
He'll make your Paris Louvre shake for it,   132
Were it the mistress court of mighty Europe;
And be assured you'll find a difference,
As we his subjects have in wonder found,
Between the promise of his greener days
And these he masters now. Now he weighs time   137
Even to the utmost grain. That you shall read
In your own losses, if he stay in France.
KING
To-morrow shall you know our mind at full.
      Flourish.
EXETER
Dispatch us with all speed, lest that our king
Come here himself to question our delay;
For he is footed in this land already.

50 *fleshed* initiated in blood shedding   54 *struck* waged   57 *mountain* i.e. towering (?)   64 *fate* fortune, luck   69 *Turn head* stand at bay; *stop* i.e. put an end to   80 *By law . . . nations* i.e. morally and legally; *'longs* belongs   82 *all wide-stretched* i.e. the whole range of   83 *ordinance of times* decree of tradition   85 *sinister* illegitimate; *awkward* shambling   88 *line* line of descent   91 *evenly* directly   94 *indirectly* wrongfully   95 *challenger* claimant   97 *constraint* force   101 *requiring* demanding   102 *in the bowels* i.e. in the very being (Biblical metaphor)   106 *Turning* retorting, flinging back   107 *privèd* deprived (i.e. of their *betrothèd lovers*)   124 *womby vaultages* hollow caverns   126 *second accent* i.e. echo; *ordinance* cannon   131 *Paris balls* tennis balls   132 *Louvre* (pronounced 'lover' with play on *mistress* in next line)   137 *masters* governs

KING
You shall be soon dispatched with fair conditions.
A night is but small breath and little pause
To answer matters of this consequence.   *Exeunt.*

＊

III, Cho.   *Enter Chorus.*
1   Thus with imagined wing our swift scene flies,
In motion of no less celerity
Than that of thought. Suppose that you have seen
The well-appointed king at Hampton pier
Embark his royalty; and his brave fleet
6   With silken streamers the young Phoebus fanning.
Play with your fancies, and in them behold
Upon the hempen tackle shipboys climbing;
Hear the shrill whistle which doth order give
10   To sounds confused; behold the threaden sails,
Borne with th' invisible and creeping wind,
12   Draw the huge bottoms through the furrowed sea,
Breasting the lofty surge. O, do but think
14   You stand upon the rivage and behold
A city on th' inconstant billows dancing;
For so appears this fleet majestical,
Holding due course to Harfleur. Follow, follow!
18   Grapple your minds to sternage of this navy,
And leave your England as dead midnight still,
Guarded with grandsires, babies, and old women,
21   Either past or not arrived to pith and puissance;
For who is he whose chin is but enriched
With one appearing hair that will not follow
These culled and choice-drawn cavaliers to France?
Work, work your thoughts, and therein see a siege:
Behold the ordinance on their carriages,
27   With fatal mouths gaping on girded Harfleur.
Suppose th' ambassador from the French comes back;
Tells Harry that the king doth offer him
Katherine his daughter, and with her to dowry
Some petty and unprofitable dukedoms.
32   The offer likes not; and the nimble gunner
33   With linstock now the devilish cannon touches,
Alarum, and chambers go off.
And down goes all before them. Still be kind,
And eke out our performance with your mind.   *Exit.*

III, i   *Enter the King, Exeter, Bedford, and Gloucester.*
Alarum : [with Soldiers carrying] scaling ladders at
Harfleur.
KING
Once more unto the breach, dear friends, once more,
Or close the wall up with our English dead!
In peace there's nothing so becomes a man
As modest stillness and humility,
But when the blast of war blows in our ears,
Then imitate the action of the tiger:
Stiffen the sinews, summon up the blood,
Disguise fair nature with hard-favored rage;
Then lend the eye a terrible aspect:
10   Let it pry through the portage of the head
Like the brass cannon; let the brow o'erwhelm it
12   As fearfully as doth a gallèd rock
13   O'erhang and jutty his confounded base,

Swilled with the wild and wasteful ocean.   14
Now set the teeth and stretch the nostril wide,
Hold hard the breath and bend up every spirit
To his full height! On, on, you noble English,
Whose blood is fet from fathers of war-proof,   18
Fathers that like so many Alexanders
Have in these parts from morn till even fought
And sheathed their swords for lack of argument.   21
Dishonor not your mothers; now attest
That those whom you called fathers did beget you!
Be copy now to men of grosser blood   24
And teach them how to war! And you, good yeomen,
Whose limbs were made in England, show us here
The mettle of your pasture. Let us swear   27
That you are worth your breeding; which I doubt not,
For there is none of you so mean and base
That hath not noble lustre in your eyes.
I see you stand like greyhounds in the slips,   31
Straining upon the start. The game's afoot!
Follow your spirit; and upon this charge
Cry 'God for Harry! England and Saint George!'   34
          [Exeunt.] Alarum, and chambers go off.
Enter Nym, Bardolph, Pistol, and Boy.   III, ii
BARDOLPH On, on, on, on, on! to the breach, to the
breach!
NYM Pray thee, corporal, stay. The knocks are too hot;   2
and, for mine own part, I have not a case of lives. The   3
humor of it is too hot; that is the very plain-song of it.   4
PISTOL
The plain-song is most just; for humors do abound.
Knocks go and come; God's vassals drop and die;
          And sword and shield
          In bloody field
          Doth win immortal fame.
BOY Would I were in an alehouse in London! I would
give all my fame for a pot of ale and safety.
PISTOL And I:
          If wishes would prevail with me,
          My purpose should not fail with me,
          But thither would I hie.
BOY   As duly, but not as truly,
          As bird doth sing on bough.
Enter Fluellen.
FLUELLEN Up to the preach, you dogs! Avaunt, you cul-   18
lions!
          [Drives them in.]
PISTOL
Be merciful, great duke, to men of mould!   19
Abate thy rage, abate thy manly rage,
Abate thy rage, great duke!
Good bawcock, bate thy rage! Use lenity, sweet chuck!   22

III, Cho. **1** *imagined wing* wing of imagination **6** *the . . . fanning* i.e.
waving in the dawn **10** *threaden* woven of thread **12** *bottoms* hulls
14 *rivage* shore **18** *Grapple* fasten; *sternage* the wake **21** *pith* muscle,
strength **27** *girded* surrounded, besieged **32** *likes* pleases **33** *linstock*
lighting-stick
III, i Before the walls of Harfleur **10** *portage* portholes **12** *gallèd* eroded
(at base) **13** *jutty his confounded* jut over its ruined **14** *Swilled* consumed **18** *fet* fetched, derived **21** *argument* opposition **24** *copy* examples **27** *mettle . . . pasture* quality of your rearing **31** *slips* leashes
34 *Saint George* (England's patron saint)
III, ii **2** *corporal* (at II, i, 2 Bardolph was a lieutenant) **3** *case* set **4**
plain-song unelaborated melody, i.e. unadorned truth **18** *Avaunt* be
gone; *cullions* base fellows **19** *men of mould* mere mortals **22** *bawcock*
fine fellow (from 'beau coq')

23 NYM These be good humors. Your honor wins bad humors. *Exit [with all but Boy].*
25 BOY As young as I am, I have observed these three swashers. I am boy to them all three ; but all they three, though
they would serve me, could not be man to me ; for indeed
28 three such antics do not amount to a man. For Bardolph,
he is white-livered and red-faced ; by the means whereof
'a faces it out, but fights not. For Pistol, he hath a killing
tongue and a quiet sword ; by the means whereof 'a
32 breaks words and keeps whole weapons. For Nym, he
hath heard that men of few words are the best men, and
therefore he scorns to say his prayers, lest 'a should be
thought a coward ; but his few bad words are matched
with as few good deeds, for 'a never broke any man's
head but his own, and that was against a post when he
was drunk. They will steal anything, and call it purchase.
Bardolph stole a lute-case, bore it twelve leagues, and
sold it for three halfpence. Nym and Bardolph are sworn
brothers in filching, and in Calais they stole a fire-shovel.
42 I knew by that piece of service the men would carry coals.
They would have me as familiar with men's pockets as
44 their gloves or their handkerchers ; which makes much
against my manhood, if I should take from another's
pocket to put into mine ; for it is plain pocketing up of
wrongs. I must leave them and seek some better service.
Their villainy goes against my weak stomach, and therefore I must cast it up. *Exit.*
Enter Gower [and Fluellen].
GOWER Captain Fluellen, you must come presently to the
mines. The Duke of Gloucester would speak with you.
FLUELLEN To the mines ? Tell you the duke, it is not so
53 good to come to the mines ; for look you, the mines is not
54 according to the disciplines of the war. The concavities
of it is not sufficient ; for look you, th' athversary, you
56 may discuss unto the duke, look you, is digt himself four
57 yard under the countermines. By Cheshu, I think 'a will
58 plow up all, if there is not petter directions.
GOWER The Duke of Gloucester, to whom the order of
the siege is given, is altogether directed by an Irishman,
a very valiant gentleman, i' faith.
FLUELLEN It is Captain Macmorris, is it not ?
GOWER I think it be.
FLUELLEN By Cheshu, he is an ass as in the orld ! I will
65 verify as much in his peard. He has no more directions
in the true disciplines of the wars, look you, of the
Roman disciplines, than is a puppy-dog.
Enter Macmorris and Captain Jamy.
GOWER Here 'a comes, and the Scots captain, Captain
Jamy, with him.
FLUELLEN Captain Jamy is a marvellous falorous gentle-
71 man, that is certain, and of great expedition and know-
ledge in th' aunchient wars, upon my particular

knowledge of his directions. By Cheshu, he will maintain his argument as well as any military man in the orld
in the disciplines of the pristine wars of the Romans.
JAMY I say gud day, Captain Fluellen.
FLUELLEN God-den to your worship, good Captain
James.
GOWER How now, Captain Macmorris ? Have you quit
the mines ? Have the pioners given o'er ? 79
MACMORRIS By Chrish, law, tish ill done ! The work ish
give over, the trompet sound the retreat. By my hand I
swear, and my father's soul, the work ish ill done ! It ish
give over. I would have blowed up the town, so Chrish
save me, law, in an hour. O, tish ill done ! tish ill done !
By my hand, tish ill done !
FLUELLEN Captain Macmorris, I beseech you now, will
you voutsafe me, look you, a few disputations with you,
as partly touching or concerning the disciplines of the
war, the Roman wars ? In the way of argument, look you,
and friendly communication ; partly to satisfy my 90
opinion, and partly for the satisfaction, look you, of my
mind, as touching the direction of the military discipline, that is the point.
JAMY It sall be vary gud, gud feith, gud captens bath, and
I sall quit you with gud leve, as I may pick occasion. 95
That sall I, mary.
MACMORRIS It is no time to discourse, so Chrish save
me ! The day is hot, and the weather, and the wars, and
the king, and the dukes. It is no time to discourse. The
town is beseeched, and the trompet call us to the breach,
and we talk, and, be Chrish, do nothing. 'Tis shame for
us all. So God sa' me, 'tis shame to stand still, it is
shame, by my hand ! and there is throats to be cut, and
works to be done, and there ish nothing done, so Chrish
sa' me, law !
JAMY By the mess, ere theise eyes of mine take themselves 105
to slomber, ay'll de gud service, or ay'll lig i' th' grund
for it ! ay, or go to death ! And ay'll pay't as valorously as
I may, that sall I suerly do, that is the breff and the long.
Mary, I wad full fain heard some question 'tween you 109
tway.
FLUELLEN Captain Macmorris, I think, look you, under
your correction, there is not many of your nation –
MACMORRIS Of my nation ? What ish my nation ? Ish a 113
villain and a bastard, and a knave, and a rascal ! What ish
my nation ? Who talks of my nation ?
FLUELLEN Look you, if you take the matter otherwise
than is meant, Captain Macmorris, peradventure I shall
think you do not use me with that affability as in dis-
cretion you ought to use me, look you, being as good a
man as yourself, poth in the disciplines of war, and in
the derivation of my pirth, and in other particularities.
MACMORRIS I do not know you so good a man as myself.
So Chrish save me, I will cut off your head !
GOWER Gentlemen both, you will mistake each other. 124
JAMY A', that's a foul fault ! 125
A parley [sounded].
GOWER The town sounds a parley.
FLUELLEN Captain Macmorris, when there is more pet-
ter opportunity to be required, look you, I will be so
pold as to tell you I know the disciplines of war ; and
there is an end. *Exit [with others].*

*

23–24 *These . . . humors* (a cryptic utterance, even for Nym) 25 *swashers*
swashbucklers 28 *antics* fantastics, zanies 32 *breaks* i.e. fails to keep
his 42 *carry coals* i.e. put up with abuse 44 *makes* i.e. offends 53 *mines*
undermining operations 54 *disciplines* i.e. correct procedure ; *concavities*
i.e. slope, downward pitch 56 *discuss* explain 57 *Cheshu* Jesu 58 *plow*
blow 65 *in his peard* in his beard, i.e. to his face ; *directions* instruction
71 *expedition* readiness 79 *pioners* sappers 90 *communication* consultation
95 *quit* answer 105 *mess* i.e. Mass 109 *question* discussion 113 *What
ish* i.e. what about ; *Ish* i.e. someone, not exclusively Fluellen's (Macmorris'
sensitivity about his nationality makes him discharge at a general target the
insulting epithets which follow) 124 *will mistake* persist in misjudging
125 *A'* (equivalent to 'Ach')

III, iii   *Enter the King [Henry] and all his Train before the gates.*

KING

How yet resolves the governor of the town?
2   This is the latest parle we will admit:
Therefore to our best mercy give yourselves,
4   Or, like to men proud of destruction,
Defy us to our worst; for, as I am a soldier,
A name that in my thoughts becomes me best,
If I begin the batt'ry once again,
I will not leave the half-achievèd Harfleur
Till in her ashes she lie burièd.
The gates of mercy shall be all shut up,
11   And the fleshed soldier, rough and hard of heart,
In liberty of bloody hand shall range
13   With conscience wide as hell, mowing like grass
Your fresh fair virgins and your flow'ring infants.
What is it then to me if impious war,
Arrayed in flames to the prince of fiends,
17   Do with his smirched complexion all fell feats
Enlinked to waste and desolation?
What is 't to me, when you yourselves are cause,
If your pure maidens fall into the hand
Of hot and forcing violation?
What rein can hold licentious wickedness
23   When down the hill he holds his fierce career?
24   We may as bootless spend our vain command
Upon th' enragèd soldiers in their spoil
26   As send precepts to the leviathan
To come ashore. Therefore, you men of Harfleur,
Take pity of your town and of your people
Whiles yet my soldiers are in my command,
30   Whiles yet the cool and temperate wind of grace
31   O'erblows the filthy and contagious clouds
32   Of heady murder, spoil, and villainy.
If not – why, in a moment look to see
The blind and bloody soldier with foul hand
Defile the locks of your shrill-shrieking daughters;
Your fathers taken by the silver beards,
And their most reverend heads dashed to the walls;
Your naked infants spitted upon pikes,
Whiles the mad mothers with their howls confused
Do break the clouds, as did the wives of Jewry
41   At Herod's bloody-hunting slaughtermen.
What say you? Will you yield, and this avoid?
43   Or, guilty in defense, be thus destroyed?
    Enter Governor [on the wall].

GOVERNOR

Our expectation hath this day an end.
The Dauphin, whom of succors we entreated,
46   Returns us that his powers are not yet ready
To raise so great a siege. Therefore, great king,
We yield our town and lives to thy soft mercy.
Enter our gates, dispose of us and ours,
For we no longer are defensible.

KING

Open your gates. Come, uncle Exeter,
Go you and enter Harfleur; there remain
And fortify it strongly 'gainst the French.
Use mercy to them all. For us, dear uncle,
The winter coming on, and sickness growing
Upon our soldiers, we will retire to Calais.
To-night in Harfleur will we be your guest;
58   To-morrow for the march are we addrest.
    Flourish, and enter the town.

Enter Katherine and [Alice,] an old Gentlewoman.   III, iv

KATHERINE Alice, tu as esté en Angleterre, et tu bien
parles le langage.
ALICE Un peu, madame.
KATHERINE Je te prie m'enseigner; il faut que j'apprends
à parler. Comment appelez-vous le main en Anglois?
ALICE Le main? Il est appelé de hand.
KATHERINE De hand. Et les doigts?
ALICE Les doigts? Ma foi, j'oublie les doigts; mais je me
souviendrai. Les doigts? Je pense qu'ils'ont appelé de
fingres; oui, de fingres.   10
KATHERINE Le main, de hand; les doigts, de fingres. Je
pense que je suis le bon escolier; j'ai gagné deux mots
d'Anglois vistement. Comment appelez-vous les ongles?
ALICE Les ongles, les appelons de nailès.
KATHERINE De nailès. Escoute; dites-moi si je parle
bien: de hand, de fingres, et de nailès.
ALICE C'est bien dict, madame; il est fort bon Anglois.
KATHERINE Dites-moi l'Anglois pour le bras.
ALICE De arm, madame.
KATHERINE Et le coude.   20
ALICE D'elbow.
KATHERINE D'elbow. Je me'en fais le répétition de tous
les mots que vous m'avez apprins dès à présent.
ALICE Il est trop difficile, madame, comme je pense.
KATHERINE Excuse moi, Alice; escoute: d' hand, de
fingre, de nailès, d' arma, de bilbow.
ALICE D'elbow, madame.
KATHERINE O Seigneur Dieu, je m'en oublie d' elbow!
Comment appelez-vous le col?
ALICE De nick, madame.   30
KATHERINE De nick. Et le menton?
ALICE De chin.
KATHERINE De sin. Le col, de nick; le menton, de sin.
ALICE Oui. Sauf vostre honneur, en vérité, vous prononc-
ez les mots aussi droict que les natifs d'Angleterre.
KATHERINE Je ne doute point d'apprendre, par la grace
de Dieu, et en peu de temps.
ALICE N'avez-vous pas déjà oublié ce que je vous ai en-
seigné?

III, iii Before the walls of Harfleur at the gates   **2** *parle* parley   **4** *proud
of* who glory in   **11** *fleshed* hardened with killing   **13** *wide* permissive
17 *smirched* sooty   **23** *holds . . . career* maintains his fierce gallop   **24**
bootless uselessly   **26** *precepts* written summons   **30** *grace* mercy   **31**
O'erblows outblows   **32** *heady* headstrong   **41** *Herod's . . . slaughtermen*
(cf. Matthew ii, 16–18)   **43** *in defense* i.e. of reckless defense   **46** *Returns
us* replies   **58** *addrest* prepared
III, iv Within the palace of the French King   **1–58** KATH. Alice, you have
been in England, and you speak the language well. AL. A little, my lady.
KATH. I beg you teach me; I must learn to speak it. What do you call
le main in English? AL. *Le main*? It is called *de hand*. KATH. *De hand*.
And *les doigts*? AL. *Les doigts*? My faith, I forget *les doigts*; but I will
remember. *Les doigts*? I think they are called *de fingres*; yes, *de fingres*.
KATH. *Le main, de hand; les doigts, de fingres*. I think I am a good scholar;
I have learned two words of English quickly. What do you call *les ongles*?
AL. *Les ongles* we call *de nailès*. KATH. *De nailès*. Listen; tell me if I speak
well: *de hand, de fingres*, and *de nailès*. AL. Well spoken, my lady; it is
very good English. KATH. Tell me the English for *le bras*. AL. *De arm*,
my lady. KATH. And *le coude*. AL. *D'elbow*. KATH. *D'elbow*. I am going
to repeat all the words you have taught me so far. AL. It is too hard, my
lady, so I think. KATH. Excuse me, Alice; listen: *d'hand, de fingre, de
nailès, d'arma, de bilbow*. AL. *D'elbow*, my lady. KATH. O Lord God, I
can't remember *d'elbow*. What do you call *le col*? AL. *De nick*, my lady.
KATH. *De nick*. And *le menton*? AL. *De chin*. KATH. *De sin. Le col, de nick;
le menton, de sin*. AL. Yes. Save your honor, indeed you pronounce the
words as well as the native English. KATH. I trust to learn, by the grace
of God, and in short time. AL. You have not already forgotten what I have
taught you?

40 KATHERINE Non, je réciterai à vous promptement : d'
hand, de fingre, de mailès –
ALICE De nailès, madame.
KATHERINE De nailès, de arm, de ilbow –
ALICE Sauf vostre honneur, d' elbow.
KATHERINE Ainsi dis-je ; d' elbow, de nick, et de sin.
Comment appelez-vous le pied et la robe ?
ALICE De foot, madame ; et de count.
KATHERINE De foot et de count ! O Seigneur Dieu ! ils'ont
les mots de son mauvais, corruptible, gros, et impudi-
50 que, et non pour les dames d'honneur d'user : je ne
voudrais prononcer ces mots devant les seigneurs de
France pour tout le monde. Foh ! de foot et de count !
Néantmoins, je réciterai une autre fois ma leçon en-
semble : d' hand, de fingre, de nailès, d' arm, d' elbow,
de nick, de sin, de foot, de count.
ALICE Excellent, madame !
KATHERINE C'est assez pour une fois : allons-nous à
diner.   *Exit [with Alice].*

*

III, v   *Enter the King of France, the Dauphin [, Britaine],*
           the Constable of France, and others.

KING
1   'Tis certain he hath passed the river Somme.
CONSTABLE
And if he be not fought withal, my lord.
Let us not live in France ; let us quit all
And give our vineyards to a barbarous people.
DAUPHIN
5   O Dieu vivant ! Shall a few sprays of us,
6   The emptying of our fathers' luxury,
7   Our scions, put in wild and savage stock,
Spurt up so suddenly into the clouds
And overlook their grafters ?
BRITAINE
Normans, but bastard Normans, Norman bastards !
11   Mort de ma vie ! if they march along
Unfought withal, but I will sell my dukedom
13   To buy a slobb'ry and a dirty farm
14   In that nook-shotten isle of Albion.
CONSTABLE
15   Dieu de batailles ! where have they this mettle ?
Is not their climate foggy, raw, and dull,
On whom, as in despite, the sun looks pale,

KATH. No, I shall recite for you promptly : *d'hand, de fingre, de mailès* – AL.
De nailès, my lady. KATH. *De nailès, de arm, de ilbow* – AL. Save your honor,
d'elbow. KATH. So I said – *d'elbow, de nick, and de sin*. What do you call *le
pied* and *la robe* ? AL. *De foot*, my lady ; and *de count* [i.e. gown]. KATH.
De foot [which she mistakes for indecent '*foutre*'] and *de count* ! O Lord
God ! they are bad words, wicked, coarse, and immodest, and not for ladies
of honor to use : I would not speak those words before the gentlemen of
France for all the world. Foh ! *de foot* and *de count* ! Nevertheless, I will
recite once more my entire lesson : *d'hand, de fingre, de nailès, d'arm,
d'elbow, de nick, de sin, de foot, de count*. AL. Excellent, my lady ! KATH.
That's enough for one time ; let's go to dinner.
III, v The French King's quarters at Rouen   1 *passed . . . Somme* (in the
withdrawal to Calais)   5 *sprays* offshoots   6 *fathers' luxury* i.e. forefathers' lust   7 *scions* grafts   11 *Mort . . . vie* death of my life   13 *slobb'ry*
slovenly   14 *nook-shotten* full of nooks, i.e. with a ragged coastline   15
batailles battles   18 *sodden* boiled   19 *drench . . . jades* draught for exhausted horses ; *barley broth* ale (sometimes used as a drench)   20 *Decoct*
infuse   23 *roping* spun out by dripping   26 '*Poor*' . . . *lords* i.e. but not
rich in their possessors   33 *And* i.e. to ; *lavoltas* dance characterized by
leaps ; *corantos* dance characterized by running steps   34 *in our heels* (1)
as dancers, (2) as those who 'take to their heels'   47 *quit* acquit   59 *sink*
pit   60 *for achievement* i.e. instead of conquering
III, vi The English camp in Picardy

Killing their fruit with frowns ? Can sodden water,   18
A drench for sur-reined jades, their barley broth,   19
Decoct their cold blood to such valiant heat ?   20
And shall our quick blood, spirited with wine,
Seem frosty ? O, for honor of our land,
Let us not hang like roping icicles   23
Upon our houses' thatch, whiles a more frosty people
Sweat drops of gallant youth in our rich fields –
'Poor' we call them in their native lords !   26
DAUPHIN
By faith and honor,
Our madams mock at us and plainly say
Our mettle is bred out, and they will give
Their bodies to the lust of English youth
To new-store France with bastard warriors.
BRITAINE
They bid us to the English dancing schools
And teach lavoltas high, and swift corantos,   33
Saying our grace is only in our heels   34
And that we are most lofty runaways.
KING
Where is Montjoy the herald ? Speed him hence ;
Let him greet England with our sharp defiance.
Up, princes ! and with spirit of honor edged
More sharper than your swords, hie to the field.
Charles Delabreth, High Constable of France,
You Dukes of Orleans, Bourbon, and of Berri,
Alençon, Brabant, Bar, and Burgundy ;
Jacques Chatillon, Rambures, Vaudemont,
Beaumont, Grandpré, Roussi, and Faulconbridge,
Foix, Lestrale, Bouciqualt, and Charolois,
High dukes, great princes, barons, lords, and knights,
For your great seats now quit you of great shames.   47
Bar Harry England, that sweeps through our land
With pennons painted in the blood of Harfleur.
Rush on his host as doth the melted snow
Upon the valleys whose low vassal seat
The Alps doth spit and void his rheum upon.
Go down upon him – you have power enough –
And in a captive chariot into Rouen
Bring him our prisoner.
CONSTABLE   This becomes the great.
Sorry am I his numbers are so few,
His soldiers sick and famished in their march ;
For I am sure, when he shall see our army,
He'll drop his heart into the sink of fear   59
And, for achievement, offer us his ransom.   60
KING
Therefore, Lord Constable, haste on Montjoy,
And let him say to England that we send
To know what willing ransom he will give.
Prince Dauphin, you shall stay with us in Rouen.
DAUPHIN
Not so, I do beseech your majesty.
KING
Be patient, for you shall remain with us.
Now forth, Lord Constable and princes all,
And quickly bring us word of England's fall.   *Exeunt.*

*

III, vi   *Enter Captains, English and Welsh – Gower and*
          Fluellen.
GOWER How now, Captain Fluellen ? Come you from the
bridge ?

FLUELLEN I assure you there is very excellent services committed at the pridge.

GOWER Is the Duke of Exeter safe?

FLUELLEN The Duke of Exeter is as magnanimous as Agamemnon, and a man that I love and honor with my
8 soul, and my heart, and my duty, and my live, and my living, and my uttermost power. He is not – God be praised and plessed! – any hurt in the orld, but keeps the pridge most valiantly, with excellent discipline.
12 There is an aunchient lieutenant there at the pridge, I think in my very conscience he is as valiant a man as
14 Mark Anthony, and he is a man of no estimation in the
15 orld, but I did see him do as gallant service.

GOWER What do you call him?

FLUELLEN He is called Aunchient Pistol.

GOWER I know him not.

Enter Pistol.

FLUELLEN Here is the man.

PISTOL
Captain, I thee beseech to do me favors.
The Duke of Exeter doth love thee well.

FLUELLEN Ay, I praise God; and I have merited some love at his hands.

PISTOL
Bardolph, a soldier firm and sound of heart,
And of buxom valor, hath by cruel fate,
And giddy Fortune's furious fickle wheel –
That goddess blind,
That stands upon the rolling restless stone –

FLUELLEN By your patience, Aunchient Pistol. Fortune
30 is painted plind, with a muffler afore her eyes, to signify to you that Fortune is plind; and she is painted also with a wheel, to signify to you, which is the moral of it, that she is turning and inconstant, and mutability, and variation; and her foot, look you, is fixed upon a spherical stone, which rolls, and rolls, and rolls. In good truth, the poet makes a most excellent description of it.
37 Fortune is an excellent moral.

PISTOL
38 Fortune is Bardolph's foe, and frowns on him;
39 For he hath stol'n a pax, and hangèd must 'a be –
A damnèd death!
Let gallows gape for dog; let man go free,
And let not hemp his windpipe suffocate.
43 But Exeter hath given the doom of death
For pax of little price.
Therefore, go speak – the duke will hear thy voice;
And let not Bardolph's vital thread be cut
With edge of penny cord and vile reproach.
Speak, captain, for his life, and I will thee requite.

FLUELLEN Aunchient Pistol, I do partly understand your meaning.

PISTOL
Why then, rejoice therefore!

FLUELLEN Certainly, Aunchient, it is not a thing to rejoice at; for if, look you, he were my prother, I would desire the duke to use his good pleasure and put him to execution; for discipline ought to be used.

PISTOL
56 Die and be damned! and figo for thy friendship!

FLUELLEN It is well.

PISTOL
The fig of Spain!   *Exit.*

FLUELLEN Very good.

GOWER Why, this is an arrant counterfeit rascal! I remember him now – a bawd, a cutpurse.

FLUELLEN I'll assure you, 'a uttered as prave words at the pridge as you shall see in a summer's day. But it is very well. What he has spoke to me, that is well, I warrant you, when time is serve.

GOWER Why, 'tis a gull, a fool, a rogue, that now and then goes to the wars to grace himself, at his return into London, under the form of a soldier. And such fellows are
69 perfit in the great commanders' names, and they will learn you by rote where services were done: at such
71 and such a sconce, at such a breach, at such a convoy; who came off bravely, who was shot, who disgraced, what terms the enemy stood on; and this they con perfitly in the phrase of war, which they trick up with new-tuned oaths; and what a beard of the general's cut and a horrid
75 suit of the camp will do among foaming bottles and ale-washed wits is wonderful to be thought on. But you
78 must learn to know such slanders of the age, or else you may be marvellously mistook.

FLUELLEN I tell you what, Captain Gower, I do perceive he is not the man that he would gladly make show to the
82 orld he is. If I find a hole in his coat, I will tell him my mind. *[Drum within.]* Hark you, the king is coming, and I must speak with him from the pridge.

Drum and Colors. Enter the King and his poor Soldiers [and Gloucester].

God pless your majesty!

KING
How now, Fluellen? Cam'st thou from the bridge?

FLUELLEN Ay, so please your majesty. The Duke of Exeter has very gallantly maintained the pridge; the French is gone off, look you, and there is gallant and
90 most prave passages. Marry, th' athversary was have possession of the pridge, but he is enforced to retire, and the Duke of Exeter is master of the pridge. I can tell your majesty, the duke is a prave man.

KING What men have you lost, Fluellen?

FLUELLEN The perdition of th' athversary hath been very
95 great, reasonable great. Marry, for my part, I think the duke hath lost never a man but one that is like to be executed for robbing a church – one Pardolph, if your majesty know the man. His face is all bubukles and whelks,
99 and knobs, and flames o' fire, and his lips plows at his nose, and it is like a coal of fire, sometimes plue and sometimes red; but his nose is executed, and his fire 's out.

KING We would have all such offenders so cut off. And we give express charge that in our marches through the country there be nothing compelled from the villages, nothing taken but paid for; none of the French upbraided or abused in disdainful language; for when

---

8 *live* i.e. life   12 *aunchient lieutenant* (Pistol is elsewhere ranked simply as 'ancient,' i.e. ensign)   14 *estimation* fame   15 *gallant service* i.e. with words (cf. ll. 62–63)   37 *moral* i.e. emblem of instruction (the goddess Fortune figured prominently in literary and pictorial admonitions about the mutability of life)   38 *foe . . . frowns* (reminiscent of popular ballad, 'Fortune, my foe, why dost thou frown on me?')   39 *pax* metal disk engraved with crucifix, kissed during celebration of Mass   43 *doom* sentence   56 *figo* i.e. Spanish for fig (epithet and gesture of contempt)   69 *perfit* word-perfect   71 *sconce* earthwork; *convoy* transport of troops   75–76 *horrid suit* fierce attire   78 *slanders* disgraces   82 *a hole . . . coat* i.e. a means of exposing him   90 *passages* (of arms)   95 *perdition* loss, casualties   99 *bubukles and whelks* carbuncles and pimples

lenity and cruelty play for a kingdom, the gentler
109 gamester is the soonest winner.
Tucket. Enter Montjoy.
110 MONTJOY You know me by my habit.
KING Well then, I know thee. What shall I know of thee?
MONTJOY My master's mind.
KING Unfold it.
MONTJOY Thus says my king: Say thou to Harry of Eng-
115 land: Though we seemed dead, we did but sleep. Advantage is a better soldier than rashness. Tell him we
could have rebuked him at Harfleur, but that we thought
118 not good to bruise an injury till it were full ripe. Now we
speak upon our cue, and our voice is imperial. England
120 shall repent his folly, see his weakness, and admire our
sufferance. Bid him therefore consider of his ransom,
which must proportion the losses we have borne, the sub-
123 jects we have lost, the disgrace we have digested; which
in weight to re-answer, his pettiness would bow under.
For our losses, his exchequer is too poor; for th'effusion
of our blood, the muster of his kingdom too faint a number; and for our disgrace, his own person kneeling at
our feet but a weak and worthless satisfaction. To this
add defiance; and tell him for conclusion he hath betrayed his followers, whose condemnation is pronounced. So far my king and master; so much my office.
KING
132 What is thy name? I know thy quality.
MONTJOY Montjoy.
KING
Thou dost thy office fairly. Turn thee back,
And tell thy king I do not seek him now,
But could be willing to march on to Calais
137 Without impeachment: for, to say the sooth,
Though 'tis no wisdom to confess so much
139 Unto an enemy of craft and vantage,
My people are with sickness much enfeebled,
My numbers lessened, and those few I have
Almost no better than so many French,
Who when they were in health, I tell thee, herald,
I thought upon one pair of English legs
Did march three Frenchmen. Yet forgive me, God,
That I do brag thus! This your air of France
147 Hath blown that vice in me. I must repent.
Go therefore tell thy master here I am;
My ransom is this frail and worthless trunk;
My army but a weak and sickly guard;
Yet, God before, tell him we will come on,
Though France himself and such another neighbor
Stand in our way. There's for thy labor, Montjoy.
[Gives a purse.]
154 Go bid thy master well advise himself:

If we may pass, we will; if we be hind'red,
We shall your tawny ground with your red blood
Discolor; and so, Montjoy, fare you well.
The sum of all our answer is but this:
We would not seek a battle as we are,
Nor, as we are, we say we will not shun it.
So tell your master.
MONTJOY
I shall deliver so. Thanks to your highness.   *[Exit.]*
GLOUCESTER
I hope they will not come upon us now.
KING
We are in God's hand, brother, not in theirs.
March to the bridge. It now draws toward night.
Beyond the river we'll encamp ourselves,
And on to-morrow bid them march away.   *Exeunt.*

*

*Enter the Constable of France, the Lord Rambures,   III, vii
Orleans, Dauphin, with others.*
CONSTABLE Tut! I have the best armor of the world.
Would it were day!
ORLEANS You have an excellent armor; but let my horse
have his due.
CONSTABLE It is the best horse of Europe.
ORLEANS Will it never be morning?
DAUPHIN My Lord of Orleans, and my Lord High Con-
stable, you talk of horse and armor?
ORLEANS You are well provided of both as any prince in
the world.
DAUPHIN What a long night is this! I will not change my
horse with any that treads but on four pasterns. Ça, ha!
he bounds from the earth, as if his entrails were hairs; 13
le cheval volant, the Pegasus, chez les narines de feu! 14
When I bestride him, I soar, I am a hawk. He trots the
air. The earth sings when he touches it. The basest horn 16
of his hoof is more musical than the pipe of Hermes. 17
ORLEANS He's of the color of the nutmeg.
DAUPHIN And of the heat of the ginger. It is a beast for
Perseus: he is pure air and fire; and the dull elements of 20
earth and water never appear in him, but only in patient
stillness while his rider mounts him. He is indeed a
horse, and all other jades you may call beasts.
CONSTABLE Indeed, my lord, it is a most absolute and 24
excellent horse.
DAUPHIN It is the prince of palfreys. His neigh is like the 26
bidding of a monarch, and his countenance enforces
homage.
ORLEANS No more, cousin.
DAUPHIN Nay, the man hath no wit that cannot, from the
rising of the lark to the lodging of the lamb, vary de- 31
served praise on my palfrey. It is a theme as fluent as the
sea. Turn the sands into eloquent tongues, and my horse
is argument for them all. 'Tis a subject for a sovereign to
reason on, and for a sovereign's sovereign to ride on; 35
and for the world, familiar to us and unknown, to lay 36
apart their particular functions and wonder at him. I
once writ a sonnet in his praise and began thus, 'Wonder
of nature!'
ORLEANS I have heard a sonnet begin so to one's mistress.
DAUPHIN Then did they imitate that which I composed
to my courser, for my horse is my mistress.
ORLEANS Your mistress bears well.

109 s.d. *Tucket* trumpet call 110 *habit* attire 115 *Advantage* circumspection 118 *bruise* squeeze (as in treating a boil) 120–21 *admire . . .
sufferance* wonder at our patience 123–24 *which . . . under* i.e. to compensate for which his means are too small 132 *quality* rank 137
impeachment challenge 139 *vantage* superiority in numbers 147 *blown*
brought to bloom 154 *advise himself* consider
III, vii The French camp near Agincourt 13 *hairs* (like the stuffing of a
tennis ball) 14 *le cheval . . . feu* the flying horse, Pegasus, with nostrils of
fire 16 *basest horn* i.e. hoofbeat (with pun on the musical instrument)
17 *pipe* (the musical instrument with which Hermes, lulled
to sleep the monster Argus) 20 *Perseus* (in Ovid, the rider of Pegasus
while rescuing Andromeda from a dragon) 24 *absolute* perfect 26 *palfreys*
saddle-horses 31 *lodging* i.e. going to bed 35 *reason on* discourse upon
36–37 *to lay . . . functions* i.e. to combine

44 DAUPHIN Me well, which is the prescript praise and perfection of a good and particular mistress.

CONSTABLE Nay, for methought yesterday your mistress
47 shrewdly shook your back.

DAUPHIN So perhaps did yours.

CONSTABLE Mine was not bridled.

DAUPHIN O, then belike she was old and gentle, and you
51 rode like a kern of Ireland, your French hose off, and in
52 your strait strossers.

CONSTABLE You have good judgment in horsemanship.

DAUPHIN Be warned by me then. They that ride so, and
ride not warily, fall into foul bogs. I had rather have my
56 horse to my mistress.

CONSTABLE I had as lief have my mistress a jade.

DAUPHIN I tell thee, Constable, my mistress wears his
own hair.

CONSTABLE I could make as true a boast as that, if I had a
sow to my mistress.

62 DAUPHIN 'Le chien est retourné à son propre vomissement, et la truie lavée au bourbier.' Thou mak'st use of
anything.

CONSTABLE Yet do I not use my horse for my mistress,
or any such proverb so little kin to the purpose.

RAMBURES My Lord Constable, the armor that I saw in
your tent to-night – are those stars or suns upon it?

CONSTABLE Stars, my lord.

DAUPHIN Some of them will fall to-morrow, I hope.

71 CONSTABLE And yet my sky shall not want.

DAUPHIN That may be, for you bear a many superflu-
ously, and 'twere more honor some were away.

CONSTABLE Ev'n as your horse bears your praises, who
would trot as well, were some of your brags dismounted.

DAUPHIN Would I were able to load him with his desert!
Will it never be day? I will trot to-morrow a mile, and
my way shall be paved with English faces.

79 CONSTABLE I will not say so, for fear I should be faced
out of my way: but I would it were morning, for I
would fain be about the ears of the English.

82 RAMBURES Who will go to hazard with me for twenty
prisoners?

CONSTABLE You must first go yourself to hazard ere you
have them.

DAUPHIN 'Tis midnight; I'll go arm myself.   Exit.

ORLEANS The Dauphin longs for morning.

RAMBURES He longs to eat the English.

CONSTABLE I think he will eat all he kills.

ORLEANS By the white hand of my lady, he's a gallant
prince.

CONSTABLE Swear by her foot, that she may tread out
the oath.

ORLEANS He is simply the most active gentleman of
France.

95 CONSTABLE Doing is activity, and he will still be doing.

ORLEANS He never did harm, that I heard of.

CONSTABLE Nor will he do none to-morrow. He will keep
that good name still.

ORLEANS I know him to be valiant.

CONSTABLE I was told that by one that knows him better
than you.

ORLEANS What's he?

CONSTABLE Marry, he told me so himself, and he said he
cared not who knew it.

ORLEANS He needs not; it is no hidden virtue in him.

106 CONSTABLE By my faith, sir, but it is! Never anybody

saw it but his lackey. 'Tis a hooded valor; and when it 107
appears, it will bate.   108

ORLEANS Ill will never said well.

CONSTABLE I will cap that proverb with 'There is flattery in friendship.'

ORLEANS And I will take up that with 'Give the devil his
due.'

CONSTABLE Well placed! There stands your friend for 114
the devil. Have at the very eye of that proverb with 'A 115
pox of the devil!'

ORLEANS You are the better at proverbs, by how much 'a
fool's bolt is soon shot.'

CONSTABLE You have shot over.   119

ORLEANS 'Tis not the first time you were overshot.   120

        Enter a Messenger.

MESSENGER My Lord High Constable, the English lie
within fifteen hundred paces of your tents.

CONSTABLE Who hath measured the ground?

MESSENGER The Lord Grandpré.

CONSTABLE A valiant and most expert gentleman. Would
it were day! Alas, poor Harry of England! He longs not
for the dawning, as we do.

ORLEANS What a wretched and peevish fellow is this king 128
of England, to mope with his fat-brained followers so 129
far out of his knowledge!   130

CONSTABLE If the English had any apprehension, they 131
would run away.

ORLEANS That they lack; for if their heads had any intellectual armor, they could never wear such heavy head-
pieces.

RAMBURES That island of England breeds very valiant
creatures. Their mastiffs are of unmatchable courage.

ORLEANS Foolish curs, that run winking into the mouth 138
of a Russian bear and have their heads crushed like
rotten apples! You may as well say that's a valiant flea
that dare eat his breakfast on the lip of a lion.

CONSTABLE Just, just! and the men do sympathize with 142
the mastiffs in robustious and rough coming on, leaving
their wits with their wives; and then give them great
meals of beef and iron and steel, they will eat like wolves
and fight like devils.

ORLEANS Ay, but these English are shrewdly out of beef. 147

CONSTABLE Then shall we find to-morrow they have
only stomachs to eat and none to fight. Now is it time to
arm. Come, shall we about it?

ORLEANS
It is now two o'clock; but let me see – by ten
We shall have each a hundred Englishmen.   *Exeunt.*

                        *

44 *prescript* appropriate   47 *shrewdly* grievously   51 *kern* Irish bush-
fighter; *French hose* breeches   52 *strait strossers* tight trousers, i.e. bare-
legged   56 *to* as   62–63 *Le chien . . . bourbier* the dog is returned to his
own vomit and the washed sow to the mire (2 Peter ii, 22)   71 *want* be
lacking (in stars, i.e. honors)   79 *faced* braved   82 *go to hazard* play at
dice   95 *Doing* i.e. acting, pretending   106–07 *Never . . . lackey* i.e. he
is valiant only with his lackey   107 *hooded* with head covered, i.e. like a
quiescent hawk   108 *bate* flutter, i.e. like a hawk when unhooded (with
pun on 'bate' in sense of 'diminish')   114 *Well placed* well played, i.e.
appropriate   115 *Have . . . eye* i.e. right on the mark (another sporting
term evoked by this contest in proverb-capping)   119 *shot over* i.e. over
the mark   120 *overshot* i.e. defeated   128 *peevish* silly   129 *mope* grope
about   130 *out . . . knowledge* i.e. over his head   131 *apprehension* understanding   138 *winking* with eyes shut   142 *sympathize* i.e. have fellow-
feeling   147 *shrewdly* grievously

V, Cho.

Chorus.

1 Now entertain conjecture of a time
2 When creeping murmur and the poring dark
Fills the wide vessel of the universe.
From camp to camp, through the foul womb of night,
5 The hum of either army stilly sounds,
6 That the fixed sentinels almost receive
The secret whispers of each other's watch.
8 Fire answers fire, and through their paly flames
9 Each battle sees the other's umbered face.
Steed threatens steed, in high and boastful neighs
Piercing the night's dull ear; and from the tents
12 The armorers accomplishing the knights,
With busy hammers closing rivets up,
Give dreadful note of preparation.
The country cocks do crow, the clocks do toll
And the third hour of drowsy morning name.
17 Proud of their numbers and secure in soul,
18 The confident and over-lusty French
19 Do the low-rated English play at dice;
And chide the cripple tardy-gaited night
Who like a foul and ugly witch doth limp
So tediously away. The poor condemnèd English,
Like sacrifices, by their watchful fires
Sit patiently and inly ruminate
The morning's danger; and their gesture sad,
Investing lank-lean cheeks and war-worn coats,
Presenteth them unto the gazing moon
28 So many horrid ghosts. O, now, who will behold
The royal captain of this ruined band
Walking from watch to watch, from tent to tent,
Let him cry, 'Praise and glory on his head!'
For forth he goes and visits all his host,
Bids them good morrow with a modest smile
And calls them brothers, friends, and countrymen.
Upon his royal face there is no note
36 How dread an army hath enrounded him;
37 Nor doth he dedicate one jot of color
Unto the weary and all-watchèd night,
39 But freshly looks, and overbears attaint
With cheerful semblance and sweet majesty;
That every wretch, pining and pale before,
Beholding him, plucks comfort from his looks.
A largess universal, like the sun,
His liberal eye doth give to every one,
Thawing cold fear, that mean and gentle all
46 Behold, as may unworthiness define,
47 A little touch of Harry in the night.
And so our scene must to the battle fly;

Where (O for pity!) we shall much disgrace
With four or five most vile and ragged foils,
Right ill-disposed in brawl ridiculous,
The name of Agincourt. Yet sit and see,
Minding true things by what their mock'ries be.   *Exit.* 53

Enter the King, Bedford, and Gloucester.   IV, i

KING
Gloucester, 'tis true that we are in great danger;
The greater therefore should our courage be.
Good morrow, brother Bedford. God Almighty!
There is some soul of goodness in things evil,
Would men observingly distill it out;
For our bad neighbor makes us early stirrers,
Which is both healthful, and good husbandry.   7
Besides, they are our outward consciences,
And preachers to us all, admonishing
That we should dress us fairly for our end.   10
Thus may we gather honey from the weed
And make a moral of the devil himself.
  Enter Erpingham.
Good morrow, old Sir Thomas Erpingham.
A good soft pillow for that good white head
Were better than a churlish turf of France.
ERPINGHAM
Not so, my liege. This lodging likes me better,
Since I may say, 'Now lie I like a king.'
KING
'Tis good for men to love their present pains
Upon example: so the spirit is eased;   19
And when the mind is quick'ned, out of doubt   20
The organs, though defunct and dead before,
Break up their drowsy grave and newly move   22
With casted slough and fresh legerity.   23
Lend me thy cloak, Sir Thomas. Brothers both,
Commend me to the princes in our camp;
Do my good morrow to them, and anon
Desire them all to my pavilion.
GLOUCESTER
We shall, my liege.
ERPINGHAM
Shall I attend your grace?
KING   No, my good knight.
Go with my brothers to my lords of England.
I and my bosom must debate awhile,   31
And then I would no other company.
ERPINGHAM
The Lord in heaven bless thee, noble Harry!
                    Exeunt [all but the King].
KING
God-a-mercy, old heart! thou speak'st cheerfully.
  Enter Pistol.
PISTOL Che vous la?   35
KING A friend.
PISTOL
Discuss unto me, art thou officer;
Or art thou base, common, and popular?   38
KING I am a gentleman of a company.
PISTOL
Trail'st thou the puissant pike?   40
KING Even so. What are you?
PISTOL
As good a gentleman as the emperor.

IV, Cho. 1 *entertain conjecture of* imagine 2 *poring* peering 5 *stilly* quietly 6 *That* so that 8 *paly* pale (with play on heraldic meaning of alternately tinctured vertical lines?) 9 *battle* army; *umbered* shadowed (with play on 'umbred,' i.e. visored?, or on heraldic 'umbrated,' i.e. outlined, here silhouetted?) 12 *accomplishing* equipping 17 *secure in soul* confident in spirit 18 *over-lusty* over-lively 19 *play* i.e. play for 28 *horrid* fearful 36 *enrounded* surrounded 37 *dedicate* yield up 39 *overbears attaint* masters fatigue 46 *as ... define* as it may be roughly expressed 47 *touch* i.e. essence 53 *Minding* bearing in mind; *mock'ries* absurd imitations
IV, i The English camp near Agincourt 7 *husbandry* good management 10 *dress us* prepare ourselves 19 *Upon example* in exemplary fashion 20 *quick'ned* enlivened 22 *Break ... grave* break out of their grave of lethargy 23 *casted slough* discarded old skin; *legerity* briskness 31 *bosom* i.e. inner self, soul 35 *Che vous la* (Pistol's version of '*Qui va là*,' i.e. who goes there) 38 *popular* plebeian 40 *Trail'st ... pike* i.e. are you an infantryman

KING Then you are a better than the king.

PISTOL
44 The king's a bawcock, and a heart of gold,
45 A lad of life, an imp of fame,
Of parents good, of fist most valiant.
47 I kiss his dirty shoe, and from heartstring
I love the lovely bully. What is thy name?

KING Harry le Roy.

PISTOL
Le Roy? A Cornish name. Art thou of Cornish crew?

51 KING No, I am a Welshman.

PISTOL
Know'st thou Fluellen?

KING Yes.

PISTOL
Tell him I'll knock his leek about his pate
55 Upon Saint Davy's day.

KING Do not you wear your dagger in your cap that day,
lest he knock that about yours.

PISTOL
Art thou his friend?

KING And his kinsman too.

PISTOL
60 The figo for thee then!

KING I thank you. God be with you!

PISTOL
My name is Pistol called.

63 KING It sorts well with your fierceness.

           Exit [Pistol]. Manet King [aside].
          Enter Fluellen and Gower.

GOWER Captain Fluellen!

FLUELLEN So! in the name of Cheshu Christ, speak
66 fewer. It is the greatest admiration in the universal orld,
when the true and aunchient prerogatifes and laws of
the wars is not kept. If you would take the pains but to
examine the wars of Pompey the Great, you shall find, I
70 warrant you, that there is no tiddle taddle nor pibble
pabble in Pompey's camp. I warrant you, you shall find
the ceremonies of the wars, and the cares of it, and the
forms of it, and the sobriety of it, and the modesty of it,
to be otherwise.

GOWER Why, the enemy is loud; you hear him all night.

FLUELLEN If the enemy is an ass and a fool and a prating
coxcomb, is it meet, think you, that we should also, look
77 you, be an ass and a fool and a prating coxcomb? In your
own conscience now?

GOWER I will speak lower.

FLUELLEN I pray you and beseech you that you will.
                Exit [with Gower].

KING
Though it appear a little out of fashion,
There is much care and valor in this Welshman.
    Enter three Soldiers, John Bates, Alexander Court,
    and Michael Williams.

COURT Brother John Bates, is not that the morning which
breaks yonder?

BATES I think it be; but we have no great cause to desire
the approach of day.

WILLIAMS We see yonder the beginning of the day, but I
think we shall never see the end of it. Who goes there?

KING A friend.

WILLIAMS Under what captain serve you?

KING Under Sir Thomas Erpingham.

WILLIAMS A good old commander and a most kind
gentleman. I pray you, what thinks he of our estate?   93

KING Even as men wracked upon a sand, that look to be
washed off the next tide.

BATES He hath not told his thought to the king?

KING No; nor it is not meet he should. For though I speak
it to you, I think the king is but a man, as I am. The violet
smells to him as it doth to me; the element shows to him   99
as it doth to me; all his senses have but human condi-   100
tions. His ceremonies laid by, in his nakedness he ap-   101
pears but a man; and though his affections are higher   102
mounted than ours, yet when they stoop, they stoop   103
with the like wing. Therefore, when he sees reason of
fears, as we do, his fears, out of doubt, be of the same
relish as ours are. Yet, in reason, no man should possess   106
him with any appearance of fear, lest he, by showing it,
should dishearten his army.

BATES He may show what outward courage he will; but I
believe, as cold a night as 'tis, he could wish himself in
Thames up to the neck; and so I would he were, and I
by him, at all adventures, so we were quit here.   111

KING By my troth, I will speak my conscience of the
king: I think he would not wish himself anywhere but
where he is.

BATES Then I would he were here alone. So should he be
sure to be ransomed, and a many poor men's lives saved.

KING I dare say you love him not so ill to wish him here
alone, howsoever you speak this to feel other men's
minds. Methinks I could not die anywhere so contented
as in the king's company, his cause being just and his
quarrel honorable.

WILLIAMS That's more than we know.

BATES Ay, or more than we should seek after, for we know
enough if we know we are the king's subjects. If his
cause be wrong, our obedience to the king wipes the
crime of it out of us.

WILLIAMS But if the cause be not good, the king himself
hath a heavy reckoning to make when all those legs and
arms and heads, chopped off in a battle, shall join together at the latter day and cry all, 'We died at such a   130
place,' some swearing, some crying for a surgeon, some
upon their wives left poor behind them, some upon the
debts they owe, some upon their children rawly left. I   133
am afeard there are few die well that die in a battle; for
how can they charitably dispose of anything when blood   135
is their argument? Now, if these men do not die well, it
will be a black matter for the king that led them to it;
who to disobey were against all proportion of subjection.   138

KING So, if a son that is by his father sent about merchandise do sinfully miscarry upon the sea, the imputation of
his wickedness, by your rule, should be imposed upon
his father that sent him; or if a servant, under his master's
command transporting a sum of money, be assailed by

---

44 *bawcock* fine fellow (cf. III, ii, 22)   45 *imp* child   47 *heartstring* i.e. the very cords of my heart   51 *a Welshman* (technically true, like his reply 'Harry le Roy'; cf. IV, vii, 100)   55 *Saint Davy's day* March 1, the Welsh national holiday   60 *figo* (cf. III, vi, 56)   63 *sorts* suits   66 *admiration* wonder   70–71 *pibble pabble* bibble babble, chatter   77 *In* on   93 *estate* state   99 *element shows* sky appears   100 *conditions* i.e. limitations   101 *ceremonies* observances due royalty   102 *affections* emotions   103 *stoop* swoop downward (hawking term)   106 *relish* taste   106–07 *possess him with* induce in him   111 *at all adventures* by all means   130 *latter* last   133 *rawly* unprepared   135 *charitably* in Christian love   138 *proportion of subjection* due obedience

144 robbers and die in many irreconciled iniquities, you may call the business of the master the author of the servant's damnation. But this is not so. The king is not bound to answer the particular endings of his soldiers, the father of his son, nor the master of his servant; for they purpose not their death when they purpose their services. Besides, there is no king, be his cause never so spotless, if it come to the arbitrement of swords, can try it out with all unspotted soldiers. Some peradventure have on them the guilt of premeditated and contrived murder; some, of beguiling virgins with the broken seals of perjury; some, making the wars their bulwark, that have before gored the gentle bosom of peace with pillage and rob-
157 bery. Now, if these men have defeated the law and out-
158 run native punishment, though they can outstrip men, they have no wings to fly from God. War is his beadle, war is his vengeance; so that here men are punished for before-breach of the king's laws in now the king's quarrel. Where they feared the death, they have borne life away; and where they would be safe, they perish. Then
164 if they die unprovided, no more is the king guilty of their damnation than he was before guilty of those impieties for the which they are now visited. Every subject's duty is the king's, but every subject's soul is his own. Therefore should every soldier in the wars do as
169 every sick man in his bed – wash every mote out of his
170 conscience; and dying so, death is to him advantage; or not dying, the time was blessedly lost wherein such preparation was gained; and in him that escapes, it were not sin to think that, making God so free an offer, he let him outlive that day to see his greatness and to teach others how they should prepare.

WILLIAMS 'Tis certain, every man that dies ill, the ill upon his own head – the king is not to answer it.

BATES I do not desire he should answer for me, and yet I determine to fight lustily for him.

KING I myself heard the king say he would not be ransomed.

WILLIAMS Ay, he said so, to make us fight cheerfully; but when our throats are cut, he may be ransomed, and we ne'er the wiser.

KING If I live to see it, I will never trust his word after.

WILLIAMS You pay him then! That's a perilous shot out
187 of an elder-gun that a poor and a private displeasure can do against a monarch! You may as well go about to turn the sun to ice with fanning in his face with a peacock's feather. You'll never trust his word after! Come, 'tis a foolish saying.

192 KING Your reproof is something too round. I should be angry with you if the time were convenient.

WILLIAMS Let it be a quarrel between us if you live.

KING I embrace it.

---

144 *irreconciled* unabsolved   157 *defeated* broken   158 *native* in their own country   164 *unprovided* unprepared   169 *mote* small impurity   170 *advantage* a gain (in that he dies prepared)   187 *elder-gun* pop-gun   192 *round* unsparing   197 *gage* token of challenge   211 *enow* enough   212 *crowns* gold pieces (with play on 'heads' since the English are outnumbered)   214 *cut* i.e. clip edges of (a crime against the monarch's coinage classified as treason)   217 *careful* careworn   222 *wringing* suffering   225 *ceremony* royal pomp   231 *soul of adoration* i.e. true essence of, or reason for, worship   241 *flexure* bowing   245 *find thee* find thee out, expose thee   246 *balm* consecrated oil used in coronation   249 *farcèd* stuffed, padded; *the king* i.e. the king's name   251 *high shore* i.e. sea cliffs (impervious to tides)   256 *distressful* i.e. hard-earned (?)

WILLIAMS How shall I know thee again?

KING Give me any gage of thine, and I will wear it in my 197 bonnet. Then, if ever thou dar'st acknowledge it, I will make it my quarrel.

WILLIAMS Here's my glove. Give me another of thine.

KING There.

WILLIAMS This will I also wear in my cap. If ever thou come to me and say, after to-morrow, 'This is my glove,' by this hand, I will take thee a box on the ear.

KING If ever I live to see it, I will challenge it.

WILLIAMS Thou dar'st as well be hanged.

KING Well, I will do it, though I take thee in the king's company.

WILLIAMS Keep thy word. Fare thee well.

BATES Be friends, you English fools, be friends! We have French quarrels enow, if you could tell how to reckon. 211

KING Indeed the French may lay twenty French crowns to 212 one they will beat us, for they bear them on their shoulders; but it is no English treason to cut French crowns, 214 and to-morrow the king himself will be a clipper.

Exit [Bates with other] Soldiers.

Upon the king! Let us our lives, our souls,
Our debts, our careful wives,   217
Our children, and our sins, lay on the king!
We must bear all. O hard condition,
Twin-born with greatness, subject to the breath
Of every fool, whose sense no more can feel
But his own wringing! What infinite heart's-ease   222
Must kings neglect that private men enjoy!
And what have kings that privates have not too,
Save ceremony, save general ceremony?   225
And what art thou, thou idol Ceremony?
What kind of god art thou, that suffer'st more
Of mortal griefs than do thy worshippers?
What are thy rents? What are thy comings-in?
O Ceremony, show me but thy worth!
What is thy soul of adoration?   231
Art thou aught else but place, degree, and form,
Creating awe and fear in other men?
Wherein thou art less happy being feared
Than they in fearing.
What drink'st thou oft, instead of homage sweet,
But poisoned flattery? O, be sick, great greatness,
And bid thy ceremony give thee cure!
Think'st thou the fiery fever will go out
With titles blown from adulation?
Will it give place to flexure and low bending?   241
Canst thou, when thou command'st the beggar's knee,
Command the health of it? No, thou proud dream,
That play'st so subtilly with a king's repose.
I am a king that find thee; and I know   245
'Tis not the balm, the sceptre, and the ball,   246
The sword, the mace, the crown imperial,
The intertissued robe of gold and pearl,
The farcèd title running 'fore the king,   249
The throne he sits on, nor the tide of pomp
That beats upon the high shore of this world –   251
No, not all these, thrice-gorgeous ceremony,
Not all these, laid in bed majestical,
Can sleep so soundly as the wretched slave,
Who, with a body filled, and vacant mind,
Gets him to rest, crammed with distressful bread;   256
Never sees horrid night, the child of hell;

258 But like a lackey, from the rise to set,
259 Sweats in the eye of Phoebus, and all night
Sleeps in Elysium; next day after dawn,
261 Doth rise and help Hyperion to his horse;
And follows so the ever-running year
With profitable labor to his grave;
And but for ceremony, such a wretch,
Winding up days with toil and nights with sleep,
Had the forehand and vantage of a king.
267 The slave, a member of the country's peace,
Enjoys it; but in gross brain little wots
269 What watch the king keeps to maintain the peace,
270 Whose hours the peasant best advantages.
         Enter Erpingham.

ERPINGHAM
271 My lord, your nobles, jealous of your absence,
Seek through your camp to find you.
KING   Good old knight,
Collect them all together at my tent.
I'll be before thee.
ERPINGHAM   I shall do't, my lord.   *Exit.*
KING
O God of battles, steel my soldiers' hearts,
Possess them not with fear! Take from them now
277 The sense of reck'ning, if th' opposèd numbers
Pluck their hearts from them. Not to-day, O Lord,
O, not to-day, think not upon the fault
280 My father made in compassing the crown!
281 I Richard's body have interrèd new;
And on it have bestowed more contrite tears
Than from it issued forcèd drops of blood.
Five hundred poor I have in yearly pay,
Who twice a day their withered hands hold up
286 Toward heaven to pardon blood;
287 And I have built two chantries,
288 Where the sad and solemn priests sing still
For Richard's soul. More will I do:
Though all that I can do is nothing worth,
291 Since that my penitence comes after all,
Imploring pardon.
         Enter Gloucester.
GLOUCESTER
My liege!
KING
My brother Gloucester's voice. Ay.
I know thy errand; I will go with thee.
The day, my friends, and all things stay for me.   *Exeunt.*

               *

IV, ii   *Enter the Dauphin, Orleans, Rambures, and*
        Beaumont.
ORLEANS
The sun doth gild our armor. Up, my lords!
2 DAUPHIN Monte, cheval! My horse, varlet lacquais! Ha!
ORLEANS O brave spirit!
4 DAUPHIN Via les eaux et terre!
5 ORLEANS Rien puis les air et feu?
6 DAUPHIN Cieux! cousin Orleans.
         Enter Constable.
Now, my Lord Constable?
CONSTABLE
Hark how our steeds for present service neigh!

DAUPHIN
Mount them and make incision in their hides,
That their hot blood may spin in English eyes
And dout them with superfluous courage, ha!   11
RAMBURES
What, will you have them weep our horses' blood?
How shall we then behold their natural tears?
         Enter Messenger.
MESSENGER
The English are embattled, you French peers.
CONSTABLE
To horse, you gallant princes! straight to horse!
Do but behold yond poor and starvèd band,
And your fair show shall suck away their souls,
Leaving them but the shales and husks of men.   18
There is not work enough for all our hands,
Scarce blood enough in all their sickly veins
To give each naked curtle-axe a stain   21
That our French gallants shall to-day draw out
And sheathe for lack of sport. Let us but blow on them,
The vapor of our valor will o'erturn them.
'Tis positive 'gainst all exceptions, lords,   25
That our superfluous lackeys and our peasants,
Who in unnecessary action swarm
About our squares of battle, were enow
To purge this field of such a hilding foe,   29
Though we upon this mountain's basis by   30
Took stand for idle speculation: 31
But that our honors must not. What's to say?
A very little little let us do,
And all is done. Then let the trumpets sound
The tucket sonance and the note to mount;   35
For our approach shall so much dare the field   36
That England shall couch down in fear and yield.
         Enter Grandpré.
GRANDPRÉ
Why do you stay so long, my lords of France?
Yond island carrions, desperate of their bones,   39
Ill-favoredly become the morning field.
Their ragged curtains poorly are let loose,   41
And our air shakes them passing scornfully.
Big Mars seems bankrout in their beggared host   43
And faintly through a rusty beaver peeps.   44
The horsemen sit like fixèd candlesticks

258 *lackey* constant attendant   259 *Sweats . . . Phoebus* i.e. works in sight of the sun   261 *Hyperion* charioteer of the sun   267 *member* sharer   269 *watch* wakeful guard   270 *advantages* profits   271 *jealous of* concerned about   277 *sense of reck'ning* ability to count   280 *compassing* obtaining   281 *new* anew   286 *blood* sinful flesh (?), the spilling of blood (?)   287 *chantries* chapels where masses are celebrated for the souls of the dead   288 *still* continuously   291 *Since that* i.e. as shown by the fact that
IV, ii The French camp   **s.d.** *Beaumont* (a 'ghost' character, mute and appearing only in this one stage direction)   2 *Monte, cheval* soar, horse (cf. III, vii, 11–16); *varlet lacquais* rascal groom   4 *Via . . . terre* away waters and earth (i.e. streams and solid ground)   5 *Rien . . . feu?* not also air and fire? (Orleans jestingly takes the Dauphin's 'eaux' and 'terre' to refer to two of the four elements over which his horse will soar; and asks if it will not also soar above the realms of air and fire)   6 *Cieux* the heavens (to which, in the old cosmology, the realm of fire extended; the Dauphin has converted the joke into serious hyperbole)   11 *dout* extinguish; *superfluous courage* i.e. blood we can spare   18 *shales* shells   21 *curtle-axe* cutlass   25 *exceptions* objections   29 *hilding* worthless   30 *mountain's basis by* i.e. nearby foothill   31 *speculation* viewing   35 *tucket sonance* trumpet call   36 *dare* daze (as the hawk terrifies its prey)   39 *carrions* cadavers; *desperate* despairing   41 *curtains* flags   43 *bankrout* bankrupt   44 *beaver* visor

46 With torch-staves in their hand ; and their poor jades
47 Lob down their heads, dropping the hides and hips,
48 The gum down roping from their pale-dead eyes,
49 And in their pale dull mouths the gimmaled bit
Lies foul with chawed grass, still and motionless ;
51 And their executors, the knavish crows,
Fly o'er them all, impatient for their hour.
Description cannot suit itself in words
To demonstrate the life of such a battle
55 In life so lifeless as it shows itself.

CONSTABLE
56 They have said their prayers, and they stay for death.

DAUPHIN
Shall we go send them dinners and fresh suits
And give their fasting horses provender,
And after fight with them ?

CONSTABLE
60 I stay but for my guard. On to the field !
61 I will the banner from a trumpet take
And use it for my haste. Come, come away !
63 The sun is high, and we outwear the day.   *Exeunt.*

*

IV, iii   *Enter Gloucester, Bedford, Exeter, Erpingham with*
all his Host, Salisbury, and Westmoreland.

GLOUCESTER
Where is the king ?

BEDFORD
2 The king himself is rode to view their battle.

WESTMORELAND
Of fighting men they have full three-score thousand.

EXETER
There's five to one ; besides, they all are fresh.

SALISBURY
God's arm strike with us ! 'Tis a fearful odds.
God bye you, princes all ; I'll to my charge.
If we no more meet till we meet in heaven,
Then joyfully, my noble Lord of Bedford,
My dear Lord Gloucester, and my good Lord Exeter,
And my kind kinsman, warriors all, adieu !

BEDFORD
Farewell, good Salisbury, and good luck go with thee !

EXETER
Farewell, kind lord : fight valiantly to-day ;
And yet I do thee wrong to mind thee of it,
14 For thou art framed of the firm truth of valor.
                 [Exit Salisbury.]

BEDFORD
He is as full of valor as of kindness,
Princely in both.
      Enter the King.

WESTMORELAND O that we now had here
But one ten thousand of those men in England
That do no work to-day !

KING   What's he that wishes so ?
My cousin Westmoreland ? No, my fair cousin.
If we are marked to die, we are enow   20
To do our country loss ; and if to live,
The fewer men, the greater share of honor.
God's will ! I pray thee wish not one man more.
By Jove, I am not covetous for gold,
Nor care I who doth feed upon my cost ;
It yearns me not if men my garments wear ;   26
Such outward things dwell not in my desires :
But if it be a sin to covet honor,
I am the most offending soul alive.
No, faith, my coz, wish not a man from England.   30
God's peace ! I would not lose so great an honor
As one man more methinks would share from me
For the best hope I have. O, do not wish one more !
Rather proclaim it, Westmoreland, through my host,
That he which hath no stomach to this fight,
Let him depart ; his passport shall be made,
And crowns for convoy put into his purse.   37
We would not die in that man's company
That fears his fellowship to die with us.   39
This day is called the Feast of Crispian.   40
He that outlives this day, and comes safe home,
Will stand a-tiptoe when this day is namèd
And rouse him at the name of Crispian.
He that shall see this day, and live old age,
Will yearly on the vigil feast his neighbors
And say, 'To-morrow is Saint Crispian.'
Then will he strip his sleeve and show his scars,
[And say, 'These wounds I had on Crispin's day.']
Old men forget ; yet all shall be forgot,
But he'll remember, with advantages,   50
What feats he did that day. Then shall our names,
Familiar in his mouth as household words –
Harry the King, Bedford and Exeter,
Warwick and Talbot, Salisbury and Gloucester –
Be in their flowing cups freshly remem'red.
This story shall the good man teach his son ;
And Crispin Crispian shall ne'er go by,
From this day to the ending of the world,
But we in it shall be rememberèd –
We few, we happy few, we band of brothers ;
For he to-day that sheds his blood with me
Shall be my brother. Be he ne'er so vile,   62
This day shall gentle his condition ;   63
And gentlemen in England now abed
Shall think themselves accursed they were not here,
And hold their manhoods cheap whiles any speaks
That fought with us upon Saint Crispin's day.
      Enter Salisbury.

SALISBURY
My sovereign lord, bestow yourself with speed.
The French are bravely in their battles set
And will with all expedience charge on us.   70

KING
All things are ready, if our minds be so.

WESTMORELAND
Perish the man whose mind is backward now !

KING
Thou dost not wish more help from England, coz ?

WESTMORELAND
God's will, my liege ! would you and I alone,
Without more help, could fight this royal battle !

---

46 *torch-staves* tapers 47 *Lob* droop 48 *roping* (cf. III, v, 23) 49
gimmaled jointed 51 *executors* disposers of the remains 55 *In life* in
actuality 56 *stay* wait 60 *guard* (including color-bearer) 61 *trumpet*
trumpeter 63 *outwear* waste
IV, iii The English camp 2 *battle* army 14 *framed . . . truth* i.e. made of
the authentic stuff 20–21 *enow To do* enough to cause 26 *yearns* moves,
grieves 30 *coz* cousin, kinsman 37 *convoy* transport 39 *fellowship* i.e.
fraternal right 40 *Feast of Crispian* October 25 (the brothers Crispianus
and Crispinus were martyred A.D. 487 ; they became the patron saints of
shoemakers) 50 *advantages* i.e. embellishments 62 *vile* low-born 63
gentle his condition i.e. achieve gentility 70 *expedience* expedition

KING
Why, now thou hast unwished five thousand men !
Which likes me better than to wish us one.
You know your places. God be with you all !
    Tucket. Enter Montjoy.
MONTJOY
Once more I come to know of thee, King Harry,
80   If for thy ransom thou wilt now compound,
Before thy most assurèd overthrow ;
For certainly thou art so near the gulf
83   Thou needs must be englutted. Besides, in mercy,
84   The Constable desires thee thou wilt mind
Thy followers of repentance, that their souls
May make a peaceful and a sweet retire
From all these fields, where (wretches !) their poor bodies
Must lie and fester.
KING   Who hath sent thee now ?
MONTJOY
The Constable of France.
KING
I pray thee bear my former answer back :
91   Bid them achieve me, and then sell my bones.
Good God ! why should they mock poor fellows thus ?
The man that once did sell the lion's skin
While the beast lived, was killed with hunting him.
A many of our bodies shall no doubt
96   Find native graves ; upon the which, I trust,
Shall witness live in brass of this day's work ;
And those that leave their valiant bones in France,
Dying like men, though buried in your dunghills,
They shall be famed ; for there the sun shall greet them
101   And draw their honors reeking up to heaven,
Leaving their earthly parts to choke your clime,
The smell whereof shall breed a plague in France.
Mark then abounding valor in our English,
105   That, being dead, like to the bullet's crasing,
Break out into a second course of mischief,
107   Killing in relapse of mortality.
Let me speak proudly. Tell the Constable
109   We are but warriors for the working day.
Our gayness and our gilt are all besmirched
111   With rainy marching in the painful field.
112   There's not a piece of feather in our host –
Good argument, I hope, we will not fly –
And time hath worn us into slovenry.
But, by the mass, our hearts are in the trim ;
And my poor soldiers tell me, yet ere night
117   They'll be in fresher robes, or they will pluck
The gay new coats o'er the French soldiers' heads
119   And turn them out of service. If they do this,
As, if God please, they shall, my ransom then
121   Will soon be levied. Herald, save thou thy labor.
Come thou no more for ransom, gentle herald.
They shall have none, I swear, but these my joints ;
Which if they have as I will leave 'em them
Shall yield them little, tell the Constable.
MONTJOY
I shall, King Harry. And so fare thee well.
Thou never shalt hear herald any more.   *Exit.*
KING
128   I fear thou wilt once more come again for a ransom.
     Enter York.
YORK
My lord, most humbly on my knee I beg

The leading of the vaward.   130
KING
Take it, brave York. Now, soldiers, march away ;
And how thou pleasest, God, dispose the day !   *Exeunt.*

*

Alarum. Excursions. Enter Pistol, French Soldier,   IV, iv
    Boy.
PISTOL   Yield, cur !
FRENCH SOLDIER   Je pense que vous estes le gentil-   2
homme de bon qualité.
PISTOL   Qualtitie calmie custure me ! Art thou a gentle-   4
man ? What is thy name ? Discuss.   5
FRENCH SOLDIER   O Seigneur Dieu !
PISTOL
O Signieur Dew should be a gentleman.
Perpend my words, O Signieur Dew, and mark.   8
O Signieur Dew, thou diest on point of fox,   9
Except, O signieur, thou do give to me
Egregious ransom.   11
FRENCH SOLDIER   O, prenez miséricorde ! ayez pitié de   12
moi !
PISTOL
Moy shall not serve. I will have forty moys,
Or I will fetch thy rim out at thy throat   14
In drops of crimson blood.
FRENCH SOLDIER   Est-il impossible d'eschapper le force   16
de ton bras ?
PISTOL   Brass, cur ?
Thou damnèd and luxurious mountain goat,   19
Offer'st me brass ?
FRENCH SOLDIER   O, pardonnez-moi !
PISTOL
Say'st thou me so ? Is that a ton of moys ?
Come hither, boy ; ask me this slave in French
What is his name.
BOY   Escoute. Comment estes-vous appelé ?   25
FRENCH SOLDIER   Monsieur le Fer.
BOY   He says his name is Master Fer.
PISTOL   Master Fer ? I'll fer him, and firk him, and ferret   28
him ! Discuss the same in French unto him.
BOY   I do not know the French for 'fer,' and 'ferret,' and
'firk.'
PISTOL
Bid him prepare, for I will cut his throat.

---

80 *compound* come to terms   83 *englutted* swallowed up   84 *mind* remind
91 *achieve* win, capture   96 *native* i.e. English   96–97 *upon . . . work*
i.e. bearing bronze tablets commemorating their deeds at Agincourt
101 *reeking* breathing   105 *crasing* grazing, rebounding   107 *in . . .*
mortality i.e. while in the process of decaying   109 *warriors . . . day* i.e.
workaday or commonplace soldiers   111 *painful* arduous   112 *piece of*
feather decorative plume   117 *in fresher robes* i.e. new-garbed in heaven
119 *turn . . . service* i.e. dismiss them stripped of their livery   121 *levied*
collected (from the French themselves)   128 *again* (perhaps an intrusion
in the text)   130 *vaward* vanguard
IV, iv The battlefield of Agincourt   2–3 *Je . . . qualité* I think you are a
gentleman of rank   4 *Qualtitie . . . me* (gibberish, echoing *qualité* in l. 3,
together with refrain of a popular ballad, 'Callen o custare me' ; the
refrain itself derives from an Irish line 'Cailin ó chois tS'uire me, meaning
'I am a girl from beside the Suir')   5 *Discuss* declare   8 *Perpend* consider   9 *fox* sword (derived from trademark of a famous swordmaker)
11 *Egregious* extraordinary   12–13 *O . . . moi* O, have mercy ! take pity on
me   14 *rim* belly-lining   16–17 *Est-il . . . bras* is it impossible to escape the
strength of your arm   19 *luxurious* lecherous   25 *Escoute . . . appelé* listen,
what is your name   28 *firk* beat ; *ferret* worry

33 FRENCH SOLDIER Que dit-il, monsieur?

34 BOY Il me commande de vous dire que vous faites vous

35 prest; car ce soldat ici est disposé tout asture de couper
  vostre gorge.
 PISTOL
  Owy, cuppe le gorge, permafoy,
  Peasant, unless thou give me crowns, brave crowns,
  O'er-mangled shalt thou be by this my sword.
 FRENCH SOLDIER O, je vous supplie, pour l'amour de
  Dieu, me pardonner! Je suis le gentilhomme de bon
  maison. Gardez ma vie, et je vous donnerai deux cents
  escus.
 PISTOL
  What are his words?
 BOY He prays you to save his life. He is a gentleman of a
  good house, and for his ransom he will give you two
  hundred crowns.
 PISTOL
  Tell him my fury shall abate, and I
  The crowns will take.

49 FRENCH SOLDIER Petit monsieur, que dit-il?

50 BOY Encore qu'il est contre son jurement de pardonner
  aucun prisonnier; néantmoins, pour les escus que vous
  l'avez promis, il est content de vous donner le liberté, le
  franchisement.
 FRENCH SOLDIER Sur mes genoux je vous donne mille
  remercîmens; et je m'estime heureux que j'ai tombé
  entre les mains d'un chevalier, je pense, le plus brave,
  vaillant, et très-distingué seigneur d'Angleterre.
 PISTOL
  Expound unto me, boy.
 BOY He gives you, upon his knees, a thousand thanks;
  and he esteems himself happy that he hath fall'n into
  the hands of one, as he thinks, the most brave, valorous,
  and thrice-worthy signieur of England.
 PISTOL

63 As I suck blood, I will some mercy show!
  Follow me.   [Exit.]
 BOY Suivez-vous le grand capitaine. [Exit French Soldier.]
  I did never know so full a voice issue from so empty a
  heart; but the saying is true, 'The empty vessel makes
  the greatest sound.' Bardolph and Nym had ten times

69 more valor than this roaring devil i' th' old play that
  every one may pare his nails with a wooden dagger; and
  they are both hanged; and so would this be, if he durst
  steal anything adventurously. I must stay with the
  lackeys with the luggage of our camp. The French
  might have a good prey of us, if he knew of it; for there
  is none to guard it but boys.   Exit.

IV, v *Enter Constable, Orleans, Bourbon, Dauphin, and*
  Rambures.

 CONSTABLE O diable!

ORLEANS O Seigneur! le jour est perdu, tout est perdu! 2
DAUPHIN
 Mort de ma vie! all is confounded, all!   3
 Reproach and everlasting shame
 Sits mocking in our plumes.
   A short alarum.
 O meschante fortune! Do not run away.   6
CONSTABLE
 Why, all our ranks are broke.
DAUPHIN
 O perdurable shame! Let's stab ourselves.   8
 Be these the wretches that we played at dice for?
ORLEANS
 Is this the king we sent to for his ransom?
BOURBON
 Shame, and eternal shame! nothing but shame!
 Let us die in honor. Once more back again!
 And he that will not follow Bourbon now,
 Let him go hence, and with his cap in hand
 Like a base pander hold the chamber door
 Whilst by a slave, no gentler than my dog,
 His fairest daughter is contaminated.
CONSTABLE
 Disorder, that hath spoiled us, friend us now!   18
 Let us on heaps go offer up our lives.
ORLEANS
 We are enow yet living in the field
 To smother up the English in our throngs,
 If any order might be thought upon.
BOURBON
 The devil take order now! I'll to the throng.
 Let life be short; else shame will be too long. *Exeunt.*
  Alarum. Enter the King and his Train, [Exeter, and IV, vi
  others,] with Prisoners.
KING
 Well have we done, thrice-valiant countrymen;
 But all's not done, yet keep the French the field.
EXETER
 The Duke of York commends him to your majesty.
KING
 Lives he, good uncle? Thrice within this hour
 I saw him down; thrice up again and fighting.
 From helmet to the spur all blood he was.
EXETER
 In which array, brave soldier, doth he lie,
 Larding the plain; and by his bloody side,   8
 Yoke-fellow to his honor-owing wounds,
 The noble Earl of Suffolk also lies.
 Suffolk first died; and York, all haggled over,   11
 Comes to him, where in gore he lay insteepèd,
 And takes him by the beard, kisses the gashes
 That bloodily did yawn upon his face,
 And cries aloud, 'Tarry, my cousin Suffolk!
 My soul shall thine keep company to heaven.
 Tarry, sweet soul, for mine, then fly abreast;
 As in this glorious and well-foughten field
 We kept together in our chivalry!'
 Upon these words I came and cheered him up.
 He smiled me in the face, raught me his hand,   21
 And with a feeble gripe, says, 'Dear my lord,
 Commend my service to my sovereign.'
 So did he turn, and over Suffolk's neck
 He threw his wounded arm and kissed his lips;
 And so, espoused to death, with blood he sealed

---

33 *Que . . . monsieur* what does he say, sir 34–36 *Il . . . gorge* he bids me
tell you to prepare, for this soldier is disposed to cut your throat at once
35 *asture* i.e. '*à cette heure,*' at once 49 *Petit . . . dit-il* small sir, what says
he 50–53 *Encore . . . franchisement* although it is against his oath to pardon
any prisoner, still for the crowns you have promised he is willing to give
you liberty, freedom 63 *suck blood* (cf. II, iii, 50–51) 69 *roaring devil*
i.e. the devil or Vice in the old morality plays, sometimes subjected to the
indignity of having his claws pared
IV, v 2 *O . . . perdu* O Lord! the day is lost, all is lost 3 *Mort . . . vie*
death of my life; *confounded* ruined 6 *O . . . fortune* O tainted Fortune
8 *perdurable* enduring 18 *spoiled* despoiled, ruined
IV, vi 8 *Larding* fattening, fertilizing 11 *haggled* hacked 21 *raught*
reached

A testament of noble-ending love.
The pretty and sweet manner of it forced
Those waters from me which I would have stopped ;
But I had not so much of man in me,

31 And all my mother came into mine eyes
And gave me up to tears.

KING   I blame you not ;

33 For hearing this, I must perforce compound

34 With mistful eyes, or they will issue too.   *Alarum.*
But hark ! what new alarum is this same ?
The French have reinforced their scattered men.
Then every soldier kill his prisoners !
Give the word through.   *Exit [with others].*

❋

IV, vii   *Enter Fluellen and Gower.*

FLUELLEN Kill the poys and the luggage ? 'Tis expressly
against the law of arms. 'Tis as arrant a piece of knavery,
mark you now, as can be offert. In your conscience, now,
is it not ?

GOWER 'Tis certain there's not a boy left alive ; and the
cowardly rascals that ran from the battle ha' done this
slaughter. Besides, they have burned and carried away
all that was in the king's tent ; wherefore the king most
worthily hath caused every soldier to cut his prisoner's
throat. O, 'tis a gallant king !

11 FLUELLEN Ay, he was porn at Monmouth, Captain
Gower. What call you the town's name where Alexander the Pig was born.

GOWER Alexander the Great.

FLUELLEN Why, I pray you, is not 'pig' great ? The pig,
or the great, or the mighty, or the huge, or the magnanimous are all one reckonings, save the phrase is a

17 little variations.

GOWER I think Alexander the Great was born in Macedon.
His father was called Philip of Macedon, as I take it.

FLUELLEN I think it is in Macedon where Alexander is
porn. I tell you, captain, if you look in the maps of the
orld, I warrant you sall find, in the comparisons between Macedon and Monmouth, that the situations,

24 look you, is poth alike. There is a river in Macedon, and
there is also moreover a river at Monmouth. It is called
Wye at Monmouth ; but it is out of my prains what is the
name of the other river. But 'tis all one ; 'tis alike as my
fingers is to my fingers, and there is salmons in poth. If
you mark Alexander's life well, Harry of Monmouth's

30 life is come after it indifferent well ; for there is figures
in all things. Alexander, God knows and you know, in
his rages, and his furies, and his wraths, and his cholers,
and his moods, and his displeasures, and his indigna-
tions, and also being a little intoxicates in his prains, did,
in his ales and his angers, look you, kill his best friend,

35 Cleitus.

GOWER Our king is not like him in that. He never killed
any of his friends.

FLUELLEN It is not well done, mark you now, to take the
tales out of my mouth ere it is made and finished. I speak
but in the figures and comparisons of it. As Alexander
killed his friend Cleitus, being in his ales and his cups,
so also Harry Monmouth, being in his right wits and his
good judgments, turned away the fat knight with the

44 great pelly doublet. He was full of jests, and gipes, and
knaveries, and mocks. I have forgot his name.

GOWER Sir John Falstaff.

FLUELLEN That is he. I'll tell you there is good men porn
at Monmouth.

GOWER Here comes his majesty.

     Alarum. Enter King Harry and Bourbon, [Warwick,
     Gloucester, Exeter, and Herald,] with Prisoners.
     Flourish.

KING
I was not angry since I came to France

51 Until this instant. Take a trumpet, herald ;
Ride thou unto the horsemen on yond hill.
If they will fight with us, bid them come down

54 Or void the field. They do offend our sight.
If they'll do neither, we will come to them

56 And make them skirr away as swift as stones

57 Enforcèd from the old Assyrian slings.
Besides, we'll cut the throats of those we have ;
And not a man of them that we shall take
Shall taste our mercy. Go and tell them so.
     [Exeunt Herald and Gower.]
     Enter Montjoy.

EXETER
Here comes the herald of the French, my liege.

GLOUCESTER
His eyes are humbler than they used to be.

KING
How now ? What means this, herald ? Know'st thou not

64 That I have fined these bones of mine for ransom ?
Com'st thou again for ransom ?

HERALD   No, great king.
I come to thee for charitable license
That we may wander o'er this bloody field

68 To book our dead, and then to bury them ;
To sort our nobles from our common men.
For many of our princes, woe the while !

71 Lie drowned and soaked in mercenary blood.
So do our vulgar drench their peasant limbs
In blood of princes, and the wounded steeds
Fret fetlock-deep in gore and with wild rage

75 Yerk out their armèd heels at their dead masters,
Killing them twice. O, give us leave, great king,
To view the field in safety and dispose
Of their dead bodies !

KING   I tell thee truly, herald,
I know not if the day be ours or no ;

80 For yet a many of your horsemen peer
And gallop o'er the field.

HERALD   The day is yours.

KING
Praisèd be God and not our strength for it !
What is this castle called that stands hard by ?

HERALD
They call it Agincourt.

KING
Then call we this the field of Agincourt,
Fought on the day of Crispin Crispianus.

---

31 *mother* i.e. womanly tenderness   33 *compound* come to terms   34
mistful tearful ; *issue* run (tears)
IV, vii The battlefield of Agincourt   11 *Monmouth* i.e. in Wales   17 *variations* i.e. altered   24 *river* (there follows a parody of rhetorical 'comparisons')   30 *is come after* i.e. resembles ; *figures* comparisons   35
Cleitus friend of Alexander, slain in drunken rage for praising Philip
44 *great pelly* stuffed belly ; *gipes* japes   51 *trumpet* trumpeter   54 *void*
leave, depart from   56 *skirr* scurry   57 *Enforcèd* driven   64 *fined* pledged
68 *book* register   71 *mercenary blood* blood of hired soldiers   75 *Yerk*
kick   80 *peer* appear

FLUELLEN Your grandfather of famous memory, an't please your majesty, and your great-uncle Edward the Plack Prince of Wales, as I have read in the chronicles, fought a most prave pattle here in France.

KING They did, Fluellen.

FLUELLEN Your majesty says very true. If your majesties is rememb'red of it, the Welshmen did good service in a garden where leeks did grow, wearing leeks in their Monmouth caps; which your majesty know to this hour is an honorable padge of the service; and I do believe your majesty takes no scorn to wear the leek upon Saint Tavy's day.

95

KING
I wear it for a memorable honor;
For I am Welsh, you know, good countryman.

FLUELLEN All the water in Wye cannot wash your majesty's Welsh plood out of your pody, I can tell you that. God pless it and preserve it, as long as it pleases his grace, and his majesty too!

KING Thanks, good my countryman.

FLUELLEN By Cheshu, I am your majesty's countryman, I care not who know it! I will confess it to all the orld. I need not to be ashamed of your majesty, praised be God, so long as your majesty is an honest man.

KING
God keep me so! Our heralds go with him.
Enter Williams.
Bring me just notice of the numbers dead
On both our parts.   [*Exeunt Heralds with Montjoy.*]
Call yonder fellow hither.

110

EXETER Soldier, you must come to the king.

KING Soldier, why wear'st thou that glove in thy cap?

WILLIAMS An't please your majesty, 'tis the gage of one that I should fight withal, if he be alive.

KING An Englishman?

WILLIAMS An't please your majesty, a rascal that swaggered with me last night; who, if 'a live and ever dare to challenge this glove, I have sworn to take him a box o' th' ear; or if I can see my glove in his cap, which he swore, as he was a soldier, he would wear if alive, I will strike it out soundly.

120

KING What think you, Captain Fluellen? Is it fit this soldier keep his oath?

FLUELLEN He is a craven and a villain else, an't please your majesty, in my conscience.

KING It may be his enemy is a gentleman of great sort, quite from the answer of his degree.

129

FLUELLEN Though he be as good a gentleman as the devil is, as Lucifer and Belzebub himself, it is necessary, look your grace, that he keep his vow and his oath. If he be perjured, see you now, his reputation is as arrant a villain and a jack sauce as ever his plack shoe trod upon God's ground and his earth, in my conscience, law!

134

KING Then keep thy vow, sirrah, when thou meet'st the fellow.

WILLIAMS So I will, my liege, as I live.

KING Who serv'st thou under?

WILLIAMS Under Captain Gower, my liege.

FLUELLEN Gower is a good captain and is good knowledge and literatured in the wars.

142

KING Call him hither to me, soldier.

WILLIAMS I will, my liege.   *Exit.*

KING Here, Fluellen; wear thou this favor for me and stick it in thy cap. When Alençon and myself were down together, I plucked this glove from his helm. If any man challenge this, he is a friend to Alençon and an enemy to our person. If thou encounter any such, apprehend him, an thou dost me love.

FLUELLEN Your grace doo's me as great honors as can be desired in the hearts of his subjects. I would fain see the man, that has but two legs, that shall find himself aggriefed at this glove, that is all. But I would fain see it once, an please God of his grace that I might see.

153

KING Know'st thou Gower?

FLUELLEN He is my dear friend, an please you.

KING Pray thee go seek him and bring him to my tent.

FLUELLEN I will fetch him.   *Exit.*

KING
My Lord of Warwick, and my brother Gloucester,
Follow Fluellen closely at the heels.
The glove which I have given him for a favor
May haply purchase him a box o' th' ear;
It is the soldier's. I by bargain should
Wear it myself. Follow, good cousin Warwick.
If that the soldier strike him – as I judge
By his blunt bearing, he will keep his word –
Some sudden mischief may arise of it;
For I do know Fluellen valiant,
And, touched with choler, hot as gunpowder,
And quickly will return an injury.
Follow, and see there be no harm between them.
Go you with me, uncle of Exeter.   *Exeunt.*

162

170

*

Enter Gower and Williams.   IV, viii

WILLIAMS I warrant it is to knight you, captain.
Enter Fluellen.

FLUELLEN God's will and his pleasure, captain, I beseech you now, come apace to the king. There is more good toward you peradventure than is in your knowledge to dream of.

WILLIAMS Sir, know you this glove?

FLUELLEN Know the glove? I know the glove is a glove.

WILLIAMS I know this; and thus I challenge it.
Strikes him.

FLUELLEN 'Sblood! an arrant traitor as any's in the universal orld, or in France, or in England!

GOWER How now, sir? You villain!

WILLIAMS Do you think I'll be forsworn?

FLUELLEN Stand away, Captain Gower. I will give treason his payment into plows, I warrant you.

12

WILLIAMS I am no traitor.

FLUELLEN That's a lie in thy throat. I charge you in his majesty's name apprehend him. He's a friend of the Duke Alençon's.
Enter Warwick and Gloucester.

WARWICK How now, how now? What's the matter?

FLUELLEN My Lord of Warwick, here is, praised be God for it, a most contagious treason come to light, look you, as you shall desire in a summer's day. Here is his majesty.
Enter King and Exeter.

20

95 *Monmouth caps* tall tapering hats without brims   129 *from . . . degree* above responding to a challenge from one of his rank   134 *as ever* as sure as   142 *literatured* well-read, learned   153 *aggriefed* aggrieved, incensed   162 *favor* token   170 *touched . . . choler* i.e. quick-tempered   IV, viii The English camp   12 *his* its   20 *contagious* noxious

KING How now? What's the matter?

FLUELLEN My liege, here is a villain and a traitor that, look your grace, has struck the glove which your majesty is take out of the helmet of Alençon.

26 WILLIAMS My liege, this was my glove, here is the fellow
27 of it; and he that I gave it to in change promised to wear it in his cap. I promised to strike him if he did. I met this man with my glove in his cap, and I have been as good as my word.

FLUELLEN Your majesty hear now, saving your majesty's manhood, what an arrant, rascally, peggarly, lousy knave it is! I hope your majesty is pear me testimony and wit-
34 ness, and will avouchment, that this is the glove of Alen-çon that your majesty is give me, in your conscience, now.

KING
Give me thy glove, soldier. Look, here is the fellow of it.
'Twas I indeed thou promised'st to strike;
And thou hast given me most bitter terms.

FLUELLEN An please your majesty, let his neck answer for it, if there is any martial law in the orld.

KING How canst thou make me satisfaction?

WILLIAMS All offenses, my lord, come from the heart. Never came any from mine that might offend your majesty.

KING It was ourself thou didst abuse.

WILLIAMS Your majesty came not like yourself. You ap-peared to me but as a common man; witness the night,
48 your garments, your lowliness. And what your highness suffered under that shape, I beseech you take it for your own fault, and not mine; for had you been as I took you for, I made no offense. Therefore I beseech your high-ness pardon me.

KING
Here, uncle Exeter, fill this glove with crowns
And give it to this fellow. Keep it, fellow,
And wear it for an honor in thy cap
Till I do challenge it. Give him the crowns;
And captain, you must needs be friends with him.

FLUELLEN By this day and this light, the fellow has
58 mettle enough in his pelly. Hold, there is twelve pence for you; and I pray you to serve God, and keep you out of prawls, and prabbles, and quarrels, and dissensions, and, I warrant you, it is the petter for you.

WILLIAMS I will none of your money.

FLUELLEN It is with a good will. I can tell you it will serve you to mend your shoes. Come, wherefore should you be so pashful? Your shoes is not so good. 'Tis a good silling, I warrant you, or I will change it.
Enter [an English] Herald.

KING
Now, herald, are the dead numb'red?

HERALD
Here is the number of the slaught'red French.
[Gives a paper.]

KING
70 What prisoners of good sort are taken, uncle?

EXETER
Charles Duke of Orleans, nephew to the king;
John Duke of Bourbon and Lord Bouciqualt:
Of other lords and barons, knights and squires,
Full fifteen hundred, besides common men.

KING
This note doth tell me of ten thousand French

That in the field lie slain. Of princes, in this number,
And nobles bearing banners, there lie dead   77
One hundred twenty-six; added to these,
Of knights, esquires, and gallant gentlemen,
Eight thousand and four hundred; of the which,
Five hundred were but yesterday dubbed knights;
So that in these ten thousand they have lost   82
There are but sixteen hundred mercenaries;
The rest are princes, barons, lords, knights, squires,
And gentlemen of blood and quality.
The names of those their nobles that lie dead:
Charles Delabreth, High Constable of France;
Jacques of Chatillon, Admiral of France;
The master of the crossbows, Lord Rambures;
Great Master of France, the brave Sir Guichard Dauphin;
John Duke of Alençon; Anthony Duke of Brabant,
The brother to the Duke of Burgundy;
And Edward Duke of Bar; of lusty earls,
Grandpré and Roussi, Faulconbridge and Foix,
Beaumont and Marle, Vaudemont and Lestrale.
Here was a royal fellowship of death!
Where is the number of our English dead?
    [Herald gives another paper.]
Edward the Duke of York, the Earl of Suffolk,
Sir Richard Ketly, Davy Gam, esquire;   99
None else of name; and of all other men
But five-and-twenty. O God, thy arm was here!   101
And not to us, but to thy arm alone,
Ascribe we all! When, without stratagem,
But in plain shock and even play of battle,
Was ever known so great and little loss
On one part and on th' other? Take it, God,   106
For it is none but thine!

EXETER   'Tis wonderful!

KING
Come, go we in procession to the village;
And be it death proclaimèd through our host
To boast of this, or take that praise from God
Which is his only.

FLUELLEN Is it not lawful, an please your majesty, to tell how many is killed?

KING
Yes, captain; but with this acknowledgment,
That God fought for us.

FLUELLEN Yes, my conscience, he did us great good.

KING
Do we all holy rites.
Let there be sung 'Non nobis' and 'Te Deum,'   118
The dead with charity enclosed in clay,
And then to Calais; and to England then;
Where ne'er from France arrived more happy men.   121
                                Exeunt.

*

26 *fellow* mate 27 *change* exchange 34 *avouchment* i.e. avouch 48 *lowliness* i.e. humble bearing 58 *mettle* i.e. courage 70 *good sort* high rank 77 *bearing banners* (cf. IV, ii, 61–62) 82 *ten thousand* (the mortality figures are from Hall and Holinshed; the modern estimate is about 7000) 99 *Davy Gam* David ap Llewellyn 101 *five-and-twenty* (the figure given by Hall; the modern estimate is about 450) 106 *Take it* i.e. take the credit 118 *Non nobis* i.e. Psalm cxv, beginning in English 'Not unto us, O Lord, not unto us, but unto thy name give glory'; *Te Deum* song of thanksgiving beginning in English 'We praise thee, O God' 121 *happy* fortunate

V, Cho.   *Enter Chorus.*

Vouchsafe to those that have not read the story
That I may prompt them; and of such as have,
3 I humbly pray them to admit th' excuse
Of time, of numbers, and due course of things
Which cannot in their huge and proper life
Be here presented. Now we bear the king
Toward Calais. Grant him there. There seen,
Heave him away upon your wingèd thoughts
Athwart the sea. Behold, the English beach
10 Pales in the flood with men, wives, and boys,
Whose shouts and claps outvoice the deep-mouthed sea,
12 Which, like a mighty whiffler 'fore the king,
Seems to prepare his way. So let him land,
And solemnly see him set on to London.
So swift a pace hath thought that even now
You may imagine him upon Blackheath;
Where that his lords desire him to have borne
His bruisèd helmet and his bended sword
Before him through the city. He forbids it,
Being free from vainness and self-glorious pride;
21 Giving full trophy, signal, and ostent
Quite from himself to God. But now behold,
23 In the quick forge and working-house of thought,
How London doth pour out her citizens!
The mayor and all his brethren in best sort,
Like to the senators of th' antique Rome,
With the plebeians swarming at their heels,
Go forth and fetch their conqu'ring Caesar in;
29 As, by a lower but by loving likelihood,
30 Were now the general of our gracious empress,
As in good time he may, from Ireland coming,
32 Bringing rebellion broachèd on his sword,
How many would the peaceful city quit
To welcome him! Much more, and much more cause,
Did they this Harry. Now in London place him;
36 As yet the lamentation of the French
Invites the King of England's stay at home;
38 The emperor's coming in behalf of France
To order peace between them; and omit
All the occurrences, whatever chanced,
Till Harry's back-return again to France.
42 There must we bring him; and myself have played
43 The interim, by rememb'ring you 'tis past.
44 Then brook abridgment; and your eyes advance,
After your thoughts, straight back again to France.

Exit.

Enter Fluellen and Gower.   **V, i**

GOWER Nay, that's right. But why wear you your leek to-
day? Saint Davy's day is past.

FLUELLEN There is occasions and causes why and wherefore in all things. I will tell you ass my friend, Captain
Gower. The rascally, scald, peggarly, lousy, pragging 5
knave, Pistol, which you and yourself and all the orld
know to be no petter than a fellow, look you now, of no 7
merits, he is come to me and prings me pread and salt
yesterday, look you, and pid me eat my leek. It was in a
place where I could not preed no contention with him; 10
but I will be so pold as to wear it in my cap till I see him
once again, and then I will tell him a little piece of my
desires.

Enter Pistol.

GOWER Why, here he comes, swelling like a turkey cock.

FLUELLEN 'Tis no matter for his swellings nor his turkey
cocks. God pless you, Aunchient Pistol! you scurvy,
lousy knave, God pless you!

PISTOL

Ha! art thou bedlam? Dost thou thirst, base Trojan, 17
To have me fold up Parca's fatal web? 18
Hence! I am qualmish at the smell of leek.

FLUELLEN I beseech you heartily, scurvy, lousy knave, at
my desires, and my requests, and my petitions, to eat,
look you, this leek. Because, look you, you do not love it,
nor your affections and your appetites and your disges-
tions doo's not agree with it, I would desire you to eat it.

PISTOL

Not for Cadwallader and all his goats. 25

FLUELLEN There is one goat for you. (*Strikes him.*) Will
you be so good, scald knave, as eat it?

PISTOL

Base Trojan, thou shalt die!

FLUELLEN You say very true, scald knave, when God's
will is. I will desire you to live in the meantime, and eat
your victuals. Come, there is sauce for it. [*Strikes him.*]
You called me yesterday mountain-squire; but I will
make you to-day a squire of low degree. I pray you fall
to. If you can mock a leek, you can eat a leek.

GOWER Enough, captain. You have astonished him. 35

FLUELLEN I say I will make him eat some part of my leek,
or I will peat his pate four days. – Pite, I pray you. It is
good for your green wound and your ploody coxcomb. 38

PISTOL Must I bite?

FLUELLEN Yes, certainly, and out of doubt, and out of
question too, and ambiguities.

PISTOL By this leek, I will most horribly revenge. I eat
and eat, I swear.

FLUELLEN Eat, I pray you. Will you have some more
sauce to your leek? There is not enough leek to swear by.

PISTOL Quiet thy cudgel, thou dost see I eat.

FLUELLEN Much good do you, scald knave, heartily.
Nay, pray you throw none away, the skin is good for
your proken coxcomb. When you take occasions to see
leeks hereafter, I pray you mock at 'em; that is all.

PISTOL Good.

FLUELLEN Ay, leeks is good. Hold you, there is a groat to 52
heal your pate.

PISTOL Me a groat?

FLUELLEN Yes verily, and in truth you shall take it, or I
have another leek in my pocket which you shall eat.

PISTOL

I take thy groat in earnest of revenge.

V, Cho. 3 *admit th'excuse* i.e. tolerate the treatment 10 *Pales* hems
12 *whiffler* member of an armed escort clearing the way for a procession
21 *signal, and ostent* token and show (of victory) 23 *quick . . . thought*
i.e. nimble creative imagination 29 *lower . . . likelihood* i.e. less exalted
but no less longed-for possibility 30 *general* i.e. Robert Devereux, Earl
of Essex, whose inglorious campaign in Ireland ended in September, 1599
32 *broachèd* impaled 36 *As . . . lamentation* while the continuing state of
dejection 38 *emperor's coming* i.e. the Holy Roman Emperor Sigismund's
mission to England in May, 1416 42–43 *played The interim* filled up the
interval 43 *rememb'ring* reminding 44 *brook* put up with
V, i The English camp 5 *scald* scurvy 7 *fellow* i.e. groom 10 *preed* i.e.
breed, foment 17 *bedlam* mad; *Trojan* roisterer 18 *fold . . . web* i.e. complete the design of the Parcae (Fates) by ending your life 25 *Cadwallader*
(last of the British kings); *goats* (associated with Welsh poverty) 35
astonishèd dazed 38 *green* raw; *coxcomb* fool's scalp 52 *groat* fourpenny
piece

FLUELLEN If I owe you anything, I will pay you in cudgels. You shall be a woodmonger and buy nothing of me but cudgels. God bye you, and keep you, and heal your pate.   *Exit.*

PISTOL
All hell shall stir for this!

GOWER Go, go. You are a counterfeit cowardly knave. Will you mock at an ancient tradition, begun upon an
64 honorable respect and won as a memorable trophy of predeceased valor, and dare not avouch in your deeds any
66 of your words? I have seen you gleeking and galling at this gentleman twice or thrice. You thought, because he could not speak English in the native garb, he could not therefore handle an English cudgel. You find it otherwise, and henceforth let a Welsh correction teach you a good English condition. Fare ye well.   *Exit.*

PISTOL
72 Doth Fortune play the huswife with me now?
73 News have I, that my Doll is dead i' th' spital
74 Of a malady of France;
And there my rendezvous is quite cut off.
Old I do wax, and from my weary limbs
Honor is cudgelled. Well, bawd I'll turn,
78 And something lean to cutpurse of quick hand.
To England will I steal, and there I'll steal;
And patches will I get unto these cudgelled scars
81 And swear I got them in the Gallia wars.   *Exit.*

*

V, ii   *Enter, at one door, King Henry, Exeter, Bedford, [Gloucester,] Warwick, [Westmoreland,] and other Lords; at another, Queen Isabel, the [French] King, the Duke of Burgundy, [the Princess Katherine, Alice,] and other French.*

KING HENRY
Peace to this meeting, wherefore we are met.
Unto our brother France and to our sister
Health and fair time of day. Joy and good wishes
To our most fair and princely cousin Katherine.
5 And as a branch and member of this royalty,
By whom this great assembly is contrived,
We do salute you, Duke of Burgundy.
And, princes French, and peers, health to you all.

FRANCE
Right joyous are we to behold your face,
Most worthy brother England. Fairly met.
So are you, princes English, every one.

QUEEN
So happy be the issue, brother England,
Of this good day and of this gracious meeting
As we are now glad to behold your eyes –
Your eyes which hitherto have borne in them,
Against the French that met them in their bent,
17 The fatal balls of murdering basilisks.
The venom of such looks, we fairly hope,
Have lost their quality, and that this day
Shall change all griefs and quarrels into love.

KING HENRY
To cry amen to that, thus we appear.

QUEEN
You English princes all, I do salute you.

BURGUNDY
My duty to you both, on equal love,

Great Kings of France and England! That I have labored
With all my wits, my pains, and strong endeavors
To bring your most imperial majesties
Unto this bar and royal interview,   27
Your mightiness on both parts best can witness.
Since, then, my office hath so far prevailed
That, face to face and royal eye to eye,
You have congreeted, let it not disgrace me   31
If I demand before this royal view,
What rub or what impediment there is   33
Why that the naked, poor, and mangled Peace,
Dear nurse of arts, plenties, and joyful births,
Should not, in this best garden of the world,
Our fertile France, put up her lovely visage.
Alas, she hath from France too long been chased,
And all her husbandry doth lie on heaps,
Corrupting in it own fertility.   40
Her vine, the merry cheerer of the heart,
Unprunèd dies; her hedges even-pleached,   42
Like prisoners wildly overgrown with hair,
Put forth disordered twigs; her fallow leas   44
The darnel, hemlock, and rank fumitory
Doth root upon, while that the coulter rusts   46
That should deracinate such savagery.
The even mead, that erst brought sweetly forth   48
The freckled cowslip, burnet, and green clover,
Wanting the scythe, all uncorrected, rank,
Conceives by idleness, and nothing teems
But hateful docks, rough thistles, kecksies, burrs,   52
Losing both beauty and utility.
And all our vineyards, fallows, meads, and hedges,
Defective in their natures, grow to wildness.   55
Even so our houses and ourselves and children
Have lost, or do not learn for want of time,
The sciences that should become our country;
But grow like savages, as soldiers will,
That nothing do but meditate on blood,
To swearing and stern looks, diffused attire,   61
And everything that seems unnatural.
Which to reduce into our former favor   63
You are assembled; and my speech entreats
That I may know the let why gentle Peace   65
Should not expel these inconveniences
And bless us with her former qualities.

KING HENRY
If, Duke of Burgundy, you would the peace
Whose want gives growth to th' imperfections
Which you have cited, you must buy that peace
With full accord to all our just demands;
Whose tenures and particular effects   72
You have, enscheduled briefly, in your hands.

BURGUNDY
The king hath heard them; to the which as yet

64 *respect* consideration   66 *gleeking and galling* gibing and scoffing 72 *huswife* hussy   73 *Doll* (error for Nell); *spital* hospital   74 *malady of France* venereal disease   78 *something . . . hand* i.e. lean to quick-handed purse-cutting   81 *Gallia* French
V, ii Within the palace of the French king at Troyes   5 *royalty* royal family   17 *basilisks* monsters which killed with a look; here, cannons   27 *bar* court of justice   31 *congreeted* greeted each other; *disgrace* ill become   33 *rub* obstacle   40 *it* its   42 *even-pleached* evenly pleated 44 *leas* arable fields   46 *coulter* cutting wheel or blade in front of ploughshare   48 *erst* formerly   52 *kecksies* kexes, dry stems   55 *Defective* i.e. fallen, blighted by original sin   61 *diffused* disordered   63 *reduce* lead back; *favor* appearance   65 *let* hindrance   72 *tenures* gist

There is no answer made.

KING HENRY   Well then, the peace,
Which you before so urged, lies in his answer.

FRANCE

77   I have but with a cursitory eye
O'erglanced the articles. Pleaseth your grace
To appoint some of your Council presently
To sit with us once more, with better heed
To resurvey them, we will suddenly
82   Pass our accept and peremptory answer.

KING HENRY

Brother, we shall. Go, uncle Exeter,
And brother Clarence, and you, brother Gloucester,
Warwick, and Huntingdon, go with the king;
And take with you free power to ratify,
Augment, or alter, as your wisdoms best
Shall see advantageable for our dignity,
Anything in or out of our demands,
90   And we'll consign thereto. Will you, fair sister,
Go with the princes or stay here with us?

QUEEN

Our gracious brother, I will go with them.
93   Happily a woman's voice may do some good
94   When articles too nicely urged be stood on.

KING HENRY

Yet leave our cousin Katherine here with us.
96   She is our capital demand, comprised
Within the fore-rank of our articles.

QUEEN

She hath good leave.

*Exeunt omnes. Manent King [Henry] and
Katherine [with the Gentlewoman Alice].*

KING HENRY   Fair Katherine, and most fair,
Will you vouchsafe to teach a soldier terms
Such as will enter at a lady's ear
And plead his love suit to her gentle heart?

KATHERINE Your majesty shall mock at me. I cannot
speak your England.

KING HENRY O fair Katherine, if you will love me
soundly with your French heart, I will be glad to hear
you confess it brokenly with your English tongue. Do
you like me, Kate?

KATHERINE Pardonnez-moi, I cannot tell wat is 'like
me.'

KING HENRY An angel is like you, Kate, and you are like
an angel.

111 KATHERINE Que dit-il? Que je suis semblable à les
anges?

113 ALICE Oui, vraiment, sauf vostre grace, ainsi dit-il.

KING HENRY I said so, dear Katherine, and I must not
blush to affirm it.

KATHERINE O bon Dieu! les langues des hommes sont
pleine de tromperies.

KING HENRY What says she, fair one? that the tongues
of men are full of deceits?

---

77 *cursitory* cursory   82 *accept* accepted; *peremptory* authoritative   90 *consign* consent   93 *Happily* haply, perchance   94 *nicely* punctiliously   96 *capital* chief   111–12 *Que . . . anges?* what does he say? That I am like the angels?   113 *Oui . . . dit-il* yes, truly, save your grace, so he says   121 *better Englishwoman* (because disdainful of flattery)   128 *wear . . . suit* exhaust my terms of courtship   137–38 *under . . . spoken* though to say so may be reproved as bragging   141 *jackanapes* monkey   142 *greenly* wanly   148 *cook* i.e. caterer   152 *uncoined* not prepared for circulation   157 *fall* diminish   178–79 *Je quand . . . moi* (Henry's bad attempt to paraphrase ll. 172–73)

ALICE Oui, dat de tongues of de mans is be full of deceits.
Dat is de princesse.

KING HENRY The princess is the better Englishwoman. 121
I' faith, Kate, my wooing is fit for thy understanding. I
am glad thou canst speak no better English; for if thou
couldst, thou wouldst find me such a plain king that
thou wouldst think I had sold my farm to buy my crown.
I know no ways to mince it in love but directly to say, 'I
love you.' Then, if you urge me farther than to say, 'Do
you in faith?' I wear out my suit. Give me your answer, 128
i' faith, do: and so clap hands and a bargain. How say
you, lady?

KATHERINE Sauf vostre honneur, me understand well.

KING HENRY Marry, if you would put me to verses or to
dance for your sake, Kate, why, you undid me. For the
one I have neither words nor measure; and for the other
I have no strength in measure, yet a reasonable measure
in strength. If I could win a lady at leapfrog, or by vaulting into my saddle with my armor on my back, under the 137
correction of bragging be it spoken, I should quickly leap
into a wife. Or if I might buffet for my love, or bound
my horse for her favors, I could lay on like a butcher and
sit like a jackanapes, never off. But, before God, Kate, I 141
cannot look greenly, not gasp out my eloquence, nor I 142
have no cunning in protestation, only downright oaths
which I never use till urged, nor never break for urging.
If thou canst love a fellow of this temper, Kate, whose
face is not worth sunburning, that never looks in his
glass for love of anything he sees there, let thine eye be
thy cook. I speak to thee plain soldier. If thou canst love 148
me for this, take me; if not, to say to thee that I shall die,
is true; but for thy love, by the Lord, no; yet I love thee
too. And while thou liv'st, dear Kate, take a fellow of
plain and uncoined constancy, for he perforce must do 152
thee right, because he hath not the gift to woo in other
places. For these fellows of infinite tongue that can
rhyme themselves into ladies' favors, they do always
reason themselves out again. What! A speaker is but a
prater; a rhyme is but a ballad. A good leg will fall, a 157
straight back will stoop, a black beard will turn white, a
curled pate will grow bald, a fair face will wither, a full
eye will wax hollow; but a good heart, Kate, is the sun
and the moon; or rather, the sun, and not the moon, for
it shines bright and never changes, but keeps his course
truly. If thou would have such a one, take me; and take
me, take a soldier; take a soldier, take a king. And what
say'st thou then to my love? Speak, my fair, and fairly, I
pray thee.

KATHERINE Is it possible dat I sould love de ennemie of
France?

KING HENRY No, it is not possible you should love the
enemy of France, Kate; but in loving me you should
love the friend of France, for I love France so well that I 170
will not part with a village of it – I will have it all mine.
And, Kate, when France is mine and I am yours, then
yours is France and you are mine.

KATHERINE I cannot tell wat is dat.

KING HENRY No, Kate? I will tell thee in French, which
I am sure will hang upon my tongue like a new-married
wife about her husband's neck, hardly to be shook off.
Je quand sur le possession de France, et quand vous avez 178
le possession de moi (let me see, what then? Saint Denis
be my speed!), donc vostre est France et vous estes
mienne. It is as easy for me, Kate, to conquer the king-

dom as to speak so much more French. I shall never
move thee in French, unless it be to laugh at me.

184 KATHERINE Sauf vostre honneur, le François que vous
parlez, il est meilleur que l'Anglois lequel je parle.

KING HENRY No, faith, is't not, Kate. But thy speaking
of my tongue, and I thine, most truly-falsely, must
needs be granted to be much at one. But, Kate, dost
thou understand thus much English? Canst thou love
me?

KATHERINE I cannot tell.

KING HENRY Can any of your neighbors tell, Kate? I'll
ask them. Come, I know thou lovest me; and at night
193   when you come into your closet, you'll question this
gentlewoman about me, and I know, Kate, you will to
her dispraise those parts in me that you love with your
heart; but, good Kate, mock me mercifully, the rather,
gentle princess, because I love thee cruelly. If ever thou
beest mine, Kate, as I have a saving faith within me tells
199   me thou shalt, I get thee with scambling, and thou must
therefore needs prove a good soldier-breeder. Shall not
thou and I, between Saint Denis and Saint George,
compound a boy, half French, half English, that shall
go to Constantinople and take the Turk by the beard?
Shall we not? What say'st thou, my fair flower-de-
luce?

KATHERINE I do not know dat.

KING HENRY No; 'tis hereafter to know, but now to
promise. Do but now promise, Kate, you will endeavor
for your French part of such a boy, and for my English
209   moiety take the word of a king and a bachelor. How
210   answer you, la plus belle Katherine du monde, mon
trèscher et devin déesse?

KATHERINE Your majestee ave fausse French enough to
deceive de most sage demoiselle dat is en France.

KING HENRY Now, fie upon my false French! By mine
honor in true English, I love thee, Kate; by which honor
I dare not swear thou lovest me; yet my blood begins to
flatter me that thou dost, notwithstanding the poor and
218   untempering effect of my visage. Now beshrew my
father's ambition! He was thinking of civil wars when he
got me; therefore was I created with a stubborn outside,
with an aspect of iron, that when I come to woo ladies,
I fright them. But in faith, Kate, the elder I wax the better I shall appear. My comfort is that old age, that ill
layer-up of beauty, can do no more spoil upon my face.
Thou hast me, if thou hast me, at the worst; and thou
shalt wear me, if thou wear me, better and better; and
therefore tell me, most fair Katherine, will you have
me? Put off your maiden blushes; avouch the thoughts
of your heart with the looks of an empress; take me by
the hand, and say, 'Harry of England, I am thine!'
which word thou shalt no sooner bless mine ear withal
but I will tell thee aloud, 'England is thine, Ireland is
thine, France is thine, and Henry Plantagenet is thine';
234   who, though I speak it before his face, if he be not fellow
with the best king, thou shalt find the best king of good
fellows. Come, your answer in broken music! for thy
voice is music and thy English broken; therefore, queen
of all, Katherine, break thy mind to me in broken
English. Wilt thou have me?

239 KATHERINE Dat is as it sall please de roi mon père.

KING HENRY Nay, it will please him well, Kate; it shall
please him, Kate.

KATHERINE Den it sall also content me.

KING HENRY Upon that I kiss your hand and I call you
my queen.

KATHERINE Laissez, mon seigneur, laissez, laissez! Ma 245
foi, je ne veux point que vous abaissiez vostre grandeur
en baisant le main d'une de vostre seigneurie indigne
serviteur. Excusez-moi, je vous supplie, mon très-
puissant seigneur.

KING HENRY Then I will kiss your lips, Kate.

KATHERINE Les dames et demoiselles pour estre baisée
devant leur nopces, il n'est pas la coutume de France.

KING HENRY Madam my interpreter, what says she?

ALICE Dat it is not be de fashon pour le ladies of France –
I cannot tell wat is 'baiser' en Anglish.

KING HENRY To kiss.

ALICE Your majestee entendre bettre que moi.   256

KING HENRY It is not a fashion for the maids in France
to kiss before they are married, would she say?

ALICE Oui, vraiment.

KING HENRY O Kate, nice customs curtsy to great kings.
Dear Kate, you and I cannot be confined within the
weak list of a country's fashion. We are the makers of 262
manners, Kate; and the liberty that follows our places 263
stops the mouth of all findfaults, as I will do yours for
upholding the nice fashion of your country in denying 265
me a kiss. Therefore patiently, and yielding. [Kisses
her.] You have witchcraft in your lips, Kate. There is
more eloquence in a sugar touch of them than in the
tongues of the French Council, and they should sooner
persuade Harry of England than a general petition of
monarchs. Here comes your father.

Enter the French Power and the English Lords.

BURGUNDY God save your majesty! My royal cousin,
teach you our princess English?

KING HENRY I would have her learn, my fair cousin,
how perfectly I love her, and that is good English.

BURGUNDY Is she not apt?

KING HENRY Our tongue is rough, coz, and my condi- 277
tion is not smooth; so that, having neither the voice nor
the heart of flattery about me, I cannot so conjure up the
spirit of love in her that he will appear in his true likeness.

BURGUNDY Pardon the frankness of my mirth if I answer
you for that. If you would conjure in her, you must make
a circle; if conjure up love in her in his true likeness, he
must appear naked and blind. Can you blame her then, 284
being a maid yet rosed over with the virgin crimson of
modesty, if she deny the appearance of a naked blind
boy in her naked seeing self? It were, my lord, a hard
condition for a maid to consign to.   288

KING HENRY Yet they do wink and yield, as love is blind 289
and enforces.

BURGUNDY They are then excused, my lord, when they
see not what they do.

184–85 *Sauf . . . parle* save your honor, the French you speak is better than
the English I speak 193 *closet* private room 199 *scambling* scrambling
for possessions, snatching 209 *moiety* half 210–11 *la . . . déesse* the
most beautiful Katherine of the world, my very dear and divine goddess
218 *untempering* unpropitiating 234–35 *fellow with* equal to 239 *de
. . . père* the king my father 245–49 *Laissez . . . seigneur* desist, my lord,
desist, desist! My faith, I do not wish you to lower your dignity by
kissing the hand of your lordship's unworthy servant. Excuse me, I pray
you, my all-powerful lord 256 *entendre* understands 262 *list* barrier
263 *follows our places* attends our rank 265 *nice* fastidious 277 *condition*
personality 284 *blind* (1) sightless, (2) reckless, brutal 288 *consign*
consent 289 *wink* shut eyes

KING HENRY Then, good my lord, teach your cousin to consent winking.

BURGUNDY I will wink on her to consent, my lord, if you
296 will teach her to know my meaning; for maids well sum-
297 mered and warm kept are like flies at Bartholomew-tide, blind, though they have their eyes; and then they will endure handling which before would not abide looking on.

KING HENRY This moral ties me over to time and a hot summer; and so I shall catch the fly, your cousin, in the latter end, and she must be blind too.

BURGUNDY As love is, my lord, before it loves.

KING HENRY It is so; and you may, some of you, thank love for my blindness, who cannot see many a fair French city for one fair French maid that stands in my way.

307 FRANCE Yes, my lord, you see them perspectively, the cities turned into a maid; for they are all girdled with maiden walls that war hath never entered.

KING HENRY Shall Kate be my wife?

FRANCE So please you.

KING HENRY I am content, so the maiden cities you talk
313 of may wait on her. So the maid that stood in the way for my wish shall show me the way to my will.

FRANCE
We have consented to all terms of reason.

KING HENRY
Is't so, my lords of England?

WESTMORELAND
The king hath granted every article:
His daughter first; and in sequel all,
319 According to their firm proposèd natures.

EXETER Only he hath not yet subscribèd this: Where your majesty demands that the King of France, having any occasion to write for matter of grant, shall name your highness in this form and with this addition, in
323 French, 'Nostre très-cher fils Henri, Roi d'Angleterre, Héritier de France'; and thus in Latin, 'Praeclarissimus filius noster Henricus, Rex Angliae et Haeres Franciae.'

FRANCE
Nor this I have not, brother, so denied
But your request shall make me let it pass.

KING HENRY
I pray you then, in love and dear alliance,
Let that one article rank with the rest,
And thereupon give me your daughter.

FRANCE
Take her, fair son, and from her blood raise up
Issue to me, that the contending kingdoms
Of France and England, whose very shores look pale   334
With envy of each other's happiness,
May cease their hatred, and this dear conjunction
Plant neighborhood and Christian-like accord
In their sweet bosoms, that never war advance
His bleeding sword 'twixt England and fair France.

LORDS Amen!

KING HENRY
Now, welcome, Kate; and bear me witness all
That here I kiss her as my sovereign queen.

Flourish.

QUEEN
God, the best maker of all marriages,
Combine your hearts in one, your realms in one!
As man and wife, being two, are one in love,
So be there 'twixt your kingdoms such a spousal
That never may ill office, or fell jealousy,   347
Which troubles oft the bed of blessèd marriage,
Thrust in between the paction of these kingdoms   349
To make divorce of their incorporate league;
That English may as French, French Englishmen,
Receive each other! God speak this Amen!

ALL Amen!

KING HENRY
Prepare we for our marriage; on which day,
My Lord of Burgundy, we'll take your oath,
And all the peers', for surety of our leagues.
Then shall I swear to Kate, and you to me,
And may our oaths well kept and prosp'rous be!

Sennet. Exeunt.

Enter Chorus [as Epilogue].   Epi.
Thus far, with rough and all-unable pen,
    Our bending author hath pursued the story,   2
In little room confining mighty men,
    Mangling by starts the full course of their glory.   4
Small time; but in that small most greatly lived
    This Star of England. Fortune made his sword,
By which the world's best garden he achieved,   7
    And of it left his son imperial lord.
Henry the Sixth, in infant bands crowned King   9
    Of France and England, did this king succeed;
Whose state so many had the managing
    That they lost France and made his England bleed:
Which oft our stage hath shown; and for their sake,   13
In your fair minds let this acceptance take.   14

---

296 *well summered* i.e. carefully nurtured   297 *like . . . Bartholomew-tide*
i.e. sluggish in the heat of summer   307 *perspectively* i.e. through an
optic glass (which multiplies images)   313 *wait on her* i.e. come with
her as a dowry   319 *firm . . . natures* strict stipulations   323–26 *Nostre . . .
France; . . . Praeclarissimus . . . Franciae* our dear son Henry, King of
England and heir of France   334 *look pale* i.e. with their chalk cliffs   347
ill office evil dealing   349 *paction* pact
Epi.   2 *bending* bowing, humble   4 *Mangling by starts* misrepresenting in
fragments   7 *best garden* i.e. France (cf. V, ii, 36)   9 *infant bands* swaddling
clothes   13 *for their sake* i.e. inasmuch as they have pleased you   14 *this*
this play

APPENDIX: THE QUARTO AND FOLIO TEXTS

The 1600 quarto of *Henry V*, although twice reprinted, presents a curtailed and corrupt version of the play, probably obtained by memorial reconstruction of the original. It is sometimes maintained that the actors playing the parts of Exeter and Gower were the chief agents in this reconstruction, since the portions of the play where they are on stage are somewhat more accurately preserved than the rest. The quarto is useful in supplying an occasional line or reading in instances where the folio text is clearly defective. The folio text, although reliable in the main, is marred by a number of misprints and a somewhat capricious division into acts. The first act corresponds to acts I and II in modern editions, the second to III, the third to the first six scenes of IV, the fourth to the remainder of IV, and the fifth to V. The modern division is based on the position of the four internal speeches by the Chorus. The logic of this solution may be more apparent than real, since it substitutes for the inordinately long first "act" of the folio the inordinately long fourth "act" of modern editions. It is possible that the choruses were originally no more than a narrative convenience, their number formally insignificant.

In the present edition, there is a minimum of departure from the folio text except for the usual modernization of spelling and punctuation, the normalization of speech-prefixes, and occasional relineation. (In the folio, Pistol's speeches are printed in prose, apparently because his thumping iambics appear in the midst of the prose dialogue of his comic associates.) Such proper names as "Dauphin," "Burgundy," "Calais," "Harfleur," etc. have been consistently substituted for the original "Dolphin," "Burgonie" (or "Burgogne"), "Callice," "Harflew," etc. Fluellen's Welsh dialect has been normalized by the consistent use of "orld" for "world," "Cheshu" for "Jesu," and "p" for initial "b" in stressed syllables. However, Macmorris' "sh" for "s" is allowed to remain intermittent.

Contrary to general practice in modern editions of this play, the passages in French are no more extensively modified than the passages in English. Archaic and familiar grammatical forms, as well as errors in grammar and idiom, have been retained. The advantage of this kind of fidelity to the copy-text is that more of the original quality and flavour of Shakespeare's French is preserved than is possible when modern copybook correctness is substituted, and, in one instance (IV, ii, 2–6), an original meaning is restored. After expending much effort upon my attempt to restore Princess Katherine's English lesson (III, iv) to its Shakespearean form, I found that I had been anticipated in most details by Nikolaus Delius.

The following is a complete list of all substantive departures from the text of the folio of 1623 (F). The adopted readings in italics from the quarto of 1600 (Q) and from the later folios and the editors are followed by the folio readings in roman.

I, ii, 38 *succedant* (F2) succedaul   45, 52 *Elbe* (Capell) Elue   74 *Lingard* (Sisson) Lingare   82 *Ermengard* (Sisson) Ermengare   94 *imbar* (F3) imbarre   131 *blood* (F3) Bloods   163 *her* (Capell) their   209 *many several* (Q) many   213 *End* (Q) And

II, i, 22 *mare* (Q) name   26 *How... Pistol* (joined in F to preceding speech by Bardolph; assigned in Q to Nym)   39, 40 *Iceland* (Steevens) Island   68 *Coupe la* (Dyce) Couple a   69 *thee defy* (Q) defie thee   76 *enough.* (Pope) enough to   79 *you,* (Hanmer) *your*   101–02 *I ... betting* (Q) Omitted   112 *that's* (Q) that   114 *Ah* (Pope) A

II, ii, 75 *hath* (Q) have   87 *furnish him* (F2) furnish   108 *whoop* (Theobald) hoope   114 *All* (Hanmer) And   122 *lion gait* (Capell) Lyon-gate   139 *mark the* (Malone) make thee   147 *Henry* (Q) Thomas   148 *Masham* (Rowe) Marsham   159 *Which I* (F2) which   176 *have sought* (Q) sought

II, iii, 6 *earn* (Camb.) erne   16 *'a babbled* (Theobald) a Table   24 *upward and upward* (Q) vp-peer'd and vpward   44 *word* (Q) world

II, iv, 68 *followed* (Pope) followèd   79 *borrowed* (Pope) borrowèd   107 *privèd* (Walter) privy   109 *swallowed* (Pope) swallowèd   134 *difference* (Camb.) diff'rence

III, Cho., 4 *Hampton* (Theobald) Dover   6 *fanning* (Rowe) fayning   12 *furrowed* (Rowe) furrowèd

III, i, 7 *summon* (Rowe) commune   17 *noble* (Malone) noblish   24 *men* (F4) me   32 *Straining* (Rowe) Straying

III, ii, 15 *hie* (Q) high   18 *preach* (Hanmer, as also for some similar normalizations of Welsh accent following) breach   58, 127 *petter* better   64, 74 *orld* world   65 *peard* beard   100 *trompet* trumpet   106 *ay'll lig* (Camb.) Ile ligge   107 *ay'll* (Camb.) Ile   120 *poth* both   121 *pirth* birth   129 *pold* bold

III, iii, 16 *Arrayed* (Pope) Arrayèd   32 *heady* (F2) headly   35 *Defile* (Rowe) Desire

III, iv, 2 *parles* (Warburton) parlas   4 *enseigner* (F2) ensigniez   *j'apprends* (This ed.) ie apprend   6, 17, 24 *est* (F2) &   7 *Et les doigts* (misplaced in a separate speech given to *Alice* in F; corrected by Theobald) *Et les* (Capell) E le   8 *Alice* (Theobald) Kat   *Les* (Capell) Le   *les* (Capell) e   9 *souviendrai* (F2) souemeray   11 *Katherine* (Theobald) Alice (F, with proper assignment to Katherine restored at *j'ai gagné*)   *de fingres* (Capell) le Fingres   11, 13 *les* (Capell) le   14 *Les* (F2) Le   20 *Et le* (F2) E de   36 *la* (F2) de   38 *N'avez-vous pas* (F2) N'ave vos y   *déjà* (Warburton) desia   40 *Non* (Warburton) Nome   44 *Sauf* (Rowe) Sans   45 *dis-je* (Capell) de ie   46 *le* (Capell) les   *la* (Capell) de   *robe* (Rowe) roba   47, 48 *De ... de* (Capell) Le ... le   50 *les* (F2) le   51 *ces* (F2) ces   *le* (F2) le   52 *Foh!* (Camb.) fo   *de* (Capell) le   53 *Néantmoins* (F2) neant moys   55 *de count* (Warburton) le count

III, v, 7 *scions* (Var., 1803) Syens   11 *de* (F2) du   43 *Vaudemont* (F2) Vandemont   45 *Foix* (Capell) Loys   46 *knights* (Theobald conj.; Pope) Kings

III, vi, 4, 11 *pridge* Bridge   10 *plessed* blessed   10, 15, 82 *orld* world   30, 31 *plind* blind   30 *her* (Q) his   53 *prother* Brother   98 *Pardolph* Bardolph   100 *plows* blows   108 *lenity* (Q) Leuitie

III, vii, 12 *pasterns* (F2) postures   *Ça* (Theobald) ch'   57 *lief* (Capell) liue   62 *vomissement* (F2) vemissement   63 *et la truie* (Rowe) est la leuye

IV, Cho., 16 *name* (Tyrwhitt conj.; Steevens) nam'd   20 *cripple* (Theobald) creeple–   27 *Presenteth* (Hanmer) Presented

IV, i, 3 *Good* (F3) God   65 *Cheshu* Jesu   66 *orld* world   71 *pabble* babble   91 *Thomas* (Theobald) John   231 *What is* (Knight) What?   is   *adoration* (F2) Odoration   239 *Think'st* (Rowe) Thinks   261 *Hyperion* (F2) Hiperio   277 *if* (Tyrwhitt conj.; Steevens) of   282 *bestowed* (Pope) bestowèd

IV, ii, 4 *eaux* (Theobald) ewes   5 *les* (This ed.) le   6 *Cieux* (Munro, as 'cieu') Cien   11 *dout* (Rowe) doubt   25 *'gainst* (F2) against   49 *gimmaled* (Delius) Iymold

IV, iii, 13–14 *And ... valor* (after l. 11 in F; correction by Theobald supported by Q)   48 *And ... day* (Q) Omitted   59 *rememberèd* (Rowe) rememb'red   99 *buried* (Eds.) buryèd

IV, iv, 12 *pitié* (F2) pitez   14 *Or* (Hanmer) For   34 *de* (F2) a *faites* (Malone) faite   37 *cuppe le* (This ed.) cuppele   39 *O'er-* (This ed.) Or   51 *néantmoins* (F2) neant-mons   52 *l'avez promis* (Malone) layt a promets   55 *remercîmens* (F2) remercious *j'ai tombé* (This ed.) Je intombe   57 *distingué* (Capell) distinie   65 *Suivez* (Rowe) Saaue

IV, v, 2 *perdu ... est perdu* (Rowe) perdia ... et perdie   3 *Mort de* (Rowe) Mor Dieu   12 *honor* (Q) Omitted   16 *by a slave* (Q) a base slave   24 *Exeunt* (Eds.) Exit

IV, vi, 15 *And* (Q) He   34 *mistful* (Theobald) mixtful

APPENDIX

IV, vii, 24, 28 *poth* both   44 *pelly* belly   73 *the* (Capell) with   96 *padge* badge   106 *Cheshu* Jeshu   110 *God* (F3) Good   119 *'a live* (Capell) aliue   134 *plack* blacke

IV, viii, 10, 41 *orld* world   32 *peggarly* beggarly   58 *pelly* belly   61 *petter* better   94 *Foix* (Capell) Foyes   108 *me* (F2) me

V, i, 5 *peggarly* beggarly   6 *orld* world   9 *pid* bid   10 *preed* breed   11 *pold* bold   20 *beseech* peseech   37 *Pite* Bite   49 *proken* broken   81 *swear* (F3) swore

V, ii, 12 *England* (F2) Ireland   45 *fumitory* (F4) Femetary   50 *all* (Rowe) withall   77 *cursitory* (Wilson) curselarie   185 *est* (Pope) & *meilleur* (Hanmer) melius   246 *abaissiez* (Johnson) abbaise *grandeur* (F2) grandeus   247 *de vostre* (Camb.) nostre *seigneurie* (Camb.) Seigneur   252 *coutume* (Rowe) costume   255 *baiser* (Hanmer) buisse   259 *vraiment* (Hanmer) verayment   309 *never* (Rowe) Omitted   324 *Héritier* (Rowe) Heretere   349 *paction* (Theobald) Pation

THE LIFE OF KING HENRY THE EIGHTH

INTRODUCTION

There can be few serious students of Shakespeare who have not sometimes felt that possibly the hardest problem involved in their study is that which requires for its solution some reasonable and acceptable theory as to the play of *King Henry VIII*. None such has ever yet been offered....

If the situation can be said to have changed since Swinburne wrote these words over eighty years ago, it is only because it has become still more common than in his day for scholars to express their disappointment, or even to condemn the play outright. "Less interesting than any other in the Folio" and "Shakespeare has lost the impulse which gave his final stories their mellow power" are typical judgments by contemporary Shakespeareans. Those who have attempted a defense of the play as worthy of Shakespeare have but a small following.

At first thought this might seem curious considering that the play has fared quite well on the stage. Producers of almost every generation have been attracted by its color and pageantry, of which indeed *Henry VIII* has more to offer than many of Shakespeare's plays. Betterton's productions at the end of the seventeenth century were applauded for their "magnificence." In a mid-eighteenth-century staging, over 130 figures participated in the procession of IV, i. In the nineteenth century Kean employed a moving panorama of London, and a real barge in which Buckingham made his exit in II, i. Even more lavish was the coronation scene in Henry Irving's production near the end of the century; and if in modern productions there is greater reluctance to spend vast sums of money on merely pictorial or spectacular effects, one nevertheless remembers them, especially Tyrone Guthrie's, for their handling of large numbers of people on the stage and their ceremonial color.

The actors have likewise been tempted by the play's great roles. Readers may be disappointed with the character of Henry, but actors have liked impersonating a living Holbein portrait of the King, who seems as cheerful and healthy and young at the play's end as he was at the beginning, whatever has happened to Buckingham, Katherine, Wolsey, or his own troubled conscience. We all know that he will continue to tread over corpses, but mind little because it is all past history. Buckingham's role is hardly more than that of prologue, but he becomes sufficiently attractive in the opening scene for the audience to remain hushed during his farewell speech in II, i: the young, frank, congenial nobleman has been slandered, it is all so unjust, and how manly, how noble his forgiving spirit! But it is naturally the richer parts of Wolsey and Katherine that have drawn actors and actresses, from Kemble and Mrs Siddons to Irving and Ellen Terry and, in more recent times, Lewis Casson and Sibyl Thorndike. Owing

largely to the influence of these and other actors, certain set speeches and passages of dialogue from *Henry VIII* were, until recently at least, among the most widely quoted of Shakespeare's. Fifty years ago, one could hardly imagine a Shakespearean recital which did not include Wolsey's leave-taking from Cromwell in III, ii. "Scenes from Shakespeare" presented by some pair of travelling actors would inevitably include Katherine's trial, II, iv.

Why then such disenchantment with the play? Here are some of the criticisms frequently made: the play may lend itself to impressive pageantry but it is not great drama; it may contain famous speeches but most of the verse is smoothly languid rather than breathtakingly Shakespearean; we are gripped intensely by only a few scenes: dramatic tension is aroused only episodically; after the fall of the most developed and interesting characters, Katherine and Wolsey, there is only sentimentality and anticlimax; the quarrel between Cranmer and Gardiner in the final act fails to excite us because our interest in these characters has not been aroused before, and they are pale shadows after Katherine and Wolsey. The play, as one critic put it, "falls utterly away, and leaves us in the last act among persons we scarcely know, and events for which we do not care." So the complaints run. Some readers even feel morally outraged that a play which dwells so long on the tribulations of Katherine should end in a celebration of events which were only made possible by the injustice done to her. And some do not hesitate to state that they would have preferred a tragedy ending on the execution of Anne, or a historical treatment showing how Henry's personal difficulties with Katherine led to England's adopting the Protestant cause. But if the events dramatized in the play bear any relation to the Reformation, Shakespeare did his best to avoid saying so.

Against such strictures only one kind of defense of the play is possible, other than insistence upon its appeal in a good performance – namely, in terms of a purpose and dramatic form that are usually misunderstood or overlooked. But let us first deal with some facts and fancies: when it was written and when first staged, how it fits into the Shakespeare canon, and whether indeed Shakespeare should be held totally responsible for the play as we have it.

Scholars are agreed that *Henry VIII* was composed very late in Shakespeare's career and first produced in 1613. It was probably written last of all the plays included in the first folio. Originally, Shakespeare and his company may well have planned to present the play first at Whitehall during the wedding ceremonies of the Elector Palatine and Princess Elizabeth in February, 1613. The Princess often made people think of her great namesake of recent memory

– Queen Elizabeth had died only ten years before. Several passages of the play's fifth act would have fitted the occasion admirably. But the list of plays we actually know to have been presented then does not include *Henry VIII*, and it appears more probable that it was first produced at the Globe on the fateful day of June 29, 1613, when the discharge of the chambers in I, iv set the thatch of the roof on fire. Within an hour the stately building had burnt to the ground. The event was sufficient news to be given a paragraph in more than one letter of state. There was no loss of life; "nothing did perish, but a few forsaken Cloaks," according to one correspondent; presumably he did not enquire about the prompt-books or other manuscripts of the King's Men.

Is *Henry VIII* then Shakespeare's last play? If the answer were a simple yes, the implications would be challenging. But there is a rub, a complication at both ends. There is a stubborn tradition that Prospero's Epilogue in *The Tempest* represents Shakespeare's final leavetaking of his art. And in at least two recent books on Shakespeare's last plays, *Henry VIII* is virtually ignored. On the other hand we know that Shakespeare had a share, with Fletcher as the other author, in a play probably written later than *Henry VIII*, *The Two Noble Kinsmen*, and perhaps also in the lost *Cardenio*. If we primarily link *Henry VIII* to *The Winter's Tale* and *The Tempest*, plays of Shakespeare's sole authorship, then we must regard it as his last major work. But perhaps, like *The Two Noble Kinsmen*, *Henry VIII* is of divided authorship?

This has indeed been a widely held view for over a hundred years. We may place the ultimate blame – or credit – for it on the poet Tennyson, about whose sensitivity to style and rhythm, and training in the technicalities of metre, there can be little question. Tennyson intimated to his friends that the verse of large parts of *Henry VIII* seemed to him much more like Fletcher's than like Shakespeare's. James Spedding, the famous editor of Bacon, took the hint, and in 1850 published a paper which has become a classic. In an eloquent scene-by-scene examination of the style, he argued the view that only certain scenes, namely I, i–ii, II, iii–iv, III, ii (up to line 203), and V, i are by Shakespeare, and the rest by Fletcher. In the "Shakespearean" scenes, Spedding found a style similar to that of Shakespeare's other late work, thick with imagery, highly involved, remarkably free in metre, and almost careless in syntax, while the other scenes show a small "proportion of thought and fancy to words and images." He further found that in the "Fletcherian" scenes the frequency of end-stopped lines and of weak endings or redundant syllables at the end of lines – lines of 11 or even 12 syllables are indeed frequent in this play – is similar to that of *Valentinian* and other Fletcher plays, while in the "Shakespearean" scenes the proportion is quite different. To cap the whole matter, Samuel Hickson independently arrived in the same year at essentially the same conclusions. Consternation was great, especially since, according to the division, all the great speeches for which the play has become famous, except for Katherine's defense in II, iv, were here attributed to Fletcher. Yet one lonely voice apart, Swinburne's, the position remained practically unchallenged until 1930, and the voices echoing Spedding are still numerous and strong.

Spedding's thesis has since been supported with a great wealth of statistical analysis of several aspects of the play's language. Here there is room only to tell those who are skeptical in principle of the value of such statistics that the cumulative detail of the assembled evidence is more impressive than similar evidence for perhaps any other Elizabethan or Jacobean drama of doubtful authorship; that the best of the scholars participating in the debate have been impelled, as was Spedding, by a general sense of incongruity of style; and that any careful reader of the play who is sensitive to style will be bound to notice this incongruity, even if he does not necessarily wish to draw Spedding's conclusions. Let him read only the first two scenes and then continue with the third, or read II, ii after I, ii – scenes which provide a better standard of comparison, for they both include Wolsey and the King. In style the play's opening scenes remind one much of *Cymbeline* or of the first acts of *The Winter's Tale*, in their knottiness, their involutions, and, as not always acknowledged, their sometimes downright carelessness in syntax (dangling clauses beginning with *that*) and in development of imagery (see I, i, 224–26): it is as if a brilliant artist had dashed the lines down. In the "Fletcherian" scenes, on the other hand, the style is consistently clear and never careless; it also seems very competent rather than brilliant, lacking in the spark of Shakespeare.

Yet scholarly caution is in order. It seems all too convenient to place the blame for the play's weaknesses on Fletcher's shoulders, or those of a presumed imperfect partnership of the two dramatists. One needs to remember that *Henry VIII* is in the first folio, while *The Two Noble Kinsmen* is not, and that there are no other external data; that hardly anyone thought of Fletcher in connection with *Henry VIII* before the middle of the last century; that stylistic comparison with Fletcher's other plays may not be wholly trustworthy because Fletcher wrote no other history play in the least like *Henry VIII*; that Fletcher's plays provide us with plenty of evidence of the enormous influence on him of Shakespeare, while, from 1608 on at least, Shakespeare was probably somewhat influenced by his able junior. Further, one may ask whether two collaborating playwrights would be likely to divide up their share of work in the manner Spedding's division of scenes suggests. We know that the collaboration between Lady Gregory and Yeats operated in a quite different manner, and however Jonson, Marston, and Chapman divided up their labors for *Eastward Ho!*, it can hardly have been by scene. Finally, some readers well acquainted with Fletcher's work have asked themselves whether he indeed could have written the speech of Buckingham's farewell, which has all the superficial characteristics of Fletcher's style; to quote Swinburne:

Here is the same smooth and fluent declamation, the same prolonged and persistent melody, which if not monotonous is certainly not various; the same pure, lucid, perspicuous flow of simple rather than strong and elegant rather than exquisite English; and yet . . . I cannot but think that we shall perceive in it a comparative severity and elevation which will be missed when we turn back from it to the text of Fletcher. There is an aptness of phrase, an abstinence from excess, a "plentiful lack" of mere flowery and superfluous beauties, which we may rather wish than hope to find in the most famous of Shakespeare's successors.

One will either agree with this comment or not: there is no basis for argument. A better case against Fletcher's authorship can perhaps be made for the death-scene of Katherine, IV, ii, upon which Dr Johnson bestowed the highest praise, and which has been called "the glory of the play." One thinks especially of the Queen's last moment of resurgence when she firmly rebukes the Messenger: "You are a saucy fellow; / Deserve we no more reverence?" That even in her great weakness, near death, and in her humility, Katherine should so insist on her queenly dignity and its proper due, is indeed a very Shakespearean touch. One recalls Imogen's "But clay and clay differs in dignity, / Whose dust is both alike." And, no less important, the development of the entire scene seems natural, without the least sense of the artificially contrived which, in Fletcher's plays, is so rarely absent.

But let us leave this debate and boldly assume that Shakespeare at least thought of *Henry VIII* as his concluding work – he did at least write those scenes which introduce the major characters – and then ask whether we can discern significant relations to his other work. And of course two groups are bound to spring to mind: his earlier English history plays and the Romances. Like the former, *Henry VIII* is an English chronicle play, and if one considers the period of history which Shakespeare dramatized in his two historical tetralogies, from *Henry VI* to *Richard III*, and from *Richard II* to *Henry V*, then indeed *Henry VIII* looks like the completion of a pattern. It brings relevant modern English history up to the birth of England's golden Queen, and in Cranmer's final prophecy includes even a clear allusion to James I, the contemporary Stuart king. We are not exactly saying that Shakespeare thought of *Henry VIII* as in a sense completing his dramatic *epic* on English history – in that case he might indeed be blamed for making his last play too undramatic – but are implying that the play's final act may have been extremely important to him, and that Shakespeare perhaps did not mind if the play's chronicle structure was as loose as that of his earliest history plays. Indeed there are signs in Shakespeare's late work that his mind sometimes wandered back to his earliest artistic preoccupations – from *The Tempest*, for instance, to *The Comedy of Errors*.

The other significant connection is with the Romances. We have already pointed to similarities of style, at least in the "Shakespearean" scenes. Another characteristic feature of *Henry VIII*, the use of narrative rather than dramatic technique in several scenes, also reminds one of the Romances. Several times in *Henry VIII*, noblemen or gentlemen recall events which have taken place off stage, for the audience's benefit, somewhat in the manner of the last scene but one of *The Winter's Tale*. The large time-span in the Romances, *Henry VIII*, and some other chronicle plays encourages the use of narrative techniques. Striking also is the dramatist's greater than customary readiness to employ spectacular stage devices, supernatural and other colorful effects, of which the most pertinent examples are the theophanies in the Romances and Katherine's vision in IV, ii (cf. Posthumus' vision in *Cymbeline* and the appearance of Diana in *Pericles*). The scene of Katherine's trial does not merely remind one generally of Hermione's trial in *The Winter's Tale* but resembles that earlier scene in much detail. But perhaps the most significant similarity may be seen in the general pattern of the action of the Romances and *Henry VIII*, which moves from a series of misfortunes and tragic events to a conclusion of joy and promise.

If indeed there is a meaningful relation in *Henry VIII* between the sufferings of Buckingham, Katherine, and Wolsey in the early acts, and the joyful ending, one of the most common interpretations of the play must be wrong: that the first three or four acts are like a morality play in which three noble and proud characters undergo a sudden fall from fortune, become conscious of the "Vain pomp and glory of this world" (III, ii, 365), and learn how to endure their tribulations with patience and how to forgive their enemies, with the final act merely tagged on. But we will misunderstand the play if we concentrate only on Buckingham, Katherine, and Wolsey, even if the play's Prologue may encourage us to do just that. Granted that Anne Bullen's role is remarkably undeveloped, the three scenes in which she is given a part perform a function in the play's developing design. Of these the first, I, iv, the banquet at Wolsey's house where the masked Henry is attracted by Anne's youthful beauty, is certainly gay in mood. What is striking is that here the dramatist consciously departed from his sources – mainly Holinshed – for he placed an episode which occurred only in 1527 immediately before the scene of Buckingham's (reported) trial and execution, events which had occurred five years earlier. The contrast in mood between the two scenes was surely designed. When next we encounter Anne with the Old Lady in II, iii, she appears attractive in the sympathy she voices for Katherine, though it must dawn on her that she herself is on the way to becoming queen. The banter with the Old Lady on "queen" and "quean" is interrupted by the announcement of her elevation to Marchioness of Pembroke. This scene precedes that of the trial which leads to the unqueening of Katherine. Anne's next scene, IV, i, is that of her coronation. There she does not speak a single word but unquestionably becomes the centre of interest. The Third Gentleman reports how she sat down

> In a rich chair of state, opposing freely
> The beauty of her person to the people.
> Believe me, sir, she is the goodliest woman
> That every lay by man; which when the people
> Had the full view of, such a noise arose
> As the shrouds make at sea in a stiff tempest,
> As loud, and to as many tunes. Hats, cloaks
> (Doublets, I think) flew up; and had their faces
> Been loose, this day they had been lost. Such joy
> I never saw before.   (IV, i, 67–76)

Such a scene has no place in the fourth act of a morality play. A little before, the other two Gentlemen had lamented the fate of Katherine Dowager – "she was removed to Kimbolton, / Where she remains now sick" – but were interrupted in their musings by the hautboys and flourish of trumpets announcing the "order" of the coronation, which then passed in all its royal color over the stage. Katherine is momentarily forgotten. But in the next scene we meet her once more, for the last time, and hear of Wolsey's death. Again Shakespeare changed the order of history: for Holinshed and other historians had written that Wolsey died three years before the divorce and Anne's coronation. And again the change was made for the sake of an evolving dramatic pattern.

The famous Anne Bullen of history appears surprisingly little on the stage in *Henry VIII*, but the scenes in which she does enter, strategically placed as they are, and with the facts of history adjusted as we have noted, afford a hint of the mood of the play's ending. In the final act she herself does not appear; we need only the birth of her daughter Elizabeth and Cranmer's prophecy. And naturally we are given no intimation of what was to follow soon after in history: a stillborn male child and Anne's execution.

The presentation of Cranmer is perhaps less satisfactory. But we must remember that Shakespeare's contemporaries looked upon Cranmer as the founder of their own church, the Church of England. For his role in the final scenes we are prepared, though insufficiently, by the King's remarks at the very moment when Wolsey begins to fall out of favor (II, iv, 233–38). The quarrel between Gardiner and Cranmer drives home the contrast between the new archbishop and the old, and also shows the King for the first time actively exercising justice – early in the play he had leaned on the Cardinal's shoulders. Again, the change befits the mood of the play's ending, even if it does not quite fit the facts of history. The earlier acts showed Henry as a singularly neutral figure, developed in such a way as hardly to encourage us to blame him for the events. Absorbed as we were by Buckingham first, and then by Katherine and Wolsey, we neither sympathized with nor were very critical of Henry. But now in the fifth act he takes active command of his kingdom, and on the side of justice; and then he becomes the father of Elizabeth – the Elizabeth of England's golden age.

A Christian note sounds more strongly through *Henry VIII* than in any other of Shakespeare's plays – at least it receives more overt expression. It is heard first in the forgiving words of Buckingham's farewell, then very clearly in Wolsey's conversion after his fall:

> I feel within me
> A peace above all earthly dignities,
> A still and quiet conscience.   (III, ii, 378–80)

The recollection of his "virtue" strengthens Katherine in her mood of patient forgiveness and acceptance in IV, ii, but even more striking in this scene is Katherine's vision, which assures us that she will find happiness and peace in heaven. In the last act we are first made to see Cranmer's Christian humility, and then listen to his prophecy. There, of course, we are meant to feel that God is speaking through Cranmer; and we may not be wrong to remember those prophecies of Shakespeare's earlier history plays which brought upon England the series of tribulations that furnish the main material of these plays, and of which there are still some in *Henry VIII*; only that at the end we are shown justice and reconciliation, and hear the promise of a great queen followed by a peaceful reign under James.

If this was the intent of the play, Shakespeare, or Shakespeare with Fletcher, may not have completely succeeded, as indeed the reaction of so many of its readers would appear to suggest. But one can then see the work as a final bold experiment in writing a new kind of English history

play in which some of the themes and devices and even the symbolism of the Romances would be put to new use. The play would also conclude the pattern begun in the early histories by extending the view to the birth of Queen Elizabeth, in a sense even to 1613.

Victoria College   F. David Hoeniger
University of Toronto

NOTE ON THE TEXT

Henry VIII was first printed in the folio of 1623, in a good text set up from what modern textual scholars believe to have been a fair scribal copy of the author's manuscript. The general nature and elaboration of the stage directions and the considerable variation in speech-prefixes suggest author's manuscript rather than theatrical prompt-copy, but the relative absence in the folio text of known unusual Shakespearean spellings suggests scribal copy rather than direct original. The folio text is divided into acts and scenes, and this division was followed by later editors except that the folio V, ii, was divided into ii and iii and the remaining scenes were renumbered as in the division provided marginally for reference in the present edition. The folio is least trustworthy in matters of punctuation. In general its errors, relatively few, appear to have derived from either the scribe or the compositors. The present edition follows the folio text closely. All substantive departures from it are listed below, with the adopted reading in italics followed by the folio reading in roman:

I, i, 42–47 *All . . . together* (assigned to Buckingham in F)   63 *web, 'a* Web. O   69–70 *that? | . . . hell the* that, / . . . Hell? The   79–80 *council out, | . . . in he* Councell, out / . . . in, he   96 *Bordeaux* Burdeux   120 *venom-mouthed* venom'd–mouth'd   123 *chafed* chaff'd   200 *Hereford* Hertford   219 *Perk* Pecke *chancellor* Councellour   221 *Nicholas* Michaell

I, ii, 67 *business* basenesse   156 *feared* feare   164 *confession's* Commissions   170 *To win the* To the ('win' appearing in source)   180 *To* For this to   190 *Bulmer* Blumer   191 *time. Being* time, being

I, iii, 59 *wherewithal. In him* wherewithall in him;

II, i, 18 *have* him   20 *Perk* Pecke   86 *mark* make

II, iii, 14 *quarrel, fortune, do* quarrel. Fortune, do   32 *cheveril* Chiverell   59 *note 's* notes   61 *of you, and* of you, to you; and

II, iv, 131 *Exeunt* Exit   172 *A* And   197 *throe* throw   217 *summons. Unsolicited* Summons unsolicited

III, i, 23 s.d. *Campeius* Campian   61 *your* our   83 *profit. Can* profit can   124 *accursed* a curse

III, ii, 142 *glad* gald   233 *commissions, lords?* Commission? Lords,   292 *Who* Whom   343 *Chattels* Castels

IV, i, 20 *2. Gentleman* 1   34 *Kimbolton* Kymmalton   36 s.d. *Choristers* Quirristers   54–56 *2. Gentleman. Their . . . | 1. Gentleman. And . . . 2. Gentleman. No . . . | 1. Gentleman. God . . .* 2 Their . . . / And . . . 2 No . . . / 1 God . . .   78 *press* prease   101 *Stokesly* Stokeley

IV, ii, 7 *think* thank   82 s.d. *reverent* reverend

V, i, 37 *time* Lime   55 *Exeunt* Exit   139 *precipice* Precepit

V, ii, 8 *piece* Peere

V, iii, 85, 87 *Chancellor* Cham.   172 *brother-love* Brother; loue

V, iv, 79 *press* praesse

V, v, 37 *ways* way

THE LIFE OF KING HENRY THE EIGHTH

[NAMES OF THE ACTORS

King Henry the Eighth	*Cromwell, servant to Wolsey*
Cardinal Wolsey	*Griffith, gentleman usher to Queen Katherine*
Cardinal Campeius	*Three Gentlemen*
Capuchius, ambassador from the Emperor Charles V	*Dr Butts, physician to the King*
Cranmer, Archbishop of Canterbury	*Garter King-at-Arms*
Duke of Norfolk	*Surveyor to the Duke of Buckingham*
Duke of Buckingham	*Doorkeeper of the Council Chamber*
Duke of Suffolk	*Sergeant-at-Arms*
Earl of Surrey	*Porter, and his Man*
Lord Chamberlain	*Page to Gardiner*
Lord Chancellor	*Secretaries to Wolsey*
Gardiner, King's Secretary, afterwards	*A Crier*
Bishop of Winchester	*Queen Katherine, wife to King Henry, afterwards divorced*
Bishop of Lincoln	*Anne Bullen, her Maid of Honor, afterwards Queen*
Lord Abergavenny	*An Old Lady, friend to Anne Bullen*
Lord Sandys (also styled Sir Walter Sandys)	*Patience, woman to Queen Katherine*
Sir Henry Guilford	*Spirits*
Sir Thomas Lovell	*Lords, Ladies, Bishops, Judges, Gentlemen, and Priests ;*
Sir Anthony Denny	*Lord Mayor of London and Aldermen ; Vergers,*
Sir Nicholas Vaux	*Scribes, Guards, Attendants, Servants, and Common*
Brandon	*People ; Women attending upon Queen Katherine*

Scene : *London ; Kimbolton*]

*

Pro.   THE PROLOGUE

I come no more to make you laugh. Things now
That bear a weighty and a serious brow,
3   Sad, high, and working, full of state and woe,
Such noble scenes as draw the eye to flow
We now present. Those that can pity, here
May (if they think it well) let fall a tear :
The subject will deserve it. Such as give
Their money out of hope they may believe,
May here find truth too. Those that come to see
Only a show or two and so agree
The play may pass – if they be still and willing,
12   I'll undertake may see away their shilling
13   Richly in two short hours. Only they
14   That come to hear a merry bawdy play,
15   A noise of targets, or to see a fellow
16   In a long motley coat guarded with yellow,
17   Will be deceived. For, gentle hearers, know
To rank our chosen truth with such a show
19   As fool and fight is, beside forfeiting
20   Our own brains and the opinion that we bring
21   To make that only true we now intend,

Will leave us never an understanding friend.   22
Therefore, for goodness' sake, and as you are known
The first and happiest hearers of the town,   24
Be sad, as we would make ye. Think ye see   25
The very persons of our noble story
As they were living. Think you see them great,
And followed with the general throng and sweat
Of thousand friends. Then, in a moment, see
How soon this mightiness meets misery.
And if you can be merry then, I'll say
A man may weep upon his wedding day.

Names of the Actors *Brandon* (perhaps identical with the Duke of Suffolk above, whose name was Charles Brandon)

Pro. 3 *Sad . . . working* serious, lofty, and effective   12 *shilling* (for the 'twelve-penny room' next to the stage)   13 *two . . . hours* (a round number ; i.e. 2–3 hours)   14–19 *merry . . . fight is* (probably an allusion to Rowley's play on Henry VIII, *When You See Me*, 1605, which has two fools and a sword-and-buckler fight)   15 *targets* shields   16 *motley coat* coat in pied colors, worn by the fool; *guarded* trimmed   17 *deceived* disappointed   19–20 *forfeiting . . . brains* abandoning all claims to intelligence   20 *opinion* reputation   21 *make . . . intend* i.e. make the play we have in view truthful to fact   22 *understanding* (with quibble on 'understanders' or groundlings)   24 *happiest* most favored   25 *sad* serious

I, i *Enter the Duke of Norfolk at one door ; at the other,*
the Duke of Buckingham and the Lord Abergavenny.

BUCKINGHAM
Good morrow and well met. How have ye done
Since last we saw in France ?

NORFOLK   I thank your grace,
3 Healthful, and ever since a fresh admirer
Of what I saw there.

BUCKINGHAM   An untimely ague
Stayed me a prisoner in my chamber when
6 Those suns of glory, those two lights of men,
Met in the vale of Andren.

7 NORFOLK   'Twixt Guynes and Arde.
I was then present, saw them salute on horseback,
9 Beheld them when they lighted, how they clung
10 In their embracement, as they grew together ;
11 Which had they, what four throned ones could have
weighed
Such a compounded one ?

12 BUCKINGHAM   All the whole time
I was my chamber's prisoner.

NORFOLK   Then you lost
The view of earthly glory. Men might say
15 Till this time pomp was single, but now married
To one above itself. Each following day
17 Became the next day's master, till the last
18 Made former wonders, its. To-day the French,
19 All clinquant, all in gold, like heathen gods
Shone down the English ; and to-morrow they
21 Made Britain India – every man that stood
Showed like a mine. Their dwarfish pages were
23 As cherubins, all gilt. The madams too,
Not used to toil, did almost sweat to bear
25 The pride upon them, that their very labor
26 Was to them as a painting. Now this masque
27 Was cried incomparable ; and th' ensuing night
Made it a fool and beggar. The two kings,
Equal in lustre, were now best, now worst,
30 As presence did present them : him in eye
Still him in praise ; and being present both,
32 'Twas said they saw but one, and no discerner
33 Durst wag his tongue in censure. When these suns

(For so they phrase 'em) by their heralds challenged 34
The noble spirits to arms, they did perform
Beyond thought's compass, that former fabulous story, 36
Being now seen possible enough, got credit,
That Bevis was believed. 38

BUCKINGHAM   O you go far.

NORFOLK
As I belong to worship and affect 39
In honor honesty, the tract of ev'ry thing 40
Would by a good discourser lose some life
Which action's self was tongue to. All was royal.
To the disposing of it naught rebelled ;
Order gave each thing view. The office did 44
Distinctly his full function.

BUCKINGHAM   Who did guide,
I mean who set the body and the limbs
Of this great sport together ? 47

NORFOLK   As you guess :
One certes, that promises no element 48
In such a business.

BUCKINGHAM   I pray you who, my lord ?

NORFOLK
All this was ord'red by the good discretion
Of the right reverend Cardinal of York.

BUCKINGHAM
The devil speed him ! No man's pie is freed
From his ambitious finger. What had he
To do in these fierce vanities ? I wonder 54
That such a keech can with his very bulk 55
Take up the ray o' th' beneficial sun 56
And keep it from the earth.

NORFOLK   Surely, sir,
There's in him stuff that puts him to these ends ;
For, being not propped by ancestry, whose grace
Chalks successors their way, nor called upon
For high feats done to th' crown, neither allied 61
To eminent assistants, but spiderlike 62
Out of his self-drawing web, 'a gives us note, 63
The force of his own merit makes his way, 64
A gift that heaven gives for him, which buys 65
A place next to the king.

ABERGAVENNY   I cannot tell
What heaven hath given him. Let some graver eye
Pierce into that ; but I can see his pride
Peep through each part of him. Whence has he that ?
If not from hell the devil is a niggard,
Or has given all before, and he begins
A new hell in himself.

BUCKINGHAM   Why the devil,
Upon this French going out, took he upon him 73
(Without the privity o' th' king) t' appoint 74
Who should attend on him ? He makes up the file 75
Of all the gentry, for the most part such
To whom as great a charge as little honor 77
He meant to lay upon ; and his own letter, 78
The honorable board of council out,
Must fetch him in he papers.

ABERGAVENNY   I do know
Kinsmen of mine, three at the least, that have
By this so sickened their estates that never 82
They shall abound as formerly.

BUCKINGHAM   O many
Have broke their backs with laying manors on 'em 84
For this great journey. What did this vanity

86 But minister communication of
A most poor issue?

NORFOLK   Grievingly I think

88 The peace between the French and us not values
The cost that did conclude it.

BUCKINGHAM   Every man,

90 After the hideous storm that followed, was
91 A thing inspired, and not consulting broke
Into a general prophecy – that this tempest,

93 Dashing the garment of this peace, aboded
94 The sudden breach on't.

NORFOLK   Which is budded out;

95 For France hath flawed the league and hath attached
Our merchants' goods at Bordeaux.

ABERGAVENNY   Is it therefore

97 Th' ambassador is silenced?

NORFOLK   Marry is't!

ABERGAVENNY

98 A proper title of a peace, and purchased
99 At a superfluous rate!

BUCKINGHAM   Why, all this business
Our reverend cardinal carried.

100 NORFOLK   Like it your grace,
101 The state takes notice of the private difference
Betwixt you and the cardinal. I advise you
(And take it from a heart that wishes towards you

104 Honor and plenteous safety) that you read
The cardinal's malice and his potency
Together; to consider further, that

107 What his high hatred would effect wants not
A minister in his power. You know his nature,
That he's revengeful; and I know his sword
Hath a sharp edge; it's long, and 't may be said
It reaches far, and where 'twill not extend

112 Thither he darts it. Bosom up my counsel;
You'll find it wholesome. Lo where comes that rock

114 That I advise your shunning.

*Enter Cardinal Wolsey, the purse borne before him,
certain of the Guard, and two Secretaries with
papers. The Cardinal in his passage fixeth his eye on
Buckingham, and Buckingham on him, both full
of disdain.*

WOLSEY

115 The Duke of Buckingham's surveyor? Ha!
116 Where's his examination?

FIRST SECRETARY   Here, so please you.

WOLSEY

Is he in person ready?

FIRST SECRETARY   Ay, please your grace.

WOLSEY

Well, we shall then know more, and Buckingham
Shall lessen this big look.

Exeunt Cardinal and his train.

BUCKINGHAM

120 This butcher's cur is venom-mouthed, and I
Have not the power to muzzle him; therefore best

122 Not wake him in his slumber. A beggar's book
Outworths a noble's blood.

123 NORFOLK   What, are you chafed?
124 Ask God for temp'rance. That's th' appliance only
Which your disease requires.

BUCKINGHAM   I read in's looks
Matter against me, and his eye reviled

127 Me as his abject object. At this instant

He bores me with some trick. He's gone to th' king.   128
I'll follow and outstare him.

NORFOLK   Stay, my lord,
And let your reason with your choler question
What 'tis you go about. To climb steep hills
Requires slow pace at first. Anger is like
A full hot horse, who being allowed his way,
Self-mettle tires him. Not a man in England   134
Can advise me like you. Be to yourself
As you would to your friend.

BUCKINGHAM   I'll to the king
And from a mouth of honor quite cry down
This Ipswich fellow's insolence, or proclaim
There's difference in no persons.   139

NORFOLK   Be advised.
Heat not a furnace for your foe so hot
That it do singe yourself. We may outrun
By violent swiftness that which we run at,
And lose by overrunning. Know you not
The fire that mounts the liquor till't run o'er   144
In seeming to augment it wastes it? be advised.
I say again there is no English soul
More stronger to direct you than yourself,
If with the sap of reason you would quench,
Or but allay the fire of passion.

BUCKINGHAM   Sir,
I am thankful to you, and I'll go along
By your prescription. But this top-proud fellow –
Whom from the flow of gall I name not, but   152
From sincere motions – by intelligence,   153
And proofs as clear as founts in July when
We see each grain of gravel, I do know
To be corrupt and treasonous.

NORFOLK   Say not treasonous.

BUCKINGHAM

To th' king I'll say't and make my vouch as strong   157
As shore of rock. Attend. This holy fox,
Or wolf, or both (for he is equal rav'nous   159
As he is subtile, and as prone to mischief
As able to perform't), his mind and place
Infecting one another, yea reciprocally,
Only to show his pomp as well in France   164
As here at home, suggests the king our master
To this last costly treaty; th' interview
That swallowed so much treasure and like a glass
Did break i' th' wrenching.

---

86 *minister communication* furnish occasion for talk   86–87 *of . . . issue* i.e. of little consequence   88 *not values* is not worth   90 *hideous storm* (on June 18, interrupting the tournament)   91 *not consulting* without taking counsel together   93 *aboded* boded, foreshadowed (with following quibble in *budded*, l. 94)   94 *sudden* immediate; *on't* of it   95 *flawed* broken; *attached* seized   97 *silenced* (Ed. Hall reports that he was 'commaunded to kepe his house in silence')   98 *A proper . . . peace* a fine thing to call a peace   99 *a superfluous rate* too high a price   100 *Like it* if it please   101 *difference* quarrel   104 *read* consider   107–08 *wants . . . minister* does not lack an agent   112 *Bosom up* hide in your bosom   114 s.d. *purse* the bag containing the great seal, emblem of the Lord High Chancellor's office   115 *surveyor* steward, overseer of estates (Charles Knyvet, Buckingham's cousin)   116 *examination* paper containing the witness's deposition   120 *butcher's cur* (see note to l. 55)   122 *book* learning   123 *chafed* heated, angry   124 *appliance* remedy   127 *abject* spurned   128 *bores* cheats   134 *Self-mettle* his own ardor   139 *difference* distinction of rank or quality; *Be advised* take care   144 *mounts* causes to rise   152–53 *Whom . . . motions* whom I mention not out of anger but from sincere motives   153 *intelligence* secret information   157 *vouch* attestation   159 *equal* equally, as   164 *suggests* incites, tempts

NORFOLK   Faith, and so it did.

BUCKINGHAM

Pray give me favor, sir. This cunning cardinal

169   The articles o' th' combination drew

As himself pleased; and they were ratified

As he cried 'Thus let be,' to as much end

172   As give a crutch to th' dead. But our count-cardinal

Has done this, and 'tis well; for worthy Wolsey

(Who cannot err) he did it. Now this follows

(Which, as I take it, is a kind of puppy

To th' old dam, treason), Charles the emperor,

Under pretense to see the queen his aunt

178   (For 'twas indeed his color, but he came

To whisper Wolsey), here makes visitation.

His fears were that the interview betwixt

England and France might through their amity

Breed him some prejudice, for from this league

Peeped harms that menaced him: privily

184   Deals with our cardinal, and, as I trow,

Which I do well; for I am sure the emperor

Paid ere he promised, whereby his suit was granted

Ere it was asked; but when the way was made,

And paved with gold, the emperor thus desired,

That he would please to alter the king's course

And break the foresaid peace. Let the king know

(As soon he shall by me) that thus the cardinal

Does buy and sell his honor as he pleases,

And for his own advantage.

NORFOLK   I am sorry

To hear this of him, and could wish he were

195   Something mistaken in 't.

BUCKINGHAM   No, not a syllable.

196   I do pronounce him in that very shape

197   He shall appear in proof.

Enter Brandon, a Sergeant-at-arms before him,
and two or three of the Guard.

BRANDON

Your office, sergeant; execute it.

SERGEANT   Sir,

My lord the Duke of Buckingham, and Earl

Of Hereford, Stafford, and Northampton, I

Arrest thee of high treason, in the name

Of our most sovereign king.

202 BUCKINGHAM   Lo you, my lord,

The net has fall'n upon me! I shall perish

204   Under device and practice.

BRANDON   I am sorry

To see you ta'en from liberty, to look on

The business present. 'Tis his highness' pleasure

You shall to th' Tower.

BUCKINGHAM   It will help me nothing

To plead mine innocence, for that dye is on me

Which makes my whit'st part black. The will of heav'n

Be done in this and all things! I obey.

O my Lord Aberga'ny, fare you well!

BRANDON

Nay, he must bear you company.

[To Abergavenny]   The king

Is pleased you shall to th' Tower till you know

How he determines further.

ABERGAVENNY   As the duke said,

The will of heaven be done, and the king's pleasure

By me obeyed!

BRANDON   Here is a warrant from

The king t' attach Lord Montacute and the bodies   217

Of the duke's confessor, John de la Car,

One Gilbert Perk, his chancellor –

BUCKINGHAM   So, so!

These are the limbs o' th' plot. No more, I hope.

BRANDON

A monk o' th' Chartreux.

BUCKINGHAM   O, Nicholas Hopkins?

BRANDON   He.

BUCKINGHAM

My surveyor is false. The o'er-great cardinal

Hath showed him gold; my life is spanned already.   223

I am the shadow of poor Buckingham,   224

Whose figure even this instant cloud puts on

By dark'ning my clear sun. My lord, farewell.   *Exeunt.*

*

Cornets. Enter King Henry, leaning on the   I, ii
Cardinal's shoulder, the Nobles, [the Cardinal's
Secretary,] and Sir Thomas Lovell. The Cardinal
places himself under the King's feet on his right side.

KING

My life itself, and the best heart of it,   1

Thanks you for this great care. I stood i' th' level   2

Of a full-charged confederacy, and give thanks   3

To you that choked it. Let be called before us

That gentleman of Buckingham's; in person

I'll hear him his confessions justify,   6

And point by point the treasons of his master

He shall again relate.   8

A noise within, crying 'Room for the Queen!' Enter
the Queen, ushered by the Duke of Norfolk, and
Suffolk. She kneels. [The] King riseth from his
state, takes her up, kisses and placeth her by him.

KATHERINE

Nay, we must longer kneel. I am a suitor.

KING

Arise and take place by us. Half your suit

Never name to us; you have half our power.

The other moiety ere you ask is given.   12

Repeat your will, and take it.   13

KATHERINE   Thank your majesty.

That you would love yourself, and in that love

Not unconsidered leave your honor nor

The dignity of your office, is the point

Of my petition.

KING   Lady mine, proceed.

KATHERINE

I am solicited, not by a few,

And those of true condition, that your subjects   19

20 Are in great grievance. There have been commissions
21 Sent down among 'em, which hath flawed the heart
Of all their loyalties; wherein, although,
My good lord cardinal, they vent reproaches
Most bitterly on you as putter-on
Of these exactions, yet the king our master,
26 Whose honor heaven shield from soil! – even he escapes
not
27 Language unmannerly; yea such which breaks
The sides of loyalty and almost appears
In loud rebellion.

NORFOLK   Not almost appears –
It doth appear; for upon these taxations,
The clothiers all not able to maintain
32 The many to them longing, have put off
33 The spinsters, carders, fullers, weavers, who,
Unfit for other life, compelled by hunger
And lack of other means, in desperate manner
36 Daring th' event to th' teeth, are all in uproar,
37 And danger serves among them.

KING   Taxation?
Wherein? and what taxation? My lord cardinal,
You that are blamed for it alike with us,
Know you of this taxation?

WOLSEY   Please you, sir,
41 I know but of a single part in aught
42 Pertains to th' state, and front but in that file
43 Where others tell steps with me.

KATHERINE   No, my lord?
44 You know no more than others? but you frame
Things that are known alike, which are not wholesome
To those which would not know them and yet must
Perforce be their acquaintance. These exactions
48 (Whereof my sovereign would have note) – they are
Most pestilent to th' hearing; and, to bear 'em,
50 The back is sacrifice to th' load. They say
They are devised by you, or else you suffer
52 Too hard an exclamation.

KING   Still exaction!
53 The nature of it? In what kind, let's know,
Is this exaction?

KATHERINE   I am much too venturous
In tempting of your patience, but am bold'ned
56 Under your promised pardon. The subject's grief
Comes through commissions, which compels from each
The sixth part of his substance, to be levied
Without delay; and the pretense for this
Is named, your wars in France. This makes bold mouths.
Tongues spit their duties out, and cold hearts freeze
Allegiance in them. Their curses now
Live where their prayers did; and it's come to pass
64 This tractable obedience is a slave
65 To each incensèd will. I would your highness
Would give it quick consideration, for
67 There is no primer business.

KING   By my life,
This is against our pleasure.

WOLSEY   And for me,
I have no further gone in this than by
70 A single voice, and that not passed me but
By learned approbation of the judges. If I am
Traduced by ignorant tongues, which neither know
73 My faculties nor person yet will be
The chronicles of my doing, let me say

'Tis but the fate of place and the rough brake   75
That virtue must go through. We must not stint   76
Our necessary actions in the fear
To cope malicious censurers, which ever,   78
As rav'nous fishes, do a vessel follow
That is new-trimmed, but benefit no further
Than vainly longing. What we oft do best,
By sick interpreters (once weak ones) is   82
Not ours, or not allowed; what worst, as oft   83
Hitting a grosser quality, is cried up   84
For our best act. If we shall stand still,
In fear our motion will be mocked or carped at,   86
We should take root here where we sit,
Or sit state-statues only.

KING   Things done well
And with a care exempt themselves from fear;
Things done without example, in their issue   90
Are to be feared. Have you a precedent
Of this commission? I believe, not any.
We must not rend our subjects from our laws
And stick them in our will. Sixth part of each?   94
A trembling contribution! Why, we take   95
From every tree lop, bark, and part o' th' timber;
And though we leave it with a root, thus hacked,
The air will drink the sap. To every county
Where this is questioned, send our letters with
Free pardon to each man that has denied
The force of this commission. Pray look to 't.   101
I put it to your care.

WOLSEY [aside to the Secretary] A word with you.
Let there be letters writ to every shire
Of the king's grace and pardon. The grievèd commons   104
Hardly conceive of me. Let it be noised   105
That through our intercession this revokement
And pardon comes. I shall anon advise you
Further in the proceeding.   Exit Secretary.
          Enter Surveyor.

KATHERINE
I am sorry that the Duke of Buckingham
Is run in your displeasure.   110

KING   It grieves many.
The gentleman is learned and a most rare speaker,
To nature none more bound; his training such   112

20 *grievance* distress; *commissions* writs of authority (for collecting taxes)
21 *flawed* broken 26 *soil* moral stain 27–28 *breaks The sides* i.e. bursts
the bounds 32 *longing* belonging, i.e. working for them; *put off* dismissed
from employment 33 *spinsters* spinners; *carders* those who comb out
impurities from wool; *fullers* those who 'full,' i.e. clean cloth by beating
36 *Daring . . . teeth* defiantly challenging the outcome 37 *danger . . .
them* i.e. they almost welcome danger 41 *a single part* one person's share
42 *front* march in the front rank 43 *tell steps* march in step 44–47 *You
. . . acquaintance* i.e. in a sense you do not know more than others, but
rather are the instigator of measures familiar to all which those (of the
council) who regard them as undesirable and would therefore wish to reject
them are nevertheless forced to accept 48 *note* knowledge 50 *is sacrifice*
becomes a sacrifice 52 *exclamation* outcry, reproach 53 *In what kind* of
what form 56 *grief* grievance 64 *tractable* docile (in the negative sense;
one should obey reason and one's king) 65 *each incensèd will* each individual's aroused passion 67 *primer* more important 70 *single voice*
unanimous vote 73 *faculties* qualities 75 *place* office, rank; *brake*
thicket 76 *stint* cease to do 78 *cope* encounter; *censurers* judges 82
sick envious 83 *allowed* approved 84 *Hitting . . . quality* catching favor
with lower-class (and ignorant) people 86 *motion* move 90 *issue* outcome 94 *stick . . . will* i.e. deal with them according to our pleasure 95
trembling fearful 101 *force* power 104 *grace* mercy 105 *Hardly conceive* think harshly; *noised* rumored 110 *Is run in* has incurred 112
bound indebted

That he may furnish and instruct great teachers
114 And never seek for aid out of himself. Yet see,
When these so noble benefits shall prove
116 Not well disposed, the mind growing once corrupt,
117 They turn to vicious forms, ten times more ugly
118 Than ever they were fair. This man so complete,
Who was enrolled 'mongst wonders, and when we,
Almost with ravished list'ning, could not find
His hour of speech a minute – he, my lady,
122 Hath into monstrous habits put the graces
That once were his, and is become as black
As if besmeared in hell. Sit by us; you shall hear
(This was his gentleman in trust) of him
Things to strike honor sad. Bid him recount
127 The fore-recited practices, whereof
We cannot feel too little, hear too much.

WOLSEY
Stand forth, and with bold spirit relate what you
130 Most like a careful subject have collected
Out of the Duke of Buckingham.

KING   Speak freely.

SURVEYOR
First, it was usual with him – every day
It would infect his speech – that if the king
134 Should without issue die, he'll carry it so
To make the sceptre his. These very words
I've heard him utter to his son-in-law,
Lord Aberga'ny, to whom by oath he menaced
Revenge upon the cardinal.

WOLSEY   Please your highness note
This dangerous conception in this point:
140 Not friended by his wish to your high person,
His will is most malignant, and it stretches
Beyond you to your friends.

KATHERINE   My learned lord cardinal,
143 Deliver all with charity.

KING   Speak on.
How grounded he his title to the crown
145 Upon our fail? To this point hast thou heard him
At any time speak aught?

SURVEYOR   He was brought to this
147 By a vain prophecy of Nicholas Henton.

KING
What was that Henton?

SURVEYOR   Sir, a Chartreux friar,
His confessor, who fed him every minute
With words of sovereignty.

KING   How know'st thou this?

SURVEYOR
Not long before your highness sped to France,
152 The duke being at the Rose, within the parish
Saint Lawrence Poultney, did of me demand
What was the speech among the Londoners

Concerning the French journey. I replied,
Men feared the French would prove perfidious,
To the king's danger. Presently the duke   157
Said 'twas the fear indeed, and that he doubted
'Twould prove the verity of certain words
Spoke by a holy monk 'that oft,' says he,
'Hath sent to me, wishing me to permit
John de la Car, my chaplain, a choice hour
To hear from him a matter of some moment;   163
Whom after under the confession's seal
He solemnly had sworn that what he spoke
My chaplain to no creature living but
To me should utter, with demure confidence   167
This pausingly ensued: Neither the king nor 's heirs 168
(Tell you the duke) shall prosper. Bid him strive
To win the love o' th' commonalty. The duke   170
Shall govern England.'

KATHERINE   If I know you well,
You were the duke's surveyor and lost your office
On the complaint o' th' tenants. Take good heed
You charge not in your spleen a noble person   174
And spoil your nobler soul. I say, take heed;   175
Yes, heartily beseech you.

KING   Let him on.
Go forward.

SURVEYOR   On my soul, I'll speak but truth.
I told my lord the duke, by th' devil's illusions   178
The monk might be deceived; and that 'twas dangerous
To ruminate on this so far until
It forged him some design, which, being believed,   181
It was much like to do. He answered 'Tush,
It can do me no damage!' adding further
That, had the king in his last sickness failed,   184
The cardinal's and Sir Thomas Lovell's heads
Should have gone off.

KING   Ha! What, so rank? Ah, ha!   186
There's mischief in this man. Canst thou say further?

SURVEYOR
I can, my liege.

KING   Proceed.

SURVEYOR   Being at Greenwich,
After your highness had reproved the duke
About Sir William Bulmer –

KING   I remember
Of such a time. Being my sworn servant,
The duke retained him his. But on: what hence?

SURVEYOR
'If,' quoth he, 'I for this had been committed,
As to the Tower I thought, I would have played
The part my father meant to act upon
Th' usurper Richard, who, being at Salisbury,
Made suit to come in's presence, which if granted,
As he made semblance of his duty, would   198
Have put his knife into him.'

KING   A giant traitor!

WOLSEY
Now, madam, may his highness live in freedom,
And this man out of prison?

KATHERINE   God mend all.

KING
There's something more would out of thee. What say'st?

SURVEYOR
After 'the duke his father,' with the 'knife,'
He stretched him, and, with one hand on his dagger,   204

114 *out of* beyond 116 *disposed* directed 117 *vicious* evil 118 *complete*
accomplished 122 *habits* shapes (from the sense 'dresses, garments')
127 *practices* intrigues 130 *collected* gathered 134 *carry it so* manage it
in such a way as 140 *friended by* successful in 143 *Deliver* tell 145
fail (1) death, (2) failure to have issue 147 *Henton* (otherwise *Hopkins*,
cf. I, i, 221) 152 *Rose* i.e. manor of the Red Rose, belonging to Buckingham
157 *Presently* at once 163 *moment* importance 167 *demure* grave 168
pausingly with pauses between words 170 *commonalty* common people
174 *spleen* malice 175 *spoil* ruin 178 *illusions* deceptions 181–82 *being
. . . do* once believed in, was very likely to do him harm 184 *failed* died
186 *rank* haughtily rebellious (*O.E.D.*, A, I, 1) 198 *semblance . . . duty*
pretense of homage 204 *stretched him* straightened himself

205 Another spread on's breast, mounting his eyes,
He did discharge a horrible oath, whose tenor
207 Was, were he evil used, he would outgo
His father by as much as a performance
Does an irresolute purpose.
209 KING   There's his period,
210 To sheathe his knife in us. He is attached;
211 Call him to present trial. If he may
Find mercy in the law, 'tis his: if none,
Let him not seek't of us. By day and night,
214 He's traitor to th' height!   *Exeunt.*

*

I, iii   *Enter Lord Chamberlain and Lord Sandys.*
CHAMBERLAIN
1 Is't possible the spells of France should juggle
2 Men into such strange mysteries?
SANDYS   New customs,
Thou they be never so ridiculous
(Nay, let 'em be unmanly), yet are followed.
CHAMBERLAIN
As far as I see, all the good our English
Have got by the late voyage is but merely
7 A fit or two o' th' face; but they are shrewd ones,
8 For when they hold 'em, you would swear directly
Their very noses had been counsellors
10 To Pepin or Clotharius, they keep state so.
SANDYS
They have all new legs, and lame ones. One would take it,
12 That never see 'em pace before, the spavin,
13 A springhalt reigned among 'em.
CHAMBERLAIN   Death my lord,
14 Their clothes are after such a pagan cut to't
That sure th' have worn out Christendom.
     Enter Sir Thomas Lovell.   How now?
What news, Sir Thomas Lovell?
LOVELL   Faith, my lord,
I hear of none but the new proclamation
That's clapped upon the court-gate.
CHAMBERLAIN   What is't for?
LOVELL
The reformation of our travelled gallants
That fill the court with quarrels, talk and tailors.
CHAMBERLAIN
I'm glad 'tis there. Now I would pray our monsieurs
To think an English courtier may be wise
And never see the Louvre.
LOVELL   They must either
(For so run the conditions) leave those remnants
Of fool and feather that they got in France,
26 With all their honorable points of ignorance
27 Pertaining thereunto – as fights and fireworks;
Abusing better men than they can be,
Out of a foreign wisdom – renouncing clean
The faith they have in tennis and tall stockings,
31 Short blist'red breeches, and those types of travel,
32 And understand again like honest men,
33 Or pack to their old playfellows. There, I take it,
34 They may cum privilegio 'wee' away
35 The lag-end of their lewdness and be laughed at.
SANDYS
'Tis time to give 'em physic, their diseases
Are grown so catching.

CHAMBERLAIN   What a loss our ladies
Will have of these trim vanities!
LOVELL   Ay, marry,
There will be woe indeed, lords. The sly whoresons
Have got a speeding trick to lay down ladies.   40
A French song and a fiddle has no fellow.
SANDYS
The devil fiddle 'em! I am glad they are going,
For sure there's no converting of 'em. Now
An honest country lord, as I am, beaten
A long time out of play, may bring his plain-song   45
And have an hour of hearing, and, by'r Lady,
Held current music too.   47
CHAMBERLAIN   Well said, Lord Sandys.
Your colt's tooth is not cast yet?   48
SANDYS   No, my lord,
Nor shall not while I have a stump.   49
CHAMBERLAIN   Sir Thomas,
Whither were you a-going?
LOVELL   To the cardinal's.
Your lordship is a guest too.
CHAMBERLAIN   O, 'tis true;
This night he makes a supper, and a great one,   52
To many lords and ladies. There will be
The beauty of this kingdom, I'll assure you.
LOVELL
That churchman bears a bounteous mind indeed,
A hand as fruitful as the land that feeds us;
His dews fall everywhere.
CHAMBERLAIN   No doubt he's noble.
He had a black mouth that said other of him.   58
SANDYS
He may, my lord; has wherewithal. In him
Sparing would show a worse sin than ill doctrine.
Men of his way should be most liberal;   61
They are set here for examples.
CHAMBERLAIN   True, they are so;
But few now give so great ones. My barge stays;
Your lordship shall along. Come, good Sir Thomas,
We shall be late else; which I would not be,
For I was spoke to, with Sir Henry Guilford   66
This night to be comptrollers.   67
SANDYS   I am your lordship's.
                      Exeunt.

*

205 *mounting* raising 207 *evil* badly; *outgo* surpass 209 *period* end and goal 210 *attached* arrested 211 *present* immediate 214 *to th' height* in the highest degree
I, iii The royal palace s.d. *Sandys* (pronounced 'Sands') 1 *juggle* trick 2 *mysteries* i.e. artificial fashions (comically 'mysterious') 7 *A fit . . . o'* a way of screwing up; *shrewd* artful (O.E.D., 13) 8 *hold 'em* i.e. keep their grimaces 10 *Pepin, Clotharius* early kings of the Franks 12 *see* saw (an old form of the past tense); *pace* walk, strut; *spavin* tumor on a horse's leg 13 *A* even a, what's more a (but often emended to 'And' or 'Or' by editors); *springhalt* disease causing spasmodic contractions in the leg muscles 14 *to't* in addition, moreover 26 *With . . . ignorance* with what they ignorantly regard as honorable 27 *fights and fireworks* (probably) duelling and whoring (with additional allusion to the mock-battles and fireworks staged at Princess Elizabeth's wedding in 1613) 31 *blist'red* garnished with puffs; *types* marks, badges 32 *understand* (see note to Prologue, l. 22) 33 *pack* depart, clear off 34 *cum privilegio* with immunity; *'wee'* (the Englishman's aping of French 'oui') 35 *lag-end* remainder 40 *speeding* effective, successful 45 *play* (with sexual allusion); *plain-song* simple melody (see *French song*, l. 41) 47 *current* good, of full value 48 *colt's tooth* (proverbial for wantonness) 49 *stump* i.e. of a tooth (with bawdy quibble) 52 *makes* gives 58 *black* evil 61 *way* way of life 66 *spoke to* asked 67 *comptrollers* stewards

I, iv   *Hautboys. A small table under a state for the*
Cardinal, a longer table for the guests. Then enter
Anne Bullen and divers other Ladies and
Gentlemen, as guests at one door ; at another door
enter Sir Henry Guilford.

GUILFORD
Ladies, a general welcome from his grace
Salutes ye all. This night he dedicates
To fair content and you. None here, he hopes,
4   In all this noble bevy, has brought with her
One care abroad. He would have all as merry
6   As first, good company, good wine, good welcome
Can make good people.
  Enter Lord Chamberlain, Lord Sandys, and Lovell.
    O my lord, y' are tardy !
The very thought of this fair company
Clapped wings to me.
CHAMBERLAIN You are young, Sir Harry Guilford.
SANDYS
Sir Thomas Lovell, had the cardinal
11   But half my lay thoughts in him, some of these
12   Should find a running banquet ere they rested,
I think would better please 'em. By my life,
They are a sweet society of fair ones.
LOVELL
O that your lordship were but now confessor
To one or two of these !
SANDYS   I would I were.
They should find easy penance.
LOVELL   Faith, how easy ?
SANDYS
As easy as a down-bed would afford it.
CHAMBERLAIN
Sweet ladies, will it please you sit ? Sir Harry,
20   Place you that side ; I'll take the charge of this.
His grace is ent'ring. Nay, you must not freeze !
Two women placed together makes cold weather.
23   My Lord Sandys, you are one will keep 'em waking.
Pray sit between these ladies.
SANDYS   By my faith,
And thank your lordship. By your leave, sweet ladies,
  [Seats himself between Anne Bullen and another
  lady.]
If I chance to talk a little wild, forgive me ;
I had it from my father.
ANNE   Was he mad, sir ?
SANDYS
O very mad, exceeding mad, in love too.
But he would bite none. Just as I do now,
He would kiss you twenty with a breath.
  [Kisses her.]
30 CHAMBERLAIN   Well said, my lord.
So now y' are fairly seated. Gentlemen,
The penance lies on you if these fair ladies
Pass away frowning.
33 SANDYS   For my little cure,
Let me alone.

Hautboys. Enter Cardinal Wolsey, [attended,] and 34
takes his state.
WOLSEY
Y' are welcome, my fair guests. That noble lady
Or gentleman that is not freely merry
Is not my friend. This to confirm my welcome ;
And to you all, good health.
  [Drinks.]
SANDYS   Your grace is noble.
Let me have such a bowl may hold my thanks
And save me so much talking.
WOLSEY   My Lord Sandys,
I am beholding to you : cheer your neighbors : 41
Ladies, you are not merry ; gentlemen,
Whose fault is this ?
SANDYS   The red wine first must rise
In their fair cheeks, my lord ; then we shall have 'em
Talk us to silence.
ANNE   You are a merry gamester, 45
My Lord Sandys.
SANDYS   Yes, if I make my play. 46
Here's to your ladyship ; and pledge it, madam,
For 'tis to such a thing –
ANNE   You cannot show me.
SANDYS
I told your grace they would talk anon. 49
  Drum and trumpet. Chambers discharged.
WOLSEY   What's that ?
CHAMBERLAIN
Look out there, some of ye. *[Exit a Servant.]*
WOLSEY   What warlike voice,
And to what end is this ? Nay ladies, fear not.
By all the laws of war y' are privileged.
  Enter a Servant.
CHAMBERLAIN
How now, what is't ?
SERVANT   A noble troop of strangers
For so they seem. Th' have left their barge and landed,
And hither make, as great ambassadors
From foreign princes.
WOLSEY   Good lord chamberlain,
Go, give 'em welcome ; you can speak the French
  tongue ;
And pray receive 'em nobly and conduct 'em
Into our presence, where this heaven of beauty
Shall shine at full upon them. Some attend him !
    [Exit Chamberlain, attended.]
    All rise, and tables removed.
You have now a broken banquet, but we'll mend it. 61
A good digestion to you all ! and once more
I show'r a welcome on ye : welcome all.
  Hautboys. Enter King and others, as maskers,
  habited like shepherds, ushered by the Lord
  Chamberlain. They pass directly before the
  Cardinal and gracefully salute him.
A noble company ! What are their pleasures ?
CHAMBERLAIN
Because they speak no English, thus they prayed
To tell your grace : that having heard by fame 66
Of this so noble and so fair assembly
This night to meet here, they could do no less
(Out of the great respect they bear to beauty)
But leave their flocks and, under your fair conduct, 70
Crave leave to view these ladies and entreat

I, iv York Place **4** *bevy* company **6** *first* i.e. first ... then ... then **11** *lay*
secular **12** *running banquet* (with bawdy quibble) **20** *Place* assign places
23 *waking* i.e. lively **30** *said* done **33** *cure* remedy **34** s.d. *state* chair of
state **41** *beholding* beholden **45** *gamester* pleasant fellow (with bawdy
innuendo) **46** *make my play* win **49** s.d. *Chambers* small cannons used
in salutes (which probably caused the fire at the Globe in 1613) **61** *broken*
intercepted **66** *fame* report **70** *conduct* guidance

72 An hour of revels with 'em.

WOLSEY   Say, lord chamberlain,
They have done my poor house grace; for which I pay
    'em
A thousand thanks and pray 'em take their pleasures.
    Choose ladies. King and Anne Bullen.

KING
The fairest hand I ever touched: O beauty,
Till now I never knew thee!
    Music. Dance.

WOLSEY
My lord!

CHAMBERLAIN   Your grace?

WOLSEY   Pray tell 'em thus much from me:
There should be one amongst 'em, by his person,
79 More worthy this place than myself; to whom,
If I but knew him, with my love and duty
I would surrender it.

CHAMBERLAIN   I will, my lord.
    Whisper [with the Maskers].

WOLSEY
What say they?

CHAMBERLAIN   Such a one they all confess
There is indeed, which they would have your grace
84 Find out, and he will take it.

WOLSEY   Let me see then;
By all your good leaves, gentlemen; here I'll make
My royal choice.

KING [*unmasks*]   Ye have found him, cardinal.
You hold a fair assembly. You do well, lord.
You are a churchman, or I'll tell you, cardinal,
89 I should judge now unhappily.

WOLSEY   I am glad
90 Your grace is grown so pleasant.

KING   My lord chamberlain,
Prithee come hither. What fair lady 's that?

CHAMBERLAIN
An't please your grace, Sir Thomas Bullen's daughter,
The Viscount Rochford, one of her highness' women.

KING
By heaven she is a dainty one. Sweetheart,
95 I were unmannerly to take you out
And not to kiss you. [*Kisses her.*] A health, gentlemen!
97 Let it go round.

WOLSEY
Sir Thomas Lovell, is the banquet ready
I' th' privy chamber?

LOVELL   Yes, my lord.

WOLSEY   Your grace,
I fear, with dancing is a little heated.

KING
I fear, too much.

WOLSEY   There's fresher air, my lord,
In the next chamber.

KING
Lead in your ladies ev'ry one. Sweet partner,
I must not yet forsake you. Let's be merry,
Good my lord cardinal; I have half a dozen healths
106 To drink to these fair ladies, and a measure
To lead 'em once again; and then let's dream
108 Who's best in favor. Let the music knock it.
    Exeunt with Trumpets.

*

1. GENTLEMAN
Whither away so fast?

2. GENTLEMAN   O, God save ye!
Ev'n to the Hall, to hear what shall become   2
Of the great Duke of Buckingham.

1. GENTLEMAN   I'll save you
That labor, sir. All's now done but the ceremony
Of bringing back the prisoner.

2. GENTLEMAN   Were you there?

1. GENTLEMAN
Yes indeed was I.

2. GENTLEMAN   Pray speak what has happened.

1. GENTLEMAN
You may guess quickly what.

2. GENTLEMAN   Is he found guilty?

1. GENTLEMAN
Yes truly is he, and condemned upon't.

2. GENTLEMAN
I am sorry for't.

1. GENTLEMAN   So are a number more.

2. GENTLEMAN
But pray how passed it?   10

1. GENTLEMAN
I'll tell you in a little. The great duke   11
Came to the bar; where to his accusations
He pleaded still not guilty, and allegèd   13
Many sharp reasons to defeat the law.   14
The king's attorney, on the contrary,
Urged on the examinations, proofs, confessions   16
Of divers witnesses, which the duke desired
To have brought viva voce to his face;   18
At which appeared against him his surveyor,
Sir Gilbert Perk his chancellor, and John Car,
Confessor to him, with that devil monk,
Hopkins, that made this mischief.

2. GENTLEMAN   That was he
That fed him with his prophecies.

1. GENTLEMAN   The same.
All these accused him strongly, which he fain   24
Would have flung from him, but indeed he could not;
And so his peers upon this evidence
Have found him guilty of high treason. Much
He spoke, and learnedly for life; but all
Was either pitied in him or forgotten.

2. GENTLEMAN
After all this how did he bear himself?

1. GENTLEMAN
When he was brought again to th' bar, to hear
His knell rung out, his judgment, he was stirred   32
With such an agony he sweat extremely
And something spoke in choler, ill and hasty;   34
But he fell to himself again, and sweetly   35
In all the rest showed a most noble patience.

---

72 *revels* dancing 79 *this place* i.e. place of honor 84 *it* (refers to *place* in l. 79) 89 *unhappily* unfavorably 90 *pleasant* merry 95 *take you out* lead you out to a dance 97 *it* i.e. the cup 106 *measure* stately dance 108 *in favor* i.e. with the ladies; *knock it* strike up

II, i A *street* s.d. *several* different 2 *Hall* Westminster Hall 10 *passed it* did the trial proceed 11 *in a little* briefly 13 *alleged* put forward 14 *sharp reasons* acute arguments; *defeat* make void, frustrate 16 *Urged on* pressed as evidence; *proofs* written statements or evidence 18 *viva voce* (literally) with a living voice 24 *which* i.e. which accusations 32 *judgment* sentence 34 *ill* offensive 35 *fell . . . again* regained self-control

2 . GENTLEMAN
I do not think he fears death.

1 . GENTLEMAN   Sure he does not ;
He never was so womanish. The cause
He may a little grieve at.

2 . GENTLEMAN   Certainly
40 The cardinal is the end of this.

1 . GENTLEMAN   'Tis likely
41 By all conjectures : first Kildare's attendure,
42 Then Deputy of Ireland, who removed,
Earl Surrey was sent thither, and in haste too,
44 Lest he should help his father.

2 . GENTLEMAN   That trick of state
45 Was a deep envious one.

1 . GENTLEMAN   At his return
No doubt he will requite it. This is noted
47 (And generally), whoever the king favors,
48 The card'nal instantly will find employment,
And far enough from court too.

2 . GENTLEMAN   All the commons
50 Hate him perniciously, and o' my conscience
Wish him ten fathom deep. This duke as much
They love and dote on, call him bounteous Buckingham
53 The mirror of all courtesy –

Enter Buckingham from his arraignment ; Tipstaves
before him ; [Officer bearing] the [executioner's] axe
with the edge towards him ; Halberds on each side ;
accompanied with Sir Thomas Lovell, Sir Nicholas
Vaux, Sir Walter Sandys, and common people, etc.

1 . GENTLEMAN   Stay there, sir,
And see the noble ruined man you speak of.

2 . GENTLEMAN
Let's stand close and behold him.

BUCKINGHAM   All good people,
You that thus far have come to pity me,
57 Hear what I say and then go home and lose me.
58 I have this day received a traitor's judgment
And by that name must die. Yet heaven bear witness,
60 And if I have a conscience, let it sink me
Even as the axe falls, if I be not faithful !
The law I bear no malice for my death,
63 'T has done upon the premises but justice :
But those that sought it I could wish more Christians.
Be what they will, I heartily forgive 'em.
66 Yet let 'em look they glory not in mischief,
67 Nor build their evils on the graves of great men ;
For then my guiltless blood must cry against 'em.
For further life in this world I ne'er hope,

Nor will I sue, although the king have mercies
More than I dare make faults. You few that loved me   71
And dare be bold to weep for Buckingham,
His noble friends and fellows, whom to leave
Is only bitter to him, only dying,   74
Go with me like good angels to my end ;
And, as the long divorce of steel falls on me,
Make of your prayers one sweet sacrifice   77
And lift my soul to heaven. Lead on a God's name.   78

LOVELL
I do beseech your grace, for charity,   79
If ever any malice in your heart
Were hid against me, now to forgive me frankly.

BUCKINGHAM
Sir Thomas Lovell, I as free forgive you
As I would be forgiven : I forgive all.
There cannot be those numberless offenses
'Gainst me that I cannot take peace with : no black envy   85
Shall mark my grave. Commend me to his grace ;
And if he speak of Buckingham, pray tell him
You met him half in heaven. My vows and prayers
Yet are the king's, and till my soul forsake   89
Shall cry for blessings on him. May he live
Longer than I have time to tell his years ;   91
Ever beloved and loving may his rule be ;
And when old time shall lead him to his end,   93
Goodness and he fill up one monument !   94

LOVELL
To th' waterside I must conduct your grace ;
Then give my charge up to Sir Nicholas Vaux,
Who undertakes you to your end.   97

VAUX   Prepare there,
The duke is coming. See the barge be ready
And fit it with such furniture as suits   99
The greatness of his person.

BUCKINGHAM   Nay, Sir Nicholas,
Let it alone ; my state now will but mock me.
When I came hither I was Lord High Constable
And Duke of Buckingham ; now poor Edward Bohun.
Yet I am richer than my base accusers,
That never knew what truth meant : I now seal it ;   105
And with that blood will make 'em one day groan for't.
My noble father, Henry of Buckingham,
Who first raised head against usurping Richard,   108
Flying for succor to his servant Banister,
Being distressed, was by that wretch betrayed,
And without trial fell ; God's peace be with him !
Henry the Seventh succeeding, truly pitying
My father's loss, like a most royal prince
Restored me to my honors ; and out of ruins
Made my name once more noble. Now his son,
Henry the Eighth, life, honor, name, and all
That made me happy, at one stroke has taken
For ever from the world. I had my trial,
And must needs say a noble one ; which makes me
A little happier than my wretched father.
Yet thus far we are one in fortunes : both
Fell by our servants, by those men we loved most –
A most unnatural and faithless service.
Heaven has an end in all ; yet you that hear me,   124
This from a dying man receive as certain :   125
Where you are liberal of your loves and counsels
Be sure you be not loose ; for those you make friends   127
And give your hearts to, when they once perceive

40 *the end of* responsible for, at the bottom of   41 *attendure* attainder (the confiscation of the Earl of Kildare's estate, upon the death sentence)   42 *Deputy* i.e. viceroy   44 *father* (Surrey was Buckingham's son-in-law) 45 *deep envious* profoundly malicious   47 *generally* by everybody   48 *employment* employment for   50 *perniciously* to the death   53 *mirror* model ; *courtesy* courtly behavior ; **s.d.** *Tipstaves* officers who take the accused from the court into custody (so called because they carried staves tipped with silver) ; *Halberds* halberdiers (carrying long-handled battle-axes with spearpoints)   57 *lose* forget   58 *judgment* sentence   60 *sink* destroy   63 *premises* evidence   66 *look* take care   67 *build . . . graves* i.e. thrive in their evil designs on the downfalls   71 *make faults* commit offenses   74 *Is only . . . only* alone is . . . alone is   77 *sacrifice* offering   78 *a* in   79–81 *I . . . frankly* (see I, ii, 185–86)   85 *envy* malice   89 *forsake* leave the body   91 *tell* count   93 *old time* old age   94 *monument* tomb   97 *undertakes you* takes charge of you   99 *furniture* equipment   105 *seal* ratify   108 *raised head* gathered a force   124 *end* purpose   125 *receive as certain* accept as truth   127 *loose* unrestrained

793

129 The least rub in your fortunes, fall away
      Like water from ye, never found again
131 But where they mean to sink ye. All good people,
      Pray for me! I must now forsake ye; the last hour
      Of my long weary life is come upon me.
      Farewell!
      And when you would say something that is sad,
      Speak how I fell. I have done, and God forgive me!
                                        Exeunt Duke and train.

      1 . GENTLEMAN
137 O this is full of pity! Sir, it calls,
      I fear, too many curses on their heads
      That were the authors.
      2 . GENTLEMAN   If the duke be guiltless,
      'Tis full of woe. Yet I can give you inkling
      Of an ensuing evil, if it fall,
      Greater than this.
      1 . GENTLEMAN   Good angels keep it from us!
143 What may it be? you do not doubt my faith, sir?
      2 . GENTLEMAN
      This secret is so weighty 'twill require
      A strong faith to conceal it.
      1 . GENTLEMAN   Let me have it;
      I do not talk much.
146 2 . GENTLEMAN   I am confident.
      You shall, sir. Did you not of late days hear
148 A buzzing of a separation
      Between the king and Katherine?
149 1 . GENTLEMAN   Yes, but it held not;
      For when the king once heard it, out of anger
151 He sent command to the lord mayor straight
152 To stop the rumor and allay those tongues
      That durst disperse it.
      2 . GENTLEMAN   But that slander, sir,
      Is found a truth now; for it grows again
155 Fresher than e'er it was, and held for certain
      The king will venture at it. Either the cardinal,
157 Or some about him near, have out of malice
158 To the good queen possessed him with a scruple
      That will undo her. To confirm this too,
      Cardinal Campeius is arrived, and lately,
      As all think, for this business.
      1 . GENTLEMAN   'Tis the cardinal;
162 And merely to revenge him on the emperor
      For not bestowing on him at his asking
      The archbishopric of Toledo, this is purposed.
      2 . GENTLEMAN
      I think you have hit the mark. But is't not cruel
      That she should feel the smart of this? The cardinal
      Will have his will, and she must fall.
      1 . GENTLEMAN   'Tis woeful.
168 We are too open here to argue this;
      Let's think in private more.   *Exeunt.*

                              *

II, ii   *Enter Lord Chamberlain, reading this letter.*
      [CHAMBERLAIN] 'My lord – The horses your lordship
  2   sent for, with all the care I had, I saw well chosen, rid-
  3   den, and furnished. They were young and handsome
      and of the best breed in the north. When they were
      ready to set out for London, a man of my lord cardinal's
  6   by commission and main power took 'em from me, with
      this reason: his master would be served before a subject,

if not before the king; which stopped our mouths, sir.'
I fear he will indeed. Well, let him have them.
He will have all, I think.
          *Enter to the Lord Chamberlain the Dukes of Norfolk
          and Suffolk.*
NORFOLK
Well met, my lord chamberlain.
CHAMBERLAIN
Good day to both your graces.
SUFFOLK
How is the king employed?
CHAMBERLAIN   I left him private,
Full of sad thoughts and troubles.   14
NORFOLK   What's the cause?
CHAMBERLAIN
It seems the marriage with his brother's wife
Has crept too near his conscience.
SUFFOLK *[aside]*   No, his conscience
Has crept too near another lady.
NORFOLK   'Tis so.
This is the cardinal's doing: the king-cardinal,
That blind priest, like the eldest son of Fortune,   19
Turns what he list. The king will know him one day.
SUFFOLK
Pray God he do, he'll never know himself else.
NORFOLK
How holily he works in all his business
And with what zeal! for, now he has cracked the league   23
Between us and the emperor, the queen's great nephew,
He dives into the king's soul, and there scatters
Dangers, doubts, wringing of the conscience,   26
Fears, and despairs, and all these for his marriage.
And out of all these, to restore the king,
He counsels a divorce, a loss of her
That like a jewel has hung twenty years   30
About his neck, yet never lost her lustre;
Of her that loves him with that excellence   32
That angels love good men with; even of her
That, when the greatest stroke of fortune falls,
Will bless the king. And is not this course pious?
CHAMBERLAIN
Heaven keep me from such counsel! 'Tis most true
These news are everywhere, every tongue speaks 'em,
And every true heart weeps for't. All that dare
Look into these affairs see this main end –   39
The French king's sister. Heaven will one day open
The king's eyes that so long have slept upon   41
This bold bad man.
SUFFOLK   And free us from his slavery.
NORFOLK
We had need pray,
And heartily, for our deliverance,
Or this imperious man will work us all

129 *rub* check, impediment   **131** *sink* ruin   **137** *calls* summons   **143** *faith* trustworthiness   **146** *am confident* trust you   **148** *buzzing* rumor   **149** *held not* did not continue   **151** *straight* at once   **152** *allay* restrain   **155** *held* is thought   **157** *about him near* intimate with him   **158** *possessed* imbued   **162** *emperor* Charles V (Holy Roman Emperor, and nephew of Queen Katherine)   **168** *open* public, exposed to view; *argue* discuss
II, ii The royal palace   **2** *ridden* broken in   **3** *furnished* equipped   **6** *main power* superior force   **14** *sad* serious   **19–20** *blind . . . list* (an allusion to Fortune, conceived in the Middle Ages as blind, and her wheel which she turns arbitrarily)   **23** *cracked* broken   **26** *wringing* torture   **30** *jewel* costly gold chain (worn by gentlemen)   **32** *excellence* surpassing virtue   **39** *end* object   **41** *slept upon* been blind to

From princes into pages. All men's honors
47 Lie like one lump before him, to be fashioned
48 Into what pitch he please.

SUFFOLK   For me, my lords,
I love him not, nor fear him; there's my creed:
50 As I am made without him, so I'll stand,
If the king please. His curses and his blessings
Touch me alike; th' are breath I not believe in.
I knew him, and I know him: so I leave him
To him that made him proud, the pope.

NORFOLK   Let's in,
And with some other business put the king
From these sad thoughts that work too much upon him.
My lord, you'll bear us company?

CHAMBERLAIN   Excuse me.
The king has sent me otherwhere. Besides,
You'll find a most unfit time to disturb him.
Health to your lordships!

NORFOLK   Thanks, my good lord chamberlain.
       Exit Lord Chamberlain ; and the King draws
       the curtain and sits reading pensively.

SUFFOLK
61 How sad he looks; sure he is much afflicted.

KING
Who's there, ha?

NORFOLK   Pray God he be not angry.

KING
Who's there, I say? How dare you thrust yourselves
Into my private meditations?
Who am I? ha?

NORFOLK
A gracious king that pardons all offenses
67 Malice ne'er meant. Our breach of duty this way
68 Is business of estate; in which we come
To know your royal pleasure.

KING   Ye are too bold:
Go to! I'll make ye know your times of business.
Is this an hour for temporal affairs? ha?
       Enter Wolsey and Campeius with a commission.
Who's there? My good lord cardinal? O my Wolsey,
The quiet of my wounded conscience;
Thou art a cure fit for a king. *[to Campeius]* You're wel-
come,
Most learned reverend sir, into our kingdom.
Use us and it. *[to Wolsey]* My good lord, have great care
77 I be not found a talker.

WOLSEY   Sir, you cannot;
I would your grace would give us but an hour
Of private conference.

KING *[to Norfolk and Suffolk]* We are busy: go.

NORFOLK *[aside to Suffolk]*
This priest has no pride in him!

SUFFOLK *[aside to Norfolk]*   Not to speak of.
81 I would not be so sick though for his place.
But this cannot continue.

NORFOLK *[aside to Suffolk]* If it do,
I'll venture one; have at him!   83

SUFFOLK *[aside to Norfolk]*   I another.
       Exeunt Norfolk and Suffolk.

WOLSEY
Your grace has given a precedent of wisdom
Above all princes in committing freely
Your scruple to the voice of Christendom.   86
Who can be angry now? what envy reach you?   87
The Spaniard, tied by blood and favor to her,
Must now confess, if they have any goodness,
The trial just and noble. All the clerks   90
(I mean the learned ones in Christian kingdoms)
Have their free voices. Rome, the nurse of judgment,   92
Invited by your noble self, hath sent
One general tongue unto us, this good man,   94
This just and learned priest, Cardinal Campeius,
Whom once more I present unto your highness.

KING
And once more in mine arms I bid him welcome
And thank the holy conclave for their loves.   98
They have sent me such a man I would have wished for.

CAMPEIUS
Your grace must needs deserve all strangers' loves,   100
You are so noble. To your highness' hand
I tender my commission; by whose virtue,
The court of Rome commanding, you, my Lord
Cardinal of York, are joined with me their servant
In the unpartial judging of this business.

KING
Two equal men. The queen shall be acquainted   106
Forthwith for what you come. Where's Gardiner?

WOLSEY
I know your majesty has always loved her
So dear in heart, not to deny her that
A woman of less place might ask by law –   110
Scholars allowed freely to argue for her.

KING
Ay, and the best she shall have; and my favor
To him that does best, God forbid else. Cardinal,
Prithee call Gardiner to me, my new secretary.
I find him a fit fellow.   *[Exit Wolsey.]*
       Enter [Wolsey, with] Gardiner.

WOLSEY *[aside to Gardiner]*
Give me your hand. Much joy and favor to you;
You are the king's now.

GARDINER *[aside to Wolsey]* But to be commanded
For ever by your grace, whose hand has raised me.

KING
Come hither, Gardiner.
       Walks and whispers.

CAMPEIUS
My Lord of York, was not one Doctor Pace
In this man's place before him?

WOLSEY   Yes, he was.

CAMPEIUS
Was he not held a learned man?

WOLSEY   Yes, surely.

CAMPEIUS
Believe me, there's an ill opinion spread then,
Even of yourself, lord cardinal.

WOLSEY   How? of me?

CAMPEIUS
They will not stick to say you envied him,   125

---

47 *lump* i.e. lump of clay   48 *pitch* level, status   50 *stand* stand firm   61
afflicted troubled   67 *this way* in this respect   68 *estate* state   77 *I . . .
talker* i.e. that this be not found mere empty talk   81 *sick . . . place* sick with
pride even to gain his position   83 *have at him* (a challenge)   86 *voice* vote
87 *envy* malice   90 *clerks* scholars   92 *voices* votes   94 *One general tongue*
one to speak for all   98 *conclave* assembly of cardinals   100 *strangers'*
foreigners'   106 *equal* impartial   110 *less place* lower rank   125 *stick*
scruple

And fearing he would rise (he was so virtuous),
127 Kept him a foreign man still, which so grieved him
That he ran mad and died.
  WOLSEY   Heav'n's peace be with him!
129 That's Christian care enough. For living murmurers
There's places of rebuke. He was a fool,
For he would needs be virtuous. That good fellow,
132 If I command him, follows my appointment;
133 I will have none so near else. Learn this, brother,
134 We live not to be griped by meaner persons.
  KING
135 Deliver this with modesty to th' Queen. *Exit Gardiner.*
The most convenient place that I can think of
137 For such receipt of learning is Blackfriars.
There ye shall meet about this weighty business.
My Wolsey, see it furnished. O my lord,
Would it not grieve an able man to leave
So sweet a bedfellow? But conscience, conscience!
O 'tis a tender place, and I must leave her.   *Exeunt.*

                *

II, iii   *Enter Anne Bullen and an Old Lady.*
  ANNE
1 Not for that neither; here's the pang that pinches:
His highness having lived so long with her, and she
So good a lady that no tongue could ever
4 Pronounce dishonor of her – by my life,
She never knew harm-doing – O, now after
6 So many courses of the sun enthronèd,
7 Still growing in a majesty and pomp, the which
To leave a thousandfold more bitter than
9 'Tis sweet at first t' acquire – after this process
10 To give her the avaunt, it is a pity
Would move a monster.
  OLD LADY   Hearts of most hard temper
11 Melt and lament for her.
  ANNE   O God's will much better
13 She ne'er had known pomp. Though't be temporal,
14 Yet if that quarrel, fortune, do divorce
15 It from the bearer, 'tis a sufferance panging
As soul and body's severing.
  OLD LADY   Alas, poor lady,
17 She's a stranger now again.
  ANNE   So much the more
Must pity drop upon her. Verily
I swear 'tis better to be lowly born
20 And range with humble livers in content
21 Than to be perked up in a glist'ring grief
And wear a golden sorrow.
  OLD LADY   Our content
Is our best having.
  ANNE   By my troth and maidenhead,
I would not be a queen.
24   OLD LADY   Beshrew me, I would,
And venture maidenhead for't; and so would you,
26 For all this spice of your hypocrisy.
27 You that have so fair parts of women on you
Have, too, a woman's heart, which ever yet
29 Affected eminence, wealth, sovereignty;
30 Which, to say sooth, are blessings; and which gifts
31 (Saving your mincing) the capacity
32 Of your soft cheveril conscience would receive,
If you might please to stretch it.

  ANNE   Nay, good troth.   33
  OLD LADY
Yes troth, and troth; you would not be a queen?   34
  ANNE
No, not for all the riches under heaven.
  OLD LADY
'Tis strange; a threepence bowed would hire me,   36
Old as I am, to queen it. But I pray you,   37
What think you of a duchess? Have you limbs
To bear that load of title?
  ANNE   No, in truth.
  OLD LADY
Then you are weakly made. Pluck off a little;   40
I would not be a young count in your way   41
For more than blushing comes to. If your back   42
Cannot vouchsafe this burden, 'tis too weak
Ever to get a boy.
  ANNE   How you do talk!
I swear again, I would not be a queen
For all the world.
  OLD LADY   In faith, for little England   46
You'ld venture an emballing. I myself   47
Would for Carnarvonshire, although there longed   48
No more to th' crown but that. Lo, who comes here?
     Enter Lord Chamberlain.
  CHAMBERLAIN
Good morrow, ladies. What were't worth to know
The secret of your conference?   51
  ANNE   My good lord,
Not your demand; it values not your asking: 52
Our mistress' sorrows we were pitying.
  CHAMBERLAIN
It was a gentle business and becoming
The action of good women. There is hope
All will be well.
  ANNE   Now I pray God, amen.
  CHAMBERLAIN
You bear a gentle mind, and heav'nly blessings
Follow such creatures. That you may, fair lady,
Perceive I speak sincerely, and high note's
Ta'en of your many virtues, the king's majesty
Commends his good opinion of you, and   61

127 *a foreign man still* continually employed in other countries 129 *murmurers* grumblers 132 *appointment* bidding 133 *near* familiar 134 *griped* grasped by the hand 135 *Deliver . . . modesty* i.e. inform her of this without making too much of it 137 *such . . . learning* hearing such learned discourses (?), the reception of such learned men (?)
II, iii The Queen's apartments 1 *pinches* hurts, torments 4 *Pronounce* make known 6 *courses . . . enthronèd* years 7–8 *the which To leave* which to leave is 9 *process* proceeding 10 *avaunt* order to leave; *pity* cause for pity 11 *temper* disposition 13 *temporal* i.e. merely worldly, not eternal 14 *quarrel* quarreller (use of abstract noun for agent; the emendation 'quarr'lous' is plausible) 15 *sufferance panging* suffering painful 17 *stranger* foreigner 20 *range . . . livers* rank with humble people 21 *perked up* perched up, made smart 24 *Beshrew me* woe befall me (a mild oath) 26 *spice* dash 27 *fair parts* attractive qualities 29 *Affected* aspired to 30 *to say sooth* truly, indeed 31 *Saving your mincing* with all respect to your affectation 32 *cheveril* flexible, stretching (like kid-leather) 33, 34 *troth* faith (with pun on 'trot': old hag) 36 *bowed* bent (and thus worthless) (with further quibble on 'bawd') 37 *queen* (punning on 'quean') 40 *Pluck off* come lower 41 *count* i.e. one rank lower than a duke; *way* path (with sexual innuendo) 42 *For . . .* i.e. with (no) more fuss than a mere blush 46 *little England* (possibly) Pembrokeshire (see l. 63) 47 *emballing* investing with the ball as the emblem of royalty (but with sexual innuendo?) 48 *Carnarvonshire* a barren county in Wales (with quibble on its shape and on 'carnal'?); *longed* belonged 51 *conference* conversation 52 *values not* is not worth 61 *Commends . . . you* presents his compliments

Does purpose honor to you no less flowing
Than Marchioness of Pembroke ; to which title
A thousand pound a year, annual support,
Out of his grace he adds.

ANNE   I do not know
What kind of my obedience I should tender.
67 More than my all is nothing ; nor my prayers
Are not words duly hallowed, nor my wishes
More worth than empty vanities ; yet prayers and wishes
Are all I can return. Beseech your lordship,
71 Vouchsafe to speak my thanks and my obedience,
As from a blushing handmaid, to his highness ;
Whose health and royalty I pray for.

CHAMBERLAIN   Lady,
74 I shall not fail t' approve the fair conceit
The king hath of you. [aside] I have perused her well.
Beauty and honor in her are so mingled
That they have caught the king ; and who knows yet
But from this lady may proceed a gem
79 To lighten all this isle. – I'll to the king
And say I spoke with you.

ANNE   My honored lord.
          Exit Lord Chamberlain.

OLD LADY
81 Why, this it is ! See, see,
I have been begging sixteen years in court
83 (Am yet a courtier beggarly) nor could
Come pat betwixt too early and too late
85 For any suit of pounds ; and you (O fate !),
A very fresh fish here – fie, fie, fie upon
87 This compelled fortune ! – have your mouth filled up
Before you open it.

ANNE   This is strange to me.

OLD LADY
89 How tastes it ? Is it bitter ? Forty pence, no.
There was a lady once ('tis an old story)
That would not be a queen, that would she not,
92 For all the mud in Egypt ; have you heard it ?

ANNE
Come, you are pleasant.

OLD LADY   With your theme I could
O'ermount the lark. The Marchioness of Pembroke ?
A thousand pounds a year, for pure respect ?
No other obligation ? By my life,
97 That promises moe thousands ! Honor's train
Is longer than his foreskirt. By this time
I know your back will bear a duchess. Say,
Are you not stronger than you were ?

ANNE   Good lady,
Make yourself mirth with your particular fancy 101
And leave me out on 't. Would I had no being
If this salute my blood a jot ! It faints me 103
To think what follows.
The queen is comfortless, and we forgetful
In our long absence. Pray do not deliver 106
What here y' have heard to her.

OLD LADY   What do you think me ?
          Exeunt.

*

Trumpets, sennet, and cornets.   II, iv
*Enter two Vergers, with short silver wands ; next
them, two Scribes, in the habit of doctors ; after
them, the [Arch-]bishop of Canterbury alone ; after
him, the Bishops of Lincoln, Ely, Rochester, and
Saint Asaph ; next them, with some small distance,
follows a Gentleman bearing the purse, with the great
seal and a cardinal's hat ; then two Priests, bearing
each a silver cross ; then [Griffith,] a Gentleman
Usher, bareheaded, accompanied with a Sergeant-
at-arms bearing a silver mace ; then two Gentlemen
bearing two great silver pillars ; after them, side by
side, the two Cardinals, two Noblemen with the
sword and mace. The King takes place under the cloth
of state ; the two Cardinals sit under him as Judges.
The Queen takes place some distance from the King.
The Bishops place themselves on each side the court,
in manner of a consistory ; below them, the Scribes.
The Lords sit next the Bishops. The rest of the
Attendants stand in convenient order about the stage.*

WOLSEY
Whilst our commission from Rome is read,
Let silence be commanded.

KING   What's the need ?
It hath already publicly been read,
And on all sides th' authority allowed.
You may then spare that time.

WOLSEY   Be't so. Proceed.

SCRIBE
Say, 'Henry King of England, come into the court.'

CRIER
Henry King of England, etc.

KING
Here.

SCRIBE
Say, 'Katherine Queen of England, come into the court.'

CRIER
Katherine Queen of England, etc.
    *The Queen makes no answer, rises out of her chair,
    goes about the court, comes to the King, and kneels
    at his feet ; then speaks.*

[KATHERINE]
Sir, I desire you do me right and justice,
And to bestow your pity on me ; for
I am a most poor woman and a stranger, 13
Born out of your dominions : having here
No judge indifferent, nor no more assurance 15
Of equal friendship and proceeding. Alas, sir, 16
In what have I offended you ? What cause
Hath my behavior given to your displeasure
That thus you should proceed to put me off 19
And take your good grace from me ? Heaven witness, 20

I have been to you a true and humble wife,
At all times to your will conformable,
Ever in fear to kindle your dislike,
Yea, subject to your countenance – glad or sorry
As I saw it inclined. When was the hour
I ever contradicted your desire
Or made it not mine too ? Or which of your friends
Have I not strove to love, although I knew
He were mine enemy ? What friend of mine
30 That had to him derived your anger, did I
Continue in my liking ? nay, gave notice
He was from thence discharged ? Sir, call to mind
That I have been your wife in this obedience
Upward of twenty years, and have been blest
With many children by you. If in the course
And process of this time you can report,
And prove it too, against mine honor aught,
My bond to wedlock, or my love and duty
39 Against your sacred person, in God's name
Turn me away, and let the foul'st contempt
Shut door upon me, and so give me up
To the sharp'st kind of justice. Please you, sir,
The king your father was reputed for
A prince most prudent, of an excellent
45 And unmatched wit and judgment. Ferdinand,
46 My father, King of Spain, was reckoned one
The wisest prince that there had reigned by many
A year before. It is not to be questioned
That they had gathered a wise council to them
Of every realm, that did debate this business,
Who deemed our marriage lawful. Wherefore I humbly
Beseech you, sir, to spare me till I may
Be by my friends in Spain advised, whose counsel
I will implore. If not, i' th' name of God,
Your pleasure be fulfilled !
  WOLSEY   You have here, lady
(And of your choice), these reverend fathers, men
Of singular integrity and learning :
Yea, the elect o' th' land, who are assembled
59 To plead your cause. It shall be therefore bootless
60 That longer you desire the court, as well
For your own quiet as to rectify
What is unsettled in the king.
  CAMPEIUS   His grace
Hath spoken well and justly. Therefore, madam,
It's fit this royal session do proceed
And that without delay their arguments
66 Be now produced and heard.
  KATHERINE   Lord cardinal,
To you I speak.
  WOLSEY   Your pleasure, madam.
67 KATHERINE   Sir,
I am about to weep ; but, thinking that
69 We are a queen (or long have dreamed so), certain
The daughter of a king, my drops of tears
I'll turn to sparks of fire.
  WOLSEY   Be patient yet.
  KATHERINE
I will, when you are humble ; nay before,
Or God will punish me. I do believe
74 (Induced by potent circumstances) that
75 You are mine enemy ; and make my challenge
You shall not be my judge. For it is you
77 Have blown this coal betwixt my lord and me –

Which God's dew quench ! Therefore I say again
I utterly abhor, yea, from my soul   79
Refuse you for my judge, whom yet once more
I hold my most malicious foe and think not
At all a friend to truth.
  WOLSEY   I do profess   82
You speak not like yourself, who ever yet
Have stood to charity and displayed th' effects   84
Of disposition gentle, and of wisdom
O'ertopping woman's pow'r. Madam, you do me wrong.
I have no spleen against you, nor injustice   87
For you or any. How far I have proceeded,
Or how far further shall, is warranted
By a commission from the consistory,   90
Yea, the whole consistory of Rome. You charge me
That I have blown this coal : I do deny it.
The king is present. If it be known to him
That I gainsay my deed, how may he wound,   94
And worthily, my falsehood, yea, as much   95
As you have done my truth. If he know
That I am free of your report, he knows   97
I am not of your wrong. Therefore in him   98
It lies to cure me, and the cure is to
Remove these thoughts from you ; the which before
His highness shall speak in, I do beseech   101
You, gracious madam, to unthink your speaking
And to say so no more.
  KATHERINE   My lord, my lord,
I am a simple woman, much too weak
T' oppose your cunning. Y' are meek and humble-
   mouthed ;
You sign your place and calling, in full seeming,   106
With meekness and humility ; but your heart
Is crammed with arrogancy, spleen, and pride.
You have, by fortune and his highness' favors,
Gone slightly o'er low steps, and now are mounted   110
Where pow'rs are your retainers, and your words   111
(Domestics to you) serve your will as't please
Yourself pronounce their office. I must tell you
You tender more your person's honor than   114
Your high profession spiritual ; that again
I do refuse you for my judge and here,
Before you all, appeal unto the pope,
To bring my whole cause 'fore his holiness
And to be judged by him.
    She curtsies to the King and offers to depart.
  CAMPEIUS   The queen is obstinate,
Stubborn to justice, apt to accuse it, and   120
Disdainful to be tried by't. 'Tis not well.
She's going away.
  KING
Call her again.

30 *derived* drawn   39 *Against* towards   45 *one The wit* wisdom   46–47 *one The wisest* the very wisest   59 *bootless* profitless   60 *desire* i.e. to protract the business of   66 *produced* brought forward   67 ff. *Sir . . .* (cf. Hermione in *The Winter's Tale*, III, ii)   69 *certain* certainly   74 *Induced* persuaded   75 *challenge* (legal term) objection to a person, raised during a trial   77 *blown this coal* i.e. stirred up strife   79 *abhor* (legal term) protest against   82 *profess* affirm   84 *stood to* upheld   87 *spleen* strong hatred or anger   90 *consistory* assembly of cardinals   94 *gainsay my deed* deny what I have done   95 *worthily* deservedly   97 *report* (mild) accusation   98 *I . . . wrong* i.e. I have done nothing to injure you   101 *in* in reference to   106 *sign your place* mark your office   110 *slightly* easily   111 *pow'rs* i.e. powerful men   111–13 *words . . . office* i.e. his words are immediately acted upon, as if they were his 'domestics'   114 *tender* hold tenderly, cherish   120 *accuse* find fault with

CRIER
  Katherine Queen of England, come into the court.
GRIFFITH
  Madam, you are called back.
KATHERINE
126 What need you note it? pray you keep your way;
  When you are called, return. Now the Lord help,
  They vex me past my patience. Pray you pass on.
  I will not tarry; no, nor ever more
  Upon this business my appearance make
  In any of their courts. *Exeunt Queen and her Attendants.*
KING   Go thy ways, Kate.
  That man i' th' world who shall report he has
  A better wife, let him in naught be trusted
  For speaking false in that. Thou art alone
135 (If thy rare qualities, sweet gentleness,
  Thy meekness saint-like, wife-like government,
137 Obeying in commanding, and thy parts
138 Sovereign and pious else, could speak thee out)
  The queen of earthly queens. She's noble born,
  And like her true nobility she has
141 Carried herself towards me.
WOLSEY   Most gracious sir,
142 In humblest manner I require your highness
  That it shall please you to declare in hearing
  Of all these ears (for where I am robbed and bound,
  There must I be unloosed, although not there
146 At once and fully satisfied) whether ever I
  Did broach this business to your highness, or
  Laid any scruple in your way which might
149 Induce you to the question on't; or ever
  Have to you, but with thanks to God for such
151 A royal lady, spake one the least word that might
152 Be to the prejudice of her present state
153 Or touch of her good person.
KING   My lord cardinal,
154 I do excuse you; yea, upon mine honor,
  I free you from't. You are not to be taught
  That you have many enemies that know not
  Why they are so, but like to village curs
  Bark when their fellows do. By some of these
  The queen is put in anger. Y' are excused:
  But will you be more justified? you ever
  Have wished the sleeping of this business; never desired
  It to be stirred, but oft have hind'red, oft
163 The passages made toward it. On my honor,
  I speak my good lord card'nal to this point,
  And thus far clear him. Now what moved me to't,

I will be bold with time and your attention:
  Then mark th' inducement. Thus it came; give heed to't: 167
  My conscience first received a tenderness,
  Scruple and prick, on certain speeches uttered
  By th' Bishop of Bayonne, then French ambassador,
  Who had been hither sent on the debating
  A marriage 'twixt the Duke of Orleans and
  Our daughter Mary. I' th' progress of this business,
  Ere a determinate resolution, he   174
  (I mean the bishop) did require a respite,   175
  Wherein he might the king his lord advertise   176
  Whether our daughter were legitimate,
  Respecting this our marriage with the dowager,
  Sometimes our brother's wife. This respite shook   179
  The bosom of my conscience, entered me,   180
  Yea, with a spitting power, and made to tremble   181
  The region of my breast, which forced such way
  That many mazed considerings did throng   183
  And pressed in with this caution. First, methought
  I stood not in the smile of heaven, who had   185
  Commanded nature that my lady's womb,
  If it conceived a male child by me, should
  Do no more offices of life to't than   188
  The grave does to th' dead; for her male issue
  Or died where they were made or shortly after
  This world had aired them. Hence I took a thought
  This was a judgment on me, that my kingdom
  (Well worthy the best heir o' th' world) should not
  Be gladded in't by me. Then follows that
  I weighed the danger which my realms stood in
  By this my issue's fail, and that gave to me   196
  Many a groaning throe. Thus hulling in   197
  The wild sea of my conscience, I did steer
  Toward this remedy whereupon we are
  Now present here together; that's to say
  I mean to rectify my conscience, which   201
  I then did feel full sick, and yet not well,   202
  By all the reverend fathers of the land
  And doctors learned. First I began in private   204
  With you, my Lord of Lincoln. You remember
  How under my oppression I did reek   206
  When I first moved you.   207
LINCOLN   Very well, my liege.
KING
  I have spoke long. Be pleased yourself to say
  How far you satisfied me.
LINCOLN   So please your highness,
  The question did at first so stagger me,
  Bearing a state of mighty moment in't   211
  And consequence of dread, that I committed   212
  The daring'st counsel which I had to doubt
  And did entreat your highness to this course
  Which you are running here.
KING   I then moved you,
  My Lord of Canterbury, and got your leave
  To make this present summons. Unsolicited
  I left no reverend person in this court,
  But by particular consent proceeded
  Under your hands and seals. Therefore go on,   220
  For no dislike i' th' world against the person
  Of the good queen, but the sharp thorny points
  Of my allegèd reasons, drives this forward.   223
  Prove but our marriage lawful, by my life
  And kingly dignity, we are contented

---

126 *keep your way* keep going   135 *rare* excelling   137 *parts* qualities   138 *Sovereign* excellent, supreme; *speak thee out* describe you   141 *Carried herself* behaved   142 *require* request   146 *satisfied* given satisfaction   149 *on't* of it   151 *one the least* the very least   152 *prejudice* detriment   153 *touch* taint, sullying   154 *excuse* i.e. free from imputation   163 *passages* proceedings   163–65 *On . . . him* (the king now addresses the whole court)   167 *inducement* incentive   174 *determinate resolution* final settlement   175 *require* request   176 *advertise* inform   179 *Sometimes* formerly   180 *bosom* i.e. seat (cf. *The Tempest,* II, i, 271–72)   181 *spitting* piercing, and thereby transfixing   183 *mazed* perplexed   185 *smile* favor   188 *offices* functions   196 *issue's fail* lack of issue   197 *throe* pang; *hulling* drifting   201 *rectify* set right   202 *yet* which is still   204 *doctors learned* learned lawyers   206 *oppression* distress; *reek* sweat   207 *moved* appealed to   211 *Bearing . . . moment* concerning a state of affairs of great importance   212 *consequence of dread* fearful outcome   212–13 *committed . . . to doubt* i.e. distrusted . . .   220 *Under your hands* with your written consent   223 *allegèd* put forward (cf. II, i, 13–14)

226 To wear our mortal state to come with her,
Katherine our queen, before the primest creature
228 That's paragoned o' th' world.
CAMPEIUS   So please your highness,
The queen being absent, 'tis a needful fitness
230 That we adjourn this court till further day.
231 Meanwhile must be an earnest motion
Made to the queen to call back her appeal
She intends unto his holiness.
KING [aside]   I may perceive
These cardinals trifle with me. I abhor
This dilatory sloth and tricks of Rome.
My learned and well-belovèd servant Cranmer,
Prithee return. With thy approach I know
My comfort comes along. – Break up the court;
I say set on.   Exeunt, in manner as they entered.

*

III, i   Enter the Queen and her Women, as at work.
KATHERINE
Take thy lute, wench, my soul grows sad with troubles;
2 Sing, and disperse 'em if thou canst: leave working.

Song.

Orpheus with his lute made trees,
And the mountain tops that freeze,
    Bow themselves when he did sing.
To his music plants and flowers
7 Ever sprung, as sun and showers
    There had made a lasting spring.

Every thing that heard him play,
10 Even the billows of the sea,
11   Hung their heads, and then lay by.
In sweet music is such art,
Killing care and grief of heart
    Fall asleep, or hearing die.

Enter a Gentleman.
KATHERINE
How now?
GENTLEMAN
16 An't please your grace, the two great cardinals
17 Wait in the presence.
KATHERINE   Would they speak with me?
GENTLEMAN
18 They willed me say so, madam.
KATHERINE   Pray their graces
To come near.   [Exit Gentleman.]
What can be their business
With me, a poor weak woman, fall'n from favor?
I do not like their coming. Now I think on't,
22 They should be good men, their affairs as righteous;
But all hoods make not monks.
Enter the two Cardinals, Wolsey and Campeius.
WOLSEY   Peace to your highness.
KATHERINE
Your graces find me here part of a housewife
25 (I would be all) against the worst may happen.
What are your pleasures with me, reverend lords?
WOLSEY
May it please you, noble madam, to withdraw
Into your private chamber, we shall give you
The full cause of our coming.

KATHERINE   Speak it here.
There's nothing I have done yet, o' my conscience,
Deserves a corner. Would all other women   31
Could speak this with as free a soul as I do!   32
My lords, I care not (so much I am happy
Above a number) if my actions   34
Were tried by ev'ry tongue, ev'ry eye saw 'em,
Envy and base opinion set against 'em,   36
I know my life so even. If your business   37
Seek me out, and that way I am wife in,   38
Out with it boldly: truth loves open dealing.
WOLSEY Tanta est erga te mentis integritas, regina   40
serenissima –
KATHERINE
O, good my lord, no Latin!
I am not such a truant since my coming   43
As not to know the language I have lived in.
A strange tongue makes my cause more strange, sus-   45
picious.
Pray speak in English. Here are some will thank you,
If you speak truth, for their poor mistress' sake.
Believe me, she has had much wrong. Lord cardinal,
The willing'st sin I ever yet committed   49
May be absolved in English.
WOLSEY   Noble lady,
I am sorry my integrity should breed
(And service to his majesty and you)
So deep suspicion where all faith was meant.   53
We come not by the way of accusation   54
To taint that honor every good tongue blesses,
Nor to betray you any way to sorrow –   56
You have too much, good lady – but to know
How you stand minded in the weighty difference
Between the king and you, and to deliver   59
(Like free and honest men) our just opinions   60
And comforts to your cause.
CAMPEIUS   Most honored madam,
My Lord of York, out of his noble nature,
Zeal and obedience he still bore your grace,   63
Forgetting (like a good man) your late censure
Both of his truth and him (which was too far),   65
Offers, as I do, in a sign of peace,   66
His service and his counsel.
KATHERINE [aside]   To betray me. –
My lords, I thank you both for your good wills,
Ye speak like honest men (pray God ye prove so).
But how to make ye suddenly an answer   70
In such a point of weight, so near mine honor   71
(More near my life, I fear), with my weak wit,   72
And to such men of gravity and learning,

226 *our mortal state* everything that pertains to my being and majesty on earth 228 *paragoned o'* put forward as a model of excellence by 230 *further* a future 231 *motion* appeal
III, i The Queen's apartments 2 *leave* cease 7 *as* as if 10 *sea* (in Shakespeare's time pronounced 'say') 11 *lay by* rested 16 *An't* if it 17 *presence* presence-chamber 18 *willed* desired 22 *affairs* business 25 *against* in preparation for 31 *a corner* i.e. secrecy 32 *free* innocent 34 *a number* many 36 *Envy* malice; *opinion* gossip, rumor 37 *even* constant (in its uprightness) 38 *Seek . . . in* concerns me in my capacity as a wife 40–41 *Tanta . . . serenissima* such is the integrity of mind towards you, O most serene queen 43 *truant* idler 45 *strange . . . strange, suspicious* foreign . . . unfamiliar, and thus suspicious 49 *willing'st* most deliberate 53 *faith* loyalty 54 *by . . . accusation* in order to accuse you 56 *any way* in any manner 59 *deliver* declare 60 *honest* honorable 63 *still* always 65 *was* went 66 *in a sign* as a token 70 *suddenly* extempore 71, 72 *near* intimately affecting 72 *wit* understanding

74 In truth I know not. I was set at work
Among my maids, full little (God knows) looking
Either for such men or such business.
For her sake that I have been – for I feel
The last fit of my greatness – good your graces,
Let me have time and counsel for my cause.
Alas, I am a woman friendless, hopeless.

WOLSEY
Madam, you wrong the king's love with these fears ;
Your hopes and friends are infinite.

KATHERINE   In England
But little for my profit. Can you think, lords,
That any Englishman dare give me counsel ?
Or be a known friend 'gainst his highness' pleasure
86 (Though he be grown so desperate to be honest)
And live a subject ? Nay forsooth, my friends,
88 They that must weigh out my afflictions,
They that my trust must grow to, live not here.
They are (as all my other comforts) far hence
In mine own country, lords.

CAMPEIUS   I would your grace
Would leave your griefs and take my counsel.

KATHERINE   How, sir ?

CAMPEIUS
Put your main cause into the king's protection,
He's loving and most gracious. 'Twill be much
Both for your honor better and your cause ;
For if the trial of the law o'ertake ye,
97 You'll part away disgraced.

WOLSEY   He tells you rightly.

KATHERINE
Ye tell me what ye wish for both – my ruin.
Is this your Christian counsel ? Out upon ye !
Heaven is above all yet ; there sits a judge
That no king can corrupt.

101 CAMPEIUS   Your rage mistakes us.

KATHERINE
The more shame for ye ! Holy men I thought ye,
103 Upon my soul, two reverend cardinal virtues ;
But cardinal sins and hollow hearts I fear ye :
Mend 'em for shame, my lords ! Is this your comfort ?
The cordial that ye bring a wretched lady ?
107 A woman lost among ye, laughed at, scorned ?
I will not wish ye half my miseries,
I have more charity. But say I warned ye.
110 Take heed, for heaven's sake take heed, lest at once
The burthen of my sorrows fall upon ye.

WOLSEY
112 Madam, this is a mere distraction.
113 You turn the good we offer into envy.

KATHERINE
Ye turn me into nothing. Woe upon ye

And all such false professors ! Would you have me   115
(If you have any justice, any pity,
If ye be anything but churchmen's habits)   117
Put my sick cause into his hands that hates me ?
Alas, has banished me his bed already,   119
His love, too long ago. I am old, my lords,
And all the fellowship I hold now with him
Is only my obedience. What can happen
To me above this wretchedness ? All your studies   123
Make me accursed like this.   124

CAMPEIUS   Your fears are worse.

KATHERINE
Have I lived thus long (let me speak myself,
Since virtue finds no friends) a wife, a true one ?
A woman (I dare say without vainglory)
Never yet branded with suspicion ?
Have I with all my full affections   129
Still met the king ? loved him next heav'n ? obeyed him ?   130
Been (out of fondness) superstitious to him ?   131
Almost forgot my prayers to content him ?
And am I thus rewarded ? 'tis not well, lords.
Bring me a constant woman to her husband,   134
One that ne'er dreamed a joy beyond his pleasure,
And to that woman (when she has done most)
Yet will I add an honor – a great patience.

WOLSEY
Madam, you wander from the good we aim at.

KATHERINE
My lord, I dare not make myself so guilty
To give up willingly that noble title   140
Your master wed me to. Nothing but death
Shall e'er divorce my dignities.

WOLSEY   Pray hear me.

KATHERINE
Would I had never trod this English earth
Or felt the flatteries that grow upon it !
Ye have angels' faces, but heaven knows your hearts.
What will become of me now, wretched lady ?
I am the most unhappy woman living.
    [To her Women]
Alas, poor wenches, where are now your fortunes ?
Shipwracked upon a kingdom where no pity,
No friends, no hope, no kindred weep for me,
Almost no grave allowed me. Like the lily
That once was mistress of the field and flourished,
I'll hang my head and perish.

WOLSEY   If your grace
Could but be brought to know our ends are honest,   154
You'ld feel more comfort. Why should we, good lady,
Upon what cause, wrong you ? Alas, our places,   156
The way of our profession is against it.
We are to cure such sorrows, not to sow 'em.
For goodness' sake, consider what you do ;
How you may hurt yourself, ay, utterly
Grow from the king's acquaintance by this carriage.   161
The hearts of princes kiss obedience,
So much they love it ; but to stubborn spirits
They swell and grow as terrible as storms.
I know you have a gentle, noble temper,   165
A soul as even as a calm. Pray think us
Those we profess, peacemakers, friends, and servants.

CAMPEIUS
Madam, you'll find it so. You wrong your virtues
With these weak women's fears. A noble spirit,

---

74 *set* seated   86 *so . . . honest* so reckless as to say what he thinks   88
weigh out measure and share the full extent of (?), assess at their full weight
(?)   97 *part away* leave   101 *mistakes* misjudges   103 *two . . . virtues* i.e.
two personifications or models of the cardinal virtues (with obvious
quibble)   107 *lost* brought to ruin   110 *at once* all at once   112 *mere
distraction* absolute frenzy   113 *envy* malice   115 *professors* those who
profess some strong conviction or faith   117 *habits* robes   119 *has he* has
123 *studies* efforts   124 *accursed* wretched, as if smitten with a curse ;
worse i.e. than your wretchedness   129 *affections* love   130 *Still* always
131 *superstitious* excessively devoted   134 *constant woman to* woman
constant to   154 *honest* honorable   156 *places* offices   161 *Grow from*
become estranged from ; *carriage* conduct   165 *temper* disposition

170 As yours was put into you, ever casts
     Such doubts as false coin from it. The king loves you :
     Beware you lose it not. For us, if you please
     To trust us in your business, we are ready
174 To use our utmost studies in your service.
     KATHERINE
     Do what ye will, my lords ; and pray forgive me ;
176 If I have used myself unmannerly,
177 You know I am a woman, lacking wit
     To make a seemly answer to such persons.
179 Pray do my service to his majesty,
     He has my heart yet, and shall have my prayers
     While I shall have my life. Come, reverend fathers,
     Bestow your counsels on me. She now begs
     That little thought, when she set footing here,
     She should have bought her dignities so dear.   *Exeunt.*

*

III, ii   *Enter the Duke of Norfolk, Duke of Suffolk, Lord*
             Surrey, and Lord Chamberlain.
     NORFOLK
     If you will now unite in your complaints
2   And force them with a constancy, the cardinal
3   Cannot stand under them. If you omit
     The offer of this time, I cannot promise
5   But that you shall sustain moe new disgraces
     With these your bear already.
     SURREY   I am joyful
     To meet the least occasion that may give me
8   Remembrance of my father-in-law, the duke,
     To be revenged on him.
     SUFFOLK   Which of the peers
10   Have uncontemned gone by him, or at least
     Strangely neglected ? When did he regard
     The stamp of nobleness in any person
13   Out of himself ?
     CHAMBERLAIN My lords, you speak your pleasures.
     What he deserves of you and me I know.
     What we can do to him (though now the time
16   Gives way to us) I much fear. If you cannot
17   Bar his access to th' king, never attempt
     Anything on him ; for he hath a witchcraft
     Over the king in's tongue.
     NORFOLK   O fear him not,
20   His spell in that is out. The king hath found
     Matter against him that for ever mars
22   The honey of his language. No, he's settled
23   (Not to come off) in his displeasure.
     SURREY   Sir,
     I should be glad to hear such news as this
     Once every hour.
     NORFOLK   Believe it, this is true.
26   In the divorce his contrary proceedings
27   Are all unfolded ; wherein he appears
     As I would wish mine enemy.
     SURREY   How came
29   His practices to light ?
     SUFFOLK   Most strangely.
     SURREY   O how ? how ?
     SUFFOLK
30   The cardinal's letters to the pope miscarried
     And came to th' eye o' th' king, wherein was read
     How that the cardinal did entreat his holiness

To stay the judgment o' th' divorce ; for if
It did take place, 'I do,' quoth he, 'perceive
My king is tangled in affection to
A creature of the queen's, Lady Anne Bullen.'   36
SURREY
Has the king this ?
SUFFOLK   Believe it.
SURREY   Will this work ?
CHAMBERLAIN
The king in this perceives him, how he coasts   38
And hedges his own way. But in this point   39
All his tricks founder and he brings his physic   40
After his patient's death : the king already
Hath married the fair lady.
SURREY   Would he had !
SUFFOLK
May you be happy in your wish, my lord,
For I profess you have it.   44
SURREY   Now all my joy
Trace the conjunction !   45
SUFFOLK   My amen to't !
NORFOLK   All men's !
SUFFOLK
There's order given for her coronation.
Marry this is yet but young, and may be left   47
To some ears unrecounted. But, my lords,
She is a gallant creature and complete   49
In mind and feature. I persuade me, from her
Will fall some blessing to this land, which shall
In it be memorized.   52
SURREY   But will the king
Digest this letter of the cardinal's ?   53
The Lord forbid !
NORFOLK   Marry amen.
SUFFOLK   No, no ;
There be moe wasps that buzz about his nose
Will make this sting the sooner. Cardinal Campeius
Is stol'n away to Rome, hath ta'en no leave,
Has left the cause o' th' king unhandled, and
Is posted as the agent of our cardinal   59
To second all his plot. I do assure you
The king cried 'Ha' at this.   61
CHAMBERLAIN   Now God incense him
And let him cry 'Ha' louder !
NORFOLK   But, my lord,
When returns Cranmer ?
SUFFOLK
He is returned in his opinions, which   64

170 *As . . . you* i.e. such as that you are endowed with   174 *studies* efforts
176 *used myself* behaved   177 *wit* understanding   179 *do my service* pay
my respects
III, ii The King's apartments   2 *force* press home ; *constancy* persistence
3 *omit* neglect   5 *moe* more   8 *duke* i.e. of Buckingham   10 *uncontemned*
not despised   13 *Out of* except ; *speak your pleasures* say freely what you
will   16 *Gives way to* favors   17–18 *attempt Anything* make any attack
20 *out* finished   22 *he* (probably Wolsey)   23 *come off* escape ; *his* i.e. the
King's   26 *contrary* contradictory (see ll. 32–36)   27 *unfolded* disclosed
29 *practices* intrigues   30 *miscarried* went astray   36 *creature* servant, anyone employed or favored by her   38 *coasts* (the metaphor is carried on in
founder, l. 40)   39 *his own way* i.e. towards his own ends   40 *physic*
medicine   44 *profess* declare   45 *conjunction* marriage, union   47 *Marry*
to be sure (derived from 'by Mary') ; *young* new   49 *gallant* splendid ;
complete perfect   52 *memorized* made memorable   53 *Digest* i.e. put up
with   59 *posted* gone with haste   61 *Ha* (the king's favorite exclamation)
64 *is . . . opinions* has returned with his views confirmed (?), has sent in
advance the opinions he gathered before returning in person (?)

Have satisfied the king for his divorce,
Together with all famous colleges
Almost in Christendom. Shortly, I believe,
His second marriage shall be published and
Her coronation. Katherine no more
Shall be called queen, but princess dowager,
And widow to Prince Arthur.

NORFOLK   This same Cranmer's
A worthy fellow, and hath ta'en much pain
In the king's business.

SUFFOLK   He has, and we shall see him
For it an archbishop.

NORFOLK   So I hear.

SUFFOLK   'Tis so.
    Enter Wolsey and Cromwell.
The cardinal !

NORFOLK   Observe, observe, he's moody.

WOLSEY
The packet, Cromwell,
Gave't you the king ?

CROMWELL   To his own hand, in's bedchamber.

WOLSEY
Looked he o' th' inside of the paper ?

CROMWELL   Presently
He did unseal them, and the first he viewed,
He did it with a serious mind ; a heed
Was in his countenance. You he bade
Attend him here this morning.

WOLSEY   Is he ready
To come abroad ?

CROMWELL   I think by this he is.

WOLSEY
Leave me awhile.   *Exit Cromwell.*
    [*Aside*]
It shall be to the Duchess of Alençon,
The French king's sister ; he shall marry her.
Anne Bullen ? no ! I'll no Anne Bullens for him ;
There's more in't than fair visage. Bullen ?
No, we'll no Bullens ! Speedily I wish
To hear from Rome. The Marchioness of Pembroke ?

NORFOLK
He's discontented.

SUFFOLK   May be he hears the king
Does whet his anger to him.

SURREY   Sharp enough,
Lord, for thy justice !

WOLSEY [*aside*]
The late queen's gentlewoman ? a knight's daughter
To be her mistress' mistress ? the queen's queen ?
This candle burns not clear, 'tis I must snuff it ;
Then out it goes. What though I know her virtuous

And well-deserving ? yet I know her for
A spleeny Lutheran, and not wholesome to
Our cause that she should lie i' th' bosom of
Our hard-ruled king. Again there is sprung up
An heretic, an arch one – Cranmer, one
Hath crawled into the favor of the king
And is his oracle.

NORFOLK   He is vexed at something.
    Enter King, reading of a schedule [, and Lovell].

SURREY
I would 'twere something that would fret the string,
The master-cord on's heart.

SUFFOLK   The king, the king !

KING
What piles of wealth hath he accumulated
To his own portion ! and what expense by th' hour
Seems to flow from him ! How i' th' name of thrift
Does he rake this together ? – Now, my lords,
Saw you the cardinal ?

NORFOLK   My lord, we have
Stood here observing him. Some strange commotion
Is in his brain. He bites his lip, and starts,
Stops on a sudden, looks upon the ground,
Then lays his finger on his temple ; straight
Springs out into fast gait, then stops again,
Strikes his breast hard, and anon he casts
His eye against the moon : in most strange postures
We have seen him set himself.

KING   It may well be,
There is a mutiny in's mind. This morning
Papers of state he sent me to peruse
As I required ; and wot you what I found
There, on my conscience, put unwittingly ?
Forsooth an inventory, thus importing
The several parcels of his plate, his treasure,
Rich stuffs and ornaments of household ; which
I find at such proud rate that it outspeaks
Possession of a subject.

NORFOLK   It's heaven's will ;
Some spirit put this paper in the packet
To bless your eye withal.

KING   If we did think
His contemplation were above the earth
And fixed on spiritual object, he should still
Dwell in his musings ; but I am afraid
His thinkings are below the moon, not worth
His serious considering.
    *King takes his seat ; whispers Lovell, who goes to
    the Cardinal.*

WOLSEY   Heaven forgive me ;
Even God bless your highness !

KING   Good my lord,
You are full of heavenly stuff, and bear the inventory
Of your best graces in your mind ; the which
You were now running o'er. You have scarce time
To steal from spiritual leisure a brief span
To keep your earthly audit ; sure in that
I deem you an ill husband, and am glad
To have you therein my companion.

WOLSEY   Sir,
For holy offices I have a time ; a time
To think upon the part of business which
I bear i' th' state ; and nature does require
Her times of preservation, which perforce

68 *published* proclaimed   72 *pain* pains   78 *paper* wrapper with contents
inside ; *Presently* immediately   99 *spleeny* passionate ; *wholesome* suitable,
beneficial   100 *lie . . . bosom of* (1) marry, (2) share the secrets of   101
hard-ruled managed with difficulty   102 *arch one* chief   103 *Hath* who
has   104 *oracle* i.e. trusted adviser   s.d. *schedule* scroll of paper   105 *fret*
corrode (with play on the 'fret' of a stringed instrument, a bar to regulate
fingering)   106 *master-cord* (not merely a metaphor ; the Elizabethan
believed in heart-strings) ; *on's* of his   108 *portion* allotted share   112
commotion rebellion, perturbation   122 *wot* know   124 *importing* signifying   125 *several parcels* various items   127 *rate* value   127–28 *outspeaks . . . subject* describes more than what is fitting for a subject to possess
130 *withal* therewith   134 *below the moon* worldly   137 *stuff* (cf. l. 126)
140 *spiritual leisure* i.e. time devoted to religious duties   142 *ill husband*
bad manager

I, her frail son, amongst my brethren mortal,
149 Must give my tendance to.
    KING   You have said well.
    WOLSEY
And ever may your highness yoke together
(As I will lend you cause) my doing well
With my well saying!
    KING   'Tis well said again,
And 'tis a kind of good deed to say well;
And yet words are no deeds. My father loved you;
155 He said he did, and with his deed did crown
His word upon you. Since I had my office,
I have kept you next my heart; have not alone
Employed you where high profits might come home,
159 But pared my present havings to bestow
My bounties upon you.
    WOLSEY [aside]   What should this mean?
    SURREY [aside]
The Lord increase this business!
    KING   Have I not made you
162 The prime man of the state? I pray you tell me
163 If what I now pronounce you have found true;
164 And if you may confess it, say withal
If you are bound to us or no. What say you?
    WOLSEY
My sovereign, I confess your royal graces,
Showered on me daily, have been more than could
168 My studied purposes requite, which went
Beyond all man's endeavors. My endeavors
Have ever come too short of my desires,
171 Yet filled with my abilities. Mine own ends
172 Have been mine so, that evermore they pointed
To th' good of your most sacred person and
The profit of the state. For your great graces
Heaped upon me (poor undeserver) I
Can nothing render but allegiant thanks,
My prayers to heaven for you, my loyalty,
Which ever has and ever shall be growing,
Till death (that winter) kill it.
    KING   Fairly answered:
A loyal and obedient subject is
181 Therein illustrated. The honor of it
Does pay the act of it, as i' th' contrary
183 The foulness is the punishment. I presume
184 That, as my hand has opened bounty to you,
My heart dropped love, my pow'r rained honor, more
On you than any, so your hand and heart,
Your brain and every function of your power
188 Should, notwithstanding that your bond of duty,
189 As 'twere in love's particular, be more
To me, your friend, than any.
    WOLSEY   I do profess
That for your highness' good I ever labored
192 More than mine own; that am, have, and will be –
Though all the world should crack their duty to you
And throw it from their soul; though perils did
Abound as thick as thought could make 'em and
Appear in forms more horrid – yet my duty,
197 As doth a rock against the chiding flood,
Should the approach of this wild river break,
And stand unshaken yours.
    KING   'Tis nobly spoken.
Take notice, lords, he has a loyal breast,
For you have seen him open't. Read o'er this,

[Gives him papers.]
And after, this, and then to breakfast with
What appetite you have.
                  Exit King frowning upon the Cardinal.
                     The Nobles throng after him,
                          smiling and whispering.
    WOLSEY   What should this mean?
What sudden anger's this? How have I reaped it?
He parted frowning from me, as if ruin
Leaped from his eyes. So looks the chafèd lion   206
Upon the daring huntsman that has galled him;   207
Then makes him nothing. I must read this paper;   208
I fear, the story of his anger. 'Tis so;
This paper has undone me. 'Tis th' accompt
Of all that world of wealth I have drawn together
For mine own ends – indeed to gain the popedom
And fee my friends in Rome. O negligence
Fit for a fool to fall by! What cross devil   214
Made me put this main secret in the packet   215
I sent the king? Is there no way to cure this?
No new device to beat this from his brains?
I know 'twill stir him strongly; yet I know
A way, if it take right, in spite of fortune,   219
Will bring me off again. What's this? 'To th' pope'?   220
The letter (as I live) with all the business
I writ to 's holiness. Nay then, farewell!   222
I have touched the highest point of all my greatness,
And from that full meridian of my glory   224
I haste now to my setting. I shall fall
Like a bright exhalation in the evening,   226
And no man see me more.
              Enter to Wolsey the Dukes of Norfolk and Suffolk,
              the Earl of Surrey, and the Lord Chamberlain.
    NORFOLK
Hear the king's pleasure, cardinal, who commands you
To render up the great seal presently   229
Into our hands and to confine yourself
To Asher House, my Lord of Winchester's,
Till you hear further from his highness.
    WOLSEY   Stay:
Where's your commission, lords? Words cannot carry
Authority so weighty.
    SUFFOLK   Who dare cross 'em,   234
Bearing the king's will from his mouth expressly?
    WOLSEY
Till I find more than will or words to do it   236
(I mean your malice) know, officious lords,
I dare and must deny it. Now I feel
Of what coarse metal ye are moulded – envy;   239
How eagerly ye follow my disgraces
As if it fed ye, and how sleek and wanton   241

149 *tendance* attention   155 *crown* perfect, complete nobly   159 *havings* possessions   162 *prime* principal   163 *pronounce* declare   164 *withal* also, in addition   168 *studied purposes* efforts   171 *filled with* fulfilled to the best of; *ends* aims   172 *so* in such a way   181–82 *The honor . . . it* the honor of being loyal is the reward of loyalty   183 *foulness* moral impurity   184 *opened* generously made available   188 *that . . . duty* i.e. his commitment to the pope   189 *particular* special intimacy   192 *have* have been   197 *chiding* noisily scolding   206 *chafèd* angry, raging   207 *galled* wounded   208 *makes him nothing* annihilates him   214 *cross* thwarting   215 *main* chief, very important   219 *take right* succeed   220 *bring me off* rescue me, acquit me   222 *writ* wrote   224 *meridian* prime, splendor, point of highest altitude of a star   226 *exhalation* meteor   229 *presently* at once   234 *cross* oppose   236 *do it* i.e. render up the seal   239 *envy* malice   241 *wanton* reckless and willful

Ye appear in everything may bring my ruin!
Follow your envious courses, men of malice.
244 You have Christian warrant for 'em, and no doubt
245 In time will find their fit rewards. That seal
You ask with such a violence, the king
(Mine and your master) with his own hand gave me;
248 Bade me enjoy it, with the place and honors,
During my life; and to confirm his goodness
250 Ties it by letters patents. Now who'll take it?

SURREY
The king that gave it.

WOLSEY   It must be himself then.

SURREY
Thou art a proud traitor, priest.

WOLSEY   Proud lord, thou liest!
253 Within these forty hours Surrey durst better
Have burnt that tongue than said so.

SURREY   Thy ambition
255 (Thou scarlet sin) robbed this bewailing land
Of noble Buckingham, my father-in-law.
The heads of all thy brother cardinals
258 (With thee and all thy best parts bound together)
259 Weighed not a hair of his. Plague of your policy!
You sent me Deputy for Ireland,
Far from his succor, from the king, from all
262 That might have mercy on the fault thou gav'st him;
Whilst your great goodness, out of holy pity,
Absolved him with an axe.

WOLSEY   This, and all else
265 This talking lord can lay upon my credit,
I answer is most false. The duke by law
Found his deserts. How innocent I was
268 From any private malice in his end,
His noble jury and foul cause can witness.
If I loved many words, lord, I should tell you
You have as little honesty as honor,
272 That in the way of loyalty and truth
Toward the king, my ever royal master,
274 Dare mate a sounder man than Surrey can be
And all that love his follies.

SURREY   By my soul,
Your long coat, priest, protects you; thou shouldst feel
My sword i' th' lifeblood of thee else. My lords,
Can ye endure to hear this arrogance?
279 And from this fellow? If we live thus tamely,
280 To be thus jaded by a piece of scarlet,

Farewell nobility! let his grace go forward
And dare us with his cap, like larks.   282

WOLSEY   All goodness
Is poison to thy stomach.

SURREY   Yes, that goodness
Of gleaning all the land's wealth into one,
Into your own hands, cardinal, by extortion;
The goodness of your intercepted packets
You writ to th' pope against the king. Your goodness,
Since you provoke me, shall be most notorious.
My Lord of Norfolk, as you are truly noble,
As you respect the common good, the state
Of our despised nobility, our issues   291
(Who, if he live, will scarce be gentlemen),
Produce the grand sum of his sins, the articles   293
Collected from his life. I'll startle you
Worse than the sacring bell when the brown wench   295
Lay kissing in your arms, lord cardinal.

WOLSEY
How much, methinks, I could despise this man
But that I am bound in charity against it.

NORFOLK
Those articles, my lord, are in the king's hand;
But thus much – they are foul ones.   300

WOLSEY   So much fairer
And spotless shall mine innocence arise
When the king knows my truth.

SURREY   This cannot save you.
I thank my memory, I yet remember
Some of these articles, and out they shall!
Now if you can blush and cry guilty, cardinal
You'll show a little honesty.

WOLSEY   Speak on, sir,
I dare your worst objections. If I blush,   307
It is to see a nobleman want manners.

SURREY
I had rather want those than my head. Have at you!   309
First, that without the king's assent or knowledge
You wrought to be a legate, by which power   311
You maimed the jurisdiction of all bishops.

NORFOLK
Then, that all you writ to Rome, or else
To foreign princes, 'Ego et Rex meus'   314
Was still inscribed; in which you brought the king   315
To be your servant.   316

SUFFOLK   Then, that without the knowledge
Either of king or council, when you went
Ambassador to the emperor, you made bold   318
To carry into Flanders the great seal.

SURREY
Item, you sent a large commission
To Gregory de Cassado to conclude,
Without the king's will or the state's allowance,   322
A league between his highness and Ferrara.

SUFFOLK
That out of mere ambition you have caused   324
Your holy hat to be stamped on the king's coin.   325

SURREY
Then, that you have sent innumerable substance   326
(By what means got, I leave to your own conscience)
To furnish Rome and to prepare the ways   328
You have for dignities, to the mere undoing   329
Of all the kingdom. Many more there are,
Which, since they are of you, and odious,

244 *Christian warrant* (ironical) 245 *find* meet with 248 *place and honors* i.e. of the office of Lord Chancellor 250 *letters patents* open documents conferring certain rights (from French, '*lettres patentes*') 253 *forty* (used as a round number) 255 *scarlet* (alluding both to Isaiah i, 18 and to the cardinal's robes) 258 *parts* qualities 259 *Weighed not* was not worth; *Plague of* plague upon 262 *fault* offense 265 *credit* good name 268 *From of* 272 *That . . . way of* I that in 274 *mate* match 279 *fellow* (gross insult, for the term was usually used towards servants) 280 *jaded* cowed 282 *dare* dazzle (and thus render helpless; alludes to the method of catching larks with the help of a mirror and a red cloth) 291 *issues* sons 293 *articles* counts of indictment 295 *sacring* consecrating 300 *thus much* i.e. I can say this much 307 *objections* accusations 309 *Have at you* (a phrase announcing the attack) 311 *legate* pope's official representative 314 *Ego . . . meus* I and my king 315 *still* always 316 *servant* (a mistaken idea, not original in this play; the Latin phrase suggests equality) 318 *emperor* i.e. Charles V 322 *allowance* permission 324 *mere* sheer 325 *Your . . . coin* (Wolsey had the right to coin half-groats, but not groats, with his initials and the cardinal's hat upon them) 326 *innumerable substance* countless wealth 328 *furnish* supply 329 *mere undoing* complete ruin

I will not taint my mouth with.
CHAMBERLAIN   O my lord,
Press not a falling man too far ! 'Tis virtue.
His faults lie open to the laws ; let them,
Not you, correct him. My heart weeps to see him
So little of his great self.
SURREY   I forgive him.
SUFFOLK
Lord cardinal, the king's further pleasure is –
Because all those things you have done of late
339 By your power legative within this kingdom
340 Fall into th' compass of a praemunire –
341 That therefore such a writ be sued against you,
To forfeit all your goods, lands, tenements,
Chattels, and whatsoever, and to be
344 Out of the king's protection. This is my charge.
NORFOLK
And so we'll leave you to your meditations
How to live better. For your stubborn answer
About the giving back the great seal to us,
The king shall know it, and (no doubt) shall thank you.
349 So fare you well, my little good lord cardinal.
                          Exeunt all but Wolsey.
WOLSEY
So farewell to the little good you bear me.
351 Farewell ? a long farewell to all my greatness !
This is the state of man : to-day he puts forth
The tender leaves of hopes ; to-morrow blossoms
354 And bears his blushing honors thick upon him ;
The third day comes a frost, a killing frost,
356 And when he thinks, good easy man, full surely
His greatness is a-ripening, nips his root,
And then he falls as I do. I have ventured,
Like little wanton boys that swim on bladders,
This many summers in a sea of glory,
But far beyond my depth. My high-blown pride
At length broke under me, and now has left me,
Weary and old with service, to the mercy
364 Of a rude stream that must for ever hide me.
365 Vain pomp and glory of this world, I hate ye !
I feel my heart new opened. O, how wretched
Is that poor man that hangs on princes' favors !
There is betwixt that smile we would aspire to,
369 That sweet aspect of princes, and their ruin,
More pangs and fears than wars or women have ;
And when he falls, he falls like Lucifer,
Never to hope again.
                          Enter Cromwell, standing amazed.
                          Why how now, Cromwell ?
CROMWELL
I have no power to speak, sir.
WOLSEY   What, amazed
At my misfortunes ? Can thy spirit wonder
375 A great man should decline ? Nay, an you weep,
I am fall'n indeed.
CROMWELL   How does your grace ?
WOLSEY   Why well ;
Never so truly happy, my good Cromwell.
I know myself now, and I feel within me
A peace above all earthly dignities,
A still and quiet conscience. The king has cured me –
I humbly thank his grace – and from these shoulders,
These ruined pillars, out of pity taken
A load would sink a navy – too much honor.

O 'tis a burden, Cromwell, 'tis a burden
Too heavy for a man that hopes for heaven.
CROMWELL
I am glad your grace has made that right use of it.
WOLSEY
I hope I have. I am able now, methinks,
Out of a fortitude of soul I feel,
To endure more miseries and greater far
Than my weak-hearted enemies dare offer.
What news abroad ?
CROMWELL   The heaviest and the worst
Is your displeasure with the king.   392
WOLSEY   God bless him !
CROMWELL
The next is that Sir Thomas More is chosen
Lord Chancellor in your place.
WOLSEY   That's somewhat sudden.
But he's a learnèd man. May he continue
Long in his highness' favor, and do justice
For truth's sake and his conscience ; that his bones,
When he has run his course and sleeps in blessings,
May have a tomb of orphans' tears wept on him.   399
What more ?
CROMWELL   That Cranmer is returned with welcome ;
Installed Lord Archbishop of Canterbury.
WOLSEY
That's news indeed.
CROMWELL   Last, that the Lady Anne,
Whom the king hath in secrecy long married,
This day was viewed in open as his queen,
Going to chapel ; and the voice is now   405
Only about her coronation.
WOLSEY
There was the weight that pulled me down. O Cromwell,
The king has gone beyond me : all my glories   408
In that one woman I have lost for ever.
No sun shall ever usher forth mine honors
Or gild again the noble troops that waited   411
Upon my smiles. Go get thee from me, Cromwell !
I am a poor fall'n man, unworthy now
To be thy lord and master. Seek the king
(That sun, I pray, may never set). I have told him
What and how true thou art. He will advance thee :
Some little memory of me will stir him
(I know his noble nature) not to let
Thy hopeful service perish too. Good Cromwell,
Neglect him not ; make use now, and provide   420
For thine own future safety.
CROMWELL   O my lord,
Must I then leave you ? Must I needs forgo
So good, so noble, and so true a master ?
Bear witness, all that have not hearts of iron,

339 *legative* as a legate   340 *praemunire* a writ by which a person could be summoned on a charge of asserting papal jurisdiction in England   341 *sued* applied for   344 *Out . . . protection* i.e. without legal protection   349 *little good* little-good (?)   351 *Farewell?* (so in the folio ; Wolsey suddenly realizes the appropriateness of the word to his whole career ; but editors often replace the query mark by a comma)   354 *blushing* glowing   356 *easy* easygoing   364 *rude* rough   365 *Vain . . . world* (an intentional allusion to the Anglican baptismal service)   369 *their ruin* the ruin they cause   375 *decline* fall from prosperity ; *an if*   392 *your . . . king* the king's displeasure towards you   399 *tomb . . . him* (for the Lord Chancellor is the general guardian, or legal protector, of children)   405 *voice* general talk   408 *gone beyond* overreached   411 *troops* retainers   420 *make use* take advantage

With what a sorrow Cromwell leaves his lord.
The king shall have my service, but my pray'rs
For ever and for ever shall be yours.

WOLSEY
Cromwell, I did not think to shed a tear
In all my miseries; but thou hast forced me
430 (Out of thy honest truth) to play the woman.
Let's dry our eyes: and thus far hear me, Cromwell,
And when I am forgotten, as I shall be,
And sleep in dull cold marble, where no mention
Of me more must be heard of, say I taught thee;
Say, Wolsey, that once trod the ways of glory
436 And sounded all the depths and shoals of honor,
Found thee a way (out of his wrack) to rise in,
A sure and safe one, though thy master missed it.
Mark but my fall and that that ruined me.
Cromwell, I charge thee, fling away ambition!
By that sin fell the angels; how can man then
442 (The image of his Maker) hope to win by it?
443 Love thyself last, cherish those hearts that hate thee;
Corruption wins not more than honesty.
445 Still in thy right hand carry gentle peace
446 To silence envious tongues. Be just, and fear not.
Let all the ends thou aim'st at be thy country's,
448 Thy God's and truth's: then if thou fall'st, O Cromwell,
Thou fall'st a blessèd martyr.
Serve the king. And prithee lead me in:
There take an inventory of all I have
To the last penny: 'tis the king's. My robe,
And my integrity to heaven, is all
I dare now call mine own. O Cromwell, Cromwell,
Had I but served my God with half the zeal
I served my king, he would not in mine age
457 Have left me naked to mine enemies.

CROMWELL
Good sir, have patience.

WOLSEY   So I have. Farewell
The hopes of court; my hopes in heaven do dwell.

                                         Exeunt.

                    *

IV, i   *Enter two Gentlemen, meeting one another.*

1. GENTLEMAN
Y' are well met once again.

2. GENTLEMAN   So are you.

1. GENTLEMAN
You come to take your stand here, and behold
The Lady Anne pass from her coronation?

2. GENTLEMAN
'Tis all my business. At our last encounter

The Duke of Buckingham came from his trial.

1. GENTLEMAN
'Tis very true; but that time offered sorrow,
This, general joy.

2. GENTLEMAN   'Tis well. The citizens
I am sure have shown at full their royal minds –   8
As let 'em have their rights, they are ever forward –   9
In celebration of this day with shows,
Pageants, and sights of honor.

1. GENTLEMAN   Never greater,
Nor, I'll assure you, better taken, sir.   12

2. GENTLEMAN
May I be bold to ask what that contains,
That paper in your hand?

1. GENTLEMAN   Yes, 'tis the list
Of those that claim their offices this day,
By custom of the coronation.
The Duke of Suffolk is the first, and claims
To be high steward; next, the Duke of Norfolk,
He to be earl marshal. You may read the rest.

2. GENTLEMAN
I thank you, sir. Had I not known those customs,
I should have been beholding to your paper.   21
But, I beseech you, what's become of Katherine,
The princess dowager? how goes her business?

1. GENTLEMAN
That I can tell you too. The Archbishop
Of Canterbury, accompanied with other
Learnèd and reverend fathers of his order,
Held a late court at Dunstable, six miles off   27
From Ampthill, where the princess lay, to which   28
She was often cited by them, but appeared not;   29
And to be short, for not-appearance and
The king's late scruple, by the main assent   31
Of all these learnèd men she was divorced
And the late marriage made of none effect;   33
Since which she was removed to Kimbolton,   34
Where she remains now sick.

2. GENTLEMAN   Alas good lady.
                    [*Trumpets.*]
The trumpets sound. Stand close, the queen is coming.   36
Hautboys.

                    THE ORDER OF THE CORONATION

1. A lively flourish of trumpets.
2. Then two Judges.
3. Lord Chancellor, with purse and mace before him.
4. Choristers singing. Music.
5. Mayor of London, bearing the mace. Then Garter, in his coat of arms, and on his head he wore a gilt copper crown.
6. Marquess Dorset, bearing a sceptre of gold, on his head a demi-coronal of gold. With him the Earl of Surrey, bearing the rod of silver with the dove, crowned with an earl's coronet. Collars of Esses.
7. Duke of Suffolk, in his robe of estate, his coronet on his head, bearing a long white wand, as high steward. With him the Duke of Norfolk, with the rod of marshalship, a coronet on his head. Collars of Esses.
8. A canopy borne by four of the Cinque-Ports; under it the Queen in her robe; in her hair, richly adorned with pearl, crowned. On each side her the Bishops of London and Winchester.

---

430 *play the woman* shed tears **436** *sounded* fathomed **442** *win* profit
443 *Love . . . thee* (a paraphrase of Matthew v, 44) **445** *Still* constantly
446 *envious* malicious **448–49** *if . . . martyr* (a prediction of Cromwell's
fate) **457** *naked* i.e. defenseless
IV, i A street in Westminster **8** *royal minds* devotion to royalty **9** *As
. . . rights* give them their due ('As' merely introduces the parenthesis);
forward eager **12** *taken* received **21** *beholding* indebted **27** *late* recent
28 *lay* resided **29** *cited* summoned **31** *late* former; *main assent* general
agreement **33** *of none effect* null **34** *Kimbolton* (in Huntingdonshire; the
'b' is not pronounced) **36** *close* out of sight **s.d. item 3** *Lord Chancellor*
i.e. Sir Thomas More **item 5** *Garter* the chief herald, Garter King-at-
Arms **item 6** *demi-coronal* small crown-like circlet **items 6, 7** *Collars of
Esses* ornamental chains made of a series of joined letters 'S' **item 7** *estate*
state **item 8** *Cinque-Ports* barons of the five Channel ports of Hastings,
Sandwich, Dover, Romney, and Hythe; *in her hair* with her hair loosely
hanging (as customary for brides)

9. *The old Duchess of Norfolk, in a coronal of gold,*
   wrought with flowers, bearing the Queen's train.
10. *Certain ladies or countesses, with plain circlets of*
   gold without flowers.

Exeunt, first passing over the stage
in order and state, and then a
great flourish of trumpets.

2. GENTLEMAN

37 A royal train, believe me. These I know.
Who's that that bears the sceptre?

1. GENTLEMAN   Marquess Dorset,
And that the Earl of Surrey with the rod.

2. GENTLEMAN
A bold brave gentleman. That should be
The Duke of Suffolk.

1. GENTLEMAN   'Tis the same: high steward.

2. GENTLEMAN
And that my Lord of Norfolk?

1. GENTLEMAN   Yes.

2. GENTLEMAN *[looks on the Queen]* Heaven bless thee,
Thou hast the sweetest face I ever looked on.
Sir, as I have a soul, she is an angel;
45 Our king has all the Indies in his arms,
46 And more, and richer, when he strains that lady.
I cannot blame his conscience.

1. GENTLEMAN   They that bear
48 The cloth of honor over her are four barons
Of the Cinque-Ports.

2. GENTLEMAN
50 Those men are happy, and so are all are near her.
51 I take it, she that carries up the train
Is that old noble lady, Duchess of Norfolk.

1. GENTLEMAN
It is, and all the rest are countesses.

2. GENTLEMAN
54 Their coronets say so. These are stars indeed –

1. GENTLEMAN
55 And sometimes falling ones.

2. GENTLEMAN   No more of that.
           [Exit procession.]

Enter a third Gentleman.

1. GENTLEMAN
God save you, sir. Where have you been broiling?

3. GENTLEMAN
57 Among the crowd i' th' Abbey, where a finger
Could not be wedged in more. I am stifled
59 With the mere rankness of their joy.

2. GENTLEMAN   You saw
The ceremony?

3. GENTLEMAN   That I did.

1. GENTLEMAN   How was it?

3. GENTLEMAN
Well worth the seeing.

61 2. GENTLEMAN   Good sir, speak it to us.

3. GENTLEMAN
As well as I am able. The rich stream
Of lords and ladies, having brought the queen
64 To a prepared place in the choir, fell off
A distance from her; while her grace sat down
To rest awhile, some half an hour or so,
67 In a rich chair of state, opposing freely
The beauty of her person to the people.
69 Believe me, sir, she is the goodliest woman

That ever lay by man; which when the people
Had the full view of, such a noise arose
As the shrouds make at sea in a stiff tempest,   72
As loud, and to as many tunes. Hats, cloaks
(Doublets, I think) flew up; and had their faces
Been loose, this day they had been lost. Such joy
I never saw before. Great-bellied women
That had not half a week to go, like rams   77
In the old time of war, would shake the press   78
And make 'em reel before 'em. No man living
Could say 'This is my wife' there, all were woven
So strangely in one piece.   81

2. GENTLEMAN   But what followed?

3. GENTLEMAN
At length her grace rose and with modest paces   82
Came to the altar, where she kneeled, and saint-like
Cast her fair eyes to heaven and prayed devoutly;
Then rose again and bowed her to the people;
When by the Archbishop of Canterbury
She had all the royal makings of a queen,   87
As holy oil, Edward Confessor's crown,   88
The rod, and bird of peace, and all such emblems
Laid nobly on her; which performed, the choir
With all the choicest music of the kingdom   91
Together sung 'Te Deum.' So she parted,   92
And with the same full state packed back again   93
To York Place, where the feast is held.

1. GENTLEMAN   Sir,
You must no more call it York Place. That's past;
For since the cardinal fell that title 's lost;
'Tis now the king's, and called Whitehall.

3. GENTLEMAN   I know it;
But 'tis so lately altered that the old name
Is fresh about me.

2. GENTLEMAN   What two reverend bishops
Were those that went on each side of the queen?

3. GENTLEMAN
Stokesly and Gardiner; the one of Winchester,
Newly preferred from the king's secretary;   102
The other, London.

2. GENTLEMAN   He of Winchester
Is held no great good lover of the archbishop's,
The virtuous Cranmer.

3. GENTLEMAN   All the land knows that.
However, yet there is no great breach. When it comes,
Cranmer will find a friend will not shrink from him.

2. GENTLEMAN
Who may that be, I pray you?

3. GENTLEMAN   Thomas Cromwell,
A man in much esteem with th' king, and truly
A worthy friend. The king has made him
Master o' th' Jewel House,   111
And one, already, of the Privy Council.

---

37 *train* retinue   45 *Indies* i.e. abundant riches (both East and West
Indies were sources of wealth)   46 *strains* embraces   48 *cloth of honor*
canopy   50 *all* all who   51 *carries . . . train* bears the robes   54 *stars* (a
common image for nobles)   55 *falling* (with sexual quibble)   57 *Abbey*
Westminster Abbey   59 *mere rankness* sheer exuberance   61 *speak* describe   64 *fell off* withdrew   67 *opposing* exposing   69 *goodliest* most
attractive   72 *shrouds* sail-ropes   77 *rams* battering-rams   78 *press* crowd
81 *piece* i.e. of cloth   82 *modest* moderate (and therefore decorous)   87
makings i.e. ceremonial tokens and symbolic attributes   88 *As* namely
91 *music* musicians   92 *parted* departed   93 *state* pomp   102 *Newly . . .
secretary* (cf. II, ii, 114)   111 *Master . . . Jewel House* keeper of the crown
jewels, the king's silver, etc.

2 . GENTLEMAN
  He will deserve more.
3 . GENTLEMAN   Yes, without all doubt.
  Come, gentlemen, ye shall go my way,
  Which is to th' court, and there ye shall be my guests.
116   Something I can command. As I walk thither,
  I'll yell ye more.
BOTH   You may command us, sir.   *Exeunt.*

*

IV, ii   *Enter Katherine Dowager, sick ; led between Griffith,*
         her gentleman usher, and Patience, her woman.
GRIFFITH
  How does your grace ?
KATHERINE   O Griffith, sick to death.
  My legs like loaden branches bow to th' earth,
  Willing to leave their burden. Reach a chair.
  So now, methinks, I feel a little ease.
  Didst thou not tell me, Griffith, as thou led'st me,
6   That the great child of honor, Cardinal Wolsey,
7   Was dead ?
GRIFFITH   Yes, madam ; but I think your grace,
  Out of the pain you suffered, gave no ear to't.
KATHERINE
  Prithee, good Griffith, tell me how he died.
10   If well, he stepped before me happily
  For my example.
11 GRIFFITH   Well, the voice goes, madam ;
  For after the stout Earl Northumberland
  Arrested him at York and brought him forward
14   As a man sorely tainted, to his answer,
  He fell sick suddenly, and grew so ill
  He could not sit his mule.
KATHERINE   Alas, poor man.
GRIFFITH
17   At last, with easy roads, he came to Leicester,
  Lodged in the abbey ; where the reverend abbot
19   With all his covent honorably received him ;
  To whom he gave these words : 'O father abbot,
  An old man, broken with the storms of state,
  Is come to lay his weary bones among ye :
  Give him a little earth for charity !'
  So went to bed, where eagerly his sickness
  Pursued him still ; and three nights after this,

116 *Something . . . command* i.e. the cupboard is not bare
IV, ii Katherine's apartments (at Kimbolton) 6 *child* youth of noble birth (a chivalric title ; here applied though Wolsey was not of noble birth) 7 *dead* (actually Wolsey died five years before Katherine) 10 *happily* haply, perhaps (?), fortunately (?) 11 *voice* common talk 14 *sorely tainted* severely discredited ; *to his answer* to answer the charges against him 17 *roads* stages of a journey 19 *covent* convent 28 *sorrows* sighs, expressions of sorrow 30 *blessèd part* soul 32 *speak* describe 34 *stomach* ambition 35 *suggestion* evil seduction (?), underhand practice (?) (Holinshed's term is 'craftie suggestion') 36 *Tied* fettered, enslaved ; *Simony* trafficking in ecclesiastical preferments 37 *presence* presence-chamber 38 *double* deceitfully ambiguous 39 *meaning* i.e. matter, content (mere words, the ornaments of style, are contrasted with substance or matter) 43 *ill* depraved 45–46 *Men's . . . water* i.e. men's vices are remembered, their virtues forgotten 50–51 *From . . . one* (Wolsey was reputed to have been extraordinarily learned as a child) 53 *Lofty* haughty 58 *raised* built 59 *Ipswich and Oxford* (Wolsey founded a college at Ipswich, his birthplace, and also Christ Church College, Oxford) 60 *good* good man ; *did* created 62 *art* learning ; *rising* (as a structure and in influence) 65 *felt himself* knew himself (cf. III, ii, 377–80) 70 *living* while alive 74 *religious* scrupulous ; *modesty* moderation 78 *note* melody 80 *celestial harmony* the music of the spheres (believed to be too rarefied for mortal ears)

  After the hour of eight, which he himself
  Foretold should be his last, full of repentance,
  Continual meditations, tears and sorrows,   28
  He gave his honors to the world again,
  His blessèd part to heaven, and slept in peace.   30
KATHERINE
  So may he rest, his faults lie gently on him !
  Yet thus far, Griffith, give me leave to speak him,   32
  And yet with charity. He was a man
  Of an unbounded stomach, ever ranking   34
  Himself with princes ; one that by suggestion   35
  Tied all the kingdom. Simony was fair play ;   36
  His own opinion was his law. I' th' presence   37
  He would say untruths, and be ever double   38
  Both in his words and meaning. He was never   39
  (But where he meant to ruin) pitiful.
  His promises were, as he then was, mighty ;
  But his performance, as he is now, nothing.
  Of his own body he was ill, and gave   43
  The clergy ill example.
GRIFFITH   Noble madam,
  Men's evil manners live in brass ; their virtues   45
  We write in water. May it please your highness
  To hear me speak his good now ?
KATHERINE   Yes, good Griffith,
  I were malicious else.
GRIFFITH   This cardinal,
  Though from an humble stock, undoubtedly
  Was fashioned to much honor. From his cradle   50
  He was a scholar, and a ripe and good one,
  Exceeding wise, fair-spoken, and persuading ;
  Lofty and sour to them that loved him not,   53
  But to those men that sought him, sweet as summer.
  And though he were unsatisfied in getting
  (Which was a sin), yet in bestowing, madam,
  He was most princely. Ever witness for him
  Those twins of learning that he raised in you,   58
  Ipswich and Oxford ; one of which fell with him,   59
  Unwilling to outlive the good that did it ;   60
  The other, though unfinished, yet so famous,
  So excellent in art, and still so rising,   62
  That Christendom shall ever speak his virtue.
  His overthrow heaped happiness upon him ;
  For then, and not till then, he felt himself,   65
  And found the blessedness of being little.
  And, to add greater honors to his age
  Than man could give him, he died fearing God.
KATHERINE
  After my death I wish no other herald,
  No other speaker of my living actions   70
  To keep mine honor from corruption,
  But such an honest chronicler as Griffith.
  Whom I most hated living, thou hast made me,
  With thy religious truth and modesty,   74
  Now, in his ashes, honor : peace be with him !
  Patience, be near me still, and set me lower ;
  I have not long to trouble thee. Good Griffith,
  Cause the musicians play me that sad note   78
  I named my knell, whilst I sit meditating
  On that celestial harmony I go to.   80
        Sad and solemn music.
GRIFFITH
  She is asleep. Good wench, let's sit down quiet
  For fear we wake her. Softly, gentle Patience.

82

THE VISION

Enter, solemnly tripping one after another, six
personages clad in white robes, wearing on their heads
garlands of bays, and golden vizards on their faces,
branches of bays or palm in their hands. They first
congee unto her, then dance ; and, at certain changes,
the first two hold a spare garland over her head ; at
which the other four make reverent curtsies. Then the
two that held the garland deliver the same to the other
next two, who observe the same order in their changes,
and holding the garland over her head ; which done,
they deliver the same garland to the last two, who
likewise observe the same order ; at which (as it were
by inspiration) she makes (in her sleep) signs of
rejoicing and holdeth up her hands to heaven. And so
in their dancing vanish, carrying the garland with
them. The music continues.

KATHERINE
Spirit of peace, where are ye ? Are ye all gone
And leave me here in wretchedness behind ye ?

GRIFFITH
Madam, we are here.

KATHERINE   It is not you I call for.
Saw ye none enter since I slept ?

GRIFFITH   None, madam.

KATHERINE
No ? Saw you not even now a blessed troop
Invite me to a banquet, whose bright faces
Cast thousand beams upon me like the sun ?
They promised me eternal happiness
And brought me garlands, Griffith, which I feel
I am not worthy yet to wear ; I shall assuredly.

GRIFFITH
I am most joyful, madam, such good dreams
94   Possess your fancy.

KATHERINE   Bid the music leave.
95   They are harsh and heavy to me.
Music ceases.

PATIENCE   Do you note
How much her grace is altered on the sudden ?
How long her face is drawn ? how pale she looks,
98   And of an earthly cold ? Mark her eyes !

GRIFFITH
She is going, wench. Pray, pray !

PATIENCE   Heaven comfort her !
Enter a Messenger.

MESSENGER
An't like your grace –

KATHERINE   You are a saucy fellow ;
Deserve we no more reverence ?

GRIFFITH   You are to blame,
102   Knowing she will not lose her wonted greatness,
To use so rude behavior. Go to, kneel !

MESSENGER
I humbly do entreat your highness' pardon ;
105   My haste made me unmannerly. There is staying
A gentleman sent from the king, to see you.

KATHERINE
107   Admit him entrance, Griffith. But this fellow
Let me ne'er see again.   *[Exit Messenger].*
Enter Lord Capuchius.
       If my sight fail not,
You should be lord ambassador from the emperor,
My royal nephew, and your name Capuchius.

CAPUCHIUS
Madam, the same – your servant.

KATHERINE   O my lord,
The times and titles now are altered strangely
With me since first you knew me. But I pray you,
What is your pleasure with me ?

CAPUCHIUS   Noble lady,
First mine own service to your grace ; the next,
The king's request that I would visit you,
Who grieves much for your weakness, and by me
Sends you his princely commendations,   118
And heartily entreats you take good comfort.

KATHERINE
O my good lord, that comfort comes too late,
'Tis like a pardon after execution.
That gentle physic, given in time, had cured me ;
But now I am past all comforts here but prayers.
How does his highness ?

CAPUCHIUS   Madam, in good health.

KATHERINE
So may he ever do, and ever flourish,
When I shall dwell with worms, and my poor name
Banished the kingdom. Patience, is that letter
I caused you write yet sent away ?

PATIENCE   No madam.
[Gives it to Katherine.]

KATHERINE
Sir, I most humbly pray you to deliver
This to my lord the king.

CAPUCHIUS   Most willing, madam.   130

KATHERINE
In which I have commended to his goodness
The model of our chaste loves, his young daughter –   132
The dews of heaven fall thick in blessings on her ! –
Beseeching him to give her virtuous breeding –   134
She is young and of a noble modest nature ;
I hope she will deserve well – and a little
To love her for her mother's sake, that loved him,
Heaven knows how dearly. My next poor petition
Is that his noble grace would have some pity
Upon my wretched women, that so long
Have followed both my fortunes faithfully ;   141
Of which there is not one, I dare avow
(And now I should not lie), but will deserve   143
For virtue and true beauty of the soul,
For honesty and decent carriage,   145
A right good husband : let him be a noble ;
And sure those men are happy that shall have 'em.
The last is for my men – they are the poorest
(But poverty could never draw 'em from me) –
That they may have their wages duly paid 'em,
And something over to remember me by.
If heaven had pleased to have given me longer life
And able means, we had not parted thus.   153

---

82 s.d. *white robes* (symbolic of purity) ; *bays* bay leaves (in token of joy or
triumph) ; *golden vizards* (to indicate spirits ?) ; *congee* bow ; *changes* figures
in the dance   **94** *Possess* occupy ; *music* musicians ; *leave* cease playing   **95**
heavy oppressive   **98** *cold* coldness (a sign of death ; often emended to
'color')   **102** *lose* forgo   **105** *staying* waiting   **107** *Admit* allow   **118**
commendations compliments   **130** *willing* willingly   **132** *model* image, symbol   **134** *virtuous breeding* a good education   **141** *both my fortunes* my good
and bad fortunes   **143** *now . . . lie* (it was believed that people close to death
spoke truth)   **145** *honesty* integrity ; *decent carriage* proper demeanor
153 *able* sufficient, generously adequate

These are the whole contents ; and, good my lord,
By that you love the dearest in this world,
As you wish Christian peace to souls departed,
157 Stand these poor people's friend, and urge the king
To do me this last right.
CAPUCHIUS   By heaven I will,
159 Or let me lose the fashion of a man !
KATHERINE
160 I thank you, honest lord. Remember me
In all humility unto his highness.
Say his long trouble now is passing
Out of this world. Tell him in death I blessed him,
For so I will. Mine eyes grow dim. Farewell,
My lord. Griffith, farewell. Nay, Patience,
You must not leave me yet. I must to bed ;
Call in more women. When I am dead, good wench,
Let me be used with honor. Strew me over
169 With maiden flowers, that all the world may know
I was a chaste wife to my grave. Embalm me,
171 Then lay me forth. Although unqueened, yet like
A queen, and daughter to a king, inter me.
173 I can no more.   *Exeunt, leading Katherine.*

*

V, i   *Enter Gardiner, Bishop of Winchester, a Page with
a torch before him, met by Sir Thomas Lovell.*
GARDINER
It's one o'clock, boy is't not ?
BOY   It hath struck.
GARDINER
These should be hours for necessities,
3 Not for delights ; times to repair our nature
With comforting repose, and not for us
To waste these times. Good hour of night, Sir Thomas :
Whither so late ?
LOVELL   Came you from the king, my lord ?
GARDINER
7 I did, Sir Thomas, and left him at primero
With the Duke of Suffolk.
LOVELL   I must to him too
Before he go to bed. I'll take my leave.
GARDINER
Not yet, Sir Thomas Lovell. What's the matter ?
11 It seems you are in haste. An if there be
No great offense belongs to't, give your friend
13 Some touch of your late business. Affairs that walk
(As they say spirits do) at midnight have
In them a wilder nature than the business
That seeks dispatch by day.
LOVELL   My lord, I love you,

157 *Stand* be   159 *fashion* nature (literally, shape)   160 *honest* good
169 *maiden flowers* (befitting chastity ; cf. *Hamlet*, V, i, 220)   171 *lay
me forth* lay me out for burial   173 *I . . . more* i.e. I am too weak to say
more
V, i The royal palace   3 *repair* restore   7 *primero* a gambling card game
fashionable at court   11 *An if* if truly   13 *touch* hint ; *walk* (this term suggests the spirits of the following line)   17 *commend* entrust   18 *this work* i.e.
what I am about   19 *feared* i.e. it is feared that   22 *Good time* good fortune
23 *grubbed up* rooted out   24 *Cry the amen* assent   28 *way* i.e. religious
thinking (they are both anti-protestant)   33 *remarked* noted   34–35
Master . . . Rolls judge of the court of appeal   36 *gap and trade* opening and
beaten path   37 *time* course of events   43 *Incensed* set on, roused (or perhaps 'insensed,' i.e. informed)   45 *most* extreme   46 *moved* aroused   47
broken with revealed their views to   49 *fell* terrible   50 *hath* that he has
52 *convented* summoned   55 *rest* remain   62 *deliver* make known

And durst commend a secret to your ear   17
Much weightier than this work. The queen 's in labor,   18
They say in great extremity, and feared   19
She'll with the labor end.
GARDINER   The fruit she goes with
I pray for heartily, that it may find
Good time, and live ; but for the stock, Sir Thomas,   22
I wish it grubbed up now.   23
LOVELL   Methinks I could
Cry the amen, and yet my conscience says   24
She's a good creature and sweet lady, does
Deserve our better wishes.
GARDINER   But, sir, sir,
Hear me, Sir Thomas ! Y' are a gentleman
Of mine own way. I know you wise, religious ;   28
And let me tell you it will ne'er be well –
'Twill not, Sir Thomas Lovell, take't of me –
Till Cranmer, Cromwell, her two hands, and she
Sleep in their graves.
LOVELL   Now, sir, you speak of two
The most remarked i' th' kingdom. As for Cromwell,   33
Beside that of the Jewel House, is made Master   34
O' th' Rolls and the king's secretary ; further, sir,
Stands in the gap and trade of moe preferments,   36
With which the time will load him. Th' archbishop   37
Is the king's hand and tongue, and who dare speak
One syllable against him ?
GARDINER   Yes, yes, Sir Thomas,
There are that dare, and I myself have ventured
To speak my mind of him ; and indeed this day,
Sir (I may tell it you), I think I have
Incensed the lords o' th' council that he is   43
(For so I know he is, they know he is)
A most arch-heretic, a pestilence   45
That does infect the land ; with which they moved   46
Have broken with the king, who hath so far   47
Given ear to our complaint – of his great grace
And princely care, foreseeing those fell mischiefs   49
Our reasons laid before him – hath commanded   50
To-morrow morning to the council board
He be convented. He's a rank weed, Sir Thomas,   52
And we must root him out. From your affairs
I hinder you too long, good night, Sir Thomas.
LOVELL
Many good nights, my lord ; I rest your servant.   55
                    Exeunt Gardiner and Page.
          Enter King and Suffolk.
KING
Charles, I will play no more to-night,
My mind 's not on 't, you are too hard for me.
SUFFOLK
Sir, I did never win of you before.
KING
But little, Charles,
Nor shall not when my fancy 's on my play.
Now, Lovell, from the queen what is the news ?
LOVELL
I could not personally deliver to her   62
What you commanded me, but by her woman
I sent your message, who returned her thanks
In the great'st humbleness, and desired your highness
Most heartily to pray for her.
KING   What say'st thou ? Ha ?
To pray for her ? what, is she crying out ?

LOVELL
68 So said her woman, and that her suff'rance made
Almost each pang a death:
KING   Alas good lady.
SUFFOLK
70 God safely quit her of her burden, and
71 With gentle travail, to the gladding of
Your highness with an heir.
KING   'Tis midnight, Charles.
Prithee to bed, and in thy pray'rs remember
74 Th' estate of my poor queen. Leave me alone,
For I must think of that which company
Would not be friendly to.
SUFFOLK   I wish your highness
A quiet night, and my good mistress will
Remember in my prayers.
KING   Charles, good night.
                       Exit Suffolk.
Enter Sir Anthony Denny.
Well, sir, what follows?
DENNY
Sir, I have brought my lord the archbishop
As you commanded me.
KING   Ha? Canterbury?
DENNY
Ay, my good lord.
KING   'Tis true: where is he, Denny?
DENNY
He attends your highness' pleasure.
KING   Bring him to us.
                       Exit Denny.
LOVELL *[aside]*
This is about that which the bishop spake.
85 I am happily come hither.
     Enter Cranmer and Denny.
KING
86 Avoid the gallery.
     [Lovell seems to stay.] Ha! I have said. Be gone.
What!   *Exeunt Lovell and Denny.*
CRANMER *[aside]*
87   I am fearful. Wherefore frowns he thus?
88 'Tis his aspect of terror. All's not well.
KING
How now, my lord? You do desire to know
Wherefore I sent for you?
CRANMER *[kneels]*   It is my duty
T' attend your highness' pleasure.
KING   Pray you arise,
My good and gracious Lord of Canterbury.
Come, you and I must walk a turn together;
I have news to tell you. Come, come give me your hand.
Ah, my good lord, I grieve at what I speak
And am right sorry to repeat what follows.
I have, and most unwillingly, of late
Heard many grievous – I do say, my lord,
Grievous complaints of you; which being considered,
100 Have moved us and our council, that you shall
This morning come before us; where I know
102 You cannot with such freedom purge yourself
But that, till further trial in those charges
104 Which will require your answer, you must take
Your patience to you, and be well contented
106 To make your house our Tower. You, a brother of us,
107 It fits we thus proceed, or else no witness

Would come against you.
CRANMER *[kneels]*   I humbly thank your highness,
And am right glad to catch this good occasion
Most throughly to be winnowed, where my chaff   110
And corn shall fly asunder. For I know
There's none stands under more calumnious tongues   112
Than I myself, poor man.
KING   Stand up, good Canterbury,
Thy truth and thy integrity is rooted
In us, thy friend. Give me thy hand, stand up;
     [Cranmer rises.]
Prithee let's walk. Now by my holidame,   116
What manner of man are you? My lord, I looked   117
You would have given me your petition, that
I should have ta'en some pains to bring together
Yourself and your accusers, and to have heard you
Without indurance further.   121
CRANMER   Most dread liege,
The good I stand on is my truth and honesty: 122
If they shall fail, I with mine enemies
Will triumph o'er my person, which I weigh not,   124
Being of those virtues vacant. I fear nothing   125
What can be said against me.
KING   Know you not
How your state stands i' th' world, with the whole world?
Your enemies are many and not small; their practices   128
Must bear the same proportion, and not ever   129
The justice and the truth o' th' question carries   130
The due o' th' verdict with it. At what ease   131
Might corrupt minds procure knaves as corrupt
To swear against you! such things have been done.
You are potently opposed, and with a malice
Of as great size. Ween you of better luck,   135
I mean in perjured witness, than your Master,   136
Whose minister you are, whiles here he lived
Upon this naughty earth? Go to, go to,   138
You take a precipice for no leap of danger,
And woo your own destruction.
CRANMER   God and your majesty
Protect mine innocence, or I fall into
The trap is laid for me!
KING   Be of good cheer,
They shall no more prevail than we give way to.   143
Keep comfort to you, and this morning see
You do appear before them. If they shall chance
In charging you with matters to commit you,   146
The best persuasions to the contrary
Fail not to use, and with what vehemency
Th' occasion shall instruct you. If entreaties
Will render you no remedy, this ring

68 *suff'rance* suffering   70 *quit* release   71 *gladding* making happy   74 *estate* state, condition   85 *happily* by good fortune   86 *Avoid* leave; *gallery* (not necessarily the upper stage; this word is taken over from Foxe's *Acts and Monuments*)   87 *fearful* afraid   88 *aspect* expression   100 *moved* prompted   102 *freedom* ease (and therefore completeness); *purge* clear of guilt   104–05 *take . . . you* (cf. the same phrase in *The Winter's Tale*, III, ii, 229)   106 *You . . . us* i.e. you, being a fellow councillor   107 *fits* is fitting   110 *throughly* thoroughly   112 *stands under* is subject to   116 *by my holidame* i.e. by our Lady   117 *looked* expected   121 *indurance further* further hardship   122 *good* virtue   124 *weigh not* do not value   125 *vacant* devoid (of); *nothing* not at all   128 *practices* intrigues, plots   129 *bear . . . proportion* be correspondingly great; *ever* always   130 *question* cause   130–31 *carries . . . it* make for the fitting verdict   131 *At what ease* how easily   135 *Ween you of* do you imagine   136 *witness* evidence   138 *naughty* wicked   143 *give way to* give them scope   146 *commit* i.e. to the prison of the Tower

Deliver them, and your appeal to us
There make before them. Look, the good man weeps:
He's honest on mine honor! God's blest mother,
I swear he is true-hearted, and a soul
None better in my kingdom. Get you gone
And do as I have bid you.   *[Exit Cranmer.]*
               He has strangled
His language in his tears.
         Enter Old Lady.
GENTLEMAN *[within]*   Come back: what mean you?
OLD LADY
I'll not come back. The tidings that I bring
Will make my boldness manners. Now good angels
160   Fly o'er thy royal head and shade thy person
Under their blessed wings!
KING   Now by thy looks
I guess thy message. Is the queen delivered?
Say ay, and of a boy.
OLD LADY   Ay, ay, my liege,
And of a lovely boy. The God of heaven
Both now and ever bless her: 'tis a girl
Promises boys hereafter. Sir, your queen
167   Desires your visitation, and to be
Acquainted with this stranger. 'Tis as like you
As cherry is to cherry.
KING   Lovell!
       [Enter Lovell.]
LOVELL   Sir?
KING
170   Give her an hundred marks. I'll to the queen. *Exit King.*
OLD LADY
An hundred marks? By this light, I'll ha' more!
An ordinary groom is for such payment.
I will have more or scold it out of him.
Said I for this the girl was like to him?
I'll have more or else unsay't; and now, while 'tis hot,
176   I'll put it to the issue.   *Exit Lady [with Lovell].*

             *

V, ii   *Enter Cranmer, Archbishop of Canterbury*
       [; Pursuivants, Pages, and Footboys at the door].
CRANMER
I hope I am not too late, and yet the gentleman
That was sent to me from the council prayed me
3   To make great haste. All fast? What means this? Ho!
Who waits there? Sure you know me?
       Enter Keeper.
KEEPER   Yes, my lord.
But yet I cannot help you.
CRANMER
Why?

KEEPER
Your grace must wait till you be called for.
       Enter Doctor Butts.
CRANMER   So.
BUTTS *[aside]*
This is a piece of malice. I am glad
I came this way so happily. The king   9
Shall understand it presently.   *Exit.* 10
CRANMER   'Tis Butts,
The king's physician. As he passed along,
How earnestly he cast his eyes upon me:
Pray heaven he sound not my disgrace; for certain   13
This is of purpose laid by some that hate me   14
(God turn their hearts, I never sought their malice)
To quench mine honor. They would shame to make me
Wait else at door, a fellow councillor,
'Mong boys, grooms, and lackeys. But their pleasures
Must be fulfilled, and I attend with patience.   19
       Enter the King and Butts at a window above.
BUTTS
I'll show your grace the strangest sight –
KING   What's that, Butts?
BUTTS
I think your highness saw this many a day.
KING
Body a me; where is it?   22
BUTTS   There, my lord:
The high promotion of his grace of Canterbury,
Who holds his state at door 'mongst pursuivants,   24
Pages, and footboys.
KING   Ha? 'Tis he indeed.
Is this the honor they do one another?
'Tis well there's one above 'em yet. I had thought   27
They had parted so much honesty among 'em –   28
At least good manners – as not thus to suffer
A man of his place and so near our favor   30
To dance attendance on their lordships' pleasures,
And at the door too, like a post with packets.   32
By holy Mary, Butts, there's knavery!
Let 'em alone, and draw the curtain close: 34
We shall hear more anon.
       A council table brought in with chairs and stools, and   V, iii
       placed under the state. Enter Lord Chancellor, places
       himself at the upper end of the table on the left hand,
       a seat being left void above him, as for Canterbury's
       seat. Duke of Suffolk, Duke of Norfolk, Surrey,
       Lord Chamberlain, Gardiner seat themselves in order
       on each side. Cromwell at lower end, as secretary.
CHANCELLOR
Speak to the business, master secretary;
Why are we met in council?
CROMWELL   Please your honors,
The chief cause concerns his grace of Canterbury.
GARDINER
Has he had knowledge of it?   4
CROMWELL   Yes.
NORFOLK   Who waits there?
KEEPER
Without, my noble lords?   5
GARDINER   Yes.
KEEPER   My lord archbishop,
And has done half an hour to know your pleasures.
CHANCELLOR
Let him come in.

---

167 *visitation* visit   **170** *an hundred marks* about £65 (by no means a small gift)   **176** *put...issue* bring it to a head
V, ii Outside the council chamber   s.d. *Pursuivants* junior officers; *at the door* i.e. outside the door of the council chamber (but of course just inside one of the main 'doors' of the stage)   **3** *fast* shut   **9** *happily* fortunately   **10** *presently* at once   **13** *sound* make known   **14** *laid* prepared as a trap   **19** s.d. *above* (note use of upper stage; perhaps the only time in this play)   **22** *Body a me* (a mild oath; *a*: of)   **24** *holds his state* maintains his dignity   **27** *one above* God (?), Henry (?), both (?)   **28** *parted* shared; *honesty* honorable conduct, decency   **30** *place* office, rank   **32** *post* courier; *packets* mail   **34** *curtain* i.e. the upper-stage curtain (after l. 35 the action returns to the main stage)
V, iii The council chamber   s.d. *state* chair of state   **4** *had knowledge* been informed   **5** *Without* outside

KEEPER   Your grace may enter now.
Cranmer approaches the council table.

CHANCELLOR
My good lord archbishop, I'm very sorry
9   To sit here at this present and behold
That chair stand empty; but we all are men
11   In our own natures frail, and capable
Of our flesh; few are angels; out of which frailty
And want of wisdom, you, that best should teach us,
Have misdemeaned yourself, and not a little:
Toward the king first, then his laws, in filling
The whole realm by your teaching and your chaplains'
(For so we are informed) with new opinions,
18   Divers and dangerous; which are heresies,
19   And not reformed, may prove pernicious.

GARDINER
Which reformation must be sudden too,
My noble lords; for those that tame wild horses
Pace 'em not in their hands to make 'em gentle,
23   But stop their mouths with stubborn bits and spur 'em
24   Till they obey the manage. If we suffer,
25   Out of our easiness and childish pity
To one man's honor, this contagious sickness,
Farewell all physic! And what follows then?
28   Commotions, uproars, with a general taint
Of the whole state, as of late days our neighbors,
30   The upper Germany, can dearly witness,
Yet freshly pitied in our memories.

CRANMER
My good lords, hitherto, in all the progress
Both of my life and office, I have labored,
34   And with no little study, that my teaching
And the strong course of my authority
Might go one way, and safely; and the end
Was ever to do well; nor is there living
38   (I speak it with a single heart, my lords)
39   A man that more detests, more stirs against,
40   Both in his private conscience and his place,
41   Defacers of a public peace than I do.
Pray heaven the king may never find a heart
With less allegiance in it! Men that make
Envy and crookèd malice nourishment
Dare bite the best. I do beseech your lordships
That in this case of justice, my accusers,
47   Be what they will, may stand forth face to face
48   And freely urge against me.

SUFFOLK   Nay, my lord,
That cannot be. You are a councillor,
50   And by that virtue no man dare accuse you.

GARDINER
51   My lord, because we have business of more moment,
We will be short with you. 'Tis his highness' pleasure
And our consent, for better trial of you,
From hence you be committed to the Tower
Where, being but a private man again,
You shall know many dare accuse you boldly,
More than, I fear, you are provided for.

CRANMER
Ah, my good Lord of Winchester, I thank you;
You are always my good friend; if your will pass,
I shall both find your lordship judge and juror,
You are so merciful. I see your end –
62   'Tis my undoing. Love and meekness, lord,
Become a churchman better than ambition;

Win straying souls with modesty again,   64
Cast none away. That I shall clear myself,
Lay all the weight ye can upon my patience,   66
I make as little doubt as you do conscience   67
In doing daily wrongs. I could say more,
But reverence to your calling makes me modest.

GARDINER
My lord, my lord, you are a sectary,   70
That's the plain truth. Your painted gloss discovers,   71
To men that understand you, words and weakness.   72

CROMWELL
My lord of Winchester, y' are a little,
By your good favor, too sharp. Men so noble,
However faulty, yet should find respect   75
For what they have been: 'tis a cruelty
To load a falling man.

GARDINER   Good master secretary,
I cry your honor mercy. You may worst   78
Of all this table say so.

CROMWELL   Why, my lord?

GARDINER
Do not I know you for a favorer
Of this new sect? Ye are not sound.   81

CROMWELL   Not sound?

GARDINER
Not sound, I say.

CROMWELL   Would you were half so honest!
Men's prayers then would seek you, not their fears.

GARDINER
I shall remember this bold language.

CROMWELL   Do.
Remember your bold life too.

CHANCELLOR   That is too much;
Forbear for shame, my lords.

GARDINER   I have done.

CROMWELL   And I.

CHANCELLOR
Then thus for you, my lord: it stands agreed,
I take it, by all voices, that forthwith   88
You be conveyed to th' Tower a prisoner,   89
There to remain till the king's further pleasure
Be known unto us. Are you all agreed, lords?

ALL
We are.

CRANMER   Is there no other way of mercy
But I must needs to th' Tower, my lords?

GARDINER   What other
Would you expect? You are strangely troublesome: 94
Let some o' th' guard be ready there!
Enter the Guard.

CRANMER   For me?
Must I go like a traitor thither?

---

9 *present* very time   11–12 *capable . . . flesh* prone to the weaknesses of the flesh   18 *Divers* various, perverse (?)   19 *pernicious* disastrous   23 *stubborn* hard   24 *manage* handling   25 *easiness* indulgence   28 *taint* corruption   30 *upper* i.e. interior   34 *study* effort   38 *single* single-minded (cf. 'singleness of heart,' Acts ii, 46)   39 *stirs* is active   40 *place* office   41 *Defacers* destroyers   47 *Be . . . will* whoever they are   48 *urge* press their case   50 *by that virtue* by virtue of that   51 *moment* importance   62 *undoing* ruin   64 *modesty* moderation   66 *Lay . . . weight* put all the pressure   67 *do conscience* have scruples   70 *sectary* follower of an heretical sect   71 *painted gloss* specious language and behavior; *discovers* reveals   72 *words* mere words   75 *find* meet with   78 *cry . . . mercy* beg your honor's pardon; *worst* with least cause   81 *sound* loyal   88 *voices* votes   89 *conveyed* escorted   94 *strangely* extraordinarily

96 GARDINER   Receive him
And see him safe i' th' Tower.
CRANMER   Stay, good my lords,
I have a little yet so say. Look there, my lords.
By virtue of that ring I take my cause
100 Out of the gripes of cruel men and give it
To a most noble judge, the king my master.
CHAMBERLAIN
This is the king's ring.
SURREY   'Tis no counterfeit.
SUFFOLK
'Tis the right ring, by heav'n! I told ye all,
104 When we first put this dangerous stone a-rolling,
'Twould fall upon ourselves.
NORFOLK   Do you think, my lords,
The king will suffer but the little finger
Of this man to be vexed?
CHAMBERLAIN   'Tis now too certain,
108 How much more is his life in value with him.
Would I were fairly out on't!
109 CROMWELL   My mind gave me,
110 In seeking tales and informations
Against this man, whose honesty the devil
And his disciples only envy at,
113 Ye blew the fire that burns ye: now have at ye!
Enter King, frowning on them; takes his seat.
GARDINER
Dread sovereign, how much are we bound to heaven
In daily thanks, that gave us such a prince,
Not only good and wise but most religious;
One that in all obedience makes the church
The chief aim of his honor, and to strengthen
119 That holy duty out of dear respect,
His royal self in judgment comes to hear
The cause betwixt her and this great offender.
KING
122 You were ever good at sudden commendations,
Bishop of Winchester. But know I come not
To hear such flattery now, and in my presence
They are too thin and base to hide offenses;
To me you cannot reach. You play the spaniel,
And think with wagging of your tongue to win me.
But whatsoe'er thou tak'st me for, I'm sure
Thou hast a cruel nature and a bloody.
[To Cranmer]
Good man, sit down. Now let me see the proudest
131 He, that dares most, but wag his finger at thee:
132 By all that's holy, he had better starve
Than but once think his place becomes thee not.
SURREY
May it please your grace –

KING   No, sir, it does not please me.
I had thought I had had men of some understanding
And wisdom of my council; but I find none.
Was it discretion, lords, to let this man,
This good man (few of you deserve that title),
This honest man, wait like a lousy footboy
At chamber door? and one as great as you are?
Why, what a shame was this? Did my commission   141
Bid ye so far forget yourselves? I gave ye
Power as he was a councillor to try him,
Not as a groom. There's some of ye, I see,
More out of malice than integrity,
Would try him to the utmost, had ye mean,   146
Which ye shall never have while I live.
CHANCELLOR   Thus far,
My most dread sovereign, may it like your grace   148
To let my tongue excuse all. What was purposed
Concerning his imprisonment was rather
(If there be faith in men) meant for his trial
And fair purgation to the world than malice,   152
I'm sure, in me.
KING   Well, well, my lords, respect him.
Take him, and use him well; he's worthy of it.
I will say thus much for him: if a prince
May be beholding to a subject, I   156
Am for his love and service so to him.
Make me no more ado, but all embrace him.
Be friends for shame, my lords. My Lord of Canterbury,
I have a suit which you must not deny me;
That is, a fair young maid that yet wants baptism,
You must be godfather and answer for her.
CRANMER
The greatest monarch now alive may glory
In such an honor: how may I deserve it
That am a poor and humble subject to you?
KING Come, come, my lord, you'ld spare your spoons! 166
you shall have two noble partners with you, the old 167
Duchess of Norfolk and Lady Marquess Dorset. Will
these please you?
Once more, my Lord of Winchester, I charge you
Embrace and love this man.
GARDINER   With a true heart
And brother-love I do it.   172
CRANMER   And let heaven
Witness how dear I hold this confirmation
KING
Good man, those joyful tears show thy true heart.
The common voice I see is verified   175
Of thee, which says thus: 'Do my Lord of Canterbury
A shrewd turn, and he's your friend for ever.'   177
Come, lords, we trifle time away: I long
To have this young one made a Christian.
As I have made ye one, lords, one remain;
So I grow stronger, you more honor gain.   *Exeunt.*

*

Noise and tumult within. Enter Porter and his Man. V, iv
PORTER You'll leave your noise anon, ye rascals! Do you
take the court for Parish Garden? Ye rude slaves, leave 2
your gaping! 3
[ONE] *within* Good master porter, I belong to th' larder. 4
PORTER Belong to th' gallows and be hanged, ye rogue!
Is this a place to roar in? Fetch me a dozen crabtree

96 *Receive* take   100 *gripes* clutches   104–05 *stone . . . ourselves* (cf. Proverbs xxvi, 27)   108 *in value with* esteemed by   109 *My . . . me* I had a misgiving   110 *tales and informations* malicious and incriminating hearsay   113 *have at ye* prepare   119 *dear* heartfelt, zealous   122 *sudden commendations* impromptu compliments   131 *He* man, he-man   132 *starve* die   141 *shame* infliction of dishonor   146 *try* (1) put on trial, (2) afflict; *mean* means   148 *like* please   152 *purgation* clearing of himself (a law term)   156 *beholding* indebted   166 *spare your spoons* i.e. wish to be that niggardly (a gently mocking comment, alluding to the custom of giving christening or apostle spoons to god-children)   167 *partners* i.e. godparents   172 *brother-love* brotherly love   175 *voice* judgment   177 *shrewd* malicious, bad
V, iv The palace court   2 *Parish Garden* Paris Garden (great centre of bear- and bull-baiting in London)   3 *gaping* shouting, bawling   4 *belong to* i.e. am employed in

7 staves, and strong ones; these are but switches to 'em:
I'll scratch your heads. You must be seeing christenings?
9 Do you look for ale and cakes here, you rude rascals?

MAN

Pray, sir, be patient; 'tis as much impossible,
Unless we sweep 'em from the door with cannons,
To scatter 'em as 'tis to make 'em sleep
13 On May-day morning, which will never be.
14 We may as well push against Paul's as stir 'em.

PORTER How got they in, and be hanged?

MAN

Alas I know not, how gets the tide in?
As much as one sound cudgel of four foot
(You see the poor remainder) could distribute,
I made no spare, sir.

PORTER   You did nothing, sir.

MAN

20 I am not Samson, nor Sir Guy, nor Colebrand,
To mow 'em down before me; but if I spared any
That had a head to hit, either young or old,
He or she, cuckold or cuckold-maker,
24 Let me ne'er hope to see a chine again;
25 And that I would not for a cow, God save her.

[ONE] *within* Do you hear, master porter?

PORTER I shall be with you presently, good master puppy;
keep the door close, sirrah.

MAN What would you have me do?

PORTER What should you do but knock 'em down by th'
31 dozens? Is this Moorfields to muster in? Or have we
32 some strange Indian with the great tool come to court,
33 the women so besiege us? Bless me, what a fry of fornication is at door! On my Christian conscience this one
christening will beget a thousand; here will be father,
godfather, and all together.

37 MAN The spoons will be the bigger, sir. There is a fellow
38 somewhat near the door, he should be a brazier by his
39 face, for o' my conscience twenty of the dog-days now
reign in's nose. All that stand about him are under the
41 line; they need no other penance. That fire-drake did I
hit three times on the head, and three times was his nose
43 discharged against me; he stands there like a mortar-
44 piece to blow us. There was a haberdasher's wife of small
45 wit near him, that railed upon me till her pinked porringer fell off her head, for kindling such a combustion in the
47 state. I missed the meteor once and hit that woman, who
48 cried out 'Clubs,' when I might see from far some forty
49 truncheoners draw to her succor, which were the hope
50 o' th' Strond, where she was quartered. They fell on, I
51 made good my place. At length they came to th' broom-
staff to me, I defied 'em still; when suddenly a file of
53 boys behind 'em, loose shot, delivered such a shower of
54 pebbles that I was fain to draw mine honor in and let
55 'em win the work. The devil was amongst 'em I think
surely.

PORTER These are the youths that thunder at a playhouse
58 and fight for bitten apples; that no audience but the tri-
59 bulation of Tower Hill or the limbs of Limehouse, their
dear brothers, are able to endure. I have some of 'em in
61 Limbo Patrum, and there they are like to dance these
62 three days, besides the running banquet of two beadles
that is to come.

Enter Lord Chamberlain.

CHAMBERLAIN

Mercy o' me, what a multitude are here!

They grow still too; from all parts they are coming
As if we kept a fair here. Where are these porters,
65 These lazy knaves? Y' have made a fine hand, fellows!
66 There's a trim rabble let in; are all these
67 Your faithful friends o' th' suburbs? We shall have
Great store of room, no doubt, left for the ladies
When they pass back from the christening.

PORTER   An't please your honor, 69
We are but men; and what so many may do,
Not being torn a-pieces, we have done:
An army cannot rule 'em. 72

CHAMBERLAIN   As I live,
If the king blame me for't, I'll lay ye all 73
By th' heels, and suddenly; and on your heads 74
Clap round fines for neglect. Y' are lazy knaves, 75
And here ye lie baiting of bombards when 76
Ye should do service. Hark, the trumpets sound!
Th' are come already from the christening.
Go break among the press, and find a way out 79
To let the troop pass fairly, or I'll find 80
A Marshalsea shall hold ye play these two months. 81

PORTER

Make way there for the princess!

MAN   You great fellow,
Stand close up, or I'll make your head ache!

PORTER

You i' th' chamblet, get up o' th' rail, 84
I'll peck you o'er the pales else!   *Exeunt.* 85

*

7 *switches* thin shoots   9 *ale and cakes* (traditional festival fare)   13 *May-
day* May 1 (a day of great festivity)   14 *Paul's* St Paul's Cathedral   20
Samson . . . Colebrand (all noted for their strength; Guy, Earl of Warwick,
slays Colebrand, a giant, in a well-known story)   24 *chine* joint of beef
25 *not . . . cow* (a common phrase of no special meaning; here used by
association with *chine*)   31 *Moorfields* a park (seems also to have been used
as a training ground for the London militia)   32 *strange Indian* North
American Indian (Virginia was much in the news in 1612–13); *tool* (with
bawdy significance)   33 *fry of fornication* swarm of would-be fornicators
37 *spoons* christening spoons (see note on V, iii, 166)   38 *brazier* brass-
maker   39 *dog-days* hottest season (July 13–August 15, when Sirius, the
dog-star, rises about the same time as the sun)   41 *line* equator; *fire-drake*
i.e. meteor (still referring to the red-nosed brazier)   43 *like a mortar-piece*
i.e. gaping upwards   44 *blow* blast   45 *pinked porringer* round cap ornamented with perforations, and resembling a porridge dish   47 *meteor*
(still the brazier)   48 *'Clubs'* the call which summoned apprentices to
start or stop a fight   49 *truncheoners* cudgel-bearers   50 *Strond* Strand,
a main shopping street in London, then a fashionable residential area;
fell on attacked   51 *broom-staff* i.e. close quarters (fighting with staves)
53 *loose shot* marksmen not attached to a company (the term fits the humor
of the whole speech)   55 *fain* glad, obliged   58–59 *tribula-
tion . . . Hill* a local gang of ruffians (?)   59 *limbs* young lads (also a gang?);
Limehouse a dockyard town just east of what was then London   61 *Limbo
Patrum* prison (literally, a region near hell; with quibble on *limbs* and
Limehouse)   62 *running banquet* of public whipping by (running offenders
through the street; this punishment being the 'dessert' to the 'feast' of
being in *Limbo Patrum*)   65 *a find hand* a fine success of things (ironic)
66 *trim* fine (ironic)   67 *suburbs* (suggests lawlessness, because outside
the jurisdiction of the city)   69 *An't* if it   72 *rule* control   73–74 *lay . . .
heels* put you in the stocks   74 *suddenly* immediately   75 *Clap* impose;
round heavy   76 *baiting of bombards* drinking deep (out of leathern bottles)
79 *press* crowd   80 *fairly* properly   81 *Marshalsea* a prison in Southwark
84 *chamblet* camlet, a rich fabric made of goat's hair   85 *peck . . . else* pitch
you over the rails if you don't

V, v *Enter Trumpets, sounding ; then two Aldermen, Lord*
   Mayor, Garter, Cranmer, Duke of Norfolk with his
   marshal's staff, Duke of Suffolk, two Noblemen
   bearing great standing bowls for the christening gifts ;
   then four Noblemen bearing a canopy, under which
   the Duchess of Norfolk, godmother, bearing the child
   richly habited in a mantle, etc., train borne by a
   Lady ; then follows the Marchioness Dorset, the other
   godmother, and Ladies. The troop pass once about
   the stage, and Garter speaks.

1 GARTER Heaven, from thy endless goodness, send prosperous life, long and ever happy, to the high and mighty
  princess of England, Elizabeth.
   Flourish. Enter King and Guard.

CRANMER *[kneels]*
  And to your royal grace and the good queen,
5 My noble partners and myself thus pray
  All comfort, joy in this most gracious lady,
  Heaven ever laid up to make parents happy,
  May hourly fall upon ye !
KING   Thank you, good lord archbishop :
  What is her name ?
CRANMER   Elizabeth.
KING   Stand up, lord.
  [Cranmer rises. The King kisses the child.]
  With this kiss take my blessing. God protect thee,
  Into whose hand I give thy life.
CRANMER   Amen.
KING
12 My noble gossips, y' have been too prodigal ;
  I thank ye heartily. So shall this lady,
  When she has so much English.
CRANMER   Let me speak, sir,
  For heaven now bids me ; and the words I utter
  Let none think flattery, for they'll find 'em truth.
17 This royal infant – heaven still move about her ! –
  Though in her cradle, yet now promises
  Upon this land a thousand thousand blessings,
  Which time shall bring to ripeness. She shall be
  (But few now living can behold that goodness)
  A pattern to all princes living with her
23 And all that shall succeed. Saba was never
  More covetous of wisdom and fair virtue
  Than this pure soul shall be. All princely graces
26 That mould up such a mighty piece as this is,
  With all the virtues that attend the good,
  Shall still be doubled on her. Truth shall nurse her,
29 Holy and heavenly thoughts still counsel her ;
30 She shall be loved and feared ; her own shall bless her ;
  Her foes shake like a field of beaten corn
  And hang their heads with sorrow. Good grows with her ;

In her days every man shall eat in safety
Under his own vine what he plants, and sing
The merry songs of peace to all his neighbors.
God shall be truly known, and those about her
From her shall read the perfect ways of honor, 37
And by those claim their greatness, not by blood.
Nor shall this peace sleep with her ; but as when
The bird of wonder dies, the maiden phoenix, 40
Her ashes new create another heir 41
As great in admiration as herself, 42
So shall she leave her blessedness to one
(When heaven shall call her from this cloud of darkness) 44
Who from the sacred ashes of her honor
Shall starlike rise, as great in fame as she was,
And so stand fixed. Peace, plenty, love, truth, terror,
That were the servants to this chosen infant,
Shall then be his, and like a vine grow to him.
Wherever the bright sun of heaven shall shine, 50
His honor and the greatness of his name
Shall be, and make new nations. He shall flourish 52
And like a mountain cedar reach his branches
To all the plains about him. Our children's children
Shall see this, and bless heaven.
KING   Thou speakest wonders.
CRANMER
  She shall be, to the happiness of England,
  An aged princess ; many days shall see her,
  And yet no day without a deed to crown it.
  Would I had known no more ! but she must die,
  She must, the saints must have her : yet a virgin,
  A most unspotted lily shall she pass 61
  To th' ground, and all the world shall mourn her.
KING
  O lord archbishop,
  Thou hast made me now a man ; never before 64
  This happy child did I get anything. 65
  This oracle of comfort has so pleased me
  That when I am in heaven I shall desire
  To see what this child does, and praise my Maker.
  I thank ye all. To you, my good lord mayor,
  And you good brethren I am much beholding. 70
  I have received much honor by your presence,
  And ye shall find me thankful. Lead the way, lords,
  Ye must all see the queen, and she must thank ye ;
  She will be sick else. This day, no man think 74
  'Has business at his house ; for all shall stay :
  This little one shall make it Holy-day. *Exeunt.*

      THE EPILOGUE Epi.

'Tis ten to one this play can never please
All that are here. Some come to take their ease
And sleep an act or two ; but those we fear
W' have frighted with our trumpets ; so 'tis clear
They'll say 'tis naught ; others to hear the city 5
Abused extremely, and to cry 'That's witty,'
Which we have not done neither ; that I fear 7
All the expected good w' are like to hear
For this play at this time, is only in
The merciful construction of good women, 10
For such a one we showed 'em. If they smile
And say 'twill do, I know within a while
All the best men are ours ; for 'tis ill hap,
If they hold when their ladies bid 'em clap. 14

V, v The palace **s.d.** *Garter* (see note on IV, i, 36 s.d. item 5) ; *marshal's*
Earl Marshal's ; *standing bowls* bowls with legs ; *habited* clothed **1–3** *Heaven
. . . Elizabeth* (the usual formula on such occasions) **5** *partners* fellow godparents **12** *gossips* godparents **17** *heaven . . . her* God be always near her
23 *Saba* Queen of Sheba **26** *mould . . . piece* inform such a great person **29**
still always **30** *own* own people **37** *read* learn **40** *maiden phoenix* (comparisons between Queen Elizabeth and the phoenix, a mythical unique bird,
were common) **41** *heir* i.e. James I **42** *admiration* arousing wonder **44**
cloud of darkness i.e. earth **50–54** *Wherever . . . him* (cf. Genesis xvii, 4–6
and Romans iv, 17 ; the passage compliments both James I and Princess
Elizabeth, his daughter) **52** *new nations* (a probable reference to Virginia)
61 *pass* pass away **64** *a man* i.e. a successful, prospering man **65** *get*
achieve (quibbling on 'beget') **70** *beholding* indebted **74** *sick* unhappy
Epi. **5** *naught* nothing, worthless **7** *that* so that **10** *construction* interpretation **14** *hold* keep back

THE TRAGEDIES

FOREWORD

No secular works have had wider and more continuous currency than Shakespeare's tragedies, and none have stimulated such persistent efforts of analysis and evaluation. The author himself never defined tragedy, and the definitions and descriptive remarks of such

fellow-playwrights as Jonson, Chapman, and Webster are somewhat less comprehensive than Sidney's, written before there were great English tragedies to define: "high and excellent Tragedy, that openeth the greatest wounds, and sheweth forth the Ulcers that are covered with Tissue; that maketh Kinges feare to be Tyrants, and Tyrants manifest their tirranical humors; that, with sturring the affects of admiration and commiseration, teacheth the uncertainty of this world, and upon how weake foundations guilden roofes are builded. . . ." The phrase "sturring the affects of admiration and commiseration" seems an echo of Aristotle's "effecting a purgation of fear and pity" although Sidney's "admiration" means *awe* rather than *fear*. Actually neither Greek tragedy nor Aristotle's commentary upon it had much direct impact upon the Elizabethans. If Shakespearean tragedy shows an affinity with that of Aeschylus, Sophocles, and Euripides (and it does), it is owing to its universality.

Sidney's definition is a useful reminder of the medieval or "Gothic" inheritance of Elizabethan tragedy, transmitted through narrative poetry of the *contemptus mundi* and *de casibus* kinds. The most familiar examples are Chaucer's *Monk's Tale*, and *The Mirror for Magistrates* compiled by William Baldwin and his successors between 1555 and 1587 in continuation of Boccaccio's fourteenth-century *De Casibus Virorum Illustrium* and Lydgate's fifteenth-century *Fall of Princes*. A "tragedy" was a tale of the fall and wretched death of an eminent person. In combination with similar tales, it was designed to demonstrate the treachery of the goddess Fortuna, or the curse upon mankind resulting from Adam's fall, or the wages of particular sins committed by particular men. In this last and most common aspect Gothic tragedy fused with Senecan tragedy of dreadful crime and dreadful retribution, and with the theatrical spawn of novellas of villainous intrigue. One of the mines of the English playwrights was a French compilation by Belleforest leaning heavily upon Italian fiction and called *Histoires Tragiques*. In popular practise, if not in critical theory, a stage tragedy could be based upon a fiction, and could employ devices of intrigue once thought appropriate only in comedy. The usual protagonist was not Aristotle's man "better than ourselves" in most particulars, but a passionate villain superior only in social station. A typical Elizabethan tragedy was a display of transgression and punishment, two parts sensational to one part exemplary.

Shakespeare dramatized the same kinds of material as the other playwrights, although he avoided "domestic" tragedy of middle-class marital infidelity, and, when he turned to historical sources, he tended to focus upon disastrous behavior of a political rather than private kind. In most of his tragedies the intricate action and bloody extravagance of Elizabethan tragedy in general finds a parallel, while the Gothic and Senecan influences are clearly manifest. Yet his tragedies are far from typical. With the exception of *Titus Andronicus*, they transcend both their literary heredity and their theatrical environment. A strain of the heroic had mingled in anterior tragic poetry: there had been tales in honor of famous men who had sacrificed themselves in great causes. And there was, of course, a copious literature and living tradition of religious martyrdom. Shakespeare's sensitiveness to the heroic and self-sacrificial strain, along with his superior endowment as an artist, gives his tragedies their special cast. If we ask what quality his tragic protagonists come nearest to sharing in common, we must answer their *unworldliness*, their incapacity for compromise. They love whatever it is they love not wisely but too well. Macbeth generically is the familiar Elizabethan super-villain, and Antony the very epitome of those mighty ones who fall precipitously from high place, but that is not all they are. Macbeth seems the black shadow of his complete opposite, and Antony lingers in our minds neither as fallen conqueror nor decayed sensualist but as one who valued a personal relationship in heroic excess of its true worth. The term "tragic flaw" is an awkward one in connection with the remaining Shakespearean tragic heroes because the ultimate cause of their suffering is their idealism, which is impractical by definition and yet, in essence, a thing of value. Man owes to aspiration whatever he has that is good, including his human status. But the tragic nature of that status derives from the identical thing which confers it, and in its intimation of this great mystery may lie the symbolic power of Shakespearean tragedy. It treats of imperfect ones torn by their dreams of perfection, mortals with immortal longings in them.

A. H.

BIBLIOGRAPHY

Anthologies of criticism are *Shakespeare: The Tragedies*, ed. A. Harbage (1964); *Shakespeare: The Tragedies*, ed. C. Leech (1965). A pivotal work is A. C. Bradley, *Shakespearean Tragedy* (1904) since earlier criticism leads into it and later criticism out of it. The abundance of commentary upon the tragedies is indicated by the fact that a number of the works of general criticism listed in the General Introduction are largely concerned with them, and by the large number of recent books concerned with them exclusively: Lily B. Campbell, *Shakespeare's Tragic Heroes: Slaves of Passion* (1930); Willard Farnham, *The Medieval Heritage of*

Elizabethan Tragedy (1936), *Shakespeare's Tragic Frontier* (1950); H. B. Charlton, *Shakespearian Tragedy* (1948); Clifford Leech, *Shakespeare's Tragedies* (1950); J. V. Cunningham, *Woe or Wonder* (1951); G. B. Harrison, *Shakespeare's Tragedies* (1951); R. Speaight, *Nature in Shakespearian Tragedy* (1955); Brents Stirling, *Unity in Shakespearian Tragedy* (1956); Geoffrey Bush, *Shakespeare and the Natural Condition* (1956); Paul N. Siegel, *Shakespearean Tragedy and the Elizabethan Compromise* (1957); Harold S. Wilson, *On the Design of Shakespearian Tragedy* (1957); Kenneth Muir, *Shakespeare and the Tragic Pattern* (1958); William Rosen, *Shakespeare and the Craft of Tragedy* (1960); John Lawlor, *The Tragic Sense in Shakespeare* (1960); Irving Ribner, *Patterns in Shakespearian Tragedy* (1960); John Holloway, *The Story of the Night* (1961); Terence Hawkes, *Shakespeare and the Reason* (1964); Virgil K. Whitaker, *The Mirror up to Nature : the Technique of Shakespeare's Tragedies* (1965); Matthew N. Proser, *The Heroic Image in Five Shakespearean Tragedies* (1965); Thomas McFarland, *Tragic Meanings in Shakespeare* (1966); Northrop Frye, *Fools of Time* (1967). For works on individual plays, see, for HAMLET: Fredson T. Bowers, *Elizabethan Revenge Tragedy* (1940); J. Dover Wilson, *What Happens in Hamlet* (3rd ed. 1951); John E. Hankins, *The Character of Hamlet and Other Essays* (1941); Salvador de Madariaga, *On Hamlet* (1948, reprinted with new preface, 1964); Roy Walker, *The Time is Out of Joint* (1948); Bernard D. Grebanier, *The Heart of Hamlet* (1949); Francis Fergusson, *The Idea of a Theater* (1949); Ernest Jones, *Hamlet and Oedipus* (1910, new ed. 1949); G. R. Elliott, *Scourge and Minister* (1951); Peter Alexander, *Hamlet : Father and Son* (1955); Harry Levin, *The Question of Hamlet* (1959);

L. C. Knights, *An Approach to Hamlet* (1960). For TROILUS AND CRESSIDA : Oscar J. Campbell, *Comicall Satyre and Shakespeare's Troilus and Cressida* (1938); Robert Kimbrough, *Shakespeare's Troilus and Cressida and Its Setting* (1964). For OTHELLO : F. R. Leavis, *The Common Pursuit* (1952); G. R. Elliott, *Flaming Minister* (1953); Helen Gardner, *The Noble Moor* (1955); Robert B. Heilman, *Magic in the Web* (1956); Bernard Spivack, *Shakespeare and the Allegory of Evil* (1958); Marvin Rosenberg, *The Masks of Othello* (1961). For KING LEAR : Robert B. Heilman, *This Great Stage* (1948); John F. Danby, *Shakespeare's Doctrine of Nature* (1949); Richard B. Sewall, *The Vision of Tragedy* (1959); Russell A. Fraser, *Shakespeare's Poetics in Relation to King Lear* (1962); Maynard Mack, *King Lear in Our Time* (1965); William R. Elton, *King Lear and the Gods* (1966); Paul A. Jorgensen, *Lear's Self-Discovery* (1967). For MACBETH : Walter C. Curry, *Shakespeare's Philosophical Patterns* (1937); Roy Walker, *The Time is Free* (1949); Henry N. Paul, *The Royal Play of Macbeth* (1950); G. R. Elliott, *Dramatic Providence in Macbeth* (1958). For the ROMAN PLAYS, see A. C. Bradley, *Oxford Lectures on Poetry* (1909); M. W. MacCallum, *Shakespeare's Roman Plays and Their Background* (1910); James E. Phillips, *The State in Shakespeare's Greek and Roman Plays* (1940); John Palmer, *Political Characters in Shakespeare* (1945); Maurice Charney, *Shakespeare's Roman Plays* (1955); Derek Traversi, *Shakespeare : The Roman Plays* (1963); Ernest Schanzer, *The Problem Plays of Shakespeare* (1963). Works on the populace, the military, etc. listed with those on the Histories also bear upon the Roman plays. For a survey of twentieth-century criticism of the Roman plays, see J. C. Maxwell in *Shakespeare Survey*, ed. A. Nicoll, X (1957).

TITUS ANDRONICUS

INTRODUCTION

Titus Andronicus is a ridiculous play. This gallimaufry of murders, rape, lopped limbs, and heads baked in a pie, lavishly served with the rich purple sauce of rhetoric, may have been to the taste of the Elizabethans, but what is one to make of it to-day? As long ago as 1614 Ben Jonson bracketed the play with Kyd's *Spanish Tragedy* as representative of the outmoded tragic vein of some twenty-five or thirty years before, and scoffed at those who still admired it. After a brief revival of popularity in the eighteenth century (in Edward Ravenscroft's "improved" version), *Titus Andronicus* became the least performed of all Shakespeare's plays, until in 1955 a production in Stratford-upon-Avon revealed that a modern audience could be moved by it, and that it might have something to say to the twentieth century. Like the Elizabethans, modern man is no stranger to violence, and he could find mirrored in the play the crimes of the concentration camp. Here was stark horror, unrelieved by pity; human agony pitched beyond endurance, until the victim becomes insane. The arbitrariness of the action seemed to symbolize the essential absurdity of modern life: Titus was like a man thrust blindfold into a room full of whirling knives. The play could be seen as Shakespeare's one tragic contribution to the drama of the absurd, or so it seemed at Stratford, under the spell of Sir Laurence Olivier's magnificent interpretation of Titus. Stratford proved that *Titus Andronicus* is still good theatre, and almost succeeded in turning it into a good play, yet reading it again one is tempted to concur with Edward Ravenscroft, who, in the preface to his adaptation of 1678, called it not a "structure," but "a heap of rubbish."

The manifest deficiencies of *Titus Andronicus* have persuaded critics careful of Shakespeare's reputation to dismiss it altogether from the canon as unworthy of his genius. Others, for whom the external evidence pointing to Shakespeare's authorship is not so lightly to be set aside, have sought a compromise by claiming that what we have represents Shakespeare's rather perfunctory reworking of a much older play, in which the hands of Peele, Greene, Kyd, and Marlowe have been variously, but not very convincingly, detected. Others again have argued that *Titus Andronicus* was one of the first plays Shakespeare wrote, and have sought to excuse its imperfections on the grounds of the author's youthfulness and inexperience. More ingeniously, the view has been put forward that the obvious absurdities of plot and diction prove that it was part of Shakespeare's conscious intention to burlesque the conventional excesses of the then popular "tragedy of blood," the formula for which Kyd and others had derived from Seneca's Latin tragedies of revenge. The continuing debate attests to the widespread feeling that the play calls for some sort of apology. The only general agreement so far arrived at is

that in the absence of any conclusive evidence to the contrary the play must be regarded as largely, if not wholly, by Shakespeare, and that the publication of the first quarto in 1594 at least indicates that it was written at a comparatively early date in his dramatic career. An entry in Henslowe's diary records a production of "Titus & Ondronicus" as "ne" (new) by Sussex's Men on January 24, 1594. The entry probably refers to the present play, but there is some doubt as to whether the "ne" means newly written, newly revised, or newly acquired by the company named. Lending some support to the last possibility is the fact that the title page of the quarto of 1594 names Derby's Men and Pembroke's Men as well as Sussex's Men as the companies which had acted it. An original date of 1590 or even earlier is not precluded. It is hard to conceive of *Titus Andronicus* as having been written after *Richard III* and only shortly before the fine plays of Shakespeare's "lyrical period."

The play's failure to arouse any of the emotions usually associated with the tragic experience must be attributed largely to the lack of that frame of moral reference, so clearly and unequivocally established in Shakespeare's major tragedies, which might conceivably have made meaningful its gruesome catalogue

> of murders, rapes, and massacres,
> Acts of black night, abominable deeds,
> Complots of mischief, treason, villainies
> Ruthful to hear, yet piteously performed.
> (V, i, 63–66)

Without this moral framework the play is little more than an horrific entertainment, an empty exercise in revenge tragedy; the barbaric cruelty of the action, the physical shock of Lavinia's entry, "her hands cut off, and her tongue cut out, and ravished," or the monstrous spectacle of Tamora unwittingly eating her dead sons' flesh, can only give rise to feelings of revulsion, or, at best, a curiosity to see where and when the next blow will fall. When T. S. Eliot called *Titus Andronicus* "one of the stupidest and most uninspired plays ever written," it was to the casual irrelevance of these atrocities divorced from moral judgments that he referred.

Symptomatic of this lack of inner significance is the pasteboard-like quality of the protagonists. Lavinia's mutilation cannot move us, for as a character she scarcely begins to exist, while the succession of blows beneath which Titus reels until his mind gives way with grief renders him a pathetic rather than a tragic figure. Titus is no King Lear: his sufferings do not bring increased self-knowledge or greater understanding of the human condition. He is incapable of recognizing that his misfortunes stem from that stern inflexibility which at the beginning of the play caused him to brush aside Tamora's pleadings for her son, and which drove him to kill his own youngest son for venturing to interpose on Lavinia's behalf in a just quarrel. While it is true that Titus is presented initially as the selfless savior of Rome and human embodiment of all the Roman virtues, his ill-considered actions, committed in the empty name of "honor," quickly alienate our sympathies, and he never afterwards succeeds in quite regaining them.

Such wanton violence and inhumanity, unmatched elsewhere in Shakespeare, disqualify the play as a tragedy in the truest sense. Viewed closer, it abounds in minor flaws and inconsistencies such as might have escaped a careless or inexperienced dramatist. No explanation is given for the readiness of the defeated Goths to rally to their former enemy, Lucius, in order to help him free Rome from the tyranny of their queen, Tamora, and her emperor-husband, Saturnine. Tamora herself is given an ambiguous role. When her eloquent plea for mercy goes unheeded, and her son is sacrificed according to the Roman custom, Tamora vows to avenge herself on Titus, yet although she displays her tigerish qualities when the occasion offers, she does not really take an active part in the destruction of the Andronici. Instead, she figures, surprisingly, as the lustful mistress of Aaron the Moor, and it is this image of her that is kept before us while Aaron plans the rape of Lavinia and the deaths of Bassianus, Quintus, and Martius, from no other motive than his sheer delight in doing evil. Again, it is curious, to say the least, that Aaron, the demonic force behind most of the action of the play, should be silent during the entire first act. When Tamora does take a hand in the action it is unclear what she intends to do, and hard to see what dramatic purpose is served by her elaborate masquerade as Revenge in Act V, apart from delivering her sons into Titus' clutches so that he can slit their throats. Other scenes hover on the brink of absurdity: there is an air of grotesque farce about Quintus' fall into the pit from which he is trying to extricate his brother, while the spectacle of Lavinia bearing Titus' severed hand between her teeth must have aroused mixed feelings even in the 1590's.

Despite these glaring faults it must be conceded that *Titus Andronicus* anticipates, in a way which other early tragedies of blood do not, later and better works in the genre, including Shakespeare's own. It has a kind of savage energy and exuberance that carry it successfully over the rough places to its bloody conclusion. Through its imperfections we catch a glimpse of the kind of play it might have been, written ten years later by a more mature and practiced playwright. Titus is the prototype of the Shakespearean tragic hero, a brave and upright warrior, grown old and scarred in his country's service, who holds blindly to honor and justice, thereby setting in motion the forces that will destroy him. His blindness to the consequences of his actions is a condition of life in a corrupt society, where the distinction between good and evil has become blurred. Titus first falls from grace when he puts justice before mercy, and the rapid succession of events that culminate in his murder of his son accomplishes his damnation. His punishment is meted out by an incarnate devil, Aaron, the living symbol of evil itself, who is himself destroyed at the end of the play, thus implying the triumph of goodness and the restoration of true justice to a Rome governed by Titus' sole surviving son. Such an out-

line hints at the far greater plays to come, notably *Macbeth,* while Tamora is an early sketch for Macbeth's fiend-like queen. Titus, the honest soldier, used to the plain dealing of war, suggests Othello; in his anguish he foreshadows the grief-stricken Lear, while his madness, half real, half feigned, points to Hamlet. The liaison between Aaron and Tamora prefigures the intrigue between Edmund and Lear's wicked daughters, yet Aaron is very clearly a cartoon for Iago. Reading *Titus Andronicus* one is constantly reminded of what was to come. None of these tremendous possibilities are realized in the play, yet they are unmistakably there; no other early revenge play has such powerful stuff in it.

The most powerful single ingredient in *Titus Andronicus* is Aaron. Of all the characters he is the most fully developed and the most convincing. He has life and energy; an ingenious contriver of mischief, he is a descendant of the Vice of the old morality play who has learned some new tricks from Kyd's and Marlowe's Machiavellian villains. His aspirations take wing on Marlovian hyperboles:

> I will be bright and shine in pearl and gold,
> To wait upon this new-made empress.
> To wait, said I? to wanton with this queen,
> This goddess, this Semiramis, this nymph,
> This siren that will charm Rome's Saturnine
> And see his shipwrack and his commonweal's.
> (II, i, 19–24)

He can display inhuman cruelty, yet he is passionate in defense of the baby that Tamora would have callously had him destroy:

> Now by the burning tapers of the sky,
> That shone so brightly when this boy was got,
> He dies upon my scimitar's sharp point
> That touches this my first-born son and heir!
> (IV, ii, 89–92)

When captured he explains that he had no reason for what he did other than the enjoyment he took in the doing of it, and he is sorry only that in a lifetime dedicated to crime he had not time to do more. Like Iago, he is unmoved by the dreadful sentence pronounced upon him, and his last words smack of the devil himself:

> I am no baby, I, that with base prayers
> I should repent the evils I have done;
> Ten thousand worse than ever yet I did
> Would I perform if I might have my will.
> If one good deed in all my life I did,
> I do repent it from my very soul. (V, iii, 185–90)

It took a more assured genius to transfer this whole-hearted and unmotivated malignancy to such an ordinary-seeming soldier as Iago, yet Aaron the Moor is wholly credible as the human agent of the evil forces at work in the world of the play.

It is not the plot, however crudely constructed, nor the characterization that present obstacles to the contemporary reader, but the style of the play. The excessively artificial diction contrasts oddly with the violence of the events we are asked to witness. When Marcus first finds Lavinia with her tongue cut out, his ornate description of her plight is couched in the phrases of a love poet:

Alas, a crimson river of warm blood,
Like to a bubbling fountain stirred with wind,
Doth rise and fall between thy rosèd lips,
Coming and going with thy honey breath.
(II, iv, 22–25)

These are hardly the words of an uncle confronted by a niece savagely assaulted: they seem rather the description of a painting or a tapestry, and this pictorial quality recurs throughout the play. The action halts while speakers deliver themselves of passages of lyrical description, such as Tamora's hymn to nature when she greets her lover:

The birds chaunt melody on every bush,
The snake lies rollèd in the cheerful sun,
The green leaves quiver with the cooling wind,
And make a checkered shadow on the ground.
(II, iii, 12–15)

When Martius peers into the "dark, blood-drinking pit" his description of what he sees lyrically transforms the body of Bassianus:

Upon his bloody finger he doth wear
A precious ring that lightens all this hole,
Which, like a taper in some monument,
Doth shine upon the dead man's earthy cheeks,
And shows the ragged entrails of this pit.
So pale did shine the moon on Pyramus
When he by night lay bathed in maiden blood.
(II, iii, 226–32)

This static, decorative technique belongs to narrative rather than the drama, and forms a link between the play and two early works by Shakespeare which it most resembles, the narrative poems *Venus and Adonis* and *The Rape of Lucrece*, and, through them, with Ovid's *Metamorphoses*.

The immediate source of *Titus Andronicus* was most probably the prose *History of Titus Andronicus*, of which an eighteenth-century chapbook reprint is preserved in the Folger Shakespeare Library, but there can be no doubt that Shakespeare also had in mind the story of Philomela in the *Metamorphoses*, Book VI. The main plot of the play parallels that of Ovid's tale. Philomela was ravished by Tereus, her sister's husband, and her tongue cut out so that she could not inform against him. She reveals the crime to her sister, Procne, by weaving the story into a tapestry, and the pair determine on revenge. Procne kills Itys, her son by Tereus, and the sisters serve him up to his father to eat. Ovid's tale ends not with tragedy, but with wonder: as Tereus is about to kill the sisters he is transformed into a hoopoe, and they into a nightingale and a swallow. There are frequent references to this story in the play, yet more significant is Shakespeare's attempt to capture something of Ovid's manner of telling it. It was Ovid's elegance and luxuriously elaborated imagery that the young dramatist must have thought appropriate for a first tragedy ambitiously cast in the high Roman fashion, but the richly decorative style of the story-teller does not meet the dramatic demand for pace and energy. Often it is as though Shakespeare, like Ovid, were exhibiting his mangled corpses and bleeding victims not as objects of pity and terror, but of wonderment: the florid descriptions ask us to admire the sufferers' wounds as if they were precious stones. Ovid's urbanity and detachment, so admirably reflected in Shakespeare's narrative poems, conflict with the mood of tragic passion: the violence of the play stubbornly refused to be metamorphosed into poetry.

This uncertainty of treatment suggests that *Titus Andronicus* was an experimental play in which the possibilities of the tragic mode were being explored. Ovid proved an unsatisfactory model, and in subsequent tragedies Shakespeare learned to handle horrors more directly and to much more dramatic effect. He learned, moreover, to give a sense of direction to the tragic action, and was able to plumb the depths of man's moral and spiritual being. Alone of the tragedies *Titus Andronicus* does not raise profound questions about the nature of man and his relationship to the universe, nor does it, except in half-hearted fashion, ask us to consider the nature of justice. It is a wholly extrovert play, content simply to show suffering and injustice as empirical facts. A desire for revenge, or a delight in wickedness for its own sake, are sufficient motives to set the plot rolling, and it does not stop until the stage is strewn with corpses. The singleness of purpose with which this is consummated at least proclaims a dramatist who, if uncertain of his ultimate destination, knows what effect he wants to achieve in this play. *Titus Andronicus* is an exercise in woe and wonder, Senecan revenge tragedy pushed to its limits. It is neither subtle nor moving, yet it has tremendous vigor, and it is bursting with promise in a great many different directions. *Titus Andronicus* may be the least satisfactory of Shakespeare's plays, but as the work that marks the beginning of the road that leads to *Macbeth*, *Othello*, and *King Lear* it is by no means the least significant.

University of Newcastle, N.S.W.   GUSTAV CROSS

NOTE ON THE TEXT

The most Lamentable Romaine Tragedie of Titus Andronicus was first published in a quarto of 1594, a unique copy of which was discovered in Sweden in 1904 and is now in the Folger Shakespeare Library. This quarto was almost certainly printed from the author's draft, and the present edition adheres closely to its text. A list of the few departures from it, together with a description of the texts of the two later quartos and of the folio (which supplies one scene, III, ii, omitted from the quartos), is provided in the Appendix. The quarto text is not divided into acts and scenes. The folio text is divided into acts but not into scenes. The folio acts were divided into scenes by later editors, and this traditional division is supplied marginally for reference in the present edition.

TITUS ANDRONICUS

*

I, i   [Flourish.] Enter the Tribunes and Senators aloft.
     And then enter [below] Saturninus and his Followers
     at one door ; and Bassianus and his Followers [at the
     other], with Drums and Trumpets.

SATURNINUS
    Noble patricians, patrons of my right,
    Defend the justice of my cause with arms.
    And, countrymen, my loving followers,
4   Plead my successive title with your swords.
5   I am his first-born son that was the last
6   That ware the imperial diadem of Rome.
    Then let my father's honors live in me,
8   Nor wrong mine age with this indignity.

BASSIANUS
    Romans, friends, followers, favorers of my right,
    If ever Bassianus, Caesar's son,
11   Were gracious in the eyes of royal Rome,
12   Keep then this passage to the Capitol;
    And suffer not dishonor to approach
    The imperial seat, to virtue consecrate,
15   To justice, continence, and nobility;
16   But let desert in pure election shine;
    And, Romans, fight for freedom in your choice.
       [Enter] Marcus Andronicus, [aloft,] with the crown.

MARCUS
    Princes that strive by factions and by friends
19   Ambitiously for rule and empery,
    Know that the people of Rome, for whom we stand
    A special party, have by common voice
    In election for the Roman empery
    Chosen Andronicus surnamèd Pius
24   For many good and great deserts to Rome.
    A nobler man, a braver warrior,

Lives not this day within the city walls.
He by the Senate is accited home   27
From weary wars against the barbarous Goths,
That with his sons, a terror to our foes,
Hath yoked a nation strong, trained up in arms.   30
Ten years are spent since first he undertook
This cause of Rome, and chastisèd with arms
Our enemies' pride. Five times he hath returned
Bleeding to Rome, bearing his valiant sons
In coffins from the field, and at this day   35
To the monument of the Andronici
Done sacrifice of expiation,
And slain the noblest prisoner of the Goths.
And now at last, laden with honor's spoils,
Returns the good Andronicus to Rome,
Renownèd Titus, flourishing in arms.
Let us entreat by honor of his name
Whom worthily you would have now succeed,
And in the Capitol and Senate's right,   44
Whom you pretend to honor and adore,   45
That you withdraw you and abate your strength,
Dismiss your followers, and, as suitors should,
Plead your deserts in peace and humbleness.

I, i Before the Capitol in Rome **s.d.** *Flourish* trumpet fanfare **4** *successive title* claim to the succession **5** *his . . . that* the first-born son of him who **6** *ware* wore **8** *age* i.e. seniority **11** *gracious* acceptable **12** *Keep* guard **15** *continence* self-restraint **16** *let . . . shine* let worth triumph simply in election **19** *empery* dominion **24** *deserts* worthy deeds **27** *accited* summoned **30** *yoked* subjugated **35-38** *and . . . Goths* (These three and a half lines occur only in Q1, and are inconsistent with what follows since they imply that Titus has already sacrificed Alarbus. Either they have become misplaced, or Shakespeare omitted to delete them from his manuscript.) **44** *the Capitol . . . right* the right of the Capitol and of the Senate **45** *pretend* claim

SATURNINUS

49   How fair the tribune speaks to calm my thoughts.

BASSIANUS

50   Marcus Andronicus, so I do affy
     In thy uprightness and integrity,
     And so I love and honor thee and thine,
     Thy noble brother Titus and his sons,
     And her to whom my thoughts are humbled all,
     Gracious Lavinia, Rome's rich ornament,
     That I will here dismiss my loving friends:
     And to my fortune's and the people's favor
     Commit my cause in balance to be weighed.
             Exeunt Soldiers [of Bassianus].

SATURNINUS

     Friends that have been thus forward in my right,
     I thank you all and here dismiss you all,
     And to the love and favor of my country
62   Commit myself, my person, and the cause.
             [Exeunt Soldiers of Saturninus.]
     Rome, be as just and gracious unto me
64   As I am confident and kind to thee.
     Open the gates and let me in.

BASSIANUS

66   Tribunes, and me, a poor competitor.
     [Flourish.] They go up into the Senate House.
     Enter a Captain.

CAPTAIN

     Romans, make way. The good Andronicus,
68   Patron of virtue, Rome's best champion,
     Successful in the battles that he fights,
     With honor and with fortune is returned
71   From where he circumscribèd with his sword
     And brought to yoke the enemies of Rome.
     Sound drums and trumpets, and then enter two of
     Titus' sons, [Martius and Mutius;] and then two
     men bearing a coffin covered with black; then
     [Lucius and Quintus,] two other sons; then Titus
     Andronicus; and then Tamora, the Queen of Goths,
     and her two sons, Chiron and Demetrius, with Aaron
     the Moor, and others as many as can be [including
     Tamora's son Alarbus and other Goths, prisoners].
     Then set down the coffin, and Titus speaks.

TITUS

73   Hail, Rome, victorious in thy mourning weeds!
74   Lo, as the bark that hath discharged her fraught
     Returns with precious lading to the bay
76   From whence at first she weighed her anchorage,
     Cometh Andronicus, bound with laurel boughs,
     To re-salute his country with his tears,
     Tears of true joy for his return to Rome.
80   Thou great defender of this Capitol,
     Stand gracious to the rites that we intend,
     Romans, of five and twenty valiant sons,
     Half of the number that King Priam had,
     Behold the poor remains, alive and dead.

These that survive let Rome reward with love;
These that I bring unto their latest home,   86
With burial amongst their ancestors.
Here Goths have given me leave to sheathe my sword.
Titus, unkind and careless of thine own,   89
Why suffer'st thou thy sons, unburied yet,
To hover on the dreadful shore of Styx?   91
Make way to lay them by their brethren.
         They open the tomb.
There greet in silence, as the dead are wont,
And sleep in peace, slain in your country's wars.
O sacred receptacle of my joys,
Sweet cell of virtue and nobility,
How many sons hast thou of mine in store
That thou wilt never render to me more!

LUCIUS

Give us the proudest prisoner of the Goths,
That we may hew his limbs and on a pile
Ad manes fratrum sacrifice his flesh   101
Before this earthy prison of their bones,
That so the shadows be not unappeased,
Nor we disturbed with prodigies on earth.   104

TITUS

I give him you, the noblest that survives,
The eldest son of this distressèd queen.

TAMORA

Stay, Roman brethren! Gracious conqueror,
Victorious Titus, rue the tears I shed,
A mother's tears in passion for her son: 109
And if thy sons were ever dear to thee,
O, think my son to be as dear to me.
Sufficeth not that we are brought to Rome
To beautify thy triumphs and return,   113
Captive to thee and to thy Roman yoke;
But must my sons be slaught'red in the streets
For valiant doings in their country's cause?
O, if to fight for king and commonweal
Were piety in thine, it is in these.
Andronicus, stain not thy tomb with blood.
Wilt thou draw near the nature of the gods?
Draw near them then in being merciful.
Sweet mercy is nobility's true badge:
Thrice-noble Titus, spare my first-born son.

TITUS

Patient yourself, madam, and pardon me.   124
These are their brethren whom your Goths beheld
Alive and dead, and for their brethren slain
Religiously they ask a sacrifice:
To this your son is marked, and die he must,
T' appease their groaning shadows that are gone.

LUCIUS

Away with him, and make a fire straight,
And with our swords, upon a pile of wood,
Let's hew his limbs till they be clean consumed.
         Exeunt Titus' sons with Alarbus.

TAMORA

O cruel irreligious piety!

CHIRON

Was never Scythia half so barbarous.   134

DEMETRIUS

Oppose not Scythia to ambitious Rome.   135
Alarbus goes to rest, and we survive
To tremble under Titus' threat'ning look.
Then, madam, stand resolved, but hope withal   138

49 *fair* civilly   50 *affy* trust   62 *cause* matter to be decided   64 *confident* trusting; *kind* loving   66 *competitor* rival   68 *Patron* representative   71 *circumscribèd* confined within limits   73 *weeds* apparel   74 *fraught* freight   76 *anchorage* anchors   80 *Thou great defender* i.e. Jupiter   86 *latest* last   89 *unkind* unnatural   91 *Styx* river surrounding Hades   101 *Ad manes fratrum* to the ghosts of our brothers   104 *prodigies* ominous events   109 *passion* grief   113 *triumphs* triumphal processions   124 *Patient* calm   134 *Scythia* ancient name for southern Russia, the inhabitants of which were notorious for their savagery   135 *Oppose* compare   138 *withal* as well

139 The selfsame gods that armed the Queen of Troy
With opportunity of sharp revenge
Upon the Thracian tyrant in his tent
May favor Tamora, the Queen of Goths
(When Goths were Goths, and Tamora was queen),
144 To quit the bloody wrongs upon her foes.
Enter the sons of Andronicus again.

LUCIUS
See, lord and father, how we have performed
Our Roman rites. Alarbus' limbs are lopped
And entrails feed the sacrificing fire,
Whose smoke like incense doth perfume the sky.
Remaineth naught but to inter our brethren
150 And with loud 'larums welcome them to Rome.

TITUS
Let it be so, and let Andronicus
Make this his latest farewell to their souls.
Sound trumpets, and lay the coffin in the tomb.
In peace and honor rest you here, my sons;
Rome's readiest champions, repose you here in rest,
Secure from worldly chances and mishaps.
156 Here lurks no treason, here no envy swells,
157 Here grow no damnèd drugs, here are no storms,
No noise, but silence and eternal sleep.
In peace and honor rest you here, my sons.
Enter Lavinia.

LAVINIA
In peace and honor live Lord Titus long;
My noble lord and father, live in fame.
162 Lo, at this tomb my tributary tears
163 I render for my brethren's obsequies,
And at thy feet I kneel, with tears of joy
Shed on this earth for thy return to Rome.
O, bless me here with thy victorious hand,
Whose fortunes Rome's best citizens applaud.

TITUS
Kind Rome, that hast thus lovingly reserved
169 The cordial of mine age to glad my heart.
Lavinia, live; outlive thy father's days,
And fame's eternal date, for virtue's praise.

MARCUS *[aloft]*
Long live Lord Titus, my belovèd brother,
Gracious triumpher in the eyes of Rome!

TITUS
Thanks, gentle tribune, noble brother Marcus.

MARCUS
And welcome, nephews, from successful wars,
You that survive, and you that sleep in fame.
Fair lords, your fortunes are alike in all
That in your country's service drew your swords;
But safer triumph is this funeral pomp
180 That hath aspired to Solon's happiness
And triumphs over chance in honor's bed.
Titus Andronicus, the people of Rome,
Whose friend in justice thou hast ever been,
Send thee by me, their tribune and their trust,
185 This palliament of white and spotless hue,
186 And name thee in election for the empire,
With these our late-deceasèd emperor's sons.
188 Be candidatus then, and put it on,
And help to set a head on headless Rome.

TITUS
A better head her glorious body fits
Than his that shakes for age and feebleness.

What should I don this robe, and trouble you? 192
Be chosen with proclamations to-day,
To-morrow yield up rule, resign my life,
And set abroad new business for you all?
Rome, I have been thy soldier forty years,
And led my country's strength successfully,
And buried one and twenty valiant sons,
Knighted in field, slain manfully in arms,
In right and service of their noble country.
Give me a staff of honor for mine age,
But not a sceptre to control the world.
Upright he held it, lords, that held it last.

MARCUS
Titus, thou shalt obtain and ask the empery. 204

SATURNINUS
Proud and ambitious tribune, canst thou tell? 205

TITUS
Patience, Prince Saturninus.

SATURNINUS   Romans, do me right.
Patricians, draw your swords, and sheathe them not
Till Saturninus be Rome's emperor.
Andronicus, would thou were shipped to hell
Rather than rob me of the people's hearts!

LUCIUS
Proud Saturnine, interrupter of the good
That noble-minded Titus means to thee!

TITUS
Content thee, prince, I will restore to thee
The people's hearts, and wean them from themselves.

BASSIANUS
Andronicus, I do not flatter thee,
But honor thee, and will do till I die.
My faction if thou strengthen with thy friends,
I will most thankful be, and thanks to men
Of noble minds is honorable meed. 219

TITUS
People of Rome, and people's tribunes here,
I ask your voices and your suffrages.
Will ye bestow them friendly on Andronicus?

TRIBUNES
To gratify the good Andronicus,
And gratulate his safe return to Rome, 224
The people will accept whom he admits.

TITUS
Tribunes, I thank you, and this suit I make,
That you create our emperor's eldest son,
Lord Saturnine; whose virtues will, I hope,
Reflect on Rome as Titan's rays on earth, 229
And ripen justice in this commonweal.
Then, if you will elect by my advice,
Crown him and say 'Long live our emperor!'

MARCUS
With voices and applause of every sort,
Patricians and plebeians, we create

139-41 *Queen . . . tent* (Hecuba, Queen of Troy, revenged herself on Polymnestor, the Thracian tyrant who killed her son, by murdering his sons) 144 *quit* requite 150 *'larums* alarums, trumpet calls 156 *envy* ill will 157 *drugs* poisonous plants 162 *tributary* offered as tribute 163 *obsequies* funeral rites 169 *cordial* comfort 180 *aspired* risen; *Solon's happiness* (refers to Solon's saying, 'Call no man happy until he is dead') 185 *palliament* robe 186 *in election* i.e. as a candidate 188 *candidatus* candidate (in Latin, literally 'white-robed') 192 *What* why 204 *obtain and ask* i.e. obtain if only you ask 205 *canst thou tell* i.e. how can you be certain 219 *meed* reward 224 *gratulate* rejoice at 229 *Titan's* the sun god's

Lord Saturninus Rome's great emperor
And say 'Long live our emperor Saturnine!'
[A long flourish till they come down.]

SATURNINUS
Titus Andronicus, for thy favors done
238 To us in our election this day
239 I give thee thanks in part of thy deserts,
And will with deeds requite thy gentleness:
241 And for an onset, Titus, to advance
Thy name and honorable family,
Lavinia will I make my emperess,
Rome's royal mistress, mistress of my heart,
245 And in the sacred Pantheon her espouse.
246 Tell me, Andronicus, doth this motion please thee?
TITUS
It doth, my worthy lord, and in this match
I hold me highly honored of your grace;
And here in sight of Rome, to Saturnine,
King and commander of our commonweal,
The wide world's emperor, do I consecrate
My sword, my chariot, and my prisoners,
253 Presents well worthy Rome's imperious lord.
Receive them then, the tribute that I owe,
Mine honor's ensigns humbled at thy feet.
SATURNINUS
Thanks, noble Titus, father of my life.
How proud I am of thee and of thy gifts
Rome shall record, and when I do forget
259 The least of these unspeakable deserts,
260 Romans, forget your fealty to me.
TITUS *[to Tamora]*
Now, madam, are you prisoner to an emperor,
262 To him that for your honor and your state
Will use you nobly and your followers.
SATURNINUS *[aside]*
A goodly lady, trust me, of the hue
That I would choose, were I to choose anew. –
Clear up, fair queen, that cloudy countenance.
267 Though chance of war hath wrought this change of
cheer,
Thou com'st not to be made a scorn in Rome.
Princely shall be thy usage every way.
Rest on my word, and let not discontent
271 Daunt all your hopes. Madam, he comforts you
Can make you greater than the Queen of Goths.
Lavinia, you are not displeased with this?
LAVINIA
274 Not I, my lord, sith true nobility
275 Warrants these words in princely courtesy.
SATURNINUS
Thanks, sweet Lavinia. Romans, let us go.
Ransomless here we set our prisoners free.
Proclaim our honors, lords, with trump and drum.
[Flourish. Exeunt Saturninus, Tamora,
Demetrius, Chiron, and Aaron.]

BASSIANUS
Lord Titus, by your leave, this maid is mine.
[Seizes Lavinia.]
TITUS
How, sir! Are you in earnest then, my lord?
BASSIANUS
Ay, noble Titus, and resolved withal
To do myself this reason and this right.
MARCUS
'Suum cuique' is our Roman justice: 283
This prince in justice seizeth but his own.
LUCIUS
And that he will, and shall if Lucius live.
TITUS
Traitors, avaunt! Where is the emperor's guard?   286
Treason, my lord! Lavinia is surprised!   287
SATURNINUS *[re-entering]*
Surprised? By whom?
BASSIANUS   By him that justly may
Bear his betrothed from all the world away.
[Exeunt Bassianus and Marcus with Lavinia.]
MUTIUS
Brothers, help to convey her hence away,
And with my sword I'll keep this door safe.   291
[Exeunt Lucius, Quintus, and Martius.]
TITUS
Follow, my lord, and I'll soon bring her back.
[Exit Saturninus.]
MUTIUS
My lord, you pass not here.
TITUS   What, villain boy?
Barr'st me my way in Rome?
MUTIUS   Help, Lucius, help!
[Titus kills him.]
[Enter Lucius.]
LUCIUS
My lord, you are unjust, and more than so,
In wrongful quarrel you have slain your son.
TITUS
Nor thou, nor he, are any sons of mine;
My sons would never so dishonor me.
Enter aloft the Emperor with Tamora and her two
Sons, and Aaron the Moor.
Traitor, restore Lavinia to the emperor.
LUCIUS
Dead, if you will; but not to be his wife,
That is another's lawful promised love.   *[Exit.]*
SATURNINUS
No, Titus, no. The emperor needs her not,
Nor her, nor thee, nor any of thy stock.
I'll trust by leisure him that mocks me once;   304
Thee never, nor thy traitorous haughty sons,
Confederates all thus to dishonor me.
Was none in Rome to make a stale   307
But Saturnine? Full well, Andronicus,
Agree these deeds with that proud brag of thine
That said'st I begged the empire at thy hands.
TITUS
O monstrous! What reproachful words are these?
SATURNINUS
But go thy ways; go, give that changing piece   312
To him that flourished for her with his sword.
A valiant son-in-law thou shalt enjoy;
One fit to bandy with thy lawless sons,   315

238 *election* (here, as frequently in Shakespeare, the '-ion' is pronounced as
a disyllable)   239 *in part of* i.e. as partial reward for   241 *onset* beginning
245 *Pantheon* Roman temple dedicated to all the gods   246 *motion* proposal   253 *imperious* imperial   259 *unspeakable* inexpressible   260 *fealty*
loyalty   262 *for* because of   267 *cheer* countenance   271 *he* i.e. the man
who   274 *sith* since   275 *Warrants* justifies   283 *Suum cuique* to each
his own   286 *avaunt* be off   287 *surprised* taken captive   291 *door* (pronounced as a disyllable)   304 *by leisure* with caution   307 *stale* laughing-
stock   312 *changing piece* fickle wench   315 *bandy* brawl

316 To ruffle in the commonwealth of Rome.

TITUS
These words are razors to my wounded heart.

SATURNINUS
And therefore, lovely Tamora, Queen of Goths,
319 That like the stately Phoebe 'mongst her nymphs
Dost overshine the gallant'st dames of Rome,
If thou be pleased with this my sudden choice,
Behold, I choose thee, Tamora, for my bride
And will create thee Emperess of Rome.
Speak, Queen of Goths, dost thou applaud my choice?
And here I swear by all the Roman gods,
Sith priest and holy water are so near,
And tapers burn so bright, and everything
328 In readiness for Hymenaeus stand,
I will not re-salute the streets of Rome
Or climb my palace till from forth this place
I lead espoused my bride along with me.

TAMORA
And here in sight of heaven to Rome I swear,
If Saturnine advance the Queen of Goths,
She will a handmaid be to his desires,
A loving nurse, a mother to his youth.

SATURNINUS
Ascend, fair queen, Pantheon. Lords, accompany
Your noble emperor and his lovely bride,
Sent by the heavens for Prince Saturnine,
Whose wisdom hath her fortune conquerèd.
There shall we consummate our spousal rites.
Exeunt omnes. [Manet Titus.]

TITUS
341 I am not bid to wait upon this bride.
Titus, when wert thou wont to walk alone,
343 Dishonorèd thus and challengèd of wrongs?
*Enter Marcus and Titus' Sons [Lucius, Quintus,
and Martius].*

MARCUS
O Titus, see, O see what thou hast done,
In a bad quarrel slain a virtuous son.

TITUS
No, foolish tribune, no: no son of mine,
Nor thou, nor these, confederates in the deed
That hath dishonorèd all our family,
Unworthy brother, and unworthy sons!

LUCIUS
350 But let us give him burial as becomes;
Give Mutius burial with our bretheren.

TITUS
Traitors, away! He rests not in this tomb:
This monument five hundred years hath stood,
354 Which I have sumptuously re-edified.
355 Here none but soldiers and Rome's servitors
Repose in fame; none basely slain in brawls.
Bury him where you can, he comes not here.

MARCUS
My lord, this is impiety in you.
My nephew Mutius' deeds do plead for him;
He must be buried with his bretheren.
Titus' two Sons speak.

[QUINTUS, MARTIUS]
And shall, or him we will accompany.

TITUS
And shall? What villain was it spake that word?
Titus' Son speaks.

[QUINTUS]
He that would vouch it in any place but here. 363

TITUS
What, would you bury him in my despite? 364

MARCUS
No, noble Titus, but entreat of thee
To pardon Mutius and to bury him.

TITUS
Marcus, even thou hast stroke upon my crest,
And with these boys mine honor thou hast wounded.
My foes I do repute you every one, 369
So trouble me no more, but get you gone.

MARTIUS
He is not with himself, let us withdraw. 371

QUINTUS
Not I, till Mutius' bones be burièd.
The Brother and the Sons kneel.

MARCUS
Brother, for in that name doth nature plead—

QUINTUS
Father, and in that name doth nature speak—

TITUS
Speak thou no more, if all the rest will speed. 375

MARCUS
Renownèd Titus, more than half my soul—

LUCIUS
Dear father, soul and substance of us all—

MARCUS
Suffer thy brother Marcus to inter 378
His noble nephew here in virtue's nest,
That died in honor and Lavinia's cause.
Thou art a Roman, be not barbarous:
The Greeks upon advice did bury Ajax, 382
That slew himself; and wise Laertes' son 383
Did graciously plead for his funerals.
Let not young Mutius then, that was thy joy,
Be barred his entrance here.

TITUS   Rise, Marcus, rise.
The dismall'st day is this that e'er I saw,
To be dishonorèd by my sons in Rome.
Well, bury him, and bury me the next.
They put him in the tomb.

LUCIUS
There lie thy bones, sweet Mutius, with thy friends,
Till we with trophies do adorn thy tomb. 391
They all kneel and say:

[ALL]
No man shed tears for noble Mutius;
He lives in fame that died in virtue's cause.
Exeunt [i.e. stand aside] all but Marcus and Titus.

MARCUS
My lord, to step out of these dreary dumps, 394
How comes it that the subtle Queen of Goths
Is of a sudden thus advanced in Rome?

TITUS
I know not, Marcus, but I know it is:

---

316 *ruffle* swagger 319 *Phoebe* the moon goddess 328 *Hymenaeus* god of marriage 341 *bid* asked 343 *challengèd* accused 350 *as becomes* as is fitting 354 *re-edified* rebuilt 355 *servitors* armed defenders 363 *vouch* maintain 364 *in my despite* in spite of me 369 *repute* consider 371 *not with himself* demented 375 *if . . . speed* if everything is to go well 378 *Suffer* permit 382 *advice* deliberation; *Ajax* (Ajax killed himself in fury because the armor of Achilles was awarded to Odysseus) 383 *Laertes' son* Odysseus 391 *trophies* memorial tokens 394 *dumps* i.e. melancholy

398 Whether by device or no, the heavens can tell.
399 Is she not then beholding to the man
That brought her for this high good turn so far?
[Yes, and will nobly him remunerate.]
    [Flourish.] Enter the Emperor, Tamora and her two
    Sons, with the Moor, at one door. Enter at the other
    door Bassianus and Lavinia, with others.

SATURNINUS
402 So, Bassianus, you have played your prize.
God give you joy, sir, of your gallant bride.

BASSIANUS
And you of yours, my lord. I say no more
Nor wish no less, and so I take my leave.

SATURNINUS
Traitor, if Rome have law or we have power,
Thou and thy faction shall repent this rape.

BASSIANUS
Rape call you it, my lord, to seize my own,
My true betrothèd love, and now my wife?
But let the laws of Rome determine all;
411 Meanwhile am I possessed of that is mine.

SATURNINUS
'Tis good, sir. You are very short with us;
But if we live, we'll be as sharp with you.

BASSIANUS
My lord, what I have done, as best I may
Answer I must, and shall do with my life.
Only thus much I give your grace to know:
By all the duties that I owe to Rome,
This noble gentleman, Lord Titus here,
419 Is in opinion and in honor wronged,
That in the rescue of Lavinia
With his own hand did slay his youngest son,
In zeal to you, and highly moved to wrath
423 To be controlled in that he frankly gave.
Receive him then to favor, Saturnine,
That hath expressed himself in all his deeds
A father and a friend to thee and Rome.

TITUS
427 Prince Bassianus, leave to plead my deeds.
'Tis thou, and those, that have dishonorèd me.
Rome and the righteous heavens be my judge
How I have loved and honored Saturnine.

TAMORA
My worthy lord, if ever Tamora
Were gracious in those princely eyes of thine,
433 Then hear me speak indifferently for all;
And at my suit, sweet, pardon what is past.

SATURNINUS
What, madam, be dishonorèd openly
436 And basely put it up without revenge?

TAMORA
437 Not so, my lord; the gods of Rome forfend
438 I should be author to dishonor you!
439 But on mine honor dare I undertake

398 *device* plan 399 *beholding* indebted 402 *played your prize* won
your contest 411 *that* that which 419 *opinion* reputation 423 *controlled* thwarted; *frankly* freely 427 *leave to plead* refrain from pleading
433 *indifferently* impartially 436 *put it up* submit to it 437 *forfend*
forbid 438 *author* agent 439 *undertake* vouch 441 *Whose . . . griefs*
whose undisguised rage is evidence of his grievances 443 *vain suppose*
idle supposition 452 *at entreats* to entreaty; *let me alone* leave it to me
454 *race* eradicate 478 *mildly . . . might* as mild as might be (i.e. in the
circumstances) 479 *Tend'ring* having regard for 489 *churl* ill-bred
peasant 491 *part* depart

For good Lord Titus' innocence in all,
Whose fury not dissembled speaks his griefs: 441
Then at my suit look graciously on him.
Lose not so noble a friend on vain suppose, 443
Nor with sour looks afflict his gentle heart.
    [Aside to Saturninus]
My lord, be ruled by me, be won at last;
Dissemble all your griefs and discontents:
You are but newly planted in your throne;
Lest, then, the people, and patricians too,
Upon a just survey take Titus' part,
And so supplant you for ingratitude,
Which Rome reputes to be a heinous sin,
Yield at entreats: and then let me alone, 452
I'll find a day to massacre them all
And race their faction and their family, 454
The cruel father, and his traitorous sons,
To whom I suèd for my dear son's life;
And make them know what 'tis to let a queen
Kneel in the streets and beg for grace in vain.
    [Aloud]
Come, come, sweet emperor – come, Andronicus –
Take up this good old man, and cheer the heart
That dies in tempest of thy angry frown.

SATURNINUS
Rise, Titus, rise, my empress hath prevailed.

TITUS
I thank your majesty, and her, my lord.
These words, these looks, infusè new life in me.

TAMORA
Titus, I am incorporate in Rome,
A Roman now adopted happily,
And must advise the emperor for his good.
This day all quarrels die, Andronicus.
And let it be mine honor, good my lord,
That I have reconciled your friends and you. 470
For you, Prince Bassianus, I have passed
My word and promise to the emperor
That you will be more mild and tractable.
And fear not, lords, and you, Lavinia;
By my advice, all humbled on your knees
You shall ask pardon of his majesty.
    [They kneel.]

LUCIUS
We do, and vow to heaven and to his highness
That what we did was mildly as we might, 478
Tend'ring our sister's honor and our own. 479

MARCUS
That on mine honor here do I protest.

SATURNINUS
Away, and talk not, trouble us no more.

TAMORA
Nay, nay, sweet emperor, we must all be friends.
The tribune and his nephews kneel for grace.
I will not be denied. Sweet heart, look back.

SATURNINUS
Marcus, for thy sake and thy brother's here,
And at my lovely Tamora's entreats,
I do remit these young men's heinous faults.
Stand up.
    [They rise.]
Lavinia, though you left me like a churl, 489
I found a friend; and sure as death I swore
I would not part a bachelor from the priest. 491

Come, if the emperor's court can feast two brides,
You are my guest, Lavinia, and your friends.
494   This day shall be a love-day, Tamora.

TITUS

495   To-morrow, an it please your majesty
To hunt the panther and the hart with me,
497   With horn and hound we'll give your grace bonjour.

SATURNINUS

498   Be it so, Titus, and gramercy too.

Exeunt. Sound trumpets. Manet [Aaron the] Moor.

II, i AARON

1   Now climbeth Tamora Olympus' top,
Safe out of fortune's shot, and sits aloft,
3   Secure of thunder's crack or lightning flash,
4   Advanced above pale envy's threat'ning reach.
As when the golden sun salutes the morn,
And having gilt the ocean with his beams,
7   Gallops the zodiac in his glistering coach
8   And overlooks the highest-peering hills,
So Tamora.
Upon her wit doth earthly honor wait,
And virtue stoops and trembles at her frown.
Then, Aaron, arm thy heart and fit thy thoughts
To mount aloft with thy imperial mistress,
14   And mount her pitch whom thou in triumph long
Hast prisoner held, fett'red in amorous chains,
16   And faster bound to Aaron's charming eyes
17   Than is Prometheus tied to Caucasus.
18   Away with slavish weeds and servile thoughts!
I will be bright and shine in pearl and gold,
To wait upon this new-made empress.
To wait, said I ? to wanton with this queen,
22   This goddess, this Semiramis, this nymph,
This siren that will charm Rome's Saturnine
And see his shipwrack and his commonweal's.
25   Holla ! what storm is this ?

Enter Chiron and Demetrius, braving.

DEMETRIUS

26   Chiron, thy years wants wit, thy wits wants edge
27   And manners, to intrude where I am graced
28   And may, for aught thou knowest, affected be.

CHIRON

29   Demetrius, thou dost overween in all,
30   And so in this, to bear me down with braves.
'Tis not the difference of a year or two
Makes me less gracious, or thee more fortunate :
I am as able and as fit as thou
To serve, and to deserve my mistress' grace ;
35   And that my sword upon thee shall approve,
And plead my passions for Lavinia's love.

AARON

37   Clubs, clubs ! These lovers will not keep the peace.

DEMETRIUS

38   Why, boy, although our mother, unadvised,
39   Gave you a dancing rapier by your side,
Are you so desperate grown to threat your friends ?
41   Go to ! Have your lath glued within your sheath
Till you know better how to handle it.

CHIRON

Meanwhile, sir, with the little skill I have,
Full well shalt thou perceive how much I dare.

DEMETRIUS

Ay, boy, grow ye so brave ?

They draw.

AARON   Why, how now, lords ?
So near the emperor's palace dare ye draw
And maintain such a quarrel openly ?
Full well I wot the ground of all this grudge :   48
I would not for a million of gold
The cause were known to them it most concerns ;
Nor would your noble mother for much more
Be so dishonorèd in the court of Rome.
For shame, put up.   53

DEMETRIUS   Not I, till I have sheathed
My rapier in his bosom, and withal
Thrust those reproachful speeches down his throat
That he hath breathed in my dishonor here.

CHIRON

For that I am prepared and full resolved,
Foul-spoken coward, that thund'rest with thy tongue
And with thy weapon nothing dar'st perform.

AARON

Away, I say !
Now, by the gods that warlike Goths adore,
This petty brabble will undo us all.   62
Why, lords, and think you not how dangerous
It is to jet upon a prince's right ?   64
What, is Lavinia then become so loose,
Or Bassianus so degenerate,
That for her love such quarrels may be broached
Without controlment, justice, or revenge ?
Young lords, beware ! and should the empress know
This discord's ground, the music would not please.   70

CHIRON

I care not, I, knew she and all the world :
I love Lavinia more than all the world.

DEMETRIUS

Youngling, learn thou to make some meaner choice.   73
Lavinia is thine elder brother's hope.

AARON

Why, are ye mad ? or know ye not in Rome
How furious and impatient they be,
And cannot brook competitors in love ?
I tell you, lords, you do but plot your deaths
By this device.

CHIRON   Aaron, a thousand deaths
Would I propose to achieve her whom I love.   80

AARON

To achieve her ! How ?

DEMETRIUS   Why makes thou it so strange ?   81
She is a woman, therefore may be wooed ;

494 *love-day* day appointed to settle disputes (with pun on 'day of love')
495 *an* if **497** *bonjour* good day **498** *gramercy* thanks
II, i (there is clearly no break in the action, since Aaron remains on stage)
1 *Olympus* Mount Olympus (the home of the gods) **3** *of* from **4** *envy's* hatred's **7** *Gallops* gallops through **8** *overlooks* looks down upon **14** *mount her pitch* rise to the highest point of her flight (a technical term of falconry) **16** *charming* casting a magic spell **17** *Prometheus* one of the Titans of Greek myth who stole fire from heaven and was chained by Zeus to Mount Caucasus **18** *weeds* garments **22** *Semiramis* legendary Assyrian queen, renowned for her beauty and sexuality **25 s.d.** *braving* talking arrogantly **26** *wants* (the ending '-s' often occurs with a plural subject) **27** *graced* favored **28** *affected* loved **29** *overween* presume too much **30** *braves* threats **35** *approve* prove **37** *Clubs, clubs* (cry to summon the apprentices to stop a brawl in Elizabethan London) **38** *unadvised* unwisely **39** *dancing rapier* ornamental sword worn by dancers **41** *lath* wooden stage sword (contemptuous) **48** *wot* know **53** *put up* sheathe your swords **62** *brabble* brawl **64** *jet* encroach **70** *ground* reason (with a pun on the musical sense 'bass to a descant') **73** *Youngling* youngster (contemptuous) **80** *propose* gladly encounter **81** *Why . . . strange* why do you seem so surprised

She is a woman, therefore may be won;
She is Lavinia, therefore must be loved.
What, man! more water glideth by the mill
Than wots the miller of; and easy it is

87 Of a cut loaf to steal a shive, we know:
Though Bassianus be the emperor's brother,

89 Better than he have worn Vulcan's badge.

AARON *[aside]*
Ay, and as good as Saturninus may.

DEMETRIUS
Then why should he despair that knows to court it
With words, fair looks, and liberality?

93 What, hast not thou full often stroke a doe,
And borne her cleanly by the keeper's nose?

AARON

95 Why, then, it seems some certain snatch or so
96 Would serve your turns.

CHIRON   Ay, so the turn were served.

DEMETRIUS
Aaron, thou hast hit it.

AARON   Would you had hit it too!
Then should not we be tired with this ado.
Why, hark ye, hark ye, and are you such fools

100 To square for this? Would it offend you then
101 That both should speed?

CHIRON
Faith, not me.

DEMETRIUS   Nor me, so I were one.

AARON

103 For shame, be friends, and join for that you jar.
104 'Tis policy and stratagem must do
105 That you affect; and so must you resolve,
That what you cannot as you would achieve,
You must perforce accomplish as you may.

108 Take this of me: Lucrece was not more chaste
Than this Lavinia, Bassianus' love.
A speedier course than ling'ring languishment
Must we pursue, and I have found the path.

112 My lords, a solemn hunting is in hand;
There will the lovely Roman ladies troop:
The forest walks are wide and spacious,

115 And many unfrequented plots there are,
116 Fitted by kind for rape and villainy.
117 Single you thither then this dainty doe,
And strike her home by force, if not by words.
This way, or not at all, stand you in hope.
Come, come, our empress, with her sacred wit
To villainy and vengeance consecrate,
Will we acquaint withal what we intend;

123 And she shall file our engines with advice,

That will not suffer you to square yourselves,
But to your wishes' height advance you both.
The emperor's court is like the house of fame, 126
The palace full of tongues, of eyes and ears:
The woods are ruthless, dreadful, deaf, and dull. 128
There speak and strike, brave boys, and take your turns,
There serve your lust, shadowed from heaven's eye,
And revel in Lavinia's treasury.

CHIRON
Thy counsel, lad, smells of no cowardice.

DEMETRIUS
'Sit fas aut nefas,' till I find the stream 133
To cool this heat, a charm to calm these fits,
'Per Stygia, per manes vehor.'   *Exeunt.* 135

                     *

Enter Titus Andronicus and his three Sons, making   II, ii
     a noise with hounds and horns [; and Marcus].

TITUS
The hunt is up, the morn is bright and grey,
The fields are fragrant and the woods are green.
Uncouple here and let us make a bay,   3
And wake the emperor and his lovely bride,
And rouse the prince, and ring a hunter's peal,
That all the court may echo with the noise.
Sons, let it be your charge, as it is ours,
To attend the emperor's person carefully:
I have been troubled in my sleep this night,
But dawning day new comfort hath inspired.   10

     Here a cry of hounds, and wind horns in a peal, then
     enter Saturninus, Tamora, Bassianus, Lavinia,
     Chiron, Demetrius, and their Attendants.

Many good morrows to your majesty!
Madam, to you as many and as good!
I promisèd your grace a hunter's peal.

SATURNINUS
And you have rung it lustily, my lords,
Somewhat too early for new-married ladies.

BASSIANUS
Lavinia, how say you?

LAVINIA   I say, no:
I have been broad awake two hours and more.

SATURNINUS
Come on then, horse and chariots let us have,
And to our sport. Madam, now shall ye see
Our Roman hunting.

MARCUS   I have dogs, my lord,
Will rouse the proudest panther in the chase,   21
And climb the highest promontory top.

TITUS
And I have horse will follow where the game
Makes way, and runs like swallows o'er the plain.

DEMETRIUS
Chiron, we hunt not, we, with horse nor hound,
But hope to pluck a dainty doe to ground.   *Exeunt.*

                     *

Enter Aaron alone [with a bag of gold].   II, iii

AARON
He that had wit would think that I had none,
To bury so much gold under a tree,
And never after to inherit it.   3

---

87 *shive* slice   89 *Vulcan's badge* i.e. cuckold's horns (Vulcan, god of fire, was deceived by his wife, Venus)   93 *stroke* struck (with an arrow)   95 *snatch* quick catch (with probable sexual connotation)   96 *turns* purposes (with sexual meaning)   100 *square* quarrel   101 *speed* succeed   103 *join . . . jar* unite to obtain what you are quarrelling over   104 *policy* cunning   105 *affect* desire   108 *Lucrece* chaste Roman matron whose rape by Tarquin and subsequent suicide is the subject of Shakespeare's poem *The Rape of Lucrece*   112 *solemn* ceremonial   115 *plots* spots   116 *kind* nature   117 *Single* single out (a hunting term)   123 *file our engines* sharpen our wits   126 *house of fame* home of rumor (a possible allusion to Chaucer's poem *The House of Fame*)   128 *ruthless* pitiless   133 *Sit . . . nefas* be it right or wrong   135 *Per . . . vehor* I am borne through the Stygian (i.e. infernal) regions
II, ii The grounds of the Emperor's palace   3 *Uncouple* unleash the hounds; *bay* prolonged barking   10 s.d. *cry* deep barking   21 *chase* hunting ground
II, iii A forest near Rome   3 *inherit* possess

Let him that thinks of me so abjectly
5 Know that this gold must coin a stratagem,
Which, cunningly effected, will beget
A very excellent piece of villainy:
8 And so repose, sweet gold, for their unrest
[Hides the gold.]
That have their alms out of the empress' chest.
Enter Tamora alone to the Moor.

TAMORA
My lovely Aaron, wherefore look'st thou sad
11 When everything doth make a gleeful boast?
The birds chaunt melody on every bush,
The snake lies rollèd in the cheerful sun,
The green leaves quiver with the cooling wind,
And make a checkered shadow on the ground;
Under their sweet shade, Aaron, let us sit,
And whilst the babbling echo mocks the hounds,
Replying shrilly to the well-tuned horns,
As if a double hunt were heard at once,
20 Let us sit down and mark their yellowing noise;
And after conflict such as was supposed
22 The wand'ring prince and Dido once enjoyed,
When with a happy storm they were surprised,
And curtained with a counsel-keeping cave,
We may, each wreathèd in the other's arms,
Our pastimes done, possess a golden slumber,
Whiles hounds and horns and sweet melodious birds
Be unto us as is a nurse's song
Of lullaby to bring her babe asleep.

AARON
Madam, though Venus govern your desires,
31 Saturn is dominator over mine.
32 What signifies my deadly-standing eye,
My silence, and my cloudy melancholy,
My fleece of woolly hair that now uncurls
Even as an adder when she doth unroll
To do some fatal execution?
37 No, madam, these are no venereal signs.
Vengeance is in my heart, death in my hand,
Blood and revenge are hammering in my head.
Hark, Tamora, the empress of my soul,
Which never hopes more heaven than rests in thee,
This is the day of doom for Bassianus;
43 His Philomel must lose her tongue to-day,
Thy sons make pillage of her chastity
And wash their hands in Bassianus' blood.
Seest thou this letter? take it up, I pray thee,
And give the king this fatal-plotted scroll.
Now question me no more; we are espied;
49 Here comes a parcel of our hopeful booty,
Which dreads not yet their lives' destruction.
Enter Bassianus and Lavinia.

TAMORA
Ah, my sweet Moor, sweeter to me than life.

AARON
No more, great empress; Bassianus comes.
Be cross with him, and I'll go fetch thy sons
To back thy quarrels, whatsoe'er they be.   *[Exit.]*

BASSIANUS
Who have we here? Rome's royal emperess,
56 Unfurnished of her well-beseeming troop?
57 Or is it Dian, habited like her,
Who hath abandonèd her holy groves
To see the general hunting in this forest?

TAMORA
Saucy controller of my private steps!   60
Had I the pow'r that some say Dian had,
Thy temples should be planted presently   62
With horns, as was Actaeon's, and the hounds   63
Should drive upon thy new-transformèd limbs,
Unmannerly intruder as thou art!

LAVINIA
Under your patience, gentle emperess,
'Tis thought you have a goodly gift in horning,   67
And to be doubted that your Moor and you   68
Are singled forth to try experiments.
Jove shield your husband from his hounds to-day!
'Tis pity they should take him for a stag.

BASSIANUS
Believe me, queen, your swart Cimmerian   72
Doth make your honor of his body's hue,
Spotted, detested, and abominable.
Why are you sequest'red from all your train,
Dismounted from your snow-white goodly steed,
And wand'red hither to an obscure plot,
Accompanied but with a barbarous Moor,
If foul desire had not conducted you?

LAVINIA
And being intercepted in your sport,
Great reason that my noble lord be rated   81
For sauciness. I pray you let us hence,
And let her joy her raven-colored love;   83
This valley fits the purpose passing well.

BASSIANUS
The king my brother shall have note of this.

LAVINIA
Ay, for these slips have made him noted long.   86
Good king, to be so mightily abused!

TAMORA
Why I have patience to endure all this.
Enter Chiron and Demetrius.

DEMETRIUS
How now, dear sovereign and our gracious mother,
Why doth your highness look so pale and wan?

TAMORA
Have I not reason, think you, to look pale?
These two have ticed me hither to this place,   92
A barren detested vale you see it is;
The trees, though summer, yet forlorn and lean,
Overcome with moss and baleful mistletoe.
Here never shines the sun; here nothing breeds,
Unless the nightly owl or fatal raven:

5 *coin* produce (as in coining money)   8–9 *their unrest . . . chest* the discomfiture of those who find this money belonging to the empress   11 *boast* display   20 *yellowing* loudly bellowing   22 *wand'ring prince* Aeneas, legendary Trojan hero who loved Dido, Queen of Carthage   31 *dominator* the planet that has a dominant place in the horoscope (those dominated by Saturn were reputedly of sluggish, cold, and gloomy temperament)   32 *deadly-standing* fixed in a death-dealing stare (?)   37 *venereal* associated with love (Venus)   43 *Philomel* (in Greek myth Tereus raped Philomel and cut out her tongue, but she revealed his guilt by weaving the story into a tapestry; see also II, iv, 26–27, 38–39; IV, i, 47–48; V, ii, 194)   49 *parcel . . . booty* part of the prize we hope for   56 *Unfurnished of* deprived of   57 *Dian* Diana, goddess of hunting; *habited* dressed   60 *controller* censorious critic   62 *presently* immediately   63 *Actaeon* legendary hunter who spied on Diana bathing and was transformed by her into a stag and killed by his own hounds   67 *horning* (a wife's unfaithfulness was said to give her husband horns)   68 *doubted* suspected   72 *Cimmerian* legendary dweller in darkness   81 *rated* berated   83 *joy* enjoy   86 *noted* notorious   92 *ticed* enticed

834

And when they showed me this abhorrèd pit,
They told me, here, at dead time of the night,
A thousand fiends, a thousand hissing snakes,
101   Ten thousand swelling toads, as many urchins,
Would make such fearful and confusèd cries
As any mortal body hearing it
Should straight fall mad, or else die suddenly.
No sooner had they told this hellish tale
But straight they told me they would bind me here
Unto the body of a dismal yew
And leave me to this miserable death.
And then they called me foul adulteress,
Lascivious Goth, and all the bitterest terms
That ever ear did hear to such effect;
And had you not by wondrous fortune come,
This vengeance on me had they executed.
Revenge it, as you love your mother's life,
Or be ye not henceforth called my children.

DEMETRIUS
This is a witness that I am thy son.
    Stab him [Bassianus].

CHIRON
And this for me, struck home to show my strength.

LAVINIA
118 Ay, come, Semiramis, nay, barbarous Tamora,
For no name fits thy nature but thy own.

TAMORA
Give me the poniard; you shall know, my boys,
Your mother's hand shall right your mother's wrong.

DEMETRIUS
Stay, madam, here is more belongs to her:
First thrash the corn, then after burn the straw.
124 This minion stood upon her chastity,
Upon her nuptial vow, her loyalty,
126 And with that painted hope braves your mightiness;
And shall she carry this unto her grave?

CHIRON
An if she do, I would I were an eunuch.
Drag hence her husband to some secret hole,
And make his dead trunk pillow to our lust.

TAMORA
But when ye have the honey we desire,
132 Let not this wasp outlive, us both to sting.

CHIRON
I warrant you, madam, we will make that sure.
Come, mistress, now perforce we will enjoy
135 That nice-preservèd honesty of yours.

LAVINIA
O Tamora, thou bearest a woman's face –

TAMORA
I will not hear her speak, away with her!

LAVINIA
Sweet lords, entreat her hear me but a word.

DEMETRIUS
Listen, fair madam: let it be your glory
To see her tears; but be your heart to them
As unrelenting flint to drops of rain.

LAVINIA
When did the tiger's young ones teach the dam? 142
O, do not learn her wrath; she taught it thee; 143
The milk thou suck'dst from her did turn to marble;
Even at thy teat thou hadst thy tyranny.
Yet every mother breeds not sons alike.
    [To Chiron]
Do thou entreat her show a woman's pity.

CHIRON
What, wouldst thou have me prove myself a bastard?

LAVINIA
'Tis true the raven doth not hatch a lark:
Yet have I heard – O, could I find it now! –
The lion, moved with pity, did endure
To have his princely paws pared all away.
Some say that ravens foster forlorn children
The whilst their own birds famish in their nests:
O, be to me, though thy hard heart say no,
Nothing so kind, but something pitiful. 156

TAMORA
I know not what it means, away with her!

LAVINIA
O, let me teach thee for my father's sake,
That gave thee life when well he might have slain thee,
Be not obdurate, open thy deaf ears.

TAMORA
Hadst thou in person ne'er offended me,
Even for his sake am I pitiless.
Remember, boys, I poured forth tears in vain
To save your brother from the sacrifice,
But fierce Andronicus would not relent.
Therefore away with her, and use her as you will;
The worse to her, the better loved of me.

LAVINIA
O Tamora, be called a gentle queen
And with thine own hands kill me in this place,
For 'tis not life that I have begged so long.
Poor I was slain when Bassianus died.

TAMORA
What begg'st thou then? fond woman, let me go. 172

LAVINIA
'Tis present death I beg; and one thing more
That womanhood denies my tongue to tell. 174
O, keep me from their worse than killing lust,
And tumble me into some loathsome pit,
Where never man's eye may behold my body.
Do this, and be a charitable murderer.

TAMORA
So should I rob my sweet sons of their fee.
No, let them satisfice their lust on thee.

DEMETRIUS
Away! for thou hast stayed us here too long.

LAVINIA
No grace? no womanhood? Ah, beastly creature,
The blot and enemy to our general name! 183
Confusion fall – 184

CHIRON
Nay then, I'll stop your mouth. Bring thou her husband.
This is the hole where Aaron bid us hide him.
    [Demetrius throws the body of Bassianus into the pit;
               then exeunt Demetrius and Chiron,
                    dragging off Lavinia.]

TAMORA
Farewell, my sons: see that you make her sure.

---

101 *urchins* hedgehogs 118 *Semiramis* (see II, i, 22n.) 124 *minion* contemptible creature; *stood upon* made much of 126 *painted* unrealistic 132 *outlive* survive 135 *nice-preservèd honesty* carefully guarded chastity 142 *dam* mother 143 *learn* teach 156 *Nothing . . . pitiful* i.e. not so kind as the raven, yet showing some pity 172 *fond* foolish 174 *denies* forbids 183 *our general name* the name of woman 184 *Confusion* destruction

Ne'er let my heart know merry cheer indeed
189 Till all the Andronici be made away.
Now will I hence to seek my lovely Moor
191 And let my spleenful sons this trull deflow'r.   *[Exit.]*
     Enter Aaron, with two of Titus' Sons [Quintus and
     Martius].

AARON
     Come on, my lords, the better foot before.
     Straight will I bring you to the loathsome pit
     Where I espied the panther fast asleep.

QUINTUS
     My sight is very dull, whate'er it bodes.

MARTIUS
     And mine, I promise you: were it not for shame,
     Well could I leave our sport to sleep awhile.
     [Falls into the pit.]

QUINTUS
     What, art thou fallen? What subtle hole is this,
     Whose mouth is coverèd with rude-growing briers,
     Upon whose leaves are drops of new-shed blood
     As fresh as morning dew distilled on flowers?
202 A very fatal place it seems to me.
     Speak, brother, hast thou hurt thee with the fall?

MARTIUS
     O brother, with the dismall'st object hurt
     That ever eye with sight made heart lament.

AARON
     Now will I fetch the king to find them here,
     That he thereby may have a likely guess
     How these were they that made away his brother.   *Exit.*

MARTIUS
     Why dost not comfort me and help me out
     From this unhallowed and bloodstainèd hole?

QUINTUS
211 I am surprisèd with an uncouth fear;
     A chilling sweat o'erruns my trembling joints;
     My heart suspects more than mine eye can see.

MARTIUS
     To prove thou hast a true-divining heart,
     Aaron and thou look down into this den
     And see a fearful sight of blood and death.

QUINTUS
     Aaron is gone, and my compassionate heart
     Will not permit mine eyes once to behold
219 The thing whereat it trembles by surmise.
     O, tell me who it is, for ne'er till now
     Was I a child to fear I know not what.

MARTIUS
222 Lord Bassianus lies berayed in blood,
     All on a heap, like to a slaughterèd lamb,
     In this detested, dark, blood-drinking pit.

QUINTUS
     If it be dark, how dost thou know 'tis he?

MARTIUS
     Upon his bloody finger he doth wear
     A precious ring that lightens all this hole,
     Which, like a taper in some monument,
     Doth shine upon the dead man's earthy cheeks,
230 And shows the ragged entrails of this pit.
231 So pale did shine the moon on Pyramus
     When he by night lay bathed in maiden blood.
     O brother, help me with thy fainting hand,
     If fear hath made thee faint, as me it hath,

Out of this fell devouring receptacle,   235
As hateful as Cocytus' misty mouth.   236

QUINTUS
     Reach me thy hand, that I may help thee out,
     Or, wanting strength to do thee so much good,   238
     I may be plucked into the swallowing womb
     Of this deep pit, poor Bassianus' grave.
     I have no strength to pluck thee to the brink.

MARTIUS
     Nor I no strength to climb without thy help.

QUINTUS
     Thy hand once more; I will not loose again
     Till thou art here aloft, or I below.
     Thou canst not come to me: I come to thee.   *[Falls in.]*
     Enter the Emperor and Aaron the Moor.

SATURNINUS
     Along with me: I'll see what hole is here,
     And what he is that now is leaped into it.
     Say, who art thou that lately didst descend
     Into this gaping hollow of the earth?

MARTIUS
     The unhappy sons of old Andronicus,   250
     Brought hither in a most unlucky hour
     To find thy brother Bassianus dead.

SATURNINUS
     My brother dead? I know thou dost but jest.
     He and his lady both are at the lodge
     Upon the north side of this pleasant chase;
     'Tis not an hour since I left them there.

MARTIUS
     We know not where you left them all alive;
     But, out alas! here have we found him dead.
     Enter Tamora, Andronicus, and Lucius.

TAMORA
     Where is my lord the king?

SATURNINUS
     Here, Tamora; though grieved with killing grief.

TAMORA
     Where is thy brother Bassianus?

SATURNINUS
     Now to the bottom dost thou search my wound: 262
     Poor Bassianus here lies murderèd.

TAMORA
     Then all too late I bring this fatal writ,
     The complot of this timeless tragedy;   265
     And wonder greatly that man's face can fold   266
     In pleasing smiles such murderous tyranny.
     She giveth Saturnine a letter.

SATURNINUS *(reads the letter)*
     'An if we miss to meet him handsomely,   268
     Sweet huntsman, Bassianus 'tis we mean,
     Do thou so much as dig the grave for him,
     Thou know'st our meaning: look for thy reward
     Among the nettles at the elder tree
     Which overshades the mouth of that same pit
     Where we decreed to bury Bassianus.

---

189 *made away* murdered   191 *spleenful* lustful; *trull* harlot   202 *fatal*
ill-omened   211 *surprised* overcome; *uncouth* strange   219 *by surmise* to
imagine   222 *berayed* befouled   230 *ragged entrails* rough interior
231 *Pyramus* the lover of Thisbe, who killed himself because he thought
she was dead   235 *fell* savage   236 *Cocytus* a river in Hades   238 *wanting*
lacking   262 *search* probe   265 *complot* plot; *timeless* untimely   266 *fold*
conceal   268 *handsomely* conveniently

Do this, and purchase us thy lasting friends.'
O Tamora, was ever heard the like ?
This is the pit, and this the elder tree.
Look, sirs, if you can find the huntsman out
279   That should have murderèd Bassianus here.

AARON

My gracious lord, here is the bag of gold.

SATURNINUS [to Titus]

281   Two of thy whelps, fell curs of bloody kind,
Have here bereft my brother of his life.
Sirs, drag them from the pit unto the prison.
There let them bide until we have devised
Some never-heard-of torturing pain for them.

TAMORA

What, are they in this pit ? O wondrous thing !
How easily murder is discoverèd !

TITUS

High emperor, upon my feeble knee
I beg this boon, with tears not lightly shed,
That this fell fault of my accursèd sons,
Accursèd if the fault be proved in them –

SATURNINUS

292   If it be proved ? You see it is apparent.
Who found this letter ? Tamora, was it you ?

TAMORA

Andronicus himself did take it up.

TITUS

I did, my lord, yet let me be their bail ;
For by my father's reverent tomb I vow
They shall be ready at your highness' will
298   To answer their suspicion with their lives.

SATURNINUS

Thou shalt not bail them : see thou follow me.
Some bring the murderèd body, some the murderers.
Let them not speak a word ; the guilt is plain ;
For, by my soul, were there worse end than death,
That end upon them should be executed.

TAMORA

Andronicus, I will entreat the king ;
305   Fear not thy sons, they shall do well enough.

TITUS

Come, Lucius, come ; stay not to talk with them.
                          [Exeunt.]

*

II, iv   *Enter the Empress' Sons [Demetrius and Chiron],*
with Lavinia, her hands cut off, and her tongue cut
out, and ravished.

DEMETRIUS

So, now go tell, an if thy tongue can speak,
Who 'twas that cut thy tongue and ravished thee.

CHIRON

3   Write down thy mind, bewray thy meaning so,
An if thy stumps will let thee play the scribe.

DEMETRIUS

See how with signs and tokens she can scrowl.   5

CHIRON

Go home, call for sweet water, wash thy hands.   6

DEMETRIUS

She hath no tongue to call, nor hands to wash ;
And so let's leave her to her silent walks.

CHIRON

An 'twere my cause, I should go hang myself.   9

DEMETRIUS

If thou hadst hands to help thee knit the cord.
             Exeunt [Demetrius and Chiron].
      Enter Marcus, from hunting.

MARCUS

Who is this ? my niece, that flies away so fast !
Cousin, a word : where is your husband ?   12
If I do dream, would all my wealth would wake me !
If I do wake, some planet strike me down,
That I may slumber an eternal sleep !
Speak, gentle niece, what stern ungentle hand
Hath lopped and hewed and made thy body bare
Of her two branches, those sweet ornaments
Whose circling shadows kings have sought to sleep in,
And might not gain so great a happiness
As half thy love ? Why dost not speak to me ?
Alas, a crimson river of warm blood,
Like to a bubbling fountain stirred with wind,
Doth rise and fall between thy rosèd lips,
Coming and going with thy honey breath.
But sure some Tereus hath deflow'rèd thee,   26
And, lest thou shouldst detect him, cut thy tongue.   27
Ah, now thou turn'st away thy face for shame,
And, notwithstanding all this loss of blood,
As from a conduit with three issuing spouts,   30
Yet do thy cheeks look red as Titan's face   31
Blushing to be encount'red with a cloud.
Shall I speak for thee ? Shall I say 'tis so ?
O that I knew thy heart, and knew the beast,
That I might rail at him to ease my mind !
Sorrow concealèd, like an oven stopped,
Doth burn the heart to cinders where it is.
Fair Philomel, why she but lost her tongue,   38
And in a tedious sampler sewed her mind :   39
But, lovely niece, that mean is cut from thee ;
A craftier Tereus, cousin, hast thou met,
And he hath cut those pretty fingers off
That could have better sewed than Philomel.
O, had the monster seen those lily hands
Tremble like aspen leaves upon a lute
And make the silken strings delight to kiss them,
He would not then have touched them for his life.
Or had he heard the heavenly harmony
Which that sweet tongue hath made,
He would have dropped his knife, and fell asleep,
As Cerberus at the Thracian poet's feet.   51
Come, let us go and make thy father blind,
For such a sight will blind a father's eye.
One hour's storm will drown the fragrant meads ;
What will whole months of tears thy father's eyes ?
Do not draw back, for we will mourn with thee :
O, could our mourning ease thy misery !   *Exeunt.*

---

279 *should* was to 281 *kind* nature 292 *apparent* plainly visible 298 *their suspicion* the suspicion they are under 305 *Fear not* do not be afraid for

II, iv The forest 3 *bewray* reveal 5 *scrowl* scrawl 6 *sweet* perfumed 9 *cause* case 12 *Cousin* (commonly used of a relative more distant than brother or sister) 26 *Tereus* (see II, iii, 43n.) 27 *detect* expose 30 *conduit* fountain 31 *Titan's* (see I, i, 229n.) 38 *Philomel* (see II, iii 43n.) 39 *tedious* laborious; *sampler* tapestry 51 *Cerberus* three-headed dog that guarded the entrance to Hades; *Thracian poet* i.e. Orpheus, whose music lulled Cerberus asleep

III, i

*Enter the Judges and Senators, with Titus' two
Sons [Martius and Quintus], bound, passing on the
stage to the place of execution, and Titus going
before, pleading.*

TITUS

Hear me, grave fathers! noble tribunes, stay,
For pity of mine age, whose youth was spent
In dangerous wars whilst you securely slept;
For all my blood in Rome's great quarrel shed,
For all the frosty nights that I have watched,
And for these bitter tears which now you see
Filling the agèd wrinkles in my cheeks,
Be pitiful to my condemnèd sons,
Whose souls are not corrupted as 'tis thought.
For two and twenty sons I never wept,
Because they died in honor's lofty bed.

Andronicus lieth down, and the Judges pass by him.

For these, tribunes, in the dust I write

13   My heart's deep languor and my soul's sad tears.
14   Let my tears staunch the earth's dry appetite;
     My sons' sweet blood will make it shame and blush.
     O earth, I will befriend thee more with rain
17   That shall distill from these two ancient urns
     Than youthful April shall with all his show'rs.
19   In summer's drought I'll drop upon thee still,
     In winter with warm tears I'll melt the snow,
     And keep eternal spring-time on thy face,
22   So thou refuse to drink my dear sons' blood.

Enter Lucius, with his weapon drawn.

     O reverent tribunes! O gentle agèd men!
24   Unbind my sons, reverse the doom of death;
     And let me say, that never wept before,
     My tears are now prevailing orators!

LUCIUS

O noble father, you lament in vain,
The tribunes hear you not; no man is by,
And you recount your sorrows to a stone.

TITUS

Ah, Lucius, for thy brothers let me plead.
Grave tribunes, once more I entreat of you –

LUCIUS

My gracious lord, no tribune hears you speak.

TITUS

Why, 'tis no matter, man: if they did hear,
They would not mark me; or if they did mark,
They would not pity me; yet plead I must,
36   And bootless unto them.
     Therefore I tell my sorrows to the stones,
     Who, though they cannot answer my distress,
     Yet in some sort they are better than the tribunes,
40   For that they will not intercept my tale.
     When I do weep, they humbly at my feet
     Receive my tears and seem to weep with me;
43   And were they but attirèd in grave weeds,
     Rome could afford no tribunes like to these.
     A stone is soft as wax, tribunes more hard than stones:
     A stone is silent and offendeth not,
     And tribunes with their tongues doom men to death.

[Rises.]

But wherefore stand'st thou with thy weapon drawn?

LUCIUS

To rescue my two brothers from their death;
50   For which attempt the judges have pronounced
     My everlasting doom of banishment.

TITUS

O happy man! they have befriended thee.
Why, foolish Lucius, dost thou not perceive
That Rome is but a wilderness of tigers?
Tigers must prey, and Rome affords no prey
But me and mine: how happy art thou then
From these devourers to be banishèd!
But who comes with our brother Marcus here?

Enter Marcus with Lavinia.

MARCUS

Titus, prepare thy agèd eyes to weep,
Or if not so, thy noble heart to break!
I bring consuming sorrow to thine age.

TITUS

Will it consume me? let me see it then.

MARCUS

This was thy daughter.

TITUS   Why, Marcus, so she is.

LUCIUS

Ay me, this object kills me!   64

TITUS

Faint-hearted boy, arise and look upon her.
Speak, Lavinia, what accursèd hand
Hath made thee handless in thy father's sight?
What fool hath added water to the sea
Or brought a fagot to bright-burning Troy?
My grief was at the height before thou cam'st,
And now like Nilus it disdaineth bounds.   71
Give me a sword: I'll chop off my hands too;
For they have fought for Rome, and all in vain;
And they have nursed this woe in feeding life;
In bootless prayer have they been held up,
And they have served me to effectless use.
Now all the service I require of them
Is that the one will help to cut the other.
'Tis well, Lavinia, that thou hast no hands;
For hands to do Rome service is but vain.

LUCIUS

Speak, gentle sister, who hath martyred thee?   81

MARCUS

O, that delightful engine of her thoughts   82
That blabbed them with such pleasing eloquence   83
Is torn from forth that pretty hollow cage,
Where like a sweet melodious bird it sung
Sweet varied notes, enchanting every ear!

LUCIUS

O, say thou for her, who hath done this deed?

MARCUS

O, thus I found her straying in the park,
Seeking to hide herself, as doth the deer
That hath received some unrecuring wound.   90

TITUS

It was my dear, and he that wounded her
Hath hurt me more than had he killed me dead;
For now I stand as one upon a rock,
Environed with a wilderness of sea,
Who marks the waxing tide grow wave by wave,

III, i A street in Rome **13** *languor* grief **14** *staunch* satisfy **17** *urns*
i.e. his eyes **19** *still* all the time **22** *So* provided that **24** *doom* sentence
36 *bootless* in vain **40** *intercept* interrupt **43** *grave weeds* ceremonial
dress **64** *Ay me* alas; *object* spectacle **71** *Nilus* the Nile **81** *martyred*
mutilated **82** *engine* instrument **83** *blabbed* freely uttered **90** *unrecuring* incurable

96   Expecting ever when some envious surge
Will in his brinish bowels swallow him.
This way to death my wretched sons are gone ;
Here stands my other son, a banished man,
And here my brother, weeping at my woes :
101   But that which gives my soul the greatest spurn
Is dear Lavinia, dearer than my soul.
Had I but seen thy picture in this plight,
It would have madded me : what shall I do
105   Now I behold thy lively body so ?
Thou hast no hands to wipe away thy tears,
Nor tongue to tell me who hath mart'red thee.
Thy husband he is dead, and for his death
109   Thy brothers are condemned, and dead by this.
Look, Marcus ! ah, son Lucius, look on her !
When I did name her brothers, then fresh tears
Stood on her cheeks, as doth the honeydew
Upon a gath'red lily almost withered.

MARCUS
Perchance she weeps because they killed her husband ;
Perchance because she knows them innocent.

TITUS
If they did kill thy husband, then be joyful,
Because the law hath ta'en revenge on them.
No, no, they would not do so foul a deed ;
Witness the sorrow that their sister makes.
Gentle Lavinia, let me kiss thy lips,
121   Or make some sign how I may do thee ease.
Shall thy good uncle and thy brother Lucius
And thou and I sit round about some fountain,
Looking all downwards to behold our cheeks
How they are stained, like meadows yet not dry
With miry slime left on them by a flood ?
And in the fountain shall we gaze so long
128   Till the fresh taste be taken from that clearness,
And made a brine-pit with our bitter tears ?
Or shall we cut away our hands like thine ?
131   Or shall we bite our tongues, and in dumb shows
Pass the remainder of our hateful days ?
What shall we do ? let us that have our tongues
Plot some device of further misery,
To make us wond'red at in time to come.

LUCIUS
Sweet father, cease your tears ; for at your grief
See how my wretched sister sobs and weeps.

MARCUS
Patience, dear niece. Good Titus, dry thine eyes.

TITUS
Ah, Marcus, Marcus ! brother, well I wot
140   Thy napkin cannot drink a tear of mine,
141   For thou, poor man, hast drowned it with thine own.

LUCIUS
Ah, my Lavinia, I will wipe thy cheeks.

TITUS
Mark, Marcus, mark ! I understand her signs :
Had she a tongue to speak, now would she say
That to her brother which I said to thee.
His napkin, with his true tears all bewet,
Can do no service on her sorrowful cheeks.

96 *Expecting . . . when* awaiting . . . the time when ; *envious* malignant
101 *spurn* stroke   105 *lively* living   109 *by this* by now   121 *do thee ease*
bring you relief   128 *clearness* i.e. clear fountain   131 *dumb shows* mime
140 *napkin* handkerchief   141 *drowned* soaked   148 *sympathy* affinity
178 *meet* fit

O, what a sympathy of woe is this :
As far from help as Limbo is from bliss !   148
     Enter Aaron the Moor, alone.

AARON
Titus Andronicus, my lord the emperor
Sends thee this word, that, if thou love thy sons,
Let Marcus, Lucius, or thyself, old Titus,
Or any one of you, chop off your hand
And send it to the king : he for the same
Will send thee hither both thy sons alive ;
And that shall be the ransom for their fault.

TITUS
O gracious emperor ! O gentle Aaron !
Did ever raven sing so like a lark
That gives sweet tidings of the sun's uprise ?
With all my heart I'll send the emperor my hand.   160
Good Aaron, wilt thou help to chop it off ?

LUCIUS
Stay, father, for that noble hand of thine,
That hath thrown down so many enemies,
Shall not be sent : my hand will serve the turn,
My youth can better spare my blood than you,
And therefore mine shall save my brothers' lives.

MARCUS
Which of your hands hath not defended Rome
And reared aloft the bloody battle-axe,
Writing destruction on the enemy's castle ?
O, none of both but are of high desert :   170
My hand hath been but idle ; let it serve
To ransom my two nephews from their death ;
Then have I kept it to a worthy end.

AARON
Nay, come, agree whose hand shall go along,
For fear they die before their pardon come.

MARCUS
My hand shall go.

LUCIUS   By heaven, it shall not go !

TITUS
Sirs, strive no more. Such withered herbs as these
Are meet for plucking up, and therefore mine.   178

LUCIUS
Sweet father, if I shall be thought thy son,
Let me redeem my brothers both from death.

MARCUS
And for our father's sake and mother's care,
Now let me show a brother's love to thee.

TITUS
Agree between you ; I will spare my hand.

LUCIUS
Then I'll go fetch an axe.

MARCUS
But I will use the axe.   *Exeunt [Lucius and Marcus].*

TITUS
Come hither, Aaron. I'll deceive them both :
Lend me thy hand, and I will give thee mine.

AARON [*aside*]
If that be called deceit, I will be honest,
And never whilst I live deceive men so :
But I'll deceive you in another sort,
And that you'll say ere half an hour pass.
     He cuts off Titus' hand.
     Enter Lucius and Marcus again.

TITUS
Now stay your strife ; what shall be is dispatched.

Good Aaron, give his majesty my hand :

194 Tell him it was a hand that warded him

From thousand dangers ; bid him bury it ;

More hath it merited, that let it have.

As for my sons, say I account of them

As jewels purchased at an easy price ;

And yet dear too, because I bought mine own.

AARON

I go, Andronicus ; and for thy hand

201 Look by and by to have thy sons with thee.

[Aside]

Their heads, I mean. O, how this villainy

203 Doth fat me with the very thoughts of it !

Let fools do good, and fair men call for grace,

Aaron will have his soul black like his face.   *Exit.*

TITUS

O, here I lift this one hand up to heaven,

And bow this feeble ruin to the earth.

If any power pities wretched tears,

To that I call !

[To Lavinia] What, wouldst thou kneel with me ?

Do then, dear heart ; for heaven shall hear our prayers,

211 Or with our sighs we'll breathe the welkin dim

And stain the sun with fog, as sometime clouds

When they do hug him in their melting bosoms.

MARCUS

O brother, speak with possibility,

And do not break into these deep extremes.

TITUS

Is not my sorrow deep, having no bottom ?

217 Then be my passions bottomless with them !

MARCUS

But yet let reason govern thy lament.

TITUS

If there were reason for these miseries,

220 Then into limits could I bind my woes :

When heaven doth weep, doth not the earth o'erflow ?

If the winds rage, doth not the sea wax mad,

Threat'ning the welkin with his big-swoll'n face ?

224 And wilt thou have a reason for this coil ?

I am the sea ; hark how her sighs doth flow !

She is the weeping welkin, I the earth :

Then must my sea be moved with her sighs ;

Then must my earth with her continual tears

Become a deluge, overflowed and drowned ;

230 For why my bowels cannot hide her woes,

But like a drunkard must I vomit them.

Then give me leave ; for losers will have leave

233 To ease their stomachs with their bitter tongues.

Enter a Messenger, with two heads and a hand.

MESSENGER

Worthy Andronicus, ill art thou repaid

For that good hand thou sent'st the emperor.

Here are the heads of thy two noble sons,

And here's thy hand, in scorn to thee sent back,

Thy grief their sports, thy resolution mocked,

239 That woe is me to think upon thy woes

More than remembrance of my father's death.   *Exit.*

MARCUS

Now let hot Etna cool in Sicily,

And be my heart an ever-burning hell !

These miseries are more than may be borne.

244 To weep with them that weep doth ease some deal ;

245 But sorrow flouted at is double death.

LUCIUS

Ah, that this sight should make so deep a wound,

And yet detested life not shrink thereat ;   247

That ever death should let life bear his name   248

Where life hath no more interest but to breathe !

[Lavinia kisses Titus.]

MARCUS

Alas, poor heart, that kiss is comfortless

As frozen water to a starved snake.   251

TITUS

When will this fearful slumber have an end ?   252

MARCUS

Now farewell, flatt'ry ; die, Andronicus ;

Thou dost not slumber : see thy two sons' heads,

Thy warlike hand, thy mangled daughter here,

Thy other banished son with this dear sight   256

Struck pale and bloodless, and thy brother, I,

Even like a stony image, cold and numb.

Ah, now no more will I control thy griefs :

Rend off thy silver hair, thy other hand

Gnawing with thy teeth ; and be this dismal sight

The closing up of our most wretched eyes.

Now is a time to storm ; why art thou still ?

TITUS Ha, ha, ha !

MARCUS

Why dost thou laugh ? it fits not with this hour.

TITUS

Why, I have not another tear to shed ;

Besides, this sorrow is an enemy,

And would usurp upon my wat'ry eyes

And make them blind with tributary tears.   269

Then which way shall I find Revenge's cave ?

For these two heads do seem to speak to me,

And threat me I shall never come to bliss

Till all these mischiefs be returned again

Even in their throats that hath committed them.

Come, let me see what task I have to do.

You heavy people, circle me about,   276

That I may turn me to each one of you

And swear unto my soul to right your wrongs.

The vow is made. Come, brother, take a head ;

And in this hand the other will I bear.

And, Lavinia, thou shalt be employed in these arms :   281

Bear thou my hand, sweet wench, between thy teeth.

As for thee, boy, go get thee from my sight,

Thou art an exile, and thou must not stay.

Hie to the Goths and raise an army there ;

And if ye love me, as I think you do,

Let's kiss and part, for we have much to do.

Exeunt [all except Lucius].

LUCIUS

Farewell, Andronicus, my noble father,

The woefull'st man that ever lived in Rome.

194 *warded* guarded   201 *Look* expect   203 *fat* delight (literally, nourish) 211 *breathe . . . dim* make the heavens cloudy with our breath   217 *passions* passionate outbursts   220 *bind* confine   224 *coil* disturbance   230 *For why* because ; *bowels* (formerly associated with compassion)   233 *ease their stomachs* relieve their feelings   239 *That* so that   244 *some deal* somewhat   245 *flouted* mocked   247 *shrink* slip away   248 *bear his name* i.e. still be called 'life'   251 *starved* numbed by cold   252 *fearful slumber* i.e. frightful dream   256 *dear* grievous   269 *tributary* paid as tribute 276 *heavy* sorrowful   281 *employed . . . arms* (clearly corrupt : the word 'arms' may have been intended as a less grotesque substitute for *teeth* in the following line, mistakenly caught up by the compositor ; the original reading may have been 'employed in this')

Farewell, proud Rome, till Lucius come again!
He loves his pledges dearer than his life.
Farewell, Lavinia, my noble sister.
293 O, would thou wert as thou tofore hast been!
But now nor Lucius nor Lavinia lives
But in oblivion and hateful griefs.
If Lucius live, he will requite your wrongs
And make proud Saturnine and his empress
298 Beg at the gates like Tarquin and his queen.
Now will I to the Goths and raise a pow'r,
To be revenged on Rome and Saturnine.   *Exit Lucius.*

*

III, ii   *A banquet. Enter Andronicus, Marcus, Lavinia, and*
        the Boy [Lucius].
    TITUS
So, so, now sit; and look you eat no more
Than will preserve just so much strength in us
As will revenge these bitter woes of ours.
4 Marcus, unknit that sorrow-wreathen knot:
Thy niece and I, poor creatures, want our hands,
6 And cannot passionate our tenfold grief
With folded arms. This poor right hand of mine
Is left to tyrannize upon my breast;
Who, when my heart, all mad with misery,
Beats in this hollow prison of my flesh,
Then thus I thump it down.
    [To Lavinia]
12 Thou map of woe, that thus dost talk in signs,
When thy poor heart beats with outrageous beating,
Thou canst not strike it thus to make it still.
Wound it with sighing, girl, kill it with groans;
Or get some little knife between thy teeth
And just against thy heart make thou a hole,
That all the tears that thy poor eyes let fall
19 May run into that sink, and soaking in,
20 Drown the lamenting fool in sea-salt tears.
    MARCUS
Fie, brother, fie! teach her not thus to lay
Such violent hands upon her tender life.
    TITUS
How now! has sorrow made thee dote already?
Why, Marcus, no man should be mad but I.
What violent hands can she lay on her life?
Ah, wherefore dost thou urge the name of hands,
27 To bid Aeneas tell the tale twice o'er,
How Troy was burnt and he made miserable?
O, handle not the theme, to talk of hands,
Lest we remember still that we have none.
31 Fie, fie, how franticly I square my talk,
As if we should forget we had no hands
If Marcus did not name the word of hands!
Come, let's fall to; and, gentle girl, eat this.
Here is no drink! hark, Marcus, what she says.

I can interpret all her martyred signs:
She says she drinks no other drink but tears,
38 Brewed with her sorrow, meshed upon her cheeks.
Speechless complainer, I will learn thy thought.
40 In thy dumb action will I be as perfect
As begging hermits in their holy prayers.
Thou shalt not sigh, nor hold thy stumps to heaven,
43 Nor wink, nor nod, nor kneel, nor make a sign,
But I of these will wrest an alphabet
45 And by still practice learn to know thy meaning.
    BOY
Good grandsire, leave these bitter deep laments.
Make my aunt merry with some pleasing tale.
    MARCUS
Alas, the tender boy, in passion moved,
Doth weep to see his grandsire's heaviness.
    TITUS
Peace, tender sapling, thou art made of tears,
And tears will quickly melt thy life away.
    Marcus strikes the dish with a knife.
What dost thou strike at, Marcus, with thy knife?
    MARCUS
At that that I have killed, my lord – a fly.
    TITUS
Out on thee, murderer! Thou kill'st my heart;
Mine eyes are cloyed with view of tyranny.
A deed of death done on the innocent
Becomes not Titus' brother. Get thee gone!
I see thou art not for my company.
    MARCUS
Alas, my lord, I have but killed a fly.
    TITUS
'But'? How if that fly had a father and mother?
How would he hang his slender gilded wings
62 And buzz lamenting doings in the air!
Poor harmless fly,
That, with his pretty buzzing melody,
Came here to make us merry, and thou hast killed him.
    MARCUS
66 Pardon me, sir; it was a black ill-favored fly,
Like to the empress' Moor; therefore I killed him.
    TITUS
O, O, O!
Then pardon me for reprehending thee,
For thou hast done a charitable deed.
71 Give me thy knife, I will insult on him,
Flattering myself as if it were the Moor
Come hither purposely to poison me.
There's for thyself, and that's for Tamora.
75 Ah, sirrah!
Yet, I think, we are not brought so low
But that between us we can kill a fly
That comes in likeness of a coal-black Moor.
    MARCUS
Alas, poor man! Grief has so wrought on him
He takes false shadows for true substances.
    TITUS
81 Come, take away. Lavinia, go with me.
82 I'll to thy closet and go read with thee
83 Sad stories chancèd in the times of old.
Come, boy, and go with me. Thy sight is young,
And thou shalt read when mine begin to dazzle.
    [Exeunt.]

*

293 *tofore* formerly 298 *Tarquin* Roman king, deposed when his son
Tarquin raped Lucrece
III, ii The house of Titus (the quartos omit this scene, but its inclusion in
the folio is sufficient guarantee of its authenticity) 4 *knot* i.e. folded arms,
signifying sorrow 6 *passionate* express with passion 12 *map* symbol
19 *sink* receptacle 20 *fool* (here, as often, a term of affection) 27 *Aeneas*
(see Virgil, *Aeneid* II, 2) 31 *square* regulate 38 *meshed* brewed 40
perfect fully understanding 43 *wink* blink 45 *still* constant 62 *lamenting
doings* lamentations (?) 66 *ill-favored* ugly 71 *insult on* triumph over
75 *sirrah* (contemptuous term of address to inferiors) 81 *take away* clear
the table 82 *closet* private chamber 83 *chancèd* that happened

IV, i *Enter Lucius' Son and Lavinia running after him, and the Boy flies from her with his books under his arm. Enter Titus and Marcus.*

BOY
Help, grandsire, help! My aunt Lavinia
Follows me everywhere, I know not why.
Good uncle Marcus, see how swift she comes:
Alas, sweet aunt, I know not what you mean.

MARCUS
Stand by me, Lucius; do not fear thine aunt.

TITUS
She loves thee, boy, too well to do thee harm.

BOY
Ay, when my father was in Rome she did.

MARCUS
What means my niece Lavinia by these signs?

TITUS
Fear her not, Lucius. Somewhat doth she mean.
See, Lucius, see, how much she makes of thee:
Somewhither would she have thee go with her.
12 Ah, boy, Cornelia never with more care
Read to her sons than she hath read to thee
14 Sweet poetry and Tully's Orator.

MARCUS
Canst thou not guess wherefore she plies thee thus?

BOY
My lord, I know not, I, nor can I guess,
Unless some fit or frenzy do possess her;
For I have heard my grandsire say full oft,
Extremity of griefs would make men mad;
And I have read that Hecuba of Troy
Ran mad for sorrow; that made me to fear,
Although, my lord, I know my noble aunt
Loves me as dear as e'er my mother did,
24 And would not, but in fury, fright my youth;
Which made me down to throw my books, and fly,
Causeless, perhaps, but pardon me, sweet aunt;
And, madam, if my uncle Marcus go,
28 I will most willingly attend your ladyship.

MARCUS
Lucius, I will.
[Lavinia turns over with her stumps the books which Lucius has let fall.]

TITUS
How now, Lavinia? Marcus, what means this?
Some book there is that she desires to see.
Which is it, girl, of these? Open them, boy.
But thou art deeper read and better skilled:
Come and take choice of all my library,
And so beguile thy sorrow, till the heavens
Reveal the damned contriver of this deed.
37 Why lifts she up her arms in sequence thus?

MARCUS
I think she means that there were more than one
39 Confederate in the fact. Ay, more there was;
Or else to heaven she heaves them for revenge.

TITUS
41 Lucius, what book is that she tosseth so?

BOY
42 Grandsire, 'tis Ovid's Metamorphosis.
My mother gave it me.

MARCUS   For love of her that's gone
Perhaps she culled it from among the rest.

TITUS
Soft; so busily she turns the leaves!
Help her: what would she find? Lavinia, shall I read?
This is the tragic tale of Philomel   47
And treats of Tereus' treason and his rape;
And rape, I fear, was root of thine annoy.

MARCUS
See, brother, see, note how she quotes the leaves.   50

TITUS
Lavinia, wert thou thus surprised, sweet girl,
Ravished and wronged as Philomela was,
Forced in the ruthless, vast, and gloomy woods?   53
See, see!
Ay, such a place there is where we did hunt
(O had we never, never hunted there!)
Patterned by that the poet here describes,   57
By nature made for murders and for rapes.

MARCUS
O, why should nature build so foul a den,
Unless the gods delight in tragedies?

TITUS
Give signs, sweet girl, for here are none but friends,
What Roman lord it was durst do the deed.
Or slunk not Saturnine, as Tarquin erst,   63
That left the camp to sin in Lucrece' bed?

MARCUS
Sit down, sweet niece: brother, sit down by me.
Apollo, Pallas, Jove, or Mercury,
Inspire me, that I may this treason find.
My lord, look here: look here, Lavinia!
He writes his name with his staff, and guides it with feet and mouth.
This sandy plot is plain; guide, if thou canst,   69
This after me. I have writ my name   70
Without the help of any hand at all.
Cursed be that heart that forced us to this shift!   72
Write thou, good niece, and here display at last
What God will have discoverèd for revenge.   74
Heaven guide thy pen to print thy sorrows plain,
That we may know the traitors and the truth.
She takes the staff in her mouth and guides it with her stumps and writes.

TITUS
O, do ye read, my lord, what she hath writ?
'Stuprum. Chiron. Demetrius.'   78

MARCUS
What, what! the lustful sons of Tamora
Performers of this heinous bloody deed?

TITUS
'Magni dominator poli,   81
Tam lentus audis scelera? tam lentus vides?'

MARCUS
O, calm thee, gentle lord! although I know

IV, i The garden of Titus **12** *Cornelia* mother of the Gracchi, famous Roman tribunes **14** *Tully's Orator* Cicero's *De Oratore*, or his *ad M. Brutum Orator* **24** *but in fury* except in madness **28** *attend* accompany **37** *in sequence* one after the other **39** *fact* crime **41** *tosseth* turns the leaves of **42** *Ovid's Metamorphosis* (the spelling of Golding's translation of *Metamorphoses*, with which Shakespeare was familiar) **47–48** *Philomel ... Tereus* (see II, iii, 43n.) **50** *quotes* notes **53** *vast* desolate **57** *Patterned by* on the pattern of **63** *erst* once **69** *plain* level **70** *after me* as I did **72** *shift* stratagem **74** *discoverèd* revealed **78** *Stuprum* rape **81–82** *Magni ... vides* ruler of the great heavens, art thou so slow to hear and to see crimes (Seneca, *Hippolytus*, ll. 671–72)

There is enough written upon this earth
To stir a mutiny in the mildest thoughts
And arm the minds of infants to exclaims.
My lord, kneel down with me; Lavinia, kneel;
88 And kneel, sweet boy, the Roman Hector's hope;
89 And swear with me, as with the woeful fere
And father of that chaste dishonorèd dame,
91 Lord Junius Brutus sware for Lucrece' rape,
92 That we will prosecute by good advice
Mortal revenge upon these traitorous Goths,
And see their blood or die with this reproach.

TITUS
'Tis sure enough, an you knew how,
But if you hunt these bear-whelps, then beware:
97 The dam will wake, an if she wind ye once;
She's with the lion deeply still in league,
And lulls him whilst she playeth on her back,
100 And when he sleeps will she do what she list.
You are a young huntsman, Marcus; let alone;
And come, I will go get a leaf of brass,
103 And with a gad of steel will write these words,
104 And lay it by: the angry northern wind
105 Will blow these sands like Sibyl's leaves abroad,
And where's our lesson then? Boy, what say you?

BOY
I say, my lord, that if I were a man,
Their mother's bedchamber should not be safe
For these base bondmen to the yoke of Rome.

MARCUS
Ay, that's my boy! thy father hath full oft
For his ungrateful country done the like.

BOY
And, uncle, so will I, an if I live.

TITUS
Come, go with me into mine armory:
Lucius, I'll fit thee; and withal my boy
Shall carry from me to the empress' sons
Presents that I intend to send them both.
Come, come; thou'lt do my message, wilt thou not?

BOY
Ay, with my dagger in their bosoms, grandsire.

TITUS
No, boy, not so. I'll teach thee another course.
Lavinia, come. Marcus, look to my house.
121 Lucius and I'll go brave it at the court.
122 Ay, marry, will we, sir; and we'll be waited on.
Exeunt [Titus, Lavinia, and Young Lucius].

MARCUS
O heavens, can you hear a good man groan
And not relent, or not compassion him?
125 Marcus, attend him in his ecstasy,

88 *the Roman Hector* i.e. Titus, Roman counterpart of Hector of Troy
89 *fere* husband   91 *Junius Brutus* leader of the revolt against the Tarquins
92 *by good advice* after careful consideration   97 *an . . . ye* if she gets wind
of you   100 *list* please   103 *gad* spike   104 *northern* north   105 *Sibyl's
leaves* (the prophecies of the Sibyl were written on leaves which were often
scattered by the wind)   121 *brave it* act defiantly   122 *marry* (interjection
of affirmation); *waited on* attended to   125 *ecstasy* madness   129 *Revenge
the heavens* let the heavens take vengeance
IV, ii The Emperor's palace   6 *confound* destroy   7 *Gramercy* thanks
8 *deciphered* detected   16 *appointed* equipped   20–21 *Integer . . . arcu* he
who is of upright life and free from crime does not need the javelins or
bow of the Moor (Horace, *Odes*, I, xxii, 1–2)   29 *witty* quick-witted
30 *conceit* device   38 *insinuate* curry favor

That hath more scars of sorrow in his heart
Than foemen's marks upon his batt'red shield,
But yet so just that he will not revenge.
Revenge the heavens for old Andronicus!   *Exit.* 129

*

Enter Aaron, Chiron, and Demetrius at one door,   IV, ii
and at the other door Young Lucius and another,
with a bundle of weapons, and verses writ upon them.

CHIRON
Demetrius, here's the son of Lucius;
He hath some message to deliver us.

AARON
Ay, some mad message from his mad grandfather.

BOY
My lords, with all the humbleness I may,
I greet your honors from Andronicus –
   [Aside]
And pray the Roman gods confound you both.   6

DEMETRIUS
Gramercy, lovely Lucius, what's the news?   7

BOY *[aside]*
That you are both deciphered, that's the news,   8
For villains marked with rape.
   [Aloud]   May it please you,
My grandsire, well-advised, hath sent by me
The goodliest weapons of his armory
To gratify your honorable youth,
The hope of Rome, for so he bid me say;
And so I do, and with his gifts present
Your lordships, that, whenever you have need,
You may be armèd and appointed well.   16
And so I leave you both – *[aside]* like bloody villains.
   Exit [with Attendant].

DEMETRIUS
What's here? a scroll, and written round about?
Let's see.
'Integer vitae scelerisque purus   20
Non eget Mauri iaculis nec arcu.'

CHIRON
O, 'tis a verse in Horace; I know it well.
I read it in the grammar long ago.

AARON
Ay, just; a verse in Horace; right, you have it.
   [Aside]
Now what a thing it is to be an ass!
Here's no sound jest! the old man hath found their
   guilt,
And sends them weapons wrapped about with lines
That wound, beyond their feeling, to the quick.
But were our witty empress well afoot,   29
She would applaud Andronicus' conceit.   30
But let her rest in her unrest awhile. –
And now, young lords, was't not a happy star
Led us to Rome, strangers, and more than so,
Captives, to be advancèd to this height?
It did me good before the palace gate
To brave the tribune in his brother's hearing.

DEMETRIUS
But me more good to see so great a lord
Basely insinuate and send us gifts.   38

AARON
    Had he not reason, Lord Demetrius?
    Did you not use his daughter very friendly?

DEMETRIUS
    I would we had a thousand Roman dames
42 At such a bay, by turn to serve our lust.

CHIRON
    A charitable wish and full of love!

AARON
    Here lacks but your mother for to say amen.

CHIRON
    And that would she for twenty thousand more.

DEMETRIUS
    Come, let us go and pray to all the gods
    For our belovèd mother in her pains.

AARON *[aside]*
    Pray to the devils; the gods have given us over.
       Trumpets sound.

DEMETRIUS
    Why do the emperor's trumpets flourish thus?

CHIRON
50 Belike for joy the emperor hath a son.

DEMETRIUS
    Soft, who comes here?
       Enter Nurse, with a blackamoor Child.

NURSE   God morrow, lords.
    O, tell me, did you see Aaron the Moor?

AARON
    Well, more or less, or ne'er a whit at all,
    Here Aaron is; and what with Aaron now?

NURSE
    O gentle Aaron, we are all undone!
    Now help, or woe betide thee evermore!

AARON
    Why, what a caterwauling dost thou keep!
    What dost thou wrap and fumble in thine arms?

NURSE
    O, that which I would hide from heaven's eye –
    Our empress' shame and stately Rome's disgrace!
    She is delivered, lords, she is delivered.

AARON
    To whom?

NURSE   I mean she is brought a-bed.

AARON
    Well, God give her good rest! What hath he sent her?

NURSE
    A devil.

64 AARON   Why, then she is the devil's dam:
    A joyful issue!

NURSE
    A joyless, dismal, black, and sorrowful issue!
    Here is the babe, as loathsome as a toad
    Amongst the fair-faced breeders of our clime.
    The empress sends it thee, thy stamp, thy seal,
    And bids thee christen it with thy dagger's point.

AARON
71 Zounds, ye whore! is black so base a hue?
72 Sweet blowse, you are a beauteous blossom sure.

DEMETRIUS
    Villain, what hast thou done?

AARON
    That which thou canst not undo.

CHIRON
    Thou hast undone our mother.

AARON
    Villain, I have done thy mother.   76

DEMETRIUS
    And therein, hellish dog, thou hast undone her.
    Woe to her chance, and damned her loathèd choice! 78
    Accursed the offspring of so foul a fiend!

CHIRON
    It shall not live.

AARON
    It shall not die.

NURSE
    Aaron, it must; the mother wills it so.

AARON
    What, must it, nurse? then let no man but I
    Do execution on my flesh and blood.

DEMETRIUS
    I'll broach the tadpole on my rapier's point.
    Nurse, give it me; my sword shall soon dispatch it.

AARON
    Sooner this sword shall plough thy bowels up.
    Stay, murderous villains! will you kill your brother?
    Now by the burning tapers of the sky,
    That shone so brightly when this boy was got,   90
    He dies upon my scimitar's sharp point
    That touches this my first-born son and heir!
    I tell you, younglings, not Enceladus,   93
    With all his threat'ning band of Typhon's brood,
    Nor great Alcides, nor the god of war,   95
    Shall seize this prey out of his father's hands.
    What, what, ye sanguine, shallow-hearted boys! 97
    Ye white-limed walls! ye alehouse painted signs! 98
    Coal-black is better than another hue
    In that it scorns to bear another hue;
    For all the water in the ocean
    Can never turn the swan's black legs to white,
    Although she lave them hourly in the flood.   103
    Tell the emperess from me I am of age
    To keep mine own, excuse it how she can.

DEMETRIUS
    Wilt thou betray thy noble mistress thus?

AARON
    My mistress is my mistress; this myself,
    The vigor and the picture of my youth.
    This before all the world do I prefer;
    This maugre all the world will I keep safe,   110
    Or some of you shall smoke for it in Rome!   111

DEMETRIUS
    By this our mother is for ever shamed.

CHIRON
    Rome will despise her for this foul escape.   113

NURSE
    The emperor in his rage will doom her death.

CHIRON
    I blush to think upon this ignomy.   115

AARON
    Why, there's the privilege your beauty bears.

---

42 *At . . . bay* thus cornered 50 *Belike* probably 64 *dam* mother 71 *Zounds* (an oath; a contraction of 'by God's wounds') 72 *blowse* red-cheeked wench (ironical) 76 *done* had sexual intercourse with 78 *chance* luck 90 *got* begotten 93 *Enceladus* one of the Titans, sons of Typhon, who fought the Olympians 95 *Alcides* Hercules 97 *sanguine* red-cheeked 98 *white-limed walls* i.e. 'whited sepulchres' (Matthew xxiii, 27) 103 *lave* wash 110 *maugre* in spite of 111 *smoke* suffer 113 *escape* escapade 115 *ignomy* ignominy

Fie, treacherous hue, that will betray with blushing
118 The close enacts and counsels of thy heart!
119 Here's a young lad framed of another leer.
Look how the black slave smiles upon the father,
As who should say 'Old lad, I am thine own.'
122 He is your brother, lords, sensibly fed
Of that self blood that first gave life to you;
And from that womb where you imprisoned were
He is enfranchisèd and come to light.
126 Nay, he is your brother by the surer side,
Although my seal be stampèd in his face.

NURSE
Aaron, what shall I say unto the empress?

DEMETRIUS
Advise thee, Aaron, what is to be done,
130 And we will all subscribe to thy advice:
Save thou the child, so we may all be safe.

AARON
Then sit we down and let us all consult.
133 My son and I will have the wind of you:
Keep there; now talk at pleasure of your safety.

DEMETRIUS
How many women saw this child of his?

AARON
Why, so, brave lords! when we join in league,
I am a lamb; but if you brave the Moor,
138 The chafèd boar, the mountain lioness,
The ocean swells not so as Aaron storms.
But say again, how many saw the child?

NURSE
Cornelia the midwife and myself,
And no one else but the deliverèd empress.

AARON
The emperess, the midwife, and yourself:
Two may keep counsel when the third's away.
Go to the empress, tell her this I said.
        He kills her.
Weeke, weeke!
So cries a pig preparèd to the spit.

DEMETRIUS
What mean'st thou, Aaron? wherefore didst thou this?

AARON
O Lord, sir, 'tis a deed of policy!
Shall she live to betray this guilt of ours,
A long-tongued babbling gossip? no, lords, no.
And now be it known to you my full intent.
153 Not far one Muliteus my countryman
His wife but yesternight was brought to bed;
His child is like to her, fair as you are:
156 Go pack with him, and give the mother gold,
And tell them both the circumstance of all;
And how by this their child shall be advanced,
And be receivèd for the emperor's heir
And substituted in the place of mine,

To calm this tempest whirling in the court;
And let the emperor dandle him for his own.
Hark ye, lords: you see I have given her physic,   163
And you must needs bestow her funeral.
The fields are near, and you are gallant grooms.   165
This done, see that you take no longer days,   166
But send the midwife presently to me.
The midwife and the nurse well made away,
Then let the ladies tattle what they please.

CHIRON
Aaron, I see thou wilt not trust the air
With secrets.

DEMETRIUS   For this care of Tamora,
Herself and hers are highly bound to thee.
        Exeunt [Demetrius and Chiron,
              bearing off the dead Nurse].

AARON
Now to the Goths, as swift as swallow flies,
There to dispose this treasure in mine arms
And secretly to greet the empress' friends.
Come on, you thick-lipped slave, I'll bear you hence;
For it is you that puts us to our shifts.   177
I'll make you feed on berries and on roots,
And feed on curds and whey, and suck the goat,
And cabin in a cave, and bring you up   180
To be a warrior and command a camp.   *Exit.*

                    *

Enter Titus, Old Marcus, Young Lucius, and other   IV, iii
Gentlemen, with bows, and Titus bears the arrows
with letters on the ends of them.

TITUS
Come, Marcus, come; kinsmen, this is the way.
Sir boy, let me see your archery:
Look ye draw home enough, and 'tis there straight.   3
'Terras Astraea reliquit.'   4
Be you rememb'red, Marcus. She's gone, she's fled.   5
Sirs, take you to your tools. You, cousins, shall
Go sound the ocean, and cast your nets;
Happily you may catch her in the sea.   8
Yet there's as little justice as at land.
No, Publius and Sempronius, you must do it.
'Tis you must dig with mattock and with spade
And pierce the inmost centre of the earth;
Then, when you come to Pluto's region,   13
I pray you deliver him this petition.
Tell him it is for justice and for aid,
And that it comes from old Andronicus,
Shaken with sorrows in ungrateful Rome.
Ah, Rome! Well, well, I made thee miserable
What time I threw the people's suffrages
On him that thus doth tyrannize o'er me.
Go, get you gone, and pray be careful all,
And leave you not a man-of-war unsearched:
This wicked emperor may have shipped her hence;
And, kinsmen, then we may go pipe for justice.   24

MARCUS
O Publius, is not this a heavy case,
To see thy noble uncle thus distract?

PUBLIUS
Therefore, my lords, it highly us concerns
By day and night t' attend him carefully,
And feed his humor kindly as we may,   29
Till time beget some careful remedy.

118 *close enacts* secret resolutions   119 *leer* complexion   122 *sensibly* perceptibly to the senses   126 *the surer side* i.e. the mother's side   130 *subscribe* agree   133 *have the wind of* keep watch upon (as game is watched, down wind)   138 *chafèd* enraged   153–54 *my countryman His wife* i.e. my countryman's wife   156 *pack* come to an arrangement   163 *physic* medicine   165 *grooms* fellows   166 *days* time   177 *puts . . . shifts* makes us resort to stratagems   180 *cabin* dwell
IV, iii *A public place in Rome*   3 *home* to the full extent   4 *Terras Astraea reliquit* Astraea, goddess of justice, has left the earth (Ovid, *Metamorphoses*, I, 150)   5 *Be you rememb'red* remember   8 *Happily* perhaps   13 *Pluto's region* Hades   24 *pipe* whistle (i.e. seek vainly)   29 *humor* mood

MARCUS
  Kinsmen, his sorrows are past remedy.
  Join with the Goths, and with revengeful war
33 Take wreak on Rome for this ingratitude,
  And vengeance on the traitor Saturnine.
TITUS
  Publius, how now? how now, my masters?
  What, have you met with her?
PUBLIUS
  No, my good lord; but Pluto sends you word,
  If you will have Revenge from hell, you shall.
  Marry, for Justice, she is so employed,
  He thinks, with Jove in heaven, or somewhere else,
  So that perforce you must needs stay a time.
TITUS
  He doth me wrong to feed me with delays.
  I'll dive into the burning lake below,
44 And pull her out of Acheron by the heels.
46 Marcus, we are but shrubs, no cedars we,
  No big-boned men framed of the Cyclops' size;
  But metal, Marcus, steel to the very back,
  Yet wrung with wrongs more than our backs can bear;
49 And, sith there's no justice in earth nor hell,
  We will solicit heaven, and move the gods
51 To send down Justice for to wreak our wrongs.
52 Come, to this gear. You are a good archer, Marcus.
         He gives them the arrows.
53 'Ad Jovem,' that's for you: here, 'ad Apollinem.'
  'Ad Martem,' that's for myself.
  Here, boy, 'to Pallas': here, 'to Mercury.'
  'To Saturn,' Caius, not to Saturnine;
57 You were as good to shoot against the wind.
  To it, boy! Marcus, loose when I bid.
  Of my word, I have written to effect;
  There's not a god left unsolicited.
MARCUS
  Kinsmen, shoot all your shafts into the court:
  We will afflict the emperor in his pride.
TITUS
  Now, masters, draw. O, well said, Lucius!
64 Good boy, in Virgo's lap; give it Pallas.
MARCUS
  My lord, I aim a mile beyond the moon.
  Your letter is with Jupiter by this.
TITUS Ha, ha!
  Publius, Publius, what hast thou done?
  See, see, thou hast shot off one of Taurus' horns!
MARCUS
  This was the sport, my lord: when Publius shot,
  The Bull, being galled, gave Aries such a knock
  That down fell both the Ram's horns in the court;
  And who should find them but the empress' villain?
  She laughed, and told the Moor he should not choose
  But give them to his master for a present.
TITUS
76 Why, there it goes! God give his lordship joy!
        Enter the Clown, with a basket, and two pigeons in it.
  News, news from heaven! Marcus, the post is come.
  Sirrah, what tidings? Have you any letters?
  Shall I have justice? what says Jupiter?
80 CLOWN Who? the gibbet-maker? He says that he hath
  taken them down again, for the man must not be hanged
  till the next week.
TITUS But what says Jupiter I ask thee?

CLOWN Alas, sir, I know not Jubiter; I never drank with
  him in all my life.
TITUS Why, villain, art not thou the carrier?
CLOWN Ay, of my pigeons, sir; nothing else.
TITUS Why, didst thou not come from heaven?
CLOWN From heaven? alas, sir, I never came there. God
  forbid I should be so bold to press to heaven in my young
  days. Why, I am going with my pigeons to the tribunal 91
  plebs, to take up a matter of brawl betwixt my uncle and
  one of the emperal's men.
MARCUS Why, sir, that is as fit as can be to serve for your
  oration; and let him deliver the pigeons to the emperor
  from you.
TITUS Tell me, can you deliver an oration to the emperor
  with a grace?
CLOWN Nay, truly, sir, I could never say grace in all my
  life.
TITUS
  Sirrah, come hither: make no more ado,
  But give your pigeons to the emperor:
  By me thou shalt have justice at his hands.
  Hold, hold, meanwhile here's money for thy charges. 103
  Give me pen and ink.
  Sirrah, can you with a grace deliver a supplication?
CLOWN Ay, sir.
TITUS Then here is a supplication for you. And when you
  come to him, at the first approach you must kneel; then
  kiss his foot; then deliver up your pigeons; and then look
  for your reward. I'll be at hand, sir: see you do it bravely. 110
CLOWN I warrant you, sir, let me alone.
TITUS
  Sirrah, hast thou a knife? Come, let me see it.
  Here, Marcus, fold it in the oration;
  For thou hast made it like an humble suppliant.
  And when thou hast given it to the emperor,
  Knock at my door and tell me what he says.
CLOWN God be with you, sir; I will.   *Exit.*
TITUS Come, Marcus, let us go. Publius, follow me.
                            Exeunt.
               *

Enter Emperor and Empress, and her two Sons. The   IV, iv
Emperor brings the arrows in his hand that Titus shot
at him.
SATURNINUS
  Why, lords, what wrongs are these! Was ever seen
  An emperor in Rome thus overborne,
  Troubled, confronted thus; and, for the extent   3
  Of egal justice, used in such contempt?   4
  My lords, you know, as know the mightful gods,
  However these disturbers of our peace
  Buzz in the people's ears, there naught hath passed,
  But even with law, against the willful sons   8
  Of old Andronicus. And what an if
  His sorrows have so overwhelmed his wits?

---

33 *wreak* vengeance   44 *Acheron* river in Hades   46 *Cyclops* giants in
Homer's *Odyssey*, IX   49 *sith* since   51 *wreak* avenge   52 *gear* business
53–54 *Ad Jovem . . . ad Apollinem. Ad Martem* to Jove . . . to Apollo.
To Mars   57 *were . . . shoot* would do as much good by shooting   64 *Virgo*
the Virgin (sign of the Zodiac; *Taurus*, l. 69, is the Bull, and *Aries*, l. 71, the
Ram)   76 s.d. *Clown* yokel   80 *gibbet-maker* (the Clown hears *Jupiter* as
'gibbeter': gibbet-maker)   91–92 *tribunal plebs* (properly '*tribunus plebis,*'
i.e. tribune of the people; *emperal*, l. 93, is another of the Clown's malapropisms)   103 *charges* i.e. pigeons   110 *bravely* well
IV, iv Before the Emperor's palace   3 *extent* exercise   4 *egal* equal
8 *even* in agreement

11 Shall we be thus afflicted in his wreaks,
His fits, his frenzy, and his bitterness?
And now he writes to heaven for his redress.
See, here's 'to Jove,' and this 'to Mercury';
This 'to Apollo'; this 'to the god of war':
Sweet scrolls to fly about the streets of Rome!
What's this but libelling against the Senate
18 And blazoning our unjustice everywhere?
A goodly humor, is it not, my lords?
As who would say, in Rome no justice were.
21 But if I live, his feignèd ecstasies
Shall be no shelter to these outrages;
But he and his shall know that justice lives
In Saturninus' health; whom, if he sleep,
He'll so awake as he in fury shall
Cut off the proud'st conspirator that lives.

TAMORA
My gracious lord, my lovely Saturnine,
Lord of my life, commander of my thoughts,
Calm thee, and bear the faults of Titus' age,
Th' effects of sorrow for his valiant sons,
Whose loss hath pierced him deep and scarred his heart;
And rather comfort his distressèd plight
Than prosecute the meanest or the best
For these contempts. [aside] Why, thus it shall become
35 High-witted Tamora to gloze with all.
But, Titus, I have touched thee to the quick;
37 Thy lifeblood out, if Aaron now be wise,
Then is all safe, the anchor in the port.
Enter Clown.
How now, good fellow? Wouldst thou speak with us?

CLOWN Yea, forsooth, an your mistress-ship be emperial.

TAMORA
Empress I am, but yonder sits the emperor.

42 CLOWN 'Tis he. God and Saint Stephen give you godden.
I have brought you a letter and a couple of pigeons here.
He [Saturninus] reads the letter.

SATURNINUS
Go take him away, and hang him presently.

CLOWN How much money must I have?

TAMORA Come, sirrah, you must be hanged.

47 CLOWN Hanged? By' lady, then I have brought up a
neck to a fair end.   *Exit.*

SATURNINUS
Despiteful and intolerable wrongs!
Shall I endure this monstrous villainy?
I know from whence this same device proceeds.
May this be borne as if his traitorous sons,
That died by law for murder of our brother,
Have by my means been butcherèd wrongfully?
Go drag the villain hither by the hair;
56 Nor age nor honor shall shape privilege.
For this proud mock I'll be thy slaughterman,
Sly frantic wretch, that holp'st to make me great
59 In hope thyself should govern Rome and me!
Enter Nuntius Aemilius.
What news with thee, Aemilius?

AEMILIUS
Arm, my lords! Rome never had more cause.
62 The Goths have gatherèd head, and with a power
Of high-resolvèd men, bent to the spoil,
64 They hither march amain, under conduct
Of Lucius, son to old Andronicus;
Who threats in course of this revenge to do
67 As much as ever Coriolanus did.

SATURNINUS
Is warlike Lucius general of the Goths?
These tidings nip me, and I hang the head
As flowers with frost or grass beat down with storms.
Ay, now begins our sorrows to approach.
'Tis he the common people love so much;
Myself hath often overheard them say,
When I have walkèd like a private man,
That Lucius' banishment was wrongfully,
And they have wished that Lucius were their emperor.

TAMORA
Why should you fear? is not your city strong?

SATURNINUS
Ay, but the citizens favor Lucius
And will revolt from me to succor him.

TAMORA
King, be thy thoughts imperious like thy name.
Is the sun dimmed, that gnats do fly in it?
The eagle suffers little birds to sing,
83 And is not careful what they mean thereby,
Knowing that with the shadow of his wings
85 He can at pleasure stint their melody:
Even so mayest thou the giddy men of Rome.
Then cheer thy spirit; for know thou, emperor,
I will enchant the old Andronicus
With words more sweet, and yet more dangerous,
90 Than baits to fish or honey stalks to sheep,
When as the one is wounded with the bait,
The other rotted with delicious feed.

SATURNINUS
But he will not entreat his son for us.

TAMORA
If Tamora entreat him, then he will;
For I can smooth, and fill his agèd ears
With golden promises, that, were his heart
Almost impregnable, his old ears deaf,
Yet should both ear and heart obey my tongue.
[To Aemilius]
Go thou before to be our ambassador;
Say that the emperor requests a parley
Of warlike Lucius, and appoint the meeting
Even at his father's house, the old Andronicus.

SATURNINUS
Aemilius, do this message honorably,
104 And if he stand on hostage for his safety,
Bid him demand what pledge will please him best.

AEMILIUS
Your bidding shall I do effectually.   *Exit.*

TAMORA
Now will I to that old Andronicus
108 And temper him with all the art I have,
To pluck proud Lucius from the warlike Goths.
And now, sweet emperor, be blithe again
And bury all thy fear in my devices.

SATURNINUS
Then go successantly, and plead to him.   *Exeunt.* 112

11 *wreaks* vindictive acts 18 *blazoning* proclaiming 21 *ecstasies* fits of
madness 35 *gloze* use fair words 37 *Thy lifeblood out* once thy lifeblood
is out 42 *godden* good evening (used at any time after noon) 47 *By' lady*
(interjection, from 'by Our Lady') 56 *shape privilege* create immunity 59
s.d. *Nuntius* messenger 62 *gatherèd head* raised an army 64 *conduct*
leadership 67 *Coriolanus* Roman hero who led an army against Rome 83
careful mindful 85 *stint* stop 90 *honey stalks* clover stalks 104 *stand on*
insist upon 108 *temper* work upon 112 *successantly* in succession (?)

*Enter Lucius, with an army of Goths, with Drum
and Soldiers.*

LUCIUS
Approvèd warriors and my faithful friends,
I have receivèd letters from great Rome
Which signifies what hate they bear their emperor
And how desirous of our sight they are.
Therefore, great lords, be as your titles witness,
Imperious, and impatient of your wrongs;
7   And wherein Rome hath done you any scath,
Let him make treble satisfaction.

1 . GOTH
9   Brave slip sprung from the great Andronicus,
Whose name was once our terror, now our comfort,
Whose high exploits and honorable deeds
Ingrateful Rome requites with foul contempt,
13 Be bold in us: we'll follow where thou lead'st,
Like stinging bees in hottest summer's day,
Led by their master to the flow'rèd fields,
And be avenged on cursèd Tamora.

[ALL]
And as he saith, so say we all with him.

LUCIUS
I humbly thank him, and I thank you all.
But who comes here, led by a lusty Goth?

*Enter a Goth, leading of Aaron with his Child in his
arms.*

2 . GOTH
Renownèd Lucius, from our troops I strayed
To gaze upon a ruinous monastery;
And as I earnestly did fix mine eye
23 Upon the wasted building, suddenly
I heard a child cry underneath a wall.
I made unto the noise, when soon I heard
The crying babe controlled with this discourse:
27 'Peace, tawny slave, half me and half thy dame.
28 Did not thy hue bewray whose brat thou art,
Had nature lent thee but thy mother's look,
Villain, thou mightst have been an emperor:
But where the bull and cow are both milk-white,
They never do beget a coal-black calf.
33 Peace, villain, peace!' even thus he rates the babe,
'For I must bear thee to a trusty Goth,
Who, when he knows thou art the empress' babe,
Will hold thee dearly for thy mother's sake.'
With this, my weapon drawn, I rushed upon him,
Surprised him suddenly, and brought him hither
To use as you think needful of the man.

LUCIUS
O worthy Goth, this is the incarnate devil
That robbed Andronicus of his good hand:
This is the pearl that pleased your empress' eye;
And here's the base fruit of her burning lust.
44 Say, wall-eyed slave, whither wouldst thou convey
This growing image of thy fiend-like face?
Why dost not speak? What, deaf? not a word?
A halter, soldiers! Hang him on this tree,
And by his side his fruit of bastardy.

AARON
Touch not the boy, he is of royal blood.

LUCIUS
Too like the sire for ever being good.
First hang the child, that he may see it sprawl –
A sight to vex the father's soul withal.

Get me a ladder.

[A ladder brought, which Aaron is made to climb.]

AARON   Lucius, save the child,
And bear it from me to the emperess.
If thou do this, I'll show thee wondrous things
That highly may advantage thee to hear;
If thou wilt not, befall what may befall,
I'll speak no more – but vengeance rot you all!

LUCIUS
Say on; and if it please me which thou speak'st,
Thy child shall live, and I will see it nourished.   60

AARON
And if it please thee! why, assure thee, Lucius,
'Twill vex thy soul to hear what I shall speak;
For I must talk of murders, rapes, and massacres,
Acts of black night, abominable deeds,
Complots of mischief, treason, villainies
Ruthful to hear, yet piteously performed;   66
And this shall all be buried in my death
Unless thou swear to me my child shall live.

LUCIUS
Tell on thy mind; I say thy child shall live.

AARON
Swear that he shall, and then I will begin.

LUCIUS
Who should I swear by? thou believest no god.
That granted, how canst thou believe an oath?

AARON
What if I do not? as indeed I do not.
Yet, for I know thou art religious
And hast a thing within thee callèd conscience,
With twenty popish tricks and ceremonies
Which I have seen thee careful to observe,
Therefore I urge thy oath; for that I know
An idiot holds his bauble for a god   79
And keeps the oath which by that god he swears,
To that I'll urge him: therefore thou shalt vow
By that same god, what god soe'er it be,
That thou adorest and hast in reverence,
To save my boy, to nourish and bring him up,
Or else I will discover naught to thee.

LUCIUS
Even by my god I swear to thee I will.

AARON
First know thou, I begot him on the empress.

LUCIUS
O most insatiate and luxurious woman!   88

AARON
Tut, Lucius, this was but a deed of charity
To that which thou shalt hear of me anon.   90
'Twas her two sons that murderèd Bassianus;
They cut thy sister's tongue, and ravished her,
And cut her hands, and trimmed her as thou sawest.

LUCIUS
O detestable villain! call'st thou that trimming?

AARON
Why, she was washed and cut and trimmed, and 'twas
Trim sport for them which had the doing of it.

V, i Fields near Rome 7 *scath* harm 9 *slip* offshoot 13 *bold* confident
23 *wasted* devastated 27 *tawny* black; *dame* mother 28 *bewray* make
known; *brat* child 33 *rates* reproves 44 *wall-eyed* glaring (literally, having
a discolored eye) 66 *Ruthful* lamentable; *piteously* so as to arouse pity
79 *bauble* jester's baton 88 *luxurious* lustful 90 *To* compared with

LUCIUS
O barbarous beastly villains like thyself!

AARON
Indeed, I was their tutor to instruct them.

99 That codding spirit had they from their mother,
100 As sure a card as ever won the set;
That bloody mind I think they learned of me,
102 As true a dog as ever fought at head.
Well, let my deeds be witness of my worth.
104 I trained thy brethren to that guileful hole
Where the dead corpse of Bassianus lay.
I wrote the letter that thy father found
And hid the gold within that letter mentioned,
Confederate with the queen and her two sons;
And what not done, that thou hast cause to rue,
Wherein I had no stroke of mischief in it?
111 I played the cheater for thy father's hand,
And when I had it, drew myself apart
And almost broke my heart with extreme laughter.
I pried me through the crevice of a wall
When for his hand he had his two sons' heads,
Beheld his tears, and laughed so heartily
That both mine eyes were rainy like to his;
And when I told the empress of this sport,
119 She sounded almost at my pleasing tale
And for my tidings gave me twenty kisses.

GOTH
What, canst thou say all this and never blush?

AARON
Ay, like a black dog, as the saying is.

LUCIUS
Art thou not sorry for these heinous deeds?

AARON
Ay, that I had not done a thousand more.
Even now I curse the day, and yet I think
Few come within the compass of my curse,
Wherein I did not some notorious ill:
As kill a man, or else devise his death;
Ravish a maid, or plot the way to do it;
130 Accuse some innocent, and forswear myself;
Set deadly enmity between two friends;
Make poor men's cattle break their necks;
133 Set fire on barns and haystalks in the night
And bid the owners quench them with their tears.
Oft have I digged up dead men from their graves
And set them upright at their dear friends' door
Even when their sorrows almost was forgot,
And on their skins, as on the bark of trees,
Have with my knife carvèd in Roman letters
140 'Let not your sorrow die, though I am dead.'
But I have done a thousand dreadful things
As willingly as one would kill a fly,
And nothing grieves me heartily indeed
But that I cannot do ten thousand more.

LUCIUS
Bring down the devil, for he must not die
So sweet a death as hanging presently.

[Aaron is brought down from the ladder.]

AARON
If there be devils, would I were a devil,
To live and burn in everlasting fire,
So I might have your company in hell
But to torment you with my bitter tongue! 150

LUCIUS
Sirs, stop his mouth and let him speak no more.
Enter Aemilius.

GOTH
My lord, there is a messenger from Rome
Desires to be admitted to your presence.

LUCIUS
Let him come near.
Welcome, Aemilius: what's the news from Rome?

AEMILIUS
Lord Lucius, and you princes of the Goths,
The Roman emperor greets you all by me;
And, for he understands you are in arms,
He craves a parley at your father's house,
Willing you to demand your hostages, 160
And they shall be immediately delivered.

GOTH
What says our general?

LUCIUS
Aemilius, let the emperor give his pledges
Unto my father and my uncle Marcus,
And we will come. March, away. *[Exeunt.]*

*

Enter Tamora and her two Sons, disguised. V, ii

TAMORA
Thus, in this strange and sad habiliment, 1
I will encounter with Andronicus,
And say I am Revenge, sent from below
To join with him and right his heinous wrongs.
Knock at his study, where they say he keeps 5
To ruminate strange plots of dire revenge.
Tell him Revenge is come to join with him
And work confusion on his enemies.
They knock, and Titus opens his study door.

TITUS
Who doth molest my contemplation?
Is it your trick to make me ope the door,
That so my sad decrees may fly away 11
And all my study be to no effect?
You are deceived; for what I mean to do
See here in bloody lines I have set down;
And what is written shall be executed.

TAMORA
Titus, I am come to talk with thee.

TITUS
No, not a word; how can I grace my talk,
Wanting a hand to give it that accord? 18
Thou hast the odds of me, therefore no more. 19

TAMORA
If thou didst know me, thou wouldst talk with me.

TITUS
I am not mad; I know thee well enough.
Witness this wretched stump, witness these crimson
lines,
Witness these trenches made by grief and care,
Witness the tiring day and heavy night,

99 *codding* lustful   100 *set* game   102 *at head* (a brave bulldog seized the bull by the nose)   104 *trained* enticed   111 *cheater* officer appointed to look after escheats (property forfeited to the Crown)   119 *sounded* swooned   130 *forswear* perjure   133 *haystalks* haystacks (dialect)
V, ii Before the house of Titus   1 *sad habiliment* sombre clothing   5 *keeps* stays   11 *sad decrees* serious resolutions   18 *Wanting . . . accord* lacking a hand to make appropriate gestures   19 *odds of* advantage over

Witness all sorrow, that I know thee well
For our proud empress, mighty Tamora.
Is not thy coming for my other hand ?

TAMORA

Know, thou sad man, I am not Tamora ;
She is thy enemy, and I thy friend.
I am Revenge, sent from th' infernal kingdom
To ease the gnawing vulture of thy mind
32   By working wreakful vengeance on thy foes.
Come down and welcome me to this world's light ;
Confer with me of murder and of death.
There's not a hollow cave or lurking place,
No vast obscurity or misty vale,
Where bloody murder or detested rape
38   Can couch for fear, but I will find them out,
And in their ears tell them my dreadful name,
Revenge, which makes the foul offender quake.

TITUS

Art thou Revenge ? and art thou sent to me
To be a torment to mine enemies ?

TAMORA

I am ; therefore come down and welcome me.

TITUS

Do me some service ere I come to thee.
Lo, by thy side where Rape and Murder stands ;
46   Now give some surance that thou art Revenge :
Stab them, or tear them on thy chariot wheels,
And then I'll come and be thy wagoner
And whirl along with thee about the globe.
50   Provide thee two proper palfreys, black as jet,
To hale thy vengeful wagon swift away
And find out murd'rers in their guilty caves ;
53   And when thy car is loaden with their heads,
I will dismount, and by thy wagon wheel
Trot like a servile footman all day long,
56   Even from Hyperion's rising in the east
Until his very downfall in the sea ;
And day by day I'll do this heavy task,
59   So thou destroy Rapine and Murder there.

TAMORA

These are my ministers and come with me.

TITUS

Are they thy ministers ? what are they called ?

TAMORA

Rape and Murder ; therefore callèd so
'Cause they take vengeance of such kind of men.

TITUS

Good Lord, how like the empress' sons they are !
65   And you the empress ! but we worldly men
Have miserable, mad, mistaking eyes.
O sweet Revenge, now do I come to thee ;
And, if one arm's embracement will content thee,
I will embrace thee in it by and by.   [Exit.]

TAMORA

70   This closing with him fits his lunacy.
71   Whate'er I forge to feed his brainsick humors
Do you uphold and maintain in your speeches,
For now he firmly takes me for Revenge ;
And, being credulous in this mad thought,
I'll make him send for Lucius his son,
And whilst I at a banquet hold him sure,
77   I'll find some cunning practice out of hand
To scatter and disperse the giddy Goths,
Or at the least make them his enemies.

See, here he comes, and I must ply my theme.
    [Enter Titus.]

TITUS

Long have I been forlorn, and all for thee.
Welcome, dread Fury, to my woeful house.
Rapine and Murder, you are welcome too.
How like the empress and her sons you are !
Well are you fitted, had you but a Moor.
Could not all hell afford you such a devil ?
For well I wot the empress never wags   87
But in her company there is a Moor ;
And, would you represent our queen aright,
It were convenient you had such a devil.   90
But welcome as you are : what shall we do ?

TAMORA

What wouldst thou have us do, Andronicus ?

DEMETRIUS

Show me a murderer, I'll deal with him.

CHIRON

Show me a villain that hath done a rape,
And I am sent to be revenged on him.

TAMORA

Show me a thousand that hath done thee wrong,
And I will be revengèd on them all.

TITUS

Look round about the wicked streets of Rome,
And when thou find'st a man that's like thyself,
Good Murder, stab him ; he's a murderer.
Go thou with him, and when it is thy hap   101
To find another that is like to thee,
Good Rapine, stab him ; he is a ravisher.
Go thou with them ; and in the emperor's court
There is a queen, attended by a Moor.
Well shalt thou know her by thine own proportion,
For up and down she doth resemble thee.
I pray thee do on them some violent death ;
They have been violent to me and mine.

TAMORA

Well hast thou lessoned us ; this shall we do.   110
But would it please thee, good Andronicus,
To send for Lucius, thy thrice-valiant son,
Who leads towards Rome a band of warlike Goths,
And bid him come and banquet at thy house :
When he is here, even at thy solemn feast,
I will bring in the empress and her sons,
The emperor himself, and all thy foes,
And at thy mercy shall they stoop and kneel,
And on them shalt thou ease thy angry heart.
What says Andronicus to this device ?

TITUS

Marcus, my brother, 'tis sad Titus calls.
    Enter Marcus.
Go, gentle Marcus, to thy nephew Lucius ;
Thou shalt enquire him out among the Goths.
Bid him repair to me and bring with him   124
Some of the chiefest princes of the Goths.
Bid him encamp his soldiers where they are.
Tell him the emperor and the empress too

---

32 *wreakful* avenging   38 *couch* lie hidden   46 *surance* assurance   50 *proper palfreys* handsome horses   53 *car* chariot   56 *Hyperion* the sun god   59 *So* provided that; *Rapine* rape   65 *worldly* mortal   70 *closing* agreeing   71 *forge* invent   77 *practice* plan of action ; *out of hand* on the spur of the moment   87 *wags* moves   90 *convenient* fitting   101 *hap* chance   110 *lessoned* instructed   124 *repair* come

Feast at my house, and he shall feast with them.
This do thou for my love; and so let him,
As he regards his agèd father's life.

MARCUS
This will I do and soon return again.   *[Exit.]*

TAMORA
Now will I hence about thy business
And take my ministers along with me.

TITUS
Nay, nay, let Rape and Murder stay with me,
Or else I'll call my brother back again
And cleave to no revenge but Lucius.

TAMORA *[aside to her sons]*
What say you, boys? will you abide with him
Whiles I go tell my lord the emperor
139   How I have governed our determined jest?
140   Yield to his humor, smooth and speak him fair,
And tarry with him till I turn again.

TITUS *[aside]*
I knew them all, though they supposed me mad,
143   And will o'erreach them in their own devices,
A pair of cursèd hellhounds and their dame.

DEMETRIUS
Madam, depart at pleasure; leave us here.

TAMORA
Farewell, Andronicus: Revenge now goes
147   To lay a complot to betray thy foes.

TITUS
I know thou dost; and, sweet Revenge, farewell.
                 [Exit Tamora.]

CHIRON
Tell us, old man, how shall we be employed?

TITUS
Tut, I have work enough for you to do.
Publius, come hither, Caius and Valentine.
    [Enter Publius, Caius, and Valentine.]

PUBLIUS
What is your will?

TITUS
Know you these two?

PUBLIUS
The empress' sons, I take them, Chiron and Demetrius.

TITUS
Fie, Publius, fie! thou art too much deceived.
The one is Murder, and Rape is the other's name;
And therefore bind them, gentle Publius:
Caius and Valentine, lay hands on them.
Oft have you heard me wish for such an hour,
160   And now I find it. Therefore bind them sure,
And stop their mouths if they begin to cry.   *[Exit.]*

CHIRON
Villains, forbear! we are the empress' sons.

PUBLIUS
And therefore do we what we are commanded.
Stop close their mouths, let them not speak a word.

Is he sure bound? look that you bind them fast.
    Enter Titus Andronicus with a knife, and Lavinia
    with a basin.

TITUS
Come, come, Lavinia; look, thy foes are bound.
Sirs, stop their mouths, let them not speak to me,
But let them hear what fearful words I utter.
O villains, Chiron and Demetrius!
Here stands the spring whom you have stained with   *170*
   mud,
This goodly summer with your winter mixed.
You killed her husband, and for that vile fault
Two of her brothers were condemned to death,
My hand cut off and made a merry jest;
Both her sweet hands, her tongue, and that more dear
Than hands or tongue, her spotless chastity,
Inhuman traitors, you constrained and forced.
What would you say if I should let you speak?
Villains, for shame you could not beg for grace.
Hark, wretches, how I mean to martyr you.   *180*
This one hand yet is left to cut your throats
Whiles that Lavinia 'tween her stumps doth hold
The basin that receives your guilty blood.
You know your mother means to feast with me,
And calls herself Revenge, and thinks me mad.
Hark, villains, I will grind your bones to dust,
And with your blood and it I'll make a paste,
And of the paste a coffin I will rear,   *188*
And make two pasties of your shameful heads,
And bid that strumpet, your unhallowed dam,
Like to the earth, swallow her own increase.   *191*
This is the feast that I have bid her to,
And this the banquet she shall surfeit on;
For worse than Philomel you used my daughter,   *194*
And worse than Progne I will be revenged.   *195*
And now prepare your throats. Lavinia, come,
Receive the blood; and when that they are dead,
Let me go grind their bones to powder small
And with this hateful liquor temper it;   *199*
And in that paste let their vile heads be baked.
Come, come, be every one officious   *201*
To make this banquet, which I wish may prove
More stern and bloody than the Centaurs' feast.   *203*
      He cuts their throats.
So, now bring them in, for I'll play the cook
And see them ready against their mother comes.   *205*
                 Exeunt.

                *

    Enter Lucius, Marcus, and the Goths [with Aaron   V, iii
    prisoner, and his Child in the arms of an Attendant].

LUCIUS
Uncle Marcus, since 'tis my father's mind
That I repair to Rome, I am content.   *2*

GOTH
And ours with thine, befall what fortune will.

LUCIUS
Good uncle, take you in this barbarous Moor,
This ravenous tiger, this accursèd devil.
Let him receive no sust'nance, fetter him,
Till he be brought unto the empress' face
For testimony of her foul proceedings.
And see the ambush of our friends be strong;
I fear the emperor means no good to us.

139 *governed . . . jest* contrived the jest we determined on   140 *smooth . . . fair* flatter and humor him   143 *o'erreach* outwit   147 *complot* plot   180 *martyr* kill   188 *coffin* pie crust   191 *increase* offspring   194 *Philomel* (see II, iii, 43n.)   195 *Progne* Procne, sister of Philomel and wife of Tereus: to avenge her sister's rape and mutilation by Tereus, Procne killed her son Itys and served him to his father Tereus at a meal   199 *temper* blend   201 *officious* busy   203 *Centaurs' feast* (the wedding feast of Pirithous and Hippodamia, to which the Lapiths invited the Centaurs, ended with the slaughter of the latter)   205 *against* by the time that
V, iii The house of Titus   2 *repair* return

AARON

Some devil whisper curses in mine ear
And prompt me that my tongue may utter forth
The venomous malice of my swelling heart!

LUCIUS

Away, inhuman dog, unhallowèd slave!
Sirs, help our uncle to convey him in.
                 [Exeunt Goths with Aaron.]
The trumpets show the emperor is at hand.
    Sound trumpets. Enter Emperor and Empress, with
    [Aemilius,] Tribunes, and others.

SATURNINUS

17   What, hath the firmament moe suns than one?

LUCIUS

18   What boots it thee to call thyself a sun?

MARCUS

19   Rome's emperor, and nephew, break the parle;
These quarrels must be quietly debated.

21   The feast is ready which the careful Titus
Hath ordained to an honorable end,
For peace, for love, for league, and good to Rome.
Please you therefore draw nigh and take your places.

SATURNINUS

Marcus, we will.
    [A table brought in.] Trumpets sounding, enter Titus
    like a cook, placing the dishes, and Lavinia with a
    veil over her face.

TITUS

Welcome, my lord; welcome, dread queen;
Welcome, ye warlike Goths; welcome, Lucius;

28   And welcome all: although the cheer be poor,
'Twill fill your stomachs; please you eat of it.

SATURNINUS

Why art thou thus attired, Andronicus?

TITUS

Because I would be sure to have all well
To entertain your highness and your empress.

TAMORA

We are beholding to you, good Andronicus.

TITUS

An if your highness knew my heart, you were.

35   My lord the emperor, resolve me this:
36   Was it well done of rash Virginius
To slay his daughter with his own right hand,

38   Because she was enforced, stained, and deflow'red?

SATURNINUS

It was, Andronicus.

TITUS

Your reason, mighty lord?

SATURNINUS

Because the girl should not survive her shame,
And by her presence still renew his sorrows.

TITUS

A reason mighty, strong, and effectual;

44   A pattern, precedent, and lively warrant
For me, most wretched, to perform the like.
Die, die, Lavinia, and thy shame with thee,
And with thy shame thy father's sorrow die!
        [He kills her.]

SATURNINUS

48   What hast thou done, unnatural and unkind?

TITUS

Killed her for whom my tears have made me blind.
I am as woeful as Virginius was,

And have a thousand times more cause than he
To do this outrage; and it now is done.

SATURNINUS

What, was she ravished? tell who did the deed.

TITUS

Will't please you eat? will't please your highness feed?

TAMORA

Why hast thou slain thine only daughter thus?

TITUS

Not I: 'twas Chiron and Demetrius,
They ravished her and cut away her tongue;
And they, 'twas they, that did her all this wrong.

SATURNINUS

Go fetch them hither to us presently.   59

TITUS

Why, there they are, both bakèd in this pie,
Whereof their mother daintily hath fed,
Eating the flesh that she herself hath bred.
'Tis true, 'tis true; witness my knife's sharp point!
        He stabs the Empress.

SATURNINUS

Die, frantic wretch, for this accursèd deed!
        [He stabs Titus.]

LUCIUS

Can the son's eye behold his father bleed?
There's meed for meed, death for a deadly deed!   66
        [He stabs Saturninus.]

MARCUS

You sad-faced men, people and sons of Rome,
By uproar severed, as a flight of fowl
Scattered by winds and high tempestuous gusts,
O, let me teach you how to knit again   70
This scattered corn into one mutual sheaf,
These broken limbs again into one body;
Lest Rome herself be bane unto herself,   73
And she whom mighty kingdoms curtsy to,
Like a forlorn and desperate castaway,
Do shameful execution on herself,
But if my frosty signs and chaps of age,   77
Grave witnesses of true experience,
Cannot induce you to attend my words,
        [To Lucius]
Speak, Rome's dear friend, as erst our ancestor,   · 80
When with his solemn tongue he did discourse
To lovesick Dido's sad-attending ear   82
The story of that baleful burning night   83
When subtle Greeks surprised King Priam's Troy.
Tell us what Sinon hath bewitched our ears,   85
Or who hath brought the fatal engine in
That gives our Troy, our Rome, the civil wound.   87
My heart is not compact of flint nor steel;   88
Nor can I utter all our bitter grief,
But floods of tears will drown my oratory
And break my utt'rance, even in the time

17 *moe* more   18 *boots* avails   19 *break the parle* break off the dispute   21 *careful* full of cares, sorrowful   28 *cheer* entertainment   35 *resolve* answer   36 *Virginius* Roman who killed his daughter to save her from rape   38 *enforced* raped   44 *lively* striking   48 *unkind* cruel   59 *presently* immediately   66 *meed for meed* measure for measure (i.e. fitting reward)   70 *knit* bind together   73 *bane* death   77 *But if* unless; *frosty signs* white hair; *chaps* wrinkles   80 *erst* formerly; *our ancestor* i.e. Aeneas   82 *sad-attending* seriously listening   83 *baleful* evil   85 *Sinon* cunning Greek who persuaded the Trojans to admit the wooden horse   87 *civil* incurred in civil war   88 *compact* composed

When it should move ye to attend me most,
And force you to commiseration.
Here's Rome's young captain, let him tell the tale,
While I stand by and weep to hear him speak.

LUCIUS

96 Then, gracious auditory, be it known to you
That Chiron and the damned Demetrius
Were they that murd'red our emperor's brother,
And they it were that ravishèd our sister.
100 For their fell faults our brothers were beheaded,
101 Our father's tears despised, and basely cozened
Of that true hand that fought Rome's quarrel out
And sent her enemies unto the grave.
104 Lastly, myself unkindly banishèd,
The gates shut on me, and turned weeping out
To beg relief among Rome's enemies;
Who drowned their enmity in my true tears
And oped their arms to embrace me as a friend:
109 I am the turnèd-forth, be it known to you,
That have preserved her welfare in my blood
And from her bosom took the enemy's point,
Sheathing the steel in my advent'rous body.
113 Alas, you know I am no vaunter, I;
My scars can witness, dumb although they are,
That my report is just and full of truth.
116 But soft, methinks I do digress too much,
Citing my worthless praise. O, pardon me!
For when no friends are by, men praise themselves.

MARCUS

Now is my turn to speak. Behold the child:
Of this was Tamora deliverèd,
The issue of an irreligious Moor,
Chief architect and plotter of these woes.
The villain is alive in Titus' house,
And as he is to witness, this is true.
Now judge what cause had Titus to revenge
These wrongs unspeakable, past patience,
Or more than any living man could bear.
Now you have heard the truth, what say you, Romans?
Have we done aught amiss, show us wherein,
And, from the place where you behold us pleading,
The poor remainder of Andronici
Will hand in hand all headlong hurl ourselves
133 And on the ragged stones beat forth our souls,
134 And make a mutual closure of our house.
Speak, Romans, speak, and if you say we shall,
Lo, hand in hand, Lucius and I will fall.

AEMILIUS

Come, come, thou reverent man of Rome,
And bring our emperor gently in thy hand –
Lucius our emperor; for well I know
The common voice do cry it shall be so.

ALL

Lucius, all hail, Rome's royal emperor!

MARCUS

Go, go into old Titus' sorrowful house,
And hither hale that misbelieving Moor
To be adjudged some direful slaught'ring death,

As punishment for his most wicked life.

[Exeunt Attendants.]

ALL

Lucius, all hail, Rome's gracious governor!

LUCIUS

Thanks, gentle Romans: may I govern so
To heal Rome's harms and wipe away her woe.
149 But, gentle people, give me aim awhile,
For nature puts me to a heavy task.
Stand all aloof; but, uncle, draw you near
152 To shed obsequious tears upon this trunk.
O, take this warm kiss on thy pale cold lips,
These sorrowful drops upon thy bloodstained face,
The last true duties of thy noble son!

MARCUS

Tear for tear, and loving kiss for kiss,
Thy brother Marcus tenders on thy lips.
O, were the sum of these that I should pay
Countless and infinite, yet would I pay them.

LUCIUS

Come hither, boy; come, come and learn of us
To melt in showers: thy grandsire loved thee well.
Many a time he danced thee on his knee,
Sung thee asleep, his loving breast thy pillow.
Many a story hath he told to thee,
And bid thee bear his pretty tales in mind
And talk of them when he was dead and gone.

MARCUS

How many thousand times hath these poor lips,
When they were living, warmed themselves on thine!
169 O, now, sweet boy, give them their latest kiss.
Bid him farewell; commit him to the grave;
171 Do them that kindness, and take leave of them.

BOY

O grandsire, grandsire! ev'n with all my heart
Would I were dead, so you did live again!
O Lord, I cannot speak to him for weeping;
My tears will choke me if I ope my mouth.

[Enter Attendants with Aaron.]

ROMAN

You sad Andronici, have done with woes.
Give sentence on this execrable wretch
That hath been breeder of these dire events.

LUCIUS

Set him breast-deep in earth, and famish him.
There let him stand and rave and cry for food.
If any one relieves or pities him,
182 For the offense he dies. This is our doom.
Some stay to see him fast'ned in the earth.

AARON

Ah, why should wrath be mute and fury dumb?
I am no baby, I, that with base prayers
I should repent the evils I have done;
Ten thousand worse than ever yet I did
Would I perform if I might have my will.
If one good deed in all my life I did,
I do repent it from my very soul.

LUCIUS

Some loving friends convey the emperor hence,
And give him burial in his father's grave.
My father and Lavinia shall forthwith
Be closèd in our household's monument.
As for that ravenous tiger, Tamora,
No funeral rite, nor man in mourning weeds,

---

96 *auditory* audience   100 *fell* savage   101 *cozened* cheated   104 *unkindly*
unnaturally   109 *turnèd-forth* exile   113 *vaunter* braggart   116 *soft* stay
(common interjection used to enjoin silence)   133 *ragged* rugged   134
mutual closure common end   149 *give me aim* bear with me   152 *obsequious*
mourning   169 *latest* last   171 *them* i.e. Titus' lips   182 *doom* sentence

No mournful bell shall ring her burial ;
But throw her forth to beasts and birds to prey.
Her life was beastly and devoid of pity,
200   And being dead, let birds on her take pity !

[See justice done on Aaron, that damned Moor,
By whom our heavy haps had their beginning.
Then, afterwards, to order well the state,
That like events may ne'er it ruinate.]   *Exeunt.*

APPENDIX: THE QUARTO AND FOLIO TEXTS

The only authoritative text of *Titus Andronicus* is that of the first quarto, printed in 1594. Apart from its deficient punctuation and a few obvious errors it provides a remarkably accurate text, and it is moreover the sole source for a number of lines which were omitted or altered in subsequent editions. The wording of some of the stage directions (e.g. I, i, 72, *enter . . . others as many as can be*) and some irregularities in the speech-prefixes (e.g. *Saturninus* is also given as *Emperor* or *King*) suggest that the first quarto was set up from the author's "foul papers" or working manuscript of the play, rather than from a clean copy prepared for use in the theatre.

The second quarto, printed in 1600, was set up from a copy of the first quarto that must have been slightly damaged at the foot of the last three leaves, for six passages towards the end of Act V (including the last four lines of the play) are clearly conjectural. Whoever prepared this copy for the printer also removed the three and a half lines at I, i, 35–38 which are contradicted by the subsequent action, and which may well have been struck out of the original manuscript and printed in the first quarto by mistake. He also made a number of minor corrections and considerably improved the punctuation, but the text incorporated a great many new errors. There is no reason to suppose that the emendations were the work of anyone other than the compositor, and the text therefore has no authority.

A third quarto, printed in 1611, was set up from a copy of the second quarto, and contains far more corruptions than corrections. It would be of little interest but for the fact that it provided the copy for the first folio. .

The folio text is even more corrupt than the third quarto, but it adds many new stage directions, as well as an entire new scene, III, ii, which must have derived from a manuscript source. The authenticity of this new scene cannot be disputed, for it is of a piece with the rest of the play. Its most probable source is the playhouse prompt-book, which would also have furnished the additional stage directions, but since the folio does not restore the conjectural readings of the second quarto it must be assumed that the prompt-book used was not the original but a printed copy to which corrections and additions had been made. Only the most perfunctory use can have been made of such new material as the prompt-book made available, for the folio elsewhere follows the text of the third quarto.

The present edition is based on the first quarto, except for III, ii, which is necessarily based on the folio. Speech-prefixes have been regularized throughout, and spelling and punctuation modernized. The act divisions are those introduced by the folio; the scene divisions are those of the later editors.

The following are the only readings in the present edition departing materially from the text of the first quarto (Q1). Corrections of simple literal errors, punctuation, and mislineation of verse are not noted unless the sense is affected. The adopted reading in italics is followed by the Q1 reading in roman. Where the adopted reading derives from the second quarto (Q2), the

third quarto (Q3), or the folio (F), that fact is recorded in parentheses following the reading; where there is no such indication, the reading is an emendation, usually one suggested quite early in the history of Shakespearean scholarship.

I, i, 36 *the Andronici* that Andronicy   58 s.d. *Exeunt* Exit   74 *her* (F4) his   92 *bretheren* (Q3) brethren   101 *manes* (F3) manus   115 *slaught'red* (F) slaughtered   132 s.d. *Exeunt* Exit   229 *Titan's* (Q2) Tytus   243 *emperess* Empresse   245 *Pantheon* (F2) Pathan   267 *chance* (Q2) change   283 *cuique* (F2) cuiqum   319 *Phoebe* (F2) Thebe   360 *bretheren* (Q3) brethren   s.d. *speak* speakes   393 s.d. *Exeunt* Exit   401 *Yes . . . remunerate* (F; omitted in QQ)   477–79 *We do . . . our own* (assigned as in F; printed as part of Tamora's speech in QQ)

II, i, 110 *than* this   130 *shadowed* shadowèd

II, ii, 1 *morn* (Q3) Moone

II, iii, 13 *snake* (Q3) snakes   22 *enjoyed* enjoyèd   55, 66 *emperess* Empresse   69 *try experiments* (Q2) trie thy experimens   72 *swart* swartie   85 *note* notice   110 *Lascivious* (Q3) Lauicious   118 *Ay, I*   132 *outlive, us* out live us   144 *suck'dst* suck'st   160 *ears* (Q3) yeares   198 *What,* (F4) What   210 *unhallowed* unhollow   222 *berayed* bereaud   231 *Pyramus* (Q2) Priamus   236 *Cocytus'* (F2) Ocitus   286 *What,* What   291 *fault* faults   296 *father's* fathers

II, iv, 27 *him* them   30 *three* their   38 *Philomel* Philomela

III, i, 9 *are* (F2) is   17 *urns* ruines   34 *or* (Q2; omitted in Q1)   113 *withered* witherèd   146 *with his* (F4) with her   297 *empress* Emperesse

III, ii (this scene is found only in F)   39 *complainer* complainet   52 *thy* (omitted in F)   53 *fly* Flys   54 *thee,* (F3) the   55 *are* (omitted in F)   72 *myself* my selfes

IV, i, 15 *Marcus* (speech-prefix omitted in Q)   50 *quotes* (Q2) coats   77 *Titus* (F; speech-prefix omitted in QQ)   88 *hope* (Q2) hop (?) I op (?)   91 *sware* (F3) sweare

IV, ii, 95 *Alcides* (Q2) Alciades   104, 143 *emperess* Empresse

IV, iii, 56 *Saturn,' Caius* Saturnine, to Caius   77 *News . . . come* (assigned in Q to Clown)   80 *Who* Ho

IV, iv, 5 *know, as know* know   47 *By' lady* be Lady   59 s.d. *Nuntius* (Q2) Nutius   92 *feed* (Q3) seed   97 *ears* (F) yeares   104 *on* (F4) in

V, i, 16 *avenged* (Q3) adveng'd   53 *Get . . . ladder* (assigned to Aaron in Q)   54 *emperess* Empresse

V, ii, 18 *it* (omitted in QQ; F has 'it action' for QQ 'that accord')   49 *globe* globes   52 *murd'rers* murder   *caves* (F2) cares   56 *Hyperion's* (F2) Epeons   61 *Are they* (F2) Are them   65 *worldly* (Q2) wordlie

V, iii, 73 *Lest* Roman Lord. Let   125 *cause* (F4) course   144 *adjudged* (Q3) adiudge   154 *bloodstained* (F3) blood slaine   163 *Sung* (Q2) Song   201–04 *See . . . ruinate* (not in Q1, but in Q2, Q3, F)   Q concludes "Finis the Tragedy of Titus Andronicus"

ROMEO AND JULIET

INTRODUCTION

Romeo and Juliet is a play of young love. No other conveys so well the impetuous, idealistic passion of youth. The hero and heroine are not remarkable except in the overwhelming strength of their love for each other. Readers who love deeply may find here the idealized utterance of their feelings, and those who do not love deeply are led to wish that they could. The universal longing for a perfect romantic love, for the union of physical desire with selfless self-surrender, finds full expression in this play and makes it what Georg Brandes has called the great typical love-tragedy of the world.

That this appeal to a universal longing in human nature is the true secret of the play's success is witnessed by the great popularity of the balcony scene in Act II, which is not at all the dramatic climax of the play but is usually the scene most clearly remembered. In former centuries the Library of Oxford University kept its folio copy of Shakespeare's works chained to a desk at which students could stand and read. The well-thumbed pages of the balcony scene and of the parting scene in Act III give mute evidence that for young Oxonians these utterances of love were the most popular passages in all of Shakespeare's works.

Indeed, Shakespeare's finest achievement in this play is the successful portrayal of passionate physical love in terms of purity and innocence. The suggestive wink and the salacious leer are present in the jestings of the Nurse and the innuendoes of Mercutio, but these merely serve as contrasts to what Romeo and Juliet feel within themselves. When Juliet, soliloquizing, expresses her eager anticipation of her wedding night, she does not appear immodest but innocent in the best sense. Her passion for Romeo is ennobling, and the same is true of Romeo's love for her. The completeness of their devotion to each other leads them to ironic, untimely death; yet we cannot feel that this is wholly a defeat, for their love has risen superior to the storms of circumstance. In the words of Professor van Kranendonk, late of Amsterdam: "The poet has placed this springtime love in so intense a poetic light that an afterglow still remains over the somber ending. When we hear the names of Romeo and Juliet, we do not think first of all (as with Othello and Desdemona) about their pain, their misery, and their terrible undoing, but about their happiness together."

In style and manner, *Romeo and Juliet* seems nearer to *A Midsummer Night's Dream* than to Shakespeare's other plays. One finds the same intense lyricism, the same dependence upon rhymed couplets, the same enchantment of moonlight scenes, and the same interest in fairy lore. Finally, in *A Midsummer Night's Dream* there occurs a passage which seems to contain the theme enlarged upon in *Romeo and Juliet*. Lysander laments that in stories of the past the "course of true love never did run smooth" and that mutual happiness seldom endured, passing like a sound, a shadow, a dream, a flash of lightning swallowed up in darkness. "So quick bright things come to confusion," Lysander concludes, to which Hermia replies, "If then true lovers have been ever crossed, / It stands as an edict in destiny." These lines anticipate the "star-crossed lovers" of the Prologue to *Romeo and Juliet* and suggest that the evanescence of "bright things," particularly of young love, is a key to the mood in which the later play was written.

For some years scholars have debated the relative dates of these two plays. Internal evidence, while indicating 1594–95 as the date of *A Midsummer Night's Dream*, seemed to place *Romeo and Juliet* in 1591. In the Nurse's first scene, she says, "'Tis since the earthquake now eleven years," a line which has the earmarks of a topical allusion. If she refers to the much-publicized earthquake which shook England on April 6, 1580, then the play should be dated in 1591, a date which on other grounds seems much too early. Recent scholarship, however, has given us a choice of earthquakes, since one occurred in Dorsetshire in 1583 and one in Kent in 1585. A "terrible earthquake" which occurred on the Continent on March 1, 1584, is described in William Covell's *Polimanteia* (1595), a book which also praised "Sweet Shakspeare." It is therefore obvious that the earthquake could date *Romeo and Juliet* in 1594, 1595, or 1596, just as well as in 1591.

Other methods of establishing the date have been attempted. The play opens "a fortnight and odd days" before Lammas Tide (August 1). Calculating the position of the moon as described in the play yields 1596 as the only year that will fit astronomically. The first edition of the play, the quarto of 1597, is described on the title page as having been acted by "Lord Hunsdon's servants." Shakespeare's company was known by this title only from July 1596 to March 1597. A scholar who has compared the type face of this edition with other books issued by its printer, John Danter, concludes that the quarto was printed in February or March of 1597. Since it was a reported edition and was presumably not authorized by Shakespeare, it probably represented an attempt to exploit the popularity of a new play. We may therefore with some confidence assign the composition of the play to the middle of 1596, in which case the earthquake recalled by the Nurse would be the one which occurred in Kent on August 4, 1585. The play followed *A Midsummer Night's Dream* by slightly more than a year.

Shakespeare's source for this play was *The Tragicall Historye of Romeus and Iuliet, written first in Italian by*

Bandell, and now in Englishe by Ar. Br. (1562). This work by Arthur Broke, or Brooke, is a long narrative poem based on the prose of Bandello (1554) through an intermediate French version by Pierre Boaistuau (1559). Before Bandello, elements of the story were used by Luigi da Porto (1525) and Masuccio Salernitano (1476). Brooke's poem apparently created in England a vogue for "tragical histories" translated from Bandello, Boccaccio, and other prose romancers. In the two decades following 1562, extensive collections of these were published in prose by William Painter, Geoffrey Fenton, and George Pettie, and in verse by James Sandford, George Turbervile, Robert Smyth, and Richard Tarleton. Painter's work included a prose translation of the Romeo-Juliet story, but Shakespeare seems not to have used it. Brooke tells us in his preface that he had recently seen a play on the same subject acted on the stage (probably at the Inns of Court), but it seems unlikely that this play came to Shakespeare's attention thirty years later, since no further performances or printings of it are recorded. His obvious source, and probably his only one, was Brooke's poem.

Shakespeare's dramatic genius may be studied in the changes which he has made from Brooke's narrative. He has shortened the duration of the action from nine months to less than a week. Thus the hasty march of events becomes a major cause of the tragedy; there is not time to settle problems which greater leisure would have simplified. He has expanded Mercutio's role from a mere reference in Brooke and has invented the two duels involving Tybalt, thereby enhancing Romeo's dilemma of love against honor; for in Brooke's poem Romeo kills Tybalt accidentally while defending himself in a street brawl. He has taken from Brooke almost every incident involving the Nurse, yet he has created in her affectionate, vulgar, easy-going personality one of his most original characters. Finally, he has portrayed in the Capulet household a remarkable study in family psychology.

In Bandello's story Juliet is eighteen years old, in Brooke's poem she is sixteen, and in Shakespeare's play she is nearing her fourteenth birthday. Since Renaissance physiologists generally considered fourteen to mark the beginning of puberty (cf. *The Winter's Tale*, II, i, 147), Shakespeare apparently intended to picture Juliet's love for Romeo as first love, strengthened by the fact that she is just becoming emotionally aware of the meaning of love itself. (A similar purpose is evident in *The Tempest*, where Miranda is approximately the same age as Juliet.) In her emotions Juliet has suddenly become a woman, while in other respects she is still a child. Neither she nor her parents can quite understand this change; they consider her refusal to marry Paris childish willfulness, and she is too much in awe of them to tell them the truth.

Capulet is an old man married to a young woman. In spite of Lady Capulet's reference to her "old age," she is twenty-eight, only twice the age of her daughter. Capulet, however, had last attended a masquerade more than thirty years before and is now probably in his sixties. Since the earth had "swallowèd all my hopes" but Juliet, and since she is the only child born to Lady Capulet, Capulet must have had children by a former marriage. Lady Capulet has retained something of the awe of the child-bride for her older husband and defers to his judgment – and to his temper – in hastening the marriage with Paris. Her habit of deference to his wishes may have caused her to withhold

from Juliet sympathy which she normally would have given. Capulet assumes the management of the household duties and dearly loves to plan big parties. Even among his laments for Juliet's death is a regret that it should "murder our solemnity," i.e., spoil the feast which he had planned. His domestic ménage is hardly that of a great Italian nobleman and perhaps more nearly resembles that of a wealthy burgher of Stratford, recalled from Shakespeare's youth.

The play also represents an advance in Shakespeare's ability to reproduce the language of young gentlemen. The badinage of Mercutio, Romeo, and Benvolio is a decided improvement over similar conversations in earlier plays. Mercutio's unique blend of critical acumen, delicate fancy, and obscene levity makes him a remarkable character creation. One critic suggests that Shakespeare was forced to kill Mercutio lest he "steal the show" from the major figures of the plot. Like Jaques and Falstaff in later plays, he exists more as a character portrayed for its own innate interest than as an essential participant in the dramatic action.

Unlike Shakespeare's later tragedies, *Romeo and Juliet* is a play of externals, of characters portrayed in their relationships with each other. Their motives and feelings are readily understandable. There is a minimum of introspective brooding, enigmatic utterance, and puzzlement over moral problems; instead, all is quick decision and rapid action. In later tragedies Shakespeare undertook to explore the secret recesses of the soul, but here he shows people in conflict with external circumstance. Their errors of judgment are not errors involving a consciousness of sin but are attributable to impetuous haste and unkind fate. Nothing is withheld from the reader; characters and their motives are revealed as completely as possible. The same lack of reticence is evident in the literary style, which abounds in conceits, plays on words, and luxuriant poetic descriptions. Perhaps it is the quality of complete representations of emotions and moods that has made the play a favorite with musical composers: Gounod, Berlioz, Tchaikovsky, Prokofiev, and Milhaud, among others.

In *Romeo and Juliet* Shakespeare exploits dramatic irony in abrupt reversals of situation. Romeo, despondent, goes unwillingly to Capulet's ball and is quickly raised to joy by his encounter with Juliet, only to find that she is his hereditary enemy. This obstacle overcome, his joy reaches a height with his wedding, but within a half hour he is plunged into despair after his duel with Tybalt. At the beginning of Act V, Romeo is cheerful because of a dream which seems to foretell his reunion with Juliet, but his hopes are quickly dashed by Balthasar's news of her death. The supreme instance of irony comes as he stands beside her in the sepulchre, observing that she looks as though alive, and then drinks the poison to join her in death. The audience knows that she really is alive and will awake in a few minutes. In David Garrick's acting version of the play (as in Bandello's story) Juliet awakes before Romeo dies, and he thus realizes the bitter irony of his situation. The questionable dramatic propriety of this ending has caused considerable debate among students of the play.

Shakespeare makes one other effective use of irony. When Capulet and his wife are scolding Juliet for her refusal to marry Paris, each petulantly expresses a wish for her death. "I would the fool were married to her grave," says Lady Capulet. Capulet says that they have only one child, "But now I see this one is one too much." They do not intend these statements seriously, as Juliet doubtless realizes, but their words are ominous of what is to come. They get what they ask for.

In recent years numerous attempts have been made to state a central theme for the play. One critic views it as a tragedy of unawareness. Capulet and Montague are unaware of the fateful issues which may hang upon their quarrel. Romeo and Juliet fall in love while unaware that they are hereditary enemies. Mercutio and Tybalt are both unaware of the true state of affairs when they fight their duel. In the chain of events leading to the final tragedy, even the servants play a part and are unaware of the results of their actions. The final scene, with Friar Laurence's long explanation, is dramatically justified because it brings Montague, Capulet, Lady Capulet, and the Prince to at least a partial awareness of their responsibility for what has happened. Supplementing this view of the play is one which finds it to be a study of the wholeness and complexity of things in human affairs. The issues of the feud may appear to be simple and clear, but in reality they are highly complex, giving rise to results which are completely unforeseen. The goodness or badness of human actions is relative, not absolute, an idea symbolically set forth in Friar Laurence's opening speech on herbs which are medicinal or poisonous according to the manner of their use.

Other clues to the meaning of the play may be found in the repetitive imagery employed by Shakespeare. The images of haste, of events rushing to a conclusion, are found throughout. When Romeo says, "I stand on sudden haste," Friar Laurence answers, "They stumble that run fast," and thus expresses one moral to be drawn from the play. Romeo and Mercutio symbolize their wit-combat by the wild-goose chase, a reckless cross-country horse race. "Swits and spurs," cries Romeo, using the imagery of speed. Numerous other instances may be found.

Closely allied to the imagery of haste is the violence expressed in the gunpowder image. The Friar warns that too impetuous love is like fire and powder, which, "as they kiss, consume." Romeo desires a poison that will expel life from his body, like powder fired from a cannon. This may identify the Apothecary's poison as aconite, since elsewhere Shakespeare compares the action of aconite with that of "rash gunpowder" (*2 Henry IV*, IV, iv, 48). Violence is also expressed in the image of shipwreck which may end the voyage of life. Capulet compares Juliet weeping to a bark in danger from tempests. Romeo describes his death as the shipwreck of his "seasick weary bark." Earlier, after expressing a premonition that attendance at Capulet's party will cause his death, he resigns himself to him "that hath the steerage of my course," anticipating his later images of the ship and the voyage of life.

Also repeated in the play is the image of Death as the lover of Juliet. She herself uses it, her father uses it beside her bier, and Romeo uses it most effectively in the final scene. The effect of this repeated image is to suggest that Juliet is foredoomed to die, that Death, personified, has claimed her for his own. It thus strengthens the ominous note of fate which is felt throughout the play.

That *Romeo and Juliet* is a tragedy of fate can hardly be doubted. Shakespeare says as much in the Prologue. The lovers are marked for death; their fortunes are "crossed" by the stars. The reason for their doom is likewise given: only the shock of their deaths can force their parents to end the senseless feud. At the end of the play Capulet calls the lovers "Poor sacrifices of our enmity," and the Prince describes their deaths as Heaven's punishment of their parents' hate. Romeo's premonition of death before going to the party attributes it to some "consequence yet hanging in the stars." The note of fate is struck repeatedly during the play. "A greater power than we can contradict / Hath thwarted our intents," says Friar Laurence to Juliet in the tomb. The numerous mischances experienced by the lovers are not fortuitous bad luck but represent the working out of some hidden design. Critics who attack the play for lacking inevitability have misunderstood Shakespeare's dramatic technique. Like Hamlet's adventure with the pirates, the sequence of mishaps here is deliberately made so improbable that chance alone cannot explain it. Fate, or the will of Heaven, must be invoked.

One finds it difficult to interpret this tragedy in Aristotelian terms, since the parents are really the ones who have the "tragic flaw" and suffer the results of their folly, as Lear does, in the deaths of their children. Yet the children, not the parents, are the major figures of the play. Some critics have named impetuosity as Romeo's "tragic flaw," but Romeo is less impetuous than Tybalt or Mercutio, and one can hardly name as a "flaw" a quality which is pictured as common to youth. It is true that greater placidity of temperament and more deliberate speed might have averted the tragedy under the given circumstances, yet the pattern of circumstances might easily have been different and the will of fate accomplished just the same.

Shakespeare makes it clear that society is partly responsible for the tragedy. The feud between noble families was a matter of social convention. So was the necessity to take personal revenge for an insult to one's honor. Here there seems to be a topical allusion. Prince Escalus represents the view of Queen Elizabeth, whose government decreed that homicide in a duel should be punishable as murder. She was determined to stamp out duelling. Furthermore, the evil arising from any form of civil strife is a constantly reiterated theme in Elizabethan literature. Current social attitudes may be noted both in the Prince's edict against street fighting and in the cavalier disregard of it.

As might be expected, *Romeo and Juliet* has been a popular stage play, never more so than now, when each year sees from ten to twenty new productions by professional and amateur groups. What Hamlet is for the actor, Juliet is for the actress, a role which offers the fullest scope for the display of female histrionics. In past centuries Mrs Betterton and Fanny Kemble made great successes in the part. In the present century Julia Marlowe, Eva Le Gallienne, Jane Cowl, and Katherine Cornell are among those who have played Juliet. The producer of this play always has a problem, for very few great actresses achieve eminence by the age of fourteen, and most of them are recognizably mature women trying to look young. To a lesser extent the same problem exists in casting the masculine roles. The producer must choose between the verisimilitude of a youthful cast and the more sophisticated acting of experienced players. Nevertheless, despite all difficulties, *Romeo and Juliet* is still constantly staged with success, and most of us can recall productions in which it proved as vivid and moving in the theatre as it always proves on the printed page.

University of Maine   JOHN E. HANKINS

NOTE ON THE TEXT

An abridged and inaccurate version of *Romeo and Juliet*, evidently "reporting" the play in performance, was published in quarto in 1597. In 1599 appeared a good quarto, probably printed from Shakespeare's draft with some reference to the earlier quarto. A third quarto was printed from the second in 1609, and this was used as copy for the fourth quarto (1622?) and the text of the first folio, 1623. The present edition follows the quarto of 1599, with faulty readings corrected with caution by reference to the quarto of 1597, and with few emendations. (All material departures from the text of the 1599 quarto are listed in an appendix, with the exception of added stage directions and adjusted cancellations; the two latter classes of departure are noted as they occur.) None of the early texts, including that of the folio, are divided into acts and scenes. The division supplied marginally in the present edition is "editorial" and is for purposes of reference only.

ROMEO AND JULIET

[NAMES OF THE ACTORS

Chorus
Escalus, *Prince of Verona*
Paris, *a young count, kinsman to the Prince*
Montague
Capulet
An old Man, *of the Capulet family*
Romeo, *son to Montague*
Mercutio, *kinsman to the Prince, and friend to Romeo*
Benvolio, *nephew to Montague, and friend to Romeo*
Tybalt, *nephew to Lady Capulet*
Friar Laurence ⎫ *Franciscans*
Friar John ⎭
Balthasar, *servant to Romeo*
Abram, *servant to Montague*

Sampson ⎫ *servants to Capulet*
Gregory ⎭
Peter, *servant to Juliet's nurse*
An Apothecary
Three Musicians
An Officer
Lady Montague, *wife to Montague*
Lady Capulet, *wife to Capulet*
Juliet, *daughter to Capulet*
Nurse *to Juliet*
Citizens *of Verona,* Gentlemen *and* Gentlewomen *of both
houses,* Maskers, Torchbearers, Pages, Guards,
Watchmen, Servants, *and* Attendants

Scene : *Verona, Mantua*]

*

Pro.

THE PROLOGUE

[Enter] Chorus.

CHORUS

Two households, both alike in dignity,
    In fair Verona, where we lay our scene,
3 From ancient grudge break to new mutiny,
4   Where civil blood makes civil hands unclean.
From forth the fatal loins of these two foes
6   A pair of star-crossed lovers take their life ;
Whose misadventured piteous overthrows
    Doth with their death bury their parents' strife.
9 The fearful passage of their death-marked love,
    And the continuance of their parents' rage,
Which, but their children's end, naught could remove,
12   Is now the two hours' traffic of our stage ;
The which if you with patient ears attend,
What here shall miss, our toil shall strive to mend.

                                    [Exit.]

Pro. 3 *mutiny* outbursts of violence **4** *civil . . . civil* citizens' . . . fellow citizens' **6** *star-crossed* thwarted by adverse stars **9** *death-marked* foredoomed to death **12** *two . . . stage* our stage-business for the next two hours
I, i A street in Verona **1** *carry coals* i.e. suffer insults **2** *colliers* coal dealers **3** *an* if; *choler* anger; *draw* draw our swords **4** *collar* hangman's noose **11** *take the wall* pass on the inner and cleaner part of the sidewalk **12–13** *the weakest . . . wall* i.e. is pushed from his place (proverbial) **15** *weaker vessels* (cf. 1 Peter iii, 7) **25–26** *sense . . . sense* meaning . . . physical sensation **28, 29** *flesh, fish* (alluding to the proverb 'Neither fish nor flesh') **30** *poor-John* dried hake, the cheapest fish; *tool* sword (with ribald innuendo)

*Enter Sampson and Gregory, with swords and
bucklers, of the house of Capulet.*

I, i

SAMPSON Gregory, on my word, we'll not carry coals.   1
GREGORY No, for then we should be colliers.   2
SAMPSON I mean, an we be in choler, we'll draw.   3
GREGORY Ay, while you live, draw your neck out of collar.   4
SAMPSON I strike quickly, being moved.
GREGORY But thou art not quickly moved to strike.
SAMPSON A dog of the house of Montague moves me.
GREGORY To move is to stir, and to be valiant is to stand.
  Therefore, if thou art moved, thou runn'st away.
SAMPSON A dog of that house shall move me to stand. I
  will take the wall of any man or maid of Montague's.   11
GREGORY That shows thee a weak slave; for the weakest   12
  goes to the wall.
SAMPSON 'Tis true; and therefore women, being the
  weaker vessels, are ever thrust to the wall. Therefore I   15
  will push Montague's men from the wall and thrust his
  maids to the wall.
GREGORY The quarrel is between our masters, and us
  their men.
SAMPSON 'Tis all one. I will show myself a tyrant. When
  I have fought with the men, I will be cruel with the
  maids – I will cut off their heads.
GREGORY The heads of the maids?
SAMPSON Ay, the heads of the maids, or their maidenheads. Take it in what sense thou wilt.   25
GREGORY They must take it in sense that feel it.
SAMPSON Me they shall feel while I am able to stand; and
  'tis known I am a pretty piece of flesh.   28
GREGORY 'Tis well thou art not fish; if thou hadst, thou   29
  hadst been poor-John. Draw thy tool! Here comes two   30
  of the house of Montagues.

Enter two other Servingmen [Abram and Balthasar].

SAMPSON My naked weapon is out. Quarrel! I will back thee.

GREGORY How? turn thy back and run?

SAMPSON Fear me not.

36 GREGORY No, marry. I fear thee!

37 SAMPSON Let us take the law of our sides; let them begin.

GREGORY I will frown as I pass by, and let them take it as they list.

40 SAMPSON Nay, as they dare. I will bite my thumb at them, which is disgrace to them if they bear it.

ABRAM Do you bite your thumb at us, sir?

SAMPSON I do bite my thumb, sir.

ABRAM Do you bite your thumb at us, sir?

SAMPSON *[aside to Gregory]* Is the law of our side if I say ay?

GREGORY *[aside to Sampson]* No.

SAMPSON No, sir, I do not bite my thumb at you, sir; but I bite my thumb, sir.

GREGORY Do you quarrel, sir?

50 ABRAM Quarrel, sir? No, sir.

SAMPSON But if you do, sir, I am for you. I serve as good a man as you.

ABRAM No better.

SAMPSON Well, sir.

Enter Benvolio.

GREGORY *[aside to Sampson]* Say 'better.' Here comes one of my master's kinsmen.

SAMPSON Yes, better, sir.

ABRAM You lie.

SAMPSON Draw, if you be men. Gregory, remember thy
60 swashing blow.

They fight.

BENVOLIO Part, fools!

Put up your swords. You know not what you do.

Enter Tybalt.

TYBALT

63   What, art thou drawn among these heartless hinds?

Turn thee, Benvolio! look upon thy death.

BENVOLIO

I do but keep the peace. Put up thy sword,

Or manage it to part these men with me.

TYBALT

What, drawn, and talk of peace? I hate the word

As I hate hell, all Montagues, and thee.

Have at thee, coward!

[They fight.]

Enter [an Officer, and] three or four Citizens with clubs or partisans.

70 OFFICER Clubs, bills, and partisans! Strike! beat them down!

CITIZENS Down with the Capulets! Down with the Montagues!

Enter old Capulet in his gown, and his Wife.

CAPULET

What noise is this? Give me my long sword, ho!

WIFE

A crutch, a crutch! Why call you for a sword?

CAPULET

My sword, I say! Old Montague is come
76 And flourishes his blade in spite of me.

Enter old Montague and his Wife.

MONTAGUE

Thou villain Capulet! – Hold me not, let me go.

MONTAGUE'S WIFE

Thou shalt not stir one foot to seek a foe.

Enter Prince Escalus, with his Train.

PRINCE

Rebellious subjects, enemies to peace,

Profaners of this neighbor-stainèd steel –

Will they not hear? What, ho! you men, you beasts,

That quench the fire of your pernicious rage

With purple fountains issuing from your veins!

On pain of torture, from those bloody hands

Throw your mistemp'red weapons to the ground   85

And hear the sentence of your movèd prince.

Three civil brawls, bred of an airy word   87

By thee, old Capulet, and Montague,

Have thrice disturbed the quiet of our streets

And made Verona's ancient citizens   90

Cast by their grave beseeming ornaments   91

To wield old partisans, in hands as old,

Cank'red with peace, to part your cank'red hate.   93

If ever you disturb our streets again,

Your lives shall pay the forfeit of the peace.

For this time all the rest depart away.

You, Capulet, shall go along with me;

And, Montague, come you this afternoon,

To know our farther pleasure in this case,

To old Freetown, our common judgment place.   100

Once more, on pain of death, all men depart.

Exeunt [all but Montague, his Wife, and Benvolio].

MONTAGUE

Who set this ancient quarrel new abroach?   102

Speak, nephew, were you by when it began?

BENVOLIO

Here were the servants of your adversary

And yours, close fighting ere I did approach.

I drew to part them. In the instant came

The fiery Tybalt, with his sword prepared;

Which, as he breathed defiance to my ears,

He swung about his head and cut the winds,

Who, nothing hurt withal, hissed him in scorn.   110

While we were interchanging thrusts and blows,

Came more and more, and fought on part and part,

Till the Prince came, who parted either part.

MONTAGUE'S WIFE

O, where is Romeo? Saw you him to-day?

Right glad I am he was not at this fray.

BENVOLIO

Madam, an hour before the worshipped sun

Peered forth the golden window of the East,

A troubled mind drave me to walk abroad;

Where, underneath the grove of sycamore

That westward rooteth from this city side,

So early walking did I see your son.

Towards him I made, but he was ware of me   122

36 *marry* indeed (originally an oath by the Virgin Mary); *I fear thee* to suppose me afraid of you is ridiculous   37 *take . . . of* have the law on 40 *bite my thumb* (an insulting gesture)   60 *swashing* smashing   63 *heartless hinds* cowardly servants   70 *bills, partisans* long-shafted weapons with combined spear-head and cutting-blade   76 *in spite of* in defiance of 85 *mistemp'red* (1) badly made, (2) used for a bad purpose   87 *airy* made with breath   90 *ancient citizens* a volunteer guard of older men   91 *grave beseeming ornaments* staffs and costumes appropriate for the aged   93 *Cank'red . . . cank'red* rusted . . . malignant   100 *Freetown* (Brooke's translation of *Villafranca*)   102 *set . . . abroach* reopened this quarrel of long standing   110 *Who* which; *nothing* not at all; *withal* therewith 122 *ware* aware, wary

And stole into the covert of the wood.
124 I, measuring his affections by my own,
125 Which then most sought where most might not be found,
Being one too many by my weary self,
Pursued my humor, not pursuing his,
And gladly shunned who gladly fled from me.

MONTAGUE
Many a morning hath he there been seen,
With tears augmenting the fresh morning's dew,
Adding to clouds more clouds with his deep sighs;
But all so soon as the all-cheering sun
Should in the farthest East begin to draw
134 The shady curtains from Aurora's bed,
135 Away from light steals home my heavy son
And private in his chamber pens himself,
Shuts up his windows, locks fair daylight out,
And makes himself an artificial night.
139 Black and portentous must this humor prove
Unless good counsel may the cause remove.

BENVOLIO
My noble uncle, do you know the cause?

MONTAGUE
I neither know it nor can learn of him.

BENVOLIO
Have you importuned him by any means?

MONTAGUE
Both by myself and many other friends;
But he, his own affections' counsellor,
Is to himself – I will not say how true –
But to himself so secret and so close,
148 So far from sounding and discovery,
As is the bud bit with an envious worm
Ere he can spread his sweet leaves to the air
Or dedicate his beauty to the sun.
Could we but learn from whence his sorrows grow,
We would as willingly give cure as know.
Enter Romeo.

BENVOLIO
See, where he comes. So please you step aside,
I'll know his grievance, or be much denied.

MONTAGUE
I would thou wert so happy by thy stay
157 To hear true shrift. Come, madam, let's away.
Exeunt [Montague and Wife].

BENVOLIO
158 Good morrow, cousin.

ROMEO   Is the day so young?

BENVOLIO
But new struck nine.

ROMEO   Ay me! sad hours seem long.
Was that my father that went hence so fast?

BENVOLIO
It was. What sadness lengthens Romeo's hours?

ROMEO
Not having that which having makes them short.

BENVOLIO In love?

ROMEO Out –

BENVOLIO Of love?

ROMEO
Out of her favor where I am in love.

BENVOLIO
167 Alas that love, so gentle in his view,
168 Should be so tyrannous and rough in proof!

ROMEO
169 Alas that love, whose view is muffled still,
Should without eyes see pathways to his will!
Where shall we dine? O me! What fray was here?
Yet tell me not, for I have heard it all.
173 Here's much to do with hate, but more with love.
Why then, O brawling love, O loving hate,
O anything, of nothing first create!
O heavy lightness, serious vanity,
Misshapen chaos of well-seeming forms,
Feather of lead, bright smoke, cold fire, sick health,
Still-waking sleep, that is not what it is!
This love feel I, that feel no love in this.
Dost thou not laugh?

BENVOLIO   181 No, coz, I rather weep.

ROMEO
Good heart, at what?

BENVOLIO   At thy good heart's oppression.

ROMEO
Why, such is love's transgression.
184 Griefs of mine own lie heavy in my breast,
Which thou wilt propagate, to have it prest
With more of thine. This love that thou hast shown
Doth add more grief to too much of mine own.
Love is a smoke raised with the fume of sighs;
Being purged, a fire sparkling in lovers' eyes;
Being vexed, a sea nourished with lovers' tears.
What is it else? A madness most discreet,
A choking gall, and a preserving sweet.
Farewell, my coz.

BENVOLIO   Soft! I will go along.
An if you leave me so, you do me wrong.

ROMEO
195 Tut! I have lost myself; I am not here;
This is not Romeo, he's some other where.

BENVOLIO
197 Tell me in sadness, who is that you love?

ROMEO
What, shall I groan and tell thee?

BENVOLIO   Groan? Why, no;
But sadly tell me who.

ROMEO
Bid a sick man in sadness make his will.
Ah, word ill urged to one that is so ill!
In sadness, cousin, I do love a woman.

BENVOLIO
I aimed so near when I supposed you loved.

ROMEO
A right good markman. And she's fair I love.

BENVOLIO
205 A right fair mark, fair coz, is soonest hit.

ROMEO
Well, in that hit you miss. She'll not be hit
207 With Cupid's arrow. She hath Dian's wit,

124 *affections* inclinations, feelings   125 *most sought . . . found* i.e. desired solitude   134 *Aurora* the dawn   135 *heavy* melancholy   139 *humor* mood   148 *sounding* being measured (as water-depth is measured with a plummet line)   157 *shrift* confession   158 *morrow* morning   167 *view* appearance   168 *in proof* in being experienced   169 *view* sight; *muffled* blindfolded   173–80 *Here's . . . this* (the rhetorical name for such paradoxes is oxymoron; cf. III, ii, 73–85)   181 *coz* cousin   184–87 *Griefs . . . own* your sorrow for my grief grieves me further to have caused you sorrow   195 *lost* (so both Q2 and Q1, but the emendation 'left,' has been cogently suggested)   197 *in sadness* seriously   205 *fair mark* bright clean target   207 *Dian* Diana, virgin goddess and huntress

861

208 And, in strong proof of chastity well armed,
209 From Love's weak childish bow she lives unharmed.
210 She will not stay the siege of loving terms,
Nor bide th' encounter of assailing eyes,
Nor ope her lap to saint-seducing gold.
O, she is rich in beauty; only poor
214 That, when she dies, with beauty dies her store.

BENVOLIO
215 Then she hath sworn that she will still live chaste?

ROMEO
216 She hath, and in that sparing makes huge waste;
For beauty, starved with her severity,
Cuts beauty off from all posterity.
She is too fair, too wise, wisely too fair,
220 To merit bliss by making me despair.
She hath forsworn to love, and in that vow
Do I live dead that live to tell it now.

BENVOLIO
Be ruled by me; forget to think of her.

ROMEO
O, teach me how I should forget to think!

BENVOLIO
By giving liberty unto thine eyes.
Examine other beauties.

ROMEO   'Tis the way
227 To call hers (exquisite) in question more.
These happy masks that kiss fair ladies' brows,
Being black puts us in mind they hide the fair.
He that is strucken blind cannot forget
The precious treasure of his eyesight lost.
232 Show me a mistress that is passing fair,
What doth her beauty serve but as a note
Where I may read who passed that passing fair?
Farewell. Thou canst not teach me to forget.

BENVOLIO
236 I'll pay that doctrine, or else die in debt.   *Exeunt.*

*

I, ii   *Enter Capulet, County Paris, and the Clown*
                 [a Servant].

CAPULET
1 But Montague is bound as well as I,
In penalty alike; and 'tis not hard, I think,
For men so old as we to keep the peace.

PARIS
4 Of honorable reckoning are you both,
And pity 'tis you lived at odds so long.
But now, my lord, what say you to my suit?

CAPULET
But saying o'er what I have said before:
8 My child is yet a stranger in the world,
She hath not seen the change of fourteen years;
Let two more summers wither in their pride
Ere we may think her ripe to be a bride.

PARIS
Younger than she are happy mothers made.

CAPULET
13 And too soon marred are those so early made.
14 Earth hath swallowèd all my hopes but she;
She is the hopeful lady of my earth.
But woo her, gentle Paris, get her heart;
My will to her consent is but a part.
18 An she agree, within her scope of choice
19 Lies my consent and fair according voice.

This night I hold an old accustomed feast,   20
Whereto I have invited many a guest,
Such as I love; and you among the store,
One more, most welcome, makes my number more.
At my poor house look to behold this night
Earth-treading stars that make dark heaven light.   25
Such comfort as do lusty young men feel
When well-apparelled April on the heel   27
Of limping Winter treads, even such delight
Among fresh fennel buds shall you this night   29
Inherit at my house. Hear all, all see,
And like her most whose merit most shall be;
Which, on more view of many, mine, being one,   32
May stand in number, though in reck'ning none.
Come, go with me.
      [To Servant, giving him a paper]
             Go, sirrah, trudge about   34
Through fair Verona; find those persons out
Whose names are written there, and to them say,
My house and welcome on their pleasure stay.
                  Exit [with Paris].

SERVANT Find them out whose names are written here?
It is written that the shoemaker should meddle with his
yard and the tailor with his last, the fisher with his pen-   40
cil and the painter with his nets; but I am sent to find   41
those persons whose names are here writ, and can never
find what names the writing person hath here writ. I   43
must to the learned. In good time!   44
      Enter Benvolio and Romeo.

BENVOLIO
Tut, man, one fire burns out another's burning;   45
    One pain is less'ned by another's anguish;   46
Turn giddy, and be holp by backward turning;   47
    One desperate grief cures with another's languish.
Take thou some new infection to thy eye,   49
And the rank poison of the old will die.

ROMEO
Your plantain leaf is excellent for that.

BENVOLIO
For what, I pray thee?

ROMEO   For your broken shin.

BENVOLIO
Why, Romeo, art thou mad?

ROMEO
Not mad, but bound more than a madman is;   54

---

208 *proof* armor   **209** *unharmed* (from Q1; Q2 reads 'uncharmed,' perhaps correctly)   **210–11** *She . . . eyes* i.e. she gives me no chance to woo her   **214** *with . . . store* she will leave no children to perpetuate her beauty   **215** *still* always   **216** *sparing* miserly economy   **220** *bliss* heaven   **227** *in question* to my mind   **232** *passing* surpassingly   **236** *pay that doctrine* convince you otherwise
I, ii A street in Verona   **1** *bound* under bond   **4** *reckoning* reputation   **8** *world* world of society   **13** *marred* disfigured by childbirth   **14** *hopes* children   **18** *scope* range   **19** *according* harmoniously agreeing   **20** *old accustomed* by custom of long standing   **25** *stars* i.e. maidens   **27** *April* (Venus' month, the season of lovemaking)   **29** *fennel* a flowering herb associated with stimulation and enticement   **32–33** *Which . . . none* my daughter will be numerically counted among those present, but possibly not among those you would wish to marry after seeing them all (cf. the common saying 'One is no number')   **34** *sirrah* (a familiar form of address, used with servants and sometimes with friends)   **40, 41** *yard, last, pencil, nets* (occupational tools humorously reversed)   **43** *find* find out (since I cannot read)   **44** *In good time* help comes just when I need it   **45** *one . . . burning* (proverb used often by Shakespeare)   **46** *another's anguish* anguish from another pain   **47** *Turn . . . turning* when giddy from whirling around, be helped by reversing direction   **49** *infection* (figuratively used, but taken literally by Romeo)   **54–56** *bound . . . tormented* (customary treatment of madmen)

Shut up in prison, kept without my food,
56 Whipped and tormented and – God-den, good fellow.
SERVANT God gi' go-den. I pray, sir, can you read?
ROMEO
Ay, mine own fortune in my misery.
SERVANT Perhaps you have learned it without book. But
I pray, can you read anything you see?
ROMEO
61 Ay, if I know the letters and the language.
SERVANT Ye say honestly. Rest you merry.
ROMEO Stay, fellow; I can read.
    He reads the letter.
'Signior Martino and his wife and daughters;
County Anselmo and his beauteous sisters;
The lady widow of Vitruvio;
Signior Placentio and his lovely nieces;
Mercutio and his brother Valentine;
Mine uncle Capulet, his wife, and daughters;
70 My fair niece Rosaline and Livia;
Signior Valentio and his cousin Tybalt;
Lucio and the lively Helena.'
A fair assembly. Whither should they come?
SERVANT Up.
ROMEO Whither? To supper?
SERVANT To our house.
ROMEO Whose house?
SERVANT My master's.
ROMEO
Indeed I should have asked you that before.
SERVANT Now I'll tell you without asking. My master is
the great rich Capulet; and if you be not of the house of
82 Montagues, I pray come and crush a cup of wine. Rest
you merry.   *[Exit.]*
BENVOLIO
At this same ancient feast of Capulet's
Sups the fair Rosaline whom thou so loves;
With all the admirèd beauties of Verona.
87 Go thither, and with unattainted eye
Compare her face with some that I shall show,
And I will make thee think thy swan a crow.
ROMEO
When the devout religion of mine eye
Maintains such falsehood, then turn tears to fires;
92 And these, who, often drowned, could never die,
Transparent heretics, be burnt for liars!
One fairer than my love? The all-seeing sun
Ne'er saw her match since first the world begun.
BENVOLIO
Tut! you saw her fair, none else being by,
Herself poised with herself in either eye;
98 But in that crystal scales let there be weighed
Your lady's love against some other maid
That I will show you shining at this feast,
101 And she shall scant show well that now seems best.

---

56 *God-den* good evening (used after 12 noon; cf. II, iv, 105)   61 *if I know*
(the servant takes this to mean 'only if I have memorized the appearance of')
82 *crush* drink   87 *unattainted* unprejudiced   92 *these* these eyes; *drowned*
i.e. in tears   98 *crystal scales* (Romeo's two eyes are compared to the two
ends of a pair of balances)   101 *scant* scarcely
I, iii Within Capulet's house   7 *give leave* leave us   9 *thou's* thou shalt
13 *teen* sorrow   15 *Lammastide* August 1   23 *earthquake* (see Introduction)
29 *bear a brain* keep my mental powers   32 *tetchy* fretful   33 *Shake* . . .
dovehouse i.e. the dovehouse creaked from the earthquake; *trow* believe
34 *trudge* run away   36 *high-lone* alone; *rood* cross   43 *holidam* halidom,
holy relic

ROMEO
I'll go along, no such sight to be shown,
But to rejoice in splendor of my own.   *[Exeunt.]*

*

Enter Capulet's Wife, and Nurse.   I, iii
WIFE
Nurse, where's my daughter? Call her forth to me.
NURSE
Now, by my maidenhead at twelve year old,
I bade her come. What, lamb! what, ladybird!
God forbid, where's this girl? What, Juliet!
    Enter Juliet.
JULIET
How now? Who calls?
NURSE   Your mother.
JULIET   Madam, I am here.
What is your will?
WIFE
This is the matter – Nurse, give leave awhile,   7
We must talk in secret. Nurse, come back again;
I have rememb'red me, thou's hear our counsel.   9
Thou knowest my daughter's of a pretty age.
NURSE
Faith, I can tell her age unto an hour.
WIFE
She's not fourteen.
NURSE   I'll lay fourteen of my teeth –
And yet, to my teen be it spoken, I have but four –   13
She's not fourteen. How long is it now
To Lammastide?   15
WIFE   A fortnight and odd days.
NURSE
Even or odd, of all days in the year,
Come Lammas Eve at night shall she be fourteen.
Susan and she (God rest all Christian souls!)
Were of an age. Well, Susan is with God;
She was too good for me. But, as I said,
On Lammas Eve at night shall she be fourteen;
That shall she, marry; I remember it well.
'Tis since the earthquake now eleven years;   23
And she was weaned (I never shall forget it),
Of all the days of the year, upon that day;
For I had then laid wormwood to my dug,
Sitting in the sun under the dovehouse wall.
My lord and you were then at Mantua.
Nay, I do bear a brain. But, as I said,   29
When it did taste the wormwood on the nipple
Of my dug and felt it bitter, pretty fool,
To see it tetchy and fall out with the dug!   32
Shake, quoth the dovehouse! 'Twas no need, I trow,   33
To bid me trudge.   34
And since that time it is eleven years,
For then she could stand high-lone; nay, by th' rood,   36
She could have run and waddled all about;
For even the day before, she broke her brow;
And then my husband (God be with his soul!
'A was a merry man) took up the child.
'Yea,' quoth he, 'dost thou fall upon thy face?
Thou wilt fall backward when thou hast more wit;
Wilt thou not, Jule?' and, by my holidam,   43
The pretty wretch left crying and said 'Ay.'
To see now how a jest shall come about!
I warrant, an I should live a thousand years,

I never should forget it. 'Wilt thou not, Jule?' quoth he,
48   And, pretty fool, it stinted and said 'Ay.'
WIFE
Enough of this. I pray thee hold thy peace.
NURSE
Yes, madam. Yet I cannot choose but laugh
To think it should leave crying and say 'Ay.'
52   And yet, I warrant, it had upon it brow
A bump as big as a young cock'rel's stone;
A perilous knock; and it cried bitterly.
'Yea,' quoth my husband, 'fall'st upon thy face?
Thou wilt fall backward when thou comest to age;
Wilt thou not, Jule?' It stinted and said 'Ay.'
JULIET
58   And stint thou too, I pray thee, nurse, say I.
NURSE
Peace, I have done. God mark thee to his grace!
Thou wast the prettiest babe that e'er I nursed.
An I might live to see thee married once,
I have my wish.
WIFE
Marry, that 'marry' is the very theme
I came to talk of. Tell me, daughter Juliet,
How stands your disposition to be married?
JULIET
It is an honor that I dream not of.
NURSE
An honor? Were not I thine only nurse,
I would say thou hadst sucked wisdom from thy teat.
WIFE
Well, think of marriage now. Younger than you,
Here in Verona, ladies of esteem,
Are made already mothers. By my count,
72   I was your mother much upon these years
That you are now a maid. Thus then in brief:
The valiant Paris seeks you for his love.
NURSE
A man, young lady! lady, such a man
76   As all the world – why he's a man of wax.
WIFE
Verona's summer hath not such a flower.
NURSE
Nay, he's a flower, in faith – a very flower.
WIFE
What say you? Can you love the gentleman?
This night you shall behold him at our feast.
Read o'er the volume of young Paris' face,
And find delight writ there with beauty's pen;
83   Examine every married lineament,
And see how one another lends content;
85   And what obscured in this fair volume lies
86   Find written in the margent of his eyes.
This precious book of love, this unbound lover,
88   To beautify him only lacks a cover.
89   The fish lives in the sea, and 'tis much pride
For fair without the fair within to hide.
That book in many's eyes doth share the glory,
That in gold clasps locks in the golden story;
So shall you share all that he doth possess,
By having him making yourself no less.
NURSE
95   No less? Nay, bigger! Women grow by men.
WIFE
Speak briefly, can you like of Paris' love?

JULIET
I'll look to like, if looking liking move;
But no more deep will I endart mine eye   98
Than your consent gives strength to make it fly.
        Enter Servingman.
SERVINGMAN Madam, the guests are come, supper
served up, you called, my young lady asked for, the
nurse cursed in the pantry, and everything in extremity.   102
I must hence to wait. I beseech you follow straight.
WIFE
We follow thee.   [*Exit Servingman.*]
        Juliet, the County stays.
NURSE
Go, girl, seek happy nights to happy days.   *Exeunt.*

                              *

        Enter Romeo, Mercutio, Benvolio, with five or six   I, iv
        other Maskers; Torchbearers.
ROMEO
What, shall this speech be spoke for our excuse?   1
Or shall we on without apology?
BENVOLIO
The date is out of such prolixity.   3
We'll have no Cupid hoodwinked with a scarf,   4
Bearing a Tartar's painted bow of lath,   5
Scaring the ladies like a crowkeeper;   6
[Nor no without-book prologue, faintly spoke   7
After the prompter, for our entrance;]   8
But, let them measure us by what they will,
We'll measure them a measure and be gone.   10
ROMEO
Give me a torch. I am not for this ambling.
Being but heavy, I will bear the light.   12
MERCUTIO
Nay, gentle Romeo, we must have you dance.
ROMEO
Not I, believe me. You have dancing shoes
With nimble soles; I have a soul of lead
So stakes me to the ground I cannot move.
MERCUTIO
You are a lover. Borrow Cupid's wings
And soar with them above a common bound.   18
ROMEO
I am too sore enpiercèd with his shaft
To soar with his light feathers; and so bound

48 *stinted* stopped   52 *it brow* its brow   58 *say I* (a pun on 'ay' and 'I';
cf. III, ii, 45–50)   72 *much . . . years* at much the same age (indicating that
Lady Capulet's age is now twenty-eight)   76 *a man of wax* handsome,
as a wax model   83 *married lineament* harmonious feature   85 *what . . .
lies* i.e. his concealed inner qualities of character   86 *margent* marginal
gloss   88 *a cover* i.e. a wife   89–94 *The fish . . . no less* i.e. as the sea enfolds the fish and the cover enfolds the book, so you shall enfold Paris
(in your arms), enhancing your good qualities by sharing his   95 *bigger*
i.e. through pregnancy   98 *endart mine eye* shoot my eye-glance (as an
arrow; cf. III, ii, 47)   102 *cursed in the pantry* i.e. the other servants
swear because the Nurse is not helping
I, iv Before Capulet's house   1 *this speech* (Romeo has prepared a set
speech, such as customarily introduced visiting maskers)   3 *The date . . .
prolixity* such superfluous speeches are now out of fashion   4 *hoodwinked*
blindfolded   5 *Tartar's . . . lath* (the Tartar's bow, used from horseback,
was much shorter than the English longbow)   6 *crowkeeper* scarecrow
7–8 (added from Q1)   7 *without-book* memorized   8 *entrance* (pronounced
'en-ter-ance'   10 *measure . . . measure* dance one dance   12 *heavy* sad, hence
'weighted down'   18 *bound* a leap, required in some dances

21 I cannot bound a pitch above dull woe.
   Under love's heavy burden do I sink.
MERCUTIO
   And, to sink in it, should you burden love –
   Too great oppression for a tender thing.
ROMEO
   Is love a tender thing ? It is too rough,
   Too rude, too boist'rous, and it pricks like thorn.
MERCUTIO
   If love be rough with you, be rough with love,
   Prick love for pricking, and you beat love down.
   Give me a case to put my visage in.
30 A visor for a visor ! What care I
31 What curious eye doth quote deformities ?
32 Here are the beetle brows shall blush for me.
BENVOLIO
   Come, knock and enter ; and no sooner in
34 But every man betake him to his legs.
ROMEO
   A torch for me ! Let wantons light of heart
36 Tickle the senseless rushes with their heels ;
37 For I am proverbed with a grandsire phrase,
38 I'll be a candle-holder and look on ;
39 The game was ne'er so fair, and I am done.
MERCUTIO
40 Tut ! dun 's the mouse, the constable's own word !
41 If thou art Dun, we'll draw thee from the mire
42 Of this sir-reverence love, wherein thou stickest
43 Up to the ears. Come, we burn daylight, ho !
ROMEO
   Nay, that's not so.
MERCUTIO   I mean, sir, in delay
   We waste our lights in vain, like lamps by day.
   Take our good meaning, for our judgments sits
47 Five times in that ere once in our five wits.
ROMEO
   And we mean well in going to this masque,
49 But 'tis no wit to go.
MERCUTIO   Why, may one ask ?
ROMEO
   I dreamt a dream to-night.
MERCUTIO   And so did I.

ROMEO
   Well, what was yours ?
MERCUTIO   That dreamers often lie.
ROMEO
   In bed asleep, while they do dream things true.
MERCUTIO
   O, then I see Queen Mab hath been with you.   53
   She is the fairies' midwife, and she comes
   In shape no bigger than an agate stone   55
   On the forefinger of an alderman,
   Drawn with a team of little atomies   57
   Over men's noses as they lie asleep ;
   Her wagon spokes made of long spinners' legs,   59
   The cover, of the wings of grasshoppers ;
   Her traces, of the smallest spider web ;   61
   Her collars, of the moonshine's wat'ry beams ;   62
   Her whip, of cricket's bone ; the lash, of film ;   63
   Her wagoner, a small grey-coated gnat,
   Not half so big as a round little worm   65
   Pricked from the lazy finger of a maid ;
   Her chariot is an empty hazelnut,
   Made by the joiner squirrel or old grub,
   Time out o' mind the fairies' coachmakers.
   And in this state she gallops night by night
   Through lovers' brains, and then they dream of love ;
   O'er courtiers' knees, that dream on curtsies straight ;
   O'er lawyers' fingers, who straight dream on fees ;
   O'er ladies' lips, who straight on kisses dream,
   Which oft the angry Mab with blisters plagues,
   Because their breaths with sweetmeats tainted are.   76
   Sometime she gallops o'er a courtier's nose,
   And then dreams he of smelling out a suit ;   78
   And sometime comes she with a tithe-pig's tail   79
   Tickling a parson's nose as 'a lies asleep,
   Then dreams he of another benefice.   81
   Sometimes she driveth o'er a soldier's neck,
   And then dreams he of cutting foreign throats,
   Of breaches, ambuscadoes, Spanish blades,
   Of healths five fathom deep ; and then anon   85
   Drums in his ear, at which he starts and wakes,
   And being thus frighted, swears a prayer or two
   And sleeps again. This is that very Mab
   That plats the manes of horses in the night
   And bakes the elflocks in foul sluttish hairs,   90
   Which once untangled much misfortune bodes.
   This is the hag, when maids lie on their backs,   92
   That presses them and learns them first to bear,
   Making them women of good carriage.
   This is she –
ROMEO   Peace, peace, Mercutio, peace !
   Thou talk'st of nothing.   96
MERCUTIO   True, I talk of dreams ;
   Which are the children of an idle brain,
   Begot of nothing but vain fantasy ;   98
   Which is as thin of substance as the air,
   And more inconstant than the wind, who woos
   Even now the frozen bosom of the North
   And, being angered, puffs away from thence,
   Turning his side to the dew-dropping South.
BENVOLIO
   This wind you talk of blows us from ourselves.
   Supper is done, and we shall come too late.
ROMEO
   I fear, too early ; for my mind misgives

21 *pitch* height (falconry)   30 *A visor . . . visor* a mask for a face ugly
enough to be itself a mask   31 *quote* note   32 *beetle brows* beetling eyebrows (of the mask)   34 *betake . . . legs* join the dance   36 *rushes* (used
as floor coverings)   37 *grandsire phrase* old saying   38 *candle-holder*
i.e. non-participant   39 *The game . . . done* best quit a game at the height
of enjoyment (proverbial; cf. I, v, 119)   40 *dun 's the mouse* be quiet
as a mouse (proverbial); *constable's own word* i.e. the caution to be quiet
41 *Dun* (stock name for a horse); *mire* (alluding to a winter game, 'Dun is
in the mire,' in which the players lifted a heavy log representing a horse
caught in the mud)   42 *sir-reverence* filthy (literally 'save-your-rever-
ence,' a euphemism associated with physical functions)   43 *burn daylight*
waste time (proverbial)   47 *five wits* mental faculties : common sense (the
perceptive power common to all five physical senses), fantasy, imagination, judgment (reason), memory   49 *no wit* not intelligent   53 *Mab* (a
Celtic folk name for the fairy queen)   55 *agate stone* jewel carved with
figures and set in a ring   57 *atomies* tiny creatures   59 *spinners* spiders
61, 62 *traces, collars* parts of the harness   63 *film* any filament   65–66
worm . . . maid (alluding to the proverbial saying that worms breed in
idle fingers)   76 *with sweetmeats* i.e. as a result of eating sweetmeats
78 *smelling . . . suit* discovering a petitioner who will pay for his influence
with government officials   79 *tithe-pig* the parson's tithe (tenth) of
his parishioner's livestock   81 *another benefice* an additional 'living'
in the church   85 *healths . . . deep* drinking toasts from glasses thirty
feet deep   90 *elflocks* knots of tangled hair   92 *hag* night hag, or nightmare   96 *nothing* no tangible thing   98 *fantasy* (cf. l. 47 and note)

107 Some consequence, yet hanging in the stars,
Shall bitterly begin his fearful date
With this night's revels and expire the term
Of a despisèd life, closed in my breast,
By some vile forfeit of untimely death.
112 But he that hath the steerage of my course
Direct my sail ! On, lusty gentlemen !

BENVOLIO Strike, drum.

I, v   *They march about the stage, and Servingmen come*
forth with napkins.

1 1. SERVINGMAN Where's Potpan, that he helps not to
2 take away ? He shift a trencher ! he scrape a trencher !
3 2. SERVINGMAN When good manners shall lie all in one
or two men's hands, and they unwashed too, 'tis a foul
thing.
6 1. SERVINGMAN Away with the joint-stools, remove the
7 court-cupboard, look to the plate. Good thou, save me
8 a piece of marchpane and, as thou loves me, let the
9 porter let in Susan Grindstone and Nell. *[Exit second*
Servingman.] Anthony, and Potpan !
[Enter two more Servingmen.]
11 3. SERVINGMAN Ay, boy, ready.
1. SERVINGMAN You are looked for and called for, asked
for and sought for, in the great chamber.
14 4. SERVINGMAN We cannot be here and there too.
15 Cheerly, boys ! Be brisk awhile, and the longer liver take
all.   *[Exeunt third and fourth Servingmen.]*
Enter [Capulet, his Wife, Juliet, Tybalt, Nurse, and]
all the Guests and Gentlewomen to the Maskers.

CAPULET
Welcome, gentlemen ! Ladies that have their toes
17 Unplagued with corns will walk a bout with you.
Ah ha, my mistresses ! which of you all
19 Will now deny to dance ? She that makes dainty,
She I'll swear hath corns. Am I come near ye now ?
Welcome, gentlemen ! I have seen the day
That I have worn a visor and could tell
A whispering tale in a fair lady's ear,
Such as would please. 'Tis gone, 'tis gone, 'tis gone !
You are welcome, gentlemen ! Come, musicians, play.
Music plays, and they dance.
26 A hall, a hall ! give room ! and foot it, girls.
More light, you knaves ! and turn the tables up,
And quench the fire, the room is grown too hot.
29 Ah, sirrah, this unlooked-for sport comes well.
Nay, sit, nay, sit, good cousin Capulet,
For you and I are past our dancing days.
How long is't now since last yourself and I
Were in a mask ?
33 2. CAPULET   By'r Lady, thirty years.
CAPULET
What, man ? 'Tis not so much, 'tis not so much ;
'Tis since the nuptial of Lucentio,
Come Pentecost as quickly as it will,
Some five-and-twenty years, and then we masked.
2. CAPULET
'Tis more, 'tis more. His son is elder, sir ;
His son is thirty.
CAPULET   Will you tell me that ?
40 His son was but a ward two years ago.
ROMEO *[to a Servingman]*
What lady's that, which doth enrich the hand
Of yonder knight ?
SERVINGMAN I know not, sir.

ROMEO
O, she doth teach the torches to burn bright !
It seems she hangs upon the cheek of night
As a rich jewel in an Ethiop's ear –
Beauty too rich for use, for earth too dear !
So shows a snowy dove trooping with crows   48
As yonder lady o'er her fellows shows.
The measure done, I'll watch her place of stand
And, touching hers, make blessèd my rude hand.   51
Did my heart love till now ? Forswear it, sight !
For I ne'er saw true beauty till this night.
TYBALT
This, by his voice, should be a Montague.
Fetch me my rapier, boy. What, dares the slave
Come hither, covered with an antic face,   56
To fleer and scorn at our solemnity ?   57
Now, by the stock and honor of my kin,
To strike him dead I hold it not a sin.
CAPULET
Why, how now, kinsman ? Wherefore storm you so ?
TYBALT
Uncle, this is a Montague, our foe ;
A villain, that is hither come in spite
To scorn at our solemnity this night.
CAPULET
Young Romeo is it ?
TYBALT   'Tis he, that villain Romeo.
CAPULET
Content thee, gentle coz, let him alone.
'A bears him like a portly gentleman,   66
And, to say truth, Verona brags of him
To be a virtuous and well-governed youth.
I would not for the wealth of all this town
Here in my house do him disparagement.
Therefore be patient, take no note of him.
It is my will, the which if thou respect,
Show a fair presence and put off these frowns,
An ill-beseeming semblance for a feast.
TYBALT
It fits when such a villain is a guest.
I'll not endure him.
CAPULET   He shall be endured.
What, goodman boy ! I say he shall. Go to !
Am I the master here, or you ? Go to !

107 *consequence* future chain of events ; *hanging* (in astrology, future events are said to 'hang' – '*dependere*' – from the stars)   112 *he* God
I, v Within Capulet's house   s.d. (Q2 adds 'Enter Romeo,' altered in folio to 'Enter Servant.' It is not certain that the Maskers leave the stage at this point ; 'marching about' itself sometimes signalled a change in locale.) 1, 3 *1. Servingman, 2. Servingman* (designated 'Servingman', '1. Servingman' in Q2)   2 *trencher* wooden platter   3–5 *When . . . thing* (a complaint that household decorum, 'good manners,' is sustained by too few, and too unwashed, servants)   6 *joint-stools* stools made by a joiner   7 *court-cupboard* sideboard ; *plate* silverware   8 *marchpane* sweetmeat with almonds   9 *Susan . . . Nell* (girls evidently invited for a servants' party in the kitchen after the banquet)   11, 14 *3. Servingman, 4. Servingman* (designated '2.' and '3.' in Q2, but presumably they are Anthony and Potpan, now arrived)   15 *longer . . . all* i.e. the spoils to the survivor (proverbial, but often used in contexts like the above, advocating enjoyment of life)   17 *walk a bout* dance a turn   19 *makes dainty* pretends to hesitate   26 *A hall* clear the hall for dancing   29 *unlooked-for sport* (a dance was not originally planned)   33 *2. Capulet* (an old man of the Capulet family) ; *thirty years* (indicating Capulet's advanced age)   40 *His son . . . ago* it seems only two years since his son was a minor   48 *with crows* (cf. I, ii, 89)   51 *rude* coarse-skinned   56 *antic face* comic mask   57 *fleer* mock ; *solemnity* dignified feast   66 *portly* of good carriage

79 You'll not endure him, God shall mend my soul!
80 You'll make a mutiny among my guests!
81 You will set cock-a-hoop, you'll be the man!

TYBALT
Why, uncle, 'tis a shame.

CAPULET   Go to, go to!
You are a saucy boy. Is't so, indeed?
84 This trick may chance to scathe you. I know what.
85 You must contrary me! Marry, 'tis time –
86 Well said, my hearts! – You are a princox – go!
Be quiet, or – More light, more light! – For shame!
I'll make you quiet; what! – Cheerly, my hearts!

TYBALT
89 Patience perforce with willful choler meeting
Makes my flesh tremble in their different greeting.
I will withdraw; but this intrusion shall,
Now seeming sweet, convert to bitt'rest gall.   *Exit.*

ROMEO
93 If I profane with my unworthiest hand
94   This holy shrine, the gentle sin is this;
95 My lips, two blushing pilgrims, ready stand
To smooth that rough touch with a tender kiss.

JULIET
97 Good pilgrim, you do wrong your hand too much,
Which mannerly devotion shows in this;
For saints have hands that pilgrims' hands do touch,
100   And palm to palm is holy palmers' kiss.

ROMEO
Have not saints lips, and holy palmers too?

JULIET
Ay, pilgrim, lips that they must use in prayer.

ROMEO
103 O, then, dear saint, let lips do what hands do!
They pray; grant thou, lest faith turn to despair.

JULIET
105 Saints do not move, though grant for prayers' sake.

ROMEO
Then move not while my prayer's effect I take.
Thus from my lips, by thine my sin is purged.
    [*Kisses her.*]

JULIET
Then have my lips the sin that they have took.

ROMEO
Sin from my lips? O trespass sweetly urged!
Give me my sin again.
    [*Kisses her.*]

110 JULIET   You kiss by th' book.

NURSE
Madam, your mother craves a word with you.

ROMEO
What is her mother?

NURSE   Marry, bachelor,
Her mother is the lady of the house,
And a good lady, and a wise and virtuous.
I nursed her daughter that you talked withal.   115
I tell you, he that can lay hold of her
Shall have the chinks.   117

ROMEO   Is she a Capulet?
O dear account! my life is my foe's debt.   118

BENVOLIO
Away, be gone; the sport is at the best.   119

ROMEO
Ay, so I fear; the more is my unrest.

CAPULET
Nay, gentlemen, prepare not to be gone;
We have a trifling foolish banquet towards.   122
Is it e'en so? Why then, I thank you all.
I thank you, honest gentlemen. Good night.
More torches here! Come on then, let's to bed.
Ah, sirrah, by my fay, it waxes late;   126
I'll to my rest.   [*Exeunt all but Juliet and Nurse.*]

JULIET
Come hither, nurse. What is yond gentleman?

NURSE
The son and heir of old Tiberio.

JULIET
What's he that now is going out of door?

NURSE
Marry, that, I think, be young Petruchio.

JULIET
What's he that follows there, that would not dance?

NURSE
I know not.

JULIET
Go ask his name. – If he be marrièd,
My grave is like to be my wedding bed.

NURSE
His name is Romeo, and a Montague,
The only son of your great enemy.

JULIET
My only love, sprung from my only hate!
Too early seen unknown, and known too late!
Prodigious birth of love it is to me   140
That I must love a loathèd enemy.

NURSE
What's tis? what's tis?   142

JULIET   A rhyme I learnt even now
Of one I danced withal.
    One calls within, 'Juliet.'

NURSE   Anon, anon!   143
Come, let's away; the strangers all are gone.   *Exeunt.*

*

[*Enter*] *Chorus.*   II, Cho.

CHORUS
Now old desire doth in his deathbed lie,   1
   And young affection gapes to be his heir;   2
That fair for which love groaned for and would die,
   With tender Juliet matched, is now not fair.

---

79 *God . . . soul* (an expression of impatience)   **80** *mutiny* violent disturbance   **81** *set cock-a-hoop* i.e. take the lead; *be the man* play the big man   **84** *scathe* injure; *what* what I'm doing   **85** *'tis time* it's time you learned your place (?)   **86** *said* done; *my hearts* (addressed to the dancers); *princox* saucy boy   **89** *Patience perforce* enforced self-restraint; *choler* anger   **93–110** (these lines form an English-style sonnet and the first quatrain of another)   **94** *shrine* i.e. Juliet's hand; *sin* i.e. roughening her soft hand with his coarser one (cf. l. 51)   **95** *pilgrims* (so called because pilgrims visit shrines)   **97–100** *Good . . . kiss* your touch is not rough, to heal it with a kiss is unnecessary, a handclasp is sufficient greeting   **100** *palmers* religious pilgrims   **103** *do what hands do* i.e. press each other (in a kiss)   **105** *move* take the initiative; *grant* give permission   **110** *book* book of etiquette   **115** *withal* with   **117** *chinks* money   **118** *my foe's debt* owed to my foe   **119** *Away . . . best* (cf. I, iv, 39)   **122** *banquet* light refreshments; *towards* in preparation   **126** *fay* faith   **140** *Prodigious* monstrous   **142** *tis* this   **143** *Anon* i.e. we are coming right away   **II, Cho.** **1** *old desire* i.e. Romeo's love of Rosaline   **2** *young affection* new love; *gapes* opens his mouth hungrily

Now Romeo is beloved and loves again,
  Alike bewitchèd by the charm of looks;
7 But to his foe supposed he must complain,
8   And she steal love's sweet bait from fearful hooks.
Being held a foe, he may not have access
10   To breathe such vows as lovers use to swear,
And she as much in love, her means much less
  To meet her new belovèd anywhere;
But passion lends them power, time means, to meet,
Temp'ring extremities with extreme sweet.   *[Exit.]*

II, i   *Enter Romeo alone.*

ROMEO
1 Can I go forward when my heart is here?
2 Turn back, dull earth, and find thy centre out.
    Enter Benvolio with Mercutio. [Romeo retires.]

BENVOLIO
Romeo! my cousin Romeo! Romeo!

MERCUTIO   He is wise,
And, on my life, hath stol'n him home to bed.

BENVOLIO
He ran this way and leapt this orchard wall.
Call, good Mercutio.

6 MERCUTIO   Nay, I'll conjure too.
7 Romeo! humors! madman! passion! lover!
Appear thou in the likeness of a sigh;
Speak but one rhyme, and I am satisfied!
Cry but 'Ay me!' pronounce but 'love' and 'dove';
11 Speak to my gossip Venus one fair word,
12 One nickname for her purblind son and heir
13 Young Abraham Cupid, he that shot so true
14 When King Cophetua loved the beggar maid!
He heareth not, he stirreth not, he moveth not;
16 The ape is dead, and I must conjure him.
I conjure thee by Rosaline's bright eyes,
By her high forehead and her scarlet lip,
By her fine foot, straight leg, and quivering thigh,
20 And the demesnes that there adjacent lie,
That in thy likeness thou appear to us!

BENVOLIO
An if he hear thee, thou wilt anger him.

MERCUTIO
This cannot anger him. 'Twould anger him
24 To raise a spirit in his mistress' circle
Of some strange nature, letting it there stand
Till she had laid it and conjured it down.
That were some spite; my invocation
Is fair and honest: in his mistress' name,
I conjure only but to raise up him.

BENVOLIO
Come, he hath hid himself among these trees
31 To be consorted with the humorous night.
Blind is his love and best befits the dark.

MERCUTIO
If love be blind, love cannot hit the mark.
Now will he sit under a medlar tree
And wish his mistress were that kind of fruit
36 As maids call medlars when they laugh alone.
O, Romeo, that she were, O that she were
38 An open et cetera, thou a pop'rin pear!
39 Romeo, good night. I'll to my truckle-bed;
This field-bed is too cold for me to sleep.
Come, shall we go?

BENVOLIO   Go then, for 'tis in vain
To seek him here that means not to be found.
    Exit [with Mercutio].

ROMEO *[coming forward]*   II, ii
He jests at scars that never felt a wound.
    [Enter Juliet above at a window.]
But soft! What light through yonder window breaks?
It is the East, and Juliet is the sun!
Arise, fair sun, and kill the envious moon,   4
Who is already sick and pale with grief
That thou her maid art far more fair than she.   6
Be not her maid, since she is envious.
Her vestal livery is but sick and green,   8
And none but fools do wear it. Cast it off.
It is my lady; O, it is my love!
O that she knew she were!
She speaks, yet she says nothing. What of that?
Her eye discourses; I will answer it.
I am too bold; 'tis not to me she speaks.
Two of the fairest stars in all the heaven,
Having some business, do entreat her eyes
To twinkle in their spheres till they return.   17
What if her eyes were there, they in her head?
The brightness of her cheek would shame those stars
As daylight doth a lamp; her eyes in heaven
Would through the airy region stream so bright
That birds would sing and think it were not night.
See how she leans her cheek upon her hand!
O that I were a glove upon that hand,
That I might touch that cheek!

JULIET   Ay me!
ROMEO   She speaks.
O, speak again, bright angel! for thou art
As glorious to this night, being o'er my head,
As is a wingèd messenger of heaven
Unto the white-upturnèd wond'ring eyes   29
Of mortals that fall back to gaze on him
When he bestrides the lazy-pacing clouds
And sails upon the bosom of the air.

JULIET
O Romeo, Romeo! wherefore art thou Romeo?
Deny thy father and refuse thy name;
Or, if thou wilt not, be but sworn my love,
And I'll no longer be a Capulet.

ROMEO *[aside]*
Shall I hear more, or shall I speak at this?

7 *complain* make a lover's plaints 8 *steal . . . hooks* (a popular conceit: the lover 'fishes' for his beloved. For Juliet to be 'caught' is dangerous because of the family feud.) 10 *use* are accustomed
II, i Within Capulet's walled orchard 1 *my heart is here* (the Neo-Platonic fancy that the heart or soul of the lover dwells in the beloved) 2 *earth* i.e. my body; *centre* i.e. my heart or soul 6 *Nay . . . too* (printed as part of preceding speech in Q2) 7 *humors* whims 11 *gossip* female crony 12 *purblind* dim-sighted 13 *Young Abraham* youthful, yet patriarchal (Cupid, or Love, was both the youngest and the oldest of the gods) 14 *King Cophetua . . . beggar maid* (from a popular ballad) 16 *The ape . . . him* (probably recalling a showman's ape who 'played dead' until called with the right word-formula) 20 *demesnes* domains 24 *circle* the conjurer's circle in which an evoked spirit supposedly appears (Mercutio intends a ribald pun) 31 *humorous* damp; also, capricious 36, 38 *medlars, pop'rin pear* fruits (used vulgarly in reference to the sex organs) 39 *truckle-bed* trundle bed
II, ii 4 *kill* make invisible by more intense light 6 *her maid* (Diana, moon-goddess, was patroness of virgins) 8 *vestal livery* virginity (after Vesta, another virgin goddess); *green* anemic 17 *spheres* orbits 29 *white-upturnèd* (the whites show when the eyes are turned upward)

JULIET
'Tis but thy name that is my enemy.
Thou art thyself, though not a Montague.
What's Montague ? It is nor hand, nor foot,
Nor arm, nor face, nor any other part
Belonging to a man. O, be some other name !
What's in a name ? That which we call a rose
44 By any other name would smell as sweet,
So Romeo would, were he not Romeo called,
46 Retain that dear perfection which he owes
Without that title. Romeo, doff thy name ;
And for thy name, which is no part of thee,
Take all myself.
ROMEO   I take thee at thy word.
Call me but love, and I'll be new baptized ;
Henceforth I never will be Romeo.
JULIET
What man art thou that, thus bescreened in night,
So stumblest on my counsel ?
ROMEO   By a name
I know not how to tell thee who I am.
My name, dear saint, is hateful to myself,
Because it is an enemy to thee.
Had I it written, I would tear the word.
JULIET
My ears have yet not drunk a hundred words
Of thy tongue's uttering, yet I know the sound.
Art thou not Romeo, and a Montague ?
ROMEO
61 Neither, fair maid, if either thee dislike.
JULIET
How camest thou hither, tell me, and wherefore ?
The orchard walls are high and hard to climb,
And the place death, considering who thou art,
If any of my kinsmen find thee here.
ROMEO
66 With love's light wings did I o'erperch these walls ;
For stony limits cannot hold love out,
And what love can do, that dares love attempt.
Therefore thy kinsmen are no stop to me.
JULIET
If they do see thee, they will murder thee.
ROMEO
Alack, there lies more peril in thine eye
Than twenty of their swords ! Look thou but sweet,
73 And I am proof against their enmity.
JULIET
I would not for the world they saw thee here.
ROMEO
I have night's cloak to hide me from their eyes ;
And but thou love me, let them find me here.
My life were better ended by their hate
78 Than death prorogued, wanting of thy love.
JULIET
By whose direction found'st thou out this place ?
ROMEO
By love, that first did prompt me to inquire.
He lent me counsel, and I lent him eyes.

I am no pilot ; yet, wert thou as far
As that vast shore washed with the farthest sea,   83
I should adventure for such merchandise.   84
JULIET
Thou knowest the mask of night is on my face ;
Else would a maiden blush bepaint my cheek
For that which thou hast heard me speak to-night.
Fain would I dwell on form – fain, fain deny
What I have spoke ; but farewell compliment !   89
Dost thou love me ? I know thou wilt say 'Ay' ;
And I will take thy word. Yet, if thou swear'st,
Thou mayst prove false. At lovers' perjuries,
They say Jove laughs. O gentle Romeo,
If thou dost love, pronounce it faithfully.
Or if thou thinkest I am too quickly won,
I'll frown, and be perverse, and say thee nay,
So thou wilt woo ; but else, not for the world.
In truth, fair Montague, I am too fond,
And therefore thou mayst think my havior light ;   99
But trust me, gentleman, I'll prove more true
Than those that have more cunning to be strange.   101
I should have been more strange, I must confess,
But that thou overheard'st, ere I was ware,   103
My true-love passion. Therefore pardon me,
And not impute this yielding to light love,
Which the dark night hath so discovered.   106
ROMEO
Lady, by yonder blessèd moon I vow,
That tips with silver all these fruit-tree tops –
JULIET
O, swear not by the moon, th' inconstant moon,
That monthly changes in her circled orb,
Lest that thy love prove likewise variable.
ROMEO
What shall I swear by ?
JULIET   Do not swear at all ;
Or if thou wilt, swear by thy gracious self,
Which is the god of my idolatry,
And I'll believe thee.
ROMEO   If my heart's dear love –
JULIET
Well, do not swear. Although I joy in thee,
I have no joy of this contract to-night.
It is too rash, too unadvised, too sudden ;
Too like the lightning, which doth cease to be
Ere one can say 'It lightens.' Sweet, good night !   120
This bud of love, by summer's ripening breath,
May prove a beauteous flow'r when next we meet.
Good night, good night ! As sweet repose and rest
Come to thy heart as that within my breast !
ROMEO
O, wilt thou leave me so unsatisfied ?
JULIET
What satisfaction canst thou have to-night ?
ROMEO
Th' exchange of thy love's faithful vow for mine.
JULIET
I gave thee mine before thou didst request it ;
And yet I would it were to give again.
ROMEO
Wouldst thou withdraw it ? For what purpose, love ?
JULIET
But to be frank and give it thee again.   131
And yet I wish but for the thing I have.

---

44 *name* (from Q1 ; Q2 reads 'word,' perhaps correctly)   46 *owes* owns
61 *dislike* displease   66 *o'erperch* fly over   73 *proof* armored   78 *pro-roguèd* postponed ; *wanting of* lacking   83 *farthest sea* the Pacific   84
adventure risk a voyage   89 *compliment* etiquette   99 *havior* behavior
101 *strange* aloof, distant   103 *ware* aware of you   106 *discoverèd* revealed
131 *frank* generous

133 My bounty is as boundless as the sea,
My love as deep ; the more I give to thee,
135 The more I have, for both are infinite.
I hear some noise within. Dear love, adieu !
    [Nurse calls within.]
Anon, good nurse ! Sweet Montague, be true.
Stay but a little, I will come again.   *[Exit.]*

ROMEO
O blessèd, blessèd night ! I am afeard,
Being in night, all this is but a dream,
Too flattering-sweet to be substantial.
    [Enter Juliet above.]

JULIET
Three words, dear Romeo, and good night indeed.
143 If that thy bent of love be honorable,
Thy purpose marriage, send me word to-morrow,
By one that I'll procure to come to thee,
Where and what time thou wilt perform the rite ;
And all my fortunes at thy foot I'll lay
And follow thee my lord throughout the world.

NURSE *[within]* Madam !

JULIET
I come, anon. – But if thou meanest not well,
I do beseech thee –

NURSE *[within]*
Madam !

152 JULIET   By and by I come. –
To cease thy suit and leave me to my grief.
To-morrow will I send.

ROMEO   So thrive my soul –

JULIET
A thousand times good night !   *[Exit.]*

ROMEO
A thousand times the worse, to want thy light !
Love goes toward love as schoolboys from their books ;
But love from love, toward school with heavy looks.
    Enter Juliet [above] again.

JULIET
Hist ! Romeo, hist ! O for a falc'ner's voice
160 To lure this tassel-gentle back again !
161 Bondage is hoarse and may not speak aloud,
Else would I tear the cave where Echo lies
And make her airy tongue more hoarse than mine
With repetition of 'My Romeo !'

ROMEO
165 It is my soul that calls upon my name.
How silver-sweet sound lovers' tongues by night,
167 Like softest music to attending ears !

JULIET
Romeo !

ROMEO   My sweet ?

JULIET   At what o'clock to-morrow
Shall I send to thee ?

ROMEO   By the hour of nine.

JULIET
I will not fail. 'Tis twenty years till then.
I have forgot why I did call thee back.

ROMEO
Let me stand here till thou remember it.

JULIET
I shall forget, to have thee still stand there,
Rememb'ring how I love thy company.

ROMEO
And I'll still stay, to have thee still forget,

Forgetting any other home but this.

JULIET
'Tis almost morning. I would have thee gone –
And yet no farther than a wanton's bird,   178
That lets it hop a little from her hand,
Like a poor prisoner in his twisted gyves,   180
And with a silken thread plucks it back again,
So loving-jealous of his liberty.

ROMEO
I would I were thy bird.

JULIET   Sweet, so would I.
Yet I should kill thee with much cherishing.   184
Good night, good night ! Parting is such sweet sorrow
That I shall say good night till it be morrow. *[Exit.]* 186

ROMEO
Sleep dwell upon thine eyes, peace in thy breast ! 187
Would I were sleep and peace, so sweet to rest !
Hence will I to my ghostly father's cell,   189
His help to crave and my dear hap to tell. *Exit.* 190

             *

    Enter Friar [Laurence] alone, with a basket. II, iii

FRIAR
The grey-eyed morn smiles on the frowning night,
Check'ring the Eastern clouds with streaks of light ;
And fleckèd darkness like a drunkard reels   3
From forth day's path and Titan's fiery wheels. 4
Now, ere the sun advance his burning eye
The day to cheer and night's dank dew to dry,
I must up-fill this osier cage of ours   7
With baleful weeds and precious-juicèd flowers.
The earth that's nature's mother is her tomb.
What is her burying grave, that is her womb ;
And from her womb children of divers kind
We sucking on her natural bosom find,
Many for many virtues excellent,
None but for some, and yet all different.
O, mickle is the powerful grace that lies   15
In plants, herbs, stones, and their true qualities ;
For naught so vile that on the earth doth live
But to the earth some special good doth give ;
Nor aught so good but, strained from that fair use,
Revolts from true birth, stumbling on abuse.   20
Virtue itself turns vice, being misapplied,
And vice sometime 's by action dignified.   22
    Enter Romeo.
Within the infant rind of this weak flower

133 *bounty* wish to give (love) **135** *The more I have* (scholastic theologians debated how love could be given away and yet the giver have more than before ; cf. Dante, *Purgatorio,* XV 61 ff.) **143** *bent* purpose **152** *By and by* immediately **160** *tassel-gentle* tercel-gentle, or male falcon **161** *Bondage* (she feels 'imprisoned' by the nearness of her kinsmen) **165** *my soul* (cf. II, i, 1 and note) **167** *attending* paying attention **178** *wanton* spoiled child **180** *gyves* fetters **184** *cherishing* caressing **186** *morrow* morning **187–90** (In Q2 the speech-prefix 'Juliet' is mistakenly placed before the first of these lines, and they are followed by four lines that are nearly identical with those at II, iii, 1–4. Perhaps Shakespeare decided to let the Friar announce the dawn instead of Romeo, and the cancelled lines in the manuscript were printed in error.) **189** *ghostly* spiritual **190** *dear hap* good luck
II, iii Before Friar Laurence's cell **3** *fleckèd* spotted, dappled **4** *Titan's fiery wheels* the sun's chariot wheels **7** *osier cage* willow basket **15** *mickle* much **20** *true birth* its true nature **22** *dignified* made worthy ; **s.d.** (this entrance seems premature, but cf. entrance of Nurse at III, iii, 70)

Poison hath residence, and medicine power;
25 For this, being smelt, with that part cheers each part;
Being tasted, slays all senses with the heart.
27 Two such opposèd kings encamp them still
28 In man as well as herbs – grace and rude will;
And where the worser is predominant,
30 Full soon the canker death eats up that plant.

ROMEO
31 Good morrow, father.

FRIAR   Benedicite!
What early tongue so sweet saluteth me?
Young son, it argues a distempered head
So soon to bid good morrow to thy bed.
Care keeps his watch in every old man's eye,
And where care lodges, sleep will never lie;
37 But where unbruisèd youth with unstuffed brain
Doth couch his limbs, there golden sleep doth reign.
Therefore thy earliness doth me assure
Thou art uproused with some distemp'rature;
Or if not so, then here I hit it right –
Our Romeo hath not been in bed to-night.

ROMEO
That last is true – the sweeter rest was mine.

FRIAR
God pardon sin! Wast thou with Rosaline?

ROMEO
With Rosaline, my ghostly father? No.
I have forgot that name and that name's woe.

FRIAR
That's my good son! But where hast thou been then?

ROMEO
I'll tell thee ere thou ask it me again.
I have been feasting with mine enemy,
Where on a sudden one hath wounded me
That's by me wounded. Both our remedies
52 Within thy help and holy physic lies.
I bear no hatred, blessèd man, for, lo,
54 My intercession likewise steads my foe.

FRIAR
55 Be plain, good son, and homely in thy drift.
56 Riddling confession finds but riddling shrift.

ROMEO
Then plainly know my heart's dear love is set
On the fair daughter of rich Capulet;
As mine on hers, so hers is set on mine,
And all combined, save what thou must combine
By holy marriage. When, and where, and how
We met, we wooed, and made exchange of vow,
I'll tell thee as we pass; but this I pray,
That thou consent to marry us to-day.

FRIAR
Holy Saint Francis! What a change is here!

Is Rosaline, that thou didst love so dear,
So soon forsaken? Young men's love then lies
Not truly in their hearts, but in their eyes.
Jesu Maria! What a deal of brine
Hath washed thy sallow cheeks for Rosaline!
How much salt water thrown away in waste
To season love, that of it doth not taste!   72
The sun not yet thy sighs from heaven clears,
Thy old groans ring yet in mine ancient ears.
Lo, here upon thy cheek the stain doth sit
Of an old tear that is not washed off yet.
If e'er thou wast thyself, and these woes thine,
Thou and these woes were all for Rosaline.
And art thou changed? Pronounce this sentence then:
Women may fall when there's no strength in men.   80

ROMEO
Thou chid'st me oft for loving Rosaline.

FRIAR
For doting, not for loving, pupil mine.

ROMEO
And bad'st me bury love.

FRIAR   Not in a grave
To lay one in, another out to have.

ROMEO
I pray thee chide not. She whom I love now
Doth grace for grace and love for love allow.   86
The other did not so.

FRIAR   O, she knew well
Thy love did read by rote, that could not spell.   88
But come, young waverer, come go with me.
In one respect I'll thy assistant be;
For this alliance may so happy prove
To turn your households' rancor to pure love.

ROMEO
O, let us hence! I stand on sudden haste.   93

FRIAR
Wisely and slow. They stumble that run fast. *Exeunt.*

*

Enter Benvolio and Mercutio.   II, iv

MERCUTIO
Where the devil should this Romeo be?
Came he not home to-night?

BENVOLIO
Not to his father's. I spoke with his man.

MERCUTIO
Why, that same pale hard-hearted wench, that Rosaline,
Torments him so that he will sure run mad.

BENVOLIO
Tybalt, the kinsman to old Capulet,
Hath sent a letter to his father's house.

MERCUTIO A challenge, on my life.

BENVOLIO Romeo will answer it.

MERCUTIO Any man that can write may answer a letter.   10

BENVOLIO Nay, he will answer the letter's master, how
he dares, being dared.

MERCUTIO Alas, poor Romeo, he is already dead!
stabbed with a white wench's black eye; run through the
ear with a love song; the very pin of his heart cleft with 15
the blind bow-boy's butt-shaft; and is he a man to en- 16
counter Tybalt?

BENVOLIO Why, what is Tybalt?

MERCUTIO More than Prince of Cats, I can tell you. O, 19

25–26 *being . . . heart* i.e. being smelt, stimulates; being tasted, kills   **27** *still* always   **28** *grace* power of goodness; *rude will* coarse impulses of the flesh   **30** *canker* the worm in the bud   **31** *morrow* morning; *Benedicite* bless you   **37** *unstuffed* carefree   **52** *physic* medicine   **54** *intercession* request; *steads* benefits   **55** *homely* simple; *drift* explanation   **56** *shrift* absolution   **72** *season* flavor; *doth not taste* i.e. now has no savor   **80** *strength* constancy   **86** *grace* favor   **88** *by rote . . . spell* like a child repeating words without understanding them   **93** *on* in need of

II, iv A street in Verona   **10** *answer* accept   **15** *pin* peg in the centre of a target, bull's eye   **16** *bow-boy's butt-shaft* Cupid's arrow (jestingly identified as a barbless target-arrow)   **16–17** *is . . . Tybalt* (Mercutio has doubts of Romeo's prowess while he is despondent and low-spirited)   **19** *Prince of Cats* (Tybalt, or Tybert, is the cat's name in medieval stories of Reynard the Fox)

20 he's the courageous captain of compliments. He fights as
21 you sing pricksong – keeps time, distance, and propor-
22 tion; he rests his minim rests, one, two, and the third in
23 your bosom! the very butcher of a silk button, a duellist,
24 a duellist! a gentleman of the very first house, of the first
25 and second cause. Ah, the immortal passado! the punto
26 reverso! the hay!

BENVOLIO The what?

28 MERCUTIO The pox of such antic, lisping, affecting fantasticoes – these new tuners of accent! 'By Jesu, a very
30 good blade! a very tall man! a very good whore!' Why,
31 is not this a lamentable thing, grandsir, that we should be
thus afflicted with these strange flies, these fashion-
33 mongers, these pardon-me's, who stand so much on the
34 new form that they cannot sit at ease on the old bench?
35 O, their bones, their bones!

Enter Romeo.

BENVOLIO Here comes Romeo! here comes Romeo!

37 MERCUTIO Without his roe, like a dried herring. O flesh,
38 flesh, how art thou fishified! Now is he for the numbers
39 that Petrarch flowed in. Laura, to his lady, was a
kitchen wench (marry, she had a better love to berhyme
41 her), Dido a dowdy, Cleopatra a gypsy, Helen and Hero
42 hildings and harlots, Thisbe a grey eye or so, but not to
43 the purpose. Signior Romeo, bon jour! There's a French
44 salutation to your French slop. You gave us the counter-
45 feit fairly last night.

ROMEO Good morrow to you both. What counterfeit did
I give you?

48 MERCUTIO The slip, sir, the slip. Can you not conceive?

ROMEO Pardon, good Mercutio. My business was great,
and in such a case as mine a man may strain courtesy.

51 MERCUTIO That's as much as to say, such a case as yours
52 constrains a man to bow in the hams.

ROMEO Meaning, to curtsy.

54 MERCUTIO Thou hast most kindly hit it.

ROMEO A most courteous exposition.

MERCUTIO Nay, I am the very pink of courtesy.

57 ROMEO Pink for flower.

MERCUTIO Right.

59 ROMEO Why, then is my pump well-flowered.

MERCUTIO Sure wit, follow me this jest now till thou
hast worn out thy pump, that, when the single sole of it
62 is worn, the jest may remain, after the wearing, solely
singular.

64 ROMEO O single-soled jest, solely singular for the singleness!

66 MERCUTIO Come between us, good Benvolio! My wits
faint.

67 ROMEO Swits and spurs, swits and spurs! or I'll cry a
match.

68 MERCUTIO Nay, if our wits run the wild-goose chase, I
am done; for thou hast more of the wild goose in one of
70 thy wits than, I am sure, I have in my whole five. Was I
with you there for the goose?

72 ROMEO Thou wast never with me for anything when
thou wast not there for the goose.

MERCUTIO I will bite thee by the ear for that jest.

75 ROMEO Nay, good goose, bite not!

76 MERCUTIO Thy wit is a very bitter sweeting; it is a most
sharp sauce.

78 ROMEO And is it not, then, well served in to a sweet goose?

79 MERCUTIO O, here's a wit of cheveril, that stretches from
80 an inch narrow to an ell broad!

ROMEO I stretch it out for that word 'broad,' which, added
to the goose, proves thee far and wide a broad goose. 82

MERCUTIO Why, is not this better now than groaning for
love? Now art thou sociable, now art thou Romeo; now
art thou what thou art, by art as well as by nature. For
this drivelling love is like a great natural that runs lolling 86
up and down to hide his bauble in a hole. 87

BENVOLIO Stop there, stop there!

MERCUTIO Thou desirest me to stop in my tale against 89
the hair.

BENVOLIO Thou wouldst else have made thy tale large. 91

MERCUTIO O, thou art deceived! I would have made it
short; for I was come to the whole depth of my tale, and
meant indeed to occupy the argument no longer. 94

ROMEO Here's goodly gear! 95

Enter Nurse and her Man [Peter].

MERCUTIO A sail, a sail!

BENVOLIO Two, two! a shirt and a smock. 97

NURSE Peter!

PETER Anon.

NURSE My fan, Peter.

MERCUTIO Good Peter, to hide her face; for her fan 's
the fairer face.

NURSE God ye good morrow, gentlemen.

MERCUTIO God ye good-den, fair gentlewoman.

NURSE Is it good-den? 105

MERCUTIO 'Tis no less, I tell ye; for the bawdy hand of
the dial is now upon the prick of noon. 107

NURSE Out upon you! What a man are you!

ROMEO One, gentlewoman, that God hath made for himself to mar.

NURSE By my troth, it is well said. 'For himself to mar,'
quoth 'a? Gentlemen, can any of you tell me where I 112
may find the young Romeo?

---

20 *compliments* etiquette 21 *pricksong* written music 22 *minim rests* shortest rests (in the old musical notation); *third* third rapier thrust 23 *button* i.e. on his opponent's shirt 24 *first house* finest fencing school 24–25 *first and second cause* causes for a challenge (in the duellist's code) 25 *passado* lunge 25–26 *punto reverso* backhanded stroke 26 *hay* home-thrust (from 'hai,' 'I have it'; a new term to Benvolio) 28 *fantasticoes* coxcombs 30 *tall* brave 31 *grandsir* good sir 33 *pardon-me's* i.e. sticklers for etiquette 34 *form* (1) fashion, (2) school-bench; *old bench* i.e. native manners and learning 35 *bones* Fr. 'good's': '*bon's*' 37 *Without his roe* i.e. 'shot' 38 *numbers* verses 39 *Laura* Petrarch's beloved; *to* in comparison with 41 *Dido* Queen of Carthage who fell in love with Aeneas; *Helen* Helen of Troy; *Hero* beloved of Leander 42 *hildings* worthless creatures; *Thisbe* (Pyramus and Thisbe were young lovers whose story resembles that of Romeo and Juliet) 42–43 *not to the purpose* not worth mentioning 43 *bon jour* good day 44 *slop* trousers 45 *fairly* effectively 48 *slip* (1) escape, (2) counterfeit coin 51 *such . . . yours* the pox (implied) 52 *hams* hips 54 *kindly hit it* interpreted it in your own way 57 *flower* ('flower of courtesy' was the usual complimentary form; cf. II, v, 43) 59 *pump* shoe; *well-flowered* (because pinked, or punched, with an orna-mental design) 62–63 *solely singular* uniquely remarkable 64 *single-soled* weak; *singleness* weakness 66 *My wits faint* my mind fails in this intricate word play 67 *Swits and spurs* switches and spurs, i.e. keep your horse (wit) running; *cry a match* claim victory 68 *wild-goose chase* cross-country horse race of 'follow the leader' 70–71 *Was . . . goose* was I accurate in calling you a goose 72–73 *Thou . . . goose* you were never in my company for any purpose when you weren't looking for a prostitute (goose) 75 *good . . . not* spare me (proverbial) 76 *bitter sweeting* a tart species of apple 78 *sweet* tasty, tender 79 *cheveril* kid-skin, easily stretched 80 *ell* forty-five inches (English measure) 82 *broad goose* possibly, a goose from the Broads, shallow Norfolk lakes (?) 86 *natural* idiot 87 *bauble* jester's wand, here a phallic symbol 89–90 *against the hair* with my hair rubbed the wrong way, against my inclination 91 *large* broad, indecent 94 *occupy the argument* pursue the subject 95 *gear* stuff 97 *shirt, smock* male and female garments 105 *Is it good-den* is it already afternoon 107 *prick* (1) indented point on a clock-face or sundial, (2) phallus 112 *quoth 'a* said he

ROMEO I can tell you; but young Romeo will be older
when you have found him than he was when you sought
116 him. I am the youngest of that name, for fault of a worse.
NURSE You say well.
118 MERCUTIO Yea, is the worst well? Very well took, i'
faith! wisely, wisely.
120 NURSE If you be he, sir, I desire some confidence with you.
121 BENVOLIO She will endite him to some supper.
122 MERCUTIO A bawd, a bawd, a bawd! So ho!
ROMEO What hast thou found?
124 MERCUTIO No hare, sir; unless a hare, sir, in a lenten pie,
125 that is something stale and hoar ere it be spent.
[He walks by them and sings.]
An old hare hoar,
And an old hare hoar,
Is very good meat in Lent;
But a hare that is hoar
Is too much for a score
When it hoars ere it be spent.
Romeo, will you come to your father's? We'll to dinner
thither.
ROMEO I will follow you.
135 MERCUTIO Farewell, ancient lady. Farewell, *[sings]* lady,
lady, lady.   *Exeunt [Mercutio, Benvolio].*
NURSE I pray you, sir, what saucy merchant was this that
138 was so full of his ropery?
ROMEO A gentleman, nurse, that loves to hear himself
talk and will speak more in a minute than he will stand
to in a month.
NURSE An 'a speak anything against me, I'll take him
down, an 'a were lustier than he is, and twenty such
Jacks; and if I cannot, I'll find those that shall. Scurvy
145 knave! I am none of his flirt-gills; I am none of his
146 skains-mates. And thou must stand by too, and suffer
every knave to use me at his pleasure!
148 PETER I saw no man use you at his pleasure. If I had, my
weapon should quickly have been out, I warrant you. I
dare draw as soon as another man, if I see occasion in a
good quarrel, and the law on my side.
NURSE Now, afore God, I am so vexed that every part
about me quivers. Scurvy knave! Pray you, sir, a word;
and, as I told you, my young lady bid me inquire you
out. What she bid me say, I will keep to myself; but
156 first let me tell ye, if ye should lead her into a fool's
paradise, as they say, it were a very gross kind of behavior, as they say; for the gentlewoman is young; and
therefore, if you should deal double with her, truly it

were an ill thing to be offered to any gentlewoman, and
very weak dealing.   161
ROMEO Nurse, commend me to thy lady and mistress. I
protest unto thee –
NURSE Good heart, and i' faith I will tell her as much.
Lord, Lord! she will be a joyful woman.
ROMEO What wilt thou tell her, nurse? Thou dost not
mark me.
NURSE I will tell her, sir, that you do protest, which, as I
take it, is a gentlemanlike offer.
ROMEO
Bid her devise
Some means to come to shrift this afternoon;
And there she shall at Friar Laurence' cell
Be shrived and married. Here is for thy pains.
NURSE No, truly, sir; not a penny.
ROMEO Go to! I say you shall.
NURSE This afternoon, sir? Well, she shall be there.
ROMEO
And stay, good nurse, behind the abbey wall.
Within this hour my man shall be with thee
And bring thee cords made like a tackled stair,   178
Which to the high topgallant of my joy   179
Must be my convoy in the secret night.   180
Farewell. Be trusty, and I'll quit thy pains.   181
Farewell. Commend me to thy mistress.
NURSE
Now God in heaven bless thee! Hark you, sir.
ROMEO
What say'st thou, my dear nurse?
NURSE
Is your man secret? Did you ne'er hear say,
Two may keep counsel, putting one away?
ROMEO
I warrant thee my man's as true as steel.
NURSE Well, sir, my mistress is the sweetest lady. Lord,
Lord! when 'twas a little prating thing – O, there is a
nobleman in town, one Paris, that would fain lay knife   190
aboard; but she, good soul, had as lieve see a toad, a   191
very toad, as see him. I anger her sometimes, and tell her
that Paris is the properer man; but I'll warrant you,
when I say so, she looks as pale as any clout in the versal   194
world. Doth not rosemary and Romeo begin both with a
letter?
ROMEO Ay, nurse; what of that? Both with an R.
NURSE Ah, mocker! that's the dog's name. R is for the –   197
No; I know it begins with some other letter; and she
hath the prettiest sententious of it, of you and rosemary,   199
that it would do you good to hear it.
ROMEO Commend me to thy lady.
NURSE Ay, a thousand times. *[Exit Romeo.]* Peter!
PETER Anon.
NURSE *[Peter, take my fan, and go]* before, and apace.   204
                   Exit [after Peter].

*

Enter Juliet.   II, v
JULIET
The clock struck nine when I did send the nurse;
In half an hour she promised to return.
Perchance she cannot meet him. That's not so.
O, she is lame! Love's heralds should be thoughts,
Which ten times faster glide than the sun's beams
Driving back shadows over low'ring hills.
Therefore do nimble-pinioned doves draw Love,   7

116 *for . . . worse* (parodying 'for want of a better') 118 *took* understood
120 *confidence* conference (malapropism) 121 *endite* invite (anticipating
a malapropism) 122 *So ho* (hunter's cry on sighting game) 124 *hare*
i.e. prostitute; *lenten pie* meat pie eaten sparingly during Lent 125
hoar (1) grey with mould, (2) grey-haired; with wordplay on 'whore';
s.d. (from Q1) 135–36 *lady, lady, lady* (ballad refrain from *Chaste Susanna*)
138 *ropery* vulgar jesting 145 *flirt-gills* flirting Jills 146 *skains-mates*
outlaws, gangster molls 148–49 *my weapon . . . out* (cf. I, i, 30 and n.)
156–57 *lead . . . paradise* seduce her (proverbial) 161 *weak* unmanly
178 *tackled stair* rope ladder 179 *topgallant* mast and sail above the
mainmast 180 *convoy* conveyance 181 *quit thy pains* reward your
efforts 190–91 *lay knife aboard* i.e. partake of this dish 191 *lieve* willingly
194 *clout* cloth; *versal* universal 197 *dog's name* (R was called 'the dog's
letter,' since the sound 'r-r-r-r' supposedly resembles a dog's growl.
The Nurse thinks it an ugly sound.) 199 *sententious* sentences 204
Peter . . . go (from Q1)
II, v The Capulet orchard 7 *nimble-pinioned* swift-winged; *doves* (Venus'
birds, who draw her chariot)

And therefore hath the wind-swift Cupid wings.
9   Now is the sun upon the highmost hill
Of this day's journey, and from nine till twelve
Is three long hours ; yet she is not come.
Had she affections and warm youthful blood,
She would be as swift in motion as a ball ;
14 My words would bandy her to my sweet love,
And his to me.
16 But old folks, many feign as they were dead –
Unwieldy, slow, heavy and pale as lead.
      Enter Nurse [and Peter].
O God, she comes ! O honey nurse, what news ?
Hast thou met with him ? Send thy man away.

NURSE
Peter, stay at the gate.   *[Exit Peter.]*

JULIET
Now, good sweet nurse – O Lord, why lookest thou sad ?
Though news be sad, yet tell them merrily ;
If good, thou shamest the music of sweet news
By playing it to me with so sour a face.

NURSE
25 I am aweary, give me leave awhile.
26 Fie, how my bones ache ! What a jaunce have I had !

JULIET
I would thou hadst my bones, and I thy news.
Nay, come, I pray thee speak. Good, good nurse, speak.

NURSE
29 Jesu, what haste ! Can you not stay awhile ?
Do you not see that I am out of breath ?

JULIET
How art thou out of breath when thou hast breath
To say to me that thou art out of breath ?
The excuse that thou dost make in this delay
Is longer than the tale thou dost excuse.
Is thy news good or bad ? Answer to that.
36 Say either, and I'll stay the circumstance.
Let me be satisfied, is't good or bad ?

38 NURSE Well, you have made a simple choice ; you know
not how to choose a man. Romeo ? No, not he. Though
his face be better than any man's, yet his leg excels all
men's ; and for a hand and a foot, and a body, though
they be not to be talked on, yet they are past compare.
He is not the flower of courtesy, but, I'll warrant him, as
gentle as a lamb. Go thy ways, wench ; serve God. What,
have you dined at home ?

JULIET
No, no. But all this did I know before.
What says he of our marriage ? What of that ?

NURSE
Lord, how my head aches ! What a head have I !
It beats as it would fall in twenty pieces.
50 My back a t' other side – ah, my back, my back !
51 Beshrew your heart for sending me about
To catch my death with jauncing up and down !

JULIET
I' faith, I am sorry that thou art not well.
Sweet, sweet, sweet nurse, tell me, what says my love ?

NURSE Your love says, like an honest gentleman, and a
courteous, and a kind, and a handsome, and, I warrant,
a virtuous – Where is your mother ?

JULIET
Where is my mother ? Why, she is within.
Where should she be ? How oddly thou repliest !
'Your love says, like an honest gentleman,

"Where is your mother ?"'

NURSE   O God's Lady dear !
Are you so hot ? Marry come up, I trow.   62
Is this the poultice for my aching bones ?
Henceforward do your messages yourself.

JULIET
Here's such a coil ! Come, what says Romeo ?   65

NURSE
Have you got leave to go to shrift to-day ?

JULIET
I have.

NURSE
Then hie you hence to Friar Laurence' cell ;
There stays a husband to make you a wife.
Now comes the wanton blood up in your cheeks :
They'll be in scarlet straight at any news.   71
Hie you to church ; I must another way,
To fetch a ladder, by the which your love
Must climb a bird's nest soon when it is dark.   74
I am the drudge, and toil in your delight ;
But you shall bear the burden soon at night.
Go ; I'll to dinner ; hie you to the cell.

JULIET
Hie to high fortune ! Honest nurse, farewell.   *Exeunt.*

*

     Enter Friar [Laurence] and Romeo.   II, vi

FRIAR
So smile the heavens upon this holy act
That after-hours with sorrow chide us not !

ROMEO
Amen, amen ! But come what sorrow can,
It cannot countervail the exchange of joy   4
That one short minute gives me in her sight.
Do thou but close our hands with holy words,
Then love-devouring death do what he dare –
It is enough I may but call her mine.

FRIAR
These violent delights have violent ends
And in their triumph die, like fire and powder,
Which, as they kiss, consume. The sweetest honey
Is loathsome in his own deliciousness   12
And in the taste confounds the appetite.
Therefore love moderately : long love doth so ;
Too swift arrives as tardy as too slow.   15
     Enter Juliet.
Here comes the lady. O, so light a foot
Will ne'er wear out the everlasting flint.   17
A lover may bestride the gossamer   18
That idles in the wanton summer air,
And yet not fall ; so light is vanity.   20

9 *upon . . . hill* at the zenith **14** *bandy* speed, as in tennis **16** *old . . . dead* many persons speak figuratively of old folks as being dead **25** *give me leave* let me alone **26** *jaunce* jolting **29** *stay* wait **36** *stay the circumstance* wait for details **38** *simple* foolish **50** *a* on **51** *Beshrew* shame on **62** *hot* angry ; *Marry come up* by the Virgin Mary, take your come-uppance (penalty) ; *trow* trust **65** *coil* fuss **71** *in scarlet* (Juliet blushes easily – cf. II, ii, 86 ; III, ii, 14) ; *straight* straightway **74** *climb . . . nest* i.e. climb to Juliet's room
II, vi Before Friar Laurence's cell **4** *countervail* outweigh **12** *Is loathsome* i.e. if eaten to excess **15** *Too . . . slow* (proverbial ; cf. II, iii, 94) **17** *wear . . . flint* (suggested by the proverb 'In time small water drops will wear away the stone') **18** *gossamer* spider's web **20** *vanity* transitory earthly love (cf. Ecclesiastes ix, 9)

JULIET
21 Good even to my ghostly confessor.

FRIAR
Romeo shall thank thee, daughter, for us both.

JULIET
23 As much to him, else is his thanks too much.

ROMEO
Ah, Juliet, if the measure of thy joy
25 Be heaped like mine, and that thy skill be more
26 To blazon it, then sweeten with thy breath
This neighbor air, and let rich music's tongue
Unfold the imagined happiness that both
Receive in either by this dear encounter.

JULIET
30 Conceit, more rich in matter than in words,
Brags of his substance, not of ornament.
They are but beggars that can count their worth;
33 But my true love is grown to such excess
I cannot sum up sum of half my wealth.

FRIAR
Come, come with me, and we will make short work;
For, by your leaves, you shall not stay alone
Till Holy Church incorporate two in one.   *[Exeunt.]*

*

III, i   *Enter Mercutio, Benvolio, and Men.*

BENVOLIO
I pray thee, good Mercutio, let's retire.
The day is hot, the Capulets abroad,
And, if we meet, we shall not 'scape a brawl,
For now, these hot days, is the mad blood stirring.

MERCUTIO Thou art like one of these fellows that, when
he enters the confines of a tavern, claps me his sword
upon the table and says 'God send me no need of thee!'
8 and by the operation of the second cup draws him on
the drawer, when indeed there is no need.

BENVOLIO Am I like such a fellow?

MERCUTIO Come, come, thou art as hot a Jack in thy
12 mood as any in Italy; and as soon moved to be moody,
and as soon moody to be moved.

BENVOLIO And what to?

MERCUTIO Nay, an there were two such, we should have
none shortly, for one would kill the other. Thou! why,
thou wilt quarrel with a man that hath a hair more or a
hair less in his beard than thou hast. Thou wilt quarrel
with a man for cracking nuts, having no other reason
but because thou hast hazel eyes. What eye but such an
21 eye would spy out such a quarrel? Thy head is as full of

quarrels as an egg is full of meat; and yet thy head hath
been beaten as addle as an egg for quarrelling. Thou
hast quarrelled with a man for coughing in the street,
because he hath wakened thy dog that hath lain asleep in
the sun. Didst thou not fall out with a tailor for wearing
his new doublet before Easter? with another for tying 27
his new shoes with old riband? And yet thou wilt tutor 28
me from quarrelling!

BENVOLIO An I were so apt to quarrel as thou art, any
man should buy the fee simple of my life for an hour and 31
a quarter.

MERCUTIO The fee simple? O simple!   33
    Enter Tybalt and others.

BENVOLIO By my head, here come the Capulets.

MERCUTIO By my heel, I care not.

TYBALT
Follow me close, for I will speak to them.
Gentlemen, good-den. A word with one of you.   37

MERCUTIO
And but one word with one of us?
Couple it with something; make it a word and a blow.

TYBALT You shall find me apt enough to that, sir, an you
will give me occasion.

MERCUTIO Could you not take some occasion without
giving?

TYBALT Mercutio, thou consortest with Romeo.

MERCUTIO Consort? What, dost thou make us minstrels? 45
An thou make minstrels of us, look to hear nothing but
discords. Here's my fiddlestick; here's that shall make 47
you dance. Zounds, consort!   48

BENVOLIO
We talk here in the public haunt of men.
Either withdraw unto some private place,
Or reason coldly of your grievances,
Or else depart. Here all eyes gaze on us.

MERCUTIO
Men's eyes were made to look, and let them gaze.
I will not budge for no man's pleasure, I.
    Enter Romeo.

TYBALT
Well, peace be with you, sir. Here comes my man.

MERCUTIO
But I'll be hanged, sir, if he wear your livery.   56
Marry, go before to field, he'll be your follower!   57
Your worship in that sense may call him man.

TYBALT
Romeo, the love I bear thee can afford
No better term than this: thou art a villain.

ROMEO
Tybalt, the reason that I have to love thee
Doth much excuse the appertaining rage   62
To such a greeting. Villain am I none.
Therefore farewell. I see thou knowest me not.

TYBALT
Boy, this shall not excuse the injuries
That thou hast done me; therefore turn and draw.

ROMEO
I do protest I never injured thee,
But love thee better than thou canst devise   68
Till thou shalt know the reason of my love;
And so, good Capulet, which name I tender   70
As dearly as mine own, be satisfied.

MERCUTIO
O calm, dishonorable, vile submission!

---

21 *ghostly* spiritual   23 *As much* the same greeting   25 *that* if; *thy ... more*
you sing better than I   26 *blazon* set forth   30–31 *Conceit ... ornament* my
understanding is fixed upon the reality of my great love, not upon a vocal
expression of it   33 *love ... excess* (cf. II, ii, 135 and n.)
III, i A public place in Verona   8–9 *by the operation ... drawer* after drinking
only two cups of wine, draws his sword against the waiter   12 *moody*
angry   21 *spy out* see occasion for   27 *doublet* jacket   28 *riband* ribbon
31 *fee simple* permanent lease   31–32 *hour and a quarter* probable duration
of the lease, i.e. of my life   33 *O simple* O stupid; s.d. (Q2 includes the
name 'Petruchio')   37 *good-den* good afternoon   45 *Consort* (1) associate
with, (2) accompany in vocal or instrumental music; *minstrels* (a more
disreputable title than 'musicians'; cf. IV, v, 111–12)   47 *fiddlestick* i.e.
rapier   48 *Zounds* by God's wounds   56 *livery* servant's uniform (*my
man* could mean 'my manservant')   57 *field* duelling ground   62 *appertaining rage* suitably angry reaction   68 *devise* understand   70 *tender* value

73 Alla stoccata carries it away.
[Draws.]
Tybalt, you ratcatcher, will you walk?

TYBALT
What wouldst thou have with me?

MERCUTIO Good King of Cats, nothing but one of your
77 nine lives. That I mean to make bold withal, and, as you
78 shall use me hereafter, dry-beat the rest of the eight. Will
79 you pluck your sword out of his pilcher by the ears?
Make haste, lest mine be about your ears ere it be out.

TYBALT I am for you.
[Draws.]

ROMEO
Gentle Mercutio, put thy rapier up.

83 MERCUTIO Come, sir, your passado!
[They fight.]

ROMEO
Draw, Benvolio; beat down their weapons.
Gentlemen, for shame! forbear this outrage!
Tybalt, Mercutio, the Prince expressly hath
Forbid this bandying in Verona streets.
88 Hold, Tybalt! Good Mercutio!
[Tybalt under Romeo's arm thrusts Mercutio in,
and flies with his Followers.]

MERCUTIO I am hurt.
89 A plague a both your houses! I am sped.
Is he gone and hath nothing?

BENVOLIO What, art thou hurt?

MERCUTIO
Ay, ay, a scratch, a scratch. Marry, 'tis enough.
Where is my page? Go, villain, fetch a surgeon.
[Exit Page.]

ROMEO
Courage, man. The hurt cannot be much.

MERCUTIO No, 'tis not so deep as a well, nor so wide as a
church door; but 'tis enough, 'twill serve. Ask for me
96 to-morrow, and you shall find me a grave man. I am
peppered, I warrant, for this world. A plague a both
your houses! Zounds, a dog, a rat, a mouse, a cat, to
scratch a man to death! a braggart, a rogue, a villain,
100 that fights by the book of arithmetic! Why the devil
came you between us? I was hurt under your arm.

ROMEO
I thought all for the best.

MERCUTIO
Help me into some house, Benvolio,
Or I shall faint. A plague a both your houses!
105 They have made worms' meat of me. I have it,
And soundly too. Your houses!
Exit [supported by Benvolio].

ROMEO
This gentleman, the Prince's near ally,
108 My very friend, hath got this mortal hurt
In my behalf – my reputation stained
With Tybalt's slander – Tybalt, that an hour
Hath been my cousin. O sweet Juliet,
Thy beauty hath made me effeminate
And in my temper soft'ned valor's steel!
Enter Benvolio.

BENVOLIO
O Romeo, Romeo, brave Mercutio is dead!
115 That gallant spirit hath aspired the clouds,
Which too untimely here did scorn the earth.

ROMEO
This day's black fate on moe days doth depend; 117
This but begins the woe others must end.
[Enter Tybalt.]

BENVOLIO
Here comes the furious Tybalt back again.

ROMEO
Alive in triumph, and Mercutio slain?
Away to heaven respective lenity, 121
And fire-eyed fury be my conduct now! 122
Now, Tybalt, take the 'villain' back again
That late thou gavest me; for Mercutio's soul
Is but a little way above our heads,
Staying for thine to keep him company.
Either thou or I, or both, must go with him.

TYBALT
Thou, wretched boy, that didst consort him here,
Shalt with him hence.

ROMEO This shall determine that.
They fight. Tybalt falls.

BENVOLIO
Romeo, away, be gone!
The citizens are up, and Tybalt slain.
Stand not amazed. The Prince will doom thee death
If thou art taken. Hence, be gone, away!

ROMEO
O, I am fortune's fool! 134

BENVOLIO Why dost thou stay? *Exit Romeo.*
Enter Citizens.

CITIZEN
Which way ran he that killed Mercutio?
Tybalt, that murderer, which way ran he?

BENVOLIO
There lies that Tybalt.

CITIZEN Up, sir, go with me.
I charge thee in the Prince's name obey.
Enter Prince [attended], old Montague, Capulet,
their Wives, and all.

PRINCE
Where are the vile beginners of this fray?

BENVOLIO
O noble Prince, I can discover all 140
The unlucky manage of this fatal brawl. 141
There lies the man, slain by young Romeo,
That slew thy kinsman, brave Mercutio.

CAPULET'S WIFE
Tybalt, my cousin! O my brother's child!
O Prince! O husband! O, the blood is spilled
Of my dear kinsman! Prince, as thou art true,
For blood of ours shed blood of Montague.
O cousin, cousin!

PRINCE
Benvolio, who began this bloody fray?

73 *Alla stoccata* 'at the thrust'; i.e. Tybalt; *carries it away* triumphs, gets away with it 77 *nine lives* (proverbial: a cat has nine lives) 78 *dry-beat* thrash 79 *pilcher* scabbard 83 *passado* lunge 88 s.d. (from Q1; Q2 reads 'Away Tybalt.') 89 *a* on; *sped* mortally wounded 96 *grave* (1) serious, (2) inhabiting a grave 100 *by . . . arithmetic* by timing his strokes (cf. II, iv, 21) 105 *worms' meat* i.e. a corpse; *I have it* I am wounded 108 *very* true 115 *aspired* climbed toward 117 *moe* more; *depend* hang down over (cf. I, iv, 107 and note) 121 *respective lenity* reasoned gentleness (personified as an angel) 122 *fire-eyed fury* (fury personified); *conduct* guide 134 *fool* dupe, victim 140 *discover* reveal 141 *manage* course

BENVOLIO

    Tybalt, here slain, whom Romeo's hand did slay.

    Romeo, that spoke him fair, bid him bethink

152   How nice the quarrel was, and urged withal

    Your high displeasure. All this – utterèd

    With gentle breath, calm look, knees humbly bowed –

155   Could not take truce with the unruly spleen

    Of Tybalt deaf to peace, but that he tilts

    With piercing steel at bold Mercutio's breast;

    Who, all as hot, turns deadly point to point,

    And, with a martial scorn, with one hand beats

    Cold death aside and with the other sends

    It back to Tybalt, whose dexterity

    Retorts it. Romeo, he cries aloud,

    'Hold, friends! friends, part!' and swifter than his

      tongue,

    His agile arm beats down their fatal points,

    And 'twixt them rushes; underneath whose arm

166   An envious thrust from Tybalt hit the life

    Of stout Mercutio, and then Tybalt fled;

    But by and by comes back to Romeo,

169   Who had but newly entertained revenge,

    And to't they go like lightning; for, ere I

    Could draw to part them, was stout Tybalt slain;

    And, as he fell, did Romeo turn and fly.

    This is the truth, or let Benvolio die.

CAPULET'S WIFE

    He is a kinsman to the Montague;

    Affection makes him false, he speaks not true.

    Some twenty of them fought in this black strife,

    And all those twenty could but kill one life.

    I beg for justice, which thou, Prince, must give.

    Romeo slew Tybalt; Romeo must not live.

PRINCE

    Romeo slew him; he slew Mercutio.

    Who now the price of his dear blood doth owe?

MONTAGUE

    Not Romeo, Prince; he was Mercutio's friend;

    His fault concludes but what the law should end,

    The life of Tybalt.

PRINCE   And for that offense

    Immediately we do exile him hence.

    I have an interest in your hate's proceeding,

    My blood for your rude brawls doth lie a-bleeding;

188   But I'll amerce you with so strong a fine

    That you shall all repent the loss of mine.

    I will be deaf to pleading and excuses;

    Nor tears nor prayers shall purchase out abuses.

    Therefore use none. Let Romeo hence in haste,

    Else, when he is found, that hour is his last.

152 *nice* trivial   155 *spleen* temper   166 *envious* malicious   169 *entertained* harbored thoughts of   188 *amerce* penalize   194 *attend our will* come to be judged

III, ii Capulet's house   1 *steeds* horses drawing the chariot of the sun   2 *Phoebus* the sun-god; *lodging* (below the western horizon)   3 *Phaeton* Phoebus' son, with whom the horses of the sun ran away   6 *runaways' eyes* eyes of the sun's horses (?); *wink* close   9 *love* Cupid   14 *Hood* cover with a hood (falconry); *unmanned* untamed; *bating* fluttering   15 *strange* unfamiliar   16 *true love acted* the act of true love   37 *weraday* welladay, alas   40 *heaven . . . envious* (cf. III, v, 211)   45–50 *I* (with the alternate meaning 'ay')   47 *cockatrice* basilisk (a fabulous serpent which killed with eye-glances)   49 *those eyes' shot* the Nurse's eye-glance, which may inadvertently reveal her unspoken answer (see supplementary note on page 894)

    Bear hence this body, and attend our will.   194

    Mercy but murders, pardoning those that kill.

                       Exit [with others].

                       *

    Enter Juliet alone.   III, ii

JULIET

    Gallop apace, you fiery-footed steeds,   1

    Towards Phoebus' lodging! Such a wagoner   2

    As Phaeton would whip you to the west   3

    And bring in cloudy night immediately.

    Spread thy close curtain, love-performing night,

    That runaways' eyes may wink, and Romeo   6

    Leap to these arms untalked of and unseen.

    Lovers can see to do their amorous rites

    By their own beauties; or, if love be blind,   9

    It best agrees with night. Come, civil night,

    Thou sober-suited matron, all in black,

    And learn me how to lose a winning match,

    Played for a pair of stainless maidenhoods.

    Hood my unmanned blood, bating in my cheeks,   14

    With thy black mantle till strange love grow bold,   15

    Think true love acted simple modesty.   16

    Come, night; come, Romeo; come, thou day in night;

    For thou wilt lie upon the wings of night

    Whiter than new snow upon a raven's back.

    Come, gentle night; come, loving, black-browed night;

    Give me my Romeo; and, when he shall die,

    Take him and cut him out in little stars,

    And he will make the face of heaven so fine

    That all the world will be in love with night

    And pay no worship to the garish sun.

    O, I have bought the mansion of a love,

    But not possessed it; and though I am sold,

    Not yet enjoyed. So tedious is this day

    As is the night before some festival

    To an impatient child that hath new robes   30

    And may not wear them. O, here comes my nurse,

          Enter Nurse, with cords.

    And she brings news; and every tongue that speaks

    But Romeo's name speaks heavenly eloquence.

    Now, nurse, what news? What hast thou there, the cords

    That Romeo bid thee fetch?

NURSE   Ay, ay, the cords.

      [Throws them down.]

JULIET

    Ay me! what news? Why dost thou wring thy hands?

NURSE

    Ah, weraday! he's dead, he's dead, he's dead!   37

    We are undone, lady, we are undone!

    Alack the day! he's gone, he's killed, he's dead!

JULIET

    Can heaven be so envious?   40

NURSE   Romeo can,

    Though heaven cannot. O Romeo, Romeo!

    Who ever would have thought it? Romeo!

JULIET

    What devil art thou that dost torment me thus?

    This torture should be roared in dismal hell.

    Hath Romeo slain himself? Say thou but 'I,'   45

    And that bare vowel 'I' shall poison more

    Than the death-darting eye of cockatrice.   47

    I am not I, if there be such an 'I'

    Or those eyes' shot that makes the answer 'I.'   49

If he be slain, say 'I'; or if not, 'no.'
Brief sounds determine of my weal or woe.

NURSE
I saw the wound, I saw it with mine eyes,
53 (God save the mark!) here on his manly breast.
A piteous corse, a bloody piteous corse;
Pale, pale as ashes, all bedaubed in blood,
56 All in gore-blood. I swounded at the sight.

JULIET
57 O, break, my heart! poor bankrout, break at once!
To prison, eyes; ne'er look on liberty!
59 Vile earth, to earth resign; end motion here,
And thou and Romeo press one heavy bier!

NURSE
O Tybalt, Tybalt, the best friend I had!
O courteous Tybalt! honest gentleman!
That ever I should live to see thee dead!

JULIET
What storm is this that blows so contrary?
Is Romeo slaught'red, and is Tybalt dead?
My dearest cousin, and my dearer lord?
67 Then, dreadful trumpet, sound the general doom!
For who is living, if those two are gone?

NURSE
Tybalt is gone, and Romeo banishèd;
Romeo that killed him, he is banishèd.

JULIET
O God! Did Romeo's hand shed Tybalt's blood?

NURSE
72 It did, it did! alas the day, it did!

JULIET
73 O serpent heart, hid with a flow'ring face!
Did ever dragon keep so fair a cave?
75 Beautiful tyrant! fiend angelical!
76 Dove-feathered raven! wolvish-ravening lamb!
Despisèd substance of divinest show!
Just opposite to what thou justly seem'st –
A damnèd saint, an honorable villain!
O nature, what hadst thou to do in hell
81 When thou didst bower the spirit of a fiend
In mortal paradise of such sweet flesh?
Was ever book containing such vile matter
So fairly bound? O, that deceit should dwell
In such a gorgeous palace!

NURSE   There's no trust,
No faith, no honesty in men; all perjured,
All forsworn, all naught, all dissemblers.
88 Ah, where's my man? Give me some aqua vitae.
These griefs, these woes, these sorrows make me old.
Shame come to Romeo!

JULIET   Blistered be thy tongue
For such a wish! He was not born to shame.
Upon his brow shame is ashamed to sit;
For 'tis a throne where honor may be crowned
Sole monarch of the universal earth.
O, what a beast was I to chide at him!

NURSE
Will you speak well of him that killed your cousin?

JULIET
Shall I speak ill of him that is my husband?
Ah, poor my lord, what tongue shall smooth thy name
When I, thy three-hours wife, have mangled it?
But wherefore, villain, didst thou kill my cousin?
That villain cousin would have killed my husband.

Back, foolish tears, back to your native spring!
Your tributary drops belong to woe,   103
Which you, mistaking, offer up to joy.
My husband lives, that Tybalt would have slain;
And Tybalt's dead, that would have slain my husband.
All this is comfort; wherefore weep I then?
Some word there was, worser than Tybalt's death,
That murd'red me. I would forget it fain;
But O, it presses to my memory
Like damnèd guilty deeds to sinners' minds!
'Tybalt is dead, and Romeo – banishèd.'
That 'banishèd,' that one word 'banishèd,'
Hath slain ten thousand Tybalts. Tybalt's death
Was woe enough, if it had ended there;
Or, if sour woe delights in fellowship
And needly will be ranked with other griefs,   117
Why followèd not, when she said 'Tybalt's dead,'
Thy father, or thy mother, nay, or both,
Which modern lamentation might have moved?   120
But with a rearward following Tybalt's death,   121
'Romeo is banishèd' – to speak that word
Is father, mother, Tybalt, Romeo, Juliet,
All slain, all dead. 'Romeo is banishèd' –
There is no end, no limit, measure, bound,
In that word's death; no words can that woe sound.
Where is my father and my mother, nurse?

NURSE
Weeping and wailing over Tybalt's corse.   128
Will you go to them? I will bring you thither.

JULIET
Wash they his wounds with tears? Mine shall be spent,
When theirs are dry, for Romeo's banishment.
Take up those cords. Poor ropes, you are beguiled,
Both you and I, for Romeo is exiled.
He made you for a highway to my bed;
But I, a maid, die maiden-widowèd.
Come, cords; come, nurse. I'll to my wedding bed;
And death, not Romeo, take my maidenhead!

NURSE
Hie to your chamber. I'll find Romeo
To comfort you. I wot well where he is.   139
Hark ye, your Romeo will be here at night.
I'll to him; he is hid at Laurence' cell.

JULIET
O, find him! give this ring to my true knight
And bid him come to take his last farewell.

Exit [with Nurse].

＊

Enter Friar [Laurence].   III, iii

FRIAR
Romeo, come forth; come forth, thou fearful man.   1
Affliction is enamored of thy parts,   2

53 *God . . . mark* God avert the evil omen   56 *gore-blood* clotted blood;
swounded swooned   57 *bankrout* bankrupt   59 *Vile earth* i.e. my body;
resign return   67 *trumpet* i.e. the 'last trumpet'; *general doom* Judgment
Day   72, 73 (in Q2 l. 72 is mistakenly assigned to Juliet, l. 73 to the Nurse)
73 *flow'ring face* (traditionally, the Serpent in Eden appeared to Eve
with the face of a young girl, wreathed in flowers)   75 *fiend angelical*
(cf. 2 Corinthians xi, 14)   76 *wolvish-ravening lamb* (cf. Matthew vii,
15)   81–82 *spirit . . . paradise* i.e. the Serpent in Eden   88 *aqua vitae*
alcoholic spirits   103 *tributary* tribute-paying   117 *needly* necessarily   120
modern ordinary, conventional   121 *rearward* rearguard   128 *corse* body
139 *wot* know
III, iii Friar Laurence's cell   s.d. (separate entrances in Q1; Q2 reads 'Enter
Friar and Romeo.')   1 *fearful* full of fear   2 *parts* qualities

And thou art wedded to calamity.
Enter Romeo.

ROMEO
Father, what news ? What is the Prince's doom ?
What sorrow craves acquaintance at my hand
That I yet know not ?

FRIAR   Too familiar
Is my dear son with such sour company.
8   I bring thee tidings of the Prince's doom.

ROMEO
9   What less than doomsday is the Prince's doom ?

FRIAR
10 A gentler judgment vanished from his lips –
Not body's death, but body's banishment.

ROMEO
Ha, banishment ? Be merciful, say 'death' ;
For exile hath more terror in his look,
Much more than death. Do not say 'banishment.'

FRIAR
Hence from Verona art thou banishèd.
Be patient, for the world is broad and wide.

ROMEO
There is no world without Verona walls,
But purgatory, torture, hell itself.
Hence banishèd is banished from the world,
And world's exile is death. Then 'banishèd'
Is death mistermed. Calling death 'banishèd,'
Thou cut'st my head off with a golden axe
And smilest upon the stroke that murders me.

FRIAR
O deadly sin ! O rude unthankfulness !
Thy fault our law calls death ; but the kind Prince,
26 Taking thy part, hath rushed aside the law,
And turned that black word 'death' to banishment.
This is dear mercy, and thou seest it not.

ROMEO
'Tis torture, and not mercy. Heaven is here,
Where Juliet lives ; and every cat and dog
And little mouse, every unworthy thing,
Live here in heaven and may look on her ;
33 But Romeo may not. More validity,
34 More honorable state, more courtship lives
In carrion flies than Romeo. They may seize
On the white wonder of dear Juliet's hand
And steal immortal blessing from her lips,
38 Who, even in pure and vestal modesty,
39 Still blush, as thinking their own kisses sin ;
40 But Romeo may not, he is banishèd.
Flies may do this but I from this must fly ;
They are freemen, but I am banishèd.
And sayest thou yet that exile is not death ?
Hadst thou no poison mixed, no sharp-ground knife,
45 No sudden mean of death, though ne'er so mean,
But 'banishèd' to kill me – 'banishèd' ?

O friar, the damnèd use that word in hell ;
Howling attends it ! How hast thou the heart,
Being a divine, a ghostly confessor,
A sin-absolver, and my friend professed,
To mangle me with that word 'banishèd' ?

FRIAR
Thou fond mad man, hear me a little speak.   52

ROMEO
O, thou wilt speak again of banishment.

FRIAR
I'll give thee armor to keep off that word ;
Adversity's sweet milk, philosophy,
To comfort thee, though thou art banishèd.

ROMEO
Yet 'banishèd' ? Hang up philosophy !
Unless philosophy can make a Juliet,
Displant a town, reverse a prince's doom,
It helps not, it prevails not. Talk no more.

FRIAR
O, then I see that madmen have no ears.

ROMEO
How should they, when that wise men have no eyes ?

FRIAR
Let me dispute with thee of thy estate.   63

ROMEO
Thou canst not speak of that thou dost not feel.
Wert thou as young as I, Juliet thy love,
An hour but married, Tybalt murderèd,
Doting like me, and like me banishèd,
Then mightst thou speak, then mightst thou tear thy
    hair,
And fall upon the ground, as I do now,
Taking the measure of an unmade grave.   70
Enter Nurse and knock.

FRIAR
Arise ; one knocks. Good Romeo, hide thyself.

ROMEO
Not I ; unless the breath of heartsick groans
Mist-like infold me from the search of eyes.   73
[Knock.]

FRIAR
Hark, how they knock ! Who's there ? Romeo, arise ;
Thou wilt be taken. – Stay awhile ! – Stand up ;   75
[Knock.]
Run to my study. – By and by ! – God's will,   76
What simpleness is this. – I come, I come !   77
Knock.
Who knocks so hard ? Whence come you ? What's your
    will ?
Enter Nurse.

NURSE
Let me come in, and you shall know my errand.
I come from Lady Juliet.

FRIAR   Welcome then.

NURSE
O holy friar, O, tell me, holy friar,
Where is my lady's lord, where's Romeo ?

FRIAR
There on the ground, with his own tears made drunk.

NURSE
O, he is even in my mistress' case,
Just in her case ! O woeful sympathy !
Piteous predicament ! Even so lies she,
Blubb'ring and weeping, weeping and blubb'ring.

---

8 *Prince's doom* punishment decreed by the Prince   9 *doomsday* i.e. death
10 *vanished* disappeared into air   26 *rushed* pushed   33 *validity* value
34 *courtship* privilege of wooing   38 *vestal* virgin   39 *kisses* (when her
lips touch each other)   40–42 (in Q2 these lines are preceded by 'This
may flies do when I from this must fly' – evidently a cancelled line printed
in error – and by l. 43, evidently misplaced)   45 *mean . . . mean* means
. . . lowly   52 *fond* foolish   63 *dispute* reason ; *estate* situation   70 *Taking
the measure* providing the measurements ; **s.d.** (so Q2, with another
entrance for Nurse at l. 78)   73 **s.d.** (Q2 reads 'They knock.')   75 **s.d.**
(Q2 reads 'Slud knock.')   76 *By and by* in a moment   77 *simpleness*
stupid conduct

Stand up, stand up! Stand, an you be a man.
For Juliet's sake, for her sake, rise and stand!
90 Why should you fall into so deep an O?

ROMEO [rises] Nurse –

NURSE
  Ah sir! ah sir! Death's the end of all.

ROMEO
  Spakest thou of Juliet? How is it with her?
94 Doth not she think me an old murderer,
  Now I have stained the childhood of our joy
  With blood removed but little from her own?
  Where is she? and how doth she! and what says
98 My concealed lady to our cancelled love?

NURSE
  O, she says nothing, sir, but weeps and weeps;
  And now falls on her bed, and then starts up,
  And Tybalt calls; and then on Romeo cries,
  And then down falls again.

ROMEO   As if that name,
103 Shot from the deadly level of a gun,
  Did murder her; as that name's cursèd hand
  Murdered her kinsman. O, tell me, friar, tell me,
106 In what vile part of this anatomy
  Doth my name lodge? Tell me, that I may sack
108 The hateful mansion.

[He offers to stab himself, and Nurse snatches the
dagger away.]

FRIAR   Hold thy desperate hand.
  Art thou a man? Thy form cries out thou art;
  Thy tears are womanish, thy wild acts denote
111 The unreasonable fury of a beast.
112 Unseemly woman in a seeming man!
113 And ill-beseeming beast in seeming both!
  Thou hast amazed me. By my holy order,
  I thought thy disposition better tempered.
  Hast thou slain Tybalt? Wilt thou slay thyself?
117 And slay thy lady that in thy life lives,
  By doing damnèd hate upon thyself?
  Why railest thou on thy birth, the heaven, and earth?
120 Since birth and heaven and earth, all three do meet
  In thee at once; which thou at once wouldst lose.
  Fie, fie, thou shamest thy shape, thy love, thy wit,
123 Which, like a usurer, abound'st in all,
124 And usest none in that true use indeed
  Which should bedeck thy shape, thy love, thy wit.
126 Thy noble shape is but a form of wax,
  Digressing from the valor of a man;
  Thy dear love sworn but hollow perjury,
129 Killing that love which thou hast vowed to cherish;
130 Thy wit, that ornament to shape and love,
131 Misshapen in the conduct of them both,
132 Like powder in a skilless soldier's flask,
  Is set afire by thine own ignorance,
134 And thou dismemb'red with thine own defense.
  What, rouse thee, man! Thy Juliet is alive,
136 For whose dear sake thou wast but lately dead.
137 There art thou happy. Tybalt would kill thee,
  But thou slewest Tybalt. There art thou happy too.
  The law, that threat'ned death, becomes thy friend
  And turns it to exile. There art thou happy.
  A pack of blessings light upon thy back;
  Happiness courts thee in her best array;
  But, like a misbehaved and sullen wench,
  Thou pout'st upon thy fortune and thy love.

  Take heed, take heed, for such die miserable.
  Go get thee to thy love, as was decreed,
  Ascend her chamber, hence and comfort her.
  But look thou stay not till the watch be set,
  For then thou canst not pass to Mantua,
  Where thou shalt live till we can find a time
  To blaze your marriage, reconcile your friends,   151
  Beg pardon of the Prince, and call thee back
  With twenty hundred thousand times more joy
  Than thou went'st forth in lamentation.
  Go before, nurse. Commend me to thy lady,
  And bid her hasten all the house to bed,
  Which heavy sorrow makes them apt unto.
  Romeo is coming.

NURSE
  O Lord, I could have stayed here all the night
  To hear good counsel. O, what learning is!
  My lord, I'll tell my lady you will come.

ROMEO
  Do so, and bid my sweet prepare to chide.

NURSE
  Here is a ring she bid me give you, sir.
  Hie you, make haste, for it grows very late.   [Exit.]

ROMEO
  How well my comfort is revived by this!

FRIAR
  Go hence; good night; and here stands all your state: 166
  Either be gone before the watch be set,
  Or by the break of day disguised from hence.
  Sojourn in Mantua. I'll find out your man,
  And he shall signify from time to time
  Every good hap to you that chances here.
  Give me thy hand. 'Tis late. Farewell; good night.

ROMEO
  But that a joy past joy calls out on me,
  It were a grief so brief to part with thee.
  Farewell.   Exeunt.

*

Enter old Capulet, his Wife, and Paris.   III, iv

CAPULET
  Things have fall'n out, sir, so unluckily
  That we have had no time to move our daughter.   2
  Look you, she loved her kinsman Tybalt dearly,
  And so did I. Well, we were born to die.
  'Tis very late; she'll not come down to-night.
  I promise you, but for your company,
  I would have been abed an hour ago.

PARIS
  These times of woe afford no times to woo.
  Madam, good night. Commend me to your daughter.

90 *an O* a fit of groaning 94 *old* hardened 98 *concealed . . . cancelled* hidden from me . . . invalidated by my act (the two words were given almost the same pronunciation) 103 *level* aim 106 *anatomy* body 108 s.d. (from Q1) 111 *unreasonable* irrational 112 *Unseemly . . . seeming* disorderly . . . apparent 113 *ill-beseeming . . . both* inappropriate . . . man and woman 117 *in . . . lives* (cf. II, i, 1 and n.) 120 *all . . . meet* the soul comes from heaven, the body from earth; they unite in man at his birth 123 *Which* (you) who; *all* all capabilities 124 *true use* proper handling of wealth 126 *form of wax* waxwork, outward appearance 129 *Killing that love* (cf. l. 117) 130 *wit* intellect 131 *Misshapen* distorted; *conduct* guidance 132 *flask* powder horn 134 *defense* i.e. intellect 136 *dead* as one dead 137 *happy* fortunate 151 *blaze* publish 166 *here . . . state* here is your situation
III, iv Capulet's house 2 *move* talk with

LADY
I will, and know her mind early to-morrow ;
11 To-night she's mewed up to her heaviness.

CAPULET
12 Sir Paris, I will make a desperate tender
Of my child's love. I think she will be ruled
In all respects by me ; nay more, I doubt it not.
Wife, go you to her ere you go to bed ;
Acquaint her here of my son Paris' love
And bid her (mark you me ?) on Wednesday next –
But soft ! what day is this ?

PARIS   Monday, my lord.

CAPULET
Monday ! ha, ha ! Well, Wednesday is too soon.
20 A Thursday let it be – a Thursday, tell her,
She shall be married to this noble earl.
Will you be ready ? Do you like this haste ?
We'll keep no great ado – a friend or two ;
For hark you, Tybalt being slain so late,
It may be thought we held him carelessly,
Being our kinsman, if we revel much.
Therefore we'll have some half a dozen friends,
And there an end. But what say you to Thursday ?

PARIS
My lord, I would that Thursday were to-morrow.

CAPULET
Well, get you gone. A Thursday be it then.
Go you to Juliet ere you go to bed ;
Prepare her, wife, against this wedding day.
Farewell, my lord. – Light to my chamber, ho !
34 Afore me, it is so very very late
35 That we may call it early by and by.
Good night.   *Exeunt.*

*

III, v *Enter Romeo and Juliet aloft [at the window].*

JULIET
Wilt thou be gone ? It is not yet near day.
It was the nightingale, and not the lark,
3 That pierced the fearful hollow of thine ear.
Nightly she sings on yond pomegranate tree.
Believe me, love, it was the nightingale.

ROMEO
It was the lark, the herald of the morn ;
No nightingale. Look, love, what envious streaks
Do lace the severing clouds in yonder East.
9 Night's candles are burnt out, and jocund day
Stands tiptoe on the misty mountain tops.
I must be gone and live, or stay and die.

JULIET
Yond light is not daylight ; I know it, I.
13 It is some meteor that the sun exhales

11 *mewed up* shut up (falconry); *heaviness* grief 12 *desperate tender* risk-taking offer 20 *A* on 34 *Afore me* (a light oath) 35 *by and by* immediately III, v The Capulet orchard s.d. *at the window* (from Q1) 3 *fearful* apprehensive 9 *Night's candles* the stars 13 *meteor* nocturnal light, such as the will-o'-the-wisp, supposedly of luminous gas given off by the sun or drawn by his power (*exhales*) out of marshy ground 20 *reflex . . . brow* reflection of the moon 25 *my soul* (cf. II, ii, 165) 29 *division* melody 31 *change* exchange (a folk belief) 33 *affray* frighten 34 *hunt's-up* morning song to awaken huntsmen 36 s.d. *hastily* (from Q1 ; Q2 reads 'Enter Madam and Nurse.') 41 *life* (cf. III, iii, 117) 42 s.d. (from Q1) 43 *friend* clandestine lover 46 *much* advanced 54 *ill-divining* prophetic of evil 59 *Dry . . . blood* (the presumed effect of grief was to dry up the blood)

To be to thee this night a torchbearer
And light thee on thy way to Mantua.
Therefore stay yet ; thou need'st not to be gone.

ROMEO
Let me be ta'en, let me be put to death.
I am content, so thou wilt have it so.
I'll say yon grey is not the morning's eye,
'Tis but the pale reflex of Cynthia's brow ; 20
Nor that is not the lark whose notes do beat
The vaulty heaven so high above our heads.
I have more care to stay than will to go.
Come, death, and welcome ! Juliet wills it so.
How is't, my soul ? Let's talk ; it is not day. 25

JULIET
It is, it is ! Hie hence, be gone, away !
It is the lark that sings so out of tune,
Straining harsh discords and unpleasing sharps.
Some say the lark makes sweet division ; 29
This doth not so, for she divideth us.
Some say the lark and loathèd toad change eyes ; 31
O, now I would they had changed voices too,
Since arm from arm that voice doth us affray, 33
Hunting thee hence with hunt's-up to the day. 34
O, now be gone ! More light and light it grows.

ROMEO
More light and light – more dark and dark our woes. 36
Enter Nurse [hastily].

NURSE Madam !

JULIET Nurse ?

NURSE
Your lady mother is coming to your chamber.
The day is broke ; be wary, look about. *[Exit.]*

JULIET
Then, window, let day in, and let life out. 41

ROMEO
Farewell, farewell ! One kiss, and I'll descend. 42
[He goeth down.]

JULIET
Art thou gone so, love-lord, ay husband-friend ? 43
I must hear from thee every day in the hour,
For in a minute there are many days.
O, by this count I shall be much in years 46
Ere I again behold my Romeo !

ROMEO
Farewell !
I will omit no opportunity
That may convey my greetings, love, to thee.

JULIET
O, think'st thou we shall ever meet again ?

ROMEO
I doubt it not ; and all these woes shall serve
For sweet discourses in our times to come.

JULIET
O God, I have an ill-divining soul ! 54
Methinks I see thee, now thou art so low,
As one dead in the bottom of a tomb.
Either my eyesight fails, or thou lookest pale.

ROMEO
And trust me, love, in my eye so do you.
Dry sorrow drinks our blood. Adieu, adieu ! *Exit.* 59

JULIET
O Fortune, Fortune ! all men call thee fickle.
If thou art fickle, what dost thou with him
That is renowned for faith ? Be fickle, Fortune,

For then I hope thou wilt not keep him long
64   But send him back.
> *[She goeth down from the window.]*
> *Enter Mother.*

LADY
Ho, daughter! are you up?

JULIET
Who is't that calls? It is my lady mother.
67   Is she not down so late, or up so early?
What unaccustomed cause procures her hither?

LADY
Why, how now, Juliet?

JULIET   Madam, I am not well.

LADY
Evermore weeping for your cousin's death?
What, wilt thou wash him from his grave with tears?
An if thou couldst, thou couldst not make him live.
Therefore have done. Some grief shows much of love;
But much of grief shows still some want of wit.

JULIET
75   Yet let me weep for such a feeling loss.

LADY
So shall you feel the loss, but not the friend
Which you weep for.

JULIET   Feeling so the loss,
I cannot choose but ever weep the friend.

LADY
Well, girl, thou weep'st not so much for his death
As that the villain lives which slaughtered him.

JULIET
What villain, madam?

LADY   That same villain Romeo.

JULIET *[aside]*
Villain and he be many miles asunder. –
God pardon him! I do, with all my heart;
84   And yet no man like he doth grieve my heart.

LADY
That is because the traitor murderer lives.

JULIET
Ay, madam, from the reach of these my hands.
Would none but I might venge my cousin's death!

LADY
We will have vengeance for it, fear thou not.
Then weep no more. I'll send to one in Mantua,
90   Where that same banished runagate doth live,
Shall give him such an unaccustomed dram
That he shall soon keep Tybalt company;
And then I hope thou wilt be satisfied.

JULIET
Indeed I never shall be satisfied
With Romeo till I behold him – dead –
Is my poor heart so for a kinsman vexed.
Madam, if you could find out but a man
98   To bear a poison, I would temper it;
That Romeo should, upon receipt thereof,
Soon sleep in quiet. O, how my heart abhors
To hear him named and cannot come to him,
To wreak the love I bore my cousin
Upon his body that hath slaughtered him!

LADY
Find thou the means, and I'll find such a man.
But now I'll tell thee joyful tidings, girl!

JULIET
And joy comes well in such a needy time.

What are they, beseech your ladyship?

LADY
Well, well, thou hast a careful father, child;
One who, to put thee from thy heaviness,
Hath sorted out a sudden day of joy   110
That thou expects not nor I looked not for.

JULIET
Madam, in happy time! What day is that?   112

LADY
Marry, my child, early next Thursday morn
The gallant, young, and noble gentleman,
The County Paris, at Saint Peter's Church,
Shall happily make thee there a joyful bride.

JULIET
Now by Saint Peter's Church, and Peter too,
He shall not make me there a joyful bride!
I wonder at this haste, that I must wed
Ere he that should be husband comes to woo.
I pray you tell my lord and father, madam,
I will not marry yet; and when I do, I swear
It shall be Romeo, whom you know I hate,
Rather than Paris. These are news indeed!

LADY
Here comes your father. Tell him so yourself,
And see how he will take it at your hands.
> *Enter Capulet and Nurse.*

CAPULET
When the sun sets the earth doth drizzle dew,
But for the sunset of my brother's son
It rains downright.
How now? a conduit, girl? What, still in tears?   130
Evermore show'ring? In one little body
Thou counterfeit'st a bark, a sea, a wind:
For still thy eyes, which I may call the sea,
Do ebb and flow with tears; the bark thy body is,
Sailing in this salt flood; the winds, thy sighs,
Who, raging with thy tears and they with them,
Without a sudden calm will overset   137
Thy tempest-tossèd body. How now, wife?
Have you deliverèd to her our decree?

LADY
Ay, sir; but she will none, she gives you thanks.   140
I would the fool were married to her grave!   141

CAPULET
Soft! take me with you, take me with you, wife.   142
How? Will she none? Doth she not give us thanks?
Is she not proud? Doth she not count her blest,
Unworthy as she is, that we have wrought   145
So worthy a gentleman to be her bride?   146

JULIET
Not proud you have, but thankful that you have.
Proud can I never be of what I hate,
But thankful even for hate that is meant love.

---

64 s.d. (from Q1, and so placed that it might apply only to the Nurse; but since the Q1 stage direction immediately following is 'Enter Juliet's Mother, Nurse,' the indications are that the subsequent action takes place below, where Juliet joins her mother; hence the orchard into which Romeo has descended now becomes an interior) 67 *down* abed 75 *feeling* deeply felt 84 *like* so much as 90 *runagate* renegade 98 *temper* prepare or concoct (with play on 'moderate') 110 *sorted* chosen 112 *in happy time* opportunely 130 *conduit* water pipe 137 *sudden* immediate 140 *gives you thanks* says 'No, thank you' 141 *married . . . grave* (a petulant but prophetic comment, like l. 167 below) 142 *take . . . you* let me understand you 145 *wrought* arranged for 146 *bride* bridegroom

CAPULET

150 How, how, how, how, chopped-logic? What is this?
'Proud' – and 'I thank you' – and 'I thank you not' –
And yet 'not proud'? Mistress minion you,
Thank me no thankings, nor proud me no prouds,
154 But fettle your fine joints 'gainst Thursday next
To go with Paris to Saint Peter's Church,
156 Or I will drag thee on a hurdle thither.
157 Out, you green-sickness carrion! out, you baggage!
158 You tallow-face!

LADY   Fie, fie! what, are you mad?

JULIET

Good father, I beseech you on my knees,
Hear me with patience but to speak a word.

CAPULET

Hang thee, young baggage! disobedient wretch!
162 I tell thee what – get thee to church a Thursday
Or never after look me in the face.
Speak not, reply not, do not answer me!
My fingers itch. Wife, we scarce thought us blest
That God had lent us but this only child;
But now I see this one is one too much,
And that we have a curse in having her.
169 Out on her, hilding!

NURSE   God in heaven bless her!
170 You are to blame, my lord, to rate her so.

CAPULET

And why, my Lady Wisdom? Hold your tongue,
172 Good Prudence. Smatter with your gossips, go!

NURSE

I speak no treason.

173 CAPULET   O, God-i-god-en!

NURSE

May not one speak?

CAPULET   Peace, you mumbling fool!
Utter your gravity o'er a gossip's bowl,
For here we need it not.

LADY   You are too hot.

CAPULET

177 God's bread! it makes me mad.
178 Day, night; hour, tide, time; work, play;
Alone, in company; still my care hath been
To have her matched; and having now provided
A gentleman of noble parentage,
182 Of fair demesnes, youthful, and nobly trained,
Stuffed, as they say, with honorable parts,
Proportioned as one's thought would wish a man –
185 And then to have a wretched puling fool,
186 A whining mammet, in her fortune's tender,
To answer 'I'll not wed, I cannot love';

I am too young, I pray you pardon me'!
But, an you will not wed, I'll pardon you!   189
Graze where you will, you shall not house with me.
Look to't, think on't; I do not use to jest.   191
Thursday is near; lay hand on heart, advise: 192
An you be mine, I'll give you to my friend;
An you be not, hang, beg, starve, die in the streets,
For, by my soul, I'll ne'er acknowledge thee,
Nor what is mine shall never do thee good.
Trust to't. Bethink you. I'll not be forsworn.   *Exit.*

JULIET

Is there no pity sitting in the clouds
That sees into the bottom of my grief?
O sweet my mother, cast me not away!
Delay this marriage for a month, a week;
Or if you do not, make the bridal bed
In that dim monument where Tybalt lies.

LADY

Talk not to me, for I'll not speak a word.
Do as thou wilt, for I have done with thee.   *Exit.*

JULIET

O God! – O nurse, how shall this be prevented?
My husband is on earth, my faith in heaven.   207
How shall that faith return again to earth   208
Unless that husband send it me from heaven
By leaving earth? Comfort me, counsel me.
Alack, alack, that heaven should practise stratagems
Upon so soft a subject as myself!
What say'st thou? Hast thou not a word of joy?
Some comfort, nurse.

NURSE   Faith, here it is.
Romeo is banished; and all the world to nothing   215
That he dares ne'er come back to challenge you;   216
Or if he do, it needs must be by stealth.
Then, since the case so stands as now it doth,
I think it best you married with the County.
O, he's a lovely gentleman!
Romeo's a dishclout to him. An eagle, madam,   221
Hath not so green, so quick, so fair an eye
As Paris hath. Beshrew my very heart,
I think you are happy in this second match,
For it excels your first; or if it did not,
Your first is dead – or 'twere as good he were
As living here and you no use of him.

JULIET

Speak'st thou from thy heart?

NURSE

And from my soul too; else beshrew them both.   229

JULIET Amen!

NURSE What?

JULIET

Well, thou hast comforted me marvellous much.
Go in; and tell my lady I am gone,
Having displeased my father, to Laurence' cell,
To make confession and to be absolved.

NURSE

Marry, I will; and this is wisely done.   *[Exit.]*

JULIET

Ancient damnation! O most wicked fiend!   237
Is it more sin to wish me thus forsworn,
Or to dispraise my lord with that same tongue
Which she hath praised him with above compare
So many thousand times? Go, counsellor!
Thou and my bosom henceforth shall be twain.   242

150 *chopped-logic* hair-splitting 154 *fettle* prepare 156 *hurdle* sledge on which criminals were carried to execution 157 *green-sickness* anemic; *baggage* worthless woman 158 *tallow-face* pale-face; *are you mad* (addressed to Capulet) 162 *a* on 169 *hilding* worthless creature 170 *rate* scold 172 *Smatter . . . gossips* chatter with your cronies 173 *God-i-god-en* for God's sake 177 *bread* bread of the Sacrament 178–79 *Day . . . company* (in Q1 the equivalent matter occupies two separate lines: 'Day, night; early, late; at home, abroad: Alone, in company; waking or sleeping;' – more logical, but irreconcilable with the Q2 passage except by guesswork) 182 *demesnes* domains 185 *puling* whining 186 *mammet* doll; *tender* offer 189 *I'll pardon you* (ironic) 191 *do not use* am not accustomed 192 *advise* consider 207 *my faith in heaven* my marriage vow is recorded in heaven 208–10 *How . . . earth* how can I marry unless I am first widowed 215 *all . . . nothing* i.e. it is a safe bet 216 *challenge* demand possession of 221 *dishclout* dishcloth 229 *beshrew* a curse on 237 *Ancient damnation* damnable old woman 242 *bosom* confidence; *twain* separated

I'll to the friar to know his remedy.
If all else fail, myself have power to die.   *Exit.*

*

IV, i   *Enter Friar [Laurence] and County Paris.*

FRIAR
   On Thursday, sir? The time is very short.
PARIS
   My father Capulet will have it so,
   And I am nothing slow to slack his haste.
FRIAR
   You say you do not know the lady's mind.
5 Uneven is the course; I like it not.
PARIS
   Immoderately she weeps for Tybalt's death,
   And therefore have I little talked of love;
8 For Venus smiles not in a house of tears.
   Now, sir, her father counts it dangerous
   That she do give her sorrow so much sway,
   And in his wisdom hastes our marriage
   To stop the inundation of her tears,
13 Which, too much minded by herself alone,
   May be put from her by society.
   Now do you know the reason of this haste.
FRIAR *[aside]*
   I would I knew not why it should be slowed. –
   Look, sir, here comes the lady toward my cell.
            Enter Juliet.
PARIS
   Happily met, my lady and my wife!
JULIET
   That may be, sir, when I may be a wife.
PARIS
20 That 'may be' must be, love, on Thursday next.
JULIET
   What must be shall be.
FRIAR   That's a certain text.
PARIS
   Come you to make confession to this father?
JULIET
   To answer that, I should confess to you.
PARIS
   Do not deny to him that you love me.
JULIET
   I will confess to you that I love him.
PARIS
   So will ye, I am sure, that you love me.
JULIET
   If I do so, it will be of more price,
   Being spoke behind your back, than to your face.
PARIS
   Poor soul, thy face is much abused with tears.
JULIET
30 The tears have got small victory by that,
   For it was bad enough before their spite.
PARIS
   Thou wrong'st it more than tears with that report.
JULIET
   That is no slander, sir, which is a truth;
   And what I spake, I spake it to my face.
PARIS
   Thy face is mine, and thou hast sland'red it.

JULIET
   It may be so, for it is not mine own.
   Are you at leisure, holy father, now,
   Or shall I come to you at evening mass?
FRIAR
   My leisure serves me, pensive daughter, now.
   My lord, we must entreat the time alone.
PARIS
   God shield I should disturb devotion!   41
   Juliet, on Thursday early will I rouse ye.
   Till then, adieu, and keep this holy kiss.   *Exit.*
JULIET
   O, shut the door! and when thou hast done so,
   Come weep with me – past hope, past cure, past help!
FRIAR
   Ah, Juliet, I already know thy grief;
   It strains me past the compass of my wits.   47
   I hear thou must, and nothing may prorogue it,   48
   On Thursday next be married to this County.
JULIET
   Tell me not, friar, that thou hearest of this,
   Unless thou tell me how I may prevent it.
   If in thy wisdom thou canst give no help,
   Do thou but call my resolution wise
   And with this knife I'll help it presently.
   God joined my heart and Romeo's, thou our hands;
   And ere this hand, by thee to Romeo's sealed,
   Shall be the label to another deed,   57
   Or my true heart with treacherous revolt
   Turn to another, this shall slay them both.
   Therefore, out of thy long-experienced time,   60
   Give me some present counsel; or, behold,
   'Twixt my extremes and me this bloody knife   62
   Shall play the umpire, arbitrating that
   Which the commission of thy years and art   64
   Could to no issue of true honor bring.
   Be not so long to speak. I long to die
   If what thou speak'st speak not of remedy.
FRIAR
   Hold, daughter. I do spy a kind of hope,
   Which craves as desperate an execution
   As that is desperate which we would prevent.
   If, rather than to marry County Paris,
   Thou hast the strength of will to slay thyself,
   Then it is likely thou wilt undertake
   A thing like death to chide away this shame,
   That cop'st with death himself to scape from it;   75
   And, if thou darest, I'll give thee remedy.
JULIET
   O, bid me leap, rather than marry Paris,
   From off the battlements of any tower,
   Or walk in thievish ways, or bid me lurk   79
   Where serpents are; chain me with roaring bears,
   Or hide me nightly in a charnel house,   81

IV, i *Friar Laurence's cell* 5 *course* i.e. racecourse 8 *Venus . . . tears*
the influence of the planet Venus is unfavorable when she appears in the
'house' of a 'moist' constellation, such as Pisces or Aquarius; i.e, one
cannot talk of love amidst grief 13 *minded* thought about 41 *shield*
forbid 47 *the compass . . . wits* my wit's end 48 *prorogue* postpone 57
label i.e. strip of parchment bearing the seal, attached to a deed 60 *time*
age 62 *extremes* difficulties 64 *commission . . . art* authority of your age
and skill 75 *cop'st* encounterest 79 *thievish ways* roads frequented by
robbers 81 *charnel house* depository of human bones

O'ercovered quite with dead men's rattling bones,
83 With reeky shanks and yellow chapless skulls;
Or bid me go into a new-made grave
And hide me with a dead man in his shroud –
Things that, to hear them told, have made me tremble –
And I will do it without fear or doubt,
To live an unstained wife to my sweet love.

FRIAR
Hold, then. Go home, be merry, give consent
To marry Paris. Wednesday is to-morrow.
To-morrow night look that thou lie alone;
Let not the nurse lie with thee in thy chamber.
Take thou this vial, being then in bed,
94 And this distilling liquor drink thou off;
When presently through all thy veins shall run
96 A cold and drowsy humor; for no pulse
97 Shall keep his native progress, but surcease;
No warmth, no breath, shall testify thou livest;
The roses in thy lips and cheeks shall fade
100 To wanny ashes, thy eyes' windows fall
Like death when he shuts up the day of life;
102 Each part, deprived of supple government,
Shall, stiff and stark and cold, appear like death;
And in this borrowèd likeness of shrunk death
Thou shalt continue two-and-forty hours,
And then awake as from a pleasant sleep.
Now, when the bridegroom in the morning comes
To rouse thee from thy bed, there art thou dead.
Then, as the manner of our country is,
In thy best robes uncoverèd on the bier
111 Thou shalt be borne to that same ancient vault
Where all the kindred of the Capulets lie.
113 In the mean time, against thou shalt awake,
114 Shall Romeo by my letters know our drift;
And hither shall he come; and he and I
Will watch thy waking, and that very night
Shall Romeo bear thee hence to Mantua.
And this shall free thee from this present shame,
119 If no inconstant toy nor womanish fear
Abate thy valor in the acting it.

JULIET
Give me, give me! O, tell not me of fear!

FRIAR
Hold! Get you gone, be strong and prosperous
In this resolve. I'll send a friar with speed
To Mantua, with my letters to thy lord.

JULIET
Love give me strength! and strength shall help afford.
Farewell, dear father.   Exit [with Friar].

*

83 reeky smelly; chapless jawless 94 distilling infusing 96 humor moisture
97 surcease cease 100 wanny pale, shrunken; windows i.e. eyelids (the
figure derives from the covering of shop-fronts at the close of the day)
102 supple government the life force that keeps the body supple 111 (in
Q2 this line is preceded by 'Be borne to burial in thy kindred's grave,'
evidently a cancelled version of the line, printed in error) 113 against
. . . awake in preparation for your awaking 114 drift intention 119 toy
whim
IV, ii Capulet's house 5 try test 6–7 'tis . . . fingers it's a poor cook
who doesn't like to taste the food which he prepares (proverbial) 10
unfurnished unprovided 14 harlotry hussy 24 to-morrow morning (i.e.
Wednesday, one day earlier than planned) 32 bound indebted

Enter Father Capulet, Mother, Nurse, and   IV, ii
Servingmen, two or three.

CAPULET
So many guests invite as here are writ.
                              [Exit a Servingman.]
Sirrah, go hire me twenty cunning cooks.

SERVINGMAN You shall have none ill, sir; for I'll try if
they can lick their fingers.

CAPULET
How canst thou try them so?   5

SERVINGMAN Marry, sir, 'tis an ill cook that cannot lick 6
his own fingers. Therefore he that cannot lick his fingers
goes not with me.

CAPULET Go, begone.   [Exit Servingman.]
We shall be much unfurnished for this time.   10
What, is my daughter gone to Friar Laurence?

NURSE Ay, forsooth.

CAPULET
Well, he may chance to do some good on her.
A peevish self-willed harlotry it is.   14

                Enter Juliet.

NURSE
See where she comes from shrift with merry look.

CAPULET
How now, my headstrong? Where have you been gadding?

JULIET
Where I have learnt me to repent the sin
Of disobedient opposition
To you and your behests, and am enjoined
By holy Laurence to fall prostrate here
To beg your pardon. Pardon, I beseech you!
Henceforward I am ever ruled by you.

CAPULET
Send for the County. Go tell him of this.
I'll have this knot knit up to-morrow morning.   24

JULIET
I met the youthful lord at Laurence' cell
And gave him what becomèd love I might,
Not stepping o'er the bounds of modesty.

CAPULET
Why, I am glad on't. This is well. Stand up.
This is as't should be. Let me see the County.
Ay, marry, go, I say, and fetch him hither.
Now, afore God, this reverend holy friar,
All our whole city is much bound to him.   32

JULIET
Nurse, will you go with me into my closet
To help me sort such needful ornaments
As you think fit to furnish me to-morrow?

MOTHER
No, not till Thursday. There is time enough.

CAPULET
Go, nurse, go with her. We'll to church to-morrow.
                        Exeunt [Juliet and Nurse].

MOTHER
We shall be short in our provision.
'Tis now near night.

CAPULET   Tush, I will stir about,
And all things shall be well, I warrant thee, wife.
Go thou to Juliet, help to deck up her.
I'll not to bed to-night; let me alone.
I'll play the housewife for this once. What, ho!
They are all forth; well, I will walk myself

To County Paris, to prepare up him
Against to-morrow. My heart is wondrous light,
Since this same wayward girl is so reclaimed.
                              Exit [with Mother].

                              *

IV, iii   *Enter Juliet and Nurse.*

JULIET
     Ay, those attires are best ; but, gentle nurse,
     I pray thee leave me to myself to-night ;
3   For I have need of many orisons
     To move the heavens to smile upon my state,
5   Which, well thou knowest, is cross and full of sin.
                    Enter Mother.
MOTHER
     What, are you busy, ho ? Need you my help ?
JULIET
7   No, madam ; we have culled such necessaries
8   As are behoveful for our state to-morrow.
     So please you, let me now be left alone,
     And let the nurse this night sit up with you ;
     For I am sure you have your hands full all
     In this so sudden business.
MOTHER   Good night.
     Get thee to bed, and rest ; for thou hast need.
                    Exeunt [Mother and Nurse].
JULIET
     Farewell ! God knows when we shall meet again.
15   I have a faint cold fear thrills through my veins
     That almost freezes up the heat of life.
     I'll call them back again to comfort me.
     Nurse ! – What should she do here ?
     My dismal scene I needs must act alone.
     Come, vial.
     What if this mixture do not work at all ?
     Shall I be married then to-morrow morning ?
     No, no ! This shall forbid it. Lie thou there.
                    [Lays down a dagger.]
     What if it be a poison which the friar
25   Subtly hath minist'red to have me dead,
     Lest in this marriage he should be dishonored
     Because he married me before to Romeo ?
     I fear it is ; and yet methinks it should not,
29   For he hath still been tried a holy man.
     How if, when I am laid into the tomb,
     I wake before the time that Romeo
     Come to redeem me ? There's a fearful point !
     Shall I not then be stifled in the vault,
     To whose foul mouth no healthsome air breathes in,
     And there die strangled ere my Romeo comes ?
     Or, if I live, is it not very like
37   The horrible conceit of death and night,
     Together with the terror of the place –
     As in a vault, an ancient receptacle
     Where for this many hundred years the bones
     Of all my buried ancestors are packed ;
42   Where bloody Tybalt, yet but green in earth,
     Lies fest'ring in his shroud ; where, as they say,
     At some hours in the night spirits resort –
45   Alack, alack, is it not like that I,
     So early waking – what with loathsome smells,
47   And shrieks like mandrakes torn out of the earth,
     That living mortals, hearing them, run mad –
     O, if I wake, shall I not be distraught,

Environèd with all these hideous fears,
And madly play with my forefathers' joints,
And pluck the mangled Tybalt from his shroud,
And, in this rage, with some great kinsman's bone
As with a club dash out my desp'rate brains ?
O, look ! methinks I see my cousin's ghost
Seeking out Romeo, that did spit his body
Upon a rapier's point. Stay, Tybalt, stay !
Romeo, I come ! this do I drink to thee.   58
          [She falls upon her bed within the curtains.]

                              *

          Enter Lady of the House and Nurse.   IV, iv
LADY
     Hold, take these keys and fetch more spices, nurse.
NURSE
     They call for dates and quinces in the pastry.
               Enter old Capulet.
CAPULET
     Come, stir, stir, stir ! The second cock hath crowed,
     The curfew bell hath rung, 'tis three o'clock.
     Look to the baked meats, good Angelica ;   5
     Spare not for cost.
NURSE   Go, you cot-quean, go,   6
     Get you to bed ! Faith, you'll be sick to-morrow
     For this night's watching.   8
CAPULET
     No, not a whit. What, I have watched ere now
     All night for lesser cause, and ne'er been sick.
LADY
     Ay, you have been a mouse-hunt in your time ;   11
     But I will watch you from such watching now.
                         Exit Lady and Nurse.
CAPULET
     A jealous hood, a jealous hood !   13
          Enter three or four [Fellows] with
          spits and logs and baskets.
                              Now, fellow,
     What is there ?
1. FELLOW
     Things for the cook, sir ; but I know not what.   15
CAPULET
     Make haste, make haste.   *[Exit first Fellow.]*
                         Sirrah, fetch drier logs.
     Call Peter ; he will show thee where they are.
2. FELLOW
     I have a head, sir, that will find out logs   18
     And never trouble Peter for the matter.
CAPULET
     Mass, and well said ; a merry whoreson, ha !   20
     Thou shalt be loggerhead.   21
               [Exit second Fellow, with the others.]
                         Good Father ! 'tis day.

IV, iii *Juliet's chamber*   3 *orisons* prayers   5 *cross* perverse   7 *culled*
picked out   8 *behoveful* fitting ; *state* ceremony   15 *faint* causing faintness   25 *minist'red* administered   29 *tried* proved (after this line, Q1
inserts 'I will not entertain so bad a thought')   37 *conceit* imagination
42 *green* new   45 *like* likely   47 *mandrakes* mandragora (a narcotic plant
with a forked root resembling the human form, supposed to utter maddening shrieks when uprooted)   58 s.d. (from Q1)
IV, iv *Within Capulet's house*   5 *baked meats* meat pies   6 *cot-quean* a man
who plays housewife   8 *watching* staying awake   11 *mouse-hunt* i.e. a nocturnal prowler after women   13 *A jealous hood* you wear the cap (or hood) of
jealousy   15, 18 *1. Fellow, 2. Fellow* (Q2 reads 'Fellow' in both instances)
18 *1 . . . logs* i.e. my head is wooden and has an affinity for logs   20 *Mass*
by the Mass ; *whoreson* bastard, rascal   21 *loggerhead* blockhead

The County will be here with music straight,
For so he said he would.
     Play music.   I hear him near.
Nurse ! Wife ! What, ho ! What, nurse, I say !
     Enter Nurse.

25   Go waken Juliet ; go and trim her up.
I'll go and chat with Paris. Hie, make haste,
Make haste ! The bridegroom he is come already :
Make haste, I say.   *[Exit.]*

IV, v   *[Nurse goes to curtains.]*

NURSE
1   Mistress ! what, mistress ! Juliet ! Fast, I warrant her, she.
2   Why, lamb ! why, lady ! Fie, you slug-abed.
     Why, love, I say ! madam ! sweetheart ! Why, bride !
4   What, not a word ? You take your pennyworths now ;
     Sleep for a week ; for the next night, I warrant,
6   The County Paris hath set up his rest
     That you shall rest but little. God forgive me !
     Marry, and amen. How sound is she asleep !
     I needs must wake her. Madam, madam, madam !
     Ay, let the County take you in your bed ;
     He'll fright you up, i' faith. Will it not be ?
      [Draws aside the curtains.]
12   What, dressed, and in your clothes, and down again ?
     I must needs wake you. Lady ! lady ! lady !
     Alas, alas ! Help, help ! my lady 's dead !
15   O weraday that ever I was born !
16   Some aqua vitae, ho ! My lord ! my lady !
      [Enter Mother.]

MOTHER
     What noise is here ?
NURSE
                O lamentable day !
MOTHER
     What is the matter ?
NURSE
                Look, look ! O heavy day !
MOTHER
     O me, O me ! My child, my only life !
20   Revive, look up, or I will die with thee !
     Help, help ! Call help.
      Enter Father.
FATHER
     For shame, bring Juliet forth ; her lord is come.
NURSE
     She's dead, deceased ; she's dead, alack the day !
MOTHER
     Alack the day, she's dead, she's dead, she's dead !
CAPULET
     Ha ! let me see her. Out alas ! she's cold,
     Her blood is settled, and her joints are stiff ;
     Life and these lips have long been separated.
     Death lies on her like an untimely frost
     Upon the sweetest flower of all the field.
NURSE
30   O lamentable day !
MOTHER   O woeful time !

---

25 *trim her up* dress her neatly
IV, v 1 *Fast* fast asleep 2 *slug-abed* sleepyhead 4 *pennyworths* small
portions 6 *set . . . rest* i.e. made his firm decision (from primero, a card
game) 12 *down* back to bed 15 *weraday* welladay, alas 16 *aqua vitae*
alcoholic spirits 45 *lasting labor* continuous toil 46 *But one* (cf. III,
v, 166) 61 *To murder . . . solemnity* to spoil our ceremony 69 *Your part*
her mortal body, generated by her parents 70 *his part* her immortal soul,
created directly by God 79 *rosemary* plant symbolizing remembrance 82
fond nature foolish human nature 83 *merriment* cause for optimism

CAPULET
     Death, that hath ta'en her hence to make me wail,
     Ties up my tongue and will not let me speak.
      Enter Friar [Laurence] and the County [Paris, with
      Musicians].
FRIAR
     Come, is the bride ready to go to church ?
CAPULET
     Ready to go, but never to return.
     O son, the night before thy wedding day
     Hath Death lain with thy wife. There she lies,
     Flower as she was, deflowerèd by him.
     Death is my son-in-law, Death is my heir ;
     My daughter he hath wedded. I will die
     And leave him all. Life, living, all is Death's.
PARIS
     Have I thought long to see this morning's face,
     And doth it give me such a sight as this ?
MOTHER
     Accursed, unhappy, wretched, hateful day !
     Most miserable hour that e'er time saw
     In lasting labor of his pilgrimage !   45
     But one, poor one, one poor and loving child,   46
     But one thing to rejoice and solace in,
     And cruel Death hath catched it from my sight.
NURSE
     O woe ! O woeful, woeful, woeful day !
     Most lamentable day, most woeful day
     That ever ever I did yet behold !
     O day, O day, O day ! O hateful day !
     Never was seen so black a day as this.
     O woeful day ! O woeful day !
PARIS
     Beguiled, divorcèd, wrongèd, spited, slain !
     Most detestable Death, by thee beguiled,
     By cruel cruel thee quite overthrown.
     O love ! O life ! not life, but love in death !
CAPULET
     Despised, distressèd, hated, martyred, killed !
     Uncomfortable time, why cam'st thou now
     To murder, murder our solemnity ?   61
     O child, O child ! my soul, and not my child !
     Dead art thou – alack, my child is dead,
     And with my child my joys are burièd !
FRIAR
     Peace, ho, for shame ! Confusion's cure lives not
     In these confusions. Heaven and yourself
     Had part in this fair maid – now heaven hath all,
     And all the better is it for the maid.
     Your part in her you could not keep from death,   69
     But heaven keeps his part in eternal life.   70
     The most you sought was her promotion,
     For 'twas your heaven she should be advanced ;
     And weep ye now, seeing she is advanced
     Above the clouds, as high as heaven itself ?
     O, in this love, you love your child so ill
     That you run mad, seeing that she is well.
     She's not well married that lives married long,
     But she's best married that dies married young.
     Dry up your tears and stick your rosemary   79
     On this fair corse, and, as the custom is,
     In all her best array bear her to church ;
     For though fond nature bids us all lament,   82
     Yet nature's tears are reason's merriment.   83

CAPULET

All things that we ordainèd festival
Turn from their office to black funeral –
Our instruments to melancholy bells,
Our wedding cheer to a sad burial feast;
Our solemn hymns to sullen dirges change;
Our bridal flowers serve for a buried corse;
And all things change them to the contrary.

FRIAR

Sir, go you in; and, madam, go with him;
And go, Sir Paris. Every one prepare
To follow this fair corse unto her grave.

94   The heavens do low'r upon you for some ill;
95   Move them no more by crossing their high will.
         Exeunt [casting rosemary on her and shutting the
         curtains]. Manet [the Nurse with Musicians].

1. MUSICIAN

Faith, we may put up our pipes and be gone.

NURSE

Honest good fellows, ah, put up, put up!
98   For well you know this is a pitiful case.   *[Exit.]*

1. MUSICIAN

99   Ay, by my troth, the case may be amended.
         Enter Peter.

100 PETER Musicians, O, musicians, 'Heart's ease,' 'Heart's
         ease'! O, an you will have me live, play 'Heart's ease.'

1. MUSICIAN Why 'Heart's ease'?

103 PETER O, musicians, because my heart itself plays 'My
104   heart is full of woe.' O, play me some merry dump to
         comfort me.

1. MUSICIAN Not a dump we! 'Tis no time to play now.

PETER You will not then?

1. MUSICIAN No.

PETER I will then give it you soundly.

1. MUSICIAN What will you give us?

111 PETER No money, on my faith, but the gleek. I will give
         you the minstrel.

1. MUSICIAN Then will I give you the serving-creature.

PETER Then will I lay the serving-creature's dagger on
115   your pate. I will carry no crotchets. I'll re you, I'll fa
         you. Do you note me?

1. MUSICIAN An you re us and fa us, you note us.

118 2. MUSICIAN Pray you put up your dagger, and put out
         your wit.

120 PETER Then have at you with my wit! I will dry-beat you
         with an iron wit, and put up my iron dagger. Answer
         me like men.

123   'When griping grief the heart doth wound,
             And doleful dumps the mind oppress,
         Then music with her silver sound' –
         Why 'silver sound'? Why 'music with her silver sound'?

127 What say you, Simon Catling?

1. MUSICIAN Marry, sir, because silver hath a sweet
         sound.

129 PETER Pretty! What say you, Hugh Rebeck?

2. MUSICIAN I say 'silver sound' because musicians
         sound for silver.

132 PETER Pretty too! What say you, James Soundpost?

3. MUSICIAN Faith, I know not what to say.

134 PETER O, I cry you mercy! you are the singer. I will say
         for you. It is 'music with her silver sound' because
         musicians have no gold for sounding.
         'Then music with her silver sound
             With speedy help doth lend redress.'   *Exit.*

1. MUSICIAN What a pestilent knave is this same!

2. MUSICIAN Hang him, Jack! Come, we'll in here, tarry
         for the mourners, and stay dinner.   *Exit [with others].* 141

*

Enter Romeo.   V, i

ROMEO

If I may trust the flattering truth of sleep,   1
My dreams presage some joyful news at hand.
My bosom's lord sits lightly in his throne,   3
And all this day an unaccustomed spirit
Lifts me above the ground with cheerful thoughts.
I dreamt my lady came and found me dead
(Strange dream that gives a dead man leave to think!)
And breathed such life with kisses in my lips
That I revived and was an emperor.
Ah me! how sweet is love itself possessed,
When but love's shadows are so rich in joy!   11
    Enter Romeo's man [Balthasar, booted].
News from Verona! How now, Balthasar?
Dost thou not bring me letters from the friar?
How doth my lady? Is my father well?
How fares my Juliet? That I ask again,
For nothing can be ill if she be well.

MAN

Then she is well, and nothing can be ill.
Her body sleeps in Capel's monument,
And her immortal part with angels lives.
I saw her laid low in her kindred's vault
And presently took post to tell it you.   21
O, pardon me for bringing these ill news,
Since you did leave it for my office, sir.

ROMEO

Is it e'en so? Then I defy you, stars!   24
Thou knowest my lodging. Get me ink and paper
And hire posthorses. I will hence to-night.

MAN

I do beseech you, sir, have patience.
Your looks are pale and wild and do import   28
Some misadventure.

ROMEO   Tush, thou art deceived.
Leave me and do the thing I bid thee do.
Hast thou no letters to me from the friar?

MAN

No, my good lord.

ROMEO   No matter. Get thee gone
And hire those horses. I'll be with thee straight.
    Exit [Balthasar].

94 *low'r* look angrily; *ill* sin   95 s.d. *casting . . . curtains* (from Q1)   98 s.d. (Q2 reads 'Exit omnes.')   99 *case* instrument case; *amended* repaired; s.d. *Enter Peter* (Q2 has 'Enter Will Kemp,' the actor playing Peter's role) 100, 103–04 *Heart's ease, My heart is full of woe* (old ballad tunes)   104 *dump* slow dance melody   111 *gleek* mock   111–12 *give you* insultingly call you   115 *carry* put up with; *crotchets* (1) whims, (2) quarter notes in music; *re, fa* (musical notes)   118 *put out* display   120 *Then . . . wit* (added to preceding speech in Q2); *dry-beat* thrash   123–25 (The second line is missing in Q2 but appears in Q1. The song is from Richard Edwards' 'In Commendation of Music,' in *The Paradise of Dainty Devices*, 1576.) 127 *Catling* (lutestring)   129 *Rebeck* (three-stringed fiddle)   132 *Soundpost* (wooden peg in a violin, supporting the bridge)   134 *cry you mercy* beg your pardon   141 *stay* await
V, i A street in Mantua   1 *flattering* favorable to me; *truth of sleep* (cf. I, iv, 52)   3 *bosom's lord* heart   11 *shadows* dream-images   21 *presently* at once; *took post* hired posthorses   24 *stars* (cf. I, iv, 107)   28 *import* suggest

Well, Juliet, I will lie with thee to-night.
Let's see for means. O mischief, thou art swift
To enter in the thoughts of desperate men !
I do remember an apothecary,
And hereabouts 'a dwells, which late I noted
39 In tatt'red weeds, with overwhelming brows,
40 Culling of simples. Meagre were his looks,
Sharp misery had worn him to the bones ;
And in his needy shop a tortoise hung,
An alligator stuffed, and other skins
Of ill-shaped fishes ; and about his shelves
45 A beggarly account of empty boxes,
Green earthen pots, bladders, and musty seeds,
47 Remnants of packthread, and old cakes of roses
Were thinly scatterèd, to make up a show.
Noting this penury, to myself I said,
'An if a man did need a poison now
Whose sale is present death in Mantua,
52 Here lives a caitiff wretch would sell it him.'
O, this same thought did but forerun my need,
And this same needy man must sell it me.
As I remember, this should be the house.
Being holiday, the beggar's shop is shut.
What, ho ! apothecary !
    [Enter Apothecary.]
APOTHECARY   Who calls so loud ?
ROMEO
Come hither, man. I see that thou art poor.
Hold, there is forty ducats. Let me have
60 A dram of poison, such soon-speeding gear
As will disperse itself through all the veins
That the life-weary taker may fall dead,
And that the trunk may be discharged of breath
As violently as hasty powder fired
65 Doth hurry from the fatal cannon's womb.
APOTHECARY
66 Such mortal drugs I have ; but Mantua's law
67 Is death to any he that utters them.
ROMEO
Art thou so bare and full of wretchedness
And fearest to die ? Famine is in thy cheeks,
70 Need and oppression starveth in thy eyes,
Contempt and beggary hangs upon thy back :
The world is not thy friend, nor the world's law ;
The world affords no law to make thee rich ;
Then be not poor, but break it and take this.
APOTHECARY
My poverty but not my will consents.
ROMEO
I pay thy poverty and not thy will.
APOTHECARY
Put this in any liquid thing you will
And drink it off, and if you had the strength
Of twenty men, it would dispatch you straight.

ROMEO
There is thy gold – worse poison to men's souls,
Doing more murder in this loathsome world,
Than these poor compounds that thou mayst not sell.
I sell thee poison ; thou hast sold me none.
Farewell. Buy food and get thyself in flesh.
Come, cordial and not poison, go with me
To Juliet's grave ; for there must I use thee.   *Exeunt.*

                              *

      Enter Friar John to Friar Laurence.   V, ii
JOHN
Holy Franciscan friar, brother, ho !
      Enter [Friar] Laurence.
LAURENCE
This same should be the voice of Friar John.
Welcome from Mantua. What says Romeo ?
Or, if his mind be writ, give me his letter.
JOHN
Going to find a barefoot brother out,   5
One of our order, to associate me   6
Here in this city visiting the sick,
And finding him, the searchers of the town,   8
Suspecting that we both were in a house
Where the infectious pestilence did reign,   10
Sealed up the doors, and would not let us forth,
So that my speed to Mantua there was stayed.
LAURENCE
Who bare my letter, then, to Romeo ?
JOHN
I could not send it – here it is again –
Nor get a messenger to bring it thee,
So fearful were they of infection.
LAURENCE
Unhappy fortune ! By my brotherhood,   17
The letter was not nice, but full of charge,   18
Of dear import ; and the neglecting it
May do much danger. Friar John, go hence,
Get me an iron crow and bring it straight   21
Unto my cell.
JOHN   Brother, I'll go and bring it thee.   *Exit.*
LAURENCE
Now must I to the monument alone.
Within this three hours will fair Juliet wake.
She will beshrew me much that Romeo   25
Hath had no notice of these accidents ;   26
But I will write again to Mantua,
And keep her at my cell till Romeo come –
Poor living corse, closed in a dead man's tomb ! *Exit.*

                              *

    Enter Paris and his Page [with flowers and sweet   V, iii
    water].
PARIS
Give me thy torch, boy. Hence, and stand aloof.
Yet put it out, for I would not be seen.
Under yond yew tree lay thee all along,   3
Holding thy ear close to the hollow ground.
So shall no foot upon the churchyard tread
(Being loose, unfirm, with digging up of graves)

39 *weeds* garments; *overwhelming* overhanging 40 *simples* herbs 45
account quantity 47 *cakes of roses* compressed rose petals, used for
perfume 52 *caitiff* miserable 60 *gear* stuff 65 *womb* i.e. barrel 66 *mortal*
deadly 67 *utters* gives out 70 *starveth* are revealed by the starved look
V, ii Friar Laurence's cell 5 *a barefoot brother* another friar 6 *associate*
accompany 8 *searchers* health officers 10 *pestilence* plague 17 *brother-*
hood order (Franciscans) 18 *nice* trivial; *charge* important matters
21 *crow* crowbar 25 *beshrew* reprove 26 *accidents* occurrences
V, iii A churchyard in Verona s.d. *with . . . water* (from Q1); *sweet*
perfumed 3 *all along* at full length

But thou shalt hear it. Whistle then to me,
As signal that thou hearest something approach.
Give me those flowers. Do as I bid thee, go.

PAGE [aside]
I am almost afraid to stand alone
Here in the churchyard ; yet I will adventure.   [Retires.]

PARIS
Sweet flower, with flowers thy bridal bed I strew
  (O woe ! thy canopy is dust and stones)
Which with sweet water nightly I will dew ;
  Or, wanting that, with tears distilled by moans.
The obsequies that I for thee will keep
Nightly shall be to strew thy grave and weep.
         Whistle Boy.
The boy gives warning something doth approach.
What cursèd foot wanders this way to-night

20 To cross my obsequies and true love's rite ?
21 What, with a torch ? Muffle me, night, awhile.   [Retires.]
      Enter Romeo [and Balthasar with a torch, a mattock,
      and a crow of iron].

ROMEO
Give me that mattock and the wrenching iron.
Hold, take this letter. Early in the morning
See thou deliver it to my lord and father.
Give me the light. Upon thy life I charge thee,
Whate'er thou hearest or seest, stand all aloof
And do not interrupt me in my course.
Why I descend into this bed of death
Is partly to behold my lady's face,
But chiefly to take thence from her dead finger

31 A precious ring – a ring that I must use
In dear employment. Therefore hence, be gone.

33 But if thou, jealous, dost return to pry
In what I farther shall intend to do,
By heaven, I will tear thee joint by joint
And strew this hungry churchyard with thy limbs.
The time and my intents are savage-wild,
More fierce and more inexorable far
Than empty tigers or the roaring sea.

BALTHASAR
I will be gone, sir, and not trouble you.

ROMEO
41 So shalt thou show me friendship. Take thou that.
Live, and be prosperous ; and farewell, good fellow.

BALTHASAR [aside]
For all this same, I'll hide me hereabout.
His looks I fear, and his intents I doubt.   [Retires.]

ROMEO
Thou detestable maw, thou womb of death,
Gorged with the dearest morsel of the earth,
Thus I enforce thy rotten jaws to open,
48 And in despite I'll cram thee with more food.
      [Romeo opens the tomb.]

PARIS
This is that banished haughty Montague
That murd'red my love's cousin – with which grief
It is supposèd the fair creature died –
And here is come to do some villainous shame
53 To the dead bodies. I will apprehend him.
Stop thy unhallowèd toil, vile Montague !
Can vengeance be pursued further than death ?
Condemnèd villain, I do apprehend thee.
Obey, and go with me ; for thou must die.

ROMEO
I must indeed ; and therefore came I hither.
Good gentle youth, tempt not a desp'rate man.
Fly hence and leave me. Think upon these gone ;   60
Let them affright thee. I beseech thee, youth,
Put not another sin upon my head
By urging me to fury. O, be gone !
By heaven, I love thee better than myself,
For I come hither armed against myself.
Stay not, be gone. Live, and hereafter say
A madman's mercy bid thee run away.

PARIS
I do defy thy conjuration   68
And apprehend thee for a felon here.

ROMEO
Wilt thou provoke me ? Then have at thee, boy !
      [They fight.]

PAGE
O Lord, they fight ! I will go call the watch.
         [Exit. Paris falls.]

PARIS
O, I am slain ! If thou be merciful,
Open the tomb, lay me with Juliet.
      [Dies.]

ROMEO
In faith, I will. Let me peruse this face.   74
Mercutio's kinsman, noble County Paris !
What said my man when my betossèd soul
Did not attend him as we rode ? I think   77
He told me Paris should have married Juliet.
Said he not so ? or did I dream it so ?
Or am I mad, hearing him talk of Juliet,
To think it was so ? O, give me thy hand,
One writ with me in sour misfortune's book !
I'll bury thee in a triumphant grave.
A grave ? O, no, a lanthorn, slaught'red youth,   84
For here lies Juliet, and her beauty makes
This vault a feasting presence full of light.   86
Death, lie thou there, by a dead man interred.
      [Lays him in the tomb.]
How oft when men are at the point of death
Have they been merry ! which their keepers call   89
A lightning before death. O, how may I   90
Call this a lightning ? O my love ! my wife !
Death, that hath sucked the honey of thy breath,
Hath had no power yet upon thy beauty.
Thou are not conquered. Beauty's ensign yet   94
Is crimson in thy lips and in thy cheeks,
And death's pale flag is not advancèd there.
Tybalt, liest thou there in thy bloody sheet ?
O, what more favor can I do to thee
Than with that hand that cut thy youth in twain
To sunder his that was thine enemy ?
Forgive me, cousin ! Ah, dear Juliet,

---

20 *cross* interfere with   **21 s.d.** *and Balthasar . . . iron* (from Q1 ; Q2 reads 'Enter Romeo and Peter.') ; *mattock* pickaxe   **31** *A precious ring* (a false excuse to assure Balthasar's non-interference)   **33** *jealous* curious, jealous of my privacy   **41** *that* (a purse)   **48** *in despite* to spite you ; **s.d.** (from Q1)   **53** *apprehend* arrest   **60** *gone* dead   **68** *conjuration* threatening appeal   **74** *peruse* read, look at   **77** *attend* pay attention to   **84** *lanthorn* lantern (a many-windowed turret room)   **86** *presence* presence chamber   **89** *keepers* jailers   **90** *A lightning before death* (a common phrase for the phenomenon described)   **94** *ensign* banner

102 Why art thou yet so fair? Shall I believe
That unsubstantial Death is amorous,
And that the lean abhorrèd monster keeps
Thee here in dark to be his paramour?
For fear of that I still will stay with thee
And never from this pallet of dim night
108 Depart again. Here, here will I remain
With worms that are thy chambermaids. O, here
110 Will I set up my everlasting rest
111 And shake the yoke of inauspicious stars
From this world-wearied flesh. Eyes, look your last!
Arms, take your last embrace! and, lips, O you
The doors of breath, seal with a righteous kiss
115 A dateless bargain to engrossing death!
116 Come, bitter conduct; come, unsavory guide!
117 Thou desperate pilot, now at once run on
118 The dashing rocks thy seasick weary bark!
119 Here's to my love! *[Drinks.]* O true apothecary!
Thy drugs are quick. Thus with a kiss I die.
[Falls.]
Enter Friar [Laurence], with lanthorn, crow, and spade.

FRIAR
121 Saint Francis be my speed! how oft to-night
122 Have my old feet stumbled at graves! Who's there?
BALTHASAR
Here's one, a friend, and one that knows you well.
FRIAR
Bliss be upon you! Tell me, good my friend,
What torch is yond that vainly lends his light
To grubs and eyeless skulls? As I discern,
It burneth in the Capels' monument.
BALTHASAR
It doth so, holy sir; and there's my master,
One that you love.
FRIAR   Who is it?
BALTHASAR   Romeo.
FRIAR
How long hath he been there?
BALTHASAR   Full half an hour.
FRIAR
Go with me to the vault.
BALTHASAR   I dare not, sir.
My master knows not but I am gone hence,
And fearfully did menace me with death
If I did stay to look on his intents.
FRIAR
Stay then; I'll go alone. Fear comes upon me.
136 O, much I fear some ill unthrifty thing.
BALTHASAR
As I did sleep under this yew tree here,

I dreamt my master and another fought,
And that my master slew him.
FRIAR   Romeo!
Alack, alack, what blood is this which stains
The stony entrance of this sepulchre?
What mean these masterless and gory swords
To lie discolored by this place of peace?
[Enters the tomb.]
Romeo! O, pale! Who else? What, Paris too?
And steeped in blood? Ah, what an unkind hour
Is guilty of this lamentable chance!
The lady stirs.
[Juliet rises.]
JULIET
O comfortable friar! where is my lord?   148
I do remember well where I should be,
And there I am. Where is my Romeo?
FRIAR
I hear some noise. Lady, come from that nest
Of death, contagion, and unnatural sleep.
A greater power than we can contradict
Hath thwarted our intents. Come, come away.
Thy husband in thy bosom there lies dead;
And Paris too. Come, I'll dispose of thee
Among a sisterhood of holy nuns.
Stay not to question, for the watch is coming.
Come, go, good Juliet. I dare no longer stay.
JULIET
Go, get thee hence, for I will not away.   *Exit [Friar].*
What's here? A cup, closed in my true love's hand?
Poison, I see, hath been his timeless end.   162
O churl! drunk all, and left no friendly drop
To help me after? I will kiss thy lips.
Haply some poison yet doth hang on them
To make me die with a restorative.   166
[Kisses him.]
Thy lips are warm!
CHIEF WATCHMAN *[within]* Lead, boy. Which way?
JULIET
Yea, noise? Then I'll be brief. O happy dagger!   169
[Snatches Romeo's dagger.]
This is thy sheath; there rust, and let me die.   170
[She stabs herself and falls.]
Enter [Paris's] Boy and Watch.
BOY
This is the place. There, where the torch doth burn.
CHIEF WATCHMAN
The ground is bloody. Search about the churchyard.
Go, some of you; whoe'er you find attach.
[Exeunt some of the Watch.]
Pitiful sight! here lies the County slain;
And Juliet bleeding, warm, and newly dead,
Who here hath lain this two days burièd.
Go, tell the Prince; run to the Capulets;
Raise up the Montagues; some others search.
[Exeunt others of the Watch.]
We see the ground whereon these woes do lie,
But the true ground of all these piteous woes   180
We cannot without circumstance descry.   181
Enter [some of the Watch, with] Romeo's Man
[Balthasar].
2. WATCHMAN
Here's Romeo's man. We found him in the churchyard.

102 *Why . . . fair* (followed in Q2 by a superfluous 'I will believe,' evidently another manuscript cancellation printed in error) 108 *again. Here* (Q2 prints between these words the following material, obviously cancelled in the manuscript because it appears in substance later in the speech: 'come lie thou in my arm. Here's to thy health, where e'er thou tumblest in. O true Apothecary! Thy drugs are quick. Thus with a kiss I die. Depart again.') 110 *set . . . rest* make my decision to stay forever (cf. IV, v, 6) 111 *inauspicious stars* (cf. V, i, 24) 115 *dateless* in perpetuity; *engrossing* taking everything 116 *conduct* guide, i.e. the poison 117 *pilot* i.e. Romeo's soul 118 *bark* i.e. Romeo's body 119 *Here's to my love* (cf. IV, iii, 58) 121 *speed* aid 122 *stumbled at graves* (a bad omen) 136 *unthrifty* unfortunate 148 *comfortable* comfort-giving 162 *timeless* untimely 166 *restorative* i.e. restoring me to you 169 *happy* opportune 170 *rust* (Q1 'rest') 180 *ground* basis 181 *circumstance* details

CHIEF WATCHMAN
Hold him in safety till the Prince come hither.
Enter Friar [Laurence] and another Watchman.

3. WATCHMAN
Here is a friar that trembles, sighs, and weeps.
We took this mattock and this spade from him
As he was coming from this churchyard side.

CHIEF WATCHMAN
A great suspicion! Stay the friar too.
Enter the Prince [and Attendants].

PRINCE
What misadventure is so early up,
189   That calls our person from our morning rest?
Enter Capulet and his Wife [with others].

CAPULET
What should it be, that is so shrieked abroad?

WIFE
O the people in the street cry 'Romeo,'
Some 'Juliet,' and some 'Paris'; and all run,
With open outcry, toward our monument.

PRINCE
What fear is this which startles in your ears?

CHIEF WATCHMAN
Sovereign, here lies the County Paris slain;
And Romeo dead; and Juliet, dead before,
Warm and new killed.

PRINCE
Search, seek, and know how this foul murder comes.

CHIEF WATCHMAN
Here is a friar, and slaughtered Romeo's man,
With instruments upon them fit to open
These dead men's tombs.

CAPULET
O heavens! O wife, look how our daughter bleeds!
203   This dagger hath mista'en, for, lo, his house
Is empty on the back of Montague,
And it missheathèd in my daughter's bosom!

WIFE
O me! this sight of death is as a bell
207   That warns my old age to a sepulchre.
Enter Montague [and others].

PRINCE
Come, Montague; for thou art early up
To see thy son and heir more early down.

MONTAGUE
Alas, my liege, my wife is dead to-night!
Grief of my son's exile hath stopped her breath.
What further woe conspires against mine age?

PRINCE
Look, and thou shalt see.

MONTAGUE
O thou untaught! what manners is in this,
To press before thy father to a grave?

PRINCE
216   Seal up the mouth of outrage for a while,
Till we can clear these ambiguities
And know their spring, their head, their true descent;
219   And then will I be general of your woes
220   And lead you even to death. Meantime forbear,
And let mischance be slave to patience.
Bring forth the parties of suspicion.

FRIAR
I am the greatest, able to do least,
Yet most suspected, as the time and place

Doth make against me, of this direful murder;
And here I stand, both to impeach and purge   226
Myself condemnèd and myself excused.

PRINCE
Then say at once what thou dost know in this.

FRIAR
I will be brief, for my short date of breath   229
Is not so long as is a tedious tale.
Romeo, there dead, was husband to that Juliet;
And she, there dead, that Romeo's faithful wife.
I married them; and their stol'n marriage day
Was Tybalt's doomsday, whose untimely death
Banished the new-made bridegroom from this city;
For whom, and not for Tybalt, Juliet pined.
You, to remove that siege of grief from her,
Betrothed and would have married her perforce   238
To County Paris. Then comes she to me
And with wild looks bid me devise some mean
To rid her from this second marriage,
Or in my cell there would she kill herself.
Then gave I her (so tutored by my art)
A sleeping potion; which so took effect
As I intended, for it wrought on her
The form of death. Meantime I writ to Romeo
That he should hither come as this dire night   247
To help to take her from her borrowèd grave,
Being the time the potion's force should cease.
But he which bore my letter, Friar John,
Was stayed by accident, and yesternight
Returned my letter back. Then all alone
At the prefixèd hour of her waking
Came I to take her from her kindred's vault;
Meaning to keep her closely at my cell   255
Till I conveniently could send to Romeo.
But when I came, some minute ere the time
Of her awakening, here untimely lay
The noble Paris and true Romeo dead.
She wakes; and I entreated her come forth
And bear this work of heaven with patience;
But then a noise did scare me from the tomb,
And she, too desperate, would not go with me,
But, as it seems, did violence on herself.
All this I know, and to the marriage
Her nurse is privy; and if aught in this   266
Miscarried by my fault, let my old life
Be sacrificed, some hour before his time,
Unto the rigor of severest law.

PRINCE
We still have known thee for a holy man.   270
Where's Romeo's man? What can he say in this?

BALTHASAR
I brought my master news of Juliet's death;
And then in post he came from Mantua
To this same place, to this same monument.
This letter he early bid me give his father,

---

189 s.d. *Enter ... Wife* (in Q2 'Enter Capels' appears here, with the present stage direction after l. 201) 203 *his house* its sheath 207 *my old age* (she is only twenty-eight – I, iii, 72–73 – but she feels old and ready for death; cf. III, ii, 89) 216 *mouth of outrage* violent outcries 219 *general ... woes* your leader in lamentation 220 *even to death* even if grief kills us 226 *impeach and purge* accuse and exonerate 229 *date of breath* life expectancy 238 *perforce* by force 247 *as* on 255 *closely* secretly 266 *privy* in the secret 270 *still* always

And threat'ned me with death, going in the vault,
If I departed not and left him there.

PRINCE
Give me the letter. I will look on it.
Where is the County's page that raised the watch?
280   Sirrah, what made your master in this place?

BOY
He came with flowers to strew his lady's grave;
And bid me stand aloof, and so I did.
283   Anon comes one with light to ope the tomb;
284   And by and by my master drew on him;
And then I ran away to call the watch.

PRINCE
This letter doth make good the friar's words,
Their course of love, the tidings of her death;
And here he writes that he did buy a poison
Of a poor pothecary, and therewithal
Came to this vault to die, and lie with Juliet.
Where be these enemies? Capulet, Montague,
See what a scourge is laid upon your hate,
That heaven finds means to kill your joys with love.   293
And I, for winking at your discords too,   294
Have lost a brace of kinsmen. All are punished.

CAPULET
O brother Montague, give me thy hand.
This is my daughter's jointure, for no more   297
Can I demand.

MONTAGUE   But I can give thee more;
For I will raise her statue in pure gold,
That whiles Verona by that name is known,
There shall no figure at such rate be set   301
As that of true and faithful Juliet.

CAPULET
As rich shall Romeo's by his lady's lie –
Poor sacrifices of our enmity!

PRINCE
A glooming peace this morning with it brings.   305
   The sun for sorrow will not show his head.
Go hence, to have more talk of these sad things;
   Some shall be pardoned, and some punishèd;
For never was a story of more woe
Than this of Juliet and her Romeo.   *[Exeunt omnes.]*

280 *made* did   283 *Anon* soon   284 *by and by* almost at once; *drew* drew his
sword   293 *with* by means of   294 *winking at* shutting my eyes to   297
jointure marriage portion   301 *rate* value   305 *glooming* cloudy, overcast

APPENDIX: DEPARTURES FROM THE 1599 QUARTO

The only departures from the copy-text (second quarto, 1599) are listed below, except for relineations, corrections of obvious typographical errors, added stage directions (in brackets), and the treatment of cancelled passages (explained in the notes). Variants in speech prefixes within a scene have been regularized without comment. All the listed readings have been adopted from the first quarto, 1597, except those marked Q3 (third quarto, 1609), Q4 (fourth quarto, n.d.), F1 (first folio, 1623), F2 (second folio, 1632), F4 (fourth folio, 1683), and Eds (emendation, usually made quite early in the history of Shakespearean textual study and still generally accepted by modern editors). The adopted reading in italics is followed by the reading of the copy-text in roman.

I, i, 21 *cruel* (Q4) civil   26 *in sense* sense   30 *comes two* comes   60 *swashing* (Q4) washing   85 *mistemp'red* mistemperèd   118 *drave* (F1) drive   151 *sun* (Eds) same   175 *create* created   177 *well-seeming* well-seeing   188 *raised* made   190 *lovers'* loving   200 *Bid a sick* A sick   *make* makes   201 *Ah* A   209 *unharmed* uncharmed   216 *makes* (Q4) make
I, ii, 32 *on more view* (Q4) one more view   70 *and Livia* Livia
I, iii, 66, 67 *honor* hour   99 *make it fly* make fly
I, iv, 39 *done* dum   42 *Of this sir-reverence* Or save your reverence   45 *like lamps* lights lights   47 *five wits* fine wits   66 *maid* man   72 *O'er courtiers'* On courtiers   81 *dreams he* he dreams   113 *sail* suit
I, v, 18 *Ah ha* Ah   95 *ready* did ready
II, i, 10 *pronounce* prouaunt   *dove* day   12 *heir* her   38 *et cetera,* or
II, ii, 31 *pacing* puffing   41 *nor any other part* (omitted in Q2)   44 *name* word   83 *washed* (F2) washeth   99 *havior* behavior   101 *more cunning* coying   110 *circled* circle   153 *suit* (Q4) strife   163 *mine* (omitted in Q2)   168 *sweet* (F2) Neece   *At what* What   179 *her* his   189 *father's* friar's close
II, iii, 4 *fiery* burning   22 *sometime's* sometime   74 *ring yet* yet ringing   85 *She whom* Her
II, iv, 19 *I can tell you* (omitted in Q2)   28 *fantasticoes* fantasies   96 (spoken by Romeo in Q2)   97 (spoken by Mercutio in Q2)   109 *for* (omitted in Q2)   187 *I warrant* (F2) Warrant   197 *Ah* (Eds) A
II, v, 26 *have I had* (F2) have I
III, i, 106 *soundly too. Your* (Eds) soundly, to your   120 *Alive He gan*   122 *eyed* end   145 *O husband* (Eds) O cousin, husband   164 *agile* aged   186 *hate's* hearts
III, ii, 9 *By* (F2) And by   21 *he* (Q4) I   49 *the* (F2) thee   51 *determine of* (F1) determine   76 *Dove-feathered* (Eds) Ravenous dove-feathered   79 *damnèd* (F2) dimme
III, iii, 15 *Hence* Here   52 *Thou* Then   117 *lives* (F4) lies   138 *happy too* happy   143 *misbehaved* mishavèd   144 *pout'st upon* (Eds) puts up   163 *is* sir
III, iv, 34 *very very* very
III, v, 13 *exhales* exhale   83 *pardon him* (F2) pardon   182 *trained* liand
IV, i, 7 *talked* talk   45 *cure* care   46 *Ah* O   72 *slay* stay   83 *chapless* chapels   85 *his shroud* (Q4) his   98 *breath* breast   100 *wanny* (Eds) many   116 *waking* (Q3) walking
IV, iii, 58 *Romeo . . . thee* Romeo, Romeo, Romeo, here's drink, I drink to thee
IV, v, 41 *long* love   65 *cure* (Eds) care   81 *In all* And in   82 *fond* (F2) some   104 *full of woe* (Q4) full   129, 132 *Pretty* Prates

V, i, 15 *fares my* doth my Lady   24 *defy* deny   76 *pay* pray
V, iii, 3 *yew tree* young trees   68 *conjuration* commiration   137 *yew* (Q3) young   190 *shrieked* (Eds) shrike   209 *more early* now earling   232 *that* that's

SUPPLEMENTARY NOTE

III, ii, 49 *Or those eyes' shot that makes the answer 'I'*

Almost every editor since Capell except H. R. Hoppe (Crofts, 1943) has accepted his emendation *shut* for *shot*, reading "Or those eyes shut that make(s) thee answer 'I' [Ay]." Our copy-text, Q2, reads: "Or those eyes shot, that makes thee answer I." This reading is retained by the later quartos and folios, except that *thee* is emended to *the* in F2, F3, and F4.

I have supplied the apostrophe which makes *eyes* a possessive. Since Q2 regularly omits the apostrophe, as in "eyes windows" (IV, i, 100), supplying it does no violence to the text. *Shot* becomes a noun instead of a past participle. A usage similar to this appears in *Cymbeline*, I, i, 89–90, when Imogen says, "And I shall here abide the hourly shot / Of angry eyes."

If we interpret the passage as emended by Capell, Juliet refers to Romeo's eyes closed in death; or else she refers to the Nurse's eyes which, if shut, will indicate *ay*. If, as I think, the Nurse's eyes are meant, *shot* is the more logical reading. Juliet is studying the Nurse's face and may receive her answer from the Nurse's voice or, failing that, from the Nurse's eyes. Either form of affirmative, the spoken *ay* or the revelatory eye-glance (*eyes' shot*), will slay Juliet, who feels that her life is bound up with that of Romeo. As the eye-glance of the cockatrice (basilisk) darts death, so will the spoken *ay* or the eye-glance of the Nurse. This implies no malice on the part of the Nurse, since it is her message which may be fatal to Juliet.

Involved here is the Elizabethan theory of vision, or the act of seeing. It was believed that the eye darted forth a stream of very fine particles which pierced or fastened upon the beheld object and then relayed impulses back to the sender. The arrow was the appropriate image for such an eye-glance. Thus, Juliet promises her mother to look at Paris, "But no more deep will I endart mine eye" than her mother wishes (I, iii, 98). Such imagery is very common in the works of Shakespeare and his contemporaries.

If one retains *thee* as the correct reading, Juliet's meaning is as follows: "I am not myself if there be such a spoken *ay* or if there be your eye-glance that forces you to answer 'Ay.'" This makes sense after a fashion, but I have adopted the less tortuous reading of the later folios, changing *thee* to *the*. Juliet's meaning then becomes: "I am not myself if there be such a spoken *ay* or if there be your eye-glance that forms the answer 'Ay.'"

In support of the interpretation here given, we may notice that Mercutio pictures Romeo as being "dead," pierced by vision and by sound: "stabbed with a white wench's black eye; run through the ear with a love song" (II, iv, 14–15). So it is with Juliet. The spoken *ay* of the Nurse may slay her through the ear as effectively as the visual eye-dart of the cockatrice. Likewise, the Nurse's "eyes' shot," if it reveals the unspoken *ay*, will kill visually as effectively as her voice would kill through the ear.

JULIUS CAESAR

INTRODUCTION

Despite its apparent simplicity, this play has occasioned opposite interpretations. For some critics, Caesar is, in Antony's words, "the noblest man / That ever livèd in the tide of times" and the assassination a senseless act of criminal folly, while for others Caesar is an ambitious tyrant and the assassination a valiant attempt by patriotic Romans to preserve the Republic. These views of the play correspond to contrasting views of the historical events it dramatizes – the medieval condemnation of Brutus and Cassius, as in Dante and Chaucer, and the Renaissance condemnation of Caesar, as in Machiavelli, Elyot, Montaigne, Sidney, Marlowe, Harington, and Jonson. Shakespeare himself reflects the medieval view in his early trilogy on the reign of Henry VI and the Renaissance view in plays written in the late 1590's and after. As a practical dramatist, however, he was not concerned to teach his audience a particular interpretation of history, as he had to some extent been forced to do in his English chronicle plays; rather, he knew that the more and less educated members of his audience would tend to hold, respectively, the Renaissance and medieval views, and he chose to fashion his play in such a way that it should take advantage of the preconceptions of both sections of his audience. The result is a structure of sustained dramatic ambiguities that are resolved only in the latter part of the play, a method of construction that he was to use with even more brilliant and controversial effect in his next tragedy, *Hamlet*.

Julius Caesar was probably first produced at the new Globe Theatre in the fall of 1599, some months after the appearance of *Henry V*, the last of the nine English histories that Shakespeare wrote in the 1590's, and shortly before the appearance of a comedy with the significant title *As You Like It*. The history and the comedy are culminations of established interests on Shakespeare's part; *The Tragedy of Julius Caesar*, although Shakespeare had already written highly popular tragedies, is a new departure, an important turning-point midway in his career as England's most popular dramatist. He had abandoned English history, was soon to abandon romantic comedy, and was about to undertake his series of great heroic tragedies, to be framed, as it turned out, by four tragedies based on Sir Thomas North's translation of Plutarch's *Lives*, the literary source that Shakespeare seems most to have respected and admired.

With *Julius Caesar* he turned for the first time from Holinshed's *Chronicles* of English history to Plutarch's comparative studies of the careers of great men of Greece and Rome. He was turning from English to Roman history for subject matter, but more significantly he was turning from history to tragedy. His earlier English histories had indeed been tragical, although the later ones must more

aptly be termed comical, and they had finally to take an intensely patriotic view of the civil wars that led to the accession of Henry VII, the first of the Tudors. Even his other tragedies, unlike those drawn from Plutarch, end with the destruction of the forces of evil and the belated victory of the good forces that survive. The Plutarchan tragedies, particularly those concerned with the Roman civil wars, with the decline and fall of the Roman Republic, are more ironic; the forces that prevail at the ends of these tragedies cannot easily be seen as forces of good, and they are, in each case, forces hostile to the tragic heroes. For Brutus is the tragic hero of *Julius Caesar*; Caesar himself, or more properly "the spirit of Caesar" as embodied in Octavius, is the historic victor.

To men of the Renaissance, Republican Rome was the apex of human achievement in civilization and political organization, although without benefit of Christianity. Its heroes, whether legendary or historical, were held in reverence as notable examples of patriotism, military valor, and the pagan virtues. In his popular poem *The Rape of Lucrece* Shakespeare had written of two of the legendary figures, the chaste Lucrece and the patriot Junius Brutus, founder of the Republic and reputed ancestor of Marcus Brutus. In *Julius Caesar* the names of two other admired Romans, Pompey and Cato of Utica, are invoked to lend moral weight to the Republican cause, for both had been destroyed by Caesar as the renowned Cicero was to be destroyed by Caesar's followers.

The play opens with the tribunes of the people, whose function it was to safeguard and maintain popular liberties, using Pompey's memory to dissuade the fickle plebeians from participating in Caesar's triumph over fellow Romans; they express the Republican fear that Caesar seeks to rob the Romans of their ancient liberties. In the next scene, Caesar's ambition to be crowned, a move which if successful would reduce the Republic to a monarchy, is vividly communicated as an off-stage action accompanying Cassius' attempt to persuade Brutus to lead a conspiracy against Caesar. Caesar's scheme to have himself crowned by popular acclaim would surely have reminded many in Shakespeare's audience of the similar scheme used by the usurping tyrant Richard III, as Shakespeare had dramatized it. In both cases, the unwillingness of the people to go along with the scheme frustrates it, and the schemers must resort to other devices to get themselves crowned. The center of interest in this play, however, is not the progress of Caesar and his followers; it is the impact of "the spirit of Caesar" on his fellow Romans, particularly on Brutus, who must choose between his personal friendship for Caesar and his public responsibility, both as a Roman and as a praetor, to prevent the subversion of the Republic. This is his tragic dilemma and Shakespeare's major interest in the first two acts of the play.

Brutus, from the first, is "with himself at war" and deeply concerned for "the general good." His soliloquy at the beginning of Act II, the first of Shakespeare's famous deliberative soliloquies, dramatizes his attempt to resolve his inner conflict. The question is not whether or not Caesar must be killed for the general good – Brutus has already decided that he must be – but how Brutus can reconcile his political decision as a public man with his conscience as a private man: "I know no personal cause to spurn at him, / But for the general." In the rest of the soliloquy, as Coleridge failed to perceive but as Kittredge points out, Brutus considers Caesar as a private man and can find nothing to justify his assassination. By means of the commonplace, however, that absolute power usually corrupts absolutely, he is able to bring his personal feelings into line with his sense of public duty. Yet he is not comfortable with his decision – "all the interim is / Like a phantasma or a hideous dream" – and he continues to distinguish between Caesar the man and Caesar the would-be king and probable tyrant:

> Let's be sacrificers, but not butchers, Caius.
> We all stand up against the spirit of Caesar,
> And in the spirit of men there is no blood.
> O that we then could come by Caesar's spirit
> And not dismember Caesar! But, alas,
> Caesar must bleed for it.

That is what he says privately to the other conspirators; it is an essential part of his public explanation to the plebeians in the Forum: "Not that I loved Caesar less, but that I loved Rome more. . . . As Caesar loved me, I weep for him ; . . . as he was ambitious, I slew him."

Cassius and Antony, unlike Brutus, are unscrupulous politicians of the sort that the Elizabethans called Machiavellian. Both place personal gain above the general good. They are, respectively, the dominant villains of the first and second halves of the play. Cassius' soliloquy at the end of Act I, scene ii, is quite as much like the soliloquies of Iago as is Antony's brief soliloquy after he has delivered his masterpiece of demagogic rhetoric: "Now let it work. Mischief, thou art afoot, / Take thou what course thou wilt." Cassius, for all his political shrewdness, must defer to Brutus – as Antony must later defer to Octavius – since Brutus had been chosen to lead the conspiracy just because his known integrity, "like richest alchemy," would make it seem worthy and virtuous. Plutarch analyzes Brutus' failure to preserve the Republic as the result of two major political "mistakes": his refusal to kill Caesar's chief supporters, notably Antony, along with Caesar, and his permission that Antony speak at Caesar's funeral. Some critics find a third "mistake" in Brutus' decision to meet the enemy at Philippi instead of letting them search out the Republican forces. Shakespeare has Cassius propose shrewder alternatives to each of these choices, but in each case Cassius is a foil to Brutus, whose nobility as tragic hero is only the more enhanced by his rejections of Cassius' politic proposals.

The one episode in which Cassius passionately stands up to Brutus, though he is as usual overridden by him, is the famous quarrel scene in Act IV. Here Brutus is most nearly disillusioned about the motives of his fellow conspirators:

> Did not great Julius bleed for justice sake?
> What villain touched his body that did stab
> And not for justice? What, shall one of us,
> That struck the foremost man of all this world
> But for supporting robbers – shall we now
> Contaminate our fingers with base bribes . . . ?

Shakespeare has shown us, at the beginning of Act IV, those robbers, the triumvirate, about their work, with Antony cast in the most villainous role of the three. Many in Shakespeare's audience must have been reminded of the proverbial lack of honor among thieves, which finally, as Shakespeare was to dramatize it in *Antony and Cleopatra*, works to the advantage of Octavius Caesar, the coldest, youngest, and most cunning of the three. In this play, Octavius overrides Antony, much as Brutus overrides Cassius, and the fact that Octavius is given the final speech of the play, generally assigned in both the tragedies and the histories to the highest-ranking of the surviving figures, foreshadows his defeat of Antony.

Antony is at least capable of feeling, and his lamentation over the corpse of Caesar makes him highly sympathetic in Act III, scene i. He and Cassius are opposite types, both of them foils for Brutus, who in some respects stands as a mean between their extremes. Antony is too "gamesome," "a masker and a reveller," and far from having Cassius' "lean and hungry look." Cassius "loves no plays," "hears no music," "reads much," and is envious. They are, respectively, excessive and deficient in their capacities for feeling, for "love," one of the key-words of the play. Brutus loves, and inspires love in others:

> My heart doth joy that yet in all my life
> I found no man but he was true to me.

Like Cassius he reads, like Antony he loves music, but he is not dissolute like the latter, nor envious like the former. His integrity, his honor, contrasts sharply with the conniving of Antony and Cassius. His love for Portia and his concern for the welfare of his servants (notably Lucius, who has no counterpart in Plutarch) heighten our sympathetic admiration of him. Antony's final speech in praise of Brutus directs our proper response to the tragic hero defeated by the spirit of Caesar:

> This was the noblest Roman of them all.
> All the conspirators save only he
> Did that they did in envy of great Caesar;
> He, only in a general honest thought
> And common good to all, made one of them.

Caesar himself is almost enigmatic. Brutus, after the assassination, calls him "the foremost man of all this world," yet Shakespeare presents him in his own person as a pompous, arrogant usurper, and in Cassius' description as a Colossus afflicted with unmanly weaknesses. He sees himself as the polestar and as Mount Olympus, yet he is associated with sterility, epilepsy, and deafness. He insists that he is unshakeable, yet Cassius tells us "How he did shake" and we see how he is shaken. Cassius sees him as a wolf, ferociously carnivorous, Antony as a hart, harmlessly herbivorous. Other images are applied to him, but the concept of Caesar as a diseased statue is the most powerful in the first movement of the play, where he is not so much an active force for evil as a static center of corruption. Even many of the medieval glorifiers of Caesar condemned him for the inordinate ambition that led to his assassination and the ultimate decline of Rome. Even the majority of Renaissance glorifiers of Brutus recognized Caesar's earlier greatness while condemning him for the subversion of the Republic. Shakespeare, while he is careful to disabuse his audience of the vulgar error that Caesar was actually the first of the Roman Emperors, gives the spirit of Caesar its historical due, but he seems to have thought to show Caesar himself as a victim of that blind infatuation, "security," that leads great men to their destruction. Caesar's *hubris* is more extraordinary than that of any other major figure in Shakespeare's plays.

After Brutus, Caesar, Cassius, and Antony, the plebeians are the most important "character" in the play. It is their corruption that defeats the Republican cause from the start. Brutus' major disillusionment, if this had been a history play, should have occurred at the very moment of his greatest apparent success – the moment when, after his plain and honest speech in the Forum, the plebeians shout "Let him be Caesar." "Caesar's better parts / Shall be crowned in Brutus." At this point Shakespeare's audience knew that the Roman mob was no longer capable of Republicanism, that the Romans, like themselves, might best be governed by a king. It is Brutus' nobility as a tragic hero, and his weakness as a political leader, not to have perceived this fact, of which Antony and Octavius will take such advantage. Yet the less politic Brutus is, the more heroic he can be made. Indeed Shakespeare, in transmuting the material he found in Plutarch's lives of Caesar, Antony, and Brutus, selected from and augmented that material in such a way as to make Brutus his centrally admirable figure, the high-minded man in a corrupt world.

Julius Caesar has been widely acclaimed for its essential truth to the spirit of ancient Rome, despite such evident anachronisms as chimney tops, striking clocks, and books with leaves. The contrast between Stoicism and Epicureanism, two of the dominant philosophic systems of the Romans, is clearly brought out. In fact, it is Cassius' shift from Epicureanism (which to the Elizabethans meant atheism) to a belief in portents that helps to make him a sympathetic figure at the end of the play. The anachronisms are not important. To the Elizabethans, excepting such purists as Ben Jonson, the play must have seemed pretty thoroughly Roman. Although there are certain homely references to details of costume that can only have been Elizabethan, there was probably, as we can surmise from a contemporary illustration of the staging of *Titus Andronicus*, an attempt to clothe the major figures in costumes that the Elizabethans thought of as Roman.

Even the style of the play seems to reflect a similar intention. It is unusually straightforward, having neither the lyric floridity of the earlier tragedies nor the condensed metaphoric texture of the later plays. The animal and hunting imagery is as forthright in its application as the frequent use of monosyllabic lines is forceful in its simplicity. Shakespeare subordinated poetry to rhetoric to gain his Roman effects. Rhetoric, the art of persuasion, is structural as well as stylistic in this play: the tribunes persuade the people not to honor Caesar, Cassius persuades Brutus to lead the conspiracy, Brutus persuades himself of the justice of his cause, Portia persuades Brutus to reveal his secret to her, Calphurnia persuades Caesar not to go forth, Decius persuades him to go, Brutus persuades the people to support the Republicans, Antony persuades them to mutiny. This persuasion and counter-persuasion reaches its climax with the speeches in the Forum, the turning-point of the play, after which the spirit of Caesar dominates and the Republic, along with the Republicans, is destroyed.

Shakespeare compresses events of three years into five dramatic "days," the first two of which account for the first three acts of the play, and he compresses the complexities of motives, as Plutarch discussed them, in order to gain momentum for his powerful rhetorical construction. Despite this compression, Shakespeare, following Plutarch, is concerned less with what happens than with why it happens, less with events than with interacting purposes, and this remains his major interest in his later plays. *Julius Caesar* never mounts to the passionate intensity of the greater tragedies that followed it – in this respect it is more stoically Roman than they – but it anticipates their pattern of heroic disillusionment, inner conflict, and the attempt to set right a time which is out of joint. Unlike his legendary ancestor, Junius Brutus, and unlike his immediate successor, Hamlet, Brutus does not accomplish his purpose. Elizabethans may have seen the triumph of Caesarism as Plutarch saw it – "the state of Rome (in my opinion) . . . could not more abide to be governed by many lords, but required one only absolute governor" – or even as an Elizabethan publisher saw it – "an evident demonstration that peoples' rule must give place, and Prince's power prevail." As the play presents it, however, the triumph of Caesarism is a matter of history making tragedy ironic. There is no restoration of a positive moral order to relieve the sense of tragic waste. Only the memory of Brutus' nobility, as his corpse is carried off, transcends the bleak facts of history at the end of the play:

> His life was gentle, and the elements
> So mixed in him that Nature might stand up
> And say to all the world, 'This was a man!'

Columbia University   S. F. JOHNSON

NOTE ON THE TEXT

Julius Caesar was first published in the folio of 1623, evidently from the playhouse prompt-book or a careful transcript of it. The folio text is divided into acts but not into scenes. The act–scene division supplied marginally for reference in the present edition is that of the later editors, and it needlessly indicates a break in the action at IV, iii, 1. The action in V, here printed continuously as in the folio, takes place in various parts of the plains of Philippi. Certain character names have here been normalized in the text as well as in speech-prefixes:

I, i, s.d. *Marullus* (F Murellus)
I, ii, s.d. *Marullus* (F Murellus)   282 *Marullus* (F Murrellus)   3, 4, 6, 190 *Antonius* (F Antonio)
I, iii, 37 *Antonius* (F Antonio)
III, i, 275 s.d. *Octavius* (F Octavio)
IV, iii, 242, 244, 244 s.d., 289 *Claudius* (F Claudio)   244, 244 s.d., 289 *Varro* (F Varrus)

V, ii, 4 *Octavius* (F Octavio)
V, iii, 108 *Labeo, Flavius* (F Labio, Flavio)

Throughout the play Caska is changed to *Casca*, and Lucillius to *Lucilius*. Otherwise the present edition adheres closely to the folio text, and admits only the following emendations in addition to the correction of obvious typographical errors. The adopted reading in italics is followed by the folio reading in roman.

I, iii, 129 *fev'rous* Fauors
II, i, 40 *ides* first
II, ii, 19 *fought* fight   23 *did neigh* do neigh   46 *are* heare
III, i, 113 *states* State   115 *lies* lye   283 *for* from
III, ii, 104 *art* are
V, iii, 104 *Thasos* Tharsus
V, iv, 17 *the news* thee news
V, v, 33 *to thee too, Strato. Countrymen,* to thee, to Strato, Countreymen:

JULIUS CAESAR

❋

I, i   Enter Flavius, Marullus, and certain Commoners
over the stage.

FLAVIUS
Hence! home, you idle creatures, get you home!
Is this a holiday? What, know you not,
3   Being mechanical, you ought not walk
4   Upon a laboring day without the sign
Of your profession? Speak, what trade art thou?
CARPENTER Why, sir, a carpenter.
MARULLUS
Where is thy leather apron and thy rule?
What dost thou with thy best apparel on?
You, sir, what trade are you?
10 COBBLER Truly, sir, in respect of a fine workman I am
11 but, as you would say, a cobbler.
MARULLUS
12 But what trade art thou? Answer me directly.

COBBLER A trade, sir, that I hope I may use with a safe
conscience, which is indeed, sir, a mender of bad soles.   14
FLAVIUS
What trade, thou knave? Thou naughty knave, what 15
trade?
COBBLER Nay, I beseech you, sir, be not out with me. 16
Yet if you be out, sir, I can mend you.   17
MARULLUS
What mean'st thou by that? Mend me, thou saucy
fellow?
COBBLER Why, sir, cobble you.
FLAVIUS
Thou art a cobbler, art thou?
COBBLER Truly, sir, all that I live by is with the awl. I
meddle with no tradesman's matters nor women's mat- 22
ters; but withal – I am indeed, sir, a surgeon to old shoes. 23
When they are in great danger, I recover them. As proper 24
men as ever trod upon neat's leather have gone upon my 25
handiwork.
FLAVIUS
But wherefore art not in thy shop to-day?
Why dost thou lead these men about the streets?
COBBLER Truly, sir, to wear out their shoes, to get my-
self into more work. But indeed, sir, we make holiday to
see Caesar and to rejoice in his triumph.   31
MARULLUS
Wherefore rejoice? What conquest brings he home?
What tributaries follow him to Rome   33

I, i A street in Rome   s.d. over the stage who cross the stage before halting
3 mechanical workers   4 sign tools and costume (which indicate a man's
trade)   10 in . . . workman as far as skilled work is concerned   11 cobbler
(with pun on 'bungler')   12 directly plainly   14 soles (with pun on
'souls')   15 naughty worthless   16 out angry   17 be out have worn-
out shoes; mend (with pun on 'reform')   22 meddle (with pun on 'am intimate')   23 withal nevertheless (with puns on 'all' and 'awl')   24 recover
re-sole (with pun on 'cure'); proper handsome   25 neat's cattle's (the
phrase is proverbial); gone walked   31 triumph victory procession   33
tributaries captives

To grace in captive bonds his chariot wheels?
You blocks, you stones, you worse than senseless
    things!
O you hard hearts, you cruel men of Rome.
37 Knew you not Pompey? Many a time and oft
Have you climbed up to walls and battlements,
To tow'rs and windows, yea, to chimney tops,
Your infants in your arms, and there have sat
The livelong day, with patient expectation,
To see great Pompey pass the streets of Rome.
And when you saw his chariot but appear,
Have you not made an universal shout,
45 That Tiber trembled underneath her banks
46 To hear the replication of your sounds
47 Made in her concave shores?
And do you now put on your best attire?
And do you now cull out a holiday?
And do you now strew flowers in his way
51 That comes in triumph over Pompey's blood?
Be gone!
Run to your houses, fall upon your knees,
54 Pray to the gods to intermit the plague
That needs must light on this ingratitude.

FLAVIUS
Go, go, good countrymen, and for this fault
Assemble all the poor men of your sort;
Draw them to Tiber banks, and weep your tears
Into the channel, till the lowest stream
60 Do kiss the most exalted shores of all.
                 Exeunt all the Commoners.
61 See, whe'r their basest mettle be not moved.
They vanish tongue-tied in their guiltiness.
Go you down that way towards the Capitol;
64 This way will I. Disrobe the images
65 If you do find them decked with ceremonies.

MARULLUS
May we do so?
67 You know it is the feast of Lupercal.

FLAVIUS
It is no matter. Let no images
69 Be hung with Caesar's trophies. I'll about
70 And drive away the vulgar from the streets.
So do you too, where you perceive them thick.
These growing feathers plucked from Caesar's wing
73 Will make him fly an ordinary pitch,
74 Who else would soar above the view of men
And keep us all in servile fearfulness.   *Exeunt.*

                 *

I, ii   *[Music.] Enter Caesar, Antony (for the course),*
       Calphurnia, Portia, Decius, Cicero, Brutus,
       Cassius, Casca, [a great crowd following, among
       them] a Soothsayer; after them, Marullus and
       Flavius.

CAESAR
Calphurnia.
CASCA   Peace, ho! Caesar speaks.
     [Music ceases.]
CAESAR   Calphurnia.
CALPHURNIA
Here, my lord.
CAESAR
Stand you directly in Antonius' way
4 When he doth run his course. Antonius.

ANTONY
Caesar, my lord?
CAESAR
Forget not in your speed, Antonius,
To touch Calphurnia; for our elders say
The barren, touchèd in this holy chase,
Shake off their sterile curse.
ANTONY   I shall remember.
When Caesar says 'Do this,' it is performed.
CAESAR
Set on, and leave no ceremony out.
     [Music.]
SOOTHSAYER Caesar!
CAESAR Ha! Who calls?
CASCA
Bid every noise be still. Peace yet again!
     [Music ceases.]
CAESAR
Who is it in the press that calls on me?   15
I hear a tongue shriller than all the music
Cry 'Caesar!' Speak. Caesar is turned to hear.
SOOTHSAYER
Beware the ides of March.   18
CAESAR   What man is that?
BRUTUS
A soothsayer bids you beware the ides of March.
CAESAR
Set him before me; let me see his face.
CASSIUS
Fellow, come from the throng; look upon Caesar.
CAESAR
What say'st thou to me now? Speak once again.
SOOTHSAYER
Beware the ides of March.
CAESAR
He is a dreamer. Let us leave him. Pass.   24
           Sennet. Exeunt. Mane[n]t Brutus and Cassius.
CASSIUS
Will you go see the order of the course?   25
BRUTUS Not I.
CASSIUS I pray you do.
BRUTUS
I am not gamesome. I do lack some part   28
Of that quick spirit that is in Antony.   29
Let me not hinder, Cassius, your desires.
I'll leave you.
CASSIUS
Brutus, I do observe you now of late;
I have not from your eyes that gentleness   33
And show of love as I was wont to have.   34

37 *Pompey* (defeated by Caesar in 48 B.C., later murdered) 45 *That*
such that 46 *replication* reverberation 47 *concave shores* hollowed-
out banks 51 *blood* i.e. sons (also the blood of Pompey and his followers)
54 *intermit* withhold 60 *most exalted shores* highest flood level, verge
of heavens 61 *whe'r* whether; *their basest* even their very base; *mettle*
substance, temperament 64 *images* statues 65 *ceremonies* ornaments
67 *Lupercal* fertility festival held on February 15 69 *trophies* ornaments
70 *vulgar* plebeians, common people 73 *pitch* height 74 *above . . . men*
i.e. like the gods
I, ii A public place 4 *run his course* i.e. race naked through the city striking
bystanders with a goatskin thong 15 *press* crowd 18 *ides* the half-way
point in the month, the fifteenth day in March, May, July, and October
24 s.d. *Sennet* trumpet call 25 *order* events 28 *gamesome* sport-loving
29 *quick spirit* lively nature 33 *gentleness* well-bred politeness 34 *love*
friendship; *wont* accustomed

35 You bear too stubborn and too strange a hand
Over your friend that loves you.
BRUTUS   Cassius,
37 Be not deceived. If I have veiled my look,
I turn the trouble of my countenance
39 Merely upon myself. Vexèd I am
40 Of late with passions of some difference,
41 Conceptions only proper to myself,
42 Which give some soil, perhaps, to my behaviors;
But let not therefore my good friends be grieved
(Among which number, Cassius, be you one)
45 Nor construe any further my neglect
Than that poor Brutus, with himself at war,
47 Forgets the shows of love to other men.
CASSIUS
48 Then, Brutus, I have much mistook your passion;
49 By means whereof this breast of mine hath buried
Thoughts of great value, worthy cogitations.
Tell me, good Brutus, can you see your face?
BRUTUS
No, Cassius; for the eye sees not itself
But by reflection, by some other things.
54 CASSIUS 'Tis just.
And it is very much lamented, Brutus,
56 That you have no such mirrors as will turn
57 Your hidden worthiness into your eye,
58 That you might see your shadow. I have heard
59 Where many of the best respect in Rome
(Except immortal Caesar), speaking of Brutus
And groaning underneath this age's yoke,
Have wished that noble Brutus had his eyes.
BRUTUS
Into what dangers would you lead me, Cassius,
That you would have me seek into myself
For that which is not in me?
CASSIUS
Therefore, good Brutus, be prepared to hear;
And since you know you cannot see yourself
68 So well as by reflection, I, your glass,
69 Will modestly discover to yourself
That of yourself which you yet know not of.
71 And be not jealous on me, gentle Brutus.
72 Were I a common laughter, or did use
73 To stale with ordinary oaths my love

To every new protester; if you know   74
That I do fawn on men and hug them hard,
And after scandal them; or if you know   76
That I profess myself in banqueting   77
To all the rout, then hold me dangerous.   78
Flourish and shout.
BRUTUS
What means this shouting? I do fear the people
Choose Caesar for their king.
CASSIUS   Ay, do you fear it?
Then must I think you would not have it so.
BRUTUS
I would not, Cassius; yet I love him well.
But wherefore do you hold me here so long?
What is it that you would impart to me?
If it be aught toward the general good,   85
Set honor in one eye and death i' th' other,
And I will look on both indifferently;   87
For let the gods so speed me as I love   88
The name of honor more than I fear death.
CASSIUS
I know that virtue to be in you, Brutus,
As well as I do know your outward favor.   91
Well, honor is the subject of my story.
I cannot tell what you and other men
Think of this life; but for my single self,   94
I had as lief not be as live to be   95
In awe of such a thing as I myself.   96
I was born free as Caesar; so were you.
We both have fed as well, and we can both
Endure the winter's cold as well as he.
For once, upon a raw and gusty day,
The troubled Tiber chafing with her shores,   101
Caesar said to me, 'Dar'st thou, Cassius, now
Leap in with me into this angry flood
And swim to yonder point?' Upon the word,
Accoutred as I was, I plungèd in   105
And bade him follow. So indeed he did.
The torrent roared, and we did buffet it
With lusty sinews, throwing it aside
And stemming it with hearts of controversy.   109
But ere we could arrive the point proposed,   110
Caesar cried, 'Help me, Cassius, or I sink!'
I, as Aeneas, our great ancestor,   112
Did from the flames of Troy upon his shoulder
The old Anchises bear, so from the waves of Tiber
Did I the tirèd Caesar. And this man
Is now become a god, and Cassius is
A wretched creature and must bend his body
If Caesar carelessly but nod on him.
He had a fever when he was in Spain,
And when the fit was on him, I did mark   120
How he did shake. 'Tis true, this god did shake.
His coward lips did from their color fly,   122
And that same eye whose bend doth awe the world   123
Did lose his luster. I did hear him groan.   124
Ay, and that tongue of his that bade the Romans
Mark him and write his speeches in their books,
'Alas,' it cried, 'give me some drink, Titinius,'
As a sick girl! Ye gods, it doth amaze me
A man of such a feeble temper should   129
So get the start of the majestic world   130
And bear the palm alone.   131
Shout. Flourish.

35-36 *bear . . . Over* behave roughly and unnaturally to   37 *veiled my look* i.e. concealed my true friendship   39 *Merely* wholly   40 *passions . . . difference* conflicting emotions   41 *proper to* concerning   42 *soil* blemish   45 *construe* interpret (accent on first syllable)   47 *shows* manifestations   48 *passion* feelings   49 *buried* concealed   54 *just* true   56 *turn* reflect   57 *hidden worthiness* true nobility, inner worth   58 *shadow* image   59 *best respect* highest repute   68 *glass* mirror   69 *modestly* without exaggeration   71 *jealous on* suspicious of   72 *laughter* object of ridicule; *did use* were accustomed   73 *stale* cheapen; *ordinary* tavern (?), commonplace (?)   74 *protester* one who easily declares friendship   76 *scandal* slander   77 *profess myself* declare my friendship   78 *rout* rabble   s.d. *Flourish* elaborate trumpet call   85 *general good* welfare of the state   87 *indifferently* impartially   88 *speed me* make me prosper   91 *favor* appearance   94 *single* particular   95 *as lief . . . as* rather than   96 *such . . . myself* i.e. a mere mortal   101 *chafing with* raging against   105 *Accoutred* fully armed   109 *stemming . . . controversy* making headway with keen competition   110 *arrive* attain   112 *Aeneas* founder of the Roman state and hero of Virgil's *Aeneid*; Anchises was his father   120 *fit* periodic chills; *mark* observe   122 *color* i.e. the color fled from his lips like cowardly soldiers deserting their flag   123 *bend* glance   124 *his* its   129 *temper* constitution   130 *get the start of* outstrip all others in   131 *palm* victor's prize

BRUTUS
Another general shout?
I do believe that these applauses are
For some new honors that are heaped on Caesar.

CASSIUS
Why, man, he doth bestride the narrow world
136 Like a Colossus, and we petty men
Walk under his huge legs and peep about
To find ourselves dishonorable graves.
139 Men at some time are masters of their fates.
The fault, dear Brutus, is not in our stars,
But in ourselves, that we are underlings.
'Brutus,' and 'Caesar.' What should be in that 'Caesar'?
143 Why should that name be sounded more than yours?
Write them together: yours is as fair a name.
Sound them: it doth become the mouth as well.
Weigh them: it is as heavy. Conjure with 'em:
147 'Brutus' will start a spirit as soon as 'Caesar.'
Now in the names of all the gods at once,
Upon what meat doth this our Caesar feed
That he is grown so great? Age, thou art shamed.
Rome, thou hast lost the breed of noble bloods.
152 When went there by an age since the great Flood
But it was famed with more than with one man?
When could they say (till now) that talked of Rome
155 That her wide walks encompassed but one man?
156 Now is it Rome indeed, and room enough,
When there is in it but one only man.
O, you and I have heard our fathers say
159 There was a Brutus once that would have brooked
160 Th' eternal devil to keep his state in Rome
161 As easily as a king.

BRUTUS
162 That you do love me I am nothing jealous.
163 What you would work me to, I have some aim.
How I have thought of this, and of these times,
I shall recount hereafter. For this present,
166 I would not so (with love I might entreat you)
Be any further moved. What you have said
I will consider; what you have to say
I will with patience hear, and find a time
170 Both meet to hear and answer such high things.
171 Till then, my noble friend, chew upon this:
Brutus had rather be a villager
Than to repute himself a son of Rome
174 Under these hard conditions as this time
Is like to lay upon us.

CASSIUS   I am glad
That my weak words have struck but thus much show
177 Of fire from Brutus.
Enter Caesar and his Train.

BRUTUS
The games are done, and Caesar is returning.

CASSIUS
As they pass by, pluck Casca by the sleeve,
180 And he will (after his sour fashion) tell you
What hath proceeded worthy note to-day.

BRUTUS
I will do so. But look you, Cassius,
The angry spot doth glow on Caesar's brow,
And all the rest look like a chidden train.
Calphurnia's cheek is pale, and Cicero
186 Looks with such ferret and such fiery eyes
As we have seen him in the Capitol,

Being crossed in conference by some senators.   188

CASSIUS
Casca will tell us what the matter is.

CAESAR Antonius.

ANTONY Caesar?

CAESAR
Let me have men about me that are fat,   192
Sleek-headed men, and such as sleep a-nights.   193
Yond Cassius has a lean and hungry look.   194
He thinks too much. Such men are dangerous.

ANTONY
Fear him not, Caesar; he's not dangerous.
He is a noble Roman, and well given.   197

CAESAR
Would he were fatter! But I fear him not.
Yet if my name were liable to fear,   199
I do not know the man I should avoid
So soon as that spare Cassius. He reads much,
He is a great observer, and he looks
Quite through the deeds of men. He loves no plays   203
As thou dost, Antony; he hears no music.   204
Seldom he smiles, and smiles in such a sort   205
As if he mocked himself and scorned his spirit
That could be moved to smile at anything.
Such men as he be never at heart's ease
Whiles they behold a greater than themselves,
And therefore are they very dangerous.
I rather tell thee what is to be feared
Than what I fear; for always I am Caesar.
Come on my right hand, for this ear is deaf,
And tell me truly what thou think'st of him.
Sennet. Exeunt Caesar and his Train.
[Manet Casca.]

CASCA
You pulled me by the cloak. Would you speak with me?

BRUTUS
Ay, Casca. Tell us what hath chanced to-day
That Caesar looks so sad.   217

CASCA
Why, you were with him, were you not?

BRUTUS
I should not then ask Casca what had chanced.

CASCA Why, there was a crown offered him; and being
offered him, he put it by with the back of his hand thus;
and then the people fell a-shouting.

BRUTUS What was the second noise for?

CASCA Why, for that too.

---

136 *Colossus* gigantic statue; *petty* inconsiderable   139 *some* a particular
143 *sounded* pronounced (with pun on 'proclaimed')   147 *start* raise up
152 *Flood* Deucalion's flood, the classical analogue to Noah's   155 *walks*
parks and gardens surrounding ancient Rome   156 *Rome, room* (homo-
nyms)   159 *a Brutus* Lucius Junius Brutus, founder of the Roman Republic in 509 B.C.; *brooked* tolerated   160 *eternal* i.e. eternally damned;
devil (pronounced 'deil'); *his* the devil's   161 *As . . . king* as soon as tolerate
a king's doing so   162 *am nothing jealous* have no doubt   163 *work* persuade; *aim* idea   166 *so* that way   170 *meet* fitting; *high* serious   171
chew upon consider   174 *these* such   177 s.d. *Train* followers   180 *sour*
harsh   186 *ferret* like those of a ferret, a weasel-like animal with red eyes
188 *crossed* opposed; *conference* debate   192 *fat* plump (not 'obese')
193 *Sleek-headed* well-groomed   194 *lean* (proverbially associated with
envy)   197 *given* disposed   199 *my name . . . to* I were capable of   203
through . . . men i.e. to the motivations behind men's actions   204 *hears
no music* (cf. *Merchant of Venice*, V, i, 83–88: 'The man that hath no music
in himself . . . Is fit for treasons . . . . Let no such man be trusted.')   205
sort manner   217 *sad* serious

CASSIUS
They shouted thrice. What was the last cry for?

CASCA Why, for that too.

BRUTUS Was the crown offered him thrice?

228 **CASCA** Ay, marry, was't! and he put it by thrice, every
time gentler than other; and at every putting-by mine
230 honest neighbors shouted.

CASSIUS
Who offered him the crown?

CASCA   Why, Antony.

BRUTUS
233 Tell us the manner of it, gentle Casca.

CASCA I can as well be hanged as tell the manner of it. It
was mere foolery; I did not mark it. I saw Mark Antony
offer him a crown – yet 'twas not a crown neither, 'twas
237 one of these coronets – and, as I told you, he put it by
238 once; but for all that, to my thinking, he would fain
have had it. Then he offered it to him again; then he put
it by again; but to my thinking, he was very loath to lay
his fingers off it. And then he offered it the third time.
242 He put it the third time by; and still as he refused it, the
243 rabblement hooted, and clapped their chopt hands, and
244 threw up their sweaty nightcaps, and uttered such a deal
of stinking breath because Caesar refused the crown that
246 it had, almost, choked Caesar; for he swounded and fell
down at it. And for mine own part, I durst not laugh, for
fear of opening my lips and receiving the bad air.

CASSIUS
249 But soft, I pray you. What, did Caesar swound?

CASCA He fell down in the market place and foamed at
mouth and was speechless.

BRUTUS
252 'Tis very like he hath the falling sickness.

CASSIUS
No, Caesar hath it not; but you, and I,
254 And honest Casca, we have the falling sickness.

CASCA I know not what you mean by that, but I am sure
256 Caesar fell down. If the tag-rag people did not clap him
and hiss him, according as he pleased and displeased
258 them, as they use to do the players in the theatre, I am
no true man.

BRUTUS
What said he when he came unto himself?

CASCA Marry, before he fell down, when he perceived the
262 common herd was glad he refused the crown, he plucked
263 me ope his doublet and offered them his throat to cut.

An I had been a man of any occupation, if I would not 264
have taken him at a word I would I might go to hell
among the rogues. And so he fell. When he came to
himself again, he said, if he had done or said anything
amiss, he desired their worships to think it was his
infirmity. Three or four wenches where I stood cried
'Alas, good soul!' and forgave him with all their hearts.
But there's no heed to be taken of them. If Caesar had
stabbed their mothers, they would have done no less.

BRUTUS
And after that, he came thus sad away?   273

CASCA Ay.

CASSIUS
Did Cicero say anything?

CASCA Ay, he spoke Greek.

CASSIUS To what effect?

CASCA Nay, an I tell you that, I'll ne'er look you i' th'
face again. But those that understood him smiled at one
another and shook their heads; but for mine own part,
it was Greek to me. I could tell you more news too.
Marullus and Flavius, for pulling scarfs off Caesar's
images, are put to silence. Fare you well. There was more 283
foolery yet, if I could remember it.

CASSIUS Will you sup with me to-night, Casca?

CASCA No, I am promised forth.   286

CASSIUS Will you dine with me to-morrow?

CASCA Ay, if I be alive, and your mind hold, and your 288
dinner worth eating.

CASSIUS Good. I will expect you.

CASCA Do so. Farewell both.   *Exit.*

BRUTUS
What a blunt fellow is this grown to be!
He was quick mettle when he went to school.   293

CASSIUS
So is he now in execution
Of any bold or noble enterprise,
However he puts on this tardy form.   296
This rudeness is a sauce to his good wit,   297
Which gives men stomach to disgest his words   298
With better appetite.

BRUTUS
And so it is. For this time I will leave you.
To-morrow, if you please to speak with me,
I will come home to you; or if you will,
Come home to me, and I will wait for you.   302

CASSIUS
I will do so. Till then, think of the world.   *Exit Brutus.* 304
Well, Brutus, thou art noble; yet I see
Thy honorable mettle may be wrought   306
From that it is disposed. Therefore it is meet
That noble minds keep ever with their likes;
For who so firm that cannot be seduced?
Caesar doth bear me hard; but he loves Brutus.   310
If I were Brutus now and he were Cassius,
He should not humor me. I will this night,   312
In several hands, in at his windows throw,   313
As if they came from several citizens,
Writings, all tending to the great opinion   315
That Rome holds of his name; wherein obscurely
Caesar's ambition shall be glancèd at.   317
And after this let Caesar seat him sure,   318
For we will shake him, or worse days endure.   *Exit.* 319

228 *marry* indeed (originally an oath by the Virgin Mary)   230 *honest*
worthy   233 *gentle* noble   237 *coronets* small crowns wreathed with
laurel   238 *fain* willingly   242 *still* each time   243 *chopt* chapped
244 *nightcaps* i.e. the citizens' caps (contemptuous)   246 *swounded* fainted
249 *soft* slowly   252 *like* likely that (Plutarch suggests Caesar feigned an
attack); *falling sickness* epilepsy   254 *we . . . sickness* i.e. we are declining
(into subjection)   256 *tag-rag people* ragged rabble   258 *use* are accustomed
262–63 *plucked me* i.e. plucked (a colloquialism)   263 *doublet* short jacket
264 *An* if; *man . . . occupation* workingman (also 'man of action'?)   273
sad seriously   283 *put to silence* deprived of their tribuneships and exiled
(?) or executed (?) (the tribunes were the guardians of the rights of the
plebeians)   286 *promised forth* previously engaged   288 *hold* change
not   293 *quick mettle* of a lively temperament   296 *tardy form* sluggish
pose   297 *wit* intellect   298 *stomach* appetite, disposition; *disgest* digest
302 *come home* to visit   304 *the world* i.e. the times we are experiencing
306–07 *wrought . . . disposed* so worked upon as to change its natural
qualities   310 *bear me hard* bear a grudge against me   312 *He* i.e. Brutus;
humor persuade by flattery   313 *several hands* different handwritings
315 *tending . . . opinion* concerning the high respect   317 *glancèd* hinted
318 *him sure* himself firmly in power   319 *shake him* i.e. from his dominant
position

I, iii   *Thunder and lightning. Enter, [from opposite sides,]*
Casca, [with his sword drawn,] and Cicero.

CICERO

1   Good even, Casca. Brought you Caesar home?
   Why are you breathless? and why stare you so?

CASCA

3   Are not you moved when all the sway of earth
   Shakes like a thing unfirm? O Cicero,
   I have seen tempests when the scolding winds
6   Have rived the knotty oaks, and I have seen
   Th' ambitious ocean swell and rage and foam
8   To be exalted with the threat'ning clouds;
   But never till to-night, never till now,
   Did I go through a tempest dropping fire.
   Either there is a civil strife in heaven,
12   Or else the world, too saucy with the gods,
   Incenses them to send destruction.

CICERO

   Why, saw you any thing more wonderful?

CASCA

   A common slave (you know him well by sight)
   Held up his left hand, which did flame and burn
   Like twenty torches joined; and yet his hand,
18   Not sensible of fire, remained unscorched.
   Besides (I ha' not since put up my sword),
20   Against the Capitol I met a lion,
21   Who glazed upon me, and went surly by
22   Without annoying me. And there were drawn
23   Upon a heap a hundred ghastly women,
   Transformèd with their fear, who swore they saw
   Men, all in fire, walk up and down the streets.
26   And yesterday the bird of night did sit
   Even at noonday upon the market place,
28   Hooting and shrieking. When these prodigies
   Do so conjointly meet, let not men say
   'These are their reasons – they are natural,'
   For I believe they are portentous things
32   Unto the climate that they point upon.

CICERO

   Indeed it is a strange-disposèd time.
34   But men may construe things after their fashion,
35   Clean from the purpose of the things themselves.
   Comes Caesar to the Capitol to-morrow?

CASCA

   He doth; for he did bid Antonius
   Send word to you he would be there to-morrow.

CICERO

   Good night then, Casca. This disturbèd sky
   Is not to walk in.

CASCA   Farewell, Cicero.   *Exit Cicero.*
     Enter Cassius.

CASSIUS

   Who's there?

CASCA   A Roman.

CASSIUS   Casca, by your voice.

CASCA

   Your ear is good. Cassius, what night is this?

CASSIUS

   A very pleasing night to honest men.

CASCA

   Who ever knew the heavens menace so?

CASSIUS

   Those that have known the earth so full of faults.
   For my part, I have walked about the streets,

   Submitting me unto the perilous night,
   And, thus unbracèd, Casca, as you see,   48
   Have bared my bosom to the thunder-stone;   49
   And when the cross blue lightning seemed to open   50
   The breast of heaven, I did present myself
   Even in the aim and very flash of it.

CASCA

   But wherefore did you so much tempt the heavens?
   It is the part of men to fear and tremble   54
   When the most mighty gods by tokens send
   Such dreadful heralds to astonish us.   56

CASSIUS

   You are dull, Casca, and those sparks of life
   That should be in a Roman you do want,   58
   Or else you use not. You look pale, and gaze,
   And put on fear, and cast yourself in wonder;   60
   To see the strange impatience of the heavens;
   But if you would consider the true cause –
   Why all these fires, why all these gliding ghosts,
   Why birds and beasts, from quality and kind;   64
   Why old men, fools, and children calculate;   65
   Why all these things change from their ordinance,   66
   Their natures, and preformèd faculties,   67
   To monstrous quality – why, you shall find   68
   That heaven hath infused them with these spirits   69
   To make them instruments of fear and warning
   Unto some monstrous state.
   Now could I, Casca, name to thee a man
   Most like this dreadful night
   That thunders, lightens, opens graves, and roars
   As doth the lion in the Capitol;
   A man no mightier than thyself or me
   In personal action, yet prodigious grown
   And fearful, as these strange eruptions are.   78

CASCA

   'Tis Caesar that you mean. It is not, Cassius?

CASSIUS

   Let it be who it is. For Romans now
   Have thews and limbs like to their ancestors;
   But woe the while, our fathers' minds are dead,   82
   And we are governed with our mothers' spirits;
   Our yoke and sufferance show us womanish.   84

CASCA

   Indeed, they say the senators to-morrow
   Mean to establish Caesar as a king,
   And he shall wear his crown by sea and land
   In every place save here in Italy.   88

I, iii A street   **1** *Brought* accompanied, escorted   **3** *sway* established order   **6** *rived* split   **8** *exalted with* raised to the level of   **12** *saucy* insolent   **18** *sensible of* feeling   **20** *Against* opposite   **21** *glazed* stared   **22–23** *drawn . . . heap* crowded together   **23** *ghastly* pale as ghosts   **26** *bird of night* screech owl (proverbially ill-omened)   **28** *prodigies* monstrous events   **32** *climate* region   **34** *construe* (cf. I, ii, 45n.); *after their fashion* each in his own way   **35** *Clean . . . purpose* contrary to the meaning   **48** *unbracèd* with doublet unbuttoned, i.e. exposed   **49** *thunder-stone* thunderbolt, lightning   **50** *cross* forked   **54** *part* appropriate action   **56** *heralds* precursors; *astonish* terrify   **58** *want* lack   **60** *put on* manifest; *cast . . . wonder* are astonished   **64** *from . . . kind* contrary to their nature (in behavior)   **65** *old men* i.e. in their second childhood; *calculate* compute future events (proverbially children and fools speak truth, without discourse of reason)   **66** *ordinance* established modes of behavior   **67** *preformèd faculties* congenital qualities   **68** *monstrous* unnatural   **69** *spirits* powers (?), demons (?)   **78** *fearful* causing fear; *eruptions* disturbances of natural and accustomed order   **82** *woe the while* alas for the times   **84** *yoke and sufferance* i.e. meek endurance of tyranny   **88** *every place* all parts of the Roman Empire

CASSIUS
I know where I will wear this dagger then;
Cassius from bondage will deliver Cassius.
91 Therein, ye gods, you make the weak most strong;
Therein, ye gods, you tyrants do defeat.
Nor stony tower, nor walls of beaten brass,
Nor airless dungeon, nor strong links of iron,
95 Can be retentive to the strength of spirit;
But life, being weary of these worldly bars,
Never lacks power to dismiss itself.
98 If I know this, know all the world besides,
That part of tyranny that I do bear
100 I can shake off at pleasure.
Thunder still.
CASCA   So can I.
So every bondman in his own hand bears
The power to cancel his captivity.
CASSIUS
And why should Caesar be a tyrant then?
Poor man! I know he would not be a wolf
But that he sees the Romans are but sheep;
106 He were no lion, were not Romans hinds.
Those that with haste will make a mighty fire
Begin it with weak straws. What trash is Rome,
What rubbish and what offal, when it serves
For the base matter to illuminate
So vile a thing as Caesar! But, O grief,
Where hast thou led me? I, perhaps, speak this
Before a willing bondman. Then I know
My answer must be made. But I am armed,
115 And dangers are to me indifferent.
CASCA
You speak to Casca, and to such a man
117 That is no fleering telltale. Hold, my hand.
118 Be factious for redress of all these griefs,
And I will set this foot of mine as far
As who goes farthest.
[They shake hands.]
CASSIUS   There's a bargain made.
Now know you, Casca, I have moved already
Some certain of the noblest-minded Romans
123 To undergo with me an enterprise
124 Of honorable dangerous consequence;
125 And I do know, by this they stay for me
126 In Pompey's Porch; for now, this fearful night,
There is no stir or walking in the streets,

And the complexion of the element   128
Is fev'rous, like the work we have in hand,   129
Most bloody, fiery, and most terrible.
Enter Cinna.
CASCA
Stand close awhile, for here comes one in haste.   131
CASSIUS
'Tis Cinna. I do know him by his gait.
He is a friend. Cinna, where haste you so?
CINNA
To find out you. Who's that? Metellus Cimber?   134
CASSIUS
No, it is Casca, one incorporate   135
To our attempts. Am I not stayed for, Cinna?
CINNA
I am glad on't. What a fearful night is this!   137
There's two or three of us have seen strange sights.
CASSIUS
Am I not stayed for? Tell me.
CINNA   Yes, you are.
O Cassius, if you could
But win the noble Brutus to our party –
CASSIUS
Be you content. Good Cinna, take this paper
And look you lay it in the praetor's chair,   143
Where Brutus may but find it. And throw this
In at his window. Set this up with wax
Upon old Brutus' statue. All this done,   146
Repair to Pompey's Porch, where you shall find us.
Is Decius Brutus and Trebonius there?   148
CINNA
All but Metellus Cimber, and he's gone
To seek you at your house. Well, I will hie   150
And so bestow these papers as you bade me.   151
CASSIUS
That done, repair to Pompey's Theatre.   *Exit Cinna.* 152
Come, Casca, you and I will yet ere day   153
See Brutus at his house. Three parts of him   154
Is ours already, and the man entire
Upon the next encounter yields him ours.   156
CASCA
O, he sits high in all the people's hearts;
And that which would appear offense in us,
His countenance, like richest alchemy,   159
Will change to virtue and to worthiness.
CASSIUS
Him and his worth and our great need of him
You have right well conceited. Let us go,   162
For it is after midnight; and ere day
We will awake him and be sure of him.   *Exeunt.*

*

91 *Therein* i.e. in suicide   95 *be retentive to* confine   98 *know all . . . besides* let everyone else know   100 *s.d. still* continually   106 *hinds* does (with pun on 'peasants')   115 *indifferent* a matter of indifference   117 *fleering* mocking, flattering   118 *factious* politically active   123 *undergo* undertake   124 *honorable* honorably   125 *by . . . stay* by this time they are waiting   126 *Pompey's Porch* the colonnade of the great theatre built by Pompey   128 *complexion . . . element* appearance of the sky   129 *fev'rous* feverish (the folio 'Fauors' is sometimes otherwise emended to 'favored,' i.e. featured)   131 *close* concealed   134 *find out* look for   135 *incorporate* closely associated   137 *on't* of it   143 *praetor's chair* official seat of the highest judicial magistrate, at that time Brutus (see II, iv, 35n.)   146 *old Brutus' statue* (see I, ii, 159n.)   148 *Decius Brutus* a kinsman of Marcus Brutus; his name was really Decimus   150 *hie* hasten   151 *bestow* distribute   152 *repair* return   153 *ere* before   154 *Three parts* three-quarters (?), three of the four humours in man (?) (see V, v, 73n.)   156 *yields him ours* i.e. will join our faction   159 *countenance* support; *alchemy* the proto-science devoted to transmuting base metals into gold   162 *conceited* conceived (with pun on 'expressed in a fanciful simile')

II, i By the house of Brutus   *s.d. orchard* garden   5 *When* (exclamation of impatience)

Enter Brutus in his orchard.   II, i
BRUTUS
What, Lucius, ho!
I cannot by the progress of the stars
Give guess how near to day. Lucius, I say!
I would it were my fault to sleep so soundly.
When, Lucius, when? Awake, I say! What, Lucius!   5
Enter Lucius.
LUCIUS Called you, my lord?

BRUTUS

Get me a taper in my study, Lucius.

When it is lighted, come and call me here.

LUCIUS I will, my lord.   *Exit.*

BRUTUS

It must be by his death ; and for my part,

11   I know no personal cause to spurn at him,

12   But for the general. He would be crowned.

How that might change his nature, there's the question.

It is the bright day that brings forth the adder,

15   And that craves wary walking. Crown him that,

And then I grant we put a sting in him

17   That at his will he may do danger with.

Th' abuse of greatness is, when it disjoins

19   Remorse from power. And to speak truth of Caesar,

20   I have not known when his affections swayed

21   More than his reason. But 'tis a common proof

22   That lowliness is young ambition's ladder,

Whereto the climber upward turns his face ;

But when he once attains the upmost round,

He then unto the ladder turns his back,

26   Looks in the clouds, scorning the base degrees

By which he did ascend. So Caesar may.

28   Then lest he may, prevent. And since the quarrel

29   Will bear no color for the thing he is,

30   Fashion it thus : that what he is, augmented,

31   Would run to these and these extremities ;

And therefore think him as a serpent's egg,

33   Which, hatched, would as his kind grow mischievous,

And kill him in the shell.

Enter Lucius.

LUCIUS

35   The taper burneth in your closet, sir.

Searching the window for a flint, I found

This paper, thus sealed up ; and I am sure

It did not lie there when I went to bed.

Gives him the letter.

BRUTUS

Get you to bed again ; it is not day.

Is not to-morrow, boy, the ides of March ?

LUCIUS I know not, sir.

BRUTUS

42   Look in the calendar and bring me word.

LUCIUS I will, sir.   *Exit.*

BRUTUS

44   The exhalations, whizzing in the air,

Give so much light that I may read by them.

Opens the letter and reads.

'Brutus, thou sleep'st. Awake, and see thyself !

47   Shall Rome, &c. Speak, strike, redress !'

'Brutus, thou sleep'st. Awake !'

Such instigations have been often dropped

Where I have took them up.

51   'Shall Rome, &c.' Thus must I piece it out :

52   Shall Rome stand under one man's awe ? What, Rome ?

53   My ancestors did from the streets of Rome

The Tarquin drive when he was called a king.

'Speak, strike, redress !' Am I entreated

To speak and strike ? O Rome, I make thee promise,

57   If the redress will follow, thou receivest

58   Thy full petition at the hand of Brutus !

Enter Lucius.

LUCIUS

59   Sir, March is wasted fifteen days.

Knock within.

BRUTUS

'Tis good. Go to the gate ; somebody knocks.

[Exit Lucius.]

Since Cassius first did whet me against Caesar,

I have not slept.

Between the acting of a dreadful thing

And the first motion, all the interim is   64

Like a phantasma or a hideous dream.   65

The genius and the mortal instruments   66

Are then in council, and the state of a man,   67

Like to a little kingdom, suffers then

The nature of an insurrection.

Enter Lucius.

LUCIUS

Sir, 'tis your brother Cassius at the door,   70

Who doth desire to see you.

BRUTUS   Is he alone ?

LUCIUS

No, sir, there are moe with him.   72

BRUTUS   Do you know them ?

LUCIUS

No, sir. Their hats are plucked about their ears

And half their faces buried in their cloaks,

That by no means I may discover them   75

By any mark of favor.   76

BRUTUS   Let 'em enter.   *[Exit Lucius.]*

They are the faction. O conspiracy,

Sham'st thou to show thy dang'rous brow by night,

When evils are most free ? O, then by day   79

Where wilt thou find a cavern dark enough

To mask thy monstrous visage ? Seek none, conspiracy.

Hide it in smiles and affability :

For if thou path, thy native semblance on,   83

Not Erebus itself were dim enough   84

To hide thee from prevention.   85

Enter the Conspirators, Cassius, Casca, Decius,

Cinna, Metellus [Cimber], and Trebonius.

CASSIUS

I think we are too bold upon your rest.   86

Good morrow, Brutus. Do we trouble you ?

BRUTUS

I have been up this hour, awake all night.

Know I these men that come along with you ?

---

11 *spurn at* kick against   12 *general* public welfare, health of the state   15 *craves* calls for ; *Crown him that* i.e. king (a word Brutus here avoids)   17 *danger* harm   19 *Remorse* mercy   20 *affections swayed* passions ruled   21 *common proof* commonplace, conventional observation based on experience   22 *lowliness* apparent humility   26 *base degrees* lower rungs of the ladder (with pun on 'lower grades of office,' possibly referring to the Roman *'cursus honorum'*)   28 *prevent* take measures to forestall ; *quarrel* case (against Caesar)   29 *bear no color* carry no conviction   30 *Fashion it* put the case   31 *extremities* extremes (of tyranny)   33 *his kind* its nature is   35 *closet* study   42 *calendar* (the Julian calendar, instituted by Caesar in 46 B.C.)   44 *exhalations* meteors   47, 51 *&c.* (read *'et cetera'*)   52 *under . . . awe* in fear of one man   53 *ancestors* (see I, ii, 159n.)   57 *redress* i.e. correction of abuses in the Republic   58 *Thy full petition* all you ask   59 *fifteen* (the Romans counted both the day from which and the day to which they reckoned)   64 *motion* proposal   65 *phantasma* hallucination, nightmare   66 *genius* guardian spirit ; *mortal instruments* intellectual and emotional faculties   67 *in council* deliberating ; *of a man* (many editors delete 'a')   70 *brother* i.e. brother-in-law (Cassius was married to Brutus' sister, Junia)   72 *moe* more   75 *discover* recognize, identify   76 *favor* appearance   79 *evils . . . free* evil things range abroad most freely   83 *path* walk ; *native semblance* true form   84 *Erebus* region of primeval darkness between the upper Earth and Hades   85 *prevention* being forestalled   86 *upon* in intruding on

CASSIUS
Yes, every man of them; and no man here
But honors you; and every one doth wish
You had but that opinion of yourself
Which every noble Roman bears of you.
This is Trebonius.
BRUTUS   He is welcome hither.
CASSIUS
This, Decius Brutus.
BRUTUS   He is welcome too.
CASSIUS
This, Casca; this, Cinna; and this, Metellus Cimber.
BRUTUS
They are all welcome.
98 What watchful cares do interpose themselves
Betwixt your eyes and night?
CASSIUS
Shall I entreat a word?
     They whisper.
DECIUS
Here lies the east. Doth not the day break here?
CASCA No.
CINNA
O, pardon, sir, it doth; and yon grey lines
104 That fret the clouds are messengers of day.
CASCA
You shall confess that you are both deceived.
Here, as I point my sword, the sun arises,
107 Which is a great way growing on the south,
108 Weighing the youthful season of the year.
Some two months hence, up higher toward the north
110 He first presents his fire; and the high east
Stands as the Capitol, directly here.
BRUTUS
Give me your hands all over, one by one.
CASSIUS
And let us swear our resolution.
BRUTUS
114 No, not an oath. If not the face of men,
115 The sufferance of our souls, the time's abuse –
116 If these be motives weak, break off betimes,
117 And every man hence to his idle bed.
118 So let high-sighted tyranny range on
119 Till each man drop by lottery. But if these
120 (As I am sure they do) bear fire enough

To kindle cowards and to steel with valor
The melting spirits of women, then, countrymen, 122
What need we any spur but our own cause 123
To prick us to redress? what other bond 124
Than secret Romans that have spoke the word 125
And will not palter? and what other oath 126
Than honesty to honesty engaged 127
That this shall be, or we will fall for it?
Swear priests and cowards and men cautelous, 129
Old feeble carrions and such suffering souls 130
That welcome wrongs; unto bad causes swear
Such creatures as men doubt; but do not stain
The even virtue of our enterprise, 133
Nor th' insuppressive mettle of our spirits, 134
To think that or our cause or our performance 135
Did need an oath; when every drop of blood
That every Roman bears, and nobly bears,
Is guilty of a several bastardy 138
If he do break the smallest particle
Of any promise that hath passed from him.
CASSIUS
But what of Cicero? Shall we sound him? 141
I think he will stand very strong with us.
CASCA
Let us not leave him out.
CINNA   No, by no means.
METELLUS
O, let us have him, for his silver hairs
Will purchase us a good opinion 145
And buy men's voices to commend our deeds.
It shall be said his judgment ruled our hands.
Our youths and wildness shall no whit appear, 148
But all be buried in his gravity. 149
BRUTUS
O, name him not. Let us not break with him; 150
For he will never follow anything
That other men begin.
CASSIUS   Then leave him out.
CASCA
Indeed he is not fit.
DECIUS
Shall no man else be touched but only Caesar?
CASSIUS
Decius, well urged. I think it is not meet 155
Mark Antony, so well beloved of Caesar,
Should outlive Caesar. We shall find of him 157
A shrewd contriver; and you know, his means, 158
If he improve them, may well stretch so far 159
As to annoy us all; which to prevent, 160
Let Antony and Caesar fall together.
BRUTUS
Our course will seem too bloody, Caius Cassius,
To cut the head off and then hack the limbs,
Like wrath in death and envy afterwards; 164
For Antony is but a limb of Caesar. 165
Let's be sacrificers, but not butchers, Caius.
We all stand up against the spirit of Caesar, 167
And in the spirit of men there is no blood.
O that we then could come by Caesar's spirit 169
And not dismember Caesar! But, alas,
Caesar must bleed for it. And, gentle friends, 171
Let's kill him boldly, but not wrathfully;
Let's carve him as a dish fit for the gods,
Not hew him as a carcass fit for hounds.

---

98 *watchful cares* concerns that keep you awake 104 *fret* ornamentally interlace 107 *growing on* toward 108 *Weighing* considering 110 *high* due, exact 114 *face* appearance (which should be identical with reality), i.e. the serious manner of the conspirators and the anxious manner of their fellow citizens 115 *sufferance* distress; *time's abuse* corruption of these days (i.e. Caesar's violation of the laws of the Republic) 116 *betimes* at once 117 *idle* unused 118 *high-sighted* looking down from on high (like a falcon), i.e. arrogant 119 *lottery* whim 120 *fire* i.e. spirit, courage 122 *melting* yielding 123 *What* why 124 *prick* spur 125 *secret Romans* the mere fact that we are Romans able to hold our tongues (?), sharing a secret (?); *spoke the word* given one another our word of honor 126 *palter* quibble 127 *honesty* personal honor; *engaged* pledged 129 *Swear* make swear, bind by oath; *cautelous* crafty, deceitful 130 *carrions* physical wrecks, practically corpses 133 *even* uniform, unblemished 134 *insuppressive* indomitable; *mettle* (see I, i, 61n.) 135 *or ... or* either ... or 138 *several* separate, individual 141 *sound* feel out 145 *purchase* procure; *opinion* reputation 148 *no whit* not at all 149 *gravity* sobriety and authority of character 150 *break with* put the matter to 155 *urged* recommended 157 *of* in 158 *shrewd contriver* formidable plotter; *means* capacity (to harm us) 159 *improve* exploit 160 *annoy* injure; *prevent* forestall 164 *envy* malice 165 *limb* mere appendage 167 *spirit* principles (i.e. Caesarism) 169 *come by* get at 171 *gentle* noble

175 And let our hearts, as subtle masters do,
Stir up their servants to an act of rage
And after seem to chide 'em. This shall make
178 Our purpose necessary, and not envious ;
Which so appearing to the common eyes,
180 We shall be called purgers, not murderers.
And for Mark Antony, think not of him ;
For he can do no more than Caesar's arm
When Caesar's head is off.

CASSIUS   Yet I fear him ;
184 For in the ingrafted love he bears to Caesar –

BRUTUS
Alas, good Cassius, do not think of him !
If he love Caesar, all that he can do
187 Is to himself – take thought, and die for Caesar.
188 And that were much he should ; for he is given
To sports, to wildness, and much company.

TREBONIUS
190 There is no fear in him. Let him not die ;
For he will live, and laugh at this hereafter.
Clock strikes.

BRUTUS
Peace ! Count the clock.

CASSIUS   The clock hath stricken three.

TREBONIUS
'Tis time to part.

CASSIUS   But it is doubtful yet
194 Whether Caesar will come forth to-day or no ;
For he is superstitious grown of late,
196 Quite from the main opinion he held once
197 Of fantasy, of dreams, and ceremonies.
198 It may be these apparent prodigies,
The unaccustomed terror of this night,
200 And the persuasion of his augurers
May hold him from the Capitol to-day.

DECIUS
Never fear that. If he be so resolved,
203 I can o'ersway him ; for he loves to hear
204 That unicorns may be betrayed with trees
205 And bears with glasses, elephants with holes,
206 Lions with toils, and men with flatterers ;
But when I tell him he hates flatterers,
He says he does, being then most flatterèd.
Let me work ;
210 For I can give his humor the true bent
And I will bring him to the Capitol.

CASSIUS
212 Nay, we will all of us be there to fetch him.

BRUTUS
213 By the eight hour. Is that the uttermost ?

CINNA
Be that the uttermost, and fail not then.

METELLUS
215 Caius Ligarius doth bear Caesar hard,
216 Who rated him for speaking well of Pompey.
I wonder none of you have thought of him.

BRUTUS
218 Now, good Metellus, go along by him.
He loves me well, and I have given him reasons.
220 Send him but hither, and I'll fashion him.

CASSIUS
The morning comes upon's. We'll leave you, Brutus.
And, friends, disperse yourselves ; but all remember
What you have said and show yourselves true Romans.

BRUTUS
Good gentlemen, look fresh and merrily.   224
Let not our looks put on our purposes,   225
But bear it as our Roman actors do,   226
With untired spirits and formal constancy.   227
And so good morrow to you every one.
           Exeunt. Manet Brutus.
Boy ! Lucius ! Fast asleep ? It is no matter.
Enjoy the honey-heavy dew of slumber.   230
Thou hast no figures nor no fantasies   231
Which busy care draws in the brains of men ;
Therefore thou sleep'st so sound.
      Enter Portia.

PORTIA   Brutus, my lord.

BRUTUS
Portia ! What mean you ? Wherefore rise you now ?
It is not for your health thus to commit   235
Your weak condition to the raw cold morning.

PORTIA
Nor for yours neither. Y' have ungently, Brutus,   237
Stole from my bed. And yesternight at supper
You suddenly arose and walked about,
Musing and sighing with your arms across ;   240
And when I asked you what the matter was,
You stared upon me with ungentle looks.
I urged you further ; then you scratched your head
And too impatiently stamped with your foot.
Yet I insisted ; yet you answered not,
But with an angry wafter of your hand   246
Gave sign for me to leave you. So I did,
Fearing to strengthen that impatience
Which seemed too much enkindled, and withal
Hoping it was but an effect of humor,   250
Which sometime hath his hour with every man.   251
It will not let you eat not talk nor sleep,
And could it work so much upon your shape
As it hath much prevailed on your condition,   254
I should not know you Brutus. Dear my lord,   255
Make me acquainted with your cause of grief.

BRUTUS
I am not well in health, and that is all.

PORTIA
Brutus is wise and, were he not in health,
He would embrace the means to come by it.   259

BRUTUS
Why, so I do. Good Portia, go to bed.

175–77 *And . . . chide 'em* i.e. let us not be wrathful in our hearts although our hands must be made to perform this violent act (in order to preserve the Republic)   178 *envious* malicious   180 *purgers* healers   184 *ingrafted* deeply implanted   187 *take thought* fall into a melancholy state   188 *that . . . should* it is unlikely that he would   190 *no fear* nothing to fear   194 *Whether* (pronounced, and often spelled, 'where' or 'whe'r')   196 *from the main* contrary to the strong   197 *fantasy* fancy, i.e. imaginary fears; *ceremonies* portents   198 *apparent prodigies* manifest signs of disaster   200 *augurers* augurs (priests who interpreted omens)   203 *o'ersway* persuade   204 *betrayed with trees* tricked into running their horns into tree trunks, thence easily captured   205 *glasses* mirrors; *holes* pits   206 *toils* snares   210 *humor* disposition ; *bent* direction   212 *fetch* escort   213 *eight* eighth ; *uttermost* latest   215 *bear Caesar hard* (see I, ii, 310n.)   216 *rated* upbraided   218 *him* his house   220 *fashion* shape (to our purposes)   224 *fresh* brightly   225 *put on* display   226 *bear it* play your roles   227 *untired* alert ; *formal constancy* proper self-possession   230 *honey-heavy dew* i.e. sweetly drowsy refreshment   231 *figures* figments of imagination   235 *commit* expose   237 *ungently* ignobly, discourteously   240 *across* folded across your chest (a sign of melancholy)   246 *wafter* wafture, gesture   250 *effect of humor* symptom of a temporary mood   251 *his* its   254 *condition* disposition   255 *know you* recognize you as   259 *embrace* adopt ; *come by* regain

PORTIA

261 Is Brutus sick, and is it physical
262 To walk unbracèd and suck up the humors
Of the dank morning? What, is Brutus sick,
And will he steal out of his wholesome bed
265 To dare the vile contagion of the night,
266 And tempt the rheumy and unpurgèd air,
To add unto his sickness? No, my Brutus.
268 You have some sick offense within your mind,
269 Which by the right and virtue of my place
       [Kneels.]
I ought to know of; and upon my knees
271 I charm you, by my once commended beauty,
By all your vows of love, and that great vow
273 Which did incorporate and make us one,
274 That you unfold to me, your self, your half,
275 Why you are heavy – and what men to-night
Have had resort to you; for here have been
Some six or seven, who did hide their faces
Even from darkness.

BRUTUS   Kneel not, gentle Portia.
       [Raises her.]

PORTIA

I should not need if you were gentle Brutus.
Within the bond of marriage, tell me, Brutus,
281 Is it excepted I should know no secrets
That appertain to you? Am I your self
283 But, as it were, in sort or limitation?
284 To keep with you at meals, comfort your bed,
285 And talk to you sometimes? Dwell I but in the suburbs
Of your good pleasure? If it be no more,
Portia is Brutus' harlot, not his wife.

BRUTUS

You are my true and honorable wife,
As dear to me as are the ruddy drops
That visit my sad heart.

PORTIA

If this were true, then should I know this secret.
I grant I am a woman; but withal
A woman that Lord Brutus took to wife.
I grant I am a woman; but withal
295 A woman well-reputed, Cato's daughter.
Think you I am no stronger than my sex,
Being so fathered and so husbanded?
298 Tell me your counsels; I will not disclose 'em.
299 I have made strong proof of my constancy,

---

261 *physical* healthful   262 *unbracèd* (see I, iii, 48n.); *humors* mists, dews
265 *vile . . . night* (night air was thought to be poisonous)   266 *tempt* risk;
rheumy moist; *unpurgèd* not purified (by the sun)   268 *sick offense* harmful
illness   269 *virtue* power; *place* (as your wife)   271 *charm* solemnly entreat
273 *incorporate* make us one flesh   274 *unfold* disclose; *self* other self; *half*
i.e. wife   275 *heavy* sad   281 *excepted* made an exception that   283 *in . . .
limitation* after a fashion or under restriction (a legalism)   284 *keep*
keep company   285 *suburbs* outlying districts (notorious for their brothels
and other disreputable haunts)   295 *Cato* (Cato of Utica, famous for
absolute moral integrity, fought with Pompey against Caesar and killed
himself to avoid capture in 46 B.C.; he was Brutus' uncle as well as father-
in-law)   298 *counsels* secrets   299 *proof* trial; *constancy* fortitude   307
engagements commitments; *construe* explain fully   308 *the charactery of*
that which is written in shorthand upon (accent 'charàctery')   312 *how*
how are you   313 *Vouchsafe* deign to accept   314 *brave* noble   315
To . . . kerchief i.e. to be sick   322 *derived . . . loins* (see I, ii, 159n.)   323
exorcist conjurer   324 *mortifièd* deadened, as if dead   327 *whole* healthy
328 *make sick* i.e. kill   330 *unfold* disclose   331 *To whom* to the house of
him to whom; *Set on* advance
II, ii Within the house of Caesar   s.d. *nightgown* dressing gown   1 *Nor . . .
nor* neither . . . nor   3 *Who's within* which of the servants is about

---

Giving myself a voluntary wound
Here, in the thigh. Can I bear that with patience,
And not my husband's secrets?

BRUTUS   O ye gods,
Render me worthy of this noble wife!
       Knock.
Hark, hark! One knocks. Portia, go in awhile,
And by and by thy bosom shall partake
The secrets of my heart.
All my engagements I will construe to thee,   307
All the charactery of my sad brows.   308
Leave me with haste.   *Exit Portia.*
        Lucius, who's that knocks?
    Enter Lucius and [Caius] Ligarius.

LUCIUS

Here is a sick man that would speak with you.

BRUTUS

Caius Ligarius, that Metellus spake of.
Boy, stand aside. Caius Ligarius, how?   312

CAIUS

Vouchsafe good morrow from a feeble tongue.   313

BRUTUS

O, what a time have you chose out, brave Caius,   314
To wear a kerchief! Would you were not sick.   315

CAIUS

I am not sick if Brutus have in hand
Any exploit worthy the name of honor.

BRUTUS

Such an exploit have I in hand, Ligarius,
Had you a healthful ear to hear of it.

CAIUS

By all the gods that Romans bow before,
I here discard my sickness.
    [Throws off his kerchief.]   Soul of Rome,
Brave son derived from honorable loins,   322
Thou like an exorcist hast conjured up   323
My mortifièd spirit. Now bid me run,   324
And I will strive with things impossible;
Yea, get the better of them. What's to do?

BRUTUS

A piece of work that will make sick men whole.   327

CAIUS

But are not some whole that we must make sick?   328

BRUTUS

That must we also. What it is, my Caius,
I shall unfold to thee as we are going   330
To whom it must be done.   331

CAIUS   Set on your foot,
And with a heart new-fired I follow you,
To do I know not what; but it sufficeth
That Brutus leads me on.
    Thunder.

BRUTUS   Follow me then.   *Exeunt.*

              *

   Thunder and lightning. Enter Julius Caesar, in his   II, ii
   nightgown.

CAESAR

Nor heaven nor eath have been at peace to-night.   1
Thrice hath Calphurnia in her sleep cried out
'Help, ho! They murder Caesar!' Who's within?   3
   Enter a Servant.

SERVANT My lord?

CAESAR

5　Go bid the priests do present sacrifice,
6　And bring me their opinions of success.

SERVANT I will, my lord.　　　　　　　　　*Exit.*

Enter Calphurnia.

CALPHURNIA

What mean you, Caesar? Think you to walk forth?
You shall not stir out of your house to-day.

CAESAR

Caesar shall forth. The things that threatened me
Ne'er looked but on my back. When they shall see
The face of Caesar, they are vanishèd.

CALPHURNIA

13　Caesar, I never stood on ceremonies,
Yet now they fright me. There is one within,
Besides the things that we have heard and seen,
16　Recounts most horrid sights seen by the watch.
A lioness hath whelpèd in the streets,
And graves have yawned and yielded up their dead.
Fierce fiery warriors fought upon the clouds
20　In ranks and squadrons and right form of war,
Which drizzled blood upon the Capitol.
22　The noise of battle hurtled in the air,
Horses did neigh, and dying men did groan,
And ghosts did shriek and squeal about the streets.
25　O Caesar, these things are beyond all use,
And I do fear them.

CAESAR　　　　　　　　What can be avoided
Whose end is purposed by the mighty gods?
Yet Caesar shall go forth; for these predictions
29　Are to the world in general as to Caesar.

CALPHURNIA

When beggars die there are no comets seen;
31　The heavens themselves blaze forth the death of princes.

CAESAR

Cowards die many times before their deaths;
The valiant never taste of death but once.
Of all the wonders that I yet have heard,
It seems to me most strange that men should fear,
Seeing that death, a necessary end,
Will come when it will come.

Enter a Servant.　　　　What say the augurers?

SERVANT

They would not have you to stir forth to-day.
Plucking the entrails of an offering forth,
They could not find a heart within the beast.

CAESAR

The gods do this in shame of cowardice.
42　Caesar should be a beast without a heart
If he should stay at home to-day for fear.
No, Caesar shall not. Danger knows full well
That Caesar is more dangerous than he.
We are two lions littered in one day,
And I the elder and more terrible,
And Caesar shall go forth.

CALPHURNIA　　　　　　　Alas, my lord,
49　Your wisdom is consumed in confidence!
Do not go forth to-day! Call it my fear
That keeps you in the house and not your own.
We'll send Mark Antony to the Senate House,
And he shall say you are not well to-day.
Let me upon my knee prevail in this.

CAESAR

Mark Antony shall say I am not well,
And for thy humor I will stay at home.　　　56

Enter Decius.

Here's Decius Brutus; he shall tell them so.

DECIUS

Caesar, all hail! Good morrow, worthy Caesar;
I come to fetch you to the Senate House.　　　59

CAESAR

And you are come in very happy time　　　60
To bear my greeting to the senators
And tell them that I will not come to-day.
Cannot, is false; and that I dare not, falser:
I will not come to-day. Tell them so, Decius.

CALPHURNIA

Say he is sick.

CAESAR　　　　　Shall Caesar send a lie?
Have I in conquest stretched mine arm so far
To be afeard to tell greybeards the truth!
Decius, go tell them Caesar will not come.

DECIUS

Most mighty Caesar, let me know some cause,
Lest I be laughed at when I tell them so.

CAESAR

The cause is in my will: I will not come.
That is enough to satisfy the Senate;
But for your private satisfaction,
Because I love you, I will let you know.
Calphurnia here, my wife, stays me at home.　　　75
She dreamt to-night she saw my statue,　　　76
Which, like a fountain with an hundred spouts,
Did run pure blood; and many lusty Romans　　　78
Came smiling and did bathe their hands in it.
And these does she apply for warnings and portents　　　80
And evil imminent, and on her knee
Hath begged that I will stay at home to-day.

DECIUS

This dream is all amiss interpreted;
It was a vision fair and fortunate.
Your statue spouting blood in many pipes,
In which so many smiling Romans bathed,
Signifies that from you great Rome shall suck
Reviving blood, and that great men shall press
For tinctures, stains, relics, and cognizance.　　　89
This by Calphurnia's dream is signified.

CAESAR

And this way have you well expounded it.

DECIUS

I have, when you have heard what I can say;
And know it now. The Senate have concluded　　　93
To give this day a crown to mighty Caesar.
If you shall send them word you will not come,
Their minds may change. Besides, it were a mock　　　96
Apt to be rendered, for some one to say

5 *priests* augurs (see II, i, 200n.); *present* immediate　6 *opinions of success* judgments of the success or failure of my plans　13 *stood on ceremonies* heeded portents　16 *watch* nightwatchmen　20 *right form* regular order　22 *hurtled* clashed　25 *use* normal experience　29 *Are to* are as applicable to　31 *blaze forth* i.e. proclaim　42 *should* would indeed　49 *consumed in confidence* destroyed by overconfidence　56 *humor* whim　59 *fetch* escort　60 *in . . . time* at a most opportune moment　75 *stays* keeps　76 *statue* (trisyllabic)　78 *lusty* vigorous, gallant　80 *apply for* interpret as; *portents* (accent 'portènts')　89 *tinctures* stains (with heraldic and alchemical associations); *relics* (as of holy martyrs); *cognizance* an identifying emblem worn by a nobleman's followers　93 *concluded* formally determined　96–97 *mock . . . rendered* sarcastic remark likely to be made

'Break up the Senate till another time,
When Caesar's wife shall meet with better dreams.'
100 If Caesar hide himself, shall they not whisper
'Lo, Caesar is afraid'?
Pardon me, Caesar; for my dear dear love
103 To your proceeding bids me tell you this,
104 And reason to my love is liable.

CAESAR
How foolish do your fears seem now, Calphurnia!
I am ashamèd I did yield to them.
107 Give me my robe, for I will go.
Enter Brutus, Ligarius, Metellus, Casca,
Trebonius, Cinna, and Publius.
And look where Publius is come to fetch me.

PUBLIUS
Good morrow, Caesar.

CAESAR   Welcome, Publius.
What, Brutus, are you stirred so early too?
Good morrow, Casca. Caius Ligarius,
112 Caesar was ne'er so much your enemy
113 As that same ague which hath made you lean.
What is't o'clock?

BRUTUS   Caesar, 'tis strucken eight.

CAESAR
I thank you for your pains and courtesy.
Enter Antony.
See, Antony, that revels long a-nights,
Is notwithstanding up. Good morrow, Antony.

ANTONY
118 So to most noble Caesar.

CAESAR   Bid them prepare within.
I am to blame to be thus waited for.
Now, Cinna. Now, Metellus. What, Trebonius!
I have an hour's talk in store for you;
Remember that you call on me to-day;
Be near me, that I may remember you.

TREBONIUS
124 Caesar, I will. *[aside]* And so near will I be
That your best friends shall wish I had been further.

CAESAR
Good friends, go in and taste some wine with me,
And we (like friends) will straightway go together.

BRUTUS *[aside]*
128 That every like is not the same, O Caesar,
129 The heart of Brutus erns to think upon.   *Exeunt.*

*

Enter Artemidorus [reading a paper].   II, iii

[ARTEMIDORUS] 'Caesar, beware of Brutus; take heed
of Cassius; come not near Casca; have an eye to Cinna;
trust not Trebonius; mark well Metellus Cimber;
Decius Brutus loves thee not; thou hast wronged Caius
Ligarius. There is but one mind in all these men, and it
is bent against Caesar. If thou beest not immortal, look   6
about you. Security gives way to conspiracy. The   7
mighty gods defend thee!

'Thy lover,   9
'Artemidorus.'

Here will I stand till Caesar pass along
And as a suitor will I give him this.   12
My heart laments that virtue cannot live
Out of the teeth of emulation.   14
If thou read this, O Caesar, thou mayest live;
If not, the Fates with traitors do contrive.   *Exit.* 16

*

Enter Portia and Lucius.   II, iv

PORTIA
I prithee, boy, run to the Senate House.
Stay not to answer me, but get thee gone!
Why dost thou stay?

LUCIUS   To know my errand, madam.

PORTIA
I would have had thee there and here again
Ere I can tell thee what thou shouldst do there.
[Aside]
O constancy, be strong upon my side,   6
Set a huge mountain 'tween my heart and tongue!
I have a man's mind, but a woman's might.   8
How hard it is for women to keep counsel!   9
Art thou here yet?

LUCIUS   Madam, what should I do?
Run to the Capitol and nothing else?
And so return to you and nothing else?

PORTIA
Yes, bring me word, boy, if thy lord look well,
For he went sickly forth; and take good note   14
What Caesar doth, what suitors press to him.
Hark, boy! What noise is that?

LUCIUS
I hear none, madam.

PORTIA   Prithee listen well.
I heard a bustling rumor like a fray,   18
And the wind brings it from the Capitol.

LUCIUS
Sooth, madam, I hear nothing.   20
Enter the Soothsayer.

PORTIA
Come hither, fellow. Which way hast thou been?

SOOTHSAYER
At mine own house, good lady.

PORTIA
What is't o'clock?

SOOTHSAYER   About the ninth hour, lady.

PORTIA
Is Caesar yet gone to the Capitol?

SOOTHSAYER
Madam, not yet. I go to take my stand,
To see him pass on to the Capitol.

---

100 *shall* will indeed   103 *proceeding* advancement (?), career (?)   104
reason . . . liable i.e. my love outweighs my judgment in speaking thus
freely to you   107 *robe* toga   112 *enemy* (Ligarius, like Brutus, Cassius,
and Cicero, had supported Pompey against Caesar)   113 *lean* (apparently
the same actor took the parts of Cassius and Ligarius)   118 *So* likewise;
prepare i.e. set out the wine   124–25 *And . . . further* (actually Trebonius
lures Antony out of the way before the assassination)   128 *every . . . same*
i.e. appearance is not always the same as reality   129 *erns* grieves
II, iii A street near the Capitol   6 *bent* directed   7 *Security* overconfidence;
way path, opportunity   9 *lover* friend   12 *as a suitor* pretending to be a
petitioner   14 *Out . . . emulation* i.e. beyond the reach of envious rivalry
16 *contrive* conspire
II, iv Before the house of Brutus   6 *constancy* self-control, fortitude
8 *might* strength   9 *counsel* a secret (i.e. Brutus' secret which he has told
her according to his promise; that he has had no opportunity to do so is
irrelevant by the Elizabethan theatrical convention of 'double time')
14 *take good note* observe well   18 *bustling . . . fray* confused noise as in
battle   20 *Sooth* truly   s.d. *Soothsayer* (the same who had warned Caesar
at I, ii, 18)

PORTIA

Thou hast some suit to Caesar, hast thou not?

SOOTHSAYER

That I have, lady, if it will please Caesar
To be so good to Caesar as to hear me:
I shall beseech him to befriend himself.

PORTIA

Why, know'st thou any harm's intended towards him?

SOOTHSAYER

32   None that I know will be, much that I fear may chance.
Good morrow to you. Here the street is narrow.
The throng that follows Caesar at the heels,
35   Of Senators, of praetors, common suitors,
Will crowd a feeble man almost to death.
37   I'll get me to a place more void and there
Speak to great Caesar as he comes along.   *Exit.*

PORTIA

I must go in. Ay me, how weak a thing
The heart of woman is! O Brutus,
The heavens speed thee in thine enterprise!
Sure the boy heard me. – Brutus hath a suit
That Caesar will not grant. – O, I grow faint. –
44   Run, Lucius, and commend me to my lord;
45   Say I am merry. Come to me again
And bring me word what he doth say to thee.

                        Exeunt [severally].

*

III, i   *Flourish. Enter Caesar, Brutus, Cassius, Casca,*
Decius, Metellus, Trebonius, Cinna, Antony,
Lepidus, Artemidorus, [Popilius,] Publius, and the
Soothsayer.

CAESAR

The ides of March are come.

SOOTHSAYER

Ay, Caesar, but not gone.

ARTEMIDORUS

3   Hail, Caesar! Read this schedule.

DECIUS

Trebonius doth desire you to o'erread
(At your best leisure) this his humble suit.

ARTEMIDORUS

O Caesar, read mine first; for mine's a suit
7   That touches Caesar nearer. Read it, great Caesar!

CAESAR

8   What touches us ourself shall be last served.

ARTEMIDORUS

Delay not, Caesar! Read it instantly!

CAESAR

What, is the fellow mad?

10 PUBLIUS   Sirrah, give place.

CASSIUS

What, urge you your petitions in the street?
12   Come to the Capitol.

     [Caesar goes to the Capitol, the rest following.]

POPILIUS

13   I wish your enterprise to-day may thrive.

CASSIUS

What enterprise, Popilius?

POPILIUS   Fare you well.

     [Advances to Caesar.]

BRUTUS

What said Popilius Lena?

CASSIUS

He wished to-day our enterprise might thrive.
I fear our purpose is discoverèd.

BRUTUS

Look how he makes to Caesar. Mark him.   18

CASSIUS

Casca, be sudden, for we fear prevention.   19
Brutus, what shall be done? If this be known,
Cassius or Caesar never shall turn back,   21
For I will slay myself.

BRUTUS   Cassius, be constant.   22
Popilius Lena speaks not of our purposes;
For look, he smiles, and Caesar doth not change.   24

CASSIUS

Trebonius knows his time; for look you, Brutus,
He draws Mark Antony out of the way.

          [Exeunt Antony and Trebonius.]

DECIUS

Where is Metellus Cimber? Let him go
And presently prefer his suit to Caesar.   28

BRUTUS

He is addressed. Press near and second him.   29

CINNA

Casca, you are the first that rears your hand.

CAESAR

Are we all ready? What is now amiss
That Caesar and his Senate must redress?

METELLUS

Most high, most mighty, and most puissant Caesar,
Metellus Cimber throws before thy seat
An humble heart.

     [Kneels.]

CAESAR   I must prevent thee, Cimber.   35
These couchings and these lowly courtesies   36
Might fire the blood of ordinary men
And turn preordinance and first decree   38
Into the lane of children. Be not fond   39
To think that Caesar bears such rebel blood   40
That will be thawed from the true quality   41
With that which melteth fools – I mean, sweet words,
Low-crookèd curtsies, and base spaniel fawning.   43
Thy brother by decree is banishèd.
If thou dost bend and pray and fawn for him,
I spurn thee like a cur out of my way.

32 *chance* happen   35 *praetors* high-ranking judges in the administration of Roman law (Caesar increased their number from eight to sixteen. Brutus, Cassius, and Cinna were praetors in 44 B.C., Brutus being '*praetor urbanus*,' the chief justice of the state and second only in authority to the two consuls – Caesar, who had been appointed Dictator for life, and Antony. Cassius, as '*praetor peregrinus*,' ranked immediately below Brutus.)   37 *void* empty, spacious   44 *commend me* give my best love and wishes   45 *merry* in good spirits
III, i Before the Capitol   3 *schedule* document   7 *touches* concerns   8 *served* attended to   10 *Sirrah* (contemptuous form of address); *give place* get out of the way   12 **s.d.** *the Capitol* (possibly the 'inner stage,' probably just before it)   13 *enterprise* undertaking   18 *makes to* advances toward   19 *sudden* quick; *prevention* being forestalled   21 *turn back* return alive   22 *constant* unshaken   24 *Caesar . . . change* i.e. his expression does not change   28 *presently* immediately; *prefer* present   29 *addressed* ready   35 *prevent* forestall   36 *couchings* bowings; *courtesies* curtsies, bowings   38 *preordinance . . . decree* the original, time-honored laws by which men organized themselves into societies, i.e. the laws of man in accordance with the laws of nature and of God   39 *lane* path, byway (many editors emend to 'law'); *fond* so foolish as   40 *rebel* untrue to its own nature   41 *thawed* i.e. altered; *true* proper   43 *spaniel* i.e. hypocritically flattering

47   Know, Caesar doth not wrong, nor without cause
Will he be satisfied.

METELLUS
Is there no voice more worthy than my own,
To sound more sweetly in great Caesar's ear
51   For the repealing of my banished brother?

BRUTUS
I kiss thy hand, but not in flattery, Caesar,
Desiring thee that Publius Cimber may
54   Have an immediate freedom of repeal.

CAESAR
What, Brutus?

CASSIUS   Pardon, Caesar! Caesar, pardon!
As low as to thy foot doth Cassius fall
To beg enfranchisement for Publius Cimber.

CAESAR
I could be well moved, if I were as you;
If I could pray to move, prayers would move me:
60   But I am constant as the Northern Star,
61   Of whose true-fixed and resting quality
62   There is no fellow in the firmament.
63   The skies are painted with unnumb'red sparks,
They are all fire, and every one doth shine;
65   But there's but one in all doth hold his place.
So in the world: 'tis furnished well with men,
67   And men are flesh and blood, and apprehensive;
Yet in the number I do know but one
69   That unassailable holds on his rank,
Unshaked of motion; and that I am he,
Let me a little show it, even in this –
72   That I was constant Cimber should be banished
And constant do remain to keep him so.

CINNA
O Caesar.
74 CAESAR   Hence! Wilt thou lift up Olympus?

DECIUS
Great Caesar.
75 CAESAR   Doth not Brutus bootless kneel?

CASCA
Speak hands for me.
They stab Caesar [– Casca first, Brutus last].

CAESAR
77   *Et tu, Brutè?* – Then fall Caesar.
Dies.

CINNA
Liberty! Freedom! Tyranny is dead!

Run hence, proclaim, cry it about the streets!

CASSIUS
Some to the common pulpits and cry out   80
'Liberty, freedom, and enfranchisement!'

BRUTUS
People and senators, be not affrighted.
Fly not; stand still. Ambition's debt is paid.   83

CASCA
Go to the pulpit, Brutus.

DECIUS   And Cassius too.

BRUTUS
Where's Publius?   85

CINNA
Here, quite confounded with this mutiny.   86

METELLUS
Stand fast together, lest some friend of Caesar's   87
Should chance –

BRUTUS
Talk not of standing! Publius, good cheer.   89
There is no harm intended to your person
Nor to no Roman else. So tell them, Publius.

CASSIUS
And leave us, Publius, lest that the people,
Rushing on us, should do your age some mischief.   93

BRUTUS
Do so; and let no man abide this deed   94
But we the doers.
Enter Trebonius.

CASSIUS   Where is Antony?

TREBONIUS
Fled to his house amazed.   96
Men, wives, and children stare, cry out, and run,
As it were doomsday.

BRUTUS   Fates, we will know your pleasures.
That we shall die, we know; 'tis but the time,
And drawing days out, that men stand upon.   100

CASCA
Why, he that cuts off twenty years of life
Cuts off so many years of fearing death.

BRUTUS
Grant that, and then is death a benefit.
So are we Caesar's friends, that have abridged
His time of fearing death. Stoop, Romans, stoop,
And let us bathe our hands in Caesar's blood
Up to the elbows and besmear our swords.
Then walk we forth, even to the market place,   108
And waving our red weapons o'er our heads,
Let's all cry 'Peace, freedom, and liberty!'

CASSIUS
Stoop then and wash. How many ages hence
Shall this our lofty scene be acted over
In states unborn and accents yet unknown!

BRUTUS
How many times shall Caesar bleed in sport,   114
That now on Pompey's basis lies along   115
No worthier than the dust!

CASSIUS   So oft as that shall be,
So often shall the knot of us be called   117
The men that gave their country liberty.

DECIUS
What, shall we forth?   119

CASSIUS   Ay, every man away.
Brutus shall lead, and we will grace his heels   120
With the most boldest and best hearts of Rome.

47–48 *Know . . . satisfied* (it is possible that Shakespeare first wrote, 'Caesar did never wrong, but with just cause, Nor without cause will he be satisfied,' but altered it out of deference to the criticism of Ben Jonson) **51** *repealing* recalling from banishment **54** *freedom of repeal* permission to be recalled **60** *constant . . . Star* as fixed as the polestar (an ultimate symbol of constancy) **61** *resting* immovable **62** *fellow* equal **63** *painted* adorned **65** *hold* remain fixed in **67** *apprehensive* capable of knowing and reasoning **69** *holds . . . rank* remains fixed in his position **72** *constant* determined (resolutely) **74** *Olympus* a mountain in Greece, the home of the gods **75** *bootless* unavailingly **77** *Et tu, Brutè* and thou, Brutus (cf. Caesar's remark at III, i, 55) **80** *pulpits* platforms for delivering public speeches **83** *Ambition's debt* what was due to Caesar's ambition **85** *Publius* an old senator, too confused to flee **86** *mutiny* tumult **87** *fast* close **89** *standing* organizing resistance **93** *your age* i.e. you as an old man **94** *abide* stand the consequences of, be responsible for **96** *amazed* full of consternation **100** *drawing . . . upon* prolonging life, that men attach importance to **108** *market place* the Roman Forum **114** *in sport* for entertainment, i.e. as plays **115** *basis* pedestal of statue; *along* stretched out prostrate **117** *knot* group (of conspirators) **119** *forth* go out into the city **120** *grace* do honor to

Enter a Servant.

BRUTUS

122   Soft! who comes here? A friend of Antony's.

SERVANT

Thus, Brutus, did my master bid me kneel;
Thus did Mark Antony bid me fall down;
And being prostrate, thus he bade me say:

126   Brutus is noble, wise, valiant, and honest;

127   Caesar was mighty, bold, royal, and loving.
Say I love Brutus and I honor him;
Say I feared Caesar, honored him, and loved him.
If Brutus will vouchsafe that Antony

131   May safely come to him and be resolved
How Caesar hath deserved to lie in death,
Mark Antony shall not love Caesar dead
So well as Brutus living; but will follow
The fortunes and affairs of noble Brutus

136   Thorough the hazards of this untrod state
With all true faith. So says my master Antony.

BRUTUS

Thy master is a wise and valiant Roman.
I never thought him worse.

140   Tell him, so please him come unto this place,
He shall be satisfied and, by my honor,
Depart untouched.

SERVANT   I'll fetch him presently.   *Exit.*

BRUTUS

143   I know that we shall have him well to friend.

CASSIUS

144   I wish we may. But yet have I a mind

145   That fears him much; and my misgiving still

146   Falls shrewdly to the purpose.

Enter Antony.

BRUTUS

But here comes Antony. Welcome, Mark Antony.

ANTONY

O mighty Caesar! dost thou lie so low?
Are all thy conquests, glories, triumphs, spoils,
Shrunk to this little measure? Fare thee well.
I know not, gentlemen, what you intend,

152   Who else must be let blood, who else is rank.
If I myself, there is no hour so fit
As Caesar's death's hour; nor no instrument
Of half that worth as those your swords, made rich
With the most noble blood of all this world.

157   I do beseech ye, if you bear me hard,

158   Now, whilst your purpled hands do reek and smoke,

159   Fulfil your pleasure. Live a thousand years,

160   I shall not find myself so apt to die;

161   No place will please me so, no mean of death,
As here by Caesar, and by you cut off,
The choice and master spirits of this age.

BRUTUS

O Antony, beg not your death of us!
Though now we must appear bloody and cruel,
As by our hands and this our present act
You see we do, yet see you but our hands
And this the bleeding business they have done.

169   Our hearts you see not. They are pitiful;
And pity to the general wrong of Rome

171   (As fire drives out fire, so pity pity)
Hath done this deed on Caesar. For your part,
To you our swords have leaden points, Mark Antony.

174   Our arms in strength of malice, and our hearts

Of brothers' temper, do receive you in
With all kind love, good thoughts, and reverence.

CASSIUS

Your voice shall be as strong as any man's   177
In the disposing of new dignities.   178

BRUTUS

Only be patient till we have appeased
The multitude, beside themselves with fear,
And then we will deliver you the cause   181
Why I, that did love Caesar when I struck him,
Have thus proceeded.

ANTONY   I doubt not of your wisdom.
Let each man render me his bloody hand.
First, Marcus Brutus, will I shake with you;
Next, Caius Cassius, do I take your hand;
Now, Decius Brutus, yours; now yours, Metellus;
Yours, Cinna; and, my valiant Casca, yours.
Though last, not least in love, yours, good Trebonius.
Gentlemen all – Alas, what shall I say?
My credit now stands on such slippery ground   191
That one of two bad ways you must conceit me,   192
Either a coward or a flatterer.
That I did love thee, Caesar, O, 'tis true!
If then thy spirit look upon us now,
Shall it not grieve thee dearer than thy death   196
To see thy Antony making his peace,
Shaking the bloody fingers of thy foes,
Most noble! in the presence of thy corse?
Had I as many eyes as thou hast wounds,
Weeping as fast as they stream forth thy blood,
It would become me better than to close   202
In terms of friendship with thine enemies.
Pardon me, Julius! Here wast thou bayed, brave hart;   204
Here didst thou fall; and here thy hunters stand,
Signed in thy spoil, and crimsoned in thy lethe.   206
O world, thou wast the forest to this hart;
And this indeed, O world, the heart of thee!
How like a deer, stroken by many princes,   209
Dost thou here lie!

CASSIUS

Mark Antony –

ANTONY   Pardon me, Caius Cassius.
The enemies of Caesar shall say this;
Then, in a friend, it is cold modesty.   213

CASSIUS

I blame you not for praising Caesar so;
But what compact mean you to have with us?   215

---

122 *Soft* wait a moment, slowly   **126** *honest* honorable   **127** *royal* nobly munificent   **131** *be resolved* have satisfactorily explained to him (?), be fully informed (?)   **136** *Thorough* (common dissyllabic form of 'through'); *untrod state* novel state of affairs (?), uncertain future (?)   **140** *so* if it should   **143** *to* as a   **144** *mind* presentiment   **145** *fears* distrusts; *still* always   **146** *Falls . . . purpose* turns out to be very near the truth   **152** *let blood* i.e. put to death; *rank* diseased (with pun on 'grown too strong')   **157** *bear me hard* bear me a grudge   **158** *purpled* i.e. with blood; *reek and smoke* i.e. steam (with warm blood)   **159** *Live* if I should live   **160** *apt* ready   **161** *so* so well; *mean* manner, means   **169** *pitiful* full of pity   **171** *pity pity* pity for the general wrong drove out pity for Caesar   **174–75** *Our arms . . . temper* both our arms, strong in the appearance of enmity, and our hearts, full of brotherly feeling   **177** *voice* vote   **178** *dignities* offices of state   **181** *deliver* report to   **191** *My credit* my reputation as Caesar's friend (?), trust in me (?)   **192** *conceit* judge   **196** *dearer* more keenly   **202** *close* conclude an agreement   **204** *bayed* brought to bay; *hart* deer (with pun on 'heart')   **206** *Signed . . . spoil* marked with the signs of your slaughter; *lethe* deer's blood, marked on all who were in at the kill (disyllabic)   **209** *stroken* struck down   **213** *modesty* moderation   **215** *compact* agreement (accented on second syllable)

216 Will you be pricked in number of our friends,
Or shall we on, and not depend on you?

ANTONY
Therefore I took your hands, but was indeed
Swayed from the point by looking down on Caesar.
Friends am I with you all, and love you all,
Upon this hope, that you shall give me reasons
Why and wherein Caesar was dangerous.

BRUTUS
Or else were this a savage spectacle.
224 Our reasons are so full of good regard
That were you, Antony, the son of Caesar,
You should be satisfied.

ANTONY   That's all I seek;
And am moreover suitor that I may
228 Produce his body to the market place
And in the pulpit, as becomes a friend,
230 Speak in the order of his funeral.

BRUTUS
You shall, Mark Antony.

CASSIUS   Brutus, a word with you.
[Aside to Brutus]
You know not what you do. Do not consent
That Antony speak in his funeral.
Know you how much the people may be moved
By that which he will utter?

BRUTUS *[aside to Cassius]*   By your pardon –
I will myself into the pulpit first
And show the reason of our Caesar's death.
238 What Antony shall speak, I will protest
He speaks by leave and by permission;
And that we are contented Caesar shall
241 Have all true rites and lawful ceremonies.
242 It shall advantage more than do us wrong.

CASSIUS *[aside to Brutus]*
243 I know not what may fall. I like it not.

BRUTUS
Mark Antony, here, take you Caesar's body.
You shall not in your funeral speech blame us,
But speak all good you can devise of Caesar;
And say you do't by our permission.
Else shall you not have any hand at all
About his funeral. And you shall speak
In the same pulpit whereto I am going,
After my speech is ended.

ANTONY   Be it so.
I do desire no more.

BRUTUS
Prepare the body then, and follow us.
Exeunt. Manet Antony.

ANTONY
O, pardon me, thou bleeding piece of earth,

That I am meek and gentle with these butchers!
Thou art the ruins of the noblest man
That ever livèd in the tide of times.   257
Woe to the hand that shed this costly blood!
Over thy wounds now do I prophesy
(Which, like dumb mouths, do ope their ruby lips
To beg the voice and utterance of my tongue),
A curse shall light upon the limbs of men;
Domestic fury and fierce civil strife
Shall cumber all the parts of Italy;   264
Blood and destruction shall be so in use   265
And dreadful objects so familiar
That mothers shall but smile when they behold
Their infants quarterèd with the hands of war,
All pity choked with custom of fell deeds;   269
And Caesar's spirit, ranging for revenge,   270
With Atè by his side come hot from hell,   271
Shall in these confines with a monarch's voice   272
Cry 'Havoc!' and let slip the dogs of war,   273
That this foul deed shall smell above the earth   274
With carrion men, groaning for burial.   275
      Enter Octavius' Servant.
You serve Octavius Caesar, do you not?

SERVANT
I do, Mark Antony.

ANTONY
Caesar did write for him to come to Rome.

SERVANT
He did receive his letters and is coming,
And bid me say to you by word of mouth –
O Caesar!

ANTONY
Thy heart is big. Get thee apart and weep.   282
Passion, I see, is catching; for mine eyes,   283
Seeing those beads of sorrow stand in thine,
Began to water. Is thy master coming?

SERVANT
He lies to-night within seven leagues of Rome.

ANTONY
Post back with speed and tell him what hath chanced.   287
Here is a mourning Rome, a dangerous Rome,
No Rome of safety for Octavius yet.   289
Hie hence and tell him so. Yet stay awhile.   290
Thou shalt not back till I have borne this corse
Into the market place. There shall I try   292
In my oration how the people take
The cruel issue of these bloody men;   294
According to the which thou shalt discourse   295
To young Octavius of the state of things.
Lend me your hand.   *Exeunt [with Caesar's body].*

              ✻

---

216 *pricked* marked down   224 *good regard* sound considerations   228 *Produce* bring forth   230 *order* ritual, ceremony   238 *protest* proclaim   241 *true* proper   242 *advantage* benefit (us)   243 *fall* happen   257 *tide of times* course of history   264 *cumber* burden   265 *in use* common   269 *custom . . . deeds* being accustomed to cruel deeds   270 *ranging* roving (in search of prey)   271 *Atè* Greek goddess of discord   272 *confines* regions   273 *Havoc* signal for unlimited slaughter; *let slip* unleash   274 *That* so that   275 *carrion* dead and rotting   282 *big* full of grief   283 *Passion* grief   287 *chanced* happened   289 *Rome* (see I, ii, 156n.)   290 *Hie* hasten   292 *try* test   294 *cruel issue* result of the cruelty   295 *the which* the result of my test

III, ii The Forum   1 *will be satisfied* demand a full explanation   2 *audience* a hearing   4 *part* divide

     Enter Brutus and [presently] goes into the pulpit,   III, ii
     and Cassius, with the Plebeians.

PLEBEIANS
We will be satisfied! Let us be satisfied!   1

BRUTUS
Then follow me and give me audience, friends.   2
Cassius, go you into the other street
And part the numbers.   4
Those that will hear me speak, let 'em stay here;
Those that will follow Cassius, go with him;

7 And public reasons shall be renderèd
Of Caesar's death.

1 . PLEBEIAN   I will hear Brutus speak.

2 . PLEBEIAN
I will hear Cassius, and compare their reasons
10 When severally we hear them renderèd.
           [Exit Cassius, with some of the Plebeians.]

3 . PLEBEIAN
The noble Brutus is ascended. Silence!

12 BRUTUS   Be patient till the last.

13 Romans, countrymen, and lovers, hear me for my cause,
and be silent, that you may hear. Believe me for mine
15 honor, and have respect to mine honor, that you may
16 believe. Censure me in your wisdom, and awake your
17 senses, that you may the better judge. If there be any in
this assembly, any dear friend of Caesar's, to him I say
that Brutus' love to Caesar was no less than his. If then
that friend demand why Brutus rose against Caesar, this
is my answer: Not that I loved Caesar less, but that I
loved Rome more. Had you rather Caesar were living,
and die all slaves, than that Caesar were dead, to live all
freemen? As Caesar loved me, I weep for him; as he was
fortunate, I rejoice at it; as he was valiant, I honor him;
but – as he was ambitious, I slew him. There is tears for
his love; joy for his fortune; honor for his valor; and
death for his ambition. Who is here so base that would
29 be a bondman? If any, speak; for him have I offended.
30 Who is here so rude that would not be a Roman? If any,
speak; for him have I offended. Who is here so vile that
will not love his country? If any, speak; for him have I
offended. I pause for a reply.

ALL   None, Brutus, none!

BRUTUS   Then none have I offended. I have done no more
36 to Caesar than you shall do to Brutus. The question of
37 his death is enrolled in the Capitol; his glory not extenu-
38 ated, wherein he was worthy; nor his offenses enforced,
for which he suffered death.
      Enter Mark Antony [and others], with Caesar's
      body.
Here comes his body, mourned by Mark Antony, who,
though he had no hand in his death, shall receive the
42 benefit of his dying, a place in the commonwealth, as
which of you shall not? With this I depart, that, as I slew
44 my best lover for the good of Rome, I have the same
dagger for myself when it shall please my country to
need my death.

ALL   Live, Brutus! live, live!

1 . PLEBEIAN
Bring him with triumph home unto his house.

2 . PLEBEIAN
49 Give him a statue with his ancestors.

3 . PLEBEIAN
Let him be Caesar.

4 . PLEBEIAN   Caesar's better parts
Shall be crowned in Brutus.

1 . PLEBEIAN
We'll bring him to his house with shouts and clamors.

BRUTUS
My countrymen –

2 . PLEBEIAN   Peace! silence! Brutus speaks.

1 . PLEBEIAN   Peace, ho!

BRUTUS
Good countrymen, let me depart alone,
And, for my sake, stay here with Antony.

Do grace to Caesar's corpse, and grace his speech   57
Tending to Caesar's glories which Mark Antony,   58
By our permission, is allowed to make.
I do entreat you, not a man depart,
Save I alone, till Antony have spoke.   *Exit.*

1 . PLEBEIAN
Stay, ho! and let us hear Mark Antony.

3 . PLEBEIAN
Let him go up into the public chair.   63
We'll hear him. Noble Antony, go up.

ANTONY
For Brutus' sake I am beholding to you.   65
     [Antony goes into the pulpit.]

4 . PLEBEIAN
What does he say of Brutus?

3 . PLEBEIAN   He says for Brutus' sake
He finds himself beholding to us all.

4 . PLEBEIAN
'Twere best he speak no harm of Brutus here!

1 . PLEBEIAN
This Caesar was a tyrant.

3 . PLEBEIAN   Nay, that's certain.
We are blest that Rome is rid of him.

2 . PLEBEIAN
Peace! Let us hear what Antony can say.

ANTONY
You gentle Romans –

ALL   Peace, ho! Let us hear him.

ANTONY
Friends, Romans, countrymen, lend me your ears;
I come to bury Caesar, not to praise him.
The evil that men do lives after them;
The good is oft interrèd with their bones.
So let it be with Caesar. The noble Brutus
Hath told you Caesar was ambitious.
If it were so, it was a grievous fault,
And grievously hath Caesar answered it.   80
Here under leave of Brutus and the rest
(For Brutus is an honorable man;
So are they all, all honorable men),
Come I to speak in Caesar's funeral.
He was my friend, faithful and just to me;   85
But Brutus says he was ambitious,
And Brutus is an honorable man.
He hath brought many captives home to Rome,
Whose ransoms did the general coffers fill.   89
Did this in Caesar seem ambitious?
When that the poor have cried, Caesar hath wept;
Ambition should be made of sterner stuff.
Yet Brutus says he was ambitious;
And Brutus is an honorable man.
You all did see that on the Lupercal
I thrice presented him a kingly crown,

---

7 *public reasons* reasons having to do with the general good (?), reasons in explanation to the public (?)   10 *severally* separately   12 *last* end of my speech   13 *lovers* dear friends; *my cause* i.e. the cause of freedom   15 *have . . . honor* remember that I am honorable   16 *Censure* judge   17 *senses* reason   29 *bondman* slave   30 *rude* barbarous   36 *shall do* i.e. if Brutus should so offend; *question of* considerations that led to   37 *enrolled in* recorded in the archives of; *extenuated* understated   38 *enforced* over-stated   42 *place* i.e. as a free Roman   44 *lover* friend   49 *ancestors* (see I, ii, 159n.)   57 *Do . . . speech* show due respect to Caesar's corpse and listen respectfully to Antony's speech   58 *Tending* relating   63 *chair* pulpit, rostrum   65 *beholding* obliged   80 *answered it* paid the penalty   85 *just* entirely reliable   89 *general coffers* public treasury

Which he did thrice refuse. Was this ambition?
Yet Brutus says he was ambitious;
And sure he is an honorable man.
100 I speak not to disprove what Brutus spoke,
But here I am to speak what I do know.
You all did love him once, not without cause.
What cause withholds you then to mourn for him?
O judgment, thou art fled to brutish beasts,
And men have lost their reason! Bear with me.
My heart is in the coffin there with Caesar,
And I must pause till it come back to me.

1. PLEBEIAN
Methinks there is much reason in his sayings.

2. PLEBEIAN
If thou consider rightly of the matter,
Caesar has had great wrong.

3. PLEBEIAN   Has he, masters?
I fear there will a worse come in his place.

4. PLEBEIAN
Marked ye his words? He would not take the crown;
Therefore 'tis certain he was not ambitious.

1. PLEBEIAN
114 If it be found so, some will dear abide it.

2. PLEBEIAN
Poor soul! his eyes are red as fire with weeping.

3. PLEBEIAN
There's not a nobler man in Rome than Antony.

4. PLEBEIAN
Now mark him. He begins again to speak.

ANTONY
But yesterday the word of Caesar might
Have stood against the world. Now lies he there,
120 And none so poor to do him reverence.
O masters! If I were disposed to stir
122 Your hearts and minds to mutiny and rage,
I should do Brutus wrong, and Cassius wrong,
Who, you all know, are honorable men.
I will not do them wrong. I rather choose
To wrong the dead, to wrong myself and you,
Than I will wrong such honorable men.
But here's a parchment with the seal of Caesar.
129 I found it in his closet; 'tis his will.
130 Let but the commons hear this testament,
Which (pardon me) I do not mean to read,
And they would go and kiss dead Caesar's wounds
133 And dip their napkins in his sacred blood;
Yea, beg a hair of him for memory,
And dying, mention it within their wills,
Bequeathing it as a rich legacy
Unto their issue.

4. PLEBEIAN
We'll hear the will! Read it, Mark Antony.

ALL
The will, the will! We will hear Caesar's will!

ANTONY
Have patience, gentle friends; I must not read it.
It is not meet you know how Caesar loved you.   141
You are not wood, you are not stones, but men;
And being men, hearing the will of Caesar,
It will inflame you, it will make you mad.
'Tis good you know not that you are his heirs;
For if you should, O, what would come of it?

4. PLEBEIAN
Read the will! We'll hear it, Antony!
You shall read us the will, Caesar's will!

ANTONY
Will you be patient? Will you stay awhile?   149
I have o'ershot myself to tell you of it.   150
I fear I wrong the honorable men
Whose daggers have stabbed Caesar; I do fear it.

4. PLEBEIAN
They were traitors. Honorable men!

ALL
The will! the testament!

2. PLEBEIAN   They were villains,
Murderers! The will! Read the will!

ANTONY
You will compel me then to read the will?
Then make a ring about the corpse of Caesar
And let me show you him that made the will.
Shall I descend? and will you give me leave?

ALL   Come down.

2. PLEBEIAN   Descend.

3. PLEBEIAN   You shall have leave.
[Antony comes down.]

4. PLEBEIAN   A ring! Stand round.

1. PLEBEIAN
Stand from the hearse! Stand from the body!   165

2. PLEBEIAN
Room for Antony, most noble Antony!

ANTONY
Nay, press not so upon me. Stand far off.   167

ALL   Stand back! Room! Bear back!   168

ANTONY
If you have tears, prepare to shed them now.
You all do know this mantle. I remember   170
The first time ever Caesar put it on.
'Twas on a summer's evening in his tent,
That day he overcame the Nervii.   173
Look, in this place ran Cassius' dagger through.
See what a rent the envious Casca made.   175
Through this the well-belovèd Brutus stabbed;
And as he plucked his cursèd steel away,
Mark how the blood of Caesar followed it,
As rushing out of doors to be resolved   179
If Brutus so unkindly knocked or no;   180
For Brutus, as you know, was Caesar's angel.   181
Judge, O you gods, how dearly Caesar loved him!
This was the most unkindest cut of all;   183
For when the noble Caesar saw him stab,
Ingratitude, more strong than traitors' arms,
Quite vanquished him. Then burst his mighty heart;
And in his mantle muffling up his face,
Even at the base of Pompey's statue   188
(Which all the while ran blood) great Caesar fell.
O, what a fall was there, my countrymen!
Then I, and you, and all of us fell down,
Whilst bloody treason flourished over us.   192

---

114 *dear abide it* pay a heavy penalty for it   120 *so poor* base enough   122 *mutiny* riot   129 *closet* study (?), cabinet for private papers (?)   130 *commons* plebeians   133 *napkins* handkerchiefs   141 *meet* fitting that   149 *stay* wait   150 *o'ershot myself* gone further than I intended   165 *hearse* bier   167 *far* farther   168 *Bear* move   170 *mantle* cloak (here toga)   173 *Nervii* a tribe defeated in 57 B.C. in one of the most decisive victories in the Gallic Wars   175 *envious* malicious   179 *be resolved* learn for certain   180 *unkindly* unnaturally and cruelly   181 *angel* 'darling,' i.e. favorite who could do no wrong   183 *most unkindest* cruelest and most unnatural   188 *base* pedestal; *statue* (trisyllabic)   192 *flourished* swaggered and brandished its sword in triumph

O, now you weep, and I perceive you feel
194 The dint of pity. These are gracious drops.
195 Kind souls, what weep you when you but behold
196 Our Caesar's vesture wounded? Look you here!
197 Here is himself, marred as you see with traitors.
  1. PLEBEIAN O piteous spectacle!
  2. PLEBEIAN O noble Caesar!
  3. PLEBEIAN O woeful day!
  4. PLEBEIAN O traitors, villains!
  1. PLEBEIAN O most bloody sight!
  2. PLEBEIAN We will be revenged.
204 [ALL] Revenge! About! Seek! Burn! Fire! Kill! Slay!
  Let not a traitor live!
206 ANTONY Stay, countrymen.
  1. PLEBEIAN Peace there! Hear the noble Antony.
  2. PLEBEIAN We'll hear him, we'll follow him, we'll die
  with him!
ANTONY
  Good friends, sweet friends, let me not stir you up
  To such a sudden flood of mutiny.
  They that have done this deed are honorable.
213 What private griefs they have, alas, I know not,
  That made them do it. They are wise and honorable,
  And will no doubt with reasons answer you.
  I come not, friends, to steal away your hearts.
  I am no orator, as Brutus is,
  But (as you know me all) a plain blunt man
  That love my friend; and that they know full well
220 That gave me public leave to speak of him.
221 For I have neither writ, nor words, nor worth,
222 Action, nor utterance, nor the power of speech
223 To stir men's blood. I only speak right on.
  I tell you that which you yourselves do know,
  Show you sweet Caesar's wounds, poor poor dumb
    mouths,
  And bid them speak for me. But were I Brutus,
  And Brutus Antony, there were an Antony
228 Would ruffle up your spirits, and put a tongue
  In every wound of Caesar that should move
  The stones of Rome to rise and mutiny.
ALL
  We'll mutiny.
  1. PLEBEIAN We'll burn the house of Brutus.
  3. PLEBEIAN
  Away then! Come, seek the conspirators.
ANTONY
  Yet hear me, countrymen. Yet hear me speak.
ALL
  Peace, ho! Hear Antony, most noble Antony!
ANTONY
  Why, friends, you go to do you know not what.
  Wherein hath Caesar thus deserved your loves?
  Alas, you know not! I must tell you then.
  You have forgot the will I told you of.
ALL
  Most true! The will! Let's stay and hear the will.
ANTONY
  Here is the will, and under Caesar's seal.
  To every Roman citizen he gives,
242 To every several man, seventy-five drachmas.
  2. PLEBEIAN
  Most noble Caesar! We'll revenge his death!
244 3. PLEBEIAN O royal Caesar!
  ANTONY Hear me with patience.

ALL Peace, ho!
ANTONY
  Moreover, he hath left you all his walks,   247
  His private arbors, and new-planted orchards,   248
  On this side Tiber; he hath left them you,
  And to your heirs for ever – common pleasures,   250
  To walk abroad and recreate yourselves.
  Here was a Caesar! When comes such another?
1. PLEBEIAN
  Never, never! Come, away, away!
  We'll burn his body in the holy place   254
  And with the brands fire the traitors' houses.
  Take up the body.
2. PLEBEIAN Go fetch fire!
3. PLEBEIAN Pluck down benches!   258
4. PLEBEIAN Pluck down forms, windows, anything!   259
                    Exit Plebeians [with the body].
ANTONY
  Now let it work. Mischief, thou art afoot,   260
  Take thou what course thou wilt.
     Enter Servant.   How now, fellow?   261
SERVANT
  Sir, Octavius is already come to Rome.
ANTONY Where is he?
SERVANT
  He and Lepidus are at Caesar's house.
ANTONY
  And thither will I straight to visit him.   265
  He comes upon a wish. Fortune is merry,   266
  And in this mood will give us anything.
SERVANT
  I heard him say Brutus and Cassius
  Are rid like madmen through the gates of Rome.   269
ANTONY
  Belike they had some notice of the people,   270
  How I had moved them. Bring me to Octavius.   *Exeunt.*   271

                          *

    Enter Cinna the Poet, and after him the Plebeians.   III, iii
CINNA
  I dreamt to-night that I did feast with Caesar,   1
  And things unluckily charge my fantasy.   2
  I have no will to wander forth of doors,   3
  Yet something leads me forth.
1. PLEBEIAN What is your name?

194 *dint* impression; *gracious* full of grace, becoming 195 *what* why
196 *vesture* i.e. the mantle 197 *marred* mangled; *with* by 204 *About* to
work 206 *Stay* wait 213 *private griefs* personal grievances 220 *public
... speak* permission to speak in public 221 *writ* a written-out speech
(most editors emend to 'wit,' i.e. invention, which accords with the rest
of the list of qualities of a good orator that follows); *words* fluency; *worth*
stature as a public figure, authority 222 *Action* skilful use of gesture;
utterance good delivery 223 *right on* straight out, just as I think it 228
ruffle up stir to rage 242 *several* individual; *seventy-five drachmas* (at least
£12 to-day) 244 *royal* nobly munificent 247 *walks* (see I, ii, 155n.)
248 *orchards* gardens 250 *common pleasures* public parks 254 *holy place*
where the most sacred temples were in Rome 258 *Pluck down* wrench
loose, tear out 259 *forms* long benches; *windows* shutters 260 *work*
have its full effect 261 *fellow* (form of address to inferiors) 265 *straight*
at once 266 *upon a wish* exactly as I might have wished; *merry* in a good
mood (toward us) 269 *Are rid* have ridden 270 *Belike* probably;
notice of news about 271 *Bring* escort
III, iii A street 1 *to-night* last night 2 *things ... fantasy* what has happened
gives my dream a bad interpretation 3 *forth* out

                         918

2. PLEBEIAN Whither are you going?

3. PLEBEIAN Where do you dwell?

4. PLEBEIAN Are you a married man or a bachelor?

9 2. PLEBEIAN Answer every man directly.

1. PLEBEIAN Ay, and briefly.

4. PLEBEIAN Ay, and wisely.

3. PLEBEIAN Ay, and truly, you were best.

CINNA What is my name? Whither am I going? Where do I dwell? Am I a married man or a bachelor? Then, to answer every man directly and briefly, wisely and truly: wisely I say, I am a bachelor.

17 2. PLEBEIAN That's as much as to say they are fools that
18 marry. You'll bear me a bang for that, I fear. Proceed directly.

CINNA Directly I am going to Caesar's funeral.

1. PLEBEIAN As a friend or an enemy?

CINNA As a friend.

2. PLEBEIAN That matter is answered directly.

4. PLEBEIAN For your dwelling – briefly.

CINNA Briefly, I dwell by the Capitol.

3. PLEBEIAN Your name, sir, truly.

CINNA Truly, my name is Cinna.

1. PLEBEIAN Tear him to pieces! He's a conspirator.

CINNA I am Cinna the poet! I am Cinna the poet!

4. PLEBEIAN Tear him for his bad verses! Tear him for his bad verses!

CINNA I am not Cinna the conspirator.

33 4. PLEBEIAN It is no matter; his name 's Cinna! Pluck
34 but his name out of his heart, and turn him going.

3. PLEBEIAN Tear him, tear him! *[They kill him.]* Come, brands, ho! firebrands! To Brutus', to Cassius'! Burn all! Some to Decius' house and some to Casca's; some to Ligarius'! Away, go!

Exeunt all the Plebeians [with the body of Cinna].

*

IV, i   *Enter Antony, Octavius, and Lepidus.*

ANTONY

1   These many, then, shall die; their names are pricked.

OCTAVIUS

Your brother too must die. Consent you, Lepidus?

LEPIDUS

I do consent –

OCTAVIUS   Prick him down, Antony.

LEPIDUS

Upon condition Publius shall not live,

Who is your sister's son, Mark Antony.

ANTONY

He shall not live. Look, with a spot I damn him.   6

But, Lepidus, go you to Caesar's house.

Fetch the will hither, and we shall determine

How to cut off some charge in legacies.   9

LEPIDUS

What? shall I find you here?

OCTAVIUS

Or here or at the Capitol.   *Exit Lepidus.* 11

ANTONY

This is a slight unmeritable man,   12

Meet to be sent on errands. Is it fit,

The threefold world divided, he should stand   14

One of the three to share it?

OCTAVIUS   So you thought him,

And took his voice who should be pricked to die   16

In our black sentence and proscription.   17

ANTONY

Octavius, I have seen more days than you;   18

And though we lay these honors on this man

To ease ourselves of divers sland'rous loads,   20

He shall but bear them as the ass bears gold,

To groan and sweat under the business,   22

Either led or driven as we point the way;

And having brought our treasure where we will,

Then take we down his load, and turn him off   25

(Like to the empty ass) to shake his ears   26

And graze in commons.   27

OCTAVIUS   You may do your will;

But he's a tried and valiant soldier.   28

ANTONY

So is my horse, Octavius, and for that

I do appoint him store of provender.   30

It is a creature that I teach to fight,

To wind, to stop, to run directly on,   32

His corporal motion governed by my spirit.   33

And, in some taste, is Lepidus but so.   34

He must be taught, and trained, and bid go forth:

A barren-spirited fellow; one that feeds   36

On objects, arts, and imitations

Which, out of use and staled by other men,   38

Begin his fashion. Do not talk of him   39

But as a property. And now, Octavius,   40

Listen great things. Brutus and Cassius   41

Are levying powers. We must straight make head.   42

Therefore let our alliance be combined,   43

Our best friends made, our means stretched;   44

And let us presently go sit in council

How covert matters may be best disclosed   46

And open perils surest answerèd.   47

OCTAVIUS

Let us do so; for we are at the stake   48

And bayed about with many enemies;

And some that smile have in their hearts, I fear,

Millions of mischiefs.   *Exeunt.* 51

---

9 *directly* plainly   **17–18** *they . . . marry* (proverbial)   **18** *bear me a bang* get a beating from me   **33** *Pluck* tear   **34** *turn him going* send him packing

IV, i The house of Antony   **1** *pricked* marked down on a list   **6** *spot* mark; *damn* condemn   **9** *cut . . . charge* reduce the outlay of the estate (by altering the will)   **11** *Or* either   **12** *slight unmeritable* insignificant and unworthy   **14** *The . . . divided* the world being divided among the three triumvirs into three parts (Europe, Africa, and Asia)   **16** *voice* vote   **17** *black* i.e. death; *proscription* condemnation to death or exile   **18** *have . . . days* am older, i.e. more experienced   **20** *ease . . . loads* lighten for ourselves some of the charges that will be brought against us   **22** *business* work done by beasts   **25** *turn him off* send him packing   **26** *empty* unburdened   **27** *commons* public pasture   **28** *soldier* (trisyllabic)   **30** *appoint* assign; *store* a supply   **32** *To wind . . . on* to turn, to stop suddenly, to resume running immediately   **33** *corporal* bodily   **34** *taste* degree; *so* the same   **36** *barren-spirited* without initiative, unoriginal   **36–37** *feeds . . . imitations* nourishes his spirit with curiosities, artificial contrivances, and following of fashions   **38** *staled* cheapened, worn-out   **39** *Begin his fashion* he then adopts as fashionable   **40** *property* chattel (?), tool (?)   **41** *Listen* hear   **42** *straight make head* immediately raise an army   **43** *combined* strengthened   **44** *made* mustered; *stretched* used to their fullest advantage   **46** *How . . . disclosed* to determine how hidden dangers may best be discovered   **47** *surest answerèd* most safely met   **48** *at the stake* i.e. like a bear at the stake bayed by dogs   **51** *mischiefs* schemes to harm us

*

IV, ii   *Drum. Enter Brutus, Lucilius, [Lucius,] and the*
    Army. Titinius and Pindarus meet them.

BRUTUS Stand ho!

LUCILIUS Give the word, ho! and stand!

BRUTUS
    What now, Lucilius! Is Cassius near?

LUCILIUS
    He is at hand, and Pindarus is come
    To do you salutation from his master.

BRUTUS
6   He greets me well. Your master, Pindarus,
7   In his own change, or by ill officers,
8   Hath given me some worthy cause to wish
    Things done undone; but if he be at hand,
10 I shall be satisfied.

PINDARUS   I do not doubt
    But that my noble master will appear
12 Such as he is, full of regard and honor.

BRUTUS
13 He is not doubted. A word, Lucilius,
14 How he received you. Let me be resolved.

LUCILIUS
    With courtesy and with respect enough,
16 But not with such familiar instances
17 Nor with such free and friendly conference
    As he hath used of old.

BRUTUS   Thou hast described
19 A hot friend cooling. Ever note, Lucilius,
    When love begins to sicken and decay
21 It useth an enforcèd ceremony.
    There are no tricks in plain and simple faith;
23 But hollow men, like horses hot at hand,
24 Make gallant show and promise of their mettle;
    Low march within.
    But when they should endure the bloody spur,
26 They fall their crests, and like deceitful jades
27 Sink in the trial. Comes his army on?

LUCILIUS
28 They mean this night in Sardis to be quartered.
29 The greater part, the horse in general,
    Are come with Cassius.

BRUTUS   Hark! He is arrived.
31 March gently on to meet him.
    Enter Cassius and his Powers.

CASSIUS Stand, ho!

BRUTUS Stand, ho! Speak the word along.

1. SOLDIER Stand!

2. SOLDIER Stand!

3. SOLDIER Stand!

CASSIUS
    Most noble brother, you have done me wrong.

BRUTUS
    Judge me, you gods! wrong I mine enemies?
    And if not so, how should I wrong a brother.

CASSIUS
40 Brutus, this sober form of yours hides wrongs;
    And when you do them –

41 BRUTUS   Cassius, be content.
42 Speak your griefs softly. I do know you well.
    Before the eyes of both our armies here
    (Which should perceive nothing but love from us)
    Let us not wrangle. Bid them move away.
46 Then in my tent, Cassius, enlarge your griefs,

    And I will give you audience.   47

CASSIUS   Pindarus,
    Bid our commanders lead their charges off   48
    A little from this ground.

BRUTUS
    Lucilius, do you the like; and let no man
    Come to our tent till we have done our conference.
    Let Lucius and Titinius guard our door.   *Exeunt.*
    Mane[n]t Brutus and Cassius.   IV, iii

CASSIUS
    That you have wronged me doth appear in this:
    You have condemned and noted Lucius Pella   2
    For taking bribes here of the Sardians;
    Wherein my letters, praying on his side,   4
    Because I knew the man, was slighted off.   5

BRUTUS
    You wronged yourself to write in such a case.

CASSIUS
    In such a time as this it is not meet
    That every nice offense should bear his comment. 8

BRUTUS
    Let me tell you, Cassius, you yourself
    Are much condemned to have an itching palm,   10
    To sell and mart your offices for gold   11
    To undeservers.

CASSIUS   I an itching palm?
    You know that you are Brutus that speaks this,
    Or, by the gods, this speech were else your last!

BRUTUS
    The name of Cassius honors this corruption,   15
    And chastisement doth therefore hide his head.

CASSIUS Chastisement?

BRUTUS
    Remember March; the ides of March remember.
    Did not great Julius bleed for justice sake?
    What villain touched his body that did stab
    And not for justice? What, shall one of us,   21
    That struck the foremost man of all this world
    But for supporting robbers – shall we now   23
    Contaminate our fingers with base bribes,
    And sell the mighty space of our large honors 25
    For so much trash as may be graspèd thus?   26

IV, ii The camp of Brutus (near Sardis) **6** *greets me well* sends his greetings by a worthy man **7** *In . . . officers* whether from changed feelings on his part or through the acts of unworthy subordinates **8** *worthy* justifiable **10** *be satisfied* receive a full explanation **12** *Such* exactly; *full . . . honor* regardful (of your interests) and honorable **13** *A word* i.e. tell me **14** *resolved* fully informed **16** *familiar instances* signs of friendship **17** *conference* conversation **19** *Ever note* always observe **21** *enforcèd* forced **23** *hollow* insincere; *hot at hand* spirited at the start **24** *mettle* high spirit **26** *fall* let fall; *crests* ridges of horses' necks; *jades* horses (contemptuous) **27** *Sink . . . trial* fail when they are put to the test **28** *Sardis* (the capital of the ancient kingdom of Lydia, in western Asia Minor; Brutus had requested Cassius to join forces with him there) **29** *horse in general* all the cavalry **31** *gently* slowly **40** *sober form* serious and restrained manner **41** *content* calm **42** *griefs* grievances **46** *enlarge* expound fully **47** *audience* a hearing **48** *charges* troops

IV, iii **2** *noted* publicly disgraced, slandered **4** *letters* (singular in meaning) **5** *slighted off* contemptuously dismissed **8** *nice . . . comment* trivial offense should be criticized **10** *condemned to have* accused of having; *itching palm* i.e. a covetous disposition **11** *mart* traffic in **15** *honors* lends an appearance of honor to **21** *And not* except **23** *supporting robbers* i.e. having backed those who desire to rob the Romans of their freedom (see I, ii, 283n.) **25** *the mighty . . . honors* our great power to confer honorable public offices **26** *trash* money (contemptuous)

27   I had rather be a dog and bay the moon
      Than such a Roman.
28   CASSIUS   Brutus, bait not me!
      I'll not endure it. You forget yourself
30   To hedge me in. I am a soldier, I,
      Older in practice, abler than yourself
32   To make conditions.
      BRUTUS   Go to! You are not Cassius.
      CASSIUS I am.
      BRUTUS I say you are not.
      CASSIUS
35   Urge me no more! I shall forget myself.
36   Have mind upon your health. Tempt me no farther.
37   BRUTUS Away, slight man!
      CASSIUS
      Is't possible?
      BRUTUS   Hear me, for I will speak.
39   Must I give way and room to your rash choler?
40   Shall I be frighted when a madman stares?
      CASSIUS
      O ye gods, ye gods! Must I endure all this?
      BRUTUS
      All this? Ay, more! Fret till your proud heart break.
      Go show your slaves how choleric you are
44   And make your bondmen tremble. Must I budge?
45   Must I observe you? Must I stand and crouch
46   Under your testy humor? By the gods,
47   You shall digest the venom of your spleen,
      Though it do split you; for from this day forth
49   I'll use you for my mirth, yea, for my laughter,
      When you are waspish.
      CASSIUS   Is it come to this?
      BRUTUS
      You say you are a better soldier.
52   Let it appear so; make your vaunting true,
      And it shall please me well. For mine own part,
54   I shall be glad to learn of noble men.
      CASSIUS
      You wrong me every way! You wrong me, Brutus!
      I said an elder soldier, not a better.
      Did I say 'better'?
      BRUTUS   If you did, I care not.
      CASSIUS
58   When Caesar lived he durst not thus have moved me.
      BRUTUS
59   Peace, peace! You durst not so have tempted him.
      CASSIUS I durst not?
      BRUTUS No.

      CASSIUS
      What, durst not tempt him?
      BRUTUS   For your life you durst not.
      CASSIUS
      Do not presume too much upon my love.
      I may do that I shall be sorry for.
      BRUTUS
      You have done that you should be sorry for.
      There is no terror, Cassius, in your threats;
      For I am armed so strong in honesty   67
      That they pass by me as the idle wind,
      Which I respect not. I did send to you   69
      For certain sums of gold, which you denied me;
      For I can raise no money by vile means.
      By heaven, I had rather coin my heart
      And drop my blood for drachmas than to wring
      From the hard hands of peasants their vile trash
      By any indirection. I did send   75
      To you for gold to pay my legions,
      Which you denied me. Was that done like Cassius?
      Should I have answered Caius Cassius so?
      When Marcus Brutus grows so covetous
      To lock such rascal counters from his friends,   80
      Be ready, gods, with all your thunderbolts,
      Dash him to pieces!
      CASSIUS   I denied you not.
      BRUTUS You did.
      CASSIUS
      I did not. He was but a fool that brought
      My answer back. Brutus hath rived my heart.   85
      A friend should bear his friend's infirmities,
      But Brutus makes mine greater than they are.
      BRUTUS
      I do not, till you practise them on me.
      CASSIUS
      You love me not.
      BRUTUS   I do not like your faults.
      CASSIUS
      A friendly eye could never see such faults.
      BRUTUS
      A flatterer's would not, though they do appear
      As huge as high Olympus.
      CASSIUS
      Come, Antony, and young Octavius, come!
      Revenge yourselves alone on Cassius.   94
      For Cassius is aweary of the world:
      Hated by one he loves; braved by his brother;   96
      Checked like a bondman; all his faults observed,   97
      Set in a notebook, learned and conned by rote
      To cast into my teeth. O, I could weep   99
      My spirit from mine eyes! There is my dagger,
      And here my naked breast; within, a heart
      Dearer than Pluto's mine, richer than gold.   102
      If that thou be'st a Roman, take it forth.
      I, that denied thee gold, will give my heart.
      Strike as thou didst at Caesar; for I know,
      When thou didst hate him worst, thou lovedst him better
      Than ever thou lovedst Cassius.
      BRUTUS   Sheathe your dagger.
      Be angry when you will; it shall have scope.   108
      Do what you will; dishonor shall be humor.   109
      O Cassius, you are yokèd with a lamb
      That carries anger as the flint bears fire;

---

27 *bay* howl at   28 *bait* harass   30 *hedge me in* i.e. limit my authority   32 *make conditions* manage affairs   35 *Urge* drive   36 *health* safety; *Tempt* provoke   37 *slight* worthless   39 *way . . . choler* course and scope to your rash anger   40 *stares* glares   44 *budge* flinch   45 *observe* wait upon obsequiously; *crouch* bow   46 *testy humor* irritable temper   47 *digest the venom* swallow the poison; *spleen* i.e. hot temper   49 *laughter* object of ridicule   52 *vaunting* boasting   54 *learn of* hear of the existence of (with pun on 'take lessons from')   58 *moved* angered   59 *tempted* provoked   67 *honesty* integrity   69 *respect not* ignore   75 *indirection* irregular means   80 *rascal counters* base coins   85 *rived* split in two   94 *alone* solely   96 *braved* defied   97 *Checked* scolded   99 *cast . . . teeth* i.e. throw up to me   102 *Dearer . . . mine* more precious than the riches within the earth (Pluto, god of the underworld, probably confused with Plutus, god of riches)   108 *it* i.e. your anger; *scope* free play   109 *dishonor . . . humor* I shall take your insults as an effect of your hot temper

112 Who, much enforcèd, shows a hasty spark,
113 And straight is cold again.

CASSIUS   Hath Cassius lived
To be but mirth and laughter to his Brutus
115 When grief and blood ill-tempered vexeth him?

BRUTUS
When I spoke that, I was ill-tempered too.

CASSIUS
Do you confess so much? Give me your hand.

BRUTUS
And my heart too.

CASSIUS   O Brutus!

BRUTUS   What's the matter?

CASSIUS
Have you not love enough to bear with me
120 When that rash humor which my mother gave me
Makes me forgetful?

BRUTUS   Yes, Cassius; and from henceforth,
When you are over-earnest with your Brutus,
123 He'll think your mother chides, and leave you so.

*Enter a Poet [followed by Lucilius, Titinius, and
Lucius].*

POET
Let me go in to see the generals!
125 There is some grudge between 'em. 'Tis not meet
They be alone.

LUCILIUS   You shall not come to them.

POET
Nothing but death shall stay me.

CASSIUS   How now? What's the matter?

POET
For shame, you generals! What do you mean?
Love and be friends, as two such men should be;
For I have seen more years, I'm sure, than ye.

CASSIUS
133 Ha, ha! How vilely doth this cynic rhyme!

BRUTUS
134 Get you hence, sirrah! Saucy fellow, hence!

CASSIUS
Bear with him, Brutus. 'Tis his fashion.

BRUTUS
136 I'll know his humor when he knows his time.
137 What should the wars do with these jigging fools?
138 Companion, hence!

CASSIUS   Away, away, be gone!   *Exit Poet.*

BRUTUS
Lucilius and Titinius, bid the commanders
Prepare to lodge their companies to-night.

CASSIUS
And come yourselves, and bring Messala with you
Immediately to us.   *[Exeunt Lucilius and Titinius.]*

BRUTUS   Lucius, a bowl of wine. *[Exit Lucius.]*

CASSIUS
I did not think you could have been so angry.

BRUTUS
O Cassius, I am sick of many griefs.

CASSIUS
Of your philosophy you make no use
146 If you give place to accidental evils.

BRUTUS
No man bears sorrow better. Portia is dead.

CASSIUS   Ha! Portia?

BRUTUS   She is dead.

CASSIUS
How scaped I killing when I crossed you so?   150
O insupportable and touching loss!   151
Upon what sickness?   152

BRUTUS   Impatient of my absence,
And grief that young Octavius with Mark Antony
Have made themselves so strong; for with her death   154
That tidings came. With this she fell distract,   155
And (her attendants absent) swallowed fire.   156

CASSIUS
And died so?

BRUTUS   Even so.

CASSIUS   O ye immortal gods!

Enter Boy [Lucius], with wine and tapers.

BRUTUS
Speak no more of her. Give me a bowl of wine.
In this I bury all unkindness, Cassius.   159
Drinks.

CASSIUS
My heart is thirsty for that noble pledge.
Fill, Lucius, till the wine o'erswell the cup.
I cannot drink too much of Brutus' love.
          [Drinks. Exit Lucius.]
Enter Titinius and Messala.

BRUTUS
Come in, Titinius! Welcome, good Messala.
Now sit we close about this taper here
And call in question our necessities.   165

CASSIUS
Portia, art thou gone?

BRUTUS   No more, I pray you.
Messala, I have here receivèd letters
That young Octavius and Mark Antony
Come down upon us with a mighty power,   169
Bending their expedition toward Philippi.   170

MESSALA
Myself have letters of the selfsame tenure.   171

BRUTUS
With what addition?

MESSALA
That by proscription and bills of outlawry   173
Octavius, Antony, and Lepidus
Have put to death an hundred senators.

BRUTUS
Therein our letters do not well agree.

112 *enforcèd* worked upon   113 *straight* at once   115 *blood ill-tempered* unbalanced disposition   120 *rash humor* choleric or splenetic temperament   123 *mother* i.e. inherited temperament (also hysteria ?); *leave you so* leave it at that   125 *grudge* ill-feeling   133 *cynic* boorish fellow   134 *sirrah* (contemptuous form of address); *Saucy* insolent   136 *I'll . . . time* I'll accept his fashion of behavior when he knows the proper time and place for it   137 *jigging* rhyming (contemptuous), doggerel versifying   138 *Companion* fellow (contemptuous)   146 *place* way; *accidental evils* evils caused by chance (i.e. Brutus, as a Stoic, should not be affected by those external adversities caused by Fortune)   150 *killing* being killed by you; *crossed* opposed   151 *touching* grievous   152 *Upon* as a result of; *Impatient of* unable to endure (also desperate at ?)   154-55 *for . . . came* for together with the news of her death came the news of their strength   155 *distract* distraught   156 *swallowed fire* (according to Plutarch, as translated by North, she cast 'hot burning coals [from a charcoal brazier] . . . into her mouth, and kept her mouth so close that she choked herself')   159 *In . . . unkindness* in this wine I'll drown all our differences   165 *call in question* deliberate upon   169 *upon* against; *power* army   170 *Bending* directing; *expedition* rapid march   171 *tenure* tenor, purport   173 *proscription* condemnation to death; *bills of outlawry* proscription lists

Mine speak of seventy senators that died
By their proscriptions, Cicero being one.

CASSIUS
Cicero one?

MESSALA   Cicero is dead,
And by that order of proscription.

181   Had you your letters from your wife, my lord?

BRUTUS No, Messala.

MESSALA
Nor nothing in your letters writ of her?

BRUTUS
Nothing, Messala.

MESSALA   That methinks is strange.

BRUTUS
Why ask you? Hear you aught of her in yours?

MESSALA No, my lord.

BRUTUS
Now as you are a Roman, tell me true.

MESSALA
Then like a Roman bear the truth I tell;
For certain she is dead, and by strange manner.

BRUTUS
Why, farewell, Portia. We must die, Messala.
191   With meditating that she must die once,
I have the patience to endure it now.

MESSALA
Even so great men great losses should endure.

CASSIUS
194   I have as much of this in art as you,
195   But yet my nature could not bear it so.

BRUTUS
196   Well, to our work alive. What do you think
Of marching to Philippi presently?

CASSIUS
I do not think it good.

BRUTUS   Your reason?

CASSIUS   This it is:
'Tis better that the enemy seek us.
So shall he waste his means, weary his soldiers,
201   Doing himself offense, whilst we, lying still,
Are full of rest, defense, and nimbleness.

BRUTUS
203   Good reasons must of force give place to better.
The people 'twixt Philippi and this ground
205   Do stand but in a forced affection;
For they have grudged us contribution.
The enemy, marching along by them,
By them shall make a fuller number up,
209   Come on refreshed, new added, and encouraged;
From which advantage shall we cut him off
If at Philippi we do face him there,
These people at our back.

181–95 (some editors, assuming revision, bracket or delete this episode as contradictory and redundant of ll. 143–58 and 166) 191 *once* at some time 194 *this in art* i.e. this stoical fortitude in philosophical theory 195 *nature* natural emotions 196 *alive* that concerns us as living men 201 *offense* injury 203 *of force* of necessity 205 *Do ... affection* favor us only by compulsion 209 *new added* reinforced 220 *Omitted* not taken 221 *bound in* confined to 224 *ventures* investments risked on the high seas; *with your will* as you wish 228 *niggard* stint, i.e. sleep only a short time 230 *hence* go from here 231 *gown* dressing gown 239 *instrument* lute or cithern 241 *knave* lad (affectionate); *o'erwatched* tired from lack of sleep 247 *raise* rouse; *by and by* soon 249 *watch your pleasure* await your commands 251 *otherwise bethink me* change my mind

CASSIUS   Hear me, good brother.

BRUTUS
Under your pardon. You must note beside
That we have tried the utmost of our friends,
Our legions are brimful, our cause is ripe.
The enemy increaseth every day;
We, at the height, are ready to decline.
There is a tide in the affairs of men
Which, taken at the flood, leads on to fortune;
Omitted, all the voyage of their life   220
Is bound in shallows and in miseries.   221
On such a full sea are we now afloat,
And we must take the current when it serves
Or lose our ventures.   224

CASSIUS   Then, with your will, go on.
We'll along ourselves and meet them at Philippi.

BRUTUS
The deep of night is crept upon our talk
And nature must obey necessity,
Which we will niggard with a little rest.   228
There is no more to say?

CASSIUS   No more. Good night.
Early to-morrow will we rise and hence.   230

BRUTUS
Lucius! (*Enter Lucius.*) My gown.   [*Exit Lucius.*] 231
                                   Farewell, good Messala.
Good night, Titinius. Noble, noble Cassius,
Good night and good repose.

CASSIUS   O my dear brother,
This was an ill beginning of the night!
Never come such division 'tween our souls!
Let it not, Brutus.

Enter Lucius, with the gown.

BRUTUS   Everything is well.

CASSIUS
Good night, my lord.

BRUTUS   Good night, good brother.

TITINIUS, MESSALA
Good night, Lord Brutus.

BRUTUS   Farewell every one.
Exeunt [Cassius, Titinius, and Messala].
Give me the gown. Where is thy instrument?   239

LUCIUS
Here in the tent.

BRUTUS   What, thou speak'st drowsily?
Poor knave, I blame thee not; thou art o'erwatched.   241
Call Claudius and some other of my men;
I'll have them sleep on cushions in my tent.

LUCIUS Varro and Claudius!
Enter Varro and Claudius.

VARRO Calls my lord?

BRUTUS
I pray you, sirs, lie in my tent and sleep.
It may be I shall raise you by and by   247
On business to my brother Cassius.

VARRO
So please you, we will stand and watch your pleasure.   249

BRUTUS
I will not have it so. Lie down, good sirs.
It may be I shall otherwise bethink me.   251
    [*Varro and Claudius lie down.*]
Look, Lucius, here's the book I sought for so;
I put it in the pocket of my gown.

LUCIUS
I was sure your lordship did not give it me.

BRUTUS
Bear with me, good boy, I am much forgetful.
Canst thou hold up thy heavy eyes awhile,
257 And touch thy instrument a strain or two ?

LUCIUS
258 Ay, my lord, an't please you.

BRUTUS   It does, my boy.
I trouble thee too much, but thou art willing.

LUCIUS It is my duty, sir.

BRUTUS
I should not urge thy duty past thy might.
262 I know young bloods look for a time of rest.

LUCIUS I have slept, my lord, already.

BRUTUS
It was well done ; and thou shalt sleep again ;
265 I will not hold thee long. If I do live,
266 I will be good to thee.
Music, and a song. [Lucius falls asleep.]
267 This is a sleepy tune. O murd'rous slumber !
268 Layest thou thy leaden mace upon my boy,
That plays thee music ? Gentle knave, good night.
I will not do thee so much wrong to wake thee.
If thou dost nod, thou break'st thy instrument ;
I'll take it from thee ; and, good boy, good night.
Let me see, let me see. Is not the leaf turned down
Where I left reading ? Here it is, I think.
[Sits.] Enter the Ghost of Caesar.
275 How ill this taper burns ! Ha, who comes here ?
276 I think it is the weakness of mine eyes
That shapes this monstrous apparition.
278 It comes upon me. Art thou any thing ?
Art thou some god, some angel, or some devil,
280 That mak'st my blood cold and my hair to stare ?
Speak to me what thou art.

GHOST
Thy evil spirit, Brutus.

BRUTUS   Why com'st thou ?

GHOST
To tell thee thou shalt see me at Philippi.

BRUTUS Well ; then I shall see thee again ?

GHOST Ay, at Philippi.

BRUTUS
Why, I will see thee at Philippi then.   *[Exit Ghost.]*
Now I have taken heart thou vanishest.
Ill spirit, I would hold more talk with thee.
Boy. Lucius ! Varro, Claudius. Sirs ! Awake !
Claudius !

291 **LUCIUS** The strings, my lord, are false.

BRUTUS
He thinks he still is at his instrument.
Lucius, awake !

LUCIUS My lord ?

BRUTUS
Didst thou dream, Lucius, that thou so criedst out ?

LUCIUS
My lord, I do not know that I did cry.

BRUTUS
Yes, that thou didst. Didst thou see anything ?

LUCIUS Nothing, my lord.

BRUTUS
Sleep again, Lucius. Sirrah Claudius !
[To Varro]

Fellow thou, awake !

VARRO My lord ?

CLAUDIUS My lord ?

BRUTUS
Why did you so cry out, sirs, in your sleep ?

BOTH
Did we, my lord ?

BRUTUS   Ay. Saw you anything ?

VARRO
No, my lord, I saw nothing.

CLAUDIUS   Nor I, my lord.

BRUTUS
Go and commend me to my brother Cassius.   306
Bid him set on his pow'rs betimes before,   307
And we will follow.

BOTH   It shall be done, my lord.   *Exeunt.*

*

Enter Octavius, Antony, and their Army.   V, i

OCTAVIUS
Now, Antony, our hopes are answerèd.
You said the enemy would not come down
But keep the hills and upper regions.
It proves not so. Their battles are at hand ;   4
They mean to warn us at Philippi here,   5
Answering before we do demand of them.   6

ANTONY
Tut ! I am in their bosoms and I know   7
Wherefore they do it. They could be content   8
To visit other places, and come down
With fearful bravery, thinking by this face   10
To fasten in our thoughts that they have courage.   11
But 'tis not so.
Enter a Messenger.

MESSENGER   Prepare you, generals.
The enemy comes on in gallant show ;   13
Their bloody sign of battle is hung out,   14
And something to be done immediately.

ANTONY
Octavius, lead your battle softly on   16
Upon the left hand of the even field.

OCTAVIUS
Upon the right hand I. Keep thou the left.

ANTONY
Why do you cross me in this exigent ?   19

257 *touch* play on; *strain* musical composition   258 *an't* if it   262 *young bloods* youthful constitutions   265 *hold* detain   266 s.d. *Music, and a song* (stage tradition prescribes the use of 'Orpheus with his lute,' from *Henry VIII*; more appropriate is 'Come, heavy sleep,' from John Dowland's *First Book of Songs*, 1597)   267 *murd'rous* giving the appearance of death   268 *leaden* heavy (lead was associated with death); *mace* staff of office with which a man was touched on the shoulder when arrested   275 *How . . . burns* (it was commonly held that lights burned dim or blue in the presence of a ghost or spirit)   276 *weakness . . . eyes* i.e. possibly a hallucination   278 *upon* toward   280 *stare* stand on end   291 *false* out of tune   306 *commend me* give my greetings   307 *set on* advance ; *betimes before* early in the morning before me
V, i The plains of Philippi   4 *proves* turns out to be ; *battles* armies   5 *warn* challenge   6 *Answering . . . them* appearing against us before we call them to combat   7 *in their bosoms* aware of their secrets (i.e. he has spies in their army)   8–9 *could . . . places* would prefer to be elsewhere   10 *fearful bravery* display that inspires (with pun on 'is full of') fear; *face* show   11 *fasten* fix the idea   13 *gallant* splendid   14 *bloody sign* red flag   16 *battle* army; *softly* slowly   19 *cross* oppose; *exigent* critical moment

OCTAVIUS
I do not cross you ; but I will do so.
March. Drum. Enter Brutus, Cassius, and their Army
[; Lucilius, Titinius, Messala, and others].

BRUTUS
They stand and would have parley.

CASSIUS
Stand fast, Titinius. We must out and talk.

OCTAVIUS
Mark Antony, shall we give sign of battle ?

ANTONY
24   No, Caesar, we will answer on their charge.
25   Make forth. The generals would have some words.

OCTAVIUS
Stir not until the signal.

BRUTUS
Words before blows. Is it so, countrymen ?

OCTAVIUS
Not that we love words better, as you do.

BRUTUS
Good words are better than bad strokes, Octavius.

ANTONY
In your bad strokes, Brutus, you give good words ;
Witness the hole you made in Caesar's heart,
Crying 'Long live ! Hail, Caesar !'

CASSIUS   Antony,
33   The posture of your blows are yet unknown ;
34   But for your words, they rob the Hybla bees,
And leave them honeyless.

ANTONY   Not stingless too.

BRUTUS
O yes, and soundless too !
For you have stol'n their buzzing, Antony,
And very wisely threat before you sting.

ANTONY
39   Villains ! you did not so when your vile daggers
Hacked one another in the sides of Caesar.
41   You showed your teeth like apes, and fawned like hounds,
And bowed like bondmen, kissing Caesar's feet ;
Whilst damnèd Casca, like a cur, behind
Struck Caesar on the neck. O you flatterers !

CASSIUS
Flatterers ? Now, Brutus, thank yourself !
This tongue had not offended so to-day
47   If Cassius might have ruled.

OCTAVIUS
48   Come, come, the cause ! If arguing make us sweat,
49   The proof of it will turn to redder drops.

---

24 *on their charge* when they attack   25 *Make forth* go forward   33 *posture* fashion, quality   34 *Hybla* a Sicilian town famous for the sweetness of its honey   39 *so* i.e. give warning   41 *showed your teeth* grinned obsequiously   47 *ruled* had his way (at II, i, 155–61)   48 *the cause* to our business   49 *proof* trial   52 *goes up* will be sheathed   54 *another Caesar* i.e. himself   55 *Have . . . to* has also been killed by   59 *strain* line of descent   61 *peevish* childish (Octavius was twenty-one) ; *worthless* unworthy   62 *masker . . . reveller* (see II, i, 189 ; II, ii, 116)   66 *stomachs* appetite (for battle)   68 *on the hazard* at stake   74 *As Pompey was* (at Pharsalus, where he was persuaded to give battle to Caesar against his will ; see I, i, 37n.) ; *set* stake, gamble   76–77 *held . . . opinion* was a convinced follower of the Epicurean philosophy, i.e. a materialist, who thought it foolishly superstitious to believe in omens (cf. II, i, 193–201)   78 *credit* believe in   79 *former* foremost ; *ensign* standard, banner   80 *fell* swooped down   82 *consorted* accompanied   84 *ravens . . . kites* scavengers which proverbially anticipate death   86 *sickly* dying   87 *fatal* foreboding death   89 *but* only   91 *constantly* resolutely   93 *The . . . friendly* may the gods be well-disposed toward us to-day

---

Look,
I draw a sword against conspirators.
When think you that the sword goes up again ?   52
Never, till Caesar's three-and-thirty wounds
Be well avenged, or till another Caesar   54
Have added slaughter to the sword of traitors.   55

BRUTUS
Caesar, thou canst not die by traitors' hands
Unless thou bring'st them with thee.

OCTAVIUS   So I hope.
I was not born to die on Brutus' sword.

BRUTUS
O, if thou wert the noblest of thy strain,   59
Young man, thou couldst not die more honorable.

CASSIUS
A peevish schoolboy, worthless of such honor,   61
Joined with a masker and a reveller !   62

ANTONY
Old Cassius still.

OCTAVIUS   Come, Antony. Away !
Defiance, traitors, hurl we in your teeth.
If you dare fight to-day, come to the field ;
If not, when you have stomachs.   66
Exit Octavius, [with] Antony, and Army.

CASSIUS
Why, now blow wind, swell billow, and swim bark !
The storm is up, and all is on the hazard.   68

BRUTUS
Ho, Lucilius ! Hark, a word with you.
Lucilius stands forth.

LUCILIUS   My lord ?
[Brutus and Lucilius converse apart.]

CASSIUS
Messala.
Messala stands forth.

MESSALA   What says my general ?

CASSIUS   Messala,
This is my birthday ; as this very day
Was Cassius born. Give me thy hand, Messala.
Be thou my witness that against my will
(As Pompey was) am I compelled to set   74
Upon one battle all our liberties.
You know that I held Epicurus strong   76
And his opinion. Now I change my mind
And partly credit things that do presage.   78
Coming from Sardis, on our former ensign   79
Two mighty eagles fell ; and there they perched,   80
Gorging and feeding from our soldiers' hands,
Who to Philippi here consorted us.   82
This morning are they fled away and gone,
And in their steads do ravens, crows, and kites   84
Fly o'er our heads and downward look on us
As we were sickly prey. Their shadows seem   86
A canopy most fatal, under which   87
Our army lies, ready to give up the ghost.

MESSALA
Believe not so.

CASSIUS   I but believe it partly ;   89
For I am fresh of spirit and resolved
To meet all perils very constantly.   91

BRUTUS
Even so, Lucilius.

CASSIUS   Now, most noble Brutus,
The gods to-day stand friendly, that we may,   93

94 Lovers in peace, lead on our days to age!
95 But since the affairs of men rests still incertain,
96 Let's reason with the worst that may befall.
If we do lose this battle, then is this
The very last time we shall speak together.
99 What are you then determinèd to do?

BRUTUS

100 Even by the rule of that philosophy
101 By which I did blame Cato for the death
Which he did give himself – I know not how,
But I do find it cowardly and vile,
104 For fear of what might fall, so to prevent
105 The time of life – arming myself with patience
106 To stay the providence of some high powers
That govern us below.

CASSIUS   Then, if we lose this battle,
108 You are contented to be led in triumph
Thorough the streets of Rome.

BRUTUS

No, Cassius, no. Think not, thou noble Roman,
111 That ever Brutus will go bound to Rome.
He bears too great a mind. But this same day
Must end that work the ides of March begun,
And whether we shall meet again I know not.
Therefore our everlasting farewell take.
For ever and for ever farewell, Cassius!
If we do meet again, why, we shall smile;
If not, why then this parting was well made.

CASSIUS

For ever and for ever farewell, Brutus!
If we do meet again, we'll smile indeed;
If not, 'tis true this parting was well made.

BRUTUS

Why then, lead on. O that a man might know
The end of this day's business ere it come!
But it sufficeth that the day will end,
And then the end is known. Come, ho! Away!   *Exeunt.*

V, ii   *Alarum. Enter Brutus and Messala.*

BRUTUS

1 Ride, ride, Messala, ride, and give these bills
2 Unto the legions on the other side.
     Loud alarum.
3 Let them set on at once; for I perceive
4 But cold demeanor in Octavius' wing,
5 And sudden push gives them the overthrow.
6 Ride, ride, Messala! Let them all come down.   *Exeunt.*

V, iii   *Alarums. Enter Cassius and Titinius.*

CASSIUS

1 O, look, Titinius, look! The villains fly!
2 Myself have to mine own turned enemy.
3 This ensign here of mine was turning back;
4 I slew the coward and did take it from him.

TITINIUS

O Cassius, Brutus gave the word too early,
6 Who, having some advantage on Octavius,
7 Took it too eagerly. His soldiers fell to spoil,
Whilst we by Antony are all enclosed.
     Enter Pindarus.

PINDARUS

Fly further off, my lord! fly further off!
10 Mark Antony is in your tents, my lord.
11 Fly, therefore, noble Cassius, fly far off!

CASSIUS

This hill is far enough. Look, look, Titinius!

Are those my tents where I perceive the fire?

TITINIUS

They are, my lord.

CASSIUS   Titinius, if thou lovest me,
Mount thou my horse and hide thy spurs in him
Till he have brought thee up to yonder troops
And here again, that I may rest assured
Whether yond troops are friend or enemy.

TITINIUS

I will be here again even with a thought.   *Exit.* 19

CASSIUS

Go, Pindarus, get higher on that hill.
My sight was ever thick. Regard Titinius,   21
And tell me what thou not'st about the field.   22
     [Pindarus goes up.]
This day I breathèd first. Time is come round,
And where I did begin, there shall I end.
My life is run his compass. Sirrah, what news?   25

PINDARUS *(above)* O my lord!   26

CASSIUS What news?

PINDARUS *[above]*

Titinius is enclosèd round about
With horsemen that make to him on the spur.   29
Yet he spurs on. Now they are almost on him.
Now Titinius. Now some light. O, he lights too!   31
He's ta'en. *(Shout.)* And hark! They shout for joy.   32

CASSIUS

Come down; behold no more.
O coward that I am to live so long
To see my best friend ta'en before my face!
     Enter Pindarus [from above].
Come hither, sirrah.
In Parthia did I take thee prisoner;
And then I swore thee, saving of thy life,   38
That whatsoever I did bid thee do,
Thou shouldst attempt it. Come now, keep thine oath.
Now be a freeman, and with this good sword,
That ran through Caesar's bowels, search this bosom.   42
Stand not to answer. Here, take thou the hilts;   43
And when my face is covered, as 'tis now,
Guide thou the sword.
     [Pindarus stabs him.] Caesar, thou art revenged
Even with the sword that killed thee.
     [Dies.]

PINDARUS

So, I am free; yet would not so have been,   47

---

94 *Lovers* dear friends   95 *rests still* remain always   96 *reason . . . befall* consider what to do if the worst should happen   99 *then* i.e. if we should lose   100 *that philosophy* i.e. Stoicism   101 *Cato* (see II, i, 295n.)   104 *fall* happen; *prevent* anticipate   105 *time* natural limit   106 *stay* wait for; *providence* destiny; *some* whatever (i.e. Brutus does not believe in the Roman gods, but he does believe in 'powers' whose nature he cannot exactly define)   108 *in triumph* in a victory procession (as a captive)   111 *bound* in chains (as a captive)
V, ii *s.d. Alarum* a drum signal calling to arms   1 *bills* written orders   2 *side* wing (of the army), i.e. Cassius' forces   3 *set on* attack   4 *cold demeanor* lack of spirit (in battle)   5 *push* assault; *gives . . . overthrow* will defeat them   6 *them . . . down* the whole army attack
V, iii   1 *villains* i.e. his own troops   2 *mine own* my own men   3 *ensign* standard-bearer   4 *it* i.e. the standard he was bearing   6 *on* over   7 *spoil* looting   10 *tents* encampment   11 *far* farther   19 *even . . . thought* in the twinkling of an eye   21 *thick* dim, i.e. near-sighted; *Regard* observe   22 *not'st* observe   25 *is . . . compass* has completed its full circuit   26 *s.d. above* (on the 'upper stage')   29 *make to* approach; *on the spur* rapidly   31 *light* dismount   32 *ta'en* captured   38 *swore thee* made you swear; *saving of* when I spared   42 *search* probe, penetrate into   43 *Stand* delay   47 *not so* not in such circumstances

48   Durst I have done my will. O Cassius !
       Far from this country Pindarus shall run,
       Where never Roman shall take note of him.   *[Exit.]*
       Enter Titinius and Messala.

MESSALA

51   It is but change, Titinius ; for Octavius
       Is overthrown by noble Brutus' power,
       As Cassius' legions are by Antony.

TITINIUS

54   These tidings will well comfort Cassius.

MESSALA

       Where did you leave him ?

TITINIUS   All disconsolate,
       With Pindarus his bondman, on this hill.

MESSALA

       Is not that he that lies upon the ground ?

TITINIUS

       He lies not like the living. O my heart !

MESSALA

       Is not that he ?

TITINIUS   No, this was he, Messala,
60   But Cassius is no more. O setting sun,
       As in thy red rays thou dost sink to night,
       So in his red blood Cassius' day is set !
       The sun of Rome is set. Our day is gone ;
64   Clouds, dews, and dangers come ; our deeds are done !
65   Mistrust of my success hath done this deed.

MESSALA

       Mistrust of good success hath done this deed.
67   O hateful Error, Melancholy's child,
68   Why dost thou show to the apt thoughts of men
       The things that are not ? O Error, soon conceived,
       Thou never com'st unto a happy birth,
71   But kill'st the mother that engend'red thee !

TITINIUS

       What, Pindarus ! Where art thou, Pindarus ?

MESSALA

       Seek him, Titinius, whilst I go to meet
       The noble Brutus, thrusting this report
       Into his ears. I may say 'thrusting' it ;
       For piercing steel and darts envenomèd
       Shall be as welcome to the ears of Brutus
       As tidings of this sight.
78 TITINIUS   Hie you, Messala,
       And I will seek for Pindarus the while.   *[Exit Messala.]*
80   Why didst thou send me forth, brave Cassius ?
       Did I not meet thy friends, and did not they

       Put on my brows this wreath of victory
       And bid me give it thee ? Didst thou not hear their
         shouts ?
       Alas, thou hast misconstrued everything !   84
       But hold thee, take this garland on thy brow.   85
       Thy Brutus bid me give it thee, and I
       Will do his bidding. Brutus, come apace
       And see how I regarded Caius Cassius.   88
       By your leave, gods. This is a Roman's part.   89
       Come, Cassius' sword, and find Titinius' heart.
       Dies.
       Alarum. Enter Brutus, Messala, Young Cato,
       Strato, Volumnius, and Lucilius.

BRUTUS

       Where, where, Messala, doth his body lie ?

MESSALA

       Lo, yonder, and Titinius mourning it.

BRUTUS

       Titinius' face is upward.

CATO   He is slain.

BRUTUS

       O Julius Caesar, thou art mighty yet !
       Thy spirit walks abroad and turns our swords
       In our own proper entrails.   96
       Low alarums.

CATO   Brave Titinius !
       Look whe'r he have not crowned dead Cassius.

BRUTUS

       Are yet two Romans living such as these ?
       The last of all the Romans, fare thee well !
       It is impossible that ever Rome
       Should breed thy fellow. Friends, I owe moe tears   101
       To this dead man than you shall see me pay.
       I shall find time, Cassius ; I shall find time.
       Come therefore, and to Thasos send his body.   104
       His funerals shall not be in our camp,
       Lest it discomfort us. Lucilius, come ;   106
       And come, young Cato. Let us to the field.
       Labeo and Flavius set our battles on.   108
       'Tis three o'clock ; and, Romans, yet ere night
       We shall try fortune in a second fight.
                      Exeunt.
       Alarum. Enter Brutus, Messala, [Young] Cato,   V, iv
       Lucilius, and Flavius.

BRUTUS

       Yet, countrymen, O, yet hold up your heads !
         [Exit, followed by Messala and Flavius.]

CATO

       What bastard doth not ? Who will go with me ?   2
       I will proclaim my name about the field.
       I am the son of Marcus Cato, ho !   4
       A foe to tyrants, and my country's friend.   5
       I am the son of Marcus Cato, ho !
       Enter Soldiers and fight.

LUCILIUS

       And I am Brutus, Marcus Brutus I !   7
       Brutus, my country's friend ! Know me for Brutus !
       [Young Cato falls.]
       O young and noble Cato, art thou down ?
       Why, now thou diest as bravely as Titinius,   10
       And mayst be honored, being Cato's son.

[1.] SOLDIER

       Yield, or thou diest.

LUCILIUS   Only I yield to die.   12

---

48 *my will* (rather than Cassius' will, which he was sworn to do)   51 *change* an exchange, 'quid pro quo'   54 *comfort* encourage   60 *setting sun* (a figurative comparison : actually it is mid-afternoon – see l. 109)   64 *dews* (see II, i, 262n., 265n.)   65 *Mistrust . . . success* fear as to how I should make out   67 *Melancholy's child* (melancholy persons fear unreal dangers)   68 *apt* impressionable   71 *mother* i.e. the melancholy person who conceived the error   78 *Hie* hurry   80 *brave* noble   84 *misconstrued* (accented on second syllable)   85 *hold thee* wait a minute   88 *regarded* respected, honored   89 *leave* permission ; *part* role, function (in such circumstances)   96 *own proper* very own ; *Brave* noble   101 *moe* more   104 *Thasos* an island near Philippi where, according to Plutarch, Cassius was buried   106 *discomfort us* dishearten our army   108 *battles* forces
V, iv   2 *What bastard* who is so low-born that he   4 *Cato* (see II, i, 295n.)   5 *tyrants* (such as Caesar and his followers)   7 *Lucilius* (in the folio this speech-prefix appears at l. 9, but Lucilius, as indicated in Plutarch, also speaks ll. 7–8, impersonating Brutus, though some editors give ll. 7–8 to Brutus)   10 *bravely* nobly   12 *Only . . . die* I surrender only in order to die

13   There is so much that thou wilt kill me straight.
Kill Brutus, and be honored in his death.

[1.] SOLDIER
We must not. A noble prisoner!
Enter Antony.

2. SOLDIER
Room ho! Tell Antony Brutus is ta'en.

1. SOLDIER
I'll tell the news. Here comes the general.
Brutus is ta'en! Brutus is ta'en, my lord!

ANTONY   Where is he?

LUCILIUS
Safe, Antony; Brutus is safe enough.
I dare assure thee that no enemy
Shall ever take alive the noble Brutus.
The gods defend him from so great a shame!
When you do find him, or alive or dead,
25   He will be found like Brutus, like himself.

ANTONY
This is not Brutus, friend; but, I assure you,
A prize no less in worth. Keep this man safe;
Give him all kindness. I had rather have
Such men my friends than enemies. Go on,
And see whe'r Brutus be alive or dead;
And bring us word unto Octavius' tent
32   How every thing is chanced.   *Exeunt.*

V, v   *Enter Brutus, Dardanius, Clitus, Strato, and*
Volumnius.

BRUTUS
1   Come, poor remains of friends, rest on this rock.

CLITUS
2   Statilius showed the torchlight; but, my lord,
He came not back. He is or ta'en or slain.

BRUTUS
Sit thee down, Clitus. Slaying is the word.
It is a deed in fashion. Hark thee, Clitus.
[Whispers.]

CLITUS
What, I, my lord? No, not for all the world!

BRUTUS
Peace then. No words.

CLITUS   I'll rather kill myself.

BRUTUS
Hark thee, Dardanius.
[Whispers.]

DARDANIUS   Shall I do such a deed?

CLITUS   O Dardanius!

DARDANIUS   O Clitus!

CLITUS
What ill request did Brutus make to thee?

DARDANIUS
To kill him, Clitus. Look, he meditates.

CLITUS
13   Now is that noble vessel full of grief,
That it runs over even at his eyes.

BRUTUS
Come hither, good Volumnius. List a word.

VOLUMNIUS
What says my lord?

BRUTUS   Why this, Volumnius.
The ghost of Caesar hath appeared to me
18   Two several times by night – at Sardis once,
And this last night here in Philippi fields.
I know my hour is come.

VOLUMNIUS   Not so, my lord.

BRUTUS
Nay, I am sure it is, Volumnius.
Thou seest the world, Volumnius, how it goes.
Our enemies have beat us to the pit.   23
Low alarums.
It is more worthy to leap in ourselves   24
Than tarry till they push us. Good Volumnius,
Thou know'st that we two went to school together.
Even for that our love of old, I prithee
Hold thou my sword-hilts whilst I run on it.

VOLUMNIUS
That's not an office for a friend, my lord.
Alarum still.

CLITUS
Fly, fly, my lord! There is no tarrying here.

BRUTUS
Farewell to you; and you; and you, Volumnius.
Strato, thou hast been all this while asleep.
Farewell to thee too, Strato. Countrymen,
My heart doth joy that yet in all my life
I found no man but he was true to me.
I shall have glory by this losing day
More than Octavius and Mark Antony
By this vile conquest shall attain unto.   38
So fare you well at once; for Brutus' tongue   39
Hath almost ended his life's history.
Night hangs upon mine eyes; my bones would rest,
That have but labored to attain this hour.   42
Alarum. Cry within: Fly, fly, fly!

CLITUS
Fly, my lord, fly!

BRUTUS   Hence! I will follow.
[Exeunt Clitus, Dardanius, and Volumnius.]
I prithee, Strato, stay thou by thy lord.
Thou art a fellow of a good respect;   45
Thy life hath had some smatch of honor in it.   46
Hold then my sword, and turn away thy face
While I do run upon it. Wilt thou, Strato?

STRATO
Give me your hand first. Fare you well, my lord.

BRUTUS
Farewell, good Strato. Caesar, now be still.
I killed not thee with half so good a will.
[He runs on his sword and] dies.
Alarum. Retreat. Enter Octavius, Antony,
Messala, Lucilius, and the Army.

OCTAVIUS
What man is that?

MESSALA
My master's man. Strato, where is thy master?   53

---

13 *so much* so great an inducement to honor and fame (?), so much that I can be blamed for (?) (some editors suppose an offer of money); *straight* at once   25 *like himself* true to his noble nature   32 *is chanced* has happened
V, v   1 *poor remains* pitiful survivors   2 *Statilius . . . torchlight* i.e. a scout who got as far as Cassius' encampment, occupied by Antony's troops, from which he signalled   13 *noble vessel* completely noble man (also a sacred vessel for holding the tears of devout mourners)   18 *several* different   23 *the pit* (into which a wild animal is driven in order to be captured; with pun on 'the grave')   24 *more worthy* nobler   38 *vile conquest* i.e. the destruction of Republican Rome   39 *at once* all together   42 *but labored* experienced only pain   45 *respect* reputation   46 *smatch* taste   53 *man* servant

STRATO
Free from the bondage you are in, Messala.
55 The conquerors can but make a fire of him ;
56 For Brutus only overcame himself,
And no man else hath honor by his death.

LUCILIUS
So Brutus should be found. I thank thee, Brutus,
59 That thou hast proved Lucilius' saying true.

OCTAVIUS
60 All that served Brutus, I will entertain them.
61 Fellow, wilt thou bestow thy time with me ?

STRATO
62 Ay, if Messala will prefer me to you.

OCTAVIUS
Do so, good Messala.

MESSALA
How died my master, Strato ?

STRATO
I held the sword, and he did run on it.

MESSALA
Octavius, then take him to follow thee,   66
That did the latest service to my master.   67

ANTONY
This was the noblest Roman of them all.
All the conspirators save only he
Did that they did in envy of great Caesar ;
He, only in a general honest thought   71
And common good to all, made one of them.   72
His life was gentle, and the elements   73
So mixed in him that Nature might stand up   74
And say to all the world, 'This was a man !'   75

OCTAVIUS
According to his virtue let us use him,   76
With all respect and rites of burial.
Within my tent his bones to-night shall lie,
Most like a soldier, orderèd honorably.   79
So call the field to rest, and let's away   80
To part the glories of this happy day.   *Exeunt omnes.* 81

---

55 *make a fire of* cremate 56 *Brutus only overcame* only Brutus defeated
59 *saying* (see V, iv, 21–25) 60 *entertain them* take them into my service
61 *Fellow* (addressed to Strato) ; *bestow* spend 62 *prefer* recommend 66
follow serve 67 *latest* last, final 71–72 *general . . . all* honorable purpose
to the whole society and for the good of all Romans 72 *made . . . them*
joined the conspiracy 73 *gentle* noble ; *elements* the four elements (earth,
water, air, fire) of which all matter was thought to be composed, or the four
humors (melancholic, phlegmatic, sanguine, choleric) 74 *So mixed* i.e.
equally balanced 75 *a man* i.e. an ideal man 76 *use* treat 79 *orderèd*
treated 80 *field* army 81 *part* share, divide

HAMLET PRINCE OF DENMARK

INTRODUCTION

Vicissitudes of literary taste and temper in the present age have not weakened the hold of *Hamlet* upon viewer and reader, however much they have changed it. Probably they have made it stronger than ever before, stronger even than it was for the last age of men, in the nineteenth century. This is saying much, for men in the nineteenth century helped mightily to make *Hamlet* the most acted and most written-about of Shakespeare's plays. They earnestly accepted its challenge to understanding.

That from which this challenge issues, stamped with a name in words given by Shakespeare to Hamlet himself – "you would pluck out the heart of my mystery" (III, ii, 351–52) – has come to be called the Hamlet mystery by many. Here and there it has been called so with resignation, sometimes hopelessly, but even in its guise of insolubility it can still command critical statement about its being.

It is already plain that the twentieth century will add perception that will matter to the Hamlet tradition in our culture. What it adds will be, like such an addition by any other age, a characteristic enlargement of Shakespeare's dramatic achievement. After a lapse of centuries an extension of perception for a constantly lived-with and experienced work of art like *Hamlet* is an extension of the original creation much to be reckoned with for its revelation of a complex vitality. The new creation comes about not only because the author has conceived form capable of long-continuing growth but also because a late age of posterity, despite the variety of contributions made by former ages, has conceived form into which growth can proceed.

What we in this age seem bent on giving to *Hamlet* is greatly enlarged scope. We are sure enough of ourselves to think of this as meaning a new breadth, and we may hope that it will mean also a new depth. For a long time after Shakespeare there was no generally recognized Hamlet mystery; Hamlet seems to have been for most men a courageous prince who found it understandably hard to take revenge on a shrewd and powerful king. By the nineteenth century the mystery was well established. It was troublesome enough but it could usually be kept within close bounds – that is, within the outlines of Hamlet the man realistically considered as someone who in all essential qualities, however exceptional they might be, could be judged by common sense as a walking and talking inhabitant of the critic's own age. A further limitation came from much thinking that the key to Hamlet's tragedy was probably some one dominant thing such as unstable nervous quality, or shock from his father's death and his mother's hasty remarriage, or melancholy pessimism, or sensitivity unfitting him for the crass burden of his duty to take revenge, or delight in thought unfitting him for

crucial action. Such ideas were all, of course, well worth the having, and they shook down into a corpus that will be a lasting part of the Hamlet tradition. But they did not offer enough satisfaction to keep critics from hastening on to other searchings.

Our twentieth-century searchings have become less and less confined, even when they have been within the personal creation that is Hamlet. Hamlet psychology, still very much alive in an age that has produced Freud and Jung, is now not content with merely a homely reading of Hamlet's character by everyday use of heart and mind. The field of Elizabethan psychology has been carefully explored for principles applicable to Hamlet, and thus there has been a fitting of his creation into the history of ideas. With the application of modern psychological theories – especially and most inevitably those having to do with the ancient family triad of father, mother, and child – there has been an expansion of his persona to take account of a dark abysm of the human self from which can come to anyone, as is thought, tensely opposed feelings for both father and mother, and from which, we are to understand, there comes to Hamlet so much emotional conflict with regard to his uncle the King as a substitute father image, married to his mother, that his hate cannot achieve the murder of the King before his bringing, by hesitation, of death to both his mother and himself. Hamlet, indeed, may seem to have been shaped to order for psychoanalysis. In modern psychology an extension of the Hamlet creation, truly meaningful whether one responds to it or not, has been made by the coming together with a startling show of affinity of something in us and something in Shakespeare.

Elizabethan, nineteenth-century, and twentieth-century psychologies often invite us to see within Hamlet some severe seizure of the soul which is close to disease, if not actually disease, and is the more easily thought of in these terms because of the dominant disease imagery running through the play. A Hamlet viewed as thus stricken can be found to have the tragic flaw in an extreme form. Frequently enough an idea has been held that Hamlet shows an exceptionally noble nature and that in this there is, and should be, a classic flaw to make his drama a tragedy. Sometimes the flaw has seemed by no means to be disease-like or wholly undesirable but to take a paradoxical coloring of good from the nobility in which it appears. Yet it has been conceived to be no less an explanatory flaw for all that and necessarily to be delimited, even in the face of mounting disagreement as to what it is exactly.

A part of the present releasing of the Hamlet mystery from its former bounds takes Hamlet the created personality into a realm of criticism where the time-honored idea of the tragic flaw suddenly loses validity. Here there is the thought that imperfection in the hero cannot yield even a part of the meaning in his tragedy by providing some show of justice for what happens to him as an individual. But here at the same time a conception of Hamlet's having nobility of nature remains, and it may go so far as to make him into a type of human perfection. The Hamlet mystery may thus turn into something like a mystery of Hamlet's martyrdom, where whatever makes it mystery tends to be found outside the character of an individual Hamlet in the character of man in general and in the character of the universe which produces the common predicament of man. Man must act, but all action involves him in evil. It is a finding in the content of *Hamlet* that our age has perhaps been qualified to make by its rediscovery of some forgotten powers of evil in human life and by its interpretation of these in recent literature. In such an area of criticism the question is bound to rise, and does rise, whether *Hamlet* is after all a tragedy, whether it is not a drama worthy perhaps to stand with the greatest tragedies but of a kind peculiar to itself. Yet most critics still seem not of a mind to release *Hamlet* from an obligation to show tragic form.

It is remarkable that *Hamlet* should so perplex the mind and at the same time work so little confusion in the heart. It has supremely that which can make us forget our questions when we give ourselves over to it. Probably no other tragic hero of Shakespeare's equals Hamlet in drawing from the observer that most profound pity which is really as much admiration as pity, and is perfectly tragic because there is no condescension in it. It seems impossible not to forgive Hamlet his brutalities to Ophelia, Polonius, or Rosencrantz and Guildenstern, for they are washed out in our feeling if not in our thinking. He should not be made, we believe, to suffer fools gladly, he the superior spirit to add that suffering to his load.

Perhaps more strongly than anything else pity senses the terrible loneliness of Hamlet. The idealism which moves him to a life-and-death struggle with imprisoning evil is so complex, including even a composition of low comedy with high seriousness, that his single companion, the good but all too solemn Horatio, must always be alien to it. The way in which Horatio fails him in the gravediggers' scene – "'Twere to consider too curiously" (V, i, 193) – is a part of the tragedy, and no minor one. Love desired is always falling away from Hamlet – love in father, in mother, in Ophelia. The poetry that circles about him makes us know that the Prince of Denmark goes through darkness and waste places "most dreadfully attended."

A part of the *Hamlet* that troubles the mind's eye seems to come from Shakespeare's absorption, with sympathies not at all narrow, of a story that had already had a development of meaning at different depths in different ages. This development had taken place in some rather widespread folklore, in a sophisticated literary account of "Amlethus" in the twelfth-century *Historia Danica* of Saxo Grammaticus (printed in 1514), in a very free version of Saxo's account in the fifth volume of the *Histoires Tragiques* of François de Belleforest (1576), and in an old play about Hamlet on the English stage. Concerning the pre-Shakespearean *Hamlet* we know little. A not very revelatory passage in Thomas Nashe's epistle to Robert Greene's *Menaphon* contains a reference to "whole Hamlets, I should say handfuls, of tragicall speeches" as being lifted from Seneca, which indicates that a *Hamlet* was on the

stage by 1589, the date of *Menaphon*, and that it was a Senecan tragedy. Some even more tantalizing words of Nashe's in the same passage have led many to believe that Thomas Kyd, the author of the Senecan *Spanish Tragedy*, wrote this old *Hamlet*. A performance of it is recorded for 1594 and a glimpse of a part of its action comes in 1596 in Thomas Lodge's *Wits Miserie* with a description of a countenance "pale as the Visard of ye ghost which cried so miserally at ye Theator like an oister wife, *Hamlet, revenge.*" Shakespeare's *Hamlet*, in the present state of our knowledge, may be dated 1600–1601. Mainly its story follows that in Belleforest. An English translation of Belleforest, *The Hystorie of Hamblet*, was published in 1608 and seems to have been affected somewhat by Shakespeare's play. It remains to mention one more Hamlet play, the unpraiseworthy German piece *Der Bestrafte Brudermord*, the origin of which is problematic, but which seems to have derived mainly from an early acting version of Shakespeare's *Hamlet*. The German play was printed as late as 1781 from a manuscript dated 1710.

Some have thought that the Hamlet mystery has been put forever beyond our understanding by the loss of the older English *Hamlet*, the so-called *Ur-Hamlet*. Some have gone so far as to make out that Shakespeare was overwhelmed by matter drawn from the *Ur-Hamlet*, which turned out to be so unmanageable as he built around it that the result was incomprehensibility for his joined whole. That way lies an accusation that *Hamlet* is a failure as a piece of dramatic art, and the accusation has been made more than once. Doubtless Shakespeare found the *Ur-Hamlet* of some avail, and doubtless the *Ur-Hamlet* was a rude play befitting the dramatic immaturity of its time, with a quality very different from the mature Shakespearean. But it would seem probable that when he wrote *Hamlet* Shakespeare was beyond being overwhelmed by an old play he wanted to use. He was almost ready to melt and recast one with complete mastery to make *King Lear*. As for *Hamlet*'s being a dramatic or literary failure, the answer of course is that our western culture has forcefully refused to have it so, and on the contrary has given it esteem of the highest. It is for western man to keep on asking why, as there seems to be no danger of his ceasing to do.

As he asks why, it is for western man to realize that he is posing questions about truth itself, about the glorious but also terrifying lack of simplicity that truth shows – and shows in special ways within his own culture – according to a Shakespearean structure of dramatic and poetic images. Here, I would say, is the Hamlet problem of Hamlet problems, one whose recognition lets us know why, after all, there must be many Hamlet problems and various answers to them, yet a gathering together of these into some containing oneness.

The theme of unsimple truth comes early into the Hamlet story. Saxo's Amlethus pretends madness to protect himself until he can get revenge upon the uncle who has killed his father and married his mother. There is no complication of soul-searching and delay in his taking of revenge. He merely bides his time. But there is complication in his procedure of saying things that will make those around him think he does not have the wit to accomplish his revenge. He has not merely that wit but the greater wit to deceive only by being truthful, by turning toward the simple swordsmen who surround him faces of the truth that they do not recognize. He has compulsion never in deepest consequence to destroy truth and he delights in following truth toward a mastery of its complexity. He mingles "craft and candor" to let no word of his "lack truth." There is in him something of primitive riddling, but that is not all. When his uncle's followers think to have sport with Amlethus on the seashore as with a simpleton and bid him look at the meal, meaning the sand, they fully expect that he will take the sand for meal. He not only takes it so; he makes it so in truth. His reply is that it has "been ground small by hoary tempests of the ocean." Here we suddenly know that we are witnessing in fully acceptable form a demonstration of the wide division between the truth of things and the truth of spirit, and the annihilation of this division in the truth of poetry. Such matter as this is largely replaced in Belleforest by a too simple moralizing but not, certainly, in Shakespeare.

In *Hamlet* the theme of unsimple truth is so abundantly restored and so subtly extended that it is everywhere in the action and the poetry. Hamlet at his first appearance begins a searching of the complexity of truth by means of word play and idea play that is carried on throughout the drama; the craft and candor of his dark rejection of sonship to the King and of royal sun-like favor from him, in the punning words "I am too much in the sun" (I, ii, 67), are right Hamlet substance and right introduction to much of the tragedy that comes later. It is by no means only in words and ideas of the moment that Hamlet stands between truths both to divide and unite them. In the large he stands thus between whole worlds of truths in our culture: between the world of an uncivilized heroic past going back even behind Christianity and that of a civilized present; between the world of medieval faith and other-worldliness and that of modern doubt and this-worldliness. In the same way he stands between the truth of angel-like and god-like man and that of man the quintessence of dust, or, in a realm of complete abstraction, between the truth of love and that of hate. There are, needless to say, countless variations in *Hamlet* on the theme of unsimple truth.

It may be said that *Hamlet* is indeed about the pursuit of revenge but most deeply about the pursuit of truth, and that the two pursuits come together to give form to the action of the tragedy. By meeting and testing his father's ghost Hamlet gains truth that seems adequate. It proves on second thought to be not enough. By testing the King with the play within the play he gains truth "more relative than this." Here is the high point of a rising action. Now comes a testing by circumstance of truth that Hamlet has gained with his own testing. He has the chance to kill the praying King. For some reason (we ourselves never stop testing to find it) he loses at this moment of opportunity all truth he has won about revenge as a crying *immediate* need. He fails to kill the King and thus makes possible the killing of Polonius, which starts a falling action that carries him to death – and ironically to attainment of his revenge, a revenge that takes being from tragic defeat, not a revenge in simple truth such as the revenger seeks. Just before the end, to sharpen the irony, Hamlet uneasily tests his need for revenge against the King all over again, showing inability to make secure in simplicity whatever of lost truth he has regained:

> ... is't not perfect conscience
> To quit him with this arm? And is't not to be damned
> To let this canker of our nature come
> In further evil?

Hamlet dies on the search for truth that all men die on. But his tragedy has a richness of texture all its own, not only within and around the seeker but also within and around what is sought.

University of California   WILLARD FARNHAM
at Berkeley

NOTE ON THE TEXT

Hamlet is preserved in three distinct but related early texts: first, the corrupt and abbreviated acting version in the "bad" quarto of 1603; second, the version "newly imprinted and enlarged to almost as much again as it was, according to the true and perfect coppie" in the "good" quarto of 1604–05 (now usually regarded, but without complete assurance, as printed from Shakespeare's own draft); and third, the version in the 1623 folio (now usually regarded, but again without complete assurance, as printed from the prompt-book of Shakespeare's acting company or from the good quarto altered after reference to such a prompt-book). The present edition is based on the quarto of 1604–05 with a minimum of emendation, but, in view of the manifest faultiness of the quarto printing, with occasional deference to readings in the folio, and even with an eye on the 1603 quarto. Enclosed in square brackets are all additions to the quarto stage directions, as well as additions of whole lines or more of dialogue from the folio. (The longer passages thus added are II, ii, 237–66, 330–54; IV, v, 161–63; V, i, 32–35; V, ii, 68–80.) The texts of the quartos are undivided, and that of the folio almost so since there is no scene division in the first act after I, iii, 1, and no division of any kind after II, ii, 1. It is a common complaint that the editorial act–scene division superimposed on the text in modern times is mechanical and inorganic, but, as explained in the general foreword, it is supplied in the present edition only for reference purposes. A list of departures from the text of the quarto of 1604–05 is supplied in the Appendix along with a few Supplementary Notes.

HAMLET PRINCE OF DENMARK

[NAMES OF THE ACTORS

Claudius, King of Denmark
Hamlet, son to the late, and nephew to the present,
    King
Polonius, Lord Chamberlain
Horatio, friend to Hamlet
Laertes, son to Polonius
Voltemand
Cornelius
Rosencrantz } *courtiers*
Guildenstern
Osric
A Gentleman
A Priest

Marcellus }
Bernardo } *officers*
Francisco, a soldier
Reynaldo, servant to Polonius
Players
Two Clowns, gravediggers
Fortinbras, Prince of Norway
A Norwegian Captain
English Ambassadors
Gertrude, Queen of Denmark, mother to Hamlet
Ophelia, daughter to Polonius
Ghost of Hamlet's Father
Lords, Ladies, Officers, Soldiers, Sailors,
    Messengers, Attendants

Scene : *Elsinore*]

*

I, i   *Enter Bernardo and Francisco, two sentinels.*

BERNARDO Who's there ?

FRANCISCO
  Nay, answer me. Stand and unfold yourself.

BERNARDO Long live the king !

FRANCISCO Bernardo ?

BERNARDO He.

FRANCISCO
  You come most carefully upon your hour.

BERNARDO
  'Tis now struck twelve. Get thee to bed, Francisco.

FRANCISCO
  For this relief much thanks. 'Tis bitter cold,
  And I am sick at heart.

BERNARDO
  Have you had quiet guard ?

FRANCISCO   Not a mouse stirring.

BERNARDO
  Well, good night.
  If you do meet Horatio and Marcellus,
13   The rivals of my watch, bid them make haste.
    Enter Horatio and Marcellus.

FRANCISCO
  I think I hear them. Stand, ho ! Who is there ?

HORATIO
  Friends to this ground.

15 MARCELLUS   And liegemen to the Dane.

FRANCISCO
  Give you good night.

MARCELLUS   O, farewell, honest soldier.

  Who hath relieved you ?

FRANCISCO   Bernardo hath my place.
  Give you good night.   *Exit Francisco.*

MARCELLUS   Holla, Bernardo !

BERNARDO   Say –
  What, is Horatio there ?

HORATIO   A piece of him.

BERNARDO
  Welcome, Horatio. Welcome, good Marcellus.

HORATIO
  What, has this thing appeared again to-night ?

BERNARDO
  I have seen nothing.

MARCELLUS
  Horatio says 'tis but our fantasy,
  And will not let belief take hold of him
  Touching this dreaded sight twice seen of us.
  Therefore I have entreated him along
  With us to watch the minutes of this night,
  That, if again this apparition come,
  He may approve our eyes and speak to it.   29

HORATIO
  Tush, tush, 'twill not appear.

BERNARDO   Sit down awhile,
  And let us once again assail your ears,
  That are so fortified against our story,
  What we two nights have seen.

HORATIO   Well, sit we down,
  And let us hear Bernardo speak of this.

BERNARDO
  Last night of all,
  When yond same star that's westward from the pole 36
  Had made his course t' illume that part of heaven

I, i Elsinore Castle: a sentry-post   13 *rivals* sharers   15 *Dane* King of
Denmark   29 *approve* confirm   36 *pole* polestar

Where now it burns, Marcellus and myself,
The bell then beating one –

Enter Ghost.

MARCELLUS

Peace, break thee off. Look where it comes again.

BERNARDO

In the same figure like the king that's dead.

MARCELLUS

Thou art a scholar ; speak to it, Horatio.

BERNARDO

Looks 'a not like the king ? Mark it, Horatio.

HORATIO

Most like. It harrows me with fear and wonder.

BERNARDO

It would be spoke to.

MARCELLUS   Speak to it, Horatio.

HORATIO

What art thou that usurp'st this time of night
Together with that fair and warlike form
48   In which the majesty of buried Denmark
49   Did sometimes march ? By heaven I charge thee, speak.

MARCELLUS

It is offended.

BERNARDO   See, it stalks away.

HORATIO   –

Stay. Speak, speak. I charge thee, speak.   *Exit Ghost.*

MARCELLUS

'Tis gone and will not answer.

BERNARDO

How now, Horatio ? You tremble and look pale.
Is not this something more than fantasy ?
What think you on't ?

HORATIO

Before my God, I might not this believe
Without the sensible and true avouch
Of mine own eyes.

MARCELLUS   Is it not like the king ?

HORATIO

As thou art to thyself.
Such was the very armor he had on
61   When he th' ambitious Norway combated.
62   So frowned he once when, in an angry parle,
He smote the sledded Polacks on the ice.
'Tis strange.

MARCELLUS

65   Thus twice before, and jump at this dead hour,
With martial stalk hath he gone by our watch.

HORATIO

In what particular thought to work I know not ;
68   But, in the gross and scope of my opinion,
This bodes some strange eruption to our state.

MARCELLUS

Good now, sit down, and tell me he that knows,
Why this same strict and most observant watch
72   So nightly toils the subject of the land,
And why such daily cast of brazen cannon
74   And foreign mart for implements of war,
75   Why such impress of shipwrights, whose sore task
Does not divide the Sunday from the week.
77   What might be toward that this sweaty haste
Doth make the night joint-laborer with the day ?
Who is't that can inform me ?

HORATIO   That can I.
At least the whisper goes so. Our last king,

Whose image even but now appeared to us,
Was as you know by Fortinbras of Norway,
Thereto pricked on by a most emulate pride,   83
Dared to the combat ; in which our valiant Hamlet
(For so this side of our known world esteemed him)
Did slay this Fortinbras ; who, by a sealed compact
Well ratified by law and heraldry,   87
Did forfeit, with his life, all those his lands
Which he stood seized of to the conqueror ;   89
Against the which a moiety competent   90
Was gagèd by our king, which had returned   91
To the inheritance of Fortinbras
Had he been vanquisher, as, by the same comart   93
And carriage of the article designed,   94
His fell to Hamlet. Now, sir, young Fortinbras,
Of unimprovèd mettle hot and full,   96
Hath in the skirts of Norway here and there
Sharked up a list of lawless resolutes   98
For food and diet to some enterprise
That hath a stomach in't ; which is no other,   100
As it doth well appear unto our state,
But to recover of us by strong hand
And terms compulsatory those foresaid lands
So by his father lost ; and this, I take it,
Is the main motive of our preparations,
The source of this our watch, and the chief head   106
Of this posthaste and romage in the land.   107

BERNARDO

I think it be no other but e'en so.
Well may it sort that this portentous figure   109
Comes armèd through our watch so like the king
That was and is the question of these wars.

HORATIO

A mote it is to trouble the mind's eye.   112
In the most high and palmy state of Rome,
A little ere the mightiest Julius fell,
The graves stood tenantless and the sheeted dead   115
Did squeak and gibber in the Roman streets ;
As stars with trains of fire and dews of blood,   117
Disasters in the sun ; and the moist star   118
Upon whose influence Neptune's empire stands
Was sick almost to doomsday with eclipse.
And even the like precurse of feared events,   121
As harbingers preceding still the fates   122
And prologue to the omen coming on,   123
Have heaven and earth together demonstrated
Unto our climatures and countrymen.   125

Enter Ghost.

But soft, behold, lo where it comes again !
I'll cross it, though it blast me. – Stay, illusion.   127

He spreads his arms.

48 *buried Denmark* the buried King of Denmark   **49** *sometimes* formerly
61 *Norway* King of Norway   **62** *parle* parley   **65** *jump* just, exactly   **68**
gross and scope gross scope, general view   **72** *toils* makes toil ; *subject* subjects   **74** *mart* trading   **75** *impress* conscription   **77** *toward* in preparation
83 *emulate* jealously rivalling   **87** *law and heraldry* law of heralds regulating
combat   **89** *seized* possessed   **90** *moiety competent* sufficient portion   **91**
gagèd engaged, staked   **93** *comart* joint bargain   **94** *carriage* purport
96 *unimprovèd* unused   **98** *Sharked* snatched indiscriminately as the shark
takes prey ; *resolutes* desperadoes   **100** *stomach* show of venturesomeness
106 *head* fountainhead, source   **107** *romage* intense activity   **109** *sort*
suit   **112** *mote* speck of dust   **115** *sheeted* in shrouds   **117** *As* (see Appendix : Supplementary Notes)   **118** *Disasters* ominous signs ; *moist star*
moon   **121** *precurse* foreshadowing   **122** *harbingers* forerunners ; *still* constantly   **123** *omen* calamity   **125** *climatures* regions   **127** *cross it* cross its
path

If thou hast any sound or use of voice,
Speak to me.
If there be any good thing to be done
That may to thee do ease and grace to me,
Speak to me.
If thou art privy to thy country's fate,
134   Which happily foreknowing may avoid,
O, speak!
Or if thou hast uphoarded in thy life
Extorted treasure in the womb of earth,
For which, they say, you spirits oft walk in death,
    The cock crows.
Speak of it. Stay and speak. Stop it, Marcellus.

MARCELLUS
140   Shall I strike at it with my partisan?

HORATIO
Do, if it will not stand.

BERNARDO   'Tis here.

HORATIO   'Tis here.

MARCELLUS
'Tis gone.   *[Exit Ghost.]*
We do it wrong, being so majestical,
To offer it the show of violence,
For it is as the air invulnerable,
And our vain blows malicious mockery.

BERNARDO
It was about to speak when the cock crew.

HORATIO
And then it started, like a guilty thing
Upon a fearful summons. I have heard
The cock, that is the trumpet to the morn,
Doth with his lofty and shrill-sounding throat
Awake the god of day, and at his warning,
Whether in sea or fire, in earth or air,
154   Th' extravagant and erring spirit hies
To his confine; and of the truth herein
156   This present object made probation.

MARCELLUS
It faded on the crowing of the cock.
158   Some say that ever 'gainst that season comes
Wherein our Saviour's birth is celebrated,
This bird of dawning singeth all night long,
And then, they say, no spirit dare stir abroad,
162   The nights are wholesome, then no planets strike,
163   No fairy takes, nor witch hath power to charm.
So hallowed and so gracious is that time.

HORATIO
So have I heard and do in part believe it.
But look, the morn in russet mantle clad
Walks o'er the dew of yon high eastward hill.
Break we our watch up, and by my advice
Let us impart what we have seen to-night
Unto young Hamlet, for upon my life
This spirit, dumb to us, will speak to him.
Do you consent we shall acquaint him with it,
As needful in our loves, fitting our duty?

MARCELLUS
Let's do't, I pray, and I this morning know
Where we shall find him most conveniently.   *Exeunt.*

*

Flourish. Enter Claudius, King of Denmark,   I, ii
*Gertrude the Queen, Councillors, Polonius and his
son Laertes, Hamlet, cum aliis [including Voltemand
and Cornelius].*

KING
Though yet of Hamlet our dear brother's death
The memory be green, and that it us befitted
To bear our hearts in grief, and our whole kingdom
To be contracted in one brow of woe,
Yet so far hath discretion fought with nature
That we with wisest sorrow think on him
Together with remembrance of ourselves.
Therefore our sometime sister, now our queen,
Th' imperial jointress to this warlike state,   9
Have we, as 'twere with a defeated joy,
With an auspicious and a dropping eye,
With mirth in funeral and with dirge in marriage,
In equal scale weighing delight and dole,
Taken to wife. Nor have we herein barred   14
Your better wisdoms, which have freely gone
With this affair along. For all, our thanks.
Now follows, that you know, young Fortinbras,
Holding a weak supposal of our worth,
Or thinking by our late dear brother's death
Our state to be disjoint and out of frame,
Colleaguèd with this dream of his advantage,   21
He hath not failed to pester us with message
Importing the surrender of those lands
Lost by his father, with all bands of law,
To our most valiant brother. So much for him.
Now for ourself and for this time of meeting.
Thus much the business is: we have here writ
To Norway, uncle of young Fortinbras –
Who, impotent and bedrid, scarcely hears
Of this his nephew's purpose – to suppress
His further gait herein, in that the levies,   31
The lists, and full proportions are all made   32
Out of his subject; and we here dispatch
You, good Cornelius, and you, Voltemand,
For bearers of this greeting to old Norway,
Giving to you no further personal power
To business with the king, more than the scope
Of these delated articles allow.   38
Farewell, and let your haste commend your duty.

CORNELIUS, VOLTEMAND
In that, and all things, will we show our duty.

KING
We doubt it nothing. Heartily farewell.
        [Exeunt Voltemand and Cornelius.]
And now, Laertes, what's the news with you?
You told us of some suit. What is't, Laertes?
You cannot speak of reason to the Dane   44
And lose your voice. What wouldst thou beg, Laertes,   45
That shall not be my offer, not thy asking?
The head is not more native to the heart,   47
The hand more instrumental to the mouth,   48
Than is the throne of Denmark to thy father.
What wouldst thou have, Laertes?

134 *happily* haply, perchance   140 *partisan* pike   154 *extravagant* wandering beyond bounds; *erring* wandering   156 *probation* proof   158 *'gainst* just before   162 *strike* work evil by influence   163 *takes* bewitches
I, ii Elsinore Castle: a room of state   s.d. *cum aliis* with others   9 *jointress* a woman who has a jointure, or joint tenancy of an estate   14 *barred* excluded   21 *Colleaguèd* united   31 *gait* going   32 *proportions* amounts of forces and supplies   38 *delated* detailed   44 *Dane* King of Denmark   45 *lose your voice* speak in vain   47 *native* joined by nature   48 *instrumental* serviceable

LAERTES   My dread lord,
    Your leave and favor to return to France,
    From whence though willingly I came to Denmark
    To show my duty in your coronation,
    Yet now I must confess, that duty done,
    My thoughts and wishes bend again toward France
    And bow them to your gracious leave and pardon.
KING
    Have you your father's leave? What says Polonius?
POLONIUS
    He hath, my lord, wrung from me my slow leave
    By laborsome petition, and at last
    Upon his will I sealed my hard consent.
    I do beseech you give him leave to go.
KING
    Take thy fair hour, Laertes. Time be thine,
    And thy best graces spend it at thy will.
64   But now, my cousin Hamlet, and my son –
HAMLET [aside]
65   A little more than kin, and less than kind!
KING
    How is it that the clouds still hang on you?
HAMLET
67   Not so, my lord. I am too much in the sun.
QUEEN
    Good Hamlet, cast thy nighted color off,
    And let thine eye look like a friend on Denmark.
70   Do not for ever with thy vailèd lids
    Seek for thy noble father in the dust.
    Thou know'st 'tis common. All that lives must die,
    Passing through nature to eternity.
HAMLET
    Ay, madam, it is common.
QUEEN   If it be,
    Why seems it so particular with thee?
HAMLET
    Seems, madam? Nay, it is. I know not 'seems.'
    'Tis not alone my inky cloak, good mother,
    Nor customary suits of solemn black,
    Nor windy suspiration of forced breath,
80   No, nor the fruitful river in the eye,
    Nor the dejected havior of the visage,
    Together with all forms, moods, shapes of grief,
    That can denote me truly. These indeed seem,
    For they are actions that a man might play,
    But I have that within which passeth show –
    These but the trappings and the suits of woe.
KING
    'Tis sweet and commendable in your nature, Hamlet,
    To give these mourning duties to your father,
    But you must know your father lost a father,
    That father lost, lost his, and the survivor bound
    In filial obligation for some term
92   To do obsequious sorrow. But to persever
    In obstinate condolement is a course
    Of impious stubbornness. 'Tis unmanly grief.
    It shows a will most incorrect to heaven,
    A heart unfortified, a mind impatient,
    An understanding simple and unschooled.
    For what we know must be and is as common
    As any the most vulgar thing to sense,
100   Why should we in our peevish opposition
    Take it to heart? Fie, 'tis a fault to heaven,
    A fault against the dead, a fault to nature,

    To reason most absurd, whose common theme
    Is death of fathers, and who still hath cried,
    From the first corse till he that died to-day,
    'This must be so.' We pray you throw to earth
    This unprevailing woe, and think of us
    As of a father, for let the world take note
    You are the most immediate to our throne,
    And with no less nobility of love
    Than that which dearest father bears his son
    Do I impart toward you. For your intent
    In going back to school in Wittenberg,
    It is most retrograde to our desire,   114
    And we beseech you, bend you to remain
    Here in the cheer and comfort of our eye,
    Our chiefest courtier, cousin, and our son.
QUEEN
    Let not thy mother lose her prayers, Hamlet.
    I pray thee stay with us, go not to Wittenberg.
HAMLET
    I shall in all my best obey you, madam.
KING
    Why, 'tis a loving and a fair reply.
    Be as ourself in Denmark. Madam, come.
    This gentle and unforced accord of Hamlet
    Sits smiling to my heart, in grace whereof
    No jocund health that Denmark drinks to-day
    But the great cannon to the clouds shall tell,
    And the king's rouse the heaven shall bruit again,   127
    Respeaking earthly thunder. Come away.
                      Flourish. Exeunt all but Hamlet.
HAMLET
    O that this too too sullied flesh would melt,   129
    Thaw, and resolve itself into a dew,
    Or that the Everlasting had not fixed
    His canon 'gainst self-slaughter. O God, God,   132
    How weary, stale, flat, and unprofitable
    Seem to me all the uses of this world!
    Fie on't, ah, fie, 'tis an unweeded garden
    That grows to seed. Things rank and gross in nature
    Possess it merely. That it should come to this,   137
    But two months dead, nay, not so much, not two,
    So excellent a king, that was to this
    Hyperion to a satyr, so loving to my mother   140
    That he might not beteem the winds of heaven   141
    Visit her face too roughly. Heaven and earth,
    Must I remember? Why, she would hang on him
    As if increase of appetite had grown
    By what it fed on, and yet within a month –
    Let me not think on't; frailty, thy name is woman –
    A little month, or ere those shoes were old
    With which she followed my poor father's body
    Like Niobe, all tears, why she, even she –   149

64 *cousin* kinsman more distant than parent, child, brother, or sister
65 *kin* related as nephew; *kind* kindly in feeling, as by kind, or nature,
a son would be to his father 67 *sun* sunshine of the king's undesired
favor (with the punning additional meaning of 'place of a son') 70
vailèd downcast 92 *obsequious* proper to obsequies or funerals; *persever* persevere (accented on the second syllable, as always in Shakespeare)
114 *retrograde* contrary 127 *rouse* toast drunk in wine; *bruit* echo 129
sullied (see Appendix: Supplementary Notes) 132 *canon* law 137
merely completely 140 *Hyperion* the sun god 141 *beteem* allow 149
Niobe the proud mother who boasted of having more children than Leto
and was punished when they were slain by Apollo and Artemis, children
of Leto; the grieving Niobe was changed by Zeus into a stone, which
continually dropped tears

150 O God, a beast that wants discourse of reason
Would have mourned longer – married with my uncle,
My father's brother, but no more like my father
Than I to Hercules. Within a month,
Ere yet the salt of most unrighteous tears
155 Had left the flushing in her gallèd eyes,
She married. O, most wicked speed, to post
With such dexterity to incestuous sheets!
It is not nor it cannot come to good.
But break my heart, for I must hold my tongue.

Enter Horatio, Marcellus, and Bernardo.

HORATIO
Hail to your lordship!

HAMLET   I am glad to see you well.
Horatio – or I do forget myself.

HORATIO
The same, my lord, and your poor servant ever.

HAMLET
163 Sir, my good friend, I'll change that name with you.
164 And what make you from Wittenberg, Horatio?
Marcellus?

MARCELLUS My good lord!

HAMLET
I am very glad to see you. *[to Bernardo]* Good even, sir.
But what, in faith, make you from Wittenberg?

HORATIO
A truant disposition, good my lord.

HAMLET
I would not hear your enemy say so,
Nor shall you do my ear that violence
To make it truster of your own report
Against yourself. I know you are no truant.
But what is your affair in Elsinore?
We'll teach you to drink deep ere you depart.

HORATIO
My lord, I came to see your father's funeral.

HAMLET
I prithee do not mock me, fellow student.
I think it was to see my mother's wedding.

HORATIO
Indeed, my lord, it followed hard upon.

HAMLET
Thrift, thrift, Horatio. The funeral baked meats
Did coldly furnish forth the marriage tables.
182 Would I had met my dearest foe in heaven
Or ever I had seen that day, Horatio!
My father – methinks I see my father.

HORATIO
Where, my lord?

HAMLET   In my mind's eye, Horatio.

HORATIO
I saw him once. 'A was a goodly king.

HAMLET
'A was a man, take him for all in all,
I shall not look upon his like again.

HORATIO
My lord, I think I saw him yesternight.

HAMLET Saw? who?

HORATIO
My lord, the king your father.

HAMLET   The king my father?

HORATIO
Season your admiration for a while   192
With an attent ear till I may deliver
Upon the witness of these gentlemen
This marvel to you.

HAMLET   For God's love let me hear!

HORATIO
Two nights together had these gentlemen,
Marcellus and Bernardo, on their watch
In the dead waste and middle of the night
Been thus encountered. A figure like your father,
Armèd at point exactly, cap-a-pe,   200
Appears before them and with solemn march
Goes slow and stately by them. Thrice he walked
By their oppressed and fear-surprisèd eyes
Within his truncheon's length, whilst they, distilled   204
Almost to jelly with the act of fear,
Stand dumb and speak not to him. This to me
In dreadful secrecy impart they did,
And I with them the third night kept the watch,
Where, as they had delivered, both in time,
Form of the thing, each word made true and good,
The apparition comes. I knew your father.
These hands are not more like.

HAMLET   But where was this?

MARCELLUS
My lord, upon the platform where we watched.

HAMLET
Did you not speak to it?

HORATIO   My lord, I did,
But answer made it none. Yet once methought
It lifted up it head and did address   216
Itself to motion like as it would speak.
But even then the morning cock crew loud,
And at the sound it shrunk in haste away
And vanished from our sight.

HAMLET   'Tis very strange.

HORATIO
As I do live, my honored lord, 'tis true,
And we did think it writ down in our duty
To let you know of it.

HAMLET
Indeed, indeed, sirs, but this troubles me.
Hold you the watch to-night?

ALL   We do, my lord.

HAMLET Armed, say you?

ALL Armed, my lord.

HAMLET
From top to toe?

ALL   My lord, from head to foot.

HAMLET
Then saw you not his face?

HORATIO
O, yes, my lord. He wore his beaver up.   230

HAMLET
What, looked he frowningly?

HORATIO
A countenance more in sorrow than in anger.

HAMLET Pale or red?

HORATIO
Nay, very pale.

---

150 *discourse* logical power or process   155 *gallèd* irritated   163 *change* exchange   164 *make* do   182 *dearest* direst, bitterest   192 *Season your admiration* control your wonder   200 *at point* completely; *cap-a-pe* from head to foot   204 *truncheon* military commander's baton   216 *it* its   230 *beaver* visor or movable face-guard of the helmet

HAMLET   And fixed his eyes upon you?

HORATIO
   Most constantly.

HAMLET   I would I had been there.

HORATIO
   It would have much amazed you.

HAMLET
   Very like, very like. Stayed it long?

HORATIO
238 While one with moderate haste might tell a hundred.

BOTH Longer, longer.

HORATIO
   Not when I saw't.

240 HAMLET   His beard was grizzled, no?

HORATIO
   It was as I have seen it in his life,

242 A sable silvered.

HAMLET   I will watch to-night.
   Perchance 'twill walk again.

HORATIO   I warr'nt it will.

HAMLET
   If it assume my noble father's person,
   I'll speak to it though hell itself should gape
   And bid me hold my peace. I pray you all,
   If you have hitherto concealed this sight,
248 Let it be tenable in your silence still,
   And whatsomever else shall hap to-night,
   Give it an understanding but no tongue.
   I will requite your loves. So fare you well.
   Upon the platform, 'twixt eleven and twelve
   I'll visit you.

ALL   Our duty to your honor.

HAMLET
   Your loves, as mine to you. Farewell.
                    Exeunt [all but Hamlet].
   My father's spirit – in arms? All is not well.
256 I doubt some foul play. Would the night were come!
   Till then sit still, my soul. Foul deeds will rise,
   Though all the earth o'erwhelm them, to men's eyes.
                                        Exit.

                    *

I, iii   *Enter Laertes and Ophelia, his sister.*

LAERTES
   My necessaries are embarked. Farewell.
   And, sister, as the winds give benefit
3 And convoy is assistant, do not sleep,
   But let me hear from you.

OPHELIA   Do you doubt that?

LAERTES
   For Hamlet, and the trifling of his favor,
   Hold it a fashion and a toy in blood,
7 A violet in the youth of primy nature,
   Forward, not permanent, sweet, not lasting,
9 The perfume and suppliance of a minute,
   No more.

OPHELIA No more but so?

LAERTES   Think it no more.
11 For nature crescent does not grow alone
12 In thews and bulk, but as this temple waxes
   The inward service of the mind and soul
   Grows wide withal. Perhaps he loves you now,
15 And now no soil nor cautel doth besmirch
16 The virtue of his will, but you must fear,

His greatness weighed, his will is not his own.   17
[For he himself is subject to his birth.]
He may not, as unvalued persons do,
Carve for himself, for on his choice depends
The safety and health of this whole state,
And therefore must his choice be circumscribed
Unto the voice and yielding of that body   23
Whereof he is the head. Then if he says he loves you,
It fits your wisdom so far to believe it
As he in his particular act and place
May give his saying deed, which is no further
Than the main voice of Denmark goes withal.
Then weigh what loss your honor may sustain
If with too credent ear you list his songs,   30
Or lose your heart, or your chaste treasure open
To his unmastered importunity.
Fear it, Ophelia, fear it, my dear sister,
And keep you in the rear of your affection,   34
Out of the shot and danger of desire.
The chariest maid is prodigal enough
If she unmask her beauty to the moon.
Virtue itself scapes not calumnious strokes.
The canker galls the infants of the spring   39
Too oft before their buttons be disclosed,   40
And in the morn and liquid dew of youth
Contagious blastments are most imminent.   42
Be wary then; best safety lies in fear.
Youth to itself rebels, though none else near.

OPHELIA
I shall the effect of this good lesson keep
As watchman to my heart, but, good my brother,
Do not as some ungracious pastors do,
Show me the steep and thorny way to heaven,
Whiles like a puffed and reckless libertine
Himself the primrose path of dalliance treads
And recks not his own rede.   51

          Enter Polonius.

LAERTES   O, fear me not.
I stay too long. But here my father comes.
A double blessing is a double grace;
Occasion smiles upon a second leave.

POLONIUS
Yet here, Laertes? Aboard, aboard, for shame!
The wind sits in the shoulder of your sail,
And you are stayed for. There – my blessing with thee,
And these few precepts in thy memory
Look thou character. Give thy thoughts no tongue,   59
Nor any unproportioned thought his act.   60
Be thou familiar, but by no means vulgar.
Those friends thou hast, and their adoption tried,
Grapple them unto thy soul with hoops of steel,
But do not dull thy palm with entertainment
Of each new-hatched, unfledged courage. Beware   65
Of entrance to a quarrel; but being in,

---

238 *tell* count   240 *grizzled* grey   242 *sable silvered* black mixed with white
248 *tenable* held firmly   256 *doubt* suspect, fear
I, iii Elsinore Castle: the chambers of Polonius   3 *convoy* means of transport   7 *primy* of the springtime   9 *perfume and suppliance* filling sweetness   11 *crescent* growing   12 *this temple* the body   15 *cautel* deceit
16 *will* desire   17 *greatness weighed* high position considered   23 *yielding* assent   30 *credent* credulous   34 *affection* feelings, which rashly lead forward into dangers   39 *canker* rose worm; *galls* injures   40 *buttons* buds
42 *blastments* blights   51 *recks* regards; *rede* counsel   59 *character* inscribe
60 *unproportioned* unadjusted to what is right   65 *courage* man of spirit, young blood

Bear't that th' opposèd may beware of thee.
Give every man thine ear, but few thy voice;
69   Take each man's censure, but reserve thy judgment.
Costly thy habit as thy purse can buy,
But not expressed in fancy; rich, not gaudy,
For the apparel oft proclaims the man,
And they in France of the best rank and station
74   Are of a most select and generous chief in that.
Neither a borrower nor a lender be,
For loan oft loses both itself and friend,
77   And borrowing dulleth edge of husbandry.
This above all, to thine own self be true,
And it must follow as the night the day
Thou canst not then be false to any man.
81   Farewell. My blessing season this in thee!

LAERTES
Most humbly do I take my leave, my lord.

POLONIUS
83   The time invites you. Go, your servants tend.

LAERTES
Farewell, Ophelia, and remember well
What I have said to you.

OPHELIA   'Tis in my memory locked,
And you yourself shall keep the key of it.

LAERTES Farewell.   *Exit Laertes.*

POLONIUS
What is't, Ophelia, he hath said to you?

OPHELIA
So please you, something touching the Lord Hamlet.

POLONIUS
90   Marry, well bethought.
'Tis told me he hath very oft of late
Given private time to you, and you yourself
Have of your audience been most free and bounteous.
If it be so – as so 'tis put on me,
And that in way of caution – I must tell you
You do not understand yourself so clearly
As it behooves my daughter and your honor.
What is between you? Give me up the truth.

OPHELIA
99   He hath, my lord, of late made many tenders
Of his affection to me.

POLONIUS
Affection? Pooh! You speak like a green girl,
102   Unsifted in such perilous circumstance.
Do you believe his tenders, as you call them?

OPHELIA
I do not know, my lord, what I should think.

POLONIUS
Marry, I will teach you. Think yourself a baby
That you have ta'en these tenders for true pay   106
Which are not sterling. Tender yourself more dearly,
Or (not to crack the wind of the poor phrase,   108
Running it thus) you'll tender me a fool.

OPHELIA
My lord, he hath importuned me with love
In honorable fashion.

POLONIUS
Ay, fashion you may call it. Go to, go to.   112

OPHELIA
And hath given countenance to his speech, my lord,
With almost all the holy vows of heaven.

POLONIUS
Ay, springes to catch woodcocks. I do know,   115
When the blood burns, how prodigal the soul
Lends the tongue vows. These blazes, daughter,
Giving more light than heat, extinct in both
Even in their promise, as it is a-making,
You must not take for fire. From this time
Be something scanter of your maiden presence.
Set your entreatments at a higher rate   122
Than a command to parley. For Lord Hamlet,   123
Believe so much in him that he is young,
And with a larger tether may he walk
Than may be given you. In few, Ophelia,
Do not believe his vows, for they are brokers,   127
Not of that dye which their investments show,   128
But mere implorators of unholy suits,
Breathing like sanctified and pious bawds,
The better to beguile. This is for all:
I would not, in plain terms, from this time forth
Have you so slander any moment leisure   133
As to give words or talk with the Lord Hamlet.
Look to't, I charge you. Come your ways.

OPHELIA
I shall obey, my lord.   *Exeunt.*

*

Enter Hamlet, Horatio, and Marcellus.   I, iv

HAMLET
The air bites shrewdly; it is very cold.   1

HORATIO
It is a nipping and an eager air.   2

HAMLET
What hour now?

HORATIO   I think it lacks of twelve.

MARCELLUS No, it is struck.

HORATIO
Indeed? I heard it not. It then draws near the season
Wherein the spirit held his wont to walk.
     A flourish of trumpets, and two pieces goes off.
What does this mean, my lord?

HAMLET
The king doth wake to-night and takes his rouse,   8
Keeps wassail, and the swaggering upspring reels,   9
And as he drains his draughts of Rhenish down   10
The kettledrum and trumpet thus bray out
The triumph of his pledge.   12

HORATIO   Is it a custom?

HAMLET
Ay, marry, is't,
But to my mind, though I am native here

---

69 *censure* judgment   74 *chief* eminence   77 *husbandry* thriftiness   81 *season* ripen and make fruitful   83 *tend* wait   90 *Marry* by Mary   99 *tenders* offers   102 *Unsifted* untested   106–09 *tenders . . . Tender . . . tender* offers . . . hold in regard . . . present (a word play going through three meanings, the last use of the word yielding further complexity with its valid implications that she will show herself to him as a fool, will show him to the world as a fool, and may go so far as to present him with a baby, which would be a fool because 'fool' was an Elizabethan term of endearment especially applicable to an infant as a 'little innocent')   108 *crack . . . of* make wheeze like a horse driven too hard   112 *Go to* go away, go on (expressing impatience)   115 *springes* snares; *woodcocks* birds believed foolish   122 *entreatments* military negotiations for surrender   123 *parley* confer with a besieger   127 *brokers* middlemen, panders   128 *investments* clothes   133 *slander* use disgracefully; *moment* momentary
I, iv The sentry-post   1 *shrewdly* wickedly   2 *eager* sharp   8 *rouse* carousal   9 *upspring* a German dance   10 *Rhenish* Rhine wine   12 *triumph* achievement, feat (in downing a cup of wine at one draught)

And to the manner born, it is a custom
16 More honored in the breach than the observance.
This heavy-headed revel east and west
18 Makes us traduced and taxed of other nations.
19 They clepe us drunkards and with swinish phrase
20 Soil our addition, and indeed it takes
From our achievements, though performed at height,
22 The pith and marrow of our attribute.
So oft it chances in particular men
24 That (for some vicious mole of nature in them,
As in their birth, wherein they are not guilty,
26 Since nature cannot choose his origin)
27 By the o'ergrowth of some complexion,
28 Oft breaking down the pales and forts of reason,
29 Or by some habit that too much o'erleavens
30 The form of plausive manners – that (these men
Carrying, I say, the stamp of one defect,
32 Being nature's livery, or fortune's star)
Their virtues else, be they as pure as grace,
As infinite as man may undergo,
Shall in the general censure take corruption
From that particular fault. The dram of evil
37 Doth all the noble substance of a doubt,
To his own scandal.

Enter Ghost.

HORATIO   Look, my lord, it comes.
HAMLET
Angels and ministers of grace defend us!
40 Be thou a spirit of health or goblin damned,
Bring with thee airs from heaven or blasts from hell,
Be thy intents wicked or charitable,
Thou com'st in such a questionable shape
That I will speak to thee. I'll call thee Hamlet,
King, father, royal Dane. O, answer me!
Let me not burst in ignorance, but tell
47 Why thy canonized bones, hearsèd in death,
48 Have burst their cerements, why the sepulchre
Wherein we saw thee quietly interred
Hath oped his ponderous and marble jaws
To cast thee up again. What may this mean
That thou, dead corse, again in complete steel,
Revisits thus the glimpses of the moon,
54 Making night hideous, and we fools of nature
So horridly to shake our disposition
With thoughts beyond the reaches of our souls?
Say, why is this? wherefore? what should we do?
[Ghost] beckons.
HORATIO
It beckons you to go away with it,
As if it some impartment did desire
To you alone.
MARCELLUS   Look with what courteous action
It waves you to a more removèd ground.
But do not go with it.
HORATIO   No, by no means.
HAMLET
It will not speak. Then will I follow it.
HORATIO
Do not, my lord.
HAMLET   Why, what should be the fear?
I do not set my life at a pin's fee,
And for my soul, what can it do to that,
Being a thing immortal as itself?
It waves me forth again. I'll follow it.

HORATIO
What if it tempt you toward the flood, my lord,
Or to the dreadful summit of the cliff
That beetles o'er his base into the sea,   71
And there assume some other horrible form,
Which might deprive your sovereignty of reason   73
And draw you into madness? Think of it.
The very place puts toys of desperation,   75
Without more motive, into every brain
That looks so many fathoms to the sea
And hears it roar beneath.
HAMLET   It waves me still.
Go on. I'll follow thee.
MARCELLUS
You shall not go, my lord.
HAMLET   Hold off your hands.
HORATIO
Be ruled. You shall not go.
HAMLET   My fate cries out
And makes each petty artere in this body   82
As hardy as the Nemean lion's nerve.   83
Still am I called. Unhand me, gentlemen.
By heaven, I'll make a ghost of him that lets me! 85
I say, away! Go on. I'll follow thee.
Exit Ghost, and Hamlet.
HORATIO
He waxes desperate with imagination.
MARCELLUS
Let's follow. 'Tis not fit thus to obey him.
HORATIO
Have after. To what issue will this come?
MARCELLUS
Something is rotten in the state of Denmark.
HORATIO
Heaven will direct it.
MARCELLUS   Nay, let's follow him.   *Exeunt.*

*

Enter Ghost and Hamlet.   I, v
HAMLET
Whither wilt thou lead me? Speak. I'll go no further.
GHOST
Mark me.
HAMLET   I will.
GHOST   My hour is almost come,
When I to sulph'rous and tormenting flames   3
Must render up myself.
HAMLET   Alas, poor ghost!

16 *More . . . observance* better broken than observed   18 *taxed of* censured by   19 *clepe* call   20 *addition* reputation, title added as a distinction   22 *attribute* reputation, what is attributed   24 *mole* blemish, flaw   26 *his* its   27 *complexion* part of the make-up, combination of humors   28 *pales* barriers, fences   29 *o'erleavens* works change throughout, as yeast ferments dough   30 *plausive* pleasing   32 *livery* characteristic equipment or provision; *star* make-up as formed by stellar influence   37 *Doth . . . doubt* (see Appendix: Supplementary Notes)   40 *of health* sound, good; *goblin* fiend   47 *canonized* buried with the established rites of the Church   48 *cerements* waxed grave-cloths   54 *fools of nature* men made conscious of natural limitations by a supernatural manifestation   71 *beetles* juts out   73 *deprive* take away; *sovereignty of reason* state of being ruled by reason   75 *toys* fancies   82 *artere* artery   83 *Nemean lion* a lion slain by Hercules in the performance of one of his twelve labors; *nerve* sinew   85 *lets* hinders
I, v Another part of the fortifications   3 *flames* sufferings in purgatory (not hell)

GHOST
Pity me not, but lend thy serious hearing
To what I shall unfold.

HAMLET   Speak. I am bound to hear.

GHOST
So art thou to revenge, when thou shalt hear.

HAMLET What?

GHOST
I am thy father's spirit,
Doomed for a certain term to walk the night,
11 And for the day confined to fast in fires,
Till the foul crimes done in my days of nature
Are burnt and purged away. But that I am forbid
To tell the secrets of my prison house,
I could a tale unfold whose lightest word
Would harrow up thy soul, freeze thy young blood,
17 Make thy two eyes like stars start from their spheres,
Thy knotted and combinèd locks to part,
19 And each particular hair to stand an end
20 Like quills upon the fretful porpentine.
21 But this eternal blazon must not be
To ears of flesh and blood. List, list, O, list!
If thou didst ever thy dear father love –

HAMLET O God!

GHOST
Revenge his foul and most unnatural murder.

HAMLET Murder?

GHOST
Murder most foul, as in the best it is,
But this most foul, strange, and unnatural.

HAMLET
Haste me to know't, that I, with wings as swift
30 As meditation or the thoughts of love,
May sweep to my revenge.

GHOST   I find thee apt,
And duller shouldst thou be than the fat weed
33 That roots itself in ease on Lethe wharf,
Wouldst thou not stir in this. Now, Hamlet, hear.
'Tis given out that, sleeping in my orchard,
A serpent stung me. So the whole ear of Denmark
37 Is by a forgèd process of my death
Rankly abused. But know, thou noble youth,
The serpent that did sting thy father's life
Now wears his crown.

HAMLET   O my prophetic soul!
My uncle?

GHOST
42 Ay, that incestuous, that adulterate beast,
With witchcraft of his wit, with traitorous gifts –
O wicked wit and gifts, that have the power
So to seduce! – won to his shameful lust
The will of my most seeming-virtuous queen.

O Hamlet, what a falling-off was there,
From me, whose love was of that dignity
That it went hand in hand even with the vow
I made to her in marriage, and to decline
Upon a wretch whose natural gifts were poor
To those of mine!
But virtue, as it never will be moved,
Though lewdness court it in a shape of heaven,   54
So lust, though to a radiant angel linked,
Will sate itself in a celestial bed
And prey on garbage.
But soft, methinks I scent the morning air.
Brief let me be. Sleeping within my orchard,
My custom always of the afternoon,
Upon my secure hour thy uncle stole   61
With juice of cursed hebona in a vial,   62
And in the porches of my ears did pour
The leperous distilment, whose effect
Holds such an enmity with blood of man
That swift as quicksilver it courses through
The natural gates and alleys of the body,
And with a sudden vigor it doth posset   68
And curd, like eager droppings into milk,   69
The thin and wholesome blood. So did it mine,
And a most instant tetter barked about   71
Most lazar-like with vile and loathsome crust   72
All my smooth body.
Thus was I sleeping by a brother's hand
Of life, of crown, of queen at once dispatched,
Cut off even in the blossoms of my sin,
Unhouseled, disappointed, unaneled,   77
No reck'ning made, but sent to my account
With all my imperfections on my head.
O, horrible! O, horrible! most horrible!
If thou hast nature in thee, bear it not.
Let not the royal bed of Denmark be
A couch for luxury and damnèd incest.   83
But howsomever thou pursues this act,
Taint not thy mind, nor let thy soul contrive
Against thy mother aught. Leave her to heaven
And to those thorns that in her bosom lodge
To prick and sting her. Fare thee well at once.
The glowworm shows the matin to be near   89
And gins to pale his uneffectual fire.
Adieu, adieu, adieu. Remember me.   [Exit.]

HAMLET
O all you host of heaven! O earth! What else?
And shall I couple hell? O fie! Hold, hold, my heart,
And you, my sinews, grow not instant old,
But bear me stiffly up. Remember thee?
Ay, thou poor ghost, while memory holds a seat
In this distracted globe. Remember thee?   97
Yea, from the table of my memory   98
I'll wipe away all trivial fond records,
All saws of books, all forms, all pressures past   100
That youth and observation copied there,
And thy commandment all alone shall live
Within the book and volume of my brain,
Unmixed with baser matter. Yes, by heaven!
O most pernicious woman!
O villain, villain, smiling, damnèd villain!
My tables – meet it is I set it down
That one may smile, and smile, and be a villain.
At least I am sure it may be so in Denmark.

11 *fast* do penance   17 *spheres* transparent revolving shells in each of which, according to the Ptolemaic astronomy, a planet or other heavenly body was placed   19 *an* on   20 *porpentine* porcupine   21 *eternal blazon* revelation of eternity   30 *meditation* thought   33 *Lethe* the river in Hades which brings forgetfulness of past life to a spirit who drinks of it   37 *forgèd process* falsified official report   42 *adulterate* adulterous   54 *shape of heaven* angelic disguise   61 *secure* carefree, unsuspecting   62 *hebona* some poisonous plant   68 *posset* curdle   69 *eager* sour   71 *tetter* eruption; *barked* covered as with a bark   72 *lazar-like* leper-like   77 *Unhouseled* without the Sacrament; *disappointed* unprepared spiritually; *unaneled* without extreme unction   83 *luxury* lust   89 *matin* morning   97 *globe* head   98 *table* writing tablet, record book   100 *saws* wise sayings; *forms* mental images, concepts; *pressures* impressions

[Writes.]
So, uncle, there you are. Now to my word :
It is 'Adieu, adieu, remember me.'
I have sworn't.
       Enter Horatio and Marcellus.

HORATIO
My lord, my lord !

MARCELLUS   Lord Hamlet !

HORATIO   Heavens secure him !

HAMLET So be it !

MARCELLUS
115   Illo, ho, ho, my lord !

HAMLET
Hillo, ho, ho, boy ! Come, bird, come.

MARCELLUS
How is't, my noble lord ?

HORATIO   What news, my lord ?

HAMLET O, wonderful !

HORATIO
Good my lord, tell it.

HAMLET   No, you will reveal it.

HORATIO
Not I, my lord, by heaven.

MARCELLUS   Nor I, my lord.

HAMLET
How say you then ? Would heart of man once think it ?
But you'll be secret ?

BOTH   Ay, by heaven, my lord.

HAMLET
There's never a villain dwelling in all Denmark
But he's an arrant knave.

HORATIO
There needs no ghost, my lord, come from the grave
To tell us this.

HAMLET   Why, right, you are in the right,
127   And so, without more circumstance at all,
I hold it fit that we shake hands and part :
You, as your business and desires shall point you,
For every man hath business and desire
Such as it is, and for my own poor part,
Look you, I'll go pray.

HORATIO
These are but wild and whirling words, my lord.

HAMLET
I am sorry they offend you, heartily ;
Yes, faith, heartily.

HORATIO   There's no offense, my lord.

HAMLET
Yes, by Saint Patrick, but there is, Horatio,
And much offense too. Touching this vision here,
138   It is an honest ghost, that let me tell you.
For your desire to know what is between us,
O'ermaster't as you may. And now, good friends,
As you are friends, scholars, and soldiers,
Give me one poor request.

HORATIO
What is't, my lord ? We will.

HAMLET
Never make known what you have seen to-night.

BOTH
My lord, we will not.

HAMLET   Nay, but swear't.

HORATIO   In faith,
My lord, not I.

MARCELLUS   Nor I, my lord – in faith.

HAMLET
Upon my sword.   147

MARCELLUS   We have sworn, my lord, already.

HAMLET
Indeed, upon my sword, indeed.
      Ghost cries under the stage.

GHOST Swear.

HAMLET
Ha, ha, boy, say'st thou so ? Art thou there, truepenny ?   150
Come on. You hear this fellow in the cellarage.
Consent to swear.

HORATIO   Propose the oath, my lord.

HAMLET
Never to speak of this that you have seen,
Swear by my sword.

GHOST *[beneath]* Swear.

HAMLET
Hic et ubique ? Then we'll shift our ground.   156
Come hither, gentlemen,
And lay your hands again upon my sword.
Swear by my sword
Never to speak of this that you have heard.

GHOST *[beneath]* Swear by his sword.

HAMLET
Well said, old mole ! Canst work i' th' earth so fast ?
A worthy pioner ! Once more remove, good friends.   163

HORATIO
O day and night, but this is wondrous strange !

HAMLET
And therefore as a stranger give it welcome.
There are more things in heaven and earth, Horatio,
Than are dreamt of in your philosophy.   167
But come :
Here as before, never, so help you mercy,
How strange or odd some'er I bear myself
(As I perchance hereafter shall think meet
To put an antic disposition on),   172
That you, at such times seeing me, never shall,
With arms encumb'red thus, or this head-shake,   174
Or by pronouncing of some doubtful phrase,
As 'Well, well, we know,' or 'We could, an if we would,'   176
Or 'If we list to speak,' or 'There be, an if they might,'
Or such ambiguous giving out, to note
That you know aught of me – this do swear,
So grace and mercy at your most need help you.

GHOST *[beneath]* Swear.
      [They swear.]

HAMLET
Rest, rest, perturbèd spirit ! So, gentlemen,
With all my love I do commend me to you,   183
And what so poor a man as Hamlet is
May do t' express his love and friending to you,
God willing, shall not lack. Let us go in together,
And still your fingers on your lips, I pray.   187
The time is out of joint. O cursèd spite
That ever I was born to set it right !
Nay, come, let's go together.   *Exeunt.*
               *

115 *Illo, ho, ho* cry of the falconer to summon his hawk   127 *circumstance*
ceremony   138 *honest* genuine (not a disguised demon)   147 *sword* i.e.
upon the cross formed by the sword hilt   150 *truepenny* honest old fellow
156 *Hic et ubique* here and everywhere   163 *pioner* pioneer, miner   167
your philosophy this philosophy one hears about   172 *antic* grotesque, mad
174 *encumb'red* folded   176 *an if* if   183 *commend* entrust   187 *still* always

II, i   *Enter old Polonius, with his man [Reynaldo].*

POLONIUS
Give him this money and these notes, Reynaldo.

REYNALDO
I will, my lord.

POLONIUS
You shall do marvellous wisely, good Reynaldo,
Before you visit him, to make inquire
Of his behavior.

REYNALDO   My lord, I did intend it.

POLONIUS
Marry, well said, very well said. Look you, sir,
7   Enquire me first what Danskers are in Paris,
8   And how, and who, what means, and where they keep,
     What company, at what expense ; and finding
10   By this encompassment and drift of question
     That they do know my son, come you more nearer
12   Than your particular demands will touch it.
     Take you as 'twere some distant knowledge of him,
     As thus, 'I know his father and his friends,
     And in part him' – do you mark this, Reynaldo ?

REYNALDO
Ay, very well, my lord.

POLONIUS
'And in part him, but,' you may say, 'not well,
But if 't be he I mean, he's very wild
Addicted so and so.' And there put on him
20   What forgeries you please ; marry, none so rank
     As may dishonor him – take heed of that –
     But, sir, such wanton, wild, and usual slips
     As are companions noted and most known
     To youth and liberty.

REYNALDO   As gaming, my lord.

POLONIUS
Ay, or drinking, fencing, swearing, quarrelling,
26   Drabbing. You may go so far.

REYNALDO
My lord, that would dishonor him.

POLONIUS
28   Faith, no, as you may season it in the charge.
     You must not put another scandal on him,
30   That he is open to incontinency.
31   That's not my meaning. But breathe his faults so quaintly
     That they may seem the taints of liberty,
     The flash and outbreak of a fiery mind,
34   A savageness in unreclaimèd blood,
35   Of general assault.

REYNALDO   But, my good lord –

POLONIUS
Wherefore should you do this ?

REYNALDO   Ay, my lord,
I would know that.

POLONIUS   Marry, sir, here's my drift,
And I believe it is a fetch of warrant.   38
You laying these slight sullies on my son
As 'twere a thing a little soiled i' th' working,
Mark you,
Your party in converse, him you would sound,
Having ever seen in the prenominate crimes   43
The youth you breathe of guilty, be assured
He closes with you in this consequence :   45
'Good sir,' or so, or 'friend,' or 'gentleman' –
According to the phrase or the addition   47
Of man and country –

REYNALDO   Very good, my lord.

POLONIUS
And then, sir, does 'a this – 'a does –
What was I about to say ? By the mass, I was about to
say something ! Where did I leave ?

REYNALDO At 'closes in the consequence,' at 'friend or
so,' and 'gentleman.'

POLONIUS
At 'closes in the consequence' – Ay, marry !
He closes thus : 'I know the gentleman ;
I saw him yesterday, or t' other day,
Or then, or then, with such or such, and, as you say,
There was 'a gaming, there o'ertook in 's rouse,   58
There falling out at tennis' ; or perchance,   59
'I saw him enter such a house of sale,'
Videlicet, a brothel, or so forth.   61
See you now –
Your bait of falsehood takes this carp of truth,
And thus do we of wisdom and of reach,   64
With windlasses and with assays of bias,   65
By indirections find directions out.   66
So, by my former lecture and advice,
Shall you my son. You have me, have you not ?

REYNALDO
My lord, I have.

POLONIUS   God bye ye, fare ye well.   69

REYNALDO Good my lord.

POLONIUS
Observe his inclination in yourself.

REYNALDO I shall, my lord.

POLONIUS
And let him ply his music.

REYNALDO   Well, my lord.

POLONIUS
Farewell.   *Exit Reynaldo.*
     Enter Ophelia.
     How now, Ophelia, what's the matter ?

OPHELIA
O my lord, my lord, I have been so affrighted !

POLONIUS
With what, i' th' name of God ?

OPHELIA
My lord, as I was sewing in my closet,   77
Lord Hamlet, with his doublet all unbraced,   78
No hat upon his head, his stockings fouled,
Ungartered, and down-gyvèd to his ankle,   80
Pale as his shirt, his knees knocking each other,
And with a look so piteous in purport
As if he had been loosèd out of hell
To speak of horrors – he comes before me.

POLONIUS
Mad for thy love ?

II, i The chambers of Polonius   7 *Danskers* Danes   8 *what means* what their
wealth ; *keep* dwell   10 *encompassment* circling about   12 *particular
demands* definite questions   20 *forgeries* invented wrongdoings   26 *Drabbing* whoring   28 *season* soften   30 *incontinency* extreme sensuality   31
quaintly expertly, gracefully   34 *unreclaimèd* untamed   35 *Of general
assault* assailing all young men   38 *fetch of warrant* allowable trick   43
Having ever if he has ever ; *prenominate* aforementioned   45 *closes with you*
follows your lead to a conclusion ; *consequence* following way   47 *addition*
title   58 *o'ertook* overcome with drunkenness ; *rouse* carousal   59 *falling
out* quarrelling   61 *Videlicet* namely   64 *reach* far-reaching comprehension   65 *windlasses* roundabout courses ; *assays of bias* devious attacks   66
directions ways of procedure   69 *God bye ye* God be with you, good-bye
77 *closet* private living-room   78 *doublet* jacket ; *unbraced* unlaced   80
down-gyvèd fallen down like gyves or fetters on a prisoner's legs

OPHELIA   My lord, I do not know,
But truly I do fear it.
POLONIUS   What said he?
OPHELIA
He took me by the wrist and held me hard.
Then goes he to the length of all his arm,
And with his other hand thus o'er his brow
90   He falls to such perusal of my face
As 'a would draw it. Long stayed he so.
At last, a little shaking of mine arm
And thrice his head thus waving up and down,
He raised a sigh so piteous and profound
As it did seem to shatter all his bulk
And end his being. That done, he lets me go,
And with his head over his shoulder turned
He seemed to find his way without his eyes,
For out o' doors he went without their helps
And to the last bended their light on me.
POLONIUS
Come, go with me. I will go seek the king.
102   This is the very ecstasy of love,
103   Whose violent property fordoes itself
And leads the will to desperate undertakings
As oft as any passion under heaven
That does afflict our natures. I am sorry.
What, have you given him any hard words of late?
OPHELIA
No, my good lord; but as you did command
I did repel his letters and denied
His access to me.
POLONIUS   That hath made him mad.
I am sorry that with better heed and judgment
112   I had not quoted him. I feared he did but trifle
113   And meant to wrack thee; but beshrew my jealousy.
By heaven, it is as proper to our age
115   To cast beyond ourselves in our opinions
As it is common for the younger sort
To lack discretion. Come, go we to the king.
118   This must be known, which, being kept close, might
move
119   More grief to hide than hate to utter love.
Come.   Exeunt.

                    *

II, ii   Flourish. Enter King and Queen, Rosencrantz, and
          Guildenstern [with others].
     KING
Welcome, dear Rosencrantz and Guildenstern.
2   Moreover that we much did long to see you,
The need we have to use you did provoke
Our hasty sending. Something have you heard
Of Hamlet's transformation – so call it,
6   Sith nor th' exterior nor the inward man
Resembles that it was. What it should be,
More than his father's death, that thus hath put him
So much from th' understanding of himself,
I cannot dream of. I entreat you both
That, being of so young days brought up with him,
12   And sith so neighbored to his youth and havior,
That you vouchsafe your rest here in our court
Some little time, so by your companies
To draw him on to pleasures, and to gather
So much as from occasion you may glean,

Whether aught to us unknown afflicts him thus,
That opened lies within our remedy.   18
QUEEN
Good gentlemen, he hath much talked of you,
And sure I am two men there are not living
To whom he more adheres. If it will please you   21
To show us so much gentry and good will   22
As to expend your time with us awhile
For the supply and profit of our hope,
Your visitation shall receive such thanks
As fits a king's remembrance.
ROSENCRANTZ   Both your majesties
Might, by the sovereign power you have of us,
Put your dread pleasures more into command
Than to entreaty.
GUILDENSTERN   But we both obey,
And here give up ourselves in the full bent   30
To lay our service freely at your feet,
To be commanded.
KING
Thanks, Rosencrantz and gentle Guildenstern.
QUEEN
Thanks, Guildenstern and gentle Rosencrantz.
And I beseech you instantly to visit
My too much changèd son. – Go, some of you,
And bring these gentlemen where Hamlet is.
GUILDENSTERN
Heavens make our presence and our practices
Pleasant and helpful to him!
QUEEN   Ay, amen!
          Exeunt Rosencrantz and Guildenstern
                    [with some Attendants].
     Enter Polonius.
POLONIUS
Th' ambassadors from Norway, my good lord,
Are joyfully returned.
KING
Thou still hast been the father of good news.   42
POLONIUS
Have I, my lord? Assure you, my good liege,
I hold my duty as I hold my soul,
Both to my God and to my gracious king,
And I do think – or else this brain of mine
Hunts not the trail of policy so sure
As it hath used to do – that I have found
The very cause of Hamlet's lunacy.
KING
O, speak of that! That do I long to hear.
POLONIUS
Give first admittance to th' ambassadors.
My news shall be the fruit to that great feast.   52
KING
Thyself do grace to them and bring them in.   53
                         [Exit Polonius.]

102 *ecstasy* madness 103 *property* quality; *fordoes* destroys 112 *quoted*
observed 113 *beshrew* curse 115 *cast beyond ourselves* find by calculation
more significance in something than we ought to 118 *close* secret; *move*
cause 119 *to hide . . . love* by such hiding of love than there would be hate
moved by a revelation of it (a violently condensed putting of the case which
is a triumph of special statement for Polonius)
II, ii A chamber in the Castle 2 *Moreover that* besides the fact that 6
Sith since 12 *youth and havior* youthful ways of life 18 *opened* revealed
21 *more adheres* is more attached 22 *gentry* courtesy 30 *in the full bent*
at the limit of bending (of a bow), to full capacity 42 *still* always 52 *fruit*
dessert 53 *grace* honor

He tells me, my dear Gertrude, he hath found
The head and source of all your son's distemper.

QUEEN

56 I doubt it is no other but the main,
His father's death and our o'erhasty marriage.

KING

Well, we shall sift him.
*Enter Ambassadors [Voltemand and Cornelius,
with Polonius].* Welcome, my good friends.
Say, Voltemand, what from our brother Norway?

VOLTEMAND

Most fair return of greetings and desires.

61 Upon our first, he sent out to suppress
His nephew's levies, which to him appeared
To be a preparation 'gainst the Polack,
But better looked into, he truly found
It was against your highness, whereat grieved,
That so his sickness, age, and impotence

67 Was falsely borne in hand, sends out arrests
On Fortinbras; which he in brief obeys,

69 Receives rebuke from Norway, and in fine
Makes vow before his uncle never more

71 To give th' assay of arms against your majesty.
Whereon old Norway, overcome with joy,
Gives him threescore thousand crowns in annual fee
And his commission to employ those soldiers,
So levied as before, against the Polack,
With an entreaty, herein further shown,
[Gives a paper.]
That it might please you to give quiet pass
Through your dominions for this enterprise,

79 On such regards of safety and allowance
As therein are set down.

KING It likes us well;

81 And at our more considered time we'll read,
Answer, and think upon this business.
Meantime we thank you for your well-took labor.
Go to your rest; at night we'll feast together.
Most welcome home! *Exeunt Ambassadors.*

POLONIUS This business is well ended.

86 My liege and madam, to expostulate
What majesty should be, what duty is,
Why day is day, night night, and time is time,
Were nothing but to waste night, day, and time.

90 Therefore, since brevity is the soul of wit,
And tediousness the limbs and outward flourishes,
I will be brief. Your noble son is mad.
Mad call I it, for, to define true madness,
What is't but to be nothing else but mad?
But let that go.

QUEEN More matter, with less art.

POLONIUS

Madam, I swear I use no art at all.
That he is mad, 'tis true: 'tis true 'tis pity,

98 And pity 'tis 'tis true – a foolish figure.

---

56 *doubt* suspect **61** *our first* our first words about the matter **67** *borne in hand* deceived **69** *in fine* in the end **71** *assay* trial **79** *regards* terms **81** *considered time* convenient time for consideration **86** *expostulate* discuss **90** *wit* understanding **98** *figure* figure in rhetoric **105** *Perpend* ponder **118** *Doubt* suspect **120** *numbers* verses **124** *machine* body; *to* attached to **126** *above* besides **136** *desk or table book* i.e. silent receiver **137** *winking* closing of the eyes **139** *round* roundly, plainly **141** *star* condition determined by stellar influence **142** *prescripts* instructions **148** *watch* sleepless state **149** *lightness* lightheadedness

But farewell it, for I will use no art.
Mad let us grant him then, and now remains
That we find out the cause of this effect –
Or rather say, the cause of this defect,
For this effect defective comes by cause.
Thus it remains, and the remainder thus.
Perpend. 105
I have a daughter (have while she is mine),
Who in her duty and obedience, mark,
Hath given me this. Now gather, and surmise.
[Reads the] letter.
'To the celestial, and my soul's idol, the most beautified
Ophelia,' –
That's an ill phrase, a vile phrase; 'beautified' is a vile
phrase. But you shall hear. Thus:
[Reads.]
'In her excellent white bosom, these, &c.'

QUEEN

Came this from Hamlet to her?

POLONIUS

Good madam, stay awhile. I will be faithful.
[Reads.]
'Doubt thou the stars are fire;
Doubt that the sun doth move;
Doubt truth to be a liar; 118
But never doubt I love.
'O dear Ophelia, I am ill at these numbers. I have not 120
art to reckon my groans, but that I love thee best, O
most best, believe it. Adieu.
'Thine evermore, most dear lady,
whilst this machine is to him, Hamlet.' 124

This in obedience hath my daughter shown me,
And more above hath his solicitings, 126
As they fell out by time, by means, and place,
All given to mine ear.

KING But how hath she
Received his love?

POLONIUS What do you think of me?

KING

As of a man faithful and honorable.

POLONIUS

I would fain prove so. But what might you think,
When I had seen this hot love on the wing
(As I perceived it, I must tell you that,
Before my daughter told me), what might you,
Or my dear majesty your queen here, think,
If I had played the desk or table book, 136
Or given my heart a winking, mute and dumb, 137
Or looked upon this love with idle sight?
What might you think? No, I went round to work 139
And my young mistress thus I did bespeak:
'Lord Hamlet is a prince, out of thy star. 141
This must not be.' And then I prescripts gave her, 142
That she should lock herself from his resort,
Admit no messengers, receive no tokens.
Which done, she took the fruits of my advice,
And he, repellèd, a short tale to make,
Fell into a sadness, then into a fast,
Thence to a watch, thence into a weakness, 148
Thence to a lightness, and, by this declension, 149
Into the madness wherein now he raves,
And all we mourn for.

KING Do you think 'tis this?

QUEEN
It may be, very like.

POLONIUS
Hath there been such a time – I would fain know that –
That I have positively said ''Tis so,'
When it proved otherwise ?

KING   Not that I know.

POLONIUS [pointing to his head and shoulder]
Take this from this, if this be otherwise.
If circumstances lead me, I will find
Where truth is hid, though it were hid indeed
159   Within the center.

KING   How may we try it further ?

POLONIUS
You know sometimes he walks four hours together
Here in the lobby.

QUEEN   So he does indeed.

POLONIUS
At such a time I'll loose my daughter to him.
163   Be you and I behind an arras then.
Mark the encounter. If he love her not,
165   And be not from his reason fallen thereon,
Let me be no assistant for a state
But keep a farm and carters.

KING   We will try it.

Enter Hamlet [reading on a book].

QUEEN
But look where sadly the poor wretch comes reading.

POLONIUS
Away, I do beseech you both, away.

Exit King and Queen [with Attendants].

170   I'll board him presently. O, give me leave.
How does my good Lord Hamlet ?

172 HAMLET Well, God-a-mercy.

POLONIUS Do you know me, my lord ?

174 HAMLET Excellent well. You are a fishmonger.

POLONIUS Not I, my lord.

HAMLET Then I would you were so honest a man.

POLONIUS Honest, my lord ?

HAMLET Ay, sir. To be honest, as this world goes, is to be
one man picked out of ten thousand.

POLONIUS That's very true, my lord.

HAMLET For if the sun breed maggots in a dead dog,
182   being a good kissing carrion – Have you a daughter ?

POLONIUS I have, my lord.

HAMLET Let her not walk i' th' sun. Conception is a
blessing, but as your daughter may conceive, friend,
look to't.

POLONIUS [aside] How say you by that ? Still harping on
my daughter. Yet he knew me not at first. 'A said I was a
fishmonger. 'A is far gone, far gone. And truly in my
youth I suffered much extremity for love, very near this.
I'll speak to him again. – What do you read, my lord ?

HAMLET Words, words, words.

POLONIUS What is the matter, my lord ?

193 HAMLET Between who ?

POLONIUS I mean the matter that you read, my lord.

HAMLET Slanders, sir, for the satirical rogue says here
that old men have grey beards, that their faces are
wrinkled, their eyes purging thick amber and plum-tree
gum, and that they have a plentiful lack of wit, together
with most weak hams. All which, sir, though I most
powerfully and potently believe, yet I hold it not
honesty to have it thus set down, for you yourself, sir,

should be old as I am if, like a crab, you could go backward.

POLONIUS [aside] Though this be madness, yet there is
method in't. – Will you walk out of the air, my lord ?

HAMLET Into my grave ?

POLONIUS Indeed, that's out of the air. [aside] How preg- 206
nant sometimes his replies are ! a happiness that often 207
madness hits on, which reason and sanity could not so
prosperously be delivered of. I will leave him and suddenly contrive the means of meeting between him and
my daughter. – My honorable lord, I will most humbly
take my leave of you.

HAMLET You cannot, sir, take from me anything that I
will more willingly part withal – except my life, except 214
my life, except my life.

Enter Guildenstern and Rosencrantz.

POLONIUS Fare you well, my lord.

HAMLET These tedious old fools !

POLONIUS You go to seek the Lord Hamlet. There he is.

ROSENCRANTZ [to Polonius] God save you, sir !

[Exit Polonius.]

GUILDENSTERN My honored lord !

ROSENCRANTZ My most dear lord !

HAMLET My excellent good friends ! How dost thou,
Guildenstern ? Ah, Rosencrantz ! Good lads, how do ye
both ?

ROSENCRANTZ
As the indifferent children of the earth.   224

GUILDENSTERN
Happy in that we are not over-happy.
On Fortune's cap we are not the very button.

HAMLET Nor the soles of her shoe ?

ROSENCRANTZ Neither, my lord.

HAMLET Then you live about her waist, or in the middle
of her favors ?

GUILDENSTERN Faith, her privates we.   231

HAMLET In the secret parts of Fortune ? O, most true !
she is a strumpet. What news ?

ROSENCRANTZ None, my lord, but that the world 's
grown honest.

HAMLET Then is doomsday near. But your news is not
true. [Let me question more in particular. What have
you, my good friends, deserved at the hands of Fortune
that she sends you to prison hither ?

GUILDENSTERN Prison, my lord ?

HAMLET Denmark 's a prison.

ROSENCRANTZ Then is the world one.

HAMLET A goodly one ; in which there are many con- 243
fines, wards, and dungeons, Denmark being one o' th' 244
worst.

ROSENCRANTZ We think not so, my lord.

HAMLET Why, then 'tis none to you, for there is nothing
either good or bad but thinking makes it so. To me it is a
prison.

---

159 *center* center of the earth and also of the Ptolemaic universe   163 *arras*
hanging tapestry   165 *thereon* on that account   170 *board* accost ; *presently*
at once   172 *God-a-mercy* thank you (literally, 'God have mercy !')   174
fishmonger seller of harlots, procurer (a cant term used here with a glance at
the fishing Polonius is doing when he offers Ophelia as bait)   182 *good
kissing carrion* good bit of flesh for kissing   193 *Between who* matter for a
quarrel between what persons (Hamlet's willful misunderstanding)   206
pregnant full of meaning   207 *happiness* aptness of expression   214 *withal*
with   224 *indifferent* average   231 *privates* ordinary men in private, not
public, life (with obvious play upon the sexual term 'private parts')   243
confines places of imprisonment   244 *wards* cells

ROSENCRANTZ Why, then your ambition makes it one. 'Tis too narrow for your mind.

HAMLET O God, I could be bounded in a nutshell and count myself a king of infinite space, were it not that I have bad dreams.

GUILDENSTERN Which dreams indeed are ambition, for the very substance of the ambitious is merely the shadow of a dream.

HAMLET A dream itself is but a shadow.

ROSENCRANTZ Truly, and I hold ambition of so airy and light a quality that it is but a shadow's shadow.

260 HAMLET Then are our beggars bodies, and our monarchs
261 and outstretched heroes the beggars' shadows. Shall we
262 to th' court? for, by my fay, I cannot reason.

263 BOTH We'll wait upon you.

HAMLET No such matter. I will not sort you with the rest of my servants, for, to speak to you like an honest man, I am most dreadfully attended.] But in the beaten way of
267 friendship, what make you at Elsinore?

ROSENCRANTZ To visit you, my lord; no other occasion.

HAMLET Beggar that I am, I am even poor in thanks, but I thank you; and sure, dear friends, my thanks are too
271 dear a halfpenny. Were you not sent for? Is it your own inclining? Is it a free visitation? Come, come, deal justly with me. Come, come. Nay, speak.

GUILDENSTERN What should we say, my lord?

HAMLET Why, anything – but to th' purpose. You were sent for, and there is a kind of confession in your looks, which your modesties have not craft enough to color. I know the good king and queen have sent for you.

ROSENCRANTZ To what end, my lord?

HAMLET That you must teach me. But let me conjure you
281 by the rights of our fellowship, by the consonancy of our youth, by the obligation of our ever-preserved love, and
283 by what more dear a better proposer can charge you
284 withal, be even and direct with me whether you were sent for or no.

ROSENCRANTZ [aside to Guildenstern] What say you?

HAMLET [aside] Nay then, I have an eye of you. – If you love me, hold not off.

GUILDENSTERN My lord, we were sent for.

290 HAMLET I will tell you why. So shall my anticipation pre-
291 vent your discovery, and your secrecy to the king and

queen moult no feather. I have of late – but wherefore I 292 know not – lost all my mirth, forgone all custom of ex-ercises; and indeed, it goes so heavily with my disposi-tion that this goodly frame the earth seems to me a sterile promontory; this most excellent canopy, the air, look you, this brave o'erhanging firmament, this majestical 297 roof fretted with golden fire – why, it appeareth nothing 298 to me but a foul and pestilent congregation of vapors. What a piece of work is a man, how noble in reason, how infinite in faculties; in form and moving how ex- 301 press and admirable, in action how like an angel, in ap-prehension how like a god: the beauty of the world, the paragon of animals! And yet to me what is this quint- 304 essence of dust? Man delights not me – nor woman neither, though by your smiling you seem to say so.

ROSENCRANTZ My lord, there was no such stuff in my thoughts.

HAMLET Why did ye laugh then, when I said 'Man de-lights not me'?

ROSENCRANTZ To think, my lord, if you delight not in man, what lenten entertainment the players shall re- 311 ceive from you. We coted them on the way, and hither 312 are they coming to offer you service.

HAMLET He that plays the king shall be welcome – his majesty shall have tribute of me – , the adventurous knight shall use his foil and target, the lover shall not 316 sigh gratis, the humorous man shall end his part in 317 peace, the clown shall make those laugh whose lungs are tickle o' th' sere, and the lady shall say her mind freely, 319 or the blank verse shall halt for't. What players are 320 they?

ROSENCRANTZ Even those you were wont to take such delight in, the tragedians of the city.

HAMLET How chances it they travel? Their residence, 323 both in reputation and profit, was better both ways.

ROSENCRANTZ I think their inhibition comes by the 325 means of the late innovation. 326

HAMLET Do they hold the same estimation they did when I was in the city? Are they so followed?

ROSENCRANTZ No indeed, are they not.

[HAMLET How comes it? Do they grow rusty?

ROSENCRANTZ Nay, their endeavor keeps in the wonted pace, but there is, sir, an eyrie of children, little eyases, 332 that cry out on the top of question and are most tyran- 333 nically clapped for't. These are now the fashion, and so berattle the common stages (so they call them) that 335 many wearing rapiers are afraid of goosequills and dare 336 scarce come thither.

HAMLET What, are they children? Who maintains 'em? How are they escoted? Will they pursue the quality no 339 longer than they can sing? Will they not say afterwards, 340 if they should grow themselves to common players (as it is most like, if their means are no better), their writers do them wrong to make them exclaim against their own succession?

ROSENCRANTZ Faith, there has been much to do on both sides, and the nation holds it no sin to tarre them to con- 346 troversy. There was, for a while, no money bid for argu- 347 ment unless the poet and the player went to cuffs in the question.

HAMLET Is't possible?

GUILDENSTERN O, there has been much throwing about of brains.

HAMLET Do the boys carry it away?

260 *bodies* solid substances, not shadows (because beggars lack ambition) 261 *outstretched* elongated as shadows (with a corollary implication of far-reaching with respect to the ambitions that make both heroes and monarchs into shadows) 262 *fay* faith 263 *wait upon* attend 267 *make* do 271 *a halfpenny* at a halfpenny 281 *consonancy* accord (in sameness of age) 283 *proposer* propounder 284 *withal* with; *even* straight 290 *prevent* forestall 291 *discovery* disclosure 292 *moult no feather* be left whole 297 *firmament* sky 298 *fretted* decorated with fretwork 301 *express* well framed 304 *quintessence* fifth or last and finest essence (an alchemical term) 311 *lenten* scanty 312 *coted* overtook 316 *foil and target* sword and shield 317 *humorous man* eccentric character dominated by one of the humours 319 *tickle o' th' sere* hair-triggered for the discharge of laughter ('sere': part of a gunlock) 320 *halt* go lame 323 *residence* residing at the capital 325 *inhibition* impediment to acting in residence (formal prohibition?) 326 *innovation* new fashion of having companies of boy actors play on the 'private' stage (?), political up-heaval (?) 332 *eyrie* nest; *eyases* nestling hawks 333 *on the top of question* above others on matter of dispute 335 *berattle* berate; *common stages* 'public' theatres of the 'common' players, who were organized in companies mainly composed of adult actors (allusion being made to the 'War of the Theatres' in Shakespeare's London) 336 *goosequills* pens (of satirists who made out that the London public stage showed low taste) 339 *escoted* supported; *quality* profession of acting 340 *sing* i.e. with unchanged voices 346 *tarre* incite 347 *argument* matter of a play

ROSENCRANTZ Ay, that they do, my lord – Hercules and
354 his load too.]
HAMLET It is not very strange, for my uncle is King of
356 Denmark, and those that would make mows at him
while my father lived give twenty, forty, fifty, a hundred
358 ducats apiece for his picture in little. 'Sblood, there is
something in this more than natural, if philosophy
could find it out.
A flourish.
GUILDENSTERN There are the players.
HAMLET Gentlemen, you are welcome to Elsinore. Your
hands, come then. Th' appurtenance of welcome is
fashion and ceremony. Let me comply with you in this
364 garb, lest my extent to the players (which I tell you must
show fairly outwards) should more appear like entertainment than yours. You are welcome. But my uncle-
father and aunt-mother are deceived.
GUILDENSTERN In what, my dear lord?
HAMLET I am but mad north-north-west. When the
370 wind is southerly I know a hawk from a handsaw.
Enter Polonius.
POLONIUS Well be with you, gentlemen.
HAMLET Hark you, Guildenstern – and you too – at each
ear a hearer. That great baby you see there is not yet out
374 of his swaddling clouts.
375 ROSENCRANTZ Happily he is the second time come to
them, for they say an old man is twice a child.
HAMLET I will prophesy he comes to tell me of the
players. Mark it. – You say right, sir; a Monday morning, 'twas then indeed.
POLONIUS My lord, I have news to tell you.
381 HAMLET My lord, I have news to tell you. When Roscius
was an actor in Rome –
POLONIUS The actors are come hither, my lord.
HAMLET Buzz, buzz.
POLONIUS Upon my honor –
HAMLET Then came each actor on his ass –
POLONIUS The best actors in the world, either for tragedy, comedy, history, pastoral, pastoral-comical, historical-pastoral, tragical-historical, tragical-comical-
390 historical-pastoral; scene individable, or poem unlimi-
391 ted. Seneca cannot be too heavy, nor Plautus too light.
392 For the law of writ and the liberty, these are the only men.
393 HAMLET O Jephthah, judge of Israel, what a treasure
hadst thou!
POLONIUS What treasure had he, my lord?
HAMLET Why,
'One fair daughter, and no more,
398 The which he lovèd passing well.'
POLONIUS [aside] Still on my daughter.
HAMLET Am I not i' th' right, old Jephthah?
POLONIUS If you call me Jephthah, my lord, I have a
daughter that I love passing well.
HAMLET Nay, that follows not.
POLONIUS What follows then, my lord?
HAMLET Why,
'As by lot, God wot,'
and then, you know,
'It came to pass, as most like it was.'
409 The first row of the pious chanson will show you more,
410 for look where my abridgment comes.
Enter the Players.
You are welcome, masters, welcome, all. – I am glad to
see thee well. – Welcome, good friends. – O, old friend,

why, thy face is valanced since I saw thee last. Com'st 413
thou to beard me in Denmark? – What, my young lady 414
and mistress? By'r Lady, your ladyship is nearer to
heaven than when I saw you last by the altitude of a
chopine. Pray God your voice, like a piece of uncurrent 417
gold, be not cracked within the ring. – Masters, you are 418
all welcome. We'll e'en to't like French falconers, fly at
anything we see. We'll have a speech straight. Come,
give us a taste of your quality. Come, a passionate speech.
PLAYER What speech, my good lord?
HAMLET I heard thee speak me a speech once, but it was
never acted, or if it was, not above once, for the play, I
remember, pleased not the million; 'twas caviary to the 425
general, but it was (as I received it, and others, whose 426
judgments in such matters cried in the top of mine) an 427
excellent play, well digested in the scenes, set down with
as much modesty as cunning. I remember one said there
were no sallets in the lines to make the matter savory, 430
nor no matter in the phrase that might indict the author
of affectation, but called it an honest method, as wholesome as sweet, and by very much more handsome than
fine. One speech in't I chiefly loved. 'Twas Aeneas' tale
to Dido, and thereabout of it especially where he speaks
of Priam's slaughter. If it live in your memory, begin at 436
this line – let me see, let me see:
'The rugged Pyrrhus, like th' Hyrcanian beast –' 438
'Tis not so; it begins with Pyrrhus:
'The rugged Pyrrhus, he whose sable arms, 440
Black as his purpose, did the night resemble
When he lay couchèd in the ominous horse, 442
Hath now this dread and black complexion smeared
With heraldry more dismal. Head to foot 444
Now is he total gules, horridly tricked 445
With blood of fathers, mothers, daughters, sons,
Baked and impasted with the parching streets, 447
That lend a tyrannous and a damnèd light
To their lord's murder. Roasted in wrath and fire,
And thus o'ersizèd with coagulate gore, 450
With eyes like carbuncles, the hellish Pyrrhus
Old grandsire Priam seeks.'
So, proceed you.

354 *load* i.e. the whole world (with a topical reference to the sign of the Globe Theatre, a representation of Hercules bearing the world on his shoulders) 356 *mows* grimaces 358 *'Sblood* by God's blood 364 *garb* fashion; *extent* showing of welcome 370 *hawk* mattock or pickaxe (also called 'hack'; here used apparently with a play on 'hawk': a bird); *handsaw* carpenter's tool (apparently with a play on some corrupt form of 'hern-shaw'; heron, a bird often hunted with the hawk) 374 *clouts* clothes 375 *Happily* haply, perhaps 381 *Roscius* the greatest of Roman comic actors 390 *scene individable* drama observing the unities; *poem unlimited* drama not observing the unities 391 *Seneca* Roman writer of tragedies; *Plautus* Roman writer of comedies 392 *law of writ* orthodoxy determined by critical rules of the drama; *liberty* freedom from such orthodoxy 393 *Jephthah* the compelled sacrificer of a dearly beloved daughter (Judges xi) 398 *passing* surpassingly (verses are from a ballad on Jephthah) 409 *row* stanza; *chanson* song 410 *my abridgment* that which shortens my talk 413 *valanced* fringed (with a beard) 414 *young lady* boy who plays women's parts 417 *chopine* women's thick-soled shoe; *uncurrent* not legal tender 418 *within the ring* from the edge through the line circling the design on the coin (with a play on 'ring': a sound) 425 *caviary* caviare 426 *general* multitude 427 *in the top of* more authoritatively than 430 *sallets* salads, highly seasoned passages 436 *Priam's slaughter* i.e. at the fall of Troy (Aeneid II, 506 ff.) 438 *Hyrcanian beast* tiger 440 *sable* black 442 *ominous* fateful; *horse* the wooden horse by which the Greeks gained entrance to Troy 444 *dismal* ill-omened 445 *gules* red (heraldic term); *tricked* decorated in color (heraldic term) 447 *parching* i.e. because Troy was burning 450 *o'ersizèd* covered as with size, a glutinous material used for filling pores of plaster, etc.; *coagulate* clotted

POLONIUS Fore God, my lord, well spoken, with good accent and good discretion.

PLAYER   'Anon he finds him,
Striking too short at Greeks. His antique sword,
Rebellious to his arms, lies where it falls,
Repugnant to command. Unequal matched,
Pyrrhus at Priam drives, in rage strikes wide,
461 But with the whiff and wind of his fell sword
462 Th' unnervèd father falls. Then senseless Ilium,
Seeming to feel this blow, with flaming top
464 Stoops to his base, and with a hideous crash
Takes prisoner Pyrrhus' ear. For lo! his sword,
Which was declining on the milky head
Of reverend Priam, seemed i' th' air to stick.
468 So as a painted tyrant Pyrrhus stood,
469 And like a neutral to his will and matter
Did nothing.
471 But as we often see, against some storm,
472 A silence in the heavens, the rack stand still,
The bold winds speechless, and the orb below
As hush as death, anon the dreadful thunder
475 Doth rend the region, so after Pyrrhus' pause,
Aroused vengeance sets him new awork,
477 And never did the Cyclops' hammers fall
478 On Mars' armor, forged for proof eterne,
With less remorse than Pyrrhus' bleeding sword
Now falls on Priam.
Out, out, thou strumpet Fortune! All you gods,
In general synod take away her power,
483 Break all the spokes and fellies from her wheel,
484 And bowl the round nave down the hill of heaven,
As low as to the fiends.'
POLONIUS This is too long.
HAMLET It shall to the barber's, with your beard. –
488 Prithee say on. He's for a jig or a tale of bawdry, or he sleeps. Say on; come to Hecuba.
PLAYER
490 'But who (ah woe!) had seen the mobled queen –'
HAMLET 'The mobled queen'?
POLONIUS That's good. 'Mobled queen' is good.
PLAYER
'Run barefoot up and down, threat'ning the flames
494 With bisson rheum; a clout upon that head
Where late the diadem stood, and for a robe,
496 About her lank and all o'erteemèd loins,
A blanket in the alarm of fear caught up –
Who this had seen, with tongue in venom steeped
499 'Gainst Fortune's state would treason have pronounced.
But if the gods themselves did see her then,
When she saw Pyrrhus make malicious sport

In mincing with his sword her husband's limbs,
The instant burst of clamor that she made
(Unless things mortal move them not at all)
505 Would have made milch the burning eyes of heaven
And passion in the gods.'
507 POLONIUS Look, whe'r he has not turned his color, and has tears in's eyes. Prithee no more.
HAMLET 'Tis well. I'll have thee speak out the rest of this
510 soon. – Good my lord, will you see the players well bestowed? Do you hear? Let them be well used, for they are the abstract and brief chronicles of the time. After your death you were better have a bad epitaph than their ill report while you live.
POLONIUS My lord, I will use them according to their desert.
516 HAMLET God's bodkin, man, much better! Use every man after his desert, and who shall scape whipping? Use them after your own honor and dignity. The less they deserve, the more merit is in your bounty. Take them in.
POLONIUS Come, sirs.
HAMLET Follow him, friends. We'll hear a play tomorrow. [aside to Player] Dost thou hear me, old friend? Can you play 'The Murder of Gonzago'?
PLAYER Ay, my lord.
HAMLET We'll ha't to-morrow night. You could for a need study a speech of some dozen or sixteen lines which I would set down and insert in't, could you not?
PLAYER Ay, my lord.
HAMLET Very well. Follow that lord, and look you mock
530 him not. – My good friends, I'll leave you till night. You are welcome to Elsinore.   *Exeunt Polonius and Players.*
ROSENCRANTZ Good my lord.
                         Exeunt [Rosencrantz and Guildenstern].
HAMLET
Ay, so, God bye to you. – Now I am alone.
O, what a rogue and peasant slave am I!
Is it not monstrous that this player here,
But in a fiction, in a dream of passion,
537 Could force his soul so to his own conceit
That from her working all his visage wanned,
Tears in his eyes, distraction in his aspect,
540 A broken voice, and his whole function suiting
With forms to his conceit? And all for nothing,
For Hecuba!
What's Hecuba to him, or he to Hecuba,
That he should weep for her? What would he do
Had he the motive and the cue for passion
That I have? He would drown the stage with tears
And cleave the general ear with horrid speech,
Make mad the guilty and appal the free,
Confound the ignorant, and amaze indeed
The very faculties of eyes and ears.
Yet I,
552 A dull and muddy-mettled rascal, peak
553 Like John-a-dreams, unpregnant of my cause,
And can say nothing. No, not for a king,
Upon whose property and most dear life
A damned defeat was made. Am I a coward?
Who calls me villain? breaks my pate across?
Plucks off my beard and blows it in my face?
Tweaks me by the nose? gives me the lie i' th' throat
As deep as to the lungs? Who does me this?
561 Ha, 'swounds, I should take it, for it cannot be

---

461 *fell* cruel 462 *senseless* without feeling 464 *his* its 468 *painted* pictured 469 *will and matter* purpose and its realization (between which he stands motionless) 471 *against* just before 472 *rack* clouds 475 *region* sky 477 *Cyclops* giant workmen who made armor in the smithy of Vulcan 478 *proof eterne* eternal protection 483 *fellies* segments of the rim 484 *nave* hub 488 *jig* short comic piece with singing and dancing often presented after a play 490 *mobled* muffled 494 *bisson rheum* blinding tears; *clout* cloth 496 *o'erteemèd* overproductive of children 499 *state* government of worldly events 505 *milch* tearful (milk-giving); *eyes* i.e. stars 507 *whe'r* whether 510 *bestowed* lodged 516 *God's bodkin* by God's little body 537 *conceit* conception, idea 540 *function* action of bodily powers 552 *muddy-mettled* dull-spirited; *peak* mope 553 *John-a-dreams* a sleepy dawdler; *unpregnant* barren of realization 561 *'swounds* by God's wounds

562 But I am pigeon-livered and lack gall
　　　To make oppression bitter, or ere this
564 I should ha' fatted all the region kites
565 With this slave's offal. Bloody, bawdy villain!
566 Remorseless, treacherous, lecherous, kindless villain!
　　　O, vengeance!
　　　Why, what an ass am I! This is most brave,
　　　That I, the son of a dear father murdered,
　　　Prompted to my revenge by heaven and hell,
　　　Must like a whore unpack my heart with words
　　　And fall a-cursing like a very drab,
573 A stallion! Fie upon't, foh! About, my brains.
　　　Hum –
　　　I have heard that guilty creatures sitting at a play
　　　Have by the very cunning of the scene
577 Been struck so to the soul that presently
　　　They have proclaimed their malefactions.
　　　For murder, though it have no tongue, will speak
　　　With most miraculous organ. I'll have these players
　　　Play something like the murder of my father
　　　Before mine uncle. I'll observe his looks.
583 I'll tent him to the quick. If 'a do blench,
　　　I know my course. The spirit that I have seen
　　　May be a devil, and the devil hath power
　　　T' assume a pleasing shape, yea, and perhaps
　　　Out of my weakness and my melancholy,
　　　As he is very potent with such spirits,
589 Abuses me to damn me. I'll have grounds
590 More relative than this. The play 's the thing
　　　Wherein I'll catch the conscience of the king.　　　*Exit.*

*

III, i　　Enter King, Queen, Polonius, Ophelia, Rosencrantz,
　　　　　Guildenstern, Lords.

KING
1　And can you by no drift of conference
　　Get from him why he puts on this confusion,
　　Grating so harshly all his days of quiet
　　With turbulent and dangerous lunacy?
ROSENCRANTZ
　　He does confess he feels himself distracted,
　　But from what cause 'a will by no means speak.
GUILDENSTERN
　　Nor do we find him forward to be sounded,
　　But with a crafty madness keeps aloof
　　When we would bring him on to some confession
　　Of his true state.
QUEEN　　　　　Did he receive you well?
ROSENCRANTZ
　　Most like a gentleman.
GUILDENSTERN
　　But with much forcing of his disposition.
ROSENCRANTZ
　　Niggard of question, but of our demands
　　Most free in his reply.
14 QUEEN　　　　　Did you assay him
　　To any pastime?
ROSENCRANTZ
　　Madam, it so fell out that certain players
17 We o'erraught on the way. Of these we told him,
　　And there did seem in him a kind of joy
　　To hear of it. They are here about the court,
　　And, as I think, they have already order

This night to play before him.
POLONIUS　　　　　　　　'Tis most true,
　　And he beseeched me to entreat your majesties
　　To hear and see the matter.
KING
　　With all my heart, and it doth much content me
　　To hear him so inclined.
　　Good gentlemen, give him a further edge　　　26
　　And drive his purpose into these delights.
ROSENCRANTZ
　　We shall, my lord. *Exeunt Rosencrantz and Guildenstern.*
KING　　　　　Sweet Gertrude, leave us too,
　　For we have closely sent for Hamlet hither,　　　29
　　That he, as 'twere by accident, may here
　　Affront Ophelia.　　　　　　　　　　　　31
　　Her father and myself (lawful espials)　　　　32
　　Will so bestow ourselves that, seeing unseen,
　　We may of their encounter frankly judge
　　And gather by him, as he is behaved,
　　If't be th' affliction of his love or no
　　That thus he suffers for.
QUEEN　　　　　　　I shall obey you. –
　　And for your part, Ophelia, I do wish
　　That your good beauties be the happy cause
　　Of Hamlet's wildness. So shall I hope your virtues
　　Will bring him to his wonted way again,
　　To both your honors.
OPHELIA　　　　　Madam, I wish it may. *[Exit Queen.]*
POLONIUS
　　Ophelia, walk you here. – Gracious, so please you,
　　We will bestow ourselves. –
　　　[To Ophelia]　　　Read on this book,
　　That show of such an exercise may color　　　45
　　Your loneliness. We are oft to blame in this,
　　'Tis too much proved, that with devotion's visage
　　And pious action we do sugar o'er
　　The devil himself.
KING *[aside]*　　　O, 'tis too true.
　　How smart a lash that speech doth give my conscience!
　　The harlot's cheek, beautied with plast'ring art,
　　Is not more ugly to the thing that helps it　　　52
　　Than is my deed to my most painted word.
　　O heavy burthen!
POLONIUS
　　I hear him coming. Let's withdraw, my lord.
　　　　　　　　　[Exeunt King and Polonius.]
　　Enter Hamlet.
HAMLET
　　To be, or not to be – that is the question:
　　Whether 'tis nobler in the mind to suffer
　　The slings and arrows of outrageous fortune
　　Or to take arms against a sea of troubles
　　And by opposing end them. To die, to sleep –
　　No more – and by a sleep to say we end

562 *pigeon-livered* of dove-like gentleness　564 *region kites* kites of the air
565 *offal* guts　566 *kindless* unnatural　573 *stallion* prostitute (male or
female)　577 *presently* immediately　583 *tent* probe; *blench* flinch　589
Abuses deludes　590 *relative* pertinent
III, i A chamber in the Castle　1 *drift of conference* direction of conversation　14 *assay* try to win　17 *o'erraught* overtook　26 *edge* keenness
of desire　29 *closely* privately　31 *Affront* come face to face with　32
espials spies　45 *exercise* religious exercise (the book being obviously one
of devotion); *color* give an appearance of naturalness to　52 *to* compared
to

The heartache, and the thousand natural shocks
That flesh is heir to. 'Tis a consummation
Devoutly to be wished. To die, to sleep –
65   To sleep – perchance to dream : ay, there's the rub,
For in that sleep of death what dreams may come
67   When we have shuffled off this mortal coil,
68   Must give us pause. There's the respect
69   That makes calamity of so long life.
For who would bear the whips and scorns of time,
Th' oppressor's wrong, the proud man's contumely
The pangs of despised love, the law's delay,
The insolence of office, and the spurns
That patient merit of th' unworthy takes,
75   When he himself might his quietus make
76   With a bare bodkin ? Who would fardels bear,
To grunt and sweat under a weary life,
But that the dread of something after death,
79   The undiscovered country, from whose bourn
No traveller returns, puzzles the will,
And makes us rather bear those ills we have
Than fly to others that we know not of ?
Thus conscience does make cowards of us all,
And thus the native hue of resolution
Is sicklied o'er with the pale cast of thought,
86   And enterprises of great pitch and moment
87   With this regard their currents turn awry
And lose the name of action. – Soft you now,
89   The fair Ophelia ! – Nymph, in thy orisons
Be all my sins remembered.

OPHELIA   Good my lord,
How does your honor for this many a day ?

HAMLET
I humbly thank you, well, well, well.

OPHELIA
My lord, I have remembrances of yours
That I have longèd long to re-deliver.
I pray you, now receive them.

HAMLET   No, not I,
I never gave you aught.

OPHELIA
My honored lord, you know right well you did,
And with them words of so sweet breath composed
As made the things more rich. Their perfume lost,
Take these again, for to the noble mind
Rich gifts wax poor when givers prove unkind.
There, my lord.

103 HAMLET Ha, ha ! Are you honest ?

OPHELIA My lord ?

HAMLET Are you fair ?

OPHELIA What means your lordship ?

HAMLET That if you be honest and fair, your honesty
should admit no discourse to your beauty.

OPHELIA Could beauty, my lord, have better commerce 109
than with honesty ?

HAMLET Ay, truly ; for the power of beauty will sooner
transform honesty from what it is to a bawd than the
force of honesty can translate beauty into his likeness.
This was sometime a paradox, but now the time gives it 114
proof. I did love you once.

OPHELIA Indeed, my lord, you made me believe so.

HAMLET You should not have believed me, for virtue
cannot so inoculate our old stock but we shall relish of it. 118
I loved you not.

OPHELIA I was the more deceived.

HAMLET Get thee to a nunnery. Why wouldst thou be a
breeder of sinners ? I am myself indifferent honest, but 122
yet I could accuse me of such things that it were better
my mother had not borne me : I am very proud,
revengeful, ambitious, with more offenses at my beck
than I have thoughts to put them in, imagination to give
them shape, or time to act them in. What should such
fellows as I do crawling between earth and heaven ? We
are arrant knaves all ; believe none of us. Go thy ways to
a nunnery. Where's your father ?

OPHELIA At home, my lord.

HAMLET Let the doors be shut upon him, that he may
play the fool nowhere but in's own house. Farewell.

OPHELIA O, help him, you sweet heavens !

HAMLET If thou dost marry, I'll give thee this plague for
thy dowry : be thou as chaste as ice, as pure as snow, thou
shalt not escape calumny. Get thee to a nunnery. Go,
farewell. Or if thou wilt needs marry, marry a fool, for
wise men know well enough what monsters you make 139
of them. To a nunnery, go, and quickly too. Farewell.

OPHELIA O heavenly powers, restore him !

HAMLET I have heard of your paintings too, well enough.
God hath given you one face, and you make yourselves
another. You jig, you amble, and you lisp ; you nickname
God's creatures and make your wantonness your igno- 145
rance. Go to, I'll no more on't ; it hath made me mad.
I say we will have no more marriage. Those that are
married already – all but one – shall live. The rest shall
keep as they are. To a nunnery, go.   *Exit.*

OPHELIA
O, what a noble mind is here o'erthrown !
The courtier's, soldier's, scholar's, eye, tongue, sword,
Th' expectancy and rose of the fair state,   152
The glass of fashion and the mould of form,   153
Th' observed of all observers, quite, quite down !
And I, of ladies most deject and wretched,
That sucked the honey of his music vows,
Now see that noble and most sovereign reason
Like sweet bells jangled, out of time and harsh,
That unmatched form and feature of blown youth
Blasted with ecstasy. O, woe is me   160
T' have seen what I have seen, see what I see !
Enter King and Polonius.

KING
Love ? his affections do not that way tend,   162
Nor what he spake, though it lacked form a little,
Was not like madness. There's something in his soul
O'er which his melancholy sits on brood,
And I do doubt the hatch and the disclose   166
Will be some danger ; which for to prevent,
I have in quick determination
Thus set it down : he shall with speed to England

65 *rub* obstacle (literally, obstruction encountered by a bowler's ball)
67 *shuffled off* cast off as an encumbrance ; *coil* to-do, turmoil 68 *respect*
consideration 69 *of so long life* so long-lived 75 *quietus* settlement
(literally, release from debt) 76 *bodkin* dagger ; *fardels* burdens 79
bourn confine, region 86 *pitch* height (of a soaring falcon's flight) 87
regard consideration 89 *orisons* prayers (because of the book of devotion
she reads) 103 *honest* chaste 109 *commerce* intercourse 114 *paradox*
idea contrary to common opinion 118 *inoculate* graft ; *relish* have a flavor
(because of original sin) 122 *indifferent honest* moderately respectable
139 *monsters* i.e. unnatural combinations of wisdom and uxorious folly
145 *wantonness* affectation ; *your ignorance* a matter for which you offer
the excuse that you don't know any better 152 *expectancy and rose* fair
hope 153 *glass* mirror 160 *ecstasy* madness 162 *affections* emotions
166 *doubt* fear

For the demand of our neglected tribute.
Haply the seas, and countries different,
With variable objects, shall expel
173　This something-settled matter in his heart,
Whereon his brains still beating puts him thus
From fashion of himself. What think you on't?
POLONIUS
It shall do well. But yet do I believe
The origin and commencement of his grief
Sprung from neglected love. – How now, Ophelia?
You need not tell us what Lord Hamlet said.
We heard it all. – My lord, do as you please,
But if you hold it fit, after the play
Let his queen mother all alone entreat him
183　To show his grief. Let her be round with him,
And I'll be placed, so please you, in the ear
Of all their conference. If she find him not,
To England send him, or confine him where
Your wisdom best shall think.
KING　　　　　　　　　It shall be so.
Madness in great ones must not unwatched go. *Exeunt.*

*

III, ii　　　*Enter Hamlet and three of the Players.*
　HAMLET Speak the speech, I pray you, as I pronounced it
2　　to you, trippingly on the tongue. But if you mouth it, as
　　many of our players do, I had as lief the town crier spoke
　　my lines. Nor do not saw the air too much with your
　　hand, thus, but use all gently, for in the very torrent,
　　tempest, and (as I may say) whirlwind of your passion,
　　you must acquire and beget a temperance that may give
8　　it smoothness. O, it offends me to the soul to hear a ro-
9　　bustious periwig-pated fellow tear a passion to tatters,
10　to very rags, to split the ears of the groundlings, who for
　　the most part are capable of nothing but inexplicable
12　dumb shows and noise. I would have such a fellow
13　whipped for o'erdoing Termagant. It out-herods Herod.
　　Pray you avoid it.
　PLAYER I warrant your honor.
　HAMLET Be not too tame neither, but let your own dis-
　　cretion be your tutor. Suit the action to the word, the
　　word to the action, with this special observance, that you
　　o'erstep not the modesty of nature. For anything so over-
19　done is from the purpose of playing, whose end, both at
　　the first and now, was and is, to hold, as 'twere, the mirror
　　up to nature, to show virtue her own feature, scorn her
　　own image, and the very age and body of the time his
23　form and pressure. Now this overdone, or come tardy off,
　　though it make the unskillful laugh, cannot but make
25　the judicious grieve, the censure of the which one must
　　in your allowance o'erweigh a whole theatre of others.
　　O, there be players that I have seen play, and heard others
　　praise, and that highly (not to speak it profanely), that
　　neither having th' accent of Christians, nor the gait of
　　Christian, pagan, nor man, have so strutted and bellowed
31　that I have thought some of Nature's journeymen had
　　made men, and not made them well, they imitated hu-
　　manity so abominably.
34　PLAYER I hope we have reformed that indifferently with
　　us, sir.
　HAMLET O, reform it altogether! And let those that play
　　your clowns speak no more than is set down for them, for
38　there be of them that will themselves laugh, to set on

some quantity of barren spectators to laugh too, though
in the mean time some necessary question of the play be
then to be considered. That's villainous and shows a
most pitiful ambition in the fool that uses it. Go make
you ready.　　　　　　　　　　　　　*[Exeunt Players.]*
　　　Enter Polonius, Guildenstern, and Rosencrantz.
How now, my lord? Will the king hear this piece of
work?
POLONIUS And the queen too, and that presently.　　45
HAMLET Bid the players make haste.　　*[Exit Polonius.]*
　　Will you two help to hasten them?
ROSENCRANTZ Ay, my lord.　　　　　　*Exeunt they two.*
HAMLET What, ho, Horatio!
　　　Enter Horatio.
HORATIO
Here, sweet lord, at your service.
HAMLET
Horatio, thou art e'en as just a man
As e'er my conversation coped withal.　　　　　　52
HORATIO
O, my dear lord –
HAMLET　　　　　Nay, do not think I flatter.
For what advancement may I hope from thee,
That no revenue hast but thy good spirits
To feed and clothe thee? Why should the poor be
　flattered?
No, let the candied tongue lick absurd pomp,
And crook the pregnant hinges of the knee　　　　　58
Where thrift may follow fawning. Dost thou hear?　　59
Since my dear soul was mistress of her choice
And could of men distinguish her election,
S' hath sealed thee for herself, for thou hast been　　62
As one in suff'ring all that suffers nothing,
A man that Fortune's buffets and rewards
Hast ta'en with equal thanks; and blest are those
Whose blood and judgment are so well commeddled　66
That they are not a pipe for Fortune's finger
To sound what stop she please. Give me that man
That is not passion's slave, and I will wear him
In my heart's core, ay, in my heart of heart,
As I do thee. Something too much of this –
There is a play to-night before the king.
One scene of it comes near the circumstance
Which I have told thee, of my father's death.
I prithee, when thou seest that act afoot,
Even with the very comment of thy soul　　　　　　76
Observe my uncle. If his occulted guilt　　　　　　77
Do not itself unkennel in one speech, ·
It is a damnèd ghost that we have seen,　　　　　　79

173 *something-settled* somewhat settled　183 *round* plain-spoken
III, ii The hall of the Castle　2 *trippingly* easily　8 *robustious* boisterous
9 *periwig-pated* wig-wearing (after the custom of actors)　10 *groundlings*
spectators who paid least and stood on the ground in the pit or yard of
the theatre　12 *dumb shows* brief actions without words, forecasting dramatic matter to follow (the play presented later in this scene giving an old-
fashioned example)　13 *Termagant* a Saracen 'god' in medieval romance
and drama; *Herod* the raging tyrant of old Biblical plays　19 *from* apart
from　23 *pressure* impressed or printed character; *come tardy off* brought
off slowly and badly　25 *the censure of the which one* the judgment of even
one of whom　31 *journeymen* workmen not yet masters of their trade
34 *indifferently* fairly well　38 *of them* some of them　45 *presently* at once
52 *conversation coped withal* intercourse with men encountered　58 *pregnant* quick to move　59 *thrift* profit　62 *sealed* marked　66 *blood* passion;
commeddled mixed together　76 *the very . . . soul* thy deepest sagacity　77
occulted hidden　79 *damnèd ghost* evil spirit, devil (as thought of in II, ii,
584 ff.)

And my imaginations are as foul
81   As Vulcan's stithy. Give him heedful note,
For I mine eyes will rivet to his face,
And after we will both our judgments join
84   In censure of his seeming.

HORATIO   Well, my lord.
If 'a steal aught the while this play is playing,
And scape detecting, I will pay the theft.

*Enter Trumpets and Kettledrums, King, Queen,
Polonius, Ophelia [, Rosencrantz, Guildenstern, and
other Lords attendant].*

87 HAMLET They are coming to the play. I must be idle.
Get you a place.

89 KING How fares our cousin Hamlet?

90 HAMLET Excellent, i' faith, of the chameleon's dish. I eat
the air, promise-crammed. You cannot feed capons so.

KING I have nothing with this answer, Hamlet. These
93   words are not mine.

HAMLET No, nor mine now. *[to Polonius]* My lord, you
played once i' th' university, you say?

POLONIUS That did I, my lord, and was accounted a
good actor.

HAMLET What did you enact?

POLONIUS I did enact Julius Caesar. I was killed i' th'
Capitol; Brutus killed me.

HAMLET It was a brute part of him to kill so capital a calf
there. Be the players ready?

103 ROSENCRANTZ Ay, my lord. They stay upon your
patience.

QUEEN Come hither, my dear Hamlet, sit by me.

HAMLET No, good mother. Here's metal more attractive.

POLONIUS *[to the King]* O ho! do you mark that?

HAMLET Lady, shall I lie in your lap?

[He lies at Ophelia's feet.]

OPHELIA No, my lord.

HAMLET I mean, my head upon your lap?

OPHELIA Ay, my lord.

111 HAMLET Do you think I meant country matters?

OPHELIA I think nothing, my lord.

HAMLET That's a fair thought to lie between maids' legs.

OPHELIA What is, my lord?

HAMLET Nothing.

OPHELIA You are merry, my lord.

HAMLET Who, I?

OPHELIA Ay, my lord.

119 HAMLET O God, your only jig-maker! What should a
man do but be merry? For look you how cheerfully my
mother looks, and my father died within's two hours.

OPHELIA Nay, 'tis twice two months, my lord.

HAMLET So long? Nay then, let the devil wear black, for
124   I'll have a suit of sables. O heavens! die two months

ago, and not forgotten yet? Then there's hope a great
man's memory may outlive his life half a year. But, by'r
Lady, 'a must build churches then, or else shall 'a
suffer not thinking on, with the hobby-horse, whose 128
epitaph is 'For O, for O, the hobby-horse is forgot!'

*The trumpets sound. Dumb show follows:
Enter a King and a Queen [very lovingly], the Queen embracing him, and he her. [She kneels; and makes show of
protestation unto him.] He takes her up, and declines his head
upon her neck. He lies him down upon a bank of flowers. She,
seeing him asleep, leaves him. Anon come in another man:
takes off his crown, kisses it, pours poison in the sleeper's ears,
and leaves him. The Queen returns, finds the King dead,
makes passionate action. The poisoner, with some three or
four, come in again, seem to condole with her. The dead body
is carried away. The poisoner woos the Queen with gifts; she
seems harsh awhile, but in the end accepts love.   [Exeunt.]*

OPHELIA What means this, my lord?

HAMLET Marry, this is miching mallecho; it means mis- 131
chief.

OPHELIA Belike this show imports the argument of the
play.

Enter Prologue.

HAMLET We shall know by this fellow. The players cannot keep counsel; they'll tell all.

OPHELIA Will 'a tell us what this show meant?

HAMLET Ay, or any show that you'll show him. Be not
you ashamed to show, he'll not shame to tell you what it
means.

OPHELIA You are naught, you are naught. I'll mark the 139
play.

PROLOGUE For us and for our tragedy,
Here stooping to your clemency,
We beg your hearing patiently.   *[Exit.]*

HAMLET Is this a prologue, or the posy of a ring?   143

OPHELIA 'Tis brief, my lord.

HAMLET As woman's love.

Enter [two Players as] King and Queen.

KING
Full thirty times hath Phoebus' cart gone round   146
Neptune's salt wash and Tellus' orbèd ground,   147
And thirty dozen moons with borrowed sheen   148
About the world have times twelve thirties been,
Since love our hearts, and Hymen did our hands,   150
Unite commutual in most sacred bands.   151

QUEEN
So many journeys may the sun and moon
Make us again count o'er ere love be done!
But woe is me, you are so sick of late,
So far from cheer and from your former state,
That I distrust you. Yet, though I distrust,   156
Discomfort you, my lord, it nothing must.
For women fear too much, even as they love,
And women's fear and love hold quantity,   159
In neither aught, or in extremity.
Now what my love is, proof hath made you know,
And as my love is sized, my fear is so.
Where love is great, the littlest doubts are fear;
Where little fears grow great, great love grows there.

KING
Faith, I must leave thee, love, and shortly too;
My operant powers their functions leave to do.   166

---

81 *stithy* smithy   84 *censure of* sentence upon   87 *be idle* be foolish, act the madman   89 *cousin* nephew   90 *chameleon's dish* i.e. air (which was believed the chameleon's food; Hamlet willfully takes *fares* in the sense of 'feeds')   93 *not mine* not for me as the asker of my question   103–04 *stay upon your patience* await your indulgence   111 *country matters* rustic goings-on, barnyard mating (with a play upon a sexual term)   119 *jig-maker* writer of jigs (see II, ii, 488)   124 *sables* black furs (luxurious garb, not for mourning)   128 *hobby-horse* traditional figure strapped round the waist of a performer in May games and morris dances   131 *miching mal-lecho* sneaking iniquity   139 *naught* indecent   143 *posy* brief motto in rhyme ('poesy'); *ring finger* ring   146 *Phoebus' cart* the sun's chariot   147 *Tellus* Roman goddess of the earth   148 *borrowed* i.e. taken from the sun   150 *Hymen* Greek god of marriage   151 *commutual* mutually   156 *distrust you* fear for you   159 *quantity* proportion   166 *operant powers* active bodily forces

And thou shalt live in this fair world behind,
Honored, beloved, and haply one as kind
For husband shalt thou –

QUEEN   O, confound the rest!
Such love must needs be treason in my breast.
In second husband let me be accurst!
None wed the second but who killed the first.

173 HAMLET *[aside]* That's wormwood.

QUEEN

174   The instances that second marriage move
Are base respects of thrift, but none of love.
A second time I kill my husband dead
When second husband kisses me in bed.

KING
I do believe you think what now you speak,
But what we do determine oft we break.

180   Purpose is but the slave to memory,
181   Of violent birth, but poor validity,
Which now like fruit unripe sticks on the tree,
But fall unshaken when they mellow be.
Most necessary 'tis that we forget
To pay ourselves what to ourselves is debt.
What to ourselves in passion we propose,
The passion ending, doth the purpose lose.
The violence of either grief or joy

189   Their own enactures with themselves destroy.
Where joy most revels, grief doth most lament;
Grief joys, joy grieves, on slender accident.
This world is not for aye, nor 'tis not strange
That even our loves should with our fortunes change,
For 'tis a question left us yet to prove,
Whether love lead fortune, or else fortune love.
The great man down, you mark his favorite flies,
The poor advanced makes friends of enemies;
And hitherto doth love on fortune tend,
For who not needs shall never lack a friend,
And who in want a hollow friend doth try,

201   Directly seasons him his enemy.
But, orderly to end where I begun,
Our wills and fates do so contrary run

204   That our devices still are overthrown;
Our thoughts are ours, their ends none of our own.
So think thou wilt no second husband wed,
But die thy thoughts when thy first lord is dead.

QUEEN
Nor earth to me give food, nor heaven light,
Sport and repose lock from me day and night,
To desperation turn my trust and hope,

211   An anchor's cheer in prison be my scope,
212   Each opposite that blanks the face of joy
Meet what I would have well, and it destroy,

214   Both here and hence pursue me lasting strife,
If, once a widow, ever I be wife!

HAMLET If she should break it now!

KING
'Tis deeply sworn. Sweet, leave me here awhile.
My spirits grow dull, and fain I would beguile
The tedious day with sleep. *[He sleeps.]*

QUEEN   Sleep rock thy brain,
And never come mischance between us twain!   *Exit.*

HAMLET Madam, how like you this play?
QUEEN The lady doth protest too much, methinks.

HAMLET O, but she'll keep her word.
KING Have you heard the argument? Is there no offense 224
in't?
HAMLET No, no, they do but jest, poison in jest; no
offense i' th' world.
KING What do you call the play?
HAMLET 'The Mousetrap.' Marry, how? Tropically. 229
This play is the image of a murder done in Vienna. Gon-
zago is the duke's name; his wife, Baptista. You shall see
anon. 'Tis a knavish piece of work, but what o' that?
Your majesty, and we that have free souls, it touches us 233
not. Let the galled jade winch; our withers are unwrung. 234
Enter Lucianus.
This is one Lucianus, nephew to the king.
OPHELIA You are as good as a chorus, my lord.   236
HAMLET I could interpret between you and your love, if I
could see the puppets dallying.   238
OPHELIA You are keen, my lord, you are keen.
HAMLET It would cost you a groaning to take off my edge.
OPHELIA Still better, and worse.
HAMLET So you must take your husbands. – Begin, mur-
derer. Leave thy damnable faces and begin. Come, the
croaking raven doth bellow for revenge.

LUCIANUS
Thoughts black, hands apt, drugs fit, and time agreeing,
Confederate season, else no creature seeing,   246
Thou mixture rank, of midnight weeds collected,
With Hecate's ban thrice blasted, thrice infected,   248
Thy natural magic and dire property
On wholesome life usurps immediately.
[Pours the poison in his ears.]

HAMLET 'A poisons him i' th' garden for his estate. His
name 's Gonzago. The story is extant, and written in
very choice Italian. You shall see anon how the mur-
derer gets the love of Gonzago's wife.
OPHELIA The king rises.
HAMLET What, frighted with false fire?   256
QUEEN How fares my lord?
POLONIUS Give o'er the play.
KING Give me some light. Away!
POLONIUS Lights, lights, lights!
         Exeunt all but Hamlet and Horatio.
HAMLET Why, let the strucken deer go weep,
       The hart ungallèd play.
       For some must watch, while some must sleep;
       Thus runs the world away.
Would not this, sir, and a forest of feathers – if the rest of 265
my fortunes turn Turk with me – with two Provincial 266
roses on my razed shoes, get me a fellowship in a cry of 267
players, sir?

173 *wormwood* a bitter herb   174 *instances* motives   180 *slave to* i.e.
dependent upon for life   181 *validity* strength   189 *enactures* fulfillments
201 *seasons him* ripens him into   204 *still* always   211 *anchor's* hermit's
212 *blanks* blanches, makes pale   214 *hence* in the next world   224 *argument* plot summary   229 *Tropically* in the way of a trope or figure (with
a play on 'trapically')   233 *free* guiltless   234 *galled* sore-backed; *jade*
horse; *winch* wince; *withers* shoulders   236 *chorus* one in a play who
explains the action   238 *puppets* i.e. you and your lover as in a puppet
show   246 *Confederate season* the occasion being my ally   248 *Hecate*
goddess of witchcraft and black magic; *ban* curse   256 *false fire* a firing
of a gun charged with powder but no shot, a blank-discharge   265 *feathers*
plumes for actors' costumes   266 *turn Turk* turn renegade, like a Christian
turning Mohammedan   266–67 *Provincial roses* ribbon rosettes   267
razed decorated with cut patterns; *cry* pack

HORATIO Half a share.

HAMLET A whole one, I.
For thou dost know, O Damon dear,
    This realm dismantled was
Of Jove himself; and now reigns here
    A very, very – peacock.

HORATIO You might have rhymed.

HAMLET O good Horatio, I'll take the ghost's word for a thousand pound. Didst perceive?

HORATIO Very well, my lord.

HAMLET Upon the talk of the poisoning?

HORATIO I did very well note him.

281 HAMLET Aha! Come, some music! Come, the recorders!
For if the king like not the comedy,
283   Why then, belike he likes it not, perdy.
Come, some music!

Enter Rosencrantz and Guildenstern.

GUILDENSTERN Good my lord, vouchsafe me a word with you.

HAMLET Sir, a whole history.

GUILDENSTERN The king, sir –

HAMLET Ay, sir, what of him?

289 GUILDENSTERN Is in his retirement marvellous distempered.

HAMLET With drink, sir?

291 GUILDENSTERN No, my lord, with choler.

HAMLET Your wisdom should show itself more richer to signify this to the doctor, for for me to put him to his purgation would perhaps plunge him into more choler.

GUILDENSTERN Good my lord, put your discourse into
296 some frame, and start not so wildly from my affair.

HAMLET I am tame, sir; pronounce.

GUILDENSTERN The queen, your mother, in most great affliction of spirit hath sent me to you.

HAMLET You are welcome.

GUILDENSTERN Nay, good my lord, this courtesy is not of the right breed. If it shall please you to make me a wholesome answer, I will do your mother's commandment. If not, your pardon and my return shall be the end of my business.

HAMLET Sir, I cannot.

ROSENCRANTZ What, my lord?

HAMLET Make you a wholesome answer; my wit 's diseased. But, sir, such answer as I can make, you shall command, or rather, as you say, my mother. Therefore no more, but to the matter. My mother, you say –

ROSENCRANTZ Then thus she says: your behavior hath
313 struck her into amazement and admiration.

HAMLET O wonderful son, that can so stonish a mother! But is there no sequel at the heels of this mother's admiration? Impart.

317 ROSENCRANTZ She desires to speak with you in her closet ere you go to bed.

---

281 *recorders* musical instruments of the flute class   283 *perdy* by God ('*par dieu*')   289 *distempered* out of temper, vexed (twisted by Hamlet into 'deranged')   291 *choler* anger (twisted by Hamlet into 'biliousness')   296 *frame* logical order   313 *admiration* wonder   317 *closet* private room   322 *pickers and stealers* i.e. hands   329 *while the grass grows* (a proverb, ending: 'the horse starves')   331 *recorders* (see III, ii, 281n.); *withdraw* step aside   332 *recover the wind* come up to windward like a hunter   333 *toil* snare   335 *is too unmannerly* leads me beyond the restraint of good manners   343 *ventages* holes, vents   357 *fret* irritate (with a play on the fret-fingering of certain stringed musical instruments)   360 *presently* at once   368 *by and by* immediately   369 *bent* (see II, ii, 30n.)   379 *Nero* murderer of his mother

---

HAMLET We shall obey, were she ten times our mother. Have you any further trade with us?

ROSENCRANTZ My lord, you once did love me.

HAMLET And do still, by these pickers and stealers.   322

ROSENCRANTZ Good my lord, what is your cause of distemper? You do surely bar the door upon your own liberty, if you deny your griefs to your friend.

HAMLET Sir, I lack advancement.

ROSENCRANTZ How can that be, when you have the voice of the king himself for your succession in Denmark?

HAMLET Ay, sir, but 'while the grass grows' – the proverb 329 is something musty.

Enter the Player with recorders.

O, the recorders. Let me see one. To withdraw with 331 you – why do you go about to recover the wind of me, as 332 if you would drive me into a toil?   333

GUILDENSTERN O my lord, if my duty be too bold, my 335 love is too unmannerly.

HAMLET I do not well understand that. Will you play upon this pipe?

GUILDENSTERN My lord, I cannot.

HAMLET I pray you.

GUILDENSTERN Believe me, I cannot.

HAMLET I do beseech you.

GUILDENSTERN I know no touch of it, my lord.

HAMLET It is as easy as lying. Govern these ventages 343 with your fingers and thumb, give it breath with your mouth, and it will discourse most eloquent music. Look you, these are the stops.

GUILDENSTERN But these cannot I command to any utt'rance of harmony. I have not the skill.

HAMLET Why, look you now, how unworthy a thing you make of me! You would play upon me, you would seem to know my stops, you would pluck out the heart of my mystery, you would sound me from my lowest note to the top of my compass; and there is much music, excellent voice, in this little organ, yet cannot you make it speak. 'Sblood, do you think I am easier to be played on than a pipe? Call me what instrument you will, though you can fret me, you cannot play upon me.   357

Enter Polonius.

God bless you, sir!

POLONIUS My lord, the queen would speak with you, and presently.   360

HAMLET Do you see yonder cloud that's almost in shape of a camel?

POLONIUS By th' mass and 'tis, like a camel indeed.

HAMLET Methinks it is like a weasel.

POLONIUS It is backed like a weasel.

HAMLET Or like a whale.

POLONIUS Very like a whale.

HAMLET Then I will come to my mother by and by. 368 *[aside]* They fool me to the top of my bent. – I will come 369 by and by.

POLONIUS I will say so.   *[Exit.]*

HAMLET 'By and by' is easily said. Leave me, friends.
            [Exeunt all but Hamlet.]
'Tis now the very witching time of night,
When churchyards yawn, and hell itself breathes out
Contagion to this world. Now could I drink hot blood
And do such bitter business as the day
Would quake to look on. Soft, now to my mother.
O heart, lose not thy nature; let not ever
The soul of Nero enter this firm bosom.   379

Let me be cruel, not unnatural;
I will speak daggers to her, but use none.
My tongue and soul in this be hypocrites:
383 How in my words somever she be shent,
384 To give them seals never, my soul, consent!   *Exit.*

*

III, iii   *Enter King, Rosencrantz, and Guildenstern.*

KING
I like him not, nor stands it safe with us
To let his madness range. Therefore prepare you.
I your commission will forthwith dispatch,
And he to England shall along with you.
5 The terms of our estate may not endure
Hazard so near's as doth hourly grow
7 Out of his brows.
GUILDENSTERN   We will ourselves provide.
Most holy and religious fear it is
To keep those many many bodies safe
That live and feed upon your majesty.
ROSENCRANTZ
11 The single and peculiar life is bound
With all the strength and armor of the mind
13 To keep itself from noyance, but much more
That spirit upon whose weal depends and rests
15 The lives of many. The cess of majesty
16 Dies not alone, but like a gulf doth draw
What's near it with it; or 'tis a massy wheel
Fixed on the summit of the highest mount,
To whose huge spokes ten thousand lesser things
Are mortised and adjoined, which when it falls,
Each small annexment, petty consequence,
22 Attends the boist'rous ruin. Never alone
Did the king sigh, but with a general groan.
KING
24 Arm you, I pray you, to this speedy voyage,
For we will fetters put upon this fear,
Which now goes too free-footed.
ROSENCRANTZ   We will haste us. *Exeunt Gentlemen.*
    Enter Polonius.
POLONIUS
My lord, he's going to his mother's closet.
Behind the arras I'll convey myself
29 To hear the process. I'll warrant she'll tax him home,
And, as you said, and wisely was it said,
'Tis meet that some more audience than a mother,
Since nature makes them partial, should o'erhear
33 The speech, of vantage. Fare you well, my liege.
I'll call upon you ere you go to bed
And tell you what I know.
KING   Thanks, dear my lord. *Exit [Polonius].*
O, my offense is rank, it smells to heaven;
37 It hath the primal eldest curse upon't,
A brother's murder. Pray can I not,
Though inclination be as sharp as will.
My stronger guilt defeats my strong intent,
And like a man to double business bound
I stand in pause where I shall first begin,
And both neglect. What if this cursèd hand
Were thicker than itself with brother's blood,
Is there not rain enough in the sweet heavens
To wash it white as snow? Whereto serves mercy
47 But to confront the visage of offense?

And what's in prayer but this twofold force,
To be forestallèd ere we come to fall,
Or pardoned being down? Then I'll look up.
My fault is past. But, O, what form of prayer
Can serve my turn? 'Forgive me my foul murder'?
That cannot be, since I am still possessed
Of those effects for which I did the murder,   54
My crown, mine own ambition, and my queen.
May one be pardoned and retain th' offense?
In the corrupted currents of this world
Offense's gilded hand may shove by justice,   58
And oft 'tis seen the wicked prize itself
Buys out the law. But 'tis not so above.
There is no shuffling; there the action lies   61
In his true nature, and we ourselves compelled,
Even to the teeth and forehead of our faults,   63
To give in evidence. What then? What rests?
Try what repentance can. What can it not?
Yet what can it when one cannot repent?
O wretched state! O bosom black as death!
O limèd soul, that struggling to be free   68
Art more engaged! Help, angels! Make assay.   69
Bow, stubborn knees, and, heart with strings of steel,
Be soft as sinews of the new-born babe.
All may be well.
    [He kneels.]
    Enter Hamlet.
HAMLET
Now might I do it pat, now 'a is a-praying,   73
And now I'll do't. And so 'a goes to heaven,
And so am I revenged. That would be scanned.
A villain kills my father, and for that
I, his sole son, do this same villain send
To heaven.
Why, this is hire and salary, not revenge.
'A took my father grossly, full of bread,   80
With all his crimes broad blown, as flush as May;   81
And how his audit stands, who knows save heaven?   82
But in our circumstance and course of thought,
'Tis heavy with him; and am I then revenged,
To take him in the purging of his soul,
When he is fit and seasoned for his passage?
No.
Up, sword, and know thou a more horrid hent.   88
When he is drunk asleep, or in his rage,
Or in th' incestuous pleasure of his bed,
At game a-swearing, or about some act
That has no relish of salvation in't –   92
Then trip him, that his heels may kick at heaven,
And that his soul may be as damned and black

383 *shent* reproved   384 *seals* authentications in actions
III, iii A chamber in the Castle   5 *terms* circumstances; *estate* royal
position   7 *brows* effronteries (apparently with an implication of knitted
brows)   11 *peculiar* individual   13 *noyance* harm   15 *cess* cessation,
decease   16 *gulf* whirlpool   22 *Attends* joins in (like a royal attendant)
24 *Arm* prepare   29 *process* proceedings; *tax him home* thrust home in
reprimanding him   33 *of vantage* from an advantageous position   37
primal eldest curse that of Cain, who also murdered a brother   47 *offense* sin
54 *effects* things acquired   58 *gilded* gold-laden   61 *shuffling* sharp practice, double-dealing; *action* legal proceeding (in heaven's court)   63 *teeth
and forehead* face-to-face recognition   68 *limèd* caught in birdlime, a gluey
material spread as a bird-snare   69 *engaged* embedded; *assay* an attempt
73 *pat* opportunely   80 *grossly* in a state of gross unpreparedness; *bread*
i.e. worldly sense gratification   81 *broad blown* fully blossomed; *flush*
vigorous   82 *audit* account   88 *more horrid hent* grasping by me on a more
horrid occasion   92 *relish* flavor

As hell, whereto it goes. My mother stays.
This physic but prolongs thy sickly days.   *Exit.*
KING [*rises*]
My words fly up, my thoughts remain below.
Words without thoughts never to heaven go.   *Exit.*

                                    *

III, iv   *Enter [Queen] Gertrude and Polonius.*
    POLONIUS
1   'A will come straight. Look you lay home to him.
2   Tell him his pranks have been too broad to bear with,
        And that your grace hath screened and stood between
        Much heat and him. I'll silence me even here.
5   Pray you be round with him.
        [HAMLET (*within*) Mother, mother, mother!]
        QUEEN I'll warrant you; fear me not. Withdraw; I hear
        him coming.   [*Polonius hides behind the arras.*]
            Enter Hamlet.
    HAMLET
        Now, mother, what's the matter?
    QUEEN
        Hamlet, thou hast thy father much offended.
    HAMLET
        Mother, you have my father much offended.
    QUEEN
12   Come, come, you answer with an idle tongue.
    HAMLET
        Go, go, you question with a wicked tongue.
    QUEEN
        Why, how now, Hamlet?
    HAMLET   What's the matter now?
    QUEEN
        Have you forgot me?
15 HAMLET   No, by the rood, not so!
        You are the queen, your husband's brother's wife,
        And (would it were not so) you are my mother.
    QUEEN
        Nay, then I'll set those to you that can speak.
    HAMLET
        Come, come, and sit you down. You shall not budge.
        You go not till I set you up a glass
        Where you may see the inmost part of you.
    QUEEN
        What wilt thou do? Thou wilt not murder me?
        Help, ho!
    POLONIUS [*behind*] What, ho! help!
    HAMLET [*draws*]
        How now? a rat? Dead for a ducat, dead!
            [*Makes a pass through the arras and kills Polonius.*]
    POLONIUS [*behind*]
        O, I am slain!
    QUEEN   O me, what hast thou done?

III, iv The private chamber of the Queen 1 *lay* thrust 2 *broad* unrestrained 5 *round* plain-spoken 12 *idle* foolish 15 *rood* cross 38 *custom*
habit; *brazed* hardened like brass 39 *proof* armor; *sense* feeling 45
blister brand (of degradation) 47 *contraction* the marriage contract 48
religion i.e. sacred marriage vows 50 *compound mass* the earth as compounded of the four elements 51 *against* in expectation of; *doom* Day of
Judgment 53 *index* table of contents preceding the body of a book 55
counterfeit presentment portrayed representation 57 *Hyperion* the sun god;
front forehead 59 *station* attitude in standing 68 *batten* feed greedily 70
heyday excitement of passion 71 *waits upon* yields to 72 *Sense* feeling
73 *motion* desire, impulse 74 *apoplexed* paralyzed 75 *ecstasy* madness
78 *cozened* cheated; *hoodman-blind* blindman's buff 80 *sans* without

---

    HAMLET
        Nay, I know not. Is it the king?
    QUEEN
        O, what a rash and bloody deed is this!
    HAMLET
        A bloody deed – almost as bad, good mother,
        As kill a king, and marry with his brother.   30
    QUEEN
        As kill a king?
    HAMLET   Ay, lady, it was my word.
        [*Lifts up the arras and sees Polonius.*]
        Thou wretched, rash, intruding fool, farewell!
        I took thee for thy better. Take thy fortune.
        Thou find'st to be too busy is some danger. –
        Leave wringing of your hands. Peace, sit you down
        And let me wring your heart, for so I shall
        If it be made of penetrable stuff,
        If damnèd custom have not brazed it so   38
        That it is proof and bulwark against sense.   39
    QUEEN
        What have I done that thou dar'st wag thy tongue
        In noise so rude against me?
    HAMLET   Such an act
        That blurs the grace and blush of modesty,
        Calls virtue hypocrite, takes off the rose
        From the fair forehead of an innocent love,
        And sets a blister there, makes marriage vows   45
        As false as dicers' oaths. O, such a deed
        As from the body of contraction plucks   47
        The very soul, and sweet religion makes   48
        A rhapsody of words! Heaven's face does glow,
        And this solidity and compound mass,   50
        With heated visage, as against the doom,   51
        Is thought-sick at the act.
    QUEEN   Ay me, what act,
        That roars so loud and thunders in the index?   53
    HAMLET
        Look here upon this picture, and on this,
        The counterfeit presentment of two brothers.   55
        See what a grace was seated on this brow:
        Hyperion's curls, the front of Jove himself,   57
        An eye like Mars, to threaten and command,
        A station like the herald Mercury   59
        New lighted on a heaven-kissing hill –
        A combination and a form indeed
        Where every god did seem to set his seal
        To give the world assurance of a man.
        This was your husband. Look you now what follows.
        Here is your husband, like a mildewed ear
        Blasting his wholesome brother. Have you eyes?
        Could you on this fair mountain leave to feed,
        And batten on this moor? Ha! have you eyes?   68
        You cannot call it love, for at your age
        The heyday in the blood is tame, it's humble,   70
        And waits upon the judgment, and what judgment   71
        Would step from this to this? Sense sure you have,   72
        Else could you not have motion, but sure that sense   73
        Is apoplexed, for madness would not err,   74
        Nor sense to ecstasy was ne'er so thralled   75
        But it reserved some quantity of choice
        To serve in such a difference. What devil was't
        That thus hath cozened you at hoodman-blind?   78
        Eyes without feeling, feeling without sight,
        Ears without hands or eyes, smelling sans all,   80

Or but a sickly part of one true sense
82   Could not so mope.
     O shame, where is thy blush ? Rebellious hell,
84   If thou canst mutine in a matron's bones,
     To flaming youth let virtue be as wax
     And melt in her own fire. Proclaim no shame
87   When the compulsive ardor gives the charge,
     Since frost itself as actively doth burn,
89   And reason panders will.
     QUEEN   O Hamlet, speak no more.
     Thou turn'st mine eyes into my very soul,
91   And there I see such black and grainèd spots
92   As will not leave their tinct.
     HAMLET   Nay, but to live
93   In the rank sweat of an enseamèd bed,
     Stewed in corruption, honeying and making love
     Over the nasty sty –
     QUEEN   O, speak to me no more.
     These words like daggers enter in mine ears.
     No more, sweet Hamlet.
     HAMLET   A murderer and a villain,
98   A slave that is not twentieth part the tithe
99   Of your precedent lord, a vice of kings,
100 A cutpurse of the empire and the rule,
     That from a shelf the precious diadem stole
     And put it in his pocket –
102 QUEEN   No more.
           Enter [the] Ghost [in his nightgown].
     HAMLET
     A king of shreds and patches –
     Save me and hover o'er me with your wings,
     You heavenly guards ? What would your gracious figure ?
     QUEEN
     Alas, he's mad.
     HAMLET
     Do you not come your tardy son to chide,
108 That, lapsed in time and passion, lets go by
     Th' important acting of your dread command ?
     O, say !
     GHOST
     Do not forget. This visitation
     Is but to whet thy almost blunted purpose.
     But look, amazement on thy mother sits.
     O, step between her and her fighting soul !
115 Conceit in weakest bodies strongest works.
     Speak to her, Hamlet.
     HAMLET   How is it with you, lady ?
     QUEEN
     Alas, how is't with you,
     That you do bend your eye on vacancy,
119 And with th' incorporal air do hold discourse ?
     Forth at your eyes your spirits wildly peep,
     And as the sleeping soldiers in th' alarm
122 Your bedded hairs like life in excrements
123 Start up and stand an end. O gentle son,
124 Upon the heat and flame of thy distemper
     Sprinkle cool patience. Whereon do you look ?
     HAMLET
     On him, on him ! Look you, how pale he glares !
     His form and cause conjoined, preaching to stones,
128 Would make them capable. – Do not look upon me,
     Lest with this piteous action you convert
130 My stern effects. Then what I have to do
     Will want true color – tears perchance for blood.

QUEEN
     To whom do you speak this ?
HAMLET   Do you see nothing there ?
QUEEN
     Nothing at all ; yet all that is I see.
HAMLET
     Nor did you nothing hear ?
QUEEN   No, nothing but ourselves.
HAMLET
     Why, look you there ! Look how it steals away !
     My father, in his habit as he lived !
     Look where he goes even now out at the portal !
                              Exit Ghost.
QUEEN
     This is the very coinage of your brain.
     This bodiless creation ecstasy   139
     Is very cunning in.
HAMLET   Ecstasy ?
     My pulse as yours doth temperately keep time
     And makes as healthful music. It is not madness
     That I have uttered. Bring me to the test,
     And I the matter will reword, which madness
     Would gambol from. Mother, for love of grace,   145
     Lay not that flattering unction to your soul,   146
     That not your trespass but my madness speaks.
     It will but skin and film the ulcerous place
     Whiles rank corruption, mining all within,   149
     Infects unseen. Confess yourself to heaven,
     Repent what's past, avoid what is to come,
     And do not spread the compost on the weeds   152
     To make them ranker. Forgive me this my virtue.
     For in the fatness of these pursy times   154
     Virtue itself of vice must pardon beg,
     Yea, curb and woo for leave to do him good.   156
QUEEN
     O Hamlet, thou hast cleft my heart in twain.
HAMLET
     O, throw away the worser part of it,
     And live the purer with the other half.
     Good night – but go not to my uncle's bed.
     Assume a virtue, if you have it not.
     That monster custom, who all sense doth eat,   162
     Of habits devil, is angel yet in this,
     That to the use of actions fair and good
     He likewise gives a frock or livery   165
     That aptly is put on. Refrain to-night,
     And that shall lend a kind of easiness
     To the next abstinence ; the next more easy ;
     For use almost can change the stamp of nature,   169
     And either . . . the devil, or throw him out   170
     With wondrous potency. Once more, good night,

82 *mope* be stupid   84 *mutine* mutiny   87 *compulsive* compelling ; *gives the charge* delivers the attack   89 *panders will* acts as procurer for desire   91 *grainèd* dyed in grain   92 *tinct* color   93 *enseamèd* grease-laden   98 *tithe* tenth part   99 *vice* clownish rogue (like the Vice of the morality plays)   100 *cutpurse* skulking thief   102 **s.d.** *nightgown* dressing gown   108 *lapsed . . . passion* having let the moment slip and passion cool   115 *Conceit* imagination   119 *incorporal* bodiless   122 *excrements* outgrowths   123 *an on*   124 *distemper* mental disorder   128 *capable* susceptible   130 *effects* manifestations of emotion and purpose   139 *ecstasy* madness   145 *gambol* shy (like a startled horse)   146 *unction* ointment   149 *mining* undermining   152 *compost* fertilizing mixture   154 *fatness* gross slackness ; *pursy* corpulent   156 *curb* bow to   162–63 *all sense . . . devil* (see Appendix : Supplementary Notes)   165 *livery* characteristic dress (accompanying the suggestion of 'garb' in *habits*)   169 *use* habit ; *stamp* impression, form   170 *And . . . out* (see Appendix : Supplementary Notes)

And when you are desirous to be blest,
I'll blessing beg of you. – For this same lord,
I do repent ; but heaven hath pleased it so,
To punish me with this, and this with me,
That I must be their scourge and minister.
177 I will bestow him and will answer well
The death I gave him. So again, good night.
I must be cruel only to be kind.
180 Thus bad begins, and worse remains behind.
One word more, good lady.
QUEEN   What shall I do ?
HAMLET
Not this, by no means, that I bid you do :
183 Let the bloat king tempt you again to bed,
Pinch wanton on your cheek, call you his mouse,
185 And let him, for a pair of reechy kisses,
Or paddling in your neck with his damned fingers,
187 Make you to ravel all this matter out,
That I essentially am not in madness,
But mad in craft. 'Twere good you let him know,
For who that's but a queen, fair, sober, wise,
191 Would from a paddock, from a bat, a gib,
192 Such dear concernings hide ? Who would do so ?
No, in despite of sense and secrecy,
Unpeg the basket on the house's top,
195 Let the birds fly, and like the famous ape,
196 To try conclusions, in the basket creep
And break your own neck down.
QUEEN
Be thou assured, if words be made of breath,
And breath of life, I have no life to breathe
What thou hast said to me.
HAMLET
I must to England ; you know that ?
QUEEN   Alack,
I had forgot. 'Tis so concluded on.
HAMLET
There's letters sealed, and my two schoolfellows,
Whom I will trust as I will adders fanged,
205 They bear the mandate ; they must sweep my way
And marshal me to knavery. Let it work.
207 For 'tis the sport to have the enginer
208 Hoist with his own petar, and 't shall go hard
But I will delve one yard below their mines
And blow them at the moon. O, 'tis most sweet
When in one line two crafts directly meet.
212 This man shall set me packing.
I'll lug the guts into the neighbor room.
Mother, good night. Indeed, this counsellor
Is now most still, most secret, and most grave,
Who was in life a foolish prating knave.

177 *bestow* stow, hide   180 *behind* to come   183 *bloat* bloated with sense
gratification   185 *reechy* filthy   187 *ravel . . . out* disentangle   191 *paddock* toad ; *gib* tomcat   192 *dear concernings* matters of great personal significance   195 *famous ape* (one in a story now unknown)   196 *conclusions*
experiments   205 *mandate* order   207 *enginer* engineer, constructor of
military engines or works   208 *Hoist* blown up ; *petar* petard, bomb or
mine   212 *packing* travelling in a hurry (with a play upon his 'packing' or
shouldering of Polonius' body and also upon his 'packing' in the sense
of 'plotting' or 'contriving')
IV, i   A chamber in the Castle   11 *brainish apprehension* headstrong conception   17 *providence* foresight   18 *haunt* association with others   22
divulging becoming known   25 *ore* vein of gold   26 *mineral* mine   40 *And
. . . done* (see Appendix : Supplementary Notes)   42 *As level* with as direct
aim ; *blank* mark, central white spot on a target

Come, sir, to draw toward an end with you.
Good night, mother.
                    [*Exit the Queen. Then*] *exit* [*Hamlet,
                            tugging in Polonius*].
                            *

Enter King and Queen, with Rosencrantz and   IV, i
Guildenstern.
KING
There's matter in these sighs. These profound heaves
You must translate ; 'tis fit we understand them.
Where is your son ?
QUEEN
Bestow this place on us a little while.
                [*Exeunt Rosencrantz and Guildenstern.*]
Ah, mine own lord, what have I seen to-night !
KING
What, Gertrude ? How does Hamlet ?
QUEEN
Mad as the sea and wind when both contend
Which is the mightier. In his lawless fit,
Behind the arras hearing something stir,
Whips out his rapier, cries, 'A rat, a rat !'
And in this brainish apprehension kills   11
The unseen good old man.
KING   O heavy deed !
It had been so with us, had we been there.
His liberty is full of threats to all,
To you yourself, to us, to every one.
Alas, how shall this bloody deed be answered ?
It will be laid to us, whose providence   17
Should have kept short, restrained, and out of haunt   18
This mad young man. But so much was our love
We would not understand what was most fit,
But, like the owner of a foul disease,
To keep it from divulging, let it feed
Even on the pith of life. Where is he gone ?   22
QUEEN
To draw apart the body he hath killed ;
O'er whom his very madness, like some ore   25
Among a mineral of metals base,   26
Shows itself pure. 'A weeps for what is done.
KING
O Gertrude, come away !
The sun no sooner shall the mountains touch
But we will ship him hence, and this vile deed
We must with all our majesty and skill
Both countenance and excuse. Ho, Guildenstern !
        Enter Rosencrantz and Guildenstern.
Friends both, go join you with some further aid.
Hamlet in madness hath Polonius slain,
And from his mother's closet hath he dragged him.
Go seek him out ; speak fair, and bring the body
Into the chapel. I pray you haste in this.
                [*Exeunt Rosencrantz and Guildenstern.*]
Come, Gertrude, we'll call up our wisest friends
And let them know both what we mean to do
And what's untimely done . . .   40
Whose whisper o'er the world's diameter,
As level as the cannon to his blank   42
Transports his poisoned shot, may miss our name
And hit the woundless air. O, come away !
My soul is full of discord and dismay.   *Exeunt.*
                            *

IV, ii   *Enter Hamlet.*

HAMLET Safely stowed.

GENTLEMEN *(within)* Hamlet! Lord Hamlet!

HAMLET But soft, what noise? Who calls on Hamlet? O, here they come.

          [Enter] Rosencrantz, [Guildenstern,] and others.

ROSENCRANTZ
     What have you done, my lord, with the dead body?

HAMLET
     Compounded it with dust, whereto 'tis kin.

ROSENCRANTZ
     Tell us where 'tis, that we may take it thence
     And bear it to the chapel.

HAMLET Do not believe it.

ROSENCRANTZ Believe what?

HAMLET That I can keep your counsel and not mine own.

12   Besides, to be demanded of a sponge, what replication should be made by the son of a king?

ROSENCRANTZ Take you me for a sponge, my lord?

15 HAMLET Ay, sir, that soaks up the king's countenance, his rewards, his authorities. But such officers do the king best service in the end. He keeps them, like an ape, in the corner of his jaw, first mouthed, to be last swallowed. When he needs what you have gleaned, it is but squeezing you and, sponge, you shall be dry again.

ROSENCRANTZ I understand you not, my lord.

22 HAMLET I am glad of it. A knavish speech sleeps in a foolish ear.

ROSENCRANTZ My lord, you must tell us where the body is and go with us to the king.

HAMLET The body is with the king, but the king is not with the body. The king is a thing –

GUILDENSTERN A thing, my lord?

29 HAMLET Of nothing. Bring me to him. Hide fox, and all after.   *Exeunt.*

                              *

IV, iii   *Enter King, and two or three.*

KING
     I have sent to seek him and to find the body.
     How dangerous is it that this man goes loose!
     Yet must not we put the strong law on him;
4   He's loved of the distracted multitude,
     Who like not in their judgment, but their eyes,
6   And where 'tis so, th' offender's scourge is weighed,
     But never the offense. To bear all smooth and even,
     This sudden sending him away must seem
9   Deliberate pause. Diseases desperate grown
     By desperate appliance are relieved,
     Or not at all.

          Enter Rosencrantz, [Guildenstern,] and all the rest.
          How now? What hath befallen?

ROSENCRANTZ
     Where the dead body is bestowed, my lord,
     We cannot get from him.

KING   But where is he?

ROSENCRANTZ
     Without, my lord; guarded, to know your pleasure.

KING
     Bring him before us.

ROSENCRANTZ   Ho! Bring in the lord.
          They enter [with Hamlet].

KING Now, Hamlet, where's Polonius?

HAMLET At supper.

KING At supper? Where?

HAMLET Not where he eats, but where 'a is eaten. A certain convocation of politic worms are e'en at him. 20 Your worm is your only emperor for diet. We fat 21 all creatures else to fat us, and we fat ourselves for maggots. Your fat king and your lean beggar is but variable service – two dishes, but to one table. That's 24 the end.

KING Alas, alas!

HAMLET A man may fish with the worm that hath eat of a king, and eat of the fish that hath fed of that worm.

KING What dost thou mean by this?

HAMLET Nothing but to show you how a king may go a progress through the guts of a beggar.   31

KING Where is Polonius?

HAMLET In heaven. Send thither to see. If your messenger find him not there, seek him i' th' other place yourself. But if indeed you find him not within this month, you shall nose him as you go up the stairs into the lobby.

KING *[to Attendants]* Go seek him there.

HAMLET 'A will stay till you come.   *[Exeunt Attendants.]*

KING
     Hamlet, this deed, for thine especial safety,
     Which we do tender as we dearly grieve   40
     For that which thou hast done, must send thee hence
     With fiery quickness. Therefore prepare thyself.
     The bark is ready and the wind at help,
     Th' associates tend, and everything is bent   44
     For England.

HAMLET   For England?

KING   Ay, Hamlet.

HAMLET   Good.

KING
     So is it, if thou knew'st our purposes.

HAMLET I see a cherub that sees them. But come, for 47 England! Farewell, dear mother.

KING Thy loving father, Hamlet.

HAMLET My mother – father and mother is man and wife, man and wife is one flesh, and so, my mother. Come, for England!   *Exit.*

KING
     Follow him at foot; tempt him with speed aboard. 53
     Delay it not; I'll have him hence to-night.
     Away! for everything is sealed and done
     That else leans on th' affair. Pray you make haste. 56
                        [Exeunt all but the King.]
     And, England, if my love thou hold'st at aught – 57
     As my great power thereof may give thee sense,

IV, ii A passage in the Castle   12 *replication* reply   15 *countenance* favor   22 *sleeps in* means nothing to   29 *Of nothing* (cf. Prayer Book, Psalm cxliv, 4, 'Man is like a thing of naught: his time passeth away like a shadow')   29–30 *Hide . . . after* (apparently well-known words from some game of hide-and-seek)
IV, iii A chamber in the Castle   4 *distracted* confused   6 *scourge* punishment   9 *Deliberate pause* something done with much deliberation   20 *politic worms* political and craftily scheming worms (such as Polonius might well attract)   21 *diet* food and drink (perhaps with a play upon a famous 'convocation,' the Diet of Worms opened by the Emperor Charles V on January 28, 1521, before which Luther appeared)   24 *variable service* different servings of one food   31 *progress* royal journey of state   40 *tender* hold dear; *dearly* intensely   44 *tend* wait; *bent* set in readiness (like a bent bow)   47 *cherub* one of the cherubim (angels with a distinctive quality of knowledge)   53 *at foot* at heel, close   56 *leans on* is connected with   57 *England* King of England

60   Since yet thy cicatrice looks raw and red

60   After the Danish sword, and thy free awe

61   Pays homage to us – thou mayst not coldly set

62   Our sovereign process, which imports at full

63   By letters congruing to that effect

64   The present death of Hamlet. Do it, England,

65   For like the hectic in my blood he rages,

     And thou must cure me. Till I know 'tis done,

67   Howe'er my haps, my joys were ne'er begun.   *Exit.*

*

IV, iv   *Enter Fortinbras with his Army over the stage.*

FORTINBRAS

     Go, captain, from me greet the Danish king.

     Tell him that by his license Fortinbras

3   Craves the conveyance of a promised march

     Over his kingdom. You know the rendezvous.

     If that his majesty would aught with us,

6   We shall express our duty in his eye ;

     And let him know so.

CAPTAIN   I will do't, my lord.

FORTINBRAS

8   Go softly on.   *[Exeunt all but the Captain.]*

     Enter Hamlet, Rosencrantz, [Guildenstern,] and

     others.

HAMLET

9   Good sir, whose powers are these ?

CAPTAIN

     They are of Norway, sir.

HAMLET

     How purposed, sir, I pray you ?

CAPTAIN

     Against some part of Poland.

HAMLET

     Who commands them, sir ?

CAPTAIN

     The nephew to old Norway, Fortinbras.

HAMLET

15   Goes it against the main of Poland, sir,

     Or for some frontier ?

CAPTAIN

17   Truly to speak, and with no addition,

     We go to gain a little patch of ground

     That hath in it no profit but the name.

20   To pay five ducats, five, I would not farm it,

     Nor will it yield to Norway or the Pole

22   A ranker rate, should it be sold in fee.

HAMLET

     Why, then the Polack never will defend it.

CAPTAIN

     Yes, it is already garrisoned.

HAMLET

     Two thousand souls and twenty thousand ducats

     Will not debate the question of this straw.

     This is th' imposthume of much wealth and peace,   27

     That inward breaks, and shows no cause without

     Why the man dies. I humbly thank you, sir.

CAPTAIN

     God bye you, sir.   *[Exit.]*

ROSENCRANTZ   Will't please you go, my lord ?

HAMLET

     I'll be with you straight. Go a little before.

               [Exeunt all but Hamlet.]

     How all occasions do inform against me   32

     And spur my dull revenge ! What is a man,

     If his chief good and market of his time   34

     Be but to sleep and feed ? A beast, no more.

     Sure he that made us with such large discourse,   36

     Looking before and after, gave us not

     That capability and godlike reason

     To fust in us unused. Now, whether it be   39

     Bestial oblivion, or some craven scruple   40

     Of thinking too precisely on th' event –   41

     A thought which, quartered, hath but one part wisdom

     And ever three parts coward – I do not know

     Why yet I live to say, 'This thing 's to do,'

     Sith I have cause, and will, and strength, and means

     To do't. Examples gross as earth exhort me.   46

     Witness this army of such mass and charge,   47

     Led by a delicate and tender prince,

     Whose spirit, with divine ambition puffed,

     Makes mouths at the invisible event,   50

     Exposing what is mortal and unsure

     To all that fortune, death, and danger dare,

     Even for an eggshell. Rightly to be great

     Is not to stir without great argument,

     But greatly to find quarrel in a straw   55

     When honor 's at the stake. How stand I then,

     That have a father killed, a mother stained,

     Excitements of my reason and my blood,

     And let all sleep, while to my shame I see

     The imminent death of twenty thousand men

     That for a fantasy and trick of fame   61

     Go to their graves like beds, fight for a plot

     Whereon the numbers cannot try the cause,   63

     Which is not tomb enough and continent   64

     To hide the slain ? O, from this time forth,

     My thoughts be bloody, or be nothing worth !   *Exit.*

*

         Enter Horatio, [Queen] Gertrude, and a Gentleman.   IV, v

QUEEN

     I will not speak with her.

GENTLEMAN

     She is importunate, indeed distract.   2

     Her mood will needs be pitied.

QUEEN   What would she have ?

GENTLEMAN

     She speaks much of her father, says she hears

     There's tricks i' th' world, and hems, and beats her heart,   5

     Spurns enviously at straws, speaks things in doubt   6

     That carry but half sense. Her speech is nothing,

60 *free awe* voluntary show of respect   **61** *set* esteem   **62** *process* formal command   **63** *congruing* agreeing   **64** *present* instant   **65** *hectic* a continuous fever   **67** *haps* fortunes

IV, iv A coastal highway   **3** *conveyance* escort   **6** *eye* presence   **8** *softly* slowly   **9** *powers* forces   **15** *main* main body   **17** *addition* exaggeration   **20** *To pay* i.e. for a yearly rental of   **22** *ranker* more abundant ; *in fee* outright   **27** *imposthume* abscess   **32** *inform* take shape   **34** *market of* compensation for   **36** *discourse* power of thought   **39** *fust* grow mouldy   **40** *oblivion* forgetfulness   **41** *event* outcome (as also in l. 50)   **46** *gross* large and evident   **47** *charge* expense   **50** *Makes mouths* makes faces scornfully   **55** *greatly . . . straw* to recognize the great argument even in some small matter   **61** *fantasy* fanciful image ; *trick* toy   **63** *try the cause* find space in which to settle the issue by battle   **64** *continent* receptacle

IV, v A chamber in the Castle   **2** *distract* insane   **5** *tricks* deceits   **6** *Spurns enviously* kicks spitefully, takes offense ; *straws* trifles

8   Yet the unshapèd use of it doth move
9   The hearers to collection ; they aim at it,
10   And botch the words up fit to their own thoughts,
    Which, as her winks and nods and gestures yield them,
    Indeed would make one think there might be thought,
    Though nothing sure, yet much unhappily.

HORATIO
    'Twere good she were spoken with, for she may strew
    Dangerous conjectures in ill-breeding minds.

QUEEN
    Let her come in.   *[Exit Gentleman.]*
    [Aside]
    To my sick soul (as sin's true nature is)
18   Each toy seems prologue to some great amiss.
19   So full of artless jealousy is guilt
20   It spills itself in fearing to be spilt.
      Enter Ophelia [distracted].

OPHELIA
    Where is the beauteous majesty of Denmark ?

QUEEN How now, Ophelia ?

OPHELIA
    She sings.   How should I your true-love know
              From another one ?
25   By his cockle hat and staff
26   And his sandal shoon.

QUEEN
    Alas, sweet lady, what imports this song ?

OPHELIA Say you ? Nay, pray you mark.

         Song.

      He is dead and gone, lady,
        He is dead and gone ;
      At his head a grass-green turf,
        At his heels a stone.

    O, ho !

QUEEN Nay, but Ophelia –

OPHELIA Pray you mark.
    [Sings] White his shroud as the mountain snow –
      Enter King.

QUEEN Alas, look here, my lord.

OPHELIA   *Song.*
38   Larded all with sweet flowers ;
        Which bewept to the grave did not go
           With true-love showers.

KING How do you, pretty lady ?

42 OPHELIA Well, God dild you ! They say the owl was a
    baker's daughter. Lord, we know what we are, but know
    not what we may be. God be at your table !

45 KING Conceit upon her father.

OPHELIA Pray let's have no words of this, but when they
    ask you what it means, say you this :

         Song.

      To-morrow is Saint Valentine's day.
49   All in the morning betime,
      And I a maid at your window,
        To be your Valentine.
      Then up he rose and donned his clo'es
53   And dupped the chamber door,
      Let in the maid, that out a maid
        Never departed more.

KING Pretty Ophelia !

OPHELIA Indeed, la, without an oath, I'll make an end on 't :

    [Sings] By Gis and by Saint Charity,   58
         Alack, and fie for shame !
    Young men will do't if they come to't.
      By Cock, they are to blame.   61
    Quoth she, 'Before you tumbled me,
      You promised me to wed.'
   He answers :
      'So would I 'a' done, by yonder sun,
        And thou hadst not come to my bed.'

KING How long hath she been thus ?

OPHELIA I hope all will be well. We must be patient, but
    I cannot choose but weep to think they would lay him i'
    th' cold ground. My brother shall know of it ; and so I 70
    thank you for your good counsel. Come, my coach !
    Good night, ladies, good night. Sweet ladies, good
    night, good night.   *[Exit.]*

KING
    Follow her close ; give her good watch, I pray you.
                      [Exit Horatio.]
    O, this is the poison of deep grief ; it springs
    All from her father's death – and now behold !
    O Gertrude, Gertrude,
    When sorrows come, they come not single spies,
    But in battalions : first, her father slain ;
    Next, your son gone, and he most violent author
    Of his own just remove ; the people muddied,   81
    Thick and unwholesome in their thoughts and whispers
    For good Polonius' death, and we have done but greenly 83
    In hugger-mugger to inter him ; poor Ophelia   84
    Divided from herself and her fair judgment,
    Without the which we are pictures or mere beasts ;
    Last, and as much containing as all these,
    Her brother is in secret come from France,
    Feeds on his wonder, keeps himself in clouds,   89
    And wants not buzzers to infect his ear   90
    With pestilent speeches of his father's death,
    Wherein necessity, of matter beggared,   92
    Will nothing stick our person to arraign   93
    In ear and ear. O my dear Gertrude, this,
    Like to a murd'ring piece, in many places   95
    Gives me superfluous death.
      A noise within.
      Enter a Messenger.

QUEEN   Alack, what noise is this ?

KING
    Attend, where are my Switzers ? Let them guard the 97
    door.
    What is the matter ?

MESSENGER   Save yourself, my lord.
    The ocean, overpeering of his list,   99

---

8 *unshapèd use* disordered manner   9 *collection* attempts at shaping meaning ; *aim* guess   10 *botch* patch   18 *toy* trifle ; *amiss* calamity   19 *artless* unskillfully managed ; *jealousy* suspicion   20 *spills* destroys   25 *cockle hat* hat bearing a cockle shell, worn by a pilgrim who had been to the shrine of St James of Compostela   26 *shoon* shoes   38 *Larded* garnished   42 *dild* yield, repay ; *the owl* an owl into which, according to a folk-tale, a baker's daughter was transformed because of her failure to show wholehearted generosity when Christ asked for bread in the baker's shop   45 *Conceit* thought   49 *betime* early   53 *dupped* opened   58 *Gis* Jesus   61 *Cock* God (with a perversion of the name not uncommon in oaths)   81 *muddied* stirred up and confused   83 *greenly* foolishly   84 *hugger-mugger* secrecy and disorder   89 *clouds* obscurity   90 *wants* lacks ; *buzzers* whispering talebearers   92 *of matter beggared* unprovided with facts   93 *nothing stick* in no way hesitate ; *arraign* accuse   95 *murd'ring piece* cannon loaded with shot meant to scatter   97 *Switzers* hired Swiss guards   99 *overpeering of* rising to look over and pass beyond ; *list* boundary

100 Eats not the flats with more impiteous haste
101 Than young Laertes, in a riotous head,
O'erbears your officers. The rabble call him lord,
And, as the world were now but to begin,
Antiquity forgot, custom not known,
105 The ratifiers and props of every word,
They cry, 'Choose we! Laertes shall be king!'
Caps, hands, and tongues applaud it to the clouds,
'Laertes shall be king! Laertes king!'
    A noise within.

QUEEN
How cheerfully on the false trail they cry!
110 O, this is counter, you false Danish dogs!
KING
The doors are broke.
    Enter Laertes with others.

LAERTES
Where is this king? – Sirs, stand you all without.
ALL
No, let's come in.
LAERTES   I pray you give me leave.
ALL   We will, we will.
LAERTES
I thank you. Keep the door.   *[Exeunt his Followers.]*
                O thou vile king,
Give me my father.
QUEEN   Calmly, good Laertes.
LAERTES
That drop of blood that's calm proclaims me bastard,
Cries cuckold to my father, brands the harlot
Even here between the chaste unsmirchèd brows
Of my true mother.
KING   What is the cause, Laertes,
That thy rebellion looks so giant-like?
122 Let him go, Gertrude. Do not fear our person.
There's such divinity doth hedge a king
124 That treason can but peep to what it would,
Acts little of his will. Tell me, Laertes,
Why thou art thus incensed. Let him go, Gertrude.
Speak, man.
LAERTES
Where is my father?
KING   Dead.
QUEEN   But not by him.
KING
Let him demand his fill.
LAERTES
How came he dead? I'll not be juggled with.
To hell allegiance, vows to the blackest devil,
Conscience and grace to the profoundest pit!
I dare damnation. To this point I stand,
134 That both the worlds I give to negligence,

Let come what comes, only I'll be revenged
Most throughly for my father.   136
KING   Who shall stay you?
LAERTES
My will, not all the world's.
And for my means, I'll husband them so well
They shall go far with little.
KING   Good Laertes,
If you desire to know the certainty
Of your dear father, is't writ in your revenge
That swoopstake you will draw both friend and foe,   142
Winner and loser?
LAERTES
None but his enemies.
KING   Will you know them then?
LAERTES
To his good friends thus wide I'll ope my arms
And like the kind life-rend'ring pelican
Repast them with my blood.   146
KING   Why, now you speak
Like a good child and a true gentleman.
That I am guiltless of your father's death,
And am most sensibly in grief for it,   150
It shall as level to your judgment 'pear   151
As day does to your eye.
    A noise within : 'Let her come in.'
LAERTES
How now? What noise is that?
    Enter Ophelia.
O heat, dry up my brains; tears seven times salt
Burn out the sense and virtue of mine eye!
By heaven, thy madness shall be paid by weight
Till our scale turn the beam. O rose of May,   157
Dear maid, kind sister, sweet Ophelia!
O heavens, is't possible a young maid's wits
Should be as mortal as an old man's life?
[Nature is fine in love, and where 'tis fine,   161
It sends some precious instance of itself   162
After the thing it loves.]

OPHELIA   *Song.*
They bore him barefaced on the bier
     [Hey non nony, nony, hey nony]
     And in his grave rained many a tear –
Fare you well, my dove!
LAERTES
Hadst thou thy wits, and didst persuade revenge,
It could not move thus.
OPHELIA You must sing 'A-down a-down, and you call
him a-down-a.' O, how the wheel becomes it! It is the   171
false steward, that stole his master's daughter.
LAERTES This nothing's more than matter.   173
OPHELIA There's rosemary, that's for remembrance.
Pray you, love, remember. And there is pansies, that's
for thoughts.
LAERTES A document in madness, thoughts and re-   177
membrance fitted.
OPHELIA There's fennel for you, and columbines.   179
There's rue for you, and here's some for me. We may   180
call it herb of grace o' Sundays. O, you must wear your
rue with a difference. There's a daisy. I would give you   182
some violets, but they withered all when my father died.   183
They say 'a made a good end.
[Sings] For bonny sweet Robin is all my joy.

100 *impiteous* pitiless   101 *head* armed force   105 *word* promise   110 *counter* hunting backward on the trail   122 *fear* fear for   124 *peep to* i.e. through the barrier   134 *both the worlds* whatever may result in this world or the next; *give to negligence* disregard   136 *throughly* thoroughly   142 *swoopstake* sweepstake, taking all stakes on the gambling table   146 *life-rend'ring* life-yielding (because the mother pelican supposedly took blood from her breast with her bill to feed her young)   150 *sensibly* feelingly   151 *level* plain   157 *beam* bar of a balance   161 *fine* refined to purity   162 *instance* token   171 *wheel* burden, refrain   173 *more than matter* more meaningful than sane speech   177 *document* lesson   179 *fennel* symbol of flattery; *columbines* symbol of thanklessness (?)   180 *rue* symbol of repentance   182 *daisy* symbol of dissembling   183 *violets* symbol of faithfulness

LAERTES
Thought and affliction, passion, hell itself,
187   She turns to favor and to prettiness.

OPHELIA   *Song.*

And will 'a not come again?
And will 'a not come again?
No, no, he is dead;
Go to thy deathbed;
He never will come again.
His beard was as white as snow,
194   All flaxen was his poll.
He is gone, he is gone,
And we cast away moan.
God 'a' mercy on his soul!

198   And of all Christian souls, I pray God. God bye you.
                                [Exit.]

LAERTES
Do you see this, O God?

KING
Laertes, I must commune with your grief,
Or you deny me right. Go but apart,
Make choice of whom your wisest friends you will,
And they shall hear and judge 'twixt you and me.
204   If by direct or by collateral hand
205   They find us touched, we will our kingdom give,
Our crown, our life, and all that we call ours,
To you in satisfaction; but if not,
Be you content to lend your patience to us,
And we shall jointly labor with your soul
To give it due content.

LAERTES   Let this be so.
His means of death, his obscure funeral –
212   No trophy, sword, nor hatchment o'er his bones,
213   No noble rite nor formal ostentation –
Cry to be heard, as 'twere from heaven to earth,
215   That I must call't in question.

KING   So you shall;
And where th' offense is, let the great axe fall.
I pray you go with me.   *Exeunt.*

*

IV, vi   *Enter Horatio and others.*

HORATIO What are they that would speak with me?
GENTLEMAN Seafaring men, sir. They say they have
   letters for you.
HORATIO Let them come in.   *[Exit Attendant.]*
I do not know from what part of the world
I should be greeted, if not from Lord Hamlet.
     Enter Sailors.
SAILOR God bless you, sir.
HORATIO Let him bless thee too.
SAILOR 'A shall, sir, an't please him. There's a letter for
   you, sir – it came from th' ambassador that was bound
   for England – if your name be Horatio, as I am let to
   know it is.
HORATIO *[reads the letter]* 'Horatio, when thou shalt have
14   overlooked this, give these fellows some means to the
   king. They have letters for him. Ere we were two days
16   old at sea, a pirate of very warlike appointment gave us
   chase. Finding ourselves too slow of sail, we put on a
   compelled valor, and in the grapple I boarded them. On
   the instant they got clear of our ship; so I alone became

their prisoner. They have dealt with me like thieves of 20
mercy, but they knew what they did: I am to do a good
turn for them. Let the king have the letters I have sent,
and repair thou to me with as much speed as thou
wouldest fly death. I have words to speak in thine ear will
make thee dumb; yet are they much too light for the bore 25
of the matter. These good fellows will bring thee where I
am. Rosencrantz and Guildenstern hold their course for
England. Of them I have much to tell thee. Farewell.

         'He that thou knowest thine, Hamlet.'
Come, I will give you way for these your letters,
And do't the speedier that you may direct me
To him from whom you brought them.   *Exeunt.*

*

         Enter King and Laertes.   IV, vii

KING
Now must your conscience my acquittance seal,
And you must put me in your heart for friend,
Sith you have heard, and with a knowing ear,
That he which hath your noble father slain
Pursued my life.

LAERTES   It well appears. But tell me
Why you proceeded not against these feats   6
So crimeful and so capital in nature,   7
As by your safety, wisdom, all things else,
You mainly were stirred up.   9

KING   O, for two special reasons,
Which may to you perhaps seem much unsinewed,
But yet to me they're strong. The queen his mother
Lives almost by his looks, and for myself –
My virtue or my plague, be it either which –
She is so conjunctive to my life and soul   14
That, as the star moves not but in his sphere,
I could not but by her. The other motive
Why to a public count I might not go   17
Is the great love the general gender bear him,   18
Who, dipping all his faults in their affection,
Would, like the spring that turneth wood to stone,
Convert his gyves to graces; so that my arrows,   21
Too slightly timbered for so loud a wind,
Would have reverted to my bow again,
And not where I had aimed them.

LAERTES
And so have I a noble father lost,
A sister driven into desp'rate terms,   26
Whose worth, if praises may go back again,   27
Stood challenger on mount of all the age   28
For her perfections. But my revenge will come.

KING
Break not your sleeps for that. You must not think
That we are made of stuff so flat and dull
That we can let our beard be shook with danger,

---

187 *favor* charm   194 *poll* head   198 *of* on   204 *collateral* indirect   205
touched i.e. with the crime   212 *trophy* memorial; *hatchment* coat of arms
213 *ostentation* ceremony   215 *That* so that
IV, vi A chamber in the Castle   14 *overlooked* surveyed, scanned; *means*
i.e. of access   16 *appointment* equipment   20–21 *thieves of mercy* merciful
thieves   25 *bore* caliber (as of a gun)
IV, vii A chamber in the Castle   6 *feats* deeds   7 *capital* punishable by
death   9 *mainly* powerfully   14 *conjunctive* closely united   17 *count* trial,
accounting   18 *general gender* common people   21 *gyves* fetters   26 *terms*
circumstances   27 *back again* i.e. to her better circumstances   28 *on mount*
on a height

And think it pastime. You shortly shall hear more.
I loved your father, and we love ourself,
And that, I hope, will teach you to imagine –
Enter a Messenger with letters.
[How now ? What news ?]

MESSENGER   [Letters, my lord, from Hamlet :]
These to your majesty, this to the queen.

KING
From Hamlet ? Who brought them ?

MESSENGER
Sailors, my lord, they say ; I saw them not.
They were given me by Claudio ; he received them
Of him that brought them.

KING   Laertes, you shall hear them. –
Leave us.   *[Exit Messenger.]*

43   *[Reads]* 'High and mighty, you shall know I am set naked
on your kingdom. To-morrow shall I beg leave to see
your kingly eyes ; when I shall (first asking your pardon
thereunto) recount the occasion of my sudden and more
strange return.   Hamlet.'
What should this mean ? Are all the rest come back ?

49   Or is it some abuse, and no such thing ?

LAERTES
Know you the hand ?

50 KING   'Tis Hamlet's character. 'Naked' !
And in a postscript here, he says 'alone.'

52   Can you devise me ?

LAERTES
I am lost in it, my lord. But let him come.
It warms the very sickness in my heart
That I shall live and tell him to his teeth,
'Thus diddest thou.'

KING   If it be so, Laertes,
(As how should it be so ? how otherwise ?)
Will you be ruled by me ?

LAERTES   Ay, my lord,
So you will not o'errule me to a peace.

KING
To thine own peace. If he be now returned,
61   As checking at his voyage, and that he means
No more to undertake it, I will work him
To an exploit now ripe in my device,
Under the which he shall not choose but fall ;
And for his death no wind of blame shall breathe,
66   But even his mother shall uncharge the practice
And call it accident.

LAERTES   My lord, I will be ruled ;
The rather if you could devise it so
69   That I might be the organ.

KING   It falls right.
You have been talked of since your travel much,

And that in Hamlet's hearing, for a quality
Wherein they say you shine. Your sum of parts
Did not together pluck such envy from him
As did that one, and that, in my regard,
Of the unworthiest siege.   75

LAERTES   What part is that, my lord ?

KING
A very riband in the cap of youth,   76
Yet needful too, for youth no less becomes
The light and careless livery that it wears   78
Than settled age his sables and his weeds,   79
Importing health and graveness. Two months since   80
Here was a gentleman of Normandy.
I have seen myself, and served against, the French,
And they can well on horseback, but this gallant   83
Had witchcraft in't. He grew unto his seat,
And to such wondrous doing brought his horse
As had he been incorpsed and demi-natured   86
With the brave beast. So far he topped my thought   87
That I, in forgery of shapes and tricks,   88
Come short of what he did.

LAERTES   A Norman was't ?

KING   A Norman.

LAERTES
Upon my life, Lamord.

KING   The very same.

LAERTES
I know him well. He is the brooch indeed   92
And gem of all the nation.

KING
He made confession of you,   94
And gave you such a masterly report
For art and exercise in your defense,
And for your rapier most especial,
That he cried out 'twould be a sight indeed
If one could match you. The scrimers of their nation   99
He swore had neither motion, guard, nor eye,
If you opposed them. Sir, this report of his
Did Hamlet so envenom with his envy
That he could nothing do but wish and beg
Your sudden coming o'er to play with you.
Now, out of this –

LAERTES   What out of this, my lord ?

KING
Laertes, was your father dear to you ?
Or are you like the painting of a sorrow,
A face without a heart ?

LAERTES   Why ask you this ?

KING
Not that I think you did not love your father,
But that I know love is begun by time,
And that I see, in passages of proof,   111
Time qualifies the spark and fire of it.   112
There lives within the very flame of love
A kind of wick or snuff that will abate it,   114
And nothing is at a like goodness still,   115
For goodness, growing to a plurisy,   116
Dies in his own too-much. That we would do
We should do when we would, for this 'would' changes,
And hath abatements and delays as many
As there are tongues, are hands, are accidents,
And then this 'should' is like a spendthrift sigh,
That hurts by easing. But to the quick o' th' ulcer –   122
Hamlet comes back ; what would you undertake

---

43 *naked* destitute   49 *abuse* imposture   50 *character* handwriting   52 *devise* explain to   61 *checking at* turning aside from (like a falcon turning from its quarry for other prey)   66 *uncharge the practice* acquit the stratagem of being a plot   69 *organ* instrument   75 *siege* seat, rank   76 *riband* decoration   78 *livery* distinctive attire   79 *sables* dignified robes richly furred with sable ; *weeds* distinctive garments   80 *health* welfare, prosperity   83 *can well* can perform well   86 *incorpsed* made one body ; *demi-natured* made sharer of nature half and half (as man shares with horse in the centaur)   87 *topped* excelled ; *thought* imagination of possibilities   88 *forgery* invention   92 *brooch* ornament   94 *made confession* admitted the rival accomplishments   99 *scrimers* fencers   111 *passages of proof* incidents of experience   112 *qualifies* weakens   114 *snuff* unconsumed portion of the burned wick   115 *still* always   116 *plurisy* excess   122 *hurts* i.e. shortens life by drawing blood from the heart (as was believed) ; *quick* sensitive flesh

To show yourself your father's son in deed
More than in words?

LAERTES   To cut his throat i' th' church!

KING
126   No place indeed should murder sanctuarize;
     Revenge should have no bounds. But, good Laertes,
     Will you do this? Keep close within your chamber.
     Hamlet returned shall know you are come home.
130   We'll put on those shall praise your excellence
     And set a double varnish on the fame
132   The Frenchman gave you, bring you in fine together
133   And wager on your heads. He, being remiss,
     Most generous, and free from all contriving,
135   Will not peruse the foils, so that with ease,
     Or with a little shuffling, you may choose
137   A sword unbated, and, in a pass of practice,
     Requite him for your father.

LAERTES   I will do't,
     And for that purpose I'll anoint my sword.
140   I bought an unction of a mountebank,
     So mortal that, but dip a knife in it,
142   Where it draws blood no cataplasm so rare,
143   Collected from all simples that have virtue
     Under the moon, can save the thing from death
145   That is but scratched withal. I'll touch my point
146   With this contagion, that, if I gall him slightly,
     It may be death.

KING   Let's further think of this,
     Weigh what convenience both of time and means
149   May fit us to our shape. If this should fail,
150   And that our drift look through our bad performance,
     'Twere better not assayed. Therefore this project
     Should have a back or second, that might hold
153   If this did blast in proof. Soft, let me see.
     We'll make a solemn wager on your cunnings –
     I ha't!
     When in your motion you are hot and dry –
     As make your bouts more violent to that end –
158   And that he calls for drink, I'll have preferred him
159   A chalice for the nonce, whereon but sipping,
160   If he by chance escape your venomed stuck,
     Our purpose may hold there. – But stay, what noise?

Enter Queen.

QUEEN
     One woe doth tread upon another's heel,
     So fast they follow. Your sister's drowned, Laertes.

LAERTES Drowned! O, where?

QUEEN
165   There is a willow grows askant the brook,
166   That shows his hoar leaves in the glassy stream.
     Therewith fantastic garlands did she make
     Of crowflowers, nettles, daisies, and long purples,
169   That liberal shepherds give a grosser name,
     But our cold maids do dead men's fingers call them.
171   There on the pendent boughs her crownet weeds
     Clamb'ring to hang, an envious sliver broke,
     When down her weedy trophies and herself
     Fell in the weeping brook. Her clothes spread wide,
     And mermaid-like awhile they bore her up,
176   Which time she chanted snatches of old lauds,
177   As one incapable of her own distress,
178   Or like a creature native and indued
     Unto that element. But long it could not be

Till that her garments, heavy with their drink,
Pulled the poor wretch from her melodious lay
To muddy death.

LAERTES   Alas, then she is drowned?

QUEEN Drowned, drowned.

LAERTES
Too much of water hast thou, poor Ophelia,
And therefore I forbid my tears; but yet
It is our trick; nature her custom holds,   186
Let shame say what it will. When these are gone,
The woman will be out. Adieu, my lord.   188
I have a speech o' fire, that fain would blaze
But that this folly drowns it.   *Exit.*

KING   Let's follow, Gertrude.
How much I had to do to calm his rage!
Now fear I this will give it start again;
Therefore let's follow.   *Exeunt.*

*

Enter two Clowns.   V, i

CLOWN Is she to be buried in Christian burial when she   1
     willfully seeks her own salvation?

OTHER I tell thee she is. Therefore make her grave straight.   3
     The crowner hath sate on her, and finds it Christian   4
     burial.

CLOWN How can that be, unless she drowned herself in
     her own defense?

OTHER Why, 'tis found so.

CLOWN It must be *se offendendo*; it cannot be else. For   8
     here lies the point: if I drown myself wittingly, it argues
     an act, and an act hath three branches – it is to act, to do,
     and to perform. Argal, she drowned herself wittingly.   11

OTHER Nay, but hear you, Goodman Delver.   12

CLOWN Give me leave. Here lies the water – good. Here
     stands the man – good. If the man go to this water and
     drown himself, it is, will he nill he, he goes, mark you   15
     that. But if the water come to him and drown him, he
     drowns not himself. Argal, he that is not guilty of his
     own death shortens not his own life.

OTHER But is this law?

CLOWN Ay marry, is't – crowner's quest law.   20

OTHER Will you ha' the truth on't? If this had not been a
     gentlewoman, she should have been buried out o'
     Christian burial.

CLOWN Why, there thou say'st. And the more pity that   24
     great folk should have count'nance in this world to   25

---

126 *sanctuarize* protect from punishment, give sanctuary to   130 *put on* instigate   132 *in fine* finally   133 *remiss* negligent   135 *peruse* scan   137 *unbated* not blunted; *pass of practice* thrust made effective by trickery   140 *unction* ointment; *mountebank* quack-doctor   142 *cataplasm* poultice   143 *simples* herbs   145 *withal* with it   146 *gall* scratch   149 *shape* plan   150 *drift* intention; *look* show   153 *blast in proof* burst during trial (like a faulty cannon)   158 *preferred* offered   159 *nonce* occasion   160 *stuck* thrust   165 *askant* alongside   166 *hoar* grey   169 *liberal* free-spoken, licentious   171 *crownet* coronet   176 *lauds* hymns   177 *incapable of* insensible to   178 *indued* endowed   186 *trick* way (i.e. to shed tears when sorrowful)   188 *woman* unmanly part of nature
V, i A churchyard **s.d.** *Clowns* rustics   1 *in Christian burial* in consecrated ground with the prescribed service of the Church (a burial denied to suicides)   3 *straight* straightway, at once   4 *crowner* coroner   8 *se offendendo* a clownish transformation of 'se defendendo,' 'in self-defense'   11 *Argal* for 'ergo,' 'therefore'   12 *Delver* Digger   15 *will he nill he* willy-nilly   20 *quest* inquest   24 *thou say'st* you have it right   25 *count'nance* privilege

26 drown or hang themselves more than their even-Christen. Come, my spade. There is no ancient gentle-men but gard'ners, ditchers, and grave-makers. They hold up Adam's profession.

OTHER Was he a gentleman?

CLOWN 'A was the first that ever bore arms.

32 [OTHER Why, he had none.

CLOWN What, art a heathen? How dost thou understand the Scripture? The Scripture says Adam digged. Could he dig without arms?] I'll put another question to thee. If thou answerest me not to the purpose, confess thy-self –

OTHER Go to.

CLOWN What is he that builds stronger than either the mason, the shipwright, or the carpenter?

OTHER The gallows-maker, for that frame outlives a thousand tenants.

CLOWN I like thy wit well, in good faith. The gallows does well. But how does it well? It does well to those that do ill. Now thou dost ill to say the gallows is built stronger than the church. Argal, the gallows may do well to thee. To't again, come.

OTHER Who builds stronger than a mason, a shipwright, or a carpenter?

49 CLOWN Ay, tell me that, and unyoke.

OTHER Marry, now I can tell.

CLOWN To't.

52 OTHER Mass, I cannot tell.

CLOWN Cudgel thy brains no more about it, for your dull ass will not mend his pace with beating. And when you are asked this question next, say 'a grave-maker.' The houses he makes last till doomsday. Go, get thee in, and 57 fetch me a stoup of liquor.   [Exit Other Clown.]
        Enter Hamlet and Horatio [as Clown digs and sings].

                    Song.

    In youth when I did love, did love,
        Methought it was very sweet
60 To contract – O – the time for – a – my behove,
    O, methought there – a – was nothing – a – meet.

HAMLET Has this fellow no feeling of his business, that 'a sings at grave-making?

64 HORATIO Custom hath made it in him a property of easi-ness.

HAMLET 'Tis e'en so. The hand of little employment 66 hath the daintier sense.

---

26 even-Christen fellow Christian   32 had none i.e. had no gentleman's coat of arms   49 unyoke i.e. unharness your powers of thought after a good day's work   52 Mass by the Mass   57 stoup large mug   60 behove behoof, benefit   64 property peculiarity; easiness easy acceptability   66 daintier sense more delicate feeling (because the hand is less calloused)   69 intil into   72 jowls hurls   74 politician crafty schemer; o'erreaches gets the better of (with a play upon the literal meaning)   82 chapless lacking the lower chap or jaw   83 mazzard head   86 loggets small pieces of wood thrown in a game   88 For and and   92 quiddities subtleties (from scholastic 'quidditas,' meaning the distinctive nature of anything); quillities nice distinctions   93 tenures holdings of property   94 sconce head   97 statutes, recognizances legal documents or bonds acknowledging debt   98 fines, recoveries modes of converting estate tail into fee simple; vouchers persons vouched or called on to warrant a title; fine end (introducing a word play involving four meanings of 'fine')   102 pair of indentures deed or legal agreement in duplicate; conveyances deeds   118 quick living

CLOWN   Song.
    But age with his stealing steps
        Hath clawed me in his clutch,
    And hath shipped me intil the land,   69
        As if I had never been such.

    [Throws up a skull.]

HAMLET That skull had a tongue in it, and could sing once. How the knave jowls it to the ground, as if 'twere 72 Cain's jawbone, that did the first murder! This might be the pate of a politician, which this ass now o'erreaches; 74 one that would circumvent God, might it not?

HORATIO It might, my lord.

HAMLET Or of a courtier, which could say 'Good mor-row, sweet lord! How dost thou, sweet lord?' This might be my Lord Such-a-one, that praised my Lord Such-a-one's horse when 'a meant to beg it, might it not?

HORATIO Ay, my lord.

HAMLET Why, e'en so, and now my Lady Worm's, chap- 82 less, and knocked about the mazzard with a sexton's 83 spade. Here's fine revolution, an we had the trick to see't. Did these bones cost no more the breeding but to play at loggets with 'em? Mine ache to think on't.   86

CLOWN   Song.
    A pickaxe and a spade, a spade,
        For and a shrouding sheet;   88
    O, a pit of clay for to be made
        For such a guest is meet.

    [Throws up another skull.]

HAMLET There's another. Why may not that be the skull of a lawyer? Where be his quiddities now, his quillities, 92 his cases, his tenures, and his tricks? Why does he suffer 93 this mad knave now to knock him about the sconce with 94 a dirty shovel, and will not tell him of his action of battery? Hum! This fellow might be in's time a great buyer of land, with his statutes, his recognizances, his 97 fines, his double vouchers, his recoveries. [Is this the fine 98 of his fines, and the recovery of his recoveries,] to have his fine pate full of fine dirt? Will his vouchers vouch him no more of his purchases, and double ones too, than the length and breadth of a pair of indentures? The very con- 102 veyances of his lands will scarcely lie in this box, and must th' inheritor himself have no more, ha?

HORATIO Not a jot more, my lord.

HAMLET Is not parchment made of sheepskins?

HORATIO Ay, my lord, and of calveskins too.

HAMLET They are sheep and calves which seek out as-surance in that. I will speak to this fellow. Whose grave's this, sirrah?

CLOWN Mine, sir.

[Sings] O, a pit of clay for to be made
            For such a guest is meet.

HAMLET I think it be thine indeed, for thou liest in't.

CLOWN You lie out on't, sir, and therefore 'tis not yours. For my part, I do not lie in't, yet it is mine.

HAMLET Thou dost lie in't, to be in't and say it is thine. 'Tis for the dead, not for the quick; therefore thou liest. 118

CLOWN 'Tis a quick lie, sir; 'twill away again from me to you.

HAMLET What man dost thou dig it for?

CLOWN For no man, sir.

HAMLET What woman then?

CLOWN For none neither.

HAMLET Who is to be buried in't?

CLOWN One that was a woman, sir; but, rest her soul, she's dead.

128 HAMLET How absolute the knave is! We must speak by
129 the card, or equivocation will undo us. By the Lord, Horatio, this three years I have taken note of it, the age
131 is grown so picked that the toe of the peasant comes so
132 near the heel of the courtier he galls his kibe. – How long hast thou been a grave-maker?

CLOWN Of all the days i' th' year, I came to't that day that our last king Hamlet overcame Fortinbras.

HAMLET How long is that since?

CLOWN Cannot you tell that? Every fool can tell that. It was the very day that young Hamlet was born – he that is mad, and sent into England.

140 HAMLET Ay, marry, why was he sent into England?

CLOWN Why, because 'a was mad. 'A shall recover his wits there; or, if 'a do not, 'tis no great matter there.

HAMLET Why?

CLOWN 'Twill not be seen in him there. There the men are as mad as he.

HAMLET How came he mad?

CLOWN Very strangely, they say.

HAMLET How strangely?

CLOWN Faith, e'en with losing his wits.

HAMLET Upon what ground?

CLOWN Why, here in Denmark. I have been sexton here, man and boy, thirty years.

HAMLET How long will a man lie i' th' earth ere he rot?

CLOWN Faith, if 'a be not rotten before 'a die (as we have
155 many pocky corses now-a-days that will scarce hold the laying in), 'a will last you some eight year or nine year. A tanner will last you nine year.

HAMLET Why he more than another?

CLOWN Why, sir, his hide is so tanned with his trade that 'a will keep out water a great while, and your water is a sore decayer of your whoreson dead body. Here's a skull now hath lien you i' th' earth three-and-twenty years.

HAMLET Whose was it?

CLOWN A whoreson mad fellow's it was. Whose do you think it was?

HAMLET Nay, I know not.

CLOWN A pestilence on him for a mad rogue! 'A poured a
168 flagon of Rhenish on my head once. This same skull, sir, was – sir – Yorick's skull, the king's jester.

HAMLET This?

CLOWN E'en that.

HAMLET Let me see. *[Takes the skull.]* Alas, poor Yorick! I knew him, Horatio, a fellow of infinite jest, of most excellent fancy. He hath borne me on his back a thousand times. And now how abhorred in my imagination it is! My gorge rises at it. Here hung those lips that I have kissed I know not how oft. Where be your gibes now? Your gambols, your songs, your flashes of merriment that were wont to set the table on a roar? Not one now to
180 mock your own grinning? Quite chapfall'n? Now get you to my lady's chamber, and tell her, let her paint an
182 inch thick, to this favor she must come. Make her laugh at that. Prithee, Horatio, tell me one thing.

HORATIO What's that, my lord?

HAMLET Dost thou think Alexander looked o' this fashion i' th' earth?

HORATIO E'en so.

HAMLET And smelt so? Pah!
[Puts down the skull.]

HORATIO E'en so, my lord.

HAMLET To what base uses we may return, Horatio! Why may not imagination trace the noble dust of Alexander till 'a find it stopping a bunghole?

HORATIO 'Twere to consider too curiously, to consider so. 193

HAMLET No, faith, not a jot, but to follow him thither with 195 modesty enough, and likelihood to lead it; as thus: Alexander died, Alexander was buried, Alexander returneth to dust; the dust is earth; of earth we make loam; and why of that loam whereto he was converted might they not stop a beer barrel?

Imperious Caesar, dead and turned to clay,   200
Might stop a hole to keep the wind away.
O, that that earth which kept the world in awe
Should patch a wall t' expel the winter's flaw!   203
But soft, but soft awhile! Here comes the king –
    Enter King, Queen, Laertes, and the Corse [with
    Lords attendant and a Doctor of Divinity as Priest].
The queen, the courtiers. Who is this they follow?
And with such maimèd rites? This doth betoken
The corse they follow did with desp'rate hand
Fordo it own life. 'Twas of some estate.   208
Couch we awhile, and mark.   209
    [Retires with Horatio.]

LAERTES
What ceremony else?

HAMLET   That is Laertes,
A very noble youth. Mark.

LAERTES
What ceremony else?

DOCTOR
Her obsequies have been as far enlarged
As we have warranty. Her death was doubtful,
And, but that great command o'ersways the order,
She should in ground unsanctified have lodged
Till the last trumpet. For charitable prayers,
Shards, flints, and pebbles should be thrown on her.   218
Yet here she is allowed her virgin crants,   219
Her maiden strewments, and the bringing home   220
Of bell and burial.

LAERTES
Must there no more be done?

DOCTOR   No more be done.
We should profane the service of the dead
To sing a requiem and such rest to her
As to peace-parted souls.

LAERTES   Lay her i' th' earth,
And from her fair and unpolluted flesh
May violets spring! I tell thee, churlish priest,
A minist'ring angel shall my sister be
When thou liest howling.

HAMLET   What, the fair Ophelia?

128 *absolute* positive   128–29 *by the card* by the card on which the points of the mariner's compass are marked, absolutely to the point   129 *equivocation* ambiguity   131 *picked* refined, spruce   132 *galls* chafes; *kibe* chilblain   155 *pocky* rotten (literally, corrupted by pox, or syphilis)   168 *Rhenish* Rhine wine   180 *chapfall'n* lacking the lower chap, or jaw (with a play on the sense 'down in the mouth,' 'dejected')   182 *favor* countenance, aspect   193 *curiously* minutely   195 *modesty* moderation   200 *Imperious* imperial   203 *flaw* gust of wind   208 *Fordo* destroy; *it* its; *estate* rank   209 *Couch* hide   218 *Shards* broken pieces of pottery   219 *crants* garland   220 *strewments* strewings of the grave with flowers; *bringing home* laying to rest

QUEEN
Sweets to the sweet! Farewell.
[Scatters flowers.]
I hoped thou shouldst have been my Hamlet's wife.
I thought thy bride-bed to have decked, sweet maid,
And not have strewed thy grave.
LAERTES   O, treble woe
Fall ten times treble on that cursèd head
235   Whose wicked deed thy most ingenious sense
Deprived thee of! Hold off the earth awhile,
Till I have caught her once more in mine arms.
[Leaps in the grave.]
Now pile your dust upon the quick and dead
Till of this flat a mountain you have made
240   T' o'ertop old Pelion or the skyish head
Of blue Olympus.
HAMLET *[coming forward]* What is he whose grief
Bears such an emphasis? whose phrase of sorrow
243   Conjures the wand'ring stars, and makes them stand
Like wonder-wounded hearers? This is I,
Hamlet the Dane.
[Leaps in after Laertes.]
LAERTES   The devil take thy soul!
[Grapples with him.]
HAMLET
Thou pray'st not well.
I prithee take thy fingers from my throat,
248   For, though I am not splenitive and rash,
Yet have I in me something dangerous,
Which let thy wisdom fear. Hold off thy hand.
KING
Pluck them asunder.
QUEEN   Hamlet, Hamlet!
ALL
Gentlemen!
HORATIO   Good my lord, be quiet.
[Attendants part them, and they come out of the grave.]
HAMLET
Why, I will fight with him upon this theme
Until my eyelids will no longer wag.
QUEEN
O my son, what theme?
HAMLET
I loved Ophelia. Forty thousand brothers
Could not with all their quantity of love
Make up my sum. What wilt thou do for her?
KING
O, he is mad, Laertes.
QUEEN
For love of God, forbear him.

HAMLET
'Swounds, show me what thou't do.
Woo't weep? woo't fight? woo't fast? woo't tear thyself? 262
Woo't drink up esill? eat a crocodile?   263
I'll do't. Dost thou come here to whine?
To outface me with leaping in her grave?
Be buried quick with her, and so will I.   266
And if thou prate of mountains, let them throw
Millions of acres on us, till our ground,
Singeing his pate against the burning zone,
Make Ossa like a wart! Nay, an thou'lt mouth,
I'll rant as well as thou.
QUEEN   This is mere madness;   271
And thus a while the fit will work on him.
Anon, as patient as the female dove
When that her golden couplets are disclosed,   274
His silence will sit drooping.
HAMLET   Hear you, sir.
What is the reason that you use me thus?
I loved you ever. But it is no matter.
Let Hercules himself do what he may,
The cat will mew, and dog will have his day.
KING
I pray thee, good Horatio, wait upon him.
              Exit Hamlet and Horatio.
[To Laertes]
Strengthen your patience in our last night's speech.   281
We'll put the matter to the present push. –   282
Good Gertrude, set some watch over your son. –
This grave shall have a living monument.
An hour of quiet shortly shall we see;
Till then in patience our proceeding be.   *Exeunt.*

            *

Enter Hamlet and Horatio.   V, ii
HAMLET
So much for this, sir; now shall you see the other.
You do remember all the circumstance?
HORATIO
Remember it, my lord!
HAMLET
Sir, in my heart there was a kind of fighting
That would not let me sleep. Methought I lay
Worse than the mutines in the bilboes. Rashly,   6
And praised be rashness for it – let us know,
Our indiscretion sometime serves us well
When our deep plots do pall, and that should learn us   9
There's a divinity that shapes our ends,
Rough-hew them how we will –   11
HORATIO   That is most certain.
HAMLET
Up from my cabin,
My sea-gown scarfed about me, in the dark
Groped I to find out them, had my desire,
Fingered their packet, and in fine withdrew   15
To mine own room again, making so bold,
My fears forgetting manners, to unseal
Their grand commission; where I found, Horatio –
Ah, royal knavery! – an exact command,
Larded with many several sorts of reasons,   20
Importing Denmark's health, and England's too,   21
With, ho! such bugs and goblins in my life,   22
That on the supervise, no leisure bated,   23

235 *most ingenious* of quickest apprehension   240 *Pelion* a mountain in Thessaly, like Olympus and also Ossa (the allusion being to the war in which the Titans fought the gods and attempted to heap Ossa and Olympus on Pelion, or Pelion and Ossa on Olympus, in order to scale heaven)   243 *Conjures* charms, puts a spell upon; *wand'ring stars* planets   248 *splenitive* of fiery temper (the spleen being considered the seat of anger)   262 *Woo't* wilt (thou)   263 *esill* vinegar   266 *quick* alive   271 *mere* absolute   274 *couplets* pair of fledglings; *disclosed* hatched   281 *in* by calling to mind   282 *present push* immediate trial
V, ii The hall of the Castle   6 *mutines* mutineers; *bilboes* fetters   9 *pall* fail   11 *Rough-hew* shape roughly in trial form   15 *Fingered* filched; *in fine* finally   20 *Larded* enriched   21 *Importing* relating to   22 *bugs* bugbears; *in my life* to be encountered as dangers if I should be allowed to live   23 *supervise* perusal; *bated* deducted, allowed

No, not to stay the grinding of the axe,
My head should be struck off.
HORATIO   Is't possible?
HAMLET
Here's the commission; read it at more leisure.
But wilt thou hear me how I did proceed?
HORATIO   I beseech you.
HAMLET
Being thus benetted round with villainies,
30   Or I could make a prologue to my brains,
They had begun the play. I sat me down,
Devised a new commission, wrote it fair.
33   I once did hold it, as our statists do,
34   A baseness to write fair, and labored much
How to forget that learning, but, sir, now
36   It did me yeoman's service. Wilt thou know
37   Th' effect of what I wrote?
HORATIO   Ay, good my lord.
HAMLET
An earnest conjuration from the king,
As England was his faithful tributary,
As love between them like the palm might flourish,
41   As peace should still her wheaten garland wear
42   And stand a comma 'tween their amities,
43   And many such-like as's of great charge,
That on the view and knowing of these contents,
Without debatement further, more or less,
He should the bearers put to sudden death,
47   Not shriving time allowed.
HORATIO   How was this sealed?
HAMLET
48   Why, even in that was heaven ordinant.
I had my father's signet in my purse,
50   Which was the model of that Danish seal,
Folded the writ up in the form of th' other,
52   Subscribed it, gave't th' impression, placed it safely,
The changeling never known. Now, the next day
54   Was our sea-fight, and what to this was sequent
Thou know'st already.
HORATIO
So Guildenstern and Rosencrantz go to't.
HAMLET
[Why, man, they did make love to this employment.]
They are not near my conscience; their defeat
59   Does by their own insinuation grow.
'Tis dangerous when the baser nature comes
61   Between the pass and fell incensèd points
Of mighty opposites.
HORATIO   Why, what a king is this!
HAMLET
63   Does it not, think thee, stand me now upon –
He that hath killed my king, and whored my mother,
65   Popped in between th' election and my hopes,
66   Thrown out his angle for my proper life,
67   And with such coz'nage – is't not perfect conscience
68   [To quit him with this arm? And is't not to be damned
69   To let this canker of our nature come
In further evil?
HORATIO
It must be shortly known to him from England
What is the issue of the business there.
HAMLET
It will be short; the interim is mine,
And a man's life 's no more than to say 'one.'

But I am very sorry, good Horatio,
That to Laertes I forgot myself,
For by the image of my cause I see
The portraiture of his. I'll court his favors.
But sure the bravery of his grief did put me   79
Into a tow'ring passion.
HORATIO   Peace, who comes here?]
       Enter [Osric,] a courtier.
OSRIC Your lordship is right welcome back to Denmark.
HAMLET I humbly thank you, sir. *[aside to Horatio]* Dost know this waterfly?
HORATIO *[aside to Hamlet]* No, my good lord.
HAMLET *[aside to Horatio]* Thy state is the more gracious, for 'tis a vice to know him. He hath much land, and fertile. Let a beast be lord of beasts, and his crib shall stand at the king's mess. 'Tis a chough, but, as I say,   88
spacious in the possession of dirt.
OSRIC Sweet lord, if your lordship were at leisure, I should impart a thing to you from his majesty.
HAMLET I will receive it, sir, with all diligence of spirit. Put your bonnet to his right use. 'Tis for the head.
OSRIC I thank your lordship, it is very hot.
HAMLET No, believe me, 'tis very cold; the wind is northerly.
OSRIC It is indifferent cold, my lord, indeed.   97
HAMLET But yet methinks it is very sultry and hot for my complexion.   99
OSRIC Exceedingly, my lord; it is very sultry, as 'twere – I cannot tell how. But, my lord, his majesty bade me signify to you that 'a has laid a great wager on your head. Sir, this is the matter –
HAMLET I beseech you remember.   104
      [Hamlet moves him to put on his hat.]
OSRIC Nay, good my lord; for mine ease, in good faith.   105
Sir, here is newly come to court Laertes – believe me, an absolute gentleman, full of most excellent differences,   107
very soft society and great showing. Indeed, to speak   108
feelingly of him, he is the card or calendar of gentry; for   109
you shall find in him the continent of what part a   110
gentleman would see.
HAMLET Sir, his definement suffers no perdition in you,   112
though, I know, to divide him inventorially would dozy   113
th' arithmetic of memory, and yet but yaw neither in re-   114

30 *Or* ere   33 *statists* statesmen   34 *fair* with professional clarity (like a clerk or a scrivener, not like a gentleman)   36 *yeoman's service* stout service such as yeomen footsoldiers gave as archers   37 *effect* purport   41 *wheaten garland* adornment of fruitful agriculture   42 *comma* connective (because it indicates continuity of thought in a sentence)   43 *charge* burden (with a double meaning to fit a play that makes *as's* into 'asses')   47 *shriving time* time for confession and absolution   50 *model* counterpart   52 *impression* i.e. of the signet   54 *sequent* subsequent   59 *insinuation* intrusion   61 *pass* thrust; *fell* fierce   63 *stand* rest incumbent   65 *election* i.e. to the kingship (the Danish kingship being elective)   66 *angle* fishing line; *proper* own   67 *coz'nage* cozenage, trickery   68 *quit* repay   69 *canker* cancer, ulcer   79 *bravery* ostentatious display   88 *mess* table; *chough* jackdaw, chatterer   97 *indifferent* somewhat   99 *complexion* temperament   104 *remember* i.e. remember you have done all that courtesy demands   105 *for mine ease* i.e. I keep my hat off just for comfort (a conventional polite phrase)   107 *differences* differentiating characteristics, special qualities   108 *soft society* gentle manners; *great showing* noble appearance   109 *feelingly* appropriately; *card* map; *calendar* guide; *gentry* gentlemanliness   110 *continent* all-containing embodiment (with an implication of geographical continent to go with *card*)   112 *definement* definition; *perdition* loss   113 *dozy* dizzy, stagger   114 *yaw* hold to a course unsteadily like a ship that steers wild; *neither* for all that   114-15 *in respect of* in comparison with

spect of his quick sail. But, in the verity of extolment, I
116 take him to be a soul of great article, and his infusion of
117 such dearth and rareness as, to make true diction of him,
118 his semblable is his mirror, and who else would trace
119 him, his umbrage, nothing more.

OSRIC Your lordship speaks most infallibly of him.

121 HAMLET The concernancy, sir? Why do we wrap the
122 gentleman in our more rawer breath?

OSRIC Sir?

HORATIO Is't not possible to understand in another
125 tongue? You will to't, sir, really.

126 HAMLET What imports the nomination of this gentleman?

OSRIC Of Laertes?

HORATIO [aside to Hamlet] His purse is empty already.
All's golden words are spent.

HAMLET Of him, sir.

OSRIC I know you are not ignorant –

HAMLET I would you did, sir; yet, in faith, if you did, it
133 would not much approve me. Well, sir?

OSRIC You are not ignorant of what excellence Laertes is –

135 HAMLET I dare not confess that, lest I should compare
with him in excellence; but to know a man well were to
know himself.

OSRIC I mean, sir, for his weapon; but in the imputation
139 laid on him by them, in his meed he's unfellowed.

HAMLET What's his weapon?

OSRIC Rapier and dagger.

HAMLET That's two of his weapons – but well.

OSRIC The king, sir, hath wagered with him six Barbary
144 horses, against the which he has impawned, as I take it,
145 six French rapiers and poniards, with their assigns, as
146 girdle, hangers, and so. Three of the carriages, in faith,
147 are very dear to fancy, very responsive to the hilts, most
148 delicate carriages, and of very liberal conceit.

HAMLET What call you the carriages?

HORATIO [aside to Hamlet] I knew you must be edified by
151 the margent ere you had done.

OSRIC The carriages, sir, are the hangers.

HAMLET The phrase would be more germane to the matter if we could carry a cannon by our sides. I would it
might be hangers till then. But on! Six Barbary horses
against six French swords, their assigns, and three
liberal-conceited carriages – that's the French bet
against the Danish. Why is this all impawned, as you
call it?

OSRIC The king, sir, hath laid, sir, that in a dozen passes
between yourself and him he shall not exceed you three
hits; he hath laid on twelve for nine, and it would come
to immediate trial if your lordship would vouchsafe
the answer.

HAMLET How if I answer no?

OSRIC I mean, my lord, the opposition of your person in
trial.

HAMLET Sir, I will walk here in the hall. If it please his
majesty, it is the breathing time of day with me. Let the 168
foils be brought, the gentleman willing, and the king
hold his purpose, I will win for him an I can; if not, I 170
will gain nothing but my shame and the odd hits.

OSRIC Shall I redeliver you e'en so?

HAMLET To this effect, sir, after what flourish your
nature will.

OSRIC I commend my duty to your lordship.

HAMLET Yours, yours. [Exit Osric.] He does well to commend it himself; there are no tongues else for's turn.

HORATIO This lapwing runs away with the shell on his 178
head.

HAMLET 'A did comply, sir, with his dug before 'a sucked 179
it. Thus has he, and many more of the same bevy that I 180
know the drossy age dotes on, only got the tune of the 181
time and, out of an habit of encounter, a kind of yeasty
collection, which carries them through and through the
most fanned and winnowed opinions; and do but blow 184
them to their trial, the bubbles are out.

Enter a Lord.

LORD My lord, his majesty commended him to you by
young Osric, who brings back to him that you attend
him in the hall. He sends to know if your pleasure hold
to play with Laertes, or that you will take longer time.

HAMLET I am constant to my purposes; they follow the
king's pleasure. If his fitness speaks, mine is ready; now
or whensoever, provided I be so able as now.

LORD The king and queen and all are coming down.

HAMLET In happy time.   194

LORD The queen desires you to use some gentle enter- 195
tainment to Laertes before you fall to play.

HAMLET She well instructs me.   [Exit Lord.]

HORATIO You will lose this wager, my lord.

HAMLET I do not think so. Since he went into France I
have been in continual practice. I shall win at the odds.
But thou wouldst not think how ill all's here about my
heart. But it is no matter.

HORATIO Nay, good my lord –

HAMLET It is but foolery, but it is such a kind of gain- 204
giving as would perhaps trouble a woman.

HORATIO If your mind dislike anything, obey it. I will
forestall their repair hither and say you are not fit.

HAMLET Not a whit, we defy augury. There is special
providence in the fall of a sparrow. If it be now, 'tis not
to come; if it be not to come, it will be now; if it be not
now, yet it will come. The readiness is all. Since no man 211
of aught he leaves knows, what is't to leave betimes? Let
be.

A table prepared. [Enter] Trumpets, Drums, and
Officers with cushions; King, Queen, [Osric,] and all
the State, [with] foils, daggers, [and stoups of wine
borne in;] and Laertes.

KING
Come, Hamlet, come, and take this hand from me.
[The King puts Laertes' hand into Hamlet's.]

HAMLET
Give me your pardon, sir. I have done you wrong,
But pardon't, as you are a gentleman.
This presence knows, and you must needs have heard, 217
How I am punished with a sore distraction.

---

116 *article* scope, importance; *infusion* essence   117 *dearth* scarcity   118 *semblable* likeness (i.e. only true likeness); *trace* follow   119 *umbrage* shadow   121 *concernancy* relevance   122 *rawer breath* cruder speech   125 *to't* i.e. get to an understanding   126 *nomination* mention   133 *approve me* be to my credit   135 *compare* compete   139 *meed* worth   144 *impawned* staked   145 *assigns* appurtenances   146 *hangers* straps by which the sword hangs from the belt   147 *dear to fancy* finely designed; *respon-sive* corresponding closely   148 *liberal conceit* tasteful design, refined conception   151 *margent* margin (i.e. explanatory notes there printed)   168 *breathing time* exercise hour   170 *an* if   178 *lapwing* a bird reputed to be so precocious as to run as soon as hatched   179 *comply* observe formalities of courtesy; *dug* mother's nipple   180 *bevy* company   181 *drossy* frivolous   184 *fanned and winnowed* select and refined   194 *In happy time* I am happy (a polite response)   195 *entertainment* words of reception or greeting   204 *gaingiving* misgiving   211 *all* all that matters   217 *presence* assembly

What I have done
220 That might your nature, honor, and exception
Roughly awake, I here proclaim was madness.
Was't Hamlet wronged Laertes? Never Hamlet.
If Hamlet from himself be ta'en away,
And when he's not himself does wrong Laertes,
Then Hamlet does it not, Hamlet denies it.
Who does it then? His madness. If't be so,
227 Hamlet is of the faction that is wronged;
His madness is poor Hamlet's enemy.
Sir, in this audience,
Let my disclaiming from a purposed evil
Free me so far in your most generous thoughts
That I have shot my arrow o'er the house
And hurt my brother.
233 LAERTES   I am satisfied in nature,
Whose motive in this case should stir me most
235 To my revenge. But in my terms of honor
I stand aloof, and will no reconcilement
Till by some elder masters of known honor
238 I have a voice and precedent of peace
239 To keep my name ungored. But till that time
I do receive your offered love like love,
And will not wrong it.
HAMLET   I embrace it freely,
And will this brother's wager frankly play.
Give us the foils. Come on.
LAERTES   Come, one for me.
HAMLET
244 I'll be your foil, Laertes. In mine ignorance
Your skill shall, like a star i' th' darkest night,
246 Stick fiery off indeed.
LAERTES   You mock me, sir.
HAMLET
No, by this hand.
KING
Give them the foils, young Osric. Cousin Hamlet,
You know the wager?
HAMLET   Very well, my lord.
Your grace has laid the odds o' th' weaker side.
KING
I do not fear it, I have seen you both;
But since he is bettered, we have therefore odds.
LAERTES
This is too heavy; let me see another.
HAMLET
This likes me well. These foils have all a length?
[Prepare to play.]
OSRIC
Ay, my good lord.
KING
Set me the stoups of wine upon that table.
If Hamlet give the first or second hit,
258 Or quit in answer of the third exchange,
Let all the battlements their ordnance fire.
The king shall drink to Hamlet's better breath,
261 And in the cup an union shall he throw
Richer than that which four successive kings
In Denmark's crown have worn. Give me the cups,
264 And let the kettle to the trumpet speak,
The trumpet to the cannoneer without,
The cannons to the heavens, the heaven to earth,
'Now the king drinks to Hamlet.' Come, begin.
Trumpets the while.

And you, the judges, bear a wary eye.
HAMLET
Come on, sir.
LAERTES   Come, my lord.
[They play.]
HAMLET   One.
LAERTES   No.
HAMLET   Judgment?
OSRIC
A hit, a very palpable hit.
Drum, trumpets, and shot. Flourish; a piece goes off.
LAERTES   Well, again.
KING
Stay, give me drink. Hamlet, this pearl is thine.
Here's to thy health. Give him the cup.
HAMLET
I'll play this bout first; set it by awhile.
Come. [They play.] Another hit. What say you?
LAERTES
A touch, a touch; I do confess't.
KING
Our son shall win.
QUEEN   He's fat, and scant of breath.   276
Here, Hamlet, take my napkin, rub thy brows.   277
The queen carouses to thy fortune, Hamlet.   278
HAMLET
Good madam!
KING   Gertrude, do not drink.
QUEEN
I will, my lord; I pray you pardon me.
[Drinks.]
KING [aside]
It is the poisoned cup; it is too late.
HAMLET
I dare not drink yet, madam – by and by.
QUEEN
Come, let me wipe thy face.
LAERTES
My lord, I'll hit him now.
KING   I do not think't.
LAERTES [aside]
And yet it is almost against my conscience.
HAMLET
Come for the third, Laertes. You but dally.
I pray you pass with your best violence;
I am afeard you make a wanton of me.   288
LAERTES
Say you so? Come on.
[They play.]
OSRIC
Nothing neither way.
LAERTES
Have at you now!
[In scuffling they change rapiers, and both are
wounded with the poisoned weapon.]
KING   Part them. They are incensed.

220 *exception* disapproval 227 *faction* body of persons taking a side in a
contention 233 *nature* natural feeling as a person 235 *terms of honor*
position as a man of honor 238 *voice* authoritative statement 239
ungored uninjured 244 *foil* setting that displays a jewel advantageously
(with a play upon the meaning 'weapon') 246 *Stick fiery off* show in brilliant relief 258 *quit* repay by a hit 261 *union* pearl 264 *kettle* kettledrum
276 *fat* not physically fit, out of training 277 *napkin* handkerchief 278
carouses drinks a toast 288 *wanton* pampered child

HAMLET
Nay, come – again !
[The Queen falls.]
OSRIC   Look to the queen there, ho !
HORATIO
They bleed on both sides. How is it, my lord ?
OSRIC
How is't, Laertes ?
LAERTES
295 Why, as a woodcock to mine own springe, Osric.
I am justly killed with mine own treachery.
HAMLET
How does the queen ?
297 KING   She sounds to see them bleed.
QUEEN
No, no, the drink, the drink ! O my dear Hamlet !
The drink, the drink ! I am poisoned.
[Dies.]
HAMLET
O villainy ! Ho ! let the door be locked.
Treachery ! Seek it out.
[Laertes falls.]
LAERTES
It is here, Hamlet. Hamlet, thou art slain ;
No med'cine in the world can do thee good.
In thee there is not half an hour's life.
The treacherous instrument is in thy hand,
306 Unbated and envenomed. The foul practice
Hath turned itself on me. Lo, here I lie,
Never to rise again. Thy mother 's poisoned.
I can no more. The king, the king 's to blame.
HAMLET
The point envenomed too ?
Then venom, to thy work.
[Hurts the King.]
ALL Treason ! treason !
KING
O, yet defend me, friends. I am but hurt.
HAMLET
Here, thou incestuous, murd'rous, damnèd Dane,
Drink off this potion. Is thy union here ?
Follow my mother.
[King dies.]
LAERTES   He is justly served.
317 It is a poison tempered by himself.
Exchange forgiveness with me, noble Hamlet.
Mine and my father's death come not upon thee,
Nor thine on me !
[Dies.]
HAMLET
Heaven make thee free of it ! I follow thee.
I am dead, Horatio. Wretched queen, adieu !
You that look pale and tremble at this chance,
324 That are but mutes or audience to this act,

---

295 *woodcock* a bird reputed to be stupid and easily trapped ; *springe* trap
297 *sounds* swoons 306 *Unbated* unblunted ; *practice* stratagem 317
tempered mixed 324 *mutes* actors in a play who speak no lines 325
sergeant sheriff's officer 342 *o'ercrows* triumphs over (like a victor in a
cockfight) 344 *election* i.e. to the throne 345 *voice* vote 346 *occurrents*
occurrences 347 *solicited* incited, provoked 353 *quarry* pile of dead
(literally, of dead deer gathered after the hunt) ; *cries on* proclaims loudly ;
havoc indiscriminate killing and destruction such as would follow the order
'havoc,' or 'pillage,' given to an army 354 *toward* forthcoming 364 *jump*
precisely 367 *stage* platform 371 *judgments* retributions ; *casual* not
humanly planned (reinforcing *accidental*) 372 *put on* instigated

---

Had I but time – as this fell sergeant, Death,   325
Is strict in his arrest – O, I could tell you –
But let it be. Horatio, I am dead ;
Thou livest ; report me and my cause aright
To the unsatisfied.
HORATIO   Never believe it.
I am more an antique Roman than a Dane.
Here's yet some liquor left.
HAMLET   As th' art a man,
Give me the cup. Let go. By heaven, I'll ha't !
O God, Horatio, what a wounded name,
Things standing thus unknown, shall live behind me !
If thou didst ever hold me in thy heart,
Absent thee from felicity awhile,
And in this harsh world draw thy breath in pain,
To tell my story.
A march afar off.
What warlike noise is this ?
OSRIC
Young Fortinbras, with conquest come from Poland,
To the ambassadors of England gives
This warlike volley.
HAMLET   O, I die, Horatio !
The potent poison quite o'ercrows my spirit.   342
I cannot live to hear the news from England,
But I do prophesy th' election lights   344
On Fortinbras. He has my dying voice.   345
So tell him, with th' occurrents, more and less,   346
Which have solicited – the rest is silence.   347
Dies.
HORATIO
Now cracks a noble heart. Good night, sweet prince,
And flights of angels sing thee to thy rest !
[March within.]
Why does the drum come hither ?
Enter Fortinbras, with the Ambassadors [and with
his train of Drum, Colors, and Attendants].
FORTINBRAS
Where is this sight ?
HORATIO   What is it you would see ?
If aught of woe or wonder, cease your search.
FORTINBRAS
This quarry cries on havoc. O proud Death,   353
What feast is toward in thine eternal cell   354
That thou so many princes at a shot
So bloodily hast struck ?
AMBASSADOR   The sight is dismal ;
And our affairs from England come too late.
The ears are senseless that should give us hearing
To tell him his commandment is fulfilled,
That Rosencrantz and Guildenstern are dead.
Where should we have our thanks ?
HORATIO   Not from his mouth,
Had it th' ability of life to thank you.
He never gave commandment for their death.
But since, so jump upon this bloody question,   364
You from the Polack wars, and you from England,
Are here arrived, give order that these bodies
High on a stage be placèd to the view,   367
And let me speak to th' yet unknowing world
How these things came about. So shall you hear
Of carnal, bloody, and unnatural acts,
Of accidental judgments, casual slaughters,   371
Of deaths put on by cunning and forced cause,   372

And, in this upshot, purposes mistook
Fall'n on th' inventors' heads. All this can I
Truly deliver.
FORTINBRAS   Let us haste to hear it,
And call the noblest to the audience.
For me, with sorrow I embrace my fortune.
378 I have some rights of memory in this kingdom,
379 Which now to claim my vantage doth invite me.
HORATIO
Of that I shall have also cause to speak,
381 And from his mouth whose voice will draw on more.
382 But let this same be presently performed,
Even while men's minds are wild, lest more mischance
384 On plots and errors happen.
FORTINBRAS   Let four captains

Bear Hamlet like a soldier to the stage,
For he was likely, had he been put on,   386
To have proved most royal ; and for his passage   387
The soldiers' music and the rites of war
Speak loudly for him.
Take up the bodies. Such a sight as this
Becomes the field, but here shows much amiss.
Go, bid the soldiers shoot.
                    Exeunt [marching ; after the which
                    a peal of ordinance are shot off].

378 *of memory* traditional and kept in mind   379 *vantage* advantageous
opportunity   381 *more* i.e. more voices, or votes, for the kingship   382
presently immediately   384 *On* on the basis of   386 *put on* set to perform in
office   387 *passage* death

APPENDIX: DEPARTURES FROM THE TEXT OF THE 1604–05 QUARTO

Except for a few corrections of obvious typographical errors, all departures from the text of the 1604–05 quarto (Q2) are listed below, with the adopted reading in italics followed by the rejected Q2 reading in roman. The great majority of the adopted readings are from the 1623 folio (F) and are so designated. When the adopted reading appears also in the "bad" quarto of 1603 (Q1), the fact is indicated. When the adopted reading does not occur in Q1 or F, the name of the first to make the emendation is given in most cases; otherwise (usually when the emendation is of an obvious or minor defect) the abbreviation "Eds" for "editors" is used. Quartos other than Q1 and Q2 are occasionally cited, but only when the adopted reading does not occur in F. (Actually Q4, although not regarded as of substantive value, contains a considerable number of the readings that have been adopted from F.)

I, i, 16 *soldier* (Q1, F) souldiers   33 *two nights have* (F) haue two nights   44 *harrows* (F) horrowes   61 *th' ambitious* (F) the ambitious   63 *sledded* (F) sleaded   *Polacks* (Malone) Pollax   68 *my* (Q1, F) mine   73 *why* (Q1, F) with   *cast* (F) cost   87 *heraldry* (Q1, F) heraldy   88 *those* (Q1, F) these   91 *returned* (F) returne   94 *designed* (Pope) desseigne   108 *e'en so* (Eds) enso   121 *feared* (Collier) feare   127 s.d. *He* (Q '76) It (Q2) s.d. omitted   138 *you* (Q1, F) your   140 *at* (F) omitted   164 *hallowed* (F) hallowèd   175 *conveniently* (Q1, F) conuenient

I, ii, s.d. *Councillors,* (Eds) Counsaile : as   16 *all,* (Johnson) all   58 *He hath* (Q1, Q4) Hath   67 *so* (F) so much   77 *good* (F) coold   82 *shapes* (Q4) chapes (Q2) shewes (F)   85 *passes* (F) passeth   96 *a* (F) or   129 *sullied* (anon.) sallied   132 *self* (F) seale   133 *weary* (F) wary   137 *to this* (F) thus   143 *would* (Q1, F) should   148 *followed* (Rowe) followèd   149 *even she* (F) omitted   175 *to drink deep* (F) for to drinke   178 *see* (Q1, F) omitted   179 *followed* (Eds) followèd   199 *encountered* (Eds) incountred   209 *Where, as* (Q1) Whereas   *delivered* (Q1, F) deliuerèd   213 *watched* (F) watch   224 *Indeed, indeed* (Q1, F) Indeede   237 *Very like, very like* (Q1, F) Very like   257 *Foul* (Q1, F) fonde

I, iii, 1 *embarked* (F) inbarckt   3 *convoy is* (F) conuay, in   12 *bulk* (F) bulkes   32 *unmastered* (Eds) vnmastred   49 *like* (F) omitted   51 *recks* (Pope) reakes   68 *thine* (F) thy   74 *Are* (F) Or   75 *be* (F) boy   76 *loan* (F) loue   83 *invites* (F) inuests   109 *Running* (Collier) Wrong   125 *tether* (F) tider   129 *implorators* (F) imploratotors   130 *bawds* (Theobald) bonds   131 *beguile* (F) beguide

I, iv, 2 *a* (F) omitted   9 *swaggering* (Q1, F) swaggring   17 *revel* (Q4) reueale (Q2) ll. 17–38 omitted (F)   18 *taxed* (Pope) taxèd   27 *the* (Pope) their   33 *Their* (Theobald) His   36 *evil* (Keightley conjecture, withdrawn) eale   63 *will I* (Q1, F) I will   69 *lord* (Q1, F) omitted   87 *imagination* (Q1, F) imagion

I, v, 20 *fretful* (Q1, F) fearefull   43 *wit* (Pope) wits   47 *a* (F) omitted   53 *moved* (Eds) moouèd   55 *lust* (Q1, F) but   56 *sate* (Q1, F) sort   62 *cursed* (Eds) cursèd   64 *leperous* (F) leaprous   68 *posset* (F) possesse   77 *Unhouseled* (Theobald) Vnhuzled (Q2) Vnhouzzled (F)   95 *stiffly* (F) swiftly   96 *while* (F) whiles   116 *bird* (F) and   122 *my lord* (Q1, F) omitted   129 *desires* (Q1, F) desire   132 *Look you, I'll* (F) I will   170 *some'er* (Eds) so mere

II, i, s.d. *man* (Eds) man or two   3 *marvellous* (Q4) meruiles (Q2) maruels (F)   28 *no* (F) omitted   38 *warrant* (F) wit   39 *sullies* (Q4) sallies (Q2) sulleyes (F)   40 *i' th'* (F) with   52–53 as *'friend . . . gentleman'* (F) omitted   56 *t'other* (Q1, F) th' other   58 *gaming,* (F) gaming   *o'ertook* (F) or tooke   63 *takes* (F) take   79 *fouled* (F) foulèd   80 *Ungartered* (Eds) Vngartred   105 *passion* (F) passions

II, ii, 20 *are* (F) is   43 *Assure you,* (F) I assure   57 *o'erhasty* (F) hastie   76 *shown* (Q1, F) shone   81 *considered* (F) considerèd   90 *since* (F) omitted   97 *he is* (F) hee's   108 s.d. *letter* (placed here as in F; at line 116 in Q2)   112 *Thus :* (Malone, from Jennens substantially) thus   126 *above* (F) about   137 *winking* (F) working   143 *his* (F) her   146 *repelled* (Eds) repell'd   148 *watch*

(F) wath   149 *a* (F) omitted   151 *'tis* (F) omitted   165 *fallen* (Eds) falne   189 *far gone, far gone* (F) farre gone   190 *suffered* (Eds) suffred   201 *you* (F) omitted   202 *should be* (F) shall grow   208 *sanity* (F) sancity   209–10 *and . . . him* (F) omitted   211 *honorable* (F) omitted   *most humbly* (F) omitted   213 *sir* (F) omitted   214 *will* (F) will not   222 *excellent* (F) extent   223 *ye* (F) you   225 *over-* (F) euer   226 *cap* (F) lap   234 *that* (F) omitted   269 *even* (F) euer   275 *Why, anything – but* (F) Anything but   300 *a piece* (F) peece   301 *moving how* (F) moouing, how   302 *admirable,* (F) admirable   *action* (F) action,   *angel,* (F) Angell   *apprehension* (Eds) apprehension,   305 *woman* (Q1, F) women   315 *of* (F) on   318–19 *the clown . . . sere* (F) omitted   320 *blank* (Q1, F) black   356 *mows* (Q1, F) mouths   364 *lest my* (F) let me   389–90 *tragical-historical . . . -pastoral* (F) omitted   395 *treasure* (Walker) a treasure   415 *By'r* (F) by   419 *e'en to't* (Rowe) ento't (Q2) e'ne to't (F)   *French falconers* (Q1, F) friendly Fankners   432 *affectation* (F) affection   434 *tale* (Q1, F) talke   435 *where* (Q1, F) when   442 *the* (Q1, F) th'   462 *Then . . . Ilium* (F) omitted   469 *And* (F) omitted   483 *fellies* (Eds) follies   492 *Mobled . . . good* (F2) omitted   502 *husband's* (Q1, F) husband   507 *whe'r* (Capell) where   526 *ha't* (F) hate   527 *dozen* (Q1, F) dosen   lines   538 *his* (F) the   540 *and* (F) an   543 *to Hecuba* (Q1, F) to her   545 *the cue* (F) that   564 *ha'* (Eds) a   567 *O, vengeance!* (F) omitted   569 *father* (Q1, Q4) omitted (Q2, F)   *murdered* (Eds) murtherèd   573 *About,* (Theobald) About   585 *devil . . . devil* (F) deale . . . deale

III, i, 1 *And* (F) An   28 *too* (F) two   32 *lawful espials* (F) omitted   33 *Will I* (F) Wee'le   46 *loneliness* (F) lowlines   55 *Let's* (F) omitted   79 *bourn* (Capell) borne (Q2) bourne (Pope)   83 *of us all* (Q1, F) omitted   85 *sickled* (F) sickled   90 *remembered* (Eds) remembred   92 *well, well, well* (F) well   99 *the* (F) these   107 *your honesty* (F) you   121 *to* (F) omitted   121, 130, 137, 140, 149 *nunnery* (Q1, F) Nunry   129 *all* (Q1, F) omitted   137 *Go* (Q1, F) omitted   141 *O* (F) omitted   144 *you amble* (Q1, F) & amble   *lisp* (F) list   145–46 *your ignorance* (F) ignorance   147 *more* (F) mo   152 *expectancy* (F) expectation   156 *music* (F) musickt (Q2)   157 *that* (F) what   159 *feature* (F) stature   161 *see!* (F) see.   Exit   188 *unwatched* (F) vnmatcht

III, ii, 9 *tatters* (F) totters   10 *split* (Q1, F) spleet   18 *overdone* (F) ore-doone   21 *own* (F) omitted   24 *make* (F) makes   25 *the which* (F) which   28 *praise* (F) praysd   35 *sir* (F) omitted   49 *ho* (F) howe   86 *detecting* (F) detected   94 *now.* (Johnson) now   110 *I mean . . . lord* (these two lines are present in F, omitted in Q2)   123 *devil* (F) deule   129 s.d. *sound* (Q4) sounds   DUMB SHOW (ll. 8, 10) *poisoner* (F) poysner   131 *is* (Q1, F) omitted   *miching* (Q1, F) munching   136 *counsel* (Q1, F) omitted   138 *you'll* (Q1, F) you will   147 *orbèd* (F) orb'd   the   148 *borrowed* (Capell) borrowèd   155 *your* (F) you   160 *In neither* (F) Eyther none, in neither   161 *love* (F) Lord   182 *like* (F) the   191 *joys* (F) ioy   211 *An* (Theobald) And   215 *once a* (Q1, F) once I be a   be (Q1, F) be a   220 s.d. *Exit* (Q1, F) Exeunt   232 *o'* (Q1, F) of   240 *my* (F) mine   242 *must take* (Q1) mistake   246 *Confederate* (Q1, F) Considerat   248 *infected* (Q1, F) inuected   256 (this line is present in F, omitted in Q2)   266 *two* (F) omitted   268 *sir* (F) omitted   274 *peacock* (Pope) paiock (Q2) pecock (Q '95)   279 *poisoning* (F) poysning   289 *distempered* (F) distempred   296 *start* (F) stare   305 *of my* (F) of   330 s.d. *Player* (Eds) Players   344 *and thumb* (F) & the vmber   353 *the top of* (F) omitted   357 *can fret me* (Q1, F) fret me not   371–72 *Polonius. I . . . friends.* (F) Leaue me friends. / I will, say so. By and by is easily said,   374 *breathes* (F) breakes   376 *bitter business as the day* (F) busines as the bitter day   381 *daggers* (Q1, F) dagger

III, iii, 17 *'tis* (Dyce ii) is   19 *huge* (F) hough   22 *ruin* (F) raine   23 *with* (F) omitted   25 *upon* (F) about   50 *pardoned* (F) pardon   58 *shove* (F) showe   69 *engaged* (F) ingagèd   73 *pat* (F) but   75 *revenged* (F) reuendge   79 *hire and salary* (F) base and silly   84 *revenged* (F) reuendgèd   89 *drunk* (F) drunke,

III, iv, 5 *with him* (F) omitted 7 *warrant* (F) wait 21 *inmost* (F) most 23, 24 *ho* (Q1, F) how 39 *is* (F) be 50 *And* (Eds) Ore 54 *Hamlet* (placed as in F; comes one line earlier in Q2) 60 *heaven-kissing* (F) heaue, a kissing 65 *mildewed* (F) mildewèd 80 *sans* (Eds) sance 89 *panders* (F) pardons 90 *mine* (F) my very *very* (F) omitted (Q2) 91 *grainèd* (F) greeued 92 *not leave* (F) leaue there 94 *Stewed* (F) Stewèd 96 *mine* (F) my 98 *tithe* (F) kyth 122 *hairs* (Rowe) haire 136 *lived* (Eds) liuèd 140 *Ecstasy* (F) omitted 143 *uttered* (Eds) vttred 144 *I* (F) omitted 159 *live* (F) leaue 166 *Refrain to-night* (F) to refraine night 171 *wondrous* (Q5) wonderous (Q2) lines omitted (F) 180 *Thus* (F) This 187 *ravel* (F) rouell 216 *foolish* (F) most foolish

IV, i, 35 *dragged* (F) dreg'd 43 *poisoned* (Eds) poysned

IV, ii, 2 (this line is present in F, omitted in Q2) 6 *Compounded* (F) Compound 17 *ape* (F) apple 29–30 *Hide . . . after* (F) omitted

IV, iii, 6 *weighed* (F) wayed 11 *befallen* (Eds) befalne 15 *Ho* (F) Howe 29 *King* (F) King. King. 42 *With fiery quickness* (F) omitted 51 *and so* (F) so 67 *were ne'er begun* (F) will nere begin

IV, v, 9 *aim* (F) yawne 16 *Queen* (Blackstone) omitted 39 *grave* (F) ground 42 *God* (F) good 57 *la,* (F) omitted 82 *their* (F) omitted 89 *his* (F) this 96 *Queen . . . this?* (F) omitted 97 *are* (F) is 106 *They* (F) The 119 *brows* (Q '76) browe 152 s.d. *Let her come in* (as in F, given as a speech to Laertes in Q2, at l. 153) 156 *by* (F) with 160 *an old* (Q1, F) a poore 164 *barefaced* (F) bare-faste 181 *O* (F) omitted *must* (Q1, F) may 186 *affliction* (F) afflictions 194 *All* (F) omitted 198 *Christian* (F) Christians *I pray God* (F) omitted 199 *see* (F) omitted

IV, vi, 21 *good* (F) omitted 25 *bore* (F) bord 29 *He* (F) So 30 *give* (F) omitted

IV, vii, 6 *proceeded* (F) proceede 7 *crimeful* (F) criminall 8 *safety,* (F) safetie, greatnes, 11 *they're* (Q '76) tha'r (Q2) they are (F) 14 *conjunctive* (F) concliue 20 *Would* (F) Worke 22 *loud a wind* (F) loued Arm'd 24 *And* (F) But *had* (F) haue 40 *received* (F) receiuèd 45 *your pardon* (F) you pardon 46–47 *and more strange* (F) omitted 55 *shall* (F) omitted 56 *diddest* (F) didst 60 *returned* (F) returnèd 61 *checking* (F) the King 87 *my* (F) me 114 *wick* (Rowe ii) weeke 121 *spendthrift* (Q '76) spend thrifts (Q2) ll. 113–22 omitted (F) 122 *o'* (Eds) of 124 *yourself . . . deed* (F) your selfe indeede your fathers sonne 133 *on* (F) ore 139 *that* (F) omitted 155 *ha't* (F) hate 166 *hoar* (F) horry 170 *cold* (F) cull-cold

V, i, 8 *se offendendo* (F) so offended 10–11 *do, and* (F) doe, 11 *Argal* (F) or all 41 *frame* (F) omitted 56 *last* (Q1, Q4) lasts (Q2, F) 57 *stoup* (Q1, F) soope 62 *that* (F) omitted 63 *at* (F) in 66 *daintier* (F) dintier 68 *clawed* (Pope) clawèd 69 *shipped* (Eds) shippèd *intil* (F) into 80 *meant* (F) went 82 *chapless* (F) Choples 83 *mazzard* (F) massene 84 *an* (Capell) and 86 *'em* (F) them 100 *his vouchers* (F) vouchers 101 *double ones too* (F) doubles 112 *O* (F) or 113 (line is present in F, omitted in Q2) 130 *taken* (F) tooke 133 *a* (F) omitted 134 *all* (F) omitted 138 *the* (F) that 155 *now-a-days* (F) omitted 162 *three-and-twenty* (F) 23. 169 *sir – Yorick's* (Eds) sir Yoricks 172 *Let me see* (F) omitted 174 *borne* (F) bore 181 *chamber* (Q1, F) table 195 *as thus* (Q1, F) omitted 203 *winter's* (F) waters 216 *have* (F) been 218 *Shards* (F) omitted 234 *treble* (F) double 236 *Deprived* (F) Depriuèd 248 *and* (F) omitted 256 *loved* (Q1, F) louèd 264 *thou* (Q1, F) omitted 272 *thus* (F) this 274 *disclosed* (F) disclosèd 285 *shortly* (F) thirtie

V, ii, 5 *Methought* (F) my thought 6 *bilboes* (F) bilbo 17 *unseal* (F) vnfold 27 *me* (F) now 29 *villainies* (Capell) villaines 43 *as's* (Eds) as sir 46 *the* (F) those 52 *Subscribed* (F) Subscribe 55 *know'st* (F) knowest 93 *Put* (F) omitted 98 *sultry* (F) sully *for* (F) or 100 *sultry* (F) soultery 101 *But* (F) omitted 105 *mine* (F) my 109 *feelingly* (Q4) sellingly (Q2) omitted (F) 138 *his* (Q '76) this (Q2) omitted (F) 146 *hangers* (F) hanger 152 *carriages* (F) carriage 155 *might* (F) omitted *Barbary* (F) Barbry (Q2) 158 *impawned, as* (Eds) omitted (Q2) impon'd as (F) 170 *an* (Capell) and 172 *redeliver* (F) deliuer *e'en* (F) omitted 176 *yours.* (F) omitted 179 *comply* (F) omitted 180 *bevy* (F) breede 182 *yeasty* (F) histy 184 *fanned . . . win-*

nowed (Warburton) prophane . . . trennowed 198 *this wager* (F) omitted 201 *But* (F) omitted 204 *gaingiving* (F) gamgiuing 209 *now* (F) omitted 222 *wronged* (F) wrongèd 227 *wronged* (F) wrongèd 229 (this line is present in F, omitted in Q2) 239 *keep* (F) omitted *till* (F) all 243 *Come on* (F) omitted 252 *bettered* (F) better 261 *union* (F) Vnice 275 *A touch, a touch* (F) omitted 281 *poisoned* (F) poysned 286 *but* (F) doe but 288 *afeard* (F) sure 292 *ho* (F) howe 299 *poisoned* (F) poysned 300 *Ho* (Q4) how (Q2, F) 302 *Hamlet. Hamlet.* (F) Hamlet 305 *thy* (Q1, F) my 308 *poisoned* (F) poysned 314 *murd'rous* (F) omitted 315 *thy* (Q1, F) the *union* (Q1, F) Onixe 316 *served* (F) seruèd 332 *ha't* (Capell) hate 334 *live* (F) I leaue 338 (all quartos and folios give a s.d. here: Enter Osrick) 340 *the* (Eds) th' 347 s.d. *Dies* (Q1, F) omitted 366 *arrived* (Eds) arriuèd 368 *th'* (F) omitted 372 *forced* (F) for no 381 *on* (F) no 387 *proved* (Q1, F) proouèd 388 *rites* (F) right

SUPPLEMENTARY NOTES

I, i, 117 *As* Something is obviously wrong with the transition of thought. The conjecture that some preceding matter has been left out of the text is perhaps as good as any.

I, ii, 129 *sullied* Use of this emendation of the 'sallied' of the 1604–05 quarto instead of the widely accepted 'solid' of the 1623 folio is strongly recommended by: (1) the implications of the interestingly corrupt 'too much grieu'd and sallied flesh' of the 1603 quarto, into which the intrusive participle 'grieu'd' cannot be thought to have come at the call of an original 'solid' standing in the place of 'sallied'; (2) the example of the 'sallies' in a later passage of the 1604–05 quarto (II, i, 39), which in its context is most certainly to be taken as 'sullies' and which in the folio appears as 'sulleyes.'

I, iv, 37 *Doth . . . doubt* This difficult and often altered line is here printed without emendation. In the famous crux of which it is a key part the intent of what Hamlet is saying had perhaps best be taken as a close rewording of what he has just been saying; he may be taken to say that the dram of evil imparts a doubtful quality to all the noble human substance, to his (its) own scandal, i.e. to the detriment of the nobility itself because of the general censure that he has mentioned before in developing at involved length what he offers here with the emphasis of brevity.

III, iv, 162 *all sense doth eat* absorbs and lives upon all human sense, not only that made up of the bodily faculties but also the contrasting 'inward' sense made up of the faculties of the mind and soul – all sense, whether low or high and whether bad or good in use (looking forward to completion of the image of custom as a monster of double form, part devil and part angel; see the *Oxford English Dictionary* under 'Sense,' I, 3 and 7). The crux of which these words make a part has also produced frequent emendation. See the note following.

III, iv, 163 *Of habits devil* being a devil in, or in respect of, habits (with a play on 'habits,' as meaning both settled practices and garments, which by looking forward to 'actions fair and good' and to 'frock or livery' is subtly involved in the opposition and monstrous combination within the passage of devil and angel, and which contributes to an essential poetic image that tends to be destroyed by a finding of need to emend the phrase, especially when 'devil' is changed to 'evil'; see the *Oxford English Dictionary* under 'Of,' XI, 37, for a showing of the use of the preposition in the sense here given, as in the example, dated 1535, 'he y^t is a blabbe of his tonge').

III, iv, 170 *And . . . out* This line is usually taken to suffer from an omission after 'either' of some such word as 'master,' 'curb,' or 'quell.'

IV, i, 40 *And . . . done* It would seem that after this fragmentary line there is an omission. Capell's insertion of 'So, haply, slander,' a purely conjectural completion of the line, has often been accepted as providing desired clarification of thought.

THE HISTORY OF TROILUS AND CRESSIDA

INTRODUCTION

Troilus and Cressida remains an enigma. Complications surrounded its first publication; our only clues to its first performance are a puzzle; the customary dramatic categories will neither explain nor include it; and its fascination for the intellect cannot conceal its defects as art.

On February 7, 1603, there was entered in the Stationers' Register for copyright "The booke of Troilus and Cresseda as yt is acted by my lord Chamberlens men." There is a second entry in 1609 for different publishers, whose quarto edition shortly appeared under the title "The Historie of Troylus and Cresseida. As it was acted by the Kings Maiesties seruants at the Globe. Written by William Shakespeare." But the same text was immediately reissued with the original title page cut away and two new leaves substituted. The first bore a different title: "The Famous Historie of Troylus and Cresseid. Excellently expressing the beginning of their loues, with the conceited wooing of Pandarus Prince of Licia. Written by William Shakespeare." The second leaf contained the preface, "A Never Writer, to an Ever Reader. News," which heads the present edition. In conjunction with the new title, this preface looks like an attempt to urge as a selling point that the play had never been "clapper-clawed with the palms of the vulgar" – that is, had never been performed in the public theatre. The subsequent sentences also imply that the play, having displeased the witless, is now being offered to its proper patrons, the witty.

Still further complications ensued when the first folio was being prepared. Three pages of the play were actually printed for inclusion among the tragedies after *Romeo and Juliet*. Then, presumably because of copyright difficulties, these were withdrawn and *Timon of Athens* was substituted. Finally the play was printed without pagination, too late for inclusion in the preliminary list of plays, and placed between the histories and the tragedies in the complete folio.

The facts just related provide our best clues to the date and performance of the play. Most critics date it about 1602 on the basis of style and allusions in the text, although dissenters have placed it in the late 1590's. One may perhaps conjecture that, shortly before February 7, 1603, it was performed by Shakespeare's company, then the Lord Chamberlain's Men, but for a special audience rather than before the "vulgar" in the Globe Theatre. The character of the play suggests performance before one of the Inns of Court, where wit might be found, if anywhere. It was not unusual for plays to be performed before special audiences at the time, but it must be conceded that it was quite unusual for plays to be especially written for such performances.

Hence we are dealing here not with an established fact, as is sometimes assumed, but with a hypothesis only, although it comes as near as any to explaining the peculiar characteristics of *Troilus and Cressida*: the play is a unique combination of learned subject matter, all-inclusive satire, and something close to smut; and it is neither comedy nor tragedy – nor, in fact, well-constructed drama. A subject with the most respectable literary antecedents has been treated disrespectfully enough to appeal to the sophisticated and cynical.

Of the two plot-threads of the play, the story of Troilus and Cressida is drawn from Chaucer's *Troilus and Criseyde*. In the background, though little used in the play, lurks Robert Henryson's *Testament of Cresseid*, a sequel in which Cresseid becomes a leper and a beggar. For the military episodes Shakespeare drew upon Caxton's *Recuyell of the Historyes of Troye*, upon Homer in Chapman's translation, and, for such details as the romantic motive of Hector's challenge, upon his own familiarity with tales of chivalry. But the knightly trappings of the Trojan War are thoroughly in accord with the medieval versions of the Troy story that lay behind all his sources but Homer. The subject was dramatically timely. In 1599 Dekker and Chettle had written a play on Troilus and Cressida for the Admiral's Men, a rival company; and Chapman's *Sir Giles Goosecap*, a comedy contemporary with Shakespeare's play, adapted some of the story elements to English characters in an English setting. Shakespeare, too, may have been trying to give the story a novel treatment, partly by his dissection of the moral issues involved in the war. For this ethical analysis he may have found precedent in Robert Greene's *Euphues His Censure to Philautus* (1587).

Either the classical subject matter or a learned audience may account for the style of the play. Passages in *Troilus and Cressida* come closer than anything else in Shakespeare to the epic style that Milton developed, on the precedent of Latin epic, for *Paradise Lost*. This is true not only of the Latinate diction but also of the figurative language, extreme even by Elizabethan standards and particularly prone to such devices as personification, hyperbole, or substituting an abstraction for a plural noun:

> But let the ruffian Boreas once enrage
> The gentle Thetis, and anon behold
> The strong-ribbed bark through liquid mountains cut.
> (I, iii, 38–40)

> The specialty of rule hath been neglected.　(I, iii, 78)

Either the audience or Shakespeare's own preoccupation with philosophic ideas must account for the long passages in the two council scenes that make the play almost a summary of Shakespeare's cosmology and ethics. These will be discussed below.

If Shakespeare finds a grand style appropriate to his re-telling of a great love story and the greatest of all war stories, his treatment nevertheless results in a total deflation of both romance and glory. Troilus is an estimable young man, but he is an erotic gourmet nonetheless:

> I am giddy; expectation whirls me round.
> Th' imaginary relish is so sweet
> That it enchants my sense. What will it be
> When that the wat'ry palates taste indeed
> Love's thrice-repurèd nectar? Death, I fear me,
> Sounding destruction, or some joy too fine,
> Too subtle, potent, tuned too sharp in sweetness
> For the capacity of my ruder powers.   (III, ii, 16–23)

This is human enough, but it is not romantic love. As to Cressida, if we have any doubts after her exchange of wit with Pandarus at the end of the second scene, they are immediately dispelled by her own words. She is a practiced "daughter of the game," as Ulysses later calls her. She sums herself up:

> Ah, poor our sex! this fault in us I find,
> The error of our eye directs our mind.
> What error leads must err. O, then conclude
> Minds swayed by eyes are full of turpitude.
>   (V, ii, 105–08)

When Troilus discovers his mistake in supposing that the woman he has seduced is proof against other men, he is pathetic in his grief, but he is not tragic.

The Trojan War is even more thoroughly deflated. Thersites sums the matter up in his scurrilous way: "All the argument is a whore and a cuckold, a good quarrel to draw emulous factions and bleed to death upon" (II, iii, 68–70). Helen's own character and the atmosphere that surrounds her are perfectly suggested by Pandarus' long scene with her, and particularly by the tone of the song that concludes it (III, i). Diomedes gets down to cases:

> For every false drop in her bawdy veins
> A Grecian's life hath sunk; for every scruple
> Of her contaminated carrion weight
> A Troyan hath been slain. Since she could speak,
> She hath not given so many good words breath
> As for her Greeks and Troyans suff'red death.
>   (IV, i, 69–74)

The Greeks, therefore, are trying to recover what is not worth fighting for; but they quarrel like spoiled and selfish children, and Achilles, their hero, is a vainglorious muscle-man. He pouts in his tent with his favorite and, in defiance of Homer's account, has his Myrmidons ambush Hector, who is unarmed. He is, in short, a bully and a coward. The Trojans are very different but equally flawed. They know their cause is wrong. Hector proves all too clearly that

>   these moral laws
> Of nature and of nations speak aloud
> To have her [Helen] back returned.   (II, ii, 184–86)

He knows that Troilus, in arguing for keeping her, is driven by passion as against judgment:

>   Or is your blood
> So madly hot that no discourse of reason,
> Nor fear of bad success in a bad cause,
> Can qualify the same?   (II, ii, 115–18)

But, after enunciating the soundest moral principles, he reverses himself and concludes:

>   Hector's opinion
> Is this in way of truth; yet ne'ertheless,
> My spritely brethren, I propend to you
> In resolution to keep Helen still;
> For 'tis a cause that hath no mean dependence
> Upon our joint and several dignities.
>   (II, ii, 188–93)

As a fighter, he is as reckless in his chivalry as Achilles is cowardly. He is playing foolishly in a foolish war. The rational norm of bravery is not in either man. In this play (though nowhere else in Shakespeare) war is what it is in much modern fiction – a bloody mess from which no one emerges with glory or even integrity.

The intention of the play is therefore ambiguous. Apparently it puzzled Shakespeare's contemporaries. The second entry in the Stationers' Register and the quarto title pages call it a history – that is, a dramatic narrative of historical events which is not definitely tragedy. The folio editors intended to place it among the tragedies and called it "The Tragedie of Troylus and Cressida." Elizabethan literary theory restricted comedy to non-historical subject matter. But the play is simply not tragedy, even though it ends with the death of Troilus' illusions and of Hector himself. Its subject matter, unlike its style, is never heroic, and in Thersites it descends to obscene raillery. The war plot has only the loosest narrative organization, and the two great council scenes have no dramatic function at all proportionate to the pains that Shakespeare lavished upon them. Perhaps the best hypothesis is that he tried to adapt the well-known story to the satiric mood then in fashion in the theatre and to make it especially palatable to a learned and sophisticated audience by seasoning it with large, unassimilated chunks of philosophy and a liberal sprinkling of innuendo or even outright scurrility. But, if so, his attempt to turn what was for his audience a great historical theme into comical satire was unique in the Elizabethan theatre.

What has the play to offer the modern reader? The answer, despite what precedes, is that it is Shakespeare's own key to his greatest plays and that it is a powerful, if unconventional, mirror of human nature.

Shakespeare, like most of his contemporaries, believed that God the Creator had imposed upon all nature a universal and hierarchical order, in accordance with which all things performed their part in achieving His ultimate purposes. This order resulted from the obedience of all creation to laws that governed not only the physical universe but also social and political institutions and man the individual. As a rational being and the highest of created things on earth, man shared with God and the angels the possession of free will. He was free to live rationally – that is, to obey the commands of God and conform to the laws of nature. But he was also free to violate "the moral laws of nature and of nations" and, by so doing, to bring suffering upon himself and disruption to the social and even cosmic order of which he was a part. This view is present throughout the plays; it is fundamental to the great tragedies. Shakespeare's concept of universal order is stated fully and explicitly in Ulysses' great speech to the Greek council (I, iii, 75–137). His explanation of human disorder is summarized, more succinctly, in Hector's parallel argument to the Trojan council in the next act (II, ii, 163–93). The decision of the council and of Hector himself is, moreover, an example of "those raging appetites" that overcome the reason and will, and lead men to corrupt the law of nature. And the play is filled with short passages that echo or clarify the same system of ideas, as the psychology and ethics of love and war are analyzed explicitly and fully. In the tragedies Shakespeare presents in action what here he explains in theoretical terms. Always, as in *Othello* and *Macbeth*, we see man's will "benumbed" in sin; in *Macbeth* and *King Lear* we also see "what discord follows" the destruction of "degree," and in *King Lear* the "appetite" that disrupts nature

> Must make perforce an universal prey
> And last eat up himself. (I, iii, 123–24)

So evil becomes self-destructive, and order is restored to a suffering world. In short, the lover of Shakespeare must know *Troilus and Cressida* thoroughly, or he does not know Shakespeare at all.

But *Troilus and Cressida* itself portrays a very different world from that of tragedy, the world of all-too-human nature. The satire is sharp, but it is justified. The modern reader of the play does not need to be told that what passes for love is often lust, and that what motivates much patriotism has nothing to do with love of country. Modern literature has made these points in wearisome detail. But Shakespeare has intensified and clarified even this aspect of human nature with all the matchless resources of his imagination. His eye has roved from the councils of the mighty to the backbiting of their hangers-on. Modern fiction has done much better, moreover, at giving us Cressidas, or a Pandarus and Thersites, than at showing us a Hector betraying his intellect under pressure of the moment or a Ulysses expending his wisdom on an intrigue to end a petty broil. And Shakespeare has summarized these insights in unforgettable lines of verse. *Troilus and Cressida* is certainly not his greatest play, but it is in some respects his most modern. We may not like its people, but they are with us everywhere. Shakespeare often tells us what we can be or should be. Here he tells us what, unfortunately, we all too often are.

Stanford University   VIRGIL K. WHITAKER

NOTE ON THE TEXT

The present edition is based on the quarto of 1609, which is believed to have been printed from a private transcript of Shakespeare's own draft made by himself or a scribe. The folio text was printed from the quarto, perhaps collated with the original draft after it had been prepared for performance. A few brief passages supplied by the folio have been included in square brackets, and a number of readings from the folio have been adopted at points where the text of the quarto seems corrupt or obviously inferior. These, and the limited number of emendations, are listed in the Appendix. The stage directions are those of the quarto, with bracketed additions and amplifications suggested usually by the folio. Both the quarto and folio are without act–scene divisions, and those of the later editors have been supplied marginally.

THE HISTORY OF TROILUS AND CRESSIDA

A NEVER WRITER, TO AN EVER READER. NEWS.

Eternal reader, you have here a new play, never staled with the stage, never clapper-clawed with the palms of the vulgar, and yet passing full of the palm comical; for it is a birth of your brain that never undertook anything comical vainly. And were but the vain names of comedies changed for the titles of commodities, or of plays for pleas, you should see all those grand censors, that now style them such vanities, flock to them for the main grace of their gravities, especially this author's comedies, that are so framed to the life that they serve for the most common commentaries of all the actions of our lives, showing such a dexterity and power of wit that the most displeased with plays are pleased with his comedies. And all such dull and heavy-witted worldlings as were never capable of the wit of a comedy, coming by report of them to his representations, have found that wit there that they never found in themselves and have parted better witted than they came, feeling an edge of wit set upon them more than ever they dreamed they had brain to grind it on. So much and such savored salt of wit is in his comedies that they seem, for their height of pleasure, to be born in that sea that brought forth Venus. Amongst all there is none more witty than this: and had I time I would comment upon it, though I know it needs not, for so much as will make you think your testern well bestowed, but for so much worth as even poor I know to be stuffed in it. It deserves such a labor as well as the best comedy in Terence or Plautus. And believe this, that when he is gone and his comedies out of sale, you will scramble for them and set up a new English Inquisition. Take this for a warning, and at the peril of your pleasure's loss, and judgment's, refuse not, nor like this the less for not being sullied with the smoky breath of the multitude; but thank fortune for the 'scape it hath made amongst you, since by the grand possessors' wills I believe you should have prayed for them rather than been prayed. And so I leave all such to be prayed for, for the state of their wits' healths, that will not praise it. Vale.

*

[NAMES OF THE ACTORS

Priam, King of Troy
Hector ⎫
Troilus ⎪
Paris ⎬ his sons
Deiphobus ⎪
Helenus ⎭
Margarelon, a bastard son of Priam
Aeneas ⎫
Antenor ⎬ Trojan commanders
Calchas, a Trojan priest, taking part with the Greeks
Pandarus, uncle to Cressida
Agamemnon, the Greek general
Menelaus, his brother
Achilles ⎫
Ajax ⎬ Greek commanders

Ulysses ⎫
Nestor ⎪
Diomedes ⎬ Greek commanders
Patroclus ⎭
Thersites, a deformed and scurrilous Greek
Alexander, servant to Cressida
Servant to Troilus
Servant to Paris
Servant to Diomedes
Helen, wife to Menelaus
Andromache, wife to Hector
Cassandra, daughter to Priam; a prophetess
Cressida, daughter to Calchas
Trojan and Greek Soldiers and Attendants

Scene: Troy, and the Greek Camp before it]

*

[THE PROLOGUE

Pro. In Troy there lies the scene. From isles of Greece
  2 The princes orgulous, their high blood chafed,
     Have to the port of Athens sent their ships,
     Fraught with the ministers and instruments
     Of cruel war. Sixty and nine, that wore
     Their crownets regal, from th' Athenian bay
  7 Put forth toward Phrygia; and their vow is made
  8 To ransack Troy, within whose strong immures
     The ravished Helen, Menelaus' queen,

With wanton Paris sleeps; and that's the quarrel.
To Tenedos they come,
And the deep-drawing barks do there disgorge
Their warlike fraughtage. Now on Dardan plains 13

Preface 21 *Venus* (the Latin goddess was identified with the Greek Aphrodite, who sprang from the sea foam) 24 *testern* sixpence 33 *grand possessors* (the actor-sharers of the King's Men, who apparently were trying to prevent the publication of their plays)
Pro. 2 *orgulous* proud 7 *Phrygia* western Asia Minor 8 *immures* walls 13 *fraughtage* cargo, i.e. warriors; *Dardan* Trojan, Dardanus being a mythical ancestor

980

The fresh and yet unbruisèd Greeks do pitch
Their brave pavilions. Priam's six-gated city,
16 Dardan, and Timbria, Helias, Chetas, Troien,
And Antenonidus, with massy staples
18 And corresponsive and fulfilling bolts,
19 Sperr up the sons of Troy.
Now expectation, tickling skittish spirits,
On one and other side, Troyan and Greek,
Sets all on hazard. And hither am I come,
23 A prologue armed, but not in confidence
24 Of author's pen or actor's voice, but suited
25 In like conditions as our argument,
To tell you, fair beholders, that our play
27 Leaps o'er the vaunt and firstlings of those broils,
Beginning in the middle, starting thence away
To what may be digested in a play.
Like or find fault; do as your pleasures are:
Now good or bad, 'tis but the chance of war.]

I, i	*Enter Pandarus and Troilus.*
TROILUS
1	Call here my varlet, I'll unarm again.
Why should I war without the walls of Troy
That find such cruel battle here within?
Each Troyan that is master of his heart,
Let him to field; Troilus, alas, hath none.
PANDARUS
6	Will this gear ne'er be mended?
TROILUS
7	The Greeks are strong, and skillful to their strength,
Fierce to their skill, and to their fierceness valiant;
But I am weaker than a woman's tear,
10	Tamer than sleep, fonder than ignorance,
Less valiant than the virgin in the night,
And skilless as unpractised infancy.
PANDARUS Well, I have told you enough of this. For my
part, I'll not meddle nor make no farther. He that will
have a cake out of the wheat must tarry the grinding.
TROILUS Have I not tarried?
PANDARUS Ay, the grinding; but you must tarry the
17	bolting.
TROILUS Have I not tarried?
PANDARUS Ay, the bolting; but you must tarry the
leavening.
TROILUS Still have I tarried.
PANDARUS Ay, to the leavening; but here's yet in the
word 'hereafter' the kneading, the making of the cake,
the heating of the oven, and the baking; nay, you must
stay the cooling too, or you may chance to burn your lips.
TROILUS
Patience herself, what goddess e'er she be,
26	Doth lesser blench at suff'rance than I do.

At Priam's royal table do I sit,
And when fair Cressid comes into my thoughts –
So, traitor, then she comes when she is thence.	29
PANDARUS Well, she looked yesternight fairer than ever
I saw her look, or any woman else.
TROILUS
I was about to tell thee, when my heart,
As wedgèd with a sigh, would rive in twain,	33
Lest Hector or my father should perceive me:
I have, as when the sun doth light a-scorn,	35
Buried this sigh in wrinkle of a smile;
But sorrow, that is couched in seeming gladness,
Is like that mirth fate turns to sudden sadness.
PANDARUS An her hair were not somewhat darker than	39
Helen's – well, go to – there were no more comparison
between the women: but, for my part, she is my kins-
woman; I would not, as they term it, praise her, but I
would somebody had heard her talk yesterday, as I did.
I will not dispraise your sister Cassandra's wit, but –
TROILUS
O Pandarus! I tell thee, Pandarus –
When I do tell thee, there my hopes lie drowned,
Reply not in how many fathoms deep
They lie indrenched. I tell thee I am mad
In Cressid's love; thou answer'st she is fair;
Pour'st in the open ulcer of my heart
Her eyes, her hair, her cheek, her gait, her voice;
Handlest in thy discourse, O, that her hand,	52
In whose comparison all whites are ink,
Writing their own reproach; to whose soft seizure
The cygnet's down is harsh, and spirit of sense	55
Hard as the palm of ploughman. This thou tell'st me,
As true thou tell'st me, when I say I love her;
But, saying thus, instead of oil and balm,
Thou lay'st in every gash that love hath given me
The knife that made it.
PANDARUS I speak no more than truth.
TROILUS Thou dost not speak so much.
PANDARUS Faith, I'll not meddle in it. Let her be as she
is. If she be fair, 'tis the better for her; an she be not, she
has the mends in her own hands.	65
TROILUS Good Pandarus, how now, Pandarus?
PANDARUS I have had my labor for my travail; ill-
thought-on of her, and ill-thought-on of you; gone be-
tween and between, but small thanks for my labor.
TROILUS What, art thou angry, Pandarus? what, with
me?
PANDARUS Because she's kin to me, therefore she's not so
fair as Helen. An she were not kin to me, she would be as	72
fair on Friday as Helen is on Sunday. But what care I?
I care not an she were a blackamoor; 'tis all one to me.	74
TROILUS Say I she is not fair?
PANDARUS I do not care whether you do or no. She's a
fool to stay behind her father. Let her to the Greeks, and	77
so I'll tell her the next time I see her. For my part, I'll
meddle nor make no more i' th' matter.
TROILUS Pandarus –
PANDARUS Not I.
TROILUS Sweet Pandarus –
PANDARUS Pray you, speak no more to me. I will leave all
as I found it, and there an end.	*Exit. Sound alarum.*	84
TROILUS
Peace, you ungracious clamors! Peace, rude sounds!
Fools on both sides! Helen must needs be fair,

16–17 *Dardan . . . Antenonidus* (i.e. Antenorides) names of the gates
18 *fulfilling* filling full, i.e. tightly 19 *Sperr* shut 23 *armed* in armor
24 *suited* dressed 25 *argument* theme, subject 27 *vaunt* first part
I, i Before the palace of Priam in Troy 1 *varlet* servant 6 *gear* business
7 *to* in addition to 10 *fonder* more foolish 17 *bolting* sifting 26 *blench*
flinch 29 *traitor* (a rebuke for implying that she may ever be absent)
33 *rive* split 35 *a-scorn* grudgingly (?) 39 *An* if 52 *that her hand* that
hand of hers 55 *cygnet's* young swan's; *spirit* a very thin bodily substance that was believed to transmit sense impressions through the nerves
65 *mends* remedies, i.e. cosmetics 72–73 *as fair . . . Sunday* as fair in
ordinary clothes as Helen in her Sunday best 74 *blackamoor* Negro
77 *father* Calchas, a seer who anticipated the Trojan defeat and deserted
to the Greeks 84 s.d. *alarum* signal to arms

When with your blood you daily paint her thus.
88 I cannot fight upon this argument;
It is too starved a subject for my sword.
But Pandarus – O gods, how do you plague me!
I cannot come to Cressid but by Pandar;
92 And he's as tetchy to be wooed to woo
As she is stubborn, chaste, against all suit.
94 Tell me, Apollo, for thy Daphne's love,
What Cressid is, what Pandar, and what we.
Her bed is India; there she lies, a pearl.
97 Between our Ilium and where she resides
Let it be called the wild and wand'ring flood,
Ourself the merchant, and this sailing Pandar
Our doubtful hope, our convoy and our bark.
    Alarum. Enter Aeneas.

AENEAS
How now, Prince Troilus, wherefore not afield?
TROILUS
Because not there. This woman's answer sorts,
For womanish it is to be from thence.
What news, Aeneas, from the field to-day?
AENEAS
That Paris is returnèd home, and hurt.
TROILUS
By whom, Aeneas?
AENEAS   Troilus, by Menelaus.
TROILUS
Let Paris bleed; 'tis but a scar to scorn.
108 Paris is gored with Menelaus' horn.
    Alarum.
AENEAS
Hark what good sport is out of town to-day!
TROILUS
Better at home, if 'would I might' were 'may.'
But to the sport abroad. Are you bound thither?
AENEAS
In all swift haste.
TROILUS   Come, go we then together.   *Exeunt.*

                *

I, ii   *Enter Cressida and [Alexander,] her man.*
CRESSIDA
Who were those went by?
MAN   Queen Hecuba and Helen.
CRESSIDA
And whither go they?
MAN   Up to the eastern tower,
Whose height commands as subject all the vale,
To see the battle. Hector, whose patience
Is as a virtue fixed, to-day was moved.
He chid Andromache, and struck his armorer,
7 And, like as there were husbandry in war,
8 Before the sun rose he was harnessed light,
And to the field goes he, where every flower
Did, as a prophet, weep what it foresaw
In Hector's wrath.
CRESSIDA   What was his cause of anger?
MAN
The noise goes, this: there is among the Greeks
A lord of Troyan blood, nephew to Hector;
They call him Ajax.
CRESSIDA   Good; and what of him?

MAN
They say he is a very man per se
And stands alone.
CRESSIDA So do all men unless they are drunk, sick, or
have no legs.
MAN This man, lady, hath robbed many beasts of their particular additions: he is as valiant as the lion, churlish as 20
the bear, slow as the elephant; a man into whom nature
hath so crowded humors that his valor is crushed into 22
folly, his folly sauced with discretion. There is no man
hath a virtue that he hath not a glimpse of, nor any man 24
an attaint but he carries some stain of it. He is melan- 25
choly without cause and merry against the hair. He hath 26
the joints of everything, but everything so out of joint
that he is a gouty Briareus, many hands and no use, or 28
purblind Argus, all eyes and no sight. 29
CRESSIDA But how should this man that makes me smile
make Hector angry?
MAN They say he yesterday coped Hector in the battle 32
and struck him down, the disdain and shame whereof
hath ever since kept Hector fasting and waking.
    [Enter Pandarus.]
CRESSIDA Who comes here?
MAN Madam, your uncle Pandarus.
CRESSIDA Hector's a gallant man.
MAN As may be in the world, lady.
PANDARUS What's that? What's that?
CRESSIDA Good morrow, uncle Pandarus.
PANDARUS Good morrow, cousin Cressid. What do you 41
talk of? Good morrow, Alexander. How do you,
cousin? When were you at Ilium?
CRESSIDA This morning, uncle.
PANDARUS What were you talking of when I came? Was
Hector armed and gone ere ye came to Ilium? Helen
was not up, was she?
CRESSIDA Hector was gone, but Helen was not up.
PANDARUS E'en so, Hector was stirring early.
CRESSIDA That were we talking of, and of his anger.
PANDARUS Was he angry?
CRESSIDA So he says here. 52
PANDARUS True, he was so. I know the cause too. He'll
lay about him to-day, I can tell them that; and there's
Troilus will not come far behind him. Let them take
heed of Troilus, I can tell them that too.
CRESSIDA What, is he angry too?
PANDARUS Who, Troilus? Troilus is the better man of
the two.
CRESSIDA O Jupiter! there's no comparison.
PANDARUS What, not between Troilus and Hector? Do
you know a man if you see him?
CRESSIDA Ay, if I ever saw him before and knew him.
PANDARUS Well, I say Troilus is Troilus.
CRESSIDA Then you say as I say, for I am sure he is not
Hector.

88 *argument* subject of contention   92 *tetchy* fretful   94 *Daphne* a nymph
beloved of Apollo, who was changed into a bay tree to escape his pursuit
97 *Ilium* here, Priam's palace   108 *horn* (symbol of a cuckold, a man whose
wife had been unfaithful. Paris had stolen Helen from Menelaus.)
I, ii Before the house of Cressida   7 *husbandry* thrift   8 *harnessed* in
armor   20 *additions* indications of rank or distinction added to a man's
name   22 *humors* bodily fluids the excess of which caused emotional disorders   24 *glimpse* spark   25 *attaint* stain on honor   26 *hair* natural
tendency   28 *Briareus* a hundred-handed giant   29 *Argus* a herdsman
who had eyes all over his body   32 *coped* came to blows with   41 *cousin*
i.e. niece   52 *he* i.e. Alexander

67 PANDARUS No, nor Hector is not Troilus in some degrees.

CRESSIDA 'Tis just to each of them; he is himself.

69 PANDARUS Himself? Alas, poor Troilus, I would he were.

CRESSIDA So he is.

71 PANDARUS Condition, I had gone barefoot to India.

CRESSIDA He is not Hector.

PANDARUS Himself? no, he's not himself. Would 'a were himself! Well, the gods are above; time must friend or end. Well, Troilus, well, I would my heart were in her body. No, Hector is not a better man than Troilus.

CRESSIDA Excuse me.

PANDARUS He is elder.

CRESSIDA Pardon me, pardon me.

80 PANDARUS Th' other's not come to't; you shall tell me another tale when th' other's come to't. Hector shall not

82 have his wit this year.

CRESSIDA He shall not need it if he have his own.

PANDARUS Nor his qualities.

CRESSIDA No matter.

PANDARUS Nor his beauty.

CRESSIDA 'Twould not become him; his own's better.

PANDARUS You have no judgment, niece. Helen herself

89 swore th' other day that Troilus, for a brown favor – for so 'tis, I must confess, not brown neither –

CRESSIDA No, but brown.

PANDARUS Faith, to say truth, brown and not brown.

CRESSIDA To say the truth, true and not true.

PANDARUS She praised his complexion above Paris.

CRESSIDA Why, Paris hath color enough.

PANDARUS So he has.

CRESSIDA Then Troilus should have too much. If she praised him above, his complexion is higher than his. He having color enough, and the other higher, is too flaming a praise for a good complexion. I had as lief Helen's golden tongue had commended Troilus for a copper nose.

PANDARUS I swear to you, I think Helen loves him better than Paris.

104 CRESSIDA Then she's a merry Greek indeed.

PANDARUS Nay, I am sure she does. She came to him th'

106 other day into the compassed window, and, you know, he has not past three or four hairs on his chin –

CRESSIDA Indeed, a tapster's arithmetic may soon bring his particulars therein to a total.

PANDARUS Why, he is very young; and yet will he, within three pound, lift as much as his brother Hector.

112 CRESSIDA Is he so young a man, and so old a lifter?

PANDARUS But to prove to you that Helen loves him, she came and puts me her white hand to his cloven chin –

CRESSIDA Juno have mercy! how came it cloven?

PANDARUS Why, you know 'tis dimpled. I think his smiling becomes him better than any man in all Phrygia.

CRESSIDA O, he smiles valiantly.

PANDARUS Does he not?

CRESSIDA O, yes, an 'twere a cloud in autumn.

PANDARUS Why, go to then. But to prove to you that Helen loves Troilus –

CRESSIDA Troilus will stand to the proof, if you'll prove it so.

PANDARUS Troilus? Why, he esteems her no more than I esteem an addle egg. 125

CRESSIDA If you love an addle egg as well as you love an idle head, you would eat chickens i' th' shell.

PANDARUS I cannot choose but laugh to think how she tickled his chin. Indeed, she has a marvell's white hand, I must needs confess.

CRESSIDA Without the rack. 131

PANDARUS And she takes upon her to spy a white hair on his chin.

CRESSIDA Alas poor chin, many a wart is richer.

PANDARUS But there was such laughing: Queen Hecuba laughed that her eyes ran o'er.

CRESSIDA With millstones. 137

PANDARUS And Cassandra laughed.

CRESSIDA But there was a more temperate fire under the pot of her eyes. Did her eyes run o'er too?

PANDARUS And Hector laughed.

CRESSIDA At what was all this laughing?

PANDARUS Marry, at the white hair that Helen spied on Troilus' chin.

CRESSIDA An't had been a green hair, I should have laughed too.

PANDARUS They laughed not so much at the hair as at his pretty answer.

CRESSIDA What was his answer?

PANDARUS Quoth she, 'Here's but two-and-fifty hairs 150 on your chin, and one of them is white.'

CRESSIDA This is her question.

PANDARUS That's true; make no question of that. 'Two-and-fifty hairs,' quoth he, 'and one white. That white hair is my father, and all the rest are his sons.' 'Jupiter!' quoth she, 'which of these hairs is Paris, my husband?' 'The forked one,' quoth he; 'pluck't out, and give it 157 him.' But there was such laughing, and Helen so blushed, and Paris so chafed, and all the rest so laughed, that it passed.

CRESSIDA So let it now, for it has been a great while going by.

PANDARUS Well, cousin, I told you a thing yesterday; think on't.

CRESSIDA So I do.

PANDARUS I'll be sworn 'tis true; he will weep you, an 164 'twere a man born in April. 165

Sound a retreat.

CRESSIDA And I'll spring up in his tears, an 'twere a nettle against May.

PANDARUS Hark, they are coming from the field. Shall we stand up here and see them as they pass toward Ilium? Good niece, do; sweet niece, Cressida.

CRESSIDA At your pleasure.

PANDARUS Here, here, here's an excellent place; here we may see most bravely. I'll tell you them all by their 173 names as they pass by, but mark Troilus above the rest.

Enter Aeneas [passing across the stage].

CRESSIDA Speak not so loud.

PANDARUS That's Aeneas. Is not that a brave man? He's one of the flowers of Troy, I can tell you. But mark Troilus; you shall see anon.

Enter Antenor [passing across the stage].

---

67 *in some degrees* by some distance   69 *I would he were* i.e. himself, and not in love   71 *Condition . . . India* even though it meant my going barefoot to India   80 *come to't* come to manhood   82 *wit* intelligence   89 *favor* complexion   104 *a merry Greek* i.e. light of heart and morals   106 *compassed* bay   112 *lifter* thief   125 *addle* rotten, spoiled   131 *rack* torture   137 *millstones* i.e. obviously not tears   157 *forked* (like a cuckold's horns)   164 *an* as if   165–67 *April . . . May* i.e. April showers bring May flowers   173 *bravely* excellently

CRESSIDA Who's that?

PANDARUS That's Antenor. He has a shrewd wit, I can tell you; and he's a man good enough: he's one o' th' sound-
182 est judgments in Troy whosoever, and a proper man of person. When comes Troilus? I'll show you Troilus anon. If he see me, you shall see him nod at me.

185 CRESSIDA Will he give you the nod?

PANDARUS You shall see.

187 CRESSIDA If he do, the rich shall have more.

Enter Hector [passing across the stage].

PANDARUS That's Hector, that, that, look you, that; there's a fellow! Go thy way, Hector! There's a brave man, niece. O brave Hector! Look how he looks; there's a countenance! Is't not a brave man?

CRESSIDA O, a brave man!

PANDARUS Is 'a not? It does a man's heart good. Look you what hacks are on his helmet. Look you yonder, do you see? Look you there. There's no jesting; there's
196 laying on, take't off who will, as they say. There be hacks!

CRESSIDA Be those with swords?

PANDARUS Swords, anything; he cares not; an the devil come to him, it's all one. By God's lid, it does one's heart good.

Enter Paris [passing across the stage].

Yonder comes Paris, yonder comes Paris. Look ye
202 yonder, niece. Is't not a gallant man too, is't not? Why, this is brave now. Who said he came hurt home to-day? He's not hurt. Why, this will do Helen's heart good now, ha! Would I could see Troilus now. You shall see Troilus anon.

CRESSIDA Who's that?

Enter Helenus [passing across the stage].

PANDARUS That's Helenus. I marvel where Troilus is. That's Helenus. I think he went not forth to-day. That's Helenus.

210 CRESSIDA Can Helenus fight, uncle?

PANDARUS Helenus? No. Yes, he'll fight indifferent well. I marvel where Troilus is. Hark, do you not hear the people cry 'Troilus'? Helenus is a priest.

CRESSIDA What sneaking fellow comes yonder?

Enter Troilus [passing across the stage].

PANDARUS Where? Yonder? That's Deiphobus. 'Tis Troilus! There's a man, niece! Hem! Brave Troilus, the prince of chivalry!

CRESSIDA Peace, for shame, peace!

PANDARUS Mark him, note him. O brave Troilus! Look well upon him, niece. Look you how his sword is blood-ied, and his helm more hacked than Hector's; and how he looks, and how he goes. O admirable youth! he never saw three-and-twenty. Go thy way, Troilus, go thy
224 way! Had I a sister were a grace, or a daughter a god-dess, he should take his choice. O admirable man! Paris? Paris is dirt to him; and I warrant Helen, to change, would give an eye to boot.

[Enter Common Soldiers.]

CRESSIDA Here comes more.

PANDARUS Asses, fools, dolts; chaff and bran, chaff and bran; porridge after meat. I could live and die in the eyes of Troilus. Ne'er look, ne'er look. The eagles are gone; crows and daws, crows and daws. I had rather be such a man as Troilus than Agamemnon and all Greece.

CRESSIDA There is amongst the Greeks Achilles, a better man than Troilus.

PANDARUS Achilles? A drayman, a porter, a very camel.

CRESSIDA Well, well.

PANDARUS 'Well, well'? Why, have you any discretion, have you any eyes, do you know what a man is? Is not birth, beauty, good shape, discourse, manhood, learn-ing, gentleness, virtue, youth, liberality, and such like, the spice and salt that season a man?

CRESSIDA Ay, a minced man; and then to be baked with 243 no date in the pie, for then the man's date is out.

PANDARUS You are such a woman a man knows not at what ward you lie. 246

CRESSIDA Upon my back, to defend my belly; upon my wit, to defend my wiles; upon my secrecy, to defend mine honesty; my mask, to defend my beauty; and you, 249 to defend all these: and at all these wards I lie, at a thousand watches.

PANDARUS Say one of your watches. 252

CRESSIDA Nay, I'll watch you for that; and that's one of the chiefest of them too. If I cannot ward what I would not have hit, I can watch you for telling how I took the 255 blow; unless it swell past hiding, and then it's past watching.

PANDARUS You are such another!

Enter [Troilus'] Boy.

BOY Sir, my lord would instantly speak with you.

PANDARUS Where?

BOY At your own house. There he unarms him.

PANDARUS Good boy, tell him I come. *[Exit Boy.]* I doubt he be hurt. Fare ye well, good niece.

CRESSIDA Adieu, uncle.

PANDARUS I will be with you, niece, by and by.

CRESSIDA To bring, uncle? 265

PANDARUS Ay, a token from Troilus.

CRESSIDA By the same token, you are a bawd.

[Exit Pandarus.]

Words, vows, gifts, tears, and love's full sacrifice
He offers in another's enterprise;
But more in Troilus thousandfold I see
Than in the glass of Pandar's praise may be.
Yet hold I off: women are angels, wooing; 272
Things won are done, joy's soul lies in the doing.
That she beloved knows nought that knows not this:
Men prize the thing ungained more than it is; 275
That she was never yet, that ever knew
Love got so sweet as when desire did sue. 277
Therefore this maxim out of love I teach: 278
Achievement is command; ungained, beseech. 279
Then, though my heart's content firm love doth bear,
Nothing of that shall from mine eyes appear.

Exit.

*

182 *proper* good-looking   185 *nod* (quibble on 'noddy,' simpleton) 187 *the rich . . . more* the simple-minded will become simpler   196 *laying on* fighting; *take't off who will* i.e. regardless of circumstances ('take off' being a proverbial tag to 'lay on')   202 *gallant* (a general epithet of praise) 210 *Can Helenus fight* i.e. being a priest   224 *grace* subordinate and attendant goddess   243 *minced* simpering   246 *ward* posture of defense (fencing term)   249 *honesty* chastity   252 *watches* i.e. at night   255 *watch you* i.e. make sure that you do not tell (this passage fully establishes Cressida's moral level)   265 *bring* get even   272 *wooing* while being wooed   275 *it is* its value   277 *got* i.e. by men   278 *out of love* as taught by love   279 *Achievement . . . beseech* having achieved love, men command; when trying to gain it, they beseech

I, iii   *[Sennet.] Enter Agamemnon, Nestor, Ulysses,*
         Diomedes, Menelaus, with others.

AGAMEMNON
    Princes,
    What grief hath set the jaundice on your cheeks?
    The ample proposition that hope makes
    In all designs begun on earth below
    Fails in the promised largeness. Checks and disasters
    Grow in the veins of actions highest reared,
7   As knots, by the conflux of meeting sap,
    Infects the sound pine and diverts his grain
9   Tortive and errant from his course of growth.
    Nor, princes, is it matter new to us
11 That we come short of our suppose so far
    That after seven years' siege yet Troy walls stand;
    Sith every action that hath gone before,
    Whereof we have record, trial did draw
15 Bias and thwart, not answering the aim
    And that unbodied figure of the thought
    That gave't surmisèd shape. Why then, you princes,
    Do you with cheeks abashed behold our works
    And call them shames, which are indeed nought else
    But the protractive trials of great Jove
    To find persistive constancy in men?
    The fineness of which metal is not found
    In Fortune's love; for then, the bold and coward,
24 The wise and fool, the artist and unread,
25 The hard and soft, seem all affined and kin.
    But, in the wind and tempest of her frown,
    Distinction, with a broad and powerful fan,
    Puffing at all, winnows the light away;
    And what hath mass or matter by itself
30 Lies rich in virtue and unmingled.
NESTOR
    With due observance of thy godlike seat,
    Great Agamemnon, Nestor shall apply
    Thy latest words. In the reproof of chance
    Lies the true proof of men. The sea being smooth,
    How many shallow bauble boats dare sail
    Upon her patient breast, making their way
    With those of nobler bulk?
38 But let the ruffian Boreas once enrage
39 The gentle Thetis, and anon behold
    The strong-ribbed bark through liquid mountains cut,
    Bounding between the two moist elements
42 Like Perseus' horse, where's then the saucy boat,
    Whose weak untimbered sides but even now
    Co-rivalled greatness? Either to harbor fled,
45 Or made a toast for Neptune. Even so
    Doth valor's show and valor's worth divide
    In storms of fortune. For in her ray and brightness

    The herd hath more annoyance by the breese   48
    Than by the tiger; but when the splitting wind
    Makes flexible the knees of knotted oaks,
    And flies fled under shade, why then the thing of courage,
    As roused with rage, with rage doth sympathize,
    And with an accent tuned in self-same key
    Returns to chiding fortune.   54
ULYSSES   Agamemnon,
    Thou great commander, nerves and bone of Greece,   55
    Heart of our numbers, soul and only spirit,
    In whom the tempers and the minds of all
    Should be shut up, hear what Ulysses speaks.   58
    Besides th' applause and approbation
    The which, *[to Agamemnon]* most mighty for thy place
        and sway,
        [To Nestor]
    And thou most reverend for thy stretched-out life,
    I give to both your speeches, which were such
    As Agamemnon and the hand of Greece
    Should hold up high in brass; and such again
    As venerable Nestor, hatched in silver,   65
    Should with a bond of air, strong as the axle-tree
    On which heaven rides, knit all the Greekish ears
    To his experienced tongue; yet let it please both,
    Thou great, and wise, to hear Ulysses speak.
[AGAMEMNON
    Speak, Prince of Ithaca; and be't of less expect
    That matter needless, of importless burden,
    Divide thy lips than we are confident,
    When rank Thersites opes his mastic jaws,   73
    We shall hear music, wit, and oracle.]
ULYSSES
    Troy, yet upon his basis, had been down,
    And the great Hector's sword had lacked a master,
    But for these instances.
    The specialty of rule hath been neglected;   78
    And look, how many Grecian tents do stand
    Hollow upon this plain, so many hollow factions.
    When that the general is not like the hive
    To whom the foragers shall all repair,
    What honey is expected? Degree being vizarded,   83
    Th' unworthiest shows as fairly in the mask.
    The heavens themselves, the planets, and this centre
    Observe degree, priority, and place,
    Insisture, course, proportion, season, form,   87
    Office, and custom, in all line of order.
    And therefore is the glorious planet Sol   89
    In noble eminence enthroned and sphered
    Amidst the other; whose med'cinable eye   91
    Corrects the influence of evil planets,   92
    And posts, like the commandment of a king,
    Sans check to good and bad. But when the planets
    In evil mixture to disorder wander,
    What plagues, and what portents, what mutiny,
    What raging of the sea, shaking of earth,
    Commotion in the winds, frights, changes, horrors,
    Divert and crack, rend and deracinate   99
    The unity and married calm of states
    Quite from their fixure? O, when degree is shaked,
    Which is the ladder of all high designs,
    The enterprise is sick. How could communities,
    Degrees in schools, and brotherhoods in cities,
    Peaceful commerce from dividable shores,
    The primogenity and due of birth,   106

I, iii The Grecian camp   s.d. *Sennet* a conventional sequence of trumpet
notes to indicate a procession   7 *conflux* flowing together   9 *Tortive
and errant* distorted and wandering   11 *suppose* expectation   15 *Bias and
thwart* to one side and crosswise   24 *artist* scholar in the liberal arts
25 *affined* in affinity   30 *unmingled* unalloyed   38 *Boreas* north wind
39 *Thetis* a Nereid or sea-maiden, mother of Achilles, here personifying
the sea   42 *Perseus' horse* the winged horse Pegasus, which sprang from
Medusa's blood after Perseus beheaded her   45 *toast* a piece of toast put
into liquor   48 *breese* gadfly   54 *Returns* answers back   55 *nerves* sinews
58 *shut up* gathered in   65 *hatched in silver* with silver lines in his hair
73 *mastic* abusive (from Greek 'scourge')   78 *specialty of rule* particular
rights of supreme authority   83 *Degree being vizarded* the hierarchy of
authority being hidden   87 *Insisture* regularity of position   89 *Sol* sun
91 *other* others   92 *influence* astrological effect   99 *deracinate* uproot
106 *primogenity* right of the eldest son to succeed

Prerogative of age, crowns, sceptres, laurels,
But by degree, stand in authentic place?
Take but degree away, untune that string,
And hark what discord follows. Each thing meets
111 In mere oppugnancy. The bounded waters
Should lift their bosoms higher than the shores
113 And make a sop of all this solid globe;
114 Strength should be lord of imbecility,
And the rude son should strike his father dead;
Force should be right, or rather right and wrong,
117 Between whose endless jar justice resides,
Should lose their names, and so should justice too;
119 Then everything include itself in power,
Power into will, will into appetite.
And appetite, an universal wolf,
So doubly seconded with will and power,
Must make perforce an universal prey
And last eat up himself. Great Agamemnon,
125 This chaos, when degree is suffocate,
Follows the choking.
127 And this neglection of degree it is
128 That by a pace goes backward with a purpose
It hath to climb. The general's disdained
By him one step below, he by the next,
That next by him beneath; so every step,
132 Exampled by the first pace that is sick
Of his superior, grows to an envious fever
Of pale and bloodless emulation:
And 'tis this fever that keeps Troy on foot,
Not her own sinews. To end a tale of length,
Troy in our weakness stands, not in her strength.

NESTOR
Most wisely hath Ulysses here discovered
The fever whereof all our power is sick.

AGAMEMNON
The nature of the sickness found, Ulysses,
What is the remedy?

ULYSSES
The great Achilles, whom opinion crowns
The sinew and the forehand of our host,
Having his ear full of his airy fame,
145 Grows dainty of his worth, and in his tent
Lies mocking our designs. With him Patroclus
Upon a lazy bed the livelong day
Breaks scurril jests,
And with ridiculous and silly action
(Which, slanderer, he imitation calls)
151 He pageants us. Sometime, great Agamemnon,
152 Thy topless deputation he puts on
And, like a strutting player, whose conceit
154 Lies in his hamstring, and doth think it rich
To hear the wooden dialogue and sound
156 'Twixt his stretched footing and the scaffoldage,
Such to-be-pitied and o'er-wrested seeming
He acts thy greatness in; and when he speaks,
159 'Tis like a chime a-mending, with terms unsquared,
160 Which, from the tongue of roaring Typhon dropped,
Would seem hyperboles. At this fusty stuff
The large Achilles, on his pressed bed lolling,
From his deep chest laughs out a loud applause,
Cries, 'Excellent! 'tis Agamemnon right.
Now play me Nestor; hem, and stroke thy beard,
As he being drest to some oration.'
That's done, as near as the extremest ends

Of parallels, as like as Vulcan and his wife, 168
Yet god Achilles still cries, 'Excellent!
'Tis Nestor right. Now play him me, Patroclus,
Arming to answer in a night alarm.'
And then, forsooth, the faint defects of age
Must be the scene of mirth; to cough and spit,
And with a palsy fumbling on his gorget, 174
Shake in and out the rivet; and at this sport
Sir Valor dies; cries, 'O! enough, Patroclus,
Or give me ribs of steel; I shall split all
In pleasure of my spleen.' And in this fashion 178
All our abilities, gifts, natures, shapes,
Severals and generals of grace exact, 180
Achievements, plots, orders, preventions,
Excitements to the field or speech for truce,
Success or loss, what is or is not, serves
As stuff for these two to make paradoxes. 184

NESTOR
And in the imitation of these twain,
Who, as Ulysses says, opinion crowns
With an imperial voice, many are infect.
Ajax is grown self-willed, and bears his head
In such a rein, in full as proud a place 189
As broad Achilles; keeps his tent like him;
Makes factious feasts; rails on our state of war,
Bold as an oracle, and sets Thersites,
A slave whose gall coins slanders like a mint, 193
To match us in comparisons with dirt,
To weaken and discredit our exposure,
How rank soever rounded in with danger. 196

ULYSSES
They tax our policy and call it cowardice,
Count wisdom as no member of the war,
Forestall prescience, and esteem no act 199
But that of hand. The still and mental parts
That do contrive how many hands shall strike
When fitness calls them on, and know by measure
Of their observant toil the enemies' weight –
Why, this hath not a finger's dignity.
They call this bed-work, mapp'ry, closet-war; 205
So that the ram that batters down the wall,
For the great swinge and rudeness of his poise, 207
They place before his hand that made the engine,
Or those that with the fineness of their souls
By reason guide his execution.

NESTOR
Let this be granted, and Achilles' horse 211

---

111 *mere oppugnancy* total strife 113 *sop* pulp 114 *imbecility* weakness 117 *jar* collision 119 *include itself in* should confine itself within, i.e. convert itself into 125 *chaos* raw matter without form or order 127 *neglection* neglect 128–29 *by a pace … climb* step by step goes backward when it is trying to climb 132–33 *Exampled … superior* taking its example from the first step that someone takes against his superior 145 *dainty of* particular about 151 *pageants* acts or mimics 152 *topless deputation* supreme authority 154 *hamstring* tendon at the back of the knee 156 *scaffoldage* stage 159 *unsquared* unsuited 160 *Typhon* a monster with serpents' heads and a tremendous voice, overwhelmed by Zeus with thunderbolts 168 *Vulcan and his wife* (the beautiful Venus cuckolded Vulcan, who was lame and sooty, with Mars) 174 *gorget* throat armor 178 *spleen* (regarded as the seat of the emotions of anger and hilarity) 180 *Severals and generals* individual and common excellences 184 *paradoxes* absurdities 189 *In such a rein* so high 193 *gall* source of bile, a humor conducive to rancor 196 *rank* abundantly 199 *Forestall prescience* discount foresight 205 *mapp'ry* map-making 207 *swinge* impetus 211 *horse* (either literally or collectively for his horsemen, i.e. Myrmidons)

212 Makes many Thetis' sons.
Tucket.

AGAMEMNON
What trumpet? Look, Menelaus.

MENELAUS
From Troy.
Enter Aeneas.

AGAMEMNON
What would you 'fore our tent?

AENEAS
Is this great Agamemnon's tent, I pray you?

AGAMEMNON
Even this.

AENEAS
May one that is a herald and a prince
219 Do a fair message to his kingly eyes?

AGAMEMNON
With surety stronger than Achilles' arm
'Fore all the Greekish heads, which with one voice
Call Agamemnon head and general.

AENEAS
Fair leave and large security. How may
A stranger to those most imperial looks
Know them from eyes of other mortals?

AGAMEMNON   How?

AENEAS
Ay.
I ask, that I might waken reverence,
And bid the cheek be ready with a blush
Modest as morning when she coldly eyes
230 The youthful Phoebus,
Which is that god in office, guiding men?
Which is the high and mighty Agamemnon?

AGAMEMNON
This Troyan scorns us, or the men of Troy
Are ceremonious courtiers.

AENEAS
Courtiers as free, as debonair, unarmed,
As bending angels; that's their fame in peace.
But when they would seem soldiers, they have galls,
238 Good arms, strong joints, true swords; and, Jove's
    accord,
Nothing so full of heart. But peace, Aeneas;
Peace, Troyan; lay thy finger on thy lips.
The worthiness of praise distains his worth,
If that the praised himself bring the praise forth.
But what the repining enemy commends,
That breath fame blows; that praise, sole pure, trans-
    cends.

AGAMEMNON
Sir, you of Troy, call you yourself Aeneas?

AENEAS
Ay, Greek, that is my name.

AGAMEMNON
What's your affair, I pray you?

AENEAS
Sir, pardon; 'tis for Agamemnon's ears.

AGAMEMNON
He hears nought privately that comes from Troy.

AENEAS
Nor I from Troy come not to whisper him:
I bring a trumpet to awake his ear,
To set his seat on the attentive bent,   252
And then to speak.

AGAMEMNON   Speak frankly as the wind;
It is not Agamemnon's sleeping hour.
That thou shalt know, Troyan, he is awake,
He tells thee so himself.

AENEAS   Trumpet, blow loud,
Send thy brass voice through all these lazy tents;
And every Greek of mettle, let him know,
What Troy means fairly shall be spoke aloud.
Sound trumpet.
We have, great Agamemnon, here in Troy
A prince called Hector – Priam is his father –
Who in this dull and long-continued truce
Is rusty grown. He bade me take a trumpet,
And to this purpose speak: Kings, princes, lords,
If there be one among the fair'st of Greece
That holds his honor higher than his ease,
That seeks his praise more than he fears his peril,
That knows his valor and knows not his fear,
That loves his mistress more than in confession   269
With truant vows to her own lips he loves,
And dare avow her beauty and her worth
In other arms than hers – to him this challenge.
Hector, in view of Troyans and of Greeks,
Shall make it good, or do his best to do it,
He hath a lady wiser, fairer, truer,
Than ever Greek did compass in his arms;
And will to-morrow with his trumpet call,
Midway between your tents and walls of Troy,
To rouse a Grecian that is true in love.
If any come, Hector shall honor him;
If none, he'll say in Troy when he retires,
The Grecian dames are sunburnt and not worth   282
The splinter of a lance. Even so much.

AGAMEMNON
This shall be told our lovers, Lord Aeneas;
If none of them have soul in such a kind,
We left them all at home. But we are soldiers;
And may that soldier a mere recreant prove,
That means not, hath not, or is not in love!
If then one is, or hath, or means to be,
That one meets Hector; if none else, I am he.

NESTOR
Tell him of Nestor, one that was a man
When Hector's grandsire sucked. He is old now,
But if there be not in our Grecian host
A noble man that hath one spark of fire
To answer for his love, tell him from me,
I'll hide my silver beard in a gold beaver,   296
And in my vantbrace put this withered brawn,   297
And, meeting him, will tell him that my lady
Was fairer than his grandam, and as chaste
As may be in the world. His youth in flood,
I'll prove this troth with my three drops of blood.

AENEAS
Now heavens forfend such scarcity of youth!

ULYSSES
Amen.

---

212 **s.d.** *Tucket* preparatory signal on a trumpet   **219** *to . . . eyes* i.e. in his presence   **230** *Phoebus* Apollo, the sun god   **238** *Jove's accord* if Jove favor them, i.e. with God on their side   **252** *To set . . . bent* i.e. to make him sit up and take notice   **269–70** *more . . . loves* more than enough to swear false vows that he loves her   **282** *sunburnt* dark, i.e. ugly   **296** *beaver* face-guard of a helmet   **297** *vantbrace* armor for the forearm

AGAMEMNON
For Lord Aeneas, let me touch your hand ;
To our pavilion shall I lead you first.
Achilles shall have word of this intent ;
So shall each lord of Greece, from tent to tent.
Yourself shall feast with us before you go,
And find the welcome of a noble foe.
              [Exeunt. Manent Ulysses and Nestor.]

ULYSSES
Nestor.

NESTOR
What says Ulysses ?

ULYSSES
312   I have a young conception in my brain ;
Be you my time to bring it to some shape.

NESTOR
What is 't ?

ULYSSES
[This 'tis :]
Blunt wedges rive hard knots ; the seeded pride
That hath to this maturity blown up
In rank Achilles, must or now be cropped
319   Or, shedding, breed a nursery of like evil
To overbulk us all.

NESTOR   Well, and how ?

ULYSSES
This challenge that the gallant Hector sends,
However it is spread in general name,
Relates in purpose only to Achilles.

NESTOR
True, the purpose is perspicuous as substance
325   Whose grossness little characters sum up ;
326   And, in the publication, make no strain
But that Achilles, were his brain as barren
As banks of Libya – though, Apollo knows,
'Tis dry enough – will with great speed of judgment,
Ay with celerity, find Hector's purpose
Pointing on him.

ULYSSES
And wake him to the answer, think you ?

NESTOR
Why, 'tis most meet. Who may you else oppose
That can from Hector bring his honor off,
If not Achilles ? Though 't be a sportful combat,
336   Yet in this trial much opinion dwells ;
For here the Troyans taste our dear'st repute
With their fin'st palate ; and trust to me, Ulysses,
339   Our imputation shall be oddly poised
340   In this vild action. For the success,
341   Although particular, shall give a scantling
342   Of good or bad unto the general ;
343   And in such indexes, although small pricks
To their subsequent volumes, there is seen
The baby figure of the giant mass
Of things to come at large. It is supposed
He that meets Hector issues from our choice ;
And choice, being mutual act of all our souls,
349   Makes merit her election, and doth boil,
As 'twere from forth us all, a man distilled
Out of our virtues ; who miscarrying,
What heart receives from hence a conquering part,
To steel a strong opinion to themselves !
354   [Which entertained, limbs are his instruments,

In no less working than are swords and bows
Directive by the limbs.]

ULYSSES
Give pardon to my speech : therefore 'tis meet
Achilles meet not Hector. Let us, like merchants,
First show foul wares, and think perchance they'll sell ;
If not, the lustre of the better shall exceed
By showing the worse first. Do not consent
That ever Hector and Achilles meet ;
For both our honor and our shame in this
Are dogged with two strange followers.   364

NESTOR
I see them not with my old eyes. What are they ?

ULYSSES
What glory our Achilles shares from Hector,
Were he not proud, we all should share with him.
But he already is too insolent,
And we were better parch in Afric sun
Than in the pride and salt scorn of his eyes,   370
Should he 'scape Hector fair. If he were foiled,
Why then we did our main opinion crush   372
In taint of our best man. No, make a lott'ry ;
And by device let blockish Ajax draw
The sort to fight with Hector ; among ourselves
Give him allowance for the better man,
For that will physic the great Myrmidon   377
Who broils in loud applause, and make him fall   378
His crest that prouder than blue Iris bends.   379
If the dull brainless Ajax comes safe off,
We'll dress him up in voices ; if he fail,
Yet go we under our opinion still
That we have better men. But, hit or miss,
Our project's life this shape of sense assumes :
Ajax employed plucks down Achilles' plumes.

NESTOR
Now, Ulysses, I begin to relish thy advice,
And I will give a taste thereof forthwith
To Agamemnon. Go we to him straight.
Two curs shall tame each other ; pride alone
Must tarre the mastiffs on, as 'twere a bone.   *Exeunt.* 390

              *

        Enter Ajax and Thersites.   II, i

AJAX   Thersites !

THERSITES   Agamemnon, how if he had biles – full, all   2
over, generally ?

AJAX   Thersites !

THERSITES   And those biles did run ? – say so. Did not   5
the general run then ? Were not that a botchy core ?   6

AJAX   Dog !

312–13 *I have . . . shape* I have conceived a bright idea ; listen while I develop it   319 *shedding* i.e. scattering its seed   325 *grossness . . . up* great size little figures describe   326 *make no strain* have no difficulty in understanding   336 *opinion* reputation   339 *imputation* reputation ; *oddly poised* unequally balanced   340 *vild* trivial   341 *scantling* sample   342 *general* entire army   343–44 *small . . . volumes* small marks in comparison to the volumes that follow   349 *election* basis of choice   354 *his* its, i.e. the strong opinion's   364 *followers* consequences   370 *salt* bitter   372 *our main opinion* the chief source of our reputation   377 *Myrmidon* Achilles, son of Peleus, whose subjects, created by Zeus out of ants (myrmekes), were called Myrmidons   378 *broils* i.e. suns himself   379 *Iris* the rainbow   390 *tarre* incite to fight
II, i The Grecian camp   **2, 5** *biles* boils   **6** *botchy core* inflamed boil

THERSITES Then would come some matter from him. I see none now.

AJAX Thou bitch-wolf's son, canst thou not hear? Feel then.

[Strikes him.]

11 THERSITES The plague of Greece upon thee, thou mongrel beef-witted lord!

13 AJAX Speak then, thou vinewed'st leaven, speak. I will beat thee into handsomeness.

THERSITES I shall sooner rail thee into wit and holiness;
16 but I think thy horse will sooner con an oration than
17 thou learn a prayer without book. Thou canst strike,
18 canst thou? A red murrain o' thy jade's tricks!

19 AJAX Toadstool, learn me the proclamation.

THERSITES Dost thou think I have no sense, thou strikest me thus?

AJAX The proclamation!

THERSITES Thou art proclaimed fool, I think.

24 AJAX Do not, porpentine, do not; my fingers itch.

THERSITES I would thou didst itch from head to foot; an I had the scratching of thee, I would make thee the loathsomest scab in Greece. When thou art forth in the
28 incursions, thou strikest as slow as another.

AJAX I say, the proclamation!

THERSITES Thou grumblest and railest every hour on Achilles, and thou art as full of envy at his greatness as
32 Cerberus is at Proserpina's beauty, ay that thou bark'st at him.

AJAX Mistress Thersites!

THERSITES Thou shouldst strike him.

35 AJAX Cobloaf!

36 THERSITES He would pun thee into shivers with his fist, as a sailor breaks a biscuit.

AJAX You whoreson cur!

[Beating him.]

THERSITES Do, do.

AJAX Thou stool for a witch!

THERSITES Ay, do, do, thou sodden-witted lord! thou
42 hast no more brain than I have in mine elbows; an asinico may tutor thee. Thou scurvy-valiant ass, thou art here
44 but to thrash Troyans, and thou art bought and sold among those of any wit like a barbarian slave. If thou use to beat me, I will begin at thy heel, and tell what thou
47 art by inches, thou thing of no bowels, thou!

AJAX You dog!

THERSITES You scurvy lord!

AJAX You cur!

[Beating him.]

51 THERSITES Mars his idiot! Do, rudeness; do, camel; do, do.

[Enter Achilles and Patroclus.]

ACHILLES Why, how now, Ajax, wherefore do ye thus? How now, Thersites, what's the matter, man?

THERSITES You see him there, do you?

ACHILLES Ay, what's the matter?

THERSITES Nay, look upon him.

ACHILLES So I do. What's the matter?

THERSITES Nay, but regard him well.

ACHILLES 'Well' – why so I do.

THERSITES But yet you look not well upon him; for, whosomever you take him to be, he is Ajax.   61

ACHILLES I know that, fool.

THERSITES Ay, but that fool knows not himself.   63

AJAX Therefore I beat thee.

THERSITES Lo, lo, lo, lo, what modicums of wit he utters! His evasions have ears thus long. I have bobbed 66 his brain more than he has beat my bones. I will buy nine sparrows for a penny, and his pia mater is not 68 worth the ninth part of a sparrow. This lord, Achilles, Ajax, who wears his wit in his belly and his guts in his head, I'll tell you what I say of him.

ACHILLES What?

THERSITES I say, this Ajax –

[Ajax offers to strike him.]

ACHILLES Nay, good Ajax.

THERSITES Has not so much wit –

[Ajax again offers to strike him.]

ACHILLES Nay, I must hold you.

THERSITES As will stop the eye of Helen's needle, for whom he comes to fight.

ACHILLES Peace, fool!

THERSITES I would have peace and quietness, but the fool will not – he there, that he. Look you there.

AJAX O thou damned cur, I shall –

ACHILLES Will you set your wit to a fool's?   83

THERSITES No, I warrant you; the fool's will shame it.

PATROCLUS Good words, Thersites.

ACHILLES What's the quarrel?

AJAX I bade the vile owl go learn me the tenor of the proclamation, and he rails upon me.

THERSITES I serve thee not.

AJAX Well, go to, go to.

THERSITES I serve here voluntary.

ACHILLES Your last service was sufferance, 'twas not voluntary; no man is beaten voluntary. Ajax was here the voluntary, and you as under an impress.   94

THERSITES E'en so. A great deal of your wit, too, lies in your sinews, or else there be liars. Hector shall have a great catch if he knock out either of your brains. 'A were as good crack a fusty nut with no kernel.

ACHILLES What, with me too, Thersites?

THERSITES There's Ulysses and old Nestor, whose wit was mouldy ere your grandsires had nails on their toes, yoke you like draught-oxen and make you plough up the wars.

ACHILLES What, what?

THERSITES Yes, good sooth. To, Achilles; to, Ajax; to – 104

AJAX I shall cut out your tongue.

THERSITES 'Tis no matter; I shall speak as much as thou afterwards.

PATROCLUS No more words, Thersites; peace!

THERSITES I will hold my peace when Achilles' brach 109 bids me, shall I?

---

11 *plague of Greece* (probably an allusion to a plague sent by Apollo upon the Greek army) 13 *vinewed'st* most mouldy 16 *con* learn by heart 17 *without book* by heart 18 *murrain* plague; *jade's* broken-down horse's 19 *learn me* find out for me 24 *porpentine* porcupine 28 *incursions* attacks upon the Trojans 32 *Cerberus* watchdog of Hades; *Proserpina* a beautiful goddess carried off by Hades or Pluto for his bride 35 *Cobloaf* a crusty uneven loaf of bread 36 *pun* thumped 42 *asinico* little ass 44 *bought and sold* i.e. made sport of 47 *bowels* i.e. bowels of mercy 51 *Mars his* Mars's 61 *whosomever* whomsoever 63 *that fool* (Thersites pretends that Achilles said, 'I know that fool') 66 *have ears thus long* i.e. are those of an ass; *bobbed* thumped 68 *pia mater* (here the brain itself) 83 *set . . . fool's* match wits with a fool 94 *impress* (pun on impressment into military service) 104 *To . . . Ajax* (Achilles and Ajax are compared to horses being urged on by a driver) 109 *brach* bitch

ACHILLES There's for you, Patroclus.

112 THERSITES I will see you hanged, like clotpoles, ere I
come any more to your tents. I will keep where there is
wit stirring and leave the faction of fools.   *Exit.*

PATROCLUS A good riddance.

ACHILLES

116 Marry, this, sir, is proclaimed through all our host :
117 That Hector, by the fifth hour of the sun,
Will, with a trumpet, 'twixt our tents and Troy
To-morrow morning call some knight to arms
That hath a stomach, and such a one that dare
Maintain – I know not what ; 'tis trash. Farewell.

AJAX
Farewell ? Who shall answer him ?

ACHILLES
I know not. 'Tis put to lott'ry. Otherwise,
He knew his man.

AJAX
O, meaning you ? I will go learn more of it.   *[Exeunt.]*

*

II, ii   *Enter Priam, Hector, Troilus, Paris, and Helenus.*

PRIAM
After so many hours, lives, speeches spent,
Thus once again says Nestor from the Greeks :
'Deliver Helen, and all damage else,
As honor, loss of time, travail, expense,
Wounds, friends, and what else dear that is consumed
6 In hot digestion of this cormorant war,
Shall be struck off.' Hector, what say you to't ?

HECTOR
Though no man lesser fears the Greeks than I,
9 As far as toucheth my particular,
Yet, dread Priam,
There is no lady of more softer bowels,
More spongy to suck in the sense of fear,
More ready to cry out, 'Who knows what follows ?'
14 Than Hector is. The wound of peace is surety,
Surety secure ; but modest doubt is called
16 The beacon of the wise, the tent that searches
To th' bottom of the worst. Let Helen go.
Since the first sword was drawn about this question,
19 Every tithe soul, 'mongst many thousand dismes,
Hath been as dear as Helen ; I mean, of ours.
If we have lost so many tenths of ours
To guard a thing not ours nor worth to us,
Had it our name, the value of one ten,
What merit 's in that reason which denies
The yielding of her up ?

TROILUS   Fie, fie, my brother !
Weigh you the worth and honor of a king
So great as our dread father in a scale
28 Of common ounces ? Will you with counters sum
29 The past proportion of his infinite,
And buckle in a waist most fathomless
31 With spans and inches so diminutive
As fears and reasons ? Fie, for godly shame !

HELENUS
No marvel, though you bite so sharp at reasons,
You are so empty of them. Should not our father
Bear the great sway of his affairs with reason,
Because your speech hath none that tell him so ?

TROILUS
You are for dreams and slumbers, brother priest ;
You fur your gloves with reason. Here are your reasons : 38
You know an enemy intends you harm ;
You know a sword employed is perilous,
And reason flies the object of all harm.
Who marvels then, when Helenus beholds
A Grecian and his sword, if he do set
The very wings of reason to his heels
And fly like chidden Mercury from Jove,
Or like a star disorbed ? Nay, if we talk of reason, 46
Let's shut our gates and sleep. Manhood and honor
Should have hare-hearts, would they but fat their
    thoughts
With this crammed reason. Reason and respect
Make livers pale and lustihood deject. 50

HECTOR
Brother, she is not worth what she doth cost
The keeping.

TROILUS   What's aught but as 'tis valued ?

HECTOR
But value dwells not in particular will ; 53
It holds his estimate and dignity 54
As well wherein 'tis precious of itself
As in the prizer. 'Tis mad idolatry 56
To make the service greater than the god ;
And the will dotes that is attributive 58
To what infectiously itself affects, 59
Without some image of th' affected merit.

TROILUS
I take to-day a wife, and my election
Is led on in the conduct of my will –
My will enkindled by mine eyes and ears,
Two traded pilots 'twixt the dangerous shores 64
Of will and judgment. How may I avoid,
Although my will distaste what it elected,
The wife I chose ? There can be no evasion
To blench from this and to stand firm by honor. 68
We turn not back the silks upon the merchant
When we have soiled them, nor the remainder viands
We do not throw in unrespective sieve 71
Because we now are full. It was thought meet
Paris should do some vengeance on the Greeks.
Your breath with full consent bellied his sails ;
The seas and winds, old wranglers, took a truce
And did him service ; he touched the ports desired,
And for an old aunt whom the Greeks held captive 77
He brought a Grecian queen, whose youth and freshness
Wrinkles Apollo's and makes stale the morning.

112 *clotpoles* blockheads   116 *Marry* why, indeed (originally an oath by
the Virgin Mary)   117 *fifth hour* i.e. 11 a.m.
II, ii The palace of Priam   6 *cormorant* ravenous   9 *my particular* me
personally   14 *The . . . surety* our sense of security imperils peace   16
tent lint for probing wounds   19 *Every . . . dismes* every soul taken by
war as its tenth among many thousand such tenths   28 *counters* worthless
tokens used for counting   29 *The . . . infinite* his infinite greatness past
comparing by measurement   31 *spans* measures of nine inches   38 *fur . . .
reason* use reason in your speech as fur is used to ornament gloves or to
give them a soft, warm lining   46 *disorbed* thrown from its sphere   50
livers (regarded as seats of the passions)   53 *particular will* the individual's
inclination   54 *dignity* worth   56 *prizer* appraiser   58 *attributive* i.e.
subservient as is one who pays tribute   59–60 *To what . . . merit* to what
it inclines toward, as if diseased, without some idea of the value it is seeking
  64 *traded* experienced   68 *blench* shrink   71 *unrespective sieve* receptacle
which does not care what is put into it   77 *aunt* Hesione, Priam's sister
and mother of Ajax

Why keep we her ? The Grecians keep our aunt.
Is she worth keeping ? Why, she is a pearl
82   Whose price hath launched above a thousand ships
And turned crowned kings to merchants.
If you'll avouch 'twas wisdom Paris went –
As you must needs, for you all cried, 'Go, go' –
If you'll confess he brought home worthy prize –
As you must needs, for you all clapped your hands,
And cried, 'Inestimable !' – why do you now
89   The issue of your proper wisdoms rate,
And do a deed that never Fortune did,
91   Beggar the estimation which you prized
Richer than sea and land ? O theft most base,
That we have stol'n what we do fear to keep !
But thieves unworthy of a thing so stol'n,
95   That in their country did them that disgrace
96   We fear to warrant in our native place.
CASSANDRA [within]
97   Cry, Troyans, cry !
PRIAM   What noise ? what shriek is this ?
TROILUS
'Tis our mad sister. I do know her voice.
CASSANDRA [within]   Cry, Troyans !
HECTOR   It is Cassandra.
       Enter Cassandra raving [with her hair about her ears].
CASSANDRA
Cry, Troyans, cry ! Lend me ten thousand eyes,
And I will fill them with prophetic tears.
HECTOR
Peace, sister, peace !
CASSANDRA
Virgins and boys, mid-age and wrinkled elders,
Soft infancy, that nothing canst but cry,
Add to my clamors ! Let us pay betimes
107   A moiety of that mass of moan to come.
Cry, Troyans, cry ! Practise your eyes with tears !
Troy must not be, nor goodly Ilion stand ;
110   Our firebrand brother, Paris, burns us all.
Cry, Troyans, cry ! A Helen and a woe !
Cry, cry ! Troy burns, or else let Helen go.   Exit.
HECTOR
Now, youthful Troilus, do not these high strains
Of divination in our sister work
Some touches of remorse ? Or is your blood
So madly hot that no discourse of reason,
Nor fear of bad success in a bad cause,
Can qualify the same ?
TROILUS   Why, brother Hector,
We may not think the justness of each act
120   Such and no other than event doth form it,

Nor once deject the courage of our minds
Because Cassandra 's mad. Her brainsick raptures   122
Cannot distaste the goodness of a quarrel   123
Which hath our several honors all engaged
To make it gracious. For my private part,
I am no more touched than all Priam's sons ;
And Jove forbid there should be done amongst us
Such things as might offend the weakest spleen   128
To fight for and maintain.
PARIS
Else might the world convince of levity   130
As well my undertakings as your counsels ;
But I attest the gods, your full consent
Gave wings to my propension and cut off   133
All fears attending on so dire a project.
For what, alas, can these my single arms ?
What propugnation is in one man's valor   136
To stand the push and enmity of those
This quarrel would excite ? Yet, I protest,
Were I alone to pass the difficulties,   139
And had as ample power as I have will,
Paris should ne'er retract what he hath done
Nor faint in the pursuit.
PRIAM   Paris, you speak
Like one besotted on your sweet delights.
You have the honey still, but these the gall ;
So to be valiant is no praise at all.
PARIS
Sir, I propose not merely to myself
The pleasures such a beauty brings with it ;
But I would have the soil of her fair rape   148
Wiped off in honorable keeping her.
What treason were it to the ransacked queen,   150
Disgrace to your great worths, and shame to me,
Now to deliver her possession up
On terms of base compulsion ! Can it be
That so degenerate a strain as this
Should once set footing in your generous bosoms ?   155
There's not the meanest spirit on our party
Without a heart to dare or sword to draw
When Helen is defended, nor none so noble
Whose life were ill bestowed or death unfamed
Where Helen is the subject. Then, I say,
Well may we fight for her, whom we know well
The world's large spaces cannot parallel.
HECTOR
Paris and Troilus, you have both said well ;
And on the cause and question now in hand
Have glozed, but superficially ; not much   165
Unlike young men, whom Aristotle thought
Unfit to hear moral philosophy.   167
The reasons you allege do more conduce
To the hot passion of distemp'red blood
Than to make up a free determination
'Twixt right and wrong, for pleasure and revenge
Have ears more deaf than adders to the voice   172
Of any true decision. Nature craves
All dues be rend'red to their owners. Now,
What nearer debt in all humanity
Than wife is to the husband ? If this law
Of nature be corrupted through affection,   177
And that great minds, of partial indulgence   178
To their benumbèd wills, resist the same,   179
There is a law in each well-ordered nation

---

82 *Whose . . . ships* (cf. Marlowe, 'Was this the face that launched a thousand ships?')   89 *your . . . rate* your own wisdom condemn   91 *estimation* thing esteemed   95 *disgrace* i.e. the rape of Helen   96 *warrant* justify by defense   97 *Cassandra* (when she resisted the love of Apollo, he nullified his former gift of prophecy by causing her never to be believed)   107 *moiety* part   110 *firebrand* (his mother dreamed that she was delivered of a firebrand when Paris was born)   120 *event* outcome   122 *raptures* prophetic seizures   123 *distaste* make distasteful   128 *spleen* temper   130 *convince* convict   133 *propension* inclination   136 *propugnation* defense   139 *pass* undergo   148 *rape* carrying off   150 *ransacked* carried off   155 *generous* of noble birth, and therefore of noble nature   165 *glozed* commented, glossed   167 *moral* (Aristotle wrote 'political,' but Shakespeare's 'moral' is paralleled in contemporary translations of the passage)   172 *more deaf than adders* (cf. Psalms lviii, 4–5)   177 *affection* movement of appetite   178 *partial* favoring   179 *benumbèd* hypnotized by appetite and insensitive to reason

To curb those raging appetites that are
Most disobedient and refractory.
If Helen, then, be wife to Sparta's king,
As it is known she is, these moral laws
Of nature and of nations speak aloud
To have her back returned. Thus to persist
187 In doing wrong extenuates not wrong,
But makes it much more heavy. Hector's opinion
Is this in way of truth; yet ne'ertheless,
190 My spritely brethren, I propend to you
In resolution to keep Helen still;
For 'tis a cause that hath no mean dependence
Upon our joint and several dignities.

TROILUS
Why, there you touched the life of our design.
Were it not glory that we more affected
196 Than the performance of our heaving spleens,
I would not wish a drop of Troyan blood
Spent more in her defense. But, worthy Hector,
She is a theme of honor and renown,
A spur to valiant and magnanimous deeds,
Whose present courage may beat down our foes
And fame in time to come canonize us;
For I presume brave Hector would not lose
So rich advantage of a promised glory
As smiles upon the forehead of this action
For the wide world's revenue.

HECTOR   I am yours,
You valiant offspring of great Priamus.
208 I have a roisting challenge sent amongst
The dull and factious nobles of the Greeks
Will strike amazement to their drowsy spirits.
211 I was advertised their great general slept
212 Whilst emulation in the army crept.
This, I presume, will wake him.   *Exeunt.*

*

II, iii   *Enter Thersites solus.*
THERSITES How now, Thersites? What, lost in the laby-
2   rinth of thy fury? Shall the elephant Ajax carry it thus?
He beats me, and I rail at him. O worthy satisfaction!
Would it were otherwise – that I could beat him, whilst
5   he railed at me. 'Sfoot, I'll learn to conjure and raise
6   devils, but I'll see some issue of my spiteful execrations.
Then there's Achilles, a rare enginer. If Troy be not
taken till these two undermine it, the walls will stand till
they fall of themselves. O thou great thunder-darter of
Olympus, forget that thou art Jove, the king of gods;
11   and, Mercury, lose all the serpentine craft of thy caduceus, if ye take not that little, little, less than little wit from
them that they have; which short-armed ignorance itself knows is so abundant scarce it will not in circumvention deliver a fly from a spider, without drawing their
massy irons and cutting the web. After this, the ven-
17   geance on the whole camp! or, rather, the Neapolitan
bone-ache, for that, methinks, is the curse depending on
19   those that war for a placket. I have said my prayers, and
devil Envy say 'Amen.' What ho, my Lord Achilles!
    Enter Patroclus.
PATROCLUS Who's there? Thersites? Good Thersites,
come in and rail.
THERSITES If I could 'a' remembered a gilt counterfeit,
24   thou wouldst not have slipped out of my contemplation.

But it is no matter; thyself upon thyself! The common
curse of mankind, folly and ignorance, be thine in great
revenue. Heaven bless thee from a tutor, and discipline 27
come not near thee. Let thy blood be thy direction till 28
thy death. Then, if she that lays thee out says thou art a
fair corse, I'll be sworn and sworn upon't she never
shrouded any but lazars. Amen. Where's Achilles?   31
PATROCLUS What, art thou devout? Wast thou in
prayer?
THERSITES Ay; the heavens hear me!
PATROCLUS Amen.
    Enter Achilles.
ACHILLES Who's there?
PATROCLUS Thersites, my lord.
ACHILLES Where, where, O, where? Art thou come?
Why, my cheese, my digestion, why hast thou not
served thyself in to my table so many meals? Come,
what's Agamemnon?
THERSITES Thy commander, Achilles. Then tell me,
Patroclus, what's Achilles?
PATROCLUS Thy lord, Thersites. Then tell me, I pray
thee, what's thyself?
THERSITES Thy knower, Patroclus. Then tell me, Pat-
roclus, what art thou?
PATROCLUS Thou must tell that knowest.
ACHILLES O tell, tell.
THERSITES I'll decline the whole question. Agamemnon 49
commands Achilles, Achilles is my lord, I am Patroclus'
knower, and Patroclus is a fool.
[PATROCLUS You rascal!
THERSITES Peace, fool! I have not done.
ACHILLES He is a privileged man. Proceed, Thersites.
THERSITES Agamemnon is a fool, Achilles is a fool, Ther-
sites is a fool, and, as aforesaid, Patroclus is a fool.]
ACHILLES Derive this; come.
THERSITES Agamemnon is a fool to offer to command
Achilles, Achilles is a fool to be commanded of Aga-
memnon, Thersites is a fool to serve such a fool, and
this Patroclus is a fool positive.
PATROCLUS Why am I a fool?
THERSITES Make that demand of the Creator. It suffices
me thou art. Look you, who comes here?
    Enter [at a distance] Agamemnon, Ulysses, Nestor,
    Diomedes, Ajax, and Calchas.
ACHILLES Come, Patroclus, I'll speak with nobody.
Come in with me, Thersites.   *Exit.*
THERSITES Here is such patchery, such juggling, and 67
such knavery. All the argument is a whore and a cuck-
old, a good quarrel to draw emulous factions and bleed
to death upon. [Now, the dry serpigo on the subject, 70
and war and lechery confound all!]   *[Exit.]*
AGAMEMNON Where is Achilles?
PATROCLUS
Within his tent, but ill-disposed, my lord.

187 *extenuates* lessens 190 *spritely* spirited; *propend* incline 196 *heaving*
spleens aroused passions 208 *roisting* roistering 211 *advertised* informed
212 *emulation* quarrelsome rivalry
II, iii Before the tent of Achilles 2 *carry it* carry off the honors 5
'*Sfoot* God's foot 6 *but I'll see* rather than not see 11 *caduceus* Mercury's
staff of office, twined with snakes 17–18 *Neapolitan bone-ache* syphilis
19 *placket* petticoat, i.e. woman 24 *slipped* (pun on 'slip,' a counterfeit coin of brass covered with silver or gold) 27 *bless* save 28 *blood*
violent passion 31 *lazars* lepers 49 *decline* go through (as in declining
a noun) 67 *patchery* roguery 70 *serpigo* impetigo or similar skin
eruption

AGAMEMNON
Let it be known to him that we are here.
75 He shent our messengers, and we lay by
76 Our appertainings, visiting of him.
Let him be told so, lest perchance he think
78 We dare not move the question of our place
Or know not what we are.

PATROCLUS   I shall so say to him.   *[Exit.]*

ULYSSES We saw him at the opening of his tent. He is not
sick.

AJAX Yes, lion-sick, sick of proud heart. You may call it
melancholy if you will favor the man ; but, by my head,
'tis pride. But why, why ? Let him show us a cause. [A
word, my lord.]
    [Takes Agamemnon aside.]

NESTOR What moves Ajax thus to bay at him ?

ULYSSES Achilles hath inveigled his fool from him.

NESTOR Who, Thersites ?

ULYSSES He.

90 NESTOR Then will Ajax lack matter, if he have lost his argument.

ULYSSES No, you see, he is his argument that has his
argument, Achilles.

94 NESTOR All the better ; their fraction is more our wish
95 than their faction. But it was a strong composure a fool
could disunite.

ULYSSES The amity that wisdom knits not, folly may
easily untie.
    [Enter Patroclus.]
Here comes Patroclus.

NESTOR No Achilles with him ?

ULYSSES
The elephant hath joints, but none for courtesy.
102 His legs are legs for necessity, not for flexure.

PATROCLUS
Achilles bids me say, he is much sorry
If anything more than your sport and pleasure
105 Did move your greatness and this noble state
To call upon him ; he hopes it is no other
But, for your health and your digestion sake,
108 An after-dinner's breath.

AGAMEMNON   Hear you, Patroclus.
We are too well acquainted with these answers ;
But his evasion, winged thus swift with scorn,
Cannot outfly our apprehensions.
Much attribute he hath, and much the reason
Why we ascribe it to him ; yet all his virtues,
114 Not virtuously on his own part beheld,
Do in our eyes begin to lose their gloss,
Yea, like fair fruit in an unwholesome dish,
Are like to rot untasted. Go and tell him,
We come to speak with him ; and you shall not sin

If you do say we think him over-proud
And under-honest, in self-assumption greater   120
Than in the note of judgment ; and worthier than   121
himself
Here tend the savage strangeness he puts on,   122
Disguise the holy strength of their command,   123
And underwrite in an observing kind
His humorous predominance ; yea, watch
His course and time, his ebbs and flows, as if
The passage and whole carriage of this action
Rode on his tide. Go tell him this, and add
That, if he overhold his price so much,   129
We'll none of him ; but let him, like an engine   130
Not portable, lie under this report :
'Bring action hither, this cannot go to war.'
A stirring dwarf we do allowance give   133
Before a sleeping giant. Tell him so.

PATROCLUS
I shall, and bring his answer presently.   *[Exit.]*

AGAMEMNON
In second voice we'll not be satisfied ;
We come to speak with him. Ulysses, enter you.
    [Exit Ulysses.]

AJAX What is he more than another ?

AGAMEMNON No more than what he thinks he is.

AJAX Is he so much ? Do you not think he thinks himself a
better man than I am ?

AGAMEMNON No question.

AJAX Will you subscribe his thought, and say he is ?

AGAMEMNON No, noble Ajax ; you are as strong, as
valiant, as wise, no less noble, much more gentle, and
altogether more tractable.

AJAX Why should a man be proud ? How doth pride
grow ? I know not what pride is.

AGAMEMNON Your mind is the clearer and your virtues
the fairer. He that is proud eats up himself. Pride is his
own glass, his own trumpet, his own chronicle ; and   151
whatever praises itself but in the deed, devours the
deed in the praise.

AJAX I do hate a proud man, as I do hate the engendering
of toads.

NESTOR *[aside]* And yet he loves himself. Is't not strange ?
    Enter Ulysses.

ULYSSES
Achilles will not to the field to-morrow.

AGAMEMNON
What's his excuse ?

ULYSSES   He doth rely on none,
But carries on the stream of his dispose   158
Without observance or respect of any,
In will peculiar and in self-admission.   160

AGAMEMNON
Why will he not upon our fair request
Untent his person and share th' air with us ?

ULYSSES
Things small as nothing, for request's sake only,   163
He makes important. Possessed he is with greatness,
And speaks not to himself but with a pride
That quarrels at self-breath. Imagined worth   166
Holds in his blood such swoln and hot discourse
That 'twixt his mental and his active parts
Kingdomed Achilles in commotion rages   169
And batters down himself. What should I say ?
He is so plaguy proud that the death-tokens of it   171

---

75 *shent* reviled   76 *appertainings* rights of rank   78 *move . . . place* raise
the question of our authority   90 *argument* subject matter   94 *fraction*
break   95 *faction* union; *composure* union   102 *flexure* bending   105
state accompanying noblemen   108 *breath* exercise   114 *Not . . . beheld*
not modestly borne   120 *under-honest* lacking in open dealing   121
note of judgment esteem of men of judgment   122 *tend . . . strangeness*
wait upon the rude aloofness   123–25 *Disguise . . . predominance* hide
their god-given authority and acquiesce obediently in his eccentric claim to
superiority   129 *overhold* overvalue   130 *engine* mechanical contrivance
(here military)   133 *allowance* approbation , 151 *glass* mirror   158 *dispose*
bent of mind   160 *self-admission* self-approval   163 *for . . . only* only
because they are requested   166 *That . . . self-breath* that quarrels with
itself for speaking   169 *Kingdomed* i.e. Achilles is like a kingdom in
civil war   171 *death-tokens* symptoms of the plague on the body

Cry 'No recovery.'

AGAMEMNON   Let Ajax go to him.
Dear lord, go you and greet him in his tent:
'Tis said he holds you well, and will be led
At your request a little from himself.

ULYSSES
O Agamemnon, let it not be so!
We'll consecrate the steps that Ajax makes
When they go from Achilles. Shall the proud lord
179   That bastes his arrogance with his own seam
And never suffers matter of the world
Enter his thoughts, save such as doth revolve
And ruminate himself, shall he be worshipped
Of that we hold an idol more than he?
No, this thrice-worthy and right valiant lord
185   Shall not so stale his palm, nobly acquired,
186   Nor, by my will, assubjugate his merit,
As amply titled as Achilles' is,
By going to Achilles.
That were to enlard his fat-already pride,
190   And add more coals to Cancer when he burns
191   With entertaining great Hyperion.
This lord go to him! Jupiter forbid,
And say in thunder, 'Achilles, go to him.'

NESTOR [aside]
194   O, this is well. He rubs the vein of him.

DIOMEDES [aside]
And how his silence drinks up his applause!

AJAX
If I go to him, with my armèd fist
197   I'll pash him o'er the face.

AGAMEMNON
O, no! you shall not go.

AJAX
199   An he be proud with me, I'll pheese his pride.
Let me go to him.

ULYSSES
Not for the worth that hangs upon our quarrel.

AJAX   A paltry, insolent fellow!

NESTOR [aside]   How he describes himself!

AJAX   Can he not be sociable?

ULYSSES [aside]   The raven chides blackness.
206   AJAX   I'll let his humorous blood.

AGAMEMNON [aside]   He will be the physician that should
be the patient.

AJAX   An all men were of my mind –

ULYSSES [aside]   Wit would be out of fashion.
211   AJAX   'A should not bear it so, 'a should eat swords first.
Shall pride carry it?

NESTOR [aside]   An 'twould, you'd carry half.

ULYSSES [aside]   'A would have ten shares.

AJAX   I will knead him; I'll make him supple.
216   NESTOR [aside]   He's not yet through warm. Force him
with praises; pour in, pour in; his ambition is dry.

ULYSSES [to Agamemnon]
My lord, you feed too much on this dislike.

NESTOR
Our noble general, do not do so.

DIOMEDES
You must prepare to fight without Achilles.

ULYSSES
Why, 'tis this naming of him does him harm.
Here is a man – but 'tis before his face;
I will be silent.

NESTOR   Wherefore should you so?
He is not emulous, as Achilles is.   224

ULYSSES
Know the whole world, he is as valiant –

AJAX
A whoreson dog, that shall palter with us thus!   226
Would he were a Troyan!

NESTOR   What a vice were it in Ajax now –

ULYSSES   If he were proud –

DIOMEDES   Or covetous of praise –

ULYSSES   Ay, or surly borne –

DIOMEDES   Or strange, or self-affected!   232

ULYSSES
Thank the heavens, lord, thou art of sweet composure;
Praise him that got thee, she that gave thee suck;
Famed be thy tutor, and thy parts of nature
Thrice-famed beyond all erudition;   236
But he that disciplined thine arms to fight,
Let Mars divide eternity in twain
And give him half; and, for thy vigor,
Bull-bearing Milo his addition yield   240
To sinewy Ajax. I will not praise thy wisdom,
Which, like a bourn, a pale, a shore, confines   242
Thy spacious and dilated parts. Here's Nestor,
Instructed by the antiquary times,   244
He must, he is, he cannot but be wise;
But pardon, father Nestor, were your days
As green as Ajax, and your brain so tempered,
You should not have the eminence of him,
But be as Ajax.

AJAX   Shall I call you father?

NESTOR
Ay, my good son.

DIOMEDES   Be ruled by him, Lord Ajax.

ULYSSES
There is no tarrying here; the hart Achilles
Keeps thicket. Please it our great general
To call together all his state of war;   253
Fresh kings are come to Troy. To-morrow,
We must with all our main of power stand fast.   255
And here's a lord – come knights from east to west,
And cull their flower, Ajax shall cope the best.

AGAMEMNON
Go we to council. Let Achilles sleep:
Light boats sail swift, though greater hulks draw deep.
          Exeunt.

          *

[Music sounds within.] Enter Pandarus [and a   III, i
Servant].

PANDARUS   Friend you, pray you a word. Do you not follow the young Lord Paris?

SERVANT   Ay, sir, when he goes before me.

PANDARUS   You depend upon him, I mean.   4

179 *seam* fat   185 *stale his palm* sully his glory   186 *assubjugate* debase
190 *Cancer* i.e. summer, which begins under this sign of the Zodiac   191
Hyperion the sun   194 *vein* mood   197 *pash* batter   199 *pheese* settle the
matter of   206 *let . . . blood* cure his humors by letting blood   211 *'A* he
216 *through* thoroughly   224 *emulous* envious   226 *palter* dodge   232
strange, or self-affected distant or caring only for himself   236 *erudition*
knowledge   240 *Milo* a famous Greek athlete; *addition* i.e. his epithet
(*Bull-bearing*)   242 *bourn* boundary; *pale* fence   244 *antiquary* i.e. studied
by antiquaries   253 *state* nobles in council   255 *main* might of military power
III, i The palace of Priam   4 *depend* are in a position of dependence

SERVANT Sir, I do depend upon the Lord.

PANDARUS You depend upon a noble gentleman; I must needs praise him.

SERVANT The Lord be praised!

PANDARUS You know me, do you not?

SERVANT Faith, sir, superficially.

PANDARUS Friend, know me better. I am the Lord Pandarus.

SERVANT I hope I shall know your honor better.

PANDARUS I do desire it.

14 SERVANT You are in the state of grace.

15 PANDARUS Grace? Not so, friend. Honor and lordship are my titles. What music is this?

SERVANT I do but partly know, sir. It is music in parts.

PANDARUS Know you the musicians?

SERVANT Wholly, sir.

PANDARUS Who play they to?

SERVANT To the hearers, sir.

PANDARUS At whose pleasure, friend?

SERVANT At mine, sir, and theirs that love music.

PANDARUS Command, I mean, friend.

SERVANT Who shall I command, sir?

PANDARUS Friend, we understand not one another. I am too courtly, and thou too cunning. At whose request do these men play?

SERVANT That's to't, indeed, sir. Marry, sir, at the re-
30 quest of Paris, my lord, who is there in person; with him the mortal Venus, the heart-blood of beauty, love's invisible soul.

PANDARUS Who? My cousin Cressida?

SERVANT No, sir, Helen. Could you not find out that by her attributes?

PANDARUS It should seem, fellow, that thou hast not seen the Lady Cressid. I come to speak with Paris from the Prince Troilus. I will make a complimental assault
39 upon him, for my business seethes.

40 SERVANT Sodden business! There's a stewed phrase, indeed.

Enter Paris and Helen.

PANDARUS Fair be to you, my lord, and to all this fair company. Fair desires in all fair measure fairly guide
43 them. Especially to you, fair queen, fair thoughts be your fair pillow.

HELEN Dear lord, you are full of fair words.

PANDARUS You speak your fair pleasure, sweet queen.
47 Fair prince, here is good broken music.

PARIS You have broke it, cousin; and, by my life, you shall make it whole again; you shall piece it out with a piece of your performance. Nell, he is full of harmony.

PANDARUS Truly, lady, no.

HELEN O, sir!

PANDARUS Rude, in sooth; in good sooth, very rude.

54 PARIS Well said, my lord. Well, you say so in fits.

PANDARUS I have business to my lord, dear queen. My lord, will you vouchsafe me a word?

HELEN Nay, this shall not hedge us out. We'll hear you 57 sing, certainly.

PANDARUS Well, sweet queen, you are pleasant with me. But, marry, thus, my lord: my dear lord and most esteemed friend, your brother Troilus –

HELEN My Lord Pandarus, honey-sweet lord –

PANDARUS Go to, sweet queen, go to – commends himself most affectionately to you.

HELEN You shall not bob us out of our melody. If you do, 65 our melancholy upon your head!

PANDARUS Sweet queen, sweet queen; that's a sweet queen, i' faith.

HELEN And to make a sweet lady sad is a sour offense.

PANDARUS Nay, that shall not serve your turn; that shall it not, in truth, la. Nay, I care not for such words; no, no. And, my lord, he desires you that, if the king call for him at supper, you will make his excuse.

HELEN My Lord Pandarus –

PANDARUS What says my sweet queen, my very, very sweet queen?

PARIS What exploit's in hand? Where sups he to-night?

HELEN Nay, but my lord –

PANDARUS What says my sweet queen? My cousin will fall out with you.

HELEN You must not know where he sups.

PARIS I'll lay my life, with my disposer Cressida. 82

PANDARUS No, no; no such matter; you are wide. Come, 83 your disposer is sick.

PARIS Well, I'll make excuse.

PANDARUS Ay, good my lord. Why should you say Cressida? No, your poor disposer's sick.

PARIS I spy.

PANDARUS You spy? What do you spy? Come, give me an instrument now, sweet queen.

HELEN Why, this is kindly done.

PANDARUS My niece is horribly in love with a thing you have, sweet queen.

HELEN She shall have it, my lord, if it be not my Lord Paris.

PANDARUS He? No, she'll none of him; they two are twain. 95

HELEN Falling in, after falling out, may make them three.

PANDARUS Come, come, I'll hear no more of this. I'll sing you a song now.

HELEN Ay, ay, prithee. Now by my troth, sweet lord, thou hast a fine forehead.

PANDARUS Ay, you may, you may. 101

HELEN Let thy song be love. This love will undo us all. O Cupid, Cupid, Cupid!

PANDARUS Love! ay, that it shall, i' faith.

PARIS Ay, good, now 'Love, love, nothing but love.'

PANDARUS [In good troth, it begins so:]
    [Sings.]
Love, love, nothing but love, still love still more!
For, O, love's bow shoots buck and doe.
The shaft confounds not that it wounds,
But tickles still the sore. 110
These lovers cry, O ho! they die!
Yet that which seems the wound to kill
Doth turn O ho! to Ha, ha, he!
So dying love lives still.
O ho! a while, but Ha, ha, ha!
O ho! groans out for Ha, ha, ha! – Heigh ho!

HELEN In love, i' faith, to the very tip of the nose.

---

14 *You . . . grace* (he pretends that Pandarus meant 'I desire to be better')
15 *Grace* the title of a duke, etc.   39 *seethes* is at full boil, i.e. in haste
40 *stewed* (1) boiled, (2) pertaining to stews (brothels)   43 *queen* possible quibble on 'quean': slut (Helen was queen to Menelaus, not to Paris)
47 *broken music* music by a group of different instruments   54 *fits* parts of a song   57 *hedge* shut   65 *bob* cheat   82 *my disposer* i.e. who manages me   83 *wide* wide of the mark   95 *twain* at odds   101 *you may* i.e. have your joke   110 *sore* wound, or buck of fourth year

PARIS He eats nothing but doves, love, and that breeds
     hot blood, and hot blood begets hot thoughts, and hot
120   thoughts beget hot deeds, and hot deeds is love.

PANDARUS Is this the generation of love – hot blood, hot
     thoughts, and hot deeds? Why, they are vipers. Is love a
     generation of vipers? Sweet lord, who's a-field to-day?

PARIS Hector, Deiphobus, Helenus, Antenor, and all the
     gallantry of Troy. I would fain have armed to-day, but
     my Nell would not have it so. How chance my brother
     Troilus went not?

HELEN He hangs the lip at something. You know all,
     Lord Pandarus.

130 PANDARUS Not I, honey-sweet queen. I long to hear how
     they sped to-day. You'll remember your brother's ex-
     cuse?

PARIS To a hair.

PANDARUS Farewell, sweet queen.

HELEN Commend me to your niece.

PANDARUS I will, sweet queen.   *[Exit.] Sound a retreat.*

PARIS
     They're come from the field. Let us to Priam's hall
     To greet the warriors. Sweet Helen, I must woo you
     To help unarm our Hector. His stubborn buckles,
     With these your white enchanting fingers touched,
     Shall more obey than to the edge of steel
     Or force of Greekish sinews. You shall do more
143   Than all the island kings – disarm great Hector.

HELEN
     'Twill make us proud to be his servant, Paris;
     Yea, what he shall receive of us in duty
     Gives us more palm in beauty than we have,
     Yea, overshines ourself.

PARIS
     Sweet, above thought I love thee.   *Exeunt.*

*

III, ii   *Enter Pandarus [and] Troilus' Man.*

PANDARUS How now, where's thy master? At my cousin
     Cressida's?

MAN No, sir; he stays for you to conduct him thither.
     [Enter Troilus.]

PANDARUS O, here he comes. How now, how now?

TROILUS Sirrah, walk off.   *[Exit Man.]*

PANDARUS Have you seen my cousin?

TROILUS
     No, Pandarus. I stalk about her door
8   Like a strange soul upon the Stygian banks
9   Staying for waftage. O, be thou my Charon,
     And give me swift transportance to those fields
     Where I may wallow in the lily-beds
12   Proposed for the deserver. O gentle Pandar,
     From Cupid's shoulder pluck his painted wings,
     And fly with me to Cressid.

PANDARUS
15   Walk here i' th' orchard. I'll bring her straight.   *[Exit.]*

TROILUS
     I am giddy; expectation whirls me round.
     Th' imaginary relish is so sweet
     That it enchants my sense. What will it be
19   When that the wat'ry palates taste indeed
     Love's thrice-repurèd nectar? Death, I fear me,
21   Sounding destruction, or some joy too fine,
     Too subtle, potent, tuned too sharp in sweetness
     For the capacity of my ruder powers.

     I fear it much; and I do fear besides
     That I shall lose distinction in my joys,   *25*
     As doth a battle, when they charge on heaps
     The enemy flying.
     [Enter Pandarus.]

PANDARUS She's making her ready; she'll come straight;
     you must be witty now. She does so blush, and fetches   *29*
     her wind so short as if she were frayed with a spirit. I'll   *30*
     fetch her. It is the prettiest villain; she fetches her   *31*
     breath as short as a new-ta'en sparrow.   *[Exit.]*

TROILUS
     Even such a passion doth embrace my bosom.
     My heart beats thicker than a feverous pulse,
     And all my powers do their bestowing lose,   *35*
     Like vassalage at unawares encount'ring   *36*
     The eye of majesty.
     Enter Pandarus and Cressida.

PANDARUS Come, come, what need you blush? Shame 's
     a baby. Here she is now; swear the oaths now to her that
     you have sworn to me. What! are you gone again? You
     must be watched ere you be made tame, must you?   *41*
     Come your ways, come your ways; an you draw back-
     ward, we'll put you i' th' fills. Why do you not speak to   *43*
     her? Come, draw this curtain, and let's see your picture.   *44*
     Alas the day, how loath you are to offend daylight! An
     'twere dark, you'd close sooner. So, so; rub on, and kiss   *46*
     the mistress. How now, a kiss in fee-farm! Build there,   *47*
     carpenter; the air is sweet. Nay, you shall fight your
     hearts out ere I part you. The falcon as the tercel, for all   *49*
     the ducks i' th' river. Go to, go to.

TROILUS You have bereft me of all words, lady.

PANDARUS Words pay no debts, give her deeds; but
     she'll bereave you o' th' deeds too if she call your activity
     in question. What, billing again? Here's 'In witness   *54*
     whereof the parties interchangeably' – Come in, come
     in. I'll go get a fire.   *[Exit.]*

CRESSIDA Will you walk in, my lord?

TROILUS O Cressid, how often have I wished me thus!

CRESSIDA Wished, my lord? The gods grant – O my lord!

TROILUS What should they grant? What makes this
     pretty abruption? What too curious dreg espies my   *61*
     sweet lady in the fountain of our love?

CRESSIDA More dregs than water, if my fears have eyes.

TROILUS Fears make devils of cherubins; they never see
     truly.

CRESSIDA Blind fear, that seeing reason leads, finds safer
     footing than blind reason stumbling without fear. To
     fear the worst oft cures the worse.

TROILUS O, let my lady apprehend no fear. In all Cupid's
     pageant there is presented no monster.

---

143 *island* i.e. Greek
III, ii Pandarus' orchard   8 *Stygian* (the Styx was a river of the underworld)   9 *waftage* passage by water; *Charon* ferryman of the dead across the
Styx to Hades   12 *Proposed* promised   15 *orchard* garden   19 *wat'ry*
watering (cf. 'mouth waters')   21 *Sounding* swooning   25 *distinction*
power of distinguishing   29 *be witty* have your wits about you   30 *frayed
with a spirit* frightened by a ghost   31 *villain* (a term of endearment here)
35 *bestowing* proper use   36 *vassalage* vassals   41 *watched* kept awake (a
method used in taming a hawk)   43 *fills* shafts   44 *curtain* i.e. veil
46–47 *rub . . . mistress* (in bowling, 'to rub' was to meet obstacles in the
way of the object-ball or 'mistress')   47 *in fee-farm* in perpetuity   49–50
The falcon . . . river i.e. I will bet on the falcon (female hawk, i.e. Cressida)
against the tercel (male hawk) to bring down any amount of game   54–55
In witness . . . interchangeably (a legal formula completed by the words
'have set their hands and seals')   61 *abruption* breaking off; *curious*
causing care or anxiety

70 CRESSIDA Nor nothing monstrous neither?

TROILUS Nothing but our undertakings when we vow to weep seas, live in fire, eat rocks, tame tigers, thinking it harder for our mistress to devise imposition enough than for us to undergo any difficulty imposed. This is the monstruosity in love, lady, that the will is infinite and the execution confined; that the desire is boundless and the act a slave to limit.

CRESSIDA They say all lovers swear more performance than they are able, and yet reserve an ability that they never perform, vowing more than the perfection of ten and discharging less than the tenth part of one. They that have the voice of lions and the act of hares, are they not monsters?

TROILUS Are there such? Such are not we. Praise us as
85 we are tasted, allow us as we prove; our head shall go
86 bare till merit crown it. No perfection in reversion shall have a praise in present; we will not name desert before his birth, and, being born, his addition shall be humble. Few words to fair faith. Troilus shall be such to Cressid,
90 as what envy can say worst shall be a mock for his truth, and what truth can speak truest not truer than Troilus.

CRESSIDA Will you walk in, my lord?

Enter Pandarus.

PANDARUS What, blushing still? Have you not done talking yet?

CRESSIDA Well, uncle, what folly I commit, I dedicate to you.

PANDARUS I thank you for that. If my lord get a boy of you, you'll give him me. Be true to my lord; if he flinch, chide me for it.

100 TROILUS You know now your hostages, your uncle's word and my firm faith.

PANDARUS Nay, I'll give my word for her too. Our kindred, though they be long ere they be wooed, they are constant being won. They are burrs, I can tell you; they'll stick where they are thrown.

CRESSIDA
Boldness comes to me now and brings me heart.
Prince Troilus, I have loved you night and day
For many weary months.

TROILUS
Why was my Cressid then so hard to win?

CRESSIDA
110 Hard to seem won; but I was won, my lord,
With the first glance that ever – pardon me:
If I confess much you will play the tyrant.
I love you now, but not, till now, so much
But I might master it. In faith, I lie;
My thoughts were like unbridled children grown
Too headstrong for their mother. See, we fools!
Why have I blabbed? Who shall be true to us
When we are so unsecret to ourselves?
But, though I loved you well, I wooed you not;
120 And yet, good faith, I wished myself a man,

Or that we women had men's privilege
Of speaking first. Sweet, bid me hold my tongue,
For in this rapture I shall surely speak
The thing I shall repent. See, see! your silence,
Cunning in dumbness, from my weakness draws
My very soul of counsel. Stop my mouth.   126

TROILUS
And shall, albeit sweet music issues thence.

PANDARUS Pretty, i' faith.

CRESSIDA
My lord, I do beseech you, pardon me;
'Twas not my purpose thus to beg a kiss.
I am ashamed. O heavens, what have I done?
For this time will I take my leave, my lord.

TROILUS
Your leave, sweet Cressid?

PANDARUS Leave! An you take leave till to-morrow morning –

CRESSIDA
Pray you, content you.

TROILUS   What offends you, lady?

CRESSIDA
Sir, mine own company.

TROILUS
You cannot shun yourself.

CRESSIDA
Let me go and try.
I have a kind of self resides with you;
But an unkind self, that itself will leave
To be another's fool. I would be gone.
Where is my wit? I know not what I speak.   142

TROILUS
Well know they what they speak that speak so wisely.

CRESSIDA
Perchance, my lord, I show more craft than love,
And fell so roundly to a large confession   146
To angle for your thoughts. But you are wise,   147
Or else you love not, for to be wise and love
Exceeds man's might; that dwells with gods above.

TROILUS
O! that I thought it could be in a woman –
As, if it can, I will presume in you –
To feed for aye her lamp and flames of love;
To keep her constancy in plight and youth,   153
Outliving beauty's outward, with a mind
That doth renew swifter than blood decays;
Or that persuasion could but thus convince me
That my integrity and truth to you
Might be affronted with the match and weight   158
Of such a winnowed purity in love;
How were I then uplifted! But, alas,
I am as true as truth's simplicity,
And simpler than the infancy of truth.

CRESSIDA
In that I'll war with you.

TROILUS   O virtuous fight,
When right with right wars who shall be most right!
True swains in love shall in the world to come
Approve their truth by Troilus. When their rhymes,   166
Full of protest, of oath, and big compare,
Wants similes, truth tired with iteration,
'As true as steel, as plantage to the moon,   169
As sun to day, as turtle to her mate,   170
As iron to adamant, as earth to th' centre,'   171

Yet, after all comparisons of truth,
As truth's authentic author to be cited,
'As true as Troilus' shall crown up the verse
175 And sanctify the numbers.
　CRESSIDA　　　　　　　　Prophet may you be!
If I be false or swerve a hair from truth,
When time is old and hath forgot itself,
When waterdrops have worn the stones of Troy,
And blind oblivion swallowed cities up,
180 And mighty states characterless are grated
To dusty nothing, yet let memory,
From false to false among false maids in love,
Upbraid my falsehood! When th' have said, 'as false
As air, as water, wind or sandy earth,
As fox to lamb, as wolf to heifer's calf,
186 Pard to the hind, or stepdame to her son,'
Yea, let them say, to stick the heart of falsehood,
'As false as Cressid.'
　PANDARUS　Go to, a bargain made; seal it, seal it; I'll be
the witness. Here I hold your hand, here my cousin's. If
ever you prove false one to another, since I have taken
such pains to bring you together, let all pitiful goers-
between be called to the world's end after my name; call
194 them all Pandars; let all constant men be Troiluses, all
false women Cressids, and all brokers-between Pandars! Say, 'Amen.'
　TROILUS　Amen.
　CRESSIDA　Amen.
　PANDARUS　Amen. Whereupon I will show you a cham-
199 ber which bed, because it shall not speak of your pretty
encounters, press it to death. Away!
　　　　　　　　　　Exeunt [Troilus and Cressida].
And Cupid grant all tongue-tied maidens here
Bed, chamber, Pandar to provide this gear!　　　Exit.

*

III, iii　　[Flourish of trumpets.] Enter Ulysses, Diomedes,
Nestor, Agamemnon, [Menelaus, Ajax, and]
Calchas.
　CALCHAS
Now, princes, for the service I have done,
Th' advantage of the time prompts me aloud
To call for recompense. Appear it to mind
That through the sight I bear in things to love,
5 I have abandoned Troy, left my possession,
Incurred a traitor's name, exposed myself,
From certain and possessed conveniences,
8 To doubtful fortunes, sequest'ring from me all
That time, acquaintance, custom, and condition
10 Made tame and most familiar to my nature;
And here, to do you service, am become
As new into the world, strange, unacquainted.
13 I do beseech you, as in way of taste,
To give me now a little benefit
Out of those many regist'red in promise,
Which, you say, live to come in my behalf.
　AGAMEMNON
What wouldst thou of us, Troyan? Make demand.
　CALCHAS
You have a Troyan prisoner, called Antenor,
Yesterday took; Troy holds him very dear.
Oft have you – often have you thanks therefor –
21 Desired my Cressid in right great exchange,

Whom Troy hath still denied; but this Antenor
I know is such a wrest in their affairs　　23
That their negotiations all must slack,
Wanting his manage; and they will almost
Give us a prince of blood, a son of Priam,
In change of him. Let him be sent, great princes,
And he shall buy my daughter; and her presence
Shall quite strike off all service I have done
In most accepted pain.　　　　　　　30
　AGAMEMNON　　　　　Let Diomedes bear him,
And bring us Cressid hither. Calchas shall have
What he requests of us. Good Diomed,
Furnish you fairly for his interchange.
Withal bring word if Hector will to-morrow
Be answered in his challenge. Ajax is ready.
　DIOMEDES
This shall I undertake, and 'tis a burden
Which I am proud to bear.　　　Exit [with Calchas].
　　Achilles and Patroclus stand in their tent.
　ULYSSES
Achilles stands i' th' entrance of his tent.
Please it our general to pass strangely by him,
As if he were forgot; and, princes all,
Lay negligent and loose regard upon him.
I will come last. 'Tis like he'll question me
Why such unplausive eyes are bent, why turned, on him. 43
If so, I have derision med'cinable
To use between your strangeness and his pride,
Which his own will shall have desire to drink.
It may do good; pride hath no other glass
To show itself but pride, for supple knees　　48
Feed arrogance and are the proud man's fees.
　AGAMEMNON
We'll execute your purpose, and put on
A form of strangeness as we pass along.
So do each lord, and either greet him not
Or else disdainfully, which shall shake him more
Than if not looked on. I will lead the way.
　ACHILLES
What comes the general to speak with me?
You know my mind; I'll fight no more 'gainst Troy.
　AGAMEMNON
What says Achilles? Would he aught with us?
　NESTOR
Would you, my lord, aught with the general?
　ACHILLES　No.
　NESTOR　Nothing, my lord.　　　　　　60
　AGAMEMNON　The better.
　ACHILLES　Good day, good day.
　MENELAUS　How do you? How do you?
　ACHILLES　What, does the cuckold scorn me?
　AJAX　How now, Patroclus?
　ACHILLES　Good morrow, Ajax.
　AJAX　Ha?
　ACHILLES　Good morrow.

175 *numbers* verses　180 *characterless* without a mark　186 *Pard* panther
or leopard; *hind* doe　194 *constant* (the context demands 'inconstant,'
but the text foretells the outcome of the play)　199 *which bed* in which the
bed; *because* in order that
III, iii The Grecian camp　5 *abandoned* (cf. I, i, 77)　8 *sequest'ring*
putting away　10 *tame* familiar　13 *taste* foretaste　21 *right great exchange* exchange for someone very great　23 *wrest* key for tuning a harp,
i.e. key to harmony in Troy　30 *accepted* cheerfully endured　43 *unplausive* disapproving　48 *show* mirror

AJAX Ay, and good next day too.   *Exeunt.*

ACHILLES
70   What mean these fellows? Know they not Achilles?

PATROCLUS
They pass by strangely. They were used to bend,
To send their smiles before them to Achilles,
To come as humbly as they used to creep
To holy altars.

ACHILLES   What, am I poor of late?
'Tis certain, greatness, once fall'n out with fortune,
Must fall out with men too. What the declined is
He shall as soon read in the eyes of others
As feel in his own fall; for men, like butterflies,
79   Show not their mealy wings but to the summer,
And not a man, for being simply man,
Hath any honor, but honor for those honors
82   That are without him, as place, riches, and favor,
Prizes of accident as oft as merit;
Which when they fall, as being slippery standers,
The love that leaned on them as slippery too,
Doth one pluck down another, and together
Die in the fall. But 'tis not so with me;
Fortune and I are friends. I do enjoy
89   At ample point all that I did possess,
Save these men's looks; who do, methinks, find out
Something not worth in me such rich beholding
As they have often given. Here is Ulysses;
I'll interrupt his reading.
How now, Ulysses.

ULYSSES   Now, great Thetis' son.

ACHILLES
What are you reading?

ULYSSES   A strange fellow here
96   Writes me that man, how dearly ever parted,
97   How much in having, or without or in,
Cannot make boast to have that which he hath,
99   Nor feels not what he owes but by reflection;
As when his virtues aiming upon others
Heat them, and they retort that heat again
To the first giver.

ACHILLES   This is not strange, Ulysses.
The beauty that is borne here in the face
The bearer knows not, but commends itself
To others' eyes; nor doth the eye itself,
That most pure spirit of sense, behold itself,
Not going from itself; but eye to eye opposed
Salutes each other with each other's form;
109   For speculation turns not to itself
Till it hath travelled and is married there
Where it may see itself. This is not strange at all.

ULYSSES
112   I do not strain at the position,
It is familiar, but at the author's drift;

Who in his circumstance expressly proves   114
That no man is the lord of anything –
Though in and of him there be much consisting –   116
Till he communicate his parts to others;
Nor doth he of himself know them for aught
Till he behold them formèd in th' applause
Where th' are extended; who, like an arch, reverb'rate   120
The voice again, or, like a gate of steel
Fronting the sun, receives and renders back
His figure and his heat. I was much rapt in this,
And apprehended here immediately
Th' unknown Ajax.
Heavens, what a man is there! A very horse,
That has he knows not what. Nature, what things there
    are
Most abject in regard and dear in use!   128
What things again most dear in the esteem
And poor in worth! Now shall we see to-morrow,
An act that very chance doth throw upon him,
Ajax renowned. O heavens, what some men do,
While some men leave to do!
How some men creep in skittish Fortune's hall,   134
Whiles others play the idiots in her eyes!
How one man eats into another's pride,
While pride is fasting in his wantonness!   137
To see these Grecian lords – why, even already
They clap the lubber Ajax on the shoulder,
As if his foot were on brave Hector's breast,
And great Troy shrinking.

ACHILLES
I do believe it; for they passed by me
As misers do by beggars, neither gave to me
Good word nor look. What, are my deeds forgot?

ULYSSES
Time hath, my lord, a wallet at his back,
Wherein he puts alms for oblivion,
A great-sized monster of ingratitudes.
Those scraps are good deeds past, which are devoured
As fast as they are made, forgot as soon
As done. Perseverance, dear my lord,
Keeps honor bright; to have done, is to hang
Quite out of fashion, like a rusty mail   152
In monumental mock'ry. Take the instant way;   153
For honor travels in a strait so narrow
Where one but goes abreast. Keep, then, the path;
For emulation hath a thousand sons
That one by one pursue. If you give way,
Or hedge aside from the direct forthright,   158
Like to an ent'red tide they all rush by
And leave you hindmost;
[Or, like a gallant horse fall'n in first rank,
Lie there for pavement to the abject rear,   162
O'errun and trampled on.] Then what they do in present,
Though less than yours in past, must o'ertop yours;
For time is like a fashionable host,
That slightly shakes his parting guest by th' hand,
And with his arms outstretched, as he would fly,
Grasps in the comer. The welcome ever smiles,
And farewell goes out sighing. Let not virtue seek
Remuneration for the thing it was. For beauty, wit,
High birth, vigor of bone, desert in service,
Love, friendship, charity, are subjects all
To envious and calumniating time.
One touch of nature makes the whole world kin,   174

175   That all with one consent praise new-born gawds,
Though they are made and moulded of things past,
And give to dust that is a little gilt
More laud than gilt o'er-dusted.
The present eye praises the present object.
Then marvel not, thou great and complete man,
That all the Greeks begin to worship Ajax;
Since things in motion sooner catch the eye
183   Than what not stirs. The cry went once on thee,
And still it might, and yet it may again,
If thou wouldst not entomb thyself alive
And case thy reputation in thy tent;
Whose glorious deeds, but in these fields of late,
188   Made emulous missions 'mongst the gods themselves
189   And drave great Mars to faction.

ACHILLES   Of this my privacy
I have strong reasons.

ULYSSES   But 'gainst your privacy
The reasons are more potent and heroical.
'Tis known, Achilles, that you are in love
193   With one of Priam's daughters.

ACHILLES   Ha! known!

ULYSSES
Is that a wonder?
196   The providence that's in a watchful state
197   Knows almost every grain of Pluto's gold,
198   Finds bottom in th' uncomprehensive deeps,
Keeps place with thought, and almost, like the gods,
Does thoughts unveil in their dumb cradles.
201   There is a mystery – with whom relation
Durst never meddle – in the soul of state,
Which hath an operation more divine
Than breath or pen can give expressure to.
All the commerce that you have had with Troy
As perfectly is ours as yours, my lord;
And better would it fit Achilles much
To throw down Hector than Polyxena.
209   But it must grieve young Pyrrhus now at home,
When fame shall in our islands sound her trump,
And all the Greekish girls shall tripping sing,
'Great Hector's sister did Achilles win,
But our great Ajax bravely beat down him.'
Farewell, my lord; I as your lover speak;
The fool slides o'er the ice that you should break. *[Exit.]*

PATROCLUS
To this effect, Achilles, have I moved you.
A woman impudent and mannish grown
Is not more loathed than an effeminate man
In time of action. I stand condemned for this.
They think my little stomach to the war
And your great love to me restrains you thus.
Sweet, rouse yourself; and the weak wanton Cupid
Shall from your neck unloose his amorous fold
And, like a dew-drop from the lion's mane,
Be shook to air.

ACHILLES   Shall Ajax fight with Hector?

PATROCLUS
Ay, and perhaps receive much honor by him.

ACHILLES
I see my reputation is at stake;
228   My fame is shrewdly gored.

PATROCLUS   O, then, beware!
Those wounds heal ill that men do give themselves.
Omission to do what is necessary

Seals a commission to a blank of danger;   231
And danger, like an ague, subtly taints
Even then when we sit idly in the sun.

ACHILLES
Go call Thersites hither, sweet Patroclus.
I'll send the fool to Ajax and desire him
T' invite the Troyan lords after the combat
To see us here unarmed. I have a woman's longing,   237
An appetite that I am sick withal,
To see great Hector in his weeds of peace,   239
To talk with him and to behold his visage,
Even to my full of view. A labor saved!
       Enter Thersites.

THERSITES   A wonder!

ACHILLES   What?

THERSITES   Ajax goes up and down the field, asking for
himself.   245

ACHILLES   How so?

THERSITES   He must fight singly to-morrow with Hector, and is so prophetically proud of an heroical cudgelling that he raves in saying nothing.

ACHILLES   How can that be?

THERSITES   Why, 'a stalks up and down like a peacock – a stride and a stand; ruminates like an hostess that hath no arithmetic but her brain to set down her reckoning; bites his lip with a politic regard, as who should say, 'There 254 were wit in this head an 'twould out'; and so there is, but it lies as coldly in him as fire in a flint, which will not show without knocking. The man's undone for ever, for if Hector break not his neck i' th' combat, he'll break't himself in vainglory. He knows not me. I said, 'Good morrow, Ajax'; and he replies, 'Thanks, Agamemnon.' What think you of this man that takes me for the general? He's grown a very land-fish, languageless, a monster. A plague of opinion! A man may wear it on both sides like a leather jerkin.   264

ACHILLES   Thou must be my ambassador to him, Thersites.

THERSITES   Who, I? Why, he'll answer nobody; he professes not answering. Speaking is for beggars; he wears his tongue in's arms. I will put on his presence; let 268 Patroclus make demands to me, you shall see the pageant of Ajax.

ACHILLES   To him, Patroclus. Tell him I humbly desire the valiant Ajax to invite the most valorous Hector to come unarmed to my tent, and to procure safe-conduct for his person of the magnanimous and most illustrious, six-or-seven-times-honored captain-general of the Grecian army, Agamemnon, et caetera. Do this.

PATROCLUS   Jove bless great Ajax!

THERSITES   Hum!

175 *gawds* toys, gewgaws   183 *cry* public acclaim   188 *emulous missions* (the gods joined in the fighting, taking opposing sides)   189 *to faction* to become a partisan   193 *one . . . daughters* Polyxena (with whom, in one legend, Achilles was keeping a tryst when Paris shot him in his vulnerable heel)   196 *providence* (here, timely care rather than foresight)   197 *Pluto's* (Shakespeare confused Pluto, god of the underworld, with Plutus, god of wealth)   198 *uncomprehensive* unfathomable   201 *relation* open statement 209 *Pyrrhus* son of Achilles (also called Neoptolemus), who came to the siege after his father's death   228 *shrewdly gored* seriously wounded 231 *Seals . . . danger* binds one to encounter unknown dangers (royal agents were given blank commissions, already sealed, to use for arrests or exactions)   237 *woman's* i.e. pregnant woman's   239 *weeds* dress   245 *himself* ('Ajax,' i.e. a jakes, was slang for a privy)   254 *politic regard* expression of wisdom   264 *jerkin* close-fitting jacket   268 *put on* imitate

PATROCLUS I come from the worthy Achilles –

THERSITES Ha!

280 PATROCLUS Who most humbly desires you to invite Hector to his tent –

THERSITES Hum!

PATROCLUS And to procure safe-conduct from Agamemnon.

THERSITES Agamemnon?

PATROCLUS Ay, my lord.

THERSITES Ha!

PATROCLUS What say you to't?

THERSITES God be wi' you, with all my heart.

PATROCLUS Your answer, sir.

290 THERSITES If to-morrow be a fair day, by eleven of the clock it will be one way or other; howsoever, he shall pay for me ere he has me.

PATROCLUS Your answer, sir.

THERSITES Fare ye well, with all my heart.

ACHILLES Why, but he is not in this tune, is he?

THERSITES No, but out of tune thus. What music will be in him when Hector has knocked out his brains, I know not; but I am sure none, unless the fiddler Apollo get

299 his sinews to make catlings on.

ACHILLES Come, thou shalt bear a letter to him straight.

THERSITES Let me bear another to his horse, for that's

302 the more capable creature.

ACHILLES
My mind is troubled, like a fountain stirred;
And I myself see not the bottom of it.
[Exeunt Achilles and Patroclus.]

THERSITES Would the fountain of your mind were clear again, that I might water an ass at it! I had rather be a tick in a sheep than such a valiant ignorance. *[Exit.]*

*

IV, i   *Enter, at one door, Aeneas with a torch; at another,*
Paris, Deiphobus, Antenor, Diomed the Grecian,
[and others,] with torches.

PARIS
See, ho! who is that there?

DEIPHOBUS   It is the Lord Aeneas.

AENEAS
Is the prince there in person?
Had I so good occasion to lie long
As you, Prince Paris, nothing but heavenly business
Should rob my bed-mate of my company.

DIOMEDES
That's my mind too. Good morrow, Lord Aeneas.

PARIS
A valiant Greek, Aeneas; take his hand.

8 Witness the process of your speech, wherein

9 You told how Diomed, a whole week by days,
Did haunt you in the field.

AENEAS   Health to you, valiant sir,

11 During all question of the gentle truce;

But when I meet you armed, as black defiance
As heart can think or courage execute.

DIOMEDES
The one and other Diomed embraces.
Our bloods are now in calm, and, so long, health!
But when contention and occasion meet,   16
By Jove, I'll play the hunter for thy life
With all my force, pursuit, and policy.

AENEAS
And thou shalt hunt a lion that will fly
With his face backward. In humane gentleness,
Welcome to Troy! Now, by Anchises' life,   21
Welcome indeed! By Venus' hand I swear,   22
No man alive can love in such a sort
The thing he means to kill more excellently.

DIOMEDES
We sympathize. Jove, let Aeneas live,
If to my sword his fate be not the glory,
A thousand complete courses of the sun!
But, in mine emulous honor, let him die
With every joint a wound, and that to-morrow!

AENEAS
We know each other well.

DIOMEDES
We do, and long to know each other worse.

PARIS
This is the most despiteful gentle greeting,
The noblest hateful love, that e'er I heard of.
What business, lord, so early?

AENEAS
I was sent for to the king; but why, I know not.

PARIS
His purpose meets you; 'twas to bring this Greek
To Calchas' house, and there to render him,
For the enfreed Antenor, the fair Cressid.
Let's have your company; or, if you please,
Haste there before us. I constantly do think –   40
Or rather call my thought a certain knowledge –
My brother Troilus lodges there to-night.
Rouse him and give him note of our approach,
With the whole quality wherefore. I fear   44
We shall be much unwelcome.

AENEAS   That I assure you.
Troilus had rather Troy were borne to Greece
Than Cressid borne from Troy.

PARIS   There is no help.
The bitter disposition of the time
Will have it so. On, lord; we'll follow you.

AENEAS
Good morrow, all.   *[Exit Aeneas.]*

PARIS
And tell me, noble Diomed; faith, tell me true,
Even in the soul of sound good-fellowship,
Who, in your thoughts, deserves fair Helen best,
Myself or Menelaus?

DIOMEDES   Both alike.
He merits well to have her that doth seek her,
Not making any scruple of her soilure,
With such a hell of pain and world of charge;   57
And you as well to keep her that defend her,
Not palating the taste of her dishonor,   59
With such a costly loss of wealth and friends.
He, like a puling cuckold, would drink up
The lees and dregs of a flat tamèd piece;   62

299 *catlings* strings of catgut   302 *capable* intelligent
IV, i *Within the gates of Troy*   8 *process* drift, gist   9 *by days* day by day   11 *question . . . truce* conversation made possible by the truce   16 *occasion* opportunity   21 *Anchises* Aeneas' father   22 *By Venus' hand* (Diomedes had wounded Venus, mother of Aeneas, in the hand)   40 *constantly* firmly   44 *quality* explanation   57 *charge* cost   59 *Not palating* insensible of   62 *flat tamèd piece* cask so long opened that the wine is flat; also piece of flesh

1001

You, like a lecher, out of whorish loins
Are pleased to breed out your inheritors.
65   Both merits poised, each weighs nor less nor more ;
But he as he, the heavier for a whore.

PARIS
You are too bitter to your countrywoman.

DIOMEDES
She's bitter to her country. Hear me, Paris :
For every false drop in her bawdy veins
70   A Grecian's life hath sunk ; for every scruple
Of her contaminated carrion weight
A Troyan hath been slain. Since she could speak,
She hath not given so many good words breath
As for her Greeks and Troyans suff'red death.

PARIS
75   Fair Diomed, you do as chapmen do,
Dispraise the thing that you desire to buy ;
But we in silence hold this virtue well,
We'll not commend what we intend to sell.
Here lies our way.   *Exeunt.*

        *

IV, ii   *Enter Troilus and Cressida.*

TROILUS
Dear, trouble not yourself ; the morn is cold.

CRESSIDA
Then, sweet my lord, I'll call mine uncle down ;
He shall unbolt the gates.

TROILUS   Trouble him not ;
4   To bed, to bed. Sleep kill those pretty eyes,
And give as soft attachment to thy senses
As infants' empty of all thought !

CRESSIDA   Good morrow then.

TROILUS
I prithee now, to bed.

CRESSIDA   Are you aweary of me ?

TROILUS
O Cressida, but that the busy day,
Waked by the lark, hath roused the ribald crows,
And dreaming night will hide our joys no longer,
I would not from thee.

CRESSIDA   Night hath been too brief.

TROILUS
12   Beshrew the witch ! with venomous wights she stays
As tediously as hell, but flies the grasps of love
With wings more momentary-swift than thought.
You will catch cold and curse me.

CRESSIDA   Prithee, tarry ;
You men will never tarry.
O foolish Cressid ! I might have still held off,
And then you would have tarried. Hark, there's one up.

PANDARUS *[within]* What's all the doors open here ?

TROILUS It is your uncle.

CRESSIDA A pestilence on him ! Now will he be mocking.
I shall have such a life.
        Enter Pandarus.

PANDARUS How now, how now ! How go maidenheads ?
Here, you maid, where's my cousin Cressid ?

CRESSIDA
Go hang yourself, you naughty mocking uncle.
You bring me to do – and then you flout me too.

PANDARUS To do what ? To do what ? Let her say what.
What have I brought you to do ?

CRESSIDA
Come, come ; beshrew your heart ! You'll ne'er be good,
Nor suffer others.

PANDARUS Ha, ha ! Alas, poor wretch ! A poor capoc- 31
chia ! Hast not slept to-night ? Would he not, a naughty
man, let it sleep ? A bugbear take him !

CRESSIDA
Did not I tell you ? Would he were knocked i' th' head !
      One knocks.
Who's that at door ? Good uncle, go and see.
My lord, come you again into my chamber.
You smile and mock me, as if I meant naughtily.

TROILUS Ha, ha !

CRESSIDA
Come, you are deceived, I think of no such thing.
      Knock.
How earnestly they knock ! Pray you, come in.
I would not for half Troy have you seen here.
        Exeunt [Troilus and Cressida].

PANDARUS Who's there ? What's the matter ? Will you
beat down the door ? How now, what's the matter ?
      [Enter Aeneas.]

AENEAS
Good morrow, lord, good morrow.

PANDARUS Who's there ? My Lord Aeneas ! By my troth,
I knew you not. What news with you so early ?

AENEAS
Is not Prince Troilus here ?

PANDARUS Here ? What should he do here ?

AENEAS
Come, he is here, my lord. Do not deny him.
It doth import him much to speak with me.   50

PANDARUS Is he here, say you ? 'Tis more than I know,
I'll be sworn. For my own part, I came in late. What
should he do here ?

AENEAS Who ! nay, then. Come, come, you'll do him
wrong ere you are ware. You'll be so true to him, to be
false to him. Do not you know of him, but yet go fetch
him hither ; go.
      [Enter Troilus.]

TROILUS How now, what's the matter ?

AENEAS
My lord, I scarce have leisure to salute you,
My matter is so rash. There is at hand   60
Paris your brother, and Deiphobus,
The Grecian Diomed, and our Antenor
Delivered to us ; and for him forthwith,
Ere the first sacrifice, within this hour,
We must give up to Diomedes' hand
The Lady Cressida.

TROILUS   Is it concluded so ?

AENEAS
By Priam, and the general state of Troy.
They are at hand and ready to effect it.

TROILUS
How my achievements mock me !
I will go meet them. And, my Lord Aeneas,   70
We met by chance ; you did not find me here.

---

65 *poised* weighed   70 *scruple* the smallest unit of weight   75 *chapmen*
merchants
IV, ii The house of Pandarus   4 *kill* overpower   12 *venomous* poisonous,
i.e. doing evil   31 *capocchia* simpleton   50 *doth import* is important to
60 *rash* urgent

AENEAS
    Good, good, my lord ; the secrets of nature
    Have not more gift in taciturnity.
                        Exeunt [Troilus and Aeneas].
PANDARUS Is't possible ? No sooner got but lost ? The
    devil take Antenor ! The young prince will go mad. A
    plague upon Antenor ! I would they had broke 's neck !
        Enter Cressida.
CRESSIDA
    How now ? What's the matter ? Who was here ?
PANDARUS Ah, ah !
CRESSIDA
    Why sigh you so profoundly ? Where's my lord ?
80 Gone ? Tell me, sweet uncle, what's the matter ?
PANDARUS Would I were as deep under the earth as I am
    above !
CRESSIDA O the gods ! what's the matter ?
PANDARUS Pray thee, get thee in. Would thou hadst
    ne'er been born ! I knew thou wouldst be his death. O
    poor gentleman ! A plague upon Antenor !
CRESSIDA Good uncle, I beseech you on my knees,
    what's the matter ?
PANDARUS Thou must be gone, wench, thou must be
    gone ; thou art changed for Antenor. Thou must to thy
    father and be gone from Troilus. 'Twill be his death ;
92 'twill be his bane ; he cannot bear it.
CRESSIDA
    O you immortal gods ! I will not go.
PANDARUS Thou must.
CRESSIDA
    I will not, uncle. I have forgot my father ;
    I know no touch of consanguinity –
    No kin, no love, no blood, no soul so near me
    As the sweet Troilus. O you gods divine,
    Make Cressid's name the very crown of falsehood
    If ever she leave Troilus ! Time, force, and death,
    Do to this body what extremes you can ;
    But the strong base and building of my love
    Is as the very centre of the earth,
    Drawing all things to it. I'll go in and weep.
PANDARUS Do, do.
CRESSIDA
    Tear my bright hair, and scratch my praisèd cheeks,
    Crack my clear voice with sobs, and break my heart
    With sounding Troilus. I will not go from Troy.
                        [Exeunt.]

                        *

IV, iii   *Enter Paris, Troilus, Aeneas, Deiphobus, Antenor,*
            Diomedes.
    PARIS
1   It is great morning, and the hour prefixed
    For her delivery to this valiant Greek
    Comes fast upon. Good my brother Troilus,
    Tell you the lady what she is to do,
    And haste her to the purpose.
        TROILUS   Walk into her house.

92 *bane* destruction
IV, iii Outside the house of Pandarus   1 *great morning* broad daylight
6 *presently* at once
IV, iv The house of Pandarus   4 *violenteth* rages   7 *palate* taste   13
spectacles (a pun)   23 *strained* filtered, purified   24 *fancy* love   32 *injury
of chance* injurious accident   35 *rejoindure* joining again

    I'll bring her to the Grecian presently ;   6
    And to his hand when I deliver her,
    Think it an altar, and thy brother Troilus
    A priest there off'ring to it his own heart.
PARIS
    I know what 'tis to love ;
    And would, as I shall pity, I could help !
    Please you walk in, my lords.   *Exeunt.*

                        *

            Enter Pandarus and Cressida.   IV, iv
PANDARUS Be moderate, be moderate.
CRESSIDA
    Why tell you me of moderation ?
    The grief is fine, full, perfect, that I taste,
    And violenteth in a sense as strong   4
    As that which causeth it. How can I moderate it ?
    If I could temporize with my affections,
    Or brew it to a weak and colder palate,   7
    The like allayment could I give my grief.
    My love admits no qualifying dross ;
    No more my grief, in such a precious loss.
        Enter Troilus.
PANDARUS Here, here, here he comes. Ah, sweet ducks !
CRESSIDA *[embracing him]* O Troilus ! Troilus !
PANDARUS What a pair of spectacles is here ! Let me em- 13
    brace too. 'O heart,' as the goodly saying is –
            O heart, heavy heart,
            Why sigh'st thou without breaking ?
    where he answers again,
            Because thou canst not ease thy smart
            By friendship nor by speaking.
    There was never a truer rhyme. Let us cast away noth-
    ing, for we may live to have need of such a verse. We see
    it, we see it. How now, lambs !
TROILUS
    Cressid, I love thee in so strained a purity,   23
    That the blest gods, as angry with my fancy,   24
    More bright in zeal than the devotion which
    Cold lips blow to their deities, take thee from me.
CRESSIDA Have the gods envy ?
PANDARUS Ay, ay, ay, ay ; 'tis too plain a case.
CRESSIDA
    And is it true that I must go from Troy ?
TROILUS
    A hateful truth.
CRESSIDA   What, and from Troilus too ?
TROILUS
    From Troy and Troilus.
CRESSIDA   Is't possible ?
TROILUS
    And suddenly, where injury of chance   32
    Puts back leave-taking, justles roughly by
    All time of pause, rudely beguiles our lips
    Of all rejoindure, forcibly prevents   35
    Our locked embrasures, strangles our dear vows
    Even in the birth of our own laboring breath.
    We two, that with so many thousand sighs
    Did buy each other, must poorly sell ourselves
    With the rude brevity and discharge of one.
    Injurious time now with a robber's haste
    Crams his rich thiev'ry up, he knows not how.
    As many farewells as be stars in heaven,

44 With distinct breath and consigned kisses to them,
45 He fumbles up into a loose adieu,
And scants us with a single famished kiss,
47 Distasted with the salt of broken tears.

AENEAS *(within)* My lord, is the lady ready?

TROILUS
49 Hark! you are called. Some say the Genius
Cries so to him that instantly must die.
Bid them have patience; she shall come anon.

PANDARUS Where are my tears? Rain, to lay this wind,
or my heart will be blown up by the root!   *[Exit.]*

CRESSIDA
I must, then, to the Grecians?

TROILUS   No remedy.

CRESSIDA
A woeful Cressid 'mongst the merry Greeks!
When shall we see again?

TROILUS
Hear me, love. Be thou but true of heart –

CRESSIDA
58 I true! How now! What wicked deem is this?

TROILUS
Nay, we must use expostulation kindly,
60 For it is parting from us.
I speak not 'be thou true' as fearing thee,
62 For I will throw my glove to Death himself
63 That there's no maculation in thy heart;
64 But 'be thou true,' say I, to fashion in
My sequent protestation; be thou true,
And I will see thee.

CRESSIDA
O, you shall be exposed, my lord, to dangers
As infinite as imminent; but I'll be true.

TROILUS
And I'll grow friend with danger. Wear this sleeve.

CRESSIDA
And you this glove. When shall I see you?

TROILUS
I will corrupt the Grecian sentinels,
To give thee nightly visitation.
But yet, be true.

CRESSIDA   O heavens! 'be true' again!

TROILUS
Hear why I speak it, love.
75 The Grecian youths are full of quality;
[They're loving, well composed, with gift of nature,]
77 And swelling o'er with arts and exercise.
78 How novelty may move, and parts with person,
Alas! a kind of godly jealousy –
Which, I beseech you, call a virtuous sin –
Makes me afeared.

CRESSIDA   O heavens, you love me not!

TROILUS
Die I a villain, then!
In this I do not call your faith in question
So mainly as my merit. I cannot sing,
85 Nor heel the high lavolt, nor sweeten talk,
Nor play at subtle games – fair virtues all,
87 To which the Grecians are most prompt and pregnant;
But I can tell that in each grace of these
89 There lurks a still and dumb-discoursive devil
That tempts most cunningly. But be not tempted.

CRESSIDA Do you think I will?

TROILUS No.

But something may be done that we will not;
And sometimes we are devils to ourselves
When we will tempt the frailty of our powers,
Presuming on their changeful potency.   96

AENEAS *(within)*
Nay, good my lord!

TROILUS   Come, kiss; and let us part.

PARIS *(within)*
Brother Troilus!

TROILUS   Good brother, come you hither;
And bring Aeneas and the Grecian with you.

CRESSIDA
My lord, will you be true?

TROILUS
Who? I? Alas, it is my vice, my fault.
Whiles others fish with craft for great opinion,   102
I with great truth catch mere simplicity;
Whilst some with cunning gild their copper crowns,
With truth and plainness I do wear mine bare.
Fear not my truth; the moral of my wit   106
Is 'plain and true'; there's all the reach of it.
     [Enter Aeneas, Paris, Antenor, Deiphobus, and
     Diomedes.]
Welcome, Sir Diomed. Here is the lady
Which for Antenor we deliver you.
At the port, lord, I'll give her to thy hand,   110
And by the way possess thee what she is.   111
Entreat her fair; and, by my soul, fair Greek,   112
If e'er thou stand at mercy of my sword,
Name Cressid, and thy life shall be as safe
As Priam is in Ilion.

DIOMEDES   Fair Lady Cressid,
So please you, save the thanks this prince expects.
The lustre in your eye, heaven in your cheek,
Pleads your fair usage; and to Diomed
You shall be mistress, and command him wholly.

TROILUS
Grecian, thou dost not use me courteously,
To shame the seal of my petition here   121
In praising her. I tell thee, lord of Greece,
She is as far high-soaring o'er thy praises
As thou unworthy to be called her servant.
I charge thee use her well, even for my charge;   125
For, by the dreadful Pluto, if thou dost not,
Though the great bulk Achilles be thy guard,
I'll cut thy throat.

DIOMEDES   O, be not moved, Prince Troilus.
Let me be privileged by my place and message
To be a speaker free. When I am hence,
I'll answer to my lust; and know you, lord,   131
I'll nothing do on charge. To her own worth
She shall be prized; but that you say 'be 't so,'

44 *With . . . them* with the words of farewell and kisses that should ratify each   45 *fumbles* wraps up clumsily   47 *Distasted* tasting bad   49 *Genius* a man's attendant spirit   58 *deem* thought   60 *it . . . us* we are saying goodbye   62 *throw my glove* give a challenge   63 *maculation* taint of disloyalty   64–65 *fashion . . . protestation* furnish a pattern for my own promise that follows   75 *quality* good qualities   77 *arts and exercise* i.e. theory and practice   78 *parts with person* accomplishments with personal charm   85 *lavolt* a lively dance   87 *pregnant* ready   89 *dumb-discoursive* speakingly in silence   96 *changeful potency* power that may change (to failure)   102 *opinion* reputation for wisdom   106 *moral* maxim   110 *port* gate   111 *possess* make known to   112 *Entreat* treat   121 *shame the seal of* treat disdainfully my promise given in exchange for   125 *even for my charge* merely because I tell you to   131 *answer . . . lust* do as I please

I'll speak it in my spirit and honor, 'no.'

TROILUS

Come, to the port. I'll tell thee, Diomed,

136   This brave shall oft make thee to hide thy head.
Lady, give me your hand, and, as we walk,
To our own selves bend we our needful talk.
           [Exeunt Troilus, Cressida, and Diomedes.]
       Sound trumpet.

PARIS

Hark ! Hector's trumpet.

AENEAS   How have we spent this morning !
The prince must think me tardy and remiss,
That swore to ride before him to the field.

PARIS

'Tis Troilus' fault. Come, come, to field with him.

[DEIPHOBUS

Let us make ready straight.

AENEAS

Yea, with a bridegroom's fresh alacrity,
Let us address to tend on Hector's heels.
The glory of our Troy doth this day lie
On his fair worth and single chivalry.]   *Exeunt.*

*

IV, v   *Enter Ajax, armed ; Achilles, Patroclus, Agamem-*
       non, Menelaus, Ulysses, Nestor, Calchas, &c.

AGAMEMNON

1   Here art thou in appointment fresh and fair,
2   Anticipating time. With starting courage,
Give with thy trumpet a loud note to Troy,
Thou dreadful Ajax, that the appallèd air
May pierce the head of the great combatant
And hale him hither.

6 AJAX   Thou, trumpet, there's my purse.
Now crack thy lungs, and split thy brazen pipe.
8   Blow, villain, till thy spherèd bias cheek
9   Outswell the colic of puffed Aquilon.
Come, stretch thy chest, and let thy eyes spout blood ;
Thou blowest for Hector.
       [Trumpet sounds.]

ULYSSES

No trumpet answers.

12 ACHILLES   'Tis but early days.

AGAMEMNON

Is not yond Diomed with Calchas' daughter ?

ULYSSES

'Tis he, I ken the manner of his gait ;
He rises on the toe. That spirit of his
In aspiration lifts him from the earth.
       [Enter Diomedes, with Cressida.]

AGAMEMNON

Is this the Lady Cressid ?

DIOMEDES   Even she.

AGAMEMNON

Most dearly welcome to the Greeks, sweet lady.

NESTOR

Our general doth salute you with a kiss.

ULYSSES

Yet is the kindness but particular.   20
'Twere better she were kissed in general.   21

NESTOR

And very courtly counsel. I'll begin.
So much for Nestor.

ACHILLES

I'll take that winter from your lips, fair lady.
Achilles bids you welcome.

MENELAUS

I had good argument for kissing once.

PATROCLUS

But that's no argument for kissing now ;
For thus popped Paris in his hardiment,   28
And parted thus you and your argument.   29

ULYSSES

O, deadly gall, and theme of all our scorns !
For which we lose our heads to gild his horns.

PATROCLUS

The first was Menelaus' kiss ; this, mine :
Patroclus kisses you.

MENELAUS   O, this is trim.

PATROCLUS

Paris and I kiss evermore for him.

MENELAUS

I'll have my kiss, sir. Lady, by your leave.

CRESSIDA

In kissing, do you render or receive ?

PATROCLUS

Both take and give.

CRESSIDA   I'll make my match to live,   37
The kiss you take is better than you give ;
Therefore no kiss.

MENELAUS

I'll give you boot ; I'll give you three for one.   40

CRESSIDA

You are an odd man ; give even, or give none.   41

MENELAUS

An odd man, lady ? Every man is odd.

CRESSIDA

No, Paris is not, for you know 'tis true
That you are odd and he is even with you.

MENELAUS

You fillip me o' th' head.   45

CRESSIDA   No, I'll be sworn.

ULYSSES

It were no match, your nail against his horn.   46
May I, sweet lady, beg a kiss of you ?

CRESSIDA

You may.

ULYSSES   I do desire it.

CRESSIDA   Why, beg then.

ULYSSES

Why, then, for Venus' sake, give me a kiss,
When Helen is a maid again, and his –

CRESSIDA

I am your debtor ; claim it when 'tis due.

ULYSSES

Never's my day, and then a kiss of you.

DIOMEDES

Lady, a word. I'll bring you to your father.
       [Exeunt Diomedes and Cressida.]

---

136 *brave* boast
IV, v The Grecian camp 1 *appointment* equipment 2 *starting* active
6 *trumpet* trumpeter 8 *bias* puffed-out 9 *colic . . . Aquilon* the north
wind, personified, distended by colic 12 *days* in the day 20 *particular*
single 21 *in general* (1) by the general, (2) universally 28 *hardiment*
boldness 29 *argument* i.e. Helen 37 *make . . . live* wager my life 40
boot odds 41 *odd* i.e. singular and single 45 *fillip* tap 46 *It . . . horn*
your nail, in tapping, would be no match for his hard horn

NESTOR
A woman of quick sense.

ULYSSES   Fie, fie upon her!
There's language in her eye, her cheek, her lip;
Nay, her foot speaks. Her wanton spirits look out
57   At every joint and motive of her body.
O, these encounterers, so glib of tongue,
59   That give a coasting welcome ere it comes,
60   And wide unclasp the tables of their thoughts
To every ticklish reader, set them down
62   For sluttish spoils of opportunity
And daughters of the game.
     Flourish. Enter all of Troy [Hector, Paris, Aeneas,
     Helenus, Troilus, and Attendants].

ALL
The Troyans' trumpet.

AGAMEMNON   Yonder comes the troop.

AENEAS
Hail, all the state of Greece. What shall be done
To him that victory commands? Or do you purpose
A victor shall be known? Will you the knights
Shall to the edge of all extremity
Pursue each other, or shall they be divided
By any voice or order of the field?
Hector bade ask.

AGAMEMNON   Which way would Hector have it?

AENEAS
He cares not; he'll obey conditions.

ACHILLES
73   'Tis done like Hector; but securely done,
A little proudly, and great deal misprising
The knight opposed.

AENEAS   If not Achilles, sir,
What is your name?

ACHILLES   If not Achilles, nothing.

AENEAS
Therefore Achilles; but, whate'er, know this:
In the extremity of great and little,
Valor and pride excel themselves in Hector:
The one almost as infinite as all,
The other blank as nothing. Weigh him well,
And that which looks like pride is courtesy.
83   This Ajax is half made of Hector's blood,
In love whereof half Hector stays at home;
Half heart, half hand, half Hector comes to seek
This blended knight, half Troyan, and half Greek.

ACHILLES
87   A maiden battle, then? O, I perceive you.
     [Enter Diomedes.]

AGAMEMNON
Here is Sir Diomed. Go, gentle knight,
Stand by our Ajax. As you and Lord Aeneas
90   Consent upon the order of their fight,
So be it; either to the uttermost,
92   Or else a breath. The combatants being kin
Half stints their strife before their strokes begin.
     [Ajax and Hector enter the lists.]

[ULYSSES
They are opposed already.]

AGAMEMNON
95   What Troyan is that same that looks so heavy?

ULYSSES
The youngest son of Priam, a true knight,
Not yet mature, yet matchless, firm of word,

Speaking in deeds and deedless in his tongue,   98
Not soon provoked, nor being provoked soon calmed;
His heart and hand both open and both free,   100
For what he has he gives, what thinks he shows;
Yet gives he not till judgment guide his bounty,
Nor dignifies an impare thought with breath;   103
Manly as Hector, but more dangerous;
For Hector, in his blaze of wrath, subscribes   105
To tender objects, but he in heat of action
Is more vindicative than jealous love.
They call him Troilus, and on him erect
A second hope as fairly built as Hector.
Thus says Aeneas, one that knows the youth
Even to his inches, and with private soul   111
Did in great Ilion thus translate him to me.
     Alarum. [Hector and Ajax fight.]

AGAMEMNON
They are in action.

NESTOR
Now, Ajax, hold thine own!

TROILUS   Hector, thou sleep'st; awake thee!

AGAMEMNON
His blows are well disposed. There, Ajax!

DIOMEDES
You must no more.
     Trumpets cease.

AENEAS   Princes, enough, so please you.

AJAX
I am not warm yet; let us fight again.

DIOMEDES
As Hector pleases.

HECTOR   Why, then will I no more.
Thou art, great lord, my father's sister's son,
A cousin-german to great Priam's seed;
The obligation of our blood forbids
A gory emulation 'twixt us twain.
Were thy commixtion Greek and Troyan so   123
That thou couldst say, 'This hand is Grecian all,
And this is Troyan; the sinews of this leg
All Greek, and this all Troy; my mother's blood
Runs on the dexter cheek, and this sinister   127
Bounds in my father's,' by Jove multipotent,   128
Thou shouldst not bear from me a Greekish member
Wherein my sword had not impressure made
[Of our rank feud.] But the just gods gainsay
That any drop thou borrowedst from thy mother,
My sacred aunt, should by my mortal sword
Be drained! Let me embrace thee, Ajax;
By him that thunders, thou hast lusty arms;   135
Hector would have them fall upon him thus.   136
Cousin, all honor to thee!

AJAX   I thank thee, Hector.
Thou art too gentle and too free a man.
I came to kill thee, cousin, and bear hence
A great addition earnèd in thy death.

---

57 *motive* moving part   59 *coasting* sidelong   60 *tables* tablets   62–63 *For . . . game* for harlots who yield at every opportunity   73 *securely* over-confidently   83 *Hector's blood* (cf. II, ii, 77)   87 *maiden* bloodless, like that of men in training   90 *Consent* agree   92 *a breath* merely exercise   95 *heavy* heavy-hearted   98 *deedless . . . tongue* not boastful   100 *free* open, generous   103 *impare* unequal to his judgment   105–06 *subscribes . . . objects* grants terms to the defenseless   111 *Even to his inches* from top to toe; *with private soul* in confidence   123 *commixtion* composition   127 *dexter, sinister* right, left   128 *multipotent* of many powers   135 *him that thunders* Zeus   136 *thus* in an embrace

HECTOR

141 Not Neoptolemus so mirable,
142 On whose bright crest Fame with her loud'st 'Oyes'
Cries, 'This is he !' could promise to himself
A thought of added honor torn from Hector.

AENEAS

There is expectance here from both the sides,
What further you will do.

HECTOR   We'll answer it ;

147 The issue is embracement. Ajax, farewell.

AJAX

If I might in entreaties find success –
149 As seld I have the chance – I would desire
My famous cousin to our Grecian tents.

DIOMEDES

'Tis Agamemnon's wish, and great Achilles
Doth long to see unarmed the valiant Hector.

HECTOR

Aeneas, call my brother Troilus to me,
And signify this loving interview
155 To the expecters of our Troyan part.
156 Desire them home. Give me thy hand, my cousin ;
I will go eat with thee and see your knights.
[Agamemnon and the rest approach them.]

AJAX

Great Agamemnon comes to meet us here.

HECTOR

The worthiest of them tell me name by name ;
But for Achilles, mine own searching eyes
Shall find him by his large and portly size.

AGAMEMNON

Worthy all arms *[embraces him]*, as welcome as to one
That would be rid of such an enemy –
[But that's no welcome. Understand more clear,
What's past and what's to come is strewed with husks
And formless ruin of oblivion ;
167 But in this extant moment, faith and troth,
168 Strained purely from all hollow bias-drawing,
Bids thee, with most divine integrity,]
From heart of very heart, great Hector, welcome.

HECTOR

I thank thee, most imperious Agamemnon.

AGAMEMNON *[to Troilus]*

My well-famed lord of Troy, no less to you.

MENELAUS

Let me confirm my princely brother's greeting.
You brace of warlike brothers, welcome hither.

HECTOR

Who must we answer ?

AENEAS   The noble Menelaus.

HECTOR

O, you, my lord ? By Mars his gauntlet, thanks !
177 Mock not that I affect th' untraded oath ;
Your quondam wife swears still by Venus' glove.
She's well, but bade me not commend her to you.

MENELAUS

Name her not now, sir ; she's a deadly theme.

HECTOR

O, pardon ! I offend.

NESTOR

I have, thou gallant Troyan, seen thee oft,
Laboring for destiny, make cruel way   183
Through ranks of Greekish youth, and I have seen thee,
As hot as Perseus, spur thy Phrygian steed,
Despising many forfeits and subduements,   186
When thou hast hung thy advancèd sword i' th' air,   187
Not letting it decline on the declinèd,
That I have said to some my standers-by,
'Lo, Jupiter is yonder, dealing life !'   190
And I have seen thee pause and take thy breath,
When that a ring of Greeks have shraped thee in,   192
Like an Olympian wrestling. This have I seen ;
But this thy countenance, still locked in steel,   194
I never saw till now. I knew thy grandsire,   195
And once fought with him. He was a soldier good ;
But, by great Mars, the captain of us all,
Never like thee. Let an old man embrace thee ;
And, worthy warrior, welcome to our tents.

AENEAS

'Tis the old Nestor.

HECTOR

Let me embrace thee, good old chronicle,
That hast so long walked hand in hand with time.
Most reverend Nestor, I am glad to clasp thee.

NESTOR

I would my arms could match thee in contention,
[As they contend with thee in courtesy.]

HECTOR

I would they could.

NESTOR

Ha,
By this white beard, I'd fight with thee to-morrow.
Well, welcome, welcome. I have seen the time –

ULYSSES

I wonder now how yonder city stands,
When we have here her base and pillar by us.

HECTOR

I know your favor, Lord Ulysses, well.   212
Ah, sir, there's many a Greek and Troyan dead,
Since first I saw yourself and Diomed
In Ilion, on your Greekish embassy.

ULYSSES

Sir, I foretold you then what would ensue.
My prophecy is but half his journey yet,
For yonder walls, that pertly front your town,
Yon towers, whose wanton tops do buss the clouds,
Must kiss their own feet.

HECTOR   I must not believe you.   220
There they stand yet, and modestly I think,
The fall of every Phrygian stone will cost
A drop of Grecian blood. The end crowns all,
And that old common arbitrator, Time,
Will one day end it.

ULYSSES   So to him we leave it.
Most gentle and most valiant Hector, welcome.
After the general, I beseech you next
To feast with me and see me at my tent.

ACHILLES

I shall forestall thee, Lord Ulysses, thou !

---

141 *Neoptolemus* (cf. III, iii, 209n. ; but perhaps Achilles is meant here); *mirable* wonderful   142 *Oyes* cry beginning a herald's proclamation   147 *issue* outcome   149 *seld* seldom   155 *expecters . . . part* Trojans waiting for news   156 *Desire them home* ask them to go home   167 *extant* present   168 *bias-drawing* tortuous dealings (like the course given by the bias to the bowl in bowling)   177 *untraded* unused   183 *Laboring for destiny* i.e. causing destined deaths   186 *Despising . . . subduements* ignoring the vanquished whose lives were forfeit   187 *hung* held suspended   190 *dealing life* i.e. by not dealing death   192 *shraped* trapped   194 *still* always   195 *grandsire* Laomedon, who built the walls of Troy   212 *favor* face

Now, Hector, I have fed mine eyes on thee;
I have with exact view perused thee, Hector,
232 And quoted joint by joint.
HECTOR   Is this Achilles?
ACHILLES
  I am Achilles.
HECTOR
  Stand fair, I prithee; let me look on thee.
ACHILLES
  Behold thy fill.
HECTOR   Nay, I have done already.
ACHILLES
  Thou art too brief. I will the second time,
  As I would buy thee, view thee limb by limb.
HECTOR
  O, like a book of sport thou'lt read me o'er;
  But there's more in me than thou understand'st.
  Why dost thou so oppress me with thine eye?
ACHILLES
  Tell me, you heavens, in which part of his body
  Shall I destroy him, whether there, or there, or there?
  That I may give the local wound a name,
  And make distinct the very breach whereout
  Hector's great spirit flew. Answer me, heavens!
HECTOR
  It would discredit the blessed gods, proud man,
  To answer such a question. Stand again.
248 Think'st thou to catch my life so pleasantly
249 As to prenominate in nice conjecture
  Where thou wilt hit me dead?
ACHILLES   I tell thee, yea.
HECTOR
  Wert thou an oracle to tell me so,
  I'd not believe thee. Henceforth guard thee well,
  For I'll not kill thee there, nor there, nor there;
254 But, by the forge that stithied Mars his helm,
  I'll kill thee everywhere, yea, o'er and o'er.
  You wisest Grecians, pardon me this brag.
  His insolence draws folly from my lips;
  But I'll endeavor deeds to match these words,
  Or may I never –
AJAX   Do not chafe thee, cousin;
  And you, Achilles, let these threats alone,
  Till accident or purpose bring you to't.
  You may have every day enough of Hector,
263 If you have stomach. The general state, I fear,
  Can scarce entreat you to be odd with him.
HECTOR
  I pray you, let us see you in the field.
266 We have had pelting wars since you refused
  The Grecians' cause.
ACHILLES   Dost thou entreat me, Hector?
268 To-morrow do I meet thee, fell as death;
  To-night all friends.
HECTOR   Thy hand upon that match.
AGAMEMNON
  First, all you peers of Greece, go to my tent;
271 There in the full convive we. Afterwards,
  As Hector's leisure and your bounties shall
273 Concur together, severally entreat him
  To taste your bounties. Let the trumpets blow,
  That this great soldier may his welcome know.
        Exeunt [all except Troilus and Ulysses].

TROILUS
  My Lord Ulysses, tell me, I beseech you,
  In what place of the field doth Calchas keep?   277
ULYSSES
  At Menelaus' tent, most princely Troilus.
  There Diomed doth feast with him to-night;
  Who neither looks upon the heaven nor earth,
  But gives all gaze and bent of amorous view
  On the fair Cressid.
TROILUS
  Shall I, sweet lord, be bound to thee so much,
  After we part from Agamemnon's tent,
  To bring me thither?
ULYSSES   You shall command me, sir.
  As gentle tell me, of what honor was
  This Cressida in Troy? Had she no lover there
  That wails her absence?
TROILUS
  O, sir, to such as boasting show their scars
  A mock is due. Will you walk on, my lord?
  She was beloved, she loved; she is, and doth:
  But still sweet love is food for fortune's tooth.   *Exeunt.*

                               *

        Enter Achilles and Patroclus.   V, i
ACHILLES
  I'll heat his blood with Greekish wine to-night,
  Which with my scimitar I'll cool to-morrow.
  Patroclus, let us feast him to the height.
PATROCLUS
  Here comes Thersites.
    Enter Thersites.
ACHILLES   How now, thou cur of envy!
  Thou crusty batch of nature, what's the news?   5
THERSITES Why, thou picture of what thou seemest, and
  idol of idiot-worshippers, here's a letter for thee.
ACHILLES From whence, fragment?
THERSITES Why, thou full dish of fool, from Troy.
PATROCLUS Who keeps the tent now?   10
THERSITES The surgeon's box or the patient's wound. 11
PATROCLUS Well said, adversity, and what need these
  tricks?
THERSITES Prithee, be silent, boy; I profit not by thy
  talk. Thou art said to be Achilles' male varlet.
PATROCLUS Male varlet, you rogue! What's that?
THERSITES Why, his masculine whore. Now, the rotten
  diseases of the south, the guts-griping ruptures, catarrhs,
  loads o' gravel in the back, lethargies, cold palsies, raw 18
  eyes, dirt-rotten livers, wheezing lungs, bladders full of
  imposthume, sciaticas, lime-kilns i' th' palm, incurable 20
  bone-ache, and the rivelled fee-simple of the tetter, and 21

232 *quoted* marked 248 *pleasantly* merrily 249 *prenominate* name
beforehand; *nice* precise 254 *stithied* forged 263 *stomach* inclination
263–64 *The general . . . him* i.e. you will have to do it on private impulse,
since you will not do it when the Greek leaders ask you 266 *pelting*
petty 268 *fell* fierce 271 *convive* feast 273 *severally entreat* individually
invite 277 *keep* dwell
V, i Before the tent of Achilles 5 *batch* bread of the same baking 10
Who . . . now (Thersites can no longer taunt Achilles for keeping to his tent)
11 *surgeon's box . . . wound* (play on *tent* in the sense of a lancet for probing
a wound) 18 *back* kidney; *lethargies* apoplexies; *cold palsies* paralysis
20 *imposthume* abscess; *lime-kilns* burnings 21 *rivelled* wrinkled; *tetter*
possibly chronic ringworm

the like, take and take again such preposterous discoveries!

PATROCLUS Why, thou damnable box of envy, thou,
what means thou to curse thus?

THERSITES Do I curse thee?

27 PATROCLUS Why, no, you ruinous butt, you whoreson
28 indistinguishable cur, no.

THERSITES No? Why art thou then exasperate, thou idle
30 immaterial skein of sleave silk, thou green sarcenet flap
for a sore eye, thou tassel of a prodigal's purse, thou?
Ah, how the poor world is pestered with such waterflies, diminutives of nature.

PATROCLUS Out, gall!

THERSITES Finch egg!

ACHILLES
My sweet Patroclus, I am thwarted quite
From my great purpose in to-morrow's battle.
Here is a letter from Queen Hecuba,
A token from her daughter, my fair love,
40 Both taxing me and gaging me to keep
An oath that I have sworn. I will not break it.
Fall Greeks, fail fame, honor or go or stay,
My major vow lies here; this I'll obey.
Come, come, Thersites, help to trim my tent;
This night in banqueting must all be spent.
Away, Patroclus!   Exit [with Patroclus].

THERSITES With too much blood and too little brain,
these two may run mad; but if with too much brain and
too little blood they do, I'll be a curer of madmen. Here's
Agamemnon, an honest fellow enough, and one that
51 loves quails, but he has not so much brain as ear-wax; and
52 the goodly transformation of Jupiter there, his brother,
53 the bull, the primitive statue and oblique memorial of
54 cuckolds; a thrifty shoeing-horn in a chain, hanging at
his brother's leg, to what form but that he is should wit
56 larded with malice and malice forced with wit turn him
to? To an ass, were nothing; he is both ass and ox: to an
ox, were nothing; he is both ox and ass. To be a dog, a
59 mule, a cat, a fitchew, a toad, a lizard, an owl, a puttock,
or a herring without a roe, I would not care; but to be
Menelaus! I would conspire against destiny. Ask me not
62 what I would be, if I were not Thersites, for I care not to
63 be the louse of a lazar, so I were not Menelaus. Hey-day,
spirits and fires!
        Enter Agamemnon, Ulysses, Nestor, [Hector, Ajax,
        Troilus, Menelaus,] and Diomedes, with lights.

AGAMEMNON
We go wrong, we go wrong.

AJAX   No, yonder 'tis;
There, where we see the lights.

HECTOR   I trouble you.

AJAX
No, not a whit.

---

27 *ruinous butt* dilapidated cask 28 *indistinguishable* shapeless 30
sleave silk silk floss; *sarcenet* silk 40 *taxing* censuring; *gaging* binding to
a promise 51 *quails* loose women 52 *Jupiter* (who changed himself into
a bull to seduce Europa) 53 *primitive . . . memorial* i.e. in having horns,
the symbol of a cuckold 54 *thrifty* stingy 54–55 *hanging . . . leg* (so that
he cannot be shaken off) 56 *forced* stuffed 59 *fitchew* polecat; *puttock*
kite (opprobrious, as feeding on carrion) 62–63 *I care not to be* I wouldn't
mind being 63 *lazar* leper 74 *draught* privy 82 *tide* time 95 *leave to
see* miss seeing
V, ii Before the tent of Calchas

ULYSSES   Here comes himself to guide you.
        [Enter Achilles.]

ACHILLES
Welcome, brave Hector; welcome, princes all.

AGAMEMNON
So now, fair prince of Troy, I bid good night.
Ajax commands the guard to tend on you.

HECTOR
Thanks and good night to the Greeks' general.

MENELAUS
Good night, my lord.

HECTOR
Good night, sweet Lord Menelaus.

THERSITES Sweet draught! 'Sweet,' quoth 'a! Sweet 74
sink, sweet sewer.

ACHILLES
Good night and welcome both at once, to those
That go or tarry.

AGAMEMNON Good night.
                    Exeunt Agamemnon [and] Menelaus.

ACHILLES
Old Nestor tarries, and you too, Diomed,
Keep Hector company an hour or two.

DIOMEDES
I cannot, lord; I have important business,
The tide whereof is now. Good night, great Hector. 82

HECTOR
Give me your hand.

ULYSSES [aside to Troilus] Follow his torch; he goes
To Calchas' tent. I'll keep you company.

TROILUS
Sweet sir, you honor me.

HECTOR   And so, good night.
        [Exeunt Diomedes, then Ulysses and Troilus.]

ACHILLES
Come, come, enter my tent.
                Exeunt [Achilles, Hector, Ajax, and Nestor].

THERSITES That same Diomed's a false-hearted rogue, a
most unjust knave; I will no more trust him when he
leers than I will a serpent when he hisses. He will spend
his mouth and promise like Brabbler the hound; but
when he performs, astronomers foretell it, it is prodigious, there will come some change. The sun borrows of
the moon when Diomed keeps his word. I will rather
leave to see Hector than not to dog him. They say he 95
keeps a Troyan drab, and uses the traitor Calchas' tent.
I'll after – nothing but lechery! All incontinent varlets!
                                                    Exit.

                         *

        Enter Diomed.   V, ii

DIOMEDES What, are you up here, ho? Speak.

CALCHAS [within] Who calls?

DIOMEDES Diomed. Calchas, I think. Where's your
daughter?

CALCHAS [within] She comes to you.
        Enter Troilus and Ulysses[; after them Thersites].

ULYSSES
Stand where the torch may not discover us.
        Enter Cressid.

TROILUS
Cressid comes forth to him.

DIOMEDES   How now, my charge!

CRESSIDA
Now, my sweet guardian ! Hark, a word with you.
[Whispers.]
TROILUS Yea, so familiar !
ULYSSES She will sing any man at first sight.
THERSITES And any man may sing her, if he can take her
11 cliff ; she's noted.
DIOMEDES Will you remember ?
CRESSIDA Remember ? Yes.
DIOMEDES Nay, but do, then ;
And let your mind be coupled with your words.
TROILUS What shall she remember ?
ULYSSES List !
CRESSIDA
Sweet honey Greek, tempt me no more to folly.
THERSITES Roguery !
DIOMEDES
Nay, then –
20 CRESSIDA I'll tell you what –
DIOMEDES
Foh, foh ! come, tell a pin. You are forsworn.
CRESSIDA
In faith, I cannot. What would you have me do ?
THERSITES A juggling trick – to be secretly open.
DIOMEDES
What did you swear you would bestow on me ?
CRESSIDA
I prithee, do not hold me to mine oath ;
Bid me do anything but that, sweet Greek.
DIOMEDES Good night.
TROILUS Hold, patience !
ULYSSES How now, Troyan ?
30 CRESSIDA Diomed –
DIOMEDES
No, no, good night ; I'll be your fool no more.
TROILUS
Thy better must.
CRESSIDA Hark, a word in your ear.
TROILUS
O plague and madness !
ULYSSES
You are movèd, prince ; let us depart, I pray you,
Lest your displeasure should enlarge itself
To wrathful terms. This place is dangerous ;
The time right deadly. I beseech you, go.
TROILUS
Behold, I pray you !
ULYSSES Nay, good my lord, go off ;
You flow to great distraction ; come, my lord.
TROILUS
I prithee, stay.
40 ULYSSES You have not patience ; come.
TROILUS
I pray you, stay. By hell, and all hell's torments,
I will not speak a word !
DIOMEDES And so, good night.
CRESSIDA
Nay, but you part in anger.
TROILUS Doth that grieve thee ?
O withered truth !
ULYSSES How now, my lord !
TROILUS By Jove,
I will be patient.
CRESSIDA Guardian ! Why, Greek !

DIOMEDES
Foh, foh ! adieu ; you palter.
CRESSIDA
In faith, I do not. Come hither once again.
ULYSSES
You shake, my lord, at something. Will you go ?
You will break out.
TROILUS She strokes his cheek !
ULYSSES Come, come.
TROILUS
Nay, stay ; by Jove, I will not speak a word.
There is between my will and all offenses
A guard of patience. Stay a little while.
THERSITES How the devil Luxury, with his fat rump and 53
potato finger, tickles these together. Fry, lechery, fry ! 54
DIOMEDES But will you, then ?
CRESSIDA
In faith, I will, la ; never trust me else.
DIOMEDES
Give me some token for the surety of it.
CRESSIDA
I'll fetch you one. *Exit.*
ULYSSES
You have sworn patience.
TROILUS Fear me not, my lord ;
I will not be myself, nor have cognition
Of what I feel. I am all patience.
Enter Cressid.
THERSITES Now the pledge ; now, now, now !
CRESSIDA Here, Diomed, keep this sleeve.
TROILUS
O beauty, where is thy faith ?
ULYSSES My lord –
[TROILUS
I will be patient ; outwardly I will.]
CRESSIDA
You look upon that sleeve ; behold it well.
He loved me – O false wench ! Give't me again.
DIOMEDES
Whose was't ?
CRESSIDA It is no matter, now I have't again.
I will not meet with you to-morrow night.
I prithee, Diomed, visit me no more.
THERSITES Now she sharpens. Well said, whetstone ! 71
DIOMEDES
I shall have it. 72
CRESSIDA What, this ?
DIOMEDES Ay, that.
CRESSIDA
O, all you gods ! O pretty, pretty pledge !
Thy master now lies thinking in his bed
Of thee and me, and sighs, and takes my glove,
And gives memorial dainty kisses to it, 76
As I kiss thee. Nay, do not snatch it from me ;
He that takes that doth take my heart withal.
DIOMEDES
I had your heart before ; this follows it.
TROILUS
I did swear patience.

11 *cliff* musical clef ; *noted* (pun on notes of music) 53 *Luxury* lechery
54 *potato* (considered to stimulate lechery) 71 *sharpens* whets his desire
72 *shall* am determined to 76 *memorial* i.e. of remembrance

CRESSIDA
You shall not have it, Diomed ; faith, you shall not ;
I'll give you something else.
DIOMEDES
I will have this. Whose was it ?
CRESSIDA   It is no matter.
DIOMEDES
Come, tell me whose it was.
CRESSIDA
'Twas one's that loved me better than you will.
But, now you have it, take it.
DIOMEDES   Whose was it ?
CRESSIDA
87   By all Diana's waiting-women yond,
And by herself, I will not tell you whose.
DIOMEDES
To-morrow will I wear it on my helm,
And grieve his spirit that dares not challenge it.
TROILUS
Wert thou the devil, and wor'st it on thy horn,
It should be challenged.
CRESSIDA
Well, well, 'tis done, 'tis past. And yet it is not ;
I will not keep my word.
DIOMEDES   Why then, farewell ;
Thou never shalt mock Diomed again.
CRESSIDA
You shall not go. One cannot speak a word
97   But it straight starts you.
DIOMEDES   I do not like this fooling.
98   THERSITES Nor I, by Pluto ; but that that likes not you
pleases me best.
DIOMEDES
What, shall I come ? The hour ?
CRESSIDA   Ay, come – O Jove ! –
101   Do come – I shall be plagued.
DIOMEDES   Farewell till then.
CRESSIDA
Good night. I prithee, come.   [Exit Diomedes.]
Troilus, farewell. One eye yet looks on thee,
But with my heart the other eye doth see.
105   Ah, poor our sex ! this fault in us I find,
106   The error of our eye directs our mind.
What error leads must err. O, then conclude
Minds swayed by eyes are full of turpitude.   Exit.
THERSITES
109   A proof of strength she could not publish more,
Unless she say, 'My mind is now turned whore.'

ULYSSES
All's done, my lord.
TROILUS   It is.
ULYSSES   Why stay we, then ?
TROILUS
To make a recordation to my soul
Of every syllable that here was spoke.
But if I tell how these two did co-act,
Shall I not lie in publishing a truth ?
Sith yet there is a credence in my heart,
An esperance so obstinately strong,   117
That doth invert th' attest of eyes and ears,   118
As if those organs had deceptious functions,   119
Created only to calumniate.
Was Cressid here ?
ULYSSES   I cannot conjure, Troyan.   121
TROILUS
She was not, sure.
ULYSSES   Most sure she was.
TROILUS
Why, my negation hath no taste of madness.
ULYSSES
Nor mine, my lord. Cressid was here but now.
TROILUS
Let it not be believed for womanhood !   125
Think we had mothers ; do not give advantage
To stubborn critics, apt, without a theme,
For depravation, to square the general sex   128
By Cressid's rule. Rather think this not Cressid.
ULYSSES
What hath she done, prince, that can soil our mothers ?
TROILUS
Nothing at all, unless that this were she.
THERSITES Will 'a swagger himself out on's own eyes ?   132
TROILUS
This she ? No, this is Diomed's Cressida.
If beauty have a soul, this is not she ;
If souls guide vows, if vows be sanctimonies,
If sanctimony be the gods' delight,
If there be rule in unity itself,   137
This was not she. O madness of discourse,   138
That cause sets up with and against itself ;
Bi-fold authority, where reason can revolt   140
Without perdition, and loss assume all reason
Without revolt. This is, and is not, Cressid.
Within my soul there doth conduce a fight   143
Of this strange nature that a thing inseparate   144
Divides more wider than the sky and earth ;
And yet the spacious breadth of this division
Admits no orifice for a point as subtle
As Ariachne's broken woof to enter.   148
Instance, O instance, strong as Pluto's gates ;   149
Cressid is mine, tied with the bonds of heaven.
Instance, O instance, strong as heaven itself ;
The bonds of heaven are slipped, dissolved, and loosed ;
And with another knot, five-finger-tied,
The fractions of her faith, orts of her love,   154
The fragments, scraps, the bits, and greasy relics
Of her o'er-eaten faith, are bound to Diomed.   156
ULYSSES
May worthy Troilus be half attachèd   157
With that which here his passion doth express ?
TROILUS
Ay, Greek ; and that shall be divulgèd well

---

87 *Diana's waiting-women* stars attending the moon   97 *starts you* makes
you start off (angry)   98 *likes* pleases   101 *plagued* punished   105 *poor
our sex* our poor sex   106 *error* wandering (both physical and moral here)
109 *proof of strength* strong proof ; *publish more* confess more clearly   117
esperance hope   118 *attest* witness   119 *deceptious* deceiving   121 *conjure*
raise spirits (instead of Cressida)   125 *for* for the sake of   128–29 *square
. . . rule* measure all women by Cressida's standard (cf. 'carpenter's rule')
132 *swagger . . . eyes* (cf. 'walk out on his own eyes')   137 *If . . . itself* if it
is a principle that Cressida must be one   138 *discourse* reason   140–42
where reason . . . revolt where reason can revolt against itself without self-
destruction, and destruction can take control of reason without its revolting
143 *conduce* go on   144 *thing inseparate* i.e. Cressida, as herself indivisible
148 *Ariachne* (Minerva tore up her fine-spun web in
jealousy and turned her into a spider)   149 *Instance* evidence, argument
154 *orts* scraps (properly of food)   156 *o'er-eaten* i.e. she has swallowed
her word   157 *half attachèd* half as much affected (as his passion indicates)

In characters as red as Mars his heart
Inflamed with Venus. Never did young man fancy
With so eternal and so fixed a soul.
Hark, Greek : as much as I do Cressid love,
So much by weight hate I her Diomed ;
That sleeve is mine that he'll bear on his helm ;
Were it a casque composed by Vulcan's skill,
My sword should bite it. Not the dreadful spout
Which shipmen do the hurricano call,
169   Constringed in mass by the almighty sun,
Shall dizzy with more clamor Neptune's ear
In his descent than shall my prompted sword
Falling on Diomed.
173 THERSITES He'll tickle it for his concupy.
TROILUS
O Cressid ! O false Cressid ! false, false, false !
Let all untruths stand by thy stainèd name,
And they'll seem glorious.
ULYSSES   O, contain yourself ;
Your passion draws ears hither.
     Enter Aeneas.
AENEAS
I have been seeking you this hour, my lord.
Hector, by this, is arming him in Troy ;
Ajax, your guard, stays to conduct you home.
TROILUS
181   Have with you, prince. My courteous lord, adieu.
Farewell, revolted fair ; and Diomed,
Stand fast, and wear a castle on thy head !
ULYSSES
I'll bring you to the gates.
TROILUS
Accept distracted thanks.
     Exeunt Troilus, Aeneas, and Ulysses.
THERSITES Would I could meet that rogue Diomed. I
187   would croak like a raven ; I would bode, I would bode.
Patroclus will give me anything for the intelligence of
this whore. The parrot will not do more for an almond
than he for a commodious drab. Lechery, lechery ; still
wars and lechery ; nothing else holds fashion. A burning
devil take them !   *Exit.*

     *

V, iii   *Enter Hector and Andromache.*
ANDROMACHE
When was my lord so much ungently tempered,
To stop his ears against admonishment ?
Unarm, unarm, and do not fight to-day.
HECTOR
4   You train me to offend you ; get you in.
By all the everlasting gods, I'll go.
ANDROMACHE
6   My dreams will, sure, prove ominous to the day.
HECTOR
No more, I say.
     Enter Cassandra.
CASSANDRA   Where is my brother Hector ?
ANDROMACHE
Here, sister ; armed and bloody in intent.
Consort with me in loud and dear petition ;
Pursue we him on knees, for I have dreamed
Of bloody turbulence, and this whole night
Hath nothing been but shapes and forms of slaughter.

CASSANDRA
O, 'tis true.
HECTOR   Ho, bid my trumpet sound.
CASSANDRA
No notes of sally, for the heavens, sweet brother.
HECTOR
Be gone, I say ; the gods have heard me swear.
CASSANDRA
The gods are deaf to hot and peevish vows.   16
They are polluted off'rings, more abhorred
Than spotted livers in the sacrifice.
ANDROMACHE
O, be persuaded ! Do not count it holy
[To hurt by being just. It is as lawful,
For we would give much, to use violent thefts,   21
And rob in the behalf of charity.
CASSANDRA]
It is the purpose that makes strong the vow ;
But vows to every purpose must not hold.
Unarm, sweet Hector.
HECTOR   Hold you still, I say ;
Mine honor keeps the weather of my fate.   26
Life every man holds dear ; but the dear man   27
Holds honor far more precious-dear than life.
     Enter Troilus.
How now, young man ; mean'st thou to fight to-day ?
ANDROMACHE
Cassandra, call my father to persuade.   *Exit Cassandra.*
HECTOR
No, faith, young Troilus ; doff thy harness, youth ;
I am to-day i' th' vein of chivalry.
Let grow thy sinews till their knots be strong,
And tempt not yet the brushes of the war.   34
Unarm thee, go, and doubt thou not, brave boy,
I'll stand to-day for thee and me and Troy.
TROILUS
Brother, you have a vice of mercy in you,
Which better fits a lion than a man.
HECTOR
What vice is that, good Troilus ? Chide me for it.
TROILUS
When many times the captive Grecian falls,
Even in the fan and wind of your fair sword,
You bid them rise and live.
HECTOR
O, 'tis fair play.
TROILUS   Fool's play, by heaven, Hector.
HECTOR
How now, how now ?
TROILUS   For th' love of all the gods,
Let's leave the hermit pity with our mother,
And when we have our armors buckled on,
The venomed vengeance ride upon our swords,
Spur them to ruthful work, rein them from ruth.   48
HECTOR
Fie, savage, fie !

169 *Constringed* drawn together   173 *it* i.e. Diomedes (contemptuous);
concupy concupiscence, lust   181 *Have with you* come along   187 *bode*
portend (like a raven, a bird of ill omen)
V, iii Before the palace of Priam   4 *train* tempt ; *offend* injure   6 *ominous to*
the day omens of the day's events   16 *peevish* perverse   21 *For* because   26
keeps the weather keeps to windward (the position of advantage)   27 *dear*
man worthy man   34 *brushes* encounters   48 *ruthful* pitiful ; *ruth* pity

49 TROILUS   Hector, then 'tis wars.
HECTOR
    Troilus, I would not have you fight to-day.
TROILUS
    Who should withhold me?
    Not fate, obedience, nor the hand of Mars
53 . Beck'ning with fiery truncheon my retire;
    Not Priamus and Hecuba on knees,
55 Their eyes o'ergallèd with recourse of tears;
    Nor you, my brother, with your true sword drawn,
    Opposed to hinder me, should stop my way,
    [But by my ruin.]
            Enter Priam and Cassandra.
CASSANDRA
    Lay hold upon him, Priam, hold him fast;
60 He is thy crutch. Now if thou lose thy stay,
    Thou on him leaning, and all Troy on thee,
    Fall all together.
PRIAM   Come, Hector, come; go back.
    Thy wife hath dreamed, thy mother hath had visions,
    Cassandra doth foresee, and I myself
    Am like a prophet suddenly enrapt
    To tell thee that this day is ominous:
    Therefore, come back.
HECTOR   Aeneas is a-field;
    And I do stand engaged to many Greeks,
69 Even in the faith of valor, to appear
    This morning to them.
PRIAM   Ay, but thou shalt not go.
HECTOR
    I must not break my faith.
    You know me dutiful; therefore, dear sir,
73 Let me not shame respect, but give me leave
    To take that course by your consent and voice,
    Which you do here forbid me, royal Priam.
CASSANDRA
    O Priam, yield not to him!
ANDROMACHE   Do not, dear father.
HECTOR
    Andromache, I am offended with you.
    Upon the love you bear me, get you in.
            Exit Andromache.
TROILUS
    This foolish, dreaming, superstitious girl
80 Makes all these bodements.
CASSANDRA   O farewell, dear Hector!
    Look, how thou diest; look, how thy eye turns pale;
    Look, how thy wounds do bleed at many vents!
    Hark, how Troy roars, how Hecuba cries out,
    How poor Andromache shrills her dolors forth!
    Behold, distraction, frenzy, and amazement,
86 Like witless antics, one another meet,
    And all cry Hector! Hector's dead! O Hector!
TROILUS
    Away! Away!

49 *then 'tis wars* war is like that   53 *truncheon* staff used to signal the end
of a combat between two champions   55 *o'ergallèd* inflamed; *recourse*
coursing down   60 *stay* prop   69 *faith of valor* word of honor of a brave
man   73 *shame respect* disgrace the respect due a parent   80 *bodements*
ill omens   86 *antics* lunatics   101 *tisick* cough
V, iv Field before the walls of Troy   8 *sleeveless* fruitless   9 *crafty swearing*
i.e. crafty to the extent of perjury   15–16 *proclaim barbarism* set up the
authority of ignorance   20–21 *advantageous . . . multitude* care for my
own advantage led me to avoid facing heavy odds   23–24 *Hold . . . sleeve*
(Thersites is urging both men on impartially)

CASSANDRA
    Farewell. Yet, soft: Hector, I take my leave.
    Thou dost thyself and all our Troy deceive.   *[Exit.]*
HECTOR
    You are amazed, my liege, at her exclaim.
    Go in and cheer the town. We'll forth and fight;
    Do deeds worth praise and tell you them at night.
PRIAM
    Farewell. The gods with safety stand about thee.
            [Exeunt Priam and Hector.] Alarum.
TROILUS
    They are at it, hark. Proud Diomed, believe,
    I come to lose my arm, or win my sleeve.
            Enter Pandar.
PANDARUS Do you hear, my lord? Do you hear?
TROILUS What now?
PANDARUS Here's a letter come from yond poor girl.
TROILUS Let me read.
PANDARUS A whoreson tisick, a whoreson rascally tisick 101
    so troubles me, and the foolish fortune of this girl; and
    what one thing, what another, that I shall leave you one
    o' these days; and I have a rheum in mine eyes too, and
    such an ache in my bones that, unless a man were
    cursed, I cannot tell what to think on't. What says she
    there?
TROILUS
    Words, words, mere words, no matter from the heart;
    Th' effect doth operate another way.
            [Tearing the letter.]
    Go, wind to wind, there turn and change together.
    My love with words and errors still she feeds,
    But edifies another with her deeds.   *Exeunt.*

                    *

    [Alarum.] Excursions. Enter Thersites [in excursion]. V, iv
THERSITES Now they are clapper-clawing one another;
    I'll go look on. That dissembling abominable varlet,
    Diomed, has got that same scurvy doting foolish young
    knave's sleeve of Troy there in his helm. I would fain
    see them meet, that that same young Troyan ass, that
    loves the whore there, might send that Greekish whore-
    masterly villain with the sleeve back to the dissembling
    luxurious drab, of a sleeveless errand. O' th' t' other 8
    side, the policy of those crafty swearing rascals – that 9
    stale old mouse-eaten dry cheese, Nestor, and that same
    dog-fox, Ulysses – is not proved worth a blackberry.
    They set me up, in policy, that mongrel cur, Ajax,
    against that dog of as bad a kind, Achilles. And now is
    the cur Ajax prouder than the cur Achilles, and will not
    arm to-day. Whereupon the Grecians begin to proclaim 15
    barbarism, and policy grows into an ill opinion.
            [Enter Diomedes and Troilus.]
    Soft! here comes sleeve, and t' other.
TROILUS
    Fly not; for shouldst thou take the river Styx,
    I would swim after.
DIOMEDES   Thou dost miscall retire.
    I do not fly, but advantageous care   20
    Withdrew me from the odds of multitude.
    Have at thee!
THERSITES Hold thy whore, Grecian! Now for thy 23
    whore, Troyan! Now the sleeve, now the sleeve!
            [Exeunt Troilus and Diomedes, fighting.]

Enter Hector.

HECTOR
  What art thou, Greek ? Art thou for Hector's match ?
  Art thou of blood and honor ?

THERSITES No, no. I am a rascal, a scurvy railing knave,
  a very filthy rogue.

HECTOR
  I do believe thee ; live.   *[Exit.]*

THERSITES God-a-mercy, that thou wilt believe me ; but
  a plague break thy neck – for frighting me. What's become of the wenching rogues ? I think they have swallowed one another. I would laugh at that miracle – yet,
  in a sort, lechery eats itself. I'll seek them.   *Exit.*

V, v   *Enter Diomed and Servant.*

DIOMEDES
  Go, go, my servant, take thou Troilus' horse ;
  Present the fair steed to my Lady Cressid.
  Fellow, commend my service to her beauty ;
  Tell her I have chastised the amorous Troyan,
  And am her knight by proof.

SERVANT   I go, my lord.   *[Exit.]*

     Enter Agamemnon.

AGAMEMNON
  Renew, renew ! The fierce Polydamas
  Hath beat down Menon ; bastard Margarelon
  Hath Doreus prisoner,
9   And stands colossus-wise, waving his beam,
10   Upon the pashèd corses of the kings
  Epistrophus and Cedius ; Polixenes is slain,
  Amphimachus and Thoas deadly hurt,
  Patroclus ta'en or slain, and Palamedes
14   Sore hurt and bruisèd. The dreadful Sagittary
  Appals our numbers. Haste we, Diomed,
  To reinforcement, or we perish all.

     Enter Nestor.

NESTOR
  Go, bear Patroclus' body to Achilles,
  And bid the snail-paced Ajax arm for shame.
  There is a thousand Hectors in the field.
  Now here he fights on Galathe his horse,
  And there lacks work ; anon he's there afoot,
22   And there they fly or die, like scalèd sculls
  Before the belching whale ; then is he yonder,
24   And there the strawy Greeks, ripe for his edge,
  Fall down before him, like a mower's swath.
  Here, there, and everywhere, he leaves and takes,
  Dexterity so obeying appetite
  That what he will he does, and does so much
29   That proof is called impossibility.

     Enter Ulysses.

ULYSSES
  O, courage, courage, princes ! Great Achilles
  Is arming, weeping, cursing, vowing vengeance.
  Patroclus' wounds have roused his drowsy blood,
  Together with his mangled Myrmidons,
  That noseless, handless, hacked and chipped, come to
    him,
  Crying on Hector. Ajax hath lost a friend,
  And foams at mouth, and he is armed and at it,
  Roaring for Troilus, who hath done to-day
  Mad and fantastic execution,
  Engaging and redeeming of himself
  With such a careless force and forceless care

As if that luck, in very spite of cunning,
Bade him win all.

     Enter Ajax.

AJAX
  Troilus, thou coward Troilus !   *Exit.*

DIOMEDES   Ay, there, there.

NESTOR
  So, so, we draw together.   *Exit.*

     Enter Achilles.

ACHILLES   Where is this Hector ?
  Come, come, thou boy-queller, show thy face ;   45
  Know what it is to meet Achilles angry.
  Hector, where's Hector ? I will none but Hector.   *Exit.*

     Enter Ajax.   V, vi

AJAX
  Troilus, thou coward Troilus, show thy head.

     Enter Diomedes.

DIOMEDES
  Troilus, I say, where's Troilus ?

AJAX   What wouldst thou ?

DIOMEDES
  I would correct him.

AJAX
  Were I the general, thou shouldst have my office
  Ere that correction. Troilus, I say ; what, Troilus !   5

     Enter Troilus.

TROILUS
  O traitor Diomed ! Turn thy false face, thou traitor,
  And pay thy life thou owest me for my horse.

DIOMEDES
  Ha, art thou there ?

AJAX
  I'll fight with him alone. Stand, Diomed.

DIOMEDES
  He is my prize ; I will not look upon.   10

TROILUS
  Come, both you cogging Greeks ; have at you both !   11
                    [Exeunt, fighting.]

     [Enter Hector.]

HECTOR
  Yea, Troilus ? O, well fought, my youngest brother !

     Enter Achilles.

ACHILLES
  Now do I see thee. Have at thee, Hector !
     [They fight.]

HECTOR
  Pause, if thou wilt.

ACHILLES
  I do disdain thy courtesy, proud Troyan.
  Be happy that my arms are out of use.
  My rest and negligence befriends thee now,
  But thou anon shalt hear of me again ;
  Till when, go seek thy fortune.   *Exit.*

HECTOR   Fare thee well :
  I would have been much more a fresher man,
  Had I expected thee. How now, my brother !

     Enter Troilus.

V, v   9 *beam* lance 10 *pashèd corses* battered corpses 14 *Sagittary* a
Centaur (half man, half horse) who aided the Trojans 22 *scalèd sculls*
scaly schools of fish 24 *strawy* i.e. like straw ripe for the mower's scythe
29 *proof* fact 45 *boy-queller* boy-killer
V, vi 5 *correction* privilege of correcting Troilus 10 *look upon* remain a
bystander 11 *cogging* deceitful

TROILUS

22   Ajax hath ta'en Aeneas ! Shall it be ?
No, by the flame of yonder glorious heaven,
He shall not carry him ; I'll be ta'en too,
Or bring him off. Fate, hear me what I say !
I reck not though thou end my life to-day.   *Exit.*
    Enter one in armor.

HECTOR
Stand, stand, thou Greek ; thou art a goodly mark.
No ? Wilt thou not ? I like thy armor well ;
29   I'll frush it and unlock the rivets all,
But I'll be master of it. Wilt thou not, beast, abide ?
Why then, fly on, I'll hunt thee for thy hide.
    Exit [in pursuit].

V, vii   *Enter Achilles with Myrmidons.*

ACHILLES
Come here about me, you my Myrmidons ;
Mark what I say. Attend me where I wheel ;
Strike not a stroke, but keep yourselves in breath ;
And when I have the bloody Hector found,
5   Empale him with your weapons round about ;
6   In fellest manner execute your arms.
Follow me, sirs, and my proceedings eye.
It is decreed, Hector the great must die.
    Exit [with Myrmidons].
    Enter Thersites, Menelaus, Paris [the last two
    fighting].

THERSITES   The cuckold and the cuckold-maker are at it.
10   Now, bull ! now, dog ! 'Loo, Paris, 'loo ! Now, my
11   double-horned Spartan ! 'Loo, Paris, 'loo ! The bull has
the game ; 'ware horns, ho ! *Exeunt Paris and Menelaus.*
    Enter Bastard [Margarelon].

BASTARD   Turn, slave, and fight.

THERSITES   What art thou ?

BASTARD   A bastard son of Priam's.

THERSITES   I am a bastard too ; I love bastards. I am a
bastard begot, bastard instructed, bastard in mind,
bastard in valor, in everything illegitimate. One bear
will not bite another, and wherefore should one bastard ? Take heed, the quarrel 's most ominous to us. If
the son of a whore fight for a whore, he tempts judgment. Farewell, bastard.

BASTARD   The devil take thee, coward !   *Exit.*

V, viii   *Enter Hector.*

HECTOR
Most putrefièd core, so fair without,
Thy goodly armor thus hath cost thy life.
Now is my day's work done ; I'll take my breath.
Rest, sword ; thou hast thy fill of blood and death.
    [Puts off his helmet, and hangs his shield behind him.]
    Enter Achilles and his Myrmidons.

ACHILLES
Look, Hector, how the sun begins to set,
How ugly night comes breathing at his heels.
7   Even with the vail and dark'ning of the sun,

To close the day up, Hector's life is done.

HECTOR
I am unarmed ; forgo this vantage, Greek.

ACHILLES
Strike, fellows, strike ; this is the man I seek.
    [Hector falls.]
So, Ilion, fall thou next ! Come, Troy, sink down !
Here lies thy heart, thy sinews, and thy bone.
On, Myrmidons, and cry you all amain,
'Achilles hath the mighty Hector slain !'
    Retreat.
Hark, a retire upon our Grecian part.

GREEK
The Troyan trumpets sound the like, my lord.

ACHILLES
The dragon wing of night o'erspreads the earth,
And, stickler-like, the armies separates.   18
My half-supped sword, that frankly would have fed,   19
Pleased with this dainty bait, thus goes to bed.
    [Sheathes his sword.]
Come, tie his body to my horse's tail ;
Along the field I will the Troyan trail.   *Exeunt.*
    Enter Agamemnon, Ajax, Menelaus, Nestor,   V, ix
    Diomed, and the rest, marching. [Sound retreat.
    Shout.]

AGAMEMNON
Hark, hark, what shout is that ?

NESTOR   Peace, drums !

SOLDIERS *(within)*   Achilles !
Achilles ! Hector 's slain ! Achilles !

DIOMEDES
The bruit is, Hector 's slain, and by Achilles.   3

AJAX
If it be so, yet bragless let it be ;
Great Hector was as good a man as he.

AGAMEMNON
March patiently along. Let one be sent
To pray Achilles see us at our tent.
If in his death the gods have us befriended,
Great Troy is ours, and our sharp wars are ended.
    Exeunt.
    Enter Aeneas, Paris, Antenor, and Deiphobus.   V, x

AENEAS
Stand, ho ! yet are we masters of the field.
Never go home ; here starve we out the night.
    Enter Troilus.

TROILUS
Hector is slain.

ALL   Hector ! The gods forbid !

TROILUS
He's dead and at the murderer's horse's tail,
In beastly sort, dragged through the shameful field.
Frown on, you heavens, effect your rage with speed ;
Sit, gods, upon your thrones, and smile at Troy.   7
I say, at once let your brief plagues be mercy,   8
And linger not our sure destructions on.

AENEAS
My lord, you do discomfort all the host.

TROILUS
You understand me not that tell me so.
I do not speak of flight, of fear, of death,
But dare all imminence that gods and men   13
Address their dangers in. Hector is gone.

22 *ta'en* taken captive   29 *frush* batter
V, vii   5 *Empale him* fence him in   6 *execute* give effect to   10 *'Loo* (a
cry to excite dogs)   11–12 *has the game* wins
V, viii   7 *vail* going down   18 *stickler-like* like umpires parting combatants   19 *frankly* freely
V, ix   3 *bruit* rumor
V, x   7 *smile* i.e. in derision   8 *let . . . mercy* show mercy by letting your
plagues destroy quickly   13–14 *But . . . dangers in* but dare whatever
imminent dangers gods and men may be preparing

Who shall tell Priam so, or Hecuba?
Let him that will a screech-owl aye be called
Go in to Troy, and say there Hector's dead.
There is a word will Priam turn to stone,
19   Make wells and Niobes of the maids and wives,
Cold statues of the youth, and in a word
Scare Troy out of itself. [But march away.
Hector is dead;] there is no more to say.
Stay yet. You vile abominable tents,
24   Thus proudly pight upon our Phrygian plains,
25   Let Titan rise as early as he dare,
26   I'll through and through you! And, thou great-sized
     coward,
No space of earth shall sunder our two hates.
I'll haunt thee like a wicked conscience still,
That mouldeth goblins swift as frenzy's thoughts.
Strike a free march to Troy. With comfort go;
Hope of revenge shall hide our inward woe.
       Enter Pandarus.

PANDARUS
But hear you, hear you!

TROILUS
Hence, broker lackey! Ignomy and shame
Pursue thy life, and live aye with thy name.
       Exeunt all but Pandarus.
PANDARUS A goodly medicine for my aching bones! O
world, world! thus is the poor agent despised. O traitors
and bawds, how earnestly are you set a-work, and

how ill requited! Why should our endeavor be so
loved, and the performance so loathed? What verse for
it? What instance for it? Let me see.
    Full merrily the humble-bee doth sing,
    Till he hath lost his honey and his sting;
    And being once subdued in armèd tail,
    Sweet honey and sweet notes together fail.
Good traders in the flesh, set this in your painted cloths: 45
'As many as be here of Pandar's hall,
Your eyes, half out, weep out at Pandar's fall;
Or if you cannot weep, yet give some groans,
Though not for me, yet for your aching bones.
Brethren and sisters of the hold-door trade,   50
Some two months hence my will shall here be made.
It should be now, but that my fear is this,
Some gallèd goose of Winchester would hiss.   53
Till then I'll sweat and seek about for eases,   54
And at that time bequeath you my diseases.'   *[Exit.]*

19 *Niobes* (Niobe, whose seven sons and seven daughters were slain, wept and was turned into a stone that still wept) 24 *pight* pitched 25 *Titan* (Helios, the sun, was one of the Titans) 26 *coward* i.e. Achilles 45 *painted cloths* painted cloth hangings (used like tapestries, and sometimes to advertise wares) 50 *hold-door trade* prostitution 53 *gallèd goose* irritated prostitute; *Winchester* (the brothels of Southwark had once been under the jurisdiction of the Bishop of Winchester, a prostitute being called a Winchester goose) 54 *sweat* (a treatment for venereal diseases)

APPENDIX: THE QUARTO AND FOLIO TEXTS

As indicated in the "Note on the text", both the quarto and folio texts have substantive value. In addition to the passages bracketed, a number of readings in the present text have been adopted from the folio. These are noted below, along with all other material departures from the quarto text. The adopted reading in italics is followed by the quarto reading in roman.

Preface   17 *witted* wittied   30 *judgment's* Iudgements   36 *state* states
Pro. (supplied from F) 8 *immures* emures   12 *barks* barke   19 *Sperr* Stirre
I, i, 23 *of* (F) Omitted (Q)   25 *you* (F) yea   *to* (F) Omitted (Q)   39 *An* And   50 *Pour'st* (F) Powrest   64 *an* And   67–68 *ill-thought-on* (F) ill thought   72 *An* and   *not* (F) Omitted (Q)   73 *on* (F) a   *care* (F) Omitted (Q)   74 *an* and   92 *tetchy* teachy
I, ii, 17 *they* (F) the   43 *Ilium* (F) Illum   46 *ye* yea   82 *wit* will   111 *lift* (F) liste   120 *an* and   123 *the* thee   145 *An't* And t'   181 *a* (F) Omitted (Q)   193 *man's* (F) man   199 *anything;* anything   *an* and   200 s.d. (after l. 198 in Q)   211–12 *indifferent well.* indifferent, well,   275 *prize* (F) price
I, iii, 2 *the jaundice on* the Iaundies on (F) these Iaundies ore (Q)   13 *every* (F) ever   31 *thy* (F) the   36 *patient* (F) ancient   54 *Returns* Retires   56 *spirit* (F) spright   61 *thy* (F) the   72 *lips than* lips; then   75 *basis* (F) bases   87 *Insisture* (F) In sisture   110 *meets* (F) melts   156 *scaffoldage* scoaffollage   157 *o'er-wrested* ore-rested   159 *unsquared* (F) unsquare   176 *natures,* (F) natures   188 *self-willed* (F) selfe-wild   195 *and* (F) our   209 *fineness* (F) finesse   212 s.d. (F) Omitted (Q)   214 s.d. (F) Omitted (Q)   238 *Jove's* (F) great Ioues   247 *affair* (F) affaires   250 *him* (F) with him   252 *that* (F) the   256 *loud* (F) alowd   262 *this* (F) his   263 *rusty* (F) restie   267 *That seeks* (F) And feeds   276 *compass* (F) couple   289 *or means* (F) a meanes   294

one (F) no   297 *vantbrace* (F) vambrace   *this withered brawn* (F) my withered braunes   298 *will* (F) Omitted (Q)   302 *youth* (F) men   304 *Agamemnon* (F) Omitted (Q)   305 *first* (F) sir   327 *Achilles, were* (F) Achilles weare   334 *his honor* (F) those honours   336 *this* (F) the   354 *his* in his   369 *we* (F) it   372 *did* (F) do   390 *tarre* (F) arre
II, i, 13 *vinewed'st* whinid'st (F) unsalted (Q)   16 *oration* (F) oration without booke   17 *a* (F) Omitted (Q)   18 *murrain* murren (F) murrion (Q)   *o'* ath   25 *an* and   36, 38, 39 *Thersites, Ajax, Thersites* (F) Omitted (Q)   43 *Thou* (F) you   67 *I* (F) It   71 *I'll* (F) I   92 *sufferance* (F) suffrance   97 *if he* (F) and out* (F) at   101 *your* their   *on their toes* (F) Omitted (Q)   109 *brach* brooch   117 *fifth* (F) first
II, ii, 14, 15 *surety* (F) surely   17 *worst.* (F) worst   27 *father* (F) fathers   33 *at* (F) of   47 *Let's* (F) Sets   64 *shores* (F) shore   79 *stale* (F) pale   82 *launched* (F) lansh't   100 s.d. (after l. 96 in Q)   210 *strike* (F) shrike
II, iii, 1 *Thersites* [s.p.] (F) Omitted (Q)   20 s.d. (F) Omitted (Q)   24 *wouldst* (F) couldst   29 *art* (F) art not   30 *corse* course   45 *thyself* (F) Thersites   59 *of Agamemnon* (F) Omitted (Q)   63 *Creator* (F) Prover   66 s.d. (F) Omitted (Q)   75 *shent* sent (F) sate (Q)   79 *so say* (F) say so   110 *winged* wingèd   126 *as* (F) and   127 *carriage of this action* (F) streame of his commencement   137 *enter you* (F) entertaine   156 s.d. (after l. 153 in Q)   187 *titled* (F) liked   197 *pash* (F) push   199 *An* and   206 *let* (F) tell   209, 213 *An* And   214 *Ulysses* (F) Aiax   215 *Ajax* (F) Omitted (Q)   216 *Nestor* (after *warm* in l. 216 in Q)   217 *praises* (F) praiers *pour in, pour in* (F) poure in, poure   234 *got* (F) gat   236 *all* (F) all thy   242 *bourn* (F) boord   243 *Thy* (F) This   257 *cull* (F) call
III, i, 6 *noble* (F) notable   24 *friend* (F) Omitted (Q)   34 *you not* (F) not you   36 *that* (F) Omitted (Q)   87 *poor* (F) Omitted (Q)

99 *lord* (F) lad   109 *shaft confounds* (F) shafts confound   140 *these* (F) this   148 *thee* (F) her
III, ii, 3 *he* (F) Omitted (Q)   8 *a* to a   10 *those* (F) these   42, 45 *an* and   63 *fears* teares   75 *is* (F) Omitted (Q)   86 *crown it. No perfection* (F) lover part no affection   92 s.d. (F) Omitted (Q)   111 *glance that ever –* glance ; that ever   113 *not, till now* (F) till now not   125 *Cunning* Comming   134 *An* and   149 *might ;* might   152 *aye* (F) age   159 *winnowed* winnow'd   168 *similes,* (F) simele's   172 *Yet* (F) Omitted (Q)   177 *and* (F) or   185 *as* (F) or   192 *pains* (F) paine
III, iii 33 *his* this   39 *to* (F) Omitted (Q)   44 *med'cinable* medecinable   102 *giver* (F) givers   119 *th'* (F) the   128 *abject* (F) obiect   140 *on* (F) one   141 *shrinking* (F) shriking   155 *one* (F) on   158 *hedge* (F) turne   160 *hindmost ;* (F) him, most,   162 *rear* neere   164 *past* (F) passe   177 *give* goe   197 *grain of Pluto's gold* (F) thing   198 *th'* (F) the   *deeps* (F) depth   200 *Does* Do   224 *a* (F) Omitted (Q)   233 *we* (F) they   255 *an* and   265 *to him* (F) Omitted (Q)   272 *most* (F) Omitted (Q)   276 *Grecian* (F) Omitted (Q)   *et caetera* (F) Omitted (Q)   288 *be wi'* buy
IV, i, s.d. *with a torch* (F) Omitted (Q)   4 *you* (F) your   15 *and, so long,* and so long   16 *But* (F) Lul'd   40 *do think* (F) beleeve   52 *the* (F) Omitted (Q)   56 *soilure* (F) soyle   76 *you* (F) they
IV, ii, 6 *infants'* infants   22 s.d. (F) Omitted (Q)   31 *capocchia* chipochia   51 *'Tis* (F) its   63 *us* (F) him   *for him* (F) Omitted (Q)   66 *concluded so* (F) so concluded   72 *nature* (F) neighbor Pandar   77 *Cressida* (F) Omitted (Q)
IV, iv, 4 *as* (F) is   53 *the root* (F) my throate   63 *there's* (F) there is   76 *They're* Their   78 *person* (F) portion   134 *I'll* (F) I   138 s.d. *Sound trumpet* (F) Omitted (Q)
IV, v, 95 *Agamemnon* (F) Ulisses [not a s.p.]   97 *matchless,* (F) matchlesse   98 *in deeds* (F) deeds   115 *disposed* (F) dispo'd   132 *drop* (F) day   142 *O yes* O yes   160 *mine* (F) my   177 *that I affect* (F) that I   *untraded oath* (F) thy affect, the untraded earth   187 *thy,* (F) th'   192 *shraped* shrupd   198 *Let* (F) O let   234 *prithee* (F) pray thee   254 *stithied* (F) stichied   283 *thee* (F) you   286 *As* (F) But   291 *she loved* (F) my Lord
V, i, 12 *need these* (F) needs this   14 *boy* (F) box   17 *catarrhs* (F)

Omitted (Q)   18 *o'* a   19 *wheezing* whissing   20 *lime-kilns* lime-kills   21–22 *and the like* (F) Omitted (Q)   31 *tassel* (F) toslell   32 *pestered* pestred   37 *in to-morrow's* (F) into morrowes   46 s.d. (F) Omitted (Q)   52 *brother* (F) be   54 *hanging* (F) Omitted (Q)   55 *brother's* (F) bare   56 *forced* (F) faced   58 *he is* (F) her's   *dog* (F) day   59 *mule* (F) Moyle   *fitchew* (F) Fichooke   61 *Menelaus !* Menelaus   *not* (F) Omitted (Q)   64 *spirits* (F) sprites   75 *sewer* sure   76 *at once* (F) Omitted (Q)   97 s.d. *Exit* Exeunt (F) Omitted (Q)
V, ii, 5 s.d. (F) Omitted (Q)   13 *Cressida.* Cal.   34 *you* (F) Omitted (Q)   38 *Nay* (F) Now   39 *distraction* (F) distruction   44 *withered* wither'd   45 *Why, Greek !* why Greeke ?   46 *adieu* (F) Omitted (Q)   54 *these* (F) Omitted (Q)   55 *But* (F) Omitted (Q)   56 *la* lo   66 *Cressida* (F) Troy :   68 *have't* (F) ha't   74 *in* (F) on   77 *Nay* Dio : [s.p.] Nay   78 *He* Cres : [s.p.] He   81 *Cressida* (F) Omitted (Q)   85 *one's* on's   87 *By* (F) And by   100 *Ay,* (F) I   101 *plagued* (F) plagu'd   110 *say* (F) said   114 *co-act* (F) Court   119 *had deceptious* (F) were deceptions   130 *soil* (F) spoile   147 *orifice* orifex   148 *Ariachne's* (F) Ariachna's   153 *five-* (F) finde   156 *bound* (F) given   163 *as I* I
V, iii, 14 *Cassandra* (F) Cres.   21 *give* count give   *use* as   29 *mean'st* (F) meanest   39 *that, good Troilus ?* that ? good Troylus   85 *distraction* (F) destruction   104 *o' these* ath's
V, iv, 3 *young* (F) Omitted (Q)   15 *begin* began   25 *art thou* (F) art
V, v, 22 *scaled* (F) scaling   41 *luck* (F) lust   43 *Ajax* (F) Omitted (Q)
V, vi, 1 *Ajax* (F) Omitted (Q)   2 *Diomedes* (F) Omitted (Q)   13 *Achilles* (F) Omitted (Q)   *thee* thee ha   26 *reck* wreake   *thou* (F) I
V, vii, 1 *Achilles* (F) Omitted (Q)   10 *'Loo* lowe   *'loo* lowe   11 *-horned* hen'd   *'Loo, Paris, 'loo* lowe Paris, lowe   12 s.d. *Exeunt* Exit   16 *am a bastard* (F) am bastard
V, viii, 4 s.d. *his* (F) Omitted (Q)   15 *part* (F) prat   16 *Greek* (F) One   *Troyan trumpets* (F) Troyans trumpet
V, ix, 1 *shout is that* (F) is this
V, x, s.d. *and* (F) Omitted (Q)   3 *Troilus* (F) before l. 2 in Q   8 *say, say*   12 *fear, of* (F) feare of   17 *there* (F) their   23 *vile* (F) proud   24 *pight* (F) pitcht   29 *frenzy's* (F) frienzes   33 *broker lackey !* broker, lacky,   *Ignomy and* (F) ignomyny   49 *your* (F) my

OTHELLO THE MOOR OF VENICE

INTRODUCTION

Of the four tragedies commonly thought to be Shakespeare's greatest and the most distinguished examples of this form in the English language – *Hamlet, Othello, King Lear*, and *Macbeth* – *Othello* is the most tightly constructed and the narrowest in scope. The resultant concentration of emotion and action makes it a play of unusual forcefulness, powerful not only on the stage but in the study, sweeping from the confident and brilliant opening to the tragic close. All four tragedies came within a six- or seven-year span; *Othello*, the second, was probably written not long before November 1, 1604, when it was performed by the King's Men at Court, and it is interesting that it alone has this tight construction and headlong action.

Shakespeare gains this concentration in several ways. For one thing, here the time of action is condensed so that the events of only two or three nights and days appear to be set forth on the stage, and the only emphasized time-lapse is that required for the voyage from Venice to Cyprus. The other three tragedies span months or even years, and time-consuming events which occur between scenes have to be pointed out to the audience: for example, in *Hamlet* Laertes' trip from Elsinore to Paris and return; in *King Lear* Cordelia's sojourn in France; and in *Macbeth* Malcolm and Macduff's flight to England, the recruitment of an army there, and then the march of that army to Dunsinane. The elimination in *Othello* of all but one such emphasized space-breaks and time-breaks helps to give the play its headlong rush from the arrival in Cyprus to Othello's death.

Not only by a limitation of time has Shakespeare intensified the effect of rushing events, but also by an unusual concentration of the action in the three main characters, Othello, Desdemona, and Iago. One or more of these three is on the stage in each of the fifteen scenes of the play except for the brief proclamation scene (II, ii), whereas Macbeth and Lady Macbeth are absent from nine scenes of their play, Lear and his daughters fail to appear in six scenes of *King Lear*, and even in the one-man play of *Hamlet* both the protagonist and Ophelia are off-stage during four scenes totalling nearly five hundred lines. These observations afford, of course, no evidence of the comparative merits of the four tragedies, but they do point to Shakespeare's deviation from his customary practice in achieving the distinctive concentration of *Othello*. He has denied himself the development of any subsidiary interests in order to concentrate on the tragic destruction of Othello and Desdemona through the diabolism of Iago.

To the same end Shakespeare has minimized the number of characters in this play. Not only is the cast of *Othello* smaller than those of the other three tragedies – it has half to two-thirds the number of characters – but in it the secondary characters, Brabantio, Cassio, Roderigo, and Emilia, are undeveloped save for their relations to the plotting of Iago or the downfall of Othello and Desdemona. Even Iago's gulling of Roderigo, which might at first glance seem to be an underplot, is really only an instrument in the destruction of Othello; Roderigo is given little individuality beyond that of the uncomprehending gull to whom Iago may speak freely (thus further revealing for the audience his own character and plans) and who will carry out Iago's schemes for the disgrace and assassination of Cassio. Roderigo has no unrelated or parallel existence, like that of Lady Macduff in *Macbeth*, or Polonius and Fortinbras in *Hamlet*. All such secondary concerns, which add variety and depth of character-interest to Shakespeare's other major tragedies, and to *Romeo and Juliet, Julius Caesar, Antony and Cleopatra*, and *Coriolanus* as well, have been sacrificed in this play to give *Othello* that unique concentration and simplicity which make it more like modern tragedies in structure than any of Shakespeare's other tragic masterpieces.

Othello differs again from the usual Shakespearean pattern in the extent to which the power of evil is concentrated in one figure. The conflict of good and evil in an ostensibly Christian world was always a basic element in Elizabethan tragedies, and Shakespeare's presentation of the conflict is everywhere more subtle and complex than that of any of his contemporaries, but in the other Shakespearean tragedies the evil is more dispersed through various characters or even, as in *King Lear*, through the entire world of the play. Here the inherent weaknesses of Desdemona and Othello are made fatal through the maneuvering of Iago, whose cunning of the devil makes the finally disabused Othello look for his cloven hoof (V, ii, 286). This further simplification of the structure of the play not only makes possible the creation of Shakespeare's supreme stage villain – one of the most coveted roles in the history of the theatre – but it provides yet another device for the concentration of emotions in the tragedy. The play's excellence in structure and vividness in characterization seem even more impressive when *Othello* is compared with its source, a mediocre Italian tale by "Cinthio" (Giovanni Baptista Giraldi) told in the *Hecatommithi*, a collection of 1565.

Having planned his scenario to reduce the scope and variety made possible by the Elizabethan stage and familiarly exploited in tragedies like his own *Antony and Cleopatra* and Marlowe's *Doctor Faustus*, Shakespeare could lavish his dramatic and poetic genius on the painful degeneration of the noble and assured Othello of Act I, scenes ii and iii, to the pitiful dupe and the figure of passionate remorse we see in V, ii; on the battering of the proud and confident Desdemona of I, iii into the childlike and uncomprehending victim of Acts IV and V – all by means of the terrifyingly casual and joyous evil of "honest Iago." All the seeds of these tragic events are displayed to the audience in the first act, but they are so adroitly overlaid by a romantic and optimistic tone that the prosperity of the love of Othello and Desdemona is made to seem superficially possible.

Othello is a man of action whose achievement was immediately obvious to an Elizabethan audience, in spite of his exotic color and background, because of his position as the commanding general for the greatest commercial power of the preceding century. He is first presented in a situation in which his experience and reputation make him easily the dominant figure on the stage. In the second scene of the play, as the drawn swords flash about him, Othello, the object of the attack, stands quietly confident, his weapon still in its scabbard, and speaks to these incensed men like a veteran to excited boys: "Keep up your bright swords, for the dew will rust them."

At Othello's second appearance, in the third scene of the play, he dominates not a mere cluster of street fighters but the Duke and senators of a powerful Renaissance state assembled in formal council. The scene is skillfully contrived at the beginning to draw the audience into the crisis of a national emergency; then a principal senator arrives who focuses the attention of the council on his just indignation against the unnamed seducer of his daughter. Unhesitatingly the Duke accepts Brabantio's story and unhesitatingly promises him the bloody punishment of the culprit, though the man be the Duke's own son. But when Brabantio explains that the unnamed seducer is their great general, the attitude of Duke and senators changes sharply. Respectfully they listen as the black Othello describes his courtship of the daughter of a great Venetian magnifico; they watch sympathetically as Desdemona confesses her duty and obedience to the Moor above her duty and obedience to her father; the Duke in the presence of the other senators advises Brabantio to make the best of his new son-in-law; and Duke and senators proceed to reiterate their confidence in Othello by assigning him the command at Cyprus as though Brabantio had never spoken. Again, as in scene ii, the assured power of Othello over great men in council as well as over lesser men in action is dramatized before the audience.

Yet under this dominating impression of a commanding and unshakeable personality the weaknesses of Othello have been less vividly suggested. In the second scene he speaks confidentially to Iago as to a trusted friend, and toward the end of the third scene he commits his beloved wife to the protection of Iago, whom he calls a man "of honesty and trust." But the audience had been introduced to Iago before they had been to Othello. In the opening scene of the play Iago was heard to admit his hatred of Othello, to declare his moral code as unscrupulous self-aggrandizement, and to assert his policy of consistent insincerity. And in the council chamber scene, immediately after the exit of Othello, the trusted Iago again declares his principles of calculated self-seeking and closes the act with a soliloquy in which he reasserts his hatred of Othello and plots the general's betrayal. Can Othello's assured mastery of threatening situations be so unshakeable as it has seemed

in the two big dramatic scenes of the act if he is so naive in his judgment of Iago?

And what of the romantic marriage with Desdemona so touchingly presented? Othello says of his wife that

> She loved me for the dangers I had passed,
> And I loved her that she did pity them.

The lines are beautifully evocative, but many members of the audience might have an uneasy feeling that Desdemona really knew very little about Othello. And they would feel uneasy again at Brabantio's bitter parting jibe at Othello,

> Look to her, Moor, if thou hast eyes to see:
> She has deceived her father, and may thee,

a jibe made in a spirit of animosity and not of thoughtful analysis, yet reminding us that romantic ignorance often prepares the way for deception. The Elizabethan ideal of respect for parents was much stronger than ours, and this emphatic couplet was calculated to make a sharper impression on an audience than a more elaborately rational statement would have made. Even the phrase "if thou hast eyes to see" has an ominous relevance, for Othello has already shown he has no eyes to see the true character of Iago. Does he know more of Desdemona?

And so carefully planned concentration on Iago, Othello, and Desdemona in the first act of the play leaves a dominant impression of a resourceful and confident general, triumphant in a seriously threatened love affair, off for new triumphs in the field of his greatest competence, so fortunate that as he sets out to meet the challenge of a military emergency he is not even required to forgo the company of his bride. And yet here, less dominantly presented in this opening movement, are all the seeds of the fifth act. Othello is a proud and confident man, but his experience, as he himself points out, is almost exclusively military; his appealing new wife knows little of him save for his military honors and adventures, and he knows little of her save for her admiration of his exploits; his trusted ensign is an unscrupulous opportunist who prides himself on his insincerity. In these terms the play is to develop.

The transfer of the action to Cyprus for the developments of the last four acts is significant. From Desdemona's native world of wealthy, sophisticated, pampered Venice, where Othello is out of his usual campaign environment, the action moves to an outpost under martial law, a setting alien to Desdemona. Here, like most of Shakespeare's tragic heroines, she is isolated from her accustomed friends and supporters, while Othello is in a setting familiar, as he has said, from childhood:

> For since these arms of mine had seven years' pith
> Till now some nine moons wasted, they have used
> Their dearest action in the tented field.

In such an environment one would expect Othello to be even more effortlessly dominant than in worldly Venice, and the first two hundred lines of the Cyprus action suggest that he will be, for all on stage are relieved at his arrival and eager to trust and serve him; even the fortunate dispersal of the Turkish fleet seems another triumph for lucky Othello. But it only seems so, for Othello's accustomed environment of war is suddenly removed, and in the last hundred lines of II, i Iago establishes the cynical, lecherous, intriguing tone of a decadent

Renaissance court more vividly than it was ever set in the first act at Venice itself. Othello's apparent good fortune in the transfer of the action from sophisticated Venice, where, as he says, "little of this great world can I speak," to the familiar setting of a town at war, with the added good fortune of the company of his bride, is a completely illusory triumph. Cyprus is not really an honest camp but an outpost of Venetian intrigue in which Othello is a helpless child; his new wife is not even a typical Venetian, for she is more naive and imperceptive than Othello, as her actions in the third and fourth acts and her conversation with Emilia in the last part of IV, iii so vividly show; Iago is not the trusty ensign who will fight at his commander's side but a Venetian devil incarnate, adept at hellish insinuations. As in so many Shakespearean tragedies, the great man of the first act enters a new set of circumstances and becomes "no more but such a poor, bare, forked animal as thou art."

It is only Iago who prospers in the new environment. The declared villain satisfies his hatred of his general and his lieutenant by creating for Othello the vivid illusion of Desdemona's infidelity with Cassio, and in the terrifying grip of this illusion Othello destroys his reputation, his happiness, his bride, and himself. Perhaps the most tragically terrifying aspect of this irrational destruction is the fact that Othello, like all mortals who only know in part, dimly realizes what he is doing at each step, but in the grip of the illusion he always misunderstands why he is doing it. As early as the middle of the third act he knows that his suspicious uncertainty of Desdemona has destroyed his peace of mind and his cherished professional career.

> O, now for ever
> Farewell the tranquil mind ! farewell content !
> Farewell the plumèd troop, and the big wars
> That make ambition virtue ! O, farewell !
> Farewell the neighing steed and the shrill trump,
> The spirit-stirring drum, th' ear-piercing fife,
> The royal banner, and all quality,
> Pride, pomp, and circumstance of glorious war !
> And O you mortal engines whose rude throats
> Th' immortal Jove's dread clamors counterfeit,
> Farewell ! Othello's occupation 's gone !

When he comes in to kill Desdemona he is painfully aware that his love for her is as deep as ever, that he destroys what he loves best. He kisses the sleeping girl.

> O balmy breath, that dost almost persuade
> Justice to break her sword ! One more, one more !
> Be thus when thou art dead, and I will kill thee,
> And love thee after. One more, and that's the last !
> So sweet was ne'er so fatal. I must weep,
> But they are cruel tears. This sorrow 's heavenly ;
> It strikes where it doth love.

And a few lines later when she protests her innocence he partially and confusedly understands what he does :

> O perjured woman ! thou dost stone my heart,
> And mak'st me call what I intend to do
> A murder, which I thought a sacrifice.

When, immediately after the stifling of Desdemona, Emilia enters the death chamber with news of the street murder, Othello again vaguely recognizes what he has done in the madness of his illusion, though he speaks in general terms :

> It is the very error of the moon.
> She comes more nearer earth than she was wont
> And makes men mad.

And when Emilia roundly asserts the fidelity of her dead mistress, Othello protests in half-realization of his illusion,

> Cassio did top her. Ask thy husband else.
> O, I were damned beneath all depth in hell
> But that I did proceed upon just grounds
> To this extremity. Thy husband knew it all.

Only in the last hundred lines of the play does he clearly begin to see himself and to comprehend what has happened to him :

> with this little arm and this good sword
> I have made my way through more impediments
> Than twenty times your stop. But O vain boast !
> Who can control his fate ? 'Tis not so now.
> Be not afraid, though you do see me weaponed.
> Here is my journey's end.

And only in his final speech to the emissaries from the Duke and senators, just before he stabs himself, does the great general of Venice, like the great King Lear, truly know himself :

> I pray you, in your letters,
> When you shall these unlucky deeds relate,
> Speak of me as I am. Nothing extenuate,
> Nor set down aught in malice. Then must you speak
> Of one that loved not wisely, but too well ;
> Of one not easily jealous, but, being wrought,
> Perplexed in the extreme ; of one whose hand,
> Like the base Judean, threw a pearl away
> Richer than all his tribe.

This is the tragedy, then, of another deluded mortal who destroys what he loves best, so that his own death is only an appropriate corollary. King Lear and Coriolanus and Brutus do likewise, but they destroy themselves in a context of troubled kingdoms and empires, while the little world of Othello's tragedy is his own marriage and his false friend, "honest Iago." This narrowed scope of the tragedy reduces the generalized philosophic comments which characterize plays of more varied situation and looser structure like *King Lear* and *Hamlet*, but it intensifies the emotional impact of blind self-destruction.

Princeton University　　　　GERALD EADES BENTLEY

NOTE ON THE TEXT

Two versions of *Othello* have come down to us, one in a quarto of 1622 and another in the folio of 1623. Both are good, although they vary somewhat in details and their precise relationship is still subject to debate. The folio version is the fuller (by about 160 lines) and has been used as the basis of the present text ; however, a number of readings from the quarto have been admitted, especially in contractions, oaths, and stage directions, where the corresponding words in the folio suggest editorial intervention. A few lines and brief passages of dialogue (I, iii, 372–75 ; III, iv, 92–93) omitted from the folio have been added from the quarto in square brackets. The act–scene division supplied marginally for reference is identical with that of the folio except for the indication of a new scene (II, iii) after the reading of the proclamation. (Unlike earlier quartos, that of *Othello* is partially divided into acts, with headings at II, IV, and V.) The extent of the use made of the quarto text is indicated in the Appendix as well as a listing of emendations.

OTHELLO THE MOOR OF VENICE

*

I, i   *Enter Roderigo and Iago.*

RODERIGO

Tush, never tell me ! I take it much unkindly
That thou, Iago, who hast had my purse

3   As if the strings were thine, shouldst know of this.

IAGO

4   'Sblood, but you'll not hear me !
If ever I did dream of such a matter,
Abhor me.

RODERIGO

Thou told'st me thou didst hold him in thy hate.

IAGO

Despise me if I do not. Three great ones of the city,
In personal suit to make me his lieutenant,

10   Off-capped to him ; and, by the faith of man,
I know my price ; I am worth no worse a place.
But he, as loving his own pride and purposes,

13   Evades them with a bombast circumstance.
Horribly stuffed with epithets of war ;
[And, in conclusion,]

16   Nonsuits my mediators ; for, 'Certes,' says he,
'I have already chose my officer.'
And what was he ?

19   Forsooth, a great arithmetician,
One Michael Cassio, a Florentine

21   (A fellow almost damned in a fair wife)
That never set a squadron in the field,
Nor the division of a battle knows
More than a spinster ; unless the bookish theoric,
Wherein the togèd consuls can propose
As masterly as he. Mere prattle without practice

Is all his soldiership. But he, sir, had th' election ;
And I (of whom his eyes had seen the proof
At Rhodes, at Cyprus, and on other grounds

30   Christian and heathen) must be belee'd and calmed

31   By debitor and creditor ; this counter-caster,
He, in good time, must his lieutenant be,

33   And I – God bless the mark ! – his Moorship's ancient.

RODERIGO

By heaven, I rather would have been his hangman.

IAGO

Why, there's no remedy ; 'tis the curse of service.

36   Preferment goes by letter and affection,
And not by old gradation, where each second
Stood heir to th' first. Now, sir, be judge yourself,

39   Whether I in any just term am affined
To love the Moor.

RODERIGO   I would not follow him then.

IAGO

O, sir, content you ;
I follow him to serve my turn upon him.
We cannot all be masters, nor all masters
Cannot be truly followed. You shall mark
Many a duteous and knee-crooking knave
That, doting on his own obsequious bondage,
Wears out his time, much like his master's ass,

48   For naught but provender ; and when he's old, cashiered.
Whip me such honest knaves ! Others there are

50   Who, trimmed in forms and visages of duty,
Keep yet their hearts attending on themselves ;
And, throwing but shows of service on their lords,
Do well thrive by them, and when they have lined their
          coats,
Do themselves homage. These fellows have some soul ;
And such a one do I profess myself. For, sir,
It is as sure as you are Roderigo,
Were I the Moor, I would not be Iago.
In following him, I follow but myself ;
Heaven is my judge, not I for love and duty,

But seeming so, for my peculiar end;
For when my outward action doth demonstrate
62   The native act and figure of my heart
63   In compliment extern, 'tis not long after
But I will wear my heart upon my sleeve
For daws to peck at; I am not what I am.

RODERIGO
66   What a full fortune does the thick-lips owe
If he can carry't thus!

IAGO   Call up her father,
Rouse him. Make after him, poison his delight,
Proclaim him in the streets. Incense her kinsmen,
And though he in a fertile climate dwell,
Plague him with flies; though that his joy be joy,
Yet throw such changes of vexation on't
As it may lose some color.

RODERIGO
Here is her father's house. I'll call aloud.

IAGO
75   Do, with like timorous accent and dire yell
As when, by night and negligence, the fire
Is spied in populous cities.

RODERIGO
What, ho, Brabantio! Signior Brabantio, ho!

IAGO
Awake! What, ho, Brabantio! Thieves! thieves! thieves!
Look to your house, your daughter, and your bags!
81   Thieves! thieves!

        Brabantio at a window.

BRABANTIO *(above)*
What is the reason of this terrible summons?
What is the matter there?

RODERIGO
Signior, is all your family within?

IAGO
Are your doors locked?

BRABANTIO   Why, wherefore ask you this?

IAGO
Zounds, sir, y' are robbed! For shame, put on your
     gown!
Your heart is burst; you have lost half your soul.
Even now, now, very now, an old black ram
Is tupping your white ewe. Arise, arise!
90   Awake the snorting citizens with the bell,
Or else the devil will make a grandsire of you.
Arise, I say!

BRABANTIO   What, have you lost your wits?

RODERIGO
Most reverend signior, do you know my voice?

BRABANTIO
Not I. What are you?

RODERIGO
My name is Roderigo.

BRABANTIO   The worser welcome!
I have charged thee not to haunt about my doors.
In honest plainness thou hast heard me say
My daughter is not for thee; and now, in madness,
Being full of supper and distemp'ring draughts,
Upon malicious knavery dost thou come
To start my quiet.

RODERIGO
Sir, sir, sir —

BRABANTIO   But thou must needs be sure
My spirit and my place have in them power

To make this bitter to thee.

RODERIGO   Patience, good sir.

BRABANTIO
What tell'st thou me of robbing? This is Venice;
My house is not a grange.   106

RODERIGO   Most grave Brabantio,
In simple and pure soul I come to you.

IAGO Zounds, sir, you are one of those that will not serve
God if the devil bid you. Because we come to do you
service, and you think we are ruffians, you'll have your
daughter covered with a Barbary horse; you'll have
your nephews neigh to you; you'll have coursers for 112
cousins, and gennets for germans.   113

BRABANTIO
What profane wretch art thou?

IAGO I am one, sir, that comes to tell you your daughter
and the Moor are now making the beast with two backs.

BRABANTIO
Thou art a villain.

IAGO   You are — a senator.

BRABANTIO
This thou shalt answer. I know thee, Roderigo.

RODERIGO
Sir, I will answer anything. But I beseech you,
If 't be your pleasure and most wise consent,
As partly I find it is, that your fair daughter,
At this odd-even and dull watch o' th' night,   122
Transported, with no worse nor better guard
But with a knave of common hire, a gondolier,
To the gross clasps of a lascivious Moor —
If this be known to you, and your allowance,   126
We then have done you bold and saucy wrongs;
But if you know not this, my manners tell me
We have your wrong rebuke. Do not believe
That, from the sense of all civility,   130
I thus would play and trifle with your reverence.
Your daughter, if you have not given her leave,
I say again, hath made a gross revolt,
Tying her duty, beauty, wit, and fortunes
In an extravagant and wheeling stranger   135
Of here and everywhere. Straight satisfy yourself.
If she be in her chamber, or your house,
Let loose on me the justice of the state
For thus deluding you.

BRABANTIO   Strike on the tinder, ho!
Give me a taper! Call up all my people!
This accident is not unlike my dream.   141
Belief of it oppresses me already.
Light, I say! light!   *Exit [above].*

IAGO   Farewell, for I must leave you.
It seems not meet, nor wholesome to my place,
To be produced — as, if I stay, I shall —
Against the Moor. For I do know the state,
However this may gall him with some check,   147
Cannot with safety cast him; for he's embarked   148

---

62 *The . . . heart* what I really believe and intend   63 *compliment extern*
outward appearance   66 *thick-lips* (Elizabethans made no clear distinction
between Moors and Negroes); *owe* own   75 *timorous* terrifying   81 **s.d.**
Brabantio at a window (added from quarto)   90 *snorting* snoring   106
grange isolated farmhouse   112 *nephews* i.e. grandsons   113 *gennets for*
germans Spanish horses for near kinsmen   122 *odd-even* between night
and morning   126 *allowance* approval   130 *from the sense* in violation
135 *extravagant and wheeling* expatriate and roving   141 *accident* occurrence   147 *check* reprimand   148 *cast* discharge

With such loud reason to the Cyprus wars,
150   Which even now stand in act, that for their souls
151   Another of his fathom they have none
To lead their business; in which regard,
Though I do hate him as I do hell-pains,
Yet, for necessity of present life,
I must show out a flag and sign of love,
Which is indeed but sign. That you shall surely find him,
157   Lead to the Sagittary the raisèd search;
158   And there will I be with him. So farewell.   *Exit.*
Enter [below] Brabantio in his nightgown, and
Servants with torches.

BRABANTIO
It is too true an evil. Gone she is;
And what's to come of my despisèd time
Is naught but bitterness. Now, Roderigo,
Where didst thou see her? – O unhappy girl! –
With the Moor, say'st thou? – Who would be a father? –
How didst thou know 'twas she? – O, she deceives me
165   Past thought! – What said she to you? – Get moe tapers!
Raise all my kindred! – Are they married, think you?

RODERIGO
Truly I think they are.

BRABANTIO
O heaven! How got she out? O treason of the blood!
Fathers, from hence trust not your daughters' minds
By what you see them act. Is there not charms
171   By which the property of youth and maidhood
May be abused? Have you not read, Roderigo,
Of some such thing?

RODERIGO   Yes, sir, I have indeed.

BRABANTIO
Call up my brother. – O, would you had had her! –
Some one way, some another. – Do you know
Where we may apprehend her and the Moor?

RODERIGO
I think I can discover him, if you please
To get good guard and go along with me.

BRABANTIO
Pray you lead on. At every house I'll call;
I may command at most. – Get weapons, ho!
And raise some special officers of night. –
182   On, good Roderigo; I'll deserve your pains.   *Exeunt.*

*

I, ii   *Enter Othello, Iago, and Attendants with torches.*
IAGO
Though in the trade of war I have slain men,
Yet do I hold it very stuff o' th' conscience
To do no contrived murther. I lack iniquity
Sometimes to do me service. Nine or ten times
5   I had thought t' have yerked him here under the ribs.

OTHELLO
'Tis better as it is.

IAGO   Nay, but he prated,
And spoke such scurvy and provoking terms
Against your honor
That with the little godliness I have
I did full hard forbear him. But I pray you, sir,
Are you fast married? Be assured of this,   11
That the magnifico is much beloved,   12
And hath in his effect a voice potential   13
As double as the Duke's. He will divorce you,   14
Or put upon you what restraint and grievance
The law, with all his might to enforce it on,
Will give him cable.

OTHELLO   Let him do his spite.
My services which I have done the signiory   18
Shall out-tongue his complaints. 'Tis yet to know –   19
Which, when I know that boasting is an honor,
I shall promulgate – I fetch my life and being
From men of royal siege; and my demerits   22
May speak unbonneted to as proud a fortune   23
As this that I have reached. For know, Iago,
But that I love the gentle Desdemona,
I would not my unhousèd free condition   26
Put into circumscription and confine
For the sea's worth. But look, what lights come yond?

IAGO
Those are the raisèd father and his friends.
You were best go in.

OTHELLO   Not I; I must be found.
My parts, my title, and my perfect soul   31
Shall manifest me rightly. Is it they?

IAGO
By Janus, I think no.
Enter Cassio, with torches, Officers.

OTHELLO
The servants of the Duke, and my lieutenant.
The goodness of the night upon you, friends!
What is the news?

CASSIO   The Duke does greet you, general;
And he requires your haste-post-haste appearance
Even on the instant.

OTHELLO   What's the matter, think you?

CASSIO
Something from Cyprus, as I may divine.
It is a business of some heat. The galleys
Have sent a dozen sequent messengers   41
This very night at one another's heels,
And many of the consuls, raised and met,
Are at the Duke's already. You have been hotly called for;
When, being not at your lodging to be found,
The Senate hath sent about three several quests
To search you out.

OTHELLO   'Tis well I am found by you.
I will but spend a word here in the house,
And go with you.   *[Exit.]*

CASSIO   Ancient, what makes he here?

IAGO
Faith, he to-night hath boarded a land carack.   50
If it prove lawful prize, he's made for ever.

CASSIO
I do not understand.

IAGO   He's married.

CASSIO   To who?

---

150 *stand in act* are going on   151 *fathom* capacity   157 *Sagittary* an inn   158 *s.d. nightgown* dressing gown   165 *moe* more   171 *property* nature   182 *deserve* show gratitude for
I, ii *Before the lodgings of Othello*   5 *yerked* stabbed   11 *fast* securely   12 *magnifico* grandee (Brabantio)   13 *potential* powerful   14 *double* doubly influential   18 *signiory* Venetian government   19 *yet to know* still not generally known   22 *siege* rank; *demerits* deserts   23–24 *May speak . . . reached* are equal, I modestly assert, to those of Desdemona's family   26 *unhousèd* unrestrained   31 *perfect soul* stainless conscience   41 *sequent* consecutive   50 *carack* treasure ship

[Enter Othello.]

IAGO
Marry, to – Come, captain, will you go?

OTHELLO   Have with you.

CASSIO
Here comes another troop to seek for you.
Enter Brabantio, Roderigo, and others with lights and weapons.

IAGO
It is Brabantio. General, be advised.
He comes to bad intent.

OTHELLO   Holla! stand there!

RODERIGO
Signior, it is the Moor.

BRABANTIO   Down with him, thief!
[They draw on both sides.]

IAGO
You, Roderigo! Come, sir, I am for you.

OTHELLO
59   Keep up your bright swords, for the dew will rust them.
Good signior, you shall more command with years
Than with your weapons.

BRABANTIO
O thou foul thief, where hast thou stowed my daughter?
Damned as thou art, thou hast enchanted her!
For I'll refer me to all things of sense,
If she in chains of magic were not bound,
Whether a maid so tender, fair, and happy,
So opposite to marriage that she shunned
The wealthy curlèd darlings of our nation,
Would ever have, t' incur a general mock,
Run from her guardage to the sooty bosom
Of such a thing as thou – to fear, not to delight.
72   Judge me the world if 'tis not gross in sense
That thou hast practiced on her with foul charms,
Abused her delicate youth with drugs or minerals
75   That weaken motion. I'll have 't disputed on;
'Tis probable, and palpable to thinking.
77   I therefore apprehend and do attach thee
For an abuser of the world, a practicer
Of arts inhibited and out of warrant.
Lay hold upon him. If he do resist,
Subdue him at his peril.

OTHELLO   Hold your hands,
Both you of my inclining and the rest.
Were it my cue to fight, I should have known it
Without a prompter. Where will you that I go
To answer this your charge?

BRABANTIO   To prison, till fit time
86   Of law and course of direct session
Call thee to answer.

OTHELLO   What if I do obey?
How may the Duke be therewith satisfied,
Whose messengers are here about my side
Upon some present business of the state
To bring me to him?

OFFICER   'Tis true, most worthy signior.
The Duke 's in council, and your noble self
I am sure is sent for.

BRABANTIO   How? The Duke in council?
In this time of the night? Bring him away.
95   Mine's not an idle cause. The Duke himself,
Or any of my brothers of the state,
Cannot but feel this wrong as 'twere their own;

For if such actions may have passage free,
Bondslaves and pagans shall our statesmen be.   *Exeunt.*

*

Enter Duke and Senators, set at a table, with lights   I, iii
and Attendants.

DUKE
There is no composition in these news   1
That gives them credit.

1. SENATOR   Indeed they are disproportionèd.
My letters say a hundred and seven galleys.

DUKE
And mine a hundred forty.

2. SENATOR   And mine two hundred.
But though they jump not on a just account –   5
As in these cases where the aim reports   6
'Tis oft with difference – yet do they all confirm
A Turkish fleet, and bearing up to Cyprus.

DUKE
Nay, it is possible enough to judgment.
I do not so secure me in the error   10
But the main article I do approve   11
In fearful sense.

SAILOR *(within)* What, ho! what, ho! what, ho!

OFFICER
A messenger from the galleys.
Enter Sailor.

DUKE   Now, what's the business?

SAILOR
The Turkish preparation makes for Rhodes.
So was I bid report here to the state
By Signior Angelo.

DUKE
How say you by this change?

1. SENATOR   This cannot be
By no assay of reason. 'Tis a pageant   18
To keep us in false gaze. When we consider   19
Th' importancy of Cyprus to the Turk,
And let ourselves again but understand
That, as it more concerns the Turk than Rhodes,
So may he with more facile question bear it,   23
For that it stands not in such warlike brace,   24
But altogether lacks th' abilities
That Rhodes is dressed in – if we make thought of this,
We must not think the Turk is so unskillful
To leave that latest which concerns him first,
Neglecting an attempt of ease and gain
To wake and wage a danger profitless.   30

DUKE
Nay, in all confidence, he's not for Rhodes.

OFFICER
Here is more news.
Enter a Messenger.

MESSENGER
The Ottomites, reverend and gracious,
Steering with due course toward the isle of Rhodes,

---

59 *Keep up* i.e. sheath   72 *gross in sense* obvious   75 *motion* perception
77 *attach* arrest   86 *direct session* regular trial   95 *idle* trifling
I, iii The Venetian Senate Chamber   1 *composition* consistency   5 *jump*
agree   6 *aim* conjecture   10 *so secure me* take such comfort   11 *article*
substance; *approve* accept   18 *assay* test   19 *in false gaze* looking the
wrong way   23 *with . . . bear* more easily capture   24 *brace* posture of
defense   30 *wake and wage* rouse and risk

Have there injointed them with an after fleet.

1. SENATOR
Ay, so I thought. How many, as you guess?

MESSENGER
37 Of thirty sail; and now they do restem
Their backward course, bearing with frank appearance
Their purposes toward Cyprus. Signior Montano,
Your trusty and most valiant servitor,
With his free duty recommends you thus,
And prays you to believe him.

DUKE
'Tis certain then for Cyprus.
44 Marcus Luccicos, is not he in town?

1. SENATOR
He's now in Florence.

DUKE
Write from us to him; post, post-haste dispatch.

1. SENATOR
Here comes Brabantio and the valiant Moor.
    Enter Brabantio, Othello, Cassio, Iago, Roderigo,
    and Officers.

DUKE
Valiant Othello, we must straight employ you
Against the general enemy Ottoman.
    [To Brabantio]
I did not see you. Welcome, gentle signior.
We lacked your counsel and your help to-night.

BRABANTIO
So did I yours. Good your grace, pardon me.
Neither my place, nor aught I heard of business,
Hath raised me from my bed; nor doth the general care
Take hold on me; for my particular grief
56 Is of so floodgate and o'erbearing nature
57 That it engluts and swallows other sorrows,
And it is still itself.

DUKE   Why, what's the matter?

BRABANTIO
My daughter! O, my daughter!

ALL   Dead?

BRABANTIO   Ay, to me.
She is abused, stol'n from me, and corrupted
By spells and medicines bought of mountebanks;
For nature so prepost'rously to err,
63 Being not deficient, blind, or lame of sense,
Sans witchcraft could not.

DUKE
Whoe'er he be that in this foul proceeding
Hath thus beguiled your daughter of herself,
And you of her, the bloody book of law
You shall yourself read in the bitter letter
69 After your own sense; yea, though our proper son
70 Stood in your action.

BRABANTIO   Humbly I thank your grace.
Here is the man – this Moor, whom now, it seems,
Your special mandate for the state affairs
Hath hither brought.

ALL   We are very sorry for't.

DUKE *[to Othello]*
What, in your own part, can you say to this?

BRABANTIO
Nothing, but this is so.

OTHELLO
Most potent, grave, and reverend signiors,
My very noble, and approved good masters,   77
That I have ta'en away this old man's daughter,
It is most true; true I have married her.
The very head and front of my offending
Hath this extent, no more. Rude am I in my speech,   81
And little blessed with the soft phrase of peace;
For since these arms of mine had seven years' pith   83
Till now some nine moons wasted, they have used
Their dearest action in the tented field;
And little of this great world can I speak
More than pertains to feats of broil and battle;
And therefore little shall I grace my cause
In speaking for myself. Yet, by your gracious patience,
I will a round unvarnished tale deliver   90
Of my whole course of love – what drugs, what charms,
What conjuration, and what mighty magic
(For such proceeding am I charged withal)
I won his daughter.

BRABANTIO   A maiden never bold;
Of spirit so still and quiet that her motion   95
Blushed at herself; and she – in spite of nature,
Of years, of country, credit, everything –
To fall in love with what she feared to look on!
It is a judgment maimed and most imperfect
That will confess perfection so could err
Against all rules of nature, and must be driven
To find out practices of cunning hell   102
Why this should be. I therefore vouch again   103
That with some mixtures pow'rful o'er the blood,   104
Or with some dram, conjured to this effect,
He wrought upon her.

DUKE   To vouch this is no proof,
Without more certain and more overt test
Than these thin habits and poor likelihoods   108
Of modern seeming do prefer against him.   109

1. SENATOR
But, Othello, speak.
Did you by indirect and forcèd courses   111
Subdue and poison this young maid's affections?
Or came it by request, and such fair question   113
As soul to soul affordeth?

OTHELLO   I do beseech you,
Send for the lady to the Sagittary
And let her speak of me before her father.
If you do find me foul in her report,
The trust, the office, I do hold of you
Not only take away, but let your sentence
Even fall upon my life.

DUKE   Fetch Desdemona hither.

OTHELLO
Ancient, conduct them; you best know the place.
    Exit [Iago, with] two or three [Attendants].
And till she come, as truly as to heaven
I do confess the vices of my blood,
So justly to your grave ears I'll present
How I did thrive in this fair lady's love,
And she in mine.

---

37 *restem* steer again   44 *Marcus Luccicos* (presumably a Venetian envoy)
56 *floodgate* torrential   57 *engluts* devours   63 *deficient* feeble-minded
69 *our proper* my own   70 *Stood in your action* were accused by you   77
approved tested by experience   81 *Rude* unpolished   83 *pith* strength
90 *round* plain   95–96 *her motion Blushed* her own emotions caused her
to blush   102 *practices* plots   103 *vouch* assert   104 *blood* passions
108 *thin habits* slight appearances   109 *modern seeming* everyday supposition   111 *forcèd* violent   113 *question* conversation

DUKE
Say it, Othello.

OTHELLO
Her father loved me, oft invited me;
129 Still questioned me the story of my life
From year to year – the battles, sieges, fortunes
That I have passed.
I ran it through, even from my boyish days
To th' very moment that he bade me tell it.
Wherein I spoke of most disastrous chances,
Of moving accidents by flood and field;
Of hairbreadth scapes i' th' imminent deadly breach;
Of being taken by the insolent foe
And sold to slavery; of my redemption thence
139 And portance in my travels' history;
140 Wherein of anters vast and deserts idle,
Rough quarries, rocks, and hills whose heads touch
    heaven,
142 It was my hint to speak – such was the process;
And of the Cannibals that each other eat,
144 The Anthropophagi, and men whose heads
Do grow beneath their shoulders. This to hear
Would Desdemona seriously incline;
But still the house affairs would draw her thence;
Which ever as she could with haste dispatch,
She'ld come again, and with a greedy ear
Devour up my discourse. Which I observing,
151 Took once a pliant hour, and found good means
To draw from her a prayer of earnest heart
153 That I would all my pilgrimage dilate,
154 Whereof by parcels she had something heard,
155 But not intentively. I did consent,
And often did beguile her of her tears
When I did speak of some distressful stroke
That my youth suffered. My story being done,
She gave me for my pains a world of sighs.
She swore, i' faith, 'twas strange, 'twas passing strange;
'Twas pitiful, 'twas wondrous pitiful.
She wished she had not heard it; yet she wished
That heaven had made her such a man. She thanked me;
And bade me, if I had a friend that loved her,
I should but teach him how to tell my story,
166 And that would woo her. Upon this hint I spake.
She loved me for the dangers I had passed,
And I loved her that she did pity them.
This only is the witchcraft I have used.
Here comes the lady. Let her witness it.
    Enter Desdemona, Iago, Attendants.

DUKE
I think this tale would win my daughter too.
Good Brabantio,
Take up this mangled matter at the best.
Men do their broken weapons rather use
Than their bare hands.

BRABANTIO   I pray you hear her speak.
If she confess that she was half the wooer,
Destruction on my head if my bad blame
Light on the man! Come hither, gentle mistress.
Do you perceive in all this noble company
Where most you owe obedience?

DESDEMONA   My noble father,
I do perceive here a divided duty.
182 To you I am bound for life and education;
My life and education both do learn me

How to respect you: you are the lord of duty;
I am hitherto your daughter. But here's my husband;
And so much duty as my mother showed
To you, preferring you before her father,
So much I challenge that I may profess   188
Due to the Moor my lord.

BRABANTIO   God be with you! I have done.
Please it your grace, on to the state affairs.
I had rather to adopt a child than get it.   191
Come hither, Moor.
I here do give thee that with all my heart
Which, but thou hast already, with all my heart
I would keep from thee. For your sake, jewel,   195
I am glad at soul I have no other child;
For thy escape would teach me tyranny,   197
To hang clogs on them. I have done, my lord.

DUKE
Let me speak like yourself and lay a sentence   199
Which, as a grise or step, may help these lovers   200
[Into your favor.]
When remedies are past, the griefs are ended
By seeing the worst, which late on hopes depended.
To mourn a mischief that is past and gone
Is the next way to draw new mischief on.
What cannot be preserved when fortune takes,
Patience her injury a mock'ry makes.
The robbed that smiles steals something from the thief;
He robs himself that spends a bootless grief.

BRABANTIO
So let the Turk of Cyprus us beguile: 210
We lose it not so long as we can smile.
He bears the sentence well that nothing bears
But the free comfort which from thence he hears;
But he bears both the sentence and the sorrow
That to pay grief must of poor patience borrow.
These sentences, to sugar, or to gall,
Being strong on both sides, are equivocal.
But words are words. I never yet did hear
That the bruised heart was piercèd through the ear.
Beseech you, now to the affairs of state.

DUKE The Turk with a most mighty preparation makes
for Cyprus. Othello, the fortitude of the place is best   222
known to you; and though we have there a substitute
of most allowed sufficiency, yet opinion, a more sover-   224
eign mistress of effects, throws a more safer voice on you.
You must therefore be content to slubber the gloss of   226
your new fortunes with this more stubborn and
boist'rous expedition.

OTHELLO
The tyrant custom, most grave senators,
Hath made the flinty and steel couch of war
My thrice-driven bed of down. I do agnize   231
A natural and prompt alacrity
I find in hardness; and do undertake
These present wars against the Ottomites.

129 *Still* continually   139 *portance* behavior   140 *anters* caves   142 *hint* occasion   144 *Anthropophagi* man-eaters   151 *pliant* propitious   153 *dilate* recount in full   154 *parcels* portions   155 *intentively* with full attention   166 *hint* opportunity   182 *education* upbringing   188 *challenge* claim the right   191 *get* beget   195 *For your sake* because of you   197 *escape* escapade   199 *like yourself* as you should; *sentence* maxim   200 *grise* step   222 *fortitude* fortification   224 *allowed* acknowledged; *opinion* public opinion   226 *slubber* sully   231-33 *agnize . . . hardness* recognize in myself a natural and easy response to hardship

Most humbly, therefore, bending to your state,
I crave fit disposition for my wife,
237 Due reference of place, and exhibition,
238 With such accommodation and besort
239 As levels with her breeding.

DUKE   If you please,
Be't at her father's.

BRABANTIO   I will not have it so.

OTHELLO
Nor I.

DESDEMONA Nor I. I would not there reside,
To put my father in impatient thoughts
By being in his eye. Most gracious Duke,
244 To my unfolding lend your prosperous ear,
And let me find a charter in your voice,
246 T' assist my simpleness.

DUKE
What would you, Desdemona?

DESDEMONA
That I did love the Moor to live with him,
My downright violence, and storm of fortunes,
May trumpet to the world. My heart's subdued
Even to the very quality of my lord.
I saw Othello's visage in his mind,
And to his honors and his valiant parts
Did I my soul and fortunes consecrate.
So that, dear lords, if I be left behind,
A moth of peace, and he go to the war,
The rites for which I love him are bereft me,
And I a heavy interim shall support
By his dear absence. Let me go with him.

OTHELLO
Let her have your voice.
Vouch with me, heaven, I therefore beg it not
To please the palate of my appetite,
263 Not to comply with heat – the young affects
In me defunct – and proper satisfaction;
But to be free and bounteous to her mind;
And heaven defend your good souls that you think
I will your serious and great business scant
When she is with me. No, when light-winged toys
269 Of feathered Cupid seel with wanton dullness
270 My speculative and officed instruments,
271 That my disports corrupt and taint my business,
Let housewives make a skillet of my helm,
273 And all indign and base adversities
274 Make head against my estimation!

DUKE
Be it as you shall privately determine,
Either for her stay or going. Th' affair cries haste,
And speed must answer it.

1. SENATOR
You must away to-night.

OTHELLO   With all my heart.

DUKE
At nine i' th' morning here we'll meet again.
Othello, leave some officer behind,
And he shall our commission bring to you,
With such things else of quality and respect
As doth import you.   283

OTHELLO   So please your grace, my ancient;
A man he is of honesty and trust.
To his conveyance I assign my wife,
With what else needful your good grace shall think
To be sent after me.

DUKE   Let it be so.
Good night to every one.
     [To Brabantio]   And, noble signior,
If virtue no delighted beauty lack,   289
Your son-in-law is far more fair than black.

1. SENATOR
Adieu, brave Moor. Use Desdemona well.

BRABANTIO
Look to her, Moor, if thou hast eyes to see:
She has deceived her father, and may thee.
       Exeunt [Duke, Senators, Officers, &c.].

OTHELLO
My life upon her faith! – Honest Iago,
My Desdemona must I leave to thee.
I prithee let thy wife attend on her,
And bring them after in the best advantage.   297
Come, Desdemona. I have but an hour
Of love, of worldly matters and direction,
To spend with thee. We must obey the time.
       Exit Moor and Desdemona.

RODERIGO Iago, –

IAGO What say'st thou, noble heart?

RODERIGO What will I do, think'st thou?

IAGO Why, go to bed and sleep.

RODERIGO I will incontinently drown myself.   305

IAGO If thou dost, I shall never love thee after. Why, thou silly gentleman!

RODERIGO It is silliness to live when to live is torment; and then have we a prescription to die when death is our physician.

IAGO O villainous! I have looked upon the world for four times seven years; and since I could distinguish betwixt a benefit and an injury, I never found man that knew how to love himself. Ere I would say I would drown myself for the love of a guinea hen, I would change my humanity with a baboon.

RODERIGO What should I do? I confess it is my shame to be so fond, but it is not in my virtue to amend it.

IAGO Virtue? a fig! 'Tis in ourselves that we are thus or thus. Our bodies are our gardens, to the which our wills are gardeners; so that if we will plant nettles or sow lettuce, set hyssop and weed up thyme, supply it with one gender of herbs or distract it with many – either to 323 have it sterile with idleness or manured with industry – why, the power and corrigible authority of this lies in 325 our wills. If the balance of our lives had not one scale of reason to poise another of sensuality, the blood and 327 baseness of our natures would conduct us to most preposterous conclusions. But we have reason to cool our raging motions, our carnal stings, our unbitted lusts; 330 whereof I take this that you call love to be a sect or scion. 331

RODERIGO It cannot be.

IAGO It is merely a lust of the blood and a permission of

237 *exhibition* allowance of money   238 *besort* suitable company   239 *levels* corresponds   244 *prosperous* favorable   246 *simpleness* lack of skill   263 *heat* passions; *young affects* tendencies of youth   269 *seel* blind   270 *My . . . instruments* my perceptive and responsible faculties   271 *That* so that   273 *indign* unworthy   274 *estimation* reputation   283 *import* concern   289 *delighted* delightful   297 *in the best advantage* at the best opportunity   305 *incontinently* forthwith   323 *gender* species   325 *corrigible authority* corrective power   327 *poise* counterbalance   327–28 *blood and baseness* animal instincts   330 *motions* appetites; *unbitted* uncontrolled   331 *sect or scion* offshoot, cutting

1027

the will. Come, be a man! Drown thyself? Drown cats and blind puppies! I have professed me thy friend, and I confess me knit to thy deserving with cables of perdurable toughness. I could never better stead thee than now. Put
338 money in thy purse. Follow thou the wars; defeat thy favor with an usurped beard. I say, put money in thy purse. It cannot be that Desdemona should long continue her love to the Moor – put money in thy purse – nor he his to her. It was a violent commencement in her, and
343 thou shalt see an answerable sequestration – put but money in thy purse. These Moors are changeable in their wills – fill thy purse with money. The food that to him now is as luscious as locusts shall be to him shortly as bit-
347 ter as coloquintida. She must change for youth: when she is sated with his body, she will find the error of her choice. [She must have change, she must.] Therefore put money in thy purse. If thou wilt needs damn thyself, do it a more
351 delicate way than drowning. Make all the money thou
352 canst. If sanctimony and a frail vow betwixt an erring barbarian and a supersubtle Venetian be not too hard for my wits and all the tribe of hell, thou shalt enjoy her. Therefore make money. A pox of drowning thyself! 'Tis clean out of the way. Seek thou rather to be hanged in compassing thy joy than to be drowned and go without her.

RODERIGO Wilt thou be fast to my hopes, if I depend on the issue?

IAGO Thou art sure of me. Go, make money. I have told thee often, and I retell thee again and again, I hate the
362 Moor. My cause is hearted; thine hath no less reason. Let us be conjunctive in our revenge against him. If thou canst cuckold him, thou dost thyself a pleasure, me a sport. There are many events in the womb of time,
366 which will be delivered. Traverse, go, provide thy money! We will have more of this to-morrow. Adieu.

RODERIGO Where shall we meet i' th' morning?

IAGO At my lodging.

RODERIGO I'll be with thee betimes.

IAGO Go to, farewell. – Do you hear, Roderigo?

[RODERIGO What say you?

IAGO No more of drowning, do you hear?

RODERIGO I am changed.

IAGO Go to, farewell. Put money enough in your purse.]

RODERIGO I'll sell all my land.   Exit.

IAGO
Thus do I ever make my fool my purse;
For I mine own gained knowledge should profane
379 If I would time expend with such a snipe
But for my sport and profit. I hate the Moor;
And it is thought abroad that 'twixt my sheets
H'as done my office. I know not if't be true;
But I, for mere suspicion in that kind,
384 Will do as if for surety. He holds me well;
The better shall my purpose work on him.
Cassio's a proper man. Let me see now:
387 To get his place, and to plume up my will
In double knavery – How, how? – Let's see: –
After some time, to abuse Othello's ears
That he is too familiar with his wife.
391 He hath a person and a smooth dispose
To be suspected – framed to make women false.
393 The Moor is of a free and open nature
That thinks men honest that but seem to be so;
And will as tenderly be led by th' nose

As asses are.
I have't! It is engend'red! Hell and night
Must bring this monstrous birth to the world's light.
                                        Exit.

                    *

Enter Montano and two Gentlemen.   II, i

MONTANO
What from the cape can you discern at sea?

1. GENTLEMAN
Nothing at all: it is a high-wrought flood.
I cannot 'twixt the heaven and the main
Descry a sail.

MONTANO
Methinks the wind hath spoke aloud at land;
A fuller blast ne'er shook our battlements.
If it hath ruffianed so upon the sea,
What ribs of oak, when mountains melt on them,
Can hold the mortise? What shall we hear of this?   9

2. GENTLEMAN
A segregation of the Turkish fleet.   10
For do but stand upon the foaming shore,
The chidden billow seems to pelt the clouds;
The wind-shaked surge, with high and monstrous mane,
Seems to cast water on the burning Bear
And quench the Guards of th' ever-fixèd pole.   15
I never did like molestation view   16
On the enchafèd flood.

MONTANO   If that the Turkish fleet
Be not ensheltered and embayed, they are drowned;
It is impossible to bear it out.
                    Enter a third Gentleman.

3. GENTLEMAN
News, lads! Our wars are done.
The desperate tempest hath so banged the Turks
That their designment halts. A noble ship of Venice   22
Hath seen a grievous wrack and sufferance   23
On most part of their fleet.

MONTANO
How? Is this true?

3. GENTLEMAN   The ship is here put in,
A Veronesa; Michael Cassio,   26
Lieutenant to the warlike Moor Othello,
Is come on shore; the Moor himself at sea,
And is in full commission here for Cyprus.

MONTANO
I am glad on't. 'Tis a worthy governor.

3. GENTLEMAN
But this same Cassio, though he speak of comfort
Touching the Turkish loss, yet he looks sadly
And prays the Moor be safe, for they were parted
With foul and violent tempest.

MONTANO   Pray heaven he be;
For I have served him, and the man commands

338–39 *defeat thy favor* spoil thy appearance   343 *sequestration* estrangement   347 *coloquintida* a medicine   351 *Make* raise   352 *erring* wandering
362 *My cause is hearted* my heart is in it   366 *Traverse* forward march
379 *snipe* fool   384 *well* in high regard   387 *plume up* gratify   391 *dispose* manner   393 *free* frank
II, i An open place in Cyprus, near the harbor   9 *hold the mortise* hold their joints together   10 *segregation* scattering   15 *Guards* stars near the North Star; *pole* polestar   16 *molestation* tumult   22 *designment halts* plan is crippled   23 *sufferance* disaster   26 *Veronesa* ship furnished by Verona

Like a full soldier. Let's to the seaside, ho!
As well to see the vessel that's come in
As to throw out our eyes for brave Othello,
Even till we make the main and th' aerial blue

40 An indistinct regard.

3 . GENTLEMAN   Come, let's do so;
For every minute is expectancy
Of more arrivance.
      Enter Cassio.

CASSIO

Thanks, you the valiant of this warlike isle,
That so approve the Moor! O, let the heavens
Give him defense against the elements,
For I have lost him on a dangerous sea!

MONTANO

Is he well shipped?

CASSIO

His bark is stoutly timbered, and his pilot
Of very expert and approved allowance;

50 Therefore my hopes, not surfeited to death,
51 Stand in bold cure.
      (Within) A sail, a sail, a sail!
      Enter a Messenger.

CASSIO

What noise?

MESSENGER

The town is empty; on the brow o' th' sea
Stand ranks of people, and they cry 'A sail!'

CASSIO

My hopes do shape him for the governor.
      A shot.

2 . GENTLEMAN

They do discharge their shot of courtesy:
Our friends at least.

CASSIO   I pray you, sir, go forth
And give us truth who 'tis that is arrived.

2 . GENTLEMAN

I shall.   *Exit.*

MONTANO

But, good lieutenant, is your general wived?

CASSIO

Most fortunately. He hath achieved a maid

62 That paragons description and wild fame;
63 One that excels the quirks of blazoning pens,
64 And in th' essential vesture of creation
Does tire the ingener.
      Enter Second Gentleman.
             How now? Who has put in?

2 . GENTLEMAN

'Tis one Iago, ancient to the general.

CASSIO

H'as had most favorable and happy speed:
Tempests themselves, high seas, and howling winds,

69 The guttered rocks and congregated sands,
70 Traitors ensteeped to clog the guiltless keel,
As having sense of beauty, do omit

Their mortal natures, letting go safely by
The divine Desdemona.   72

MONTANO   What is she?

CASSIO

She that I spake of, our great captain's captain,
Left in the conduct of the bold Iago,
Whose footing here anticipates our thoughts   76
A se'nnight's speed. Great Jove, Othello guard,   77
And swell his sail with thine own pow'rful breath,
That he may bless this bay with his tall ship,
Make love's quick pants in Desdemona's arms,
Give renewed fire to our extinced spirits,
[And bring all Cyprus comfort!]
      Enter Desdemona, Iago, Roderigo, and Emilia [with
        Attendants].   O, behold!
The riches of the ship is come on shore!
You men of Cyprus, let her have your knees.   84
Hail to thee, lady! and the grace of heaven,
Before, behind thee, and on every hand,
Enwheel thee round!

DESDEMONA   I thank you, valiant Cassio.
What tidings can you tell me of my lord?

CASSIO

He is not yet arrived; nor know I aught
But that he's well and will be shortly here.

DESDEMONA

O but I fear! How lost you company?

CASSIO

The great contention of the sea and skies
Parted our fellowship.
      (Within) A sail, a sail! *[A shot.]*
             But hark. A sail!

2 . GENTLEMAN

They give their greeting to the citadel;
This likewise is a friend.

CASSIO   See for the news.
             [Exit Gentleman.]
Good ancient, you are welcome.
      [To Emilia]   Welcome, mistress. –
Let it not gall your patience, good Iago,
That I extend my manners. 'Tis my breeding
That gives me this bold show of courtesy.   99
      [Kisses Emilia.]

IAGO

Sir, would she give you so much of her lips
As of her tongue she oft bestows on me,
You would have enough.

DESDEMONA   Alas, she has no speech!

IAGO

In faith, too much.
I find it still when I have list to sleep.
Marry, before your ladyship, I grant,
She puts her tongue a little in her heart
And chides with thinking.

EMILIA

You have little cause to say so.

IAGO

Come on, come on! You are pictures out of doors,
Bells in your parlors, wildcats in your kitchens,
Saints in your injuries, devils being offended,
Players in your housewifery, and housewives in your   112
beds.

DESDEMONA

O, fie upon thee, slanderer!

---

40 *An indistinct regard* indistinguishable   50 *surfeited to death* over-
indulged   51 *in bold cure* a good chance of fulfillment   62 *paragons*
surpasses   63 *quirks* ingenuities; *blazoning* describing   64–65 *And . . .*
ingener merely to describe her as God made her exhausts her praiser
69 *guttered* jagged   70 *ensteeped* submerged   72 *mortal* deadly   76
footing landing   77 *se'nnight's* week's   84 *knees* i.e. kneeling   99 s.d.
Kisses Emilia (kissing was a common Elizabethan form of social courtesy)
112 *housewifery* housekeeping; *housewives* hussies

IAGO
Nay, it is true, or else I am a Turk :
You rise to play, and go to bed to work.

EMILIA
You shall not write my praise.

IAGO   No, let me not.

DESDEMONA
What wouldst thou write of me, if thou shouldst praise
me ?

IAGO
O gentle lady, do not put me to't,
For I am nothing if not critical.

DESDEMONA
120   Come on, assay. – There's one gone to the harbor ?

IAGO
Ay, madam.

DESDEMONA
I am not merry ; but I do beguile
The thing I am by seeming otherwise. –
Come, how wouldst thou praise me ?

IAGO
I am about it ; but indeed my invention
126   Comes from my pate as birdlime does from frieze –
It plucks out brains and all. But my Muse labors,
And thus she is delivered :
If she be fair and wise, fairness and wit –
The one's for use, the other useth it.

DESDEMONA
131   Well praised ! How if she be black and witty ?

IAGO
If she be black, and thereto have a wit,
She'll find a white that shall her blackness fit.

DESDEMONA
Worse and worse !

EMILIA
How if fair and foolish ?

IAGO
She never yet was foolish that was fair,
137   For even her folly helped her to an heir.

138 DESDEMONA These are old fond paradoxes to make fools
laugh i' th' alehouse. What miserable praise hast thou
140   for her that's foul and foolish ?

IAGO
There's none so foul, and foolish thereunto,
But does foul pranks which fair and wise ones do.

DESDEMONA O heavy ignorance ! Thou praisest the
worst best. But what praise couldst thou bestow on a
deserving woman indeed – one that in the authority of
146   her merit did justly put on the vouch of very malice
itself ?

IAGO
She that was ever fair, and never proud ;
Had tongue at will, and yet was never loud ;
Never lacked gold, and yet went never gay ;
Fled from her wish, and yet said 'Now I may' ;
She that, being ang'red, her revenge being nigh,
Bade her wrong stay, and her displeasure fly ;
She that in wisdom never was so frail
154   To change the cod's head for the salmon's tail ;
She that could think, and ne'er disclose her mind ;
See suitors following, and not look behind :
She was a wight (if ever such wight were) –

DESDEMONA To do what ?

IAGO
To suckle fools and chronicle small beer.   159

DESDEMONA O most lame and impotent conclusion ! Do
not learn of him, Emilia, though he be thy husband.
How say you, Cassio ? Is he not a most profane and   162
liberal counsellor ?

CASSIO He speaks home, madam. You may relish him   164
more in the soldier than in the scholar.

IAGO [aside] He takes her by the palm. Ay, well said,
whisper ! With as little a web as this will I ensnare as
great a fly as Cassio. Ay, smile upon her, do ! I will gyve   168
thee in thine own courtship. – You say true ; 'tis so, indeed ! – If such tricks as these strip you out of your lieutenantry, it had been better you had not kissed your
three fingers so oft – which now again you are most apt
to play the sir in. Very good ! well kissed ! an excellent   173
courtesy ! 'Tis so, indeed. Yet again your fingers to your
lips ? Would they were clyster pipes for your sake !   175
(Trumpet within.) The Moor ! I know his trumpet.

CASSIO 'Tis truly so.

DESDEMONA Let's meet him and receive him.

CASSIO Lo, where he comes.
       Enter Othello and Attendants.

OTHELLO
O my fair warrior !

DESDEMONA   My dear Othello !

OTHELLO
It gives me wonder great as my content
To see you here before me. O my soul's joy !
If after every tempest come such calms,
May the winds blow till they have wakened death !
And let the laboring bark climb hills of seas
Olympus-high, and duck again as low
As hell's from heaven ! If it were now to die,
'Twere now to be most happy ; for I fear   188
My soul hath her content so absolute
That not another comfort like to this
Succeeds in unknown fate.

DESDEMONA   The heavens forbid
But that our loves and comforts should increase
Even as our days do grow.

OTHELLO   Amen to that, sweet powers !
I cannot speak enough of this content ;
It stops me here ; it is too much of joy.
And this, and this, the greatest discords be
      They kiss.
That e'er our hearts shall make !

IAGO [aside]   O, you are well tuned now !
But I'll set down the pegs that make this music,   198
As honest as I am.

OTHELLO   Come, let us to the castle.
News, friends ! Our wars are done ; the Turks are
drowned.
How does my old acquaintance of this isle ? –
Honey, you shall be well desired in Cyprus ;   202

---

120 *assay* try   126 *birdlime* a sticky paste; *frieze* rough cloth   131 *black*
brunette   137 *folly* wantonness   138 *fond* foolish   140 *foul* ugly   146 *put
on the vouch* compel the approval   154 *To . . . tail* i.e. to exchange the good
for the poor but expensive   159 *chronicle small beer* keep petty household
accounts   162–63 *profane and liberal* worldly and licentious   164 *home*
bluntly   168–69 *gyve . . . courtship* manacle you by means of your courtly
manners   173 *sir* courtly gentleman   175 *clyster pipes* syringes   188
happy fortunate   198 *set down* loosen   202 *well desired* warmly welcomed

I have found great love amongst them. O my sweet,
I prattle out of fashion, and I dote
In mine own comforts. I prithee, good Iago,
Go to the bay and disembark my coffers.
207 Bring thou the master to the citadel;
He is a good one, and his worthiness
209 Does challenge much respect. – Come, Desdemona,
Once more well met at Cyprus.
           Exit Othello [with all but Iago and Roderigo].
IAGO *[to an Attendant, who goes out]* Do thou meet me
presently at the harbor. *[to Roderigo]* Come hither. If
thou be'st valiant (as they say base men being in love
have then a nobility in their natures more than is native
to them), list me. The lieutenant to-night watches on
216 the court of guard. First, I must tell thee this: Desdemona is directly in love with him.
RODERIGO With him? Why, 'tis not possible.
219 IAGO Lay thy finger thus, and let thy soul be instructed.
Mark me with what violence she first loved the Moor,
but for bragging and telling her fantastical lies; and will
she love him still for prating? Let not thy discreet heart
think it. Her eye must be fed; and what delight shall she
have to look on the devil? When the blood is made dull
with the act of sport, there should be, again to inflame it
and to give satiety a fresh appetite, loveliness in favor,
sympathy in years, manners, and beauties; all which the
Moor is defective in. Now for want of these required
229 conveniences, her delicate tenderness will find itself
230 abused, begin to heave the gorge, disrelish and abhor the
Moor. Very nature will instruct her in it and compel her
to some second choice. Now sir, this granted – as it is a
233 most pregnant and unforced position – who stands so
eminent in the degree of this fortune as Cassio does? A
235 knave very voluble; no further conscionable than in put-
236 ting on the mere form of civil and humane seeming for
237 the better compassing of his salt and most hidden loose
238 affection? Why, none! why, none! A slipper and subtle
knave; a finder-out of occasions; that has an eye can
stamp and counterfeit advantages, though true advantage never present itself; a devilish knave! Besides, the
knave is handsome, young, and hath all those requisites
in him that folly and green minds look after. A pestilent
complete knave! and the woman hath found him already.
RODERIGO I cannot believe that in her; she's full of most
246 blessed condition.
IAGO Blessed fig's-end! The wine she drinks is made of
grapes. If she had been blessed, she would never have
loved the Moor. Blessed pudding! Didst thou not see
her paddle with the palm of his hand? Didst not mark
that?
RODERIGO Yes, that I did; but that was but courtesy.

IAGO Lechery, by this hand! an index and obscure prologue to the history of lust and foul thoughts. They met
so near with their lips that their breaths embraced together. Villainous thoughts, Roderigo! When these mu- 255
tualities so marshal the way, hard at hand comes the
master and main exercise, th' incorporate conclusion. 257
Pish! But, sir, be you ruled by me: I have brought you
from Venice. Watch you to-night; for the command,
I'll lay't upon you. Cassio knows you not. I'll not be far
from you: do you find some occasion to anger Cassio,
either by speaking too loud, or tainting his discipline, or 262
from what other course you please which the time shall
more favorably minister.
RODERIGO Well.
IAGO Sir, he's rash and very sudden in choler, and haply 266
with his truncheon may strike at you. Provoke him that
he may; for even out of that will I cause these of Cyprus
to mutiny; whose qualification shall come into no true 269
taste again but by the displanting of Cassio. So shall you
have a shorter journey to your desires by the means I
shall then have to prefer them; and the impediment 272
most profitably removed without the which there were
no expectation of our prosperity.
RODERIGO I will do this if you can bring it to any oppor-
tunity.
IAGO I warrant thee. Meet me by and by at the citadel; I
must fetch his necessaries ashore. Farewell.
RODERIGO Adieu.   *Exit.*
IAGO
That Cassio loves her, I do well believe't;
That she loves him, 'tis apt and of great credit.   281
The Moor, howbeit that I endure him not,
Is of a constant, loving, noble nature,
And I dare think he'll prove to Desdemona
A most dear husband. Now I do love her too;
Not out of absolute lust, though peradventure
I stand accountant for as great a sin,   287
But partly led to diet my revenge,   288
For that I do suspect the lusty Moor
Hath leaped into my seat; the thought whereof
Doth, like a poisonous mineral, gnaw my inwards;
And nothing can or shall content my soul
Till I am evened with him, wife for wife;
Or failing so, yet that I put the Moor
At least into a jealousy so strong
That judgment cannot cure. Which thing to do,
If this poor trash of Venice, whom I trash   297
For his quick hunting, stand the putting on,   298
I'll have our Michael Cassio on the hip,   299
Abuse him to the Moor in the rank garb   300
(For I fear Cassio with my nightcap too),
Make the Moor thank me, love me, and reward me
For making him egregiously an ass
And practicing upon his peace and quiet   304
Even to madness. 'Tis here, but yet confused:
Knavery's plain face is never seen till used.   *Exit.*

*

---

207 *master* ship captain   **209** *challenge* deserve   **216** *court of guard* head-
quarters   **219** *thus* i.e. on your lips   **229** *conveniences* compatibilities
230 *heave the gorge* be nauseated   **233** *pregnant* evident   **235** *conscionable*
conscientious   **236** *humane* polite   **237** *salt* lecherous   **238** *slipper* slippery
246 *condition* character   **255** *mutualities* exchanges   **257** *incorporate*
carnal   **262** *tainting* discrediting   **266** *sudden in choler* violent in anger
269 *qualification* appeasement   **269–70** *true taste* satisfactory state   **272**
prefer advance   **281** *apt* probable   **287** *accountant* accountable   **288** *diet*
feed   **297** *I trash* I weight down (in order to keep under control)   **298**
For in order to develop; *stand the putting on* responds to my inciting
299 *on the hip* at my mercy   **300** *rank garb* gross manner   **304** *practicing*
upon plotting against
II, ii A street in Cyprus   **3** *mere perdition* complete destruction

Enter Othello's Herald, with a proclamation.   II, ii
HERALD It is Othello's pleasure, our noble and valiant
general, that, upon certain tidings now arrived, importing the mere perdition of the Turkish fleet, every man   3

put himself into triumph ; some to dance, some to make bonfires, each man to what sport and revels his addiction leads him. For, besides these beneficial news, it is the celebration of his nuptial. So much was his pleasure

8   should be proclaimed. All offices are open, and there is full liberty of feasting from the present hour of five till the bell have told eleven. Heaven bless the isle of Cyprus and our noble general Othello !   *Exit.*

*

II, iii   *Enter Othello, Desdemona, Cassio, and Attendants.*

OTHELLO
Good Michael, look you to the guard to-night.
Let's teach ourselves that honorable stop,
Not to outsport discretion.

CASSIO
Iago hath direction what to do ;
But not withstanding, with my personal eye
Will I look to't.

OTHELLO   Iago is most honest.
Michael, good night. To-morrow with your earliest
Let me have speech with you.
     [To Desdemona]   Come, my dear love.
The purchase made, the fruits are to ensue ;
That profit's yet to come 'tween me and you. –
Good night.
        Exit [Othello with Desdemona and Attendants].
        Enter Iago.

CASSIO Welcome, Iago. We must to the watch.

IAGO Not this hour, lieutenant ; 'tis not yet ten o' th'

14   clock. Our general cast us thus early for the love of his Desdemona ; who let us not therefore blame. He hath not yet made wanton the night with her, and she is sport for Jove.

CASSIO She's a most exquisite lady.

IAGO And, I'll warrant her, full of game.

CASSIO Indeed, she's a most fresh and delicate creature.

IAGO What an eye she has ! Methinks it sounds a parley to provocation.

CASSIO An inviting eye ; and yet methinks right modest.

IAGO And when she speaks, is it not an alarum to love ?

CASSIO She is indeed perfection.

IAGO Well, happiness to their sheets ! Come, lieutenant, I

27   have a stoup of wine, and here without are a brace of Cyprus gallants that would fain have a measure to the health of black Othello.

CASSIO Not to-night, good Iago. I have very poor and unhappy brains for drinking ; I could well wish courtesy would invent some other custom of entertainment.

IAGO O, they are our friends. But one cup ! I'll drink for you.

CASSIO I have drunk but one cup to-night, and that was

36   craftily qualified too ; and behold what innovation it makes here. I am unfortunate in the infirmity and dare not task my weakness with any more.

IAGO What, man ! 'Tis a night of revels : the gallants desire it.

CASSIO Where are they ?

IAGO Here at the door ; I pray you call them in.

CASSIO I'll do't, but it dislikes me.   *Exit.*

IAGO
If I can fasten but one cup upon him
With that which he hath drunk to-night already,

He'll be as full of quarrel and offense
As my young mistress' dog. Now my sick fool Roderigo,
Whom love hath turned almost the wrong side out,
To Desdemona hath to-night caroused
Potations pottle-deep ; and he's to watch.   50
Three lads of Cyprus – noble swelling spirits,
That hold their honors in a wary distance,   52
The very elements of this warlike isle –   53
Have I to-night flustered with flowing cups,
And they watch too. Now, 'mongst this flock of drunkards
Am I to put our Cassio in some action
That may offend the isle.
     Enter Cassio, Montano, and Gentlemen [; Servants following with wine].
           But here they come.
If consequence do but approve my dream,
My boat sails freely, both with wind and stream.

CASSIO 'Fore God, they have given me a rouse already.   60

MONTANO Good faith, a little one ; not past a pint, as I am a soldier.

IAGO Some wine, ho !
    [Sings]   And let me the canakin clink, clink ;
               And let me the canakin clink.
                  A soldier's a man ;
                  A life's but a span,
              Why then, let a soldier drink.
Some wine, boys !   70

CASSIO 'Fore God, an excellent song !

IAGO I learned it in England, where indeed they are most potent in potting. Your Dane, your German, and your swag-bellied Hollander – Drink, ho ! – are nothing to your English.

CASSIO Is your Englishman so expert in his drinking ?

IAGO Why, he drinks you with facility your Dane dead drunk ; he sweats not to overthrow your Almain ; he gives your Hollander a vomit ere the next pottle can be filled.

CASSIO To the health of our general !

MONTANO I am for it, lieutenant, and I'll do you justice.

IAGO O sweet England !
    [Sings]   King Stephen was a worthy peer ;
               His breeches cost him but a crown ;
               He held 'em sixpence all too dear,
                  With that he called the tailor lown.   87
               He was a wight of high renown,
                  And thou art but of low degree.
             'Tis pride that pulls the country down ;
               Then take thine auld cloak about thee.
Some wine, ho !

CASSIO 'Fore God, this is a more exquisite song than the other.

IAGO Will you hear't again ?

CASSIO No, for I hold him to be unworthy of his place that does those things. Well, God's above all ; and there   97 be souls must be saved, and there be souls must not be saved.

---

8 *offices* kitchens and storerooms
II, iii The Cyprian castle   **14** *cast* dismissed   **27** *stoup* two-quart tankard   **36** *qualified* diluted ; *innovation* disturbance   **50** *pottle-deep* bottoms up   **52** *That ... distance* very sensitive about their honor   **53** *very elements* true representatives   **60** *rouse* bumper   **87** *lown* rascal   **97** *does ... things* i.e. behaves in this fashion

IAGO It's true, good lieutenant.

CASSIO For mine own part – no offense to the general,
nor any man of quality – I hope to be saved.

IAGO And so do I too, lieutenant.

CASSIO Ay, but, by your leave, not before me. The lieutenant is to be saved before the ancient. Let's have no
more of this; let's to our affairs. – God forgive us our
sins! – Gentlemen, let's look to our business. Do not
think, gentlemen, I am drunk. This is my ancient; this
is my right hand, and this is my left. I am not drunk now.
110 I can stand well enough, and I speak well enough.

ALL Excellent well!

CASSIO Why, very well then. You must not think then
that I am drunk.   *Exit.*

MONTANO
To th' platform, masters. Come, let's set the watch.

IAGO
You see this fellow that is gone before.
He's a soldier fit to stand by Caesar
And give direction; and do but see his vice.
118 'Tis to his virtue a just equinox,
The one as long as th' other. 'Tis pity of him.
I fear the trust Othello puts him in,
On some odd time of his infirmity,
Will shake this island.

MONTANO   But is he often thus?

IAGO
'Tis evermore his prologue to his sleep:
124 He'll watch the horologe a double set
If drink rock not his cradle.

MONTANO   It were well
The general were put in mind of it.
Perhaps he sees it not, or his good nature
Prizes the virtue that appears in Cassio
And looks not on his evils. Is not this true?
     Enter Roderigo.

IAGO *[aside to him]*
How now, Roderigo?
I pray you after the lieutenant, go!   *Exit Roderigo.*

MONTANO
And 'tis great pity that the noble Moor
Should hazard such a place as his own second
134 With one of an ingraft infirmity.
It were an honest action to say
So to the Moor.

IAGO   Not I, for this fair island!
I do love Cassio well and would do much
To cure him of this evil.
    (Within) Help! help!
                But hark! What noise?
    Enter Cassio, driving in Roderigo.

CASSIO
Zounds, you rogue! you rascal!

MONTANO
What's the matter, lieutenant?

CASSIO   A knave teach me my duty?
141 I'll beat the knave into a twiggen bottle.

---

118 *just equinox* exact equivalent 124 *watch . . . set* stay awake twice
around the clock 134 *ingraft* i.e. ingrained 141 *twiggen* wicker-covered
144 *mazzard* head 151 *rise* grow riotous 163 *carve for* indulge 166
propriety proper self 170 *quarter* friendliness 175 *peevish odds* childish
quarrel 183 *censure* judgment 184 *unlace* undo 185 *rich opinion* high
reputation

RODERIGO
Beat me?

CASSIO   Dost thou prate, rogue?
    [Strikes him.]

MONTANO   Nay, good lieutenant!
    [Stays him.]
I pray you, sir, hold your hand.

CASSIO   Let me go, sir,
Or I'll knock you o'er the mazzard.   144

MONTANO   Come, come, you're drunk!

CASSIO Drunk?
    They fight.

IAGO *[aside to Roderigo]*
Away, I say! Go out and cry a mutiny!   *Exit Roderigo.*
Nay, good lieutenant. God's will, gentlemen!
Help, ho! – lieutenant – sir – Montano – sir –
Help, masters! – Here's a goodly watch indeed!
    A bell rung.
Who's that which rings the bell? Diablo, ho!
The town will rise. God's will, lieutenant, hold!   151
You'll be shamed for ever.
    Enter Othello and Gentlemen with weapons.

OTHELLO   What is the matter here?

MONTANO
Zounds, I bleed still. I am hurt to th' death.
He dies!

OTHELLO
Hold for your lives!

IAGO
Hold, hold! Lieutenant – sir – Montano – gentlemen!
Have you forgot all sense of place and duty?
Hold! The general speaks to you. Hold, for shame!

OTHELLO
Why, how now, ho? From whence ariseth this?
Are we turned Turks, and to ourselves do that
Which heaven hath forbid the Ottomites?
For Christian shame put by this barbarous brawl!
He that stirs next to carve for his own rage   163
Holds his soul light; he dies upon his motion.
Silence that dreadful bell! It frights the isle
From her propriety. What is the matter, masters?   166
Honest Iago, that looks dead with grieving,
Speak. Who began this? On thy love, I charge thee.

IAGO
I do not know. Friends all, but now, even now,
In quarter, and in terms like bride and groom   170
Devesting them for bed; and then, but now –
As if some planet had unwitted men –
Swords out, and tilting one at other's breast
In opposition bloody. I cannot speak
Any beginning to this peevish odds,   175
And would in action glorious I had lost
Those legs that brought me to a part of it!

OTHELLO
How comes it, Michael, you are thus forgot?

CASSIO
I pray you pardon me; I cannot speak.

OTHELLO
Worthy Montano, you were wont to be civil;
The gravity and stillness of your youth
The world hath noted, and your name is great
In mouths of wisest censure. What's the matter   183
That you unlace your reputation thus   184
And spend your rich opinion for the name   185

Of a night-brawler? Give me answer to it.

MONTANO
Worthy Othello, I am hurt to danger.
Your officer, Iago, can inform you,
189 While I spare speech, which something now offends me,
Of all that I do know; nor know I aught
By me that's said or done amiss this night,
Unless self-charity be sometimes a vice,
And to defend ourselves it be a sin
When violence assails us.

OTHELLO   Now, by heaven,
195 My blood begins my safer guides to rule,
196 And passion, having my best judgment collied,
197 Assays to lead the way. If I once stir
Or do but lift this arm, the best of you
Shall sink in my rebuke. Give me to know
How this foul rout began, who set it on;
201 And he that is approved in this offense,
Though he had twinned with me, both at a birth,
Shall lose me. What! in a town of war,
Yet wild, the people's hearts brimful of fear,
205 To manage private and domestic quarrel?
In night, and on the court and guard of safety?
'Tis monstrous. Iago, who began't?

MONTANO
208 If partially affined, or leagued in office,
Thou dost deliver more or less than truth,
Thou art no soldier.

IAGO   Touch me not so near.
I had rather have this tongue cut from my mouth
Than it should do offense to Michael Cassio;
Yet I persuade myself, to speak the truth
Shall nothing wrong him. This it is, general.
Montano and myself being in speech,
There comes a fellow crying out for help,
And Cassio following him with determined sword
218 To execute upon him. Sir, this gentleman
Steps in to Cassio and entreats his pause.
Myself the crying fellow did pursue,
Lest by his clamor – as it so fell out –
The town might fall in fright. He, swift of foot,
Outran my purpose; and I returned then rather
For that I heard the clink and fall of swords,
225 And Cassio high in oath; which till to-night
I ne'er might say before. When I came back –
For this was brief – I found them close together
At blow and thrust, even as again they were
When you yourself did part them.
More of this matter cannot I report;
But men are men; the best sometimes forget.
Though Cassio did some little wrong to him,
As men in rage strike those that wish them best,
Yet surely Cassio I believe received
From him that fled some strange indignity,
236 Which patience could not pass.

OTHELLO   I know, Iago,
Thy honesty and love doth mince this matter,
Making it light to Cassio. Cassio, I love thee;
But never more be officer of mine.

Enter Desdemona, attended.

Look if my gentle love be not raised up!
I'll make thee an example.

DESDEMONA   What's the matter?

OTHELLO
All's well now, sweeting; come away to bed.
[To Montano]
Sir, for your hurts, myself will be your surgeon.
Lead him off.
[Montano is led off.]
Iago, look with care about the town
And silence those whom this vile brawl distracted. 246
Come, Desdemona; 'tis the soldiers' life
To have their balmy slumbers waked with strife.
         Exit [with all but Iago and Cassio].

IAGO What, are you hurt, lieutenant?

CASSIO Ay, past all surgery.

IAGO Marry, God forbid!

CASSIO Reputation, reputation, reputation! O, I have lost my reputation! I have lost the immortal part of myself, and what remains is bestial. My reputation, Iago, my reputation!

IAGO As I am an honest man, I thought you had received some bodily wound. There is more sense in that than in reputation. Reputation is an idle and most false imposition; oft got without merit and lost without deserving. You have lost no reputation at all unless you repute yourself such a loser. What, man! there are ways to recover 261 the general again. You are but now cast in his mood – a 262 punishment more in policy than in malice, even so as one would beat his offenseless dog to affright an imperious lion. Sue to him again, and he's yours.

CASSIO I will rather sue to be despised than to deceive so good a commander with so slight, so drunken, and so indiscreet an officer. Drunk! and speak parrot! and 268 squabble! swagger! swear! and discourse fustian with 269 one's own shadow! O thou invisible spirit of wine, if thou hast no name to be known by, let us call thee devil!

IAGO What was he that you followed with your sword? What had he done to you?

CASSIO I know not.

IAGO Is't possible?

CASSIO I remember a mass of things, but nothing distinctly; a quarrel, but nothing wherefore. O God, that men should put an enemy in their mouths to steal away their brains! that we should with joy, pleasance, revel, and applause transform ourselves into beasts! 280

IAGO Why, but you are now well enough. How came you thus recovered?

CASSIO It hath pleased the devil drunkenness to give place to the devil wrath. One unperfectness shows me another, to make me frankly despise myself.

IAGO Come, you are too severe a moraler. As the time, the place, and the condition of this country stands, I could heartily wish this had not so befall'n; but since it is as it is, mend it for your own good.

CASSIO I will ask him for my place again: he shall tell me I am a drunkard! Had I as many mouths as Hydra, such 291 an answer would stop them all. To be now a sensible

189 *offends* pains   195 *blood* passion   196 *collied* darkened   197 *Assays* tries   201 *approved in* proved guilty of   205 *manage* carry on   208 *partially . . . office* prejudiced by comradeship or official relations   218 *execute* work his will   225 *high in oath* cursing   236 *pass* pass over, ignore   246 *distracted* excited   261 *recover* regain favor with   262 *cast in his mood* dismissed because of his anger   268 *parrot* meaningless phrases   269 *fustian* bombastic nonsense   280 *applause* desire to please   291 *Hydra* monster with many heads

man, by and by a fool, and presently a beast ! O strange !
294 Every inordinate cup is unblest, and the ingredient is a
devil.

IAGO Come, come, good wine is a good familiar creature
if it be well used. Exclaim no more against it. And, good
lieutenant, I think you think I love you.

298 CASSIO I have well approved it, sir. I drunk !

IAGO You or any man living may be drunk at some time,
man. I'll tell you what you shall do. Our general's wife is
now the general. I may say so in this respect, for that he
hath devoted and given up himself to the contemplation,
mark, and denotement of her parts and graces. Confess
yourself freely to her ; importune her help to put you in
305 your place again. She is of so free, so kind, so apt, so
blessed a disposition she holds it a vice in her goodness
not to do more than she is requested. This broken joint
308 between you and her husband entreat her to splinter ;
309 and my fortunes against any lay worth naming, this
crack of your love shall grow stronger than it was before.

CASSIO You advise me well.

IAGO I protest, in the sincerity of love and honest kindness.

CASSIO I think it freely ; and betimes in the morning will
I beseech the virtuous Desdemona to undertake for me.
I am desperate of my fortunes if they check me here.

IAGO You are in the right. Good night, lieutenant ; I must
to the watch.

CASSIO Good night, honest Iago.   *Exit Cassio.*

IAGO
And what's he then that says I play the villain,
When this advice is free I give and honest,
321 Probal to thinking, and indeed the course
To win the Moor again ? For 'tis most easy
323 Th' inclining Desdemona to subdue
In any honest suit ; she's framed as fruitful
As the free elements. And then for her
To win the Moor – were't to renounce his baptism,
All seals and symbols of redeemèd sin –
His soul is so enfettered to her love
That she may make, unmake, do what she list,
Even as her appetite shall play the god
With his weak function. How am I then a villain
332 To counsel Cassio to this parallel course,
333 Directly to his good ? Divinity of hell !
334 When devils will the blackest sins put on,
They do suggest at first with heavenly shows,
As I do now. For whiles this honest fool
Plies Desdemona to repair his fortunes,
And she for him pleads strongly to the Moor,
I'll pour this pestilence into his ear,
340 That she repeals him for his body's lust ;
And by how much she strives to do him good,
She shall undo her credit with the Moor.
So will I turn her virtue into pitch,

294 *ingredient* contents 298 *approved* proved 305 *free* bounteous
308 *splinter* bind up with splints 309 *lay* wager 321 *Probal* probable
323 *subdue* persuade 332 *parallel* corresponding 333 *Divinity* theology
334 *put on* incite 340 *repeals him* seeks his recall 347 *cry* pack 357
cashiered Cassio maneuvered Cassio's discharge 368 *jump* at the exact
moment
III, i Before the chamber of Othello and Desdemona 1 *content* reward
4 *Naples* (notorious for its association with venereal disease) 23 *quillets*
quips

And out of her own goodness make the net
That shall enmesh them all.
        Enter Roderigo.   How, now, Roderigo ?

RODERIGO I do follow here in the chase, not like a hound
that hunts, but one that fills up the cry. My money is al- 347
most spent ; I have been to-night exceedingly well cudgelled ; and I think the issue will be – I shall have so
much experience for my pains ; and so, with no money
at all, and a little more wit, return again to Venice.

IAGO
How poor are they that have not patience !
What wound did ever heal but by degrees ?
Thou know'st we work by wit, and not by witchcraft ;
And wit depends on dilatory time.
Does't not go well ? Cassio hath beaten thee,
And thou by that small hurt hast cashiered Cassio. 357
Though other things grow fair against the sun,
Yet fruits that blossom first will first be ripe.
Content thyself awhile. By the mass, 'tis morning !
Pleasure and action make the hours seem short.
Retire thee ; go where thou art billeted.
Away, I say ! Thou shalt know more hereafter.
Nay, get thee gone !   *Exit Roderigo.*
            Two things are to be done :
My wife must move for Cassio to her mistress ;
I'll set her on ;
Myself the while to draw the Moor apart
And bring him jump when he may Cassio find 368
Soliciting his wife. Ay, that's the way !
Dull not device by coldness and delay.   *Exit.*

                    *

        Enter Cassio, with Musicians and the Clown.   III, i

CASSIO
Masters, play here, I will content your pains : 1
Something that's brief ; and bid 'Good morrow, general.'
        [They play.]

CLOWN Why, masters, ha' your instruments been in
Naples, that they speak i' th' nose thus ? 4

MUSICIAN How, sir, how ?

CLOWN Are these, I pray you, called wind instruments ?

MUSICIAN Ay, marry, are they, sir.

CLOWN O, thereby hangs a tail.

MUSICIAN Whereby hangs a tale, sir ?

CLOWN Marry, sir, by many a wind instrument that I
know. But, masters, here's money for you ; and the
general so likes your music that he desires you, for love's
sake, to make no more noise with it.

MUSICIAN Well, sir, we will not.

CLOWN If you have any music that may not be heard, to't
again : but, as they say, to hear music the general does
not greatly care.

MUSICIAN We have none such, sir.

CLOWN Then put up your pipes in your bag, for I'll away.
Go, vanish into air, away !
                Exit Musician [with his fellows].

CASSIO Dost thou hear, my honest friend ?

CLOWN No, I hear not your honest friend. I hear you.

CASSIO Prithee keep up thy quillets. There's a poor piece 23
of gold for thee. If the gentlewoman that attends the
general's wife be stirring, tell her there's one Cassio
entreats her a little favor of speech. Wilt thou do this ?

CLOWN She is stirring sir. If she will stir hither, I shall
seem to notify unto her.

CASSIO

[Do, good my friend.]   *Exit Clown.*

29   *Enter Iago.*   In happy time, Iago.

IAGO

You have not been abed then?

CASSIO

Why, no; the day had broke
Before we parted. I have made bold, Iago,
To send in to your wife: my suit to her
Is that she will to virtuous Desdemona
Procure me some access.

IAGO   I'll send her to you presently;
And I'll devise a mean to draw the Moor
Out of the way, that your converse and business
May be more free.

CASSIO

I humbly thank you for't.   *Exit [Iago].*
                                   I never knew
40   A Florentine more kind and honest.
                Enter Emilia.

EMILIA

Good morrow, good lieutenant. I am sorry
For your displeasure; but all will sure be well.
The general and his wife are talking of it,
And she speaks for you stoutly. The Moor replies
That he you hurt is of great fame in Cyprus
46   And great affinity, and that in wholesome wisdom
He might not but refuse you; but he protests he loves
   you,
And needs no other suitor but his likings
49   [To take the safest occasion by the front]
To bring you in again.

CASSIO   Yet I beseech you,
If you think fit, or that it may be done,
Give me advantage of some brief discourse
With Desdemona alone.

EMILIA   Pray you come in.
I will bestow you where you shall have time
55   To speak your bosom freely.

CASSIO   I am much bound to you.
                                        Exeunt.

                          *

III, ii   *Enter Othello, Iago, and Gentlemen.*

OTHELLO

These letters give, Iago, to the pilot
And by him do my duties to the Senate.
3   That done, I will be walking on the works;
Repair there to me.

IAGO   Well, my good lord, I'll do't.

OTHELLO

This fortification, gentlemen, shall we see't?

GENTLEMEN

We'll wait upon your lordship.   *Exeunt.*

                          *

III, iii   *Enter Desdemona, Cassio, and Emilia.*

DESDEMONA

Be thou assured, good Cassio, I will do
All my abilities in thy behalf.

EMILIA

Good madam, do. I warrant it grieves my husband
As if the cause were his.

DESDEMONA

O, that's an honest fellow. Do not doubt, Cassio,
But I will have my lord and you again
As friendly as you were.

CASSIO   Bounteous madam,
Whatever shall become of Michael Cassio,
He's never anything but your true servant.

DESDEMONA

I know't; I thank you. You do love my lord;
You have known him long; and be you well assured
He shall in strangeness stand no farther off   12
Than in a politic distance.   13

CASSIO   Ay, but, lady,
That policy may either last so long,
Or feed upon such nice and waterish diet,   15
Or breed itself so out of circumstance,
That, I being absent, and my place supplied,
My general will forget my love and service.

DESDEMONA

Do not doubt that; before Emilia here   19
I give thee warrant of thy place. Assure thee,
If I do vow a friendship, I'll perform it
To the last article. My lord shall never rest;
I'll watch him tame and talk him out of patience;   23
His bed shall seem a school, his board a shrift;   24
I'll intermingle everything he does
With Cassio's suit. Therefore be merry, Cassio,
For thy solicitor shall rather die
Than give thy cause away.
                Enter Othello and Iago [at a distance].

EMILIA

Madam, here comes my lord.

CASSIO

Madam, I'll take my leave.   30

DESDEMONA

Why, stay, and hear me speak.

CASSIO

Madam, not now: I am very ill at ease,
Unfit for mine own purposes.

DESDEMONA

Well, do your discretion.   *Exit Cassio.*

IAGO

Ha! I like not that.

OTHELLO   What dost thou say?

IAGO

Nothing, my lord; or if – I know not what.

OTHELLO

Was not that Cassio parted from my wife?

IAGO

Cassio, my lord? No, sure, I cannot think it,
That he would steal away so guilty-like,
Seeing your coming.

OTHELLO   I do believe 'twas he.   40

29 *In happy time* well met   40 *Florentine* i.e. even a Florentine (like
Cassio; Iago was a Venetian)   46 *affinity* family connections   49 *occasion*
opportunity; *front* forelock   55 *your bosom* your inmost thoughts
III, ii The castle   3 *works* fortifications
III, iii The castle grounds   12 *strangeness* aloofness   13 *Than . . . distance*
than wise policy requires   15 *Or . . . diet* or be continued for such slight
reasons   19 *doubt* fear   23 *watch him tame* keep him awake until he gives
in   24 *shrift* confessional

DESDEMONA
How now, my lord?
I have been talking with a suitor here,
A man that languishes in your displeasure.

OTHELLO
Who is't you mean?

DESDEMONA
Why, your lieutenant, Cassio. Good my lord,
If I have any grace or power to move you,
47   His present reconciliation take;
For if he be not one that truly loves you,
That errs in ignorance, and not in cunning,
I have no judgment in an honest face.
I prithee call him back.

OTHELLO   Went he hence now?

DESDEMONA
Yes, faith; so humbled
That he hath left part of his grief with me
To suffer with him. Good love, call him back.

OTHELLO
Not now, sweet Desdemon; some other time.

DESDEMONA
But shall't be shortly?

OTHELLO   The sooner, sweet, for you.

DESDEMONA
Shall't be to-night at supper?

OTHELLO   No, not to-night.

DESDEMONA
To-morrow dinner then?

OTHELLO   I shall not dine at home;
I meet the captains at the citadel.

DESDEMONA
Why then, to-morrow night, or Tuesday morn,
On Tuesday noon or night, or Wednesday morn.
I prithee name the time, but let it not
Exceed three days. I' faith, he's penitent;
And yet his trespass, in our common reason
(Save that, they say, the wars must make examples
66   Out of their best), is not almost a fault
67   T' incur a private check. When shall he come?
Tell me, Othello. I wonder in my soul
What you could ask me that I should deny
70   Or stand so mamm'ring on. What? Michael Cassio,
That came a-wooing with you, and so many a time,
When I have spoke of you dispraisingly,
Hath ta'en your part – to have so much to do
To bring him in? By'r Lady, I could do much –

OTHELLO
Prithee no more. Let him come when he will!
I will deny thee nothing.

DESDEMONA   Why, this is not a boon;
'Tis as I should entreat you wear your gloves,
Or feed on nourishing dishes, or keep you warm,
Or sue to you to do a peculiar profit
To your own person. Nay, when I have a suit
Wherein I mean to touch your love indeed,
It shall be full of poise and difficult weight,
83   And fearful to be granted.

OTHELLO   I will deny thee nothing!
Whereon I do beseech thee grant me this,
To leave me but a little to myself.

DESDEMONA
Shall I deny you? No. Farewell, my lord.

OTHELLO
Farewell, my Desdemon: I'll come to thee straight.

DESDEMONA
Emilia, come. – Be as your fancies teach you;
Whate'er you be, I am obedient.   *Exit [with Emilia].*

OTHELLO
Excellent wretch! Perdition catch my soul   90
But I do love thee! and when I love thee not,
Chaos is come again.

IAGO
My noble lord –

OTHELLO   What dost thou say, Iago?

IAGO
Did Michael Cassio, when you wooed my lady,
Know of your love?

OTHELLO
He did, from first to last. Why dost thou ask?

IAGO
But for a satisfaction of my thought;
No further harm.

OTHELLO   Why of thy thought, Iago?

IAGO
I did not think he had been acquainted with her.

OTHELLO
O, yes, and went between us very oft.   100

IAGO
Indeed?

OTHELLO
Indeed? Ay, indeed! Discern'st thou aught in that?
Is he not honest?

IAGO   Honest, my lord?

OTHELLO   Honest. Ay, honest.

IAGO
My lord, for aught I know.

OTHELLO
What dost thou think?

IAGO   Think, my lord?

OTHELLO   Think, my lord?
By heaven, he echoes me,
As if there were some monster in his thought
Too hideous to be shown. Thou dost mean something:
I heard thee say even now, thou lik'st not that,
When Cassio left my wife. What didst not like?
And when I told thee he was of my counsel
In my whole course of wooing, thou cried'st 'Indeed?'
And didst contract and purse thy brow together,
As if thou then hadst shut up in thy brain
Some horrible conceit. If thou dost love me,   115
Show me thy thought.

IAGO
My lord, you know I love you.

OTHELLO   I think thou dost;
And, for I know thou'rt full of love and honesty
And weigh'st thy words before thou giv'st them breath,
Therefore these stops of thine fright me the more;
For such things in a false disloyal knave
Are tricks of custom; but in a man that's just
They are close dilations, working from the heart   123
That passion cannot rule.

47 *present* immediate **66** *not almost* hardly **67** *a private check* even a
private reprimand **70** *mamm'ring on* hesitating about **83** *fearful* dangerous **90** *wretch* (a term of endearment) **100** *went . . . us* (i.e. as messenger)
115 *conceit* fancy **123–24** *close dilations . . . rule* secret emotions which
well up in spite of restraint

IAGO   For Michael Cassio,
I dare be sworn I think that he is honest.

OTHELLO
I think so too.

IAGO   Men should be what they seem ;
127   Or those that be not, would they might seem none !

OTHELLO
Certain, men should be what they seem.

IAGO
Why then, I think Cassio 's an honest man.

OTHELLO
Nay, yet there's more in this.
I prithee speak to me as to thy thinkings,
As thou dost ruminate, and give thy worst of thoughts
The worst of words.

IAGO   Good my lord, pardon me :
Though I am bound to every act of duty,
135   I am not bound to that all slaves are free to.
Utter my thoughts ? Why, say they are vile and false,
As where's that palace whereinto foul things
Sometimes intrude not ? Who has a breast so pure
But some uncleanly apprehensions
140   Keep leets and law days, and in Sessions sit
With meditations lawful ?

OTHELLO
Thou dost conspire against thy friend, Iago,
If thou but think'st him wronged, and mak'st his ear
A stranger to thy thoughts.

IAGO   I do beseech you –
Though I perchance am vicious in my guess
(As I confess it is my nature's plague
147   To spy into abuses, and oft my jealousy
Shapes faults that are not), that your wisdom yet
149   From one that so imperfectly conjects
Would take no notice, nor build yourself a trouble
Out of his scattering and unsure observance.
It were not for your quiet nor your good,
Nor for my manhood, honesty, and wisdom,
To let you know my thoughts.

OTHELLO   What dost thou mean ?

IAGO
Good name in man and woman, dear my lord,
156   Is the immediate jewel of their souls.
Who steals my purse steals trash ; 'tis something,
     nothing ;
'Twas mine, 'tis his, and has been slave to thousands ;
But he that filches from me my good name
Robs me of that which not enriches him
And makes me poor indeed.

OTHELLO
By heaven, I'll know thy thoughts !

IAGO
You cannot, if my heart were in your hand ;
Nor shall not whilst 'tis in my custody.

OTHELLO
Ha !

IAGO O, beware, my lord, of jealousy !
166   It is the green-eyed monster, which doth mock
The meat it feeds on. That cuckold lives in bliss
Who, certain of his fate, loves not his wronger ;
But O, what damnèd minutes tells he o'er
Who dotes, yet doubts – suspects, yet strongly loves !

OTHELLO
O misery !

IAGO
Poor and content is rich, and rich enough ;
But riches fineless is as poor as winter   173
To him that ever fears he shall be poor.
Good God, the souls of all my tribe defend
From jealousy !

OTHELLO   Why, why is this ?
Think'st thou I'ld make a life of jealousy,
To follow still the changes of the moon
With fresh suspicions ? No ! To be once in doubt
Is once to be resolved. Exchange me for a goat
When I shall turn the business of my soul
To such exsufflicate and blown surmises,   182
Matching this inference. 'Tis not to make me jealous
To say my wife is fair, feeds well, loves company,
Is free of speech, sings, plays, and dances ;
Where virtue is, these are more virtuous.
Nor from mine own weak merits will I draw
The smallest fear or doubt of her revolt,   188
For she had eyes, and chose me. No, Iago ;
I'll see before I doubt ; when I doubt, prove ;
And on the proof there is no more but this –
Away at once with love or jealousy !

IAGO
I am glad of this ; for now I shall have reason
To show the love and duty that I bear you
With franker spirit. Therefore, as I am bound,
Receive it from me. I speak not yet of proof.
Look to your wife ; observe her well with Cassio ;
Wear your eyes thus, not jealous nor secure :   198
I would not have your free and noble nature,
Out of self-bounty, be abused. Look to't.   200
I know our country disposition well :
In Venice they do let God see the pranks
They dare not show their husbands ; their best
     conscience
Is not to leave't undone, but keep't unknown.

OTHELLO
Dost thou say so ?

IAGO
She did deceive her father, marrying you ;
And when she seemed to shake and fear your looks,
She loved them most.

OTHELLO   And so she did.

IAGO   Why, go to then !
She that, so young, could give out such a seeming
To seel her father's eyes up close as oak –   210
He thought 'twas witchcraft – but I am much to blame.
I humbly do beseech you of your pardon
For too much loving you.

OTHELLO   I am bound to thee for ever.

IAGO
I see this hath a little dashed your spirits.

OTHELLO
Not a jot, not a jot.

IAGO   I' faith, I fear it has.

---

127 *seem none* i.e. not pretend to be men when they are really monsters 135 *bound . . . free to* bound to tell that which even slaves are allowed to keep to themselves 140 *leets and law days* sittings of the courts 147 *jealousy* suspicion 149 *conjects* conjectures 156 *immediate* nearest the heart 166 *mock* play with, like a cat with a mouse 173 *fineless* unlimited 182 *exsufflicate and blown* spat out and flyblown 188 *revolt* unfaithfulness 198 *secure* overconfident 200 *self-bounty* natural goodness 210 *seel* close ; *oak* oak grain

I hope you will consider what is spoke
Comes from my love. But I do see y' are moved.
I am to pray you not to strain my speech
219 To grosser issues nor to larger reach
Than to suspicion.

OTHELLO
I will not.

IAGO   Should you do so, my lord,
222 My speech should fall into such vile success
As my thoughts aim not at. Cassio 's my worthy friend –
My lord, I see y' are moved.

OTHELLO   No, not much moved :
225 I do not think but Desdemona 's honest.

IAGO
Long live she so ! and long live you to think so !

OTHELLO
And yet, how nature erring from itself –

IAGO
Ay, there 's the point ! as (to be bold with you)
Not to affect many proposèd matches
Of her own clime, complexion, and degree,
Whereto we see in all things nature tends –
Foh ! one may smell in such a will most rank,
Foul disproportions, thoughts unnatural –
234 But pardon me – I do not in position
Distinctly speak of her ; though I may fear
236 Her will, recoiling to her better judgment,
237 May fall to match you with her country forms,
238 And happily repent.

OTHELLO   Farewell, farewell !
If more thou dost perceive, let me know more.
Set on thy wife to observe. Leave me, Iago.

IAGO
My lord, I take my leave.   [Going.]

OTHELLO
Why did I marry ? This honest creature doubtless
Sees and knows more, much more, than he unfolds.

IAGO [returns]
My lord, I would I might entreat your honor
To scan this thing no further : leave it to time.
Although 'tis fit that Cassio have his place,
For sure he fills it up with great ability,
Yet, if you please to hold him off awhile,
You shall by that perceive him and his means.
250 Note if your lady strain his entertainment
With any strong or vehement importunity ;
Much will be seen in that. In the mean time
253 Let me be thought too busy in my fears
(As worthy cause I have to fear I am)
255 And hold her free, I do beseech your honor.

OTHELLO
256 Fear not my government.

IAGO
I once more take my leave.   Exit.

OTHELLO
This fellow 's of exceeding honesty,
And knows all qualities, with a learned spirit   259
Of human dealings. If I do prove her haggard,   260
Though that her jesses were my dear heartstrings,   261
I 'd whistle her off and let her down the wind   262
To prey at fortune. Haply, for I am black
And have not those soft parts of conversation   264
That chamberers have, or for I am declined   265
Into the vale of years – yet that 's not much –
She 's gone. I am abused, and my relief
Must be to loathe her. O curse of marriage,
That we can call these delicate creatures ours,
And not their appetites ! I had rather be a toad
And live upon the vapor of a dungeon
Than keep a corner in the thing I love
For others' uses. Yet 'tis the plague of great ones ;   273
Prerogatived are they less than the base.   274
'Tis destiny unshunnable, like death.
Even then this forkèd plague is fated to us   276
When we do quicken. Look where she comes.   277
          Enter Desdemona and Emilia.
If she be false, O, then heaven mocks itself !
I 'll not believe 't.

DESDEMONA   How now, my dear Othello ?
Your dinner, and the generous islanders   280
By you invited, do attend your presence.

OTHELLO
I am to blame.

DESDEMONA   Why do you speak so faintly ?
Are you not well ?

OTHELLO
I have a pain upon my forehead, here.

DESDEMONA
Faith, that 's with watching ; 'twill away again.   285
Let me but bind it hard, within this hour
It will be well.

OTHELLO   Your napkin is too little ;   287
          [He pushes the handkerchief from him, and it falls
          unnoticed.]
Let it alone. Come, I 'll go in with you.   288

DESDEMONA
I am very sorry that you are not well. Exit [with Othello].

EMILIA
I am glad I have found this napkin ;
This was her first remembrance from the Moor,
My wayward husband hath a hundred times
Wooed me to steal it ; but she so loves the token
(For he conjured her she should ever keep it)
That she reserves it evermore about her
To kiss and talk to. I 'll have the work ta'en out   296
And give 't Iago.
What he will do with it heaven knows, not I ;
I nothing but to please his fantasy.   299
          Enter Iago.

IAGO
How now ? What do you here alone ?

EMILIA
Do not you chide ; I have a thing for you.

IAGO
A thing for me ? It is a common thing –

EMILIA Ha ?

219 To grosser issues to mean something more monstrous   222 vile success evil outcome   225 honest chaste   234 position definite assertion   236 recoiling reverting   237 fall to match happen to compare   238 happily haply, perhaps   250 strain his entertainment urge his recall   253 busy meddlesome   255 hold her free consider her guiltless   256 government self-control   259 qualities natures   259–60 learned spirit Of mind informed about   260 haggard a wild hawk   261 jesses thongs for controlling a hawk 262–63 whistle . . . fortune turn her out and let her take care of herself   264 soft . . . conversation ingratiating manners   265 chamberers courtiers   273 great ones prominent men   274 Prerogatived privileged   276 forkèd plague i.e. horns of a cuckold   277 do quicken are born   280 generous noble 285 watching working late   287 napkin handkerchief   288 it i.e. his forehead   296 work ta'en out pattern copied   299 fantasy whim

IAGO
　　To have a foolish wife.
EMILIA
　　O, is that all? What will you give me now
　　For that same handkerchief?
IAGO　　　　　　　　　　　　What handkerchief?
EMILIA
　　What handkerchief!
　　Why, that the Moor first gave to Desdemona;
　　That which so often you did bid me steal.
IAGO
　　Hast stol'n it from her?
EMILIA
　　No, faith; she let it drop by negligence,
312　And to th' advantage, I, being here, took't up.
　　Look, here it is.
IAGO　　　　　　　A good wench! Give it me.
EMILIA
　　What will you do with't, that you have been so earnest
　　To have me filch it?
IAGO　　　　　　　　Why, what is that to you?
　　　[Snatches it.]
EMILIA
316　If it be not for some purpose of import,
　　Give't me again. Poor lady, she'll run mad
　　When she shall lack it.
IAGO
319　Be not acknown on't; I have use for it.
　　Go, leave me.　　　　　　　　　　　　Exit Emilia.
　　I will in Cassio's lodgings lose this napkin
　　And let him find it. Trifles light as air
　　Are to the jealous confirmations strong
　　As proofs of holy writ. This may do something.
　　The Moor already changes with my poison:
326　Dangerous conceits are in their natures poisons,
　　Which at the first are scarce found to distaste,
　　But with a little act upon the blood
　　Burn like the mines of sulphur.
　　　　Enter Othello.　　　　　　I did say so.
330　Look where he comes! Not poppy nor mandragora,
　　Nor all the drowsy syrups of the world,
　　Shall ever med'cine thee to that sweet sleep
　　Which thou owedst yesterday.
OTHELLO　　　　　　　　　Ha! ha! false to me?
IAGO
　　Why, how now, general? No more of that!
OTHELLO
　　Avaunt! be gone! Thou hast set me on the rack.
　　I swear 'tis better to be much abused
　　Than but to know't a little.
IAGO　　　　　　　　　　How now, my lord?
OTHELLO
　　What sense had I of her stol'n hours of lust?
　　I saw't not, thought it not, it harmed not me;
340　I slept the next night well, fed well, was free and merry;
　　I found not Cassio's kisses on her lips.
342　He that is robbed, not wanting what is stol'n,
　　Let him not know't, and he's not robbed at all.
IAGO
　　I am sorry to hear this.
OTHELLO
　　I had been happy if the general camp,
346　Pioners and all, had tasted her sweet body,
　　So I had nothing known. O, now for ever

　　Farewell the tranquil mind! farewell content!
　　Farewell the plumèd troop, and the big wars　　349
　　That make ambition virtue! O, farewell!
　　Farewell the neighing steed and the shrill trump,
　　The spirit-stirring drum, th' ear-piercing fife,
　　The royal banner, and all quality,
　　Pride, pomp, and circumstance of glorious war!　　354
　　And O you mortal engines whose rude throats　　355
　　Th' immortal Jove's dread clamors counterfeit,　　356
　　Farewell! Othello's occupation's gone!
IAGO
　　Is't possible, my lord?
OTHELLO
　　Villain, be sure thou prove my love a whore!
　　Be sure of it; give me the ocular proof;
　　Or, by the worth of mine eternal soul,
　　Thou hadst been better have been born a dog
　　Than answer my waked wrath!
IAGO　　　　　　　　　　　　Is't come to this?
OTHELLO
　　Make me to see't; or at the least so prove it
　　That the probation bear no hinge nor loop　　365
　　To hang a doubt on – or woe upon thy life!
IAGO
　　My noble lord –
OTHELLO
　　If thou dost slander her and torture me,
　　Never pray more; abandon all remorse;
　　On horror's head horrors accumulate;
　　Do deeds to make heaven weep, all earth amazed;
　　For nothing canst thou to damnation add
　　Greater than that.
IAGO　　　　　　　O grace! O heaven forgive me!
　　Are you a man? Have you a soul or sense? –
　　God b' wi' you! take mine office. O wretched fool,
　　That liv'st to make thine honesty a vice!
　　O monstrous world! Take note, take note, O world,
　　To be direct and honest is not safe.
　　I thank you for this profit; and from hence　　379
　　I'll love no friend, sith love breeds such offense.
OTHELLO
　　Nay, stay. Thou shouldst be honest.
IAGO
　　I should be wise; for honesty 's a fool
　　And loses that it works for.
OTHELLO　　　　　　　　By the world,
　　I think my wife be honest, and think she is not;
　　I think that thou art just, and think thou art not.
　　I'll have some proof. Her name, that was as fresh
　　As Dian's visage, is now begrimed and black
　　As mine own face. If there be cords, or knives,
　　Poison, or fire, or suffocating streams,
　　I'll not endure it. Would I were satisfied!　　390
IAGO
　　I see, sir, you are eaten up with passion:
　　I do repent me that I put it to you.
　　You would be satisfied?
OTHELLO　　　　　　　　Would? Nay, I will.

312 *to th' advantage* opportunely　316 *import* importance　319 *Be . . . on't* do not acknowledge it　326 *conceits* ideas　330 *mandragora* a narcotic　340 *free* carefree　342 *wanting* missing　346 *Pioners* sappers, laborers　349 *big* stately　354 *circumstance* pageantry　355 *mortal engines* deadly artillery　356 *counterfeit* imitate　365 *probation* proof　379 *profit* profitable lesson　390 *satisfied* completely informed

IAGO
And may ; but how ? how satisfied, my lord ?
395 Would you, the supervisor, grossly gape on ?
Behold her topped ?
OTHELLO   Death and damnation ! O !
IAGO
It were a tedious difficulty, I think,
To bring them to that prospect. Damn them then,
399 If ever mortal eyes do see them bolster
More than their own ! What then ? How then ?
What shall I say ? Where's satisfaction ?
It is impossible you should see this,
403 Were they as prime as goats, as hot as monkeys,
404 As salt as wolves in pride, and fools as gross
As ignorance made drunk. But yet, I say,
If imputation and strong circumstances
Which lead directly to the door of truth
Will give you satisfaction, you may have't.
OTHELLO
Give me a living reason she's disloyal.
IAGO
410 I do not like the office.
But sith I am ent'red in this cause so far,
Pricked to't by foolish honesty and love,
I will go on. I lay with Cassio lately,
And being troubled with a raging tooth,
I could not sleep.
There are a kind of men so loose of soul
That in their sleeps will mutter their affairs.
One of this kind is Cassio.
In sleep I heard him say, 'Sweet Desdemona,
420 Let us be wary, let us hide our loves !'
And then, sir, would he gripe and wring my hand,
Cry 'O sweet creature !' and then kiss me hard,
As if he plucked up kisses by the roots
That grew upon my lips ; then laid his leg
Over my thigh, and sighed, and kissed, and then
Cried 'Cursèd fate that gave thee to the Moor !'
OTHELLO
O monstrous ! monstrous !
IAGO   Nay, this was but his dream.
OTHELLO
428 But this denoted a foregone conclusion :
429 'Tis a shrewd doubt, though it be but a dream.
IAGO
And this may help to thicken other proofs
That do demonstrate thinly.
OTHELLO   I'll tear her all to pieces !
IAGO
Nay, but be wise. Yet we see nothing done ;
She may be honest yet. Tell me but this –
Have you not sometimes seen a handkerchief
Spotted with strawberries in your wife's hand ?
OTHELLO
I gave her such a one ; 'twas my first gift.
IAGO
I know not that ; but such a handkerchief –

I am sure it was your wife's – did I to-day
See Cassio wipe his beard with.
OTHELLO   If it be that –
IAGO
If it be that, or any that was hers,
It speaks against her with the other proofs.   440
OTHELLO
O, that the slave had forty thousand lives !
One is too poor, too weak for my revenge.
Now do I see 'tis true. Look here, Iago :
All my fond love thus do I blow to heaven.
'Tis gone.
Arise, black vengeance, from the hollow hell !
Yield up, O love, thy crown and hearted throne
To tyrannous hate ! Swell, bosom, with thy fraught,   449
For 'tis of aspics' tongues !   450
IAGO   Yet be content.
OTHELLO
O, blood, blood, blood !
IAGO
Patience, I say. Your mind perhaps may change.
OTHELLO
Never, Iago. Like to the Pontic sea,   453
Whose icy current and compulsive course
Ne'er feels retiring ebb, but keeps due on
To the Propontic and the Hellespont,
Even so my bloody thoughts, with violent pace,
Shall ne'er look back, ne'er ebb to humble love,
Till that a capable and wide revenge   459
Swallow them up.
     He kneels.   Now, by yond marble heaven,
In the due reverence of a sacred vow
I here engage my words.
IAGO   Do not rise yet.
     Iago kneels.
Witness, you ever-burning lights above,
You elements that clip us round about,   464
Witness that here Iago doth give up
The execution of his wit, hands, heart   466
To wronged Othello's service ! Let him command,
And to obey shall be in me remorse,   468
What bloody business ever.
     [They rise.]
OTHELLO   I greet thy love,
Not with vain thanks but with acceptance bounteous,
And will upon the instant put thee to't.
Within these three days let me hear thee say
That Cassio's not alive.
IAGO
My friend is dead ; 'tis done at your request.
But let her live.
OTHELLO
Damn her, lewd minx ! O, damn her ! damn her !
Come, go with me apart. I will withdraw
To furnish me with some swift means of death
For the fair devil. Now art thou my lieutenant.
IAGO
I am your own for ever.   *Exeunt.*

---

395 *supervisor* spectator   399 *bolster* lie together   403 *prime* lustful
404 *salt* lecherous ; *pride* heat   428 *foregone conclusion* previous experience
429 *a shrewd doubt* cursedly suspicious   449 *fraught* burden   450 *aspics*
deadly poisonous snakes   453 *Pontic sea* Black Sea   459 *capable* all-
embracing   464 *clip* encompass   466 *execution* activities ; *wit* mind   468
remorse pity
III, iv The environs of the castle   2 *lies* lives, lodges

                       *

     Enter Desdemona, Emilia, and Clown.   III, iv
DESDEMONA Do you know, sirrah, where Lieutenant
Cassio lies ?   2
CLOWN I dare not say he lies anywhere.

DESDEMONA Why, man?

CLOWN He's a soldier, and for me to say a soldier lies is stabbing.

DESDEMONA Go to. Where lodges he?

CLOWN To tell you where he lodges is to tell you where I lie.

DESDEMONA Can anything be made of this?

CLOWN I know not where he lodges; and for me to devise a lodging, and say he lies here or he lies there, were to lie in mine own throat.

DESDEMONA Can you enquire him out, and be edified by report?

CLOWN I will catechize the world for him; that is, make questions, and by them answer.

DESDEMONA Seek him, bid him come hither. Tell him I
19 have moved my lord on his behalf and hope all will be well.

CLOWN To do this is within the compass of man's wit, and therefore I'll attempt the doing of it.   *Exit.*

DESDEMONA
Where should I lose that handkerchief, Emilia?

EMILIA
I know not, madam.

DESDEMONA
Believe me, I had rather have lost my purse
26 Full of crusadoes; and but my noble Moor
Is true of mind, and made of no such baseness
As jealous creatures are, it were enough
To put him to ill thinking.

EMILIA   Is he not jealous?

DESDEMONA
Who? he? I think the sun where he was born
31 Drew all such humors from him.
          Enter Othello.

EMILIA   Look where he comes.

DESDEMONA
I will not leave him now till Cassio
Be called to him. – How is't with you, my lord?

OTHELLO
Well, my good lady. *[aside]* O, hardness to dissemble! –
How do you, Desdemona?

DESDEMONA   Well, my good lord.

OTHELLO
Give me your hand. This hand is moist, my lady.

DESDEMONA
It yet hath felt no age nor known no sorrow.

OTHELLO
This argues fruitfulness and liberal heart.
Hot, hot, and moist. This hand of yours requires
40 A sequester from liberty, fasting and prayer,
Much castigation, exercise devout;
For here's a young and sweating devil here
That commonly rebels. 'Tis a good hand,
A frank one.

DESDEMONA You may, indeed, say so;
For 'twas that hand that gave away my heart.

OTHELLO
A liberal hand! The hearts of old gave hands;
47 But our new heraldry is hands, not hearts.

DESDEMONA
I cannot speak of this. Come now, your promise!

OTHELLO
What promise, chuck?

DESDEMONA
I have sent to bid Cassio come speak with you.

OTHELLO
I have a salt and sorry rheum offends me.   51
Lend me thy handkerchief.

DESDEMONA   Here, my lord.

OTHELLO
That which I gave you.

DESDEMONA   I have it not about me.

OTHELLO
Not?

DESDEMONA No, faith, my lord.

OTHELLO   That's a fault.
That handkerchief
Did an Egyptian to my mother give.   56
She was a charmer, and could almost read   57
The thoughts of people. She told her, while she kept it,
'Twould make her amiable and subdue my father   59
Entirely to her love; but if she lost it
Or made a gift of it, my father's eye
Should hold her loathèd, and his spirits should hunt
After new fancies. She, dying, gave it me,
And bid me, when my fate would have me wive,
To give it her. I did so; and take heed on't;
Make it a darling like your precious eye.
To lose't or give't away were such perdition   67
As nothing else could match.

DESDEMONA   Is't possible?

OTHELLO
'Tis true. There's magic in the web of it.
A sibyl that had numb'red in the world
The sun to course two hundred compasses,   71
In her prophetic fury sewed the work;
The worms were hallowed that did breed the silk;
And it was dyed in mummy which the skillful
Conserved of maidens' hearts.

DESDEMONA   I' faith? Is't true?

OTHELLO
Most veritable. Therefore look to't well.

DESDEMONA
Then would to God that I had never seen't!

OTHELLO Ha! Wherefore?

DESDEMONA
Why do you speak so startingly and rash?

OTHELLO
Is't lost? Is't gone? Speak, is it out o' th' way?

DESDEMONA Heaven bless us!

OTHELLO Say you?

DESDEMONA
It is not lost. But what an if it were?

OTHELLO How?

DESDEMONA
I say it is not lost.

OTHELLO   Fetch't, let me see't!

DESDEMONA
Why, so I can, sir; but I will not now.
This is a trick to put me from my suit: 87
Pray you let Cassio be received again.

---

19 *moved* made proposals 26 *crusadoes* Portuguese gold coins 31 *humors* inclinations 40 *sequester* removal 47 *heraldry* heraldic symbolism 51 *salt . . . rheum* distressing head-cold ·56 *Egyptian* gypsy 57 *charmer* sorceress 59 *amiable* lovable 67 *perdition* disaster 71 *compasses* annual rounds 74 *mummy* a drug made from mummies 87 *put* divert

OTHELLO
Fetch me the handkerchief! My mind misgives.

DESDEMONA
Come, come!
You'll never meet a more sufficient man.

OTHELLO
The handkerchief!

[**DESDEMONA**   I pray talk me of Cassio.

OTHELLO
The handkerchief!]

93 **DESDEMONA**   A man that all his time
Hath founded his good fortunes on your love,
Shared dangers with you –

OTHELLO
The handkerchief!

DESDEMONA
I' faith, you are to blame.

OTHELLO Zounds!   *Exit Othello.*

EMILIA Is not this man jealous?

DESDEMONA
I ne'er saw this before.
Sure there's some wonder in this handkerchief;
I am most unhappy in the loss of it.

EMILIA
'Tis not a year or two shows us a man.
They are all but stomachs, and we all but food;
They eat us hungerly, and when they are full,
They belch us.
     Enter Iago and Cassio.
       Look you – Cassio and my husband!

IAGO
There is no other way; 'tis she must do't.

108 And lo the happiness! Go and importune her.

DESDEMONA
How now, good Cassio? What's the news with you?

CASSIO
Madam, my former suit. I do beseech you
That by your virtuous means I may again
Exist, and be a member of his love
Whom I with all the office of my heart
Entirely honor. I would not be delayed.
If my offense be of such mortal kind
That neither service past, nor present sorrows,
Nor purposed merit in futurity,
Can ransom me into his love again,
But to know so must be my benefit.
So shall I clothe me in a forced content,

121 And shut myself up in some other course,
To fortune's alms.

DESDEMONA   Alas, thrice-gentle Cassio!

123 My advocation is not now in tune.
My lord is not my lord; nor should I know him,

125 Were he in favor as in humor altered.
So help me every spirit sanctified
As I have spoken for you all my best

128 And stood within the blank of his displeasure

For my free speech! You must awhile be patient.
What I can do I will; and more I will
Than for myself I dare. Let that suffice you.

IAGO
Is my lord angry?

EMILIA   He went hence but now,
And certainly in strange unquietness.

IAGO
Can he be angry? I have seen the cannon
When it hath blown his ranks into the air
And, like the devil, from his very arm
Puffed his own brother – and is he angry?
Something of moment then. I will go meet him.
There's matter in't indeed if he be angry.

DESDEMONA
I prithee do so.   *Exit [Iago].*
       Something sure of state,   140
Either from Venice or some unhatched practice   141
Made demonstrable here in Cyprus to him,
Hath puddled his clear spirit; and in such cases   143
Men's natures wrangle with inferior things,
Though great ones are their object. 'Tis even so;
For let our finger ache, and it endues   146
Our other, healthful members even to a sense
Of pain. Nay, we must think men are not gods,
Nor of them look for such observancy
As fits the bridal. Beshrew me much, Emilia,
I was, unhandsome warrior as I am,   151
Arraigning his unkindness with my soul;   152
But now I find I had suborned the witness,
And he's indicted falsely.

EMILIA
Pray heaven it be state matters, as you think,
And no conception nor no jealous toy   156
Concerning you.

DESDEMONA
Alas the day! I never gave him cause.

EMILIA
But jealous souls will not be answered so;
They are not ever jealous for the cause,
But jealous for they're jealous. 'Tis a monster
Begot upon itself, born on itself.   162

DESDEMONA
Heaven keep that monster from Othello's mind!

EMILIA Lady, amen.

DESDEMONA
I will go seek him. Cassio, walk here about:
If I do find him fit, I'll move your suit
And seek to effect it to my uttermost.

CASSIO
I humbly thank your ladyship.
       Exeunt Desdemona and Emilia.
     Enter Bianca.

BIANCA
Save you, friend Cassio!

CASSIO   What make you from home?
How is't with you, my most fair Bianca?
I' faith, sweet love, I was coming to your house.

BIANCA
And I was going to your lodging, Cassio.
What, keep a week away? seven days and nights?
Eightscore eight hours? and lovers' absent hours,
More tedious than the dial eightscore times?   175

93 *all . . . time* during his whole career **108** *happiness* good luck **121** *shut myself up in* confine myself to **123** *advocation* advocacy **125** *favor* appearance **128** *blank* bull's-eye of the target **140** *state* public affairs **141** *unhatched practice* budding plot **143** *puddled* muddied **146** *endues* brings **151** *unhandsome warrior* inadequate soldier **152** *Arraigning . . . soul* indicting his unkindness before the bar of my soul **156** *toy* fancy **162** *Begot . . . itself* self-engendered **175** *dial* clock

    O weary reck'ning!

CASSIO   Pardon me, Bianca:
    I have this while with leaden thoughts been pressed;
178   But I shall in a more continuate time
    Strike off this score of absence. Sweet Bianca,
    [Gives her Desdemona's handkerchief.]
180   Take me this work out.

BIANCA   O Cassio, whence came this?
    This is some token from a newer friend.
    To the felt absence now I feel a cause.
    Is't come to this? Well, well.

CASSIO   Go to, woman!
    Throw your vile guesses in the devil's teeth,
    From whence you have them. You are jealous now
    That this is from some mistress, some remembrance.
    No, by my faith, Bianca.

BIANCA   Why, whose is it?

CASSIO
    I know not, sweet; I found it in my chamber.
189   I like the work well; ere it be demanded,
    As like enough it will, I'd have it copied.
    Take it and do't, and leave me for this time.

BIANCA
    Leave you? Wherefore?

CASSIO
    I do attend here on the general
    And think it no addition, nor my wish,
    To have him see me womaned.

BIANCA   Why, I pray you?

CASSIO
    Not that I love you not.

BIANCA   But that you do not love me!
    I pray you bring me on the way a little,
    And say if I shall see you soon at night.

CASSIO
    'Tis but a little way that I can bring you,
    For I attend here; but I'll see you soon.

BIANCA
201   'Tis very good. I must be circumstanced.   *Exeunt.*

                   *

IV, i   *Enter Othello and Iago.*

IAGO
    Will you think so?

OTHELLO   Think so, Iago?

IAGO   What,
    To kiss in private?

OTHELLO   An unauthorized kiss.

IAGO
    Or to be naked with her friend in bed
    An hour or more, not meaning any harm?

OTHELLO
    Naked in bed, Iago, and not mean harm?
6   It is hypocrisy against the devil.
    They that mean virtuously, and yet do so,
    The devil their virtue tempts, and they tempt heaven.

IAGO
    So they do nothing, 'tis a venial slip.
    But if I give my wife a handkerchief –

OTHELLO
    What then?

IAGO
    Why, then 'tis hers, my lord; and being hers,
    She may, I think, bestow't on any man.

OTHELLO
    She is protectress of her honor too;
    May she give that?

IAGO
    Her honor is an essence that's not seen;
    They have it very oft that have it not.
    But for the handkerchief –

OTHELLO
    By heaven, I would most gladly have forgot it!
    Thou said'st – O, it comes o'er my memory
    As doth the raven o'er the infected house,   21
    Boding to all! – he had my handkerchief.

IAGO
    Ay, what of that?

OTHELLO   That's not so good now.

IAGO   What
    If I had said I had seen him do you wrong?
    Or heard him say – as knaves be such abroad
    Who having, by their own importunate suit,
    Or voluntary dotage of some mistress,
    Convincèd or supplied them, cannot choose   28
    But they must blab –

OTHELLO   Hath he said anything?

IAGO
    He hath, my lord; but be you well assured,
    No more than he'll unswear.

OTHELLO   What hath he said?

IAGO
    Faith, that he did – I know not what he did.

OTHELLO What? what?

IAGO
    Lie –

OTHELLO With her?

IAGO   With her, on her; what you will.

OTHELLO Lie with her? lie on her? – We say lie on her
    when they belie her. – Lie with her! Zounds, that's ful-
    some. – Handkerchief – confessions – handkerchief! –
    To confess, and be hanged for his labor – first to be
    hanged, and then to confess! I tremble at it. Nature 39
    would not invest herself in such shadowing passion
    without some instruction. It is not words that shakes me
    thus. – Pish! Noses, ears, and lips? Is't possible? – Con-
    fess? – Handkerchief? – O devil!
    Falls in a trance.

IAGO Work on,
    My med'cine, work! Thus credulous fools are caught,
    And many worthy and chaste dames even thus,
    All guiltless, meet reproach. – What, ho! my lord!
    My lord, I say! Othello!
    Enter Cassio.   How now, Cassio?

CASSIO
    What's the matter?

IAGO
    My lord is fall'n into an epilepsy.
    This is his second fit; he had one yesterday.

CASSIO
    Rub him about the temples.

178 *continuate* uninterrupted   180 *Take . . . out* copy this embroidery for me   189 *work* needlework   201 *circumstanced* governed by circumstances   **IV, i** The environs of the castle   6 *hypocrisy . . . devil* i.e. feigned sin instead of feigned virtue   21 *infected* plague-stricken   28 *Convincèd or supplied* overcome or gratified   39–41 *Nature . . . instruction* my natural faculties would not be so overcome by passion without reason

IAGO   No, forbear.
53 The lethargy must have his quiet course.
If not, he foams at mouth, and by and by
Breaks out to savage madness. Look, he stirs.
Do you withdraw yourself a little while.
He will recover straight. When he is gone,
I would on great occasion speak with you. *[Exit Cassio.]*
How is it, general? Have you not hurt your head?

OTHELLO
Dost thou mock me?

IAGO   I mock you? No, by heaven.
Would you would bear your fortune like a man!

OTHELLO
62 A hornèd man's a monster and a beast.

IAGO
There's many a beast then in a populous city,
And many a civil monster.

OTHELLO
Did he confess it?

IAGO   Good sir, be a man.
Think every bearded fellow that's but yoked
May draw with you. There's millions now alive
68 That nightly lie in those unproper beds
69 Which they dare swear peculiar: your case is better.
O, 'tis the spite of hell, the fiend's arch-mock,
71 To lip a wanton in a secure couch,
And to suppose her chaste! No, let me know;
And knowing what I am, I know what she shall be.

OTHELLO
O, thou art wise! 'Tis certain.

IAGO   Stand you awhile apart;
75 Confine yourself but in a patient list.
Whilst you were here, o'erwhelmèd with your grief –
A passion most unsuiting such a man –
Cassio came hither. I shifted him away
79 And laid good 'scuse upon your ecstasy;
Bade him anon return, and here speak with me;
81 The which he promised. Do but encave yourself
And mark the fleers, the gibes, and notable scorns
That dwell in every region of his face;
For I will make him tell the tale anew –
Where, how, how oft, how long ago, and when
86 He hath, and is again to cope your wife.
I say, but mark his gesture. Marry, patience!
88 Or I shall say y'are all in all in spleen,
And nothing of a man.

OTHELLO   Dost thou hear, Iago?
I will be found most cunning in my patience;
But – dost thou hear? – most bloody.

IAGO   That's not amiss;
But yet keep time in all. Will you withdraw?
           [Othello retires.]
Now will I question Cassio of Bianca,
94 A huswife that by selling her desires
Buys herself bread and clothes. It is a creature
That dotes on Cassio, as 'tis the strumpet's plague

To beguile many and be beguiled by one.
He, when he hears of her, cannot refrain
From the excess of laughter. Here he comes.
      Enter Cassio.
As he shall smile, Othello shall go mad;
And his unbookish jealousy must conster   101
Poor Cassio's smiles, gestures, and light behavior
Quite in the wrong. How do you now, lieutenant?

CASSIO
The worser that you give me the addition   104
Whose want even kills me.

IAGO
Ply Desdemona well, and you are sure on't.
Now, if this suit lay in Bianca's power,
How quickly should you speed!

CASSIO   Alas, poor caitiff!   108

OTHELLO
Look how he laughs already!

IAGO
I never knew a woman love man so.

CASSIO
Alas, poor rogue! I think, i' faith, she loves me.

OTHELLO
Now he denies it faintly, and laughs it out.

IAGO
Do you hear, Cassio?

OTHELLO   Now he importunes him
To tell it o'er. Go to! Well said, well said!

IAGO
She gives it out that you shall marry her.
Do you intend it?

CASSIO Ha, ha, ha!

OTHELLO
Do you triumph, Roman? Do you triumph?

CASSIO I marry her? What, a customer? Prithee bear 119
some charity to my wit; do not think it so unwholesome.
Ha, ha, ha!

OTHELLO So, so, so, so! They laugh that win!

IAGO
Faith, the cry goes that you shall marry her.

CASSIO Prithee say true.

IAGO I am a very villain else.

OTHELLO Have you scored me? Well.   126

CASSIO This is the monkey's own giving out. She is persuaded I will marry her out of her own love and flattery,
not out of my promise.

OTHELLO Iago beckons me; now he begins the story.   130

CASSIO She was here even now; she haunts me in every
place. I was t' other day talking on the sea bank with certain Venetians, and thither comes the bauble, and, by 133
this hand, she falls me thus about my neck –

OTHELLO Crying 'O dear Cassio!' as it were. His gesture
imports it.

CASSIO So hangs, and lolls, and weeps upon me; so
shakes and pulls me! Ha, ha, ha!

OTHELLO Now he tells how she plucked him to my
chamber. O, I see that nose of yours, but not that dog I
shall throw it to.

CASSIO Well, I must leave her company.
      Enter Bianca.

IAGO Before me! Look where she comes.

CASSIO 'Tis such another fitchew! marry, a perfumed 144
one. What do you mean by this haunting of me?

BIANCA Let the devil and his dam haunt you! What did

---

53 *lethargy* coma   62 *hornèd man* cuckold   68 *unproper* not exclusively
their own   69 *peculiar* exclusively their own   71 *secure* free from fear of
rivalry   75 *in a patient list* within the limits of self-control   79 *ecstasy*
trance   81 *encave* conceal   86 *cope* meet   88 *all in all in spleen* wholly
overcome by your passion   94 *huswife* hussy   101 *unbookish* uninstructed;
conster construe, interpret   104 *addition* title   108 *caitiff* wretch   119
customer prostitute   126 *scored me* settled my account (?)   130 *beckons*
signals   133 *bauble* plaything   144 *fitchew* polecat (slang for whore)

you mean by that same handkerchief you gave me even now? I was a fine fool to take it. I must take out the whole work? A likely piece of work that you should find it in your chamber and know not who left it there! This is some minx's token, and I must take out the work?
152 There! Give it your hobby-horse. Wheresoever you had it, I'll take out no work on't.

CASSIO How now, my sweet Bianca? How now? how now?

OTHELLO By heaven, that should be my handkerchief!

BIANCA An you'll come to supper to-night, you may; an you will not, come when you are next prepared for. *Exit.*

IAGO After her, after her!

CASSIO Faith, I must; she'll rail in the street else.

IAGO Will you sup there?

CASSIO Yes, I intend so.

IAGO Well, I may chance to see you; for I would very fain speak with you.

CASSIO Prithee come. Will you?

IAGO Go to! say no more. *Exit Cassio.*

OTHELLO *[comes forward]* How shall I murder him, Iago?

168 IAGO Did you perceive how he laughed at his vice?

OTHELLO O Iago!

IAGO And did you see the handkerchief?

OTHELLO Was that mine?

172 IAGO Yours, by this hand! And to see how he prizes the foolish woman your wife! She gave it him, and he hath giv'n it his whore.

OTHELLO I would have him nine years a-killing! – A fine woman! a fair woman! a sweet woman!

IAGO Nay, you must forget that.

OTHELLO Ay, let her rot, and perish, and be damned to-night; for she shall not live. No, my heart is turned to stone; I strike it, and it hurts my hand. O, the world hath not a sweeter creature! She might lie by an emperor's side and command him tasks.

IAGO Nay, that's not your way.

OTHELLO Hang her! I do but say what she is. So delicate with her needle! an admirable musician! O, she will sing the savageness out of a bear! Of so high and plente-
187 ous wit and invention –

IAGO She's the worse for all this.

OTHELLO O, a thousand thousand times! And then, of so
190 gentle a condition!

IAGO Ay, too gentle.

OTHELLO Nay, that's certain. But yet the pity of it, Iago! O Iago, the pity of it, Iago!

194 IAGO If you are so fond over her iniquity, give her patent to offend; for if it touch not you, it comes near nobody.

OTHELLO I will chop her into messes! Cuckold me!

IAGO O, 'tis foul in her.

OTHELLO With mine officer!

IAGO That's fouler.

OTHELLO Get me some poison, Iago, this night. I'll not
201 expostulate with her, lest her body and beauty unprovide my mind again. This night, Iago!

IAGO Do it not with poison. Strangle her in her bed, even the bed she hath contaminated.

OTHELLO Good, good! The justice of it pleases. Very good!

206 IAGO And for Cassio, let me be his undertaker: you shall hear more by midnight.

OTHELLO
Excellent good!

A trumpet. What trumpet is that same?

IAGO
I warrant something from Venice.
Enter Lodovico, Desdemona, and Attendants.
'Tis Lodovico.
This comes from the Duke; and see, your wife is with 210 him.

LODOVICO
God save you, worthy general!

OTHELLO   With all my heart, sir.

LODOVICO
The Duke and senators of Venice greet you.
[Gives him a letter.]

OTHELLO
I kiss the instrument of their pleasures.
[Opens the letter and reads.]

DESDEMONA
And what's the news, good cousin Lodovico?

IAGO
I am very glad to see you, signior.
Welcome to Cyprus.

LODOVICO
I thank you. How does Lieutenant Cassio?

IAGO   Lives, sir.

DESDEMONA
Cousin, there's fall'n between him and my lord
An unkind breach; but you shall make all well.

OTHELLO Are you sure of that?   220

DESDEMONA My lord?

OTHELLO *[reads]* 'This fail you not to do, as you will –'

LODOVICO
He did not call; he's busy in the paper.
Is there division 'twixt thy lord and Cassio?

DESDEMONA
A most unhappy one. I would do much
T'atone them, for the love I bear to Cassio.   226

OTHELLO
Fire and brimstone!

DESDEMONA   My lord?

OTHELLO   Are you wise?

DESDEMONA
What, is he angry?

LODOVICO   May be the letter moved him;
For, as I think, they do command him home,
Deputing Cassio in his government.

DESDEMONA
By my troth, I am glad on't.

OTHELLO   Indeed?

DESDEMONA   My lord?

OTHELLO
I am glad to see you mad.   232

DESDEMONA   Why, sweet Othello –

OTHELLO Devil!
[Strikes her.]

DESDEMONA I have not deserved this.

LODOVICO
My lord, this would not be believed in Venice,
Though I should swear I saw't. 'Tis very much.
Make her amends; she weeps.

---

152 *hobby-horse* harlot   168 *vice* i.e. vicious conduct   172 *prizes* values
187 *invention* imagination   190 *condition* disposition   194 *patent* license
201 *unprovide* disarm   206 *be his undertaker* undertake to deal with him
226 *atone* reconcile   232 *mad* i.e. waggish

OTHELLO   O devil, devil!

238   If that the earth could teem with woman's tears,

239   Each drop she falls would prove a crocodile.
Out of my sight!

DESDEMONA   I will not stay to offend you.   *[Going.]*

LODOVICO
Truly, an obedient lady.
I do beseech your lordship call her back.

OTHELLO
Mistress!

DESDEMONA   My lord?

OTHELLO   What would you with her, sir?

LODOVICO
Who? I, my lord?

OTHELLO
Ay! You did wish that I would make her turn.
Sir, she can turn, and turn, and yet go on
And turn again; and she can weep, sir, weep;
And she's obedient; as you say, obedient,
Very obedient. – Proceed you in your tears. –

250   Concerning this, sir – O well-painted passion! –
I am commanded home. – Get you away;
I'll send for you anon. – Sir, I obey the mandate
And will return to Venice. – Hence, avaunt!

               [Exit Desdemona.]

Cassio shall have my place. And, sir, to-night
I do entreat that we may sup together.
You are welcome, sir, to Cyprus. – Goats and monkeys!

                 Exit.

LODOVICO
Is this the noble Moor whom our full Senate
Call all in all sufficient? Is this the nature
Whom passion could not shake? whose solid virtue
The shot of accident nor dart of chance
Could neither graze nor pierce?

IAGO   He is much changed.

LODOVICO
Are his wits safe? Is he not light of brain?

IAGO
He's that he is; I may not breathe my censure.
What he might be – if what he might he is not –
I would to heaven he were!

LODOVICO   What, strike his wife?

IAGO
Faith, that was not so well; yet would I knew
That stroke would prove the worst!

267 LODOVICO   Is it his use?
Or did the letters work upon his blood
And new-create this fault?

IAGO   Alas, alas!
It is not honesty in me to speak
What I have seen and known. You shall observe him,
And his own courses will denote him so
That I may save my speech. Do but go after
And mark how he continues.

LODOVICO
I am sorry that I am deceived in him.   *Exeunt.*

              *

Enter Othello and Emilia.   IV, ii

OTHELLO
You have seen nothing then?

EMILIA
Nor ever heard, nor ever did suspect.

OTHELLO
Yes, you have seen Cassio and she together.

EMILIA
But then I saw no harm, and then I heard
Each syllable that breath made up between them.

OTHELLO
What, did they never whisper?

EMILIA   Never, my lord.

OTHELLO
Nor send you out o' th' way?

EMILIA   Never.

OTHELLO
To fetch her fan, her gloves, her mask, nor nothing?

EMILIA   Never, my lord.

OTHELLO   That's strange.

EMILIA
I durst, my lord, to wager she is honest,
Lay down my soul at stake. If you think other,
Remove your thought; it doth abuse your bosom.   14
If any wretch have put this in your head,
Let heaven requite it with the serpent's curse!   16
For if she be not honest, chaste, and true,
There's no man happy; the purest of their wives
Is foul as slander.

OTHELLO   Bid her come hither. Go.   *Exit Emilia.*
She says enough; yet she's a simple bawd
That cannot say as much. This is a subtle whore,
A closet lock and key of villainous secrets;
And yet she'll kneel and pray; I have seen her do't.

         Enter Desdemona and Emilia.

DESDEMONA
My lord, what is your will?

OTHELLO   Pray, chuck, come hither.

DESDEMONA
What is your pleasure?

OTHELLO   Let me see your eyes.
Look in my face.

DESDEMONA   What horrible fancy 's this?

OTHELLO *[to Emilia]*
Some of your function, mistress.
Leave procreants alone and shut the door;   28
Cough or cry hem if anybody come.
Your mystery, your mystery! Nay, dispatch!   30

              Exit Emilia.

DESDEMONA
Upon my knees, what doth your speech import?
I understand a fury in your words,
[But not the words.]

OTHELLO
Why, what art thou?

DESDEMONA   Your wife, my lord; your true
And loyal wife.

OTHELLO   Come, swear it, damn thyself;
Lest, being like one of heaven, the devils themselves   36
Should fear to seize thee. Therefore be double-damned –
Swear thou art honest.   38

DESDEMONA   Heaven doth truly know it.

OTHELLO
Heaven truly knows that thou art false as hell.

---

238 *teem* breed   239 *crocodile* (crocodiles were supposed to shed hypocritical tears to lure men to destruction)   250 *passion* grief   267 *use* custom
IV, ii *Within the castle*   14 *abuse . . . bosom* deceive your heart   16 *serpent's curse* (cf. Genesis iii, 14)   28 *procreants* mating couples   30 *mystery* trade, occupation   36 *being . . . heaven* looking like an angel   38 *honest* chaste

DESDEMONA
To whom, my lord ? With whom ? How am I false ?

OTHELLO
Ah, Desdemon ! away ! away ! away !

DESDEMONA
Alas the heavy day ! Why do you weep ?
Am I the motive of these tears, my lord ?
If haply you my father do suspect
45 An instrument of this your calling back,
Lay not your blame on me. If you have lost him,
Why, I have lost him too.

OTHELLO   Had it pleased heaven
To try me with affliction, had they rained
All kinds of sores and shames on my bare head,
Steeped me in poverty to the very lips,
Given to captivity me and my utmost hopes,
I should have found in some place of my soul
A drop of patience. But, alas, to make me
54 A fixèd figure for the time of scorn
To point his slow unmoving finger at !
Yet could I bear that too ; well, very well.
But there where I have garnered up my heart,
Where either I must live or bear no life,
The fountain from the which my current runs
Or else dries up – to be discarded thence,
Or keep it as a cistern for foul toads
62 To knot and gender in – turn thy complexion there,
Patience, thou young and rose-lipped cherubin !
Ay, there look grim as hell !

DESDEMONA
I hope my noble lord esteems me honest.

OTHELLO
66 O, ay ; as summer flies are in the shambles,
67 That quicken even with blowing. O thou weed,
Who art so lovely fair, and smell'st so sweet,
That the sense aches at thee, would thou hadst ne'er
    been born !

DESDEMONA
Alas, what ignorant sin have I committed ?

OTHELLO
Was this fair paper, this most goodly book,
Made to write 'whore' upon ? What committed ?
73 Committed ? O thou public commoner !
I should make very forges of my cheeks
That would to cinders burn up modesty,
Did I but speak thy deeds. What committed ?
77 Heaven stops the nose at it, and the moon winks ;
The bawdy wind, that kisses all it meets,
Is hushed within the hollow mine of earth
And will not hear it. What committed ?
Impudent strumpet !

DESDEMONA   By heaven, you do me wrong !

OTHELLO
Are not you a strumpet ?

DESDEMONA   No, as I am a Christian !
If to preserve this vessel for my lord
From any other foul unlawful touch
Be not to be a strumpet, I am none.

OTHELLO
What, not a whore ?

DESDEMONA   No, as I shall be saved !

OTHELLO   Is't possible ?

DESDEMONA
O, heaven forgive us !

OTHELLO   I cry you mercy then.   88
I took you for that cunning whore of Venice
That married with Othello. – [calling] You, mistress,
That have the office opposite to Saint Peter
And keep the gate of hell !
    Enter Emilia.   You, you, ay, you !
We have done our course ; there's money for your pains :
I pray you turn the key, and keep our counsel.   Exit.

EMILIA
Alas, what does this gentleman conceive ?
How do you, madam ? How do you, my good lady ?

DESDEMONA Faith, half asleep.   97

EMILIA
Good madam, what's the matter with my lord ?

DESDEMONA With who ?

EMILIA Why, with my lord, madam.

DESDEMONA
Who is thy lord ?

EMILIA   He that is yours, sweet lady.

DESDEMONA
I have none. Do not talk to me, Emilia.
I cannot weep ; nor answers have I none
But what should go by water. Prithee to-night
Lay on my bed my wedding sheets, remember ;
And call thy husband hither.

EMILIA   Here's a change indeed ! Exit.

DESDEMONA
'Tis meet I should be used so, very meet.
How have I been behaved, that he might stick
The small'st opinion on my least misuse ?   109
    Enter Iago and Emilia.

IAGO
What is your pleasure, madam ? How is't with you ?

DESDEMONA
I cannot tell. Those that do teach young babes
Do it with gentle means and easy tasks :
He might have chid me so ; for, in good faith,
I am a child to chiding.

IAGO   What is the matter, lady ?

EMILIA
Alas, Iago, my lord hath so bewhored her,
Thrown such despite and heavy terms upon her
As true hearts cannot bear.

DESDEMONA
Am I that name, Iago ?

IAGO   What name, fair lady ?

DESDEMONA
Such as she said my lord did say I was.

EMILIA
He called her whore. A beggar in his drink
Could not have laid such terms upon his callet.   121

IAGO
Why did he so ?

DESDEMONA
I do not know ; I am sure I am none such.

IAGO
Do not weep, do not weep. Alas the day !

45 *An instrument* to be the cause   54 *time of scorn* scornful world   62 *turn thy complexion there* change thy color at that point   66 *shambles* slaughterhouse   67 *quicken* come to life   73 *commoner* harlot   77 *winks* closes her eyes   88 *cry you mercy* beg your pardon   97 *half asleep* i.e. stunned   109 *small'st opinion* least suspicion ; *least misuse* slightest misconduct   121 *callet* whore

EMILIA
Hath she forsook so many noble matches,
Her father and her country, and her friends,
To be called whore ? Would it not make one weep ?

DESDEMONA
It is my wretched fortune.

IAGO   Beshrew him for't !

129   How comes this trick upon him ?

DESDEMONA   Nay, heaven doth know.

EMILIA
I will be hanged if some eternal villain,
Some busy and insinuating rogue,
132   Some cogging, cozening slave, to get some office,
Have not devised this slander. I'll be hanged else.

IAGO
Fie, there is no such man ! It is impossible.

DESDEMONA
If any such there be, heaven pardon him !

EMILIA
A halter pardon him ! and hell gnaw his bones !
Why should he call her whore ? Who keeps her
company ?
What place ? what time ? what form ? what likelihood ?
The Moor 's abused by some most villainous knave,
Some base notorious knave, some scurvy fellow.
141   O heaven, that such companions thou'dst unfold,
And put in every honest hand a whip
To lash the rascals naked through the world
Even from the east to th' west !

144 IAGO   Speak within door.

EMILIA
O, fie upon them ! Some such squire he was
That turned your wit the seamy side without
And made you to suspect me with the Moor.

IAGO
You are a fool. Go to.

DESDEMONA   Alas, Iago,
What shall I do to win my lord again ?
Good friend, go to him ; for, by this light of heaven,
I know not how I lost him. Here I kneel :
If e'er my will did trespass 'gainst his love
153   Either in discourse of thought or actual deed,
Or that mine eyes, mine ears, or any sense
Delighted them in any other form,
Or that I do not yet, and ever did,
And ever will (though he do shake me off
To beggarly divorcement) love him dearly,
159   Comfort forswear me ! Unkindness may do much ;
160   And his unkindness may defeat my life,
But never taint my love. I cannot say 'whore.'
It does abhor me now I speak the word ;
To do the act that might the addition earn
Not the world's mass of vanity could make me.

IAGO
I pray you be content. 'Tis but his humor.
The business of the state does him offense,

129 *trick* freakish behavior   132 *cogging, cozening* cheating, defrauding   141 *companions* rogues ; *unfold* expose   144 *within door* with restraint   153 *discourse* course   159 *Comfort forswear* happiness forsake   160 *defeat* destroy   175 *thou . . . device* you put me off with some trick   177 *conveniency* favorable opportunities   188 *votarist* nun   189 *sudden respect* immediate notice   194 *fopped* duped   207 *directly* straightforwardly   215 *engines for* plots against   222–23 *abode . . . here* stay here be extended   223 *determinate* effective

[And he does chide with you.]

DESDEMONA
If 'twere no other –

IAGO   'Tis but so, I warrant.
[Trumpets within.]
Hark how these instruments summon you to supper.
The messengers of Venice stay the meat :
Go in, and weep not. All things shall be well.
                 Exeunt Desdemona and Emilia.
     Enter Roderigo.
How now, Roderigo ?

RODERIGO   I do not find that thou deal'st justly with me.

IAGO   What in the contrary ?

RODERIGO   Every day thou daff'st me with some device, 175
Iago, and rather, as it seems to me now, keep'st from me
all conveniency than suppliest me with the least ad- 177
vantage of hope. I will indeed no longer endure it ; nor
am I yet persuaded to put up in peace what already I
have foolishly suffered.

IAGO   Will you hear me, Roderigo ?

RODERIGO   Faith, I have heard too much ; for your words
and performances are no kin together.

IAGO   You charge me most unjustly.

RODERIGO   With naught but truth. I have wasted myself
out of my means. The jewels you have had from me to
deliver to Desdemona would half have corrupted a
votarist. You have told me she hath received them, and 188
returned me expectations and comforts of sudden re- 189
spect and acquaintance ; but I find none.

IAGO   Well, go to ; very well.

RODERIGO   Very well ! go to ! I cannot go to, man ; nor
'tis not very well. By this hand, I say 'tis very scurvy,
and begin to find myself fopped in it.   194

IAGO   Very well.

RODERIGO   I tell you 'tis not very well. I will make myself
known to Desdemona. If she will return me my jewels,
I will give over my suit and repent my unlawful solicitation ; if not, assure yourself I will seek satisfaction of you.

IAGO   You have said now.

RODERIGO   Ay, and said nothing but what I protest intendment of doing.

IAGO   Why, now I see there's mettle in thee ; and even
from this instant do build on thee a better opinion than
ever before. Give me thy hand, Roderigo. Thou hast
taken against me a most just exception ; but yet I protest
I have dealt most directly in thy affair.   207

RODERIGO   It hath not appeared.

IAGO   I grant indeed it hath not appeared, and your suspicion is not without wit and judgment. But, Roderigo, if
thou hast that in thee indeed which I have greater reason
to believe now than ever, I mean purpose, courage, and
valor, this night show it. If thou the next night following
enjoy not Desdemona, take me from this world with
treachery and devise engines for my life.   215

RODERIGO   Well, what is it ? Is it within reason and compass ?

IAGO   Sir, there is especial commission come from Venice
to depute Cassio in Othello's place.

RODERIGO   Is that true ? Why, then Othello and Desdemona return again to Venice.

IAGO   O, no ; he goes into Mauritania and takes away with
him the fair Desdemona, unless his abode be lingered 222
here by some accident ; wherein none can be so deter- 223
minate as the removing of Cassio.

RODERIGO How do you mean removing of him?

IAGO Why, by making him uncapable of Othello's place –
knocking out his brains.

RODERIGO And that you would have me to do?

IAGO Ay, if you dare do yourself a profit and a right. He
sups to-night with a harlotry, and thither will I go to
him. He knows not yet of his honorable fortune. If you
will watch his going thence, which I will fashion to fall
out between twelve and one, you may take him at your
pleasure. I will be near to second your attempt, and he
shall fall between us. Come, stand not amazed at it, but
go along with me. I will show you such a necessity in his
death that you shall think yourself bound to put it on
him. It is now high supper time, and the night grows to
waste. About it!

RODERIGO I will hear further reason for this.

IAGO And you shall be satisfied.   *Exeunt.*

*

IV, iii   *Enter Othello, Lodovico, Desdemona, Emilia, and*
        Attendants.

LODOVICO
    I do beseech you, sir, trouble yourself no further.

OTHELLO
    O, pardon me; 'twill do me good to walk.

LODOVICO
    Madam, good night. I humbly thank your ladyship.

DESDEMONA
    Your honor is most welcome.

OTHELLO   Will you walk, sir?
    O, Desdemona –

DESDEMONA My lord?

OTHELLO Get you to bed on th' instant; I will be returned forthwith. Dismiss your attendant there. Look't
be done.

DESDEMONA I will, my lord.
        Exit [Othello, with Lodovico and Attendants].

EMILIA How goes it now? He looks gentler than he did.

DESDEMONA
11   He says he will return incontinent.
    He hath commanded me to go to bed,
    And bade me to dismiss you.

EMILIA   Dismiss me?

DESDEMONA
    It was his bidding; therefore, good Emilia,
    Give me my nightly wearing, and adieu.
    We must not now displease him.

EMILIA I would you had never seen him!

DESDEMONA
    So would not I. My love doth so approve him
19   That even his stubbornness, his checks, his frowns –
    Prithee unpin me – have grace and favor in them.

EMILIA I have laid those sheets you bade me on the bed.

DESDEMONA
    All's one. Good faith, how foolish are our minds!
    If I do die before thee, prithee shroud me
    In one of those same sheets.

EMILIA   Come, come! You talk.

DESDEMONA
    My mother had a maid called Barbary.
26   She was in love; and he she loved proved mad
    And did forsake her. She had a song of 'Willow';
    An old thing 'twas; but it expressed her fortune,

    And she died singing it. That song to-night
    Will not go from my mind; I have much to do
    But to go hang my head all at one side
    And sing it like poor Barbary. Prithee dispatch.

EMILIA
    Shall I go fetch your nightgown?   33

DESDEMONA   No, unpin me here.
    This Lodovico is a proper man.

EMILIA A very handsome man.

DESDEMONA He speaks well.

EMILIA I know a lady in Venice would have walked barefoot to Palestine for a touch of his nether lip.

DESDEMONA *(sings)*
    'The poor soul sat sighing by a sycamore tree,
       Sing all a green willow;
    Her hand on her bosom, her head on her knee,
       Sing willow, willow, willow.
    The fresh streams ran by her and murmured her
       moans;
       Sing willow, willow, willow;
    Her salt tears fell from her, and soft'ned the stones' –
    Lay by these.
       'Sing willow, willow, willow' –
    Prithee hie thee; he'll come anon.   48
    'Sing all a green willow must be my garland.
    Let nobody blame him; his scorn I approve' –
    Nay, that's not next. Hark! who is't that knocks?

EMILIA It's the wind.

DESDEMONA *[sings]*
    'I called my love false love; but what said he then?
       Sing willow, willow, willow:
    If I court moe women, you'll couch with moe men.'
    So, get thee gone; good night. Mine eyes do itch.
    Doth that bode weeping?

EMILIA   'Tis neither here nor there.

DESDEMONA
    I have heard it said so. O, these men, these men!
    Dost thou in conscience think – tell me, Emilia –
    That there be women do abuse their husbands   60
    In such gross kind?

EMILIA   There be some such, no question.

DESDEMONA
    Wouldst thou do such a deed for all the world?

EMILIA
    Why, would not you?

DESDEMONA   No, by this heavenly light!

EMILIA
    Nor I neither by this heavenly light.
    I might do't as well i' th' dark.

DESDEMONA
    Wouldst thou do such a deed for all the world?

EMILIA The world's a huge thing; it is a great price for a
small vice.

DESDEMONA
    In troth, I think thou wouldst not.

EMILIA In troth, I think I should; and undo't when I
had done it. Marry, I would not do such a thing for a
joint-ring, nor for measures of lawn, nor for gowns, 72
petticoats, nor caps, nor any petty exhibition; but, for 73

IV, iii Within the castle   11 *incontinent* at once   19 *stubbornness* roughness; *checks* rebukes   26 *mad* wild, faithless   33 *nightgown* dressing
gown   48 *hie thee* hurry   72 *joint-ring* ring made in separable halves
73 *exhibition* gift

all the whole world – 'Ud's pity! who would not make
her husband a cuckold to make him a monarch? I
should venture purgatory for't.

DESDEMONA
Beshrew me if I would do such a wrong
For the whole world.

EMILIA Why, the wrong is but a wrong i' th' world; and
having the world for your labor, 'tis a wrong in your
own world, and you might quickly make it right.

DESDEMONA I do not think there is any such woman.

83 EMILIA Yes, a dozen; and as many to th' vantage as
84   would store the world they played for.
But I do think it is their husbands' faults
If wives do fall. Say that they slack their duties
And pour our treasures into foreign laps;
88 Or else break out in peevish jealousies,
Throwing restraint upon us; or say they strike us,
90 Or scant our former having in despite –
91 Why, we have galls; and though we have some grace,
Yet have we some revenge. Let husbands know
Their wives have sense like them. They see, and smell,
And have their palates both for sweet and sour,
As husbands have. What is it that they do
When they change us for others? Is it sport?
I think it is. And doth affection breed it?
I think it doth. Is't frailty that thus errs?
It is so too. And have not we affections,
Desires for sport, and frailty, as men have?
Then let them use us well; else let them know,
The ills we do, their ills instruct us so.

DESDEMONA
103 Good night, good night. God me such usage send,
Not to pick bad from bad, but by bad mend!   *Exeunt.*

*

V, i   *Enter Iago and Roderigo.*

IAGO
1 Here, stand behind this bulk; straight will he come.
Wear thy good rapier bare, and put it home.
Quick, quick! Fear nothing; I'll be at thy elbow.
It makes us, or it mars us – think on that,
And fix most firm thy resolution.

RODERIGO
Be near at hand; I may miscarry in't.

IAGO
Here, at thy hand. Be bold, and take thy stand.
[Stands aside.]

RODERIGO
I have no great devotion to the deed,
And yet he hath given me satisfying reasons.
'Tis but a man gone. Forth my sword! He dies!

IAGO
11 I have rubbed this young quat almost to the sense,
And he grows angry. Now whether he kill Cassio,
Or Cassio him, or each do kill the other,
Every way makes my gain. Live Roderigo,
He calls me to a restitution large

Of gold and jewels that I bobbed from him   16
As gifts to Desdemona.
It must not be. If Cassio do remain,
He hath a daily beauty in his life
That makes me ugly; and besides, the Moor
May unfold me to him; there stand I in much peril.
No, he must die. Be't so! I hear him coming.
Enter Cassio.

RODERIGO
I know his gait. 'Tis he. Villain, thou diest!
[Makes a pass at Cassio.]

CASSIO
That thrust had been mine enemy indeed
But that my coat is better than thou know'st.   25
I will make proof of thine.
[Draws, and wounds Roderigo.]

RODERIGO   O, I am slain!
*[Iago darts from concealment behind Cassio,
wounds him in the leg, and exit.]*

CASSIO
I am maimed for ever. Help, ho! Murder! murder!
[Falls.]
Enter Othello.

OTHELLO
The voice of Cassio. Iago keeps his word.

RODERIGO
O, villain that I am!

OTHELLO   It is even so.

CASSIO
O, help, ho! light! a surgeon!

OTHELLO
'Tis he. O brave Iago, honest and just,
That hast such noble sense of thy friend's wrong!
Thou teachest me. Minion, your dear lies dead,   33
And your unblest fate hies. Strumpet, I come.   34
Forth of my heart those charms, thine eyes, are blotted.
Thy bed, lust-stained, shall with lust's blood be spotted.
           Exit Othello.
Enter Lodovico and Gratiano.

CASSIO
What, ho? No watch? No passage? Murder! murder!   37

GRATIANO
'Tis some mischance. The cry is very direful.

CASSIO O, help!

LODOVICO Hark!

RODERIGO O wretched villain!

LODOVICO
Two or three groan. It is a heavy night.   42
These may be counterfeits. Let's think't unsafe
To come in to the cry without more help.

RODERIGO
Nobody come? Then shall I bleed to death.

LODOVICO Hark!
Enter Iago, with a light.

GRATIANO
Here's one comes in his shirt, with light and weapons.

IAGO
Who's there? Whose noise is this that cries on murder?   48

LODOVICO
We do not know.

IAGO   Did not you hear a cry?

CASSIO
Here, here! For heaven's sake, help me!

IAGO   What's the matter?

83 *to th' vantage* besides   84 *store* populate   88 *peevish* senseless   90 *having* allowance   91 *galls* spirits to resent   103 *usage* habits
V, i A street in Cyprus   1 *bulk* projecting shop-front   11 *quat* pimple; *sense* quick   16 *bobbed* swindled   25 *coat* under-shirt of mail   33 *Minion* mistress   34 *hies* hurries on   37 *passage* passers-by   42 *heavy* cloudy, dark   48 *cries on* raises the cry of

GRATIANO
This is Othello's ancient, as I take it.
LODOVICO
The same indeed, a very valiant fellow.
IAGO
What are you here that cry so grievously?
CASSIO
Iago? O, I am spoiled, undone by villains!
Give me some help.
IAGO
O me, lieutenant! What villains have done this?
CASSIO
I think that one of them is hereabout
58   And cannot make away.
IAGO   O treacherous villains!
       [To Lodovico and Gratiano]
What are you there? Come in, and give some help.
RODERIGO
O, help me here!
CASSIO
That's one of them.
IAGO   O murd'rous slave! O villain!
       [Stabs Roderigo.]
RODERIGO
O damned Iago! O inhuman dog!
IAGO
Kill men i' th' dark? – Where be these bloody thieves? –
How silent is this town! – Ho! murder! murder! –
What may you be? Are you of good or evil?
LODOVICO
As you shall prove us, praise us.
IAGO Signior Lodovico?
LODOVICO He, sir.
IAGO
I cry you mercy. Here's Cassio hurt by villains.
GRATIANO Cassio?
IAGO How is't, brother?
CASSIO
My leg is cut in two.
72 IAGO   Marry, heaven forbid!
Light, gentleman. I'll bind it with my shirt.
       Enter Bianca.
BIANCA
What is the matter, ho? Who is't that cried?
IAGO
Who is't that cried?
BIANCA
O my dear Cassio! my sweet Cassio!
O Cassio, Cassio, Cassio!
IAGO
O notable strumpet! – Cassio, may you suspect
Who they should be that have thus mangled you?
CASSIO No.
GRATIANO I am sorry to find you thus. I have been to
seek you.
IAGO
82   Lend me a garter. So. O for a chair
To bear him easily hence!
BIANCA
Alas, he faints! O Cassio, Cassio, Cassio!
IAGO
Gentlemen all, I do suspect this trash
To be a party in this injury. –
Patience awhile, good Cassio. – Come, come!

Lend me a light. Know we this face or no?
Alas, my friend and my dear countryman
Roderigo? No. – Yes, sure. – O heaven, Roderigo!
GRATIANO What, of Venice?
IAGO
Even he, sir. Did you know him?
GRATIANO   Know him? Ay.
IAGO
Signior Gratiano? I cry your gentle pardon.
These bloody accidents must excuse my manners
That so neglected you.
GRATIANO   I am glad to see you.
IAGO
How do you, Cassio? – O, a chair, a chair!
GRATIANO Roderigo?
IAGO
He, he, 'tis he!
       [A chair brought in.] O, that's well said; the chair.   98
Some good man bear him carefully from hence.
I'll fetch the general's surgeon.
       [To Bianca]   For you, mistress,
Save you your labor. – He that lies slain here, Cassio,
Was my dear friend. What malice was between you?
CASSIO
None in the world; nor do I know the man.
IAGO *[to Bianca]*
What, look you pale? – O, bear him out o' th' air.
                 [Cassio and Roderigo are borne off.]
Stay you, good gentlemen. – Look you pale, mistress? –
Do you perceive the gastness of her eye? –   106
Nay, if you stare, we shall hear more anon.
Behold her well; I pray you look upon her.
Do you see, gentlemen? Nay, guiltiness will speak,
Though tongues were out of use.
       Enter Emilia.
EMILIA
'Las, what's the matter? What's the matter, husband?
IAGO
Cassio hath here been set on in the dark
By Roderigo, and fellows that are scaped.
He's almost slain, and Roderigo dead.
EMILIA
Alas, good gentleman! alas, good Cassio!
IAGO
This is the fruits of whoring. Prithee, Emilia,
Go know of Cassio where he supped to-night.
       [To Bianca]
What, do you shake at that?
BIANCA
He supped at my house; but I therefore shake not.
IAGO
O, did he so? I charge you go with me.
EMILIA
Fie, fie upon thee, strumpet!
BIANCA
I am no strumpet, but of life as honest   122
As you that thus abuse me.
EMILIA   As I? Foh! fie upon thee!
IAGO
Kind gentlemen, let's go see poor Cassio dressed.
       [To Bianca]

58 *make* get   72 *Marry* (from By Mary)   82 *chair* litter   98 *well said*
well done   106 *gastness* terror   122 *honest* chaste

Come, mistress, you must tell's another tale.
Emilia, run you to the citadel
And tell my lord and lady what hath happed.

                                     [Exit Emilia.]

Will you go on afore ?   *Exeunt [all but Iago].*
         This is the night

129   That either makes me or fordoes me quite.   *[Exit.]*

                     *

V, ii   *Desdemona [asleep] in her bed. Enter Othello with a*
             light.

    OTHELLO
1   It is the cause, it is the cause, my soul.
     Let me not name it to you, you chaste stars !
     It is the cause. Yet I'll not shed her blood,
     Nor scar that whiter skin of hers than snow,
     And smooth as monumental alabaster.
     Yet she must die, else she'll betray more men.
     Put out the light, and then put out the light.
8   If I quench thee, thou flaming minister,
     I can again thy former light restore,
     Should I repent me ; but once put out thy light,
     Thou cunning'st pattern of excelling nature,
12   I know not where is that Promethean heat
13   That can thy light relume. When I have plucked the rose,
     I cannot give it vital growth again ;
     It needs must wither. I'll smell thee on the tree.
           He kisses her.
     O balmy breath, that dost almost persuade
     Justice to break her sword ! One more, one more !
     Be thus when thou art dead, and I will kill thee,
     And love thee after. One more, and that's the last !
     So sweet was ne'er so fatal. I must weep,
     But they are cruel tears. This sorrow's heavenly ;
     It strikes where it doth love. She wakes.
    DESDEMONA
     Who's there ? Othello ?
    OTHELLO   Ay, Desdemona.
    DESDEMONA
     Will you come to bed, my lord ?
    OTHELLO
     Have you prayed to-night, Desdemon ?
    DESDEMONA   Ay, my lord.
    OTHELLO
26   If you bethink yourself of any crime
     Unreconciled as yet to heaven and grace,
     Solicit for it straight.
    DESDEMONA
     Alack, my lord, what may you mean by that ?
    OTHELLO
     Well, do it, and be brief ; I will walk by.
     I would not kill thy unprepar'd spirit.
32   No, heaven forfend ! I would not kill thy soul.
    DESDEMONA
     Talk you of killing ?
    OTHELLO   Ay, I do.
    DESDEMONA   Then heaven
     Have mercy on me !

OTHELLO   Amen, with all my heart !
DESDEMONA
     If you say so, I hope you will not kill me.
OTHELLO Hum !
DESDEMONA
     And yet I fear you ; for you're fatal then
     When your eyes roll so. Why I should fear I know not,
     Since guiltiness I know not ; but yet I feel I fear.
OTHELLO
     Think on thy sins.
DESDEMONA   They are loves I bear to you.
OTHELLO
     Ay, and for that thou diest.
DESDEMONA
     That death 's unnatural that kills for loving.
     Alas, why gnaw you so your nether lip ?
     Some bloody passion shakes your very frame.
     These are portents ; but yet I hope, I hope,   45
     They do not point on me.
OTHELLO   Peace and be still !
DESDEMONA
     I will so. What's the matter ?
OTHELLO
     That handkerchief which I so loved and gave thee
     Thou gav'st to Cassio.
DESDEMONA   No, by my life and soul !
     Send for the man and ask him.
OTHELLO   Sweet soul, take heed,
     Take heed of perjury ; thou art on thy deathbed.
DESDEMONA
     Ay, but not yet to die.
OTHELLO   Yes, presently.   52
     Therefore confess thee freely of thy sin ;
     For to deny each article with oath
     Cannot remove nor choke the strong conception   55
     That I do groan withal. Thou art to die.
DESDEMONA
     Then Lord have mercy on me !
OTHELLO   I say amen.
DESDEMONA
     And have you mercy too ! I never did
     Offend you in my life ; never loved Cassio   59
     But with such general warranty of heaven
     As I might love. I never gave him token.
OTHELLO
     By heaven, I saw my handkerchief in's hand !
     O perjured woman ! thou dost stone my heart,   63
     And mak'st me call what I intend to do
     A murder, which I thought a sacrifice.
     I saw the handkerchief.
DESDEMONA   He found it then.
     I never gave it him. Send for him hither.
     Let him confess a truth.
OTHELLO   He hath confessed.
DESDEMONA
     What, my lord ?
OTHELLO
     That he hath used thee.
DESDEMONA   How ? unlawfully ?
OTHELLO   Ay.
DESDEMONA
     He will not say so.
OTHELLO   No, his mouth is stopped.
     Honest Iago hath ta'en order for't.   72

---

129 *fordoes* destroys

V, ii A bedchamber in the castle   1 *cause* cause of justice   8 *minister*
servant   12 *Promethean heat* divine fire   13 *relume* relight   26 *crime* sin
32 *forfend* forbid   45 *portents* signs of impending violence   52 *presently*
at once   55 *conception* belief   59 *Offend* wrong   63 *stone my heart* turn
my heart to stone   72 *ta'en order* taken measures

DESDEMONA
O, my fear interprets. What, is he dead?
OTHELLO
Had all his hairs been lives, my great revenge
Had stomach for them all.
DESDEMONA
Alas, he is betrayed, and I undone!
OTHELLO
Out, strumpet! Weep'st thou for him to my face?
DESDEMONA
O, banish me, my lord, but kill me not!
OTHELLO
Down, strumpet!
DESDEMONA
80   Kill me to-morrow; let me live to-night!
OTHELLO
Nay, if you strive –
DESDEMONA
But half an hour!
OTHELLO   Being done, there is no pause.
DESDEMONA
But while I say one prayer!
OTHELLO   It is too late.
    Smothers her.
[DESDEMONA O Lord, Lord, Lord!]
    Emilia at the door.
EMILIA *(calls within)*
My lord, my lord! What, ho! my lord, my lord!
OTHELLO
What noise is this? Not dead? not yet quite dead?
I that am cruel am yet merciful;
I would not have thee linger in thy pain.
So, so.
EMILIA *(within)*
What, ho! my lord, my lord!
OTHELLO   Who's there?
EMILIA *[within]*
O, good my lord, I would speak a word with you!
OTHELLO
92   Yes, 'tis Emilia. – By and by. – She's dead. –
'Tis like she comes to speak of Cassio's death.
The noise was here. Ha! no more moving?
Still as the grave. – Shall she come in? Were't good? –
I think she stirs again. No. – What's best to do?
If she come in, she'll sure speak to my wife.
My wife! my wife! what wife? I have no wife.
O, insupportable! O heavy hour!
Methinks it should be now a huge eclipse
Of sun and moon, and that th' affrighted globe
102   Should yawn at alteration.
EMILIA *[within]*   I do beseech you
That I may speak with you, O good my lord!
OTHELLO
I had forgot thee. O, come in, Emilia.
Soft, by and by. – Let me the curtains draw. –
    [Closes the bed-curtains.]
Where art thou?
    [Opens the door.]
    Enter Emilia.
                What's the matter with thee now?
EMILIA
O my good lord, yonder's foul murder done!
OTHELLO What? Now?
EMILIA But now, my lord.

OTHELLO
It is the very error of the moon.   110
She comes more nearer earth than she was wont
And makes men mad.
EMILIA
Cassio, my lord, hath killed a young Venetian
Called Roderigo.
OTHELLO   Roderigo killed?
And Cassio killed?
EMILIA   No, Cassio is not killed.
OTHELLO
Not Cassio killed? Then murder's out of tune,
And sweet revenge grows harsh.
DESDEMONA
O, falsely, falsely murdered!
EMILIA   O Lord! what cry is that?
OTHELLO That? What?
EMILIA
Out and alas! that was my lady's voice.
Help! help, ho! help! O lady, speak again!
Sweet Desdemona! O sweet mistress, speak!
DESDEMONA
A guiltless death I die.
EMILIA
O, who hath done this deed?
DESDEMONA
Nobody – I myself. Farewell.
Commend me to my kind lord. O, farewell!   126
    She dies.
OTHELLO
Why, how should she be murd'red?
EMILIA   Alas, who knows?
OTHELLO
You heard her say herself, it was not I.
EMILIA
She said so. I must needs report the truth.
OTHELLO
She's like a liar gone to burning hell!
'Twas I that killed her.
EMILIA   O, the more angel she,
And you the blacker devil!
OTHELLO
She turned to folly, and she was a whore.
EMILIA
Thou dost belie her, and thou art a devil.
OTHELLO
She was false as water.   135
EMILIA   Thou art rash as fire to say
That she was false. O, she was heavenly true!
OTHELLO
Cassio did top her. Ask thy husband else.
O, I were damned beneath all depth in hell
But that I did proceed upon just grounds
To this extremity. Thy husband knew it all.
EMILIA My husband?
OTHELLO Thy husband.
EMILIA
That she was false to wedlock?
OTHELLO
Ay, with Cassio. Nay, had she been true,

---

92 *By and by* just a moment (addressed to Emilia)   **102** *yawn* open, as in an earthquake   **110** *error* straying off course   **126** *Commend* remember   **135** *water* (which is yielding)

If heaven would make me such another world
146 Of one entire and perfect chrysolite,
I'ld not have sold her for it.

EMILIA
My husband?

OTHELLO   Ay, 'twas he that told me first.
An honest man he is, and hates the slime
That sticks on filthy deeds.

EMILIA   My husband?

OTHELLO
151 What needs this iterance, woman? I say thy husband.

EMILIA
O mistress, villainy hath made mocks with love!
My husband say that she was false?

OTHELLO   He, woman.
I say, thy husband. Dost understand the word?
My friend, thy husband; honest, honest Iago.

EMILIA
If he say so, may his pernicious soul
Rot half a grain a day! he lies to th' heart.
She was too fond of her most filthy bargain.

OTHELLO Ha!

EMILIA Do thy worst.
This deed of thine is no more worthy heaven
Than thou wast worthy her.

OTHELLO   Peace, you were best.

EMILIA
Thou hast not half the power to do me harm
164 As I have to be hurt. O gull! O dolt!
As ignorant as dirt! thou hast done a deed –
I care not for thy sword; I'll make thee known,
Though I lost twenty lives. Help! help! Ho! help!
The Moor hath killed my mistress! Murder! murder!
Enter Montano, Gratiano, Iago, and others.

MONTANO
What is the matter? How now, general?

EMILIA
170 O, are you come, Iago? You have done well,
That men must lay their murders on your neck.

GRATIANO
What is the matter?

EMILIA
Disprove this villain, if thou be'st a man.
He says thou told'st him that his wife was false.
I know thou didst not; thou'rt not such a villain.
Speak, for my heart is full.

IAGO
I told him what I thought, and told no more
Than what he found himself was apt and true.

EMILIA
But did you ever tell him she was false?

IAGO I did.

EMILIA
You told a lie, an odious damnèd lie!
Upon my soul, a lie! a wicked lie!
She false with Cassio? Did you say with Cassio?

IAGO
184 With Cassio, mistress. Go to, charm your tongue.

---

146 *chrysolite* (precious topaz) 151 *iterance* repetition 164 *to be hurt* to endure hurt 184 *charm* cast a spell on 204 *shows* appears 208 *turn* act 210 *reprobation* rejection by God, damnation 214 *gratify* reward 215 *recognizance* token 221 *liberal as the north* unchecked as the north wind blows

EMILIA
I will not charm my tongue; I am bound to speak:
My mistress here lies murdered in her bed –

ALL
O heavens forfend!

EMILIA
And your reports have set the murder on.

OTHELLO
Nay, stare not, masters. It is true indeed.

GRATIANO
'Tis a strange truth.   190

MONTANO
O monstrous act!

EMILIA   Villainy, villainy, villainy!
I think upon't – I think I smell't! – O villainy!
I thought so then. – I'll kill myself for grief. –
O villainy, villainy!

IAGO
What, are you mad? I charge you get you home.

EMILIA
Good gentlemen, let me have leave to speak.
'Tis proper I obey him, but not now.
Perchance, Iago, I will ne'er go home.

OTHELLO
O! O! O!
Falls on the bed.

EMILIA   Nay, lay thee down and roar!
For thou hast killed the sweetest innocent
That e'er did lift up eye.

OTHELLO   O, she was foul!
[Rises.]
I scarce did know you, uncle. There lies your niece,
Whose breath, indeed, these hands have newly stopped.
I know this act shows horrible and grim.   204

GRATIANO
Poor Desdemon! I am glad thy father's dead.
Thy match was mortal to him, and pure grief
Shore his old thread in twain. Did he live now,
This sight would make him do a desperate turn;   208
Yea, curse his better angel from his side,
And fall to reprobation.   210

OTHELLO
'Tis pitiful; but yet Iago knows
That she with Cassio hath the act of shame
A thousand times committed. Cassio confessed it;
And she did gratify his amorous works   214
With that recognizance and pledge of love   215
Which I first gave her. I saw it in his hand.
It was a handkerchief, an antique token
My father gave my mother.

EMILIA
O God! O heavenly God!

IAGO
Zounds, hold your peace!

EMILIA   'Twill out, 'twill out! I peace?
No, I will speak as liberal as the north.   221
Let heaven and men and devils, let them all,
All, all, cry shame against me, yet I'll speak.

IAGO
Be wise, and get you home.

EMILIA   I will not.
[Iago draws and threatens Emilia.]

GRATIANO   Fie!
Your sword upon a woman?

EMILIA
O thou dull Moor, that handkerchief thou speak'st of
I found by fortune, and did give my husband;
For often with a solemn earnestness –
More than indeed belonged to such a trifle –
He begged of me to steal't.

IAGO   Villainous whore!

EMILIA
She give it Cassio? No, alas, I found it,
And I did give't my husband.

IAGO   Filth, thou liest!

EMILIA
By heaven, I do not, I do not, gentlemen.
O murd'rous coxcomb! what should such a fool
Do with so good a wife?

235 OTHELLO   Are there no stones in heaven
But what serves for the thunder? Precious villain!
The Moor runs at Iago [but is disarmed by Montano].
Iago kills his wife.

GRATIANO
The woman falls. Sure he hath killed his wife.

EMILIA
Ay, ay. O, lay me by my mistress' side.   *Exit Iago.*

GRATIANO
He's gone, but his wife's killed.

MONTANO
240 'Tis a notorious villain. Take you this weapon,
Which I have here recovered from the Moor.
Come, guard the door without. Let him not pass,
But kill him rather. I'll after that same villain,
For 'tis a damnèd slave.
     Exit [Montano, with all but Othello and Emilia].

OTHELLO   I am not valiant neither;
245 But every puny whipster gets my sword.
But why should honor outlive honesty?
Let it go all.

EMILIA   What did thy song bode, lady?
Hark, canst thou hear me? I will play the swan,
And die in music. *[Sings]* 'Willow, willow, willow.'
Moor, she was chaste. She loved thee, cruel Moor:
So come my soul to bliss as I speak true.
So speaking as I think, alas, I die.
     She dies.

OTHELLO
I have another weapon in this chamber;
254 It is a sword of Spain, the ice brook's temper.
O, here it is. – Uncle, I must come forth.

GRATIANO *(within)*
If thou attempt it, it will cost thee dear.
Thou hast no weapon, and perforce must suffer.

OTHELLO
Look in upon me then and speak with me,
259 Or, naked as I am, I will assault thee.
     [Enter Gratiano.]

GRATIANO
What is the matter?

OTHELLO   Behold, I have a weapon;
A better never did itself sustain
Upon a soldier's thigh. I have seen the day
That with this little arm and this good sword
I have made my way through more impediments
265 Than twenty times your stop. But O vain boast!
Who can control his fate? 'Tis not so now.
Be not afraid, though you do see me weaponed.

Here is my journey's end, here is my butt,   268
And very seamark of my utmost sail: 269
Do you go back dismayed? 'Tis a lost fear.   270
Man but a rush against Othello's breast,   271
And he retires. Where should Othello go?
Now, how dost thou look now? O ill-starred wench!
Pale as thy smock! When we shall meet at compt,   274
This look of thine will hurl my soul from heaven,
And fiends will snatch at it. Cold, cold, my girl?
Even like thy chastity.
O cursèd, cursèd slave! Whip me, ye devils,
From the possession of this heavenly sight!
Blow me about in winds! roast me in sulphur!
Wash me in steep-down gulfs of liquid fire!
Oh Desdemon! dead Desdemon! dead! Oh! Oh!
     Enter Lodovico, Montano, Iago [as prisoner,] and
     Officers; Cassio in a chair.

LODOVICO
Where is this rash and most unfortunate man?

OTHELLO
That's he that was Othello. Here I am.

LODOVICO
Where is that viper? Bring the villain forth.

OTHELLO
I look down towards his feet – but that's a fable.   286
If that thou be'st a devil, I cannot kill thee.
     [Wounds Iago.]

LODOVICO
Wrench his sword from him.
     [Othello is disarmed.]

IAGO   I bleed, sir, but not killed.

OTHELLO
I am not sorry neither. I'ld have thee live;
For in my sense, 'tis happiness to die.

LODOVICO
O thou Othello that wert once so good,
Fall'n in the practice of a damnèd slave,   292
What shall be said to thee?

OTHELLO   Why, anything:
An honorable murderer, if you will;
For naught did I in hate, but all in honor.

LODOVICO
This wretch hath part confessed his villainy.
Did you and he consent in Cassio's death?   297

OTHELLO Ay.

CASSIO
Dear general, I never gave you cause.

OTHELLO
I do believe it, and I ask your pardon.
Will you, I pray, demand that demi-devil
Why he hath thus ensnared my soul and body?

IAGO
Demand me nothing. What you know, you know.
From this time forth I never will speak word.

LODOVICO
What, not to pray?

GRATIANO   Torments will ope your lips.

235 *stones* bolts like those used for thunderbolts   240 *notorious* notable
245 *puny whipster* top-whipping boy   254 *ice brook's* i.e. a Spanish blade,
tempered in cold running water   259 *naked* disarmed   265 *stop* power
to stop   268 *butt* limit   269 *seamark* beacon, destination   270 *lost*
wasted   271 *Man but a rush* wield only a reed   274 *compt* final accounting,
Last Judgment   286 *I . . . feet* i.e. to see if they are cloven, like the Devil's
292 *practice* plot   297 *consent in* agree upon

OTHELLO
Well, thou dost best.

LODOVICO
Sir, you shall understand what hath befall'n,
Which, as I think, you know not. Here is a letter
Found in the pocket of the slain Roderigo ;
310   And here another. The one of them imports
The death of Cassio to be undertook
By Roderigo.

OTHELLO
O villain !

CASSIO   Most heathenish and most gross !

LODOVICO
Now here's another discontented paper
Found in his pocket too ; and this, it seems,
Roderigo meant t' have sent this damnèd villain ;
317   But that, belike, Iago in the nick
Came in and satisfied him.

OTHELLO   O thou pernicious caitiff ! –
How came you, Cassio, by that handkerchief
That was my wife's ?

CASSIO   I found it in my chamber ;
And he himself confessed but even now
That there he dropped it for a special purpose
Which wrought to his desire.

OTHELLO   O fool ! fool ! fool !

CASSIO
There is besides in Roderigo's letter,
How he upbraids Iago that he made him
Brave me upon the watch ; whereon it came
327   That I was cast ; and even but now he spake,
After long seeming dead – Iago hurt him,
Iago set him on.

LODOVICO
You must forsake this room and go with us.
Your power and your command is taken off,
And Cassio rules in Cyprus. For this slave,
If there be any cunning cruelty
That can torment him much and hold him long,

---

317 *nick* nick of time 327 *cast* dismissed 341 *unlucky* fatal 346 *Perplexed* distracted 347 *Judean* Judas Iscariot (?) (quarto reads 'Indian')
348 *subdued* i.e. conquered by grief 357 *period* ending 362 *fell* cruel
365 *Let it be hid* i.e. draw the bed curtains 366 *seize upon* take legal
possession of 368 *censure* judicial sentence

It shall be his. You shall close prisoner rest
Till that the nature of your fault be known
To the Venetian state. Come, bring away.

OTHELLO
Soft you ! a word or two before you go.
I have done the state some service, and they know't.
No more of that. I pray you, in your letters,
When you shall these unlucky deeds relate,   341
Speak of me as I am. Nothing extenuate,
Nor set down aught in malice. Then must you speak
Of one that loved not wisely, but too well ;
Of one not easily jealous, but, being wrought,
Perplexed in the extreme ; of one whose hand,   346
Like the base Judean, threw a pearl away   347
Richer than all his tribe ; of one whose subdued eyes, 348
Albeit unusèd to the melting mood,
Drop tears as fast as the Arabian trees
Their med'cinable gum. Set you down this.
And say besides that in Aleppo once,
Where a malignant and a turbaned Turk
Beat a Venetian and traduced the state,
I took by th' throat the circumcisèd dog
And smote him – thus.
        He stabs himself.

LODOVICO
O bloody period !   357

GRATIANO   All that's spoke is marred.

OTHELLO
I kissed thee ere I killed thee. No way but this,
Killing myself, to die upon a kiss.
        He [falls upon the bed and] dies.

CASSIO
This did I fear, but thought he had no weapon ;
For he was great of heart.

LODOVICO *[to Iago]*   O Spartan dog,
More fell than anguish, hunger, or the sea !   362
Look on the tragic loading of this bed.
This is thy work. The object poisons sight ;
Let it be hid. Gratiano, keep the house,   365
And seize upon the fortunes of the Moor,   366
For they succeed on you. To you, lord governor,
Remains the censure of this hellish villain,   368
The time, the place, the torture. O, enforce it !
Myself will straight aboard, and to the state
This heavy act with heavy heart relate.   *Exeunt.*

Listed below are all departures from the folio text (F) except for the correction of a few obvious typographical errors and the addition of the bracketed lines mentioned in the "Note on the text." The great majority of these departures represent readings in the quarto (Q), the copy for which may have been a transcript of Shakespeare's draft. Although not printed until 1622, the quarto text remains totally unaffected by the Parliamentary ruling against the use of oaths in stage plays theoretically in force since 1606. On the other hand the folio text, which appears to have derived from the quarto collated with a prompt-book, reveals an unusual scrupulousness in observing this ruling. Perhaps the chief interest in the following list of variants in quarto and folio is the indication of the great variety of expressions which the acting company feared might be considered "oaths." Also of interest is the list of substitutes found for them. The adopted reading in italics is followed by the folio reading in roman.

The Names of the Actors (printed at the end of the play in F)

I, i, 1 *Tush* (Q) Omitted 4 *'Sblood* (Q) Omitted 25 *togèd* (Q) Tongued 30 *Christian* (Q) Christen'd 33 *God* (Q) Omitted 66 *full* (Q) fall 72 *changes* (Q) chances 79 *Thieves! thieves! thieves!* (Q) Theeues, Theeues 81 s.d. *Brabantio at a window* (Q) Omitted 86 *Zounds* (Q) Omitted 103 *spirit* (Q) spirits *them* (Q) their 108 *Zounds* (Q) Omitted 116 *now* (Q) Omitted 122 *odd-even* (Malone) odde Euen 145 *produced* (Q) produced 150 *stand* (Pope) stands 153 *hell-pains* (Dyce) hell apines (F) hells paines (Q) 158 s.d. *and ... with* (Q) with ... and *in his nightgown* (Q) Omitted 181 *night* (Q) might 182 *I'll* (Q) I Will

I, ii, s.d. *and* (Q) Omitted 4 *Sometimes* (Q) Sometime 15 *and* (Q) or 33 s.d. *Officers* (Q) Omitted 34 *Duke* (Q) Dukes 38 *What's* (Q) What is 54 s.d. *and others ... weapons* (Q) with Officers, and Torches 68 *darlings* (Q) Deareling 75 *weaken* (Rowe) weakens 84 *Where* (Q) Whether

I, iii, s.d. *and Senators ... Attendants* (Q) Senators, and Officers 1 *There is* (Q) There's *these* (Q) this 87 *broil* (Q) Broiles 93 *am I* (Q) I am 106 *Duke* (Q) Omitted 107 *certain* (Q) wider 121 s.d. *Exit ... two or three* (Q) Omitted 130 *fortunes* (Q) Fortune 139 *travels'* (Q) Trauellours 141 *and* (Q) Omitted 142 *the* (Q) my 145 *Do grow* (Q) Grew *This* (Q) These things 147 *thence* (Q) hence 155 *intentively* (Q) instinctiuely 159 *sighs* (Q) kisses 160 *i' faith* (Q) in faith 201 *Into your favor* (Q) Omitted 219 *ear* (Q) eares 220 *Beseech you, now* (Q) I humbly beseech you *the affairs* (Q) th' Affaires 230 *couch* (Pope) Coach 234 *These* (Malone) This 239–40 *If you please, | Be't at her father's.* (Q) Why at her Fathers? 241 *Nor I. I would not* (Q) Nor would I 248 *did* (Q) Omitted 257 *which* (Q) why 263–64 *heat – the young affects | In me defunct –* (Capell) heat the yong affects / In my defunct, 270 *instruments* (Q) Instrument 293 s.d. *Exeunt* (Q) Exit 299 *matters* (Q) matter 300 s.d. *Moor and Desdemona* (Q) Omitted 322 *thyme* (Pope) Time 326 *balance* (Q) braine 330 *our unbitted* (Q) or vnbitted 340 *be that Desdemona should long continue* (Q) be long that Desdemona should continue 348 *error* (Q) errors 355 *'Tis* (Q) it is 379 *a snipe* (Q) snpe 382 *H'as* (Q) She ha's 398 s.d. *Exit* (Q) Omitted

II, i, 13 *mane* (Knight) Maine 19 s.d. *third* (Q) Omitted 33 *prays* (Q) praye 34 *heaven* (Q) Heauens 42 *arrivance* (Q) arrivancie 43 *this* (Q) the 50 *hopes* (F3) hope's 51 s.d. *Enter a Messenger* (Q) Omitted 53 *Messenger* (Q) Gent. 55 s.d. *A shot* Omitted 65 *ingener* (Knight) Ingeniuer s.d. *Second* (Q) Omitted 70 *clog* (Q) enclogge 88 *me* (Q) Omitted 92 *the sea* (Q) Sea 93 *(Within) A sail, a sail! [A shot.] But hark. A sail!* (Collier) But hearke, a Saile. / Within. A Saile, a Saile. 94 *their* (Q) this 104 *list* (Q) leaue 117 *thou write* (Q) write 157 *such wight* (Q) such wightes 168 *gyve* (F2) giue 173 *an* (Q) and 174 *courtesy* (Q) curtsy 176 s.d. *Trumpet within* (Q2) Omitted 196 s.d. *They*

kiss (Q) Omitted 210 s.d. *Exit Othello* (Eds) Exit Othello and Desdemona 212 *hither* (Q) thither 221–22 *and will she* (Q) To 225 *again* (Q) a game 237 *compassing* (Q) compasse 239 *finder-out* (Q) finder *occasions* (Q) occasion *has* (Q) he's 255 *mutualities* (Q) mutabilities 267 *with his truncheon* (Q) Omitted 293 *for wife* (Q) wift 297 *I trash* (Stevens) I trace 300 *rank* (Q) right

II, ii, 5 *addiction* (Q2) addition 10 *Heaven* (Q) Omitted

II, iii (Capell first begins a new scene here) 37 *unfortunate* (Q) infortunate 51 *lads* (Q) else 56 *to put* (Q) put to 60 *God* (Q) heauen 67 *A life's* (Q) Oh, mans life's 71 *God* (Q) Heauen 76 *expert* (Q) exquisite 84 *a* (Q) and-a 86 *'em* (Q) them 91 *Then* (Q) And *auld* (Q) awl'd 93 *'Fore God* (Q) Why 97 *God's* (Q) heau'ns 106 *God* (Q) Omitted 131 s.d. *Exit Roderigo* (Q) Omitted 138 *(Within) Help! help!* (Q) Omitted s.d. *driving in* (Q) pursuing 139 *Zounds* (Q) Omitted 145 s.d. *They fight* (Q) Omitted 146 s.d. *Exit Roderigo* (Q) Omitted 147 *God's will* (Q2) Alas 148 *sir – Montano – sir –* (Capell) Sir Montano (F) Sir, Montanio, sir (Q2) 149 s.d. *A bell rung* (Q) Omitted 151 *God's will, lieutenant, hold!* (Q) Fie, fie Lieutenant, 152 *shamed* (Q) asham'd s.d. *and Gentlemen with weapons* (Q) and Attendants 153 *Zounds* (Q) Omitted 156 *Hold, hold* (Q) Hold hoa *sir – Montano –* (Rowe) Sir Montano 157 *sense of place* (Hanmer) place of sense 173 *breast* (Q) breastes 208 *leagued* (Pope) league 241 *What's* (Q2) What is *matter* (Q) matter (Deere?) 242 *now* (Q) Omitted 246 *vile* (Q) vil'd 251 *God* (Q) Heauen 256 *thought* (Q) had thought 261 *ways* (Q) more wayes 277 *God* (Q) Omitted 281 *Why,* (Q) Why? 288 *so* (Q) Omitted 299 *some* (Q) a 300 *I'll* (Q) I 303 *denotement* (Theobald) deuotement 316 *here* (Q) Omitted 326 *were't* (Q) were 337 *fortunes* (Q) Fortune 357 *hast* (Q) hath 360 *By the mass* (Q) Introth 366 *on;* (Q) on 367 *the while* (Theobald) a while

III, i, 3 *ha'* (Q) haue 21 *hear, my* (Capell) heare me, mine (F) hear my (Q) 25 *general's wife* (Q2) Generall 29 *Cassio. Do, good my friend* (Q) Omitted 53 *Desdemona* (Q) Desdemon 55 s.d. *Exeunt* (Q) Omitted

III, ii, 6 *We'll* (F3) well

III, iii, 16 *circumstance* (Q) circumstances 52 *Yes, faith* (Q) I sooth 60 *or* (Q) on 61 *or Wednesday* (Q) on Wensday 63 *I' faith* (Q) Infaith 65 *examples* (Q) example 66 *their* (Rowe) her 69 *could* (Q) would 74 *By'r Lady* (Q) Trust me 87 *Desdemon* (Dyce iii) Desdemona 94 *you* (Q) Alas 106 *By heaven* (Q) Alas *he echoes* (Q) thou eccho's 107 *his* (Q) thy 112 *In* (Q) Of 135 *that all* (Q) that : All *free to* (Q) free 136 *vile* (Q) vild 138 *a* (Q) that 139 *But some* (Q) Wherein 147 *oft* (Q) of 148 *yet* (Q2) Omitted 149 *conjects* (Q) conceits 162 *By heaven* (Q) Omitted 170 *strongly* (Q) soundly 175 *God* (Q) Heauen 180 *once* (Q) Omitted 182 *blown* (Q) blow'd 202 *God* (Q) Heauen 204 *keep't* (Q) kept 215 *I' faith* (Q) Trust me 217 *my* (Q) your 222 *vile* (Q) vilde 223 *As* (Q) Which *aim not at* (Q) aym'd not 248 *hold* (Q) Omitted 259 *qualities* (Q) Quantities *learned* (Q) learn'd 262 *I'd* (Q) I'ld 273 *of* (Q) to 278 *O, then* (Q) Omitted *mocks* (Q) mock'd 285 *Faith* (Q) Why 302 *A thing* (Q) You haue a thing 311 *No, faith; she* (Q) No : but she 313 *it is* (Q) 'tis 332 *med'cine* (Eds) medicine 338 *of her* (Q) in her 349 *troop* (Q) Troopes 375 *b' wi'* (F4) buy 376 *liv'st* (Eds) lou'st (F) liuest (Q) 386 *Her* (Q2) My 391 *sir* (Q) Omitted 393 *I* (Q) and 1 395 *supervisor* (Q) supervision 408 *may* (Q) might 422 *and* (Q) Omitted 424 *then* (Q) Omitted 425 *Over* (Q) ore *sighed* (Q) sigh *kissed* (Eds) kisse (F) kissèd (Q) 426 *Cried* (Q) cry 432 *but* (Q) yet 440 *that was* (Malone) it was 452 *perhaps* (Q) Omitted 455 *feels* (Q2) keepes 460 s.d. *He kneels* Omitted (F) (in Rowe after l. 461, in Q after l. 450) 462 s.d. *Iago kneels* (Q2) Omitted

III, iv, 5 *is* (Q) 'tis 22 *I'll* (Q) I will *of* (Q) Omitted s.d. *Exit* (Q) Exit Clo. 23 *that* (Q) the 37 *yet* (Q) Omitted 48 *Come now,* (Capell) Come, now 54 *faith* (Q) indeed 64 *wive* (Q) wiu'd 73 *hallowed* (Capell) hallowèd 75 *I' faith* (Q) Indeed 77 *God* (Q) Heauen 80 *is it* (Q) is't 81 *Heaven* (Q) Omitted 86 *sir* (Q) Omitted 97 *I' faith* (Q) Insooth 98 *Zounds* (Q) Away 116 *neither* (Q) nor my 161 *'Tis* (Q) It is 163 *that* (Q) the 168 s.d. *Exeunt Desdemona and Emilia* (Q) Exit 171 *I' faith* (Q) Indeed 182 *absence now* (Capell) Absence : now 184 *vile* (Q) vilde 187 *by my faith* (Q) in good troth 188 *sweet* (Q) neither 190 *I'd* (Q) I would 201 s.d. *Exeunt* (Q) Exeunt omnes

IV, i, 9 *So* (Q) If 21 *infected* (Q) infectious 32 *Faith* (Q) Why 36 *Zounds* (Q) Omitted 45 *med'cine* (Eds) Medicine *work* (Q) workes 52 *No, forbear* (Q) Omitted 60 *you?* (Q) you not 77 *unsuiting* (Q) resulting 79 *'scuse* (Q) scuses 95 *clothes* (Q) Cloath 98 *refrain* (Q) restraine 101 *conster* (Q) conserue 102 *behavior* (Q) behauiours 103 *now* (Q) Omitted 107 *power* (Q) dowre 110 *a* (Q) Omitted 111 *i' faith* (Q) indeed 118 *you triumph, Roman* (Q) ye triumph, Romaine 119 *her* (Q) Omitted 122 *win* (F4) winnes 123 *Faith* (Q) Why *shall* (Q) Omitted 130 *beckons* (Q) becomes 133–34 *by this hand, she* (Q) Omitted 149 *whole* (Q) Omitted 157 *An . . . an* (Q) If . . . if 160 *Faith* (Q) Omitted *street* (Q) streets 166 s.d. *Exit Cassio* (Q) Omitted 189 *thousand thousand* (Q) thousand, a thousand 208 s.d. *A trumpet* (Q) Omitted 210 *and* (Q) Omitted *wife is* (Q) wife's 211 *God* (Q) Omitted 212 *senators* (Q) the Senators 224 *thy* (Q) my 228 *the letter* (Q) th Letter 231 *By my troth* (Q) Trust me 241 *an* (Q) Omitted 269 *this* (Q) his

IV, ii, 24 *Pray* (Q) Pray you 30 *Nay* (Q) May 31 *knees* (Q) knee 47 *Why* (Q) Omitted 54 *A* (Q) The 55 *unmoving* (Q) and mouing 64 *Ay, there* (Theobald) I heere 69 *ne'er* (Q) neuer 71 *paper,* (Q) Paper ? 80 *hear it* (Steevens) hear't 81 *Impudent strumpet* (Q) Omitted 92 *keep* (Rowe) keepes 117 *As* (Q) That *bear* (Q) beare it 133 *I'll* (Q) I will 141 *heaven* (Q) heauens 155 *them in* (Q2) them : or 168 *'Tis* (Q) It is 169 *you* (Q) Omitted 170 *stay* (Q) staies 175 *daff'st* (Collier) dafts 180 *suffered* (Q) suffred 182 *Faith* (Q) Omitted *for* (Q) and 187 *deliver to* (Q) deliuer 193 *By this hand, I say 'tis very* (Q) Nay I think it is 221 *takes* (Q) taketh 222 *lingered* (Q) lingred 225 *of* (Q) Omitted

IV, iii, 12 *He* (Q) And 13 *bade* (Q) bid 20 *in them* (Q) Omitted 22 *faith* (Q) Father 23 *thee* (Q) Omitted 24 *those* (Q) these 39 s.d. *sings* (Q2) Omitted *sighing* (Q2) singing 46–47 *Lay . . . willow'* (Eds) Sing Willough, &c. (Lay by these) 48–49 *Prithee . . . garland* (Eds) Willough, Willough. (Prythee high thee : he'le come anon) 71 *it* (Q) Omitted 74 *'Ud's pity* (Q) why 103 *God* (Q) Heauen *usage* (Q) uses

V, i, 1 *bulk* (Q) Barke 22 *Be't* (Q) But *hear* (Q) heard 35 *Forth* (Q) For 38 *cry* (Q) voyce 42 *It is a* (Q) 'Tis 46 s.d. *with a light* (Q) Omitted 49 *Did* (Q) Do 50 *heaven's* (Q) heauen 60 *here* (Q) there 90 *O heaven* (Q) Yes, 'tis 104 *out* (Q) Omitted 110 s.d. *Enter Emilia* (Q) Omitted 111 *'Las, what's . . . What's* (Q) Alas, what is . . . What is 114 *dead* (Q) quite dead 121 *Fie, fie* (Q) Oh fie 123 *Foh* (Q) Omitted

V, ii, s.d. *Desdemona [asleep] in her bed. Enter Othello with a light* (Eds) Enter Othello, and Desdemona in her bed (F) Enter Othello with a light, and Desdemona in her bed (Q2) 15 s.d. *He kisses her* (Q, after ll. 19–20) Omitted (F) Kisses her (Q2) 32 *heaven* (Q) Heauens 35 *so* (Q) Omitted 41 *diest* (Q) dy'st 52 *Yes* (Q) Omitted 57 *Then Lord* (Q) O Heauen 64 *mak'st* (Q2) makes 85 s.d. *calls within* (Q) Omitted 87 *that am* (Q) am that 94 *here* (Q) high 102 *Should* (Q) Did 107 *murder* (Theobald) murthers 118 *O Lord* (Q) Alas 126 s.d. *She dies* (Q) Omitted 128 *heard* (Q) heare 144 *Nay* (Q) Omitted 148 *me* (Q) me on her 153 *that* (Q2) me on me 163 *the* (Q) that 168 s.d. *Gratiano, Iago, and others* (Q) Gratiano, and Iago 186 *murdered* (Pope) murthered 199 s.d. *Falls on the bed* (Eds) Omitted (F) Oth. fals on the bed (Q) 210 *reprobation* (Q) Reprobance 219 *O God ! O heavenly God* (Q) Oh Heauen ! oh heauenly Powres 220 *Zounds* (Q) Come 236 s.d. *The Moor . . . wife* (Q) Omitted 238 s.d. *Exit Iago* (Q) Omitted 241 *here* (Q) Omitted 252 s.d. *She dies* (Q) Omitted 254 *is* (Q) was 256 s.d. *within* (Q) Omitted 282 s.d. *Enter . . . chair* (Q) Enter Lodouico, Cassio, Montano, and Iago, with Officers 291 *wert* (Q) was 292 *damnèd* (Q) cursed 295 *did I* (Q) I did 317 *nick* (Q) interim 321 *but* (Capell) it but 346 *Perplexed* (Q) Perplexèd 350 *Drop* (Q2) Drops 351 *med'cinable* (Capell) Medicinable 356 s.d. *He stabs himself* (Q) Omitted 357 *that's* (Q) that is 359 s.d. *He . . . dies* (Q) Dyes

KING LEAR

INTRODUCTION

The play begins with a moment of prose "exposition," an idle conversation about the partition of a kingdom and the bastardy of a son. Its tone is casual, jocular, polite. The son responds decorously to a social introduction. The speakers are wearing familiar masks. It is then as if these murmurs by the portal subsided at the opening of some old but half-remembered ceremony. All is ritual – heralding trumpet, formal procession, symbolic objects in coronet and map, a sequence of arbitrary yet strangely predictable acts. What can be made of it? Why should that patriarch who wishes to yield up his power and possessions require of the receivers declarations of love? Why should that maiden who honestly loves him respond only with declarations of her love of honesty? No logical reasons appear – ritual is ritual, its logic its own. Prose is yielding to poetry, "realism" to reality. *King Lear* is not true. It is an allegory of truth.

That its truths are not literal is the first thing about it discerned by the budding critical faculty. Everything is initially *patterned* – this one making obvious errors which he obviously will rue, these others emerging as the good and the evil in almost geometrical symmetry, with the inevitable sisters-three, the two elder chosen though wicked, the younger rejected though virtuous. Surely these are childish things! A defense has been offered by Tolstoy, in his valedictory judgment that the only truths conveyable in literature can be conveyed in the simplest folk-tale. But *King Lear* is not simple, and Tolstoy himself failed to see its relevance to his doctrine. Freud noticed its primitive features, and compared Goneril, Regan, and Cordelia to the caskets of lead, silver, and gold in *The Merchant of Venice*. He identified Cordelia as the benign, though resisted, call of death. Cordelia as the death-wish – *lovely and soothing death* – how suggestive this is! until we recognize that her identification as the life-wish might be equally suggestive. The value of such reflections lies in their reminder that the oldest story-patterns have the greatest power to touch off reverberations. No other framework than this parable-myth could have borne so well the weight of what Shakespeare was compelled to say.

The story of Lear and his three daughters was given written form four centuries before Shakespeare's birth. How much older its components may be we do not know. Cordelia in one guise or another, including Cinderella's, has figured in the folklore of most cultures, perhaps originally expressing what Emerson saw as the conviction of every human being of his worthiness to be loved and chosen, if only his *true* self were truly known. The figure of the ruler asking a question, often a riddle, with disastrous consequences to himself is equally old and dispersed. In his *Historia Regum Britanniae* (1136) Geoffrey of Mon-

mouth converted folklore to history and established Lear and his daughters as rulers of ancient Britain, thus bequeathing them to the chronicles. Raphael Holinshed's (1587) declared that "Leir, the sonne of Baldud," came to the throne "in the yeare of the world 3105, at what time Joas reigned in Juda," but belief in the historicity of such British kings was now beginning to wane, and Shakespeare could deal freely with the record. He read the story also in John Higgins' lamentable verses in *The Firste part of the Mirour for Magistrates* (1574), and in Edmund Spenser's *Faerie Queene*, II, 10, 27–32. He knew, and may even have acted in, a bland dramatic version, *The True Chronicle History of King Leir*, published anonymously in 1605 but staged at least as early as 1594.

The printing of the old play may mark an effort to capitalize upon the staging of Shakespeare's, performed at court on December 26, 1606, and probably first brought out at the Globe playhouse sometime in 1605, although its allusion to "these late eclipses of the sun and moon" was not necessarily suggested by those of September and October of that year. The only certain anterior limit of date is March 16, 1603, when Samuel Harsnett's *Declaration of Egregious Popishe Impostures* was registered for publication. That this excursion in "pseudo-demonology" was available to Shakespeare is evident in various ways, most clearly in the borrowed inventory of devils imbedded in Edgar's jargon as Tom o' Bedlam. It is of small consequence to fix the date of *King Lear* so far as its relation to the older play is concerned, which must be reckoned as analogue rather than source, but if, as seems certain, it was composed in 1605 or early 1606, it belongs to the same season of the poet's growth as *The Tragedy of Macbeth*.

In its pre-Shakespearean forms, both those mentioned above and others, the Lear story remains rudimentary. The emphasis may vary in various recensions, depending upon whether the author was most interested in the inexpedience of subdividing a kingdom, the mutability of fortune, or, as in the older play, the rewards of Christian virtue; but all are alike in that they end happily for Lear, who is reconciled to Cordelia and restored to his throne. The fact that the story was sometimes followed by a sequel in which Cordelia was finally hounded to suicide by the broodlings of her wicked sisters has little bearing on a remarkable fact: Shakespeare alone and in defiance of precedent conducted Lear to ultimate misery. *Enter Lear, with Cordelia in his arms. . . . He dies.* These directions enclose a scene which demonstrates beyond any other in tragic literature the intransigence of poetic art – inventing the inevitable, investing horrifying things with beauty.

Compared with the tragedies of ancient Greece – and it is with these alone that one is tempted to compare it – *King*

Lear suggests the Gothic order. Its form is irregular and organic, determined seemingly by a series of upward thrusts of mounting internal energy. There is even a Gothic element of the grotesque, as when mock-beggar, jester, and king, reduced to common condition, hold their mad juridical proceedings in a storm-lashed shelter, or when crazed king and blinded subject exchange lamentations and puns! In the method of Lear's madness there is often a savage humor, more remarkable when all is said than his companioning with a Fool. It was the Fool, however, who seemed to the next age the unpardonable sin against classical decorum. In the 1680 adaptation by Nahum Tate he was expunged from the play, along with the tragic ending. Tate capped the concluding felicities of the pre-Shakespearean versions by huddling up a marriage between Edgar and Cordelia; yet his work held the stage throughout the eighteenth century. It is always ruefully remarked that the greatest critic of the age approved the adaptation, but in fairness we should add that it was not for literary reasons. The pain of Shakespeare's concluding scenes was simply too much for Dr Johnson; his response is preferable to that of those – fit for treasons, stratagems, and spoils – who can read these scenes unmoved.

The original play, or its approximation, was restored to the stage in the early nineteenth century, after it had begun to receive its critical due from the romantic essayists and poets. It is a poet's play. Keats saw in it the warrant for his conviction that truth and beauty are one, and, more surprisingly, recognized the choral and catalytic function of Lear's jester for the stroke of genius it is. Coleridge, Lamb, and Hazlitt also recorded illuminating judgments, and many critics since, of many different "schools," have said fine things about it.

The question now most frequently debated is whether the play is Christian and affirmative in spirit, or pagan and pessimistic. No work of art could endure the tugs of such a debate without being somewhat torn. "Pessimistic," like "optimistic," is a small word for a small thing, and *King Lear* is not small. It is sad, as all tragedies are sad. It is religious, as all great tragedies are religious. The exclusion of specific Christian reference, more consistent than in any other Shakespearean play of non-Christian setting, is in harmony with its Old Testament atmosphere (when "Joas reigned in Juda"), but it may reflect nothing more than evasion, in the printed text, of a recent Parliamentary ruling, which in effect labelled *God* in stage speech as blasphemy, *gods* as mere classical allusion. Although the play is rather inclusively than exclusively Christian, which can scarcely be deemed a fault, it shows obvious signs of its genesis in a Christian culture. To cite those involving a single character (other than Cordelia, who has often been viewed as a Christ-symbol), there is Edgar's persistence in returning good for evil, his preachments against the sin of despair, and his reluctance to kill except in trial by combat with its implied religious sanctions. Great questions are asked of the unseen powers – "Is there any cause in nature that makes these hard hearts?" – and these questions remain unanswered, but the silence which follows them should be viewed, here as in other contexts, as the substance of faith. On the human level, the implications of the play are more comforting than the data it abstracts. In our actual world, suffering is not always ennobling, evil not always self-consuming. In every scene where there is pain, there is someone who strives to relieve that pain. At the close, the merciless have all perished; the last sound we hear is the choral voices of the merciful.

The workers of evil are stylized in a way not quite typical of Shakespeare. He could not love these characters even as characters, except perhaps Edmund a little. To imitate the dominant animal imagery of the style, Cornwall is less repellent than Goneril and Regan only as the mad bull is less repellent than the hyena, they less repellent than Oswald only as the hyena is less repellent than the jackal. To the latter he failed to give even that engaging touch of the ludicrous he usually reserved for assistant villains. It is useless to speak of their "motivation." Like other aged parents Lear is no gift to good housewifery, and there is something poignantly familiar about such a one's trudging resentfully to the home of a second daughter. "Age is unnecessary." But to see a causal relationship between what he does to Goneril and Regan and what they do to him, or to interpret their aggression as normal revolt against parental domination, is simply to be perverse. The play deals directly, and in both its stories, with one indissoluble bond:

> We'll no more meet, no more see one another.
> But yet thou art my flesh, my blood, my daughter....

Eroded, it leaves no human bond secure. To argue that Edmund's conduct is attributable to humiliating illegitimacy, we must supply him with an "unconscious" and invoke its spectral evidence; there is no sign of sensitivity in his lines. Even that curious product of our times, the liberalism-gone-to-seed which automatically defends anything from treachery to sadism providing it savors of non-conformity, has found little to say for this insatiable quintet.

Shakespeare is not normally associated with hatred, but "a fierce hatred of cruelty and deceitful wickedness" informs *King Lear* – this the opinion of so pure an aesthetician as Benedetto Croce. Hazlitt has said, "It is then the best of all Shakespeare's plays, for it is the one in which he was most in earnest." A non-sequitur may lurk in this assertion, but we cannot deny its relevance. Our inescapable impression of the play is of its overwhelming sincerity. It says everything powerfully and everything twice – and always "what we feel, not what we ought to say." The language varies from the cryptic allusiveness of Lear's "mad" speeches to the biblical plainness of his pleas for forgiveness; and though it is often difficult, it is never ambiguous. Lamb has been much taken to task for declaring that "*Lear* is essentially impossible to be represented on a stage," but more often than not our experiences in the theatre confirm his view. There have been fine productions, but not very many: one touch of insincerity can rot everything away.

Those who now "introduce" this play must wish with Hazlitt, and with much more likelihood of greeting the wish of the reader, that they might resort to silence, since all that can be said will "fall short of the subject, or even what we ourselves conceive of it." Yet an effort must be made to state its theme, and to the present editor there seems no way of doing this except by focussing the gaze directly and continuously upon Lear himself.

"The King is coming." These words announce the first entrance of the tragic hero. Let us see him as he is, no preconceptions or critical rumors spoiling the innocence of our vision. Nothing about him suggests infirmity or decay. His magnitude and force are far greater than one's own. He issues commands with the assurance of instinct and lifelong custom. He holds a map in his hands like a Titan holding a kingdom. The kingdom spreads before us in his spacious utterance:

> Of all these bounds, even from this line to this,
> With shadowy forests and with champains riched,
> With plenteous rivers and wide-skirted meads,
> We make thee lady.

We make thee lady! Thus he disposes of a sector of the earth, this ring-giver, this warrior-leader, this chosen one, his only landlord God! Is it not passing fine . . .? Here is no soft-brained *Senex*, but the archetypal *King*.

As such Lear symbolizes Mankind, and we will say nothing essential about him by reckoning up his years and growing glib about the symptoms of senile dementia. The king-figure surrogate is an understandable product of the human mind in its early attempts at abstraction, since the most imposing of single men best lends his image to the difficult concept of Man. His vicissitudes best epitomize the vicissitudes of all, since upon the highest altitude the sun shines brightest and the cold snow lies most deep. Early Renaissance drama was steeped in the tradition of this symbolic figure, sometimes still called *King* as well as *Mankind*, *Everyman*, *Genus Humanum*, and the like. He is always identifiable by his centrality in the action, and the mixed company he keeps – vices or flatterers on the one hand, virtues or truth-speakers on the other. And there stands Lear – Goneril and Regan to the left, Kent and Cordelia to the right.

But this is also a family gathering. There is the father, and there the servants and children of his house. The central figure is, and seems always more so as the play weaves its spell, not only archetypal King, Man, and Father, but particular king, man, and father. No symbol that remained purely symbol could so touch our emotions. To have children of his flesh and blood, the father must be flesh and blood – such as can be old, grow weary, feel cold and wet.

Only a few days of fictional time elapse, only a few hours in the theatre, so that Lear's first words still echo in our ears as we hear his last.

We make thee lady. . . . Let it be so, thy truth then be thy dower! . . . Peace, Kent! Come not between the dragon and his wrath. . . . The bow is bent and drawn; make from the shaft. . . . Therefore be gone. . . . Let me not stay a jot for dinner; go get it ready. . . . Call the clotpoll back.

Such are Lear's accents at the beginning. And at the close –

You must bear with me. . . . I am old and foolish. . . . Her voice was ever soft, gentle, and low. . . . Pray you undo this button. Thank you, sir.

He has learned a new language. We are required to accept this learning as good, but we are forbidden to rejoice.

The play is Lear's gethsemane, its great reality his suffering, which so draws us into itself that our conception of the work as a whole is formed in the crucible of our fear and pity. His anguish is kin with the anguish of Job, Prometheus, Oedipus, and other tragic projections of spirits in agony, but it retains its own peculiar quality. Its cause, its nature, and its meaning will always remain the imperfectly resolved crux of the play; and one can do no more than explain, with such confidence as one is able to muster, how these things appear to him.

To say that Lear gets what he deserves is to share the opinion of Goneril and Regan. (Some have even implied that Cordelia gets what she deserves, anaesthetizing their heads and hearts with obtuse moralisms suggested by the doctrine of "poetic justice.") What does Lear deserve? He is proud and peremptory, and it is better to be humble and temporizing, but there are occupational hazards in being a king, perhaps even in being a father. Is his charge not true that the world has lied to him, telling him he was wise before he was bearded, returning "yea and nay" to everything he said? His guilt is widely shared, and his "flaw" like that of Oedipus seems mysteriously hereditary. And it is linked inextricably with his virtues. We applaud the resurgence of youthful might that cuts down Cordelia's assassin. We admire the valor of his attempts (and they come quite early) to be patient, to compromise, to hold back womanish tears, to cling to his reason. Nothing is more moving than his bewildered attempts to meet "social" obligations as he kneels by Cordelia's body. We love his *manliness*. Pride has its value too.

Lear's errors stem from no corruption of heart. His rejection of Kent and Cordelia is the reflex of his attachment to them. The errors are not the man. The man is one who has valued and been valued by such as they. The things he wants – fidelity and love – are good things. That he should find them in his servant and his child seems to him an aspect of universal order. In his vocabulary, as distinct from Edmund's, such things are *natural*. His inability to distinguish between the false and the true, and his craving for visible displays, are not failings peculiar to him. "How much do you love me?" – few parents suppress this bullying question, spoken or unspoken, however much they may have felt its burden as children. It seems in the nature of some things that they always are learned too late, that as children we might have offered more, as parents demanded less. To punish a thankless child has the appearance of justice, to withdraw in one's age from the cares of state the appearance of wisdom, to dispose of one's goods by gift instead of testament the appearance of generosity. Plain men in their prime have been similarly deceived. Gloucester shakes his head sadly over Lear's injustice, folly, and selfishness as he duplicates his actions.

In the maimed but agile mind of the Fool faithfully dogging Lear's steps, his errors stand as an *idée fixe* and are harped upon with terrible iteration. We should not imitate the example. We may find more meaning in the excess of expiation. The purely physical suffering – denial of rest, exposure to wind and rain – is real, but it strikes the sufferer himself as little more than a metaphor. We may say that his spiritual suffering is in excess of his actual afflictions, that it is selfish and centrifugal, or a mere symptom of aged petulance, but if we do so, we are stopping our ears to the voice of Shakespeare and all his decent spokesmen. Lear's curse of Goneril is still alienating, like his treatment of Cordelia, but when he stands weeping before his cormorant daughters in whom he has put his faith, and they coolly and relentlessly strip him of every vestige of dignity, our hearts turn over. Humility may be good, but this humiliation is evil.

There is no *need* that this man be attended by a hundred knights, that his messenger be deferentially treated, or that his children offer him more than subsistence. His cause rests upon no more rational grounds than our powers of sympathy and imagination. "O reason not the need." As his every expectation is brutally defeated, and he looks in dazed recognition upon the world as it is instead of what he thought it was, of himself as he is instead of what he thought he was, we defer to his past illusions. He had never identified prestige merely as power, had never imagined that the visages of respect, kindliness, and love could contort into the hideous lines of icy contempt and sour indifference.

Lear's anguish now represents for us Man's horror and sense of helplessness at the discovery of evil – the infiltration of animality in the human world, naked cruelty and appetite. It is a fissure that threatens to widen infinitely, and we see Lear at the center of turbulence as it works its breakage in minds, in families, in nations, in the heavens themselves, interacting in dreadful concatenation.

The significance of Lear's response to his discovery is best seen in the light of Gloucester's. In Sidney's *Arcadia*, II, 10, the "storie of the Paphlagonian unkind King and his kinde sonne" repeats in essence the Lear legend, except that the children, false and true, are sons instead of daughters. By reducing the rank of Sidney's king and interweaving his parallel fate in alternate scenes, Shakespeare is able, amazingly, both further to universalize and further to particularize the experience of Lear. Gloucester also represents Man, but his distinction from Lear suggests the distinction between ordinary and extraordinary men. Gloucester is amiably confused about the tawdriness of his past, of which Edmund is the product, and sentimentally fumbling in the present. What appears in Lear as heroic error appears in him as gullibility. His fine moments are identical with those of a nameless serf of Cornwall's and an ancient tenant of his own – in the presence of cruelty he becomes kind and brave:

GLOUCESTER I am tied to th' stake, and I must stand the course.
REGAN Wherefore to Dover?
GLOUCESTER Because I would not see thy cruel nails
　　Pluck out his poor old eyes.

Like Lear he is incorrupt of heart, and he grows in dignity, but his total response to vicious encroachment is something akin to apathy and surrender; his instinct is to retreat.

Not so with Lear. He batters himself to pieces against the fact of evil. Granted that its disruptive power has been unleashed by his own error, so that error itself partakes of evil, as he is shudderingly aware, yet he remains the great antagonist. Falsity, cruelty, injustice, corruption – their appalling forms swirl about him in phantasmic patterns. His instinct is to rip them from the universe, to annihilate all things if it is the only way to annihilate these things. His charges of universal hypocrisy: "handy-dandy, which is the justice, which is the thief?" – his denial of human responsibility: "None does offend, none – I say none!" – his indictment of life itself:

Thou know'st, the first time that we smell the air
We wawl and cry –

cancel their own nihilism, because they sound no acquiescence. Lear is the voice of protest. The grandeur of his spirit supplies the impotence of his body as he opposes to evil all that is left him to oppose – his molten indignation, his huge invectives, his capacity for feeling pain.

This quality of Lear seen in retrospect, his hunger after righteousness, gives magnitude to the concluding scenes. His spirit has been doubly lacerated by his own sense of guilt. He has failed "poor naked wretches" no different from himself, and he has wronged Cordelia. His remorse has found expression only in brief occasional utterances, welling up as it were against desperate efforts of containment, but its scalding power is revealed in his acts of abasement when he and Cordelia meet. The final episodes are all vitally linked. When the two are led in captive, we are made to look back upon their reunion, which he dreams of endlessly reenacting:

When thou dost ask me blessing, I'll kneel down
And ask of thee forgiveness;

then forward to their death:

Upon such sacrifices, my Cordelia,
The gods themselves throw incense.

The words help to effect that perfect coalescence of particular and general tragic experience achieved as he kneels beside her body. This is a father and his child who will come no more, the father remembering his own unkindness and the child's endearing ways. There is no melioration in his dying delusion that she still lives, no mention of an after-life. It is unspeakably sad. But it merges with a larger yet less devastating sadness. This is also a sacrifice, and although the somber tones of the survivors as they take up the burden of survival give it relevance to the future as well as the past, it is such a sacrifice as obliquely vindicates the gods if upon it they throw incense.

We know, not as an item of faith but of simple demonstrable fact, that we are greatly indebted for such wisdom as we have, that it was bought with "sacrifices." In the struggle of our kind against brutality, the great casualties, spiritual and even physical, have always been among those who have been best and those who have cared most. In the world of this play Cordelia has brought us the truest sense of human goodness, her words "No cause, no cause" the truest sense of moral beauty. She is the perfect offering. And so is Lear. She is best. He cares most for what is best. The play ends as it begins in an allegorical grouping, commemorating humanity's long, agonized, and continuing struggle to be human. This larger meaning gives our tears the dignity of an act of ratification and gratitude: to these still figures we have pitied we owe the gift of feeling pity.

Harvard University　　　　　　ALFRED HARBAGE

NOTE ON THE TEXT

In 1608 a version of *King Lear* appeared in a quarto volume sold by Nathaniel Butter at his shop at the Pied Bull. Its text was reproduced in 1619 in a quarto falsely dated 1608. Various theories have been offered to explain the nature of the Pied Bull text, the most recent being that it represents Shakespeare's rough draft carelessly copied, and corrupted by the faulty memories of actors who were party to the copying. In 1623 a greatly improved though "cut" version of the play appeared in the first folio, evidently printed from the quarto after it had been carefully collated with the official playhouse manuscript. The present edition follows the folio text, and although it adds in square brackets the passages appearing only in the quarto, and accepts fifty-three quarto readings, it follows the chosen text more closely than do most recent editions. However, deference to the quarto is paid in an appendix, where its alternative readings, both those accepted and those rejected, are listed. Few editorial emendations have been retained, but see I, ii, 21 *top* (Q & F 'to'), II, ii, 138 *contemnèd'st* (Q 'temnest'), III, vi, 25 *bourn* (Q 'broom'), III, vi, 67 *lym* (Q & F 'him'), IV, ii, 57 *to threat* (Q 'thereat'), IV, iii, 20 *seemed* (Q 'seeme'), 31 *moistened* (Q 'moistened her'). The quarto text is not divided into acts and scenes. The act and scene division here supplied marginally for reference purposes is that of the folio except that Act II, Scene ii of the latter has been subdivided into Scenes ii, iii, and iv. The continuity of the action here, and at several other misleadingly divided sections of the play, is indicated in the manner explained in the Preface.

KING LEAR

Lear, King of Britain	*Edmund, bastard son to Gloucester*	*A Gentleman attending on Cordelia*
King of France	*Curan, a courtier*	*A Herald*
Duke of Burgundy	*Old Man, tenant to Gloucester*	*Servants to Cornwall*
Duke of Cornwall	*Doctor*	*Goneril*
Duke of Albany	*Lear's Fool*	*Regan* } *daughters to Lear*
Earl of Kent	*Oswald, steward to Goneril*	*Cordelia*
Earl of Gloucester	*A Captain under Edmund's command*	*Knights attending on Lear, Officers, Messengers,*
Edgar, son to Gloucester	*Gentlemen loyal to Lear*	*Soldiers, Attendants*

Scene : *Britain*]

*

I, i   *Enter Kent, Gloucester, and Edmund.*

1 KENT I thought the King had more affected the Duke of
2 Albany than Cornwall.

GLOUCESTER It did always seem so to us ; but now, in the
division of the kingdom, it appears not which of the
5 dukes he values most, for equalities are so weighed that
6 curiosity in neither can make choice of either's moiety.

KENT Is not this your son, my lord ?

8 GLOUCESTER His breeding, sir, hath been at my charge.
I have so often blushed to acknowledge him that now I
10 am brazed to't.

11 KENT I cannot conceive you.

GLOUCESTER Sir, this young fellow's mother could ;
whereupon she grew round-wombed, and had indeed,
sir, a son for her cradle ere she had a husband for her
her bed. Do you smell a fault ?

KENT I cannot wish the fault undone, the issue of it being
17 so proper.

GLOUCESTER But I have a son, sir, by order of law, some
19 year elder than this who yet is no dearer in my account :
20 though this knave came something saucily to the world
before he was sent for, yet was his mother fair, there was
22 good sport at his making, and the whoreson must be
acknowledged. Do you know this noble gentleman,
Edmund ?

EDMUND No, my lord.

GLOUCESTER My Lord of Kent. Remember him hereafter as my honorable friend.

EDMUND My services to your lordship.

KENT I must love you, and sue to know you better.

EDMUND Sir, I shall study deserving.

GLOUCESTER He hath been out nine years, and away he 31
shall again. 32

[Sound a] sennet.

The King is coming.

*Enter [one bearing a coronet, then] King Lear, [then
the Dukes of] Cornwall, [and] Albany, [next]
Goneril, Regan, Cordelia, and Attendants.*

LEAR
Attend the lords of France and Burgundy, Gloucester.

GLOUCESTER
' I shall, my lord. *Exit [with Edmund].*

LEAR
Meantime we shall express our darker purpose. 36
Give me the map there. Know that we have divided
In three our kingdom ; and 'tis our fast intent 38
To shake all cares and business from our age,
Conferring them on younger strengths while we
Unburdened crawl toward death. Our son of Cornwall,
And you our no less loving son of Albany,
We have this hour a constant will to publish 43
Our daughters' several dowers, that future strife 44
May be prevented now. The princes, France and
Burgundy,
Great rivals in our youngest daughter's love ;
Long in our court have made their amorous sojourn, 47
And here are to be answered. Tell me, my daughters
(Since now we will divest us both of rule,
Interest of territory, cares of state), 50
Which of you shall we say doth love us most,
That we our largest bounty may extend
Where nature doth with merit challenge. Goneril, 53
Our eldest-born, speak first.

I, i Room of state within King Lear's palace 1 *affected* warmly regarded
2 *Albany* i.e. Scotland (once ruled by 'Albanacte') 5 *equalities . . .
weighed* i.e. the portions weigh so equally 6 *curiosity . . . moiety* careful
analysis by neither can make him prefer the other's portion 8 *breeding*
rearing 10 *brazed* brazened 11 *conceive* understand (with pun following)
17 *proper* handsome 19 *account* estimation 20 *saucily* (1) impertinently,
(2) bawdily 22 *whoreson* (affectionate abuse, but literally applicable,
like *knave* above) 31 *out* away (for training, or in military service) 32
s.d. *sennet* trumpet flourish (heralding a procession) 36 *darker purpose*
more secret intention (to require declarations of affection) 38 *fast* firm
43 *constant . . . publish* fixed intention to announce 44 *several* individual
47 *amorous sojourn* i.e. visit of courtship 50 *Interest* legal possession 53
nature . . . challenge natural affection matches other merits

GONERIL
55 Sir, I love you more than word can wield the matter;
56 Dearer than eyesight, space, and liberty;
Beyond what can be valuèd, rich or rare;
No less than life, with grace, health, beauty, honor;
As much as child e'er loved, or father found;
60 A love that makes breath poor, and speech unable.
Beyond all manner of so much I love you.
CORDELIA *[aside]*
What shall Cordelia speak? Love, and be silent.
LEAR
Of all these bounds, even from this line to this,
64 With shadowy forests and with champains riched,
65 With plenteous rivers and wide-skirted meads,
66 We make thee lady. To thine and Albany's issues
67 Be this perpetual. – What says our second daughter,
Our dearest Regan, wife of Cornwall?
REGAN
I am made of that self mettle as my sister,
70 And prize me at her worth. In my true heart
71 I find she names my very deed of love;
Only she comes too short, that I profess
Myself an enemy to all other joys
74 Which the most precious square of sense possesses,
75 And find I am alone felicitate
In your dear Highness' love.
CORDELIA *[aside]*   Then poor Cordelia;
And yet not so, since I am sure my love's
78 More ponderous than my tongue.
LEAR
To thee and thine hereditary ever
Remain this ample third of our fair kingdom,
81 No less in space, validity, and pleasure
Than that conferred on Goneril. – Now, our joy,
83 Although our last and least; to whose young love
84 The vines of France and milk of Burgundy
85 Strive to be interest; what can you say to draw
A third more opulent than your sisters? Speak.
CORDELIA
Nothing, my lord.
LEAR Nothing?
CORDELIA Nothing.
LEAR
Nothing will come of nothing. Speak again.
CORDELIA
Unhappy that I am, I cannot heave
My heart into my mouth. I love your Majesty
93 According to my bond, no more nor less.
LEAR
How, how, Cordelia? Mend your speech a little,
Lest you may mar your fortunes.
CORDELIA   Good my lord,
You have begot me, bred me, loved me. I
97 Return those duties back as are right fit,
Obey you, love you, and most honor you.
Why have my sisters husbands if they say
They love you all? Haply, when I shall wed,
101 That lord whose hand must take my plight shall carry
Half my love with him, half my care and duty.
Sure I shall never marry like my sisters,
[To love my father all.]
LEAR
But goes thy heart with this?
CORDELIA   Ay, my good lord.

LEAR
So young, and so untender?
CORDELIA
So young, my lord, and true.
LEAR
Let it be so, thy truth then be thy dower!
For, by the sacred radiance of the sun,
The mysteries of Hecate and the night,   110
By all the operation of the orbs   111
From whom we do exist and cease to be,
Here I disclaim all my paternal care,
Propinquity and property of blood,   114
And as a stranger to my heart and me
Hold thee from this for ever. The barbarous Scythian,   116
Or he that makes his generation messes   117
To gorge his appetite, shall to my bosom
Be as well neighbored, pitied, and relieved,
As thou my sometime daughter.   120
KENT   Good my liege –
LEAR
Peace, Kent!
Come not between the dragon and his wrath.   122
I loved her most, and thought to set my rest   123
On her kind nursery. – Hence and avoid my sight! –   124
So be my grave my peace as here I give   125
Her father's heart from her! Call France. Who stirs!
Call Burgundy. Cornwall and Albany,
With my two daughters' dowers digest the third;
Let pride, which she calls plainness, marry her.
I do invest you jointly with my power,
Preeminence, and all the large effects   131
That troop with majesty. Ourself, by monthly course,   132
With reservation of an hundred knights,
By you to be sustained, shall our abode
Make with you by due turn. Only we shall retain
The name, and all th' addition to a king. The sway,   136
Revenue, execution of the rest,
Belovèd sons, be yours; which to confirm,
This coronet part between you.   139
KENT   Royal Lear,
Whom I have ever honored as my king,
Loved as my father, as my master followed,
As my great patron thought on in my prayers –
LEAR
The bow is bent and drawn; make from the shaft.   143
KENT
Let it fall rather, though the fork invade   144

---

55 *wield* handle   **56** *space* scope (for the exercise of *liberty*)   **60** *breath* voice; *unable* inadequate   **64** *champains riched* plains enriched   **65** *wide-skirted* far spreading   **66** *issues* descendants   **67** *perpetual* in perpetuity   **70** *prize . . . worth* value me at her value   **71** *my very deed of* the true fact of my   **74** *Which . . . possesses* which the most precise measurement by the senses holds to be most precious   **75** *felicitate* made happy   **78** *ponderous* weighty   **81** *validity* value; *pleasure* pleasing qualities   **83** *least* smallest, youngest   **84** *vines* vineyards; *milk* pasture-lands (?)   **85** *interest* concerned as interested parties   **93** *bond* obligation   **97** *Return . . . fit* i.e. am fittingly dutiful in return   **101** *plight* pledge, troth-plight   **110** *Hecate* infernal goddess, patroness of witches   **111** *operation . . . orbs* astrological influences   **114** *Propinquity* relationship; *property* i.e. common property, something shared   **116** *Scythian* (proverbially barbarous)   **117** *makes . . . messes* makes meals of his offspring   **120** *sometime* former   **122** *his* its   **123** *set my rest* (1) risk my stake (a term in the card game primero), (2) rely for my repose   **124** *nursery* nursing, care   **125** *So . . . peace as* let me rest peacefully in my grave only as   **131** *effects* tokens   **132** *Ourself* I (royal plural)   **136** *th' addition* honors and prerogatives   **139** *coronet* (symbol of rule; not necessarily the royal crown)   **143** *make* make away   **144** *fall* strike; *fork* two-pronged head

The region of my heart. Be Kent unmannerly
When Lear is mad. What wouldst thou do, old man?
Think'st thou that duty shall have dread to speak
When power to flattery bows? To plainness honor 's
    bound

149 When majesty falls to folly. Reserve thy state,
150 And in thy best consideration check
151 This hideous rashness. Answer my life my judgment,
Thy youngest daughter does not love thee least,
Nor are those empty-hearted whose low sounds
154 Reverb no hollowness.

LEAR   Kent, on thy life, no more!

KENT
155 My life I never held but as a pawn
156 To wage against thine enemies; ne'er fear to lose it,
157 Thy safety being motive.

LEAR   Out of my sight!

KENT
158 See better, Lear, and let me still remain
159 The true blank of thine eye.

LEAR
Now by Apollo —

KENT   Now by Apollo, King,
Thou swear'st thy gods in vain.

161 **LEAR**   O vassal! Miscreant!
    [Grasping his sword.]

ALBANY, CORNWALL Dear sir, forbear!

KENT
Kill thy physician, and thy fee bestow
Upon the foul disease. Revoke thy gift,
Or, whilst I can vent clamor from my throat,
I'll tell thee thou dost evil.

166 **LEAR**   Hear me, recreant,
On thine allegiance, hear me!
168 That thou hast sought to make us break our vows,
169 Which we durst never yet, and with strained pride
170 To come betwixt our sentence and our power,
Which nor our nature nor our place can bear,
172 Our potency made good, take thy reward.
Five days we do allot thee for provision
174 To shield thee from disasters of the world,
And on the sixth to turn thy hated back
Upon our kingdom. If, on the tenth day following,
177 Thy banished trunk be found in our dominions,
The moment is thy death. Away. By Jupiter,
This shall not be revoked.

149 *Reserve thy state* retain your kingly authority   150 *best consideration* most careful deliberation   151 *Answer my life* i.e. I'll stake my life on   154 *Reverb no hollowness* i.e. do not reverberate (like a drum) as a result of hollowness   155 *pawn* stake   156 *wage* wager, pit   157 *motive* the moving cause   158 *still* always   159 *blank* center of the target (to guide your aim truly)   161 *Miscreant* (1) rascal, (2) infidel   166 *recreant* traitor   168 *That* in that, since   169 *strained* excessive   170 *To come . . . power* i.e. to oppose my power to sentence   172 *Our . . . good* if my power is to be demonstrated as real   174 *disasters* accidents   177 *trunk* body   180 *Sith* since   184 *approve* confirm   185 *effects* consequences   187 *shape . . . course* keep to his customary ways (of honesty)   198 *seeming substance* i.e. nothing, mere shell   199 *pieced* joined   202 *owes* owns   204 *strangered* with made alien by   206 *Election . . . conditions* no choice is possible on such terms   209 *make . . . stray* stray so far as   211 *avert* turn   214 *best favorite*   215 *argument* theme   217 *to dismantle* so to strip off   220 *That monsters it* as makes it monstrous (i.e. abnormal, freakish); *fore-vouched* previously sworn   221 *taint* decay (with the implication that the affection, and the oath attesting it, were tainted in the first place)   222 *reason . . . miracle* i.e. rational, unaided by miraculous, means of persuasion   225 *purpose not* i.e. without intending to act in accordance with my words

KENT
Fare thee well, King. Sith thus thou wilt appear,   180
Freedom lives hence, and banishment is here.
    [To Cordelia]
The gods to their dear shelter take thee, maid,
That justly think'st and hast most rightly said.
    [To Regan and Goneril]
And your large speeches may your deeds approve,   184
That good effects may spring from words of love.   185
Thus Kent, O princes, bids you all adieu;
He'll shape his old course in a country new.   *Exit.* 187
    Flourish. Enter Gloucester, with France and
    Burgundy; Attendants.

GLOUCESTER
Here's France and Burgundy, my noble lord.

LEAR
My Lord of Burgundy,
We first address toward you, who with this king
Hath rivalled for our daughter. What in the least
Will you require in present dower with her,
Or cease your quest of love?

BURGUNDY   Most royal Majesty,
I crave no more than hath your Highness offered,
Nor will you tender less.

LEAR   Right noble Burgundy,
When she was dear to us, we did hold her so;
But now her price is fallen. Sir, there she stands.
If aught within that little seeming substance,   198
Or all of it, with our displeasure pieced   199
And nothing more, may fitly like your Grace,
She's there, and she is yours.

BURGUNDY   I know no answer.

LEAR
Will you, with those infirmities she owes,   202
Unfriended, new adopted to our hate,
Dow'red with our curse, and strangered with our oath,   204
Take her, or leave her?

BURGUNDY   Pardon me, royal sir.
Election makes not up on such conditions.   206

LEAR
Then leave her, sir, for by the pow'r that made me
I tell you all her wealth. *[to France]* For you, great King,
I would not from your love make such a stray   209
To match you where I hate; therefore beseech you
T' avert your liking a more worthier way   211
Than on a wretch whom Nature is ashamed
Almost t' acknowledge hers.

FRANCE   This is most strange,
That she whom even but now was your best object,   214
The argument of your praise, balm of your age,   215
The best, the dearest, should in this trice of time
Commit a thing so monstrous to dismantle   217
So many folds of favor. Sure her offense
Must be of such unnatural degree
That monsters it, or your fore-vouched affection   220
Fall'n into taint; which to believe of her   221
Must be a faith that reason without miracle   222
Should never plant in me.

CORDELIA   I yet beseech your Majesty,
If for I want that glib and oily art
To speak and purpose not since what I well intend   225
I'll do 't before I speak, that you make known
It is no vicious blot, murder or foulness,
No unchaste action or dishonorèd step,

That hath deprived me of your grace and favor;
But even for want of that for which I am richer –
231 A still-soliciting eye, and such a tongue
That I am glad I have not, though not to have it
Hath lost me in your liking.

LEAR   Better thou
Hadst not been born than not t' have pleased me better.

FRANCE
235 Is it but this? A tardiness in nature
236 Which often leaves the history unspoke
That it intends to do. My Lord of Burgundy,
What say you to the lady? Love 's not love
239 When it is mingled with regards that stands
Aloof from th' entire point. Will you have her?
She is herself a dowry.

BURGUNDY   Royal King,
Give but that portion which yourself proposed,
And here I take Cordelia by the hand,
Duchess of Burgundy.

LEAR
Nothing. I have sworn. I am firm.

BURGUNDY
I am sorry then you have so lost a father
That you must lose a husband.

CORDELIA   Peace be with Burgundy.
248 Since that respects of fortune are his love,
I shall not be his wife.

FRANCE
Fairest Cordelia, that art most rich being poor,
Most choice forsaken, and most loved despised,
Thee and thy virtues here I seize upon.
Be it lawful I take up what's cast away.
Gods, gods! 'Tis strange that from their cold'st neglect
255 My love should kindle to inflamed respect.
Thy dow'rless daughter, King, thrown to my chance,
Is queen of us, of ours, and our fair France.
258 Not all the dukes of wat'rish Burgundy
259 Can buy this unprized precious maid of me.
Bid them farewell, Cordelia, though unkind.
261 Thou losest here, a better where to find.

LEAR
Thou hast her, France; let her be thine, for we
Have no such daughter, nor shall ever see
That face of hers again. Therefore be gone
265 Without our grace, our love, our benison.
Come, noble Burgundy.

Flourish. Exeunt [Lear, Burgundy, Cornwall,
Albany, Gloucester, and Attendants].

FRANCE
Bid farewell to your sisters.

CORDELIA
268 The jewels of our father, with washed eyes
Cordelia leaves you. I know you what you are;
270 And, like a sister, am most loath to call
271 Your faults as they are named. Love well our father.
272 To your professèd bosoms I commit him;
But yet, alas, stood I within his grace,
274 I would prefer him to a better place.
So farewell to you both.

REGAN
Prescribe not us our duty.

GONERIL   Let your study
Be to content your lord, who hath received you
278 At fortune's alms. You have obedience scanted,

And well are worth the want that you have wanted.   279

CORDELIA
Time shall unfold what plighted cunning hides,   280
Who covers faults, at last with shame derides.   281
Well may you prosper.

FRANCE   Come, my fair Cordelia.

Exit France and Cordelia.

GONERIL Sister, it is not little I have to say of what most
nearly appertains to us both. I think our father will
hence to-night.

REGAN That's most certain, and with you; next month
with us.

GONERIL You see how full of changes his age is. The observation we have made of it hath not been little. He
always loved our sister most, and with what poor judgment he hath now cast her off appears too grossly.   291

REGAN 'Tis the infirmity of his age; yet he hath ever but
slenderly known himself.   293

GONERIL The best and soundest of his time hath been but 294
rash; then must we look from his age to receive not alone
the imperfections of long-ingraffed condition, but there- 296
withal the unruly waywardness that infirm and choleric
years bring with them.

REGAN Such unconstant starts are we like to have from 299
him as this of Kent's banishment.

GONERIL There is further compliment of leave-taking 301
between France and him. Pray you let us hit together; if 302
our father carry authority with such disposition as he
bears, this last surrender of his will but offend us.   304

REGAN We shall further think of it.

GONERIL We must do something, and i' th' heat. *Exeunt.* 306

                              *

Enter Bastard [Edmund, solus, with a letter].   I, ii

EDMUND
Thou, Nature, art my goddess; to thy law   1
My services are bound. Wherefore should I
Stand in the plague of custom, and permit   3
The curiosity of nations to deprive me,   4
For that I am some twelve or fourteen moonshines   5
Lag of a brother? Why bastard? Wherefore base,   6
When my dimensions are as well compact,   7
My mind as generous, and my shape as true,   8

231 *still-soliciting* always-begging 235 *tardiness in nature* natural reticence
236 *history unspoke* actions unannounced 239-40 *mingled . . . point*
i.e. mixed with irrelevant considerations 248 *respects* considerations
255 *inflamed respect* ardent regard 258 *wat'rish* (1) watery, weak, (2)
watered, diluted 259 *unprized* unvalued 261 *here* this place; *where*
other place 265 *benison* blessing 268 *jewels* i.e. things held precious
(cf. l. 259); *washed* tear-washed 270 *like a sister* i.e with sisterly loyalty
271 *as . . . named* by their true names 272 *professèd* i.e. love-professing
274 *prefer* promote 278 *alms* small offerings 279 *worth . . . wanted*
i.e. deserving no affection since you have shown no affection 280 *plighted*
pleated, enfolded 281 *Who . . . derides* i.e. time at first conceals faults,
then exposes them to shame 291 *grossly* crudely conspicuous 293
known himself i.e. been aware of what he truly is 294 *of his time* period
of his past life 296 *long-ingraffed* ingrown, chronic; *therewithal* along with
that 299 *unconstant starts* impulsive moves 301 *compliment* formality
302 *hit* agree 304 *surrender* i.e. yielding up of authority; *offend* harm
306 *i' th' heat* i.e. while the iron is hot
I, ii Within the Earl of Gloucester's castle 1 *Nature* i.e. the material and
mechanistic as distinct from the spiritual and heaven-ordained 3 *Stand*
. . . custom submit to the affliction of convention 4 *curiosity* nice distinctions 5 *For that* because; *moonshines* months 6 *Lag of* behind (in age)
7 *compact* fitted, matched 8 *generous* befitting the high-born

9   As honest madam's issue ? Why brand they us
With base ? with baseness ? Bastardy base ? Base ?
11   Who, in the lusty stealth of nature, take
12   More composition and fierce quality
Than doth, within a dull, stale, tirèd bed,
14   Go to th' creating a whole tribe of fops
15   Got 'tween asleep and wake ? Well then,
Legitimate Edgar, I must have your land.
Our father's love is to the bastard Edmund
As to th' legitimate. Fine word, 'legitimate.'
Well, my legitimate, if this letter speed,
20   And my invention thrive, Edmund the base
Shall top th' legitimate. I grow, I prosper.
Now, gods, stand up for bastards.

Enter Gloucester.

GLOUCESTER
Kent banished thus ? and France in choler parted ?
24   And the King gone to-night ? prescribed his pow'r ?
25   Confined to exhibition ? All this done
26   Upon the gad ? – Edmund, how now ? What news ?

EDMUND
So please your lordship, none.

GLOUCESTER
28   Why so earnestly seek you to put up that letter ?

EDMUND
I know no news, my lord.

GLOUCESTER
What paper were you reading ?

EDMUND Nothing, my lord.

GLOUCESTER No ? What needed then that terrible dispatch of it into your pocket ? The quality of nothing hath not such need to hide itself. Let's see. Come, if it be nothing, I shall not need spectacles.

EDMUND I beseech you, sir, pardon me. It is a letter from my brother that I have not all o'er-read ; and for so much
38   as I have perused, I find it not fit for your o'erlooking.

GLOUCESTER Give me the letter, sir.

EDMUND I shall offend, either to detain or give it. The
41   contents, as in part I understand them, are to blame.

GLOUCESTER Let's see, let's see.

EDMUND I hope, for my brother's justification, he wrote
44   this but as an essay or taste of my virtue.

45 GLOUCESTER (*reads*) 'This policy and reverence of age
46   makes the world bitter to the best of our times ; keeps our

fortunes from us till our oldness cannot relish them. I
begin to find an idle and fond bondage in the oppression 48
of aged tyranny, who sways, not as it hath power, but as 49
it is suffered. Come to me, that of this I may speak more. 50
If our father would sleep till I waked him, you should
enjoy half his revenue for ever, and live the beloved of 52
your brother,   Edgar.'

Hum ! Conspiracy ? 'Sleep till I waked him, you should
enjoy half his revenue.' My son Edgar ! Had he a hand to
write this ? A heart and brain to breed it in ? When came
you to this ? Who brought it ?   57

EDMUND It was not brought me, my lord ; there's the
cunning of it. I found it thrown in at the casement of my 59
closet.   60

GLOUCESTER You know the character to be your 61
brother's ?

EDMUND If the matter were good, my lord, I durst swear 62
it were his ; but in respect of that, I would fain think it 63
were not.

GLOUCESTER It is his.

EDMUND It is his hand, my lord ; but I hope his heart is
not in the contents.

GLOUCESTER Has he never before sounded you in this 68
business ?

EDMUND Never, my lord. But I have heard him oft maintain it to be fit that, sons at perfect age, and fathers 71
declined, the father should be as ward to the son, and
the son manage his revenue.

GLOUCESTER O villain, villain ! His very opinion in the
letter. Abhorred villain, unnatural, detested, brutish
villain ; worse than brutish ! Go, sirrah, seek him. I'll 76
apprehend him. Abominable villain ! Where is he ?

EDMUND I do not well know, my lord. If it shall please
you to suspend your indignation against my brother till
you can derive from him better testimony of his intent,
you should run a certain course ; where, if you violently 81
proceed against him, mistaking his purpose, it would
make a great gap in your own honor and shake in pieces
the heart of his obedience. I dare pawn down my life for
him that he hath writ this to feel my affection to your 85
honor, and to no other pretense of danger.   86

GLOUCESTER Think you so ?

EDMUND If your honor judge it meet, I will place you 88
where you shall hear us confer of this and by an auri- 89
cular assurance have your satisfaction, and that without
any further delay than this very evening.

GLOUCESTER He cannot be such a monster.

[EDMUND Nor is not, sure.

GLOUCESTER To his father, that so tenderly and entirely
loves him. Heaven and earth !] Edmund, seek him out ;
wind me into him, I pray you ; frame the business after 96
your own wisdom. I would unstate myself to be in a due 97
resolution.

EDMUND I will seek him, sir, presently ; convey the busi- 99
ness as I shall find means, and acquaint you withal.   100

GLOUCESTER These late eclipses in the sun and moon 101
portend no good to us. Though the wisdom of nature can 102
reason it thus and thus, yet nature finds itself scourged by 103
the sequent effects. Love cools, friendship falls off, 104
brothers divide. In cities, mutinies ; in countries, dis- 105
cord ; in palaces, treason ; and the bond cracked 'twixt
son and father. This villain of mine comes under the pre- 107
diction, there's son against father ; the King falls from

---

9 *honest* chaste   11 *lusty . . . nature* secrecy of natural lust   12 *composition* completeness of constitution, robustness ; *fierce* mettlesome, thoroughbred   14 *fops* fools   15 *Got* begotten   20 *invention* thrive plot succeed   24 *prescribed* limited   25 *exhibition* an allowance, a pension   26 *gad* spur   28 *put up* put away   38 *o'erlooking* examination   41 *to blame* blameworthy   44 *essay* trial ; *taste* test   45 *policy and reverence* policy of reverencing   46 *the best of our times* our best years   48 *idle, fond* foolish (synonyms)   49 *who sways* which rules   50 *suffered* allowed   52 *revenue* income   57 *to this* upon this   59 *casement* window   60 *closet* room   61 *character* handwriting   62 *matter* contents   63 *in respect of that* i.e. considering what those contents are ; *fain* prefer to   68 *sounded you* sounded you out   71 *perfect age* prime of life   76 *sirrah* sir (familiar, or contemptuous, form)   81 *run . . . course* i.e. know where you are going   85 *feel* feel out, test ; *affection* attachment, loyalty   86 *pretense of danger* dangerous intention   88 *judge it meet* consider it fitting   89–90 *by . . . assurance* i.e. by the proof of your own ears   96 *wind me* worm ; *frame* plan   97–98 *unstate . . . resolution* i.e. give everything to know for certain   99 *presently* at once ; *convey* conduct   100 *withal* therewith   101 *late* recent   102 *wisdom of nature* natural lore, science   102–04 *can . . . effects* i.e. can supply explanations, yet punitive upheavals in nature (such as earthquakes) follow   103 *scourged* whipped   104 *sequent* following   105 *mutinies* rebellions   107 *comes . . . prediction* i.e. is included among these ill-omened things

109 bias of nature, there's father against child. We have seen
the best of our time. Machinations, hollowness, treachery, and all ruinous disorders follow us disquietly to our
112 graves. Find out this villain, Edmund; it shall lose thee
nothing; do it carefully. And the noble and true-hearted
Kent banished; his offense, honesty. 'Tis strange. *Exit.*
115 EDMUND This is the excellent foppery of the world, that
116 when we are sick in fortune, often the surfeits of our own
behavior, we make guilty of our disasters the sun, the
moon, and stars; as if we were villains on necessity; fools
119 by heavenly compulsion; knaves, thieves, and treachers
120 by spherical predominance; drunkards, liars, and adul-
terers by an enforced obedience of planetary influence;
and all that we are evil in, by a divine thrusting on. An
123 admirable evasion of whoremaster man, to lay his goatish
124 disposition on the charge of a star. My father compoun-
125 ded with my mother under the Dragon's Tail, and my
126 nativity was under Ursa Major, so that it follows I am
rough and lecherous. Fut! I should have been that I am,
had the maidenliest star in the firmament twinkled on
my bastardizing. Edgar –
    Enter Edgar.
130 and pat he comes, like the catastrophe of the old comedy.
131 My cue is villainous melancholy, with a sigh like Tom o'
Bedlam. – O, these eclipses do portend these divisions.
Fa, sol, la, mi.
  EDGAR How now, brother Edmund; what serious contemplation are you in?
  EDMUND I am thinking, brother, of a prediction I read
this other day, what should follow these eclipses.
  EDGAR Do you busy yourself with that?
139 EDMUND I promise you, the effects he writes of succeed
140 unhappily: [as of unnaturalness between the child and
the parent; death, dearth, dissolutions of ancient amities; divisions in state, menaces and maledictions
143 against king and nobles; needless diffidences, banish-
144 ment of friends, dissipation of cohorts, nuptial breaches,
and I know not what.
146 EDGAR How long have you been a sectary astronomical?
  EDMUND Come, come,] when saw you my father last?
  EDGAR The night gone by.
  EDMUND Spake you with him?
  EDGAR Ay, two hours together.
  EDMUND Parted you in good terms? Found you no dis-
152 pleasure in him by word nor countenance?
  EDGAR None at all.
  EDMUND Bethink yourself wherein you may have offended him; and at my entreaty forbear his presence until
156 some little time hath qualified the heat of his displeasure,
157 which at this instant so rageth in him that with the mis-
158 chief of your person it would scarcely allay.
  EDGAR Some villain hath done me wrong.
160 EDMUND That's my fear. I pray you have a continent forbearance till the speed of his rage goes slower; and, as I
say, retire with me to my lodging, from whence I will
163 fitly bring you to hear my lord speak. Pray ye, go;
there's my key. If you do stir abroad, go armed.
  EDGAR Armed, brother?
  EDMUND Brother, I advise you to the best. Go armed. I
am no honest man if there be any good meaning toward
you. I have told you what I have seen and heard; but
169 faintly, nothing like the image and horror of it. Pray
you, away.
170 EDGAR Shall I hear from you anon?

EDMUND I do serve you in this business.   *Exit [Edgar].*
A credulous father, and a brother noble,
Whose nature is so far from doing harms
That he suspects none; on whose foolish honesty
My practices ride easy. I see the business.   175
Let me, if not by birth, have lands by wit;   176
All with me's meet that I can fashion fit.   *Exit.* 177

                *

   Enter Goneril and Steward [Oswald].   I, iii
GONERIL
Did my father strike my gentleman for chiding of his
   fool?
OSWALD Ay, madam.
GONERIL
By day and night he wrongs me. Every hour
He flashes into one gross crime or other   4
That sets us all at odds. I'll not endure it.
His knights grow riotous, and himself upbraids us   6
On every trifle. When he returns from hunting,
I will not speak with him. Say I am sick.
If you come slack of former services,   9
You shall do well; the fault of it I'll answer.   10
   [Horns within.]
OSWALD He's coming, madam; I hear him.
GONERIL
Put on what weary negligence you please,
You and your fellows. I'd have it come to question.   13
If he distaste it, let him to my sister,   14
Whose mind and mine I know that are one,
[Not to be overruled. Idle old man,   16
That still would manage those authorities
That he hath given away. Now, by my life,
Old fools are babes again, and must be used
With checks as flatteries, when they are seen abused.]   20
Remember what I have said.
OSWALD   Well, madam.
GONERIL
And let his knights have colder looks among you.
What grows of it, no matter; advise your fellows so.
[I would breed from hence occasions, and I shall,   24
That I may speak.] I'll write straight to my sister
To hold my course. Prepare for dinner.   *Exeunt.*

109 *bias of nature* natural tendency 112–13 *lose thee nothing* i.e. you
will not lose by it 115 *foppery* foolishness 116 *we are sick ... surfeits*
i.e. our fortunes grow sickly, often from the excesses 119 *treachers*
traitors 120 *spherical predominance* i.e. ascendancy, or rule, of a particular
sphere 123 *goatish* lecherous 124 *compounded* (1) came to terms, (2)
created 125, 126 *Dragon's Tail, Ursa Major* (constellations, cited because of the suggestiveness of their names) 126 *nativity* birthday 130
catastrophe conclusion. 131–32 *Tom o' Bedlam* (a type of beggar, mad
or pretending to be, so named from the London madhouse, Bethlehem
or 'Bedlam' Hospital) 139–40 *succeed unhappily* unluckily follow 140
unnaturalness unkindness, enmity 143 *diffidences* instances of distrust
 144 *dissipation of cohorts* melting away of supporters 146 *sectary astronomical* of the astrological sect 152 *countenance* expression, look 156
qualified moderated 157 *mischief* injury 158 *allay* be appeased 160
continent forbearance cautious inaccessibility 163 *fitly* conveniently
 169 *image and horror* horrible true picture 170 *anon* soon 175 *practices*
plots 176 *wit* intelligence 177 *meet* proper, acceptable; *fashion fit* i.e.
rig up, shape to the purpose
I, iii Within the Duke of Albany's palace 4 *crime* offense 6 *riotous*
boisterous 9 *come ... services* i.e. serve him less well than formerly
 10 *answer* answer for 13 *question* i.e. open issue, a thing discussed
 14 *distaste* dislike 16 *Idle* foolish 20 *checks ... abused* restraints in
place of cajolery when they (the old men) are seen to be deceived (about
their true state) 24–25 *breed ... speak* i.e. make an issue of it so that I
may speak

I, iv *Enter Kent [disguised].*

KENT
If but as well I other accents borrow
2 That can my speech defuse, my good intent
3 May carry through itself to that full issue
4 For which I razed my likeness. Now, banished Kent,
If thou canst serve where thou dost stand condemned,
So may it come thy master whom thou lov'st
Shall find thee full of labors.

Horns within. Enter Lear, [Knight,] and Attendants.

8 LEAR Let me not stay a jot for dinner; go get it ready.
[Exit an Attendant.] How now, what art thou?

KENT A man, sir.

11 LEAR What dost thou profess? What wouldst thou with us?

12 KENT I do profess to be no less than I seem, to serve him truly that will put me in trust, to love him that is honest,
14 to converse with him that is wise and says little, to fear
15 judgment, to fight when I cannot choose, and to eat no fish.

LEAR What art thou?

KENT A very honest-hearted fellow, and as poor as the King.

LEAR If thou be'st as poor for a subject as he's for a king, thou art poor enough. What wouldst thou?

KENT Service.

LEAR Who wouldst thou serve?

KENT You.

LEAR Dost thou know me, fellow?

KENT No, sir, but you have that in your countenance
27 which I would fain call master.

LEAR What's that?

KENT Authority.

LEAR What services canst thou do?

31 KENT I can keep honest counsel, ride, run, mar a curious tale in telling it, and deliver a plain message bluntly. That which ordinary men are fit for I am qualified in, and the best of me is diligence.

LEAR How old art thou?

KENT Not so young, sir, to love a woman for singing, nor so old to dote on her for anything. I have years on my back forty-eight.

LEAR Follow me; thou shalt serve me. If I like thee no worse after dinner, I will not part from thee yet. Dinner,
41 ho, dinner! Where's my knave? my fool? Go you and call my fool hither. *[Exit an Attendant.]*

Enter Steward [Oswald].

You, you, sirrah, where's my daughter?

OSWALD So please you – *Exit.*

LEAR What says the fellow there? Call the clotpoll back. 45
[Exit Knight.] Where's my fool? Ho, I think the world's asleep. *[Enter Knight.]* How now? Where's that mongrel?

KNIGHT He says, my lord, your daughter is not well.

LEAR Why came not the slave back to me when I called him?

KNIGHT Sir, he answered me in the roundest manner, he would not.

LEAR He would not?

KNIGHT My lord, I know not what the matter is; but to my judgment your Highness is not entertained with 56 that ceremonious affection as you were wont. There's a great abatement of kindness appears as well in the general dependants as in the Duke himself also and your daughter.

LEAR Ha? Say'st thou so?

KNIGHT I beseech you pardon me, my lord, if I be mistaken; for my duty cannot be silent when I think your Highness wronged.

LEAR Thou but rememb'rest me of mine own conception. 64 I have perceived a most faint neglect of late, which I have 65 rather blamed as mine own jealous curiosity than as a 66 very pretense and purpose of unkindness. I will look 67 further into't. But where's my fool? I have not seen him this two days.

KNIGHT Since my young lady's going into France, sir, the fool hath much pined away.

LEAR No more of that; I have noted it well. Go you and tell my daughter I would speak with her. *[Exit Knight.]* Go you, call hither my fool. *[Exit an Attendant.]*

Enter Steward [Oswald].

O, you, sir, you! Come you hither, sir. Who am I, sir?

OSWALD My lady's father.

LEAR 'My lady's father'? My lord's knave, you whoreson dog, you slave, you cur!

OSWALD I am none of these, my lord; I beseech your pardon.

LEAR Do you bandy looks with me, you rascal? 80
[Strikes him.]

OSWALD I'll not be strucken, my lord. 81

KENT Nor tripped neither, you base football player. 82
[Trips up his heels.]

LEAR I thank thee, fellow. Thou serv'st me, and I'll love thee.

KENT Come, sir, arise, away. I'll teach you differences. 85 Away, away. If you will measure your lubber's length again; but tarry. Go to! Have you wisdom? So. 87
[Pushes him out.]

LEAR Now, my friendly knave, I thank thee. There's ear- 88 nest of thy service.
[Gives money.] Enter Fool.

FOOL Let me hire him too. Here's my coxcomb. 90
[Offers Kent his cap.]

LEAR How now, my pretty knave? How dost thou?

FOOL Sirrah, you were best take my coxcomb.

KENT Why, fool?

FOOL Why? For taking one's part that's out of favor. Nay, an thou canst not smile as the wind sits, thou'lt catch 95 cold shortly. There, take my coxcomb. Why, this fellow has banished two on's daughters, and did the third a 97 blessing against his will. If thou follow him, thou must needs wear my coxcomb. – How now, nuncle? Would I 99 had two coxcombs and two daughters.

I, iv 2 *defuse* disorder, disguise 3 *full issue* perfect result 4 *razed my likeness* erased my natural appearance 8 *stay* wait 11 *profess* do, work at (with pun following) 12 *profess* claim 14 *converse* associate 15 *judgment* i.e. God's judgment 15–16 *eat no fish* be a Protestant (anachronism) (?), avoid unmanly diet (?) 27 *fain* like to 31 *keep honest counsel* keep counsel honestly, i.e. respect confidences; *curious* elaborate, embroidered (as contrasted with *plain*) 41 *knave* boy 45 *clotpoll* clodpoll, dolt 56 *entertained* rendered hospitality 64 *rememb'rest* remind 65 *faint neglect* i.e. the *weary negligence* of I, iii, 12 66 *jealous curiosity* i.e. suspicious concern about trifles 67 *very pretense* true intention 80 *bandy* volley, exchange 81 *strucken* struck 82 *football* (an impromptu street and field game, held in low esteem) 85 *differences* distinctions in rank 87 *Go to! ... wisdom* i.e. Get along! Do you know what's good for you? 88 *earnest* part payment 90 *coxcomb* (cap of the professional fool, topped with an imitation comb) 95 *smile ... sits* i.e. adapt yourself to prevailing forces 97 *banished* i.e. provided the means for them to become alien to him 99 *nuncle* mine uncle

LEAR Why, my boy?

FOOL If I gave them all my living, I'd keep my coxcombs myself. There's mine; beg another of thy daughters.

LEAR Take heed, sirrah – the whip.

106 FOOL Truth's a dog must to kennel; he must be whipped out, when the Lady Brach may stand by th' fire and stink.

108 LEAR A pestilent gall to me.

FOOL Sirrah, I'll teach thee a speech.

LEAR Do.

FOOL Mark it, nuncle.

Have more than thou showest,
Speak less than thou knowest,
114 Lend less than thou owest,
115 Ride more than thou goest,
116 Learn more than thou trowest,
117 Set less than thou throwest;
Leave thy drink and thy whore,
And keep in-a-door,
120 And thou shalt have more
Than two tens to a score.

KENT This is nothing, fool.

123 FOOL Then 'tis like the breath of an unfee'd lawyer – you gave me nothing for't. Can you make no use of nothing, nuncle?

LEAR Why, no, boy. Nothing can be made out of nothing.

127 FOOL [to Kent] Prithee tell him, so much the rent of his land comes to; he will not believe a fool.

LEAR A bitter fool.

FOOL Dost thou know the difference, my boy, between a
131 bitter fool and a sweet one?

LEAR No, lad; teach me.

FOOL   [That lord that counselled thee
To give away thy land,
Come place him here by me –
136 Do thou for him stand.
The sweet and bitter fool
Will presently appear;
The one in motley here,
140 The other found out there.

LEAR Dost thou call me fool, boy?

FOOL All thy other titles thou hast given away; that thou wast born with.

KENT This is not altogether fool, my lord.

145 FOOL No, faith; lords and great men will not let me. If I had a monopoly out, they would have part on't. And ladies too, they will not let me have all the fool to my-
148 self; they'll be snatching.] Nuncle, give me an egg, and I'll give thee two crowns.

LEAR What two crowns shall they be?

FOOL Why, after I have cut the egg i' th' middle and eat up the meat, the two crowns of the egg. When thou clovest thy crown i' th' middle and gav'st away both
154 parts, thou bor'st thine ass on thy back o'er the dirt. Thou hadst little wit in thy bald crown when thou
156 gav'st thy golden one away. If I speak like myself in
157 this, let him be whipped that first finds it so.

158 [Sings] Fools had ne'er less grace in a year,
159 For wise men are grown foppish,
160 And know not how their wits to wear,
Their manners are so apish.

LEAR When were you wont to be so full of songs, sirrah?

163 FOOL I have used it, nuncle, e'er since thou mad'st thy daughters thy mothers; for when thou gav'st them the rod, and put'st down thine own breeches,

[Sings] Then they for sudden joy did weep,
And I for sorrow sung,
That such a king should play bo-peep   168
And go the fools among.

Prithee, nuncle, keep a schoolmaster that can teach thy fool to lie. I would fain learn to lie.

LEAR An you lie, sirrah, we'll have you whipped.   172

FOOL I marvel what kin thou and thy daughters are. They'll have me whipped for speaking true; thou'lt have me whipped for lying; and sometimes I am whipped for holding my peace. I had rather be any kind o' thing than a fool, and yet I would not be thee, nuncle: thou hast pared thy wit o' both sides and left nothing i' th' middle.   178 Here comes one o' the parings.

Enter Goneril.

LEAR How now, daughter? What makes that frontlet on?   180 You are too much of late i' th' frown.

FOOL Thou wast a pretty fellow when thou hadst no need to care for her frowning. Now thou art an O without a   183 figure. I am better than thou art now: I am a fool, thou art nothing. [to Goneril] Yes, forsooth, I will hold my tongue. So your face bids me, though you say nothing. Mum, mum,

He that keeps nor crust nor crum,   188
Weary of all, shall want some. –   189

[Points at Lear.]

That's a shealed peascod.   190

GONERIL

Not only, sir, this your all-licensed fool,   191
But other of your insolent retinue
Do hourly carp and quarrel, breaking forth   193
In rank and not-to-be-endurèd riots. Sir,
I had thought by making this well known unto you
To have found a safe redress, but now grow fearful,   196
By what yourself too late have spoke and done,
That you protect this course, and put it on   198
By your allowance; which if you should, the fault   199
Would not 'scape censure, nor the redresses sleep,   200
Which, in the tender of a wholesome weal,   201

106 *Brach* hound bitch 108 *gall* sore, source of irritation 114 *owest* borrow (?), own, keep (?) 115 *goest* walk 116 *Learn* hear, listen to; *trowest* believe 117 *Set . . . throwest* stake less than you throw for (i.e. play for odds) 120–21 *have . . . score* i.e. do better than break even 123 *breath* voice, counsel (reliable only when paid for) 127–28 *rent . . . land* (nothing, since he has no land) 131 *bitter, sweet* satirical, non-satirical 136 *Do . . . stand* (the Fool thus identifying Lear as his own foolish counsellor) 140 *found out* revealed (since Lear is the *born* fool as distinct from himself, the fool in *motley*, professionally satirical) 145 *let me* (i.e. be all fool, since they seek a share of folly) 148 *snatching* (like greedy courtiers seeking shares in royal patents of monopoly) 154 *bor'st . . . dirt* (thus foolishly reversing normal behavior) 156 *like myself* i.e. like a fool 157 *let . . . so* i.e. let him be whipped (as a fool) who mistakes this truth as my typical folly 158 *grace . . . year* favor at any time 159 *foppish* foolish 160 *their wits to wear* i.e. to use their intelligence 163 *used* practiced 168 *play bo-peep* i.e. act like a child 172 *An* if 178 *pared . . . middle* i.e. completely disposed of your wits (in disposing of your power) 180 *frontlet* band worn across the brow; frown 183–84 *O . . . figure* cipher without a digit to give it value 188 *crum* soft bread within the crust 189 *want* need 190 *shealed* shelled, empty; *peascod* pea-pod 191 *all-licensed* all privileged 193 *carp* complain 196 *safe* sure 198 *put it on* instigate it 199 *allowance* approval 200 *redresses sleep* correction lie dormant 201 *tender of* care for; *weal* state

202 Might in their working do you that offense,
Which else were shame, that then necessity
Will call discreet proceeding.
FOOL For you know, nuncle,
206   The hedge-sparrow fed the cuckoo so long
207   That it's had it head bit off by it young.
208 So out went the candle, and we were left darkling.
LEAR Are you our daughter?
GONERIL
I would you would make use of your good wisdom
211 (Whereof I know you are fraught) and put away
212 These dispositions which of late transport you
From what you rightly are.
FOOL May not an ass know when the cart draws the horse?
215 Whoop, Jug, I love thee!
LEAR
Does any here know me? This is not Lear.
Does Lear walk thus? speak thus? Where are his eyes?
218 Either his notion weakens, his discernings
219 Are lethargied – Ha! Waking? 'Tis not so.
Who is it that can tell me who I am?
FOOL Lear's shadow.
[LEAR
222 I would learn that; for, by the marks of sovereignty,
Knowledge, and reason, I should be false persuaded
I had daughters.
FOOL Which they will make an obedient father.]
LEAR Your name, fair gentlewoman?
GONERIL
227 This admiration, sir, is much o' th' savor
Of other your new pranks. I do beseech you
To understand my purposes aright.
As you are old and reverend, should be wise.
Here do you keep a hundred knights and squires,
232 Men so disordered, so deboshed and bold
That this our court, infected with their manners,
234 Shows like a riotous inn. Epicurism and lust
Makes it more like a tavern or a brothel
236 Than a graced palace. The shame itself doth speak
For instant remedy. Be then desired
By her that else will take the thing she begs ·
239 A little to disquantity your train,
240 And the remainders that shall still depend

To be such men as may besort your age,   241
Which know themselves, and you.   242
LEAR   Darkness and devils!
Saddle my horses; call my train together.
Degenerate bastard, I'll not trouble thee: 244
Yet have I left a daughter.
GONERIL
You strike my people, and your disordered rabble
Make servants of their betters.
      Enter Albany.
LEAR
Woe that too late repents. – [O, sir, are you come?]
Is it your will? Speak, sir. – Prepare my horses.
Ingratitude! thou marble-hearted fiend,
More hideous when thou show'st thee in a child
Than the sea-monster.
ALBANY   Pray, sir, be patient.
LEAR
Detested kite, thou liest.   253
My train are men of choice and rarest parts,   254
That all particulars of duty know
And in the most exact regard support   256
The worships of their name. O most small fault,   257
How ugly didst thou in Cordelia show!
Which, like an engine, wrenched my frame of nature   259
From the fixed place; drew from my heart all love
And added to the gall. O Lear, Lear, Lear!   261
Beat at this gate that let thy folly in
      [Strikes his head.]
And thy dear judgment out. Go, go, my people.
ALBANY
My lord, I am guiltless, as I am ignorant
Of what hath moved you.
LEAR   It may be so, my lord.
Hear, Nature, hear; dear goddess, hear:
Suspend thy purpose if thou didst intend
To make this creature fruitful.
Into her womb convey sterility,
Dry up in her the organs of increase,
And from her derogate body never spring   271
A babe to honor her. If she must teem,   272
Create her child of spleen, that it may live   273
And be a thwart disnatured torment to her.   274
Let it stamp wrinkles in her brow of youth,
With cadent tears fret channels in her cheeks,   276
Turn all her mother's pains and benefits   277
To laughter and contempt, that she may feel
How sharper than a serpent's tooth it is
To have a thankless child. Away, away!   *Exit.*
ALBANY
Now, gods that we adore, whereof comes this?
GONERIL
Never afflict yourself to know more of it,
But let his disposition have that scope   283
As dotage gives it.
      Enter Lear.
LEAR
What, fifty of my followers at a clap?
Within a fortnight?
ALBANY   What's the matter, sir?
LEAR
I'll tell thee. *[to Goneril]* Life and death, I am ashamed
That thou hast power to shake my manhood thus!

202–04 *Might . . . proceeding* in their operation might be considered humiliating to you but, under the circumstances, are merely prudent 206 *cuckoo* (an image suggesting illegitimacy as well as voraciousness, since the cuckoo lays its eggs in the nests of other birds) 207 *it* its 208 *darkling* in the dark (like the dead hedge-sparrow and the threatened Lear) 211 *fraught* freighted, laden 212 *dispositions* moods 215 *Jug* Joan (evidently part of some catch-phrase) 218 *notion* understanding 219 *Ha! Waking* i.e. so I am really awake (presumably accompanied by the 'business' of pinching himself) 222 *marks of sovereignty* evidences that I am King (and hence the father of the princesses) 227 *admiration* air of wonderment 232 *deboshed* debauched 234 *Epicurism* loose living 236 *graced* honored; *shame* disgrace 239 *disquantity your train* reduce the size of your retinue 240 *depend* be attached 241 *besort* befit 242 *Which know* i.e. who are aware of the status of 244 *Degenerate* unnatural, fallen away from kind 253 *Detested kite* detestable bird of prey 254 *parts* accomplishments 256 *exact regard* careful attention, punctiliousness 257 *worships* honor 259 *engine* destructive contrivance of war 259–60 *wrenched . . . place* set askew my natural structure, distorted my normal self 261 *gall* bitterness 271 *derogate* degraded 272 *teem* increase 273 *spleen* ill-humor, spitefulness 274 *thwart disnatured* perverse unnatural 276 *cadent* falling; *fret* wear 277 *pains and benefits* care and offerings 283 *disposition* mood

289 That these hot tears, which break from me perforce,
Should make thee worth them. Blasts and fogs upon thee!
291 Th' untented woundings of a father's curse
292 Pierce every sense about thee! Old fond eyes,
293 Beweep this cause again I'll pluck ye out
294 And cast you, with the waters that you loose,
295 To temper clay. [Yea, is it come to this?]
Ha! Let it be so. I have another daughter,
297 Who I am sure is kind and comfortable.
When she shall hear this of thee, with her nails
She'll flay thy wolvish visage. Thou shalt find
300 That I'll resume the shape which thou dost think
I have cast off for ever.

Exit [Lear with Kent and Attendants].

GONERIL   Do you mark that?

ALBANY
302 I cannot be so partial, Goneril,
To the great love I bear you –

GONERIL
Pray you, content. – What, Oswald, ho!
[To Fool]
You, sir, more knave than fool, after your master!
306 FOOL Nuncle Lear, nuncle Lear, tarry. Take the fool with thee.
A fox, when one has caught her,
And such a daughter,
310 Should sure to the slaughter,
311 If my cap would buy a halter.
312 So the fool follows after.   *Exit.*

GONERIL
313 This man hath had good counsel – a hundred knights!
314 'Tis politic and safe to let him keep
315 At point a hundred knights – yes, that on every dream,
316 Each buzz, each fancy, each complaint, dislike,
He may enguard his dotage with their pow'rs
318 And hold our lives in mercy. – Oswald, I say!

ALBANY
Well, you may fear too far.

GONERIL   Safer than trust too far.
320 Let me still take away the harms I fear,
321 Not fear still to be taken. I know his heart.
What he hath uttered I have writ my sister.
If she sustain him and his hundred knights,
When I have showed th' unfitness –

Enter Steward [Oswald].   How now, Oswald?
What, have you writ that letter to my sister?

OSWALD Ay, madam.

GONERIL
327 Take you some company, and away to horse.
328 Inform her full of my particular fear,
And thereto add such reasons of your own
330 As may compact it more. Get you gone,
And hasten your return. *[Exit Oswald.]* No, no, my lord,
332 This milky gentleness and course of yours,
Though I condemn not, yet under pardon,
334 You are much more atasked for want of wisdom
335 Than praised for harmful mildness.

ALBANY
How far your eyes may pierce I cannot tell;
Striving to better, oft we mar what's well.

GONERIL Nay then –

339 ALBANY Well, well; th' event.   *Exeunt.*

                            *

Enter Lear, Kent, and Fool.   I, v

LEAR Go you before to Gloucester with these letters. Acquaint my daughter no further with anything you know than comes from her demand out of the letter. If your 3 diligence be not speedy, I shall be there afore you.

KENT I will not sleep, my lord, till I have delivered your letter.   *Exit.*

FOOL If a man's brains were in's heels, were't not in danger of kibes?   8

LEAR Ay, boy.

FOOL Then I prithee be merry. Thy wit shall not go slip- 10 shod.

LEAR Ha, ha, ha.

FOOL Shalt see thy other daughter will use thee kindly; 12 for though she's as like this as a crab 's like an apple, yet 13 I can tell what I can tell.

LEAR What canst tell, boy?

FOOL She will taste as like this as a crab does to a crab. Thou canst tell why one's nose stands i' th' middle on's face?

LEAR No.

FOOL Why, to keep one's eyes of either side 's nose, that what a man cannot smell out he may spy into.

LEAR I did her wrong.   21

FOOL Canst tell how an oyster makes his shell?

LEAR No.

FOOL Nor I neither; but I can tell why a snail has a house.

LEAR Why?

FOOL Why, to put 's head in; not to give it away to his daughters, and leave his horns without a case.   27

LEAR I will forget my nature. So kind a father! – Be my 28 horses ready?

FOOL Thy asses are gone about 'em. The reason why the seven stars are no moe than seven is a pretty reason.   31

LEAR Because they are not eight.

FOOL Yes indeed. Thou wouldst make a good fool.

LEAR To take 't again perforce – Monster ingratitude!   34

FOOL If thou wert my fool, nuncle, I'ld have thee beaten for being old before thy time.

LEAR How's that?

FOOL Thou shouldst not have been old till thou hadst been wise.

289 *perforce* by force, against my will 291 *untented* untentable, too deep for treatment by a probe 292 *sense about* faculty possessed by; *fond* foolish 293 *Beweep this cause* if you weep over this matter 294 *loose* let loose 295 *temper* soften 297 *comfortable* ready to comfort 300 *shape* i.e. role of authority 302–03 *partial . . . To* made partial . . . by 306 *the fool* i.e. both your fool and your folly 310 *slaughter* hanging and quartering 311, 312 *halter, after* (pronounced 'hauter,' 'auter') 313 *good counsel* i.e. from such company (ironic) 314 *politic* prudent 315 *At point* in arms 316 *buzz* murmur 318 *in mercy* at his mercy 320 *still . . . harms* always eliminate the sources of injury 321 *still . . . taken* always to be overtaken (by them) 327 *some company* an escort 328 *particular* own 330 *compact it more* substantiate it further 332 *milky . . . course* mildly gentle way 334 *atasked* censured, taken to task 335 *harmful mildness* mildness that proves harmful 339 *th' event* the outcome, i.e. we shall see what happens
I, v The courtyard of Albany's palace 3 *demand out of* i.e. questioning provoked by reading 8 *kibes* chilblains 10 *wit . . . slipshod* intelligence (brains) shall not go slippered (because of *kibes*) 12 *Shalt* thou shalt; *kindly* after her kind, i.e. in the same way as this daughter 13 *crab* crab apple 21 *her* i.e. Cordelia (the first of the remarkable intimations of Lear's inner thoughts in this scene) 27 *horns* i.e. snail's horns (with pun on cuckold's horns; the legitimacy of Goneril and Regan being, figuratively, suspect throughout); *case* covering 28 *nature* i.e. fatherly instincts 31 *moe* more 34 *perforce* by force

LEAR
O, let me not be mad, not mad, sweet heaven!
41 Keep me in temper; I would not be mad!
    [Enter a Gentleman.]
How now, are the horses ready?
GENTLEMAN Ready, my lord.
LEAR Come, boy.
FOOL
45 She that's a maid now, and laughs at my departure,
Shall not be a maid long, unless things be cut shorter.
                Exeunt.

             *

II, i   *Enter Bastard [Edmund] and Curan severally.*
1 **EDMUND** Save thee, Curan.
CURAN And you, sir. I have been with your father, and
given him notice that the Duke of Cornwall and Regan
his Duchess will be here with him this night.
EDMUND How comes that?
CURAN Nay, I know not. You have heard of the news
abroad – I mean the whispered ones, for they are yet but
8 ear-kissing arguments?
EDMUND Not I. Pray you, what are they?
10 **CURAN** Have you heard of no likely wars toward, 'twixt
the Dukes of Cornwall and Albany?
EDMUND Not a word.
CURAN You may do, then, in time. Fare you well, sir. *Exit.*
EDMUND
14 The Duke be here to-night? The better best!
15 This weaves itself perforce into my business.
My father hath set guard to take my brother,
17 And I have one thing of a queasy question
18 Which I must act. Briefness and fortune, work!
Brother, a word: descend. Brother, I say!
    Enter Edgar.
My father watches. O sir, fly this place.
Intelligence is given where you are hid.
You have now the good advantage of the night.
Have you not spoken 'gainst the Duke of Cornwall?
He's coming hither; now i' th' night, i' th' haste,
And Regan with him. Have you nothing said
26 Upon his party 'gainst the Duke of Albany?
27 Advise yourself.
EDGAR   I am sure on't, not a word.
EDMUND
I hear my father coming. Pardon me:

In cunning I must draw my sword upon you.   29
Draw, seem to defend yourself; now quit you well. –   30
Yield! Come before my father! Light ho, here! –
Fly, brother. – Torches, torches! – So farewell.
              Exit Edgar.
Some blood drawn on me would beget opinion
Of my more fierce endeavor.
    [Wounds his arm.]   I have seen drunkards
Do more than this in sport. – Father, father!
Stop, stop! No help?
    Enter Gloucester, and Servants with torches.
GLOUCESTER
Now, Edmund, where's the villain?
EDMUND
Here stood he in the dark, his sharp sword out,
Mumbling of wicked charms, conjuring the moon
To stand auspicious mistress.
GLOUCESTER   But where is he?
EDMUND
Look, sir, I bleed.
GLOUCESTER   Where is the villain, Edmund?
EDMUND
Fled this way, sir, when by no means he could –
GLOUCESTER
Pursue him, ho! Go after.   *[Exeunt some Servants.]*
            By no means what?
EDMUND
Persuade me to the murder of your lordship;
But that I told him the revenging gods
'Gainst parricides did all the thunder bend;   46
Spoke with how manifold and strong a bond
The child was bound to th' father – sir, in fine,   48
Seeing how loathly opposite I stood   49
To his unnatural purpose, in fell motion   50
With his preparèd sword he charges home
My unprovided body, latched mine arm;   52
And when he saw my best alarumed spirits   53
Bold in the quarrel's right, roused to th' encounter,   54
Or whether gasted by the noise I made,   55
Full suddenly he fled.
GLOUCESTER   Let him fly far.
Not in this land shall he remain uncaught;
And found – dispatch. The noble Duke my master,   58
My worthy arch and patron, comes to-night: 59
By his authority I will proclaim it
That he which finds him shall deserve our thanks,
Bringing the murderous coward to the stake;
He that conceals him, death.
EDMUND
When I dissuaded him from his intent
And found him pight to do it, with curst speech   65
I threatened to discover him. He replied,   66
'Thou unpossessing bastard, dost thou think,   67
If I would stand against thee, would the reposal   68
Of any trust, virtue, or worth in thee
Make thy words faithed? No. What I should deny   70
(As this I would, ay, though thou didst produce
My very character) I'ld turn it all   72
To thy suggestion, plot, and damnèd practice;   73
And thou must make a dullard of the world,   74
If they not thought the profits of my death   75
Were very pregnant and potential spirits   76
To make thee seek it.'
GLOUCESTER   O strange and fast'ned villain!   77

41 *in temper* properly balanced   **45–46** *She . . . shorter* (an indecent gag addressed to the audience, calculated to embarrass the maids who joined in the laughter)
II, i The Earl of Gloucester's castle   1 *Save* God save   8 *ear-kissing arguments* whispered topics   10 *likely* probable; *toward* impending   14 *better best* (hyperbole)   15 *perforce* of necessity (?), of its own accord (?)   17 *of . . . question* delicately balanced as to outcome, touch-and-go   18 *Briefness and fortune* decisive speed and good luck   26 *Upon his party 'gainst* i.e. reflecting upon his feud against   27 *Advise yourself* take thought; *on't* of it   29 *In cunning* i.e. as a ruse   30 *quit you* acquit yourself   46 *bend* aim   48 *in fine* finally   49 *loathly opposite* in loathing opposition   50 *fell* deadly   52 *unprovided* undefended; *latched* lanced, pierced   53 *best alarumed* fully aroused   54 *Bold . . . right* confident in the justice of the cause   55 *gasted* struck aghast   58 *dispatch* (equivalent to 'death' or 'finis')   59 *arch* superior   65 *pight* determined, set; *curst* angry   66 *discover* expose   67 *unpossessing* having no claim, landless   68 *reposal* placing   70 *faithed* believed   72 *character* written testimony   73 *suggestion* instigation; *practice* devices   74 *make . . . world* i.e. consider everyone stupid   75 *not thought* did not think   76 *pregnant . . . spirits* teeming and powerful spirits, i.e. the devils which 'possess' him   77 *fast'ned* confirmed

78   Would he deny his letter, said he ? [I never got him.]
     Tucket within.
   Hark, the Duke's trumpets. I know not why he comes.
   All ports I'll bar ; the villain shall not 'scape ;
   The Duke must grant me that. Besides, his picture
   I will send far and near, that all the kingdom
   May have due note of him ; and of my land,
   Loyal and natural boy, I'll work the means
85   To make thee capable.
     Enter Cornwall, Regan, and Attendants.

CORNWALL
   How now, my noble friend ? Since I came hither
87   (Which I can call but now) I have heard strange news.

REGAN
   If it be true, all vengeance comes too short
   Which can pursue th' offender. How dost, my lord ?

GLOUCESTER
   O madam, my old heart is cracked, it's cracked.

REGAN
   What, did my father's godson seek your life ?
   He whom my father named, your Edgar ?

GLOUCESTER
   O lady, lady, shame would have it hid.

REGAN
   Was he not companion with the riotous knights
   That tended upon my father ?

GLOUCESTER
   I know not, madam. 'Tis too bad, too bad.

EDMUND
97   Yes, madam, he was of that consort.

REGAN
98   No marvel then though he were ill affected.
99   'Tis they have put him on the old man's death,
100   To have th' expense and waste of his revenues.
   I have this present evening from my sister
   Been well informed of them, and with such cautions
   That, if they come to sojourn at my house,
   I'll not be there.

CORNWALL   Nor I, assure thee, Regan.
   Edmund, I hear that you have shown your father
106   A childlike office.

EDMUND   It was my duty, sir.

GLOUCESTER
107   He did bewray his practice, and received
   This hurt you see, striving to apprehend him.

CORNWALL
   Is he pursued ?

GLOUCESTER   Ay, my good lord.

CORNWALL
   If he be taken, he shall never more
111   Be feared of doing harm. Make your own purpose,
   How in my strength you please. For you, Edmund,
113   Whose virtue and obedience doth this instant
   So much commend itself, you shall be ours.
   Natures of such deep trust we shall much need ;
   You we first seize on.

EDMUND   I shall serve you, sir,
   Truly, however else.

GLOUCESTER   For him I thank your Grace.

CORNWALL
   You know not why we came to visit you ?

REGAN
   Thus out of season, threading dark-eyed night.
120   Occasions, noble Gloucester, of some prize,

   Wherein we must have use of your advice.
   Our father he hath writ, so hath our sister,
   Of differences, which I best thought it fit   123
   To answer from our home. The several messengers   124
   From hence attend dispatch. Our good old friend,   125
   Lay comforts to your bosom, and bestow   126
   Your needful counsel to our businesses,   127
   Which craves the instant use.   128

GLOUCESTER   I serve you, madam.
   Your Graces are right welcome.   *Exeunt. Flourish.*

*

     Enter Kent and Steward [Oswald], severally.   II, ii

OSWALD   Good dawning to thee, friend. Art of this house ?   1
KENT   Ay.
OSWALD   Where may we set our horses ?
KENT   I' th' mire.
OSWALD   Prithee, if thou lov'st me, tell me.
KENT   I love thee not.
OSWALD   Why then, I care not for thee.
KENT   If I had thee in Lipsbury Pinfold, I would make   8
   thee care for me.
OSWALD   Why dost thou use me thus ? I know thee not.
KENT   Fellow, I know thee.
OSWALD   What dost thou know me for ?
KENT   A knave, a rascal, an eater of broken meats ; a base,   13
   proud, shallow, beggarly, three-suited, hundred-pound,   14
   filthy worsted-stocking knave ; a lily-livered, action-   15
   taking, whoreson, glass-gazing, superserviceable, finical   16
   rogue ; one-trunk-inheriting slave ; one that wouldst be a   17
   bawd in way of good service, and art nothing but the
   composition of a knave, beggar, coward, pander, and the   19
   son and heir of a mongrel bitch ; one whom I will beat
   into clamorous whining if thou deny'st the least syllable
   of thy addition.   22
OSWALD   Why, what a monstrous fellow art thou, thus to
   rail on one that is neither known of thee nor knows thee !
KENT   What a brazen-faced varlet art thou to deny thou
   knowest me ! Is it two days ago since I tripped up thy
   heels and beat thee before the King ? *[Draws his sword.]*
   Draw, you rogue, for though it be night, yet the moon
   shines. I'll make a sop o' th' moonshine of you. You   29
   whoreson cullionly barbermonger, draw !   30

---

78 *got* begot ; **s.d.** *Tucket* (personal signature in trumpet notes)   85 *capable* i.e. legitimate, able to inherit   87 *call* i.e. say was   97 *consort* company, set   98 *affected* disposed   99 *put* set   100 *expense and waste* wasteful expenditure   106 *childlike* filial   107 *bewray his practice* expose his plot   111 *of doing* lest he do   111–12 *Make . . . please* i.e. accomplish your purpose, making free use of my powers   113 *virtue and obedience* virtuous obedience   120 *prize* price, importance   123 *differences* quarrels ; *which* (refers, indefinitely, to the whole situation)   124 *answer . . . home* cope with away from home (where she need not receive Lear)   125 *attend dispatch* i.e. await settlement of the business   126 *Lay . . . bosom* be consoled (about your own trouble)   127 *needful* needed   128 *craves . . . use* requires immediate transaction (?), requires use of your counsel (?)
II, ii Before Gloucester's castle   1 *dawning* (perhaps indicating that it is too early for 'good morning') ; *Art . . . house* i.e. do you belong to this household   8 *Lipsbury Pinfold* i.e. between the teeth (cant term : 'pen in the region of the lips')   13 *broken meats* scraps   14 *three-suited* with three suits (the wardrobe allowed serving-men) ; *hundred-pound* (the minimal estate for anyone aspiring to gentility)   15 *worsted-stocking* (serving-men's attire)   15–16 *action-taking* i.e. cowardly (resorting to law instead of fighting)   16 *glass-gazing, superserviceable, finical* i.e. conceited, toadying, foppish   17 *inheriting* possessing   17–18 *a bawd . . . service* i.e. a pander, if pleasing your employer required it   19 *composition* composite   22 *addition* titles   29 *sop o' th' moonshine* i.e. something that sops up moonshine through its perforations   30 *cullionly barbermonger* vile fop (i.e. always dealing with hairdressers)

OSWALD Away, I have nothing to do with thee.

KENT Draw, you rascal. You come with letters against the
33 King, and take Vanity the puppet's part against the
34 royalty of her father. Draw, you rogue, or I'll so car-
35 bonado your shanks. Draw, you rascal. Come your ways!

OSWALD Help, ho! Murder! Help!

37 KENT Strike, you slave! Stand, rogue! Stand, you neat
slave! Strike!
[Beats him.]

OSWALD Help, ho! Murder, murder!
Enter Bastard [Edmund, with his rapier drawn],
Cornwall, Regan, Gloucester, Servants.

EDMUND How now? What's the matter? Part!

41 KENT With you, goodman boy, if you please! Come, I'll
42 flesh ye; come on, young master.

GLOUCESTER Weapons? Arms? What's the matter here?

CORNWALL Keep peace, upon your lives. He dies that
strikes again. What is the matter?

REGAN The messengers from our sister and the King.

CORNWALL What is your difference? Speak.

OSWALD I am scarce in breath, my lord.

49 KENT No marvel, you have so bestirred your valor. You
50 cowardly rascal, Nature disclaims in thee. A tailor made
thee.

CORNWALL Thou art a strange fellow. A tailor make a
man?

53 KENT A tailor, sir. A stonecutter or a painter could not
have made him so ill, though they had been but two
years o' th' trade.

CORNWALL
Speak yet, how grew your quarrel?

OSWALD This ancient ruffian, sir, whose life I have
58 spared at suit of his gray beard –

59 KENT Thou whoreson zed, thou unnecessary letter! My
60 lord, if you will give me leave, I will tread this unbolted
61 villain into mortar and daub the wall of a jakes with him.
62 Spare my gray beard? you wagtail.

CORNWALL
Peace, sirrah!

You beastly knave, know you no reverence?   64

KENT
Yes, sir, but anger hath a privilege.

CORNWALL
Why art thou angry?

KENT
That such a slave as this should wear a sword,
Who wears no honesty. Such smiling rogues as these
Like rats oft bite the holy cords atwain   69
Which are too intrinse t' unloose; smooth every passion   70
That in the natures of their lords rebel,   71
Being oil to fire, snow to the colder moods;   72
Renege, affirm, and turn their halcyon beaks   73
With every gale and vary of their masters,   74
Knowing naught, like dogs, but following.
A plague upon your epileptic visage!   76
Smile you my speeches, as I were a fool?   77
Goose, if I had you upon Sarum Plain,   78
I'ld drive ye cackling home to Camelot.   79

CORNWALL
What, art thou mad, old fellow?

GLOUCESTER
How fell you out? Say that.

KENT
No contraries hold more antipathy   82
Than I and such a knave.

CORNWALL
Why dost thou call him knave? What is his fault?

KENT
His countenance likes me not.

CORNWALL
No more perchance does mine, nor his, nor hers.

KENT
Sir, 'tis my occupation to be plain:
I have seen better faces in my time
Than stands on any shoulder that I see
Before me at this instant.

CORNWALL   This is some fellow
Who, having been praised for bluntness, doth affect
A saucy roughness, and constrains the garb   92
Quite from his nature. He cannot flatter, he;
An honest mind and plain – he must speak truth.
An they will take it, so; if not, he's plain.
These kind of knaves I know which in this plainness
Harbor more craft and more corrupter ends
Than twenty silly-ducking observants   98
That stretch their duties nicely.   99

KENT
Sir, in good faith, in sincere verity,
Under th' allowance of your great aspect,   101
Whose influence, like the wreath of radiant fire   102
On flick'ring Phoebus' front –   103

CORNWALL   What mean'st by this?

KENT To go out of my dialect, which you discommend so   104
much. I know, sir, I am no flatterer. He that beguiled   105
you in a plain accent was a plain knave, which, for my
part, I will not be, though I should win your displeasure   107
to entreat me to 't.

CORNWALL
What was th' offense you gave him?

OSWALD
I never gave him any.
It pleased the King his master very late   111
To strike at me, upon his misconstruction;   112

---

33 *Vanity the puppet* i.e. Goneril (here equated with a stock figure in morality plays, now dwindled into puppet shows) 34 *carbonado* (cut into strips or cubes) 35 *your ways* get along 37 *neat* primping 41 *goodman boy* (doubly contemptuous, since peasants were addressed as 'goodmen') 42 *flesh ye* give you your first taste of blood 49 *bestirred* exercised 50 *disclaims* claims no part 53 *stonecutter* sculptor 58 *at suit of* on the plea of, moved to mercy by 59 *zed* (last and least useful of letters) 60 *unbolted* unsifted, crude 61 *jakes* privy 62 *wagtail* (any of several birds whose tail-feathers wag or bob, suggesting obsequiousness or effeminacy) 64 *beastly* beast-like, irrational 69 *holy cords* sacred bonds (between parents and children, husbands and wives, man and God) 70 *intrinse* intrinsic, inextricable; *smooth* flatter, cater to 71 *rebel* (i.e. against reason and moral restraint) 72 *Being . . . moods* (i.e. feeders of intemperance) 73 *Renege* deny; *halcyon beaks* kingfisher beaks (supposedly serving as weather vanes when the birds were hung up by their necks) 74 *gale and vary* varying wind 76 *epileptic* contorted in a grin (?) 77 *Smile you* smile you at, mock you 78 *Sarum Plain* Salisbury Plain (said to have been associated with geese, but the allusion remains cryptic) 79 *Camelot* legendary seat of King Arthur, variously sited at Winchester, near Cadbury, in Wales, etc. 82 *contraries* opposites 92–93 *constrains . . . nature* distorts the plain fashion from its true nature, caricatures it 98 *silly-ducking observants* ludicrously bowing form-servers 99 *nicely* fussily 101 *allowance* approval; *aspect* (1) appearance, (2) heavenly position 102 *influence* astrological force 103 *Phoebus' front* sun's forehead (i.e. face) 104 *go . . . dialect* depart from my way of speaking 105 *He* (the type of plain-speaker Cornwall has condemned) 107–08 *though . . . to't* though I should persuade your disapproving self to beg me to do so (? with *displeasure* sarcastically substituted for 'grace') 111 *very late* quite recently 112 *misconstruction* misunderstanding

113 When he, compact, and flattering his displeasure,
Tripped me behind; being down, insulted, railed,
115 And put upon him such a deal of man
116 That worthied him, got praises of the King
117 For him attempting who was self-subdued;
118 And, in the fleshment of this dread exploit,
Drew on me here again.
119 KENT   None of these rogues and cowards
But Ajax is their fool.
CORNWALL   Fetch forth the stocks!
121 You stubborn ancient knave, you reverent braggart,
We'll teach you.
KENT   Sir, I am too old to learn.
Call not your stocks for me, I serve the King –
On whose employment I was sent to you;
125 You shall do small respect, show too bold malice
126 Against the grace and person of my master,
Stocking his messenger.
CORNWALL
Fetch forth the stocks. As I have life and honor,
There shall he sit till noon.
REGAN
Till noon? Till night, my lord, and all night too.
KENT
Why, madam, if I were your father's dog,
You should not use me so.
REGAN   Sir, being his knave, I will.
CORNWALL
133 This is a fellow of the selfsame color
134 Our sister speaks of. Come, bring away the stocks.
Stocks brought out.
GLOUCESTER
Let me beseech your Grace not to do so.
[His fault is much, and the good King his master
137 Will check him for't. Your purposed low correction
138 Is such as basest and contemnèd'st wretches
For pilf'rings and most common trespasses
Are punished with.]
The King his master needs must take it ill
142 That he, so slightly valued in his messenger,
Should have him thus restrained.
143 CORNWALL   I'll answer that.
REGAN
My sister may receive it much more worse,
To have her gentleman abused, assaulted,
[For following her affairs. Put in his legs.]
[Kent is put in the stocks.]
CORNWALL
Come, my lord, away!
Exit [with all but Gloucester and Kent].
GLOUCESTER
I am sorry for thee, friend. 'Tis the Duke's pleasure,
149 Whose disposition all the world well knows
150 Will not be rubbed nor stopped. I'll entreat for thee.
KENT
151 Pray do not, sir. I have watched and travelled hard.
Some time I shall sleep out, the rest I'll whistle.
153 A good man's fortune may grow out at heels.
154 Give you good morrow.
GLOUCESTER
155 The Duke's to blame in this. 'Twill be ill taken. *Exit.*
KENT
156 Good King, that must approve the common saw,
157 Thou out of heaven's benediction com'st

To the warm sun.
Approach, thou beacon to this under globe,   159
That by thy comfortable beams I may
Peruse this letter. Nothing almost sees miracles   161
But misery. I know 'tis from Cordelia,
Who hath most fortunately been informed
Of my obscurèd course. And shall find time   164
From this enormous state, seeking to give   165
Losses their remedies. – All weary and o'erwatched,   166
Take vantage, heavy eyes, not to behold   167
This shameful lodging. Fortune, good night;   168
Smile once more; turn thy wheel.   169
[Sleeps.]
Enter Edgar.   II, iii
EDGAR
I heard myself proclaimed,
And by the happy hollow of a tree   2
Escaped the hunt. No port is free, no place
That guard and most unusual vigilance
Does not attend my taking. Whiles I may 'scape,   5
I will preserve myself; and am bethought   6
To take the basest and most poorest shape
That ever penury, in contempt of man,
Brought near to beast: my face I'll grime with filth,
Blanket my loins, elf all my hairs in knots,   10
And with presented nakedness outface   11
The winds and persecutions of the sky.
The country gives me proof and precedent   13
Of Bedlam beggars, who, with roaring voices,   14
Strike in their numbed and mortified bare arms   15
Pins, wooden pricks, nails, sprigs of rosemary;   16
And with this horrible object, from low farms,   17
Poor pelting villages, sheepcotes, and mills,   18
Sometimes with lunatic bans, sometime with prayers,   19
Enforce their charity. Poor Turlygod, poor Tom,   20
That's something yet: Edgar I nothing am.   21
Exit.
Enter Lear, Fool, and Gentleman.   II, iv
LEAR
'Tis strange that they should so depart from home,
And not send back my messenger.

113 *compact* in league with   115 *And put . . . man* i.e. affected such excessive manliness   116 *worthied* enhanced his worth   117 *For him . . . self-subdued* for assailing him (Oswald) who chose not to resist   118 *fleshment of* bloodthirstiness induced by   119–20 *None . . . fool* i.e. the Ajax type, stupidly belligerent, is the favorite butt of cowardly rogues like Oswald   121 *stubborn* rude; *reverent* aged   125 *malice* ill will   126 *grace* royal honor   133 *color* kind   134 *away* along   137 *check* rebuke; *purposed* intended   138 *contemnèd'st* most harshly sentenced   142 *slightly valued in* i.e. little respected in the person of   143 *answer* answer for   149 *disposition* inclination   150 *rubbed* deflected (bowling term)   151 *watched* gone sleepless   153 *A good . . . heels* i.e. it is no disgrace to decline in fortune   154 *Give* God give   155 *taken* received   156 *approve* demonstrate the truth of; *saw* saying, proverb   157–58 *Thou . . . sun* (proverb, meaning from better to worse, i.e. from heavenly shelter to earthly exposure – 'the heat of the day')   159 *beacon . . . globe* i.e. the sun (here viewed as benign)   161–62 *Nothing . . . misery* i.e. miraculous aid is seldom seen (or searched for?) except by the miserable   164 *obscurèd* disguised   164–66 *And . . . remedies* (incoherent: perhaps corrupt, or perhaps snatches read from the letter)   165 *enormous state* monstrous situation   166 *Losses* reverses   167 *vantage* i.e. advantage of sleep   168 *lodging* (in the stocks)   169 *wheel* (Fortune's wheel was represented as vertical. Kent is at its bottom.)
II, iii   2 *happy hollow* i.e. lucky hiding-place   5 *attend my taking* contemplate my capture   6 *bethought* in mind   10 *elf* tangle (into 'elf-locks')   11 *presented* a show of   13 *proof* example   14 *Bedlam* (see I, ii, 131–32n.)   15 *Strike* stick; *mortified* deadened to pain   16 *pricks* skewers   17 *object* picture   18 *pelting* paltry   19 *bans* curses   20 *Turlygod* (unidentified, but evidently another name for a Tom o' Bedlam)   21 *Edgar* i.e. as Edgar

GENTLEMAN   As I learned,
3   The night before there was no purpose in them
4   Of this remove.
KENT   Hail to thee, noble master.
LEAR Ha!
   Mak'st thou this shame thy pastime?
KENT   No, my lord.
7 FOOL Ha, ha, he wears cruel garters. Horses are tied by
   the heads, dogs and bears by th' neck, monkeys by th'
9   loins, and men by th' legs. When a man 's over-lusty at
10   legs, then he wears wooden nether-stocks.
LEAR
   What's he that hath so much thy place mistook
   To set thee here?
KENT   It is both he and she,
   Your son and daughter.
LEAR No.
KENT Yes.
LEAR No, I say.
KENT I say yea.
[LEAR No, no, they would not.
KENT Yes, they have.]
LEAR
   By Jupiter, I swear no!
KENT
   By Juno, I swear ay!
LEAR   They durst not do't;
   They could not, would not do't. 'Tis worse than murder
23 To do upon respect such violent outrage.
24 Resolve me with all modest haste which way
   Thou mightst deserve or thy impose this usage,
   Coming from us.
KENT   My lord, when at their home
27 I did commend your Highness' letters to them,
   Ere I was risen from the place that showed
   My duty kneeling, came there a reeking post,
30 Stewed in his haste, half breathless, panting forth
   From Goneril his mistress salutations;
32 Delivered letters, spite of intermission,
33 Which presently they read; on whose contents
34 They summoned up their meiny, straight took horse,
   Commanded me to follow and attend
   The leisure of their answer, gave me cold looks;

And meeting here the other messenger,
Whose welcome I perceived had poisoned mine,
Being the very fellow which of late
Displayed so saucily against your Highness,   40
Having more man than wit about me, drew;   41
He raised the house with loud and coward cries.   42
Your son and daughter found this trespass worth
The shame which here it suffers.
FOOL Winter's not gone yet, if the wild geese fly that way.   45
     Fathers that wear rags
       Do make their children blind,   47
     But fathers that bear bags   48
       Shall see their children kind.
     Fortune, that arrant whore,   50
     Ne'er turns the key to th' poor.   51
But for all this, thou shalt have as many dolors for thy   52
daughters as thou canst tell in a year.   53
LEAR
   O, how this mother swells up toward my heart!   54
   Hysterica passio, down, thou climbing sorrow;   55
   Thy element's below. Where is this daughter?   56
KENT
   With the Earl, sir, here within.
LEAR   Follow me not;
   Stay here.   *Exit.*
GENTLEMAN
   Made you no more offense but what you speak of?
KENT None.
   How chance the King comes with so small a number?
FOOL An thou hadst been set i' th' stocks for that ques-
   tion, thou'dst well deserved it.
KENT Why, fool?
FOOL We'll set thee to school to an ant, to teach thee
   there's no laboring i' th' winter. All that follow their   66
   noses are led by their eyes but blind men, and there's not
   a nose among twenty but can smell him that's stinking.
   Let go thy hold when a great wheel runs down a hill, lest
   it break thy neck with following. But the great one that
   goes upward, let him draw thee after. When a wise man
   gives thee better counsel, give me mine again. I would
   have none but knaves follow it since a fool gives it.   73
       That sir which serves and seeks for gain,
         And follows but for form,   75
       Will pack when it begins to rain   76
         And leave thee in the storm.
       But I will tarry; the fool will stay,
         And let the wise man fly.
       The knave turns fool that runs away;   80
         The fool no knave, perdy.   81
KENT Where learned you this, fool?
FOOL Not i' th' stocks, fool.   83
     Enter Lear and Gloucester.
LEAR
   Deny to speak with me? They are sick, they are weary,
   They have travelled all the night? Mere fetches,   85
   The images of revolt and flying off!   86
   Fetch me a better answer.
GLOUCESTER   My dear lord,
   You know the fiery quality of the Duke,   88
   How unremovable and fixed he is
   In his own course.
LEAR   Vengeance, plague, death, confusion!
   Fiery? What quality? Why, Gloucester, Gloucester,
   I'ld speak with the Duke of Cornwall and his wife.

II, iv   **3** *purpose* intention   **4** *remove* removal   **7** *cruel* painful (with pun on 'crewel,' a yarn used in garters)   **9–10** *over-lusty at legs* i.e. too much on the go (?), or too much given to kicking (?)   **10** *nether-stocks* stockings (as distinct from 'upper-stocks' or breeches)   **23** *To . . . outrage* i.e. to show such outrageous disrespect   **24** *Resolve* enlighten; *modest* seemly   **27** *commend* entrust   **30** *Stewed* steaming   **32** *spite of intermission* in disregard of its being an interruption   **33** *presently* immediately; *on* on the strength of   **34** *meiny* attendants   **40** *Displayed* showed off   **41** *man* manhood; *wit* sense   **42** *raised* aroused   **45** *Winter's . . . way* i.e. the ill season continues according to these signs (with Cornwall and Regan equated with *wild geese*, proverbially evasive)   **47** *blind* (to their fathers' needs)   **48** *bags* (of gold)   **50** *Fortune . . . whore* (because so fickle and callous)   **51** *turns the key* i.e. opens the door   **52** *dolors* sorrows (with pun on 'dollars,' continental coins)   **53** *tell* count   **54, 55** *mother, Hysterica passio* hysteria (the popular and the medical terms)   **56** *element* proper place   **66** *no laboring . . . winter* (Lear, accompanied by *so small a number*, is equated with winter bereft of workers, such as ants)   **66–68** *All . . . stinking* i.e. almost anyone can smell out a person decayed in fortune   **73** *none but knaves* (here and in what follows the Fool repudiates his advice to abandon Lear)   **75** *form* show   **76** *pack* be off   **80** *The knave . . . away* i.e. faithlessness is the true folly   **81** *perdy* I swear (from '*par dieu*')   **83** *fool* (persiflage, but also a term of honor; cf. V, iii, 306n.)   **85** *fetches* counterfeit reasons, false likenesses of truth   **86** *images* true likenesses; *flying off* revolt   **88** *quality* disposition

GLOUCESTER
Well, my good lord, I have informed them so.

LEAR
Informed them? Dost thou understand me, man?

GLOUCESTER
Ay, my good lord.

LEAR
The King would speak with Cornwall. The dear father
97 Would with his daughter speak, commands – tends –
service.
Are they informed of this? My breath and blood!
Fiery? The fiery Duke, tell the hot Duke that –
No, but not yet. May be he is not well.
101 Infirmity doth still neglect all office
102 Whereto our health is bound. We are not ourselves
When nature, being oppressed, commands the mind
To suffer with the body. I'll forbear;
105 And am fallen out with my more headier will
To take the indisposed and sickly fit
For the sound man. – Death on my state! Wherefore
108 Should he sit here? This act persuades me
109 That this remotion of the Duke and her
110 Is practice only. Give me my servant forth.
Go tell the Duke and 's wife I'ld speak with them!
112 Now, presently! Bid them come forth and hear me,
Or at their chamber door I'll beat the drum
114 Till it cry sleep to death.

GLOUCESTER
I would have all well betwixt you.   *Exit.*

LEAR
O me, my heart, my rising heart! But down!
117 FOOL Cry to it, nuncle, as the cockney did to the eels when
118 she put 'em i' th' paste alive. She knapped 'em o' th' cox-
119 combs with a stick and cried, 'Down, wantons, down!'
'Twas her brother that, in pure kindness to his horse,
121 buttered his hay.
Enter Cornwall, Regan, Gloucester, Servants.

LEAR
Good morrow to you both.

CORNWALL   Hail to your Grace.
Kent here set at liberty.

REGAN
I am glad to see your Highness.

LEAR
Regan, I think you are. I know what reason
I have to think so. If thou shouldst not be glad,
126 I would divorce me from thy mother's tomb,
Sepulchring an adultress. [*to Kent*] O, are you free?
Some other time for that. – Beloved Regan,
Thy sister's naught. O Regan, she hath tied
Sharp-toothed unkindness, like a vulture, here.
I can scarce speak to thee. Thou'lt not believe
132 With how depraved a quality – O Regan!

REGAN
133 I pray you, sir, take patience. I have hope
You less know how to value her desert
135 Than she to scant her duty.

LEAR   Say? How is that?

REGAN
I cannot think my sister in the least
Would fail her obligation. If, sir, perchance
She have restrained the riots of your followers,
'Tis on such ground, and to such wholesome end,
As clears her from all blame.

LEAR
My curses on her!

REGAN   O, sir, you are old;
Nature in you stands on the very verge   142
Of his confine. You should be ruled, and led
By some discretion that discerns your state   144
Better than you yourself. Therefore I pray you
That to our sister you do make return;
Say you have wronged her.

LEAR   Ask her forgiveness?
Do you but mark how this becomes the house: 148
'Dear daughter, I confess that I am old.
[*Kneels.*]
Age is unnecessary. On my knees I beg
That you'll vouchsafe me raiment, bed, and food.'

REGAN
Good sir, no more. These are unsightly tricks.
Return you to my sister.

LEAR [*rises*]   Never, Regan.
She hath abated me of half my train,   154
Looked black upon me, struck me with her tongue
Most serpent-like upon the very heart.
All the stored vengeances of heaven fall
On her ingrateful top! Strike her young bones,   158
You taking airs, with lameness.   159

CORNWALL   Fie, sir, fie!

LEAR
You nimble lightnings, dart your blinding flames
Into her scornful eyes! Infect her beauty,
You fen-sucked fogs drawn by the pow'rful sun   162
To fall and blister –   163

REGAN   O the blessed gods!
So will you wish on me when the rash mood is on.

LEAR
No, Regan, thou shalt never have my curse.
Thy tender-hefted nature shall not give   166
Thee o'er to harshness. Her eyes are fierce, but thine
Do comfort, and not burn. 'Tis not in thee
To grudge my pleasures, to cut off my train,
To bandy hasty words, to scant my sizes,   170
And, in conclusion, to oppose the bolt   171
Against my coming in. Thou better know'st
The offices of nature, bond of childhood,   173
Effects of courtesy, dues of gratitude.   174
Thy half o' th' kingdom hast thou not forgot,
Wherein I thee endowed.

97 *tends* attends, awaits (?), tenders, offers (?) **101** *all office* duties **102** *Whereto . . . bound* to which, in health, we are bound **105** *headier* headstrong **108** *he* i.e. Kent **109** *remotion* remaining remote, inaccessible **110** *practice* trickery **112** *presently* immediately **114** *cry* pursue with noise (like a pack or 'cry' of hounds) **117** *cockney* city-dweller **118** *paste* pastry pie; *knapped* rapped **119** *wantons* i.e. frisky things **121** *buttered his hay* (another example of rustic humor at the expense of cockney inexperience) **126–27** *divorce . . . adultress* i.e. refuse to be buried with your mother since such a child as you must have been conceived in adultery **132** *how . . . quality* i.e. what innate depravity **133** *have hope* i.e. suspect **135** *scant* (in effect, a double negative; 'do' would be more logical though less emphatic) **142–43** *Nature . . . confine* i.e. your life nears the limit of its tenure **144** *some discretion . . . state* someone discerning enough to recognize your condition **148** *the house* household or family decorum **154** *abated* curtailed **158** *ingrateful top* ungrateful head **159** *taking* infectious **162** *fen-sucked* drawn up from swamps **163** *fall and blister* strike and raise blisters (such as those of smallpox) **166** *tender-hefted* swayed by tenderness, gently disposed **170** *bandy* volley; *sizes* allowances **171** *oppose the bolt* i.e. bar the door **173** *offices of nature* natural duties **174** *Effects* actions

176 REGAN   Good sir, to th' purpose.
          Tucket within.
    LEAR
      Who put my man i' th' stocks?
    CORNWALL   What trumpet's that?
    REGAN
178   I know't – my sister's. This approves her letter,
      That she would soon be here.
          Enter Steward [Oswald].   Is your lady come?
    LEAR
180   This is a slave, whose easy-borrowèd pride
181   Dwells in the fickle grace of her he follows.
182   Out, varlet, from my sight.
    CORNWALL   What means your Grace?
    LEAR
      Who stocked my servant? Regan, I have good hope
      Thou didst not know on't.
          Enter Goneril.   Who comes here? O heavens!
      If you do love old men, if your sweet sway
186   Allow obedience, if you yourselves are old,
187   Make it your cause. Send down, and take my part.
          [To Goneril]
      Art not ashamed to look upon this beard?
      O Regan, will you take her by the hand?
    GONERIL
      Why not by th' hand, sir? How have I offended?
191   All's not offense that indiscretion finds
      And dotage terms so.
192   LEAR   O sides, you are too tough!
      Will you yet hold? How came my man i' th' stocks?
    CORNWALL
      I set him there, sir; but his own disorders
195   Deserved much less advancement.
    LEAR   You? Did you?
    REGAN
196   I pray you, father, being weak, seem so.
      If till the expiration of your month
      You will return and sojourn with my sister,
      Dismissing half your train, come then to me.
      I am now from home, and out of that provision
201   Which shall be needful for your entertainment.
    LEAR
      Return to her, and fifty men dismissed?
      No, rather I abjure all roofs, and choose
204   To wage against the emnity o' th' air,
      To be a comrade with the wolf and owl,
206   Necessity's sharp pinch. Return with her?
207   Why, the hot-blooded France, that dowerless took
      Our youngest born, I could as well be brought
209   To knee his throne, and, squire-like, pension beg

      To keep base life afoot. Return with her?
      Persuade me rather to be slave and sumpter   211
      To this detested groom.   212
    GONERIL   At your choice, sir.
    LEAR
      I prithee, daughter, do not make me mad.
      I will not trouble thee, my child; farewell.
      We'll no more meet, no more see one another.
      But yet thou art my flesh, my blood, my daughter;
      Or rather a disease that's in my flesh,
      Which I must needs call mine. Thou art a boil,
      A plague-sore, or embossèd carbuncle   219
      In my corrupted blood. But I'll not chide thee.
      Let shame come when it will, I do not call it.
      I do not bid the thunder-bearer shoot,   222
      Nor tell tales of thee to high-judging Jove.   223
      Mend when thou canst, be better at thy leisure;
      I can be patient, I can stay with Regan,
      I and my hundred knights.
    REGAN   Not altogether so.
      I looked not for you yet, nor am provided
      For your fit welcome. Give ear, sir, to my sister;
      For those that mingle reason with your passion   229
      Must be content to think you old and so –
      But she knows what she does.
    LEAR   Is this well spoken?
    REGAN
      I dare avouch it, sir. What, fifty followers?   232
      Is it not well? What should you need of more?
      Yea, or so many, sith that both charge and danger 234
      Speak 'gainst so great a number? How in one house
      Should many people, under two commands,
      Hold amity? 'Tis hard, almost impossible.
    GONERIL
      Why might not you, my lord, receive attendance
      From those that she calls servants, or from mine?
    REGAN
      Why not, my lord? If then they chanced to slack ye, 240
      We could control them. If you will come to me
      (For now I spy a danger), I entreat you
      To bring but five-and-twenty. To no more
      Will I give place or notice.   244
    LEAR
      I gave you all.
    REGAN   And in good time you gave it.
    LEAR
      Made you my guardians, my depositaries,   246
      But kept a reservation to be followèd   247
      With such a number. What, must I come to you
      With five-and-twenty? Regan, said you so?
    REGAN
      And speak't again, my lord. No more with me.
    LEAR
      Those wicked creatures yet do look well-favored 251
      When others are more wicked; not being the worst
      Stands in some rank of praise.   253
          [To Goneril]   I'll go with thee.
      Thy fifty yet doth double five-and-twenty,
      And thou art twice her love.   255
    GONERIL   Hear me, my lord.
      What need you five-and-twenty? ten? or five?
      To follow in a house where twice so many
      Have a command to tend you?
    REGAN   What need one?

---

176 *purpose* point   178 *approves* confirms   180 *easy-borrowèd* acquired
on small security   181 *grace* favor   182 *varlet* low fellow   186 *Allow*
approve   187 *Make . . . cause* i.e. make my cause yours   191 *indiscretion
finds* ill judgment detects as such   192 *sides* breast (which should burst
with grief)   195 *less advancement* i.e. more abasement   196 *seem so*
i.e. act the part   201 *entertainment* lodging   204 *wage* fight   206 *Necessity's sharp pinch* (a summing up of the hardships previously listed)   207
hot-blooded choleric (cf. I, ii, 23)   209 *knee* kneel at; *squire-like* like an
attendant   211 *sumpter* packhorse   212 *groom* i.e. Oswald   219 *embossèd* risen to a head   222 *thunder-bearer* i.e. Jupiter   223 *high-judging*
judging from on high   229 *mingle . . . passion* interpret your passion in
the light of reason   232 *avouch* swear by   234 *sith that* since; *charge*
expense   240 *slack* neglect   244 *notice* recognition   246 *depositaries*
trustees   247 *kept . . . to be* stipulated that I be   251 *well-favored* comely
253 *Stands . . . praise* i.e. is at least relatively praiseworthy   255 *her love*
i.e. as loving as she

LEAR

259 O reason not the need ! Our basest beggars
260 Are in the poorest thing superfluous.
261 Allow not nature more than nature needs,
     Man's life is cheap as beast's. Thou art a lady :
263 If only to go warm were gorgeous,
     Why, nature needs not what thou gorgeous wear'st,
     Which scarcely keeps thee warm. But, for true need –
     You heavens, give me that patience, patience I need.
     You see me here, you gods, a poor old man,
     As full of grief as age, wretched in both.
     If it be you that stirs these daughters' hearts
270 Against their father, fool me not so much
     To bear it tamely ; touch me with noble anger,
     And let not women's weapons, water drops,
     Stain my man's cheeks. No, you unnatural hags !
     I will have such revenges on you both
     That all the world shall – I will do such things –
     What they are, yet I know not ; but they shall be
     The terrors of the earth. You think I'll weep.
     No, I'll not weep.
           Storm and tempest.
     I have full cause of weeping, but this heart
280 Shall break into a hundred thousand flaws
281 Or ere I'll weep. O fool, I shall go mad !
        Exeunt [Lear, Fool, Kent, and Gloucester].

CORNWALL

     Let us withdraw ; 'twill be a storm.

REGAN

     This house is little ; the old man and 's people
     Cannot be well bestowed.

GONERIL

285 'Tis his own blame ; hath put himself from rest
     And must needs taste his folly.

REGAN

287 For his particular, I'll receive him gladly,
     But not one follower.

288 GONERIL   So am I purposed.
     Where is my Lord of Gloucester ?

CORNWALL

     Followèd the old man forth.
       [Enter Gloucester.]   He is returned.

GLOUCESTER

     The King is in high rage.

CORNWALL   Whither is he going ?

GLOUCESTER

     He calls to horse, but will I know not whither.

CORNWALL

     'Tis best to give him way ; he leads himself.

GONERIL

     My lord, entreat him by no means to stay.

GLOUCESTER

     Alack, the night comes on, and the high winds
296 Do sorely ruffle. For many miles about
     There's scarce a bush.

REGAN   O, sir, to willful men
     The injuries that they themselves procure
     Must be their schoolmasters. Shut up your doors.
     He is attended with a desperate train,
301 And what they may incense him to, being apt
     To have his ear abused, wisdom bids fear.

CORNWALL

     Shut up your doors, my lord ; 'tis a wild night.
     My Regan counsels well. Come out o' th' storm. *Exeunt.*

KENT

     Who's there besides foul weather ?

GENTLEMAN

     One minded like the weather, most unquietly.   2

KENT

     I know you. Where's the King ?

GENTLEMAN

     Contending with the fretful elements ;   4
     Bids the wind blow the earth into the sea,
     Or swell the curlèd waters 'bove the main,   6
     That things might change or cease ; [tears his white hair,   7
     Which the impetuous blasts, with eyeless rage,   8
     Catch in their fury and make nothing of ;
     Strives in his little world of man to outscorn   10
     The to-and-fro-conflicting wind and rain.
     This night, wherein the cub-drawn bear would couch,   12
     The lion and the belly-pinchèd wolf   13
     Keep their fur dry, unbonneted he runs,
     And bids what will take all.]   15

KENT   But who is with him ?

GENTLEMAN

     None but the fool, who labors to outjest
     His heart-struck injuries.

KENT   Sir, I do know you,
     And dare upon the warrant of my note   18
     Commend a dear thing to you. There is division,   19
     Although as yet the face of it is covered
     With mutual cunning, 'twixt Albany and Cornwall ;
     Who have – as who have not, that their great stars   22
     Throned and set high ? – servants, who seem no less,   23
     Which are to France the spies and speculations   24
     Intelligent of our state. What hath been seen,   25
     Either in snuffs and packings of the Dukes,   26
     Or the hard rein which both of them have borne   27
     Against the old kind King, or something deeper,
     Whereof, perchance, these are but furnishings –   29
     [But, true it is, from France there comes a power   30
     Into this scatterèd kingdom, who already,   31
     Wise in our negligence, have secret feet
     In some of our best ports and are at point
     To show their open banner. Now to you :
     If on my credit you dare build so far   35
     To make your speed to Dover, you shall find

---

259 *reason* analyze   260 *Are . . . superfluous* i.e. have some poor possession not utterly indispensable   261 *than nature needs* i.e. than life needs for mere survival   263–65 *If . . . warm* i.e. if to be dressed warmly (i.e. for need) were considered sufficiently gorgeous, you would not need your present attire, which is gorgeous rather than warm   270 *fool* play with, humiliate   280 *flaws* fragments   281 *Or ere* before   285 *hath . . . rest* i.e. he himself is responsible for leaving his resting place with her (?), he is self-afflicted (?)   287 *particular* own person   288 *purposed* determined   296 *ruffle* rage   301–02 *apt . . . abused* i.e. predisposed to listen to ill counsel

III, i An open heath   2 *minded . . . unquietly* i.e. in disturbed mood   4 *Contending* quarrelling   6 *main* mainland   7 *change* revert to chaos (?), improve (?)   8 *eyeless* (1) blind, (2) invisible   10 *little world* (the 'microcosm,' which is disturbed like the great world or 'macrocosm')   12 *cub-drawn* cub-sucked (and hence ravenous)   13 *belly-pinchèd* famished   15 *take all* (the cry of the desperate gambler in staking his last)   18 *warrant . . . note* assurance of my knowledge   19 *Commend . . . thing* entrust a precious matter   22 *that* whom ; *stars* destinies   23 *Throned* have throned ; *no less* i.e. truly so   24 *speculations* spies   25 *Intelligent* supplying intelligence   26 *snuffs* quarrels ; *packings* intrigues   27 *hard rein . . . borne* i.e. harsh curbs . . . exercised   29 *furnishings* pretexts   30 *power* army   31 *scatterèd* divided   35 *my credit* trust in me ; *build* take constructive action

Some that will thank you, making just report
38 Of how unnatural and bemadding sorrow
39 The King hath cause to plain.
I am a gentleman of blood and breeding,
And from some knowledge and assurance offer
42 This office to you.]

GENTLEMAN
I will talk further with you.

KENT   No, do not.
For confirmation that I am much more
45 Than my out-wall, open this purse and take
What it contains. If you shall see Cordelia,
As fear not but you shall, show her this ring,
And she will tell you who that fellow is
That yet you do not know. Fie on this storm!
I will go seek the King.

GENTLEMAN
Give me your hand. Have you no more to say?

KENT
52 Few words, but, to effect, more than all yet:
53 That when we have found the King – in which your pain
That way, I'll this – he that first lights on him
Holla the other.   *Exeunt [severally].*

*

III, ii   *Storm still. Enter Lear and Fool.*

LEAR
Blow, winds, and crack your cheeks. Rage, blow.
2 You cataracts and hurricanoes, spout
3 Till you have drenched our steeples, drowned the cocks.
4 You sulph'rous and thought-executing fires,
5 Vaunt-couriers of oak-cleaving thunderbolts,
Singe my white head. And thou, all-shaking thunder,
Strike flat the thick rotundity o' th' world,
8 Crack Nature's moulds, all germains spill at once,
That makes ingrateful man.
10 FOOL O nuncle, court holy-water in a dry house is better
than this rain-water out o' door. Good nuncle, in; ask
thy daughters blessing. Here's a night pities neither
wise men nor fools.

38 *bemadding sorrow* maddening grievances   39 *plain* lament   42 *office* service   45 *out-wall* surface appearance   52 *to effect* in their import   53 *pain* pains, care
III, ii The same   2 *hurricanoes* water-spouts   3 *cocks* weathercocks   4 *thought-executing fires* i.e. flashes of lightning swift as thought (?), dazing, benumbing the mind (?)   5 *Vaunt-couriers* heralds   8 *moulds* (in which Nature's creations are formed); *germains* seeds   10 *court holy-water* flattery (slang)   16 *tax* charge   18 *subscription* deference   19 *pleasure* will   21 *ministers* agents   23 *high-engendered battles* heavenly battalions   27–30 *The codpiece . . . many* (the moral of the rime is that improvident cohabitation spells penury)   27 *codpiece* padded gusset at the crotch of the breeches (slang for penis)   29 *he* it   30 *many* (head-lice and body-lice, accompanying poverty)   31–34 *The man . . . wake* (a parallel instance of misery deriving from reckless impulse: to transpose the tender and precious heart and the tough and base toe is to invite injury; with *heart* also suggesting Cordelia)   35–36 *made . . . glass* i.e. before a mirror (irrelevant, except as vanity is a form of folly, the Fool's general theme)   44 *Gallow* frighten   45 *keep their caves* i.e. keep under cover   46 *horrid* horrible   48 *carry* bear   50 *pudder* turmoil   51 *Find . . . enemies* i.e. discover sinners (by their show of fear)   54 *simular* counterfeit   56 *seeming* hypocrisy   57 *practiced on* plotted against; *Close* secret   58 *Rive* split, break through; *continents* containers, covers   59 *summoners* arresting officers of ecclesiastical courts; *grace* mercy   61 *Gracious my lord* my gracious lord   63 *house* household (both building and occupants)   65 *demanding after* inquiring for   67 *scanted* stinted   70 *art* magic skill (as in alchemy)

LEAR
Rumble thy bellyful. Spit, fire. Spout, rain.
Nor rain, wind, thunder, fire are my daughters.
I tax not you, you elements, with unkindness.   16
I never gave you kingdom, called you children;
You owe me no subscription. Then let fall   18
Your horrible pleasure. Here I stand your slave,   19
A poor, infirm, weak, and despised old man.
But yet I call you servile ministers,   21
That will with two pernicious daughters join
Your high-engendered battles 'gainst a head   23
So old and white as this. O, ho! 'tis foul.
FOOL He that has a house to put 's head in has a good
headpiece.
         The codpiece that will house   27
            Before the head has any,
         The head and he shall louse: 29
            So beggars marry many.   30
         The man that makes his toe   31
            What he his heart should make
         Shall of a corn cry woe,
            And turn his sleep to wake.
For there was never yet fair woman but she made   35
mouths in a glass.
     Enter Kent.

LEAR
No, I will be the pattern of all patience;
I will say nothing.
KENT Who's there?
FOOL Marry, here's grace and a codpiece; that's a wise
man and a fool.
KENT
Alas, sir, are you here? Things that love night
Love not such nights as these. The wrathful skies
Gallow the very wanderers of the dark   44
And make them keep their caves. Since I was man,   45
Such sheets of fire, such bursts of horrid thunder,   46
Such groans of roaring wind and rain, I never
Remember to have heard. Man's nature cannot carry   48
Th' affliction nor the fear.
LEAR   Let the great gods
That keep this dreadful pudder o'er our heads   50
Find out their enemies now. Tremble, thou wretch,   51
That hast within thee undivulgèd crimes
Unwhipped of justice. Hide thee, thou bloody hand,
Thou perjured, and thou simular of virtue   54
That art incestuous. Caitiff, to pieces shake,
That under covert and convenient seeming   56
Has practiced on man's life. Close pent-up guilts,   57
Rive your concealing continents and cry   58
These dreadful summoners grace. I am a man   59
More sinned against than sinning.
KENT   Alack, bareheaded?
Gracious my lord, hard by here is a hovel;   61
Some friendship will it lend you 'gainst the tempest.
Repose you there, while I to this hard house   63
(More harder than the stones whereof 'tis raised,
Which even but now, demanding after you,   65
Denied me to come in) return, and force
Their scanted courtesy.   67
LEAR   My wits begin to turn.
Come on, my boy. How dost, my boy? Art cold?
I am cold myself. Where is this straw, my fellow?
The art of our necessities is strange,   70

And can make vile things precious. Come, your hovel.
Poor fool and knave, I have one part in my heart
That's sorry yet for thee.

FOOL [sings]
     He that has and a little tiny wit,
       With, heigh-ho, the wind and the rain,
76   Must make content with his fortunes fit
     Though the rain it raineth every day.

LEAR True, boy. Come, bring us to this hovel.
                     Exit [with Kent].

79 FOOL This is a brave night to cool a courtesan. I'll speak a
    prophecy ere I go:
81   When priests are more in word than matter;
82   When brewers mar their malt with water;
83   When nobles are their tailors' tutors;
84   No heretics burned, but wenches' suitors;
     When every case in law is right,
     No squire in debt nor no poor knight;
     When slanders do not live in tongues,
     Nor cutpurses come not to throngs;
89   When usurers tell their gold i' th' field,
     And bawds and whores do churches build –
91   Then shall the realm of Albion
92   Come to great confusion.
     Then comes the time, who lives to see 't,
94   That going shall be used with feet.
95 This prophecy Merlin shall make, for I live before his
    time.   *Exit.*

                    *

III, iii   *Enter Gloucester and Edmund.*

GLOUCESTER Alack, alack, Edmund, I like not this un-
    natural dealing. When I desired their leave that I might
3   pity him, they took from me the use of mine own house,
    charged me on pain of perpetual displeasure neither to
5   speak of him, entreat for him, or any way sustain him.

EDMUND Most savage and unnatural.

7 GLOUCESTER Go to; say you nothing. There is division
8   between the Dukes, and a worse matter than that. I have
    received a letter this night – 'tis dangerous to be spoken
10   – I have locked the letter in my closet. These injuries the
11   King now bears will be revenged home; there is part of a
12   power already footed; we must incline to the King. I will
13   look him and privily relieve him. Go you and maintain
    talk with the Duke, that my charity be not of him per-
    ceived. If he ask for me, I am ill and gone to bed. If I die
    for it, as no less is threatened me, the King my old mas-
17   ter must be relieved. There is strange things toward,
    Edmund; pray you be careful.   *Exit.*

EDMUND
19   This courtesy forbid thee shall the Duke
    Instantly know, and of that letter too.
21   This seems a fair deserving, and must draw me
    That which my father loses – no less than all.
    The younger rises when the old doth fall.   *Exit.*

                    *

III, iv   *Enter Lear, Kent, and Fool.*

KENT
1   Here is the place, my lord. Good my lord, enter.
    The tyranny of the open night's too rough
    For nature to endure.
              Storm still.

LEAR   Let me alone.

KENT
    Good my lord, enter here.

LEAR   Wilt break my heart?   4

KENT
    I had rather break mine own. Good my lord, enter.

LEAR
    Thou think'st 'tis much that this contentious storm
    Invades us to the skin. So 'tis to thee,
    But where the greater malady is fixed   8
    The lesser is scarce felt. Thou'dst shun a bear;
    But if thy flight lay toward the roaring sea,
    Thou'dst meet the bear i' th' mouth. When the mind's 11
    free,
    The body's delicate. The tempest in my mind
    Doth from my senses take all feeling else
    Save what beats there. Filial ingratitude,
    Is it not as this mouth should tear this hand
    For lifting food to 't? But I will punish home.   16
    No, I will weep no more. In such a night
    To shut me out! Pour on; I will endure.
    In such a night as this! O Regan, Goneril,
    Your old kind father, whose frank heart gave all –   20
    O, that way madness lies; let me shun that.
    No more of that.

KENT   Good my lord, enter here.

LEAR
    Prithee go in thyself; seek thine own ease.
    This tempest will not give me leave to ponder
    On things would hurt me more, but I'll go in.
       [To the Fool]
    In, boy; go first. You houseless poverty –   26
    Nay, get thee in. I'll pray, and then I'll sleep. *Exit [Fool].*
    Poor naked wretches, wheresoe'er you are,
    That bide the pelting of this pitiless storm,
    How shall your houseless heads and unfed sides,
    Your looped and windowed raggedness, defend you   31
    From seasons such as these? O, I have ta'en
    Too little care of this! Take physic, pomp;   33
    Expose thyself to feel what wretches feel,
    That thou mayst shake the superflux to them   35
    And show the heavens more just.

EDGAR *[within]* Fathom and half, fathom and half! Poor 37
Tom!

---

76 *make . . . fit* i.e. reconcile himself to his fortunes   79 *brave* fine   81
are . . . matter i.e. can outshine the gospel message (At present their ability
to speak is quite unworthy of their theme.)   82 *mar* i.e. dilute (At present
they dilute water with malt, producing very small beer.)   83 *are . . . tutors*
i.e. are no longer subservient to fashion (Each subsequent line also reverses
the present state of affairs.)   84 *burned* (pun on contracting venereal
disease); *wenches' suitors* i.e. libertines   89 *tell* count; *i' th' field* (instead
of in secret places)   91 *Albion* England   92 *confusion* ruin (ironic: an
edifice of abuses is 'ruined' by reform)   94 *going . . . feet* walking will
be done with feet (the humor of anticlimax, but suggesting a return to
normality)   95 *Merlin* (a legendary magician associated with King Arthur,
who reigned later than King Lear)
III, iii Within Gloucester's castle   3 *pity* have mercy upon   5 *entreat*
plead   7 *division* contention   8 *worse* more serious   10 *closet* chamber
11 *home* thoroughly   12 *power* army; *footed* landed; *incline to* side with
13 *look* search for; *privily* secretly   17 *toward* imminent   19 *courtesy* kind
attention (to Lear)   21 *fair deserving* i.e. action that should win favor
III, iv Before a hovel on the heath   1 *Good my lord* my good lord   4 *break
my heart* i.e. by removing the distraction of mere physical distress   8
fixed lodged   11 *i' th' mouth* i.e. in the teeth; *free* free of care   16 *home*
i.e. to the hilt   20 *frank* liberal   26 *houseless* unsheltered   31 *looped*
loopholed   33 *Take physic, pomp* i.e. cure yourself, you vainglorious
ones   35 *superflux* superfluities   37 *Fathom and half* (nautical cry in
taking soundings, perhaps suggested by the deluge)

Enter Fool.

FOOL Come not in here, nuncle; here's a spirit. Help me, help me!

KENT

Give me thy hand. Who's there?

FOOL A spirit, a spirit. He says his name 's poor Tom.

KENT

What art thou that dost grumble there i' th' straw? Come forth.

Enter Edgar [as Tom o' Bedlam].

45
46 EDGAR Away! the foul fiend follows me. Through the sharp hawthorn blow the winds. Humh! go to thy bed and warm thee.

LEAR Didst thou give all to thy daughters? And art thou come to this?

EDGAR Who gives anything to poor Tom? whom the foul fiend hath led through fire and through flame, through ford and whirlpool, o'er bog and quagmire; that hath
53 laid knives under his pillow and halters in his pew, set
54 ratsbane by his porridge, made him proud of heart, to
55 ride on a bay trotting horse over four-inched bridges, to
56 course his own shadow for a traitor. Bless thy five wits, Tom 's acold. O, do, de, do, de, do, de. Bless thee from
58 whirlwinds, star-blasting, and taking. Do poor Tom some charity, whom the foul fiend vexes. There could I have him now – and there – and there again – and there –
Storm still.

LEAR

61 Has his daughters brought him to this pass? Couldst thou save nothing? Wouldst thou give 'em all?

63 FOOL Nay, he reserved a blanket, else we had been all shamed.

LEAR

65 Now all the plagues that in the pendulous air
66 Hang fated o'er men's faults light on thy daughters!

KENT

He hath no daughters, sir.

LEAR

Death, traitor! Nothing could have subdued nature
To such a lowness but his unkind daughters.
Is it the fashion that discarded fathers
Should have thus little mercy on their flesh? 71
Judicious punishment – 'twas this flesh begot
Those pelican daughters. 73

EDGAR Pillicock sat on Pillicock Hill. Alow, alow, loo, loo! 74

FOOL This cold night will turn us all to fools and madmen.

EDGAR Take heed o' th' foul fiend; obey thy parents; keep thy words' justice; swear not; commit not with 77 man's sworn spouse; set not thy sweet heart on proud array. Tom 's acold.

LEAR What hast thou been?

EDGAR A servingman, proud in heart and mind; that curled my hair, wore gloves in my cap; served the lust of 82 my mistress' heart, and did the act of darkness with her; swore as many oaths as I spake words, and broke them in the sweet face of heaven. One that slept in the contriving of lust, and waked to do it. Wine loved I deeply, dice dearly; and in woman out-paramoured the Turk. False 87 of heart, light of ear, bloody of hand; hog in sloth, fox in 88 stealth, wolf in greediness, dog in madness, lion in prey. Let not the creaking of shoes nor the rustling of silks be- 90 tray thy poor heart to woman. Keep thy foot out of brothels, thy hand out of plackets, thy pen from lenders' 92 books, and defy the foul fiend. Still through the haw- thorn blows the cold wind; says suum, mun, nonny. 94 Dolphin my boy, boy, sessa! let him trot by. 95
Storm still.

LEAR Thou wert better in a grave than to answer with thy 96 uncovered body this extremity of the skies. Is man no more than this? Consider him well. Thou ow'st the 98 worm no silk, the beast no hide, the sheep no wool, the cat no perfume. Ha! here's three on's are sophisticated. 100 Thou art the thing itself; unaccommodated man is no 101 more but such a poor, bare, forked animal as thou art. 102 Off, off, you lendings! Come, unbutton here. 103
[Begins to disrobe.]

FOOL Prithee, nuncle, be contented; 'tis a naughty night 104 to swim in. Now a little fire in a wild field were like an 105 old lecher's heart – a small spark, all the rest on's body cold. Look, here comes a walking fire.

Enter Gloucester with a torch.

EDGAR This is the foul Flibbertigibbet. He begins at cur- 108 few, and walks till the first cock. He gives the web and 109 the pin, squints the eye, and makes the harelip; mildews 110 the white wheat, and hurts the poor creature of earth. 111
Swithold footed thrice the 'old; 112
He met the nightmare, and her nine fold; 113
Bid her alight 114
And her troth plight, 115
And aroint thee, witch, aroint thee! 116

KENT

How fares your Grace?

LEAR What's he?

KENT

Who's there? What is't you seek?

GLOUCESTER

What are you there? Your names?

EDGAR Poor Tom, that eats the swimming frog, the toad, the todpole, the wall-newt and the water; that in the fury 122 of his heart, when the foul fiend rages, eats cow-dung for sallets, swallows the old rat and the ditch-dog, drinks 124

45–46 *Through . . . winds* (cf. ll. 93–94; a line from a ballad) 46–47 *go . . . thee* (evidently a popular retort; cf. *Taming of the Shrew*, Ind., i, 7–8) 53, 54 *knives, halters, ratsbane* (temptations to suicide) 53 *pew* a gallery or balcony 55 *ride . . . bridges* i.e. take mad risks 56 *course . . . traitor* chase his own shadow as an enemy 58 *star-blasting* i.e. becoming the victim of malignant stars; *taking* pestilence 61 *pass* evil condition 63 *blanket* (to cover his nakedness) 65 *pendulous* omin- ously suspended 66 *Hang . . . faults* i.e. destined to chastise sins 71 *have . . . flesh* i.e. torture themselves 73 *pelican* i.e. feeding upon the parent's blood (a supposed habit of this species of bird) 74 *Pillicock . . . Hill* (probably from a nursery rhyme; 'Pillicock' is a pet name for a child); *Alow . . . loo* (hunting cry?) 77 *justice* i.e. dependability; *commit not* (i.e. adultery) 82 *gloves . . . cap* (a fashion with Elizabethan gallants) 87 *out-paramoured the Turk* outdid the Sultan in mistress- keeping 88 *light of ear* i.e. attentive to flattery and slander 90 *creaking, rustling* (both considered seductively fashionable sounds) 92 *plackets* slits in skirts 92–93 *pen . . . books* (in signing for loans) 94 *suum . . . nonny* (the refrain of the wind?) 95 *Dolphin . . . trot by* (variously ex- plained as cant phrases or ballad refrain, equivalent to 'Let it go') 96 *answer* bear the brunt of 98 *ow'st* have borrowed from 100 *cat* civet cat; *sophisticated* altered by artifice 101 *unaccommodated* unpampered 102 *forked* two-legged 103 *lendings* borrowed coverings 104 *naughty* evil 105 *wild* barren 108 *Flibbertigibbet* (a dancing devil); *curfew* (9 p.m.) 109 *first cock* (midnight) 109–10 *web . . . pin* cataract of the eye 110 *squints* crosses 111 *white* ripening 112 *Swithold* St Withold (Anglo-Saxon exorcist); *footed* walked over; *'old* wold, uplands 113 *nightmare* incubus, demon; *fold* offspring 114 *alight* i.e. come from the horse she was afflicting 115 *her troth plight* plight her troth, pledge her good intentions 116 *aroint thee* be gone (a direct command, concluding the charm) 122 *todpole* tadpole; *water* water-newt 124 *sallets* salads; *ditch- dog* (carcass)

125 the green mantle of the standing pool; who is whipped
126 from tithing to tithing, and stock-punished and imprisoned; who hath had three suits to his back, six
shirts to his body,
Horse to ride, and weapon to wear,
130 But mice and rats, and such small deer,
Have been Tom's food for seven long year.
132 Beware my follower! Peace, Smulkin, peace, thou fiend!

GLOUCESTER
What, hath your Grace no better company?

EDGAR
The prince of darkness is a gentleman.
135 Modo he's called, and Mahu.

GLOUCESTER
Our flesh and blood, my lord, is grown so vile
137 That it doth hate what gets it.

EDGAR Poor Tom's acold.

GLOUCESTER
139 Go in with me. My duty cannot suffer
T' obey in all your daughters' hard commands.
Though their injunction be to bar my doors
And let this tyrannous night take hold upon you,
Yet have I ventured to come seek you out
And bring you where both fire and food is ready.

LEAR
First let me talk with this philosopher.
What is the cause of thunder?

KENT
Good my lord, take his offer; go into th' house.

LEAR
148 I'll talk a word with this same learnèd Theban.
149 What is your study?

EDGAR
150 How to prevent the fiend, and to kill vermin.

LEAR
Let me ask you one word in private.

KENT
Importune him once more to go, my lord.
His wits begin t' unsettle.

GLOUCESTER   Canst thou blame him?
    Storm still.
His daughters seek his death. Ah, that good Kent,
He said it would be thus, poor banished man!
Thou sayest the King grows mad – I'll tell thee, friend,
I am almost mad myself. I had a son,
158 Now outlawed from my blood; he sought my life
But lately, very late. I loved him, friend,
No father his son dearer. True to tell thee,
The grief hath crazed my wits. What a night's this!
I do beseech your Grace –
162 LEAR   O, cry you mercy, sir.
Noble philosopher, your company.

EDGAR Tom's acold.

GLOUCESTER
In, fellow, there, into th' hovel; keep thee warm.

LEAR
Come, let's in all.

KENT   This way, my lord.

LEAR   With him!
I will keep still with my philosopher.

KENT
168 Good my lord, soothe him; let him take the fellow.

GLOUCESTER
169 Take him you on.

KENT
Sirrah, come on; go along with us.

LEAR
Come, good Athenian.   171

GLOUCESTER
No words, no words! Hush.

EDGAR   Child Rowland to the dark tower came;   173
        His word was still, 'Fie, foh, and fum,   174
        I smell the blood of a British man.'   *Exeunt.*

*

Enter Cornwall and Edmund.   III, v

CORNWALL I will have my revenge ere I depart his house.

EDMUND How, my lord, I may be censured, that nature   2
thus gives way to loyalty, something fears me to think of.   3

CORNWALL I now perceive it was not altogether your
brother's evil disposition made him seek his death; but a   5
provoking merit, set awork by a reproveable badness in
himself.

EDMUND How malicious is my fortune that I must repent
to be just! This is the letter which he spoke of, which
approves him an intelligent party to the advantages of   10
France. O heavens, that this treason were not! or not I
the detector!

CORNWALL Go with me to the Duchess.

EDMUND If the matter of this paper be certain, you have
mighty business in hand.

CORNWALL True or false, it hath made thee Earl of
Gloucester. Seek out where thy father is, that he may be
ready for our apprehension.

EDMUND *[aside]* If I find him comforting the King, it   19
will stuff his suspicion more fully. – I will persever in   20
my course of loyalty, though the conflict be sore between that and my blood.   22

CORNWALL I will lay trust upon thee, and thou shalt find   23
a dearer father in my love.   *Exeunt.*

*

Enter Kent and Gloucester.   III, v

GLOUCESTER Here is better than the open air; take it
thankfully. I will piece out the comfort with what addition I can. I will not be long from you.

KENT All the power of his wits have given way to his
impatience. The gods reward your kindness.   5
                Exit [Gloucester].

125 *mantle* scum; *standing* stagnant   126 *tithing* a ten-family district within a parish; *stock-punished* placed in the stocks   130 *deer* game (adapted from lines in the romance *Bevis of Hampton*)   132, 135 *Smulkin, Modo, Mahu* (devils described in Harsnett's *Declaration*, 1603)   137 *gets* begets (a reference to Edgar, Goneril, and Regan)   139 *suffer* permit   148 *Theban* (an unexplained association of Thebes with philosophy, i.e. science)   149 *study* i.e. scientific specialty   150 *prevent* thwart   158 *outlawed . . . blood* proscribed as no child of mine   162 *cry you mercy* I beg your pardon   168 *soothe* humor   169 *you on* along with you   171 *Athenian* i.e. philosopher   173 *Child* (i.e. a candidate for knighthood); *Rowland* Roland of the Charlemagne legends (the line perhaps from a lost ballad)   174 *His word was still* i.e. his repeated word, his motto, was always   174–75 *Fie . . . man* (absurdly heroic)
III, v Within Gloucester's castle   2 *censured* judged   3 *something fears me* frightens me somewhat   5–7 *a provoking . . . himself* i.e. evil justice incited by evil (a case of poison driving out poison)   10 *approves* proves; *intelligent . . . advantages* spying partisan on behalf   19 *comforting* aiding   20 *persever* persevere   22 *blood* natural feelings   23 *lay . . . thee* trust you (?), reward you with a place of trust (?)
III, vi Within a cottage near Gloucester's castle   5 *impatience* rage

Enter Lear, Edgar, and Fool.

6 EDGAR Frateretto calls me, and tells me Nero is an angler
7 in the lake of darkness. Pray, innocent, and beware the
foul fiend.

FOOL Prithee, nuncle, tell me whether a madman be a
10 gentleman or a yeoman.

LEAR
A king, a king.

FOOL No, he's a yeoman that has a gentleman to his son;
13 for he's a mad yeoman that sees his son a gentleman
before him.

LEAR
To have a thousand with red burning spits
16 Come hizzing in upon 'em –
[EDGAR The foul fiend bites my back.

FOOL He's mad that trusts in the tameness of a wolf, a
horse's health, a boy's love, or a whore's oath.

LEAR
20 It shall be done; I will arraign them straight.
    [To Edgar]
Come, sit thou here, most learned justice.
    [To the Fool]
Thou, sapient sir, sit here. Now, you she-foxes –
23 EDGAR Look, where he stands and glares. Want'st thou
24 eyes at trial, madam?
25   Come o'er the bourn, Bessy, to me.
FOOL   Her boat hath a leak,
       And she must not speak
    Why she dares not come over to thee.
EDGAR The foul fiend haunts poor Tom in the voice of a
30 nightingale. Hoppedance cries in Tom's belly for two
31 white herring. Croak not, black angel; I have no food
for thee.

KENT
33 How do you, sir? Stand you not so amazed.
Will you lie down and rest upon the cushions?

LEAR
I'll see their trial first. Bring in their evidence.
    [To Edgar]
Thou, robèd man of justice, take thy place.
    [To the Fool]
And thou, his yokefellow of equity,

Bench by his side. *[to Kent]* You are o' th' commission; 38
Sit you too.
EDGAR Let us deal justly.
    Sleepest or wakest thou, jolly shepherd?
      Thy sheep be in the corn;   42
      And for one blast of thy minikin mouth   43
      Thy sheep shall take no harm.
Purr, the cat is gray.   45
LEAR Arraign her first. 'Tis Goneril, I here take my oath
before this honorable assembly, kicked the poor king
her father.
FOOL Come hither, mistress. Is your name Goneril?
LEAR She cannot deny it.
FOOL Cry you mercy, I took you for a joint-stool.   51
LEAR
And here's another, whose warped looks proclaim
What store her heart is made on. Stop her there!
Arms, arms, sword, fire! Corruption in the place!   54
False justicer, why hast thou let her 'scape?]
EDGAR Bless thy five wits!
KENT
O pity! Sir, where is the patience now
That you so oft have boasted to retain?
EDGAR *[aside]*
My tears begin to take his part so much   59
They mar my counterfeiting.   60
LEAR
The little dogs and all,
Tray, Blanch, and Sweetheart – see, they bark at me.
EDGAR Tom will throw his head at them. Avaunt, you curs.
    Be thy mouth or black or white,
    Tooth that poisons if it bite;
    Mastiff, greyhound, mongrel grim,
    Hound or spaniel, brach or lym,   67
    Or bobtail tike, or trundle-tail –   68
    Tom will make him weep and wail;
    For, with throwing thus my head,
    Dogs leaped the hatch, and all are fled.   71
Do, de, de, de. Sessa! Come, march to wakes and fairs 72
and market towns. Poor Tom, thy horn is dry.   73
LEAR Then let them anatomize Regan. See what breeds
about her heart. Is there any cause in nature that makes
these hard hearts? *[to Edgar]* You, sir, I entertain for
one of my hundred; only I do not like the fashion of
your garments. You will say they are Persian; but let 78
them be changed.
KENT
Now, good my lord, lie here and rest awhile.
LEAR
Make no noise, make no noise; draw the curtains.
So, so. We'll go to supper i' th' morning.
FOOL And I'll go to bed at noon.
    Enter Gloucester.
GLOUCESTER
Come hither, friend. Where is the King my master?
KENT
Here, sir, but trouble him not; his wits are gone.
GLOUCESTER
Good friend, I prithee take him in thy arms.
I have o'erheard a plot of death upon him.
There is a litter ready; lay him in't
And drive toward Dover, friend, where thou shalt meet
Both welcome and protection. Take up thy master.
If thou shouldst dally half an hour, his life,

---

6 *Frateretto* (a devil mentioned in Harsnett's *Declaration*); *Nero* (in Rabelais, Trajan was the angler, Nero a fiddler, in Hades) **7** *innocent* hapless victim, plaything **10** *yeoman* a property owner, next in rank to a gentleman (The allusion is to self-penalizing indulgence of one's children.) **13** *sees* i.e. sees to it **16** *hizzing* hissing (Lear is musing on vicious military retaliation) **20** *arraign* bring to trial **23** *he* Lear (?), one of Edgar's 'devils' (?) **24** *eyes* such eyes (?), spectators (?) **25** *bourn* brook (Edgar's line is from a popular song; the Fool's are a ribald improvisation) **30** *nightingale* i.e. the fool; *Hoppedance* (a devil mentioned in Harsnett's *Declaration* as 'Hobberdidance') **31** *white* unsmoked (in contrast with *black angel*, i.e. smoked devil) **33** *amazed* bewildered **38** *commission* those commissioned as King's justices **42** *corn* wheatfield **43** *one . . . mouth* one strain on your delicate shepherd's pipe (?) **45** *gray* (gray cats were among the forms supposedly assumed by devils) **51** *Cry . . . joint-stool* (a cant expression for 'Pardon me for failing to notice you,' but two joint-stools – cf. *warped*, l. 52 – were probably the actual stage objects arraigned as Goneril and Regan) **54** *Corruption . . . place* i.e. bribery in the court **59** *take his part* i.e. fall on his behalf **60** *counterfeiting* i.e. simulating madness **67** *brach* hound bitch; *lym* bloodhound **68** *bobtail . . . trundle-tail* short-tailed cur or long-tailed **71** *hatch* lower half of a 'Dutch door' **72** *Sessa* (interjection, equivalent to 'Away!'); *wakes* parish feasts **73** *Poor . . . dry* (Edgar expresses his exhaustion in his role, by an allusion to the horns proffered by Toms o' Bedlam in begging drink) **78** *Persian* (Persian costume was reputedly gorgeous. Ironically, or in actual delusion, Lear refers thus to Edgar's rags, as he refers to bed curtains in l. 81.)

        With thine and all that offer to defend him,
        Stand in assurèd loss. Take up, take up,
94   And follow me, that will to some provision
95   Give thee quick conduct.

[KENT   Oppressèd nature sleeps.
96   This rest might yet have balmed thy broken sinews,
97   Which, if convenience will not allow,
98   Stand in hard cure.
         [To the Fool] Come, help to bear thy master.
         Thou must not stay behind.]

GLOUCESTER   Come, come, away!
                   Exeunt [all but Edgar].

[EDGAR
100   When we our betters see bearing our woes,
101   We scarcely think our miseries our foes.
        Who alone suffers suffers most i' th' mind,
103   Leaving free things and happy shows behind;
104   But then the mind much sufferance doth o'erskip
105   When grief hath mates, and bearing fellowship.
106   How light and portable my pain seems now,
        When that which makes me bend makes the King bow.
        He childed as I fatherèd. Tom, away.
109   Mark the high noises, and thyself bewray
110   When false opinion, whose wrong thoughts defile thee,
111   In thy just proof repeals and reconciles thee.
112   What will hap more to-night, safe 'scape the King!
113   Lurk, lurk.]   *[Exit.]*

                 *

III, vii   *Enter Cornwall, Regan, Goneril, Bastard [Edmund], and Servants.*

CORNWALL *[to Goneril]* Post speedily to my lord your husband; show him this letter. The army of France is landed. *[to Servants]* Seek out the traitor Gloucester.
                 [Exeunt some Servants.]

REGAN Hang him instantly.

GONERIL Pluck out his eyes.

CORNWALL Leave him to my displeasure. Edmund, keep
7   you our sister company. The revenges we are bound to take upon your traitorous father are not fit for your be-holding. Advise the Duke where you are going, to a most
10   festinate preparation. We are bound to the like. Our
11   posts shall be swift and intelligent betwixt us. Farewell,
12   dear sister; farewell, my Lord of Gloucester.
         Enter Steward [Oswald].
         How now? Where's the King?

OSWALD
        My Lord of Gloucester hath conveyed him hence.
        Some five or six and thirty of his knights,
16   Hot questrists after him, met him at gate;
        Who, with some other of the lord's dependants,
        Are gone with him toward Dover, where they boast
        To have well-armèd friends.

CORNWALL   Get horses for your mistress.
                  Exit [Oswald].

GONERIL
        Farewell, sweet lord, and sister.

CORNWALL
        Edmund, farewell.   *[Exeunt Goneril and Edmund.]*
        Go seek the traitor Gloucester,
        Pinion him like a thief, bring him before us.
                 [Exeunt other Servants.]
23   Though well we may not pass upon his life
        Without the form of justice, yet our power

        Shall do a court'sy to our wrath, which men   25
        May blame, but not control.
         Enter Gloucester and Servants.
                 Who's there, the traitor?

REGAN
Ingrateful fox, 'tis he.

CORNWALL
Bind fast his corky arms.   28

GLOUCESTER
What means your Graces? Good my friends, consider
You are my guests. Do me no foul play, friends.

CORNWALL
Bind him, I say.
         [Servants bind him.]

REGAN   Hard, hard! O filthy traitor.

GLOUCESTER
Unmerciful lady as you are, I'm none.

CORNWALL
To this chair bind him. Villain, thou shalt find –
         [Regan plucks his beard.]

GLOUCESTER
By the kind gods, 'tis most ignobly done
To pluck me by the beard.

REGAN
So white, and such a traitor?

GLOUCESTER   Naughty lady,   36
These hairs which thou dost ravish from my chin
Will quicken and accuse thee. I am your host.   38
With robber's hands my hospitable favors   39
You should not ruffle thus. What will you do?   40

CORNWALL
Come, sir, what letters had you late from France?   41

REGAN
Be simple-answered, for we know the truth.   42

CORNWALL
And what confederacy have you with the traitors
Late footed in the kingdom?   44

REGAN
To whose hands you have sent the lunatic King.
Speak.

GLOUCESTER
I have a letter guessingly set down,   47
Which came from one that's of a neutral heart,
And not from one opposed.

CORNWALL   Cunning.

REGAN   And false.

CORNWALL
Where hast thou sent the king?

---

94 *provision* supplies   95 *conduct* guidance   96 *balmed* healed; *sinews* nerves   97 *convenience* propitious circumstances   98 *Stand . . . cure* will be hard to cure   100 *our woes* woes like ours   101 *our foes* i.e. our peculiar foes (they seem rather a part of universal misery)   103 *free* carefree; *shows* scenes   104 *sufferance* suffering   105 *bearing fellowship* enduring has company   106 *portable* bearable   109 *Mark . . . noises* i.e. heed the rumors concerning those in power (?); *bewray* reveal   110 *wrong thoughts* misconceptions   111 *In . . . reconciles thee* i.e. upon your vindication recalls you and makes peace with you   112 *What . . . more* whatever more happens   113 *Lurk* i.e. keep covered   **III, vii** Within Gloucester's castle   7 *bound* required   10 *festinate* speedy   11 *intelligent* informative   12 *Lord of Gloucester* (as now endowed with his father's title and estates)   16 *questrists* seekers   23 *pass upon* issue a sentence against   25 *do a court'sy to* i.e. defer to, act in conformity with   28 *corky* (because aged)   36 *Naughty* evil   38 *quicken* come to life   39 *favors* features   40 *ruffle* tear at   41 *late* of late   42 *Be simple-answered* i.e. give plain answers   44 *footed* landed   47 *guessingly* i.e. tentatively, not stated as an assured fact

GLOUCESTER
  To Dover.
REGAN
52   Wherefore to Dover? Wast thou not charged at peril –
CORNWALL
  Wherefore to Dover? Let him answer that.
GLOUCESTER
54   I am tied to th' stake, and I must stand the course.
REGAN
  Wherefore to Dover?
GLOUCESTER
  Because I would not see thy cruel nails
  Pluck out his poor old eyes; nor thy fierce sister
58   In his anointed flesh stick boarish fangs.
  The sea, with such a storm as his bare head
60   In hell-black night endured, would have buoyed up
61   And quenched the stellèd fires.
62   Yet, poor old heart, he holp the heavens to rain.
  If wolves had at thy gate howled that stern time,
64   Thou shouldst have said, 'Good porter, turn the key.'
65   All cruels else subscribe. But I shall see
66   The wingèd vengeance overtake such children.
CORNWALL
  See't shalt thou never. Fellows, hold the chair.
  Upon these eyes of thine I'll set my foot.
GLOUCESTER
69   He that will think to live till he be old,
  Give me some help. – O cruel! O you gods!
REGAN
71   One side will mock another. Th' other too.
CORNWALL
  If you see vengeance –
1. SERVANT   Hold your hand, my lord!
  I have served you ever since I was a child;
  But better service have I never done you
  Than now to bid you hold.
REGAN   How now, you dog?
1. SERVANT
  If you did wear a beard upon your chin,
77   I'ld shake it on this quarrel. What do you mean!
CORNWALL
78   My villain!
    [Draw and fight.]

1. SERVANT
  Nay, then, come on, and take the chance of anger.
REGAN
  Give me thy sword. A peasant stand up thus?
    [She takes a sword and runs at him behind,] kills him.
1. SERVANT
  O, I am slain! My lord, you have one eye left
  To see some mischief on him. O!   82
CORNWALL
  Lest it see more, prevent it. Out, vile jelly.
  Where is thy lustre now?
GLOUCESTER
  All dark and comfortless. Where's my son Edmund?
  Edmund, enkindle all the sparks of nature   86
  To quit this horrid act.   87
REGAN   Out, treacherous villain;
  Thou call'st on him that hates thee. It was he
  That made the overture of thy treasons to us;   89
  Who is too good to pity thee.
GLOUCESTER
  O my follies! Then Edgar was abused.   91
  Kind gods, forgive me that, and prosper him.
REGAN
  Go thrust him out at gates, and let him smell
  His way to Dover.   *Exit [one] with Gloucester.*
       How is't, my lord? How look you?   94
CORNWALL
  I have received a hurt. Follow me, lady.
  Turn out that eyeless villain. Throw this slave
  Upon the dunghill. Regan, I bleed apace.
  Untimely comes this hurt. Give me your arm.   *Exeunt.*
[2. SERVANT
  I'll never care what wickedness I do,
  If this man come to good.
3. SERVANT   If she live long,
  And in the end meet the old course of death,   101
  Women will all turn monsters.
2. SERVANT
  Let's follow the old Earl, and get the bedlam
  To lead him where he would. His roguish madness   104
  Allows itself to anything.   *[Exit.]*
3. SERVANT
  Go thou. I'll fetch some flax and whites of eggs
  To apply to his bleeding face. Now heaven help him.
         Exit.]

          *

       Enter Edgar.   IV, i
EDGAR
  Yet better thus, and known to be contemned,   1
  Than still contemned and flattered. To be worst,
  The lowest and most dejected thing of fortune,   3
  Stands still in esperance, lives not in fear.   4
  The lamentable change is from the best;
  The worst returns to laughter. Welcome then,   6
  Thou unsubstantial air that I embrace:
  The wretch that thou hast blown unto the worst
  Owes nothing to thy blasts.   9
     Enter Gloucester and an Old Man.
         But who comes here?
  My father, poorly led? World, world, O world!   10
  But that thy strange mutations make us hate thee,   11
  Life would not yield to age.
OLD MAN   O my good lord,
  I have been your tenant, and your father's tenant,

---

52 *charged at peril* ordered on peril of your life   54 *course* coursing (as by a string of dogs baiting a bear or bull tied in the pit)   58 *anointed* (as king)   60 *buoyed* surged   61 *stellèd* starry   62 *holp* helped   64 *turn the key* i.e. let them come in to shelter   65 *All . . . subscribe* i.e. at such times all other cruel creatures give way, agree to renounce their cruelty (?)   66 *wingèd* heavenly (?), swift (?)   69 *will think* hopes, expects   71 *mock* i.e. subject to ridicule (because of the contrast)   71 *shake it* (as Regan has done with Gloucester's – an act of extreme defiance); *on this quarrel* in this cause; *What . . . mean* i.e. how dare you (The words are given to Regan by most editors, but they are no more 'un-servantlike,' than those which precede them.)   78 *My villain* i.e. my serf (with play on its more modern meaning)   82 *mischief* injury   86 *nature* natural feeling   87 *quit* requite, avenge; *horrid* horrible   89 *overture* disclosure   91 *abused* wronged   94 *How look you* i.e. how looks it with you, what is your condition   101 *meet . . . death* i.e. die a natural death   104–05 *His roguish . . . anything* i.e. his being an irresponsible wanderer allows him to do anything

IV, i A path leading from Gloucester's castle   1 *contemned* despised   3 *dejected* cast down, abased   4 *esperance* hope   6 *The worst . . . laughter* i.e. the worst extreme is the point of return to happiness   9 *nothing* i.e. nothing good (and hence he is free of debt)   10 *poorly* poor-like, i.e. like a blind beggar (?)   11–12 *But . . . age* i.e. were it not for your hateful mutability, we would never be reconciled to old age and death

These fourscore years.

GLOUCESTER
Away, get thee away. Good friend, be gone.
16 Thy comforts can do me no good at all ;
17 Thee they may hurt.

OLD MAN   You cannot see your way.

GLOUCESTER
18 I have no way, and therefore want no eyes ;
I stumbled when I saw. Full oft 'tis seen
20 Our means secure us, and our mere defects
Prove our commodities. O dear son Edgar,
22 The food of thy abusèd father's wrath,
23 Might I but live to see thee in my touch
I'ld say I had eyes again !

OLD MAN   How now ? Who's there ?

EDGAR *[aside]*
O gods ! Who is't can say 'I am at the worst' ?
I am worse than e'er I was.

OLD MAN   'Tis poor mad Tom.

EDGAR *[aside]*
27 And worse I may be yet. The worst is not
So long as we can say 'This is the worst.'

OLD MAN
Fellow, where goest ?

GLOUCESTER   Is it a beggarman ?

OLD MAN
Madman and beggar too.

GLOUCESTER
31 He has some reason, else he could not beg.
I' th' last night's storm I such a fellow saw,
33 Which made me think a man a worm. My son
Came then into my mind, and yet my mind
Was then scarce friends with him. I have heard more
since.
36 As flies to wanton boys are we to th' gods ;
They kill us for their sport.

EDGAR *[aside]*   How should this be ?
Bad is the trade that must play fool to sorrow,
39 Ang'ring itself and others. – Bless thee, master.

GLOUCESTER
Is that the naked fellow ?

OLD MAN   Ay, my lord.

GLOUCESTER
Then prithee get thee gone. If for my sake
Thou wilt o'ertake us hence a mile or twain
43 I' th' way toward Dover, do it for ancient love ;
And bring some covering for this naked soul,
Which I'll entreat to lead me.

OLD MAN   Alack, sir, he is mad.

GLOUCESTER
46 'Tis the time's plague when madmen lead the blind.
47 Do as I bid thee, or rather do thy pleasure.
Above the rest, be gone.

OLD MAN
49 I'll bring him the best 'parel that I have,
Come on 't what will.   *Exit.*

GLOUCESTER
Sirrah naked fellow –

EDGAR
52 Poor Tom 's acold. *[aside]* I cannot daub it further.

GLOUCESTER
Come hither, fellow.

EDGAR *[aside]*
And yet I must. – Bless thy sweet eyes, they bleed.

GLOUCESTER
Know'st thou the way to Dover ?

EDGAR Both stile and gate, horseway and footpath. Poor
Tom hath been scared out of his good wits. Bless thee,
good man's son, from the foul fiend. [Five fiends have
been in poor Tom at once : of lust, as Obidicut ; Hobbi- 59
didence, prince of dumbness ; Mahu, of stealing ; Modo, 60
of murder ; Flibbertigibbet, of mopping and mowing, 61
who since possesses chambermaids and waiting women.
So, bless thee, master.]

GLOUCESTER
Here, take this purse, thou whom the heavens' plagues
Have humbled to all strokes. That I am wretched   65
Makes thee the happier. Heavens, deal so still !   66
Let the superfluous and lust-dieted man,   67
That slaves your ordinance, that will not see   68
Because he does not feel, feel your pow'r quickly ;
So distribution should undo excess,
And each man have enough. Dost thou know Dover ?

EDGAR Ay, master.

GLOUCESTER
There is a cliff, whose high and bending head   73
Looks fearfully in the confinèd deep.   74
Bring me but to the very brim of it,
And I'll repair the misery thou dost bear
With something rich about me. From that place
I shall no leading need.

EDGAR   Give me thy arm.
Poor Tom shall lead thee.   *Exeunt.*

*

Enter Goneril, Bastard [Edmund], and Steward   IV, ii
[Oswald].

GONERIL
Welcome, my lord. I marvel our mild husband
Not met us on the way.   2
[To Oswald]   Now, where's your master ?

OSWALD
Madam, within, but never man so changed.
I told him of the army that was landed :
He smiled at it. I told him you were coming :
His answer was, 'The worse.' Of Gloucester's treachery
And of the loyal service of his son
When I informed him, then he called me sot   8
And told me I had turned the wrong side out.

16 *comforts* ministrations **17** *hurt* do injury (since they are forbidden)
18 *want* need **20–21** *Our means . . . commodities* i.e. prosperity makes us
rash, and sheer affliction proves a boon **22** *food* i.e. the object fed upon ;
abusèd deceived **23** *in* i.e. by means of **27–28** *The worst . . . worst* (because
at the very worst there will be no such comforting thought) **31** *reason*
powers of reason **33–34** *My son . . . mind* (because it was actually he –
a natural touch) **36** *wanton* irresponsibly playful **39** *Ang'ring* offending
43 *ancient love* i.e. such love as formerly bound master and man (nostalgic)
46 *time's plague* i.e. malady characteristic of these times **47** *thy pleasure*
as you please **49** *'parel* apparel **52** *daub it* lay it on, act the part **59**
Obidicut Hoberdicut (a devil mentioned in Harsnett's *Declaration*, as are
the four following) **60** *dumbness* muteness (Shakespeare identifies each
devil with some form of possession) **61** *mopping and mowing* grimaces,
affected facial expressions **65** *humbled to* reduced to bearing humbly
66 *happier* i.e. less wretched **67** *superfluous* possessed of superfluities ;
lust-dieted i.e. whose desires are feasted **68** *slaves your ordinance* subordinates your injunction (to share) **73** *bending* overhanging **74** *in* . . .
deep i.e. to the sea hemmed in below
IV, ii Before Albany's palace **2** *Not met* has not met **8** *sot* fool

What most he should dislike seems pleasant to him;
11 What like, offensive.
   GONERIL [to Edmund] Then shall you go no further.
12 It is the cowish terror of his spirit,
13 That dares not undertake. He'll not feel wrongs
14 Which tie him to an answer. Our wishes on the way
   May prove effects. Back, Edmund, to my brother.
16 Hasten his musters and conduct his pow'rs.
17 I must change names at home, and give the distaff
   Into my husband's hands. This trusty servant
   Shall pass between us. Ere long you are like to hear
   (If you dare venture in your own behalf)
21 A mistress's command. Wear this. Spare speech.
      [Gives a favor.]
   Decline your head. This kiss, if it durst speak,
   Would stretch thy spirits up into the air.
24 Conceive, and fare thee well.
   EDMUND
   Yours in the ranks of death.   Exit.
   GONERIL   My most dear Gloucester.
   O, the difference of man and man:
   To thee a woman's services are due;
28 My fool usurps my body.
   OSWALD   Madam, here comes my lord.
                                          [Exit.]
       Enter Albany.
   GONERIL
29 I have been worth the whistle.
   ALBANY   O Goneril,
   You are not worth the dust which the rude wind
31 Blows in your face. [I fear your disposition:
   That nature which contemns its origin
33 Cannot be bordered certain in itself.
34 She that herself will sliver and disbranch
35 From her material sap, perforce must wither
   And come to deadly use.

GONERIL
No more; the text is foolish.
ALBANY
Wisdom and goodness to the vile seem vile;
Filths savor but themselves. What have you done?   39
Tigers not daughters, what have you performed?
A father, and a gracious agèd man,
Whose reverence even the head-lugged bear would lick,   42
Most barbarous, most degenerate, have you madded.   43
Could my good brother suffer you to do it?
A man, a prince, by him so benefited!
If that the heavens do not their visible spirits   46
Send quickly down to tame these vile offenses,
It will come,   48
Humanity must perforce prey on itself,
Like monsters of the deep.]
GONERIL   Milk-livered man,   50
That bear'st a cheek for blows, a head for wrongs;
Who hast not in thy brows an eye discerning   52
Thine honor from thy suffering; [that not know'st
Fools do those villains pity who are punished   54
Ere they have done their mischief. Where's thy drum?   55
France spreads his banners in our noiseless land,   56
With plumèd helm thy state begins to threat,   57
Whilst thou, a moral fool, sits still and cries   58
'Alack, why does he so?']
ALBANY   See thyself, devil:
Proper deformity seems not in the fiend   60
So horrid as in woman.
GONERIL   O vain fool!
[ALBANY
Thou changèd and self-covered thing, for shame   62
Bemonster not thy feature. Were't my fitness   63
To let these hands obey my blood,   64
They are apt enough to dislocate and tear
Thy flesh and bones. Howe'er thou art a fiend,
A woman's shape doth shield thee.
GONERIL
Marry, your manhood – mew!]   68
      Enter a Messenger.
[ALBANY What news?]
MESSENGER
O, my good lord, the Duke of Cornwall's dead,
Slain by his servant, going to put out   71
The other eye of Gloucester.
ALBANY   Gloucester's eyes?
MESSENGER
A servant that he bred, thrilled with remorse,   73
Opposed against the act, bending his sword
To his great master; who, thereat enraged,
Flew on him, and amongst them felled him dead;   76
But not without that harmful stroke which since
Hath plucked him after.   78
ALBANY   This shows you are above,
You justicers, that these our nether crimes   79
So speedily can venge. But, O poor Gloucester,   80
Lost he his other eye?
MESSENGER   Both, both, my lord.
This letter, madam, craves a speedy answer.   82
'Tis from your sister.
GONERIL [aside]   One way I like this well;
But being widow, and my Gloucester with her,
May all the building in my fancy pluck   85
Upon my hateful life. Another way   86

11 *What like* what he should like 12 *cowish* cowardly 13 *undertake* engage 14 *an answer* retaliation 14–15 *Our wishes . . . effects* i.e. our wishes, that you might supplant Albany, may materialize 16 *musters* enlistments; *conduct his pow'rs* lead his army 17 *change names* i.e. exchange the name of 'mistress' for 'master'; *distaff* spinning-staff (symbol of the housewife) 21 *mistress's* (at present she plays the role of master, but, mated with Edmund, she would again *change names*) 24 *Conceive* (1) understand, (2) quicken (with the seed I have planted in you) 28 *usurps* wrongfully occupies 29 *worth the whistle* i.e. valued enough to be welcomed home ('not worth the whistle' applying proverbially to a 'poor dog') 31 *fear your disposition* distrust your nature 33 *bordered certain* safely contained (it will be unpredictably licentious) 34 *sliver, disbranch* cut off 35 *material sap* sustaining stock, nourishing trunk 39 *savor* relish 42 *head-lugged* dragged with a head-chain (hence, surly); *lick* i.e. treat with affection 43 *degenerate* unnatural; *madded* maddened 46 *visible* made visible, material 48 *It* i.e. chaos 50 *Milk-livered* i.e. spiritless 52–53 *discerning . . . suffering* distinguishing between dishonor and tolerance 54 *Fools* i.e. only fools 55 *drum* i.e. military preparation 56 *noiseless* i.e. unaroused 57 *helm* war-helmet 58 *moral* moralizing 60 *Proper* fair-surfaced 62 *changèd* transformed (diabolically, as in witchcraft); *self-covered* i.e. your natural self overwhelmed by evil (?), devil disguised as woman (?) 63 *Bemonster . . . feature* i.e. do not exchange your human features for a monster's; *my fitness* fit for me 64 *blood* passion 68 *Marry* (oath, derived from 'By Mary'); *your manhood – mew* i.e. 'What a man!' followed by a contemptuous interjection (?), mew up (contain) this display of manliness (?) 71 *going to* about to 73 *bred* reared; *thrilled with remorse* in the throes of pity 76 *amongst them* i.e. aided by the others 78 *plucked him after* drawn him along (to death) 79 *justicers* dispensers of justice; *nether crimes* sins committed here below 80 *venge* avenge 82 *craves* requires 85–86 *May . . . life* i.e. may make my life hateful by destroying my dream-castles 86 *Another way* the other way (alluded to in l. 83, probably the removal of Cornwall as an obstacle to sole reign with Edmund)

87 The news is not so tart. – I'll read, and answer.   *[Exit.]*

ALBANY

Where was his son when they did take his eyes?

MESSENGER

Come with my lady hither.

ALBANY   He is not here.

MESSENGER

90 No, my good lord; I met him back again.

ALBANY

Knows he the wickedness?

MESSENGER

Ay, my good lord. 'Twas he informed against him,

And quit the house on purpose, that their punishment

Might have the freer course.

ALBANY   Gloucester, I live

To thank thee for the love thou show'dst the King,

And to revenge thine eyes. Come hither, friend.

Tell me what more thou know'st.   *Exeunt.*

✳

IV, iii   *[Enter Kent and a Gentleman.*

KENT Why the King of France is so suddenly gone back

'know you no reason?

3 GENTLEMAN Something he left imperfect in the state,

4 which since his coming forth is thought of, which imports

5 to the kingdom so much fear and danger that his per-

6 sonal return was most required and necessary.

KENT

Who hath he left behind him general?

GENTLEMAN The Marshal of France, Monsieur La Far.

9 KENT Did your letters pierce the Queen to any demon-

stration of grief?

GENTLEMAN

Ay, sir. She took them, read them in my presence,

12 And now and then an ample tear trilled down

Her delicate cheek. It seemed she was a queen

14 Over her passion, who, most rebel-like,

Sought to be king o'er her.

KENT   O, then it movèd her?

GENTLEMAN

Not to a rage. Patience and sorrow strove

17 Who should express her goodliest. You have seen

Sunshine and rain at once – her smiles and tears

19 Were like, a better way: those happy smilets

That played on her ripe lip seemed not to know

What guests were in her eyes, which parted thence

As pearls from diamonds dropped. In brief,

23 Sorrow would be a rarity most belovèd,

If all could so become it.

KENT   Made she no verbal question?

GENTLEMAN

25 Faith, once or twice she heaved the name of father

Pantingly forth, as if it pressed her heart;

Cried 'Sisters, sisters, shame of ladies, sisters!

Kent, father, sisters? What, i' th' storm i' th' night?

29 Let pity not be believed!' There she shook

The holy water from her heavenly eyes,

31 And clamor moistened; then away she started

To deal with grief alone.

KENT   It is the stars,

33 The stars above us govern our conditions;

34 Else one self mate and make could not beget

35 Such different issues. You spoke not with her since?

GENTLEMAN No.

KENT

Was this before the King returned?

GENTLEMAN   No, since.

KENT

Well, sir, the poor distressèd Lear's i' th' town;

Who sometime, in his better tune, remembers   39

What we are come about, and by no means

Will yield to see his daughter.

GENTLEMAN   Why, good sir?

KENT

A sovereign shame so elbows him; his own unkindness,   42

That stripped her from his benediction, turned her   43

To foreign casualties, gave her dear rights   44

To his dog-hearted daughters – these things sting

His mind so venomously that burning shame

Detains him from Cordelia.

GENTLEMAN   Alack, poor gentleman.

KENT

Of Albany's and Cornwall's powers you heard not?

GENTLEMAN

'Tis so; they are afoot.   49

KENT

Well, sir, I'll bring you to our master Lear

And leave you to attend him. Some dear cause   51

Will in concealment wrap me up awhile.

When I am known aright, you shall not grieve

Lending me this acquaintance. I pray you go

Along with me.   *Exeunt.]*

✳

Enter, with Drum and Colors, Cordelia, Gentleman   IV, iv

[Doctor], and Soldiers.

CORDELIA

Alack, 'tis he! Why, he was met even now

As mad as the vexed sea, singing aloud,

Crowned with rank fumiter and furrow weeds,   3

With hardocks, hemlock, nettles, cuckoo flow'rs,   4

Darnel, and all the idle weeds that grow   5

In our sustaining corn. A century send forth!   6

Search every acre in the high-grown field

And bring him to our eye.   *[Exit an Officer.]*

               What can man's wisdom   8

In the restoring his bereavèd sense?   9

He that helps him take all my outward worth.   10

DOCTOR

There is means, madam.

---

87 *tart* distasteful   **90** *back* going back

IV, iii A meeting place at Dover   **3** *imperfect . . . state* i.e. rift in affairs of state   **4** *imports* means   **5** *fear* uneasiness   **6** *most* most urgently   **9** *pierce* goad   **12** *trilled* trickled   **14** *who* which   **17** *goodliest* i.e. most becomingly   **19** *Were . . . way* i.e. improved upon that spectacle   **23** *rarity* gem   **25–26** *heaved . . . forth* uttered . . . chokingly   **29** *Let pity* let it for pity (?)   **31** *clamor moistened* i.e. mixed, and thus muted, lamentation with tears   **33** *govern our conditions* determine our characters   **34** *Else . . . make* otherwise the same husband and wife   **35** *issues* children   **39** *better tune* i.e. more rational state, less jangled   **42** *sovereign* overruling; *elbows* jogs   **43** *stripped* cut off (cf. *disbranch*, IV, ii, 34); *benediction* blessing   **44** *casualties* chances   **49** *'Tis so* i.e. I have to this extent   **51** *dear cause* important purpose

IV, iv A field near Dover   **3** *fumiter* fumitory; *furrow weeds* (those that appear after ploughing?)   **4** *hardocks* (variously identified as burdock, 'hoar dock,' 'harlock,' etc.)   **5** *Darnel* tares; *idle* useless   **6** *sustaining corn* life-giving wheat; *century* troop of a hundred men   **8** *can* i.e. can accomplish   **9** *bereavèd* bereft   **10** *outward worth* material possessions

12 Our foster nurse of nature is repose,
13 The which he lacks. That to provoke in him
14 Are many simples operative, whose power
   Will close the eye of anguish.
   CORDELIA   All blessed secrets,
16 All you unpublished virtues of the earth,
17 Spring with my tears ; be aidant and remediate
   In the good man's distress. Seek, seek for him,
   Lest his ungoverned rage dissolve the life
20 That wants the means to lead it.
               Enter Messenger
   MESSENGER   News, madam.
   The British pow'rs are marching hitherward.
   CORDELIA
   'Tis known before. Our preparation stands
   In expectation of them. O dear father,
   It is thy business that I go about.
25 Therefore great France
26 My mourning, and importuned tears hath pitied.
27 No blown ambition doth our arms incite,
   But love, dear love, and our aged father's right.
   Soon may I hear and see him !   *Exeunt.*

                              ✻

IV, v   *Enter Regan and Steward [Oswald].*
   REGAN
   But are my brother's pow'rs set forth ?
   OSWALD   Ay, madam.
   REGAN
   Himself in person there ?
2 OSWALD   Madam, with much ado.
   Your sister is the better soldier.
   REGAN
   Lord Edmund spake not with your lord at home ?
   OSWALD No, madam.
   REGAN
6 What might import my sister's letter to him ?
   OSWALD I know not, lady.
   REGAN
8 Faith, he is posted hence on serious matter.
9 It was great ignorance, Gloucester's eyes being out,
   To let him live. Where he arrives he moves
   All hearts against us. Edmund, I think, is gone,
   In pity of his misery, to dispatch
13 His nighted life ; moreover, to descry
   The strength o' th' enemy.
   OSWALD
   I must needs after him, madam, with my letter.
   REGAN
   Our troops set forth to-morrow. Stay with us.

   The ways are dangerous.
   OSWALD   I may not, madam.
   My lady charged my duty in this business.   18
   REGAN
   Why should she write to Edmund ? Might not you
   Transport her purposes by word ? Belike,   20
   Some things – I know not what. I'll love thee much,
   Let me unseal the letter.
   OSWALD   Madam, I had rather –
   REGAN
   I know your lady does not love her husband,
   I am sure of that ; and at her late being here   24
   She gave strange eliads and most speaking looks   25
   To noble Edmund. I know you are of her bosom.   26
   OSWALD I, madam ?
   REGAN
   I speak in understanding – y' are, I know't –
   Therefore I do advise you take this note :   29
   My lord is dead ; Edmund and I have talked,
   And more convenient is he for my hand   31
   Than for your lady's. You may gather more.   32
   If you do find him, pray you give him this ;   33
   And when your mistress hears thus much from you,
   I pray desire her call her wisdom to her.   35
   So fare you well.
   If you do chance to hear of that blind traitor,
   Preferment falls on him that cuts him off.   38
   OSWALD
   Would I could meet him, madam ! I should show
   What party I do follow.
   REGAN   Fare thee well.   *Exeunt.*

                              ✻

            Enter Gloucester and Edgar.   IV, vi
   GLOUCESTER
   When shall I come to th' top of that same hill ?
   EDGAR
   You do climb up it now. Look how we labor.
   GLOUCESTER
   Methinks the ground is even.
   EDGAR   Horrible steep.
   Hark, do you hear the sea ?
   GLOUCESTER   No, truly.
   EDGAR
   Why, then, your other senses grow imperfect
   By your eyes' anguish.   6
   GLOUCESTER   So may it be indeed.
   Methinks thy voice is altered, and thou speak'st
   In better phrase and matter than thou didst.
   EDGAR
   Y' are much deceived. In nothing am I changed
   But in my garments.
   GLOUCESTER   Methinks y' are better spoken.
   EDGAR
   Come on, sir ; here's the place. Stand still. How fearful
   And dizzy 'tis to cast one's eyes so low !
   The crows and choughs that wing the midway air   13
   Show scarce so gross as beetles. Halfway down   14
   Hangs one that gathers sampire – dreadful trade ;   15
   Methinks he seems no bigger than his head.
   The fishermen that walk upon the beach
   Appear like mice ; and yond tall anchoring bark,   18

19 Diminished to her cock; her cock, a buoy
Almost too small for sight. The murmuring surge
21 That on th' unnumb'red idle pebble chafes
Cannot be heard so high. I'll look no more,
23 Lest my brain turn, and the deficient sight
24 Topple down headlong.

GLOUCESTER   Set me where you stand.

EDGAR
Give me your hand. You are now within a foot
Of th' extreme verge. For all beneath the moon
27 Would I not leap upright.

GLOUCESTER   Let go my hand.
Here, friend, 's another purse; in it a jewel
29 Well worth a poor man's taking. Fairies and gods
Prosper it with thee. Go thou further off;
Bid me farewell, and let me hear thee going.

EDGAR
Now fare ye well, good sir.

GLOUCESTER   With all my heart.

EDGAR [aside]
33 Why I do trifle thus with his despair
Is done to cure it.

GLOUCESTER   O you mighty gods!
[He kneels.]
This world I do renounce, and in your sights
Shake patiently my great affliction off.
37 If I could bear it longer and not fall
38 To quarrel with your great opposeless wills,
39 My snuff and loathèd part of nature should
Burn itself out. If Edgar live, O bless him!
Now, fellow, fare thee well.
[He falls forward and swoons.]

EDGAR   Gone, sir – farewell.
42 And yet I know not how conceit may rob
The treasury of life when life itself
44 Yields to the theft. Had he been where he thought,
By this had thought been past. Alive or dead?
Ho you, sir! Friend! Hear you, sir? Speak!
Thus might he pass indeed. Yet he revives.
What are you, sir?

GLOUCESTER   Away, and let me die.

EDGAR
Hadst thou been aught but gossamer, feathers, air,
50 So many fathom down precipitating,
Thou'dst shivered like an egg; but thou dost breathe,
Hast heavy substance, bleed'st not, speak'st, art sound.
53 Ten masts at each make not the altitude
Which thou hast perpendicularly fell.
55 Thy life 's a miracle. Speak yet again.

GLOUCESTER
But have I fall'n, or no?

EDGAR
57 From the dread summit of this chalky bourn.
58 Look up a-height. The shrill-gorged lark so far
Cannot be seen or heard. Do but look up.

GLOUCESTER
Alack, I have no eyes.
Is wretchedness deprived that benefit
To end itself by death? 'Twas yet some comfort
When misery could beguile the tyrant's rage
63 And frustrate his proud will.

EDGAR   Give me your arm.
65 Up – so. How is't? Feel you your legs? You stand.

GLOUCESTER
Too well, too well.

EDGAR   This is above all strangeness.
Upon the crown o' th' cliff what thing was that
Which parted from you?

GLOUCESTER   A poor unfortunate beggar.

EDGAR
As I stood here below, methought his eyes
Were two full moons; he had a thousand noses,
Horns whelked and waved like the enridgèd sea. 71
It was some fiend. Therefore, thou happy father, 72
Think that the clearest gods, who make them honors 73
Of men's impossibilities, have preservèd thee.

GLOUCESTER
I do remember now. Henceforth I'll bear
Affliction till it do cry out itself
'Enough, enough, and die.' That thing you speak of,
I took it for a man. Often 'twould say
'The fiend, the fiend' – he led me to that place.

EDGAR
Bear free and patient thoughts. 80
Enter Lear [mad, bedecked with weeds].
         But who comes here?
The safer sense will ne'er accommodate 81
His master thus. 82

LEAR No, they cannot touch me for coining; I am the 83
King himself.

EDGAR
O thou side-piercing sight!

LEAR Nature 's above art in that respect. There's your 86
press money. That fellow handles his bow like a crow- 87
keeper. Draw me a clothier's yard. Look, look, a mouse! 88
Peace, peace; this piece of toasted cheese will do't.
There's my gauntlet; I'll prove it on a giant. Bring up 90
the brown bills. O, well flown, bird. I' th' clout, i' th' 91
clout – hewgh! Give the word. 92

EDGAR Sweet marjoram. 93

LEAR Pass.

GLOUCESTER
I know that voice.

LEAR Ha! Goneril with a white beard? They flattered me
like a dog, and told me I had the white hairs in my beard 97

19 *Diminished . . . cock* reduced to the size of her cockboat   21 *unnumb'red idle pebble* i.e. barren reach of countless pebbles   23 *the deficient sight* i.e. my dizziness   24 *Topple* topple me   27 *upright* i.e. even upright, let alone forward   29 *Fairies* (the usual wardens of treasure)   33 *Why . . . trifle* i.e. the reason I toy with (*done* in l. 34 being redundant)   37–38 *fall . . . with* i.e. rebel against (irreligiously)   38 *opposeless* not to be opposed   39 *My snuff . . . nature* i.e. the guttering and hateful tag end of my life   42 *conceit* imagination   44 *Yields to* i.e. welcomes   50 *precipitating* falling   53 *at each* end to end   55 *life* survival   57 *bourn* boundary, headland   58 *a-height* on high; *gorged* throated   63 *beguile* outwit   65 *Feel* test   71 *whelked* corrugated; *enridgèd* blown into ridges   72 *happy father* lucky old man   73 *clearest* purest   73–74 *who . . . impossibilities* i.e. whose glory it is to do for man what he cannot do for himself   80 *free* (of despair)   81 *safer* saner; *accommodate* accoutre   82 *His* its   83 *touch* i.e. interfere with; *coining* minting coins (a royal prerogative)   86 *Nature . . . respect* i.e. a born king is above a made king in legal immunity (cf. the coeval debate on the relative merits of poets of nature, i.e. born, and poets of art, i.e. made by self-effort)   87 *press money* i.e. the 'king's shilling' (token payment on military impressment or enlistment)   87–88 *crow-keeper* i.e. farmhand warding off crows   88 *clothier's yard* i.e. arrow (normally a yard long)   90 *gauntlet* armored glove (hurled as challenge); *prove it on* maintain it against   91 *brown bills* varnished halberds; *well flown* (hawking cry); *clout* bull's-eye (archery term)   92 *word* password   93 *Sweet marjoram* (herb, associated with treating madness?)   97 *like a dog* i.e. fawningly; *I . . . beard* i.e. I was wise

98 ere the black ones were there. To say 'ay' and 'no' to
99 everything that I said! 'Ay' and 'no' too was no good
divinity. When the rain came to wet me once, and the
wind to make me chatter; when the thunder would not
peace at my bidding; there I found 'em, there I smelt
'em out. Go to, they are not men o' their words. They
104 told me I was everything. 'Tis a lie – I am not ague-proof.

GLOUCESTER
105 The trick of that voice I do well remember.
Is't not the King?

LEAR   Ay, every inch a king.
When I do stare, see how the subject quakes.
108 I pardon that man's life. What was thy cause?
Adultery?
Thou shalt not die. Die for adultery? No.
The wren goes to't, and the small gilded fly
112 Does lecher in my sight.
Let copulation thrive; for Gloucester's bastard son
Was kinder to his father than my daughters
115 Got 'tween the lawful sheets.
116 To't, luxury, pell-mell, for I lack soldiers.
Behold yond simp'ring dame,
118 Whose face between her forks presages snow,
119 That minces virtue, and does shake the head
120 To hear of pleasure's name.
121 The fitchew nor the soilèd horse goes to't
With a more riotous appetite.
123 Down from the waist they are Centaurs,
Though women all above.
125 But to the girdle do the gods inherit,
Beneath is all the fiend's.
There's hell, there's darkness, there is the sulphurous
pit; burning, scalding, stench, consumption. Fie, fie,
129 fie! pah, pah! Give me an ounce of civet; good apothecary, sweeten my imagination! There's money for thee.

GLOUCESTER
O, let me kiss that hand.

132 LEAR Let me wipe it first; it smells of mortality.

GLOUCESTER
133 O ruined piece of nature; this great world
Shall so wear out to naught. Dost thou know me?

LEAR I remember thine eyes well enough. Dost thou
squiny at me? No, do thy worst, blind Cupid; I'll not 136
love. Read thou this challenge; mark but the penning of it.

GLOUCESTER
Were all thy letters suns, I could not see.

EDGAR [aside]
I would not take this from report – it is, 139
And my heart breaks at it.

LEAR Read.

GLOUCESTER
What, with the case of eyes? 142

LEAR O, ho, are you there with me? No eyes in your head, 143
nor no money in your purse? Your eyes are in a heavy
case, your purse in a light; yet you see how this world 145
goes.

GLOUCESTER
I see it feelingly. 147

LEAR What, art mad? A man may see how this world goes
with no eyes. Look with thine ears. See how yond justice
rails upon yond simple thief. Hark in thine ear: change 150
places and, handy-dandy, which is the justice, which is 151
the thief? Thou hast seen a farmer's dog bark at a beggar?

GLOUCESTER Ay, sir.

LEAR And the creature run from the cur. There thou
mightst behold the great image of authority – a dog's 155
obeyed in office.
Thou rascal beadle, hold thy bloody hand! 157
Why dost thou lash that whore? Strip thy own back.
Thou hotly lusts to use her in that kind 159
For which thou whip'st her. The usurer hangs the 160
   cozener.
Through tattered clothes small vices do appear; 161
Robes and furred gowns hide all. Plate sin with gold,
And the strong lance of justice hurtless breaks; 163
Arm it in rags, a pygmy's straw does pierce it. 164
None does offend, none – I say none! I'll able 'em. 165
Take that of me, my friend, who have the power 166
To seal th' accuser's lips. Get thee glass eyes
And, like a scurvy politician, seem 168
To see the things thou dost not. Now, now, now, now!
Pull off my boots. Harder, harder! So.

EDGAR
O, matter and impertinency mixed; 171
Reason in madness.

LEAR
If thou wilt weep my fortunes, take my eyes.
I know thee well enough; thy name is Gloucester.
Thou must be patient. We came crying hither;
Thou know'st, the first time that we smell the air
We wawl and cry. I will preach to thee. Mark.

GLOUCESTER
Alack, alack the day.

LEAR
When we are born, we cry that we are come
To this great stage of fools. – This' a good block. 180
It were a delicate stratagem to shoe 181
A troop of horse with felt. I'll put't in proof, 182
And when I have stol'n upon these son-in-laws,
Then kill, kill, kill, kill, kill, kill!

     Enter a Gentleman [with Attendants].

GENTLEMAN
O, here he is! Lay hand upon him. – Sir,
Your most dear daughter –

98 *To say . . . 'no'* i.e. to agree   99–100 *no good divinity* i.e. bad theology
(For 'good divinity' cf. 2 Corinthians i, 18: 'But as God is true, our word
to you was not yea and nay'; also Matthew v, 36–37, James v, 12.)   104
ague-proof proof against chills and fever   105 *trick* peculiarity   108 *cause*
case   112 *lecher* copulate   115 *Got* begotten   116 *luxury* lechery; *for
. . . soldiers* (and therefore a higher birth rate)   118 *Whose . . . snow* i.e.
whose face (mien) presages snow (frigidity) between her forks (legs)
119 *minces* mincingly affects   120 *pleasure's name* i.e. the very name of
sexual indulgence   121 *fitchew* polecat, prostitute; *soilèd* pastured   123
Centaurs (lustful creatures of mythology, half-human and half-beast)
125 *girdle* waist; *inherit* possess   129 *civet* musk perfume   132 *mortality*
death   133–34 *this . . . naught* i.e. the universe (macrocosm) will decay
like this man (microcosm) (cf. III, i, 10n.)   136 *squiny* squint   139 *take*
accept   142 *case* sockets   143 *are . . . me* is that the situation   145 *case*
plight (pun)   147 *feelingly* (1) only by touch, (2) by feeling pain   150
simple mere   151 *handy-dandy* (old formula used in the child's game of
choosing which hand)   155 *great image* universal symbol   155–56 *a dog's
. . . office* i.e. man bows to authority regardless of who exercises it   157
beadle parish constable   159 *lusts* wish (suggestive form of 'lists'); *kind*
i.e. same act   160 *The usurer . . . cozener* i.e. the great cheat, some money-
lending judge, sentences to death the little cheat   161 *appear* show plainly
163 *hurtless* without hurting   164 *Arm . . . rags* i.e. armored (cf. *Plate,*
l. 162) only in rags   165 *able* authorize   166 *that* (i.e. the assurance of
immunity)   168 *scurvy politician* vile opportunist   171 *matter and
impertinency* sense and nonsense   180 *block* felt hat (?)   181 *delicate*
subtle   182 *in proof* to the test

LEAR
No rescue ? What, a prisoner ? I am even
188   The natural fool of fortune. Use me well ;
You shall have ransom. Let me have surgeons ;
190   I am cut to th' brains.
GENTLEMAN   You shall have anything.
LEAR
No seconds ? All myself ?
192   Why, this would make a man a man of salt,
To use his eyes for garden waterpots,
[Ay, and laying autumn's dust.] I will die bravely,
195   Like a smug bridegroom. What, I will be jovial !
Come, come, I am a king ; masters, know you that ?
GENTLEMAN
You are a royal one, and we obey you.
198 LEAR Then there's life in 't. Come, an you get it, you shall
199   get it by running. Sa, sa, sa, sa !
                        Exit [running, followed by Attendants].
GENTLEMAN
A sight most pitiful in the meanest wretch,
Past speaking of in a king. Thou hast one daughter
202   Who redeems Nature from the general curse
203   Which twain have brought her to.
EDGAR
Hail, gentle sir.
204 GENTLEMAN   Sir, speed you. What's your will ?
EDGAR
205   Do you hear aught, sir, of a battle toward ?
GENTLEMAN
206   Most sure and vulgar. Every one hears that
Which can distinguish sound.
EDGAR   But, by your favor,
How near's the other army ?
GENTLEMAN
209   Near and on speedy foot. The main descry
Stands on the hourly thought.
EDGAR   I thank you, sir. That's all.
GENTLEMAN
Though that the Queen on special cause is here,
Her army is moved on.
EDGAR   I thank you, sir. *Exit [Gentleman]*.
GLOUCESTER
You ever-gentle gods, take my breath from me ;
214   Let not my worser spirit tempt me again
To die before you please.
EDGAR   Well pray you, father.
GLOUCESTER
Now, good sir, what are you ?
EDGAR
217   A most poor man, made tame to fortune's blows,
218   Who, by the art of known and feeling sorrows,
219   Am pregnant to good pity. Give me your hand ;
220   I'll lead you to some biding.
GLOUCESTER   Hearty thanks.
221   The bounty and the benison of heaven
To boot, and boot.
          Enter Steward [Oswald].
222 OSWALD   A proclaimed prize ! Most happy ;
223   That eyeless head of thine was first framed flesh
To raise my fortunes. Thou old unhappy traitor,
225   Briefly thyself remember. The sword is out
That must destroy thee.
226 GLOUCESTER   Now let thy friendly hand
Put strength enough to 't.

          [Edgar interposes.]
OSWALD   Wherefore, bold peasant,
Dar'st thou support a published traitor ? Hence,   228
Lest that th' infection of his fortune take
Like hold on thee. Let go his arm.
EDGAR
Chill not let go, zir, without vurther 'casion.   231
OSWALD
Let go, slave, or thou diest.
EDGAR Good gentleman, go your gait, and let poor voke 233
pass. An chud ha' bin zwaggered out of my life, 'twould 234
not ha' bin zo long as 'tis by a vortnight. Nay, come not
near th' old man. Keep out, che vore ye, or Ise try   236
whether your costard or my ballow be the harder. Chill 237
be plain with you.
OSWALD Out, dunghill !
          [They fight.]
EDGAR Chill pick your teeth, zir. Come. No matter vor 240
your foins.   241
          [Oswald falls.]
OSWALD
Slave, thou hast slain me. Villain, take my purse.   242
If ever thou wilt thrive, bury my body,
And give the letters which thou find'st about me   244
To Edmund Earl of Gloucester. Seek him out
Upon the English party. O, untimely death !   246
Death !
          [He dies.]
EDGAR
I know thee well. A serviceable villain,   248
As duteous to the vices of thy mistress   249
As badness would desire.
GLOUCESTER   What, is he dead ?
EDGAR
Sit you down, father ; rest you.
Let's see these pockets ; the letters that he speaks of
May be my friends. He's dead ; I am only sorry
He had no other deathsman. Let us see.   254
Leave, gentle wax and manners : blame us not   255
To know our enemies' minds. We rip their hearts ;   256
Their papers is more lawful.   257
          Reads the letter.
'Let our reciprocal vows be remembered. You have
many opportunities to cut him off. If your will want not, 259

188 *natural fool* born plaything 190 *cut* wounded 192 *salt* i.e. all tears
195 *smug bridegroom* spruce bridegroom (the image suggested by the
secondary meaning of *bravely*, i.e. handsomely, and the sexual suggestion
of *will die*) 198 *life* (and therefore 'hope') 199 *Sa . . . sa* (hunting and
rallying cry) 202 *general curse* universal condemnation 203 *twain* i.e.
the other two 204 *speed* God speed 205 *toward* impending 206 *sure
and vulgar* commonly known certainty 209 *on speedy foot* rapidly marching 209-10 *main . . . thought* sight of the main body is expected hourly
214 *worser spirit* i.e. bad angel 217 *tame* submissive 218 *art . . . sorrows*
i.e. lesson of sorrows painfully experienced 219 *pregnant* prone 220
biding biding place 221 *benison* blessing 222 *proclaimed prize* i.e. one
with a price on his head ; *happy* lucky 223 *framed flesh* born, created
225 *thyself remember* i.e. pray, think of your soul 226 *friendly* i.e. unconsciously befriending 228 *published* proclaimed 231 *Chill* I'll (rustic
dialect) ; *vurther 'casion* further occasion 233 *gait* way ; *voke* folk 234
An chud if I could ; *zwaggered* swaggered, bluffed 236 *che vore* I warrant,
assure ; *Ise* I shall 237 *costard* head ; *ballow* cudgel 240 *Chill pick* i.e.
I'll knock out 241 *foins* thrusts 242 *Villain* serf 244 *letters* letter ;
about upon 246 *party* side 248 *serviceable* usable 249 *duteous* ready
to serve 254 *deathsman* executioner 255 *Leave, gentle wax* by your
leave, kind seal (formula used in opening sealed documents) 256 *To
know* i.e. for growing intimate with 257 *Their papers* i.e. to rip their
papers 259 *want not* is not lacking

time and place will be fruitfully offered. There is nothing done, if he return the conqueror. Then am I the
262 prisoner, and his bed my gaol ; from the loathed warmth
whereof deliver me, and supply the place for your labor.
264   'Your (wife, so I would say) affectionate servant,
                               'Goneril.'
266 O indistinguished space of woman's will –
A plot upon her virtuous husband's life,
268 And the exchange my brother ! Here in the sands
269 Thee I'll rake up, the post unsanctified
270 Of murderous lechers ; and in the mature time
271 With this ungracious paper strike the sight
272 Of the death-practiced Duke. For him 'tis well
That of thy death and business I can tell.
     GLOUCESTER
274 The King is mad. How stiff is my vile sense,
275 That I stand up, and have ingenious feeling
276 Of my huge sorrows ! Better I were distract ;
So should my thoughts be severed from my griefs,
278 And woes by wrong imaginations lose
The knowledge of themselves.
          Drum afar off.
   EDGAR   Give me your hand.
Far off methinks I hear the beaten drum.
281 Come, father, I'll bestow you with a friend.   *Exeunt.*

                         *

IV, vii   *Enter Cordelia, Kent, [Doctor,] and Gentleman.*
     CORDELIA
O thou good Kent, how shall I live and work
To match thy goodness ? My life will be too short
And every measure fail me.
     KENT
To be acknowledged, madam, is o'erpaid.
5 All my reports go with the modest truth ;
6 Nor more nor clipped, but so.
     CORDELIA   Be better suited.
7 These weeds are memories of those worser hours.
I prithee put them off.
     KENT   Pardon, dear madam.
9 Yet to be known shortens my made intent.
10 My boon I make it that you know me not
11 Till time and I think meet.
     CORDELIA
Then be't so, my good lord.
       [To the Doctor]   How does the King ?

262 *gaol* jail   264 *would* wish to   266 *indistinguished* unlimited ; *will*
desire   268 *exchange* substitute   269 *rake up* cover, bury   270 *in the
mature* at the ripe   271 *strike* blast   272 *death-practiced* whose death is
plotted   274 *stiff* obstinate ; *vile sense* i.e. hateful consciousness   275
ingenious feeling i.e. awareness   276 *distract* distracted   278 *wrong
imaginations* i.e. delusions   281 *bestow* lodge
IV, vii The French camp near Dover   5 *go* conform   6 *clipped* i.e. less
(curtailed) ; *suited* attired   7 *weeds* clothes ; *memories* reminders   9 *Yet
. . . intent* i.e. to reveal myself just yet would mar my plan   10 *My boon
. . . it* the reward I ask is   11 *meet* proper   15 *abused* confused, disturbed
16 *jarring* discordant ; *wind up* tune   17 *child-changèd* (1) changed to a
child, (2) changed by his children (suggesting 'changeling,' wherein
mental defect is associated with the malignance of witches)   20 *I' th'
sway of* according to   28 *harms* wounds   29 *reverence* reverend person
30 *flakes* strands of hair   31 *challenge* demand   33 *deep dread-bolted*
deep-voiced and full of dreadful bolts   35 *perdu* (1) expendable outpost
(military term), (2) lost one   36 *helm* military helmet ; here, thin hair
38 *fain* glad   40 *short* scanty (?), tramped to fragments (?)   47 *wheel of
fire* (implement combining the tortures of breaking and burning, figuring
in medieval visions of hell)   50 *wide* off the mark   53 *abused* confused

     DOCTOR
Madam, sleeps still.
     CORDELIA
O you kind gods,
Cure this great breach in his abusèd nature !   15
Th' untuned and jarring senses, O, wind up   16
Of this child-changèd father !   17
     DOCTOR   So please your Majesty
That we may wake the King ? He hath slept long.
     CORDELIA
Be governed by your knowledge, and proceed
I' th' sway of your own will. Is he arrayed ?   20
        Enter Lear in a chair carried by Servants.
     GENTLEMAN
Ay, madam. In the heaviness of sleep
We put fresh garments on him.
     DOCTOR
Be by, good madam, when we do awake him.
I doubt not of his temperance.
[CORDELIA   Very well.
       [Music.]
     DOCTOR
Please you draw near. Louder the music there.]
     CORDELIA
O my dear father, restoration hang
Thy medicine on my lips, and let this kiss
Repair those violent harms that my two sisters   28
Have in thy reverence made.   29
     KENT   Kind and dear princess.
     CORDELIA
Had you not been their father, these white flakes   30
Did challenge pity of them. Was this a face   31
To be opposed against the jarring winds ?
[To stand against the deep dread-bolted thunder ?   33
In the most terrible and nimble stroke
Of quick cross lightning to watch, poor perdu,   35
With this thin helm ?] Mine enemy's dog,   36
Though he had bit me, should have stood that night
Against my fire ; and wast thou fain, poor father,   38
To hovel thee with swine and rogues forlorn
In short and musty straw ? Alack, alack,   40
'Tis wonder that thy life and wits at once
Had not concluded all. – He wakes. Speak to him.
     DOCTOR
Madam, do you ; 'tis fittest.
     CORDELIA
How does my royal lord ? How fares your Majesty ?
     LEAR
You do me wrong to take me out o' th' grave.
Thou art a soul in bliss ; but I am bound
Upon a wheel of fire, that mine own tears   47
Do scald like molten lead.
     CORDELIA   Sir, do you know me ?
     LEAR
You are a spirit, I know. Where did you die ?
     CORDELIA
Still, still, far wide !   50
     DOCTOR
He's scarce awake. Let him alone awhile.
     LEAR
Where have I been ? Where am I ? Fair daylight ?
I am mightily abused. I should e'en die with pity   53
To see another thus. I know not what to say.
I will not swear these are my hands. Let's see –

I feel this pin prick. Would I were assured
Of my condition.

CORDELIA   O look upon me, sir,
And hold your hand in benediction o'er me.
You must not kneel.

LEAR   Pray, do not mock me.

60 I am a very foolish fond old man,
Fourscore and upward, not an hour more nor less;
And, to deal plainly,
I fear I am not in my perfect mind.
Methinks I should know you, and know this man;
Yet I am doubtful, for I am mainly ignorant
What place this is; and all the skill I have
Remembers not these garments; nor I know not
Where I did lodge last night. Do not laugh at me;
For, as I am a man, I think this lady
To be my child Cordelia.

70 CORDELIA   And so I am! I am!

LEAR
Be your tears wet? Yes, faith. I pray weep not.
If you have poison for me, I will drink it.
I know you do not love me; for your sisters
Have (as I do remember) done me wrong.
You have some cause, they have not.

CORDELIA   No cause, no cause.

LEAR
Am I in France?

KENT   In your own kingdom, sir.

LEAR
77 Do not abuse me.

DOCTOR
Be comforted, good madam. The great rage
You see is killed in him; [and yet it is danger
80 To make him even o'er the time he has lost.]
Desire him to go in. Trouble him no more
82 Till further settling.

CORDELIA
Will't please your Highness walk?

LEAR   You must bear with me.
Pray you now, forget and forgive. I am old and foolish.
                Exeunt. [Manent Kent and Gentleman.]

[GENTLEMAN Holds it true, sir, that the Duke of Cornwall was so slain?

KENT Most certain, sir.

GENTLEMAN Who is conductor of his people?

KENT As 'tis said, the bastard son of Gloucester.

GENTLEMAN They say Edgar, his banished son, is with
the Earl of Kent in Germany.

KENT Report is changeable. 'Tis time to look about; the
93 powers of the kingdom approach apace.

94 GENTLEMAN The arbitrement is like to be bloody. Fare
you well, sir.   [Exit.]

KENT
96 My point and period will be throughly wrought,
97 Or well or ill, as this day's battle's fought.   Exit.]

                *

V, i   Enter, with Drum and Colors, Edmund, Regan,
          Gentleman, and Soldiers.

EDMUND
1   Know of the Duke if his last purpose hold,
2   Or whether since he is advised by aught
To change the course. He's full of alteration

And self-reproving. Bring his constant pleasure.   4
                [Exit an Officer.]

REGAN
Our sister's man is certainly miscarried.   5

EDMUND
'Tis to be doubted, madam.   6

REGAN   Now, sweet lord,
You know the goodness I intend upon you.   7
Tell me, but truly – but then speak the truth –
Do you not love my sister?

EDMUND   In honored love.   9

REGAN
But have you never found my brother's way
To the forfended place?   11

[EDMUND   That thought abuses you.

REGAN
I am doubtful that you have been conjunct   12
And bosomed with her, as far as we call hers.]

EDMUND
No, by mine honor, madam.

REGAN
I never shall endure her. Dear my lord,
Be not familiar with her.

EDMUND   Fear me not.
She and the Duke her husband!
          Enter, with Drum and Colors, Albany, Goneril,
          Soldiers.

[GONERIL [aside]
I had rather lose the battle than that sister
Should loosen him and me.]   19

ALBANY
Our very loving sister, well bemet.   20
Sir, this I heard: the King is come to his daughter,
With others whom the rigor of our state   22
Forced to cry out. [Where I could not be honest,   23
I never yet was valiant. For this business,
It touches us as France invades our land,   25
Not bolds the King with others, whom I fear   26
Most just and heavy causes make oppose.

EDMUND
Sir, you speak nobly.]

REGAN   Why is this reasoned?   28

GONERIL
Combine together 'gainst the enemy;
For these domestic and particular broils   30
Are not the question here.   31

ALBANY   Let's then determine
With th' ancient of war on our proceeding.   32

[EDMUND
I shall attend you presently at your tent.]   33

REGAN
  Sister, you'll go with us?
GONERIL No.
REGAN
36 'Tis most convenient. Pray go with us.
GONERIL
37 O ho, I know the riddle. – I will go.
                                        Exeunt both the Armies.
        Enter Edgar.
EDGAR *[to Albany]*
38 If e'er your Grace had speech with man so poor,
    Hear me one word.
ALBANY *[to those departing]*
                            I'll overtake you. *[to Edgar]* Speak.
EDGAR
    Before you fight the battle, ope this letter.
41 If you have victory, let the trumpet sound
    For him that brought it. Wretched though I seem,
43 I can produce a champion that will prove
44 What is avouchèd there. If you miscarry,
    Your business of the world hath so an end,
46 And machination ceases. Fortune love you.
ALBANY
    Stay till I have read the letter.
EDGAR   I was forbid it.
    When time shall serve, let but the herald cry,
    And I'll appear again.
ALBANY
50 Why, fare thee well. I will o'erlook thy paper.
                                        Exit [Edgar].
        Enter Edmund.
EDMUND
51 The enemy's in view; draw up your powers.
52 Here is the guess of their true strength and forces
53 By diligent discovery; but your haste
    Is now urged on you.
54 ALBANY   We will greet the time.   *Exit.*
EDMUND
    To both these sisters have I sworn my love;
56 Each jealous of the other, as the stung
    Are of the adder. Which of them shall I take?
    Both? One? Or neither? Neither can be enjoyed,
    If both remain alive. To take the widow

Exasperates, makes mad her sister Goneril;
And hardly shall I carry out my side,   61
Her husband being alive. Now then, we'll use
His countenance for the battle, which being done,   63
Let her who would be rid of him devise
His speedy taking off. As for the mercy
Which he intends to Lear and to Cordelia –
The battle done, and they within our power,
Shall never see his pardon; for my state   68
Stands on me to defend, not to debate.   *Exit.*

                            *

        Alarum within. Enter, with Drum and Colors, Lear,   V, ii
        [held by the hand by] Cordelia; and Soldiers [of
        France], over the stage and exeunt.
        Enter Edgar and Gloucester.
EDGAR
    Here, father, take the shadow of this tree
    For your good host. Pray that the right may thrive.
    If ever I return to you again,
    I'll bring you comfort.
GLOUCESTER   Grace go with you, sir.   4
                                        Exit [Edgar].
        Alarum and retreat within. Enter Edgar.
EDGAR
    Away, old man! Give me thy hand. Away!
    King Lear hath lost, he and his daughter ta'en.   6
    Give me thy hand. Come on.
GLOUCESTER
    No further, sir. A man may rot even here.   8
EDGAR
    What, in ill thoughts again? Men must endure   9
    Their going hence, even as their coming hither;
    Ripeness is all. Come on.   11
GLOUCESTER   And that's true too.   *Exeunt.*
        Enter, on conquest, with Drum and Colors, Edmund;   V, iii
        Lear and Cordelia as prisoners; Soldiers, Captain.
EDMUND
    Some officers take them away. Good guard
    Until their greater pleasures first be known   2
    That are to censure them.   3
CORDELIA   We are not the first
    Who with best meaning have incurred the worst.   4
    For thee, oppressèd king, I am cast down;
    Myself could else outfrown false Fortune's frown.
    Shall we not see these daughters and these sisters?
LEAR
    No, no, no, no! Come, let's away to prison.
    We two alone will sing like birds i' th' cage.
    When thou dost ask me blessing, I'll kneel down   10
    And ask of thee forgiveness. So we'll live,
    And pray, and sing, and tell old tales, and laugh   12
    At gilded butterflies, and hear poor rogues
    Talk of court news; and we'll talk with them too –
    Who loses and who wins; who's in, who's out –
    And take upon's the mystery of things   16
    As if we were God's spies; and we'll wear out,   17
    In a walled prison, packs and sects of great ones 18
    That ebb and flow by th' moon.
EDMUND   Take them away.
LEAR
    Upon such sacrifices, my Cordelia,   20
    The gods themselves throw incense. Have I caught thee?

<hr/>

36 *convenient* fitting; *with us* (i.e. with her rather than Edmund as each leads an 'army' from the stage) 37 *riddle* (i.e. the reason for Regan's strange demand) 38 *had speech* i.e. has condescended to speak 41 *sound* sound a summons 43 *prove* (in trial by combat) 44 *avouchèd* charged 46 *machination* i.e. all plots and counterplots 50 *o'erlook* look over 51 *powers* troops 52 *guess* estimate 53 *discovery* reconnoitering 54 *greet* i.e. meet the demands of 56 *jealous* suspicious 61 *hardly . . . side* with difficulty shall I play my part (as Goneril's lover, or as a great power in England?) 63 *countenance* backing 68–69 *my state . . . debate* i.e. my status depends upon my strength, not my arguments
V, ii An open place near the field of battle 4 s.d. *Alarum and retreat* (trumpet sounds, signalling the beginning and the ending of a battle) 6 *ta'en* captured 8 *rot* i.e. die 9 *ill* i.e. suicidal; *endure* put up with, suffer through 11 *Ripeness* i.e. the time decreed by the gods for the fruit to fall from the branch
V, iii 2 *greater pleasures* i.e. the desires of those in higher command 3 *censure* judge 4 *meaning* intentions 10–11 *When . . . forgiveness* (cf. IV, vii, 57–59) 12–14 *laugh . . . news* view with amusement bright ephemera, such as gallants preoccupied with court gossip 16–17 *take . . . spies* i.e. contemplate the wonder of existence as if with divine insight, seek eternal rather than temporal truths 17 *wear out* outlast 18–19 *packs . . . moon* i.e. partisan and intriguing clusters of *great ones* who gain and lose power monthly 20–21 *Upon . . . incense* i.e. the gods themselves are the the celebrants at such sacrificial offerings to love as we are

22 He that parts us shall bring a brand from heaven
And fire us hence like foxes. Wipe thine eyes.
24 The goodyears shall devour them, flesh and fell,
Ere they shall make us weep! We'll see 'em starved first.
Come.   *Exeunt [Lear and Cordelia, guarded].*
EDMUND   Come hither, captain; hark.
Take thou this note.
      [Gives a paper.] Go follow them to prison.
One step I have advanced thee. If thou dost
As this instructs thee, thou dost make thy way
To noble fortunes. Know thou this, that men
31 Are as the time is. To be tender-minded
32 Does not become a sword. Thy great employment
33 Will not bear question. Either say thou'lt do't,
Or thrive by other means.
CAPTAIN   I'll do't, my lord.
EDMUND
35 About it; and write happy when th' hast done.
Mark, I say instantly, and carry it so
As I have set it down.
[CAPTAIN
I cannot draw a cart, nor eat dried oats –
If it be man's work, I'll do't.]   *Exit*
Flourish. Enter Albany, Goneril, Regan, Soldiers.
ALBANY
Sir, you have showed to-day your valiant strain,
And fortune led you well. You have the captives
42 Who were the opposites of this day's strife.
I do require them of you, so to use them
44 As we shall find their merits and our safety
May equally determine.
EDMUND   Sir, I thought it fit
To send the old and miserable King
47 To some retention [and appointed guard];
Whose age had charms in it, whose title more,
49 To pluck the common bosom on his side
50 And turn our impressed lances in our eyes
Which do command them. With him I sent the Queen,
My reason all the same; and they are ready
53 To-morrow, or at further space, t' appear
54 Where you shall hold your session. [At this time
We sweat and bleed, the friend hath lost his friend,
56 And the best quarrels, in the heat, are cursed
57 By those that feel their sharpness.
The question of Cordelia and her father
Requires a fitter place.]
ALBANY   Sir, by your patience,
60 I hold you but a subject of this war,
Not as a brother.
61 REGAN   That's as we list to grace him.
Methinks our pleasure might have been demanded
Ere you had spoke so far. He led our powers,
Bore the commission of my place and person,
65 The which immediacy may well stand up
And call itself your brother.
GONERIL   Not so hot!
In his own grace he doth exalt himself
68 More than in your addition.
REGAN   In my rights
69 By me invested, he compeers the best.
ALBANY
70 That were the most if he should husband you.
REGAN
Jesters do oft prove prophets.

GONERIL   Holla, holla!
That eye that told you so looked but asquint.   72
REGAN
Lady, I am not well; else I should answer
From a full-flowing stomach. General,   74
Take thou my soldiers, prisoners, patrimony;   75
Dispose of them, of me; the walls is thine.   76
Witness the world that I create thee here
My lord and master.
GONERIL   Mean you to enjoy him?
ALBANY
The let-alone lies not in your good will.   79
EDMUND
Nor in thine, lord.
ALBANY   Half-blooded fellow, yes.   80
REGAN *[to Edmund]*
Let the drum strike, and prove my title thine.   81
ALBANY
Stay yet; hear reason. Edmund, I arrest thee
On capital treason; and, in thy attaint,   83
This gilded serpent.
     [Points to Goneril.] For your claim, fair sister,
I bar it in the interest of my wife.
'Tis she is subcontracted to this lord,   86
And I, her husband, contradict your banes.   87
If you will marry, make your loves to me;   88
My lady is bespoke.
GONERIL   An interlude!   89
ALBANY
Thou art armed, Gloucester. Let the trumpet sound.
If none appear to prove upon thy person
Thy heinous, manifest, and many treasons,
There is my pledge.
     [Throws down a glove.] I'll make it on thy heart,   93
Ere I taste bread, thou art in nothing less   94
Than I have here proclaimed thee.
REGAN   Sick, O sick!
GONERIL *[aside]*
If not, I'll ne'er trust medicine.   96
EDMUND
There's my exchange.
     [Throws down a glove.] What in the world he is

22–23 *He . . . foxes* i.e. to separate us, as foxes are smoked out and scattered, would require not a human but a heavenly torch   24 *goodyears* (undefined forces of evil); *fell* hide   31 *as the time is* (i.e. ruthless in war) 32 *become* befit   33 *bear question* admit discussion   35 *write happy* consider yourself fortunate   42 *opposites of* enemies in   44 *merits* deserts 47 *some . . . guard* detention under duly appointed guards   49 *pluck . . . bosom* draw popular sympathy   50 *turn . . . eyes* i.e. make our conscripted lancers turn on us   53 *space* interval   54 *session* trials   56 *best quarrels* worthiest causes   57 *sharpness* i.e. painful effects   60 *subject of* subordinate in   61 *list to grace* please to honor   65 *immediacy* i.e. present status (as my deputy)   68 *your addition* honors conferred by you   69 *compeers* equals   70 *most* i.e. most complete investiture in your rights; *husband* wed   72 *asquint* cross-eyed, crookedly   74 *stomach* anger   75 *patrimony* inheritance   76 *walls is thine* i.e. you have stormed the citadel (myself)   79 *let-alone* permission   80 *Half-blooded* i.e. by birth only half noble   81 *Let . . . thine* i.e. fight and win for yourself my rights in the kingdom   83 *in thy attaint* i.e. as party to your corruption (cf. the *serpent* of Eden)   86 *subcontracted* i.e. engaged, though previously married (sarcastic play on 'precontracted,' a legal term applied to one facing an impediment to marriage because previously engaged to another)   87 *contradict your banes* forbid your banns, i.e. declare an impediment   88 *loves* love-suits   89 *An interlude* a quaint playlet (equivalent to saying 'How dramatic!' or 'How comical!') 93 *make* prove   94 *nothing less* i.e. no respect less guilty   96 *medicine* i.e. poison

That names me traitor, villain-like he lies.
99   Call by the trumpet. He that dares approach,
On him, on you, who not? I will maintain
My truth and honor firmly.
ALBANY
A herald, ho!
[EDMUND   A herald, ho, a herald!]
ALBANY
103   Trust to thy single virtue; for thy soldiers,
All levied in my name, have in my name
Took their discharge.
REGAN   My sickness grows upon me.
ALBANY
She is not well. Convey her to my tent.
                                    [Exit Regan, attended.]
        Enter a Herald.
Come hither, herald. Let the trumpet sound,
And read out this.
[CAPTAIN   Sound, trumpet!]
        A trumpet sounds.
110   HERALD (reads) 'If any man of quality or degree within
111   the lists of the army will maintain upon Edmund, sup-
      posed Earl of Gloucester, that he is a manifold traitor,
      let him appear by the third sound of the trumpet. He is
      bold in his defense.'
[EDMUND   Sound!]
        First trumpet.
HERALD   Again!
        Second trumpet.
Again!
        Third trumpet.
        Trumpet answers within.
        Enter Edgar, armed [at the third sound, a Trumpeter
        before him].
ALBANY
Ask him his purposes, why he appears
Upon this call o' th' trumpet.
HERALD   What are you?
Your name, your quality, and why you answer
This present summons?
EDGAR   Know my name is lost,
122   By treason's tooth bare-gnawn and canker-bit;
Yet am I noble as the adversary
I come to cope.
ALBANY   Which is that adversary?
EDGAR
What's he that speaks for Edmund Earl of Gloucester?

EDMUND
Himself. What say'st thou to him?
EDGAR   Draw thy sword.
That, if my speech offend a noble heart,
Thy arm may do thee justice. Here is mine.
Behold it is my privilege,   129
The privilege of mine honors,
My oath, and my profession. I protest –
Maugre thy strength, place, youth, and eminence,   132
Despite thy victor sword and fire-new fortune,   133
Thy valor and thy heart – thou art a traitor,   134
False to thy gods, thy brother, and thy father,
Conspirant 'gainst this high illustrious prince,   136
And from th' extremest upward of thy head   137
To the descent and dust below thy foot   138
A most toad-spotted traitor. Say thou 'no,'   139
This sword, this arm, and my best spirits are bent 140
To prove upon thy heart, whereto I speak,
Thou liest.
EDMUND   In wisdom I should ask thy name,   142
But since thy outside looks so fair and warlike,
And that thy tongue some say of breeding breathes, 144
What safe and nicely I might well delay   145
By rule of knighthood I disdain and spurn.
Back do I toss these treasons to thy head,   147
With the hell-hated lie o'erwhelm thy heart,   148
Which – for they yet glance by and scarcely bruise – 149
This sword of mine shall give them instant way
Where they shall rest for ever. Trumpets, speak!
        Alarums. Fight. [Edmund falls.]
ALBANY
Save him, save him.   152
GONERIL   This is practice, Gloucester.
By th' law of war thou wast not bound to answer
An unknown opposite. Thou art not vanquished,
But cozened and beguiled.   155
ALBANY   Shut your mouth, dame,
Or with this paper shall I stop it. – Hold, sir. – 156
        [To Goneril]
Thou worse than any name, read thine own evil.
No tearing, lady! I perceive you know it.
GONERIL
Say if I do – the laws are mine, not thine.   159
Who can arraign me for't?
ALBANY   Most monstrous! O,
Know'st thou this paper?
GONERIL   Ask me not what I know. Exit.
ALBANY
Go after her. She's desperate; govern her.   162
                                    [Exit an Officer.]
EDMUND
What you have charged me with, that have I done,
And more, much more. The time will bring it out.
'Tis past, and so am I. – But what art thou
That hast this fortune on me? If thou'rt noble,   166
I do forgive thee.
EDGAR   Let's exchange charity.   167
I am no less in blood than thou art, Edmund;
If more, the more th' hast wronged me.   169
My name is Edgar and thy father's son.
The gods are just, and of our pleasant vices   171
Make instruments to plague us.
The dark and vicious place where thee he got   173
Cost him his eyes.

99 trumpet trumpeter   103 single virtue unaided prowess   110 degree
rank   111 lists muster   122 canker-bit eaten, as by the rose-caterpillar
129-31 it . . . profession i.e. wielding this sword is the privilege of my
knightly honor, oath, and function   132 Maugre in spite of   133 fire-
new brand-new   134 heart courage   136 Conspirant in conspiracy   137
extremest upward uppermost extreme   138 descent and dust i.e. all that
intervenes from the head to the dust   139 toad-spotted i.e. exuding venom
like a toad   140 bent directed   142 wisdom prudence   144 some say
some assay, i.e. proof (?), one might say (?)   145 safe and nicely cautiously
and punctiliously   147 treasons accusations of treason   148 hell-hated
hateful as hell   149-51 Which . . . ever i.e. the accusations of treason,
now flying about harmlessly, will be routed into you with my sword-thrust
and lodge there permanently   152 Save him spare him (cf. l. 156); practice
trickery   155 cozened cheated   156 Hold wait (If addressed to Edmund,
this suggests a motive for the Save him of l. 152: i.e. Albany hopes to
obtain a confession.)   159 mine (i.e. as ruler)   162 govern control   166
fortune on i.e. victory over   167 charity forgiveness and love   169 If
more if greater (since legitimate)   171 of our pleasant out of our pleasurable
173 place i.e. the bed of adultery; got begot

EDMUND   Th' hast spoken right ; 'tis true.
175   The wheel is come full circle ; I am here.
ALBANY
176   Methought thy very gait did prophesy
       A royal nobleness. I must embrace thee.
       Let sorrow split my heart if ever I
       Did hate thee, or thy father.
EDGAR   Worthy prince, I know't.
ALBANY
       Where have you hid yourself ?
       How have you known the miseries of your father ?
EDGAR
       By nursing them, my lord. List a brief tale ;
       And when 'tis told, O that my heart would burst !
       The bloody proclamation to escape
185   That followed me so near (O our lives' sweetness,
       That we the pain of death would hourly die
       Rather than die at once !) taught me to shift
       Into a madman's rags, t' assume a semblance
189   That very dogs disdained ; and in this habit
190   Met I my father with his bleeding rings,
       Their precious stones new lost ; became his guide,
       Led him, begged for him, saved him from despair ;
       Never – O fault ! – revealed myself unto him
194   Until some half hour past, when I was armed,
       Not sure, though hoping of this good success,
       I asked his blessing, and from first to last
197   Told him our pilgrimage. But his flawed heart –
       Alack, too weak the conflict to support –
       'Twixt two extremes of passion, joy and grief,
       Burst smilingly.
EDMUND   This speech of yours hath moved me,
       And shall perchance do good ; but speak you on –
       You look as you had something more to say.
ALBANY
       If there be more, more woeful, hold it in,
204   For I am almost ready to dissolve,
       Hearing of this.
205   [EDGAR   This would have seemed a period
206   To such as love not sorrow ; but another,
       To amplify too much, would make much more,
       And top extremity.
209   Whilst I was big in clamor, came there in a man,
210   Who, having seen me in my worst estate,
       Shunned my abhorred society ; but then, finding
       Who 'twas that so endured, with his strong arms
       He fastened on my neck, and bellowed out
       As he'd burst heaven, threw him on my father,
       Told the most piteous tale of Lear and him
       That ever ear received ; which in recounting
217   His grief grew puissant, and the strings of life
       Began to crack. Twice then the trumpets sounded,
219   And there I left him tranced.
ALBANY   But who was this ?
EDGAR
       Kent, sir, the banished Kent ; who in disguise
221   Followed his enemy king and did him service
       Improper for a slave.]
       Enter a Gentleman [with a bloody knife].
GENTLEMAN
       Help, help ! O, help !
EDGAR   What kind of help ?
ALBANY   Speak, man.

EDGAR
       What means this bloody knife ?
GENTLEMAN   'Tis hot, it smokes.   224
       It came even from the heart of – O, she's dead.
ALBANY
       Who dead ? Speak, man.
GENTLEMAN
       Your lady, sir, your lady ; and her sister
       By her is poisonèd ; she confesses it.
EDMUND
       I was contracted to them both. All three   229
       Now marry in an instant.   230
EDGAR   Here comes Kent.
       Enter Kent.
ALBANY
       Produce the bodies, be they alive or dead.
                              [Exit Gentleman.]
       This judgment of the heavens, that makes us tremble,
       Touches us not with pity. – O, is this he ?
       The time will not allow the compliment   234
       Which very manners urges.   235
KENT   I am come
       To bid my king and master aye good night.
       Is he not here ?
ALBANY   Great thing of us forgot !   237
       Speak, Edmund, where's the King ? and where's
         Cordelia ?
       Goneril and Regan's bodies brought out.
       Seest thou this object, Kent ?   239
KENT
       Alack, why thus ?
EDMUND   Yet Edmund was beloved.   240
       The one the other poisoned for my sake,
       And after slew herself.
ALBANY
       Even so. Cover their faces.
EDMUND
       I pant for life. Some good I mean to do,   244
       Despite of mine own nature. Quickly send –
       Be brief in it – to th' castle, for my writ   246
       Is on the life of Lear and on Cordelia.
       Nay, send in time.
ALBANY   Run, run, O run !
EDGAR
       To who, my lord ? Who has the office ? Send   249
       Thy token of reprieve.
EDMUND
       Well thought on. Take my sword ;
       Give it the captain.
EDGAR   Haste thee for thy life. *[Exit Officer.]*
EDMUND
       He hath commission from thy wife and me

175 *wheel* (of fortune); *here* (at its bottom)   176 *prophesy* promise   185–86
O . . . die i.e. how sweet is life that we would prefer to suffer death-pangs
hourly   189 *habit* attire   190 *rings* sockets   194 *armed* in armor   197
our pilgrimage of our journey ; *flawed* cracked   204 *dissolve* melt into
tears   205 *a period* the limit   206–08 *another . . . extremity* i.e. another
sorrow, too fully described, would exceed the limit   209 *big in clamor*
loud in lamentation   210 *estate* state   217 *puissant* powerful   219
tranced insensible   221 *enemy* inimical   224 *smokes* steams   229 *contracted* engaged   230 *marry* (i.e. in death)   234 *compliment* ceremony
235 *very manners* i.e. sheer decency   237 *thing* matter ; *of* by   239 *object*
sight   240 *Yet* despite all   244 *pant for life* i.e. gasp for life's breath
246 *writ* i.e. order of execution   249 *office* commission

To hang Cordelia in the prison and
To lay the blame upon her own despair
256   That she fordid herself.

ALBANY
The gods defend her ! Bear him hence awhile.
                     [Edmund is borne off.]
    Enter Lear, with Cordelia in his arms [, Gentleman,
    and others following].

LEAR
Howl, howl, howl ! O, you are men of stones.
Had I your tongues and eyes, I'd use them so
That heaven's vault should crack. She's gone for ever.
I know when one is dead, and when one lives.
She's dead as earth. Lend me a looking glass.
263   If that her breath will mist or stain the stone,
Why then she lives.
264 KENT   Is this the promised end ?

EDGAR
265   Or image of that horror ?

ALBANY   Fall and cease.

LEAR
This feather stirs ; she lives ! If it be so,
267   It is a chance which does redeem all sorrows
That ever I have felt.

KENT   O my good master.

LEAR
Prithee away.

EDGAR   'Tis noble Kent, your friend.

LEAR
A plague upon you murderers, traitors all ;
I might have saved her ; now she's gone for ever.
Cordelia, Cordelia, stay a little. Ha,
What is't thou say'st ? Her voice was ever soft,
Gentle, and low – an excellent thing in woman.
I killed the slave that was a-hanging thee.

GENTLEMAN
'Tis true, my lords, he did.

LEAR   Did I not, fellow ?
277   I have seen the day, with my good biting falchion
I would have made them skip. I am old now,
279   And these same crosses spoil me. Who are you ?
280   Mine eyes are not o' th' best, I'll tell you straight.

KENT
281   If Fortune brag of two she loved and hated,
One of them we behold.

LEAR
This is a dull sight. Are you not Kent ?   283

KENT   The same :
Your servant Kent ; where is your servant Caius ?   284

LEAR
He's a good fellow, I can tell you that.
He'll strike, and quickly too. He's dead and rotten.

KENT
No, my good lord ; I am the very man.

LEAR
I'll see that straight.   288

KENT
That from your first of difference and decay   289
Have followed your sad steps.

LEAR   You are welcome hither.

KENT
Nor no man else. All's cheerless, dark, and deadly.   291
Your eldest daughters have fordone themselves,   292
And desperately are dead.   293

LEAR   Ay, so I think.

ALBANY
He knows not what he says ; and vain is it
That we present us to him.

EDGAR   Very bootless.   295
          Enter a Messenger.

MESSENGER
Edmund is dead, my lord.

ALBANY   That's but a trifle here.
You lords and noble friends, know our intent.
What comfort to this great decay may come   298
Shall be applied. For us, we will resign,
During the life of this old Majesty,
To him our absolute power ; *[to Edgar and Kent]* you to
    your rights,
With boot and such addition as your honors   302
Have more than merited. All friends shall taste
The wages of their virtue, and all foes
The cup of their deservings. – O, see, see !

LEAR
And my poor fool is hanged : no, no, no life ?   306
Why should a dog, a horse, a rat, have life,
And thou no breath at all ? Thou'lt come no more,
Never, never, never, never, never.
Pray you undo this button. Thank you, sir.
Do you see this ? Look on her ! Look her lips,
Look there, look there –
         He dies.

EDGAR   He faints. My lord, my lord –

KENT
Break, heart, I prithee break !

EDGAR   Look up, my lord.

KENT
Vex not his ghost. O, let him pass ! He hates him   314
That would upon the rack of this tough world   315
Stretch him out longer.

EDGAR   He is gone indeed.

KENT
The wonder is he hath endured so long ;
He but usurped his life.   318

ALBANY
Bear them from hence. Our present business
Is general woe.
      [To Kent and Edgar] Friends of my soul, you twain

---

256 *fordid* destroyed   **263** *stone* i.e. glass   **264** *promised end* i.e. doomsday **265** *image* duplicate; *Fall and cease* i.e. strike once and for all, make an end of things   **267** *redeem* atone for   **277** *falchion* small sword slightly hooked   **279** *crosses* adversities; *spoil me* i.e. sap my strength   **280** *tell you straight* admit (?), recognize you in a moment (?)   **281** *two* (i.e. Lear, and a hypothetical second extreme example of Fortune's cruelty with whom he may be equated); *loved and hated* i.e. favored, then victimized **283** *sight* eyesight (instinctively Lear shuns the admission that he is dazed and weeping)   **284** *Caius* (Kent's alias)   **288** *see that straight* understand that in a moment   **289** *difference and decay* change and decline in fortune **291** *Nor no man else* i.e. no, nor anyone else   **292** *fordone* destroyed   **293** *desperately* in a state of despair   **295** *bootless* useless   **298** *What . . . come* i.e. whatever means of aiding this ruined great one presents itself   **302** *boot* good measure; *addition* titles, advancement in rank   **306** *fool* i.e. Cordelia ('Fool' was often a term of affection, and sometimes, as in Erasmus and elsewhere in Shakespeare, of praise – an ironic commentary upon self-seeking 'worldly wisdom.')   **314** *Vex . . . ghost* do not trouble his departing spirit   **315** *rack* instrument of torture   **318** *usurped* possessed contrary to (natural) law

Rule in this realm, and the gored state sustain.

KENT

I have a journey, sir, shortly to go.

My master calls me ; I must not say no.

EDGAR

324   The weight of this sad time we must obey,

Speak what we feel, not what we ought to say.

The oldest hath borne most ; we that are young

Shall never see so much, nor live so long.

Exeunt with a dead march.

324 *obey* i.e. accept

APPENDIX : THE QUARTO TEXT

The present edition, as explained in the "Note on the text," adheres closely to the folio version of the play. The quarto version, although inferior in the main, is of great literary interest. The essential material for a comparison of the verbal features of the two versions is here supplied.

Mechanically, the quarto text is very defective : stage directions are often lacking and the speakers are confusingly designated ; the punctuation is bad ; and the verse is often printed as prose, the prose as verse. Omitted from the quarto but included in the folio are passages totalling approximately 100 lines, appearing in the present edition at the following points :

I, i, 40–45 *while . . . now*   49–50 *Since . . . state*   64–65 *and . . . rivers*   83–85 *to whose . . . interest*   88–89 *Nothing . . . Nothing*   162 *Dear sir, forbear*
I, ii 107–12 *This villain . . . graves*   160–65 *I pray . . . brother*
I, iv, 252 *Pray . . . patient*   265 *Of . . . you*   313–24 *This man . . . Oswald*
II, iv, 6 *No, my lord*   21 *By Juno . . . ay*   45–53 *Winter's . . . year*   93–94 *Well . . . man*   98 *Are . . . blood*   135–40 *Say . . . blame*   291–92 *Whither . . . horse*
III, i, 22–29 *Who have . . . furnishings*
III, ii, 79–96 *This . . . time*
III, iv, 17–18 *In . . . endure*   26–27 *In, boy . . . sleep*   37–38 *Fathom . . . Tom*
III, vi, 12–14 *No . . . him*   83 *And . . . noon*
IV, i, 6–9 *Welcome . . . blasts*
IV, ii, 25 *My . . . Gloucester*
IV, vi, 162–67 *Plate . . . lips*
V, ii, 11 *And . . . too*
V, iii, 76 *Dispose . . . thine*   89 *An interlude*   145 *What . . . delay*   223 *Speak, man*   311–12 *Do . . . there*

On the other hand, included in the quarto but omitted from the folio are passages totalling approximately 283 lines – inserted in square brackets in the present edition at the following points :

I, i, 104   I, ii, 93–95, 140–47   I, iii, 16–20, 24–25   I, iv, 133–48, 222–25, 248, 295   II, i, 78   II, ii, 136–40, 146   II, iv, 18–19 III, i, 7–15, 30–42   III, vi, 17–55, 95–99, 100–13   III, vii, 99–107   IV, i, 58–63   IV, ii, 31–50, 53–59, 62–68, 69   IV, iii, 1–55 IV, vi, 194   IV, vii, 24–25, 33–36, 79–80, 85–97   V, i, 11–13, 18–19, 23–28, 33   V, iii, 38–39, 47, 54–59, 102, 109, 115, 205–22.

In addition, the following words in the present edition represent insertions from the quarto : I, i, 214 *best*   289 *not*   I, ii, 127 *Fut* 129 *Edgar*   130 *and*   166 *Go armed*   II, i, 71 *ay*   II, iii, 15 *bare* III, iv, 127 *had*   IV, vii, 24 *not*   V, i, 16 *me*

The wording of the quarto text differs from that of the folio in hundreds of instances. In the present edition a quarto reading has been substituted for a folio reading only when the latter makes poor or obviously inferior sense. The list of such substitutions follows, with the adopted quarto readings in italics followed by the folio readings in roman. (In this appendix the readings of the quarto as well as the folio are given in modern spelling.)

I, i, 5 *equalities* qualities   74 *possesses* professes   170 *sentence* sentences   188 *Gloucester* Cordelia   206 *on* in   221 *Fall'n* Fall 225 *well* will   248 *respects of fortune* respect and fortunes   302 *hit* sit
I, iv, 1 *well* will   93 *Kent. Why, fool* Lear. Why, my boy   163 *e'er* (from '*euer*') ere   169 *fools* fool   194 *endurèd* endured   334 *atasked* at task
II, i, 70 *I should* should I   79 *why* where   87 *strange news* strangeness   115 *Natures* Nature's
II, ii, 21 *clamorous* clamors   70 *too* t'   73 *Renege* Revenge   74 *gale* gall   118 *dread* dead   125 *respect* respects
II, iv, 2 *messenger* messengers   30 *panting* painting   33 *whose* those   126 *mother's* mother   181 *fickle* 'fickly'
III, ii, 3 *drowned* drown
III, iv, 52 *ford* sword   86 *deeply* dearly   109 *till the* at   126 *stock-punished* stocked, punished
III, v, 24 *dearer* dear
III, vi, 68 *tike* tight   75 *makes* make
IV, i, 41 *Then prithee get thee gone* Get thee away
IV, ii, 75 *thereat enraged* threat-enraged   79 *justicers* justices
IV, iv, 18 *distress* desires
IV, vi, 17 *walk* walked   71 *enridgèd* enragèd   83 *coining* crying   161 *small* great   201 *one* a
V, i, 46 *love* loves
V, iii, 83 *attaint* arrest   84 *sister* sisters   97 *he is* he's   161 *Goneril* Bastard (i.e. Edmund)   278 *them* him

Omitted from the above list are a few instances of variation in which a folio misprint would have been detectable without reference to the quarto. Omitted from the following list are numerous instances of slight variation between quarto and folio in the use of articles, prepositions, elision, number, tense, etc., in which the literary interest is small. In all such instances the folio has been followed in the present edition, as well as in the variations listed below. Here the adopted folio readings are in italics followed by the quarto readings in roman. The great majority of the latter are, by common consent, inferior, but while these cast suspicion upon all, the fact remains that a certain number are not inferior to the folio readings and may represent what Shakespeare actually wrote. Marked with stars are the quarto readings which seem to the present editor best able to compete with the folio readings when judged from a purely literary point of view.

I, i, 20 *to* into   34 *the* my   35 *lord* liege   37 *Give me the map there. Know that we have divided* *The map there. Know we have divided   38 *fast* first   39 *from our age of our state* 40 *Conferring* Confirming   *strengths* years   45 *The princes* The two great princes   53 *Where nature doth with merit challenge* Where merit doth most challenge it   55 *love* do love   62 *speak* do   64 *shadowy* shady   68 *of Cornwall* *to Cornwall ? Speak 69 *of that self mettle as my sister* of the selfsame mettle that my sister is   72 *comes too* came   78 *ponderous* richer   82 *conferred* confirmed   83 *our last and least* the last, not least in our dear love   85 *draw* win   86 *sisters ? Speak* sisters   90 *Nothing will* How ? Nothing can   94 *How, how, Cordelia* Go to, Go to   95 *you* it   108 *Let* Well, let   118 *shall to my bosom* shall   130 *with* in 135 *shall* still 149 *falls* *stoops *Reserve thy state* *Reverse thy doom 156 *ne'er* nor 157 *motive* the motive 161 *Miscreant* Recreant 163 *Kill* Do. Kill 164 *gift* doom 166 *Hear me, recreant* Hear me 168 *That* Since *vows* vow 169 *strained* strayed 173 *Five* Four 174 *disasters* *diseases 175 *sixth* fifth 180 *Fare* Why, fare 181 *Freedom* Friendship 182 *dear shelter* protection 190 *this* a 193 *Most royal* Royal 194 *hath* what 200 *more* else 202 *Will* Sir, will 204 *Dow'red* Covered 214 *whom* that 216 *The best, the dearest* Most best, most dearest 223 *Should* Could 226 *make known* may know 228 *unchaste* *unclean 230 *richer* rich 232 *That* As 233 *Better* Go, to, go to. Better 235 *but* no more but 239 *regards* respects 241 *a dowry* and dower *King* Lear 258 *of* in 259 *Can* Shall 271 *Love* Use 276 *duty* duties 280 *plighted* pleated 281 *with shame* shame them 283 *not little* not a little 291 *grossly* gross 305 *of it* on't

I, ii, 10 *With base? with baseness? Bastardy base? Base* With base, base bastardy 15 *then* the 18 *legitimate. Fine word, 'legitimate'* legitimate 24 *prescribed* subscribed 38 *o'erlooking* liking 45 *policy and reverence* policy 68 *before* heretofore 70 *heard him oft* often heard him 72 *declined* declining 76 *sirrah* sir *I'll* I 85 *that he hath writ* he hath wrote 86 *other* further 100 *find* see 103 *reason it* reason 118 *on* by 120 *spherical* spiritual 124 *on to a star* stars 129 *bastardizing* bastardy 130 *pat* out 131 *Tom o'* them of 132–33 *divisions. Fa, sol, la, mi* divisions 138 *with* about 139 *writes* writ 148 *The night* Why, the night 150 *Ay, two* Two

I, iii, 13 *fellows* fellow servants *to* in 14 *distaste* dislike 18 *my* our 21 *have said* tell you *Well* Very well 26 *course* *very course *Prepare* Go prepare

I, iv, 20 *be't* be 30 *canst thou* canst 43 *You, you* You 68 *my* this 72 *noted it well* noted it 75 *you, sir, you* you sir, you sir *hither, sir* hither 78–79 *your pardon* you pardon me 81 *strucken* struck 85 *sir, arise, away* sir 87 *Go to! Have you wisdom? So You have wisdom* 97 *did* done 106 *the Lady Brach* Lady o' the Brach 111 *nuncle* uncle 122 *Kent* Lear 123 *'tis like* like 125 *nuncle* uncle 131 *sweet one* sweet fool 158 *grace* wit 160 *And* They *to wear* do wear 172 *lie, sirrah* lie 181 *You* *Methinks you 183 *frowning* *frown 188 *nor crust* neither crust 204 *Will* Must 205 *know* trow 210 *I would* Come, sir, I would *your* that 212 *transport* transform 216 *This Why, this* 219 *Ha! Waking? 'Tis Sleeping or waking? Ha! Sure 'tis* 227 *This admiration, sir* Come, sir, this admiration 229 *To understand* Understand 236 *graced* great 237 *then* thou 248 *Woe repents* repent's 261 *Lear, Lear, Lear* Lear, Lear 266 *Hear* Hark 280 *Away, away* Go, go, my people 282 *more of it* the cause 294 *loose* make 296 *Ha! Let it be so. I have another daughter* *Let it be so. Yet have I left a daughter 301 *ever* ever. Thou shalt, I warrant thee *that* that, my lord 304 *Pray you, content. – What, Oswald, ho* Come, sir, no more 306 *tarry* tarry and 331 *No, no, Now* 333 *condemn* dislike

I, v, 4 *afore* before 10 *not* ne'er 14 *can tell what* can what 15 *What canst tell, boy* Why, what canst thou tell, my boy 17 *canst* canst not *i' th' middle on's* in the middle of his 31 *moe* more 33 *Yes indeed* Yes 38 *till* before 40 *O, let me not be mad, not mad, sweet heaven* O, let me not be mad, sweet heaven. I would not be mad 42 *How now, are* Are 45 *that's a* that is 46 *unless* except

II, i, 3–4 *Regan his Duchess* his Duchess 4 *this* to 7 *they* there 8 *ear-kissing* *ear-bussing 13 *the* the two 13 *may do* may 18 *I must act. Briefness* must ask briefness *work* help 23 *Cornwall* Cornwall ought 27 *yourself* your – 30 *Draw, seem* Seem 31 *ho* here 32 *Fly, brother* Fly, brother, fly 39 *Mumbling* Warbling 40 *stand* stand's 43 *him, ho* him 46 *the thunder* *their thunders 52 *latched* lanched 56 *Full* But 62 *coward* caitiff 68 *would the reposal* could the reposure 73 *practice* pretence 76 *spirits* *spurs 77 *O strange* *Strong 78 *letter, said he* letter 90 *O madam* Madam *it's cracked* *is cracked 97 *he was of that consort* he was 100 *th' expense and waste* the waste and spoil 120 *prize* poise

II, ii, 1 *dawning* even 5 *lov'st* love 15–16 *action-taking* action-taking knave. A 16 *superserviceable, finical* superfinical 21 *deny'st* deny 28 *night, yet* night 29 *You* Draw, you 32 *come with* bring 39 *Murder, murder* Murder! help 40 *matter? Part* matter 54 *they* he 55 *years o' th' trade* hours at the trade 64 *know you* you have 69 *atwain* in twain 72 *Being* *Bring *the* *their 79 *drive* send 84 *fault* offense 90 *some* a 94 *An honest mind and plain* He must be plain 100 *faith* sooth 101 *great* grand 103 *mean'st* mean'st thou 113 *compact* conjunct 120 *Fetch* Bring 121 *ancient* miscreant 122 *Sir, I* I 127 *Stocking* Stopping 133 *color* nature 141 *King his master needs must* King must 142 *he* he's 147 *Cornwall. Come, my lord, away* *Regan. Come, my good lord, away 152 *out* on't 155 *taken* took

II, iii, 1 *heard* hear 10 *hairs in* hair with 19 *Sometimes* Sometime

II, iv, 3 *purpose in them* purpose 5 *Ha* How 7 *he* look, he 8 *heads* heels 25 *impose* purpose 34 *meiny* men 57 *here within* within 58 *here* there 59 *but* than 60 *None* no 61 *number train* 68 *twenty* a hundred 70 *following* following it 71 *upward* up the hill 74 *which serves and seeks* that serves 83 *stocks, fool* stocks 85 *have travelled all the night* travelled hard to-night 91 *Fiery? What quality* What fiery quality 97 *commands – tends – service* *commands her service 99 *Fiery? The fiery Duke* Fiery Duke *that* that Lear 111 *Go tell* Tell 116 *O me, my heart, my rising heart! But down* O my heart, my heart 118 *knapped* rapped 132 *With* Of 135 *scant* slack 143 *his* *her 148 *you but* you 153 *Never* No 163 *blister* blast her pride 164 *mood is on* *mood – 186 *you yourselves* yourselves 189 *will you* wilt thou 217 *that's in* that lies within 227 *looked* look 230 *you* you are 251 *look* seem 258 *need* needs 267 *man* fellow 272 *And let* O let 293 *best* good 295 *high* *bleak 296 *ruffle* rustle 297 *scarce* not

III, i, s.d. *severally* at several doors 1 *Who's there besides* What's there beside 4 *elements* element 18 *note* art 20 *is* be 48 *that* *your 53–54 *King – in which your pain* That way, I'll this King – I'll this way, you that

III, ii, 5 *of* *to 7 *Strike* Smite 16 *tax* task 18 *Then* Now then 22 *will* have *join* joined 42 *are* sit 49 *fear* force 50 *pudder* pother 54 *simular* simular man 55 *to* in 58 *concealing continents* concealed centers 64 *harder than the stones* hard than is the stone 73 *And* *That 73 *That's sorry* That sorrows 74 *has and* has 77 *Though* For 78 *boy* my good boy

III, iii, 4 *perpetual* their 12 *footed* landed 13 *look* seek 15 *If I Though I* 17 *strange things* some strange thing 23 *The* Then *doth* do

III, iv, 4 *enter here* enter 6 *contentious* tempestuous 16 *home sure* 22 *enter here* enter 29 *storm* night 46 *blow the winds* *blows the cold wind *Humh! go* Go *bed* *cold bed 48 *Didst thou give all to thy* Hast given all to thy two 54 *porridge* pottage 57 *acold. O, do, de, do, de, do, de* acold 60 *there – and there again – and there* and there again 61 *Has his* What, his 62 *Wouldst* Didst 66 *light* fall 74 *Alow, alow, loo, loo* Alo, lo, lo 77 *words' justice* *words justly 94 *says suum, mun* hay 96 *Thou* Why, thou *a* thy 98 *more than* *more but 100 *Ha! here's* here's 104 *contented; 'tis* content; this is 108 *foul* foul fiend 110 *squints* *squemes (i.e. squinies?) 132 *Smulkin* Snulbug 148 *same* most 152 *him once more* him 162 *mercy, sir* mercy 173 *tower came* town come

III, v, 9 *letter which* *letter 11 *this* his

III, vi, 68 *Or bobtail* *Bobtail 69 *him* them 71 *leaped* *leap 72 *Do, de, de, de. Sessa* Loudla doodla 76 *these hard hearts* this hardness 78 *You will* You'll *Persian* Persian attire 80 *here and rest* here 82 *So, so. We'll go to supper i' th' morning* So, so, so. We'll go to supper i' th' morning. So, so, so 93 *up, take up* up the King

III, vii, 3 *traitor* villain 23 *Though well* Though 32 *I'm none I am true* 42 *answered* answerer 53 *answer* first answer 58 *stick* *rash (meaning 'rip') 59 *bare* lowed 62 *rain* rage 63 *stern* *dearn (meaning 'drear') 65 *subscribe* *subscribed 73 *served you* served 79 *Nay* Why 81 *you have* *yet have you 86 *enkindle* unbridle 87 *treacherous villain* villain

IV, i, 4 *esperance* experience 9 *But who comes* Who's 10 *poorly led* parti, eyd (*sic*) 14 *These fourscore years* This fourscore – 17 *You* Alack, sir, you 36 *flies to* flies are to th' 45 *Which* Who 52 *daub* dance 54 *And yet I must. – Bless* Bless 57–58 *thee, good man's son* the good man
IV, ii, 17 *names* *arms 28 *My fool* A fool *body* bed 29 *whistle* whistling 60 *seems* *shows 73 *thrilled* thralled
IV, iv, 10 *helps* can help 26 *importuned* important
IV, v, 15 *him, madam* him 40 *party* Lady
IV, vi, 1 *I* we 8 *In* With 46 *sir!* Friend sir 51 *Thou'dst* Thou hadst 65 *How is't* How 73 *make them* made their 78 *'twould* would it 89 *this piece of* this 91–92 *I' th' clout, i' th' clout* in the air, hah 96 *Goneril with a white beard* Goneril, ha Regan 104 *ague-proof* argue-proof 127 *sulphurous* sulphury 128 *consumption* consummation 130 *sweeten* *to sweeten 132 *Let me* Here 138 *thy* the *see* see one 148 *this* the 150–51 *change places and, handy-dandy* Handy-dandy 159 *Thou* Thy blood 161 *clothes* rags 169 *Now, now, now, now* No, now 177 *wawl* wail *Mark* Mark me 182 *felt. I'll put't in proof* felt 186 *dear daughter* – dear – 192 *a man a man* a man 195 *smug bridegroom* bridegroom 198 *Come* Nay 199 *running. Sa, sa, sa, sa* running 207 *sound* sense 217 *tame to* lame by 224 *old* most 237 *ballow* bat 246 *English* *British 252 *these* his 264 *servant* *servant, and for you her own for venture (*sic*) 277 *severed* *fencèd
IV, vii, 16 *jarring* hurrying 32 *opposed* exposed *jarring* *warring 36 *enemy's* injurious 58 *hand* hands 59 *You* No, sir, you *mock me* mock 61 *upward, not an hour more nor less* upward 70 *I am! I am* I am 79 *killed* cured 84 *Pray you* Pray
V, i, 21 *heard* hear 36 *Pray* Pray you 46 *And machination ceases. Fortune* Fortune 52 *true* great
V, ii, 1 *tree* bush
V, iii, 8 *No, no, no, no* No, no 25 *starved* starve 43 *I* We 62 *might* should 68 *addition* advancement 78 *him* him then 81 *thine* good 90 *Gloucester. Let the trumpet sound* Gloucester 91 *person* head 93 *make* prove 96 *medicine* poison 99 *the* thy 105 *My* This 110–11 *within the lists* in the host 113 *by* at 120 *name, your* name and 124 *cope* *cope withal 129–30 *my privilege, The privilege of mine honors* the privilege of my tongue 136 *Conspirant* Conspicuate 138 *below thy foot* beneath thy feet 144 *tongue* being 146 *rule* right 147 *Back* Here 152 *practice* *mere practice 153 *war* *arms 155 *Shut* *Stop 156 *stop* *stopple *it. – Hold, sir* it 157 *name* thing 172 *plague* *scourge 174 *right; 'tis true* truth 186 *we* with 191 *Their* The 197 *our* my 223 *help! O, help* help 225 *of* – O, she's dead *of* 226 *Who dead? Speak, man* Who, man? Speak 228 *poisoned; she confesses* poisoned; she hath confessed 232 *judgment* justice 233 *is this* 'tis 252 *Edgar* Albany 258 *Howl, howl, howl* Howl, howl, howl, howl 270 *you murderers* your murderous 274 *woman* women 281 *brag* bragged *and* or 283 *This is a dull sight. Are* Are 289 *first* life 306 *no, no, no* no, no 308 *Thou'lt* O, thou wilt 309 *Never, never, never, never, never* Never, never, never 310 *sir* sir. 0, 0, 0, 0 316 *He* O, he 324 *Edgar* Albany 326 *hath* *have

MACBETH

INTRODUCTION

Macbeth is the shortest of Shakespeare's tragedies and the simplest in its statement: *Thou shalt not kill*. In the words of Coleridge, it contains "no reasonings of equivocal morality, . . . no sophistry of self-delusion." With eyes wide open to the hideousness of his offense, a brave, imaginative, and morally sensitive man commits a stealthy murder for gain. His victim is his guest, his benefactor, his kinsman, and his king; and to shield himself from detection he incontinently sacrifices the lives and reputation of two innocent underlings. The retribution is as appalling as the crime – his soul's slow death in self-horror, degradation, loneliness, and despair, then his bloody extermination.

Why should such a man do such evil? That we ask the question instead of dismissing the play as an incredible fiction is our tribute to the poet's vision and artistry. The question reshapes itself on our lips, Why is there evil for men to do? and we realize that there can be no answer. The core of *Macbeth* is a religious mystery, its moral clarity a testament of faith. Evil may be recognized, loathed, and combated without being understood: " . . . in these cases / We still have judgment here."

The earliest mention of the play occurs in notes on a performance at the Globe, April 20, 1611, by the spectator Simon Forman, but the style and a few shreds of literary evidence suggest 1605–06 as the period of composition; hence it followed *Hamlet*, *Othello*, and possibly also *Lear*, those other tragedies in which destruction is wrought by naked evil, not mere domestic or political strife. *Macbeth* differs from the other three in that the evil works through the protagonist as well as upon him. The one with whom we identify is the one who is possessed; this citadel crumbles from within. The supernatural soliciting of the Weird Sisters, the strenuous persuasions of the wife, do not explain Macbeth's guilt. They enhance its power over our imagination by revealing stages in its course and suggesting forces in perilous balance.

In Holinshed's *Chronicle*, from which Shakespeare drew his material, adding to the sins of the semi-legendary Macbeth those of Donwald, slayer of King Duff, the Weird Sisters are "goddesses of destinie" derived from a heathen fatalism. In the play they are Elizabethan witches, their prescriptive powers subtly curtailed; they predict, abet, and symbolize damnation but do not determine it. Any sense that Macbeth is a helpless victim, his crime predestined, his will bound, is canceled as the play proceeds. We may seem to see in the encounter on the heath the very inception of his lethal designs, but we should ask with Banquo,

> Good sir, why do you start and seem to fear
> Things that do sound so fair?

Nothing in the witches' prophecies would have suggested to an untainted mind that to "be King hereafter" meant to be murderer first. That Macbeth was already tainted would have been apparent to the original audience. In another play of the era, *The Witch of Edmonton*, the black dog appears at her side only when the wish for his presence is wrung from old Mother Sawyer's lips. The stars could influence but could not govern, the devils could come but only upon summons. At some unknown time for some unknown reason Macbeth has corrupted in pride, and has contemplated the sale of his soul as certainly as Faustus. When we later discover through the words of his Lady that plans to murder Duncan had preceded the meeting on the heath, we should not bring charges of inconsistency, speculate about "lost scenes," or complain that we have been tricked.

The prophecies, nevertheless, without explaining or excusing Macbeth's crimes, impress us as mitigation: powerful and wily forces are speeding him on his course. The more earthly influence of his Lady's persuasions impresses us in a similar way. They provide, moreover, an occasion for the display of his aversion for what he is about to do, and convert it, at least in some measure, from utter self-serving into an offering to her. Lady Macbeth's own behavior is not totally alienating. In a perverted way she is doing what all loyal wives are expected to do, urging her husband on to what she deems his good; here, as in the period of danger that follows, she at least is *all for him*. This is one of the marvels of the play, the manner in which this frightful collusion proceeds in an atmosphere of domestic virtue without the effect of irony. If the evil is great it is also limited, even in respect to the malefactors. After the Lady's collapse, her initial ferocity is remembered as something false to her nature, and the solicitude of her wise and kindly physician seems to us not misplaced.

Macbeth himself is as humane in his reflections as he is inhuman in his acts. Like Iago he is a moralizing villain, but his moralizing is not clever aphoristic display. It comes from his heart, sometimes like an echo of ancient folk beliefs,

> It will have blood, they say: blood will have blood.
> Stones have been known to move and trees to speak;
> Augures and understood relations have
> By maggot-pies and choughs and rooks brought forth
> The secret'st man of blood –

sometimes like religious revelation,

> [Duncan's] virtues
> Will plead like angels, trumpet-tongued against
> The deep damnation of his taking-off;
> And pity, like a naked new-born babe

Striding the blast, or heaven's cherubin horsed
Upon the sightless couriers of the air,
Shall blow the horrid deed in every eye
That tears shall drown the wind.

No voice in literature has sounded with greater sadness:

I have lived long enough. My way of life
Is fall'n into the sear, the yellow leaf,
And that which should accompany old age,
As honor, love, obedience, troops of friends,
I must not look to have; but, in their stead,
Curses not loud but deep, mouth-honor, breath,
Which the poor heart would fain deny, and dare not.

To say that no one who has become a bloody tyrant would speak in this way is pointless; he would *feel* in this way, or so we are convinced.

By feeling the pangs that we would feel if we were in his place, and by passing our judgments upon himself, Macbeth attaches us to him and consequently himself to us. We cannot view him with cold objectivity as something strange and apart. The unnaturalness of his acts is always counterpoised by the naturalness of his actions: his hesitant overtures to Banquo, his volubility after Duncan's death, his dazed petulance at the appearance of the ghost,

The time has been
That, when the brains were out, the man would die,
And there an end. But now they rise again,
With twenty mortal murders on their crowns,
And push us from our stools.

There is something here both grimly humorous and affecting, this killer's speaking in the accents of a hurt child. We should not ascribe Macbeth's humanity to the automatic working of Shakespeare's sympathetic nature. There is nothing casual about it. If Macbeth were other than he is, less like ourselves, he would be a less powerful symbol of our own worst potentialities and the abyss we have escaped. There is nothing of him in Edmund or Iago for all of Shakespeare's sympathetic nature.

It is hard to believe that so universal a work was calculated to the meridian of any particular person, but there are arguments favoring the possibility. James Stuart, who had ascended the English throne and become the nominal patron of Shakespeare's company a few years before *Macbeth* was written, was supposedly descended from Banquo and was intensely interested in witchcraft; moreover he had assumed in 1605 the prerogative of curing the "king's evil" instituted by Edward the Confessor and mentioned somewhat irrelevantly in the play. On the other hand, one may argue that, had Shakespeare's primary concern been to please the monarch, he might have dramatized more creditable episodes in Scottish history, might have drawn a more flattering portrait of Banquo, and might have seized the opportunity to eulogize James as first holder of the "treble sceptres" mentioned in the show of kings (IV, i). Possibly Shakespeare was responding in his own way to the urgings of his dramatic company; he was in some respects the most reticent writer of his times, and his allusions even to Elizabeth had been few and restrained.

Whether or not *Macbeth* may be considered in a sense "topical" it contains elements that are, or might have been, mere theatrical entertainment. It combines with its great theme the working out of a puzzle, and affords us the pleasure of watching pieces dropping into place. That

Macbeth would be king but no father of kings, that he would reign until Birnam Wood marched to Dunsinane, that he would be unconquerable by any man born of woman were riddling prophecies included in Holinshed, but the manner of presenting them through apparitions was Shakespeare's invention: the "Armed Head" instigating the aggression against Macduff probably represents Macbeth himself; the "Child Crowned, with a tree in his hand" certainly represents young Malcolm, deviser of the tactics at Birnam Wood; the "Bloody Child" represents Macduff, who was "from his mother's womb / Untimely ripped." These ingenuities might well have been intrusive in a play so elemental; as handled by Shakespeare they contribute to the master plan by allowing us to watch Macbeth gradually stripped of hope by those "juggling fiends" upon whom he has relied.

The opportunities for spectacularity offered by the play were seized early, and alterations had already been made in the single version that has come down to us, that printed in the folio of 1623. The Hecate scenes (III, v; IV, i, 39–43, 125–32) are interpolations obviously designed in order to introduce songs and dances by the witches. The first words of the songs, "Come away" and "Black spirits," permit us to identify them as having been borrowed from Thomas Middleton's *The Witch*, where their texts appear in full. Who wrote the surrounding matter we do not know, but its quality serves one useful purpose. Such lines as

O, well done! I commend your pains,
And every one shall share i' th' gains.
And now about the cauldron sing
Like elves and fairies in a ring

make us appreciate the more the magical raucousness of the language that Shakespeare himself gave his witches. The authenticity of the Porter's speech was questioned by Coleridge in one of his critical lapses; this too served a useful purpose, in evoking from De Quincey a gem of literary appreciation. At the Restoration the tradition of spectacular amplification was in full bloom, and on January 7, 1667, Samuel Pepys pronounced a revival as especially excellent "in *divertissement*, though it be a deep tragedy, which is a strange perfection in a tragedy." This "strange perfection" afflicts us still; no other Shakespearean play has provoked more recklessness in the invention of "effects."

Whatever intrudes upon the stark simplicity of this work of art is an offense. It needs no help. Its brevity makes us wonder if there have been cuts as well as additions in the text printed in the folio, but it is hard to imagine any extension that would not have marred its present compact structure. The physical and spiritual terror rises in swift crescendos until Macduff's child is slaughtered at Fife and the universe seems riven in two; then comes the resting place of the scene in England like the still moment at the core of a hurricane; when the blast resumes, it is not to compound chaos but to orchestrate the restoration of moral order. No one who has read the play will ever forget the hardy characters who struggle to readmit light into their murky world, and certainly not that incandescent couple who kill together and die apart. The style has the vigor, condensation, and imaginative splendor of Shakespeare at his greatest, when he seems to be pressing upon the very bounds of the expressible.

Blood and darkness are constantly invoked, and jarring antitheses, violent hyperbole, and chaotic imagery give the lines the quality demanded by the action. But there are also moments of unforgettable hush. Some of the speeches seem to express the agony of all mankind:

> Canst thou not minister to a mind diseased,
> Pluck from the memory a rooted sorrow,
> Raze out the written troubles of the brain,
> And with some sweet oblivious antidote
> Cleanse the stuffed bosom of that perilous stuff
> Which weighs upon the heart?

Over the centuries comes the quiet answer, convincing us, as so often the words of this poet so strangely do, that nothing further can be said,

> Therein the patient
> Must minister to himself.

Harvard University Alfred Harbage

NOTE ON THE TEXT

The present edition follows closely the only substantive text (folio, 1623), which is mechanically defective but not corrupt in the sense of misrepresenting, in general, Shakespeare's language. The copy was evidently provided by a transcript of a prompt-book. The act–scene division here supplied marginally coincides with the division of the folio text except that V, vii of the latter is subdivided into vii and viii. A more rational point of subdivision comes later (at V, viii, 35) and is marked by some modern editors as scene ix. A stage direction in the folio text indicates that Macbeth was slain in sight of the audience, and this direction is retained in the present text. The body could have been carried offstage by Macduff or another. Except for extensive relineation, the following list of emendations indicates the only material departures from the folio text. The adopted reading in italics is followed by the folio reading in roman.

I, i, 1 *again* again? 9–11 2. *Witch . . . air* (in the folio these lines form a single speech attributed to "All")
I, ii, 13 *gallowglasses* Gallowgrosses 14 *quarrel* Quarry 26 *thunders break* Thunders 56 *point rebellious, arm* point, rebellious arm
I, iii, 32 *weird* weyward 39 *Forres* Soris 98 *Came* Can 109 *borrowed* borrowèd
I, iv, 1 *Are* Or
I, v, 7 *weird* weyward
I, vi, 4 *martlet* Barlet 5 *loved* lovèd 9 *most* must
I, vii, 6 *shoal* Schoole 47 *do* no
II, i, 20 *weird* weyward 55 *strides* sides 56 *sure* sowre 57 *way they* they may
II, ii, 13 s.d. *Enter Macbeth* (appears after line 8 in folio)
III, i, 2 *weird* weyard
III, iv, 78 *time* times 133 *weird* weyard 135 *worst. For* worst, for 144 *in deed* indeed
III, vi, 24 *son* Sonnes 38 *the* their
IV, i, 59 *all together* altogether 93 *Dunsinane* Dunsmane 98 *Birnam* Byrnan 111 s.d. *Kings and Banquo, last* Kings, and Banquo last 119 *eighth* eight 136 *weird* weyard
IV, ii, 22 *none* move 30 s.d. *Exit* Exit Rosse 72 s.d. *Exit* Exit Messenger
IV, iii, 4 *downfall'n* downfall 15 *deserve* discerne 107 *accursed* accust 133 *thy here-approach* they here approach 235 *tune* time
V, i, 1 *two* too
V, ii, 5, 31 *Birnam* Byrnan
V, iii, 2, 60 *Birnam* Byrnan 55 *senna* Cyme
V, iv, 3 *Birnam* Byrnan 11 *gone* given
V, v, 34, 44 *Birnam* Byrnan 39 *shalt* shall
V, vii, 19 *unbattered* unbatterèd
V, viii, 30 *Birnam* Byrnan

MACBETH

[NAMES OF THE ACTORS

Duncan, King of Scotland
Malcolm } *his sons*
Donalbain
Macbeth
Banquo
Macduff
Lennox
Ross } *noblemen of Scotland*
Menteith
Angus
Caithness
Fleance, son to Banquo
Siward, Earl of Northumberland
Young Siward, his son
Seyton, an officer attending on Macbeth

Boy, son to Macduff
A Captain
An English Doctor
A Scottish Doctor
A Porter
An Old Man
Three Murderers
Lady Macbeth
Lady Macduff
A Gentlewoman, attending on Lady Macbeth
The Weird Sisters
Hecate
The Ghost of Banquo
Apparitions
Lords, Officers, Soldiers, Messengers, Attendants

Scene : *Scotland and England*]

I, i *Thunder and lightning. Enter three Witches.*

1. WITCH When shall we three meet again
In thunder, lightning, or in rain ?

2. WITCH When the hurlyburly 's done,
When the battle 's lost and won.

3. WITCH That will be ere the set of sun.

1. WITCH Where the place ?

2. WITCH Upon the heath.

3. WITCH There to meet with Macbeth.

8 1. WITCH I come, Graymalkin !

9 2. WITCH Paddock calls.

3. WITCH Anon !

ALL Fair is foul, and foul is fair.
Hover through the fog and filthy air. *Exeunt.*

I, ii *Alarum within. Enter King [Duncan], Malcolm,*
Donalbain, Lennox, with Attendants, meeting a
bleeding Captain.

KING
What bloody man is that ? He can report,
As seemeth by his plight, of the revolt
The newest state.

3 MALCOLM This is the sergeant
Who like a good and hardy soldier fought
'Gainst my captivity. Hail, brave friend !
Say to the King the knowledge of the broil
As thou didst leave it.

CAPTAIN Doubtful it stood,
As two spent swimmers that do cling together

And choke their art. The merciless Macdonwald
(Worthy to be a rebel, for to that
The multiplying villainies of nature
Do swarm upon him) from the Western Isles 12
Of kerns and gallowglasses is supplied ; 13
And Fortune, on his damnèd quarrel smiling,
Showed like a rebel's whore. But all's too weak :
For brave Macbeth (well he deserves that name),
Disdaining Fortune, with his brandished steel,
Which smoked with bloody execution,
Like valor's minion carved out his passage 19
Till he faced the slave ;
Which ne'er shook hands nor bade farewell to him
Till he unseamed him from the nave to th' chops 22
And fixed his head upon our battlements.

KING
O valiant cousin ! worthy gentleman !

CAPTAIN
As whence the sun 'gins his reflection
Shipwracking storms and direful thunders break,
So from that spring whence comfort seemed to come
Discomfort swells. Mark, King of Scotland, mark.
No sooner justice had, with valor armed,
Compelled these skipping kerns to trust their heels

I, i An open place 8 *Graymalkin* her familiar spirit, a gray cat 9 *Paddock*
a toad ; *Anon* at once
I, ii A field near Forres 3 *sergeant* so designated, apparently, as a staff-
officer ; he ranks as a captain 12 *Western Isles* Hebrides (and Ireland ?)
13 *kerns* Irish bush-fighters ; *gallowglasses* Irish regulars, armored infantry-
men 19 *minion* darling 22 *nave* navel

31 But the Norweyan lord, surveying vantage,
With furbished arms and new supplies of men,
Began a fresh assault.

KING   Dismayed not this
Our captains, Macbeth and Banquo ?

CAPTAIN   Yes,
As sparrows eagles, or the hare the lion.
If I say sooth, I must report they were
37 As cannons overcharged with double cracks,
So they doubly redoubled strokes upon the foe.
Except they meant to bathe in reeking wounds,
40 Or memorize another Golgotha,
I cannot tell –
But I am faint ; my gashes cry for help.

KING
So well thy words become thee as thy wounds,
They smack of honor both. Go get him surgeons.
                              [Exit Captain, attended.]
          Enter Ross and Angus.
Who comes here ?

45 MALCOLM   The worthy Thane of Ross.

LENNOX
What a haste looks through his eyes ! So should he look
47 That seems to speak things strange.

ROSS   God save the King !

KING
Whence cam'st thou, worthy Thane ?

ROSS   From Fife, great King,
Where the Norweyan banners flout the sky
And fan our people cold.
Norway himself, with terrible numbers,
Assisted by that most disloyal traitor
53 The Thane of Cawdor, began a dismal conflict,
54 Till that Bellona's bridegroom, lapped in proof,
55 Confronted him with self-comparisons,
Point against point rebellious, arm 'gainst arm,
Curbing his lavish spirit : and to conclude,
The victory fell on us.

KING   Great happiness !

ROSS   That now
59 Sweno, the Norways' king, craves composition ;
Nor would we deign him burial of his men
61 Till he disbursèd, at Saint Colme's Inch,
62 Ten thousand dollars to our general use.

KING
No more that Thane of Cawdor shall deceive
64 Our bosom interest. Go pronounce his present death
And with his former title greet Macbeth.

ROSS
I'll see it done.

KING
What he hath lost noble Macbeth hath won.   Exeunt.

                              *

31 *surveying vantage* seeing opportunity 37 *cracks* explosives 40 *memorize
another Golgotha* make memorable as another 'place of the dead' 45 *Thane*
a Scottish lord 47 *seems to* seems about to 53 *dismal* ominous 54 *Bellona*
goddess of war ; *lapped in proof* clad in proven armor 55 *self-comparisons*
cancelling powers 59 *composition* terms of surrender 61 *Inch* island 62
dollars Spanish or Dutch coins 64 *bosom interest* heart's trust
I, iii A heath 6 *Aroint thee* get thee gone ; *rump-fed ronyon* fat-rumped
scab 15 *very ports they blow* i.e. their power to blow ships to ports 17 *card*
compass card 20 *penthouse lid* eyelid 21 *forbid* accursed 32 *weird* fate-
serving 33 *Posters* swift travellers 43 *question* confer with 44 *choppy*
chapped

Thunder. Enter the three Witches.   I, iii

1. WITCH Where hast thou been, sister ?
2. WITCH Killing swine.
3. WITCH Sister, where thou ?
1. WITCH A sailor's wife had chestnuts in her lap
          And mounched and mounched and mounched.
          'Give me,' quoth I.
          'Aroint thee, witch !' the rump-fed ronyon 6
          cries.
          Her husband 's to Aleppo gone, master o' th'
          Tiger :
          But in a sieve I'll thither sail
          And, like a rat without a tail,
          I'll do, I'll do, and I'll do.
2. WITCH I'll give thee a wind.
1. WITCH Th' art kind.
3. WITCH And I another.
1. WITCH I myself have all the other,
          And the very ports they blow,   15
          All the quarters that they know
          I' th' shipman's card.   17
          I'll drain him dry as hay.
          Sleep shall neither night nor day
          Hang upon his penthouse lid.   20
          He shall live a man forbid.   21
          Weary sev'nights, nine times nine,
          Shall he dwindle, peak, and pine.
          Though his bark cannot be lost,
          Yet it shall be tempest-tost.
          Look what I have.
2. WITCH Show me, show me.
1. WITCH Here I have a pilot's thumb,
          Wracked as homeward he did come.
          Drum within.
3. WITCH A drum, a drum !
          Macbeth doth come.
ALL   The weird sisters, hand in hand,   32
          Posters of the sea and land,   33
          Thus do go about, about,
          Thrice to thine, and thrice to mine,
          And thrice again, to make up nine.
          Peace ! The charm 's wound up.
          Enter Macbeth and Banquo.

MACBETH
So foul and fair a day I have not seen.

BANQUO
How far is 't called to Forres ? What are these,
So withered and so wild in their attire
That look not like th' inhabitants o' th' earth
And yet are on 't ? Live you, or are you aught
That man may question ? You seem to understand me, 43
By each at once her choppy finger laying   44
Upon her skinny lips. You should be women,
And yet your beards forbid me to interpret
That you are so.

MACBETH   Speak, if you can. What are you ?

1. WITCH
All hail, Macbeth ! Hail to thee, Thane of Glamis !

2. WITCH
All hail, Macbeth ! Hail to thee, Thane of Cawdor !

3. WITCH
All hail, Macbeth, that shalt be King hereafter !

BANQUO
Good sir, why do you start and seem to fear

Things that do sound so fair ? I' th' name of truth,
53 Are ye fantastical, or that indeed
Which outwardly ye show ? My noble partner
55 You greet with present grace and great prediction
Of noble having and of royal hope,
57 That he seems rapt withal. To me you speak not.
58 If you can look into the seeds of time
And say which grain will grow and which will not,
Speak then to me, who neither beg nor fear
Your favors nor your hate.

1. WITCH Hail !

2. WITCH Hail !

3. WITCH Hail !

1. WITCH
Lesser than Macbeth, and greater.

2. WITCH
66 Not so happy, yet much happier.

3. WITCH
67 Thou shalt get kings, though thou be none.
So all hail, Macbeth and Banquo !

1. WITCH
Banquo and Macbeth, all hail !

MACBETH
70 Stay, you imperfect speakers, tell me more :
71 By Sinel's death I know I am Thane of Glamis,
But how of Cawdor ? The Thane of Cawdor lives,
A prosperous gentleman ; and to be King
Stands not within the prospect of belief,
No more than to be Cawdor. Say from whence
You owe this strange intelligence, or why
Upon this blasted heath you stop our way
With such prophetic greeting. Speak, I charge you.
Witches vanish.

BANQUO
The earth hath bubbles as the water has,
And these are of them. Whither are they vanished ?

MACBETH
81 Into the air, and what seemed corporal melted
As breath into the wind. Would they had stayed!

BANQUO
Were such things here as we do speak about ?
84 Or have we eaten on the insane root
That takes the reason prisoner ?

MACBETH
Your children shall be kings.

BANQUO   You shall be King.

MACBETH
And Thane of Cawdor too. Went it not so ?

BANQUO
To th' selfsame tune and words. Who's here ?
Enter Ross and Angus.

ROSS
The King hath happily received, Macbeth,
90 The news of thy success ; and when he reads
Thy personal venture in the rebels' fight,
92 His wonders and his praises do contend
Which should be thine or his. Silenced with that,
In viewing o'er the rest o' th' selfsame day,
He finds thee in the stout Norweyan ranks,
Nothing afeard of what thyself didst make,
97 Strange images of death. As thick as tale
98 Came post with post, and every one did bear
Thy praises in his kingdom's great defense
And poured them down before him.

ANGUS   We are sent
To give thee from our royal master thanks ;
Only to herald thee into his sight,
Not pay thee.

ROSS
And for an earnest of a greater honor,
He bade me, from him, call thee Thane of Cawdor ;
In which addition, hail, most worthy Thane,   106
For it is thine.

BANQUO   What, can the devil speak true ?

MACBETH
The Thane of Cawdor lives. Why do you dress me
In borrowed robes ?

ANGUS   Who was the Thane lives yet,
But under heavy judgment bears that life
Which he deserves to lose. Whether he was combined   111
With those of Norway, or did line the rebel   112
With hidden help and vantage, or that with both   113
He labored in his country's wrack, I know not ;
But treasons capital, confessed and proved,
Have overthrown him.

MACBETH [*aside*]   Glamis, and Thane of Cawdor –
The greatest is behind !   117
[*To Ross and Angus*] Thanks for your pains.
[*Aside to Banquo*]
Do you not hope your children shall be kings,
When those that gave the Thane of Cawdor to me
Promised no less to them ?

BANQUO [*to Macbeth*]   That, trusted home,   120
Might yet enkindle you unto the crown,
Besides the Thane of Cawdor. But 'tis strange :
And oftentimes, to win us to our harm,
The instruments of darkness tell us truths,
Win us with honest trifles, to betray's
In deepest consequence. –   126
Cousins, a word, I pray you.   127

MACBETH [*aside*]   Two truths are told,
As happy prologues to the swelling act   128
Of the imperial theme. – I thank you, gentlemen. –
[*Aside*]
This supernatural soliciting   130
Cannot be ill, cannot be good. If ill,
Why hath it given me earnest of success,
Commencing in a truth ? I am Thane of Cawdor.
If good, why do I yield to that suggestion
Whose horrid image doth unfix my hair
And make my seated heart knock at my ribs   136
Against the use of nature ? Present fears   137
Are less than horrible imaginings.
My thought, whose murder yet is but fantastical,   139
Shakes so my single state of man that function   140
Is smothered in surmise and nothing is

53 *fantastical* creatures of fantasy   55 *grace* honor   57 *rapt withal* spellbound at the thought   58 *seeds of time* genesis of events   66 *happy* fortunate   67 *get* beget   70 *imperfect* incomplete   71 *Sinel* i.e. Macbeth's father   81 *corporal* corporeal   84 *insane* madness-inducing   90 *reads* considers   92–93 *His wonders . . . or his* i.e. dumbstruck admiration makes him keep your praises to himself   97 *thick as tale* i.e. as fast as they can be counted   98 *post with post* messenger after messenger   106 *addition* title   111 *combined* leagued   112 *line* support   113 *vantage* assistance   117 *is behind* is to come   120 *home* all the way   126 *deepest consequence* i.e. in the vital sequel   127 *Cousins* i.e. fellow lords   128–29 *swelling act . . . imperial theme* i.e. stately drama of rise to sovereignty   130 *soliciting* inviting, beckoning   136 *seated* fixed   137 *use* way   139 *fantastical* imaginary   140 *single* unaided, weak ; *function* normal powers

But what is not.

142 BANQUO   Look how our partner 's rapt.

MACBETH [aside]
If chance will have me King, why chance may crown me
Without my stir.

BANQUO   New honors come upon him,
145 Like our strange garments, cleave not to their mould
But with the aid of use.

MACBETH [aside]   Come what come may,
Time and the hour runs through the roughest day.

BANQUO
Worthy Macbeth, we stay upon your leisure.

MACBETH
149 Give me your favor. My dull brain was wrought
With things forgotten. Kind gentlemen, your pains
Are regist'red where every day I turn
The leaf to read them. Let us toward the King.
[Aside to Banquo]
Think upon what hath chanced, and at more time,
The interim having weighed it, let us speak
155 Our free hearts each to other.

BANQUO   Very gladly.

MACBETH
Till then, enough. – Come, friends.   Exeunt.

*

I, iv   Flourish. Enter King [Duncan], Lennox, Malcolm,
            Donalbain, and Attendants.

KING
Is execution done on Cawdor ? Are not
2 Those in commission yet returned ?

MALCOLM   My liege,
They are not yet come back. But I have spoke
With one that saw him die ; who did report
That very frankly he confessed his treasons,
Implored your Highness' pardon, and set forth
A deep repentance. Nothing in his life
Became him like the leaving it. He died
9 As one that had been studied in his death
10 To throw away the dearest thing he owed
As 'twere a careless trifle.

KING   There's no art
To find the mind's construction in the face.
He was a gentleman on whom I built
An absolute trust.
            Enter Macbeth, Banquo, Ross, and Angus.
                    O worthiest cousin,
The sin of my ingratitude even now
16 Was heavy on me. Thou art so far before
That swiftest wing of recompense is slow
To overtake thee. Would thou hadst less deserved,
19 That the proportion both of thanks and payment
Might have been mine ! Only I have left to say,
More is thy due than more than all can pay.

MACBETH
The service and the loyalty I owe,
In doing it pays itself. Your Highness' part
Is to receive our duties, and our duties
Are to your throne and state children and servants,
Which do but what they should by doing everything
Safe toward your love and honor.   27

KING   Welcome hither.
I have begun to plant thee and will labor   28
To make thee full of growing. Noble Banquo,
That hast no less deserved nor must be known
No less to have done so, let me enfold thee
And hold thee to my heart.

BANQUO   There if I grow,
The harvest is your own.

KING   My plenteous joys,
Wanton in fullness, seek to hide themselves   34
In drops of sorrow. Sons, kinsmen, thanes,
And you whose places are the nearest, know
We will establish our estate upon
Our eldest, Malcolm, whom we name hereafter
The Prince of Cumberland ; which honor must
Not unaccompanied invest him only,
But signs of nobleness, like stars, shall shine
On all deservers. From hence to Inverness,
And bind us further to you.

MACBETH
The rest is labor which is not used for you.
I'll be myself the harbinger, and make joyful
The hearing of my wife with your approach ;
So, humbly take my leave.

KING   My worthy Cawdor !

MACBETH [aside]
The Prince of Cumberland – that is a step
On which I must fall down or else o'erleap,
For in my way it lies. Stars, hide your fires ;
Let not light see my black and deep desires.
The eye wink at the hand ; yet let that be   52
Which the eye fears, when it is done, to see.   Exit.

KING
True, worthy Banquo : he is full so valiant,
And in his commendations I am fed ;
It is a banquet to me. Let's after him,
Whose care is gone before to bid us welcome.
It is a peerless kinsman.   Flourish. Exeunt.

*

Enter Macbeth's Wife, alone, with a letter.   I, v

LADY [reads] 'They met me in the day of success ; and I
have learned by the perfect'st report they have more in
them than mortal knowledge. When I burned in desire
to question them further, they made themselves air, into
which they vanished. Whiles I stood rapt in the wonder
of it, came missives from the King, who all-hailed me 6
Thane of Cawdor, by which title, before, these weird
sisters saluted me, and referred me to the coming on of
time with "Hail, King that shalt be !" This have I
thought good to deliver thee, my dearest partner of
greatness, that thou mightst not lose the dues of rejoicing by being ignorant of what greatness is promised
thee. Lay it to thy heart, and farewell.'

Glamis thou art, and Cawdor, and shalt be
What thou art promised. Yet do I fear thy nature.

142 rapt bemused 145 strange new 149 favor pardon 155 Our free
hearts our thoughts freely
I, iv A field near Forres as before, or a place in the palace itself 2 in
commission commissioned to carry out the execution 9 studied rehearsed
10 owed owned 16 before ahead in deserving 19 proportion preponder-
ance 27 Safe fitting 28 plant nurture 34 Wanton unrestrained 52
wink at the hand blind itself to what the hand does
I, v Within Macbeth's castle at Inverness 6 missives messengers

It is too full o' th' milk of human kindness
To catch the nearest way. Thou wouldst be great,
Art not without ambition, but without
18 The illness should attend it. What thou wouldst highly,
That wouldst thou holily ; wouldst not play false,
And yet wouldst wrongly win. Thou'ldst have, great Glamis,
That which cries 'Thus thou must do' if thou have it ;
And that which rather thou dost fear to do
Than wishest should be undone. Hie thee hither,
That I may pour my spirits in thine ear
And chastise with the valor of my tongue
26 All that impedes thee from the golden round
27 Which fate and metaphysical aid doth seem
28 To have thee crowned withal.
    Enter Messenger.   What is your tidings ?
MESSENGER
The King comes here to-night.
LADY   Thou'rt mad to say it !
Is not thy master with him ? who, were't so,
Would have informed for preparation.
MESSENGER
So please you, it is true. Our Thane is coming.
One of my fellows had the speed of him,
34 Who, almost dead for breath, had scarcely more
Than would make up his message.
LADY   Give him tending ;
He brings great news.   *Exit Messenger.*
             The raven himself is hoarse
That croaks the fatal entrance of Duncan
Under my battlements. Come, you spirits
39 That tend on mortal thoughts, unsex me here,
And fill me from the crown to the toe top-full
Of direst cruelty. Make thick my blood ;
42 Stop up th' access and passage to remorse,
43 That no compunctious visitings of nature
44 Shake my fell purpose nor keep peace between
Th' effect and it. Come to my woman's breasts
46 And take my milk for gall, you murd'ring ministers,
47 Wherever in your sightless substances
48 You wait on nature's mischief. Come, thick night,
49 And pall thee in the dunnest smoke of hell,
That my keen knife see not the wound it makes,
Nor heaven peep through the blanket of the dark
To cry 'Hold, hold !'
    Enter Macbeth.   Great Glamis ! worthy Cawdor !
Greater than both, by the all-hail hereafter !
Thy letters have transported me beyond
55 This ignorant present, and I feel now
The future in the instant.
MACBETH   My dearest love,
Duncan comes here to-night.
LADY   And when goes hence ?
MACBETH
To-morrow, as he purposes.
LADY   O, never
Shall sun that morrow see !
Your face, my Thane, is as a book where men
61 May read strange matters. To beguile the time,
62 Look like the time ; bear welcome in your eye,
Your hand, your tongue ; look like th' innocent flower,
But be the serpent under't. He that's coming
Must be provided for ; and you shall put
66 This night's great business into my dispatch,

Which shall to all our nights and days to come
Give solely sovereign sway and masterdom.
MACBETH
We will speak further.
LADY   Only look up clear.   69
To alter favor ever is to fear.   70
Leave all the rest to me.   *Exeunt.*

                  *

    Hautboys and torches. Enter King [Duncan],   I, vi
    Malcolm, Donalbain, Banquo, Lennox, Macduff,
    Ross, Angus, and Attendants.
KING
This castle hath a pleasant seat. The air   1
Nimbly and sweetly recommends itself
Unto our gentle senses.   3
BANQUO   This guest of summer,
The temple-haunting martlet, does approve   4
By his loved mansionry that the heaven's breath   5
Smells wooingly here. No jutty, frieze,   6
Buttress, nor coign of vantage, but this bird   7
Hath made his pendent bed and procreant cradle.   8
Where they most breed and haunt, I have observed
The air is delicate.
    Enter Lady [Macbeth].
KING   See, see, our honored hostess !
The love that follows us sometime is our trouble,   11
Which still we thank as love. Herein I teach you
How you shall bid God 'ield us for your pains   13
And thank us for your trouble.
LADY   All our service
In every point twice done, and then done double,
Were poor and single business to contend
Against those honors deep and broad wherewith
Your Majesty loads our house. For those of old,
And the late dignities heaped up to them,
We rest your hermits.   20
KING   Where's the Thane of Cawdor ?
We coursed him at the heels and had a purpose
To be his purveyor ; but he rides well,   22
And his great love, sharp as his spur, hath holp him
To his home before us. Fair and noble hostess,
We are your guest to-night.
LADY   Your servants ever
Have theirs, themselves, and what is theirs, in compt,   26
To make their audit at your Highness' pleasure,
Still to return your own.   28
KING   Give me your hand.

18 *illness* ruthlessness 26 *round* crown 27 *metaphysical* supernatural 28 *withal* with 34 *breath* want of breath 39 *mortal* deadly 42 *remorse* pity 43 *nature* natural feeling 44 *fell* fierce 44–45 *keep peace . . . and it* i.e. lull it from achieving its end 46 *for gall* in exchange for gall; *ministers* agents 47 *sightless* invisible 48 *wait on* aid 49 *pall thee* shroud thyself; *dunnest* darkest 55 *ignorant* i.e. ordinarily unaware 61 *beguile the time* make sly use of the occasion 62 *Look like the time* play up to the occasion 66 *dispatch* swift management 69 *look up clear* appear untroubled 70 *alter favor* change countenance ; *fear* incur risk
I, vi At the portal of Inverness **s.d.** *Hautboys* oboes 1 *seat* site 3 *gentle* soothed 4 *temple-haunting* nesting in church spires ; *martlet* martin, swallow ; *approve* prove 5 *loved mansionry* beloved nests 6 *jutty* projection 7 *coign of vantage* convenient corner 8 *procreant* breeding 11–12 *The love . . . as love* the love that sometimes inconveniences us we still hold precious 13 *God 'ield us* God reward me 20 *hermits* beadsmen 22 *purveyor* advance agent of supplies 26 *Have theirs* have their servants ; *what is theirs* their possessions ; *in compt* in trust 28 *Still* always

Conduct me to mine host; we love him highly.
And shall continue our graces towards him.
By your leave, hostess.   *Exeunt.*

*

I, vii   *Hautboys. Torches. Enter a Sewer, and divers*
    Servants with dishes and service over the stage. Then
    enter Macbeth.

MACBETH

1 If it were done when 'tis done, then 'twere well
It were done quickly. If th' assassination
3 Could trammel up the consequence, and catch
4 With his surcease success, that but this blow
Might be the be-all and the end-all –; here,
But here upon this bank and shoal of time,
7 We'ld jump the life to come. But in these cases
We still have judgment here, that we but teach
9 Bloody instructions, which, being taught, return
To plague th' inventor. This even-handed justice
Commends th' ingredience of our poisoned chalice
To our own lips. He's here in double trust:
First, as I am his kinsman and his subject,
Strong both against the deed; then, as his host,
Who should against his murderer shut the door,
Not bear the knife myself. Besides, this Duncan
17 Hath borne his faculties so meek, hath been
18 So clear in his great office, that his virtues
Will plead like angels, trumpet-tongued against
The deep damnation of his taking-off;
And pity, like a naked new-born babe
Striding the blast, or heaven's cherubin horsed
23 Upon the sightless couriers of the air,
Shall blow the horrid deed in every eye
That tears shall drown the wind. I have no spur
To prick the sides of my intent, but only
Vaulting ambition, which o'erleaps itself
And falls on th' other –
    Enter Lady [Macbeth].
                How now? What news?

LADY

He has almost supped. Why have you left the chamber?

MACBETH

Hath he asked for me?

LADY   Know you not he has?

MACBETH

We will proceed no further in this business.
32 He hath honored me of late, and I have bought
Golden opinions from all sorts of people,
Which would be worn now in their newest gloss,
Not cast aside so soon.

LADY   Was the hope drunk
Wherein you dressed yourself? Hath it slept since?
And wakes it now to look so green and pale   37
At what it did so freely? From this time
Such I account thy love. Art thou afeard
To be the same in thine own act and valor
As thou art in desire? Wouldst thou have that
Which thou esteem'st the ornament of life,
And live a coward in thine own esteem,
Letting 'I dare not' wait upon 'I would,'
Like the poor cat i' th' adage?   45

MACBETH   Prithee peace!
I dare do all that may become a man;
Who dares do more is none.

LADY   What beast was't then
That made you break this enterprise to me?   48
When you durst do it, then you were a man;
And to be more than what you were, you would
Be so much more the man. Nor time nor place
Did then adhere, and yet you would make both.   52
They have made themselves, and that their fitness now   53
Does unmake you. I have given suck, and know
How tender 'tis to love the babe that milks me:
I would, while it was smiling in my face,
Have plucked my nipple from his boneless gums
And dashed the brains out, had I so sworn as you
Have done to this.

MACBETH   If we should fail?

LADY   We fail?
But screw your courage to the sticking place   60
And we'll not fail. When Duncan is asleep
(Whereto the rather shall his day's hard journey
Soundly invite him), his two chamberlains
Will I with wine and wassail so convince   64
That memory, the warder of the brain,
Shall be a fume, and the receipt of reason   66
A limbeck only. When in swinish sleep   67
Their drenchèd natures lies as in a death,
What cannot you and I perform upon
Th' unguarded Duncan? what not put upon
His spongy officers, who shall bear the guilt
Of our great quell?   72

MACBETH   Bring forth men-children only;
For thy undaunted mettle should compose   73
Nothing but males. Will it not be received,
When we have marked with blood those sleepy two
Of his own chamber and used their very daggers,
That they have done't?

LADY   Who dares receive it other,   77
As we shall make our griefs and clamor roar
Upon his death?

MACBETH   I am settled, and bend up
Each corporal agent to this terrible feat.
Away, and mock the time with fairest show;   81
False face must hide what the false heart doth know.
                              Exeunt.

*

    Enter Banquo, and Fleance, with a torch before him.   **II, i**

BANQUO

How goes the night, boy?

FLEANCE

The moon is down; I have not heard the clock.

I, vii The courtyard of Inverness from which open the chambers of the castle **s.d.** *Sewer* chief waiter **1** *done* done with **3** *trammel up the consequence* enclose the consequences in a net **4** *his surcease* its (the assassination's) completion; *success* all that follows **7** *jump* risk **9** *instructions* lessons **17** *faculties* powers **18** *clear* untainted **23** *sightless couriers* invisible coursers (the winds) **32** *bought* acquired **37** *green* bilious **45** *cat i' th' adage* (who wants the fish but doesn't want to get its paws wet) **48** *break* broach **52** *adhere* lend themselves to the occasion **53** *that their fitness* their very fitness **60** *sticking place* notch (holding the string of a crossbow cranked taut for shooting) **64** *convince* overcome **66** *receipt* container **67** *limbeck* cap of a still (to which the fumes rise) **72** *quell* killing **73** *mettle* vital substance **77** *other* otherwise **81** *mock* delude **II, i** The same

BANQUO
And she goes down at twelve.

FLEANCE   I take 't, 'tis later, sir.

BANQUO
4   Hold, take my sword. There's husbandry in heaven;
Their candles are all out. Take thee that too.
6   A heavy summons lies like lead upon me,
And yet I would not sleep. Merciful powers,
Restrain in me the cursèd thoughts that nature
Gives way to in repose.
Enter Macbeth, and a Servant with a torch.
Give me my sword!
Who's there?

MACBETH
A friend.

BANQUO
What, sir, not yet at rest? The King's abed.
He hath been in unusual pleasure and
14   Sent forth great largess to your offices.
This diamond he greets your wife withal
16   By the name of most kind hostess, and shut up
In measureless content.

MACBETH   Being unprepared,
18   Our will became the servant to defect,
Which else should free have wrought.

BANQUO   All's well.
I dreamt last night of the three weird sisters.
To you they have showed some truth.

MACBETH   I think not of them.
Yet when we can entreat an hour to serve,
We would spend it in some words upon that business,
If you would grant the time.

BANQUO   At your kind'st leisure.

MACBETH
25   If you shall cleave to my consent, when 'tis,
It shall make honor for you.

BANQUO   So I lose none
In seeking to augment it, but still keep
28   My bosom franchised and allegiance clear,
29   I shall be counselled.

MACBETH   Good repose the while.

BANQUO
Thanks, sir. The like to you.
Exeunt Banquo [and Fleance].

MACBETH
Go bid thy mistress, when my drink is ready,
She strike upon the bell. Get thee to bed. *Exit [Servant].*
Is this a dagger which I see before me,
The handle toward my hand? Come, let me clutch thee!
I have thee not, and yet I see thee still.
Art thou not, fatal vision, sensible
To feeling as to sight? or art thou but
A dagger of the mind, a false creation
Proceeding from the heat-oppressèd brain?
I see thee yet, in form as palpable
As this which now I draw.
Thou marshall'st me the way that I was going,
And such an instrument I was to use.
Mine eyes are made the fools o' th' other senses,
Or else worth all the rest. I see thee still,
46   And on thy blade and dudgeon gouts of blood,
Which was not so before. There's no such thing.
48   It is the bloody business which informs
Thus to mine eyes. Now o'er the one half-world

Nature seems dead, and wicked dreams abuse   50
The curtained sleep. Witchcraft celebrates
Pale Hecate's offerings; and withered murder,   52
Alarumed by his sentinel, the wolf,   53
Whose howl's his watch, thus with his stealthy pace,
With Tarquin's ravishing strides, towards his design   55
Moves like a ghost. Thou sure and firm-set earth,
Hear not my steps which way they walk, for fear
Thy very stones prate of my whereabout
And take the present horror from the time,   59
Which now suits with it. Whiles I threat, he lives;
Words to the heat of deeds too cold breath gives.
A bell rings.
I go, and it is done. The bell invites me.
Hear it not, Duncan, for it is a knell
That summons thee to heaven, or to hell.   *Exit.*
Enter Lady [Macbeth].   II, ii

LADY
That which hath made them drunk hath made me bold;
What hath quenched them hath given me fire. Hark!
Peace!
It was the owl that shrieked, the fatal bellman   3
Which gives the stern'st good-night. He is about it.
The doors are open, and the surfeited grooms
Do mock their charge with snores. I have drugged their   6
possets,
That death and nature do contend about them
Whether they live or die.

MACBETH *[within]*   Who's there? What, ho?

LADY
Alack, I am afraid they have awaked,
And 'tis not done! Th' attempt, and not the deed,
Confounds us. Hark! I laid their daggers ready –   11
He could not miss 'em. Had he not resembled
My father as he slept, I had done 't.
Enter Macbeth.   My husband!

MACBETH
I have done the deed. Didst thou not hear a noise?

LADY
I heard the owl scream and the crickets cry.
Did not you speak?

MACBETH   When?

LADY   Now.

MACBETH   As I descended?

LADY Ay.

MACBETH Hark!
Who lies i' th' second chamber?

LADY   Donalbain.

MACBETH This is a sorry sight.

LADY
A foolish thought, to say a sorry sight.

MACBETH
There's one did laugh in's sleep, and one cried 'Murder!'

4 *husbandry* economy   **6** *summons* signal to sleep   **14** *largess to your offices*
gratuities to your household departments   **16** *shut up* concluded   **18** *will*
good will; *defect* deficient means   **25** *cleave . . . when 'tis* favor my cause at
the proper time   **28** *franchised* free from guilt   **29** *counselled* open to
persuasion   **46** *dudgeon* wooden hilt; *gouts* blobs   **48** *informs* creates impressions   **50** *abuse* deceive   **52** *Hecate's offerings* worship of Hecate
(Goddess of sorcery)   **53** *Alarumed* given the signal   **55** *Tarquin* Roman
tyrant, ravisher of Lucrece   **59–60** *take . . . suits with it* delay, by prating,
the commission of the deed at this suitably horrible moment (?), reduce, by
breaking the silence, the suitable horror of this moment (?)
II, ii   3–4 *fatal bellman . . . good-night* i.e. like the night-watch cry to felons
scheduled for execution in the morning   **6** *possets* bedtime drinks   **11**
Confounds ruins

23 That they did wake each other. I stood and heard them.
But they did say their prayers and addressed them
Again to sleep.
LADY   There are two lodged together.
MACBETH
One cried 'God bless us!' and 'Amen!' the other,
27 As they had seen me with these hangman's hands,
List'ning their fear. I could not say 'Amen!'
When they did say 'God bless us!'
LADY   Consider it not so deeply.
MACBETH
But wherefore could not I pronounce 'Amen'?
I had most need of blessing, and 'Amen'
Stuck in my throat.
LADY   These deeds must not be thought
After these ways; so, it will make us mad.
MACBETH
Methought I heard a voice cry 'Sleep no more!
Macbeth does murder sleep' – the innocent sleep,
36 Sleep that knits up the ravelled sleave of care,
The death of each day's life, sore labor's bath,
38 Balm of hurt minds, great nature's second course,
Chief nourisher in life's feast.
LADY   What do you mean?
MACBETH
Still it cried 'Sleep no more!' to all the house;
'Glamis hath murdered sleep, and therefore Cawdor
Shall sleep no more, Macbeth shall sleep no more.'
LADY
Who was it that thus cried? Why, worthy Thane,
44 You do unbend your noble strength to think
So brainsickly of things. Go get some water
46 And wash this filthy witness from your hand.
Why did you bring these daggers from the place?
They must lie there: go carry them and smear
The sleepy grooms with blood.
MACBETH   I'll go no more.
I am afraid to think what I have done;
Look on't again I dare not.
LADY   Infirm of purpose!
Give me the daggers. The sleeping and the dead
53 Are but as pictures. 'Tis the eye of childhood
That fears a painted devil. If he do bleed,
55 I'll gild the faces of the grooms withal,
For it must seem their guilt.   *Exit.*
Knock within.
MACBETH
Whence is that knocking?
How is't with me when every noise appals me?
What hands are here? Ha! they pluck out mine eyes.
Will all great Neptune's ocean wash this blood
Clean from my hand? No, this my hand will rather

The multitudinous seas incarnadine,   61
Making the green one red.   62
Enter Lady [Macbeth].
LADY
My hands are of your color, but I shame
To wear a heart so white. *(Knock.)* I hear a knocking
At the south entry. Retire we to our chamber.
A little water clears us of this deed.
How easy is it then! Your constancy
Hath left you unattended.   68
Knock.   Hark! more knocking.
Get on your nightgown, lest occasion call us   69
And show us to be watchers. Be not lost   70
So poorly in your thoughts.   71
MACBETH
To know my deed, 'twere best not know myself.
Knock.
Wake Duncan with thy knocking! I would thou couldst.
      Exeunt.

Enter a Porter. Knocking within.   II, iii
PORTER Here's a knocking indeed! If a man were porter of
hell gate, he should have old turning the key. *(Knock.)*   2
Knock, knock, knock. Who's there, i' th' name of Belzebub? Here's a farmer that hanged himself on th' expecta-   4
tion of plenty. Come in time! Have napkins enow about   5
you; here you'll sweat for't. *(Knock.)* Knock, knock.
Who's there, in th' other devil's name? Faith, here's an
equivocator, that could swear in both the scales against   8
either scale; who committed treason enough for God's
sake, yet could not equivocate to heaven. O come in,
equivocator. *(Knock.)* Knock, knock, knock. Who's
there? Faith, here's an English tailor come hither for
stealing out of a French hose. Come in, tailor. Here you   13
may roast your goose. *(Knock.)* Knock, knock. Never at   14
quiet! What are you? – But this place is too cold for hell.
I'll devil-porter it no further. I had thought to have let
in some of all professions that go the primrose way to th'
everlasting bonfire. *(Knock.)* Anon, anon! [*Opens the
way.*] I pray you remember the porter.
Enter Macduff and Lennox.
MACDUFF
Was it so late, friend, ere you went to bed,
That you do lie so late?
PORTER Faith, sir, we were carousing till the second cock;   22
and drink, sir, is a great provoker of three things.
MACDUFF What three things does drink especially provoke?
PORTER Marry, sir, nose-painting, sleep, and urine.
Lechery, sir, it provokes, and unprovokes: it provokes
the desire, but it takes away the performance. Therefore
much drink may be said to be an equivocator with lechery: it makes him, and it mars him; it sets him on, and it
takes him off; it persuades him, and disheartens him;
makes him stand to, and not stand to; in conclusion,   31
equivocates him in a sleep, and, giving him the lie,
leaves him.
MACDUFF I believe drink gave thee the lie last night.   33
PORTER That it did, sir, i' the very throat on me; but I
requited him for his lie; and, I think, being too strong
for him, though he took up my legs sometime, yet I
made a shift to cast him.   37
MACDUFF Is thy master stirring?
Enter Macbeth.
Our knocking has awaked him: here he comes.

---

23 *That* so that   27 *hangman's hands* i.e. bloody, like an executioner's   36 *knits up . . . sleave* smooths out the tangled skein   38 *second course* i.e. sleep, after food   44 *unbend* relax   46 *witness* evidence   53 *as pictures* like pictures (since without motion)   55 *gild* paint   61 *incarnadine* redden   62 *one* uniformly   68 *unattended* deserted   69 *nightgown* dressing gown   70 *watchers* i.e. awake   71 *poorly* weakly
II, iii   2 *old* much   4 *farmer* i.e. one who has hoarded crops   4–5 *expectation of plenty* prospect of a crop surplus (which will lower prices)   5 *enow* enough   8 *equivocator* (usually considered an allusion to the Jesuits tried for political conspiracy)   13 *French hose* close-fitting breeches   14 *roast your goose* heat your pressing-iron   22 *second cock* second cockcrow (3 a.m.)   31 *stand to* stand his guard   33 *gave thee the lie* called you a liar (i.e. unable to stand)   37 *cast* throw

LENNOX
Good morrow, noble sir.
MACBETH   Good morrow, both.
MACDUFF
Is the King stirring, worthy Thane?
MACBETH   Not yet.
MACDUFF
42   He did command me to call timely on him;
43   I have almost slipped the hour.
MACBETH   I'll bring you to him.
MACDUFF
I know this is a joyful trouble to you;
But yet 'tis one.
MACBETH
46   The labor we delight in physics pain.
This is the door.
MACDUFF   I'll make so bold to call,
48   For 'tis my limited service.   *Exit Macduff.*
LENNOX
Goes the King hence to-day?
MACBETH   He does; he did appoint so.
LENNOX
The night has been unruly. Where we lay,
Our chimneys were blown down; and, as they say,
Lamentings heard i' th' air, strange screams of death,
And prophesying, with accents terrible,
54   Of dire combustion and confused events
55   New hatched to th' woeful time. The obscure bird
Clamored the livelong night. Some say the earth
Was feverous and did shake.
MACBETH   'Twas a rough night.
LENNOX
My young remembrance cannot parallel
A fellow to it.
     Enter Macduff.
MACDUFF
O horror, horror, horror! Tongue nor heart
Cannot conceive nor name thee!
MACBETH AND LENNOX   What's the matter?
MACDUFF
62   Confusion now hath made his masterpiece:
Most sacrilegious murder hath broke ope
The Lord's anointed temple and stole thence
The life o' th' building!
MACBETH   What is't you say? the life?
LENNOX
Mean you his Majesty?
MACDUFF
Approach the chamber and destroy your sight
68   With a new Gorgon. Do not bid me speak.
See, and then speak yourselves.
     Exeunt Macbeth and Lennox.
     Awake, awake!
Ring the alarum bell! Murder and treason!
Banquo and Donalbain! Malcolm, awake!
Shake off this downy sleep, death's counterfeit,
And look on death itself. Up, up, and see
74   The great doom's image. Malcolm! Banquo!
As from your graves rise up and walk like sprites
76   To countenance this horror. Ring the bell!
     Bell rings. Enter Lady [Macbeth].
LADY
What's the business,
That such a hideous trumpet calls to parley

The sleepers of the house? Speak, speak!
MACDUFF   O gentle lady,
'Tis not for you to hear what I can speak:
The repetition in a woman's ear   81
Would murder as it fell.
     Enter Banquo.   O Banquo, Banquo,
Our royal master's murdered!
LADY   Woe, alas!
What, in our house?
BANQUO   Too cruel anywhere.
Dear Duff, I prithee contradict thyself
And say it is not so.
     Enter Macbeth, Lennox, and Ross.
MACBETH
Had I but died an hour before this chance,
I had lived a blessèd time; for from this instant
There's nothing serious in mortality: 89
All is but toys. Renown and grace is dead,   90
The wine of life is drawn, and the mere lees   91
Is left this vault to brag of.   92
     Enter Malcolm and Donalbain.
DONALBAIN
What is amiss?
MACBETH   You are, and do not know't.
The spring, the head, the fountain of your blood
Is stopped, the very source of it is stopped.
MACDUFF
Your royal father's murdered.
MALCOLM   O, by whom?
LENNOX
Those of his chamber, as it seemed, had done't.
Their hands and faces were all badged with blood;   98
So were their daggers, which unwiped we found
Upon their pillows. They stared and were distracted.
No man's life was to be trusted with them.
MACBETH
O, yet I do repent me of my fury
That I did kill them.
MACDUFF   Wherefore did you so?
MACBETH
Who can be wise, amazed, temp'rate and furious,   104
Loyal and neutral, in a moment? No man.
The expedition of my violent love   106
Outrun the pauser, reason. Here lay Duncan,
His silver skin laced with his golden blood;
And his gashed stabs looked like a breach in nature
For ruin's wasteful entrance: there, the murderers,
Steeped in the colors of their trade, their daggers
Unmannerly breeched with gore. Who could refrain   112
That had a heart to love, and in that heart
Courage to make's love known?
LADY   Help me hence, ho!
MACDUFF
Look to the lady.   115
MALCOLM *[aside to Donalbain]*
     Why do we hold our tongues,

42 *timely* early   43 *slipped* let slip   46 *physics pain* cures trouble   48 *limited* appointed   54 *combustion* tumult   55 *obscure bird* i.e. the owl   62 *Confusion* destruction   68 *a new Gorgon* a new Medusa (capable of turning the beholder's eyes to stone)   74 *great doom's image* resemblance of the day of judgment   76 *countenance* appear in keeping with   81 *repetition* recital   89 *serious in mortality* worthwhile in human life   90 *toys* trifles   91 *lees* dregs   92 *vault* wine-vault   98 *badged* marked   104 *amazed* confused   106 *expedition* haste   112 *Unmannerly . . . gore* crudely wearing breeches of blood; *refrain* restrain oneself   115 *Look to* look after

116   That most may claim this argument for ours?

DONALBAIN *[to Malcolm]*
   What should be spoken here,
118   Where our fate, hid in an auger hole,
   May rush and seize us? Let's away:
   Our tears are not yet brewed.

MALCOLM *[To Donalbain]*   Nor our strong sorrow
121   Upon the foot of motion.

BANQUO   Look to the lady.
                [Lady Macbeth is carried out.]
122   And when we have our naked frailties hid,
   That suffer in exposure, let us meet
124   And question this most bloody piece of work,
125   To know it further. Fears and scruples shake us.
   In the great hand of God I stand, and thence
127   Against the undivulged pretense I fight
   Of treasonous malice.

MACDUFF   And so do I.

ALL   So all.

MACBETH
   Let's briefly put on manly readiness
   And meet i' th' hall together.

ALL   Well contented.
         Exeunt [all but Malcolm and Donalbain].

MALCOLM
   What will you do? Let's not consort with them.
   To show an unfelt sorrow is an office
   Which the false man does easy. I'll to England.

DONALBAIN
   To Ireland I. Our separated fortune
   Shall keep us both the safer. Where we are
136   There's daggers in men's smiles; the near in blood,
   The nearer bloody.

MALCOLM   This murderous shaft that's shot
   Hath not yet lighted, and our safest way
   Is to avoid the aim. Therefore to horse,
   And let us not be dainty of leave-taking
141   But shift away. There's warrant in that theft
   Which steals itself when there's no mercy left.   *Exeunt.*

*

II, iv   *Enter Ross with an Old Man.*

OLD MAN
   Threescore and ten I can remember well;
   Within the volume of which time I have seen
   Hours dreadful and things strange, but this sore night
4   Hath trifled former knowings.

ROSS   Ha, good father,
5   Thou seest the heavens, as troubled with man's act,
   Threatens his bloody stage. By th' clock 'tis day,

And yet dark night strangles the travelling lamp.   7
Is't night's predominance, or the day's shame,   8
That darkness does the face of earth entomb
When living light should kiss it?

OLD MAN   'Tis unnatural,
Even like the deed that's done. On Tuesday last
A falcon, tow'ring in her pride of place,   12
Was by a mousing owl hawked at and killed.   13

ROSS
And Duncan's horses (a thing most strange and certain),   14
Beauteous and swift, the minions of their race,   15
Turned wild in nature, broke their stalls, flung out,   16
Contending 'gainst obedience, as they would make
War with mankind.

OLD MAN   'Tis said they eat each other.   18

ROSS
They did so, to th' amazement of mine eyes
That looked upon't.
      Enter Macduff.   Here comes the good Macduff.
How goes the world, sir, now?

MACDUFF   Why, see you not?

ROSS
Is't known who did this more than bloody deed?

MACDUFF
Those that Macbeth hath slain.

ROSS   Alas the day,
What good could they pretend?   24

MACDUFF   They were suborned.
Malcolm and Donalbain, the King's two sons,
Are stol'n away and fled, which puts upon them
Suspicion of the deed.

ROSS   'Gainst nature still.
Thriftless ambition, that will ravin up   28
Thine own live's means! Then 'tis most like
The sovereignty will fall upon Macbeth.

MACDUFF
He is already named, and gone to Scone
To be invested.   32

ROSS   Where is Duncan's body?

MACDUFF
Carried to Colmekill,
The sacred storehouse of his predecessors
And guardian of their bones.

ROSS   Will you to Scone?

MACDUFF
No, cousin, I'll to Fife.

ROSS   Well, I will thither.

MACDUFF
Well, may you see things well done there. Adieu,
Lest our old robes sit easier than our new!

ROSS
Farewell, father.

OLD MAN
God's benison go with you, and with those   40
That would make good of bad, and friends of foes.
                   Exeunt omnes.

*

        Enter Banquo.   III, i

BANQUO
Thou hast it now – King, Cawdor, Glamis, all,
As the weird women promised; and I fear
Thou play'dst most foully for't. Yet it was said   3

116 *argument for ours* topic as chiefly our concern   118 *auger hole* i.e. any tiny cranny   121 *Upon the foot of motion* yet in motion   122 *frailties hid* bodies clothed   124 *question* discuss   125 *scruples* doubts   127 *undivulged pretense* secret stratagems   136 *near* nearer   141 *warrant* justification

II, iv Outside Inverness castle   4 *trifled former knowings* made former experiences seem trifling   5 *man's act* the human drama   7 *travelling lamp* i.e. of Phoebus, the sun   8 *predominance* supernatural ascendancy   12 *tow'ring* soaring   13 *mousing* i.e. ordinarily preying on mice; *hawked at* swooped upon   14 *certain* significant   15 *minions* darlings   16 *flung out* lunged about   18 *eat* ate   24 *pretend* expect; *suborned* bribed   28 *Thriftless* wasteful; *ravin up* bolt, swallow   32 *invested* crowned   40 *benison* blessing

III, i Within the royal palace (at Forres)   3 *foully* cheatingly

4   It should not stand in thy posterity,
       But that myself should be the root and father
       Of many kings. If there come truth from them
7   (As upon thee, Macbeth, their speeches shine),
       Why, by the verities on thee made good,
       May they not be my oracles as well
10   And set me up in hope? But hush, no more!
                Sennet sounded. Enter Macbeth as King, Lady
                [Macbeth], Lennox, Ross, Lords, and Attendants.
       MACBETH
       Here's our chief guest.
       LADY   If he had been forgotten,
       It had been as a gap in our great feast,
13   And all-thing unbecoming.
       MACBETH
14   To-night we hold a solemn supper, sir,
       And I'll request your presence.
       BANQUO   Let your Highness
       Command upon me, to the which my duties
       Are with a most indissoluble tie
       For ever knit.
       MACBETH   Ride you this afternoon?
       BANQUO
       Ay, my good lord.
       MACBETH
       We should have else desired your good advice
21   (Which still hath been both grave and prosperous)
       In this day's council; but we'll take to-morrow.
       Is't far you ride?
       BANQUO
       As far, my lord, as will fill up the time
25   'Twixt this and supper. Go not my horse the better,
26   I must become a borrower of the night
       For a dark hour or twain.
       MACBETH   Fail not our feast.
       BANQUO
       My lord, I will not.
       MACBETH
       We hear our bloody cousins are bestowed
       In England and in Ireland, not confessing
       Their cruel parricide, filling their hearers
32   With strange invention. But of that to-morrow,
33   When therewithal we shall have cause of state
       Craving us jointly. Hie you to horse. Adieu,
       Till you return at night. Goes Fleance with you?
       BANQUO
       Ay, my good lord. Our time does call upon's.
       MACBETH
       I wish your horses swift and sure of foot,
       And so I do commend you to their backs.
       Farewell.   *Exit Banquo.*
       Let every man be master of his time
       Till seven at night. To make society
       The sweeter welcome, we will keep ourself
43   Till supper time alone. While then, God be with you!
                              Exeunt Lords [and others].
44   Sirrah, a word with you. Attend those men
       Our pleasure?
       SERVANT
       They are, my lord, without the palace gate.
       MACBETH
       Bring them before us.   *Exit Servant.*
48   To be thus is nothing, but to be safely thus –
49   Our fears in Banquo stick deep,

       And in his royalty of nature reigns that
       Which would be feared. 'Tis much he dares;   51
       And to that dauntless temper of his mind
       He hath a wisdom that doth guide his valor
       To act in safety. There is none but he
       Whose being I do fear; and under him
       My genius is rebuked, as it is said   56
       Mark Antony's was by Caesar. He chid the sisters
       When first they put the name of King upon me,
       And bade them speak to him. Then, prophet-like,
       They hailed him father to a line of kings.
       Upon my head they placed a fruitless crown
       And put a barren sceptre in my gripe,   62
       Thence to be wrenched with an unlineal hand,
       No son of mine succeeding. If't be so,
       For Banquo's issue have I filed my mind;   65
       For them the gracious Duncan have I murdered;
       Put rancors in the vessel of my peace   67
       Only for them, and mine eternal jewel   68
       Given to the common enemy of man   69
       To make them kings – the seeds of Banquo kings.
       Rather than so, come, Fate, into the list,   71
       And champion me to th' utterance! Who's there?   72
                Enter Servant and two Murderers.
       Now go to the door and stay there till we call.
                                        Exit Servant.
       Was it not yesterday we spoke together?
       MURDERERS
       It was, so please your Highness.
       MACBETH   Well then, now
       Have you considered of my speeches? Know
       That it was he, in the times past, which held you
       So under fortune, which you thought had been   78
       Our innocent self. This I made good to you
       In our last conference, passed in probation with you   80
       How you were borne in hand, how crossed; the   81
          instruments;
       Who wrought with them; and all things else that might
       To half a soul and to a notion crazed   83
       Say 'Thus did Banquo.'
       1. MURDERER   You made it known to us.
       MACBETH
       I did so; and went further, which is now
       Our point of second meeting. Do you find   86
       Your patience so predominant in your nature
       That you can let this go? Are you so gospelled   88
       To pray for this good man and for his issue,
       Whose heavy hand hath bowed you to the grave
       And beggared yours for ever?
       1. MURDERER   We are men, my liege.

4 *stand* continue as a legacy   7 *shine* are brilliantly substantiated   10 s.d.
Sennet trumpet salute   13 *all-thing* altogether   14 *solemn* state   21 *still*
always; *prosperous* profitable   25 *Go not my horse the better* i.e. unless my
horse goes faster than anticipated   26 *borrower of* i.e. borrower of time from
32 *invention* falsehoods   33–34 *cause . . . jointly* state business requiring
our joint attention   43 *While* until   44 *Sirrah* form used in addressing
inferiors; *Attend* await   48 *but* unless   49 *in Banquo* about Banquo; *stick
deep* are deeply imbedded in me   51 *would be* deserves to be   56 *genius is
rebuked* controlling spirit is daunted   62 *gripe* grasp   65 *filed* defiled
67 *rancors* bitter enmities   68 *jewel* soul   69 *common enemy of man* i.e.
Satan   71 *list* lists, field of combat   72 *champion . . . utterance* engage with
me to the death   78 *under fortune* out of favor with fortune   80 *passed in
probation* reviewed the evidence   81 *borne in hand* manipulated; *crossed*
thwarted; *instruments* agents   83 *half a soul* a halfwit; *notion* mind   86
Our point of the point of our   88 *gospelled* tamed by gospel precepts

MACBETH

92 Ay, in the catalogue ye go for men,
As hounds and greyhounds, mongrels, spaniels, curs,
94 Shoughs, water-rugs, and demi-wolves are clept
95 All by the name of dogs. The valued file
Distinguishes the swift, the slow, the subtle,
97 The housekeeper, the hunter, every one
According to the gift which bounteous nature
99 Hath in him closed, whereby he does receive
100 Particular addition, from the bill
That writes them all alike ; and so of men.
Now, if you have a station in the file,
Not i' th' worst rank of manhood, say't ;
104 And I will put that business in your bosoms
Whose execution takes your enemy off,
Grapples you to the heart and love of us,
Who wear our health but sickly in his life,
Which in his death were perfect.
2. MURDERER   I am one, my liege,
Whom the vile blows and buffets of the world
Have so incensed that I am reckless what
I do to spite the world.
1. MURDERER   And I another,
So weary with disasters, tugged with fortune,
113 That I would set my life on any chance
To mend it or be rid on't.
MACBETH   Both of you
Know Banquo was your enemy.
MURDERERS   True, my lord.
MACBETH
116 So is he mine, and in such bloody distance
That every minute of his being thrusts
118 Against my near'st of life ; and though I could
With barefaced power sweep him from my sight
120 And bid my will avouch it, yet I must not,
121 For certain friends that are both his and mine,
122 Whose loves I may not drop, but wail his fall
Who I myself struck down. And thence it is
That I to your assistance do make love,
Masking the business from the common eye
For sundry weighty reasons.
2. MURDERER   We shall, my lord,
Perform what you command us.
1. MURDERER   Though our lives –
MACBETH
Your spirits shine through you. Within this hour at most
I will advise you where to plant yourselves,
130 Acquaint you with the perfect spy o' th' time
The moment on't, for't must be done to-night
132 And something from the palace (always thought
133 That I require a clearness) ; and with him,

134 To leave no rubs nor botches in the work,
Fleance his son, that keeps him company,
Whose absence is no less material to me
Than is his father's, must embrace the fate
Of that dark hour. Resolve yourselves apart ;
I'll come to you anon.
MURDERERS   We are resolved, my lord.
MACBETH
I'll call upon you straight. Abide within.
It is concluded. Banquo, thy soul's flight,
If it find heaven, must find it out to-night.   Exeunt.

*

Enter Macbeth's Lady and a Servant.   III, ii
LADY
Is Banquo gone from court ?
SERVANT
Ay, madam, but returns again to-night.
LADY
Say to the King I would attend his leisure
For a few words.
SERVANT   Madam, I will.   *Exit.*
LADY   Naught's had, all's spent,
Where our desire is got without content.
'Tis safer to be that which we destroy
Than by destruction dwell in doubtful joy.
Enter Macbeth.
How now, my lord ? Why do you keep alone,
Of sorriest fancies your companions making,   9
Using those thoughts which should indeed have died
With them they think on ? Things without all remedy   11
Should be without regard. What's done is done.
MACBETH
We have scorched the snake, not killed it.   13
She'll close and be herself, whilst our poor malice   14
Remains in danger of her former tooth.
But let the frame of things disjoint, both the worlds 16
suffer,
Ere we will eat our meal in fear, and sleep
In the affliction of these terrible dreams
That shake us nightly. Better be with the dead,
Whom we, to gain our peace, have sent to peace,
Than on the torture of the mind to lie   21
In restless ecstasy. Duncan is in his grave ;   22
After life's fitful fever he sleeps well.
Treason has done his worst : nor steel nor poison,
Malice domestic, foreign levy, nothing,   25
Can touch him further.
LADY   Come on.
Gentle my lord, sleek o'er your rugged looks ;
Be bright and jovial among your guests to-night.
MACBETH
So shall I, love ; and so, I pray, be you.
Let your remembrance apply to Banquo ;   30
Present him eminence both with eye and tongue :   31
Unsafe the while, that we must lave   32
Our honors in these flattering streams
And make our faces vizards to our hearts,   34
Disguising what they are.
LADY   You must leave this.
MACBETH
O, full of scorpions is my mind, dear wife !
Thou know'st that Banquo, and his Fleance, lives.

92 *catalogue* inventory, classification   94 *Shoughs* shaggy pet dogs ; *water-rugs* long-haired water-dogs ; *clept* named   95 *valued file* classification according to valuable traits   97 *housekeeper* watchdog   99 *closed* invested   100 *addition, from the bill* distinction, contrary to the listing   104 *in your bosoms* in your trust   113 *set* risk   116 *distance* enmity   118 *near'st of life* vital parts   120 *avouch* justify   121 *For* because of   122 *wail* I must wail   130 *with the perfect spy o' th' time* by means of a perfect look-out (?), with precise timing (?)   132 *thought* borne in mind   133 *clearness* alibi   134 *rubs* defects
III, ii The same   9 *sorriest* most contemptible   11 *all remedy* any form of remedy   13 *scorched* slashed   14 *close* heal ; *poor malice* feeble opposition   16 *frame of things disjoint* structure of the universe collapse ; *both the worlds* i.e. heaven and earth   21 *torture* rack   22 *ecstasy* frenzy   25 *Malice domestic* civil war   30 *remembrance* i.e. awareness of the necessity   31 *Present him eminence* exalt him   32 *lave* dip   34 *vizards* masks

LADY
38 But in them Nature's copy 's not eterne.
MACBETH
There's comfort yet ; they are assailable.
Then be thou jocund. Ere the bat hath flown
His cloistered flight, ere to black Hecate's summons
42 The shard-borne beetle with his drowsy hums
Hath rung night's yawning peal, there shall be done
A deed of dreadful note.
LADY   What's to be done ?
MACBETH
Be innocent of the knowledge, dearest chuck,
46 Till thou applaud the deed. Come, seeling night,
47 Scarf up the tender eye of pitiful day,
And with thy bloody and invisible hand
49 Cancel and tear to pieces that great bond
Which keeps me pale. Light thickens, and the crow
51 Makes wing to th' rooky wood.
Good things of day begin to droop and drowse,
Whiles night's black agents to their preys do rouse.
Thou marvell'st at my words, but hold thee still ;
Things bad begun make strong themselves by ill.
So prithee go with me.   *Exeunt.*

*

III, iii   *Enter three Murderers.*
1 . MURDERER
But who did bid thee join with us ?
3 . MURDERER   Macbeth.
2 . MURDERER
2 He needs not our mistrust, since he delivers
3 Our offices and what we have to do
To the direction just.
1 . MURDERER   Then stand with us.
The west yet glimmers with some streaks of day.
6 Now spurs the lated traveller apace
To gain the timely inn, and near approaches
The subject of our watch.
3 . MURDERER   Hark, I hear horses.
BANQUO *(within)*
Give us a light there, ho !
2 . MURDERER   Then 'tis he : the rest
10 That are within the note of expectation
Already are i' th' court.
1 . MURDERER   His horses go about.
3 . MURDERER
Almost a mile ; but he does usually,
So all men do, from hence to th' palace gate
Make it their walk.
      Enter Banquo and Fleance, with a torch.
2 . MURDERER
A light, a light !
3 . MURDERER   'Tis he.
1 . MURDERER   Stand to't.
BANQUO
It will be rain to-night.
1 . MURDERER   Let it come down !
BANQUO
O, treachery ! Fly, good Fleance, fly, fly, fly !
           [Exit Fleance.]
Thou mayst revenge – O slave !
      [Banquo slain.]

3 . MURDERER
Who did strike out the light ?
1 . MURDERER   Was't not the way ?   19
3 . MURDERER
There's but one down : the son is fled.
2 . MURDERER
We have lost best half of our affair.
1 . MURDERER
Well, let's away, and say how much is done.   *Exeunt.*

*

      Banquet prepared. Enter Macbeth, Lady [Macbeth], III, iv
      Ross, Lennox, Lords, and Attendants.
MACBETH
You know your own degrees – sit down :   1
At first and last the hearty welcome.
LORDS
Thanks to your Majesty.
MACBETH
Ourself will mingle with society   4
And play the humble host.
Our hostess keeps her state, but in best time   6
We will require her welcome.
LADY
Pronounce it for me, sir, to all our friends,
For my heart speaks they are welcome.
      Enter First Murderer.
MACBETH
See, they encounter thee with their hearts' thanks.   10
Both sides are even. Here I'll sit i' th' midst.
Be large in mirth ; anon we'll drink a measure
The table round.
      [Goes to Murderer.]
There's blood upon thy face.
MURDERER   'Tis Banquo's then.
MACBETH
'Tis better thee without than he within.
Is he dispatched ?
MURDERER   My lord, his throat is cut :
That I did for him.
MACBETH   Thou are the best o' th' cut-throats.
Yet he's good that did the like for Fleance :
If thou didst it, thou art the nonpareil.
MURDERER
Most royal sir, Fleance is 'scaped.
MACBETH *[aside]*
Then comes my fit again. I had else been perfect ;   21
Whole as the marble, founded as the rock,   22
As broad and general as the casing air.   23
But now I am cabined, cribbed, confined, bound in   24
To saucy doubts and fears. – But Banquo's safe ?   25

38 *Nature's copy* Nature's copyhold, lease on life   **42** *shard-borne* borne on scaly wings   **46** *seeling* sewing together the eyelids (from falconry)   **47** *Scarf up* blindfold   **49** *great bond* i.e. Banquo's lease on life (with suggestion also of the bond of human feeling)   **51** *rooky* harboring rooks
III, iii An approach to the palace   **2** *He needs not our mistrust* i.e. we need not mistrust this man   **3** *offices* duties   **6** *lated* belated   **10** *within the note of expectation* on the list of those expected (invited)   **19** *Was't not the way* i.e. was it not the right thing to do
III, iv The hall of the palace   **1** *degrees* relative rank, order of precedence   **4** *society* the company   **6** *keeps her state* remains seated in her chair of state   **10** *encounter* greet   **21** *perfect* sound of health   **22** *founded* solidly based   **23** *broad and general* unconfined ; *casing* enveloping   **24** *cribbed* boxed in   **25** *saucy* insolent

MURDERER
Ay, my good lord. Safe in a ditch he bides,
27 With twenty trenchèd gashes on his head,
The least a death to nature.
MACBETH   Thanks for that. –
   [Aside]
29 There the grown serpent lies ; the worm that's fled
Hath nature that in time will venom breed,
No teeth for th' present. – Get thee gone. To-morrow
32 We'll hear ourselves again.   Exit Murderer.
LADY   My royal lord,
33 You do not give the cheer. The feast is sold
34 That is not often vouched, while 'tis a-making,
35 'Tis given with welcome. To feed were best at home ;
36 From thence, the sauce to meat is ceremony :
37 Meeting were bare without it.
   Enter the Ghost of Banquo, and sits in Macbeth's
   place.
MACBETH   Sweet remembrancer !
Now good digestion wait on appetite,
And health on both !
LENNOX   May't please your Highness sit.
MACBETH
Here had we now our country's honor roofed
Were the graced person of our Banquo present –
42 Who may I rather challenge for unkindness
Than pity for mischance !
ROSS   His absence, sir,
Lays blame upon his promise. Please't your Highness
To grace us with your royal company ?
MACBETH
The table 's full.
LENNOX   Here is a place reserved, sir.
MACBETH
Where ?
LENNOX
Here, my good lord. What is't that moves your
   Highness ?
MACBETH
Which of you have done this ?
LORDS   What, my good lord ?
MACBETH
Thou canst not say I did it. Never shake
Thy gory locks at me.
ROSS
Gentlemen, rise. His Highness is not well.
LADY
Sit, worthy friends. My lord is often thus,
And hath been from his youth. Pray you keep seat.
The fit is momentary ; upon a thought

He will again be well. If much you note him,
You shall offend him and extend his passion.   57
Feed, and regard him not. – Are you a man ?
MACBETH
Ay, and a bold one, that dare look on that
Which might appal the devil.
LADY   O proper stuff !
This is the very painting of your fear.
This is the air-drawn dagger which you said   62
Led you to Duncan. O, these flaws and starts   63
(Impostors to true fear) would well become   64
A woman's story at a winter's fire,
Authorized by her grandam. Shame itself !   66
Why do you make such faces ? When all's done,
You look but on a stool.
MACBETH   Prithee see there !
Behold ! Look ! Lo ! – How say you ?
Why, what care I ? If thou canst nod, speak too.
If charnel houses and our graves must send
Those that we bury back, our monuments   72
Shall be the maws of kites.   [Exit Ghost.]   73
LADY   What, quite unmanned in folly ?
MACBETH
If I stand here, I saw him.
LADY   Fie, for shame !
MACBETH
Blood hath been shed ere now, i' th' olden time,
Ere humane statute purged the gentle weal ;   76
Ay, and since too, murders have been performed
Too terrible for the ear. The time has been
That, when the brains were out, the man would die,
And there an end. But now they rise again,
With twenty mortal murders on their crowns,   81
And push us from our stools. This is more strange
Than such a murder is.
LADY   My worthy lord,
Your noble friends do lack you.
MACBETH   I do forget.
Do not muse at me, my most worthy friends :
I have a strange infirmity, which is nothing
To those that know me. Come, love and health to all !
Then I'll sit down. Give me some wine, fill full.
   Enter Ghost.
I drink to th' general joy o' th' whole table,
And to our dear friend Banquo, whom we miss.
Would he were here ! To all, and him, we thirst,   91
And all to all.   92
LORDS   Our duties, and the pledge.
MACBETH
Avaunt, and quit my sight ! Let the earth hide thee !
Thy bones are marrowless, thy blood is cold ;
Thou hast no speculation in those eyes   95
Which thou dost glare with !
LADY   Think of this, good peers,
But as a thing of custom. 'Tis no other.
Only it spoils the pleasure of the time.
MACBETH
What man dare, I dare.
Approach thou like the rugged Russian bear,
The armed rhinoceros, or th' Hyrcan tiger ;   101
Take any shape but that, and my firm nerves
Shall never tremble. Or be alive again
And dare me to the desert with thy sword.   104
If trembling I inhabit then, protest me   105

27 trenchèd deep, trench-like   29 worm serpent   32 hear ourselves confer
33 cheer tokens of convivial hospitality; sold i.e. not freely given   34
vouched sworn   35 To feed . . . home i.e. mere eating is best done at home
36 meat food   37 bare barren, pointless; remembrancer prompter   42
Who may . . . challenge whom I hope I may reprove   57 extend his passion
prolong his seizure   62 air-drawn fashioned of air   63 flaws outbursts
64 Impostors to true fear (i.e. because they are authentic signs of false or
unjustified fear)   66 Authorized sanctioned   72 monuments i.e. our only
tombs   73 maws of kites bellies of ravens   76 purged the gentle weal i.e.
purged the state of savagery   81 murders on their crowns murderous
gashes on their heads   91 thirst are eager to drink   92 all to all let everyone drink to everyone   95 speculation intelligence, power of rational
observation   101 Hyrcan from Hyrcania, anciently a region near the
Caspian Sea   104 the desert a solitary place   105 If trembling I inhabit
if I tremble

106 The baby of a girl. Hence, horrible shadow!
    Unreal mock'ry, hence!   [*Exit Ghost.*]
                        Why, so; being gone,
    I am a man again. Pray you sit still.
        LADY
    You have displaced the mirth, broke the good meeting
110 With most admired disorder.
        MACBETH   Can such things be,
111 And overcome us like a summer's cloud
112 Without our special wonder? You make me strange
    Even to the disposition that I owe,
    When now I think you can behold such sights
    And keep the natural ruby of your cheeks
116 When mine is blanched with fear.
        ROSS   What sights, my lord?
        LADY
    I pray you speak not: he grows worse and worse;
    Question enrages him. At once, good night.
    Stand not upon the order of your going,
    But go at once.
        LENNOX   Good night and better health
    Attend his Majesty.
        LADY   A kind good night to all. *Exeunt Lords.*
        MACBETH
    It will have blood, they say: blood will have blood.
    Stones have been known to move and trees to speak;
124 Augures and understood relations have
125 By maggot-pies and choughs and rooks brought forth
    The secret'st man of blood. What is the night?
        LADY
    Almost at odds with morning, which is which.
        MACBETH
    How say'st thou, that Macduff denies his person
    At our great bidding?
        LADY   Did you send to him, sir?
        MACBETH
130 I hear it by the way; but I will send.
    There's not a one of them but in his house
132 I keep a servant fee'd. I will to-morrow
133 (And betimes I will) to the weird sisters.
134 More shall they speak, for now I am bent to know
    By the worst means the worst. For mine own good
    All causes shall give way. I am in blood
    Stepped in so far that, should I wade no more,
    Returning were as tedious as go o'er.
    Strange things I have in head, that will to hand,
140 Which must be acted ere they may be scanned.
        LADY
141 You lack the season of all natures, sleep.
        MACBETH
142 Come, we'll to sleep. My strange and self-abuse
143 Is the initiate fear that wants hard use.
    We are yet but young in deed.   *Exeunt.*

                                *

III, v   [*Thunder. Enter the three Witches, meeting Hecate.*
        1. WITCH
    Why, how now, Hecate? You look angerly.
        HECATE
2   Have I not reason, beldams as you are,
    Saucy and overbold? How did you dare
    To trade and traffic with Macbeth
    In riddles and affairs of death;

And I, the mistress of your charms,
The close contriver of all harms,   7
Was never called to bear my part
Or show the glory of our art?
And, which is worse, all you have done
Hath been but for a wayward son,
Spiteful and wrathful, who, as others do,
Loves for his own ends, not for you.
But make amends now: get you gone
And at the pit of Acheron   15
Meet me i' th' morning. Thither he
Will come to know his destiny.
Your vessels and your spells provide,
Your charms and everything beside.
I am for th' air. This night I'll spend
Unto a dismal and a fatal end.
Great business must be wrought ere noon.
Upon the corner of the moon
There hangs a vap'rous drop profound;   24
I'll catch it ere it come to ground:
And that, distilled by magic sleights,   26
Shall raise such artificial sprites   27
As by the strength of their illusion
Shall draw him on to his confusion.
He shall spurn fate, scorn death, and bear
His hopes 'bove wisdom, grace, and fear:
And you all know security   32
Is mortals' chiefest enemy.
            Music, and a song.
Hark! I am called. My little spirit, see,
Sits in a foggy cloud and stays for me.   [*Exit.*]
    Sing within, 'Come away, come away,' &c.
    1. WITCH
Come, let's make haste: she'll soon be back again.
                                [*Exeunt.*]

                                *

    Enter Lennox and another Lord.   III,
    LENNOX
My former speeches have but hit your thoughts,   1
Which can interpret farther. Only I say   2
Things have been strangely borne. The gracious Duncan
Was pitied of Macbeth. Marry, he was dead.
And the right valiant Banquo walked too late;
Whom, you may say (if't please you) Fleance killed,
For Fleance fled. Men must not walk too late.
Who cannot want the thought how monstrous   8
It was for Malcolm and for Donalbain
To kill their gracious father? Damnèd fact,   10
How it did grieve Macbeth! Did he not straight,

106 *The baby of a girl* a baby girl   110 *admired* wondered at   111 *overcome us* come over us   112–13 *You make . . . I owe* you oust me from my proper role (as a brave man)   116 *blanched* made pale   124 *Augures* auguries; *relations* utterances   125 *maggot-pies* magpies; *choughs* jackdaws (capable of 'utterances,' as are magpies and rooks)   130 *by the way* casually   132 *fee'd* paid to spy   133 *betimes* speedily   134 *bent* inclined, determined   140 *ere they may be scanned* i.e. without being closely studied   141 *season* seasoning, preservative   142 *self-abuse* delusion   143 *initiate fear* beginner's fear; *wants hard use* lacks toughening practice
III, v An open place (an interpolated scene, by a different author)   2 *beldams* old crones   7 *close* secret   15 *Acheron* a river of Hades   24 *profound* weighty   26 *sleights* devices   27 *artificial sprites* spirits created by magic arts   32 *security* over-confidence
III, vi Any meeting place in Scotland   1 *My former speeches* what I have just said; *hit* matched   2 *interpret farther* draw further conclusions   8 *cannot want the thought* can avoid thinking   10 *fact* deed

In pious rage, the two delinquents tear
13 That were the slaves of drink and thralls of sleep?
Was not that nobly done? Ay, and wisely too,
For 'twould have angered any heart alive
To hear the men deny't. So that I say
17 He has borne all things well; and I do think
That, had he Duncan's sons under his key
19 (As, an't please heaven, he shall not), they should find
What 'twere to kill a father. So should Fleance.
21 But peace! for from broad words, and 'cause he failed
His presence at the tyrant's feast, I hear
Macduff lives in disgrace. Sir, can you tell
Where he bestows himself?

LORD   The son of Duncan,
25 From whom this tyrant holds the due of birth,
Lives in the English court, and is received
Of the most pious Edward with such grace
That the malevolence of fortune nothing
29 Takes from his high respect. Thither Macduff
30 Is gone to pray the holy King upon his aid
31 To wake Northumberland and warlike Siward;
That by the help of these (with Him above
To ratify the work) we may again
Give to our tables meat, sleep to our nights,
Free from our feasts and banquets bloody knives,
36 Do faithful homage and receive free honors –
All which we pine for now. And this report
Hath so exasperate the King that he
Prepares for some attempt of war.

LENNOX   Sent he to Macduff?
LORD
He did; and with an absolute 'Sir, not I,'
41 The cloudy messenger turns me his back
And hums, as who should say, 'You'll rue the time
43 That clogs me with this answer.'

LENNOX   And that well might
44 Advise him to a caution t' hold what distance
His wisdom can provide. Some holy angel
Fly to the court of England and unfold
His message ere he come, that a swift blessing
May soon return to this our suffering country
Under a hand accursed!

LORD   I'll send my prayers with him.
                               Exeunt.

*

IV, i   *Thunder. Enter the three Witches.*
1 1. WITCH Thrice the brinded cat hath mewed.
2. WITCH Thrice, and once the hedge-pig whined.
3 3. WITCH Harpier cries. – 'Tis time, 'tis time!
1. WITCH Round about the cauldron go;

---

13 *thralls* slaves   17 *borne* carried off   19 *an't* if it   21 *from broad words* through plain speaking   25 *due of birth* birthright   29 *his high respect* high respect for him   30 *upon his aid* upon Malcolm's behalf   31 *wake* arouse; *Northumberland* (English county bordering Scotland)   36 *free* untainted   41 *cloudy* angry   43 *clogs* encumbers   44–45 *Advise him . . . can provide* warn him to keep at as safe a distance as he can devise
IV, i A cave (cf. III, v, 15)   1 *brinded* brindled, striped   3 *Harpier* (name of familiar spirit, suggestive of harpy)   8 *Swelt'red venom, sleeping got* exuded venom formed while sleeping   12 *fenny* swamp   16 *blindworm* a lizard, popularly supposed poisonous   23 *mummy* mummified flesh; *maw and gulf* stomach and gullet   24 *ravined* insatiable   31 *drab* harlot   32 *slab* sticky   33 *chaudron* guts   38 s.d.–43 s.d. (an interpolation)   44 *By* i.e. I know by   53 *yesty* yeasty, foamy   54 *Confound* destroy   55 *bladed corn be lodged* ripe grain be beaten to earth   57 *slope* incline   59 *Nature's germains* seeds of creation   60 *sicken* shall surfeit

In the poisoned entrails throw.
Toad, that under cold stone
Days and nights has thirty-one
Swelt'red venom, sleeping got,   8
Boil thou first i' th' charmèd pot.

ALL   Double, double, toil and trouble,
Fire burn and cauldron bubble.

2. WITCH Fillet of a fenny snake,   12
In the cauldron boil and bake;
Eye of newt, and toe of frog,
Wool of bat, and tongue of dog,
Adder's fork, and blindworm's sting,   16
Lizard's leg, and howlet's wing –
For a charm of pow'rful trouble,
Like a hell-broth boil and bubble.

ALL   Double, double, toil and trouble,
Fire burn and cauldron bubble.

3. WITCH Scale of dragon, tooth of wolf,
Witch's mummy, maw and gulf   23
Of the ravined salt-sea shark,   24
Root of hemlock digged i' th' dark,
Liver of blaspheming Jew,
Gall of goat, and slips of yew
Slivered in the moon's eclipse,
Nose of Turk, and Tartar's lips,
Finger of birth-strangled babe
Ditch-delivered by a drab   31
Make the gruel thick and slab.   32
Add thereto a tiger's chaudron   33
For th' ingredience of our cauldron.

ALL   Double, double, toil and trouble,
Fire burn and cauldron bubble.

2. WITCH Cool it with a baboon's blood,
Then the charm is firm and good.   38

[Enter Hecate and the other three Witches.

HECATE   O, well done! I commend your pains,
And every one shall share i' th' gains.
And now about the cauldron sing
Like elves and fairies in a ring,
Enchanting all that you put in.
Music and a song, 'Black spirits,' &c.]
               [Exeunt Hecate and singers.]

2. WITCH By the pricking of my thumbs,   44
Something wicked this way comes.
Open locks,
Whoever knocks!

Enter Macbeth.

MACBETH
How now, you secret, black, and midnight hags,
What is't you do?

ALL   A deed without a name.

MACBETH
I conjure you by that which you profess,
Howe'er you come to know it, answer me.
Though you untie the winds and let them fight
Against the churches, though the yesty waves   53
Confound and swallow navigation up,   54
Though bladed corn be lodged and trees blown down,   55
Though castles topple on their warders' heads,
Though palaces and pyramids do slope   57
Their heads to their foundations, though the treasure
Of Nature's germains tumble all together   59
Even till destruction sicken, answer me   60
To what I ask you.

1 . WITCH   Speak.

2 . WITCH   Demand.

3 . WITCH   We'll answer.

1 . WITCH

Say if th' hadst rather hear it from our mouths

Or from our masters.

MACBETH   Call 'em. Let me see 'em.

1 . WITCH Pour in sow's blood, that hath eaten

65   Her nine farrow ; grease that's sweaten

From the murderer's gibbet throw

Into the flame.

ALL   Come, high or low,

68   Thyself and office deftly show !

Thunder. First Apparition, an Armed Head.

MACBETH

Tell me, thou unknown power –

1 . WITCH   He knows thy thought :

Hear his speech, but say thou naught.

1 . APPARITION

Macbeth, Macbeth, Macbeth, beware Macduff !

Beware the Thane of Fife ! Dismiss me. – Enough.

He descends.

MACBETH

Whate'er thou art, for thy good caution thanks :

74   Thou hast harped my fear aright. But one word more –

1 . WITCH

He will not be commanded. Here's another,

More potent than the first.

Thunder. Second Apparition, a Bloody Child.

2 . APPARITION

Macbeth, Macbeth, Macbeth –

MACBETH

Had I three ears, I'ld hear thee.

2 . APPARITION

Be bloody, bold, and resolute ! Laugh to scorn

The pow'r of man, for none of woman born

Shall harm Macbeth.   *Descends.*

MACBETH

Then live, Macduff, – what need I fear of thee ?

But yet I'll make assurance double sure

84   And take a bond of fate. Thou shalt not live ;

That I may tell pale-hearted fear it lies

And sleep in spite of thunder.

Thunder. Third Apparition, a Child Crowned, with

a tree in his hand.

                    What is this

That rises like the issue of a king

88   And wears upon his baby-brow the round

And top of sovereignty ?

ALL   Listen, but speak not to't.

3 . APPARITION

Be lion-mettled, proud, and take no care

Who chafes, who frets, or where conspirers are !

Macbeth shall never vanquished be until

Great Birnam Wood to high Dunsinane Hill

Shall come against him.   *Descends.*

MACBETH   That will never be.

95   Who can impress the forest, bid the tree

96   Unfix his earth-bound root ? Sweet bodements, good !

Rebellious dead rise never till the Wood

Of Birnam rise, and our high-placed Macbeth

99   Shall live the lease of nature, pay his breath

100   To time and mortal custom. Yet my heart

Throbs to know one thing. Tell me, if your art

Can tell so much : Shall Banquo's issue ever   102

Reign in this kingdom ?

ALL   Seek to know no more.

MACBETH

I will be satisfied. Deny me this,

And an eternal curse fall on you ! Let me know.

Why sinks that cauldron ? and what noise is this ?   106

Hautboys.

1 . WITCH Show !

2 . WITCH Show !

3 . WITCH Show !

ALL   Show his eyes, and grieve his heart !

Come like shadows, so depart !

A show of eight Kings and Banquo, last [King] with a

glass in his hand.

MACBETH

Thou art too like the spirit of Banquo. Down !

Thy crown does sear mine eyeballs. And thy hair,

Thou other gold-bound brow, is like the first.

A third is like the former. Filthy hags,

Why do you show me this ? A fourth ? Start, eyes !   116

What, will the line stretch out to th' crack of doom ?

Another yet ? A seventh ? I'll see no more.

And yet the eighth appears, who bears a glass

Which shows me many more ; and some I see

That twofold balls and treble sceptres carry.   121

Horrible sight ! Now I see 'tis true ;

For the blood-boltered Banquo smiles upon me   123

And points at them for his. What ? Is this so ?

[1 . WITCH Ay, sir, all this is so. But why   125

Stands Macbeth thus amazedly ?

Come, sisters, cheer we up his sprites   127

And show the best of our delights.

I'll charm the air to give a sound

While you perform your antic round,   130

That this great king may kindly say

Our duties did his welcome pay.

Music. The Witches dance, and vanish.]

MACBETH

Where are they ? Gone ? Let this pernicious hour

Stand aye accursèd in the calendar !

Come in, without there !

Enter Lennox.

LENNOX   What's your Grace's will ?

MACBETH

Saw you the weird sisters ?

LENNOX   No, my lord.

MACBETH

Came they not by you ?

LENNOX   No indeed, my lord.

MACBETH

Infected be the air whereon they ride,

And damned all those that trust them ! I did hear

The galloping of horse. Who was't came by ?

LENNOX

'Tis two or three, my lord, that bring you word

---

65 *nine farrow* litter of nine   68 *office* function   74 *harped* hit the tune of 84 *take a bond of* secure a guarantee from   88 *round* crown   95 *impress* conscript   96 *bodements* prophecies   99 *lease of nature* i.e. the full life-span   100 *mortal custom* normal death   102 *issue* offspring   106 *noise* music   116 *Start* bulge   121 *twofold balls and treble sceptres* (English coronation insignia)   123 *blood-boltered* matted with blood   125–32 (an interpolation)   127 *sprites* spirits   130 *antic round* grotesque circular dance

Macduff is fled to England.

MACBETH   Fled to England?

LENNOX

Ay, my good lord.

MACBETH [aside]

144 Time, thou anticipat'st my dread exploits.
145 The flighty purpose never is o'ertook
Unless the deed go with it. From this moment
147 The very firstlings of my heart shall be
The firstlings of my hand. And even now,
To crown my thoughts with acts, be it thought and done:
The castle of Macduff I will surprise,
Seize upon Fife, give to th' edge o' th' sword
His wife, his babes, and all unfortunate souls
153 That trace him in his line. No boasting like a fool;
This deed I'll do before this purpose cool.
But no more sights! – Where are these gentlemen?
Come, bring me where they are.   Exeunt.

*

IV, ii   Enter Macduff's Wife, her Son, and Ross.

WIFE

What had he done to make him fly the land?

ROSS

2 You must have patience, madam.

WIFE   He had none.
His flight was madness. When our actions do not,
4 Our fears do make us traitors.

ROSS   You know not
Whether it was his wisdom or his fear.

WIFE

Wisdom? To leave his wife, to leave his babes,
His mansion and his titles in a place
From whence himself does fly? He loves us not,
9 He wants the natural touch. For the poor wren
(The most diminutive of birds) will fight,
Her young ones in her nest, against the owl.
All is the fear and nothing is the love,
As little is the wisdom, where the flight
So runs against all reason.

14 ROSS   My dearest coz,
I pray you school yourself. But for your husband,
He is noble, wise, judicious, and best knows
17 The fits o' th' season. I dare not speak much further,
But cruel are the times when we are traitors
19 And do not know ourselves; when we hold rumor
From what we fear, yet know not what we fear
But float upon a wild and violent sea
Each way and none. I take my leave of you.
Shall not be long but I'll be here again.

144 *anticipat'st* forestall 145 *flighty* fleeting 147–48 *firstlings ... my hand*
i.e. I shall act at the moment I feel the first impulse 153 *trace* follow; *line*
family line
IV, ii Within the castle at Fife 2 *patience* self-control 4 *traitors* i.e.
traitors to ourselves 9 *wants* lacks 14 *coz* cousin, kinswoman 17 *fits*
o' th' season present disorders 19 *know ourselves* know ourselves to be so
19–20 *hold rumor ... we fear* are credulous in accordance with our fears
24 *will cease* i.e. must cease descending 29 *would be my* would be to my
(i.e. his weeping) 34 *lime* birdlime 35 *gin* trap 41 *sell* betray 42–43
Thou speak'st ... for thee i.e. you use all the intelligence you have, and it is
quite enough 56 *enow* enough 65 *in your state ... perfect* I am informed
of your noble identity 66 *doubt* fear 67 *homely* plain 70–71 *To do*
worse ... your person i.e. not to frighten you were to do worse, expose you
to that fierce cruelty which is impending

Things at the worst will cease, or else climb upward   24
To what they were before. – My pretty cousin,
Blessing upon you!

WIFE

Fathered he is, and yet he's fatherless.

ROSS

I am so much a fool, should I stay longer
It would be my disgrace and your discomfort.   29
I take my leave at once.   Exit.

WIFE   Sirrah, your father's dead;
And what will you do now? How will you live?

SON

As birds do, mother.

WIFE   What, with worms and flies?

SON

With what I get, I mean; and so do they.

WIFE

Poor bird! thou'dst never fear the net nor lime,   34
The pitfall nor the gin.   35

SON

Why should I, mother? Poor birds they are not set for.
My father is not dead for all your saying.

WIFE

Yes, he is dead. How wilt thou do for a father?

SON Nay, how will you do for a husband?

WIFE Why, I can buy me twenty at any market.

SON Then you'll buy 'em to sell again.   41

WIFE

Thou speak'st with all thy wit; and yet, i' faith,   42
With wit enough for thee.

SON

Was my father a traitor, mother?

WIFE Ay, that he was!

SON What is a traitor?

WIFE Why, one that swears and lies.

SON And be all traitors that do so?

WIFE Every one that does so is a traitor and must be
hanged.

SON And must they all be hanged that swear and lie?

WIFE Every one.

SON Who must hang them?

WIFE Why, the honest men.

SON Then the liars and swearers are fools, for there are
liars and swearers enow to beat the honest men and   56
hang up them.

WIFE Now God help thee, poor monkey! But how wilt
thou do for a father?

SON If he were dead, you'ld weep for him. If you would
not, it were a good sign that I should quickly have a new
father.

WIFE Poor prattler, how thou talk'st!
              Enter a Messenger.

MESSENGER

Bless you, fair dame! I am not to you known,
Though in your state of honor I am perfect. ·   65
I doubt some danger does approach you nearly.   66
If you will take a homely man's advice,   67
Be not found here. Hence with your little ones!
To fright you thus methinks I am too savage;
To do worse to you were fell cruelty,   70
Which is too nigh your person. Heaven preserve you!
I dare abide no longer.   Exit.

WIFE   Whither should I fly?
I have done no harm. But I remember now

I am in this earthly world, where to do harm
Is often laudable, to do good sometime
Accounted dangerous folly. Why then, alas,
Do I put up that womanly defense
To say I have done no harm?
Enter Murderers.   What are these faces?

MURDERER
Where is your husband?

WIFE
I hope in no place so unsanctified
Where such as thou mayst find him.

MURDERER   He's a traitor.

SON
82   Thou liest, thou shag-eared villain!

MURDERER   What, you egg!
     [Stabs him.]
83   Young fry of treachery!

SON   He has killed me, mother.
Run away, I pray you!
     [Dies.]

                        Exit [Wife], crying 'Murder!'
                        [pursued by Murderers].

                              *

IV, iii   *Enter Malcolm and Macduff.*

MALCOLM
Let us seek out some desolate shade, and there
Weep our sad bosoms empty.

MACDUFF   Let us rather
3   Hold fast the mortal sword and, like good men,
4   Bestride our downfall'n birthdom. Each new morn
New widows howl, new orphans cry, new sorrows
Strike heaven on the face, that it resounds
As if it felt with Scotland and yelled out
8   Like syllable of dolor.

MALCOLM   What I believe, I'll wail;
What know, believe; and what I can redress,
10   As I shall find the time to friend, I will.
What you have spoke, it may be so perchance.
12   This tyrant, whose sole name blisters our tongues,
Was once thought honest; you have loved him well;
14   He hath not touched you yet. I am young; but something
15   You may deserve of him through me, and wisdom
To offer up a weak, poor, innocent lamb
T' appease an angry god.

MACDUFF
I am not treacherous.

MALCOLM   But Macbeth is.
19   A good and virtuous nature may recoil
In an imperial charge. But I shall crave your pardon.
21   That which you are, my thoughts cannot transpose:
22   Angels are bright still though the brightest fell;
Though all things foul would wear the brows of grace,
Yet grace must still look so.

MACDUFF   I have lost my hopes.

MALCOLM
Perchance even there where I did find my doubts.
26   Why in that rawness left you wife and child,
Those precious motives, those strong knots of love,
Without leave-taking? I pray you,
29   Let not my jealousies be your dishonors,
But mine own safeties. You may be rightly just
Whatever I shall think.

MACDUFF   Bleed, bleed, poor country!
Great tyranny, lay thou thy basis sure,   32
For goodness dare not check thee; wear thou thy wrongs,
The title is affeered! Fare thee well, lord.   34
I would not be the villain that thou think'st
For the whole space that's in the tyrant's grasp
And the rich East to boot.

MALCOLM   Be not offended.
I speak not as in absolute fear of you.   38
I think our country sinks beneath the yoke,
It weeps, it bleeds, and each new day a gash
Is added to her wounds. I think withal   41
There would be hands uplifted in my right;
And here from gracious England have I offer
Of goodly thousands. But, for all this,
When I shall tread upon the tyrant's head
Or wear it on my sword, yet my poor country
Shall have more vices than it had before,
More suffer, and more sundry ways than ever,
By him that shall succeed.

MACDUFF   What should he be?

MALCOLM
It is myself I mean, in whom I know
All the particulars of vice so grafted   51
That, when they shall be opened, black Macbeth   52
Will seem as pure as snow, and the poor state
Esteem him as a lamb, being compared
With my confineless harms.   55

MACDUFF   Not in the legions
Of horrid hell can come a devil more damned
In evils to top Macbeth.

MALCOLM   I grant him bloody,
Luxurious, avaricious, false, deceitful,   58
Sudden, malicious, smacking of every sin   59
That has a name. But there's no bottom, none,
In my voluptuousness. Your wives, your daughters,
Your matrons, and your maids could not fill up
The cistern of my lust; and my desire
All continent impediments would o'erbear   64
That did oppose my will. Better Macbeth
Than such an one to reign.

MACDUFF   Boundless intemperance
In nature is a tyranny. It hath been   67
Th' untimely emptying of the happy throne
And fall of many kings. But fear not yet
To take upon you what is yours. You may
Convey your pleasures in a spacious plenty   71
And yet seem cold – the time you may so hoodwink.
We have willing dames enough. There cannot be
That vulture in you to devour so many
As will to greatness dedicate themselves,
Finding it so inclined.

82 *shag-eared* i.e. with shaggy hair falling about the ears   83 *fry* spawn
IV, iii The grounds of the King's palace in England   3 *mortal* deadly
4 *Bestride* i.e. stand over protectively; *birthdom* place of birth   8 *Like
syllable of dolor* a similar cry of pain   10 *time to friend* time propitious
12 *sole name* very name   14 *young* i.e. young and inexperienced   15 *wisdom*
i.e. it may be wise   19–20 *recoil . . . imperial charge* reverse itself under
royal pressure   21 *transpose* alter   22 *the brightest* i.e. Lucifer   26 *rawness* unprotected state   29 *jealousies* suspicions   32 *basis* foundation   34
affeered confirmed by law   38 *absolute* complete   41 *withal* furthermore
51 *particulars* varieties; *grafted* implanted   52 *opened* revealed   55 *confineless harms* unlimited vices   58 *Luxurious* lecherous   59 *Sudden* violent
64 *continent* containing, restraining   67 *In nature* in one's nature   71
Convey obtain by stealth

MALCOLM   With this there grows
77   In my most ill-composed affection such
78   A stanchless avarice that, were I King,
I should cut off the nobles for their lands,
Desire his jewels, and this other's house,
And my more-having would be as a sauce
82   To make me hunger more, that I should forge
Quarrels unjust against the good and loyal,
Destroying them for wealth.
MACDUFF   This avarice
Sticks deeper, grows with more pernicious root
86   Than summer-seeming lust, and it hath been
87   The sword of our slain kings. Yet do not fear.
88   Scotland hath foisons to fill up your will
89   Of your mere own. All these are portable,
With other graces weighed.
MALCOLM
But I have none. The king-becoming graces,
As justice, verity, temp'rance, stableness,
93   Bounty, perseverance, mercy, lowliness,
Devotion, patience, courage, fortitude,
95   I have no relish of them, but abound
96   In the division of each several crime,
Acting in many ways. Nay, had I pow'r, I should
Pour the sweet milk of concord into hell,
99   Uproar the universal peace, confound
All unity on earth.
MACDUFF   O Scotland, Scotland !
MALCOLM
If such a one be fit to govern, speak.
I am as I have spoken.
MACDUFF   Fit to govern ?
No, not to live ! O nation miserable,
With an untitled tyrant bloody-sceptred,
When shalt thou see thy wholesome days again,
Since that the truest issue of thy throne
107 By his own interdiction stands accursed
And does blaspheme his breed ? Thy royal father
Was a most sainted king ; the queen that bore thee,
Oft'ner upon her knees than on her feet,
111 Died every day she lived. Fare thee well.
These evils thou repeat'st upon thyself
Hath banished me from Scotland. O my breast,
Thy hope ends here !
MALCOLM   Macduff, this noble passion,
Child of integrity, hath from my soul
116 Wiped the black scruples, reconciled my thoughts
To thy good truth and honor. Devilish Macbeth
118 By many of these trains hath sought to win me
119 Into his power ; and modest wisdom plucks me
From over-credulous haste ; but God above

Deal between thee and me, for even now
I put myself to thy direction and
Unspeak mine own detraction, here abjure
The taints and blames I laid upon myself
For strangers to my nature. I am yet   125
Unknown to woman, never was forsworn,
Scarcely have coveted what was mine own,
At no time broke my faith, would not betray
The devil to his fellow, and delight
No less in truth than life. My first false speaking
Was this upon myself. What I am truly,   131
Is thine and my poor country's to command ;
Whither indeed, before thy here-approach,
Old Siward with ten thousand warlike men
Already at a point was setting forth.   135
Now we'll together ; and the chance of goodness   136
Be like our warranted quarrel ! Why are you silent ?
MACDUFF
Such welcome and unwelcome things at once
'Tis hard to reconcile.
     Enter a Doctor.
MALCOLM
Well, more anon. Comes the King forth, I pray you ?   140
DOCTOR
Ay, sir. There are a crew of wretched souls
That stay his cure. Their malady convinces   142
The great assay of art ; but at his touch,   143
Such sanctity hath heaven given his hand,
They presently amend.
MALCOLM   I thank you, doctor. Exit [Doctor].
MACDUFF
What's the disease he means ?
MALCOLM   'Tis called the evil.   146
A most miraculous work in this good King,
Which often since my here-remain in England
I have seen him do : how he solicits heaven
Himself best knows, but strangely-visited people,   150
All swol'n and ulcerous, pitiful to the eye,
The mere despair of surgery, he cures,   152
Hanging a golden stamp about their necks,   153
Put on with holy prayers ; and 'tis spoken,
To the succeeding royalty he leaves
The healing benediction. With this strange virtue,
He hath a heavenly gift of prophecy,
And sundry blessings hang about his throne
That speak him full of grace.
     Enter Ross.
MACDUFF   See who comes here.
MALCOLM
My countryman ; but yet I know him not.
MACDUFF
My ever gentle cousin, welcome hither.
MALCOLM
I know him now. Good God betimes remove   162
The means that makes us strangers !
ROSS   Sir, amen.
MACDUFF
Stands Scotland where it did ?
ROSS   Alas, poor country,
Almost afraid to know itself. It cannot
Be called our mother but our grave, where nothing   166
But who knows nothing is once seen to smile ;
Where sighs and groans, and shrieks that rent the air,
Are made, not marked ; where violent sorrow seems   169

77 ill-composed affection disordered disposition 78 stanchless insatiable
82 forge fabricate 86 summer-seeming i.e. seasonal, transitory 87 sword
of our slain cause of death of our 88–89 foisons . . . mere own riches of your
own enough to satisfy you 89 portable bearable 93 lowliness humility
95 relish trace 96 division subdivisions 99 Uproar blast 107 interdiction curse 111 Died i.e. turned away from this life 116 scruples doubts
118 trains plots 119 modest cautious ; plucks holds 125 For as 131
upon against 135 at a point armed 136–37 the chance . . . warranted
quarrel i.e. let the chance of success equal the justice of our cause 140
anon soon 142 stay await ; convinces baffles 143 assay of art resources of
medical science 146 evil scrofula (king's evil) 150 strangely-visited
unusually afflicted 152 mere utter 153 stamp coin 162 betimes quickly
166 nothing no one 169 marked noticed

170   A modern ecstasy. The dead man's knell
171   Is there scarce asked for who, and good men's lives
      Expire before the flowers in their caps,
      Dying or ere they sicken.
173 MACDUFF   O, relation
174   Too nice, and yet too true!
    MALCOLM   What's the newest grief?
    ROSS
175   That of an hour's age doth hiss the speaker;
176   Each minute teems a new one.
    MACDUFF   How does my wife?
    ROSS
      Why, well.
    MACDUFF   And all my children?
    ROSS   Well too.
    MACDUFF
      The tyrant has not battered at their peace?
    ROSS
      No, they were well at peace when I did leave 'em.
    MACDUFF
      Be not a niggard of your speech. How goes 't?
    ROSS
      When I came hither to transport the tidings
182   Which I have heavily borne, there ran a rumor
183   Of many worthy fellows that were out,
184   Which was to my belief witnessed the rather
      For that I saw the tyrant's power afoot.
      Now is the time of help. Your eye in Scotland
      Would create soldiers, make our women fight
      To doff their dire distresses.
    MALCOLM   Be't their comfort
      We are coming thither. Gracious England hath
      Lent us good Siward and ten thousand men,
      An older and a better soldier none
192   That Christendom gives out.
    ROSS   Would I could answer
      This comfort with the like. But I have words
      That would be howled out in the desert air,
195   Where hearing should not latch them.
    MACDUFF   What concern they,
196   The general cause or is it a fee-grief
197   Due to some single breast?
    ROSS   No mind that's honest
      But in it shares some woe, though the main part
      Pertains to you alone.
    MACDUFF   If it be mine,
      Keep it not from me; quickly let me have it.
    ROSS
      Let not your ears despise my tongue for ever,
      Which shall possess them with the heaviest sound
      That ever yet they heard.
    MACDUFF   Humh! I guess at it.
    ROSS
204   Your castle is surprised, your wife and babes
      Savagely slaughtered. To relate the manner
206   Were, on the quarry of these murdered deer,
      To add the death of you.
    MALCOLM   Merciful heaven!
      What, man! Ne'er pull your hat upon your brows.
209   Give sorrow words. The grief that does not speak
210   Whispers the o'erfraught heart and bids it break.
    MACDUFF
      My children too?
    ROSS   Wife, children, servants, all

      That could be found.
    MACDUFF   And I must be from thence?
      My wife killed too?
    ROSS   I have said.
    MALCOLM   Be comforted.
      Let's make us med'cines of our great revenge
      To cure this deadly grief.
    MACDUFF
      He has no children. All my pretty ones?
      Did you say all? O hell-kite! All?
      What, all my pretty chickens and their dam
      At one fell swoop?
    MALCOLM
      Dispute it like a man.   220
    MACDUFF   I shall do so;
      But I must also feel it as a man.
      I cannot but remember such things were
      That were most precious to me. Did heaven look on
      And would not take their part? Sinful Macduff,
      They were all struck for thee! Naught that I am,   225
      Not for their own demerits but for mine
      Fell slaughter on their souls. Heaven rest them now!
    MALCOLM
      Be this the whetstone of your sword. Let grief
      Convert to anger; blunt not the heart, enrage it.
    MACDUFF
      O, I could play the woman with mine eyes
      And braggart with my tongue. But, gentle heavens,
      Cut short all intermission. Front to front   232
      Bring thou this fiend of Scotland and myself.
      Within my sword's length set him. If he scape,
      Heaven forgive him too!
    MALCOLM   This tune goes manly.
      Come, go we to the King. Our power is ready;   236
      Our lack is nothing but our leave. Macbeth   237
      Is ripe for shaking, and the pow'rs above
      Put on their instruments. Receive what cheer you may.   239
      The night is long that never finds the day.   *Exeunt.*

*

Enter a Doctor of Physic and a Waiting Gentlewoman. V, i

DOCTOR I have two nights watched with you, but can
perceive no truth in your report. When was it she last
walked?

GENTLEWOMAN Since his Majesty went into the field I
have seen her rise from her bed, throw her nightgown 5
upon her, unlock her closet, take forth paper, fold it, 6
write upon't, read it, afterwards seal it, and again return
to bed; yet all this while in a most fast sleep.

DOCTOR A great perturbation in nature, to receive at once
the benefit of sleep and do the effects of watching! In this 10

170 *modern ecstasy* commonplace emotion 171 *Is there . . . for who* scarcely calls forth an inquiry about identity 173 *relation* report 174 *nice* precise 175 *doth hiss the speaker* causes the speaker to be hissed (for stale repetition) 176 *teems* brings forth 182 *heavily borne* sadly carried 183 *out* up in arms 184 *witnessed* attested 192 *gives out* reports 195 *latch* catch hold of 196 *fee-grief* i.e. a grief possessed in private 197 *Due* belonging 204 *surprised* attacked 206 *quarry* heap of game 209 *speak* speak aloud 210 *Whispers* whispers to 220 *Dispute* revenge 225 *Naught* wicked 232 *intermission* interval; *Front to front* face to face 236 *power* army 237 *Our lack . . . our leave* i.e. nothing remains but to say farewell 239 *Put on their instruments* urge on their agents
V, i Within Macbeth's castle at Dunsinane 5 *nightgown* dressing gown 6 *closet* a chest, or desk 10 *do the effects of watching* act as if awake

slumb'ry agitation, besides her walking and other actual performances, what (at any time) have you heard her say?

GENTLEWOMAN That, sir, which I will not report after her.

14 DOCTOR You may to me, and 'tis most meet you should.

GENTLEWOMAN Neither to you nor any one, having no witness to confirm my speech.

Enter Lady [Macbeth], with a taper.

17 Lo you, here she comes! This is her very guise, and,
18 upon my life, fast asleep! Observe her; stand close.

DOCTOR How came she by that light?

GENTLEWOMAN Why, it stood by her. She has light by her continually. 'Tis her command.

DOCTOR You see her eyes are open.

23 GENTLEWOMAN Ay, but their sense are shut.

DOCTOR What is it she does now? Look how she rubs her hands.

GENTLEWOMAN It is an accustomed action with her, to seem thus washing her hands. I have known her continue in this a quarter of an hour.

LADY Yet here's a spot.

DOCTOR Hark, she speaks. I will set down what comes from her, to satisfy my remembrance the more strongly.

LADY Out, damned spot! Out, I say! One – two – why then 'tis time to do't. Hell is murky. Fie, my lord, fie! a soldier and afeard? What need we fear who knows it,
35 when none can call our power to accompt? Yet who would have thought the old man to have had so much blood in him?

DOCTOR Do you mark that?

LADY The Thane of Fife had a wife. Where is she now? What, will these hands ne'er be clean? No more o' that, my lord, no more o' that! You mar all with this
42 starting.

DOCTOR Go to, go to! You have known what you should not.

GENTLEWOMAN She has spoke what she should not, I am sure of that. Heaven knows what she has known.

LADY Here's the smell of the blood still. All the perfumes of Arabia will not sweeten this little hand. Oh, oh, oh!

49 DOCTOR What a sigh is there! The heart is sorely charged.

GENTLEWOMAN I would not have such a heart in my bosom for the dignity of the whole body.

DOCTOR Well, well, well.

GENTLEWOMAN Pray God it be, sir.

54 DOCTOR This disease is beyond my practice. Yet I have known those which have walked in their sleep who have died holily in their beds.

LADY Wash your hands, put on your nightgown, look not so pale! I tell you yet again, Banquo 's buried. He cannot come out on 's grave.

DOCTOR Even so?

LADY To bed, to bed! There's knocking at the gate.

Come, come, come, come, give me your hand! What's done cannot be undone. To bed, to bed, to bed! *Exit.*

DOCTOR Will she go now to bed?

GENTLEWOMAN Directly.

DOCTOR
Foul whisp'rings are abroad. Unnatural deeds
Do breed unnatural troubles. Infected minds
To their deaf pillows will discharge their secrets.
More needs she the divine than the physician.
God, God forgive us all! Look after her;
Remove from her the means of all annoyance,   71
And still keep eyes upon her. So good night.
My mind she has mated, and amazed my sight.   73
I think, but dare not speak.

GENTLEWOMAN   Good night, good doctor.

Exeunt.

*

Drum and Colors. Enter Menteith, Caithness,   V, ii
Angus, Lennox, Soldiers.

MENTEITH
The English pow'r is near, led on by Malcolm,
His uncle Siward, and the good Macduff.
Revenges burn in them; for their dear causes
Would to the bleeding and the grim alarm   4
Excite the mortified man.   5

ANGUS   Near Birnam Wood
Shall we well meet them; that way are they coming.   6

CAITHNESS
Who knows if Donalbain be with his brother?

LENNOX
For certain, sir, he is not. I have a file   8
Of all the gentry. There is Siward's son
And many unrough youths that even now   10
Protest their first of manhood.   11

MENTEITH   What does the tyrant?

CAITHNESS
Great Dunsinane he strongly fortifies.
Some say he's mad; others, that lesser hate him,
Do call it valiant fury; but for certain
He cannot buckle his distempered cause   15
Within the belt of rule.   16

ANGUS   Now does he feel
His secret murders sticking on his hands.
Now minutely revolts upbraid his faith-breach.   18
Those he commands move only in command,
Nothing in love. Now does he feel his title
Hang loose about him, like a giant's robe
Upon a dwarfish thief.

MENTEITH   Who then shall blame
His pestered senses to recoil and start,   23
When all that is within him does condemn
Itself for being there?

CAITHNESS   Well, march we on
To give obedience where 'tis truly owed.
Meet we the med'cine of the sickly weal;   27
And with him pour we in our country's purge
Each drop of us.

LENNOX   Or so much as it needs
To dew the sovereign flower and drown the weeds.   30
Make we our march towards Birnam. *Exeunt, marching.*

---

14 *meet* fitting   17 *guise* habit   18 *close* concealed   23 *sense* powers of sensation   35 *call our power to accompt* call to account anyone so powerful as we   42 *starting* startled movements   49 *charged* laden   54 *practice* professional competence   71 *annoyance* self-injury   73 *mated* bemused
V, ii Open country near Birnam Wood and Dunsinane   4 *bleeding* blood of battle   5 *Excite* incite; *mortified* dead   6 *well* surely   8 *file* list   10 *unrough* unbearded   11 *Protest* assert   15 *distempered* disease-swollen   16 *rule* reason   18 *minutely* every minute; *revolts* rebellions   23 *pestered* tormented   27 *med'cine* cure (i.e. Malcolm); *weal* commonwealth   30 *dew* water

V, iii   *Enter Macbeth, Doctor, and Attendants.*

MACBETH
Bring me no more reports. Let them fly all !
Till Birnam Wood remove to Dunsinane,
3   I cannot taint with fear. What's the boy Malcolm ?
Was he not born of woman ? The spirits that know
5   All mortal consequences have pronounced me thus :
'Fear not, Macbeth. No man that's born of woman
Shall e'er have power upon thee.' Then fly, false thanes,
8   And mingle with the English epicures.
9   The mind I sway by and the heart I bear
Shall never sag with doubt nor shake with fear.
        Enter Servant.
11   The devil damn thee black, thou cream-faced loon !
Where got'st thou that goose look ?

SERVANT
There is ten thousand –

MACBETH   Geese, villain ?

SERVANT   Soldiers, sir.

MACBETH
14   Go prick thy face and over-red thy fear,
15   Thou lily-livered boy. What soldiers, patch ?
Death of thy soul ! those linen cheeks of thine
Are counsellors to fear. What soldiers, whey-face ?

SERVANT
The English force, so please you.

MACBETH
Take thy face hence.   *[Exit Servant.]*
        Seyton ! – I am sick at heart,
20   When I behold – Seyton, I say ! – This push
Will cheer me ever, or disseat me now.
I have lived long enough. My way of life
23   Is fall'n into the sear, the yellow leaf,
And that which should accompany old age,
As honor, love, obedience, troops of friends,
I must not look to have ; but, in their stead,
Curses not loud but deep, mouth-honor, breath,
Which the poor heart would fain deny, and dare not.
Seyton !
        Enter Seyton.
SEYTON
What's your gracious pleasure ?

MACBETH   What news more ?

SEYTON
All is confirmed, my lord, which was reported.

MACBETH
I'll fight till from my bones my flesh be hacked.
Give me my armor.

SEYTON   'Tis not needed yet.

MACBETH
I'll put it on.
35   Send out moe horses, skirr the country round,
Hang those that talk of fear. Give me mine armor.
How does your patient, doctor ?

DOCTOR   Not so sick, my lord,
As she is troubled with thick-coming fancies
That keep her from her rest.

MACBETH   Cure her of that !
Canst thou not minister to a mind diseased,
Pluck from the memory a rooted sorrow,
42   Raze out the written troubles of the brain,
43   And with some sweet oblivious antidote
44   Cleanse the stuffed bosom of that perilous stuff
Which weighs upon the heart ?

DOCTOR   Therein the patient
Must minister to himself.

MACBETH
Throw physic to the dogs, I'll none of it !   47
Come, put mine armor on. Give me my staff.
Seyton, send out. – Doctor, the thanes fly from me. –
Come, sir, dispatch. – If thou couldst, doctor, cast   50
The water of my land, find her disease,
And purge it to a sound and pristine health,
I would applaud thee to the very echo,
That should applaud again. – Pull't off, I say. –
What rhubarb, senna, or what purgative drug
Would scour these English hence ? Hear'st thou of them ?

DOCTOR
Ay, my good lord. Your royal preparation
Makes us hear something.

MACBETH   Bring it after me !   58
I will not be afraid of death and bane   59
Till Birnam Forest come to Dunsinane.
                Exeunt [all but the Doctor].

DOCTOR
Were I from Dunsinane away and clear,
Profit again should hardly draw me here.   *[Exit.]*

*

Drum and Colors. Enter Malcolm, Siward,   V, iv
Macduff, Siward's Son, Menteith, Caithness,
Angus, [Lennox, Ross,] and Soldiers, marching.

MALCOLM
Cousins, I hope the days are near at hand
That chambers will be safe.   2

MENTEITH   We doubt it nothing.

SIWARD
What wood is this before us ?

MENTEITH   The Wood of Birnam.

MALCOLM
Let every soldier hew him down a bough
And bear't before him. Thereby shall we shadow
The numbers of our host and make discovery   6
Err in report of us.

SOLDIERS   It shall be done.

SIWARD
We learn no other but the confident tyrant
Keeps still in Dunsinane and will endure
Our setting down before't.

MALCOLM   'Tis his main hope,
For where there is advantage to be gone   11
Both more and less have given him the revolt,   12
And none serve with him but constrainèd things
Whose hearts are absent too.

MACDUFF   Let our just censures   14

V, iii Within Dunsinane Castle **3** *taint* become tainted **5** *consequences*
sequence of events **8** *English epicures* (i.e. as compared with the austerely-
living Scots) **9** *sway* direct myself **11** *loon* lout **14** *over-red thy fear*
i.e. paint red over your fearful pallor **15** *patch* fool **20** *push* struggle
23 *sear* dry, withered **35** *moe* more ; *skirr* scour **42** *Raze* erase **43**
oblivious antidote opiate, medicine of forgetfulness **44** *stuffed* choked up
47 *physic* medicine **50** *dispatch* hasten **50–51** *cast . . . water* analyze the
urine **58** *it* i.e. the remainder of the armor **59** *bane* destruction
V, iv Birnam Wood **2** *That chambers* when sleeping-chambers ; *nothing*
not at all **6** *discovery* i.e. reports by scouts **11** *advantage* opportunity **12**
more and less high and low **14** *just censures* impartial judgment

15 Attend the true event, and put we on
Industrious soldiership.
SIWARD   The time approaches
That will with due decision make us know
What we shall say we have and what we owe.
19 Thoughts speculative their unsure hopes relate,
20 But certain issue strokes must arbitrate –
21 Towards which advance the war.   *Exeunt, marching.*

*

V, v   *Enter Macbeth, Seyton, and Soldiers, with Drum
and Colors.*
MACBETH
Hang out our banners on the outward walls.
2 The cry is still, 'They come!' Our castle's strength
Will laugh a siege to scorn. Here let them lie
Till famine and the ague eat them up.
5 Were they not forced with those that should be ours,
We might have met them dareful, beard to beard,
And beat them backward home.
A cry within of women.   What is that noise?
SEYTON
It is the cry of women, my good lord.   *[Exit.]*
MACBETH
I have almost forgot the taste of fears.
The time has been my senses would have cooled
11 To hear a night-shriek, and my fell of hair
12 Would at a dismal treatise rouse and stir
As life were in't. I have supped full with horrors.
14 Direness, familiar to my slaughterous thoughts,
15 Cannot once start me.
[Enter Seyton.] Wherefore was that cry?
SEYTON
The Queen, my lord, is dead.
MACBETH
She should have died hereafter:
There would have been a time for such a word.
To-morrow, and to-morrow, and to-morrow
Creeps in this petty pace from day to day
To the last syllable of recorded time,
And all our yesterdays have lighted fools
The way to dusty death. Out, out, brief candle!
Life's but a walking shadow, a poor player
That struts and frets his hour upon the stage
And then is heard no more. It is a tale
Told by an idiot, full of sound and fury,
Signifying nothing.
Enter a Messenger.
Thou com'st to use thy tongue: thy story quickly!
MESSENGER
Gracious my lord,
31 I should report that which I say I saw,
But know not how to do't.

MACBETH   Well, say, sir.
MESSENGER
As I did stand my watch upon the hill,
I looked toward Birnam, and anon methought
The wood began to move.
MACBETH   Liar and slave!
MESSENGER
Let me endure your wrath if't be not so.
Within this three mile may you see it coming.
I say, a moving grove.
MACBETH   If thou speak'st false,
Upon the next tree shalt thou hang alive
Till famine cling thee. If thy speech be sooth,
I care not if thou dost for me as much.   **40**
I pull in resolution, and begin   **42**
To doubt th' equivocation of the fiend,   **43**
That lies like truth. 'Fear not, till Birnam Wood
Do come to Dunsinane!' and now a wood
Comes toward Dunsinane. Arm, arm, and out!
If this which he avouches does appear,   **47**
There is nor flying hence nor tarrying here.
I 'gin to be aweary of the sun,
And wish th' estate o' th' world were now undone.
Ring the alarum bell! Blow wind, come wrack,
At least we'll die with harness on our back.   *Exeunt.* **52**

*

Drum and Colors. Enter Malcolm, Siward,   V, vi
Macduff, and their Army, with boughs.
MALCOLM
Now near enough. Your leavy screens throw down
And show like those you are. You, worthy uncle,
Shall with my cousin, your right noble son,
Lead our first battle. Worthy Macduff and we   **4**
Shall take upon's what else remains to do,
According to our order.   **6**
SIWARD   Fare you well.
Do we but find the tyrant's power to-night,   **7**
Let us be beaten if we cannot fight.
MACDUFF
Make all our trumpets speak, give them all breath,
Those clamorous harbingers of blood and death.
Exeunt. Alarums continued.

*

Enter Macbeth.   V, vii
MACBETH
They have tied me to a stake. I cannot fly,
But bear-like I must fight the course. What's he   **2**
That was not born of woman? Such a one
Am I to fear, or none.
Enter Young Siward.
YOUNG SIWARD
What is thy name?
MACBETH   Thou'lt be afraid to hear it.
YOUNG SIWARD
No, though thou call'st thyself a hotter name
Than any is in hell.
MACBETH   My name's Macbeth.
YOUNG SIWARD
The devil himself could not pronounce a title
More hateful to mine ear.
MACBETH   No, nor more fearful.

---

15 *Attend* await; *put we on* let us put on **19** *relate* convey **20** *certain issue*
the definite outcome; *arbitrate* decide **21** *war* army
V, v Within Dunsinane Castle **2** *still* always **5** *forced* reinforced **11**
fell pelt **12** *treatise* story **14** *Direness* horror **15** *start me* make me start
31 *say* i.e. affirm **40** *cling* shrivel; *sooth* truth **42** *pull in* curb, check
43 *doubt* suspect; *equivocation* double-talk **47** *avouches* affirms **52** *harness* armor
V, vi Fields outside Dunsinane Castle **4** *battle* battalion **6** *order* battle-plan **7** *power* forces
V, vii The same **2** *course* attack (like a bear tied to a stake and baited by dogs or men)

YOUNG SIWARD
Thou liest, abhorrèd tyrant ! With my sword
I'll prove the lie thou speak'st.
Fight, and Young Siward slain.

MACBETH   Thou wast born of woman.
But swords I smile at, weapons laugh to scorn,
Brandished by man that's of a woman born.   *Exit.*
Alarums. Enter Macduff.

MACDUFF
That way the noise is. Tyrant, show thy face !
If thou beest slain and with no stroke of mine,
My wife and children's ghosts will haunt me still.
17   I cannot strike at wretched kerns, whose arms
18   Are hired to bear their staves. Either thou, Macbeth,
Or else my sword with an unbattered edge
20   I sheathe again undeeded. There thou shouldst be :
By this great clatter one of greatest note
22   Seems bruited. Let me find him, Fortune,
And more I beg not !   *Exit. Alarums.*
Enter Malcolm and Siward.

SIWARD
24   This way, my lord. The castle 's gently rend'red :
The tyrant's people on both sides do fight,
The noble thanes do bravely in the war,
27   The day almost itself professes yours
And little is to do.

MALCOLM   We have met with foes
29   That strike beside us.

SIWARD   Enter, sir, the castle.
Exeunt. Alarum.

V, viii   *Enter Macbeth.*

MACBETH
Why should I play the Roman fool and die
2   On mine own sword ? Whiles I see lives, the gashes
Do better upon them.
Enter Macduff.

MACDUFF   Turn, hellhound, turn !

MACBETH
Of all men else I have avoided thee.
5   But get thee back ! My soul is too much charged
With blood of thine already.

MACDUFF   I have no words ;
My voice is in my sword, thou bloodier villain
Than terms can give thee out !
Fight. Alarum.

MACBETH   Thou losest labor.
9   As easy mayst thou the intrenchant air
10   With thy keen sword impress as make me bleed.
Let fall thy blade on vulnerable crests.
I bear a charmèd life, which must not yield
To one of woman born.

13 MACDUFF   Despair thy charm,
14   And let the angel whom thou still hast served
Tell thee, Macduff was from his mother's womb
Untimely ripped.

MACBETH
Accursèd be that tongue that tells me so,
18   For it hath cowed my better part of man !
And be these juggling fiends no more believed,
20   That palter with us in a double sense,
That keep the word of promise to our ear
And break it to our hope. I'll not fight with thee.

MACDUFF
Then yield thee, coward,

And live to be the show and gaze o' th' time.   24
We'll have thee, as our rarer monsters are,   25
Painted upon a pole, and underwrit   26
'Here may you see the tyrant.'

MACBETH   I will not yield,
To kiss the ground before young Malcolm's feet
And to be baited with the rabble's curse.
Though Birnam Wood be come to Dunsinane,
And thou opposed, being of no woman born,
Yet I will try the last. Before my body
I throw my warlike shield. Lay on, Macduff,
And damned be him that first cries 'Hold, enough !'   34
Exeunt fighting. Alarums.
[Re-]enter fighting, and Macbeth slain.
[Exit Macduff.]

*

*Retreat and flourish. Enter, with Drum and Colors,
Malcolm, Siward, Ross, Thanes, and Soldiers.*

MALCOLM
I would the friends we miss were safe arrived.

SIWARD
Some must go off ; and yet, by these I see,   36
So great a day as this is cheaply bought.

MALCOLM
Macduff is missing, and your noble son.

ROSS
Your son, my lord, has paid a soldier's debt.
He only lived but till he was a man,
The which no sooner had his prowess confirmed
In the unshrinking station where he fought   42
But like a man he died.

SIWARD   Then he is dead ?

ROSS
Ay, and brought off the field. Your cause of sorrow
Must not be measured by his worth, for then
It hath no end.

SIWARD   Had he his hurts before ?

ROSS
Ay, on the front.

SIWARD   Why then, God's soldier be he.
Had I as many sons as I have hairs,
I would not wish them to a fairer death :
And so his knell is knolled.

MALCOLM   He's worth more sorrow,
And that I'll spend for him.

SIWARD   He's worth no more.
They say he parted well and paid his score,   52
And so, God be with him. Here comes newer comfort.
Enter Macduff, with Macbeth's head.

MACDUFF
Hail, King, for so thou art. Behold where stands

17 *kerns* soldiers of meanest rank   18 *staves* spears   20 *undeeded* not glorified by deeds   22 *bruited* reported   24 *rend'red* surrendered   27 *itself
professes* declares itself   29 *beside us* at our side (?), without trying to hit
us (?)
V, viii   2 *lives* living bodies   5 *charged* burdened   9 *intrenchant* incapable of being trenched (gashed)   10 *impress* leave a mark on   13
Despair despair of   14 *angel* i.e. of the host of Lucifer ; *still* always   18
better part of man most manly side   20 *palter* quibble   24 *gaze* sight
25 *monsters* freaks   26 *Painted upon a pole* pictured on a showman's banner
34 *s.d. Exeunt . . . slain* (after this action the scene apparently shifts to
within Dunsinane Castle ; cf. V, vii, 29)   36 *go off* perish ; *these* i.e. these
here assembled   42 *unshrinking station* place from which he did not retreat
52 *parted* departed ; *score* reckoning

55 Th' usurper's cursèd head. The time is free.
56 I see thee compassed with thy kingdom's pearl,
That speak my salutation in their minds,
Whose voices I desire aloud with mine –
Hail, King of Scotland!

ALL   Hail, King of Scotland!
Flourish.

MALCOLM
We shall not spend a large expense of time
61 Before we reckon with your several loves

And make us even with you. My Thanes and kinsmen, 62
Henceforth be Earls, the first that ever Scotland
In such an honor named. What's more to do
Which would be planted newly with the time – 65
As calling home our exiled friends abroad
That fled the snares of watchful tyranny,
Producing forth the cruel ministers 68
Of this dead butcher and his fiend-like queen,
Who (as 'tis thought) by self and violent hands 70
Took off her life – this, and what needful else
That calls upon us, by the grace of Grace
We will perform in measure, time, and place. 73
So thanks to all at once and to each one,
Whom we invite to see us crowned at Scone.

Flourish. Exeunt omnes.

---

55 *free* released from tyranny   **56** *compassed* surrounded   **61** *reckon* come to an accounting   **62** *make us even with you* repay you   **65** *would be planted newly with the time* i.e. should be done at the outset of this new era   **68** *ministers* agents   **70** *self and violent* her own violent   **73** *in measure* with decorum; *time, and place* at the proper time and place

THE LIFE OF TIMON OF ATHENS

INTRODUCTION

Critical responses to *Timon of Athens* have been extremely varied, and have not always been characterized by moderation. Commentators seeking in this play exactly the qualities they most value in such undeniable masterpieces as *Macbeth* and *King Lear* have condemned it as an abortive piece of work at best, un-Shakespearean, a failure, not worth the modern reader's serious attention. Other critics, recognizing that not all its differences from these great tragedies need be regarded as weaknesses, and insisting that *Timon* ought, like *Troilus and Cressida,* to be judged by quite different standards, have found it at least as rewarding as that remarkable if also somewhat dissatisfying play. Others still, extravagant admirers indeed, have professed to see in *Timon* one of the final triumphs of the world's dramatic art, an archetypal tragedy so compulsively emotional as to make the voices in *Hamlet, Othello,* and even *Lear* sound childish in comparison. Apparently *Timon* encourages hyperbole. But while in each of these views there is no doubt some measure of truth, it seems folly to regard the play either as one of the very best of Shakespeare's tragedies or as so bad that it cannot even be thought wholly his. The fact is that *Timon,* more strikingly than most other plays, "is of a mingled yarn, good and ill together." From several points of view it must surely be considered less effective than any other of Shakespeare's "mature" tragedies; but at least occasionally, and especially in its last two acts, *Timon* rivals *Lear* in eloquence and power.

In many ways – in tone and temper, in poetic merit, in dramatic technique – the first three acts of *Timon of Athens* differ widely from Acts IV and V. The salient qualities of I–III can best be shown by an examination of the opening scene of the play, which consists of four more or less distinct yet admirably fused parts. In the first of these we hear a conversation in which a poet, a painter, a jeweller, and a merchant discuss the incomparable virtues of Lord Timon, from whose "bounty" it is immediately plain they all hope to profit. The principal speakers are first the painter, who has brought a flattering portrait of Timon to present to him, and then, more important still, the poet. After a momentary interruption which effectively shows the greatest men of Athens, her senators, flocking to the enjoyment of Timon's liberality, the poet describes the instrument with which he hopes to win Timon's favor: an allegorical poem which, while its primary intent is to magnify Timon's glory, is evidently indebted to the old fickleness-of-Fortune tradition and ends by showing the hero betrayed by his erstwhile friends

When Fortune in her shift and change of mood
Spurns down her late beloved.

The poet's offering, in short, has a double function. As but the last in a series of gifts which insincere men are pressing on Timon in order to exploit him, it is a principal means of establishing the atmosphere of designing falsehood with which the appearance of Timon is meant to be prefaced; but it has a subtler and more important purpose as well, since it in fact provides the initial statement of the play's theme.

No sooner has the inevitable downfall of the Fortunate Man been thus adumbrated than trumpets sound and Lord Timon, surrounded by admirers and followed by a retinue of servants, makes his grand first entry. The stage direction calls for some ceremony of compliment, and the formality and courtliness of this makes for an effective contrast with what has gone before. But the most essential thing now is the impression we first get of Timon himself, of a man nobly but unwisely generous – though what is emphasized at this point in the play is rather the nobility than the rashness of his bounty. Not a man to desert a friend in his adversity, he redeems Ventidius from prison by paying his heavy debt; and he then endows a mere servant, though an honest one, with a fortune sufficiently large to enable him to marry the girl he truly loves. This is Timon at his best, and there is nothing with which to find fault in these two instances of his goodness, in the very first view we have of him. Cause for dissatisfaction is then at once provided, however, by his behavior toward the poet and his fellows; and it is manifestly the function of the carping Apemantus, who is now introduced, not only to inveigh against the falseness of all such men, whether artists or merchants or great lords, but to insist on the folly of Timon's indiscriminate liberality toward them. Alcibiades, perhaps because he is not meant to be tarred with the same brush, makes his first appearance only very late in the scene – which is then rounded off with a brief colloquy between two Athenian lords about Timon's excessive prodigality. They pay lip service, as it would be out of character for Apemantus to do, to Timon's kindness and nobility; but the chief purpose of their dialogue is to provide choric comment on all that has gone before. The emphasis is again on Timon's folly; and the second lord's "Long may he live / In fortunes" sounds, as the scene ends, the unmistakably ominous note of tragedy to come.

In almost every respect this is an admirable beginning. It is lively, colorful, full of both movement and matter. It has abundant variety, yet its numerous components are coherently interrelated and form a unified whole. The economy with which so much is so quickly imparted is striking: in less than three hundred lines the atmosphere in which the action of the first part of the play is to take

1136

place is well established; the theme of this action is both announced and in due course vigorously restated; all the most important characters save one – Timon's steward, Flavius, who is to appear in the next scene – are introduced; the essential qualities of Timon, or at any rate of Timon in his prosperity, are already fairly clear; and the likelihood of future disaster is made plain. Even in *King Lear* (to which *Timon* is so similar as regards the general structure of its opening scene) the exposition, the initial presentation of situation and character, is hardly managed more adroitly.

To point out these virtues is of course not to affirm that there are no defects whatever. On the contrary, the most serious faults with which the play as a whole can be charged (to be noticed more particularly later) are to some extent shared by its initial scene. Alcibiades' part here seems slighted, for example, and the relationship between him and Timon is not made clear; nor is Timon's nobility of soul, though frequently mentioned, made convincing. Notwithstanding these weaknesses, however, the many-faceted excellence of this scene is hardly to be denied; and one may add at once that dramaturgical skill of a high order is evident throughout *Timon*. Still, there are some notable lapses. The passage of approximately seventy lines devoted to the fool and the page (see II, ii, 47–119) is dramatically unnecessary, has small intrinsic merit, and seems at best an infelicitous interruption of the serious business in hand. But this particular kind of artlessness, of which there are instances enough in other Shakespearean plays, is rare, whereas examples of superior craftmanship abound. The various ingredients that make up the long second scene of Act I are as skillfully combined as those in the first; and what immediately follows, the very short contrasting scene in which the imminence of Timon's fall is made plain (II, i), is equally effective in its very different way. Especially illuminating are the three consecutive scenes at the beginning of Act III which, collectively, provide the play's crucial demonstration of its central figure's betrayal by his fair-weather friends. Here, each of the lords most deeply in Timon's debt is in turn appealed to for help, which he declines to give. The scenes in question are all short, and precisely the same story is told in each. Yet monotony is skillfully avoided. In less than two hundred lines Lords Lucullus, Lucius, and Sempronius become distinct individuals, each loathsome in his own special way; and even Timon's three servants are to some extent individualized. The second, who is much meeker than the other two (one notes that he is called Servilius), is appropriately denied a final speech of passionate denunciation like that given each of his fellows. The vileness of Lord Lucius receives its full share of castigation, however, from the "three strangers" whose presence effectively differentiates the second of these scenes from the first and the third. There is no doubt some artificiality in this, but there is art as well. And there is more art and less trickery later on. It must be acknowledged that the misanthropic tirades of Timon in his latter days (Acts IV and V) are long-drawn-out; but while in aim and mood they are all alike, the virtuosity they nonetheless show as a succession of variations on a single theme is remarkable indeed.

More remarkable still, to be sure, is the poetry in this part of the play. What above all else makes *Timon of Athens* an extraordinary work of art is the magnificence of the

language in which its hero, to whom life at its best has become no more than a long disease, pours out his bitterness of soul, his anguished contempt for all humanity, and his longing for the nothingness of death. But the poetic excellence of Acts IV and V has long been recognized, whereas the lesser merits of the play, though both pervasive and real, have tended to be overlooked. Critical interest has usually been directed instead to the reasons for *Timon's* failure to produce at last, despite the eloquence of its concluding scenes, the kind of effect we regard as essential to all really great tragedy. And much attention has also been given to certain peculiarities in the only authoritative text that has come down to us, peculiarities that are without parallel elsewhere. These are especially interesting, and are not without relevance to questions about the play's literary qualities, as indications that Shakespeare left *Timon of Athens* unfinished.

"Unfinished," however, is a misleading term. *Timon* is a whole play. That there is a marked difference between Acts I–III and IV–V does not imply incoherence or betray any lack of plan. What may be called the two movements of the play are evidently intended to produce the very striking before-and-after contrast that we find: the first three acts are a necessary preparation for the last two; progress is systematic throughout; and when the last speech of Alcibiades comes to a close ("Let our drums strike") there can be no more doubt that a conclusion has been reached than when Fortinbras issues a similar command ("Go, bid the soldiers shoot") and *Hamlet* ends.

Emphatically, then, *Timon* is not a mere fragment. It is complete, or at least very nearly so. But the manuscript from which the Folio text was printed was evidently one that still needed a good deal of revision, larded as it was with inconsistencies and irregularities of various kinds. There is one, for instance, in the very first entry direction. The "mercer" who is mentioned here is a "ghost" character. He neither speaks nor is ever referred to again; and the text proper quickly makes it clear (see I, i, 8, where the painter says to the poet, "I know them both") that we cannot even infer his mute presence. What we can infer is an original intention of having five speakers in the opening passage, then the failure to remove all trace of the mercer when only four were actually used. Much more striking anomalies are found in the text proper, however, and the following are but a few of many.

(1) The first fifty-odd lines of the passage which introduces Timon are devoted to two instances of his generosity (see I, i, 94–151). He gives five talents to redeem Ventidius, then settles three talents on Lucilius. A talent being worth, in terms of today's values, something like $2,000, these are impressive gifts – about $10,000 and $6,000 respectively – as of course they were meant to be. However, later in the play (at II, ii, 189–90, 195 and III, i, 17–18) we hear of fifty and a thousand talents: very large sums indeed, especially the latter, since by the same reckoning as before a thousand talents would be equivalent to about $2,000,000. Now there are similar discrepancies in Shakespeare's sources. The play is based mainly on North's translation of Plutarch's *Life of Antony* and, though through precisely what intermediary is uncertain, Lucian's *Timon the Misanthrope*. Relatively small numbers of talents are mentioned in Lucian, much larger ones in Plutarch. Especially interesting, therefore, is what we find in III, ii (lines 12, 23, 35, and 37): three consecutive mentions of no

specific number but only of "so many talents" and then, according to the Folio, of "fifty five hundred Talents" ($11,000,000). Or, as the present text gives it, "fifty – five hundred – talents" – as if the author had set down two alternative sums and had never got around to striking out one or the other. For the repeated use of the manifestly unsatisfactory "so many" in the preceding lines is hardly understandable except as an indication that the writer had become uncertain whether "fifty" or "five hundred" should eventually be used to specify a very large but yet not an altogether preposterous sum.

(2) At IV, iii, 349 the approach of the poet and the painter is announced. Next to appear, however, are first "the Banditti" (after line 394) and then Timon's steward (after line 453). The poet and the painter in due course appear (see V, i), but two major episodes and nearly two hundred lines later than, apparently, they were originally meant to.

(3) There is some inconsistency in Alcibiades' three statements about his knowledge of Timon's misfortunes in IV, iii (compare line 57 with lines 77 and 93–96), but there is grosser inconsistency in the two couplets which Alcibiades later reads out as Timon's epitaph (see V, iv, 70–73). Plutarch gives two epitaphs, first the one he supposes to have been made by Timon himself and, later, one "not his, but made by the poet Callimachus." Though they are quite contradictory ("Seek not my name.... Here lie I, Timon"), Shakespeare set down both, one immediately after the other – apparently not yet having decided which to use and which to cancel.

(4) The compositor who set the type for the Folio text of *Timon* was undoubtedly responsible for some misrepresentation of the manuscript from which he worked, but this manuscript must nevertheless have contained a considerable amount of very imperfect verse. In fact it must have contained many passages which, though they represented something nearly complete, something more than rough sketches, could not yet be regarded by Shakespeare as in their final form. For, while there are various kinds of irregularity in the authoritative texts of a number of Shakespeare's plays, the deficiencies of the verse in *Timon* are without parallel elsewhere. Sometimes a single speech is partly in prose, partly in rhymed couplets, and partly in blank verse (as in I, ii, 36–50); and passages wholly in verse often contain some lines with too many stresses and some with too few (as in III, v or IV, ii, 30–50). Examples are to be found throughout the play, even in the great poetic utterances of Acts IV and V (for instance in Timon's soliloquy at IV, iii, 1–48).

There is now pretty general agreement that *Timon of Athens* is not a collaborated work, partly by someone other than Shakespeare. It is consistent in mood and temper; the execution of all its parts seems firmly governed by a single general scheme; the same patterns of image and idea recur throughout; details which all critics have found characteristically if not uniquely Shakespearean are scattered through the very passages which are in other respects so far below the expected standard, and the flaws which mar these are by no means peculiar to them alone. The play is of a piece, and Shakespearean. Yet it undeniably contains hosts of such relatively small anomalies as have been noticed above – metrical irregularities, small inconsistencies of various kinds, signs of false starts and of alterations planned but not made. The simplest and most

satisfactory explanation of these is that the manuscript used by the Folio printers was, in the sense of the word already suggested, unfinished: substantially complete but not yet what could forthwith be made the basis of a prompt-book and so of stage presentation. Parts of this manuscript, indeed, seem to have required transcription before serving as printers' copy (as is suggested in the Note on the Text to the present edition).

Anomalies of the kind we have been considering cannot be said to increase the value of *Timon of Athens* as a work of art. They are not merits but defects, explain them how we may. If we have accounted for them correctly, however, they are matters to which literary criticism can hardly be altogether indifferent. The peculiarities in question may not, it is true, provide a sound basis for generalization about Shakespeare's usual working methods, about the procedures he followed when writing his other plays; but they probably give us the clearest view we are ever likely to get of a Shakespearean manuscript in process of completion. That Shakespeare seldom blotted a line, pious fiction though it essentially is, may not be completely without foundation: much of the time, no doubt, "his mind and his hand went together" and he composed with rapidity and ease – relatively speaking; as compared, say, with Ben Jonson. Yet there are plenty of indications (for instance in *Love's Labor's Lost* and *Romeo and Juliet* and *Julius Caesar*) that the very firstlings of his heart were not invariably the lastlings of his pen as well – as they evidently were not when he was working on *Timon of Athens*.

The imperfections which suggest that Shakespeare left the play unfinished are very numerous but are also relatively trifling. Such faults in *Macbeth* and *King Lear* would not much obscure their essential greatness, and if *Timon* lacks this greatness the reasons must be sought in more serious shortcomings, in weaknesses which nothing short of wholesale rewriting could well obviate. One of these is centered in Alcibiades. Some of the problems associated with his character and function are minor. Though we are given no real opportunity to know him in the first part of the play, what kind of man he is may be sufficiently revealed in the scene which ends in his banishment (III, v) and which in some measure prepares us for the dominant role he will have at the end, where, by sweeping away the old and establishing the new order and by providing the final summary comment on Timon's tragedy, he resolves the action. Again, there is perhaps no absolute need for any more detailed indications than we are given of the nature of the bond between Alcibiades and Timon. But what can be made of their entirely different reactions to Athenian ingratitude? Does this contrast really show that Timon has far greater spiritual worth than his less sensitive but more successful friend, or is this only its imperfectly realized aim? Does it not in fact rather diminish than augment the stature of the protagonist in our eyes? One has only to think of the differing responses of Gloucester and Lear to ingratitude, and of what their tragedy gains from these differences, to appreciate how much less is achieved by the corresponding contrast in *Timon*.

Unless we come to feel that the evils with which a tragedy deals are of the deepest concern to humanity in general, and unless in contending with these evils the protagonist increasingly reveals qualities of mind and spirit which we regard as heroic, the play may fail to produce in us that sense of exaltation which is always evoked by the tragedies we value most. And so it is, for many readers, with this play. For one thing Timon's errors seem more ridiculous than frightening, and it is hard to take very seriously the disaster to which they lead. The crimes of Macbeth and the follies of King Lear precipitate evils which plague all mankind, and are the more terrible because committed by men who have impressive intellectual and spiritual capabilities. The Timon of Acts I–III reveals no such qualities, and his foolishness is of a comparatively trivial kind. Do we really believe that the lure of money is the root of all evil? or that the loss of false friends is a calamity? To be sure there is a certain imaginative grandeur in Timon's vilification, later on, of "Yellow, glittering, precious gold" (IV, iii, 26–48). Evil is generalized here. Indeed a vastly enlarged range of vision and emotion is evident throughout the various indictments of human bestiality that fill Acts IV and V. Yet there are important difficulties here too. One is that, as Apemantus trenchantly observes (IV, iii, 299–300), Timon is now as immoderate in his misanthropy as he was earlier in his bounty. He is foolish still. His transformation, though striking, has not been accompanied by any increase in self-knowledge. His sufferings have not brought him to an awareness of his own imperfections; they have embittered but not magnified him. One of his chief deficiencies as a tragic hero is certainly his incapacity for spiritual growth. Finally, Timon's response to misfortune is not only unheroic but undramatic. He simply withdraws from the world of men. Far from becoming the champion of aspiring humanity in its endless struggle against evil, he rather "slinks out of the race, where that immortal garland is to be run for, not without dust and heat." Dust and heat – involvement and conflict – are the life-blood of drama. As Timon's story is conceived, however, the second half of it must for the most be sustained by other means, by the sheer eloquence of the maledictions with which he belabors a long succession of unwelcome visitors; and, high though the poetic quality of Acts IV and V unquestionably is, it yet fails to make Timon himself an entirely satisfactory protagonist.

There is general agreement that *Timon of Athens* must have been written sometime between 1604 and 1609 (after *Othello* but before the late romances), though whether it is really "the still-born twin of *Lear*" (1605–06) or belongs rather to the period of *Antony and Cleopatra* and *Coriolanus* (1607–08) is by no means clear. It was almost certainly not staged before the Restoration, nor has it ever been successful in the theatre since. Its very survival, by virtue of being printed in 1623, is a little surprising. It is assuredly not one of the great tragedies of a great age. Yet it has rewarding qualities throughout, and parts of it challenge comparison with the supreme manifestations of Shakespeare's maturest art. And if it is also a play which its author never quite finished, as it seems indeed to be, its very imperfections should be of interest to students of Shakespeare.

University of Kansas   CHARLTON HINMAN

NOTE ON THE TEXT

Timon of Athens was first printed in the Folio of 1623, evidently from an author's draft, the peculiar nature of which is discussed below. In the Folio the play is not divided into acts and scenes. The division supplied marginally for reference in the present edition is that given currency by later editors.

In the Folio *Timon* immediately follows *Romeo and Juliet*. Its appearance just here, as the fourth of the Tragedies, was not originally planned. *Troilus and Cressida* had been meant for this position; but difficulties arose (apparently over copyright), the printing of *Troilus* as the next play after *Romeo* was abruptly given over, and *Timon of Athens* was later used to fill the space which had been allotted to the other play. Thus at least the position of *Timon* in the 1623 collection is anomalous; and we cannot even be sure that its inclusion anywhere in the volume was contemplated from the beginning. This much, however, is plain: the "copy" from which the Folio printers were obliged to work was most unusual. It seems to have represented a full but not yet finally revised text, a version antecedent to "foul papers," as an author's last draft of a play is rather misleadingly called. Many of the peculiarities of the copy for *Timon* (including such unnecessarily descriptive details in stage directions as " . . . *Then comes, drooping after all, Apemantus, discontentedly, like himself.*") are indeed of the kind thought characteristic of foul papers, and much of this copy was very likely in Shakespeare's own handwriting. But numerous oddities in spelling that cannot be attributed to the printers demonstrate the presence of a second hand as well; and perhaps the best explanation that can at present be offered is that various parts of Shakespeare's incompletely revised autograph version were found so untidy and illegible that the services of a scribe had to be enlisted to make them sufficiently "clean" for printing-house use. That in any event the second hand did not belong to a second author but only to a transcriber seems clear enough, since it is sometimes found in the most peculiarly Shakespearean passages in the play.

Except for extensive relineation, the following list shows all the material departures from the Folio text, which is often manifestly corrupt. The adopted reading in italics is followed by the Folio reading in roman. Most of the corrections first appeared in eighteenth-century editions (along with many other emendations which may now be rejected as unnecessary) and have generally been accepted since.

The Actors' Names (printed at the end of the play in F)

I, i, 21 *gum . . . oozes* Gowne . . . vses 25 *chafes* chases 40 *man* men 87 *hands . . . slip* hand . . . sit 101 *most needs* must neede 166 *satiety* society 210 *cost* cast 221 *feigned* fegin'd 257 *more* most

I, ii, s.d. *drooping* dropping 29 *ever* verie 78 *these* those 99 *joy* ioyes 118 *Th' ear* There 119 *smell, all* all 145 *Lady* Lord 164 *accept* accept it

II, i, 33 *Take* I go sir? / Take 34 *in compt* in. Come

II, ii, 4 *resumes* resume 38 *broken* debt, broken 72, 99 *mistress'* Masters 125 *proposed* propose 132 *found* sound 152 *of* or 182 *Flaminius* Flauius

III, ii, 37 *fifty – five hundred –* fifty five hundred 64 *spirit* sport

III, iii, 12 *Thrice* Thriue 21 *and I* and

III, iv, 110 *Sempronius* Sempronius Vllorxa 113 *There is* there's

III, v, 4 *him* 'em 14 *this fault* his Fate 17 *An* And 22 *behave* behooue 49 *felon* fellow 63 *I say* say 67 *'em* him 70 *no more* no

III, vi, 19 *here's* heares 78 *foes* fees 79 *lag* legge

IV, i, 6 *steads* steeds 13 *Son* Some

IV, ii, 41 *does* do

IV, iii, 10 *senator* Senators 12 *pasture . . . wether's* Pastour . . . Brothers 13 *lean* leaue 117 *window-bars* window Barne 122, 185 *thy* the 204 *fortune* future 223 *mossed* moyst 283 *my* thy 394 *them* then 430 *villainy* Villaine 470 *grant'st* grunt'st 488 *mild* wilde 505 *A* If not a 521 *Have* Ha's

V, i, 50 *worship* worship 69 *men* man 124 *chance* chanc'd 143 *And* Which 145 *sense* since 146 *fail* fall 180 *reverend'st* reuerends 218 *sour* four

V, ii, 8 *had* made

V, iv, 24 *griefs* greefe 44 *all together* altogether 55 *Descend* Defend 62 *rendered* remedied

THE LIFE OF TIMON OF ATHENS

THE ACTORS' NAMES

Timon of Athens
Lucius
Lucullus ⎬ flattering lords
Sempronius
Ventidius, one of Timon's false friends
Apemantus, a churlish philosopher
Alcibiades, an Athenian captain
[Flavius, steward to Timon]
Poet, Painter, Jeweller, Merchant [, Mercer]
[An old Athenian]
Flaminius
[Lucilius] ⎬ Timon's servants
Servilius

Caphis
Philotus
Titus ⎬ several servants [to Timon's creditors]
Hortensius
[Others]
[A Page]
[A Fool]
[Three Strangers]
[Phrynia ⎬ mistresses to Alcibiades]
[Timandra
Certain Maskers [as] Cupid [and Amazons]
[Lords, Ladies,] Senators, [Officers, Messengers, Soldiers,]
Thieves, Servants [to Lucius and Lucullus], and Attendants

[Scene : Athens, and the woods nearby]

*

I, i   *Enter Poet, Painter, Jeweller, Merchant, and
Mercer, at several doors.*

POET
  Good day, sir.
PAINTER   I am glad y' are well.
POET
2 I have not seen you long ; how goes the world ?
PAINTER
3 It wears, sir, as it grows.
POET   Ay, that's well known.
  But what particular rarity ? What strange,
5 Which manifold record not matches ? See,
6 Magic of bounty, all these spirits thy power
  Hath conjured to attend ! I know the merchant.
PAINTER
  I know them both. Th' other's a jeweller.
MERCHANT
  O, 'tis a worthy lord !
9 JEWELLER   Nay, that's most fixed.
MERCHANT
10 A most incomparable man ; breathed, as it were,
11 To an untirable and continuate goodness.
12 He passes.

JEWELLER   I have a jewel here –
MERCHANT
  O, pray let's see't. For the Lord Timon, sir ?
JEWELLER
  If he will touch the estimate ; but for that –   14
POET *[Recites.]*
  'When we for recompense have praised the vile,   15
  It stains the glory in that happy verse
  Which aptly sings the good.'
MERCHANT *[Looks at the jewel.]* 'Tis a good form.
JEWELLER
  And rich. Here is a water, look ye.   18
PAINTER
  You are rapt, sir, in some work, some dedication   19
  To the great lord.
POET   A thing slipped idly from me.
  Our poesy is as a gum which oozes   21
  From whence 'tis nourishèd. The fire i' th' flint
  Shows not till it be struck ; our gentle flame
  Provokes itself and like the current flies   24
  Each bound it chafes. What have you there ?
PAINTER
  A picture, sir. When comes your book forth ?
POET
  Upon the heels of my presentment, sir.   27
  Let's see your piece.
PAINTER   'Tis a good piece.
POET
  So 'tis. This comes off well and excellent.   29
PAINTER
  Indifferent.
POET   Admirable. How this grace
  Speaks his own standing ! What a mental power   31

This eye shoots forth ! How big imagination
33 Moves in this lip ! To th' dumbness of the gesture
One might interpret.
PAINTER
It is a pretty mocking of the life.
Here is a touch ; is't good ?
POET   I will say of it,
37 It tutors nature. Artificial strife
Lives in these touches, livelier than life.
Enter certain Senators [and pass over].
PAINTER
How this lord is followed !
POET
The senators of Athens. Happy man !
PAINTER
41 Look, moe !
POET
You see this confluence, this great flood of visitors :
I have in this rough work shaped out a man
45 Whom this beneath world doth embrace and hug
46 With amplest entertainment. My free drift
Halts not particularly, but moves itself
48 In a wide sea of wax ; no levelled malice
49 Infects one comma in the course I hold,
50 But flies an eagle flight, bold and forth on,
Leaving no tract behind.
PAINTER
How shall I understand you ?
51 POET   I will unbolt to you.
52 You see how all conditions, how all minds,
As well of glib and slipp'ry creatures as
Of grave and austere quality, tender down
Their services to Lord Timon. His large fortune,
Upon his good and gracious nature hanging,
57 Subdues and properties to his love and tendance
All sorts of hearts ; yea, from the glass-faced flatterer
To Apemantus, that few things loves better
Than to abhor himself – even he drops down
The knee before him and returns in peace
Most rich in Timon's nod.
PAINTER   I saw them speak together.
POET
Sir, I have upon a high and pleasant hill
Feigned Fortune to be throned. The base o' th' mount
65 Is ranked with all deserts, all kind of natures
That labor on the bosom of this sphere
67 To propagate their states. Amongst them all
Whose eyes are on this sovereign lady fixed
69 One do I personate of Lord Timon's frame,
Whom Fortune with her ivory hand wafts to her,
71 Whose present grace to present slaves and servants
72 Translates his rivals.
PAINTER   'Tis conceived to scope.
This throne, this Fortune, and this hill, methinks,
With one man beckoned from the rest below,
Bowing his head against the steepy mount
76 To climb his happiness, would be well expressed
In our condition.
POET   Nay, sir, but hear me on.
All those which were his fellows but of late
(Some better than his value) on the moment
Follow his strides, his lobbies fill with tendance,
Rain sacrificial whisperings in his ear,
82 Make sacred even his stirrup, and through him

Drink the free air.
PAINTER   Ay, marry, what of these ?   83
POET
When Fortune in her shift and change of mood
Spurns down her late beloved, all his dependants,
Which labored after him to the mountain's top
Even on their knees and hands, let him slip down,
Not one accompanying his declining foot.
PAINTER
'Tis common.
A thousand moral paintings I can show   90
That shall demonstrate these quick blows of Fortune's
More pregnantly than words. Yet you do well   92
To show Lord Timon that mean eyes have seen   93
The foot above the head.
*Trumpets sound. Enter Lord Timon, addressing
himself courteously to every suitor [; a Messenger
from Ventidius talking with him ; Lucilius and other
Servants following].*
TIMON   Imprisoned is he, say you ?
MESSENGER
Ay, my good lord. Five talents is his debt,   95
His means most short, his creditors most strait.   96
Your honorable letter he desires
To those have shut him up, which failing
Periods his comfort.   99
TIMON   Noble Ventidius ! Well,
I am not of that feather to shake off
My friend when he most needs me. I do know him
A gentleman that well deserves a help,
Which he shall have. I'll pay the debt and free him.
MESSENGER
Your lordship ever binds him.   104
TIMON
Commend me to him. I will send his ransom ;
And, being enfranchised, bid him come to me.   106
'Tis not enough to help the feeble up,
But to support him after. Fare you well.
MESSENGER
All happiness to your honor !   *Exit.*
Enter an old Athenian.
OLD MAN
Lord Timon, hear me speak.
TIMON   Freely, good father.   110
OLD MAN
Thou hast a servant named Lucilius.
TIMON
I have so. What of him ?

---

33 *Moves in* is suggested by   33–34 *To th' dumbness . . . interpret* i.e. it
'can almost talk'   37 *Artificial strife* the struggle of art to outdo nature
41 *moe* more   45 *entertainment* welcome ; *drift* aim   46 *particularly* on any
individual   46–47 *moves . . . wax* i.e. has great scope (though 'wax' has
not been altogether satisfactorily explained)   48 *comma* i.e. detail   49
flies my course is   50 *tract* trace, track   51 *unbolt* explain   52 *conditions*
social levels   57 *properties* appropriates ; *tendance* care, service   65
ranked . . . deserts filled with men of all degrees of merit   67 *states* fortunes,
estates   69 *personate* represent   71 *to present* immediately to   72 *Translates* transforms, changes ; *to scope* aptly   76–77 *would . . . condition*
would be closely paralleled by our situation in the real world   82–83
through . . . air act as if indebted to him even for breathing   83 *marry* to
be sure   90 *moral* allegorical   92 *pregnantly* cogently   93 *mean* lowly
95 *talents* sums of silver or gold (each worth about $2,000 by modern
standards)   96 *strait* exacting, strict   99 *Periods* ends   104 *binds* attaches
by ties of gratitude (but with quibble on *free* in l. 103)   106 *enfranchised*
freed   110 *father* (respectful form of address to an old man)

OLD MAN
Most noble Timon, call the man before thee.

TIMON
Attends he here or no? Lucilius!

LUCILIUS
Here, at your lordship's service.

OLD MAN
116   This fellow here, Lord Timon, this thy creature,
By night frequents my house. I am a man
118   That from my first have been inclined to thrift,
And my estate deserves an heir more raised
120   Than one which holds a trencher.

TIMON   Well; what further?

OLD MAN
One only daughter have I, no kin else
On whom I may confer what I have got.
123   The maid is fair, o' th' youngest for a bride,
124   And I have bred her at my dearest cost
125   In qualities of the best. This man of thine
126   Attempts her love. I prithee, noble lord,
127   Join with me to forbid him her resort;
Myself have spoke in vain.

TIMON   The man is honest.

OLD MAN
129   Therefore he will be, Timon.
His honesty rewards him in itself;
131   It must not bear my daughter.

TIMON   Does she love him?

OLD MAN
132   She is young and apt.
Our own precedent passions do instruct us
What levity 's in youth.

TIMON   Love you the maid?

LUCILIUS
Ay, my good lord, and she accepts of it.

OLD MAN
If in her marriage my consent be missing,
I call the gods to witness I will choose
Mine heir from forth the beggars of the world
139   And dispossess her all.

TIMON   How shall she be endowed
If she be mated with an equal husband?

OLD MAN
141   Three talents on the present; in future, all.

TIMON
This gentleman of mine hath served me long;
To build his fortune I will strain a little,
144   For 'tis a bond in men. Give him thy daughter:
What you bestow, in him I'll counterpoise,
And make him weigh with her.

OLD MAN   Most noble lord,

Pawn me to this your honor, she is his.   147

TIMON
My hand to thee; mine honor on my promise.

LUCILIUS
Humbly I thank your lordship. Never may
That state or fortune fall into my keeping
Which is not owed to you!   151
                Exit [Lucilius, with old Athenian].

POET *[Presents his poem.]*
Vouchsafe my labor, and long live your lordship!   152

TIMON
I thank you; you shall hear from me anon.   153
Go not away. – What have you there, my friend?

PAINTER
A piece of painting, which I do beseech
Your lordship to accept.

TIMON   Painting is welcome.
The painting is almost the natural man;   157
For since dishonor traffics with man's nature
He is but outside; these pencilled figures are
Even such as they give out. I like your work,
And you shall find I like it. Wait attendance
Till you hear further from me.

PAINTER   The gods preserve ye!

TIMON
Well fare you, gentleman. Give me your hand;
We must needs dine together. – Sir, your jewel
Hath suffered under praise.   165

JEWELLER   What, my lord? Dispraise?

TIMON
A mere satiety of commendations.
If I should pay you for't as 'tis extolled,
It would unclew me quite.   168

JEWELLER   My lord, 'tis rated
As those which sell would give; but you well know   169
Things of like value, differing in the owners,
Are prizèd by their masters. Believe't, dear lord,   171
You mend the jewel by the wearing it.

TIMON
Well mocked.
            Enter Apemantus.

MERCHANT
No, my good lord; he speaks the common tongue
Which all men speak with him.

TIMON   Look who comes here.
Will you be chid?

JEWELLER   We'll bear, with your lordship.   176

MERCHANT
He'll spare none.

TIMON
Good morrow to thee, gentle Apemantus.

APEMANTUS
Till I be gentle stay thou for thy good morrow –   179
When thou art Timon's dog, and these knaves honest.   180

TIMON
Why dost thou call them knaves? Thou know'st them
not.

APEMANTUS   Are they not Athenians?

TIMON   Yes.

APEMANTUS   Then I repent not.

JEWELLER   You know me, Apemantus?

APEMANTUS   Thou know'st I do; I called thee by thy
name.

TIMON   Thou art proud, Apemantus.

---

116 *creature* dependent (contemptuous) 118 *first* earliest days, youth 120 *holds a trencher* i.e. waits table 123 *o' th' youngest for* barely old enough to be 124 *bred* brought up, educated 125 *qualities* accomplishments 126 *Attempts* seeks to win 127 *her resort* access to her 129 *will be* i.e. will act the part (and stop pursuing my daughter against my wishes?) 131 *bear* win 132 *apt* impressionable 139 *all* wholly 141 *Three talents* (about $6,000) 144 *bond* obligation 147 *Pawn . . . honor* if you'll pledge, on your honor, to do so 151 *owed* (acknowledged as) due to 152 *Vouchsafe* deign to accept 153 *anon* soon 157–60 *The painting . . . out* i.e. painting can almost be said to represent what man is instead of what he pretends to be 165 *suffered under* been overwhelmed with (complimentary, but the jeweller takes it otherwise) 168 *unclew* ruin (undo, as in unwinding a ball of yarn) 169 *As . . . give* i.e. at cost price 171 *by* according to 176 *We'll . . . lordship* i.e. we can stand it if you can 179 *stay . . . morrow* expect such greeting from me 180 *When . . . honest* i.e. never

APEMANTUS Of nothing so much as that I am not like Timon.

TIMON Whither art going?

APEMANTUS To knock out an honest Athenian's brains.

TIMON That's a deed thou'lt die for.

APEMANTUS Right, if doing nothing be death by th' law.

TIMON How lik'st thou this picture, Apemantus?

195 APEMANTUS The best for the innocence.

TIMON Wrought he not well that painted it?

APEMANTUS He wrought better that made the painter, and yet he's but a filthy piece of work.

PAINTER Y' are a dog.

200 APEMANTUS Thy mother 's of my generation. What's she, if I be a dog?

TIMON Wilt dine with me, Apemantus?

APEMANTUS No, I eat not lords.

204 TIMON An thou shouldst, thou'dst anger ladies.

APEMANTUS O, they eat lords. So they come by great bellies.

206 TIMON That's a lascivious apprehension.

APEMANTUS So thou apprehend'st it; take it for thy labor.

TIMON How dost thou like this jewel, Apemantus?

APEMANTUS Not so well as plain-dealing, which will not
210 cost a man a doit.

TIMON What dost thou think 'tis worth?

APEMANTUS Not worth my thinking. How now, poet?

POET How now, philosopher?

APEMANTUS Thou liest.

POET Art not one?

APEMANTUS Yes.

POET Then I lie not.

APEMANTUS Art not a poet?

POET Yes.

220 APEMANTUS Then thou liest. Look in thy last work, where thou hast feigned him a worthy fellow.

POET That's not feigned; he is so.

APEMANTUS Yes, he is worthy of thee, and to pay thee for thy labor. He that loves to be flattered is worthy o' th' flatterer. Heavens, that I were a lord!

TIMON What wouldst do then, Apemantus?

APEMANTUS E'en as Apemantus does now – hate a lord with my heart.

TIMON What, thyself?

APEMANTUS Ay.

TIMON Wherefore?

232 APEMANTUS That I had no angry wit to be a lord. Art not thou a merchant?

MERCHANT Ay, Apemantus.

235 APEMANTUS Traffic confound thee, if the gods will not!

MERCHANT If traffic do it, the gods do it.

APEMANTUS Traffic 's thy god; and thy god confound thee!

Trumpet sounds. Enter a Messenger.

TIMON
What trumpet 's that?

MESSENGER
'Tis Alcibiades and some twenty horse,
240 All of companionship.

TIMON
Pray entertain them; give them guide to us.

[Exeunt some Attendants.]

You must needs dine with me. Go not you hence
Till I have thanked you. When dinner 's done,

Show me this piece. – I am joyful of your sights.   244

Enter Alcibiades with the rest.

Most welcome, sir!

[They salute.]

APEMANTUS   So; so; there!
Aches contract and starve your supple joints!   246
That there should be small love 'mongst these sweet knaves,
And all this courtesy! The strain of man 's bred out   248
Into baboon and monkey.

ALCIBIADES
Sir, you have saved my longing, and I feed   250
Most hungerly on your sight.

TIMON   Right welcome, sir!
Ere we depart we'll share a bounteous time
In different pleasures. Pray you, let us in.

Exeunt [all but Apemantus].

Enter two Lords.

1. LORD What time o' day is't, Apemantus?

APEMANTUS Time to be honest.

1. LORD That time serves still.   256

APEMANTUS The more accursèd thou that still omit'st it.

2. LORD Thou art going to Lord Timon's feast?

APEMANTUS Ay, to see meat fill knaves and wine heat fools.

2. LORD Fare thee well, fare thee well.

APEMANTUS Thou art a fool to bid me farewell twice.

2. LORD Why, Apemantus?

APEMANTUS Shouldst have kept one to thyself, for I mean to give thee none.

1. LORD Hang thyself!

APEMANTUS No, I will do nothing at thy bidding. Make thy requests to thy friend.

2. LORD Away, unpeaceable dog, or I'll spurn thee hence!

APEMANTUS I will fly, like a dog, the heels o' th' ass.

[Exit.]

1. LORD
He's opposite to humanity. Come, shall we in   270
And taste Lord Timon's bounty? He outgoes
The very heart of kindness.

2. LORD
He pours it out. Plutus, the god of gold,
Is but his steward. No meed but he repays   274
Sevenfold above itself; no gift to him
But breeds the giver a return exceeding
All use of quittance.   277

1. LORD   The noblest mind he carries
That ever governed man.

2. LORD   Long may he live
In fortunes! Shall we in?   279

1. LORD   I'll keep you company. *Exeunt.*

*

195 *innocence* silliness 200 *generation* breed, species 204 *An* if 206 *apprehension* (1) idea, (2) capture (of men by women) 210 *doit* half a farthing, an eighth of a penny 220 *Then thou liest* (because it is necessary for poets to 'feign,' hence to be liars) 232 *had . . . lord* had, in my anger, no more sense than to wish to be a lord (perhaps: the line may be corrupt but has not been convincingly emended) 235 *Traffic* trade 240 *of companionship* of the same party 244 *of your sights* to see you 246 *Aches* (pronounced 'aitches') 248 *bred out* degenerated 250 *saved my* kept me from further 256 *still* always 270 *opposite* hostile 274 *meed* (1) gift, (2) merit 277 *use of quittance* customary repayment 279 *In fortunes* fortunate, prosperous (but possibly we should read 'In Fortune's,' in the goddess Fortune's mind)

I, ii

Hautboys playing loud music. A great banquet served in [, Flavius the Steward and others attending]; and then enter Lord Timon, the States, the Athenian Lords, Ventidius (which Timon redeemed from prison). Then comes, drooping after all, Apemantus, discontentedly, like himself.

VENTIDIUS

Most honored Timon,
It hath pleased the gods to remember my father's age
And call him to long peace.
He is gone happy, and has left me rich.
Then, as in grateful virtue I am bound

6   To your free heart, I do return those talents,
Doubled with thanks and service, from whose help
I derived liberty.

TIMON   O, by no means,
Honest Ventidius. You mistake my love:
I gave it freely ever; and there's none
Can truly say he gives, if he receives.

12 If our betters play at that game, we must not dare
13 To imitate them; faults that are rich are fair.

VENTIDIUS

A noble spirit!

TIMON

Nay, my lords, ceremony was but devised at first
To set a gloss on faint deeds, hollow welcomes,
Recanting goodness, sorry ere 'tis shown;
But where there is true friendship, there needs none.
Pray sit. More welcome are ye to my fortunes
Than my fortunes to me.

[They sit.]

1. LORD

My lord, we always have confessed it.

APEMANTUS

22 Ho, ho, confessed it? Hanged it, have you not?

TIMON

O, Apemantus, you are welcome.

APEMANTUS   No,
You shall not make me welcome;
I come to have thee thrust me out of doors.

TIMON

26 Fie, thou'rt a churl; ye've got a humor there
Does not become a man; 'tis much to blame.

28 They say, my lords, *Ira furor brevis est;* but yon man is
ever angry. Go, let him have a table by himself; for he

30 does neither affect company nor is he fit for't indeed.

31 APEMANTUS Let me stay at thine apperil, Timon. I come
to observe; I give thee warning on't.

TIMON I take no heed of thee. Thou'rt an Athenian,

therefore welcome. I myself would have no power; 34
prithee let my meat make thee silent.

APEMANTUS I scorn thy meat. 'Twould choke me; for I
should ne'er flatter thee. O you gods, what a number of
men eats Timon, and he sees 'em not! It grieves me to
see so many dip their meat in one man's blood; and all
the madness is, he cheers them up too.   40
I wonder men dare trust themselves with men.
Methinks they should invite them without knives: 42
Good for their meat, and safer for their lives.
There's much example for't. The fellow that sits next
him now, parts bread with him, pledges the breath of
him in a divided draft, is the readiest man to kill him. 46
'T has been proved. If I were a huge man, I should fear 47
to drink at meals,
Lest they should spy my windpipe's dangerous notes. 49
Great men should drink with harness on their throats. 50

TIMON *[to a Lord who drinks to him]*
My lord, in heart! and let the health go round.   51

2. LORD
Let it flow this way, my good lord.

APEMANTUS Flow this way? A brave fellow! He keeps
his tides well. Those healths will make thee and thy 54
state look ill, Timon.
Here's that which is too weak to be a sinner:
Honest water, which ne'er left man i' th' mire.
This and my food are equals; there's no odds.
Feasts are too proud to give thanks to the gods.   59

Apemantus' Grace.

Immortal gods, I crave no pelf;
I pray for no man but myself;
Grant I may never prove so fond   62
To trust man on his oath or bond,
Or a harlot for her weeping,
Or a dog that seems a-sleeping,
Or a keeper with my freedom,   66
Or my friends, if I should need 'em.
Amen. So; fall to't;
Rich men sin, and I eat root.

[Eats and drinks.]

Much good dich thy good heart, Apemantus!   70

TIMON Captain Alcibiades, your heart's in the field now.

ALCIBIADES My heart is ever at your service, my lord.

TIMON You had rather be at a breakfast of enemies than a
dinner of friends.

ALCIBIADES So they were bleeding new, my lord, there's
no meat like 'em; I could wish my best friend at such a
feast.

APEMANTUS Would all these flatterers were thine
enemies then, that then thou mightst kill 'em – and bid
me to 'em!

1. LORD Might we but have that happiness, my lord, that
you would once use our hearts, whereby we might ex- 80
press some part of our zeals, we should think ourselves
for ever perfect.   82

TIMON O no doubt, my good friends, but the gods themselves have provided that I shall have much help from
you: how had you been my friends else? Why have you
that charitable title from thousands, did not you chiefly 86
belong to my heart? I have told more of you to myself
than you can with modesty speak in your own behalf;
and thus far I confirm you. O you gods, think I, what 89
need we have any friends if we should ne'er have need

I, ii The hall in Timon's house   **s.d.** *Hautboys* oboes; *States* rulers of the state; senators   **6** *free* generous   **12** *If* i.e. even if   **13** *that are rich* i.e. in the rich   **22** *confessed . . . not* (bitter allusion to proverbial 'confess and be hanged')   **26** *humor* mood   **28** *Ira . . . est* anger is a brief madness   **30** *affect* like, seek   **31** *thine apperil* your own risk   **34** *power* i.e. to keep you quiet   **40** *cheers . . . too* encourages them as well (though possibly 'too' should be 'to't,' to do it)   **42** *without knives* (Elizabethan if not ancient Athenian guests normally brought their own)   **46** *divided draft* shared drink   **47** *huge* great (in rank, not physical size)   **49** *my . . . notes* indications on my throat of where my windpipe is   **50** *harness* armor   **51** *in heart* heartily   **54** *tides* (1) tides, which *flow,* (2) times, seasons   **54–55** *Those healths . . . ill* (cf. proverbial 'to drink healths is to drink sickness')   **59** *Feasts* feasters   **62** *fond* foolish   **66** *keeper* jailer   **70** *dich* may it do   **80** *use our hearts* put our love to the test   **82** *perfect* completely happy   **86** *from thousands* i.e. you alone of all the thousands I know   **89** *confirm you* vouch for your worthiness

of 'em? They were the most needless creatures living,
should we ne'er have use for 'em; and would most resemble sweet instruments hung up in cases, that keeps
their sounds to themselves. Why, I have often wished
95 myself poorer, that I might come nearer to you. We are
born to do benefits; and what better or properer can we
call our own than the riches of our friends? O what a
precious comfort 'tis to have so many like brothers com-
99 manding one another's fortunes! O joy, e'en made away
100 ere't can be born! Mine eyes cannot hold out water,
methinks. To forget their faults, I drink to you.

APEMANTUS Thou weep'st to make them drink, Timon.

2. LORD
Joy had the like conception in our eyes
And at that instant like a babe sprung up.

APEMANTUS
Ho, ho! I laugh to think that babe a bastard.

3. LORD
I promise you, my lord, you moved me much.

107 APEMANTUS Much!
    Sound tucket.

TIMON
What means that trump?
    Enter Servant.   How now?

SERVANT Please you, my lord, there are certain ladies
most desirous of admittance.

TIMON Ladies? What are their wills?

SERVANT There comes with them a forerunner, my lord,
113 which bears that office to signify their pleasures.

TIMON I pray let them be admitted.   *[Exit Servant.]*
    Enter Cupid.

CUPID
Hail to thee, worthy Timon, and to all
That of his bounties taste! The five best senses
Acknowledge thee their patron, and come freely
118 To gratulate thy plenteous bosom. Th' ear,
Taste, touch, smell, all, pleased from thy table rise;
They only now come but to feast thine eyes.

TIMON
They're welcome all; let 'em have kind admittance.
Music, make their welcome!   *[Exit Cupid.]*

1. LORD
You see, my lord, how ample y' are beloved.
    [Music.] Enter Cupid, with the Masque of Ladies
    [as] Amazons with lutes in their hands, dancing and
    playing.

APEMANTUS
Hoy-day!
What a sweep of vanity comes this way!
They dance? They are madwomen.
127 Like madness is the glory of this life
128 As this pomp shows to a little oil and root.
We make ourselves fools to disport ourselves
130 And spend our flatteries to drink those men
131 Upon whose age we void it up again
With poisonous spite and envy.
Who lives that's not depravèd or depraves?
Who dies that bears not one spurn to their graves
135 Of their friends' gift?
I should fear those that dance before me now
Would one day stamp upon me. 'T has been done.
Men shut their doors against a setting sun.
    The Lords rise from table, with much adoring of
    Timon, and to show their loves, each single out an

Amazon, and all dance, men with women, a lofty
strain or two to the hautboys, and cease.

TIMON
You have done our pleasures much grace, fair ladies,
Set a fair fashion on our entertainment,
Which was not half so beautiful and kind;   141
You have added worth unto't and lustre,
And entertained me with mine own device.   143
I am to thank you for't.   144

1. LADY
My lord, you take us even at the best.   145

APEMANTUS Faith, for the worst is filthy, and would not
hold taking, I doubt me.   147

TIMON
Ladies, there is an idle banquet attends you;
Please you to dispose yourselves.   149

ALL LADIES
Most thankfully, my lord.   *Exeunt [Cupid and Ladies].*

TIMON   Flavius.

FLAVIUS
My lord?

TIMON   The little casket bring me hither.

FLAVIUS
Yes, my lord. *[aside]* More jewels yet?
There is no crossing him in's humor;   154
Else I should tell him well, i' faith I should;
When all's spent, he'd be crossed then, an he could.   156
'Tis pity bounty had not eyes behind,
That man might ne'er be wretched for his mind.   *Exit.* 158

1. LORD
Where be our men?

SERVANT
Here, my lord, in readiness.

2. LORD
Our horses!
    Enter Flavius [with the casket].

TIMON   O my friends, I have one word
To say to you. Look you, my good lord,
I must entreat you honor me so much
As to advance this jewel; accept and wear it,   164
Kind my lord.

1. LORD
I am so far already in your gifts –

ALL
So are we all.
    Enter a Servant.

SERVANT
My lord, there are certain nobles of the senate
Newly alighted and come to visit you.

TIMON
They are fairly welcome.   *[Exit Servant.]*

95 *come nearer to* try   99 *made away* destroyed, turned to tears   100 *cannot . . . water* are leaky   107 s.d. *tucket* trumpet call   113 *which . . . office* whose function is   118 *gratulate . . . bosom* greet thy generous heart   118–20 *Th' ear . . . eyes* i.e. though your feast has gratified all the senses, the masquers can hope to please your sense of sight only   127 *Like* just such   128 *As . . . shows to* in the same sense as this lavishness is when compared with; *a little . . . root* i.e. sane frugality   130 *drink* drink healths to   131 *age* old age   135 *Of . . . gift* given them by their friends   141 *was not* i.e. before you came   143 *mine own device* (apparently Timon has himself composed the masque)   144 *am to* should and do   145 *take . . . best* i.e. give us most generous praise   147 *hold taking* bear handling (in an obscene sense)   149 *dispose yourselves* take your places   154 *humor* frame of mind   156 *crossed* (1) freed of debt, (2) thwarted (as in l. 154)   158 *for his mind* because of his (generosity of) spirit   164 *advance* add value to (by possessing; cf. I, i, 170–71)

FLAVIUS I beseech your honor,
171 Vouchsafe me a word; it does concern you near.
TIMON
Near? Why then, another time I'll hear thee. I prithee
Let's be provided to show them entertainment.
FLAVIUS [aside]
I scarce know how.
Enter another Servant.
SERVANT
May it please your honor, Lord Lucius,
Out of his free love, hath presented to you
177 Four milk-white horses trapped in silver.
TIMON
I shall accept them fairly. Let the presents
179 Be worthily entertained. *[Exit Servant.]*
Enter a third Servant.
How now? What news?
SERVANT Please you, my lord, that honorable gentleman,
Lord Lucullus, entreats your company to-morrow to
hunt with him and has sent your honor two brace of
greyhounds.
TIMON
I'll hunt with him; and let them be received,
Not without fair reward. *[Exit Servant.]*
FLAVIUS [aside] What will this come to?
He commands us to provide and give great gifts,
And all out of an empty coffer;
Nor will he know his purse, or yield me this,
To show him what a beggar his heart is,
190 Being of no power to make his wishes good.
191 His promises fly so beyond his state
That what he speaks is all in debt; he owes
For every word. He is so kind that he now
194 Pays interest for't; his land's put to their books.
Well, would I were gently put out of office
Before I were forced out!
Happier is he that has no friend to feed
198 Than such that do e'en enemies exceed.
I bleed inwardly for my lord. *Exit.*
TIMON You do yourselves
200 Much wrong; you bate too much of your own merits.
Here, my lord – a trifle of our love.
2. LORD
With more than common thanks I will receive it.
3. LORD
O, he's the very soul of bounty!

171 *Vouchsafe* allow 177 *trapped in silver* in silver-mounted trappings
179 *entertained* taken care of 190 *Being of* (the desires of his heart) having
191 *state* means 194 *put ... books* mortgaged to them 198 *such ...
exceed* such (friends) as do more harm than even his enemies 200 *bate ... of*
reduce, undervalue 204–05 *gave good words* spoke well 207 *pardon ...
that* i.e. don't ask me to accept such a gift as that 209 *but* anything except;
affect like 211 *call to* visit (?), ask your help in return should I need it (?)
212 *all ... several* both your joint and separate · 217 *It ... thee* giving to you
is real charity (since you have no property of your own); *living* (1) life, (2)
property 219 *defiled* (1) having, like a battlefield, files of soldiers on it, (2)
contaminated (since 'pitch ... doth defile'; see 1 *Henry IV*, II, iv, 394–95)
222 *All to you* all the obligation is mine, to you 224 *coil* fuss 225 *Serving
of becks* bowing (and scraping) 226 *legs* (1) limbs, (2) bows 234–35 *Thou
... shortly* you've so long been squandering your tangible assets that I
fear you'll soon be giving away all that's left of yourself in such unreal
property as promises, mere worthless notes 241 *thy heaven* i.e. my good
counsel
II, i The house of a Senator of Athens 1 *late* recently; *five thousand* (presumably 'crowns' as in III, iv, 29; a very large sum is evidently meant)
3–4 *Still ... Of* constantly engaged in 5 *steal but* I have only to steal

TIMON And now I remember, my lord, you gave good 204
words the other day of a bay courser I rode on. 'Tis
yours because you liked it.
3. LORD
O, I beseech you pardon me, my lord, in that! 207
TIMON
You may take my word, my lord, I know no man
Can justly praise but what he does affect. 209
I weigh my friends' affection with mine own.
I'll tell you true; I'll call to you. 211
ALL LORDS O none so welcome!
TIMON
I take all and your several visitations 212
So kind to heart 'tis not enough to give.
Methinks I could deal kingdoms to my friends
And ne'er be weary. Alcibiades,
Thou art a soldier, therefore seldom rich.
It comes in charity to thee; for all thy living 217
Is 'mongst the dead, and all the lands thou hast
Lie in a pitched field.
ALCIBIADES Ay, defiled land, my lord. 219
1. LORD We are so virtuously bound –
TIMON And so
Am I to you.
2. LORD So infinitely endeared –
TIMON
All to you. Lights, more lights! 222
1. LORD The best of happiness,
Honor, and fortunes keep with you, Lord Timon!
TIMON
Ready for his friends. *Exeunt Lords [and others.*
Manent Apemantus and Timon].
APEMANTUS What a coil's here! 224
Serving of becks and jutting-out of bums! 225
I doubt whether their legs be worth the sums 226
That are given for 'em. Friendship's full of dregs.
Methinks false hearts should never have sound legs.
Thus honest fools lay out their wealth on curtsies.
TIMON
Now, Apemantus, if thou wert not sullen,
I would be good to thee.
APEMANTUS No, I'll nothing; for if I should be bribed
too, there would be none left to rail upon thee, and then
thou wouldst sin the faster. Thou giv'st so long, Timon, 234
I fear me thou wilt give away thyself in paper shortly.
What needs these feasts, pomps, and vainglories?
TIMON Nay, an you begin to rail on society once, I am
sworn not to give regard to you. Farewell, and come
with better music. *Exit.*
APEMANTUS So. Thou wilt not hear me now; thou shalt
not then. I'll lock thy heaven from thee. 241
O that men's ears should be
To counsel deaf but not to flattery! *Exit.*

*

Enter a Senator [with papers in his hand]. II, i
SENATOR
And late five thousand. To Varro and to Isidore 1
He owes nine thousand, besides my former sum,
Which makes it five-and-twenty. Still in motion 3
Of raging waste! It cannot hold; it will not.
If I want gold, steal but a beggar's dog 5
And give it Timon – why, the dog coins gold.

If I would sell my horse and buy twenty moe
Better than he – why, give my horse to Timon ;
9   Ask nothing, give it him – it foals me straight,
10 And able horses. No porter at his gate,
But rather one that smiles and still invites
12 All that pass by. It cannot hold ; no reason
Can sound his state in safety. Caphis, ho !
Caphis, I say !
    Enter Caphis.
    CAPHIS   Here, sir. What is your pleasure ?
    SENATOR
Get on your cloak and haste you to Lord Timon.
16 Importune him for my moneys. Be not ceased
17 With slight denial, nor then silenced when
'Commend me to your master' and the cap
Plays in the right hand, thus ; but tell him
My uses cry to me ; I must serve my turn
Out of mine own ; his days and times are past,
22 And my reliances on his fracted dates
Have smit my credit. I love and honor him,
But must not break my back to heal his finger.
Immediate are my needs, and my relief
Must not be tossed and turned to me in words
But find supply immediate. Get you gone.
Put on a most importunate aspect,
A visage of demand ; for I do fear,
30 When every feather sticks in his own wing,
31 Lord Timon will be left a naked gull,
32 Which flashes now a phoenix. Get you gone.
    CAPHIS
I go, sir.
    SENATOR Take the bonds along with you
34 And have the dates in compt.
    CAPHIS   I will, sir.
    SENATOR   Go.   *Exeunt.*

                    *

II, ii   *Enter [Flavius, Timon's] Steward, with many bills*
            in his hand.
    STEWARD
No care, no stop ; so senseless of expense
That he will neither know how to maintain it
Nor cease his flow of riot ; takes no account
4   How things go from him nor resumes no care
5   Of what is to continue. Never mind
Was to be so unwise to be so kind.
What shall be done ? He will not hear till feel.
8   I must be round with him, now he comes from hunting.
Fie, fie, fie, fie !
    Enter Caphis [and the Servants of] Isidore and Varro.
    CAPHIS
Good even, Varro. What, you come for money ?
    VARRO'S SERVANT
Is't not your business too ?
    CAPHIS
It is ; and yours too, Isidore ?
    ISIDORE'S SERVANT   It is so.
    CAPHIS
Would we were all discharged !
13 VARRO'S SERVANT   I fear it.
    CAPHIS
Here comes the lord.
    Enter Timon and his Train [with Alcibiades].

    TIMON
So soon as dinner's done we'll forth again,
My Alcibiades. – With me ? What is your will ?
    CAPHIS
My lord, here is a note of certain dues.
    TIMON
Dues ? Whence are you ?
    CAPHIS   Of Athens here, my lord.
    TIMON
Go to my steward.
    CAPHIS
Please it your lordship, he hath put me off
To the succession of new days this month.   21
My master is awaked by great occasion   22
To call upon his own, and humbly prays you   23
That with your other noble parts you'll suit   24
In giving him his right.
    TIMON   Mine honest friend,
I prithee but repair to me next morning.
    CAPHIS
Nay, good my lord –
    TIMON   Contain thyself, good friend.
    VARRO'S SERVANT
One Varro's servant, my good lord –
    ISIDORE'S SERVANT
From Isidore ; he humbly prays your speedy payment.
    CAPHIS
If you did know, my lord, my master's wants –
    VARRO'S SERVANT
'Twas due on forfeiture, my lord, six weeks and past.   31
    ISIDORE'S SERVANT
Your steward puts me off, my lord, and I
Am sent expressly to your lordship.
    TIMON
Give me breath.
I do beseech you, good my lords, keep on ;   35
I'll wait upon you instantly.
                    [Exeunt Alcibiades, Lords, etc.]
    [To Flavius]   Come hither. Pray you,
How goes the world that I am thus encount'red
With clamorous demands of broken bonds
And the detention of long-since-due debts,   39
Against my honor ?   40
    STEWARD   Please you, gentlemen,
The time is unagreeable to this business.
Your importunacy cease till after dinner,
That I may make his lordship understand
Wherefore you are not paid.
    TIMON
Do so, my friends – See them well entertained.   *[Exit.]*

9 *straight* forthwith 10 *able* good, strong (as foals are not) 12–13 *no
. . . safety* no reasonable man can investigate his estate and find it financially
secure 16 *ceased* stopped 17–19 *when . . . thus* when with . . . thus (he
tries to put you off) 22 *fracted* broken 30 *every . . . wing* i.e. when all
property is in the hands of its rightful owner 31 *gull* (1) unfledged bird,
(2) dupe 32 *phoenix* i.e. uniquely glorious thing 34 *in compt* noted
down
II, ii Before Timon's house 4 *resumes* takes 5 *what . . . continue* what
will serve future needs 8 *round* blunt 13 *it* i.e. that we won't be 21 *To
. . . days* i.e. from one day to the next 22 *awaked . . . occasion* aroused by
serious need 23 *call . . . own* liquidate his assets (?), ask payment of what
he is owed (?) 24 *suit* be consistent 31 *on forfeiture* under penalty if not
paid 35–36 *keep on . . . instantly* go ahead (without me); I'll be with you
again in no time 39 *the detention* withholding payment 40 *Against my
honor* thus calling my honor into question

STEWARD

46 Pray draw near.   *Exit.*

      Enter Apemantus and Fool.

CAPHIS

  Stay, stay; here comes the fool with Apemantus.
  Let's ha' some sport with 'em.

VARRO'S SERVANT Hang him, he'll abuse us.

ISIDORE'S SERVANT A plague upon him, dog!

VARRO'S SERVANT How dost, fool?

APEMANTUS Dost dialogue with thy shadow?

VARRO'S SERVANT I speak not to thee.

APEMANTUS No, 'tis to thyself. *[to the Fool]* Come
  away.

ISIDORE'S SERVANT *[to Varro's Servant]* There's the
56 fool hangs on your back already.

57 APEMANTUS No, thou stand'st single; thou'rt not on
  him yet.

CAPHIS Where's the fool now?

59 APEMANTUS He last asked the question. Poor rogues and
  usurers' men; bawds between gold and want!

ALL SERVANTS What are we, Apemantus?

APEMANTUS Asses.

ALL SERVANTS Why?

APEMANTUS That you ask me what you are, and do not
  know yourselves. Speak to 'em, fool.

FOOL How do you, gentlemen?

67 ALL SERVANTS Gramercies, good fool. How does your
  mistress?

FOOL She's e'en setting on water to scald such chickens
70 as you are. Would we could see you at Corinth!

APEMANTUS Good! Gramercy.

      Enter Page.

FOOL Look you, here comes my mistress' page.

PAGE *[to the Fool]* Why, how now, captain? What do you
  in this wise company? How dost thou, Apemantus?

APEMANTUS Would I had a rod in my mouth, that I
  might answer thee profitably.

77 PAGE Prithee, Apemantus, read me the superscription of
  these letters; I know not which is which.

APEMANTUS Canst not read?

PAGE No.

APEMANTUS There will little learning die then that day
  thou art hanged. This is to Lord Timon, this to
  Alcibiades. Go; thou wast born a bastard and thou'lt
  die a bawd.

PAGE Thou wast whelped a dog and thou shalt famish a
  dog's death. Answer not; I am gone.   *Exit.*

86 APEMANTUS E'en so thou outrun'st grace. Fool, I will go
  with you to Lord Timon's.

FOOL Will you leave me there?

APEMANTUS If Timon stay at home – You three serve 89
  three usurers?

ALL SERVANTS Ay. Would they served us!

APEMANTUS So would I – as good a trick as ever hangman served thief.

FOOL Are you three usurers' men?

ALL SERVANTS Ay, fool.

FOOL I think no usurer but has a fool to his servant. My
  mistress is one, and I am her fool. When men come to
  borrow of your masters, they approach sadly and go
  away merry; but they enter my mistress' house merrily
  and go away sadly. The reason of this?

VARRO'S SERVANT I could render one.   101

APEMANTUS Do it then, that we may account thee a
  whoremaster and a knave; which notwithstanding,
  thou shalt be no less esteemed.

VARRO'S SERVANT What is a whoremaster, fool?

FOOL A fool in good clothes, and something like thee. 'Tis
  a spirit; sometime 't appears like a lord, sometime like a
  lawyer, sometime like a philosopher, with two stones 108
  moe than 's artificial one. He is very often like a knight; 109
  and, generally, in all shapes that man goes up and down
  in, from fourscore to thirteen, this spirit walks in.

VARRO'S SERVANT Thou art not altogether a fool.

FOOL Nor thou altogether a wise man. As much foolery
  as I have, so much wit thou lack'st.

APEMANTUS That answer might have become Apemantus.

ALL SERVANTS Aside, aside; here comes Lord Timon.

      Enter Timon and [Flavius, his] Steward.

APEMANTUS Come with me, fool, come.

FOOL I do not always follow lover, elder brother, and 118
  woman; sometime the philosopher.

      [Exeunt Apemantus and Fool.]

STEWARD

  Pray you walk near; I'll speak with you anon.

                          Exeunt [Servants].

TIMON

  You make me marvel wherefore ere this time

  Had you not fully laid my state before me,   122

  That I might so have rated my expense   123

  As I had leave of means.

STEWARD   You would not hear me;

  At many leisures I proposed –

TIMON   Go to!

  Perchance some single vantages you took,   126

  When my indisposition put you back,

  And that unaptness made your minister   128

  Thus to excuse yourself.

STEWARD   O my good lord,

  At many times I brought in my accounts,

  Laid them before you. You would throw them off

  And say you found them in mine honesty.   132

  When for some trifling present you have bid me

  Return so much, I have shook my head and wept;

  Yea, 'gainst th' authority of manners prayed you

  To hold your hand more close. I did endure

  Not seldom, nor no slight checks, when I have   137

  Prompted you in the ebb of your estate   138

  And your great flow of debts. My lovèd lord,

  Though you hear now too late, yet now's a time: 140

  The greatest of your having lacks a half   141

  To pay your present debts.

---

46 *draw near* come this way 56 *hangs . . . back* i.e. equated with you
57-58 *thou'rt . . . yet* you haven't yet been identified with *him* (Isidore's
servant) 59-60 *Poor . . . want* (perhaps misplaced, as this characterization
seems to belong after *yourselves* in l. 65) 67 *Gramercies* many thanks 70
Corinth (where the brothels were) 77 *superscription* address 86 *grace* i.e.
the blessing of being chastised by me 89 *If . . . home* i.e. as long as Timon
is there, a fool will be present 101 *one* (for instance that they are now
poorer – and probably diseased as well) 108 *stones* testicles 109 *artificial
one* i.e. the philosophers' stone 118-19 *lover . . . woman* i.e. people likely,
for one reason or another, to prove generous 122 *state* financial position
123-24 *rated . . . means* adjusted my expenditures to my actual wealth
126 *vantages* opportunities 128-29 *And . . . excuse yourself* and made that
indisposition serve you as an excuse thereafter 132 *found . . . honesty* had
all the information you wanted in knowing me to be honest 137 *seldom*
infrequent (an adjective, modifying *checks*) 138 *in* about 140 *now's a
time* i.e. better late than never 141-42 *The greatest . . . debts* what you own
won't, at best, pay half what you owe

TIMON Let all my land be sold.
STEWARD
143 'Tis all engaged, some forfeited and gone ;
And what remains will hardly stop the mouth
145 Of present dues. The future comes apace ;
146 What shall defend the interim ? and at length
How goes our reck'ning ?
TIMON
148 To Lacedaemon did my land extend.
STEWARD
O my good lord, the world is but a word ;
Were it all yours to give it in a breath,
How quickly were it gone !
TIMON You tell me true.
STEWARD
152 If you suspect my husbandry of falsehood,
Call me before th' exactest auditors
154 And set me on the proof. So the gods bless me,
155 When all our offices have been oppressed
With riotous feeders, when our vaults have wept
157 With drunken spilth of wine, when every room
Hath blazed with lights and brayed with minstrelsy,
159 I have retired me to a wasteful cock
160 And set mine eyes at flow.
TIMON Prithee no more.
STEWARD
Heavens, have I said, the bounty of this lord !
162 How many prodigal bits have slaves and peasants
163 This night englutted ! Who is not Timon's ?
What heart, head, sword, force, means, but is Lord
Timon's ?
Great Timon ; noble, worthy, royal Timon !
Ah, when the means are gone that buy this praise,
The breath is gone whereof this praise is made.
Feast-won, fast-lost : one cloud of winter show'rs,
169 These flies are couched.
TIMON Come, sermon me no further.
No villainous bounty yet hath passed my heart ;
Unwisely, not ignobly, have I given.
172 Why, dost thou weep ? Canst thou the conscience lack
173 To think I shall lack friends ? Secure thy heart ;
If I would broach the vessels of my love
175 And try the argument of hearts by borrowing,
Men and men's fortunes could I frankly use
As I can bid thee speak.
177 STEWARD Assurance bless your thoughts !
TIMON
And in some sort these wants of mine are crowned,
179 That I account them blessings ; for by these
Shall I try friends. You shall perceive how you
Mistake my fortunes ; I am wealthy in my friends.
Within there ! Flaminius ! Servilius !
*Enter three Servants [Flaminius, Servilius, and
another].*
SERVANTS My lord ? My lord ?
TIMON I will dispatch you severally – *[to Servilius]* you to
Lord Lucius ; *[to Flaminius]* to Lord Lucullus you ; I
hunted with his honor to-day ; *[to the other]* you to
Sempronius. Commend me to their loves ; and I am
proud, say, that my occasions have found time to use 'em
189 toward a supply of money. Let the request be fifty
talents.
FLAMINIUS As you have said, my lord. *[Exeunt Servants.]*
STEWARD *[aside]* Lord Lucius and Lucullus ? Humh.

TIMON
Go you, sir, to the senators,
Of whom, even to the state's best health, I have 193
Deserved this hearing. Bid 'em send o' th' instant
A thousand talents to me. 195
STEWARD I have been bold,
For that I knew it the most general way,
To them to use your signet and your name ;
But they do shake their heads, and I am here
No richer in return.
TIMON Is't true ? Can't be ?
STEWARD
They answer in a joint and corporate voice
That now they are at fall, want treasure, cannot 201
Do what they would, are sorry : you are honorable,
But yet they could have wished – they know not –
Something hath been amiss – a noble nature
May catch a wrench – would all were well – 'tis pity – 205
And so, intending other serious matters, 206
After distasteful looks and these hard fractions, 207
With certain half-caps and cold-moving nods 208
They froze me into silence.
TIMON You gods, reward them !
Prithee, man, look cheerily. These old fellows
Have their ingratitude in them hereditary.
Their blood is caked, 'tis cold, it seldom flows ;
'Tis lack of kindly warmth they are not kind ; 213
And nature, as it grows again toward earth, 214
Is fashioned for the journey, dull and heavy.
Go to Ventidius. Prithee be not sad ;
Thou art true and honest ; ingeniously I speak, 217
No blame belongs to thee. Ventidius lately
Buried his father, by whose death he's stepped
Into a great estate. When he was poor,
Imprisoned, and in scarcity of friends,
I cleared him with five talents. Greet him from me.
Bid him suppose some good necessity 223
Touches his friend, which craves to be rememb'red 224
With those five talents. That had, give't these fellows
To whom 'tis instant due. Ne'er speak or think
That Timon's fortunes 'mong his friends can sink.
STEWARD
I would I could not think it. That thought is bounty's foe ; 229
Being free itself, it thinks all others so. *Exeunt.* 230

*

143 *engaged* mortgaged 145 *present dues* immediate obligations 146–47
What . . . reck'ning what shall we meanwhile use to ward off disaster, and
what will our eventual fate be 148 *Lacedaemon* Sparta 152 *husbandry*
household management 154 *set me on* put me to 155 *offices* kitchens,
pantries, etc. 157 *spilth* spilling 159 *wasteful cock* leaky tap (of a wine
barrel) 160 *set . . . flow* wept 162 *prodigal bits* lavish morsels 163 *englutted* swallowed ; *is not* does not profess to be 169 *couched* gone into
hiding 172 *conscience* judgment 173 *Secure* set at ease 175 *try the
argument* test the protestations 177 *Assurance . . . thoughts* may it prove so
179 *That* so that 189–90, 195 *fifty . . . A thousand talents* (large sums
indeed : see I, i, 95n.) 193 *even . . . health* the very soundness of the state's
treasury being due to me 201 *fall* low ebb ; *want treasure* lack funds 205
catch a wrench suffer a reverse 206 *intending* giving their attention to 207
hard fractions callous fragments of sentences 208 *half-caps* grudging
salutations 213 *lack* i.e. from lack ; *kindly* (1) natural, (2) generous 214
grows . . . earth nears the grave 217 *ingeniously* sincerely 223 *good*
genuine 224–25 *craves . . . talents* i.e. asks that Ventidius recall the gift
which restored his freedom – and reciprocate 229–30 *That thought . . . so*
(obscure, metrically odd ; perhaps corrupt) 230 *free* liberal

III,i *Flaminius waiting to speak with a Lord, [Lucullus,] from his Master ; enters a Servant to him.*

SERVANT I have told my lord of you ; he is coming down to you.

FLAMINIUS I thank you, sir.

Enter Lucullus.

SERVANT Here's my lord.

6 LUCULLUS *[aside]* One of Lord Timon's men ? A gift, I warrant. Why, this hits right ; I dreamt of a silver basin 8 and ewer to-night. – Flaminius, honest Flaminius, you are very respectively welcome, sir. Fill me some wine. *[Exit Servant.]* And how does that honorable, complete, freehearted gentleman of Athens, thy very bountiful good lord and master ?

FLAMINIUS His health is well, sir.

LUCULLUS I am right glad that his health is well, sir. And what hast thou there under thy cloak, pretty Flaminius ?

17 FLAMINIUS Faith, nothing but an empty box, sir, which in my lord's behalf I come to entreat your honor to supply ; who, having great and instant occasion to use fifty talents, hath sent to your lordship to furnish him, nothing doubting your present assistance therein.

22 LUCULLUS La, la, la, la ! 'Nothing doubting,' says he ? Alas, good lord ! a noble gentleman 'tis, if he would not keep so good a house. Many a time and often I ha' dined with him and told him on't, and come again to supper to 26 him of purpose to have him spend less ; and yet he would embrace no counsel, take no warning by my coming. Every man has his fault, and honesty is his. I ha' told him on't, but I could ne'er get him from't.

Enter Servant with wine.

SERVANT Please your lordship, here is the wine.

30 LUCULLUS Flaminius, I have noted thee always wise. Here's to thee.

31 FLAMINIUS Your lordship speaks your pleasure.

32 LUCULLUS I have observed thee always for a towardly prompt spirit, give thee thy due, and one that knows what belongs to reason, and canst use the time well if the time use thee well. Good parts in thee ! *[to Servant]* Get you gone, sirrah. *[Exit Servant.]* Draw nearer, honest Flaminius. Thy lord's a bountiful gentleman ; but thou art wise, and thou know'st well enough, although thou com'st to me, that this is no time to lend money, espe-cially upon bare friendship without security. Here's 41 three solidares for thee. Good boy, wink at me and say thou saw'st me not. Fare thee well.

III, i The house of Lucullus 6 *hits right* is just as it should be 8 *re-spectively* particularly 17 *supply* fill 22 *keep . . . house* be so hospitable 26 *honesty* generosity 30 *Here's to thee* (drinking the wine originally meant for Flaminius) 31 *speaks your pleasure* is pleased to say so 32–33 *towardly prompt* friendly and well-disposed 41 *solidares* (of Shakespeare's invention but evidently for coins of no great worth) 43–44 *Is't . . . lived* can we possibly have lived long enough to see the world so much changed 49 *Let . . . damnation* i.e. may you be sent to hell by having melted gold poured down your throat 53 *passion* anger (?), suffering (?) (with religi-ous overtones, as in *my lord's meat* in the next line) ; *slave . . . honor* (a better characterization of Sempronius : see III, iii, 26. Many editors follow Pope in emending 'unto his honor' to 'unto this hour' as more suitable to both sense and metre.) 58 *of nature* i.e. of his body 60 *hour* time of suffering

III, ii A public place in Athens 12, 23, 35 *so many* (probably expressions which the author intended to change later to specific numbers : see Intro-duction) 21–22 *mistook . . . me* made the mistake of sending to me, a man who owed him less 22–23 *denied his occasion* refused him in his need 33 *Has* he has ; *his present occasion* word of his urgent need 37 *fifty – five hundred* (indicating the author's uncertainty as to which number he should use ; see Introduction)

FLAMINIUS

Is't possible the world should so much differ, 43 And we alive that lived ? Fly, damnèd baseness, To him that worships thee !

[Throws the money back.]

LUCULLUS Ha ! Now I see thou art a fool, and fit for thy master. *Exit Lucullus.*

FLAMINIUS

May these add to the number that may scald thee ! Let molten coin be thy damnation, 49 Thou disease of a friend, and not himself ! Has friendship such a faint and milky heart It turns in less than two nights ? O you gods, I feel my master's passion. This slave unto his honor 53 Has my lord's meat in him. Why should it thrive and turn to nutriment When he is turned to poison ? O may diseases only work upon't ; And when he's sick to death, let not that part of nature 58 Which my lord paid for be of any power To expel sickness, but prolong his hour ! *Exit.* 60

*

Enter Lucius with three Strangers. III, ii

LUCIUS Who ? the Lord Timon ? He is my very good friend and an honorable gentleman.

1. STRANGER We know him for no less, though we are but strangers to him. But I can tell you one thing, my lord, and which I hear from common rumors : now Lord Timon's happy hours are done and past, and his estate shrinks from him.

LUCIUS Fie, no, do not believe it ; he cannot want for money.

2. STRANGER But believe you this, my lord, that not long ago one of his men was with the Lord Lucullus to borrow so many talents ; nay, urged extremely for't, 12 and showed what necessity belonged to't, and yet was denied.

LUCIUS How ?

2. STRANGER I tell you denied, my lord.

LUCIUS What a strange case was that ! Now before the gods, I am ashamed on't. Denied that honorable man ? There was very little honor showed in't. For my own part, I must needs confess, I have received some small kindnesses from him, as money, plate, jewels, and such-like trifles – nothing comparing to his ; yet had he mis- 21 took him and sent to me, I should ne'er have denied his 22 occasion so many talents. 23

Enter Servilius.

SERVILIUS See, by good hap, yonder's my lord. I have sweat to see his honor. – My honored lord !

LUCIUS Servilius ? You are kindly met, sir. Fare thee well ; commend me to thy honorable virtuous lord, my very exquisite friend.

SERVILIUS May it please your honor, my lord hath sent –

LUCIUS Ha ! What has he sent ? I am so much endeared to that lord ! He's ever sending. How shall I thank him, think'st thou ? And what has he sent now ?

SERVILIUS Has only sent his present occasion now, my 33 lord, requesting your lordship to supply his instant use with so many talents. 35

LUCIUS

I know his lordship is but merry with me ; He cannot want fifty – five hundred – talents. 37

SERVILIUS
But in the mean time he wants less, my lord.
If his occasion were not virtuous,
I should not urge it half so faithfully.
LUCIUS
Dost thou speak seriously, Servilius?
SERVILIUS
Upon my soul, 'tis true, sir.
LUCIUS What a wicked beast was I to disfurnish myself
44 against such a good time, when I might ha' shown
myself honorable! How unluckily it happ'ned that I
46 should purchase the day before for a little part and undo
a great deal of honor! Servilius, now before the gods, I
am not able to do – the more beast, I say – I was sending
49 to use Lord Timon myself, these gentlemen can witness;
but I would not for the wealth of Athens I had done't
now. Commend me bountifully to his good lordship;
and I hope his honor will conceive the fairest of me,
because I have no power to be kind. And tell him this
from me: I count it one of my greatest afflictions, say,
that I cannot pleasure such an honorable gentleman.
Good Servilius, will you befriend me so far as to use
mine own words to him?
SERVILIUS Yes, sir, I shall.
LUCIUS
59 I'll look you out a good turn, Servilius.   *Exit Servilius.*
True, as you said, Timon is shrunk indeed;
61 And he that's once denied will hardly speed.   *Exit.*
1. STRANGER
Do you observe this, Hostilius?
2. STRANGER   Ay, too well.
1. STRANGER
63 Why, this is the world's soul, and just of the same piece
Is every flatterer's spirit. Who can call him
His friend that dips in the same dish? For in
66 My knowing Timon has been this lord's father
67 And kept his credit with his purse,
Supported his estate. Nay, Timon's money
Has paid his men their wages. He ne'er drinks
But Timon's silver treads upon his lip;
And yet – O, see the monstrousness of man
72 When he looks out in an ungrateful shape! –
73 He does deny him, in respect of his,
What charitable men afford to beggars.
3. STRANGER
Religion groans at it.
1. STRANGER   For mine own part,
76 I never tasted Timon in my life,
Nor came any of his bounties over me
To mark me for his friend; yet I protest,
For his right noble mind, illustrious virtue,
80 And honorable carriage,
Had his necessity made use of me,
82 I would have put my wealth into donation
And the best half should have returned to him,
So much I love his heart. But I perceive
Men must learn now with pity to dispense;
For policy sits above conscience.   *Exeunt.*

Enter a third Servant [of Timon's] with Sempronius, **III,**
another of Timon's Friends.
SEMPRONIUS
Must he needs trouble me in't – hum! – 'bove all others?
He might have tried Lord Lucius or Lucullus;
And now Ventidius is wealthy too,
Whom he redeemed from prison. All these
Owes their estates unto him.
SERVANT   My lord,
They have all been touched and found base metal,   6
For they have all denied him.
SEMPRONIUS   How? Have they denied him? 7
Has Ventidius and Lucullus denied him,
And does he send to me? Three? Humh!   9
It shows but little love or judgment in him.
Must I be his last refuge? His friends, like physicians,
Thrice give him over. Must I take th' cure upon me?
Has much disgraced me in't; I'm angry at him,   13
That might have known my place. I see no sense for't
But his occasions might have wooed me first;
For, in my conscience, I was the first man   16
That e'er received gift from him;
And does he think so backwardly of me now
That I'll requite it last? No.
So it may prove an argument of laughter   20
To th' rest, and I 'mongst lords be thought a fool.
I'd rather than the worth of thrice the sum
Had sent to me first, but for my mind's sake;   23
I'd such a courage to do him good. But now return,   24
And with their faint reply this answer join:
Who bates mine honor shall not know my coin.   *Exit.* 26
SERVANT Excellent! Your lordship's a goodly villain.
The devil knew not what he did when he made man
politic. He crossed himself by't; and I cannot think but 29
in the end the villainies of man will set him clear. How 30
fairly this lord strives to appear foul! takes virtuous
copies to be wicked, like those that under hot ardent
zeal would set whole realms on fire. Of such a nature is
his politic love.
This was my lord's best hope; now all are fled
Save only the gods. Now his friends are dead.
Doors that were ne'er acquainted with their wards   37
Many a bounteous year must be employed
Now to guard sure their master.   39
And this is all a liberal course allows:
Who cannot keep his wealth must keep his house.   *Exit.* 41

---

44 *against . . . time* for dealing with such an opportunity   46–47 *for . . . honor* (probably somewhat corrupt, but Lucius is evidently saying that only his present lack of funds keeps him from treating Timon handsomely)   49 *use* i.e. borrow from   59 *look you out* find a way to do you   61 *speed* prosper   63 *world's soul* essence of this corrupt world   66 *father* sponsor, protector   67 *his . . . his* Lucius' . . . Timon's   72 *looks out in* shows himself as   73–74 *in respect . . . afford* considering his wealth, even the pittance good men give   76 *tasted Timon* i.e. sampled his liberality   80 *carriage* conduct   82 *put . . . donation* treated my wealth as a gift from Timon

III, iii The house of Sempronius   6 *touched* tested (as with a touchstone)   7 *denied* refused   9 *Three* (Lucius as well as Ventidius and Lucullus)   13 *Has* he has   16 *in my conscience* to my knowledge   20 *argument of* subject for   23 *Had* he had   24 *courage* inclination   26 *bates* detracts from   29 *crossed* thwarted (since man thus becomes his superior in evil)   30 *set him clear* make the devil look innocent   37 *wards* locks   39 *guard sure* (lest he be arrested for debt)   41 *keep . . . keep* preserve . . . stay inside

III, iv

Enter [two of] Varro's Men, meeting [Lucius' Servant and] others, all [being servants of] Timon's creditors, to wait for his coming out. Then enter Titus and Hortensius.

1. VARRO'S MAN
Well met; good morrow, Titus and Hortensius.

TITUS
The like to you, kind Varro.

HORTENSIUS   Lucius!
What, do we meet together?

LUCIUS' SERVANT   Ay, and I think
One business does command us all, for mine
Is money.

TITUS
So is theirs and ours.
Enter Philotus.

LUCIUS' SERVANT   And Sir Philotus too!

PHILOTUS
7   Good day at once.

LUCIUS' SERVANT Welcome, good brother.
What do you think the hour?

8 PHILOTUS   Laboring for nine.

LUCIUS' SERVANT
So much?

PHILOTUS Is not my lord seen yet?

LUCIUS' SERVANT   Not yet.

PHILOTUS
I wonder on't; he was wont to shine at seven.

LUCIUS' SERVANT
11   Ay, but the days are waxèd shorter with him.
You must consider that a prodigal course
Is like the sun's,
14   But not, like his, recoverable. I fear
'Tis deepest winter in Lord Timon's purse;
16   That is, one may reach deep enough and yet
Find little.

PHILOTUS I am of your fear for that.

TITUS
I'll show you how t' observe a strange event.
Your lord sends now for money.

HORTENSIUS   Most true, he does.

TITUS
And he wears jewels now of Timon's gift,
21   For which I wait for money.

HORTENSIUS
It is against my heart.

LUCIUS' SERVANT   Mark how strange it shows:
Timon in this should pay more than he owes,
24   And e'en as if your lord should wear rich jewels
And send for money for 'em.

HORTENSIUS
I'm weary of this charge, the gods can witness;

I know my lord hath spent of Timon's wealth,
And now ingratitude makes it worse than stealth.   28

1. VARRO'S MAN
Yes, mine's three thousand crowns; what's yours?

LUCIUS' SERVANT
Five thousand mine.

1. VARRO'S MAN
'Tis much deep; and it should seem by th' sum   31
Your master's confidence was above mine,   32
Else surely his had equalled.   33
Enter Flaminius.

TITUS One of Lord Timon's men.

LUCIUS' SERVANT Flaminius? Sir, a word. Pray, is my
lord ready to come forth?

FLAMINIUS No, indeed he is not.

TITUS We attend his lordship; pray signify so much.

FLAMINIUS I need not tell him that; he knows you are
too diligent.   [Exit.]
Enter [Timon's] Steward, [Flavius,] in a cloak, muffled.

LUCIUS' SERVANT
Ha, is not that his steward muffled so?
He goes away in a cloud. Call him, call him!   42

TITUS Do you hear, sir?

2. VARRO'S MAN By your leave, sir—

STEWARD
What do ye ask of me, my friend?

TITUS
We wait for certain money here, sir.

STEWARD   Ay,
If money were as certain as your waiting,
'Twere sure enough.
Why then preferred you not your sums and bills   49
When your false masters ate of my lord's meat?
Then they could smile, and fawn upon his debts,
And take down th' int'rest into their glutt'nous maws.   52
You do yourselves but wrong to stir me up;
Let me pass quietly.
Believe't, my lord and I have made an end;
I have no more to reckon, he to spend.

LUCIUS' SERVANT
Ay, but this answer will not serve.

STEWARD
If 'twill not serve, 'tis not so base as you,
For you serve knaves.   [Exit.]

1. VARRO'S MAN How? What does his cashiered wor-   60
ship mutter?

2. VARRO'S MAN No matter what; he's poor, and that's
revenge enough. Who can speak broader than he that   63
has no house to put his head in? Such may rail against
great buildings.
Enter Servilius.

TITUS O, here's Servilius; now we shall know some
answer.

SERVILIUS If I might beseech you, gentlemen, to repair   67
some other hour, I should derive much from't. For
take't of my soul, my lord leans wondrously to discontent. His comfortable temper has forsook him; he's
much out of health and keeps his chamber.

LUCIUS' SERVANT
Many do keep their chambers are not sick;
And if it be so far beyond his health,   72
Methinks he should the sooner pay his debts   73
And make a clear way to the gods.
    75

III, iv The house of Timon   7 *at once* to all of you   8 *Laboring for* slowly approaching   11 *waxèd* become (not here, as often, 'grown larger')   14 *recoverable* retraceable (with quibble on idea of financial recovery)   16 *reach deep enough* (as do animals digging deep in the snow for food)   21 *For . . . money* for buying which Timon borrowed the money I now seek from him   24–25 *wear . . . 'em* not only wear the rich jewels given him but also ask for the money that bought them   28 *stealth* theft   31 *much* very   32 *above mine* greater than my master's   33 *his* my master's loan   42 *in a cloud* (1) disguised, (2) gloomily   49 *preferred* presented   52 *th' int'rest* i.e. the food Timon provided was one kind of interest they got on their loans   60 *cashiered* dismissed   63 *broader* more freely (with quibble on idea of being abroad)   67 *repair* come back   72 *are* who are   73 *it be . . . health* his state is so unhealthy   75 *And . . . gods* i.e. and so prepare himself for death

SERVILIUS Good gods!

TITUS
We cannot take this for answer, sir.

FLAMINIUS (within)
Servilius, help! My lord, my lord!
Enter Timon, in a rage.

TIMON
What, are my doors opposed against my passage?
79 Have I been ever free, and must my house
Be my retentive enemy, my jail?
The place which I have feasted, does it now,
Like all mankind, show me an iron heart?

LUCIUS' SERVANT Put in now, Titus.

TITUS My lord, here is my bill.

LUCIUS' SERVANT Here's mine.

HORTENSIUS And mine, my lord.

BOTH VARRO'S MEN And ours, my lord.

PHILOTUS All our bills.

TIMON
89 Knock me down with 'em; cleave me to the girdle!

LUCIUS' SERVANT Alas, my lord –

TIMON Cut my heart in sums!

TITUS Mine, fifty talents.

93 TIMON Tell out my blood!

LUCIUS' SERVANT Five thousand crowns, my lord.

TIMON Five thousand drops pays that. What yours? and
yours?

1. VARRO'S MAN My lord –

2. VARRO'S MAN My lord –

TIMON Tear me, take me, and the gods fall upon you!
Exit.

99 HORTENSIUS Faith, I perceive our masters may throw
their caps at their money. These debts may well be
called desperate ones, for a madman owes 'em. *Exeunt.*
Enter Timon [and Flavius, his Steward].

TIMON They have e'en put my breath from me, the
slaves! Creditors? Devils!

STEWARD My dear lord –

105 TIMON What if it should be so?

STEWARD My lord –

TIMON I'll have it so. My steward!

STEWARD Here, my lord.

TIMON
109 So fitly? Go, bid all my friends again,
Lucius, Lucullus, and Sempronius – all.
I'll once more feast the rascals.

STEWARD O my lord,
You only speak from your distracted soul;
113 There is not so much left to furnish out
A moderate table.

TIMON Be it not in thy care. Go,
I charge thee, invite them all; let in the tide
Of knaves once more; my cook and I'll provide. *Exeunt.*

*

III, v *Enter three Senators at one door, Alcibiades meeting
them, with Attendants.*

1. SENATOR
1 My lord, you have my voice to't; the fault's
Bloody; 'tis necessary he should die.
Nothing emboldens sin so much as mercy.

2. SENATOR
Most true. The law shall bruise him.

ALCIBIADES
Honor, health, and compassion to the senate!

1. SENATOR
Now, Captain?

ALCIBIADES
I am an humble suitor to your virtues;
For pity is the virtue of the law, 8
And none but tyrants use it cruelly.
It pleases time and fortune to lie heavy
Upon a friend of mine, who in hot blood
Hath stepped into the law, which is past depth 12
To those that without heed do plunge into't.
He is a man, setting this fault aside,
Of comely virtues;
Nor did he soil the fact with cowardice 16
(An honor in him which buys out his fault)
But with a noble fury and fair spirit,
Seeing his reputation touched to death, 19
He did oppose his foe;
And with such sober and unnoted passion 21
He did behave his anger, ere 'twas spent, 22
As if he had but proved an argument.

1. SENATOR
You undergo too strict a paradox, 24
Striving to make an ugly deed look fair.
Your words have took such pains as if they labored
To bring manslaughter into form and set 27
Quarrelling upon the head of valor; which indeed 28
Is valor misbegot, and came into the world
When sects and factions were newly born.
He's truly valiant that can wisely suffer
The worst that man can breathe, and make his wrongs
His outsides, to wear them like his raiment, carelessly, 33
And ne'er prefer his injuries to his heart, 34
To bring it into danger.
If wrongs be evils, and enforce us kill, 36
What folly 'tis to hazard life for ill!

ALCIBIADES
My lord –

1. SENATOR You cannot make gross sins look clear. 38
To revenge is no valor, but to bear. 39

ALCIBIADES
My lords, then, under favor, pardon me
If I speak like a captain.
Why do fond men expose themselves to battle 42
And not endure all threats? sleep upon't, 43
And let the foes quietly cut their throats
Without repugnancy? If there be 45
Such valor in the bearing, what make we

79 *free* (1) at liberty, (2) generous   89 *Knock . . . girdle* (since *bills* also meant
weapons which could split a man to his belt)   93 *Tell out* count out drops of
99–100 *throw . . . at* give up hoping for   105 *What . . . so* I wonder if it
would work (Timon has just thought of giving his mock banquet: see
ll. 109–11; also III, vi)   109 *fitly* opportunely   113 *to* as to
III, v The senate house   1 *my voice to't* my vote for it (the death sentence
we are considering)   8 *virtue* chief merit   12 *stepped into* i.e. to some
extent violated; *past depth* overwhelming   16 *soil the fact* blemish his deed
19 *touched to death* fatally threatened   21 *sober and unnoted* serious and
unmarked by excess   22 *behave* govern   24 *undergo . . . paradox* are trying
to maintain too highly strained an argument   27–28 *set . . . head* make
duelling the highest manifestation   28 *which* i.e. *Quarrelling*, fighting duels
33 *His outsides* mere externals, nothing vital to him   34 *prefer* present
36–37 *If . . . ill* (some senators are less lucid than sententious)   38 *clear*
innocent   39 *bear* put up with wrongs   42 *fond* foolish   43 *sleep* why do
they not sleep   45 *repugnancy* resistance

Abroad? Why then, women are more valiant
48 That stay at home, if bearing carry it;
And the ass more captain than the lion; the felon
Loaden with irons wiser than the judge,
If wisdom be in suffering. O my lords,
As you are great, be pitifully good.
Who cannot condemn rashness in cold blood?
54 To kill, I grant, is sin's extremest gust;
55 But in defense, by mercy, 'tis most just.
To be in anger is impiety;
57 But who is man that is not angry?
Weigh but the crime with this.

2. SENATOR
You breathe in vain.

ALCIBIADES   In vain? His service done
At Lacedaemon and Byzantium
Were a sufficient briber for his life.

1. SENATOR
What's that?

ALCIBIADES
Why, I say, my lords, he's done fair service
And slain in fight many of your enemies.
How full of valor did he bear himself
In the last conflict, and made plenteous wounds!

2. SENATOR
He has made too much plenty with 'em.
68 He's a sworn rioter; he has a sin that often
Drowns him and takes his valor prisoner.
70 If there were no more foes, that were enough
To overcome him. In that beastly fury
He has been known to commit outrages
73 And cherish factions. 'Tis inferred to us
His days are foul and his drink dangerous.

1. SENATOR
He dies.

ALCIBIADES Hard fate! He might have died in war.
76 My lords, if not for any parts in him –
77 Though his right arm might purchase his own time,
And be in debt to none – yet, more to move you,
Take my deserts to his and join 'em both;
And, for I know your reverend ages love
81 Security, I'll pawn my victories, all
My honor to you, upon his good returns.
If by this crime he owes the law his life,
84 Why, let the war receive't in valiant gore;
For law is strict, and war is nothing more.

1. SENATOR
We are for law. He dies. Urge it no more,
87 On height of our displeasure. Friend or brother,

He forfeits his own blood that spills another.   88

ALCIBIADES
Must it be so? It must not be. My lords,
I do beseech you know me.

2. SENATOR   How?

ALCIBIADES
Call me to your remembrances.

3. SENATOR   What!

ALCIBIADES
I cannot think but your age has forgot me;
It could not else be I should prove so base,
To sue and be denied such common grace.   94
My wounds ache at you.

1. SENATOR   Do you dare our anger?
'Tis in few words but spacious in effect:
We banish thee for ever.

ALCIBIADES   Banish me?
Banish your dotage, banish usury,
That makes the senate ugly!

1. SENATOR
If after two days' shine Athens contain thee,
Attend our weightier judgment. And, not to swell our 101
spirit,
He shall be executed presently.   *Exeunt [Senators].* 102

ALCIBIADES
Now the gods keep you old enough that you may live 103
Only in bone, that none may look on you!
I'm worse than mad: I have kept back their foes
While they have told their money and let out 106
Their coin upon large interest, I myself
Rich only in large hurts. All those for this?
Is this the balsam that the usuring senate
Pours into captains' wounds? Banishment!
It comes not ill; I hate not to be banished;
It is a cause worthy my spleen and fury,
That I may strike at Athens. I'll cheer up
My discontented troops and lay for hearts.   114
'Tis honor with most lands to be at odds;   115
Soldiers should brook as little wrongs as gods.   *Exit.* 116

*

[Music. Tables set out, Servants attending.] Enter   III, vi
divers Friends [of Timon, being Senators and Lords,]
at several doors.

1. FRIEND The good time of day to you, sir.

2. FRIEND I also wish it to you. I think this honorable
lord did but try us this other day.

1. FRIEND Upon that were my thoughts tiring when we 4
encount'red. I hope it is not so low with him as he made
it seem in the trial of his several friends.

2. FRIEND It should not be, by the persuasion of his new 7
feasting.

1. FRIEND I should think so. He hath sent me an earnest
inviting, which many my near occasions did urge me to 10
put off; but he hath conjured me beyond them, and I 11
must needs appear.

2. FRIEND In like manner was I in debt to my importu- 13
nate business, but he would not hear my excuse. I am
sorry, when he sent to borrow of me, that my provision
was out.

1. FRIEND I am sick of that grief too, as I understand
how all things go.

2. FRIEND Every man here's so. What would he have
borrowed of you?

---

48 *bearing* enduring (with pun on the meaning 'childbearing')   54 *gust*
indulgence   55 *by mercy* if we but take a merciful view of it   57 *not* never
68 *sworn rioter* confirmed debauchee   70 *that* i.e. the sin of drunkenness
73 *cherish factions* foster dissension; *inferred* alleged   76 *parts* good
qualities   77 *his own time* the right to a natural death when his time comes
81 *Security* (1) safety, (2) collateral (hence *pawn* and *good returns*)   84
let . . . gore i.e. let him give it in battle   87 *On height of our* on pain of our
highest   88 *another* i.e. another's blood   94 *To . . . denied* that I should
ask for and be refused   101 *Attend . . . judgment* expect our more severe
sentence; *spirit* anger   102 *presently* immediately   103–04 *live . . . bone*
be mere skeletons   106 *told* counted   114 *lay for hearts* try to win their
loyalty   115 *most lands* (meaning unclear; probably corrupt)   116 *as gods*
as do gods
III, vi The hall of Timon's house   4 *tiring* feeding (a term in falconry)
7 *persuasion* evidence   10 *my near occasions* pressing interests of mine
11 *put off* decline; *conjured . . . them* enticed me away from them   13–14
was . . . business did my own affairs make urgent demands of me

1 . FRIEND A thousand pieces.

2 . FRIEND A thousand pieces!

1 . FRIEND What of you?

2 . FRIEND He sent to me, sir – Here he comes.

Enter Timon and Attendants.

25 TIMON With all my heart, gentlemen both! And how fare you?

1 . FRIEND Ever at the best, hearing well of your lordship.

2 . FRIEND The swallow follows not summer more willing than we your lordship.

TIMON *[aside]* Nor more willingly leaves winter; such summer birds are men. – Gentlemen, our dinner will not recompense this long stay. Feast your ears with the

33 music awhile, if they will fare so harshly o' th' trumpets' sound; we shall to't presently.

35 1 . FRIEND I hope it remains not unkindly with your lordship that I returned you an empty messenger.

TIMON O sir, let it not trouble you.

2 . FRIEND My noble lord –

TIMON Ah, my good friend, what cheer?

2 . FRIEND My most honorable lord, I am e'en sick of shame that when your lordship this other day sent to me

42 I was so unfortunate a beggar.

TIMON Think not on't, sir.

2 . FRIEND If you had sent two hours before –

45 TIMON Let it not cumber your better remembrance. *(The banquet brought in.)* Come, bring in all together.

47 2 . FRIEND All covered dishes!

1 . FRIEND Royal cheer, I warrant you.

3 . FRIEND Doubt not that, if money and the season can yield it.

1 . FRIEND How do you? What's the news?

3 . FRIEND Alcibiades is banished. Hear you of it?

BOTH Alcibiades banished?

3 . FRIEND 'Tis so, be sure of it.

1 . FRIEND How? how?

56 2 . FRIEND I pray you, upon what?

TIMON My worthy friends, will you draw near?

3 . FRIEND I'll tell you more anon. Here's a noble feast

59 toward.

2 . FRIEND This is the old man still.

61 3 . FRIEND Will't hold? Will't hold?

2 . FRIEND It does; but time will – and so –

63 3 . FRIEND I do conceive.

TIMON Each man to his stool, with that spur as he would

65 to the lip of his mistress. Your diet shall be in all places alike; make not a City feast of it, to let the meat cool ere we can agree upon the first place; sit, sit. The gods require our thanks.

You great benefactors, sprinkle our society with thankfulness. For your own gifts make yourselves

71 praised; but reserve still to give, lest your deities be despised. Lend to each man enough, that one need not lend to another; for were your godheads to borrow of men, men would forsake the gods. Make the meat beloved more than the man that gives it. Let no assembly of twenty be without a score of villains. If there is twelve women at the table, let a dozen of them be – as they are. The rest of your foes, O gods – the senators of Athens,

79 together with the common lag of people – what is amiss

80 in them, you gods, make suitable for destruction. For these my present friends, as they are to me nothing, so in nothing bless them, and to nothing are they welcome.

Uncover, dogs, and lap.

[The dishes are uncovered, and seen to be full of warm water and stones.]

SOME SPEAK What does his lordship mean?

SOME OTHER I know not.

TIMON

May you a better feast never behold,

You knot of mouth-friends! Smoke and lukewarm water 86

Is your perfection. This is Timon's last; 87

Who, stuck and spangled with your flatteries,

Washes it off and sprinkles in your faces

[Throws the water in their faces.]

Your reeking villainy. Live loathed and long,

Most smiling, smooth, detested parasites,

Courteous destroyers, affable wolves, meek bears,

You fools of fortune, trencher-friends, time's flies, 93

Cap-and-knee slaves, vapors, and minute-jacks! 94

Of man and beast the infinite malady 95

Crust you quite o'er! What, dost thou go?

Soft, take thy physic first; thou too, and thou! 97

Stay, I will lend thee money, borrow none.

[Throws stones and drives them out.]

What, all in motion? Henceforth be no feast

Whereat a villain's not a welcome guest.

Burn house! Sink Athens! Henceforth hated be

Of Timon man and all humanity! *Exit.*

Enter [the Friends –] the Senators with other Lords [, returning].

1 . FRIEND How now, my lords?

2 . FRIEND Know you the quality of Lord Timon's fury?

3 . FRIEND Push! Did you see my cap? 105

4 . FRIEND I have lost my gown.

1 . FRIEND He's but a mad lord and naught but humors 107 sways him. He gave me a jewel th' other day, and now he has beat it out of my hat. Did you see my jewel?

3 . FRIEND Did you see my cap?

2 . FRIEND Here 'tis.

4 . FRIEND Here lies my gown.

1 . FRIEND Let's make no stay.

2 . FRIEND
Lord Timon 's mad.

3 . FRIEND I feel't upon my bones.

4 . FRIEND
One day he gives us diamonds, next day stones. *Exeunt.*

*

Enter Timon. IV,

TIMON

Let me look back upon thee. O thou wall

That girdles in those wolves, dive in the earth

---

25 *With . . . heart* my cordial greetings 33 *so harshly o'* on such rough fare as 35–36 *it remains . . . messenger* you don't harbor unkind thoughts toward me because I sent your man back without any money 42 *so . . . beggar* so unlucky as to be out of funds 45 *cumber . . . remembrance* trouble you 47 *covered* (implying especially good food) 56 *upon what* why 59 *toward* in prospect 61 *hold* last 63 *conceive* get your idea 65–67 *Your . . . place* i.e. let's be informal and not waste time arguing about who is entitled by rank to sit where, as at an official state dinner 71 *reserve still* always keep something more 79 *lag* dregs 80 *For* as for 86 *Smoke* steam ('hot air') 87 *Is your perfection* suits you best 93 *time's flies* fair-weather insects 94 *vapors* creatures without substance; *minute-jacks* time-servers 95–96 *the infinite . . . o'er* every possible disease cover you wholly with scabs 97 *physic* medicine 105 *Push* tush 107 *humors* caprice

IV, i Outside the walls of Athens

And fence not Athens! Matrons, turn incontinent!
Obedience fail in children! Slaves and fools,
Pluck the grave wrinkled senate from the bench

6 And minister in their steads! To general filths
Convert o' th' instant, green virginity!
Do't in your parents' eyes! Bankrupts, hold fast;
Rather than render back, out with your knives
And cut your trusters' throats! Bound servants, steal:

11 Large-handed robbers your grave masters are
12 And pill by law. Maid, to thy master's bed:
Thy mistress is o' th' brothel. Son of sixteen,

14 Pluck the lined crutch from thy old limping sire;
With it beat out his brains! Piety and fear,

16 Religion to the gods, peace, justice, truth,
17 Domestic awe, night-rest and neighborhood,
18 Instruction, manners, mysteries and trades,
19 Degrees, observances, customs and laws,
20 Decline to your confounding contraries,
And yet confusion live! Plagues incident to men,
Your potent and infectious fevers heap
On Athens, ripe for stroke! Thou cold sciatica,

24 Cripple our senators, that their limbs may halt
25 As lamely as their manners! Lust and liberty
Creep in the minds and marrows of our youth,
That 'gainst the stream of virtue they may strive

28 And drown themselves in riot! Itches, blains,
Sow all th' Athenian bosoms, and their crop
Be general leprosy! Breath infect breath,
That their society, as their friendship, may

32 Be merely poison! Nothing I'll bear from thee
But nakedness, thou detestable town;

34 Take thou that too, with multiplying bans!
Timon will to the woods, where he shall find
Th' unkindest beast more kinder than mankind.
The gods confound – hear me, you good gods all –
Th' Athenians both within and out that wall;
And grant, as Timon grows, his hate may grow
To the whole race of mankind, high and low!
Amen.   *Exit.*

*

V, ii   *Enter [Flavius the] Steward with two or three*
        Servants.

I . SERVANT
Hear you, Master Steward, where's our master?
Are we undone? cast off? nothing remaining?

STEWARD
Alack, my fellows, what should I say to you?

---

6 *general filths* common whores   11 *Large-handed* i.e. sticky-fingered
12 *pill* rob   14 *lined* padded   16 *Religion to* veneration of   17 *Domestic
awe* respect for parents; *neighborhood* neighborliness   18 *mysteries* crafts
19 *Degrees* ranks   20–21 *Decline . . . live* degenerate into chaos, and may
confusion then persist   24 *halt* limp   25 *liberty* license   28 *blains* blisters
32 *merely* pure   34 *that too* (another article of clothing); *bans* curses
IV, ii The house of Timon   7 *his fortune* i.e. him, in his misfortune   9
From . . . grave from the grave of a newly buried friend   13 *dedicated
. . . air* beggar who has pledged himself to the open air   15 *like contempt*
as if he were contempt itself   20 *dying* i.e. sinking   21–22 *part . . . air*
depart into this expanse of nothingness, death   23 *The latest* what remains
28 *put out all* all of you put out   35 *what state compounds* that splendor
consists of   36 *But only* nothing more than   38 *blood* nature   40 *again*
hereafter   42 *to be* only to be   46–47 *to Supply* what is needed to sustain
47 *that . . . it* i.e. money
IV, iii Before Timon's cave in a wood by the sea   2 *thy sister's* the
moon's

Let me be recorded by the righteous gods,
I am as poor as you.

I . SERVANT   Such a house broke?
So noble a master fall'n; all gone, and not
One friend to take his fortune by the arm   7
And go along with him?

2 . SERVANT   As we do turn our backs
From our companion thrown into his grave,   9
So his familiars to his buried fortunes
Slink all away; leave their false vows with him,
Like empty purses picked; and his poor self,
A dedicated beggar to the air,   13
With his disease of all-shunned poverty,
Walks, like contempt, alone. More of our fellows.   15
     Enter other Servants.

STEWARD
All broken implements of a ruined house.

3 . SERVANT
Yet do our hearts wear Timon's livery;
That see I by our faces. We are fellows still,
Serving alike in sorrow. Leaked is our bark;
And we, poor mates, stand on the dying deck,   20
Hearing the surges threat. We must all part   21
Into this sea of air.

STEWARD   Good fellows all,
The latest of my wealth I'll share amongst you.   23
Wherever we shall meet, for Timon's sake
Let's yet be fellows; let's shake our heads and say,
As 'twere a knell unto our master's fortunes,
'We have seen better days.' Let each take some.
     [Gives money.]
Nay, put out all your hands. Not one word more;   28
Thus part we rich in sorrow, parting poor.
     Embrace, and part several ways.
O the fierce wretchedness that glory brings us!
Who would not wish to be from wealth exempt,
Since riches point to misery and contempt?
Who would be so mocked with glory, or to live
But in a dream of friendship,
To have his pomp and all what state compounds   35
But only painted, like his varnished friends?   36
Poor honest lord, brought low by his own heart,
Undone by goodness! Strange, unusual blood,   38
When man's worst sin is he does too much good!
Who then dares to be half so kind again?   40
For bounty, that makes gods, does still mar men.
My dearest lord, blest to be most accurst,   42
Rich only to be wretched, thy great fortunes
Are made thy chief afflictions. Alas, kind lord,
He's flung in rage from this ingrateful seat
Of monstrous friends; nor has he with him to   46
Supply his life, or that which can command it.   47
I'll follow and inquire him out.
I'll ever serve his mind with my best will;
Whilst I have gold, I'll be his steward still.   *Exit.*

*

     Enter Timon in the woods.   IV, iii
TIMON
O blessed breeding sun, draw from the earth
Rotten humidity; below thy sister's orb   2
Infect the air! Twinned brothers of one womb –
Whose procreation, residence, and birth

5   Scarce is dividant – touch them with several fortunes,
6   The greater scorns the lesser. Not nature,
    To whom all sores lay siege, can bear great fortune
8   But by contempt of nature.
9   Raise me this beggar and deny't that lord ;
10   The senator shall bear contempt hereditary,
    The beggar native honor.
12   It is the pasture lards the wether's sides,
    The want that makes him lean. Who dares, who dares
    In purity of manhood stand upright
    And say 'This man 's a flatterer' ? If one be,
16   So are they all ; for every grise of fortune
    Is smoothed by that below. The learnèd pate
18   Ducks to the golden fool. All's obliquy ;
19   There's nothing level in our cursèd natures
    But direct villainy. Therefore be abhorred
    All feasts, societies, and throngs of men.
22   His semblable, yea himself, Timon disdains.
23   Destruction fang mankind ! Earth, yield me roots ;
    [Digs.]
    Who seeks for better of thee, sauce his palate
25   With thy most operant poison. What is here ?
    Gold ? Yellow, glittering, precious gold !
27   No, gods, I am no idle votarist :
28   Roots, you clear heavens ! Thus much of this will make
    Black white, foul fair, wrong right,
    Base noble, old young, coward valiant.
    Ha, you gods, why this ? What this, you gods ? Why, this
    Will lug your priests and servants from your sides,
    Pluck sick men's pillows from below their heads.
    This yellow slave
    Will knit and break religions, bless th' accursed,
36   Make the hoar leprosy adored, place thieves
37   And give them title, knee, and approbation
    With senators on the bench. This is it
39   That makes the wappened widow wed again ;
40   She whom the spital-house and ulcerous sores
    Would cast the gorge at, this embalms and spices
42   To th' April day again. Come, damnèd earth,
43   Thou common whore of mankind, that puts odds
    Among the rout of nations, I will make thee
45   Do thy right nature.
    March afar off. Ha ! a drum ? Thou'rt quick ;
46   But yet I'll bury thee. Thou'lt go, strong thief,
    When gouty keepers of thee cannot stand.
48   Nay, stay thou out for earnest.
    [Keeps some gold.]
    Enter Alcibiades, with Drum and Fife, in warlike
    manner ; and Phrynia and Timandra.
ALCIBIADES   What art thou there ?
Speak.
TIMON
50   A beast, as thou art. The canker gnaw thy heart
    For showing me again the eyes of man !
ALCIBIADES
    What is thy name ? Is man so hateful to thee
    That art thyself a man ?
TIMON
    I am Misanthropos and hate mankind.
    For thy part, I do wish thou wert a dog,
56   That I might love thee something.
ALCIBIADES   I know thee well,
57   But in thy fortunes am unlearned and strange.

TIMON
    I know thee too ; and more than that I know thee
    I not desire to know. Follow thy drum ;
    With man's blood paint the ground, gules, gules !   60
    Religious canons, civil laws are cruel ;
    Then what should war be ? This fell whore of thine   62
    Hath in her more destruction than thy sword
    For all her cherubin look.   64
PHRYNIA   Thy lips rot off !
TIMON
    I will not kiss thee ; then the rot returns
    To thine own lips again.
ALCIBIADES
    How came the noble Timon to this change ?
TIMON
    As the moon does, by wanting light to give.   68
    But then renew I could not, like the moon ;
    There were no suns to borrow of.
ALCIBIADES   Noble Timon,
    What friendship may I do thee ?
TIMON   None, but to
    Maintain my opinion.
ALCIBIADES   What is it, Timon ?
TIMON Promise me friendship, but perform none. If thou   73
    wilt not promise, the gods plague thee, for thou art a
    man ! if thou dost perform, confound thee, for thou art
    a man !
ALCIBIADES
    I have heard in some sort of thy miseries.   77
TIMON
    Thou saw'st them when I had prosperity.
ALCIBIADES
    I see them now ; then was a blessèd time.
TIMON
    As thine is now, held with a brace of harlots.
TIMANDRA
    Is this th' Athenian minion whom the world   81
    Voiced so regardfully ?   82
TIMON   Art thou Timandra ?
TIMANDRA Yes.
TIMON
    Be a whore still. They love thee not that use thee ;
    Give them diseases, leaving with thee their lust.
    Make use of thy salt hours. Season the slaves   86

---

5 *dividant* divisible   6 *The* so that the   6–7 *Not nature . . . can* human nature . . . cannot   8 *nature* natural ties   9 *deny't* withhold such elevation from   10–11 *The senator . . . honor* i.e. let each be treated as if born to what he now merits   12 *lards . . . sides* fattens the sheep   16–17 *every . . . below* each rank is flattered by the next lower one   18 *golden* rich ; *obliquy* indirectness   19 *level* straightforward   22 *His semblable* anything like him 23 *fang* seize   25 *operant* potent   27 *idle votarist* insincere worshipper (I meant it when I asked for roots)   28 *clear* pure   36 *hoar* white (as lepers' skins are) ; *place* give high office to   37 *knee* deference (shown by kneeling to)   39 *wappened* worn out   40–41 *whom . . . gorge at* at the mere sight of whom hospital patients with running sores would vomit   42 *damnèd earth* i.e. gold   43–44 *puts odds Among* sets at each other's throats   45 *thy right nature* your proper work (of corrupting mankind) ; *quick* (1) swift, (2) alive (hence unburied)   46 *go* walk   48 *for earnest* as a token   50 *canker* cancerous disease   56 *something* a little   57 *unlearned and strange* uninformed and ignorant (but cf. ll. 77, 93–96)   60 *gules* red (in heraldry) 62 *fell* deadly   64 *cherubin* angelic   68 *wanting* lacking   73–76 *If . . . man* if you are a man you deserve damnation even if you do not make false promises, and also even if you do what you promise to   77 *in some sort* a little (though even with this qualification the speech seems inconsistent with the statement in l. 57 ; see also ll. 93–96)   81 *minion* darling   82 *Voiced* spoke of   86 *salt* lustful

87   For tubs and baths ; bring down rose-cheekèd youth
    To the tub-fast and the diet.

TIMANDRA   Hang thee, monster !

ALCIBIADES
    Pardon him, sweet Timandra ; for his wits
    Are drowned and lost in his calamities.
    I have but little gold of late, brave Timon,
    The want whereof doth daily make revolt
93   In my penurious band. I have heard, and grieved,
    How cursèd Athens, mindless of thy worth,
    Forgetting thy great deeds when neighbor states,
    But for thy sword and fortune, trod upon them –

TIMON
    I prithee beat thy drum and get thee gone.

ALCIBIADES
    I am thy friend and pity thee, dear Timon.

TIMON
    How dost thou pity him whom thou dost trouble ?
    I had rather be alone.

ALCIBIADES   Why, fare thee well.
    Here is some gold for thee.

TIMON   Keep it ; I cannot eat it.

ALCIBIADES
102   When I have laid proud Athens on a heap –

TIMON
    Warr'st thou 'gainst Athens ?

ALCIBIADES   Ay, Timon, and have cause.

TIMON
    The gods confound them all in thy conquest,
    And thee after, when thou hast conquerèd !

ALCIBIADES
    Why me, Timon ?

TIMON   That by killing of villains
    Thou wast born to conquer my country.
    Put up thy gold. Go on. Here's gold. Go on.
109   Be as a planetary plague when Jove
    Will o'er some high-viced city hang his poison
    In the sick air. Let not thy sword skip one.
    Pity not honored age for his white beard ;
113   He is an usurer. Strike me the counterfeit matron ;
114   It is her habit only that is honest,
    Herself 's a bawd. Let not the virgin's cheek

Make soft thy trenchant sword ; for those milk paps   116
That through the window-bars bore at men's eyes   117
Are not within the leaf of pity writ,   118
But set them down horrible traitors. Spare not the babe
Whose dimpled smiles from fools exhaust their mercy ;
Think it a bastard whom the oracle
Hath doubtfully pronounced thy throat shall cut,   122
And mince it sans remorse. Swear against objects ;   123
Put armor on thine ears and on thine eyes,
Whose proof nor yells of mothers, maids, nor babes,   125
Nor sight of priests in holy vestments bleeding,
Shall pierce a jot. There's gold to pay thy soldiers ;
Make large confusion ; and, thy fury spent,   128
Confounded be thyself ! Speak not ; be gone.

ALCIBIADES
Hast thou gold yet ? I'll take the gold thou givest me,
Not all thy counsel.

TIMON
Dost thou, or dost thou not, heaven's curse upon thee !

BOTH [WOMEN]
Give us some gold, good Timon. Hast thou more ?

TIMON
Enough to make a whore forswear her trade,
And, to make whores, a bawd. Hold up, you sluts,   135
Your aprons mountant. You are not oathable,   136
Although I know you'll swear, terribly swear,   137
Into strong shudders and to heavenly agues,
Th' immortal gods that hear you. Spare your oaths ;
I'll trust to your conditions. Be whores still ;   140
And he whose pious breath seeks to convert you –
Be strong in whore, allure him, burn him up,
Let your close fire predominate his smoke,   143
And be no turncoats. Yet may your pains six months   144
Be quite contrary ! And thatch your poor thin roofs   145
With burdens of the dead – some that were hanged,
No matter ; wear them, betray with them. Whore still ;
Paint till a horse may mire upon your face.   148
A pox of wrinkles !

BOTH   Well, more gold ! What then ?
Believe 't that we'll do anything for gold.

TIMON
Consumption sow
In hollow bones of man ; strike their sharp shins,
And mar men's spurring. Crack the lawyer's voice,
That he may never more false title plead
Nor sound his quillets shrilly. Hoar the flamen,   155
That scolds against the quality of flesh   156
And not believes himself. Down with the nose –   157
Down with it flat ; take the bridge quite away –
Of him that, his particular to foresee,   159
Smells from the general weal. Make curled-pate
    ruffians bald,
And let the unscarred braggarts of the war
Derive some pain from you. Plague all,
That your activity may defeat and quell   163
The source of all erection. There's more gold.   164
Do you damn others and let this damn you,
And ditches grave you all !   166

BOTH
More counsel with more money, bounteous Timon.

TIMON
More whore, more mischief first ; I have given you
    earnest.   168

---

87 *tubs and baths* (used to treat venereal disease ; cf. in l. 88 *tub-fast*, abstinence during the treatment)   93 *penurious* poverty-stricken   102 *on a heap* in ruins   109 *planetary* (the plagues London suffered were often attributed to the baleful influence of planets 'in opposition')   113 *counterfeit matron* woman pretending married respectability   114 *habit* garb ; *honest* chaste   116 *trenchant* sharp   117 *window-bars* latticework of the bodice (?)   118 *Are . . . writ* have nothing to do with pity   122 *doubtfully* ambiguously ; *thy . . . cut* shall cut thy throat   123 *mince* chop it to bits ; *objects* things that evoke pity   125 *proof* tested strength (the armor's)   128 *large confusion* wholesale ruin   135 *to . . . bawd* to make a bawd give over making whores   136 *mountant* i.e. in such a way as to hold what I am about to give you (with a bawdy quibble on heraldic jargon ; cf. *erection* in l. 164) ; *oathable* believable though on oath   137 *swear* (to do what I shall ask)   140 *your conditions* what you are   143 *Let . . . smoke* let the hidden flames of desire overcome his pious 'hot air' (cf. III, vi, 86)   144–45 *Yet . . . contrary* (obscure and commonly supposed corrupt ; is painful miscarriage being spoken of ?)   145–46 *thatch . . . dead* cover your baldness with hair taken from corpses   148 *mire upon* bog down in   155 *quillets* quibbles ; *Hoar the flamen* whiten (with leprosy) the priest   156 *the . . . flesh* fleshly desire   157–59 *Down . . . Of* i.e. let syphilis afflict   159–60 *his . . . weal* in hunting after private gain loses scent of the common good   163 *quell* destroy   164 *erection* advancement (with an obvious bawdy pun)   166 *grave* entomb   168 *earnest* a token payment

ALCIBIADES
Strike up the drum towards Athens! Farewell, Timon;
If I thrive well, I'll visit thee again.

TIMON
171   If I hope well, I'll never see thee more.

ALCIBIADES
I never did thee harm.

TIMON
Yes, thou spok'st well of me.

ALCIBIADES   Call'st thou that harm?

TIMON
174   Men daily find it. Get thee away and take
Thy beagles with thee.

ALCIBIADES   We but offend him. Strike!
[Drum beats.] Exeunt [all but Timon].

TIMON
That nature, being sick of man's unkindness,
Should yet be hungry! Common mother, thou
[Digs.]
Whose womb unmeasurable and infinite breast
179   Teems and feeds all; whose selfsame mettle
Whereof thy proud child, arrogant man, is puffed
Engenders the black toad and adder blue,
The gilded newt and eyeless venomed worm,
With all th' abhorrèd births below crisp heaven
184   Whereon Hyperion's quick'ning fire doth shine –
Yield him who all thy human sons doth hate,
From forth thy plenteous bosom, one poor root!
187   Ensear thy fertile and conceptious womb;
Let it no more bring out ingrateful man!
189   Go great with tigers, dragons, wolves, and bears;
190   Teem with new monsters whom thy upward face
Hath to the marbled mansion all above
Never presented! – O, a root! Dear thanks! –
Dry up thy marrows, vines, and plough-torn leas,
194   Whereof ingrateful man with liquorish drafts
195   And morsels unctuous greases his pure mind,
196   That from it all consideration slips –
Enter Apemantus.
More man? Plague, plague!

APEMANTUS
I was directed hither. Men report
199   Thou dost affect my manners and dost use them.

TIMON
'Tis then because thou dost not keep a dog,
Whom I would imitate. Consumption catch thee!

APEMANTUS
This is in thee a nature but infected,
A poor unmanly melancholy sprung
From change of fortune. Why this spade? this place?
205   This slave-like habit and these looks of care?
Thy flatterers yet wear silk, drink wine, lie soft,
207   Hug their diseased perfumes, and have forgot
That ever Timon was. Shame not these woods
209   By putting on the cunning of a carper.
Be thou a flatterer now and seek to thrive
By that which has undone thee; hinge thy knee
212   And let his very breath whom thou'lt observe
Blow off thy cap; praise his most vicious strain
And call it excellent. Thou wast told thus;
Thou gav'st thine ears, like tapsters that bade welcome,
To knaves and all approachers. 'Tis most just
That thou turn rascal; hadst thou wealth again,
Rascals should have't. Do not assume my likeness.

TIMON
Were I like thee, I'd throw away myself.

APEMANTUS
Thou hast cast away thyself, being like thyself;
A madman so long, now a fool. What, think'st
That the bleak air, thy boisterous chamberlain,   222
Will put thy shirt on warm? Will these mossed trees,
That have outlived the eagle, page thy heels   224
And skip when thou point'st out? Will the cold brook,
Candied with ice, caudle thy morning taste   226
To cure thy o'er-night's surfeit? Call the creatures   227
Whose naked natures live in all the spite   228
Of wreakful heaven, whose bare unhousèd trunks,   229
To the conflicting elements exposed,
Answer mere nature; bid them flatter thee.   231
O, thou shalt find –

TIMON   A fool of thee. Depart.   232

APEMANTUS
I love thee better now than e'er I did.

TIMON
I hate thee worse.

APEMANTUS   Why?

TIMON   Thou flatter'st misery.

APEMANTUS
I flatter not, but say thou art a caitiff.

TIMON
Why dost thou seek me out?

APEMANTUS   To vex thee.

TIMON
Always a villain's office or a fool's.
Dost please thyself in't?

APEMANTUS   Ay.

TIMON   What, a knave too?   238

APEMANTUS
If thou didst put this sour cold habit on   239
To castigate thy pride, 'twere well; but thou
Dost it enforcedly. Thou'dst courtier be again
Wert thou not beggar. Willing misery
Outlives incertain pomp, is crowned before;   243
The one is filling still, never complete,   244
The other at high wish; best state, contentless,   245
Hath a distracted and most wretched being,
Worse than the worst, content.   247
Thou shouldst desire to die, being miserable.   248

TIMON
Not by his breath that is more miserable.   249

171 *If . . . well* if my hopes are realized **174** *find it* learn that it is **179** *Teems* prolifically brings forth; *mettle* essence **184** *Hyperion's quick'ning* the sun's life-giving **187** *Ensear* dry up **189** *Go great* be pregnant **190–92** *whom . . . presented* i.e. hitherto unknown **194** *liquorish* appetizing **195** *greases* (1) oils, (2) makes lewd **196** *consideration* ability to think **199** *affect* assume **205** *habit* garb (cf. IV, i, 32–34) **207** *diseased perfumes* perfumed but diseased mistresses **209** *putting on . . . carper* pretending to a cynic's art **212** *observe* court **222–23** *chamberlain . . . warm* valet will warm your shirt before you put it on **224** *eagle* (proverbially long-lived) **224–25** *page . . . out* serve you as a page and jump to do your bidding **226** *Candied* crusted over; *caudle . . . taste* warm your breakfast drink **227** *o'er-night's surfeit* last night's overindulgence **227–31** *creatures . . . nature* (cf. *Lear* III, iv, 28–36, 96–103) **228** *live in* a continually exposed to **229** *wreakful* vengeful **231** *Answer mere nature* must cope with nature in its crudest form **232** *of* in **238** *too* i.e. as well as a fool (see l. 237) **239** *put . . . habit on* adopt . . . manner of living **243** *is crowned before* achieves glory sooner **244** *still* always **245** *at high wish* just as desired; *best state, contentless* pomp, which does not bring content **247** *the worst, content* misery, if it is accepted contentedly **248** *miserable* discontented **249** *Not . . . miserable* i.e. not when you are the one recommending this desire

Thou art a slave whom Fortune's tender arm
251 With favor never clasped, but bred a dog.
252 Hadst thou, like us from our first swath, proceeded
The sweet degrees that this brief world affords
254 To such as may the passive drugs of it
Freely command, thou wouldst have plunged thyself
In general riot, melted down thy youth
In different beds of lust, and never learned
The icy precepts of respect, but followed
The sug'red game before thee. But myself,
Who had the world as my confectionary,
The mouths, the tongues, the eyes, and hearts of men
262 At duty, more than I could frame employment;
That numberless upon me stuck, as leaves
264 Do on the oak, have, with one winter's brush,
265 Fell from their boughs and left me open, bare
266 For every storm that blows – I to bear this,
That never knew but better, is some burden.
268 Thy nature did commence in sufferance; time
Hath made thee hard in't. Why shouldst thou hate men?
They never flattered thee. What hast thou given?
If thou wilt curse, thy father, that poor rag,
Must be thy subject, who in spite put stuff
To some she-beggar and compounded thee
Poor rogue hereditary. Hence; be gone!
If thou hadst not been born the worst of men,
Thou hadst been a knave and flatterer.

APEMANTUS   Art thou proud yet?
TIMON
  Ay, that I am not thee.
APEMANTUS   I, that I was
No prodigal.
TIMON   I, that I am one now.
Were all the wealth I have shut up in thee,
280 I'd give thee leave to hang it. Get thee gone.
That the whole life of Athens were in this!
Thus would I eat it.
    [Gnaws a root.]
282 APEMANTUS   Here! I will mend thy feast.
    [Offers him food.]
TIMON
  First mend my company; take away thyself.
APEMANTUS
  So I shall mend mine own, by th' lack of thine.
TIMON
285 'Tis not well mended so; it is but botched.
286 If not, I would it were.
APEMANTUS
  What wouldst thou have to Athens?
TIMON
  Thee thither in a whirlwind. If thou wilt,

Tell them there I have gold. Look, so I have.
APEMANTUS
  Here is no use for gold.
TIMON   The best and truest;
For here it sleeps, and does no hirèd harm.
APEMANTUS
  Where liest a-nights, Timon?
TIMON   Under that's above me. 292
Where feed'st thou a-days, Apemantus?
APEMANTUS Where my stomach finds meat; or rather,
  where I eat it.
TIMON
  Would poison were obedient and knew my mind!
APEMANTUS
  Where wouldst thou send it?
TIMON
  To sauce thy dishes.
APEMANTUS The middle of humanity thou never knew-
  est, but the extremity of both ends. When thou wast in
  thy gilt and thy perfume, they mocked thee for too much
  curiosity; in thy rags thou know'st none, but art de- 302
  spised for the contrary. There's a medlar for thee; eat it. 303
TIMON On what I hate I feed not.
APEMANTUS Dost hate a medlar?
TIMON
  Ay, though it look like thee. 306
APEMANTUS An thou'dst hated meddlers sooner, thou 307
  shouldst have loved thyself better now. What man didst
  thou ever know unthrift that was beloved after his 309
  means?
TIMON Who, without those means thou talk'st of, didst
  thou ever know beloved?
APEMANTUS Myself.
TIMON I understand thee. Thou hadst some means to
  keep a dog.
APEMANTUS What things in the world canst thou nearest
  compare to thy flatterers?
TIMON Women nearest; but men – men are the things
  themselves. What wouldst thou do with the world,
  Apemantus, if it lay in thy power? 320
APEMANTUS Give it the beasts, to be rid of the men.
TIMON Wouldst thou have thyself fall in the confusion of
  men, and remain a beast with the beasts?
APEMANTUS Ay, Timon.
TIMON A beastly ambition, which the gods grant thee
  t' attain to! If thou wert the lion, the fox would beguile
  thee; if thou wert the lamb, the fox would eat thee; if
  thou wert the fox, the lion would suspect thee when
  peradventure thou wert accused by the ass; if thou wert
  the ass, thy dullness would torment thee, and still thou
  livedst but as a breakfast to the wolf. If thou wert the 331
  wolf, thy greediness would afflict thee, and oft thou
  shouldst hazard thy life for thy dinner. Wert thou the
  unicorn, pride and wrath would confound thee and 334
  make thine own self the conquest of thy fury; wert thou
  a bear, thou wouldst be killed by the horse; wert thou a
  horse, thou wouldst be seized by the leopard; wert thou
  a leopard, thou wert germane to the lion, and the spots 338
  of thy kindred were jurors on thy life: all thy safety were
  remotion and thy defense absence. What beast couldst 340
  thou be that were not subject to a beast? And what a
  beast art thou already, that seest not thy loss in trans- 342
  formation!
APEMANTUS If thou couldst please me with speaking to

---

251 *bred a dog* have been a dog from birth   252 *swath* swaddling clothes
254 *drugs* drudges, servants   262 *At duty* serving me; *frame* provide with
264 *have* and that have; *winter's brush* onslaught of winter   265 *Fell*
fallen   266 *I* for me   268 *sufferance* suffering   280 *it* i.e. yourself   282
mend improve the quality of   285 *botched* badly patched (since you are
still in your own company)   286 *If not* i.e. if not mended to this extent,
by your leaving   292 *that's* what's   302 *curiosity* fastidiousness   303
medlar small apple, eaten when decayed (often used, as here, in quibbles
on *meddlers* in others' affairs)   306 *like thee* i.e. well decayed   307 *An* if
309 *unthrift* (to be a) spendthrift; *after* in accordance with (?), after the
dissipation of (?)   331 *livedst* would live   334 *unicorn* (supposed captured
by goading it to drive its horn deeply into a tree trunk)   338 *germane* akin
338–39 *spots . . . life* sins that are yours only 'by association' would condemn
you to death   340 *remotion* going elsewhere   342–43 *thy . . . transformation*
what you would lose by the change

me, thou mightst have hit upon it here. The commonwealth of Athens is become a forest of beasts.

TIMON How has the ass broke the wall, that thou art out
of the city?

349 APEMANTUS Yonder comes a poet and a painter. The
plague of company light upon thee! I will fear to catch
it, and give way. When I know not what else to do, I'll
see thee again.

TIMON When there is nothing living but thee, thou shalt
be welcome. I had rather be a beggar's dog than
Apemantus.

APEMANTUS

355 Thou art the cap of all the fools alive.

TIMON

Would thou wert clean enough to spit upon!

APEMANTUS

A plague on thee! thou art too bad to curse.

TIMON

358 All villains that do stand, by thee, are pure.

APEMANTUS

There is no leprosy but what thou speak'st.

TIMON

If I name thee.

361 I'll beat thee, but I should infect my hands.

APEMANTUS

I would my tongue could rot them off!

TIMON

Away, thou issue of a mangy dog!
Choler does kill me that thou art alive;
I swoon to see thee.

APEMANTUS   Would thou wouldst burst!

TIMON   Away,
Thou tedious rogue! I am sorry I shall lose
A stone by thee.
                    [Throws a stone at him.]

APEMANTUS Beast!

TIMON Slave!

APEMANTUS Toad!

TIMON

Rogue, rogue, rogue!
I am sick of this false world, and will love naught
373 But even the mere necessities upon't.
Then, Timon, presently prepare thy grave.
Lie where the light foam of the sea may beat
Thy gravestone daily. Make thine epitaph,
377 That death in me at others' lives may laugh.
                    [To the gold.]
O thou sweet king-killer, and dear divorce
'Twixt natural son and sire; thou bright defiler
380 Of Hymen's purest bed; thou valiant Mars;
Thou ever young, fresh, loved, and delicate wooer,
382 Whose blush doth thaw the consecrated snow
383 That lies on Dian's lap; thou visible god,
384 That sold'rest close impossibilities
And mak'st them kiss; that speak'st with every tongue
386 To every purpose! O thou touch of hearts!
Think thy slave man rebels; and by thy virtue
388 Set them into confounding odds, that beasts
May have the world in empire!

APEMANTUS   Would 'twere so,
But not till I am dead. I'll say thou'st gold.
Thou wilt be thronged to shortly.

TIMON   Thronged to?

APEMANTUS   Ay.

TIMON

Thy back, I prithee.

APEMANTUS   Live, and love thy misery.

TIMON

Long live so, and so die. I am quit.

APEMANTUS

Moe things like men! Eat, Timon, and abhor them.
                                    Exit Apemantus.
    Enter the Banditti.

1. BANDIT Where should he have this gold? It is some 395
poor fragment, some slender ort of his remainder. The 396
mere want of gold and the falling-from of his friends
drove him into this melancholy.

2. BANDIT It is noised he hath a mass of treasure.

3. BANDIT Let us make the assay upon him. If he care not 400
for't, he will supply us easily; if he covetously reserve
it, how shall's get it? 402

2. BANDIT True; for he bears it not about him; 'tis hid.

1. BANDIT Is not this he?

ALL Where?

2. BANDIT 'Tis his description.

3. BANDIT He! I know him.

ALL Save thee, Timon!

TIMON ·Now, thieves?

ALL

Soldiers, not thieves.

TIMON   Both too, and women's sons. 410

ALL

We are not thieves, but men that much do want.

TIMON

Your greatest want is, you want much of meat. 412
Why should you want? Behold, the earth hath roots;
Within this mile break forth a hundred springs;
The oaks bear mast, the briers scarlet hips; 415
The bounteous housewife Nature on each bush
Lays her full mess before you. Want? Why want? 417

1. BANDIT

We cannot live on grass, on berries, water,
As beasts and birds and fishes.

TIMON

Nor on the beasts themselves, the birds and fishes;
You must eat men. Yet thanks I must you con 421
That you are thieves professed, that you work not
In holier shapes; for there is boundless theft
In limited professions. Rascal thieves, 424
Here's gold. Go, suck the subtle blood o' th' grape
Till the high fever seethe your blood to froth, 426
And so scape hanging. Trust not the physician;
His antidotes are poison, and he slays
Moe than you rob. Take wealth and lives together.
Do villainy, do, since you protest to do't, 430

349 Yonder ... painter (they don't in fact appear until about 190 lines later:
see Introduction) 355 cap i.e. top dog 358 by compared with 361
I'll I'd 373 But even save only; necessities (of which death is the chief:
see next line) 377 death in me I, though dead 380 Hymen the god of
marriage; Mars the adulterous god of war 382 blush glow (of the gold,
not of Mars) 383 Dian a virgin goddess, patroness of chastity 384 close
firmly together 386 touch touchstone 388 them all men 395 should he
have can he have got (?), can he be keeping (?) 396 ort ... remainder
scrap of what he had left 400 make ... him try him (in the language of
gold miners) 402 shall's shall we 410 Both too, and both indeed, and
also 412 Your ... meat what you really need is merely plenty of food
415 mast acorns; hips fruit of the rose 417 full mess complete menu 421
con tender 424 limited regular, legal 426 high fever seethe drunkenness
boil 430 protest profess

431 Like workmen. I'll example you with thievery:
The sun 's a thief, and with his great attraction
Robs the vast sea; the moon 's an arrant thief,
And her pale fire she snatches from the sun;
The sea 's a thief, whose liquid surge resolves
The moon into salt tears; the earth 's a thief,
437 That feeds and breeds by a composture stol'n
From gen'ral excrement. Each thing 's a thief.
The laws, your curb and whip, in their rough power
Has unchecked theft. Love not yourselves: away,
Rob one another. There's more gold. Cut throats.
All that you meet are thieves. To Athens go;
Break open shops; nothing can you steal
444 But thieves do lose it. Steal less for this I give you,
445 And gold confound you howsoe'er! Amen.
3. BANDIT Has almost charmed me from my profession
by persuading me to it.
1. BANDIT 'Tis in the malice of mankind that he thus
449 advises us, not to have us thrive in our mystery.
450 2. BANDIT I'll believe him as an enemy, and give over
my trade.
452 1. BANDIT Let us first see peace in Athens; there is no
time so miserable but a man may be true.

Exit [with the other] Thieves.
Enter [Flavius] the Steward, to Timon.

STEWARD
O you gods!
Is yon despised and ruinous man my lord?
Full of decay and failing? O monument
And wonder of good deeds evilly bestowed!
What an alteration of honor has desp'rate want made!
What viler thing upon the earth than friends,
Who can bring noblest minds to basest ends!
461 How rarely does it meet with this time's guise
When man was wished to love his enemies!
Grant I may ever love, and rather woo
464 Those that would mischief me than those that do!
Has caught me in his eye; I will present
My honest grief unto him, and as my lord
Still serve him with my life. My dearest master!

TIMON
Away! What art thou?

STEWARD   Have you forgot me, sir?

TIMON
Why dost ask that? I have forgot all men;
Then if thou grant'st thou'rt a man, I have forgot thee.

STEWARD
An honest poor servant of yours.

TIMON
Then I know thee not.
I never had honest man about me; ay, all
I kept were knaves, to serve in meat to villains.

STEWARD
The gods are witness,
Ne'er did poor steward wear a truer grief
For his undone lord than mine eyes for you.

TIMON
What, dost thou weep? Come nearer then; I love thee
Because thou art a woman and disclaim'st
Flinty mankind, whose eyes do never give   480
But thorough lust and laughter. Pity 's sleeping.   481
Strange times, that weep with laughing, not with
weeping!

STEWARD
I beg of you to know me, good my lord,
T' accept my grief, and whilst this poor wealth lasts
To entertain me as your steward still.   485

TIMON
Had I a steward
So true, so just, and now so comfortable?   487
It almost turns my dangerous nature mild.
Let me behold thy face. Surely this man
Was born of woman.
Forgive my general and exceptless rashness,   491
You perpetual-sober gods! I do proclaim
One honest man – mistake me not, but one;
No more, I pray – and he's a steward.
How fain would I have hated all mankind,
And thou redeem'st thyself. But all save thee
I fell with curses.
Methinks thou art more honest now than wise;
For by oppressing and betraying me
Thou mightst have sooner got another service;
For many so arrive at second masters,
Upon their first lord's neck. But tell me true –
For I must ever doubt, though ne'er so sure –
Is not thy kindness subtle-covetous,
A usuring kindness, and as rich men deal gifts,   505
Expecting in return twenty for one?

STEWARD
No, my most worthy master, in whose breast
Doubt and suspect, alas, are placed too late.   508
You should have feared false times when you did feast.
Suspect still comes where an estate is least.   510
That which I show, heaven knows, is merely love,   511
Duty, and zeal to your unmatchèd mind,
Care of your food and living; and believe it,   513
My most honored lord,
For any benefit that points to me,   515
Either in hope or present, I'd exchange   516
For this one wish, that you had power and wealth
To requite me by making rich yourself.

TIMON
Look thee, 'tis so! Thou singly honest man,   519
Here, take. The gods out of my misery
Have sent thee treasure. Go, live rich and happy,
But thus conditioned: thou shalt build from men,   522
Hate all, curse all, show charity to none,
But let the famished flesh slide from the bone
Ere thou relieve the beggar. Give to dogs
What thou deniest to men. Let prisons swallow 'em,
Debts wither 'em to nothing; be men like blasted
woods,
And may diseases lick up their false bloods!
And so farewell, and thrive.

STEWARD   O let me stay

431 *example you with* give some examples to justify your   437 *composture*
manure   444 *for* because you have   445 *howsoe'er* anyhow   449 *mystery*
profession   450 *as as I would*   452 *peace* (when thievery is less easy)   452–
53 *there . . . true* i.e. since one may reform at any time, let's not make any
radical changes while the pickings are so good   461–62 *rarely . . . wished*
especially apt for to-day's world is the admonition to man   464 *Those . . .
do* professed enemies than those who harm me though pretending friendship   480 *give* yield tears   481 *But thorough* except through   485 *entertain*
employ   487 *comfortable* comforting   491 *exceptless* making no exceptions
505 *as* as we have when   508 *suspect* suspicion   510 *still* ever   511
merely purely   513 *Care of* concern for   515 *points to* may be indicated for
516 *in . . . present* later or now   519 *singly* (1) uniquely, (2) truly   522 *thus
conditioned* with those provisos; *from* remote from

And comfort you, my master.
TIMON   If thou hat'st curses,
Stay not; fly, whilst thou art blest and free;
Ne'er see thou man, and let me ne'er see thee.
                    [Timon withdraws.] Exit [Flavius].

＊

V, i   *Enter Poet and Painter. [Timon watches them from*
               his cave.]
PAINTER As I took note of the place, it cannot be far
where he abides.
POET What's to be thought of him? Does the rumor hold
for true that he's so full of gold?
PAINTER Certain. Alcibiades reports it; Phrynia and
Timandra had gold of him. He likewise enriched poor
straggling soldiers with great quantity. 'Tis said he
gave unto his steward a mighty sum.
9 POET Then this breaking of his has been but a try for his
friends?
PAINTER Nothing else. You shall see him a palm in
Athens again, and flourish with the highest. Therefore
'tis not amiss we tender our loves to him in this sup-
14 posed distress of his; it will show honestly in us and is
15 very likely to load our purposes with what they travail
16 for, if it be a just and true report that goes of his having.
POET What have you now to present unto him?
PAINTER Nothing at this time but my visitation. Only I
will promise him an excellent piece.
20 POET I must serve him so too, tell him of an intent that's
coming toward him.
PAINTER Good as the best. Promising is the very air o'
th' time; it opens the eyes of expectation. Performance
24 is ever the duller for his act; and, but in the plainer and
25 simpler kind of people, the deed of saying is quite out of
use. To promise is most courtly and fashionable; performance is a kind of will or testament which argues a
great sickness in his judgment that makes it.
          Enter Timon from his cave.
TIMON *[aside]* Excellent workman! Thou canst not paint
a man so bad as is thyself.
POET I am thinking what I shall say I have provided for
32 him. It must be a personating of himself; a satire against
33 the softness of prosperity, with a discovery of the infinite flatteries that follow youth and opulency.
35 TIMON *[aside]* Must thou needs stand for a villain in
thine own work? Wilt thou whip thine own faults in
other men? Do so, I have gold for thee.
POET Nay, let's seek him.
Then do we sin against our own estate
When we may profit meet, and come too late.
PAINTER True.
42 When the day serves, before black-cornered night,
Find what thou want'st by free and offered light.
Come.
TIMON *[aside]*
45 I'll meet you at the turn. What a god's gold
That he is worshipped in a baser temple
Than where swine feed!
'Tis thou that rigg'st the bark and plough'st the foam,
49 Settlest admirèd reverence in a slave.
To thee be worship, and thy saints for aye
Be crowned with plagues, that thee alone obey!
52 Fit I meet them.
          [Comes forward.]

POET
Hail, worthy Timon!
PAINTER   Our late noble master!
TIMON
Have I once lived to see two honest men?   54
POET Sir,
Having often of your open bounty tasted,
Hearing you were retired, your friends fall'n off,
Whose thankless natures – O abhorrèd spirits! –
Not all the whips of heaven are large enough –
What, to you,
Whose starlike nobleness gave life and influence
To their whole being? – I am rapt, and cannot cover   62
The monstrous bulk of this ingratitude
With any size of words.   64
TIMON
Let it go naked; men may see't the better.
You that are honest, by being what you are
Make them best seen and known.   67
PAINTER   He and myself
Have travelled in the great show'r of your gifts,   68
And sweetly felt it.
TIMON   Ay, you are honest men.
PAINTER
We are hither come to offer you our service.
TIMON
Most honest men! Why, how shall I requite you?
Can you eat roots and drink cold water? No?
BOTH
What we can do, we'll do, to do you service.
TIMON
Y' are honest men. Ye've heard that I have gold?
I am sure you have. Speak truth; y' are honest men.
PAINTER
So it is said, my noble lord; but therefore   76
Came not my friend, nor I.
TIMON
Good honest men! Thou draw'st a counterfeit   78
Best in all Athens. Thou'rt indeed the best;
Thou counterfeit'st most lively.   80
PAINTER   So so, my lord.
TIMON
E'en so, sir, as I say. *[to the Poet]* And for thy fiction, 81
Why, thy verse swells with stuff so fine and smooth
That thou art even natural in thine art.   83
But for all this, my honest-natured friends,
I must needs say you have a little fault.
Marry, 'tis not monstrous in you; neither wish I
You take much pains to mend.

V, i Before Timon's cave **9** *breaking* going bankrupt; *try* test **14** *show
honestly* seem honorable **15** *travail* strive **16** *having* wealth **20–21** *an
intent . . . him* what I have in mind for him **24** *for his act* for its being
realized; *but except* **25** *deed of saying* fulfillment of promises **32** *a
personating of himself* an allegorical representation of his own case **33**
discovery disclosure **35** *stand* serve as a model **42** *black-cornered* (presumably because night has the attributes of dark corners) **45** *meet . . .
turn* i.e. give you a little of your own dishonest game (as he presently
does) **49** *Settlest . . .* slave makes slaves admire and revere their masters
52 *Fit I* I'd better **54** *once* actually, after all **62** *rapt* bemused **64**
size of i.e. adequate **67** *them* i.e. the ingrates you speak of **68** *travelled
in* experienced **76–77** *therefore Came not* not for this reason came **78**
counterfeit (1) portrait, (2) spurious imitation (the verb, as in l. 80, being
likewise equivocal) **80** *lively* (1) in lifelike fashion, (2) actively **81** *fiction*
imaginative work **83** *thou . . . thine art* the products of your art are like
nature itself (but *natural* also meant 'like a born fool')

BOTH   Beseech your honor
To make it known to us.
TIMON   You'll take it ill.
BOTH
Most thankfully, my lord.
TIMON   Will you, indeed?
BOTH
Doubt it not, worthy lord.
TIMON
There's never a one of you but trusts a knave
That mightily deceives you.
BOTH   Do we, my lord?
TIMON
93   Ay, and you hear him cog, see him dissemble,
94   Know his gross patchery, love him, feed him,
95   Keep in your bosom; yet remain assured
96   That he's a made-up villain.
PAINTER
I know none such, my lord.
POET   Nor I.
TIMON
Look you, I love you well; I'll give you gold,
Rid me these villains from your companies.
100   Hang them or stab them, drown them in a draught,
Confound them by some course, and come to me,
I'll give you gold enough.
BOTH
Name them, my lord; let's know them.
TIMON
104   You that way, and you this, but two in company;
Each man apart, all single and alone,
Yet an arch-villain keeps him company.
    [To Painter]
If, where thou art, two villains shall not be,
Come not near him.
    [To Poet]   If thou wouldst not reside
But where one villain is, then him abandon. –
110   Hence, pack! There's gold; you came for gold, ye slaves.
    [To Painter]
111   You have work for me; there's payment.
Hence!
    [To Poet]
112   You are an alchemist; make gold of that. –
Out, rascal dogs!   *Exeunt [both, beaten out by Timon,*
                         who retires to his cave].
    Enter [Flavius the] Steward and two Senators.
STEWARD
It is vain that you would speak with Timon;
115   For he is set so only to himself

That nothing but himself which looks like man
Is friendly with him.
1. SENATOR   Bring us to his cave.
It is our part and promise to th' Athenians   118
To speak with Timon.
2. SENATOR   At all times alike
Men are not still the same. 'Twas time and griefs   120
That framed him thus. Time, with his fairer hand
Offering the fortunes of his former days,
The former man may make him. Bring us to him,
And chance it as it may.
STEWARD   Here is his cave.
Peace and content be here! Lord Timon! Timon!
Look out, and speak to friends. Th' Athenians
By two of their most reverend senate greet thee.
Speak to them, noble Timon.
    Enter Timon out of his cave.
TIMON
Thou sun that comforts, burn! Speak and be hanged!
For each true word a blister, and each false
Be as a cauterizing to the root o' th' tongue,
Consuming it with speaking!   131
1. SENATOR   Worthy Timon –
TIMON
Of none but such as you, and you of Timon.
1. SENATOR
The senators of Athens greet thee, Timon.
TIMON
I thank them; and would send them back the plague,
Could I but catch it for them.
1. SENATOR   O, forget
What we are sorry for ourselves in thee.   137
The senators with one consent of love
Entreat thee back to Athens, who have thought
On special dignities, which vacant lie
For thy best use and wearing.
2. SENATOR   They confess
Toward thee forgetfulness too general-gross;
And now the public body, which doth seldom
Play the recanter, feeling in itself
A lack of Timon's aid, hath sense withal
Of it own fail, restraining aid to Timon,   146
And send forth us to make their sorrowed render,   147
Together with a recompense more fruitful
Than their offense can weigh down by the dram;   149
Ay, even such heaps and sums of love and wealth
As shall to thee blot out what wrongs were theirs   151
And write in thee the figures of their love,   152
Ever to read them thine.   153
TIMON   You witch me in it;
Surprise me to the very brink of tears.
Lend me a fool's heart and a woman's eyes,
And I'll beweep these comforts, worthy senators.
1. SENATOR
Therefore so please thee to return with us   157
And of our Athens, thine and ours, to take
The captainship, thou shalt be met with thanks,
Allowed with absolute power, and thy good name   160
Live with authority. So soon we shall drive back   161
Of Alcibiades th' approaches wild,
Who like a boar too savage doth root up
His country's peace.
2. SENATOR   And shakes his threat'ning sword
Against the walls of Athens.

---

93 *cog* cheat   94 *patchery* roguery   95 *Keep . . . bosom* cherish him   96 *made-up* complete   100 *draught* privy   104–06 *You . . . company* i.e. each of you is a thorough villain (riddlingly spelled out further in ll. 107–09)   110 *pack* be off   111 *there's payment* (since Timon now strikes him)   112 *alchemist* i.e. one who strives by art to improve on nature, out of common things to produce precious; *that* (the blow Timon now gives him as well)   115 *set . . . to* so completely wrapped up in   118 *part and promise* promised part   120 *still the same* 'at all times alike' (as before: senators sometimes repeat themselves)   131 *cauterizing* searing with acid or a hot iron   137 *What . . . thee* the wrongs we are sorry to have done you   146 *it own fail* its own fault   147 *sorrowed render* amends for regretted wrongs   149 *can . . . dram* can, weighed scrupulously, outbalance   151 *were theirs* they did you   152 *write . . . figures* enter you in the ledgers (the imagery is persistently commercial though the subject is love)   153 *Ever . . . thine* thus providing a permanent record of their esteem for you   157 *so if it*   160 *Allowed with* given   161 *Live with authority* shall remain authoritative

1 . SENATOR   Therefore, Timon –
TIMON
Well, sir, I will ; therefore I will, sir, thus :
If Alcibiades kill my countrymen,
Let Alcibiades know this of Timon,
That Timon cares not. But if he sack fair Athens
And take our goodly agèd men by th' beards,
Giving our holy virgins to the stain

172 Of contumelious, beastly, mad-brained war,
Then let him know (and tell him Timon speaks it
In pity of our agèd and our youth)
I cannot choose but tell him that I care not –
And let him take't at worst – for their knives care not,

177 While you have throats to answer. For myself,
178 There's not a whittle in th' unruly camp
179 But I do prize it at my love before
The reverend'st throat in Athens. So I leave you
181 To the protection of the prosperous gods,
182 As thieves to keepers.
STEWARD   Stay not ; all's in vain.
TIMON
Why, I was writing of my epitaph.
It will be seen to-morrow. My long sickness
185 Of health and living now begins to mend,
186 And nothing brings me all things. Go, live still ;
Be Alcibiades your plague, you his,
And last so long enough !
1 . SENATOR   We speak in vain.
TIMON
But yet I love my country and am not
One that rejoices in the common wrack,
191 As common bruit doth put it.
1 . SENATOR   That's well spoke.
TIMON
Commend me to my loving countrymen –
1 . SENATOR
These words become your lips as they pass through
them.
2 . SENATOR
And enter in our ears like great triumphers
In their applauding gates.
TIMON   Commend me to them,
And tell them that, to ease them of their griefs,
Their fears of hostile strokes, their aches, losses,
Their pangs of love, with other incident throes
That nature's fragile vessel doth sustain
In life's uncertain voyage, I will some kindness do
them :
201 I'll teach them to prevent wild Alcibiades' wrath.
1 . SENATOR
I like this well. He will return again.
TIMON
203 I have a tree which grows here in my close
That mine own use invites me to cut down,
And shortly must I fell it. Tell my friends,
Tell Athens, in the sequence of degree
From high to low throughout, that whoso please
To stop affliction, let him take his haste,
Come hither ere my tree hath felt the axe –
And hang himself ! I pray you do my greeting.
STEWARD
Trouble him no further ; thus you still shall find him.

TIMON
Come not to me again ; but say to Athens,
Timon hath made his everlasting mansion
Upon the beachèd verge of the salt flood,   214
Who once a day with his embossèd froth   215
The turbulent surge shall cover. Thither come,
And let my gravestone be your oracle.   217
Lips, let sour words go by and language end.
What is amiss, plague and infection mend !
Graves only be men's works, and death their gain.
Sun, hide thy beams ; Timon hath done his reign.
     Exit Timon [into his cave].
1 . SENATOR
His discontents are unremovably
Coupled to nature.   223
2 . SENATOR
Our hope in him is dead. Let us return
And strain what other means is left unto us
In our dear peril.   226
1 . SENATOR   It requires swift foot.   *Exeunt.*

           *

Enter two other Senators with a Messenger.   V, ii
3 . SENATOR
Thou hast painfully discovered ; are his files   1
As full as thy report ?
MESSENGER   I have spoke the least.   2
Besides, his expedition promises   3
Present approach.
4 . SENATOR
We stand much hazard if they bring not Timon.   5
MESSENGER
I met a courier, one mine ancient friend ;
Whom, though in general part we were opposed,   7
Yet our old love had a particular force
And made us speak like friends. This man was riding
From Alcibiades to Timon's cave
With letters of entreaty, which imported
His fellowship i' th' cause against your city,
In part for his sake moved.   13
     Enter the other Senators [from Timon].
3 . SENATOR   Here come our brothers.
1 . SENATOR
No talk of Timon ; nothing of him expect.
The enemy's drum is heard, and fearful scouring   15
Doth choke the air with dust. In, and prepare.
Ours is the fall, I fear ; our foe's the snare.   *Exeunt.* 17

           *

172 *contumelious* insolent   177 *answer* suffer the consequences   178 *whittle* clasp-knife   179 *at* in   181 *prosperous* propitious   182 *keepers* jailers   185 *health and living* healthful life   186 *nothing* oblivion, death   191 *bruit* rumor   201 *prevent* anticipate   203 *in my close* i.e. alongside my cave ('close' ordinarily meaning 'enclosure,' 'yard')   214 *beachèd verge of* beach that edges (is the limit of)   215 *embossèd* foaming   217 *oracle* source of wisdom   223 *Coupled to nature* part and parcel of his being   226 *dear* grievous
V, ii Before the walls of Athens   1 *painfully discovered* reconnoitered with great care (?), revealed distressing facts (?) ; *files* ranks (of Alcibiades' army)   2 *spoke the least* given a conservative estimate   3 *expedition* speed   5 *they* (the senators, designated 1 and 2, sent out for this purpose)   7 *general part* public affairs   13 *moved* undertaken   15 *scouring* scurrying about in preparation for battle   17 *Ours ... snare* i.e. I fear we are about to fall into our enemy's trap

V, iii   *Enter a Soldier in the woods, seeking Timon for*
                Alcibiades.

SOLDIER

    By all description this should be the place.
    Who's here ? Speak, ho ! No answer ? What is this ?
    [Reads.]
    'Timon is dead, who hath outstretched his span.
4   Some beast read this ; there does not live a man.'
    Dead, sure, and this his grave. What's on this tomb
6   I cannot read ; the character I'll take with wax.
    Our captain hath in every figure skill,
    An aged interpreter, though young in days.
    Before proud Athens he's set down by this,
10   Whose fall the mark of his ambition is.   *Exit.*

＊

V, iv   *Trumpets sound. Enter Alcibiades with his Powers*
                before Athens.

ALCIBIADES

    Sound to this coward and lascivious town
    Our terrible approach.
          Sound a parley. The Senators appear upon the walls.
    Till now you have gone on and filled the time
4   With all licentious measure, making your wills
5   The scope of justice. Till now myself and such
    As slept within the shadow of your power
7   Have wandered with our traversed arms and breathed
8   Our sufferance vainly. Now the time is flush,
9   When crouching marrow in the bearer strong
    Cries, of itself, 'No more !' Now breathless wrong
    Shall sit and pant in your great chairs of ease,
12   And pursy insolence shall break his wind
    With fear and horrid flight.

I . SENATOR   Noble and young,
14   When thy first griefs were but a mere conceit,
    Ere thou hadst power or we had cause of fear,
    We sent to thee, to give thy rages balm,
    To wipe out our ingratitude with loves
    Above their quantity.

2 . SENATOR   So did we woo
    Transformèd Timon to our city's love

By humble message and by promised means.
We were not all unkind, nor all deserve   21
The common stroke of war.

I . SENATOR   These walls of ours
Were not erected by their hands from whom
You have received your griefs ; nor are they such   24
That these great tow'rs, trophies, and schools should fall
For private faults in them.   26

2 . SENATOR   Nor are they living
Who were the motives that you first went out.   27
Shame, that they wanted cunning, in excess   28
Hath broke their hearts. March, noble lord,
Into our city with thy banners spread.
By decimation and a tithèd death,   31
If thy revenges hunger for that food
Which nature loathes, take thou the destined tenth,
And by the hazard of the spotted die   34
Let die the spotted.   35

I . SENATOR   All have not offended.
For those that were, it is not square to take,   36
On those that are, revenge ; crimes, like lands,
Are not inherited. Then, dear countryman,
Bring in thy ranks, but leave without thy rage ;   39
Spare thy Athenian cradle, and those kin
Which in the bluster of thy wrath must fall
With those that have offended. Like a shepherd
Approach the fold and cull th' infected forth,
But kill not all together.

2 . SENATOR   What thou wilt,
Thou rather shalt enforce it with thy smile
Than hew to't with thy sword.

I . SENATOR   Set but thy foot
Against our rampired gates and they shall ope,   47
So thou wilt send thy gentle heart before   48
To say thou'lt enter friendly.

2 . SENATOR   Throw thy glove,
Or any token of thine honor else,
That thou wilt use the wars as thy redress
And not as our confusion, all thy powers   52
Shall make their harbor in our town till we
Have sealed thy full desire.   54

ALCIBIADES   Then there's my glove ;
Descend, and open your unchargèd ports.   55
Those enemies of Timon's and mine own
Whom you yourselves shall set out for reproof
Fall, and no more ; and, to atone your fears   58
With my more noble meaning, not a man   59
Shall pass his quarter or offend the stream
Of regular justice in your city's bounds
But shall be rendered to your public laws
At heaviest answer.   63

BOTH   'Tis most nobly spoken.

ALCIBIADES

Descend, and keep your words.
     [The Senators descend and open the gates.]
     Enter [Soldier as] a Messenger.

MESSENGER

    My noble general, Timon is dead,
    Entombed upon the very hem o' th' sea,
    And on his gravestone this insculpture, which   67
    With wax I brought away, whose soft impression
    Interprets for my poor ignorance.   69

V, iii Before Timon's cave *4 read . . . man* will read this, since human
beings are not men but beasts *6 cannot read* (apparently because in a
strange language, as a Latin epitaph would be to an Elizabethan soldier) ;
character lettering *10 the mark . . . is* is his goal
V, iv Before the walls of Athens *4 all licentious measure* every form of
licentiousness *5 scope* determinants *7 our traversed arms* our weapons
not borne as if for battle *7–8 breathed . . . vainly* spoken in vain of our
sufferings *8 flush* ripe *9 crouching marrow* latent courage *12 pursy*
short-winded *14 conceit* fancy *21 all* altogether *24 they* (your griefs)
26 them those who wronged you *27 the motives . . . out* responsible for
your original banishment *28 Shame . . . excess* excessive shame over their
folly *31 tithèd death* death to every tenth person (an explanation of
decimation) *34 die* (singular of dice) *35 die the spotted* perish the guilty
(with quibble on preceding phrase) *36 square* just *39 without* outside
47 rampired barricaded *48 So* if only *52 confusion* ruin *54 sealed* completely satisfied *55 ports* gates *58 atone* appease *59 meaning* intentions *59–60 not . . . quarter* not one of my soldiers shall leave his prescribed
duty-area *63 At heaviest answer* for severest punishment *67 insculpture*
inscription *69 Interprets . . . ignorance* will yield you the meaning which I
am too ignorant to get from it (cf. V, iii, 5–8 and V, iii, 6n.)

ALCIBIADES *(Reads the epitaph.)*

70   'Here lies a wretched corse, of wretched soul bereft;
    Seek not my name. A plague consume you wicked
      caitiffs left!
    Here lie I, Timon, who alive all living men did hate.
73   Pass by and curse thy fill; but pass, and stay not here thy
      gait.'

    These well express in thee thy latter spirits.
    Though thou abhorred'st in us our human griefs,
76   Scorned'st our brains' flow and those our droplets which
77   From niggard nature fall, yet rich conceit
    Taught thee to make vast Neptune weep for aye

On thy low grave, on faults forgiven. Dead
Is noble Timon, of whose memory
Hereafter more. Bring me into your city,
And I will use the olive with my sword,   82
Make war breed peace, make peace stint war, make each 83
Prescribe to other, as each other's leech.   84
Let our drums strike.   *Exeunt.*

70–73 *Here . . . gait* (one of these two contradictory couplets was probably meant for cancellation: see Introduction) 73 *gait* steps 76 *brains' flow* tears 77 *niggard* (since our tears are *droplets* indeed when compared with the seas which now wash Timon's grave); *conceit* imagination 82 *use . . . sword* combine peace with war 83 *stint* stop 84 *leech* physician

ANTONY AND CLEOPATRA

INTRODUCTION

Critics have been known to speak of *Macbeth*, *King Lear*, and *Antony and Cleopatra* as Shakespeare's *Inferno*, *Purgatorio*, and *Paradiso*. The comparison is misleading if taken as a guide to Shakespeare's states of mind, of which we know nothing, or even as a guide to the order of the three plays, the consensus of modern opinion being that *Macbeth* (ca. 1606) falls between *King Lear* (ca. 1605) and *Antony and Cleopatra* (ca. 1607). But the notion has a certain merit if taken solely as a guide to tone.

Macbeth and *King Lear*, like *Othello* earlier, are dark plays, filled with actions taking place in what can only be called "dramatic" as well as literal night, a dark night of the soul engulfed by evil. *Antony and Cleopatra*, on the other hand, is a bright play. *Macbeth* and *King Lear*, too, are savage – if one fully responds to them, terrifying. There is no savagery in *Antony and Cleopatra*; it is moving, exhilarating, even exalting, but contains nothing that should tear an audience to tatters. The humor of *Macbeth* and *King Lear* is either grim or pitiful: a drunken porter at the gate of hell, a court jester shivering on a stormy heath. The humor of *Antony and Cleopatra* is neither grim nor pitiful, although sometimes acrid enough. Cleopatra is given qualities that make her a very unqueenly queen: she lies, wheedles, sulks, screams, and makes love, all with equal abandon. Antony is given qualities that make him in some senses more like an elderly playboy than a tragic hero. We are encouraged by Shakespeare in this play to disengage ourselves from the protagonists, to feel superior to them, even to laugh at them, as we rarely are with his earlier tragic persons.

Against laughter, however, the playwright poises sympathy and even admiration. Tawdry though he has made these seasoned old campaigners in love and war, he has also magnified and idealized them, to the point at which their mutual passion becomes glorious as well as cheap. Antony, the play tells us, has "infinite virtue," Cleopatra "infinite variety." He is the "triple pillar of the world," she is the "day o' th' world." He seems a "plated Mars," she more beautiful than Venus. His guardian spirit is called "unmatchable," she is called a "lass unparalleled." He descends from the god Hercules, she from the moon-goddess Isis. She sees him as the sun and moon, lighting this "little O, th' earth"; Charmian sees her as the "Eastern star." When Antony cries Ho! "Like boys unto a muss, kings would start forth"; Cleopatra has a hand that "kings Have lipped, and trembled kissing." When Antony will swear an oath, he cries, "Let Rome in Tiber melt and the wide arch Of the ranged empire fall!" When Cleopatra will swear, she cries, "Melt Egypt into Nile! and kindly creatures Turn all to serpents." Antony, about to die, thinks of death as a continuing amour with Cleopatra: "Where souls do couch on flowers, we'll hand in hand, And with our sprightly port make the ghosts gaze." When Cleopatra is about to die, she sees death in the same transcendent terms: "Go fetch My best attires. I am again for Cydnus, To meet Mark Antony."

Traces of Shakespeare's duality of attitude toward his lovers may be found in Plutarch, whose *Lives of the Noble Grecians and Romans Compared Together* he had read in Thomas North's magnificent English rendering (1579) of Jacques Amyot's translation of the original into French (1559). So eloquent was North's prose that in certain instances it could be assumed into blank verse with a minimum of change, as in the following well-known description of Cleopatra going to meet Antony in her barge, which should be compared with the lines of Enobarbus (II, ii, 191–241) in Shakespeare's play.

... She went to Antonius at the age when a woman's beauty is at the prime, and she also of best judgment.... She disdained to set forward otherwise but to take her barge in the river of Cydnus, the poop whereof was of gold, the sails of purple, and the oars of silver, which kept stroke in rowing after the sound of the music of flutes, hautboys, cithers, viols, and such other instruments as they played upon in the barge. And now for the person of herself: She was laid under a pavilion of cloth-of-gold of tissue, apparelled and attired like the goddess Venus commonly drawn in picture; and hard by her, on either hand of her, pretty fair boys, apparelled as painters do set forth god Cupid, with little fans in their hands, with the which they fanned wind upon her. Her ladies and gentlewomen also, the fairest of them, were apparelled like the nymphs Nereides (which are the mermaids of the waters) and like the Graces, some steering the helm, others tending the tackle and ropes of the barge, out of the which there came a wonderful passing sweet savor of perfumes that perfumed the wharf's side, pestered with innumerable multitudes of people. Some of them followed the barge all alongest the river's side, others also ran out of the city to see her coming in, so that in the end there ran such multitudes of people one after another to see her that Antonius was left post-alone in the market place in his imperial seat to give audience. And there went a rumor in the people's mouths that the goddess Venus was come to play with the god Bacchus for the general good of all Asia.

Shakespeare's play owes to Plutarch's life of Antony many of its incidents, and to North's prose the wording of occasional passages like the lines of Enobarbus referred to above. It precipitates, however, an interpretation of these materials that is spectacularly Shakespeare's own. Plutarch's narrative, for all its stress on the baffling blends of vice and virtue in great minds, is at bottom the relatively familiar story of the Great Man and the Temptress. His Antony loses the world for love, not wisely but too well, and his Cleopatra, though possibly she rises to genuine love before the end (Plutarch leaves this point undecided), is rather the instrument of a great man's downfall than a tragic figure in herself. To understand the distinctiveness of Shakespeare's treatment of her, we have only to return to the passage in Plutarch and the lines of Enobarbus already cited. Plutarch's Cleopatra is all siren, every effect calculated to ensnare the senses of the conquering Roman. Shakespeare's Cleopatra is all siren too, but she is more. The repeated paradoxes in Enobarbus' language serve notice on us that everything about her is impossible, mysteriously contradictory. Her page-boys cool her cheeks only to make them burn, "and what they undid did." Her gentlewomen are seeming mermaids, half human, half sea-creature. The silken tackle swells with a life of its own at "the touches of those flower-soft hands." The wharves come alive and have "sense," quickened by her "strange invisible perfume." The city comes alive, to "cast" its people out upon her. Antony is left sitting in the market place, whistling to the air, and the air itself, except that nature abhors a vacuum, would have "gone to gaze on Cleopatra too" and left a gap behind. She is a creature, says Enobarbus in conclusion, who makes defect perfection, and, when breathless, power breathes forth. Other women cloy the appetites they feed, "but she makes hungry Where most she satisfies." Even the vilest things are so becoming when she does them that "the holy priests Bless her when she is riggish."

This is clearly not a portrait of a mere intriguing woman, but a kind of absolute oxymoron: Cleopatra is glimpsed here as a force like the Lucretian Venus, whose vitality resists both definition and regulation. Yet enveloped as she is by Enobarbus' mocking tones, wise and faintly world-weary, calculating amusedly the effects of his words on these uninitiated Romans, she remains the more a trollop for that. His reliable anti-romanticism undercuts the picture he draws of her, and at the same time confirms it, because it comes from him.

The ambiguity of these lines extends to almost everything in the play. In the world the dramatist has given his lovers, nothing is stable, fixed, or sure, not even ultimate values; all is in motion. Seen from one point of view, the motion may be discerned as process, the inexorable march of causes and effects, exemplified in Antony's fall and epitomized by Caesar in commenting to Octavia on the futility of her efforts to preserve the peace: "But let determined things to destiny Hold unbewailed their way." Seen from another angle, the motion reveals itself as flux, the restless waxing and waning of tides, of moons, of human feeling. Especially of human feeling. Antony pursued Brutus to his death, we are reminded by Enobarbus, yet wept when he found him slain. So within the play itself Caesar weeps, having pursued Antony to his death; and Antony, desiring that Fulvia die, finds her "good, being gone"; and Enobarbus, seeking some way to leave his master, is heart-struck when he succeeds; and the Roman populace, always fickle, "Like to a vagabond flag upon the stream, Goes to and back, lackeying the varying tide, To rot itself with motion."

In such a context, it is not surprising that the lovers' passion is subject to vicissitudes, going to and back in ever more violent oscillations of attraction and recoil. Shakespeare nowhere disguises the unstable and ultimately destructive character of their relationship, and those who, like Shaw, have belabored him for not giving sexual

infatuation the satiric treatment it deserves have read too carelessly. It is likewise not surprising that the play's structure should reflect, in its abrupt and numerous shifts of scene, so marked a quality of its leading characters – their emotional and psychological vacillation. Though these shifts have also met with criticism, some finding in them a serious threat to unity, they are easily seen in the theatre to be among the dramatist's means of conveying to us an awareness of the competing values by which the lovers, and particularly Antony, are torn. "Kingdoms are clay," he declares in Egypt; "The nobleness of life Is to do thus," and embraces Cleopatra. A few hours later, however, he says with equal earnestness, "These strong Egyptian fetters I must break Or lose myself in dotage," and he departs for Rome. Again, he declares to Octavia in Rome, hereafter everything shall "be done by th' rule," yet scarcely thirty lines later, after his interview with the soothsayer, he has added, "I will to Egypt." From this point on follows a succession of fluctuations in both war and love. In war, confidence of victory shifting to despair at loss, then to new confidence, then to new despair. In love, adorings of Cleopatra changing to recriminations, then to renewed adorings, then to fresh disgust. This aspect of the play's rhythm is vividly summed up in two speeches in the third act (III, xi). "I have offended reputation," Antony says after the first sea defeat, "A most unnoble swerving": there is the voice of Rome and the soldier. A few seconds after, he says to Cleopatra, "Fall not a tear, I say: one of them rates All that is won and lost": this is the voice of Egypt and the lover.

"All that is won *and* lost" is of course the crucial ambiguity of this tragedy. Perhaps it is one about which no two readers are likely finally to agree. Much is obviously lost by the lovers in the course of the play, and Shakespeare underscores this fact, as Plutarch had done, by placing their deaths in Cleopatra's monument – that is to say, a tomb. All those imperial ambitions that once mustered the "kings o' th' earth for war" have shrunk now to this narrow stronghold, which is also a waiting grave. Antony had said as he put his arms about Cleopatra in the opening scene, "Here is my space." Now that challenge has been taken up. This is his space indeed.

But what then, if anything, has been won? The answer to this question depends as much on what one brings to *Antony and Cleopatra* as on what one finds there, for the evidence is mixed. Antony does give his life for his love before the play ends, and we observe that there are no recriminations at his final meeting with Cleopatra; only his quiet hope that she will remember him for what was noblest in him, and her acknowledgment that he was, and is, her man of men. But then, too, his death has been precipitated by her duplicity in the false report of hers; it has among its motives a self-interested desire to evade Caesar's triumph; and the suicide is even bungled in the doing: if this is a hero's death, it is a humiliating one. Likewise, Cleopatra seems to give her life for love. As Antony will be a bridegroom in his death, "and run into't As to a lover's bed," so Cleopatra will be a bride in hers, calling, "Husband, I come," receiving darkness as if it were "a lover's pinch, Which hurts, and is desired," and breathing out, in words that could equally be describing the union of life with death or the union of lover with lover, "As sweet as balm, as soft as air, as gentle – O

Antony!" This, however, is the same woman who has long studied "easy ways to die," who ends her life only after becoming convinced that Caesar means to lead her in triumph, and who has cached away with her treasurer Seleucus more than half her valuables in case of need. True, the scene with Seleucus can be so played as to indicate that she is using his confession to dupe Caesar about her intention to die. But that is precisely the point. What the actor or reader makes of her conduct here will be conditioned by what he has made of her elsewhere, by what he makes of the play as a whole, and even, perhaps, by his beliefs about human nature and the depiction of human nature in art.

Are we to take the high-sounding phrases which introduce us to this remarkable love affair in the play's first scene as amorous rant?

CLEOPATRA
  If it be love indeed, tell me how much.
ANTONY
  There's beggary in the love that can be reckoned.
CLEOPATRA
  I'll set a bourn how far to be beloved.
ANTONY
  Then must thou needs find out new heaven, new earth.

Or is there a prophetic resonance in that reference to "new heaven, new earth," which we are meant to remember when Cleopatra, dreaming of a transcendent Antony –

His face was as the heav'ns, and therein stuck
A sun and moon, which kept their course and lighted
The little O, th' earth....
His legs bestrid the ocean : his reared arm
Crested the world : his voice was propertied
As all the tunèd spheres –

consigns her baser elements to "baser life"? Does the passion of these two remain a destructive element to the bitter end, doomed like all the feeling in the play to "rot itself with motion"? Or, as the world slips from them, have they a glimmering of something they could not have earlier understood, of another power besides death "Which shackles accidents and bolts up change"? Is it "paltry to be Caesar," as Cleopatra claims, since "Not being Fortune, he's but Fortune's knave"? Or is it more paltry to be Antony, and, as Caesar sees it, "give a kingdom for a mirth," as well as, eventually, the world?

To such questions, *Antony and Cleopatra*, like life itself, gives no clear-cut answers. Shakespeare holds the balance even, and does not decide for us who finally is the strumpet of the play, Antony's Cleopatra, or Caesar's Fortune, and who, therefore, is the "strumpet's fool." Those who would have it otherwise, who are "hot for certainties in this our life," as Meredith phrased it, should turn to other authors than Shakespeare, and should have been born into some other world than this.

Yale University   MAYNARD MACK

Antony and Cleopatra was first published in the folio of 1623, in a good text with full stage directions, evidently printed from Shakespeare's own draft after it had been prepared for stage production. The folio text is undivided into acts and scenes. The division appearing marginally in the present edition is editorial, and supplied only for reference purposes. The following list of departures from the folio text, amplified from the one supplied by the editor, perhaps errs on the side of inclusiveness; it omits only the most obvious typographical errors, the instances of mislineation, and the variations in speech-prefixes and proper names, including several instances of "Cleopater" which may indicate an alternative pronunciation. The adopted reading in italics is followed by the folio reading in roman.

I, i, 18 *me!* me, 39 *On* One 50 *whose* who

I, ii, 4 *charge* change 37 *fertile* foretell 58 *Charmian* Alexas 76 *Saw* Save 106 *minds* windes 108 s.d. Omitted (in F: Enter another Messenger) 110 *1. Attendant* 1. Mes. 111 *2. Attendant* 2. Mes. 114 *Messenger* 3. Mes. 134 *occasion* an occasion 175 *leave* love 180 *Hath* Have 189 *hair* heire 191 *place is* places *requires* require

I, iii, 20 *What,* What 24 *know* – know. 25 *betrayed* betrayèd 33 *sued* suèd 43 *services* Servicles 51 *thrived* thrivèd 80 *blood: no more.* blood no more? 82 *my* (not in F)

I, iv, 3 *Our* One 8 *Vouchsafed* vouchsafe 9 *the abstract* th' abstracts 21 *smell* smels 44 *deared* fear'd 46 *lackeying* lacking 49 *Make* Makes 56 *wassails* Vassailes 75 *me* me

I, v, 5 *time* time: 29 *time?* time. 34 s.d. *Alexas* Alexas from Caesar 50 *dumbed* dumbe 61 *man* mans

II, i, 41 *warred* wan'd 43 *greater.* greater, 44 *all,* all:

II, ii, 71–72 *you . . . Alexandria;* you, . . . Alexandria 107 *soldier* Souldier, 115–16 *staunch, . . . world* staunch . . . world: 120 *so* say 121 *reproof* proofe 122 *deserved* deservèd 146–47 *hand: | Further* hand | Further 171 s.d. *[Exeunt.]* Exit omnes. 195 *lovesick with* Love-sicke. | With 205 *glow* glove 207 *gentlewomen* Gentlewoman 224 *'no'* no *heard* hard 229 *ploughed* ploughèd 233 *And, breathless,* And breathlesse

II, iii, 8 *Octavia* (not in F) 20 *high, unmatchable* high unmatchable 24 *thee, no more but when to thee.* thee no more but: when to thee, 30 *away* alway

II, v, 10–11 *river: there, | My . . . off,* River there | My . . . off. 12 *finned* fine 28 *him,* him. 43 *is* 'tis 96 *face, to me* face to me, 111 *Alexas;* Alexas 115 *not! – Charmian,* not Charmian,

II, vi, 19 *is his* 30 *present) how you take* present how you take) 43 *telling,* telling. 52 *gained* gainèd 58 *composition* composion 66 *meanings* meaning 69 *of* (not in F) 81 s.d. *Manent* Manet

II, vii, 91 *is he* is 99 *grows* grow 101 *all four days* all, foure dayes, 110 *bear* beate 119 *off* of 123 *Splits* Spleet's 127 *father's* Father 128–29 *not. | Menas* not Menas

III, i, 3 *body* body, 4 *army.* Army

III, ii, 10 *Agrippa* Ant. 16 *figures* Figure 20 *beetle.* [. . .] *So –* Beetle, so: 49 *full* the full 59 *wept* weepe

III, iii, 21 *lookedst* look'st

III, iv, 8 *them* then 9 *took't* look't 24 *yours* your 30 *Your* You 38 *has* he's

III, v, 12 *world* would *hast* hadst *chaps,* chaps 14 *the one* (not in F)

III, vi, 13 *he there proclaimed the kings* hither proclaimèd the King 19 *reported,* reported 22 *know* knowes 28 *triumvirate* Triumpherate 29 *being, that* being that, 78 *do* does

III, vii, 4 *it is* it it 5 *Is't not,* If not, 23 *Toryne* Troine 35 *muleters* Militers 51 *Actium* Action 72 *Canidius* Ven. 78 *Well* Well,

III, x, s.d. *Enobarbus* Enobarbus and Scarus 14 *June* Inne 28 *he* his

III, xi, 19 *that* them 22 *pray,* pray 44 *He is* Hee's 47 *seize* cease 56 *followed* followèd 58 *tow* stowe 59 *Thy* The

III, xiii, 10 *meered* meered 55 *Caesar* Caesars 57 *feared* fearèd 60 *deserved* deservèd 74 *this:* this *deputation* disputation, 90 *me. Of late,* me of late. 103 *again. This* againe, the 112–13 *eyes, | In . . . filth* eyes | In . . . filth, 132 *'a* a 137 *whipped for . . . him.* whipt. For . . . him, 162 *smite* smile 165 *discandying* discandering 168 *sits* sets 178 *sinewed* sinewèd 199 *on* in 201 s.d. *Exit* Exeunt

IV, i, 3 *combat,* combat.

IV, ii, 1 *No.* No? 12 *And thou* Thou

IV, iii, 8 *4. Soldier* 2 10 *3. Soldier* 1 15 *loved* lovèd 17 *Omnes (speak together)* Speak together. / Omnes.

IV, iv, 5–6 *too. | What's* too, Anthony. / What's 6 *Antony* (not in F) 8 *Cleopatra* (not in F) 24 *Captain* Alex. 32 *thee* thee. 33 *steel.* Steele,

IV, v, 1, 3, 6 *Soldier* Eros 17 *Dispatch.* Dispatch

IV, vi, 20 *more* mote 36 *do't, I feel.* doo't. I feele

IV, vii, 8 s.d. *far off* (in F after 'heads', line 6)

IV, viii, 18 *My* Mine 23 *favoring* savouring 26 *Destroyed* Destroyèd

IV, xii, 4 *augurers* Auguries 9 s.d. *Alarum . . . sea-fight* (in F before line 1) 10 *betrayed* betrayèd 21 *spanieled* pannelled

IV, xiii, 10 *death.* death

IV, xiv, 4 *towered* toward 10 *dislimns* dislimes 19 *Caesar* Caesars 77 *ensued* ensuèd 95 s.d. *Kills himself* (in F after line 93) 104 *ho* how

IV, xv, 54 *lived the* lived. The 76 *e'en* in 86 *What, what!* What, what

V, i, s.d. *Maecenas* Menas 28 *Agrippa* Dol. 31 *Agrippa* Dola. 36 *followed* followèd 48 s.d. *Enter an Egyptian* (in F after 'says', line 51) 53 *all she has,* all, she has 54 *intents desires* intents, desires, 59 *live* leave 68 s.d. *Exit* Exit Proculeius

V, ii, 35 *You* Pro. [s.p.] You 56 *varletry* Varlotarie 66 *me* (not in F) 81 *O, o'* 87 *autumn 'twas* Anthony it was 104 *smites* suites 139 *valued* valewèd 151 *followed* followèd 216 *Ballad us out o'* Ballads us out a 223 *my* mine 317 *awry* away 318 s.d. *in.* in, and Dolabella. 324 *here!* Charmian here Charmian 340 *diadem* diadem; 341 *mistress;* Mistris

ANTONY AND CLEOPATRA

[NAMES OF THE ACTORS

Mark Antony ⎫
Octavius Caesar ⎬ triumvirs
M. Aemilius Lepidus ⎭
Sextus Pompeius
Domitius Enobarbus ⎫
Ventidius ⎜
Eros ⎜
Scarus ⎬ friends to Antony
Decretas ⎜
Demetrius ⎜
Philo ⎭
Canidius, lieutenant-general to Antony
Maecenas ⎫
Agrippa ⎜
Dolabella ⎬ friends to Caesar
Proculeius ⎜
Thidias ⎜
Gallus ⎭

Taurus, lieutenant-general to Caesar
Menas ⎫
Menecrates ⎬ friends to Pompey
Varrius ⎭
Roman Officer under Ventidius
A Schoolmaster, ambassador from Antony to Caesar
Alexas ⎫
Mardian ⎜
Seleucus ⎬ attendants on Cleopatra
Diomedes ⎭
A Soothsayer
A Clown
Cleopatra, Queen of Egypt
Octavia, sister to Caesar and wife to Antony
Charmian ⎫
Iras ⎬ attendants on Cleopatra
Officers, Soldiers, Messengers, Attendants

Scene : The Roman Empire]

*

I, i *Enter Demetrius and Philo.*

PHILO

1 Nay, but this dotage of our general's
O'erflows the measure : those his goodly eyes
That o'er the files and musters of the war
4 Have glowed like plated Mars, now bend, now turn
5 The office and devotion of their view
6 Upon a tawny front. His captain's heart,
Which in the scuffles of great fights hath burst
8 The buckles on his breast, reneges all temper
And is become the bellows and the fan
10 To cool a gypsy's lust.
Flourish. Enter Antony, Cleopatra, her Ladies, the Train, with Eunuchs fanning her.
Look where they come :
Take but good note, and you shall see in him
12 The triple pillar of the world transformed
13 Into a strumpet's fool. Behold and see.

I, i The palace of Cleopatra in Alexandria   1 *dotage* (applicable not only to the aged; Antony 'dotes' on Cleopatra)   4 *plated* armored   5 *office* service   6 *front* face (with pun on military sense)   8 *reneges* rejects; *temper* moderation   10 *gypsy* (1) native of Egypt (gypsies were thought to originate thence), (2) slut   12 *The triple . . . world* one of the three 'pillars' of the world (the others being Octavius Caesar and Lepidus)   13 *fool* dupe   16 *bourn* limit   18 *Grates . . . sum* it annoys me; be brief   20 *Fulvia* Antony's wife   21 *scarce-bearded* hardly grown up (Octavius was twenty-three)   23 *Take in* seize; *enfranchise* set free   26 *dismission* recall   28 *process* summons   31 *Is Caesar's homager* pays respect to Caesar's authority; *else* or else

CLEOPATRA
If it be love indeed, tell me how much.
ANTONY
There's beggary in the love that can be reckoned.
CLEOPATRA
I'll set a bourn how far to be beloved.   16
ANTONY
Then must thou needs find out new heaven, new earth.
Enter a Messenger.
MESSENGER
News, my good lord, from Rome.
ANTONY   Grates me ! The sum. 18
CLEOPATRA
Nay, hear them, Antony.
Fulvia perchance is angry ; or who knows   20
If the scarce-bearded Caesar have not sent   21
His pow'rful mandate to you, 'Do this, or this ;
Take in that kingdom, and enfranchise that.   23
Perform't, or else we damn thee.'
ANTONY   How, my love ?
CLEOPATRA
Perchance ? Nay, and most like :
You must not stay here longer, your dismission   26
Is come from Caesar ; therefore hear it, Antony.
Where's Fulvia's process ? Caesar's I would say ? both ? 28
Call in the messengers. As I am Egypt's Queen,
Thou blushest, Antony, and that blood of thine
Is Caesar's homager : else so thy cheek pays shame   31
When shrill-tongued Fulvia scolds. The messengers !

ANTONY
Let Rome in Tiber melt and the wide arch
34   Of the ranged empire fall! Here is my space,
Kingdoms are clay : our dungy earth alike
Feeds beast as man. The nobleness of life
37   Is to do thus; when such a mutual pair
And such a twain can do't, in which I bind,
39   On pain of punishment, the world to weet
We stand up peerless.
CLEOPATRA   Excellent falsehood!
Why did he marry Fulvia, and not love her?
42   I'll seem the fool I am not. Antony
Will be himself.
ANTONY   But stirred by Cleopatra.
Now for the love of Love and her soft hours,
45   Let's not confound the time with conference harsh.
46   There's not a minute of our lives should stretch
Without some pleasure now. What sport to-night?
CLEOPATRA
Hear the ambassadors.
ANTONY   Fie, wrangling queen!
Whom every thing becomes – to chide, to laugh,
50   To weep; whose every passion fully strives
To make itself, in thee, fair and admired.
No messenger but thine, and all alone
To-night we'll wander through the streets and note
The qualities of people. Come, my queen ;
Last night you did desire it. – Speak not to us.
     Exeunt [Antony and Cleopatra] with the Train.
DEMETRIUS
56   Is Caesar with Antonius prized so slight?
PHILO
Sir, sometimes when he is not Antony
58   He comes too short of that great property
Which still should go with Antony.
DEMETRIUS   I am full sorry
60   That he approves the common liar, who
Thus speaks of him at Rome ; but I will hope
Of better deeds to-morrow. Rest you happy!   *Exeunt.*

                    *

I, ii   *Enter Enobarbus, Lamprius, a Soothsayer, Rannius,*
        Lucillius, Charmian, Iras, Mardian the Eunuch, and
        Alexas.
CHARMIAN Lord Alexas, sweet Alexas, most anything
2   Alexas, almost most absolute Alexas, where's the sooth-
sayer that you praised so to th' Queen? O that I knew
4   this husband which, you say, must charge his horns
with garlands!
ALEXAS Soothsayer!
SOOTHSAYER Your will?
CHARMIAN Is this the man? Is't you, sir, that know
things?
SOOTHSAYER
In nature's infinite book of secrecy
A little I can read.
ALEXAS Show him your hand.
ENOBARBUS
Bring in the banquet quickly : wine enough
Cleopatra's health to drink.
CHARMIAN Good sir, give me good fortune.
SOOTHSAYER
I make not, but foresee.

CHARMIAN Pray then, foresee me one.
SOOTHSAYER
You shall be yet far fairer than you are.
CHARMIAN He means in flesh.   17
IRAS No, you shall paint when you are old.
CHARMIAN Wrinkles forbid!
ALEXAS Vex not his prescience, be attentive.
CHARMIAN Hush!
SOOTHSAYER
You shall be more beloving than beloved.
CHARMIAN I had rather heat my liver with drinking.   23
ALEXAS Nay, hear him.
CHARMIAN Good now, some excellent fortune. Let me
be married to three kings in a forenoon and widow them
all. Let me have a child at fifty, to whom Herod of Jewry 27
may do homage. Find me to marry me with Octavius
Caesar, and companion me with my mistress.   29
SOOTHSAYER
You shall outlive the lady whom you serve.
CHARMIAN O excellent! I love long life better than figs.
SOOTHSAYER
You have seen and proved a fairer former fortune   32
Than that which is to approach.
CHARMIAN Then belike my children shall have no names. 34
Prithee, how many boys and wenches must I have?   35
SOOTHSAYER
If every of your wishes had a womb,
And fertile every wish, a million.
CHARMIAN Out, fool! I forgive thee for a witch.   38
ALEXAS You think none but your sheets are privy to your 39
wishes.
CHARMIAN Nay, come, tell Iras hers.
ALEXAS We'll know all our fortunes.
ENOBARBUS Mine, and most of our fortunes, to-night,
shall be – drunk to bed.
IRAS There's a palm presages chastity, if nothing else.
CHARMIAN E'en as the o'erflowing Nilus presageth
famine.
IRAS Go, you wild bedfellow, you cannot soothsay.
CHARMIAN Nay, if an oily palm be not a fruitful prog- 48
nostication, I cannot scratch mine ear. Prithee tell her
but a workyday fortune.   50
SOOTHSAYER Your fortunes are alike.
IRAS But how, but how? Give me particulars.
SOOTHSAYER I have said.
IRAS Am I not an inch of fortune better than she?

34 *ranged* well-ordered (?), wide-ranging (?)   37 *thus* (perhaps indicating
an embrace; perhaps a general reference to their way of life)   39 *weet*
know   42 *the fool . . . not* i.e. foolish enough to believe you   45 *confound*
destroy, waste   46 *stretch* pass   50 *passion* mood   56 *prized* valued
58 *property* distinction   60 *approves* confirms

I, ii The chambers of Cleopatra   s.d. *Enter Enobarbus . . . Alexas* (thus in
folio, but Lamprius, Rannius, and Lucillius do not speak in the scene and
do not appear elsewhere in the play. Possibly Lamprius is the name of the
Soothsayer.)   2 *absolute* perfect   4–5 *must . . . garlands* i.e. must be not
only a cuckold and grow horns (as cuckolds – husbands of unfaithful
wives – were humorously said to do) but a champion cuckold, wearing a
winner's garland   17 *He . . . flesh* he means that you will put on weight
23 *heat . . . drinking* i.e. rather than with unreciprocated love (the liver
being regarded as love's residence)   27–28 *to . . . homage* i.e. to whom even
King Herod (who massacred the infants of Judea) would do homage   29
companion me with give me as my servant   32 *proved* experienced   34
have no names illegitimate   35 *wenches* girls   38 *I . . . witch* i.e. I can
see that you have no prophetic powers   39 *privy to* in on the secret of
48 *oily palm* (symptom of sensuality); *fruitful prognostication* prophetic
sign of fertility   50 *workyday* ordinary

CHARMIAN Well, if you were but an inch of fortune better than I, where would you choose it?

IRAS Not in my husband's nose.

CHARMIAN Our worser thoughts Heavens mend! Alexas
– come, his fortune, his fortune. O, let him marry a
60 woman that cannot go, sweet Isis, I beseech thee, and
let her die too, and give him a worse, and let worse
follow worse till the worst of all follow him laughing
to his grave, fiftyfold a cuckold. Good Isis, hear me this
prayer, though thou deny me a matter of more weight:
good Isis, I beseech thee.

IRAS Amen, dear goddess, hear that prayer of the people.
67 For, as it is a heartbreaking to see a handsome man loose-
wived, so it is a deadly sorrow to behold a foul knave
69 uncuckolded. Therefore, dear Isis, keep decorum, and
fortune him accordingly.

CHARMIAN Amen.

ALEXAS Lo now, if it lay in their hands to make me a
cuckold, they would make themselves whores but
74 they'ld do't.

Enter Cleopatra.

ENOBARBUS
Hush, here comes Antony.

CHARMIAN   Not he, the Queen.

CLEOPATRA
Saw you my lord?

ENOBARBUS   No, lady.

CLEOPATRA   Was he not here?

CHARMIAN No, madam.

CLEOPATRA
He was disposed to mirth; but on the sudden
A Roman thought hath struck him. Enobarbus!

ENOBARBUS Madam?

CLEOPATRA
Seek him, and bring him hither. Where's Alexas?

ALEXAS
Here at your service. My lord approaches.

Enter Antony with a Messenger [and Attendants].

CLEOPATRA
We will not look upon him. Go with us.

*Exeunt [all but Antony, Messenger,
and Attendants].*

MESSENGER
Fulvia thy wife first came into the field.

ANTONY
Against my brother Lucius?

MESSENGER Ay.
87 But soon that war had end, and the time's state
Made friends of them, jointing their force 'gainst Caesar,

Whose better issue in the war from Italy   89
Upon the first encounter drave them.   90

ANTONY   Well, what worst?

MESSENGER
The nature of bad news infects the teller.

ANTONY
When it concerns the fool or coward. On.
Things that are past are done with me. 'Tis thus:
Who tells me true, though in his tale lie death,
I hear him as he flattered.   95

MESSENGER   Labienus
(This is stiff news) hath with his Parthian force
Extended Asia: from Euphrates,   97
His conquering banner shook, from Syria
To Lydia and to Ionia,
Whilst –

ANTONY Antony, thou wouldst say.

MESSENGER   O, my lord.

ANTONY
Speak to me home, mince not the general tongue,   101
Name Cleopatra as she is called in Rome:
Rail thou in Fulvia's phrase, and taunt my faults
With such full license as both truth and malice   104
Have power to utter. O, then we bring forth weeds
When our quick minds lie still, and our ills told us   106
Is as our earing. Fare thee well awhile.   107

MESSENGER
At your noble pleasure.   *Exit Messenger.*

ANTONY
From Sicyon, how the news? Speak there!

1. ATTENDANT
The man from Sicyon – is there such an one?

2. ATTENDANT
He stays upon your will.   111

ANTONY   Let him appear.
These strong Egyptian fetters I must break
Or lose myself in dotage.

Enter another Messenger, with a letter.
                                   What are you?

MESSENGER
Fulvia thy wife is dead.

ANTONY   Where died she?

MESSENGER
In Sicyon.
Her length of sickness, with what else more serious
Importeth thee to know, this bears.   117

[Gives a letter.]

ANTONY   Forbear me. *[Exit Messenger.]*
There's a great spirit gone! Thus did I desire it:
What our contempts doth often hurl from us,
We wish it ours again. The present pleasure,
By revolution low'ring, does become   121
The opposite of itself: she's good, being gone;
The hand could pluck her back that shoved her on.
I must from this enchanting queen break off: 124
Ten thousand harms, more than the ills I know,
My idleness doth hatch.   126

Enter Enobarbus.
How now, Enobarbus!

ENOBARBUS What's your pleasure, sir?

ANTONY I must with haste from hence.

ENOBARBUS Why, then we kill all our women. We see
how mortal an unkindness is to them. If they suffer our
departure, death's the word.

60 *go* bear children (?), give – or receive – sexual satisfaction (?); *Isis*
Egyptian goddess of earth, fertility, and the moon 67 *loose-wived* married
to a loose woman 69 *keep decorum* i.e. act as suits his quality 74 s.d.
(this, the folio's, placing of Cleopatra's entrance suggests either that the
sound of her approach is heard before she can be seen, thus causing
Enobarbus' error, or that his remark is ironical, alluding to her power over
Antony's will) 87 *time's state* conditions of the moment 89 *issue* success
90 *drave* drove 95 *as* as if; *Labienus* Quintus Labienus, who had been sent
by Brutus and Cassius to seek aid against Antony and Octavius Caesar
from Orodes, King of Parthia, and was now commanding a Parthian army
97 *Extended* seized 101 *home* plainly; *mince . . . tongue* don't soften what
everybody is saying 104 *license* freedom 106 *quick* live, fertile 107
earing being ploughed (to uproot the weeds) 111 *stays upon* awaits
117 *Importeth* concerns; *Forbear* leave 121 *By revolution low'ring* i.e.
moving downward on the revolving wheel of our opinions 124 *enchanting*
(Cleopatra is felt by the Romans in the play to have witchlike powers of
seduction) 126 *idleness* trifling

ANTONY I must be gone.

ENOBARBUS Under a compelling occasion let women die: It were pity to cast them away for nothing, though between them and a great cause they should be esteemed nothing. Cleopatra, catching but the least noise of this, dies instantly: I have seen her die twenty times
139 upon far poorer moment. I do think there is mettle in death, which commits some loving act upon her, she hath such a celerity in dying.

ANTONY She is cunning past man's thought.

ENOBARBUS Alack, sir, no; her passions are made of nothing but the finest part of pure love. We cannot call her winds and waters sighs and tears: they are greater storms and tempests than almanacs can report. This
147 cannot be cunning in her; if it be, she makes a shower of
148 rain as well as Jove.

ANTONY Would I had never seen her!

ENOBARBUS O, sir, you had then left unseen a wonderful piece of work, which not to have been blest withal would have discredited your travel.

ANTONY Fulvia is dead.

ENOBARBUS Sir?

ANTONY Fulvia is dead.

ENOBARBUS Fulvia?

ANTONY Dead.

ENOBARBUS Why, sir, give the gods a thankful sacrifice. When it pleaseth their deities to take the wife of a man
160 from him, it shows to man the tailors of the earth; comforting therein, that when old robes are worn out, there are members to make new. If there were no more
163 women but Fulvia, then had you indeed a cut, and the
164 case to be lamented. This grief is crowned with consolation, your old smock brings forth a new petticoat, and indeed the tears live in an onion that should water this sorrow.

ANTONY
167 The business she hath broachèd in the state Cannot endure my absence.

169 ENOBARBUS And the business you have broached here cannot be without you; especially that of Cleopatra's,
171 which wholly depends on your abode.

ANTONY
No more light answers. Let our officers
173 Have notice what we purpose. I shall break
174 The cause of our expedience to the Queen And get her leave to part. For not alone
176 The death of Fulvia, with more urgent touches, Do strongly speak to us, but the letters too
178 Of many our contriving friends in Rome
179 Petition us at home. Sextus Pompeius Hath given the dare to Caesar and commands The empire of the sea. Our slippery people, Whose love is never linked to the deserver
183 Till his deserts are past, begin to throw Pompey the Great and all his dignities Upon his son; who, high in name and power,
186 Higher than both in blood and life, stands up
187 For the main soldier; whose quality, going on,
188 The sides o' th' world may danger. Much is breeding,
189 Which, like the courser's hair, hath yet but life And not a serpent's poison. Say, our pleasure,
191 To such whose place is under us, requires Our quick remove from hence.

ENOBARBUS I shall do't.   [Exeunt.]

Enter Cleopatra, Charmian, Alexas, and Iras.   I, iii

CLEOPATRA
Where is he?

CHARMIAN   I did not see him since.

CLEOPATRA
See where he is, who's with him, what he does: I did not send you. If you find him sad,   3
Say I am dancing; if in mirth, report That I am sudden sick. Quick, and return. [Exit Alexas.]

CHARMIAN
Madam, methinks, if you did love him dearly, You do not hold the method to enforce The like from him.

CLEOPATRA   What should I do, I do not?   8

CHARMIAN
In each thing give him way, cross him in nothing.

CLEOPATRA
Thou teachest like a fool: the way to lose him!

CHARMIAN
Tempt him not so too far. I wish, forbear.   11
In time we hate that which we often fear.
    Enter Antony.
But here comes Antony.

CLEOPATRA   I am sick and sullen.

ANTONY
I am sorry to give breathing to my purpose –   14

CLEOPATRA
Help me away, dear Charmian! I shall fall. It cannot be thus long; the sides of nature   16
Will not sustain it.

ANTONY   Now, my dearest queen –

CLEOPATRA
Pray you stand farther from me.

ANTONY   What's the matter?

CLEOPATRA
I know by that same eye there's some good news. What, says the married woman you may go?   20
Would she had never given you leave to come! Let her not say 'tis I that keep you here. I have no power upon you: hers you are.

ANTONY
The gods best know –

CLEOPATRA   O, never was there queen So mightily betrayed: yet at the first I saw the treasons planted.

ANTONY   Cleopatra –

CLEOPATRA
Why should I think you can be mine, and true, (Though you in swearing shake the thronèd gods) Who have been false to Fulvia? Riotous madness,

139 *moment* cause; *mettle* vigor   147 *makes* manufactures   148 *Jove* i.e. Jupiter Pluvius, Roman god of rain   160 *the tailors* i.e. that the gods are the tailors   163, 164, 169 (in *cut, case, business,* and *broached*, Enobarbus puns bawdily)   167 *broachèd* opened up   171 *abode* staying   173 *break tell*   174 *expedience* haste   176 *touches* motives   178 *contriving* i.e. acting in my interest   179 *at home* to return home; *Sextus Pompeius* son of Pompey the Great, who had been outlawed, but, owing to the division between Antony and Octavius Caesar, was able to seize Sicily and command the Roman sea-routes   183 *throw* transfer   186 *blood and life* vital energy   187 *quality* character and position; *going on* evolving   188 *danger* endanger   189 *courser's hair* (horse hairs in water were thought to come to life as small serpents)   191 *place* rank
I, iii The chambers of Cleopatra   3 *sad* serious   8 *I do not* that I am not doing   11 *Tempt* try; *I wish* I wish you would   14 *breathing* utterance   16 *sides of nature* human body   20 *the married woman* i.e. Fulvia

To be entangled with those mouth-made vows
Which break themselves in swearing.

ANTONY   Most sweet queen –

CLEOPATRA

32   Nay, pray you seek no color for your going,
33   But bid farewell, and go : when you sued staying,
    Then was the time for words : no going then,
    Eternity was in our lips and eyes,
36   Bliss in our brows' bent : none our parts so poor
37   But was a race of heaven. They are so still,
    Or thou, the greatest soldier of the world,
    Art turned the greatest liar.

ANTONY   How now, lady ?

CLEOPATRA

    I would I had thy inches ; thou shouldst know
41   There were a heart in Egypt.

ANTONY   Hear me, Queen :
    The strong necessity of time commands
    Our services awhile, but my full heart
44   Remains in use with you. Our Italy
45   Shines o'er with civil swords ; Sextus Pompeius
    Makes his approaches to the port of Rome ;
    Equality of two domestic powers
48   Breed scrupulous faction ; the hated, grown to strength,
    Are newly grown to love ; the condemned Pompey,
    Rich in his father's honor, creeps apace
    Into the hearts of such as have not thrived
52   Upon the present state, whose numbers threaten ;
53   And quietness, grown sick of rest, would purge
54   By any desperate change. My more particular,
55   And that which most with you should safe my going,
    Is Fulvia's death.

CLEOPATRA

    Though age from folly could not give me freedom,
    It does from childishness. Can Fulvia die ?

ANTONY

    She's dead, my queen.
    Look here, and at thy sovereign leisure read
61   The garboils she awaked. At the last, best,
    See when and where she died.

CLEOPATRA   O most false love !
63   Where be the sacred vials thou shouldst fill
    With sorrowful water ? Now I see, I see,
    In Fulvia's death, how mine received shall be.

ANTONY

    Quarrel no more, but be prepared to know
    The purposes I bear : which are, or cease,
    As you shall give th' advice. By the fire   68
    That quickens Nilus' slime, I go from hence   69
    Thy soldier, servant, making peace or war
    As thou affects.   71

CLEOPATRA   Cut my lace, Charmian, come ;
    But let it be, I am quickly ill, and well –
    So Antony loves.   73

ANTONY   My precious queen, forbear,
    And give true evidence to his love, which stands   74
    An honorable trial.

CLEOPATRA   So Fulvia told me.   75
    I prithee turn aside and weep for her ;
    Then bid adieu to me, and say the tears
    Belong to Egypt. Good now, play one scene
    Of excellent dissembling, and let it look,
    Like perfect honor.

ANTONY   You'll heat my blood : no more.

CLEOPATRA

    You can do better yet ; but this is meetly.   81

ANTONY

    Now by my sword –

CLEOPATRA   And target. Still he mends.   82
    But this is not the best. Look, prithee, Charmian,
    How this Herculean Roman does become   84
    The carriage of his chafe.

ANTONY

    I'll leave you, lady.

CLEOPATRA   Courteous lord, one word.
    Sir, you and I must part, but that's not it :
    Sir, you and I have loved, but there's not it :
    That you know well. Something it is I would –
    O, my oblivion is a very Antony,   90
    And I am all forgotten.   91

ANTONY   But that your royalty
    Holds idleness your subject, I should take you
    For idleness itself.

CLEOPATRA   'Tis sweating labor
    To bear such idleness so near the heart
    As Cleopatra this. But, sir, forgive me,
    Since my becomings kill me when they do not   96
    Eye well to you. Your honor calls you hence ;   97
    Therefore be deaf to my unpitied folly,
    And all the gods go with you. Upon your sword
    Sit laurel victory, and smooth success
    Be strewed before your feet !

ANTONY   Let us go. Come :
    Our separation so abides and flies
    That thou residing here goes yet with me,
    And I hence fleeting here remain with thee.
    Away !   *Exeunt.*

*

Enter Octavius [Caesar], reading a letter, Lepidus,   I, iv
and their Train.

CAESAR

    You may see, Lepidus, and henceforth know
    It is not Caesar's natural vice to hate
    Our great competitor. From Alexandria   3
    This is the news : he fishes, drinks, and wastes
    The lamps of night in revel ; is not more manlike
    Than Cleopatra, nor the queen of Ptolemy   6

32 *color* pretext   **33** *sued* begged for   **36** *bent* curve   **37** *a race of heaven*
of heavenly origin (?), of heavenly flavor (?)   **41** *Egypt* Cleopatra   **44**
in . . . you for you to keep and use   **45** *civil swords* i.e. civil war   **48**
scrupulous faction contest over trifles   **52** *state* government   **53–54**
grown . . . change i.e. ill through peace, would cure itself by letting blood
54 *particular* personal concern   **55** *safe* make safe   **61** *garboils* commotions ;
best best news of all   **63–64** *sacred vials . . . water* (a reference to the practice
of consecrating bottles of tears to the dead)   **68** *fire* i.e. the sun   **69**
quickens vivifies ; *Nilus' slime* fertile mud left by the Nile's annual overflow
71 *forbear* desist   **73** *So* provided (?), with
sudden changes like my own change now (?) ; *forbear* desist   **74** *stands*
will sustain   **75** *told* taught (through my observing how faithful you were
to her)   **81** *meetly* well suited to the occasion   **82** *target* shield   **84–85**
How . . . chafe i.e. how becomingly he plays his role of angry Hercules
(from whom Antony was supposed to be descended)   **90** *my . . . Antony*
my forgetfulness is like Antony, who is now leaving, i.e. forgetting, me
91 *I . . . forgotten* (1) I have forgotten what I was going to say, (2) I am all
forgotten by Antony   **91–92** *But . . . subject* if you were not the queen of
trifling   **96** *my becomings* the emotions that become me (in my situation
of abandoned lover)   **97** *Eye* look
I, iv The house of Octavius Caesar in Rome   **3** *competitor* partner   **6**
Ptolemy Cleopatra's dead husband

1177

7   More womanly than he ; hardly gave audience, or
    Vouchsafed to think he had partners. You shall find there
9   A man who is the abstract of all faults
    That all men follow.

LEPIDUS   I must not think there are
11   Evils enow to darken all his goodness :
12   His faults, in him, seem as the spots of heaven,
    More fiery by night's blackness ; hereditary
14   Rather than purchased, what he cannot change
    Than what he chooses.

CAESAR
    You are too indulgent. Let's grant it is not
    Amiss to tumble on the bed of Ptolemy,
    To give a kingdom for a mirth, to sit
19   And keep the turn of tippling with a slave,
20   To reel the streets at noon, and stand the buffet
    With knaves that smell of sweat. Say this becomes him
22   (As his composure must be rare indeed
    Whom these things cannot blemish), yet must Antony
24   No way excuse his foils when we do bear
    So great weight in his lightness. If he filled
26   His vacancy with his voluptuousness,
27   Full surfeits and the dryness of his bones
28   Call on him for't. But to confound such time
29   That drums him from his sport and speaks as loud
    As his own state and ours, 'tis to be chid
31   As we rate boys who, being mature in knowledge,
    Pawn their experience to their present pleasure
33   And so rebel to judgment.

Enter a Messenger.

LEPIDUS   Here's more news.

MESSENGER
    Thy biddings have been done, and every hour,
    Most noble Caesar, shalt thou have report
    How 'tis abroad. Pompey is strong at sea,
    And it appears he is beloved of those
    That only have feared Caesar : to the ports
39   The discontents repair, and men's reports
40   Give him much wronged.

CAESAR   I should have known no less.
41   It hath been taught us from the primal state
    That he which is was wished until he were ;
    And the ebbed man, ne'er loved till ne'er worth love,
44   Comes deared by being lacked. This common body,
45   Like to a vagabond flag upon the stream,
46   Goes to and back, lackeying the varying tide,
    To rot itself with motion.

MESSENGER   Caesar, I bring thee word
    Menecrates and Menas, famous pirates,
    Make the sea serve them, which they ear and wound
    With keels of every kind. Many hot inroads
    They make in Italy ; the borders maritime
52   Lack blood to think on't, and flush youth revolt.
    No vessel can peep forth but 'tis as soon
54   Taken as seen ; for Pompey's name strikes more
    Than could his war resisted.

CAESAR   Antony,
56   Leave thy lascivious wassails. When thou once
    Was beaten from Modena, where thou slew'st
    Hirtius and Pansa, consuls, at thy heel
    Did famine follow, whom thou fought'st against
    (Though daintily brought up) with patience more
    Than savages could suffer. Thou didst drink
62   The stale of horses and the gilded puddle

Which beasts would cough at. Thy palate then did deign
The roughest berry on the rudest hedge.
Yea, like the stag when snow the pasture sheets,
The barks of trees thou browsed. On the Alps
It is reported thou didst eat strange flesh,
Which some did die to look on. And all this
(It wounds thine honor that I speak it now)
Was borne so like a soldier that thy cheek
So much as lanked not.   71

LEPIDUS   'Tis pity of him.

CAESAR
    Let his shames quickly
    Drive him to Rome. 'Tis time we twain
    Did show ourselves i' th' field ; and to that end
    Assemble we immediate council. Pompey
    Thrives in our idleness.

LEPIDUS   To-morrow, Caesar,
    I shall be furnished to inform you rightly
    Both what by sea and land I can be able   78
    To front this present time.   79

CAESAR   Till which encounter,
    It is my business too. Farewell.

LEPIDUS
    Farewell, my lord. What you shall know meantime
    Of stirs abroad, I shall beseech you, sir,
    To let me be partaker.

CAESAR   Doubt not, sir ;
    I knew it for my bond.   *Exeunt.* 84

*

Enter Cleopatra, Charmian, Iras, and Mardian.   I, v

CLEOPATRA Charmian !

CHARMIAN Madam ?

CLEOPATRA
    Ha, ha.   3
    Give me to drink mandragora.   4

CHARMIAN   Why, madam ?

CLEOPATRA
    That I might sleep out this great gap of time
    My Antony is away.

CHARMIAN   You think of him too much.

CLEOPATRA
    O, 'tis treason !

CHARMIAN   Madam, I trust, not so.

7 *audience* i.e. to Caesar's messengers (cf. I, i) 9 *is the abstract of* sums up 11 *enow* enough 12–13 *His . . . blackness* i.e. like stars that show the brighter by night's blackness, Antony's faults stand out the more in the present dark political situation 14 *purchased* acquired 19 *keep . . . of* take turns 20 *stand the buffet* trade blows 22 *his composure* that man's make-up 24 *foils* disgraces 24–25 *when . . . lightness* when his levity puts so heavy a burden upon us 26 *vacancy* leisure 27–28 *Full . . . him* i.e. let his own physical symptoms be the reckoning 28 *confound* destroy, waste 29–30 *speaks . . . ours* calls urgently for decisions affecting the political futures of all of us 31 *rate* berate ; *mature in knowledge* old enough to know better 33 *to judgment* against good sense 39 *discontents* discontented 40 *Give* declare 41 *from . . . state* since government began 44 *Comes deared* becomes beloved ; *common body* common people 45 *flag* iris 46 *lackeying* following obsequiously 52 *Lack blood* grow pale ; *flush* vigorous 54–55 *strikes . . . resisted* is more effective than his forces would be if opposed 56 *wassails* carousings 62 *stale* urine ; *gilded* yellow-colored 71 *lanked* thinned 78 *be able* muster 79 *front* cope with 84 *bond* duty
I, v The chambers of Cleopatra 3 *Ha, ha* (perhaps indicating a yawn) 4 *mandragora* mandrake (a narcotic)

CLEOPATRA
Thou, eunuch Mardian!

MARDIAN   What's your Highness' pleasure?

CLEOPATRA
Not now to hear thee sing. I take no pleasure
In aught an eunuch has : 'tis well for thee
11   That, being unseminared, thy freer thoughts
May not fly forth of Egypt. Hast thou affections?

MARDIAN   Yes, gracious madam.

CLEOPATRA   Indeed?

MARDIAN
Not in deed, madam; for I can do nothing
But what indeed is honest to be done :
Yet have I fierce affections, and think
What Venus did with Mars.

CLEOPATRA   O Charmian,
Where think'st thou he is now? Stands he, or sits he?
Or does he walk? or is he on his horse?
O happy horse, to bear the weight of Antony!
22   Do bravely, horse! for wot'st thou whom thou mov'st?
23   The demi-Atlas of this earth, the arm
24   And burgonet of men. He's speaking now,
Or murmuring, 'Where's my serpent of old Nile?'
(For so he calls me). Now I feed myself
With most delicious poison. Think on me,
28   That am with Phoebus' amorous pinches black
29   And wrinkled deep in time? Broad-fronted Caesar,
When thou wast here above the ground, I was
A morsel for a monarch; and great Pompey
Would stand and make his eyes grow in my brow;
33   There would he anchor his aspect, and die
With looking on his life.
     Enter Alexas.

ALEXAS   Sovereign of Egypt, hail!

CLEOPATRA
How much unlike art thou Mark Antony!
36   Yet, coming from him, that great med'cine hath
With his tinct gilded thee.
38   How goes it with my brave Mark Antony?

ALEXAS
Last thing he did, dear Queen,
He kissed – the last of many doubled kisses –
41   This orient pearl. His speech sticks in my heart.

CLEOPATRA
Mine ear must pluck it thence.

ALEXAS   'Good friend,' quoth he,
43   'Say the firm Roman to great Egypt sends
This treasure of an oyster; at whose foot,
To mend the petty present, I will piece
Her opulent throne with kingdoms. All the East
(Say thou) shall call her mistress.' So he nodded,

And soberly did mount an arm-gaunt steed,   48
Who neighed so high that what I would have spoke
Was beastly dumbed by him.   50

CLEOPATRA   What was he, sad or merry?

ALEXAS
Like to the time o' th' year between the extremes
Of hot and cold, he was nor sad nor merry.

CLEOPATRA
O well-divided disposition! Note him,
Note him, good Charmian, 'tis the man; but note him.   54
He was not sad, for he would shine on those
That make their looks by his; he was not merry,
Which seemed to tell them his remembrance lay
In Egypt with his joy; but between both.
O heavenly mingle! Be'st thou sad or merry,
The violence of either thee becomes,
So does it no man else. – Met'st thou my posts?   61

ALEXAS
Ay, madam, twenty several messengers.
Why do you send so thick?

CLEOPATRA   Who's born that day
When I forget to send to Antony
Shall die a beggar. Ink and paper, Charmian.
Welcome, my good Alexas. Did I, Charmian,
Ever love Caesar so?

CHARMIAN   O that brave Caesar!

CLEOPATRA
Be choked with such another emphasis!
Say 'the brave Antony.'

CHARMIAN   The valiant Caesar!

CLEOPATRA
By Isis, I will give thee bloody teeth
If thou with Caesar paragon again   71
My man of men.

CHARMIAN   By your most gracious pardon,
I sing but after you.

CLEOPATRA   My salad days,   73
When I was green in judgment, cold in blood,
To say as I said then. But come, away,
Get me ink and paper.
He shall have every day a several greeting,
Or I'll unpeople Egypt.   *Exeunt.* 78

*

     Enter Pompey, Menecrates, and Menas, in warlike   II, i
     manner.

POMPEY
If the great gods be just, they shall assist
The deeds of justest men.

MENECRATES   Know, worthy Pompey,
That what they do delay, they not deny.

POMPEY
Whiles we are suitors to their throne, decays   4
The thing we sue for.

MENECRATES   We, ignorant of ourselves,
Beg often our own harms, which the wise pow'rs
Deny us for our good : so find we profit
By losing of our prayers.

POMPEY   I shall do well :
The people love me, and the sea is mine;
My powers are crescent, and my auguring hope   10
Says it will come to th' full. Mark Antony   11
In Egypt sits at dinner, and will make

---

11 *unseminared* unsexed   22 *wot'st* knowest   23 *demi-Atlas* i.e. Antony and Caesar, like Atlas, support the world between them (Lepidus being of no importance)   24 *burgonet* helmet   28 *Phoebus'* the sun's   29 *Broad-fronted* with broad forehead; *Caesar* Julius Caesar   33 *aspect* gaze   36–37 *that . . . thee* (Cleopatra playfully compares Antony to the 'great medicine' of the alchemists which turned baser metals to gold : even Alexas shows some effect)   38 *brave* splendid   41 *orient* i.e. bright as the east   43 *firm* constant   48 *arm-gaunt* toughened for war (?), battle-hungry (?)   50 *dumbed* silenced   54 *the man* i.e. the real Antony   61 *posts* messengers   71 *paragon* compare   73 *salad days* green youth   78 *unpeople* i.e. by sending messengers to Antony
II, i Pompey's house in Messina   4–5 *Whiles . . . for* i.e. the thing we pray for loses its worth even while we pray   10 *crescent* increasing   11 *it* i.e. my fortunes (imaged as a crescent moon)

No wars without doors. Caesar gets money where
He loses hearts. Lepidus flatters both,
Of both is flattered; but he neither loves,
Nor either cares for him.

MENAS   Caesar and Lepidus
Are in the field; a mighty strength they carry.

POMPEY
Where have you this? 'Tis false.

MENAS   From Silvius, sir.

POMPEY
He dreams: I know they are in Rome together,
Looking for Antony. But all the charms of love,
21 Salt Cleopatra, soften thy waned lip!
Let witchcraft join with beauty, lust with both!
Tie up the libertine in a field of feasts,
Keep his brain fuming. Epicurean cooks
25 Sharpen with cloyless sauce his appetite,
26 That sleep and feeding may prorogue his honor
27 Even till a Lethe'd dulness –
    Enter Varrius.   How now, Varrius?

VARRIUS
This is most certain that I shall deliver:
Mark Antony is every hour in Rome
Expected. Since he went from Egypt 'tis
31 A space for farther travel.

POMPEY   I could have given less matter
A better ear. Menas, I did not think
33 This amorous surfeiter would have donned his helm
For such a petty war. His soldiership
Is twice the other twain. But let us rear
36 The higher our opinion, that our stirring
Can from the lap of Egypt's widow pluck
The ne'er-lust-wearied Antony.

38 MENAS   I cannot hope
39 Caesar and Antony shall well greet together;
His wife that's dead did trespasses to Caesar;
41 His brother warred upon him; although I think
Not moved by Antony.

POMPEY   I know not, Menas,
How lesser enmities may give way to greater.
Were't not that we stand up against them all,
45 'Twere pregnant they should square between them-
      selves,
For they have entertainèd cause enough
To draw their swords; but how the fear of us
May cement their divisions and bind up
The petty difference, we yet not know.
50 Be't as our gods will have't! It only stands
Our lives upon to use our strongest hands.
Come, Menas.   *Exeunt.*

                         *

II, ii   *Enter Enobarbus and Lepidus.*

LEPIDUS
Good Enobarbus, 'tis a worthy deed,
And shall become you well, to entreat your captain
To soft and gentle speech.

ENOBARBUS   I shall entreat him
4   To answer like himself. If Caesar move him,
Let Antony look over Caesar's head
And speak as loud as Mars. By Jupiter,
Were I the wearer of Antonio's beard,
8   I would not shave't to-day!

LEPIDUS   'Tis not a time
For private stomaching.   9

ENOBARBUS   Every time
Serves for the matter that is then born in't.

LEPIDUS
But small to greater matters must give way.

ENOBARBUS
Not if the small come first.

LEPIDUS   Your speech is passion;
But pray you stir no embers up. Here comes
The noble Antony.
    Enter Antony and Ventidius.

ENOBARBUS   And yonder, Caesar.
    Enter Caesar, Maecenas, and Agrippa.

ANTONY
If we compose well here, to Parthia.   15
Hark, Ventidius.

CAESAR   I do not know,
Maecenas; ask Agrippa.

LEPIDUS   Noble friends,
That which combined us was most great, and let not
A leaner action rend us. What's amiss,
May it be gently heard. When we debate
Our trivial difference loud, we do commit
Murder in healing wounds. Then, noble partners,
The rather for I earnestly beseech,   23
Touch you the sourest points with sweetest terms,
Nor curstness grow to th' matter.   25

ANTONY   'Tis spoken well.
Were we before our armies, and to fight,
I should do thus.   27
    Flourish.

CAESAR
Welcome to Rome.

ANTONY   Thank you.

CAESAR   Sit.

ANTONY   Sit, sir.

CAESAR   Nay then.
    [They sit.]

ANTONY
I learn you take things ill which are not so,
Or being, concern you not.

CAESAR   I must be laughed at
If, or for nothing or a little, I   31
Should say myself offended, and with you
Chiefly i' th' world; more laughed at that I should
Once name you derogately, when to sound your name   34
It not concerned me.

ANTONY   My being in Egypt, Caesar,
What was't to you?

CAESAR
No more than my residing here at Rome

21 *Salt* lustful; *waned* faded   25 *cloyless* which never cloys   26 *prorogue* suspend   27 *Lethe'd dulness* i.e. an oblivion as deep as that which comes from drinking of the river Lethe in the underworld   31 *A space . . . travel* time enough for even a longer journey   33 *surfeiter* one who indulges to excess   36 *opinion* i.e. of ourselves   38 *hope* expect   39 *greet* get on   41 *brother* (cf. I, ii, 84–90)   45 *pregnant* likely; *square* quarrel   50–51 *stands . . . upon* is a matter of life and death
II, ii The house of Lepidus in Rome   4 *like himself* as befits his greatness   8 *I . . . shave't* i.e. I would dare Caesar to pluck it   9 *stomaching* resentment   15 *compose* reach agreement   23 *The rather for* all the more because   25 *Nor . . . matter* and let not ill temper make matters worse   27 *thus* (Antony makes some courteous gesture)   31 *or . . . or* either . . . or   34 *derogately* disparagingly

        Might be to you in Egypt : yet if you there
39   Did practice on my state, your being in Egypt
40   Might be my question.
ANTONY   How intend you ? practiced ?
CAESAR
        You may be pleased to catch at mine intent
        By what did here befall me. Your wife and brother
        Made wars upon me, and their contestation
44   Was theme for you ; you were the word of war.
ANTONY
        You do mistake your business : my brother never
46   Did urge me in his act. I did inquire it
47   And have my learning from some true reports
        That drew their swords with you. Did he not rather
        Discredit my authority with yours,
50   And make the wars alike against my stomach,
51   Having alike your cause ? Of this my letters
52   Before did satisfy you. If you'll patch a quarrel,
        As matter whole you have to make it with,
        It must not be with this.
CAESAR   You praise yourself
        By laying defects of judgment to me, but
        You patched up your excuses.
ANTONY   Not so, not so :
        I know you could not lack, I am certain on't,
        Very necessity of this thought, that I,
        Your partner in the cause 'gainst which he fought,
60   Could not with graceful eyes attend those wars
        Which fronted mine own peace. As for my wife,
        I would you had her spirit in such another ;
63   The third o' th' world is yours, which with a snaffle
64   You may pace easy, but not such a wife.
ENOBARBUS Would we had all such wives, that the men
        might go to wars with the women.
ANTONY
67   So much uncurbable, her garboils, Caesar,
        Made out of her impatience – which not wanted
        Shrewdness of policy too – I grieving grant
        Did you too much disquiet : for that you must
        But say I could not help it.
CAESAR   I wrote to you
        When rioting in Alexandria ; you
        Did pocket up my letters, and with taunts
74   Did gibe my missive out of audience.
ANTONY   Sir,
        He fell upon me, ere admitted, then :
76   Three kings I had newly feasted, and did want
        Of what I was i' th' morning ; but next day
78   I told him of myself, which was as much
        As to have asked him pardon. Let this fellow

        Be nothing of our strife : if we contend,
        Out of our question wipe him.   81
CAESAR   You have broken
        The article of your oath, which you shall never
        Have tongue to charge me with.
LEPIDUS   Soft, Caesar.
ANTONY   No,
        Lepidus ; let him speak.
        The honor is sacred which he talks on now,   85
        Supposing that I lacked it. But on, Caesar,
        The article of my oath –
CAESAR
        To lend me arms and aid when I required them,
        The which you both denied.
ANTONY   Neglected rather :
        And then when poisonèd hours had bound me up   90
        From mine own knowledge. As nearly as I may,
        I'll play the penitent to you. But mine honesty   92
        Shall not make poor my greatness, nor my power
        Work without it. Truth is, that Fulvia,
        To have me out of Egypt, made wars here,
        For which myself, the ignorant motive, do
        So far ask pardon as befits mine honor
        To stoop in such a case.
LEPIDUS   'Tis noble spoken.
MAECENAS
        If it might please you, to enforce no further
        The griefs between ye : to forget them quite
        Were to remember that the present need
        Speaks to atone you.   102
LEPIDUS   Worthily spoken, Maecenas.
ENOBARBUS Or, if you borrow one another's love for the
        instant, you may, when you hear no more words of
        Pompey, return it again : you shall have time to wrangle
        in when you have nothing else to do.
ANTONY
        Thou art a soldier only, speak no more.
ENOBARBUS That truth should be silent I had almost
        forgot.
ANTONY
        You wrong this presence, therefore speak no more.   109
ENOBARBUS Go to, then ; your considerate stone.   110
CAESAR
        I do not much dislike the matter, but
        The manner of his speech ; for't cannot be
        We shall remain in friendship, our conditions
        So diff'ring in their acts. Yet if I knew
        What hoop should hold us staunch, from edge to edge
        O' th' world I would pursue it.
AGRIPPA   Give me leave, Caesar.
CAESAR
        Speak, Agrippa.
AGRIPPA
        Thou hast a sister by the mother's side,
        Admired Octavia : great Mark Antony
        Is now a widower.
CAESAR   Say not so, Agrippa :
        If Cleopatra heard you, your reproof
        Were well deserved of rashness.   122
ANTONY
        I am not married, Caesar : let me hear
        Agrippa further speak.
AGRIPPA
        To hold you in perpetual amity,

---

39 *practice on* plot against   **40** *question* concern   **44** *you were . . . war* the war was carried on in your name   **46** *urge me* use my name   **47** *reports* reporters   **50** *stomach* desire   **51** *Having . . . cause* i.e. I having as much cause as you to resent it   **52–54** *If . . . this* i.e. if you are determined to patch a quarrel out of pieces, when you actually have whole cloth to fashion it from (cf. ll. 81–98), this is not the right piece   **60** *with . . . attend* regard with pleasure   **63** *snaffle* bridle bit   **64** *pace* manage   **67** *garboils* commotions   **74** *missive* messenger   **76–77** *did . . . morning* was not myself   **78** *myself* my condition   **81** *question* argument   **85** *honor* i.e. keeping an oath   **90–91** *bound . . . knowledge* i.e. prevented my realizing what I was doing   **92–94** *mine . . . it* i.e. my actions will be prompted by my honesty (which makes me willing to apologize) but also by my power (which does not intend to grovel)   **102** *atone* reconcile   **109** *presence* company   **110** *your considerate stone* i.e. I'll be dumb as a stone, but still thinking (considering)   **122** *of rashness* because of your rashness (in ignoring Antony's bond to Cleopatra)

To make you brothers, and to knit your hearts
With an unslipping knot, take Antony
Octavia to his wife ; whose beauty claims
No worse a husband than the best of men ;
Whose virtue and whose general graces speak
That which none else can utter. By this marriage
132 All little jealousies, which now seem great,
And all great fears, which now import their dangers,
134 Would then be nothing : truths would be tales,
Where now half-tales be truths : her love to both
Would each to other, and all loves to both,
Draw after her. Pardon what I have spoke ;
For 'tis a studied, not a present thought,
By duty ruminated.

ANTONY   Will Caesar speak ?

CAESAR
Not till he hears how Antony is touched
With what is spoke already.

ANTONY   What power is in Agrippa,
If I would say, 'Agrippa, be it so,'
To make this good ?

CAESAR   The power of Caesar, and
His power unto Octavia.

ANTONY   May I never
145 To this good purpose, that so fairly shows,
Dream of impediment : let me have thy hand :
147 Further this act of grace, and from this hour
The heart of brothers govern in our loves
And sway our great designs.

CAESAR   There's my hand.
A sister I bequeath you, whom no brother
Did ever love so dearly. Let her live
152 To join our kingdoms and our hearts ; and never
Fly off our loves again.

LEPIDUS   Happily, amen.

ANTONY
I did not think to draw my sword 'gainst Pompey,
155 For he hath laid strange courtesies and great
Of late upon me. I must thank him only,
157 Lest my remembrance suffer ill report :
At heel of that, defy him.

LEPIDUS   Time calls upon 's.
159 Of us must Pompey presently be sought,
Or else he seeks out us.

ANTONY   Where lies he ?

CAESAR
161 About the Mount Mesena.

ANTONY
What is his strength by land ?

CAESAR
Great and increasing ; but by sea
He is an absolute master.

164 ANTONY   So is the fame.
Would we had spoke together ! Haste we for it,
Yet, ere we put ourselves in arms, dispatch we
The business we have talked of.

CAESAR   With most gladness ;
And do invite you to my sister's view,
Whither straight I'll lead you.

ANTONY   Let us, Lepidus,
Not lack your company.

LEPIDUS   Noble Antony,
Not sickness should detain me.   *Flourish. [Exeunt.]*
Mane[n]t Enobarbus, Agrippa, Maecenas.

MAECENAS Welcome from Egypt, sir.

ENOBARBUS Half the heart of Caesar, worthy Maecenas. 173
My honorable friend, Agrippa.

AGRIPPA Good Enobarbus.

MAECENAS We have cause to be glad that matters are so
well disgested. You stayed well by't in Egypt. 177

ENOBARBUS Ay, sir, we did sleep day out of countenance 178
and made the night light with drinking.

MAECENAS Eight wild boars roasted whole at a breakfast,
and but twelve persons there. Is this true ?

ENOBARBUS This was but as a fly by an eagle : we had 182
much more monstrous matter of feast, which worthily
deserved noting.

MAECENAS She's a most triumphant lady, if report be
square to her. 186

ENOBARBUS When she first met Mark Antony, she pursed 187
up his heart, upon the river of Cydnus.

AGRIPPA There she appeared indeed ; or my reporter de- 189
vised well for her.

ENOBARBUS
I will tell you.
The barge she sat in, like a burnished throne,
Burned on the water : the poop was beaten gold ;
Purple the sails, and so perfumèd that
The winds were lovesick with them ; the oars were
    silver,
Which to the tune of flutes kept stroke, and made
The water which they beat to follow faster,
As amorous of their strokes. For her own person,
It beggared all description : she did lie
In her pavilion, cloth-of-gold of tissue, 200
O'erpicturing that Venus where we see 201
The fancy outwork nature. On each side her 202
Stood pretty dimpled boys, like smiling Cupids,
With divers-colored fans, whose wind did seem
To glow the delicate cheeks which they did cool, 205
And what they undid did.

AGRIPPA   O, rare for Antony.

ENOBARBUS
Her gentlewomen, like the Nereides, 207
So many mermaids, tended her i' th' eyes, 208
And made their bends adornings. At the helm 209
A seeming mermaid steers : the silken tackle
Swell with the touches of those flower-soft hands,
That yarely frame the office. From the barge 212
A strange invisible perfume hits the sense
Of the adjacent wharfs. The city cast
Her people out upon her ; and Antony,
Enthroned i' th' market place, did sit alone,

---

132 *jealousies* misunderstandings   134–35 *would be . . . be* would be taken for . . . are taken for   145 *so fairly shows* looks so hopeful   147 *grace* reconciliation   152–53 *never . . . loves* never may we be estranged   155 *strange* unusual   157 *remembrance* readiness to acknowledge favors   159 *presently* at once   161 *Mesena* i.e. Misenum, an Italian port   164 *fame* report   173 *Half* i.e. sharing it with Agrippa   177 *disgested* digested, arranged ; *stayed . . . by't* kept at it, 'lived it up'   178–79 *we . . . drinking* i.e. we ruffled the dignity of day (personified) by sleeping through it, and made night light (i.e. bright, lightheaded, and wanton) with drinking parties   182 *by* compared to   186 *square* fair   187–88 *pursed up* pocketed (but with a suggestion of pursed lips for kissing)   189 *appeared* came before the public ; *devised* invented   200 *cloth-of-gold of tissue* cloth interwoven with gold threads   201 *O'erpicturing* outdoing the picture of   202 *fancy* i.e. the painter's imagination   205 *glow* make glow (as if heated)   207 *Nereides* sea nymphs   208 *tended* . . . *eyes* waited on her every glance   209 *made . . . adornings* made their postures of submission decorative (as in a tableau)   212 *yarely frame* nimbly perform

217   Whistling to th' air ; which, but for vacancy,
Had gone to gaze on Cleopatra too,
And made a gap in nature.

AGRIPPA   Rare Egyptian !

ENOBARBUS
Upon her landing, Antony sent to her,
Invited her to supper. She replied,
It should be better he became her guest ;
Which she entreated. Our courteous Antony,
Whom ne'er the word of 'no' woman heard speak,
Being barbered ten times o'er, goes to the feast,
226   And for his ordinary pays his heart
For what his eyes eat only.

AGRIPPA   Royal wench !
She made great Caesar lay his sword to bed ;
229   He ploughed her, and she cropped.

ENOBARBUS   I saw her once
Hop forty paces through the public street ;
And having lost her breath, she spoke, and panted,
232   That she did make defect perfection
And, breathless, pow'r breathe forth.

MAECENAS
Now Antony must leave her utterly.

ENOBARBUS
Never ; he will not :
Age cannot wither her, nor custom stale
Her infinite variety : other women cloy
The appetites they feed, but she makes hungry
Where most she satisfies. For vilest things
240   Become themselves in her, that the holy priests
241   Bless her when she is riggish.

MAECENAS
If beauty, wisdom, modesty, can settle
The heart of Antony, Octavia is
244   A blessèd lottery to him.

AGRIPPA   Let us go.
Good Enobarbus, make yourself my guest
Whilst you abide here.

ENOBARBUS   Humbly, sir, I thank you. *Exeunt.*

*

II, iii   *Enter Antony, Caesar, Octavia between them.*

ANTONY
The world and my great office will sometimes
Divide me from your bosom.

OCTAVIA   All which time
Before the gods my knee shall bow my prayers
To them for you.

ANTONY   Good night, sir. My Octavia,
Read not my blemishes in the world's report :
6   I have not kept my square, but that to come
Shall all be done by th' rule. Good night, dear lady.

217 *but for vacancy* except that it would have left a vacuum   226 *ordinary* meal   229 *cropped* bore fruit (i.e. Julius Caesar's son, Caesarion)   232 *defect* i.e. the resulting breathlessness   240 *Become . . . her* are so becoming to her   241 *riggish* lewd   244 *lottery* gift of fortune
II, iii The house of Octavius Caesar   6 *square* carpenter's square (i.e. I have not followed the straight and narrow)   14 *motion* mind   19 *demon* guardian angel   22 *a fear* i.e. timorous   27 *thickens* dims   32 *art or hap* skill or chance   34 *cunning* skill   35 *chance* luck ; *speeds* wins   36 *still* always   37 *it . . . naught* i.e. the odds are everything to nothing in my favor   38 *inhooped* i.e. fighting confined within a hoop
II, iv Before the house of Lepidus   8 *Mount* (cf. II, ii, 161)   10 *about* roundabout

OCTAVIA   Good night, sir.
CAESAR   Good night.   *Exit [with Octavia].*
      Enter Soothsayer.

ANTONY
Now, sirrah : you do wish yourself in Egypt ?

SOOTHSAYER
Would I had never come from thence, nor you thither.

ANTONY
If you can, your reason ?

SOOTHSAYER
I see it in my motion, have it not in my tongue,   14
But yet hie you to Egypt again.

ANTONY   Say to me,
Whose fortunes shall rise higher, Caesar's or mine ?

SOOTHSAYER   Caesar's.
Therefore, O Antony, stay not by his side.
Thy demon, that thy spirit which keeps thee, is   19
Noble, courageous, high, unmatchable,
Where Caesar's is not. But near him thy angel
Becomes a fear, as being o'erpow'red. Therefore   22
Make space enough between you.

ANTONY   Speak this no more.

SOOTHSAYER
To none but thee, no more but when to thee.
If thou dost play with him at any game,
Thou art sure to lose ; and of that natural luck
He beats thee 'gainst the odds. Thy lustre thickens   27
When he shines by : I say again, thy spirit
Is all afraid to govern thee near him ;
But he away, 'tis noble.

ANTONY   Get thee gone.
Say to Ventidius I would speak with him.
                        Exit [Soothsayer].
He shall to Parthia. – Be it art or hap,   32
He hath spoken true. The very dice obey him,
And in our sports my better cunning faints   34
Under his chance : if we draw lots, he speeds ;   35
His cocks do win the battle still of mine   36
When it is all to naught, and his quails ever   37
Beat mine, inhooped, at odds. I will to Egypt :   38
And though I make this marriage for my peace,
I' th' East my pleasure lies.
      Enter Ventidius.   O, come, Ventidius,
You must to Parthia. Your commission 's ready :
Follow me, and receive't.   *Exeunt.*

*

      Enter Lepidus, Maecenas, and Agrippa.   II, iv

LEPIDUS   Trouble yourselves no further : pray you,
hasten your generals after.

AGRIPPA   Sir, Mark Antony will e'en but kiss Octavia,
and we'll follow.

LEPIDUS   Till I shall see you in your soldier's dress,
which will become you both, farewell.

MAECENAS   We shall, as I conceive the journey, be at
Mount before you, Lepidus.   8

LEPIDUS   Your way is shorter ; my purposes do draw me
much about : you'll win two days upon me.   10

BOTH   Sir, good success.

LEPIDUS   Farewell.   *Exeunt.*

*

II, v   *Enter Cleopatra, Charmian, Iras, and Alexas.*

CLEOPATRA
Give me some music : music, moody food
Of us that trade in love.

OMNES   The music, ho !
    Enter Mardian the Eunuch.

CLEOPATRA
Let it alone, let's to billiards : come, Charmian.

CHARMIAN
My arm is sore ; best play with Mardian.

CLEOPATRA
As well a woman with an eunuch played
As with a woman. Come, you'll play with me, sir ?

MARDIAN   As well as I can, madam.

CLEOPATRA
And when good will is showed, though't come too
    short,
The actor may plead pardon. I'll none now.
10 Give me mine angle, we'll to th' river : there,
My music playing far off, I will betray
Tawny-finned fishes. My bended hook shall pierce
Their slimy jaws ; and as I draw them up,
I'll think them every one an Antony,
And say, 'Ah, ha ! y' are caught !'

CHARMIAN   'Twas merry when
You wagered on your angling, when your diver
17 Did hang a salt fish on his hook, which he
With fervency drew up.

CLEOPATRA   That time – O times ! –
I laughed him out of patience ; and that night
I laughed him into patience ; and next morn
Ere the ninth hour I drunk him to his bed ;
22 Then put my tires and mantles on him, whilst
23 I wore his sword Philippan.
    Enter a Messenger.   O, from Italy !
Ram thou thy fruitful tidings in mine ears,
That long time have been barren.

MESSENGER   Madam, madam –

CLEOPATRA
Antonio 's dead : if thou say so, villain,
Thou kill'st thy mistress : but well and free,
If thou so yield him, there is gold and here
My bluest veins to kiss, a hand that kings
Have lipped, and trembled kissing.

MESSENGER
First, madam, he is well.

CLEOPATRA   Why, there's more gold.
But, sirrah, mark, we use
33 To say the dead are well : bring it to that,
The gold I give thee will I melt and pour
Down thy ill-uttering throat.

MESSENGER
Good madam, hear me.

CLEOPATRA   Well, go to, I will :
37 But there's no goodness in thy face if Antony
38 Be free and healthful ; so tart a favor
To trumpet such good tidings ? If not well,
Thou shouldst come like a Fury crowned with snakes,
41 Not like a formal man.

MESSENGER   Will't please you hear me ?

CLEOPATRA
I have a mind to strike thee ere thou speak'st :
Yet, if thou say Antony lives, is well,
Or friends with Caesar, or not captive to him,
I'll set thee in a shower of gold, and hail
Rich pearls upon thee.

MESSENGER   Madam, he's well.

CLEOPATRA   Well said.

MESSENGER
And friends with Caesar.

CLEOPATRA   Th' art an honest man.

MESSENGER
Caesar and he are greater friends than ever.

CLEOPATRA
Make thee a fortune from me.

MESSENGER   But yet, madam –

CLEOPATRA
I do not like 'but yet,' it does allay   50
The good precedence : fie upon 'but yet,'
'But yet' is as a jailer to bring forth
Some monstrous malefactor. Prithee, friend,
Pour out the pack of matter to mine ear,
The good and bad together : he's friends with Caesar,
In state of health, thou say'st, and thou say'st, free.

MESSENGER
Free, madam, no : I made no such report,
He's bound unto Octavia.

CLEOPATRA   For what good turn ?

MESSENGER
For the best turn i' th' bed.

CLEOPATRA   I am pale, Charmian.

MESSENGER
Madam, he's married to Octavia.

CLEOPATRA
The most infectious pestilence upon thee !
    Strikes him down.

MESSENGER
Good madam, patience.

CLEOPATRA   What say you ?
    Strikes him.   Hence,
Horrible villain ! or I'll spurn thine eyes   63
Like balls before me : I'll unhair thy head,   64
    She hales him up and down.
Thou shalt be whipped with wire and stewed in brine,
Smarting in ling'ring pickle.   66

MESSENGER   Gracious madam,
I that do bring the news made not the match.

CLEOPATRA
Say 'tis not so, a province I will give thee,
And make thy fortunes proud : the blow thou hadst
Shall make thy peace for moving me to rage,
And I will boot thee with what gift beside   71
Thy modesty can beg.   72

MESSENGER   He's married, madam.

CLEOPATRA
Rogue, thou hast lived too long.
    Draw a knife.

MESSENGER   Nay, then I'll run.
What mean you, madam ? I have made no fault.   *Exit.*

II, v The chambers of Cleopatra in her palace at Alexandria 10 *angle* fishing tackle 17 *salt* dried 22 *tires* headdresses 23 *Philippan* (so called because he had beaten Brutus and Cassius with it at Philippi) 33 *well* i.e. in heaven ; *bring . . . that* say that you mean that 37 *goodness* i.e. truth 38 *tart a favor* sour a face 41 *Not . . . man* not in human shape 50–51 *allay . . . precedence* spoil the good that preceded it 63 *spurn* kick 64 s.d. *hales* drags 66 *pickle* pickling solution 71 *boot* benefit 72 *modesty* humble condition

CHARMIAN
Good madam, keep yourself within yourself,
The man is innocent.

CLEOPATRA
Some innocents 'scape not the thunderbolt.
Melt Egypt into Nile! and kindly creatures
Turn all to serpents! Call the slave again:
Though I am mad, I will not bite him. Call!

CHARMIAN
He is afeard to come.

CLEOPATRA   I will not hurt him. *[Exit Charmian.]*
These hands do lack nobility, that they strike
A meaner than myself; since I myself
84   Have given myself the cause.
     Enter [Charmian and] the Messenger again.
               Come hither, sir.
Though it be honest, it is never good
To bring bad news: give to a gracious message
An host of tongues, but let ill tidings tell
Themselves when they be felt.

MESSENGER   I have done my duty.

CLEOPATRA
Is he married?
I cannot hate thee worser than I do
If thou again say 'Yes.'

MESSENGER   He's married, madam.

CLEOPATRA
92   The gods confound thee! Dost thou hold there still?

MESSENGER
Should I lie, madam?

CLEOPATRA   O, I would thou didst,
94   So half my Egypt were submerged and made
A cistern for scaled snakes! Go get thee hence;
96   Hadst thou Narcissus in thy face, to me
Thou wouldst appear most ugly. He is married?

MESSENGER
I crave your Highness' pardon.

CLEOPATRA   He is married?

MESSENGER
99   Take no offense that I would not offend you:
To punish me for what you make me do
101   Seems much unequal: he's married to Octavia.

CLEOPATRA
O, that his fault should make a knave of thee,
103   That art not what th' art sure of! Get thee hence,
The merchandise which thou hast brought from Rome
105   Are all too dear for me. Lie they upon thy hand,
106   And be undone by 'em!   *[Exit Messenger.]*

CHARMIAN   Good your Highness, patience.

CLEOPATRA
In praising Antony I have dispraised Caesar.

---

84 *cause* i.e. by loving Antony   92 *confound* destroy   94 *So* even though
96 *Hadst . . . face* were you as handsome as Narcissus (in Greek legend,
the youth who fell in love with his image reflected in a stream)   99 *Take
. . . you* don't be angry that I'd rather not anger you (i.e. by answering)
101 *unequal* unjust   103 *That . . . of* i.e. who are not really hateful, like
the news you bring   105 *upon thy hand* i.e. unsold   106 *undone* bankrupt
116 *Gorgon* Medusa (the sight of whose ugly face turned men to stone)
II, vi An open place near Misenum   2 *meet* suitable   7 *tall* bold   10
factors agents   13 *ghosted* haunted   24 *fear* frighten   25 *speak* contest
26 *o'ercount* outnumber   27 *o'ercount* cheat; *house* (Plutarch says that
Antony had bought this house but not paid for it)   28 *cuckoo* (which
never builds its own nest but lays its eggs in the nests of other birds)
29 *as thou mayst* as long as you can   30 *from the present* off the topic   33
embraced if accepted

CHARMIAN
Many times, madam.

CLEOPATRA   I am paid for't now.
Lead me from hence,
I faint. O Iras, Charmian! 'Tis no matter.
Go to the fellow, good Alexas; bid him
Report the feature of Octavia: her years,
Her inclination, let him not leave out
The color of her hair. Bring me word quickly.
                 [Exit Alexas.]
Let him for ever go!—let him not!—Charmian,
Though he be painted one way like a Gorgon,   116
The other way's a Mars. *[to Mardian]* Bid you Alexas
Bring me word how tall she is.—Pity me, Charmian,
But do not speak to me. Lead me to my chamber.
                   Exeunt.

                 *

Flourish. Enter Pompey at one door, with Drum and   II, vi
*Trumpet: at another, Caesar, Lepidus, Antony,
Enobarbus, Maecenas, Agrippa, Menas, with
Soldiers marching.*

POMPEY
Your hostages I have, so have you mine;
And we shall talk before we fight.

CAESAR   Most meet   2
That first we come to words, and therefore have we
Our written purposes before us sent;
Which if thou hast considerèd, let us know
If 'twill tie up thy discontented sword
And carry back to Sicily much tall youth   7
That else must perish here.

POMPEY   To you all three,
The senators alone of this great world,
Chief factors for the gods: I do not know   10
Wherefore my father should revengers want,
Having a son and friends, since Julius Caesar,
Who at Philippi the good Brutus ghosted,   13
There saw you laboring for him. What was't
That moved pale Cassius to conspire? And what
Made all-honored, honest, Roman Brutus,
With the armed rest, courtiers of beauteous freedom,
To drench the Capitol, but that they would
Have one man but a man? And that is it
Hath made me rig my navy, at whose burden
The angered ocean foams; with which I meant
To scourge th' ingratitude that despiteful Rome
Cast on my noble father.

CAESAR   Take your time.

ANTONY
Thou canst not fear us, Pompey, with thy sails.   24
We'll speak with thee at sea. At land thou know'st   25
How much we do o'ercount thee.   26

POMPEY   At land indeed
Thou dost o'ercount me of my father's house: 27
But since the cuckoo builds not for himself,   28
Remain in't as thou mayst.   29

LEPIDUS   Be pleased to tell us
(For this is from the present) how you take   30
The offers we have sent you.

CAESAR   There's the point.

ANTONY
Which do not be entreated to, but weigh
What it is worth embraced.   33

CAESAR   And what may follow,
34 To try a larger fortune.
POMPEY   You have made me offer
Of Sicily, Sardinia ; and I must
Rid all the sea of pirates ; then, to send
Measures of wheat to Rome ; this 'greed upon,
38 To part with unhacked edges and bear back
39 Our targes undinted.
OMNES   That's our offer.
POMPEY   Know then
I came before you here a man prepared
To take this offer ; but Mark Antony
Put me to some impatience. Though I lose
The praise of it by telling, you must know,
When Caesar and your brother were at blows,
Your mother came to Sicily and did find
Her welcome friendly.
ANTONY   I have heard it, Pompey,
47 And am well studied for a liberal thanks,
Which I do owe you.
POMPEY   Let me have your hand :
I did not think, sir, to have met you here.
ANTONY
The beds i' th' East are soft ; and thanks to you,
That called me timelier than my purpose hither ;
For I have gained by 't.
CAESAR   Since I saw you last
There's a change upon you.
POMPEY   Well, I know not
54 What counts harsh fortune casts upon my face,
But in my bosom shall she never come
To make my heart her vassal.
LEPIDUS   Well met here.
POMPEY
I hope so, Lepidus. Thus we are agreed.
58 I crave our composition may be written,
And sealed between us.
CAESAR   That's the next to do.
POMPEY
We'll feast each other ere we part, and let's
Draw lots who shall begin.
ANTONY   That will I, Pompey.
POMPEY
No, Antony, take the lot :
But, first or last, your fine Egyptian cookery
Shall have the fame. I have heard that Julius Caesar
Grew fat with feasting there.
ANTONY   You have heard much.
POMPEY
I have fair meanings, sir.
ANTONY   And fair words to them.
POMPEY
Then so much have I heard,
And I have heard Apollodorus carried –
ENOBARBUS
No more of that : he did so.
POMPEY   What, I pray you ?
ENOBARBUS
A certain queen to Caesar in a mattress.
POMPEY
I know thee now ; how far'st thou, soldier ?
ENOBARBUS   Well ;
And well am like to do, for I perceive
73 Four feasts are toward.

POMPEY   Let me shake thy hand,
I never hated thee : I have seen thee fight
When I have envied thy behavior.
ENOBARBUS   Sir,
I never loved you much ; but I ha' praised ye
When you have well deserved ten times as much
As I have said you did.
POMPEY   Enjoy thy plainness,
It nothing ill becomes thee.   79
Aboard my galley I invite you all :
Will you lead, lords ?
ALL   Show 's the way, sir.
POMPEY   Come.
Exeunt. Manent Enobarbus and Menas.
MENAS *[aside]* Thy father, Pompey, would ne'er have
made this treaty. – You and I have known, sir.   83
ENOBARBUS At sea, I think.
MENAS We have, sir.
ENOBARBUS You have done well by water.
MENAS And you by land.
ENOBARBUS I will praise any man that will praise me ;
though it cannot be denied what I have done by land.
MENAS Nor what I have done by water.
ENOBARBUS Yes, something you can deny for your own
safety : you have been a great thief by sea.
MENAS And you by land.
ENOBARBUS There I deny my land service. But give me
your hand, Menas : if our eyes had authority, here they   95
might take two thieves kissing.
MENAS All men's faces are true, whatsome'er their hands
are.
ENOBARBUS But there is never a fair woman has a true   99
face.
MENAS No slander, they steal hearts.
ENOBARBUS We came hither to fight with you.
MENAS For my part, I am sorry it is turned to a drinking.
Pompey doth this day laugh away his fortune.
ENOBARBUS If he do, sure he cannot weep 't back again.
MENAS Y' have said, sir. We looked not for Mark Antony   105
here. Pray you, is he married to Cleopatra ?
ENOBARBUS Caesar's sister is called Octavia.
MENAS True, sir, she was the wife of Caius Marcellus.
ENOBARBUS But she is now the wife of Marcus Antonius.
MENAS Pray ye, sir ?   110
ENOBARBUS 'Tis true.
MENAS Then is Caesar and he for ever knit together.
ENOBARBUS If I were bound to divine of this unity, I
would not prophesy so.
MENAS I think the policy of that purpose made more in   115
the marriage than the love of the parties.
ENOBARBUS I think so too. But you shall find the band
that seems to tie their friendship together will be the
very strangler of their amity : Octavia is of a holy, cold,
and still conversation.   120
MENAS Who would not have his wife so ?
ENOBARBUS Not he that himself is not so ; which is Mark
Antony. He will to his Egyptian dish again : then shall

---

34 *a larger fortune* i.e. war with the triumvirs   38 *edges* swords   39
targes shields ; *Omnes* all (Antony, Caesar, Lepidus)   47 *studied for*
prepared with   54 *counts* tallies (as on a scoring stick)   58 *composition*
agreement   73 *toward* coming up   79 *nothing* not at all   83 *known* met
95 *had* were in   99 *true* honest   105 *Y' have said* i.e. you are quite right
110 *Pray ye* i.e. how's that again   115 *made more* played more part   120
conversation way of life

the sighs of Octavia blow the fire up in Caesar, and, as I
said before, that which is the strength of their amity shall
prove the immediate author of their variance. Antony
127 will use his affection where it is. He married but his
128 occasion here.

MENAS And thus it may be. Come, sir, will you aboard?
I have a health for you.

ENOBARBUS I shall take it, sir: we have used our throats
in Egypt.

MENAS Come, let's away.   *Exeunt.*

*

, vii   *Music plays. Enter two or three Servants, with a
         banquet.*

1 1. SERVANT Here they'll be, man. Some o' their plants
   are ill-rooted already; the least wind i' th' world will
   blow them down.

2. SERVANT Lepidus is high-colored.

5 1. SERVANT They have made him drink alms-drink.

2. SERVANT As they pinch one another by the disposi-
7 tion, he cries out 'No more,' reconciles them to his entreaty, and himself to th' drink.

1. SERVANT But it raises the greater war between him
   and his discretion.

2. SERVANT Why, this it is to have a name in great
12 men's fellowship. I had as live have a reed that will do
13 me no service as a partisan I could not heave.

14 1. SERVANT To be called into a huge sphere and not to
   be seen to move in't, are the holes where eyes should be,
16 which pitifully disaster the cheeks.

         *A sennet sounded. Enter Caesar, Antony, Pompey,
         Lepidus, Agrippa, Maecenas, Enobarbus, Menas,
         with other Captains.*

   ANTONY
   Thus do they, sir: they take the flow o' th' Nile
18 By certain scales i' th' pyramid. They know
19 By th' height, the lowness, or the mean, if dearth
   Or foison follow. The higher Nilus swells,
   The more it promises; as it ebbs, the seedsman
   Upon the slime and ooze scatters his grain,
   And shortly comes to harvest.

   LEPIDUS Y' have strange serpents there.

   ANTONY Ay, Lepidus.

   LEPIDUS Your serpent of Egypt is bred now of your mud
   by the operation of your sun: so is your crocodile.

   ANTONY They are so.

   POMPEY Sit – and some wine! A health to Lepidus!

LEPIDUS I am not so well as I should be, but I'll ne'er out. 30

ENOBARBUS Not till you have slept. I fear me you'll be in 31
till then.

LEPIDUS Nay, certainly, I have heard the Ptolemies' pyra- 33
mises are very goodly things: without contradiction I
have heard that.

MENAS
Pompey, a word.

POMPEY   Say in mine ear. What is't?

MENAS
Forsake thy seat, I do beseech thee, captain,
And hear me speak a word.

POMPEY   Forbear me till anon.
   [Menas] whispers in's ear.
This wine for Lepidus!

LEPIDUS What manner o' thing is your crocodile?

ANTONY It is shaped, sir, like itself, and it is as broad as it
hath breadth; it is just so high as it is, and moves with it 42
own organs. It lives by that which nourisheth it, and
the elements once out of it, it transmigrates.   44

LEPIDUS What color is it of?

ANTONY Of it own color too.   46

LEPIDUS 'Tis a strange serpent.

ANTONY 'Tis so, and the tears of it are wet.   48

CAESAR Will this description satisfy him?

ANTONY With the health that Pompey gives him; else he
is a very epicure.
   [Menas whispers again.]

POMPEY
Go hang, sir, hang! Tell me of that? Away!
Do as I bid you. – Where's this cup I called for?

MENAS
If for the sake of merit thou wilt hear me,
Rise from thy stool.

POMPEY   I think th' art mad.
   [Rises and walks aside.]   The matter?

MENAS
I have ever held my cap off to thy fortunes.   56

POMPEY
Thou hast served me with much faith. What's else to
   say? –
Be jolly, lords.

ANTONY   These quicksands, Lepidus,
Keep off them, for you sink.

MENAS
Wilt thou be lord of all the world?

POMPEY   What say'st thou?

MENAS
Wilt thou be lord of the whole world? That's twice.

POMPEY
How should that be?

MENAS   But entertain it,   62
And though thou think me poor, I am the man
Will give thee all the world.

POMPEY   Hast thou drunk well?

MENAS
No, Pompey, I have kept me from the cup.
Thou art, if thou dar'st be, the earthly Jove:
Whate'er the ocean pales, or sky inclips,   67
Is thine, if thou wilt ha't.

POMPEY   Show me which way.

MENAS
These three world-sharers, these competitors,   69
Are in thy vessel. Let me cut the cable;

---

127 *where it is* i.e. in Egypt 128 *occasion* convenience
II, vii Aboard Pompey's galley in the port of Misenum 1 *plants* feet (with
pun on the usual sense: cf. *ill-rooted*) 5 *alms-drink* drink drunk on behalf
of one too far gone to continue his part in a round of toasts (Lepidus
has been tricked into drinking more than the rest) 7 *No more* i.e. no more
quarrelling 12 *live* lief 13 *partisan* spear 14–16 *To . . . cheeks* (Lepidus,
a little man in a part too big for him, is compared first to a heavenly body
that fails to perform its function in its *sphere*, and then to a face without
eyes; *disaster*, carrying the image back on itself, likens the face without
eyes to a heaven without stars) 16 s.d. *sennet* distinctive set of trumpet
notes announcing persons of importance 18 *scales* graduations 19–20
dearth Or foison famine or plenty 30 *ne'er out* never give up 31 *in*
drunk 33 *pyramises* (Lepidus's drunken rendering of 'pyramides,' i.e.
pyramids) 42–43, 46 *it own* its own 44 *transmigrates* i.e. its soul takes
over the body of some other creature (Antony is teasing the drunken
Lepidus) 48 *tears* i.e. its 'crocodile tears' 56 *held . . . off* i.e. been
devoted 62 *Bı entertain it* only accept the idea 67 *pales* encloses
69 *competitors* paı ners

And when we are put off, fall to their throats.
All there is thine.
POMPEY   Ah, this thou shouldst have done,
And not have spoke on't. In me 'tis villainy,
In thee't had been good service. Thou must know,
'Tis not my profit that does lead mine honor ;
76   Mine honor, it. Repent that e'er thy tongue
Hath so betrayed thine act. Being done unknown,
I should have found it afterwards well done,
But must condemn it now. Desist, and drink.
MENAS [aside]
For this,
81   I'll never follow thy palled fortunes more.
Who seeks, and will not take when once 'tis offered,
Shall never find it more.
POMPEY   This health to Lepidus !
ANTONY
84   Bear him ashore. I'll pledge it for him, Pompey.
ENOBARBUS
Here's to thee, Menas.
MENAS   Enobarbus, welcome.
POMPEY Fill till the cup be hid.
ENOBARBUS There's a strong fellow, Menas.
       [Points to the Servant who carries off Lepidus.]
MENAS Why ?
ENOBARBUS 'A bears the third part of the world, man ;
seest not ?
MENAS
The third part then is drunk. Would it were all,
92   That it might go on wheels !
ENOBARBUS
93   Drink thou : increase the reels.
MENAS Come.
POMPEY
This is not yet an Alexandrian feast.
ANTONY
96   It ripens towards it. Strike the vessels, ho !
Here's to Caesar !
97 CAESAR   I could well forbear't.
It's monstrous labor when I wash my brain
And it grows fouler.
ANTONY   Be a child o' th' time.
CAESAR
100   Possess it, I'll make answer ;
But I had rather fast from all four days
Than drink so much in one.
ENOBARBUS   Ha, my brave emperor !
Shall we dance now the Egyptian Bacchanals
And celebrate our drink ?
POMPEY   Let's ha't, good soldier.
ANTONY
Come, let's all take hands
Till that the conquering wine hath steeped our sense
107 In soft and delicate Lethe.
ENOBARBUS   All take hands :
Make battery to our ears with the loud music ;
The while I'll place you ; then the boy shall sing.
110 The holding every man shall bear as loud
As his strong sides can volley.
    Music plays. Enobarbus places them hand in hand.

        The Song.

     Come, thou monarch of the vine,
113   Plumpy Bacchus with pink eyne !

In thy fats our cares be drowned,   114
With thy grapes our hairs be crowned.
Cup us till the world go round,
Cup us till the world go round !
CAESAR
What would you more ? Pompey, good night.
Good brother,
Let me request you off : our graver business   119
Frowns at this levity. Gentle lords, let's part ;
You see we have burned our cheeks. Strong Enobarb
Is weaker than the wine, and mine own tongue
Splits what it speaks : the wild disguise hath almost 123
Anticked us all. What needs more words ? Good night. 124
Good Antony, your hand.
POMPEY   I'll try you on the shore. 125
ANTONY
And shall, sir. – Give's your hand.
POMPEY   O Antony,
You have my father's house. But what, we are friends !
Come down into the boat.
ENOBARBUS   Take heed you fall not.
    [Exeunt all but Enobarbus and Menas.]
Menas, I'll not on shore.
MENAS   No, to my cabin.
These drums ! these trumpets, flutes ! what !
Let Neptune hear we bid a loud farewell
To these great fellows. Sound and be hanged, sound
out !
    Sound a flourish, with drums.
ENOBARBUS
Hoo ! says 'a. There's my cap.
MENAS
Hoo ! Noble captain, come.   Exeunt.

                 *

    Enter Ventidius as it were in triumph, the dead body III,
    of Pacorus borne before him [by Romans].
VENTIDIUS
Now, darting Parthia, art thou struck, and now   1
Pleased fortune does of Marcus Crassus' death
Make me revenger. Bear the King's son's body
Before our army. Thy Pacorus, Orodes,
Pays this for Marcus Crassus.   5
ROMAN [SILIUS]   Noble Ventidius,
Whilst yet with Parthian blood thy sword is warm,
The fugitive Parthians follow. Spur through Media,
Mesopotamia, and the shelters whither
The routed fly : so thy grand captain, Antony,
Shall set thee on triumphant chariots and
Put garlands on thy head.
VENTIDIUS   O Silius, Silius,
I have done enough. A lower place, note well,   12
May make too great an act. For learn this, Silius,

76 Mine honor, it i.e. my honor comes before my profit 81 palled decayed
84 I'll . . . him (cf. l. 5 : Antony is now taking an alms-drink) 92 go on
wheels whirl smoothly 93 reels whirls 96 Strike the vessels broach the
casks 97 forbear't i.e. pass up this toast 100 Possess it down it 107
Lethe (cf. II, i, 27n.) 110 holding refrain 113 pink half-closed 114
fats vats 119 off to come away 123 disguise dancing and drinking
124 Anticked made fools of 125 try you take you on in a drinking bout
III, i A field in Syria 1 darting i.e. famous for its bowmen 5 Marcus
Crassus (member of the first triumvirate with Pompey the Great and Julius
Caesar, who was killed by the Parthians and who is now avenged by the
death of Pacorus, son to Orodes the Parthian king) 12 A lower place an
underling

Better to leave undone, than by our deed
Acquire too high a fame when him we serve's away.
Caesar and Antony have ever won
More in their officer than person. Sossius,
One of my place in Syria, his lieutenant,
For quick accumulation of renown,
Which he achieved by th' minute, lost his favor.
Who does i' th' wars more than his captain can
Becomes his captain's captain; and ambition
(The soldier's virtue) rather makes choice of loss
Than gain which darkens him.
I could do more to do Antonius good,
26 But 'twould offend him. And in his offense
Should my performance perish.
27 ROMAN [SILIUS]   Thou hast, Ventidius, that
Without the which a soldier and his sword
Grants scarce distinction. Thou wilt write to Antony?
VENTIDIUS
I'll humbly signify what in his name,
That magical word of war, we have effected;
How with his banners and his well-paid ranks
The ne'er-yet-beaten horse of Parthia
34 We have jaded out o' th' field.
ROMAN [SILIUS]   Where is he now?
VENTIDIUS
He purposeth to Athens; whither, with what haste
The weight we must convey with's will permit,
We shall appear before him. – On, there, pass along.
                               Exeunt.

                          *

III, ii   *Enter Agrippa at one door, Enobarbus at another.*
AGRIPPA
1   What, are the brothers parted?
ENOBARBUS
They have dispatched with Pompey; he is gone;
3   The other three are sealing. Octavia weeps
To part from Rome; Caesar is sad, and Lepidus
Since Pompey's feast, as Menas says, is troubled
6   With the green-sickness.
AGRIPPA   'Tis a noble Lepidus.
ENOBARBUS
A very fine one. O, how he loves Caesar!
AGRIPPA
Nay, but how dearly he adores Mark Antony!
ENOBARBUS
Caesar? Why, he's the Jupiter of men.
AGRIPPA
What's Antony? The god of Jupiter.
ENOBARBUS
Spake you of Caesar? How! the nonpareil!
AGRIPPA
12   O Antony! O thou Arabian bird!

---

26 *in his offense* in offending him   27 *that* i.e. discretion   34 *jaded* driven
weary
III, ii The house of Octavius Caesar in Rome   1 *parted* departed   3
sealing concluding agreements   6 *green-sickness* (traditionally the disease
of lovesick girls: Lepidus is likened to one in his relations to Caesar and
Antony)   12 *Arabian bird* i.e. unique (like the mythical phoenix, of which
only one was supposed to exist at a time)   20 *shards* wings   26–27 *as my
farthest . . . approof* such as I will give my uttermost bond that you will
prove to be   28 *piece* paragon   32 *mean* intermediary   35 *curious*
punctiliously exacting   48–50 *the swan's . . . inclines* i.e. her feelings
for husband and brother are evenly balanced   51–59 (Enobarbus and
Agrippa talk aside)   52 *horse* (horses without white markings on the face
were thought to be ill-tempered)

ENOBARBUS
Would you praise Caesar, say 'Caesar': go no further.
AGRIPPA
Indeed he plied them both with excellent praises.
ENOBARBUS
But he loves Caesar best, yet he loves Antony:
Hoo! hearts, tongues, figures, scribes, bards, poets,
   cannot
Think, speak, cast, write, sing, number – hoo! –
His love to Antony. But as for Caesar,
Kneel down, kneel down, and wonder.
AGRIPPA   Both he loves
ENOBARBUS
They are his shards, and he their beetle.   20
     [Trumpet within.]   So –
This is to horse. Adieu, noble Agrippa.
AGRIPPA
Good fortune, worthy soldier, and farewell!
      Enter Caesar, Antony, Lepidus, and Octavia.
ANTONY
No further, sir.
CAESAR
You take from me a great part of myself;
Use me well in't. Sister, prove such a wife
As my thoughts make thee, and as my farthest band   26
Shall pass on thy approof. Most noble Antony,
Let not the piece of virtue which is set   28
Betwixt us as the cement of our love
To keep it builded, be the ram to batter
The fortress of it: for better might we
Have loved without this mean, if on both parts   32
This be not cherished.
ANTONY   Make me not offended
In your distrust.
CAESAR   I have said.
ANTONY   You shall not find,
Though you be therein curious, the least cause   35
For what you seem to fear. So the gods keep you
And make the hearts of Romans serve your ends!
We will here part.
CAESAR
Farewell, my dearest sister, fare thee well.
The elements be kind to thee, and make
Thy spirits all of comfort: fare thee well.
OCTAVIA
My noble brother!
ANTONY
The April's in her eyes: it is love's spring,
And these the showers to bring it on. Be cheerful.
OCTAVIA
Sir, look well to my husband's house; and –
CAESAR   What,
Octavia?
OCTAVIA   I'll tell you in your ear.
ANTONY
Her tongue will not obey her heart, nor can
Her heart inform her tongue – the swan's down-feather   48
That stands upon the swell at full of tide,
And neither way inclines.
ENOBARBUS
Will Caesar weep?   51
AGRIPPA   He has a cloud in's face.
ENOBARBUS
He were the worse for that, were he a horse;   52

So is he, being a man.

AGRIPPA   Why, Enobarbus,
When Antony found Julius Caesar dead,
He cried almost to roaring ; and he wept
When at Philippi he found Brutus slain.

ENOBARBUS
57   That year indeed he was troubled with a rheum.
58   What willingly he did confound he wailed,
Believe't, till I wept too.

CAESAR   No, sweet Octavia,
60   You shall hear from me still : the time shall not
Outgo my thinking on you.

ANTONY   Come, sir, come,
I'll wrestle with you in my strength of love :
Look, here I have you ; thus I let you go,
And give you to the gods.

CAESAR   Adieu, be happy !

LEPIDUS
Let all the number of the stars give light
To thy fair way !

CAESAR   Farewell, farewell !
        Kisses Octavia.

ANTONY   Farewell !
                    Trumpets sound. Exeunt.

                    ✻

III, iii   *Enter Cleopatra, Charmian, Iras, and Alexas.*
CLEOPATRA
Where is the fellow ?
ALEXAS   Half afeard to come.
CLEOPATRA
Go to, go to.
        Enter the Messenger as before.
            Come hither, sir.
ALEXAS   Good Majesty,
3   Herod of Jewry dare not look upon you
But when you are well pleased.
CLEOPATRA   That Herod's head
I'll have : but how, when Antony is gone
Through whom I might command it ? Come thou near.
MESSENGER
Most gracious Majesty !
CLEOPATRA
Didst thou behold Octavia ?
MESSENGER   Ay, dread Queen.
CLEOPATRA   Where.
MESSENGER
Madam, in Rome.
I looked her in the face, and saw her led
Between her brother and Mark Antony.
CLEOPATRA
Is she as tall as me ?
MESSENGER   She is not, madam.
CLEOPATRA
Didst hear her speak ? Is she shrill-tongued or low ?
MESSENGER
Madam, I heard her speak ; she is low-voiced.
CLEOPATRA
17   That's not so good. He cannot like her long.
CHARMIAN
Like her ? O Isis ! 'tis impossible.
CLEOPATRA
I think so, Charmian. Dull of tongue, and dwarfish.

What majesty is in her gait ? Remember,
If e'er thou lookedst on majesty.
MESSENGER   She creeps :
Her motion and her station are as one.   22
She shows a body rather than a life,
A statue than a breather.
CLEOPATRA   Is this certain ?
MESSENGER
Or I have no observance.
CHARMIAN   Three in Egypt
Cannot make better note.
CLEOPATRA   He's very knowing,
I do perceive't. There's nothing in her yet.
The fellow has good judgment.
CHARMIAN   Excellent.
CLEOPATRA
Guess at her years, I prithee.
MESSENGER   Madam,
She was a widow –
CLEOPATRA   Widow ? Charmian, hark.
MESSENGER
And I do think she's thirty.
CLEOPATRA
Bear'st thou her face in mind ? is't long or round ?   32
MESSENGER
Round even to faultiness.
CLEOPATRA
For the most part, too, they are foolish that are so.
Her hair, what color ?
MESSENGER
Brown, madam ; and her forehead
As low as she would wish it.
CLEOPATRA   There's gold for thee.
Thou must not take my former sharpness ill ;
I will employ thee back again : I find thee
Most fit for business. Go, make thee ready ;
Our letters are prepared.   *[Exit Messenger.]*
CHARMIAN   A proper man.   41
CLEOPATRA
Indeed he is so : I repent me much
That so I harried him. Why, methinks, by him,   43
This creature 's no such thing.   44
CHARMIAN   Nothing, madam.
CLEOPATRA
The man hath seen some majesty, and should know.
CHARMIAN
Hath he seen majesty ? Isis else defend,
And serving you so long !
CLEOPATRA
I have one thing more to ask him yet, good Charmian ;
But 'tis no matter, thou shalt bring him to me
Where I will write. All may be well enough.
CHARMIAN
I warrant you, madam.   *Exeunt.*

                    ✻

57 *rheum* running at the eyes 58 *confound* destroy 60–61 *the time . . . you*
i.e. my thoughts of you will not be left behind (as in a race) by time
III, iii The chambers of Cleopatra in her palace at Alexandria **3** *Herod*
i.e. even Herod (traditionally represented as a tyrant) **17** *good* i.e. as
I am **22** *Her . . . one* even in motion she is still **32** *long or round* (thought
to be signs, respectively, of prudence and folly) **41** *proper* attractive
43 *harried* mistreated **44** *no such thing* nothing much

I, iv   *Enter Antony and Octavia.*

ANTONY

Nay, nay, Octavia, not only that,
That were excusable, that and thousands more
3   Of semblable import – but he hath waged
4   New wars 'gainst Pompey ; made his will, and read it
To public ear ;
Spoke scantly of me : when perforce he could not
But pay me terms of honor, cold and sickly
8   He vented them, most narrow measure lent me ;
When the best hint was given him, he not took't,
10 Or did it from his teeth.

OCTAVIA   O, my good lord,
Believe not all, or if you must believe,
12 Stomach not all. A more unhappy lady,
If this division chance, ne'er stood between,
Praying for both parts.
15 The good gods will mock me presently
When I shall pray 'O, bless my lord and husband !'
Undo that prayer by crying out as loud
'O, bless my brother !' Husband win, win brother,
Prays, and destroys the prayer ; no midway
'Twixt these extremes at all.

ANTONY   Gentle Octavia,
Let your best love draw to that point which seeks
Best to preserve it. If I lose mine honor,
I lose myself : better I were not yours
24 Than yours so branchless. But as you requested,
Yourself shall go between's : the mean time, lady,
I'll raise the preparation of a war
27 Shall stain your brother. Make your soonest haste ;
So your desires are yours.

OCTAVIA   Thanks to my lord.
The Jove of power make me most weak, most weak,
Your reconciler ! Wars 'twixt you twain would be
As if the world should cleave, and that slain men
Should solder up the rift.

ANTONY

When it appears to you where this begins,
Turn your displeasure that way, for our faults
Can never be so equal that your love
Can equally move with them. Provide your going ;
Choose your own company, and command what cost
Your heart has mind to.   *Exeunt.*

II, v   *Enter Enobarbus and Eros.*

ENOBARBUS How now, friend Eros ?
EROS There's strange news come, sir.
ENOBARBUS What, man ?
EROS Caesar and Lepidus have made wars upon Pompey.
5   ENOBARBUS This is old. What is the success ?
6   EROS Caesar, having made use of him in the wars 'gainst
7   Pompey, presently denied him rivality, would not let
him partake in the glory of the action ; and not resting

here, accuses him of letters he had formerly wrote to
Pompey ; upon his own appeal, seizes him ; so the poor 10
third is up till death enlarge his confine.   11

ENOBARBUS

Then, world, thou hast a pair of chaps, no more ;   12
And throw between them all the food thou hast,
They'll grind the one the other. Where's Antony ?

EROS

He's walking in the garden – thus, and spurns
The rush that lies before him ; cries 'Fool Lepidus !'
And threats the throat of that his officer   17
That murd'red Pompey.

ENOBARBUS   Our great navy 's rigged.

EROS

For Italy and Caesar. More, Domitius :
My lord desires you presently. My news
I might have told hereafter.

ENOBARBUS   'Twill be naught ;
But let it be. Bring me to Antony.

EROS Come, sir.   *Exeunt.*

＊

Enter Agrippa, Maecenas, and Caesar.   **III, vi**

CAESAR

Contemning Rome, he has done all this and more   1
In Alexandria. Here's the manner of't :
I' th' market place on a tribunal silvered,
Cleopatra and himself in chairs of gold
Were publicly enthroned ; at the feet sat
Caesarion, whom they call my father's son,   6
And all the unlawful issue that their lust
Since then hath made between them. Unto her
He gave the stablishment of Egypt ; made her   9
Of lower Syria, Cyprus, Lydia,
Absolute queen.

MAECENAS   This in the public eye ?

CAESAR

I' th' common show-place, where they exercise.
His sons he there proclaimed the kings of kings :
Great Media, Parthia, and Armenia
He gave to Alexander ; to Ptolemy he assigned
Syria, Cilicia, and Phoenicia. She
In th' habiliments of the goddess Isis   17
That day appeared, and oft before gave audience,
As 'tis reported, so.

MAECENAS   Let Rome be thus
Informed.

AGRIPPA   Who, queasy with his insolence   20
Already, will their good thoughts call from him.

CAESAR

The people know it, and have now received
His accusations.

AGRIPPA   Who does he accuse ?

CAESAR

Caesar, and that, having in Sicily
Sextus Pompeius spoiled, we had not rated him   25
His part o' th' isle. Then does he say he lent me   26
Some shipping unrestored. Lastly, he frets
That Lepidus of the triumvirate
Should be deposed ; and, being, that we detain
All his revenue.

AGRIPPA   Sir, this should be answered.

CAESAR

'Tis done already, and the messenger gone.

III, iv The house of Antony in Athens 3 *semblable* like 4 *read it* (to
show the public what benefactions they might expect from him) 8
narrow measure little credit 10 *from his teeth* grudgingly 12 *Stomach*
resent 15 *presently* at once 24 *branchless* pruned (of my honors) 27
stain eclipse
III, v 5 *success* sequel 6 *wars* (a new outbreak, in which Pompey was
defeated) 7 *rivality* partnership 10 *appeal* accusation 11 *up* jailed
12 *chaps* jaws 17 *that his officer* that officer of his
III, vi The house of Octavius Caesar in Rome 1 *Contemning* scorning
6 *my father's* (Octavius, though actually a nephew, had been adopted by
Julius Caesar) 9 *stablishment* rule 17 *Isis* (cf. I, ii, 60n.) 20 *queasy*
nauseated 25 *spoiled* despoiled ; *rated* allotted 26 *isle* i.e. Sicily

I have told him Lepidus was grown too cruel,
That he his high authority abused
And did deserve his change. For what I have conquered,
I grant him part; but then in his Armenia,
And other of his conquered kingdoms, I
Demand the like.

MAECENAS   He'll never yield to that.

CAESAR

Nor must not then be yielded to in this.

Enter Octavia with her Train.

OCTAVIA

Hail, Caesar, and my lord, hail, most dear Caesar!

CAESAR

40   That ever I should call thee castaway!

OCTAVIA

You have not called me so, nor have you cause.

CAESAR

Why have you stol'n upon us thus? You come not
Like Caesar's sister. The wife of Antony
Should have an army for an usher, and
The neighs of horse to tell of her approach
Long ere she did appear. The trees by th' way
Should have borne men, and expectation fainted,
Longing for what it had not. Nay, the dust
Should have ascended to the roof of heaven,
Raised by your populous troops. But you are come
A market-maid to Rome, and have prevented
The ostentation of our love; which, left unshown,
53   Is often left unloved. We should have met you
By sea and land, supplying every stage
With an augmented greeting.

OCTAVIA   Good my lord,
To come thus was I not constrained, but did it
On my free will. My lord, Mark Antony,
Hearing that you prepared for war, acquainted
My grievèd ear withal; whereon I begged
His pardon for return.

CAESAR   Which soon he granted,
61   Being an abstract 'tween his lust and him.

OCTAVIA

Do not say so, my lord.

CAESAR   I have eyes upon him,
And his affairs come to me on the wind.
Where is he now?

OCTAVIA   My lord, in Athens.

CAESAR

No, my most wrongèd sister, Cleopatra
Hath nodded him to her. He hath given his empire
Up to a whore, who now are levying
The kings o' th' earth for war. He hath assembled
Bocchus, the king of Libya; Archelaus,
Of Cappadocia; Philadelphos, king
Of Paphlagonia; the Thracian king, Adallas;
72   King Mauchus of Arabia; King of Pont;
Herod of Jewry; Mithridates, king
Of Comagene; Polemon and Amyntas,
The kings of Mede and Lycaonia; with a
More larger list of sceptres.

OCTAVIA   Ay me most wretched,
That have my heart parted betwixt two friends
That do afflict each other!

CAESAR   Welcome hither.
Your letters did withhold our breaking forth,
Till we perceived both how you were wrong led

And we in negligent danger. Cheer your heart: 81
Be you not troubled with the time, which drives
O'er your content these strong necessities;
But let determined things to destiny
Hold unbewailed their way. Welcome to Rome,
Nothing more dear to me. You are abused   86
Beyond the mark of thought: and the high gods,   87
To do you justice, makes his ministers   88
Of us and those that love you. Best of comfort,
And ever welcome to us.

AGRIPPA   Welcome, lady.

MAECENAS

Welcome, dear madam.
Each heart in Rome does love and pity you.
Only th' adulterous Antony, most large   93
In his abominations, turns you off
And gives his potent regiment to a trull   95
That noises it against us.   96

OCTAVIA   Is it so, sir?

CAESAR

Most certain. Sister, welcome. Pray you
Be ever known to patience. My dear'st sister!   *Exeunt.* 98

*

Enter Cleopatra and Enobarbus.   III,

CLEOPATRA

I will be even with thee, doubt it not.

ENOBARBUS

But why, why, why?

CLEOPATRA

Thou hast forspoke my being in these wars,   3
And say'st it is not fit.

ENOBARBUS   Well, is it, is it?

CLEOPATRA

Is't not denounced against us? Why should not we 5
Be there in person?

ENOBARBUS *[aside]* Well, I could reply:
If we should serve with horse and mares together,
The horse were merely lost; the mares would bear 8
A soldier and his horse.

CLEOPATRA   What is't you say?

ENOBARBUS

Your presence needs must puzzle Antony;   10
Take from his heart, take from his brain, from's time,
What should not then be spared. He is already
Traduced for levity; and 'tis said in Rome
That Photinus an eunuch and your maids
Manage this war.

CLEOPATRA   Sink Rome, and their tongues rot
That speak against us! A charge we bear i' th' war, 16
And as the president of my kingdom will
Appear there for a man. Speak not against it,
I will not stay behind.

Enter Antony and Canidius.

---

53 *left unloved* thought to be unfelt   61 *abstract* short-cut   72 *Mauchus*
(so spelled in folio; Plutarch reads 'Malchus,' and North's translation
'Manchus')   81 *negligent danger* danger through negligence   86 *abused*
betrayed (by Antony)   87 *mark* reach   88 *makes his* make their   93 *large*
uninhibited   95 *regiment* rule; *trull* harlot   96 *noises it* clamors   98 *Be
... patience* be always calm
III, vii Antony's camp near Actium   3 *forspoke* opposed   5 *denounced*
declared   8 *merely* entirely   10 *puzzle* paralyze   16 *charge* responsibility

ENOBARBUS   Nay, I have done.
 Here comes the Emperor.
ANTONY   Is it not strange, Canidius,
 That from Tarentum and Brundusium
 He could so quickly cut the Ionian sea
23 And take in Toryne? – You have heard on't, sweet?
CLEOPATRA
 Celerity is never more admired
 Than by the negligent.
ANTONY   A good rebuke,
 Which might have well becomed the best of men
 To taunt at slackness. Canidius, we
 Will fight with him by sea.
CLEOPATRA   By sea; what else?
CANIDIUS
 Why will my lord do so?
29 ANTONY   For that he dares us to't.
ENOBARBUS
 So hath my lord dared him to single fight.
CANIDIUS
 Ay, and to wage this battle at Pharsalia,
 Where Caesar fought with Pompey. But these offers,
 Which serve not for his vantage, he shakes off;
 And so should you.
ENOBARBUS   Your ships are not well manned;
35 Your mariners are muleters, reapers, people
36 Ingrossed by swift impress. In Caesar's fleet
 Are those that often have 'gainst Pompey fought;
38 Their ships are yare; yours, heavy: no disgrace
39 Shall fall you for refusing him at sea,
 Being prepared for land.
ANTONY   By sea, by sea.
ENOBARBUS
 Most worthy sir, you therein throw away
 The absolute soldiership you have by land,
43 Distract your army, which doth most consist
 Of war-marked footmen, leave unexecuted
 Your own renownèd knowledge, quite forgo
 The way which promises assurance, and
 Give up yourself merely to chance and hazard
 From firm security.
ANTONY   I'll fight at sea.
CLEOPATRA
 I have sixty sails, Caesar none better.
ANTONY
 Our overplus of shipping will we burn,
 And with the rest full-manned, from th' head of Actium
 Beat th' approaching Caesar. But if we fail,
 We then can do't at land.
 Enter a Messenger. Thy business?
MESSENGER
 The news is true, my lord, he is descried;
 Caesar has taken Toryne.
ANTONY
 Can he be there in person? 'Tis impossible;

Strange that his power should be. Canidius,   57
 Our nineteen legions thou shalt hold by land
 And our twelve thousand horse. We'll to our ship.
 Away, my Thetis!   60
 Enter a Soldier.   How now, worthy soldier?
SOLDIER
 O noble Emperor, do not fight by sea,
 Trust not to rotten planks. Do you misdoubt
 This sword and these my wounds? Let th' Egyptians
 And the Phoenicians go a-ducking: we
 Have used to conquer standing on the earth
 And fighting foot to foot.
ANTONY   Well, well, away!
 Exit Antony [with] Cleopatra and Enobarbus.
SOLDIER
 By Hercules, I think I am i' th' right.
CANIDIUS
 Soldier, thou art; but his whole action grows   68
 Not in the power on't: so our leader's led,
 And we are women's men.
SOLDIER   You keep by land
 The legions and the horse whole, do you not?
CANIDIUS
 Marcus Octavius, Marcus Justeius,
 Publicola, and Caelius are for sea;
 But we keep whole by land. This speed of Caesar's
 Carries beyond belief.   75
SOLDIER   While he was yet in Rome,
 His power went out in such distractions as   76
 Beguiled all spies.   77
CANIDIUS   Who's his lieutenant, hear you?
SOLDIER
 They say, one Taurus.
CANIDIUS   Well I know the man.
 Enter a Messenger.
MESSENGER
 The Emperor calls Canidius.
CANIDIUS
 With news the time's with labor and throws forth   80
 Each minute some.   *Exeunt.*

*

 Enter Caesar, with his Army, marching.   III, viii
CAESAR Taurus!
TAURUS My lord?
CAESAR
 Strike not by land; keep whole, provoke not battle
 Till we have done at sea. Do not exceed
 The prescript of this scroll. Our fortune lies
 Upon this jump.   *Exit [with Taurus and the Army].*   6
 Enter Antony and Enobarbus.   III, ix
ANTONY
 Set we our squadrons on yond side o' th' hill
 In eye of Caesar's battle; from which place   2
 We may the number of the ships behold,
 And so proceed accordingly.   *Exit [with Enobarbus].*
 Canidius marcheth with his land army one way over   III, x
 the stage, and Taurus, the lieutenant of Caesar, the
 other way. After their going in is heard the noise of a
 sea-fight. Alarum. Enter Enobarbus.
ENOBARBUS
 Naught, naught, all naught! I can behold no longer.   1
 Th' Antoniad, the Egyptian admiral,   2

---

23 *take in* seize 29 *For that* because 35 *muleters* mule-drivers, i.e.
peasants 36 *Ingrossed* collected wholesale; *impress* draft 38 *yare* nimble
39 *you* to you 43 *Distract* divide 57 *power* army 60 *Thetis* name of a sea
goddess 68–69 *his . . . on't* his plan of action does not spring from a right
estimate of the nature of his strength 75 *Carries* i.e. like an arrow 76
distractions detachments 77 *Beguiled* deceived 80 *throws* i.e. as an
animal 'throws,' gives birth to, its young
III, viii A field near Actium 6 *jump* chance
III, ix 2 *battle* battle-line
III, x 1 *Naught* i.e. all's come to naught 2 *admiral* flagship

With all their sixty, fly and turn the rudder:
To see't mine eyes are blasted.
    Enter Scarus.
SCARUS   Gods and goddesses,
5 All the whole synod of them!
ENOBARBUS   What's thy passion?
SCARUS
6 The greater cantle of the world is lost
With very ignorance; we have kissed away
Kingdoms and provinces.
ENOBARBUS   How appears the fight?
SCARUS
9 On our side like the tokened pestilence
10 Where death is sure. Yon ribaudred nag of Egypt –
Whom leprosy o'ertake! – i' th' midst o' th' fight,
When vantage like a pair of twins appeared,
13 Both as the same, or rather ours the elder,
14 The breese upon her, like a cow in June,
Hoists sails, and flies.
ENOBARBUS
That I beheld:
Mine eyes did sicken at the sight, and could not
Endure a further view.
18 SCARUS   She once being loofed,
The noble ruin of her magic, Antony,
20 Claps on his sea-wing, and (like a doting mallard)
Leaving the fight in heighth, flies after her.
I never saw an action of such shame;
Experience, manhood, honor, ne'er before
Did violate so itself.
ENOBARBUS   Alack, alack!
    Enter Canidius.
CANIDIUS
Our fortune on the sea is out of breath,
And sinks most lamentably. Had our general
27 Been what he knew himself, it had gone well.
O, he has given example for our flight
Most grossly by his own.
29 ENOBARBUS   Ay, are you thereabouts?
Why then, good night indeed.
CANIDIUS
Toward Peloponnesus are they fled.
SCARUS
'Tis easy to't; and there I will attend
What further comes.
CANIDIUS   To Caesar will I render
My legions and my horse; six kings already
Show me the way of yielding.
ENOBARBUS   I'll yet follow
36 The wounded chance of Antony, though my reason
37 Sits in the wind against me.   *[Exeunt.]*

                  *

III, xi   *Enter Antony with Attendants.*
ANTONY
Hark! the land bids me tread no more upon't,
It is ashamed to bear me. Friends, come hither.
3 I am so lated in the world that I
Have lost my way for ever. I have a ship
Laden with gold: take that, divide it. Fly,
And make your peace with Caesar.
OMNES   Fly? Not we.

ANTONY
I have fled myself, and have instructed cowards
To run and show their shoulders. Friends, be gone.
I have myself resolved upon a course
Which has no need of you. Be gone.
My treasure's in the harbor. Take it! O,
I followed that I blush to look upon.   12
My very hairs do mutiny: for the white
Reprove the brown for rashness, and they them
For fear and doting. Friends, be gone, you shall
Have letters from me to some friends that will
Sweep your way for you. Pray you look not sad   17
Nor make replies of loathness; take the hint
Which my despair proclaims. Let that be left   19
Which leaves itself. To the seaside straightway!
I will possess you of that ship and treasure.
Leave me, I pray, a little: pray you now,
Nay, do so; for indeed I have lost command,   23
Therefore I pray you. I'll see you by and by.
    Sits down.
    Enter Cleopatra led by Charmian, [Iras,] and Eros.
EROS Nay, gentle madam, to him, comfort him.
IRAS Do, most dear Queen.
CHARMIAN Do? Why, what else?
CLEOPATRA Let me sit down. O Juno!
ANTONY No, no, no, no, no.
EROS See you here, sir?
ANTONY O fie, fie, fie!
CHARMIAN Madam!
IRAS Madam, O good Empress!
EROS Sir, sir!
ANTONY
Yes, my lord, yes. He at Philippi kept   35
His sword e'en like a dancer, while I struck
The lean and wrinkled Cassius; and 'twas I
That the mad Brutus ended: he alone
Dealt on lieutenantry, and no practice had   39
In the brave squares of war: yet now – No matter.   40
CLEOPATRA Ah, stand by.
EROS The Queen, my lord, the Queen.
IRAS
Go to him, madam, speak to him;
He is unqualitied with very shame.   44
CLEOPATRA
Well then, sustain me. O!
EROS
Most noble sir, arise. The Queen approaches.
Her head's declined, and death will seize her, but   47
Your comfort makes the rescue.
ANTONY
I have offended reputation,
A most unnoble swerving.

5 *synod* assembly 6 *cantle* piece 9 *like . . . pestilence* like the plague when its certain symptoms have been seen 10 *ribaudred* foul, obscene (many editors read 'ribald-rid,' but the meaning is the same) 13 *elder* i.e. superior 14 *breese* stinging fly (with pun on 'breeze') 18 *loofed* luffed, turned to the wind to fly (?), disengaged (?) 20 *doting mallard* lovesick wild duck 27 *what . . . himself* his true self (as a great soldier) 29 *are you thereabouts* i.e. is that where your thoughts are 36 *chance* fortunes 37 *Sits . . . me* dissuades me
III, xi The palace of Cleopatra in Alexandria 3 *so . . . world* i.e. like a traveller after nightfall 12 *that* what 17 *Sweep* i.e. with Caesar 19 *that* i.e. himself 23–24 *I . . . pray you* i.e. I have lost the right to order you, so I entreat you 35–36 *kept . . . dancer* i.e. never drew his sword 39 *Dealt on lieutenantry* relied on subordinates 40 *squares* squadrons 44 *unqualitied* unmanned 47 *but* unless

EROS   Sir, the Queen.

ANTONY
O, whither hast thou led me, Egypt? See
How I convey my shame out of thine eyes
53   By looking back what I have left behind
'Stroyed in dishonor.

CLEOPATRA   O my lord, my lord,
Forgive my fearful sails: I little thought
You would have followed.

ANTONY   Egypt, thou knew'st too well
My heart was to thy rudder tied by th' strings,
And thou shouldst tow me after. O'er my spirit
Thy full supremacy thou knew'st, and that
60   Thy beck might from the bidding of the gods
Command me.

CLEOPATRA   O, my pardon!

ANTONY   Now I must
62   To the young man send humble treaties, dodge
63   And palter in the shifts of lowness, who
With half the bulk o' th' world played as I pleased,
Making and marring fortunes. You did know
How much you were my conqueror, and that
My sword, made weak by my affection, would
Obey it on all cause.

CLEOPATRA   Pardon, pardon!

ANTONY
69   Fall not a tear, I say: one of them rates
All that is won and lost. Give me a kiss;
71   Even this repays me. We sent our schoolmaster.
72   Is 'a come back? Love, I am full of lead.
Some wine, within there, and our viands! Fortune
    knows
We scorn her most when most she offers blows. *Exeunt.*

*

III, xii   *Enter Caesar, Agrippa, Dolabella, [Thidias,]*
        with others.

CAESAR
Let him appear that's come from Antony.
Know you him?

DOLABELLA   Caesar, 'tis his schoolmaster:
An argument that he is plucked, when hither
He sends so poor a pinion of his wing,
Which had superfluous kings for messengers
Not many moons gone by.
    Enter Ambassador from Antony.

CAESAR   Approach and speak.

AMBASSADOR
Such as I am, I come from Antony.
I was of late as petty to his ends
As is the morn-dew on the myrtle leaf

To his grand sea.   10

CAESAR   Be't so. Declare thine office.

AMBASSADOR
Lord of his fortunes he salutes thee, and
Requires to live in Egypt; which not granted,   12
He lessons his requests, and to thee sues   13
To let him breathe between the heavens and earth,   14
A private man in Athens: this for him.
Next, Cleopatra does confess thy greatness,
Submits her to thy might, and of thee craves
The circle of the Ptolemies for her heirs,   18
Now hazarded to thy grace.   19

CAESAR   For Antony,
I have no ears to his request. The Queen
Of audience nor desire shall fail, so she   21
From Egypt drive her all-disgracèd friend
Or take his life there. This if she perform,
She shall not sue unheard. So to them both.

AMBASSADOR
Fortune pursue thee!

CAESAR   Bring him through the bands.   25
                  [Exit Ambassador.]
    [To Thidias]
To try thy eloquence now 'tis time. Dispatch.
From Antony win Cleopatra: promise,
And in our name, what she requires; add more,
From thine invention, offers. Women are not
In their best fortunes strong, but want will perjure
The ne'er-touched Vestal. Try thy cunning, Thidias;
Make thine own edict for thy pains, which we   32
Will answer as a law.

THIDIAS   Caesar, I go.

CAESAR
Observe how Antony becomes his flaw,   34
And what thou think'st his very action speaks   35
In every power that moves.

THIDIAS   Caesar, I shall.   *Exeunt.*

*

III, xiii   *Enter Cleopatra, Enobarbus, Charmian, and Iras.*

CLEOPATRA
What shall we do, Enobarbus?

ENOBARBUS   Think, and die.

CLEOPATRA
Is Antony or we in fault for this?

ENOBARBUS
Antony only, that would make his will   3
Lord of his reason. What though you fled
From that great face of war, whose several ranges   5
Frighted each other? Why should he follow?
The itch of his affection should not then
Have nicked his captainship, at such a point,   8
When half to half the world opposed, he being
The merèd question. 'Twas a shame no less   10
Than was his loss, to course your flying flags   11
And leave his navy gazing.

CLEOPATRA   Prithee peace.
    Enter the Ambassador, with Antony.

ANTONY
Is that his answer?

AMBASSADOR
Ay, my lord.

---

53 *By looking back* i.e. by averting my eyes from yours and looking back at
60 *beck* beckoning 62 *treaties* proposals 63 *palter . . . lowness* i.e. use
the tricks to which a man brought low is reduced 69 *Fall* let fall; *rates*
equals 71 *schoolmaster* i.e. his children's tutor 72 *lead* i.e. grief
III, xii The camp of Octavius Caesar in Egypt 10 *sea* i.e. the ultimate
source of dew 12 *Requires* requests 13 *lessons* disciplines 14 *breathe*
i.e. go on living 18 *circle* crown 19 *hazarded . . . grace* dependent on
your mercy 21 *audience* a hearing; *so* provided 25 *bands* troops 32 *Make
. . . edict* name your own price (as reward) 34 *becomes his flaw* takes his
fall 35–36 *And . . . moves* and what you think his every move reveals
III, xiii The palace of Cleopatra 3 *will* desire 5 *ranges* battle-lines
8 *nicked* got the better of 10 *merèd question* sole cause (?), decisive factor
(?) 11 *course* chase

ANTONY
　The Queen shall then have courtesy, so she
　Will yield us up.
AMBASSADOR　　He says so.
ANTONY　　　　　　　　　　Let her know't.
　To the boy Caesar send this grizzled head,
　And he will fill thy wishes to the brim
　With principalities.
CLEOPATRA　　　　That head, my lord?
ANTONY
　To him again! Tell him he wears the rose
　Of youth upon him; from which the world should note
22　Something particular. His coin, ships, legions
　May be a coward's, whose ministers would prevail
　Under the service of a child as soon
　As i' th' command of Caesar. I dare him therefore
26　To lay his gay comparisons apart
27　And answer me declined, sword against sword,
　Ourselves alone. I'll write it: follow me.
　　　　　　　　　[Exeunt Antony and Ambassador.]
　　ENOBARBUS [aside]
29　Yes, like enough: high-battled Caesar will
30　Unstate his happiness and be staged to th' show
　Against a sworder! I see men's judgments are
32　A parcel of their fortunes, and things outward
33　Do draw the inward quality after them
34　To suffer all alike. That he should dream,
35　Knowing all measures, the full Caesar will
　Answer his emptiness! Caesar, thou has subdued
　His judgment too.
　　　　Enter a Servant.
SERVANT　　　　A messenger from Caesar.
CLEOPATRA
　What, no more ceremony? See, my women,
　Against the blown rose may they stop their nose
　That kneeled unto the buds. Admit him, sir.
　　　　　　　　　　　　[Exit Servant.]

　ENOBARBUS [aside]
41　Mine honesty and I begin to square.
　The loyalty well held to fools does make
　Our faith mere folly: yet he that can endure
　To follow with allegiance a fall'n lord
　Does conquer him that did his master conquer
　And earns a place i' th' story.
　　　　Enter Thidias.
CLEOPATRA　　　　Caesar's will?
THIDIAS
　Hear it apart.
CLEOPATRA　　None but friends: say boldly.
THIDIAS
48　So, haply, are they friends to Antony.
ENOBARBUS
　He needs as many, sir, as Caesar has,
　Or needs not us. If Caesar please, our master
　Will leap to be his friend; for us, you know,
52　Whose he is we are, and that is Caesar's.
THIDIAS　　　　　　　　So.
　Thus then, thou most renowned, Caesar entreats
54　Not to consider in what case thou stand'st
　Further than he is Caesar.
CLEOPATRA　　　　Go on: right royal.
THIDIAS
　He knows that you embrace not Antony
　As you did love, but as you feared him.

CLEOPATRA　　　　　　　　　　O!
THIDIAS
　The scars upon your honor therefore he
　Does pity, as constrainèd blemishes,
　Not as deserved.
CLEOPATRA　　　He is a god, and knows
　What is most right. Mine honor was not yielded,
　But conquered merely.
ENOBARBUS *[aside]*　　To be sure of that,
　I will ask Antony. Sir, sir, thou art so leaky
　That we must leave thee to thy sinking, for
　Thy dearest quit thee.　　*Exit Enobarbus.*
THIDIAS　　　　　　Shall I say to Caesar
　What you require of him? For he partly begs　66
　To be desired to give. It much would please him
　That of his fortunes you should make a staff
　To lean upon. But it would warm his spirits
　To hear from me you had left Antony,
　And put yourself under his shroud,　　　　71
　The universal landlord.
CLEOPATRA　　　　What's your name?
THIDIAS
　My name is Thidias.
CLEOPATRA　　　　Most kind messenger,
　Say to great Caesar this: in deputation　　74
　I kiss his conqu'ring hand; tell him I am prompt
　To lay my crown at's feet, and there to kneel.
　Tell him, from his all-obeying breath, I hear　77
　The doom of Egypt.
THIDIAS　　　　　'Tis your noblest course:
　Wisdom and fortune combating together,
　If that the former dare but what it can,　　80
　No chance may shake it. Give me grace to lay
　My duty on your hand.　　　　　　　82
CLEOPATRA　　　　Your Caesar's father oft,
　When he hath mused of taking kingdoms in,
　Bestowed his lips on that unworthy place,
　As it rained kisses.
　　　　Enter Antony and Enobarbus.
ANTONY　　　　Favors? by Jove that thunders!
　What art thou, fellow?
THIDIAS　　　　One that but performs
　The bidding of the fullest man, and worthiest
　To have command obeyed.
ENOBARBUS *[aside]*　　You will be whipped.
ANTONY
　Approach there! Ah, you kite! Now, gods and devils!
　Authority melts from me. Of late, when I cried 'Ho!'
　Like boys unto a muss, kings would start forth,　91
　And cry 'Your will?' Have you no ears? I am
　Antony yet.

22 *Something particular* i.e. some personal heroism　26 *comparisons* i.e. all things which give him the advantage when he compares his position with mine　27 *declined* i.e. in years and fortune　29 *high-battled* lifted high in strength and mood by successful armies　30 *Unstate* abdicate　30–31 *be . . . sworder* be exposed as a public spectacle in a gladiatorial duel　32 *A parcel* i.e. part and parcel　33 *quality* nature　34 *To . . . alike* so that both decline together　35 *Knowing all measures* being a good judge (of men and things)　41 *square* quarrel　48 *haply* most likely　52 *Whose . . . are* i.e. whomever Antony belongs to, we belong to (?)　54–55 *Not . . . Caesar* i.e. not to think about your situation beyond realizing that you have to do with (a generous conqueror like) Caesar　66 *require* request　71 *shroud* shelter　74 *in deputation* i.e. through you as deputy　77 *all-obeying* that all obey　80 *If . . . can* if discretion confines itself to the possible　82 *My duty* i.e. a kiss　91 *muss* scramble

Enter a Servant.

93   Take hence this Jack and whip him.

ENOBARBUS *[aside]*
'Tis better playing with a lion's whelp
Than with an old one dying.

ANTONY   Moon and stars!
Whip him. Were't twenty of the greatest tributaries
That do acknowledge Caesar, should I find them
98 So saucy with the hand of she here – what's her name
Since she was Cleopatra? Whip him, fellows,
Till like a boy you see him cringe his face
And whine aloud for mercy. Take him hence.

THIDIAS
Mark Antony –

ANTONY   Tug him away. Being whipped,
Bring him again. This Jack of Caesar's shall
Bear us an errand to him. *Exeunt [Servants] with Thidias.*
You were half blasted ere I knew you. Ha!
Have I my pillow left unpressed in Rome,
Forborne the getting of a lawful race,
108 And by a gem of women, to be abused
109 By one that looks on feeders?

CLEOPATRA   Good my lord –

ANTONY
110 You have been a boggler ever:
But when we in our viciousness grow hard
112 (O misery on't!) the wise gods seel our eyes,
In our own filth drop our clear judgments, make us
Adore our errors, laugh at's while we strut
To our confusion.

CLEOPATRA   O, is't come to this?

ANTONY
I found you as a morsel cold upon
117 Dead Caesar's trencher: nay, you were a fragment
Of Gneius Pompey's, besides what hotter hours,
119 Unregist'red in vulgar fame, you have
120 Luxuriously picked out. For I am sure,
Though you can guess what temperance should be,
You know not what it is.

CLEOPATRA   Wherefore is this?

ANTONY
To let a fellow that will take rewards
124 And say 'God quit you!' be familiar with
My playfellow, your hand, this kingly seal
126 And plighter of high hearts. O that I were
Upon the hill of Basan to outroar
The hornèd herd! for I have savage cause,
129 And to proclaim it civilly were like
A haltered neck which does the hangman thank
131 For being yare about him.

---

93 *Jack* conceited upstart **98–99** *what's . . . Cleopatra* (Antony implies that this common trafficker in kisses cannot be the imperial Cleopatra) **108** *abused* betrayed **109** *feeders* menials **110** *boggler* shifty one **112** *seel* sew up **117** *trencher* plate; *fragment* leftover **119** *vulgar fame* common gossip **120** *Luxuriously* lustfully **124** *quit* repay **126–28** *O . . . herd* (Antony thinks of himself as chief among the herd of bulls of Bashan whose roaring is described in Psalms xxii, 12–13 – i.e. as chief cuckold among all the lovers cuckolded by Cleopatra) **129** *like* to act like **131** *yare* nimble **140** *entertainment* reception (here) **146** *orbs* the spheres in which they turn **149** *Hipparchus* (who had earlier revolted to Caesar); *enfranchèd* freed **153** *our . . . moon* i.e. Cleopatra, our terrestrial Isis or moon-goddess **155** *stay his time* wait out his fury **157** *one . . . points* his valet **161** *determines* melts **163** *the memory . . . womb* i.e. my offspring **165** *discandying* melting (as if it were hard candy) **171** *fleet* are afloat **172** *heart* courage **174** *in blood* (1) bloody, (2) with blood up, spirited **175** *our chronicle* our place in history

---

Enter a Servant with Thidias.

               Is he whipped?

SERVANT
Soundly, my lord.

ANTONY   Cried he? and begged 'a pardon?

SERVANT
He did ask favor.

ANTONY
If that thy father live, let him repent
Thou wast not made his daughter; and be thou sorry
To follow Caesar in his triumph, since
Thou hast been whipped for following him. Henceforth
The white hand of a lady fever thee,
Shake thou to look on't. Get thee back to Caesar,
Tell him thy entertainment: look thou say   140
He makes me angry with him. For he seems
Proud and disdainful, harping on what I am,
Not what he knew I was. He makes me angry,
And at this time most easy 'tis to do't,
When my good stars that were my former guides
Have empty left their orbs and shot their fires   146
Into th' abysm of hell. If he mislike
My speech and what is done, tell him he has
Hipparchus, my enfranchèd bondman, whom   149
He may at pleasure whip, or hang, or torture,
As he shall like, to quit me. Urge it thou.
Hence with thy stripes, be gone!   *Exit Thidias.*

CLEOPATRA
Have you done yet?

ANTONY   Alack, our terrene moon   153
Is now eclipsed, and it portends alone
The fall of Antony.

CLEOPATRA   I must stay his time.   155

ANTONY
To flatter Caesar, would you mingle eyes
With one that ties his points?   157

CLEOPATRA   Not know me yet?

ANTONY
Cold-hearted toward me?

CLEOPATRA   Ah, dear, if I be so,
From my cold heart let heaven engender hail,
And poison it in the source, and the first stone
Drop in my neck: as it determines, so   161
Dissolve my life! The next Caesarion smite,
Till by degrees the memory of my womb,   163
Together with my brave Egyptians all,
By the discandying of this pelleted storm,   165
Lie graveless, till the flies and gnats of Nile
Have buried them for prey!

ANTONY   I am satisfied.
Caesar sits down in Alexandria, where
I will oppose his fate. Our force by land
Hath nobly held; our severed navy too
Have knit again, and fleet, threat'ning most sea-like.   171
Where hast thou been, my heart? Dost thou hear, lady?   172
If from the field I shall return once more
To kiss these lips, I will appear in blood;   174
I and my sword will earn our chronicle.   175
There's hope in't yet.

CLEOPATRA
That's my brave lord!

ANTONY
I will be treble-sinewed, hearted, breathed,
And fight maliciously; for when mine hours

180 Were nice and lucky, men did ransom lives
Of me for jests ; but now I'll set my teeth
And send to darkness all that stop me. Come,
183 Let's have one other gaudy night : call to me
All my sad captains ; fill our bowls once more ;
Let's mock the midnight bell.

CLEOPATRA   It is my birthday.
I had thought t' have held it poor. But since my lord
Is Antony again, I will be Cleopatra.

ANTONY
We will yet do well.

CLEOPATRA
Call all his noble captains to my lord.

ANTONY
Do so, we'll speak to them ; and to-night I'll force
The wine peep through their scars. Come on, my queen,
192 There's sap in't yet ! The next time I do fight,
I'll make death love me, for I will contend
Even with his pestilent scythe.

                         Exeunt [all but Enobarbus].

ENOBARBUS
Now he'll outstare the lightning. To be furious
Is to be frighted out of fear, and in that mood
197 The dove will peck the estridge ; and I see still
A diminution in our captain's brain
Restores his heart. When valor preys on reason,
It eats the sword it fights with : I will seek
Some way to leave him.   *Exit.*

*

IV, i   *Enter Caesar, Agrippa, and Maecenas, with his
Army, Caesar reading a letter.*

CAESAR
He calls me boy, and chides as he had power
To beat me out of Egypt. My messenger
He hath whipped with rods ; dares me to personal
     combat,
Caesar to Antony. Let the old ruffian know
I have many other ways to die, meantime
Laugh at his challenge.

MAECENAS   Caesar must think,
When one so great begins to rage, he's hunted
Even to falling. Give him no breath, but now
9 Make boot of his distraction : never anger
Made good guard for itself.

CAESAR   Let our best heads
Know that to-morrow the last of many battles
12 We mean to fight. Within our files there are,
Of those that served Mark Antony but late,
14 Enough to fetch him in. See it done,
And feast the army ; we have store to do't,
And they have earned the waste. Poor Antony !

                                   Exeunt.

*

IV, ii   *Enter Antony, Cleopatra, Enobarbus, Charmian,
Iras, Alexas, with others.*

ANTONY
He will not fight with me, Domitius ?

ENOBARBUS   No.

ANTONY
Why should he not ?

ENOBARBUS
He thinks, being twenty times of better fortune,
He is twenty men to one.

ANTONY   To-morrow, soldier,
By sea and land I'll fight : or I will live,   5
Or bathe my dying honor in the blood
Shall make it live again. Woo't thou fight well ?

ENOBARBUS
I'll strike, and cry 'Take all !'   8

ANTONY   Well said, come on ;
Call forth my household servants ; let's to-night
Be bounteous at our meal.
     Enter three or four Servitors.
                         Give me thy hand,
Thou hast been rightly honest, so hast thou,
And thou, and thou, and thou : you have served me well,
And kings have been your fellows.

CLEOPATRA   What means this ?   13

ENOBARBUS
'Tis one of those odd tricks which sorrow shoots
Out of the mind.

ANTONY   And thou art honest too.
I wish I could be made so many men,   16
And all of you clapped up together in
An Antony, that I might do you service
So good as you have done.

OMNES   The gods forbid !

ANTONY
Well, my good fellows, wait on me to-night :
Scant not my cups, and make as much of me
As when mine empire was your fellow too
And suffered my command.

CLEOPATRA   What does he mean ?

ENOBARBUS
To make his followers weep.

ANTONY   Tend me to-night ;
May be it is the period of your duty.   25
Haply you shall not see me more ; or if,   26
A mangled shadow. Perchance to-morrow
You'll serve another master. I look on you
As one that takes his leave. Mine honest friends,
I turn you not away, but like a master
Married to your good service, stay till death.
Tend me to-night two hours, I ask no more,
And the gods yield you for't !   33

ENOBARBUS   What mean you, sir,
To give them this discomfort ? Look, they weep,
And I, an ass, am onion-eyed ; for shame !
Transform us not to women.

ANTONY   Ho, ho, ho !
Now the witch take me if I meant it thus !
Grace grow where those drops fall ! My hearty friends,   38
You take me in too dolorous a sense,
For I spake to you for your comfort, did desire you
To burn this night with torches. Know, my hearts,

180 *nice* able to be 'choosy'   183 *gaudy* joyous   192 *sap* i.e. life, hope
197 *estridge* species of hawk
IV, i The camp of Octavius Caesar   9 *boot* advantage   12 *files* troops
14 *fetch him in* capture him
IV, ii The palace of Cleopatra   5 *or* either   8 *Take all* winner take all
13–15 (here and in ll. 23–24 Enobarbus and Cleopatra talk aside)   16 *so
many men* i.e. so many men as you are   25 *period* end   26 *Haply* most
likely   33 *yield* repay   38 *Grace grow* may virtues spring up (with a pun on
'grace' as one name for the herb rue)

I hope well of to-morrow, and will lead you
Where rather I'll expect victorious life
Than death and honor. Let's to supper, come,
And drown consideration.   *Exeunt.*

*

IV, iii   *Enter a Company of Soldiers.*

1. SOLDIER
Brother, good night: to-morrow is the day.
2. SOLDIER
It will determine one way: fare you well.
Heard you of nothing strange about the streets?
1. SOLDIER
Nothing. What news?
2. SOLDIER
Belike 'tis but a rumor. Good night to you.
1. SOLDIER
Well, sir, good night.
        They meet other Soldiers.
2. SOLDIER   Soldiers, have careful watch.
3. SOLDIER
And you. Good night, good night.
        They place themselves in every corner of the stage.
4. SOLDIER
8   Here we; and if to-morrow
Our navy thrive, I have an absolute hope
Our landmen will stand up.
3. SOLDIER   'Tis a brave army,
And full of purpose.
        Music of the hautboys is under the stage.
2. SOLDIER   Peace! What noise?
1. SOLDIER   List, list!
2. SOLDIER
Hark!
1. SOLDIER   Music i' th' air.
3. SOLDIER   Under the earth.
4. SOLDIER
13 It signs well, does it not?
3. SOLDIER   No.
1. SOLDIER   Peace, I say!
What should this mean?
2. SOLDIER
15 'Tis the god Hercules, whom Antony loved,
Now leaves him.
1. SOLDIER   Walk; let's see if other watchmen
Do hear what we do.
2. SOLDIER   How now, masters?
OMNES *(speak together)*   How now?
How now? Do you hear this?
1. SOLDIER   Ay. Is't not strange?
3. SOLDIER
Do you hear, masters? do you hear?
1. SOLDIER
20 Follow the noise so far as we have quarter.

Let's see how it will give off.
OMNES
Content. 'Tis strange.   *Exeunt.*

*

        Enter Antony and Cleopatra, with others.   IV, iv
ANTONY
Eros! mine armor, Eros!
CLEOPATRA   Sleep a little.
ANTONY
No, my chuck. Eros, come; mine armor, Eros.
        Enter Eros [with armor].
Come, good fellow, put thine iron on.   3
If fortune be not ours to-day, it is
Because we brave her. Come.
CLEOPATRA   Nay, I'll help too.
What's this for?
ANTONY   Ah, let be, let be! Thou art
The armorer of my heart. False, false; this, this.   7
CLEOPATRA
Sooth, la, I'll help: thus it must be.
ANTONY   Well, well,
We shall thrive now. Seest thou, my good fellow?
Go, put on thy defenses.
EROS   Briefly, sir.   10
CLEOPATRA
Is not this buckled well?
ANTONY   Rarely, rarely:
He that unbuckles this, till we do please
To daff 't for our repose, shall hear a storm.   13
Thou fumblest, Eros, and my queen 's a squire
More tight at this than thou. Dispatch. O love,   15
That thou couldst see my wars to-day, and knew'st
The royal occupation: thou shouldst see
A workman in't.   18
        Enter an armed Soldier.
        Good morrow to thee, welcome,
Thou look'st like him that knows a warlike charge.   19
To business that we love we rise betime   20
And go to't with delight.
SOLDIER   A thousand, sir,
Early though't be, have on their riveted trim,   22
And at the port expect you.   23
        Shout. Trumpets flourish. Enter Captains and Soldiers.
CAPTAIN
The morn is fair. Good morrow, General.
ALL
Good morrow, General.
ANTONY   'Tis well blown, lads.   25
This morning, like the spirit of a youth
That means to be of note, begins betimes.
So, so. Come, give me that: this way. Well said.   28
Fare thee well, dame; whate'er becomes of me,
This is a soldier's kiss. Rebukable
And worthy shameful check it were to stand   31
On more mechanic compliment. I'll leave thee
Now like a man of steel. You that will fight,
Follow me close; I'll bring you to't. Adieu.
        Exeunt [Antony, Eros, Captains, and Soldiers].
CHARMIAN
Please you retire to your chamber?
CLEOPATRA   Lead me.

IV, iii An open place in Alexandria **8** *Here we* i.e. here is our post **13** *signs* signifies **15** *Hercules* (cf. I, iii, 84–85n.) **20** *as . . . quarter* as our watch extends
IV, iv The palace of Cleopatra **3** *thine iron* i.e. this armor of mine **7** *False* wrong **10** *Briefly* in a moment **13** *daff 't* take it off **15** *tight* deft **18** *workman* craftsman, expert **19** *charge* duty **20** *betime* early **22** *riveted trim* armor **23** *port* gate **25** *blown* opened (i.e. the morning) **28** *said* done (spoken to Cleopatra, who is arming him) **31** *check* reproof **31–32** *stand . . . compliment* use more elaborate ceremony

He goes forth gallantly. That he and Caesar might
Determine this great war in single fight!
Then Antony – but now – Well, on.   *Exeunt.*

*

IV, v   *Trumpets sound. Enter Antony and Eros [, a Soldier*
      meeting them].

SOLDIER
The gods make this a happy day to Antony!

ANTONY
Would thou and those thy scars had once prevailed
To make me fight at land!

SOLDIER   Hadst thou done so,
The kings that have revolted and the soldier
That has this morning left thee would have still
Followèd thy heels.

ANTONY   Who's gone this morning?

SOLDIER   Who?
One ever near thee: call for Enobarbus,
He shall not hear thee, or from Caesar's camp
Say 'I am none of thine.'

ANTONY   What sayest thou?

SOLDIER   Sir,
He is with Caesar.

EROS   Sir, his chests and treasure
He has not with him.

ANTONY   Is he gone?

SOLDIER   Most certain.

ANTONY
Go, Eros, send his treasure after; do it;
Detain no jot, I charge thee. Write to him
14   (I will subscribe) gentle adieus and greetings;
Say that I wish he never find more cause
To change a master. O, my fortunes have
Corrupted honest men! Dispatch. Enobarbus!
      Exit [with Eros and Soldier].

*

IV, vi   *Flourish. Enter Agrippa, Caesar, with Enobarbus,*
      and Dolabella.

CAESAR
Go forth, Agrippa, and begin the fight.
Our will is Antony be took alive:
Make it so known.

AGRIPPA
Caesar, I shall.   *[Exit.]*

CAESAR
The time of universal peace is near.
6   Prove this a prosp'rous day, the three-nooked world
Shall bear the olive freely.
      Enter a Messenger.

MESSENGER   Antony
Is come into the field.

CAESAR   Go charge Agrippa
9   Plant those that have revolted in the vant,
That Antony may seem to spend his fury
11   Upon himself.   *Exeunt [all but Enobarbus].*

ENOBARBUS
Alexas did revolt and went to Jewry on
13   Affairs of Antony; there did dissuade
Great Herod to incline himself to Caesar

And leave his master Antony. For this pains
Caesar hath hanged him. Canidius and the rest
That fell away have entertainment, but   17
No honorable trust. I have done ill,
Of which I do accuse myself so sorely
That I will joy no more.
      Enter a Soldier of Caesar's.

SOLDIER   Enobarbus, Antony
Hath after thee sent all thy treasure, with
His bounty overplus. The messenger
Came on my guard, and at thy tent is now
Unloading of his mules.

ENOBARBUS   I give it you.

SOLDIER
Mock not, Enobarbus.
I tell you true. Best you safed the bringer   26
Out of the host; I must attend mine office
Or would have done't myself. Your emperor
Continues still a Jove.   *Exit.*

ENOBARBUS
I am alone the villain of the earth,
And feel I am so most. O Antony,
Thou mine of bounty, how wouldst thou have paid
My better service, when my turpitude
Thou dost so crown with gold! This blows my heart.   34
If swift thought break it not, a swifter mean   35
Shall outstrike thought; but thought will do't, I feel.
I fight against thee? No, I will go seek
Some ditch wherein to die: the foul'st best fits
My latter part of life.   *Exit.*

*

      Alarum. Drums and Trumpets. Enter Agrippa   IV, vi
      [and Soldiers].

AGRIPPA
Retire. We have engaged ourselves too far.   1
Caesar himself has work, and our oppression   2
Exceeds what we expected.   *Exit [with Soldiers].*
      Alarums. Enter Antony, and Scarus wounded.

SCARUS
O my brave Emperor, this is fought indeed!
Had we done so at first, we had droven them home
With clouts about their heads.   6

ANTONY   Thou bleed'st apace.

SCARUS
I had a wound here that was like a T,
But now 'tis made an H.   8
      [Sound retreat] far off.

ANTONY   They do retire.

SCARUS
We'll beat 'em into bench-holes. I have yet   9
Room for six scotches more.   10
      Enter Eros.

IV, v An open place in Alexandria   14 *subscribe* sign
IV, vi The camp of Octavius Caesar   6 *three-nooked* three-cornered
(Africa, Asia, Europe)   9 *vant* front lines   11 *himself* i.e. his own former
soldiers   13 *dissuade* i.e. from Antony   17 *entertainment* employment
26 *safed* gave safe conduct to   34 *blows* makes swell   35 *thought* grief
IV, vii A field near Alexandria   1 *engaged* entangled (with the enemy)
2 *our oppression* the pressure on us   6 *clouts* bandages   8 *H* (pun on
'ache,' which was pronounced 'aitch')   9 *bench-holes* privy holes   10
scotches gashes

EROS
They are beaten, sir, and our advantage serves
For a fair victory.

12 **SCARUS** Let us score their backs
And snatch 'em up, as we take hares, behind :
'Tis sport to maul a runner.

ANTONY I will reward thee
Once for thy sprightly comfort, and tenfold
For thy good valor. Come thee on.

16 **SCARUS** I'll halt after.
Exeunt.

IV, viii *Alarum. Enter Antony again in a march ; Scarus,*
with others.

ANTONY
We have beat him to his camp. Run one before
2 And let the Queen know of our gests. To-morrow,
Before the sun shall see 's, we'll spill the blood
That has to-day escaped. I thank you all,
For doughty-handed are you, and have fought
Not as you served the cause, but as 't had been
7 Each man's like mine : you have shown all Hectors.
8 Enter the city, clip your wives, your friends,
Tell them your feats, whilst they with joyful tears
Wash the congealment from your wounds, and kiss
The honored gashes whole.
Enter Cleopatra.
[*To Scarus*] Give me thy hand ;
12 To this great fairy I'll commend thy acts,
Make her thanks bless thee. – O thou day o' th' world,
Chain mine armed neck ; leap thou, attire and all,
15 Through proof of harness to my heart, and there
16 Ride on the pants triumphing.

CLEOPATRA Lord of lords !
17 O infinite virtue, com'st thou smiling from
18 The world's great snare uncaught ?

ANTONY My nightingale,
We have beat them to their beds. What, girl ! though
gray
Do something mingle with our younger brown, yet ha'
we
A brain that nourishes our nerves, and can
22 Get goal for goal of youth. Behold this man :
Commend unto his lips thy favoring hand. –
Kiss it, my warrior. – He hath fought to-day
As if a god in hate of mankind had
Destroyed in such a shape.

CLEOPATRA I'll give thee, friend,
An armor all of gold ; it was a king's.

ANTONY
28 He has deserved it, were it carbuncled
29 Like holy Phoebus' car. Give me thy hand.

---

12 *score* mark   16 *halt* limp
IV, viii Before the gates of Alexandria   2 *gests* deeds   7 *shown* proved
8 *clip* hug   12 *fairy* enchantress   15 *proof of harness* i.e. impenetrable
armor   16 *Ride . . . pants* i.e. as if his heart were a panting steed   17
virtue valor   18 *snare* i.e. death in war   22 *Get . . . of* hold our own with
28 *carbuncled* jewelled   29 *holy Phoebus' car* the sun-god's chariot   31
targets shields ; *owe* own
IV, ix The camp of Octavius Caesar   5 *shrewd* wicked   8–9 *When . . .*
memory when traitors go down in history shamed   12 *mistress* i.e. the moon
13 *disponge* squeeze (as from a sponge)   17 *Which* (refers to *heart*); *dried*
(sorrow was thought to dry up the blood)   20 *in . . . particular* i.e. yourself
21 *in register* in its records   22 *master leaver* (1) runaway servant, (2) outstanding traitor   26 *Swoonds* faints   27 *for sleep* conducive to sleep   29
raught reached   30 *Demurely* softly

Through Alexandria make a jolly march ;
Bear our hacked targets like the men that owe them. 31
Had our great palace the capacity
To camp this host, we all would sup together
And drink carouses to the next day's fate,
Which promises royal peril. Trumpeters,
With brazen din blast you the city's ear,
Make mingle with our rattling tabourines,
That heaven and earth may strike their sounds together,
Applauding our approach. *Exeunt.*

✷

Enter a Sentry and his Company. Enobarbus IV, ix
follows.

SENTRY
If we be not relieved within this hour,
We must return to th' court of guard. The night
Is shiny, and they say we shall embattle
By th' second hour i' th' morn.

1 . **WATCHMAN** This last day was
A shrewd one to's. 5

ENOBARBUS O, bear me witness, night –

2 . **WATCHMAN**
What man is this ?

1 . **WATCHMAN** Stand close, and list him.

ENOBARBUS
Be witness to me, O thou blessèd moon,
When men revolted shall upon record
Bear hateful memory, poor Enobarbus did 8
Before thy face repent !

SENTRY Enobarbus ?

2 . **WATCHMAN** Peace :
Hark further.

ENOBARBUS
O sovereign mistress of true melancholy, 12
The poisonous damp of night disponge upon me, 13
That life, a very rebel to my will,
May hang no longer on me. Throw my heart
Against the flint and hardness of my fault,
Which, being dried with grief, will break to powder, 17
And finish all foul thoughts. O Antony,
Nobler than my revolt is infamous,
Forgive me in thine own particular, 20
But let the world rank me in register 21
A master leaver and a fugitive. 22
O Antony ! O Antony !
[*Dies.*]

1 . **WATCHMAN** Let's speak
To him.

SENTRY Let's hear him, for the things he speaks
May concern Caesar.

2 . **WATCHMAN** Let's do so. But he sleeps.

SENTRY
Swoonds rather, for so bad a prayer as his 26
Was never yet for sleep. 27

1 . **WATCHMAN** Go we to him.

2 . **WATCHMAN**
Awake, sir, awake, speak to us.

1 . **WATCHMAN** Hear you, sir ?

SENTRY
The hand of death hath raught him. 29
Drums afar off. Hark ! The drums
Demurely wake the sleepers. Let us bear him 30

To th' court of guard : he is of note. Our hour
Is fully out.
2 . WATCHMAN
  Come on then,
He may recover yet.   *Exeunt [with the body].*

*

IV, x   *Enter Antony and Scarus, with their Army.*
ANTONY
  Their preparation is to-day by sea ;
  We please them not by land.
SCARUS   For both, my lord.
ANTONY
  I would they'ld fight i' th' fire or i' th' air ;
4 We'ld fight there too. But this it is, our foot
  Upon the hills adjoining to the city
  Shall stay with us – Order for sea is given ;
  They have put forth the haven –
8 Where their appointment we may best discover
  And look on their endeavor.   *Exeunt.*

IV, xi   *Enter Caesar and his Army.*
  CAESAR
1 But being charged, we will be still by land,
  Which, as I take't, we shall ; for his best force
  Is forth to man his galleys. To the vales,
  And hold our best advantage.   *Exeunt.*

IV, xii   *Enter Antony and Scarus.*
ANTONY
  Yet they are not joined. Where yond pine does stand
  I shall discover all. I'll bring thee word
  Straight how 'tis like to go.   *Exit.*
SCARUS   Swallows have built
  In Cleopatra's sails their nests. The augurers
  Say they know not, they cannot tell, look grimly,
  And dare not speak their knowledge. Antony
  Is valiant, and dejected, and by starts
8 His fretted fortunes give him hope and fear
  Of what he has, and has not.
    Alarum afar off, as at a sea-fight.
    Enter Antony.
ANTONY   All is lost !
  This foul Egyptian hath betrayed me :
  My fleet hath yielded to the foe, and yonder
  They cast their caps up and carouse together
13 Like friends long lost. Triple-turned whore ! 'tis thou
  Hast sold me to this novice, and my heart
  Makes only wars on thee. Bid them all fly ;
16 For when I am revenged upon my charm,
  I have done all. Bid them all fly, be gone. *[Exit Scarus.]*
  O sun, thy uprise shall I see no more.
  Fortune and Antony part here, even here
  Do we shake hands. All come to this ? The hearts
  That spanieled me at heels, to whom I gave
22 Their wishes, do discandy, melt their sweets
23 On blossoming Caesar ; and this pine is barked,
  That overtopped them all. Betrayed I am.
25 O this false soul of Egypt ! this grave charm,
  Whose eye becked forth my wars, and called them home,
27 Whose bosom was my crownet, my chief end,
28 Like a right gypsy hath at fast and loose
  Beguiled me to the very heart of loss.
  What, Eros, Eros !
    Enter Cleopatra.
30   Ah, thou spell ! Avaunt !

CLEOPATRA
  Why is my lord enraged against his love ?
ANTONY
  Vanish, or I shall give thee thy deserving
  And blemish Caesar's triumph. Let him take thee 33
  And hoist thee up to the shouting plebeians ;
  Follow his chariot, like the greatest spot
  Of all thy sex. Most monster-like be shown
  For poor'st diminitives, for dolts, and let 37
  Patient Octavia plough thy visage up
  With her prepared nails.   *Exit Cleopatra.*
            'Tis well th' art gone,
  If it be well to live ; but better 'twere
  Thou fell'st into my fury, for one death
  Might have prevented many. Eros, ho !
  The shirt of Nessus is upon me ; teach me, 43
  Alcides, thou mine ancestor, thy rage. 44
  Let me lodge Lichas on the horns o' th' moon
  And with those hands that grasped the heaviest club
  Subdue my worthiest self. The witch shall die.
  To the young Roman boy she hath sold me, and I fall
  Under this plot : she dies for't. Eros, ho !   *Exit.*

*

    Enter Cleopatra, Charmian, Iras, Mardian.
CLEOPATRA
  Help me, my women : O, he's more mad
  Than Telamon for his shield ; the boar of Thessaly 2
  Was never so embossed. 3
CHARMIAN   To th' monument !
  There lock yourself, and send him word you are dead.
  The soul and body rive not more in parting 5
  Than greatness going off.
CLEOPATRA   To th' monument !
  Mardian, go tell him I have slain myself :
  Say that the last I spoke was 'Antony'
  And word it, prithee, piteously. Hence, Mardian,
  And bring me how he takes my death. To th' monument !
                      Exeunt.

*

    Enter Antony and Eros.
ANTONY
  Eros, thou yet behold'st me ?
EROS   Ay, noble lord.

IV, x A *field near Alexandria* 4 *foot* infantry 8 *appointment* arrangement
IV, xi 1 *But being* unless we are
IV, xii 8 *fretted* shifting 13 *Triple-turned* i.e. from Pompey, from Julius Caesar, and now from himself 16 *charm* enchantress 22 *discandy* melt 23 *barked* stripped 25 *grave* deadly 27 *my crownet . . . end* the crown and purpose of my life 28 *right* true ; *fast and loose* (a game) 30 *Avaunt* be gone 33 *triumph* triumphal procession (in Rome) 37 *diminitives* little people, i.e. the populace 43 *Nessus* (Fatally wounded by Hercules with a poisoned arrow, the centaur Nessus persuaded Hercules' wife to give his blood-stained shirt to her husband, telling her it would assure his love for her. The shirt so poisoned Hercules that in his agony he threw his page Lichas, who had brought it, to the skies and set about destroying himself.) 44 *Alcides* Hercules
IV, xiii The *palace of Cleopatra* 2 *Telamon* Ajax Telamon, who went mad when Achilles' shield was not given to him but to his rival, Ulysses ; *boar of Thessaly* (sent by Artemis to ravage Thessaly in punishment for omitted sacrifices) 3 *embossed* infuriated ; *monument* tomb (which like other Egyptian rulers Cleopatra had prepared in advance) 5 *rive* rend
IV, xiv Near the *palace of Cleopatra*

ANTONY
Sometime we see a cloud that's dragonish;
A vapor sometime like a bear or lion,
A towered citadel, a pendant rock,
A forkèd mountain, or blue promontory
With trees upon't that nod unto the world
And mock our eyes with air. Thou hast seen these signs;
8 They are black Vesper's pageants.

EROS   Ay, my lord.

ANTONY
That which is now a horse, even with a thought
10 The rack dislimns, and makes it indistinct
As water is in water.

EROS   It does, my lord.

ANTONY
My good knave Eros, now thy captain is
Even such a body: here I am Antony,
Yet cannot hold this visible shape, my knave.
15 I made these wars for Egypt, and the Queen,
Whose heart I thought I had, for she had mine,
Which, whilst it was mine, had annexed unto't
18 A million moe, now lost – she, Eros, has
19 Packed cards with Caesar, and false-played my glory
20 Unto an enemy's triumph.
Nay, weep not, gentle Eros, there is left us
Ourselves to end ourselves.
     Enter Mardian.   O, thy vile lady!
23 She has robbed me of my sword.

MARDIAN   No, Antony.
My mistress loved thee and her fortunes mingled
With thine entirely.

ANTONY   Hence, saucy eunuch, peace!
She hath betrayed me and shall die the death.

MARDIAN
Death of one person can be paid but once,
And that she has discharged. What thou wouldst do
Is done unto thy hand. The last she spake
Was 'Antony! most noble Antony!'
Then in the midst a tearing groan did break
The name of Antony; it was divided
Between her heart and lips: she rend'red life,
Thy name so buried in her.

ANTONY   Dead, then?

MARDIAN   Dead.

ANTONY
Unarm, Eros. The long day's task is done,
And we must sleep.
     [To Mardian] That thou depart'st hence safe
Does pay thy labor richly: go.   *Exit Mardian.*
          Off, pluck off:

---

8 *black Vesper's pageants* i.e. shows heralding the coming of night (as pageants used to herald the coming of a king or queen) 10 *rack* cloud; *dislimns* unshapes 15 *Egypt* i.e. Cleopatra 18 *moe* more 19 *Packed* i.e. stacked the deck; *false-played* falsely played away 20 *triumph* (1) victory, (2) trump 23 *sword* manhood and soldiership 38 *sevenfold* having seven thicknesses 39 *battery* the battering (of grief) 40 *continent* i.e. that which contains thee 46 *length* i.e. of life 47–49 *labor . . . strength* i.e. force is defeated by its own strength, labor by its own effort 49 *seal* bring all to a close (as in sealing a document or will) 51 *Where . . . flowers* i.e. in the Elysian fields 52 *port* behavior 53 *want troops* lack admirers (i.e. in comparison with us as faithful lovers – since Aeneas deserted Dido for Roman greatness whereas Antony is deserting Roman greatness for Cleopatra) 59 *to lack* for lacking 63 *exigent* need 65 *prosecution* pursuit 72 *windowed* i.e. watching from a window 73 *pleached* folded 74 *corrigible* submissive 75 *penetrative* penetrating 77 *His . . . ensued* the baseness of him that followed 83 *precedent* former

---

The sevenfold shield of Ajax cannot keep   38
The battery from my heart. O, cleave, my sides!   39
Heart, once be stronger than thy continent,   40
Crack thy frail case! Apace, Eros, apace.
No more a soldier. Bruisèd pieces, go;
You have been nobly borne. – From me awhile. *Exit Eros.*
I will o'ertake thee, Cleopatra, and
Weep for my pardon. So it must be, for now
All length is torture: since the torch is out,   46
Lie down, and stray no farther. Now all labor   47
Mars what it does; yea, very force entangles
Itself with strength: seal then, and all is done.   49
Eros! – I come, my queen. – Eros! – Stay for me.
Where souls do couch on flowers, we'll hand in hand,   51
And with our sprightly port make the ghosts gaze: 52
Dido and her Aeneas shall want troops,   53
And all the haunt be ours. – Come, Eros, Eros!
     Enter Eros.

EROS
What would my lord?

ANTONY   Since Cleopatra died
I have lived in such dishonor that the gods
Detest my baseness. I, that with my sword
Quartered the world and o'er green Neptune's back
With ships made cities, condemn myself to lack   59
The courage of a woman – less noble mind
Than she which by her death our Caesar tells
'I am conqueror of myself.' Thou art sworn, Eros,
That, when the exigent should come, which now   63
Is come indeed, when I should see behind me
Th' inevitable prosecution of   65
Disgrace and horror, that on my command
Thou then wouldst kill me. Do't, the time is come.
Thou strik'st not me, 'tis Caesar thou defeat'st.
Put color in thy cheek.

EROS   The gods withhold me!
Shall I do that which all the Parthian darts,
Though enemy, lost aim and could not?

ANTONY   Eros,
Wouldst thou be windowed in great Rome and see   72
Thy master thus with pleached arms, bending down   73
His corrigible neck, his face subdued   74
To penetrative shame, whilst the wheeled seat   75
Of fortunate Caesar, drawn before him, branded
His baseness that ensued?   77

EROS   I would not see't.

ANTONY
Come then: for with a wound I must be cured.
Draw thou thy honest sword, which thou hast worn
Most useful for thy country.

EROS   O sir, pardon me.

ANTONY
When I did make thee free, swor'st thou not then
To do this when I bade thee? Do it at once,
Or thy precedent services are all   83
But accidents unpurposed. Draw, and come.

EROS
Turn from me then that noble countenance
Wherein the worship of the whole world lies.

ANTONY
Lo thee!
     [Turns from him.]

EROS
My sword is drawn.

ANTONY   Then let it do at once
The thing why thou hast drawn it.

EROS   My dear master,
My captain, and my emperor, let me say,
Before I strike this bloody stroke, farewell.

ANTONY
'Tis said, man, and farewell.

EROS
Farewell, great chief. Shall I strike now?

ANTONY   Now, Eros.

EROS
Why, there then! Thus I do escape the sorrow
Of Antony's death.
          Kills himself.

ANTONY   Thrice-nobler than myself!
Thou teachest me, O valiant Eros, what
I should, and thou couldst not. My queen and Eros

98   Have by their brave instruction got upon me
A nobleness in record. But I will be
A bridegroom in my death, and run into't
As to a lover's bed. Come then; and, Eros,
Thy master dies thy scholar. To do thus
          [Falls on his sword.]
I learned of thee. How? not dead? not dead?

104 The guard, ho! O, dispatch me!
          Enter [Decretas and] a [Company of the] Guard.

1. GUARDSMAN   What's the noise?

ANTONY
I have done my work ill, friends. O, make an end
Of what I have begun.

2. GUARDSMAN   The star is fall'n.

1. GUARDSMAN

107 And time is at his period.

ALL   Alas, and woe!

ANTONY
Let him that loves me strike me dead.

1. GUARDSMAN
Not I.

2. GUARDSMAN   Nor I.

3. GUARDSMAN   Nor any one.
          Exeunt [the Guardsmen].

DECRETAS
Thy death and fortunes bid thy followers fly.
This sword but shown to Caesar, with this tidings,

113 Shall enter me with him.
          Enter Diomedes.

DIOMEDES
Where's Antony?

DECRETAS   There, Diomed, there.

DIOMEDES   Lives he?
Wilt thou not answer, man?   *[Exit Decretas.]*

ANTONY
Art thou there, Diomed? Draw thy sword, and give me
Sufficing strokes for death.

DIOMEDES   Most absolute lord,
My mistress Cleopatra sent me to thee.

ANTONY
When did she send thee?

DIOMEDES   Now, my lord.

ANTONY   Where is she?

DIOMEDES
Locked in her monument. She had a prophesying fear
Of what hath come to pass; for when she saw
(Which never shall be found) you did suspect

She had disposed with Caesar, and that your rage   123
Would not be purged, she sent you word she was dead;   124
But, fearing since how it might work, hath sent
Me to proclaim the truth, and I am come,
I dread, too late.

ANTONY
Too late, good Diomed. Call my guard, I prithee.

DIOMEDES
What ho! the Emperor's guard! the guard, what ho!
Come, your lord calls!
          Enter four or five of the Guard of Antony.

ANTONY
Bear me, good friends, where Cleopatra bides;
'Tis the last service that I shall command you.

1. GUARDSMAN
Woe, woe are we, sir, you may not live to wear
All your true followers out.

ALL   Most heavy day!

ANTONY
Nay, good my fellows, do not please sharp fate
To grace it with your sorrows. Bid that welcome
Which comes to punish us, and we punish it,
Seeming to bear it lightly. Take me up:
I have led you oft; carry me now, good friends,
And have my thanks for all.
          Exit [the Guard,] bearing Antony.

                              *

          Enter Cleopatra and her Maids aloft, with Charmian   IV, x
          and Iras.

CLEOPATRA
O Charmian, I will never go from hence.

CHARMIAN
Be comforted, dear madam.

CLEOPATRA   No, I will not.
All strange and terrible events are welcome,
But comforts we despise. Our size of sorrow,
Proportioned to our cause, must be as great
As that which makes it.
          Enter Diomed [below].
                      How now? Is he dead?

DIOMEDES
His death's upon him, but not dead.
Look out o' th' other side your monument;
His guard have brought him thither.
          Enter [below,] Antony, and the Guard [bearing him].

CLEOPATRA   O sun,
Burn the great sphere thou mov'st in, darkling stand   10
The varying shore o' th' world! O Antony,
Antony, Antony! Help, Charmian, help, Iras, help:
Help, friends below, let's draw him hither.

ANTONY   Peace!
Not Caesar's valor hath o'erthrown Antony,
But Antony's hath triumphed on itself.

CLEOPATRA
So it should be, that none but Antony
Should conquer Antony, but woe 'tis so!

98–99 *got . . . record* beaten me to a noble name in history   **104 s.d.** *Decretas* (the usual folio spelling of a name which also appears in the folio as 'Dercetus' and is sometimes revised by editors to 'Dercetas')   **107** *period* end   **113** *enter* recommend   **123** *disposed* made terms   **124** *purged* expelled   **IV, xv** Before the monument of Cleopatra   **10** *darkling* darkened

ANTONY
    I am dying, Egypt, dying; only
19   I here importune death awhile, until
    Of many thousand kisses the poor last
    I lay upon thy lips.
21 CLEOPATRA   I dare not, dear;
    Dear my lord, pardon: I dare not,
    Lest I be taken. Not th' imperious show
    Of the full-fortuned Caesar ever shall
25   Be brooched with me, if knife, drugs, serpents have
    Edge, sting, or operation. I am safe:
    Your wife Octavia, with her modest eyes
28   And still conclusion, shall acquire no honor
29   Demuring upon me. But come, come, Antony!
    Help me, my women, we must draw thee up:
    Assist, good friends.
ANTONY   O, quick, or I am gone.
CLEOPATRA
    Here's sport indeed! How heavy weighs my lord!
33   Our strength is all gone into heaviness:
    That makes the weight. Had I great Juno's power,
    The strong-winged Mercury should fetch thee up
    And set thee by Jove's side. Yet come a little,
    Wishers were ever fools. O, come, come, come.
      They heave Antony aloft to Cleopatra.
    And welcome, welcome! Die when thou hast lived,
39   Quicken with kissing. Had my lips that power,
    Thus would I wear them out.
ALL   A heavy sight!
ANTONY
    I am dying, Egypt, dying.
    Give me some wine, and let me speak a little.
CLEOPATRA
    No, let me speak, and let me rail so high
44   That the false huswife Fortune break her wheel,
    Provoked by my offense.
ANTONY   One word, sweet queen.
    Of Caesar seek your honor, with your safety. O!
CLEOPATRA
    They do not go together.
ANTONY   Gentle, hear me:
    None about Caesar trust but Proculeius.
CLEOPATRA
    My resolution and my hands I'll trust,
    None about Caesar.
ANTONY
    The miserable change now at my end
    Lament nor sorrow at; but please your thoughts
    In feeding them with those my former fortunes,
    Wherein I lived the greatest prince o' th' world,
    The noblest: and do now not basely die,
    Not cowardly put off my helmet to
    My countryman. A Roman, by a Roman
    Valiantly vanquished. Now my spirit is going,
    I can no more.

CLEOPATRA   Noblest of men, woo't die?   59
    Hast thou no care of me? Shall I abide
    In this dull world, which in thy absence is
    No better than a sty? O, see, my women,
      [Antony dies.]
    The crown o' th' earth doth melt. My lord!
    O, withered is the garland of the war,   64
    The soldier's pole is fall'n: young boys and girls   65
    Are level now with men. The odds is gone,   66
    And there is nothing left remarkable
    Beneath the visiting moon.
      [Swoons.]
CHARMIAN O, quietness, lady!
IRAS She's dead too, our sovereign.
CHARMIAN Lady!
IRAS Madam!
CHARMIAN O madam, madam, madam!
IRAS Royal Egypt! Empress!
CHARMIAN Peace, peace, Iras!
CLEOPATRA
    No more but e'en a woman, and commanded
    By such poor passion as the maid that milks
    And does the meanest chares. It were for me   78
    To throw my sceptre at the injurious gods,
    To tell them that this world did equal theirs
    Till they had stol'n our jewel. All's but naught.
    Patience is sottish, and impatience does   82
    Become a dog that's mad: then is it sin
    To rush into the secret house of death
    Ere death dare come to us? How do you, women?
    What, what! good cheer! Why, how now, Charmian?
    My noble girls! Ah, women, women, look!
    Our lamp is spent, it's out! Good sirs, take heart: 88
    We'll bury him; and then, what's brave, what's noble,
    Let's do't after the high Roman fashion,
    And make death proud to take us. Come away.
    This case of that huge spirit now is cold.
    Ah, women, women! Come; we have no friend
    But resolution, and the briefest end.
      Exeunt, bearing off Antony's body.

                *

    Enter Caesar, Agrippa, Dolabella, Maecenas,   V, i
    [Gallus, Proculeius,] with his Council of War.
CAESAR
    Go to him, Dolabella, bid him yield:
    Being so frustrate, tell him he mocks   2
    The pauses that he makes.
DOLABELLA   Caesar, I shall.   *[Exit.]*
    Enter Decretas, with the sword of Antony.
CAESAR
    Wherefore is that? And what art thou that dar'st
    Appear thus to us?
DECRETAS   I am called Decretas.
    Mark Antony I served, who best was worthy
    Best to be served. Whilst he stood up and spoke,
    He was my master, and I wore my life
    To spend upon his haters. If thou please
    To take me to thee, as I was to him
    I'll be to Caesar; if thou pleasest not,
    I yield thee up my life.
CAESAR   What is't thou say'st?

---

19 *importune* beg to delay **21** *dare not* i.e. dare not descend to Antony's side **25** *brooched* adorned **28** *still conclusion* wordless censure **29** *Demuring* looking demurely **33** *heaviness* (with pun on 'grief') **39** *Quicken* come back to life **44** *huswife* jilt **59** *woo't* wilt thou **64** *garland . . . war* flower of all soldiers **65** *pole* North Star (?) **66** *odds* standard of measurement **78** *chares* chores **82–83** *Patience . . . mad* both patience and sorrow are now beside the point **88** *sirs* i.e. Cleopatra's women
V, i The camp of Octavius Caesar **2** *frustrate* helpless **2–3** *he mocks . . . makes* i.e. to delay surrendering is ridiculous

DECRETAS
I say, O Caesar, Antony is dead.

CAESAR
The breaking of so great a thing should make
A greater crack. The round world
16 Should have shook lions into civil streets
And citizens to their dens. The death of Antony
Is not a single doom, in the name lay
19 A moiety of the world.

DECRETAS   He is dead, Caesar,
Not by a public minister of justice
21 Nor by a hirèd knife ; but that self hand
Which writ his honor in the acts it did
Hath, with the courage which the heart did lend it,
Splitted the heart. This is his sword,
I robbed his wound of it : behold it stained
With his most noble blood.

CAESAR   Look you sad, friends ?
The gods rebuke me, but it is tidings
To wash the eyes of kings.

AGRIPPA   And strange it is
That nature must compel us to lament
30 Our most persisted deeds.

MAECENAS   His taints and honors
31 Waged equal with him.

AGRIPPA   A rarer spirit never
Did steer humanity ; but you, gods, will give us
Some faults to make us men. Caesar is touched.

MAECENAS
When such a spacious mirror 's set before him,
He needs must see himself.

CAESAR   O Antony,
36 I have followed thee to this. But we do launch
Diseases in our bodies. I must perforce
Have shown to thee such a declining day
39 Or look on thine : we could not stall together
In the whole world. But yet let me lament
41 With tears as sovereign as the blood of hearts
42 That thou, my brother, my competitor
43 In top of all design, my mate in empire,
Friend and companion in the front of war,
The arm of mine own body, and the heart
46 Where mine his thoughts did kindle – that our stars,
Unreconciliable, should divide
Our equalness to this. Hear me, good friends –
Enter an Egyptian.
But I will tell you at some meeter season.
50 The business of this man looks out of him ;
We'll hear him what he says. Whence are you ?

EGYPTIAN
A poor Egyptian yet. The Queen my mistress,
Confined in all she has, her monument,
Of thy intents desires instruction,
That she preparèdly may frame herself
To th' way she's forced to.

CAESAR   Bid her have good heart :
She soon shall know of us, by some of ours,
How honorable and how kindly we
Determine for her. For Caesar cannot live
To be ungentle.

EGYPTIAN   So the gods preserve thee !   *Exit.*

CAESAR
Come hither, Proculeius. Go and say
We purpose her no shame : give her what comforts

The quality of her passion shall require,
Lest, in her greatness, by some mortal stroke
She do defeat us. For her life in Rome
Would be eternal in our triumph. Go,
And with your speediest bring us what she says
And how you find of her.

PROCULEIUS   Caesar, I shall.   *Exit.*

CAESAR
Gallus, go you along. *[Exit Gallus.]* Where's Dolabella,
To second Proculeius ?

ALL   Dolabella !

CAESAR
Let him alone, for I remember now
How he's employed. He shall in time be ready.
Go with me to my tent, where you shall see
How hardly I was drawn into this war,
How calm and gentle I proceeded still
In all my writings. Go with me, and see
What I can show in this.   *Exeunt.*

*

Enter Cleopatra, Charmian, Iras, and Mardian.   V

CLEOPATRA
My desolation does begin to make
A better life. 'Tis paltry to be Caesar :
Not being Fortune, he's but Fortune's knave,
A minister of her will. And it is great
To do that thing that ends all other deeds,
Which shackles accidents and bolts up change ;
Which sleeps, and never palates more the dung,
The beggar's nurse and Caesar's.
Enter [to the gates of the monument] Proculeius.

PROCULEIUS
Caesar sends greeting to the Queen of Egypt,
And bids thee study on what fair demands
Thou mean'st to have him grant thee.

CLEOPATRA   What's thy name ?

PROCULEIUS
My name is Proculeius.

CLEOPATRA   Antony
Did tell me of you, bade me trust you, but
I do not greatly care to be deceived,
That have no use for trusting. If your master
Would have a queen his beggar, you must tell him
That majesty, to keep decorum, must
No less beg than a kingdom : if he please
To give me conquered Egypt for my son,
He gives me so much of mine own as I
Will kneel to him with thanks.

PROCULEIUS   Be of good cheer :
Y' are fall'n into a princely hand, fear nothing.
Make your full reference freely to my lord,
Who is so full of grace that it flows over

16 *civil* city   19 *moiety* half   21 *self* same   30 *persisted* i.e. persisted in
31 *Waged equal with* were evenly balanced in   36 *launch* lance   39 *stall*
dwell   41 *sovereign* potent   42 *competitor* partner   43 *In . . . design* in
every lofty enterprise   46 *his* its   50 *looks . . . him* shows in his eyes   63
passion grief   66 *eternal* eternally memorable   76 *writings* dispatches (to
Antony)
V, ii Before the monument of Cleopatra   2 *A better life* i.e. a truer estimate
of values   3 *knave* servant   7 *dung* i.e. the fruits of earth, which is everybody's nurse   14 *to be deceived* whether I am deceived or not   20 *as that*
23 *Make . . . reference* entrust your case

On all that need. Let me report to him
Your sweet dependency, and you shall find
27 A conqueror that will pray in aid for kindness,
Where he for grace is kneeled to.

CLEOPATRA   Pray you, tell him
I am his fortune's vassal, and I send him
30 The greatness he has got. I hourly learn
A doctrine of obedience, and would gladly
Look him i' th' face.

PROCULEIUS   This I'll report, dear lady.
Have comfort, for I know your plight is pitied
Of him that caused it.
        [Enter Roman Soldiers into the monument.]
You see how easily she may be surprised.
        [They seize Cleopatra.]
Guard her till Caesar come.

IRAS Royal Queen!

CHARMIAN O Cleopatra! thou art taken, Queen.

CLEOPATRA
Quick, quick, good hands!
        [Draws a dagger.]

PROCULEIUS   Hold, worthy lady, hold!
        [Disarms her.]
Do not yourself such wrong, who are in this
41 Relieved, but not betrayed.

CLEOPATRA   What, of death too,
42 That rids our dogs of languish?

PROCULEIUS   Cleopatra,
Do not abuse my master's bounty by
Th' undoing of yourself: let the world see
45 His nobleness well acted, which your death
Will never let come forth.

CLEOPATRA   Where art thou, death?
Come hither, come: come, come, and take a queen
Worth many babes and beggars!

PROCULEIUS   O, temperance, lady!

CLEOPATRA
Sir, I will eat no meat, I'll not drink, sir –
50 If idle talk will once be necessary –
I'll not sleep neither. This mortal house I'll ruin,
Do Caesar what he can. Know, sir, that I
Will not wait pinioned at your master's court
Nor once be chastised with the sober eye
Of dull Octavia. Shall they hoist me up
56 And show me to the shouting varletry
Of censuring Rome? Rather a ditch in Egypt
Be gentle grave unto me! Rather on Nilus' mud
Lay me stark-nak'd and let the waterflies
60 Blow me into abhorring! Rather make
My country's high pyramides my gibbet
And hang me up in chains!

27 *pray . . . kindness* ask your aid in naming kindnesses he can do for you
30 *got* i.e. won from me 41 *Relieved* rescued 42 *languish* pain 45 *acted*
put into effect 50 *If . . . necessary* even if I must for the present moment
resort to words, not acts 56 *varletry* mob 60 *Blow me* make me swell
81 *Th' . . . earth* (the generally accepted rendering of a folio reading which
may possibly mean something quite different: 'The little o' th' earth')
83–84 *was propertied As* i.e. made music like 85 *quail* cow; *orb* earth
88–90 *his . . . lived in* i.e. he rose above the pleasures that he lived in as the
dolphin rises above the surface of the sea 91 *crowns and crownets* i.e.
kings and princes 92 *plates* coins 97–100 *nature . . . quite* i.e. nature
rarely can compete with man's imagination in creating outstanding forms of
excellence, but if she created an Antony, he would be her masterpiece,
outdoing the unreal images of imagination altogether 102–03 *Would . . . do*
i.e. may I never have success if I do not

PROCULEIUS   You do extend
These thoughts of horror further than you shall
Find cause in Caesar.
        Enter Dolabella.

DOLABELLA   Proculeius,
What thou hast done thy master Caesar knows,
And he hath sent me for thee. For the Queen,
I'll take her to my guard.

PROCULEIUS   So, Dolabella,
It shall content me best: be gentle to her.
        [*To Cleopatra*]
To Caesar I will speak what you shall please,
If you'll employ me to him.

CLEOPATRA   Say, I would die. 70
        Exit Proculeius [with Soldiers].

DOLABELLA
Most noble Empress, you have heard of me?

CLEOPATRA
I cannot tell.

DOLABELLA Assuredly you know me.

CLEOPATRA
No matter, sir, what I have heard or known.
You laugh when boys or women tell their dreams;
Is't not your trick?

DOLABELLA   I understand not, madam.

CLEOPATRA
I dreamt there was an Emperor Antony.
O, such another sleep, that I might see
But such another man.

DOLABELLA   If it might please ye –

CLEOPATRA
His face was as the heav'ns, and therein stuck
A sun and moon, which kept their course and lighted
The little O, th' earth. 81

DOLABELLA   Most sovereign creature –

CLEOPATRA
His legs bestrid the ocean: his reared arm
Crested the world: his voice was propertied 83
As all the tunèd spheres, and that to friends;
But when he meant to quail and shake the orb, 85
He was as rattling thunder. For his bounty,
There was no winter in't: an autumn 'twas
That grew the more by reaping: his delights 88
Were dolphin-like, thy showed his back above
The element they lived in: in his livery
Walked crowns and crownets: realms and islands were 91
As plates dropped from his pocket. 92

DOLABELLA   Cleopatra –

CLEOPATRA
Think you there was or might be such a man
As this I dreamt of?

DOLABELLA   Gentle madam, no.

CLEOPATRA
You lie, up to the hearing of the gods.
But if there be nor ever were one such,
It's past the size of dreaming: nature wants stuff 97
To vie strange forms with fancy, yet t' imagine
An Antony were nature's piece 'gainst fancy,
Condemning shadows quite.

DOLABELLA   Hear me, good madam.
Your loss is as yourself, great; and you bear it
As answering to the weight. Would I might never 102
O'ertake pursued success but I do feel,
By the rebound of yours, a grief that smites

My very heart at root.

CLEOPATRA   I thank you, sir.
Know you what Caesar means to do with me?

DOLABELLA
I am loath to tell you what I would you knew.

CLEOPATRA
Nay, pray you, sir.

DOLABELLA   Though he be honorable –

CLEOPATRA
He'll lead me, then, in triumph?

DOLABELLA
Madam, he will. I know't.
    Flourish. Enter Proculeius, Caesar, Gallus,
    Maecenas, [Seleucus,] and others of his Train.

ALL
Make way there! Caesar!

CAESAR
Which is the Queen of Egypt?

DOLABELLA
It is the Emperor, madam.
    Cleopatra kneels.

CAESAR
Arise! You shall not kneel:
I pray you rise, rise, Egypt.

CLEOPATRA   Sir, the gods
Will have it thus. My master and my lord
I must obey.

CAESAR   Take to you no hard thoughts.
The record of what injuries you did us,
Though written in our flesh, we shall remember
As things but done by chance.

CLEOPATRA   Sole sir o' th' world,
121   I cannot project mine own cause so well
To make it clear, but do confess I have
Been laden with like frailties which before
Have often shamed our sex.

CAESAR   Cleopatra, know,
125   We will extenuate rather than enforce.
126   If you apply yourself to our intents,
Which towards you are most gentle, you shall find
A benefit in this change; but if you seek
To lay on me a cruelty by taking
Antony's course, you shall bereave yourself
Of my good purposes, and put your children
To that destruction which I'll guard them from
If thereon you rely. I'll take my leave.

CLEOPATRA
And may, through all the world: 'tis yours, and we,
135   Your scutcheons and your signs of conquest, shall
Hang in what place you please. Here, my good lord.
    [Offering a scroll.]

CAESAR
You shall advise me in all for Cleopatra.

CLEOPATRA
138   This is the brief of money, plate, and jewels
I am possessed of. 'Tis exactly valued,
Not petty things admitted. Where's Seleucus?

SELEUCUS
Here, madam.

CLEOPATRA
This is my treasurer; let him speak, my lord,
Upon his peril, that I have reserved
To myself nothing. Speak the truth, Seleucus.

SELEUCUS
Madam,
I had rather seel my lips than to my peril   146
Speak that which is not.

CLEOPATRA   What have I kept back?

SELEUCUS
Enough to purchase what you have made known.

CAESAR
Nay, blush not, Cleopatra, I approve
Your wisdom in the deed.

CLEOPATRA   See, Caesar: O, behold,
How pomp is followed! Mine will now be yours,   151
And should we shift estates, yours would be mine.   152
The ingratitude of this Seleucus does
Even make me wild. O slave, of no more trust
Than love that's hired! What, goest thou back? Thou
   shalt
Go back, I warrant thee; but I'll catch thine eyes,
Though they had wings. Slave, soulless villain, dog!
O rarely base!

CAESAR   Good Queen, let us entreat you.

CLEOPATRA
O Caesar, what a wounding shame is this,
That thou vouchsafing here to visit me,
Doing the honor of thy lordliness
To one so meek, that mine own servant should
Parcel the sum of my disgraces by   163
Addition of his envy. Say, good Caesar,
That I some lady trifles have reserved,   165
Immoment toys, things of such dignity   166
As we greet modern friends withal; and say   167
Some nobler token I have kept apart
For Livia and Octavia, to induce
Their mediation – must I be unfolded
With one that I have bred? The gods! It smites me   171
Beneath the fall I have. *[to Seleucus]* Prithee go hence,
Or I shall show the cinders of my spirits   173
Through th' ashes of my chance. Wert thou a man,   174
Thou wouldst have mercy on me.

CAESAR   Forbear, Seleucus.
    [Exit Seleucus.]

CLEOPATRA
Be it known that we, the greatest, are misthought   176
For things that others do; and, when we fall,
We answer others' merits in our name,   178
Are therefore to be pitied.

CAESAR   Cleopatra,
Not what you have reserved, nor what acknowledged,
Put we i' th' roll of conquest: still be't yours,
Bestow it at your pleasure, and believe   182
Caesar's no merchant, to make prize with you   183
Of things that merchants sold. Therefore be cheered,
Make not your thoughts your prisons: no, dear Queen,   185
For we intend so to dispose you as   186

---

121 *project* set forth   125 *enforce* emphasize (them)   126 *apply* conform
135 *scutcheons* victor's trappings   138 *brief* résumé   146 *seel* sew up   151
Mine i.e. my followers   152 *estates* positions   163 *Parcel* piece out further
165 *lady* feminine   166 *Immoment* of no moment   167 *modern* common
171 *With* by   173 *cinders* burning coals   174 *chance* fortune   176 *mis-*
thought misjudged   178 *merits . . . name* misdeeds done in our name (as if
Seleucus had falsified the inventory for his own gain)   182 *Bestow* use
183 *make prize* haggle   185 *Make . . . prisons* i.e. only in your own conception are you a prisoner   186 *you* of you

Yourself shall give us counsel. Feed and sleep :
Our care and pity is so much upon you
That we remain your friend ; and so adieu.

CLEOPATRA
My master, and my lord !

CAESAR   Not so. Adieu.
       Flourish. Exeunt Caesar, and his Train.

CLEOPATRA
191 He words me, girls, he words me, that I should not
192 Be noble to myself ! But hark thee, Charmian.
       [Whispers Charmian.]

IRAS
Finish, good lady, the bright day is done,
And we are for the dark.

CLEOPATRA   Hie thee again :
I have spoke already, and it is provided ;
Go put it to the haste.

CHARMIAN   Madam, I will.
       Enter Dolabella.

DOLABELLA
Where's the Queen ?

CHARMIAN   Behold, sir.   *[Exit.]*

CLEOPATRA   Dolabella !

DOLABELLA
Madam, as thereto sworn, by your command
(Which my love makes religion to obey)
200 I tell you this : Caesar through Syria
Intends his journey, and within three days
You with your children will he send before.
Make your best use of this. I have performed
Your pleasure, and my promise.

CLEOPATRA   Dolabella,
I shall remain your debtor.

DOLABELLA   I your servant.
Adieu, good Queen ; I must attend on Caesar.

CLEOPATRA
Farewell, and thanks.   *Exit [Dolabella].*
         Now, Iras, what think'st thou ?
Thou, an Egyptian puppet, shall be shown
In Rome as well as I : mechanic slaves
With greasy aprons, rules, and hammers shall
Uplift us to the view. In their thick breaths,
212 Rank of gross diet, shall we be enclouded,
And forced to drink their vapor.

IRAS   The gods forbid !

CLEOPATRA
214 Nay, 'tis most certain, Iras. Saucy lictors
215 Will catch at us like strumpets, and scald rhymers
Ballad us out o' tune. The quick comedians
Extemporally will stage us, and present
Our Alexandrian revels : Antony
Shall be brought drunken forth, and I shall see
220 Some squeaking Cleopatra boy my greatness
I' th' posture of a whore.

IRAS   O the good gods !

CLEOPATRA
Nay, that's certain.

IRAS
I'll never see't ! for I am sure my nails
Are stronger than mine eyes.

CLEOPATRA   Why, that's the way
To fool their preparation, and to conquer
Their most absurd intents.
     Enter Charmian.   Now, Charmian !
Show me, my women, like a queen : go fetch
My best attires. I am again for Cydnus,
To meet Mark Antony. Sirrah Iras, go.
Now, noble Charmian, we'll dispatch indeed,
And when thou hast done this chare, I'll give thee leave 231
To play till doomsday. – Bring our crown and all.
      [Exit Iras.] A noise within.
Wherefore's this noise ?
     Enter a Guardsman.

GUARDSMAN   Here is a rural fellow
That will not be denied your Highness' presence :
He brings you figs.

CLEOPATRA
Let him come in.   *Exit Guardsman.*
         What poor an instrument
May do a noble deed ! He brings me liberty.
My resolution 's placed, and I have nothing 238
Of woman in me : now from head to foot
I am marble-constant : now the fleeting moon
No planet is of mine. 241
     Enter Guardsman and Clown [with basket].

GUARDSMAN   This is the man.

CLEOPATRA
Avoid, and leave him.   *Exit Guardsman.* 242
Hast thou the pretty worm of Nilus there, 243
That kills and pains not ?

CLOWN Truly I have him ; but I would not be the party
that should desire you to touch him, for his biting is
immortal : those that do die of it do seldom or never 247
recover.

CLEOPATRA Remember'st thou any that have died on't ?

CLOWN Very many, men and women too. I heard of one
of them no longer than yesterday ; a very honest woman, 251
but something given to lie, as a woman should not do
but in the way of honesty – how she died of the biting
of it, what pain she felt. Truly, she makes a very good
report o' th' worm ; but he that will believe all that they
say shall never be saved by half that they do ; but this is
most falliable, the worm 's an odd worm. 257

CLEOPATRA Get thee hence, farewell.

CLOWN I wish you all joy of the worm.
     [Sets down his basket.]

CLEOPATRA Farewell.

CLOWN You must think this, look you, that the worm
will do his kind. 262

CLEOPATRA Ay, ay ; farewell.

CLOWN Look you, the worm is not to be trusted but in the
keeping of wise people : for indeed there is no goodness
in the worm.

CLEOPATRA Take thou no care, it shall be heeded.

CLOWN Very good. Give it nothing, I pray you, for it is
not worth the feeding.

CLEOPATRA Will it eat me ?

CLOWN You must not think I am so simple but I know the

---

191 *words* deceives with words 192 *noble* i.e. by suicide 212 *Rank of* offensive because of 214 *lictors* officers 215 *scald* scabby 220 *squeaking* i.e. because women's parts were acted by young boys ; *boy* satirize 231 *chare* chore 238 *placed* fixed 241 s.d. *Clown* rustic 242 *Avoid* go 243 *worm* serpent (asp) 247 *immortal* mortal, i.e. deadly (the rustic blunders in speech here and below) 251 *honest* respectable 257 *falliable* (an error for 'infallible') 262 *his kind* i.e. what may be expected from his species

devil himself will not eat a woman : I know that a
273   woman is a dish for the gods, if the devil dress her not.
But truly, these same whoreson devils do the gods great
harm in their women ; for in every ten that they make,
the devils mar five.

CLEOPATRA Well, get thee gone, farewell.

CLOWN Yes, forsooth. I wish you joy o' th' worm.   *Exit.*
     [*Enter Iras with a robe, crown, etc.*]

CLEOPATRA
Give me my robe, put on my crown, I have
Immortal longings in me. Now no more
The juice of Egypt's grape shall moist this lip.
282   Yare, yare, good Iras ; quick. Methinks I hear
Antony call : I see him rouse himself
To praise my noble act. I hear him mock
The luck of Caesar, which the gods give men
To excuse their after wrath. Husband, I come :
Now to that name my courage prove my title !
288   I am fire, and air ; my other elements
I give to baser life. So, have you done ?
Come then, and take the last warmth of my lips.
Farewell, kind Charmian, Iras, long farewell.
     [*Kisses them. Iras falls and dies.*]
292   Have I the aspic in my lips ? Dost fall ?
If thou and nature can so gently part,
The stroke of death is as a lover's pinch,
Which hurts, and is desired. Dost thou lie still ?
If thus thou vanishest, thou tell'st the world
It is not worth leave-taking.

CHARMIAN
Dissolve, thick cloud, and rain, that I may say
The gods themselves do weep.

CLEOPATRA   This proves me base :
If she first meet the curlèd Antony,
He'll make demand of her, and spend that kiss
Which is my heaven to have. Come, thou mortal wretch,
     [*To an asp, which she applies to her breast.*]
303   With thy sharp teeth this knot intrinsicate
Of life at once untie. Poor venomous fool,
305   Be angry, and dispatch. O, couldst thou speak,
That I might hear thee call great Caesar ass
307   Unpolicied !

CHARMIAN   O Eastern star !

CLEOPATRA   Peace, peace !
Dost thou not see my baby at my breast,
That sucks the nurse asleep ?

CHARMIAN   O, break ! O, break !

CLEOPATRA
As sweet as balm, as soft as air, as gentle –
O Antony ! Nay, I will take thee too :
     [*Applies another asp to her arm.*]
What should I stay –
     Dies.

CHARMIAN
In this wild world ? So, fare thee well.
Now boast thee, death, in thy possession lies
A lass unparalleled. Downy windows, close ;
And golden Phoebus never be beheld
Of eyes again so royal ! Your crown 's awry ;
I'll mend it, and then play –
     Enter the Guard, rustling in.

1. GUARDSMAN
Where's the Queen ?

CHARMIAN   Speak softly, wake her not.

1. GUARDSMAN
Caesar hath sent –

CHARMIAN   Too slow a messenger.
     [*Applies an asp.*]
O, come apace, dispatch, I partly feel thee.

1. GUARDSMAN
Approach, ho ! All's not well : Caesar 's beguiled.   322

2. GUARDSMAN
There's Dolabella sent from Caesar. Call him.

1. GUARDSMAN
What work is here ! Charmian, is this well done ?

CHARMIAN
It is well done, and fitting for a princess
Descended of so many royal kings.
Ah, soldier !
     Charmian dies.
     Enter Dolabella.

DOLABELLA
How goes it here ?

2. GUARDSMAN   All dead.

DOLABELLA   Caesar, thy thoughts
Touch their effects in this : thyself art coming   329
To see performed the dreaded act which thou
So sought'st to hinder.
     Enter Caesar and all his Train, marching.

ALL   A way there, a way for Caesar !

DOLABELLA
O sir, you are too sure an augurer :
That you did fear is done.

CAESAR   Bravest at the last,
She levelled at our purposes, and being royal,   334
Took her own way. The manner of their deaths ?
I do not see them bleed.

DOLABELLA   Who was last with them ?

1. GUARDSMAN
A simple countryman, that brought her figs.
This was his basket.

CAESAR   Poisoned, then.

1. GUARDSMAN   O Caesar,
This Charmian lived but now, she stood and spake ;
I found her trimming up the diadem
On her dead mistress ; tremblingly she stood,
And on the sudden dropped.

CAESAR   O noble weakness !
If they had swallowed poison, 'twould appear
By external swelling ; but she looks like sleep,
As she would catch another Antony
In her strong toil of grace.   346

DOLABELLA   Here on her breast
There is a vent of blood, and something blown ;   347
The like is on her arm.

1. GUARDSMAN
This is an aspic's trail, and these fig leaves
Have slime upon them, such as th' aspic leaves
Upon the caves of Nile.

273 *dress* (with pun on the culinary sense)   282 *Yare* nimbly   288 *fire, and air* (the lighter of the four elements, thought of as belonging to immortality) ; *other elements* i.e. water and earth, the heavier elements, bequeathed by Cleopatra to mortality   292 *aspic* asp   303 *intrinsicate* intricate   305 *dispatch* make haste   307 *Unpolicied* outwitted   322 *beguiled* tricked   329 *Touch their effects* meet fulfillment   334 *levelled at* guessed   346 *toil* net   347 *vent* discharge ; *blown* swelled

CAESAR   Most probable
          That so she died : for her physician tells me
353   She hath pursued conclusions infinite
          Of easy ways to die. Take up her bed,
          And bear her women from the monument.
          She shall be buried by her Antony.

353 *conclusions* experiments   357 *clip* clasp   359 *Strike* touch

No grave upon the earth shall clip in it   357
A pair so famous. High events as these
Strike those that make them ; and their story is   359
No less in pity than his glory which
Brought them to be lamented. Our army shall
In solemn show attend this funeral,
And then to Rome. Come, Dolabella, see
High order in this great solemnity.   *Exeunt omnes.*

CORIOLANUS

INTRODUCTION

This play, which must have seen its first performance in 1608 or thereabouts, may be the last of Shakespeare's tragedies as we define them to-day. Criticism has tended to range it beside his greatest for its power, its amplitude, and its craftsmanship. But it has never been so popular as the others; and that is by no means surprising, since it so expressly calls into question the equivocal values of popularity. On an elementary human basis, Shakespeare's appeal has always been exerted through his characters, and through the bonds of sympathy that ally them with the spectator or the reader. From the outset of *Coriolanus*, however, such an identification is harshly repelled; and modern ideology, which disposes us to sympathize less readily with the hero than with the viewpoint of his antagonists, has slanted and colored our understanding of both. Yet recent history, by grimly reviving the very issues that Shakespeare dramatized, has greatly increased the importance and the impressiveness of his dramatization. *Coriolanus* has been found, on revival, to be more fraught with significance for our time than any other drama in the Shakespearean repertory. Max Reinhardt's production in Germany was turbulently prophetic. French crowds rioted when, in the years between the wars, it was performed at the Comédie Française.

Shakespeare's audiences, on occasion, could be quite as explosive. His England must often have seemed to be rifted internally, as well as externally menaced. Even while he was writing *Coriolanus*, outcries over the scarcity of grain were daily reaching London from the Midlands. A Stuart monarch, recently enthroned, claimed more and wielded less authority than his Tudor predecessors had done. Strong-willed men could make spectacular bids for power; Sir Walter Ralegh was being held in the Tower on charges of conspiracy; the Earl of Essex had incited Londoners to fight in the streets a few years before; and for that insurrection *Richard II* had been utilized as propaganda. Such, of course, had not been Shakespeare's purpose. His mounting sequence of histories had made England's coming-of-age coincide with his own, and had subsumed – along with the English past – the most triumphant decade of the first Elizabeth's reign. Therefore his chronicle plays had been somewhat controlled by considerations of patriotism, royal prerogative, and the relative familiarity of the facts. Seeking a freer field of political observation, pushing toward profounder formulations of statecraft, shifting his concern from the ruler's duties and rights to those of the citizen, Shakespeare was inevitably led to a point where more distant roads converge: the archetype of city-states, the keystone of western traditions, Rome.

At the beginning of his tragic period – the opening years of the seventeenth century – he essayed this republican theme in *Julius Caesar*. He resumed it with an even grander sequel, *Antony and Cleopatra*, but not until after completing his exhaustive explorations of personality in *Hamlet*, *Othello*, *Macbeth*, and *King Lear*. Thus *Coriolanus* rounds out a trilogy, though it stands somewhat apart from the other two Roman plays, possibly nearer to *Antony and Cleopatra* in scope and to *Julius Caesar* in subject. All three, taken together, constitute a great debate on ethics, in which the statement of private interests is balanced against the counter-statement of public responsibilities. *Julius Caesar* lays the dialectical groundwork by showing a group of individuals in conflict over the state. *Antony and Cleopatra* shows its individualistic hero and heroine rejecting their obligations to their respective states and behaving as if they were laws unto themselves. *Coriolanus* explores the extreme situation of the individual who pits himself against the state. Here Julius Caesar might have proved a monumental counterpart; but Shakespeare's portrait was brief and enigmatic, registering the impact of Caesarism on others, notably on the conscience of Marcus Brutus; and Brutus, acting in the "common good to all," presented the obverse of the Roman coin whereon Coriolanus is stamped incisively.

The historical Caius Marcius Coriolanus, figuring in the earliest annals of the Republic, had won his victory at Corioli in 493 B.C. He may indeed have been a half-legendary embodiment of patrician resistance to the increasing demands of the plebeians and especially their newly appointed spokesmen, the tribunes. Hence, instead of being elected to the consulate, he was banished, and went over to the enemy as the hero does in the play. In the end, as the historian Mommsen sums it up, "he expiated his first treason by a second, and both by death." Poetic justice was better served than either side. Shakespeare drew his version of these episodes from Plutarch's *Lives*, the source that inspired him most, that treasury of ancient biography which comprises a series of comparative studies in heroic citizenship. Plutarch, the Greek moralist, saw Coriolanus as an outstanding example of the peculiarly Roman conception of virtue: *virtus*, which is translated "valiantness." The vice that attended and finally defeated this salient quality was "willfulness." Plutarch's contrasting parallel is the career of Alcibiades, whose ingratiating suppleness – like Antony's – throws the intransigent arrogance of Coriolanus into bold relief. That the latter was brought up by his widowed mother, and was chiefly animated by the desire to please her, Plutarch is at pains to emphasize.

Shakespeare follows Plutarch so very closely that he often echoes the phraseology of the magnificent Elizabethan translation by Sir Thomas North. Volumnia's plea to her son in Act V, eloquently massive as it is, is scarcely more than a metrical adaptation of North's prose. On the other hand, her appeal to him in Act III is Shakespeare's interpolation; he has reserved his right to modify and augment his material in the interests of psychological motivation and dramatic equilibrium; and those two interventions of Volumnia, in each case changing the mind of Coriolanus, are the turning-points of the plot. Rhetoric, the art of persuasion, determined not only the style but also the structure of *Julius Caesar*: Cassius persuades Brutus, Brutus persuades the people, Mark Antony persuades them otherwise. *Coriolanus* is not less Roman in its recourse to public speech; and speech-making triumphs ironically over war-mongering; but now the forensic mode is that of dissuasion. The candidate actually dissuades the people from voting for him; the general at length is dissuaded from pursuing his revenge. His vein is negation: curses, threats, and invectives from first to last. Once he rallies his men; many times he scolds them. When he girds the gods, his rant sounds more like the misanthropic Timon than the iconoclastic Tamburlaine. Yet how narrowly it misses the tone of Hotspur!

Coriolanus to the contrary, the word is not "mildly." The language of the play reverberates with the dissonance of its subject-matter and the thunder-like percussion of its protagonist. The words are so tensely involved in the situation that they do not lend themselves much to purple passages or quotations out of context. Reflecting a stylistic transition, they seem to combine the serried diction of Shakespeare's middle period with the flowing rhythm of his later plays. The speeches frequently begin and break off in the middle of a line; but the cadence of the blank verse persists through occasional setbacks; and sometimes the overlapping pentameters are more evident to the ear than on the page. This has been a problem for editors, many of whom have regarded the difficulties of the text as invitations to change it. The present edition assumes that the unique redaction of *Coriolanus*, which has come down to us through the folios, is more or less authoritative; and that, except for some obvious readjustments and a few unavoidable emendations, it simply needs to be modernized in spelling and punctuation. The original stage directions, which are unusually explicit, convey a suggestion of pageantry commanding the full resources of the resplendent Globe. And from a contemporary sketch of *Titus Andronicus*, we know that the Elizabethans could approximate Roman dress.

Though the scenes march by in swift continuity, moving from camp to camp and faction to faction, the acts are sharply divided, as if to stress the division among the characters. Act I presents the hero in his proper field of action, the battlefield, where heroism can be demonstrated in its simplest terms as valiantness. Act II brings him reluctantly home to his triumph, and even more grudgingly into the electoral campaign. This goes against him in Act III and leads, after another disastrous attempt at propitiation, to the decree of banishment. Act IV pursues the exiled Coriolanus traversing the distance between Rome and Antium, and betraying himself and his fellow Romans to the Volscian general, Aufidius. Act V witnesses his capitulation and consummates his tragedy: military commitment, resisting civic pressure, yields to domestic. Throughout these vicissitudes he sustains his predomi-

nating role, the central figure when he is on stage, the topic of discussion when he is not. His monolithic character is measured by no single foil of comparable stature – least of all by his rival, Aufidius, who has failed to square accounts with him honorably, and vowed to do so through dishonorable means if necessary – but by his dynamic relations with all the others, on the diverging levels of family, city, and enemy.

The one is accordingly weighed against the many; and the tendency toward monodrama is counterpoised by an unusual number of choric roles – citizens, officers, soldiers, servants, other ranks of society. The scales tip during the roadside interview between a Roman and a Volscian, with its implication that Coriolanus is taking the same road to espionage and betrayal. As for the populace, the tribunes can hardly speak for it because it is so vocal on its own behalf; the mistake of Coriolanus is to believe that its "voices" are merely votes. Generalization soon breaks down into Hob and Dick, and the types are individualized, loudly insisting upon their individuality. There are some ugly mob-scenes and one violent outbreak of street-fighting, but mother-wit is the characteristic weapon. The humorous mediator, Menenius Agrippa, can handle this pithy prose idiom. The crowd in turn can rise to the pitch of blank verse, while their shrewd heckling enlivens his tale of the belly and the members. The First Citizen, "great toe" though he may be, accepts the question-begging metaphor that identifies the organ of digestion with the deliberation of the Senate. But, logically enough, he presses the claims of the other parts, including the soldierly arm. The parable will apply to the choleric hero as much as to the angry mob.

In a subsequent argument, when Coriolanus is compared to a disease, Menenius retorts that he is rather a diseased limb which can be cured. By this time many sores and wounds have been metaphorically and literally probed, thereby revealing other aspects of the body politic. The age-old fable expounded by Menenius, appeasing the uproar of the introductory scene, has served to establish an ideal of social order – the concept of commonweal, *res publica* – more honored in the breach than the observance. It has also concretely grounded the imagery of the play in the matter at hand, the dearth of corn, the fundamental problem of nourishment. The struggling classes seek to feed on each other; Menenius is a self-confessed epicure; the poor justify themselves by hungry proverbs; and Coriolanus finds himself in their desperate position when he appears at the feast of Aufidius. In close association with these images of food, battle is described as if it were harvest, with the swords of destruction figuratively turning into the ploughshares of fertility. Another associated train of thought runs to animals, always an inspiration for name-calling. The hero is introduced as a dog to the people, who are curs to him then and crucially later. The prevailing code is dog-eat-dog.

Menenius points the moral succinctly when he demands: "On both sides more respect." Since both sides indulge in such embittered polemics, interpretation has varied between the extremes of left and right, now underlining the dangers of dictatorship and now the weaknesses of democracy, according to the political adherence of the interpreters. Nothing could better attest what Coleridge, in this connection, called "the wonderful philosophic impartiality in Shakespeare's politics." His portrayal of the multitude, whose sedition he arms with a grievance, is anti-demagogic rather than anti-democratic. The demagogues are the tribunes, portrayed in unequivocal cynicism, dissuading the plebs from the suffrage they have already pledged to Coriolanus. Coriolanus, on his side, is no friend of the people; and it is to the credit of his integrity that he cannot act a part he does not feel. He earns, with an authoritarian vengeance, the title that Ibsen would bestow in irony upon his humanitarian Dr Stockmann – *An Enemy of the People*. All men are enemies, rivals if not foes, to Coriolanus. His aggressive temperament could never be happy until it had lurched all other swords of the garland. His fight against the world is not for booty nor praise nor office, but for acknowledged superiority; he does not want to dominate but to excel; and he cannot bear the thought of subordination.

We need not look far afield for the school that nurtured that spirit of single-minded competitiveness. The Roman matron, the masculine dowager, the statuesque Volumnia, is both father and mother to her son; and she has taught him aristocratic scorn along with martial courage. His wife, the gracious Virgilia, in contrast is sheer femininity; and her main attribute, like Cordelia's, is silence. His young son chases butterflies with congenital resolution; subsequently Coriolanus commands a Volscian army as eager as boys chasing butterflies. No man can withstand him and only one woman can plead with him. In yielding to her, in feeling this ultimate modicum of feminine tenderness, the strong man becomes again – as it were – a child. Thence the sting in the last taunt of Aufidius. Under the epithet "traitor" Coriolanus has slightly flinched. But "boy!" "Thou boy of tears!" In significant contradistinction, we are reminded continually that the tribunes are elderly men. Leadership, as Volumnia's boy had learned it in the wars, was largely an individual matter of athletic prowess, having little to do with the sort of maturity that peaceful civilian government requires. Perhaps the trouble, as analyzed by Aufidius, lay in a soldier's inability to move "from th' casque to th' cushion." The virtues of war may well be the vices of peace; the man on horseback, dismounted, a sorry creature.

T. S. Eliot's modernized *Coriolan* consists of two poems: "Triumphal March" and "Difficulties of a Statesman." These headings suggest the dilemma of Shakespeare's protagonist. His is not an internal struggle; so far as his two short soliloquies indicate, the treason causes him less mental anguish than the election; and, what is even worse, at Antium he employs the flatteries he has despised at Rome. Rather it is the external manifestation of his colossal pride that exalts him, all but deifies him, and renders the slippery turns of fortune more precipitous than the Tarpeian Rock. "Rome or I! One or the other must fall!" Such is the climax, verbalized by Wagner, to Beethoven's orchestration of this theme. "The note of banishment," the note that James Joyce kept hearing in Shakespeare's plays, is never more plangently sounded than in the parting denunciation of Coriolanus to the Romans: "I banish you!" Never was man more alienated than he, as the gates of Rome close behind him and he is forced to seek "a world elsewhere." The scene reverses his initial triumph, when the gates of Corioli shut him in alone of all the Romans. The ironic pattern is completed, on his return to the hostile town, by his fatal words to its citizens. And note the emphatic position of the first personal pronoun:

> If you have writ your annals true, 'tis there
> That, like an eagle in a dovecote, I
> Fluttered your Volscians in Corioles.
> Alone I did it.

Othello, at a similar moment, had the satisfaction of recalling his services to the state. Caius Marcius – Coriolanus no longer – can only glory in his isolation. The word "alone" is repeated more than in any other Shakespearean work; and, from the welter of similes, the most memorable is "a lonely dragon." We end by realizing the ambiguity of the foreign name this Roman has proudly flaunted. How can he expect it to be anything but a target of hatred for the orphans and widows and comrades-in-arms of men he has killed? After the combat in which he gained it, he had generously tried to befriend a certain Volscian, and had characteristically forgotten the poor man's name – a touch which Shakespeare added to Plutarch's anecdote. Shakespeare's insight, detailed as it is, confirms an observation cited from Plato by Plutarch: that such overriding egoism can only terminate in "desolation." This must be that desolation of solitude which the American imagination has paralleled in the career of another tragic captain, Melville's Ahab.

Harvard University   HARRY LEVIN

NOTE ON THE TEXT

Coriolanus was first published in the folio of 1623, evidently from the author's own manuscript. The present edition follows the folio text, with emendation confined as a rule to the most generally recognized instances of misprinting and mislineation. The folio text is divided into acts but not into scenes. The division provided marginally for reference in the present edition represents the folio acts as divided into scenes by later editors. This play is exceptional in the large number of speakers given only generic names in the speech-prefixes. These have been spelled out *First Citizen* etc. instead of *1. Citizen* etc. as in the other plays of the present edition. All material departures from the folio text are listed below, with the adopted reading in italics followed by the folio reading in roman.

I, i, 60 *First Citizen* 2 Cit. (and so through rest of scene) 62 *you*. *For* you for 105 *tauntingly* taintingly 110 *crownèd* crown'd 179 *vile* vilde 209 *Shouting* Shooting 221 s.d. *Junius* Annius 234 *Lartius* Lucius 239, 243 *First Senator* Sen.

I, ii, 4 *on* one

I, iii, 34 *that's* that 81 *Ithaca* Athica 108 s.d. *Exeunt* Exeunt Ladies

I, iv, 42 *Follow me* followes 45 s.d. *gates* Gati 57 *Cato's* Calues

I, v, 3 s.d. *Alarum* exeunt. Alarum *Titus Lartius* Titus

I, vi, 24 s.d. *Enter Marcius* (at l. 21 in F) 32 *burned* burnt 53 *Antiates* Antients 70 *Lesser* Lessen 81 *select* select from all

I, vii, 7 s.d. *Exeunt* Exit

I, ix, s.d. *Flourish* (not in F) 46 *coverture* Ouerture 49 *shout* shoot 66 *All* Omnes *Caius Marcius* Marcus Caius 67, 78, 81, 89 *Coriolanus* Martius

I, x, 2, 16, 29, 33 *First Soldier* Sould 22 *Embargements* Embarquements

II, i, 16 *with all* withall 52 *cannot* can 57 *you you* you 59 *bisson* beesome 155 *Coriolanus* Martius Caius Coriolanus 179 *relish* Rallish 193 s.d. *Brutus . . . forward* Enter Brutus and Sicinius 244 *touch* teach 249 *to th'* to the

II, ii, 44 *Caius Marcius* Martius Caius 65, 121, 128 *First Senator* Senat 79 *one on's* on ones 89 *chin* Shinne 90 *bristled* brizled 106 *took. From face to foot* tooke from face to foote: 136 *suffrage* sufferage 152 *Senators* Senat s.d. *Manent* Manet

II, iii, 26 *wedged* wadg'd 35 *it. I say, if* it, I say. If 39 *all together* altogether 59 s.d. *Enter . . . Citizens* (at l. 58 in F) 65 *not* but 84, 87, 101 *Fourth Citizen* 1. 100 *Fifth Citizen* 2. 109 *hire* higher 110 *toge* tongue 113 *do't,* doo't? 116 *t' o'erpeer* to or'epeere 121, 125 *voices!* voyces? 221 *th'* the 238 *And Censorinus nobly* And nobly *namèd* nam'd 239 *being by the people chosen* being chosen

III, i, s.d. *Lartius* Latius 10 *vilely* vildly 63, 75 *First Senator* Senat. 91 *O good* O God! 143 *Where one* Whereon 172 s.d. *Enter an Aedile* (at l. 171 in F) 185 *All* (at l. 187 in F) 198, 233, 335 *First Senator* Sena. 231 *Coriolanus* Com. 237 *Cominius* Corio. 238 *Coriolanus* Mene. 287 *our* one 305 *Sicinius* Menen. 323 *bring him* bring him in peace

III, ii, 13 s.d. *Enter Volumnia* (at l. 6 in F) 25 *taxings* things 26 *First Senator* Sen. 32 *th' herd* th' heart 101 *bear? Well, I* beare Well? I 115 *lulls* lull

III, iii, 32 *for th'* fourth 36 *Throng* Through 55 *accents* Actions 99 *i' th' name* In the Name 110 *for* from 136 s.d. *Menenius Cumalijs* 138 *Hoo! hoo!* Hoo, oo.

IV, i, 34 *wilt* will

IV, ii, 9 s.d. *Enter . . . Menenius* (at l. 7 in F) 36 *let us* let's 44 s.d. *Exeunt* Exit 53 *Exeunt* (at end of preceding speech in F, with *Exit* here)

IV, iii, 31 *will* well

IV, iv, 23 *hate* haue

IV, v, 108 *thy* that 151 *strucken* strocken 164 *on* one 178 *lief* liue 203 *sowl* sole 225 *sprightly, waking* spightly walking 227 *sleepy* sleepe 229 *war* warres

IV, vi, 10 s.d. *Enter Menenius* (at l. 9 in F) 25 *Citizens* All

IV, vii, 15 *Had* haue 37 *'twas* 'was 49 *virtues* Vertue 55 *founder* fouler

V, i, 41 *toward* towards

V, ii, s.d. *on* or 16 *haply* happely 56 s.d. *and with* 58 *errand* arrant 61 *by my* my 72 *our* your 83 *pity note* pitty : Note 90 s.d. *Manent* Manet

V, iii, 48 *prate* pray 56 *What is* What's 63 *holp* hope 79 *you'd* youl'd 149 *fine* fiue 154 *noble man* Nobleman 163 *clucked* clock'd 169 *him* him with him 179 *this* his

V, v, 4 *Unshout* Unshoot

V, vi, 48 s.d. *sound* sounds 72 *That* Then, 99 *other* others 114 *Fluttered* Flatter'd 115 *it. Boy?* it, Boy. 129 s.d. *Draw* Draw both *kill* kils 153 s.d. *Coriolanus* Martius

CORIOLANUS

Caius Marcius, afterwards Caius Marcius Coriolanus
Titus Lartius ⎫
Cominius ⎬ Generals against the Volscians
Menenius Agrippa, friend to Coriolanus
Sicinius Velutus ⎫
Junius Brutus ⎬ Tribunes of the People
Young Marcius, son to Coriolanus
Nicanor, a Roman
Senators ⎫
Officers ⎪
Aediles ⎬ of Rome
Heralds ⎪
Messengers ⎪
Soldiers ⎭

Citizens of Rome
Tullus Aufidius, General of the Volscians
Adrian, a Volscian
Lieutenant to Aufidius
Conspirators with Aufidius
Servants to Aufidius
Senators ⎫
Lords ⎬ of Corioli
Soldiers ⎭
A Citizen of Antium
Volumnia, mother to Coriolanus
Virgilia, wife to Coriolanus
Valeria, friend to Virgilia
Gentlewoman, attending on Virgilia

Scene : *Rome and the neighborhood ; the Volscian towns of Corioli and Antium*]

*

I, i *Enter a company of mutinous Citizens, with staves, clubs, and other weapons.*

FIRST CITIZEN Before we proceed any further, hear me speak.

ALL Speak, speak.

FIRST CITIZEN You are all resolved rather to die than to famish?

ALL Resolved, resolved.

FIRST CITIZEN First, you know Caius Marcius is chief enemy to the people.

ALL We know't, we know't.

FIRST CITIZEN Let us kill him, and we'll have corn at
10 our own price. Is't a verdict?

11 ALL No more talking on't! Let it be done! Away, away!

SECOND CITIZEN One word, good citizens.

FIRST CITIZEN We are accounted poor citizens, the
14 patricians good. What authority surfeits on would re-
15 lieve us. If they would yield us but the superfluity while it were wholesome, we might guess they relieved us
17 humanely; but they think we are too dear. The leanness
18 that afflicts us, the object of our misery, is as an in-
19 ventory to particularize their abundance; our sufferance
20 is a gain to them. Let us revenge this with our pikes ere
21 we become rakes; for the gods know I speak this in hunger for bread, not in thirst for revenge.

SECOND CITIZEN Would you proceed especially against Caius Marcius?

FIRST CITIZEN Against him first. He's a very dog to the
26 commonalty.

SECOND CITIZEN Consider you what services he has done for his country?

FIRST CITIZEN Very well, and could be content to give him good report for't, but that he pays himself with being proud.

SECOND CITIZEN Nay, but speak not maliciously.

FIRST CITIZEN I say unto you, what he hath done famously, he did it to that end. Though soft-conscienced 34 men can be content to say it was for his country, he did it to please his mother and to be partly proud, which he is, even to the altitude of his virtue. 37

SECOND CITIZEN What he cannot help in his nature, you account a vice in him. You must in no way say he is covetous.

FIRST CITIZEN If I must not, I need not be barren of accusations. He hath faults, with surplus, to tire in repetition.

Shouts within.

What shouts are these? The other side o' th' city is risen. Why stay we prating here? To th' Capitol! 44

ALL Come, come!

FIRST CITIZEN Soft! who comes here? 46

Enter Menenius Agrippa.

SECOND CITIZEN Worthy Menenius Agrippa, one that hath always loved the people.

FIRST CITIZEN He's one honest enough. Would all the rest were so!

I, i A street in Rome 10 *verdict* agreement 11 *on't* about it 14 *patricians* aristocrats; *good* substantial; *authority* the ruling class 15 *superfluity* surplus 17 *dear* expensive 18 *object* spectacle 19 *sufferance* suffering 20 *pikes* pitchforks 21 *rakes* lean as rakes 26 *commonalty* common people 34 *to that end* i.e. to achieve fame 37 *altitude of his virtue* height of his valor 44 *Capitol* Temple of Jupiter, Capitoline Hill 46 *Soft* stay

MENENIUS
What work 's, my countrymen, in hand? Where go you
With bats and clubs? The matter? Speak, I pray you.

FIRST CITIZEN Our business is not unknown to th'
Senate. They have had inkling this fortnight what we
intend to do, which now we'll show 'em in deeds. They
56 say poor suitors have strong breaths; they shall know
we have strong arms too.

MENENIUS
Why, masters, my good friends, mine honest neighbors,
Will you undo yourselves?

FIRST CITIZEN We cannot, sir, we are undone already.

MENENIUS
I tell you, friends, most charitable care
62 Have the patricians of you. For your wants,
63 Your suffering in this dearth, you may as well
Strike at the heaven with your staves as lift them
65 Against the Roman state, whose course will on
The way it takes, cracking ten thousand curbs
Of more strong link asunder than can ever
68 Appear in your impediment. For the dearth,
The gods, not the patricians, make it, and
Your knees to them, not arms, must help. Alack,
71 You are transported by calamity
Thither where more attends you, and you slander
73 The helms o' th' state, who care for you like fathers,
When you curse them as enemies.

FIRST CITIZEN Care for us? True, indeed! They ne'er
cared for us yet: suffer us to famish, and their store-
houses crammed with grain; make edicts for usury, to
support usurers; repeal daily any wholesome act estab-
79 lished against the rich, and provide more piercing
statutes daily to chain up and restrain the poor. If the
wars eat us not up, they will; and there's all the love
they bear us.

MENENIUS
Either you must
83 Confess yourselves wondrous malicious,
Or be accused of folly. I shall tell you
A pretty tale. It may be you have heard it;
But, since it serves my purpose, I will venture
87 To stale 't a little more.

FIRST CITIZEN Well, I'll hear it, sir; yet you must not
89 think to fob off our disgrace with a tale. But, an't please
you, deliver.

MENENIUS
There was a time when all the body's members
Rebelled against the belly, thus accused it:
That only like a gulf it did remain
I' th' midst o' th' body, idle and unactive,
95 Still cupboarding the viand, never bearing
96 Like labor with the rest, where th' other instruments
Did see and hear, devise, instruct, walk, feel,

And mutually participate, did minister   98
Unto the appetite and affection common
Of the whole body. The belly answered –   99

FIRST CITIZEN Well, sir, what answer made the belly?

MENENIUS
Sir, I shall tell you. With a kind of smile,
Which ne'er came from the lungs, but even thus –   103
For, look you, I may make the belly smile
As well as speak – it tauntingly replied
To th' discontented members, the mutinous parts
That envied his receipt; even so most fitly   107
As you malign our senators, for that   108
They are not such as you.

FIRST CITIZEN   Your belly's answer? What?
The kingly crownèd head, the vigilant eye,
The counsellor heart, the arm our soldier,
Our steed the leg, the tongue our trumpeter,
With other muniments and petty helps   113
In this our fabric, if that they –

MENENIUS   What then?
'Fore me, this fellow speaks! What then? what then?   115

FIRST CITIZEN
Should by the cormorant belly be restrained,
Who is the sink o' th' body –

MENENIUS   Well, what then?

FIRST CITIZEN
The former agents, if they did complain,
What could the belly answer?

MENENIUS   I will tell you;
If you'll bestow a small – of what you have little –
Patience awhile, you'st hear the belly's answer.   121

FIRST CITIZEN
Y' are long about it.   122

MENENIUS   Note me this, good friend;
Your most grave belly was deliberate,   123
Not rash like his accusers, and thus answered:
'True is it, my incorporate friends,' quoth he,
'That I receive the general food at first,
Which you do live upon; and fit it is,
Because I am the storehouse and the shop   128
Of the whole body. But, if you do remember,
I send it through the rivers of your blood
Even to the court, the heart, to th' seat o' th' brain;
And, through the cranks and offices of man,   132
The strongest nerves and small inferior veins
From me receive that natural competency   134
Whereby they live. And though that all at once' –
You, my good friends! This says the belly. Mark me.

FIRST CITIZEN
Ay, sir, well, well.

MENENIUS   'Though all at once cannot
See what I do deliver out to each,
Yet I can make my audit up, that all
From me do back receive the flour of all,
And leave me but the bran.' What say you to 't?

FIRST CITIZEN
It was an answer. How apply you this?

MENENIUS
The senators of Rome are this good belly,
And you the mutinous members. For examine
Their counsels and their cares, disgest things rightly   145
Touching the weal o' th' common, you shall find   146
No public benefit which you receive
But it proceeds or comes from them to you,

56 *suitors* petitioners **62** *For* as for **63** *dearth* famine **65** *on* go on
68 *your impediment* the obstruction you raise **71** *transported* carried
away **73** *helms* pilots **79** *piercing* far-reaching **83** *wondrous* extraordinarily **87** *stale 't* make it stale **89** *fob off* elude; *disgrace* hardship;
an't if it **95** *Still* always **96** *Like* similar; *instruments* organs **98** *participate* taking part **99** *affection* inclination **103** *lungs* i.e. organ of laughter
107 *his receipt* what he received **108** *for that* because **113** *muniments*
furnishings **115** *'Fore me* upon my soul **121** *you'st* you'll (provincial)
122 *Y' are* you're **123** *Your* this **128** *shop* workshop **132** *cranks*
windings; *offices* servants' quarters **134** *competency* sufficiency **145**
disgest digest **146** *weal o' th' common* public welfare

And no way from yourselves. What do you think,
You, the great toe of this assembly?

FIRST CITIZEN
I the great toe! Why the great toe?

MENENIUS
For that, being one o' th' lowest, basest, poorest
Of this most wise rebellion, thou goest foremost.
154 Thou rascal, that art worst in blood to run,
155 Lead'st first to win some vantage.
But make you ready your stiff bats and clubs.
Rome and her rats are at the point of battle;
158 The one side must have bale.
    Enter Caius Marcius.   Hail, noble Marcius!

MARCIUS
159 Thanks. What's the matter, you dissentious rogues,
That, rubbing the poor itch of your opinion,
Make yourselves scabs?

FIRST CITIZEN   We have ever your good word.

MARCIUS
He that will give good words to thee will flatter
Beneath abhorring. What would you have, you curs,
164 That like nor peace nor war? The one affrights you,
165 The other makes you proud. He that trusts to you,
Where he should find you lions, finds you hares;
Where foxes, geese. You are no surer, no,
Than is the coal of fire upon the ice,
Or hailstone in the sun. Your virtue is
170 To make him worthy whose offense subdues him
171 And curse that justice did it. Who deserves greatness
Deserves your hate; and your affections are
A sick man's appetite, who desires most that
Which would increase his evil. He that depends
Upon your favors swims with fins of lead
And hews down oaks with rushes. Hang ye! Trust ye?
With every minute you do change a mind,
And call him noble that was now your hate,
Him vile that was your garland. What's the matter,
That in these several places of the city
You cry against the noble Senate, who,
Under the gods, keep you in awe, which else
183 Would feed on one another? What's their seeking?

MENENIUS
For corn at their own rates, whereof they say
The city is well stored.

MARCIUS   Hang 'em! They say?
They'll sit by th' fire and presume to know
What's done i' th' Capitol, who's like to rise,
188 Who thrives and who declines; side factions and give
    out
Conjectural marriages, making parties strong
190 And feebling such as stand not in their liking
191 Below their cobbled shoes. They say there's grain
    enough?
192 Would the nobility lay aside their ruth,
193 And let me use my sword, I'd make a quarry
194 With thousands of these quartered slaves as high
195 As I could pick my lance.

MENENIUS
Nay, these are almost thoroughly persuaded;
For though abundantly they lack discretion,
198 Yet are they passing cowardly. But, I beseech you,
What says the other troop?

MARCIUS   They are dissolved. Hang 'em!
200 They said they were anhungry, sighed forth proverbs –

That hunger broke stone walls, that dogs must eat,
That meat was made for mouths, that the gods sent not
Corn for the rich men only. With these shreds
They vented their complainings, which being answered
And a petition granted them, a strange one,
To break the heart of generosity,   206
And make bold power look pale, they threw their caps
As they would hang them on the horns o' th' moon,
Shouting their emulation.   209

MENENIUS   What is granted them?

MARCIUS
Five tribunes to defend their vulgar wisdoms,   210
Of their own choice. One's Junius Brutus,
Sicinius Velutus, and I know not – 'Sdeath!   212
The rabble should have first unroofed the city
Ere so prevailed with me; it will in time
Win upon power, and throw forth greater themes   215
For insurrection's arguing.   216

MENENIUS   This is strange.

MARCIUS
Go, get you home, you fragments!
    Enter a Messenger hastily.

MESSENGER
Where's Caius Marcius?

MARCIUS   Here. What's the matter?

MESSENGER
The news is, sir, the Volsces are in arms.

MARCIUS
I am glad on't. Then we shall ha' means to vent   220
Our musty superfluity. See, our best elders.
    Enter Sicinius Velutus, Junius Brutus, Cominius,
    Titus Lartius, with other Senators.

FIRST SENATOR
Marcius, 'tis true that you have lately told us:
The Volsces are in arms.

MARCIUS   They have a leader,
Tullus Aufidius, that will put you to't.   224
I sin in envying his nobility;
And were I any thing but what I am,
I would wish me only he.

COMINIUS   You have fought together?   227

MARCIUS
Were half to half the world by th' ears and he
Upon my party, I'd revolt, to make   229
Only my wars with him. He is a lion
That I am proud to hunt.

FIRST SENATOR   Then, worthy Marcius,
Attend upon Cominius to these wars.

COMINIUS
It is your former promise.

MARCIUS   Sir, it is,
And I am constant. Titus Lartius, thou
Shalt see me once more strike at Tullus' face.

---

154 *rascal* worthless deer; *blood* condition 155 *vantage* advantage 158 *bale* destruction 159 *dissentious* seditious 164 *nor . . . nor* neither . . . nor; *The one* i.e. war 165 *The other* i.e. peace 170 *make him worthy* glorify that man; *subdues* degrades 171 *that justice* that justice which 183 *seeking* petition 188 *side* take sides with 190 *feebling* making weak 191 *cobbled* mended 192 *ruth* pity 193 *quarry* heap of slaughtered 194 *quartered* cut in four like criminals 195 *pick* pitch 198 *passing* extremely 200 *anhungry* hungry 206 *generosity* aristocracy 209 *emulation* envy 210 *tribunes* official protectors of the people's interests 212 *'Sdeath* (modified oath) 215 *Win upon power* gain authority 216 *For insurrection's arguing* for revolution to fight over 220 *vent* get rid of 224 *to't* to the test 227 *together* one another 229 *party* side

236   What, art thou stiff? Stand'st out?

TITUS   No, Caius Marcius,
I'll lean upon one crutch and fight with t' other,
Ere stay behind this business.

MENENIUS   O, true-bred!

FIRST SENATOR
Your company to th' Capitol, where I know
240   Our greatest friends attend us.

TITUS [to Cominius]   Lead you on.
            [To Marcius]
Follow Cominius. We must follow you.
242   Right worthy you priority.

COMINIUS   Noble Marcius!

FIRST SENATOR [to the Citizens]
Hence to your homes, be gone!

MARCIUS   Nay, let them follow.
The Volsces have much corn. Take these rats thither
To gnaw their garners. Worshipful mutineers,
246   Your valor puts well forth. Pray follow.
                  Exeunt. Citizens steal away.
                  Manent Sicinius and Brutus.

SICINIUS
Was ever man so proud as is this Marcius?

BRUTUS
He has no equal.

SICINIUS
When we were chosen tribunes for the people –

BRUTUS
Marked you his lip and eyes?

SICINIUS   Nay, but his taunts.

BRUTUS
251   Being moved, he will not spare to gird the gods.

SICINIUS
Bemock the modest moon.

BRUTUS
The present wars devour him. He is grown
Too proud to be so valiant.

SICINIUS   Such a nature,
Tickled with good success, disdains the shadow
Which he treads on at noon. But I do wonder
His insolence can brook to be commanded
Under Cominius.

BRUTUS   Fame, at the which he aims,
259   In whom already he's well graced, cannot
Better be held nor more attained than by
A place below the first; for what miscarries
Shall be the general's fault, though he perform
To th' utmost of a man, and giddy censure
Will then cry out of Marcius, 'O, if he
Had borne the business!'

SICINIUS   Besides, if things go well,
266   Opinion, that so sticks on Marcius, shall
267   Of his demerits rob Cominius.

BRUTUS   Come.
268   Half all Cominius' honors are to Marcius,

Though Marcius earned them not; and all his faults
To Marcius shall be honors, though indeed
In aught he merit not.

SICINIUS   Let's hence and hear
How the dispatch is made, and in what fashion,
More than his singularity, he goes   272
Upon this present action.   273

BRUTUS   Let's along.   *Exeunt.*

                        *

       Enter Tullus Aufidius, with Senators of Corioles.   I, ii

FIRST SENATOR
So, your opinion is, Aufidius,
That they of Rome are entered in our counsels   2
And know how we proceed.

AUFIDIUS   Is it not yours?
What ever have been thought on in this state,   4
That could be brought to bodily act ere Rome
Had circumvention? 'Tis not four days gone   6
Since I heard thence. These are the words. I think
I have the letter here. Yes, here it is:
'They have pressed a power, but it is not known   9
Whether for east or west. The dearth is great,
The people mutinous; and it is rumored,
Cominius, Marcius your old enemy,
Who is of Rome worse hated than of you,
And Titus Lartius, a most valiant Roman,
These three lead on this preparation
Whither 'tis bent. Most likely 'tis for you.
Consider of it.'

FIRST SENATOR   Our army's in the field.
We never yet made doubt but Rome was ready
To answer us.

AUFIDIUS   Nor did you think it folly
To keep your great pretenses veiled till when   20
They needs must show themselves, which in the
    hatching,
It seemed, appeared to Rome. By the discovery   22
We shall be shortened in our aim, which was   23
To take in many towns ere almost Rome   24
Should know we were afoot.

SECOND SENATOR   Noble Aufidius,
Take your commission; hie you to your bands;
Let us alone to guard Corioles.
If they set down before's, for the remove   28
Bring up your army; but, I think, you'll find
Th' have not prepared for us.   30

AUFIDIUS   O, doubt not that,
I speak from certainties. Nay more,
Some parcels of their power are forth already,   32
And only hitherward. I leave your honors.
If we and Caius Marcius chance to meet,
'Tis sworn between us we shall ever strike
Till one can do no more.

ALL   The gods assist you!

AUFIDIUS
And keep your honors safe!

FIRST SENATOR   Farewell.

SECOND SENATOR   Farewell.

ALL
Farewell.   *Exeunt omnes.*

---

236 *Stand'st out* do you keep aloof   240 *attend* await   242 *worthy you priority* you are worthy of precedence   246 *puts . . . forth* blossoms   251 *spare to gird* desist from taunting   259 *whom* which   266 *so sticks* is so set   267 *demerits* merits   268 *are to* belong to   272 *dispatch* completion   273 *More than his singularity* personal considerations aside
I, ii The senate house in Corioli   2 *entered in* initiated into   4 *What* what counsels   6 *circumvention* means of foiling   9 *pressed a power* raised an army   20 *pretenses* designs   22 *appeared* became visible   23 *shortened* reduced   24 *take in* capture   28 *for the remove* to force their departure   30 *Th'* they   32 *parcels* parts

                        *

I, iii *Enter Volumnia and Virgilia, mother and wife to Marcius. They set them down on two low stools and sew.*

VOLUMNIA I pray you, daughter, sing, or express your-
2 self in a more comfortable sort. If my son were my husband, I should freelier rejoice in that absence wherein he won honor than in the embracements of his bed where he would show most love. When yet he was but tender-bodied and the only son of my womb, when
7 youth with comeliness plucked all gaze his way, when for a day of kings' entreaties a mother should not sell
9 him an hour from her beholding, I, considering how
10 honor would become such a person, that it was no better than picture-like to hang by th' wall, if renown made it not stir, was pleased to let him seek danger where he was like to find fame. To a cruel war I sent him, from
14 whence he returned, his brows bound with oak. I tell thee, daughter, I sprang not more in joy at first hearing he was a man-child than now in first seeing he had proved himself a man.

VIRGILIA But had he died in the business, madam, how then?

VOLUMNIA Then his good report should have been my son; I therein would have found issue. Hear me profess sincerely: had I a dozen sons, each in my love alike, and none less dear than thine and my good Marcius, I had rather had eleven die nobly for their country than one
23 voluptuously surfeit out of action.

Enter a Gentlewoman.

GENTLEWOMAN
Madam, the Lady Valeria is come to visit you.

VIRGILIA
25 Beseech you, give me leave to retire myself.

VOLUMNIA
Indeed, you shall not.
Methinks I hear hither your husband's drum;
See him pluck Aufidius down by th' hair;
As children from a bear, the Volsces shunning him.
Methinks I see him stamp thus, and call thus:
31 'Come on, you cowards! You were got in fear,
Though you were born in Rome.' His bloody brow
With his mailed hand then wiping, forth he goes,
34 Like to a harvest-man that's tasked to mow
35 Or all or lose his hire.

VIRGILIA
His bloody brow? O Jupiter, no blood!

VOLUMNIA
Away, you fool! it more becomes a man
38 Than gilt his trophy. The breasts of Hecuba,
39 When she did suckle Hector, looked not lovelier
Than Hector's forehead when it spit forth blood
41 At Grecian sword, contemning. Tell Valeria,
We are fit to bid her welcome. *Exit Gentlewoman.*

VIRGILIA
43 Heavens bless my lord from fell Aufidius!

VOLUMNIA
He'll beat Aufidius' head below his knee
And tread upon his neck.

Enter Valeria, with an Usher and a Gentlewoman.

VALERIA My ladies both, good day to you.
VOLUMNIA Sweet madam.
VIRGILIA I am glad to see your ladyship.
49 VALERIA How do you both? You are manifest house-
50 keepers. What are you sewing here? A fine spot, in good faith. How does your little son?

VIRGILIA I thank your ladyship; well, good madam.
VOLUMNIA He had rather see the swords and hear a drum than look upon his schoolmaster.
VALERIA O' my word, the father's son! I'll swear 'tis a 55 very pretty boy. O' my troth, I looked upon him o' Wednesday half an hour together. 'Has such a con- 57 firmed countenance! I saw him run after a gilded butterfly, and when he caught it, he let it go again, and after it again, and over and over he comes, and up again; catched it again; or whether his fall enraged him, or how 'twas, he did so set his teeth and tear it! O, I I warrant, how he mammocked it! 62
VOLUMNIA One on's father's moods.
VALERIA Indeed, la, 'tis a noble child.
VIRGILIA A crack, madam. 65
VALERIA Come, lay aside your stitchery. I must have you play the idle housewife with me this afternoon.
VIRGILIA No, good madam, I will not out of doors.
VALERIA Not out of doors?
VOLUMNIA She shall, she shall.
VIRGILIA Indeed, no, by your patience. I'll not over the threshold till my lord return from the wars.
VALERIA Fie, you confine yourself most unreasonably. Come, you must go visit the good lady that lies in. 74
VIRGILIA I will wish her speedy strength and visit her with my prayers, but I cannot go thither.
VOLUMNIA Why, I pray you?
VIRGILIA 'Tis not to save labor, nor that I want love. 78
VALERIA You would be another Penelope; yet they say 79 all the yarn she spun in Ulysses' absence did but fill Ithaca full of moths. Come; I would your cambric were sensible as your finger, that you might leave pricking it 82 for pity. Come, you shall go with us.
VIRGILIA No, good madam, pardon me; indeed I will not forth.
VALERIA In truth, la, go with me, and I'll tell you excellent news of your husband.
VIRGILIA O, good madam, there can be none yet.
VALERIA Verily, I do not jest with you. There came news from him last night.
VIRGILIA Indeed, madam?
VALERIA In earnest, it's true; I heard a senator speak it. Thus it is: the Volsces have an army forth, against whom Cominius the general is gone, with one part of our Roman power. Your lord and Titus Lartius are set down before their city Corioles. They nothing doubt prevailing and to make it brief wars. This is true, on mine honor; and so, I pray, go with us.
VIRGILIA Give me excuse, good madam. I will obey you 99 in everything hereafter.
VOLUMNIA Let her alone, lady. As she is now, she will but disease our better mirth. 102

I, iii Within the house of Marcius **2** *comfortable sort* cheerful manner **7** *plucked all gaze* attracted the attention of all **9** *from her beholding* out of her sight **10** *person* body **14** *bound with oak* crowned for saving a Roman citizen in battle **23** *surfeit* overindulge himself **25** *Beseech* I beseech **31** *got* begotten **34** *tasked* employed **35** *Or . . . or* either . . . or **38** *gilt his trophy* gilding becomes his monument; *Hecuba* queen of Troy **39** *Hector* Trojan champion **41** *contemning* despising **43** *bless* protect **49–50** *manifest house-keepers* well known for staying at home **50** *spot* embroidered figure **55** *O'* on **57** *confirmed* resolute **62** *mammocked* tore to pieces **65** *crack* imp **74** *lies in* expects a child **78** *want* am lacking in **79** *Penelope* faithful wife of Ulysses, who put off suitors by weaving **82** *sensible* capable of sensation; *leave* stop **99** *Give me excuse* excuse me **102** *disease* make uneasy; *better mirth* enjoyment which will be greater without her

VALERIA In troth, I think she would. Fare you well, then. Come, good sweet lady. Prithee, Virgilia, turn thy solemnness out o' door and go along with us.

VIRGILIA No, at a word, madam. Indeed, I must not. I wish you much mirth.

VALERIA Well, then, farewell.   *Exeunt.*

*

I, iv   *Enter Marcius, Titus Lartius, with Drum and*
           Colors, with Captains and Soldiers, as before the city
           Corioles. To them a Messenger.

MARCIUS
Yonder comes news. A wager they have met.

LARTIUS
My horse to yours, no.

MARCIUS   'Tis done.

LARTIUS   Agreed.

MARCIUS
Say, has our general met the enemy?

MESSENGER
4   They lie in view, but have not spoke as yet.

LARTIUS
So, the good horse is mine.

MARCIUS   I'll buy him of you.

LARTIUS
No, I'll nor sell nor give him. Lend you him I will
For half a hundred years. Summon the town.

MARCIUS
How far off lie these armies?

MESSENGER   Within this mile and half.

MARCIUS
9   Then shall we hear their 'larum, and they ours.
Now, Mars, I prithee, make us quick in work,
That we with smoking swords may march from hence,
12   To help our fielded friends! Come, blow thy blast.
           They sound a parley.
           Enter two Senators, with others, on the walls of
           Corioles.
Tullus Aufidius, is he within your walls?

FIRST SENATOR
No, nor a man that fears you less than he:
15   That's lesser than a little.
           Drum afar off.   Hark! our drums
Are bringing forth our youth. We'll break our walls
17   Rather than they shall pound us up. Our gates,
Which yet seem shut, we have but pinned with rushes;
They'll open of themselves.
           Alarum afar off.   Hark you, far off!
There is Aufidius. List what work he makes
21   Amongst your cloven army.

MARCIUS   O, they are at it!

LARTIUS
22   Their noise be our instruction. Ladders, ho!
           Enter the army of the Volsces.

MARCIUS
They fear us not, but issue forth their city.
Now put your shields before your hearts, and fight
With hearts more proof than shields. Advance, brave   25
Titus.
They do disdain us much beyond our thoughts,
Which makes me sweat with wrath. Come on, my
fellows.
He that retires, I'll take him for a Volsce,
And he shall feel mine edge.   29
           Alarum. The Romans are beat back to their trenches.
           Enter Marcius, cursing.

MARCIUS
All the contagion of the south light on you,
You shames of Rome! you herd of – Boils and plagues
Plaster you o'er, that you may be abhorred
Farther than seen, and one infect another
Against the wind a mile! You souls of geese,
That bear the shapes of men, how have you run
From slaves that apes would beat! Pluto and hell!
All hurt behind! backs red, and faces pale
With flight and agued fear! Mend and charge home,   38
Or, by the fires of heaven, I'll leave the foe
And make my wars on you! Look to't. Come on!
If you'll stand fast, we'll beat them to their wives,
As they us to our trenches. Follow me!
           Another alarum and Marcius follows them to gates
           and is shut in.
So, now the gates are ope. Now prove good seconds.   43
'Tis for the followers fortune widens them,   44
Not for the fliers. Mark me, and do the like.   45
           Enter the gates.

FIRST SOLDIER
Foolhardiness, not I.

SECOND SOLDIER   Nor I.

FIRST SOLDIER
See, they have shut him in.
           Alarum continues.

ALL   To th' pot, I warrant him.   47
           Enter Titus Lartius.

LARTIUS
What is become of Marcius?

ALL   Slain, sir, doubtless.

FIRST SOLDIER
Following the fliers at the very heels,
With them he enters, who upon the sudden
Clapped to their gates; he is himself alone,
To answer all the city.

LARTIUS   O noble fellow!
Who sensibly outdares his senseless sword,   53
And, when it bows, stand'st up. Thou art left, Marcius.
A carbuncle entire, as big as thou art,
Were not so rich a jewel. Thou wast a soldier
Even to Cato's wish, not fierce and terrible   57
Only in strokes; but with thy grim looks and
The thunder-like percussion of thy sounds,
Thou mad'st thine enemies shake, as if the world
Were feverous and did tremble.   61
           Enter Marcius, bleeding, assaulted by the Enemy.

FIRST SOLDIER   Look, sir.

LARTIUS   O, 'tis Marcius!
Let's fetch him off, or make remain alike.   62
           They fight, and all enter the City.

I, iv Before the gates of Corioli   4 *spoke* encountered   9 *'larum* call to
arms   12 *fielded* in the battlefield   15 *lesser than a* little next to nothing
17 *pound* pen   21 *cloven* split   22 *our instruction* a lesson to us   25 *proof*
impenetrable   29 *edge* sword   38 *agued* trembling; *home* to the utmost
43 *ope* open; *seconds* supporters   44 *followers* pursuers   45 *fliers* pursued
47 *To th' pot* to destruction   53 *sensibly* feelingly; *senseless* insensate
57 *Cato* the Censor, exponent of Roman ethics   61 *feverous* feverish
62 *make remain alike* stay there similarly

*

I, v   *Enter certain Romans, with spoils.*

FIRST ROMAN   This will I carry to Rome.

SECOND ROMAN   And I this.

3   THIRD ROMAN   A murrain on't! I took this for silver.
Alarum continues still afar off.
Enter Marcius and Titus Lartius, with a Trumpet.

MARCIUS

4   See here these movers that do prize their hours

5   At a cracked drachma! Cushions, leaden spoons,

6   Irons of a doit, doublets that hangmen would
Bury with those that wore them, these base slaves,
Ere yet the fight be done, pack up. Down with them!
And hark, what noise the general makes! To him!
There is the man of my soul's hate, Aufidius,
Piercing our Romans. Then, valiant Titus, take
Convenient numbers to make good the city;
Whilst I, with those that have the spirit, will haste
To help Cominius.

LARTIUS   Worthy sir, thou bleed'st.
Thy exercise hath been too violent

16   For a second course of fight.

MARCIUS   Sir, praise me not.
My work hath yet not warmed me. Fare you well.

18   The blood I drop is rather physical
Than dangerous to me. To Aufidius thus
I will appear and fight.

LARTIUS   Now the fair goddess Fortune
Fall deep in love with thee, and her great charms
Misguide thy opposers' swords! Bold gentleman,
Prosperity be thy page!

MARCIUS   Thy friend no less

24   Than those she placeth highest. So, farewell.

LARTIUS

Thou worthiest Marcius!   *[Exit Marcius.]*
Go sound thy trumpet in the market-place.
Call thither all the officers o' th' town,
Where they shall know our mind. Away!   *Exeunt.*

*

I, vi   *Enter Cominius, as it were in retire, with Soldiers.*

COMINIUS

Breathe you, my friends. Well fought! We are come off
Like Romans, neither foolish in our stands

3   Nor cowardly in retire. Believe me, sirs,
We shall be charged again. Whiles we have struck,

5   By interims and conveying gusts we have heard
The charges of our friends. The Roman gods

7   Lead their successes as we wish our own,
That both our powers, with smiling fronts encount'ring,
May give you thankful sacrifice.
Enter a Messenger.   Thy news?

MESSENGER

10   The citizens of Corioles have issued,
And given to Lartius and to Marcius battle.
I saw our party to their trenches driven,
And then I came away.

COMINIUS   Though thou speakest truth,
Methinks thou speak'st not well. How long is't since?

MESSENGER

Above an hour, my lord.

COMINIUS

16   'Tis not a mile; briefly we heard their drums.

17   How couldst thou in a mile confound an hour,

And bring thy news so late?

MESSENGER   Spies of the Volsces
Held me in chase, that I was forced to wheel   19
Three or four miles about; else had I, sir,
Half an hour since brought my report.

COMINIUS   Who's yonder,
That does appear as he were flayed? O gods!
He has the stamp of Marcius, and I have
Beforetime seen him thus.   24
Enter Marcius.

MARCIUS   Come I too late?

COMINIUS

The shepherd knows not thunder from a tabor   25
More than I know the sound of Marcius' tongue
From every meaner man.

MARCIUS   Come I too late?

COMINIUS

Ay, if you come not in the blood of others,
But mantled in your own.

MARCIUS   O, let me clip ye   29
In arms as sound as when I wooed, in heart
As merry as when our nuptial day was done,
And tapers burned to bedward!   32

COMINIUS   Flower of warriors!
How is't with Titus Lartius?

MARCIUS

As with a man busied about decrees:
Condemning some to death, and some to exile;
Ransoming him or pitying, threatening th' other;   36
Holding Corioles in the name of Rome,
Even like a fawning greyhound in the leash,
To let him slip at will.   39

COMINIUS   Where is that slave
Which told me they had beat you to your trenches?
Where is he? Call him hither.

MARCIUS   Let him alone.
He did inform the truth. But for our gentlemen,
The common file, – a plague! tribunes for them! –   43
The mouse ne'er shunned the cat as they did budge
From rascals worse than they.

COMINIUS   But how prevailed you?

MARCIUS

Will the time serve to tell? I do not think.
Where is the enemy? Are you lords o' th' field?
If not, why cease you till you are so?

COMINIUS   Marcius,
We have at disadvantage fought and did
Retire to win our purpose.

MARCIUS

How lies their battle? Know you on which side
They have placed their men of trust?

COMINIUS   As I guess, Marcius,
Their bands i' th' vaward are the Antiates,   53

I, v A street in Corioli   3 *murrain* cattle plague; s.d. *Trumpet* trumpeter 4 *movers* active men; *prize their hours* value their time   5 *drachma* Greek coin   6 *of a doit* worth the smallest sum; *hangmen* (whose perquisites included the clothes of the hanged)   16 *course* round; *praise* appraise 18 *physical* curative   24 *those* friend to those
I, vi An open place near the Roman camp   3 *retire* withdrawal   5 *conveying* carrying the noise of battle   7 *successes* fortunes   10 *issued* sallied forth 16 *briefly* a short while ago   17 *confound* waste   19 *that* so that   24 *Beforetime* in former time   25 *tabor* small drum   29 *clip* embrace   32 *tapers burned to bedward* candles indicated bedtime   36 *Ransoming* releasing   39 *let him slip* unleash him   43 *common file* rank and file   53 *vaward* vanguard

Of their best trust; o'er them Aufidius,
Their very heart of hope.

MARCIUS   I do beseech you
By all the battles wherein we have fought,
By th' blood we have shed together, by th' vows
58   We have made to endure friends, that you directly
Set me against Aufidius and his Antiates;
And that you not delay the present, but,
Filling the air with swords advanced and darts,
62   We prove this very hour.

COMINIUS   Though I could wish
You were conducted to a gentle bath
And balms applied to you, yet dare I never
Deny your asking. Take your choice of those
That best can aid your action.

MARCIUS   Those are they
That most are willing. If any such be here –
As it were sin to doubt – that love this painting
69   Wherein you see me smeared; if any fear
Lesser his person than an ill report;
If any think brave death outweighs bad life,
And that his country's dearer than himself;
Let him alone, or so many so minded,
Wave thus, to express his disposition,
And follow Marcius.

They all shout and wave their swords, take him up in
their arms, and cast up their caps.

O, me alone! Make you a sword of me?
77   If these shows be not outward, which of you
But is four Volsces? None of you but is
Able to bear against the great Aufidius
A shield as hard as his. A certain number,
Though thanks to all, must I select. The rest
Shall bear the business in some other fight,
83   As cause will be obeyed. Please you to march;
And four shall quickly draw out my command,
Which men are best inclined.

COMINIUS   March on, my fellows.
86   Make good this ostentation, and you shall
Divide in all with us.   *Exeunt.*

*

I, vii   *Titus Lartius, having set a guard upon Corioles,*
going with Drum and Trumpet toward Cominius and
Caius Marcius, enters with a Lieutenant, other
Soldiers, and a Scout.

LARTIUS
1   So, let the ports be guarded. Keep your duties,
As I have set them down. If I do send, dispatch
3   Those centuries to our aid; the rest will serve
For a short holding. If we lose the field,
We cannot keep the town.

---

58 *endure* remain   62 *prove* test   69–70 *fear Lesser* fear less for   77
shows gestures   83 *cause will be obeyed* circumstances require   86 *ostenta-*
tion showing
I, vii Before the gates of Corioli   1 *ports* gates   3 *centuries* companies of a
hundred   5 *Fear not* do not worry about   7 *guider* guide
I, viii An open place near the Roman camp   s.d. *at several doors* from
different entrances   3 *Afric* Africa   4 *fame and envy* enviable fame   7
Hollo hunt down   12 *whip* champion; *bragged progeny* boasted progenitors
13 *scape* escape   14 *Officious* meddling   15 *condemnèd seconds* ineffectual aid
I, ix   2 *Thou't* thou wouldst   6 *quaked* made to tremble   7 *fusty* mouldy;
plebeians lowest class   10 *of* in   12 *caparison* trappings   14 *charter*
privilege   18 *effected his good will* accomplished his intention   19–20
You . . . deserving you shall not bury your merit

LIEUTENANT   Fear not our care, sir.   5
LARTIUS
Hence, and shut your gates upon's.
Our guider, come; to th' Roman camp conduct us.   7
                                    Exeunt.

*

Alarum, as in battle. Enter Marcius and Aufidius at   I, viii
several doors.

MARCIUS
I'll fight with none but thee, for I do hate thee
Worse than a promise-breaker.

AUFIDIUS   We hate alike.
Not Afric owns a serpent I abhor   3
More than thy fame and envy. Fix thy foot.   4

MARCIUS
Let the first budger die the other's slave,
And the gods doom him after!

AUFIDIUS   If I fly, Marcius,
Hollo me like a hare.   7

MARCIUS   Within these three hours, Tullus,
Alone I fought in your Corioles walls,
And made what work I pleased. 'Tis not my blood
Wherein thou seest me masked. For thy revenge
Wrench up thy power to th' highest.

AUFIDIUS   Wert thou the Hector
That was the whip of your bragged progeny,   12
Thou shouldst not scape me here.   13

Here they fight, and certain Volsces come in the aid of
Aufidius. Marcius fights till they be driven in
breathless.

Officious and not valiant, you have shamed me   14
In your condemnèd seconds.   15
                                    [*Exeunt.*]

Flourish. Alarum. A retreat is sounded. Flourish.   I, ix
Enter, at one door, Cominius, with the Romans; at
another door, Marcius, with his arm in a scarf.

COMINIUS
If I should tell thee o'er this thy day's work,
Thou't not believe thy deeds. But I'll report it   2
Where senators shall mingle tears with smiles;
Where great patricians shall attend and shrug,
I' th' end admire; where ladies shall be frighted,
And, gladly quaked, hear more; where the dull tribunes,   6
That with the fusty plebeians hate thine honors,   7
Shall say against their hearts, 'We thank the gods
Our Rome hath such a soldier.'
Yet camest thou to a morsel of this feast,   10
Having fully dined before.

Enter Titus [Lartius], with his Power, from the
pursuit.

LARTIUS   O general,
Here is the steed, we the caparison.   12
Hadst thou beheld –

MARCIUS   Pray now, no more. My mother,
Who has a charter to extol her blood,   14
When she does praise me grieves me. I have done
As you have done – that's what I can; induced
As you have been – that's for my country.
He that has but effected his good will   18
Hath overta'en mine act.

COMINIUS   You shall not be   19
The grave of your deserving. Rome must know
The value of her own. 'Twere a concealment

22 Worse than a theft, no less than a traducement,
To hide your doings and to silence that
24 Which, to the spire and top of praises vouched,
25 Would seem but modest. Therefore, I beseech you –
26 In sign of what you are, not to reward
What you have done – before our army hear me.
MARCIUS
I have some wounds upon me, and they smart
To hear themselves rememb'red.
COMINIUS   Should they not,
30 Well might they fester 'gainst ingratitude
31 And tent themselves with death. Of all the horses,
32 Whereof we have ta'en good and good store, of all
The treasure in this field achieved and city,
We render you the tenth, to be ta'en forth
Before the common distribution at
Your only choice.
MARCIUS   I thank you, general,
But cannot make my heart consent to take
A bribe to pay my sword. I do refuse it,
And stand upon my common part with those
That have beheld the doing.
A long flourish. They all cry, 'Marcius! Marcius!',
cast up their caps and lances. Cominius and Lartius
stand bare.
MARCIUS
May these same instruments which you profane
Never sound more! When drums and trumpets shall
I' th' field prove flatterers, let courts and cities be
44 Made all of false-faced soothing! When steel grows
45 Soft as the parasite's silk, let him be made
46 A coverture for th' wars. No more, I say!
For that I have not washed my nose that bled,
48 Or foiled some debile wretch, which without note
Here's many else have done, you shout me forth
In acclamations hyperbolical,
51 As if I loved my little should be dieted
In praises sauced with lies.
COMINIUS   Too modest are you,
More cruel to your good report than grateful
54 To us that give you truly. By your patience,
If 'gainst yourself you be incensed, we'll put you,
56 Like one that means his proper harm, in manacles,
Then reason safely with you. Therefore be it known,
As to us, to all the world, that Caius Marcius
Wears this war's garland; in token of the which,
My noble steed, known to the camp, I give him,
61 With all his trim belonging; and from this time,
For what he did before Corioles, call him,
With all th' applause and clamor of the host,
Caius Marcius Coriolanus. Bear
65 Th' addition nobly ever!
Flourish. Trumpets sound, and drums.
ALL
Caius Marcius Coriolanus!
CORIOLANUS
I will go wash;
And when my face is fair, you shall perceive
Whether I blush or no. Howbeit, I thank you.
I mean to stride your steed, and at all times
71 To undercrest your good addition
72 To th' fairness of my power.
COMINIUS   So, to our tent,
Where, ere we do repose us, we will write

To Rome of our success. You, Titus Lartius,
Must to Corioles back. Send us to Rome
The best, with whom we may articulate,   76
For their own good and ours.
LARTIUS   I shall, my lord.
CORIOLANUS
The gods begin to mock me. I, that now
Refused most princely gifts, am bound to beg
Of my lord general.
COMINIUS   Take't, 'tis yours. What is't?
CORIOLANUS
I sometime lay here in Corioles   81
At a poor man's house; he used me kindly.   82
He cried to me; I saw him prisoner;   83
But then Aufidius was within my view,
And wrath o'erwhelmed my pity. I request you
To give my poor host freedom.
COMINIUS   O, well begged!
Were he the butcher of my son, he should
Be free as is the wind. Deliver him, Titus.
LARTIUS
Marcius, his name?
CORIOLANUS   By Jupiter, forgot!
I am weary; yea, my memory is tired.
Have we no wine here?
COMINIUS   Go we to our tent.
The blood upon your visage dries; 'tis time
It should be looked to. Come.   *Exeunt.*

*

A flourish. Cornets. Enter Tullus Aufidius, bloody,   I, x
with two or three Soldiers.
AUFIDIUS
The town is ta'en.
FIRST SOLDIER
'Twill be delivered back on good condition.   2
AUFIDIUS
Condition?
I would I were a Roman; for I cannot,
Being a Volsce, be that I am. Condition?
What good condition can a treaty find
I' th' part that is at mercy? Five times, Marcius,   7
I have fought with thee; so often hast thou beat me,
And wouldst do so, I think, should we encounter
As often as we eat. By th' elements,
If e'er again I meet him beard to beard,
He's mine or I am his. Mine emulation   12
Hath not that honor in't it had; for where
I thought to crush him in an equal force,
True sword to sword, I'll potch at him some way;   15
Or wrath or craft may get him.

22 *traducement* slander   24 *vouched* attested   25 *modest* moderate   26 *sign* token   30 *'gainst* exposed to   31 *tent* cure by probing   32 *good and good store* good in quality and quantity   44 *false-faced soothing* hypocritical flattery   45 *him* i.e. the silk   46 *coverture* covering   48 *foiled* have defeated; *debile* weak; *without note* unnoticed   51 *little* small share; *dieted* fed   54 *give* represent   56 *means* intends; *proper* own   61 *trim belonging* appertaining equipment   65 *addition* title   71 *undercrest* adopt and justify (heraldic)   72 *To . . . power* as fairly as I can   76 *articulate* come to terms   81 *sometime lay* once lodged   82 *used* treated   83 *cried* cried out
I, x The camp of the Volsces   2 *good condition* favorable terms   7 *I' th' part* for the side; *at mercy* in the victor's power   12 *emulation* rivalry   15 *potch* make a stab

1224

FIRST SOLDIER   He's the devil.
AUFIDIUS
   Bolder, though not so subtle. My valor 's poisoned
   With only suffering stain by him; for him
19 Shall fly out of itself. Nor sleep nor sanctuary,
20 Being naked, sick, nor fane nor capitol,
   The prayers of priests nor times of sacrifice,
22 Embargements all of fury, shall lift up
   Their rotten privilege and custom 'gainst
   My hate to Marcius. Where I find him, were it
25 At home, upon my brother's guard, even there,
26 Against the hospitable canon, would I
   Wash my fierce hand in's heart. Go you to th' city.
   Learn how 'tis held, and what they are that must
   Be hostages for Rome.
FIRST SOLDIER   Will not you go?
AUFIDIUS
   I am attended at the cypress grove: I pray you –
   'Tis south the city mills – bring me word thither
   How the world goes, that to the pace of it
   I may spur on my journey.
FIRST SOLDIER   I shall, sir.   *[Exeunt.]*

*

II, i   *Enter Menenius, with the two Tribunes of the People,*
         Sicinius and Brutus.
1 MENENIUS The augurer tells me we shall have news to-
   night.
   BRUTUS Good or bad?
   MENENIUS Not according to the prayer of the people, for
   they love not Marcius.
   SICINIUS Nature teaches beasts to know their friends.
   MENENIUS Pray you, who does the wolf love?
   SICINIUS The lamb.
   MENENIUS Ay, to devour him, as the hungry plebeians
   would the noble Marcius.
   BRUTUS He's a lamb indeed, that baas like a bear.
   MENENIUS He's a bear indeed, that lives like a lamb. You
   two are old men: tell me one thing that I shall ask you.
   BOTH Well, sir.
14 MENENIUS In what enormity is Marcius poor in, that you
   two have not in abundance?
   BRUTUS He's poor in no one fault, but stored with all.
   SICINIUS Especially in pride.
   BRUTUS And topping all others in boasting.
   MENENIUS This is strange now. Do you two know how
20 you are censured here in the city, I mean of us o' th'
21 right-hand file? Do you?
   BOTH Why, how are we censured?

MENENIUS Because you talk of pride now – will you not
   be angry?
BOTH Well, well, sir, well.
MENENIUS Why, 'tis no great matter; for a very little 26
   thief of occasion will rob you of a great deal of patience.
   Give your dispositions the reins and be angry at your
   pleasures – at the least, if you take it as a pleasure to you
   in being so. You blame Marcius for being proud?
BRUTUS We do it not alone, sir.
MENENIUS I know you can do very little alone; for your
   helps are many, or else your actions would grow won- 33
   drous single. Your abilities are too infant-like for doing
   much alone. You talk of pride: O that you could turn
   your eyes toward the napes of your necks, and make but
   an interior survey of your good selves! O that you could!
BRUTUS What then, sir?
MENENIUS Why, then you should discover a brace of un-
   meriting, proud, violent, testy magistrates, alias fools,
   as any in Rome.
SICINIUS Menenius, you are known well enough too.
MENENIUS I am known to be a humorous patrician, and 43
   one that loves a cup of hot wine with not a drop of allay- 44
   ing Tiber in't; said to be something imperfect in favor- 45
   ing the first complaint; hasty and tinder-like upon too
   trivial motion; one that converses more with the buttock 47
   of the night than with the forehead of the morning.
   What I think, I utter, and spend my malice in my
   breath. Meeting two such wealsmen as you are, – I can- 50
   not call you Lycurguses – if the drink you give me touch 51
   my palate adversely, I make a crooked face at it. I cannot
   say your worships have delivered the matter well, when
   I find the ass in compound with the major part of your 54
   syllables; and though I must be content to bear with
   those that say you are reverend grave men, yet they lie
   deadly that tell you you have good faces. If you see this
   in the map of my microcosm, follows it that I am known 58
   well enough too? What harm can your bisson conspec- 59
   tuities glean out of this character, if I be known well
   enough too?
BRUTUS Come, sir, come, we know you well enough.
MENENIUS You know neither me, yourselves, nor anything. You are ambitious for poor knaves' caps and legs. 63
   You wear out a good wholesome forenoon in hearing a
   cause between an orange-wife and a forset-seller, and 65
   then rejourn the controversy of threepence to a second 66
   day of audience. When you are hearing a matter between party and party, if you chance to be pinched with
   the colic, you make faces like mummers; set up the 69
   bloody flag against all patience; and, in roaring for a
   chamber-pot, dismiss the controversy bleeding, the 71
   more entangled by your hearing. All the peace you
   make in their cause is, calling both the parties knaves.
   You are a pair of strange ones.
BRUTUS Come, come, you are well understood to be a 74
   perfecter giber for the table than a necessary bencher in
   the Capitol.
MENENIUS Our very priests must become mockers, if
   they shall encounter such ridiculous subjects as you are.
   When you speak best unto the purpose, it is not worth
   the wagging of your beards; and your beards deserve
   not so honorable a grave as to stuff a botcher's cushion 81
   or to be entombed in an ass's pack-saddle. Yet you
   must be saying Marcius is proud; who, in a cheap estimation, is worth all your predecessors since Deucalion, 84

19 *Shall . . . itself* it shall deviate from its nature **20** *fane* shrine **22**
Embargements restraints **25** *upon* under **26** *hospitable canon* law of
hospitality
II, i A public place in Rome **1** *augurer* soothsayer **14** *enormity* vice **20**
censured judged **21** *right-hand file* ruling class **26–27** *a very . . . patience*
you get very impatient upon the slightest pretext **33–34** *wondrous single*
extraordinarily feeble **43** *humorous* whimsical **44–45** *allaying Tiber*
diluting river-water **45–46** *imperfect . . . complaint* prone to sympathize
47 *motion* motive **47–48** *one . . . morning* more used to staying up late than
rising early **50** *wealsmen* statesmen **51** *Lycurgus* Spartan lawgiver **54**
ass in compound phrases beginning 'whereas' **58** *map* face; *microcosm* body
59 *bisson conspectuities* blinded eyesights **63** *caps* doffing of hats; *legs* bows
65 *orange-wife* street-vendor; *forset* wine-tap **66** *rejourn* postpone **69**
mummers masqueraders **69–70** *set . . . against* declare war on **71** *bleeding*
unhealed **74–76** *a perfecter . . . Capitol* rather a dinner-table wit than a
serious judge **81** *botcher* clothes-mender **84** *Deucalion* survivor of the Flood

though peradventure some of the best of 'em were hereditary hangmen. Good-e'en to your worships.
87 More of your conversation would infect my brain, being the herdsmen of the beastly plebeians. I will be bold to take my leave of you.

Brutus and Sicinius aside.
Enter Volumnia, Virgilia, and Valeria.

How now, my as fair as noble ladies, – and the moon, were she earthly, no nobler – whither do you follow your eyes so fast?

VOLUMNIA Honorable Menenius, my boy Marcius approaches. For the love of Juno, let's go.

MENENIUS Ha? Marcius coming home?

VOLUMNIA Ay, worthy Menenius, and with most prosperous approbation.

97 MENENIUS Take my cap, Jupiter, and I thank thee. Hoo! Marcius coming home!

TWO LADIES Nay, 'tis true.

VOLUMNIA Look, here's a letter from him. The state hath another, his wife another; and, I think, there's one at home for you.

MENENIUS I will make my very house reel to-night. A letter for me!

VIRGILIA Yes, certain, there's a letter for you; I saw't.

MENENIUS A letter for me! It gives me an estate of seven
107 years' health, in which time I will make a lip at the
108 physician. The most sovereign prescription in Galen is
109 but empiricutic and, to this preservative, of no better
110 report than a horse-drench. Is he not wounded? He was wont to come home wounded.

VIRGILIA O, no, no, no.

VOLUMNIA O, he is wounded; I thank the gods for't.

114 MENENIUS So do I too, if it be not too much. Brings 'a victory in his pocket? The wounds become him.

VOLUMNIA On's brows. Menenius, he comes the third time home with the oaken garland.

MENENIUS Has he disciplined Aufidius soundly?

VOLUMNIA Titus Lartius writes they fought together, but Aufidius got off.

MENENIUS And 'twas time for him too, I'll warrant him that. An he had stayed by him, I would not have been so
123 fidiused for all the chests in Corioles and the gold that's
124 in them. Is the Senate possessed of this?

VOLUMNIA Good ladies, let's go. Yes, yes, yes! The Senate has letters from the general, wherein he gives my
127 son the whole name of the war. He hath in this action outdone his former deeds doubly.

129 VALERIA In troth, there's wondrous things spoke of him.

MENENIUS Wondrous? Ay, I warrant you, and not with-
131 out his true purchasing.

VIRGILIA The gods grant them true!

133 VOLUMNIA True? pow waw!

MENENIUS True? I'll be sworn they are true. Where is he wounded? *[to the Tribunes]* God save your good worships! Marcius is coming home. He has more cause to be proud. – Where is he wounded?

VOLUMNIA I' th' shoulder and i' th' left arm. There will be
139 large cicatrices to show the people, when he shall stand
140 for his place. He received in the repulse of Tarquin seven hurts i' th' body.

MENENIUS One i' th' neck and two i' th' thigh – there's nine that I know.

VOLUMNIA He had, before this last expedition, twenty-five wounds upon him.

MENENIUS Now it's twenty-seven. Every gash was an enemy's grave. *(A shout and flourish.)* Hark! the trumpets.

VOLUMNIA These are the ushers of Marcius. Before him he carries noise, and behind him he leaves tears. Death, that dark spirit, in's nervy arm doth lie; 150 Which, being advanced, declines, and then men die. 151

A sennet. Trumpets sound. Enter Cominius the General and Titus Lartius; between them, Coriolanus, crowned with an oaken garland; with Captains and Soldiers and a Herald.

HERALD
Know, Rome, that all alone Marcius did fight Within Corioles gates, where he hath won, With fame, a name to Caius Marcius. These 154 In honor follows Coriolanus. Welcome to Rome, renownèd Coriolanus!
Sound. Flourish.

ALL
Welcome to Rome, renownèd Coriolanus!

CORIOLANUS
No more of this; it does offend my heart. Pray now, no more.

COMINIUS   Look, sir, your mother!

CORIOLANUS   O,
You have, I know, petitioned all the gods For my prosperity!
Kneels.

VOLUMNIA   Nay, my good soldier, up.
My gentle Marcius, worthy Caius, and By deed-achieving honor newly named – 163 What is it? – Coriolanus must I call thee? – But, O, thy wife!

CORIOLANUS   My gracious silence, hail!
Wouldst thou have laughed had I come coffined home, That weep'st to see me triumph? Ah, my dear, Such eyes the widows in Corioles wear, And mothers that lack sons.

MENENIUS   Now, the gods crown thee!

CORIOLANUS
And live you yet? *[to Valeria]* O my sweet lady, pardon.

VOLUMNIA
I know not where to turn. O, welcome home! And welcome, General! and y' are welcome all!

MENENIUS
A hundred thousand welcomes! I could weep And I could laugh; I am light and heavy. Welcome. 174 A curse begin at very root on's heart 175 That is not glad to see thee! You are three That Rome should dote on; yet, by the faith of men, We have some old crab-trees here at home that will not Be grafted to your relish. Yet welcome, warriors! 179 We call a nettle but a nettle and The faults of fools but folly.

87 *being* since you are   97 *Take ... Jupiter* I throw my cap in the air   107 *make a lip at* mock   108 *sovereign* efficacious; *Galen* Greek medical authority   109 *empiricutic* quackish; *to* compared to   110 *drench* dose 114 *'a* he (familiar)   123 *fidiused* treated like Aufidius   124 *possessed* fully informed   127 *name* credit   129 *troth* truth   131 *purchasing* winning 133 *pow waw* pooh   139 *cicatrices* scars; *stand* be a candidate   140 *Tarquin* deposed Roman tyrant   150 *nervy* sinewy   151 *declines* sinks down; **s.d.** *sennet* trumpet signal   154 *With* along with; *to* in addition to   163 *deed-achieving* achieved by deeds   174 *light* joyful; *heavy* sad   175 *begin at* penetrate to; *on's* of his   179 *grafted to your relish* implanted with a liking for you

COMINIUS   Ever right.

CORIOLANUS
182   Menenius, ever, ever.

HERALD
Give way there, and go on !

CORIOLANUS *[to Volumnia and Virgilia]*
      Your hand, and yours.
Ere in our own house I do shade my head,
The good patricians must be visited ;
From whom I have received not only greetings,
187   But with them change of honors.

VOLUMNIA   I have lived
188   To see inherited my very wishes
And the buildings of my fancy. Only
There's one thing wanting, which I doubt not but
Our Rome will cast upon thee.

CORIOLANUS   Know, good mother,
I had rather be their servant in my way,
193   Than sway with them in theirs.

COMINIUS   On, to the Capitol !
*Flourish. Cornets. Exeunt in state, as before. Brutus
and Sicinius [come forward].*

BRUTUS
194   All tongues speak of him, and the blearèd sights
Are spectacled to see him. Your prattling nurse
196   Into a rapture lets her baby cry,
197   While she chats him ; the kitchen malkin pins
198   Her richest lockram 'bout her reechy neck,
199   Clamb'ring the walls to eye him. Stalls, bulks, windows
200   Are smothered up, leads filled, and ridges horsed
201   With variable complexions, all agreeing
202   In earnestness to see him. Seld-shown flamens
Do press among the popular throngs, and puff
204   To win a vulgar station. Our veiled dames
205   Commit the war of white and damask in
206   Their nicely-gawded cheeks to th' wanton spoil
207   Of Phoebus' burning kisses – such a pother
As if that whatsoever god who leads him
Were slily crept into his human powers
And gave him graceful posture.

SICINIUS   On the sudden,
211   I warrant him consul.

BRUTUS   Then our office may,
During his power, go sleep.

SICINIUS
He cannot temp'rately transport his honors
214   From where he should begin and end, but will
Lose those he hath won.

BRUTUS   In that there's comfort.

SICINIUS   Doubt not

The commoners, for whom we stand, but they
Upon their ancient malice will forget   217
With the least cause these his new honors, which
That he will give them make I as little question
As he is proud to do't.   220

BRUTUS   I heard him swear,
Were he to stand for consul, never would he
Appear i' th' market-place nor on him put
The napless vesture of humility ;   223
Nor, showing, as the manner is, his wounds
To th' people, beg their stinking breaths.

SICINIUS   'Tis right.

BRUTUS
It was his word : O, he would miss it rather
Than carry it but by the suit of the gentry to him   227
And the desire of the nobles.

SICINIUS   I wish no better
Than have him hold that purpose and to put it
In execution.

BRUTUS   'Tis most like he will.   230

SICINIUS
It shall be to him then as our good wills,   231
A sure destruction.

BRUTUS   So it must fall out
To him or our authorities for an end.
We must suggest the people in what hatred   234
He still hath held them ; that to's power he would
Have made them mules, silenced their pleaders, and
Dispropertied their freedoms, holding them,   237
In human action and capacity,
Of no more soul nor fitness for the world
Than camels in their war, who have their provand   240
Only for bearing burthens, and sore blows   241
For sinking under them.

SICINIUS   This, as you say, suggested
At some time when his soaring insolence
Shall touch the people – which time shall not want,   244
If he be put upon't, and that's as easy   245
As to set dogs on sheep – will be his fire
To kindle their dry stubble ; and their blaze
Shall darken him for ever.

Enter a Messenger.

BRUTUS   What's the matter ?

MESSENGER
You are sent for to th' Capitol. 'Tis thought
That Marcius shall be consul.
I have seen the dumb men throng to see him, and
The blind to hear him speak. Matrons flung gloves,
Ladies and maids their scarfs and handkerchers,
Upon him as he passed. The nobles bended,
As to Jove's statue, and the commons made
A shower and thunder with their caps and shouts.
I never saw the like.

BRUTUS   Let's to the Capitol,
And carry with us ears and eyes for th' time,   258
But hearts for the event.   259

SICINIUS   Have with you.   *Exeunt.*

*

*Enter two Officers, to lay cushions, as it were in the
Capitol.*   II, ii

FIRST OFFICER Come, come, they are almost here. How
many stand for consulships ?

182 *ever* still the same   187 *change of honors* promotion   188 *inherited* realized   193 *sway* rule   194 *sights* eyesights   196 *rapture* fit   197 *chats* gossips about; *malkin* slattern   198 *lockram* coarse linen ; *reechy* grimy   199 *bulks* shop-fronts   200 *leads* leaden roofs ; *ridges horsed* roof-tops bestridden   201 *variable complexions* different types   202 *Seld-shown flamens* priests who rarely appear   204 *vulgar station* place in the crowd   205 *damask* red   206 *nicely-gawded* daintily adorned   207 *Phoebus* the sun; *pother* turmoil   211 *consul* one of Rome's two chief magistrates   214 *and end* to where he should end   217 *Upon . . . malice* because of their longstanding hostility   220 *As* as that   223 *napless* threadbare   227 *carry* win   230 *like* likely   231 *good wills* advantage requires   234 *suggest* insinuate to   237 *Dispropertied* dispossessed   240 *provand* provender   241 *burthens* burdens   244 *which . . . want* and that time will come   245 *put upon't* provoked   258 *time* situation   259 *event* outcome
II, ii The Roman senate house in the Capitol   s.d. *cushions* used on stage for seats

3 SECOND OFFICER Three, they say; but 'tis thought of every one Coriolanus will carry it.

5 FIRST OFFICER That's a brave fellow; but he's vengeance proud, and loves not the common people.

SECOND OFFICER Faith, there hath been many great men that have flattered the people, who ne'er loved them; and there be many that they have loved, they know not wherefore; so that, if they love they know not why, they hate upon no better a ground. Therefore, for Coriolanus neither to care whether they love or hate
13 him manifests the true knowledge he has in their dis-
14 position, and out of his noble carelessness lets them plainly see't.

FIRST OFFICER If he did not care whether he had their
16 love or no, he waved indifferently 'twixt doing them neither good nor harm; but he seeks their hate with greater devotion than they can render it him, and leaves
19 nothing undone that may fully discover him their
20 opposite. Now to seem to affect the malice and dis-pleasure of the people is as bad as that which he dislikes – to flatter them for their love.

SECOND OFFICER He hath deserved worthily of his country; and his ascent is not by such easy degrees as those who, having been supple and courteous to the
26 people, bonneted, without any further deed to have them at all into their estimation and report. But he hath so planted his honors in their eyes and his actions in their hearts that for their tongues to be silent and not confess so much were a kind of ingrateful injury; to re-port otherwise were a malice that, giving itself the lie, would pluck reproof and rebuke from every ear that heard it.

FIRST OFFICER No more of him; he's a worthy man.
34 Make way, they are coming.

A sennet. Enter the Patricians and the Tribunes of the People, Lictors before them : Coriolanus, Menenius, Cominius the Consul. Sicinius and Brutus take their places by themselves. Coriolanus stands.

MENENIUS
35 Having determined of the Volsces and
To send for Titus Lartius, it remains,
37 As the main point of this our after-meeting,
38 To gratify his noble service that
Hath thus stood for his country. Therefore, please you,
Most reverend and grave elders, to desire
The present consul, and last general
42 In our well-found successes, to report
A little of that worthy work performed
By Caius Marcius Coriolanus, whom
We met here both to thank and to remember
With honors like himself.

FIRST SENATOR Speak, good Cominius.
Leave nothing out for length, and make us think
48 Rather our state 's defective for requital
49 Than we to stretch it out. 		*[To the Tribunes]* 	Masters o' th' people,
We do request your kindest ears, and after,
51 Your loving motion toward the common body
52 To yield what passes here.

SICINIUS 		We are convented
53 Upon a pleasing treaty, and have hearts
Inclinable to honor and advance
The theme of our assembly.

BRUTUS 		Which the rather 		55
We shall be blest to do, if he remember 		56
A kinder value of the people than
He hath hereto prized them at.

MENENIUS 		That's off, that's off! 		58
I would you rather had been silent. Please you
To hear Cominius speak?

BRUTUS 		Most willingly;
But yet my caution was more pertinent
Than the rebuke you give it.

MENENIUS 		He loves your people;
But tie him not to be their bedfellow.
Worthy Cominius, speak.
Coriolanus rises, and offers to go away.
		Nay, keep your place.

FIRST SENATOR
Sit, Coriolanus. Never shame to hear
What you have nobly done.

CORIOLANUS 		Your honors' pardon.
I had rather have my wounds to heal again
Than hear say how I got them.

BRUTUS 		Sir, I hope
My words disbenched you not. 		69

CORIOLANUS 		No, sir. Yet oft,
When blows have made me stay, I fled from words.
You soothed not, therefore hurt not : but your people, 		71
I love them as they weigh –

MENENIUS 		Pray now, sit down.

CORIOLANUS
I had rather have one scratch my head i' th' sun 		73
When the alarum were struck than idly sit
To hear my nothings monstered. 		*Exit Coriolanus.* 		75

MENENIUS 		Masters of the people,
Your multiplying spawn how can he flatter –
That's thousand to one good one – when you now see
He'd rather venture all his limbs for honor
Than one on's ears to hear it? Proceed, Cominius. 		79

COMINIUS
I shall lack voice. The deeds of Coriolanus
Should not be uttered feebly. It is held
That valor is the chiefest virtue, and
Most dignifies the haver. If it be,
The man I speak of cannot in the world
Be singly counterpoised. At sixteen years, 		85
When Tarquin made a head for Rome, he fought 		86
Beyond the mark of others. Our then dictator, 		87
Whom with all praise I point at, saw him fight,
When with his Amazonian chin he drove 		89
The bristled lips before him; he bestrid 		90
An o'erpressed Roman and i' th' consul's view 		91

3 *of* by 	5 *vengeance* terribly 	13 *in* of 	14 *carelessness* indifference 	16 *waved* wavered 	19–20 *discover . . . opposite* show that he is opposed to them 	20 *affect* cultivate 	26–27 *bonneted . . . report* did nothing but doff their hats to attain popularity 	34 s.d. *Lictors* magistrates' attendants 	35 *of* concerning 	37 *after-meeting* later meeting 	38 *gratify* requite 	42 *well-found* fortunately encountered 	48 *defective for requital* unable to reward adequately 	49 *stretch it out* extend it 	51 *Your . . . body* your kind media-tion with the people 	52 *yield* grant; *convented* summoned 	53 *Upon* to consider 	55 *rather* sooner 	56 *blest* happy 	58 *off* beside the point 	69 *disbenched you* made you get up 	71 *soothed* flattered 	73–74 *have . . . struck* be idle during battle 	75 *monstered* made marvels of 	79 *Than . . . hear it* than venture one of his ears to hear about it 	85 *singly counterpoised* equalled by another individual 	86 *made . . . for* raised an army to reconquer 	87 *dictator* wartime leader 	89 *Amazonian* unbearded (like a female warrior) 	90 *bestrid* protected 	91 *o'erpressed* overwhelmed

Slew three opposers; Tarquin's self he met,
93   And struck him on his knee. In that day's feats,
When he might act the woman in the scene,
He proved best man i' th' field, and for his meed
Was brow-bound with the oak. His pupil age
97   Man-entered thus, he waxèd like a sea,
And in the brunt of seventeen battles since
99   He lurched all swords of the garland. For this last,
Before and in Corioles, let me say,
101   I cannot speak him home. He stopped the fliers,
And by his rare example made the coward
Turn terror into sport. As weeds before
A vessel under sail, so men obeyed
105   And fell below his stem; his sword, death's stamp,
Where it did mark, it took. From face to foot
He was a thing of blood, whose every motion
108   Was timed with dying cries. Alone he entered
109   The mortal gate of th' city, which he painted
110   With shunless destiny; aidless came off,
And with a sudden reinforcement struck
Corioles like a planet. Now all's his,
113   When by and by the din of war gan pierce
114   His ready sense; then straight his doubled spirit
115   Requickened what in flesh was fatigate,
And to the battle came he; where he did
117   Run reeking o'er the lives of men, as if
'Twere a perpetual spoil, and till we called
119   Both field and city ours, he never stood
To ease his breast with panting.
MENENIUS   Worthy man!
FIRST SENATOR
121   He cannot but with measure fit the honors
Which we devise him.
COMINIUS   Our spoils he kicked at,
And looked upon things precious as they were
The common muck of the world. He covets less
125   Than misery itself would give; rewards
His deeds with doing them; and is content
127   To spend the time to end it.
MENENIUS   He's right noble.
Let him be called for.
FIRST SENATOR   Call Coriolanus.
OFFICER
He doth appear.
        Enter Coriolanus.
MENENIUS
The Senate, Coriolanus, are well pleased
To make thee consul.
CORIOLANUS   I do owe them still
My life and services.
MENENIUS   It then remains
That you do speak to the people.

CORIOLANUS   I do beseech you,
Let me o'erleap that custom; for I cannot
Put on the gown, stand naked, and entreat them   135
For my wounds' sake to give their suffrage. Please you
That I may pass this doing.
SICINIUS   Sir, the people
Must have their voices; neither will they bate   138
One jot of ceremony.
MENENIUS   Put them not to't.
Pray you, go fit you to the custom and
Take to you, as your predecessors have,
Your honor with your form.   142
CORIOLANUS   It is a part
That I shall blush in acting, and might well
Be taken from the people.
BRUTUS [to Sicinius]   Mark you that?
CORIOLANUS
To brag unto them, 'Thus I did, and thus!'
Show them th' unaching scars which I should hide,
As if I had received them for the hire
Of their breath only!
MENENIUS   Do not stand upon't.   148
We recommend to you, tribunes of the people,
Our purpose to them; and to our noble consul
Wish we all joy and honor.
SENATORS
To Coriolanus come all joy and honor!
            Flourish. Cornets. Then exeunt.
            Manent Sicinius and Brutus.
BRUTUS
You see how he intends to use the people.
SICINIUS
May they perceive's intent! He will require them   154
As if he did contemn what he requested   155
Should be in them to give.   156
BRUTUS   Come, we'll inform them
Of our proceedings here. On th' market-place   157
I know they do attend us.   [*Exeunt.*]

                        *

        Enter seven or eight Citizens.   II, iii
FIRST CITIZEN Once if he do require our voices, we
ought not to deny him.
SECOND CITIZEN We may, sir, if we will.
THIRD CITIZEN We have power in ourselves to do it, but 4
it is a power that we have no power to do; for if he show 5
us his wounds and tell us his deeds, we are to put our
tongues into those wounds and speak for them. So, if he
tell us his noble deeds, we must also tell him our noble
acceptance of them. Ingratitude is monstrous; and for
the multitude to be ingrateful were to make a monster
of the multitude; of the which we being members,
should bring ourselves to be monstrous members.
FIRST CITIZEN And to make us no better thought of, a 13
little help will serve; for once we stood up about the corn, 14
he himself stuck not to call us the many-headed multi- 15
tude.
THIRD CITIZEN We have been called so of many; not 16
that our heads are some brown, some black, some abram, 17
some bald, but that our wits are so diversely colored;
and truly I think if all our wits were to issue out of one
skull, they would fly east, west, north, south, and their

---

93 *on* to   97 *Man-entered* initiated into manhood; *waxèd* grew   99
lurched robbed   101 *home* sufficiently   105 *stem* bow   108 *timed* rhyth-
mically accompanied   109 *mortal* fatal   110 *shunless* inevitable   113 *gan*
began to   114 *ready* alert; *doubled* strengthened   115 *fatigate* weary   117
reeking steaming   119 *stood* stopped   121 *with measure* in proportion
125 *misery* poverty   127 *spend . . . it* pass his time in killing time   135
naked exposed   138 *voices* votes; *bate* abate   142 *form* formality   148
stand insist   154 *require* ask   155 *contemn* despise   156 *Should . . . give*
that they should be willing to give   157 *market-place* the Forum
II, iii The Roman Forum   4 *power* authority   5 *no power* no right   13–14
a little . . . serve not much is needed   14 *once* when   15 *stuck not* did not
hesitate   16 *of* by   17 *abram* auburn

21 consent of one direct way should be at once to all the points o' th' compass.

SECOND CITIZEN Think you so? Which way do you judge my wit would fly?

THIRD CITIZEN Nay, your wit will not so soon out as another man's will; 'tis strongly wedged up in a block-head; but if it were at liberty, 'twould, sure, southward.

SECOND CITIZEN Why that way?

THIRD CITIZEN To lose itself in a fog; where being three
30 parts melted away with rotten dews, the fourth would return for conscience sake, to help to get thee a wife.

SECOND CITIZEN You are never without your tricks.
33 You may, you may!

THIRD CITIZEN Are you all resolved to give your voices?
35 But that's no matter, the greater part carries it. I say, if he would incline to the people, there was never a worthier man.

Enter Coriolanus in a gown of humility, with Menenius.

Here he comes, and in the gown of humility. Mark his behavior. We are not to stay all together, but to come by him where he stands, by ones, by twos, and by threes.
41 He's to make his requests by particulars; wherein every one of us has a single honor, in giving him our own voices with our own tongues. Therefore follow me, and I'll direct you how you shall go by him.

ALL Content, content.   *[Exeunt Citizens.]*

MENENIUS
O sir, you are not right. Have you not known
The worthiest men have done't?

CORIOLANUS   What must I say?
'I pray, sir' – Plague upon't! I cannot bring
My tongue to such a pace. 'Look, sir, my wounds!
I got them in my country's service, when
Some certain of your brethren roared and ran
From th' noise of our own drums.'

MENENIUS   O me, the gods!
You must not speak of that. You must desire them
To think upon you.

CORIOLANUS   Think upon me? Hang 'em!
I would they would forget me, like the virtues
56 Which our divines lose by 'em.

MENENIUS   You'll mar all.
I'll leave you. Pray you, speak to 'em, I pray you,
58 In wholesome manner.   *Exit.*

CORIOLANUS   Bid them wash their faces
And keep their teeth clean.

Enter three of the Citizens.

59   So, here comes a brace.
You know the cause, sir, of my standing here.

THIRD CITIZEN We do, sir. Tell us what hath brought you to't.

CORIOLANUS Mine own desert.

SECOND CITIZEN Your own desert?

CORIOLANUS Ay, not mine own desire.

THIRD CITIZEN How not your own desire?

CORIOLANUS No, sir, 'twas never my desire yet to trouble the poor with begging.

THIRD CITIZEN You must think, if we give you any-thing, we hope to gain by you.

CORIOLANUS Well then, I pray, your price o' th' consul-ship?

FIRST CITIZEN The price is to ask it kindly.

CORIOLANUS Kindly, sir, I pray, let me ha't. I have wounds to show you, which shall be yours in private. 74 Your good voice, sir. What say you?

SECOND CITIZEN You shall ha't, worthy sir.

CORIOLANUS A match, sir. There's in all two worthy 77 voices begged. I have your alms. Adieu.

THIRD CITIZEN But this is something odd.

SECOND CITIZEN An 'twere to give again – but 'tis no matter.   *Exeunt.*

Enter two other Citizens.

CORIOLANUS Pray you now, if it may stand with the tune 81 of your voices that I may be consul, I have here the cus-tomary gown.

FOURTH CITIZEN You have deserved nobly of your country, and you have not deserved nobly.

CORIOLANUS Your enigma?

FOURTH CITIZEN You have been a scourge to her enemies; you have been a rod to her friends. You have not indeed loved the common people.

CORIOLANUS You should account me the more virtuous that I have not been common in my love. I will, sir, flat-ter my sworn brother, the people, to earn a dearer esti- 92 mation of them. 'Tis a condition they account gentle; 93 and since the wisdom of their choice is rather to have my hat than my heart, I will practice the insinuating nod and be off to them most counterfeitly: that is, sir, I will 96 counterfeit the bewitchment of some popular man and 97 give it bountiful to the desirers. Therefore, beseech you, I may be consul.

FIFTH CITIZEN We hope to find you our friend, and therefore give you our voices heartily.

FOURTH CITIZEN You have received many wounds for your country.

CORIOLANUS I will not seal your knowledge with show- 103 ing them. I will make much of your voices, and so trouble you no farther.

BOTH The gods give you joy, sir, heartily!   *[Exeunt.]*

CORIOLANUS
Most sweet voices!
Better it is to die, better to starve,
Than crave the hire which first we do deserve.   109
Why in this wolvish toge should I stand here,   110
To beg of Hob and Dick that does appear   111
Their needless vouches? Custom calls me to't.   112
What custom wills, in all things should we do't,
The dust on antique time would lie unswept
And mountainous error be too highly heaped
For truth t' o'erpeer. Rather than fool it so,   116
Let the high office and the honor go
To one that would do thus. I am half through;
The one part suffered, the other will I do.

Enter three Citizens more.

Here come moe voices.   120

---

21 *consent . . . way* agreement to go straight   30 *rotten* unwholesome
33 *You may* go on   35 *greater part* majority   41 *by particulars* to individuals
56 *lose by* fail to inculcate in   58 *wholesome* decent   59 *brace* pair   74 *yours* available to you   77 *match* agreement   81 *stand* accord   92–93 *dearer estimation of* higher opinion from   93 *condition* quality; *gentle* amiable 96 *be off* take my hat off   97 *bewitchment* witchery; *popular man* man of the people   103 *seal* confirm   109 *hire* reward; *first* beforehand   110 *toge* toga   111 *Hob* rustic nickname for Robert; *that does appear* as they come by 112 *vouches* attestations   116 *o'erpeer* overtop; *fool it* play the fool   120 *moe* more

Your voices! For your voices I have fought;
122   Watched for your voices; for your voices bear
     Of wounds two dozen odd; battles thrice six
     I have seen and heard of; for your voices have
     Done many things, some less, some more. Your voices!
     Indeed, I would be consul.
FIRST CITIZEN He has done nobly, and cannot go with-
     out any honest man's voice.
SECOND CITIZEN Therefore let him be consul. The gods
     give him joy, and make him good friend to the people!
ALL Amen, amen. God save thee, noble consul! *[Exeunt.]*
CORIOLANUS Worthy voices!
     Enter Menenius, with Brutus and Sicinius.
MENENIUS
133   You have stood your limitation, and the tribunes
134   Endue you with the people's voice. Remains
135   That, in th' official marks invested, you
     Anon do meet the Senate.
CORIOLANUS   Is this done?
SICINIUS
     The custom of request you have discharged.
     The people do admit you, and are summoned
139   To meet anon upon your approbation.
CORIOLANUS
     Where? at the Senate House?
SICINIUS   There, Coriolanus.
CORIOLANUS
     May I change these garments?
SICINIUS   You may, sir.
CORIOLANUS
     That I'll straight do; and, knowing myself again,
     Repair to th' Senate House.
MENENIUS
144   I'll keep you company. Will you along?
BRUTUS
     We stay here for the people.
SICINIUS   Fare you well.
         Exeunt Coriolanus and Menenius.
     He has it now; and by his looks, methinks,
     'Tis warm at's heart.
BRUTUS
     With a proud heart he wore his humble weeds.
     Will you dismiss the people?
     Enter the Plebeians.
SICINIUS
150   How now, my masters! Have you chose this man?
FIRST CITIZEN
     He has our voices, sir.
BRUTUS
     We pray the gods he may deserve your loves.
SECOND CITIZEN
     Amen, sir. To my poor unworthy notice,

     He mocked us when he begged our voices.
THIRD CITIZEN   Certainly
     He flouted us downright.
FIRST CITIZEN
     No, 'tis his kind of speech; he did not mock us.
SECOND CITIZEN
     Not one amongst us, save yourself, but says
     He used us scornfully. He should have showed us
     His marks of merit, wounds received for's country.   159
SICINIUS
     Why, so he did, I am sure.
ALL   No, no! No man saw 'em.
THIRD CITIZEN
     He said he had wounds, which he could show in private;
     And with his hat, thus waving it in scorn,
     'I would be consul,' says he. 'Aged custom,   163
     But by your voices, will not so permit me.
     Your voices therefore.' When we granted that,
     Here was 'I thank you for your voices, thank you!
     Your most sweet voices! Now you have left your voices,
     I have no further with you.' Was not this mockery?   168
SICINIUS
     Why either were you ignorant to see it,   169
     Or, seeing it, of such childish friendliness
     To yield your voices?
BRUTUS   Could you not have told him
     As you were lessoned? When he had no power,   172
     But was a petty servant to the state,
     He was your enemy, ever spake against
     Your liberties and the charters that you bear   175
     I' th' body of the weal; and now, arriving   176
     A place of potency and sway o' th' state,
     If he should still malignantly remain
     Fast foe to th' plebeii, your voices might   179
     Be curses to yourselves. You should have said
     That as his worthy deeds did claim no less
     Than what he stood for, so his gracious nature
     Would think upon you for your voices and   183
     Translate his malice towards you into love,   184
     Standing your friendly lord.
SICINIUS   Thus to have said,
     As you were fore-advised, had touched his spirit   186
     And tried his inclination; from him plucked
     Either his gracious promise, which you might,
     As cause had called you up, have held him to;   189
     Or else it would have galled his surly nature,
     Which easily endures not article   191
     Tying him to aught; so putting him to rage,
     You should have ta'en the advantage of his choler
     And passed him unelected.
BRUTUS   Did you perceive
     He did solicit you in free contempt   195
     When he did need your loves, and do you think
     That his contempt shall not be bruising to you
     When he hath power to crush? Why, had your bodies
     No heart among you? Or had you tongues to cry   199
     Against the rectorship of judgment?   200
SICINIUS   Have you,
     Ere now, denied the asker? And now again,
     Of him that did not ask but mock, bestow   202
     Your sued-for tongues!   203
THIRD CITIZEN
     He's not confirmed; we may deny him yet.

---

122 *Watched* stayed awake   **133** *limitation* appointed time   **134** *Endue* endow; *Remains* it remains   **135** *official marks* insignia   **139** *upon your approbation* to confirm your election   **144** *along* come along   **150** *my masters* gentlemen   **159** *for's* for his   **163** *Aged* ancient   **168** *no further* nothing further to do   **169** *ignorant* too unobservant   **172** *lessoned* taught   **175** *charters* rights   **176** *body of the weal* commonwealth; *arriving* attaining   **179** *plebeii* plebeians (Latin)   **183** *Would think upon* should remember   **184** *Translate* change   **186** *fore-advised* previously advised; *had* would have   **189** *As . . . up* as occasion aroused you   **191–92** *article . . . aught* any conditions   **195** *free* open   **199** *heart* courage; *cry* protest   **200** *rectorship* rule   **202** *bestow* to bestow   **203** *sued-for* solicited

SECOND CITIZEN
And will deny him.
I'll have five hundred voices of that sound.
FIRST CITIZEN
207   I twice five hundred, and their friends to piece 'em.
BRUTUS
Get you hence instantly, and tell those friends
They have chose a consul that will from them take
Their liberties; make them of no more voice
Than dogs, that are as often beat for barking
212   As therefore kept to do so.
SICINIUS   Let them assemble,
And on a safer judgment all revoke
214   Your ignorant election. Enforce his pride,
215   And his old hate unto you. Besides, forget not
With what contempt he wore the humble weed,
How in his suit he scorned you; but your loves,
Thinking upon his services, took from you
219   Th' apprehension of his present portance,
Which most gibingly, ungravely, he did fashion
After th' inveterate hate he bears you.
221   **BRUTUS**   Lay
A fault on us, your tribunes: that we labored,
223   No impediment between, but that you must
Cast your election on him.
SICINIUS   Say you chose him
225   More after our commandment than as guided
By your own true affections, and that your minds,
Preoccupied with what you rather must do
Than what you should, made you against the grain
229   To voice him consul. Lay the fault on us.
BRUTUS
Ay, spare us not. Say we read lectures to you,
How youngly he began to serve his country,
How long continued, and what stock he springs of,
The noble house o' th' Marcians, from whence came
234   That Ancus Marcius, Numa's daughter's son,
Who after great Hostilius here was king;
Of the same house Publius and Quintus were,
237   That our best water brought by conduits hither;
And [Censorinus,] nobly naméd so,
239   Twice being [by the people chosen] censor,
Was his great ancestor.
SICINIUS   One thus descended,
That hath beside well in his person wrought
To be set high in place, we did commend
To your remembrances; but you have found,
244   Scaling his present bearing with his past,
That he's your fixèd enemy, and revoke
Your sudden approbation.
BRUTUS   Say, you ne'er had done 't –
247   Harp on that still – but by our putting on;
248   And presently, when you have drawn your number,
Repair to th' Capitol.
ALL   We will so: almost all
Repent in their election.   *Exeunt Plebeians.*
BRUTUS   Let them go on.
251   This mutiny were better put in hazard
252   Than stay past doubt, for greater.
If, as his nature is, he fall in rage
254   With their refusal, both observe and answer
The vantage of his anger.
SICINIUS   To th' Capitol, come.
We will be there before the stream o' th' people;

And this shall seem, as partly 'tis, their own,
Which we have goaded onward.   *Exeunt.*

*

Cornets. Enter Coriolanus, Menenius, all the   III
Gentry, Cominius, Titus Lartius, and other
Senators.
CORIOLANUS
Tullus Aufidius then had made new head?   1
LARTIUS
He had, my lord, and that it was which caused
Our swifter composition.   3
CORIOLANUS
So then the Volsces stand but as at first,
Ready, when time shall prompt them, to make road   5
Upon's again.
COMINIUS   They are worn, lord consul, so,
That we shall hardly in our ages see
Their banners wave again.
CORIOLANUS   Saw you Aufidius?
LARTIUS
On safeguard he came to me; and did curse   9
Against the Volsces, for they had so vilely   10
Yielded the town. He is retired to Antium.   11
CORIOLANUS
Spoke he of me?
LARTIUS   He did, my lord.
CORIOLANUS   How? what?
LARTIUS
How often he had met you, sword to sword;
That of all things upon the earth he hated
Your person most; that he would pawn his fortunes
To hopeless restitution, so he might   16
Be called your vanquisher.
CORIOLANUS   At Antium lives he?
LARTIUS
At Antium.
CORIOLANUS
I wish I had a cause to seek him there,
To oppose his hatred fully. Welcome home.
     Enter Sicinius and Brutus.
Behold, these are the tribunes of the people,
The tongues o' th' common mouth. I do despise them;
For they do prank them in authority   23
Against all noble sufferance.   24
SICINIUS   Pass no further.
CORIOLANUS
Ha! What is that?
BRUTUS
It will be dangerous to go on. No further.

---

207 *piece* supplement   **212** *therefore* for that reason   **214** *Enforce* emphasize   **215** *forget not* do not ignore   **219** *apprehension* observation; *portance* bearing   **221–22** *Lay . . . on* blame   **223** *No impediment between* that there should be no obstacle   **225** *after* according to   **229** *voice* vote   **234** *Numa* second king of Rome   **237** *conduits* aqueducts   **239** *censor* keeper of public records   **244** *Scaling* weighing   **247** *putting on* instigation   **248** *presently* immediately; *drawn your number* gathered a crowd   **251** *put in hazard* risked   **252** *for greater* and run a greater risk   **254–55** *answer The vantage* take advantage

III, i A Roman street   **1** *made new head* raised another army   **3** *swifter composition* coming to terms the more speedily   **5** *road* inroads   **9** *safeguard* safe-conduct   **10** *for* because   **11** *Antium* Volscian capital   **16** *To hopeless restitution* beyond hope of recovery   **23** *prank* dress up   **24** *noble sufferance* patrician endurance

CORIOLANUS
What makes this change?

MENENIUS
The matter?

COMINIUS
29 Hath he not passed the noble and the common?

BRUTUS
Cominius, no.

CORIOLANUS   Have I had children's voices?

FIRST SENATOR
Tribunes, give way. He shall to th' market-place.

BRUTUS
The people are incensed against him.

SICINIUS   Stop,
Or all will fall in broil.

CORIOLANUS   Are these your herd?
Must these have voices, that can yield them now
And straight disclaim their tongues? What are your
   offices?
36 You being their mouths, why rule you not their teeth?
Have you not set them on?

MENENIUS   Be calm, be calm.

CORIOLANUS
It is a purposed thing, and grows by plot,
To curb the will of the nobility.
40 Suffer't, and live with such as cannot rule
Nor ever will be ruled.

BRUTUS   Call't not a plot:
The people cry you mocked them; and of late,
43 When corn was given them gratis, you repined;
44 Scandaled the suppliants for the people, called them
45 Time-pleasers, flatterers, foes to nobleness.

CORIOLANUS
Why, this was known before.

BRUTUS   Not to them all.

CORIOLANUS
47 Have you informed them sithence?

BRUTUS   How! I inform them!

CORIOLANUS
You are like to do such business.

BRUTUS   Not unlike,
49 Each way, to better yours.

CORIOLANUS
Why then should I be consul? By yond clouds,
Let me deserve so ill as you, and make me
Your fellow tribune.

SICINIUS   You show too much of that
53 For which the people stir. If you will pass
To where you are bound, you must inquire your way,
55 Which you are out of, with a gentler spirit,
Or never be so noble as a consul,
57 Nor yoke with him for tribune.

MENENIUS   Let's be calm.

COMINIUS
The people are abused, set on. This paltering   58
Becomes not Rome, nor has Coriolanus
Deserved this so dishonored rub, laid falsely   60
I' th' plain way of his merit.

CORIOLANUS   Tell me of corn!
This was my speech, and I will speak't again—

MENENIUS
Not now, not now.

FIRST SENATOR   Not in this heat, sir, now.

CORIOLANUS
Now, as I live, I will. My nobler friends,
I crave their pardons.
For the mutable, rank-scented meiny, let them   66
Regard me as I do not flatter, and
Therein behold themselves. I say again,
In soothing them we nourish 'gainst our Senate
The cockle of rebellion, insolence, sedition,   70
Which we ourselves have ploughed for, sowed, and
   scattered
By mingling them with us, the honored number,
Who lack not virtue, no, nor power, but that
Which they have given to beggars.

MENENIUS   Well, no more.

FIRST SENATOR
No more words, we beseech you.

CORIOLANUS   How? no more?
As for my country I have shed my blood,
Not fearing outward force, so shall my lungs
Coin words till their decay against those measles   78
Which we disdain should tetter us, yet sought   79
The very way to catch them.

BRUTUS   You speak o' th' people
As if you were a god to punish, not
A man of their infirmity.

SICINIUS   'Twere well
We let the people know't.

MENENIUS   What, what? His choler?

CORIOLANUS
Choler!
Were I as patient as the midnight sleep,
By Jove, 'twould be my mind!

SICINIUS   It is a mind
That shall remain a poison where it is,
Not poison any further.

CORIOLANUS   Shall remain!
Hear you this Triton of the minnows? Mark you   89
His absolute 'shall'?

COMINIUS   'Twas from the canon.   90

CORIOLANUS   'Shall'?
O good but most unwise patricians! Why,
You grave but reckless senators, have you thus
Given Hydra here to choose an officer,   93
That with his peremptory 'shall,' being but
The horn and noise o' th' monster's, wants not spirit   95
To say he'll turn your current in a ditch,
And make your channel his? If he have power,
Then vail your ignorance; if none, awake   98
Your dangerous lenity. If you are learned,   99
Be not as common fools; if you are not,
Let them have cushions by you. You are plebeians   101
If they be senators; and they are no less
When, both your voices blended, the great'st taste   103
Most palates theirs. They choose their magistrate;   104

---

29 *passed* been approved by   36 *rule* control   40 *live* you will live   43 *repined* expressed regret   44 *Scandaled* defamed   45 *nobleness* aristocracy   47 *sithence* since   49 *better yours* do better than you would do as consul   53 *For . . . stir* which disturbs the people   55 *are out of* have strayed from   57 *yoke* cooperate   58 *abused* deceived; *paltering* equivocating   60 *dishonored rub* shameful obstacle   66 *For* as for; *meiny* multitude   70 *cockle* weed   78 *those measles* that leprosy   79 *tetter* break out in; *sought* have sought   89 *Triton* god who calms the waves   90 *from the canon* contrary to rule   93 *Given* allowed; *Hydra* many-headed monster   95 *horn* (attribute of Triton)   98 *vail your ignorance* let your negligence bow down   99 *lenity* mildness   101 *have cushions by you* sit with you in the Senate   103 *great'st taste* taste of the greatest   104 *palates* smacks of

And such a one as he, who puts his 'shall,'
His popular 'shall,' against a graver bench
Than ever frowned in Greece. By Jove himself,
It makes the consuls base ! and my soul aches
109 To know, when two authorities are up,
Neither supreme, how soon confusion
May enter 'twixt the gap of both and take
The one by th' other.
COMINIUS   Well, on to th' market-place.
CORIOLANUS
Whoever gave that counsel, to give forth
The corn o' th' storehouse gratis, as 'twas used
Sometime in Greece –
MENENIUS   Well, well, no more of that.
CORIOLANUS
Though there the people had more absolute power –
I say they nourished disobedience, fed
The ruin of the state.
BRUTUS   Why, shall the people give
One that speaks thus their voice ?
CORIOLANUS   I'll give my reasons,
More worthier than their voices. They know the corn
121 Was not our recompense, resting well assured
122 They ne'er did service for't. Being pressed to th' war,
123 Even when the navel of the state was touched,
124 They would not thread the gates. This kind of service
Did not deserve corn gratis. Being i' th' war,
Their mutinies and revolts, wherein they showed
Most valor, spoke not for them. Th' accusation
Which they have often made against the Senate,
129 All cause unborn, could never be the native
130 Of our so frank donation. Well, what then ?
131 How shall this bosom multiplied digest
The Senate's courtesy ? Let deeds express
What's like to be their words : 'We did request it ;
134 We are the greater poll, and in true fear
They gave us our demands.' Thus we debase
The nature of our seats, and make the rabble
Call our cares fears ; which will in time
Break ope the locks o' th' Senate, and bring in
The crows to peck the eagles.
MENENIUS   Come, enough.
BRUTUS
Enough, with over-measure.
CORIOLANUS   No, take more !
What may be sworn by, both divine and human,
142 Seal what I end withal ! This double worship,
Where one part does disdain with cause, the other
144 Insult without all reason ; where gentry, title, wisdom,
Cannot conclude but by the yea and no
146 Of general ignorance – it must omit
Real necessities, and give way the while
148 To unstable slightness. Purpose so barred, it follows,
Nothing is done to purpose. Therefore, beseech you, –
150 You that will be less fearful than discreet ;
That love the fundamental part of state
152 More than you doubt the change on't ; that prefer
A noble life before a long, and wish
154 To jump a body with a dangerous physic
That's sure of death without it – at once pluck out
The multitudinous tongue ; let them not lick
157 The sweet which is their poison. Your dishonor
Mangles true judgment, and bereaves the state
159 Of that integrity which should become't,

Not having the power to do the good it would
For th' ill which doth control't.
BRUTUS   'Has said enough.   161
SICINIUS
'Has spoken like a traitor, and shall answer
As traitors do.
CORIOLANUS   Thou wretch, despite o'erwhelm thee !   163
What should the people do with these bald tribunes ?
On whom depending, their obedience fails
To th' greater bench. In a rebellion,   166
When what's not meet, but what must be, was law,
Then were they chosen. In a better hour,
Let what is meet be said it must be meet,   169
And throw their power i' th' dust.
BRUTUS
Manifest treason !
SICINIUS   This a consul ? No.
BRUTUS
The aediles, ho !   172
        Enter an Aedile.
                 Let him be apprehended.
SICINIUS
Go, call the people ; [exit Aedile] in whose name myself
Attach thee as a traitorous innovator,   174
A foe to th' public weal. Obey, I charge thee,
And follow to thine answer.   176
CORIOLANUS   Hence, old goat !
ALL [PATRICIANS]
We'll surety him.   177
COMINIUS   Ag'd sir, hands off.
CORIOLANUS
Hence, rotten thing ! or I shall shake thy bones
Out of thy garments.
SICINIUS   Help, ye citizens !
        Enter a rabble of Plebeians, with the Aediles.
MENENIUS
On both sides more respect.
SICINIUS
Here's he that would take from you all your power.
BRUTUS
Seize him, aediles !
ALL [PLEBEIANS]
Down with him ! down with him !
SECOND SENATOR
Weapons, weapons, weapons !
        They all bustle about Coriolanus.
ALL
Tribunes ! – Patricians ! – Citizens ! – What, ho !
Sicinius ! – Brutus ! – Coriolanus ! – Citizens !
Peace, peace, peace ! – Stay, hold, peace !
MENENIUS
What is about to be ? I am out of breath ;
Confusion's near ; I cannot speak. You, tribunes   189
To th' people ! – Coriolanus, patience ! –

---

109 *up* in action   121 *recompense* reward to them   122 *pressed* conscripted
123 *navel* center   124 *thread* pass through   129 *All cause unborn* without
justification ; *native* origin   130 *frank* free   131 *bosom multiplied* many-
breasted crowd   134 *greater poll* majority   142 *Seal* confirm ; *withal* with ;
double worship divided authority   144 *without* beyond   146 *omit* neglect
148 *Purpose so barred* when planning thus becomes impossible   150 *discreet*
wise   152 *doubt* fear   154 *jump* risk   157 *sweet* flattery   159 *integrity*
wholeness ; *become't* befit it   161 *'Has* he has   163 *despite* scorn   166
greater bench Senate   169 *Let . . . be meet* let it be said that what is proper
should be done   172 *aediles* police officers   174 *Attach* arrest   176 *answer*
interrogation   177 *surety* stand pledged for   189 *Confusion* ruin

Speak, good Sicinius.

SICINIUS   Hear me, people. Peace!

ALL [PLEBEIANS] Let's hear our tribune. Peace! Speak,
speak, speak!

SICINIUS

194 You are at point to lose your liberties.
Marcius would have all from you, Marcius,
Whom late you have named for consul.

MENENIUS   Fie, fie, fie!
This is the way to kindle, not to quench.

FIRST SENATOR
To unbuild the city and to lay all flat.

SICINIUS
What is the city but the people?

ALL [PLEBEIANS]   True,
The people are the city.

BRUTUS
By the consent of all we were established
The people's magistrates.

ALL [PLEBEIANS]   You so remain.

MENENIUS
And so are like to do.

COMINIUS
That is the way to lay the city flat,
To bring the roof to the foundation,
206 And bury all, which yet distinctly ranges,
In heaps and piles of ruin.

SICINIUS   This deserves death.

BRUTUS
Or let us stand to our authority,
Or let us lose it. We do here pronounce,
Upon the part o' th' people, in whose power
We were elected theirs, Marcius is worthy
212 Of present death.

SICINIUS   Therefore lay hold of him;
213 Bear him to th' Rock Tarpeian, and from thence
Into destruction cast him.

BRUTUS   Aediles, seize him!

ALL [PLEBEIANS]
Yield, Marcius, yield!

MENENIUS   Hear me one word.
Beseech you, tribunes, hear me but a word.

AEDILES
Peace, peace!

MENENIUS [to Brutus]
Be that you seem, truly your country's friend,
And temp'rately proceed to what you would
Thus violently redress.

BRUTUS   Sir, those cold ways,
That seem like prudent helps, are very poisonous
Where the disease is violent. Lay hands upon him,
And bear him to the Rock.

      Coriolanus draws his sword.

CORIOLANUS   No, I'll die here.
There's some among you have beheld me fighting:
Come, try upon yourselves what you have seen me.

MENENIUS
Down with that sword! Tribunes, withdraw awhile.

BRUTUS
Lay hands upon him.

MENENIUS   Help Marcius, help!
You that be noble, help him, young and old!

ALL [PLEBEIANS]
Down with him! down with him!   *Exeunt.*
      *In this mutiny the Tribunes, the Aediles, and the
People are beat in.*

MENENIUS
Go, get you to your house! be gone, away!
All will be naught else.   231

SECOND SENATOR   Get you gone.

CORIOLANUS   Stand fast!
We have as many friends as enemies.

MENENIUS
Shall it be put to that?

FIRST SENATOR   The gods forbid!
I prithee, noble friend, home to thy house;
Leave us to cure this cause.

MENENIUS   For 'tis a sore upon us
You cannot tent yourself. Be gone, beseech you.   236

COMINIUS
Come, sir, along with us.

CORIOLANUS
I would they were barbarians, as they are,
Though in Rome littered; not Romans, as they are not,
Though calvèd i' th' porch o' th' Capitol –

MENENIUS   Be gone;
Put not your worthy rage into your tongue.
One time will owe another.   242

CORIOLANUS   On fair ground
I could beat forty of them.

MENENIUS   I could myself
Take up a brace o' th' best of them; yea, the two tribunes. 244

COMINIUS
But now 'tis odds beyond arithmetic,
And manhood is called foolery when it stands
Against a falling fabric. Will you hence   247
Before the tag return? whose rage doth rend   248
Like interrupted waters, and o'erbear   249
What they are used to bear.

MENENIUS   Pray you, be gone.
I'll try whether my old wit be in request   251
With those that have but little. This must be patched
With cloth of any color.

COMINIUS   Nay, come away.
      Exeunt Coriolanus and Cominius [with others].

PATRICIAN
This man has marred his fortune.

MENENIUS
His nature is too noble for the world.
He would not flatter Neptune for his trident,   256
Or Jove for's power to thunder. His heart's his mouth. 257
What his breast forges, that his tongue must vent;
And, being angry, does forget that ever
He heard the name of death.   260
      A noise within.
Here's goodly work!

PATRICIAN   I would they were abed!

MENENIUS
I would they were in Tiber! What the vengeance!
Could he not speak 'em fair?   263

194 *at point to lose* on the point of losing   206 *distinctly ranges* is ranked
separately   212 *present* immediate   213 *Rock Tarpeian* Capitoline cliff
from which state criminals were hurled   231 *naught* ruined   236 *tent* treat
242 *One . . . another* another time will make up for this   244 *Take up* cope
with   247 *fabric* building   248 *tag* rabble   249 *o'erbear* overpower   251
request demand   256 *trident* three-pronged fork symbolizing sea-power
257 *His . . . mouth* he speaks what he feels   260 s.d. *within* backstage
263 *speak 'em fair* address them graciously

Enter Brutus and Sicinius, with the Rabble again.

SICINIUS   Where is this viper
That would depopulate the city and
265   Be every man himself?
MENENIUS   You worthy tribunes –
SICINIUS
He shall be thrown down the Tarpeian Rock
With rigorous hands. He hath resisted law;
And therefore law shall scorn him further trial
Than the severity of the public power,
Which he so sets at nought.
FIRST CITIZEN   He shall well know
The noble tribunes are the people's mouths,
And we their hands.
272 ALL [PLEBEIANS]   He shall, sure on't.
MENENIUS   Sir, sir, –
SICINIUS
Peace!
MENENIUS
274   Do not cry havoc, where you should but hunt
275   With modest warrant.
SICINIUS   Sir, how comes't that you
276   Have holp to make this rescue?
MENENIUS   Hear me speak:
As I do know the consul's worthiness,
So can I name his faults –
SICINIUS   Consul! what consul?
MENENIUS
The consul Coriolanus.
BRUTUS   He consul!
ALL [PLEBEIANS]
No, no, no, no, no!
MENENIUS
If, by the tribunes' leave, and yours, good people,
I may be heard, I would crave a word or two;
283   The which shall turn you to no further harm
Than so much loss of time.
SICINIUS   Speak briefly then;
285   For we are peremptory to dispatch
This viperous traitor. To eject him hence
Were but our danger, and to keep him here
Our certain death. Therefore it is decreed
He dies to-night.
MENENIUS   Now the good gods forbid
That our renownèd Rome, whose gratitude
291   Towards her deservèd children is enrolled
In Jove's own book, like an unnatural dam
Should now eat up her own!
SICINIUS
He's a disease that must be cut away.
MENENIUS
O, he's a limb that has but a disease:
Mortal, to cut it off; to cure it, easy.
297   What has he done to Rome that's worthy death?
Killing our enemies, the blood he hath lost –
Which, I dare vouch, is more than that he hath,
By many an ounce – he dropped it for his country;
And what is left, to lose it by his country
Were to us all that do't and suffer it
A brand to th' end o' th' world.
303 SICINIUS   This is clean kam.
BRUTUS
304   Merely awry. When he did love his country,
It honored him.

SICINIUS   The service of the foot,
Being once gangrened, is not then respected
For what before it was.
BRUTUS   We'll hear no more.
Pursue him to his house and pluck him thence,
Lest his infection, being of catching nature,
Spread further.
MENENIUS   One word more, one word.
This tiger-footed rage, when it shall find
The harm of unscanned swiftness, will too late   3▮
Tie leaden pounds to's heels. Proceed by process,   3▮
Lest parties, as he is beloved, break out
And sack great Rome with Romans.
BRUTUS   If it were so –
SICINIUS
What do ye talk?
Have we not had a taste of his obedience?
Our aediles smote? ourselves resisted? Come.   3▮
MENENIUS
Consider this: he has been bred i' th' wars
Since 'a could draw a sword, and is ill schooled
In bolted language; meal and bran together   32▮
He throws without distinction. Give me leave,
I'll go to him and undertake to bring him
Where he shall answer by a lawful form,   32▮
In peace, to his utmost peril.
FIRST SENATOR   Noble tribunes,
It is the humane way. The other course
Will prove too bloody, and the end of it
Unknown to the beginning.
SICINIUS   Noble Menenius,
Be you then as the people's officer.
Masters, lay down your weapons.
BRUTUS   Go not home.
SICINIUS
Meet on the market-place. We'll attend you there;   33
Where, if you bring not Marcius, we'll proceed
In our first way.
MENENIUS   I'll bring him to you.
[To the Senators]
Let me desire your company. He must come,
Or what is worst will follow.
FIRST SENATOR   Pray you, let's to him.   33
                       Exeunt omnes.

*

Enter Coriolanus, with Nobles.   II
CORIOLANUS
Let them pull all about mine ears, present me
Death on the wheel or at wild horses' heels,   2
Or pile ten hills on the Tarpeian Rock,
That the precipitation might down stretch   4
Below the beam of sight, yet will I still   5

---

265 *Be . . . himself* constitute himself the whole population   272 *sure on't* for certain   274 *cry havoc* call for slaughter   275 *modest* moderate   276 *holp* helped   283 *turn you to* cause you   285 *peremptory* resolved   291 *deservèd* meritorious   291–92 *enrolled . . . book* recorded in the Capitol   297 *worthy* deserving of   303 *clean kam* quite wrong   304 *Merely awry* completely twisted   312 *unscanned swiftness* thoughtless haste   313 *to's* to its; *process* course of law   318 *smote* smitten   321 *bolted* sifted   324–25 *answer . . . peril* peacefully face judgment, however severe   331 *attend* await   335 *to* go to
III, ii The house of Coriolanus   2 *wheel* instrument of torture   4 *precipitation* precipitousness   5 *Below . . . sight* beyond eyesight

Be thus to them.

NOBLE   You do the nobler.

CORIOLANUS

7   I muse my mother
Does not approve me further, who was wont
To call them woollen vassals, things created
10 To buy and sell with groats, to show bare heads
11 In congregations, to yawn, be still and wonder,
12 When one but of my ordinance stood up
To speak of peace or war.
      Enter Volumnia.   I talk of you:
Why did you wish me milder? Would you have me
False to my nature? Rather say I play
The man I am.

VOLUMNIA   O, sir, sir, sir,
I would have had you put your power well on,
Before you had worn it out.

18 CORIOLANUS   Let go.

VOLUMNIA
You might have been enough the man you are
With striving less to be so. Lesser had been
21 The taxings of your dispositions, if
You had not showed them how ye were disposed
23 Ere they lacked power to cross you.

CORIOLANUS   Let them hang!

VOLUMNIA
Ay, and burn too!
      Enter Menenius, with the Senators.

MENENIUS
25 Come, come, you have been too rough, something too
    rough.
You must return and mend it.

FIRST SENATOR   There's no remedy,
Unless, by not so doing, our good city
28 Cleave in the midst, and perish.

VOLUMNIA   Pray, be counselled.

29 I have a heart as little apt as yours,
But yet a brain that leads my use of anger
31 To better vantage.

MENENIUS   Well said, noble woman!
Before he should thus stoop to th' herd, but that
33 The violent fit o' th' time craves it as physic
For the whole state, I would put mine armor on,
Which I can scarcely bear.

CORIOLANUS   What must I do?

MENENIUS
Return to th' tribunes.

CORIOLANUS   Well, what then? what then?

MENENIUS
Repent what you have spoke.

CORIOLANUS
For them? I cannot do it to the gods.
Must I then do't to them?

VOLUMNIA   You are too absolute;
Though therein you can never be too noble,
But when extremities speak. I have heard you say,   41
Honor and policy, like unsevered friends,   42
I' th' war do grow together. Grant that, and tell me,
In peace what each of them by th' other lose,
That they combine not there.

CORIOLANUS   Tush, tush!

MENENIUS   A good demand.

VOLUMNIA
If it be honor in your wars to seem
The same you are not, – which, for your best ends,
You adopt your policy – how is it less or worse,   48
That it shall hold companionship in peace
With honor, as in war; since that to both   50
It stands in like request?

CORIOLANUS   Why force you this?   51

VOLUMNIA
Because that now it lies you on to speak   52
To th' people, not by your own instruction,
Nor by th' matter which your heart prompts you,
But with such words that are but roted in   55
Your tongue, though but bastards and syllables
Of no allowance to your bosom's truth.   57
Now, this no more dishonors you at all
Than to take in a town with gentle words,   59
Which else would put you to your fortune and
The hazard of much blood.
I would dissemble with my nature where
My fortunes and my friends at stake required
I should do so in honor. I am in this   64
Your wife, your son, these senators, the nobles;
And you will rather show our general louts   66
How you can frown than spend a fawn upon 'em,   67
For the inheritance of their loves and safeguard   68
Of what that want might ruin.   69

MENENIUS   Noble lady! –
Come, go with us. Speak fair. You may salve so,
Not what is dangerous present, but the loss   71
Of what is past.

VOLUMNIA   I prithee now, my son,
Go to them, with this bonnet in thy hand;
And thus far having stretched it, – here be with them –   74
Thy knee bussing the stones, – for in such business   75
Action is eloquence, and the eyes of th' ignorant
More learned than the ears – waving thy head,   77
Which, often thus correcting thy stout heart,   78
Now humble as the ripest mulberry   79
That will not hold the handling; or say to them
Thou art their soldier, and being bred in broils
Hast not the soft way which, thou dost confess,
Were fit for thee to use as they to claim,
In asking their good loves; but thou wilt frame
Thyself, forsooth, hereafter theirs, so far   85
As thou hast power and person.

MENENIUS   This but done,
Even as she speaks, why, their hearts were yours;   87
For they have pardons, being asked, as free
As words to little purpose.   89

VOLUMNIA   Prithee now,
Go, and be ruled; although I know thou hadst rather   90

91 Follow thine enemy in a fiery gulf
92 Than flatter him in a bower.
    Enter Cominius.   Here is Cominius.

COMINIUS
I have been i' th' market-place; and, sir, 'tis fit
You make strong party, or defend yourself
By calmness or by absence. All's in anger.

MENENIUS
Only fair speech.

COMINIUS   I think 'twill serve, if he
Can thereto frame his spirit.

VOLUMNIA   He must, and will.
Prithee now, say you will, and go about it.

CORIOLANUS
99 Must I go show them my unbarbed sconce? Must I
With my base tongue give to my noble heart
A lie that it must bear? Well, I will do't.
102 Yet, were there but this single plot to lose,
103 This mould of Marcius, they to dust should grind it
And throw't against the wind. To th' market-place!
You have put me now to such a part which never
106 I shall discharge to th' life.

COMINIUS   Come, come, we'll prompt you.

VOLUMNIA
I prithee now, sweet son, as thou hast said
My praises made thee first a soldier, so,
To have my praise for this, perform a part
Thou hast not done before.

CORIOLANUS   Well, I must do't.
Away, my disposition, and possess me
Some harlot's spirit! My throat of war be turned,
113 Which quired with my drum, into a pipe
Small as an eunuch, or the virgin voice
115 That babies lulls asleep! The smiles of knaves
116 Tent in my cheeks, and schoolboys' tears take up
117 The glasses of my sight! A beggar's tongue
Make motion through my lips, and my armed knees,
Who bowed but in my stirrup, bend like his
That hath received an alms! I will not do't,
121 Lest I surcease to honor mine own truth
And by my body's action teach my mind
123 A most inherent baseness.

VOLUMNIA   At thy choice, then.
To beg of thee, it is my more dishonor
Than thou of them. Come all to ruin! Let
Thy mother rather feel thy pride than fear
127 Thy dangerous stoutness; for I mock at death
128 With as big heart as thou. Do as thou list.
Thy valiantness was mine, thou suck'st it from me;
130 But owe thy pride thyself.

CORIOLANUS   Pray, be content.
Mother, I am going to the market-place.
132 Chide me no more. I'll mountebank their loves,
133 Cog their hearts from them, and come home beloved
Of all the trades in Rome. Look, I am going.
Commend me to my wife. I'll return consul,
Or never trust to what my tongue can do
I' th' way of flattery further.

VOLUMNIA   Do your will. *Exit Volumnia.*

COMINIUS
Away! The tribunes do attend you. Arm yourself
To answer mildly; for they are prepared
With accusations, as I hear, more strong
Than are upon you yet.

CORIOLANUS
The word is 'mildly.' Pray you, let us go.   142
Let them accuse me by invention, I   143
Will answer in mine honor.   144

MENENIUS   Ay, but mildly.

CORIOLANUS
Well, mildly be't then. Mildly!   *Exeunt.*

*

Enter Sicinius and Brutus.   III,

BRUTUS
In this point charge him home, that he affects   1
Tyrannical power. If he evade us there,
Enforce him with his envy to the people,   3
And that the spoil got on the Antiates
Was ne'er distributed.
    Enter an Aedile.   What, will he come?

AEDILE
He's coming.

BRUTUS   How accompanied?

AEDILE
With old Menenius, and those senators
That always favored him.

SICINIUS   Have you a catalogue
Of all the voices that we have procured
Set down by th' poll?   10

AEDILE   I have; 'tis ready.

SICINIUS
Have you collected them by tribes?

AEDILE   I have.

SICINIUS
Assemble presently the people hither;
And when they hear me say, 'It shall be so
I' th' right and strength o' th' commons,' be it either
For death, for fine, or banishment, then let them,
If I say fine, cry 'Fine!' – if death, cry 'Death!',
Insisting on the old prerogative
And power i' th' truth o' th' cause.   18

AEDILE   I shall inform them.

BRUTUS
And when such time they have begun to cry,   19
Let them not cease, but with a din confused
Enforce the present execution
Of what we chance to sentence.

AEDILE   Very well.

SICINIUS
Make them be strong, and ready for this hint   23
When we shall hap to give't them.   24

BRUTUS   Go about it. *[Exit Aedile.]*
Put him to choler straight. He hath been used
Ever to conquer, and to have his worth   26

91 *in* into   92 *bower* boudoir   99 *unbarbed sconce* uncovered head   102 *plot* piece of earth   103 *mould* form   106 *discharge . . . life* enact convincingly   113 *quired* sang in chorus   115 *babies lulls* lulls dolls   116 *Tent* encamp; *take up* occupy   117 *glasses . . . sight* eyeballs   121 *surcease* cease   123 *inherent* irremovable   127 *dangerous stoutness* danger provoked by your obstinacy   128 *thou list* you please   130 *owe* you own   132 *mountebank* gain by artful speeches   133 *Cog* cheat   142 *word* watchword   143 *accuse . . . invention* invent accusations against me   144 *in* according to   III, iii The Roman Forum   1 *charge him home* press the charge against him; *affects* aims at   3 *Enforce* confront; *envy to* ill-will toward   10 *poll* registry of voters   18 *truth . . . cause* justice of the case   19 *when such time* in such time as; *cry* shout   23 *hint* occasion   24 *hap* chance   26 *worth* pennyworth

Óf contradiction. Being once chafed, he cannot
Be reined again to temperance; then he speaks
29   What's in his heart, and that is there which looks
With us to break his neck.

*Enter Coriolanus, Menenius, and Cominius, with
others.*

SICINIUS   Well, here he comes.

MENENIUS
Calmly, I do beseech you.

CORIOLANUS
32   Ay, as an ostler, that for th' poorest piece
33   Will bear the knave by th' volume. Th' honored gods
Keep Rome in safety, and the chairs of justice
Supplied with worthy men! plant love among's!
36   Throng our large temples with the shows of peace,
And not our streets with war!

FIRST SENATOR   Amen, amen.

MENENIUS
A noble wish.

Enter the Aedile, with the Plebeians.

SICINIUS
Draw near, ye people.

AEDILE
40   List to your tribunes. Audience! Peace, I say!

CORIOLANUS
First hear me speak.

BOTH TRIBUNES   Well, say. Peace, ho!

CORIOLANUS
42   Shall I be charged no further than this present?
43   Must all determine here?

SICINIUS   I do demand,
If you submit you to the people's voices,
45   Allow their officers, and are content
To suffer lawful censure for such faults
As shall be proved upon you?

CORIOLANUS   I am content.

MENENIUS
Lo, citizens, he says he is content.
The warlike service he has done, consider; think
50   Upon the wounds his body bears, which show
Like graves i' th' holy churchyard.

CORIOLANUS   Scratches with briars,
Scars to move laughter only.

MENENIUS   Consider further,
That when he speaks not like a citizen,
You find him like a soldier. Do not take
His rougher accents for malicious sounds,
But, as I say, such as become a soldier,
57   Rather than envy you.

COMINIUS   Well, well, no more.

CORIOLANUS
What is the matter
That being passed for consul with full voice,
I am so dishonored that the very hour
You take it off again?

SICINIUS   Answer to us.   61

CORIOLANUS
Say, then. 'Tis true, I ought so.   62

SICINIUS
We charge you that you have contrived to take
From Rome all seasoned office, and to wind   64
Yourself into a power tyrannical,
For which you are a traitor to the people.

CORIOLANUS
How? traitor?

MENENIUS   Nay, temperately! your promise.

CORIOLANUS
The fires i' th' lowest hell fold in the people!   68
Call me their traitor, thou injurious tribune!   69
Within thine eyes sat twenty thousand deaths,   70
In thy hands clutched as many millions, in
Thy lying tongue both numbers, I would say
'Thou liest' unto thee with a voice as free
As I do pray the gods.

SICINIUS   Mark you this, people?

ALL
To th' Rock, to th' Rock with him!

SICINIUS   Peace!
We need not put new matter to his charge.
What you have seen him do and heard him speak,
Beating your officers, cursing yourselves,
Opposing laws with strokes, and here defying
Those whose great power must try him – even this,
So criminal and in such capital kind,   81
Deserves th' extremest death.

BRUTUS   But since he hath
Served well for Rome –

CORIOLANUS   What do you prate of service?

BRUTUS
I talk of that, that know it.

CORIOLANUS
You?

MENENIUS
Is this the promise that you made your mother?

COMINIUS
Know, I pray you –

CORIOLANUS   I'll know no further.
Let them pronounce the steep Tarpeian death,
Vagabond exile, flaying, pent to linger   89
But with a grain a day – I would not buy
Their mercy at the price of one fair word;
Nor check my courage for what they can give,   92
To have't with saying 'Good morrow.'

SICINIUS   For that he has,   93
As much as in him lies, from time to time   94
Envied against the people, seeking means   95
To pluck away their power; as now at last   96
Given hostile strokes, and that not in the presence
Of dreaded justice, but on the ministers
That doth distribute it: i' th' name o' th' people
And in the power of us the tribunes, we,
Even from this instant, banish him our city,
In peril of precipitation   102
From off the Rock Tarpeian, never more
To enter our Rome gates. I' th' people's name,
I say it shall be so.

ALL
It shall be so! it shall be so! Let him away!
He's banished, and it shall be so!

COMINIUS
Hear me, my masters, and my common friends –
SICINIUS
He's sentenced. No more hearing.
COMINIUS   Let me speak.
I have been consul, and can show for Rome
Her enemies' marks upon me. I do love
My country's good with a respect more tender,
More holy and profound, than mine own life,
114 My dear wife's estimate, her womb's increase,
And treasure of my loins. Then if I would
Speak that –
SICINIUS   We know your drift. Speak what?
BRUTUS
117 There's no more to be said, but he is banished
As enemy to the people and his country.
It shall be so.
ALL
It shall be so! it shall be so!
CORIOLANUS
121 You common cry of curs, whose breath I hate
122 As reek o' th' rotten fens, whose loves I prize
As the dead carcasses of unburied men
That do corrupt my air, I banish you!
And here remain with your uncertainty.
Let every feeble rumor shake your hearts!
Your enemies, with nodding of their plumes,
Fan you into despair! Have the power still
To banish your defenders, till at length
130 Your ignorance – which finds not till it feels,
131 Making but reservation of yourselves,
Still your own foes – deliver you as most
133 Abated captives to some nation
That won you without blows! Despising,
135 For you, the city, thus I turn my back.
There is a world elsewhere.
            Exeunt Coriolanus, Cominius, with Menenius
            [and the other Senators].
AEDILE
The people's enemy is gone, is gone!
ALL
Our enemy is banished! he is gone!
            They all shout, and throw up their caps.
                                        Hoo! hoo!
SICINIUS
Go, see him out at gates, and follow him
As he hath followed you, with all despite;
141 Give him deserved vexation. Let a guard
Attend us through the city.
ALL
Come, come, let's see him out at gates! Come.
The gods preserve our noble tribunes! Come.   *Exeunt.*

                        *

IV, i   *Enter Coriolanus, Volumnia, Virgilia, Menenius,*
            Cominius, with the young Nobility of Rome.
CORIOLANUS
Come, leave your tears. A brief farewell. The beast
With many heads butts me away. Nay, mother,
3   Where is your ancient courage? You were used
To say extremities was the trier of spirits;
That common chances common men could bear;
That when the sea was calm all boats alike

Showed mastership in floating; fortune's blows
When most struck home, being gentle wounded craves 8
A noble cunning. You were used to load me
With precepts that would make invincible
The heart that conned them.   11
VIRGILIA
O heavens! O heavens!
CORIOLANUS   Nay, I prithee, woman –
VOLUMNIA
Now the red pestilence strike all trades in Rome,
And occupations perish!
CORIOLANUS   What, what, what!
I shall be loved when I am lacked. Nay, mother,   15
Resume that spirit when you were wont to say,
If you had been the wife of Hercules,
Six of his labors you'd have done, and saved
Your husband so much sweat. Cominius,
Droop not; adieu. Farewell, my wife, my mother.
I'll do well yet. Thou old and true Menenius,
Thy tears are salter than a younger man's,   22
And venomous to thine eyes. My sometime general, 23
I have seen thee stern, and thou hast oft beheld
Heart-hard'ning spectacles. Tell these sad women
'Tis fond to wail inevitable strokes,   26
As 'tis to laugh at 'em. My mother, you wot well 27
My hazards still have been your solace; and   28
Believe't not lightly – though I go alone,
Like to a lonely dragon, that his fen   30
Makes feared and talked of more than seen – your son
Will or exceed the common or be caught   32
With cautelous baits and practice.   33
VOLUMNIA   My first son,
Whither wilt thou go? Take good Cominius
With thee awhile. Determine on some course,
More than a wild exposure to each chance   36
That starts i' th' way before thee.
CORIOLANUS   O the gods!
COMINIUS
I'll follow thee a month, devise with thee
Where thou shalt rest, that thou mayst hear of us
And we of thee. So, if the time thrust forth
A cause for thy repeal, we shall not send   41
O'er the vast world to seek a single man,
And lose advantage, which doth ever cool
I' th' absence of the needer.
CORIOLANUS   Fare ye well.
Thou hast years upon thee, and thou art too full
Of the wars' surfeits to go rove with one   46
That's yet unbruised. Bring me but out at gate.   47
Come, my sweet wife, my dearest mother, and
My friends of noble touch. When I am forth,   49
Bid me farewell, and smile. I pray you, come.
While I remain above the ground, you shall
Hear from me still, and never of me aught

114 *estimate* value 117 *but* except that 121 *cry* pack 122 *reek* vapor
130 *finds . . . feels* learns only through experience 131 *Making . . . of*
seeking to preserve only 133 *Abated* humbled 135 *For* because of
141 *vexation* mortification
IV, i Before a gate of Rome 3 *ancient* earlier 8 *being . . . craves* to bear
one's wounds like a gentleman requires 11 *conned* studied 15 *lacked*
missed 22 *salter* saltier 23 *sometime* former 26 *fond* foolish 27 *wot*
know 28 *still* always 30 *fen* marsh 32 *or . . . common* either be exceptional 33 *cautelous* crafty; *practice* stratagem 36 *exposure* exposure 41
repeal recall 46 *surfeits* excesses 47 *Bring . . . gate* just accompany me
to the gate 49 *noble touch* tested nobility

But what is like me formerly.

MENENIUS   That's worthily
As any ear can hear. Come, let's not weep.
If I could shake off but one seven-years
From these old arms and legs, by the good gods,
I'd with thee every foot.

CORIOLANUS   Give me thy hand.
Come.   *Exeunt.*

*

IV, ii   *Enter the two Tribunes, Sicinius and Brutus, with*
               the Aedile.

  SICINIUS
1   Bid them all home. He's gone, and we'll no further.
    The nobility are vexed, whom we see have sided
    In his behalf.

  BRUTUS   Now we have shown our power,
    Let us seem humbler after it is done
5   Than when it was a-doing.

  SICINIUS   Bid them home.
    Say their great enemy is gone, and they
7   Stand in their ancient strength.

  BRUTUS   Dismiss them home. *[Exit Aedile.]*
    Here comes his mother.

  SICINIUS   Let's not meet her.

  BRUTUS   Why?

  SICINIUS
    They say she's mad.
              Enter Volumnia, Virgilia, and Menenius.

  BRUTUS
    They have ta'en note of us. Keep on your way.

  VOLUMNIA
11 O, y' are well met. The hoarded plague o' th' gods
    Requite your love!

  MENENIUS   Peace, peace. Be not so loud.

  VOLUMNIA
    If that I could for weeping, you should hear –
    Nay, and you shall hear some.
        [To Brutus]   Will you be gone?

  VIRGILIA *[to Sicinius]*
    You shall stay too. I would I had the power
    To say so to my husband.

16 SICINIUS   Are you mankind?

  VOLUMNIA
    Ay, fool, is that a shame? Note but this fool.
18 Was not a man my father? Hadst thou foxship
    To banish him that struck more blows for Rome
    Than thou hast spoken words?

  SICINIUS   O blessed heavens!

  VOLUMNIA
21 Moe noble blows than ever thou wise words,
    And for Rome's good. I'll tell thee what – Yet go.
    Nay, but thou shalt stay too. I would my son
24 Were in Arabia, and thy tribe before him,
    His good sword in his hand.

  SICINIUS   What then?

  VIRGILIA   What then?

He'ld make an end of thy posterity.

VOLUMNIA
Bastards and all.
Good man, the wounds that he does bear for Rome!

MENENIUS
Come, come, peace.

SICINIUS
I would he had continued to his country
As he began, and not unknit himself   31
The noble knot he made.

BRUTUS   I would he had.

VOLUMNIA
'I would he had'?'Twas you incensed the rabble.
Cats, that can judge as fitly of his worth
As I can of those mysteries which heaven
Will not have earth to know!

BRUTUS   Pray, let us go.

VOLUMNIA
Now, pray, sir, get you gone.
You have done a brave deed. Ere you go, hear this:
As far as doth the Capitol exceed
The meanest house in Rome, so far my son, –
This lady's husband here, this, do you see? –
Whom you have banished, does exceed you all.

BRUTUS
Well, well, we'll leave you.

SICINIUS   Why stay we to be baited
With one that wants her wits? *Exeunt Tribunes.* 44

VOLUMNIA   Take my prayers with you.
I would the gods had nothing else to do
But to confirm my curses. Could I meet 'em
But once a day, it would unclog my heart
Of what lies heavy to't.

MENENIUS   You have told them home;   48
And, by my troth, you have cause. You'll sup with me?

VOLUMNIA
Anger's my meat. I sup upon myself,
And so shall starve with feeding. Come, let's go.
Leave this faint puling, and lament as I do,   52
In anger, Juno-like. Come, come, come.

MENENIUS   Fie, fie, fie! *Exeunt.*

*

          Enter a Roman and a Volsce.   IV, iii

ROMAN I know you well, sir, and you know me. Your
name, I think, is Adrian.

VOLSCE It is so, sir. Truly, I have forgot you.

ROMAN I am a Roman; and my services are, as you are,
against 'em. Know you me yet?

VOLSCE Nicanor, no?

ROMAN The same, sir.

VOLSCE You had more beard when I last saw you; but
your favor is well appeared by your tongue. What's the 9
news in Rome? I have a note from the Volscian state to
find you out there. You have well saved me a day's
journey.

ROMAN There hath been in Rome strange insurrections:
the people against the senators, patricians, and nobles.

VOLSCE Hath been? is it ended then? Our state thinks
not so. They are in a most warlike preparation, and hope
to come upon them in the heat of their division.

ROMAN The main blaze of it is past, but a small thing
would make it flame again; for the nobles receive so to

IV, ii A street in Rome   1 *home* go home   5 *a-doing* being done   7 *ancient*
previous   11 *hoarded* accumulated   16 *mankind* masculine, human   18
foxship animal cunning   21 *Moe* more   24 *Arabia* the desert   31–32
unknit . . . knot himself undone the patriotic ties   44 *wants* lacks   48 *home*
off   52 *puling* whimpering
IV, iii The highway to Antium   9 *favor* face; *appeared* made apparent

1241

heart the banishment of that worthy Coriolanus that
they are in a ripe aptness to take all power from the
people and to pluck from them their tribunes for ever.
This lies glowing, I can tell you, and is almost mature
for the violent breaking out.

VOLSCE Coriolanus banished?

ROMAN Banished, sir.

VOLSCE You will be welcome with this intelligence, Nicanor.

28 ROMAN The day serves well for them now. I have heard it
said, the fittest time to corrupt a man's wife is when she's
fall'n out with her husband. Your noble Tullus Aufidius
will appear well in these wars, his great opposer, Coriolanus, being now in no request of his country.

33 VOLSCE He cannot choose. I am most fortunate, thus
accidentally to encounter you. You have ended my
business, and I will merrily accompany you home.

36 ROMAN I shall, between this and supper, tell you most
strange things from Rome, all tending to the good of
their adversaries. Have you an army ready, say you?

39 VOLSCE A most royal one: the centurions and their
40 charges, distinctly billeted, already in th' entertainment,
and to be on foot at an hour's warning.

ROMAN I am joyful to hear of their readiness, and am the
man, I think, that shall set them in present action. So,
sir, heartily well met, and most glad of your company.

VOLSCE You take my part from me, sir. I have the most
cause to be glad of yours.

ROMAN Well, let us go together.   *Exeunt.*

*

IV, iv   *Enter Coriolanus in mean apparel, disguised and*
         muffled.

CORIOLANUS
   A goodly city is this Antium. City,
   'Tis I that made thy widows. Many an heir
3   Of these fair edifices 'fore my wars
   Have I heard groan and drop. Then know me not,
   Lest that thy wives with spits and boys with stones
6   In puny battle slay me.
       Enter a Citizen.   Save you, sir.

CITIZEN
   And you.

CORIOLANUS Direct me, if it be your will,
8   Where great Aufidius lies. Is he in Antium?

CITIZEN
   He is, and feasts the nobles of the state
   At his house this night.

CORIOLANUS   Which is his house, beseech you?

CITIZEN
   This, here before you.

CORIOLANUS   Thank you, sir. Farewell.
                          Exit Citizen.
   O world, thy slippery turns! Friends now fast sworn,
   Whose double bosoms seems to wear one heart,
   Whose hours, whose bed, whose meal and exercise
15   Are still together; who twin, as 'twere, in love
   Unseparable, shall within this hour,
17   On a dissension of a doit, break out
18   To bitterest enmity. So, fellest foes,
   Whose passions and whose plots have broke their sleep
   To take the one the other, by some chance,
21   Some trick not worth an egg, shall grow dear friends

And interjoin their issues. So with me.   22
My birthplace hate I, and my love's upon
This enemy town. I'll enter. If he slay me,
He does fair justice; if he give me way,   25
I'll do his country service.   *Exit.*

*

      Music plays. Enter a Servingman.   IV,

FIRST SERVINGMAN Wine, wine, wine! What service is
here? I think our fellows are asleep.   *[Exit.]* 2
      Enter another Servingman.

SECOND SERVINGMAN Where's Cotus? My master calls
for him. Cotus!   *Exit.*
      Enter Coriolanus.

CORIOLANUS
   A goodly house. The feast smells well, but I
   Appear not like a guest.
      Enter the first Servingman.

FIRST SERVINGMAN What would you have, friend?
Whence are you? Here's no place for you. Pray, go to
the door.   *Exit.*

CORIOLANUS
   I have deserved no better entertainment,
   In being Coriolanus.
      Enter second Servant.

SECOND SERVINGMAN Whence are you, sir? Has the
porter his eyes in his head, that he gives entrance to such
companions? Pray, get you out.

CORIOLANUS Away!

SECOND SERVINGMAN Away? get you away!

CORIOLANUS Now th' art troublesome.

SECOND SERVINGMAN Are you so brave? I'll have you
talked with anon.   18
      Enter third Servingman; the first meets him.

THIRD SERVINGMAN What fellow's this?

FIRST SERVINGMAN A strange one as ever I looked on. I
cannot get him out o' th' house. Prithee, call my master
to him.

THIRD SERVINGMAN What have you to do here, fellow?
Pray you, avoid the house.   23

CORIOLANUS Let me but stand; I will not hurt your
hearth.

THIRD SERVINGMAN What are you?

CORIOLANUS A gentleman.

THIRD SERVINGMAN A marv'llous poor one.   27

CORIOLANUS True, so I am.

THIRD SERVINGMAN Pray you, poor gentleman, take up
some other station. Here's no place for you. Pray you,
avoid. Come.

CORIOLANUS Follow your function, go, and batten on 32
cold bits.
      Pushes him away from him.

THIRD SERVINGMAN What, you will not? Prithee, tell
my master what a strange guest he has here.

---

28 *them* the Volscians   33 *choose* help appearing well   36 *this* now   39
centurions officers each commanding a century, i.e. a hundred men   40
distinctly separately; *entertainment* service

IV, iv Before the house of Aufidius in Antium   3 *'fore* before   6 *puny*
petty; *Save God* save   8 *lies* lodges   15 *still* always   17 *dissension* . . .
doit trivial dispute   18 *fellest* fiercest   21 *trick* trifle   22 *interjoin their*
issues join fortunes   25 *give me way* grant my request

IV, v Within the house of Aufidius   2 *fellows* companions   18 *anon* at once
23 *avoid* leave   27 *marv'llous* curiously   32 *batten* grow fat

SECOND SERVINGMAN And I shall.

Exit second Servingman.

THIRD SERVINGMAN Where dwell'st thou?

38 CORIOLANUS Under the canopy.

THIRD SERVINGMAN Under the canopy?

CORIOLANUS Ay.

THIRD SERVINGMAN Where's that?

42 CORIOLANUS I' th' city of kites and crows.

THIRD SERVINGMAN I' th' city of kites and crows?
44   What an ass it is! Then thou dwell'st with daws too?

CORIOLANUS No, I serve not thy master.

THIRD SERVINGMAN How, sir? Do you meddle with
my master?

CORIOLANUS Ay, 'tis an honester service than to meddle
with thy mistress.

50   Thou prat'st, and prat'st. Serve with thy trencher.
Hence!

Beats him away.

Enter Aufidius with the [second] Servingman.

AUFIDIUS Where is this fellow?

SECOND SERVINGMAN Here, sir. I'd have beaten him
like a dog, but for disturbing the lords within.

AUFIDIUS
Whence com'st thou? What wouldst thou? Thy name?
Why speak'st not? Speak, man. What's thy name?

CORIOLANUS   If, Tullus,
Not yet thou know'st me, and, seeing me, dost not
57 Think me for the man I am, necessity
58 Commands me name myself.

AUFIDIUS   What is thy name?

CORIOLANUS
A name unmusical to the Volscians' ears,
And harsh in sound to thine.

AUFIDIUS   Say, what's thy name?
Thou hast a grim appearance, and thy face
Bears a command in't; though thy tackle 's torn,
Thou show'st a noble vessel. What's thy name?

CORIOLANUS
Prepare thy brow to frown. Know'st thou me yet?

AUFIDIUS
I know thee not. Thy name?

CORIOLANUS
My name is Caius Marcius, who hath done
To thee particularly and to all the Volsces
Great hurt and mischief; thereto witness may
69 My surname, Coriolanus. The painful service,
The extreme dangers, and the drops of blood
Shed for my thankless country are requited
72 But with that surname – a good memory,
And witness of the malice and displeasure
Which thou shouldst bear me. Only that name remains.
75 The cruelty and envy of the people,
Permitted by our dastard nobles, who
Have all forsook me, hath devoured the rest;

And suffered me by th' voice of slaves to be
Whooped out of Rome. Now this extremity   79
Hath brought me to thy hearth, not out of hope –
Mistake me not – to save my life; for if
I had feared death, of all the men i' th' world
I would have 'voided thee; but in mere spite,   83
To be full quit of those my banishers,   84
Stand I before thee here. Then if thou hast
A heart of wreak in thee, that wilt revenge   86
Thine own particular wrongs, and stop those maims
Of shame seen through thy country, speed thee straight,
And make my misery serve thy turn. So use it
That my revengeful services may prove
As benefits to thee; for I will fight
Against my cank'red country with the spleen   92
Of all the under fiends. But if so be   93
Thou dar'st not this, and that to prove more fortunes   94
Th' art tired, then, in a word, I also am
Longer to live most weary; and present
My throat to thee and to thy ancient malice;
Which not to cut would show thee but a fool,
Since I have ever followed thee with hate,
Drawn tuns of blood out of thy country's breast,
And cannot live but to thy shame, unless
It be to do thee service.

AUFIDIUS   O Marcius, Marcius!
Each word thou hast spoke hath weeded from my heart
A root of ancient envy. If Jupiter
Should from yond cloud speak divine things,
And say ''Tis true,' I'd not believe them more
Than thee, all-noble Marcius. Let me twine
Mine arms about thy body, whereagainst   108
My grainèd ash an hundred times hath broke,   109
And scarred the moon with splinters. Here I clip   110
The anvil of my sword, and do contest
As hotly and as nobly with thy love
As ever in ambitious strength I did
Contend against thy valor. Know thou first,
I loved the maid I married; never man
Sighed truer breath. But that I see thee here,
Thou noble thing, more dances my rapt heart   117
Than when I first my wedded mistress saw
Bestride my threshold. Why, thou Mars, I tell thee,   119
We have a power on foot; and I had purpose
Once more to hew thy target from thy brawn,   121
Or lose mine arm for't. Thou hast beat me out   122
Twelve several times, and I have nightly since   123
Dreamt of encounters 'twixt thyself and me.
We have been down together in my sleep,
Unbuckling helms, fisting each other's throat,
And waked half dead with nothing. Worthy Marcius,   127
Had we no other quarrel else to Rome, but that   128
Thou art thence banished, we would muster all
From twelve to seventy, and, pouring war
Into the bowels of ungrateful Rome,
Like a bold flood o'erbeat. O, come, go in,   132
And take our friendly senators by th' hands,
Who now are here, taking their leaves of me,
Who am prepared against your territories,
Though not for Rome itself.

CORIOLANUS   You bless me, gods!

AUFIDIUS
Therefore, most absolute sir, if thou wilt have   137
The leading of thine own revenges, take

139 Th' one half of my commission; and set down –
As best thou art experienced, since thou know'st
Thy country's strength and weakness – thine own ways,
Whether to knock against the gates of Rome,
Or rudely visit them in parts remote,
144 To fright them ere destroy. But come in.
Let me commend thee first to those that shall
Say yea to thy desires. A thousand welcomes!
And more a friend than e'er an enemy;
Yet, Marcius, that was much. Your hand. Most welcome!   *Exeunt.*

Enter two of the Servingmen.

FIRST SERVINGMAN Here's a strange alteration!

SECOND SERVINGMAN By my hand, I had thought to
151 have strucken him with a cudgel; and yet my mind gave
me his clothes made a false report of him.

FIRST SERVINGMAN What an arm he has! He turned
me about with his finger and his thumb as one would set
up a top.

SECOND SERVINGMAN Nay, I knew by his face that
there was something in him. He had, sir, a kind of face,
methought – I cannot tell how to term it.

FIRST SERVINGMAN He had so, looking as it were –
Would I were hanged, but I thought there was more in
him than I could think.

SECOND SERVINGMAN So did I, I'll be sworn. He is
simply the rarest man i' th' world.

FIRST SERVINGMAN I think he is. But a greater soldier
164 than he you wot on.

SECOND SERVINGMAN Who, my master?

166 FIRST SERVINGMAN Nay, it's no matter for that.

SECOND SERVINGMAN Worth six on him.

FIRST SERVINGMAN Nay, not so neither. But I take him
to be the greater soldier.

SECOND SERVINGMAN Faith, look you, one cannot tell
how to say that. For the defense of a town, our general is
excellent.

FIRST SERVINGMAN Ay, and for an assault too.

Enter the third Servingman.

THIRD SERVINGMAN O slaves, I can tell you news.
News, you rascals!

BOTH [FIRST AND SECOND] What, what, what? Let's
partake.

THIRD SERVINGMAN I would not be a Roman, of all
nations. I had as lief be a condemned man.

BOTH Wherefore? Wherefore?

180 THIRD SERVINGMAN Why, here's he that was wont to
thwack our general, Caius Marcius.

FIRST SERVINGMAN Why do you say, 'thwack our
general'?

THIRD SERVINGMAN I do not say, 'thwack our general,'
but he was always good enough for him.

SECOND SERVINGMAN Come, we are fellows and friends.
He was ever too hard for him; I have heard him say so
himself.

FIRST SERVINGMAN He was too hard for him directly,
189 to say the troth on't. Before Corioles he scotched him
190 and notched him like a carbonado.

191 SECOND SERVINGMAN An he had been cannibally given,
he might have boiled and eaten him too.

FIRST SERVINGMAN But more of thy news?

194 THIRD SERVINGMAN Why, he is so made on here within,
as if he were son and heir to Mars; set at upper end o' th'
196 table; no question asked him by any of the senators, but

they stand bald before him. Our general himself makes a 197
mistress of him; sanctifies himself with's hand, and 198
turns up the white o' th' eye to his discourse. But the
bottom of the news is, our general is cut i' th' middle
and but one half of what he was yesterday; for the other
has half, by the entreaty and grant of the whole table.
He'll go, he says, and sowl the porter of Rome gates by 203
th' ears. He will mow all down before him, and leave
his passage polled. 205

SECOND SERVINGMAN And he's as like to do't as any
man I can imagine.

THIRD SERVINGMAN Do't? he will do't! for, look you,
sir, he has as many friends as enemies; which friends,
sir, as it were, durst not, look you, sir, show themselves,
as we term it, his friends whilst he's in directitude. 211

FIRST SERVINGMAN Directitude? what's that?

THIRD SERVINGMAN But when they shall see, sir, his
crest up again, and the man in blood, they will out of
their burrows like conies after rain, and revel all with him. 215

FIRST SERVINGMAN But when goes this forward?

THIRD SERVINGMAN To-morrow, to-day, presently. 217
You shall have the drum struck up this afternoon. 'Tis,
as it were, a parcel of their feast, and to be executed ere 219
they wipe their lips.

SECOND SERVINGMAN Why, then we shall have a stirring world again. This peace is nothing but to rust iron,
increase tailors, and breed ballad-makers.

FIRST SERVINGMAN Let me have war, say I. It exceeds
peace as far as day does night. It's sprightly, waking,
audible, and full of vent. Peace is a very apoplexy, 226
lethargy; mulled, deaf, sleepy, insensible; a getter of 227
more bastard children than war 's a destroyer of men.

SECOND SERVINGMAN 'Tis so; and as war, in some sort,
may be said to be a ravisher, so it cannot be denied but
peace is a great maker of cuckolds.

FIRST SERVINGMAN Ay, and it makes men hate one another.

THIRD SERVINGMAN Reason: because they then less
need one another. The wars for my money. I hope to see
Romans as cheap as Volscians. They are rising, they are
rising.

BOTH [FIRST AND SECOND] In, in, in, in!   *Exeunt.*

                     *

Enter the two Tribunes, Sicinius and Brutus.   IV

SICINIUS
We hear not of him, neither need we fear him;
His remedies are tame: the present peace 2
And quietness of the people, which before
Were in wild hurry. Here do we make his friends
Blush that the world goes well, who rather had,
Though they themselves did suffer by't, behold 6
Dissentious numbers pest'ring streets than see 7

139 *commission* command; *set down* decide   144 *ere destroy* before destroying them   151 *gave* suggested to   164 *wot on* know of   166 *it's . . . that* never mind about names   189 *troth* truth; *scotched* slashed   190 *carbonado* meat cut for broiling   191 *An* if   194 *made on* made much of   196 *but* unless   197 *bald* bareheaded   198 *sanctifies . . . hand* touches his hand as if it were a sacred relic   203 *sowl* pull roughly   205 *polled* stripped bare   211 *directitude* discredit (verbal blunder)   215 *conies* rabbits   217 *presently* immediately   219 *parcel* part   226 *audible* capable of hearing; *apoplexy* paralysis   227 *mulled* stupefied; *getter* begetter
IV, vi A public place in Rome   2 *His remedies* the remedies against him; *tame* mild   6 *behold* beheld   7 *pest'ring* crowding

Our tradesmen singing in their shops and going
About their functions friendly.

BRUTUS
10 We stood to't in good time.
       Enter Menenius.   Is this Menenius?

SICINIUS
'Tis he, 'tis he! O, he is grown most kind of late. –
Hail, sir!

MENENIUS Hail to you both!

SICINIUS   Your Coriolanus
Is not much missed, but with his friends.
The commonwealth doth stand, and so would do,
Were he more angry at it.

MENENIUS
All's well; and might have been much better, if
17 He could have temporized.

SICINIUS   Where is he, hear you?

MENENIUS
Nay, I hear nothing. His mother and his wife
Hear nothing from him.
       Enter three or four Citizens.

ALL
The gods preserve you both!

20 SICINIUS   Good-e'en, our neighbors.

BRUTUS
Good-e'en to you all, good-e'en to you all.

FIRST CITIZEN
Ourselves, our wives, and children, on our knees,
Are bound to pray for you both.

SICINIUS   Live, and thrive!

BRUTUS
Farewell, kind neighbors. We wished Coriolanus
Had loved you as we did.

CITIZENS   Now the gods keep you!

BOTH TRIBUNES
Farewell, farewell.   *Exeunt Citizens.*

SICINIUS
27 This is a happier and more comely time
Than when these fellows ran about the streets,
Crying confusion.

BRUTUS   Caius Marcius was
A worthy officer i' th' war, but insolent,
O'ercome with pride, ambitious past all thinking,
Self-loving –

SICINIUS   And affecting one sole throne
33 Without assistance.

MENENIUS   I think not so.

SICINIUS
34 We should by this, to all our lamentation,
If he had gone forth consul, found it so.

BRUTUS
The gods have well prevented it, and Rome
Sits safe and still without him.
       Enter an Aedile.

AEDILE   Worthy tribunes,
There is a slave whom we have put in prison

Reports the Volsces with two several powers   39
Are ent'red in the Roman territories,
And with the deepest malice of the war
Destroy what lies before 'em.

MENENIUS   'Tis Aufidius,
Who, hearing of our Marcius' banishment,
Thrusts forth his horns again into the world;
Which were inshelled when Marcius stood for Rome,   45
And durst not once peep out.

SICINIUS   Come, what talk you
Of Marcius?

BRUTUS
Go see this rumorer whipped. It cannot be
The Volsces dare break with us.

MENENIUS   Cannot be!
We have record that very well it can,
And three examples of the like hath been
Within my age. But reason with the fellow,   52
Before you punish him, where he heard this,
Lest you shall chance to whip your information   54
And beat the messenger who bids beware
Of what is to be dreaded.

SICINIUS   Tell not me.
I know this cannot be.

BRUTUS   Not possible.
       Enter a Messenger.

MESSENGER
The nobles in great earnestness are going
All to the Senate House. Some news is coming
That turns their countenances.   60

SICINIUS   'Tis this slave –
Go whip him 'fore the people's eyes – his raising,   61
Nothing but his report.

MESSENGER   Yes, worthy sir.
The slave's report is seconded; and more,   63
More fearful, is delivered.   64

SICINIUS   What more fearful?

MESSENGER
It is spoke freely out of many mouths –
How probable I do not know – that Marcius,
Joined with Aufidius, leads a power 'gainst Rome,
And vows revenge as spacious as between   68
The young'st and oldest thing.

SICINIUS   This is most likely!

BRUTUS
Raised only, that the weaker sort may wish   70
Good Marcius home again.

SICINIUS   The very trick on't.

MENENIUS
This is unlikely.
He and Aufidius can no more atone   73
Than violent'st contrariety.   74
       Enter [another] Messenger.

MESSENGER
You are sent for to the Senate.
A fearful army, led by Caius Marcius
Associated with Aufidius, rages
Upon our territories; and have already
O'erborne their way, consumed with fire, and took   79
What lay before them.
       Enter Cominius.

COMINIUS   O, you have made good work!

MENENIUS
What news? What news?

---

10 *stood to't* took a stand   17 *temporized* compromised   20 *Good-e'en* good evening   27 *comely* decent   33 *assistance* partners   34 *this* this time   39 *several* separate   45 *inshelled* drawn in; *stood* stood up   52 *reason* discuss   54 *information* source of information   60 *turns* changes   61 *raising* incitement   63 *seconded* confirmed   64 *delivered* reported   68–69 *as spacious . . . thing* embracing all   70 *Raised* set going   73 *atone* be reconciled   74 *violent'st contrariety* opposite extremes   79 *O'erborne* crushed down

COMINIUS
82 You have holp to ravish your own daughters and
83 To melt the city leads upon your pates,
To see your wives dishonored to your noses, –

MENENIUS
What's the news? What's the news?

COMINIUS
Your temples burnèd in their cement, and
87 Your franchises, whereon you stood, confined
88 Into an auger's bore.

MENENIUS   Pray now, your news? –
You have made fair work, I fear me. – Pray, your news? –
If Marcius should be joined with Volscians –

COMINIUS   If?
He is their god. He leads them like a thing
Made by some other deity than nature,
That shapes man better; and they follow him
Against us brats with no less confidence
Than boys pursuing summer butterflies
Or butchers killing flies.

MENENIUS   You have made good work,
You and your apron-men! you that stood so much
98 Upon the voice of occupation and
The breath of garlic-eaters!

COMINIUS   He'll shake
Your Rome about your ears.

MENENIUS   As Hercules
101 Did shake down mellow fruit. You have made fair work!

BRUTUS
But is this true, sir?

COMINIUS   Ay, and you'll look pale
Before you find it other. All the regions
104 Do smilingly revolt; and who resists
Are mocked for valiant ignorance,
106 And perish constant fools. Who is't can blame him?
Your enemies and his find something in him.

MENENIUS
We are all undone, unless
The noble man have mercy.

COMINIUS   Who shall ask it?
The tribunes cannot do't for shame; the people
Deserve such pity of him as the wolf
Does of the shepherds. For his best friends, if they
113 Should say, 'Be good to Rome,' they charged him even
As those should do that had deserved his hate,
115 And therein showed like enemies.

MENENIUS   'Tis true.
If he were putting to my house the brand
That should consume it, I have not the face
118 To say, 'Beseech you, cease.' You have made fair hands,
119 You and your crafts! You have crafted fair!

COMINIUS   You have brought
A trembling upon Rome, such as was never
S' incapable of help.

TRIBUNES   Say not we brought it.

MENENIUS
How? Was 't we? We loved him; but, like beasts
123 And cowardly nobles, gave way unto your clusters,
Who did hoot him out o' th' city.

COMINIUS   But I fear
They'll roar him in again. Tullus Aufidius,
126 The second name of men, obeys his points
As if he were his officer. Desperation
Is all the policy, strength, and defense

That Rome can make against them.
Enter a troop of Citizens.

MENENIUS   Here come the clusters.
And is Aufidius with him? – You are they
That made the air unwholesome, when you cast
Your stinking greasy caps in hooting at
Coriolanus' exile. Now he's coming;
And not a hair upon a soldier's head
Which will not prove a whip. As many coxcombs   135
As you threw caps up will he tumble down,
And pay you for your voices. 'Tis no matter.
If he could burn us all into one coal,
We have deserved it.

OMNES
Faith, we hear fearful news.

FIRST CITIZEN   For mine own part,   140
When I said banish him, I said 'twas pity.

SECOND CITIZEN And so did I.

THIRD CITIZEN And so did I; and, to say the truth, so
did very many of us. That we did, we did for the best;
and though we willingly consented to his banishment,
yet it was against our will.

COMINIUS
Y' are goodly things, you voices!

MENENIUS   You have made
Good work, you and your cry! Shall's to the Capitol?   148

COMINIUS
O, ay, what else?   *Exeunt both.*

SICINIUS
Go, masters, get you home; be not dismayed.
These are a side that would be glad to have
This true, which they so seem to fear. Go home,
And show no sign of fear.

FIRST CITIZEN The gods be good to us! Come, masters,
let's home. I ever said we were i' th' wrong when we
banished him.

SECOND CITIZEN So did we all. But come, let's home.
Exeunt Citizens.

BRUTUS
I do not like this news.

SICINIUS   Nor I.

BRUTUS
Let's to the Capitol. Would half my wealth   160
Would buy this for a lie!

SICINIUS   Pray, let us go.
Exeunt Tribunes.

*

Enter Aufidius, with his Lieutenant.   IV, v

AUFIDIUS
Do they still fly to th' Roman?

LIEUTENANT
I do not know what witchcraft 's in him, but
Your soldiers use him as the grace 'fore meat,

82 *holp* helped 83 *leads* leaden roofs 87 *franchises* political rights;
whereon you stood on which you insisted 88 *auger's bore* smallest aperture
98 *voice of occupation* mechanics' suffrage 101 *fruit* apples of Hesperides
104 *who* whoever 106 *constant* loyal 113 *charged* would enjoin 115
showed would appear 118 *made fair hands* done a fine job (ironic) 119
crafted fair intrigued beautifully 123 *clusters* crowds 126 *of* among;
points directions 135 *coxcombs* fool's caps 140 *For . . . part* speaking for
myself 148 *cry* pack; *Shall's* shall us 160–61 *Would . . . lie* I would
give half my fortune if this were untrue
IV, vii A camp near Rome

Their talk at table, and their thanks at end ;
5   And you are dark'ned in this action, sir,
Even by your own.
AUFIDIUS   I cannot help it now,
7   Unless by using means I lame the foot
Of our design. He bears himself more proudlier,
Even to my person, than I thought he would
When first I did embrace him. Yet his nature
11 In that's no changeling, and I must excuse
What cannot be amended.
LIEUTENANT   Yet I wish, sir, –
13 I mean for your particular – you had not
Joined in commission with him ; but either
Had borne the action of yourself, or else
To him had left it solely.
AUFIDIUS
I understand thee well ; and be thou sure,
When he shall come to his account, he knows not
What I can urge against him. Although it seems,
And so he thinks, and is no less apparent
To th' vulgar eye, that he bears all things fairly,
22 And shows good husbandry for the Volscian state,
23 Fights dragon-like, and does achieve as soon
As draw his sword : yet he hath left undone
That which shall break his neck or hazard mine,
Whene'er we come to our account.
LIEUTENANT
27 Sir, I beseech you, think you he'll carry Rome ?
AUFIDIUS
28 All places yield to him ere he sits down,
And the nobility of Rome are his ;
The senators and patricians love him too.
The tribunes are no soldiers, and their people
Will be as rash in the repeal as hasty
To expel him thence. I think he'll be to Rome
34 As is the osprey to the fish, who takes it
35 By sovereignty of nature. First he was
A noble servant to them, but he could not
37 Carry his honors even. Whether 'twas pride,
38 Which out of daily fortune ever taints
The happy man ; whether defect of judgment,
40 To fail in the disposing of those chances
41 Which he was lord of ; or whether nature,
Not to be other than one thing, not moving
43 From th' casque to th' cushion, but commanding peace
Even with the same austerity and garb
As he controlled the war ; but one of these,
46 As he hath spices of them all, – not all,
47 For I dare so far free him – made him feared,

So hated, and so banished. But he has a merit,
To choke it in the utt'rance. So our virtues   49
Lie in th' interpretation of the time ;   50
And power, unto itself most commendable,
Hath not a tomb so evident as a chair   52
T' extol what it hath done.
One fire drives out one fire ; one nail, one nail ;
Rights by rights founder, strengths by strengths do fail.
Come, let's away. When, Caius, Rome is thine,
Thou art poor'st of all ; then shortly art thou mine.   57
                          Exeunt.

*

Enter Menenius, Cominius ; Sicinius, Brutus, the   V, i
   two Tribunes ; with others.
MENENIUS
No, I'll not go. You hear what he hath said
Which was sometime his general, who loved him   2
In a most dear particular. He called me father.   3
But what o' that ? Go, you that banished him ;
A mile before his tent fall down, and knee   5
The way into his mercy. Nay, if he coyed   6
To hear Cominius speak, I'll keep at home.   7
COMINIUS
He would not seem to know me.   8
MENENIUS   Do you hear ?
COMINIUS
Yet one time he did call me by my name.
I urged our old acquaintance, and the drops
That we have bled together. Coriolanus
He would not answer to ; forbade all names.
He was a kind of nothing, titleless,
Till he had forged himself a name o' th' fire   14
Of burning Rome.
MENENIUS   Why, so. – You have made good work !
A pair of tribunes that have racked for Rome,   16
To make coals cheap ! A noble memory !
COMINIUS
I minded him how royal 'twas to pardon   18
When it was less expected. He replied,
It was a bare petition of a state   20
To one whom they had punished.
MENENIUS   Very well.
Could he say less ?
COMINIUS
I offered to awaken his regard   23
For's private friends. His answer to me was,
He could not stay to pick them in a pile   25
Of noisome musty chaff. He said 'twas folly,
For one poor grain or two, to leave unburnt
And still to nose th' offense.   28
MENENIUS   For one poor grain or two ?
I am one of those ! His mother, wife, his child,
And this brave fellow too, we are the grains ;
You are the musty chaff, and you are smelt
Above the moon. We must be burnt for you.
SICINIUS
Nay, pray, be patient. If you refuse your aid
In this so-never-needed help, yet do not   34
Upbraid's with our distress. But, sure, if you
Would be your country's pleader, your good tongue,
More than the instant army we can make,
Might stop our countryman.
MENENIUS   No, I'll not meddle.

5 *dark'ned* eclipsed   7 *means* means whereby   11 *In . . . changeling* is not inconstant in that respect   13 *for your particular* in your own interests   22 *husbandry* management   23 *achieve* carry out his intention   27 *carry* win   28 *ere . . . down* before he lays siege   34 *osprey* fish-hawk   35 *sovereignty* predominance   37 *even* without losing his equilibrium   38 *daily fortune* uninterrupted success ; *taints* corrupts   40 *disposing* making good use of   41 *nature* character   43 *casque* general's helmet ; *cushion* senator's seat   46 *spices . . . all* a tincture of each   47 *free* absolve   49 *To . . . utt'rance* enough to suppress the recital of his faults   50 *the time* our contemporaries   52 *not . . . chair* no memorial so certain as a public rostrum   57 *shortly* soon
V, i A public place in Rome   2 *Which* who ; *sometime* formerly   3 *In . . . particular* with warmest personal affection   5 *knee* crawl   6 *coyed* disdained   7 *keep* stay   8 *would not seem* pretended not   14 *o'* out of   16 *racked* striven   18 *minded* reminded   20 *bare* mere   23 *offered* attempted   25 *stay . . . them* stop to pick them out   28 *nose* smell ; *offense* offensive matter   34 *so-never-needed* never so much needed

SICINIUS
Pray you, go to him.
MENENIUS   What should I do?
BRUTUS
Only make trial what your love can do
For Rome toward Marcius.
MENENIUS   Well, and say that Marcius
42 Return me, as Cominius is returned,
Unheard – what then?
44 But as a discontented friend, grief-shot
With his unkindness? Say't be so?
SICINIUS   Yet your good will
46 Must have that thanks from Rome, after the measure
As you intended well.
MENENIUS   I'll undertake't:
I think he'll hear me. Yet, to bite his lip
49 And hum at good Cominius much unhearts me.
50 He was not taken well; he had not dined.
The veins unfilled, our blood is cold, and then
We pout upon the morning, are unapt
To give or to forgive; but when we have stuffed
54 These pipes and these conveyances of our blood
With wine and feeding, we have supper souls
56 Than in our priest-like fasts. Therefore I'll watch him
57 Till he be dieted to my request,
And then I'll set upon him.
BRUTUS
You know the very road into his kindness,
And cannot lose your way.
MENENIUS   Good faith, I'll prove him,
Speed how it will. I shall ere long have knowledge
62 Of my success.   *Exit.*
COMINIUS   He'll never hear him.
SICINIUS   Not?
COMINIUS
63 I tell you, he does sit in gold, his eye
64 Red as 'twould burn Rome, and his injury
The jailer to his pity. I kneeled before him.
'Twas very faintly he said, 'Rise'; dismissed me
Thus, with his speechless hand. What he would do
He sent in writing after me; what he would not
69 Bound with an oath to yield to his conditions;
So that all hope is vain
71 Unless his noble mother and his wife,
Who, as I hear, mean to solicit him
For mercy to his country. Therefore let's hence,
74 And with our fair entreaties haste them on.   *Exeunt.*

*

V, ii   *Enter Menenius to the Watch on guard.*
FIRST WATCH
Stay. Whence are you?
SECOND WATCH   Stand, and go back.
MENENIUS
You guard like men; 'tis well. But, by your leave,
I am an officer of state, and come
To speak with Coriolanus.
FIRST WATCH   From whence?
MENENIUS   From Rome.
FIRST WATCH
You may not pass; you must return. Our general
Will no more hear from thence.

SECOND WATCH
You'll see your Rome embraced with fire before
You'll speak with Coriolanus.
MENENIUS   Good my friends,   8
If you have heard your general talk of Rome
And of his friends there, it is lots to blanks   10
My name hath touched your ears. It is Menenius.
FIRST WATCH
Be't so; go back. The virtue of your name
Is not here passable.
MENENIUS   I tell thee, fellow,
Thy general is my lover. I have been   14
The book of his good acts, whence men have read
His fame unparalleled, haply amplified;   16
For I have ever verified my friends,   17
Of whom he's chief, with all the size that verity
Would without lapsing suffer. Nay, sometimes,
Like to a bowl upon a subtle ground,   20
I have tumbled past the throw; and in his praise
Have almost stamped the leasing. Therefore, fellow,   22
I must have leave to pass.
FIRST WATCH Faith, sir, if you had told as many lies in
his behalf as you have uttered words in your own, you
should not pass here; no, though it were as virtuous to
lie as to live chastely. Therefore go back.   27
MENENIUS Prithee, fellow, remember my name is
Menenius, always factionary on the party of your   29
general.
SECOND WATCH Howsoever you have been his liar, as
you say you have, I am one that, telling true under him,
must say you cannot pass. Therefore go back.
MENENIUS Has he dined, canst thou tell? For I would
not speak with him till after dinner.
FIRST WATCH You are a Roman, are you?
MENENIUS I am, as thy general is.
FIRST WATCH Then you should hate Rome, as he does.
Can you, when you have pushed out your gates the very   38
defender of them, and in a violent popular ignorance
given your enemy your shield, think to front his re-   40
venges with the easy groans of old women, the virginal
palms of your daughters, or with the palsied intercession
of such a decayed dotant as you seem to be? Can you   43
think to blow out the intended fire your city is ready to
flame in, with such weak breath as this? No, you are
deceived; therefore back to Rome, and prepare for your
execution. You are condemned; our general has sworn
you out of reprieve and pardon.   48
MENENIUS Sirrah, if thy captain knew I were here, he
would use me with estimation.   50
FIRST WATCH Come, my captain knows you not.
MENENIUS I mean thy general.
FIRST WATCH My general cares not for you. Back, I say,

42 *Return* send away   44 *grief-shot* sorrow-stricken   46–47 *after . . . As*
to the extent that   49 *unhearts* disheartens   50 *taken well* approached
opportunely   54 *conveyances* channels   56 *watch* wait for   57 *dieted to*
fed to the point of entertaining   62 *success* result   63 *does . . . gold* is
enthroned   64 *injury* sense of injury   69 *Bound* he bound; *to yield* that
we should yield   71 *Unless* except for   74 *fair* courteous
V, ii The Volscian camp before Rome   8 *Good my friends* my good friends
10 *lots* prizes; *blanks* lottery tickets without value   14 *lover* well-wisher
16 *haply* possibly   17 *verified* supported the credit of   20 *bowl* wooden
ball; *subtle* deceptive   22 *stamped* attested; *leasing* falsehood   27 *chastely*
honestly   29 *factionary* partisan   38 *out* out of   40 *front* meet   43 *dotant*
dotard   48 *out of* beyond   50 *use* treat; *estimation* esteem

go! lest I let forth your half-pint of blood, – back! –
55 that's the utmost of your having. Back!
MENENIUS Nay, but, fellow, fellow –
     Enter Coriolanus and Aufidius.
CORIOLANUS What's the matter?
MENENIUS Now, you companion, I'll say an errand for
  you. You shall know now that I am in estimation; you
60 shall perceive that a Jack guardant cannot office me
61 from my son Coriolanus. Guess but by my entertainment with him. If thou stand'st not i' th' state of hang-
63 ing, or of some death more long in spectatorship and
  crueler in suffering, behold now presently, and swound
  for what's to come upon thee. *[to Coriolanus]* The
  glorious gods sit in hourly synod about thy particular
  prosperity, and love thee no worse than thy old father
  Menenius does! O my son, my son! Thou art preparing
  fire for us. Look thee, here's water to quench it. I was
70 hardly moved to come to thee; but being assured none
  but myself could move thee, I have been blown out of
  our gates with sighs; and conjure thee to pardon Rome
73 and thy petitionary countrymen. The good gods assuage
  thy wrath, and turn the dregs of it upon this varlet here
75 – this, who, like a block, hath denied my access to thee.
CORIOLANUS Away!
MENENIUS How? away?
CORIOLANUS
Wife, mother, child, I know not. My affairs
79 Are servanted to others. Though I owe
80 My revenge properly, my remission lies
  In Volscian breasts. That we have been familiar,
82 Ingrate forgetfulness shall poison, rather
  Than pity note how much. Therefore be gone.
  Mine ears against your suits are stronger than
85 Your gates against my force. Yet, for I loved thee,
  Take this along. I writ it for thy sake,
     [Gives a letter.]
  And would have sent it. Another word, Menenius,
  I will not hear thee speak. This man, Aufidius,
  Was my beloved in Rome; yet thou behold'st!
AUFIDIUS
You keep a constant temper.
     Exeunt. Manent the Guard and Menenius.
FIRST WATCH Now, sir, is your name Menenius?
SECOND WATCH 'Tis a spell, you see, of much power.
  You know the way home again.
94 FIRST WATCH Do you hear how we are shent for keeping
  your greatness back?
SECOND WATCH What cause do you think I have to
  swound?
MENENIUS I neither care for th' world nor your general.
  For such things as you, I can scarce think there's any,
99 y' are so slight. He that hath a will to die by himself fears

it not from another. Let your general do his worst. For
you, be that you are, long; and your misery increase 101
with your age! I say to you, as I was said to, 'Away!'
     Exit.
FIRST WATCH A noble fellow, I warrant him.
SECOND WATCH The worthy fellow is our general. He's
the rock, the oak not to be wind-shaken.   *Exit Watch.*

         *

    Enter Coriolanus and Aufidius [with others].   V, iii
CORIOLANUS
We will before the walls of Rome to-morrow
Set down our host. My partner in this action,   2
You must report to th' Volscian lords how plainly
I have borne this business.   3
AUFIDIUS   Only their ends
You have respected; stopped your ears against
The general suit of Rome; never admitted
A private whisper, no, not with such friends
That thought them sure of you.
CORIOLANUS   This last old man,
Whom with a cracked heart I have sent to Rome,
Loved me above the measure of a father;
Nay, godded me indeed. Their latest refuge   11
Was to send him; for whose old love I have –
Though I showed sourly to him – once more offered   13
The first conditions, which they did refuse
And cannot now accept. To grace him only,   15
That thought he could do more, a very little
I have yielded to. Fresh embassies and suits,   17
Nor from the state nor private friends, hereafter
Will I lend ear to.
    Shout within. Ha! What shout is this?
Shall I be tempted to infringe my vow
In the same time 'tis made? I will not.
    Enter Virgilia, Volumnia, Valeria, young Marcius,
    with Attendants.
My wife comes foremost; then the honored mould   22
Wherein this trunk was framed, and in her hand   23
The grandchild to her blood. But out, affection!
All bond and privilege of nature, break!
Let it be virtuous to be obstinate.
What is that curt'sy worth? or those doves' eyes,
Which can make gods forsworn? I melt, and am not
Of stronger earth than others. My mother bows,
As if Olympus to a molehill should   30
In supplication nod; and my young boy
Hath an aspect of intercession which
Great nature cries, 'Deny not!' Let the Volsces
Plough Rome and harrow Italy! I'll never
Be such a gosling to obey instinct, but stand
As if a man were author of himself
And knew no other kin.
VIRGILIA   My lord and husband!
CORIOLANUS
These eyes are not the same I wore in Rome.
VIRGILIA
The sorrow that delivers us thus changed
Makes you think so.   39
CORIOLANUS   Like a dull actor now,
I have forgot my part, and I am out,
Even to a full disgrace. Best of my flesh,   41

---

55 *the . . . having* as much as you have   60 *Jack guardant* knave on guard; *office* officiously keep   61 *entertainment* reception   63 *spectatorship* watching   70 *hardly* with difficulty   73 *petitionary* entreating   75 *block* obstruction, blockhead   79 *servanted* made subservient; *owe* possess   80 *properly* as my own; *remission* power to pardon   82 *Ingrate forgetfulness* your ingratitude in failing to defend me   85 *for* because   94 *shent* taken to task   99 *by himself* at his own hands   101 *long* tedious, long-lived
V, iii Before the tent of Coriolanus   2 *host* army   3 *plainly* straightforwardly   11 *godded* idolized; *latest* last   13 *showed* acted   15 *grace* gratify   17–18 *Fresh . . . friends* neither fresh embassies from the state nor suits from private friends   22 *mould* matrix   23 *trunk* body   30 *Olympus* sacred mountain   39 *delivers* shows   41 *out* at fault

Forgive my tyranny; but do not say
For that, 'Forgive our Romans.' O, a kiss
Long as my exile, sweet as my revenge!
46   Now, by the jealous queen of heaven, that kiss
47   I carried from thee dear; and my true lip
48   Hath virgined it e'er since. You gods! I prate,
And the most noble mother of the world
Leave unsaluted. Sink, my knee, i' th' earth;
    Kneels.
Of thy deep duty more impression show
Than that of common sons.
VOLUMNIA   O, stand up blest!
Whilst with no softer cushion than the flint
I kneel before thee, and unproperly
Show duty as mistaken all this while
Between the child and parent.
CORIOLANUS   What is this?
57   Your knees to me? to your corrected son?
58   Then let the pebbles on the hungry beach
59   Fillip the stars! Then let the mutinous winds
Strike the proud cedars 'gainst the fiery sun,
61   Murd'ring impossibility, to make
What cannot be, slight work.
VOLUMNIA   Thou art my warrior;
63   I holp to frame thee. Do you know this lady?
CORIOLANUS
64   The noble sister of Publicola,
The moon of Rome, chaste as the icicle
66   That's curded by the frost from purest snow
67   And hangs on Dian's temple – dear Valeria!
VOLUMNIA
68   This is a poor epitome of yours,
Which by th' interpretation of full time
70   May show like all yourself.
CORIOLANUS   The god of soldiers,
With the consent of supreme Jove, inform
Thy thoughts with nobleness, that thou mayst prove
73   To shame unvulnerable, and stick i' th' wars
74   Like a great sea-mark, standing every flaw
And saving those that eye thee!
75   VOLUMNIA   Your knee, sirrah.
CORIOLANUS
That's my brave boy!
VOLUMNIA
Even he, your wife, this lady, and myself,
Are suitors to you.
CORIOLANUS   I beseech you, peace!
Or, if you'd ask, remember this before:
80   The thing I have forsworn to grant may never
Be held by you denials. Do not bid me
82   Dismiss my soldiers, or capitulate
Again with Rome's mechanics. Tell me not
Wherein I seem unnatural. Desire not
T' allay my rages and revenges with
Your colder reasons.
VOLUMNIA   O, no more, no more!
You have said you will not grant us anything;
For we have nothing else to ask but that
Which you deny already; yet we will ask,
90   That, if you fail in our request, the blame
May hang upon your hardness. Therefore hear us.
CORIOLANUS
Aufidius, and you Volsces, mark; for we'll
Hear naught from Rome in private. – Your request?

VOLUMNIA
Should we be silent and not speak, our raiment
And state of bodies would bewray what life
We have led since thy exile. Think with thyself
How more unfortunate than all living women
Are we come hither; since that thy sight, which should
Make our eyes flow with joy, hearts dance with comforts,
Constrains them weep and shake with fear and sorrow,   100
Making the mother, wife, and child to see
The son, the husband, and the father tearing
His country's bowels out. And to poor we   103
Thine enmity's most capital. Thou barr'st us   104
Our prayers to the gods, which is a comfort
That all but we enjoy. For how can we,
Alas, how can we for our country pray,
Whereto we are bound, together with thy victory,
Whereto we are bound? Alack, or we must lose   109
The country, our dear nurse, or else thy person,
Our comfort in the country. We must find
An evident calamity, though we had   112
Our wish which side should win. For either thou
Must as a foreign recreant be led   114
With manacles through our streets, or else
Triumphantly tread on thy country's ruin,
And bear the palm for having bravely shed   117
Thy wife and children's blood. For myself, son,
I purpose not to wait on fortune till
These wars determine. If I cannot persuade thee   120
Rather to show a noble grace to both parts   121
Than seek the end of one, thou shalt no sooner
March to assault thy country than to tread –
Trust to't, thou shalt not – on thy mother's womb
That brought thee to this world.
VIRGILIA   Ay, and mine,
That brought you forth this boy, to keep your name
Living to time.
BOY   A' shall not tread on me!   127
I'll run away till I am bigger, but then I'll fight.
CORIOLANUS
Not of a woman's tenderness to be
Requires nor child nor woman's face to see.
I have sat too long.
    [Rises.]
VOLUMNIA   Nay, go not from us thus.
If it were so that our request did tend
To save the Romans, thereby to destroy
The Volsces whom you serve, you might condemn us
As poisonous of your honor. No, our suit
Is, that you reconcile them while the Volsces
May say, 'This mercy we have showed,' the Romans,
'This we received,' and each in either side
Give the all-hail to thee and cry, 'Be blest   139
For making up this peace!' Thou know'st, great son,

---

46 *queen of heaven* Juno   47 *dear* cherished   48 *virgined it* kept it intact
57 *corrected* chastised   58 *hungry* barren   59 *Fillip* snap with a finger
61 *Murd'ring impossibility* making nothing seem impossible   63 *holp*
helped   64 *Publicola* a famous consul   66 *curded* congealed   67 *Dian*
virgin goddess   68 *epitome* miniature   70 *show* appear   73 *To shame
unvulnerable* incapable of disgrace; *stick* be fixed   74 *sea-mark* point
serving as guide for navigators; *flaw* gust   75 *sirrah* sir   80 *forsworn*
sworn not   82 *capitulate* come to terms   90 *fail in* fail to grant   100 *weep*
to weep   103 *poor we* our poor selves   104 *capital* deadly; *barr'st us* keep
us from   109 *or* either   112 *evident* certain   114 *recreant* traitor   117
palm emblem of triumph   120 *determine* end   121 *grace* mercy; *parts*
sides   127 *'A* he (familiar)   139 *all-hail* salutation of honor

The end of war 's uncertain, but this certain,
That, if thou conquer Rome, the benefit
Which thou shalt thereby reap is such a name
Whose repetition will be dogged with curses,
145 Whose chronicle thus writ: 'The man was noble,
146 But with his last attempt he wiped it out,
Destroyed his country; and his name remains
To th' ensuing age abhorred,' Speak to me, son.
149 Thou hast affected the fine strains of honor,
To imitate the graces of the gods;
To tear with thunder the wide cheeks o' th' air,
152 And yet to change thy sulphur with a bolt
153 That should but rive an oak. Why dost not speak?
Think'st thou it honorable for a noble man
Still to remember wrongs? Daughter, speak you.
He cares not for your weeping. Speak thou, boy.
Perhaps thy childishness will move him more
Than can our reasons. There's no man in the world
More bound to 's mother; yet here he lets me prate
160 Like one i' th' stocks. Thou hast never in thy life
161 Showed thy dear mother any courtesy,
162 When she, poor hen, fond of no second brood,
Has clucked thee to the wars, and safely home
Loaden with honor. Say my request 's unjust,
And spurn me back; but if it be not so,
166 Thou art not honest, and the gods will plague thee
167 That thou restrain'st from me the duty which
To a mother's part belongs. He turns away.
Down, ladies! Let us shame him with our knees.
170 To his surname Coriolanus 'longs more pride
Than pity to our prayers. Down! An end!
This is the last. So, we will home to Rome,
173 And die among our neighbors. Nay, behold 's!
This boy, that cannot tell what he would have
But kneels and holds up hands for fellowship,
176 Does reason our petition with more strength
Than thou hast to deny 't. Come, let us go.
178 This fellow had a Volscian to his mother;
His wife is in Corioles, and this child
Like him by chance. Yet give us our dispatch.
I am hushed until our city be afire,
182 And then I'll speak a little.
    [Coriolanus] holds her by the hand, silent.
CORIOLANUS   O mother, mother!
183 What have you done? Behold, the heavens do ope,
The gods look down, and this unnatural scene
They laugh at. O my mother, mother! O!
You have won a happy victory to Rome;
But for your son – believe it, O believe it! –
Most dangerously you have with him prevailed,
189 If not most mortal to him. But let it come.

Aufidius, though I cannot make true wars,
I'll frame convenient peace. Now, good Aufidius,   191
Were you in my stead, would you have heard
A mother less? or granted less, Aufidius?
AUFIDIUS
I was moved withal.   194
CORIOLANUS   I dare be sworn you were!
And, sir, it is no little thing to make
Mine eyes to sweat compassion. But, good sir,
What peace you'll make, advise me. For my part,
I'll not to Rome, I'll back with you; and pray you,
Stand to me in this cause. O mother! wife!   199
AUFIDIUS *[aside]*
I am glad thou hast set thy mercy and thy honor
At difference in thee. Out of that I'll work
Myself a former fortune.   202
CORIOLANUS *[to Volumnia]*
            Ay, by and by.
But we will drink together; and you shall bear
A better witness back than words, which we,   204
On like conditions, will have counter-sealed.
Come, enter with us. Ladies, you deserve
To have a temple built you. All the swords   207
In Italy, and her confederate arms,   208
Could not have made this peace.   *Exeunt.*

                      *

      Enter Menenius and Sicinius.   V, iv
MENENIUS See you yond coign o' th' Capitol, yond   1
    cornerstone?
SICINIUS Why, what of that?
MENENIUS If it be possible for you to displace it with
    your little finger, there is some hope the ladies of Rome,
    especially his mother, may prevail with him. But I say
    there is no hope in 't; our throats are sentenced and stay   7
    upon execution.
SICINIUS Is 't possible that so short a time can alter the
    condition of a man?
MENENIUS There is difference between a grub and a   11
    butterfly; yet your butterfly was a grub. This Marcius
    is grown from man to dragon. He has wings; he's more
    than a creeping thing.
SICINIUS He loved his mother dearly.
MENENIUS So did he me; and he no more remembers his
    mother now than an eight-year-old horse. The tartness
    of his face sours ripe grapes. When he walks, he moves
    like an engine, and the ground shrinks before his tread-   19
    ing. He is able to pierce a corslet with his eye; talks like   20
    a knell and his hum is a battery. He sits in his state, as a   21
    thing made for Alexander. What he bids be done is   22
    finished with his bidding. He wants nothing of a god but   23
    eternity, and a heaven to throne in.
SICINIUS Yes, mercy, if you report him truly.
MENENIUS I paint him in the character. Mark what   26
    mercy his mother shall bring from him. There is no
    more mercy in him than there is milk in a male tiger.
    That shall our poor city find; and all this is long of you.   29
SICINIUS The gods be good unto us!
MENENIUS No, in such a case the gods will not be good
    unto us. When we banished him, we respected not
    them; and, he returning to break our necks, they respect
    not us.
      Enter a Messenger.

145 *writ* will be written   146 *it* his nobility   149 *fine strains* refinements   152 *sulphur* lightning; *with* for; *bolt* thunderbolt   153 *rive* split   160 *i' th' stocks* publicly humiliated   161 *courtesy* special consideration   162 *When* while; *fond* desirous   166 *honest* just   167 *That* because   170 *'longs* belongs   173 *behold 's* behold us   176 *reason* argue for   178 *to* for   182 *a little* i.e. a dying curse   183 *ope* open   189 *mortal* fatally   191 *convenient* appropriate   194 *withal* by it   199 *Stand to* support   202 *former fortune* fortune like my former one   204 *which* i.e. the treaty   207 *a temple* i.e. the Temple of Women's Fortune   208 *confederate arms* military allies
V, iv A street in Rome   1 *coign* corner   7–8 *stay upon* wait for   11 *difference* difference   19 *engine* instrument of war   20 *corslet* body-armor   21 *battery* assault; *state* throne   22 *thing . . . Alexander* statue of Alexander the Great   23 *finished . . . bidding* accomplished as soon as ordered; *wants* lacks   26 *in the character* according to his personality   29 *long of* owing to

MESSENGER
Sir, if you'd save your life, fly to your house.
The plebeians have got your fellow-tribune,
36   And hale him up and down ; all swearing, if
The Roman ladies bring not comfort home,
They'll give him death by inches.
Enter another Messenger.
SICINIUS   What's the news ?
MESSENGER
Good news, good news ! The ladies have prevailed,
40   The Volscians are dislodged, and Marcius gone.
A merrier day did never yet greet Rome,
42   No, not th' expulsion of the Tarquins.
SICINIUS   Friend,
Art thou certain this is true ? is't most certain ?
MESSENGER
As certain as I know the sun is fire.
45   Where have you lurked that you make doubt of it ?
46   Ne'er through an arch so hurried the blown tide
47   As the recomforted through th' gates. Why, hark you !
Trumpets, hautboys ; drums beat ; all together.
48   The trumpets, sackbuts, psalteries, and fifes,
49   Tabors and cymbals and the shouting Romans
Make the sun dance. Hark you !
A shout within.
MENENIUS   This is good news.
I will go meet the ladies. This Volumnia
Is worth of consuls, senators, patricians,
A city full ; of tribunes, such as you,
A sea and land full. You have prayed well to-day.
This morning for ten thousand of your throats
56   I'd not have given a doit. Hark, how they joy !
Sound still, with the shouts.
SICINIUS
First, the gods bless you for your tidings ; next,
Accept my thankfulness.
MESSENGER   Sir, we have all
Great cause to give great thanks.
SICINIUS   They are near the city ?
MESSENGER
60   Almost at point to enter.
SICINIUS   We will meet them,
And help the joy.   *Exeunt.*
V, v   *Enter two Senators with Ladies [Volumnia, Virgilia,*
Valeria] passing over the stage, with other Lords.
SENATOR
Behold our patroness, the life of Rome !
Call all your tribes together, praise the gods,
And make triumphant fires ; strew flowers before them.
Unshout the noise that banished Marcius ;
5   Repeal him with the welcome of his mother.
Cry, 'Welcome, ladies, welcome !'
ALL   Welcome, ladies,
Welcome !
A flourish with drums and trumpets. [Exeunt.]

*

V, vi   *Enter Tullus Aufidius, with Attendants.*
AUFIDIUS
Go tell the lords o' th' city I am here.
2   Deliver them this paper. Having read it,
Bid them repair to th' market-place, where I,
4   Even in theirs and in the commons' ears,

Will vouch the truth of it. Him I accuse   5
The city ports by this hath entered and
Intends t' appear before the people, hoping
To purge himself with words. Dispatch.
[Exeunt Attendants.]
Enter three or four Conspirators of Aufidius' faction.
Most welcome !
FIRST CONSPIRATOR
How is it with our general ?
AUFIDIUS   Even so
As with a man by his own alms empoisoned
And with his charity slain.
SECOND CONSPIRATOR   Most noble sir,
If you do hold the same intent wherein
You wished us parties, we'll deliver you   13
Of your great danger.
AUFIDIUS   Sir, I cannot tell.
We must proceed as we do find the people.
THIRD CONSPIRATOR
The people will remain uncertain whilst
'Twixt you there's difference ; but the fall of either
Makes the survivor heir of all.
AUFIDIUS   I know it ;
And my pretext to strike at him admits
A good construction. I raised him, and I pawned 20
Mine honor for his truth ; who being so heightened, 21
He watered his new plants with dews of flattery,
Seducing so my friends ; and to this end
He bowed his nature, never known before
But to be rough, unswayable, and free.
THIRD CONSPIRATOR
Sir, his stoutness   26
When he did stand for consul, which he lost
By lack of stooping –
AUFIDIUS   That I would have spoke of.
Being banished for't, he came unto my hearth ;
Presented to my knife his throat. I took him ;
Made him joint-servant with me ; gave him way   31
In all his own desires ; nay, let him choose
Out of my files, his projects to accomplish,   33
My best and freshest men ; served his designments 34
In mine own person ; holp to reap the fame   35
Which he did end all his ; and took some pride   36
To do myself this wrong ; till at the last
I seemed his follower, not partner, and
He waged me with his countenance as if   39
I had been mercenary.
FIRST CONSPIRATOR   So he did, my lord.
The army marvelled at it ; and in the last,
When he had carried Rome and that we looked
For no less spoil than glory –
AUFIDIUS   There was it !   43
For which my sinews shall be stretched upon him. 44

36 *hale* pull   40 *dislodged* retired   42 *Tarquins* dynasty of tyrants   45
lurked been hiding   46 *blown* swollen   47 s.d. *hautboys* oboes   48
sackbuts trombones ; *psalteries* stringed instruments   49 *Tabors* small
drums   56 *doit* smallest possible sum   60 *at . . . enter* on the point of entering
V, v   5 *Repeal him* recall him from exile
V, vi A public place in Corioli   2 *them* to them   4 *theirs* their ears   5
Him he whom   13 *parties* to be allies   20 *construction* interpretation
21 *truth* loyalty ; *heightened* exalted   26 *stoutness* obstinacy   31 *joint-
servant* colleague ; *gave him way* gave way to him   33 *files* ranks   34
designments enterprises   35 *holp* help   36 *end* gather in as a harvest
39 *waged* remunerated ; *countenance* patronage   43 *There* that   44 *sinews
. . . upon* strength shall be exerted against

45 At a few drops of women's rheum, which are
46 As cheap as lies, he sold the blood and labor
Of our great action ; therefore shall he die,
48 And I'll renew me in his fall. But, hark !

Drums and trumpets sound, with great shouts of the People.

FIRST CONSPIRATOR
49 Your native town you entered like a post,
And had no welcomes home ; but he returns,
Splitting the air with noise.

SECOND CONSPIRATOR   And patient fools,
Whose children he hath slain, their base throats tear
With giving him glory.

53 THIRD CONSPIRATOR Therefore, at your vantage,
Ere he express himself or move the people
With what he would say, let him feel your sword !
56 Which we will second. When he lies along,
57 After your way his tale pronounced shall bury
58 His reasons with his body.

AUFIDIUS   Say no more.
Here come the lords.

Enter the Lords of the city.

ALL LORDS
You are most welcome home.

AUFIDIUS   I have not deserved it.
But, worthy lords, have you with heed perused
What I have written to you ?

ALL   We have.

FIRST LORD   And grieve to hear't.
63 What faults he made before the last, I think
64 Might have found easy fines ; but there to end
Where he was to begin, and give away
66 The benefit of our levies, answering us
67 With our own charge, making a treaty where
There was a yielding – this admits no excuse.

AUFIDIUS
He approaches. You shall hear him.

Enter Coriolanus, marching with Drum and Colors, the Commoners being with him.

CORIOLANUS
Hail, lords ! I am returned your soldier ;
No more infected with my country's love
That when I parted hence, but still subsisting
Under your great command. You are to know
74 That prosperously I have attempted,
75 With bloody passage led your wars even to
76 The gates of Rome. Our spoils we have brought home
77 Do more than counterpoise a full third part
The charges of the action. We have made peace
With no less honor to the Antiates
Than shame to th' Romans ; and we here deliver,
Subscribed by th' consuls and patricians,
Together with the seal o' th' Senate, what
83 We have compounded on.

AUFIDIUS   Read it not, noble lords ;
But tell the traitor in the highest degree
He hath abused your powers.

CORIOLANUS
Traitor ? how now ?

AUFIDIUS   Ay, traitor, Marcius !

CORIOLANUS   Marcius ?

AUFIDIUS
Ay, Marcius, Caius Marcius ! Dost thou think
I'll grace thee with that robbery, thy stol'n name
Coriolanus in Corioles ?
You lords and heads o' th' state, perfidiously
He has betrayed your business and given up,
For certain drops of salt, your city Rome –
I say 'your city' – to his wife and mother ;
Breaking his oath and resolution like
A twist of rotten silk ; never admitting
Counsel o' th' war ; but at his nurse's tears
He whined and roared away your victory,
That pages blushed at him and men of heart   98
Looked wond'ring each at other.

CORIOLANUS   Hear'st thou, Mars ?

AUFIDIUS
Name not the god, thou boy of tears !

CORIOLANUS   Ha !

AUFIDIUS   No more.

CORIOLANUS
Measureless liar, thou hast made my heart
Too great for what contains it. Boy ? O slave !   102
Pardon me, lords, 'tis the first time that ever
I was forced to scold. Your judgments, my grave lords,
Must give this cur the lie ; and his own notion –   105
Who wears my stripes impressed upon him, that
Must bear my beating to his grave – shall join
To thrust the lie unto him.

FIRST LORD
Peace, both, and hear me speak.

CORIOLANUS
Cut me to pieces, Volsces. Men and lads,
Stain all your edges on me. Boy ? False hound !   111
If you have writ your annals true, 'tis there   112
That, like an eagle in a dovecote, I
Fluttered your Volscians in Corioles.
Alone I did it. Boy ?

AUFIDIUS   Why, noble lords,
Will you be put in mind of his blind fortune,   116
Which was your shame, by this unholy braggart,
'Fore your own eyes and ears ?

ALL CONSPIRATORS   Let him die for't.

ALL PEOPLE Tear him to pieces ! – Do it presently ! –   119
He killed my son ! – My daughter ! – He killed my
cousin Marcus ! He killed my father !

SECOND LORD
Peace, ho ! No outrage. Peace !
The man is noble and his fame folds in   123
This orb o' th' earth. His last offenses to us
Shall have judicious hearing. Stand, Aufidius,   125
And trouble not the peace.

CORIOLANUS   O that I had him,
With six Aufidiuses, or more, his tribe,
To use my lawful sword !

AUFIDIUS   Insolent villain !

ALL CONSPIRATORS
Kill, kill, kill, kill, kill him !

---

45 *rheum* tears   46 *blood and labor* bloody labor   48 *renew me* be restored
49 *post* messenger   53 *at your vantage* seizing your opportunity   56
along prone   57 *After . . . pronounced* your own version of the affair   58
reasons justification   63 *made* committed   64 *fines* punishments   66 *levies*
forces raised ; *answering* repaying   67 *charge* expenses   74 *prosperously
. . . attempted* my endeavors have been fortunate   75 *passage* course   76
spoils plunder which   77 *Do . . . counterpoise* outweigh   83 *compounded*
reached an agreement   98 *That* so that ; *heart* courage   102 *Too . . . it* too
swollen for my breast   105 *notion* understanding   111 *edges* swords   112
there recorded there   116 *blind fortune* mere luck   119 *presently* at once
123 *folds in* enfolds   125 *judicious* judicial

Draw the Conspirators, and kill Marcius, who falls.
Aufidius stands on him.

LORDS   Hold, hold, hold, hold!

AUFIDIUS
My noble masters, hear me speak.

FIRST LORD   O Tullus –

SECOND LORD
Thou hast done a deed whereat valor will weep.

THIRD LORD
Tread not upon him. Masters all, be quiet!
Put up your swords.

AUFIDIUS
My lords, when you shall know – as in this rage
Provoked by him you cannot – the great danger
136   Which this man's life did owe you, you'll rejoice
137   That he is thus cut off. Please it your honors
To call me to your Senate. I'll deliver
Myself your loyal servant, or endure
Your heaviest censure.

FIRST LORD   Bear from hence his body,
And mourn you for him. Let him be regarded
As the most noble corse that ever herald   142
Did follow to his urn.

SECOND LORD   His own impatience
Takes from Aufidius a great part of blame.
Let's make the best of it.

AUFIDIUS   My rage is gone,
And I am struck with sorrow. Take him up.
Help, three o' th' chiefest soldiers; I'll be one.
Beat thou the drum, that it speak mournfully.
Trail your steel pikes. Though in this city he
Hath widowed and unchilded many a one,   150
Which to this hour bewail the injury,
Yet he shall have a noble memory.   152
Assist.   *Exeunt, bearing the body of Coriolanus.*
                    A dead march sounded.

136 *did owe you* possessed for you   137 *Please it* may it please   142 *corse*
corpse   150 *unchilded* deprived of children   152 *memory* memorial

THE ROMANCES

FOREWORD

Pericles, Cymbeline, The Winter's Tale, and *The Tempest* are separately grouped, not because they belong to a distinct category generally recognized in their day, but because they share certain characteristics which the grouping helps to emphasize. The earliest of them was first published as "The late and much admired play called Pericles Prince of Tyre. With the true relation of the whole historie, adventures, and fortunes of the said Prince; as also the no lesse strange and worthy accidents in the birth and life of his daughter Mariana." Evidently the proprietors wished to avoid the term "comedy" since the tone of the play is prevailingly serious and certain characters die in its course; however, since it ends happily, it could scarcely be termed a "tragedy." Had they consulted Polonius, they might have settled for "tragical-pastoral." Since *Pericles* was not printed in the first folio, the editors were spared the problem of classification. *Cymbeline* was included, and grouped with the Tragedies in spite of its happy ending, no doubt because of its gravity and the occurrence in it of actual deaths. In the interest of consistency, *The Winter's Tale* should have been similarly grouped since it, too, is grave, and Antigonus perishes in it, not to mention an entire crew of sailors. At this point we might say that what distinguishes these plays is the fact that deaths precede the happy endings, but the criterion fails us with *The Tempest*. However, if we compare *The Tempest* with *A Midsummer Night's Dream*, *As You Like It*, and *Twelfth Night* on the one hand, and with *Pericles, Cymbeline*, and *The Winter's Tale* on the other, we recognize that its affinity is with the latter. We are really dealing with affinities. The affinity of the early romantic plays is with comedy, that of the late ones with tragedy. The forces of evil overcome in them are truly formidable, indeed identical with those appearing in the great tragedies; and whether or not deaths occur in them, the shadow of death lies on them.

Since the term "romance" is here being used of a particular kind of romance, it might seem that "tragi-comedy" might be more apt, but the connotations of this troublesome label render it unavailable. Although as ancient as Plautus' *Amphitruo*, it was most often used in a pejorative sense, as when Sidney called "mongrel tragi-comedy" all plays which combined the tragic episodes and upper-class characters deemed proper to tragedy with the comic episodes and lower-class characters deemed proper to comedy. (In this sense of the term nearly all of Shakespeare's tragedies would be "tragi-comedies.") John Fletcher, following the lead of the Italian critic-dramatist Guarini, author of the pastoral "tragi-comedy" *Il Pastor Fido*, tried to dignify the term and the kind of play to which it might properly be applied. He strove for unity of tone in his *Faithful Shepherdess* and affirmed that it "wants deaths, which is enough to make it no tragedy, yet brings some near it, which is enough to make it no comedy." Here he may seem to come close to providing a definition for Shakespeare's late romances. Their relation to Fletcherian tragi-comedy has been much debated, but there is in fact a crucial distinction. Fletcher was concerned with certain aesthetic and theatrical effects as an end in themselves. With Shakespeare the effects seem a means to an end, philosophic or semi-religious in character.

The four plays have a number of features in common. Their happy endings come less as a pleasant surprise than as a joyous revelation. All contain elements of the supernatural or mystical, and something resembling resurrection. The themes of transgression, expiation, redemption are mutually conspicuous. Age and youth are juxtaposed in the father–daughter relationships, and in each case the daughter evokes in our minds the figure of the vernal maiden, symbol of eternal renewal. *The Winter's Tale* proves to be a tale of Spring. Like the other three plays it ends in a family reunion, and Paulina addresses the "resurrected" Hermione,

> Bequeath to death your numbness, for from him
> Dear life redeems you.

The "dear life" is Perdita, and beside her stands her lover. In the comedies the perpetuation of life seems a merry business. In the romances it seems sacred.

A. H.

BIBLIOGRAPHY

The relative sparsity of books about the romances is deceptive. Comment has become copious in periodicals and in works of miscellaneous content. *Shakespeare: The Comedies*, ed. K. Muir (1965), includes a few essays on the romances and a brief bibliography. An exercise in depreciation by Lytton Strachey in his *Books and Characters* (1922) has proved a stimulant to defenders. Books on the romances are E. M. W. Tillyard, *Shakespeare's Last Plays* (1938); G. Wilson Knight, *The Crown of Life* (1947); S. L. Bethell, *The Winter's Tale* (1947); Derek Traversi, *Shakespeare: The Last Phase* (1954); *Later Plays*, ed. John R. Brown & Bernard Harris, *Stratford-upon-Avon Studies*, Vol. 8 (1966); D. G. James, *The Dream of Prospero* (1967). For a survey of twentieth-century criticism of the romances, see Philip Edwards in *Shakespeare Survey*, ed. A. Nicoll, XI (1958).

PERICLES PRINCE OF TYRE

INTRODUCTION

About the time when he wrote his greatest tragedy, in which King Lear endures almost intolerable evil at the hands of his two wicked daughters and learns truth through suffering of body and agony of spirit, Shakespeare was concerned with another play that deals with aspects of ill fortune and evil. Its hero, young Pericles, is as royal a figure as old Lear. His every action is magnanimous. Not once does he err in judgment or fail in the exercise of prudence and moderation. There are no outbursts of rage, no imprecations against man or fate. Storm-buffeted on the moor, Lear defies the elements and calls down destruction on mankind:

> And thou, all-shaking thunder,
> Strike flat the thick rotundity o' th' world,
> Crack Nature's moulds, all germains spill at once,
> That makes ingrateful man.

Pericles, on the deck of his tempest-tossed ship, sees his newborn daughter and, hearing that the mother has died in childbirth, utters his only remonstrance against fate:

> O you gods!
> Why do you make us love your goodly gifts
> And snatch them straight away? We here below
> Recall not what we give.

King Lear is the tragedy of a titanic old king with tremendous passions who defies the worst that human evil and the forces of nature can bring against him, and is driven to madness and death in the very process of achieving compassion and humility. *Pericles* is the story of a virtuous youth who is pursued by the wicked, betrayed by those he has benefited, buffeted by the sea, and scourged by the fickleness of Fortune until melancholy and grief reduce him to apathy. Yet, because like Job he will not curse God, the wicked receive their deserts, Fortune smiles at last, and Pericles has daughter and wife restored to him. *Pericles Prince of Tyre* is not Tragedy but Romance.

The story, with a few differences in names, appears in ninth-century Latin manuscripts as *Historia Apollonii Regis Tyri*. It is alluded to as early as the fifth or sixth century, and probably originated much earlier as a Greek romance, like those of Heliodorus and Achilles Tatius that enjoyed such wide popularity in Tudor translations. Numerous medieval manuscripts have survived, in several languages, and modern folk versions in Greek have been recorded. From Godfrey de Viterbo's *Pantheon* (ca. 1186), the English poet John Gower borrowed the tale for his *Confessio Amantis* (ca. 1383–93). A prose history of Apollonius by Thomas Twine was ready for publication in 1576; it is known only in the reprints of about 1595 and of 1607. Twine translated a French version of the story as

it appears in *Gesta Romanorum*, an age-old collection of tales that circulated all over Europe and enjoyed fresh popularity in England about 1600.

The romances of chivalry such as *Amadis of Gaul* and *Morte d'Arthur* were disdained by moralists and literary critics, but the high seriousness of Sidney's *Arcadia* and Spenser's *The Faerie Queene*, and the exotic settings and marvellous incidents of *Daphnis and Chloe*, *The Aethiopica*, *Clitophon and Leucippe*, and other Greek romances, brought into favor again the kind of story that would tease Shakespeare into writing *The Winter's Tale* and *The Tempest*.

In the romances, there is little attempt at narrative logic or probability; incident appears for its own sake. Characters are two-dimensional and static: the good are very good, and the evil have no redeeming feature. In a setting that is remote in time or place, or both, there are shipwrecks, rescues from the sea, miraculous restorations from apparent death, infants exposed to the elements, and, above all, recognitions and reconciliations and the healing of breaches or the righting of ancient injuries, usually through the agency of splendid young people, but with the direct intervention of the gods. The themes are patience, constancy, and forgiveness, and the dramatic interest is focused upon recognition scenes. Shakespeare had used some of these romantic elements as early as *The Comedy of Errors*, which owes its framework to the story of Apollonius of Tyre, but in his late romances he treated the age-old themes and incidents with a seriousness which spiritualizes and transforms them.

Partly because *Pericles*, first published in quarto form in 1609, was not included in the first folio (1623), but chiefly because the first two acts are markedly inferior to the last three, it has been argued that Shakespeare is not the sole author. According to one hypothesis, Shakespeare took a play of unknown authorship, touched up Acts I and II lightly, and revised or rewrote Acts III–V. Another hypothesis is that a collaborator (John Day, George Wilkins, and Thomas Heywood are among those proposed) wrote the inferior part of the play. A third hypothesis accepts Shakespeare as the sole author and explains the differences between the two segments of the play by supposing that the very corrupt text of the printed version was set down from memory, with much patching and improvising, by two reporters of unequal ability. The one reporter's reconstruction of Acts I and II is a feeble approximation of the play as written and acted at the Globe; while the second reporter's version of the rest of the play comes much nearer to the Shakespearean original.

Shakespeare's hand in the second half of the play can hardly be denied. Throughout the first two acts there are frequent echoes of his plays, especially *Lear*, *Macbeth*,

Measure for Measure, Richard II, and even *Henry VI*, and there are some anticipations of the plays not yet written. The former may be recollections of a reporter whose memory was crammed with scraps of Shakespeare, but they may equally be instances of a busy playwright's repeating his own phrases and ideas. Gower's structural function throughout the play is almost unique in Tudor–Stuart drama, although in Barnabe Barnes' *The Divil's Charter* (performed at court early in 1607 and entered for publication late in the year) Francesco Guicciardini is brought on stage to present the dramatization of part of his *Historie of Italie*. His choruses resemble those of Gower in Acts I and II of *Pericles*. One play imitates the other, but there are no documents to prove which came first. The combined narrative and choral function of Gower is likely to be the invention of a single mind, rather than the product of collaboration. The choruses, especially the later ones, are of the same fabric as those in *Henry V*.

To complicate the problem, a prose history by George Wilkins with the title *The Painfull Adventures of Pericles, Prince of Tyre* was published in 1608. On the title-page Wilkins called it "The true History of the Play of Pericles, as it was lately presented by the worthy and ancient Poet John Gower." At one time Wilkins' novel was considered to be evidence that he had written an *Ur-Pericles* or was Shakespeare's collaborator. Current opinion is that the writing of the novel was inspired by the play, much as the prose *History of Titus Andronicus the Renowned Roman General* had been inspired by *Titus Andronicus* and the prose *History of Hamblet* by *Hamlet Prince of Denmark*. It has been suggested that Wilkins intended to pirate the play but, finding his notes inadequate, wrote the prose version instead. To eke out the narrative he turned to the recent reprint of Twine's *Apollonius*, from which he borrowed liberally. What he remembered of the play calls up a picture of stage performance; the borrowings from Twine are simple prose narrative. Sometimes Wilkins gives duplicate versions, one from the play and the other from Twine. Where Wilkins differs from the play and is not using Twine, he may preserve details that the reporters of *Pericles* omitted. In such a scene as II, ii, where the knights parade before Simonides and Thaisa, Wilkins gives a fuller and more coherent account than the play. Scattered through the novel are bits of verse, some of it similar to corresponding lines in *Pericles*, and some that may represent lines omitted or garbled by the reporters. Some of the verse, however, like certain passages of prose, may be of Wilkins' invention, for he was a facile writer. Obviously Wilkins did not have access to a manuscript of the play (it had not yet been put in print), and his knowledge of it was far too meagre for him to have been a part-author. The novel has its uses, however, for frequently it throws light on obscure passages in the play and helps in the recovery of authentic readings.

The earliest recorded performance of *Pericles* was that which Zorzi Giustinian, the Venetian ambassador to England (from January 5, 1606, until November 23, 1608), saw in company with the French ambassador, Antoine de la Boderie (who was in England from May, 1606), and his wife (known to have been in England at least as early as April, 1607, when she had already become a favorite at court). Since the plague was active in London from mid-July to mid-November in 1606, and Twine's *Apollonius*

was reprinted in 1607, the performance in question may have been in the late autumn of 1606 or early in 1607; it could not have been later than July, 1608, when the plague closed the theatres again. It is not unlikely that the popularity of *Pericles* at the Globe in late 1606 or early 1607 motivated the reprinting of Twine in 1607 and the writing of Wilkins' *Painfull Adventures of Pericles* in 1608.

The popularity of *Pericles* in the seventeenth century is unquestioned. The pirated first quarto (1609) sold so rapidly that the type used in printing its title page was available for printing that of the second quarto. Four other reprints followed by 1635. The play was given an extraordinary performance at Whitehall in 1619 for the entertainment of the French ambassador. The record is preserved in a letter to Sir Dudley Carleton at the Hague on May 24, 1619:

In the kinges great Chamber they went to see the play of Pirrocles, Prince of Tyre, which lasted till 2 a-clocke. After two actes, the players ceased till the French all refreshed them with sweetmeates brought on Chinay voiders, & wyne & ale in bottells, after the players begann anewe.

The occurrence of the break in the performance at the end of Act II is not without interest. *Pericles* may have been the first Shakespearean play revived after the restoration of Charles II in 1660.

Although the play was added to the third folio in 1664 and was included in the fourth in 1685, the eighteenth-century editors felt uncomfortable about it. The obvious differences between it and the other plays in the canon troubled them, for they had no knowledge of how the text had been transmitted. The *dramatis personae* lacked the qualities critics expected in a Shakespearean play. The brothel scenes were considered unworthy of Shakespeare, as was the porter scene in *Macbeth*. The attitude of the age is illustrated by George Lillo's *Marina* (produced in 1738), which is built chiefly on Acts IV and V on the assumption that only the last part of the play is by Shakespeare. Edmund Malone restored the play in his edition of 1780 but with some reluctance. And critics and producers have continued to find the incest and brothel scenes highly objectionable until recent years. Now their kinship with the brothel scenes in *Measure for Measure* is generally recognized. Since the successful revival of the play by the Birmingham Repertory Theatre in 1954, audiences have had more frequent opportunities to experience the theatrical effectiveness and the emotional power of the concluding scenes.

Pericles is an experimental play in its content and in its form. It consists of striking incidents selected from a long romance with small regard for causality. These have to do with the adventures of a family, with attention focused on a father and a daughter. The events are introduced, explained, and evaluated by a presenter, old John Gower, author of the poem that supplied the fable, who gives in narrative form the links that hold the play together. Shakespeare had used a presenter, but only indirectly, in the mouse-trap scene in *Hamlet*, which also has a dumb show. Early in this scene, Ophelia asks the Prince, "What means this, my lord?"; and later, after Hamlet explains to Claudius that "This play is the image of a murder done in Vienna. Gonzago is the duke's name...," she remarks: "You are as good as a chorus." Like Hamlet, Gower introduces and bridges gaps in the action as the chorus-presenter does in *Henry V*; like Hamlet he supplies information needed to understand the play, and like Hamlet he interprets. The play, in fact, turns about Gower as on an axis. In addition to serving as presenter, prologue, chorus, and epilogue, he gives by his archaic mode of speech (which frequently lapses into normal Elizabethan English) a remoteness to the action, a fairy-tale, dreamlike quality that disarms criticism and induces belief.

This seldom-acted play is very moving in performance. In the great recognition scene, Shakespeare, with consummate skill, brings father and daughter together and helps them stumble toward the truth. From the outset the audience knows that these two are Pericles and Marina; but they have not come seeking each other, and the recognition, bit by bit, of their relationship lags far behind the wishes of the impatient audience. How differently Shakespeare had managed the meeting of Cordelia with Lear, just waking after madness. The later recognition scenes in *Cymbeline* and *The Winter's Tale* never rise to the emotional intensity of that in *Pericles*.

In the study *Pericles* is less effective than on stage. The archaisms of Gower and the colloquial speech of the fishermen and the brothel keepers make difficult reading. The reporters who compiled the text omit words, phrases, and whole lines. They transpose words and phrases. The omission of relative pronouns is frequent, with the result that the expression is too compact and the syntax obscure. Some lines retain their music and beauty, but they are outnumbered by those made commonplace by the introduction of obvious and unnecessary words.

These deficiencies in diction, grammar, and metrics are less serious than some of the other sins against the original play. There is good reason to suspect that incidents are garbled and that much has been omitted in the reporting. At II, iv, 17 ff., for example, there are indications that there was jealousy of Escanes in the court of Tyre, but the matter is dropped. At II, v, 25–28, Simonides speaks of the musical skill Pericles had displayed on the previous evening, though in the play Pericles has no occasion to play or sing. The account of the knights and their impresas seems to be both incomplete and confused. The events in I, ii

make good sense only if there is considerable rearrangement of the text. And, worst of all, the heart of Marina's discourse with Lysimachus in IV, vi is lost. A sermon there must have been, for he exclaims, "I did not think / Thou couldst have spoke so well; ne'er dreamt thou couldst," but in the play as we have it she is more eloquent in dealing with Boult.

The character of Pericles has already received attention. His daughter Marina is cast in the same mould. Despite her youth, she is calm, resolute, unrebellious. Unlike other heroines in Shakespeare, she is never properly wooed; there is no hint of what she thought of Lysimachus; and she goes to her appointed marriage like other fairy-tale princesses to their Prince Charmings because such is journey's end in romance. The character of Lysimachus is left ambiguous: he is well known to the Bawd, who receives him as a customer; yet after Marina talks with him he disavows immoral intent. The other characters, even Thaisa, function as the plot requires.

Like *Love's Labor's Lost*, but in a wholly different vein, *Pericles* is a mannered play. Its extraordinary episodes are patterned against a background of antiquated theatrical conventions: presenter, chorus, dumb show. The play should be enacted as formally as a minuet. It is a pity that the surviving text is so imperfect a vestige of the original.

The Folger Shakespeare   JAMES G. MCMANAWAY
Library

NOTE ON THE TEXT

Pericles first appeared in a quarto (1609) printed from a highly defective reportorial copy of the original play. Although providing only a debased version, the quarto is our only substantive text, and it has been followed as closely as feasible in the present edition. A discussion of this text and a list of the emendations adopted are provided in the Appendix. The quarto is not divided into acts and scenes. In the second issue of the third folio (1664), which was the first of the folios to include *Pericles*, the play is divided into acts but not into scenes. The act–scene division supplied marginally for reference in the present edition is that of the later editors.

PERICLES PRINCE OF TYRE

[NAMES OF THE ACTORS

Gower, as Chorus
Antiochus, King of Antioch
Pericles, Prince of Tyre
Helicanus }
Escanes } two lords of Tyre
Simonides, King of Pentapolis
Cleon, Governor of Tharsus
Lysimachus, Governor of Mytilene
Cerimon, a lord of Ephesus
Thaliard, a lord of Antioch
Philemon, servant to Cerimon
Leonine, servant to Dionyza
Marshal

A Pander
Boult, his servant
Fishermen
Sailors
Pirates
Daughter of Antiochus
Dionyza, wife to Cleon
Thaisa, daughter to Simonides
Marina, daughter to Pericles and Thaisa
Lychorida, nurse to Marina
A Bawd
Diana
Lords, Ladies, Knights, Gentlemen, Messengers

Scene: Coastal lands of the Aegean and eastern Mediterranean]

*

I, Cho.   *Enter Gower [as Chorus].*
To sing a song that old was sung,
From ashes ancient Gower is come,
Assuming man's infirmities
To glad your ear and please your eyes.
6 It hath been sung at festivals,
On ember-eves and holy-ales;
And lords and ladies in their lives
9 Have read it for restoratives.
The purchase is to make men glorious,
10 Et bonum quo antiquius, eo melius.
If you, born in these latter times
When wit's more ripe, accept my rhymes,
And that to hear an old man sing
May to your wishes pleasure bring,
I life would wish, and that I might
Waste it for you, like taper light.
This Antioch, then; Antiochus the Great
Built up this city for his chiefest seat,
The fairest in all Syria –
I tell you what mine authors say.
21 This king unto him took a peer,
Who died and left a female heir,
23 So buxom, blithe, and full of face
As heaven had lent her all his grace;
With whom the father liking took
And her to incest did provoke.
Bad child; worse father! to entice his own
To evil should be done by none.
By custom what they did begin
Was with long use accounted no sin.
The beauty of this sinful dame
32 Made many princes thither frame,

To seek her as a bedfellow,
In marriage pleasures, playfellow;
Which to prevent he made a law –
To keep her still, and men in awe –
That whoso asked her for his wife,
His riddle told not, lost his life.
So for her many a wight did die,
As yon grim looks do testify.   40
[Pointing to the heads.]
What now ensues, to the judgment of your eye
I give, my cause who best can justify.   *Exit.*

Enter Antiochus, Prince Pericles, and Followers.   I, i
ANTIOCHUS
Young Prince of Tyre, you have at large received
The danger of the task you undertake.
PERICLES
I have, Antiochus, and, with a soul
Embold'ned with the glory of her praise,
Think death no hazard in this enterprise.
ANTIOCHUS
Music!
Bring in our daughter, clothèd like a bride
For the embracements even of Jove himself;
At whose conception, till Lucina reigned,   9

I, Cho. **6** *ember-eves* evenings before days of fasting; *holy-ales* rural festivals **9** *purchase* profit **10** *Et . . . melius* and the more ancient a good thing is, the better **21** *peer* mate **23** *full of face* beautiful **32** *frame* journey **40** *yon grim looks* i.e. on the faces of the slain suitors who have failed to solve the riddle; see I, i, 35–41
I, i The palace of Antiochus **9** *Lucina* goddess of childbirth

10 Nature this dowry gave : to glad her presence,
The senate house of planets all did sit
To knit in her their best perfections.
    Enter Antiochus' Daughter.

PERICLES

See where she comes, apparelled like the spring,
Graces her subjects, and her thoughts the king
Of every virtue gives renown to men !
16 Her face the book of praises, where is read
17 Nothing but curious pleasures, as from thence
18 Sorrow were ever rased, and testy wrath
Could never be her mild companion.
You gods that made me man, and sway in love,
That have inflamed desire in my breast
To taste the fruit of yon celestial tree
Or die in the adventure, be my helps,
As I am son and servant to your will,
To compass such a boundless happiness !

ANTIOCHUS

Prince Pericles –

PERICLES

That would be son to great Antiochus.

ANTIOCHUS

28 Before thee stands this fair Hesperides,
With golden fruit, but dangerous to be touched ;
For death-like dragons here affright thee hard.
Her face, like heaven, enticeth thee to view
Her countless glory, which desert must gain ;
33 And which, without desert because thine eye
Presumes to reach, all the whole heap must die.
Yon sometime famous princes, like thyself,
Drawn by report, advent'rous by desire,
Tell thee, with speechless tongues and semblance pale,
That, without covering save yon field of stars,
Here they stand martyrs slain in Cupid's wars ;
And with dead cheeks advise thee to desist
41 For going on death's net, whom none resist.

PERICLES

Antiochus, I thank thee, who hath taught
My frail mortality to know itself,
And by those fearful objects to prepare
45 This body, like to them, to what I must ;
For death remembered should be like a mirror,
Who tells us life 's but breath, to trust it error.
I'll make my will then, and, as sick men do,
49 Who know the world, see heaven, but, feeling woe,
50 Gripe not at earthly joys as erst they did,
So I bequeath a happy peace to you
And all good men, as every prince should do :
My riches to the earth, from whence they came ;

[To the Princess]

But my unspotted fire of love to you.
Thus ready for the way of life or death,
I wait the sharpest blow, Antiochus.

ANTIOCHUS

Scorning advice, read the conclusion then ;   57
Which read and not expounded, 'tis
As these before thee, thou thyself shalt bleed.

DAUGHTER

Of all 'sayed yet, mayst thou prove prosperous !   60
Of all 'sayed yet, I wish thee happiness !   61

PERICLES

Like a bold champion I assume the lists,
Nor ask advice of any other thought
But faithfulness and courage.
    [Reads.]   *The Riddle.*
'I am no viper, yet I feed
On mother's flesh which did me breed.
I sought a husband, in which labor
I found that kindness in a father.
He's father, son, and husband mild ;
I mother, wife, and yet his child.
How they may be, and yet in two,   71
As you will live, resolve it you.'

Sharp physic is the last ! but, O you powers
That gives heaven countless eyes to view men's acts,   74
Why cloud they not their sights perpetually
If this be true which makes me pale to read it ?
Fair glass of light, I loved you, and could still,
Were not this glorious casket stored with ill,
But I must tell you, now my thoughts revolt ;
For he's no man on whom perfections wait
That, knowing sin within, will touch the gate.
You are a fair viol, and your sense the strings ;
Who, fingered to make man his lawful music,
Would draw heaven down, and all the gods, to hearken ;
But being played upon before your time,
Hell only danceth at so harsh a chime.
Good sooth, I care not for you.

ANTIOCHUS

Prince Pericles, touch not, upon thy life,
For that's an article within our law,
As dangerous as the rest. Your time 's expired.
Either expound now, or receive your sentence.

PERICLES

Great king,
Few love to hear the sins they love to act.
'Twould braid yourself too near for me to tell it.   94
Who has a book of all that monarchs do,
He's more secure to keep it shut than shown ;
For vice repeated is like the wand'ring wind,   97
Blows dust in others' eyes, to spread itself ;.
And yet the end of all is bought thus dear,
The breath is gone, and the sore eyes see clear
To stop the air would hurt them. The blind mole casts
Copped hills towards heaven, to tell the earth is thronged   102
By man's oppression, and the poor worm doth die for't.   103
Kings are earth's gods ; in vice their law 's their will ;
And if Jove stray, who dares say Jove doth ill ?
It is enough you know ; and it is fit,   106
What being more known grows worse, to smother it.
All love the womb that their first being bred.
Then give my tongue like leave to love my head.

10–11 *Nature . . . sit* i.e. Nature's dowry was that the planets should sit
in favorable aspect during gestation so as to make the daughter's presence
gladsome   16 *book* summation   17 *curious* exquisite   18 *rased* erased
28 *Hesperides* one of several nymphs who, with a dragon, guarded a tree
bearing golden apples   33–34 *And . . . die* i.e. because the eye presumes,
without desert, to look at the daughter, the whole body of Pericles must
die   41 *For* from   45 *what I must* i.e. death   49–50 *Who . . . did* i.e. who
loose their grip on earthly joys because woe changes their sense of values
50 *Gripe* grasp   57 *conclusion* i.e. riddle   60, 61 *'sayed* assayed   71
How . . . two i.e. how all these may be only two people   74 *eyes* i.e. stars
94 *braid* upbraid   97–101 *For . . . them* i.e. talking about vice irritates
like dust blown in the eyes, but the consequence of talking is expensive :
the vicious see clearly enough to stop the breath of scandalmongers
102 *Copped* peaked ; *thronged* crushed   103 *worm* creature   106–07 *fit . . .
it* fitting to smother what grows worse by being widely known

ANTIOCHUS *[aside]*
  Heaven, that I had thy head ! He has found the meaning.
111 But I will gloze with him. – Young Prince of Tyre,
  Though by the tenor of our strict edict,
  Your exposition misinterpreting,
114 We might proceed to cancel of your days,
115 Yet hope, succeeding from so fair a tree
  As your fair self, doth tune us otherwise.
  Forty days longer we do respite you ;
  If by which time our secret be undone,
  This mercy shows we'll joy in such a son ;
  And until then your entertain shall be
121 As doth befit our honor and your worth.
                [Exeunt.] Manet Pericles solus.

PERICLES
  How courtesy would seem to cover sin,
  When what is done is like an hypocrite,
124 The which is good in nothing but in sight !
  If it be true that I interpret false,
  Then were it certain you were not so bad
  As with foul incest to abuse your soul ;
  Where now you're both a father and a son
  By your uncomely claspings with your child
  (Which pleasures fits a husband, not a father),
  And she an eater of her mother's flesh
  By the defiling of her parents' bed ;
  And both like serpents are, who though they feed
  On sweetest flowers, yet they poison breed.
  Antioch, farewell ! for wisdom sees, those men
  Blush not in actions blacker than the night,
137 Will 'schew no course to keep them from the light.
  One sin, I know, another doth provoke ;
  Murder 's as near to lust as flame to smoke.
  Poison and treason are the hands of sin ;
141 Ay, and the targets to put off the shame.
  Then, lest my life be cropped to keep you clear,
  By flight I'll shun the danger which I fear.   *Exit.*
    Enter Antiochus.

ANTIOCHUS
  He hath found the meaning,
  For which we mean to have his head. He must
  Not live to trumpet forth my infamy,
  Nor tell the world Antiochus doth sin
  In such a loathèd manner ;
  And therefore instantly this prince must die ;
  For by his fall my honor must keep high.
  Who attends us there ?
    Enter Thaliard.

THALIARD   Doth your Highness call ?
ANTIOCHUS
  Thaliard,
153 You are of our chamber, Thaliard, and our mind
    partakes
  Her private actions to your secrecy ;
  And for your faithfulness we will advance you.
  Thaliard, behold, here's poison, and here's gold.
  We hate the Prince of Tyre, and thou must kill him.
  It fits thee not to ask the reason why :
  Because we bid it. Say, is it done ?
THALIARD   My lord,
  'Tis done.
ANTIOCHUS
  Enough.
    Enter a Messenger.

  Let your breath cool yourself, telling your haste.   162
MESSENGER
  My lord, Prince Pericles is fled.   *[Exit.]*
ANTIOCHUS As thou wilt live, fly after ; and, like an arrow
  shot from a well-experienced archer hits the mark his
  eye doth level at, so thou ne'er return unless thou say
  Prince Pericles is dead.
THALIARD My lord, if I can get him within my pistol's
  length, I'll make him sure enough. So farewell to your
  Highness.
ANTIOCHUS
  Thaliard, adieu ! *[Exit Thaliard.]* Till Pericles be dead
  My heart can lend no succor to my head.   *[Exit.]*

            *

    Enter Pericles with his Lords.   I, ii
PERICLES
  Let none disturb us. *[Exeunt Lords.]* Why should this 1
    change of thoughts,
  The sad companion, dull-eyed melancholy,
  Be my so used a guest as not an hour
  In the day's glorious walk or peaceful night,
  The tomb where grief should sleep, can breed me quiet ?
  Here pleasures court mine eyes, and mine eyes shun
    them,
  And danger, which I feared, is at Antioch,
  Whose arm seems far too short to hit me here.   8
  Yet neither pleasure's art can joy my spirits,
  Nor yet the other's distance comfort me.
  Then it is thus : the passions of the mind,
  That have their first conception by misdread,
  Have after-nourishment and life by care ;
  And what was first but fear what might be done,
  Grows elder now, and cares it be not done.   15
  And so with me. The great Antiochus,
  'Gainst whom I am too little to contend,
  Since he's so great can make his will his act,
  Will think me speaking, though I swear to silence ;
  Nor boots it me to say I honor him   20
  If he suspect I may dishonor him.
  And what may make him blush in being known,
  He'll stop the course by which it might be known.
  With hostile forces he'll o'erspread the land,
  And with th' ostent of war will look so huge   25
  Amazement shall drive courage from the state,
  Our men be vanquished ere they do resist,
  And subjects punished that ne'er thought offense ;
  Which care of them, not pity of myself –
  Who am no more but as the tops of trees,
  Which fence the roots they grow by and defend them –   31
  Makes both my body pine and soul to languish,
  And punish that before that he would punish.
    Enter [Helicanus and] all the Lords to Pericles.
I. LORD
  Joy and all comfort in your sacred breast !

111 *gloze* use fair words   114 *cancel* the cancelling   115 *succeeding* proceeding   121 s.d. *solus* alone   124 *sight* appearance   137 *'schew* eschew   141 *targets* light shields ; *put off* turn aside   153 *of our chamber* our chamberlain   162 *Let . . . haste* i.e. as you pant, tell your message   I, ii The palace of Pericles at Tyre s.d. *Enter . . . Lords* (a formal entry locates the scene in Tyre, but the lines seem wildly disordered ; see Appendix)   1 *change of thoughts* i.e. unaccustomed melancholy   8 *arm . . . short* (proverbial : kings have long arms)   15 *cares* takes care   20 *boots it* does it help   25 *ostent* display   31 *fence* protect

2 . LORD
And keep your mind, till you return to us,
Peaceful and comfortable!
HELICANUS
Peace, peace, and give experience tongue!
They do abuse the king that flatter him.
For flattery is the bellows blows up sin;
40   The thing the which is flattered, but a spark
To which that blast gives heat and stronger glowing;
Whereas reproof, obedient and in order,
Fits kings as they are men, for they may err.
When Signior Sooth here does proclaim a peace,
He flatters you, makes war upon your life.
Prince, pardon me; or strike me, if you please.
I cannot be much lower than my knees.
        [Kneels.]
PERICLES
All leave us else; but let your cares o'erlook
What shipping and what lading's in our haven,
50   And then return to us. [Exeunt Lords.] Helicanus, thou
Hast moved us. What seest thou in our looks?
HELICANUS
An angry brow, dread lord.
PERICLES
If there be such a dart in princes' frowns,
How durst thy tongue move anger to our face?
HELICANUS
How dares the plants look up to heaven, from whence
They have their nourishment?
PERICLES   Thou know'st I have power
To take thy life from thee.
HELICANUS   I have ground the axe myself.
Do but you strike the blow.
PERICLES   Rise, prithee, rise.
        [He rises.]
Sit down. Thou art no flatterer.
I thank thee for't; and heaven forbid
61   That kings should let their ears hear their faults hid!
Fit counsellor and servant for a prince,
Who by thy wisdom makes a prince thy servant,
What wouldst thou have me do?
HELICANUS   To bear with patience
Such griefs as you do lay upon yourself.
PERICLES
Thou speak'st like a physician, Helicanus,
That ministers a potion unto me
That thou wouldst tremble to receive thyself.
Attend me then. I went to Antioch,
Where, as thou know'st, against the face of death
I sought the purchase of a glorious beauty,
72   From whence an issue I might propagate
73   Are arms to princes and bring joys to subjects.
Her face was to mine eye beyond all wonder;
The rest (hark in thine ear) as black as incest;
Which by my knowledge found, the sinful father
Seemed not to strike, but smooth. But thou know'st this,
'Tis time to fear when tyrants seem to kiss.

Which fear so grew in me I hither fled
Under the covering of a careful night,
Who seemed my good protector; and being here,
Bethought me what was past, what might succeed.
I knew him tyrannous; and tyrants' fears
Decrease not, but grow faster than the years;
And should he doubt it, as no doubt he doth,
That I should open to the list'ning air
How many worthy princes' bloods were shed
To keep his bed of blackness unlaid ope,
To lop that doubt, he'll fill this land with arms
And make pretense of wrong that I have done him;
When all, for mine, if I may call offense,   91
Must feel war's blow, who spares not innocence;
Which love to all, of which thyself art one,
Who now reproved'st me for't –   94
HELICANUS   Alas, sir!
PERICLES
Drew sleep out of mine eyes, blood from my cheeks,
Musings into my mind, with thousand doubts
How I might stop this tempest ere it came;
And finding little comfort to relieve them,
I thought it princely charity to grieve them.   99
HELICANUS
Well, my lord, since you have given me leave to speak,
Freely will I speak. Antiochus you fear,
And justly too I think you fear the tyrant,
Who either by public war or private treason
Will take away your life.
Therefore, my lord, go travel for a while,
Till that his rage and anger be forgot,
Or till the Destinies do cut his thread of life.
Your rule direct to any; if to me,   108
Day serves not light more faithful than I'll be.
PERICLES
I do not doubt thy faith;
But should he wrong my liberties in my absence?   111
HELICANUS
We'll mingle our bloods together in the earth,
From whence we had our being and our birth.
PERICLES
Tyre, I now look from thee then and to Tharsus
Intend my travel, where I'll hear from thee;   115
And by whose letters I'll dispose myself.
The care I had and have of subjects' good
On thee I lay, whose wisdom's strength can bear it.
I'll take thy word for faith, not ask thine oath.
Who shuns not to break one will crack both:
But in our orbs we'll live so round and safe   121
That time of both this truth shall ne'er convince,   122
Thou show'dst a subject's shine, I a true prince'. Exeunt.

*

Enter Thaliard solus.   I, iii
THALIARD So, this is Tyre, and this the court. Here must
I kill King Pericles; and if I do it not, I am sure to be   2
hanged at home. 'Tis dangerous. Well, I perceive he
was a wise fellow and had good discretion that, being
bid to ask what he would of the king, desired he might
know none of his secrets. Now do I see he had some
reason for't; for if a king bid a man be a villain, he's
bound by the indenture of his oath to be one. Husht!
here comes the lords of Tyre.

61 *let . . . hid* listen to flattery   72 *an issue* offspring   73 *Are arms* which
are a source of strength   91 *mine* i.e. my offense   94 *now* just now   99
grieve grieve for   108 *direct* assign   111 *liberties* rights, privileges   115
Intend direct   121 *orbs* orbits   122 *convince* confute
I, iii The palace of Pericles   2–3 *kill . . . home* (perhaps a line is lost:
if I kill Pericles, I shall be hanged here; and if I do not, etc.)

Enter Helicanus, Escanes, with other Lords.

HELICANUS
You shall not need, my fellow peers of Tyre,
Further to question me of your king's departure.
His sealed commission, left in trust with me,
Does speak sufficiently he's gone to travel.

THALIARD *[aside]* How? the King gone?

HELICANUS
If further yet you will be satisfied
16 Why (as it were unlicensed of your loves)
He would depart, I'll give some light unto you.
Being at Antioch –

THALIARD *[aside]* What from Antioch?

HELICANUS
Royal Antiochus, on what cause I know not,
Took some displeasure at him; at least he judged so;
And doubting lest he had erred or sinned,
To show his sorrow, he'd correct himself;
So puts himself unto the shipman's toil,
With whom each minute threatens life or death.

THALIARD *[aside]*
Well, I perceive
26 I shall not be hanged now, although I would;
But since he's gone, the King's ears it must please
He scaped the land to perish at the seas.
I'll present myself. – Peace to the lords of Tyre!

HELICANUS
Lord Thaliard from Antiochus is welcome.

THALIARD
From him I come
With message unto princely Pericles;
But since my landing I have understood
Your lord has betook himself to unknown travels.
Now message must return from whence it came.

HELICANUS
We have no reason to desire it,
Commended to our master, not to us.
Yet, ere you shall depart, this we desire –
As friends to Antioch, we may feast in Tyre.

Exit [with Thaliard and Lords].

＊

I, iv   *Enter Cleon, the Governor of Tharsus, with his*
          wife [Dionyza] and others.

CLEON
My Dionyza, shall we rest us here,
And by relating tales of others' griefs,
See if 'twill teach us to forget our own?

DIONYZA
That were to blow at fire in hope to quench it;
For who digs hills because they do aspire
Throws down one mountain to cast up a higher.
O my distressèd lord, even such our griefs are!
Here they are but felt and seen with mischief's eyes,
But like to groves, being topped, they higher rise.

CLEON
O Dionyza,
Who wanteth food, and will not say he wants it,
Or can conceal his hunger till he famish?
13 Our tongues and sorrows to sound deep
Our woes into the air; our eyes to weep
Till lungs fetch breath that may proclaim them louder;

That, if heaven slumber while their creatures want,
They may awake their helps to comfort them.
I'll then discourse our woes, felt several years,
And, wanting breath to speak, help me with tears.   19

DIONYZA
I'll do my best, sir.

CLEON
This Tharsus, o'er which I have the government,
A city on whom Plenty held full hand,
For Riches strewed herself even in her streets;   23
Whose towers bore heads so high they kissed the clouds,
And strangers ne'er beheld but wond'red at;
Whose men and dames so jetted and adorned,   26
Like one another's glass to trim them by;
Their tables were stored full, to glad the sight,
And not so much to feed on as delight;
All poverty was scorned, and pride so great
The name of help grew odious to repeat.

DIONYZA
O, 'tis too true!

CLEON
But see what heaven can do! By this our change
Those mouths who, but of late, earth, sea, and air
Were all too little to content and please,
Although they gave their creatures in abundance,
As houses are defiled for want of use,
They are now starved for want of exercise.
Those palates who, not yet two savors younger,   39
Must have inventions to delight the taste,
Would now be glad of bread, and beg for it.
Those mothers who to nuzzle up their babes   42
Thought naught too curious, are ready now
To eat those little darlings whom they loved.
So sharp are hunger's teeth that man and wife
Draw lots who first shall die to lengthen life.   46
Here stands a lord, and there a lady weeping;
Here many sink, yet those which see them fall
Have scarce strength left to give them burial.
Is not this true?

DIONYZA
Our cheeks and hollow eyes do witness it.

CLEON
O, let those cities that of Plenty's cup
And her prosperities so largely taste
With their superfluous riots hear these tears!   54
The misery of Tharsus may be theirs.

Enter a Lord.

LORD
Where's the Lord Governor?

CLEON
Here.
Speak out thy sorrows which thou bring'st in haste,
For comfort is too far for us to expect.

LORD
We have descried, upon our neighboring shore,
A portly sail of ships make hitherward.   61

---

16 *unlicensed . . . loves* without your loving assent   26 *although I would* (the text is corrupt; see ll. 2–3 above)
I, iv The house of the Governor of Tharsus   13–15 *Our . . . louder* (an obscure passage, owing probably to a missing line)   19 *wanting* i.e. when I lack; *help me* help thou me   23 *her* i.e. this city's   26–27 *men . . . by* i.e. each was as a mirror for others   26 *jetted* strutted   39 *savors* mouthfuls   42 *nuzzle up* bring up, rear   46 *life* i.e. the other's life   54 *superfluous riots* immoderate self-indulgence   61 *portly sail* stately fleet

CLEON
    I thought as much.
    One sorrow never comes but brings an heir
    That may succeed as his inheritor;
    And so in ours, some neighboring nation,
    Taking advantage of our misery,
    Hath stuffed the hollow vessels with their power,
    To beat us down, the which are down already;
    And make a conquest of unhappy me,
70   Whereas no glory's got to overcome.
LORD
    That's the least fear; for, by the semblance
    Of their white flags displayed, they bring us peace
    And come to us as favorers, not as foes.
CLEON
74   Thou speak'st like him 's untutored to repeat:
    Who makes the fairest show means most deceit.
    But bring they what they will and what they can,
    What need we fear?
    On ground 's the lowest, and we are halfway there.
79   Go tell their general we attend him here,
    To know for what he comes, and whence he comes,
    And what he craves.
LORD
    I go, my lord.   *[Exit.]*
CLEON
83   Welcome is peace, if he on peace consist;
    If wars, we are unable to resist.
    Enter Pericles with [Lord and] Attendants.
PERICLES
    Lord Governor, for so we hear you are,
    Let not our ships and number of our men
    Be like a beacon fired t' amaze your eyes.
    We have heard your miseries as far as Tyre,
    And seen the desolation of your streets;
    Nor come we to add sorrow to your tears,
    But to relieve them of their heavy load;
92   And these our ships you happily may think
94   Are like the Troyan horse was stuffed within
95   With bloody veins, expecting overthrow,
    Are stored with corn to make your needy bread
    And give them life whom hunger starved half dead.
OMNES
    The gods of Greece protect you!
    And we'll pray for you.
    [They kneel.]
PERICLES   Arise, I pray you, rise.
    We do not look for reverence, but for love,
    And harborage for ourself, our ships, and men.
CLEON
    The which when any shall not gratify,
    Or pay you with unthankfulness in thought –
    Be it our wives, our children, or ourselves –
    The curse of heaven and men succeed their evils!
    Till when (the which, I hope, shall ne'er be seen)
    Your Grace is welcome to our town and us.

PERICLES
    Which welcome we'll accept, feast here awhile,
    Until our stars that frown lend us a smile.   *Exeunt.*

                          *

       Enter Gower.   II, Cho.
    Here have you seen a mighty king
    His child i-wis to incest bring;
    A better prince and benign lord,
    That will prove awful both in deed and word.
    Be quiet then, as men should be,
    Till he hath passed necessity.
    I'll show you those in trouble's reign,
    Losing a mite, a mountain gain.
    The good in conversation,   9
    To whom I give my benison,   10
    Is still at Tharsus, where each man
    Thinks all is writ he spoken can;   12
    And, to remember what he does,   13
    Build his statue to make him glorious.
    But tidings to the contrary   15
    Are brought your eyes. What need speak I?
          Dumb Show.
 Enter at one door Pericles, talking with Cleon; all the Train
 with them. Enter at another door a Gentleman with a letter
 to Pericles. Pericles shows the letter to Cleon. Pericles gives
 the Messenger a reward and knights him. Exit Pericles at
 one door and Cleon at another [with their Trains].

    Good Helicane, that stayed at home –
    Not to eat honey like a drone
    From others' labors, though he strive
    To killen bad, keep good alive,
    And to fulfill his prince' desire –
    Sends word of all that haps in Tyre:
    How Thaliard came full bent with sin
    And hid intent to murder him;
    And that in Tharsus was not best
    Longer for him to make his rest.
    He, doing so, put forth to seas,   27
    Where when men been, there's seldom ease;
    For now the wind begins to blow;
    Thunder above, and deeps below,
    Makes such unquiet that the ship
    Should house him safe is wracked and split,
    And he, good prince, having all lost,
    By waves from coast to coast is tost.
    All perishen of man, of pelf,   35
    Ne aught escapend but himself;   36
    Till fortune, tired with doing bad,
    Threw him ashore, to give him glad.
    And here he comes. What shall be next
    Pardon old Gower; this 'longs the text.   *[Exit.]* 40

                          *

      Enter Pericles, wet.   II, i
PERICLES
    Yet cease your ire, you angry stars of heaven!
    Wind, rain, and thunder, remember earthly man
    Is but a substance that must yield to you;
    And I, as fits my nature, do obey you.
    Alas! the seas hath cast me on the rocks,

70 *Whereas* where   **74** *repeat* recite   **79** *attend* await   **83** *if . . . consist* if
his intent is peace   **92** *happily* haply, perhaps   **94** *bloody veins* i.e. bloodthirsty warriors   **95** *corn* grain
II, Cho. 9 *The good* i.e. Pericles; *conversation* conduct   **10** *benison*
blessing   **12** *writ* Holy Writ   **13** *remember* memorialize   **15** *tidings . . .
contrary* adverse tidings   **27** *doing so* acting accordingly   **35** *pelf* goods
36 *escapend* escaping, or escape   **40** *'longs* belongs to
II, i The seaside at Pentapolis

Washed me from shore to shore, and left me breath
Nothing to think on but ensuing death.
Let it suffice the greatness of your powers
To have bereft a prince of all his fortunes,
And having thrown him from your wat'ry grave,
Here to have death in peace is all he'll crave.
Enter three Fishermen.

1. FISHERMAN What ho, Pilch!

2. FISHERMAN Ha, come and bring away the nets!

1. FISHERMAN What, Patchbreech, I say!

3. FISHERMAN What say you, master?

16 1. FISHERMAN Look how thou stirr'st now! Come away,
17 or I'll fetch th' with a wanion.

3. FISHERMAN Faith, master, I am thinking of the poor
men that were cast away before us even now.

1. FISHERMAN Alas, poor souls! It grieved my heart to
hear what pitiful cries they made to us to help them,
when (well-a-day!) we could scarce help ourselves.

3. FISHERMAN Nay, master, said not I as much when I
saw the porpoise, how he bounced and tumbled? They
say they're half fish, half flesh. A plague on them! They
ne'er come but I look to be washed. Master, I marvel
how the fishes live in the sea.

28 1. FISHERMAN Why, as men do a-land – the great ones
eat up the little ones. I can compare our rich misers to
nothing so fitly as to a whale. 'A plays and tumbles,
driving the poor fry before him, and at last devours
32 them all at a mouthful. Such whales have I heard on o'
th' land, who never leave gaping till they swallowed the
whole parish – church, steeple, bells, and all.

PERICLES *[aside]* A pretty moral.

3. FISHERMAN But, master, if I had been the sexton, I
would have been that day in the belfry.

2. FISHERMAN Why, man?

39 3. FISHERMAN Because he should have swallowed me
too; and when I had been in his belly, I would have kept
such a jangling of the bells that he should never have
42 left till he cast bells, steeple, church, and parish up
again. But if the good King Simonides were of my
mind –

PERICLES *[aside]* Simonides?

3. FISHERMAN We would purge the land of these drones
that rob the bee of her honey.

PERICLES *[aside]*
47 How from the finny subject of the sea
These fishers tell the infirmities of men,
And from their wat'ry empire recollect
50 All that may men approve or men detect! –
Peace be at your labor, honest fishermen.

52 2. FISHERMAN Honest, good fellow? What's that? If it
be a day fits you, scratch't out of the calendar, and nobody look after it.

PERICLES
May see the sea hath cast upon your coast –

2. FISHERMAN What a drunken knave was the sea to cast
thee in our way!

PERICLES
A man, whom both the waters and the wind
In that vast tennis court have made the ball
For them to play upon, entreats you pity him.
He asks of you that never used to beg.

1. FISHERMAN No, friend? Cannot you beg? Here's
them in our country of Greece gets more with begging
than we can do with working.

2. FISHERMAN Canst thou catch any fishes then?

PERICLES I never practiced it.

2. FISHERMAN Nay, then thou wilt starve sure; for
here's nothing to be got nowadays unless thou canst
fish for't.

PERICLES
What I have been I have forgot to know;
But what I am, want teaches me to think on:
A man thronged up with cold; my veins are chill, 71
And have no more of life than may suffice
To give my tongue that heat to ask your help;
Which if you shall refuse, when I am dead,
For that I am a man, pray you see me buried.

1. FISHERMAN Die, koth-a? Now gods forbid't, an I 76
have a gown here; come put it on; keep thee warm. Now,
afore me, a handsome fellow! Come, thou shalt go 78
home, and we'll have flesh for holidays, fish for fasting
days, and moreo'er puddings and flapjacks; and thou
shalt be welcome.

PERICLES I thank you, sir.

2. FISHERMAN Hark you, my friend. You said you could
not beg?

PERICLES I did but crave.

2. FISHERMAN But crave? Then I'll turn craver too,
and so I shall 'scape whipping. 87

PERICLES Why, are your beggars whipped then?

2. FISHERMAN O, not all, my friend, not all! For if all
your beggars were whipped, I would wish no better
office than to be beadle. But, master, I'll go draw up the
net. *[Exit with Third Fisherman.]*

PERICLES *[aside]*
How well this honest mirth becomes their labor!

1. FISHERMAN Hark you, sir. Do you know where ye
are?

PERICLES Not well.

1. FISHERMAN Why, I'll tell you. This is called Pentapolis, and our king the good Simonides.

PERICLES The good Simonides do you call him?

1. FISHERMAN Ay, sir; and he deserves so to be called
for his peacable reign and good government.

PERICLES He is a happy king, since he gains from his 100
subjects the name of good by his government. How far
is his court distant from this shore?

1. FISHERMAN Marry, sir, half a day's journey. And I'll
tell you, he hath a fair daughter, and to-morrow is her
birthday, and here are princes and knights come from
all parts of the world to just and tourney for her love.

PERICLES Were my fortunes equal to my desires, I could
wish to make one there.

1. FISHERMAN O, sir, things must be as they may; and
what a man cannot get, he may lawfully deal for his 110
wife's soul.

Enter the two [other] Fishermen, drawing up a net.

2. FISHERMAN Help, master, help! Here's a fish hangs
in the net like a poor man's right in the law. 'Twill

---

16 *Look . . . now* get moving 17 *fetch th'* deal thee a blow; *wanion*
vengeance 28 *a-land* on land 32 *heard on* heard of 39 *Because* so that
42 *cast* vomited 47 *subject* citizens 50 *approve* commend; *detect* expose
52–54 *If . . . after it* (perhaps a line is missing in which Pericles mentions
the present day, in which case the Fisherman's sentence would mean,
'If the day matches your bedraggled appearance, scratch it out of the
calendar, and no one will miss it.') 71 *thronged up* overwhelmed 76
koth-a quoth he, said he; *an if* 78 *afore me* by my soul 87 *'scape* escape
110–11 *deal . . . soul* buy from the proceeds of selling his wife's body

114 hardly come out. Ha! bots on't! 'tis come at last, and
'tis turned to a rusty armor.

PERICLES
An armor, friends? I pray you let me see it.
Thanks, Fortune, yet, that, after all thy crosses,
Thou givest me somewhat to repair myself!
And though it was mine own, part of my heritage
Which my dead father did bequeath to me,
With this strict charge, even as he left his life,
'Keep it, my Pericles. It hath been a shield
123 'Twixt me and death' – and pointed to this brace –
'For that it saved me, keep it. In like necessity
(The which the gods protect thee from!) may defend
thee.'
It kept where I kept, I so dearly loved it;
Till the rough seas, that spares not any man,
Took it in rage – though, calmed, have given't again –
I thank thee for't. My shipwrack now's no ill,
130 Since I have here my father gave in his will.

1. FISHERMAN What mean you, sir?

PERICLES
To beg of you, kind friends, this coat of worth,
133 For it was sometime target to a king.
I know it by this mark. He loved me dearly,
And for his sake I wish the having of it;
And that you'd guide me to your sovereign's court,
Where with it I may appear a gentleman;
And if that ever my low fortune's better,
I'll pay your bounties; till then rest your debtor.

1. FISHERMAN Why, wilt thou tourney for the lady?

PERICLES
I'll show the virtue I have borne in arms.

1. FISHERMAN Why, do'ee take it, and the gods give thee
good on't!

2. FISHERMAN Ay, but hark you, my friend! 'Twas we
that made up this garment through the rough seams of
146 the waters. There are certain condolements, certain
147 vails. I hope, sir, if you thrive, you'll remember from
whence you had it.

PERICLES
Believe't, I will.
By your furtherance I am clothed in steel;
151 And, spite of all the rapture of the sea,
This jewel holds his building on my arm.
Unto thy value I will mount myself
Upon a courser whose delightful steps
Shall make the gazer joy to see him tread.
Only, my friend, I yet am unprovided
157 Of a pair of bases.

2. FISHERMAN We'll sure provide. Thou shalt have my
best gown to make thee a pair; and I'll bring thee to the
court myself.

PERICLES
Then honor be but equal to my will,   161
This day I'll rise, or else add ill to ill.   [Exeunt.]

*

Enter [King] Simonides, with attendance, and   II, ii
Thaisa.

KING
Are the knights ready to begin the triumph?

1. LORD
They are, my liege,
And stay your coming to present themselves.

KING
Return them, we are ready; and our daughter,   4
In honor of whose birth these triumphs are,
Sits here like beauty's child, whom nature gat   6
For men to see, and seeing wonder at.   [Exit a Lord.]

THAISA
It pleaseth you, my royal father, to express
My commendations great, whose merit's less.

KING
It's fit it should be so, for princes are
A model which heaven makes like to itself.
As jewels lose their glory if neglected,
So princes their renowns if not respected.
'Tis now your honor, daughter, to entertain   14
The labor of each knight in his device.   15

THAISA
Which, to preserve mine honor, I'll perform.
The First Knight passes by [and his Squire shows his
shield to the Princess].

KING
Who is the first that doth prefer himself?

THAISA
A knight of Sparta, my renownèd father;
And the device he bears upon his shield
Is a black Ethiope reaching at the sun;
The word, 'Lux tua vita mihi.'   21

KING
He loves you well that holds his life of you.
The Second Knight.
Who is the second that presents himself?

THAISA
A prince of Macedon, my royal father;
And the device he bears upon his shield
Is an armed knight that's conquered by a lady;
The motto thus in Spanish, 'Piu por dulzura que por 27
fuerza.'
Third Knight.

KING
And what's the third?

THAISA   The third of Antioch;
And his device, a wreath of chivalry;   29
The word, 'Me pompae provexit apex.'   30
Fourth Knight.

KING
What is the fourth?

THAISA
A burning torch that's turnèd upside down;
The word, 'Qui me alit, me extinguit.'
                                                          33
KING
Which shows that beauty hath his power and will,
Which can as well inflame as it can kill.

---

114 bots on't plague on it 123 brace mailed arm piece 130 my father
gave i.e. what my father gave 133 target light shield 146 condolements
i.e. proceeds to be doled, or shared (a malapropism) 147 vails tailor's remnants 151 rapture raping, plundering 157 bases a pleated skirt worn
by knights on horseback 161 Then . . . will i.e. if I attain the honor I
purpose to win
II, ii Before the palace of King Simonides 4 Return inform, answer
6 gat begot 14 entertain receive and describe 15 device impresa, emblematic figure with a motto 21 Lux . . . mihi thy light is life to me 27 Piu
. . . fuerza more by gentleness than by force 29 wreath of chivalry chaplet
of two differently colored silks wound about each other (heraldic term)
30 Me . . . apex the crown of the triumph has led me on 33 Qui . . . extinguit
who feeds me extinguishes me

Fifth Knight.

THAISA
The fifth, an hand environed with clouds,
Holding out gold that's by the touchstone tried ;
38 The motto thus, 'Sic spectanda fides.'
Sixth Knight [Pericles].

KING
And what's
The sixth and last, the which the knight himself
With such a graceful courtesy delivered ?

THAISA
He seems to be a stranger ; but his present is
A withered branch that's only green at top ;
44 The motto, 'In hac spe vivo.'

KING
A pretty moral.
From the dejected state wherein he is
He hopes by you his fortunes yet may flourish.

I . LORD
He had need mean better than his outward show
Can any way speak in his just commend ;
For by his rusty outside he appears
51 To have practiced more the whipstock than the lance.

2 . LORD
He well may be a stranger, for he comes
To an honored triumph strangely furnishèd.

3 . LORD
And on set purpose let his armor rust
Until this day, to scour it in the dust.

KING
Opinion 's but a fool, that makes us scan
The outward habit for the inward man.
But stay, the knights are coming. We will withdraw
Into the gallery.   *[Exeunt.]*
Great shouts [within,] and all cry 'The mean knight !'

*

II, iii   *Enter the King [Simonides, Thaisa, Marshal,*
            Ladies, Lords,] and Knights from tilting.

KING
Knights,
To say you're welcome were superfluous.
To place upon the volume of your deeds,
As in a title-page, your worth in arms
Were more than you expect, or more than's fit,
6   Since every worth in show commends itself.
Prepare for mirth, for mirth becomes a feast.
You are princes and my guests.

THAISA
But you, my knight and guest ;
To whom this wreath of victory I give,
And crown you king of this day's happiness.

PERICLES
'Tis more by fortune, lady, than my merit.

KING
Call it by what you will, the day is yours ;
And here, I hope, is none that envies it.
In framing an artist, art hath thus decreed,
To make some good, but others to exceed ;
And you are her labored scholar. Come, queen o' th'
     feast,
For, daughter, so you are ; here take your place.
19 Marshal, the rest as they deserve their grace.

KNIGHTS
We are honored much by good Simonides.

KING
Your presence glads our days. Honor we love ;
For who hates honor hates the gods above.

MARSHAL
Sir, yonder is your place.

PERICLES   Some other is more fit.

I . KNIGHT
Contend not, sir ; for we are gentlemen
Have neither in our hearts nor outward eyes   25
Envied the great nor shall the low despise.

PERICLES
You are right courteous knights.

KING   Sit, sir, sit.
          [Aside]
By Jove, I wonder, that is king of thoughts,
These cates resist me, he not thought upon.   29

THAISA *[aside]*
By Juno, that is queen of marriage,
All viands that I eat do seem unsavory,   31
Wishing him my meat. – Sure he's a gallant gentleman.

KING *[aside]*
He's but a country gentleman.
Has done no more than other knights have done ;
Has broken a staff or so ; so let it pass.

THAISA *[aside]*
To me he seems like diamond to glass.

PERICLES *[aside]*
Yon king 's to me like to my father's picture,
Which tells me in that glory once he was';
Had princes sit like stars about his throne,
And he the sun for them to reverence ;
None that beheld him but, like lesser lights,
Did vail their crowns to his supremacy ;   42
Where now his son 's like a glowworm in the night,
The which hath fire in darkness, none in light.
Whereby I see that Time 's the king of men ;
He's both their parent, and he is their grave,
And gives them what he will, not what they crave.

KING
What, are you merry, knights ?

KNIGHTS
Who can be other in this royal presence ?

KING
Here, with a cup that's stored unto the brim –
As you do love, fill to your mistress' lips –
We drink this health to you.

KNIGHTS   We thank your Grace.

KING
Yet pause awhile.
Yon knight doth sit too melancholy,
As if the entertainment in our court
Had not a show might countervail his worth.   56
Note it not you, Thaisa ?

THAISA   What is 't to me, my father ?

KING
O, attend, my daughter.

38 *Sic . . . fides* thus is faith to be tried   44 *In . . . vivo* in this hope I live
51 *practiced . . . whipstock* used a whip, i.e. driven a cart
II, iii The palace of Simonides   6 *show* action   19 *the rest* i.e. place the
others   25 *Have* who have   29 *cates resist* delicacies do not appeal to
31 *unsavory* tasteless   42 *vail* take off   56 *might countervail* which could
equal

Princes, in this, should live like gods above,
Who freely give to every one that come
To honor them;

62   And princes not doing so are like to gnats,
Which make a sound, but killed are wond'red at.

64   Therefore to make his entrance more sweet,
Here, say we drink this standing bowl of wine to him.

THAISA
Alas, my father, it befits not me
Unto a stranger knight to be so bold!
He may my proffer take for an offense,
Since men take women's gifts for impudence.

KING
How?
Do as I bid you, or you'll move me else.

THAISA *[aside]*
Now, by the gods, he could not please me better.

KING
And furthermore tell him we desire to know
Of whence he is, his name and parentage.

THAISA
The King my father, sir, has drunk to you –

PERICLES
I thank him.

THAISA
Wishing it so much blood unto your life.

PERICLES
I thank both him and you, and pledge him freely.

THAISA
And further, he desires to know of you
Of whence you are, your name and parentage.

PERICLES
A gentleman of Tyre; my name, Pericles;

82   My education been in arts and arms;
Who, looking for adventures in the world,
Was by the rough seas reft of ships and men
And, after shipwrack, driven upon this shore.

THAISA
He thanks your Grace; names himself Pericles,
A gentleman of Tyre,
Who only by misfortune of the seas
Bereft of ships and men, cast on this shore.

KING
Now, by the gods, I pity his misfortune
And will awake him from his melancholy.
Come, gentlemen, we sit too long on trifles
And waste the time which looks for other revels.

94   Even in your armors, as you are addressed,
Will you well become a soldier's dance.

96   I will not have excuse with saying this:
Loud music is too harsh for ladies' heads,
Since they love men in arms as well as beds.
They dance.

99   So, this was well asked, 'twas so well performed.

Come, sir.
Here is a lady that wants breathing too;
And I have heard, you knights of Tyre
Are excellent in making ladies trip,   103
And that their measures are as excellent.   104

PERICLES
In those that practice them they are, my lord.

KING
O, that's as much as you would be denied   106
Of your fair courtesy.
They dance.   Unclasp, unclasp!
Thanks, gentlemen, to all; all have done well,
[To Pericles]
But you the best. – Pages and lights, to conduct
These knights unto their several lodgings! – Yours, sir,
We have given order to be next our own.

PERICLES
I am at your Grace's pleasure.

KING
Princes, it is too late to talk of love;
And that's the mark I know you level at.
Therefore each one betake him to his rest;
To-morrow all for speeding do their best.   *[Exeunt.]*

*

Enter Helicanus and Escanes.   II, iv

HELICANUS
No, Escanes; know this of me –
Antiochus from incest lived not free;
For which, the most high gods not minding longer
To withhold the vengeance that they had in store,
Due to this heinous capital offense,
Even in the height and pride of all his glory,
When he was seated in a chariot
Of an inestimable value, and his daughter with him,
A fire from heaven came and shrivelled up
Their bodies, even to loathing; for they so stunk
That all those eyes adored them ere their fall
Scorn now their hand should give them burial.

ESCANES
'Twas very strange.

HELICANUS   And yet but justice; for though
This king were great, his greatness was no guard
To bar heaven's shaft, but sin had his reward.

ESCANES
'Tis very true.
Enter two or three Lords.

1. LORD
See, not a man in private conference
Or council has respect with him but he.   18

2. LORD
It shall no longer grieve without reproof.

3. LORD
And cursed be he that will not second it!

1. LORD
Follow me then. Lord Helicane, a word.

HELICANUS
With me? and welcome. Happy day, my lords.

1. LORD
Know that our griefs are risen to the top
And now at length they overflow their banks.

HELICANUS
Your griefs? for what? Wrong not your prince you love.

62–63 *gnats . . . wond'red at* i.e. after gnats are dead, one wonders so small a thing made so much noise   **64** *entrance* (Pericles is one of those who came to do honor)   **82** *been* has been   **94** *addressed* costumed, accoutered **96–97** *I . . . heads* I will not accept your excuses that loud music is too harsh for ladies' heads   **99** *So . . . performed* i.e. it was proper to invite the dance, which was well performed   **103** *trip* do a light dance (perhaps with 'double entendre')   **104** *measures* formal dances (perhaps with 'double entendre')   **106–07** *that's . . . courtesy* i.e. that is as if, out of modesty, you should excuse yourself from dancing
II, iv The house of the Governor of Tyre   **18** *he* i.e. Escanes

1 . LORD
Wrong not yourself then, noble Helicane ;
But if the prince do live, let us salute him,
Or know what ground 's made happy by his breath.
If in the world he live, we'll seek him out ;
If in his grave he rest, we'll find him there
31   And be resolved he lives to govern us,
32   Or, dead, gives cause to mourn his funeral,
And leaves us to our free election.
2 . LORD
34   Whose death 's indeed the strongest in our censure ;
And knowing this kingdom is without a head –
Like goodly buildings left without a roof
Soon fall to ruin – your noble self,
That best know how to rule and how to reign,
We thus submit unto, our sovereign.
OMNES
Live, noble Helicane !
HELICANUS
41   Try honor's cause : forbear your suffrages.
If that you love Prince Pericles, forbear.
43   Take I your wish, I leap into the seas,
44   Where's hourly trouble for a minute's ease.
A twelvemonth longer let me entreat you
46   To forbear the absence of your king ;
If in which time expired he not return,
I shall with agèd patience bear your yoke.
But if I cannot win you to this love,
Go search like nobles, like noble subjects,
And in your search spend your adventurous worth ;
Whom if you find and win unto return,
You shall like diamonds sit about his crown.
1 . LORD
To wisdom he's a fool that will not yield ;
And since Lord Helicane enjoineth us,
We with our travels will endeavor it.
HELICANUS
Then you love us, we you, and we'll clasp hands.
When peers thus knit, a kingdom ever stands.   *Exeunt.*

*

II, v   *Enter the King [Simonides], reading of a letter at*
         one door. The Knights meet him.
1 . KNIGHT
Good morrow to the good Simonides.
KING
Knights, from my daughter this I let you know,
That for this twelvemonth she'll not undertake
A married life.
Her reason to herself is only known,
Which from her by no means can I get.
2 . KNIGHT
May we not get access to her, my lord ?
KING
Faith, by no means. She hath so strictly tied her
To her chamber that 'tis impossible.
10   One twelve moons more she'll wear Diana's livery.
This by the eye of Cynthia hath she vowed,
And on her virgin honor will not break it.
3 . KNIGHT
Loath to bid farewell, we take our leaves.

                      [Exeunt Knights.]

KING
So,
They are well dispatched. Now to my daughter's letter.
She tells me here, she'll wed the stranger knight,
Or never more to view nor day nor light.
'Tis well, mistress ; your choice agrees with mine ;
I like that well. Nay, how absolute she's in't,
Not minding whether I dislike or no !   20
Well, I do commend her choice ;
And will no longer have it be delayed.
Soft ! here he comes ; I must dissemble it.
       Enter Pericles.
PERICLES
All fortune to the good Simonides !
KING
To you as much ; sir, I am beholding to you
For your sweet music this last night. I do
Protest my ears were never better fed
With such delightful pleasing harmony.
PERICLES
It is your Grace's pleasure to commend ;
Not my desert.
KING   Sir, you are music's master.   30
PERICLES
The worst of all her scholars, my good lord.
KING
Let me ask you one thing :
What do you think of my daughter, sir ?
PERICLES
A most virtuous princess.
KING
And she is fair too, is she not ?
PERICLES
As a fair day in summer – wondrous fair.
KING
Sir, my daughter thinks very well of you ;
Ay, so well that you must be her master
And she will be your scholar. Therefore look to it.
PERICLES
I am unworthy for her schoolmaster.
KING
She thinks not so. Peruse this writing else.   41
PERICLES *[aside]*
What's here ?
A letter, that she loves the knight of Tyre ?
'Tis the King's subtlety to have my life. –
O, seek not to entrap me, gracious lord,
A stranger and distressèd gentleman,
That never aimed so high to love your daughter,   47
But bent all offices to honor her.   48
KING
Thou hast bewitched my daughter, and thou art
A villain.
PERICLES   By the gods, I have not !
Never did thought of mine levy offense ;   52
Nor never did my actions yet commence

31 *be resolved* satisfy our minds whether   32 *dead* if dead   34 *the strongest* the more likely alternative ; *censure* opinion   41 *Try honor's cause* i.e. follow the path of honor   43 *Take I* if I accede to   44 *hourly . . . ease* i.e. a momentary pleasure of acceptance will bring continuous troubles   46 *forbear* endure
II, v The palace of Simonides, Pentapolis   10 *wear Diana's livery* i.e. continue a maid   41 *else* if you do not believe me   47 *to* as to   48 *bent all offices* devoted all my duty   52 *levy* aim at

A deed might gain her love or your displeasure.

KING
Traitor, thou liest!

PERICLES   Traitor?

KING   Ay, traitor.

PERICLES
Even in his throat – unless it be the King –
That calls me traitor, I return the lie.

KING [aside]
Now, by the gods, I do applaud his courage.

PERICLES
My actions are as noble as my thoughts,
60 That never relished of a base descent.
I came unto your court for honor's cause,
And not to be a rebel to her state;
And he that otherwise accounts of me,
This sword shall prove he's honor's enemy.

KING
No?
Here comes my daughter, she can witness it.
    Enter Thaisa.

PERICLES
Then, as you are as virtuous as fair,
Resolve your angry father if my tongue
Did e'er solicit, or my hand subscribe
70 To any syllable that made love to you.

THAISA
Why, sir, say if you had,
Who takes offense at that would make me glad?

KING
Yea, mistress, are you so peremptory?
(Aside) I am glad on't with all my heart. –
I'll tame you; I'll bring you in subjection!
Will you, not having my consent,
Bestow your love and your affections
Upon a stranger? – (aside) who, for aught I know,
May be (nor can I think the contrary)
80 As great in blood as I myself. –
Therefore hear you, mistress: either frame
Your will to mine – and you, sir, hear you,
Either be ruled by me, or I'll make you –
Man and wife.
Nay, come, your hands and lips must seal it too;
And being joined, I'll thus your hopes destroy,
And for further grief – God give you joy! –
What, are you both pleased?

THAISA   Yes, if you love me, sir.

PERICLES
89 Even as my life my blood that fosters it!

KING
What, are you both agreed?

91 AMBO
Yes, if't please your Majesty.

KING
It pleaseth me so well that I will see you wed;
And then, with what haste you can, get you to bed.
                                    Exeunt.

                        *

89 my life i.e. my life loves   91 Ambo both
III, Cho.   13 eche eke   15 dern dark, wild; perch a measure of land
17 coigns corners   21 stead aid   22 Fame . . . inquire i.e. rumor answering
inquiry in least-known places   32 dooms judgments   36 can sound began
to proclaim   45–46 half . . . cut i.e. the voyage is half done   47 grizzled
grey   51 well-a-near alas   52 travail labor

    Enter Gower.   III, Cho.

GOWER
Now sleep yslackèd hath the rout;
No din but snores the house about,
Made louder by the o'erfed breast
Of this most pompous marriage feast.
The cat, with eyne of burning coal,
Now couches fore the mouse's hole;
And crickets sing at the oven's mouth,
E'er the blither for their drouth.
Hymen hath brought the bride to bed,
Where, by the loss of maidenhead,
A babe is moulded. Be attent,
And time that is so briefly spent
With your fine fancies quaintly eche.   13
What's dumb in show I'll plain with speech.

                [Dumb Show.]
Enter Pericles and Simonides at one door, with Attendants;
a Messenger meets them, kneels, and gives Pericles a letter.
Pericles shows it Simonides. The Lords kneel to him [Peri-
cles]. Then enter Thaisa with child, with Lychorida, a
nurse. The King shows her the letter; she rejoices. She and
Pericles take leave of her father, and depart [with Lychorida
and their Attendants. Then exeunt Simonides and the rest].

By many a dern and painful perch   15
Of Pericles the careful search,
By the four opposing coigns   17
Which the world together joins,
Is made with all due diligence
That horse and sail and high expense
Can stead the quest. At last from Tyre,   21
Fame answering the most strange inquire,   22
To th' court of King Simonides
Are letters brought, the tenor these:
Antiochus and his daughter dead,
The men of Tyrus on the head
Of Helicanus would set on
The crown of Tyre, but he will none.
The mutiny he there hastes t' appease;
Says to 'em, if King Pericles
Come not home in twice six moons,
He, obedient to their dooms,   32
Will take the crown. The sum of this,
Brought hither to Pentapolis,
Y-ravishèd the regions round,
And every one with claps can sound,   36
'Our heir apparent is a king!
Who dreamt, who thought of such a thing?'
Brief, he must hence depart to Tyre.
His queen, with child, makes her desire
(Which who shall cross?) along to go.
Omit we all their dole and woe.
Lychorida her nurse she takes,
And so to sea. Their vessel shakes
On Neptune's billow; half the flood   45
Hath their keel cut: but fortune's mood
Varies again; the grizzled North   47
Disgorges such a tempest forth
That, as a duck for life that dives,
So up and down the poor ship drives.
The lady shrieks, and, well-a-near,   51
Does fall in travail with her fear;   52
And what ensues in this fell storm

Shall for itself itself perform.

55 I nill relate, action may
Conveniently the rest convey,
57 Which might not what by me is told.
In your imagination hold
This stage the ship, upon whose deck
The sea-tossed Pericles appears to speak.   *Exit.*

*

III, i   *Enter Pericles a-shipboard.*

PERICLES
The god of this great vast, rebuke these surges,
Which wash both heaven and hell; and thou that hast
Upon the winds command, bind them in brass,
Having called them from the deep! O, still
Thy deaf'ning dreadful thunders; gently quench
Thy nimble sulphurous flashes! – O, how, Lychorida,
How does my queen? – Thou stormest venomously;
Wilt thou spit all thyself? The seaman's whistle
Is as a whisper in the ears of death,
10 Unheard. – Lychorida! – Lucina, O
Divinest patroness and midwife gentle
To those that cry by night, convey thy deity
Aboard our dancing boat; make swift the pangs
Of my queen's travails!
          Enter Lychorida [with an Infant].
                    Now, Lychorida!

LYCHORIDA
Here is a thing too young for such a place,
Who, if it had conceit, would die, as I
Am like to do. Take in your arms this piece
Of your dead queen.

PERICLES   How? how, Lychorida?

LYCHORIDA
Patience, good sir; do not assist the storm.
Here's all that is left living of your queen –
A little daughter. For the sake of it,
Be manly and take comfort.

PERICLES   O you gods!
Why do you make us love your goodly gifts
And snatch them straight away? We here below
25 Recall not what we give, and therein may
26 Vie honor with you.

LYCHORIDA   Patience, good sir,
27 Even for this charge.

PERICLES   Now mild may be thy life!
For a more blusterous birth had never babe;
Quiet and gentle thy conditions! for
Thou art the rudeliest welcomed to this world
That ever was prince's child. Happy what follows!
Thou hast as chiding a nativity
As fire, air, water, earth, and heaven can make,
To herald thee from the womb. [Poor inch of nature.]
35 Even at the first thy loss is more than can
Thy portage quit with all thou canst find here.
Now the good gods throw their best eyes upon't!
          Enter two Sailors.

1. SAILOR What courage, sir? God save you!

PERICLES
39 Courage enough. I do not fear the flaw;
It hath done to me the worst. Yet for the love
Of this poor infant, this fresh new seafarer,
I would it would be quiet.

1. SAILOR Slack the bolins there! Thou wilt not, wilt 43
thou? Blow, and split thyself.

2. SAILOR But searoom, an the brine and cloudy billow 45
kiss the moon, I care not.

1. SAILOR Sir, your queen must overboard. The sea
works high, the wind is loud, and will not lie till the 48
ship be cleared of the dead.

PERICLES That's your superstition.

1. SAILOR Pardon us, sir. With us at sea it hath been still 51
observed, and we are strong in custom. Therefore
briefly yield 'er; for she must overboard straight.

PERICLES
As you think meet. Most wretched queen!

LYCHORIDA Here she lies, sir.

PERICLES
A terrible childbed hast thou had, my dear;
No light, no fire. Th' unfriendly elements
Forgot thee utterly; nor have I time
To give thee hallowed to thy grave, but straight
Must cast thee, scarcely coffined, in the ooze;
Where, for a monument upon thy bones   61
And e'er-remaining lamps, the belching whale   62
And humming water must o'erwhelm thy corpse,
Lying with simple shells. O Lychorida,
Bid Nestor bring me spices, ink and paper,
My casket and my jewels; and bid Nicander
Bring me the satin coffin. Lay the babe   67
Upon the pillow. Hie thee, whiles I say
A priestly farewell to her. Suddenly, woman.
          [Exit Lychorida.]

2. SAILOR Sir, we have a chest beneath the hatches,
caulked and bitumed ready.   71

PERICLES
I thank thee. Mariner, say, what coast is this?

2. SAILOR We are near Tharsus.

PERICLES
Thither, gentle mariner,
Alter thy course from Tyre. When canst thou reach it?

2. SAILOR By break of day, if the wind cease.

PERICLES
O, make for Tharsus!
There will I visit Cleon, for the babe
Cannot hold out to Tyrus. There I'll leave it
At careful nursing. Go thy ways, good mariner;
I'll bring the body presently.   *Exit [with Sailors].*

*

          Enter Lord Cerimon, with a Servant [and other   III,
          Persons in distress].

CERIMON
Philemon, ho!
          Enter Philemon.

55 *nill* will not   57 *Which . . . told* i.e. what I have related could not easily
be enacted on the stage
III, i The deck of a ship at sea   25 *therein* in that respect   26 *Vie . . .
you* consider ourselves as honorable as you, place our honor in open competition with yours   27 *for this charge* i.e. for the sake of the infant
35–36 *Even . . . here* i.e. your loss at birth is greater than the rest of life
can compensate   39 *flaw* sudden gust of wind   43 *bolins* bowlines
45 *But searoom* so long as we have room to maneuver the vessel without
going aground; *an if*   48 *works high* rages   51 *still* always   61 *for* instead
of   62 *e'er-remaining* ever-burning   67 *coffin* coffer   71 *bitumed* made
watertight with bitumen
III, ii The house of Cerimon at Ephesus

PHILEMON
Doth my lord call?
CERIMON
Get fire and meat for these poor men.   *[Exit Philemon.]*
'T 'as been a turbulent and stormy night.
SERVANT
I have been in many ; but such a night as this
Till now I ne'er endured.
CERIMON
Your master will be dead ere you return.
There's nothing can be minist'red to nature
That can recover him.
9   *[To another]*   Give this to the pothecary,
And tell me how it works.   *[Exeunt all but Cerimon.]*
      Enter two Gentlemen.
1. GENTLEMAN   Good morrow.
2. GENTLEMAN
Good morrow to your lordship.
CERIMON   Gentlemen,
Why do you stir so early?
1. GENTLEMAN
Sir,
Our lodgings, standing bleak upon the sea,
15   Shook as the earth did quake. The very principals
Did seem to rend, and all to topple.
Pure surprise and fear made me to quit the house.
2. GENTLEMAN
That is the cause we trouble you so early ;
19   'Tis not our husbandry.
CERIMON   O, you say well.
1. GENTLEMAN
20   But I much marvel that your lordship, having
Rich tire about you, should at these early hours
Shake off the golden slumber of repose.
'Tis most strange
24   Nature should be so conversant with pain,
Being thereto not compelled.
CERIMON   I hold it ever
Virtue and cunning were endowments greater
27   Than nobleness and riches. Careless heirs
May the two latter darken and expend ;
But immortality attends the former,
Making a man a god. 'Tis known, I ever
Have studied physic, through which secret art,
By turning o'er authorities, I have,
Together with my practice, made familiar
34   To me and to my aid the blest infusions
35   That dwell in vegetives, in metals, stones ;
And can speak of the disturbances
That nature works, and of her cures ; which doth give me
A more content in course of true delight
Than to be thirsty after tottering honor,
Or tie my treasure up in silken bags,
To please the fool and death.
2. GENTLEMAN
Your honor has through Ephesus poured forth
Your charity, and hundreds call themselves

Your creatures, who by you have been restored ;
And not your knowledge, your personal pain, but even
Your purse, still open, hath built Lord Cerimon
Such strong renown as time shall never raze.
     Enter two or three [Servants] with a chest.
SERVANT
So, lift there.
CERIMON   What's that?
SERVANT   Sir, even now
Did the sea toss up upon our shore this chest.
'Tis of some wrack.
CERIMON   Set 't down ; let's look upon 't.
2. GENTLEMAN
'Tis like a coffin, sir.
CERIMON   Whate'er it be,
'Tis wondrous heavy. Wrench it open straight.
If the sea's stomach be o'ercharged with gold,
'Tis a good constraint of fortune it belches upon us.   54
2. GENTLEMAN
'Tis so, my lord.
CERIMON   How close 'tis caulked and bitumed.
Did the sea cast it up?
SERVANT
I never saw so huge a billow, sir,
As tossed it upon shore.
CERIMON   Wrench it open.
Soft ! It smells most sweetly in my sense.
2. GENTLEMAN
A delicate odor.
CERIMON
As ever hit my nostril. So, up with it !
O you most potent gods ! what's here ? a corse !
2. GENTLEMAN
Most strange !
CERIMON
Shrouded in cloth of state ; balmed and entreasured
With full bags of spices ! A passport too !
Apollo, perfect me in the characters !   66
     [Reads from a scroll.]
     'Here I give to understand –
     If e'er this coffin drives a-land –
     I, King Pericles, have lost
     This queen, worth all our mundane cost.
     Who finds her, give her burying ;
     She was the daughter of a king.
     Besides this treasure for a fee,
     The gods requit his charity !'   74
If thou livest, Pericles, thou hast a heart
That even cracks for woe ! This chanced to-night.
2. GENTLEMAN
Most likely, sir.
CERIMON   Nay, certainly to-night ;
For look how fresh she looks ! They were too rough
That threw her in the sea. Make a fire within.
Fetch hither all my boxes in my closet. *[Exit a Servant.]*
Death may usurp on nature many hours,
And yet the fire of life kindle again
The o'erpressed spirits. I heard of an Egyptian
That had nine hours lien dead,   84
Who was by good appliance recoverèd.
     Enter one with [boxes,] napkins, and fire.
Well said, well said ! the fire and cloths.   86
The still and woeful music that we have,
Cause it to sound, beseech you.

---

9 *pothecary* apothecary   **15** *as* as if ; *principals* chief rafters   **19** *husbandry*
zeal for work   **20–21** *having . . . you* i.e. enjoying luxury   **24** *pain* trouble
27 *nobleness* noble birth   **34** *my aid* i.e. Philemon   **35** *vegetives* herbs and
plants   **54** *constraint of fortune* act of control by fortune   **66** *Apollo*
(the patron of learning as well as of medicine) ; *perfect* instruct   **74** *requit*
repay   **84** *lien* lain   **86** *Well said* well done

89 The viol once more. How thou stirr'st, thou block!
The music there! I pray you give her air.
Gentlemen, this queen will live;
Nature awakes a warm breath out of her.
She hath not been entranced above five hours.
94 See how she gins to blow into life's flower again!

1. GENTLEMAN
The heavens,
Through you, increase our wonder, and sets up
Your fame for ever.

CERIMON   She is alive! Behold,
98 Her eyelids, cases to those heavenly jewels
Which Pericles hath lost, begin to part
100 Their fringes of bright gold. The diamonds
101 Of a most praisèd water doth appear
To make the world twice rich. Live, and make
Us weep to hear your fate, fair creature,
Rare as you seem to be!
                    She moves.

THAISA   O dear Diana,
Where am I? Where's my lord? What world is this?

2. GENTLEMAN
Is not this strange?

1. GENTLEMAN   Most rare.

CERIMON   Hush, my gentle neighbors!
Lend me your hands; to the next chamber bear her.
Get linen. Now this matter must be looked to,
110 For her relapse is mortal. Come, come!
And Aesculapius guide us!
                    They carry her away. Exeunt omnes.

*

III, iii   *Enter Pericles at Tharsus, with Cleon and Dionyza*
            [and Lychorida with Marina in her arms].

PERICLES
Most honored Cleon, I must needs be gone.
My twelve months are expired, and Tyrus stands
In a litigious peace. You and your lady
Take from my heart all thankfulness! The gods
Make up the rest upon you!

CLEON   Your strokes of fortune,
Though they hurt you mortally, yet glance
Full woundingly on us.

DIONYZA   O your sweet queen!
That the strict Fates had pleased you had brought her
    hither
To have blessed mine eyes with her!

PERICLES   We cannot but obey
The powers above us. Could I rage and roar
As doth the sea she lies in, yet the end
Must be as 'tis. My gentle babe Marina – whom,
13 For she was born at sea, I have named so – here
I charge your charity withal, leaving her
The infant of your care; beseeching you
To give her princely training, that she may
Be mannered as she is born.

CLEON   Fear not, my lord, but think
Your Grace, that fed my country with your corn,
For which the people's prayers still fall upon you,
Must in your child be thought on. If neglection
21 Should therein make me vile, the common body,
By you relieved, would force me to my duty.
But if to that my nature need a spur,

The gods revenge it upon me and mine
To the end of generation!   25

PERICLES   I believe you.
Your honor and your goodness teach me to't   26
Without your vows. Till she be married, madam,
By bright Diana, whom we honor all,
Unscissored shall this hair of mine remain,
Though I show ill in't. So I take my leave.
Good madam, make me blessèd in your care
In bringing up my child.

DIONYZA   I have one myself,
Who shall not be more dear to my respect
Than yours, my lord.

PERICLES   Madam, my thanks and prayers.

CLEON
We'll bring your Grace e'en to the edge o' th' shore,
Then give you up to the masked Neptune and   36
The gentlest winds of heaven.

PERICLES   I will embrace
Your offer. Come, dearest madam. O, no tears,
Lychorida, no tears!
Look to your little mistress, on whose grace
You may depend hereafter. Come, my lord.   *[Exeunt.]*

*

Enter Cerimon and Thaisa.   III,

CERIMON
Madam, this letter, and some certain jewels,
Lay with you in your coffer; which are
At your command. Know you the character?

THAISA
It is my lord's. That I was shipped at sea
I well remember, even on my eaning time;
But whether there delivered, by the holy gods,
I cannot rightly say. But since King Pericles,
My wedded lord, I ne'er shall see again,
A vestal livery will I take me to,   9
And never more have joy.

CERIMON
Madam, if this you purpose as ye speak,
Diana's temple is not distant far,
Where you may abide till your date expire.   13
Moreover, if you please, a niece of mine
Shall there attend you.

THAISA
My recompense is thanks, that's all;
Yet my good will is great, though the gift small.
                                Exit [with Cerimon].

*

Enter Gower.   IV,

GOWER
Imagine Pericles arrived at Tyre,
Welcomed and settled to his own desire.
His woeful queen we leave at Ephesus,
Unto Diana there's a votaress.

89 *How thou stirr'st* i.e. how slow you are   94 *gins* begins   98 *cases . . . jewels* i.e. covers to her eyes   100 *diamonds* eyes   101 *water* lustre   110 *is mortal* would be fatal
III, iii The house of Cleon   13 *For* because   21 *common body* common people   25 *end of generation* last of my posterity   26 *to't* to do so   36 *masked Neptune* calm sea
III, iv The house of Cerimon at Ephesus   9 *A vestal . . . to* I will become a priestess vowed to chastity   13 *till . . . expire* until you die

Now to Marina bend your mind,
Whom our fast-growing scene must find
At Tharsus, and by Cleon trained
8   In music's letters; who hath gained
Of education all the grace,
Which makes her both the heart and place
Of general wonder. But, alack,
That monster, Envy, oft the wrack
Of earnèd praise, Marina's life
14 Seeks to take off by treason's knife.
And in this kind hath our Cleon
One daughter, and a wench full-grown,
Even ripe for marriage rite. This maid
Hight Philoten; and it is said
For certain in our story, she
Would ever with Marina be.
21 Be't when she weaved the sleided silk
With fingers long, small, white as milk;
Or when she would with sharp needle wound
The cambric, which she made more sound
By hurting it; or when to th' lute
26 She sung, and made the night-bird mute
27 That still records with moan; or when
She would with rich and constant pen
Vail to her mistress Dian; still
This Philoten contends in skill
31 With absolute Marina. So
32 With the dove of Paphos might the crow
Vie feathers white. Marina gets
All praises, which are paid as debts,
35 And not as given. This so darks
In Philoten all graceful marks
That Cleon's wife, with envy rare,
A present murderer does prepare
For good Marina, that her daughter
Might stand peerless by this slaughter.
41 The sooner her vile thoughts to stead,
Lychorida, our nurse, is dead;
And cursèd Dionyza hath
The pregnant instrument of wrath
Prest for this blow. The unborn event
I do commend to your content:
Only I carried wingèd time
Post on the lame feet of my rhyme;
Which never could I so convey
Unless your thoughts went on my way.
Dionyza does appear,
With Leonine, a murderer.   *Exit.*

IV, i   *Enter Dionyza with Leonine.*
    DIONYZA
Thy oath remember; thou hast sworn to do't.
'Tis but a blow, which never shall be known.

IV, Cho. 8 *music's letters* the study of music 14 *treason's* treachery's
21 *sleided* divided into filaments 26 *night-bird* nightingale 27 *still*
ever, always (as also in l. 29); *records* sings the story of the rape by Tereus
of Philomela, who was turned into a nightingale 31 *absolute* perfect
in skill 32 *dove of Paphos* dove sacred to Venus 35 *darks* darkens,
obscures 41 *stead* aid
IV, i An open place in Tharsus 11 *mistress'* i.e. Lychorida's 21 *Whirring*
whirling 23 *How chance* how does it happen 25 *Have . . . me* i.e. take
me as your nurse; *favor* complexion 28 *quick* fresh 34 *With . . . heart*
i.e. as if related 36 *Our paragon . . . reports* i.e. the one who, by all report,
is peerless

Thou canst not do a thing in the world so soon
To yield thee so much profit. Let not conscience,
Which is but cold, or flaming love thy bosom
Enslave too nicely; nor let pity, which
Even women have cast off, melt thee, but be
A soldier to thy purpose.
LEONINE   I will do't.
But yet she is a goodly creature.
DIONYZA
The fitter then the gods should have her. Here
She comes weeping for her only mistress' death.   11
Thou art resolved?
LEONINE
I am resolved.
            Enter Marina, with a basket of flowers.
MARINA
No, I will rob Tellus of her weed,
To strow thy green with flowers. The yellows, blues,
The purple violets, and marigolds,
Shall, as a carpet, hang upon thy grave
While summer days do last. Ay me, poor maid,
Born in a tempest when my mother died!
This world to me is a lasting storm,
Whirring me from my friends.   21
DIONYZA
How now, Marina? Why do you keep alone?
How chance my daughter is not with you?   23
Do not consume your blood with sorrowing.
Have you a nurse of me. Lord, how your favor 's   25
Changed with this unprofitable woe!
Come give me your flowers. On the sea margent
Walk with Leonine. The air is quick there,   28
And it pierces and sharpens the stomach.
Come, Leonine, take her by the arm, walk with her.
MARINA
No, I pray you. I'll not bereave you of your servant.
DIONYZA
Come, come!
I love the King your father, and yourself,
With more than foreign heart. We every day   34
Expect him here. When he shall come and find
Our paragon to all reports thus blasted,   36
He will repent the breadth of his great voyage;
Blame both my lord and me, that we have taken
No care to your best courses. Go, I pray you.
Walk, and be cheerful once again. Resume
That excellent complexion which did steal
The eyes of young and old. Care not for me;
I can go home alone.
MARINA   Well, I will go;
But yet I have no desire to it.
DIONYZA   Come, come!
I know 'tis good for you.
Walk half an hour, Leonine, at the least.
Remember what I have said.
LEONINE   I warrant you, madam.
DIONYZA
I'll leave you, my sweet lady, for a while.
Pray walk softly; do not heat your blood.
What, I must have care of you.   50
MARINA   My thanks, sweet madam.
            [Exit Dionyza.]
    Is this wind westerly that blows?
LEONINE   Southwest.

MARINA
When I was born the wind was north.

LEONINE   Was't so?

MARINA
My father, as nurse says, did never fear,
But cried 'Good seamen!' to the sailors, galling
His kingly hands haling ropes;
And, clasping to the mast, endured a sea
That almost burst the deck.

LEONINE
When was this?

MARINA
When I was born.
Never was waves nor wind more violent;
And from the ladder tackle washes off
62   A canvas climber. 'Ha!' says one, 'wolt out?'
63   And with a dropping industry they skip
From stem to stern. The boatswain whistles, and
The master calls and trebles their confusion.

LEONINE
Come, say your prayers.

MARINA
What mean you?

LEONINE
If you require a little space for prayer,
I grant it. Pray; but be not tedious,
70   For the gods are quick of ear, and I am sworn
To do my work with haste.

MARINA   Why will you kill me?

LEONINE
To satisfy my lady.

MARINA
Why would she have me killed?
Now, as I can remember, by my troth,
I never did her hurt in all my life.
I never spake bad word nor did ill turn
To any living creature. Believe me, la,
I never killed a mouse, nor hurt a fly.
I trod upon a worm against my will,
80   But I wept for't. How have I offended
Wherein my death might yield her any profit
Or my life imply her any danger?

LEONINE
My commission
Is not to reason of the deed, but do't.

MARINA
You will not do't for all the world, I hope.
You are well-favored, and your looks foreshow
You have a gentle heart. I saw you lately
When you caught hurt in parting two that fought.
Good sooth, it showed well in you. Do so now.
90   Your lady seeks my life; come you between,
And save poor me, the weaker.

LEONINE   I am sworn,
And will dispatch.
    [Seizes her.]
    Enter Pirates.

1. **PIRATE** Hold, villain!
    [Leonine runs away.]

2. **PIRATE** A prize! a prize!

3. **PIRATE** Half part, mates, half part! Come, let's have
her aboard suddenly.
    Exit [Marina, a prisoner of the Pirates].
    Enter Leonine.

LEONINE
These roguing thieves serve the great pirate Valdes,
And they have seized Marina. Let her go.
There's no hope she will return. I'll swear she's dead
And thrown into the sea. But I'll see further.   *100*
Perhaps they will but please themselves upon her,
Not carry her aboard. If she remain,
Whom they have ravished must by me be slain.   *Exit.*

                   *

      Enter the three Bawds [Pander, Bawd, and Boult].   IV,

PANDER Boult!

BOULT Sir?

PANDER Search the market narrowly. Mytilene is full of *3*
gallants. We lost too much money this mart by being too *4*
wenchless.

BAWD We were never so much out of creatures. We have
but poor three, and they can do no more than they can
do; and they with continual action are even as good as
rotten.

PANDER Therefore let's have fresh ones, whate'er we pay *11*
for them. If there be not a conscience to be used in every
trade, we shall never prosper.

BAWD Thou say'st true. 'Tis not our bringing up of poor *13*
bastards, as, I think, I have brought up some eleven – *14*

BOULT Ay, to eleven; and brought them down again. But *15*
shall I search the market?

BAWD What else, man? The stuff we have, a strong wind
will blow it to pieces, they are so pitifully sodden. *18*

PANDER Thou sayest true; there's two unwholesome, o' *19*
conscience. The poor Transylvanian is dead that lay
with the little baggage.

BOULT Ay, she quickly pooped him; she made him roast *22*
meat for worms. But I'll go search the market.   *Exit.*

PANDER Three or four thousand checkins were as pretty *24*
a proportion to live quietly, and so give over. *25*

BAWD Why to give over, I pray you? Is it a shame to get *26*
when we are old?

PANDER O, our credit comes not in like the commodity, *28*
nor the commodity wages not with the danger. There- *29*
fore, if in our youths we could pick up some pretty
estate, 'twere not amiss to keep our door hatched. Be- *31*
sides, the sore terms we stand upon with the gods will be
strong with us for giving o'er. *33*

BAWD Come, other sorts offend as well as we. *34*

PANDER As well as we? Ay, and better too. We offend
worse. Neither is our profession any trade; it's no *36*
calling. But here comes Boult. *37*
    Enter Boult, with the Pirates and Marina.

BOULT Come your ways, my masters; you say she's a
virgin?

---

62 *wolt out* do you want to get out   63 *dropping* dripping
IV, ii A brothel in Mytilene   3 *Mytilene* a city in Lesbos   4 *mart* market-
time   11 *If . . . used* i.e. if diligence be not used   13–14 *'Tis . . . bastards*
i.e. we cannot rear bastards fast enough   14 *as* and   15 *to eleven* to the
age of eleven; *brought . . . again* i.e. debauched them   18 *sodden* i.e. stewed
in the sweating tub (as a treatment for venereal disease)   19 *there's two*
(comic understatement)   19–20 *o' conscience* i.e. I must admit   22 *pooped*
infected with venereal disease   24 *checkins* gold coins worth about eight
shillings apiece   25 *proportion* fortune; *give over* retire   26 *get* earn
money   28 *credit* reputation; *commodity* profit   29 *wages not* is not
commensurate   31 *hatched* with the hatch (the lower half of a two-part
door) closed   33 *strong* strong reason   34 *sorts* kinds of people   36 *trade*
recognized business   37 *calling* vocation

SAILOR O, sir, we doubt it not.

41 BOULT Master, I have gone through for this piece you
42 see. If you like her, so; if not, I have lost my earnest.

43 BAWD Boult, has she any qualities?

BOULT She has a good face, speaks well, and has excellent
45 good clothes. There's no farther necessity of qualities
can make her be refused.

BAWD What's her price, Boult?

48 BOULT I cannot be bated one doit of a thousand pieces.

PANDER Well, follow me, my masters; you shall have
50 your money presently. Wife, take her in; instruct her
what she has to do, that she may not be raw in her
52 entertainment.   *[Exeunt Pander and Pirates.]*

BAWD Boult, take you the marks of her – the color of her
hair, complexion, height, her age, with warrant of her
virginity; and cry, 'He that will give most shall have her
first.' Such a maidenhead were no cheap thing, if men
were as they have been. Get this done as I command you.

BOULT Performance shall follow.   *Exit.*

MARINA
Alack that Leonine was so slack, so slow!
He should have struck, not spoke; or that these pirates,
Not enough barbarous, had not o'erboard thrown me
For to seek my mother!

BAWD Why lament you, pretty one?

MARINA That I am pretty.

BAWD Come, the gods have done their part in you.

MARINA I accuse them not.

66 BAWD You are light into my hands, where you are like to
live.

MARINA
The more my fault
To scape his hands where I was like to die.

BAWD Ay, and you shall live in pleasure.

MARINA No.

BAWD Yes, indeed shall you, and taste gentlemen of all
73 fashions. You shall fare well; you shall have the differ-
74 ence of all complexions. What do you stop your ears?

MARINA Are you a woman?

76 BAWD What would you have me be, an I be not a woman?

77 MARINA An honest woman, or not a woman.

78 BAWD Marry, whip the gosling! I think I shall have something to do with you. Come, you're a young foolish
sapling, and must be bowed as I would have you.

MARINA The gods defend me!

BAWD If it please the gods to defend you by men, then
men must comfort you, men must feed you, men stir
you up. Boult's returned.
    [Enter Boult.]
Now, sir, hast thou cried her through the market?

BOULT I have cried her almost to the number of her
hairs; I have drawn her picture with my voice.

BAWD And I prithee tell me, how dost thou find the inclination of the people, especially of the younger sort?

BOULT Faith, they listened to me as they would have
hearkened to their father's testament. There was a 91
Spaniard's mouth watered, and he went to bed to her
very description.

BAWD We shall have him here to-morrow with his best
ruff on.

BOULT To-night, to-night! But, mistress, do you know
the French knight that cowers i' the hams?

BAWD Who, Monsieur Verolles?

BOULT Ay, he. He offered to cut a caper at the proclama- 99
tion; but he made a groan at it, and swore he would see
her to-morrow.

BAWD Well, well; as for him, he brought his disease
hither: here he does but repair it. I know he will come
in our shadow, to scatter his crowns in the sun.   104

BOULT Well, if we had of every nation a traveller, we
should lodge them with this sign.   106

BAWD *[to Marina]* Pray you come hither awhile. You
have fortunes coming upon you. Mark me: you must
seem to do that fearfully which you commit willingly,
despise profit where you have most gain. To weep that
you live as ye do makes pity in your lovers. Seldom but
that pity begets you a good opinion, and that opinion a
mere profit.   112

MARINA I understand you not.

BOULT O, take her home, mistress, take her home! These
blushes of hers must be quenched with some present
practice.

BAWD Thou sayest true, i' faith; so they must; for your
bride goes to that with shame which is her way to go 119
with warrant.

BOULT Faith, some do, and some do not. But, mistress, if
I have bargained for the joint –

BAWD Thou mayst cut a morsel off the spit?

BOULT I may so.

BAWD Who should deny it? Come, young one, I like the
manner of your garments well.

BOULT Ay, by my faith, they shall not be changed yet.

BAWD Boult, spend thou that in the town. Report what a
sojourner we have; you'll lose nothing by custom. 129
When Nature framed this piece, she meant thee a good
turn. Therefore say what a paragon she is, and thou
hast the harvest out of thine own report.

BOULT I warrant you, mistress, thunder shall not so
awake the beds of eels as my giving out her beauty stirs
up the lewdly inclined. I'll bring home some to-night.
                      [Exit.]

BAWD Come your ways, follow me.

MARINA
If fires be hot, knives sharp, or waters deep,
Untied I still my virgin knot will keep.
Diana aid my purpose!

BAWD What have we to do with Diana? Pray you, will
you go with us?   *Exit [with Marina].*

               *

       Enter Cleon and Dionyza.   IV, iii

DIONYZA
Why are you foolish? Can it be undone?

CLEON
O Dionyza, such a piece of slaughter   2
The sun and moon ne'er looked upon!

41 *gone through* made a deal   42 *earnest* deposit, down payment   43 *qualities* accomplishments   45–46 *There's . . . refused* i.e. there are no other requisite qualities for lack of which she might be rejected   48 *be bated* i.e. get the price reduced; *doit* very small coin; *of* below   50 *presently* at once   52 *entertainment* i.e. of customers   66 *are light* have chanced to fall   73–74 *difference . . . complexions* men of every variety of race   74 *What* why   76 *an* if   77 *honest* chaste   78 *whip the gosling* hang the greenhorn   78–79 *have . . . do* have trouble   91 *testament* will   99 *offered* attempted   104 *crowns* . . . *sun* French gold coins   106 *this sign* i.e. Marina's charms   112 *mere* downright   119–20 *which . . . warrant* i.e. to which she is entitled to go   129 *by custom* by our traffic
IV, iii The house of Cleon at Tharsus   2 *piece of slaughter* murder (of Marina)

DIONYZA

I think you'll turn a child again.

CLEON

Were I chief lord of all this spacious world,
I'd give it to undo the deed. A lady,
Much less in blood than virtue, yet a princess
To equal any single crown o' th' earth
9   I' th' justice of compare! O villain Leonine!
Whom thou hast pois'ned too.
If thou hadst drunk to him, 't had been a kindness
12   Becoming well thy fact. What canst thou say
When noble Pericles shall demand his child?

DIONYZA

That she is dead. Nurses are not the Fates,
15   To foster it, nor ever to preserve.
She died at night; I'll say so. Who can cross it?
Unless you play the pious innocent
18   And for an honest attribute cry out
'She died by foul play.'

CLEON   O, go to! Well, well,
Of all the faults beneath the heavens, the gods
Do like this worst.

21 DIONYZA   Be one of those that thinks
The petty wrens of Tharsus will fly hence
And open this to Pericles. I do shame
To think of what a noble strain you are,
And of how coward a spirit.

CLEON   To such proceeding
Who ever but his approbation added,
27   Though not his prime consent, he did not flow
From honorable sources.

DIONYZA   Be it so, then.
Yet none does know but you how she came dead,
Nor none can know, Leonine being gone.
She did distain my child and stood between
Her and her fortunes. None would look on her,
But cast their gazes on Marina's face,
34   Whilst ours was blurted at, and held a mawkin,
35   Not worth the time of day. It pierced me through;
And though you call my course unnatural,
You not your child well loving, yet I find
It greets me as an enterprise of kindness
39   Performed to your sole daughter.

CLEON   Heavens forgive it!

DIONYZA

And as for Pericles,
What should he say? We wept after her hearse,
And yet we mourn. Her monument
Is almost finished, and her epitaphs
In glitt'ring golden characters express
A general praise to her, and care in us
At whose expense 'tis done.

46 CLEON   Thou art like the harpy,
Which, to betray, dost, with thine angel's face,
48   Seize with thine eagle's talents.

DIONYZA

49   Ye're like one that superstitiously
Doth swear to th' gods that winter kills the flies;
But yet I know you'll do as I advise.   [Exeunt.]

*

IV, iv   Enter Gower.

GOWER

Thus time we waste and long leagues make short;
Sail seas in cockles, have and wish but for't;   2
Making, to take our imagination,   3
From bourn to bourn, region to region.
By you being pardoned, we commit no crime
To use one language in each several clime
Where our scenes seems to live. I do beseech you
To learn of me, who stand i' th' gaps to teach you,   8
The stages of our story. Pericles
Is now again thwarting the wayward seas,
Attended on by many a lord and knight,
To see his daughter, all his life's delight.
Old Helicanus goes along. Behind
Is left to govern it, you bear in mind,   14
Old Escanes, whom Helicanus late
Advanced in time to great and high estate.   16
Well-sailing ships and bounteous winds have brought
This king to Tharsus – think his pilot thought;   18
So with his steerage shall your thoughts groan   19
To fetch his daughter home, who first is gone.   20
Like motes and shadows see them move awhile.
Your ears unto your eyes I'll reconcile.

      [Dumb Show.]

Enter Pericles at one door, with all his Train; Cleon and
Dionyza at the other. Cleon shows Pericles the tomb [of
Marina], whereat Pericles makes lamentation, puts on
sackcloth, and in a mighty passion departs. [Then exeunt
Cleon, Dionyza, and the rest.]

See how belief may suffer by foul show!
This borrowed passion stands for true-owed woe;   24
And Pericles, in sorrow all devoured,
With sighs shot through and biggest tears o'er-showered,
Leaves Tharsus and again embarks. He swears
Never to wash his face nor cut his hairs.
He puts on sackcloth, and to sea. He bears
A tempest which his mortal vessel tears,
And yet he rides it out. Now please you wit   31
The epitaph is for Marina writ
By wicked Dionyza.

      [Reads the inscription on Marina's monument.]
'The fairest, sweetest, and best lies here,
Who withered in her spring of year.
She was of Tyrus the King's daughter,
On whom foul death hath made this slaughter;
Marina was she called, and at her birth,
Thetis, being proud, swallowed some part o' th' earth.   39
Therefore the earth, fearing to be o'erflowed,
Hath Thetis' birth-child on the heavens bestowed;
Wherefore she does (and swears she'll never stint)   42
Make raging battery upon shores of flint.'

9 I' th' . . . compare in a just comparison   12 fact deed   15 To foster . . . preserve i.e. to care for life and preserve it forever (but this is not the duty of the Fates; perhaps a line is lost)   18 attribute reputation   21–23 thinks . . . Pericles (alluding to the folk belief that birds reveal murders) 27–28 flow . . . sources i.e. descend from an honorable family   34 blurted at scorned; mawkin malkin, slut   35 the time of day i.e. a greeting   39 sole only   46–48 Thou . . . talents i.e. like the harpy, you showed Pericles a friendly face, but now you murder his daughter   48 talents talons   49–50 Ye're . . . flies i.e. you are so timorous that you protest your innocence when winter kills flies
IV, iv   2 have . . . for't i.e. have by merely wishing   3 Making travelling; take delight   8 stand . . . gaps fill up the gaps   14 it i.e. Tyre   16 time due time   18 think . . . thought i.e. think that swift thought pilots him 19 groan i.e. labor   20 first i.e. already   24 borrowed simulated (by Cleon and Dionyza); true-owed genuine   31 wit know   39 Thetis Tethys, wife to Oceanus   42 she i.e. Thetis

No visor does become black villainy
So well as soft and tender flattery.
Let Pericles believe his daughter's dead
47   And bear his courses to be orderèd
By Lady Fortune, while our scene must play
49   His daughter's woe and heavy well-a-day
In her unholy service. Patience then,
And think you now are all in Mytilen.   *Exit.*

*

IV, v   *Enter two Gentlemen [from the brothel].*

1. GENTLEMAN Did you ever hear the like?

2. GENTLEMAN No, nor never shall do in such a place as this, she being once gone.

1. GENTLEMAN But to have divinity preached there. Did you ever dream of such a thing?

2. GENTLEMAN No, no. Come, I am for no more bawdy houses. Shall's go hear the Vestals sing?

1. GENTLEMAN I'll do anything now that is virtuous, but
9   I am out of the road of rutting for ever.   *Exeunt.*

IV, vi   *Enter [Pander, Bawd, and Boult].*

PANDER Well, I had rather than twice the worth of her she had ne'er come here.

3 BAWD Fie, fie upon her! she's able to freeze the god Priapus and undo a whole generation. We must either get her ravished or be rid of her. When she should do for
6   clients her fitment, and do me the kindness of our pro-
7   fession, she has me her quirks, her reasons, her master reasons, her prayers, her knees, that she would make a
9   Puritan of the devil if he should cheapen a kiss of her.

BOULT Faith, I must ravish her, or she'll disfurnish us of
11   all our cavalleria and make our swearers priests.

12 PANDER Now the pox upon her greensickness for me!

BAWD Faith, there's no way to be rid on't but by the way
14   to the pox. Here comes the Lord Lysimachus disguised.

15 BOULT We should have both lord and lown if the peevish baggage would but give way to customers.

Enter Lysimachus.

17 LYSIMACHUS How now? How a dozen of virginities?

18 BAWD Now the gods to-bless your Honor!

BOULT I am glad to see your Honor in good health.

LYSIMACHUS You may so; 'tis the better for you that
21   your resorters stand upon sound legs. How now whole-some iniquity have you that a man may deal withal and defy the surgeon?

BAWD We have here one, sir, if she would – but there never came her like in Mytilene.

LYSIMACHUS If she'd do the deeds of darkness, thou wouldst say.

28 BAWD Your Honor knows what 'tis to say well enough.

LYSIMACHUS Well, call forth, call forth.

BOULT For flesh and blood, sir, white and red, you shall
31   see a rose; and she were a rose indeed, if she had but –

LYSIMACHUS What, prithee?

BOULT O, sir, I can be modest.

34 LYSIMACHUS That dignifies the renown of a bawd, no
35   less than it gives a good report to a number to be chaste.
[Exit Boult.]

BAWD Here comes that which grows to the stalk – never plucked yet, I can assure you.
[Enter Boult with Marina.]
Is she not a fair creature?

LYSIMACHUS Faith, she would serve after a long voyage at sea. Well, there's for you. Leave us.

BAWD I beseech your Honor give me leave a word, and I'll have done presently.   42

LYSIMACHUS I beseech you do.

BAWD *[to Marina]* First, I would have you note this is an honorable man.

MARINA I desire to find him so, that I may worthily note 46
him.

BAWD Next, he's the Governor of this country, and a man whom I am bound to.

MARINA If he govern the country, you are bound to him indeed; but how honorable he is in that, I know not.

BAWD Pray you, without any more virginal fencing, will 52
you use him kindly? He will line your apron with gold.

MARINA What he will do graciously, I will thankfully receive.

LYSIMACHUS Ha' you done?

BAWD My lord, she's not paced yet; you must take some 57
pains to work her to your manage. – Come, we will 58
leave his Honor and her together. – Go thy ways.
[Exeunt Bawd, Pander, and Boult.]

LYSIMACHUS Now, pretty one, how long have you been at this trade?

MARINA What trade, sir?

LYSIMACHUS Why, I cannot name't but I shall offend.

MARINA I cannot be offended with my trade. Please you to name it.

LYSIMACHUS How long have you been of this profession?

MARINA E'er since I can remember.

LYSIMACHUS Did you go to't so young? Were you a 68
gamester at five, or at seven?   69

MARINA Earlier too, sir, if now I be one.

LYSIMACHUS Why, the house you dwell in proclaims you to be a creature of sale.

MARINA Do you know this house to be a place of such resort, and will come into't? I hear say you're of honor-able parts, and are the Governor of this place.

LYSIMACHUS Why, hath your principal made known unto you who I am?

MARINA Who is my principal?

LYSIMACHUS Why, your herb-woman, she that sets seeds and roots of shame and iniquity. O, you have heard something of my power, and so stand aloof for more serious wooing. But I protest to thee, pretty one, my authority shall not see thee, or else look friendly upon thee. Come, bring me to some private place. Come, come!

MARINA
If you were born to honor, show it now;
If put upon you, make the judgment good   86
That thought you worthy of it.

47 *bear . . . orderèd* i.e. suffer his experiences as regulated   **49** *well-a-day* grief

IV, v The brothel at Mytilene   **9** *rutting* fornication

IV, vi   **3** *Priapus* (god of procreation)   **6** *fitment* duty   **6, 7** *do me, has me* (ethical datives)   **9** *cheapen* bargain for   **11** *cavalleria* cavaliers; *our swearers* our swearing customers (?), those who swear by us (?)   **12** *green-sickness* i.e. squeamishness; *for me* say I   **14** *pox* syphilis   **15** *lown* loon, base fellow   **17** *How a* what price for   **18** *to-bless* bless bounteously   **21–22** *How . . . iniquity* i.e. what kind of healthy prostitute   **28** *'tis to say* is to be said   **31** *but* – (the word 'thorn' is delicately omitted)   **34** *That* i.e. modesty in speech   **35** *report . . . to be chaste* i.e. reputation . . . for being chaste   **42** *presently* immediately   **46** *worthily note* bashful excuses   **57** *paced* taught her paces, broken in   **58** *manage* control (term from horsemanship)   **68** *go to't* copulate   **69** *gamester* wanton   **86** *put upon* conferred on

LYSIMACHUS
88　How's this? how's this? Some more; be sage.

MARINA　　　　　　　　　　　　　　　For me,
That am a maid, though most ungentle fortune
90　Have placed me in this sty, where, since I came,
91　Diseases have been sold dearer than physic –
That the gods
Would set me free from this unhallowed place,
Though they did change me to the meanest bird
That flies i' th' purer air!

LYSIMACHUS　　　　　　　　I did not think
Thou couldst have spoke so well; ne'er dreamt thou
　couldst.
Had I brought hither a corrupted mind,
Thy speech had altered it. Hold, here's gold for thee.
Persever in that clear way thou goest,
And the gods strengthen thee!

MARINA　　　　　　　　The good gods preserve you!

LYSIMACHUS
101　For me, be you thoughten
That I came with no ill intent; for to me
The very doors and windows savor vilely.
Fare thee well. Thou art a piece of virtue, and
I doubt not but thy training hath been noble.
Hold, here's more gold for thee.
A curse upon him, die he like a thief,
That robs thee of thy goodness! If thou dost
Hear from me, it shall be for thy good.
　　　[Enter Boult.]

110　BOULT I beseech your Honor, one piece for me.

LYSIMACHUS
Avaunt, thou damnèd doorkeeper!
Your house, but for this virgin that doth prop it,
Would sink, and overwhelm you. Away!　　　[Exit.]

BOULT How's this? We must take another course with
you! If your peevish chastity, which is not worth a
116　breakfast in the cheapest country under the cope, shall
undo a whole household, let me be gelded like a spaniel.
Come your ways.

MARINA Whither would you have me?

BOULT I must have your maidenhead taken off, or the
common hangman shall execute it. Come your ways.
We'll have no more gentlemen driven away. Come your
ways, I say.
　　　Enter Bawd.

BAWD How now? What's the matter?

BOULT Worse and worse, mistress. She has here spoken
holy words to the Lord Lysimachus.

BAWD O abominable!

BOULT She makes our profession as it were to stink afore
the face of the gods.

130　BAWD Marry hang her up for ever!

BOULT The nobleman would have dealt with her like a
nobleman, and she sent him away as cold as a snowball;
saying his prayers too.

BAWD Boult, take her away; use her at thy pleasure.
Crack the glass of her virginity and make the rest malleable.

136　BOULT An if she were a thornier piece of ground than
she is, she shall be ploughed.

MARINA Hark, hark, you gods!

139　BAWD She conjures. Away with her! Would she had never
come within my doors! – Marry hang you! – She's born
to undo us. – Will you not go the way of womenkind?

Marry come up, my dish of chastity with rosemary and　142
bays!　　　　　　　　　　　　　　　　　　　　[Exit.]

BOULT Come, mistress; come your ways with me.

MARINA Whither wilt thou have me?

BOULT To take from you the jewel you hold so dear.

MARINA Prithee tell me one thing first.

BOULT Come now, your one thing.

MARINA
What canst thou wish thine enemy to be?　　　　　　149

BOULT Why, I could wish him to be my master, or rather　150
my mistress.

MARINA
Neither of these are so bad as thou art,
Since they do better thee in their command.　　　　　153
Thou hold'st a place for which the painèd'st fiend
Of hell would not in reputation change.
Thou art the damnèd doorkeeper to every
Coistrel that comes enquiring for his Tib.　　　　　157
To the choleric fisting of every rogue　　　　　　　158
Thy ear is liable. Thy food is such
As hath been belched on by infected lungs.

BOULT What would you have me do? go to the wars,
would you? where a man may serve seven years for the
loss of a leg, and have not money enough in the end to
buy him a wooden one?

MARINA
Do anything but this thou doest. Empty
Old receptacles, or common shores, of filth;　　　　166
Serve by indenture to the common hangman.
Any of these ways are yet better than this;
For what thou professest, a baboon, could he speak,
Would own a name too dear. That the gods　　　　170
Would safely deliver me from this place!
Here, here's gold for thee.
If that thy master would gain by me,
Proclaim that I can sing, weave, sew, and dance,
With other virtues, which I'll keep from boast;
And I will undertake all these to teach.
I doubt not but this populous city will
Yield many scholars.

BOULT But can you teach all this you speak of?

MARINA
Prove that I cannot, take me home again
And prostitute me to the basest groom　　　　　　181
That doth frequent your house.

BOULT Well, I will see what I can do for thee. If I can
place thee, I will.

MARINA But amongst honest women.

BOULT Faith, my acquaintance lies little amongst them.
But since my master and mistress hath bought you,
there's no going but by their consent. Therefore I will
make them acquainted with your purpose, and I doubt
not but I shall find them tractable enough. Come, I'll
do for thee what I can. Come your ways.　　　Exeunt.

*

88 be sage be wise (spoken mockingly)　90 sty pig-sty　91 physic medicine
101 be you thoughten assure yourself　110 piece piece of gold　116 cope sky
136 An if if　139 conjures calls on the gods　142–43 dish . . . bays i.e.
specially garnished dish of chastity　149 What . . . be (an obscure riddle:
what is the worst thing you could wish your enemy to be?)　150–51
master . . . mistress i.e. as bad as my master or, rather, my mistress　153
Since . . . command i.e. since you do the evil things they only command to be
done　157 Coistrel scoundrel; Tib strumpet　158 fisting punching
166 common shores i.e. the no-man's-land where filth was deposited to be
washed away by the tide　170 own . . . dear i.e. think his reputation too
honorable　181 groom stableman

V, Cho.   *Enter Gower.*

GOWER

    Marina thus the brothel scapes and chances
    Into an honest house, our story says.
    She sings like one immortal, and she dances
    As goddess-like to her admirèd lays ;
5 Deep clerks she dumbs ; and with her neele composes
    Nature's own shape of bud, bird, branch, or berry,
7 That even her art sisters the natural roses ;
8 Her inkle, silk, twin with the rubied cherry ;
    That pupils lacks she none of noble race,
    Who pour their bounty on her ; and her gain
    She gives the cursèd bawd. Here we her place ;
    And to her father turn our thoughts again.
    Where we left him on the sea, we there him lost ;
    Whence, driven before the winds, he is arrived
    Here where his daughter dwells ; and on this coast
    Suppose him now at anchor. The city strived
17 God Neptune's annual feast to keep ; from whence
    Lysimachus our Tyrian ship espies,
19 His banners sable, trimmed with rich expense,
    And to him in his barge with fervor hies.
    In your supposing once more put your sight ;
22 Of heavy Pericles think this his bark,
23 Where what is done in action (more, if might)
    Shall be discovered – please you sit and hark.   *Exit.*

V, i   *[On board Pericles' ship, off Mytilene. A pavilion on*
       deck, with a curtain before it ; Pericles within it, on a
       couch. A barge lying beside the Tyrian vessel.] Enter
       Helicanus ; to him two Sailors [, one belonging to the
       Tyrian vessel, the other to the barge].

1. SAILOR *[to the Sailor of Mytilene]*

1 Where is Lord Helicanus ? He can resolve you.
    O, here he is.
    Sir, there is a barge put off from Mytilene,
    And in it is Lysimachus the Governor,
    Who craves to come aboard. What is your will ?

HELICANUS

    That he have his. Call up some gentlemen.

1. SAILOR Ho, gentlemen ! my lord calls.
     Enter two or three Gentlemen.

1. GENTLEMAN Doth your lordship call ?

HELICANUS

    Gentlemen, there is some of worth would come aboard.
10 I pray ye greet them fairly.
     [Exeunt Gentlemen and the two Sailors.]
     Enter [from the barge] Lysimachus [and Lords, with
     the Gentlemen and the two Sailors].

1. SAILOR

    Sir, this is the man that can, in aught you would,
    Resolve you.

LYSIMACHUS Hail, reverend sir ! the gods preserve you !

HELICANUS

    And you, to outlive the age I am,
    And die as I would do.

LYSIMACHUS   You wish me well.
    Being on shore, honoring of Neptune's triumphs,
    Seeing this goodly vessel ride before us,
    I made to it, to know of whence you are.

HELICANUS

    First, what is your place ?

LYSIMACHUS   I am the Governor
    Of this place you lie before.

HELICANUS

    Sir,
    Our vessel is of Tyre, in it the King ;
    A man who for this three months hath not spoken
    To any one, nor taken sustenance
    But to prorogue his grief.   26

LYSIMACHUS

    Upon what ground is his distemperature ?

HELICANUS

    'Twould be too tedious to repeat ;
    But the main grief springs from the loss
    Of a belovèd daughter and a wife.

LYSIMACHUS

    May we not see him ?

HELICANUS

    You may ;
    But bootless is your sight. He will not speak
    To any.

LYSIMACHUS Yet let me obtain my wish.

HELICANUS

    Behold him.
     [Draws the curtain and discovers Pericles.]
          This was a goodly person
    Till the disaster that, one mortal night,   37
    Drove him to this.

LYSIMACHUS

    Sir King, all hail ! The gods preserve you !
    Hail, royal sir !

HELICANUS

    It is in vain ; he will not speak to you.

LORD

    Sir,
    We have a maid in Mytilene, I durst wager
    Would win some words of him.

LYSIMACHUS   'Tis well bethought.
    She, questionless, with her sweet harmony
    And other chosen attractions, would allure,
    And make a batt'ry through his deafened parts,   47
    Which now are midway stopped.
    She is all happy as the fairest of all,
    And, with her fellow maids, is now upon
    The leavy shelter that abuts against
    The island's side.
     [Gives an order to a Lord, who departs.]

HELICANUS

    Sure, all effectless ! yet nothing we'll omit   53
    That bears recovery's name. But since your kindness 54
    We have stretched thus far, let us beseech you
    That for our gold we may provision have,
    Wherein we are not destitute for want,   57
    But weary for the staleness.

LYSIMACHUS   O, sir, a courtesy
    Which if we should deny, the most just gods
    For every graff would send a caterpillar,   60
    And so inflict our province. Yet once more
    Let me entreat to know at large the cause

V, Cho. 5 *neele* needle 7–8 *That . . . cherry* i.e. her embroidery looks
like real roses and cherries 8 *inkle* linen thread 17 *Neptune's annual
feast* festival on July 23 19–20 *His . . . him* its . . . it 22 *heavy* sorrowful
23 *if might* if it were possible
V, i 1 *resolve* answer 26 *prorogue* prolong 37 *one mortal night* (when he
lost Thaisa) 47 *batt'ry . . . parts* i.e. assault upon his deaf ears 53 *effectless*
in vain 54 *bears recovery's name* i.e. can be called a cure 57 *Wherein . . .
for* of which . . . because of 60 *graff* grafted plant

Of your king's sorrow.

HELICANUS   Sit, sir ; I will recount it to you.
But see, I am prevented.

[Enter Lord with Marina and a Companion.]

LYSIMACHUS
O here's the lady that I sent for.
Welcome, fair one. Is't not a goodly presence ?

HELICANUS
She's a gallant lady.

LYSIMACHUS
She's such a one that, were I well assured
Came of a gentle kind and noble stock,
I'd wish no better choice, and think me rarely wed.

71   Fair one, all goodness that consists in beauty,
Expect even here, where is a kingly patient.

73   If that thy prosperous and artificial feat
Can draw him but to answer thee in aught,
Thy sacred physic shall receive such pay
As thy desires can wish.

MARINA   Sir, I will use
My utmost skill in his recovery, provided
That none but I and my companion maid
Be suffered to come near him.

LYSIMACHUS   Come, let us leave her ;

80   And the gods make her prosperous !

[They withdraw.]

The song [by Marina].

LYSIMACHUS *[advances]*
Marked he your music ?

MARINA   No, nor looked on us.

LYSIMACHUS
See, she will speak to him.

[Withdraws again.]

MARINA
Hail, sir ! my lord, lend ear.

PERICLES   Hum, ha !

[Pushes her away.]

MARINA
I am a maid,
My lord, that ne'er before invited eyes,
But have been gazed on like a comet. She speaks,
My lord, that, may be, hath endured a grief
Might equal yours, if both were justly weighed.

90   Though wayward fortune did malign my state,
My derivation was from ancestors
Who stood equivalent with mighty kings ;
But time hath rooted out my parentage,
And to the world and awkward casualties
Bound me in servitude. *[Aside]* I will desist ;
But there is something glows upon my cheek,
And whispers in mine ear 'Go not till he speak.'

PERICLES
My fortunes – parentage – good parentage –
To equal mine – Was it not thus ? What say you ?

MARINA
100   I said, my lord, if you did know my parentage,
You would not do me violence.

PERICLES
I do think so. Pray you turn your eyes upon me.
You are like something that – What country, woman ?
Here of these shores ?

MARINA   No, nor of any shores.
Yet I was mortally brought forth, and am

No other than I appear.

PERICLES
I am great with woe, and shall deliver weeping.
My dearest wife was like this maid, and such a one
My daughter might have been. My queen's square
    brows ;
Her stature to an inch ; as wand-like straight ;
As silver-voiced ; her eyes as jewel-like,
And cased as richly ; in pace another Juno ;   112
Who starves the ears she feeds, and makes them hungry,
The more she gives them speech. Where do you live ?

MARINA
Where I am but a stranger. From the deck
You may discern the place.

PERICLES   Where were you bred ?
And how achieved you these endowments which
You make more rich to owe ?   118

MARINA
If I should tell my history, it would seem
Like lies disdained in the reporting.   120

PERICLES   Prithee speak !
Falseness cannot come from thee, for thou lookest
Modest as Justice, and thou seemest a palace
For the crowned truth to dwell in. I will believe thee,
And make my senses credit thy relation
To points that seem impossible ; for thou lookest
Like one I loved indeed. What were thy friends ?
Didst thou not say, when I did push thee back
(Which was when I perceived thee), that thou cam'st
From good descending ?

MARINA   So indeed I did.

PERICLES
Report thy parentage. I think thou said'st
Thou hadst been tossed from wrong to injury,
And that thou thought'st thy griefs might equal mine,
If both were opened.

MARINA   Some such thing
I said, and said no more but what my thoughts
Did warrant me was likely.

PERICLES   Tell thy story.
If thine considered prove the thousand part   136
Of my endurance, thou art a man, and I   137
Have suffered like a girl. Yet thou dost look
Like Patience gazing on kings' graves and smiling   139
Extremity out of act. What were thy friends ?
How lost thou them ? Thy name, my most kind virgin ?
Recount, I do beseech thee. Come, sit by me.

MARINA
My name is Marina.

PERICLES   O, I am mocked,
And thou by some incensèd god sent hither
To make the world to laugh at me.

MARINA   Patience, good sir,
Or here I'll cease.

PERICLES   Nay, I'll be patient.
Thou little know'st how thou dost startle me
To call thyself Marina.

---

71 *Fair one . . . beauty* i.e. Marina ; *consists* resides   73 *artificial* skillful
112 *cased as richly* i.e. set in as beautiful a face   118 *owe* possess   120 *in
the reporting* in the act of utterance   136 *thousand* thousandth   137 *my
endurance* what I have endured   139–40 *smiling . . . act* i.e. smiling even
the grief of bereavement out of existence

MARINA
The name
Was given me by one that had some power –
My father, and a king.
PERICLES   How ? a king's daughter ?
And called Marina ?
MARINA   You said you would believe me ;
But, not to be a troubler of your peace,
I will end here.
PERICLES   But are you flesh and blood ?
Have you a working pulse ? and are no fairy ?
156   No motion ? Well, speak on. Where were you born ?
And wherefore called Marina ?
MARINA   Called Marina
For I was born at sea.
PERICLES   At sea ? What mother ?
MARINA
My mother was the daughter of a king ;
Who died the very minute I was born,
As my good nurse Lychorida hath oft
162   Delivered weeping.
PERICLES   O, stop there a little !
          [Aside]
This is the rarest dream that e'er dull sleep
Did mock sad fools withal. This cannot be
My daughter – buried ! – Well, where were you bred ?
I'll hear you more, to th' bottom of your story,
And never interrupt you.
MARINA   You scorn ; believe me,
'Twere best I did give o'er.
PERICLES
169   I will believe you by the syllable
Of what you shall deliver. Yet give me leave :
How came you in these parts ? Where were you bred ?
MARINA
The King my father did in Tharsus leave me,
Till cruel Cleon, with his wicked wife,
Did seek to murder me ; and having wooed
175   A villain to attempt it, who having drawn to do't,
A crew of pirates came and rescued me ;
Brought me to Mytilene. But, good sir,
178   Whither will you have me ? Why do you weep ? It may
be,
179   You think me an imposture. No, good faith !
I am the daughter to King Pericles,
181   If good King Pericles be.
PERICLES Ho, Helicanus !
HELICANUS Calls my lord ?
PERICLES
Thou art a grave and noble counsellor,
Most wise in general. Tell me, if thou canst,
What this maid is, or what is like to be,
That thus hath made me weep ?
HELICANUS   I know not ; but

Here's the regent, sir, of Mytilene
Speaks nobly of her.
LYSIMACHUS   She never would tell
Her parentage. Being demanded that,   190
She would sit still and weep.
PERICLES
O Helicanus, strike me, honored sir,
Give me a gash, put me to present pain,
Lest this great sea of joys rushing upon me
O'erbear the shores of my mortality
And drown me with their sweetness. O, come hither,
Thou that beget'st him that did thee beget ;
Thou that wast born at sea, buried at Tharsus,
And found at sea again ! O Helicanus,
Down on thy knees, thank the holy gods as loud   200
As thunder threatens us. This is Marina.
What was thy mother's name ? Tell me but that,
For truth can never be confirmed enough,
Though doubts did ever sleep.
MARINA   First, sir, I pray,
What is your title ?
PERICLES
I am Pericles of Tyre. But tell me now
My drowned queen's name, as in the rest you said
Thou hast been godlike perfect.
The heir of kingdoms, and another life   209
To Pericles thy father.
MARINA
Is it no more to be your daughter than   211
To say my mother's name was Thaisa ?
Thaisa was my mother, who did end
The minute I began.
PERICLES
Now blessing on thee ! Rise ; thou art my child.
Give me fresh garments. Mine own Helicanus,
She is not dead at Tharsus, as she should have been,   217
By savage Cleon. She shall tell thee all ;
When thou shalt kneel, and justify in knowledge   219
She is thy very princess. – Who is this ?
HELICANUS
Sir, 'tis the Governor of Mytilene,
Who, hearing of your melancholy state,
Did come to see you.
PERICLES   I embrace you.
Give me my robes. I am wild in my beholding.   224
O heavens bless my girl ! [Music] But hark, what music ?
Tell Helicanus, my Marina, tell him
O'er, point by point, for yet he seems to doubt,
How sure you are my daughter. But what music ?
HELICANUS
My lord, I hear none.
PERICLES
None ?
The music of the spheres ! List, my Marina.
LYSIMACHUS
It is not good to cross him. Give him way.
PERICLES
Rarest sounds ! Do ye not hear ?
LYSIMACHUS
Music, my lord ? I hear.
PERICLES   Most heavenly music !
It nips me unto list'ning, and thick slumber   235
Hangs upon mine eyes. Let me rest.
          [Sleeps.]

156 motion puppet 162 Delivered weeping told in tears 169 by the
syllable syllable by syllable, to the letter 175 drawn drawn his sword
178 Whither . . . me i.e. to what point are you drawing me 179 imposture
imposter 181 be live 209 The heir thou art the heir 211 Is . . . than
i.e. to be your daughter, is it only necessary 217 as . . . been as it was
intended she should be 219 When i.e. then ; justify in knowledge i.e.
knowingly confirm 224 wild . . . beholding i.e. strange, unkempt in
appearance (with uncut hair and beard and mean clothing) 235 nips
compels (as if by rapture)

LYSIMACHUS
A pillow for his head!
So, leave him all. Well, my companion friends,
239 If this but answer to my just belief,
240 I'll well remember you.   *[Exeunt all but Pericles.]*
Diana [appears to Pericles in a vision].

DIANA
My temple stands in Ephesus. Hie thee thither
And do upon mine altar sacrifice.
There, when my maiden priests are met together,
Before the people all
Reveal how thou at sea didst lose thy wife.
246 To mourn thy crosses, with thy daughter's, call,
And give them repetition to the life.
248 Or perform my bidding, or thou livest in woe;
Do't, and happy – by my silver bow!
Awake, and tell thy dream.   *[Vanishes.]*

PERICLES
251 Celestial Dian, goddess argentine,
I will obey thee. Helicanus!
[Enter Helicanus, Lysimachus, and Marina.]

HELICANUS   Sir?

PERICLES
My purpose was for Tharsus, there to strike
The inhospitable Cleon; but I am
For other service first. Toward Ephesus
Turn our blown sails; eftsoons I'll tell thee why.
    [To Lysimachus]
Shall we refresh us, sir, upon your shore,
And give you gold for such provision
As our intents will need?

LYSIMACHUS
Sir,
With all my heart; and, when you come ashore,
I have another suit.

PERICLES   You shall prevail,
Were it to woo my daughter; for it seems
You have been noble towards her.

LYSIMACHUS
Sir, lend me your arm.

PERICLES   Come, my Marina.   *Exeunt.*

*

V, ii   *Enter Gower.*

GOWER
Now our sands are almost run;
More a little, and then dumb.
This, my last boon, give me,
For such kindness must relieve me:
That you aptly will suppose
What pageantry, what feats, what shows,
What minstrelsy and pretty din
The regent made in Mytilin
To greet the King. So he thrived
That he is promised to be wived
To fair Marina; but in no wise
12 Till he had done his sacrifice,
As Dian bade; whereto being bound,
14 The interim, pray you, all confound.
15 In feathered briefness sails are filled,
And wishes fall out as they're willed.
At Ephesus the temple see,
Our king, and all his company.

That he can hither come so soon
Is by your fancies' thankful doom.   *[Exit.]* 20

[The Temple of Diana at Ephesus; Thaisa standing   V, ii
near the altar, as High Priestess; a number of
Virgins on each side; Cerimon and other Ephesians
attending.] Enter Pericles, Lysimachus, Helicanus,
Marina, and others.

PERICLES
Hail, Dian! To perform thy just command,
I here confess myself the King of Tyre;
Who, frighted from my country, did wed
At Pentapolis the fair Thaisa.
At sea in childbed died she, but brought forth
A maid child called Marina; who, O goddess,
Wears yet thy silver livery. She at Tharsus   7
Was nursed with Cleon; who at fourteen years
He sought to murder; but her better stars
Brought her to Mytilene; 'gainst whose shore
Riding, her fortunes brought the maid aboard us,   11
Where, by her own most clear remembrance, she
Made known herself my daughter.

THAISA   Voice and favor!
You are, you are – O royal Pericles!
    [Swoons.]

PERICLES
What means the nun? She dies! Help, gentlemen!

CERIMON
Noble sir,
If you have told Diana's altar true,
This is your wife.

PERICLES   Reverend appearer, no.
I threw her overboard with these very arms.

CERIMON
Upon this coast, I warrant you.

PERICLES   'Tis most certain.

CERIMON
Look to the lady. O, she's but overjoyed.
Early in blustering morn this lady was
Thrown upon this shore. I oped the coffin,   23
Found there rich jewels; recovered her, and placed her
Here in Diana's temple.

PERICLES   May we see them?

CERIMON
Great sir, they shall be brought you to my house,
Whither I invite you. Look, Thaisa is
Recovered.

THAISA   O, let me look!
If he be none of mine, my sanctity   29
Will to my sense bend no licentious ear,
But curb it, spite of seeing. O my lord,
Are you not Pericles? Like him you spake;
Like him you are. Did you not name a tempest,
A birth, and death?

239 *If . . . belief* i.e. if this works out as I expect it to   240 *remember* i.e.
reward   246 *crosses* misfortunes   248 *Or* either   251 *argentine* silvery
V, ii   12 *he* i.e. Pericles   14 *confound* consume to nothingness   15
feathered briefness winged speed   20 *Is . . . doom* i.e. is thanks to the decree
of your imaginations
V, iii   7 *Wears . . . livery* is still thy chaste votaress   11 *Riding* at anchor
23 *oped* opened   29–31 *If . . . seeing* i.e. if he is not my husband, my holiness
will not listen licentiously to what my eyes tell me

PERICLES   The voice of dead Thaisa!

THAISA
That Thaisa am I, supposed dead
And drowned.

PERICLES
Immortal Dian!

THAISA   Now I know you better.
38 When we with tears parted Pentapolis,
The King my father gave you such a ring.
[Points to his ring.]

PERICLES
40 This, this! No more, you gods! your present kindness
41 Makes my past miseries sports. You shall do well
That on the touching of her lips I may
Melt and no more be seen. O, come, be buried
A second time within these arms!

MARINA   My heart
Leaps to be gone into my mother's bosom.
[Kneels to Thaisa.]

PERICLES
Look who kneels here! Flesh of thy flesh, Thaisa;
Thy burden at the sea, and called Marina
For she was yielded there.

THAISA   Blest, and mine own!

HELICANUS
Hail, madam, and my queen!

THAISA   I know you not.

PERICLES
50 You have heard me say, when I did fly from Tyre,
I left behind an ancient substitute.
Can you remember what I called the man?
I have named him oft.

THAISA   'Twas Helicanus then.

PERICLES
Still confirmation!
Embrace him, dear Thaisa; this is he.
Now do I long to hear how you were found;
How possibly preserved; and who to thank,
Besides the gods, for this great miracle.

THAISA
Lord Cerimon, my lord; this man,
Through whom the gods have shown their power, that
can
From first to last resolve you.

PERICLES   Reverend sir,
The gods can have no mortal officer
More like a god than you. Will you deliver   63
How this dead queen relives?

CERIMON   I will, my lord.
Beseech you first, go with me to my house,
Where shall be shown you all was found with her;
How she came placed here in the temple;
No needful thing omitted.

PERICLES
Pure Dian, bless thee for thy vision! I
Will offer night oblations to thee. Thaisa,   70
This prince, the fair betrothèd of your daughter,
Shall marry her at Pentapolis. And now
This ornament   73
Makes me look dismal will I clip to form;
And what this fourteen years no razor touched,
To grace thy marriage day I'll beautify.

THAISA
Lord Cerimon hath letters of good credit, sir,   77
My father's dead.

PERICLES
Heavens make a star of him! Yet there, my queen,   79
We'll celebrate their nuptials, and ourselves
Will in that kingdom spend our following days.
Our son and daughter shall in Tyrus reign.
Lord Cerimon, we do our longing stay
To hear the rest untold. Sir, lead's the way.   *[Exeunt.]*

spoken by] Gower.

In Antiochus and his daughter you have heard
Of monstrous lust the due and just reward;
In Pericles, his queen, and daughter, seen,
Although assailed with fortune fierce and keen,
Virtue preserved from fell destruction's blast,
Led on by heaven, and crowned with joy at last.
In Helicanus may you well descry
A figure of truth, of faith, of loyalty.
In reverend Cerimon there well appears
The worth that learnèd charity aye wears.   10
For wicked Cleon and his wife, when fame
Had spread his cursèd deed to th' honored name
Of Pericles, to rage the city turn,
That him and his they in his palace burn.
The gods for murder seemèd so content
To punish – although not done, but meant.
So, on your patience evermore attending,
New joy wait on you! Here our play has ending.   *[Exit.]*

---

38 *parted* departed from   40 *This . . . gods* i.e. this is perfect bliss; I ask no more   41–43 *You . . . seen* i.e. if in the ecstasy of her kiss the gods end my life, it would be fitting   63 *deliver* tell   70 *oblations* offerings   73 *ornament* i.e. his hair and beard   77 *of good credit* trustworthy   79 *there* i.e. in Pentapolis

The earliest reference to *Pericles* is its entry in the Register of the Stationers' Company on May 20, 1608, to Edward Blount, the wording of which suggests that he submitted the licensed prompt-book. For reasons that can only be surmised, he did not publish an edition. The quarto issued by Henry Gosson in 1609 did not follow from Blount's entry or derive from the prompt-book. Its corrupt text indicates a surreptitious origin. From late in July, 1608, until December, 1609, the playhouses were closed by the plague, and it may have been unemployed actors who cobbled up a text (not from shorthand notes of a performance, for the systems then in use were inadequate) and sold it to Gosson. The marked difference in the quality of the verse beginning with Act III is interpreted by some as a sign of multiple authorship. Others, thinking that Shakespeare worked alone, hold that two reporters of unequal ability are responsible, one doing Acts I and II, the other Acts III–V. A third group believe that Shakespeare had little to do with the first two acts but wrote, or revised heavily, Acts III–V, and they trace much of the corruption of the text to one or more reporters. Whatever the cause, the course of events is sometimes confused (see I, ii, 1–52); many passages printed as prose were clearly intended as verse, and some that are given in verse form are really prose; and there are numerous errors based on mishearing (see, below, the textual notes to III, Cho., 8; III, i, 62; IV, iii, 1; V, i, 73). Furthermore, the compositors who set the type misread their copy frequently and may have done even more serious injury to the text. They and the reporter(s) had difficulty with the archaic language of Gower and the colloquial speech of the fishermen and the brothel keepers. Some unusual readings and several of the emendations are given support by the equivalent passages in Wilkins' *Painfull Adventures*, from which a phrase has been borrowed at III, i, 34. Several lines seem hopelessly corrupt. In consequence, editors have felt justified in re-lining much of the text and prose and emending more freely than in plays based on authoritative manuscripts. Some of the emendations originated in the second quarto of 1609 (Q2), the fourth quarto, 1619 (Q4), the third folio, 1664 (F3), and the fourth folio, 1685 (F4) – and have been accepted not because those editions have any authority but because they correct obvious errors. The present edition adheres as closely as possible to the first quarto (Q). *Pericles* was a popular play: a second quarto, with a title page printed from the same type as the first, appeared in 1609; other quartos followed in 1611, 1619, 1630, and 1635. Omitted from the first folio, *Pericles* was added in the second issue (1664) of the third folio, along with six spurious plays. The reason for its absence from F1 is debatable: the prompt-book may have been lost; there may have been copyright difficulties; it may have been thought (or known) that Shakespeare was not the sole author.

The defectiveness of the text upon which we must unfortunately rely is illustrated by an analysis of Act I, Scene ii. Pericles, newly returned from Antioch, enters with his lords, only to dismiss them with his first words. Then he rehearses in soliloquy the danger to himself and his country from Antiochus, who will never rest easy until Pericles be dead. Thought of the situation has plunged him into unaccustomed melancholy. The lords return, wishing him joy and a safe return from his journey, though no such thing has been mentioned. Helicanus interrupts to silence them, rebuke flatterers (though there has been no flattery), speak sharply to Pericles about the duty of kings to heed honest counsel, and ask pardon for his presumption. Again Pericles dismisses the lords, this time with instructions to report on the shipping in harbor. In a brief exchange, he tests Helicanus, then praises him for his candor, and asks his advice. Helicanus tells him to learn to bear with patience his self-imposed griefs. Only then does Pericles disclose that his melancholy is caused by the evil he has discovered in Antioch and the present danger to Tyre and himself. At once Helicanus advises swift flight until death end the peril. Pericles concurs, puts state affairs in order, and starts for Tharsus.

The first attempt at reconstruction of the scene as originally written was made by Professor Philip Edwards in *Shakespeare Survey* 5 (1952). Suggesting that the reporter's memory had failed him and that he had confused his notes, Edwards proposed a rearrangement of the text somewhat as follows: Pericles enters and is greeted by the lords. Anxious for the safety of Tyre, he sends them to scan the harbor (for ships from Antioch, of course). Then he soliloquizes about the dangers threatening himself and his subjects from Antiochus. Helicanus comes in and chides Pericles for his melancholy, ending with an apology for his plain speech, with the explanation that not frankness but flattery is a crime against a king. Pericles pardons him and explains the reasons for his conduct. The scene ends as in Q, but the lords know nothing about Pericles' intention of going to Tharsus until after his departure. The reconstruction has much to recommend it. It indicates gaps in the text caused by the failure of the memory of the reporter and reveals how the reporter improvised lines to link together the bits of action and the speeches he could recall. The reconstruction indicates how far inferior the play as we have it must be to the play as acted at the Globe. There are other scenes in the play that invite similar analysis and reconstruction.

There follows a list of all substantive departures from Q, with the adopted reading in italics followed by the quarto reading in roman. Unless otherwise indicated, the adopted readings have been suggested by various editors of the play from the eighteenth century to the present. Emendations which merely affect metre, as in the matter of *-ed* endings, are listed only when the quarto text is printed as verse; and there is no attempt to indicate the extensive relineation.

Names of the Actors (adapted from list printed at end of the play in F3)
I, Cho., 6 *holy-ales* Holydayes   39 *a* (F3) of
I, i, 8 *For the* For   18 *rased* racte   23 *the* th'   30 *death-like* Death like   57 *Antiochus* (omitted in Q)   112 *our* (F3) your   114 *cancel* (F3) counsell   128 *you're* (F3) you   129 *uncomely* untimely
I, ii, 3 *Be my* By me   20 *honor him* honour   25 *th' ostent* the stint   30 *am* once   41 *blast* sparke   44 *a peace* peace   50 *Helicanus* Hellicans   56 *know'st* knowest   60 *heaven* (Q2) heaue   65 *you do* you your selfe doe   70 *Where, as* (Q2) Whereas   78 *seem* seemes   82 *Bethought me* Bethought   83 *fears* (F4) feare   85 *doubt it, as* doo't, as   99 *grieve* grive for   121 *we'll* will   123 *prince'* Prince   s.d. *Exeunt* Exit
I, iii, 27 *ears it* seas   28 *seas* Sea   30 *Helicanus* (Q4) (omitted in Q)   34 *betook* (Q2) betake
I, iv, 15 *lungs* toungs   17 *helps* helpers   39 *savors* savers   58 *thou* (Q4) thee   70 *glory's* glories   74 *him's* himnes   77 *fear* (Q4) leave   78 *On ground's* our grounds   105 *ne'er* neare
II, Cho., 11 *Tharsus* (Q4) Tharstill   12 *speken* spoken   19 *though* for though   22 *Sends word* Sav'd one   24 *hid intent . . . murder* (Q2) had intent . . . murder (Q corrected)   hid in Tent . . . murdred (Q uncorrected)   36 *aught* ought   40 *'longs* long's
II, i, 6 *me breath* my breath   12 *What ho, Pilch* What, to pelch   17 *fetch th'* (this ed.) fetch 'th   31 *devours* (F4) devowre   47 *finny* fenny   53 *scratch't* Search   76 *koth-a* ke-tha   79 *holidays* all day   80 *moreo'er* more; or   88 *your* you   95 *is* (Q2) I   117 *all thy* all   125 *from* Fame   142 *do'ee* do'e (Q corrected)   di'e (Q uncorrected)   151 *rapture* rupture   154 *delightful* delight   161 *equal* a Goale
II, ii, 4 *daughter* daughter heere   27 *Piu . . . fuerza* Pue Per doleera kee per forsa   28 *what's* (Q4) with   30 *pompae* Pompey   53 *furnishèd* furnisht   57 *for* by
II, iii, 3 *To* I   13 *yours* (Q3) your   26 *Envied* Envies   37 *Yon* You   38 *tells me* tels   43 *son's* sonne   50 *stored* stur'd   51 *you do* do you   73 *know* know of him   95 *Will you* (this ed.) Will   101 *Here is* heer's   111 *to be* be   113 *King* (omitted in Q)

II, iv, 10 *Their* those   32 *gives* give's   33 *leaves* leave   34 *death's* death   56 *endeavor it* endeavour

III, Cho., 2 *the house about* about the house   6 *fore* from   7 *crickets* Cricket   8 *E'er* Are   10 *Where, by* Whereby   13 *eche* each   17 *coigns* Crignes   29 *appease* oppresse   35 *Y-ravishèd* Iranyshed   46 *fortune's mood* fortune mov'd   60 *sea-tossed* seas tost

III, i, 7 *Thou stormest* then storme   8 *spit* speat   10 *O* oh!   11 *midwife* my wife   26 *Vie* Use   30 *welcomed* welcome   34 *Poor . . . nature* (not in Q, but from Wilkins' narrative)   52 *custom* easterne   53 *for . . . straight* (inserted in l. 54 in Q)   60 *the ooze oare*   62 *e'er-remaining* ayre remayning   65 *paper* (Q2) Taper   75 *from* for

III, ii, 40 *treasure* pleasure   47 *never raze* never   55 *bitumed* bottomed   76 *even* ever   86 *cloths* clothes   87 *still* rough   92 *warm* warmth

III, iii, *at Tharsus* Atharsus   5 *strokes* shakes   6 *hurt* hant   7 *woundingly* wondringly   29 *Unscissored* unsisterd *hair* heyre   30 *ill* will

III, iv, s.d. *Thaisa* Tharsa   5 *eaning* (F3) learning   9 *vestal* (F3) vastall

IV, Cho., 10 *her . . . heart* hie . . . art   14 *Seeks* Seeke   15 *hath our Cleon* our Cleon hath   16 *wench full-grown* full growne wench   17 *ripe* (Q2) right *rite* sight   21 *she* they   26 *night-bird* night bed   32 *With . . . crow* The dove of Paphos might with the crow   48 *on* one

IV, i, 5-6 *or flaming . . . Enslave* in flaming, thy love bosome, enflame   27 *On . . . margent* ere the sea marre it   40 *Resume* reserve   64 *stem* sterne   77 *la* law

IV, ii, 4 *much* (Q2) much much   69 *was like to* (Q4) was to   70 *pleasure* peasure   97 *i' the* ethe   118 *Bawd* (F3) Mari.

IV, iii, 1 *are* (Q4) ere   6 *A* O   8 *o' th'* ath   11 *'t had* tad   12 *fact* face   15 *nor* not   17 *pious* impious   27 *prime* prince   28 *sources* courses   31 *distain* disdaine   33 *Marina's* (Q2) Marianas   35 *through* thorow

IV, iv, 8 *i' th'* with   10 *the* (Q2) thy   18 *his* this   24 *true-owed* true olde   29 *puts* put   48 *scene* Steare

IV, v, 9 s.d. *Exeunt* Exit

IV, vi, s.d. [*Pander, Bawd, and Boult*] Bawdes 3   18 *to-bless* to blesse   34 *dignifies* (Q4) dignities   63 *name't* (F3) name   81 *aloof* aloft   121 *ways* way   123 s.d. *Bawd* Bawdes   128 *She* He   144 *ways* (F3) way   157 *Coistrel* custerell   174 *sew* sow   176 *And I* and   185 *women* (Q3) woman

V, Cho., 8 *twin* Twine   13 *lost* left   14 *Whence* Where   20 *fervor* (Q corrected) former (Q uncorrected)

V, i, 7 *1. Sailor* 2. Say.   11 *1. Sailor* 1. Say. (Q corrected) Hell. (Q uncorrected)   12 *reverend* reverent   33 *sight. He* sight, hee (Q corrected) sight see (Q uncorrected)   35 *Yet . . . wish* (Q4) (part of preceding speech in Q)   36 *Helicanus* (Q4) (this line assigned to Lysimachus in Q)   47 *deafened* defend   50 *with her* her *is now* now   59 *gods* God   66 *presence* present   70 *I'd* (Q4) I do *rarely wed* (Q4) rarely to wed   71 *one* on   73 *feat* fate   94 *awkward* augward   103 *You are* your *country, woman* Countrey women   104 *Here* heare *shores . . . shores* shewes . . . shewes   112 *cased* caste   122 *palace* Pallas   124 *my senses* (Q4) senses   127 *say* stay   132 *thought'st* thoughts   141 *thou them* thou   156 *No motion* Motion   163 *dull* duld   182 *Pericles* Hell.   209 *life* like   215 *thou art* (Q4) th'art   227 *doubt* doat   247 *life* like   262 *suit* sleight

V, iii, 6 *who* (F4) whom   15 *nun* mum   37 *Immortal* (Q4) I, mortall   50 *Pericles* Hell.   61 *Reverend* Reverent   69 *I* and

Epi., 12 *their* (Q4) his *to th'* the

CYMBELINE

INTRODUCTION

In *Romeo and Juliet* (ca. 1595) Romeo, believing that Juliet is dead, enters her tomb, takes poison there, and dies. Upon awaking and finding Romeo dead, Juliet stabs herself and dies. In *Antony and Cleopatra* (ca. 1607) Antony, believing that Cleopatra is dead, falls on his sword and thus brings about his death. In consequence, Cleopatra resolves on death by the poisonous bite of the asp. Compare these roughly similar situations with certain events in *Cymbeline* (ca. 1609–10). Imogen, recovering like Juliet from a drug which has brought about her apparent death, opens her eyes upon a corpse which she believes to be her husband's. But, though she faints, she neither takes her life nor thinks of doing so. When Posthumus receives apparent evidence of Imogen's death, he too goes on living, though he has the added burden of remorse; true, he thinks of death, but only as a natural hazard of the war that he chooses to enter.

To be sure, different lovers have different personalities. But behind the variations of personality lie literary factors that influence the strikingly different outcomes of situations up to a point strikingly alike. Different conventions are at work: in *Romeo* and *Antony*, those of tragedy; in *Cymbeline*, those of dramatic romance. As it is used here, *convention* does not mean a formula, stereotype, or constricting rule, but rather a certain point of view, a way of perceiving human behavior, of understanding it and responding to it emotionally. A convention is a bond, though a flexible one, between playwright and audience; it involves a loose, unspoken agreement about attitude and procedure; it is rooted in shared expectations, though these may be unarticulated, general rather than specific, and open to great imaginative transformation by the artist. The tragic convention interprets life as a clash between, on the one hand, transcendent principles of order and, on the other, urgencies of desire and intensities of feeling that, once they are in play, lead inevitably to destructive encounters and somber catastrophes. The convention of romance approaches life in terms of the ultimate reconcilability of desires and circumstances; though ambitions and needs may be great, they tend to fall within a realm of moral possibility; and circumstances, though they may be antagonistic for a long period, eventually yield to meritorious humanity. The tragic involvement is total, reckless, irremediable; the protagonist is wholly committed to a situation which seems to enfold all of life's possibilities. In contrast, in the convention represented in *Cymbeline* the personal impulse does not become identical with, or aspire to dominate, all of reality; beyond the individuals there is an independent life that makes legitimate claims or offers alternative possibilities. For Imogen and for Posthumus, the loved one does not become the only way, a *sine qua non*; Imogen, though grief-stricken, can cling to life, and Posthumus can fight for his country. Thus both survive for an unravelling of circumstance that offers them, in the end, satisfactions unforeseen at the moment of apparent disaster. (In the matter of circumstances romance may be contrasted with two later conventions that reacted against it: whereas romance treats circumstances as being ultimately malleable or beneficent, realism regards them as independent and subject to their own laws, and naturalism treats them as either indifferent or positively hostile to human endeavor.)

In both tragedy and romance human beings are reservoirs of strong passions. Yet romance has a greater sense of limits – of the decorum or principle or rational endowment or even pragmatic awareness that balances off the passion and holds it back from the irretrievable. Tragedy is more attuned to extremes and depths, to profound conflicts within personality (as in Macbeth, Othello, and Lear). Cymbeline, caught between the Roman Empire and British loyalty, between wife and daughter, between his dynastic plans and Imogen's emotions, is potentially a tragic figure; but Shakespeare does not portray him as destroyed by irreconcilable forces. Romance either does not see the painful inner conflict or treats it as reparable this side of catastrophe; for the clash of impulses it will most often substitute the clash of persons – sometimes simply of the good ones who come out all right in the end and the bad ones who go down. Cymbeline's Queen is all unscrupulousness; she has none of Lady Macbeth's capacity for destructive inner stresses. Cloten is self-seeking and vengeful, but as a character in romance he is not credited with the brains or drive to do permanent damage. Again, the Cymbeline–Imogen relationship has interesting resemblances to the Capulet–Juliet and the Lear–Cordelia relationships. Capulet and Cymbeline both want to impose unwelcome marriages on their daughters: in the tragedy, the father is relentless and hence contributes to the daughter's despair and to his own bitter grief; in the romance, the father is unpleasant enough, but he temporizes and hopes rather than attempts force, and hence does not push things beyond repair. In response to a daughter's independence, Cymbeline banishes a son-in-law – a sentence that need not entail disaster and that can be revoked; but Lear turns political power over to forces of unlimited ruthlessness and thus tears a whole kingdom apart.

A very clear view of the ways in which tragedy and romance diverge is provided by the striking resemblances between *Cymbeline* and *Othello*: in each play an extremely clever man, for his own purposes, uses circumstantial evidence to persuade a husband that his new bride has been unfaithful, and the bitter and vengeful husband resolves to punish his wife by death. Though romance does not ignore evil, its vision does not include the fearful malice which, like Iago's, destroys one victim after another; instead, Iachimo's deception of Posthumus, indecent and dangerous though it is, is still a game rather than an expression of human depravity. (Shakespeare found some aspects of the basic wager plot, a folk-tale that appeared in many versions, in the ninth tale of the second day in Boccaccio's *Decameron*, others in the prose tale *Frederick of Jennen*, a sixteenth-century translation of a Dutch version of a German story.) Romance may deal with a murderous impulse, but it does not give that impulse sole and final authority; whereas Othello in his mad error goes right to work and commits murder, Posthumus uses an agent who saves him from the consequences of his own fury. It may be that Posthumus is simply lucky in having to use an agent, but it is also possible to suppose that he unconsciously chooses an unreliable murderer. In either case – cooperative circumstance or secret intent – the survival of Imogen illustrates the view, almost invariable in romance, that the hate and violence of which people are capable, however great these may be, do not necessarily achieve their destructive ends.

Romance is not watered-down tragedy; it is another way of looking at conduct and experience. It is equally aware of serious dangers to life and well-being and of preventives, safety devices, the means of return from the shadows. It does not fall short of something that might be expected of it; rather it adopts a different perspective, and the better the individual romance is, the greater its ability to persuade us of the validity of its perspective. Romance can move toward theatrical (and subliterary) hackwork, or toward dramatic (and literary) excellence. Because it affirms the saving graces of life, it may either drift toward hackneyed, mechanical happy endings or struggle toward a peace and reconciliation that have been won by hard experience. (In the present example Cymbeline, Belarius, and Imogen have suffered; Posthumus has had to undergo a painful self-contemplation.) Since "entertainment" regularly plays up the comforting aspects of character and events, romance has strong affiliations with the world of entertainment: as such it can either provide standardized gratifications or require the spectator and reader to respond sharply even amid apparently familiar fare. Traditionally, romantic entertainment includes much movement and variety, distant scene and change of scene, combat, disguise, plotting, patriotic appeal. *Cymbeline* gathers all of these in a rich amalgam of many sources: Imogen's adventures in Wales may have come from an anonymous drama of the 1580's, *Sir Clyomon and Sir Clamydes*; the Belarius materials from *Rare Triumphs of Love and Fortune*, an anonymous drama acted in 1582; the political and military "history" from Holinshed's *Chronicles*, with further details from the 1578 and 1587 editions of *The Mirror for Magistrates*. Yet out of this rather astonishing medley comes not so much formula entertainment as an entertaining but not inadequate or falsifying view of reality.

After his period of great tragedies Shakespeare turned, in his latter years in the theatre, to romance: he appears to have written *Pericles, Cymbeline, The Winter's Tale*, and *The Tempest*, roughly in that order, between 1608 and 1612. Dr Simon Forman saw a performance of *Cymbeline*

at the Globe not long before September, 1611, as we know from a description of it in his manuscript "Bocke of Plaies and Notes thereof. . . ." The play need not have been new when he saw it, but the consensus of scholarly opinion, based upon its style and type, places the anterior limit of date in 1608–09. Certain elements in the late plays – the maturing of main characters, conversion or even rebirth, the triumph of justice in harmony with nature and divine ordinance – suggest to some readers that Shakespeare had personally come through a period of anguish into relative hopefulness and serenity. Though the interpretation is not implausible, we have no biographical evidence to substantiate it. What is established is that the romances were in tune with a theatrical fashion that grew strong from about 1608 on, representing in part the continual quest for novelty, in part a new exploitation of an older dramatic mode that had not been fully developed, and perhaps most of all a response to the more specialized taste of genteel audiences that for various reasons became influential at this time. Shakespeare was clearly writing in this new mode, but he developed the mode differently from the very popular John Fletcher and Fletcher's part-time collaborator, Francis Beaumont. Though *Cymbeline* itself and the Beaumont–Fletcher *Philaster* have resemblances that suggest influence in one direction or the other (a moot subject; the evidence is not conclusive), the Beaumont–Fletcher method is in general to decrease the seriousness of the political plot and to exploit to the utmost the private emotional life, sometimes by shocking events and strained or even morbid situations, and regularly by an intensified and prolonged presentation of feelings (pathos, shame, jealousy, humiliation, horror, and so on). In Shakespeare the situations, allowing for all the departures from every-day reality that are sanctioned by romance, are much less eccentric and much more representative, and the emotional life presented is not an end in itself, magnified for a slow savoring, but a natural unexpanded accompaniment of the action.

The customary procedures of romance, then, may lean toward either of two extremes: one, the escapist patterns and routines, where entertainment is expected to have no ties with truth; the other, a sophisticated sensationalism, where putting the audience through an emotional wringer drifts naturally toward off-center functionings of personality. Shakespeare's later romances are in a middle position: they stay away equally from the pure stereotypes that give little sense of what human character and experience are like, and from the whipping up of emotional states by strange situations and prolonged displays of exacerbated feeling.

Cymbeline has won, on the whole, less praise than *The Winter's Tale* and *The Tempest*. In *Cymbeline*, some readers believe, Shakespeare reveals a less sure control of his "later style": we observe looser lines, with extra syllables and more frequent feminine endings; a tendency toward solid blocking in dialogue, with more syntactical denseness and grammatical ambiguity; random outbreaks of somewhat mechanical riming. (There is still active dispute as to whether certain parts of the play, notably V, iv, 30–122, are authentic.) Some critics have argued that the plots are not well integrated, that Belarius is too sententious, that there are too many awkward expository soliloquies, that the characters are too neatly divided into black and white, that the gratifying conclusion lacks metaphysical support.

On the other hand, few have failed to admire the characterization of Imogen and the ingenious construction of the last scene (V, v). Even allowing for the susceptibility of male critics to so charming and devoted a creature as Imogen, whose attractions, ranging as they do from sweetness of affection to sharpness in repartee, from blind fidelity to keen insight into motives and character, from cookery to courage, make her virtually a dream girl, there is no doubt that she is one of the most substantially characterized, and hence convincing, of Shakespeare's romantic heroines. The final revelation scene, with its unbroken, energetic, unforced movement from one disclosure to another, is one of the most skillful in all drama. Unlike Fletcher, Shakespeare does not secure his effect of almost continuous surprise by playing tricks upon the spectator, keeping him artificially in the dark and then shocking him with sudden new light. The spectator, on the contrary, knows about everything that is taking place; his surprise is simply the surprise of the characters as they make major discoveries; yet he always understands the characters. His role is not that of naive curiosity as to what is going on, or naive wonder at novelties he has not foreseen, but adult contemplation of the diverse possibilities of human nature.

The characterization of Imogen and the management of the final scene are key elements: the merits of the play lie in characterization and craftsmanship. These disclose, as the play goes on, a view of reality that carries the romance far beyond the expectable delights of painless and thoughtless entertainment.

The play is long, and an occasional scene, such as I, iv, may be somewhat drawn out, but there is an over-all vigor of movement. Though the exposition in I, i lacks finesse, the situation is introduced, and action is started, rapidly; scenes ii and iii speedily complicate the problems to be solved. In II, iii there is a good example of a scene not only providing drama in itself but pointing ahead naturally to other action: in the midst of fighting off Cloten, Imogen misses her bracelet, so that a new problem comes into view before she is finished with the one presented by Cloten. In I, vi and II, iv, which Iachimo dominates as he first tries to "seduce" Imogen and then deceives Posthumus, excellent pace and tension are created by Iachimo in his skillful maneuvers from one strategy to another. The energetic movement is supported by variety of scene; in changing locale Shakespeare can often change mood or confront us with another point of view. From the touching scene in which Pisanio tells Imogen of Posthumus' departure (I, iii) Shakespeare makes an abrupt leap to the sophistication and skepticism at Rome (I, iv), and from that back to the heavy-handed machinations of the British Queen (I, v). The courtly polish of the scene in which Imogen, in her faithful love, resists the specious appeals of Iachimo (I, vi) is followed by the rough outdoor comedy of the loutish Cloten (II, i), and this in turn by an utterly different action in Imogen's bedroom, in which danger, evil calculation, and sexual feeling are ingeniously mixed (II, ii). From the private intrigue in Rome (II, iv, v) we are thrown back to a public scene of imperial politics at the British court (III, i), and from the royal palace to an outlaws' cave in the Welsh mountains (III, iii). From sudden battlefield reversals we shift to a supernatural vision, from divine promise to death-cell ironies, from readiness for death to a reprieve (V, iii, iv).

Nothing lags; nothing stands still; the action lines hurry on, pressed by their own inner dramatic force and intermingled so expertly that something new constantly flashes into sight to alter the perspective and undercut the obvious. This is of course good entertainment in the style of romance, but it is more than that: it is a way of countering the stereotypes into which romance may slide, of announcing the variety of possibilities in human experience, and of contemplating and accepting this variety. Though variety itself may become a cliché, variety rooted in a sense of the real alternatives in feeling and action is a denial of cliché. Even in the introductory scenes Shakespeare is not willing to let Cloten be merely a laughingstock, but instead shows him through the eyes of two commentators (I, ii; II, i), the witty observer and the straight man; aside from the drama of contrast, Cloten implicitly has enough substance to attract one follower, if only a politic one. Iachimo is the treacherous Italian dear to the Elizabethan heart, but Shakespeare modifies the conventional concept of Italian character by introducing the civil and decent Philario. The vision scene in V, iv might contain only a static, decorative theophany, but Shakespeare gives it dramatic life by having the spirits attack Jupiter almost rebelliously. Belarius and his "sons" might easily be a solid family unit playing a conventional role of rustic virtue. Belarius does voice trite sentiments about the contrast between vice at court and nobility in the mountains, but in almost their first words the young men disagree; to them their cave is a prison from the world of action and knowledge (III, iii, 27 ff.). When Guiderius kills Cloten, Belarius is less laudatory than fearful (IV, ii); when Belarius wants to play safe and wait out the war, the boys override him (IV, iv). Even the boys themselves are set partly in dramatic opposition: Guiderius, the more direct and active, criticizes Arviragus, more given to savoring words and feelings, for playing Belarius' "ingenious instrument" and for drawing out his elegy for Fidele (IV, ii).

It is in the treatment of his principal characters that Shakespeare most conspicuously avoids the expected and the obvious. As masterful wife, unscrupulous mother, and sinister stepmother, the Queen is a very old and familiar character; yet Shakespeare makes her also an authentic voice of British patriotism (III, i, v). He alters the conventional villain by giving her a generally acceptable emotion; he modifies romance by observing that malicious double-dealing at court does not bar political right feeling. Cloten is defective on nearly every count: as objectionable lover, laughable "ass," and oafish courtier of dubious principles. But he too is a patriot, even though an ungraceful one (III, i, v). He is rude and overbearing to Belarius and the King's sons, but he certainly believes that he is acting in the name of the law, and he is not a coward. His dependence on his position is ludicrous, but somehow he always needs reassurance; there is a distant touch of pathos in his incompetence and hope for security, and perhaps even in his grotesque "dreams of glory" (III, v; IV, i). He tries to think, as when he expounds the cynic's view of the gold standard in moral life (II, iii, 67 ff.), or wrestles with the paradox of love and hate (III, v, 70 ff.). In other words, Cloten is complicated enough to demand more than a stereotyped response; hence the beheading may seem excessive, unpleasantly shocking. Shakespeare wants to give the audience a quick justification for the beheading; so he has Guiderius say, "Yet I not doing this, the fool had borne / My head as I do his" (IV, ii, 116–17).

Posthumus turns out to be much more than the victim of an angry king, or than the conventional romantic hero, though he is obviously to be taken as such a hero. What interests Shakespeare more than his eligibility as a lover, or his unjust banishment, is his capacity for unheroic, indeed evil, behavior: Posthumus quickly loses faith in his wife's fidelity, and then tries to arrange her murder. Romance is made to accommodate more than a little moral reality: we see both the drive for revenge and afterwards the bitter remorse. Imogen might be no more than faithful bride and pathetic victim, but Shakespeare gives her an intelligence, a spirit, and an imagination that make her seem to earn, rather than passively inherit, the good that comes her way. But he goes beyond even this achievement and at one point regards Imogen with an amused detachment that creates the most delicately ironic scene in the play. As the convention of disguise requires, Imogen takes Cloten's body for that of Posthumus, but instead of dropping the confusion at this point, Shakespeare has her go on to identify one part of the body after another as Posthumus'. Along with all the charm of her tenderness and the pathos of her apparent bereavement, there is something exquisitely comic in the assurance of her misidentifications: no one is beyond errors that evoke smiles, Shakespeare seems to say, and this implicit view makes possible a richer humanity. The impulse to humanize by stopping short of a potential idealization appears again in the final scene when Shakespeare has Imogen coolly turn her back on Lucius ("your life.../ Must shuffle for itself," V, v, 104–05), to whom she is indebted and who is embittered by her suddenly dropping him for her own business. Shakespeare is looking at the actual ways of human nature, not at pure stereotypes. Hence, though at the end he lets Cymbeline acquire greater wisdom and dignity, he makes the king a faulty enough human being, doting on his wife, misled, capable of folly and great harshness.

Iachimo appears first as an Italian rascal, a conventional source of agreeable shudders in Renaissance England, and then apparently undergoes a pleasing conversion from skepticism to faith in chaste love. This sounds like pure theatrical hokum, but the fact is that Iachimo is a fresh and lively character. Iago, whom Iachimo strikingly resembles, has a histrionic side which is a key to Iachimo: though Iago's main pleasure, of course, is in working out his malice, he also delights in acting out the different roles that he assumes. Iachimo does not have Iago's malice, but his passion for the stage is even greater than Iago's. He loves to adopt a role and to succeed in it; he is a subtle union of actor and confidence man. Having adopted the role of disbeliever in woman's virtue, he must carry it to an extreme and conquer in it; in working on Imogen, he shifts from role to role with the agility of a born actor; in working on Posthumus, he arranges his presentation like a tight one-act play, moving from quick exposition through deepening tension to one climax and then another. Finally he chooses a very popular role, that of guilty man confessing, and here he seizes stage with an elaborate and attitudinizing self-condemnation. Even in his final five lines (V, v, 412–17) he manages to act the guilty man with a histrionic sweep, and to attract attention by praising Imogen hyperbolically.

In adopting the genre of romance, then, Shakespeare exploits all its potential variety, at one level by an always lively movement of scene and plot, and in a more fundamental way by examining characters with either an amused detachment or a fullness that stops just short of tragic complications. Though the genre commits him to solutions without disaster, he does not impose an arbitrary happy ending. His characters are complex enough to be more than flat figures of evil that perish, and of good that triumph. The characters who survive have not been merely lucky; they have been modified, have learned somewhat better or wiser ways of confronting the unexpected. The initial mood of the play is created by a widespread impulse to act resentfully and vengefully: the Queen plots deaths, the King is quick to banish, Posthumus wants Imogen killed, and Rome must punish Britain. But the closing mood is one of forbearance and generosity. Jupiter signals the change in V, iv when, though bitterly assailed by Posthumus' family, he waives his power to act punitively and actually gives promise of relief. Cymbeline can acknowledge that his trust in the Queen "was folly in me"; Lucius can rise above the harshness of the death sentence and generously ask that Fidele be saved; Cymbeline can give up a conqueror's rights and grant this request. When Iachimo confesses, Posthumus attacks himself more sharply than he does Iachimo; by relinquishing the easier course of blame, he forestalls an outbreak of recriminatory bitterness. And if the earlier Cymbeline crops up again in the royal impulse to punish Guiderius on the spot, at least now the King can wait until he knows a little more of the truth. Belarius yields up the King's sons to their father, though he is in tears at the loss of them, and Cymbeline calls Belarius "brother." The new spirit is summed up in Posthumus, who once wanted to inflict the death sentence on his wife, but who now says to Iachimo, the cause of his mad rage, "The malice [I have] towards you [is] to forgive you." It is the key line of the latter part of the play. Moved by it, Cymbeline pardons the Roman captives and then, under the further impetus of the oracle, volunteers to pay the tribute to Rome. Since the history upon which Shakespeare drew is very shadowy, and since he follows it very loosely at best, there is no reason why he should not have chosen to finish off his romance with a patriotic note of triumph that would be sure-fire theatre. Yet he chose not to make this easier appeal, but instead to ask the audience to respond in a more mature and less obvious way – to approve the acknowledgment of a national obligation to a foreign conqueror. Cymbeline's decision, since in effect it says, "We have all been wrong in Britain," is an act of humility. It marks the general triumph of magnanimity – the ultimate value dramatically espoused in the play.

But magnanimity is not unveiled in a last-minute surprise whose power to please depends upon our indifference to probability. It is rather an extension of a certain generousness that, though at times inactive, has been recurrently present. The court scenes with Lucius have always an air of courteous consideration that survives the political dispute; once even the rude Cloten approaches civility (III, i, 76 ff.). Belarius, though he kidnapped the King's sons when he was unjustly banished, did not injure or kill them; instead he brought them up in a way that could give great pleasure to the King. Belarius and Posthumus did not avenge themselves upon Cymbeline, as more persistently resentful characters might, by fighting against him in war; instead they became the instruments of his victory. Imogen has much to forgive, but she seems not even to think of the need for forgiveness.

Shakespeare defines a world in which a certain discipline of the self – which may appear as forgiveness or forbearance under provocation, or as considerateness and graciousness even in difficult relationships – is always possible and can in the end triumph, though the impulse to inflict punishment and to achieve revenge is also strong. Civility, generosity, magnanimity – such qualities mark the improved way of life that the drama reveals. It is perhaps significant that these are the virtues esteemed in another dramatic genre that was just emerging in Jacobean England and would reach its fullness three quarters of a century later – comedy of manners. We began by discussing the relation between *Cymbeline* and tragedy (the play is entitled *The Tragedie of Cymbeline* in the folio of 1623); we end by noting its affinity with comedy. The genre to which it belongs is sometimes called tragicomedy. Whether it be called tragicomedy or romance, the important point is that, in a convention which lends itself easily to an entertaining escape from reality, Shakespeare always keeps a sure foothold in human reality; that where variety is a great theatrical value, he follows the fashion brilliantly without falling into banalities; that where abnormal tensions and sensationalism could, and often did, take over, his own portrayal of violence and strong emotion did not deflect him from representative impulses and motives; and that where the popular expectation of final relief might lead to mechanical repair of disorder and restoration of well-being, Shakespeare never entirely closes off our sense of the human capacity for ill-doing. Above all, he characteristically represents an improvement in life, not as a miraculous gift to make people easily happy, but as a possession earned by the mastery, in crises, of such virtues as forbearance and magnanimity.

University of Washington ROBERT B. HEILMAN

NOTE ON THE TEXT

Cymbeline was first published in the folio of 1623. Textual scholars are divided in their opinions about the nature of the copy used by the printers, whether it was the author's draft or a scribal transcript of it, and whether this draft or transcript had or had not been used as a theatrical prompt-book. In any case, the folio text is a reasonably good one, and it has been followed closely in the present edition. The act–scene division provided marginally for reference departs from the division of the folio at three points:

I, i combining folio I, i and ii; II, iv and v dividing folio II, iv; and III, vi combining folio III, vi and vii. Departures from the folio text, except for relineations, normalization of speech-prefixes, modernization of spelling and punctuation, and correction of obvious typographical errors, are listed below with the adopted reading in italics followed by the folio reading in roman.

I, i, 4 ff. *1. Gentleman* (from here on, F assigns the speeches of the two Gentlemen simply to '1' and '2'; so also for the two Lords in I, ii, II, i, and II, iii, and for the two Captains in V, iii) 70 (F begins Scene ii here) 116 *cere* seare 143 *vile* vilde
I, iii, 9 *this* his
I, iv, 42 *offend not* offend 65 *Britain* Britanie 67 *not but* not 76 *purchase* purchases 104 *too* to 118 *thousand* thousands
I, v, 3 s.d. *Exeunt* Exit
I, vi, 28 *takes* take 98 *born* borne 104 *Fixing* Fiering 108 *by-peeping* by peeping 147 *Solicit'st* Solicites 168 *men's* men 169 *descended* defended
II, i, 11 *curtail* curtall 31 *to-night* night 58 *husband, than* Husband. Then 59 *make. The* make the 62 s.d. *Exit* Exeunt
II, ii, 49 *bare* beare
II, iii, 29 *vice* voyce 47 *solicits* solicity 137 *garment* Garments 154 *you* your
II, iv, 6 *hopes* hope 24 *mingled* wing-led 34 *through* thorough 36 *tenor* tenure 37 *Philario* Post. 47 *not* note 57 *you* yon 116 *one of* one 135 *the* her
II, v, 16 *German one* Iarmen on 27 *man may name* name
III, i, 20 *rocks* Oakes
III, ii, 67 *score* store 78 *nor* not
III, iii, 2 *Stoop* Sleepe 23 *robe* Babe 28 *know* knowes 83 *wherein they bow* whereon the Bowe
III, iv, 22 *lie* lyes 79 *afore't* a-foot 90 *make* makes 102 *eyeballs out* eyeballs
III, v, 32 *looks* looke 40 *strokes* stroke 55 s.d. *Exit* (appears after *days* in F) 138 *insultment* insulment
III, vi, 28 (F begins Scene vii here) 57 *Whither* Whether
IV, i, 13 *imperceiverant* imperseuerant
IV, ii, 49–51 *He . . . dieter* (F assigns these lines to Arviragus) 50 *sauced* sawc'st 58 *patience* patient 71 *mountaineers* Mountainers 122 *thank* thanks 154 *reck* reake 186 *ingenious* ingenuous 205 *crare* care 206 *Might* Might'st 224 *ruddock* Raddocke 290 *is* are 387 *an't* and't
IV, iii, 40 *betid* betide
IV, iv, 2 *find we* we find 17 *the* their 27 *hard* heard
V, i, 1 *wished* am wisht
V, iii, 24 *harts* hearts 42 *stooped* stopt 43 *they* the
V, iv, 18 *vile* vilde 29 s.d. *follow* followes 67 *geck* geeke 81 *look out* looke, / looke out
V, v, 64 *heard* heare 134 *On* One 198 *vilely* vildely 205 *got it* got 252 *vile* vilde 261 *from* fro 311 *on's* one's 334 *mere* neere 395 *brothers* Brother 405 *so* no 468 *this yet* yet this

CYMBELINE

[NAMES OF THE ACTORS

Cymbeline, King of Britain
Cloten, son to the Queen by a former husband
Posthumus Leonatus, a gentleman, husband to Imogen
Belarius, a banished lord, disguised under the name of Morgan
Guiderius } *sons to Cymbeline, disguised under the names of*
Arviragus } *Polydore and Cadwal, supposed sons of Morgan*
Philario, friend to Posthumus }
Iachimo, friend to Philario } *Italians*
A French Gentleman, friend to Philario
Caius Lucius, General of the Roman forces
A Roman Captain
Two British Captains

Pisanio, servant to Posthumus
Cornelius, a physician
Two Lords of Cymbeline's court
Two Gentlemen of the same
Two Jailers
Queen, wife to Cymbeline
Imogen, daughter to Cymbeline by a former queen
Helen, a lady attending on Imogen
Apparitions
Lords, Ladies, Roman Senators, Tribunes, a Soothsayer,
a Dutch Gentleman, a Spanish Gentleman, Musicians,
Officers, Captains, Soldiers, Messengers, Attendants

Scene : *Britain, Rome*]

❊

I, i   *Enter two Gentlemen.*

1. GENTLEMAN
1   You do not meet a man but frowns. Our bloods
     No more obey the heavens than our courtiers
3   Still seem as does the King's.

2. GENTLEMAN   But what's the matter?

1. GENTLEMAN
     His daughter, and the heir of's kingdom, whom
5   He purposed to his wife's sole son – a widow
6   That late he married – hath referred herself
     Unto a poor but worthy gentleman. She's wedded,
     Her husband banished, she imprisoned. All
     Is outward sorrow, though I think the King
     Be touched at very heart.

2. GENTLEMAN   None but the King?

1. GENTLEMAN
     He that hath lost her too. So is the Queen,
     That most desired the match. But not a courtier,
13   Although they wear their faces to the bent
     Of the King's looks, hath a heart that is not
     Glad at the thing they scowl at.

2. GENTLEMAN   And why so?

1. GENTLEMAN
     He that hath missed the Princess is a thing

Too bad for bad report, and he that hath her –
I mean, that married her, alack good man,
And therefore banished – is a creature such
As, to seek through the regions of the earth
For one his like, there would be something failing
In him that should compare. I do not think
So fair an outward and such stuff within
Endows a man but he.

2. GENTLEMAN   You speak him far.   24

1. GENTLEMAN
I do extend him, sir, within himself,   25
Crush him together rather than unfold   26
His measure duly.

2. GENTLEMAN   What's his name and birth?

1. GENTLEMAN
I cannot delve him to the root. His father   28
Was called Sicilius, who did join his honor   29
Against the Romans with Cassibelan,
But had his titles by Tenantius, whom
He served with glory and admired success,
So gained the sur-addition Leonatus;   33
And had, besides this gentleman in question,
Two other sons, who in the wars o' th' time
Died with their swords in hand; for which their father,
Then old and fond of issue, took such sorrow   37
That he quit being, and his gentle lady,
Big of this gentleman our theme, deceased   39
As he was born. The King he takes the babe
To his protection, calls him Posthumus Leonatus,
Breeds him and makes him of his bedchamber,   42
Puts to him all the learnings that his time   43
Could make him the receiver of, which he took
As we do air, fast as 'twas minist'red,
And in's spring became a harvest, lived in court –

I, i Britain: the palace of King Cymbeline   1 *bloods* moods   3 *seem . . .
King's* adjust their demeanor to the King's mood or expression (cf. ll. 13–14)
5 *purposed to* intended for   6 *referred* given   13 *bent* tendency   24 *speak
him far* go far in praise of him   25 *extend . . . himself* expand upon his
actual qualities   26–27 *Crush . . . duly* diminish his worth rather than
reveal his true stature   28 *delve . . . root* dig to the root of his family tree
29–31 *Sicilius, Cassibelan, Tenantius* British rulers mentioned by Holinshed
or other chroniclers   29 *did . . . honor* contributed his military fame   33
sur-addition added title   37 *fond of issue* loving his children   39 *Big . . .
theme* pregnant with Posthumus   42 *of his bedchamber* a member of the
royal retinue   43 *time* age

Which rare it is to do – most praised, most loved,
48 A sample to the youngest, to th' more mature
49 A glass that feated them, and to the graver
A child that guided dotards. To his mistress,
51 For whom he now is banished – her own price
Proclaims how she esteemed him and his virtue.
53 By her election may be truly read
What kind of man he is.

2. GENTLEMAN   I honor him
Even out of your report. But pray you tell me,
Is she sole child to th' King?

1. GENTLEMAN   His only child.
He had two sons – if this be worth your hearing,
Mark it – the eldest of them at three years old,
59 I' th' swathing clothes the other, from their nursery
60 Were stol'n, and to this hour no guess in knowledge
Which way they went.

2. GENTLEMAN   How long is this ago?

1. GENTLEMAN
Some twenty years.

2. GENTLEMAN
63 That a king's children should be so conveyed,
So slackly guarded, and the search so slow
That could not trace them!

1. GENTLEMAN   Howsoe'er 'tis strange,
66 Or that the negligence may well be laughed at,
Yet is it true, sir.

2. GENTLEMAN   I do well believe you.

1. GENTLEMAN
We must forbear. Here comes the gentleman,
The Queen, and Princess.   *Exeunt.*
    Enter the Queen, Posthumus, and Imogen.

QUEEN
No, be assured you shall not find me, daughter,
After the slander of most stepmothers,
Evil-eyed unto you. You're my prisoner, but
Your jailer shall deliver you the keys
74 That lock up your restraint. For you, Posthumus,
So soon as I can win th' offended King,
I will be known your advocate. Marry, yet
The fire of rage is in him, and 'twere good
78 You leaned unto his sentence with what patience
79 Your wisdom may inform you.

POSTHUMUS   Please your Highness,
I will from hence to-day.

QUEEN   You know the peril.
81 I'll fetch a turn about the garden, pitying
The pangs of barred affections, though the King
Hath charged you should not speak together.   *Exit.*

IMOGEN   O
Dissembling courtesy! How fine this tyrant
85 Can tickle where she wounds! My dearest husband,
I something fear my father's wrath, but nothing –
87 Always reserved my holy duty – what
His rage can do on me. You must be gone,
And I shall here abide the hourly shot
Of angry eyes, not comforted to live
But that there is this jewel in the world
That I may see again.

POSTHUMUS   My queen, my mistress.
O lady, weep no more, lest I give cause
To be suspected of more tenderness
Than doth become a man. I will remain
The loyal'st husband that did e'er plight troth;

My residence in Rome at one Philario's,
Who to my father was a friend, to me
Known but by letter. Thither write, my queen,
And with mine eyes I'll drink the words you send,
Though ink be made of gall.
    Enter Queen.

QUEEN   Be brief, I pray you.
If the King come, I shall incur I know not
How much of his displeasure. *[aside]* Yet I'll move him
To walk this way. I never do him wrong
But he does buy my injuries, to be friends;
Pays dear for my offenses.   *[Exit.]*   105

POSTHUMUS   Should we be taking leave
As long a term as yet we have to live,
The loathness to depart would grow. Adieu.

IMOGEN
Nay, stay a little.
Were you but riding forth to air yourself,
Such parting were too petty. Look here, love;
This diamond was my mother's. Take it, heart,
But keep it till you woo another wife
When Imogen is dead.

POSTHUMUS   How, how? Another?
You gentle gods, give me but this I have,
And cere up my embracements from a next   116
With bonds of death!
    [Puts on the ring.] Remain, remain thou here
While sense can keep it on. And, sweetest, fairest,
As I my poor self did exchange for you
To your so infinite loss, so in our trifles
I still win of you. For my sake wear this.
It is a manacle of love; I'll place it
Upon this fairest prisoner.
    [Puts a bracelet on her arm.]

IMOGEN   O the gods!
When shall we see again?
    Enter Cymbeline and Lords.

POSTHUMUS   Alack, the King!

CYMBELINE
Thou basest thing, avoid hence, from my sight!   125
If after this command thou fraught the court   126
With thy unworthiness, thou diest. Away!
Thou'rt poison to my blood.

POSTHUMUS   The gods protect you,
And bless the good remainders of the court.   129
I am gone.   *Exit.*

IMOGEN   There cannot be a pinch in death
More sharp than this is.

CYMBELINE   O disloyal thing
That shouldst repair my youth, thou heap'st   132
A year's age on me.   133

IMOGEN   I beseech you, sir,
Harm not yourself with your vexation.

---

48 *sample* example   49 *feated* reflected flatteringly   51 *price* i.e. the price
she paid   53 *election* choice   59 *swathing* swaddling   60 *guess in knowledge* conjecture leading to knowledge   63 *conveyed* taken away (i.e. stolen)
66 *laughed at* regarded as incredible   74 *lock . . . restraint* lock up your
prison (?), lock up and restrain you (?)   78 *leaned unto* bowed to   79
inform equip   81 *fetch* take   85 *tickle* (pretend to) gratify   87 *duty* i.e.
as a wife; all she fears is a divorce   105 *buy* accept; reward; possibly,
construe as benefits (i.e. in his eyes she can do no wrong)   116 *cere up*
shroud (with waxed cloth; possible pun on sealing with wax)   125 *avoid*
go   126 *fraught* burden   129 *remainders of* those who remain at   132
repair restore   133 *A year's age* (perhaps 'A years' age,' i.e. an age of years,
is preferable)

135 I am senseless of your wrath ; a touch more rare
Subdues all pangs, all fears.

CYMBELINE   Past grace ? obedience ?

IMOGEN
Past hope, and in despair ; that way, past grace.

CYMBELINE
That mightst have had the sole son of my queen.

IMOGEN
O blessed that I might not ! I chose an eagle
140 And did avoid a puttock.

CYMBELINE
Thou took'st a beggar, wouldst have made my throne
A seat for baseness.

IMOGEN   No, I rather added
A luster to it.

CYMBELINE   O thou vile one !

IMOGEN   Sir,
It is your fault that I have loved Posthumus.
You bred him as my playfellow, and he is
146 A man worth any woman ; overbuys me
Almost the sum he pays.

CYMBELINE   What, art thou mad ?

IMOGEN
Almost, sir. Heaven restore me ! Would I were
149 A neatherd's daughter, and my Leonatus
Our neighbor shepherd's son.

Enter Queen.

CYMBELINE   Thou foolish thing !
[To Queen]
They were again together. You have done
Not after our command. Away with her
And pen her up.

153 QUEEN   Beseech your patience. Peace,
Dear lady daughter, peace ! Sweet sovereign,
Leave us to ourselves, and make yourself some comfort
156 Out of your best advice.

CYMBELINE   Nay, let her languish
A drop of blood a day and, being aged,
Die of this folly.   *Exit [with Lords].*

Enter Pisanio.

158 QUEEN   Fie, you must give way.
Here is your servant. How now, sir ? What news ?

PISANIO
160 My lord your son drew on my master.

QUEEN   Ha !
No harm, I trust, is done ?

PISANIO   There might have been
But that my master rather played than fought
163 And had no help of anger. They were parted
By gentlemen at hand.

QUEEN   I am very glad on 't.

IMOGEN
Your son 's my father's friend ; he takes his part   165
To draw upon an exile. O brave sir !
I would they were in Afric both together,
Myself by with a needle that I might prick
The goer-back. Why came you from your master ?

PISANIO
On his command. He would not suffer me   170
To bring him to the haven, left these notes
Of what commands I should be subject to
When 't pleased you to employ me.

QUEEN   This hath been
Your faithful servant. I dare lay mine honor   174
He will remain so.

PISANIO   I humbly thank your Highness.

QUEEN
Pray walk awhile.

IMOGEN
About some half-hour hence pray you speak with me.
You shall at least go see my lord aboard.
For this time leave me.   *Exeunt.*

*

Enter Cloten and two Lords.   I, ii

1. LORD   Sir, I would advise you to shift a shirt ; the violence of action hath made you reek as a sacrifice. Where   2
air comes out, air comes in ; there's none abroad so   3
wholesome as that you vent.

CLOTEN   If my shirt were bloody, then to shift it. Have I
hurt him ?

2. LORD *[aside]*   No, faith, not so much as his patience.

1. LORD   Hurt him ? His body 's a passable carcass if he be   8
not hurt. It is a throughfare for steel if it be not hurt.   9

2. LORD *[aside]*   His steel was in debt. It went o' th' back-   10
side the town.

CLOTEN   The villain would not stand me.   12

2. LORD *[aside]*   No, but he fled forward still, toward your
face.

1. LORD   Stand you ? You have land enough of your own,
but he added to your having, gave you some ground.

2. LORD *[aside]*   As many inches as you have oceans.
Puppies !   17

CLOTEN   I would they had not come between us.

2. LORD *[aside]*   So would I, till you had measured how
long a fool you were upon the ground.

CLOTEN   And that she should love this fellow and refuse
me !

2. LORD *[aside]*   If it be a sin to make a true election, she is   22
damned.

1. LORD   Sir, as I told you always, her beauty and her
brain go not together. She 's a good sign, but I have seen   25
small reflection of her wit.

2. LORD *[aside]*   She shines not upon fools, lest the reflection should hurt her.

CLOTEN   Come, I'll to my chamber. Would there had
been some hurt done !

2. LORD *[aside]*   I wish not so – unless it had been the fall
of an ass, which is no great hurt.

CLOTEN   You'll go with us ?

1. LORD   I'll attend your lordship.

CLOTEN   Nay, come, let's go together.

2. LORD   Well, my lord.   *Exeunt.*

*

---

135 *am senseless of* do not feel ; *touch more rare* more painful feeling   140
puttock kite (bird of prey ; a term of contempt)   146–47 *overbuys . . . pays*
what he pays (either in giving himself or in suffering punishment) almost
entirely exceeds my value   149 *neatherd* cowherd   153 *Beseech* I beg
156 *advice* (self-)admonition ; *languish* pine away   158 *Fie . . . way* (said to
Cymbeline to impress Imogen)   160 *drew on* (with his sword)   163 *had
. . . anger* was not angry enough to fight seriously   165 *takes his part* acts as
expected   170 *suffer* permit   174 *lay* wager
I, ii The same   2 *reek* give off vapors   3 *abroad* outside you   8 *passable*
penetrable without damage (like a fluid ; with pun on meaning 'tolerable')
9 *throughfare* thoroughfare   10 *was in debt* i.e. paid back nothing   10–11
went . . . town (like a debtor taking a back road ; i.e. the rapier missed)
12 *stand* face   17 *Puppies* vain, foolish people   22 *election* choice   25 *sign*
appearance

I, iii   *Enter Imogen and Pisanio.*

IMOGEN
I would thou grew'st unto the shores o' th' haven
2 And questionedst every sail. If he should write
And I not have it, 'twere a paper lost
As offered mercy is. What was the last
That he spake to thee?

PISANIO   It was his queen, his queen.

IMOGEN
Then waved his handkerchief?

PISANIO   And kissed it, madam.

IMOGEN
7 Senseless linen, happier therein than I!
And that was all?

PISANIO   No, madam. For so long
As he could make me with this eye or ear
Distinguish him from others, he did keep
The deck, with glove or hat or handkerchief
Still waving, as the fits and stirs of's mind
Could best express how slow his soul sailed on,
How swift his ship.

IMOGEN   Thou shouldst have made him
15 As little as a crow or less, ere left
To after-eye him.

PISANIO   Madam, so I did.

IMOGEN
I would have broke mine eyestrings, cracked them but
To look upon him till the diminution
Of space had pointed him sharp as my needle;
Nay, followed him till he had melted from
The smallness of a gnat to air, and then
Have turned mine eye and wept. But, good Pisanio,
When shall we hear from him?

PISANIO   Be assured, madam,
24 With his next vantage.

IMOGEN
I did not take my leave of him, but had
Most pretty things to say. Ere I could tell him
How I would think on him at certain hours
Such thoughts and such; or I could make him swear
The shes of Italy should not betray
Mine interest and his honor; or have charged him
At the sixth hour of morn, at noon, at midnight,
32 T' encounter me with orisons, for then
I am in heaven for him; or ere I could
Give him that parting kiss which I had set
35 Betwixt two charming words – comes in my father,
36 And like the tyrannous breathing of the north
Shakes all our buds from growing.

          Enter a Lady.

LADY   The Queen, madam,
Desires your Highness' company.

IMOGEN
Those things I bid you do, get them dispatched.
I will attend the Queen.

PISANIO   Madam, I shall.   *Exeunt.*

                    *

I, iv   *Enter Philario, Iachimo, a Frenchman, a Dutchman,
          and a Spaniard.*

IACHIMO Believe it, sir, I have seen him in Britain. He
2 was then of a crescent note, expected to prove so worthy
as since he hath been allowed the name of. But I could

then have looked on him without the help of admiration, 4
though the catalogue of his endowments had been tabled 5
by his side and I to peruse him by items.

PHILARIO You speak of him when he was less furnished
than now he is with that which makes him both without 8
and within.

FRENCHMAN I have seen him in France. We had very
many there could behold the sun with as firm eyes as 11
he.

IACHIMO This matter of marrying his king's daughter,
wherein he must be weighed rather by her value than
his own, words him, I doubt not, a great deal from the 14
matter.

FRENCHMAN And then his banishment.

IACHIMO Ay, and the approbation of those that weep this
lamentable divorce under her colors are wonderfully to 18
extend him, be it but to fortify her judgment, which else 19
an easy battery might lay flat for taking a beggar without 20
less quality. But how comes it he is to sojourn with you? 21
How creeps acquaintance?   22

PHILARIO His father and I were soldiers together, to
whom I have been often bound for no less than my life.

          Enter Posthumus.

Here comes the Briton. Let him be so entertained
amongst you as suits, with gentlemen of your knowing,
to a stranger of his quality. I beseech you all be better
known to this gentleman, whom I commend to you as
a noble friend of mine. How worthy he is I will leave to
appear hereafter, rather than story him in his own 30
hearing.

FRENCHMAN Sir, we have known together in Orleans. 31

POSTHUMUS Since when I have been debtor to you for
courtesies which I will be ever to pay and yet pay still.

FRENCHMAN Sir, you o'errate my poor kindness. I was
glad I did atone my countryman and you. It had been 35
pity you should have been put together with so mortal a 36
purpose as then each bore, upon importance of so slight 37
and trivial a nature.

POSTHUMUS By your pardon, sir, I was then a young
traveller; rather shunned to go even with what I heard 40
than in my every action to be guided by others' experiences. But upon my mended judgment, if I offend not to 42
say it is mended, my quarrel was not altogether slight.

FRENCHMAN Faith, yes, to be put to the arbitrement of 44
swords, and by such two that would by all likelihood
have confounded one the other or have fall'n both. 46

IACHIMO Can we with manners ask what was the difference?

I, iii The same 2–4 *If . . . mercy is* loss of a letter would be like loss of
mercy (offered by heaven or by king) 7 *Senseless* without feeling 15–16
ere . . . after-eye before you stopped gazing after 24 *next vantage* first
opportunity 32 *encounter . . . orisons* join me in prayers 35 *charming*
magical, protecting like a charm 36 *north* north wind
I, iv Rome: the house of Philario 2 *crescent note* growing fame 4 *without
. . . admiration* without feeling wonder and respect 5 *tabled* set down in a
list 8 *makes* is the making of 11 *behold the sun* (as eagles were supposed
to do; a metaphor for distinction; cf. I, i, 139–40) 14–15 *words . . .
matter* gives an account of him that goes beyond the facts 18 *under her
colors* as supporters of Imogen 18–19 *are . . . him* have the effect of greatly
enlarging his reputation 19 *fortify* justify 20 *without* i.e. with (in effect,
a double negative, found more than once in Shakespeare) 21 *quality* rank
22 *creeps* (suggests 'worming his way in') 30 *story* tell about 31 *known
together* been acquainted 35 *atone* reconcile 36 *put together* i.e. in a duel
37 *importance* a matter 40 *shunned . . . even* declined to agree (cf. 'go
along with') 42 *mended* improved 44 *arbitrement* settlement 46 *confounded* destroyed

FRENCHMAN Safely, I think. 'Twas a contention in pub-
49 lic, which may without contradiction suffer the report. It
was much like an argument that fell out last night, where
51 each of us fell in praise of our country mistresses; this
52 gentleman at that time vouching – and upon warrant of
bloody affirmation – his to be more fair, virtuous, wise,
54 chaste, constant, qualified, and less attemptable than
any the rarest of our ladies in France.

IACHIMO That lady is not now living, or this gentleman's
57 opinion, by this, worn out.

58 POSTHUMUS She holds her virtue still, and I my mind.

IACHIMO You must not so far prefer her 'fore ours of Italy.

POSTHUMUS Being so far provoked as I was in France, I
61 would abate her nothing, though I profess myself her
62 adorer, not her friend.

63 IACHIMO As fair and as good – a kind of hand-in-hand
comparison – had been something too fair and too good
65 for any lady in Britain. If she went before others I have
seen as that diamond of yours outlusters many I have
beheld, I could not but believe she excelled many; but
I have not seen the most precious diamond that is, nor
you the lady.

70 POSTHUMUS I praised her as I rated her. So do I my stone.

IACHIMO What do you esteem it at?

72 POSTHUMUS More than the world enjoys.

IACHIMO Either your unparagoned mistress is dead, or
74 she's outprized by a trifle.

POSTHUMUS You are mistaken. The one may be sold or
76 given, or if there were wealth enough for the purchase
or merit for the gift. The other is not a thing for sale,
and only the gift of the gods.

IACHIMO Which the gods have given you?

POSTHUMUS Which by their graces I will keep.

81 IACHIMO You may wear her in title yours, but you know
82 strange fowl light upon neighboring ponds. Your ring
83 may be stol'n too. So your brace of unprizable estima-
84 tions, the one is but frail and the other casual. A cunning
thief, or a that-way-accomplished courtier, would hazard the winning both of first and last.

POSTHUMUS Your Italy contains none so accomplished a
88 courtier to convince the honor of my mistress, if, in the
holding or loss of that, you term her frail. I do nothing

doubt you have store of thieves; notwithstanding, I fear
not my ring.

PHILARIO Let us leave here, gentlemen.   92

POSTHUMUS Sir, with all my heart. This worthy signior,
I thank him, makes no stranger of me; we are familiar at 94
first.

IACHIMO With five times so much conversation I should
get ground of your fair mistress, make her go back even to 97
the yielding, had I admittance, and opportunity to 98
friend.

POSTHUMUS No, no.

IACHIMO I dare thereupon pawn the moiety of my estate 100
to your ring, which in my opinion o'ervalues it something. But I make my wager rather against your confidence than her reputation; and, to bar your offense
herein too, I durst attempt it against any lady in the
world.

POSTHUMUS You are a great deal abused in too bold a 105
persuasion, and I doubt not you sustain what y'are 106
worthy of by your attempt.

IACHIMO What's that?

POSTHUMUS A repulse – though your attempt, as you
call it, deserve more: a punishment too.

PHILARIO Gentlemen, enough of this. It came in too
suddenly; let it die as it was born, and I pray you be
better acquainted.

IACHIMO Would I had put my estate and my neighbor's 114
on th' approbation of what I have spoke!   115

POSTHUMUS What lady would you choose to assail?

IACHIMO Yours, whom in constancy you think stands so
safe. I will lay you ten thousand ducats to your ring that,
commend me to the court where your lady is, with no 119
more advantage than the opportunity of a second con- 120
ference, and I will bring from thence that honor of hers
which you imagine so reserved.   122

POSTHUMUS I will wage against your gold, gold to it. My 123
ring I hold dear as my finger; 'tis part of it.

IACHIMO You are a friend, and therein the wiser. If you 125
buy ladies' flesh at a million a dram, you cannot preserve it from tainting. But I see you have some religion 127
in you, that you fear.   128

POSTHUMUS This is but a custom in your tongue. You 129
bear a graver purpose, I hope.

IACHIMO I am the master of my speeches, and would un- 131
dergo what's spoken, I swear.

POSTHUMUS Will you? I shall but lend my diamond till
your return. Let there be covenants drawn between's. 134
My mistress exceeds in goodness the hugeness of your
unworthy thinking. I dare you to this match: here's my
ring.

PHILARIO I will have it no lay.   138

IACHIMO By the gods, it is one. If I bring you no sufficient testimony that I have enjoyed the dearest bodily
part of your mistress, my ten thousand ducats are yours;
so is your diamond too. If I come off and leave her in
such honor as you have trust in, she your jewel, this
your jewel, and my gold are yours – provided I have
your commendation for my more free entertainment.   145

POSTHUMUS I embrace these conditions. Let us have 146
articles betwixt us. Only, thus far you shall answer: if 147
you make your voyage upon her and give me directly to 148
understand you have prevailed, I am no further your
enemy; she is not worth our debate. If she remain un-
seduced, you not making it appear otherwise, for your

---

49 *without . . . report* without objection be reported   51 *our country mistresses* loved women of our countries (cf. Partridge, *Shakespeare's Bawdy*, p. 95)   52–53 *warrant . . . affirmation* pledge to support by shedding blood   54 *qualified* having good qualities; *attemptable* vulnerable to seduction   57 *by . . . out* by now not sound   58 *mind* opinion   61 *abate her* lower her value (cf. 'downgrade')   62 *friend* lover, i.e. paramour   63 *hand-in-hand* claiming equality   65 *went before* were superior to   70 *rated* estimated   72 *enjoys* possesses   74 *outprized* surpassed in value   76 *or if* either if   81 *wear . . . title* have title to her, possess her in name   82 *ponds, ring* (see Partridge, op. cit., pp. 169, 179)   83 *unprizable estimations* inestimable values (cf. 'prize possessions')   84 *casual* open to accident (cf. 'casualty')   88 *to convince* to overcome (perhaps 'convict'); *honor* chastity   92 *leave* leave off (drop the subject)   94–95 *familiar at first* on easy terms from the first   97–98 *get ground, go back, yielding* (military and duelling terms as metaphors for sex)   98 *to* as a   100 *moiety* half   105 *abused* deceived   106 *persuasion* opinion; *sustain* will receive   114 *put* bet   115 *on th' approbation of* that I can prove   119 *commend me* recommend me, give me an introduction   120 *conference* meeting   122 *reserved* secure   123 *wage* wager; *gold to it* gold in equal amount (?)   125 *You . . . wiser* i.e. you know her well enough to know the danger of such a bet   127 *religion* (Iachimo sneers)   128 *that* since   129 *This* the bet, the point of view   131 *undergo* undertake   134 *covenants* terms of agreement   138 *lay* wager   145 *commendation* recommendation, introduction; *free entertainment* easy reception   146 *embrace* accept   147 *articles* terms (of the bet)   148 *voyage* predatory expedition (with sexual innuendo); *directly* straightforwardly, convincingly

ill opinion and the assault you have made to her chastity
you shall answer me with your sword.

IACHIMO Your hand; a covenant. We will have these
things set down by lawful counsel, and straight away for
156 Britain, lest the bargain should catch cold and starve. I
will fetch my gold and have our two wagers recorded.

POSTHUMUS Agreed. *[Exeunt Posthumus and Iachimo.]*

FRENCHMAN Will this hold, think you?

160 PHILARIO Signior Iachimo will not from it. Pray let us
follow 'em. *Exeunt.*

*

I, v   *Enter Queen, Ladies, and Cornelius.*

QUEEN
Whiles yet the dew 's on ground, gather those flowers.
2 Make haste. Who has the note of them?

LADY   I, madam.

QUEEN
3 Dispatch.   *Exeunt Ladies.*
Now, Master Doctor, have you brought those drugs?

CORNELIUS
Pleaseth your Highness, ay. Here they are, madam.
[Presents a box.]
But I beseech your Grace, without offense –
My conscience bids me ask – wherefore you have
Commanded of me these most poisonous compounds,
9 Which are the movers of a languishing death,
But though slow, deadly.

QUEEN   I wonder, Doctor,
Thou ask'st me such a question. Have I not been
12 Thy pupil long? Hast thou not learned me how
To make perfumes? distil? preserve? yea, so
That our great king himself doth woo me oft
15 For my confections? Having thus far proceeded –
16 Unless thou think'st me devilish – is't not meet
17 That I did amplify my judgment in
18 Other conclusions? I will try the forces
Of these thy compounds on such creatures as
We count not worth the hanging – but none human –
To try the vigor of them and apply
22 Allayments to their act, and by them gather
Their several virtues and effects.

CORNELIUS   Your Highness
Shall from this practice but make hard your heart.
Besides, the seeing these effects will be
But noisome and infectious.

26 QUEEN   O, content thee.
Enter Pisanio.
[Aside]
Here comes a flattering rascal. Upon him
Will I first work. He's for his master,
And enemy to my son. – How now, Pisanio?
Doctor, your service for this time is ended;
Take your own way.

CORNELIUS *[aside]*   I do suspect you, madam,
But you shall do no harm.

QUEEN *[to Pisanio]*   Hark thee, a word.

CORNELIUS *[aside]*
I do not like her. She doth think she has
Strange ling'ring poisons. I do know her spirit
And will not trust one of her malice with
A drug of such damned nature. Those she has
Will stupefy and dull the sense awhile,

Which first perchance she'll prove on cats and dogs,
Then afterward up higher; but there is
No danger in what show of death it makes,   40
More than the locking up the spirits a time,
To be more fresh, reviving. She is fooled
With a most false effect, and I the truer
So to be false with her.

QUEEN   No further service, Doctor,
Until I send for thee.

CORNELIUS   I humbly take my leave.   *Exit.*

QUEEN
Weeps she still, say'st thou? Dost thou think in time
She will not quench and let instructions enter   47
Where folly now possesses? Do thou work.
When thou shalt bring me word she loves my son,
I'll tell thee on the instant thou art then
As great as is thy master; greater, for
His fortunes all lie speechless and his name
Is at last gasp. Return he cannot nor
Continue where he is. To shift his being   54
Is to exchange one misery with another,
And every day that comes to comes to decay   56
A day's work in him. What shalt thou expect
To be depender on a thing that leans,   58
Who cannot be new built, nor has no friends
So much as but to prop him?
[Drops the box. Pisanio picks it up.]
                    Thou tak'st up
Thou know'st not what, but take it for thy labor.
It is a thing I made which hath the King
Five times redeemed from death. I do not know
What is more cordial. Nay, I prithee take it.   64
It is an earnest of a farther good   65
That I mean to thee. Tell thy mistress how   66
The case stands with her; do't as from thyself.
Think what a chance thou changest on, but think   68
Thou hast thy mistress still – to boot, my son,
Who shall take notice of thee. I'll move the King
To any shape of thy preferment such   71
As thou'lt desire; and then myself, I chiefly,
That set thee on to this desert, am bound   73
To load thy merit richly. Call my women.   74
Think on my words.   *Exit Pisanio.*
                    A sly and constant knave,
Not to be shaked; the agent for his master,   76
And the remembrancer of her to hold   77
The handfast to her lord. I have given him that   78
Which, if he take, shall quite unpeople her
Of liegers for her sweet, and which she after,   80
Except she bend her humor, shall be assured   81
To taste of too.

156 *starve* die   160 *from it* give it up
I, v Britain: the palace of King Cymbeline   2 *note* list   3 *Dispatch* do it
quickly   9 *are* . . . *of* cause   12 *learned* taught   15 *confections* compounds
(drugs)   16 *meet* fitting   17 *amplify my judgment* increase my knowledge
18 *conclusions* experiments   22 *Allayments* antidotes; *act* action; *gather* put
together (a record of)   26 *content thee* don't worry   47 *quench* cool down;
instructions admonitions   54 *being* abode   56–57 *comes to* . . . *him* brings a
day to nought for him   58 *leans* begins to fall   64 *cordial* restorative   65
earnest sample; token payment   66 *mean to* intend for   68 *chance* . . . *on*
good chance (this is) to change (service)   71 *shape* . . . *preferment* kind of
advancement   73 *desert* meritorious action   74 *load* reward   76 *shaked*
shaken (in his devotion to Posthumus)   77 *remembrancer* agent whose duty
is to remind (legal term)   78 *handfast* marriage contract   80 *liegers* . . .
sweet her husband's ambassadors   81 *bend her humor* change her mind

1300

Enter Pisanio and Ladies.

82 So, so. Well done, well done.
The violets, cowslips, and the primroses
84 Bear to my closet. Fare thee well, Pisanio.
Think on my words. *Exit Queen, and Ladies.*

PISANIO And shall do.
But when to my good lord I prove untrue,
I'll choke myself. There's all I'll do for you. *Exit.*

*

I, vi *Enter Imogen alone.*

IMOGEN
A father cruel and a stepdame false,
A foolish suitor to a wedded lady
That hath her husband banished. O, that husband,
4 My supreme crown of grief, and those repeated
Vexations of it! Had I been thief-stol'n,
As my two brothers, happy; but most miserable
7 Is the desire that's glorious. Blessed be those,
8 How mean soe'er, that have their honest wills,
9 Which seasons comfort. Who may this be? Fie!
Enter Pisanio and Iachimo.

PISANIO
Madam, a noble gentleman of Rome
Comes from my lord with letters.

11 IACHIMO Change you, madam:
The worthy Leonatus is in safety
And greets your Highness dearly.
[Presents a letter.]

IMOGEN Thanks, good sir.
You're kindly welcome.

IACHIMO *[aside]*
15 All of her that is out of door most rich!
If she be furnished with a mind so rare,
17 She is alone th' Arabian bird, and I
Have lost the wager. Boldness be my friend!
Arm me, audacity, from head to foot,
20 Or like the Parthian I shall flying fight –
Rather, directly fly.

22 IMOGEN *[reads]* 'He is one of the noblest note, to whose
23 kindnesses I am most infinitely tied. Reflect upon him
accordingly, as you value your trust.
Leonatus.'

So far I read aloud.
But even the very middle of my heart
Is warmed by th' rest and takes it thankfully.
You are as welcome, worthy sir, as I

Have words to bid you, and shall find it so
In all that I can do.

IACHIMO Thanks, fairest lady.
What, are men mad? Hath nature given them eyes
To see this vaulted arch and the rich crop 33
Of sea and land, which can distinguish 'twixt
The fiery orbs above and the twinned stones 35
Upon the numbered beach, and can we not 36
Partition make with spectacles so precious 37
'Twixt fair and foul?

IMOGEN What makes your admiration? 38
IACHIMO
It cannot be i' th' eye, for apes and monkeys,
'Twixt two such shes, would chatter this way and 40
Contemn with mows the other; nor i' th' judgment, 41
For idiots, in this case of favor, would 42
Be wisely definite; nor i' th' appetite – 43
Sluttery, to such neat excellence opposed, 44
Should make desire vomit emptiness, 45
Not so allured to feed. 46

IMOGEN
What is the matter, trow? 47
IACHIMO The cloyèd will –
That satiate yet unsatisfied desire, that tub
Both filled and running – ravening first the lamb, 49
Longs after for the garbage.

IMOGEN What, dear sir,
Thus raps you? Are you well? 51
IACHIMO Thanks, madam, well.
[To Pisanio]
Beseech you, sir, desire
My man's abode where I did leave him. 53
He's strange and peevish. 54
PISANIO I was going, sir,
To give him welcome. *Exit.*
IMOGEN
Continues well my lord? His health, beseech you?
IACHIMO
Well, madam.
IMOGEN
Is he disposed to mirth? I hope he is.
IACHIMO
Exceeding pleasant; none a stranger there
So merry and so gamesome. He is called
The Briton reveller.
IMOGEN When he was here
He did incline to sadness, and ofttimes 62
Not knowing why.
IACHIMO I never saw him sad.
There is a Frenchman his companion, one
An eminent monsieur that, it seems, much loves
A Gallian girl at home. He furnaces 66
The thick sighs from him, whiles the jolly Briton – 67
Your lord, I mean – laughs from 's free lungs, cries 'O,
Can my sides hold to think that man who knows
By history, report, or his own proof
What woman is, yea, what she cannot choose
But must be, will 's free hours languish for 72
Assurèd bondage?'
IMOGEN Will my lord say so?
IACHIMO
Ay, madam, with his eyes in flood with laughter.
It is a recreation to be by
And hear him mock the Frenchman. But heavens know

82 *So, so* good 84 *closet* room
I, vi The same 4 *repeated* which I have recounted (in ll. 1–3) 7 *glorious* for a noble thing (?), held by a person in high position (?) 8 *honest wills* plain desires 9 *seasons* adds relish to 11 *Change you* i.e. change your expression; I have good news 15 *out of door* visible 17 *Arabian bird* mythical phoenix (only one existed at a time; hence, unique) 20 *Parthian* mounted archer who fired backwards while in flight 22 *note* distinction 23 *Reflect upon* welcome 33 *crop* harvest 35 *twinned* exactly alike 36 *numbered* (with) numerous (stones) 37 *Partition* distinction; *spectacles* eyes 38 *admiration* wonder 40 *chatter this way* speak (i.e. give approval) for this one (Imogen) 41 *mows* grimaces 42 *case of favor* question of beauty 43 *Be wisely definite* make a wise decision; *appetite* physical desire 44 *neat* elegant 45 *desire* lust; *vomit emptiness* vomit though not fed 46 *so allured* attracted by this (i.e. by *Sluttery* l. 44) 47 *trow* I wonder; *will* sexual desire 49 *ravening* feeding voraciously on 51 *raps* carries away 53 *man's abode* man to await 54 *strange* a stranger; *peevish* easily distressed 62 *sadness* seriousness 66 *Gallian* French; *furnaces* blows forth like a furnace 67 *thick* close together 72 *languish* give up to languishing

Some men are much to blame.
IMOGEN   Not he, I hope.
IACHIMO
78 Not he – but yet heaven's bounty towards him might
79 Be used more thankfully. In himself 'tis much;
80 In you, which I account his, beyond all talents.
Whilst I am bound to wonder, I am bound
To pity too.
IMOGEN   What do you pity, sir?
IACHIMO
Two creatures heartily.
IMOGEN   Am I one, sir?
84 You look on me. What wrack discern you in me
Deserves your pity?
IACHIMO   Lamentable! What,
86 To hide me from the radiant sun and solace
87 I' th' dungeon by a snuff!
IMOGEN   I pray you, sir,
Deliver with more openness your answers
To my demands. Why do you pity me?
IACHIMO
That others do,
I was about to say, enjoy your – but
92 It is an office of the gods to venge it,
Not mine to speak on't.
IMOGEN   You do seem to know
Something of me or what concerns me. Pray you,
95 Since doubting things go ill often hurts more
Than to be sure they do – for certainties
97 Either are past remedies, or, timely knowing,
98 The remedy then born – discover to me
99 What both you spur and stop.
IACHIMO   Had I this cheek
To bathe my lips upon; this hand, whose touch,
Whose every touch, would force the feeler's soul
To th' oath of loyalty; this object, which
Takes prisoner the wild motion of mine eye,
Fixing it only here; should I, damned then,
Slaver with lips as common as the stairs
That mount the Capitol; join gripes with hands
107 Made hard with hourly falsehood (falsehood, as
108 With labor); then by-peeping in an eye
109 Base and illustrious as the smoky light
That's fed with stinking tallow – it were fit
That all the plagues of hell should at one time
112 Encounter such revolt.
IMOGEN   My lord, I fear,
Has forgot Britain.
113 IACHIMO   And himself. Not I
Inclined to this intelligence pronounce
115 The beggary of his change, but 'tis your graces
116 That from my mutest conscience to my tongue
Charms this report out.
IMOGEN   Let me hear no more.
IACHIMO
O dearest soul, your cause doth strike my heart
With pity that doth make me sick. A lady
120 So fair, and fastened to an empery
121 Would make the great'st king double, to be partnered
122 With tomboys hired with that self exhibition
123 Which your own coffers yield; with diseased ventures
124 That play with all infirmities for gold
125 Which rottenness can lend nature; such boiled stuff
As well might poison poison! Be revenged,

Or she that bore you was no queen, and you
Recoil from your great stock.   128
IMOGEN   Revenged?
How should I be revenged? If this be true –
As I have such a heart that both mine ears
Must not in haste abuse – if it be true,
How should I be revenged?
IACHIMO   Should he make me
Live like Diana's priest betwixt cold sheets,
Whiles he is vaulting variable ramps,   134
In your despite, upon your purse? Revenge it.
I dedicate myself to your sweet pleasure,
More noble than that runagate to your bed,   137
And will continue fast to your affection,   138
Still close as sure.   139
IMOGEN   What ho, Pisanio!
IACHIMO
Let me my service tender on your lips.
IMOGEN
Away, I do condemn mine ears that have
So long attended thee. If thou wert honorable,   142
Thou wouldst have told this tale for virtue, not
For such an end thou seek'st, as base as strange.
Thou wrong'st a gentleman who is as far
From thy report as thou from honor, and
Solicit'st here a lady that disdains
Thee and the devil alike. What ho, Pisanio!
The King my father shall be made acquainted
Of thy assault. If he shall think it fit
A saucy stranger in his court to mart   151
As in a Romish stew and to expound   152
His beastly mind to us, he hath a court
He little cares for and a daughter who
He not respects at all. What ho, Pisanio!
IACHIMO
O happy Leonatus! I may say
The credit that thy lady hath of thee   157
Deserves thy trust, and thy most perfect goodness   158
Her assured credit. Blessèd live you long,
A lady to the worthiest sir that ever
Country called his, and you his mistress, only   161
For the most worthiest fit. Give me your pardon.
I have spoke this to know if your affiance   163
Were deeply rooted, and shall make your lord
That which he is, new o'er; and he is one   165

78 *bounty* i.e. in bestowing upon him his own qualities, and Imogen 79 *'tis* i.e. heaven's bounty is 80 *talents* his own qualities (?), wealth (?) 84 *wrack* wreck, disaster 86 *solace* find pleasure 87 *snuff* partly consumed candlewick 92 *office* duty 95 *doubting* fearing 97 *timely knowing* if one knows in time 98 *then* is then; *discover* reveal 99 *spur and stop* prod on (toward disclosure) and stop 107–08 *as With* as if made hard by 108 *by-peeping* looking sidelong 109 *illustrious* (for 'illustrous,' not lustrous) 112 *Encounter such revolt* come upon (as a punishment) such inconstancy 113–14 *Not . . . pronounce* though not inclined to give this news, I report 115 *beggary* meanness, cheapness 116 *mutest conscience* most silent knowledge 120–21 *empery Would* empire which would 121–22 *partnered With tomboys* treated the same as whores 122 *that self exhibition* the very allowance money 123 *ventures* traders (?), adventuresses (?) 124 *play* gamble, toy 125 *Which* i.e. infirmities; *boiled stuff* i.e. women treated for venereal disease by sweating 128 *Recoil . . . stock* fall away from (what is natural to) your royal heredity 134 *variable ramps* various whores 137 *runagate* to truant from 138 *fast* firm 139 *close* secret 142 *attended* listened to 151 *saucy* impudent; *to mart* should bargain 152 *stew* brothel 157 *credit . . . of* faith . . . in 158 *goodness* integrity (deserves) 161 *called his* called its own 163 *affiance* loyalty 165 *new o'er* all over again (i.e. doubly so); *one* above all, uniquely

166 The truest mannered, such a holy witch
167 That he enchants societies into him.
Half all men's hearts are his.

IMOGEN   You make amends.

IACHIMO
He sits 'mongst men like a descended god.
He hath a kind of honor sets him off
171 More than a mortal seeming. Be not angry,
Most mighty Princess, that I have adventured
173 To try your taking of a false report, which hath
Honored with confirmation your great judgment
175 In the election of a sir so rare,
176 Which you know cannot err. The love I bear him
177 Made me to fan you thus, but the gods made you,
178 Unlike all others, chaffless. Pray your pardon.

IMOGEN
All's well, sir. Take my pow'r i' th' court for yours.

IACHIMO
My humble thanks. I had almost forgot
T' entreat your Grace but in a small request,
182 And yet of moment too, for it concerns
Your lord, myself, and other noble friends
Are partners in the business.

IMOGEN   Pray what is't?

IACHIMO
Some dozen Romans of us and your lord –
The best feather of our wing – have mingled sums
To buy a present for the Emperor;
188 Which I, the factor for the rest, have done
In France. 'Tis plate of rare device and jewels
Of rich and exquisite form, their values great,
191 And I am something curious, being strange,
To have them in safe stowage. May it please you
To take them in protection?

IMOGEN   Willingly;
And pawn mine honor for their safety. Since
My lord hath interest in them, I will keep them
In my bedchamber.

IACHIMO   They are in a trunk
Attended by my men. I will make bold
To send them to you, only for this night.
I must aboard to-morrow.

IMOGEN   O, no, no.

IACHIMO
200 Yes, I beseech, or I shall short my word
By length'ning my return. From Gallia
I crossed the seas on purpose and on promise
To see your Grace.

IMOGEN   I thank you for your pains.
But not away to-morrow!

IACHIMO   O, I must, madam.
Therefore I shall beseech you, if you please
To greet your lord with writing, do't to-night.
I have outstood my time, which is material   207
To th' tender of our present.   208

IMOGEN   I will write.
Send your trunk to me; it shall safe be kept
And truly yielded you. You're very welcome.   *Exeunt.*

*

Enter Cloten and the two Lords.   II, i

CLOTEN Was there ever man had such luck? When I
kissed the jack upon an upcast, to be hit away! I had a   2
hundred pound on't. And then a whoreson jackanapes   3
must take me up for swearing, as if I borrowed mine   4
oaths of him and might not spend them at my pleasure.

1. LORD What got he by that? You have broke his pate
with your bowl.

2. LORD [aside] If his wit had been like him that broke it,
it would have run all out.

CLOTEN When a gentleman is disposed to swear, it is not
for any standers-by to curtail his oaths. Ha?   11

2. LORD No, my lord; [aside] nor crop the ears of them.

CLOTEN Whoreson dog, I gave him satisfaction! Would
he had been one of my rank.

2. LORD [aside] To have smelled like a fool.   15

CLOTEN I am not vexed more at anything in th' earth. A
pox on't! I had rather not be so noble as I am. They dare   17
not fight with me because of the Queen my mother.
Every jack-slave hath his bellyful of fighting, and I must   19
go up and down like a cock that nobody can match.

2. LORD [aside] You are cock and capon too, and you   21
crow cock with your comb on.

CLOTEN Sayest thou?

2. LORD It is not fit your lordship should undertake   24
every companion that you give offense to.   25

CLOTEN No, I know that, but it is fit I should commit   26
offense to my inferiors.

2. LORD Ay, it is fit for your lordship only.

CLOTEN Why, so I say.

1. LORD Did you hear of a stranger that's come to court
to-night?

CLOTEN A stranger, and I not know on't?

2. LORD [aside] He's a strange fellow himself, and knows
it not.

1. LORD There's an Italian come, and, 'tis thought, one
of Leonatus' friends.

CLOTEN Leonatus? A banished rascal, and he's another,
whatsoever he be. Who told you of this stranger?

1. LORD One of your lordship's pages.

CLOTEN Is it fit I went to look upon him? Is there no dero-   40
gation in't?

2. LORD You cannot derogate, my lord.   42

CLOTEN Not easily, I think.

2. LORD [aside] You are a fool granted; therefore your
issues, being foolish, do not derogate.   45

CLOTEN Come, I'll go see this Italian. What I have lost
to-day at bowls I'll win to-night of him. Come, go.

2. LORD I'll attend your lordship.

Exit [Cloten with First Lord].

That such a crafty devil as is his mother
Should yield the world this ass! A woman that
Bears all down with her brain, and this her son   51

---

166 *truest mannered* most honestly behaved; *witch* charmer   167 *societies* social groups; *into* to   171 *mortal seeming* human appearance   173 *try your taking* test your reception   175 *election* choice   176 *Which* i.e. who   177 *fan* winnow, i.e. test   178 *chaffless* faultless   182 *moment* importance   188 *factor* agent   191 *curious* anxious; *strange* foreign   200 *short* not live up to   207 *outstood* outstayed   208 *tender* giving   II, i The palace grounds   2 *kissed the jack* touched the target (in game of bowls); *upcast* throw (?), chance (?)   3 *whoreson jackanapes* (terms of abuse)   4 *take me up* take me to task   11 *curtail* cut down   15 *smelled* (pun on *rank* in l. 14)   17 *pox* venereal disease (standard oath)   19 *jack-slave* lower-class person   21–22 *capon . . . on* (puns on meanings 'castration,' 'idiot,' 'coxcomb')   24 *undertake* 'take on'   25 *companion* fellow (term of contempt)   26–27 *commit offense* attack (with excretory pun)   40 *derogation* loss of dignity   42 *cannot derogate* i.e. have no dignity to lose   45 *issues* acts   51 *Bears all down* triumphs over everything

52 Cannot take two from twenty, for his heart,
And leave eighteen. Alas, poor princess,
Thou divine Imogen, what thou endur'st,
Betwixt a father by thy stepdame governed,
A mother hourly coining plots, a wooer
More hateful than the foul expulsion is
Of thy dear husband, than that horrid act
Of the divorce he'ld make. The heavens hold firm
The walls of thy dear honor, keep unshaked
That temple, thy fair mind, that thou mayst stand,
T' enjoy thy banished lord and this great land!   *Exit.*

*

II, ii   *Enter Imogen in her bed, and a Lady [attending].*

IMOGEN
Who's there? My woman Helen?
LADY   Please you, madam.
IMOGEN
What hour is it?
LADY   Almost midnight, madam.
IMOGEN
I have read three hours then. Mine eyes are weak.
Fold down the leaf where I have left. To bed.
Take not away the taper, leave it burning;
And if thou canst awake by four o' th' clock,
I prithee call me. Sleep hath seized me wholly.
                              [Exit Lady.]
To your protection I commend me, gods.
9   From fairies and the tempters of the night
Guard me, beseech ye!
              Sleeps. Iachimo [comes] from the trunk.
IACHIMO
11 The crickets sing, and man's o'erlabored sense
12 Repairs itself by rest. Our Tarquin thus
13 Did softly press the rushes ere he wakened
14 The chastity he wounded. Cytherea,
15 How bravely thou becom'st thy bed, fresh lily,
And whiter than the sheets! That I might touch!
But kiss, one kiss! Rubies unparagoned,
18 How dearly they do't! 'Tis her breathing that
Perfumes the chamber thus. The flame o' th' taper
20 Bows toward her and would underpeep her lids
To see th' enclosèd lights, now canopied
22 Under these windows, white and azure-laced
23 With blue of heaven's own tinct. But my design:
To note the chamber. I will write all down:
Such and such pictures; there the window; such
26 Th' adornment of her bed; the arras, figures,
27 Why, such and such; and the contents o' th' story.
28 Ah, but some natural notes about her body
29 Above ten thousand meaner movables
Would testify, t' enrich mine inventory.
31 O sleep, thou ape of death, lie dull upon her.
32 And be her sense but as a monument,
Thus in a chapel lying. Come off, come off –
              [Takes off her bracelet.]
34 As slippery as the Gordian knot was hard.
'Tis mine, and this will witness outwardly,
36 As strongly as the conscience does within,
37 To th' madding of her lord. On her left breast
38 A mole cinque-spotted, like the crimson drops
39 I' th' bottom of a cowslip. Here's a voucher
40 Stronger than ever law could make. This secret

Will force him think I have picked the lock and ta'en
The treasure of her honor. No more. To what end?
Why should I write this down that's riveted,
Screwed to my memory? She hath been reading late
The tale of Tereus. Here the leaf's turned down   45
Where Philomel gave up. I have enough.
To th' trunk again, and shut the spring of it.
Swift, swift, you dragons of the night, that dawning
May bare the raven's eye. I lodge in fear.   49
Though this a heavenly angel, hell is here.
              Clock strikes.
One, two, three. Time, time!   *Exit [into the trunk].*

*

Enter Cloten and Lords.   II, iii

1. LORD Your lordship is the most patient man in loss,
the most coldest that ever turned up ace.   2
CLOTEN It would make any man cold to lose.   3
1. LORD But not every man patient after the noble temper of your lordship. You are most hot and furious
when you win.
CLOTEN Winning will put any man into courage. If I
could get this foolish Imogen, I should have gold
enough. It's almost morning, is't not?
1. LORD Day, my lord.
CLOTEN I would this music would come. I am advised to
give her music a-mornings; they say it will penetrate.   12
              Enter Musicians.
Come on, tune. If you can penetrate her with your fin-   13
gering, so; we'll try with tongue too. If none will do,   14
let her remain, but I'll never give o'er. First, a very   15
excellent good-conceited thing; after, a wonderful   16
sweet air with admirable rich words to it – and then let
her consider.

                    Song.

    Hark, hark, the lark at heaven's gate sings,
          And Phoebus gins arise,   20
    His steeds to water at those springs
          On chalicèd flowers that lies;
    And winking Mary-buds begin   23
          To ope their golden eyes.
    With every thing that pretty is,
          My lady sweet, arise,
              Arise, arise!

52 *for his heart* for the life of him
II, ii The bedchamber of Imogen 9 *fairies* i.e. evil fairies 11 *o'erlabored*
overworked, worn out 12 *Our Tarquin* Roman who raped Lucretia 13
rushes floor coverings (Elizabethan) 14 *Cytherea* Venus 15 *bravely*
finely; *lily* (emblem of chastity) 18 *they do't* i.e. her lips (rubies) kiss each
other 20 *underpeep* peep under 22 *windows* eyelids; *azure-laced* i.e. with
blue veins 23 *tinct* hue 26 *arras* tapestry 27 *story* room (?), design on
arras (?) 28 *notes* marks 29 *meaner movables* less important furnishings
31 *dull* heavy 32 *monument* i.e. sculptured human form lying horizontally
on a tomb 34 *Gordian knot* intricate knot tied by Gordius, Phrygian king,
and cut by Alexander the Great with his sword 36 *conscience* knowledge or
consciousness (of Posthumus) 37 *madding* maddening 38 *cinque-spotted*
with five spots 39 *voucher* evidence 40 *secret* intimate fact 45 *Tereus*
Thracian king who raped his sister-in-law Philomela and cut out her tongue
49 *bare . . . eye* (the raven was believed to wake early)
II, iii A hall adjoining Imogen's chambers 2 *coldest* coolest, calmest;
turned up ace made the lowest dice throw (with pun on 'ass') 3 *cold* depressed 12, 13 *penetrate* affect emotionally (with sexual innuendo) 14 *so
fine* 15 *give o'er* give up 16 *good-conceited* well-wrought 20 *Phoebus*
Apollo, as the sun; *gins* begins to 23 *winking* closed; *Mary-buds* marigold
buds

28 CLOTEN So, get you gone. If this penetrate, I will con-
29 sider your music the better ; if it do not, it is a vice in her
30 ears which horsehairs and calves' guts, nor the voice of
31 unpaved eunuch to boot, can never amend.

                          [Exeunt Musicians.]
        Enter Cymbeline and Queen.

2. LORD Here comes the King.

CLOTEN I am glad I was up so late, for that's the reason I
was up so early. He cannot choose but take this service I
35 have done fatherly. Good morrow to your Majesty and
to my gracious mother.

CYMBELINE
37 Attend you here the door of our stern daughter ?
Will she not forth ?

CLOTEN I have assailed her with musics, but she vouch-
safes no notice.

CYMBELINE
41 The exile of her minion is too new ;
She hath not yet forgot him. Some more time
Must wear the print of his remembrance on't,
And then she's yours.

QUEEN   You are most bound to th' King,
45 Who lets go by no vantages that may
46 Prefer you to his daughter. Frame yourself
47 To orderly solicits, and be friended
48 With aptness of the season. Make denials
Increase your services. So seem as if
You were inspired to do those duties which
You tender to her ; that you in all obey her,
52 Save when command to your dismission tends,
53 And therein you are senseless.

CLOTEN   Senseless ? Not so.
        [Enter a Messenger.]

MESSENGER
54 So like you, sir, ambassadors from Rome.
The one is Caius Lucius.

CYMBELINE   A worthy fellow,
Albeit he comes on angry purpose now.
But that's no fault of his. We must receive him
According to the honor of his sender,
59 And towards himself, his goodness forespent on us,
We must extend our notice. Our dear son,
When you have given good morning to your mistress,
Attend the Queen and us. We shall have need
T' employ you towards this Roman. Come, our queen.

                       Exeunt [all but Cloten].

CLOTEN
If she be up, I'll speak with her ; if not,
Let her lie still and dream. *[Knocks.]* By your leave, ho !
I know her women are about her. What
67 If I do line one of their hands ? 'Tis gold

Which buys admittance – oft it doth – yea, and makes
Diana's rangers false themselves, yield up   69
Their deer to th' stand o' th' stealer ; and 'tis gold   70
Which makes the true man killed and saves the thief,
Nay, sometime hangs both thief and true man. What
Can it not do and undo ? I will make
One of her women lawyer to me, for
I yet not understand the case myself.   75
By your leave.
        Knocks. Enter a Lady.

LADY
Who's there that knocks ?

CLOTEN   A gentleman.

LADY   No more ?

CLOTEN
Yes, and a gentlewoman's son.

LADY   That's more
Than some whose tailors are as dear as yours
Can justly boast of. What's your lordship's pleasure ?

CLOTEN
Your lady's person. Is she ready ?   81

LADY   Ay,
To keep her chamber.

CLOTEN   There is gold for you.
Sell me your good report.

LADY
How ? My good name ? Or to report of you
What I shall think is good ? The Princess !
        Enter Imogen.

CLOTEN
Good morrow, fairest sister. Your sweet hand.
                      [Exit Lady.]

IMOGEN
Good morrow, sir. You lay out too much pains   87
For purchasing but trouble. The thanks I give
Is telling you that I am poor of thanks
And scarce can spare them.

CLOTEN   Still I swear I love you.

IMOGEN
If you but said so, 'twere as deep with me.   91
If you swear still, your recompense is still   92
That I regard it not.

CLOTEN   This is no answer.

IMOGEN
But that you shall not say I yield being silent,   94
I would not speak. I pray you spare me. Faith,
I shall unfold equal discourtesy   96
To your best kindness. One of your great knowing   97
Should learn, being taught, forbearance.

CLOTEN
To leave you in your madness, 'twere my sin.
I will not.

IMOGEN
Fools are not mad folks.

CLOTEN   Do you call me fool ?

IMOGEN
As I am mad, I do.
If you'll be patient, I'll no more be mad ;
That cures us both. I am much sorry, sir,
You put me to forget a lady's manners
By being so verbal ; and learn now for all   106
That I, which know my heart, do here pronounce
By th' very truth of it, I care not for you,
And am so near the lack of charity

---

28 *consider* recompense   29 *vice* flaw   30 *horsehairs* bowstrings ; *calves' guts* fiddle strings   31 *unpaved* without stones (i.e. castrated)   35 *fatherly* as a father (modifies *take*)   37 *Attend* wait at   41 *minion* darling   45 *vantages* occasions   46 *Prefer* recommend ; *Frame* prepare   47 *solicits* approaches, importunings   47–48 *be . . . season* make good use of appropriate times   48 *denials* rejections (by her)   52 *dismission* dismissal   53 *are senseless* are not to understand (or obey)   54 *So like you* if you please   59 *his . . . us* because of his earlier goodness to us   67 *line* i.e. with money   69 *rangers* gamekeepers (i.e. attendant nymphs, vowed to chastity) ; *false* turn false   70 *stand* blind (hunter's station ; with sexual innuendo)   75 *understand the case* know how to carry on the suit   81 *ready* dressed   87 *lay out* expend   91 *deep* effective   92 *still* continually   94 *But that* in order that   96 *unfold* show   97 *knowing* knowledge (ironic)   106 *verbal* talkative, i.e. Cloten (?), outspoken, i.e. Imogen (?)

110 To accuse myself I hate you – which I had rather
You felt than make't my boast.
    CLOTEN   You sin against
112 Obedience, which you owe your father. For
113 The contract you pretend with that base wretch,
One bred of alms and fostered with cold dishes,
With scraps o' th' court – it is no contract, none.
116 And though it be allowed in meaner parties –
Yet who than he more mean ? – to knit their souls,
118 On whom there is no more dependency
119 But brats and beggary, in self-figured knot ;
120 Yet you are curbed from that enlargement by
121 The consequence o' th' crown, and must not foil
122 The precious note of it with a base slave,
123 A hilding for a livery, a squire's cloth,
124 A pantler – not so eminent.
    IMOGEN   Profane fellow !
Wert thou the son of Jupiter, and no more
But what thou art besides, thou wert too base
127 To be his groom. Thou wert dignified enough,
128 Even to the point of envy, if 'twere made
Comparative for your virtues to be styled
The under-hangman of his kingdom, and hated
For being preferred so well.
131 CLOTEN   The south fog rot him !
    IMOGEN
He never can meet more mischance than come
133 To be but named of thee. His meanest garment
134 That ever hath but clipped his body is dearer
135 In my respect than all the hairs above thee,
136 Were they all made such men. How now, Pisanio ?
    Enter Pisanio.
    CLOTEN
'His garment' ? Now the devil –
    IMOGEN
To Dorothy my woman hie thee presently.
    CLOTEN
'His garment' ?
139 IMOGEN   I am sprited with a fool,
Frighted, and ang'red worse. Go bid my woman
Search for a jewel that too casually
142 Hath left mine arm. It was thy master's. Shrew me
If I would lose it for a revenue
Of any king's in Europe. I do think
I saw't this morning ; confident I am
Last night 'twas on mine arm ; I kissed it.
I hope it be not gone to tell my lord
That I kiss aught but he.
    PISANIO   'Twill not be lost.
    IMOGEN
149 I hope so. Go and search.   *[Exit Pisanio.]*
    CLOTEN   You have abused me.
'His meanest garment' ?
    IMOGEN   Ay, I said so, sir.
151 If you will make't an action, call witness to't.
    CLOTEN
I will inform your father.
    IMOGEN   Your mother too.
153 She's my good lady and will conceive, I hope,
But the worst of me. So I leave you, sir,
To th' worst of discontent.   *Exit.*
    CLOTEN   I'll be revenged.
'His meanest garment' ? Well.   *Exit.*

    *

    Enter Posthumus and Philario.   II, iv
    POSTHUMUS
Fear it not, sir. I would I were so sure
To win the King as I am bold her honor   2
Will remain hers.
    PHILARIO   What means do you make to him ?   3
    POSTHUMUS
Not any, but abide the change of time,
Quake in the present winter's state, and wish   5
That warmer days would come. In these feared hopes   6
I barely gratify your love ; they failing,   7
I must die much your debtor.
    PHILARIO
Your very goodness and your company
O'erpays all I can do. By this, your king   10
Hath heard of great Augustus ; Caius Lucius
Will do's commission throughly. And I think
He'll grant the tribute, send th' arrearages,   13
Or look upon our Romans, whose remembrance   14
Is yet fresh in their grief.   15
    POSTHUMUS   I do believe,
Statist though I am none, nor like to be,   16
That this will prove a war ; and you shall hear   17
The legion now in Gallia sooner landed
In our not-fearing Britain than have tidings
Of any penny tribute paid. Our countrymen
Are men more ordered than when Julius Caesar   21
Smiled at their lack of skill but found their courage
Worthy his frowning at. Their discipline,
Now mingled with their courages, will make known
To their approvers they are people such   25
That mend upon the world.   26
    Enter Iachimo.
    PHILARIO   See, Iachimo !
    POSTHUMUS
The swiftest harts have posted you by land,   27
And winds of all the corners kissed your sails   28
To make your vessel nimble.
    PHILARIO   Welcome, sir.
    POSTHUMUS
I hope the briefness of your answer made   30
The speediness of your return.
    IACHIMO   Your lady
Is one of the fairest that I have looked upon.

110 *To . . . hate* that I must accuse myself of hating 112 *For* as for 113 *contract* i.e. of marriage ; *pretend* offer as an excuse (for not having me) 116 *meaner parties* lower-class people 118 *On . . . dependency* with no other consequence 119 *self-figured* self-arranged 120 *curbed . . . enlargement* restrained from that freedom 121 *consequence* what follows (from your inheritance) ; *foil* foul 122 *note* distinction 123 *hilding* good-for-nothing ; *for . . . cloth* suited for servant's attire 124 *pantler* pantry man ; *not* not even 127 *dignified* given honor 128–30 *if . . . kingdom* if, according to the virtue of each of you, you were made under-hangman and he king 131 *south fog* south wind, supposedly damp and unhealthful 133 *of* by 134 *clipped* embraced 135 *respect* regard 136 *How now* (Imogen suddenly notices that the bracelet is gone) 139 *sprited* haunted 142 *Shrew* curse (mild, polite oath ; here used emphatically) 149 *so* i.e. not 151 *action* lawsuit 153 *conceive* think, believe
II, iv Rome : the house of Philario 2 *bold* certain 3 *means* approaches 5 *winter's* i.e. bitter, outcast 6 *feared* fear-laden 7 *gratify* repay 10 *this* now 13 *He* Cymbeline ; *arrearages* overdue payments of tribute 14 *Or* or else (?), before, rather than (?) 15 *their* the Britons' (as caused by the Romans) 16 *Statist* statesman 17 *prove* result in, turn out to be 21 *ordered* disciplined 25 *approvers* those who test them 26 *mend upon* improve 27 *have posted* must have sped 28 *corners* quarters 30 *your answer* (Imogen's) reply to you

POSTHUMUS
And therewithal the best, or let her beauty
Look through a casement to allure false hearts
And be false with them.
IACHIMO   Here are letters for you.
POSTHUMUS
Their tenor good, I trust.
36 IACHIMO   'Tis very like.
PHILARIO
Was Caius Lucius in the Briton court
When you were there?
IACHIMO   He was expected then,
But not approached.
POSTHUMUS   All is well yet.
Sparkles this stone as it was wont, or is't not
Too dull for your good wearing?
IACHIMO   If I have lost it,
I should have lost the worth of it in gold.
I'll make a journey twice as far t' enjoy
A second night of such sweet shortness which
Was mine in Britain – for the ring is won.
POSTHUMUS
The stone's too hard to come by.
IACHIMO   Not a whit,
Your lady being so easy.
POSTHUMUS   Make not, sir,
Your loss your sport. I hope you know that we
Must not continue friends.
IACHIMO   Good sir, we must,
50 If you keep covenant. Had I not brought
51 The knowledge of your mistress home, I grant
52 We were to question farther, but I now
Profess myself the winner of her honor,
Together with your ring, and not the wronger
Of her or you, having proceeded but
By both your wills.
POSTHUMUS   If you can make't apparent
That you have tasted her in bed, my hand
And ring is yours. If not, the foul opinion
You had of her pure honor gains or loses
60 Your sword or mine, or masterless leave both
To who shall find them.
61 IACHIMO   Sir, my circumstances,
Being so near the truth as I will make them,
63 Must first induce you to believe; whose strength
I will confirm with oath, which I doubt not
65 You'll give me leave to spare when you shall find
You need it not.
POSTHUMUS   Proceed.

---

36 *like* likely   50 *keep covenant* hold to the bargain   51 *knowledge* i.e. sexual   52 *question* dispute in a duel   60 *leave* let it leave (some editors emend to 'leaves')   61 *circumstances* circumstantial report   63 *whose* (antecedent is *circumstances*)   65 *spare* omit   68 *watching* staying awake   71 *Cydnus* river where Antony and Cleopatra met   71–72 *or . . . press* either because of the multitude   73 *bravely* finely   73–74 *did . . . value* it was a question whether form or content was better   79 *justify* prove   81 *south* on the south wall of; *piece* art work   83 *likely to report* able to identify; *cutter* sculptor   84 *as . . . dumb* like nature (in creative power) but unable to make a sculpture speak; *outwent her* surpassed nature   85 *Motion . . . out* i.e. the sculpture cannot move or breathe   86 *from . . . reap* learn at second hand   88 *fretted* adorned by carvings   89 *winking* with eyes closed (i.e. blind)   91 *Depending . . . brands* leaning on their torches   94 *nothing saves* by no means wins   96 *Be pale* stay unflushed (i.e. calm)   97 *up* put up (i.e. in his pocket)   102 *outsell* exceed in value   107 *basilisk* mythical reptile, believed to kill by look   110–11 *The vows . . . made* let women's vows no more bind them to men

IACHIMO   First, her bedchamber –
Where I confess I slept not, but profess
Had that was well worth watching – it was hanged   68
With tapestry of silk and silver; the story
Proud Cleopatra, when she met her Roman
And Cydnus swelled above the banks, or for   71
The press of boats or pride: a piece of work
So bravely done, so rich, that it did strive   73
In workmanship and value; which I wondered
Could be so rarely and exactly wrought,
Since the true life on't was –
POSTHUMUS   This is true,
And this you might have heard of here, by me
Or by some other.
IACHIMO   More particulars
Must justify my knowledge.   79
POSTHUMUS   So they must,
Or do your honor injury.
IACHIMO   The chimney
Is south the chamber, and the chimney piece   81
Chaste Dian bathing. Never saw I figures
So likely to report themselves. The cutter   83
Was as another nature, dumb; outwent her,   84
Motion and breath left out.   85
POSTHUMUS   This is a thing
Which you might from relation likewise reap,   86
Being, as it is, much spoke of.
IACHIMO   The roof o' th' chamber
With golden cherubins is fretted. Her andirons –   88
I had forgot them – were two winking Cupids   89
Of silver, each on one foot standing, nicely
Depending on their brands.   91
POSTHUMUS   This is her honor!
Let it be granted you have seen all this – and praise
Be given to your remembrance – the description
Of what is in her chamber nothing saves   94
The wager you have laid.
IACHIMO   Then, if you can
[*Shows the bracelet.*]
Be pale, I beg but leave to air this jewel. See!   96
And now 'tis up again. It must be married   97
To that your diamond; I'll keep them.
POSTHUMUS   Jove!
Once more let me behold it. Is it that
Which I left with her?
IACHIMO   Sir, I thank her, that.
She stripped it from her arm; I see her yet.
Her pretty action did outsell her gift,   102
And yet enriched it too. She gave it me and said
She prized it once.
POSTHUMUS   May be she plucked it off
To send it me.
IACHIMO   She writes so to you, doth she?
POSTHUMUS
O, no, no, no, 'tis true. Here, take this too.
[*Gives the ring.*]
It is a basilisk unto mine eye,   107
Kills me to look on't. Let there be no honor
Where there is beauty; truth, where semblance; love,
Where there's another man. The vows of women   110
Of no more bondage be to where they are made
Than they are to their virtues, which is nothing.
O, above measure false!
PHILARIO   Have patience, sir,

And take your ring again; 'tis not yet won.
115 It may be probable she lost it, or
Who knows if one of her women, being corrupted,
Hath stol'n it from her?

POSTHUMUS   Very true,
118 And so I hope he came by 't. Back my ring;
Render to me some corporal sign about her
120 More evident than this, for this was stol'n.

IACHIMO
By Jupiter, I had it from her arm.

POSTHUMUS
Hark you, he swears; by Jupiter he swears.
'Tis true – nay, keep the ring – 'tis true. I am sure
She would not lose it. Her attendants are
125 All sworn and honorable. They induced to steal it?
And by a stranger? No, he hath enjoyed her.
127 The cognizance of her incontinency
128 Is this. She hath bought the name of whore thus dearly.
129 There, take thy hire, and all the fiends of hell
Divide themselves between you!

PHILARIO   Sir, be patient.
This is not strong enough to be believed
132 Of one persuaded well of.

POSTHUMUS   Never talk on't.
133 She hath been colted by him.

IACHIMO   If you seek
For further satisfying, under her breast –
Worthy the pressing – lies a mole, right proud
Of that most delicate lodging. By my life,
137 I kissed it, and it gave me present hunger
To feed again, though full. You do remember
139 This stain upon her?

POSTHUMUS   Ay, and it doth confirm
140 Another stain, as big as hell can hold,
Were there no more but it.

IACHIMO   Will you hear more?

POSTHUMUS
142 Spare your arithmetic; never count the turns.
Once, and a million!

IACHIMO   I'll be sworn.

POSTHUMUS   No swearing.
If you will swear you have not done't, you lie,
And I will kill thee if thou dost deny
Thou'st made me cuckold.

IACHIMO   I'll deny nothing.

POSTHUMUS
147 O that I had her here, to tear her limb-meal!
I will go there and do't i' th' court, before
Her father. I'll do something.   Exit.

149 PHILARIO   Quite besides
The government of patience! You have won.
151 Let's follow him and pervert the present wrath
He hath against himself.

IACHIMO   With all my heart.   Exeunt.

II, v   *Enter Posthumus.*

POSTHUMUS
1 Is there no way for men to be, but women
2 Must be half-workers? We are all bastards,
And that most venerable man which I
Did call my father was I know not where
5 When I was stamped. Some coiner with his tools
Made me a counterfeit; yet my mother seemed
The Dian of that time. So doth my wife
8 The nonpareil of this. O, vengeance, vengeance!

Me of my lawful pleasure she restrained
And prayed me oft forbearance – did it with
A pudency so rosy, the sweet view on't   11
Might well have warmed old Saturn – that I thought her   12
As chaste as unsunned snow. O, all the devils!
This yellow Iachimo in an hour, was't not?   14
Or less? At first? Perchance he spoke not, but,   15
Like a full-acorned boar, a German one,   16
Cried 'O!' and mounted; found no opposition
But what he looked for should oppose and she
Should from encounter guard. Could I find out
The woman's part in me! For there's no motion   20
That tends to vice in man but I affirm
It is the woman's part. Be it lying, note it,
The woman's; flattering, hers; deceiving, hers;
Lust and rank thoughts, hers, hers; revenges, hers;
Ambitions, covetings, change of prides, disdain,   25
Nice longings, slanders, mutability,   26
All faults that man may name, nay, that hell knows,
Why, hers, in part or all, but rather all.
For even to vice
They are not constant, but are changing still
One vice but of a minute old for one
Not half so old as that. I'll write against them,
Detest them, curse them. Yet 'tis greater skill
In a true hate to pray they have their will;
The very devils cannot plague them better.   *Exit.*

*

Enter in state Cymbeline, Queen, Cloten, and   III, i
Lords at one door, and at another, Caius Lucius and
Attendants.

CYMBELINE
Now say, what would Augustus Caesar with us?

LUCIUS
When Julius Caesar, whose remembrance yet
Lives in men's eyes and will to ears and tongues
Be theme and hearing ever, was in this Britain
And conquered it, Cassibelan thine uncle,
Famous in Caesar's praises no whit less
Than in his feats deserving it, for him
And his succession granted Rome a tribute,
Yearly three thousand pounds, which by thee lately
Is left untendered.

QUEEN   And, to kill the marvel,   10
Shall be so ever.

CLOTEN   There be many Caesars
Ere such another Julius. Britain's a world

115 *probable* provable   118 *so* in this manner   120 *More evident* which is better evidence   125 *sworn* bound (as if) by oath   127 *cognizance* identifying mark   128 *this* i.e. the ring   129 *hire* winnings   132 *persuaded well of* well thought of   133 *been colted by* had intercourse with   137 *present* immediate   139 *stain* mark, discoloration   140 *stain* moral flaw   142 *turns* occasions, deviations   147 *limb-meal* limb from limb   149–50 *besides The government* beyond the control   151 *pervert* turn aside
II, v   1 *be* exist   2 *half-workers* i.e. in begetting   5 *stamped* minted (i.e. begotten)   8 *nonpareil* one without equal   11 *pudency* modesty   12 *Saturn* (this god was thought to be cold and gloomy; cf. 'saturnine')   14 *yellow* i.e. in complexion   15 *At first* immediately   16 *full-acorned* full of acorns; *German* (allusion not clear)   20–21 *motion . . . to* impulse toward   25 *change of prides* series of vanities   26 *Nice* finicky or lascivious; *mutability* fickleness
III, i Britain: a room of state in the palace of King Cymbeline   10 *kill the marvel* eliminate the surprise (i.e. when non-payment is standard procedure)

By itself, and we will nothing pay
For wearing our own noses.

QUEEN   That opportunity

15   Which then they had to take from's, to resume
We have again. Remember, sir, my liege,
The kings your ancestors, together with
The natural bravery of your isle, which stands

19   As Neptune's park, ribbèd and palèd in
With rocks unscalable and roaring waters,

21   With sands that will not bear your enemies' boats
But suck them up to th' topmast. A kind of conquest
Caesar made here, but made not here his brag
Of 'Came and saw and overcame.' With shame,
The first that ever touched him, he was carried
From off our coast, twice beaten; and his shipping,

27   Poor ignorant baubles on our terrible seas,
Like eggshells moved upon their surges, cracked
As easily 'gainst our rocks. For joy whereof

30   The famed Cassibelan, who was once at point –

31   O giglet fortune! – to master Caesar's sword,

32   Made Lud's town with rejoicing fires bright
And Britons strut with courage.

CLOTEN   Come, there's no more tribute to be paid. Our
kingdom is stronger than it was at that time, and, as I
said, there is no moe such Caesars. Other of them may

37   have crook'd noses, but to owe such straight arms, none.

CYMBELINE
Son, let your mother end.

39 CLOTEN We have yet many among us can gripe as hard as
Cassibelan. I do not say I am one, but I have a hand.
Why tribute? Why should we pay tribute? If Caesar can
hide the sun from us with a blanket or put the moon in
his pocket, we will pay him tribute for light; else, sir, no
more tribute, pray you now.

CYMBELINE
You must know,

46   Till the injurious Romans did extort
This tribute from us, we were free. Caesar's ambition,
Which swelled so much that it did almost stretch

49   The sides o' th' world, against all color here
Did put the yoke upon's; which to shake off
Becomes a warlike people, whom we reckon

52   Ourselves to be, we do. Say then to Caesar,

53   Our ancestor was that Mulmutius which
Ordained our laws, whose use the sword of Caesar

55   Hath too much mangled, whose repair and franchise
Shall, by the power we hold, be our good deed,

Though Rome be therefore angry. Mulmutius made our
laws,
Who was the first of Britain which did put
His brows within a golden crown and called
Himself a king.

LUCIUS   I am sorry, Cymbeline,
That I am to pronounce Augustus Caesar –   61
Caesar, that hath moe kings his servants than   62
Thyself domestic officers – thine enemy.
Receive it from me then : war and confusion   64
In Caesar's name pronounce I 'gainst thee. Look
For fury not to be resisted. Thus defied,
I thank thee for myself.

CYMBELINE   Thou art welcome, Caius.
Thy Caesar knighted me; my youth I spent
Much under him; of him I gathered honor,
Which he to seek of me again, perforce,   70
Behooves me keep at utterance. I am perfect   71
That the Pannonians and Dalmatians for   72
Their liberties are now in arms, a precedent
Which not to read would show the Britons cold.   74
So Caesar shall not find them.

LUCIUS   Let proof speak.   75

CLOTEN His Majesty bids you welcome. Make pastime
with us a day or two, or longer. If you seek us afterwards in other terms, you shall find us in our salt-water
girdle; if you beat us out of it, it is yours. If you fall in
the adventure, our crows shall fare the better for you,
and there's an end.

LUCIUS So, sir.

CYMBELINE I know your master's pleasure, and he
mine. All the remain is, welcome.   *Exeunt.* 84

*

Enter Pisanio, reading of a letter.   III, ii
PISANIO
How? Of adultery? Wherefore write you not
What monsters her accuse? Leonatus,
O master, what a strange infection
Is fall'n into thy ear! What false Italian,
As poisoned tongued as handed, hath prevailed
On thy too ready hearing? Disloyal? No.
She's punished for her truth and undergoes,   7
More goddess-like than wife-like, such assaults
As would take in some virtue. O my master,   9
Thy mind to her is now as low as were   10
Thy fortunes. How? That I should murder her,
Upon the love and truth and vows which I
Have made to thy command? I her? Her blood?
If it be so to do good service, never
Let me be counted serviceable. How look I
That I should seem to lack humanity
So much as this fact comes to? *[Reads]* 'Do't! The letter   17
That I have sent her, by her own command
Shall give thee opportunity.' O damned paper,
Black as the ink that's on thee! Senseless bauble,   20
Art thou a fedary for this act, and look'st   21
So virgin-like without? Lo, here she comes.

Enter Imogen.
I am ignorant in what I am commanded.   23
IMOGEN
How now, Pisanio?
PISANIO
Madam, here is a letter from my lord.

---

15 *resume* take back   19 *ribbèd* enclosed; *palèd* fenced   21 *sands* i.e. quicksands   27 *ignorant* silly, inexperienced   30–31 *at point . . . to master* on the
point . . . of mastering   31 *giglet* wanton, promiscuous   32 *Lud's town*
London (after Lud, legendary king)   37 *crook'd* i.e. Roman (cf. l. 14); *owe*
own   39 *gripe* grip (in combat)   46 *injurious* insolent   49 *against all color*
without any justifying pretext (with pun on 'collar'; note *yoke* in l. 50)
52 *we do* i.e. shake off (some editors begin the next sentence with 'we do')
53 *Mulmutius* earlier king, told about in chronicles   55 *whose* (the antecedent is *laws*); *franchise* free exercise   61 *pronounce* declare   62 *moe* more;
his as his   64 *confusion* destruction   70 *he to seek* since he seeks it; *perforce*
of necessity   71 *keep at utterance* to defend to the uttermost; *perfect* well
aware   72 *Pannonians and Dalmatians* inhabitants of present-day Balkan
regions   74 *cold* lacking spirit   75 *Let proof speak* let the military test settle
it   84 *the remain* that remains
III, ii A chamber in the palace   7 *truth* fidelity; *undergoes* bears   9 *take
in* conquer   10 *to* compared with   17 *fact* deed   20 *Senseless bauble*
inanimate trifle   21 *fedary* for confederate in   23 *am ignorant* will pretend
ignorance

IMOGEN
Who, thy lord? That is my lord Leonatus?
27 O, learn'd indeed were that astronomer
28 That knew the stars as I his characters;
He'ld lay the future open. You good gods,
30 Let what is here contained relish of love,
31 Of my lord's health, of his content – yet not
That we two are asunder; let that grieve him.
33 Some griefs are med'cinable; that is one of them,
34 For it doth physic love – of his content
35 All but in that. Good wax, thy leave. Blessed be
36 You bees that make these locks of counsel. Lovers
37 And men in dangerous bonds pray not alike;
38 Though forfeiters you cast in prison, yet
39 You clasp young Cupid's tables. Good news, gods!
[Reads.]
40 'Justice and your father's wrath, should he take me in
41 his dominion, could not be so cruel to me as you, O the
dearest of creatures, would even renew me with your
43 eyes. Take notice that I am in Cambria at Milford
Haven. What your own love will out of this advise you,
follow. So he wishes you all happiness that remains
46 loyal to his vow, and your increasing in love.
Leonatus Posthumus.'
O, for a horse with wings! Hear'st thou, Pisanio?
He is at Milford Haven. Read, and tell me
50 How far 'tis thither. If one of mean affairs
May plod it in a week, why may not I
Glide thither in a day? Then, true Pisanio,
Who long'st like me to see thy lord, who long'st –
54 O, let me bate – but not like me, yet long'st,
But in a fainter kind – O, not like me!
56 For mine's beyond beyond: say, and speak thick –
57 Love's counsellor should fill the bores of hearing,
58 To th' smothering of the sense – how far it is
59 To this same blessèd Milford. And by th' way
Tell me how Wales was made so happy as
T' inherit such a haven. But first of all,
62 How we may steal from hence, and for the gap
That we shall make in time from our hence-going
And our return, to excuse. But first, how get hence?
65 Why should excuse be born or ere begot?
We'll talk of that hereafter. Prithee speak,
67 How many score of miles may we well rid
'Twixt hour and hour?
PISANIO   One score 'twixt sun and sun,
Madam, 's enough for you, and too much too.
IMOGEN
Why, one that rode to's execution, man,
71 Could never go so slow. I have heard of riding wagers
Where horses have been nimbler than the sands
73 That run i' th' clock's behalf. But this is fool'ry.
Go bid my woman feign a sickness, say
75 She'll home to her father; and provide me presently
A riding suit, no costlier than would fit
77 A franklin's housewife.
PISANIO   Madam, you're best consider.
IMOGEN
78 I see before me, man. Nor here, nor here,
79 Nor what ensues, but have a fog in them
That I cannot look through. Away, I prithee;
Do as I bid thee. There's no more to say.
Accessible is none but Milford way.   Exeunt.

*

Enter [from their cave] Belarius, Guiderius, and   III, iii
Arviragus.
BELARIUS
A goodly day not to keep house with such   1
Whose roof's as low as ours! Stoop, boys. This gate
Instructs you how t' adore the heavens and bows you 3
To a morning's holy office. The gates of monarchs   4
Are arched so high that giants may jet through   5
And keep their impious turbans on without
Good morrow to the sun. Hail, thou fair heaven!
We house i' th' rock, yet use thee not so hardly   8
As prouder livers do.   9
GUIDERIUS   Hail, heaven!
ARVIRAGUS   Hail, heaven!
BELARIUS
Now for our mountain sport. Up to yond hill;
Your legs are young. I'll tread these flats. Consider,
When you above perceive me like a crow,
That it is place which lessens and sets off,   13
And you may then revolve what tales I have told you
Of courts, of princes, of the tricks in war.
This service is not service, so being done,   16
But being so allowed. To apprehend thus   17
Draws us a profit from all things we see,
And often, to our comfort, shall we find
The sharded beetle in a safer hold   20
Than is the full-winged eagle. O, this life
Is nobler than attending for a check,   22
Richer than doing nothing for a robe,   23
Prouder than rustling in unpaid-for silk:
Such gain the cap of him that makes him fine   25
Yet keeps his book uncrossed. No life to ours.   26
GUIDERIUS
Out of your proof you speak. We poor unfledged   27
Have never winged from view o' th' nest, nor know not
What air's from home. Haply this life is best   29
If quiet life be best, sweeter to you
That have a sharper known, well corresponding
With your stiff age; but unto us it is
A cell of ignorance, travelling abed,   33

27 *astronomer* astrologer 28 *characters* handwriting 30 *relish* taste 31 *not* not content 33 *are med'cinable* have medicinal value 34 *physic* medicate; increase the strength of 35 *wax* i.e. in the seal of the letter 36 *locks of counsel* seals for confidential matters 37 *in . . . bonds* under bonds imposing penalties; *pray not alike* i.e. lovers adore, bonded men hate, waxen seals 38 *forfeiters* those who do not live up to bonds 39 *clasp . . . tables* fasten love letters 40 *take* capture 41–42 *as . . . renew* that you could not restore 43 *Cambria* Wales 46 *increasing* (object of *wishes*) 50 *mean affairs* trivial business 54 *bate* abate, tone down (the statement) 56 *thick* fast 57 *counsellor* helper; *bores of hearing* ears 58 *To . . . sense* and even overwhelm the hearing 59 *by th' way* on the way 62–64 *for . . . excuse* how to account for the elapsed time, etc. 65 *or ere begot* i.e. before it is made necessary by what we do 67 *rid* get rid of, cover 71 *riding wagers* racing bets 73 *i' th' clock's behalf* i.e. in an hourglass 75 *home* go home; *presently* without delay 77 *franklin* freeholder (small land-owner); *you're best* you had better 78 *before me* i.e. the road to Milford; *Nor . . . here* i.e. neither to right nor to left 79 *what ensues* the eventual outcome
III, iii Wales: before the cave of Belarius 1 *keep house* stay in 3 *bows you* makes you bow 4 *holy office* religious service 5 *jet* strut 8 *use* treat; *hardly* badly 9 *prouder livers* people who live more resplendently 13 *place* position; *sets off* embellishes 16 *This* any act of 17 *allowed* acknowledged; *To . . . thus* to look at things in this way 20 *sharded* with scaly wing covers; *hold* stronghold 22 *attending . . . check* doing service (at court) only to get a rebuke 23 *robe* i.e. of office 25 *gain . . . fine* is respected by the elegant man 26 *keeps . . . uncrossed* does not cross off (pay the debts in) his record-book (possibly, tailor) 27 *proof* experience 29 *air's* the air is like; *from* away from; *Haply* perhaps 33 *abed* i.e. in imagination

A prison, or a debtor that not dares
35 To stride a limit.
ARVIRAGUS   What should we speak of
When we are old as you ? When we shall hear
The rain and wind beat dark December, how
38 In this our pinching cave shall we discourse
The freezing hours away ? We have seen nothing.
40 We are beastly : subtle as the fox for prey,
41 Like warlike as the wolf for what we eat.
Our valor is to chase what flies. Our cage
We make a choir, as doth the prisoned bird,
And sing our bondage freely.
BELARIUS   How you speak !
Did you but know the city's usuries
And felt them knowingly ; the art o' th' court,
47 As hard to leave as keep, whose top to climb
Is certain falling, or so slipp'ry that
The fear 's as bad as falling ; the toil o' th' war,
50 A pain that only seems to seek out danger
51 I' th' name of fame and honor, which dies i' th' search
And hath as oft a sland'rous epitaph
53 As record of fair act ; nay, many times
54 Doth ill deserve by doing well ; what's worse,
Must curtsy at the censure. O boys, this story
The world may read in me. My body 's marked
57 With Roman swords, and my report was once
58 First with the best of note. Cymbeline loved me,
And when a soldier was the theme, my name
Was not far off. Then was I as a tree
Whose boughs did bend with fruit. But in one night
A storm or robbery, call it what you will,
63 Shook down my mellow hangings, nay, my leaves,
And left me bare to weather.
GUIDERIUS   Uncertain favor !
BELARIUS
My fault being nothing, as I have told you oft,
66 But that two villains, whose false oaths prevailed
Before my perfect honor, swore to Cymbeline
I was confederate with the Romans. So
Followed my banishment, and this twenty years
70 This rock and these demesnes have been my world,
71 Where I have lived at honest freedom, paid
More pious debts to heaven than in all
73 The fore-end of my time. But up to th' mountains !
This is not hunters' language. He that strikes
The venison first shall be the lord o' th' feast ;
To him the other two shall minister,

And we will fear no poison, which attends   77
In place of greater state. I'll meet you in the valleys.
                    Exeunt [Guiderius and Arviragus].
How hard it is to hide the sparks of nature !
These boys know little they are sons to th' King,
Nor Cymbeline dreams that they are alive.
They think they are mine, and though trained up thus
    meanly
I' th' cave wherein they bow, their thoughts do hit   83
The roofs of palaces, and nature prompts them
In simple and low things to prince it much   85
Beyond the trick of others. This Polydore,   86
The heir of Cymbeline and Britain, who
The King his father called Guiderius – Jove !
When on my three-foot stool I sit and tell
The warlike feats I have done, his spirits fly out   90
Into my story ; say 'Thus mine enemy fell,   91
And thus I set my foot on's neck,' even then
The princely blood flows in his cheek, he sweats,
Strains his young nerves, and puts himself in posture   94
That acts my words. The younger brother Cadwal,
Once Arviragus, in as like a figure   96
Strikes life into my speech and shows much more
His own conceiving. Hark, the game is roused !   98
O Cymbeline, heaven and my conscience knows
Thou didst unjustly banish me ; whereon,
At three and two years old, I stole these babes,
Thinking to bar thee of succession as
Thou reft'st me of my lands. Euriphile,   103
Thou wast their nurse ; they took thee for their mother,
And every day do honor to her grave.   105
Myself, Belarius, that am Morgan called,
They take for natural father. The game is up.   *Exit.* 107

                    *

Enter Pisanio and Imogen.   III, iv
IMOGEN
Thou told'st me, when we came from horse, the place   1
Was near at hand. Ne'er longed my mother so
To see me first as I have now. Pisanio, man,   3
Where is Posthumus ? What is in thy mind
That makes thee stare thus ? Wherefore breaks that sigh
From th' inward of thee ? One but painted thus
Would be interpreted a thing perplexed   7
Beyond self-explication. Put thyself
Into a havior of less fear, ere wildness   9
Vanquish my staider senses. What's the matter ?   10
Why tender'st thou that paper to me with
A look untender ? If't be summer news,   12
Smile to't before ; if winterly, thou need'st   13
But keep that count'nance still. My husband's hand ?
That drug-damned Italy hath outcraftied him,   15
And he's at some hard point. Speak, man ! Thy tongue   16
May take off some extremity, which to read   17
Would be even mortal to me.   18
PISANIO   Please you read,
And you shall find me, wretched man, a thing
The most disdained of fortune.
IMOGEN *[reads]* 'Thy mistress, Pisanio, hath played the
strumpet in my bed, the testimonies whereof lie bleed-
ing in me. I speak not out of weak surmises, but from
proof as strong as my grief and as certain as I expect my
revenge. That part thou, Pisanio, must act for me, if thy

35 *stride a limit* cross a boundary (and thus risk arrest)   **38** *pinching* i.e. with cold   **40** *beastly* beast-like   **41** *Like* as   **47** *keep* stay in   **50** *pain* labor   **51** *which* (the antecedent may be *pain* or *fame and honor*)   **53** *fair act* fine deed   **54** *deserve* earn, get   **57** *report* reputation   **58** *best of note* most distinguished   **63** *hangings* fruit   **66–67** *prevailed Before* had more weight than   **70** *demesnes* regions   **71** *at* in   **73** *fore-end* . . . *time* early part of my my life   **77** *attends* is to be expected   **83–84** *do hit* . . . *palaces* i.e. are elevated, aspire greatly   **85** *prince it* act like a prince   **86** *trick* aptitude   **90–91** *fly out Into* (cf. 'empathize')   **91** *say* (parallel with *tell* in l. 89)   **94** *nerves* sinews   **96** *in* . . . *figure* with an equally good acting out   **98** *conceiving* interpretation ; *roused* flushed   **103** *reft'st* robbed   **105** *her* i.e. Euriphile's   **107** *game is up* (repeats l. 98)
III, iv An open place near Milford Haven   **1** *came from horse* dismounted   **3** *have* i.e. longing to see Posthumus   **7** *perplexed* troubled   **9** *havior* . . . *fear* less frightening demeanor ; *wildness* panic   **10** *staider senses* more balanced feelings   **12, 13** *summer, winterly* good, bad   **15** *drug-damned* cursed by the use of drugs ; *outcraftied* been too crafty for   **16** *hard point* (cf. 'tough spot')   **17** *take* . . . *extremity* reduce the extreme painfulness (of the news)   **18** *mortal* fatal

26 faith be not tainted with the breach of hers. Let thine
own hands take away her life. I shall give thee opportunity at Milford Haven – she hath my letter for the
purpose – where, if thou fear to strike and to make me
certain it is done, thou art the pander to her dishonor
and equally to me disloyal.'

PISANIO
What shall I need to draw my sword? The paper
Hath cut her throat already. No, 'tis slander,
Whose edge is sharper than the sword, whose tongue
35 Outvenoms all the worms of Nile, whose breath
36 Rides on the posting winds and doth belie
37 All corners of the world. Kings, queens, and states,
Maids, matrons, nay, the secrets of the grave
This viperous slander enters. What cheer, madam?

IMOGEN
False to his bed? What is it to be false?
41 To lie in watch there and to think on him?
42 To weep 'twixt clock and clock? If sleep charge nature,
43 To break it with a fearful dream of him
And cry myself awake? That's false to's bed, is it?

PISANIO
Alas, good lady!

IMOGEN
46 I false? Thy conscience witness! Iachimo,
Thou didst accuse him of incontinency.
Thou then lookedst like a villain; now, methinks,
49 Thy favor's good enough. Some jay of Italy,
50 Whose mother was her painting, hath betrayed him.
Poor I am stale, a garment out of fashion,
52 And, for I am richer than to hang by th' walls,
I must be ripped. To pieces with me! O,
54 Men's vows are women's traitors! All good seeming,
55 By thy revolt, O husband, shall be thought
56 Put on for villainy, not born where't grows,
But worn a bait for ladies.

PISANIO   Good madam, hear me.

IMOGEN
58 True honest men, being heard like false Aeneas,
59 Were in his time thought false, and Sinon's weeping
60 Did scandal many a holy tear, took pity
From most true wretchedness. So thou, Posthumus,
62 Wilt lay the leaven on all proper men;
63 Goodly and gallant shall be false and perjured
64 From thy great fail. Come, fellow, be thou honest;
Do thou thy master's bidding. When thou seest him,
66 A little witness my obedience. Look,
I draw the sword myself. Take it, and hit
The innocent mansion of my love, my heart.
Fear not, 'tis empty of all things but grief.
Thy master is not there, who was indeed
The riches of it. Do his bidding, strike!
Thou mayst be valiant in a better cause,
But now thou seem'st a coward.

PISANIO   Hence, vile instrument!
Thou shalt not damn my hand.

IMOGEN   Why, I must die,
And if I do not by thy hand, thou art
No servant of thy master's. Against self-slaughter
There is a prohibition so divine
78 That cravens my weak hand. Come, here's my heart –
79 Something's afore't; soft, soft, we'll no defense –
80 Obedient as the scabbard. What is here?
81 The scriptures of the loyal Leonatus

All turned to heresy? Away, away,
Corrupters of my faith! You shall no more
Be stomachers to my heart.   84
[Takes his letters out of her bodice.]
          Thus may poor fools
Believe false teachers. Though those that are betrayed
Do feel the treason sharply, yet the traitor
Stands in worse case of woe.   87
And thou, Posthumus, that didst set up   88
My disobedience 'gainst the King my father
And make me put into contempt the suits
Of princely fellows, shalt hereafter find
It is no act of common passage, but   92
A strain of rareness; and I grieve myself
To think, when thou shalt be disedged by her   94
That now thou tirest on, how thy memory   95
Will then be panged by me. Prithee dispatch,   96
The lamb entreats the butcher. Where's thy knife?
Thou art too slow to do thy master's bidding
When I desire it too.

PISANIO   O gracious lady,
Since I received command to do this business
I have not slept one wink.

IMOGEN   Do't, and to bed then.

PISANIO
I'll wake mine eyeballs out first.   102

IMOGEN   Wherefore then
Didst undertake it? Why hast thou abused   103
So many miles with a pretense? This place?
Mine action and thine own? Our horses' labor?
The time inviting thee? The perturbed court
For my being absent? whereunto I never
Purpose return. Why hast thou gone so far,
To be unbent when thou hast ta'en thy stand,   109
Th' elected deer before thee?   110

PISANIO   But to win time
To lose so bad employment, in the which   111
I have considered of a course. Good lady,
Hear me with patience.

IMOGEN   Talk thy tongue weary, speak.
I have heard I am a strumpet, and mine ear,
Therein false struck, can take no greater wound,   115
Nor tent to bottom that. But speak.   116

PISANIO   Then, madam,

26 *tainted* contaminated   **35** *worms* serpents   **36** *posting* speeding; *belie* spread lies over   **37** *states* people of national importance   **41** *in watch* awake   **42** *'twixt . . . clock* from hour to hour; *charge* burden   **43** *fearful . . . him* dream involving fear for him   **46** *Thy* i.e. Posthumus'   **49** *favor* countenance; *jay* whore   **50** *Whose . . . painting* i.e. produced by painting, not by nature; *false*   **52** *for . . . than* since I'm too rich   **54** *seeming* appearance   **55** *By thy revolt* because of thy turning away (infidelity)   **56** *born* i.e. natural   **58** *heard* i.e. heard to speak; *false Aeneas* (he deserted Dido)   **59** *Sinon* (who won the confidence of the Trojans by complaining of his treatment at the hands of his fellow Greeks, and was thus able to persuade them to admit the wooden horse, in which Greek warriors were concealed)   **60** *scandal* discredit   **62** *lay . . . men* destroy confidence in honest men   **63** *be* i.e. seem   **64** *From . . . fail* because of your falseness   **66** *witness* testify for   **78** *cravens* makes cowardly   **79** *Something* i.e. Posthumus' letter, which she speaks of as if it were armor   **80** *Obedient* i.e. in receiving the sword   **81** *scriptures* letter (with pun on 'Scriptures')   **84** *stomachers* decorative breast-coverings   **87** *Stands . . . woe* is worse off   **88** *set up* spur, push   **92–93** *It . . . rareness* my choice was not an every-day occurrence but the result of a rare trait   **94** *disedged* dulled (in sexual desire)   **95** *tirest on* devourest (like a bird of prey)   **96** *panged* made miserable   **102** *wake . . . out* stay awake until my eyeballs come out   **103** *abused* made bad use of   **109** *unbent* i.e. not shooting (the figure is that of a bow)   **110** *elected* chosen   **111** *which* (the antecedent is *time*)   **115** *take* receive   **116** *tent . . . that* probe that (wound) to its depths

117   I thought you would not back again.
IMOGEN   Most like,
   Bringing me here to kill me.
PISANIO   Not so, neither.
   But if I were as wise as honest, then
   My purpose would prove well. It cannot be
121   But that my master is abused. Some villain,
122   Ay, and singular in his art, hath done you both
   This cursèd injury.
IMOGEN
   Some Roman courtesan.
124 PISANIO   No, on my life.
   I'll give but notice you are dead, and send him
   Some bloody sign of it, for 'tis commanded
   I should do so. You shall be missed at court,
128   And that will well confirm it.
IMOGEN   Why, good fellow,
   What shall I do the while? Where bide? How live?
   Or in my life what comfort when I am
   Dead to my husband?
PISANIO   If you'll back to th' court –
IMOGEN
   No court, no father, nor no more ado
   With that harsh, noble, simple nothing,
   That Cloten, whose love suit hath been to me
   As fearful as a siege.
PISANIO   If not at court,
   Then not in Britain must you bide.
IMOGEN   Where then?
   Hath Britain all the sun that shines? Day, night,
   Are they not but in Britain? I' th' world's volume
139   Our Britain seems as of it, but not in't;
   In a great pool a swan's nest. Prithee think
141   There's livers out of Britain.
PISANIO   I am most glad
   You think of other place. Th' ambassador,
   Lucius the Roman, comes to Milford Haven
   To-morrow. Now if you could wear a mind
145   Dark as your fortune is, and but disguise
146   That which, t' appear itself, must not yet be
147   But by self-danger, you should tread a course
148   Pretty and full of view; yea, happily, near
   The residence of Posthumus, so nigh, at least,
   That though his actions were not visible, yet
151   Report should render him hourly to your ear
   As truly as he moves.
IMOGEN   O, for such means,

Though peril to my modesty, not death on't,   153
   I would adventure.
PISANIO   Well then, here's the point:
   You must forget to be a woman; change
   Command into obedience, fear and niceness –
   The handmaids of all women, or more truly   156
   Woman it pretty self – into a waggish courage;   158
   Ready in gibes, quick-answered, saucy, and   159
   As quarrelous as the weasel. Nay, you must   160
   Forget that rarest treasure of your cheek,
   Exposing it – but O, the harder heart!   162
   Alack, no remedy – to the greedy touch
   Of common-kissing Titan, and forget   164
   Your laborsome and dainty trims, wherein   165
   You made great Juno angry.   166
IMOGEN   Nay, be brief.
   I see into thy end and am almost   167
   A man already.
PISANIO   First, make yourself but like one.
   Forethinking this, I have already fit –   169
   'Tis in my cloak-bag – doublet, hat, hose, all
   That answer to them. Would you, in their serving,   171
   And with what imitation you can borrow
   From youth of such a season, 'fore noble Lucius   173
   Present yourself, desire his service, tell him   174
   Wherein you're happy, which will make him know,   175
   If that his head have ear in music; doubtless
   With joy he will embrace you, for he's honorable,   177
   And, doubling that, most holy. Your means abroad –   178
   You have me, rich, and I will never fail
   Beginning nor supplyment.
IMOGEN   Thou art all the comfort
   The gods will diet me with. Prithee away.
   There's more to be considered, but we'll even   182
   All that good time will give us. This attempt
   I am soldier to, and will abide it with   184
   A prince's courage. Away, I prithee.
PISANIO
   Well, madam, we must take a short farewell,
   Lest, being missed, I be suspected of
   Your carriage from the court. My noble mistress,   188
   Here is a box; I had it from the Queen.
   What's in't is precious. If you are sick at sea
   Or stomach-qualmed at land, a dram of this
   Will drive away distemper. To some shade,   192
   And fit you to your manhood. May the gods   193
   Direct you to the best.
IMOGEN   Amen. I thank thee.   *Exeunt.*

*

Enter Cymbeline, Queen, Cloten, Lucius, and Lords.   III, v
CYMBELINE
   Thus far, and so farewell.
LUCIUS   Thanks, royal sir.
   My emperor hath wrote I must from hence,
   And am right sorry that I must report ye
   My master's enemy.
CYMBELINE   Our subjects, sir,
   Will not endure his yoke, and for ourself
   To show less sovereignty than they, must needs
   Appear unkinglike.
LUCIUS   So, sir. I desire of you
   A conduct overland to Milford Haven.   8

117 *back* go back   121 *abused* deceived   122 *singular* without equal   124 *No . . . life* (repeats his assertion of l. 118)   128 *it* i.e. your death   139 *of . . . in't* belonging to it but separated from it   141 *livers* people who live   145 *Dark* unrecognizable   146 *That* i.e. her sex; *t'appear* if it be revealed   147 *tread* i.e. pursue   148 *Pretty . . . view* desirable, with good prospects; *happily* (probably for 'haply': perhaps)   151 *render* give information about   153 *modesty* chastity   156 *Command* i.e. her prerogative as the King's daughter; *niceness* fastidiousness   158 *it* its; *waggish* roguish   159 *quick-answered* quick in reply   160 *quarrelous* quarrelsome   162 *harder* too hard (different editors regard this as applying to Posthumus, Pisanio, or Imogen herself)   164 *Of . . . Titan* of the sun who kisses everything   165 *laborsome . . . trims* elaborate and tasteful attire   166 *angry* i.e. with jealousy   167 *end* purpose, plan   169 *Forethinking* planning for in advance; *fit* prepared   171 *answer to* match; *in their serving* with their assistance   173 *season* age   174 *his service* to work for him   175 *happy* gifted; *make him know* be convincing to him (?)   177 *embrace* receive   178 *means* i.e. of subsistence   182 *even* keep up with   184 *am soldier to* have courage for; *abide* face   188 *Your carriage* taking you away   192 *distemper* illness   193 *fit you to* dress yourself for   III, v The palace of Cymbeline   8 *conduct* escort

Madam, all joy befall your Grace, and you.

CYMBELINE

10 My lords, you are appointed for that office ;
The due of honor in no point omit.
So farewell, noble Lucius.

LUCIUS   Your hand, my lord.

CLOTEN

Receive it friendly, but from this time forth
I wear it as your enemy.

14 LUCIUS   Sir, the event
Is yet to name the winner. Fare you well.

CYMBELINE

Leave not the worthy Lucius, good my lords,
Till he have crossed the Severn. Happiness !

           Exit Lucius &c.

QUEEN

18 He goes hence frowning, but it honors us
That we have given him cause.

CLOTEN   'Tis all the better ;

20 Your valiant Britons have their wishes in it.

CYMBELINE

Lucius hath wrote already to the Emperor

22 How it goes here. It fits us therefore ripely
Our chariots and our horsemen be in readiness.
The pow'rs that he already hath in Gallia

25 Will soon be drawn to head, from whence he moves
His war for Britain.

26 QUEEN   'Tis not sleepy business,
But must be looked to speedily and strongly.

CYMBELINE

Our expectation that it would be thus

29 Hath made us forward. But, my gentle queen,
Where is our daughter ? She hath not appeared
Before the Roman, nor to us hath tendered

32 The duty of the day. She looks us like
A thing more made of malice than of duty.
We have noted it. Call her before us, for

35 We have been too slight in sufferance.

           [Exit a Messenger.]

QUEEN   Royal sir,

36 Since the exile of Posthumus, most retired
Hath her life been ; the cure whereof, my lord,
'Tis time must do. Beseech your Majesty,
Forbear sharp speeches to her. She's a lady

40 So tender of rebukes that words are strokes,
And strokes death to her.

           Enter a Messenger.

CYMBELINE   Where is she, sir ? How

42 Can her contempt be answered ?

MESSENGER   Please you, sir,
Her chambers are all locked, and there's no answer

44 That will be given to th' loud of noise we make.

QUEEN

My lord, when last I went to visit her,

46 She prayed me to excuse her keeping close ;

47 Whereto constrained by her infirmity,
She should that duty leave unpaid to you
Which daily she was bound to proffer. This

50 She wished me to make known, but our great court

51 Made me to blame in memory.

CYMBELINE   Her doors locked ?
Not seen of late ? Grant, heavens, that which I fear
Prove false !   *Exit.*

QUEEN   Son, I say, follow the King.

CLOTEN

That man of hers, Pisanio, her old servant,
I have not seen these two days.

QUEEN   Go, look after.

           Exit [Cloten].

Pisanio, thou that stand'st so for Posthumus –   56
He hath a drug of mine. I pray his absence
Proceed by swallowing that, for he believes   58
It is a thing most precious. But for her,
Where is she gone ? Haply despair hath seized her,   60
Or, winged with fervor of her love, she's flown
To her desired Posthumus. Gone she is
To death or to dishonor, and my end
Can make good use of either. She being down,
I have the placing of the British crown.

           Enter Cloten.

How now, my son ?

CLOTEN   'Tis certain she is fled.
Go in and cheer the King. He rages ; none
Dare come about him.

QUEEN *[aside]*   All the better. May
This night forestall him of the coming day !   *Exit.* 69

CLOTEN

I love and hate her, for she's fair and royal,   70
And that she hath all courtly parts more exquisite   71
Than lady, ladies, woman. From every one
The best she hath, and she, of all compounded,
Outsells them all. I love her therefore, but   74
Disdaining me and throwing favors on   75
The low Posthumus slanders so her judgment   76
That what's else rare is choked ; and in that point   77
I will conclude to hate her, nay, indeed,
To be revenged upon her. For, when fools
Shall –

           Enter Pisanio.

           Who is here ? What, are you packing, sirrah ?   80
Come hither. Ah, you precious pander ! Villain,
Where is thy lady ? In a word, or else
Thou art straightway with the fiends.

PISANIO   O good my lord !

CLOTEN

Where is thy lady ? Or – by Jupiter,
I will not ask again. Close villain,   85
I'll have this secret from thy heart, or rip
Thy heart to find it. Is she with Posthumus ?
From whose so many weights of baseness cannot
A dram of worth be drawn.   89

PISANIO   Alas, my lord,
How can she be with him ? When was she missed ?
He is in Rome.

10 *office* duty   14 *event* outcome   18 *it honors us* it is to our credit (i.e. we have been patriotic)   20 *have . . . it* i.e. approve our course   22 *fits* befits ; *ripely* fully (cf. 'the time is ripe')   25 *drawn to head* organized, mobilized   26 *sleepy* sleep-permitting (cf. 'asleep on the job')   29 *forward* (take) early (action)   32 *us* to us   35 *slight in sufferance* weak in tolerance (of her conduct)   36 *retired* withdrawn, unsocial   40 *tender of* sensitive to   42 *answered* accounted for   44 *loud* loudness (some editors emend *loud of* to 'loudest')   46 *close* to herself   47 *constrained* compelled ; *infirmity* ill-being, poor condition   50 *great court* important session of court   51 *to blame* faulty   56 *stand'st so for* so strongly support   58 *Proceed by* result from   60 *Haply* perhaps   69 *forestall* deprive   70 *for* because   71 *that* because ; *parts* qualities   74 *Outsells* outvalues   75 *Disdaining* her disdaining   76 *slanders* disgraces   77 *what's else rare* her other rare qualities   80 *packing* plotting   85 *Close* secretive   89 *drawn* extracted

CLOTEN   Where is she, sir? Come nearer. 91
No farther halting. Satisfy me home 92
What is become of her.
PISANIO
O my all-worthy lord!
CLOTEN   All-worthy villain!
Discover where thy mistress is at once, 95
At the next word. No more of 'worthy lord'!
Speak, or thy silence on the instant is 97
Thy condemnation and thy death.
PISANIO   Then, sir,
This paper is the history of my knowledge
Touching her flight. 100
       [Presents a letter.]
CLOTEN   Let's see't. I will pursue her
Even to Augustus' throne.
PISANIO [aside]   Or this, or perish. 101
She's far enough, and what he learns by this
May prove his travel, not her danger. 103
CLOTEN   Humh!
PISANIO [aside]
I'll write to my lord she's dead. O Imogen,
Safe mayst thou wander, safe return again!
CLOTEN Sirrah, is this letter true?
PISANIO Sir, as I think.
CLOTEN It is Posthumus' hand; I know't. Sirrah, if thou
wouldst not be a villain, but do me true service, undergo 109
those employments wherein I should have cause to use
thee with a serious industry – that is, what villainy soe'er 111
I bid thee do, to perform it directly and truly – I would
think thee an honest man. Thou shouldst neither want
my means for thy relief nor my voice for thy preferment. 114
PISANIO Well, my good lord.
CLOTEN Wilt thou serve me? For since patiently and constantly thou hast stuck to the bare fortune of that beggar
Posthumus, thou canst not, in the course of gratitude, 118
but be a diligent follower of mine. Wilt thou serve me?
PISANIO Sir, I will.
CLOTEN Give me thy hand. Here's my purse. Hast any
of thy late master's garments in thy possession?
PISANIO I have, my lord, at my lodging the same suit he
wore when he took leave of my lady and mistress.
CLOTEN The first service thou dost me, fetch that suit
hither. Let it be thy first service. Go.
PISANIO I shall, my lord.   Exit.
CLOTEN Meet thee at Milford Haven! I forgot to ask him
one thing; I'll remember't anon. Even there, thou vil-

lain Posthumus, will I kill thee. I would these garments
were come. She said upon a time – the bitterness of it I
now belch from my heart – that she held the very garment of Posthumus in more respect than my noble and
natural person, together with the adornment of my
qualities. With that suit upon my back will I ravish her; 135
first kill him, and in her eyes. There shall she see my
valor, which will then be a torment to her contempt. He 137
on the ground, my speech of insultment ended on his 138
dead body, and when my lust hath dined – which, as I
say, to vex her I will execute in the clothes that she so
praised – to the court I'll knock her back, foot her home 141
again. She hath despised me rejoicingly, and I'll be
merry in my revenge.
       Enter Pisanio [with the clothes].
Be those the garments?
PISANIO Ay, my noble lord.
CLOTEN How long is't since she went to Milford Haven?
PISANIO She can scarce be there yet.
CLOTEN Bring this apparel to my chamber; that is the
second thing that I have commanded thee. The third is
that thou wilt be a voluntary mute to my design. Be but 150
duteous, and true preferment shall tender itself to thee.
My revenge is now at Milford. Would I had wings to
follow it! Come, and be true.   Exit.
PISANIO
Thou bid'st me to my loss, for true to thee 154
Were I to prove false, which I will never be,
To him that is most true. To Milford go, 156
And find not her whom thou pursuest. Flow, flow,
You heavenly blessings, on her. This fool's speed
Be crossed with slowness; labor be his meed.   Exit. 159

              *

       Enter Imogen alone [in boy's clothes].   III, vi
IMOGEN
I see a man's life is a tedious one.
I have tired myself, and for two nights together
Have made the ground my bed. I should be sick
But that my resolution helps me. Milford,
When from the mountain top Pisanio showed thee,
Thou wast within a ken. O Jove, I think 6
Foundations fly the wretched – such, I mean, 7
Where they should be relieved. Two beggars told me
I could not miss my way. Will poor folks lie,
That have afflictions on them, knowing 'tis
A punishment or trial? Yes. No wonder, 11
When rich ones scarce tell true. To lapse in fulness 12
Is sorer than to lie for need, and falsehood 13
Is worse in kings than beggars. My dear lord,
Thou art one o' th' false ones. Now I think on thee
My hunger's gone, but even before, I was 16
At point to sink for food. But what is this? 17
Here is a path to't. 'Tis some savage hold. 18
I were best not call; I dare not call. Yet famine, 19
Ere clean it o'erthrow nature, makes it valiant. 20
Plenty and peace breeds cowards; hardness ever 21
Of hardiness is mother. Ho! Who's here? 22
If anything that's civil, speak; if savage,
Take or lend. Ho! No answer? Then I'll enter. 24
Best draw my sword, and if mine enemy
But fear the sword like me, he'll scarcely look on't.
Such a foe, good heavens!   Exit [into the cave]. 27

91 *nearer* i.e. to the point   92 *home* completely   95 *Discover* reveal
97–98 *silence . . . condemnation* silence will condemn you instantly   100
Touching concerning   101 *Or* either   103 *travel* difficulty, trouble
109 *undergo* undertake   111 *industry* application   114 *relief* assistance;
voice support; *preferment* advancement   118 *course* ordinary action
135 *qualities* talents   137 *to her contempt* to her because of her contempt
for me   138 *insultment* triumph and scorn   141 *foot* kick   150 *be . . . mute*
to be willing to keep quiet about (as if mute)   154 *to my loss* to lose my
honor   156 *him* i.e. Posthumus, whom Pisanio thinks misled rather than
untrue   159 *crossed* thwarted; *meed* reward
III, vi Wales: before the cave of Belarius   6 *ken* sight   7 *Foundations*
(pun on the meanings 'security' and 'charitable organizations')   11 *trial*
test (of faith or moral quality)   12 *lapse in fulness* lie when well-to-do
13 *sorer* worse   16 *even* just   17 *At point* about; *for* for lack of   18 *hold*
stronghold   19 *were best* had better   20 *clean* completely; *nature* i.e. a
person   21 *hardness* hardship   22 *hardiness* courage, endurance   24 *Take
or lend* i.e. she expects the civil person to speak, the savage to act, be it
to take (life or money) or give (food or blows)   27 *Such . . . heavens* heavens
grant me such a foe

Enter Belarius, Guiderius, and Arviragus.

BELARIUS

28 You, Polydore, have proved best woodman and
Are master of the feast. Cadwal and I
30 Will play the cook and servant ; 'tis our match.
The sweat of industry would dry and die
But for the end it works to. Come, our stomachs
33 Will make what's homely savory. Weariness
34 Can snore upon the flint when resty sloth
Finds the down pillow hard. Now peace be here,
36 Poor house, that keep'st thyself.

GUIDERIUS   I am throughly weary.

ARVIRAGUS
I am weak with toil, yet strong in appetite.

GUIDERIUS
38 There is cold meat i' th' cave. We'll browse on that
Whilst what we have killed be cooked.

BELARIUS *[looking into the cave]*   Stay, come not in.
But that it eats our victuals, I should think
Here were a fairy.

GUIDERIUS   What's the matter, sir ?

BELARIUS
By Jupiter, an angel ! or, if not,
An earthly paragon ! Behold divineness
No elder than a boy !

Enter Imogen.

IMOGEN
Good masters, harm me not.
Before I entered here, I called and thought
47 To have begged or bought what I have took. Good troth,
I have stol'n naught, nor would not, though I had found
Gold strewed i' th' floor. Here's money for my meat.
I would have left it on the board so soon
As I had made my meal, and parted
With pray'rs for the provider.

GUIDERIUS   Money, youth ?

ARVIRAGUS
All gold and silver rather turn to dirt,
54 An 'tis no better reckoned but of those
Who worship dirty gods.

IMOGEN   I see you're angry.
Know, if you kill me for my fault, I should
Have died had I not made it.

BELARIUS   Whither bound ?

IMOGEN
To Milford Haven.

BELARIUS
What's your name ?

IMOGEN
Fidele, sir. I have a kinsman who
Is bound for Italy ; he embarked at Milford ;
62 To whom being going, almost spent with hunger,
63 I am fall'n in this offense.

BELARIUS   Prithee, fair youth,
Think us no churls, nor measure our good minds
By this rude place we live in. Well encountered !
66 'Tis almost night ; you shall have better cheer
67 Ere you depart, and thanks to stay and eat it.
Boys, bid him welcome.

GUIDERIUS   Were you a woman, youth,
69 I should woo hard but be your groom in honesty.
70 I bid for you as I do buy.

ARVIRAGUS   I'll make 't my comfort
He is a man. I'll love him as my brother,

And such a welcome as I'ld give to him
After long absence, such is yours. Most welcome.
Be sprightly, for you fall 'mongst friends.   74

IMOGEN   'Mongst friends ?
If brothers. *[aside]* Would it had been so that they
Had been my father's sons ! Then had my prize   76
Been less, and so more equal ballasting   77
To thee, Posthumus.

BELARIUS   He wrings at some distress.   78

GUIDERIUS
Would I could free't !

ARVIRAGUS   Or I, whate'er it be,
What pain it cost, what danger. Gods !

BELARIUS   Hark, boys.
[Whispers.]

IMOGEN
Great men
That had a court no bigger than this cave,
That did attend themselves and had the virtue   83
Which their own conscience sealed them, laying by 84
That nothing-gift of differing multitudes,   85
Could not outpeer these twain. Pardon me, gods,   86
I'ld change my sex to be companion with them,
Since Leonatus' false.

BELARIUS   It shall be so.
Boys, we'll go dress our hunt. Fair youth, come in. 89
Discourse is heavy, fasting. When we have supped,   90
We'll mannerly demand thee of thy story,
So far as thou wilt speak it.

GUIDERIUS   Pray draw near.

ARVIRAGUS
The night to th' owl and morn to th' lark less welcome.

IMOGEN
Thanks, sir.

ARVIRAGUS
I pray draw near.   *Exeunt.*

*

Enter two Roman Senators, and Tribunes.   III,

1. SENATOR
This is the tenor of the Emperor's writ :   1
That since the common men are now in action
'Gainst the Pannonians and Dalmatians,
And that the legions now in Gallia are
Full weak to undertake our wars against   5
The fall'n-off Britons, that we do incite   6
The gentry to this business. He creates
Lucius proconsul, and to you the tribunes,
For this immediate levy, he commands   9
His absolute commission. Long live Caesar !   10

28 *woodman* hunter 30 *match* bargain 33 *homely* plain 34 *resty* lazy
36 *keep'st* takest care of ; *throughly* thoroughly 38 *browse* nibble 47 *Good
troth* in truth 54 *of* by 62 *spent* exhausted 63 *in* into 66 *cheer* entertainment 67 *thanks to* i.e. we'll be pleased to have you 69 *but be* but to
be 70 *I bid . . . buy* (literal meaning not clear ; the idea is that he sets a
high value on Fidele, as in making a serious bid for purchase) 74 *sprightly*
in good spirits 76 *prize* (pun on the meanings 'value' and 'captured
ship') 77 *less* i.e. she would not have been heir to the throne ; *ballasting*
weight, position 78 *wrings* writhes 83 *attend* serve 84 *laying by* disregarding 85 *nothing-gift* worthless gift (admission ? attendance ?) ; *differing*
inconsistent 86 *outpeer* excel 89 *dress our hunt* prepare our game 90
Discourse . . . fasting conversation is burdensome when we have not eaten
III, vii Rome : Senate House 1 *writ* dispatch 5 *Full* quite 6 *fall'n-off*
revolted ; *incite* summon 9 *commands* entrusts 10 *commission* authority

TRIBUNE
Is Lucius general of the forces?
2. SENATOR   Ay.
TRIBUNE
Remaining now in Gallia?
1. SENATOR   With those legions
Which I have spoke of, whereunto your levy
14 Must be supplyant. The words of your commission
15 Will tie you to the numbers and the time
Of their dispatch.
TRIBUNE   We will discharge our duty.   *Exeunt.*

*

IV, i   *Enter Cloten alone.*
CLOTEN   I am near to th' place where they should meet, if
2 Pisanio have mapped it truly. How fit his garments serve
me! Why should his mistress, who was made by him
4 that made the tailor, not be fit too? The rather, saving
5 reverence of the word, for 'tis said a woman's fitness
6 comes by fits. Therein I must play the workman. I dare
speak it to myself, for it is not vainglory for a man and
8 his glass to confer in his own chamber – I mean, the lines
of my body are as well drawn as his; no less young, more
strong, not beneath him in fortunes, beyond him in the
11 advantage of the time, above him in birth, alike con-
12 versant in general services, and more remarkable in
13 single oppositions. Yet this imperceiverant thing loves
14 him in my despite. What mortality is! Posthumus, thy
head, which now is growing upon thy shoulders, shall
16 within this hour be off, thy mistress enforced, thy gar-
17 ments cut to pieces before thy face; and all this done,
18 spurn her home to her father, who may happily be a little
angry for my so rough usage; but my mother, having
20 power of his testiness, shall turn all into my commenda-
21 tions. My horse is tied up safe. Out, sword, and to a sore
22 purpose! Fortune put them into my hand. This is the
very description of their meeting place, and the fellow
dares not deceive me.   *Exit.*

IV, ii   *Enter Belarius, Guiderius, Arviragus, and Imogen
from the cave.*
BELARIUS *[to Imogen]*
You are not well. Remain here in the cave;
We'll come to you after hunting.
ARVIRAGUS *[to Imogen]*   Brother, stay here.

Are we not brothers?
IMOGEN   So man and man should be,
But clay and clay differs in dignity,   4
Whose dust is both alike. I am very sick.   5
GUIDERIUS
Go you to hunting; I'll abide with him.
IMOGEN
So sick I am not, yet I am not well,
But not so citizen a wanton as   8
To seem to die ere sick. So please you, leave me;
Stick to your journal course; the breach of custom   10
Is breach of all. I am ill, but your being by me
Cannot amend me; society is no comfort   12
To one not sociable. I am not very sick,
Since I can reason of it. Pray you trust me here –
I'll rob none but myself – and let me die,
Stealing so poorly.   16
GUIDERIUS   I love thee – I have spoke it –
How much the quantity, the weight as much   17
As I do love my father.
BELARIUS   What? How, how?
ARVIRAGUS
If it be sin to say so, sir, I yoke me   19
In my good brother's fault. I know not why
I love this youth, and I have heard you say
Love's reason 's without reason. The bier at door,
And a demand who is 't shall die, I'd say
'My father, not this youth.'
BELARIUS *[aside]*   O noble strain!   24
O worthiness of nature, breed of greatness!
Cowards father cowards and base things sire base;   26
Nature hath meal and bran, contempt and grace.   27
I'm not their father; yet who this should be   28
Doth miracle itself, loved before me. –
'Tis the ninth hour o' th' morn.
ARVIRAGUS   Brother, farewell.
IMOGEN
I wish ye sport.
ARVIRAGUS   You health.
          [To Belarius]   So please you, sir.   31
IMOGEN *[aside]*
These are kind creatures. Gods, what lies I have heard!
Our courtiers say all 's savage but at court.
Experience, O, thou disprov'st report!
Th' imperious seas breeds monsters; for the dish   35
Poor tributary rivers as sweet fish.   36
I am sick still, heartsick. Pisanio,
I'll now taste of thy drug.
          [Swallows some.]
GUIDERIUS   I could not stir him.   38
He said he was gentle, but unfortunate;   39
Dishonestly afflicted, but yet honest.
ARVIRAGUS
Thus did he answer me, yet said hereafter
I might know more.
BELARIUS   To th' field, to th' field.
          [To Imogen]
We'll leave you for this time; go in and rest.
ARVIRAGUS
We'll not be long away.
BELARIUS   Pray be not sick,
For you must be our housewife.
IMOGEN   Well or ill,
I am bound to you.   *Exit [into the cave].* 46

14 *supplyant* supplementary   15 *tie you to* specify to you
IV, i Wales: before the cave of Belarius   2 *fit* fittingly   4 *fit* i.e. for me
(with pun on the meaning 'inclined to')   4–5 *saving reverence* with all
due respect to you (apology to audience for puns on *fit*)   5 *for* since;
fitness inclination (i.e. sexual)   6 *fits* (cf. 'fits and starts')   8 *glass* mirror
11 *of the time* in the present (social) world; *alike conversant* equally
experienced   12 *services* i.e. military   13 *oppositions* combats; *imperceiverant* unperceiving   14 *What mortality is* what a thing life is   16
enforced raped   17 *thy face* (some editors emend 'thy' to 'her')   18 *spurn*
kick; *happily* (as elsewhere, for 'haply,' perchance)   20 *power of* control
over   20 *commendations* credit   21 *sore* causing pain   22 *This is* this
place fits
IV, ii   4 *clay and clay* different persons   5 *dust* remains after death   8
citizen city-bred (cf. 'citified,' 'sissy'); *wanton* spoiled child   10 *journal*
daily, regular; *breach* disruption   12 *amend* make better   16 *poorly* i.e.
from myself only   17 *How . . . as much* as much, as deeply   19–20 *yoke . . .
fault* confess to having committed the same fault as my brother   24 *strain*
lineage, heredity   26, 27 (in the folio text, these lines are introduced by
quotation marks to identify them as maxims or well-known sayings)
28–29 *who . . . me* that this person, whoever he may be, should be loved
ahead of me is miraculous   31 *So please you* at your command   35 *imperious*
imperial   36 *rivers . . . fish* rivers (breed) just as sweet fish (as the sea does)
38 *stir* move (to tell about himself)   39 *gentle* of noble birth   46 *bound*
obligated; *shalt be* i.e. bound (by emotional ties)

BELARIUS   And shalt be ever.
This youth, howe'er distressed, appears he hath had
Good ancestors.
ARVIRAGUS   How angel-like he sings!
GUIDERIUS
49 But his neat cookery! He cut our roots in characters,
50 And sauced our broths as Juno had been sick
51 And he her dieter.
ARVIRAGUS   Nobly he yokes
A smiling with a sigh, as if the sigh
53 Was that it was for not being such a smile;
The smile mocking the sigh that it would fly
From so divine a temple to commix
With winds that sailors rail at.
GUIDERIUS   I do note
57 That grief and patience, rooted in them both,
58 Mingle their spurs together.
ARVIRAGUS   Grow patience,
59 And let the stinking elder, grief, untwine
60 His perishing root with the increasing vine.
BELARIUS
61 It is great morning. Come away. Who's there?
     Enter Cloten.
CLOTEN
62 I cannot find those runagates. That villain
63 Hath mocked me. I am faint.
BELARIUS   'Those runagates'?
Means he not us? I partly know him. 'Tis
Cloten, the son o' th' Queen. I fear some ambush.
I saw him not these many years, and yet
67 I know 'tis he. We are held as outlaws. Hence!
GUIDERIUS
He is but one. You and my brother search
69 What companies are near. Pray you, away.
Let me alone with him. *[Exeunt Belarius and Arviragus.]*
70 **CLOTEN**   Soft, what are you
That fly me thus? Some villain mountaineers?
I have heard of such. What slave art thou?
GUIDERIUS   A thing
More slavish did I ne'er than answering
74 A 'slave' without a knock.
CLOTEN   Thou art a robber,
A lawbreaker, a villain. Yield thee, thief.
GUIDERIUS
To who? To thee? What art thou? Have not I
An arm as big as thine? A heart as big?
Thy words, I grant, are bigger, for I wear not
My dagger in my mouth. Say what thou art,
Why I should yield to thee.
CLOTEN   Thou villain base,
81 Know'st me not by my clothes?
GUIDERIUS   No, nor thy tailor, rascal,
Who is thy grandfather. He made those clothes,
Which, as it seems, make thee.
83 **CLOTEN**   Thou precious varlet,
My tailor made them not.
GUIDERIUS   Hence then, and thank
The man that gave them thee. Thou art some fool;
I am loath to beat thee.
86 **CLOTEN**   Thou injurious thief,
Hear but my name and tremble.
GUIDERIUS   What's thy name?
CLOTEN
Cloten, thou villain.

GUIDERIUS
Cloten, thou double villain, be thy name,
I cannot tremble at it. Were it Toad, or Adder, Spider,
'Twould move me sooner.
CLOTEN   To thy further fear,
Nay, to thy mere confusion, thou shalt know   92
I am son to th' Queen.
GUIDERIUS   I am sorry for't; not seeming   93
So worthy as thy birth.
CLOTEN   Art not afeard?
GUIDERIUS
Those that I reverence, those I fear – the wise;
At fools I laugh, not fear them.
CLOTEN   Die the death!   96
When I have slain thee with my proper hand,   97
I'll follow those that even now fled hence
And on the gates of Lud's town set your heads.
Yield, rustic mountaineer.   *Fight and exeunt.*
     Enter Belarius and Arviragus.
BELARIUS
No company's abroad?   101
ARVIRAGUS
None in the world. You did mistake him sure.
BELARIUS
I cannot tell. Long is it since I saw him,
But time hath nothing blurred those lines of favor   104
Which then he wore. The snatches in his voice,   105
And burst of speaking, were as his. I am absolute   106
'Twas very Cloten.   107
ARVIRAGUS   In this place we left them.
I wish my brother make good time with him,   108
You say he is so fell.   109
BELARIUS   Being scarce made up,
I mean to man, he had not apprehension   110
Of roaring terrors; for defect of judgment   111
Is oft the cause of fear.
     Enter Guiderius [with Cloten's head].
     But see, thy brother.
GUIDERIUS
This Cloten was a fool, an empty purse;
There was no money in't. Not Hercules
Could have knocked out his brains, for he had none.
Yet I not doing this, the fool had borne
My head as I do his.
BELARIUS   What hast thou done?

49 *neat* fine, elegant; *characters* letters (of the alphabet), designs   50 *as*
as if   51 *dieter* dietitian   53 *that* what   57 *them* i.e. the smile and sigh
(some editors emend to 'him')   58 *spurs* roots   59 *elder* elder tree   60
perishing noxious; *with . . . vine* from the increasing vine (?), as the vine
increases (?)   61 *great morning* broad daylight   62 *runagates* runaways
63 *mocked* fooled   67 *held* regarded   69 *companies* followers   70 *Soft*
stop (exclamation; cf. 'take it easy')   74 *'slave'* (Guiderius may be quoting
Cloten's word or simply calling Cloten a slave)   81 *clothes* i.e. court
clothes   83 *varlet* knave   86 *injurious* insulting   92 *mere confusion* utter
destruction   93 *not seeming* since you do not seem   96 *Die the death* (as
if he were imposing a legal sentence)   97 *proper* own   101 *abroad* around,
in the neighborhood   104 *lines of favor* facial lines   105 *snatches* catches,
hesitations   106 *absolute* positive   107 *very Cloten* Cloten himself   108
make good time may succeed (cf. 'have a good day')   109 *fell* savage;
made up grown up (in sense of years or mental ability)   110 *apprehension*
understanding   111–12 *defect . . . fear* (1) some editors think that there is a
scribal or typographic error, such as *cause* for 'cease'; (2) other editors,
that Shakespeare wrote these words but was careless about meaning; (3)
others, that Shakespeare wrote the words and intended this meaning:
Cloten was fearless because he had no wits at all instead of some wits
defectively used (*defect of judgment*)

GUIDERIUS

118 I am perfect what : cut off one Cloten's head,
Son to the Queen, after his own report ;
Who called me traitor, mountaineer, and swore

121 With his own single hand he'ld take us in,
Displace our heads where – thank the gods – they grow,
And set them on Lud's town.

BELARIUS   We are all undone.

GUIDERIUS

Why, worthy father, what have we to lose

125 But that he swore to take, our lives ? The law

126 Protects not us. Then why should we be tender
To let an arrogant piece of flesh threat us,
Play judge and executioner all himself,

129 For we do fear the law ? What company
Discover you abroad ?

BELARIUS   No single soul
Can we set eye on, but in all safe reason

132 He must have some attendants. Though his honor
Was nothing but mutation – ay, and that
From one bad thing to worse – not frenzy, not
Absolute madness could so far have raved
To bring him here alone. Although perhaps
It may be heard at court that such as we
Cave here, hunt here, are outlaws, and in time

139 May make some stronger head ; the which he hearing –
As it is like him – might break out, and swear

141 He'ld fetch us in ; yet is't not probable

142 To come alone, either he so undertaking,

143 Or they so suffering. Then on good ground we fear,

144 If we do fear this body hath a tail
More perilous than the head.

145 **ARVIRAGUS**   Let ordinance
Come as the gods foresay it. Howsoe'er,
My brother hath done well.

BELARIUS   I had no mind
To hunt this day. The boy Fidele's sickness

149 Did make my way long forth.

GUIDERIUS   With his own sword,
Which he did wave against my throat, I have ta'en
His head from him. I'll throw't into the creek
Behind our rock, and let it to the sea
And tell the fishes he's the Queen's son, Cloten.

154 That's all I reck.   *Exit.*

BELARIUS   I fear 'twill be revenged.
Would, Polydore, thou hadst not done't, though valor
Becomes thee well enough.

ARVIRAGUS   Would I had done't,

157 So the revenge alone pursued me. Polydore,

---

118 *perfect* aware   121 *take us in* subdue us   125 *that* what   126–27 *tender To* so tolerant as to   129 *For* because   132 *honor* (implies steadfastness; ironically joined with *mutation*, changeableness. Some editors emend to 'humor.')   139 *make . . . head* become a stronger force   141 *fetch us in* capture us   142 *To come* for him to come   143 *suffering* permitting (it)   144 *tail* i.e. what comes after : followers hostile to us   145 *ordinance* whatever is ordained   149 *Did . . . forth* made my walk forth (from the cave) seem long   154 *reck* care   157 *So* so that ; *pursued* would have pursued   160 *possible* our available ; *meet* i.e. in combat ; *seek us through* come upon us   161 *put* force   165 *hasty* quick to act   167 *gain his color* restore the color (to) his (cheeks)   168 *let . . . blood* let blood for a parish of such Clotens (a medical term as a metaphor for 'kill')   170 *blazon'st* depictest   174 *enchafed* heated   177 *frame* direct   178 *royalty* kingly conduct   179 *Civility* civilized conduct   180 *wildly* spontaneously   184 *clotpoll* blockhead   186 *ingenious* skillfully constructed   188 *give it motion* play it   189 *even* just   192 *answer* correspond to ; *accidents* events   193 *lamenting toys* lamenting for trifles   198 *on* of   204 *sound thy bottom* measure thy depths   205 *crare* small boat

---

I love thee brotherly, but envy much
Thou hast robbed me of this deed. I would revenges
That possible strength might meet would seek us through   160
And put us to our answer.   161

BELARIUS   Well, 'tis done.
We'll hunt no more to-day, nor seek for danger
Where there's no profit. I prithee, to our rock ;
You and Fidele play the cooks. I'll stay
Till hasty Polydore return, and bring him   165
To dinner presently.

ARVIRAGUS   Poor sick Fidele,
I'll willingly to him. To gain his color   167
I'ld let a parish of such Clotens blood   168
And praise myself for charity.   *Exit.*

BELARIUS   O thou goddess,
Thou divine Nature, thou thyself thou blazon'st   170
In these two princely boys ! They are as gentle
As zephyrs blowing below the violet,
Not wagging his sweet head ; and yet as rough,
Their royal blood enchafed, as the rud'st wind   174
That by the top doth take the mountain pine
And make him stoop to th' vale. 'Tis wonder
That an invisible instinct should frame them   177
To royalty unlearned, honor untaught,   178
Civility not seen from other, valor   179
That wildly grows in them but yields a crop   180
As if it had been sowed. Yet still it's strange
What Cloten's being here to us portends,
Or what his death will bring us.

Enter Guiderius.

GUIDERIUS   Where's my brother ?
I have sent Cloten's clotpoll down the stream   184
In embassy to his mother ; his body's hostage
For his return.

Solemn music.

BELARIUS   My ingenious instrument !   186
Hark, Polydore, it sounds. But what occasion
Hath Cadwal now to give it motion ? Hark !   188

GUIDERIUS
Is he at home ?

BELARIUS   He went hence even now.   189

GUIDERIUS
What does he mean ? Since death of my dear'st mother
It did not speak before. All solemn things
Should answer solemn accidents. The matter ?   192
Triumphs for nothing and lamenting toys   193
Is jollity for apes and grief for boys.
Is Cadwal mad ?

Enter Arviragus, with Imogen dead, bearing her in his arms.

BELARIUS   Look, here he comes,
And brings the dire occasion in his arms
Of what we blame him for.

ARVIRAGUS   The bird is dead
That we have made so much on. I had rather   198
Have skipped from sixteen years of age to sixty,
To have turned my leaping time into a crutch,
Than have seen this.

GUIDERIUS   O sweetest, fairest lily !
My brother wears thee not the one half so well
As when thou grew'st thyself.

BELARIUS   O melancholy,
Who ever yet could sound thy bottom, find   204
The ooze, to show what coast thy sluggish crare   205

206 Might eas'liest harbor in ? Thou blessèd thing,
207 Jove knows what man thou mightst have made ; but I,
    Thou diedst, a most rare boy, of melancholy.
    How found you him ?
209 ARVIRAGUS   Stark, as you see,
210 Thus smiling, as some fly had tickled slumber,
211 Not as death's dart being laughed at ; his right cheek
    Reposing on a cushion.
    GUIDERIUS   Where ?
    ARVIRAGUS   O' th' floor ;
213 His arms thus leagued. I thought he slept, and put
214 My clouted brogues from off my feet, whose rudeness
    Answered my steps too loud.
    GUIDERIUS   Why, he but sleeps.
    If he be gone, he'll make his grave a bed ;
    With female fairies will his tomb be haunted,
    And worms will not come to thee.
    ARVIRAGUS   With fairest flowers,
    Whilst summer lasts and I live here, Fidele,
    I'll sweeten thy sad grave. Thou shalt not lack
    The flower that's like thy face, pale primrose ; nor
222 The azured harebell, like thy veins ; no, nor
    The leaf of eglantine, whom not to slander,
224 Outsweet'ned not thy breath. The ruddock would
    With charitable bill – O bill, sore shaming
    Those rich-left heirs that let their fathers lie
    Without a monument ! – bring thee all this,
    Yea, and furred moss besides. When flowers are none
229 To winter-ground thy corse –
    GUIDERIUS   Prithee have done,
230 And do not play in wench-like words with that
    Which is so serious. Let us bury him,
    And not protract with admiration what
    Is now due debt. To th' grave.
233 ARVIRAGUS   Say, where shall's lay him ?
    GUIDERIUS
    By good Euriphile, our mother.
    ARVIRAGUS   Be't so.
    And let us, Polydore, though now our voices
236 Have got the mannish crack, sing him to th' ground,
    As once to our mother ; use like note and words,
    Save that Euriphile must be Fidele.
    GUIDERIUS
    Cadwal,
240 I cannot sing. I'll weep, and word it with thee,
    For notes of sorrow out of tune are worse
242 Than priests and fanes that lie.
    ARVIRAGUS   We'll speak it then.
    BELARIUS
    Great griefs, I see, med'cine the less, for Cloten
    Is quite forgot. He was a queen's son, boys,
    And though he came our enemy, remember
246 He was paid for that. Though mean and mighty, rotting
    Together, have one dust, yet reverence,
248 That angel of the world, doth make distinction
    Of place 'tween high and low. Our foe was princely,
250 And though you took his life as being our foe,
    Yet bury him as a prince.
    GUIDERIUS   Pray you fetch him hither.
252 Thersites' body is as good as Ajax'
    When neither are alive.
    ARVIRAGUS   If you'll go fetch him,
    We'll say our song the whilst. Brother, begin.
                    [Exit Belarius.]

GUIDERIUS
    Nay, Cadwal, we must lay his head to th' east ;   255
    My father hath a reason for't.
ARVIRAGUS   'Tis true.
GUIDERIUS
    Come on then and remove him.
ARVIRAGUS   So. Begin.

Song.

GUIDERIUS   Fear no more the heat o' th' sun
               Nor the furious winter's rages ;
          Thou thy worldly task hast done,
                Home art gone and ta'en thy wages.
          Golden lads and girls all must,   262
          As chimney-sweepers, come to dust.   263
ARVIRAGUS   Fear no more the frown o' th' great ;
               Thou art past the tyrant's stroke.
          Care no more to clothe and eat ;
               To thee the reed is as the oak.
          The sceptre, learning, physic, must   268
          All follow this and come to dust.
GUIDERIUS   Fear no more the lightning flash,
ARVIRAGUS   Nor th' all-dreaded thunder-stone ;   271
GUIDERIUS   Fear no slander, censure rash ;
ARVIRAGUS   Thou hast finished joy and moan.
BOTH   All lovers young, all lovers must
          Consign to thee and come to dust.   275
GUIDERIUS   No exorciser harm thee,   276
ARVIRAGUS   Nor no witchcraft charm thee.
GUIDERIUS   Ghost unlaid forbear thee ;   278
ARVIRAGUS   Nothing ill come near thee.
BOTH   Quiet consummation have,   280
          And renownèd be thy grave.

Enter Belarius with the body of Cloten.

GUIDERIUS
    We have done our obsequies. Come, lay him down.
BELARIUS
    Here's a few flowers, but 'bout midnight, more.
    The herbs that have on them cold dew o' th' night
    Are strewings fitt'st for graves. Upon their faces.   285
    You were as flow'rs, now withered ; even so   286
    These herblets shall which we upon you strew.   287
    Come on, away ; apart upon our knees.
    The ground that gave them first has them again.

206 *thing* i.e. Fidele   207 *but I* but I know that   209 *Stark* stiff (in rigor mortis)   210 *as* as if   211 *as . . . at* as if the sting of death were being laughed at   213 *leagued* crossed   214 *clouted brogues* nail-studded boots ; *rudeness* coarseness (of the boots)   222 *azured* sky-blue   224 *ruddock* robin   229 *To winter-ground* to protect in winter (?) (or it may be a prepositional phrase belonging to uncompleted predicate of interrupted sentence)   230 *wench-like* womanish   233 *shall's* shall us (we)   236 *crack* break, tone   240 *word* speak, recite   242 *fanes* temples   246 *paid* punished   248 *angel . . . world* messenger sent from heaven to earth   250 *as being* because he was   252 *Thersites* vindictive and foul-mouthed Greek ; *Ajax* Greek hero   255 *to th' east* (the opposite of Christian practice ; a way of suggesting the non-Christian world of the play)   262 *Golden* i.e. fine   268 *As* like   268 *sceptre, learning, physic* kings, scholars, doctors   271 *thunder-stone* thunderbolt   275 *Consign* perhaps, co-sign (i.e. the same contract : meet the same fate)   276 *exorciser* conjurer   278 *unlaid* not driven out (by formal procedures) ; *forbear* leave alone   280 *consummation* fulfillment (i.e. death)   285 *Upon their faces* flowers on front of bodies (?), flowers lying face down (?)   286 *now* now you are   287 *shall* shall be (withered)

Their pleasures here are past, so is their pain.
      Exeunt [Belarius, Guiderius, and Arviragus].
      Imogen awakes:
[IMOGEN]
   Yes, sir, to Milford Haven. Which is the way?
   I thank you. By yond bush? Pray, how far thither?
293 'Ods pittikins, can it be six mile yet?
294 I have gone all night. Faith, I'll lie down and sleep.
      [Sees the body of Cloten.]
   But, soft, no bedfellow! O gods and goddesses!
   These flow'rs are like the pleasures of the world;
   This bloody man, the care on't. I hope I dream,
298 For so I thought I was a cave-keeper
   And cook to honest creatures. But 'tis not so;
300 'Twas but a bolt of nothing, shot at nothing,
301 Which the brain makes of fumes. Our very eyes
   Are sometimes like our judgments, blind. Good faith,
   I tremble still with fear, but if there be
   Yet left in heaven as small a drop of pity
305 As a wren's eye, feared gods, a part of it!
   The dream's here still. Even when I wake it is
   Without me, as within me; not imagined, felt.
   A headless man? The garments of Posthumus?
   I know the shape of's leg; this is his hand,
310 His foot Mercurial, his Martial thigh,
311 The brawns of Hercules; but his Jovial face –
   Murder in heaven? How? 'Tis gone. Pisanio,
313 All curses madded Hecuba gave the Greeks,
   And mine to boot, be darted on thee! Thou,
315 Conspired with that irregulous devil Cloten,
   Hath here cut off my lord. To write and read
   Be henceforth treacherous! Damned Pisanio
   Hath with his forgèd letters – damned Pisanio –
   From this most bravest vessel of the world
   Struck the maintop. O Posthumus, alas,
   Where is thy head? Where's that? Ay me, where's that?
   Pisanio might have killed thee at the heart
   And left this head on. How should this be? Pisanio?
324 'Tis he and Cloten. Malice and lucre in them
325 Have laid this woe here. O, 'tis pregnant, pregnant!
   The drug he gave me, which he said was precious
327 And cordial to me, have I not found it
328 Murd'rous to th' senses? That confirms it home.
329 This is Pisanio's deed, and Cloten. O,
   Give color to my pale cheek with thy blood,

That we the horrider may seem to those
Which chance to find us. O my lord, my lord!   332
      [Falls on the body.]
      Enter Lucius, Captains, and a Soothsayer.
CAPTAIN
   To them the legions garrisoned in Gallia   333
   After your will have crossed the sea, attending   334
   You here at Milford Haven with your ships.
   They are here in readiness.
LUCIUS   But what from Rome?
CAPTAIN
   The Senate hath stirred up the confiners   337
   And gentlemen of Italy, most willing spirits
   That promise noble service, and they come
   Under the conduct of bold Iachimo,
   Siena's brother.   341
LUCIUS   When expect you them?
CAPTAIN
   With the next benefit o' th' wind.
LUCIUS   This forwardness   342
   Makes our hopes fair. Command our present numbers   343
   Be mustered; bid the captains look to't. Now, sir,
   What have you dreamed of late of this war's purpose?   345
SOOTHSAYER
   Last night the very gods showed me a vision –
   I fast and prayed for their intelligence – thus: 347
   I saw Jove's bird, the Roman eagle, winged
   From the spongy south to this part of the west,   349
   There vanished in the sunbeams; which portends,
   Unless my sins abuse my divination,   351
   Success to th' Roman host.
LUCIUS   Dream often so,
   And never false. Soft, ho, what trunk is here?   353
   Without his top? The ruin speaks that sometime
   It was a worthy building. How, a page?
   Or dead or sleeping on him? But dead rather,   356
   For nature doth abhor to make his bed   357
   With the defunct or sleep upon the dead.   358
   Let's see the boy's face.
CAPTAIN   He's alive, my lord.
LUCIUS
   He'll, then, instruct us of this body. Young one,   360
   Inform us of thy fortunes, for it seems
   They crave to be demanded. Who is this   362
   Thou mak'st thy bloody pillow? Or who was he
   That, otherwise than noble nature did,   364
   Hath altered that good picture? What's thy interest
   In this sad wrack? How came't? Who is't? What art   366
   thou?
IMOGEN
   I am nothing, or if not,
   Nothing to be were better. This was my master,
   A very valiant Briton and a good,
   That here by mountaineers lies slain. Alas,
   There is no more such masters. I may wander
   From east to occident, cry out for service,
   Try many, all good, serve truly, never
   Find such another master.
LUCIUS   'Lack, good youth
   Thou mov'st no less with thy complaining than   375
   Thy master in bleeding. Say his name, good friend.
IMOGEN
   Richard du Champ. *[aside]* If I do lie and do
   No harm by it, though the gods hear, I hope

---

293 *'Ods pittikins* God's little pity (diminutive of '[I pray for] God's pity'; cf. ll. 304–05) 294 *gone* walked 298 *so* i.e. in a dream (such as this may be); *cave-keeper* cave dweller 300 *bolt* arrow 301 *fumes* vapors believed to rise from the body to the brain and cause dreams 305 *a part* i.e. grant me a part 310 *Mercurial* quick, like Mercury's; *Martial* powerful, like Mars' 311 *brawns* muscles; *Jovial* like that of Jove, king of the gods 313 *madded* maddened; *Hecuba* wife of Priam, king of Troy, destroyed by the Greeks 315 *Conspired* conspiring; *irregulous* lawless 324 *lucre* greed 325 *pregnant* clear 327 *cordial* of medicinal value 328 *home* entirely (cf. 'drives the point home') 329 *Cloten* (idiomatic for 'Cloten's') 332 *Which* who 333 *To* besides; *them* i.e. forces mentioned by officers before coming on stage 334 *After* according to; *attending* waiting for 337 *confiners* inhabitants 341 *Siena's* lord of Siena's 342 *forwardness* moving ahead (on schedule) 343 *fair* strong 345 *of late* lately; *this war's purpose* our achieving our purpose in this war 347 *fast* fasted; *their intelligence* information from them 349 *spongy* damp 351 *abuse* mislead 353 *false* (dream) falsely 356 *Or* either 357 *nature doth abhor* man naturally abhors 358 *defunct* dead 360 *instruct us of* inform us about 362 *crave* . . . *demanded* beg to be asked about (i.e. are such as to arouse curiosity or sympathy) 364 *otherwise* . . . *did* from the form given it by noble nature 366 *wrack* ruin 375 *mov'st no less* art no less moving

They'll pardon it. Say you, sir?

LUCIUS   Thy name?

IMOGEN   Fidele, sir.

LUCIUS

380 Thou dost approve thyself the very same;
Thy name well fits thy faith, thy faith thy name.
Wilt take thy chance with me? I will not say
Thou shalt be so well mastered, but be sure
No less beloved. The Roman emperor's letters
Sent by a consul to me should not sooner
386 Than thine own worth prefer thee. Go with me.

IMOGEN

I'll follow, sir. But first, an't please the gods,
I'll hide my master from the flies, as deep
389 As these poor pickaxes can dig; and when
With wild wood-leaves and weeds I ha' strewed his grave
391 And on it said a century of prayers,
392 Such as I can, twice o'er, I'll weep and sigh,
And leaving so his service, follow you,
394 So please you entertain me.

LUCIUS   Ay, good youth,
And rather father thee than master thee.
My friends,
The boy hath taught us manly duties. Let us
Find out the prettiest daisied plot we can
399 And make him with our pikes and partisans
400 A grave. Come, arm him. Boy, he's preferred
By thee to us, and he shall be interred
As soldiers can. Be cheerful; wipe thine eyes.
Some falls are means the happier to arise.   *Exeunt.*

IV, iii   *Enter Cymbeline, Lords, and Pisanio.*

CYMBELINE

Again, and bring me word how 'tis with her.
    [Exit an Attendant.]
A fever with the absence of her son,
A madness, of which her life 's in danger. Heavens,
4 How deeply you at once do touch me! Imogen,
The great part of my comfort, gone; my queen
6 Upon a desperate bed, and in a time
When fearful wars point at me; her son gone,
8 So needful for this present. It strikes me past
The hope of comfort. But for thee, fellow,
Who needs must know of her departure and
11 Dost seem so ignorant, we'll enforce it from thee
By a sharp torture.

PISANIO   Sir, my life is yours,
I humbly set it at your will; but for my mistress,
I nothing know where she remains, why gone,
Nor when she purposes return. Beseech your Highness,
16 Hold me your loyal servant.

LORD   Good my liege,
The day that she was missing he was here.
I dare be bound he's true and shall perform
19 All parts of his subjection loyally. For Cloten,
There wants no diligence in seeking him,
21 And will no doubt be found.

CYMBELINE   The time is troublesome.
    [To Pisanio]
22 We'll slip you for a season, but our jealousy
23 Does yet depend.

LORD   So please your Majesty,

The Roman legions, all from Gallia drawn,
Are landed on your coast, with a supply
Of Roman gentlemen by the senate sent.

CYMBELINE

Now for the counsel of my son and queen!   27
I am amazed with matter.   28

LORD   Good my liege,
Your preparation can affront no less   29
Than what you hear of. Come more, for more you're 30
  ready.
The want is but to put those pow'rs in motion   31
That long to move.

CYMBELINE   I thank you. Let's withdraw,
And meet the time as it seeks us. We fear not
What can from Italy annoy us, but   34
We grieve at chances here. Away.
    Exeunt [all but Pisanio].

PISANIO

I heard no letter from my master since   36
I wrote him Imogen was slain. 'Tis strange.
Nor hear I from my mistress, who did promise
To yield me often tidings. Neither know I
What is betid to Cloten, but remain   40
Perplexed in all. The heavens still must work.
Wherein I am false I am honest; not true, to be true.
These present wars shall find I love my country,
Even to the note o' th' King, or I'll fall in them.   44
All other doubts, by time let them be cleared;
Fortune brings in some boats that are not steered.   *Exit.*

    Enter Belarius, Guiderius, and Arviragus.   IV, iv

GUIDERIUS

The noise is round about us.

BELARIUS   Let us from it.

ARVIRAGUS

What pleasure, sir, find we in life, to lock it   2
From action and adventure?

GUIDERIUS   Nay, what hope
Have we in hiding us? This way the Romans   4
Must or for Britons slay us or receive us   5
For barbarous and unnatural revolts
During their use, and slay us after.

BELARIUS   Sons,
We'll higher to the mountains, there secure us.   8
To the King's party there's no going. Newness   9

380 *approve* prove 386 *prefer* recommend 389 *pickaxes* i.e. fingers
391 *century* hundred 392 *can* know 394 *So* if it; *entertain* employ
399 *partisans* long-handled weapons 400 *arm him* carry him in your
arms; *preferred* recommended
IV, iii A chamber in the palace 4 *touch* wound 6 *desperate* i.e. she is
critically ill 8 *needful* needed; *It . . . past* the blow to me is beyond 11
enforce . . . thee force you to talk, get it out of you 16 *Hold* consider
19 *subjection* duties as a subject 21 *will* he will; *troublesome* full of troubles,
seriously disturbed 22 *slip* turn loose; *jealousy* suspicion 23 *depend*
hang (over you) 27 *Now for* if only I now had 28 *amazed with matter*
confused by (all the) business 29 *preparation* armed force; *affront*
confront 29–30 *no less Than* an army as large as 30 *Come more* if more
come 31 *The . . . but* all that's needed is 34 *annoy* injure 36 *no letter*
not a whit 40 *betid* happened 44 *note o'* recognition by
IV, iv Wales: before the cave of Belarius 2 *to lock it* when it is closed
off 4 *This way* i.e. if we hide 5 *Must or* must either 5–7 *receive . . .
use* i.e. accept us and use us for a time against the British, service which
for us would be barbarous and unnatural 8 *secure us* make ourselves
safe 9 *Newness* recency

10 Of Cloten's death – we being not known, not mustered
11 Among the bands – may drive us to a render
    Where we have lived, and so extort from's that
13 Which we have done, whose answer would be death
14 Drawn on with torture.

GUIDERIUS   This is, sir, a doubt
    In such a time nothing becoming you
    Nor satisfying us.

ARVIRAGUS   It is not likely
    That when they hear the Roman horses neigh,
18 Behold their quartered fires, have both their eyes
19 And ears so cloyed importantly as now,
20 That they will waste their time upon our note,
    To know from whence we are.

BELARIUS   O, I am known
    Of many in the army. Many years,
23 Though Cloten then but young, you see, not wore him
    From my remembrance. And besides, the King
25 Hath not deserved my service nor your loves,
    Who find in my exile the want of breeding,
27 The certainty of this hard life; aye hopeless
28 To have the courtesy your cradle promised,
29 But to be still hot summer's tanlings and
    The shrinking slaves of winter.

GUIDERIUS   Than be so
    Better to cease to be. Pray, sir, to th' army.
    I and my brother are not known; yourself
33 So out of thought, and thereto so o'ergrown,
34 Cannot be questioned.

ARVIRAGUS   By this sun that shines,
    I'll thither. What thing is't that I never
    Did see man die, scarce ever looked on blood
37 But that of coward hares, hot goats, and venison!
    Never bestrid a horse, save one that had
39 A rider like myself, who ne'er wore rowel
    Nor iron on his heel! I am ashamed
    To look upon the holy sun, to have
    The benefit of his blest beams, remaining
    So long a poor unknown.

GUIDERIUS   By heavens, I'll go.
    If you will bless me, sir, and give me leave,
    I'll take the better care, but if you will not,
46 The hazard therefore due fall on me by
    The hands of Romans!

ARVIRAGUS   So say I. Amen.

BELARIUS
    No reason I, since of your lives you set   48
    So slight a valuation, should reserve
    My cracked one to more care. Have with you, boys!   50
    If in your country wars you chance to die,   51
    That is my bed too, lads, and there I'll lie.
    Lead, lead. *[aside]* The time seems long; their blood
    thinks scorn
    Till it fly out and show them princes born.   *Exeunt.*

*

      Enter Posthumus alone [with a bloody handkerchief].   V, i
POSTHUMUS
    Yea, bloody cloth, I'll keep thee, for I wished
    Thou shouldst be colored thus. You married ones,
    If each of you should take this course, how many   3
    Must murder wives much better than themselves
    For wrying but a little! O Pisanio,   5
    Every good servant does not all commands;   6
    No bond but to do just ones. Gods, if you   7
    Should have ta'en vengeance on my faults, I never
    Had lived to put on this; so had you saved   9
    The noble Imogen to repent, and struck   10
    Me, wretch more worth your vengeance. But alack,
    You snatch some hence for little faults; that's love,
    To have them fall no more; you some permit   13
    To second ills with ills, each elder worse,   14
    And make them dread it, to the doers' thrift.   15
    But Imogen is your own. Do your best wills,
    And make me blessed to obey. I am brought hither
    Among th' Italian gentry, and to fight
    Against my lady's kingdom. 'Tis enough
    That, Britain, I have killed thy mistress; peace,
    I'll give no wound to thee. Therefore, good heavens,
    Hear patiently my purpose. I'll disrobe me
    Of these Italian weeds and suit myself   23
    As does a Briton peasant. So I'll fight
    Against the part I come with; so I'll die   25
    For thee, O Imogen, even for whom my life
    Is every breath a death; and thus, unknown,
    Pitied nor hated, to the face of peril
    Myself I'll dedicate. Let me make men know
    More valor in me than my habits show.   30
    Gods, put the strength o' th' Leonati in me.
    To shame the guise o' th' world, I will begin   32
    The fashion, less without and more within.   33

                                  Exit.
    Enter Lucius, Iachimo, and the Roman Army at   V, ii
    one door, and the Briton Army at another, Leonatus
    Posthumus following like a poor soldier. They march
    over and go out. Then enter again in skirmish
    Iachimo and Posthumus. He vanquisheth and
    disarmeth Iachimo and then leaves him.
IACHIMO
    The heaviness and guilt within my bosom
    Takes off my manhood. I have belied a lady,   2
    The princess of this country, and the air on't   3
    Revengingly enfeebles me; or could this carl,   4
    A very drudge of nature's, have subdued me
    In my profession? Knighthoods and honors, borne
    As I wear mine, are titles but of scorn.
    If that thy gentry, Britain, go before   8
    This lout as he exceeds our lords, the odds
    Is that we scarce are men and you are gods.   *Exit.*

---

10 *mustered* enrolled   11 *render* account   13 *whose answer* to which the reply (i.e. the penalty)   14 *Drawn on with* led up to by   18 *quartered* camp   19 *cloyed importantly* filled with important business   20 *upon our note* in noticing us   23 *then* was then; *not wore* did not wear (i.e. erase) 25–26 *your . . . breeding* the love of you two who because of my exile meet with lack of cultivation   27 *certainty* inescapability   27–28 *hopeless . . . courtesy* without hope of having the courtly style   28 *cradle* birth   29 *tanlings* tanned persons, i.e. living in the open, unsheltered   33 *o'ergrown* bearded (?), replaced (in their thoughts) (?)   34 *questioned* i.e. on your identity   37 *hot* lecherous   39–40 *ne'er . . . heel* i.e. never had several riding equipment   46 *hazard . . . due* danger arising from being unblessed 48 *of* on   50 *cracked* i.e. with age   51 *country* country's
V, i An open place in Britain   3 *take this course* do as I have done   5 *wrying* erring   6 *does not* does not carry out   7 *No bond but* he is bound only   9 *put on* instigate (?), load myself with (?)   10 *repent* i.e. for the misdeeds he imputes to her   13 *fall* i.e. into misconduct   14 *second* duplicate, back up; *elder* i.e. later (as if evils were becoming more 'mature' with time)   15 *them* i.e. the doers; *dread it* repent the evil course; *thrift* profit, gain   23 *weeds* clothes; *suit* dress   25 *part* side   30 *habits* show clothes proclaim   32 *guise* practice   33 *fashion, less without* i.e. fashion of having less external show
V, ii   2 *off* away   3 *air on't* nature of it   4 *carl* peasant   8 *go before* excel

The battle continues. The Britons fly; Cymbeline is taken. Then enter, to his rescue, Belarius, Guiderius, and Arviragus.

BELARIUS
Stand, stand! We have th' advantage of the ground.
The lane is guarded. Nothing routs us but
The villainy of our fears.

GUIDERIUS, ARVIRAGUS   Stand, stand, and fight!
Enter Posthumus, and seconds the Britons. They rescue Cymbeline and exeunt. Then enter Lucius, Iachimo, and Imogen.

LUCIUS
Away, boy, from the troops, and save thyself,
For friends kill friends, and the disorder 's such

16   As war were hoodwinked.

IACHIMO   'Tis their fresh supplies.

LUCIUS
17   It is a day turned strangely; or betimes
Let's reinforce or fly.   *Exeunt.*

V, iii   *Enter Posthumus and a Briton Lord.*

LORD
Cam'st thou from where they made the stand?

POSTHUMUS   I did;
Though you, it seems, come from the fliers.

LORD   I did.

POSTHUMUS
No blame be to you, sir, for all was lost,
But that the heavens fought. The King himself
Of his wings destitute, the army broken,
And but the backs of Britons seen, all flying
7   Through a strait lane; the enemy full-hearted,
8   Lolling the tongue with slaught'ring, having work
More plentiful than tools to do't, struck down
10   Some mortally, some slightly touched, some falling
Merely through fear, that the strait pass was dammed
12   With dead men hurt behind, and cowards living
To die with length'ned shame.

LORD   Where was this lane?

POSTHUMUS
Close by the battle, ditched, and walled with turf;
Which gave advantage to an ancient soldier,
An honest one I warrant, who deserved
17   So long a breeding as his white beard came to,
In doing this for's country. Athwart the lane
19   He with two striplings – lads more like to run
The country base than to commit such slaughter;
21   With faces fit for masks, or rather fairer
22   Than those for preservation cased or shame –
Made good the passage, cried to those that fled,
'Our Britain's harts die flying, not our men.
25   To darkness fleet souls that fly backwards. Stand,
26   Or we are Romans and will give you that
27   Like beasts which you shun beastly, and may save
But to look back in frown. Stand, stand!' These three,
Three thousand confident, in act as many –
30   For three performers are the file when all
The rest do nothing – with this word 'Stand, stand,'
32   Accommodated by the place, more charming
With their own nobleness, which could have turned
34   A distaff to a lance, gilded pale looks,
35   Part shame, part spirit renewed; that some, turned coward
36   But by example – O, a sin in war,
37   Damned in the first beginners! – gan to look

The way that they did and to grin like lions   38
Upon the pikes o' th' hunters. Then began
A stop i' th' chaser, a retire; anon   40
A rout, confusion thick. Forthwith they fly
Chickens, the way which they stooped eagles; slaves,   42
The strides they victors made; and now our cowards,   43
Like fragments in hard voyages, became   44
The life o' th' need. Having found the backdoor open   45
Of the unguarded hearts, heavens, how they wound!
Some slain before, some dying, some their friends   47
O'erborne i' th' former wave, ten chased by one
Are now each one the slaughterman of twenty.
Those that would die or ere resist are grown   50
The mortal bugs o' th' field.   51

LORD   This was strange chance:
A narrow lane, an old man, and two boys.

POSTHUMUS
Nay, do not wonder at it. You are made
Rather to wonder at the things you hear
Than to work any. Will you rhyme upon't   55
And vent it for a mock'ry? Here is one: 56
'Two boys, an old man twice a boy, a lane,
Preserved the Britons, was the Romans' bane.'

LORD
Nay, be not angry, sir.

POSTHUMUS   'Lack, to what end?   59
Who dares not stand his foe, I'll be his friend;   60
For if he'll do as he is made to do,   61
I know he'll quickly fly my friendship too.
You have put me into rhyme.   63

LORD   Farewell. You're angry. *Exit.*

POSTHUMUS
Still going? This is a lord! O noble misery,   64
To be i' th' field, and ask 'What news?' of me!
To-day how many would have given their honors
To have saved their carcasses, took heel to do't,
And yet died too! I, in mine own woe charmed,   68
Could not find Death where I did hear him groan
Nor feel him where he struck. Being an ugly monster,
'Tis strange he hides him in fresh cups, soft beds,   71
Sweet words, or hath moe ministers than we   72

16 *hoodwinked* blindfolded   17 *or* either; *betimes* in time
V, iii   7 *strait* narrow; *full-hearted* with high morale   8 *Lolling* letting hang out   10 *touched* wounded   12 *behind* i.e. while running away   17 *breeding* life, support, cherishing   19–20 *run . . . base* play the game of prisoner's base   21 *fit for masks* delicate enough to justify protection against the sun   22 *for . . . shame* covered for such protection or for modesty   25 *fleet* hurry   26 *we are Romans* we shall play the part of Romans   27 *beastly* i.e. like cowards   27–28 *save . . . frown* prevent by looking back fiercely   30 *file* whole force   32 *Accommodated* given an advantage; *more charming* winning over others (to turn and fight)   34 *A distaff . . . lance* a housewife into a soldier; *gilded* restored color to   35 *Part . . . part* in some . . . in others   36 *by example* by imitating others   37 *gan* began   37–38 *look The way* face in the direction   38 *they* i.e. Belarius and his sons; *grin* i.e. bare the teeth   40 *chaser* pursuer; *retire* retreat   42 *Chickens* like chickens; *way* route; *stooped eagles* swooped over like eagles; *slaves* like slaves (they fly back over)   43 *victors* as victors   44 *fragments* i.e. of food   45 *life . . . need* support of life in time of need   45–46 *Having . . . hearts* i.e. having found that the Romans were not invulnerable   47 *slain* i.e. having played dead; *dying* i.e. severely wounded; *their friends* friends of those already mentioned   50 *or ere* rather than   51 *mortal bugs* deadly terrors (cf. 'bugbears')   55 *work any* perform such (things)   56 *vent it* air it, let it get around   59 *'Lack* alack, alas   60 *stand* withstand   61 *as . . . do* as it is natural for him to do   63 *put . . . rhyme* made me versify   64 *going* running away; *noble misery* wretchedness of a noble   68 *charmed* i.e. 'leading a charmed life'   71–72 *hides . . . words* i.e. appears from unexpected places   72 *moe* more

That draw his knives i' th' war. Well, I will find him,
74 For being now a favorer to the Briton,
No more a Briton. I have resumed again
76 The part I came in. Fight I will no more,
77 But yield me to the veriest hind that shall
78 Once touch my shoulder. Great the slaughter is
79 Here made by th' Roman ; great the answer be
Britons must take. For me, my ransom 's death.
81 On either side I come to spend my breath,
Which neither here I'll keep nor bear again,
But end it by some means for Imogen.
Enter two [Briton] Captains and Soldiers.

1. CAPTAIN
Great Jupiter be praised, Lucius is taken.
'Tis thought the old man and his sons were angels.

2. CAPTAIN
86 There was a fourth man, in a silly habit,
87 That gave th' affront with them.

1. CAPTAIN   So 'tis reported,
But none of 'em can be found. Stand, who's there ?

POSTHUMUS
A Roman,
90 Who had not now been drooping here if seconds
91 Had answered him.

2. CAPTAIN   Lay hands on him. A dog,
A leg of Rome shall not return to tell
What crows have pecked them here. He brags his service
As if he were of note. Bring him to th' King.
*Enter Cymbeline, Belarius, Guiderius, Arviragus,
Pisanio, and Roman Captives. The Captains present
Posthumus to Cymbeline, who delivers him over
to a jailer.   [Exeunt.]*

*

V, iv   *Enter Posthumus and [two] Jailer[s].*

1. JAILER
You shall not now be stol'n ; you have locks upon you.
So graze as you find pasture.

2. JAILER   Ay, or a stomach.
[Exeunt Jailers.]

POSTHUMUS
Most welcome, bondage, for thou art a way,
I think, to liberty. Yet am I better
Than one that's sick o' th' gout, since he had rather
Groan so in perpetuity than be cured

By th' sure physician, Death, who is the key
T' unbar these locks. My conscience, thou art fettered
More than my shanks and wrists. You good gods, give me
The penitent instrument to pick that bolt,   10
Then free for ever. Is't enough I am sorry ?   11
So children temporal fathers do appease ;   12
Gods are more full of mercy. Must I repent,
I cannot do it better than in gyves,   14
Desired more than constrained. To satisfy,   15
If of my freedom 'tis the main part, take   16
No stricter render of me than my all.   17
I know you are more clement than vile men,
Who of their broken debtors take a third,
A sixth, a tenth, letting them thrive again
On their abatement. That's not my desire.   21
For Imogen's dear life take mine ; and though
'Tis not so dear, yet 'tis a life ; you coined it.
'Tween man and man they weigh not every stamp ;   24
Though light, take pieces for the figure's sake ;   25
You rather mine, being yours. And so, great pow'rs,   26
If you will take this audit, take this life   27
And cancel these cold bonds. O Imogen,   28
I'll speak to thee in silence.
[Sleeps.]

*Solemn music. Enter, as in an apparition, Sicilius
Leonatus, father to Posthumus, an old man attired
like a warrior ; leading in his hand an ancient
Matron, his wife and mother to Posthumus, with
music before them. Then, after other music, follow
the two young Leonati, brothers to Posthumus, with
wounds as they died in the wars. They circle
Posthumus round as he lies sleeping.*

SICILIUS
No more, thou Thunder-master, show   30
Thy spite on mortal flies.
With Mars fall out, with Juno chide,
That thy adulteries   33
Rates and revenges.   34
Hath my poor boy done aught but well,
Whose face I never saw ?
I died whilst in the womb he stayed
Attending nature's law ;   38
Whose father then, as men report
Thou orphans' father art,
Thou shouldst have been, and shielded him
From this earth-vexing smart.   42

MOTHER
Lucina lent not me her aid,   43
But took me in my throes,
That from me was Posthumus ripped,
Came crying 'mongst his foes,
A thing of pity.

SICILIUS
Great Nature like his ancestry
Moulded the stuff so fair   49
That he deserved the praise o' th' world,
As great Sicilius' heir.

1. BROTHER When once he was mature for man,   52
In Britain where was he
That could stand up his parallel,
Or fruitful object be   55
In eye of Imogen, that best
Could deem his dignity ?   57

---

74 *being . . . favorer* death now favoring   76 *part . . . in* i.e. his role as a
Roman (as the way to find death, now helping the British by taking their
enemies)   77 *hind* peasant   78 *touch my shoulder* i.e. as sign of arrest
79 *answer* retaliation   81 *spend my breath* yield my life   86 *silly habit*
simple garb   87 *affront* attack   90 *seconds* supporters   91 *answered him*
acted as he did
V, iv A British stockade   10 *penitent . . . bolt* penitence to unfetter his
conscience   11 *free* i.e. in death   12 *So* i.e. by being sorry   14 *gyves*
fetters   15 *constrained* forced upon me ; *satisfy* atone   16 *If . . . part* if
it (atonement) is essential to my freedom (of conscience)   17 *stricter
render* sterner repayment ; *all* i.e. life   21 *abatement* reduced principal ;
That i.e. to *thrive again*   24 *stamp* coin   25 *figure's* i.e. of the royal
image on the coin   26 *You . . . yours* you more readily take my life (light
coin though it is) because you made it   27 *take* accept   28 *cold* heavy,
depressing   30 *Thunder-master* Jupiter   33 *That* who   34 *Rates* scolds
38 *Attending nature's law* awaiting the completion of the natural process
42 *earth-vexing smart* suffering that afflicts earthly life   43 *Lucina* goddess
of childbirth   49 *stuff* substance (cf. I, i, 23)   52 *mature for man* grown
up   55 *fruitful* fulfilling potentialities   57 *deem his dignity* judge his
worth

MOTHER With marriage wherefore was he mocked,
To be exiled and thrown
From Leonati seat and cast
From her his dearest one,
Sweet Imogen?

63 SICILIUS Why did you suffer Iachimo,
64 Slight thing of Italy,
65 To taint his nobler heart and brain
With needless jealousy,
67 And to become the geck and scorn
O' th' other's villainy?

69 2. BROTHER For this from stiller seats we came,
Our parents and us twain,
71 That striking in our country's cause
Fell bravely and were slain,
Our fealty and Tenantius' right
With honor to maintain.

75 1. BROTHER Like hardiment Posthumus hath
To Cymbeline performed.
Then, Jupiter, thou king of gods,
78 Why hast thou thus adjourned
The graces for his merits due,
80 Being all to dolors turned?

SICILIUS Thy crystal window ope; look out.
No longer exercise
Upon a valiant race thy harsh
And potent injuries.

MOTHER Since, Jupiter, our son is good,
86 Take off his miseries.

SICILIUS Peep through thy marble mansion. Help,
Or we poor ghosts will cry
89 To th' shining synod of the rest
Against thy deity.

BROTHERS Help, Jupiter, or we appeal
And from thy justice fly.

Jupiter descends in thunder and lightning, sitting upon an eagle. He throws a thunderbolt. The Ghosts fall on their knees.

JUPITER No more, you petty spirits of region low,
Offend our hearing. Hush! How dare you ghosts
Accuse the Thunderer, whose bolt, you know,
96 Sky-planted, batters all rebelling coasts?
Poor shadows of Elysium, hence, and rest
Upon your never-withering banks of flow'rs.
99 Be not with mortal accidents opprest.
No care of yours it is; you know 'tis ours.
Whom best I love I cross; to make my gift,
102 The more delayed, delighted. Be content.
Your low-laid son our godhead will uplift;
104 His comforts thrive, his trials well are spent.
105 Our Jovial star reigned at his birth, and in
Our temple was he married. Rise, and fade.
He shall be lord of Lady Imogen,
And happier much by his affliction made.
This tablet lay upon his breast, wherein
110 Our pleasure his full fortune doth confine.
And so, away; no farther with your din
Express impatience, lest you stir up mine.
Mount, eagle, to my palace crystalline. *Ascends.*

SICILIUS He came in thunder; his celestial breath
Was sulphurous to smell; the holy eagle
Stooped, as to foot us. His ascension is 116
More sweet than our blest fields; his royal bird 117
Prunes the immortal wing and cloys his beak, 118
As when his god is pleased.

ALL   Thanks, Jupiter.

SICILIUS The marble pavement closes; he is entered 120
His radiant roof. Away, and, to be blest,
Let us with care perform his great behest.
[The Ghosts] vanish.

POSTHUMUS *[waking]*
Sleep, thou hast been a grandsire and begot
A father to me, and thou hast created
A mother and two brothers; but, O scorn, 125
Gone! They went hence so soon as they were born.
And so I am awake. Poor wretches that depend
On greatness' favor, dream as I have done;
Wake, and find nothing. But, alas, I swerve. 129
Many dream not to find, neither deserve,
And yet are steeped in favors. So am I,
That have this golden chance and know not why.
What fairies haunt this ground? A book? O rare one, 133
Be not, as is our fangled world, a garment 134
Nobler than that it covers. Let thy effects 135
So follow to be most unlike our courtiers, 136
As good as promise.
Reads.
'When as a lion's whelp shall, to himself unknown, 138
without seeking find, and be embraced by a piece of 139
tender air; and when from a stately cedar shall be lopped
branches which, being dead many years, shall after
revive, be jointed to the old stock, and freshly grow;
then shall Posthumus end his miseries, Britain be for-
tunate and flourish in peace and plenty.'
'Tis still a dream, or else such stuff as madmen
Tongue, and brain not; either both, or nothing, 146
Or senseless speaking, or a speaking such 147
As sense cannot untie. Be what it is,
The action of my life is like it, which 149
I'll keep, if but for sympathy. 150
Enter Jailer.

JAILER Come, sir, are you ready for death?
POSTHUMUS Over-roasted rather; ready long ago.
JAILER Hanging is the word, sir. If you be ready for that, 153
you are well cooked.

63 *suffer* allow   64 *Slight* contemptible   65 *taint* infect   67 *geck* dupe 69 *stiller seats* quieter dwelling places (Elysium)   71 *That* who   75 *hardiment* courageous deeds   78 *adjourned* put off   80 *dolors* sorrows 86 *off* away   89 *synod . . . rest* assembly of the gods   96 *Sky-planted* growing in the sky, based in the sky   99 *accidents* events   102 *delighted* (the more) delighted in   104 *spent* ended   105 *Jovial star* planet Jupiter, supposed to bring good fortune   110 *confine* set down concisely   116 *Stooped . . . foot* swooped as if to seize (with claws)   117 *More sweet* i.e. in contrast with the sulphurous descent   118 *Prunes* trims; *cloys* claws   120 *marble pavement* i.e. heaven   125 *O scorn* what a bitter joke 129 *swerve* err (cf. 'I'm off the track')   133 *book* i.e. the *tablet* of l. 109 134 *fangled* dressy, fancy   135 *effects* fulfillment   136 *to* as to   138 *When as* when   139 *piece* creature, morsel   146 *Tongue* say; *brain* understand   147 *senseless* irrational   147–48 *such . . . untie* too cryptic for rational analysis   149 *like it* i.e. in being difficult to understand   150 *sympathy* resemblance   153 *Hanging* (pun on death by hanging and hanging up of meat)

POSTHUMUS So, if I prove a good repast to the specta-
156 tors, the dish pays the shot.

JAILER A heavy reckoning for you, sir. But the comfort is,
you shall be called to no more payments, fear no more
159 tavern bills, which are often the sadness of parting, as
the procuring of mirth. You come in faint for want of
meat, depart reeling with too much drink; sorry that
162 you have paid too much, and sorry that you are paid too
much; purse and brain both empty; the brain the heavi-
164 er for being too light, the purse too light, being drawn of
heaviness. O, of this contradiction you shall now be quit.
166 O, the charity of a penny cord! It sums up thousands in
167 a trice. You have no true debitor and creditor but it; of
168 what's past, is, and to come, the discharge. Your neck, sir,
169 is pen, book, and counters; so the acquittance follows.

170 POSTHUMUS I am merrier to die than thou art to live.

JAILER Indeed, sir, he that sleeps feels not the toothache;
172 but a man that were to sleep your sleep, and a hangman
to help him to bed, I think he would change places with
174 his officer; for look you, sir, you know not which way
you shall go.

POSTHUMUS Yes indeed do I, fellow.

JAILER Your death has eyes in's head then. I have not
178 seen him so pictured. You must either be directed by
179 some that take upon them to know, or to take upon
180 yourself that which I am sure you do not know, or jump
181 the after-inquiry on your own peril. And how you shall
182 speed in your journey's end, I think you'll never return
to tell one.

POSTHUMUS I tell thee, fellow, there are none want eyes
185 to direct them the way I am going but such as wink and
will not use them.

187 JAILER What an infinite mock is this, that a man should
have the best use of eyes to see the way of blindness! I
am sure hanging's the way of winking.

Enter a Messenger.

MESSENGER Knock off his manacles; bring your prisoner
to the King.

POSTHUMUS Thou bring'st good news; I am called to be
193 made free.

JAILER I'll be hanged then.

POSTHUMUS Thou shalt be then freer than a jailer. No
bolts for the dead. *Exeunt [Posthumus and Messenger].*

JAILER Unless a man would marry a gallows and beget
198 young gibbets, I never saw one so prone. Yet, on my
conscience, there are verier knaves desire to live, for all
he be a Roman; and there be some of them too that die
against their wills. So should I, if I were one. I would we

were all of one mind, and one mind good. O, there were
desolation of jailers and gallowses! I speak against my
present profit, but my wish hath a preferment in't.   204
[Exit.]

*

Enter Cymbeline, Belarius, Guiderius, Arviragus,   V, v
Pisanio, and Lords.

CYMBELINE
Stand by my side, you whom the gods have made
Preservers of my throne. Woe is my heart
That the poor soldier that so richly fought,
Whose rags shamed gilded arms, whose naked breast
Stepped before targes of proof, cannot be found.   5
He shall be happy that can find him, if
Our grace can make him so.

BELARIUS   I never saw
Such noble fury in so poor a thing,
Such precious deeds in one that promised naught   9
But beggary and poor looks.

CYMBELINE   No tidings of him?

PISANIO
He hath been searched among the dead and living,
But no trace of him.

CYMBELINE   To my grief, I am
The heir of his reward, *[to Belarius, Guiderius, and Ar-*
viragus] which I will add
To you, the liver, heart, and brain of Britain,   14
By whom I grant she lives. 'Tis now the time   15
To ask of whence you are. Report it.

BELARIUS   Sir,
In Cambria are we born, and gentlemen.
Further to boast were neither true nor modest,
Unless I add we are honest.

CYMBELINE   Bow your knees.
Arise my knights o' th' battle; I create you   20
Companions to our person and will fit you   21
With dignities becoming your estates.   22

Enter Cornelius and Ladies.

There's business in these faces. Why so sadly   23
Greet you our victory? You look like Romans
And not o' th' court of Britain.

CORNELIUS   Hail, great King!
To sour your happiness I must report
The Queen is dead.

CYMBELINE   Who worse than a physician   27
Would this report become? But I consider
By med'cine life may be prolonged, yet death
Will seize the doctor too. How ended she?

CORNELIUS
With horror, madly dying, like her life,
Which, being cruel to the world, concluded
Most cruel to herself. What she confessed
I will report, so please you. These her women
Can trip me if I err, who with wet cheeks   35
Were present when she finished.

CYMBELINE   Prithee say.

CORNELIUS
First, she confessed she never loved you, only
Affected greatness got by you, not you;   38
Married your royalty, was wife to your place,
Abhorred your person.   40

CYMBELINE   She alone knew this,

156 *dish* food; *shot* reckoning   159 *often* as often   162 *are paid* are paid
off, punished (by too much liquor)   164 *drawn* emptied   166 *cord* i.e.
for hanging   167 *debitor and creditor* accountant   168 *discharge* payment
169 *counters* round pieces of metal used for reckoning; *acquittance* receipt
170 *to die . . . to live* in dying . . . in living   172 *a man that were* as for
a man scheduled   174 *officer* i.e. the hangman   178 *so pictured* i.e. in the
conventional skull representing death   179 *some clergy* (?)   179–80 *take*
upon yourself decide for yourself (on your salvation)   180 *jump* gamble on
181 *after-inquiry* final judgment   182 *speed in* make out at   185 *wink*
close   187 *mock* joke   193 *made free* i.e. by death   198 *prone* inclined (to
die)   204 *hath . . . in't* includes a better position for myself
V, v The camp of King Cymbeline   5 *targes of proof* shields of proved
strength   9 *promised* offered, presented   14 *the liver . . . brain* who are the
vital parts   15 *she* Britain   20 *knights . . . battle* knights created on the
battlefield (cf. 'battlefield commission')   21 *fit* equip   22 *estates* status
as knights   23 *There's . . . faces* i.e. their looks show that these persons
have something important to tell   27 *Who* (for 'whom')   35 *trip* stop,
catch   38 *Affected* desired, loved   40 *your* you as a

41 And but she spoke it dying, I would not
42 Believe her lips in opening it. Proceed.

CORNELIUS
43 Your daughter, whom she bore in hand to love
With such integrity, she did confess
Was as a scorpion to her sight, whose life,
But that her flight prevented it, she had
47 Ta'en off by poison.

CYMBELINE   O most delicate fiend!
Who is't can read a woman? Is there more?

CORNELIUS
More, sir, and worse. She did confess she had
50 For you a mortal mineral, which, being took,
51 Should by the minute feed on life and, ling'ring,
52 By inches waste you. In which time she purposed,
53 By watching, weeping, tendance, kissing, to
54 O'ercome you with her show and, in time,
55 When she had fitted you with her craft, to work
56 Her son into th' adoption of the crown;
But failing of her end by his strange absence,
Grew shameless desperate, opened, in despite
59 Of heaven and men, her purposes, repented
The evils she hatched were not effected, so
Despairing died.

CYMBELINE   Heard you all this, her women?

LADY
We did, so please your Highness.

CYMBELINE   Mine eyes
Were not in fault, for she was beautiful;
Mine ears, that heard her flattery; nor my heart,
65 That thought her like her seeming. It had been vicious
To have mistrusted her. Yet, O my daughter,
67 That it was folly in me thou mayst say,
68 And prove it in thy feeling. Heaven mend all!

Enter Lucius, Iachimo, [the Soothsayer,] and other
Roman Prisoners, [Posthumus] Leonatus behind,
and Imogen.

Thou com'st not, Caius, now for tribute. That
70 The Britons have razed out, though with the loss
Of many a bold one; whose kinsmen have made suit
72 That their good souls may be appeased with slaughter
Of you their captives, which ourself have granted.
74 So think of your estate.

LUCIUS
Consider, sir, the chance of war. The day
76 Was yours by accident; had it gone with us,
We should not, when the blood was cool, have threatened
Our prisoners with the sword. But since the gods
Will have it thus, that nothing but our lives
May be called ransom, let it come. Sufficeth
A Roman with a Roman's heart can suffer.
Augustus lives to think on't – and so much
83 For my peculiar care. This one thing only
I will entreat: my boy, a Briton born,
Let him be ransomed. Never master had
A page so kind, so duteous, diligent,
87 So tender over his occasions, true,
88 So feat, so nurse-like. Let his virtue join
With my request, which I'll make bold your Highness
Cannot deny. He hath done no Briton harm,
Though he have served a Roman. Save him, sir,
92 And spare no blood beside.

CYMBELINE   I have surely seen him;
93 His favor is familiar to me. Boy,

Thou hast looked thyself into my grace   94
And art mine own. I know not why, wherefore,   95
To say 'Live, boy.' Ne'er thank thy master. Live,
And ask of Cymbeline what boon thou wilt,
Fitting my bounty and thy state; I'll give it,   98
Yea, though thou do demand a prisoner,
The noblest ta'en.

IMOGEN   I humbly thank your Highness.

LUCIUS
I do not bid thee beg my life, good lad,
And yet I know thou wilt.

IMOGEN   No, no, alack,
There's other work in hand. I see a thing   103
Bitter to me as death; your life, good master,
Must shuffle for itself.   105

LUCIUS   The boy disdains me;
He leaves me, scorns me. Briefly die their joys   106
That place them on the truth of girls and boys.   107
Why stands he so perplexed?   108

CYMBELINE   What wouldst thou, boy?
I love thee more and more. Think more and more
What's best to ask. Know'st him thou look'st on? Speak.
Wilt have him live? Is he thy kin? Thy friend?

IMOGEN
He is a Roman, no more kin to me
Than I to your Highness; who, being born your vassal,
Am something nearer.   114

CYMBELINE   Wherefore ey'st him so?

IMOGEN
I'll tell you, sir, in private, if you please
To give me hearing.

CYMBELINE   Ay, with all my heart,
And lend my best attention. What's thy name?

IMOGEN
Fidele, sir.

CYMBELINE Thou'rt my good youth, my page;
I'll be thy master. Walk with me; speak freely.

[Cymbeline and Imogen talk apart.]

BELARIUS
Is not this boy revived from death?

ARVIRAGUS   One sand another
Not more resembles that sweet rosy lad   121
Who died, and was Fidele. What think you?

GUIDERIUS
The same dead thing alive.

BELARIUS
Peace, peace, see further. He eyes us not; forbear.

---

41 *but* but for the fact that   42 *opening* disclosing   43 *bore in hand* pretended   47 *Ta'en off* destroyed; *delicate* subtle   50 *mortal mineral* deadly poison   51 *by the minute* minute by minute   52 *waste* consume, destroy   53 *tendance* attentiveness   54 *show* pretense (of devotion)   55 *fitted* shaped to her purpose   56 *adoption of* adoption by you as heir to   59 *repented* was bitterly sorry because   65 *seeming* appearance; *had been vicious* would have been a fault   67 *it* i.e. trusting her   68 *prove* experience; *feeling* suffering   70 *razed out* erased   72 *their* i.e. of those lost in battle   74 *estate* spiritual state   76 *had ... us* had we won   83 *my peculiar care* care for myself   87 *tender ... occasions* sensitive to his (master's)   88 *feat* skillful   92 *no blood beside* the blood of no one else   93 *favor* face   94 *looked ... grace* by your looks secured my mercy   95 *I ... wherefore* (cf. 'I don't know why I'm doing it'; hence, 'You need not thank Lucius')   98 *Fitting* appropriate to   103 *thing* (cf. ll. 135–36)   105 *shuffle* make out as best it can   106 *Briefly* soon   106–07 *their joys That* the joys of those who   107 *place ... truth* make them depend on the fidelity   108 *perplexed* troubled   114 *something nearer* somewhat closer (to you than he is to me)   121 *Not ... lad* (unusually elliptical; some words may be lost)

Creatures may be alike. Were't he, I am sure
He would have spoke to us.
126 GUIDERIUS   But we see him dead.
BELARIUS
Be silent; let's see further.
PISANIO [aside]   It is my mistress.
Since she is living, let the time run on
To good or bad.
          [Cymbeline and Imogen advance.]
CYMBELINE   Come, stand thou by our side;
Make thy demand aloud. [to Iachimo] Sir, step you forth,
Give answer to this boy, and do it freely;
132 Or, by our greatness and the grace of it,
Which is our honor, bitter torture shall
Winnow the truth from falsehood. – On, speak to him.
IMOGEN
135 My boon is that this gentleman may render
Of whom he had this ring.
POSTHUMUS [aside]   What's that to him?
CYMBELINE
That diamond upon your finger, say
How came it yours.
IACHIMO
139 Thou'lt torture me to leave unspoken that
Which to be spoke would torture thee.
CYMBELINE   How? Me?
IACHIMO
I am glad to be constrained to utter that
Which torments me to conceal. By villainy
I got this ring. 'Twas Leonatus' jewel,
Whom thou didst banish, and – which more may grieve thee,
As it doth me – a nobler sir ne'er lived
'Twixt sky and ground. Wilt thou hear more, my lord?
CYMBELINE
All that belongs to this.
IACHIMO   That paragon, thy daughter,
For whom my heart drops blood and my false spirits
Quail to remember – Give me leave; I faint.
CYMBELINE
My daughter? What of her? Renew thy strength.
151 I had rather thou shouldst live while nature will
Than die ere I hear more. Strive, man, and speak.
IACHIMO
Upon a time – unhappy was the clock
That struck the hour! – it was in Rome – accursed

The mansion where! – 'twas at a feast – O, would
Our viands had been poisoned, or at least
Those which I heaved to head! – the good Posthumus – 157
What should I say? He was too good to be
Where ill men were, and was the best of all
Amongst the rar'st of good ones – sitting sadly,
Hearing us praise our loves of Italy
For beauty that made barren the swelled boast   162
Of him that best could speak; for feature, laming   163
The shrine of Venus or straight-pight Minerva,   164
Postures beyond brief nature; for condition,   165
A shop of all the qualities that man   166
Loves woman for; besides that hook of wiving,   167
Fairness which strikes the eye –
CYMBELINE   I stand on fire.
Come to the matter.   169
IACHIMO   All too soon I shall,
Unless thou wouldst grieve quickly. This Posthumus,
Most like a noble lord in love and one
That had a royal lover, took his hint,   172
And not dispraising whom we praised – therein
He was as calm as virtue – he began
His mistress' picture; which by his tongue being made,
And then a mind put in't, either our brags   176
Were cracked of kitchen trulls, or his description 177
Proved us unspeaking sots.   178
CYMBELINE   Nay, nay, to th' purpose.
IACHIMO
Your daughter's chastity – there it begins.
He spake of her as Dian had hot dreams   180
And she alone were cold; whereat I, wretch,   181
Made scruple of his praise and wagered with him   182
Pieces of gold 'gainst this which then he wore
Upon his honored finger, to attain
In suit the place of's bed and win this ring   185
By hers and mine adultery. He, true knight,
No lesser of her honor confident
Than I did truly find her, stakes this ring;
And would so, had it been a carbuncle   189
Of Phoebus' wheel, and might so safely, had it   190
Been all the worth of's car. Away to Britain
Post I in this design. Well may you, sir,   192
Remember me at court, where I was taught
Of your chaste daughter the wide difference   194
'Twixt amorous and villainous. Being thus quenched 195
Of hope, not longing, mine Italian brain
Gan in your duller Britain operate   197
Most vilely; for my vantage, excellent.   198
And, to be brief, my practice so prevailed   199
That I returned with simular proof enough   200
To make the noble Leonatus mad
By wounding his belief in her renown   202
With tokens thus and thus; averring notes   203
Of chamber hanging, pictures, this her bracelet –
O cunning, how I got it! – nay, some marks
Of secret on her person, that he could not
But think her bond of chastity quite cracked,   207
I having ta'en the forfeit. Whereupon –   208
Methinks I see him now –
POSTHUMUS [advancing]   Ay, so thou dost,
Italian fiend! Ay me, most credulous fool,
Egregious murderer, thief, anything   211
That's due to all the villains past, in being,
To come! O, give me cord or knife or poison,

126 But . . . dead unless we see him dead (?), but what we see is a ghost (?)
132–33 grace . . . honor our honor, which embellishes (our greatness)
135 render tell   139 to leave for leaving   151 while nature will i.e. your
natural life   157 heaved to head raised to mouth   162 made . . . boast
rendered even an exaggerated boast powerless (to express)   163 feature
figure; laming making a cripple of   164 shrine image; straight-pight erect
165 Postures . . . nature; beyond brief nature of immortal beings (?), more
enduring (as art) than natural beings (?); condition character   166 shop
store   167 hook i.e. fishhook; of wiving for marriage   169 matter point
172 lover woman in love with him; hint opportunity   176 mind put in't
i.e. she had brains as well as beauty   177 cracked of boasted about; trulls
wenches   178 unspeaking sots inarticulate fools; to th' purpose (keep) to
the point   180 as as if; hot lecherous   181 cold chaste   182 Made scruple
of stated disbelief in   185 In suit by wooing   189 would so would have
done so   190 Phoebus' wheel i.e. wheel on the sun's chariot; might so
might have done so   192 Post hurry   194 Of by   195 amorous faithful
love   195–96 quenched Of cooled off in   197 duller Britain (northern
countries supposedly produced slower minds)   198 vantage profit   199
practice scheming   200 simular simulated   202 renown good name   203
averring notes affirming the marks   207 cracked broken   208 ta'en the forfeit
gained what was forfeited (by breach of bond)   211 anything i.e. any name

214 Some upright justicer! Thou, King, send out
For torturers ingenious. It is I
216 That all th' abhorrèd things o' th' earth amend
By being worse than they. I am Posthumus,
That killed thy daughter – villain-like, I lie –
That caused a lesser villain than myself,
A sacrilegious thief, to do't. The temple
221 Of virtue was she; yea, and she herself.
Spit, and throw stones, cast mire upon me, set
The dogs o' th' street to bay me; every villain
Be called Posthumus Leonatus, and
225 Be villainy less than 'twas! O Imogen!
My queen, my life, my wife! O Imogen,
Imogen, Imogen!

IMOGEN   Peace, my lord. Hear, hear –

POSTHUMUS
228 Shall's have a play of this? Thou scornful page,
229 There lie thy part.

[Thrusts her away; she falls.]

PISANIO   O gentlemen, help!
Mine and your mistress! O my lord Posthumus,
You ne'er killed Imogen till now. Help, help!
Mine honored lady!

CYMBELINE   Does the world go round?

POSTHUMUS
233 How come these staggers on me?

PISANIO   Wake, my mistress!

CYMBELINE
If this be so, the gods do mean to strike me
235 To death with mortal joy.

PISANIO   How fares my mistress?

IMOGEN
O, get thee from my sight;
Thou gav'st me poison. Dangerous fellow, hence;
Breathe not where princes are.

238 CYMBELINE   The tune of Imogen!

PISANIO
Lady,
240 The gods throw stones of sulphur on me if
That box I gave you was not thought by me
242 A precious thing; I had it from the Queen.

CYMBELINE
243 New matter still.

IMOGEN   It poisoned me.

CORNELIUS   O gods!
I left out one thing which the Queen confessed,
245 Which must approve thee honest. 'If Pisanio
246 Have,' said she, 'given his mistress that confection
Which I gave him for cordial, she is served
As I would serve a rat.'

CYMBELINE   What's this, Cornelius?

CORNELIUS
The Queen, sir, very oft importuned me
250 To temper poisons for her, still pretending
The satisfaction of her knowledge only
In killing creatures vile, as cats and dogs
253 Of no esteem. I, dreading that her purpose
254 Was of more danger, did compound for her
255 A certain stuff which, being ta'en, would cease
The present pow'r of life, but in short time
257 All offices of nature should again
Do their due functions. Have you ta'en of it?

IMOGEN
259 Most like I did, for I was dead.

BELARIUS   My boys,
There was our error.

GUIDERIUS   This is sure Fidele.

IMOGEN
Why did you throw your wedded lady from you?
Think that you are upon a rock, and now   262
Throw me again.   263

[Embraces him.]

POSTHUMUS   Hang there like fruit, my soul,
Till the tree die!

CYMBELINE   How now, my flesh, my child?
What, mak'st thou me a dullard in this act?   265
Wilt thou not speak to me?

IMOGEN *[kneeling]*   Your blessing, sir.

BELARIUS *[to Guiderius and Arviragus]*
Though you did love this youth, I blame ye not;
You had a motive for't.   268

CYMBELINE   My tears that fall
Prove holy water on thee. Imogen,
Thy mother's dead.

IMOGEN   I am sorry for't, my lord.

CYMBELINE
O, she was naught, and long of her it was   271
That we meet here so strangely; but her son
Is gone, we know not how nor where.

PISANIO   My lord,
Now fear is from me, I'll speak troth. Lord Cloten,   274
Upon my lady's missing, came to me
With his sword drawn, foamed at the mouth, and swore,
If I discovered not which way she was gone,   277
It was my instant death. By accident
I had a feignèd letter of my master's   279
Then in my pocket, which directed him
To seek her on the mountains near to Milford;
Where, in a frenzy, in my master's garments,
Which he enforced from me, away he posts
With unchaste purpose and with oath to violate
My lady's honor. What became of him
I further know not.

GUIDERIUS   Let me end the story:
I slew him there.

CYMBELINE   Marry, the gods forfend!   287
I would not thy good deeds should from my lips   288
Pluck a hard sentence. Prithee, valiant youth,
Deny't again.   290

GUIDERIUS   I have spoke it, and I did it.

CYMBELINE
He was a prince.

---

214 *justicer* judge   216 *amend* make (seem) better   221 *she herself* virtue herself   225 *Be . . . 'twas* i.e. I have made other villainies seem smaller   228 *Shall's* shall we   229 *There . . . part* lying there is your role   233 *staggers* dizziness, agitation   235 *mortal* fatal   238 *tune* voice   240 *stones of sulphur* thunderbolts   242 *precious* beneficial   243 *matter* developments   245 *approve* prove; *honest* truthful   246 *confection* mixture   250 *temper* mix; *pretending* alleging as her purpose   253 *esteem* value   254 *of more danger* more harmful   255 *cease* cut off   257 *offices of nature* bodily parts   259 *like* probably; *dead* as if dead   262 *rock* i.e. firm ground (?) (sometimes emended to 'lock' and explained as a metaphor from wrestling)   263 *Throw me again* i.e. if you can (we are now inseparable)   265 *dullard* i.e. by ignoring me (and giving me no lines to speak); *act* perhaps, play (cf. ll. 228–29)   268 *motive* cause   271 *naught* evil; *long of* because of   274 *troth* truth   277 *discovered* revealed   279 *letter* (cf. III, v, 99–100)   287 *forfend* forbid   288 *thy good deeds* (that after) thy good deeds (against the Romans, thou)   290 *again* against (what you have just said)

GUIDERIUS
A most incivil one. The wrongs he did me
Were nothing princelike, for he did provoke me
With language that would make me spurn the sea
If it could so roar to me. I cut off's head,
And am right glad he is not standing here
297 To tell this tale of mine.
CYMBELINE   I am sorrow for thee.
By thine own tongue thou art condemned and must
Endure our law. Thou'rt dead.
IMOGEN   That headless man
I thought had been my lord.
CYMBELINE   Bind the offender
And take him from our presence.
BELARIUS   Stay, sir King.
This man is better than the man he slew,
As well descended as thyself, and hath
More of thee merited than a band of Clotens
305 Had ever scar for. [to the Guard] Let his arms alone;
They were not born for bondage.
CYMBELINE   Why, old soldier,
Wilt thou undo the worth thou art unpaid for
By tasting of our wrath? How of descent
As good as we?
ARVIRAGUS   In that he spake too far.
CYMBELINE
310 And thou shalt die for't.
BELARIUS   We will die all three
311 But I will prove that two on's are as good
As I have given out him. My sons, I must
313 For mine own part unfold a dangerous speech,
Though haply well for you.
ARVIRAGUS   Your danger's ours.
GUIDERIUS
And our good his.
315 BELARIUS   Have at it then. By leave,
Thou hadst, great King, a subject who
Was called Belarius.
CYMBELINE   What of him? He is
A banished traitor.
BELARIUS   He it is that hath
319 Assumed this age; indeed a banished man,
I know not how a traitor.
CYMBELINE   Take him hence.
The whole world shall not save him.
321 BELARIUS   Not too hot.
First pay me for the nursing of thy sons,
323 And let it be confiscate all, so soon
As I have received it.
CYMBELINE   Nursing of my sons?

BELARIUS
I am too blunt and saucy; here's my knee.   325
Ere I arise I will prefer my sons;   326
Then spare not the old father. Mighty sir,
These two young gentlemen that call me father
And think they are my sons are none of mine;
They are the issue of your loins, my liege,
And blood of your begetting.
CYMBELINE   How? My issue?
BELARIUS
So sure as you your father's. I, old Morgan,
Am that Belarius whom you sometime banished.   333
Your pleasure was my mere offense, my punishment   334
Itself, and all my treason; that I suffered
Was all the harm I did. These gentle princes –
For such and so they are – these twenty years
Have I trained up; those arts they have as I   338
Could put into them. My breeding was, sir, as
Your Highness knows. Their nurse, Euriphile,
Whom for the theft I wedded, stole these children
Upon my banishment. I moved her to't,   342
Having received the punishment before
For that which I did then. Beaten for loyalty   344
Excited me to treason. Their dear loss,
The more of you 'twas felt, the more it shaped   346
Unto my end of stealing them. But, gracious sir,
Here are your sons again, and I must lose
Two of the sweet'st companions in the world.
The benediction of these covering heavens
Fall on their heads like dew, for they are worthy
To inlay heaven with stars.
CYMBELINE   Thou weep'st and speak'st.
The service that you three have done is more   353
Unlike than this thou tell'st. I lost my children;   354
If these be they, I know not how to wish
A pair of worthier sons.
BELARIUS   Be pleased awhile.
This gentleman whom I call Polydore,
Most worthy prince, as yours, is true Guiderius;
This gentleman, my Cadwal, Arviragus,
Your younger princely son. He, sir, was lapped   360
In a most curious mantle, wrought by th' hand   361
Of his queen mother, which for more probation   362
I can with ease produce.
CYMBELINE   Guiderius had
Upon his neck a mole, a sanguine star;   364
It was a mark of wonder.
BELARIUS   This is he,
Who hath upon him still that natural stamp.
It was wise Nature's end in the donation   367
To be his evidence now.   368
CYMBELINE   O, what am I?
A mother to the birth of three? Ne'er mother
Rejoiced deliverance more. Blest pray you be,
That, after this strange starting from your orbs,   371
You may reign in them now! O Imogen,
Thou hast lost by this a kingdom.
IMOGEN   No, my lord,
I have got two worlds by't. O my gentle brothers,
Have we thus met? O, never say hereafter
But I am truest speaker. You called me brother
When I was but your sister, I you brothers
When we were so indeed.
CYMBELINE   Did you e'er meet?

---

297 tell ... mine i.e. report that he cut off my head; sorrow (a possible
idiom; some editors emend to 'sorry') 305 Had ... for earned by battle
wounds 310 thou i.e. Belarius 311 But unless 313 For ... speech
make an explanatory statement dangerous to myself 315 Have at it let's
go ahead; By leave by your permission 319 Assumed this age taken
on this look of age 321 hot hasty 323 it the payment 325 saucy direct,
'fresh' 326 prefer advance 333 sometime once 334-35 Your ...
treason my whole offense, etc., existed only because it pleased you (to
declare them) 338 arts accomplishments 342 moved incited 344
Beaten being beaten 346 of by 346-47 shaped ... of served my end in
353 service i.e. in battle 354 Unlike improbable 360 lapped wrapped
361 curious artfully wrought 362 probation proof 364 sanguine blood-
red 367 end purpose; donation endowing (him with the mark) 368 his
evidence evidence of his identity 371 orbs orbits

ARVIRAGUS

  Ay, my good lord.

GUIDERIUS   And at first meeting loved,

  Continued so until we thought he died.

CORNELIUS

  By the Queen's dram she swallowed.

CYMBELINE   O rare instinct!

382   When shall I hear all through? This fierce abridgment

383   Hath to it circumstantial branches, which

  Distinction should be rich in. Where, how lived you?

  And when came you to serve our Roman captive?

  How parted with your brothers? How first met them?

  Why fled you from the court? And whither? These,

388   And your three motives to the battle, with

  I know not how much more, should be demanded,

390   And all the other by-dependences

391   From chance to chance; but nor the time nor place

392   Will serve our long interrogatories. See,

  Posthumus anchors upon Imogen,

  And she like harmless lightning throws her eye

  On him, her brothers, me, her master, hitting

396   Each object with a joy; the counterchange

397   Is severally in all. Let's quit this ground

398   And smoke the temple with our sacrifices.

    [To Belarius]

399   Thou art my brother; so we'll hold thee ever.

IMOGEN

400   You are my father too, and did relieve me

401   To see this gracious season.

CYMBELINE   All o'erjoyed

  Save these in bonds; let them be joyful too,

403   For they shall taste our comfort.

IMOGEN   My good master,

  I will yet do you service.

LUCIUS   Happy be you!

CYMBELINE

405   The forlorn soldier, that so nobly fought,

  He would have well becomed this place and graced

  The thankings of a king.

POSTHUMUS   I am, sir,

  The soldier that did company these three

409   In poor beseeming; 'twas a fitment for

410   The purpose I then followed. That I was he,

  Speak, Iachimo. I had you down and might

412   Have made you finish.

IACHIMO *[kneeling]*   I am down again,

413   But now my heavy conscience sinks my knee,

  As then your force did. Take that life, beseech you,

415   Which I so often owe; but your ring first,

  And here the bracelet of the truest princess

  That ever swore her faith.

POSTHUMUS   Kneel not to me.

  The pow'r that I have on you is to spare you;

  The malice towards you to forgive you. Live,

  And deal with others better.

420 CYMBELINE   Nobly doomed!

421   We'll learn our freeness of a son-in-law:

  Pardon's the word to all.

ARVIRAGUS   You holp us, sir,

  As you did mean indeed to be our brother.

424   Joyed are we that you are.

POSTHUMUS

  Your servant, princes. Good my lord of Rome,

  Call forth your soothsayer. As I slept, methought

  Great Jupiter, upon his eagle backed,   427

  Appeared to me, with other spritely shows   428

  Of mine own kindred. When I waked, I found

  This label on my bosom, whose containing   430

  Is so from sense in hardness that I can   431

  Make no collection of it. Let him show   432

  His skill in the construction.   433

LUCIUS   Philarmonus!

SOOTHSAYER

  Here, my good lord.

LUCIUS   Read, and declare the meaning.

SOOTHSAYER *[reads]* 'When as a lion's whelp shall, to

  himself unknown, without seeking find, and be em-

  braced by a piece of tender air; and when from a stately

  cedar shall be lopped branches which, being dead many

  years, shall after revive, be jointed to the old stock, and

  freshly grow; then shall Posthumus end his miseries,

  Britain be fortunate and flourish in peace and plenty.'

    [To Leonatus]

  Thou, Leonatus, art the lion's whelp;

  The fit and apt construction of thy name,

  Being *Leo-natus,* doth import so much.   444

    [To Cymbeline]

  The piece of tender air, thy virtuous daughter,

  Which we call 'mollis aer,' and 'mollis aer'   446

  We term it 'mulier'; which 'mulier' I divine

  Is this most constant wife, who even now

  Answering the letter of the oracle,   449

    [To Posthumus]

  Unknown to you, unsought, were clipped about   450

  With this most tender air.

CYMBELINE   This hath some seeming.   451

SOOTHSAYER

  The lofty cedar, royal Cymbeline,

  Personates thee, and thy lopped branches point   453

  Thy two sons forth; who, by Belarius stol'n,

  For many years thought dead, are now revived,

  To the majestic cedar joined, whose issue   456

  Promises Britain peace and plenty.

CYMBELINE   Well,

  My peace we will begin. And, Caius Lucius,

  Although the victor, we submit to Caesar

  And to the Roman empire, promising

  To pay our wonted tribute, from the which

  We were dissuaded by our wicked queen,

---

382 *fierce abridgment* extraordinary pastime 383 *branches* ramifications, details 383–84 *which . . . in* which, as they are distinguished, should be plentiful 388 *your three motives* what impelled you three 390 *by-dependences* related matters 391 *chance* happening 392 *Will serve* are suited to 396 *counterchange* exchange 397 *Is . . . all* i.e. all engage in it, each according to his relationship to the others 398 *smoke* fill with incense 399 *hold* regard 400 *You* i.e. Belarius; *relieve* aid 401 *gracious season* joyful occasion 403 *taste our comfort* share in our well-being 405 *forlorn* missing 409 *beseeming* appearance (i.e. garb); *fitment for* garb fitted for 410 *followed* was carrying out 412 *finish* die 413 *sinks makes bend* 415 *often* many times (because of the extent of my misdeeds) 420 *doomed* judged 421 *freeness* generosity 424 *you are* i.e. our brother 427 *upon . . . backed* on the back of his eagle 428 *spritely shows* ghostly visions 430 *label* piece of paper; *containing* contents 431 *from . . . hardness* hard to understand 432 *collection* elucidation 433 *construction* construing, interpreting (of it) 444 *Leo-natus* lion-born; *import* mean, imply 446 *mollis aer* tender air (a supposed origin of *mulier,* woman) 449 *Answering* according to 450 *were clipped about* i.e. you were embraced (the passage is grammatically incoherent) 451 *seeming* plausibility 453 *Personates* stands for 453–54 *point . . . forth* indicate 456 *issue* descendants

463 Whom heavens in justice, both on her and hers,
Have laid most heavy hand.

SOOTHSAYER
The fingers of the pow'rs above do tune
466 The harmony of this peace. The vision
Which I made known to Lucius ere the stroke
Of this yet scarce-cold battle, at this instant
Is full accomplished; for the Roman eagle,
From south to west on wing soaring aloft,
Lessened herself and in the beams o' th' sun

So vanished; which foreshowed our princely eagle,
Th' imperial Caesar, should again unite
His favor with the radiant Cymbeline,
Which shines here in the west.

CYMBELINE   Laud we the gods,   475
And let our crooked smokes climb to their nostrils   476
From our blest altars. Publish we this peace
To all our subjects. Set we forward; let   478
A Roman and a British ensign wave
Friendly together. So through Lud's town march,
And in the temple of great Jupiter
Our peace we'll ratify, seal it with feasts.
Set on there! Never was a war did cease,   483
Ere bloody hands were washed, with such a peace.

Exeunt.

---

463 *Whom* on whom; *hers* i.e. Cloten   466 *vision* (cf. IV, ii, 346 ff.)   475 *Laud* praise   476 *crooked* curling   478 *Set we forward* let us march   483 *Set on there* forward march

THE WINTER'S TALE

INTRODUCTION

For the story presented in *The Winter's Tale* no more appropriate title could have been chosen. It is a story such as might have been often told to while away a winter's evening, a story to be heard and reheard with ever increasing pleasure, its very improbabilities and even its geographical and historical inaccuracies being not, as often assumed, the defects of carelessness, but charming if not essential characteristics of an old folk-tale. It is a story of early sadness but of final joy, a story to send the hearers off to bed content with their lot and more tolerant of their fellow-men.

Surviving records attest to a performance at the Globe Theatre witnessed by a Dr Simon Forman on May 15, 1611, and to a presentation at court some six months later. Though the evidence supplied by these records is alone too indecisive to establish the date of composition as 1610–1611, it is strongly supported by evidence within the play itself. In both theme and tone, both diction and verse, *The Winter's Tale* bears the closest resemblance to *Cymbeline* and *The Tempest*. Like them it treats the theme of alienation and reconciliation, destruction and rebirth, and like them it embraces the improbabilities of romance. The language, elliptical, involved, and crammed with thought, is that of Shakespeare's latest manner ; as is also the verse, with no rhyme save in the songs and the chorus to Act IV, with many speeches beginning or ending in the middle of the line, and with a higher percentage than has any other play of lines with weak or unstressed endings.

As was his usual practice, Shakespeare in *The Winter's Tale* chose for dramatization a story which had already demonstrated its wide appeal. His source was *Pandosto : The Triumph of Time*, written in 1588 by Robert Greene, whose deathbed attack upon him in 1592 as one "beautified with our feathers" Shakespeare seems to have calmly ignored. Inasmuch as Greene's euphuistic romance was one of the most widely read stories of the day, it could hardly have been to disguise his use of it that Shakespeare changed the names of all the characters or transferred to Sicilia the action Greene had placed in Bohemia and to Bohemia what Greene had assigned to Sicilia. In general Shakespeare follows Greene's narrative quite closely through the first three acts, although both by presenting only the last day of Polixenes' visit and by freeing Hermione of the imprudent behavior of her prototype he discards the obvious motivation of Leontes' jealousy. In Greene the newborn princess is by the king's order entrusted to destiny in a boat without rudder or sail and is by fortunate winds borne to the coast where she is discovered by the Shepherd ; none corresponding to Antigonus is present to be devoured by a bear. Most of the other changes Shakespeare introduces prepare for the radical change he was to make in Act V. He has the king upon his own initiative, rather than upon the queen's entreaty, seek the verdict of Apollo's oracle, thereby presenting Leontes somewhat more sympathetically ; and he introduces Paulina to torture the jealous king and to convince us of his sincere repentance. That engaging rogue Autolycus is, as is also the Shepherd's clownish son, wholly Shakespeare's. Indeed, for the greater part of Act IV Greene's narrative is but the starting point for Shakespeare's creative imagination. For the happy "snapper-up of unconsidered trifles" *Pandosto* offers only Capnio, a colorless attendant upon the prince, who provides no comedy and serves only to make ready the ship for the lovers' escape from Bohemia and to force the old Shepherd aboard with the telltale jewels. For the prince's wooing of the supposed shepherdess, related by Greene in his characteristic imitation of current pseudo-Arcadian pastoralism and in the language of *Euphues*, Shakespeare substitutes the delightful sheep-shearing in IV, iv, with its true and charming presentation of rural life, for which he is indebted to Greene for nothing beyond the mention of "a meeting of all the farmers' daughters," held before the prince had spied the supposed shepherdess, at which the whole day was spent "in such homely pastimes as shepherds use." For little, indeed, is Shakespeare indebted in this most beautiful and memorable scene ; Polixenes' prototype does not learn of his son's love for the unrecognized princess until they have fled across the sea. In Act V Shakespeare completely changes both the denouement and the emphasis. In Greene, Bellaria (Hermione) is not revivified ; Pandosto (Leontes), having thrown Dorastus (Florizel) into prison, conceives a lustful passion for his unrecognized daughter Fawnia (Perdita), and after her identity has been established and the marriage of the lovers celebrated, he is driven to suicide by the recollection that he had betrayed his friend Egistus (Polixenes), brought death to his queen and his son Garinter (Mamillius), and incestuously desired his own daughter.

The Winter's Tale enjoyed considerable popularity during the years following the May 1611 performance witnessed by Dr Forman. Not only was it acted at court in November of that year, but eighteen months later it was chosen as one of fourteen plays to be presented as part of the festivities honoring the marriage of Princess Elizabeth to the Elector Palatine. Two later court performances are recorded before King James' death, and the play was declared "liked" when presented before King Charles in January 1634. But *The Winter's Tale* hardly suited the taste of the Restoration or the eighteenth century. The next recorded performance was more than a century later – in 1741. It was perhaps this short but not unsuccessful revival which led to there being written within the following fifteen years no fewer than three alterations which sought to adapt the play to the taste of the eighteenth century. The most successful of the three was that by David Garrick, whose *Florizel and Perdita : A Dramatic Pastoral* replaced Shakespeare's as the stage version throughout the remainder of the century. In it the events of sixteen years before are narrated by Camillo to a lord of Bohemia, where all the scenes are laid ; there Paulina with the secreted Hermione has found refuge, and there Leontes, at last repentant, comes to ask forgiveness of Polixenes. By these changes Garrick sought to avoid the transfer of action from Sicilia to Bohemia and back to Sicilia, the lapse of sixteen years between Acts III and IV, and perhaps the absence from the stage for extended periods of certain principal characters. Although Shakespeare's text regained the stage with the opening of the nineteenth century, much of the later criticism of the play may suggest that critics have found it difficult wholly to escape the prejudices inherited from the eighteenth century, for it is only within the past few decades that any have declared *The Winter's Tale* one of Shakespeare's masterpieces.

Although earlier critics recognized in *The Winter's Tale* "the golden glow of Shakespeare's genius," praised the beauty and the force of many of its speeches, and marvelled at the daring mastery of its verse, perhaps most before the 1930's found as much to lament as they did to praise. Naturally comparing the plays of his last period with the great tragedies which preceded them, they thought they recognized a decline in Shakespeare's seriousness of purpose, a lessened interest as well in dramatic technique as in the portrayal of properly motivated characters in understandable human situations ; and to explain the change they offered such suggestions as boredom or exhaustion resulting from prolonged mental strain, or eagerness to capitalize upon the popularity recently achieved by the romantic tragicomedies of Beaumont and Fletcher. They saw in *The Winter's Tale* the characteristic fault of Beaumont and Fletcher, an undue emphasis upon the highly dramatic situation even when it could be secured only by the sacrifice of character and probability. Distressed by the lapse of sixteen years between Acts III and IV, and perhaps ignoring Shakespeare's usual disregard of the unity of time, they declared *The Winter's Tale* a structural failure, an unsuccessful experiment toward the satisfactory structure of dramatized romance achieved only in *The Tempest*.

Most of those who have discussed the play in the past thirty years have seen it in a quite different light. They have reminded us that to the English Renaissance the pastoral was not escape literature, something to be read for entertainment alone, but that, as witnessed by Sir Philip Sidney's *Arcadia*, the intelligent reader was expected to discover there notable images of virtues to be imitated and vices to be shunned. When, therefore, for the plays which closed his career Shakespeare chose to use the material of romance, there is hardly reason to suspect him of being less serious ; rather the very improbability and naïveté of the plots should encourage one to expect a serious purpose. The apparent crudity of the dramatic technique – such as the introduction of Father Time to announce the passing of sixteen years, the frequent speeches of Autolycus addressed directly to the audience, the famous exit of Antigonus "pursued by a bear" –

should be viewed not as evidence that Shakespeare had become tired or bored or indifferent, but rather as a deliberate and skillful adoption of a technique which, because it was antique and outmoded, artistically became the dramatization of a remote and marvellous tale.

Far from seeking an explanation for an odd decline in Shakespeare's serious purpose, most recent writers on *The Winter's Tale* have accepted Dr E. M. W. Tillyard's view that the plays of Shakespeare's last period represent a natural development of the interests shown in his tragedies. The full tragic pattern presents three stages – prosperity, destruction, re-creation. Although the emphasis in Shakespeare's tragedies is naturally upon the first two, in most of them there is at the end at least the promise of a new order. In the tragicomedies of his last years his concern is with the final phase of the tragic pattern, Dr Tillyard thought ; in them "the old order is destroyed as thoroughly as in the main group of tragedies, and it is this destruction that altogether separates them from the realm of comedy in general and from Shakespeare's own earlier comedies in particular." While in *The Tempest* emphasis is upon the third stage of the pattern, re-creation, the earlier stages being presented only in retrospect, in *The Winter's Tale* Shakespeare presents the full pattern ; after giving a brief glimpse of earlier prosperity and happiness, he presents, with almost equal emphasis, complete destruction and happy re-creation. In it we are to recognize, also, the cycle of the seasons, Perdita identified as Spring, and perhaps the theme of the vegetation myth of Proserpina, which Shakespeare underscores by several references. When Proserpina was abducted from her mother Ceres by Pluto, the earth withered and vegetation ceased ; only upon her release from the nether world did her mother's spirits revive and fertility return to the earth.

As spring may follow fall only after the intervention of winter, so can rebirth follow destruction only after a period of gestation, and forgiveness follow sin only after proved and continuing repentance. A complete treatment of the tragic pattern demands, therefore, an extended period. The lapse of sixteen years between the first three acts of *The Winter's Tale*, sin, alienation, destruction, and the last two acts, forgiveness, reconciliation, rebirth, though it may be thought awkward dramatically, is essential to a complete treatment of the theme. *The Tempest*, with attention centered upon the last stage of the pattern, and that presented in a single day, may appear more compact, more unified, and in its avoidance of suffering more in the spirit of comedy, but to the same extent it is farther removed from the great tragedies and is, perhaps, less serious, less moral than is *The Winter's Tale* with its insistence that sin be paid for before it be forgiven. This insistence, however, in no way lessens the happiness in which the play ends. No play by Shakespeare has a happier ending, nor can a happier ending be conceived, for the happiness is earned by the characters, not merely decreed by the poet. Leontes, purified by his suffering, a sinner no more, deserves those greatest of joys, forgiveness and reunion with those he loved. Hermione, by her selfless surrender to the dictate of the oracle, has earned not only her restoration but the return of her long-lost daughter. And the lost one, Perdita, surely one of Shakespeare's most charming characters, of royal blood but of country rearing, because of her natural manners and simple honesty merits her happy future with the adoring Florizel.

As Dr Simon Forman in his account of the performance of May 1611 makes no mention of the statue scene, it has been thought by some that this happiest of endings represents a later alteration, that in Shakespeare's original version Hermione, like her prototype in Greene, actually died as reported in Act III, and that the final scene at first presented what is now only related, the identification of Perdita. Forman, however, is here, as always, an unsatisfactory reporter; stating only that the queen was by the oracle declared guiltless, he records nothing of either her death or her supposed death. But whether or not the statue scene be a later addition, it is certainly written by Shakespeare throughout and constitutes the proper – one may almost say the necessary – ending, for the return of Hermione not only completes the happiness with which the play ends but, by more closely joining its two parts, gives to the play a unity it would otherwise lack.

University of Iowa   BALDWIN MAXWELL

NOTE ON THE TEXT

The only text of *The Winter's Tale* is that of the folio of 1623. It is an excellent text, obviously prepared from clearly written copy. This copy is now believed to have been a transcript made by the scrivener Ralph Crane, perhaps from Shakespeare's own draft. A characteristic of the folio text is the almost complete absence of stage directions and, save in a few instances, the listing at the opening of each scene of all the characters who appear during the scene, generally with no indication of the exact point at which they enter. In the present text, the entries have been split and distributed to what appear to be the proper points. The act–scene division supplied marginally is identical, in the case of this play, with that of the folio.

Except for a few corrections of obvious typographical errors, all departures from the folio text are listed below, with the adopted reading in italics followed by the folio reading in roman. Most of the alterations first appeared in the later folios or in early eighteenth-century editions.

The Names of the Actors (printed at the end of the play in F)
I, i, 25 *have* hath
I, ii, 124 *heifer* Heycfer   148 *What . . . brother?* (assigned to Leontes in F)   158 *do* do's   207 *you, they say* you say   231 *th' entreaties* the Entreaties   253 *forth. In* forth in   275 *hobby-horse* Holy-Horse   315 *gallèd* gall'd   375–76 *not | Be . . . me? 'Tis* not? | Be . . . me, 'tis   407 *followed* followèd   443 *condemnèd* condemnd   460 *off hence.* off, hence:
II, i, 32 s.d. (appears before l. 1 in F)   35 *eyed* eyèd   104 *afar off* a farre-off
II, ii, 4 s.d. (appears before l. 1 in F)   49 *hammered* hammerèd   53 *let't* le't
II, iii, 4 *th' adulteress* th' Adultresse   26 s.d. (appears before l. 1 in F)   39 *What* Who   60 *good, so* good so
III, ii, 10 *Silence!* (appears as s.d. in F)   s.d. (appears before l. 1 in F)   32 *Who* Whom   122 s.d. (appears before l. 1 in F)   235–36 *unto | Our . . . perpetual.* Once (unto | Our shame perpetuall) once
III, iii, 48 *begins. Poor* beginnes, poore   57 s.d. *Shepherd* (appears before l. 1 in F)   75 s.d. (appears before l. 1 in F)   112 *made* mad
IV, ii, 52 s.d. *Exeunt* Exit
IV, iii, 7 *on an*   10 *With . . . thrush* With heigh, the Thrush   37 *currants* currence   54 *offends* offend
IV, iv, s.d. (Autolycus enters here in F)   2 *Do* Do's   12 *Digest it* Digest   13 *swoon* sworne   23 *borrowed* borrowèd   40 *dearest* deer'st   54 s.d. (appears before l. 1 in F)   98 *your* you   105 *wi' th'* with'   242 *kiln-hole* kill-hole   off *of*   292 *Get . . . go* (not assigned in F)   354 *who* whom   412 *acknowledged* acknowledge   416 *who* whom   460 *your* my   482 *gleaned* gleanèd   483 *hide* hides   493 *our* her   516–18 *direction. | If . . . project. | May . . . alteration, on* direction, | If . . . project | May . . . alteration. On   535–36 *follows: if . . . purpose | But . . . flight, make* followes, if . . . purpose | But . . . flight; make   542 *the son* there Sonne   658 s.d. *Exeunt* Exit   723 *or toaze at toaze*   732 *pheasant, cock* Pheazant Cock   824 s.d. *Exit* Exeunt
V, i, 6 *Whilst* Whilest   12 *True* (assigned to Leontes in F)   59 (Where . . . now) *appear* soul-vexed (Where . . . now appeare) Soule-vext   61 *just cause* just such Cause   75 *I have done* (assigned to Cleomenes in F)   122 s.d. *Florizel, Perdita* (appears before l. 1 in F)   159 *his, parting* his parting   168 *whilst* whilest
V, ii, 20 *haply* happily   61 *This* I   his   67 *Wrecked* Wrackt   107 s.d. *Exeunt* Exit
V, iii, 20 s.d. (*Hermione like a statue* appears before l. 1 in F; *Paulina* has no s.d. here in F)   67 *fixture* fixure   96 *Or* On

THE WINTER'S TALE

THE NAMES OF THE ACTORS

Leontes, King of Sicilia
Mamillius, young Prince of Sicilia
Camillo ⎫
Antigonus ⎪
Cleomenes ⎬ four lords of Sicilia
Dion ⎭
Polixenes, King of Bohemia
Florizel, Prince of Bohemia
Archidamus, a lord of Bohemia
Old Shepherd, reputed father of Perdita
Clown, his son
Autolycus, a rogue

[A Mariner]
[A Gaoler]
Hermione, Queen to Leontes
Perdita, daughter to Leontes and Hermione
Paulina, wife to Antigonus
Emilia, a lady [attending on Hermione]
[Mopsa ⎫
[Dorcas ⎬ shepherdesses]
Other Lords and Gentlemen, [Ladies, Officers, and]
   Servants, Shepherds, and Shepherdesses
[Time, as Chorus]

[Scene : Sicilia and Bohemia]

*

I, i   *Enter Camillo and Archidamus.*

ARCHIDAMUS If you shall chance, Camillo, to visit Bohemia on the like occasion whereon my services are now on foot, you shall see, as I have said, great difference betwixt our Bohemia and your Sicilia.

CAMILLO I think this coming summer the King of Sicilia means to pay Bohemia the visitation which he justly owes him.

8 ARCHIDAMUS Wherein our entertainment shall shame us, we will be justified in our loves; for indeed –

CAMILLO Beseech you –

ARCHIDAMUS Verily, I speak it in the freedom of my knowledge. We cannot with such magnificence – in so rare – I know not what to say. We will give you sleepy drinks, that your senses, unintelligent of our insufficience, may, though they cannot praise us, as little accuse us.

CAMILLO You pay a great deal too dear for what's given freely.

ARCHIDAMUS Believe me, I speak as my understanding instructs me and as mine honesty puts it to utterance.

CAMILLO Sicilia cannot show himself over-kind to Bohemia. They were trained together in their childhoods, and there rooted betwixt them then such an affection which 23 cannot choose but branch now. Since their more mature dignities and royal necessities made separation of their

society, their encounters, though not personal, have been royally attorneyed with interchange of gifts, let- 26 ters, loving embassies; that they have seemed to be to- 27 gether, though absent; shook hands, as over a vast; and embraced, as it were, from the ends of opposed winds. The heavens continue their loves!

ARCHIDAMUS I think there is not in the world either malice or matter to alter it. You have an unspeakable comfort of your young prince Mamillius. It is a gentleman of the greatest promise that ever came into my note.

CAMILLO I very well agree with you in the hopes of him. It is a gallant child – one that indeed physics the sub- 36 ject, makes old hearts fresh. They that went on crutches ere he was born desire yet their life to see him a man.

ARCHIDAMUS Would they else be content to die?

CAMILLO Yes – if there were no other excuse why they should desire to live.

ARCHIDAMUS If the king had no son, they would desire to live on crutches till he had one.   *Exeunt.*

*

Enter Leontes, Hermione, Mamillius, Polixenes,   I, ii
   Camillo, Lords.

POLIXENES
Nine changes of the wat'ry star hath been   1
The shepherd's note since we have left our throne   2
Without a burthen. Time as long again
Would be filled up, my brother, with our thanks,
And yet we should, for perpetuity,
Go hence in debt. And therefore, like a cipher,
Yet standing in rich place, I multiply
With one 'We thank you' many thousands moe   8
That go before it.

I, i In or near the palace of the King of Sicilia   8–9 (Compare the broken sentences in Archidamus' next speech. He wishes to say here that the love which Polixenes bears Leontes will make up for Bohemia's inability to equal the magnificent entertainment shown Polixenes in Sicilia.)   23 *branch* flourish   26 *attorneyed* performed by proxy   27 *that* so that   36 *physics* cures (presumably of melancholy)
I, ii The same   1 *wat'ry star* moon   2 *note* observation   8 *moe* more (Modern English 'more' has absorbed both Early English 'ma': greater in number, and E.E. 'mara': greater in degree)

LEONTES   Stay your thanks a while
And pay them when you part.
POLIXENES   Sir, that's to-morrow.
11   I am questioned by my fears of what may chance
Or breed upon our absence, that may blow
13   No sneaping winds at home to make us say,
'This is put forth too truly.' Besides, I have stayed
To tire your royalty.
LEONTES   We are tougher, brother,
Than you can put us to't.
POLIXENES   No longer stay.
LEONTES
One sev'n-night longer.
POLIXENES   Very sooth, to-morrow.
LEONTES
We'll part the time between's then, and in that
I'll no gainsaying.
POLIXENES   Press me not, beseech you, so.
There is no tongue that moves, none, none i' th' world,
So soon as yours could win me. So it should now
Were there necessity in your request, although
'Twere needful I denied it. My affairs
Do even drag me homeward, which to hinder
25   Were in your love a whip to me, my stay
To you a charge and trouble. To save both,
Farewell, our brother.
LEONTES   Tongue-tied our queen? Speak you.
HERMIONE
I had thought, sir, to have held my peace until
You had drawn oaths from him not to stay. You, sir,
Charge him too coldly. Tell him you are sure
All in Bohemia's well; this satisfaction
The by-gone day proclaimed. Say this to him,
33   He's beat from his best ward.
LEONTES   Well said, Hermione.
HERMIONE
To tell he longs to see his son were strong.
But let him say so then, and let him go;
But let him swear so, and he shall not stay,
We'll thwack him hence with distaffs.
Yet of your royal presence I'll adventure
The borrow of a week. When at Bohemia
You take my lord, I'll give him my commission
41   To let him there a month behind the gest
42   Prefixed for's parting. Yet, good deed, Leontes,
43   I love thee not a jar o' th' clock behind
44   What lady she her lord. You'll stay?
POLIXENES   No, madam.
HERMIONE
Nay, but you will?
POLIXENES   I may not, verily.
HERMIONE
Verily?
47   You put me off with limber vows, but I,
Though you would seek t' unsphere the stars with oaths,
Should yet say, 'Sir, no going.' Verily,
You shall not go. A lady's 'Verily' is
As potent as a lord's. Will you go yet?
Force me to keep you as a prisoner,
53   Not like a guest, so you shall pay your fees
When you depart and save your thanks. How say you?
My prisoner or my guest? By your dread 'Verily,'
One of them you shall be.
POLIXENES   Your guest, then, madam.

To be your prisoner should import offending,   57
Which is for me less easy to commit
Than you to punish.
HERMIONE   Not your gaoler, then,
But your kind hostess. Come, I'll question you
Of my lord's tricks and yours when you were boys.
You were pretty lordings then?
POLIXENES   We were, fair queen,
Two lads that thought there was no more behind
But such a day to-morrow as to-day,
And to be boy eternal.
HERMIONE   Was not my lord
The verier wag o' th' two?
POLIXENES
We were as twinned lambs that did frisk i' th' sun,
And bleat the one at th' other. What we changed   68
Was innocence for innocence; we knew not
The doctrine of ill-doing, nor dreamed
That any did. Had we pursued that life,
And our weak spirits ne'er been higher reared
With stronger blood, we should have answered heaven
Boldly 'Not guilty,' the imposition cleared   74
Hereditary ours.
HERMIONE   By this we gather
You have tripped since.
POLIXENES   O my most sacred lady,
Temptations have since then been born to's, for
In those unfledged days was my wife a girl;
Your precious self had then not crossed the eyes
Of my young playfellow.
HERMIONE   Grace to boot!   80
Of this make no conclusion, lest you say
Your queen and I are devils. Yet go on.
Th' offenses we have made you do we'll answer,
If you first sinned with us and that with us
You did continue fault and that you slipped not
With any but with us.
LEONTES   Is he won yet?
HERMIONE
He'll stay, my lord.
LEONTES   At my request he would not.
Hermione, my dearest, thou never spok'st
To better purpose.
HERMIONE   Never?
LEONTES   Never but once.
HERMIONE
What? Have I twice said well? When was't before?
I prithee tell me. Cram's with praise, and make's
As fat as tame things. One good deed dying tongueless   92
Slaughters a thousand waiting upon that.
Our praises are our wages. You may ride's
With one soft kiss a thousand furlongs ere
With spur we heat an acre. But to the goal.   96
My last good deed was to entreat his stay.

11–14 (a difficult passage; *that may blow* may express a wish or perhaps a purpose, that there may blow) 13 *sneaping* biting 25 *in* i.e. to make 33 *ward* defense 41 *let him* let him remain; *gest* place and time of a visit 42 *good deed* indeed 43 *jar* tick 44 *What lady she* any lady 47 *limber* feeble 53 *fees* payments which gaolers usually demanded of prisoners upon their release 57 *import offending* i.e. imply that I had committed an offense 68 *changed* exchanged 74–75 *the imposition . . . ours* freed even from original sin 80 *Grace to boot* Heaven help me 92–93 *One . . . that* withholding praise of one good deed discourages a thousand others 96 *heat* race; *to the goal* to come to the point

What was my first ? It has an elder sister,
Or I mistake you. O, would her name were Grace !
But once before I spoke to the purpose. When ?
Nay, let me have't ; I long.

LEONTES   Why, that was when
102 Three crabbèd months had soured themselves to death
Ere I could make thee open thy white hand
104 And clap thyself my love. Then didst thou utter
'I am yours for ever.'

HERMIONE   'Tis Grace indeed.
Why, lo you now, I have spoke to the purpose twice ;
The one for ever earned a royal husband,
Th' other for some while a friend.

[Gives her hand to Polixenes, and they walk apart.]

LEONTES [aside]   Too hot, too hot !
To mingle friendship far is mingling bloods.
I have tremor cordis on me. My heart dances,
111 But not for joy, not joy. This entertainment
May a free face put on, derive a liberty
From heartiness, from bounty, fertile bosom,
And well become the agent. 'T may, I grant.
115 But to be paddling palms and pinching fingers,
As now they are, and making practiced smiles
As in a looking-glass, and then to sigh, as 'twere
118 The mort o' th' deer – O, that is entertainment
My bosom likes not, nor my brows. Mamillius,
Art thou my boy ?

MAMILLIUS   Ay, my good lord.
120 LEONTES   I' fecks !
121 Why, that's my bawcock. What, hast smutched thy nose ?
They say it is a copy out of mine. Come, captain,
We must be neat – not neat but cleanly, captain.
And yet the steer, the heifer, and the calf
125 Are all called neat. – Still virginalling
Upon his palm ? – How now, you wanton calf ?
Art thou my calf ?

MAMILLIUS   Yes, if you will, my lord.
LEONTES
128 Thou want'st a rough pash and the shoots that I have,
To be full like me ; yet they say we are
Almost as like as eggs. Women say so,
That will say anything. But were they false
132 As o'er-dyed blacks, as wind, as waters, false
As dice are to be wished by one that fixes
No bourn 'twixt his and mine, yet were it true
To say this boy were like me. Come, sir page,
136 Look on me with your welkin eye. Sweet villain !
137 Most dear'st ! my collop ! Can thy dam ? – may't be ? –
138 Affection, thy intention stabs the center !
Thou dost make possible things not so held,

Communicat'st with dreams – how can this be ?
With what's unreal thou coactive art,
And fellow'st nothing. Then 'tis very credent
Thou may'st co-join with something ; and thou dost,
And that beyond commission, and I find it,
And that to the infection of my brains
And hard'ning of my brows.

POLIXENES   What means Sicilia ?
HERMIONE
He something seems unsettled.

POLIXENES   How, my lord ?
What cheer ? How is't with you, best brother ?   148
HERMIONE   You look
As if you held a brow of much distraction.
Are you moved, my lord ?

LEONTES   No, in good earnest.
How sometimes nature will betray its folly,
Its tenderness, and make itself a pastime
To harder bosoms ! Looking on the lines
Of my boy's face, methoughts I did recoil   154
Twenty-three years, and saw myself unbreeched,
In my green velvet coat, my dagger muzzled
Lest it should bite its master and so prove,
As ornaments oft do, too dangerous.
How like, methought, I then was to this kernel,
This squash, this gentleman. Mine honest friend,
Will you take eggs for money ?   161

MAMILLIUS   No, my lord, I'll fight.
LEONTES
You will ? Why, happy man be's dole ! My brother,   162
Are you so fond of your young prince as we
Do seem to be of ours ?

POLIXENES   If at home, sir,
He's all my exercise, my mirth, my matter,
Now my sworn friend and then mine enemy,
My parasite, my soldier, statesman, all.
He makes a July's day short as December,
And with his varying childness cures in me
Thoughts that would thick my blood.   170

LEONTES   So stands this squire
Officed with me. We two will walk, my lord,
And leave you to your graver steps. Hermione,
How thou lov'st us, show in our brother's welcome.
Let what is dear in Sicily be cheap.
Next to thyself and my young rover, he's
Apparent to my heart.   176

HERMIONE   If you would seek us,
We are yours i' th' garden. Shall's attend you there ?
LEONTES
To your own bents dispose you. You'll be found,
Be you beneath the sky. [aside] I am angling now,
Though you perceive me not how I give line.
Go to, go to !
How she holds up the neb, the bill to him,   182
And arms her with the boldness of a wife
To her allowing husband !   184

[Exeunt Polixenes, Hermione, and Attendants.]
                         Gone already !
Inch-thick, knee-deep, o'er head and ears a forked one !   185
Go play, boy, play. Thy mother plays, and I
Play too, but so disgraced a part, whose issue   187
Will hiss me to my grave. Contempt and clamor
Will be my knell. Go play, boy, play. There have been,
Or I am much deceived, cuckolds ere now ;

---

102 *crabbed* bitter   104 *clap* pledge   111–14 *This . . . agent* Hermione's gracious entertainment may well become her if it be due to a hospitable and generous nature   115 *paddling* caressing   118 *mort o' th' deer* hunter's horn announcing the death of the deer   120 *I' fecks* in faith   121 *bawcock* fine fellow (Fr. *'beau coq'*) ; *smutched* smudged   125 *neat* (1) cleanly, (2) horned cattle ; *virginalling* playing (with fingers)   128 *pash . . . shoots* head . . . horns   132 *o'er-dyed blacks* colored fabrics dyed black or weakened by too much dyeing   136 *welkin* sky-blue   137 *collop* small portion   137–46 *Can . . . brows* (the incoherency of this passage reflects Leontes' tortured mind)   138 *intention* intensity   148 *What cheer . . . brother* (Though the folio gives these words to Leontes, most editors assign them to Polixenes. Spoken by Leontes, they may suggest a forced gaiety.)   154 *methoughts* it seemed to me (variant of 'methought')   161 *take . . . money* be imposed upon   162 *dole* lot   170 *thick my blood* make me melancholy   176 *Apparent* heir apparent   182 *neb* face   184 *allowing* approving   185 *forked one* horned one (cuckold)   187 *whose issue* the result of which

And many a man there is, even at this present,
Now while I speak this, holds his wife by th' arm,
That little thinks she has been sluiced in's absence
And his pond fished by his next neighbor, by
Sir Smile, his neighbor. Nay, there's comfort in't
Whiles other men have gates and those gates opened,
As mine, against their will. Should all despair
That have revolted wives, the tenth of mankind
Would hang themselves. Physic for't there's none.
200 It is a bawdy planet, that will strike
Where 'tis predominant; and 'tis powerful, think it,
From east, west, north, and south. Be it concluded,
No barricado for a belly. Know't,
It will let in and out the enemy
205 With bag and baggage. Many thousand on's
Have the disease and feel't not. How now, boy?

MAMILLIUS
I am like you, they say.

LEONTES   Why, that's some comfort.
What, Camillo there?

CAMILLO
Ay, my good lord.

LEONTES
Go play, Mamillius. Thou'rt an honest man.
                                        [Exit Mamillius.]
Camillo, this great sir will yet stay longer.

CAMILLO
You had much ado to make his anchor hold;
213 When you cast out, it still came home.

LEONTES   Didst note it?

CAMILLO
He would not stay at your petitions, made
His business more material

LEONTES   Didst perceive it?
[Aside]
216 They're here with me already, whisp'ring, rounding
'Sicilia is a so-forth.' 'Tis far gone,
218 When I shall gust it last. How came't, Camillo,
That he did stay?

CAMILLO   At the good queen's entreaty.

LEONTES
At the queen's be't. 'Good' should be pertinent;
221 But so it is, it is not. Was this taken
By any understanding pate but thine?
223 For thy conceit is soaking, will draw in
More than the common blocks. Not noted, is't,
225 But of the finer natures, by some severals
226 Of head-piece extraordinary? Lower messes
227 Perchance are to this business purblind? Say.

CAMILLO
Business, my lord? I think most understand
Bohemia stays here longer.

LEONTES   Ha?

CAMILLO   Stays here longer.

LEONTES
Ay, but why?

CAMILLO
To satisfy your highness and th' entreaties
Of our most gracious mistress.

232 LEONTES   Satisfy
Th' entreaties of your mistress? Satisfy;
Let that suffice. I have trusted thee, Camillo,
With all the nearest things to my heart, as well
My chamber-councils, wherein, priest-like, thou

Hast cleansed my bosom, I from thee departed
Thy penitent reformed. But we have been
Deceived in thy integrity, deceived
In that which seems so.

CAMILLO   Be it forbid, my lord!

LEONTES
To bide upon't, thou art not honest; or,   241
If thou inclin'st that way, thou art a coward,
Which hoxes honesty behind, restraining   243
From course required; or else thou must be counted
A servant grafted in my serious trust   245
And therein negligent; or else a fool
That seest a game played home, the rich stake drawn,
And tak'st it all for jest.

CAMILLO   My gracious lord,
I may be negligent, foolish, and fearful.
In every one of these no man is free,
But that his negligence, his folly, fear,
Among the infinite doings of the world,
Sometime puts forth. In your affairs, my lord,   253
If ever I were willful-negligent,
It was my folly; if industriously   255
I played the fool, it was my negligence,
Not weighing well the end; if ever fearful
To do a thing where I the issue doubted,
Whereof the execution did cry out
Against the non-performance, 'twas a fear
Which oft infects the wisest. These, my lord,
Are such allowed infirmities that honesty
Is never free of. But, beseech your grace,
Be plainer with me; let me know my trespass
By its own visage. If I deny it,
'Tis none of mine.

LEONTES   Ha' not you seen, Camillo—
But that's past doubt, you have, or your eye-glass   267
Is thicker than a cuckold's horn—or heard—   268
For to a vision so apparent rumor
Cannot be mute—or thought—for cogitation
Resides not in that man that does not think—
My wife is slippery? If thou wilt confess,
Or else be impudently negative,
To have nor eyes nor ears nor thought, then say
My wife's a hobby-horse, deserves a name
As rank as any flax-wench that puts to
Before her troth-plight. Say't and justify't.

CAMILLO
I would not be a stander-by to hear
My sovereign mistress clouded so, without
My present vengeance taken. 'Shrew my heart,   280
You never spoke what did become you less
Than this, which to reiterate were sin   282
As deep as that, though true.

200–01 *It is . . . predominant* unchastity, like a baneful planet, destroys
when in ascendant 205 *on's* of us 213 *still* always 216–17 *They're
here . . . so-forth* people are already mocking me, whispering I am a so-and-so
(perhaps Leontes, unable to say 'cuckold,' puts two fingers to his head to
suggest horns) 218 *gust* realize 221 *so* as; *taken* recognized 223 *conceit
is soaking* understanding is absorbing 225 *severals* individuals 226 *Lower
messes* inferior men (who at table occupy lower seats) 227 *purblind*
wholly blind 232 *Satisfy* (Leontes fixes upon the sexual connotation)
241 *bide* dwell 243 *hoxes* disables 245 *grafted . . . trust* insinuated into
my confidence 253 *puts forth* reveals itself 255 *industriously* willfully
267 *eye-glass* crystalline lens of the eye 268 *thicker* more opaque 280
present immediate; *'Shrew* beshrew, curse 282–83 *which . . . true* to
repeat the charge against her would be a sin as great as her infidelity were
she guilty

LEONTES   Is whispering nothing?
Is leaning cheek to cheek? Is meeting noses?
285 Kissing with inside lip? stopping the career
Of laughter with a sigh? – a note infallible
287 Of breaking honesty! – horsing foot on foot?
Skulking in corners? wishing clocks more swift?
Hours, minutes? noon, midnight? and all eyes
290 Blind with the pin and web but theirs, theirs only,
That would unseen be wicked? Is this nothing?
Why, then the world and all that's in't is nothing,
The covering sky is nothing, Bohemia nothing,
My wife is nothing, nor nothing have these nothings,
If this be nothing.
CAMILLO   Good my lord, be cured
296 Of this diseased opinion, and betimes,
For 'tis most dangerous.
LEONTES   Say it be, 'tis true.
CAMILLO
No, no, my lord.
LEONTES   It is. You lie, you lie.
I say thou liest, Camillo, and I hate thee,
Pronounce thee a gross lout, a mindless slave,
301 Or else a hovering temporizer, that
Canst with thine eyes at once see good and evil,
Inclining to them both. Were my wife's liver
Infected as her life, she would not live
305 The running of one glass.
CAMILLO   Who does infect her?
LEONTES
Why, he that wears her like her medal, hanging
About his neck – Bohemia, who, if I
Had servants true about me that bare eyes
To see alike mine honor as their profits,
Their own particular thrifts, they would do that
Which should undo more doing. Ay, and thou,
312 His cupbearer – whom I from meaner form
313 Have benched and reared to worship, who may'st see
Plainly as heaven sees earth and earth sees heaven,
How I am gallèd – might'st bespice a cup
To give mine enemy a lasting wink,
Which draught to me were cordial.
CAMILLO   Sir, my lord,
I could do this, and that with no rash potion,
But with a ling'ring dram that should not work
Maliciously like poison. But I cannot
Believe this crack to be in my dread mistress,
So sovereignly being honorable.
323 I have loved thee –
LEONTES   Make that thy question, and go rot!
Dost think I am so muddy, so unsettled,
To appoint myself in this vexation, sully
The purity and whiteness of my sheets –
Which to preserve is sleep, which being spotted

Is goads, thorns, nettles, tails of wasps –
Give scandal to the blood o' th' prince my son,
Who I do think is mine and love as mine,
Without ripe moving to't? Would I do this?   331
Could man so blench?   332
CAMILLO   I must believe you, sir.
I do, and will fetch off Bohemia for't;
Provided that, when he's removed, your highness
Will take again your queen as yours at first,
Even for your son's sake, and thereby for sealing
The injury of tongues in courts and kingdoms
Known and allied to yours.
LEONTES   Thou dost advise me
Even so as I mine own course have set down.
I'll give no blemish to her honor, none.
CAMILLO   My lord,
Go then, and with a countenance as clear   341
As friendship wears at feasts, keep with Bohemia
And with your queen. I am his cupbearer.
If from me he have wholesome beverage,
Account me not your servant.
LEONTES   This is all.
Do't, and thou hast the one half of my heart;
Do't not, thou split'st thine own.
CAMILLO   I'll do't, my lord.
LEONTES
I will seem friendly, as thou hast advised me.   Exit.
CAMILLO
O miserable lady! But for me,
What case stand I in? I must be the poisoner
Of good Polixenes; and my ground to do't
Is the obedience to a master, one
Who in rebellion with himself will have
All that are his so too. To do this deed,   354
Promotion follows. If I could find example
Of thousands that had struck anointed kings
And flourished after, I'ld not do't; but since
Nor brass nor stone nor parchment bears not one,
Let villainy itself forswear't. I must
Forsake the court. To do't, or no, is certain   360
To me a break-neck. Happy star reign now!   361
Here comes Bohemia.
                    Enter Polixenes.
POLIXENES   This is strange. Methinks
My favor here begins to warp. Not speak?   363
Good day, Camillo.
CAMILLO   Hail, most royal sir!
POLIXENES
What is the news i' th' court?
CAMILLO   None rare, my lord.   365
POLIXENES
The king hath on him such a countenance
As he had lost some province and a region
Loved as he loves himself. Even now I met him   368
With customary compliment, when he,
Wafting his eyes to th' contrary and falling
A lip of much contempt, speeds from me, and
So leaves me to consider what is breeding
That changes thus his manners.
CAMILLO
I dare not know, my lord.
POLIXENES
How dare not? do not? Do you know and dare not
Be intelligent to me? 'Tis thereabouts,   376

---

285 *career* full gallop   287 *honesty* chastity   290 *pin and web* cataract
296 *betimes* at once   301 *hovering* irresolute   305 *glass* hourglass   312
meaner form humbler position   313 *benched* placed in authority; *worship*
position of honor   323 (as Camillo would hardly be expected to use *thee*
in addressing his king, some editors assign the entire line to Leontes)
331 *Without ripe moving* without good reason (the phrase goes with *appoint,*
sully, give scandal)   332 *blench* deceive himself   341 *clear* innocent
354 *so too* i.e. in rebellion against (false to) themselves   360 *To do't* to
kill Polixenes   361 *Happy star* good fortune   363 *Not speak* (Polixenes
refers to Leontes, whom he encountered on his way in)   365 *rare* unusual   368 *met* greeted   376 *intelligent* intelligible; *'Tis thereabouts* it is
something of the sort

For, to yourself, what you do know, you must,
And cannot say you dare not. Good Camillo,
Your changed complexions are to me a mirror
Which shows me mine changed too, for I must be
A party in this alteration, finding
Myself thus altered with't.

CAMILLO There is a sickness
Which puts some of us in distemper, but
I cannot name the disease, and it is caught
Of you that yet are well.

POLIXENES How caught of me?

386 Make me not sighted like the basilisk.
I have looked on thousands who have sped the better
388 By my regard, but killed none so. Camillo,
As you are certainly a gentleman, thereto
390 Clerk-like experienced – which no less adorns
Our gentry than our parents' noble names,
392 In whose success we are gentle – I beseech you,
If you know aught which does behove my knowledge
Thereof to be informed, imprison't not
In ignorant concealment.

CAMILLO I may not answer.

POLIXENES
A sickness caught of me, and yet I well?
I must be answered. Dost thou hear, Camillo?
I conjure thee by all the parts of man
Which honor does acknowledge, whereof the least
Is not this suit of mine, that thou declare
401 What incidency thou dost guess of harm
Is creeping toward me; how far off, how near;
Which way to be prevented, if to be;
If not, how best to bear it.

CAMILLO Sir, I will tell you,
Since I am charged in honor and by him
That I think honorable. Therefore mark my counsel,
Which must be even as swiftly followed as
I mean to utter it, or both yourself and me
409 Cry 'Lost,' and so good night!

POLIXENES On, good Camillo.

CAMILLO
I am appointed him to murder you.

POLIXENES
By whom, Camillo?

CAMILLO By the king.

POLIXENES For what?

CAMILLO
He thinks, nay, with all confidence he swears,
As he had seen't or been an instrument
414 To vice you to't, that you have touched his queen
Forbiddenly.

POLIXENES O, then my best blood turn
To an infected jelly and my name
Be yoked with his that did betray the Best!
Turn then my freshest reputation to
A savor that may strike the dullest nostril
Where I arrive, and my approach be shunned,
Nay, hated too, worse than the great'st infection
That e'er was heard or read!

CAMILLO Swear his thought over
By each particular star in heaven and
By all their influences, you may as well
Forbid the sea for to obey the moon
426 As or by oath remove or counsel shake
427 The fabric of his folly, whose foundation

Is piled upon his faith and will continue
The standing of his body.

POLIXENES How should this grow?

CAMILLO
I know not. But I am sure 'tis safer to
Avoid what's grown than question how 'tis born.
If therefore you dare trust my honesty,
That lies enclosèd in this trunk which you 433
Shall bear along impawned, away to-night! 434
Your followers I will whisper to the business, 435
And will by twos and threes at several posterns 436
Clear them o' th' city. For myself, I'll put
My fortunes to your service, which are here
By this discovery lost. Be not uncertain,
For, by the honor of my parents, I
Have uttered truth, which if you seek to prove,
I dare not stand by; nor shall you be safer
Than one condemnèd by the king's own mouth,
Thereon his execution sworn.

POLIXENES I do believe thee;
I saw his heart in's face. Give me thy hand.
Be pilot to me and thy places shall 446
Still neighbor mine. My ships are ready and
My people did expect my hence departure
Two days ago. This jealousy
Is for a precious creature. As she's rare,
Must it be great; and as his person's mighty,
Must it be violent; and as he does conceive
He is dishonored by a man which ever
Professed to him, why, his revenges must 454
In that be made more bitter. Fear o'ershades me. 455
Good expedition be my friend, and comfort 456
The gracious queen, part of his theme but nothing 457
Of his ill-ta'en suspicion! Come, Camillo.
I will respect thee as a father if
Thou bear'st my life off hence. Let us avoid. 460

CAMILLO
It is in mine authority to command
The keys of all the posterns. Please your highness
To take the urgent hour. Come, sir, away. *Exeunt.*

*

Enter Hermione, Mamillius, Ladies. II, i

HERMIONE
Take the boy to you. He so troubles me, 1
'Tis past enduring.

LADY Come, my gracious lord,
Shall I be your playfellow?

MAMILLIUS No, I'll none of you.

LADY
Why, my sweet lord?

386 *Make . . . basilisk* attribute not to me a sight like that of the fabulous serpent whose look or breath was fatal 388 *regard* look 390 *Clerk-like* like a scholar 392 *In whose success* in succession from whom 401 *incidency* happening 409 *good night* this is the end (as in modern slang, an expression of finality) 414 *vice* force 426 *or . . . or* either . . . or 427 *fabric* creation 433 *trunk* body 434 *impawned* as a pledge 435 *whisper to* secretly tell of 436 *posterns* back doors 446–47 *thy places . . . mine* i.e. you may always have an appointment in my household 454 *Professed* professed love 455 *o'ershades* covers 456 *expedition* prompt action 457–58 *part . . . suspicion* also object of the king's anger though innocent of wrongdoing 460 *avoid* depart
II, i In the palace of Leontes 1 *Take . . . to you* take charge of the boy

MAMILLIUS
You'll kiss me hard and speak to me as if
I were a baby still. I love you better.

SECOND LADY
And why so, my lord?

MAMILLIUS   Not for because
Your brows are blacker. Yet black brows, they say,
Become some women best, so that there be not
Too much hair there, but in a semicircle,
Or a half-moon made with a pen.

11   **SECOND LADY**   Who taught' this?

MAMILLIUS
I learned it out of women's faces. Pray now,
What color are your eyebrows?

LADY   Blue, my lord.

MAMILLIUS
Nay, that's a mock. I have seen a lady's nose
That has been blue, but not her eyebrows.

LADY   Hark ye.
The queen your mother rounds apace. We shall
Present our services to a fine new prince

18   One of these days, and then you'ld wanton with us,
If we would have you.

SECOND LADY   She is spread of late

20   Into a goodly bulk. Good time encounter her!

HERMIONE
21   What wisdom stirs amongst you? Come, sir, now
I am for you again. Pray you sit by us
And tell's a tale.

MAMILLIUS   Merry or sad shall't be?

HERMIONE
As merry as you will.

MAMILLIUS
A sad tale's best for winter. I have one
Of sprites and goblins.

HERMIONE   Let's have that, good sir.
Come on, sit down. Come on, and do your best
To fright me with your sprites; you're powerful at it.

MAMILLIUS
There was a man –

HERMIONE   Nay, come sit down; then on.

MAMILLIUS
Dwelt by a churchyard. I will tell it softly;
31   Yond crickets shall not hear it.

HERMIONE   Come on, then,
And give't me in mine ear.
       [Enter] Leontes, Antigonus, Lords [and others].

LEONTES
Was he met there? his train? Camillo with him?

LORD
Behind the tuft of pines I met them. Never
35   Saw I men scour so on their way. I eyed them
Even to their ships.

LEONTES   How blest am I
In my just censure, in my true opinion!

Alack, for lesser knowledge! how accursed   38
In being so blest! There may be in the cup
A spider steeped, and one may drink, depart,
And yet partake no venom, for his knowledge
Is not infected; but if one present
Th' abhorred ingredient to his eye, make known
How he hath drunk, he cracks his gorge, his sides,
With violent hefts. I have drunk, and seen the spider.   45
Camillo was his help in this, his pander.
There is a plot against my life, my crown.
All's true that is mistrusted. That false villain
Whom I employed was pre-employed by him.
He has discovered my design, and I   50
Remain a pinched thing – yea, a very trick   51
For them to play at will. How came the posterns
So easily open?

LORD   By his great authority,
Which often hath no less prevailed than so
On your command.

LEONTES   I know't too well.
Give me the boy. I am glad you did not nurse him.
Though he does bear some signs of me, yet you
Have too much blood in him.

HERMIONE   What is this? sport?   58

LEONTES
Bear the boy hence. He shall not come about her.
Away with him! and let her sport herself
With that she's big with, for 'tis Polixenes
Has made thee swell thus.

HERMIONE   But I'd say he had not,
And I'll be sworn you would believe my saying,
Howe'er you lean to the nayward.   64

LEONTES   You, my lords,
Look on her, mark her well. Be but about
To say 'She is a goodly lady,' and
The justice of your hearts will thereto add
''Tis pity she's not honest, honorable.'
Praise her but for this her without-door form –   69
Which on my faith deserves high speech – and straight
The shrug, the hum or ha, these petty brands
That calumny doth use – O, I am out,   72
That mercy does, for calumny will sear
Virtue itself – these shrugs, these hums and ha's,
When you have said she's goodly, come between   75
Ere you can say she's honest. But be't known,
From him that has most cause to grieve it should be,
She's an adult'ress.

HERMIONE   Should a villain say so,
The most replenished villain in the world,   79
He were as much more villain. You, my lord,
Do but mistake.

LEONTES   You have mistook, my lady,
Polixenes for Leontes. O thou thing!
Which I'll not call a creature of thy place,   83
Lest barbarism, making me the precedent,
Should a like language use to all degrees
And mannerly distinguishment leave out
Betwixt the prince and beggar. I have said
She's an adult'ress; I have said with whom.
More, she's a traitor and Camillo is
A federary with her, and one that knows   90
What she should shame to know herself
But with her most vile principal, that she's
A bed-swerver, even as bad as those   93

11 *taught'* taught thee   18 *wanton* play   20 *Good time encounter* good fortune attend   21 *wisdom stirs* wise matter is discussed   31 *crickets* i.e. the 'ladies in waiting with their tittering and chirping laughter' (Furness)   35 *scour* hasten   38 *Alack . . . knowledge* O, that my knowledge were less   45 *hefts* heavings   50 *discovered* revealed   51 *a pinched thing* 'a wretch upon the rack' (Wilson), 'a puppet' (Heath); *trick* toy   58 *sport* jesting   64 *nayward* negative   69 *without-door form* outward appearance   72 *out* mistaken   75 *come between* interfere   79 *replenished* full   83 *place* rank   90 *federary* confederate   93 *bed-swerver* adulteress

94   That vulgars give bold'st titles – ay, and privy
      To this their late escape.

HERMIONE   No, by my life,
      Privy to none of this. How will this grieve you,
      When you shall come to clearer knowledge, that
      You thus have published me! Gentle my lord,
99   You scarce can right me throughly then to say
      You did mistake.

LEONTES   No. If I mistake
      In those foundations which I build upon,
102   The center is not big enough to bear
      A schoolboy's top. Away with her to prison!
104   He who shall speak for her is afar off guilty
      But that he speaks.

HERMIONE   There's some ill planet reigns.
      I must be patient till the heavens look
      With an aspect more favorable. Good my lords,
      I am not prone to weeping, as our sex
      Commonly are; the want of which vain dew
      Perchance shall dry your pities. But I have
      That honorable grief lodged here which burns
      Worse than tears drown. Beseech you all, my lords,
113   With thoughts so qualified as your charities
114   Shall best instruct you, measure me; and so
      The king's will be performed.

LEONTES   Shall I be heard?

HERMIONE
      Who is't that goes with me? Beseech your highness,
      My women may be with me, for you see
118   My plight requires it. Do not weep, good fools;
      There is no cause. When you shall know your mistress
      Has deserved prison, then abound in tears
      As I come out. This action I now go on
      Is for my better grace. Adieu, my lord.
      I never wished to see you sorry; now
      I trust I shall. My women, come; you have leave.

LEONTES
      Go, do our bidding. Hence!
                    [Exit Queen, guarded, with Ladies.]

LORD
      Beseech your highness, call the queen again.

ANTIGONUS
      Be certain what you do, sir, lest your justice
128   Prove violence, in the which three great ones suffer,
      Yourself, your queen, your son.

LORD   For her, my lord,
      I dare my life lay down and will do't, sir,
      Please you t' accept it, that the queen is spotless
      I' th' eyes of heaven and to you – I mean,
      In this which you accuse her.

ANTIGONUS   If it prove
134   She's otherwise, I'll keep my stables where
      I lodge my wife. I'll go in couples with her,
      Than when I feel and see her no farther trust her;
      For every inch of woman in the world,
      Ay, every dram of woman's flesh is false,
      If she be.

LEONTES   Hold your peaces.

LORD   Good my lord –

ANTIGONUS
      It is for you we speak, not for ourselves.
      You are abused and by some putter-on
      That will be damned for't. Would I knew the villain,
143   I would land-damn him. Be she honor-flawed,

      I have three daughters – the eldest is eleven,
      The second and the third, nine and some five –
      If this prove true, they'll pay for't. By mine honor,
      I'll geld 'em all; fourteen they shall not see
      To bring false generations. They are co-heirs,   148
      And I had rather glib myself than they   149
      Should not produce fair issue.

LEONTES   Cease; no more.
      You smell this business with a sense as cold
      As is a dead man's nose; but I do see't and feel't,
      As you feel doing thus [pinches Antigonus], and see withal
      The instruments that feel.   154

ANTIGONUS   If it be so,
      We need no grave to bury honesty;
      There's not a grain of it the face to sweeten
      Of the whole dungy earth.

LEONTES   What? Lack I credit?

LORD
      I had rather you did lack than I, my lord,
      Upon this ground; and more it would content me   159
      To have her honor true than your suspicion,
      Be blamed for't how you might.

LEONTES   Why, what need we
      Commune with you of this, but rather follow
      Our forceful instigation? Our prerogative   163
      Calls not your counsels, but our natural goodness   164
      Imparts this, which if you – or stupified   165
      Or seeming so in skill – cannot or will not   166
      Relish a truth like us, inform yourselves
      We need no more of your advice. The matter,
      The loss, the gain, the ord'ring on't, is all
      Properly ours.

ANTIGONUS   And I wish, my liege,
      You had only in your silent judgment tried it,
      Without more overture.   172

LEONTES   How could that be?
      Either thou art most ignorant by age
      Or thou wert born a fool. Camillo's flight,
      Added to their familiarity –
      Which was as gross as ever touched conjecture,
      That lacked sight only, nought for approbation
      But only seeing, all other circumstances
      Made up to th' deed – doth push on this proceeding.
      Yet, for a greater confirmation –
      For in an act of this importance 'twere
      Most piteous to be wild – I have dispatched in post   182
      To sacred Delphos, to Apollo's temple,
      Cleomenes and Dion, whom you know
      Of stuffed sufficiency. Now from the oracle   185
      They will bring all, whose spiritual counsel had,
      Shall stop or spur me. Have I done well?

LORD
      Well done, my lord.

94 vulgars . . . titles common people call rudest names 99 throughly
thoroughly 102 center earth 104–05 He . . . speaks he is indirectly guilty
who merely speaks in her behalf 113 qualified modified 114 measure
judge 118 fools (a term of endearment) 128 violence outrage 134–35
I'll . . . her (perhaps in part the meaning of this puzzling passage is: 'I'll
guard the stables where my wife lives and never leave her alone' – stables
intended to suggest a beast to be ridden) 143 land-damn (the 'damn' reveals
the meaning of this 'mysterious compound') 148 bring . . . generations beget
bastards 149 glib geld 154 instruments that feel i.e. Leontes' fingers
159 ground matter 163 instigation incentive 164 Calls calls for 165
Imparts bestows 166 skill discernment 172 overture public revelation
182 wild rash; post haste 185 stuffed sufficiency full competence

LEONTES
Though I am satisfied and need no more
Than what I know, yet shall the oracle
Give rest to th' minds of others, such as he
Whose ignorant credulity will not
193 Come up to th' truth. So have we thought it good
194 From our free person she should be confined,
Lest that the treachery of the two fled hence
Be left her to perform. Come, follow us.
We are to speak in public, for this business
198 Will raise us all.
ANTIGONUS [aside] To laughter, as I take it,
If the good truth were known.   Exeunt.

*

II, ii   Enter Paulina, a Gentleman [and Attendants].
PAULINA
The keeper of the prison, call to him;
Let him have knowledge who I am.   [Exit Gentleman.]
                                        Good lady,
No court in Europe is too good for thee.
What dost thou then in prison?
[Enter Gentleman with the] Gaoler.
                            Now, good sir,
You know me, do you not?
GAOLER   For a worthy lady
And one who much I honor.
PAULINA   Pray you then,
Conduct me to the queen.
GAOLER   I may not, madam.
To the contrary I have express commandment.
PAULINA
Here's ado,
To lock up honesty and honor from
11 Th' access of gentle visitors. Is't lawful, pray you,
To see her women? any of them? Emilia?
GAOLER
So please you, madam,
To put apart these your attendants, I
Shall bring Emilia forth.
PAULINA   I pray now, call her.
Withdraw yourselves.
                  [Exeunt Gentleman and Attendants.]
GAOLER   And, madam,
I must be present at your conference.
PAULINA
Well, be't so, prithee.   [Exit Gaoler.]
Here's such ado to make no stain a stain
20 As passes coloring.
        [Enter Gaoler with] Emilia.
                  Dear gentlewoman,
How fares our gracious lady?
EMILIA
As well as one so great and so forlorn
May hold together. On her frights and griefs,

Which never tender lady hath borne greater,
She is something before her time delivered.   25
PAULINA
A boy?
EMILIA A daughter, and a goodly babe,
Lusty and like to live. The queen receives
Much comfort in't, says, 'My poor prisoner,
I am innocent as you.'
PAULINA   I dare be sworn.
These dangerous unsafe lunes i' th' king, beshrew them! 30
He must be told on't, and he shall. The office
Becomes a woman best; I'll take't upon me.
If I prove honey-mouthed, let my tongue blister
And never to my red-looked anger be   34
The trumpet any more. Pray you, Emilia,
Commend my best obedience to the queen.
If she dares trust me with her little babe,
I'll show't the king and undertake to be
Her advocate to th' loud'st. We do not know
How he may soften at the sight o' th' child.
The silence often of pure innocence
Persuades when speaking fails.
EMILIA   Most worthy madam,
Your honor and your goodness is so evident
That your free undertaking cannot miss   44
A thriving issue. There is no lady living
So meet for this great errand. Please your ladyship
To visit the next room, I'll presently   47
Acquaint the queen of your most noble offer,
Who but to-day hammered of this design,   49
But durst not tempt a minister of honor   50
Lest she should be denied.
PAULINA   Tell her, Emilia,
I'll use that tongue I have. If wit flow from't
As boldness from my bosom, let't not be doubted
I shall do good.
EMILIA   Now be you blest for it!
I'll to the queen. Please you, come something nearer.
GAOLER
Madam, if't please the queen to send the babe,
I know not what I shall incur to pass it,
Having no warrant.
PAULINA   You need not fear it, sir.
This child was prisoner to the womb and is
By law and process of great nature thence
Freed and enfranchised, not a party to
The anger of the king nor guilty of,
If any be, the trespass of the queen.
GAOLER
I do believe it.
PAULINA
Do not you fear. Upon mine honor, I
Will stand betwixt you and danger.   Exeunt.

*

            Enter Leontes, Servants, Antigonus, and Lords.   II, iii
LEONTES
Nor night nor day no rest. It is but weakness
To bear the matter thus – mere weakness. If
The cause were not in being – part o' th' cause,
She, th' adulteress; for the harlot king   4
Is quite beyond mine arm, out of the blank   5
And level of my brain, plot-proof. But she

193 Come up to face 194 free easily accessible 198 raise rouse to action
II, ii A prison 11 lawful permitted (satirical) 20 passes coloring surpasses belief 25 something somewhat 30 lunes fits of lunacy 34 red-
looked red-faced 44 free voluntary 47 presently at once 49 hammered of
formulated 50 tempt try to win over
II, iii The palace of Leontes 4 harlot (originally of either sex) 5–6
blank And level target and aim

I can hook to me. Say that she were gone,
8   Given to the fire, a moiety of my rest
Might come to me again. Who's there?

SERVANT   My lord.

LEONTES
How does the boy?

SERVANT   He took good rest to-night.
'Tis hoped his sickness is discharged.

LEONTES
To see his nobleness!
Conceiving the dishonor of his mother,
He straight declined, drooped, took it deeply,
15   Fastened and fixed the shame on't in himself,
Threw off his spirit, his appetite, his sleep,
17   And downright languished. Leave me solely. Go
See how he fares.   [Exit Servant.]
18   Fie, fie! no thought of him!
The very thought of my revenges that way
Recoil upon me – in himself too mighty,
And in his parties, his alliance. Let him be
Until a time may serve. For present vengeance,
Take it on her. Camillo and Polixenes
Laugh at me, make their pastime at my sorrow.
They should not laugh if I could reach them, nor
Shall she within my power.
        Enter Paulina [with a Babe].

LORD   You must not enter.

PAULINA
27   Nay, rather, good my lords, be second to me.
Fear you his tyrannous passion more, alas,
Than the queen's life? a gracious innocent soul,
30   More free than he is jealous.

ANTIGONUS   That's enough.

SERVANT
Madam, he hath not slept to-night, commanded
None should come at him.

PAULINA   Not so hot, good sir.
I come to bring him sleep. 'Tis such as you,
That creep like shadows by him and do sigh
At each his needless heavings, such as you
Nourish the cause of his awaking. I
Do come with words as medicinal as true,
38   Honest as either, to purge him of that humor
That presses him from sleep.

LEONTES   What noise there, ho?

PAULINA
No noise, my lord, but needful conference
41   About some gossips for your highness.

LEONTES   How?
Away with that audacious lady! Antigonus,
I charged thee that she should not come about me.
I knew she would.

ANTIGONUS   I told her so, my lord,
On your displeasure's peril and on mine,
She should not visit you.

LEONTES   What, canst not rule her?

PAULINA
From all dishonesty he can. In this,
Unless he take the course that you have done,
49   Commit me for committing honor, trust it,
He shall not rule me.

ANTIGONUS   La you now, you hear!
When she will take the rein I let her run,
But she'll not stumble.

PAULINA   Good my liege, I come –
And I beseech you hear me, who professes
Myself your loyal servant, your physician,
Your most obedient counsellor, yet that dares
Less appear so in comforting your evils   56
Than such as most seem yours – I say I come
From your good queen.

LEONTES   Good queen?

PAULINA   Good queen, my lord,
Good queen. I say good queen,
And would by combat make her good, so were I
A man, the worst about you.

LEONTES   Force her hence.

PAULINA
Let him that makes but trifles of his eyes
First hand me. On mine own accord I'll off,
But first I'll do my errand. The good queen,
For she is good, hath brought you forth a daughter –
Here 'tis – commends it to your blessing.
        [Lays down the child.]

LEONTES   Out!
A mankind witch! Hence with her, out o' door!   67
A most intelligencing bawd.   68

PAULINA   Not so.
I am as ignorant in that as you
In so entitling me – and no less honest
Than you are mad, which is enough, I'll warrant,
As this world goes, to pass for honest.

LEONTES   Traitors!
Will you not push her out? Give her the bastard.
Thou dotard, thou art woman-tired, unroosted   74
By thy dame Partlet here. Take up the bastard.   75
Take't up, I say. Give't to thy crone.

PAULINA   For ever
Unvenerable be thy hands, if thou
Tak'st up the princess by that forcèd baseness   78
Which he has put upon't!

LEONTES   He dreads his wife.

PAULINA
So I would you did. Then 'twere past all doubt
You'ld call your children yours.

LEONTES   A nest of traitors!

ANTIGONUS
I am none, by this good light.

PAULINA   Nor I, nor any
But one that's here, and that's himself; for he
The sacred honor of himself, his queen's,
His hopeful son's, his babe's, betrays to slander,
Whose sting is sharper than the sword's; and will not –
For, as the case now stands, it is a curse
He cannot be compelled to't – once remove
The root of his opinion, which is rotten
As ever oak or stone was sound.

LEONTES   A callet   90
Of boundless tongue, who late hath beat her husband

8 *moiety* part 15 *on't* of it 17 *solely* alone 18 *him* i.e. Polixenes 27 *be second to* assist 30 *free* innocent 38 *that humor* that of the four humors which, by having become predominant, prevented sleep 41 *gossips* godparents for the child 49 *Commit* imprison 56 *comforting* condoning 67 *mankind* masculine 68 *intelligencing* spying 74 *dotard* imbecile; *woman-tired, unroosted* henpecked, driven from the roost 75 *Partlet* Pertelote (the hen in Chaucer's Nun's Priest's Tale, whose dominance of her husband almost brought his ruin) 78 *forcèd baseness* false designation as bastard 90 *callet* scold

And now baits me ! This brat is none of mine ;
It is the issue of Polixenes.
Hence with it, and together with the dam
Commit them to the fire !
PAULINA   It is yours,
And, might we lay th' old proverb to your charge,
So like you 'tis the worse. Behold, my lords.
Although the print be little, the whole matter
And copy of the father – eye, nose, lip,
100   The trick of 's frown, his forehead, nay, the valley,
The pretty dimples of his chin and cheek, his smiles,
The very mould and frame of hand, nail, finger.
And thou, good goddess Nature, which hast made it
104   So like to him that got it, if thou hast
The ordering of the mind too, 'mongst all colors
106   No yellow in 't, lest she suspect, as he does,
107   Her children not her husband's !
LEONTES   A gross hag !
108   And, lozel, thou art worthy to be hanged
That wilt not stay her tongue.
ANTIGONUS   Hang all the husbands
That cannot do that feat, you'll leave yourself
Hardly one subject.
LEONTES   Once more, take her hence !
PAULINA
A most unworthy and unnatural lord
Can do no more.
LEONTES   I'll ha' thee burnt.
PAULINA   I care not.
It is an heretic that makes the fire,
115   Not she which burns in 't. I'll not call you tyrant ;
But this most cruel usage of your queen,
Not able to produce more accusation
Than your own weak-hinged fancy, something savors
Of tyranny and will ignoble make you,
Yea, scandalous to the world.
LEONTES   On your allegiance,
Out of the chamber with her ! Were I a tyrant,
Where were her life ? She durst not call me so
If she did know me one. Away with her !
PAULINA
I pray you do not push me ; I'll be gone.
Look to your babe, my lord ; 'tis yours. Jove send her
126   A better guiding spirit. What needs these hands ?
You that are thus so tender o'er his follies
Will never do him good, not one of you.
So, so. Farewell ; we are gone.   *Exit.*
LEONTES
130   Thou, traitor, hast set on thy wife to this.
My child ? away with 't ! Even thou, that hast
A heart so tender o'er it, take it hence
And see it instantly consumed with fire –
Even thou and none but thou. Take it up straight.

Within this hour bring me word 'tis done,
And by good testimony, or I'll seize thy life,
With what thou else call'st thine. If thou refuse
And wilt encounter with my wrath, say so.
The bastard brains with these my proper hands   139
Shall I dash out. Go, take it to the fire,
For thou set'st on thy wife.
ANTIGONUS   I did not, sir.
These lords, my noble fellows, if they please,
Can clear me in 't.
LORDS   We can. My royal liege,
He is not guilty of her coming hither.
LEONTES
You're liars all.
LORD
Beseech your highness, give us better credit.
We have always truly served you, and beseech'   147
So to esteem of us ; and on our knees we beg,
As recompense of our dear services
Past and to come, that you do change this purpose,
Which being so horrible, so bloody, must
Lead on to some foul issue. We all kneel.
LEONTES
I am a feather for each wind that blows.
Shall I live on to see this bastard kneel
And call me father ? Better burn it now
Than curse it then. But be it ; let it live.
It shall not neither. You, sir, come you hither,   156
You that have been so tenderly officious
With Lady Margery, your midwife there,   159
To save this bastard's life – for 'tis a bastard,
So sure as this beard 's grey. What will you adventure
To save this brat's life ?
ANTIGONUS   Anything, my lord,
That my ability may undergo   163
And nobleness impose. At least thus much.
I'll pawn the little blood which I have left   165
To save the innocent. Anything possible.
LEONTES
It shall be possible. Swear by this sword
Thou wilt perform my bidding.
ANTIGONUS   I will, my lord.
LEONTES
Mark and perform it, seest thou ; for the fail   169
Of any point in 't shall not only be
Death to thyself but to thy lewd-tongued wife,
Whom for this time we pardon. We enjoin thee,
As thou art liege-man to us, that thou carry
This female bastard hence, and that thou bear it
To some remote and desert place quite out
Of our dominions, and that there thou leave it,
Without more mercy, to it own protection   177
And favor of the climate. As by strange fortune   178
It came to us, I do in justice charge thee,
On thy soul's peril and thy body's torture,
That thou commend it strangely to some place   181
Where chance may nurse or end it. Take it up.
ANTIGONUS
I swear to do this, though a present death
Had been more merciful. Come on, poor babe.
Some powerful spirit instruct the kites and ravens
To be thy nurses. Wolves and bears, they say,
Casting their savageness aside, have done
Like offices of pity. Sir, be prosperous

---

100 *valley* cleft in chin (?), crease in forehead (?)   104 *got* begot   106 *yellow* (the color of jealousy)   107 (in her righteous rage Paulina fails to realize that jealousy would not in a wife engender doubts as to the father of her children)   108 *lozel* worthless person   115 *tyrant* (the worst term of abuse applied to a monarch)   126 *these hands* i.e. those which push her   130 *Thou* i.e. Antigonus   139 *proper* own   147 *beseech'* (with 'you' understood)   156 *be it* so be it   159 *Margery* hen (?) (Partridge records a cant term from ca. 1570, 'Margery-prater' hen ; cf. *Partlet,* l. 75)   163 *undergo* perform   165 *pawn* risk   169 *fail* failure   177 *it* its (an earlier form of the possessive)   178 *strange* foreign (Polixenes, whom he declares the father, a foreigner)   181 *commend . . . place* commit it to some foreign place

189 In more than this deed does require. And blessing
Against this cruelty fight on thy side,
Poor thing, condemned to loss.   *Exit [with the Babe].*
LEONTES   No, I'll not rear
Another's issue.
        Enter a Servant.
SERVANT   Please your highness, posts
From those you sent to th' oracle are come
An hour since. Cleomenes and Dion,
Being well arrived from Delphos, are both landed,
Hasting to th' court.
LORD   So please you, sir, their speed
197 Hath been beyond account.
LEONTES   Twenty-three days
They have been absent. 'Tis good speed, foretells
199 The great Apollo suddenly will have
The truth of this appear. Prepare you, lords;
Summon a session, that we may arraign
Our most disloyal lady, for, as she hath
Been publicly accused, so shall she have
A just and open trial. While she lives
My heart will be a burthen to me. Leave me,
And think upon my bidding.   *Exeunt.*

*

III, i   *Enter Cleomenes and Dion.*
CLEOMENES
The climate's delicate, the air most sweet,
2 Fertile the isle, the temple much surpassing
The common praise it bears.
DION   I shall report,
For most it caught me, the celestial habits –
Methinks I so should term them – and the reverence
Of the grave wearers. O, the sacrifice,
How ceremonious, solemn, and unearthly
It was i' th' off'ring!
CLEOMENES   But of all, the burst
And the ear-deaf'ning voice o' th' oracle,
Kin to Jove's thunder, so surprised my sense
That I was nothing.
DION   If th' event o' th' journey
Prove as successful to the queen – O be't so! –
As it hath been to us rare, pleasant, speedy,
14 The time is worth the use on't.
CLEOMENES   Great Apollo
Turn all to th' best! These proclamations,
So forcing faults upon Hermione,
I little like.
DION   The violent carriage of it
Will clear or end the business. When the oracle,
Thus by Apollo's great divine sealed up,
Shall the contents discover, something rare
Even then will rush to knowledge. Go. Fresh horses!
And gracious be the issue!   *Exeunt.*

*

III, ii   *Enter Leontes, Lords, Officers.*
LEONTES
This sessions, to our great grief we pronounce,
Even pushes 'gainst our heart – the party tried
The daughter of a king, our wife, and one
4 Of us too much beloved. Let us be cleared

Of being tyrannous, since we so openly
Proceed in justice, which shall have due course,
Even to the guilt or the purgation.   7
Produce the prisoner.
OFFICER
It is his highness' pleasure that the queen
Appear in person here in court. Silence!
        *[Enter] Hermione, as to her trial, [Paulina, and]
        Ladies.*
LEONTES
Read the indictment.
OFFICER *[reads]* Hermione, queen to the worthy Leon-
tes, king of Sicilia, thou art here accused and arraigned
of high treason, in committing adultery with Polixenes,
king of Bohemia, and conspiring with Camillo to take
away the life of our sovereign lord the king, thy royal
husband; the pretense whereof being by circumstances 17
partly laid open, thou, Hermione, contrary to the faith
and allegiance of a true subject, didst counsel and aid
them, for their better safety, to fly away by night.
HERMIONE
Since what I am to say must be but that
Which contradicts my accusation, and
The testimony on my part no other
But what comes from myself, it shall scarce boot me   24
To say, 'Not guilty.' Mine integrity,
Being counted falsehood, shall, as I express it,
Be so received. But thus: if powers divine
Behold our human actions, as they do,
I doubt not then but innocence shall make
False accusation blush and tyranny
Tremble at patience. You, my lord, best know,
Who least will seem to do so, my past life
Hath been as continent, as chaste, as true,
As I am now unhappy; which is more
Than history can pattern, though devised   35
And played to take spectators. For behold me –   36
A fellow of the royal bed, which owe   37
A moiety of the throne, a great king's daughter,   38
The mother to a hopeful prince – here standing
To prate and talk for life and honor 'fore
Who please to come and hear. For life, I prize it
As I weigh grief, which I would spare. For honor,
'Tis a derivative from me to mine,   43
And only that I stand for. I appeal
To your own conscience, sir, before Polixenes
Came to your court, how I was in your grace,
How merited to be so; since he came,
With what encounter so uncurrent I   48
Have strained t' appear thus; if one jot beyond   49
The bound of honor, or in act or will
That way inclining, hardened be the hearts
Of all that hear me, and my near'st of kin
Cry fie upon my grave!
LEONTES   I ne'er heard yet
That any of these bolder vices wanted

189 *require* deserve   197 *account* record   199 *suddenly* at once
III, i 2 *isle* (in making Delphi
an island, as in providing Bohemia with a seacoast, Shakespeare is following
Greene)   14 *worth... on't* well spent
III, ii A public tribunal in Sicilia   4 *Of* by   7 *purgation* clearing   17
pretense purpose   24 *boot* profit   35 *pattern* match   36 *take* please   37 *owe*
own   38 *moiety* share   43 *a derivative... mine* something to be inherited
by my children from me   48 *uncurrent* unlawful   49 *strained* sinned

III, i A posting inn en route to Leontes' palace

Less impudence to gainsay what they did
Than to perform it first.

HERMIONE   That's true enough,

57   Though 'tis a saying, sir, not due to me.

LEONTES
You will not own it.

58 HERMIONE   More than mistress of
Which comes to me in name of fault, I must not
At all acknowledge. For Polixenes,
With whom I am accused, I do confess

62   I loved him as in honor he required –
With such a kind of love as might become
A lady like me, with a love even such,
So and no other, as yourself commanded –
Which not to have done I think had been in me
Both disobedience and ingratitude
To you and toward your friend, whose love had spoke,
Even since it could speak, from an infant, freely
That it was yours. Now, for conspiracy,
I know not how it tastes, though it be dished
For me to try how. All I know of it
Is that Camillo was an honest man;
And why he left your court, the gods themselves,

75   Wotting no more than I, are ignorant.

LEONTES
You knew of his departure, as you know
What you have underta'en to do in's absence.

HERMIONE
Sir,
You speak a language that I understand not,

80   My life stands in the level of your dreams,
Which I'll lay down.

LEONTES   Your actions are my dreams.
You had a bastard by Polixenes,
And I but dreamed it. As you were past all shame –

84   Those of your fact are so – so past all truth,

85   Which to deny concerns more than avails; for as
Thy brat hath been cast out, like to itself,
No father owning it – which is, indeed,
More criminal in thee than it – so thou
Shalt feel our justice, in whose easiest passage
Look for no less than death.

HERMIONE   Sir, spare your threats.

91   The bug which you would fright me with I seek.

92   To me can life be no commodity.
The crown and comfort of my life, your favor,
I do give lost, for I do feel it gone,
But know not how it went. My second joy
And first-fruits of my body, from his presence
I am barred, like one infectious. My third comfort,

98   Starred most unluckily, is from my breast,
The innocent milk in it most innocent mouth,
Haled out to murder. Myself on every post

101 Proclaimed a strumpet: with immodest hatred
The child-bed privilege denied, which 'longs
To women of all fashion. Lastly, hurried
Here to this place, i' th' open air, before

I have got strength of limit. Now, my liege,   105
Tell me what blessings I have here alive,
That I should fear to die? Therefore proceed.
But yet hear this – mistake me not, no life   108
(I prize it not a straw) but for mine honor,
Which I would free. If I shall be condemned
Upon surmises, all proofs sleeping else
But what your jealousies awake, I tell you
'Tis rigor and not law. Your honors all,
I do refer me to the oracle.
Apollo be my judge!

LORD   This your request
Is altogether just. Therefore bring forth,
And in Apollo's name, his oracle.

                                        [Exeunt certain Officers.]

HERMIONE
The emperor of Russia was my father.
O that he were alive, and here beholding
His daughter's trial; that he did but see
The flatness of my misery – yet with eyes   121
Of pity, not revenge.

        [Enter Officers with] Cleomenes, [and] Dion.

OFFICER
You here shall swear upon this sword of justice,
That you, Cleomenes and Dion, have
Been both at Delphos, and from thence have brought
This sealed-up oracle, by the hand delivered
Of great Apollo's priest, and that since then
You have not dared to break the holy seal
Nor read the secrets in't.

CLEOMENES, DION   All this we swear.

LEONTES
Break up the seals and read.   130

OFFICER [reads] Hermione is chaste, Polixenes blameless, Camillo a true subject, Leontes a jealous tyrant, his
innocent babe truly begotten; and the king shall live
without an heir if that which is lost be not found.

LORDS
Now blessèd be the great Apollo!

HERMIONE   Praisèd!

LEONTES
Hast thou read truth?

OFFICER   Ay, my lord, even so
As it is here set down.

LEONTES
There is no truth at all i' th' oracle.
The sessions shall proceed. This is mere falsehood.   139
        [Enter Servant.]

SERVANT
My lord the king, the king!

LEONTES   What is the business?

SERVANT
O sir, I shall be hated to report it.
The prince your son, with mere conceit and fear   142
Of the queen's speed, is gone.   143

LEONTES   How? gone?

SERVANT   Is dead.

LEONTES
Apollo's angry, and the heavens themselves
Do strike at my injustice.

        [Hermione swoons.] How now there?

PAULINA
This news is mortal to the queen. Look down   146
And see what death is doing.

57 *due to me* applicable to my behavior 58–59 *More . . . fault* more faults
than I have 62 *required* deserved 75 *Wotting* if they know 80 *in* on
84 *fact* deed 85 *concerns* implicates 91 *bug* bugbear 92 *commodity*
comfort 98 *Starred* fated 101 *immodest* immoderate 105 *of limit*
limited 108–09 *no life . . . honor* I speak not to ask life but for my honor
121 *flatness* uniformity 130 *up* open 139 *sessions* trial 142 *conceit*
imagination; *fear* anxiety 143 *speed* success 146 *mortal* fatal

LEONTES   Take her hence.
148   Her heart is but o'ercharged; she will recover.
I have too much believed mine own suspicion.
Beseech you, tenderly apply to her
Some remedies for life.
       [Exeunt Paulina and Ladies with Hermione.]
           Apollo, pardon
My great profaneness 'gainst thine oracle!
I'll reconcile me to Polixenes,
New woo my queen, recall the good Camillo,
Whom I proclaim a man of truth, of mercy;
For, being transported by my jealousies
To bloody thoughts and to revenge, I chose
Camillo for the minister to poison
My friend Polixenes, which had been done,
But that the good mind of Camillo tardied
My swift command, though I with death and with
Reward did threaten and encourage him,
Not doing it and being done. He, most humane
And filled with honor, to my kingly guest
165   Unclasped my practice, quit his fortunes here,
Which you knew great, and to the hazard
167   Of all incertainties himself commended,
168   No richer than his honor. How he glisters
169   Through my rust! and how his piety
Does my deeds make the blacker!
       [Enter Paulina.]
170 PAULINA   Woe the while!
O, cut my lace, lest my heart, cracking it,
Break too!
LORD   What fit is this, good lady?
PAULINA
What studied torments, tyrant, hast for me?
What wheels? racks? fires? what flaying? boiling
In leads or oils? what old or newer torture
Must I receive, whose every word deserves
To taste of thy most worst? Thy tyranny,
Together working with thy jealousies,
Fancies too weak for boys, too green and idle
For girls of nine, O, think what they have done,
And then run mad indeed, stark mad, for all
182   Thy bygone fooleries were but spices of it.
That thou betrayedst Polixenes, 'twas nothing;
184   That did but show thee, of a fool, inconstant
And damnable ingrateful. Nor was't much
Thou wouldst have poisoned good Camillo's honor,
187   To have him kill a king – poor trespasses,
More monstrous standing by. Whereof I reckon
The casting forth to crows thy baby daughter
To be or none or little, though a devil
Would have shed water out of fire ere done't.
Nor is't directly laid to thee, the death
Of the young prince, whose honorable thoughts,
194   Thoughts high for one so tender, cleft the heart
That could conceive a gross and foolish sire
Blemished his gracious dam. This is not, no,
Laid to thy answer. But the last – O lords,
When I have said, cry 'Woe!' – the queen, the queen,
The sweet'st dear'st creature's dead, and vengeance for't
Not dropped down yet.
LORD   The higher powers forbid!
PAULINA
I say she's dead; I'll swear't. If word nor oath
Prevail not, go and see. If you can bring

Tincture or lustre in her lip, her eye,   203
Heat outwardly or breath within, I'll serve you
As I would do the gods. But, O thou tyrant,
Do not repent these things, for they are heavier
Than all thy woes can stir. Therefore betake thee   207
To nothing but despair. A thousand knees
Ten thousand years together, naked, fasting,
Upon a barren mountain, and still winter
In storm perpetual, could not move the gods
To look that way thou wert.   212
LEONTES   Go on, go on.
Thou canst not speak too much. I have deserved
All tongues to talk their bitt'rest.
LORD   Say no more.
Howe'er the business goes, you have made fault
I' th' boldness of your speech.
PAULINA   I am sorry for't.
All faults I make, when I shall come to know them,
I do repent. Alas, I have showed too much
The rashness of a woman. He is touched
To the noble heart. What's gone and what's past help
Should be past grief. Do not receive affliction
At my petition. I beseech you, rather
Let me be punished, that have minded you   223
Of what you should forget. Now, good my liege,
Sir, royal sir, forgive a foolish woman.
The love I bore your queen – lo, fool again! –
I'll speak of her no more, nor of your children;
I'll not remember you of my own lord,
Who is lost too. Take your patience to you,   229
And I'll say nothing.
LEONTES   Thou didst speak but well
When most the truth, which I receive much better
Than to be pitied of thee. Prithee, bring me
To the dead bodies of my queen and son.
One grave shall be for both. Upon them shall
The causes of their death appear, unto
Our shame perpetual. Once a day I'll visit
The chapel where they lie, and tears shed there
Shall be my recreation. So long as nature   238
Will bear up with this exercise, so long
I daily vow to use it. Come, and lead me
To these sorrows.   *Exeunt.*

               *

      Enter Antigonus, [and] a Mariner, [with a] Babe.   III, iii
ANTIGONUS
Thou art perfect then our ship hath touched upon   1
The deserts of Bohemia?
MARINER   Ay, my lord, and fear
We have landed in ill time. The skies look grimly
And threaten present blusters. In my conscience,   4
The heavens with that we have in hand are angry
And frown upon's.

148 *o'ercharged* too full (of grief)   165 *Unclasped my practice* revealed my evil design   167 *commended* entrusted   168 *glisters* shines   169 *Through* (pronounced as disyllable)   170 *while* time   182 *spices* small things   184 *of a fool* for a fool   187–88 *poor . . . by* slight sins compared to others you are guilty of   194 *tender* i.e. young   203 *Tincture . . . eye* color to the lip or brightness to the eye   207 *stir* alter   212 *look . . . wert* take notice of you   223 *minded* reminded   229 *Take . . . you* be patient   238 *recreation* refreshing of mind and spirit
III, iii The seacoast of Bohemia   1 *perfect* sure   4 *conscience* opinion

ANTIGONUS
Their sacred wills be done ! Go, get aboard ;
Look to thy bark. I'll not be long before
I call upon thee.
MARINER   Make your best haste, and go not
Too far i' th' land. 'Tis like to be loud weather.
Besides, this place is famous for the creatures
12 Of prey that keep upon't.
ANTIGONUS   Go thou away ;
I'll follow instantly.
MARINER   I am glad at heart
To be so rid o' th' business.   *Exit.*
ANTIGONUS   Come, poor babe.
I have heard, but not believed, the spirits o' th' dead
May walk again. If such thing be, thy mother
Appeared to me last night, for ne'er was dream
So like a waking. To me comes a creature,
Sometimes her head on one side, some another.
I never saw a vessel of like sorrow,
So filled and so becoming. In pure white robes,
Like very sanctity, she did approach
My cabin where I lay ; thrice bowed before me,
And, gasping to begin some speech, her eyes
25 Became two spouts. The fury spent, anon
Did this break her from : 'Good Antigonus,
Since fate, against thy better disposition,
Hath made thy person for the thrower-out
Of my poor babe, according to thine oath,
Places remote enough are in Bohemia ;
There weep and leave it crying. And, for the babe
32 Is counted lost for ever, Perdita,
I prithee, call't. For this ungentle business,
Put on thee by my lord, thou ne'er shalt see
Thy wife Paulina more.' And so, with shrieks,
She melted into air. Affrighted much,
I did in time collect myself, and thought
38 This was so and no slumber. Dreams are toys ;
Yet for this once, yea, superstitiously,
40 I will be squared by this. I do believe
Hermione hath suffered death, and that
Apollo would, this being indeed the issue
Of King Polixenes, it should here be laid,
Either for life or death, upon the earth
Of its right father. Blossom, speed thee well.
46 There lie, and there thy character ; there these,
47 Which may, if fortune please, both breed thee, pretty,
And still rest thine. The storm begins. Poor wretch,
That for thy mother's fault art thus exposed
To loss and what may follow. Weep I cannot,
But my heart bleeds ; and most accursed am I
To be by oath enjoined to this. Farewell !

The day frowns more and more. Thou'rt like to have
A lullaby too rough. I never saw
The heavens so dim by day. A savage clamor !
Well may I get aboard ! This is the chase.
I am gone for ever.   *Exit, pursued by a bear.*
[Enter] Shepherd.
SHEPHERD I would there were no age between ten and 58
three-and-twenty, or that youth would sleep out the rest ;
for there is nothing in the between but getting wenches
with child, wronging the ancientry, stealing, fighting. 61
Hark you now. Would any but these boiled brains of
nineteen and two-and-twenty hunt this weather ? They
have scared away two of my best sheep, which I fear the
wolf will sooner find than the master. If anywhere I have
them, 'tis by the seaside, browsing of ivy. Good luck,
an't be thy will ! What have we here ? Mercy on's, a
barne, a very pretty barne ! A boy or a child, I wonder ? 68
A pretty one, a very pretty one. Sure, some scape. 69
Though I am not bookish, yet I can read waiting-gentle-
woman in the scape. This has been some stair-work,
some trunk-work, some behind-door-work. They were 72
warmer that got this than the poor thing is here. I'll take 73
it up for pity. Yet I'll tarry till my son come. He hal-
looed but even now. Whoa, ho, hoa ! 75
Enter Clown.
CLOWN Hilloa, loa !
SHEPHERD What, art so near ? If thou'lt see a thing to
talk on when thou art dead and rotten, come hither.
What ail'st thou, man ?
CLOWN I have seen two such sights, by sea and by land –
but I am not to say it is a sea, for it is now the sky ; betwixt the firmament and it you cannot thrust a bodkin's
point.
SHEPHERD Why, boy, how is it ?
CLOWN I would you did but see how it chafes, how it
rages, how it takes up the shore. But that's not to the
point. O, the most piteous cry of the poor souls ! Sometimes to see 'em, and not to see 'em. Now the ship
boring the moon with her main-mast, and anon swallowed with yest and froth, as you'ld thrust a cork into a 89
hogshead. And then for the land-service – to see how 90
the bear tore out his shoulder-bone, how he cried to me
for help and said his name was Antigonus, a nobleman.
But to make an end of the ship – to see how the sea flap- 93
dragoned it. But, first, how the poor souls roared, and
the sea mocked them, and how the poor gentleman
roared and the bear mocked him, both roaring louder
than the sea or weather.
SHEPHERD Name of mercy, when was this, boy ?
CLOWN Now, now ; I have not winked since I saw these
sights. The men are not yet cold under water, nor the 100
bear half dined on the gentleman. He's at it now.
SHEPHERD Would I had been by, to have helped the old
man.
CLOWN I would you had been by the ship side, to have
helped her. There your charity would have lacked
footing.
SHEPHERD Heavy matters, heavy matters ! But look thee
here, boy. Now bless thyself ! thou mettest with things
dying, I with things new-born. Here's a sight for thee.
Look thee, a bearing-cloth for a squire's child. Look 108
thee here. Take up, take up, boy ; open't. So, let's see. It
was told me I should be rich by the fairies. This is some
changeling. Open't. What's within, boy ? 111

---

12 *keep* live **25** *anon* presently **32** *Perdita* i.e. the lost one (feminine)
38 *toys* trifles **40** *squared* ruled **46** *character* writing ; *these* i.e. gold and
the jewels by which she is later to be identified **47** *breed* rear **58** (As *ten*
seems too tender an age to indulge in some of the escapades referred to,
some editors change 'ten' to 'sixteen'. If written in Arabic numerals,
either 16 or 19 might easily be misread 10. Cf. l. 63.) **61** *ancientry* old
people **68** *child* girl **69** *scape* escapade **72** *trunk-work* a pun on 'trunk'
meaning (1) a secret place, (2) the body apart from head and limbs **73** *got*
begot **75** **s.d.** *Clown* country fellow **89** *yest* foam **90** *land-service* (1) a dish
of food served on land, (2) the branch of the military serving on land, not
at sea **93** *flap-dragoned* swallowed whole **100** *cold* dead **108** *bearing-
cloth* cloth or mantle in which a child is carried to baptism **111** *changeling*
child taken or left by fairies

CLOWN You're a made old man. If the sins of your youth
113   are forgiven you, you're well to live. Gold! all gold!

SHEPHERD This is fairy gold, boy, and 'twill prove so. Up
115   with't, keep it close. Home, home, the next way. We are
lucky, boy, and to be so still requires nothing but secrecy.
Let my sheep go. Come, good boy, the next way home.

CLOWN Go you the next way with your findings. I'll go
see if the bear be gone from the gentleman and how
120   much he hath eaten. They are never curst but when they
are hungry. If there be any of him left, I'll bury it.

SHEPHERD That's a good deed. If thou mayest discern by
that which is left of him what he is, fetch me to the sight
of him.

CLOWN Marry, will I; and you shall help to put him i' the
ground.

SHEPHERD 'Tis a lucky day, boy, and we'll do good deeds
on't.   *Exeunt.*

*

IV, i   *Enter Time, the Chorus.*

TIME

1   I, that please some, try all, both joy and terror
2   Of good and bad, that makes and unfolds error,
Now take upon me, in the name of Time,
To use my wings. Impute it not a crime
To me or my swift passage that I slide
6   O'er sixteen years and leave the growth untried
Of that wide gap, since it is in my power
To o'erthrow law and in one self-born hour
To plant and o'erwhelm custom. Let me pass
The same I am, ere ancient'st order was
Or what is now received. I witness to
The times that brought them in. So shall I do
To the freshest things now reigning, and make stale
14   The glistering of this present, as my tale
Now seems to it. Your patience this allowing,
I turn my glass and give my scene such growing
As you had slept between. Leontes leaving,
18   Th' effects of his fond jealousies so grieving
That he shuts up himself, imagine me,
Gentle spectators, that I now may be
In fair Bohemia. And remember well,
I mentioned a son o' th' king's, which Florizel
23   I now name to you, and with speed so pace
To speak of Perdita, now grown in grace
Equal with wond'ring. What of her ensues
26   I list not prophesy; but let Time's news
Be known when 'tis brought forth. A shepherd's daughter
28   And what to her adheres, which follows after,
29   Is th' argument of Time. Of this allow
If ever you have spent time worse ere now;
If never, yet that Time himself doth say
He wishes earnestly you never may.   *Exit.*

IV, ii   *Enter Polixenes and Camillo.*

POLIXENES I pray thee, good Camillo, be no more importunate. 'Tis a sickness denying thee anything, a
death to grant this.

CAMILLO It is fifteen years since I saw my country.
5   Though I have for the most part been aired abroad, I
desire to lay my bones there. Besides, the penitent king,
my master, hath sent for me, to whose feeling sorrows I

might be some allay – or I o'erween to think so – which 8
is another spur to my departure.

POLIXENES As thou lov'st me, Camillo, wipe not out the
rest of thy services by leaving me now. The need I have
of thee thine own goodness hath made. Better not to
have had thee than thus to want thee. Thou, having 13
made me businesses which none without thee can sufficiently manage, must either stay to execute them thyself or take away with thee the very services thou hast
done, which if I have not enough considered – as too
much I cannot – to be more thankful to thee shall be my
study, and my profit therein the heaping friendships. 19
Of that fatal country, Sicilia, prithee speak no more,
whose very naming punishes me with the remembrance
of that penitent, as thou call'st him, and reconciled
king, my brother, whose loss of his most precious queen
and children are even now to be afresh lamented. Say to
me, when saw'st thou the Prince Florizel, my son?
Kings are no less unhappy, their issue not being gracious, than they are in losing them when they have ap- 27
proved their virtues.

CAMILLO Sir, it is three days since I saw the prince.
What his happier affairs may be, are to me unknown,
but I have missingly noted he is of late much retired 30
from court and is less frequent to his princely exercises
than formerly he hath appeared.

POLIXENES I have considered so much, Camillo, and
with some care – so far that I have eyes under my service 34
which look upon his removedness, from whom I have
this intelligence, that he is seldom from the house of a 36
most homely shepherd, a man, they say, that from very 37
nothing, and beyond the imagination of his neighbors,
is grown into an unspeakable estate. 39

CAMILLO I have heard, sir, of such a man, who hath a
daughter of most rare note. The report of her is extended more than can be thought to begin from such a
cottage.

POLIXENES That's likewise part of my intelligence; but,
I fear, the angle that plucks our son thither. Thou shalt 44
accompany us to the place, where we will, not appearing
what we are, have some question with the shepherd, from
whose simplicity I think it not uneasy to get the cause of
my son's resort thither. Prithee be my present partner
in this business, and lay aside the thoughts of Sicilia.

CAMILLO I willingly obey your command.

POLIXENES My best Camillo! We must disguise ourselves.   *Exeunt.*

*

113 *well to live* well-to-do   115 *close* secret; *next* nearest   120 *curst* mean
IV, i (Because of its awkwardness in both verse and thought, some editors have accepted Heath's view that this chorus is an interpolation written by one other than Shakespeare. Professor Kittredge defends its authenticity, declaring it written to fit the character of 'Father Time – a doddering, toothless ancient, halting but fluent, senile but self-assured, ridiculous but triumphant.') 1 *try* test 1–2 *joy . . . bad* joy to good men and terror to bad 2 *unfolds* reveals 6 *growth untried* events untold 14 *glistering* brightness 18 *fond* foolish 23 *pace* proceed 26 *list not* do not wish to 28 *adheres* relates 29 *argument* story
IV, ii The palace of the King of Bohemia 5 *been aired* lived 8 *o'erween* am presumptuous 13 *want* be without 19 *heaping* full 27 *approved* proved 30 *missingly* in missing him 34 *eyes* spies 36 *intelligence* report 37 *homely* unpretentious 39 *unspeakable estate* untold wealth 44 *angle* fishhook

IV, iii   *Enter Autolycus, singing.*

1   When daffodils begin to peer,
2   With heigh! the doxy over the dale,
     Why, then comes in the sweet o' the year,
4   For the red blood reigns in the winter's pale.

     The white sheet bleaching on the hedge,
         With heigh! the sweet birds, O how they sing!
7   Doth set my pugging tooth on edge,
         For a quart of ale is a dish for a king.

     The lark, that tirra-lyra chants,
         With heigh! with heigh! the thrush and the jay,
11   Are summer songs for me and my aunts,
         While we lie tumbling in the hay.

13   I have served Prince Florizel and in my time wore three-
     pile, but now I am out of service.

     But shall I go mourn for that, my dear?
         The pale moon shines by night.
     And when I wander here and there,
         I then do most go right.

     If tinkers may have leave to live,
20   And bear the sow-skin budget,
     Then my account I well may give,
         And in the stocks avouch it.

23   My traffic is sheets; when the kite builds, look to lesser
     linen. My father named me Autolycus, who being, as I
25   am, littered under Mercury, was likewise a snapper-up
26   of unconsidered trifles. With die and drab I purchased
27   this caparison, and my revenue is the silly cheat. Gal-
     lows and knock are too powerful on the highway;
     beating and hanging are terrors to me. For the life to
30   come, I sleep out the thought of it. A prize! a prize!
         Enter Clown.
31   CLOWN Let me see; every 'leven wether tods; every tod
     yields pound and odd shilling; fifteen hundred shorn,
     what comes the wool to?
     AUTOLYCUS *[aside]* If the springe hold, the cock 's mine.
     CLOWN I cannot do 't without counters. Let me see; what
     am I to buy for our sheep-shearing feast? Three pound
     of sugar, five pound of currants, rice – what will this
     sister of mine do with rice? But my father hath made her
     mistress of the feast, and she lays it on. She hath made me
40   four and twenty nosegays for the shearers – three-man
     songmen all, and very good ones; but they are most of
42   them means and bases, but one puritan amongst them,
     and he sings psalms to hornpipes. I must have saffron to
44   color the warden pies; mace; dates? – none, that's out of
45   my note; nutmegs, seven; a race or two of ginger, but

that I may beg; four pounds of prunes, and as many of
raisins o' the sun.   47
AUTOLYCUS O that ever I was born!
     [Grovels on the ground.]
CLOWN I' the name of me –
AUTOLYCUS O, help me, help me! pluck but off these
     rags, and then death, death!
CLOWN Alack, poor soul, thou hast need of more rags to
     lay on thee, rather than have these off.
AUTOLYCUS O, sir, the loathsomeness of them offends
     me more than the stripes I have received, which are
     mighty ones and millions.
CLOWN Alas, poor man! A million of beating may come
     to a great matter.
AUTOLYCUS I am robbed, sir, and beaten, my money
     and apparel ta'en from me, and these detestable things   60
     put upon me.
CLOWN What, by a horseman, or a footman?
AUTOLYCUS A footman, sweet sir, a footman.
CLOWN Indeed, he should be a footman by the garments
     he has left with thee. If this be a horseman's coat, it hath
     seen very hot service. Lend my thy hand, I'll help thee.
     Come, lend me thy hand.
     [Helps him up.]
AUTOLYCUS O, good sir, tenderly. O!
CLOWN Alas, poor soul!
AUTOLYCUS O, good sir, softly, good sir. I fear, sir, my   70
     shoulder-blade is out.
CLOWN How now? canst stand?
AUTOLYCUS *[picking his pocket]* Softly, dear sir; good
     sir, softly. You ha' done me a charitable office.
CLOWN Dost lack any money? I have a little money for
     thee.
AUTOLYCUS No, good sweet sir; no, I beseech you, sir. I
     have a kinsman not past three quarters of a mile hence,
     unto whom I was going. I shall there have money, or
     anything I want. Offer me no money, I pray you; that
     kills my heart.
CLOWN What manner of fellow was he that robbed you?
AUTOLYCUS A fellow, sir, that I have known to go about
     with troll-my-dames. I knew him once a servant of the   83
     prince. I cannot tell, good sir, for which of his virtues it
     was, but he was certainly whipped out of the court.
CLOWN His vices, you would say. There's no virtue
     whipped out of the court. They cherish it to make it stay
     there, and yet it will no more but abide.
AUTOLYCUS Vices, I would say, sir. I know this man
     well. He hath been since an ape-bearer, then a process-
     server, a bailiff. Then he compassed a motion of the   91
     Prodigal Son, and married a tinker's wife within a mile
     where my land and living lies, and, having flown over
     many knavish professions, he settled only in rogue.
     Some call him Autolycus.
CLOWN Out upon him! Prig, for my life, prig! He haunts   96
     wakes, fairs, and bear-baitings.
AUTOLYCUS Very true, sir; he, sir, he. That's the rogue
     that put me into this apparel.
CLOWN Not a more cowardly rogue in all Bohemia. If you
     had but looked big and spit at him, he'ld have run.
AUTOLYCUS I must confess to you, sir, I am no fighter. I
     am false of heart that way, and that he knew, I warrant
     him.
CLOWN How do you now?
AUTOLYCUS Sweet sir, much better than I was. I can

IV, iii A footpath in Bohemia   1 *peer* appear   2 *doxy* female beggar, prostitute   4 *in the winter's pale* (1) instead of winter's pallor, (2) in winter's
domain   7 *pugging* pilfering (?) (cf. sweet tooth)   11 *aunts* i.e. prostitutes
13 *three-pile* the finest velvet   20 *budget* sack   23 *lesser* smaller pieces of
25 *littered under Mercury* born when the planet Mercury was in the ascendant (as Mercury was the god of thieving, both the earlier Autolycus,
father of Odysseus, and this his namesake are skilled in that art)   26–27
With . . . caparison by dice and harlots I got this attire   27 *revenue* source
of income   30 *prize* booty or one from whom it may be taken   31 *'leven
wether tods* eleven sheep yield a tod (an old weight for wool)   40–41 *three-
man songmen* men who sing catches or rounds   42 *means* tenors   44
warden pear   44–45 *out . . . note* not on my list   45 *race* root   47 *o' the sun*
sun-dried   83 *troll-my-dames* a game resembling bagatelle   91 *compassed
a motion* devised a puppet-show   96 *Prig* thief

stand and walk. I will even take my leave of you and
pace softly towards my kinsman's.

CLOWN Shall I bring thee on the way?

AUTOLYCUS No, good-faced sir; no, sweet sir.

CLOWN Then fare thee well. I must go buy spices for our
sheep-shearing.

AUTOLYCUS Prosper you, sweet sir. *Exit [Clown].*
Your purse is not hot enough to purchase your spice.
I'll be with you at your sheep-shearing too. If I make
115 not this cheat bring out another and the shearers prove
116 sheep, let me be unrolled and my name put in the book
of virtue.

Song.

Jog on, jog on, the foot-path way,
    And merrily hent the stile-a.
119 A merry heart goes all the day,
    Your sad tires in a mile-a.   *Exit.*

*

IV, iv   *Enter Florizel, Perdita.*

FLORIZEL
These your unusual weeds to each part of you
2 Do give a life – no shepherdess, but Flora
3 Peering in April's front. This your sheep-shearing
Is as a meeting of the petty gods,
And you the queen on't.

PERDITA   Sir, my gracious lord,
6 To chide at your extremes it not becomes me –
O, pardon, that I name them. Your high self,
8 The gracious mark o' th' land, you have obscured
9 With a swain's wearing, and me, poor lowly maid,
10 Most goddess-like pranked up. But that our feasts
In every mess have folly, and the feeders
Digest it with a custom, I should blush
To see you so attired, swoon, I think,
To show myself a glass.

FLORIZEL   I bless the time
When my good falcon made her flight across
Thy father's ground.

PERDITA   Now Jove afford you cause!
To me the difference forges dread; your greatness
Hath not been used to fear. Even now I tremble
To think your father, by some accident,
Should pass this way as you did. O, the Fates!
How would he look, to see his work, so noble,
Vilely bound up? What would he say? Or how
Should I, in these my borrowed flaunts, behold
The sternness of his presence?

FLORIZEL   Apprehend
Nothing but jollity. The gods themselves,
Humbling their deities to love, have taken
27 The shapes of beasts upon them. Jupiter
Became a bull, and bellowed; the green Neptune
A ram, and bleated; and the fire-robed god,
Golden Apollo, a poor humble swain,
As I seem now. Their transformations
Were never for a piece of beauty rarer,
Nor in a way so chaste, since my desires
34 Run not before mine honor, nor my lusts
Burn hotter than my faith.

PERDITA   O, but, sir,
Your resolution cannot hold when 'tis
Opposed, as it must be, by th' power of the king.

One of these two must be necessities,
Which then will speak, that you must change this
    purpose,
Or I my life.

FLORIZEL   Thou dearest Perdita,
With these forced thoughts, I prithee, darken not 41
The mirth o' th' feast. Or I'll be thine, my fair, 42
Or not my father's. For I cannot be
Mine own, nor anything to any, if
I be not thine. To this I am most constant,
Though destiny say no. Be merry, gentle;
Strangle such thoughts as these with anything
That you behold the while. Your guests are coming.
Lift up your countenance, as it were the day
Of celebration of that nuptial which
We two have sworn shall come.

PERDITA   O lady Fortune,
Stand you auspicious!

FLORIZEL   See, your guests approach.
Address yourself to entertain them sprightly,
And let's be red with mirth.

    [Enter] Shepherd, Clown, [with] Polixenes, [and]
    Camillo [disguised], Mopsa, Dorcas, Servants.

SHEPHERD
Fie, daughter! When my old wife lived, upon
This day she was both pantler, butler, cook, 56
Both dame and servant; welcomed all, served all;
Would sing her song and dance her turn; now here
At upper end o' th' table, now i' th' middle;
On his shoulder, and his; her face o' fire
With labor, and the thing she took to quench it
She would to each one sip. You are retirèd,
As if you were a feasted one and not 63
The hostess of the meeting. Pray you bid
These unknown friends to's welcome, for it is
A way to make us better friends, more known.
Come, quench your blushes and present yourself
That which you are, mistress o' th' feast. Come on,
And bid us welcome to your sheep-shearing,
As your good flock shall prosper.

PERDITA *[to Polixenes]*   Sir, welcome.
It is my father's will I should take on me
The hostess-ship o' th' day.
    [To Camillo]   You're welcome, sir.
Give me those flowers there, Dorcas. Reverend sirs,
For you there's rosemary and rue; these keep 74
Seeming and savor all the winter long.
Grace and remembrance be to you both,
And welcome to our shearing!

POLIXENES   Shepherdess –
A fair one are you – well you fit our ages
With flowers of winter.

PERDITA   Sir, the year growing ancient,
Not yet on summer's death nor on the birth

115 *bring out* lead to 116 *unrolled* removed from the roll of thieves 119
hent take hold of
IV, iv The Shepherd's garden 2 *Flora* the goddess of flowers 3 *April's
front* early April 6 *extremes* exaggerations 8 *mark* ornament 9 *wearing*
clothes 10 *pranked up* made fine 27–30 (Jupiter took the shape of a bull
to carry off Europa, Neptune that of a ram to woo Theophane; and Apollo,
exiled from heaven by Jupiter, served Admetus as a shepherd and enabled
him to win Alcestis.) 34 *Run not before* i.e. do not win a victory over
41 *forced* far-fetched 42 *Or* either 56 *pantler* pantry-servant 63
feasted one i.e. guest 74 *rosemary . . . rue* (associated respectively with
remembrance and grace)

Of trembling winter, the fairest flowers o' th' season
82 Are our carnations and streaked gillyvors,
83 Which some call nature's bastards. Of that kind
Our rustic garden's barren, and I care not
To get slips of them.

POLIXENES   Wherefore, gentle maiden,
Do you neglect them?

PERDITA   For I have heard it said
87 There is an art which in their piedness shares
With great creating nature.

POLIXENES   Say there be;
89 Yet nature is made better by no mean
But nature makes that mean. So, over that art
Which you say adds to nature, is an art
That nature makes. You see, sweet maid, we marry
A gentler scion to the wildest stock,
And make conceive a bark of baser kind
By bud of nobler race. This is an art
Which does mend nature – change it rather – but
The art itself is nature.

PERDITA   So it is.

POLIXENES
Then make your garden rich in gillyvors,
And do not call them bastards.

PERDITA   I'll not put
100 The dibble in earth to set one slip of them,
No more than, were I painted, I would wish
This youth should say 'twere well, and only therefore
Desire to breed by me. Here's flowers for you,
Hot lavender, mints, savory, marjoram,
105 The marigold, that goes to bed wi' th' sun
And with him rises weeping. These are flowers
Of middle summer, and I think they are given
To men of middle age. Y'are very welcome.

CAMILLO
I should leave grazing, were I of your flock,
And only live by gazing.

PERDITA   Out, alas!
You'd be so lean that blasts of January
Would blow you through and through. Now, my fair'st
     friend,
I would I had some flowers o' th' spring that might
Become your time of day, and yours, and yours,
That wear upon your virgin branches yet
116 Your maidenheads growing. O Proserpina,
For the flowers now that, frighted, thou let'st fall
From Dis's wagon; daffodils,
119 That come before the swallow dares, and take
The winds of March with beauty; violets dim,
121 But sweeter than the lids of Juno's eyes

Or Cytherea's breath; pale primroses,   122
That die unmarried, ere they can behold
Bright Phoebus in his strength – a malady   124
Most incident to maids; bold oxlips and
The crown imperial; lilies of all kinds,
The flower-de-luce being one. O, these I lack
To make you garlands of, and my sweet friend,
To strew him o'er and o'er!

FLORIZEL   What, like a corse?   129
PERDITA
No, like a bank for love to lie and play on.
Not like a corse; or if, not to be buried,
But quick and in mine arms. Come, take your flowers.
Methinks I play as I have seen them do
In Whitsun pastorals. Sure this robe of mine   134
Does change my disposition.

FLORIZEL   What you do
Still betters what is done. When you speak, sweet,
I'd have you do it ever. When you sing,
I'd have you buy and sell so, so give alms,
Pray so, and for the ord'ring your affairs,
To sing them too. When you do dance, I wish you
A wave o' th' sea, that you might ever do
Nothing but that, move still, still so,
And own no other function. Each your doing,   143
So singular in each particular,
Crowns what you are doing in the present deeds,
That all your acts are queens.

PERDITA   O Doricles,   146
Your praises are too large. But that your youth,
And the true blood which peeps fairly through't,   148
Do plainly give you out an unstained shepherd,
With wisdom I might fear, my Doricles,
You wooed me the false way.

FLORIZEL   I think you have
As little skill to fear as I have purpose   152
To put you to't. But come; our dance, I pray.
Your hand, my Perdita. So turtles pair   154
That never mean to part.

PERDITA   I'll swear for 'em.
POLIXENES
This is the prettiest low-born lass that ever
Ran on the greensward. Nothing she does or seems
But smacks of something greater than herself,   158
Too noble for this place.

CAMILLO   He tells her something
That makes her blood look on't. Good sooth, she is   160
The queen of curds and cream.

CLOWN   Come on, strike up!
DORCAS
Mopsa must be your mistress. Marry, garlic,
To mend her kissing with!   163

MOPSA   Now, in good time!
CLOWN
Not a word, a word! We stand upon our manners.
Come, strike up!

   [Music.] Here a dance of Shepherds and Shepherdesses.

POLIXENES
Pray, good shepherd, what fair swain is this
Which dances with your daughter?

SHEPHERD
They call him Doricles, and boasts himself
To have a worthy feeding. But I have it   169
Upon his own report and I believe it;

82 *gillyvors* gillyflowers, clove pinks   83 *nature's bastards* i.e. created by crossbreeding   87–88 *There . . . nature* i.e. the parti-color of the flower owes as much to the skill of the gardener as to nature   89 *mean* method   100 *dibble* tool for making holes for seed   105 *goes . . . sun* i.e. closes its petals at nightfall   116 *Proserpina* Ceres' daughter, who, spied by Dis (Pluto, god of the underworld) while she was gathering flowers, was seized and taken by him to the underworld to become his queen   119 *take* charm   121 *Juno* wife of Jupiter and queen of heaven   122 *Cytherea* Venus   124 *Phoebus* the sun (Phoebus Apollo the sun god)   129 *corse* corpse   134 *Whitsun pastorals* plays (or morris dances) presented around Whitsun, the seventh Sunday after Easter   143 *Each your doing* everything you do   146 *Doricles* (the name assumed by Florizel in his disguise)   148 *peeps fairly* (many editors insert 'so' in the belief that it may have been absorbed in the 's' of 'peeps')   152 *skill* reason   154 *turtles* turtledoves   158 *greater* of gentler blood   160 *blood look on't* blush   163 *mend . . . with* escape her unpleasant breath   169 *feeding* land on which sheep feed

171   He looks like sooth. He says he loves my daughter.
I think so too, for never gazed the moon
Upon the water as he'll stand and read
As 'twere my daughter's eyes; and, to be plain,
I think there is not half a kiss to choose
176   Who loves another best.

POLIXENES   She dances featly.

SHEPHERD
So she does anything, though I report it
That should be silent. If young Doricles
Do light upon her, she shall bring him that
Which he not dreams of.
    Enter Servant.

SERVANT O master, if you did but hear the pedlar at the
door, you would never dance again after a tabor and
pipe – no, the bagpipe could not move you. He sings
184   several tunes faster than you'll tell money. He utters
them as he had eaten ballads and all men's ears grew to
his tunes.

CLOWN He could never come better. He shall come in. I
love a ballad but even too well if it be doleful matter
merrily set down, or a very pleasant thing indeed and
sung lamentably.

SERVANT He hath songs for man or woman, of all sizes.
No milliner can so fit his customers with gloves. He has
the prettiest love-songs for maids, so without bawdry,
193   which is strange, with such delicate burthens of dildos
194   and fadings, 'Jump her and thump her.' And where
some stretch-mouthed rascal would, as it were, mean
mischief and break a foul gap into the matter, he makes
the maid to answer, 'Whoop, do me no harm, good
man'; puts him off, slights him, with 'Whoop, do me no
harm, good man.'

POLIXENES This is a brave fellow.

201 CLOWN Believe me, thou talkest of an admirable con-
202   ceited fellow. Has he any unbraided wares?

SERVANT He hath ribbons of all the colors i' th' rainbow,
204   points more than all the lawyers in Bohemia can learned-
205   ly handle, though they come to him by the gross – inkles,
206   caddises, cambrics, lawns. Why, he sings 'em over as
they were gods or goddesses. You would think a smock
208   were a she-angel, he so chants to the sleeve-hand and
209   the work about the square on't.

CLOWN Prithee bring him in, and let him approach singing.

PERDITA Forewarn him that he use no scurrilous words
in's tunes.   *[Exit Servant.]*

213 CLOWN You have of these pedlars that have more in them
than you'ld think, sister.

PERDITA Ay, good brother, or go about to think.
    Enter Autolycus, singing.
    Lawn as white as driven snow,
217   Cyprus black as e'er was crow,
    Gloves as sweet as damask roses,
    Masks for faces and for noses,
220   Bugle bracelet, necklace amber,
    Perfume for a lady's chamber,
222   Golden quoifs and stomachers
    For my lads to give their dears,
224   Pins and poking-sticks of steel,
    What maids lack from head to heel.
    Come buy of me, come; come buy, come buy.
    Buy, lads, or else your lasses cry.
    Come buy.

CLOWN If I were not in love with Mopsa, thou shouldst
take no money of me; but being enthralled as I am, it
will also be the bondage of certain ribbons and gloves.

MOPSA I was promised them against the feast, but they
come not too late now.

DORCAS He hath promised you more than that, or there
be liars.

MOPSA He hath paid you all he promised you. May be he
has paid you more, which will shame you to give him 237
again.

CLOWN Is there no manners left among maids? Will they
wear their plackets where they should bear their faces?
Is there not milking-time, when you are going to bed, or
kiln-hole, to whistle off these secrets, but you must be 242
tittle-tattling before all our guests? 'Tis well they are
whispering. Clamor your tongues, and not a word more. 244

MOPSA I have done. Come, you promised me a tawdry- 245
lace and a pair of sweet gloves.

CLOWN Have I not told thee how I was cozened by the 247
way and lost all my money?

AUTOLYCUS And indeed, sir, there are cozeners abroad;
therefore it behoves men to be wary.

CLOWN Fear not thou, man; thou shalt lose nothing here.

AUTOLYCUS I hope so, sir, for I have about me many
parcels of charge.   253

CLOWN What hast here? Ballads?

MOPSA Pray now, buy some. I love a ballad in print, a life, 255
for then we are sure they are true.

AUTOLYCUS Here's one to a very doleful tune, how a
usurer's wife was brought to bed of twenty money-bags
at a burthen, and how she longed to eat adders' heads
and toads carbonadoed.   260

MOPSA Is it true, think you?

AUTOLYCUS Very true, and but a month old.

DORCAS Bless me from marrying a usurer!

AUTOLYCUS Here's the midwife's name to't, one Mistress
Tale-porter, and five or six honest wives that were
present. Why should I carry lies abroad?

MOPSA Pray you now, buy it.

CLOWN Come on, lay it by. And let's first see moe
ballads; we'll buy the other things anon.

AUTOLYCUS Here's another ballad of a fish that appeared
upon the coast on Wednesday the fourscore of April, 271
forty thousand fathom above water, and sung this ballad
against the hard hearts of maids. It was thought she was
a woman and was turned into a cold fish for she would
not exchange flesh with one that loved her. The ballad
is very pitiful and as true.

DORCAS Is it true too, think you?

AUTOLYCUS Five justices' hands at it, and witnesses
more than my pack will hold.

---

171 *like sooth* honest 176 *another* the other; *featly* nimbly 184 *tell* count 193 *dildo* (a word used as a refrain in ballads) 194 *fadings* burdens of songs 201 *conceited* witty 202 *unbraided* unfaded 204 *points* (1) points in an argument, (2) laces to fasten doublet and hose together 205 *inkles* linen tape 206 *caddises* worsted ribbons 208 *sleeve-hand* cuff 209 *square* the front upper part of a dress 213 *You have* there are some 217 *Cyprus* cloth from Cyprus 220 *Bugle* bead 222 *quoifs* coifs, head-dresses 224 *poking-sticks* metal rods used to iron pleats 237–38 *to give him again* into giving back to him 242 *kiln-hole* fireplace 244 *Clamor* stop (?) (It is said to be a technical term of bell-ringing, meaning speed up and stop. Suggested emendations are 'clammer' and, recently by Professor Sisson, 'clam a.') 245 *tawdry-lace* colored neckerchief 247 *cozened* cheated 253 *charge* value 255 *a life* on my life 260 *carbonadoed* grilled 271–72 *fourscore . . . water* (parody of the kind of 'wonders' narrated in broadside ballads)

CLOWN Lay it by too. Another.

AUTOLUCUS This is a merry ballad, but a very pretty one.

MOPSA Let's have some merry ones.

AUTOLYCUS Why, this is a passing merry one and goes to the tune of 'Two maids wooing a man.' There's scarce a
285 maid westward but she sings it. 'Tis in request, I can tell you.

MOPSA We can both sing it ; if thou'lt bear a part, thou shalt hear. 'Tis in three parts.

DORCAS We had the tune on't a month ago.

AUTOLYCUS I can bear my part ; you must know 'tis my occupation. Have at it with you.

Song.

AUTOLYCUS Get you hence, for I must go
               Where it fits not you to know.
DORCAS   Whither ?
MOPSA   O, whither ?
DORCAS   Whither ?
MOPSA   It becomes thy oath full well,
               Thou to me thy secrets tell.
DORCAS   Me too ; let me go thither.
298 MOPSA Or thou goest to th' grange or mill.
DORCAS If to either, thou dost ill.
AUTOLYCUS Neither.
DORCAS   What, neither ?
AUTOLYCUS   Neither.
DORCAS Thou hast sworn my love to be.
MOPSA Thou hast sworn it more to me.
         Then whither goest ? say, whither ?

CLOWN We'll have this song out anon by ourselves. My
305 father and the gentlemen are in sad talk, and we'll not trouble them. Come, bring away thy pack after me. Wenches, I'll buy for you both. Pedlar, let's have the first choice. Follow me, girls.
         [Exit with Dorcas and Mopsa.]

AUTOLYCUS And you shall pay well for 'em.
         [Follows singing.]

Song.

         Will you buy any tape,
         Or lace for your cape,
         My dainty duck, my dear-a ?
           Any silk, any thread,
           Any toys for your head
         Of the new'st and fin'st, fin'st wear-a ?
         Come to the pedlar.
         Money 's a meddler
318   That doth utter all men's ware-a.   *Exit.*

[Enter Servant.]

SERVANT Master, there is three carters, three shepherds,
320 three neatherds, three swineherds, that have made them-
321 selves all men of hair. They call themselves Saltiers, and
322 they have a dance which the wenches say is a gallimaufry of gambols, because they are not in't ; but they them-selves are o' th' mind, if it be not too rough for some

that know little but bowling, it will please plentifully.

SHEPHERD Away ! we'll none on't. Here has been too much homely foolery already. I know, sir, we weary you. 327

POLIXENES You weary those that refresh us. Pray, let's see these four threes of herdsmen.

SERVANT One three of them, by their own report, sir, 330 hath danced before the king ; and not the worst of the three but jumps twelve foot and a half by th' squire. 332

SHEPHERD Leave your prating. Since these good men are pleased, let them come in ; but quickly now.

SERVANT Why, they stay at door, sir.   *[Exit.]*
     Here a dance of twelve Satyrs.

POLIXENES
   O, father, you'll know more of that hereafter.
     [To Camillo]
   Is it not too far gone ? 'Tis time to part them.
   He's simple and tells much. – How now, fair shepherd,
   Your heart is full of something that does take
   Your mind from feasting. Sooth, when I was young
   And handed love as you do, I was wont   341
   To load my she with knacks. I would have ransacked
   The pedlar's silken treasury and have poured it
   To her acceptance. You have let him go
   And nothing marted with him. If your lass   345
   Interpretation should abuse and call this
   Your lack of love or bounty, you were straited   347
   For a reply, at least if you make a care   348
   Of happy holding her.

FLORIZEL   Old sir, I know
   She prizes not such trifles as these are.
   The gifts she looks from me are packed and locked
   Up in my heart, which I have given already,
   But not delivered. O, hear me breathe my life   353
   Before this ancient sir, who, it should seem,
   Hath sometime loved. I take thy hand, this hand
   As soft as dove's down and as white as it,
   Or Ethiopian's tooth, or the fanned snow that's bolted   357
   By th' northern blasts twice o'er.

POLIXENES   What follows this ?
   How prettily the young swain seems to wash
   The hand was fair before ! I have put you out.
   But to your protestation ; let me hear
   What you profess.

FLORIZEL   Do, and be witness to't.

POLIXENES
   And this my neighbor too ?

FLORIZEL   And he, and more
   Than he, and men, the earth, the heavens, and all –
   That, were I crowned the most imperial monarch,
   Thereof most worthy, were I the fairest youth
   That ever made eye swerve, had force and knowledge
   More than was ever man's, I would not prize them
   Without her love ; for her employ them all ;
   Commend them and condemn them to her service   370
   Or to their own perdition.

POLIXENES   Fairly offered.

CAMILLO
   This shows a sound affection.

SHEPHERD   But, my daughter,
   Say you the like to him ?

PERDITA   I cannot speak
   So well, nothing so well ; no, nor mean better.
   By th' pattern of mine own thoughts I cut out
   The purity of his.

---

285 *westward* (in England the 'unspoiled' country)   298 *grange* farm 305 *sad* serious   318 *utter* sell   320 *neatherds* cowherds   321 *of hair* i.e. wearing skins of animals ; *Saltiers* i.e. satyrs   322 *gallimaufry* hodgepodge 327 *homely* lacking refinement   330 *One three* one group of three   332 *squire* square (cf. T-square)   341 *handed* pledged by the hand   345 *marted* traded   347 *straited* hard pressed   348 *care* serious wish   353 *breathe . . . life* vow   357 *fanned* blown ; *bolted* sifted   370 *condemn* (i.e. to *perdition*)

SHEPHERD   Take hands, a bargain!
And, friends unknown, you shall bear witness to't.
I give my daughter to him and will make
Her portion equal his.
FLORIZEL   O, that must be
I' th' virtue of your daughter. One being dead,
I shall have more than you can dream of yet,
Enough then for your wonder. But, come on,
Contract us 'fore these witnesses.
SHEPHERD   Come, your hand;
And, daughter, yours.
384 POLIXENES   Soft, swain, awhile, beseech you.
Have you a father?
FLORIZEL   I have, but what of him?
POLIXENES
Knows he of this?
FLORIZEL   He neither does nor shall.
POLIXENES
Methinks a father
Is at the nuptial of his son a guest
That best becomes the table. Pray you once more,
Is not your father grown incapable
391 Of reasonable affairs? Is he not stupid
With age and alt'ring rheums? Can he speak? hear?
393 Know man from man? dispute his own estate?
Lies he not bed-rid? and again does nothing
But what he did being childish?
FLORIZEL   No, good sir,
He has his health and ampler strength indeed
Than most have of his age.
POLIXENES   By my white beard,
You offer him, if this be so, a wrong
399 Something unfilial. Reason my son
Should choose himself a wife, but as good reason
The father, all whose joy is nothing else
But fair posterity, should hold some counsel
In such a business.
FLORIZEL   I yield all this;
But for some other reasons, my grave sir,
405 Which 'tis not fit you know, I not acquaint
My father of this business.
POLIXENES   Let him know't.
FLORIZEL
He shall not.
POLIXENES   Prithee, let him.
FLORIZEL   No, he must not.
SHEPHERD
Let him, my son. He shall not need to grieve
At knowing of thy choice.
FLORIZEL   Come, come, he must not.
Mark our contract.
POLIXENES   Mark your divorce, young sir,
      [Discovers himself.]
Whom son I dare not call. Thou art too base
To be acknowledged. Thou a sceptre's heir,
That thus affects a sheep-hook! – Thou old traitor,
I am sorry that by hanging thee I can
But shorten thy life one week. – And thou, fresh piece
416 Of excellent witchcraft, who of force must know
417 The royal fool thou cop'st with –
SHEPHERD   O, my heart!
POLIXENES
I'll have thy beauty scratched with briers, and made
419 More homely than thy state. – For thee, fond boy,

If I may ever know thou dost but sigh
That thou no more shalt see this knack – as never   421
I mean thou shalt – we'll bar thee from succession,
Not hold thee of our blood – no, not our kin –
Farre than Deucalion off. Mark thou my words.   424
Follow us to the court. – Thou churl, for this time,
Though full of our displeasure, yet we free thee
From the dead blow of it. – And you, enchantment,   427
Worthy enough a herdsman – yea, him too,
That makes himself, but for our honor therein,
Unworthy thee – if ever henceforth thou
These rural latches to his entrance open,
Or hoop his body more with thy embraces,
I will devise a death as cruel for thee
As thou art tender to't.   Exit.   434
PERDITA   Even here undone!
I was not much afeard; for once or twice
I was about to speak and tell him plainly
The selfsame sun that shines upon his court
Hides not his visage from our cottage but
Looks on alike. Will't please you, sir, be gone?
I told you what would come of this. Beseech you,
Of your own state take care. This dream of mine –
Being now awake, I'll queen it no inch farther,
But milk my ewes and weep.
CAMILLO   Why, how now, father?
Speak ere thou diest.
SHEPHERD   I cannot speak, nor think,
Nor dare to know that which I know. O sir,
You have undone a man of fourscore three,
That thought to fill his grave in quiet, yea,
To die upon the bed my father died,   448
To lie close by his honest bones; but now
Some hangman must put on my shroud and lay me
Where no priest shovels in dust. O cursèd wretch,
That knew'st this was the prince, and wouldst adventure
To mingle faith with him. Undone! undone!
If I might die within this hour, I have lived
To die when I desire.   Exit.
FLORIZEL   Why look you so upon me?
I am but sorry, not afeard; delayed,
But nothing altered. What I was, I am,
More straining on for plucking back, not following   458
My leash unwillingly.
CAMILLO   Gracious my lord,
You know your father's temper. At this time
He will allow no speech, which I do guess
You do not purpose to him; and as hardly
Will he endure your sight as yet, I fear.
Then, till the fury of his highness settle,
Come not before him.
FLORIZEL   I not purpose it.
I think Camillo?
CAMILLO   Even he, my lord.
PERDITA
How often have I told you 'twould be thus?

---

384 *Soft* not so fast   391 *reasonable affairs* affairs requiring reason   393 *dispute* discuss   399 *Something* somewhat; *Reason* it is reasonable   405 *not* i.e. can not   416 *of force* perforce   417 *cop'st with* hast to do with   419 *fond* foolish   421 *knack* trifle   424 *Farre* farther; *Deucalion* (according to Greek mythology this king of Thessaly and his wife were the only human beings to escape a flood sent by Zeus)   427 *dead* death-dealing   434 *tender* vulnerable   448 *died* i.e. died upon   458–59 *following . . . unwillingly* i.e. dragged along

468 How often said my dignity would last
But till 'twere known!

FLORIZEL   It cannot fail but by
The violation of my faith; and then
Let nature crush the sides o' th' earth together
And mar the seeds within. Lift up thy looks.
From my succession wipe me, father. I
Am heir to my affection.

CAMILLO   Be advised.

FLORIZEL
475 I am, and by my fancy. If my reason
Will thereto be obedient, I have reason;
If not, my senses, better pleased with madness,
Do bid it welcome.

CAMILLO   This is desperate, sir.

FLORIZEL
So call it, but it does fulfil my vow.
I needs must think it honesty. Camillo,
Not for Bohemia nor the pomp that may
Be thereat gleaned, for all the sun sees or
483 The close earth wombs or the profound seas hide
In unknown fathoms, will I break my oath
To this my fair beloved. Therefore, I pray you,
As you have ever been my father's honored friend,
When he shall miss me – as, in faith, I mean not
To see him any more – cast your good counsels
Upon his passion. Let myself and fortune
490 Tug for the time to come. This you may know
And so deliver: I am put to sea
With her who here I cannot hold on shore.
And most opportune to our need I have
A vessel rides fast by, but not prepared
For this design. What course I mean to hold
496 Shall nothing benefit your knowledge, nor
Concern me the reporting.

CAMILLO   O my lord,
I would your spirit were easier for advice
Or stronger for your need.

FLORIZEL   Hark, Perdita.
[Draws her aside.]
I'll hear you by and by.

CAMILLO   He's irremovable,
Resolved for flight. Now were I happy if
His going I could frame to serve my turn,
Save him from danger, do him love and honor,
Purchase the sight again of dear Sicilia
And that unhappy king, my master, whom
I so much thirst to see.

FLORIZEL   Now, good Camillo.
507 I am so fraught with curious business that
I leave out ceremony.

CAMILLO   Sir, I think
You have heard of my poor services i' th' love
That I have borne your father?

FLORIZEL   Very nobly
Have you deserved. It is my father's music

---

468 *dignity* i.e. honor of being the Prince's betrothed   475 *fancy* love
483 *wombs* encloses   490 *Tug* contend   496–97 *Shall . . . reporting* it does
not behoove you to know nor me to say   507 *curious* requiring care   516
embrace . . . direction accept my advice   525 *qualify* assuage   531–32 *unthought-on . . . do* i.e. his unforeseen discovery by his father is to blame for
what he rashly does   541 *free* hospitable   548 *color* pretext   554 *point
. . . sitting* guide you at every interview   556 *bosom* confidence   558 *sap*
element essential to life

To speak your deeds, not little of his care
To have them recompensed as thought on.

CAMILLO   Well, my lord,
If you may please to think I love the king
And, through him, what's nearest to him, which is
Your gracious self, embrace but my direction.   516
If your more ponderous and settled project
May suffer alteration, on mine honor,
I'll point you where you shall have such receiving
As shall become your highness, where you may
Enjoy your mistress, from the whom, I see,
There's no disjunction to be made but by –
As heavens forfend! – your ruin; marry her,
And, with my best endeavors in your absence,
Your discontenting father strive to qualify   525
And bring him up to liking.

FLORIZEL   How, Camillo,
May this, almost a miracle, be done?
That I may call thee something more than man,
And after that trust to thee.

CAMILLO   Have you thought on
A place whereto you'll go?

FLORIZEL   Not any yet.
But as th' unthought-on accident is guilty   531
To what we wildly do, so we profess
Ourselves to be the slaves of chance, and flies
Of every wind that blows.

CAMILLO   Then list to me.
This follows: if you will not change your purpose
But undergo this flight, make for Sicilia,
And there present yourself and your fair princess,
For so I see she must be, 'fore Leontes.
She shall be habited as it becomes
The partner of your bed. Methinks I see
Leontes opening his free arms and weeping   541
His welcomes forth; asks thee the son forgiveness,
As 'twere i' th' father's person; kisses the hands
Of your fresh princess; o'er and o'er divides him
'Twixt his unkindness and his kindness; th' one
He chides to hell and bids the other grow
Faster than thought or time.

FLORIZEL   Worthy Camillo,
What color for my visitation shall I   548
Hold up before him?

CAMILLO   Sent by the king your father
To greet him and to give him comforts. Sir,
The manner of your bearing towards him, with
What you, as from your father, shall deliver,
Things known betwixt us three, I'll write you down,
The which shall point you forth at every sitting   554
What you must say, that he shall not perceive
But that you have your father's bosom there   556
And speak his very heart.

FLORIZEL   I am bound to you.
There is some sap in this.   558

CAMILLO   A course more promising
Than a wild dedication of yourselves
To unpathed waters, undreamed shores, most certain
To miseries enough; no hope to help you,
But as you shake off one to take another;
Nothing so certain as your anchors, who
Do their best office if they can but stay you
Where you'll be loath to be. Besides, you know
Prosperity's the very bond of love,

Whose fresh complexion and whose heart together
Affliction alters.

PERDITA   One of these is true.
I think affliction may subdue the cheek
570 But not take in the mind.

CAMILLO   Yea, say you so?
571 There shall not at your father's house these seven years
Be born another such.

FLORIZEL   My good Camillo,
573 She's as forward of her breeding as
574 She is i' th' rear 'our birth.

CAMILLO   I cannot say 'tis pity
575 She lacks instructions, for she seems a mistress
To most that teach.

PERDITA   Your pardon, sir. For this
I'll blush you thanks.

FLORIZEL   My prettiest Perdita!
But O, the thorns we stand upon! Camillo,
Preserver of my father, now of me,
The medicine of our house, how shall we do?
We are not furnished like Bohemia's son,
582 Nor shall appear in Sicilia.

CAMILLO   My lord,
Fear none of this. I think you know my fortunes
Do all lie there. It shall be so my care
To have you royally appointed as if
The scene you play were mine. For instance, sir,
That you may know you shall not want, one word.

[They talk aside.] Enter Autolycus.

AUTOLYCUS Ha, ha, what a fool Honesty is! and Trust,
his sworn brother, a very simple gentleman! I have sold
all my trumpery. Not a counterfeit stone, not a ribbon,
591 glass, pomander, brooch, table-book, ballad, knife, tape,
glove, shoe-tie, bracelet, horn-ring, to keep my pack
from fasting. They throng who should buy first, as if my
trinkets had been hallowed and brought a benediction to
595 the buyer; by which means I saw whose purse was best in
picture, and what I saw, to my good use I remembered.
My clown, who wants but something to be a reasonable
man, grew so in love with the wenches' song that he
599 would not stir his pettitoes till he had both tune and
601 words, which so drew the rest of the herd to me that all
602 their other senses stuck in ears. You might have pinched
a placket, it was senseless; 'twas nothing to geld a cod-
piece of a purse; I would have filed keys off that hung in
604 chains. No hearing, no feeling, but my sir's song and admiring the nothing of it. So that in this time of lethargy I
picked and cut most of their festival purses; and had not
the old man come in with a whoo-bub against his daugh-
608 ter and the king's son and scared my choughs from the
chaff, I had not left a purse alive in the whole army.

[Camillo, Florizel, and Perdita come forward.]

CAMILLO
Nay, but my letters, by this means being there
So soon as you arrive, shall clear that doubt.

FLORIZEL
And those that you'll procure from King Leontes –

CAMILLO
Shall satisfy your father.

PERDITA   Happy be you!
All that you speak shows fair.

CAMILLO *[seeing Autolycus]*   Who have we here?
615 We'll make an instrument of this, omit
Nothing may give us aid.

AUTOLYCUS If they have overheard me now, why, hanging.

CAMILLO
How now, good fellow? Why shak'st thou so?
Fear not, man; here's no harm intended to thee.

AUTOLYCUS I am a poor fellow, sir.

CAMILLO Why, be so still; here's nobody will steal that
from thee. Yet for the outside of thy poverty we must 622
make an exchange. Therefore disease thee instantly – 623
thou must think there's a necessity in't – and change
garments with this gentleman. Though the pennyworth 625
on his side be the worst, yet hold thee, there's some boot. 626

AUTOLYCUS I am a poor fellow, sir. *[aside]* I know ye
well enough.

CAMILLO Nay, prithee, dispatch. The gentleman is half 629
flayed already. 630

AUTOLYCUS Are you in earnest, sir? *[aside]* I smell the
trick on't.

FLORIZEL Dispatch, I prithee.

AUTOLYCUS Indeed, I have had earnest, but I cannot 634
with conscience take it.

CAMILLO Unbuckle, unbuckle.

[Florizel and Autolycus exchange garments.]

Fortunate mistress – let my prophecy
Come home to ye! – you must retire yourself 638
Into some covert. Take your sweetheart's hat
And pluck it o'er your brows, muffle your face,
Dismantle you, and, as you can, disliken 641
The truth of your own seeming, that you may –
For I do fear eyes over – to shipboard 643
Get undescried.

PERDITA   I see the play so lies
That I must bear a part.

CAMILLO   No remedy.
Have you done there?

FLORIZEL   Should I now meet my father,
He would not call me son.

CAMILLO   Nay, you shall have no hat.

[Gives it to Perdita.]

Come, lady, come. Farewell, my friend.

AUTOLYCUS   Adieu, sir.

FLORIZEL
O Perdita, what have we twain forgot?
Pray you, a word.

CAMILLO *[aside]*
What I do next, shall be to tell the king
Of this escape and whither they are bound;
Wherein my hope is I shall so prevail
To force him after; in whose company
I shall review Sicilia, for whose sight
I have a woman's longing. 656

570 *take in* subdue   571 *these seven years* i.e. for a long time to come ('seven' not to be taken literally)   573 *forward of* beyond   574 *'our* of our   575 *instructions* schooling   582 *appear* i.e. as the king's son   591 *table-book* note-book (cf. Hamlet's tables)   595–96 *was best in picture* looked best   599 *pettitoes* toes (usually of a pig)   601 *stuck in ears* were devoted to listening   602 *senseless* without feeling   602–03 *geld . . . purse* remove a purse from a pocket   604 *my sir's* i.e. the clown's   608 *choughs* birds of the crow family   615 *instrument* means to an end   622 *the outside . . . poverty* thy rags   623 *disease* undress   625–26 *Though . . . worst* though he gets the worse in the exchange   626 *boot* i.e. something additional (usually to equalize an exchange)   629 *dispatch* make haste   630 *flayed* skinned   634 *earnest* partial prepayment   638 *Come . . . ye* be fulfilled   641–42 *as . . . seeming* as far as you can, alter your true appearance   643 *eyes over* spying   656 *longing* (as for particular foods during pregnancy)

FLORIZEL   Fortune speed us!
Thus we set on, Camillo, to the seaside.
CAMILLO
The swifter speed the better.
                    Exeunt [Florizel, Perdita, and Camillo].
AUTOLYCUS I understand the business, I hear it. To have
an open ear, a quick eye, and a nimble hand is necessary
for a cutpurse. A good nose is requisite also, to smell out
work for the other senses. I see this is the time that the
unjust man doth thrive. What an exchange had this been
without boot! What a boot is here with this exchange!
Sure the gods do this year connive at us, and we may do
any thing extempore. The prince himself is about a
piece of iniquity, stealing away from his father with his
667   clog at his heels. If I thought it were a piece of honesty
to acquaint the king withal, I would not do't. I hold it
the more knavery to conceal it, and therein am I
constant to my profession.
                    Enter Clown and Shepherd.
Aside, aside! Here is more matter for a hot brain. Every
lane's end, every shop, church, session, hanging, yields
a careful man work.
CLOWN See, see! What a man you are now! There is no
676   other way but to tell the king she's a changeling and
none of your flesh and blood.
SHEPHERD Nay, but hear me.
CLOWN Nay, but hear me.
680 SHEPHERD Go to, then.
CLOWN She being none of your flesh and blood, your
flesh and blood has not offended the king, and so your
flesh and blood is not to be punished by him. Show
those things you found about her, those secret things,
all but what she has with her. This being done, let the
law go whistle, I warrant you.
SHEPHERD I will tell the king all, every word – yea, and
his son's pranks too, who, I may say, is no honest man,
neither to his father nor to me, to go about to make me
the king's brother-in-law.
CLOWN Indeed, brother-in-law was the farthest off you
could have been to him, and then your blood had been
693   the dearer by I know how much an ounce.
AUTOLYCUS *[aside]* Very wisely, puppies.
SHEPHERD Well, let us to the king. There is that in this
696   fardel will make him scratch his beard.
AUTOLYCUS *[aside]* I know not what impediment this
complaint may be to the flight of my master.
699 CLOWN Pray heartily he be at' palace.
AUTOLYCUS *[aside]* Though I am not naturally honest, I
am so sometimes by chance. Let me pocket up my
702   pedlar's excrement. *[Takes off his false beard.]* How
now, rustics, whither are you bound?
704 SHEPHERD To the palace, an it like your worship.
AUTOLYCUS Your affairs there, what, with whom, the
condition of that fardel, the place of your dwelling,
707   your names, your ages, of what having, breeding, and
708   anything that is fitting to be known, discover.

CLOWN We are but plain fellows, sir.
AUTOLYCUS A lie! You are rough and hairy. Let me have
no lying. It becomes none but tradesmen, and they often
give us soldiers the lie; but we pay them for it with
stamped coin, not stabbing steel; therefore they do not
give us the lie.
CLOWN Your worship had like to have given us one, if
you had not taken yourself with the manner.   716
SHEPHERD Are you a courtier, an't like you, sir?
AUTOLYCUS Whether it like me or no, I am a courtier.
Seest thou not the air of the court in these enfoldings? 719
Hath not my gait in it the measure of the court?
Receives not thy nose court-odor from me? Reflect I
not on thy baseness, court-contempt? Thinkest thou,
for that I insinuate, or toaze from thee thy business, I 723
am therefore no courtier? I am courtier cap-a-pe, and 724
one that will either push on or pluck back thy business
there. Whereupon I command thee to open thy affair.
SHEPHERD My business, sir, is to the king.
AUTOLYCUS What advocate hast thou to him?
SHEPHERD I know not, an't like you.
CLOWN Advocate 's the court-word for a pheasant. Say 730
you have none.
SHEPHERD None, sir. I have no pheasant, cock nor hen.
AUTOLYCUS
How blessèd are we that are not simple men!
Yet nature might have made me as these are;
Therefore I will not disdain.
CLOWN This cannot be but a great courtier.
SHEPHERD His garments are rich, but he wears them not
handsomely.
CLOWN He seems to be the more noble in being fantasti-
cal. A great man, I'll warrant. I know by the picking on's 740
teeth.
AUTOLYCUS The fardel there? What's i' the fardel?
Wherefore that box?
SHEPHERD Sir, there lies such secrets in this fardel and
box, which none must know but the king, and which he
shall know within this hour if I may come to the speech
of him.
AUTOLYCUS Age, thou hast lost thy labor.   748
SHEPHERD Why, sir?
AUTOLYCUS The king is not at the palace. He is gone
aboard a new ship to purge melancholy and air himself,
for, if thou be'st capable of things serious, thou must
know the king is full of grief.
SHEPHERD So 'tis said, sir – about his son, that should
have married a shepherd's daughter.
AUTOLYCUS If that shepherd be not in hand-fast, let him 756
fly. The curses he shall have, the tortures he shall feel,
will break the back of man, the heart of monster.
CLOWN Think you so, sir?
AUTOLYCUS Not he alone shall suffer what wit can make
heavy and vengeance bitter; but those that are germane
to him, though removed fifty times, shall all come under
the hangman, which, though it be great pity, yet it is
necessary. An old sheep-whistling rogue, a ram-tender,
to offer to have his daughter come into grace! Some say 765
he shall be stoned, but that death is too soft for him, say
I. Draw our throne into a sheep-cote! All deaths are too
few, the sharpest too easy.
CLOWN Has the old man e'er a son, sir, do you hear, an't
like you, sir?
AUTOLYCUS He has a son, who shall be flayed alive; then

---

667 *clog* (anything which impedes movement)   676 *changeling* a child left (by
fairies) with other than its true parents   680 *Go to* go on   693 *the dearer* of
greater worth   696 *fardel* bundle   699 *at'* at the   702 *excrement* appendage   704 *an it like* if it please   707 *having* property   708 *discover* reveal
716 *taken . . . manner* caught in the act (?)   719 *enfoldings* clothes
723 *toaze* tear   724 *cap-a-pe* from head to foot   730 *pheasant* i.e. as a bribe
to the judge (the clown confuses the two kinds of courts)   740–41 *picking
on's teeth* (picking the teeth was an affectation of would-be gallants)
748 *Age* old man   756 *hand-fast* custody   765 *grace* honor

'nointed over with honey, set on the head of a wasp's
nest; then stand till he be three quarters and a dram
774 dead; then recovered again with aqua-vitae or some
other hot infusion. Then, raw as he is, and in the hottest
776 day prognostication proclaims, shall he be set against a
brick-wall, the sun looking with a southward eye upon
him, where he is to behold him with flies blown to death.
But what talk we of these traitorly rascals, whose miseries are to be smiled at, their offenses being so capital?
Tell me, for you seem to be honest plain men, what you
782 have to the king. Being something gently considered,
I'll bring you where he is aboard, tender your persons to
his presence, whisper him in your behalfs; and if it be in
man besides the king to effect your suits, here is man
shall do it.

786 CLOWN He seems to be of great authority. Close with him,
give him gold; and though authority be a stubborn bear,
yet he is oft led by the nose with gold. Show the inside of
your purse to the outside of his hand, and no more ado.
Remember 'stoned,' and 'flayed alive.'

SHEPHERD An't please you, sir, to undertake the business for us, here is that gold I have. I'll make it as much
more and leave this young man in pawn till I bring it
you.

AUTOLYCUS After I have done what I promised?

SHEPHERD Ay, sir.

796 AUTOLYCUS Well, give me the moiety. Are you a party
in this business?

798 CLOWN In some sort, sir. But though my case be a pitiful
one, I hope I shall not be flayed out of it.

AUTOLYCUS O, that's the case of the shepherd's son.
Hang him, he'll be made an example.

CLOWN Comfort, good comfort! We must to the king
and show our strange sights. He must know 'tis none of
804 your daughter nor my sister; we are gone else. Sir, I
will give you as much as this old man does when the
business is performed, and remain, as he says, your
pawn till it be brought you.

AUTOLYCUS I will trust you. Walk before toward the
seaside. Go on the right hand. I will but look upon the
hedge and follow you.

CLOWN We are blest in this man, as I may say, even blest.

SHEPHERD Let's before as he bids us. He was provided
to do us good.   [Exeunt Shepherd and Clown.]

AUTOLYCUS If I had a mind to be honest, I see Fortune
would not suffer me; she drops booties in my mouth. I
816 am courted now with a double occasion, gold and a
818 means to do the prince my master good, which who
819 knows how that may turn back to my advancement? I
will bring these two moles, these blind ones, aboard him.
If he think it fit to shore them again and that the complaint they have to the king concerns him nothing, let
him call me rogue for being so far officious, for I am
proof against that title and what shame else belongs to't.
To him will I present them; there may be matter in it.
                                      Exit.

*

V, i   *Enter Leontes, Cleomenes, Dion, Paulina, Servants.*

CLEOMENES
Sir, you have done enough, and have performed
A saint-like sorrow. No fault could you make
Which you have not redeemed – indeed, paid down
More penitence than done trespass. At the last,

Do as the heavens have done, forget your evil;
With them forgive yourself.   5

LEONTES   Whilst I remember
Her and her virtues, I cannot forget
My blemishes in them, and so still think of   8
The wrong I did myself, which was so much
That heirless it hath made my kingdom and
Destroyed the sweet'st companion that e'er man
Bred his hopes out of.

PAULINA   True, too true, my lord.
If one by one you wedded all the world,
Or from the all that are took something good
To make a perfect woman, she you killed
Would be unparalleled.

LEONTES   I think so. Killed?
She I killed? I did so, but thou strik'st me
Sorely to say I did. It is as bitter
Upon thy tongue as in my thought. Now, good now,   19
Say so but seldom.

CLEOMENES   Not at all, good lady.
You might have spoken a thousand things that would
Have done the time more benefit and graced   22
Your kindness better.

PAULINA   You are one of those
Would have him wed again.

DION   If you would not so,
You pity not the state nor the remembrance
Of his most sovereign name, consider little
What dangers, by his highness' fail of issue,
May drop upon his kingdom and devour
Incertain lookers on. What were more holy   29
Than to rejoice the former queen is well?
What holier than, for royalty's repair,
For present comfort and for future good,
To bless the bed of majesty again
With a sweet fellow to't?

PAULINA   There is none worthy,
Respecting her that's gone. Besides, the gods
Will have fulfilled their secret purposes;
For has not the divine Apollo said,
Is't not the tenor of his oracle,
That King Leontes shall not have an heir
Till his lost child be found? Which that it shall
Is all as monstrous to our human reason   41
As my Antigonus to break his grave
And come again to me, who, on my life,
Did perish with the infant. 'Tis your counsel
My lord should to the heavens be contrary,
Oppose against their wills. *[to Leontes]* Care not for issue;
The crown will find an heir. Great Alexander
Left his to th' worthiest; so his successor
Was like to be the best.

LEONTES   Good Paulina,
Who hast the memory of Hermione,
I know, in honor, O that ever I

774 *aqua-vitae* brandy   776 *prognostication* forecast (forecasts for the coming year were published annually)   782 *something . . . considered* given some consideration, i.e. bribe   786 *Close* come to an agreement   796 *moiety* half   798 *case* (1) position *in this business*, (2) skin   804 *gone* undone   816 *courted . . . with* tempted . . . by   818 *turn back* revert   819 *aboard him* to him aboard (the ship)
V, i The palace of Leontes   5 *evil* sin   8 *in* i.e. in relation to   19 *good now* i.e. I pray you (?) (cf. *Hamlet* I, i, 70)   22 *graced* befitted   29 *Incertain* confused (as to an heir to the throne)   41 *monstrous* incredible

52 Had squared me to thy counsel! Then even now
I might have looked upon my queen's full eyes,
Have taken treasure from her lips–

PAULINA   And left them
More rich for what they yielded.

LEONTES   Thou speak'st truth.
56 No more such wives; therefore, no wife! One worse,
And better used, would make her sainted spirit
Again possess her corpse, and on this stage
59 (Where we offenders now) appear soul-vexed,
And begin, 'Why to me?'

PAULINA   Had she such power,
She had just cause.

LEONTES   She had, and would incense me
To murder her I married.

PAULINA   I should so.
Were I the ghost that walked, I'd bid you mark
Her eye, and tell me for what dull part in't
You chose her. Then I'ld shriek, that even your ears
Should rift to hear me, and the words that followed
Should be 'Remember mine.'

LEONTES   Stars, stars,
And all eyes else dead coals! Fear thou no wife;
I'll have no wife, Paulina.

PAULINA   Will you swear
Never to marry but by my free leave?

LEONTES
Never, Paulina, so be blest my spirit.

PAULINA
Then, good my lords, bear witness to his oath.

CLEOMENES
73 You tempt him overmuch.

PAULINA   Unless another,
As like Hermione as is her picture,
75 Affront his eye.

CLEOMENES   Good madam –

PAULINA   I have done.
Yet, if my lord will marry – if you will, sir,
No remedy but you will – give me the office
To choose you a queen. She shall not be so young
As was your former, but she shall be such
As, walked your first queen's ghost, it should take joy
To see her in your arms.

LEONTES   My true Paulina,
We shall not marry till thou bid'st us.

PAULINA   That
83 Shall be when your first queen's again in breath.
Never till then.

Enter a Servant.

SERVANT
One that gives out himself Prince Florizel,
Son of Polixenes, with his princess – she
The fairest I have yet beheld – desires access
To your high presence.

LEONTES   What with him? He comes not
89 Like to his father's greatness. His approach,
90 So out of circumstance and sudden, tells us

'Tis not a visitation framed, but forced   91
By need and accident. What train?

SERVANT   But few,
And those but mean.

LEONTES   His princess, say you, with him?

SERVANT
Ay, the most peerless piece of earth, I think,
That e'er the sun shone bright on.

PAULINA   O Hermione.
As every present time doth boast itself
Above a better gone, so must thy grave
Give way to what's seen now. Sir, you yourself
Have said and writ so, but your writing now
Is colder than that theme. She had not been,   100
Nor was not to be equalled – thus your verse
Flowed with her beauty once. 'Tis shrewdly ebbed
To say you have seen a better.

SERVANT   Pardon, madam.
The one I have almost forgot – your pardon;
The other, when she has obtained your eye,
Will have your tongue too. This is a creature,
Would she begin a sect, might quench the zeal
Of all professors else, make proselytes   108
Of who she but bid follow.

PAULINA   How? not women?

SERVANT
Women will love her that she is a woman
More worth than any man; men, that she is
The rarest of all women.

LEONTES   Go, Cleomenes.
Yourself, assisted with your honored friends,
Bring them to our embracement.

                 Exit [Cleomenes with others].
                Still, 'tis strange
He thus should steal upon us.   115

PAULINA   Had our prince,
Jewel of children, seen this hour, he had paired
Well with this lord. There was not full a month
Between their births.

LEONTES   Prithee, no more; cease. Thou know'st
He dies to me again when talked of. Sure,
When I shall see this gentleman, thy speeches
Will bring me to consider that which may
Unfurnish me of reason. They are come.   122

Enter Florizel, Perdita, Cleomenes, and others.
Your mother was most true to wedlock, prince,
For she did print your royal father off,
Conceiving you. Were I but twenty-one,
Your father's image is so hit in you,
His very air, that I should call you brother,
As I did him, and speak of something wildly
By us performed before. Most dearly welcome!
And your fair princess – goddess! O, alas!
I lost a couple that 'twixt heaven and earth
Might thus have stood begetting wonder as
You, gracious couple, do. And then I lost –
All mine own folly – the society,
Amity too, of your brave father, whom,
Though bearing misery, I desire my life
Once more to look on him.

FLORIZEL   By his command
Have I here touched Sicilia, and from him
Give you all greetings that a king, at friend,   139
Can send his brother; and, but infirmity

52 *squared me to* acted in accordance with   56 *No more* there are no more
59 *now* now play our parts (? an obscure passage)   73 *tempt* urge   75 *Affront*
confront   83 *in breath* alive   89 *approach* coming   90 *out of circumstance*
without formality   91 *framed* premeditated   100 *colder* i.e. more dead
108 *professors else* those who profess other faiths   115 *steal . . . us* i.e. come
unannounced   122 *Unfurnish* deprive   139 *at friend* in friendship

141 Which waits upon worn times hath something seized
His wished ability, he had himself
The lands and waters 'twixt your throne and his
144 Measured to look upon you, whom he loves –
He bade me say so – more than all the sceptres
And those that bear them living.

LEONTES   O my brother,
Good gentleman, the wrongs I have done thee stir
148 Afresh within me, and these thy offices,
149 So rarely kind, are as interpreters
Of my behindhand slackness. Welcome hither,
As is the spring to th' earth. And hath he too
Exposed this paragon to th' fearful usage,
At least ungentle, of the dreadful Neptune,
To greet a man not worth her pains, much less
155 Th' adventure of her person?

FLORIZEL   Good my lord,
She came from Libya.

LEONTES   Where the warlike Smalus,
That noble honored lord, is feared and loved?

FLORIZEL
Most royal sir, from thence, from him, whose daughter
His tears proclaimed his, parting with her. Thence,
A prosperous south-wind friendly, we have crossed,
To execute the charge my father gave me
For visiting your highness. My best train
I have from your Sicilian shores dismissed,
Who for Bohemia bend, to signify
Not only my success in Libya, sir,
But my arrival and my wife's in safety
Here where we are.

LEONTES   The blessèd gods
Purge all infection from our air whilst you
169 Do climate here! You have a holy father,
170 A graceful gentleman, against whose person,
So sacred as it is, I have done sin,
For which the heavens, taking angry note,
Have left me issueless; and your father 's blest,
As he from heaven merits it, with you,
Worthy his goodness. What might I have been,
Might I a son and daughter now have looked on,
Such goodly things as you?

        Enter a Lord.

LORD   Most noble sir,
That which I shall report will bear no credit,
Were not the proof so nigh. Please you, great sir,
Bohemia greets you from himself by me,
181 Desires you to attach his son, who has –
His dignity and duty both cast off –
Fled from his father, from his hopes, and with
A shepherd's daughter.

LEONTES   Where's Bohemia? Speak.

LORD
Here in your city. I now came from him.
186 I speak amazedly, and it becomes
My marvel and my message. To your court
188 Whiles he was hast'ning – in the chase, it seems,
Of this fair couple – meets he on the way
The father of this seeming lady and
Her brother, having both their country quitted
With this young prince.

FLORIZEL   Camillo has betrayed me,
Whose honor and whose honesty till now
Endured all weathers.

LORD   Lay't so to his charge.
He's with the king your father.

LEONTES   Who? Camillo?

LORD
Camillo, sir. I spake with him, who now
Has these poor men in question. Never saw I
Wretches so quake. They kneel, they kiss the earth,
Forswear themselves as often as they speak.
Bohemia stops his ears, and threatens them
With divers deaths in death.   201

PERDITA   O my poor father!
The heaven sets spies upon us, will not have
Our contract celebrated.

LEONTES   You are married?

FLORIZEL
We are not, sir, nor are we like to be.
The stars, I see, will kiss the valleys first;
The odds for high and low 's alike.   206

LEONTES   My lord,
Is this the daughter of a king?

FLORIZEL   She is
When once she is my wife.

LEONTES
That 'once,' I see by your good father's speed,
Will come on very slowly. I am sorry,
Most sorry, you have broken from his liking
Where you were tied in duty, and as sorry
Your choice is not so rich in worth as beauty,   213
That you might well enjoy her.

FLORIZEL   Dear, look up.
Though Fortune, visible an enemy,   215
Should chase us with my father, power no jot
Hath she to change our loves. Beseech you, sir,
Remember since you owed no more to time   218
Than I do now. With thought of such affections,
Step forth mine advocate. At your request
My father will grant precious things as trifles.

LEONTES
Would he do so, I'ld beg your precious mistress,
Which he counts but a trifle.

PAULINA   Sir, my liege,
Your eye hath too much youth in't. Not a month
'Fore your queen died, she was more worth such gazes
Than what you look on now.

LEONTES   I thought of her
Even in these looks I made. *[to Florizel]* But your petition
Is yet unanswered. I will to your father.
Your honor not o'erthrown by your desires,   229
I am friend to them and you. Upon which errand
I now go toward him; therefore follow me
And mark what way I make. Come, good my lord.   232

                                        Exeunt.

                                *

141 *waits . . . times* accompanies old age; *something seized* somewhat taken away 144 *Measured* journeyed over 148 *offices* courtesies 149–50 *are . . . slackness* emphasize my tardy, inadequate action 155 *adventure* risk 169 *climate* dwell 170 *graceful* gracious 181 *attach* arrest 186 *amazedly* confusedly 186–87 *it . . . marvel* my confused speech suits (results from) my wonder 188 *chase* pursuit 201 *deaths in death* tortures 206 *odds . . . alike* high and low are alike subject to misfortune 213 *worth* high birth 215 *visible* clearly 218–19 *since . . . now* when you were my age 229 *Your . . . desires* if your desires have not led you to do what is dishonorable 232 *way* progress

Enter Autolycus and a Gentleman.

AUTOLYCUS Beseech you, sir, were you present at this relation?

1. GENTLEMAN I was by at the opening of the fardel, heard the old shepherd deliver the manner how he found it; whereupon, after a little amazedness, we were all commanded out of the chamber. Only this methought I heard the shepherd say, he found the child.

AUTOLYCUS I would most gladly know the issue of it.

9 1. GENTLEMAN I make a broken delivery of the business; but the changes I perceived in the king and Camillo
11 were very notes of admiration. They seemed almost, with staring on one another, to tear the cases of their eyes. There was speech in their dumbness, language in their very gesture. They looked as they had heard of a
15 world ransomed, or one destroyed. A notable passion of wonder appeared in them. But the wisest beholder, that
17 knew no more but seeing, could not say if the importance were joy or sorrow; but in the extremity of the one, it must needs be.

Enter another Gentleman.

20 Here comes a gentleman that haply knows more. The news, Rogero?

2. GENTLEMAN Nothing but bonfires. The oracle is fulfilled; the king's daughter is found. Such a deal of wonder is broken out within this hour that balladmakers cannot be able to express it.

Enter another Gentleman.

26 Here comes the Lady Paulina's steward; he can deliver you more. How goes it now, sir? This news which is called true is so like an old tale that the verity of it is in strong suspicion. Has the king found his heir?

30 3. GENTLEMAN Most true, if ever truth were pregnant by circumstance. That which you hear you'll swear you
32 see, there is such unity in the proofs. The mantle of Queen Hermione's, her jewel about the neck of it, the letters of Antigonus found with it, which they know to
35 be his character, the majesty of the creature in resem-
36 blance of the mother, the affection of nobleness which nature shows above her breeding, and many other evidences proclaim her with all certainty to be the king's daughter. Did you see the meeting of the two kings?

2. GENTLEMAN No.

3. GENTLEMAN Then have you lost a sight which was to be seen, cannot be spoken of. There might you have beheld one joy crown another, so and in such manner that it seemed sorrow wept to take leave of them, for their joy waded in tears. There was casting up of eyes, holding up of hands, with countenance of such distraction that they
47 were to be known by garment, not by favor. Our king, being ready to leap out of himself for joy of his found daughter, as if that joy were now become a loss, cries, 'O,

thy mother, thy mother!' then asks Bohemia forgiveness; then embraces his son-in-law; then again worries
52 he his daughter with clipping her; now he thanks the old
53 shepherd, which stands by like a weather-bitten conduit of many kings' reigns. I never heard of such another en-
55 counter, which lames report to follow it and undoes description to do it.

2. GENTLEMAN What, pray you, became of Antigonus, that carried hence the child?

3. GENTLEMAN Like an old tale still, which will have matter to rehearse, though credit be asleep and not an
61 ear open. He was torn to pieces with a bear. This avou-
62 ches the shepherd's son, who has not only his innocence, which seems much, to justify him, but a handkerchief and rings of his that Paulina knows.

1. GENTLEMAN What became of his bark and his followers?

3. GENTLEMAN Wrecked the same instant of their master's death and in the view of the shepherd; so that all the instruments which aided to expose the child were even then lost when it was found. But O, the noble combat that 'twixt joy and sorrow was fought in Paulina!
71 She had one eye declined for the loss of her husband, another elevated that the oracle was fulfilled. She lifted the princess from the earth, and so locks her in embracing as if she would pin her to her heart that she might no more be in danger of losing.

1. GENTLEMAN The dignity of this act was worth the audience of kings and princes, for by such was it acted.

3. GENTLEMAN One of the prettiest touches of all, and that which angled for mine eyes, caught the water though not the fish, was when, at the relation of the queen's death, with the manner how she came to't bravely con-
82 fessed and lamented by the king, how attentiveness wounded his daughter, till, from one sign of dolor to another, she did, with an 'Alas,' I would fain say, bleed tears, for I am sure my heart wept blood. Who was most marble there changed color; some swooned, all sorrowed. If all the world could have seen't, the woe had been universal.

1. GENTLEMAN Are they returned to the court?

3. GENTLEMAN No. The princess, hearing of her mother's statue, which is in the keeping of Paulina – a piece many years in doing and now newly performed by that
91 rare Italian master, Julio Romano, who, had he himself
92 eternity and could put breath into his work, would be-
93 guile Nature of her custom, so perfectly he is her ape.
94 He so near to Hermione hath done Hermione that they say one would speak to her and stand in hope of answer. Thither with all greediness of affection are they gone, and there they intend to sup.

2. GENTLEMAN I thought she had some great matter there in hand, for she hath privately twice or thrice a day, ever since the death of Hermione, visited that removed house. Shall we thither and with our company
102 piece the rejoicing?

1. GENTLEMAN Who would be thence that has the benefit of access? Every wink of an eye some new grace will
106 be born. Our absence makes us unthrifty to our knowledge. Let's along. *Exeunt [Gentlemen].*

AUTOLYCUS Now, had I not the dash of my former life in me, would preferment drop on my head. I brought the old man and his son aboard the prince, told him I heard them talk of a fardel and I know not what. But he at that

V, ii An open place near the palace of Leontes   9 *make . . . delivery* give a fragmentary account   11 *admiration* wonder   15 *passion* emotion   17 *seeing* what he saw; *importance* import   20 *haply* perhaps   26 *deliver* tell   30–31 *pregnant by circumstance* obvious from the evidence   32 *unity* agreement   35 *character* handwriting   36 *affection of* natural tendency toward   47 *favor* features   52 *clipping* embracing   53 *conduit* structure from which flows water (here tears)   55–56 *undoes . . . it* renders description incapable of describing   61 *with* by   62 *innocence* simplicity   71 *declined* cast down in sorrow   82 *attentiveness* i.e. 'the hearing of it' (Wilson)   91 *performed* finished   92 *Romano* an Italian painter and sculptor who died in 1546   93–94 *beguile . . . custom* rob Nature of her business, i.e. creating living people   94 *her ape* Nature's imitator   102 *piece* add to   106 *unthrifty to* failing to add to

time, over-fond of the shepherd's daughter – so he then
took her to be – who began to be much seasick, and
himself little better, extremity of weather continuing,
this mystery remained undiscovered. But 'tis all one to
me; for had I been the finder out of this secret, it would
117   not have relished among my other discredits.
        Enter Shepherd and Clown.
    Here come those I have done good to against my will,
    and already appearing in the blossoms of their fortune.
    SHEPHERD Come, boy. I am past moe children, but thy
    sons and daughters will be all gentlemen born.
122 CLOWN You are well met, sir. You denied to fight with
    me this other day, because I was no gentleman born.
    See you these clothes? Say you see them not and think
125   me still no gentleman born. You were best say these
    robes are not gentlemen born. Give me the lie, do, and
    try whether I am not now a gentleman born.
    AUTOLYCUS I know you are now, sir, a gentleman born.
    CLOWN Ay, and have been so any time these four hours.
    SHEPHERD And so have I, boy.
    CLOWN So you have. But I was a gentleman born before
    my father, for the king's son took me by the hand and
    called me brother; and then the two kings called my
    father brother; and then the prince my brother and the
    princess my sister called my father father; and so we
    wept, and there was the first gentleman-like tears that
    ever we shed.
    SHEPHERD We may live, son, to shed many more.
139 CLOWN Ay, or else 'twere hard luck, being in so pre-
    posterous estate as we are.
    AUTOLYCUS I humbly beseech you, sir, to pardon me all
    the faults I have committed to your worship and to give
    me your good report to the prince my master.
    SHEPHERD Prithee, son, do, for we must be gentle now
    we are gentlemen.
    CLOWN Thou wilt amend thy life?
147 AUTOLYCUS Ay, an it like your good worship.
    CLOWN Give me thy hand. I will swear to the prince thou
    art as honest a true fellow as any is in Bohemia.
    SHEPHERD You may say it, but not swear it.
151 CLOWN Not swear it, now I am a gentleman? Let boors
152   and franklins say it, I'll swear it.
    SHEPHERD How if it be false, son?
    CLOWN If it be ne'er so false, a true gentleman may swear
    it in the behalf of his friend. And I'll swear to the prince
156   thou art a tall fellow of thy hands and that thou wilt not
    be drunk; but I know thou art no tall fellow of thy
    hands and that thou wilt be drunk. But I'll swear it, and
    I would thou wouldst be a tall fellow of thy hands.
    AUTOLYCUS I will prove so, sir, to my power.
    CLOWN Ay, by any means prove a tall fellow. If I do not
    wonder how thou darest venture to be drunk, not being
    a tall fellow, trust me not. Hark! The kings and the
164   princes, our kindred, are going to see the queen's pic-
165   ture. Come, follow us. We'll be thy good masters.

                                                Exeunt.

                            *

V, iii   *Enter Leontes, Polixenes, Florizel, Perdita, Camillo,*
              Paulina, Lords, &c.
    LEONTES
    O grave and good Paulina, the great comfort
    That I have had of thee!

PAULINA   What, sovereign sir,
    I did not well, I meant well. All my services
    You have paid home. But that you have vouchsafed,   4
    With your crowned brother and these your contracted
    Heirs of your kingdoms, my poor house to visit,
    It is a surplus of your grace which never   7
    My life may last to answer.   8
LEONTES   O Paulina,
    We honor you with trouble. But we came
    To see the statue of our queen. Your gallery
    Have we passed through, not without much content
    In many singularities; but we saw not   12
    That which my daughter came to look upon,
    The statue of her mother.
PAULINA   As she lived peerless,
    So her dead likeness, I do well believe,
    Excels whatever yet you looked upon
    Or hand of man hath done. Therefore I keep it
    Lonely, apart. But here it is. Prepare
    To see the life as lively mocked as ever   19
    Still sleep mocked death. Behold, and say 'tis well.
        [Paulina reveals] Hermione [standing] like a statue.
    I like your silence; it the more shows off
    Your wonder. But yet speak; first, you, my liege.
    Comes it not something near?
LEONTES   Her natural posture!
    Chide me, dear stone, that I may say indeed
    Thou art Hermione; or rather, thou art she
    In thy not chiding, for she was as tender
    As infancy and grace. But yet, Paulina,
    Hermione was not so much wrinkled, nothing
    So aged as this seems.
POLIXENES   O, not by much.
PAULINA
    So much the more our carver's excellence,
    Which lets go by some sixteen years and makes her   31
    As she lived now.
LEONTES   As now she might have done,
    So much to my good comfort, as it is
    Now piercing to my soul. O, thus she stood,
    Even with such life of majesty – warm life,
    As now it coldly stands – when first I wooed her!
    I am ashamed. Does not the stone rebuke me
    For being more stone than it? O royal piece,   38
    There's magic in thy majesty, which has
    My evils conjured to remembrance and   40
    From thy admiring daughter took the spirits,   41
    Standing like stone with thee.
PERDITA   And give me leave,
    And do not say 'tis superstition, that   43
    I kneel and then implore her blessing. Lady,
    Dear queen, that ended when I but began,

117 *relished among* rendered acceptable 122 *denied* refused 125 *were . . .
say* i.e. might as well say 139 *preposterous* (he intends 'prosperous')
147 *an it like* if it please 151 *boors* peasants 152 *franklins* small land-
owners, farmers 156 *tall . . . hands* bold fellow, quick to act 164 *picture*
(the statue is later said to have been painted; see V, iii, 47–48, 81–83)
165 *good masters* benefactors
V, iii Within the house of Paulina 4 *paid home* rewarded handsomely
7 *surplus . . . grace* additional show of your kindness 8 *answer* repay in
kind 12 *singularities* rarities 19 *lively mocked* vividly imitated 31 *lets
go by* i.e. indicates the passage of 38 *piece* i.e. piece of sculpture 40
conjured summoned 41 *admiring* wondering; *spirits* life-giving elements
43 *superstition* (an allusion to Protestant attack upon kneeling before
images of the Virgin)

Give me that hand of yours to kiss.

PAULINA   O, patience!
The statue is but newly fixed, the color's
Not dry.

CAMILLO
My lord, your sorrow was too sore laid on,
Which sixteen winters cannot blow away,
So many summers dry. Scarce any joy
Did ever so long live; no sorrow
But killed itself much sooner.

POLIXENES   Dear my brother,
Let him that was the cause of this have power
To take off so much grief from you as he
56 Will piece up in himself.

PAULINA   Indeed, my lord,
If I had thought the sight of my poor image
Would thus have wrought you – for the stone is mine –
I'ld not have showed it.

LEONTES   Do not draw the curtain.

PAULINA
60 No longer shall you gaze on't, lest your fancy
May think anon it moves.

LEONTES   Let be, let be.
Would I were dead, but that, methinks, already –
What was he that did make it? See, my lord,
Would you not deem it breathed? and that those veins
Did verily bear blood?

POLIXENES   Masterly done.
The very life seems warm upon her lip.

LEONTES
67 The fixture of her eye has motion in't,
As we are mocked with art.

PAULINA   I'll draw the curtain.
My lord's almost so far transported that
He'll think anon it lives.

LEONTES   O sweet Paulina,
Make me to think so twenty years together!
72 No settled senses of the world can match
The pleasure of that madness. Let't alone.

PAULINA
I am sorry, sir, I have thus far stirred you; but
I could afflict you farther.

LEONTES   Do, Paulina,
For this affliction has a taste as sweet
As any cordial comfort. Still methinks
There is an air comes from her. What fine chisel
Could ever yet cut breath? Let no man mock me,
For I will kiss her.

PAULINA   Good my lord, forbear.
The ruddiness upon her lip is wet;
You'll mar it if you kiss it, stain your own
With oily painting. Shall I draw the curtain?

LEONTES
No, not these twenty years.

PERDITA   So long could I
Stand by, a looker on.

PAULINA   Either forbear,
Quit presently the chapel, or resolve you   86
For more amazement. If you can behold it,
I'll make the statue move indeed, descend
And take you by the hand. But then you'll think –
Which I protest against – I am assisted
By wicked powers.

LEONTES   What you can make her do,
I am content to look on; what to speak,
I am content to hear, for 'tis as easy
To make her speak as move.

PAULINA   It is required
You do awake your faith. Then all stand still;
Or those that think it is unlawful business   96
I am about, let them depart.

LEONTES   Proceed.
No foot shall stir.

PAULINA   Music! Awake her, strike!
[Music.]
'Tis time; descend; be stone no more; approach;
Strike all that look upon with marvel. Come,
I'll fill your grave up. Stir, nay, come away;
Bequeath to death your numbness, for from him   102
Dear life redeems you. You perceive she stirs.
[Hermione comes down.]
Start not; her actions shall be holy as
You hear my spell is lawful. Do not shun her
Until you see her die again, for then
You kill her double. Nay, present your hand.   107
When she was young you wooed her; now in age
Is she become the suitor?

LEONTES   O, she's warm!
If this be magic, let it be an art
Lawful as eating.

POLIXENES   She embraces him.

CAMILLO
She hangs about his neck.
If she pertain to life, let her speak too.   113

POLIXENES
Ay, and make it manifest where she has lived,
Or how stol'n from the dead.

PAULINA   That she is living,
Were it but told you, should be hooted at
Like an old tale; but it appears she lives,
Though yet she speak not. Mark a little while.
Please you to interpose, fair madam. Kneel
And pray your mother's blessing. Turn, good lady;
Our Perdita is found.

HERMIONE   You gods, look down,
And from your sacred vials pour your graces   122
Upon my daughter's head! Tell me, mine own,
Where hast thou been preserved? where lived? how
    found
Thy father's court? For thou shalt hear that I,
Knowing by Paulina that the oracle
Gave hope thou wast in being, have preserved
Myself to see the issue.

PAULINA   There's time enough for that,
Lest they desire upon this push to trouble   129
Your joys with like relation. Go together,   130
You precious winners all; your exultation   131
Partake to every one. I, an old turtle,   132
Will wing me to some withered bough and there
My mate, that's never to be found again,

Lament till I am lost.
LEONTES   O, peace, Paulina!
Thou shouldst a husband take by my consent,
As I by thine a wife. This is a match,
And made between's by vows. Thou hast found mine;
But how, is to be questioned, for I saw her,
As I thought, dead, and have in vain said many
A prayer upon her grave. I'll not seek far –
For him, I partly know his mind – to find thee
An honorable husband. Come, Camillo,
And take her by the hand, whose worth and honesty
145   Is richly noted and here justified

By us, a pair of kings. Let's from this place.
What! look upon my brother. Both your pardons,
That e'er I put between your holy looks   148
My ill suspicion. This your son-in-law
And son unto the king, whom heavens directing,
Is troth-plight to your daughter. Good Paulina,
Lead us from hence, where we may leisurely
Each one demand and answer to his part
Performed in this wide gap of time since first
We were dissevered. Hastily lead away.   *Exeunt.* 155

145 *justified* vouched for   148 *holy* chaste   155 *dissevered* separated

THE TEMPEST

INTRODUCTION

In the opening scene of *The Tempest* there is not only a sinking ship but a dissolving society. The storm, like the storm in *King Lear*, does not care that it is afflicting a king, and Gonzalo's protests about the deference due to royalty seem futile enough. But while everyone is unreasonable, we can distinguish Gonzalo, who is ready to meet his fate with some detachment and humor, from Antonio and Sebastian, who are merely screaming abuse at the sailors trying to save their lives. The boatswain, who comes so vividly to life in a few crisp lines, dominates this scene and leaves us with a strong sense of the superiority of personal character to social rank.

The shipwrecked characters are then divided by Ariel into three main groups: Ferdinand; the Court Party proper; Stephano and Trinculo. Each goes through a pursuit of illusions, an ordeal, and a symbolic vision. The Court Party hunts for Ferdinand with strange shapes appearing and vanishing around them; their ordeal is a labyrinth of "forthrights and meanders" in which they founder with exhaustion, and to them is presented the vision of the disappearing banquet, symbolic of deceitful desires. There follows confinement and a madness which brings them to conviction of sin, self-knowledge, and repentance. Like Hamlet, Prospero delays revenge and sets up a dramatic action to catch the conscience of a king; like Lear on a small scale, Alonso is a king who gains in dignity by suffering. The search of Stephano and Trinculo for Prospero is also misled by illusions; their ordeal is a horse-pond and their symbolic vision the "trumpery" dangled in front of them. What happens to them is external and physical rather than internal and mental: they are hunted by hounds, filled with cramps, and finally reach what might be called a conviction of inadequacy. Probably they then settle into their old roles again: if a cold-blooded sneering assassin like Antonio can be forgiven, these amusing and fundamentally likeable rascals can be too. Ferdinand, being the hero, has a better time: he is led by Ariel's music to Miranda, undergoes the ordeal of the log pile, where he takes over Caliban's role as a bearer of wood, and his symbolic vision is that of the wedding masque.

The characters thus appear to be taking their appropriate places in a new kind of social order. We soon realize that the island looks different to different people – it is a pleasanter place to Gonzalo than to Antonio or Sebastian – and that each one is stimulated to exhibit his own ideal of society. At one end, Ferdinand unwillingly resigns himself to becoming King of Naples by the death of Alonso; at the other, Sebastian plots to become King of Naples by murdering Alonso. In between come Stephano, whose ambition to be king of the island is more ridiculous but somehow less despicable than Sebastian's, and Gonzalo, who dreams of a primitive golden age of equality and leisure, not very adequate as a social theory, but simple and honest, full of good nature and good will, like Gonzalo himself.

Into the midst of this society comes the islander Caliban, who is, on one level of nature, a natural man, a primitive whose name seems to echo the "cannibals" of Montaigne's famous essay. He is not a cannibal, but his existence in the play forms an ironic comment on Gonzalo's reverie, which has been taken from a passage in the same essay. Caliban is a human being, as Ariel is not; and whatever he does, Prospero feels responsible for him: "this thing of darkness I / Acknowledge mine," Prospero says. Whether or not he is, as one hopeful critic suggested, an anticipation of Darwin's "missing link," he knows he is not like the apes "With foreheads villainous low"; his sensuality is haunted by troubled dreams of beauty; he is not taken in by the "trumpery," and we leave him with his mind on higher things. His ambitions are to kill Prospero and rape Miranda, both, considering his situation, eminently natural desires; and even these he resigns to Stephano, to whom he tries to be genuinely loyal. Nobody has a good word for Caliban: he is a born devil to Prospero, an abhorred slave to Miranda, and to others not obviously his superiors either in intelligence or virtue he is a puppy-headed monster, a mooncalf, and a plain fish. Yet he has his own dignity, and he is certainly no Yahoo, for all his ancient and fishlike smell. True, Shakespeare, like Swift, clearly does not assume that the natural man on Caliban's level is capable also of a reasonable life. But he has taken pains to make Caliban as memorable and vivid as any character in the play.

As a natural man, Caliban is *mere* nature, nature without nurture, as Prospero would say: the nature that manifests itself more as an instinctive propensity to evil than as the calculated criminality of Antonio and Sebastian, which is rationally corrupted nature. But to an Elizabethan poet "nature" had an upper level, a cosmic and moral order that may be entered through education, obedience to law, and the habit of virtue. In this expanded sense we may say that the whole society being formed on the island under Prospero's guidance is a natural society. Its top level is represented by Miranda, whose chastity and innocence put her, like her poetic descendant the Lady in *Comus*, in tune with the harmony of a higher nature. The discipline necessary to live in this higher nature is imposed on the other characters by Prospero's magic. In Shakespeare's day the occult arts, especially alchemy, whose language Prospero is using at the beginning of the fifth act, were often employed as symbols of such discipline.

Shakespeare did not select Montaigne's essay on the

cannibals as the basis for Gonzalo's "commonwealth" speech merely at random. Montaigne is no Rousseau: he is not talking about imaginary noble savages. He is saying that, despite their unconventional way of getting their proteins, cannibals have many virtues we have not, and if we pretend to greater virtues we ought to have at least theirs. They are not models for imitation; they are children of nature who can show us what is unnatural in our own lives. If we can understand that, we shall be wiser than the cannibals as well as wiser than our present selves. Prospero takes the society of Alonso's ship, immerses it in magic, and then sends it back to the world, its original ranks restored, but given a new wisdom in the light of which Antonio's previous behavior can be seen to be "unnatural." In the Epilogue Prospero hands over to the audience what his art has created, a vision of a society permeated by the virtues of tolerance and forgiveness, in the form of one of the most beautiful plays in the world. And, adds Prospero, you might start practising those virtues by applauding the play.

The Tempest is not an allegory, or a religious drama: if it were, Prospero's great "revels" speech would say, not merely that all earthly things will vanish, but that an eternal world will take their place. In a religious context, Prospero's renunciation of magic would represent the resigning of his will to a divine will, one that can do what the boatswain says Gonzalo cannot do, command the elements to silence and work the peace of the present. In Christianity the higher level of nature is God's original creation, from which man broke away with Adam's fall. It is usually symbolized by the music of the heavenly spheres, of which the one nearest us is the moon. The traditional conception of the magician was of one who could control the moon: this power is attributed to Sycorax, but it is a sinister power and is not associated with Prospero, whose magic and music belong to the sublunary world.

In the wedding masque of the fourth act and the recognition scene of the fifth, therefore, we find ourselves moving, not out of the world, but from an ordinary to a renewed and ennobled vision of nature. The masque shows the meeting of a fertile earth and a gracious sky introduced by the goddess of the rainbow, and leads up to a dance of nymphs representing the spring rains with reapers representing the autumnal harvest. The masque has about it the freshness of Noah's new world, after the tempest had receded and the rainbow promised that seedtime and harvest should not cease. There is thus a glimpse, as Ferdinand recognizes, of an Earthly Paradise, where, as in Milton's Eden, there is no winter but spring and autumn "Danced hand in hand." In the last act, as in *The Winter's Tale*, there is a curious pretense that some of the characters have died and are brought back to life. The discovery of Ferdinand is greeted by Sebastian, of all people, as "A most high miracle." But the miracles are those of a natural, and therefore also a moral and intellectual, renewal of life. Some of Shakespeare's romances feature a final revelation through a goddess or oracle, both of which Alonso expects, but in *The Tempest* goddess and oracle are represented by Miranda and Ariel (in his speech at the banquet) respectively. Ariel is a spirit of nature, and Miranda is a natural spirit, in other words a human being, greeting the "brave new world" in all the good faith of innocence.

Hence we distort the play if we think of Prospero as supernatural, just as we do if we think of Caliban as a devil. Prospero is a tempest-raiser like the witches in *Macbeth*, though morally at the opposite pole; he is a "white" magician. Anyone with Prospero's powers is an agent of fate, a cheating fate if evil, a benevolent fate or providence if motivated as he is. Great courage was required of all magicians, white or black, for the elemental spirits they controlled were both unwilling and malignant, and any sign of faltering meant terrible disaster. Ariel is loyal because of his debt of gratitude to Prospero, and because he is a very high-class spirit, too delicate to work for a black witch like Sycorax. But even he has a short memory, and has to be periodically reminded what his debt of gratitude is. Of the others Caliban says, probably with some truth, "They all do hate him / As rootedly as I." The nervous strain of dealing with such creatures shows up in Prospero's relations with human beings too; and in his tormenting of Caliban, in his lame excuse for making Ferdinand's wooing "uneasy," in his fussing over protecting Miranda from her obviously honorable lover, there is a touch of the busybody.

Still, his benevolence is genuine, and as far as the action of the play goes he seems an admirable ruler. Yet he appears to have been a remarkably incompetent Duke of Milan, and not to be promising much improvement after he returns. His talents are evidently dramatic rather than political, and he seems less of a practical magician plotting the discomfiture of his enemies than a creative artist calling spirits from their confines to enact his present fancies. It has often been thought that Prospero is a self-portrait of Shakespeare, and there may well be something in him of a harassed overworked actor-manager, scolding the lazy actors, praising the good ones in connoisseur's language, thinking up jobs for the idle, constantly aware of his limited time before his show goes on, his nerves tense and alert for breakdowns while it is going on, looking forward longingly to peaceful retirement, yet in the meantime having to go out and beg the audience for applause.

Prospero's magic, in any case, is an "art" which includes, in fact largely consists of, music and drama. Dramatists from Euripides to Pirandello have been fascinated by the paradox of reality and illusion in drama: the play is an illusion like the dream, and yet a focus of reality more intense than life affords. The action of *The Tempest* moves from sea to land, from chaos to new creation, from reality to realization. What seems at first illusory, the magic and music, becomes real, and the *Realpolitik* of Antonio and Sebastian becomes illusion. In this island the quality of one's dreaming is an index of character. When Antonio and Sebastian remain awake plotting murder, they show that they are the real dreamers, sunk in the hallucinations of greed. We find Stephano better company because his are the exuberant dreams of the stage boaster, as when he claims to have swum thirty-five leagues "off and on," when we know that he has floated to shore on a wine cask. Caliban's life is full of nightmare interspersed by strange gleams of ecstasy. When the Court Party first came to the island "no man was his own"; they had not found their "proper selves." Through the mirages of Ariel, the mops and mows of the other spirits, the vanities of Prospero's art, and the fevers of madness, reality grows up in them from inside, in response to the fertilizing influence of illusion.

Few plays are so haunted by the passing of time as *The Tempest*: it has derived even its name from a word (*tempestas*) which means time as well as tempest. Timing was important to a magician: everything depended on it when the alchemist's project gathered to a head; astrologers were exact observers of time ("The very minute bids thee ope thine ear," Prospero says to Miranda), and the most famous of all stories about magicians, the story told in Greene's play *Friar Bacon and Friar Bungay*, had the warning of "time is past" for its moral. The same preoccupation affects the other characters too, from the sailors in the storm to Ariel watching the clock for his freedom. The tide, which also waits for no man, ebbs and flows around this Mediterranean island in defiance of geography, and its imagery enters the plotting of Antonio and Sebastian and the grief of Ferdinand. When everyone is trying to make the most of his time, it seems strange that a melancholy elegy over the dissolving of all things in time should be the emotional crux of the play.

A very deliberate echo in the dialogue gives us the clue to this. Morally, *The Tempest* shows a range of will extending from Prospero's self-control, which includes his control of all the other characters, to the self-abandonment of Alonso's despair, when, crazed with guilt and grief, he resolves to drown himself "deeper than e'er plummet sounded." Intellectually, it shows a range of vision extending from the realizing of a moment in time, the zenith of Prospero's fortune, which becomes everyone else's zenith too, to the sense of the nothingness of all temporal things. When Prospero renounces his magic, his "book" falls into the vanishing world, "deeper than did ever plummet sound." He has done what his art can do; he has held the mirror up to nature. Alonso and the rest are promised many explanations after the play is over, but we are left only with the darkening mirror, the visions fading and leaving not a rack behind. Once again the Epilogue reminds us that Prospero has used up all his magic in the play, and what more he can do depends on us.

It is not difficult to see, then, why so many students of Shakespeare, rightly or wrongly, have felt that *The Tempest* is in a peculiar sense Shakespeare's play, and that there is something in it of Shakespeare's farewell to his art. Two other features of it reinforce this feeling: the fact that no really convincing general source for the play has yet been discovered, and the fact that it is probably the last play wholly written by Shakespeare.

Whether a general source turns up or not, *The Tempest* is still erudite and allusive enough, full of echoes of literature, from the classics to the pamphlets of Shakespeare's own time. The scene of the play, an island somewhere between Tunis and Naples, suggests the journey of Aeneas from Carthage to Rome. Gonzalo's identification of Tunis and Carthage, and the otherwise tedious business about "Widow Dido" in the second act, seems almost to be emphasizing the parallel. Like *The Tempest*, the *Aeneid* begins with a terrible storm and goes on to tell a story of wanderings in which a banquet with harpies figures prominently. Near the route of Aeneas' journey, according to Virgil, was the abode of Circe, of whom (at least in her Renaissance form) Sycorax is a close relative. Circe suggests Medea, whose speech in Ovid's *Metamorphoses* is the model for Prospero's renunciation speech. Echoes from the shipwreck of St Paul (Ariel's phrase "Not a hair perished" recalls Acts xxvii, 34), from St Augustine, who

also had associations with Carthage, and from Apuleius, with his interest in magic and initiation, are appropriate enough in such a play. Most of the traditional magical names of elemental spirits were of Hebrew origin, and "Ariel," a name occurring in the Bible (Isaiah xxix, 1), was among them.

The imagery of contemporary accounts of Atlantic voyages has also left strong traces in *The Tempest*, and seems almost to have been its immediate inspiration. One ship of a fleet that sailed across the ocean to reinforce Ralegh's Virginian colony in 1609 had an experience rather like that of Alonso's ship. It was driven aground on the Bermudas by a storm and given up for lost, but the passengers managed to survive the winter there and reached Virginia the following spring. William Strachey's account of this experience, *True Repertory of the Wracke*, dated July 15, 1610, was not published until after Shakespeare's death, and as Shakespeare certainly knew it, he must have read it in manuscript. Strachey's and a closely related pamphlet, Sylvester Jourdain's *Discovery of the Barmudas* (1610), lie behind Caliban's allusions to making dams for fish and to water with "berries" (i.e. cedar-berries) in it. Other details indicate Shakespeare's reading in similar accounts. Setebos is mentioned as a god ("divell") of the Patagonians in Richard Eden's *History of Travayle in the West and East Indies* (1577), and the curious "Bowgh, wawgh" refrain in Ariel's first song seems to be from a contemporary account of an Indian dance. It is a little puzzling why New World imagery should be so prominent in *The Tempest*, which really has nothing to do with the New World, beyond Ariel's reference to the "still-vexed Bermoothes" and a general, if vague, resemblance between the relation of Caliban to the other characters and that of the American Indians to the colonizers and drunken sailors who came to exterminate or enslave them.

However that may be, the dates of these pamphlets help to establish the fact that *The Tempest* is a very late play. A performance of it is recorded for November 1, 1611, in Whitehall, and it also formed part of the celebrations connected with the wedding of King James' daughter Elizabeth in the winter of 1612-13. The versification is also that of a late play, for *The Tempest* is written in the direct speaking style of Shakespeare's last period, the lines full of weak endings and so welded together that every speech is a verse paragraph in itself, often very close in its rhythm to prose, especially in the speeches of Caliban. One should read the verse as an actor would read it, attending to the natural stresses, of which there are usually four to a line, rather than the metre. Some critics have felt that a few lines are "unmetrical," but no line that can be easily spoken on the stage is unmetrical, and it is simple enough to find the four natural stresses in "You do *look*, my *son*, in a *moved sort*," or (in octosyllabics) "*Earth's in*crease, *foi*son *plen*ty." In such writing all the regular schematic forms of verse, rhyme, alliteration, assonance, and the like, fall into the background, peeping out irregularly through the texture:

> I will stand to, and feed;
> Although my last, no matter, since I feel
> The best is past. Brother, my lord the Duke,
> Stand to, and do as we.

In its genre *The Tempest* shows a marked affinity with dramatic forms outside the normal range of tragedy and comedy. Among these is the masque : besides containing an actual masque, *The Tempest* is like the masque in its use of elaborate stage machinery and music. The magician with his wand and mantle was a frequent figure in masques, and Caliban is like the "wild men" common in the farcical interludes known as antimasques. Another is the *commedia dell'arte*, which was well known in England. Some of the sketchy plots of this half-improvised type of play have been preserved, and they show extraordinary similarities to *The Tempest*, especially in the Stephano–Trinculo scenes. *The Tempest* in short is a spectacular and operatic play, and when we think of other plays like it, we are more apt to think of, say, Mozart's *Magic Flute* than of ordinary stage plays.

But more important than these affiliations is the position of *The Tempest* as the fourth and last of the great romances of Shakespeare's final period. In these plays Shakespeare seems to have distilled the essence of all his work in tragedy, comedy, and history, and to have reached the very bedrock of drama itself, with a romantic spectacle which is at once primitive and sophisticated, childlike and profound. In these plays the central structural principles of drama emerge with great clarity, and we become aware of the affinity between the happy endings of comedy and the rituals marking the great rising rhythms of life : marriage, springtime, harvest, dawn, and rebirth. In *The Tempest* there is also an emphasis on moral and spiritual rebirth which suggests rituals of initiation, like baptism or the ancient mystery dramas, as well as of festivity. And just as its poetic texture ranges from the simplicity of Ariel's incredibly beautiful songs to the haunting solemnity of Prospero's speeches, so we may come to the play on any level, as a fairy tale with unusually lifelike characters, or as an inexhaustibly profound drama that has influenced some of the most complex poems in the language, including Milton's *Comus* and Eliot's *The Waste Land*. However we take it, *The Tempest* is a play not simply to be read or seen or even studied, but possessed.

Victoria College NORTHROP FRYE
University of Toronto

NOTE ON THE TEXT

The Tempest was first printed in the folio of 1623, evidently from a transcript (made by the scrivener Ralph Crane) of Shakespeare's draft after it had been prepared for production. The play stands first in the volume, in a carefully edited and printed text, supplied with unusually full stage directions, and a list of characters (following the Epilogue). The present edition follows the folio text ; except for occasional relineation, departures from it are few and slight. The act–scene division supplied marginally is that of the folio. Below are listed all substantive departures from the folio text, with the adopted reading in italics followed by the folio reading in roman.

The Scene ... Island followed by *Names of the Actors* (appears after Epilogue in F)

I, i, 31 *Exeunt* Exit 34 *plague* plague – 46–47 *courses! Off* courses off 56–58 *Mercy . . . split* (assigned to Gonzalo in F) 59 *with th' King* with' King

I, ii, 100 *unto* into 112 *with th' King* with King 145 *prepared* preparèd 159 *divine.* divine 201 *lightnings* Lightning 230 *stowed* stowèd 248 *made no* made thee no 271 *wast* was 282 *she* he 374 s.d. *Ariel's song* Ariel Song 380 *the burden bear* beare the burthen 381 *Hark, hark!* (appears after s.d. *Burthen dispersedly* in l. 379 in F) 384 s.d. *Burden, dispersedly* (not in F) 396 s.d. *Ariel's song* Ariell Song

II, i, 5 *master* Masters 36 *Ha, ha, ha!* (assigned to Sebastian in F) 37 *So, you're paid* (assigned to Antonio in F) 62 *gloss* glosses 90 *Ay* I 106 *removed* removèd 114 *oared* oarèd 116 *bowed* bowèd

II, ii, 45 (F has s.d. *Sings*) 173 *Caliban* (omitted in F)

III, i, 2 *sets* set 15 *least* lest 93 *withal* with all

III, ii, 14 *on, by this light. Thou* on, by this light thou 51–52 *isle ; From me* Isle From me, 118 *scout* cout 149 *Wilt come?* (assigned to Trinculo in F) 150 *I'll follow, Stephano* Ile follow Stephano

III, iii, 2 *ache* akes 17 *Sebastian . . . more* (appears after s.d. *Solemne . . . depart* in F) 29 *islanders* Islands 65 *plume* plumbe

IV, i, 9 *off* of 13 *gift* guest 17 *rite* right 52 *rein* raigne 73 (F has s.d. *Iuno descends*) 74 *her* here 106 *marriage blessing* marriage, blessing 145 *anger so* anger, so 193 s.d. *Enter Ariel . . . &c.* (appears after *line* in F) *them on* on them 230 *Let't* let's 262 *Lie* Lies

V, i, 16 *run* runs 60 *boiled* boile 72 *Didst* Did 75 *entertained* entertaine 76 *who* whom 82 *lies* ly 124 *not* nor 136 *who* whom 199 *remembrance* remembrances 236 *her* our 248 *Which shall be shortly, single I'll* (Which shall be shortly single) I'le 258 *coragio* Corasio

THE TEMPEST

*

I, i *A tempestuous noise of thunder and lightning heard.*
Enter a Shipmaster and a Boatswain.

MASTER Boatswain!

BOATSWAIN Here, master. What cheer?

3 MASTER Good, speak to th' mariners; fall to't yarely, or
we run ourselves aground. Bestir, bestir! *Exit.*
Enter Mariners.

BOATSWAIN Heigh, my hearts! Cheerly, cheerly, my
6 hearts! Yare, yare! Take in the topsail! Tend to th'
7 master's whistle! Blow till thou burst thy wind, if room
enough!
Enter Alonso, Sebastian, Antonio, Ferdinand,
Gonzalo, and others.

ALONSO Good boatswain, have care. Where's the mas-
9 ter? Play the men.

BOATSWAIN I pray now, keep below.

ANTONIO Where is the master, bos'n?

BOATSWAIN Do you not hear him? You mar our labor.
Keep your cabins: you do assist the storm.

GONZALO Nay, good, be patient.

BOATSWAIN When the sea is. Hence! What cares these
15 roarers for the name of king? To cabin! Silence!
Trouble us not!

GONZALO Good, yet remember whom thou hast aboard.

BOATSWAIN None that I more love than myself. You are
a councillor: if you can command these elements to silence and work the peace of the present, we will not hand 21
a rope more; use your authority. If you cannot, give
thanks you have lived so long, and make yourself ready
in your cabin for the mischance of the hour, if it so hap.
– Cheerly, good hearts! – Out of our way, I say. *Exit.*

GONZALO I have great comfort from this fellow: methinks he hath no drowning mark upon him; his com- 27
plexion is perfect gallows. Stand fast, good Fate, to his 28
hanging! Make the rope of his destiny our cable, for
our own doth little advantage. If he be not born to be 30
hanged, our case is miserable. *Exeunt.*
Enter Boatswain.

BOATSWAIN Down with the topmast! Yare! Lower,
lower! Bring her to try with main-course! (*A cry* 33
within.) A plague upon this howling! They are louder 34
than the weather or our office. 35
Enter Sebastian, Antonio, and Gonzalo.
Yet again? What do you here? Shall we give o'er and
drown? Have you a mind to sink?

SEBASTIAN A pox o' your throat, you bawling, blas-
phemous, incharitable dog!

BOATSWAIN Work you, then.

ANTONIO Hang, cur, hang, you whoreson, insolent noise-
maker! We are less afraid to be drowned than thou art.

GONZALO I'll warrant him for drowning, though the ship 43
were no stronger than a nutshell and as leaky as an
unstanched wench. 45

BOATSWAIN Lay her ahold, ahold! Set her two courses! 46
Off to sea again! Lay her off!
Enter Mariners wet.

MARINERS All lost! To prayers, to prayers! All lost!
[Exeunt.]

BOATSWAIN What, must our mouths be cold?

I, i The deck of a ship **3** *yarely* briskly **6** *Tend* attend **7** *Blow . . . wind*
(addressed to the storm) **7–8** *if room enough* i.e. so long as we have searoom **9** *Play* (perhaps 'ply,' keep the men busy) **15** *roarers* (1) waves,
(2) blusterers or bullies **21** *hand* handle **27** *complexion* indication of
character in appearance of face **28** *gallows* (alluding to the proverb 'He
that's born to be hanged need fear no drowning') **30** *doth little advantage*
doesn't help us much **33** *try with main-course* lie hove-to with only the
mainsail **34** *plague* (followed by a dash in F; possibly the boatswain's
language was more profane than the text indicates; cf. l. 38, and V, i,
218–19) **35** *our office* (the noise we make at) our work **43** *warrant . . . for*
guarantee . . . against **45** *unstanched* i.e. loose **46** *ahold* (perhaps 'a-hull,'
without any sail. As the ship drifts to the rocks, the order is reversed and
the *two courses*, foresail and mainsail, are set up again in an effort to clear
the shore.)

GONZALO
The King and Prince at prayers! Let's assist them,
For our case is as theirs.

SEBASTIAN   I am out of patience.

ANTONIO
52 We are merely cheated of our lives by drunkards.
53 This wide-chopped rascal – would thou mightst lie drowning
54 The washing of ten tides!

GONZALO   He'll be hanged yet,
Though every drop of water swear against it
56 And gape at wid'st to glut him.

A confused noise within :
           'Mercy on us! –
We split, we split! – Farewell, my wife and children! –
Farewell, brother! – We split, we split, we split!'
           [Exit Boatswain.]

ANTONIO
Let's all sink with th' King.

SEBASTIAN   Let's take leave of him.
           Exit [with Antonio].

GONZALO Now would I give a thousand furlongs of sea
61 for an acre of barren ground – long heath, brown furze,
anything. The wills above be done, but I would fain die
a dry death.   *Exit.*

           *

I, ii   *Enter Prospero and Miranda.*

MIRANDA
If by your art, my dearest father, you have
Put the wild waters in this roar, allay them.
The sky, it seems, would pour down stinking pitch
4 But that the sea, mounting to th' welkin's cheek,
Dashes the fire out. O, I have sufferèd
6 With those that I saw suffer! a brave vessel
(Who had no doubt some noble creature in her)
Dashed all to pieces! O, the cry did knock
Against my very heart! Poor souls, they perished!
Had I been any god of power, I would
11 Have sunk the sea within the earth or ere
It should the good ship so have swallowed and
13 The fraughting souls within her.

PROSPERO   Be collected.
14 No more amazement. Tell your piteous heart
There's no harm done.

MIRANDA   O, woe the day!

PROSPERO   No harm.
I have done nothing but in care of thee,
Of thee my dear one, thee my daughter, who
Art ignorant of what thou art, naught knowing
Of whence I am; nor that I am more better
Than Prospero, master of a full poor cell,
And thy no greater father.

MIRANDA   More to know
22 Did never meddle with my thoughts.

PROSPERO   'Tis time
I should inform thee farther. Lend thy hand
And pluck my magic garment from me. So,
25 Lie there, my art. Wipe thou thine eyes; have comfort.
The direful spectacle of the wrack, which touched
27 The very virtue of compassion in thee,
28 I have with such provision in mine art
So safely orderèd that there is no soul –

No, not so much perdition as an hair   30
Betid to any creature in the vessel   31
Which thou héard'st cry, which thou saw'st sink. Sit down;
For thou must now know farther.

MIRANDA   You have often
Begun to tell me what I am; but stopped
And left me to a bootless inquisition,   35
Concluding, 'Stay : not yet.'

PROSPERO   The hour's now come;
The very minute bids thee ope thine ear.
Obey, and be attentive. Canst thou remember   38
A time before we came unto this cell?
I do not think thou canst, for then thou wast not
Out three years old.   41

MIRANDA   Certainly, sir, I can.

PROSPERO
By what? By any other house or person?
Of any thing the image tell me that   43
Hath kept with thy remembrance.

MIRANDA   'Tis far off,
And rather like a dream than an assurance
That my remembrance warrants. Had I not   46
Four or five women once that tended me?

PROSPERO
Thou hadst, and more, Miranda. But how is it
That this lives in thy mind? What seest thou else
In the dark backward and abysm of time?   50
If thou rememb'rest aught ere thou cam'st here,
How thou cam'st here thou mayst.

MIRANDA   But that I do not.

PROSPERO
Twelve year since, Miranda, twelve year since,
Thy father was the Duke of Milan and
A prince of power.

MIRANDA   Sir, are not you my father?

PROSPERO
Thy mother was a piece of virtue, and   56
She said thou wast my daughter; and thy father
Was Duke of Milan; and his only heir
A princess – no worse issuèd.   59

MIRANDA   O the heavens!
What foul play had we that we came from thence?
Or blessèd was't we did?

PROSPERO   Both, both, my girl!
By foul play, as thou say'st, were we heaved thence,
But blessedly holp hither.   63

MIRANDA   O, my heart bleeds
To think o' th' teen that I have turned you to,   64
Which is from my remembrance! Please you, farther.   65

---

52 *merely* completely   53 *wide-chopped* wide-jawed   54 *ten tides* (pirates were hanged on shore and left until three tides washed over them)   56 *glut* gobble   61 *long heath, brown furze* heather and gorse (sometimes emended to 'ling, heath, broom, furze')
I, ii Before Prospero's cell   4 *cheek* face (with perhaps a secondary meaning of 'side of a grate')   6 *brave* fine, handsome (and so elsewhere throughout the play)   11 *or ere* before   13 *fraughting* forming the cargo; *collected* composed   14 *amazement* distraction; *piteous* pitying   22 *meddle* mingle   25 *art* i.e. his robe   27 *virtue* essence   28 *provision* foresight   30 *perdition* loss   31 *Betid* happened   35 *bootless inquisition* fruitless inquiry   38 *Obey* listen   41 *Out* fully   43 *tell me* i.e. describe for me   46 *remembrance warrants* memory guarantees   50 *backward* past; *abysm* abyss   56 *piece* masterpiece   59 *no worse issuèd* no meaner in descent   63 *blessedly holp* providentially helped   64 *teen* trouble; *turned you to* put you in mind of   65 *from* out of

PROSPERO
My brother and thy uncle, called Antonio –
I pray thee mark me – that a brother should
Be so perfidious ! – he whom next thyself
69 Of all the world I loved, and to him put
The manage of my state, as at that time
71 Through all the signories it was the first
And Prospero the prime duke, being so reputed
In dignity, and for the liberal arts
Without a parallel ; those being all my study,
The government I cast upon my brother
And to my state grew stranger, being transported
And rapt in secret studies. Thy false uncle –
Dost thou attend me ?
MIRANDA   Sir, most heedfully.
PROSPERO
79 Being once perfected how to grant suits,
How to deny them, who t' advance, and who
81 To trash for over-topping, new-created
82 The creatures that were mine, I say, or changed 'em,
83 Or else new-formed 'em ; having both the key
Of officer and office, set all hearts i' th' state
To what tune pleased his ear, that now he was
The ivy which had hid my princely trunk
And sucked my verdure out on't. Thou attend'st not ?
MIRANDA
O, good sir, I do.
PROSPERO   I pray thee mark me.
I thus neglecting worldly ends, all dedicated
90 To closeness, and the bettering of my mind
With that which, but by being so retired,
92 O'er-prized all popular rate, in my false brother
Awaked an evil nature, and my trust,
94 Like a good parent, did beget of him
A falsehood in its contrary as great
As my trust was, which had indeed no limit,
97 A confidence sans bound. He being thus lorded,
98 Not only with what my revenue yielded
But what my power might else exact, like one
100 Who having unto truth, by telling of it,
Made such a sinner of his memory
102 To credit his own lie, he did believe
103 He was indeed the Duke, out o' th' substitution
And executing th' outward face of royalty
With all prerogative. Hence his ambition growing –
Dost thou hear ?
MIRANDA   Your tale, sir, would cure deafness.
PROSPERO
To have no screen between this part he played

And him he played it for, he needs will be
Absolute Milan. Me (poor man) my library   109
Was dukedom large enough. Of temporal royalties
He thinks me now incapable ; confederates   111
(So dry he was for sway) with th' King of Naples   112
To give him annual tribute, do him homage,
Subject his coronet to his crown, and bend
The dukedom yet unbowed (alas, poor Milan !)
To most ignoble stooping.
MIRANDA   O the heavens !
PROSPERO
Mark his condition, and th' event ; then tell me   117
If this might be a brother.
MIRANDA   I should sin
To think but nobly of my grandmother.
Good wombs have borne bad sons.
PROSPERO   Now the condition.
This King of Naples, being an enemy
To me inveterate, hearkens my brother's suit ;
Which was, that he, in lieu o' th' premises   123
Of homage and I know not how much tribute,
Should presently extirpate me and mine   125
Out of the dukedom and confer fair Milan,
With all the honors, on my brother. Whereon,
A treacherous army levied, one midnight
Fated to th' purpose, did Antonio open   129
The gates of Milan ; and i' th' dead of darkness,
The ministers for th' purpose hurrièd thence   131
Me and thy crying self.
MIRANDA   Alack, for pity !
I, not rememb'ring how I cried out then,
Will cry it o'er again ; it is a hint   134
That wrings mine eyes to't.   135
PROSPERO   Hear a little further,
And then I'll bring thee to the present business
Which now's upon's ; without the which this story
Were most impertinent.   138
MIRANDA   Wherefore did they not
That hour destroy us ?
PROSPERO   Well demanded, wench.
My tale provokes that question. Dear, they durst not,
So dear the love my people bore me ; nor set
A mark so bloody on the business ; but
With colors fairer painted their foul ends.
In few, they hurried us aboard a bark,   144
Bore us some leagues to sea ; where they prepared
A rotten carcass of a butt, not rigged,   146
Nor tackle, sail, nor mast ; the very rats
Instinctively have quit it. There they hoist us,
To cry to th' sea that roared to us ; to sigh
To th' winds, whose pity, sighing back again,
Did us but loving wrong.
MIRANDA   Alack, what trouble
Was I then to you !
PROSPERO   O, a cherubin
Thou wast that did preserve me ! Thou didst smile,
Infusèd with a fortitude from heaven,
When I have decked the sea with drops full salt,
Under my burden groaned : which raised in me
An undergoing stomach, to bear up   157
Against what should ensue.
MIRANDA   How came we ashore ?
PROSPERO
By providence divine.

69–70 *put … state* entrusted the control of my administration   71 *signories* states of northern Italy   79 *perfected* grown skillful   81 *trash for over-topping* (1) check, as hounds, for going too fast, (2) cut branches, as of over-tall trees   82 *or* either   83 *key* (used with pun on its musical sense, leading to the metaphor of *tune*)   90 *closeness* seclusion (?), secret studies (?)   92 *O'er-prized* outvalued ; *rate* estimation   94 *good parent* (alluding to the same proverb cited by Miranda in l. 120)   97–99 *He . . . exact* (the sense is that Antonio had the prerogatives as well as the income of the Duke)   97 *sans bound* unlimited   98 *revenue* (accent second syllable)   100 *it* i.e. the lie   102 *To* as to   103 *out* as a result   109 *Absolute Milan* Duke of Milan in fact   111 *confederates* joins in league with   112 *dry* thirsty, eager   117 *condition* pact ; *event* outcome   123 *in lieu o' th' premises* in return for the guarantees   125 *presently* immediately ; *extirpate* remove (accent second syllable)   129 *Fated* devoted   131 *ministers* agents   134 *hint* occasion   135 *wrings* constrains   138 *impertinent* irrelevant   144 *few* few words   146 *butt* tub   157 *undergoing stomach* resolution to endure

Some food we had, and some fresh water, that
A noble Neapolitan, Gonzalo,
Out of his charity, who being then appointed
Master of this design, did give us, with
Rich garments, linens, stuffs, and necessaries
165 Which since have steaded much. So, of his gentleness,
Knowing I loved my books, he furnished me
From mine own library with volumes that
I prize above my dukedom.

MIRANDA   Would I might
But ever see that man!

PROSPERO   Now I arise.
Sit still, and hear the last of our sea-sorrow.
Here in this island we arrived; and here
172 Have I, thy schoolmaster, made thee more profit
173 Than other princess can, that have more time
For vainer hours, and tutors not so careful.

MIRANDA
Heavens thank you for't! And now I pray you, sir,—
For still 'tis beating in my mind,—your reason
For raising this sea-storm?

PROSPERO   Know thus far forth.
By accident most strange, bountiful Fortune
(Now, my dear lady) hath mine enemies
Brought to this shore; and by my prescience
181 I find my zenith doth depend upon
A most auspicious star, whose influence
183 If now I court not, but omit, my fortunes
Will ever after droop. Here cease more questions.
Thou art inclined to sleep. 'Tis a good dulness,
And give it way. I know thou canst not choose.
    [Miranda sleeps.]
187 Come away, servant, come! I am ready now.
Approach, my Ariel: come!
    Enter Ariel.

ARIEL
All hail, great master! Grave sir, hail! I come
To answer thy best pleasure; be't to fly,
To swim, to dive into the fire, to ride
192 On the curled clouds. To thy strong bidding task
193 Ariel and all his quality.

PROSPERO   Hast thou, spirit,
194 Performed to point the tempest that I bade thee?

ARIEL
To every article.
196 I boarded the King's ship: now on the beak,
197 Now in the waist, the deck, in every cabin,
198 I flamed amazement: sometime I'ld divide
And burn in many places; on the topmast,
200 The yards, and boresprit would I flame distinctly,
Then meet and join. Jove's lightnings, the precursors
O' th' dreadful thunderclaps, more momentary
And sight-outrunning were not. The fire and cracks
Of sulphurous roaring the most mighty Neptune
Seem to besiege and make his bold waves tremble;
Yea, his dread trident shake.

PROSPERO   My brave spirit!
207 Who was so firm, so constant, that this coil
Would not infect his reason?

ARIEL   Not a soul
209 But felt a fever of the mad and played
Some tricks of desperation. All but mariners
Plunged in the foaming brine and quit the vessel;
212 Then all afire with me the King's son Ferdinand,

With hair up-staring (then like reeds, not hair),   213
Was the first man that leapt; cried 'Hell is empty,
And all the devils are here!'

PROSPERO   Why, that's my spirit!
But was not this nigh shore?

ARIEL   Close by, my master.

PROSPERO
But are they, Ariel, safe?

ARIEL   Not a hair perished.
On their sustaining garments not a blemish,   218
But fresher than before; and as thou bad'st me,
In troops I have dispersed them 'bout the isle.
The King's son have I landed by himself,
Whom I left cooling of the air with sighs
In an odd angle of the isle, and sitting,
His arms in this sad knot.   224

PROSPERO   Of the King's ship
The mariners say how thou hast disposed,
And all the rest o' th' fleet.

ARIEL   Safely in harbor
Is the King's ship; in the deep nook where once
Thou call'dst me up at midnight to fetch dew
From the still-vexed Bermoothes, there she's hid;   229
The mariners all under hatches stowed,
Who, with a charm joined to their suff'red labor,   231
I have left asleep; and for the rest o' th' fleet,
Which I dispersed, they all have met again,
And are upon the Mediterranean flote   234
Bound sadly home for Naples,
Supposing that they saw the King's ship wracked
And his great person perish.

PROSPERO   Ariel, thy charge
Exactly is performed; but there's more work.
What is the time o' th' day?

ARIEL   Past the mid season.   239

PROSPERO
At least two glasses. The time 'twixt six and now   240
Must by us both be spent most preciously.

ARIEL
Is there more toil? Since thou dost give me pains,
Let me remember thee what thou hast promised,   243
Which is not yet performed me.

PROSPERO   How now? moody?
What is't thou canst demand?

ARIEL   My liberty.

PROSPERO
Before the time be out? No more!   246

ARIEL   I prithee,
Remember I have done thee worthy service,
Told thee no lies, made no mistakings, served
Without or grudge or grumblings. Thou did promise
To bate me a full year.   250

---

165 *steaded* been of use   172 *more profit* profit more   173 *princess* princesses   181 *zenith* apex of fortune   183 *omit* neglect   187 *Come away* come here   192 *task* (supply 'come')   193 *quality* cohorts (Ariel is leader of a band of elemental spirits)   194 *to point* in detail   196 *beak* prow   197 *waist* middle; *deck* poop   198 *flamed amazement* struck terror by appearing as (St Elmo's) fire   200 *boresprit* bowsprit; *distinctly* in different places   207 *coil* uproar   209 *of the mad* such as madmen have   212 *afire with me* (refers either to the vessel or to Ferdinand, depending on the punctuation; F suggests the latter)   213 *up-staring* standing on end   218 *sustaining* buoying them up in the water   224 *this* (illustrated by a gesture)   229 *still-vexed Bermoothes* constantly agitated Bermudas   231 *suff'red* undergone   234 *flote* sea   239 *mid season* noon   240 *glasses* hours   243 *remember* remind   246 *time* period of service   250 *bate me* shorten my term of service

PROSPERO   Dost thou forget
From what a torment I did free thee?
ARIEL   No.
PROSPERO
Thou dost; and think'st it much to tread the ooze
Of the salt deep,
To run upon the sharp wind of the North,
255   To do me business in the veins o' th' earth
256   When it is baked with frost.
ARIEL   I do not, sir.
PROSPERO
Thou liest, malignant thing! Hast thou forgot
258   The foul witch Sycorax, who with age and envy
Was grown into a hoop? Hast thou forgot her?
ARIEL
No, sir.
PROSPERO   Thou hast. Where was she born? Speak!
Tell me!
ARIEL
261   Sir, in Argier.
PROSPERO   O, was she so? I must
Once in a month recount what thou hast been,
Which thou forget'st. This damned witch Sycorax,
For mischiefs manifold, and sorceries terrible
To enter human hearing, from Argier,
266   Thou know'st, was banished. For one thing she did
They would not take her life. Is not this true?
ARIEL
Ay, sir.
PROSPERO
This blue-eyed hag was hither brought with child
And here was left by th' sailors. Thou, my slave,
As thou report'st thyself, wast then her servant;
And, for thou wast a spirit too delicate
To act her earthy and abhorred commands,
274   Refusing her grand hests, she did confine thee,
By help of her more potent ministers,
And in her most unmitigable rage,
Into a cloven pine; within which rift
Imprisoned thou didst painfully remain
A dozen years; within which space she died
And left thee there, where thou didst vent thy groans
281   As fast as millwheels strike. Then was this island
(Save for the son that she did litter here,
A freckled whelp, hag-born) not honored with
A human shape.
ARIEL   Yes, Caliban her son.
PROSPERO
Dull thing, I say so: he, that Caliban
Whom now I keep in service. Thou best know'st
What torment I did find thee in: thy groans
Did make wolves howl and penetrate the breasts
Of ever-angry bears. It was a torment
To lay upon the damned, which Sycorax

Could not again undo. It was mine art,
When I arrived and heard thee, that made gape
The pine, and let thee out.
ARIEL   I thank thee, master.
PROSPERO
If thou more murmur'st, I will rend an oak
And peg thee in his knotty entrails till   295
Thou hast howled away twelve winters.   296
ARIEL   Pardon, master.
I will be correspondent to command   297
And do my spriting gently.   298
PROSPERO   Do so; and after two days
I will discharge thee.
ARIEL   That's my noble master!
What shall I do? Say what? What shall I do?
PROSPERO
Go make thyself like a nymph o' th' sea. Be subject
To no sight but thine and mine; invisible
To every eyeball else. Go take this shape
And hither come in't. Go! Hence with diligence!
                                        Exit [Ariel].
Awake, dear heart, awake! Thou hast slept well.
Awake!
MIRANDA   The strangeness of your story put
Heaviness in me.
PROSPERO   Shake it off. Come on.
We'll visit Caliban, my slave, who never
Yields us kind answer.
MIRANDA   'Tis a villain, sir,
I do not love to look on.
PROSPERO   But as 'tis,
We cannot miss him: he does make our fire,   311
Fetch in our wood, and serves in offices
That profit us. What, ho! slave! Caliban!
Thou earth, thou! Speak!
CALIBAN [within]   There's wood enough within.
PROSPERO
Come forth, I say! There's other business for thee.
Come, thou tortoise! When?   316
      Enter Ariel like a water nymph.
Fine apparition! My quaint Ariel,   317
Hark in thine ear.
ARIEL   My lord, it shall be done.   Exit.
PROSPERO
Thou poisonous slave, got by the devil himself
Upon thy wicked dam, come forth!
      Enter Caliban.
CALIBAN
As wicked dew as e'er my mother brushed
With raven's feather from unwholesome fen
Drop on you both! A south-west blow on ye
And blister you all o'er!
PROSPERO
For this, be sure, to-night thou shalt have cramps,
Side-stitches that shall pen thy breath up; urchins   326
Shall, for that vast of night that they may work,   327
All exercise on thee; thou shalt be pinched
As thick as honeycomb, each pinch more stinging
Than bees that made 'em.
CALIBAN   I must eat my dinner.
This island's mine by Sycorax my mother,
Which thou tak'st from me. When thou cam'st first,
Thou strok'st me and made much of me; wouldst give me
Water with berries in't; and teach me how

255 *veins* streams   256 *baked* hardened   258 *Sycorax* (name not found elsewhere; usually connected with Greek '*sys*', sow, and '*korax*', which means both raven – cf. l. 322 – and curved, hence perhaps *hoop*); *envy* malice   261 *Argier* Algiers   266 *one thing she did* (being pregnant, her sentence was commuted from death to exile)   274 *hests* commands   281 *millwheels* i.e. the clappers on the millwheels   295 *his* its   296 *twelve* (the same length of time that Ariel has been released)   297 *correspondent* obedient   298 *spriting gently* office as a spirit graciously   311 *miss* do without   316 *When* (expression of impatience)   317 *quaint* ingenious   326 *urchins* hedgehogs (i.e. goblins in that shape)   327 *vast* void; *that they may work* (referring to the belief that malignant spirits had power only during darkness)

To name the bigger light, and how the less,
That burn by day and night; and then I loved thee
337 And showed thee all the qualities o' th' isle,
The fresh springs, brine-pits, barren place and fertile.
Cursed be I that did so! All the charms
Of Sycorax – toads, beetles, bats, light on you!
For I am all the subjects that you have,
Which first was mine own king; and here you sty me
In this hard rock, whiles you do keep from me
The rest o' th' island.

PROSPERO   Thou most lying slave,
345 Whom stripes may move, not kindness! I have used thee
(Filth as thou art) with humane care, and lodged thee
In mine own cell till thou didst seek to violate
The honor of my child.

CALIBAN
O ho, O ho! Would't had been done!
Thou didst prevent me; I had peopled else
This isle with Calibans.

351 MIRANDA   Abhorrèd slave,
Which any print of goodness wilt not take,
Being capable of all ill! I pitied thee,
Took pains to make thee speak, taught thee each hour
One thing or other: when thou didst not, savage,
Know thine own meaning, but wouldst gabble like
357 A thing most brutish, I endowed thy purposes
358 With words that made them known. But thy vile race,
359 Though thou didst learn, had that in't which good
natures
Could not abide to be with; therefore wast thou
Deservedly confined into this rock, who hadst
Deserved more than a prison.

CALIBAN
You taught me language, and my profit on't
364 Is, I know how to curse. The red plague rid you
For learning me your language!

PROSPERO   Hag-seed, hence!
366 Fetch us in fuel; and be quick, thou'rt best,
To answer other business. Shrug'st thou, malice?
If thou neglect'st or dost unwillingly
369 What I command, I'll rack thee with old cramps,
370 Fill all thy bones with aches, make thee roar
That beasts shall tremble at thy din.

CALIBAN   No, pray thee.
[Aside]
I must obey. His art is of such pow'r
It would control my dam's god, Setebos,
And make a vassal of him.

PROSPERO   So, slave; hence!
Exit Caliban.
*Enter Ferdinand; and Ariel (invisible), playing and
singing.*

Ariel's song.

Come unto these yellow sands,
And then take hands.
Curtsied when you have and kissed,
378 The wild waves whist,
379 Foot it featly here and there;
380 And, sweet sprites, the burden bear.
Hark, hark!
Burden, dispersedly. Bowgh, wawgh!
The watchdogs bark.
Burden, dispersedly. Bowgh, wawgh!

Hark, hark! I hear
The strain of strutting chanticleer
Cry cock-a-diddle-dowe.

FERDINAND
Where should this music be? I' th' air or th' earth?
It sounds no more; and sure it waits upon
Some god o' th' island. Sitting on a bank,
Weeping again the King my father's wrack,
This music crept by me upon the waters,
Allaying both their fury and my passion 393
With its sweet air. Thence I have followed it,
Or it hath drawn me rather; but 'tis gone.
No, it begins again.

Ariel's song.

Full fathom five thy father lies;
Of his bones are coral made;
Those are pearls that were his eyes;
Nothing of him that doth fade
But doth suffer a sea-change
Into something rich and strange.
Sea nymphs hourly ring his knell:
Burden.   Ding-dong.
Hark! now I hear them – Ding-dong bell.

FERDINAND
The ditty does remember my drowned father. 406
This is no mortal business, nor no sound
That the earth owes. I hear it now above me. 408

PROSPERO
The fringèd curtains of thine eye advance 409
And say what thou seest yond.

MIRANDA   What is't? a spirit?
Lord, how it looks about! Believe me, sir,
It carries a brave form. But 'tis a spirit.

PROSPERO
No, wench: it eats, and sleeps, and hath such senses
As we have, such. This gallant which thou seest
Was in the wrack; and, but he's something stained 415
With grief (that's beauty's canker), thou mightst call him
A goodly person. He hath lost his fellows
And strays about to find 'em.

MIRANDA   I might call him
A thing divine; for nothing natural
I ever saw so noble.

PROSPERO [aside]   It goes on, I see,
As my soul prompts it. Spirit, fine spirit, I'll free thee 421
Within two days for this.

FERDINAND   Most sure, the goddess 422
On whom these airs attend! Vouchsafe my prayer
May know if you remain upon this island, 424
And that you will some good instruction give
How I may bear me here. My prime request, 426
Which I do last pronounce, is (O you wonder!)
If you be maid or no?

---

337 *qualities* resources   345 *stripes* lashes   351 *Miranda* (so F; some editors have given the speech to Prospero)   357 *purposes* meanings   358 *race* nature   359 *good natures* natural virtues   364 *red plague* bubonic plague; *rid* destroy   366 *thou'rt best* you'd be well advised   369 *old* i.e. such as old people have   370 *aches* (pronounced 'aitches')   378 *whist* being hushed   379 *featly* nimbly   380 *burden* undersong, refrain   393 *passion* lamentation   406 *remember* allude to   408 *owes* owns   409 *advance* raise   415 *stained* disfigured   421 *prompts* would like   422 *Most sure* this is certainly   424 *remain* dwell   426 *bear me* conduct myself

MIRANDA   No wonder, sir,
But certainly a maid.
FERDINAND   My language? Heavens!
I am the best of them that speak this speech,
Were I but where 'tis spoken.
PROSPERO   How? the best?
What wert thou if the King of Naples heard thee?
FERDINAND

433   A single thing, as I am now, that wonders
To hear thee speak of Naples. He does hear me;
435   And that he does I weep. Myself am Naples,
Who with mine eyes, never since at ebb, beheld
The King my father wracked.
MIRANDA   Alack, for mercy!
FERDINAND
Yes, faith, and all his lords, the Duke of Milan
439   And his brave son being twain.
PROSPERO [aside]   The Duke of Milan
440   And his more braver daughter could control thee,
If now 'twere fit to do't. At the first sight
442   They have changed eyes. Delicate Ariel,
I'll set thee free for this. – A word, good sir.
444   I fear you have done yourself some wrong. A word!
MIRANDA
Why speaks my father so ungently? This
Is the third man that e'er I saw; the first
That e'er I sighed for. Pity move my father
To be inclined my way!
FERDINAND   O, if a virgin,
And your affection not gone forth, I'll make you
The Queen of Naples.
PROSPERO   Soft, sir! one word more.
[Aside]
They are both in either's pow'rs. But this swift business
I must uneasy make, lest too light winning
Make the prize light. – One word more! I charge thee
That thou attend me. Thou dost here usurp
455   The name thou ow'st not, and hast put thyself
Upon this island as a spy, to win it
From me, the lord on't.
FERDINAND   No, as I am a man!
MIRANDA
There's nothing ill can dwell in such a temple.
If the ill spirit have so fair a house,
Good things will strive to dwell with't.
PROSPERO   Follow me. –
Speak not you for him; he's a traitor. – Come!
I'll manacle thy neck and feet together;
Sea water shalt thou drink; thy food shall be
The fresh-brook mussels, withered roots, and husks
Wherein the acorn cradled. Follow!
FERDINAND   No.
466   I will resist such entertainment till
Mine enemy has more pow'r.
He draws, and is charmed from moving.

MIRANDA   O dear father,
Make not too rash a trial of him, for   468
He's gentle, and not fearful.   469
PROSPERO   What, I say,
My foot my tutor? – Put thy sword up, traitor!   470
Who mak'st a show but dar'st not strike, thy conscience
Is so possessed with guilt. Come, from thy ward!   472
For I can here disarm thee with this stick
And make thy weapon drop.
MIRANDA   Beseech you, father!
PROSPERO
Hence! Hang not on my garments.
MIRANDA   Sir, have pity.
I'll be his surety.
PROSPERO   Silence! One word more
Shall make me chide thee, if not hate thee. What,
An advocate for an impostor? Hush!
Thou think'st there is no more such shapes as he,
Having seen but him and Caliban. Foolish wench!
To th' most of men this is a Caliban,
And they to him are angels.
MIRANDA   My affections   482
Are then most humble. I have no ambition
To see a goodlier man.
PROSPERO   Come on, obey!   484
Thy nerves are in their infancy again   485
And have no vigor in them.
FERDINAND   So they are.
My spirits, as in a dream, are all bound up.
My father's loss, the weakness which I feel,
The wrack of all my friends, nor this man's threats
To whom I am subdued, are but light to me,
Might I but through my prison once a day
Behold this maid. All corners else o' th' earth
Let liberty make use of. Space enough
Have I in such a prison.
PROSPERO [aside]   It works. [to Ferdinand] Come on. –
Thou hast done well, fine Ariel!
     [To Ferdinand]   Follow me.
     [To Ariel]
Hark what thou else shalt do me.
MIRANDA   Be of comfort.
My father's of a better nature, sir,
Than he appears by speech. This is unwonted
Which now came from him.
PROSPERO   Thou shalt be as free
As mountain winds; but then exactly do
All points of my command.   500
ARIEL   To th' syllable.
PROSPERO
Come, follow. – Speak not for him.   *Exeunt.*

*

Enter Alonso, Sebastian, Antonio, Gonzalo, Adrian,   II, i
Francisco, and others.
GONZALO
Beseech you, sir, be merry. You have cause
(So have we all) of joy; for our escape
Is much beyond our loss. Our hint of woe   3
Is common: every day some sailor's wife,
The master of some merchant, and the merchant,   5
Have just our theme of woe; but for the miracle,

433 *single* (1) solitary, (2) weak or helpless   **435** *Naples* King of Naples
439 *son* (Antonio's son is not elsewhere mentioned)   **440** *control* refute
442 *changed eyes* exchanged love looks   **444** *done . . . wrong* told a lie
455 *ow'st* ownest   **466** *entertainment* treatment   **468** *trial* judgment
469 *gentle* noble; *fearful* cowardly   **470** *My . . . tutor* i.e. instructed by my
underling   **472** *ward* fighting posture   **482** *affections* inclinations   **484**
obey follow   **485** *nerves* sinews, tendons   **500** *then* till then
II, i Another part of the island   **3** *hint* occasion   **5** *master of some merchant*
master of a merchant ship; *the merchant* the owner of the ship

1379

I mean our preservation, few in millions
Can speak like us. Then wisely, good sir, weigh
Our sorrow with our comfort.

ALONSO   Prithee peace.

10 SEBASTIAN He receives comfort like cold porridge.

11 ANTONIO The visitor will not give him o'er so.

SEBASTIAN Look, he's winding up the watch of his wit;
by and by it will strike.

GONZALO Sir –

15 SEBASTIAN One. Tell.

GONZALO

16 When every grief is entertained, that's offered

17 Comes to th'entertainer –

SEBASTIAN A dollar.

19 GONZALO Dolor comes to him, indeed. You have spoken
truer than you purposed.

SEBASTIAN You have taken it wiselier than I meant you
should.

GONZALO Therefore, my lord –

24 ANTONIO Fie, what a spendthrift is he of his tongue!

ALONSO I prithee spare.

GONZALO Well, I have done. But yet –

SEBASTIAN He will be talking.

ANTONIO Which, of he or Adrian, for a good wager, first
begins to crow?

30 SEBASTIAN The old cock.

31 ANTONIO The cock'rel.

SEBASTIAN Done! The wager?

33 ANTONIO A laughter.

SEBASTIAN A match!

ADRIAN Though this island seem to be desert –

ANTONIO Ha, ha, ha!

SEBASTIAN So, you're paid.

ADRIAN Uninhabitable and almost inaccessible –

SEBASTIAN Yet –

ADRIAN Yet –

ANTONIO He could not miss't.

ADRIAN It must needs be of subtle, tender, and delicate

43 temperance.

44 ANTONIO Temperance was a delicate wench.

SEBASTIAN Ay, and a subtle, as he most learnedly delivered.

ADRIAN The air breathes upon us here most sweetly.

SEBASTIAN As if it had lungs, and rotten ones.

ANTONIO Or as 'twere perfumed by a fen.

GONZALO Here is everything advantageous to life.

ANTONIO True; save means to live.

SEBASTIAN Of that there's none, or little.

GONZALO How lush and lusty the grass looks! how
green!

ANTONIO The ground indeed is tawny.

54 SEBASTIAN With an eye of green in't.

ANTONIO He misses not much.

SEBASTIAN No; he doth but mistake the truth totally.

GONZALO But the rarity of it is – which is indeed almost
beyond credit –

59 SEBASTIAN As many vouched rarities are.

GONZALO That our garments, being, as they were,
drenched in the sea, hold, notwithstanding, their freshness and gloss, being rather new-dyed than stained with
salt water.

ANTONIO If but one of his pockets could speak, would it
not say he lies?

SEBASTIAN Ay, or very falsely pocket up his report.

GONZALO Methinks our garments are now as fresh as
when we put them on first in Afric, at the marriage of
the King's fair daughter Claribel to the King of Tunis.

SEBASTIAN 'Twas a sweet marriage, and we prosper
well in our return.

ADRIAN Tunis was never graced before with such a
paragon to their queen.   72

GONZALO Not since widow Dido's time.   73

ANTONIO Widow? A pox o' that! How came that
'widow' in? Widow Dido!

SEBASTIAN What if he had said 'widower Aeneas' too?
Good Lord, how you take it!

ADRIAN 'Widow Dido,' said you? You make me study
of that. She was of Carthage, not of Tunis.

GONZALO This Tunis, sir, was Carthage.

ADRIAN Carthage?

GONZALO I assure you, Carthage.

ANTONIO His word is more than the miraculous harp.   83

SEBASTIAN He hath raised the wall and houses too.

ANTONIO What impossible matter will he make easy
next?

SEBASTIAN I think he will carry this island home in his
pocket and give it his son for an apple.

ANTONIO And, sowing the kernels of it in the sea, bring
forth more islands.

GONZALO Ay!   90

ANTONIO Why, in good time.

GONZALO Sir, we were talking that our garments seem
now as fresh as when we were at Tunis at the marriage
of your daughter, who is now Queen.

ANTONIO And the rarest that e'er came there.

SEBASTIAN Bate, I beseech you, widow Dido.   96

ANTONIO O, widow Dido? Ay, widow Dido!

GONZALO Is not, sir, my doublet as fresh as the first day I
wore it? I mean, in a sort.   99

ANTONIO That 'sort' was well fished for.

GONZALO When I wore it at your daughter's marriage.

ALONSO
You cram these words into mine ears against
The stomach of my sense. Would I had never   103
Married my daughter there! for, coming thence,
My son is lost; and, in my rate, she too,   105
Who is so far from Italy removed
I ne'er again shall see her. O thou mine heir
Of Naples and of Milan, what strange fish
Hath made his meal on thee?

FRANCISCO   Sir, he may live.
I saw him beat the surges under him
And ride upon their backs. He trod the water,
Whose enmity he flung aside, and breasted

---

10 *porridge* (pun on *peace* [pease]) 11 *visitor* spiritual adviser; *give him
o'er* let him alone 15 *Tell* count 16 *that's* that which is 17 *entertainer*
(taken by Sebastian to mean 'innkeeper') 19 *Dolor* grief (with pun on
dollar, a continental coin) 24 *spendthrift* (Antonio labors the pun) 30
old cock i.e. Gonzalo 31 *cock'rel* i.e. Adrian 33 *laughter* the winner
laughs 43 *temperance* climate 44 *Temperance* (a girl's name) 54 *eye* spot
(or perhaps Gonzalo's eye) 59 *vouched rarities* wonders guaranteed to be
true 72 *to* for 73 *widow Dido* (Dido was the widow of Sychaeus; Aeneas
was a widower, having lost his wife in the fall of Troy. The reasons for
Antonio's amusement, if that is what it is, have not been explained.)
83 *miraculous harp* (of Amphion, which raised the walls of Thebes; Tunis
and Carthage were near each other, but not the same city) 90 *Ay* (F reads
'I'; this and Antonio's rejoinder have not been satisfactorily explained)
96 *Bate* except 99 *in a sort* i.e. comparatively 103 *stomach . . . sense*
i.e. inclination of my mind 105 *rate* opinion

The surge most swol'n that met him. His bold head
'Bove the contentious waves he kept, and oared
Himself with his good arms in lusty stroke
116 To th' shore, that o'er his wave-worn basis bowed,
As stooping to relieve him. I not doubt
He came alive to land.

ALONSO   No, no, he's gone.

SEBASTIAN
Sir, you may thank yourself for this great loss,
That would not bless our Europe with your daughter,
But rather loose her to an African,
Where she, at least, is banished from your eye
Who hath cause to wet the grief on't.

ALONSO   Prithee peace.

SEBASTIAN
You were kneeled to and importuned otherwise
125 By all of us; and the fair soul herself
Weighed, between loathness and obedience, at
Which end o' th' beam should bow. We have lost your
son,
I fear, for ever. Milan and Naples have
129 Moe widows in them of this business' making
Than we bring men to comfort them:
The fault's your own.

131 ALONSO   So is the dear'st o' th' loss.

GONZALO
My Lord Sebastian,
The truth you speak doth lack some gentleness,
And time to speak it in. You rub the sore
When you should bring the plaster.

SEBASTIAN   Very well.

ANTONIO
136 And most chirurgeonly.

GONZALO
It is foul weather in us all, good sir,
When you are cloudy.

SEBASTIAN   Foul weather?

ANTONIO   Very foul.

GONZALO
139 Had I plantation of this isle, my lord –

ANTONIO
He'd sow't with nettle seed.

SEBASTIAN   Or docks, or mallows.

GONZALO
And were the king on't, what would I do?

SEBASTIAN
Scape being drunk for want of wine.

GONZALO
143 I' th' commonwealth I would by contraries
144 Execute all things; for no kind of traffic
Would I admit; no name of magistrate;
Letters should not be known; riches, poverty,

And use of service, none; contract, succession, 147
Bourn, bound of land, tilth, vineyard, none; 148
No use of metal, corn, or wine, or oil;
No occupation; all men idle, all;
And women too, but innocent and pure;
No sovereignty.

SEBASTIAN   Yet he would be king on't.

ANTONIO The latter end of his commonwealth forgets
the beginning.

GONZALO
All things in common nature should produce
Without sweat or endeavor. Treason, felony,
Sword, pike, knife, gun, or need of any engine 157
Would I not have; but nature should bring forth,
Of it own kind, all foison, all abundance, 159
To feed my innocent people.

SEBASTIAN No marrying 'mong his subjects?

ANTONIO None, man, all idle – whores and knaves.

GONZALO
I would with such perfection govern, sir,
T' excel the golden age.

SEBASTIAN   Save his Majesty!

ANTONIO
Long live Gonzalo!

GONZALO   And – do you mark me, sir?

ALONSO
Prithee no more. Thou dost talk nothing to me.

GONZALO I do well believe your Highness; and did it to
minister occasion to these gentlemen, who are of such 168
sensible and nimble lungs that they always use to laugh 169
at nothing.

ANTONIO 'Twas you we laughed at.

GONZALO Who in this kind of merry fooling am nothing
to you: so you may continue, and laugh at nothing still.

ANTONIO What a blow was there given!

SEBASTIAN An it had not fall'n flatlong. 175

GONZALO You are gentlemen of brave mettle; you
would lift the moon out of her sphere if she would continue in it five weeks without changing.

Enter Ariel, [invisible,] playing solemn music.

SEBASTIAN We would so, and then go a-batfowling. 179

ANTONIO Nay, good my lord, be not angry.

GONZALO No, I warrant you: I will not adventure my 181
discretion so weakly. Will you laugh me asleep, for I am
very heavy.

ANTONIO Go sleep, and hear us.

[All sleep except Alonso, Sebastian, and Antonio.]

ALONSO
What, all so soon asleep? I wish mine eyes
Would, with themselves, shut up my thoughts. I find
They are inclined to do so.

SEBASTIAN   Please you, sir,
Do not omit the heavy offer of it. 188
It seldom visits sorrow; when it doth,
It is a comforter.

ANTONIO   We two, my lord,
Will guard your person while you take your rest,
And watch your safety.

ALONSO   Thank you. Wondrous heavy.

[Alonso sleeps. Exit Ariel.]

SEBASTIAN
What a strange drowsiness possesses them!

ANTONIO
It is the quality o' th' climate.

---

116 *his* its; *basis* i.e. the sand   125–27 *the fair . . . bow* (the sense is that
Claribel hated the marriage, and only obedience to her father turned the
scale)   129 *Moe* more   131 *dear'st* heaviest   136 *chirurgeonly* like a
surgeon   139 *plantation* colonization (taken by Antonio in its other sense)
143 *by contraries* in contrast to usual customs   144 *traffic* trade   147 *use
of service* having a servant class; *succession* inheritance   148 *Bourn* limits
of private property   157 *engine* weapon   159 *it* its; *foison* abundance
168 *minister occasion* afford opportunity   169 *sensible* sensitive   175 *An*
if; *flatlong* struck with the flat of a sword   179 *a-batfowling* hunting birds
with sticks ('bats') at night (using the moon for a lantern)   181 *adventure*
risk (Gonzalo is saying, very politely, that their wit is too feeble for him to
take offense at it)   188 *omit* neglect; *heavy offer* opportunity its heaviness
affords

SEBASTIAN   Why
Doth it not then our eyelids sink ? I find not
Myself disposed to sleep.
ANTONIO   Nor I : my spirits are nimble.
They fell together all, as by consent.
They dropped as by a thunder-stroke. What might,
Worthy Sebastian – O, what might ? – No more !
And yet methinks I see it in thy face,
201   What thou shouldst be. Th' occasion speaks thee, and
My strong imagination sees a crown
Dropping upon thy head.
SEBASTIAN   What ? Art thou waking ?
ANTONIO
Do you not hear me speak ?
SEBASTIAN   I do ; and surely
It is a sleepy language, and thou speak'st
Out of thy sleep. What is it thou didst say ?
This is a strange repose, to be asleep
With eyes wide open ; standing, speaking, moving,
And yet so fast asleep.
ANTONIO   Noble Sebastian,
210   Thou let'st thy fortune sleep – die, rather ; wink'st
Whiles thou art waking.
SEBASTIAN   Thou dost snore distinctly ;
There's meaning in thy snores.
ANTONIO
I am more serious than my custom. You
Must be so too, if heed me ; which to do
215   Trebles thee o'er.
SEBASTIAN   Well, I am standing water.
ANTONIO
I'll teach you how to flow.
SEBASTIAN   Do so. To ebb
217   Hereditary sloth instructs me.
ANTONIO   O,
218   If you but knew how you the purpose cherish
Whiles thus you mock it ! how, in stripping it,
220   You more invest it ! Ebbing men indeed
(Most often) do so near the bottom run
By their own fear or sloth.
SEBASTIAN   Prithee say on.
The setting of thine eye and cheek proclaim
A matter from thee ; and a birth, indeed,
225   Which throes thee much to yield.
ANTONIO   Thus, sir :
226   Although this lord of weak remembrance, this
227   Who shall be of as little memory
228   When he is earthed, hath here almost persuaded
(For he's a spirit of persuasion, only
230   Professes to persuade) the King his son 's alive,
'Tis as impossible that he's undrowned
As he that sleeps here swims.
SEBASTIAN   I have no hope
That he's undrowned.
ANTONIO   O, out of that no hope
What great hope have you ! No hope that way is
Another way so high a hope that even
236   Ambition cannot pierce a wink beyond,
237   But doubt discovery there. Will you grant with me
That Ferdinand is drowned ?
SEBASTIAN   He's gone.
ANTONIO   Then tell me,
Who's the next heir of Naples ?
SEBASTIAN   Claribel.

ANTONIO
She that is Queen of Tunis ; she that dwells
Ten leagues beyond man's life ; she that from Naples   241
Can have no note, unless the sun were post –   242
The man i' th' moon 's too slow – till new-born chins
Be rough and razorable ; she that from whom
We all were sea-swallowed, though some cast again,   245
And, by that destiny, to perform an act
Whereof what's past is prologue, what to come,
In yours and my discharge.   248
SEBASTIAN   What stuff is this ? How say you ?
'Tis true my brother's daughter 's Queen of Tunis ;
So is she heir of Naples ; 'twixt which regions
There is some space.
ANTONIO   A space whose ev'ry cubit
Seems to cry out 'How shall that Claribel
Measure us back to Naples ? Keep in Tunis,   253
And let Sebastian wake !' Say this were death
That now hath seized them, why, they were no worse
Than now they are. There be that can rule Naples
As well as he that sleeps ; lords that can prate
As amply and unnecessarily
As this Gonzalo ; I myself could make
A chough of as deep chat. O, that you bore   260
The mind that I do ! What a sleep were this
For your advancement ! Do you understand me ?
SEBASTIAN
Methinks I do.
ANTONIO   And how does your content   263
Tender your own good fortune ?
SEBASTIAN   I remember
You did supplant your brother Prospero.
ANTONIO   True.
And look how well my garments sit upon me,
Much feater than before. My brother's servants   267
Were then my fellows ; now they are my men.   268
SEBASTIAN
But, for your conscience –
ANTONIO
Ay, sir, where lies that ? If 'twere a kibe,   270
'Twould put me to my slipper ; but I feel not   271
This deity in my bosom. Twenty consciences
That stand 'twixt me and Milan, candied be they   273
And melt, ere they molest ! Here lies your brother,
No better than the earth he lies upon
If he were that which now he's like – that's dead ;
Whom I with this obedient steel (three inches of it)
Can lay to bed for ever ; whiles you, doing thus,
To the perpetual wink for aye might put   279
This ancient morsel, this Sir Prudence, who
Should not upbraid our course. For all the rest,
They'll take suggestion as a cat laps milk ;

201 *speaks* speaks to, summons   210 *wink'st* dost sleep   215 *Trebles thee o'er* increases thy status threefold ; *standing water* at slack tide   217 *Hereditary sloth* natural laziness   218 *cherish* enrich   220 *invest* clothe   225 *throes thee much* costs thee much pain, like a birth   226 *remembrance* memory   227 *of . . . memory* as little remembered   228 *earthed* buried   230 *Professes* has the function   236 *wink* glimpse   237 *doubt discovery there* is uncertain of seeing accurately   241 *Ten . . . life* i.e. thirty miles from nowhere   242 *note* communication ; *post* messenger   245 *cast* thrown up (with a suggestion of its theatrical meaning which introduces the next metaphor)   248 *discharge* business   253 *us* i.e. the cubits   260 *chough* jackdaw (a bird sometimes taught to speak)   263–64 *content Tender* inclination estimate   267 *feater* more suitable   268 *fellows* equals ; *men* servants   270 *kibe* chilblain   271 *put me to* make me wear   273 *candied* frozen   279 *wink* sleep

283 They'll tell the clock to any business that
We say befits the hour.
SEBASTIAN   Thy case, dear friend,
Shall be my precedent. As thou got'st Milan,
I'll come by Naples. Draw thy sword. One stroke
Shall free thee from the tribute which thou payest,
And I the King shall love thee.
ANTONIO   Draw together;
And when I rear my hand, do you the like,
290 To fall it on Gonzalo.
     [They draw.]
SEBASTIAN   O, but one word!
     Enter Ariel, [invisible,] with music and song.
ARIEL
My master through his art foresees the danger
That you, his friend, are in, and sends me forth
(For else his project dies) to keep them living.
     Sings in Gonzalo's ear.
         While you here do snoring lie,
         Open-eyed conspiracy
           His time doth take.
         If of life you keep a care,
         Shake off slumber and beware.
           Awake, awake!
ANTONIO
Then let us both be sudden.
GONZALO *[wakes]*   Now good angels
Preserve the King!
ALONSO
Why, how now? – Ho, awake! – Why are you drawn?
Wherefore this ghastly looking?
GONZALO   What's the matter?
SEBASTIAN
304 Whiles we stood here securing your repose,
Even now, we heard a hollow burst of bellowing
Like bulls, or rather lions. Did't not wake you?
It struck mine ear most terribly.
ALONSO   I heard nothing.
ANTONIO
O, 'twas a din to fright a monster's ear,
To make an earthquake! Sure it was the roar
Of a whole herd of lions.
ALONSO   Heard you this, Gonzalo?
GONZALO
Upon mine honor, sir, I heard a humming,
And that a strange one too, which did awake me.
I shaked you, sir, and cried. As mine eyes opened,
I saw their weapons drawn. There was a noise,
That's verily. 'Tis best we stand upon our guard,
Or that we quit this place. Let's draw our weapons.
ALONSO
Lead off this ground, and let's make further search
For my poor son.
GONZALO   Heavens keep him from these beasts!
For he is sure i' th' island.
ALONSO   Lead away.

ARIEL
Prospero my lord shall know what I have done.
So, King, go safely on to seek thy son.   *Exeunt.*

*

     Enter Caliban with a burden of wood. A noise of   II, ii
     thunder heard.
CALIBAN
All the infections that the sun sucks up
From bogs, fens, flats, on Prosper fall, and make him
By inchmeal a disease! His spirits hear me,   3
And yet I needs must curse. But they'll nor pinch,   4
Fright me with urchin-shows, pitch me i' th' mire,   5
Nor lead me, like a firebrand, in the dark   6
Out of my way, unless he bid 'em; but
For every trifle are they set upon me;
Sometime like apes that mow and chatter at me,   9
And after bite me; then like hedgehogs which
Lie tumbling in my barefoot way and mount
Their pricks at my footfall; sometime am I
All wound with adders, who with cloven tongues
Do hiss me into madness.
     Enter Trinculo.   Lo, now, lo!
Here comes a spirit of his, and to torment me
For bringing wood in slowly. I'll fall flat.
Perchance he will not mind me.
     [Lies down.]
TRINCULO Here's neither bush nor shrub to bear off any   18
weather at all, and another storm brewing: I hear it sing
i' th' wind. Yond same black cloud, yond huge one,
looks like a foul bombard that would shed his liquor.   21
If it should thunder as it did before, I know not where
to hide my head. Yond same cloud cannot choose but
fall by pailfuls. What have we here? a man or a fish?
dead or alive? A fish: he smells like a fish; a very ancient
and fishlike smell; a kind of not of the newest poor-John.   26
A strange fish! Were I in England now, as once I was,
and had but this fish painted, not a holiday fool there but   28
would give a piece of silver. There would this monster
make a man: any strange beast there makes a man. When   30
they will not give a doit to relieve a lame beggar, they   31
will lay out ten to see a dead Indian. Legged like a man!
and his fins like arms! Warm, o' my troth! I do now let
loose my opinion, hold it no longer: this is no fish, but
an islander, that hath lately suffered by a thunderbolt.
[Thunder.] Alas, the storm is come again! My best way
is to creep under his gaberdine: there is no other shelter   37
hereabout. Misery acquaints a man with strange bed-
fellows. I will here shroud till the dregs of the storm be
past.
     [Creeps under Caliban's garment.]
     Enter Stephano, singing [with a bottle in his hand].
STEPHANO   I shall no more to sea, to sea;
              Here shall I die ashore.
This is a very scurvy tune to sing at a man's funeral.
Well, here's my comfort.
     Drinks.

The master, the swabber, the boatswain, and I,
    The gunner, and his mate,
Loved Mall, Meg, and Marian, and Margery,
    But none of us cared for Kate.

283 *tell the clock* answer appropriately   290 *fall it* let it fall   304 *securing* keeping watch over
II, ii A place near Prospero's cell   3 *By inchmeal* inch by inch   4 *nor* neither 5 *urchin-shows* apparitions in the form of hedgehogs   6 *like a firebrand* in the form of a will-o'-the-wisp   9 *mow* make faces   18 *bear off* ward off   21 *bombard* leather bottle; *his* its   26 *poor-John* dried hake   28 *painted* i.e. on a signboard outside a booth at a fair   30 *make a man* (also with sense of 'make a man's fortune')   31 *doit* small coin   37 *gaberdine* cloak

For she had a tongue with a tang,
50   Would cry to a sailor 'Go hang!'
She loved not the savor of tar nor of pitch;
Yet a tailor might scratch her where e'er she did itch.
Then to sea, boys, and let her go hang!

This is a scurvy tune too; but here's my comfort.
Drinks.
CALIBAN Do not torment me! O!
STEPHANO What's the matter? Have we devils here? Do
you put tricks upon's with savages and men of Inde, ha?
I have not scaped drowning to be afeard now of your
four legs; for it hath been said, 'As proper a man as ever
60   went on four legs cannot make him give ground'; and
it shall be said so again, while Stephano breathes at
nostrils.
CALIBAN The spirit torments me. O!
STEPHANO This is some monster of the isle, with four
legs, who hath got, as I take it, an ague. Where the devil
should he learn our language? I will give him some
relief, if it be but for that. If I can recover him, and keep
him tame, and get to Naples with him, he's a present
69   for any emperor that ever trod on neat's leather.
CALIBAN Do not torment me, prithee; I'll bring my
wood home faster.
STEPHANO He's in his fit now and does not talk after the
wisest. He shall taste of my bottle: if he have never
drunk wine afore, it will go near to remove his fit. If I
75   can recover him and keep him tame, I will not take too
much for him; he shall pay for him that hath him, and
that soundly.
CALIBAN
Thou dost me yet but little hurt.
79   Thou wilt anon; I know it by thy trembling.
Now Prosper works upon thee.
STEPHANO Come on your ways: open your mouth: here
82   is that which will give language to you, cat. Open your
mouth. This will shake your shaking, I can tell you, and
that soundly. *[Gives Caliban drink.]* You cannot tell
85   who's your friend. Open your chaps again.
TRINCULO I should know that voice. It should be – but
he is drowned; and these are devils. O, defend me!
STEPHANO Four legs and two voices – a most delicate
monster! His forward voice now is to speak well of his
friend; his backward voice is to utter foul speeches and
to detract. If all the wine in my bottle will recover him,
I will help his ague. Come! *[Gives drink.]* Amen! I will
pour some in thy other mouth.
TRINCULO Stephano!
STEPHANO Doth thy other mouth call me? Mercy,
mercy! This is a devil, and no monster. I will leave
97   him; I have no long spoon.
TRINCULO Stephano! If thou beest Stephano, touch me
and speak to me; for I am Trinculo – be not afeard – thy
good friend Trinculo.
STEPHANO If thou beest Trinculo, come forth. I'll pull
thee by the lesser legs. If any be Trinculo's legs, these
are they. *[Draws him out from under Caliban's garment.]*
Thou art very Trinculo indeed: how cam'st thou to be
105   the siege of this mooncalf? Can he vent Trinculos?
TRINCULO I took him to be killed with a thunder-stroke.
But art thou not drowned, Stephano? I hope now thou
art not drowned. Is the storm overblown? I hid me

under the dead mooncalf's gaberdine for fear of the
storm. And art thou living, Stephano? O Stephano,
two Neapolitans scaped!
STEPHANO Prithee do not turn me about: my stomach is
not constant.
CALIBAN *[aside]*
These be fine things, an if they be not sprites.   114
That's a brave god and bears celestial liquor.
I will kneel to him.
STEPHANO How didst thou scape? How cam'st thou
hither? Swear by this bottle how thou cam'st hither. I
escaped upon a butt of sack which the sailors heaved
o'erboard, by this bottle, which I made of the bark of a
tree with mine own hands since I was cast ashore.
CALIBAN I'll swear upon that bottle to be thy true sub-
ject, for the liquor is not earthly.
STEPHANO Here! Swear then how thou escapedst.
TRINCULO Swum ashore, man, like a duck. I can swim
like a duck, I'll be sworn.
STEPHANO Here, kiss the book. *[Gives him drink.]* Though 127
thou canst swim like a duck, thou art made like a goose. 128
TRINCULO O Stephano, hast any more of this?
STEPHANO The whole butt, man: my cellar is in a rock
by th' seaside, where my wine is hid. How now, moon-
calf? How does thine ague?
CALIBAN Hast thou not dropped from heaven?
STEPHANO Out o' th' moon, I do assure thee. I was the
Man i' th' Moon when time was.   135
CALIBAN
I have seen thee in her, and I do adore thee.
My mistress showed me thee, and thy dog, and thy bush.
STEPHANO Come, swear to that; kiss the book. I will
furnish it anon with new contents. Swear.
[Caliban drinks.]
TRINCULO By this good light, this is a very shallow mon-
ster! I afeard of him? A very weak monster! The Man
i' th' Moon? A most poor credulous monster! – Well
drawn, monster, in good sooth!
CALIBAN
I'll show thee every fertile inch o' th' island;
And I will kiss thy foot. I prithee be my god.
TRINCULO By this light, a most perfidious and drunken
monster! When's god 's asleep, he'll rob his bottle.
CALIBAN
I'll kiss thy foot. I'll swear myself thy subject.
STEPHANO Come on then. Down, and swear!
TRINCULO I shall laugh myself to death at this puppy- 150
headed monster. A most scurvy monster! I could find
in my heart to beat him –
STEPHANO Come, kiss.
TRINCULO But that the poor monster 's in drink. An
abominable monster!
CALIBAN
I'll show thee the best springs; I'll pluck thee berries;
I'll fish for thee, and get thee wood enough.
A plague upon the tyrant that I serve!

---

69 *neat's leather* cowhide **75–76** *not take too much* i.e. take all I can get
79 *anon* soon **82** *cat* (alluding to the proverb 'Liquor will make a cat talk')
85 *chaps* jaws **97** *spoon* (alluding to the proverb 'He who sups with the
devil must have a long spoon') **105** *siege* excrement; *mooncalf* monstrosity
114 *an* if **127** *book* i.e. bottle **128** *like a goose* i.e. with a long neck
135 *when time was* once upon a time

I'll bear him no more sticks, but follow thee,
Thou wondrous man.

TRINCULO A most ridiculous monster, to make a wonder
of a poor drunkard !

CALIBAN

163   I prithee let me bring thee where crabs grow ;
164   And I with my long nails will dig thee pignuts,
Show thee a jay's nest, and instruct thee how
To snare the nimble marmoset ; I'll bring thee
To clust'ring filberts, and sometimes I'll get thee
168   Young scamels from the rock. Wilt thou go with me ?

STEPHANO I prithee now, lead the way without any more
talking. Trinculo, the King and all our company else
171   being drowned, we will inherit here. Here, bear my
172   bottle. Fellow Trinculo, we'll fill him by and by again.
Caliban sings drunkenly.

CALIBAN Farewell, master ; farewell, farewell !

TRINCULO A howling monster ! a drunken monster !

CALIBAN

No more dams I'll make for fish,
Nor fetch in firing
At requiring,
178   Nor scrape trenchering, nor wash dish.
'Ban, 'Ban, Ca – Caliban
Has a new master : get a new man.

Freedom, high-day ! high-day, freedom ! freedom, high-
day, freedom !

STEPHANO O brave monster ! lead the way.   *Exeunt.*

*

III, i   *Enter Ferdinand, bearing a log.*

FERDINAND

1   There be some sports are painful, and their labor
2   Delight in them sets off ; some kinds of baseness
3   Are nobly undergone, and most poor matters
Point to rich ends. This my mean task
Would be as heavy to me as odious, but
6   The mistress which I serve quickens what's dead
And makes my labors pleasures. O, she is
Ten times more gentle than her father's crabbèd ;
And he's composed of harshness ! I must remove
Some thousands of these logs and pile them up,
11   Upon a sore injunction. My sweet mistress
Weeps when she sees me work, and says such baseness
Had never like executor. I forget ;
But these sweet thoughts do even refresh my labors
15   Most busy least, when I do it.
Enter Miranda ; and Prospero [behind, unseen].

MIRANDA   Alas, now pray you

163 *crabs* crab apples   164 *pignuts* peanuts   168 *scamels* (unexplained, but clearly either a shellfish or a rock-nesting bird ; perhaps a misprint for 'sea-mels,' sea mews)   171 *inherit* take possession   172 *by and by* soon   178 *trenchering* trenchers, wooden plates
III, i Before Prospero's cell   1 *painful* strenuous   2 *sets off* makes greater by contrast   3 *matters* affairs   6 *quickens* brings to life   11 *sore injunction* grievous command   15 *least* i.e. least conscious of being busy (F reads 'lest')   19 *weep* i.e. exude resin   32 *visitation* (1) visit, (2) attack of plague (in the metaphor of *infected*)   37 *hest* command   38 *admiration* wonder, astonishment (the name Miranda means wonderful woman ; cf. I, ii, 427)   40 *best regard* highest approval   42 *several* different   44 *With . . . soul* i.e. so wholeheartedly   45 *owed* owned   46 *foil* (1) overthrow, (2) contrast   52 *abroad* elsewhere   53 *skilless* ignorant   57 *like of* compare to   59 *condition* situation in the world

Work not so hard ! I would the lightning had
Burnt up those logs that you are enjoined to pile !
Pray set it down and rest you. When this burns,
'Twill weep for having wearied you. My father   19
Is hard at study : pray now rest yourself.
He's safe for these three hours.

FERDINAND   O most dear mistress,
The sun will set before I shall discharge
What I must strive to do.

MIRANDA   If you'll sit down,
I'll bear your logs the while. Pray give me that :
I'll carry it to the pile.

FERDINAND   No, precious creature :
I had rather crack my sinews, break my back,
Than you should such dishonor undergo
While I sit lazy by.

MIRANDA   It would become me
As well as it does you ; and I should do it
With much more ease ; for my good will is to it,
And yours it is against.

PROSPERO *[aside]*   Poor worm, thou art infected !
This visitation shows it.   32

MIRANDA   You look wearily.

FERDINAND
No, noble mistress : 'tis fresh morning with me
When you are by at night. I do beseech you,
Chiefly that I might set it in my prayers,
What is your name ?

MIRANDA   Miranda. O my father,
I have broke your hest to say so !   37

FERDINAND   Admired Miranda !
Indeed the top of admiration, worth   38
What's dearest to the world ! Full many a lady
I have eyed with best regard, and many a time   40
Th' harmony of their tongues hath into bondage
Brought my too diligent ear ; for several virtues   42
Have I liked several women ; never any
With so full soul but some defect in her   44
Did quarrel with the noblest grace she owed,   45
And put it to the foil. But you, O you,   46
So perfect and so peerless, are created
Of every creature's best.

MIRANDA   I do not know
One of my sex ; no woman's face remember,
Save, from my glass, mine own ; nor have I seen
More that I may call men than you, good friend,
And my dear father. How features are abroad   52
I am skilless of ; but, by my modesty   53
(The jewel in my dower), I would not wish
Any companion in the world but you ;
Nor can imagination form a shape,
Besides yourself, to like of. But I prattle   57
Something too wildly, and my father's precepts
I therein do forget.

FERDINAND   I am, in my condition,   59
A prince, Miranda ; I do think, a king
(I would not so), and would no more endure
This wooden slavery than to suffer
The fleshfly blow my mouth. Hear my soul speak !
The very instant that I saw you, did
My heart fly to your service ; there resides,
To make me slave to it ; and for your sake
Am I this patient log-man.

MIRANDA   Do you love me?

FERDINAND
O heaven, O earth, bear witness to this sound,
69 And crown what I profess with kind event
If I speak true! if hollowly, invert
What best is boded me to mischief! I,
Beyond all limit of what else i' th' world,
Do love, prize, honor you.

MIRANDA   I am a fool
To weep at what I am glad of.

PROSPERO [aside]   Fair encounter
Of two most rare affections! Heavens rain grace
On that which breeds between 'em!

FERDINAND   Wherefore weep you?

MIRANDA
At mine unworthiness, that dare not offer
What I desire to give, and much less take
79 What I shall die to want. But this is trifling;
And all the more it seeks to hide itself,
81 The bigger bulk it shows. Hence, bashful cunning,
And prompt me, plain and holy innocence!
I am your wife, if you will marry me;
84 If not, I'll die your maid. To be your fellow
You may deny me; but I'll be your servant,
Whether you will or no.

FERDINAND   My mistress, dearest,
And I thus humble ever.

MIRANDA   My husband then?

FERDINAND
Ay, with a heart as willing
89 As bondage e'er of freedom. Here's my hand.

MIRANDA
And mine, with my heart in't; and now farewell
Till half an hour hence.

FERDINAND   A thousand thousand!
Exeunt [Ferdinand and Miranda severally].

PROSPERO
So glad of this as they I cannot be,
93 Who are surprised withal; but my rejoicing
At nothing can be more. I'll to my book;
For yet ere supper time must I perform
96 Much business appertaining.   Exit.

III, ii   Enter Caliban, Stephano, and Trinculo.

STEPHANO Tell not me! When the butt is out, we will
2 drink water; not a drop before. Therefore bear up and
board 'em! Servant monster, drink to me.

TRINCULO Servant monster? The folly of this island!
They say there's but five upon this isle: we are three of
them. If th' other two be brained like us, the state
totters.

STEPHANO Drink, servant monster, when I bid thee:
thy eyes are almost set in thy head.

TRINCULO Where should they be set else? He were a
brave monster indeed if they were set in his tail.

STEPHANO My man-monster hath drowned his tongue
in sack. For my part, the sea cannot drown me. I swam,
13 ere I could recover the shore, five-and-thirty leagues off
and on, by this light. Thou shalt be my lieutenant,
15 monster, or my standard.

16 TRINCULO Your lieutenant, if you list; he's no standard.

17 STEPHANO We'll not run, Monsieur Monster.

TRINCULO Nor go neither; but you'll lie like dogs, and 18
yet say nothing neither.

STEPHANO Mooncalf, speak once in thy life, if thou beest
a good mooncalf.

CALIBAN
How does thy honor? Let me lick thy shoe.
I'll not serve him; he is not valiant.

TRINCULO Thou liest, most ignorant monster: I am in
case to justle a constable. Why, thou deboshed fish thou, 25
was there ever man a coward that hath drunk so much
sack as I to-day? Wilt thou tell a monstrous lie, being
but half a fish and half a monster?

CALIBAN Lo, how he mocks me! Wilt thou let him, my
lord?

TRINCULO 'Lord' quoth he? That a monster should be
such a natural! 32

CALIBAN
Lo, lo, again! Bite him to death, I prithee.

STEPHANO Trinculo, keep a good tongue in your head. If
you prove a mutineer – the next tree! The poor monster's my subject, and he shall not suffer indignity.

CALIBAN
I thank my noble lord. Wilt thou be pleased
To hearken once again to the suit I made to thee?

STEPHANO Marry, will I. Kneel and repeat it; I will
stand, and so shall Trinculo. 40
Enter Ariel, invisible.

CALIBAN
As I told thee before, I am subject to a tyrant,
A sorcerer, that by his cunning hath
Cheated me of the island.

ARIEL   Thou liest.

CALIBAN
Thou liest, thou jesting monkey thou!
I would my valiant master would destroy thee.
I do not lie.

STEPHANO Trinculo, if you trouble him any more in's
tale, by this hand, I will supplant some of your teeth.

TRINCULO Why, I said nothing.

STEPHANO Mum then, and no more. – Proceed.

CALIBAN
I say by sorcery he got this isle;
From me he got it. If thy greatness will
Revenge it on him – for I know thou dar'st,
But this thing dare not – 54

STEPHANO That's most certain.

CALIBAN
Thou shalt be lord of it, and I'll serve thee.

STEPHANO
How now shall this be compassed?
Canst thou bring me to the party? 58

CALIBAN
Yea, yea, my lord! I'll yield him thee asleep,
Where thou mayst knock a nail into his head.

69 kind event favorable outcome · 79 want lack 81 bashful cunning i.e.
coyness 84 fellow equal 89 of freedom i.e. to win freedom 93 surprised
withal taken unaware by it 96 appertaining relevant

III, ii Another part of the island 2–3 bear . . . 'em i.e. drink up (Caliban
has almost 'passed out') 13 recover reach 15 standard ensign 16 no
standard i.e. incapable of standing up 17, 18 run, lie (secondary meanings
of) make water and excrete 18 go walk 25 case fit condition; deboshed
debauched 32 natural fool 40 s.d. invisible ('a robe for to go invisible'
is listed in an Elizabethan stage account) 54 this thing i.e. himself (or
perhaps Trinculo) 58 party person

ARIEL Thou liest; thou canst not.

CALIBAN

62 What a pied ninny 's this! Thou scurvy patch!
I do beseech thy greatness give him blows
And take his bottle from him. When that's gone,
He shall drink naught but brine, for I'll not show him
66 Where the quick freshes are.

STEPHANO Trinculo, run into no further danger: interrupt the monster one word further and, by this hand, I'll
69 turn my mercy out o' doors and make a stockfish of thee.

TRINCULO Why, what did I? I did nothing. I'll go
farther off.

STEPHANO Didst thou not say he lied?

ARIEL Thou liest.

STEPHANO Do I so? Take thou that! *[Strikes Trinculo.]*
As you like this, give me the lie another time.

TRINCULO I did not give the lie. Out o' your wits, and
hearing too? A pox o' your bottle! This can sack and
77 drinking do. A murrain on your monster, and the devil
take your fingers!

CALIBAN Ha, ha, ha!

STEPHANO Now forward with your tale. – Prithee stand
further off.

CALIBAN

Beat him enough. After a little time
I'll beat him too.

STEPHANO   Stand farther. – Come, proceed.

CALIBAN

Why, as I told thee, 'tis a custom with him
I' th' afternoon to sleep; there thou mayst brain him,
Having first seized his books, or with a log
87 Batter his skull, or paunch him with a stake,
88 Or cut his wesand with thy knife. Remember
First to possess his books; for without them
90 He's but a sot, as I am, nor hath not
One spirit to command. They all do hate him
As rootedly as I. Burn but his books.
93 He has brave utensils (for so he calls them)
Which, when he has a house, he'll deck withal.
And that most deeply to consider is
The beauty of his daughter. He himself
Calls her a nonpareil. I never saw a woman
But only Sycorax my dam and she;
But she as far surpasseth Sycorax
As great'st does least.

100 STEPHANO   Is it so brave a lass?

CALIBAN

Ay, lord. She will become thy bed, I warrant,
And bring thee forth brave brood.

STEPHANO Monster, I will kill this man: his daughter
and I will be king and queen, save our Graces! and
Trinculo and thyself shall be viceroys. Dost thou like
the plot, Trinculo?

TRINCULO Excellent.

STEPHANO Give me thy hand. I am sorry I beat thee; but
while thou liv'st, keep a good tongue in thy head.

CALIBAN

Within this half hour will he be asleep.
Wilt thou destroy him then?

STEPHANO Ay, on mine honor.

ARIEL

This will I tell my master.

CALIBAN

Thou mak'st me merry; I am full of pleasure.
Let us be jocund. Will you troll the catch   114
You taught me but whilere?   115

STEPHANO At thy request, monster, I will do reason, any
reason. Come on, Trinculo, let us sing.
     Sings.

       Flout 'em and scout 'em
       And scout 'em and flout 'em!
       Thought is free.

CALIBAN

That's not the tune.   121
     Ariel plays the tune on a tabor and pipe.

STEPHANO What is this same?

TRINCULO This is the tune of our catch, played by the
picture of Nobody.   124

STEPHANO If thou beest a man, show thyself in thy likeness. If thou beest a devil, take't as thou list.   126

TRINCULO O, forgive me my sins!

STEPHANO He that dies pays all debts. I defy thee.
Mercy upon us!

CALIBAN

Art thou afeard?

STEPHANO No, monster, not I.

CALIBAN

Be not afeard: the isle is full of noises,
Sounds and sweet airs that give delight and hurt not.
Sometimes a thousand twangling instruments
Will hum about mine ears; and sometime voices
That, if I then had waked after long sleep,
Will make me sleep again; and then, in dreaming,
The clouds methought would open and show riches
Ready to drop upon me, that, when I waked,
I cried to dream again.

STEPHANO This will prove a brave kingdom to me,
where I shall have my music for nothing.

CALIBAN

When Prospero is destroyed.

STEPHANO That shall be by and by: I remember the 144
story.

TRINCULO The sound is going away: let's follow it, and
after do our work.

STEPHANO Lead, monster; we'll follow. I would I could
see this taborer: he lays it on. Wilt come?

TRINCULO I'll follow, Stephano.   *Exeunt.*

*

62 *pied ninny* motley fool (Trinculo wears a jester's costume); *patch* clown
66 *quick freshes* fresh-water springs   69 *stockfish* dried cod, prepared by
beating   77 *murrain* cattle disease   87 *paunch* stab in the belly   88
wesand windpipe   90 *sot* fool   93 *utensils* furnishings   114 *troll the
catch* sing the part-song   115 *whilere* just now   121 s.d. *tabor* small
drum worn at the side   124 *Nobody* (referring to pictures of figures with
arms and legs but no trunk, used on signs and elsewhere)   126 *take't as
thou list* i.e. suit yourself   144 *by and by* right away
III, iii Another part of the island   1 *By'r Lakin* by our Ladykin (Virgin
Mary)   3 *forthrights* straight paths

Enter Alonso, Sebastian, Antonio, Gonzalo,   III, iii
   Adrian, Francisco, &c.

GONZALO

By'r Lakin, I can go no further, sir: 1
My old bones ache: here's a maze trod indeed
Through forthrights and meanders. By your patience,   3
I needs must rest me.

ALONSO   Old lord, I cannot blame thee,

5 Who am myself attached with weariness
To th' dulling of my spirits. Sit down and rest.
Even here I will put off my hope, and keep it
No longer for my flatterer : he is drowned
Whom thus we stray to find ; and the sea mocks
Our frustrate search on land. Well, let him go.

ANTONIO *[aside to Sebastian]*
I am right glad that he's so out of hope.
Do not for one repulse forgo the purpose
That you resolved t' effect.

SEBASTIAN *[aside to Antonio]* The next advantage
14 Will we take throughly.

ANTONIO *[aside to Sebastian]* Let it be to-night ;
For, now they are oppressed with travel, they
Will not nor cannot use such vigilance
As when they are fresh.

17 SEBASTIAN *[aside to Antonio]* I say to-night. No more.
*Solemn and strange music ; and Prospero on the top
(invisible). Enter several strange Shapes, bringing in
a banquet ; and dance about it with gentle actions of
salutations ; and, inviting the King &c. to eat, they
depart.*

ALONSO
What harmony is this ? My good friends, hark !

GONZALO
Marvellous sweet music !

ALONSO
20 Give us kind keepers, heavens ! What were these ?

SEBASTIAN
21 A living drollery. Now I will believe
That there are unicorns ; that in Arabia
There is one tree, the phoenix' throne ; one phoenix
At this hour reigning there.

ANTONIO I'll believe both ;
25 And what does else want credit, come to me,
And I'll be sworn 'tis true. Travellers ne'er did lie,
Though fools at home condemn 'em.

GONZALO If in Naples
I should report this now, would they believe me
If I should say I saw such islanders ?
(For certes these are people of the island)
Who, though they are of monstrous shape, yet note,
Their manners are more gentle, kind, than of
Our human generation you shall find
Many – nay, almost any.

PROSPERO *[aside]* Honest lord,
Thou hast said well ; for some of you there present
Are worse than devils.

36 ALONSO I cannot too much muse
Such shapes, such gesture, and such sound, expressing
(Although they want the use of tongue) a kind
Of excellent dumb discourse.

39 PROSPERO *[aside]* Praise in departing.

FRANCISCO
They vanished strangely.

SEBASTIAN No matter, since
They have left their viands behind ; for we have
stomachs.
Will't please you taste of what is here ?

ALONSO Not I.

GONZALO
Faith, sir, you need not fear. When we were boys,
Who would believe that there were mountaineers
45 Dewlapped like bulls, whose throats had hanging at 'em

Wallets of flesh ? or that there were such men
Whose heads stood in their breasts ? which now we find 47
Each putter-out of five for one will bring us 48
Good warrant of.

ALONSO I will stand to, and feed ;
Although my last, no matter, since I feel
The best is past. Brother, my lord the Duke,
Stand to, and do as we. 52
*Thunder and lightning. Enter Ariel, like a harpy ;
claps his wings upon the table ; and with a quaint
device the banquet vanishes.*

ARIEL
You are three men of sin, whom destiny –
That hath to instrument this lower world 54
And what is in't – the never-surfeited sea
Hath caused to belch up you, and on this island,
Where man doth not inhabit, you 'mongst men
Being most unfit to live, I have made you mad ;
And even with such-like valor men hang and drown
Their proper selves.
[Alonso, Sebastian, &c. draw their swords.]
You fools : I and my fellows
Are ministers of Fate. The elements,
Of whom your swords are tempered, may as well
Wound the loud winds, or with bemocked-at stabs
Kill the still-closing waters, as diminish 64
One dowle that's in my plume. My fellow ministers 65
Are like invulnerable. If you could hurt, 66
Your swords are now too massy for your strengths 67
And will not be uplifted. But remember
(For that's my business to you) that you three
From Milan did supplant good Prospero ;
Exposed unto the sea, which hath requit it, 71
Him and his innocent child ; for which foul deed
The pow'rs, delaying, not forgetting, have
Incensed the seas and shores, yea, all the creatures,
Against your peace. Thee of thy son, Alonso,
They have bereft ; and do pronounce by me
Ling'ring perdition (worse than any death 77
Can be at once) shall step by step attend
You and your ways ; whose wraths to guard you from,
Which here, in this most desolate isle, else falls
Upon your heads, is nothing but heart's sorrow 81
And a clear life ensuing. 82
*He vanishes in thunder ; then, to soft music, enter the
Shapes again, and dance with mocks and mows, and
carrying out the table.*

PROSPERO
Bravely the figure of this harpy hast thou
Performed, my Ariel ; a grace it had, devouring. 84
Of my instruction hast thou nothing bated 85

5 *attached* seized 14 *throughly* thoroughly 17 s.d. *on the top* (this may
refer to an upper level of the tiring-house of the theatre) 20 *kind keepers*
guardian angels 21 *living drollery* puppet show with live figures 25
want credit lack credibility 36 *muse* wonder at 39 *Praise in departing*
save your praise for the end 45 *Dewlapped* with skin hanging from the
neck (like the goitrous Swiss *mountaineers*) 47 *in their breasts* (an ancient
travellers' tale ; cf. *Othello* I, iii, 144–45) 48 *putter-out . . . one* traveller
depositing a sum for insurance in London, to be repaid fivefold if he
returned safely and proved he had gone to his destination 52 s.d. *quaint*
ingenious 54 *to* i.e. as its 64 *still* constantly 65 *dowle* fibre of feather-
down 66 *like* also 67 *massy* massive 71 *requit* avenged ; *it* i.e. the
usurpation 77 *perdition* ruin 81 *heart's sorrow* repentance 82 *clear*
innocent ; s.d. *mocks and mows* grimaces and gestures 84 *devouring* i.e.
making the banquet disappear 85 *bated* omitted

86 In what thou hadst to say. So, with good life
87 And observation strange, my meaner ministers
88 Their several kinds have done. My high charms work,
And these, mine enemies, are all knit up
In their distractions : they now are in my pow'r ;
And in these fits I leave them, while I visit
Young Ferdinand, whom they suppose is drowned,
And his and mine loved darling.   *[Exit above.]*

GONZALO
94 I' th' name of something holy, sir, why stand you
In this strange stare ?
95 ALONSO   O, it is monstrous, monstrous !
Methought the billows spoke and told me of it ;
The winds did sing it to me ; and the thunder,
That deep and dreadful organ pipe, pronounced
99 The name of Prosper ; it did bass my trespass.
Therefore my son i' th' ooze is bedded ; and
I'll seek him deeper than e'er plummet sounded
And with him there lie mudded.   *Exit.*
SEBASTIAN   But one fiend at a time,
I'll fight their legions o'er !
ANTONIO   I'll be thy second.
            Exeunt [Sebastian and Antonio].
GONZALO
All three of them are desperate : their great guilt,
Like poison given to work a great time after,
Now gins to bite the spirits. I do beseech you,
That are of suppler joints, follow them swiftly
108 And hinder them from what this ecstasy
May now provoke them to.
ADRIAN   Follow, I pray you.
            Exeunt omnes.

                    *

IV, i   *Enter Prospero, Ferdinand, and Miranda.*
PROSPERO
If I have too austerely punished you,
Your compensation makes amends ; for I
3 Have given you here a third of mine own life,
Or that for which I live ; who once again
I tender to thy hand. All thy vexations
Were but my trials of thy love, and thou
7 Hast strangely stood the test. Here, afore heaven,
I ratify this my rich gift. O Ferdinand,
9 Do not smile at me that I boast her off,
For thou shalt find she will outstrip all praise
11 And make it halt behind her.
FERDINAND   I do believe it
12 Against an oracle.
PROSPERO
Then, as my gift, and thine own acquisition

---

86 *good life* realistic acting 87 *observation strange* wonderfully close
attention 88 *several kinds* separate parts 94 *why* (Gonzalo has not heard
Ariel's speech) 95 *it* i.e. my sin 99 *bass* proclaim in deep tones (literally,
provide the bass part for) 108 *ecstasy* madness
IV, i Before Prospero's cell 3 *third* (Prospero's love, his knowledge and
his power being the other two-thirds ?) 7 *strangely* in a rare fashion
9 *boast her off* boast about her 11 *halt* limp 12 *Against an oracle* even
if an oracle denied it 16 *sanctimonious* holy 18 *aspersion* blessing, like
rain on crops 19 *grow* become fruitful 26 *opportune* (accent second
syllable) 27 *worser genius can* bad angel can make 30 *or . . . foundered*
either the sun-god's horses are lame 37 *rabble* rank and file 41 *vanity*
show 47 *mop and mow* antics and gestures 50 *conceive* understand
51 *be true* (Prospero appears to have caught the lovers in an embrace)
56 *liver* (supposed seat of sexual passion) 57 *corollary* surplus 58 *want*
lack ; *pertly* briskly 60 *Iris* goddess of the rainbow and female messenger
of the gods 61 *fetches* vetch

Worthily purchased, take my daughter. But
If thou dost break her virgin-knot before
16 All sanctimonious ceremonies may
With full and holy rite be minist'red,
18 No sweet aspersion shall the heavens let fall
19 To make this contract grow ; but barren hate,
Sour-eyed disdain, and discord shall bestrew
The union of your bed with weeds so loathly
That you shall hate it both. Therefore take heed,
As Hymen's lamp shall light you.
FERDINAND   As I hope
For quiet days, fair issue, and long life,
With such love as 'tis now, the murkiest den,
26 The most opportune place, the strong'st suggestion
27 Our worser genius can, shall never melt
Mine honor into lust, to take away
The edge of that day's celebration
30 When I shall think or Phoebus' steeds are foundered
Or Night kept chained below.
PROSPERO   Fairly spoke.
Sit then and talk with her ; she is thine own.
What, Ariel ! My industrious servant, Ariel !
            Enter Ariel.
ARIEL
What would my potent master ? Here I am.
PROSPERO
Thou and thy meaner fellows your last service
Did worthily perform ; and I must use you
In such another trick. Go bring the rabble,
37 O'er whom I give thee pow'r, here to this place.
Incite them to quick motion ; for I must
Bestow upon the eyes of this young couple
Some vanity of mine art ; it is my promise,
41 And they expect it from me.
ARIEL   Presently ?
PROSPERO
Ay, with a twink.
ARIEL
Before you can say 'Come' and 'Go,'
And breathe twice and cry, 'So, so,'
Each one, tripping on his toe,
Will be here with mop and mow.
47 Do you love me, master ? No ?
PROSPERO
Dearly, my delicate Ariel. Do not approach
Till thou dost hear me call.
ARIEL   Well : I conceive.   *Exit.* 50
PROSPERO
51 Look thou be true : do not give dalliance
Too much the rein : the strongest oaths are straw
To th' fire i' th' blood. Be more abstemious,
Or else good night your vow !
FERDINAND   I warrant you, sir.
The white cold virgin snow upon my heart
56 Abates the ardor of my liver.
PROSPERO   Well.
57 Now come, my Ariel : bring a corollary
58 Rather than want a spirit. Appear, and pertly !
No tongue ! All eyes ! Be silent.
            Soft music. Enter Iris.
IRIS
60 Ceres, most bounteous lady, thy rich leas
61 Of wheat, rye, barley, fetches, oats, and pease ;
Thy turfy mountains, where live nibbling sheep,

63 And flat meads thatched with stover, them to keep;
64 Thy banks with pionèd and twillèd brims,
    Which spongy April at thy hest betrims
66 To make cold nymphs chaste crowns; and thy broom groves,
    Whose shadow the dismissèd bachelor loves,
68 Being lasslorn; thy pole-clipt vineyard;
69 And thy sea-marge, sterile and rocky-hard,
70 Where thou thyself dost air – the queen o' th' sky,
    Whose wat'ry arch and messenger am I,
    Bids thee leave these, and with her sovereign grace,
73 Here on this grass-plot, in this very place,
74 To come and sport: her peacocks fly amain.
    Approach, rich Ceres, her to entertain.
            Enter Ceres.

    CERES
    Hail, many-colorèd messenger, that ne'er
    Dost disobey the wife of Jupiter,
    Who, with thy saffron wings, upon my flow'rs
    Diffusest honey drops, refreshing show'rs,
    And with each end of thy blue bow dost crown
81 My bosky acres and my unshrubbed down,
    Rich scarf to my proud earth – why hath thy queen
    Summoned me hither to this short-grassed green?

    IRIS
    A contract of true love to celebrate
85 And some donation freely to estate
    On the blessed lovers.
    CERES   Tell me, heavenly bow,
87 If Venus or her son, as thou dost know,
    Do now attend the queen? Since they did plot
89 The means that dusky Dis my daughter got,
90 Her and her blind boy's scandalled company
    I have forsworn.
    IRIS   Of her society
92 Be not afraid: I met her Deity
93 Cutting the clouds towards Paphos, and her son
    Dove-drawn with her. Here thought they to have done
    Some wanton charm upon this man and maid,
    Whose vows are, that no bed-right shall be paid
    Till Hymen's torch be lighted; but in vain.
98 Mars's hot minion is returned again;
99 Her waspish-headed son has broke his arrows,
    Swears he will shoot no more, but play with sparrows
101 And be a boy right out.
            [Enter Juno.]
    CERES   Highest queen of state,
    Great Juno, comes; I know her by her gait.
    JUNO
    How does my bounteous sister? Go with me
    To bless this twain, that they may prosperous be
    And honored in their issue.
            They sing.
    JUNO   Honor, riches, marriage blessing,
                Long continuance, and increasing,
108   Hourly joys be still upon you!
                Juno sings her blessings on you.
110 [CERES]   Earth's increase, foison plenty,
                Barns and garners never empty,
                Vines with clust'ring bunches growing,
                Plants with goodly burden bowing;
                Spring come to you at the farthest
                In the very end of harvest.
                Scarcity and want shall shun you,
                Ceres' blessing so is on you.

FERDINAND
This is a most majestic vision, and
Harmonious charmingly. May I be bold
To think these spirits?
PROSPERO   Spirits, which by mine art
I have from their confines called to enact
My present fancies.
FERDINAND   Let me live here ever!
So rare a wond'red father and a wise   123
Makes this place Paradise.
        Juno and Ceres whisper, and send Iris on employment.
PROSPERO   Sweet now, silence!
Juno and Ceres whisper seriously.
There's something else to do. Hush and be mute,
Or else our spell is marred.
IRIS
You nymphs, called Naiades, of the windring brooks,   128
With your sedged crowns and ever-harmless looks,
Leave your crisp channels, and on this green land   130
Answer your summons; Juno does command.
Come, temperate nymphs, and help to celebrate
A contract of true love: be not too late.
        Enter certain Nymphs.
You sunburned sicklemen, of August weary,
Come hither from the furrow and be merry.
Make holiday: your rye-straw hats put on,
And these fresh nymphs encounter every one
In country footing.   138
        *Enter certain Reapers, properly habited. They join
        with the Nymphs in a graceful dance; towards the end
        whereof Prospero starts suddenly and speaks; after
        which, to a strange, hollow, and confused noise, they
        heavily vanish.*
PROSPERO [aside]
I had forgot that foul conspiracy
Of the beast Caliban and his confederates
Against my life: the minute of their plot
Is almost come.
        [To the Spirits] Well done! Avoid! No more!   142
FERDINAND
This is strange. Your father's in some passion
That works him strongly.
MIRANDA   Never till this day
Saw I him touched with anger so distempered.
PROSPERO
You do look, my son, in a moved sort,   146
As if you were dismayed: be cheerful, sir.
Our revels now are ended. These our actors,   148

63 *stover* winter food for stock 64 *pionèd and twillèd* dug under by the current and protected by woven layers of branches (sometimes emended to 'peonied and lilied') 66 *broom groves* clumps of gorse 68 *pole-clipt* pruned; *vineyard* (probably a trisyllable) 69 *sea-marge* shore 70 *queen* i.e. Juno 73 *Here . . . place* (in F a stage direction at this point reads 'Juno descends') 74 *peacocks* (these were sacred to Juno, as doves were to Venus [l. 94], and drew her chariot) 81 *bosky* wooded 85 *estate* bestow 87 *her son* Cupid, often represented as blind or blindfolded 89 *means* i.e. the abduction of Proserpine, Ceres' daughter, by Pluto (Dis), god of the lower (*dusky*) world 90 *scandalled* disgraceful 92 *her Deity* i.e. her Divine Majesty 93 *Paphos* (in Cyprus, center of Venus' cult) 98 *Mars's . . . again* the lustful mistress of Mars (Venus) has gone back to where she came from 99 *waspish-headed* spiteful and inclined to sting (with his arrows) 101 *right out* outright 108 *still* constantly 110 *foison* abundance 123 *wond'red* wonderful 128 *windring* winding and wandering 130 *crisp* rippling 138 s.d. *speaks* (thereby dissolving the scene, which depended on silence) 142 *Avoid* be off 146 *moved sort* troubled state 148 *revels* pageants

As I foretold you, were all spirits and
Are melted into air, into thin air ;
151 And, like the baseless fabric of this vision,
The cloud-capped tow'rs, the gorgeous palaces,
The solemn temples, the great globe itself,
154 Yea, all which it inherit, shall dissolve,
And, like this insubstantial pageant faded,
156 Leave not a rack behind. We are such stuff
157 As dreams are made on, and our little life
Is rounded with a sleep. Sir, I am vexed.
Bear with my weakness : my old brain is troubled.
Be not disturbed with my infirmity.
If you be pleased, retire into my cell
And there repose. A turn or two I'll walk
To still my beating mind.
FERDINAND, MIRANDA We wish your peace.
Exit [Ferdinand with Miranda].
Enter Ariel.
PROSPERO
Come with a thought ! I thank thee, Ariel. Come.
ARIEL
Thy thoughts I cleave to. What's thy pleasure ?
PROSPERO Spirit,
We must prepare to meet with Caliban.
ARIEL
167 Ay, my commander : when I presented Ceres,
I thought to have told thee of it, but I feared
Lest I might anger thee.
PROSPERO
170 Say again, where didst thou leave these varlets ?
ARIEL
I told you, sir, they were redhot with drinking ;
So full of valor that they smote the air
For breathing in their faces, beat the ground
For kissing of their feet ; yet always bending
Towards their project. Then I beat my tabor ;
176 At which like unbacked colts they pricked their ears,
177 Advanced their eyelids, lifted up their noses
As they smelt music. So I charmed their ears
That calf-like they my lowing followed through
180 Toothed briers, sharp furzes, pricking goss, and thorns,
Which ent'red their frail shins. At last I left them
182 I' th' filthy mantled pool beyond your cell,
There dancing up to th' chins, that the foul lake
O'erstunk their feet.
PROSPERO This was well done, my bird.
Thy shape invisible retain thou still.
The trumpery in my house, go bring it hither
187 For stale to catch these thieves.
ARIEL I go, I go. *Exit.*
PROSPERO
A devil, a born devil, on whose nature
Nurture can never stick : on whom my pains,

151 *baseless* insubstantial, non-material 154 *it inherit* occupy it 156 *rack* wisp of cloud 157 *on* of 167 *presented* acted the part of (?), introduced (?) 170 *varlets* ruffians 176 *unbacked* unbroken 177 *Advanced* lifted up 180 *goss* gorse 182 *mantled* scummed 187 *stale* decoy 192 *cankers* festers 193 *line* lime or linden-tree, or perhaps a clothesline made of hair 197 *Jack* (1) knave, (2) jack-o'-lantern, will-o'-the-wisp 205 *hoodwink* cover over 221 *peer* (referring to the song 'King Stephen was a worthy peer,' quoted in *Othello* II, iii, 84–91) 225 *frippery* old-clothes shop 230 *luggage* junk 234 ff. (the jokes are probably obscene, but their point is lost ; sailors crossing the *line* or equator proverbially lost their hair from scurvy) 238 *by line and level* according to rule (with pun on *line*) ; *an't like* if it please 242–43 *pass of pate* sally of wit

Humanely taken, all, all lost, quite lost !
And as with age his body uglier grows,
So his mind cankers. I will plague them all, 192
Even to roaring.
Enter Ariel, loaden with glistering apparel, &c.
Come, hang them on this line. 193
[Prospero and Ariel remain, invisible.] Enter Caliban,
Stephano, and Trinculo, all wet.
CALIBAN
Pray you tread softly, that the blind mole may not
Hear a foot fall. We now are near his cell.
STEPHANO Monster, your fairy, which you say is a harm-
less fairy, has done little better than played the Jack 197
with us.
TRINCULO Monster, I do smell all horse-piss, at which
my nose is in great indignation.
STEPHANO So is mine. Do you hear, monster ? If I
should take a displeasure against you, look you –
TRINCULO Thou wert but a lost monster.
CALIBAN
Good my lord, give me thy favor still.
Be patient, for the prize I'll bring thee to
Shall hoodwink this mischance. Therefore speak softly. 205
All's hushed as midnight yet.
TRINCULO Ay, but to lose our bottles in the pool –
STEPHANO There is not only disgrace and dishonor in
that, monster, but an infinite loss.
TRINCULO That's more to me than my wetting. Yet this
is your harmless fairy, monster.
STEPHANO I will fetch off my bottle, though I be o'er
ears for my labor.
CALIBAN
Prithee, my king, be quiet. Seest thou here ?
This is the mouth o' th' cell. No noise, and enter.
Do that good mischief which may make this island
Thine own for ever, and I, thy Caliban,
For aye thy foot-licker.
STEPHANO Give me thy hand. I do begin to have bloody
thoughts.
TRINCULO O King Stephano ! O peer ! O worthy Ste- 221
phano, look what a wardrobe here is for thee !
CALIBAN
Let it alone, thou fool ! It is but trash.
TRINCULO O, ho, monster ! we know what belongs to a
frippery. O King Stephano ! 225
STEPHANO Put off that gown, Trinculo : by this hand,
I'll have that gown !
TRINCULO Thy Grace shall have it.
CALIBAN
The dropsy drown this fool ! What do you mean
To dote thus on such luggage ? Let't alone, 230
And do the murder first. If he awake,
From toe to crown he'll fill our skins with pinches,
Make us strange stuff.
STEPHANO Be you quiet, monster. Mistress line, is not 234
this my jerkin ? *[Takes it down.]* Now is the jerkin under
the line. Now, jerkin, you are like to lose your hair and
prove a bald jerkin.
TRINCULO Do, do ! We steal by line and level, an't like 238
your Grace.
STEPHANO I thank thee for that jest. Here's a garment
for't. Wit shall not go unrewarded while I am king of
this country. 'Steal by line and level' is an excellent pass 242
of pate. There's another garment for't.

244 TRINCULO Monster, come put some lime upon your
fingers, and away with the rest.

CALIBAN
I will have none on't. We shall lose our time

247 And all be turned to barnacles, or to apes
With foreheads villainous low.

STEPHANO Monster, lay-to your fingers: help to bear
this away where my hogshead of wine is, or I'll turn
you out of my kingdom. Go to, carry this.

TRINCULO And this.

STEPHANO Ay, and this.

*A noise of hunters heard. Enter divers Spirits in shape
of dogs and hounds, hunting them about, Prospero and
Ariel setting them on.*

PROSPERO Hey, Mountain, hey!

ARIEL Silver! there it goes, Silver!

PROSPERO Fury, Fury! There, Tyrant, there! Hark,
hark!

[Caliban, Stephano, and Trinculo are driven out.]

Go, charge my goblins that they grind their joints

258 With dry convulsions, shorten up their sinews

259 With agèd cramps, and more pinch-spotted make them

260 Than pard or cat o' mountain.

ARIEL   Hark, they roar!

PROSPERO
Let them be hunted soundly. At this hour
Lie at my mercy all mine enemies.
Shortly shall all my labors end, and thou
Shalt have the air at freedom. For a little,
Follow, and do me service.   *Exeunt.*

*

V, i   *Enter Prospero in his magic robes, and Ariel.*

PROSPERO
Now does my project gather to a head.

2 My charms crack not, my spirits obey, and time
Goes upright with his carriage. How's the day?

ARIEL
On the sixth hour, at which time, my lord,
You said our work should cease.

PROSPERO   I did say so
When first I raised the tempest. Say, my spirit,
How fares the King and's followers?

ARIEL   Confined together
In the same fashion as you gave in charge,
Just as you left them – all prisoners, sir,

10 In the line grove which weather-fends your cell.

11 They cannot budge till your release. The King,
His brother, and yours abide all three distracted,
And the remainder mourning over them,
Brimful of sorrow and dismay; but chiefly
Him that you termed, sir, the good old Lord Gonzalo.
His tears run down his beard like winter's drops

17 From eaves of reeds. Your charm so strongly works 'em,
That if you now beheld them, your affections
Would become tender.

PROSPERO   Dost thou think so, spirit?

ARIEL
Mine would, sir, were I human.

PROSPERO   And mine shall.
Hast thou, which art but air, a touch, a feeling
Of their afflictions, and shall not myself,

23 One of their kind, that relish all as sharply

Passion as they, be kindlier moved than thou art?
Though with their high wrongs I am struck to th' quick,
Yet with my nobler reason 'gainst my fury
Do I take part. The rarer action is
In virtue than in vengeance. They being penitent,
The sole drift of my purpose doth extend
Not a frown further. Go, release them, Ariel.
My charms I'll break, their senses I'll restore,
And they shall be themselves.

ARIEL   I'll fetch them, sir.   *Exit.*

PROSPERO
Ye elves of hills, brooks, standing lakes, and groves,
And ye that on the sands with printless foot
Do chase the ebbing Neptune, and do fly him

36 When he comes back; you demi-puppets that
By moonshine do the green sour ringlets make,
Whereof the ewe not bites; and you whose pastime

39 Is to make midnight mushrumps, that rejoice
To hear the solemn curfew; by whose aid

41 (Weak masters though ye be) I have bedimmed
The noontide sun, called forth the mutinous winds,
And 'twixt the green sea and the azured vault
Set roaring war; to the dread rattling thunder

45 Have I given fire and rifted Jove's stout oak
With his own bolt; the strong-based promontory

47 Have I made shake and by the spurs plucked up
The pine and cedar; graves at my command
Have waked their sleepers, oped, and let 'em forth
By my so potent art. But this rough magic

51 I here abjure; and when I have required
Some heavenly music (which even now I do)

53 To work mine end upon their senses that
This airy charm is for, I'll break my staff,
Bury it certain fathoms in the earth,
And deeper than did ever plummet sound
I'll drown my book.

Solemn music.

*Here enters Ariel before; then Alonso, with a frantic
gesture, attended by Gonzalo; Sebastian and
Antonio in like manner, attended by Adrian and
Francisco. They all enter the circle which Prospero
had made, and there stand charmed; which Prospero
observing, speaks.*

58 A solemn air, and the best comforter
To an unsettled fancy, cure thy brains,
Now useless, boiled within thy skull! There stand,
For you are spell-stopped.
Holy Gonzalo, honorable man,

63 Mine eyes, ev'n sociable to the show of thine,

64 Fall fellowly drops. The charm dissolves apace;
And as the morning steals upon the night,
Melting the darkness, so their rising senses
Begin to chase the ignorant fumes that mantle
Their clearer reason. O good Gonzalo,

244 *lime* birdlime (sticky, hence appropriate for stealing)   247 *barnacles*
geese   258 *dry* (resulting from deficiency of 'humors' or bodily liquids)
259 *agèd* i.e. such as old people have   260 *pard or cat o' mountain* leopard
or catamount
V, i Before Prospero's cell   2–3 *time . . . carriage* time's burden is light
10 *weather-fends* protects from the weather   11 *till your release* until
you release them   17 *eaves of reeds* i.e. a thatched roof   23 *relish* feel;
all quite   36 *demi-puppets* i.e. fairies   39 *mushrumps* mushrooms   41
masters forces   45 *rifted* split   47 *spurs* roots   51 *required* asked for
53 *their senses that* the senses of those whom   58 *and* i.e. which is   63
sociable sympathetic; *show* sight   64 *Fall* let fall

My true preserver, and a loyal sir
70 To him thou follow'st, I will pay thy graces
Home both in word and deed. Most cruelly
Didst thou, Alonso, use me and my daughter.
Thy brother was a furtherer in the act.
Thou art pinched for't now, Sebastian. Flesh and blood,
You, brother mine, that entertained ambition,
76 Expelled remorse and nature; who, with Sebastian
(Whose inward pinches therefore are most strong),
Would here have killed your king, I do forgive thee,
Unnatural though thou art. Their understanding
Begins to swell, and the approaching tide
Will shortly fill the reasonable shore,
That now lies foul and muddy. Not one of them
That yet looks on me or would know me. Ariel,
Fetch me the hat and rapier in my cell.
85 I will discase me, and myself present
86 As I was sometime Milan. Quickly, spirit!
Thou shalt ere long be free.
                 [Exit Ariel and returns immediately.]
        Ariel sings and helps to attire him.
        Where the bee sucks, there suck I;
        In a cowslip's bell I lie;
        There I couch when owls do cry.
        On the bat's back I do fly
        After summer merrily.
     Merrily, merrily shall I live now
     Under the blossom that hangs on the bough.
PROSPERO
     Why, that's my dainty Ariel! I shall miss thee,
     But yet thou shalt have freedom; so, so, so.
     To the King's ship, invisible as thou art!
     There shalt thou find the mariners asleep
     Under the hatches. The master and the boatswain
     Being awake, enforce them to this place,
101 And presently, I prithee.
ARIEL
102 I drink the air before me, and return
     Or ere your pulse twice beat.   *Exit.*
GONZALO
     All torment, trouble, wonder, and amazement
     Inhabits here. Some heavenly power guide us
     Out of this fearful country!
PROSPERO   Behold, sir King,
     The wrongèd Duke of Milan, Prospero.
     For more assurance that a living prince
     Does now speak to thee, I embrace thy body,
     And to thee and thy company I bid
     A hearty welcome.
ALONSO   Whe'r thou be'st he or no,
112 Or some enchanted trifle to abuse me,
     As late I have been, I not know. Thy pulse
     Beats, as of flesh and blood; and, since I saw thee,
     Th' affliction of my mind amends, with which,
116 I fear, a madness held me. This must crave
117 (An if this be at all) a most strange story.

Thy dukedom I resign and do entreat
Thou pardon me my wrongs. But how should Prospero
Be living and be here?
PROSPERO   First, noble friend,
     Let me embrace thine age, whose honor cannot
     Be measured or confined.
GONZALO   Whether this be
     Or be not, I'll not swear.
PROSPERO   You do yet taste
     Some subtleties o' th' isle, that will not let you   124
     Believe things certain. Welcome, my friends all.
         [Aside to Sebastian and Antonio]
     But you, my brace of lords, were I so minded,
     I here could pluck his Highness' frown upon you,   127
     And justify you traitors. At this time   128
     I will tell no tales.
SEBASTIAN *[aside]*   The devil speaks in him.
PROSPERO   No.
     For you, most wicked sir, whom to call brother
     Would even infect my mouth, I do forgive
     Thy rankest fault – all of them; and require
     My dukedom of thee, which perforce I know
     Thou must restore.
ALONSO   If thou beest Prospero,
     Give us particulars of thy preservation;
     How thou hast met us here, who three hours since
     Were wracked upon this shore; where I have lost
     (How sharp the point of this remembrance is!)
     My dear son Ferdinand.
PROSPERO   I am woe for't, sir.   139
ALONSO
     Irreparable is the loss, and patience
     Says it is past her cure.
PROSPERO   I rather think
     You have not sought her help, of whose soft grace
     For the like loss I have her sovereign aid
     And rest myself content.
ALONSO   You the like loss?
PROSPERO
     As great to me as late; and, supportable   145
     To make the dear loss, have I means much weaker   146
     Than you may call to comfort you; for I
     Have lost my daughter.
ALONSO   A daughter?
     O heavens, that they were living both in Naples,
     The King and Queen there! That they were, I wish
     Myself were mudded in that oozy bed
     Where my son lies. When did you lose your daughter?
PROSPERO
     In this last tempest. I perceive these lords
     At this encounter do so much admire   154
     That they devour their reason, and scarce think
     Their eyes do offices of truth, their words   156
     Are natural breath. But, howsoev'r you have
     Been justled from your senses, know for certain
     That I am Prospero, and that very duke
     Which was thrust forth of Milan, who most strangely
     Upon this shore, where you were wracked, was landed
     To be the lord on't. No more yet of this;
     For 'tis a chronicle of day by day,
     Not a relation for a breakfast, nor
     Befitting this first meeting. Welcome, sir;
     This cell's my court. Here have I few attendants,
     And subjects none abroad. Pray you look in.

---

70 *graces* favors   76 *remorse* pity; *nature* natural feeling   85 *discase* undress   86 *sometime Milan* when I was Duke of Milan   101 *presently* right away   102 *drink the air* i.e. consume space   112 *trifle* trick; *abuse* deceive   116 *crave* require   117 *An if . . . all* if this is really happening 124 *subtleties* (secondary meaning of) elaborate pastries representing allegorical figures, used in banquets and pageants   127 *pluck* pull down 128 *justify* prove   139 *woe* sorry   145 *late* recent   146 *dear* grievous 154 *admire* wonder   156 *do offices* perform services

My dukedom since you have given me again,
I will requite you with as good a thing,
At least bring forth a wonder to content ye
171 As much as me my dukedom.
     Here Prospero discovers Ferdinand and Miranda
     playing at chess.
MIRANDA
   Sweet lord, you play me false.
FERDINAND   No, my dearest love,
   I would not for the world.
MIRANDA
174 Yes, for a score of kingdoms you should wrangle,
   And I would call it fair play.
ALONSO   If this prove
   A vision of the island, one dear son
   Shall I twice lose.
SEBASTIAN   A most high miracle !
FERDINAND
   Though the seas threaten, they are merciful.
   I have cursed them without cause.
     [Kneels.]
ALONSO   Now all the blessings
   Of a glad father compass thee about !
   Arise, and say how thou cam'st here.
MIRANDA   O, wonder !
   How many goodly creatures are there here !
   How beauteous mankind is ! O brave new world
   That has such people in't !
PROSPERO   'Tis new to thee.
ALONSO
   What is this maid with whom thou wast at play ?
186 Your eld'st acquaintance cannot be three hours.
   Is she the goddess that hath severed us
   And brought us thus together ?
FERDINAND   Sir, she is mortal ;
   But by immortal providence she's mine.
   I chose her when I could not ask my father
   For his advice, nor thought I had one. She
   Is daughter to this famous Duke of Milan,
   Of whom so often I have heard renown
   But never saw before ; of whom I have
   Received a second life ; and second father
   This lady makes him to me.
ALONSO   I am hers.
   But, O, how oddly will it sound that I
   Must ask my child forgiveness !
PROSPERO   There, sir, stop.
   Let us not burden our remembrance with
   A heaviness that's gone.
200 GONZALO   I have inly wept,
   Or should have spoke ere this. Look down, you gods,
   And on this couple drop a blessèd crown !
   For it is you that have chalked forth the way
   Which brought us hither.
ALONSO   I say amen, Gonzalo.
GONZALO
   Was Milan thrust from Milan that his issue
   Should become kings of Naples ? O, rejoice
   Beyond a common joy, and set it down
   With gold on lasting pillars : in one voyage
   Did Claribel her husband find at Tunis,
   And Ferdinand her brother found a wife
   Where he himself was lost ; Prospero his dukedom
   In a poor isle ; and all of us ourselves

When no man was his own.
ALONSO *[to Ferdinand and Miranda]*
         Give me your hands.
   Let grief and sorrow still embrace his heart   214
   That doth not wish you joy.
GONZALO   Be it so ! Amen !
     Enter Ariel, with the Master and Boatswain
     amazedly following.
   O, look, sir ; look, sir ! Here is more of us !
   I prophesied, if a gallows were on land,
   This fellow could not drown. Now, blasphemy,
   That swear'st grace o'erboard, not an oath on shore ?
   Hast thou no mouth by land ? What is the news ?
BOATSWAIN
   The best news is that we have safely found
   Our king and company ; the next, our ship,
   Which, but three glasses since, we gave out split,
   Is tight and yare and bravely rigged as when   224
   We first put out to sea.
ARIEL *[aside to Prospero]*   Sir, all this service
   Have I done since I went.
PROSPERO *[aside to Ariel]*   My tricksy spirit !   226
ALONSO
   These are not natural events ; they strengthen
   From strange to stranger. Say, how came you hither ?
BOATSWAIN
   If I did think, sir, I were well awake,
   I'ld strive to tell you. We were dead of sleep
   And (how we know not) all clapped under hatches ;
   Where, but even now, with strange and several noises   232
   Of roaring, shrieking, howling, jingling chains,
   And moe diversity of sounds, all horrible,   234
   We were awaked ; straightway at liberty ;
   Where we, in all her trim, freshly beheld   236
   Our royal, good, and gallant ship, our master
   Cap'ring to eye her. On a trice, so please you,   238
   Even in a dream, were we divided from them
   And were brought moping hither.   240
ARIEL *[aside to Prospero]*   Was't well done ?
PROSPERO *[aside to Ariel]*
   Bravely, my diligence. Thou shalt be free.
ALONSO
   This is as strange a maze as e'er men trod,
   And there is in this business more than nature
   Was ever conduct of. Some oracle   244
   Must rectify our knowledge.
PROSPERO   Sir, my liege,
   Do not infest your mind with beating on   246
   The strangeness of this business : at picked leisure,
   Which shall be shortly, single I'll resolve you   248
   (Which to you shall seem probable) of every   249
   These happened accidents ; till when, be cheerful   250
   And think of each thing well.
     [Aside to Ariel]   Come hither, spirit.
   Set Caliban and his companions free.
   Untie the spell.   *[Exit Ariel.]*
     How fares my gracious sir ?

---

171 s.d. *discovers* discloses   174 *should wrangle* i.e. playing fair, as
Ferdinand is doing, is not a test of Miranda's love for him   186 *eld'st* i.e.
longest period of   214 *still* forever   224 *yare* shipshape   226 *tricksy* i.e.
ingenious   232 *several* various   234 *moe* more   236 *trim* sail   238
Cap'ring dancing for joy; *eye* see   240 *moping* in a daze   244 *conduct*
conductor   246 *infest* tease   248 *single* privately ; *resolve* explain   249
every every one of   250 *accidents* incidents

There are yet missing of your company
Some few odd lads that you remember not.
Enter Ariel, driving in Caliban, Stephano, and
Trinculo, in their stolen apparel.

STEPHANO Every man shift for all the rest, and let no
man take care for himself; for all is but fortune.
Coragio, bully-monster, coragio!

259 TRINCULO If these be true spies which I wear in my
head, here's a goodly sight.

CALIBAN
O Setebos, these be brave spirits indeed!
How fine my master is! I am afraid
He will chastise me.

SEBASTIAN   Ha, ha!
What things are these, my Lord Antonio?
Will money buy 'em?

ANTONIO   Very like. One of them
Is a plain fish and no doubt marketable.

PROSPERO
267   Mark but the badges of these men, my lords,
268   Then say if they be true. This misshapen knave,
His mother was a witch, and one so strong
That could control the moon, make flows and ebbs,
271   And deal in her command without her power.
These three have robbed me, and this demi-devil
(For he's a bastard one) had plotted with them
To take my life. Two of these fellows you
Must know and own; this thing of darkness I
Acknowledge mine.

CALIBAN   I shall be pinched to death.

ALONSO
Is not this Stephano, my drunken butler?

SEBASTIAN
He is drunk now: where had he wine?

ALONSO
And Trinculo is reeling ripe: where should they
Find this grand liquor that hath gilded 'em?
How cam'st thou in this pickle?

282 TRINCULO I have been in such a pickle, since I saw you
last, that I fear me will never out of my bones. I shall not
fear fly-blowing.

SEBASTIAN Why, how now, Stephano?

286 STEPHANO O, touch me not! I am not Stephano, but a
cramp.

PROSPERO You'ld be king o' the isle, sirrah?

289 STEPHANO I should have been a sore one then.

ALONSO
This is a strange thing as e'er I looked on.

PROSPERO
He is as disproportioned in his manners
As in his shape. Go, sirrah, to my cell;

Take with you your companions. As you look
To have my pardon, trim it handsomely.

CALIBAN
Ay, that I will; and I'll be wise hereafter,
And seek for grace. What a thrice-double ass
Was I to take this drunkard for a god
And worship this dull fool!

PROSPERO   Go to! Away!

ALONSO
Hence, and bestow your luggage where you found it.

SEBASTIAN Or stole it rather.
[Exeunt Caliban, Stephano, and Trinculo.]

PROSPERO
Sir, I invite your Highness and your train
To my poor cell, where you shall take your rest
For this one night; which, part of it, I'll waste   302
With such discourse as, I not doubt, shall make it
Go quick away – the story of my life,
And the particular accidents gone by
Since I came to this isle; and in the morn
I'll bring you to your ship, and so to Naples,
Where I have hope to see the nuptial
Of these our dear-beloved solemnizèd;   309
And thence retire me to my Milan, where
Every third thought shall be my grave.

ALONSO   I long
To hear the story of your life, which must
Take the ear strangely.   313

PROSPERO   I'll deliver all;
And promise you calm seas, auspicious gales,
And sail so expeditious that shall catch   315
Your royal fleet far off. – My Ariel, chick,
That is thy charge. Then to the elements
Be free, and fare thou well! – Please you draw near.
Exeunt omnes.

EPILOGUE   Epi.
spoken by Prospero.

Now my charms are all o'erthrown,
And what strength I have's mine own,
Which is most faint. Now 'tis true
I must be here confined by you,
Or sent to Naples. Let me not,
Since I have my dukedom got
And pardoned the deceiver, dwell
In this bare island by your spell;   8
But release me from my bands   9
With the help of your good hands.   10
Gentle breath of yours my sails
Must fill, or else my project fails,
Which was to please. Now I want   13
Spirits to enforce, art to enchant;
And my ending is despair
Unless I be relieved by prayer,
Which pierces so that it assaults
Mercy itself and frees all faults.
As you from crimes would pardoned be,
Let your indulgence set me free.   *Exit.*

---

259 *spies* eyes   267 *badges of these men* signs of these servants   268 *true*
honest   271 *her* i.e. the moon's; *without* beyond   282 *pickle* (1) predicament, (2) preservative (from the horse-pond; hence insects will let him alone)
286 *Stephano* (this name is said to be a slang Neapolitan term for stomach)
289 *sore* (1) tyrannical, (2) aching   302 *waste* spend   309 *solemnizèd* (accent
second syllable)   313 *Take* captivate; *deliver* tell   315 *sail* sailing
Epi.   8 *spell* i.e. silence   9 *bands* bonds   10 *hands* i.e. applause to break
the spell   13 *want* lack

THE NON-DRAMATIC POETRY

FOREWORD

The sonnets and narrative poems bring us back to the earlier years of Shakespeare's creative career. Sonnets, in translation and in imitation of Petrarch's, had been introduced to English readers by Wyatt and Surrey in *Tottel's Miscellany*, 1557. The Italian two-part form, with octave rhyming *abbaabba* and sestet working variations upon two or three additional rhymes, was abandoned by most English poets, including Shakespeare, who substituted the more supple three-quatrain-couplet form: *abab cdcd efef gg*. The earliest full sonnet sequence was Thomas Watson's *Hecatompathia or The Passionate Century of Love* (1582). It was followed by Sidney's *Astrophel and Stella*, written before 1586 though not published until 1591, and this by Daniel's *Delia*, Drayton's *Idea's Mirror*, Spenser's *Amoretti*, and others. The period of greatest vogue was 1590 to 1595. Although all sonnets must presumably be personal, only Spenser's are unequivocally autobiographical, and, curiously, his are by no means the least conventional. Sidney was more successful than most in conveying a sense of genuine emotional involvement, and Shakespeare, not unexpectedly, was still more successful than Sidney. Still he was writing in an established tradition, and although the best of his sonnets transcend the tradition, the majority must be read with the nature of the shared idiom and conventions in mind; otherwise one may be only dimly aware of what the poet was actually saying. A naive and anachronistic reading of the sonnets is responsible for a number of theories, solemnly clumsy when not ridiculous, about disturbances in Shakespeare's psyche, and about his sexual and social behavior; however, recent commentary indicates an increasing prevalence of sanity.

An older tradition, Ovidian and erotic, supplies the context of *Venus and Adonis* and *Lucrece*, although the latter is affiliated with "lament" narratives and is more anti-erotic than otherwise. Marlowe's *Hero and Leander* is the most distinguished of the contemporary narratives of amorous adventure, and its excellence prevents us from saying that, in this genre, Shakespeare "transcended" the tradition; however, either one of his poems would have established the reputation of a lesser poet. As a matter of fact, *Venus and Adonis* did much to establish that of Shakespeare.

A. H.

BIBLIOGRAPHY

An excellent collotype reproduction of the first editions of the *Sonnets* and narrative poems is *Shakespeare Poems, A Facsimile of the Earliest Editions*, The Elizabethan Club Series No. 3, Yale (1964). An incomparable edition of the *Sonnets*, with a patient précis of the commentary of the ages, bizarre and otherwise, is the *New Variorum*, ed. Hyder Rollins, 2 vols (1944). Rollins has edited the *Poems* in the same series (1938). Background books on the non-dramatic poems are Hallett Smith, *Elizabethan Poetry* (1952); Thomas W. Baldwin, *On the Literary Genetics of Shakespere's Poems* (1950); and J. W. Lever, *The Elizabethan Love Sonnet* (1956). An anthology of criticism is *Discussions of Shakespeare's Sonnets*, ed. B. Herrnstein (1964). Speculation continues in Leslie Hotson, *Shakespeare's Sonnets Dated* (1949); and J. Dover Wilson, *An Introduction to the Sonnets of Shakespeare* (1964). Critical studies are Edward Hubler, *The Sense of Shakespeare's Sonnets* (1952); J. B. Leishman, *Themes and Variations in Shakespeare's Sonnets* (1961); Hilton Landry, *Interpretations in Shakespeare's Sonnets* (1963).

THE NARRATIVE POEMS

INTRODUCTION

And Shakespeare, thou whose honey-flowing vein,
Pleasing the world, thy praises doth obtain;
Whose *Venus* and whose *Lucrece*, sweet and chaste,
Thy name in fame's immortal book have placed:
  Live ever you, at least in fame live ever;
  Well may the body die, but fame dies never.

Richard Barnfield, 1598

Some poetic genera have survived in our practise, understanding, or both, and some have not. The sonnet, and even the sonnet-sequence, are still being written, and the earliest English sonnets (Shakespeare's among them) are still being read. We have, in consequence, a going sense of what the sonnet can accomplish, and also of what subjects and attitudes traditionally belong to it. But of the masque, for instance, we have no corresponding natural awareness; only the specialist in Stuart literature could say whether Robert Frost's *A Masque of Reason* is in any way a revival of the art-form, and most readers have enjoyed Milton's *Comus* without much notion of its relation to the norms of courtly entertainment. We can, of course, find an antique work good without knowing precisely how it is "good of its kind"; but much depends, in such cases, on the simplicity of the convention and on the persistence of analogous forms of poetry. The two long poems which, in Barnfield's judgment, were to assure Shakespeare's immortality are complex and confusing in relation to a number of conventions, literary and pictorial, and those conventions are dead; poems of the kind are no longer written, and few of them are still read. Since one cannot cheer without knowing what the game is, the reader of these poems today is likely to find himself wishing for some historical guidance.

The literature on the poems is extensive, but that vast machinery of mediation does not answer one's questions with the sure brevity of a computer. Some things are clear, however. The *Venus*, of which I shall speak first and most, is an Ovidian narrative poem which derives the greater part of its material from passages of the *Metamorphoses*: those on Venus and Adonis, on Narcissus, and on Salmacis and Hermaphroditus. The epigraph, moreover, is taken from Ovid's *Amores*. Shakespeare was thus promising in some measure to emulate a witty, charming, and delicately sensual Latin poet. He was also choosing to retell a tale which every literate person knew in the original, and which had already been variously treated by English poets: by Golding in his moralized translation of Ovid, by Spenser, by Lodge, and by several others.

The dedicatee of Shakespeare's poem was the Earl of Southampton, a young courtier who employed John Florio as his tutor in Italian and was presumably a sophis-

ticate. Given such a first reader, Shakespeare would doubtless be inclined to make his poem not a moral allegory (as medieval Ovidian tradition would have urged) but lightly erotic and fashionably artificial, in the manner of Marlowe's *Hero and Leander*. If these were Shakespeare's desiderata, he cannot be said to have consistently achieved them; but that he aimed well enough at the tastes of Southampton and his like is indicated both by Gabriel Harvey's reference to *Venus'* rage among the "younger sort" and by the greater assurance of Shakespeare's dedication of *Lucrece* to Southampton one year later.

The poem has been praised for its quick, decisive beginning, and it is true that the first stanza provides the time, some sense of place, the persons, their motives, and the beginning of the action: Adonis is off to hunt, and the enamored Venus comes running to intercept him. But this sort of narrative urgency does not continue; indeed, it stops right there, and we see at once that Shakespeare is not plunging into his narrative but getting some part of it over with. As Venus begins her leisured and mannered importunities in stanza 2, it is clear that her much-told story will not be told here for story's sake. There is no question, of course, of any incapacity for narrative writing, as one may tell by this later stanza in which Venus, seeking Adonis, encounters his wounded and complaining hounds:

When he hath ceased his ill-resounding noise,
Another flap-mouthed mourner, black and grim,
Against the welkin volleys out his voice.
Another and another answer him,
  Clapping their proud tails to the ground below,
  Shaking their scratched ears, bleeding as they go.

(919 ff.)

That is cleanly written, it is vivid for eye and ear, and it does not hover too much, but keeps the story in motion; the pack goes bleeding by, and Venus moves on with increased anxiety toward the discovery of Adonis. But when she does find him, when she "unfortunately spies / The foul boar's conquest on her fair delight," the event is almost parenthetical, and the poem characteristically swerves from direct narrative into a cascade of similes, in which Venus' afflicted eyes are likened to fading stars, retracting snail-horns, and the unnerved intelligence-officers of a court.

Not only are the few happenings of the plot minimized in favor of such embroidery, but no depth or intelligible development can be found in the characters or relationship of Venus and Adonis. Adonis is a boy who likes hunting and is prodigiously insusceptible to love; sullenly, and on the whole mutely, he resists Venus' pleas and caresses from beginning to end. The one other thing we know about this rudimentary person is that he does have the decency to resuscitate a woman who has fainted. Venus, for her part, is at one moment moved by pity, but everything else she does and says – her wrestlings, her sophistries, her tricks, her reproaches – is traceable to her one allotted motive: a sometimes etherealized sensual passion. The death of Adonis saddens but does not chasten her, and though we leave her "immured" in Paphos she has not conceivably become a conventual type.

The poem differs from Ovidian poetry generally in containing a very high proportion of dialogue, but its many speeches do not serve, by characteristic cadence and lexicon, or by the betrayal of emotional pattern or conflict, to give the speakers any individual savor, or psychic volume. Their attitudes have been assigned in stanza 1, and whenever they sound unlike themselves we are dealing not with the emergence or revelation of a new quality but with inconsistency on the part of the author. For example, in her prophecy that sorrow shall hereafter attend on love (1135 ff.) Venus takes high moral ground and deplores jealousy, deceit, and unrestraint in a manner which is foreign to her but convenient for the poet's local purposes. Adonis asserts (409 ff.) that he knows not love and does not care to know it, but in the next stanza argues from a quite different and more knowing position that one may be spoilt for sexual love if one experiences it too early. The fine homily on Love and Lust (like the love-persuasions of Marlowe's Leander) comes oddly from one so innocent, and the inconsistency is not removed by the fact that Adonis admits it (806).

In addition to such distortions of character, which Shakespeare seems to have permitted himself for the sake of immediate effects, the reader must cope with apparent shifts in the poet's attitude toward his material. It will be granted, I am sure, that comedy enters the poem at the end of stanza 5, where Venus pulls Adonis from his horse and lugs him off under her arm, blushing and pouting. We are amused because a female is manhandling a male, and because the goddess of Love (though later she will stress her weightlessness) here seems not merely Rubenesque but grotesquely muscular. The occurrence is a sexual assault which, if described in a different key, might invite prurience and encourage perverse or passive fantasy. But there is no Swinburnian heavy breathing here; it is vaudeville, and it is vaudeville when Venus later falls flat not once but twice (463, 593).

If the presence of broad comedy forbids a prurient response to the early stanzas, the element of slapstick is in turn refined by the graceful artifice of Venus' entreaties, by her persistent high idealization of Adonis' beauty, by Shakespeare's stress on the loveliness of Adonis' "pretty ear" or Venus' "fair immortal hand," and by the benign ambience of summer dawn. We cannot take the word "lust" very seriously in an atmosphere of violets and dive-dappers; and when Venus "devours" Adonis as an eagle its prey, we are less likely to think of *Vénus tout entière à sa proie attachée* than of the amorous commonplace "I could eat you alive." The reader, in short, feels himself to be in that special literary preserve where the erotic may freely be enjoyed because taste and humor attend and control it. This is the domain of much of Herrick's poetry, and here as there.it is understood that moral objections would be churlish.

A critic of 1823 described *Venus and Adonis* as "deficient in that delicacy which has happily been introduced by modern refinement." The eroticism of the poem, however, is never culpably gross. Venus' celebrated "deer park" speech (229 ff.) is far too clever for pornographic purposes, and such lines as the following have a Marlovian coolness and suavity:

> Who sees his true-love in her naked bed,
> Teaching the sheets a whiter hue than white,
> But, when his glutton eye so full hath fed,
> His other agents aim at like delight?
>
> (397–400)

There are also (in addition to the other alleviations I have mentioned) occasional maxims of this sort:

> Were beauty under twenty locks kept fast,
> Yet love breaks through and picks them all at last.
>
> (575–76)

This lacks the irony of Marlowe, but like his maxims in *Hero and Leander* it distances the action by amused generalization.

Nevertheless, Shakespeare's poem breaks its own contract with the reader. By line 551 Venus' eagle has become a vulture, her face "doth reek and smoke," and her "lust" is being denounced by the poet for its shamelessness and its subversion of reason. This passage endorses in advance Adonis' tirade (769 ff.) against "sweating Lust," in which that sweat which first seemed earthily matter-of-fact (25) and later erotically attractive (143–44) becomes wholly distasteful. Is the reader expected, at this point, to make such judgments retroactive, and to see the first part of the poem in a radically altered light? If so, it is too much to ask. One could no more do it than one could reconceive *Macbeth* as comedy. Shakespeare's (and Adonis') distinctions between Love and Lust are in themselves eloquent and sound, but they have no place in such a poem as *Venus* started out to be, and one is forced to consider two possible explanations: either Shakespeare thought that he could jump, with aesthetic safety, from one Ovidian tradition to another; or the poet who was soon to write Sonnet 129 ("Th' expense of spirit in a waste of shame / Is lust in action") could not temperamentally sustain a blithe and amoral approach to sexual love.

Some critics, unwilling that Shakespeare should seem imperfect even in "the first heir of" his invention, have tried to read *Venus* as a coherent moral allegory. It is not hard to guess what sort of thing such attempts would entail: the identification of Adonis with reason and ideal beauty, Venus with lust; the assumption that hunting is here, as in *A Midsummer Night's Dream*, a metaphor for the conquest of the irrational; the interpretation of Adonis' horse as ungoverned appetite running mad; the placing of special emphasis on all passages (such as 889 ff.) having to do with the hierarchy of the faculties; and so on. The poem would thus become a myth (rather like Marlowe's digression, in *Hero and Leander*, on the enmity of Love and the Fates) of the flight of true Love and Beauty to heaven – a myth in which the imperfection of love on earth is explained as the result of passion's incapacity to defer to reason. Having come so far, an allegorical interpreter might dare to construe, in accordance with his view of the poem, that dense complex of repeated images or symbols which we encounter from the first stanza onward:

suns and moons and faces red or pale, hot or cold; eye-beams or sunbeams commercing with the several elements, and with earth or heaven. By the time one finds the fatal boar being condemned for a "downward eye" imperceptive of beauty (1105 ff.) one is aware that these recurrent motifs may indeed be driving at something; but the present writer is unable, thus far, to resolve them into any structure, and finds that the chief result of so many burning faces, eyes, tears, and exhalations is an impression of close-up photography.

We are all, I hope, ambitious for Shakespeare, and would be pleased if the discovery of consistent moral allegory in his poem could be made in better conscience – with less suppression and inflation of evidence, and less disregard of tone. The moral and allegorical elements are really there; unfortunately, they are fitful and vague. It would please us, too, if the poem could be shown to have a clear pattern of attitudes embodied in its prevalent symbols; we might then hope to discover deep and powerful focal passages, as in the plays. The suns, moons, heads, and coins of *1 Henry IV*, and their attendant political conceptions, have such cumulative effect upon the reader's imagination that when, in Act IV, the Prince's troops are seen approaching Shrewsbury, "Glittering in golden coats like images . . . / And gorgeous as the sun at midsummer," those few words render the whole play simultaneous, and reverberate through all its architecture. But *Venus* is not architectural; there are no moments in which the entire work is many-dimensionally presented to the mind through a concentrative use of symbol or idea. The poem is additive, linear, spasmodic, opportunistic; it resembles a medieval episodic painting, or a series of tapestry panels deriving from one story but only tenuously related to each other. Or, to use a comparison nearer to our experience, it is like those musical comedies of the 1920's in which the "book" was a series of casual excuses for songs and dances, and the least mention of Chicago was sufficient to motivate a massive Chicago Number.

In order to enjoy *Venus and Adonis*, one must accept it as a lesser and looser thing than the more familiar plays, and not waste too much time in clucking one's tongue over its "frigid artificiality," its "remoteness from life," its deficiencies in story, character, and idea. The pleasures of the poem may be found anywhere at random, as in these lines from Venus' three-stanza vaunt about her conquest of Mars:

> Over my altars hath he hung his lance,
> His batt'red shield, his uncontrollèd crest,
> And for my sake hath learned to sport and dance,
> To toy, to wanton, dally, smile, and jest,
>   Scorning his churlish drum and ensign red,
>   Making my arms his field, his tent my bed.
>
> (103-8)

That is part of an eighteen-line development of the paradox that the god of war should surrender. Both in *Venus* and in *Lucrece* Shakespeare sometimes employs brisk and arresting paradoxes ("O modest wantons, wanton modesty!"), but the relish of this passage lies in an eloquent expansion of the paradox, and a continually varied attack upon it. Wit is not always brief; Venus offers Adonis "Ten kisses short as one, one long as twenty," and Shakespeare knows that in witty verse one must similarly divert by unexpected proportion and duration. In the

early poems, where subtlety is chiefly of the surface, he inclines to surprise more by excess than by concision, and we respond not with a jarred delight but with that growing wonder we feel when the still-strong miler lets himself out in the stretch, or the jazz trumpeter sails on into yet another chorus. We enjoy the display of resources, the prodigality, the abundance. In the stanza above, there is a fairly full inventory of Martial properties – lance, shield, helmet, drum, ensign, field, and tent; but these things are so variously tucked into the grammar as to give no impression of padding or of tiresome catalogue. And it is precisely this handling of one enumeration which permits another (the rather redundant infinitives of lines 105 and 106) to be contrastingly presented in bald sequence.

No reader with an ear can fail to note that the vowel-progressions of the stanza are melodious, and that the line, though end-stopped, is highly versatile in pace and rhythm; the movement of the whole is nervously fluent, as suits an extended poem so decoratively aloof from action and drama. It will be noticed here, as in the poem generally, that Shakespeare's lines tend to contain words, or groups of words, which balance upon some principle or other: very often, as in a line I have quoted ("The foul boar's conquest on her fair delight"), the balance involves antithesis. Line 104 above represents "balancing" at its most obvious, but in line 107 we have something subtler: a strong initial verb defers the seesaw effect, and the balanced words are inversely arranged as adjective-noun and noun-adjective. Line 108 then cleverly repeats the pattern with other grammatical elements.

Such talk is exceedingly dry, but it does bear upon the main and steadiest sources of pleasure in the poem – for us as for the artifice-loving Elizabethans: its elaborate inventiveness, its rhetorical dexterity, its technical *éclat*. There are numerous moments at which the poem creates a response to its subject, as in the beautiful stanza of the hands (361 ff.), but mostly one is reacting to an ostentatious poetic performance the artful variety of which I have scarcely begun to describe. Shakespeare has used an Ovidian story as the basis, not of a narrative, dramatic, or philosophic poem, but of a concatenation of virtuoso descriptions, comparisons, apostrophes, essays, pleas, reproaches, digressions, laments, and what have you. The same is true of *Lucrece*, that "graver labor" which Shakespeare promised in his dedication of *Venus*, and which he published a year later, in 1594.

In this case the Ovidian source is the *Fasti*, and again Shakespeare was working with a story which English writers (among them Chaucer) had helped to make familiar. A prose "argument," and a first stanza which starts the action well along in the plot, serve to curtail the narrative, and the 1855-line poem will really tell or show us only this: the inner struggles of Tarquin as he approaches Lucrece's bed; his threatening proposal, and her pleas and refusals; her lamentations, once she has been dishonored; her revelation of Tarquin's guilt to Collatine and others; her suicide, and the banishment of the Tarquins. A very large part of the poem consists of solitary lamentation by Lucrece, and it is undoubtedly true that Shakespeare was here creating a hybrid genre by combining a species of Ovidian narrative with the "complaint": it was probably from Daniel's *Complaint of Rosamond* (1593), in which the ghost of Henry II's unfortunate mistress asks our prayers and pity, that Shakespeare borrowed the stately 7-line stanza of *Lucrece*. At the same time, *Lucrece* greatly differs from *Rosamond*, the latter being a first-person account which offers neither scene nor dialogue until the poem is two-thirds done. Like *Venus*, *Lucrece* is narrated by the poet; it has access to the thoughts of its two principals, and consists in great part of rhetorical speeches which may at times suggest declamatory or Senecan drama, but seldom suggest that the poet has a future in the theatre. Critics agree that among the few moments of dramatic potentiality are those in which Lucrece countermands her agitated orders to her maid (1289 ff.) and misunderstands the blushes of her groom (1338 ff.). One also feels that the reunion of Lucrece and her husband might be touching on the stage:

> Both stood, like old acquaintance in a trance,
> Met far from home, wond'ring each other's chance.
>
> (1595–96)

Action in *Lucrece* is smothered in poetry, as when the concrete effect of Tarquin's lifted sword (505) is instantly blunted by a comparison; moreover, the action is given us in disjunct and unresolved tableaux. The sword is never lowered, and the hand remains indefinitely on the breast. Our mind's eye beholds not a cinematic continuity, but slides or tapestries which description may explore (as Lucrece explores her painting of Troy) or rhetoric at once forsake. Ideas are unimportant; the poet is not out to demonstrate the nature of chastity, or to confront the problem of evil in the world; his thought is conventional and can often be rendered by proverbs. Character in *Lucrece* is shallow, fixed, yet inconsistent, as in *Venus and Adonis*, and for the same reason: it is brilliance of the surface which has priority. Thus Tarquin is at first the "devil" to Lucrece's "saint" (85), but once alone and pondering he is provided with a better nature, so that he may be torn between conscience and lust; and this is done not for the sake of psychological revelation but for the provision of antithesis and rhetorical opportunity. Lucrece, when contemplating suicide, takes temporarily the Christian view of self-slaughter (1156 ff.) in order to divide herself for three stanzas. Divisions, vacillations, inward debates, anatomies of stimulus and response (426 ff.) and of psychic politics (288 ff.) – the poem is full of these things, and their main *raison d'être* is stylistic: they break down the characters and their thoughts into elements which can be balanced and elaborated.

The verse of *Lucrece* is even more obtrusively artificial than that of *Venus*, and its trickiness is somehow more difficult to like. Our first view of the heroine consists of a 28-line description of the "war of lilies and of roses" in her complexion (50–77), and its length and difficulty are exasperatingly disproportionate to the content. Perhaps the subject and initial tone of *Venus* make its extravagances – the egregious dimples of 241–48, for example – seem forgivably playful, while in a grave poem about rape and suicide such fiddling with red and white seems Neronian. There are, however, passages to admire, especially in the linked lamentations of Lucrece, which flow into each other with a smoothness worthy of Ovid. In contrast to Ovid and the Ovidians, Shakespeare makes little use, either in *Venus* or in *Lucrece*, of mythological reference, but when Lucrece invites Philomel to a duet (1128 ff.) a most obvious comparison of fates is made with the utmost freshness. And – to praise one passage more – Lucrece's contemplation of

the painting of Troy is far more than a standard Elizabethan descriptive exercise, written to occupy the interval between the sending of the scroll and Collatine's return. It is, for one thing, full of explicit and implicit relationships between Troy and Lucrece's Rome. We are to liken Ardea's siege to Troy's; Helen in her "rape" resembles Lucrece, but in her infidelity contrasts with her; Paris, like Tarquin, is a king's son who puts his "private pleasure" before the public good; Sinon, like Tarquin, is a dissimulator, and the entry of the Greek horse into Troy is like Tarquin's ill-intentioned entry into Collatine's house. The description is also relevant to Tarquin's moral collapse, in its several contrasts between displays of passion (such as anger or cowardice) and examples of "government" or control. Finally, the passage dwells considerably on the clear depiction and ready perception of character or emotion in physiognomy, and so builds throughout toward Lucrece's bitter reflection that such a face as Tarquin's can yet "bear a wicked mind."

I have left myself scarcely any space in which to speak of that strange and masterly metaphysical poem, "The Phoenix and Turtle." Published in 1601, the poem is a celebration of ideal love between two people, its perfect lovers being presented as symbolic birds, the phoenix and the turtledove. Poets have often made *ad hoc* revisions of mythology or conventional symbolism, and Shakespeare has done so here: while the turtledove keeps its accepted meaning of Constancy, the phoenix is assigned the feminine gender and is made to stand not for Immortality, as would be traditional, but for Love. These initial attributions, however, are in no way limiting, for since the two birds accomplish a total fusion of their natures, they have at last the one joint meaning of pure and imperishable love. The poem is undoubtedly indebted to other literary birdassemblies, such as Chaucer's *Parliament of Fowls*, but given the chaste and world-forsaking character of the love whereby they are translated "In a mutual flame from hence," I think that the lovers must owe something of their wingedness to the *Phaedrus*. There Plato describes the highest love as an absolute spiritual union through which the lovers' souls recover their lost wings, and "when the end comes . . . are light and winged for flight."

The first part of the poem, in which the phoenix and turtle go unmentioned, is a summons to the celebrants and worthy witnesses of their funeral rite. The second part, which begins at the sixth stanza, is an anthem of praise in which those assembled "chaste wings" approach the transcendent truth of ideal love by demonstrating the powerlessness of reason to describe it: that two souls should be one is an idea which defeats mathematics and logic, and forces language into violent paradox. The collective reason of the mourners, convinced by self-defeat that "Love hath reason, reason none," proceeds then to compose a "threne" or dirge which is the poem's third movement. In it, reason affirms that the lovers have embodied a truth which lies beyond reason, and which with their death is lost to the world; at the same time, in response to the spirit of renewal which concludes all obsequies, and to the phoenix's association with the idea of rebirth, the "true or fair" are quietly made heirs of the lovers' example.

The language of this poem is intellectually strict and dry; the rhythm is abrupt and rugged in the tetrameter quatrains, like that of a nursery rhyme, and just a shade more serene in the triplets of the *Threnos*. The product of this precise abstract language and these spirited trochaic lines is, for one reader at least, an impression of complete vitality. We need not ask, in this poem, what and how much is meant by predatory birds or by burning eyes; the meanings are strong and ultimately plain. The Platonic conception of love, which in *Venus and Adonis* was inchoate and momentary, is here sharply realized, and the gift of paradox, which in *Venus* and *Lucrece* was exercised for its own sake, here serves a theme which cannot be expressed without it.

Wesleyan University   RICHARD WILBUR

NOTE ON THE TEXTS

Venus and Adonis was first printed in quarto in 1593, and was often reprinted; *Lucrece* (with the head title *The Rape of Lucrece*) was first printed in quarto in 1594, and was reprinted a number of times, although less often than its predecessor. Both poems bear dedications to the Earl of Southampton subscribed "William Shakespeare," and both are well printed, probably from the author's fair copies. It is generally agreed that the later editions lack independent authority. "The Phoenix and Turtle" was first printed in a quarto of 1601: Robert Chester's *Love's Martyr,*

or Rosaline's Complaint, a volume containing, besides the quaint verses of Chester himself, variations upon the theme of the Phoenix and Turtle "by the best and chiefest of our modern writers, with their names subscribed to their particular works, never before extant. And now first consecrated by them all generally to the love and merit of the true-noble knight, Sir John Salisbury." Of the cluster of poems thus described, two are signed "Vatum Chorus," one "Ignoto," one "William Shake-speare," one "John Marston," one "George Chapman," and two "Ben Jonson." Although reprinted, the original quarto of 1601 is the sole authority for the text. The present edition of the three poems is based on the text of the original quartos, with the following material emendations. The adopted reading in italics is followed by the quarto reading in roman.

VENUS AND ADONIS 19 *satiety* society 147 *dishevelled* dishevellèd 358 *wooed* wooèd 366 *Showed* Showèd 432 *Ear's* Eares 616 *javelin's* iavelings 644 *Saw'st* Sawest 680 *overshoot* ouer-shut 754 *sons* suns 873 *twind* twin'd 940 *dost* doest 1003 *fault* fault, 1031 *as* are 1054 *was* had
THE RAPE OF LUCRECE (press-corrected Q) 23 *decayed* decayèd 50 *Collatium* (uncorrected Q) Colatia (corrected Q) 111 *heaved-up* heauèd-up 192, 392, 552 *unhallowed* vnhallowèd 395 *Showed* showèd 573, 1549 *borrowed* borrowèd 883 *mak'st* makest 884 *blow'st* blowest 1159 *swallowed* swallowèd 1416 *shadowed* shadowèd 1662 *wreathèd* wretchèd 1680 *one woe* on woe 1713 *in it* it in
The text and glossarial notes have been prepared by the general editor.

VENUS AND ADONIS

Vilia miretur vulgus : mihi flavus Apollo
Pocula Castalia plena ministret aqua.

TO THE RIGHT HONORABLE
HENRY WRIOTHESLEY
EARL OF SOUTHAMPTON, AND BARON OF TITCHFIELD

RIGHT HONORABLE,

I know not how I shall offend in dedicating my unpolished lines to your Lordship,
nor how the world will censure me for choosing so strong a prop to support so weak a
burden; only, if your Honor seem but pleased, I account myself highly praised, and
vow to take advantage of all idle hours, till I have honored you with some graver labor.
But if the first heir of my invention prove deformed, I shall be sorry it had so noble a
godfather, and never after ear so barren a land, for fear it yield me still so bad a
harvest. I leave it to your honorable survey, and your Honor to your heart's content;
which I wish may always answer your own wish and the world's hopeful expectation.

Your Honor's in all duty,
WILLIAM SHAKESPEARE

Even as the sun with purple-colored face
Had ta'en his last leave of the weeping morn,
Rose-cheeked Adonis hied him to the chase.
Hunting he loved, but love he laughed to scorn.
5   Sick-thoughted Venus makes amain unto him
And like a bold-faced suitor 'gins to woo him.

'Thrice fairer than myself,' thus she began,
'The field's chief flower, sweet above compare,
9 Stain to all nymphs, more lovely than a man,
More white and red than doves or roses are,
11 Nature that made thee, with herself at strife,
Saith that the world hath ending with thy life.

'Vouchsafe, thou wonder, to alight thy steed,
And rein his proud head to the saddlebow.
If thou wilt deign this favor, for thy meed
A thousand honey secrets shalt thou know.
Here come and sit, where never serpent hisses
And being set, I'll smother thee with kisses.

'And yet not cloy thy lips with loathed satiety,
But rather famish them amid their plenty,
21 Making them red and pale with fresh variety –
Ten kisses short as one, one long as twenty.
A summer's day will seem an hour but short,
24   Being wasted in such time-beguiling sport.'

25 With this she seizeth on his sweating palm,
26 The precedent of pith and livelihood,
And trembling in her passion, calls it balm,
Earth's sovereign salve to do a goddess good.
29   Being so enraged, desire doth lend her force
Courageously to pluck him from his horse.

Over one arm the lusty courser's rein,
Under her other was the tender boy,
Who blushed and pouted in a dull disdain,
With leaden appetite, unapt to toy;
She red and hot as coals of glowing fire,
He red for shame, but frosty in desire.

The studded bridle on a ragged bough
Nimbly she fastens. O, how quick is love!
The steed is stallèd up, and even now
To tie the rider she begins to prove.   40
Backward she pushed him, as she would be thrust,
And governed him in strength, though not in lust.

So soon was she along as he was down,   43
Each leaning on their elbows and their hips.
Now doth she stroke his cheek, now doth he frown
And 'gins to chide; but soon she stops his lips
And kissing speaks, with lustful language broken,
'If thou wilt chide, thy lips shall never open.'

Vilia . . . aqua (from Ovid's *Amores*, I, xv, 35–36: Let the cheap dazzle
the crowd; for me, may golden Apollo minister full cups from the Cas-
talian spring) **Ded.**, 2 *Henry Wriothesley* third Earl of Southampton,
1573–1624, a favorite at the court of Elizabeth until imprisoned, 1601–03,
for complicity in the Essex Rebellion 9 *first . . . invention* i.e. first work of
literary pretensions? (since a number of plays had already been written)
10 *ear* cultivate, till
1 *purple-colored* i.e. crimson ('purple' being used for a considerable range
of colors) 5 *Sick-thoughted* i.e. suffering from love-melancholy 9 *Stain
. . . nymphs* i.e. making all nymphs suffer by comparison 11 *with . . .
strife* i.e. striving to outdo herself 21 *Making . . . pale* i.e. alternately
suffused with and drained of blood 24 *wasted* spent 25 *sweating* i.e.
not parched, youthful 26 *precedent* promise, sign; *pith and livelihood*
strength and vitality 29 *enraged* aroused 40 *prove* try 43 *along* beside
him

He burns with bashful shame; she with her tears
Doth quench the maiden burning of his cheeks.
Then with her windy sighs and golden hairs
To fan and blow them dry again she seeks.
53   He saith she is immodest, blames her miss;
    What follows more she murders with a kiss.

55 Even as an empty eagle, sharp by fast,
56 Tires with her beak on feathers, flesh, and bone,
Shaking her wings, devouring all in haste,
Till either gorge be stuffed or prey be gone –
    Even so she kissed his brow, his cheek, his chin,
    And where she ends she doth anew begin.

61 Forced to content, but never to obey,
Panting he lies and breatheth in her face.
She feedeth on the steam as on a prey
And calls it heavenly moisture, air of grace,
    Wishing her cheeks were gardens full of flowers,
    So they were dewed with such distilling showers.

Look how a bird lies tangled in a net,
So fast'ned in her arms Adonis lies.
69 Pure shame and awed resistance made him fret,
Which bred more beauty in his angry eyes.
71   Rain added to a river that is rank
    Perforce will force it overflow the bank.

Still she entreats, and prettily entreats,
74 For to a pretty ear she tunes her tale.
Still is he sullen, still he low'rs and frets,
'Twixt crimson shame and anger ashy-pale.
    Being red, she loves him best; and being white,
78   Her best is bettered with a more delight.

Look how he can, she cannot choose but love;
And by her fair immortal hand she swears
From his soft bosom never to remove
82 Till he take truce with her contending tears,
    Which long have rained, making her cheeks all wet;
84   And one sweet kiss shall pay this comptless debt.

Upon this promise did he raise his chin,
86 Like a divedapper peering through a wave,
Who, being looked on, ducks as quickly in.
So offers he to give what she did crave;
    But when her lips were ready for his pay,
90 He winks and turns his lips another way.

Never did passenger in summer's heat   91
More thirst for drink than she for this good turn.
Her help she sees, but help she cannot get;
She bathes in water, yet her fire must burn.
    'O, pity,' 'gan she cry, 'flint-hearted boy!
    'Tis but a kiss I beg – why are thou coy?

'I have been wooed, as I entreat thee now,
Even by the stern and direful god of war,
Whose sinewy neck in battle ne'er did bow,
Who conquers where he comes in every jar;   100
    Yet hath he been my captive and my slave,
    And begged for that which thou unasked shalt have.

'Over my altars hath he hung his lance,
His batt'red shield, his uncontrollèd crest,   104
And for my sake hath learned to sport and dance,
To toy, to wanton, dally, smile, and jest,
    Scorning his churlish drum and ensign red,
    Making my arms his field, his tent my bed.

'Thus he that overruled I overswayèd,
Leading him prisoner in a red-rose chain.
Strong-tempered steel his stronger strength obeyèd;
Yet was he servile to my coy disdain.
    O, be not proud, nor brag not of thy might,
    For mast'ring her that foiled the god of fight!

'Touch but my lips with those fair lips of thine –
Though mine be not so fair, yet are they red –
The kiss shall be thine own as well as mine.
What seest thou in the ground? Hold up thy head.
    Look in mine eyeballs, there thy beauty lies,
    Then why not lips on lips, since eyes in eyes?

'Art thou ashamed to kiss? Then wink again,   121
And I will wink – so shall the day seem night.   122
Love keeps his revels where there are but twain.
Be bold to play; our sport is not in sight.   124
    These blue-veined violets whereon we lean
    Never can blab, nor know not what we mean.   126

'The tender spring upon thy tempting lip   127
Shows thee unripe; yet mayst thou well be tasted.
Make use of time, let not advantage slip;   129
Beauty within itself should not be wasted.   130
    Fair flowers that are not gath'red in their prime
    Rot and consume themselves in little time.

'Were I hard-favored, foul, or wrinkled old,   133
Ill-nurtured, crooked, churlish, harsh in voice,
O'erworn, despised, rheumatic, and cold,   135
Thick-sighted, barren, lean and lacking juice   136
    Then mightst thou pause, for then I were not for thee;
    But having no defects, why dost abhor me?

'Thou canst not see one wrinkle in my brow;
Mine eyes are grey and bright and quick in turning;   140
My beauty as the spring doth yearly grow,
My flesh is soft and plump, my marrow burning;
    My smooth moist hand, were it with thy hand felt,
    Would in thy palm dissolve or seem to melt.

53 *miss* misbehavior 55 *sharp by fast* hungry from fasting 56 *Tires* preys hungrily 61 *content* i.e. put up with it 69 *awed* overborne 71 *rank* teeming 74 *ear* (punning on 'air') 78 *more* greater 82 *take truce* make peace 84 *comptless* countless 86 *divedapper* dabchick, little grebe 90 *winks* shuts his eyes 91 *passenger* wayfarer 100 *jar* fight 104 *uncontrollèd crest* unbowed helmet 121, 122 *wink* shut eyes 124 *not in sight* i.e. unseen 126 *blab* tell tales; *nor know not* i.e. or know; *mean* intend to do 127 *tender spring* i.e. light down 129 *advantage* opportunity 130 *within itself* i.e. buried in itself 133 *foul* ugly 135 *O'erworn* jaded 136 *Thick-sighted* dull of sight 140 *grey* (used of a range of iris-coloring which included blue)

'Bid me discourse, I will enchant thine ear,
Or, like a fairy, trip upon the green,
Or, like a nymph, with long dishevelled hair,
148 Dance on the sands, and yet no footing seen.
149　Love is a spirit all compact of fire,
　　Not gross to sink, but light, and will aspire.

'Witness this primrose bank whereon I lie;
152 These forceless flowers like sturdy trees support me.
Two strengthless doves will draw me through the sky
From morn till night, even where I list to sport me.
　　Is love so light, sweet boy, and may it be
　　That thou should think it heavy unto thee?

157 'Is thine own heart to thine own face affected?
158 Can thy right hand seize love upon thy left?
Then woo thyself, be of thyself rejected;
Steal thine own freedom, and complain on theft.
161　Narcissus so himself himself forsook.
　　And died to kiss his shadow in the brook.

'Torches are made to light, jewels to wear,
Dainties to taste, fresh beauty for the use,
Herbs for their smell, and sappy plants to bear.
166 Things growing to themselves are growth's abuse.
　　Seeds spring from seeds, and beauty breedeth beauty.
　　Thou wast begot; to get it is thy duty.

169 'Upon the earth's increase why shouldst thou feed
Unless the earth with thy increase be fed?
By law of nature thou art bound to breed,
That thine may live when thou thyself art dead;
　　And so, in spite of death, thou dost survive,
　　In that thy likeness still is left alive.'

By this, the lovesick queen began to sweat,
For where they lay the shadow had forsook them,
177 And Titan, tirèd in the midday heat,
With burning eye did hotly over-look them,
　　Wishing Adonis had his team to guide,
180　So he were like him, and by Venus' side.

181 And now Adonis, with a lazy sprite,
And with a heavy, dark, disliking eye,
His low'ring brows o'erwhelming his fair sight,
Like misty vapors when they blot the sky,
　　Souring his cheeks, cries, 'Fie, no more of love!
　　The sun doth burn my face – I must remove.'

'Ay me,' quoth Venus, 'young, and so unkind?
What bare excuses mak'st thou to be gone!
I'll sigh celestial breath, whose gentle wind
Shall cool the heat of this descending sun.
　　I'll make a shadow for thee of my hairs;
　　If they burn too, I'll quench them with my tears.

'The sun that shines from heaven shines but warm;
And, lo, I lie between that sun and thee.
The heat I have from thence doth little harm;
Thine eye darts forth the fire that burneth me,
　　And were I not immortal, life were done
　　Between this heavenly and earthly sun.

'Art thou obdurate, flinty, hard as steel?
Nay, more than flint, for stone at rain relenteth. 200
Art thou a woman's son, and canst not feel
What 'tis to love? how want of love tormenteth?
　　O, had thy mother borne so hard a mind,
　　She had not brought forth thee, but died unkind.

'What am I that thou shouldst contemn me this? 205
Or what great danger dwells upon my suit? 206
What were thy lips the worse for one poor kiss?
Speak, fair, but speak fair words or else be mute.
　　Give me one kiss, I'll give it thee again,
　　And one for int'rest, if thou wilt have twain.

'Fie, liveless picture, cold and senseless stone,
Well-painted idol, image dull and dead,
Statue contenting but the eye alone,
Thing like a man, but of no woman bred!
　　Thou art no man, though of a man's complexion,
　　For men will kiss even by their own direction.' 216

This said, impatience chokes her pleading tongue,
And swelling passion doth provoke a pause;
Red cheeks and fiery eyes blaze forth her wrong:
Being judge in love, she cannot right her cause, 220
　　And now she weeps, and now she fain would speak,
　　And now her sobs do her intendments break. 222

Sometime she shakes her head, and then his hand;
Now gazeth she on him, now on the ground;
Sometime her arms infold him like a band –
She would, he will not in her arms be bound;
　　And when from thence he struggles to be gone,
　　She locks her lily fingers one in one.

'Fondling,' she saith, 'since I have hemmed thee here 229
Within the circuit of this ivory pale, 230
I'll be a park, and thou shalt be my deer: 231
Feed where thou wilt, on mountain or in dale;
　　Graze on my lips; and if those hills be dry,
　　Stray lower, where the pleasant fountains lie.

'Within this limit is relief enough, 235
Sweet bottom-grass, and high delightful plain, 236
Round rising hillocks, brakes obscure and rough, 237
To shelter thee from tempest and from rain.
　　Then be my deer, since I am such a park.
　　No dog shall rouse thee, though a thousand bark.' 240

148 *footing* footprint 149 *compact* composed 152 *forceless* without strength 157 *affected* devoted 158 *upon thy left* i.e. by clasping your left hand 161 *Narcissus* in classical myth, the youth in love with his own image and transformed into the narcissus 166 *to* for (i.e. with no other purpose but growth) 169 *increase* harvest 177 *Titan* the sun-god; *tirèd* attired 180 *he* i.e. Titan 181 *lazy sprite* dull spirit 200 *relenteth* yields, is worn away 205 *this* thus (old form) 206 *dwells upon* attends 216 *by . . . direction* i.e. without prompting 220 *Being . . . cause* i.e. Venus, although presiding over the court of love, cannot obtain a favorable verdict in her own case 222 *do . . . break* frustrate her intentions 229 *Fondling* fondled one, darling (?), cause of infatuation (?) 230 *pale* fence 231 *park* deer-preserve 235 *limit* boundary 236 *bottom-grass* valley-grass 237 *brakes* thickets 240 *rouse* start

At this Adonis smiles as in disdain,
242 That in each cheek appears a pretty dimple.
243 Love made those hollows, if himself were slain,
244 He might be buried in a tomb so simple,
    Foreknowing well, if there he came to lie,
    Why, there Love lived, and there he could not die.

These lovely caves, these round enchanting pits,
Opened their mouths to swallow Venus' liking.
249 Being mad before, how doth she now for wits?
Struck dead at first, what needs a second striking?
251   Poor queen of love, in thine own law forlorn,
    To love a cheek that smiles at thee in scorn!

Now which way shall she turn? what shall she say?
Her words are done, her woes the more increasing;
The time is spent, her object will away,
And from her twining arms doth urge releasing.
257 'Pity!' she cries, 'Some favor, some remorse!'
    Away he springs and hasteth to his horse.

But, lo, from forth a copse that neighbors by
260 A breeding jennet, lusty, young, and proud,
Adonis' trampling courser doth espy,
And forth she rushes, snorts, and neighs aloud.
    The strong-necked steed, being tied unto a tree,
    Breaketh his rein, and to her straight goes he.

Imperiously he leaps, he neighs, he bounds,
And now his woven girths he breaks asunder;
267 The bearing earth with his hard hoof he wounds,
Whose hollow womb resounds like heaven's thunder;
    The iron bit he crusheth 'tween his teeth,
    Controlling what he was controllèd with.

His ears up-pricked; his braided hanging mane
272 Upon his compassed crest now stand on end;
His nostrils drink the air, and forth again,
As from a furnace, vapors doth he send;
275   His eye, which scornfully glisters like fire,
276   Shows his hot courage and his high desire.

277 Sometime he trots, as if he told the steps,
With gentle majesty and modest pride;
Anon he rears upright, curvets, and leaps,
As who should say, 'Lo, thus my strength is tried,
    And this I do to captivate the eye
    Of the fair breeder that is standing by.'

What recketh he his rider's angry stir, 283
His flattering 'Holla' or his 'Stand, I say'? 284
What cares he now for curb or pricking spur?
For rich caparisons or trappings gay?
    He sees his love, and nothing else he sees,
    For nothing else with his proud sight agrees.

Look when a painter would surpass the life 289
In limning out a well-proportionèd steed, 290
His art with nature's workmanship at strife,
As if the dead the living should exceed – 292
    So did this horse excel a common one
    In shape, in courage, color, pace, and bone. 294

Round-hoofed, short-jointed, fetlocks shag and long, 295
Broad breast, full eye, small head, and nostril wide,
High crest, short ears, straight legs and passing strong, 297
Thin mane, thick tail, broad buttock, tender hide:
    Look what a horse should have he did not lack, 299
    Save a proud rider on so proud a back.

Sometimes he scuds far off, and there he stares;
Anon he starts at stirring of a feather;
To bid the wind a base he now prepares, 303
And where he run or fly they know not whether, 304
    For through his mane and tail the high wind sings,
    Fanning the hairs, who wave like feath'red wings.

He looks upon his love and neighs unto her;
She answers him, as if she knew his mind.
Being proud, as females are, to see him woo her,
She puts on outward strangeness, seems unkind, 310
    Spurns at his love and scorns the heat he feels,
    Beating his kind embracements with her heels.

Then, like a melancholy malcontent,
He vails his tail, that, like a falling plume, 314
Cool shadow to his melting buttock lent;
He stamps, and bites the poor flies in his fume. 316
    His love, perceiving how he is enragèd,
    Grew kinder, and his fury was assuaged.

His testy master goeth about to take him,
When, lo, the unbacked breeder, full of fear, 320
Jealous of catching, swiftly doth forsake him, 321
With her the horse, and left Adonis there. 322
    As they were mad, unto the woods they hie them,
    Outstripping crows that strive to overfly them. 324

All swol'n with chafing, down Adonis sits,
Banning his boist'rous and unruly beast; 326
And now the happy season once more fits
That lovesick Love by pleading may be blest; 328
    For lovers say the heart hath treble wrong
    When it is barred the aidance of the tongue.

An oven that is stopped, or river stayed, 331
Burneth more hotly, swelleth with more rage;
So of concealèd sorrow may be said:
Free vent of words love's fire doth assuage;
    But when the heart's attorney once is mute, 335
    The client breaks, as desperate in his suit. 336

242 *That* so that 243 *if* so that if 244 *tomb* i.e. grave 249 *how . . . wits* i.e. how keep her sanity now 251 *in . . . forlorn* wretched under your own rule (of love) 257 *remorse* pity 260 *jennet* small Spanish horse 267 *bearing* receiving 272 *compassed* arched 275 *scornfully glisters* (perhaps transposed by printer) 276 *courage* passion 277 *told* counted 283 *stir* bustle 284 *flattering* soothing 289 *Look when* as when 290 *limning out* portraying 292 *dead* i.e. lifeless image 294 *bone* frame 295 *shag* bushy 297 *crest* ridge of the neck 299 *Look what* whatever 303 *bid . . . base* i.e. challenge the wind to outrun him or be taken prisoner (as in game of prisoner's base) 304 *where* whether 310 *outward strangeness* show of coyness 314 *vails* lowers 316 *fume* rage 320 *unbacked* unridden, unbroken 321 *Jealous of catching* fearful of being caught 322 *horse* i.e. stallion 324 *overfly them* i.e. remain over them in flight 326 *Banning* cursing 328 *Love* i.e. Venus 331 *stopped* i.e. with door closed; *stayed* i.e. dammed 335 *attorney* pleader 336 *breaks* goes bankrupt

He sees her coming and begins to glow,
Even as a dying coal revives with wind,
And with his bonnet hides his angry brow,
Looks on the dull earth with disturbèd mind,
 Taking no notice that she is so nigh,
 For all askance he holds her in his eye.

343 O, what a sight it was, wistly to view
How she came stealing to the wayward boy!
To note the fighting conflict of her hue,
How white and red each other did destroy!
 But now her cheek was pale, and by and by
 It flashed forth fire, as lightning from the sky.

Now was she just before him as he sat,
And like a lowly lover down she kneels;
With one fair hand she heaveth up his hat,
Her other tender hand his fair cheek feels.
 His tend'rer cheek receives her soft hand's print
354 As apt as new-fall'n snow takes any dint.

O, what a war of looks was then between them,
Her eyes petitioners to his eyes suing!
357 His eyes saw her eyes as they had not seen them;
Her eyes wooed still, his eyes disdained the wooing;
359 And all this dumb play had his acts made plain
360 With tears which chorus-like her eyes did rain.

Full gently now she takes him by the hand,
A lily prisoned in a jail of snow,
363 Or ivory in an alablaster band –
So white a friend engirts so white a foe.
 This beauteous combat, willful and unwilling,
 Showed like two silver doves that sit a-billing.

367 Once more the engine of her thoughts began:
368 'O fairest mover on this mortal round,
Would thou wert as I am, and I a man,
370 My heart all whole as thine, thy heart my wound!
 For one sweet look thy help I would assure thee,
372 Though nothing but my body's bane would cure thee.'

'Give me my hand,' saith he. 'Why dost thou feel it?'
'Give me my heart,' saith she, 'and thou shalt have it.
375 O, give it me, lest thy hard heart do steel it,
376 And being steeled, soft sighs can never grave it.
 Then love's deep groans I never shall regard,
 Because Adonis' heart hath made mine hard.'

'For shame!' he cries. 'Let go, and let me go:
My day's delight is past, my horse is gone,
And 'tis your fault I am bereft him so.
I pray you hence, and leave me here alone;
 For all my mind, my thought, my busy care
 Is how to get my palfrey from the mare.'

Thus she replies: 'Thy palfrey, as he should,
Welcomes the warm approach of sweet desire.
387 Affection is a coal that must be cooled;
388 Else, suffered, it will set the heart on fire.
 The sea hath bounds, but deep desire hath none;
 Therefore no marvel though thy horse be gone.

'How like a jade he stood, tied to the tree,
Servilely mastered with a leathern rein;
But when he saw his love, his youth's fair fee, 393
He held such petty bondage in disdain,
 Throwing the base thong from his bending crest,
 Enfranchising his mouth, his back, his breast. 396

'Who sees his true-love in her naked bed,
Teaching the sheets a whiter hue than white,
But, when his glutton eye so full hath fed,
His other agents aim at like delight? 400
 Who is so faint that dares not be so bold
 To touch the fire, the weather being cold?

'Let me excuse thy courser, gentle boy;
And learn of him, I heartily beseech thee,
To take advantage on presented joy.
Though I were dumb, yet his proceedings teach thee.
 O, learn to love! The lesson is but plain,
 And once made perfect, never lost again.'

'I know not love,' quoth he, 'nor will not know it,
Unless it be a boar, and then I chase it.
'Tis much to borrow, and I will not owe it. 411
My love to love is love but to disgrace it; 412
 For I have heard it is a life in death,
 That laughs, and weeps, and all but with a breath. 414

'Who wears a garment shapeless and unfinished?
Who plucks the bud before one leaf put forth?
If springing things be any jot diminished, 417
They wither in their prime, prove nothing worth.
 The colt that's backed and burdened being young 419
 Loseth his pride and never waxeth strong.

'You hurt my hand with wringing. Let us part,
And leave this idle theme, this bootless chat. 422
Remove your siege from my unyielding heart;
To love's alarms it will not ope the gate. 424
 Dismiss your vows, your feignèd tears, your flatt'ry;
 For where a heart is hard they make no batt'ry.' 426

'What! canst thou talk?' quoth she. 'Hast thou a tongue?
O, would thou hadst not, or I had no hearing!
Thy mermaid's voice hath done me double wrong; 429
I had my load before, now pressed with bearing: 430
 Melodious discord, heavenly tune harsh sounding,
 Ear's deep-sweet music, and heart's deep-sore wounding.

343 *wistly* intently   354 *dint* impression   357 *as* as if   359 *dumb play* dumbshow, wordless drama; *his* its   360 *chorus-like* i.e. as a commentary   363 *band* bond   367 *engine* instrument, i.e. tongue   368 *mortal round* i.e. earth   370 *my wound* i.e. wounded like mine   372 *bane* death by poison   375 *steel* turn to steel   376 *grave* engrave   387 *Affection* passion   388 *suffered* disregarded   393 *fair fee* due reward   396 *Enfranchising* setting free   400 *agents* organs   411 *borrow* take on as an obligation; *owe* own, have   412 *My . . . it* i.e. my only feeling about love is the desire to belittle it   414 *all but with a* all but in one   417 *springing* sprouting   419 *backed* ridden   422 *bootless* profitless   424 *alarms* attacks   426 *batt'ry* forced entrance   429 *mermaid's* siren's   430 *pressed* oppressed, weighted down

'Had I no eyes but ears, my ears would love
That inward beauty and invisible;
Or were I deaf, thy outward parts would move
436 Each part in me that were but sensible.
  Though neither eyes nor ears, to hear nor see,
  Yet should I be in love by touching thee.

'Say that the sense of feeling were bereft me,
And that I could not see, nor hear, nor touch,
And nothing but the very smell were left me,
Yet would my love to thee be still as much;
443 For from the stillitory of thy face excelling
  Comes breath perfumed that breedeth love by smelling.

'But, O, what banquet wert thou to the taste,
Being nurse and feeder of the other four!
Would they not wish the feast might ever last
448 And bid Suspicion double-lock the door,
  Lest Jealousy, that sour unwelcome guest,
  Should by his stealing in disturb the feast?'

Once more the ruby-colored portal opened
452 Which to his speech did honey passage yield;
Like a red morn, that ever yet betokened
Wrack to the seaman, tempest to the field,
  Sorrow to shepherds, woe unto the birds,
456 Gusts and foul flaws to herdmen and to herds.

This ill presage advisedly she marketh.
Even as the wind is hushed before it raineth,
459 Or as the wolf doth grin before he barketh,
Or as the berry breaks before it staineth,
  Or like the deadly bullet of a gun,
  His meaning struck her ere his words begun.

And at his look she flatly falleth down,
For looks kill love, and love by looks reviveth;
465 A smile recures the wounding of a frown.
466 But blessèd bankrout that by loss so thriveth!
467 The silly boy, believing she is dead,
  Claps her pale cheek till clapping makes it red,

And all amazed brake off his late intent,
For sharply he did think to reprehend her,
471 Which cunning love did wittily prevent.
472 Fair fall the wit that can so well defend her!
  For on the grass she lies as she were slain
  Till his breath breatheth life in her again.

He wrings her nose, he strikes her on the cheeks,
He bends her finger, holds her pulses hard,
He chafes her lips; a thousand ways he seeks
To mend the hurt that his unkindness marred. 478
  He kisses her; and she, by her good will,
  Will never rise, so he will kiss her still.

The night of sorrow now is turned to day:
Her two blue windows faintly she upheaveth, 482
Like the fair sun when in his fresh array
He cheers the morn and all the earth relieveth;
  And as the bright sun glorifies the sky,
  So is her face illumined with her eye;

Whose beams upon his hairless face are fixed,
As if from thence they borrowèd all their shine.
Were never four such lamps together mixed,
Had not his clouded with his brow's repine; 490
  But hers, which through the crystal tears gave light,
  Shone like the moon in water seen by night.

'O, where am I?' quoth she, 'in earth or heaven,
Or in the ocean drenched, or in the fire?
What hour is this? or morn or weary even? 494
Do I delight to die, or life desire?
  But now I lived, and life was death's annoy;
  But now I died, and death was lively joy. 497

'O, thou didst kill me, kill me once again!
Thy eyes' shrewd tutor, that hard heart of thine,
Hath taught them scornful tricks, and such disdain 500
That they have murd'red this poor heart of mine;
  And these mine eyes, true leaders to their queen,
  But for thy piteous lips no more had seen. 503

'Long may they kiss each other, for this cure!
O, never let their crimson liveries wear; 506
And as they last, their verdure still endure, 507
To drive infection from the dangerous year;
  That the stargazers, having writ on death,
  May say the plague is banished by thy breath. 509

'Pure lips, sweet seals in my soft lips imprinted,
What bargains may I make, still to be sealing?
To sell myself I can be well contented, 512
So thou wilt buy, and pay, and use good dealing;
  Which purchase if thou make, for fear of slips
  Set thy seal manual on my wax-red lips. 515

'A thousand kisses buys my heart from me;
And pay them at thy leisure, one by one.
What is ten hundred touches unto thee?
Are they not quickly told and quickly gone? 519
  Say for nonpayment that the debt should double, 520
  Is twenty hundred kisses such a trouble?'

'Fair queen,' quoth he, 'if any love you owe me, 523
Measure my strangeness with my unripe years. 524
Before I know myself, seek not to know me.
No fisher but the ungrown fry forbears. 526
  The mellow plum doth fall, the green sticks fast,
  Or being early plucked is sour to taste.

436 *sensible* sensitive to impressions 443 *stillitory* still 448 *Suspicion* caution 452 *honey* honeyed, sweet 456 *flaws* squalls 459 *grin* bare its teeth 465 *recures* cures 466 *bankrout* bankrupt 467 *silly* unsophisticated 471 *wittily* cleverly 472 *Fair fall* fair fortune befall 478 *marred* i.e. inflicted (in a forced antithesis with 'mended') 482 *blue windows* i.e. eyelids 490 *repine* repining, dissatisfaction 494 *drenched* immersed 497 *annoy* harm 500 *shrewd* sharp 503 *queen* i.e. the heart 506 *liveries* vestments; *wear* wear out 507 *verdure* fresh foliage (such as was brought indoors as a fumigant) 509 *stargazers . . . death* i.e. astrologers having predicted an epidemic 512 *still* so as always 515 *slips* errors 519 *touches* i.e. kisses 520 *told* counted 523 *owe* bear 524 *Measure . . . with* i.e. account for my reserve by 526 *fry* fish

529 'Look, the world's comforter, with weary gait,
His day's hot task hath ended in the west;
The owl, night's herald, shrieks; 'tis very late;
The sheep are gone to fold, birds to their nest,
    And coal-black clouds that shadow heaven's light
    Do summon us to part and bid good night.

'Now let me say "Good night," and so say you.
If you will say so, you shall have a kiss.'
'Good night,' quoth she; and, ere he says 'Adieu,'
The honey fee of parting tend'red is:
    Her arms do lend his neck a sweet embrace;
540   Incorporate then they seem; face grows to face;

541 Till breathless he disjoined, and backward drew
The heavenly moisture, that sweet coral mouth,
Whose precious taste her thirsty lips well knew,
Whereon they surfeit, yet complain on drouth.
545   He with her plenty pressed, she faint with dearth,
    Their lips together glued, fall to the earth.

Now quick desire hath caught the yielding prey,
And glutton-like she feeds, yet never filleth.
Her lips are conquerors, his lips obey,
550 Paying what ransom the insulter willeth;
551   Whose vulture thought doth pitch the price so high
    That she will draw his lips' rich treasure dry.

And having felt the sweetness of the spoil,
With blindfold fury she begins to forage.
555 Her face doth reek and smoke, her blood doth boil,
And careless lust stirs up a desperate courage,
557   Planting oblivion, beating reason back,
558   Forgetting shame's pure blush and honor's wrack.

Hot, faint, and weary with her hard embracing,
Like a wild bird being tamed with too much handling,
Or as the fleet-foot roe that's tired with chasing,
562 Or like the froward infant stilled with dandling,
    He now obeys and now no more resisteth,
564   While she takes all she can, not all she listeth.

565 What wax so frozen but dissolves with temp'ring
And yields at last to every light impression?
567 Things out of hope are compassed oft with vent'ring,
568 Chiefly in love, whose leave exceeds commission.
569   Affection faints not like a pale-faced coward,
570   But then woos best when most his choice is froward.

When he did frown, O, had she then gave over,
Such nectar from his lips she had not sucked.
573 Foul words and frowns must not repel a lover.
What though the rose have prickles, yet 'tis plucked.
    Were beauty under twenty locks kept fast,
    Yet love breaks through and picks them all at last.

For pity now she can no more detain him;
578 The poor fool prays her that he may depart.
She is resolved no longer to restrain him;
Bids him farewell, and look well to her heart,
    The which, by Cupid's bow she doth protest,
    He carries thence incagèd in his breast.

'Sweet boy,' she says, 'this night I'll waste in sorrow,   583
For my sick heart commands mine eyes to watch.   584
Tell me, love's master, shall we meet to-morrow?
Say, shall we? shall we? wilt thou make the match?'
    He tells her no; to-morrow he intends
    To hunt the boar with certain of his friends.

'The boar!' quoth she; whereat a sudden pale,   589
Like lawn being spread upon the blushing rose,
Usurps her cheek; she trembles at his tale,
And on his neck her yoking arms she throws;
    She sinketh down, still hanging by his neck,
    He on her belly falls, she on her back.

Now is she in the very lists of love,   595
Her champion mounted for the hot encounter.
All is imaginary she doth prove,   597
He will not manage her, although he mount her;   598
    That worse than Tantalus' is her annoy,   599
    To clip Elysium and to lack her joy.   600

Even so poor birds, deceived with painted grapes,
Do surfeit by the eye and pine the maw;   602
Even so she languisheth in her mishaps
As those poor birds that helpless berries saw.
    The warm effects which she in him finds missing   605
    She seeks to kindle with continual kissing.

But all in vain. Good Queen, it will not be!
She hath assayed as much as may be proved.   608
Her pleading hath deserved a greater fee:
She's Love, she loves, and yet she is not loved.
    'Fie, fie!' he says. 'You crush me; let me go!
    You have no reason to withhold me so.'

'Thou hadst been gone,' quoth she, 'sweet boy, ere this,
But that thou told'st me thou wouldst hunt the boar.
O, be advised, thou know'st not what it is
With javelin's point a churlish swine to gore,
    Whose tushes never sheathed he whetteth still,   617
    Like to a mortal butcher bent to kill.   618

'On his bow-back he hath a battle set
Of bristly pikes that ever threat his foes;
His eyes like glowworms shine when he doth fret;
His snout digs sepulchres where'er he goes;
    Being moved, he strikes whate'er is in his way,   623
    And whom he strikes his crooked tushes slay.

529 *world's comforter* i.e. the sun 540 *Incorporate* joined in a single body 541 *disjoined* i.e. ended the incorporate state 545 *pressed* oppressed 550 *insulter* i.e. triumphant winner 551 *vulture* i.e. ravenous 555 *reek* i.e. steam 557 *Planting oblivion* i.e. implanting blind disregard of consequences 558 *wrack* wreck 562 *froward* fretful 564 *listeth* wishes 565 *temp'ring* heating 567 *out of* beyond; *compassed* accomplished; *vent'ring* venturing 568 *leave . . . commission* i.e. liberties exceed permission 569 *Affection* passion 570 *when . . . froward* i.e. when the object of his desire is most stubborn 573 *Foul* hostile 578 *fool* plaything 583 *waste* spend 584 *watch* remain open 589 *pale* pallor 595 *lists* field of combat 597 *prove* experience 598 *manage* ride 599 *That . . . annoy* i.e. so that her torment exceeds that of Tantalus (punished in Hades by sight of unobtainable food and drink) 600 *clip* embrace; *Elysium* pagan paradise (here Adonis) 602 *pine the maw* starve the stomach 605 *effects* symptoms 608 *assayed* tried; *proved* tried 617 *tushes* tusks 618 *mortal* deadly 623 *moved* angered

'His brawny sides, with hairy bristles armèd,
626 Are better proof than thy spear's point can enter;
His short thick neck cannot be easily harmèd;
628 Being ireful, on the lion he will venter.
    The thorny brambles and embracing bushes,
    As fearful of him, part; through whom he rushes.

'Alas, he naught esteems that face of thine,
To which Love's eyes pays tributary gazes;
633 Nor thy soft hands, sweet lips, and crystal eyne,
Whose full perfection all the world amazes;
635   But having thee at vantage (wondrous dread!)
636   Would root these beauties as he roots the mead.

637 'O, let him keep his loathsome cabin still:
638 Beauty hath naught to do with such foul fiends.
639 Come not within his danger by thy will:
They that thrive well take counsel of their friends.
    When thou didst name the boar, not to dissemble,
    I feared thy fortune, and my joints did tremble.

'Didst thou not mark my face? Was it not white?
Saw'st thou not signs of fear lurk in mine eye?
645 Grew I not faint? and fell I not downright?
Within my bosom, whereon thou dost lie,
647   My boding heart pants, beats, and takes no rest,
    But, like an earthquake, shakes thee on my breast.

649 'For where Love reigns, disturbing Jealousy
Doth call himself Affection's sentinel,
651 Gives false alarms, suggesteth mutiny,
And in a peaceful hour doth cry "Kill, kill!"
653   Distemp'ring gentle Love in his desire,
    As air and water do abate the fire.

655 'This sour informer, this bate-breeding spy,
656 This canker that eats up Love's tender spring,
This carry-tale, dissentious Jealousy,
That sometime true news, sometime false doth bring,
    Knocks at my heart, and whispers in mine ear
    That if I love thee, I thy death should fear;

'And more than so, presenteth to mine eye
The picture of an angry-chafing boar,
Under whose sharp fangs on his back doth lie
An image like thyself, all stained with gore;
    Whose blood upon the fresh flowers being shed
    Doth make them droop with grief and hang the head.

'What should I do, seeing thee so indeed,
That tremble at th' imagination?
The thought of it doth make my faint heart bleed,
And fear doth teach it divination.   670
    I prophesy thy death, my living sorrow,
    If thou encounter with the boar to-morrow.

'But if thou needs wilt hunt, be ruled by me;
Uncouple at the timorous flying hare,   674
Or at the fox which lives by subtlety,
Or at the roe which no encounter dare.
    Pursue these fearful creatures o'er the downs,   677
    And on thy well-breathed horse keep with thy hounds.   678

'And when thou hast on foot the purblind hare,   679
Mark the poor wretch, to overshoot his troubles,   680
How he outruns the wind, and with what care
He cranks and crosses with a thousand doubles.   682
    The many musits through the which he goes   683
    Are like a labyrinth to amaze his foes.   684

'Sometime he runs among a flock of sheep,
To make the cunning hounds mistake their smell,
And sometime where earth-delving conies keep,   687
To stop the loud pursuers in their yell;   688
    And sometime sorteth with a herd of deer.   689
    Danger deviseth shifts, wit waits on fear;   690

'For there his smell with others being mingled,
The hot scent-snuffing hounds are driven to doubt,
Ceasing their clamorous cry till they have singled
With much ado the cold fault cleanly out.   694
    Then do they spend their mouths; echo replies,
    As if another chase were in the skies.

'By this, poor Wat, far off upon a hill,   697
Stands on his hinder legs with list'ning ear,
To hearken if his foes pursue him still.
Anon their loud alarums he doth hear,
    And now his grief may be comparèd well
    To one sore sick that hears the passing bell.   702

'Then shalt thou see the dew-bedabbled wretch
Turn and return, indenting with the way.   704
Each envious brier his weary legs do scratch;   705
Each shadow makes him stop, each murmur stay;
    For misery is trodden on by many
    And, being low, never relieved by any.

'Lie quietly and hear a little more.
Nay, do not struggle, for thou shalt not rise.
To make thee hate the hunting of the boar,
Unlike myself thou hear'st me moralize,
    Applying this to that, and so to so;
    For love can comment upon every woe.

'Where did I leave?' 'No matter where,' quoth he;
'Leave me, and then the story aptly ends.
The night is spent.' 'Why, what of that?' quoth she.
'I am,' quoth he, 'expected of my friends;
    And now 'tis dark, and going I shall fall.'
    'In night,' quoth she, 'desire sees best of all.

626 *better proof* stronger armor 628 *venter* venture 633 *eyne* eyes
635 *vantage* an advantage 636 *root* root up 637 *cabin* i.e. natural sty
638 *fiends* destroyers 639 *danger* i.e. zone of danger 645 *downright* without pause 647 *boding* foreboding 649 *Jealousy* apprehension 651 *suggesteth mutiny* incites violence 653 *Distemp'ring* reducing 655 *bate-breeding* strife-breeding 656 *canker* rose-worm; *spring* shoot 670 *divination* power to prophesy 674 *Uncouple at* loose your hound upon 677 *fearful* timid 678 *well-breathed* sound-winded; *keep* keep up 679 *on foot* in chase; *purblind* dimsighted 680 *overshoot* run beyond 682 *cranks* turns 683 *musits* gaps in a hedge or fence 684 *amaze* confuse 687 *conies* rabbits 688 *yell* full cry 689 *sorteth* mingles 690 *shifts* ruses; *waits on* goes with 694 *cold fault* lost scent 697 *Wat* hare (popular term) 702 *passing* funeral 704 *indenting* zigzagging 705 *envious* malicious

'But if thou fall, O, then imagine this :
The earth, in love with thee, thy footing trips,
And all is but to rob thee of a kiss.
724 Rich preys make true men thieves. So do thy lips
725   Make modest Dian cloudy and forlorn,
726   Lest she should steal a kiss and die forsworn.

727 'Now of this dark night I perceive the reason :
728 Cynthia for shame obscures her silver shine,
729 Till forging Nature be condemned of treason
For stealing moulds from heaven that were divine ;
  Wherein she framed thee, in high heaven's despite,
732   To shame the sun by day, and her by night.

'And therefore hath she bribed the Destinies
734 To cross the curious workmanship of Nature,
To mingle beauty with infirmities
736 And pure perfection with impure defeature,
  Making it subject to the tyranny
  Of mad mischances and much misery ;

'As burning fevers, agues pale and faint,
740 Life-poisoning pestilence, and frenzies wood,
741 The marrow-eating sickness whose attaint
Disorder breeds by heating of the blood,
743   Surfeits, imposthumes, grief, and damned despair
  Swear Nature's death for framing thee so fair.

745 'And not the least of all these maladies
But in one minute's fight brings beauty under.
747 Both favor, savor, hue, and qualities,
748 Whereat th' impartial gazer late did wonder,
  Are on the sudden wasted, thawed, and done,
  As mountain snow melts with the midday sun.

751 'Therefore, despite of fruitless chastity,
752 Love-lacking vestals, and self-loving nuns,
That on the earth would breed a scarcity
And barren dearth of daughters and of sons,
755   Be prodigal. The lamp that burns by night
  Dries up his oil to lend the world his light.

'What is thy body but a swallowing grave,
Seeming to bury that posterity
759 Which by the rights of time thou needs must have
If thou destroy them not in dark obscurity ?
  If so, the world will hold thee in disdain,
762   Sith in thy pride so fair a hope is slain.

'So in thyself thyself art made away,
A mischief worse than civil home-bred strife,
Or theirs whose desperate hands themselves do slay,
766 Or butcher sire that reaves his son of life.
767   Foul cank'ring rust the hidden treasure frets,
  But gold that's put to use more gold begets.'

'Nay, then,' quoth Adon, 'you will fall again
770 Into your idle over-handled theme.
The kiss I gave you is bestowed in vain,
And all in vain you strive against the stream ;
  For, by this black-faced night, desire's foul nurse,
774   Your treatise makes me like you worse and worse.

'If love have lent you twenty thousand tongues,
And every tongue more moving than your own,
Bewitching like the wanton mermaid's songs,
Yet from mine ear the tempting tune is blown ;
  For know, my heart stands armèd in mine ear   779
  And will not let a false sound enter there,

'Lest the deceiving harmony should run
Into the quiet closure of my breast ;   782
And then my little heart were quite undone,
In his bedchamber to be barred of rest.
  No, lady, no ; my heart longs not to groan,
  But soundly sleeps while now it sleeps alone.

'What have you urged that I cannot reprove ?   787
The path is smooth that leadeth on to danger.
I hate not love, but your device in love,   789
That lends embracements unto every stranger.
  You do it for increase. O strange excuse,
  When reason is the bawd to lust's abuse !

'Call it not love, for Love to heaven is fled
Since sweating Lust on earth unsurped his name ;
Under whose simple semblance he hath fed   795
Upon fresh beauty, blotting it with blame ;
  Which the hot tyrant stains and soon bereaves,   797
  As caterpillars do the tender leaves.

'Love comforteth like sunshine after rain,
But Lust's effect is tempest after sun.
Love's gentle spring doth always fresh remain ;
Lust's winter comes ere summer half be done.
  Love surfeits not, Lust like a glutton dies ;
  Love is all truth, Lust full of forgèd lies.

'More I could tell, but more I dare not say :
The text is old, the orator too green.   806
Therefore in sadness now I will away.   807
My face is full of shame, my heart of teen ;   808
  Mine ears, that to your wanton talk attended,
  Do burn themselves for having so offended.'

With this he breaketh from the sweet embrace
Of those fair arms which bound him to her breast
And homeward through the dark laund runs apace ;   813
Leaves Love upon her back, deeply distressed.
  Look how a bright star shooteth from the sky,
  So glides he in the night from Venus' eye ;

724 *preys* spoils 725 *Dian* Diana (chaste goddess of the moon) 726 *forsworn* i.e. violating the oath of chastity 727 *of* for 728 *Cynthia* i.e. Diana 729 *forging* counterfeiting 732 *her* i.e. the moon 734 *cross* thwart; *curious* ingenious 736 *defeature* defect 740 *wood* mad 741 *attaint* infection 743 *imposthumes* abscesses 745–46 *And . . . under* i.e. the least of these maladies subdues beauty in a minute 747 *favor* features 748 *impartial* just 751 *fruitless* sterile 752 *self-loving* i.e. intent upon their own salvation (?) 755 *prodigal* i.e. outgiving 759 *rights* claims 762 *Sith* since 766 *reaves* deprives 767 *cank'ring* eating (as does the cankerworm); *frets* erodes 770 *over-handled* threadbare 774 *treatise* discourse 779 *heart* i.e. inner resolution 782 *closure* enclosure 787 *reprove* refute 789 *device* i.e. sleights 795 *simple semblance* guileless aspect 797 *hot tyrant* i.e. lust; *bereaves* impairs, spoils 806 *green* unripe, inexperienced 807 *in sadness* in all seriousness 808 *teen* grief 813 *laund* i.e. grassy fields

Which after him she darts, as one on shore
Gazing upon a late-embarkèd friend
Till the wild waves will have him seen no more,
Whose ridges with the meeting clouds contend.
    So did the merciless and pitchy night
    Fold in the object that did feed her sight.

823 Whereat amazed, as one that unaware
Hath dropped a precious jewel in the flood,
825 Or stonished as night-wand'rers often are,
826 Their light blown out in some mistrustful wood,
    Even so confounded in the dark she lay,
    Having lost the fair discovery of her way.

And now she beats her heart, whereat it groans,
That all the neighbor caves, as seeming troubled,
Make verbal repetition of her moans.
832 Passion on passion deeply is redoubled :
    'Ay me!' she cries, and twenty times, 'Woe, woe!'
    And twenty echoes twenty times cry so.

She, marking them, begins a wailing note
And sings extemporally a woeful ditty –
837 How love makes young men thrall, and old men dote ;
How love is wise in folly, foolish-witty.
    Her heavy anthem still concludes in woe,
    And still the choir of echoes answer so.

Her song was tedious and outwore the night,
For lovers' hours are long, though seeming short.
If pleased themselves, others, they think, delight
In such-like circumstance, with such-like sport.
    Their copious stories, oftentimes begun,
    End without audience and are never done.

For who hath she to spend the night withal
848 But idle sounds resembling parasits,
Like shrill-tongued tapsters answering every call,
Soothing the humor of fantastic wits ?
    She says ''Tis so.' They answer all, ''Tis so,'
    And would say after her if she said 'No.'

Lo, here the gentle lark, weary of rest,
854 From his moist cabinet mounts up on high
And wakes the morning, from whose silver breast
The sun ariseth in his majesty ;
    Who doth the world so gloriously behold
    That cedar tops and hills seem burnished gold.

Venus salutes him with this fair good-morrow :
'O thou clear god, and patron of all light,
From whom each lamp and shining star doth borrow
The beauteous influence that makes him bright,
    There lives a son that sucked an earthly mother
    May lend thee light, as thou dost lend to other.'

This said, she hasteth to a myrtle grove,
Musing the morning is so much o'erworn
And yet she hears no tidings of her love.
She hearkens for his hounds and for his horn.
    Anon she hears them chant it lustily,
    And all in haste she coasteth to the cry ;   870

And as she runs, the bushes in the way
Some catch her by the neck, some kiss her face,
Some twind about her thigh to make her stay.   873
She wildly breaketh from their strict embrace,   874
    Like a milch doe whose swelling dugs do ache
    Hasting to feed her fawn hid in some brake.

By this, she hears the hounds are at a bay ;   877
Whereat she starts, like one that spies an adder
Wreathed up in fatal folds just in his way,
The fear whereof doth make him shake and shudder.
    Even so the timorous yelping of the hounds
    Appals her senses and her spirit confounds.

For now she knows it is no gentle chase,
But the blunt boar, rough bear, or lion proud,   884
Because the cry remaineth in one place,
Where fearfully the dogs exclaim aloud.
    Finding their enemy to be so curst,   887
    They all strain court'sy who shall cope him first.   888

This dismal cry rings sadly in her ear,
Through which it enters to surprise her heart,   890
Who, overcome by doubt and bloodless fear,
With cold-pale weakness numbs each feeling part :   892
    Like soldiers when their captain once doth yield,
    They basely fly and dare not stay the field.

Thus stands she in a trembling ecstasy ;   895
Till, cheering up her senses all dismayed,
She tells them 'tis a causeless fantasy,   897
And childish error that they are afraid ;
    Bids them leave quaking, bids them fear no more ;
    And with that word she spied the hunted boar,

Whose frothy mouth, bepainted all with red,
Like milk and blood being mingled both togither,
A second fear through all her sinews spread,
Which madly hurries her she knows not whither.
    This way she runs, and now she will no further,
    But back retires to rate the boar for murther.

823 *amazed* confused, at a loss   825 *stonished* dismayed   826 *mistrustful*
mistrusted, feared   832 *Passion* lamentation ; *redoubled* re-echoed   837
thrall captive   848 *parasits* parasites, attendants   854 *moist cabinet* dewy
cottage   870 *coasteth to* runs to head off   873 *twind* wind   874 *strict* tight
877 *at a bay* i.e. confronted by their quarry   884 *blunt* crude   887 *curst*
fierce-tempered   888 *strain court'sy* i.e. are over-polite in yielding precedence ; *cope* cope with   890 *surprise* attack   892 *feeling part* organ of
sense   895 *ecstasy* fit   897 *causeless fantasy* baseless fancy   907 *spleens*
emotional starts   909 *mated* overcome   911 *respects* designs   912 *In hand
with* busy about

A thousand spleens bear her a thousand ways ;   907
She treads the path that she untreads again ;
Her more than haste is mated with delays,   909
Like the proceedings of a drunken brain,
    Full of respects, yet naught at all respecting,   911
    In hand with all things, naught at all effecting.   912

Here kennelled in a brake she finds a hound
914 And asks the weary caitiff for his master;
And there another licking of his wound,
916 'Gainst venomed sores the only sovereign plaster;
 And here she meets another, sadly scowling,
 To whom she speaks, and he replies with howling.

When he hath ceased his ill-resounding noise,
920 Another flap-mouthed mourner, black and grim,
Against the welkin volleys out his voice.
Another and another answer him,
 Clapping their proud tails to the ground below,
 Shaking their scratched ears, bleeding as they go.

925 Look how the world's poor people are amazèd
At apparitions, signs, and prodigies,
Whereon with fearful eyes they long have gazèd,
928 Infusing them with dreadful prophecies:
 So she at these sad signs draws up her breath
930 And, sighing it again, exclaims on Death.

'Hard-favored tyrant, ugly, meagre, lean,
932 Hateful divorce of love!' – thus chides she Death –
933 'Grim-grinning ghost, earth's worm, what dost thou mean
To stifle beauty and to steal his breath
 Who, when he lived, his breath and beauty set
 Gloss on the rose, smell to the violet?

'If he be dead – O no, it cannot be,
Seeing his beauty, thou shouldst strike at it!
O yes, it may! Thou hast no eyes to see,
940 But hatefully at randon dost thou hit.
 Thy mark is feeble age; but thy false dart
 Mistakes that aim and cleaves an infant's heart.

'Hadst thou but bid beware, then he had spoke,
944 And, hearing him, thy power had lost his power.
The Destinies will curse thee for this stroke.
They bid thee crop a weed; thou pluck'st a flower.
 Love's golden arrow at him should have fled,
948 And not Death's ebon dart to strike him dead.

'Dost thou drink tears, that thou provok'st such weeping?
950 What may a heavy groan advantage thee?
Why hast thou cast into eternal sleeping
Those eyes that taught all other eyes to see?
953 Now Nature cares not for thy mortal vigor,
 Since her best work is ruined with thy rigor.'

Here overcome, as one full of despair,
956 She vailed her eyelids, who, like sluices, stopped
The crystal tide that from her two cheeks fair
In the sweet channel of her bosom dropped;
 But through the floodgates breaks the silver rain
 And with his strong course opens them again.

961 O, how her eyes and tears did lend and borrow,
Her eye seen in the tears, tears in her eye,
963 Both crystals, where they viewed each other's sorrow –
Sorrow that friendly sighs sought still to dry;
 But like a stormy day, now wind, now rain,
 Sighs dry her cheeks, tears make them wet again.

Variable passions throng her constant woe,
As striving who should best become her grief. 968
All entertained, each passion labors so 969
That every present sorrow seemeth chief,
 But none is best; then join they all together
 Like many clouds consulting for foul weather. 972

By this, far off she hears some huntsman halloa.
A nurse's song ne'er pleased her babe so well.
The dire imagination she did follow
This sound of hope doth labor to expel;
 For now reviving joy bids her rejoice
 And flatters her it is Adonis' voice.

Whereat her tears began to turn their tide, 979
Being prisoned in her eye like pearls in glass; 980
Yet sometimes falls an orient drop beside,
Which her cheek melts, as scorning it should pass 982
 To wash the foul face of the sluttish ground,
 Who is but drunken when she seemeth drowned.

O hard-believing love, how strange it seems 985
Not to believe, and yet too credulous!
Thy weal and woe are both of them extremes; 987
Despair and hope makes thee ridiculous:
 The one doth flatter thee in thoughts unlikely, 989
 In likely thoughts the other kills thee quickly. 990

Now she unweaves the web that she hath wrought:
Adonis lives, and Death is not to blame;
It was not she that called him all to naught. 993
Now she adds honors to his hateful name:
 She clepes him king of graves, and grave for kings, 995
 Imperious supreme of all mortal things. 996

'No, no,' quoth she, 'sweet Death, I did but jest;
Yet pardon me I felt a kind of fear
When as I met the boar, that bloody beast
Which knows no pity but is still severe.
 Then, gentle shadow (truth I must confess), 1001
 I railed on thee, fearing my love's decesse. 1002

''Tis not my fault the boar provoked my tongue.
Be wreaked on him, invisible commander; 1004
'Tis he, foul creature, that hath done thee wrong.
I did but act; he's author of thy slander.
 Grief hath two tongues, and never woman yet
 Could rule them both without ten women's wit.'

914 *caitiff* base wretch 916 *plaster* dressing 920 *flap-mouthed* i.e. with dangling lips of a hound 925 *amazèd* perplexed 928 *Infusing . . . prophecies* i.e. converting them into dreadful omens 930 *exclaims on* inveighs against 932 *divorce* terminator 933 *worm* i.e. canker, begetter of rot 940 *randon* random 944 *his* its 948 *ebon* ebony, black 950 *advantage* profit 953 *mortal vigor* deadly strength 956 *vailed* lowered; *who . . . stopped* which, like sluices, dammed 961 *lend and borrow* i.e. reflect each other 963 *crystals* i.e. mirrors 968 *striving who* contending which 969 *entertained* admitted 972 *consulting for* i.e. planning to produce 979 *turn their tide* ebb, subside 980 *like . . . glass* i.e. with the fixed quality of a pearl-shaped glass-bubble (?) 982 *melts* i.e. reduces to mere moisture 985 *hard-believing* i.e. stubborn, wrongheaded 987 *weal* gladness 989 *The one* i.e. hope; *thoughts unlikely* i.e. cheerful fancies 990 *likely thoughts* i.e. ominous probabilities 993 *all to naught* evil 995 *clepes* names 996 *Imperious supreme* imperial ruler 1001 *shadow* shade, spectre 1002 *decesse* decease 1004 *wreaked* revenged

Thus hoping that Adonis is alive,
1010 Her rash suspect she doth extenuate;
And that his beauty may the better thrive,
1012 With Death she humbly doth insinuate;
1013   Tells him of trophies, statues, tombs; and stories
  His victories, his triumphs, and his glories.

'O Jove,' quoth she, 'how much a fool was I
To be of such a weak and silly mind
To wail his death who lives, and must not die
Till mutual overthrow of mortal kind!
  For he being dead, with him is beauty slain,
  And, beauty dead, black chaos comes again.

'Fie, fie, fond love, thou art as full of fear
As one with treasure laden hemmed with thieves.
1023 Trifles, unwitnessèd with eye or ear,
Thy coward heart with false bethinking grieves.'
  Even at this word she hears a merry horn,
  Whereat she leaps that was but late forlorn.

As falcons to the lure, away she flies.
The grass stoops not, she treads on it so light;
And in her haste unfortunately spies
The foul boar's conquest on her fair delight;
  Which seen, her eyes, as murd'red with the view,
1032 Like stars ashamed of day, themselves withdrew;

Or as the snail, whose tender horns being hit,
Shrinks backward in his shelly cave with pain,
And there, all smooth'red up, in shade doth sit,
Long after fearing to creep forth again;
  So at his bloody view her eyes are fled
  Into the deep-dark cabins of her head;

Where they resign their office and their light
To the disposing of her troubled brain;
1041 Who bids them still consort with ugly night
1042 And never wound the heart with looks again;
1043 Who, like a king perplexèd in his throne,
1044 By their suggestion gives a deadly groan,

Whereat each tributary subject quakes,
As when the wind, imprisoned in the ground,
Struggling for passage, earth's foundation shakes,
Which with cold terror doth men's minds confound.
1049 This mutiny each part doth so surprise
  That from their dark beds once more leap her eyes,

And, being opened, threw unwilling light
Upon the wide wound that the boar had trenched   1052
In his soft flank; whose wonted lily white
With purple tears that his wound wept was drenched.
  No flow'r was nigh, no grass, herb, leaf, or weed,
  But stole his blood and seemed with him to bleed.

This solemn sympathy poor Venus noteth.
Over one shoulder doth she hang her head.
Dumbly she passions, franticly she doteth: 1059
She thinks he could not die, he is not dead;
  Her voice is stopped, her joints forget to bow;
  Her eyes are mad that they have wept till now.   1062

Upon his hurt she looks so steadfastly
That her sight dazzling makes the wound seem three;   1064
And then she reprehends her mangling eye,
That makes more gashes where no breach should be.
  His face seems twain, each several limb is doubled;
  For oft the eye mistakes, the brain being troubled.

'My tongue cannot express my grief for one,
And yet,' quoth she, 'behold two Adons dead!
My sighs are blown away, my salt tears gone,
Mine eyes are turned to fire, my heart to lead.
  Heavy heart's lead, melt at mine eyes' red fire!
  So shall I die by drops of hot desire.

'Alas, poor world, what treasure hast thou lost!
What face remains alive that's worth the viewing?
Whose tongue is music now? What canst thou boast
Of things long since, or any thing ensuing?   1078
  The flowers are sweet, their colors fresh and trim;
  But true-sweet beauty lived and died with him.

'Bonnet nor veil henceforth no creature wear!
Nor sun nor wind will ever strive to kiss you.
Having no fair to lose, you need not fear.   1083
The sun doth scorn you, and the wind doth hiss you;
  But when Adonis lived, sun and sharp air
  Lurked like two thieves, to rob him of his fair;

'And therefore would he put his bonnet on,
Under whose brim the gaudy sun would peep;
The wind would blow it off, and, being gone,
Play with his locks, then would Adonis weep;
  And straight, in pity of his tender years,
  They both would strive who first should dry his tears.

'To see his face the lion walked along
Behind some hedge, because he would not fear him.   1094
To recreate himself when he hath song,
The tiger would be tame, and gently hear him.
  If he had spoke, the wolf would leave his prey
  And never fright the silly lamb that day.

'When he beheld his shadow in the brook,
The fishes spread on it their golden gills.
When he was by, the birds such pleasure took
That some would sing, some other in their bills
  Would bring him mulberries and ripe-red cherries:
  He fed them with his sight, they him with berries.

1010 *suspect* suspicion 1012 *insinuate* ingratiate herself 1013 *stories* narrates 1023 *unwitnessèd with* not perceived by 1032 *ashamed of* put to shame by 1041 *still consort* always dwell 1042 *looks* i.e. looking 1043 *Who* i.e. which; *perplexèd* tormented 1044 *suggestion* incitement 1049 *mutiny* attack 1052 *trenched* ripped 1059 *passions* grieves, displays emotion 1062 *mad* frenzied; *till* i.e. before 1064 *dazzling* i.e. losing distinctness of vision 1078 *long since* i.e. far in the past 1083 *fair* beauty 1094 *fear* frighten

1105 'But this foul, grim, and urchin-snouted boar,
Whose downward eye still looketh for a grave,
1107 Ne'er saw the beauteous livery that he wore:
1108 Witness the entertainment that he gave.
    If he did see his face, why then I know
    He thought to kiss him, and hath killed him so.

' 'Tis true, 'tis true! thus was Adonis slain:
He ran upon the boar with his sharp spear,
Who did not whet his teeth at him again,
But by a kiss thought to persuade him there;
    And nuzzling in his flank, the loving swine
    Sheathed unaware the tusk in his soft groin.

'Had I been toothèd like him, I must confess,
With kissing him I should have killed him first;
But he is dead, and never did he bless
1120 My youth with his – the more am I accurst.'
    With this, she falleth in the place she stood
    And stains her face with his congealèd blood.

She looks upon his lips, and they are pale;
She takes him by the hand, and that is cold;
She whispers in his ears a heavy tale,
As if they heard the woeful words she told;
    She lifts the coffer-lids that close his eyes,
    Where, lo, two lamps burnt out in darkness lies;

Two glasses, where herself herself beheld
A thousand times, and now no more reflect,
Their virtue lost wherein they late excelled,
And every beauty robbed of his effect.
1133   'Wonder of time,' quoth she, 'this is my spite,
    That, thou being dead, the day should yet be light.

'Since thou art dead, lo, here I prophesy
Sorrow on love hereafter shall attend.
1137 It shall be waited on with jealousy,
Find sweet beginning, but unsavory end,
    Ne'er settled equally, but high or low,
    That all love's pleasure shall not match his woe.

'It shall be fickle, false, and full of fraud,
1142 Bud and be blasted in a breathing while,
1143 The bottom poison, and the top o'erstrawed
With sweets that shall the truest sight beguile.
    The strongest body shall it make most weak,
    Strike the wise dumb, and teach the fool to speak.

'It shall be sparing, and too full of riot,
Teaching decrepit age to tread the measures;
1149 The staring ruffian shall it keep in quiet,
Pluck down the rich, enrich the poor with treasures;
    It shall be raging mad and silly mild,
    Make the young old, the old become a child.

'It shall suspect where is no cause of fear;
It shall not fear where it should most mistrust;
It shall be merciful, and too severe,
And most deceiving when it seems most just;
1157   Perverse it shall be where it shows most toward,
    Put fear to valor, courage to the coward.

'It shall be cause of war and dire events
And set dissension 'twixt the son and sire,
Subject and servile to all discontents,
As dry combustious matter is to fire.
    Sith in his prime death doth my love destroy,
    They that love best their loves shall not enjoy.'

By this, the boy that by her side lay killed
Was melted like a vapor from her sight,
And in his blood, that on the ground lay spilled,
A purple flower sprung up, check'red with white,   1168
    Resembling well his pale cheeks and the blood
    Which in round drops upon their whiteness stood.

She bows her head the new-sprung flower to smell,
Comparing it to her Adonis' breath,
And says within her bosom it shall dwell,
Since he himself is reft from her by death;
    She crops the stalk, and in the breach appears
    Green-dropping sap, which she compares to tears.

'Poor flow'r,' quoth she, 'this was thy father's guise –   1177
Sweet issue of a more sweet-smelling sire –
For every little grief to wet his eyes.
To grow unto himself was his desire,
    And so 'tis thine; but know, it is as good
    To wither in my breast as in his blood.

'Here was thy father's bed, here in my breast;
Thou art the next of blood, and 'tis thy right.
Lo, in this hollow cradle take thy rest;
My throbbing heart shall rock thee day and night.
    There shall not be one minute in an hour
    Wherein I will not kiss my sweet love's flow'r.'

Thus weary of the world, away she hies
And yokes her silver doves, by whose swift aid
Their mistress, mounted, through the empty skies
In her light chariot quickly is conveyed,
    Holding their course to Paphos, where their queen   1193
    Means to immure herself and not be seen.

FINIS

1105 *urchin-snouted* hedgehog-snouted, i.e. rooting 1107 *livery* i.e. outsides, appearance 1108 *entertainment* treatment 1133 *spite* torment
1137 *jealousy* apprehension of evil 1142 *breathing while* space of a breath
1143 *o'erstrawed* overstrewn 1149 *staring* glaring, threatening 1157
toward tractable 1168 *purple flower* i.e. the anemone (cf. Ovid, *Metamorphoses*, X, 731–39) 1177 *guise* i.e. way, manner 1193 *Paphos* (the abode
of Venus in Cyprus)

THE RAPE OF LUCRECE

TO THE RIGHT HONORABLE

HENRY WRIOTHESLEY

EARL OF SOUTHAMPTON, AND BARON OF TITCHFIELD

The love I dedicate to your Lordship is without end; whereof this pamphlet without beginning is but a superfluous moiety. The warrant I have of your honorable disposition, not the worth of my untutored lines, makes it assured of acceptance. What I have done is yours; what I have to do is yours; being part in all I have, devoted yours. Were my worth greater, my duty would show greater; meantime, as it is, it is bound to your Lordship, to whom I wish long life still lengthened with all happiness.

Your Lordship's in all duty,
WILLIAM SHAKESPEARE

THE ARGUMENT

Lucius Tarquinius (for his excessive pride surnamed Superbus), after he had caused his own father-in-law Servius Tullius to be cruelly murdered, and, contrary to the Roman laws and customs, not requiring or staying for the people's suffrages, had possessed himself of the kingdom, went, accompanied with his sons and other noblemen of Rome, to besiege Ardea; during which siege the principal men of the army meeting one evening at the tent of Sextus Tarquinius, the King's son, in their discourses after supper every one commended the virtues of his own wife; among whom Collatinus extolled the incomparable chastity of his wife Lucretia. In that pleasant humor they all posted to Rome; and intending by their secret and sudden arrival to make trial of that which every one had before avouched, only Collatinus finds his wife (though it were late in the night) spinning amongst her maids; the other ladies were all found dancing and revelling, or in several disports. Whereupon the noblemen yielded Collatinus the victory, and his wife the fame. At that time Sextus Tarquinius being inflamed with Lucrece' beauty, yet smothering his passions for the present, departed with the rest back to the camp; from whence he shortly after privily withdrew himself, and was (according to his estate) royally entertained and lodged by Lucrece at Collatium. The same night he treacherously stealeth into her chamber, violently ravished her, and early in the morning speedeth away. Lucrece, in this lamentable plight, hastily dispatcheth messengers, one to Rome for her father, another to the camp for Collatine. They came, the one accompanied with Junius Brutus, the other with Publius Valerius; and finding Lucrece attired in mourning habit, demanded the cause of her sorrow. She, first taking an oath of them for her revenge, revealed the actor and whole manner of his dealing, and withal suddenly stabbed herself. Which done, with one consent they all vowed to root out the whole hated family of the Tarquins; and bearing the dead body to Rome, Brutus acquainted the people with the doer and manner of the vile deed, with a bitter invective against the tyranny of the King; wherewith the people were so moved that with one consent and a general acclamation the Tarquins were all exiled, and the state government changed from kings to consuls.

From the besiegèd Ardea all in post,   1
Borne by the trustless wings of false desire,   2
Lust-breathèd Tarquin leaves the Roman host
And to Collatium bears the lightless fire   4
Which, in pale embers hid, lurks to aspire
 And girdle with embracing flames the waist
 Of Collatine's fair love, Lucrece the chaste.

Haply that name of 'chaste' unhap'ly set   8
This bateless edge on his keen appetite;   9
When Collatine unwisely did not let   10
To praise the clear unmatchèd red and white
Which triumphed in that sky of his delight,   12
 Where mortal stars, as bright as heaven's beauties,   13
 With pure aspects did him peculiar duties.   14

For he the night before, in Tarquin's tent,
Unlocked the treasure of his happy state:
What priceless wealth the heavens had him lent
In the possession of his beauteous mate;
Reck'ning his fortune at such high proud rate
 That kings might be espousèd to more fame,
 But king nor peer to such a peerless dame.

Ded., **4–5** *without beginning* (often explained as signifying that the story begins *in medias res*, but perhaps only a vague term of deprecation, i.e. 'maimed,' 'imperfect') **5** *superfluous moiety* i.e. uncontained portion, spillover; *warrant* assurance
1 *all in post* post-haste **2** *trustless* treacherous **4** *lightless* i.e. smouldering **8** *Haply* perchance **9** *bateless* unabated, sharp **10** *let* forbear **12** *sky* i.e. the face of Lucrece **13** *mortal stars* i.e. the eyes of Lucrece **14** *aspects* (1) gazes, (2) astrological portents; *peculiar duties* i.e. duties reserved for him

22 O happiness enjoyed but of a few,
23 And, if possessed, as soon decayed and done
As is the morning's silver-melting dew
25 Against the golden splendor of the sun!
26 An expired date, cancelled ere well begun.
 Honor and beauty, in the owner's arms,
 Are weakly fortressed from a world of harms.

29 Beauty itself doth of itself persuade
30 The eyes of men without an orator.
31 What needeth then apologies be made
32 To set forth that which is so singular?
33 Or why is Collatine the publisher
 Of that rich jewel he should keep unknown
 From thievish ears, because it is his own?

Perchance his boast of Lucrece' sov'reignty
37 Suggested this proud issue of a king;
For by our ears our hearts oft tainted be.
Perchance that envy of so rich a thing
40 Braving compare, disdainfully did sting
 His high-pitched thoughts that meaner men should vaunt
42 That golden hap which their superiors want.

But some untimely thought did instigate
44 His all too timeless speed, if none of those.
45 His honor, his affairs, his friends, his state,
Neglected all, with swift intent he goes
47 To quench the coal which in his liver glows.
48 O rash false heat, wrapped in repentant cold,
49 Thy hasty spring still blasts and ne'er grows old!

When at Collatium this false lord arrivèd,
Well was he welcomed by the Roman dame,
Within whose face Beauty and Virtue strivèd
53 Which of them both should underprop her fame.
When Virtue bragged, Beauty would blush for shame;
 When Beauty boasted blushes, in despite
 Virtue would stain that o'er with silver white.

57 But Beauty, in that white entitulèd,
58 From Venus' doves doth challenge that fair field.
Then Virtue claims from Beauty Beauty's red,
60 Which Virtue gave the Golden Age to gild
 Their silver cheeks, and called it then their shield,
 Teaching them thus to use it in the fight,
63 When shame assailed, the red should fence the white.

This heraldry in Lucrece' face was seen,
65 Argued by Beauty's red and Virtue's white.
Of either's color was the other queen,
67 Proving from world's minority their right.
Yet their ambition makes them still to fight,
69 The sovereignty of either being so great
 That oft they interchange each other's seat.

This silent war of lilies and of roses
Which Tarquin viewed in her fair face's field,
73 In their pure ranks his traitor eye encloses;
Where, lest between them both it should be killed,
The coward captive vanquishèd doth yield
 To those two armies that would let him go
 Rather than triumph in so false a foe.

Now thinks he that her husband's shallow tongue,
The niggard prodigal that praised her so,
In that high task hath done her beauty wrong,
Which far exceeds his barren skill to show. 81
Therefore that praise which Collatine doth owe
 Enchanted Tarquin answers with surmise, 83
 In silent wonder of still-gazing eyes.

This earthly saint, adorèd by this devil,
Little suspecteth the false worshipper;
For unstained thoughts do seldom dream on evil;
Birds never limed no secret bushes fear. 88
So guiltless she securely gives good cheer 89
 And reverend welcome to her princely guest,
 Whose inward ill no outward harm expressed;

For that he colored with his high estate, 92
Hiding base sin in pleats of majesty;
That nothing in him seemed inordinate, 94
Save something too much wonder of his eye,
Which, having all, all could not satisfy;
 But, poorly rich, so wanteth in his store 97
 That, cloyed with much, he pineth still for more.

But she, that never coped with stranger eyes, 99
Could pick no meaning from their parling looks, 100
Nor read the subtle-shining secrecies
Writ in the glassy margents of such books. 102
She touched no unknown baits, nor feared no hooks;
 Nor could she moralize his wanton sight, 104
 More than his eyes were opened to the light. 105

He stories to her ears her husband's fame,
Won in the fields of fruitful Italy;
And decks with praises Collatine's high name,
Made glorious by his manly chivalry,
With bruisèd arms and wreaths of victory. 110
 Her joy with heaved-up hand she doth express, 111
 And wordless so greets heaven for his success.

Far from the purpose of his coming thither
He makes excuses for his being there.
No cloudy show of stormy blust'ring weather
Doth yet in his fair welkin once appear, 116
Till sable Night, mother of dread and fear,
 Upon the world dim darkness doth display
 And in her vaulty prison stows the day.

22 *of* by 23 *done* done with 25 *Against* i.e. in face of 26 *date* term 29 *of* by 30 *orator* pleader 31 *apologies* justifications 32 *singular* unique 33 *publisher* advertiser 37 *Suggested* prompted; *issue* offspring 40 *Braving compare* defying comparisons 42 *hap* luck 44 *timeless* untimely 45 *state* i.e. royal status 47 *liver* (supposed seat of sexual desire) 48 *wrapped in* i.e. attended by 49 *blasts* is blasted 53 *underprop* bear up 57 *entitulèd* having a claim 58 *field* (1) field of combat, (2) armorial ground 60 *gild* i.e. cover with a blush of modesty 63 *fence* shield 65 *Argued* disputed 67 *minority* youth, i.e. the Golden Age 69 *sovereignty* natural superiority 73 *encloses* overwhelms 81 *show* i.e. do justice to 83 *surmise* i.e. mounting speculation 88 *limed* snared with birdlime 89 *securely* overconfidently 92 *that he colored* i.e. the harmfulness he disguised 94 *That* so that 97 *store* abundance 99 *stranger eyes* eyes of a stranger 100 *parling* speaking 102 *glassy margents* mirroring margins 104 *moralize* interpret; *sight* glance 105 *than* than that 110 *bruisèd arms* battered armor 111 *heaved-up* upreared 116 *welkin* sky

For then is Tarquin brought unto his bed,
121 Intending weariness with heavy sprite;
122 For, after supper, long he questionèd
With modest Lucrece, and wore out the night.
124 Now leaden slumber with live's strength doth fight,
And every one to rest themselves betake,
126 Save thieves, and cares, and troubled minds that wake.

As one of which doth Tarquin lie revolving
The sundry dangers of his will's obtaining;
Yet ever to obtain his will resolving,
130 Though weak-built hopes persuade him to abstaining.
131 Despair to gain doth traffic oft for gaining;
132 And when great treasure is the meed proposèd,
133 Though death be adjunct, there's no death supposèd.

134 Those that much covet are with gain so fond
135 That what they have not, that which they possess,
136 They scatter and unloose it from their bond,
And so, by hoping more, they have but less;
Or, gaining more, the profit of excess
Is but to surfeit, and such griefs sustain
140 That they prove bankrout in this poor rich gain.

The aim of all is but to nurse the life
With honor, wealth, and ease in waning age;
143 And in this aim there is such thwarting strife
144 That one for all, or all for one we gage:
As life for honor in fell battle's rage;
Honor for wealth; and oft that wealth doth cost
The death of all, and all together lost;

So that in vent'ring ill we leave to be
149 The things we are for that which we expect;
And this ambitious foul infirmity,
151 In having much, torments us with defect
152 Of that we have: so then we do neglect
The thing we have; and, all for want of wit,
Make something nothing by augmenting it.

Such hazard now must doting Tarquin make,
Pawning his honor to obtain his lust;
157 And for himself himself he must forsake.
Then where is truth, if there be no self-trust?
When shall he think to find a stranger just
160 When he himself himself confounds, betrays
To sland'rous tongues and wretched hateful days?

Now stole upon the time the dead of night,
When heavy sleep had closed up mortal eyes.
No comfortable star did lend his light,   164
No noise but owls' and wolves' death-boding cries.
Now serves the season that they may surprise
The silly lambs. Pure thoughts are dead and still,
While lust and murder wakes to stain and kill.

And now this lustful lord leapt from his bed,
Throwing his mantle rudely o'er his arm;
Is madly tossed between desire and dread:
Th' one sweetly flatters, th' other feareth harm;
But honest fear, bewitched with lust's foul charm,
Doth too too oft betake him to retire,
Beaten away by brainsick rude desire.

His falchion on a flint he softly smiteth,   176
That from the cold stone sparks of fire do fly;
Whereat a waxen torch forthwith he lighteth,
Which must be lodestar to his lustful eye;
And to the flame thus speaks advisedly: 180
'As from this cold flint I enforced this fire,
So Lucrece must I force to my desire.'

Here pale with fear he doth premeditate
The dangers of his loathsome enterprise,
And in his inward mind he doth debate
What following sorrow may on this arise;
Then looking scornfully, he doth despise
His naked armor of still-slaughterèd lust   188
And justly thus controls his thoughts unjust:

'Fair torch, burn out thy light, and lend it not
To darken her whose light excelleth thine;
And die, unhallowed thoughts, before you blot
With your uncleanness that which is divine.
Offer pure incense to so pure a shrine.
Let fair humanity abhor the deed
That spots and stains love's modest snow-white weed.   196

'O shame to knighthood and to shining arms!
O foul dishonor to my household's grave!   198
O impious act including all foul harms!
A martial man to be soft fancy's slave!
True valor still a true respect should have;   201
Then my digression is so vile, so base,
That it will live engraven in my face.

'Yea, though I die, the scandal will survive
And be an eyesore in my golden coat.   205
Some loathsome dash the herald will contrive   206
To cipher me how fondly I did dote;   207
That my posterity, shamed with the note,
Shall curse my bones, and hold it for no sin
To wish that I their father had not been.

'What win I if I gain the thing I seek?
A dream, a breath, a froth of fleeting joy.
Who buys a minute's mirth to wail a week?
Or sells eternity to get a toy?   214
For one sweet grape who will the vine destroy?
Or what fond beggar, but to touch the crown,
Would with the sceptre straight be stroken down?

121 *Intending* pretending; *sprite* spirit 122 *questionèd* discoursed 124 *live's* life's 126 *wake* keep watch 130 *weak-built hopes* i.e. small hope of true felicity 131 *traffic* barter 132 *meed proposed* i.e. reward in view 133 *supposèd* i.e. taken into consideration 134 *fond* infatuated 135 *what for what* 136 *bond* i.e. possession 140 *bankrout* bankrupt 143 *And but* 144 *gage* stake 149 *expect* i.e. hope to be 151 *defect* i.e. the inadequacy 152 *neglect* disregard 157 *himself himself* i.e. his physical self his true self 160 *confounds* ruins 164 *comfortable* comforting, propitious 176 *falchion* curved sword 180 *advisedly* deliberately 188 *His . . . lust* i.e. his transient physical potency 196 *weed* garment 198 *grave* memorial tomb 201 *respect* veneration 205 *coat* coat of arms 206 *dash* bar, armorial abatement 207 *cipher* signal 214 *toy* trifle

THE NARRATIVE POEMS

'If Collatinus dream of my intent,
Will he not wake, and in a desp'rate rage
Post hither this vile purpose to prevent?
221 This siege that hath engirt his marriage,
This blur to youth, this sorrow to the sage,
     This dying virtue, this surviving shame,
224 Whose crime will bear an ever-during blame?

'O, what excuse can my invention make
When thou shalt charge me with so black a deed?
Will not my tongue be mute, my frail joints shake,
Mine eyes forgo their light, my false heart bleed?
The guilt being great, the fear doth still exceed;
     And extreme fear can neither fight nor fly,
     But coward-like with trembling terror die.

'Had Collatinus killed my son or sire,
Or lain in ambush to betray my life,
Or were he not my dear friend, this desire
Might have excuse to work upon his wife,
236 As in revenge or quittal of such strife;
     But as he is my kinsman, my dear friend,
     The shame and fault finds no excuse nor end.

'Shameful it is. Ay, if the fact be known.
Hateful it is. There is no hate in loving.
I'll beg her love. But she is not her own.
The worst is but denial and reproving.
243 My will is strong, past reason's weak removing.
244 Who fears a sentence or an old man's saw
245 Shall by a painted cloth be kept in awe.'

Thus graceless holds he disputation
'Tween frozen conscience and hot-burning will,
248 And with good thoughts makes dispensation,
249 Urging the worser sense for vantage still;
Which in a moment doth confound and kill
251 All pure effects, and doth so far proceed
     That what is vile shows like a virtuous deed.

Quoth he, 'She took me kindly by the hand
And gazed for tidings in my eager eyes,
Fearing some hard news from the warlike band
Where her beloved Collatinus lies.
O, how her fear did make her color rise!
     First red as roses that on lawn we lay,
     Then white as lawn, the roses took away.

'And how her hand, in my hand being locked,
Forced it to tremble with her loyal fear!
Which struck her sad, and then it faster rocked
Until her husband's welfare she did hear;
Whereat she smiled with so sweet a cheer
265 That, had Narcissus seen her as she stood,
     Self-love had never drowned him in the flood.

267 'Why hunt I then for color or excuses?
All orators are dumb when beauty pleadeth;
269 Poor wretches have remorse in poor abuses;
270 Love thrives not in the heart that shadows dreadeth.
271 Affection is my captain, and he leadeth;
     And when his gaudy banner is displayed,
273 The coward fights and will not be dismayed.

'Then childish fear avaunt, debating die!
Respect and reason wait on wrinkled age! 275
My heart shall never countermand mine eye. 276
Sad pause and deep regard beseems the sage; 277
My part is youth, and beats these from the stage. 278
     Desire my pilot is, beauty my prize;
     Then who fears sinking where such treasure lies?'

As corn o'ergrown by weeds, so heedful fear 281
Is almost choked by unresisted lust.
Away he steals with open list'ning ear,
Full of foul hope and full of fond mistrust;
Both which, as servitors to the unjust,
     So cross him with their opposite persuasion 286
     That now he vows a league, and now invasion. 287

Within his thought her heavenly image sits,
And in the selfsame seat sits Collatine.
That eye which looks on her confounds his wits;
That eye which him beholds, as more divine,
Unto a view so false will not incline;
     But with a pure appeal seeks to the heart, 293
     Which once corrupted takes the worser part;

And therein heartens up his servile powers, 295
Who, flatt'red by their leader's jocund show, 296
Stuff up his lust, as minutes fill up hours;
And as their captain, so their pride doth grow, 298
Paying more slavish tribute than they owe.
     By reprobate desire thus madly led,
     The Roman lord marcheth to Lucrece' bed.

The locks between her chamber and his will,
Each one by him enforced retires his ward; 303
But, as they open, they all rate his ill, 304
Which drives the creeping thief to some regard. 305
The threshold grates the door to have him heard;
     Night-wand'ring weasels shriek to see him there; 307
     They fright him, yet he still pursues his fear.

As each unwilling portal yields him way,
Through little vents and crannies of the place
The wind wars with his torch to make him stay,
And blows the smoke of it into his face,
Extinguishing his conduct in this case; 313
     But his hot heart, which fond desire doth scorch,
     Puffs forth another wind that fires the torch;

221 *engirt* encroached upon 224 *ever-during* ever-enduring 236 *quittal* requital 243 *removing* dissuasion 244 *sentence* moral maxim 245 *painted cloth* hanging painted with biblical or moral texts and illustrations 248 *makes dispensation* dispenses 249 *vantage* advantage 251 *effects* impulses 265 *Narcissus* in classical myth, the youth who fell in love with his own image reflected in water, and was transformed into the narcissus 267 *color* disguising appearance 269 *Poor . . . abuses* i.e. only the petty in their petty transgressions feel compunction 270 *shadows* i.e. the immaterial obstacles of conscience 271 *Affection* passion 273 *The coward* i.e. even the coward 275 *Respect* circumspection; *wait on* go with, attend 276 *countermand* run counter to 277 *Sad* serious 278 *stage* platform of action or disputation 281 *corn* grain 286 *cross* thwart 287 *league* i.e. treaty of non-aggression 293 *seeks to* seeks out, applies to 295 *servile powers* i.e. physical capacities 296 *Who* which 298 *as their captain* i.e. like their captain's (the heart's) 303 *his ward* (1) its locking bolt, (2) its posture of defense 304 *rate his ill* scold his wickedness 305 *regard* caution 307 *weasels* i.e. domestic rat-catchers (themselves furtive but startled by the furtive Tarquin) 313 *conduct* conductor, i.e. the torch

1422

316 And being lighted, by the light he spies
Lucretia's glove, wherein her needle sticks.
He takes it from the rushes where it lies,
And griping it, the needle his finger pricks,
As who should say, 'This glove to wanton tricks
321   Is not inured. Return again in haste –
    Thou seest our mistress' ornaments are chaste.'

323 But all these poor forbiddings could not stay him;
324 He in the worst sense consters their denial:
The doors, the wind, the glove, that did delay him,
326 He takes for accidental things of trial;
327 Or as those bars which stop the hourly dial,
328   Who with a ling'ring stay his course doth let
    Till every minute pays the hour his debt.

'So, so,' quoth he, 'these lets attend the time,
Like little frosts that sometime threat the spring
To add a more rejoicing to the prime
333 And give the sneapèd birds more cause to sing.
334 Pain pays the income of each precious thing:
    Huge rocks, high winds, strong pirates, shelves and sands,
    The merchant fears ere rich at home he lands.'

Now is he come unto the chamber door
That shuts him from the heaven of his thought,
Which with a yielding latch, and with no more,
Hath barred him from the blessèd thing he sought.
341 So from himself impiety hath wrought
    That for his prey to pray he doth begin,
    As if the heavens should countenance his sin.

But in the midst of his unfruitful prayer,
Having solicited th' eternal power
346 That his foul thoughts might compass his fair fair,
And they would stand auspicious to the hour,
Even there he starts. Quoth he, 'I must deflow'r.
    The powers to whom I pray abhor this fact;
    How can they then assist me in the act?

'Then Love and Fortune be my gods, my guide:
My will is backed with resolution.
Thoughts are but dreams till their effects be tried;
The blackest sin is cleared with absolution;
Against love's fire fear's frost hath dissolution.
    The eye of heaven is out, and misty night
    Covers the shame that follows sweet delight.'

This said, his guilty hand plucked up the latch,
And with his knee the door he opens wide.
The dove sleeps fast that this night owl will catch.   360
Thus treason works ere traitors be espied.
Who sees the lurking serpent steps aside;
    But she, sound sleeping, fearing no such thing,
    Lies at the mercy of his mortal sting.

Into the chamber wickedly he stalks
And gazeth on her yet unstainèd bed.
The curtains being close, about he walks,
Rolling his greedy eyeballs in his head.
By their high treason is his heart misled,
    Which gives the watchword to his hand full soon
    To draw the cloud that hides the silver moon.

Look, as the fair and fiery-pointed sun,
Rushing from forth a cloud, bereaves our sight,   373
Even so, the curtain drawn, his eyes begun
To wink, being blinded with a greater light;
Whether it is that she reflects so bright
    That dazzleth them, or else some shame supposèd;   377
    But blind they are, and keep themselves enclosèd.

O, had they in that darksome prison died,
Then had they seen the period of their ill;   380
Then Collatine again, by Lucrece' side,
In his clear bed might have reposèd still.   382
But they must ope, this blessèd league to kill,
    And holy-thoughted Lucrece to their sight
    Must sell her joy, her life, her world's delight.

Her lily hand her rosy cheek lies under,
Coz'ning the pillow of a lawful kiss;   387
Who, therefore angry, seems to part in sunder,
Swelling on either side to want his bliss;   389
Between whose hills her head entombèd is;
    Where like a virtuous monument she lies,
    To be admired of lewd unhallowed eyes.

Without the bed her other fair hand was,
On the green coverlet; whose perfect white
Showed like an April daisy on the grass,
With pearly sweat resembling dew of night.
Her eyes, like marigolds, had sheathed their light,
    And canopied in darkness sweetly lay
    Till they might open to adorn the day.

Her hair like golden threads played with her breath –
O modest wantons, wanton modesty!
Showing life's triumph in the map of death,   402
And death's dim look in life's mortality.   403
Each in her sleep themselves so beautify
    As if between them twain there were no strife,
    But that life lived in death, and death in life.

Her breasts like ivory globes circled with blue,
A pair of maiden worlds unconquerèd,
Save of their lord no bearing yoke they knew,
And him by oath they truly honorèd.   410
These worlds in Tarquin new ambition bred,
    Who like a foul usurper went about
    From this fair throne to heave the owner out.

316 *lighted* i.e. relighted 321 *inured* brazened 323 *stay* restrain 324 *consters* construes 326 *accidental . . . trial* i.e. morally insignificant tests of resolution 327 *bars . . . dial* the sixty check-points on the face of a clock 328 *Who* which; *his* its; *let* stop 333 *sneapèd* frost-nipped 334 *income* gain 341 *wrought* i.e. wrought him 346 *compass his fair fair* possess his virtuous fair one 373 *bereaves* takes away 377 *supposèd* felt, apprehended 380 *period* end; *ill* evil 382 *clear* innocent 387 *Coz'ning* cheating 389 *want* lack 402 *map* image 403 *life's mortality* i.e. sleep 410 *by oath* i.e. in accordance with the marriage vow

What could he see but mightily he noted?
What did he note but strongly he desirèd?
What he beheld, on that he firmly doted,
417 And in his will his willful eye he tirèd.
With more than admiration he admirèd
  Her azure veins, her alablaster skin,
  Her coral lips, her snow-white dimpled chin.

As the grim lion fawneth o'er his prey,
Sharp hunger by the conquest satisfied,
So o'er this sleeping soul doth Tarquin stay,
His rage of lust by gazing qualified;
Slacked, not suppressed; for, standing by her side,
426   His eye, which late this mutiny restrains,
  Unto a greater uproar tempts his veins;

428 And they, like straggling slaves for pillage fighting,
Obdurate vassals fell exploits effecting,
In bloody death and ravishment delighting,
Nor children's tears nor mothers' groans respecting,
432 Swell in their pride, the onset still expecting.
  Anon his beating heart, alarum striking,
  Gives the hot charge and bids them do their liking.

His drumming heart cheers up his burning eye,
His eye commends the leading to his hand;
His hand, as proud of such a dignity,
Smoking with pride, marched on to make his stand
On her bare breast, the heart of all her land;
440   Whose ranks of blue veins, as his hand did scale,
  Left their round turrets destitute and pale.

442 They, must'ring to the quiet cabinet
Where their dear governess and lady lies,
Do tell her she is dreadfully beset
And fright her with confusion of their cries.
She, much amazed, breaks ope her locked-up eyes,
  Who, peeping forth this tumult to behold,
448   Are by his flaming torch dimmed and controlled.

Imagine her as one in dead of night,
From forth dull sleep by dreadful fancy waking,
That thinks she hath beheld some ghastly sprite,
Whose grim aspect sets every joint a-shaking.
453 What terror 'tis! but she, in worser taking,
  From sleep disturbèd, heedfully doth view
  The sight which makes supposèd terror true.

Wrapped and confounded in a thousand fears,
Like to a new-killed bird she trembling lies.
She dares not look; yet, winking, there appears
459 Quick-shifting antics ugly in her eyes.
460 Such shadows are the weak brain's forgeries,
461   Who, angry that the eyes fly from their lights,
  In darkness daunts them with more dreadful sights.

His hand, that yet remains upon her breast
464 (Rude ram, to batter such an ivory wall!)
May feel her heart (poor citizen) distressed,
Wounding itself to death, rise up and fall,
467 Beating her bulk, that his hand shakes withal.
  This moves in him more rage and lesser pity,
  To make the breach and enter this sweet city.

First like a trumpet doth his tongue begin
To sound a parley to his heartless foe; 471
Who o'er the white sheet peers her whiter chin,
The reason of this rash alarm to know,
Which he by dumb demeanor seeks to show; 474
  But she with vehement prayers urgeth still
  Under what color he commits this ill. 476

Thus he replies: 'The color in thy face,
That even for anger makes the lily pale
And the red rose blush at her own disgrace,
Shall plead for me and tell my loving tale.
Under that color am I come to scale 481
  Thy never-conquerèd fort. The fault is thine,
  For those thine eyes betray thee unto mine.

'Thus I forestall thee, if thou mean to chide:
Thy beauty hath ensnared thee to this night, 485
Where thou with patience must my will abide, 486
My will that marks thee for my earth's delight,
Which I to conquer sought with all my might;
  But as reproof and reason beat it dead,
  By thy bright beauty was it newly bred.

'I see what crosses my attempt will bring, 491
I know what thorns the growing rose defends,
I think the honey guarded with a sting;
All this beforehand counsel comprehends,
But Will is deaf and hears no heedful friends:
  Only he hath an eye to gaze on Beauty,
  And dotes on what he looks, 'gainst law or duty.

'I have debated even in my soul
What wrong, what shame, what sorrow I shall breed;
But nothing can affection's course control 500
Or stop the headlong fury of his speed.
I know repentant tears ensue the deed, 502
  Reproach, disdain, and deadly enmity;
  Yet strive I to embrace mine infamy.'

This said, he shakes aloft his Roman blade,
Which, like a falcon tow'ring in the skies,
Coucheth the fowl below with his wings' shade, 507
Whose crooked beak threats if he mount he dies.
So under his insulting falchion lies
  Harmless Lucretia, marking what he tells
  With trembling fear, as fowl hear falcons' bells.

417 *will* lust 426 *late* i.e. a moment before; *mutiny* i.e. rebellion of the blood, lust 428 *straggling* i.e. not in military order 432 *pride* lust 440 *scale* successfully mount (continuing the military imagery) 442 *must'ring* gathering; *cabinet* the heart, where veins presumably would muster (?), or the brain, where consciousness resides (?) 448 *controlled* overpowered 453 *taking* fright 459 *antics* grotesques 460 *shadows* shapes 461 *lights* i.e. sight 464 *ram* battering-ram 467 *bulk* body 471 *heartless* timorous 474 *dumb demeanor* dumbshow 476 *color* pretext 481 *color* banner 485 *to this night* i.e. into this night's meeting 486 *will* sexual desire 491 *crosses* troubles 500 *affection's* passion's 502 *ensue* follow upon 507 *Coucheth* makes cower

'Lucrece,' quoth he, 'this night I must enjoy thee.
If thou deny, then force must work my way;
For in thy bed I purpose to destroy thee.
That done, some worthless slave of thine I'll slay,
516 To kill thine honor with thy live's decay;
    And in thy dead arms do I mean to place him,
    Swearing I slew him, seeing thee embrace him.

'So thy surviving husband shall remain
The scornful mark of every open eye;
521 Thy kinsmen hang their heads at this disdain,
Thy issue blurred with nameless bastardy;
And thou, the author of their obloquy,
    Shalt have thy trespass cited up in rhymes
    And sung by children in succeeding times.

'But if thou yield, I rest thy secret friend;
The fault unknown is as a thought unacted.
A little harm done to a great good end
For lawful policy remains enacted.
530 The poisonous simple sometime is compacted
    In a pure compound; being so applied,
    His venom in effect is purified.

'Then, for thy husband and thy children's sake,
534 Tender my suit. Bequeath not to their lot
535 The shame that from them no device can take,
The blemish that will never be forgot;
537 Worse than a slavish wipe or birth-hour's blot;
    For marks descried in men's nativity
    Are nature's faults, not their own infamy.'

540 Here with a cockatrice' dead-killing eye
He rouseth up himself and makes a pause;
While she, the picture of pure piety,
543 Like a white hind under the gripe's sharp claws,
Pleads, in a wilderness where are no laws,
    To the rough beast that knows no gentle right
    Nor aught obeys but his foul appetite.

But when a black-faced cloud the world doth threat,
In his dim mist th' aspiring mountains hiding,
549 From earth's dark womb some gentle gust doth get,
Which blows these pitchy vapors from their biding,
551 Hind'ring their present fall by this dividing,
    So his unhallowed haste her words delays,
553   And moody Pluto winks while Orpheus plays.

Yet, foul night-waking cat, he doth but dally,
While in his hold-fast foot the weak mouse panteth.
Her sad behavior feeds his vulture folly,   556
A swallowing gulf that even in plenty wanteth.   557
His ear her prayers admits, but his heart granteth
    No penetrable entrance to her plaining.   559
    Tears harden lust, though marble wear with raining.

Her pity-pleading eyes are sadly fixèd
In the remorseless wrinkles of his face.   562
Her modest eloquence with sighs is mixèd,
Which to her oratory adds more grace.   564
She puts the period often from his place,   565
    And midst the sentence so her accent breaks
    That twice she doth begin ere once she speaks.

She conjures him by high almighty Jove,
By knighthood, gentry, and sweet friendship's oath,
By her untimely tears, her husband's love,
By holy human law and common troth,
By heaven and earth, and all the power of both,
    That to his borrowed bed he make retire
    And stoop to honor, not to foul desire.   574

Quoth she, 'Reward not hospitality
With such black payment as thou hast pretended;   576
Mud not the fountain that gave drink to thee;
Mar not the thing that cannot be amended.
End thy ill aim before thy shoot be ended.   579
    He is no woodman that doth bend his bow   580
    To strike a poor unseasonable doe.

'My husband is thy friend: for his sake spare me;
Thyself art mighty: for thine own sake leave me;
Myself a weakling: do not then ensnare me;
Thou look'st not like deceit: do not deceive me.
My sighs like whirlwinds labor hence to heave thee.   586
    If ever man were moved with woman's moans,
    Be movèd with my tears, my sighs, my groans;

'All which together, like a troubled ocean,
Beat at thy rocky and wrack-threat'ning heart,
To soften it with their continual motion;
For stones dissolved to water do convert.   592
O, if no harder than a stone thou art,
    Melt at my tears and be compassionate!
    Soft pity enters at an iron gate.

'In Tarquin's likeness I did entertain thee.
Hast thou put on his shape to do him shame?
To all the host of heaven I complain me.
Thou wrong'st his honor, wound'st his princely name.
Thou art not what thou seem'st; and if the same,
    Thou seem'st not what thou art, a god, a king;
    For kings like gods should govern everything.

'How will thy shame be seeded in thine age   603
When thus thy vices bud before thy spring?
If in thy hope thou dar'st do such outrage,
What dar'st thou not when once thou art a king?
O, be remem'red, no outrageous thing
    From vassal actors can be wiped away;   608
    Then kings' misdeeds cannot be hid in clay.   609

516 *live's* life's 521 *disdain* stain, disgrace 530 *simple* herb; *compacted* compounded 534 *Tender* regard 535 *device* armorial figure 537 *wipe* brand-mark; *birth-hour's blot* birthmark 540 *cockatrice'* basilisk's (legendary serpent which killed with a look) 543 *gripe's* griffin's (?) 549 *doth get* is begot 551 *dividing* dispersal 553 *Pluto* ruler of the underworld, who was charmed by the lyre of Orpheus, husband of Eurydice; *winks* sleeps 556 *sad* grave; *vulture* ravenous 557 *gulf* belly 559 *plaining* complaining, lament 562 *remorseless* pitiless 564 *oratory* pleading 565 *his place* i.e. its proper place (in broken utterance) 574 *stoop* bow, defer 576 *pretended* proposed 579 *shoot* act of shooting (perhaps with pun on homonymic 'suit') 580 *woodman* huntsman 586 *heave* move 592 *convert* change 603 *be seeded* i.e. come to fruition 608 *vassal actors* i.e. subjects who do it 609 *in clay* i.e. even in death

'This deed will make thee only loved for fear;
But happy monarchs still are feared for love.
With foul offenders thou perforce must bear
When they in thee the like offenses prove.
614 If but for fear of this, thy will remove;
　For princes are the glass, the school, the book,
　Where subjects' eyes do learn, do read, do look.

'And wilt thou be the school where Lust shall learn?
Must he in thee read lectures of such shame?
Wilt thou be glass wherein it shall discern
Authority for sin, warrant for blame,
To privilege dishonor in thy name?
622 　Thou back'st reproach against long-living laud
　And mak'st fair reputation but a bawd.

'Hast thou command? By him that gave it thee,
From a pure heart command thy rebel will!
Draw not thy sword to guard iniquity,
For it was lent thee all that brood to kill.
Thy princely office how canst thou fulfill
　When, patterned by thy fault, foul Sin may say,
　He learned to sin, and thou didst teach the way?

'Think but how vile a spectacle it were
To view thy present trespass in another.
Men's faults do seldom to themselves appear;
Their own transgressions partially they smother.
This guilt would seem death-worthy in thy brother.
　O, how are they wrapped in with infamies
637 　That from their own misdeeds askaunce their eyes!

'To thee, to thee, my heaved-up hands appeal,
639 Not to seducing lust, thy rash relier.
640 I sue for exiled majesty's repeal;
　Let him return, and flatt'ring thoughts retire.
642 His true respect will prison false desire
　And wipe the dim mist from thy doting eyne,
　That thou shalt see thy state, and pity mine.'

'Have done,' quoth he. 'My uncontrollèd tide
646 Turns not, but swells the higher by this let.
Small lights are soon blown out; huge fires abide
And with the wind in greater fury fret.
The petty streams that pay a daily debt
650 　To their salt sovereign with their fresh falls' haste,
　Add to his flow, but alter not his taste.'

'Thou art,' quoth she, 'a sea, a sovereign king;
And, lo, there falls into thy boundless flood
Black lust, dishonor, shame, misgoverning,
Who seek to stain the ocean of thy blood.
If all these petty ills shall change thy good,
657 　Thy sea within a puddle's womb is hearsèd,
　And not the puddle in thy sea dispersèd.

'So shall these slaves be king, and thou their slave;
Thou nobly base, they basely dignified;
Thou their fair life, and they thy fouler grave;
Thou loathèd in their shame, they in thy pride.
The lesser thing should not the greater hide.
　The cedar stoops not to the base shrub's foot,
　But low shrubs wither at the cedar's root.

'So let thy thoughts, low vassals to thy state.'
'No more,' quoth he. 'By heaven, I will not hear thee!
Yield to my love; if not, enforcèd hate,
Instead of love's coy touch, shall rudely tear thee.
That done, despitefully I mean to bear thee　　　　670
　Unto the base bed of some rascal groom,
　To be thy partner in this shameful doom.'

This said, he sets his foot upon the light,
For light and lust are deadly enemies;
Shame folded up in blind concealing night,
When most unseen, then most doth tyrannize.
The wolf hath seized his prey; the poor lamb cries,
　Till with her own white fleece her voice controlled　　678
　Entombs her outcry in her lips' sweet fold;

For with the nightly linen that she wears
He pens her piteous clamors in her head,
Cooling his hot face in the chastest tears
That ever modest eyes with sorrow shed.
O, that prone lust should stain so pure a bed,
　The spots whereof, could weeping purify,
　Her tears should drop on them perpetually!

But she hath lost a dearer thing than life,
And he hath won what he would lose again.
This forcèd league doth force a further strife;
This momentary joy breeds months of pain;
This hot desire converts to cold disdain;
　Pure Chastity is rifled of her store,
　And Lust, the thief, far poorer than before.

Look, as the full-fed hound or gorgèd hawk,
Unapt for tender smell or speedy flight,　　　　　　　695
Make slow pursuit, or altogether balk　　　　　　　696
The prey wherein by nature they delight,
So surfeit-taking Tarquin fares this night:
　His taste delicious, in digestion souring,
　Devours his will, that lived by foul devouring.

O, deeper sin than bottomless conceit　　　　　　　701
Can comprehend in still imagination!
Drunken Desire must vomit his receipt　　　　　　　703
Ere he can see his own abomination.
While Lust is in his pride, no exclamation　　　　　705
　Can curb his heat or rein his rash desire
　Till, like a jade, Self-will himself doth tire.

And then with lank and lean discolored cheek,
With heavy eye, knit brow, and strengthless pace,
Feeble Desire, all recreant, poor, and meek,　　　　710
Like to a bankrout beggar wails his case.　　　　　711
The flesh being proud, Desire doth fight with Grace,
　For there it revels; and when that decays,　　　　713
　The guilty rebel for remission prays.

614 *thy will remove* dissuade your lust; 622 *back'st* support; *laud* praise 637 *askaunce* avert 639 *relier* thing relied upon (?) 640 *repeal* return from exile 642 *respect* sense of decorum; *prison* imprison 646 *let* hindrance 650 *salt sovereign* i.e. the ocean; *falls'* flows' 657 *hearsèd* entombed 678 *controlled* overpowered 695 *tender smell* weak scent 696 *balk* turn from 701 *bottomless conceit* unlimited fancy 703 *his receipt* what he has received 705 *exclamation* protest 710 *recreant* beaten, cowed 711 *bankrout* bankrupt 713 *that* i.e. pride, lust

So fares it with this fault-full lord of Rome,
Who this accomplishment so hotly chasèd;
For now against himself he sounds this doom,
That through the length of times he stands disgracèd.
Besides, his soul's fair temple is defacèd;
   To whose weak ruins muster troops of cares,
721   To ask the spotted princess how she fares.

722 She says her subjects with foul insurrection
Have battered down her consecrated wall,
724 And by their mortal fault brought in subjection
Her immortality and made her thrall
To living death and pain perpetual;
727   Which in her prescience she controllèd still,
   But her foresight could not forestall their will.

Ev'n in this thought through the dark night he stealeth,
A captive victor that hath lost in gain;
Bearing away the wound that nothing healeth,
The scar that will despite of cure remain;
Leaving his spoil perplexed in greater pain.
   She bears the load of lust he left behind,
   And he the burden of a guilty mind.

He like a thievish dog creeps sadly thence;
She like a wearied lamb lies panting there.
He scowls, and hates himself for his offense;
She desperate with her nails her flesh doth tear.
He faintly flies, sweating with guilty fear;
   She stays, exclaiming on the direful night;
   He runs, and chides his vanished loathed delight.

743 He thence departs a heavy convertite;
744 She there remains a hopeless castaway.
He in his speed looks for the morning light;
She prays she never may behold the day,
747 'For day,' quoth she, 'night's scapes doth open lay,
   And my true eyes have never practiced how
   To cloak offenses with a cunning brow.

'They think not but that every eye can see
The same disgrace which they themselves behold;
And therefore would they still in darkness be,
To have their unseen sin remain untold;
For they their guilt with weeping will unfold
755   And grave, like water that doth eat in steel,
   Upon my cheeks what helpless shame I feel.'

Here she exclaims against repose and rest,
And bids her eyes hereafter still be blind.
She wakes her heart by beating on her breast,
And bids it leap from thence, where it may find
761 Some purer chest to close so pure a mind.
   Frantic with grief thus breathes she forth her spite
   Against the unseen secrecy of night:

'O comfort-killing Night, image of hell,
Dim register and notary of shame,   765
Black stage for tragedies and murders fell,
Vast sin-concealing chaos, nurse of blame,
Blind muffled bawd, dark harbor for defame!
   Grim cave of death, whisp'ring conspirator
   With close-tongued treason and the ravisher!   770

'O hateful, vaporous, and foggy Night,
Since thou art guilty of my cureless crime,
Muster thy mists to meet the eastern light,
Make war against proportioned course of time;   774
Or if thou wilt permit the sun to climb
   His wonted height, yet ere he go to bed,
   Knit poisonous clouds about his golden head.

'With rotten damps ravish the morning air;
Let their exhaled unwholesome breaths make sick
The life of purity, the supreme fair,   780
Ere he arrive his weary noontide prick;   781
And let thy musty vapors march so thick
   That in their smoky ranks his smoth'red light
   May set at noon and make perpetual night.

'Were Tarquin Night, as he is but Night's child,
The silver-shining queen he would distain;   786
Her twinkling handmaids too, by him defiled,
Through Night's black bosom should not peep again.
So should I have co-partners in my pain;
   And fellowship in woe doth woe assuage,
   As palmers' chat makes short their pilgrimage;   791

'Where now I have no one to blush with me,
To cross their arms and hang their heads with mine,
To mask their brows and hide their infamy;
But I alone, alone must sit and pine,
Seasoning the earth with show'rs of silver brine,
   Mingling my talk with tears, my grief with groans,
   Poor wasting monuments of lasting moans.

'O Night, thou furnace of foul reeking smoke,
Let not the jealous Day behold that face   800
Which underneath thy black all-hiding cloak
Immodestly lies martyred with disgrace!
Keep still possession of thy gloomy place,
   That all the faults which in thy reign are made
   May likewise be sepulchered in thy shade!

'Make me not object to the telltale Day.   806
The light will show, charactered in my brow,
The story of sweet chastity's decay,
The impious breach of holy wedlock vow.
Yea, the illiterate, that know not how
   To cipher what is writ in learnèd books,
   Will quote my loathsome trespass in my looks.   812

'The nurse, to still her child, will tell my story
And fright her crying babe with Tarquin's name.
The orator, to deck his oratory,
Will couple my reproach to Tarquin's shame.
Feast-finding minstrels, tuning my defame,   817
   Will tie the hearers to attend each line,
   How Tarquin wrongèd me, I Collatine.

721 *spotted princess* i.e. besmirched soul 722 *subjects* i.e. senses (which should be subjects to the soul) 724 *mortal* deadly; *in* into 727 *Which* who (i.e. the subject senses) 743 *convertite* penitent 744 *castaway* lost soul 747 *scapes* misdeeds 755 *grave* engrave 761 *close* enclose 765 *notary* recorder 770 *close-tongued* secretive 774 *proportioned* orderly 780 *fair* i.e. the sun 781 *noontide prick* point of noon 786 *distain* stain 791 *palmers' chat* i.e. conversation among religious pilgrims 800 *jealous* i.e. censorious 806 *object* i.e. subject matter 812 *quote* note 817 *Feast-finding minstrels* i.e. minstrels who seek out festival occasions

‑

820 'Let my good name, that senseless reputation,
For Collatine's dear love be kept unspotted.
If that be made a theme for disputation,
The branches of another root are rotted,
And undeserved reproach to him allotted
    That is as clear from this attaint of mine
    As I ere this was pure to Collatine.

'O unseen shame, invisible disgrace!
828 O unfelt sore, crest-wounding private scar!
Reproach is stamped in Collatinus' face,
830 And Tarquin's eye may read the mot afar,
How he in peace is wounded, not in war.
    Alas, how many bear such shameful blows
    Which not themselves, but he that gives them knows!

'If, Collatine, thine honor lay in me,
From me by strong assault it is bereft;
My honey lost, and I, a drone-like bee,
Have no perfection of my summer left,
But robbed and ransacked by injurious theft.
    In thy weak hive a wand'ring wasp hath crept
    And sucked the honey which thy chaste bee kept.

'Yet am I guilty of thy honor's wrack;
Yet for thy honor did I entertain him.
843 Coming from thee, I could not put him back,
For it had been dishonor to disdain him.
Besides, of weariness he did complain him
    And talked of virtue – O unlooked-for evil
    When virtue is profaned in such a devil!

'Why should the worm intrude the maiden bud?
Or hateful cuckoos hatch in sparrow's nests?
Or toads infect fair founts with venom mud?
Or tyrant folly lurk in gentle breasts?
852 Or kings be breakers of their own behests?
    But no perfection is so absolute
    That some impurity doth not pollute.

'The agèd man that coffers up his gold
Is plagued with cramps and gouts and painful fits,
And scarce hath eyes his treasure to behold,
But like still-pining Tantalus he sits
859 And useless barns the harvest of his wits,
    Having no other pleasure of his gain
    But torment that it cannot cure his pain.

'So then he hath it when he cannot use it,
And leaves it to be mast'red by his young,
Who in their pride do presently abuse it.
Their father was too weak, and they too strong,
To hold their cursèd-blessèd fortune long.
    The sweets we wish for turn to loathèd sours
    Even in the moment that we call them ours.

'Unruly blasts wait on the tender spring;
Unwholesome weeds take root with precious flow'rs;
The adder hisses where the sweet birds sing;
What Virtue breeds Iniquity devours.
We have no good that we can say is ours,
874   But ill-annexèd Opportunity
875   Or kills his life or else his quality.

'O Opportunity, thy guilt is great!
'Tis thou that execut'st the traitor's treason;
Thou sets the wolf where he the lamb may get;
Whoever plots the sin, thou point'st the season.
'Tis thou that spurn'st at right, at law, at reason;
    And in thy shady cell, where none may spy him,
    Sits Sin, to seize the souls that wander by him.

'Thou mak'st the vestal violate her oath;
Thou blow'st the fire when temperance is thawed;
Thou smother'st honesty, thou murd'rest troth.
Thou foul abettor, thou notorious bawd,
Thou plantest scandal and displacest laud.   887
    Thou ravisher, thou traitor, thou false thief,
    Thy honey turns to gall, thy joy to grief.

'Thy secret pleasure turns to open shame,
Thy private feasting to a public fast,
Thy smoothing titles to a ragged name,   892
Thy sug'red tongue to bitter wormwood taste:
Thy violent vanities can never last.
    How comes it then, vile Opportunity,
    Being so bad, such numbers seek for thee?

'When wilt thou be the humble suppliant's friend
And bring him where his suit may be obtainèd?
When wilt thou sort an hour great strifes to end?   899
Or free that soul which wretchedness hath chainèd?
Give physic to the sick, ease to the painèd?
    The poor, lame, blind, halt, creep, cry out for thee;
    But they ne'er meet with Opportunity.

'The patient dies while the physician sleeps;
The orphan pines while the oppressor feeds;
Justice is feasting while the widow weeps;
Advice is sporting while infection breeds.   907
Thou grant'st no time for charitable deeds:
    Wrath, envy, treason, rape, and murder's rages,
    Thy heinous hours wait on them as their pages.

'When Truth and Virtue have to do with thee,
A thousand crosses keep them from thy aid.   912
They buy thy help; but Sin ne'er gives a fee,
He gratis comes; and thou art well apaid
As well to hear as grant what he hath said.
    My Collatine would else have come to me
    When Tarquin did, but he was stayed by thee.

820 *senseless* impalpable, spiritual (?) 828 *crest-wounding* i.e. that which blots the escutcheon 830 *mot* motto 843 *put him back* repel him 852 *behests* commands, laws 859 *useless . . . wits* i.e. keeps uselessly in storage the product of his acumen 874 *ill-annexèd* evilly coupled 875 *Or* either; *his* its (i.e. good's) 887 *displacest laud* displant praise 892 *smoothing* flattering; *ragged* worn away, disgraced 899 *sort* appoint 907 *Advice is sporting* i.e. medical advice (or adviser) is engaged in amusement 912 *crosses* hindrances

'Guilty thou art of murder and of theft,
Guilty of perjury and subornation,
920 Guilty of treason, forgery, and shift,
Guilty of incest, that abomination –
An accessary by thine inclination
   To all sins past and all that are to come,
   From the creation to the general doom.

925 'Misshapen Time, copesmate of ugly Night,
926 Swift subtle post, carrier of grisly care,
Eater of youth, false slave to false delight,
928 Base watch of woes, sin's packhorse, virtue's snare!
Thou nursest all, and murd'rest all that are.
   O, hear me then, injurious shifting Time;
   Be guilty of my death, since of my crime.

'Why hath thy servant Opportunity
Betrayed the hours thou gav'st me to repose?
Cancelled my fortunes, and enchainèd me
To endless date of never-ending woes?
936 Time's office is to fine the hate of foes,
   To eat up errors by opinion bred,
938   Not spend the dowry of a lawful bed.

'Time's glory is to calm contending kings,
To unmask falsehood and bring truth to light,
To stamp the seal of time in agèd things,
942 To wake the morn and sentinel the night,
To wrong the wronger till he render right,
944   To ruinate proud buildings with thy hours,
   And smear with dust their glitt'ring golden tow'rs;

'To fill with wormholes stately monuments,
To feed oblivion with decay of things,
To blot old books and alter their contents,
949 To pluck the quills from ancient ravens' wings,
950 To dry the old oak's sap and cherish springs,
   To spoil antiquities of hammered steel
   And turn the giddy round of Fortune's wheel;

'To show the beldame daughters of her daughter,
To make the child a man, the man a child,
To slay the tiger that doth live by slaughter,
To tame the unicorn and lion wild,
957 To mock the subtle in themselves beguiled,
   To cheer the ploughman with increaseful crops
959   And waste huge stones with little water-drops.

'Why work'st thou mischief in thy pilgrimage,
Unless thou couldst return to make amends?
One poor retiring minute in an age   962
Would purchase thee a thousand thousand friends,
Lending him wit that to bad debtors lends.
   O this dread night, wouldst thou one hour come back,
   I could prevent this storm and shun thy wrack!

'Thou ceaseless lackey to Eternity,   967
With some mischance cross Tarquin in his flight.
Devise extremes beyond extremity   969
To make him curse this cursèd crimeful night.
Let ghastly shadows his lewd eyes affright,
   And the dire thought of his committed evil
   Shape every bush a hideous shapeless devil.

'Disturb his hours of rest with restless trances;   974
Afflict him in his bed with bedrid groans;
Let there bechance him pitiful mischances
To make him moan, but pity not his moans.
Stone him with hard'ned hearts harder than stones,
   And let mild women to him lose their mildness,
   Wilder to him than tigers in their wildness.

'Let him have time to tear his curlèd hair,
Let him have time against himself to rave,
Let him have time of Time's help to despair,
Let him have time to live a loathèd slave,
Let him have time a beggar's orts to crave,   985
   And time to see one that by alms doth live
   Disdain to him disdainèd scraps to give.

'Let him have time to see his friends his foes
And merry fools to mock at him resort;
Let him have time to mark how slow time goes
In time of sorrow, and how swift and short
His time of folly and his time of sport;
   And ever let his unrecalling crime   993
   Have time to wail th' abusing of his time.

'O Time, thou tutor both to good and bad,
Teach me to curse him that thou taught'st this ill.
At his own shadow let the thief run mad,
Himself himself seek every hour to kill.
Such wretched hands such wretched blood should spill,
   For who so base would such an office have
   As sland'rous deathsman to so base a slave?   1001

'The baser is he, coming from a king,
To shame his hope with deeds degenerate.
The mightier man, the mightier is the thing
That makes him honored or begets him hate;
For greatest scandal waits on greatest state.
   The moon being clouded presently is missed,
   But little stars may hide them when they list.

'The crow may bathe his coal-black wings in mire
And unperceived fly with the filth away;
But if the like the snow-white swan desire,
The stain upon his silver down will stay.
Poor grooms are sightless night, kings glorious day;   1013
   Gnats are unnoted wheresoe'er they fly,
   But eagles gazed upon with every eye.

920 *shift* fraud 925 *copesmate* boon companion 926 *subtle post* sly messenger 928 *watch* crier 936 *fine* end 938 *spend* waste, dissipate 942 *sentinel* keep watch over, tell the hours of 944 *ruinate* i.e. reduce to ruins (and thus teach humility) 949 *pluck . . . wings* i.e. end the life even of the long-lived raven 950 *springs* saplings, new growth 957 *subtle* crafty 959 *waste* wear away 962 *retiring minute* moment of respite (allowing opportunity for a different choice) 967 *ceaseless lackey* ever-present attendant 969 *extremes beyond extremity* i.e. inconceivably extreme occasions 974 *trances* transports, fits 985 *orts* scraps 993 *unrecalling* irrevocable 1001 *sland'rous* disgraced 1013 *sightless* unseen

'Out, idle words, servants to shallow fools,
1017 Unprofitable sounds, weak arbitrators!
1018 Busy yourselves in skill-contending schools;
Debate where leisure serves with full debaters;
To trembling clients be you mediators:
1021　For me, I force not argument a straw,
　Since that my case is past the help of law.

'In vain I rail at Opportunity,
At Time, at Tarquin, and uncheerful Night;
In vain I cavil with mine infamy;
1026 In vain I spurn at my confirmèd despite:
This helpless smoke of words doth me no right.
　The remedy indeed to do me good
　Is to let forth my foul defilèd blood.

'Poor hand, why quiver'st thou at this decree?
Honor thyself to rid me of this shame;
For if I die, my honor lives in thee;
But if I live, thou liv'st in my defame.
Since thou couldst not defend thy loyal dame
　And wast afeard to scratch her wicked foe,
　Kill both thyself and her for yielding so.'

This said, from her betumbled couch she starteth
To find some desp'rate instrument of death;
1039 But this no slaughterhouse no tool imparteth
To make more vent for passage of her breath;
Which, thronging through her lips, so vanisheth
　As smoke from Aetna that in air consumes
　Or that which from dischargèd cannon fumes.

'In vain,' quoth she, 'I live, and seek in vain
Some happy mean to end a hapless life.
1046 I feared by Tarquin's falchion to be slain,
Yet for the selfsame purpose seek a knife;
But when I feared I was a loyal wife.
　So am I now. – O no, that cannot be:
1050　Of that true type hath Tarquin rifled me.

'O, that is gone for which I sought to live,
And therefore now I need not fear to die.
To clear this spot by death, at least I give
1054 A badge of fame to slander's livery,
A dying life to living infamy.
　Poor helpless help, the treasure stol'n away,
　To burn the guiltless casket where it lay!

'Well, well, dear Collatine, thou shalt not know
The stainèd taste of violated troth.
I will not wrong thy true affection so,
To flatter thee with an infringèd oath.
1062 This bastard graff shall never come to growth:
　He shall not boast who did thy stock pollute
　That thou art doting father of his fruit.

'Nor shall he smile at thee in secret thought,
Nor laugh with his companions at thy state;
1067 But thou shalt know thy int'rest was not bought
Basely with gold, but stol'n from forth thy gate.
For me, I am the mistress of my fate,
1070　And with my trespass never will dispense
1071　Till life to death acquit my forced offense.

'I will not poison thee with my attaint
Nor fold my fault in cleanly coined excuses;　　1073
My sable ground of sin I will not paint
To hide the truth of this false night's abuses.
My tongue shall utter all; mine eyes, like sluices,
　As from a mountain spring that feeds a dale,
　Shall gush pure streams to purge my impure tale.'

By this, lamenting Philomele had ended
The well-tuned warble of her nightly sorrow,　　1080
And solemn night with slow sad gait descended
To ugly hell; when, lo, the blushing morrow
Lends light to all fair eyes that light will borrow;
　But cloudy Lucrece shames herself to see
　And therefore still in night would cloist'red be.

Revealing day through every cranny spies
And seems to point her out where she sits weeping;
To whom she sobbing speaks: 'O eye of eyes
Why pry'st thou through my window? Leave thy peeping.
Mock with thy tickling beams eyes that are sleeping.
　Brand not my forehead with thy piercing light
　For day hath naught to do what's done by night.'

Thus cavils she with everything she sees.
True grief is fond and testy as a child,　　1094
Who wayward once, his mood with naught agrees.　　1095
Old woes, not infant sorrows, bear them mild:　　1096
Continuance tames the one; the other wild,
　Like an unpracticed swimmer plunging still,
　With too much labor drowns for want of skill.

So she, deep drenchèd in a sea of care,
Holds disputation with each thing she views
And to herself all sorrow doth compare;
No object but her passion's strength renews;
And as one shifts, another straight ensues.　　1104
　Sometime her grief is dumb and hath no words;
　Sometime 'tis mad and too much talk affords.

The little birds that tune their morning's joy　　1107
Make her moans mad with their sweet melody:
For mirth doth search the bottom of annoy;　　1109
Sad souls are slain in merry company;
Grief best is pleased with grief's society;
　True sorrow then is feelingly sufficed　　1112
　When with like semblance it is sympathized.　　1113

1017 *arbitrators* i.e. compromisers 1018 *skill-contending schools* i.e. schoolmen's contests of skill 1021 *force . . . straw* i.e. place not the value of a straw upon argument 1026 *despite* wrong 1039 *imparteth* provides 1046 *falchion* curved sword 1050 *type* stamp 1054 *livery* garment, uniform (with *badge* of household worn on sleeve) 1062 *graff* graft 1067 *int'rest* claim, right 1070 *dispense* i.e. be reconciled 1071 *to death acquit* i.e. cancel by death 1073 *cleanly coined* brightly counterfeited 1094 *fond* foolish; *testy* fretful 1095 *wayward once* i.e. once out of temper 1096 *them* themselves 1104 *shifts* yields place; *ensues* follows 1107 *tune* sing 1109 *search* plumb; *annoy* sorrow 1112 *sufficed* satisfied 1113 *sympathized* matched

1114 'Tis double death to drown in ken of shore ;
He ten times pines that pines beholding food ;
To see the salve doth make the wound ache more ;
Great grief grieves most at that would do it good ;
Deep woes roll forward like a gentle flood,
    Who, being stopped, the bounding banks o'erflows ;
1120   Grief dallied with nor law nor limit knows.

'You mocking birds,' quoth she, 'your tunes entomb
Within your hollow-swelling featherèd breasts,
And in my hearing be you mute and dumb ;
1124 My restless discord loves no stops nor rests :
A woeful hostess brooks not merry guests.
1126   Relish your nimble notes to pleasing ears ;
1127   Distress likes dumps when time is kept with tears.

1128 'Come, Philomele, that sing'st of ravishment,
Make thy sad grove in my dishevelled hair.
As the dank earth weeps at thy languishment,
So I at each sad strain will strain a tear
1132 And with deep groans the diapason bear ;
    For burden-wise I'll hum on Tarquin still,
1134   While thou on Tereus descants better skill ;

1135 'And whiles against a thorn thou bear'st thy part
To keep thy sharp woes waking, wretched I,
To imitate thee well, against my heart
Will fix a sharp knife to affright mine eye ;
1139 Who, if it wink, shall thereon fall and die.
    These means, as frets upon an instrument,
    Shall tune our heartstrings to true languishment.

'And for, poor bird, thou sing'st not in the day,
As shaming any eye should thee behold,
1144 Some dark deep desert, seated from the way,
That knows not parching heat nor freezing cold,
Will we find out ; and there we will unfold
1147   To creatures stern sad tunes, to change their kinds.
    Since men prove beasts, let beasts bear gentle minds.'

1149 As the poor frighted deer that stands at gaze,
Wildly determining which way to fly,
Or one encompassed with a winding maze
That cannot tread the way out readily,
So with herself is she in mutiny,
    To live or die which of the twain were better
1155   When life is shamed and death reproach's debtor.

'To kill myself,' quoth she, 'alack, what were it
But with my body my poor soul's pollution ?
They that lose half with greater patience bear it
Than they whose whole is swallowed in confusion.   1159
That mother tries a merciless conclusion   1160
    Who, having two sweet babes, when death takes one,
    Will slay the other and be nurse to none.

'My body or my soul, which was the dearer
When the one, pure, the other made divine ?
Whose love of either to myself was nearer
When both were kept for heaven and Collatine ?
Ay me ! the bark pilled from the lofty pine,   1167
    His leaves will wither and his sap decay :
    So must my soul, her bark being pilled away.

'Her house is sacked, her quiet interrupted,
Her mansion battered by the enemy ;
Her sacred temple spotted, spoiled, corrupted,
Grossly engirt with daring infamy.   1173
Then let it not be called impiety
    If in this blemished fort I make some hole   1175
    Through which I may convey this troubled soul.

'Yet die I will not till my Collatine
Have heard the cause of my untimely death ;
That he may vow, in that sad hour of mine,
Revenge on him that made me stop my breath.
My stainèd blood to Tarquin I'll bequeath,
    Which, by him tainted, shall for him be spent
    And as his due writ in my testament.

'My honor I'll bequeath unto the knife
That wounds my body so dishonorèd.
'Tis honor to deprive dishonored life :
The one will live, the other being dead.
So of shame's ashes shall my fame be bred,
    For in my death I murder shameful scorn ;
    My shame so dead, mine honor is new born.   1190

'Dear lord of that dear jewel I have lost,
What legacy shall I bequeath to thee ?
My resolution, love, shall be thy boast,
By whose example thou revenged mayst be.
How Tarquin must be used, read it in me :
    Myself thy friend will kill myself thy foe,
    And for my sake serve thou false Tarquin so.

'This brief abridgment of my will I make :
My soul and body to the skies and ground ;
My resolution, husband, do thou take ;
Mine honor be the knife's that makes my wound ;
My shame be his that did my fame confound ;   1202
    And all my fame that lives disbursèd be
    To those that live and think no shame of me.

'Thou, Collatine, shalt oversee this will.   1205
(How was I overseen that thou shalt see it !)   1206
My blood shall wash the slander of mine ill ;   1207
My live's foul deed, my life's fair end shall free it.
Faint not, faint heart, but stoutly say, "So be it."
    Yield to my hand ; my hand shall conquer thee :
    Thou dead, both die, and both shall victors be.'

1114 *ken* sight 1120 *dallied with* teased 1124 *stops*, *rests* (1) musical pauses, (2) cessation 1126 *Relish* warble; *pleasing* i.e. capable of being pleased 1127 *dumps* mournful airs 1128 *Philomele* (in classical myth, ravished by Tereus and transformed into the nightingale) 1132 *diapason* bass accompaniment 1134 *descants better skill* i.e. sings more skillfully (?), sings the intricate melody (?) 1135 *bear'st* sing'st 1139 *Who* which (i.e. her heart); *it wink* i.e. her eye close 1144 *seated from* situated out of 1147 *kinds* species 1149 *at gaze* transfixed (hunting term) 1155 *death . . . debtor* i.e. suicide incurs reproach 1159 *confusion* destruction 1160 *conclusion* experiment 1167 *pilled* peeled 1173 *engirt* besieged; *daring* i.e. brazen 1175 *fort* i.e. body 1202 *confound* destroy 1205 *oversee* execute, deal with 1206 *overseen* i.e. dealt with 1207 *wash* wash away; *ill* sin

This plot of death when sadly she had laid
And wiped the brinish pearl from her bright eyes,
1214 With untuned tongue she hoarsely calls her maid,
Whose swift obedience to her mistress hies;
For swift-winged duty with thought's feathers flies.
    Poor Lucrece' cheeks unto her maid seem so
    As winter meads when sun doth melt their snow.

1219 Her mistress she doth give demure good-morrow
With soft-slow tongue, true mark of modesty,
1221 And sorts a sad look to her lady's sorrow,
1222 For why her face wore sorrow's livery;
But durst not ask of her audaciously
    Why her two suns were cloud-eclipsèd so,
    Nor why her fair cheeks overwashed with woe.

But as the earth doth weep, the sun being set,
Each flower moist'ned like a melting eye,
Even so the maid with swelling drops gan wet
1229 Her circled eyne, enforced by sympathy
Of those fair suns set in her mistress' sky,
    Who in a salt-waved ocean quench their light,
    Which makes the maid weep like the dewy night.

A pretty while these pretty creatures stand,
1234 Like ivory conduits coral cisterns filling.
1235 One justly weeps, the other takes in hand
No cause, but company, of her drops spilling.
Their gentle sex to weep are often willing,
1238   Grieving themselves to guess at others' smarts,
    And then they drown their eyes or break their hearts.

1240 For men have marble, women waxen minds,
1241 And therefore are they formed as marble will.
The weak oppressed, th' impression of strange kinds
Is formed in them by force, by fraud, or skill.
Then call them not the authors of their ill,
    No more than wax shall be accounted evil
    Wherein is stamped the semblance of a devil.

1247 Their smoothness, like a goodly champain plain,
1248 Lays open all the little worms that creep;
In men, as in a rough-grown grove, remain
1250 Cave-keeping evils that obscurely sleep.
1251 Through crystal walls each little mote will peep.
    Though men can cover crimes with bold stern looks,
    Poor women's faces are their own faults' books.

No man inveigh against the witherèd flow'r,
But chide rough winter that the flow'r hath killed.
Not that devoured, but that which doth devour,
1257 Is worthy blame. O, let it not be hild
1258 Poor women's faults that they are so fulfilled
1259   With men's abuses: those proud lords to blame
    Make weak-made women tenants to their shame.

1261 The precedent whereof in Lucrece view,
1262 Assailed by night with circumstances strong
Of present death, and shame that might ensue
By that her death, to do her husband wrong.
Such danger to resistance did belong
1266   That dying fear through all her body spread;
1267   And who cannot abuse a body dead?

By this, mild patience bid fair Lucrece speak   1268
To the poor counterfeit of her complaining.   1269
'My girl,' quoth she, 'on what occasion break
Those tears from thee that down thy cheeks are raining?
If thou dost weep for grief of my sustaining,   1272
    Know, gentle wench, it small avails my mood.
    If tears could help, mine own would do me good.

'But tell me, girl, when went' (and there she stayed
Till after a deep groan) 'Tarquin from hence?'
'Madam, ere I was up,' replied the maid,
'The more to blame my sluggard negligence.
Yet with the fault I thus far can dispense –
    Myself was stirring ere the break of day,
    And ere I rose was Tarquin gone away.

'But, lady, if your maid may be so bold,
She would request to know your heaviness.'   1283
'O, peace,' quoth Lucrece. 'If it should be told,
The repetition cannot make it less;
For more it is than I can well express,
    And that deep torture may be called a hell
    When more is felt than one hath power to tell.

'Go get me hither paper, ink, and pen.
Yet save that labor, for I have them here.
What should I say? One of my husband's men
Bid thou be ready, by and by, to bear
A letter to my lord, my love, my dear.
    Bid him with speed prepare to carry it;
    The cause craves haste, and it will soon be writ.'

Her maid is gone, and she prepares to write,
First hovering o'er the paper with her quill.
Conceit and grief an eager combat fight;   1298
What wit sets down is blotted straight with will.   1299
This is too curious good, this blunt and ill.   1300
    Much like a press of people at a door,
    Throng her inventions, which shall go before.

At last she thus begins: 'Thou worthy lord
Of that unworthy wife that greeteth thee,
Health to thy person. Next vouchsafe t' afford
(If ever, love, thy Lucrece thou wilt see)
Some present speed to come and visit me.
    So I commend me, from our house in grief.
    My woes are tedious, though my words are brief.'   1309

1214 *untuned* discordant 1219 *demure* meek 1221 *sorts* matches 1222
For why because 1229 *circled* dark-circled (?), rounded (?); *eyne* eyes
1234 *coral cisterns* i.e. their reddened eyes (?) 1235 *takes in hand* acknowledges 1238 *to guess at* i.e. in mere conjecture of 1240 *waxen* i.e. yielding
to impressions 1241 *will* i.e. will have them formed 1247 *champain*
level and fertile 1248 *Lays open* reveals; *worms* reptiles 1250 *Cave-
keeping* inhabiting caves 1251 *mote* speck 1257 *hild* held 1258 *fulfilled* filled 1259 *abuses* misdemeanors 1261 *precedent* example 1262
with . . . strong i.e. under threat 1266 *dying* i.e. paralyzing 1267 *abuse*
misuse 1268 *this* i.e. this time 1269 *counterfeit* copy, mirror 1272 *of
my sustaining* i.e. which I sustain 1283 *know* i.e. learn the reason for
1298 *Conceit* i.e. the conception of what she will write 1299 *wit* i.e. the
intellectual faculty; *blotted* cancelled 1300 *curious* ingeniously 1309
tedious prolonged

1310 Here folds she up the tenure of her woe,
Her certain sorrow writ uncertainly.
1312 By this short schedule Collatine may know
Her grief, but not her grief's true quality.
She dares not thereof make discovery,
1315   Lest he should hold it her own gross abuse
1316   Ere she with blood had stained her stained excuse.

Besides, the life and feeling of her passion
She hoards, to spend when he is by to hear her,
When sighs and groans and tears may grace the fashion
Of her disgrace, the better so to clear her
From that suspicion which the world might bear her.
1322   To shun this blot, she would not blot the letter
    With words till action might become them better.

To see sad sights moves more than hear them told,
For then the eye interprets to the ear
1326 The heavy motion that it doth behold
When every part a part of woe doth bear.
'Tis but a part of sorrow that we hear.
1329   Deep sounds make lesser noise than shallow fords,
    And sorrow ebbs, being blown with wind of words.

Her letter now is sealed, and on it writ,
'At Ardea to my lord with more than haste.'
The post attends, and she delivers it,
Charging the sour-faced groom to hie as fast
1335 As lagging fowls before the Northern blast.
    Speed more than speed but dull and slow she deems:
    Extremity still urgeth such extremes.

1338 The homely villain cursies to her low;
1339 And, blushing on her, with a steadfast eye,
Receives the scroll without or yea or no
And forth with bashful innocence doth hie.
But they whose guilt within their bosoms lie
    Imagine every eye beholds their blame;
    For Lucrece thought he blushed to see her shame,

1345 When, seely groom, God wot it was defect
1346 Of spirit, life, and bold audacity.
1347 Such harmless creatures have a true respect
To talk in deeds, while others saucily
Promise more speed, but do it leisurely.
1350   Even so this pattern of the worn-out age
1351   Pawned honest looks, but laid no words to gage.

His kindled duty kindled her mistrust,
That two red fires in both their faces blazèd.
She thought he blushed as knowing Tarquin's lust,
And, blushing with him, wistly on him gazèd; 1355
Her earnest eye did make him more amazèd.
    The more she saw the blood his cheeks replenish,
    The more she thought he spied in her some blemish.

But long she thinks till he return again, 1359
And yet the duteous vassal scarce is gone.
The weary time she cannot entertain, 1361
For now 'tis stale to sigh, to weep and groan.
So woe hath wearied woe, moan tirèd moan,
    That she her plaints a little while doth stay, 1364
    Pausing for means to mourn some newer way.

At last she calls to mind where hangs a piece
Of skillful painting, made for Priam's Troy, 1367
Before the which is drawn the power of Greece, 1368
For Helen's rape the city to destroy,
Threat'ning cloud-kissing Ilion with annoy; 1370
    Which the conceited painter drew so proud 1371
    As heaven, it seemed, to kiss the turrets bowed.

A thousand lamentable objects there,
In scorn of nature, art gave liveless life. 1374
Many a dry drop seemed a weeping tear
Shed for the slaught'red husband by the wife.
The red blood reeked, to show the painter's strife; 1377
    And dying eyes gleamed forth their ashy lights,
    Like dying coals burnt out in tedious nights.

There might you see the laboring pioner 1380
Begrimed with sweat, and smearèd all with dust;
And from the tow'rs of Troy there would appear
The very eyes of men through loopholes thrust,
Gazing upon the Greeks with little lust. 1384
    Such sweet observance in this work was had 1385
    That one might see those far-off eyes look sad.

In great commanders grace and majesty
You might behold triumphing in their faces;
In youth, quick bearing and dexterity; 1389
And here and there the painter interlaces
Pale cowards marching on with trembling paces,
    Which heartless peasants did so well resemble 1392
    That one would swear he saw them quake and tremble.

In Ajax and Ulysses, O, what art
Of physiognomy might one behold!
The face of either ciphered either's heart; 1396
Their face their manners most expressly told:
In Ajax' eyes blunt rage and rigor rolled;
    But the mild glance that sly Ulysses lent
    Showed deep regard and smiling government. 1400

There pleading might you see grave Nestor stand,
As 'twere encouraging the Greeks to fight,
Making such sober action with his hand 1403
That it beguiled attention, charmed the sight.
In speech it seemed his beard, all silver white,
    Wagged up and down, and from his lips did fly 1406
    Thin winding breath, which purled up to the sky. 1407

1310 *tenure* brief statement 1312 *schedule* summary 1315 *gross abuse* i.e. willful wrongdoing 1316 *stained excuse* i.e. explanation of her stain 1322 *blot . . . blot* disgrace . . . mar 1326 *heavy motion* sad action 1329 *sounds* soundings, levels of water 1335 *lagging* i.e. those tardy in their migratory flight 1338 *villain* serf; *cursies* genuflects 1339 *on her* i.e. in awe of her 1345 *seely* simple 1346 *life* liveliness 1347 *respect* care 1350 *worn-out age* i.e. the good old days (of faithful service) 1351 *Pawned* offered as security; *gage* guaranty 1355 *wistly* meaningfully 1359 *long* i.e. it is a long time 1361 *entertain* occupy 1364 *stay* restrain 1367 *made for* depicting 1368 *power* army 1370 *cloud-kissing Ilion* i.e. high-towered Troy; *annoy* injury 1371 *conceited* inventive 1374 *In scorn of* i.e. in defiant rivalry with; *liveless* inanimate 1377 *strife* effort 1380 *pioner* engineer, sapper 1384 *lust* liking 1385 *sweet observance* i.e. loving attention to detail 1389 *quick bearing* lively deportment 1392 *heartless* uncourageous 1396 *ciphered* expressed 1400 *deep regard* i.e. profundity; *smiling government* i.e. diplomatic skill 1403 *action* gesture 1406 *Wagged* waved (non-humorous) 1407 *purled* curled

About him were a press of gaping faces
Which seemed to swallow up his sound advice,
All jointly list'ning, but with several graces,
1411 As if some mermaid did their ears entice,
1412 Some high, some low – the painter was so nice.
    The scalps of many, almost hid behind,
1414   To jump up higher seemed, to mock the mind.

Here one man's hand leaned on another's head,
His nose being shadowed by his neighbor's ear;
1417 Here one, being thronged, bears back, all boll'n and red;
1418 Another, smothered, seems to pelt and swear;
And in their rage such signs of rage they bear
    As, but for loss of Nestor's golden words,
  It seemed they would debate with angry swords.

For much imaginary work was there;
1423 Conceit deceitful, so compact, so kind,
That for Achilles' image stood his spear,
Griped in an armèd hand; himself behind
Was left unseen, save to the eye of mind:
    A hand, a foot, a face, a leg, a head
  Stood for the whole to be imaginèd.

And from the walls of strong-besiegèd Troy
When their brave hope, bold Hector, marched to field,
Stood many Troyan mothers, sharing joy
To see their youthful sons bright weapons wield;
1433 And to their hope they such odd action yield
    That through their light joy seemèd to appear
  (Like bright things stained) a kind of heavy fear.

1436 And from the strond of Dardan, where they fought,
1437 To Simois' reedy banks the red blood ran,
Whose waves to imitate the battle sought
With swelling ridges; and their ranks began
1440 To break upon the gallèd shore, and than
    Retire again, till, meeting greater ranks,
  They join, and shoot their foam at Simois' banks.

To this well-painted piece is Lucrece come,
1444 To find a face where all distress is stelled.
Many she sees where cares have carvèd some,
But none where all distress and dolor dwelled
Till she despairing Hecuba beheld,
    Staring on Priam's wounds with her old eyes,
  Which bleeding under Pyrrhus' proud foot lies.

1450 In her the painter had anatomized
Time's ruin, beauty's wrack, and grim care's reign;
1452 Her cheeks with chops and wrinkles were disguised;
Of what she was no semblance did remain.
Her blue blood, changed to black in every vein,
    Wanting the spring that those shrunk pipes had fed,
  Showed life imprisoned in a body dead.

On this sad shadow Lucrece spends her eyes
1458 And shapes her sorrow to the beldame's woes,
Who nothing wants to answer her but cries
1460 And bitter words to ban her cruel foes.
    The painter was no god to lend her those;
  And therefore Lucrece swears he did her wrong
  To give her so much grief and not a tongue.

'Poor instrument,' quoth she, 'without a sound:
I'll tune thy woes with my lamenting tongue,   1465
And drop sweet balm in Priam's painted wound,
And rail on Pyrrhus that hath done him wrong,
And with my tears quench Troy that burns so long,
    And with my knife scratch out the angry eyes
  Of all the Greeks that are thine enemies.

'Show me the strumpet that began this stir,   1471
That with my nails her beauty I may tear.
Thy heat of lust, fond Paris, did incur   1473
This load of wrath that burning Troy doth bear.
Thy eye kindled the fire that burneth here,
    And here in Troy, for trespass of thine eye,
  The sire, the son, the dame and daughter die.

'Why should the private pleasure of some one
Become the public plague of many moe?   1479
Let sin, alone committed, light alone
Upon his head that hath transgressèd so;
Let guiltless souls be freed from guilty woe.
    For one's offense why should so many fall,
  To plague a private sin in general?   1484

'Lo, here weeps Hecuba, here Priam dies,
Here manly Hector faints, here Troilus sounds,   1486
Here friend by friend in bloody channel lies,
And friend to friend gives unadvisèd wounds,   1488
And one man's lust these many lives confounds.
    Had doting Priam checked his son's desire,
  Troy had been bright with fame, and not with fire.'

Here feelingly she weeps Troy's painted woes,
For sorrow, like a heavy hanging bell,
Once set on ringing, with his own weight goes;
Then little strength rings out the doleful knell.
So Lucrece, set awork, sad tales doth tell
    To pencilled pensiveness and colored sorrow: 1497
  She lends them words, and she their looks doth borrow.

She throws her eyes about the painting round,   1499
And who she finds forlorn she doth lament.
At last she sees a wretched image bound   1501
That piteous looks to Phrygian shepherds lent.   1502
His face, though full of cares, yet showed content;
    Onward to Troy with the blunt swains he goes,   1504
  So mild that patience seemed to scorn his woes.   1505

1411 *mermaid* i.e. siren 1412 *Some . . . low* some tall and some short; *nice* precise 1414 *mock* vainly tempt (so the spectator of the picture might see those hidden in the rear) 1417 *thronged* crowded; *boll'n* swollen 1418 *pelt* scold 1423 *Conceit* contrivance; *compact* economical; *kind* natural 1433 *odd action* contrary gestures; *yield* lend 1436 *strond of Dardan* shore of Troas 1437 *Simois* river flowing from Mt Ida 1440 *gallèd* eroded; *than* then 1444 *stelled* engraved 1450 *anatomized* laid open 1452 *chops* chapping; *disguised* disfigured 1458 *beldame's* aged woman's 1460 *ban* curse 1465 *tune* voice 1471 *stir* war 1473 *fond* foolish 1479 *moe* more 1484 *plague* i.e. punish; *in general* i.e. on the general public 1486 *sounds* swoons 1488 *unadvisèd* unintentional 1497 *pencilled, colored* painted 1499 *round* all around 1501 *wretched image* i.e. of the traitor Sinon 1502 *piteous . . . lent* i.e. drew looks of pity from Phrygian shepherds 1504 *blunt* rude 1505 *patience . . . scorn* i.e. his patience seemed to make light of

In him the painter labored with his skill
1507 To hide deceit, and give the harmless show
An humble gait, calm looks, eyes wailing still,
1509 A brow unbent that seemed to welcome woe,
Cheeks neither red nor pale, but mingled so
That blushing red no guilty instance gave
Nor ashy pale the fear that false hearts have;

But, like a constant and confirmèd devil,
1514 He entertained a show so seeming just,
And therein so ensconced his secret evil,
1516 That jealousy itself could not mistrust
False creeping craft and perjury should thrust
Into so bright a day such black-faced storms
Or blot with hell-born sin such saintlike forms.

The well-skilled workman this mild image drew
1521 For perjured Sinon, whose enchanting story
The credulous old Priam after slew;
Whose words like wildfire burnt the shining glory
Of rich-built Ilion, that the skies were sorry,
And little stars shot from their fixèd places
1526 When their glass fell wherein they viewed their faces.

1527 This picture she advisedly perused
And chid the painter for his wondrous skill,
1529 Saying, some shape in Sinon's was abused;
So fair a form lodged not a mind so ill.
And still on him she gazed, and gazing still,
Such signs of truth in his plain face she spied
1533 That she concludes the picture was belied.

'It cannot be,' quoth she, 'that so much guile' –
She would have said 'can lurk in such a look';
But Tarquin's shape came in her mind the while
And from her tongue 'can lurk' from 'cannot' took.
1538 'It cannot be' she in that sense forsook
And turned it thus: 'It cannot be, I find,
But such a face should bear a wicked mind;

'For even as subtile Sinon here is painted,
So sober-sad, so weary, and so mild
(As if with grief or travail he had fainted),
1544 To me came Tarquin armèd, to beguiled
With outward honesty, but yet defiled
With inward vice. As Priam him did cherish,
So did I Tarquin; so my Troy did perish.

'Look, look how list'ning Priam wets his eyes
To see those borrowed tears that Sinon sheeds!   1549
Priam, why art thou old, and yet not wise?
For every tear he falls a Troyan bleeds.
His eye drops fire, no water thence proceeds.
Those round clear pearls of his that move thy pity
Are balls of quenchless fire to burn thy city.

'Such devils steal effects from lightless hell,
For Sinon in his fire doth quake with cold
And in that cold hot burning fire doth dwell.
These contraries such unity do hold   1558
Only to flatter fools and make them bold.   1559
So Priam's trust false Sinon's tears doth flatter
That he finds means to burn his Troy with water.'

Here, all enraged, such passion her assails
That patience is quite beaten from her breast.
She tears the senseless Sinon with her nails,
Comparing him to that unhappy guest   1565
Whose deed hath made herself herself detest.
At last she smilingly with this gives o'er:
'Fool, fool!' quoth she, 'his wounds will not be sore.'

Thus ebbs and flows the current of her sorrow,
And time doth weary time with her complaining.
She looks for night, and then she longs for morrow,
And both she thinks too long with her remaining.
Short time seems long in sorrow's sharp sustaining; 1573
Though woe be heavy, yet it seldom sleeps,   1574
And they that watch see time how slow it creeps;

Which all this time hath overslipped her thought   1576
That she with painted images hath spent,
Being from the feeling of her own grief brought
By deep surmise of others' detriment,   1579
Losing her woes in shows of discontent.   1580
It easeth some, though none it ever curèd,
To think their dolor others have endurèd.

But now the mindful messenger, come back,
Brings home his lord and other company;
Who finds his Lucrece clad in mourning black,
And round about her tear-distainèd eye   1586
Blue circles streamed, like rainbows in the sky.
These water-galls in her dim element   1588
Foretell new storms to those already spent.

Which when her sad-beholding husband saw,
Amazedly in her sad face he stares.
Her eyes, though sod in tears, looked red and raw, 1592
Her lively color killed with deadly cares.
He hath no power to ask her how she fares;
Both stood, like old acquaintance in a trance,
Met far from home, wond'ring each other's chance.   1596

At last he takes her by the bloodless hand
And thus begins: 'What uncouth ill event   1598
Hath thee befall'n, that thou dost trembling stand?
Sweet love, what spite hath thy fair color spent?   1600
Why art thou thus attired in discontent?
Unmask, dear dear, this moody heaviness   1602
And tell thy grief, that we may give redress.'

1507 *show* appearance (affected by Sinon) 1509 *unbent* unfrowning 1514 *entertained a show* i.e. adopted an appearance 1516 *jealousy* suspicion 1521 *enchanting story* i.e. seductive lie 1526 *glass* mirror (i.e. glittering Troy) 1527 *advisedly* thoughtfully 1529 *some shape* i.e. the figure of someone else; *abused* traduced 1533 *belied* proved false 1538 *that sense* i.e. the sense originally intended 1544 *armèd* equipped; *beguiled* beguile (with the superfluous 'd' providing a rhyme) 1549 *borrowed* i.e. false, not truly his; *sheeds* sheds 1558 *hold* maintain 1559 *flatter . . . bold* i.e. deceive fools and give them confidence 1565 *unhappy* unlucky, fatal 1573 *in . . . sustaining* in the sharp sorrow sustained 1574 *heavy* (1) burdensome, (2) sleepy 1576 *overslipped her thought* passed unnoticed 1579 *surmise* contemplation 1580 *shows* representations (i.e. of the woes of Troy) 1586 *tear-distainèd* tear-stained 1588 *water-galls* fragmentary rainbows (presaging stormy weather); *element* sky 1592 *sod* sodden 1596 *wond'ring . . . chance* i.e. wondering at each other's fortune 1598 *uncouth* strange 1600 *spent* dispersed 1602 *Unmask* disclose

1604 Three times with sighs she gives her sorrow fire
Ere once she can discharge one word of woe.
At length addressed to answer his desire,
She modestly prepares to let them know
Her honor is ta'en prisoner by the foe,
1609   While Collatine and his consorted lords
With sad attention long to hear her words.

And now this pale swan in her wat'ry nest
1612 Begins the sad dirge of her certain ending :
'Few words,' quoth she, 'shall fit the trespass best
Where no excuse can give the fault amending.
1615 In me moe woes than words are now depending,
And my laments would be drawn out too long
To tell them all with one poor tirèd tongue.

'Then be this all the task it hath to say :
1619 Dear husband, in the interest of thy bed
A stranger came and on that pillow lay
Where thou wast wont to rest thy weary head ;
And what wrong else may be imaginèd
By foul enforcement might be done to me,
From that, alas, thy Lucrece is not free.

'For in the dreadful dead of dark midnight
With shining falchion in my chamber came
A creeping creature with a flaming light
And softly cried, "Awake, thou Roman dame,
And entertain my love ; else lasting shame
On thee and thine this night I will inflict,
1631 If thou my love's desire do contradict.

'"For some hard-favored groom of thine," quoth he,
"Unless thou yoke thy liking to my will,
I'll murder straight, and then I'll slaughter thee
And swear I found you where you did fulfill
The loathsome act of lust, and so did kill
The lechers in their deed. This act will be
My fame and thy perpetual infamy."

'With this I did begin to start and cry ;
And then against my heart he set his sword,
Swearing, unless I took all patiently,
I should not live to speak another word.
So should my shame still rest upon record,
And never be forgot in mighty Rome
Th' adulterate death of Lucrece and her groom.

'Mine enemy was strong, my poor self weak
And far the weaker with so strong a fear.
1648 My bloody judge forbod my tongue to speak ;
No rightful plea might plead for justice there.
His scarlet lust came evidence to swear
That my poor beauty had purloined his eyes ;
And when the judge is robbed, the prisoner dies.

'O, teach me how to make mine own excuse,
Or at the least this refuge let me find :
Though my gross blood be stained with this abuse,
Immaculate and spotless is my mind ;
That was not forced ; that never was inclined
To accessary yieldings, but still pure
Doth in her poisoned closet yet endure.'

Lo, here, the hopeless merchant of this loss,   1660
With head declined and voice dammed up with woe,
With sad-set eyes and wreathèd arms across,
From lips new waxen pale begins to blow
The grief away that stops his answer so.
But, wretched as he is, he strives in vain ;
What he breathes out his breath drinks up again.

As through an arch the violent roaring tide   1667
Outruns the eye that doth behold his haste,
Yet in the eddy boundeth in his pride
Back to the strait that forced him on so fast ;
In rage sent out, recalled in rage being past :
Even so his sighs, his sorrows, make a saw,   1672
To push grief on, and back the same grief draw.

Which speechless woe of his poor she attendeth
And his untimely frenzy thus awaketh :   1675
'Dear lord, thy sorrow to my sorrow lendeth
Another power, no flood by raining slaketh ;
My woe too sensible thy passion maketh   1678
More feeling-painful. Let it then suffice
To drown one woe, one pair of weeping eyes.

'And for my sake when I might charm thee so,   1681
For she that was thy Lucrece (now attend me)
Be suddenly revengèd on my foe,
Thine, mine, his own : suppose thou dost defend me
From what is past – the help that thou shalt lend me
Comes all too late, yet let the traitor die ;
For sparing justice feeds iniquity.

'But ere I name him, you fair lords,' quoth she,
Speaking to those that came with Collatine,
'Shall plight your honorable faiths to me
With swift pursuit to venge this wrong of mine ;
For 'tis a meritorious fair design
To chase injustice with revengeful arms.
Knights by their oaths should right poor ladies' harms.'

At this request, with noble disposition
Each present lord began to promise aid,
As bound in knighthood to her imposition,
Longing to hear the hateful foe bewrayed.   1698
But she, that yet her sad task hath not said,   1699
The protestation stops. 'O, speak!' quoth she,
'How may this forcèd stain be wiped from me ?   1701

1604 *fire* i.e. the ignition needed to discharge ancient firearms 1609 *consorted* associated 1612 *certain ending* impending death 1615 *moe* more ; *depending* impending 1619 *interest* possession 1631 *contradict* i.e. deny, counter 1648 *forbod* forbade 1660 *merchant . . . loss* i.e. Collatine, seen as a merchant whose ship has been wrecked 1667 *arch* (such as those of London Bridge, which provide the following image of current and back-current swirls) 1672 *saw* i.e. back-and-forth or sawlike motion 1675 *his . . . awaketh* i.e. breaks into his untimely trance 1678 *too sensible* i.e. already too sensitive 1681 *so* as such (i.e. as her former self implied in *my sake*) 1698 *bewrayed* discovered 1699 *yet . . . said* i.e. had not yet finished this sad task of saying 1701 *forcèd* imposed by force

1702 'What is the quality of my offense,
Being constrained with dreadful circumstance ?
1704 May my pure mind with the foul act dispense,
1705 My low-declinèd honor to advance ?
May any terms acquit me from this chance ?
The poisonèd fountain clears itself again ;
And why not I from this compellèd stain ?'

With this they all at once began to say,
Her body's stain her mind untainted clears ;
While with a joyless smile she turns away
The face, that map which deep impression bears
Of hard misfortune, carved in it with tears.
'No, no !' quoth she, 'no dame hereafter living
By my excuse shall claim excuse's giving.'

Here with a sigh as if her heart would break
She throws forth Tarquin's name : 'He, he !' she says,
But more than 'he' her poor tongue could not speak,
1719 Till after many accents and delays,
1720 Untimely breathings, sick and short assays,
She utters this : 'He, he ! fair lords, 'tis he
That guides this hand to give this wound to me.'

Even here she sheathèd in her harmless breast
A harmful knife, that thence her soul unsheathèd.
1725 That blow did bail it from the deep unrest
Of that polluted prison where it breathèd.
Her contrite sighs unto the clouds bequeathèd
1728 Her wingèd sprite, and through her wounds doth fly
1729 Live's lasting date from cancelled destiny.

Stone-still, astonished with this deadly deed,
Stood Collatine and all his lordly crew,
Till Lucrece' father, that beholds her bleed,
Himself on her self-slaught'red body threw,
And from the purple fountain Brutus drew
The murd'rous knife, and, as it left the place,
Her blood, in poor revenge, held it in chase ;

And bubbling from her breast, it doth divide
In two slow rivers, that the crimson blood
Circles her body in on every side,
1740 Who, like a late-sacked island, vastly stood
Bare and unpeopled in this fearful flood.
Some of her blood still pure and red remained,
And some looked black, and that false Tarquin stained.

About the mourning and congealèd face
Of that black blood a wat'ry rigoll goes,   1745
Which seems to weep upon the tainted place ;
And ever since, as pitying Lucrece' woes,
Corrupted blood some watery token shows,
And blood untainted still doth red abide,
Blushing at that which is so putrefied.

'Daughter, dear daughter !' old Lucretius cries,
'That life was mine which thou hast here deprivèd.
If in the child the father's image lies,
Where shall I live now Lucrece is unlivèd ?
Thou wast not to this end from me derivèd.
If children predecease progenitors,
We are their offspring, and they none of ours.

'Poor broken glass, I often did behold   1758
In thy sweet semblance my old age new born ;
But now that fresh fair mirror, dim and old,
Shows me a bare-boned death by time outworn.   1761
O, from thy cheeks my image thou hast torn
And shivered all the beauty of my glass,
That I no more can see what once I was.

'O time, cease thou thy course, and last no longer,
If they surcease to be that should survive.
Shall rotten death make conquest of the stronger
And leave the falt'ring feeble souls alive ?
The old bees die, the young possess their hive.
Then live, sweet Lucrece, live again and see
Thy father die, and not thy father thee.'

By this, starts Collatine as from a dream
And bids Lucretius give his sorrow place ;
And then in key-cold Lucrece' bleeding stream   1774
He falls, and bathes the pale fear in his face,   1775
And counterfeits to die with her a space ;
Till manly shame bids him possess his breath
And live to be revengèd on her death.

The deep vexation of his inward soul
Hath served a dumb arrest upon his tongue ;   1780
Who, mad that sorrow should his use control,
Or keep him from heart-easing words so long,
Begins to talk ; but through his lips do throng
Weak words, so thick come in his poor heart's aid   1784
That no man could distinguish what he said.

Yet sometime 'Tarquin' was pronouncèd plain,
But through his teeth, as if the name he tore.
This windy tempest, till it blow up rain,
Held back his sorrow's tide, to make it more.
At last it rains, and busy winds give o'er ;
Then son and father weep with equal strife
Who should weep most, for daughter or for wife.

The one doth call her his, the other his ;
Yet neither may possess the claim they lay.
The father says, 'She's mine.' 'O, mine she is !'
Replies her husband. 'Do not take away
My sorrow's interest. Let no mourner say   1797
He weeps for her ; for she was only mine,
And only must be wailed by Collatine.'

1702 *quality* nature 1704 *dispense* be reconciled 1705 *advance* raise
1719 *accents* utterances 1720 *assays* attempts 1725 *bail* release 1728
sprite spirit 1729 *Live's . . . date* i.e. eternal life ; *cancelled destiny* i.e. the
termination of earthly life 1740 *late-sacked* recently pillaged ; *vastly
stood* i.e. rose high above 1745 *wat'ry rigoll* i.e. the rim of serum which
separates from coagulated blood 1758 *glass* mirror 1761 *death* i.e.
death's-head, skull 1774 *key-cold* i.e. cold as steel 1775 *pale fear* fearful
pallor 1780 *dumb arrest* i.e. injunction of silence 1784 *so thick* so rapidly
1797 *sorrow's interest* claim to sorrow

'O,' quoth Lucretius, 'I did give that life
1801 Which she too early and too late hath spilled.'
'Woe, woe!' quoth Collatine. 'She was my wife,
1803 I owed her, and 'tis mine that she hath killed.'
'My daughter' and 'my wife' with clamors filled
1805 The dispersed air, who, holding Lucrece' life,
Answered their cries, 'my daughter' and 'my wife.'

Brutus, who plucked the knife from Lucrece' side,
Seeing such emulation in their woe,
1809 Began to clothe his wit in state and pride,
1810 Burying in Lucrece' wound his folly's show.
He with the Romans was esteemèd so
1812 As seely jeering idiots are with kings,
For sportive words and utt'ring foolish things;

1814 But now he throws that shallow habit by
Wherein deep policy did him disguise,
And armed his long-hid wits advisedly
To check the tears in Collatinus' eyes.
'Thou wrongèd lord of Rome,' quoth he, 'arise!
1819 Let my unsounded self, supposed a fool,
Now set thy long-experienced wit to school.

'Why, Collatine, is woe the cure for woe?
Do wounds help wounds, or grief help grievous deeds?
Is it revenge to give thyself a blow
For his foul act by whom thy fair wife bleeds?
Such childish humor from weak minds proceeds.
Thy wretched wife mistook the matter so,
To slay herself that should have slain her foe.

'Courageous Roman, do not steep thy heart
In such relenting dew of lamentations;
But kneel with me, and help to bear thy part
To rouse our Roman gods with invocations
1832 That they will suffer these abominations
(Since Rome herself in them doth stand disgracèd)
1834 By our strong arms from forth her fair streets chasèd.

'Now, by the Capitol that we adore,
And by this chaste blood so unjustly stainèd,
By heaven's fair sun that breeds the fat earth's store,   1837
By all our country rights in Rome maintainèd,
And by chaste Lucrece' soul that late complainèd
Her wrongs to us, and by this bloody knife,
We will revenge the death of this true wife.'

This said, he struck his hand upon his breast
And kissed the fatal knife to end his vow;
And to his protestation urged the rest,   1844
Who, wond'ring at him, did his words allow.   1845
Then jointly to the ground their knees they bow;
And that deep vow which Brutus made before
He doth again repeat, and that they swore.

When they had sworn to this advisèd doom,   1849
They did conclude to bear dead Lucrece thence,   1850
To show her bleeding body thorough Rome,
And so to publish Tarquin's foul offense;
Which being done with speedy diligence,
The Romans plausibly did give consent   1854
To Tarquin's everlasting banishment.

FINIS

1801 *late* recently   1803 *owed* owned   1805 *dispersed air* i.e. circumambient air (into which Lucrece's *life* has passed)   1809 *state and pride* i.e. dignified statesmanship   1810 *folly's show* pretense of folly   1812 *seely ... idiots* i.e. kings' jesters; *seely* simple   1814 *habit* cloak   1819 *unsounded* unplumbed   1832 *suffer* allow   1834 *chasèd* i.e. to be chased   1837 *fat* rich, fertile   1844 *to his protestation* i.e. to take a similar vow   1845 *allow* accept   1849 *advisèd doom* deliberate judgment   1850 *to bear* by bearing   1854 *plausibly* i.e. plausively, with *a general acclamation* (see Argument, line 41)

THE PHOENIX AND TURTLE

1	Let the bird of loudest lay	Hearts remote, yet not asunder;	29
2	On the sole Arabian tree	Distance, and no space was seen	
3	Herald sad and trumpet be,	'Twixt this turtle and his queen;	
4	To whose sound chaste wings obey,	But in them it were a wonder.	32

5	But thou shrieking harbinger,	So between them love did shine	
6	Foul precurrer of the fiend,	That the turtle saw his right	34
7	Augur of the fever's end,	Flaming in the phoenix' sight:	
	To this troop come thou not near.	Either was the other's mine.	36

	From this session interdict	Property was thus appallèd,	37
10	Every fowl of tyrant wing,	That the self was not the same;	
	Save the eagle, feath'red king:	Single nature's double name	39
	Keep the obsequy so strict.	Neither two nor one was callèd.	

	Let the priest in surplice white,	Reason, in itself confounded,	41
14	That defunctive music can,	Saw division grow together,	
15	Be the death-divining swan,	To themselves yet either neither,	
16	Lest the requiem lack his right.	Simple were so well compounded;	44

17	And thou treble-dated crow,	That it cried, 'How true a twain	45
18	That thy sable gender mak'st	Seemeth this concordant one!	
19	With the breath thou giv'st and tak'st,	Love hath reason, reason none,	
	'Mongst our mourners shalt thou go.	If what parts can so remain.'	48

	Here the anthem doth commence:	Whereupon it made this threne	49
	Love and constancy is dead,	To the phoenix and the dove,	
	Phoenix and the turtle fled	Co-supremes and stars of love,	
	In a mutual flame from hence.	As chorus to their tragic scene.	

25	So they loved as love in twain
	Had the essence but in one;
27	Two distincts, division none:
28	Number there in love was slain.

THRENOS

Beauty, truth, and rarity,
Grace in all simplicity,
Here enclosed, in cinders lie.   55

Death is now the phoenix' nest;
And the turtle's loyal breast
To eternity doth rest,

Leaving no posterity:
'Twas not their infirmity,   60
It was married chastity.   61

Truth may seem, but cannot be;   62
Beauty brag, but 'tis not she: 63
Truth and Beauty buried be.

To this urn let those repair
That are either true or fair;
For these dead birds sigh a prayer.

Title: *Phoenix* mythical bird which expires in flame and is reborn in its own ashes, thus symbolizing immortality; *Turtle* turtledove (symbol of true love) 1 *bird . . . lay* i.e. the bird (unidentified) having the loudest song   2 *sole Arabian tree* i.e. the only one of its kind (unidentified) in which the phoenix nests   3 *trumpet* trumpeter   4 *To whose* whose   5 *shrieking harbinger* i.e. the owl   6 *precurrer* precursor   7 *Augur . . . end* i.e. prophet of death   10 *fowl . . . wing* i.e. bird of prey   14 *defunctive music can* i.e. can provide funeral music   15 *death-divining* (in its legendary 'swan-song' occurring only before its death)   16 *his* its   17 *treble-dated* i.e. long-lived, the length of three ordinary lives   18 *thy . . . mak'st* i.e. reproduce your own black species   19 *breath* (the crow, or at least the raven, was popularly believed to engender by billing)   25 *So . . . as* i.e. they so loved that   27 *distincts* i.e. distinct persons   28 *slain* i.e. obliterated   29 *remote* i.e. separated in space   32 *But* except (i.e. in them it was simply natural)   34 *right* i.e. due of love   36 *mine* i.e. very own   37–38 *Property . . . same* i.e. the very idea of private possession was thrown into confusion by the obliteration of the distinct or individual possessor   39–40 *Single . . . callèd* i.e. the single nature composed of two persons could be called neither two nor one   41 *in itself confounded* i.e. baffled by its own logical process   44 *Simple* i.e. simples (the individual ingredients in a compound)   45 *it* i.e. Reason   48 *If . . . remain* i.e. if what divides into two can remain one   49 *threne* funeral song (*Threnos*)   55 *Here enclosed* i.e. in the *urn* (cf. line 65) enclosing the *cinders* or ashes   60 *infirmity* i.e. sterility (?)   61 *married chastity* i.e. abstinence in marriage (?)   62 *seem* i.e. appear to exist   63 *she* i.e. true Beauty

POEMS OF DOUBTFUL AUTHENTICITY

A Lover's Complaint "By William Shake-speare" was first printed in 1609 in *Shakespeare's Sonnets*, the famous quarto issued by Thomas Thorpe. The poem begins at signature K1ᵛ and concludes the volume. Although critical opinion is divided, it tends, perhaps mistakenly, to deny Shakespeare's authorship of the poem, which is often assigned to some unidentified imitator of Shakespeare, Spenser, Sidney, and Daniel. The present text is based upon the 1609 quarto, and admits only the following material emendations: 7 *sorrow's wind* sorrowes, wind 14 *lattice* lettice 18 *seasoned* seasonèd 68 *aught* ought 80 *Of* O 103 *breathe* breath 112 *manage* mannad'g 118 *Came* Can 208 *the* th' 228 *Hallowed* Hollowèd 241 *Paling* Playing 242 *unconstrainèd* unconstraind 252 *procured* procure 260 *nun* Sunne 265 *stint* sting 284 *flowed* flowèd 293 *O* Or 326 *bestowed* bestowèd 327 *borrowed* borrowèd *owed* owèd 328 *betrayed* betrayèd.

The Passionate Pilgrim "By W. Shakespeare" was printed by William Jaggard in an octavo of 1599. At C3ᵛ, preceding the poem numbered in modern editions XV, the volume has a second title page, *Sonnets to Sundry Notes of Music*. A fragment of another and probably earlier octavo is in the Folger collection, in leaves containing the poems numbered in modern editions I, II, III, IV, V, XVI, XVII, XVIII. Jaggard's volume is an unscrupulously assembled miscellany, containing (a) poems by Shakespeare available elsewhere, (b) poems known to be by writers other than he, and (c) poems of doubtful authorship, some of them reappearing in another miscellany, *England's Helicon*, 1600, or in dubious compilations associated with specific poets.

Omitted from the present edition are the following poems in *The Passionate Pilgrim*, since they are printed from better texts elsewhere in the *Pelican Shakespeare*: I, Sonnet 138; II, Sonnet 144; III, *Love's Labor's Lost*, IV, iii, 55–68; V, *ibid.*, IV, ii, 101–14; XVI, *ibid.*, IV, iii, 96–115. Omitted also is XIX, a version of Marlowe's "The Passionate Shepherd to His Love."

Included are the remaining poems in the miscellany, although some of these can be assigned, with varying degrees of confidence, to particular poets. Numbers IV, VI, IX, and XI are on the Venus and Adonis theme, but they are more likely to have been the work of Bartholomew Griffin than of Shakespeare, Number XI having already appeared in Griffin's *Fidessa*, 1596. Numbers VIII and XX had appeared in Barnfield's *Poems: In Divers Humors*, 1598. Number XII was to reappear in Thomas Deloney's *Garden of Goodwill*, 1631; and Number XVII (as well as XVI, XIX, and, in part, XX) in *England's Helicon*, 1600. Numbers VII, X, XII, XIII, XIV, XV, XVII, XVIII cannot be proved "non-Shakespearean" on the basis of external evidence, but the majority obviously are. Several have merit, but only Number XII is worth the effort to establish a Shakespearean claim.

The present edition is based upon Jaggard's octavo of 1599, with the following material emendations or readings from alternative texts: IV, 5 *ear* eares 10 *figured* figurèd VII, 11 *midst* mids X, 5 *plum* plumbe 8, 9 *left'st* lefts XIII, 9 *with'red* witherèd XIV, 24 *sighed* sight 27 *a moon* an hour XV, 3 *fair'st* fairest XVII, 5 *Love's denying* Love is dying 7 *Heart's renying* Harts nenying 19 *mourn* morn 43 *back* blacke 49 *lass* love 51 *moan* woe XVIII, 4 *fancy (partial) might* fancy (partyall might) 12 *thy* her *sell* sale 14, 17 *ere* yer 45 *be* by 51 *ear* are XX, 22 *beasts* Beares 27–28 (omitted from *The Passionate Pilgrim* and supplied from *England's Helicon*).

A LOVER'S COMPLAINT

1 From off a hill whose concave womb re-worded
2 A plaintful story from a sist'ring vale,
3 My spirits t' attend this double voice accorded,
  And down I laid to list the sad-tuned tale;
5 Ere long espied a fickle maid full pale,
6 Tearing of papers, breaking rings a-twain,
  Storming her world with sorrow's wind and rain.

8 Upon her head a platted hive of straw,
  Which fortified her visage from the sun,
10 Whereon the thought might think sometime it saw
11 The carcass of a beauty spent and done,
12 Time had not scythèd all that youth begun,
13 Nor youth all quit; but, spite of heaven's fell rage,
  Some beauty peeped through lattice of seared age.

Oft did she heave her napkin to her eyne,   15
Which on it had conceited characters,   16
Laund'ring the silken figures in the brine
That seasoned woe had pelleted in tears,   18
And often reading what contents it bears;
As often shrieking undistinguished woe   20
In clamors of all size, both high and low.

1 *womb re-worded* i.e. valley re-echoed 2 *sist'ring* i.e. matching (one similar and nearby) 3 *accorded* inclined · 5 *fickle* changeable, perturbed 6 *papers* i.e. love-letters 8 *platted hive* i.e. woven hat 10 *thought* i.e. mind 11 *carcass* remnant 12 *scythèd* cropped, cut down 13 *all quit* i.e. left everything; *fell* deadly 15 *heave* lift; *napkin* handkerchief 16 *conceited* ingenious 18 *seasoned* (1) matured, (2) salted (punning on 'brine'); *pelleted* (1) rounded, (2) prepared as seasoners (punning on 'pellet' as culinary term) 20 *undistinguished* incoherent

22 Sometime her levelled eyes their carriage ride,
23 As they did batt'ry to the spheres intend ;
Sometimes diverted their poor balls are tied
To th' orbèd earth ; sometimes they do extend
Their view right on ; anon their gazes lend
To every place at once, and, nowhere fixed,
The mind and sight distractedly commixed.

Her hair, nor loose nor tied in formal plat,
Proclaimed in her a careless hand of pride ;
31 For some, untucked, descended her sheaved hat,
Hanging her pale and pinèd cheek beside ;
33 Some in her threaden fillet still did bide
And, true to bondage, would not break from thence,
Though slackly braided in loose negligence.

36 A thousand favors from a maund she drew,
37 Of amber, crystal, and of bedded jet,
Which one by one she in a river threw,
39 Upon whose weeping margent she was set,
Like usury, applying wet to wet,
Or monarch's hands that lets not bounty fall
Where want cries some but where excess begs all.

43 Of folded schedules had she many a one
Which she perused, sighed, tore, and gave the flood ;
45 Cracked many a ring of posied gold and bone,
Bidding them find their sepulchres in mud ;
47 Found yet moe letters sadly penned in blood,
48 With sleided silk feat and affectedly
49 Enswathed and sealed to curious secrecy.

50 These often bathed she in her fluxive eyes,
51 And often kissed, and often gave to tear ;
Cried, 'O false blood, thou register of lies,
53 What unapprovèd witness dost thou bear !
Ink would have seemed more black and damnèd here !'
This said, in top of rage the lines she rents,
Big discontent so breaking their contents.

A reverend man that grazed his cattle nigh, 57
Sometime a blusterer that the ruffle knew 58
Of court, of city, and had let go by 59
The swiftest hours, observèd as they flew,
Towards this afflicted fancy fastly drew, 61
And, privileged by age, desires to know
In brief the grounds and motives of her woe.

So slides he down upon his grainèd bat, 64
And comely-distant sits he by her side ; 65
When he again desires her, being sat,
Her grievance with his hearing to divide : 67
If that from him there may be aught applied
Which may her suffering ecstasy assuage, 69
'Tis promised in the charity of age.

'Father,' she says, 'though in me you behold
The injury of many a blasting hour,
Let it not tell your judgment I am old ;
Not age, but sorrow, over me hath power :
I might as yet have been a spreading flower,
Fresh to myself, if I had self-applied
Love to myself and to no love beside.

'But, woe is me, too early I attended 78
A youthful suit – it was to gain my grace –
Of one by nature's outwards so commended
That maidens' eyes stuck over all his face :
Love lacked a dwelling, and made him her place ;
And when in his fair parts she did abide,
She was new lodged and newly deified.

'His browny locks did hang in crooked curls,
And every light occasion of the wind 86
Upon his lips their silken parcels hurls.
What's sweet to do, to do will aptly find : 88
Each eye that saw him did enchant the mind,
For on his visage was in little drawn
What largeness thinks in Paradise was sawn. 91

'Small show of man was yet upon his chin ;
His phoenix down began but to appear, 93
Like unshorn velvet, on that termless skin 94
Whose bare out-bragged the web it seemed to wear. 95
Yet showed his visage by that cost more dear ; 96
And nice affections wavering stood in doubt 97
If best were as it was, or best without.

'His qualities were beauteous as his form,
For maiden-tongued he was, and thereof free ; 100
Yet, if men moved him, was he such a storm
As oft 'twixt May and April is to see,
When winds breathe sweet, unruly though they be.
His rudeness so with his authorized youth 104
Did livery falseness in a pride of truth. 105

'Well could he ride, and often men would say,
"That horse his mettle from his rider takes.
Proud of subjection, noble by the sway,
What rounds, what bounds, what course, what stop he
And controversy hence a question takes,   [makes !" 110
Whether the horse by him became his deed, 111
Or he his manage by th' well-doing steed. 112

---

22 *levelled* (1) directed, (2) aimed ; *carriage ride* move (punning on gun-carriage) 23 *As* as if ; *batt'ry . . . spheres* i.e. to direct fire against the heavenly bodies (continuing the artillery metaphor) 31 *sheaved* straw 33 *threaden fillet* i.e. ribbon circling the head 36 *favors* love-tokens ; *maund* basket 37 *bedded* inlaid 39 *weeping margent* wet bank 43 *schedules* missives 45 *posied* i.e. inscribed with love-mottoes 47 *moe* more 48 *sleided* ravelled ; *feat and affectedly* neatly and lovingly 49 *curious* fastidious 50 *fluxive* flowing 51 *gave* i.e. shared an impulse 53 *unapprovèd* unconfirmed 57 *reverend* aged 58 *ruffle* pretentious bustle 59–60 *had . . . flew* i.e. had gained knowledge through observation during the brief time of youth 61 *fancy* i.e. lady in her love-sick mood ; *fastly* closely (?), quickly (?) 64 *grainèd bat* shepherd's staff (so worn as to show the grain) 65 *comely-distant* i.e. at appropriate distance 67 *divide* share 69 *ecstasy* fit 78 *attended* gave attention to 86 *occasion* occurrence, i.e. movement 88 *What's . . . find* i.e. what's pleasant to do is readily done 91 *largeness* i.e. in large (in opposition to *in little*) ; *thinks* i.e. one thinks ; *sawn* seen 93 *phoenix down* i.e. incipient beard signalling the inevitable birth of man from boy (?) 94 *termless* i.e. young 95 *out-bragged* out-braved 96 *by that cost* i.e. by that expense, for that very reason 97 *nice affections* fastidious taste 100 *maiden-tongued* modest-spoken ; *free* innocent 104 *His rudeness so* his turbulent behavior then ; *authorized* privileged 105 *livery falseness* i.e. cloak or conceal indecorousness ; *truth* decorum 110 *takes* takes up, becomes involved in 111 *by . . . deed* i.e. was exalted because of him 112 *his . . . steed* i.e. excelled in horsemanship because of the skill of the steed

113 'But quickly on this side the verdict went:
114 His real habitude gave life and grace
115 To appertainings and to ornament,
116 Accomplished in himself, not in his case.
    All aids, themselves made fairer by their place,
118 Came for additions; yet their purposed trim
119 Pieced not his grace but were all graced by him.

    'So on the tip of his subduing tongue
    All kinds of arguments and question deep,
122 All replication prompt and reason strong,
123 For his advantage still did wake and sleep.
    To make the weeper laugh, the laugher weep,
125 He had the dialect and different skill,
126 Catching all passions in his craft of will;

127 'That he did in the general bosom reign
128 Of young, of old, and sexes both enchanted
    To dwell with him in thoughts, or to remain
130 In personal duty, following where he haunted.
    Consents bewitched, ere he desire, have granted,
132 And dialogued for him what he would say,
133 Asked their own wills and made their wills obey.

    'Many there were that did his picture get,
135 To serve their eyes, and in it put their mind;
    Like fools that in th' imagination set
    The goodly objects which abroad they find
    Of lands and mansions, theirs in thought assigned,
139 And laboring in moe pleasures to bestow them
140 Than the true gouty landlord which doth owe them.

    'So many have, that never touched his hand,
    Sweetly supposed them mistress of his heart.
    My woeful self, that did in freedom stand
144 And was my own fee-simple, not in part,
    What with his art in youth and youth in art,
    Threw my affections in his charmèd power,
    Reserved the stalk and gave him all my flower.

148 'Yet did I not, as some my equals did,
149 Demand of him, nor being desirèd yielded.
    Finding myself in honor so forbid,
    With safest distance I mine honor shielded.
152 Experience for me many bulwarks builded
153 Of proofs new-bleeding, which remained the foil
    Of this false jewel, and his amorous spoil.

    'But, ah, who ever shunned by precedent
    The destined ill she must herself assay?
157 Or forced examples, 'gainst her own content,
158 To put the by-past perils in her way?
159 Counsel may stop awhile what will not stay;
160 For when we rage, advice is often seen
161 By blunting us to make our wits more keen.

162 'Nor gives it satisfaction to our blood
163 That we must curb it upon others' proof,
164 To be forbod the sweets that seems so good
165 For fear of harms that preach in our behoof.
166 O appetite, from judgment stand aloof!
    The one a palate hath that needs will taste,
    Though Reason weep and cry, "It is thy last."

'For further I could say this man's untrue,   169
And knew the patterns of his foul beguiling;
Heard where his plants in others' orchards grew;   171
Saw how deceits were gilded in his smiling;
Knew vows were ever brokers to defiling;   173
Thought characters and words merely but art,   174
And bastards of his foul adulterate heart.   175

'And long upon these terms I held my city,   176
Till thus he 'gan besiege me: "Gentle maid,
Have of my suffering youth some feeling pity
And be not of my holy vows afraid.
That's to ye sworn to none was ever said;   180
For feasts of love I have been called unto,   181
Till now did ne'er invite nor never woo.

'"All my offenses that abroad you see
Are errors of the blood, none of the mind.
Love made them not. With acture they may be,   185
Where neither party is nor true nor kind.
They sought their shame that so their shame did find;
And so much less of shame in me remains
By how much of me their reproach contains.   189

'"Among the many that mine eyes have seen,
Not one whose flame my heart so much as warmèd,
Or my affection put to th' smallest teen,   192
Or any of my leisures ever charmèd.
Harm have I done to them, but ne'er was harmèd;
Kept hearts in liveries, but mine own was free   195
And reigned commanding in his monarchy.

'"Look here what tributes wounded fancies sent me
Of pallid pearls and rubies red as blood,
Figuring that they their passions likewise lent me
Of grief and blushes, aptly understood
In bloodless white and the encrimsoned mood –   201
Effects of terror and dear modesty,
Encamped in hearts, but fighting outwardly.

113 *this* i.e. the following   114 *real habitude* i.e. inborn characteristics
115 *appertainings* things associated with him   116 *case* outsides   118 *Came
for additions* came in for advantages; *yet . . . trim* i.e. always their intended
improvement   119 *Pieced* mended   122 *replication prompt* quick rejoin-
ders   123 *wake and sleep* i.e. flow and ebb   125 *dialect* discourse; *different*
varying   126 *craft of will* power of persuasion   127 *That* so that   128
enchanted charmed, i.e. influenced   130 *haunted* frequented   132 *dialogued . . . say* spoke his part as well as their own   133 *Asked* made demands
upon   135 *put their mind* i.e. used their imaginations   139 *laboring . . .
them* i.e. laboring to extract more pleasure from them   140 *gouty* rheumatic, i.e. old; *owe* own   144 *my . . . part* i.e. wholly, not partly, at my own
disposal (like land in freehold)   148 *my equals* i.e. those like me, my kind
149 *Demand . . . yielded* i.e. yield to my own desires or his   152 *Experience*
knowledge, awareness; *bulwarks* i.e. restraints   153 *proofs new-bleeding*
i.e. persons recently victimized; *foil* i.e. dark ground against which he
shone   157 *forced* gave weight to; *content* presumed satisfaction   158
To . . . way i.e. to raise as obstacles the past perils (of others)   159 *stop
awhile* i.e. only check   160 *rage* i.e. are aroused   161 *By . . . keen* i.e. to
sharpen our wits by opposition (with *blunting us* used in a forced antithesis)   162 *blood* passion   163 *proof* example   164 *forbod* forbidden   165
harms . . . behoof i.e. dangers which give good counsel   166 *stand aloof*
i.e. remain ever unreconciled   169 *say . . . untrue* i.e. tell of this man's
untruth   171 *plants* i.e. adulterate offspring; *orchards* gardens   173
brokers panders   174 *characters and words* i.e. written and spoken words
175 *bastards* i.e. base offspring   176 *city* i.e. citadel of chastity   180
That's what's   181 *called unto* invited, solicited   185 *acture* i.e. mechanical action   189 *By . . . contains* i.e. the more they reproach me   192
teen stress   195 *liveries* garments of service   201 *mood* mode

204 ' "And, lo, behold these talents of their hair,
205 With twisted metal amorously empleached,
206 I have received from many a several fair,
Their kind acceptance weepingly beseeched,
208 With the annexions of fair gems enriched,
209 And deep-brained sonnets that did amplify
Each stone's dear nature, worth, and quality.

' "The diamond – why, 'twas beautiful and hard,
212 Whereto his invised properties did tend ;
213 The deep-green em'rald, in whose fresh regard
214 Weak sights their sickly radiance do amend ;
215 The heaven-hued sapphire, and the opal blend
With objects manifold : each several stone,
217 With wit well blazoned, smiled or made some moan.

218 ' "Lo, all these trophies of affections hot,
219 Of pensived and subdued desires the tender,
Nature hath charged me that I hoard them not,
But yield them up where I myself must render :
222 That is, to you, my origin and ender ;
For these of force must your oblations be,
224 Since I their altar, you enpatron me.

225 ' "O, then, advance of yours that phraseless hand
Whose white weighs down the airy scale of praise !
227 Take all these similes to your own command,
Hallowed with sighs that burning lungs did raise.
229 What me, your minister, for you obeys,
230 Works under you ; and to your audit comes
231 Their distract parcels in combinèd sums.

' "Lo, this device was sent me from a nun,
Or sister sanctified, of holiest note,
Which late her noble suit in court did shun,   234
Whose rarest havings made the blossoms dote ;   235
For she was sought by spirits of richest coat,   236
But kept cold distance, and did thence remove
To spend her living in eternal love.   238

' "But, O my sweet, what labor is't to leave   239
The thing we have not, mast'ring what not strives,
Paling the place which did no form receive,   241
Playing patient sports in unconstrainèd gyves ?   242
She that her fame so to herself contrives,   243
The scars of battle 'scapeth by the flight   244
And makes her absence valiant, not her might.   245

' "O, pardon me, in that my boast is true :
The accident which brought me to her eye
Upon the moment did her force subdue,
And now she would the cagèd cloister fly.
Religious love put out religion's eye.   250
Not to be tempted, would she be inured,   251
And now, to tempt all, liberty procured.   252

' "How mighty then you are, O hear me tell :
The broken bosoms that to me belong   254
Have emptied all their fountains in my well,
And mine I pour your ocean all among.
I strong o'er them, and you o'er me being strong,   257
Must for your victory us all congest,   258
As compound love to physic your cold breast.   259

' "My parts had pow'r to charm a sacred nun,
Who, disciplined, ay, dieted in grace,
Believed her eyes when they t' assail begun,   262
All vows and consecrations giving place.
O most potential love ! vow, bond, nor space   264
In thee hath neither stint, knot, nor confine,   265
For thou art all, and all things else are thine.

' "When thou impressest, what are precepts worth   267
Of stale example ? When thou wilt inflame,
How coldly those impediments stand forth   269
Of wealth, of filial fear, law, kindred, fame !
Love's arms are peace, 'gainst rule, 'gainst sense,   271
['gainst shame ;
And sweetens, in the suff'ring pangs it bears,
The aloes of all forces, shocks, and fears.   273

' "Now all these hearts that do on mine depend,
Feeling it break, with bleeding groans they pine ;
And supplicant their sighs to you extend,   276
To leave the batt'ry that you make 'gainst mine,
Lending soft audience to my sweet design,
And credent soul to that strong-bonded oath   279
That shall prefer and undertake my troth."   280

'This said, his wat'ry eyes he did dismount,   281
Whose sights till then were levelled on my face ;
Each cheek a river running from a fount
With brinish current downward flowed apace.
O, how the channel to the stream gave grace !
Who glazed with crystal gate the glowing roses   286
That flame through water which their hue encloses.

'O father, what a hell of witchcraft lies
In the small orb of one particular tear!
But with the inundation of the eyes
What rocky heart to water will not wear!
What breast so cold that is not warmèd here,
293 O cleft effect! cold modesty, hot wrath,
294 Both fire from hence and chill extincture hath.

'For, lo, his passion, but an art of craft,
296 Even there resolved my reason into tears;
297 There my white stole of chastity I daffed,
Shook off my sober guards and civil fears;
299 Appear to him as he to me appears,
300 All melting; though our drops this diff'rence bore:
His poisoned me, and mine did him restore.

'In him a plenitude of subtle matter,
303 Applied to cautels, all strange forms receives,
Of burning blushes, or of weeping water,
305 Or sounding paleness; and he takes and leaves,
306 In either's aptness, as it best deceives,
To blush at speeches rank, to weep at woes,
308 Or to turn white and sound at tragic shows;

'That not a heart which in his level came   309
Could 'scape the hail of his all-hurting aim,   310
Showing fair nature is both kind and tame;   311
And, veiled in them, did win whom he would maim.   312
Against the thing he sought he would exclaim:
When he most burned in heart-wished luxury,   314
He preached pure maid and praised cold chastity.

'Thus merely with the garment of a Grace
The naked and concealèd fiend he covered;
That th' unexperient gave the tempter place,   318
Which, like a cherubin, above them hovered.   319
Who, young and simple, would not be so lovered?
Ay me! I fell, and yet do question make
What I should do again for such a sake.

'O, that infected moisture of his eye,   323
O, that false fire which in his cheek so glowed,
O, that forced thunder from his heart did fly,
O, that sad breath his spongy lungs bestowed,   326
O, all that borrowed motion seeming owed,   327
Would yet again betray the fore-betrayed
And new pervert a reconcilèd maid!'   329

FINIS

THE PASSIONATE PILGRIM

IV

1 Sweet Cytherea, sitting by a brook
2 With young Adonis, lovely, fresh, and green,
3 Did court the lad with many a lovely look,
Such looks as none could look but beauty's queen.
She told him stories to delight his ear;
6 She showed him favors to allure his eye;
To win his heart she touched him here and there –
Touches so soft still conquer chastity.
9 But whether unripe years did want conceit,
10 Or he refused to take her figured proffer,
The tender nibbler would not touch the bait,
But smile and jest at every gentle offer.
13   Then fell she on her back, fair queen, and toward.
14   He rose and ran away. Ah, fool too froward!

VI

Scarce had the sun dried up the dewy morn,
And scarce the herd gone to the hedge for shade,
When Cytherea, all in love forlorn,
4 A longing tarriance for Adonis made
5 Under an osier growing by a brook,
6 A brook where Adon used to cool his spleen.
Hot was the day; she hotter that did look
For his approach that often there had been.
9 Anon he comes, and throws his mantle by,
And stood stark naked on the brook's green brim.
The sun looked on the world with glorious eye,
12 Yet not so wistly as this queen on him.
13   He, spying her, bounced in whereas he stood.
'O Jove,' quoth she, 'why was not I a flood!'

VII

Fair is my love, but not so fair as fickle;
Mild as a dove, but neither true nor trusty;

Brighter than glass, and yet as glass is, brittle;
Softer than wax, and yet as iron rusty:
    A lily pale, with damask dye, to grace her;   5
    None fairer, nor none falser, to deface her.   6

Her lips to mine how often hath she joinèd,
Between each kiss her oaths of true love swearing!
How many tales to please me hath she coinèd,   9
Dreading my love, the loss whereof still fearing!
    Yet, in the midst of all her pure protestings,
    Her faith, her oaths, her tears, and all were jestings.

She burnt with love, as straw with fire flameth;
She burnt out love, as soon as straw outburneth;
She framed the love, and yet she foiled the framing;   15
She bade love last, and yet she fell a-turning.   16
    Was this a lover, or a lecher whether?   17
    Bad in the best, though excellent in neither.

293 *cleft* divided, double   **294** *extincture* extinguishing   **296** *resolved* dissolved   **297** *daffed* doffed   **299** *Appear* I appear   **300** *drops* medicinal drops   **303** *cautels* trickeries, deceits   **305** *sounding* swooning; *takes and leaves* i.e. alternately employs   **306** *In . . . aptness* i.e. each thing's immediate usefulness   **308** *sound* swoon   **309** *level* i.e. sights   **310** *hail* i.e. bullets   **311** *Showing . . . is* i.e. appearing to be in his nature   **312** *them* i.e. kindness and tameness   **314** *luxury* lechery   **318** *th' unexperient . . . place* i.e. the inexperienced admitted the tempter   **319** *Which . . . cherubin* i.e. who, like an angel   **323** *infected* infectious   **326** *spongy* i.e. diseased   **327** *borrowed . . . owed* i.e. assumed behavior seemingly his own   **329** *reconcilèd* penitent

IV **1** *Cytherea* Venus   **2** *green* i.e. new-grown   **3** *lovely* loving   **6** *favors* charms, gracious appearances   **9** *conceit* understanding   **10** *figured* signalled   **13** *toward* tractable, willing   **14** *froward* recalcitrant
VI **4** *tarriance* period of waiting   **5** *osier* willow   **6** *spleen* heat   **9** *Anon* presently   **12** *wistly* eagerly   **13** *whereas* whereat
VII **5** *damask* mingled red and white (of the damask rose); *to . . . her* i.e. to her credit   **6** *to deface her* i.e. to her discredit   **9** *coinèd* counterfeited   **15** *framed* formed, created; *foiled* countered   **16** *fell a-turning* i.e. proved fickle   **17** *whether* i.e. which of the two

VIII

If music and sweet poetry agree,
As they must needs (the sister and the brother),
Then must the love be great 'twixt thee and me,
Because thou lov'st the one, and I the other.
5 Dowland to thee is dear, whose heavenly touch
Upon the lute doth ravish human sense;
7 Spenser to me, whose deep conceit is such
8 As, passing all conceit, needs no defense.
Thou lov'st to hear the sweet melodious sound
10 That Phoebus' lute (the queen of music) makes;
And I in deep delight am chiefly drowned
When as himself to singing he betakes.
13   One god is god of both, as poets feign;
14   One knight loves both, and both in thee remain.

IX

Fair was the morn when the fair queen of love,
2   *   *   *   *   *   *   *
Paler for sorrow than her milk-white dove,
For Adon's sake, a youngster proud and wild,
5 Her stand she takes upon a steep-up hill.
Anon Adonis comes with horn and hounds.
She, silly queen, with more than love's good will,
Forbade the boy he should not pass those grounds.
'Once,' quoth she, 'did I see a fair sweet youth
Here in these brakes deep-wounded with a boar,
11 Deep in the thigh, a spectacle of ruth!
See, in my thigh,' quoth she, 'here was the sore.'
    She showèd hers; he saw more wounds than one,
    And blushing fled and left her all alone.

X

1 Sweet rose, fair flower, untimely plucked, soon vaded,
Plucked in the bud, and vaded in the spring!
3 Bright orient pearl, alack, too timely shaded!
Fair creature, killed too soon by death's sharp sting!
    Like a green plum that hangs upon a tree,
    And falls, through wind, before the fall should be.

I weep for thee, and yet no cause I have;
8 For why, thou left'st me nothing in thy will:
And yet thou left'st me more than I did crave;
For why, I cravèd nothing of thee still.
    O yes, dear friend, I pardon crave of thee:
    Thy discontent thou didst bequeath to me.

XI

Venus, with young Adonis sitting by her
Under a myrtle shade, began to woo him.
3 She told the youngling how god Mars did try her,
4 And as he fell to her, she fell to him.
'Even thus,' quoth she, 'the warlike god embraced me,'
And then she clipped Adonis in her arms.
7 'Even thus,' quoth she, 'the warlike god unlaced me,'
As if the boy should use like loving charms.
'Even thus,' quoth she, 'he seizèd on my lips,'
And with her lips on his did act the seizure;
And as she fetchèd breath, away he skips,
12 And would not take her meaning nor her pleasure.
13   Ah, that I had my lady at this bay,
14   To kiss and clip me till I run away!

XII

Crabbed age and youth cannot live together:
2 Youth is full of pleasance, age is full of care;
Youth like summer morn, age like winter weather;
Youth like summer brave, age like winter bare.
Youth is full of sport, age's breath is short;
Youth is nimble, age is lame;
Youth is hot and bold, age is weak and cold;
Youth is wild, and age is tame.
Age, I do abhor thee; youth, I do adore thee.
O, my love, my love is young!
11 Age, I do defy thee. O sweet shepherd, hie thee,
12 For methinks thou stays too long.

XIII

Beauty is but a vain and doubtful good;
2 A shining gloss that vadeth suddenly;
A flower that dies when first it 'gins to bud;
4 A brittle glass that's broken presently;
    A doubtful good, a gloss, a glass, a flower,
    Lost, vaded, broken, dead within an hour.

And as goods lost are seld or never found,
7 As vaded gloss no rubbing will refresh,
As flowers dead lie with'red on the ground,
As broken glass no cement can redress:
10   So beauty blemished once, for ever lost,
    In spite of physic, painting, pain, and cost.
12

VIII   5 *Dowland* John Dowland, lutenist and composer   7 *Spenser* Edmund Spenser, author of *The Faerie Queene*; *deep conceit* resourceful creativeness   8 *passing all conceit* surpassing all imagination   10 *Phoebus* Apollo, musician of the gods   13 *feign* i.e. say·in their creations   14 *One knight* (conjectured to be Sir George Carey, to whom was dedicated Dowland's first book of airs, 1597, and to whose wife was dedicated Spenser's *Muiopotmos*, 1590)
IX   2 (the line rhyming with *wild* is missing)   5 *steep-up* sharply rising   11 *ruth* pity
X   1 *vaded* faded   3 *timely* soon   8 *For why* because
XI   3 *try* attempt   4 *he . . . her* i.e. he fell to her lot (with ribald pun on second *fell*   7 *unlaced* i.e. undressed   12 *pleasure* proffered gratification   13 *bay* stand   14 *clip* embrace
XII   2 *pleasance* cheer   11 *hie thee* hasten   12 *stays* delayest
XIII   2 *vadeth* fades   4 *presently* at once   7 *seld* seldom   10 *redress* repair   12 *physic* medicine; *cost* expenditures
XIV   3 *daffed* doffed, sent off; *hanged* furnished   4 *descant* enlarge, expatiate; *doubts* fears   8 *nill . . . whether* I know not which   12 *pelf* reward, booty

XIV

Good night, good rest. Ah, neither be my share!
She bade good night that kept my rest away,
And daffed me to a cabin hanged with care
3 To descant on the doubts of my decay.
4   'Farewell,' quoth she, 'and come again to-morrow.'
    Fare well I could not, for I supped with sorrow.

Yet at my parting sweetly did she smile,
In scorn or friendship, nill I conster whether.
8 'T may be she joyed to jest at my exile;
'T may be, again to make me wander thither:
    'Wander' – a word for shadows like myself
    As take the pain but cannot pluck the pelf.
12

Lord, how mine eyes throw gazes to the east!
14 My heart doth charge the watch; the morning rise
15 Doth cite each moving sense from idle rest,
Not daring trust the office of mine eyes,
17　While Philomela sits and sings, I sit and mark,
18　And wish her lays were tunèd like the lark;

For she doth welcome daylight with her ditty
And drives away dark dreaming night.
21 The night so packed, I post unto my pretty;
Heart hath his hope, and eyes their wishèd sight;
　Sorrow changed to solace and solace mixed with sorrow;
　For why, she sighed and bade me come to-morrow.

25 Were I with her, the night would post too soon,
26 But now are minutes added to the hours;
27 To spite me now, each minute seems a moon;
Yet not for me, shine sun to succor flowers!
Pack night, peep day! Good day, of night now borrow:
30 Short, night, to-night, and length thyself to-morrow.

XV

1 It was a lording's daughter, the fairest one of three,
2 That likèd of her master as well as well might be,
Till looking on an Englishman, the fair'st that eye could see,
　Her fancy fell a-turning.
Long was the combat doubtful that love with love did fight,
To leave the master loveless, or kill the gallant knight:
7 To put in practice either, alas, it was a spite
　Unto the silly damsel!
9 But one must be refusèd; more mickle was the pain
That nothing could be usèd to turn them both to gain,
For of the two the trusty knight was wounded with disdain:
　Alas, she could not help it!
13 Thus art with arms contending was victor of the day,
Which by a gift of learning did bear the maid away:
15 Then, lullaby, the learned man hath got the lady gay;
　For now my song is ended.

XVII

My flocks feed not,
My ewes breed not,
My rams speed not,
　All is amiss:
Love's denying,
6 Faith's defying,
7 Heart's renying,
　Causer of this.
All my merry jigs are quite forgot,
All my lady's love is lost, God wot.
Where her faith was firmly fixed in love,
There a nay is placed without remove.
13 One silly cross
Wrought all my loss.
　O frowning Fortune, cursèd fickle dame!
For now I see
Inconstancy
　More in women than in men remain.

In black mourn I,
All fears scorn I,
21 Love hath forlorn me,
　Living in thrall.

Heart is bleeding,
All help needing –
O cruel speeding, 25
　Fraughted with gall! 26
My shepherd's pipe can sound no deal; 27
My wether's bell rings doleful knell;
My curtail dog, that wont to have played, 29
Plays not at all, but seems afraid;
With sighs so deep
Procures to weep,
　In howling wise, to see my doleful plight.
How sighs resound
Through heartless ground, 35
　Like a thousand vanquished men in bloody fight!

Clear wells spring not,
Sweet birds sing not,
Green plants bring not
Forth their dye.
Herds stand weeping,
Flocks all sleeping,
Nymphs back peeping
　Fearfully.
All our pleasure known to us poor swains,
All our merry meetings on the plains,
All our evening sport from us is fled,
All our love is lost, for love is dead.
Farewell, sweet lass!
Thy like ne'er was
　For a sweet content, the cause of all my moan.
Poor Corydon
Must live alone.
　Other help for him I see that there is none.

XVIII

When as thine eye hath chose the dame
And stalled the deer that thou shouldst strike, 2
Let reason rule things worthy blame,
As well as fancy (partial) might; 4
　Take counsel of some wiser head,
　Neither too young, nor yet unwed.

And when thou com'st thy tale to tell,
Smooth not thy tongue with filèd talk, 8
Lest she some subtile practice smell – 9
A cripple soon can find a halt; 10
　But plainly say thou lov'st her well,
　And set thy person forth to sell.

---

14 *charge* i.e. keep watch over　15 *cite* incite　17 *Philomela* the nightingale
18 *tunèd . . . lark* i.e. attuned to the morn　21 *packed* disposed of　25 *post*
hasten on　26 *added to* i.e. made to resemble　27 *moon* month　30 *Short
. . . length* shorten . . . lengthen
xv　1 *lording's* lord's　2 *master* teacher, tutor　7 *put in practice* i.e. act
upon, come to a decision about　9 *mickle* great　13 *art* learning　15
lullaby good night
xvii　6 *defying* rejection　7 *renying* forswearing, disowning　13 *cross*
misfortune　21 *forlorn me* rendered me forlorn　25 *speeding* progress,
journey　26 *Fraughted* laden　27 *no deal* not at all　29 *curtail* dock-tailed
35 *heartless* desolate (?), pitiless (?)
xviii　2 *stalled* brought to a stand　4 *fancy (partial) might* (so punctuated
the words suggest that 'partial' affection should share rule with impartial
reason; but the passage remains obscure)　8 *filèd* polished　9 *practice*
plot　10 *A cripple . . . halt* (proverb resembling 'Set a thief to catch a
thief'); *halt* limp

What though her frowning brows be bent,
Her cloudy looks will calm ere night;
And then too late she will repent
That thus dissembled her delight,
   And twice desire, ere it be day,
   That which with scorn she put away.

What though she strive to try her strength,
And ban and brawl and say thee nay,
Her feeble force will yield at length,
When craft hath taught her thus to say:
   'Had women been so strong as men,
   In faith, you had not had it then.'

And to her will frame all thy ways.
Spare not to spend, and chiefly there
Where thy desert may merit praise
By ringing in thy lady's ear.
   The strongest castle, tower, and town,
   The golden bullet beats it down.

Serve always with assurèd trust
And in thy suit be humble-true.
Unless thy lady prove unjust,
Press never thou to choose a new.
   When time shall serve, be thou not slack
   To proffer, though she put thee back.

The wiles and guiles that women work,
Dissembled with an outward show,
The tricks and toys that in them lurk,
The cock that treads them shall not know.
   Have you not heard it said full oft,
   A woman's nay doth stand for naught?

Think women still to strive with men
To sin, and never for to saint.
There is no heaven: be holy then
When time with age shall them attaint.
   Were kisses all the joys in bed,
   One woman would another wed.

But soft, enough! too much, I fear;
Lest that my mistress hear my song.
She will not stick to round me on th'ear,
To teach my tongue to be so long.
   Yet will she blush, here be it said,
   To hear her secrets so bewrayed.

XX

As it fell upon a day
In the merry month of May,
Sitting in a pleasant shade
Which a grove of myrtles made,
Beasts did leap and birds did sing,
Trees did grow and plants did spring;
Everything did banish moan,
Save the nightingale alone.
She, poor bird, as all forlorn,
Leaned her breast up-till a thorn
And there sung the dolefull'st ditty,
That to hear it was great pity.
'Fie, fie, fie!' now would she cry;
'Tereu, tereu!' by and by;
That to hear her so complain
Scarce I could from tears refrain;
For her griefs, so lively shown,
Made me think upon mine own.
'Ah,' thought I, 'thou mourn'st in vain;
None takes pity on thy pain.
Senseless trees they cannot hear thee;
Ruthless beasts they will not cheer thee.
King Pandion, he is dead;
All thy friends are lapped in lead;
All thy fellow birds do sing,
Careless of thy sorrowing.
[Even so, poor bird, like thee,
None alive will pity me.]
Whilst as fickle Fortune smiled,
Thou and I were both beguiled.'
Every one that flatters thee
Is no friend in misery.
Words are easy, like the wind;
Faithful friends are hard to find.
Every man will be thy friend
Whilst thou hast wherewith to spend;
But if store of crowns be scant,
No man will supply thy want.
If that one be prodigal,
Bountiful they will him call,
And with such-like flattering,
'Pity but he were a king.'
If he be addict to vice,
Quickly him they will entice.
If to women he be bent,
They have at commandement.
But if fortune once do frown,
Then farewell his great renown!
They that fawned on him before
Use his company no more.
He that is thy friend indeed,
He will help thee in thy need.
If thou sorrow, he will weep;
If thou wake, he cannot sleep.
Thus of every grief in heart
He with thee doth bear a part.
These are certain signs to know
Faithful friend from flatt'ring foe.

20 *ban* curse   33 *unjust* untrue, faithless   43 *Think* believe   44 *to saint* i.e. to be saintly   45 *There* i.e. in women   51 *stick . . . ear* i.e. hesitate to scold   54 *bewrayed* revealed
XX 23 *Pandion* a king of Athens, father of the ravished Philomela, who was transformed into the nightingale; cf. Ovid, *Metamorphoses*, VI, 424–676
42 *but he* that he was not

SHAKESPEARE'S SONNETS

INTRODUCTION

Shakespeare's sonnets are an island of poetry surrounded by a barrier of icebergs and dense fog; or, in the metaphor of Sir Walter Raleigh (the modern Oxford scholar, not the poet's contemporary), they have been used like wedding cake, not to eat but to dream upon. In more prosaic terms, the sonnets, as poems, have been obscured by the huge mass of speculation, much of it uncritical or crackpot, that has grown up around the "problems" presented by the dedication and the "story" adumbrated in the text. These few pages will be concerned largely with the character of the poetry, but enough must be said to justify dismissal of the speculations as immaterial and irrelevant.

The chief external facts are these: in 1598 Francis Meres, in a roll-call of contemporary authors in his *Palladis Tamia*, mentioned a number of Shakespeare's earlier plays and also "his sugred Sonnets among his private friends"; in 1599 the piratical William Jaggard printed two of the sonnets (138 and 144) in *The Passionate Pilgrim*; and in 1609 the publisher Thomas Thorpe issued 154 sonnets entitled *Shake-speares Sonnets: Never before Imprinted*, with a dedication signed "T.T." and addressed "To the onlie begetter of these insuing sonnets Mr. W. H. . . ." Although in this period an attractive name on a title page was not a guarantee of authenticity, we have no grounds for doubting that sonnets 1–152 are Shakespeare's (the apparently alien and unrelated 153 and 154 may be a spurious appendage). But we know nothing about some other important matters.

By 1609 – when Shakespeare was near the end of his dramatic career – the main vogue of sonneteering had long passed. Sir Philip Sidney's *Astrophel and Stella* (published posthumously in 1591) had inaugurated the fashion of sonnet sequences among the Elizabethan poets, Daniel, Lodge, Drayton, Spenser, and others. None of Shakespeare's sonnets can be, or at any rate has been, dated. There has been quite unconvincing argument that all or most of them were written in or by 1589. More persuasive arguments – parallels in idea and diction (some of them rare items in the poet's vocabulary) with the narrative poems and plays – would spread the sonnets over 1593–1609 but would assign the large majority to 1593–1596.

In this period books were often published without the author's knowledge or consent, since manuscript copies circulated and multiplied and one might readily fall into a publisher's hands. Evidently the publication of the sonnets was not authorized by Shakespeare but was managed by Thomas Thorpe; and he may have followed a manuscript of the whole sequence or assembled it piecemeal from fragmentary copies. Some modern scholars have rearranged the sonnets, on either mechanical or subjective principles; these rearrangements have seldom pleased anyone except the contriver. The 1609 arrangement is unsatisfactory and strongly suspect but is the only authority we have.

General opinion divides the sonnets into two main groups, though these do not form consecutive or coherent wholes. The first comprises 1–126, which may be addressed to one young man, the poet's much loved and admired friend, his junior in years and superior in social station. Obviously the first seventeen poems – commonly if rather quaintly known as "the procreation sonnets" – are appeals to a young man to marry and circumvent mortality by perpetuating his beauty and virtue in children. This plea is perhaps not in complete harmony with sonnets 18–126, in which the poet further celebrates the young man (if it is the same one, and if the subject is always a man) and his own complete love, with more or less related themes. In sonnets 127–52, the second group, he makes a radical switch to tell of his mingled passion and loathing for a dark woman (most Elizabethan heroines were golden blondes), a forsworn wife – if one woman only is involved – who, having already had the poet as a lover, has beguiled the young man into an affair, so that the poet has encountered a double disloyalty. This brief outline passes by a number of apparent discrepancies: for example, sonnets 40–42, which reproach the young man (forgivingly, to be sure) for his as yet unexplained liaison, are followed by sonnets which carry on the earlier vein of whole-hearted eulogy, as if nothing had happened. (We do not of course know the order in which the sonnets were written – or whether we have them all.) Another element in the dramatic situation is that in sonnets 79–86 the poet is displaced in the young friend's favor by a rival poet. In general, whether the cause is fidelity to real or imagined fact or dramatic art or accidental arrangement, the sonnets have the air of being day-to-day reflections, as if the poet were living in the moment, not looking back over a closed chapter, and knowing no more than the reader of what is to come.

In contrast with the relative conventionality of the other Elizabethan sequences, this dramatic "plot" – the poet, his young friend, the rival poet, and "the dark lady" – has seemed to many critics to carry special marks of actuality, and there has been much throwing about of brains (the phrase is something of a euphemism) in the effort to identify the *dramatis personae* as figures in Shakespeare's world. One source of misguided guesswork, based on a misreading of Thorpe's dedication, was the attempt to identify Mr W. H. with the poet's friend. The leading candidates for this role were Henry Wriothesley, Earl of Southampton, to whom Shakespeare dedicated *Venus and Adonis* and *Lucrece* in 1593 and 1594, and William Herbert, third Earl of Pembroke. It is now considered probable that in his dedication Thorpe was speaking, not about the contents and "story" of the sonnets, but about the manner of their procurement; that he was – with a touch of mystification calculated to excite interest in the volume – thanking a friend, Mr W. H., for having got hold of the material. However, while the dedication drops out of the case, the two young noblemen remain candidates, Herbert apparently the favorite. But the one fact is that we know nothing, and the wise reader will ignore the whole business. The same agnostic answer must be given in regard to the dark lady and her supposed originals and to the rival poet, who has been identified with a variety of Elizabethan writers. So much for "monsters and things indigest."

But agnosticism needs to go further. We do not know if the several characters (the poet included) and their relations with one another had some basis in fact or were entirely imaginary. To say that these poems, as distinguished from most other Elizabethan sequences, have a special note of actuality and intensity is only to say that Shakespeare was a greater poet – and no one would suggest that the actuality and intensity of his major plays came from personal experience of the situations and emotions there set forth. Apart from the particular and non-poetical puzzles touched on above, there have been two main approaches to the sonnets: they have been seen as only another, and superior, literary exercise in a conventional mode, and, from the opposite pole, as an intimately confessional and profound self-revelation. To cite two names no editor can overlook, Wordsworth, writing of the sonnet form, declared "With this key Shakespeare unlocked his heart"; "If so," affirmed Browning, "the less Shakespeare he." It is best to recognize that, for poets and their readers alike, the difference between actual and imaginative experience is indefinable and meaningless, and also that Shakespeare's sonnets are, like all great poetry, at once exercises in literary form and – in a broad general sense – self-revelation. They are, to be sure, very uneven, and many are far from great.

The Italian sonnet had been inaugurated in English poetry by Sir Thomas Wyatt, whose poems, with the Earl of Surrey's, were printed in *Tottel's Miscellany* (1557). But whereas the normal Italian sonnet had two divisions, an octave and a sestet, Wyatt introduced, and Surrey developed, what is called the English or Shakespearean form (*abab cdcd efef gg*), the one used, with variations, by the Elizabethan poets generally. This form, with its three quatrains and a concluding couplet (a pattern more congenial to English because of its fuller range of rhymes), fostered a manipulation of idea and imagery different from that of the Italian. In Shakespeare's sonnets the argument normally proceeds by quatrains, each one constituting a definite step, and the summarizing couplet acquires an epigrammatic or aphoristic quality (which can be weak). Thus in the famous "When, in disgrace with Fortune and men's eyes" (29), the poet in the first quatrain bewails his own lot; in the second, contrasts that lot with other men's; in the third, thinking of his beloved friend, he rises like the lark that "sings hymns at heaven's gate"; and in the couplet his felicity is generalized in a final contrast. The same formal and logical division and progression are not quite lost even in the most explosively emotional utterances, such as "What potions have I drunk of Siren tears" (119), "Th' expense of spirit in a waste of shame" (129), or "Poor soul, the center of my sinful

earth" (146). If to the reader of more freewheeling modern poetry such logical formalism suggests artifice and insincerity, he forgets the rigorous training in rhetoric, given to every Elizabethan schoolboy, which made such processes of thought and feeling instinctive. The same schoolroom training, the handbooks of rhetoric, and mature poetic practise ensured the systematic knowledge and use of all kinds of verbal figures, patterns of both phrase and sound. Renaissance poets (and their readers) preferred, to borrow Robert Frost's phrase, to play tennis with a net.

Shakespeare, even more than most Elizabethan writers, thinks and feels in images, and his imagery is no less notable for control than for fecundity. The material of his images, like that of his plays and Elizabethan poetry in general, is drawn chiefly from nature and everyday life, from business and law and the fine arts. A sonnet may work out a single metaphor (from business in 4, the seasons in 5, the sun in 7, music in 8), or, sometimes, may use a separate metaphor in each quatrain (as in 73 decay is treated in terms of summer and winter, day and night, fire and ashes), or (as in 1 and 19) may employ a new image in almost every line. A number of sonnets elaborate one metaphor – such as the art of the painter in 24 – with the most finespun ingenuity. This control of images, like that of the divisions of progressive argument with which it is bound up, is seldom relaxed or disrupted even in what appear to be the most deeply disturbed utterances. We are not surprised when, say, the serene exaltation of "Shall I compare thee to a summer's day?" (18) receives logical development; but 147, a violent revulsion from sensual love for the dark lady, is a no less ordered exposition of a ravaging fever incurable by reason.

The structure and texture of the sonnets combine a disciplined, orthodox formalism with the passionate ratiocination that we associate with the "metaphysical" poets – a strain that was emerging in the early 1590's, notably in Donne and Chapman. On the one hand, Shakespeare's style and rhythm, "the proud full sail of his great verse" (to quote his phrase about the rival poet), are mainly in the grand manner and have a smooth Italianate amplitude and flow, the rhetorical rotundity that we find in the earlier plays. One element in that effect is the abundant but discriminating use of alliteration and assonance – "the sessions of sweet silent thought" and "the surly sullen bell," to cite two simple examples. On the other hand, Shakespeare's diction (often monosyllabic) and images can be colloquial and homely, even when his argumentative conceits are most intricate – and to say that is to recall Coleridge's comment on Donne's and other old poets' expressing fantastic ideas in pure English. But, though active cerebration is always going on (and, like Donne's, does not always make poetry), the results are seldom intellectualized through recondite allusion; annotation of the sonnets requires the explaining, not of erudition, but of obsolete words and idioms or complex density of thought. And, while Donne's forceful language does its work in its local context but carries little or no aura of suggestion, Shakespeare's sets up rich reverberations – as lines quoted in these pages remind us.

The characters and situations of Shakespeare's sonnets, in diverging widely from the restricted Petrarchan tradition, freed him from many stereotyped themes, attitudes, and images (sonnet 130 satirizes the conventional catalogue of feminine beauties). That is not to say that those themes and attitudes – of which the most central was of course the persuasive adoration of a reluctant or disdainful mistress – did not evoke many fine sonnets from other Elizabethan poets. Moreover, Shakespeare's young man, like a Petrarchan mistress, is more loved than loving, and ten dozen sonnets in praise of him and friendship can, with all their fertile and graceful invention, fall at times into a semi-Petrarchan monotony. Since modern readers are unused to such ardor in masculine friendship and are likely to leap at the notion of homosexuality (a notion sufficiently refuted by the sonnets themselves), we may remember that such an ideal – often exalted above the love of women – could exist in real life, from Montaigne to Sir Thomas Browne, and was conspicuous in Renaissance literature (*Euphues*, Sidney's *Arcadia*, the fourth book of *The Faerie Queene*, some of Shakespeare's plays), whether on the merely human level or linked with cosmic concord. The poet's young friend, though alive, familiarly known, and sometimes charged with vices, becomes a kind of equivalent of Donne's Elizabeth Drury, a symbol of living perfection. It may be further remarked that one often could not say, and does not need to ask, whether an individual sonnet is concerned with love for a man or a woman; one supreme example is "Let me not to the marriage of true minds / Admit impediments" (116).

Indeed the "story" has value only in the poet's distillation of universal emotions and values. (The few indecent sonnets, by the way, may be regretted, not because obscenity cannot be functional, as it often is in the plays, but because here the tone is brittle and jarring.) Most of the great sonnets are at once self-sufficient units and notes in a complex symphony. While the eternizing power of poetry is an especially Renaissance theme, the modern reader, even if he does not recall the proud claims of Ovid and Horace, must be stirred by the forward-looking

> Not marble nor the gilded monuments
> Of princes shall outlive this pow'rful rime,

or by the backward-looking

> When in the chronicle of wasted time
> I see descriptions of the fairest wights,
> And beauty making beautiful old rime
> In praise of ladies dead and lovely knights....

But such passages are more than themselves; they are partial expressions of the pervasive, all-embracing theme of "Devouring Time" – a theme which inspired much of the greatest poetry and prose of the English Renaissance. Even writers, from Spenser and Raleigh to Browne and Taylor, whose most earnest vision was fixed on heaven, were poignantly conscious of the much-loved earth and time and mutability. Shakespeare's voice – heard also through Hamlet in the graveyard and elsewhere – is in the sonnets mainly the outcry of the natural man against the decay and extinction of beauty and vitality and love:

> Since brass, nor stone, nor earth, nor boundless sea,
> But sad mortality o'ersways their power,
> How with this rage shall beauty hold a plea,
> Whose action is no stronger than a flower?

Moments of unclouded happiness are moments only. The objects of love – like the lover – are subject to time, from "the darling buds of May" to "precious friends hid in death's dateless night." The young friend, in his spring-time of life and pleasure, awakens thoughts of the poet's autumnal age, of leafless boughs, "Bare ruined choirs where late the sweet birds sang." Yet perhaps the greatest of all the sonnets is a defiant affirmation, the affirmation of a man who has no Platonic supports but only his human hold on the particular:

> Love's not Time's fool, though rosy lips and cheeks
> Within his bending sickle's compass come.

But the man sustained by love is still, like all human creatures, subject not only to destructive time but to inward evil. The main contrast in the sonnets, C. S. Lewis remarks, "is between the two loves, that 'of comfort' and that 'of despair'" (Sonnet 144). No conception was more deeply rooted in the Renaissance mind than the unceasing conflict in man between the bestial and the angelic elements in his nature; and, of course, the finer the individual nature the more agonizing the conflict. What was said a while ago about the voice of "the natural man" in Shakespeare's sonnets must be qualified. It seems nowadays to be agreed that Shakespeare the dramatist shared the religious beliefs of his fellow citizens, however far his imagination might transcend popular orthodoxy; the appeals in the greater plays to Christian faith and Christian values are too numerous and too significant to be brushed off. If Elizabethan sonnets, like plays, were an essentially secular and naturalistic genre, none the less religion was too much an enveloping fact of life to be kept out. One incidental and unexpected – and, if not quite certain, strongly probable – reference at the end of Shakespeare's 110th sonnet ranks the poet's love for the young man next to the Christian heaven. But there are clearer and more important things.

In *Astrophel and Stella* Sidney had felt acute conflict between the claims of illicit but ennobling love and the claims of Christian virtue, and the last group of Shakespeare's sonnets depict an illicit, intense, and far from ennobling passion for an unworthy woman. If the praises given to her charms are mostly conventional, the savage denunciations of her falsity go well beyond the considerable license permitted to sonneteers. While both attraction and repulsion are commonly painted in naturalistic terms, there are some appeals to the moral and the religious conscience. The most often-quoted testimony is "Th' expense of spirit in a waste of shame" (129), which is at once a naturalistic and rational and impassioned analysis of "lust in action"; and the sensual lover's "heaven" and "hell" are grimly ironic reminders of their religious counterparts. The religious consciousness is present likewise in 142, 144, and above all in 146 ("Poor soul, the center of my sinful earth"), a Shakespearean parallel to that detached sonnet of Sidney's, "Leave me, O love which reachest but to dust"; both combine the despair and the comfort of *contemptus mundi*. These sonnets, few in relation to the rest, still add a major dimension to the world of experience created in the series (as, to recall a very different context, a few lines add a similar dimension to the fleshly Wife of Bath). Shakespeare's world is composed of universal elements, beauty and decay, time and death, permanence and flux, truth and falsehood, and love in all its forms, from lust to "charity"; and the changes are rung on these timeless themes by an artist of supreme sensitivity to feeling and thought and word and rhythm.

Harvard University   DOUGLAS BUSH

NOTE ON THE TEXT

The only authority for the text of the sonnets other than 138 and 144, versions of which appeared in *The Passionate Pilgrim* (1599), is the quarto volume issued by Thomas Thorpe in 1609. Although this volume contains, in addition to the 154 sonnets, a poem of doubtful authenticity (*A Lover's Complaint.* "By William Shakespeare"), and although it is unlikely that it was printed from a manuscript in the author's own hand and certain that it was not proofread by him, it provides nevertheless a text which seems reliable in the main. A rearrangement of the sonnets pirated from Thorpe's quarto by John Benson in 1640 lacks independent authority. The present edition follows the text of the quarto of 1609 and retains its order of the sonnets. The following list of emendations is complete except for corrections of obvious misprints; the adopted reading is given in italics followed by the quarto reading in roman: 12:4 *all* or 13:7 *Yourself* You selfe

25: 9 *fight* worth 26: 12 *thy* their 27: 10 *thy* their 28: 14 *strength* length 31: 8 *thee* there. 34: 12 *cross* losse 35: 8 *thy* . . . *thy* their . . . their 37: 7 *thy* their 39: 12 *doth* dost 41: 8 *she* he 43: 11 *thy* their 45: 12 *thy* their 46: 3, 8, 13, 14 *thy* their 47: 11 *not* nor 50: 6 *dully* duly 51: 11 *weigh* naigh 55: 1 *monuments* monument 56: 13 *Or* As 65: 12 *of* or 69: 3 *due* end 69: 5 *Thy* Their 70: 1 *art* are 70: 6 *Thy* Their 74: 12 *remembered* remembred 76: 7 *tell* fel 77: 10 *blanks* blacks 99: 9 *One* Our 102: 8 *her* his 112: 14 *are* y'are 113: 6 *latch* lack 113: 14 *mine eye* mine 127: 9 *brows* eyes 128: 11 *thy* their 129: 11 *proved, a* proud and 132: 2 *torments* torment 132: 6 *of the* of th' 132: 9 *mourning* morning 144: 6 *side* sight 146: 2 *Fooled by* My sinfull earth 153: 14 *eyes* eye. The spelling and punctuation have been modernized as in the other works in the present edition. The glossarial notes, supplied by the general editor, are greatly indebted to the *New Variorum Edition* by Hyder Rollins (2 vols, 1944), a superb example of modern scholarship.

SHAKESPEARE'S SONNETS

TO THE ONLY BEGETTER OF
THESE ENSUING SONNETS
MR. W. H. ALL HAPPINESS
AND THAT ETERNITY
PROMISED
BY
OUR EVER-LIVING POET
WISHETH
THE WELL-WISHING
ADVENTURER IN
SETTING
FORTH
T.T.

1 From fairest creatures we desire increase,
That thereby beauty's rose might never die,
But as the riper should by time decease,
4 His tender heir might bear his memory;
But thou, contracted to thine own bright eyes,
Feed'st thy light's flame with self-substantial fuel,
Making a famine where abundance lies,
8 Thyself thy foe, to thy sweet self too cruel.
Thou that art now the world's fresh ornament
And only herald to the gaudy spring,
Within thine own bud buriest thy content
12 And, tender churl, mak'st waste in niggarding.
  Pity the world, or else this glutton be,
  To eat the world's due, by the grave and thee.

2 When forty winters shall besiege thy brow
And dig deep trenches in thy beauty's field,
Thy youth's proud livery, so gazed on now,
4 Will be a tottered weed of small worth held:
Then being asked where all thy beauty lies,
Where all the treasure of thy lusty days,
To say within thine own deep-sunken eyes
8 Were an all-eating shame and thriftless praise.
How much more praise deserved thy beauty's use
If thou couldst answer, 'This fair child of mine
Shall sum my count and make my old excuse,'
12 Proving his beauty by succession thine.
  This were to be new made when thou art old
  And see thy blood warm when thou feel'st it cold.

Look in thy glass, and tell the face thou viewest **3**
Now is the time that face should form another,
Whose fresh repair if now thou not renewest,
Thou dost beguile the world, unbless some mother. 4
For where is she so fair whose uneared womb
Disdains the tillage of thy husbandry?
Or who is he so fond will be the tomb
Of his self-love, to stop posterity? 8
Thou art thy mother's glass, and she in thee
Calls back the lovely April of her prime;
So thou through windows of thine age shalt see,
Despite of wrinkles, this thy golden time. 12
  But if thou live rememb'red not to be,
  Die single, and thine image dies with thee.

Unthrifty loveliness, why dost thou spend **4**
Upon thyself thy beauty's legacy?
Nature's bequest gives nothing but doth lend,
And, being frank, she lends to those are free. 4
Then, beauteous niggard, why dost thou abuse
The bounteous largess given thee to give?
Profitless usurer, why dost thou use
So great a sum of sums, yet canst not live? 8
For, having traffic with thyself alone,
Thou of thyself thy sweet self dost deceive:
Then how, when Nature calls thee to be gone,
What acceptable audit canst thou leave? 12
  Thy unused beauty must be tombed with thee,
  Which, usèd, lives th' executor to be.

1: 2 *rose* (capitalized and italicized in Q) 5 *contracted* betrothed 6 *self-substantial* of your own substance 10 *only* principal 11 *thy content* what you contain (i.e. potentiality for parenthood; with play on 'self-satisfaction'?) 12 *niggarding* hoarding 14 *by . . . thee* i.e. by wilfully dying without issue

2: 2 *trenches* furrows, wrinkles 3 *livery* marks, fittings 4 *tottered weed* tattered garment 8 *thriftless* unprofitable 9 *use* investment 11 *sum . . . excuse* i.e. even my account and make amends for growing old

3: 3 *fresh repair* youthful state 4 *unbless some mother* fail to bless some woman with motherhood 5 *uneared* untilled 7 *fond* foolish; *tomb* monument 8 *to stop posterity* thus bringing an end to his line 11 *windows . . . age* apertures in the enclosure of old age 13 *rememb'red . . . be* to be forgotten

4: 2 *beauty's legacy* inheritance of beauty 3–4 *Nature's . . . free* (cf. parable of the talents, Matthew xxv, 14–30, and *Measure for Measure*, I, i, 36–40) 4 *frank* generous; *free* generous 5 *niggard* miser 7 *use* invest 8 *live* (1) make a living, (2) survive through posterity 9 *traffic* commerce 10 *deceive* cheat 14 *lives* i.e. in the person of a son

5 Those hours that with gentle work did frame
   The lovely gaze where every eye doth dwell
   Will play the tyrants to the very same
4 And that unfair which fairly doth excel;
   For never-resting time leads summer on
   To hideous winter and confounds him there,
   Sap checked with frost and lusty leaves quite gone,
8 Beauty o'ersnowed and bareness everywhere.
   Then, were not summer's distillation left
   A liquid prisoner pent in walls of glass,
   Beauty's effect with beauty were bereft,
12 Nor it nor no remembrance what it was:
     But flowers distilled, though they with winter meet,
     Leese but their show; their substance still lives sweet.

6 Then let not winter's ragged hand deface
   In thee thy summer ere thou be distilled:
   Make sweet some vial; treasure thou some place
4 With beauty's treasure ere it be self-killed.
   That use is not forbidden usury
   Which happies those that pay the willing loan;
   That's for thyself to breed another thee,
8 Or ten times happier be it ten for one.
   Ten times thyself were happier than thou art,
   If ten of thine ten times refigured thee:
   Then what could death do if thou shouldst depart,
12 Leaving thee living in posterity?
     Be not self-willed, for thou art much too fair
     To be death's conquest and make worms thine heir.

7 Lo, in the orient when the gracious light
   Lifts up his burning head, each under eye
   Doth homage to his new-appearing sight,
4 Serving with looks his sacred majesty;
   And having climbed the steep-up heavenly hill,
   Resembling strong youth in his middle age,
   Yet mortal looks adore his beauty still,
8 Attending on his golden pilgrimage;
   But when from highmost pitch, with weary car,
   Like feeble age he reeleth from the day,
   The eyes, fore duteous, now converted are
12 From his low tract and look another way:
     So thou, thyself outgoing in thy noon,
     Unlooked on diest unless thou get a son.

8 Music to hear, why hear'st thou music sadly?
   Sweets with sweets war not, joy delights in joy:
   Why lov'st thou that which thou receiv'st not gladly,
4 Or else receiv'st with pleasure thine annoy?
   If the true concord of well-tunèd sounds,
   By unions married, do offend thine ear,
   They do but sweetly chide thee, who confounds
8 In singleness the parts that thou shouldst bear.
   Mark how one string, sweet husband to another,
   Strikes each in each by mutual ordering;
   Resembling sire and child and happy mother,
12 Who, all in one, one pleasing note do sing;
     Whose speechless song, being many, seeming one,
     Sings this to thee, 'Thou single wilt prove none.'

9 Is it for fear to wet a widow's eye
   That thou consum'st thyself in single life?
   Ah, if thou issueless shalt hap to die,
4 The world will wail thee like a makeless wife;
   The world will be thy widow, and still weep
   That thou no form of thee hast left behind,
   When every private widow well may keep,
8 By children's eyes, her husband's shape in mind.
   Look what an unthrift in the world doth spend
   Shifts but his place, for still the world enjoys it;
   But beauty's waste hath in the world an end,
12 And, kept unused, the user so destroys it:
     No love toward others in that bosom sits
     That on himself such murd'rous shame commits.

10 For shame, deny that thou bear'st love to any
   Who for thyself art so unprovident:
   Grant, if thou wilt, thou art beloved of many,
4 But that thou none lov'st is most evident;
   For thou art so possessed with murd'rous hate
   That 'gainst thyself thou stick'st not to conspire,
   Seeking that beauteous roof to ruinate
8 Which to repair should be thy chief desire.
   O, change thy thought, that I may change my mind;
   Shall hate be fairer lodged than gentle love?
   Be as thy presence is, gracious and kind,
12 Or to thyself at least kind-hearted prove:
     Make thee another self for love of me,
     That beauty still may live in thine or thee.

5: 2 *gaze* object of gazes, cynosure 4 *unfair* deface; *fairly* in beauty 6 *confounds* destroys 9 *summer's distillation* essence of flowers, perfumes 11 *were bereft* would be taken away 12 *Nor it* (leaving behind) neither itself 14 *Leese* lose

6: 1 *ragged* rough 3 *treasure* enrich 5 *forbidden usury* (lending money at interest – 'use' – had formerly been illegal) 6 *happies . . . loan* makes happy those who willingly pay for the loan 9 *happier* better, luckier 10 *refigured* duplicated

7: 1 *orient* east; *light* sun 2 *each under eye* each eye on earth below 5 *steep-up* precipitous 9 *highmost pitch* apex; *car* Phoebus' chariot 11 *fore* before; *converted* turned away 12 *tract* course 13 *outgoing . . . noon* i.e. passing your prime

8: 1 *Music to hear* you whom it is music to hear (a vocative); *sadly* soberly, without joy 3–4 *Why . . . annoy* i.e. you must either love what gives you no pleasure, or else take pleasure in what annoys you 7–8 *confounds . . . bear* i.e. spoils the harmony (of marriage) by performing singly instead of in concert 14 *none* no one, nothing

9: 3 *issueless* childless 4 *makeless* mateless 7 *private* particular 9 *Look what* whatever; *unthrift* prodigal 10 *his* its 14 *murd'rous shame* shameful murder

10: 6 *thou stick'st* you scruple 7 *roof* structure (your person); *ruinate* ruin 9 *change my mind* think otherwise 11 *presence* appearance 14 *still* always

11
As fast as thou shalt wane, so fast thou grow'st
In one of thine, from that which thou departest ;
And that fresh blood which youngly thou bestow'st
4 Thou mayst call thine when thou from youth convertest.
Herein lives wisdom, beauty, and increase ;
Without this, folly, age, and cold decay.
If all were minded so, the times should cease,
8 And threescore year would make the world away.
Let those whom Nature hath not made for store,
Harsh, featureless, and rude, barrenly perish :
Look whom she best endowed she gave the more,
12 Which bounteous gift thou shouldst in bounty cherish.
    She carved thee for her seal, and meant thereby
    Thou shouldst print more, not let that copy die.

12
When I do count the clock that tells the time
And see the brave day sunk in hideous night,
When I behold the violet past prime
4 And sable curls all silvered o'er with white,
When lofty trees I see barren of leaves,
Which erst from heat did canopy the herd,
And summer's green all girded up in sheaves
8 Borne on the bier with white and bristly beard ;
Then of thy beauty do I question make
That thou among the wastes of time must go,
Since sweets and beauties do themselves forsake
12 And die as fast as they see others grow ;
    And nothing 'gainst Time's scythe can make defense
    Save breed, to brave him when he takes thee hence.

13
O, that you were yourself, but, love, you are
No longer yours than you yourself here live :
Against this coming end you should prepare,
4 And your sweet semblance to some other give.
So should that beauty which you hold in lease
Find no determination ; then you were
Yourself again after yourself's decease
8 When your sweet issue your sweet form should bear.
Who lets so fair a house fall to decay,
Which husbandry in honor might uphold
Against the stormy gusts of winter's day
12 And barren rage of death's eternal cold ?
    O, none but unthrifts ! Dear my love, you know
    You had a father – let your son say so.

14
Not from the stars do I my judgment pluck,
And yet methinks I have astronomy ;
But not to tell of good or evil luck,
4 Of plagues, of dearths, or seasons' quality ;
Nor can I fortune to brief minutes tell,
Pointing to each his thunder, rain, and wind,
Or say with princes if it shall go well
8 By oft predict that I in heaven find ;
But from thine eyes my knowledge I derive,
And, constant stars, in them I read such art
As truth and beauty shall together thrive
12 If from thyself to store thou wouldst convert :
    Or else of thee this I prognosticate,
    Thy end is truth's and beauty's doom and date.

15
When I consider everything that grows
Holds in perfection but a little moment,
That this huge stage presenteth nought but shows
4 Whereon the stars in secret influence comment ;
When I perceive that men as plants increase,
Cheerèd and checked even by the selfsame sky,
Vaunt in their youthful sap, at height decrease,
8 And wear their brave state out of memory :
Then the conceit of this inconstant stay
Sets you most rich in youth before my sight,
Where wasteful Time debateth with Decay
12 To change your day of youth to sullied night ;
    And, all in war with Time for love of you,
    As he takes from you, I ingraft you new.

16
But wherefore do not you a mightier way
Make war upon this bloody tyrant, Time ?
And fortify yourself in your decay
4 With means more blessèd than my barren rime ?
Now stand you on the top of happy hours,
And many maiden gardens, yet unset,
With virtuous wish would bear your living flowers,
8 Much liker than your painted counterfeit :
So should the lines of life that life repair
Which this time's pencil or my pupil pen,
Neither in inward worth nor outward fair
12 Can make you live yourself in eyes of men.
    To give away yourself keeps yourself still,
    And you must live, drawn by your own sweet skill.

11: 1–2 *thou grow'st ... departest* i.e. you become, in one of your children, what you cease to be in yourself 3 *youngly* in youth 4 *thou ... convertest* you ... turn away 7 *times* generations of man 9 *store* replenishment 10 *featureless* ill-featured 11 *Look whom* whomever 13 *seal* stamp from which impressions are made

12: 2 *brave* splendid 4 *sable* black 6 *erst* formerly 7 *summer's green* i.e. wheat 8 *bier* i.e. the harvest cart 9 *question make* speculate 14 *breed* offspring ; *brave* defy

13: 1 *O ... yourself* i.e. O, that your eternal self and present self were one 5 *in lease* i.e. for a term 6 *determination* end 8 *issue* offspring 10 *husbandry* thrifty management (with pun on 'marriage') 13 *unthrifts* prodigals

14: 1 *judgment* opinion ; *pluck* derive 2 *astronomy* astrology 5 *fortune ... tell* i.e. foretell the events of every moment 6 *Pointing* appointing ; *his* its 8 *oft predict that* frequent prediction of what 10 *read such art* gather such lore 11 *As* that 12 *store* replenishment ; *convert* turn 14 *doom and date* prescribed end

15: 3 *stage* the world 4 *in secret ... comment* i.e. provide a silent commentary by influencing the action 6 *Cheerèd and checked* (1) applauded and hissed, (2) nourished and starved 7 *Vaunt* boast ; *sap* i.e. vigor 8 *brave* splendid ; *out of memory* i.e. until forgotten 9 *conceit* idea ; *stay* duration 11 *wasteful* destructive ; *debateth* joins forces, fights 14 *ingraft* graft, infuse new life into (with poetry)

16: 5 *on the top* at the peak 6 *unset* unplanted 7 *wish* i.e. willingness 8 *counterfeit* portrait 9 *lines of life* living lineaments (of children) 10 *this time's pencil* contemporary portraiture ; *pupil* inexpert 11 *fair* beauty 13 *give away yourself* i.e. transfer yourself into children

17 Who will believe my verse in time to come
 If it were filled with your most high deserts?
 Though yet, heaven knows, it is but as a tomb
4 Which hides your life and shows not half your parts.
 If I could write the beauty of your eyes
 And in fresh numbers number all your graces,
 The age to come would say, 'This poet lies –
8 Such heavenly touches ne'er touched earthly faces.'
 So should my papers, yellowed with their age,
 Be scorned, like old men of less truth than tongue,
 And your true rights be termed a poet's rage
12 And stretchèd metre of an antique song.
  But were some child of yours alive that time,
  You should live twice – in it and in my rime.

18 Shall I compare thee to a summer's day?
 Thou art more lovely and more temperate.
 Rough winds do shake the darling buds of May,
4 And summer's lease hath all too short a date.
 Sometime too hot the eye of heaven shines,
 And often is his gold complexion dimmed;
 And every fair from fair sometime declines,
8 By chance, or nature's changing course, untrimmed:
 But thy eternal summer shall not fade
 Nor lose possession of that fair thou ow'st,
 Nor shall Death brag thou wand'rest in his shade
12 When in eternal lines to time thou grow'st.
  So long as men can breathe or eyes can see,
  So long lives this, and this gives life to thee.

19 Devouring Time, blunt thou the lion's paws,
 And make the earth devour her own sweet brood;
 Pluck the keen teeth from the fierce tiger's jaws,
4 And burn the long-lived phoenix in her blood;
 Make glad and sorry seasons as thou fleet'st,
 And do whate'er thou wilt, swift-footed Time,
 To the wide world and all her fading sweets,
8 But I forbid thee one most heinous crime:
 O, carve not with thy hours my love's fair brow,
 Nor draw no lines there with thine antique pen;
 Him in thy course untainted do allow
12 For beauty's pattern to succeeding men.
  Yet do thy worst, old Time: despite thy wrong,
  My love shall in my verse ever live young.

20 A woman's face, with Nature's own hand painted,
 Hast thou, the master-mistress of my passion;
 A woman's gentle heart, but not acquainted
4 With shifting change, as is false women's fashion;
 An eye more bright than theirs, less false in rolling,
 Gilding the object whereupon it gazeth;
 A man in hue all hues in his controlling,
8 Which steals men's eyes and women's souls amazeth.
 And for a woman wert thou first created,
 Till Nature as she wrought thee fell a-doting,
 And by addition me of thee defeated
12 By adding one thing to my purpose nothing.
  But since she pricked thee out for women's pleasure,
  Mine be thy love, and thy love's use their treasure.

21 So is it not with me as with that Muse
 Stirred by a painted beauty to his verse,
 Who heaven itself for ornament doth use
4 And every fair with his fair doth rehearse;
 Making a couplement of proud compare
 With sun and moon, with earth and sea's rich gems,
 With April's first-born flowers, and all things rare
8 That heaven's air in this huge rondure hems.
 O let me, true in love, but truly write,
 And then believe me, my love is as fair
 As any mother's child, though not so bright
12 As those gold candles fixed in heaven's air:
  Let them say more that like of hearsay well;
  I will not praise that purpose not to sell.

22 My glass shall not persuade me I am old
 So long as youth and thou are of one date;
 But when in thee time's furrows I behold,
4 Then look I death my days should expiate.
 For all that beauty that doth cover thee
 Is but the seemly raiment of my heart,
 Which in thy breast doth live, as thine in me:
8 How can I then be elder than thou art?
 O therefore, love, be of thyself so wary
 As I, not for myself, but for thee will,
 Bearing thy heart, which I will keep so chary
12 As tender nurse her babe from faring ill.
  Presume not on thy heart when mine is slain;
  Thou gav'st me thine not to give back again.

17: 2 *deserts* merits 4 *parts* qualities 6 *numbers* verses 8 *touches* strokes of artistry 11 *true rights* due praise 12 *stretchèd metre* poetic hyperbole 13 *that time* in that future time

18: 4 *lease* allotted time; *date* duration 5 *eye* sun 6 *dimmed* clouded over 7 *fair from fair* beautiful thing from beauty 8 *untrimmed* stripped of adornment 10 *thou ow'st* you own 11 *shade* i.e. oblivion 12 *lines* poetry; *thou grow'st* you are grafted

19: 2 *brood* i.e. the children of earth 4 *phoenix* a legendary bird which lives for hundreds of years and then propagates itself from its own ashes (symbol of immortality); *in her blood* alive 10 *antique* (1) antic, capricious, (2) old 11 *untainted* unspoiled

20: 1 *with . . . hand* i.e. naturally, without cosmetics 2 *master-mistress* master and mistress; *passion* love 5 *rolling* i.e. passing from one to another 6 *Gilding* brightening (as do the rays of the sun) 7 *A man . . . controlling* i.e. a man in complexion with all complexions – 'humors' – under his control (the line may be corrupt or, as glossed thus, may contrast male constancy with feminine inconstancy); *hues* (capitalized and italicized in Q) 11 *defeated* cheated, deprived 12 *one thing* i.e. a penis

21: 1 *Muse* poet 2 *Stirred . . . beauty* inspired by artificial beauty 4 *every . . . rehearse* i.e. mentions everything beautiful in relation to his mistress 5 *couplement* combination; *compare* comparison 8 *rondure* sphere; *hems* encircles 12 *gold candles* i.e. stars 13 *that . . . well* i.e. that are fond of large and specious comparisons 14 *that* who, i.e. since I am not a huckster

22: 2 *of one date* of an age; i.e. so long as you are young 4 *expiate* wind up 5–8 *For . . . art* i.e. the friend's beautiful body encloses the poet's heart, and this transfer of hearts makes friend and poet of one age 11 *chary* carefully 13 *Presume not on* do not expect to regain

23
As an unperfect actor on the stage,
Who with his fear is put besides his part,
Or some fierce thing replete with too much rage,
4 Whose strength's abundance weakens his own heart;
So I, for fear of trust, forget to say
The perfect ceremony of love's rite,
And in mine own love's strength seem to decay,
8 O'ercharged with burden of mine own love's might.
O, let my books be then the eloquence
And dumb presagers of my speaking breast,
Who plead for love, and look for recompense,
12 More than that tongue that more hath more expressed.
        O, learn to read what silent love hath writ:
        To hear with eyes belongs to love's fine wit.

24
Mine eye hath played the painter and hath stelled
Thy beauty's form in table of my heart;
My body is the frame wherein 'tis held,
4 And perspective it is best painter's art.
For through the painter must you see his skill
To find where your true image pictured lies,
Which in my bosom's shop is hanging still,
8 That hath his windows glazèd with thine eyes.
Now see what good turns eyes for eyes have done:
Mine eyes have drawn thy shape, and thine for me
Are windows to my breast, wherethrough the sun
12 Delights to peep, to gaze therein on thee.
        Yet eyes this cunning want to grace their art;
        They draw but what they see, know not the heart.

25
Let those who are in favor with their stars
Of public honor and proud titles boast,
Whilst I, whom fortune of such triumph bars,
4 Unlooked for joy in that I honor most.
Great princes' favorites their fair leaves spread
But as the marigold at the sun's eye;
And in themselves their pride lies burièd,
8 For at a frown they in their glory die.
The painful warrior famousèd for fight,
After a thousand victories once foiled,
Is from the book of honor rasèd quite,
12 And all the rest forgot for which he toiled.
        Then happy I, that love and am beloved
        Where I may not remove nor be removed.

26
Lord of my love, to whom in vassalage
Thy merit hath my duty strongly knit,
To thee I send this written ambassage
4 To witness duty, not to show my wit;
Duty so great, which wit so poor as mine
May make seem bare, in wanting words to show it,
But that I hope some good conceit of thine
8 In thy soul's thought, all naked, will bestow it;
Till whatsoever star that guides my moving
Points on me graciously with fair aspect,
And puts apparel on my tottered loving
12 To show me worthy of thy sweet respect:
        Then may I dare to boast how I do love thee;
        Till then not show my head where thou mayst prove me.

27
Weary with toil, I haste me to my bed,
The dear repose for limbs with travel tired,
But then begins a journey in my head
4 To work my mind when body's work's expired;
For then my thoughts, from far where I abide,
Intend a zealous pilgrimage to thee,
And keep my drooping eyelids open wide,
8 Looking on darkness which the blind do see;
Save that my soul's imaginary sight
Presents thy shadow to my sightless view,
Which, like a jewel hung in ghastly night,
12 Makes black night beauteous and her old face new.
        Lo, thus, by day my limbs, by night my mind,
        For thee and for myself no quiet find.

23: 1 *unperfect actor* i.e. imperfect in his craft or in his part 2 *besides* out of 4 *heart* i.e. capacity for performance 5 *for . . . trust* in self-distrust 5–6 *forget . . . rite* i.e. am not word-perfect in love's ritual 7 *decay* i.e. falter 10 *dumb presagers* silent messengers 12 *more expressed* more often expressed 14 *wit* intelligence

24: 1 *stelled* portrayed 2 *table* tablet (?), picture (?) 4 *perspective it is* i.e. given perspective, which is (?) 8 *his* its; *glazèd* paned 13 *cunning* skill; *want* lack; *grace* enhance

25: 1 *who . . . stars* i.e. whose stars are propitious 4 *Unlooked for* unexpectedly; *that* what 6 *But* only 7 *lies burièd* i.e. is already in its grave 9 *painful* striving; *fight* (an emendation for 'worth'; some editors retain 'worth' and emend *quite* in l. 11 to 'forth') 11 *rasèd* erased

26: 3 *ambassage* overture, message (probably the present sonnet) 4 *wit* poetic powers 7 *conceit* conception 8 *all . . . bestow it* i.e. will give it lodging despite its nakedness 9 *moving* i.e. life and actions 10 *aspect* influence (astrological term) 11 *tottered* tattered 14 *prove* test

27: 2 *travel* (1) journeying, (2) travail 4 *To work* to set to work 6 *pilgrimage* journey of devotion 8 *which* such as 9 *imaginary* imagining 10 *shadow* image

28: 6 *shake hands* unite 7 *the other to complain* i.e. the night making me complain 9 *I tell . . . bright* i.e. I please the day by telling him you are bright 10 *And . . . heaven* and can shine in his place when it is cloudy 11 *swart* dark 12 *twire* peek; *thou . . . even* you make the evening bright

28
How can I then return in happy plight
That am debarred the benefit of rest,
When day's oppression is not eased by night,
4 But day by night and night by day oppressed,
And each, though enemies to either's reign,
Do in consent shake hands to torture me,
The one by toil, the other to complain
8 How far I toil, still farther off from thee?
I tell the day, to please him, thou art bright
And dost him grace when clouds do blot the heaven;
So flatter I the swart-complexioned night,
12 When sparkling stars twire not, thou gild'st the even.
        But day doth daily draw my sorrows longer,
        And night doth nightly make grief's strength seem stronger.

29 When, in disgrace with Fortune and men's eyes,
   I all alone beweep my outcast state,
   And trouble deaf heaven with my bootless cries,
4 And look upon myself and curse my fate,
   Wishing me like to one more rich in hope,
   Featured like him, like him with friends possessed,
   Desiring this man's art, and that man's scope,
8 With what I most enjoy contented least;
   Yet in these thoughts myself almost despising,
   Haply I think on thee, and then my state,
   Like to the lark at break of day arising
12 From sullen earth, sings hymns at heaven's gate;
    For thy sweet love rememb'red such wealth brings
    That then I scorn to change my state with kings.

30 When to the sessions of sweet silent thought
   I summon up remembrance of things past,
   I sigh the lack of many a thing I sought,
4 And with old woes new wail my dear time's waste:
   Then can I drown an eye, unused to flow,
   For precious friends hid in death's dateless night,
   And weep afresh love's long since cancelled woe,
8 And moan th' expense of many a vanished sight.
   Then can I grieve at grievances foregone,
   And heavily from woe to woe tell o'er
   The sad account of fore-bemoanèd moan,
12 Which I new pay as if not paid before.
    But if the while I think on thee, dear friend,
    All losses are restored and sorrows end.

31 Thy bosom is endearèd with all hearts
   Which I by lacking have supposèd dead;
   And there reigns love, and all love's loving parts,
4 And all those friends which I thought burièd.
   How many a holy and obsequious tear
   Hath dear religious love stol'n from mine eye,
   As interest of the dead, which now appear
8 But things removed that hidden in thee lie!
   Thou art the grave where buried love doth live,
   Hung with the trophies of my lovers gone,
   Who all their parts of me to thee did give;
12 That due of many now is thine alone.
    Their images I loved I view in thee,
    And thou, all they, hast all the all of me.

32 If thou survive my well-contented day
   When that churl Death my bones with dust shall cover,
   And shalt by fortune once more resurvey
4 These poor rude lines of thy deceasèd lover,
   Compare them with the bett'ring of the time,
   And though they be outstripped by every pen,
   Reserve them for my love, not for their rime,
8 Exceeded by the height of happier men.
   O, then vouchsafe me but this loving thought:
   'Had my friend's Muse grown with this growing age,
   A dearer birth than this his love had brought
12 To march in ranks of better equipage;
    But since he died, and poets better prove,
    Theirs for their style I'll read, his for his love.'

Full many a glorious morning have I seen   33
   Flatter the mountain tops with sovereign eye,
   Kissing with golden face the meadows green,
   Gilding pale streams with heavenly alchemy;   4
   Anon permit the basest clouds to ride
   With ugly rack on his celestial face,
   And from the forlorn world his visage hide,
   Stealing unseen to west with this disgrace: 8
   Even so my sun one early morn did shine
   With all-triumphant splendor on my brow;
   But, out alack, he was but one hour mine,
   The region cloud hath masked him from me now.   12
    Yet him for this my love no whit disdaineth;
    Suns of the world may stain when heaven's sun staineth.

Why didst thou promise such a beauteous day   34
   And make me travel forth without my cloak,
   To let base clouds o'ertake me in my way,
   Hiding thy brav'ry in their rotten smoke?   4
   'Tis not enough that through the cloud thou break
   To dry the rain on my storm-beaten face,
   For no man well of such a salve can speak
   That heals the wound, and cures not the disgrace: 8
   Nor can thy shame give physic to my grief;
   Though thou repent, yet I have still the loss:
   Th' offender's sorrow lends but weak relief
   To him that bears the strong offense's cross.   12
    Ah, but those tears are pearl which thy love sheeds,
    And they are rich and ransom all ill deeds.

29: 1 *disgrace* disfavor; *eyes* regard 3 *bootless* useless 6 *like him, like him* i.e. like another, like still another 7 *art* literary skill; *scope* intellectual power 10 *Haply* perchance; *state* i.e. mood, state of mind 12 *sullen* gloomy 14 *state* lot

30: 1 *sessions* sittings, as of a court 3 *sigh* lament 4 *new wail* newly bewail; *dear time's waste* time's destruction of precious things (?), the wasteful passing of precious time (?) 6 *dateless* endless 7 *cancelled* fully paid 8 *expense* loss 9 *foregone* former 10 *tell* count

31: 1 *endearèd* enriched 5 *obsequious* mourning 6 *religious* venerating 7 *interest* rightful due; *which* who 8 *removed* absent 10 *trophies* memorials; *lovers* loved ones 11 *parts* shares 12 *That . . . many* what was due to many 14 *all they* who are all of them combined

32: 1 *my well-contented day* i.e. the ripe day of my death 5 *bett'ring* improved writing 7 *Reserve* preserve; *rime* poetic skill 8 *height* superiority; *happier* more gifted 11 *dearer* more precious 12 *of better equipage* more finely equipped

33: 2 *Flatter . . . eye* i.e. honor with a royal glance of the sun 5 *Anon* soon; *basest* darkest 6 *rack* cloud streamers 7 *forlorn* sadly forsaken 11 *out alack* alas 12 *region cloud* clouds of the upper air

34: 3 *base* dark 4 *brav'ry* splendor; *rotten smoke* unwholesome vapors 8 *disgrace* shame 9 *shame* regret; *physic* remedy 13 *sheeds* sheds 14 *ransom* atone for

35 No more be grieved at that which thou hast done:
   Roses have thorns, and silver fountains mud;
   Clouds and eclipses stain both moon and sun,
4 And loathsome canker lives in sweetest bud.
   All men make faults, and even I in this,
   Authorizing thy trespass with compare,
   Myself corrupting, salving thy amiss,
8 Excusing thy sins more than thy sins are;
   For to thy sensual fault I bring in sense
   (Thy adverse party is thy advocate)
   And 'gainst myself a lawful plea commence;
12 Such civil war is in my love and hate
      That I an accessary needs must be
      To that sweet thief which sourly robs from me.

36 Let me confess that we two must be twain
   Although our undivided loves are one:
   So shall those blots that do with me remain,
4 Without thy help by me be borne alone.
   In our two loves there is but one respect,
   Though in our lives a separable spite,
   Which though it alter not love's sole effect,
8 Yet doth it steal sweet hours from love's delight.
   I may not evermore acknowledge thee,
   Lest my bewailèd guilt should do thee shame;
   Nor thou with public kindness honor me
12 Unless thou take that honor from thy name:
      But do not so; I love thee in such sort
      As, thou being mine, mine is thy good report.

35: 3 *stain* darken   4 *canker* destroying worm   5 *make faults* are faulty
6 *Authorizing* justifying; *with compare* by comparison   7 *salving thy amiss*
palliating your offense   8 *Excusing . . . are* i.e. going further in excusing
your sins than you in sinning   9 *to . . . sense* i.e. to your physical fault I add
my intellectual fault (perhaps with a pun on 'incense')   13 *accessary*
fellow sinner

36: 3 *blots* defects   5 *but one respect* a singleness of attitude   6 *separable
spite* spiteful separation   7 *sole* singleness of   10 *bewailèd* lamented   14
report reputation

37: 3 *made lame* i.e. handicapped (in a general sense); *dearest* most grievous
4 *of* in   5 *wit* intelligence   7 *Intitled . . . sit* sit enthroned among your
qualities   8 *ingrafted . . . store* i.e. fastened to and drawing upon this
abundance   10 *shadow* the idea; *substance* the actuality   13 *Look what*
whatever

38: 1 *want . . . invent* lack subject matter   3 *argument* theme   4 *vulgar
paper* common composition   5 *in me* of mine   6 *stand . . . sight* meet your
eye   8 *invention* power of creation   10 *invocate* invoke   12 *numbers* verses; *long* a distant   13 *curious* critical   14 *pain* painstaking

39: 1 *manners* modesty   5 *for* because of   6 *name* report   8 *That due*
what is owing   11 *entertain* pass   12 *thoughts* melancholy; *deceive* beguile
away   13 *And . . . twain* i.e. and were it not that you teach how to divide one
into two

40: 1 *Take . . . loves* (read in the context of later sonnets, the allusion seems
to be to the poet's mistress whom the friend has taken)   6 *for* because; *thou
usest* you enjoy   7 *this self* i.e. this one of your selves, the poet (often
emended to 'thyself' without marked improvement of the sense)   8 *wilful
taste of* i.e. capricious dalliance with (?); *thyself* i.e. your true self (?)   10 *my
poverty* my little   12 *known* open, intended   13 *Lascivious grace* you who
are gracious even in your amours

As a decrepit father takes delight   37
To see his active child do deeds of youth,
So I, made lame by Fortune's dearest spite,
Take all my comfort of thy worth and truth.   4
For whether beauty, birth, or wealth, or wit,
Or any of these all, or all, or more,
Intitled in thy parts do crownèd sit,
I make my love ingrafted to this store.   8
So then I am not lame, poor, nor despised
Whilst that this shadow doth such substance give
That I in thy abundance am sufficed
And by a part of all thy glory live.   12
   Look what is best, that best I wish in thee.
   This wish I have; then ten times happy me!

How can my Muse want subject to invent   38
While thou dost breathe, that pour'st into my verse
Thine own sweet argument, too excellent
For every vulgar paper to rehearse?   4
O, give thyself the thanks if aught in me
Worthy perusal stand against thy sight,
For who's so dumb that cannot write to thee
When thou thyself dost give invention light?   8
Be thou the tenth Muse, ten times more in worth
Than those old nine which rimers invocate;
And he that calls on thee, let him bring forth
Eternal numbers to outlive long date.   12
   If my slight Muse do please these curious days,
   The pain be mine, but thine shall be the praise.

O, how thy worth with manners may I sing   39
When thou art all the better part of me?
What can mine own praise to mine own self bring,
And what is't but mine own when I praise thee?   4
Even for this let us divided live
And our dear love lose name of single one,
That by this separation I may give
That due to thee which thou deserv'st alone.   8
O absence, what a torment wouldst thou prove
Were it not thy sour leisure gave sweet leave
To entertain the time with thoughts of love,
Which time and thoughts so sweetly doth deceive,   12
   And that thou teachest how to make one twain
   By praising him here who doth hence remain!

Take all my loves, my love, yea, take them all: 40
What hast thou then more than thou hadst before?
No love, my love, that thou mayst true love call;
All mine was thine before thou hadst this more.   4
Then, if for my love thou my love receivest,
I cannot blame thee for my love thou usest;
But yet be blamed if thou this self deceivest
By wilful taste of what thyself refusest.   8
I do forgive thy robb'ry, gentle thief,
Although thou steal thee all my poverty;
And yet love knows it is a greater grief
To bear love's wrong than hate's known injury.   12
   Lascivious grace, in whom all ill well shows,
   Kill me with spites; yet we must not be foes.

41 Those pretty wrongs that liberty commits
   When I am sometime absent from thy heart,
   Thy beauty and thy years full well befits,
 4 For still temptation follows where thou art.
   Gentle thou art, and therefore to be won ;
   Beauteous thou art, therefore to be assailed ;
   And when a woman woos, what woman's son
 8 Will sourly leave her till she have prevailed ?
   Ay me, but yet thou mightst my seat forbear,
   And chide thy beauty and thy straying youth,
   Who lead thee in their riot even there
12 Where thou art forced to break a twofold truth :
     Hers, by thy beauty tempting her to thee,
     Thine, by thy beauty being false to me.

42 That thou hast her, it is not all my grief,
   And yet it may be said I loved her dearly ;
   That she hath thee is of my wailing chief,
 4 A loss in love that touches me more nearly.
   Loving offenders, thus I will excuse ye :
   Thou dost love her because thou know'st I love her,
   And for my sake even so doth she abuse me,
 8 Suff'ring my friend for my sake to approve her.
   If I lose thee, my loss is my love's gain,
   And losing her, my friend hath found that loss :
   Both find each other, and I lose both twain,
12 And both for my sake lay on me this cross.
     But here's the joy : my friend and I are one ;
     Sweet flattery ! then she loves but me alone.

43 When most I wink, then do mine eyes best see,
   For all the day they view things unrespected ;
   But when I sleep, in dreams they look on thee
 4 And, darkly bright, are bright in dark directed.
   Then thou, whose shadow shadows doth make bright,
   How would thy shadow's form form happy show
   To the clear day with thy much clearer light
 8 When to unseeing eyes thy shade shines so !
   How would, I say, mine eyes be blessèd made
   By looking on thee in the living day,
   When in dead night thy fair imperfect shade
12 Through heavy sleep on sightless eyes doth stay !
     All days are nights to see till I see thee,
     And nights bright days when dreams do show thee me.

44 If the dull substance of my flesh were thought,
   Injurious distance should not stop my way ;
   For then, despite of space, I would be brought,
 4 From limits far remote, where thou dost stay.
   No matter then although my foot did stand
   Upon the farthest earth removed from thee ;
   For nimble thought can jump both sea and land
 8 As soon as think the place where he would be.
   But, ah, thought kills me that I am not thought,
   To leap large lengths of miles when thou art gone,
   But that, so much of earth and water wrought,
12 I must attend time's leisure with my moan,
     Receiving naught by elements so slow
     But heavy tears, badges of either's woe.

45 The other two, slight air and purging fire,
   Are both with thee, wherever I abide ;
   The first my thought, the other my desire,
 4 These present-absent with swift motion slide.
   For when these quicker elements are gone
   In tender embassy of love to thee,
   My life, being made of four, with two alone
 8 Sinks down to death, oppressed with melancholy ;
   Until life's composition be recured
   By those swift messengers returned from thee,
   Who even but now come back again, assured
12 Of thy fair health, recounting it to me.
     This told, I joy ; but then no longer glad,
     I send them back again and straight grow sad.

46 Mine eye and heart are at a mortal war
   How to divide the conquest of thy sight ;
   Mine eye my heart thy picture's sight would bar,
 4 My heart mine eye the freedom of that right.
   My heart doth plead that thou in him dost lie,
   A closet never pierced with crystal eyes ;
   But the defendant doth that plea deny
 8 And says in him thy fair appearance lies.
   To 'cide this title is impanellèd
   A quest of thoughts, all tenants to the heart,
   And by their verdict is determinèd
12 The clear eye's moiety and the dear heart's part :
     As thus : mine eye's due is thy outward part,
     And my heart's right thy inward love of heart.

41 : 1 *pretty wrongs* peccadilloes ; *liberty* license   3 *befits* makes inevitable
4 *still* always   9 *my seat forbear* forgo the place belonging to me   11 *Who*
which ; *riot* revels

42 : 3 *of my wailing chief* my chief lament   7 *abuse* betray   8 *approve*
prove, try   9 *love's* mistress's   12 *cross* affliction

43 : 1 *wink* shut my eyes in sleep   2 *unrespected* unnoticed   4 *darkly . . .
directed* i.e. mysteriously lighted, see clearly in the dark   5 *shadow
shadows* image darkness   6 *shadow's form* actual body   14 *show thee me*
show you to me

44 : 1 *dull substance* i.e. earth and water (dull as compared with the other
elements, fire and air)   2 *Injurious* spiteful   4 *limits* bounds ; *where* to
where   6 *farthest earth* earth farthest   9 *ah, thought* ah, the thought   11
wrought fashioned   12 *attend* await   14 *either's woe* (i.e. the earth supplies the weight, the water the moisture of the 'heavy tears')

45 : 1 *two* i.e. elements ; *slight* insubstantial   4 *present-absent* now here,
now there   7 *life* living body   8 *melancholy* (induced by an excess of
particular elements or 'humors,' in this case earth and water)   9 *composition* proper balance ; *recured* restored   10 *messengers* i.e. fire and air

46 : 2 *conquest . . . sight* i.e. spoils, consisting of the sight of you   3 *bar* deny
4 *freedom* free exercise   9 *'cide* decide   10 *quest* jury ; *tenants to* i.e. from
the holdings of   12 *moiety* share

47 Betwixt mine eye and heart a league is took,
   And each doth good turns now unto the other:
   When that mine eye is famished for a look,
4 Or heart in love with sighs himself doth smother,
   With my love's picture then my eye doth feast
   And to the painted banquet bids my heart;
   Another time mine eye is my heart's guest
8 And in his thoughts of love doth share a part.
   So, either by thy picture or my love,
   Thyself away are present still with me;
   For thou not farther than my thoughts canst move,
12 And I am still with them, and they with thee;
     Or, if they sleep, thy picture in my sight
     Awakes my heart to heart's and eye's delight.

48 How careful was I, when I took my way,
   Each trifle under truest bars to thrust,
   That to my use it might unusèd stay
4 From hands of falsehood, in sure wards of trust!
   But thou, to whom my jewels trifles are,
   Most worthy comfort, now my greatest grief,
   Thou best of dearest, and mine only care,
8 Art left the prey of every vulgar thief.
   Thee have I not locked up in any chest,
   Save where thou art not, though I feel thou art,
   Within the gentle closure of my breast,
12 From whence at pleasure thou mayst come and part;
     And even thence thou wilt be stol'n, I fear,
     For truth proves thievish for a prize so dear.

Against that time, if ever that time come, 49
   When I shall see thee frown on my defects,
   Whenas thy love hath cast his utmost sum,
   Called to that audit by advised respects; 4
   Against that time when thou shalt strangely pass
   And scarcely greet me with that sun, thine eye,
   When love, converted from the thing it was,
   Shall reasons find of settled gravity: 8
   Against that time do I ensconce me here
   Within the knowledge of mine own desert,
   And this my hand against myself uprear
   To guard the lawful reasons on thy part. 12
     To leave poor me thou hast the strength of laws,
     Since why to love I can allege no cause.

How heavy do I journey on the way 50
   When what I seek (my weary travel's end)
   Doth teach that ease and that repose to say,
   'Thus far the miles are measured from thy friend.' 4
   The beast that bears me, tired with my woe,
   Plods dully on, to bear that weight in me,
   As if by some instinct the wretch did know
   His rider loved not speed, being made from thee. 8
   The bloody spur cannot provoke him on
   That sometimes anger thrusts into his hide,
   Which heavily he answers with a groan,
   More sharp to me than spurring to his side; 12
     For that same groan doth put this in my mind:
     My grief lies onward and my joy behind.

Thus can my love excuse the slow offense 51
   Of my dull bearer when from thee I speed:
   From where thou art why should I haste me thence?
   Till I return, of posting is no need. 4
   O, what excuse will my poor beast then find
   When swift extremity can seem but slow?
   Then should I spur, though mounted on the wind,
   In wingèd speed no motion shall I know. 8
   Then can no horse with my desire keep pace;
   Therefore desire, of perfect'st love being made,
   Shall weigh no dull flesh in his fiery race;
   But love, for love, thus shall excuse my jade: 12
     Since from thee going he went wilful slow,
     Towards thee I'll run and give him leave to go.

So am I as the rich whose blessèd key 52
   Can bring him to his sweet up-lockèd treasure,
   The which he will not ev'ry hour survey,
   For blunting the fine point of seldom pleasure. 4
   Therefore are feasts so solemn and so rare,
   Since, seldom coming, in the long year set,
   Like stones of worth they thinly placèd are,
   Or captain jewels in the carcanet. 8
   So is the time that keeps you as my chest,
   Or as the wardrobe which the robe doth hide,
   To make some special instant special blest
   By new unfolding his imprisoned pride. 12
     Blessèd are you, whose worthiness gives scope,
     Being had, to triumph, being lacked, to hope.

47: 1 *a league is took* an agreement is reached 6 *painted banquet* i.e. visual feast 12 *still* always

48: 1 *took my way* set out on my journey 4 *hands of falsehood* thieves 5 *to* in comparison with; *jewels* prized material possessions 7 *only care* only thing valued 8 *vulgar* common 11 *closure* enclosure 14 *truth* i.e. truth (honesty) itself

49: 1 *Against* in provision for 3 *Whenas* when; *cast . . . sum* made its final reckoning 4 *advised respects* considered reasons 5 *strangely* like a stranger 8 *of settled gravity* for continued coldness (?), of sufficient weight (?) 9 *ensconce* fortify 11–12 *this . . . part* i.e. swear, to my own disadvantage, that your actions are lawful 14 *cause* i.e. lawful obligation

50: 1 *heavy* sadly 2–3 *When . . . say* i.e. when the longed-for journey's end will bring, along with its ease and repose, the reminder that 12 *sharp* painful

51: 1 *slow offense* tardiness 4 *posting* riding in haste 6 *swift extremity* extreme swiftness 8 *know* recognize 11 *weigh* consider (?), bear (?) (emendation of 'naigh' in Q) 12 *for love* for love's sake (?) 14 *go* walk

52: 4 *For* for fear of; *seldom pleasure* pleasure seldom enjoyed 8 *captain* chief; *carcanet* jewelled collar 9 *as* like 12 *his* its

53
What is your substance, whereof are you made,
That millions of strange shadows on you tend?
Since every one hath, every one, one shade,
4 And you, but one, can every shadow lend.
Describe Adonis, and the counterfeit
Is poorly imitated after you.
On Helen's cheek all art of beauty set,
8 And you in Grecian tires are painted new.
Speak of the spring and foison of the year:
The one doth shadow of your beauty show,
The other as your bounty doth appear,
12 And you in every blessèd shape we know.
    In all external grace you have some part,
    But you like none, none you, for constant heart.

54
O, how much more doth beauty beauteous seem
By that sweet ornament which truth doth give:
The rose looks fair, but fairer we it deem
4 For that sweet odor which doth in it live.
The canker blooms have full as deep a dye
As the perfumèd tincture of the roses,
Hang on such thorns, and play as wantonly
8 When summer's breath their maskèd buds discloses;
But, for their virtue only is their show,
They live unwooed and unrespected fade,
Die to themselves. Sweet roses do not so:
12 Of their sweet deaths are sweetest odors made.
    And so of you, beauteous and lovely youth,
    When that shall vade, my verse distills your truth.

55
Not marble nor the gilded monuments
Of princes shall outlive this pow'rful rime,
But you shall shine more bright in these contents
4 Than unswept stone, besmeared with sluttish time.
When wasteful war shall statues overturn,
And broils root out the work of masonry,
Nor Mars his sword nor war's quick fire shall burn
8 The living record of your memory.
'Gainst death and all oblivious enmity
Shall you pace forth; your praise shall still find room
Even in the eyes of all posterity
12 That wear this world out to the ending doom.
    So, till the judgment that yourself arise,
    You live in this, and dwell in lovers' eyes.

56
Sweet love, renew thy force; be it not said
Thy edge should blunter be than appetite,
Which but to-day by feeding is allayed,
4 To-morrow sharp'ned in his former might.
So, love, be thou: although to-day thou fill
Thy hungry eyes even till they wink with fulness,
To-morrow see again, and do not kill
8 The spirit of love with a perpetual dulness.
Let this sad int'rim like the ocean be
Which parts the shore where two contracted new
Come daily to the banks, that, when they see
12 Return of love, more blest may be the view;
    Or call it winter, which, being full of care,
    Makes summer's welcome thrice more wished, more rare.

57
Being your slave, what should I do but tend
Upon the hours and times of your desire?
I have no precious time at all to spend,
4 Nor services to do till you require.
Nor dare I chide the world-without-end hour
Whilst I, my sovereign, watch the clock for you,
Nor think the bitterness of absence sour
8 When you have bid your servant once adieu.
Nor dare I question with my jealous thought
Where you may be, or your affairs suppose,
But, like a sad slave, stay and think of nought
12 Save where you are how happy you make those.
    So true a fool is love that in your will,
    Though you do anything, he thinks no ill.

58
That god forbid that made me first your slave
I should in thought control your times of pleasure,
Or at your hand th' account of hours to crave,
4 Being your vassal bound to stay your leisure.
O, let me suffer, being at your beck,
Th' imprisoned absence of your liberty;
And patience, tame to sufferance, bide each check
8 Without accusing you of injury.
Be where you list; your charter is so strong
That you yourself may privilege your time
To what you will; to you it doth belong
12 Yourself to pardon of self-doing crime.
    I am to wait, though waiting so be hell,
    Not blame your pleasure, be it ill or well.

53: 2 *strange shadows* foreign shades (Venus, Adonis, etc.); *tend* attend 4 *And . . . lend* i.e. each *shadow* can reflect but one of your excellences (with *you* the object of *lend*) 5 *counterfeit* picture 8 *tires* attire 9 *foison* harvest

54: 2 *By* by means of 5 *canker blooms* dog-roses 6 *tincture* color 7 *wantonly* sportively 8 *maskèd* hidden 9 *for* since 14 *vade* depart; *distills your truth* i.e. preserves your essence as a distillation

55: 2 *rime* poem 3 *these contents* what is here contained 4 *Than* than in; *stone* memorial tablet; *sluttish* untidy 6 *broils* battles 7 *Nor* neither; *Mars his sword* i.e. the sword of Mars shall destroy 9 *all oblivious enmity* i.e. oblivion the enemy of all 12 *That wear* who last 13 *judgment that* judgment day when

56: 1 *love* spirit of love 2 *appetite* lust 4 *sharp'ned in* sharpened to 6 *wink* shut 9 *sad int'rim* lamentable interval 10 *parts the shore* divides the shores; *contracted new* newly betrothed 12 *love* the loved one

57: 5 *world-without-end* tedious, everlasting 9 *question* dispute; *jealous* jealous 10 *suppose* speculate about 11 *sad* sober

58: 3 *th' account of* an accounting for; *to crave* should crave 4 *stay* await 6 *Th' . . . liberty* i.e. the imprisonment that your freedom-to-be-absent brings 7 *tame to sufferance* trained to accept suffering; *bide each check* put up with each rebuke 9 *list* wish; *charter* privilege 10 *privilege* dispose of, assign 12 *self-doing* done by yourself

59 If there be nothing new, but that which is
   Hath been before, how are our brains beguiled,
   Which, laboring for invention, bear amiss
4 The second burden of a former child!
   O that record could with a backward look,
   Even of five hundred courses of the sun,
   Show me your image in some antique book,
8 Since mind at first in character was done:
   That I might see what the old world could say
   To this composèd wonder of your frame;
   Whether we are mended, or whe'r better they,
12 Or whether revolution be the same.
     O, sure I am the wits of former days
     To subjects worse have given admiring praise.

60 Like as the waves make towards the pebbled shore,
   So do our minutes hasten to their end;
   Each changing place with that which goes before,
4 In sequent toil all forwards do contend.
   Nativity, once in the main of light,
   Crawls to maturity, wherewith being crowned,
   Crooked eclipses 'gainst his glory fight,
8 And Time that gave doth now his gift confound.
   Time doth transfix the flourish set on youth
   And delves the parallels in beauty's brow,
   Feeds on the rarities of nature's truth,
12 And nothing stands but for his scythe to mow:
     And yet to times in hope my verse shall stand,
     Praising thy worth, despite his cruel hand.

Is it thy will thy image should keep open 61
My heavy eyelids to the weary night?
Dost thou desire my slumbers should be broken
While shadows like to thee do mock my sight? 4
Is it thy spirit that thou send'st from thee
So far from home into my deeds to pry,
To find out shames and idle hours in me,
The scope and tenure of thy jealousy? 8
O no, thy love, though much, is not so great;
It is my love that keeps mine eye awake,
Mine own true love that doth my rest defeat
To play the watchman ever for thy sake. 12
    For thee watch I whilst thou dost wake elsewhere,
    From me far off, with others all too near.

Sin of self-love possesseth all mine eye 62
And all my soul and all my every part;
And for this sin there is no remedy,
It is so grounded inward in my heart. 4
Methinks no face so gracious is as mine,
No shape so true, no truth of such account,
And for myself mine own worth do define
As I all other in all worths surmount. 8
But when my glass shows me myself indeed,
Beated and chopped with tanned antiquity,
Mine own self-love quite contrary I read;
Self so self-loving were iniquity: 12
    'Tis thee (myself) that for myself I praise,
    Painting my age with beauty of thy days.

Against my love shall be as I am now, 63
With Time's injurious hand crushed and o'erworn;
When hours have drained his blood and filled his brow
With lines and wrinkles, when his youthful morn 4
Hath travelled on to age's steepy night,
And all those beauties whereof now he's king
Are vanishing, or vanished out of sight,
Stealing away the treasure of his spring – 8
For such a time do I now fortify
Against confounding age's cruel knife,
That he shall never cut from memory
My sweet love's beauty, though my lover's life. 12
    His beauty shall in these black lines be seen,
    And they shall live, and he in them still green.

59: 1 *that* everything   3 *invention* novelty   3–4 *bear . . . of* i.e. merely miscarry   5 *record* memory   6 *courses . . . sun* years   8 *Since . . . done* since thought was first expressed in writing   10 *composèd wonder* wonderful composition   11 *mended* improved; *whe'r* whether   12 *revolution . . . same* one cycle repeats another

60: 4 *sequent* successive; *contend* struggle   5 *Nativity* the new-born; *the . . . light* orbit   7 *Crooked* adverse, malignant   8 *confound* destroy   10 *delves the parallels* digs the lines   13 *times in hope* hoped-for times; *stand* endure

61: 7 *shames* faults   8 *scope and tenure* aim and purport   11 *defeat* destroy

62: 5 *gracious* pleasing   8 *As* as if; *other* others   10 *chopped* seamed; *tanned antiquity* i.e. leathery old age   11 *contrary* in a different way   13 *'Tis . . . praise* i.e. I am praising you whom I identify with myself

63: 1 *Against* in expectation of the time when   5 *steepy* deep, precipitous   9 *fortify* build defenses   10 *confounding* destroying   12 *though* i.e. though he cuts

64: 2 *cost* outlay   3 *sometime* formerly   4 *brass eternal* everlasting brass; *mortal rage* ravages of mortality   6 *Advantage* inroads   8 *Increasing . . . store* i.e. one gaining by the other's loss, one losing by the other's gain   10 *confounded* reduced   14 *to have* for having

When I have seen by Time's fell hand defaced 64
The rich proud cost of outworn buried age,
When sometime lofty towers I see down-rased
And brass eternal slave to mortal rage; 4
When I have seen the hungry ocean gain
Advantage on the kingdom of the shore,
And the firm soil win of the wat'ry main,
Increasing store with loss and loss with store; 8
When I have seen such interchange of state,
Or state itself confounded to decay,
Ruin hath taught me thus to ruminate,
That Time will come and take my love away. 12
    This thought is as a death, which cannot choose
    But weep to have that which it fears to lose.

65 Since brass, nor stone, nor earth, nor boundless sea,
But sad mortality o'ersways their power,
How with this rage shall beauty hold a plea,
4 Whose action is no stronger than a flower?
O, how shall summer's honey breath hold out
Against the wrackful siege of batt'ring days,
When rocks impregnable are not so stout,
8 Nor gates of steel so strong but Time decays?
O fearful meditation : where, alack,
Shall Time's best jewel from Time's chest lie hid?
Or what strong hand can hold his swift foot back,
12 Or who his spoil of beauty can forbid?
    O, none, unless this miracle have might,
    That in black ink my love may still shine bright.

66 Tired with all these, for restful death I cry :
As, to behold desert a beggar born,
And needy nothing trimmed in jollity,
4 And purest faith unhappily forsworn,
And gilded honor shamefully misplaced,
And maiden virtue rudely strumpeted,
And right perfection wrongfully disgraced,
8 And strength by limping sway disablèd,
And art made tongue-tied by authority,
And folly (doctor-like) controlling skill,
And simple truth miscalled simplicity,
12 And captive good attending captain ill.
    Tired with all these, from these would I be gone,
    Save that, to die, I leave my love alone.

67 Ah, wherefore with infection should he live
And with his presence grace impiety,
That sin by him advantage should achieve
4 And lace itself with his society?
Why should false painting imitate his cheek
And steal dead seeing of his living hue?
Why should poor beauty indirectly seek
8 Roses of shadow, since his rose is true?
Why should he live, now Nature bankrout is,
Beggared of blood to blush through lively veins,
For she hath no exchequer now but his,
12 And, proud of many, lives upon his gains?
    O, him she stores, to show what wealth she had
    In days long since, before these last so bad.

68 Thus is his cheek the map of days outworn
When beauty lived and died as flowers do now,
Before these bastard signs of fair were born
4 Or durst inhabit on a living brow;
Before the golden tresses of the dead,
The right of sepulchers, were shorn away
To live a second life on second head,
8 Ere beauty's dead fleece made another gay :
In him those holy antique hours are seen,
Without all ornament, itself and true,
Making no summer of another's green,
12 Robbing no old to dress his beauty new;
    And him as for a map doth Nature store,
    To show false Art what beauty was of yore.

Those parts of thee that the world's eye doth view 69
Want nothing that the thought of hearts can mend;
All tongues, the voice of souls, give thee that due,
Utt'ring bare truth, even so as foes commend. 4
Thy outward thus with outward praise is crowned,
But those same tongues that give thee so thine own
In other accents do this praise confound
By seeing farther than the eye hath shown. 8
They look into the beauty of thy mind,
And that in guess they measure by thy deeds;
Then, churls, their thoughts, although their eyes were kind,
To thy fair flower add the rank smell of weeds : 12
    But why thy odor matcheth not thy show,
    The soil is this, that thou dost common grow.

That thou art blamed shall not be thy defect, 70
For slander's mark was ever yet the fair;
The ornament of beauty is suspect,
A crow that flies in heaven's sweetest air. 4
So thou be good, slander doth but approve
Thy worth the greater, being wooed of time;
For canker vice the sweetest buds doth love,
And thou present'st a pure unstainèd prime. 8
Thou hast passed by the ambush of young days,
Either not assailed, or victor being charged;
Yet this thy praise cannot be so thy praise
To tie up envy, evermore enlarged : 12
    If some suspect of ill masked not thy show,
    Then thou alone kingdoms of hearts shouldst owe.

65 : 1 *Since* since there is neither 3 *rage* destructive power; *hold* maintain 4 *action* case 6 *wrackful* wrecking 10 *from Time's chest* i.e. from being coffered up by Time 12 *spoil* spoliation

66 : 2 *As* such as, for instance 3 *needy . . . jollity* i.e. the lack-all nobody festively attired 4 *unhappily forsworn* evilly betrayed 7 *disgraced* banished from favor 8 *by . . . disablèd* i.e. weakened by incompetent leadership 9 *art . . . . authority* (possibly an allusion to state censorship of literature) 10 *doctor-like* i.e. owlishly 11 *simplicity* stupidity

67 : 1 *wherefore* why; *infection* corruption 3 *advantage* profit 4 *lace* i.e. ornament 6 *dead seeing* the lifeless appearance 7 *poor* inferior; *indirectly* by imitation 8 *Roses of shadow* i.e. pictured roses 9 *bankrout* bankrupt 10 *Beggared . . . veins* i.e. lacking the blood to blush naturally instead of by the use of cosmetics 11 *exchequer* i.e. treasury of natural beauty 12 *proud* falsely proud (?) 13 *stores* preserves

68 : 1 *map* representation; *outworn* outlived 3 *bastard signs* i.e. cosmetics; *fair* beauty 4 *inhabit* dwell 6 *The right of* belonging properly to 9 *antique hours* ancient times 13 *as . . . map* i.e. as if for a guide; *store* preserve

69 : 1 *parts* outward parts 4 *as foes commend* i.e. forced to the admission 6 *thine own* what is due you 7 *confound* destroy 10 *in guess* at a guess 13 *odor matcheth not* (cf. Sonnet 54) 14 *soil* (1) ground, (2) soilure; *common* (1) uncultivated, like weeds, (2) overfamiliar

70 : 1 *defect* fault 3 *ornament* (like a 'beauty mark'); *suspect* suspicion 5 *approve* prove 6 *wooed of time* solicited to evil by the times (?) 7 *canker* destructive worm 9 *ambush* i.e. dangerous lure, trap 10 *charged* assailed 12 *tie up envy* i.e. silence malice 13 *If . . . show* i.e. if some suspicion did not obscure your fine appearance 14 *owe* own

71 No longer mourn for me when I am dead
Than you shall hear the surly sullen bell
Give warning to the world that I am fled
4 From this vile world, with vilest worms to dwell.
Nay, if you read this line, remember not
The hand that writ it, for I love you so
That I in your sweet thoughts would be forgot
8 If thinking on me then should make you woe.
O, if, I say, you look upon this verse
When I, perhaps, compounded am with clay,
Do not so much as my poor name rehearse,
12 But let your love even with my life decay,
    Lest the wise world should look into your moan
    And mock you with me after I am gone.

72 O, lest the world should task you to recite
What merit lived in me that you should love
After my death, dear love, forget me quite,
4 For you in me can nothing worthy prove;
Unless you would devise some virtuous lie,
To do more for me than mine own desert
And hang more praise upon deceasèd I
8 Than niggard truth would willingly impart.
O, lest your true love may seem false in this,
That you for love speak well of me untrue,
My name be buried where my body is,
12 And live no more to shame nor me nor you;
    For I am shamed by that which I bring forth,
    And so should you, to love things nothing worth.

73 That time of year thou mayst in me behold
When yellow leaves, or none, or few, do hang
Upon those boughs which shake against the cold,
4 Bare ruined choirs where late the sweet birds sang.
In me thou seest the twilight of such day
As after sunset fadeth in the west,
Which by and by black night doth take away,
8 Death's second self that seals up all in rest.
In me thou seest the glowing of such fire
That on the ashes of his youth doth lie,
As the deathbed whereon it must expire,
12 Consumed with that which it was nourished by.
    This thou perceiv'st, which makes thy love more strong,
    To love that well which thou must leave ere long.

74 But be contented: when that fell arrest
Without all bail shall carry me away,
My life hath in this line some interest
4 Which for memorial still with thee shall stay.
When thou reviewest this, thou dost review
The very part was consecrate to thee:
The earth can have but earth, which is his due;
8 My spirit is thine, the better part of me.
So then thou hast but lost the dregs of life,
The prey of worms, my body being dead,
The coward conquest of a wretch's knife,
12 Too base of thee to be rememberèd.
    The worth of that is that which it contains,
    And that is this, and this with thee remains.

75 So are you to my thoughts as food to life,
Or as sweet-seasoned showers are to the ground;
And for the peace of you I hold such strife
4 As 'twixt a miser and his wealth is found:
Now proud as an enjoyer, and anon
Doubting the filching age will steal his treasure;
Now counting best to be with you alone,
8 Then bettered that the world may see my pleasure;
Sometime all full with feasting on your sight,
And by and by clean starvèd for a look,
Possessing or pursuing no delight
12 Save what is had or must from you be took.
    Thus do I pine and surfeit day by day,
    Or gluttoning on all, or all away.

76 Why is my verse so barren of new pride?
So far from variation or quick change?
Why, with the time, do I not glance aside
4 To new-found methods and to compounds strange?
Why write I still all one, ever the same,
And keep invention in a noted weed,
That every word doth almost tell my name,
8 Showing their birth, and where they did proceed?
O, know, sweet love, I always write of you,
And you and love are still my argument;
So all my best is dressing old words new,
12 Spending again what is already spent:
    For as the sun is daily new and old,
    So is my love still telling what is told.

71: **8** *make you woe* make woe for you **10** *compounded* blended **13** *wise* i.e. disdainful of foolish sentiment **14** *with* because of

72: **1** *task . . . recite* put you to the task of telling **5** *virtuous lie* noble lie (?), false attribution of virtue (?) **8** *niggard* miserly **10** *untrue* untruly **12** *nor . . . nor* either . . . or **13** *which . . . forth* (probably a deprecatory allusion to the sonnets)

73: **4** *choirs* i.e. the part of a church or monastery where services were sung **7** *by and by* shortly **8** *seals up* encloses **10** *That* as **12** *with . . . by* i.e. by life

74: **1** *fell* fatal **2** *Without all bail* i.e. irrievably **3** *line* poem; *interest* share **4** *still* always **7** *his due* its due (i.e. 'dust to dust') **11** *The . . . knife* i.e. easily cut down by the bravo Death (?) **13–14** *The worth . . . is this* i.e. the only value of the body is as a container of the soul, and the soul is in this poem

75: **2** *sweet-seasoned* of the sweet season, spring **3** *peace of you* i.e. peace you bring me; *hold such strife* i.e. exist on such uneasy terms **5** *anon* soon **6** *Doubting* fearing **8** *bettered* better pleased **14** *Or . . . away* i.e. either feeding on the full feast of your presence or having nothing in your absence

76: **1** *pride* adornment **2** *quick change* modishness **3** *the time* the times, i.e. the current styles **4** *compounds strange* i.e. literary concoctions (?), neologisms, like those being introduced by Marston (?) **5** *one* one way **6** *invention* poetic creation; *noted weed* familiar garb **10** *argument* theme **11** *So . . . best* i.e. so that the best I am capable of

77 Thy glass will show thee how thy beauties wear,
Thy dial how thy precious minutes waste;
The vacant leaves thy mind's imprint will bear,
4 And of this book this learning mayst thou taste.
The wrinkles which thy glass will truly show,
Of mouthèd graves will give thee memory.
Thou by thy dial's shady stealth mayst know
8 Time's thievish progress to eternity.
Look what thy memory cannot contain,
Commit to these waste blanks, and thou shalt find
Those children nursed, delivered from thy brain,
12 To take a new acquaintance of thy mind.
    These offices, so oft as thou wilt look,
    Shall profit thee and much enrich thy book.

78 So oft have I invoked thee for my Muse
And found such fair assistance in my verse
As every alien pen hath got my use
4 And under thee their poesy disperse.
Thine eyes, that taught the dumb on high to sing
And heavy ignorance aloft to fly,
Have added feathers to the learnèd's wing
8 And given grace a double majesty.
Yet be most proud of that which I compile,
Whose influence is thine and born of thee.
In others' works thou dost but mend the style,
12 And arts with thy sweet graces gracèd be;
    But thou art all my art and dost advance
    As high as learning my rude ignorance.

79 Whilst I alone did call upon thy aid,
My verse alone had all thy gentle grace;
But now my gracious numbers are decayed,
4 And my sick Muse doth give another place.
I grant, sweet love, thy lovely argument
Deserves the travail of a worthier pen;
Yet what of thee thy poet doth invent
8 He robs thee of, and pays it thee again.
He lends thee virtue, and he stole that word
From thy behavior; beauty doth he give,
And found it in thy cheek: he can afford
12 No praise to thee but what in thee doth live.
    Then thank him not for that which he doth say,
    Since what he owes thee thou thyself dost pay.

80 O, how I faint when I of you do write,
Knowing a better spirit doth use your name
And in the praise thereof spends all his might
4 To make me tongue-tied, speaking of your fame.
But since your worth (wide as the ocean is)
The humble as the proudest sail doth bear,
My saucy bark, inferior far to his,
8 On your broad main doth wilfully appear.
Your shallowest help will hold me up afloat
Whilst he upon your soundless deep doth ride;
Or, being wracked, I am a worthless boat,
12 He of tall building and of goodly pride.
    Then if he thrive, and I be cast away,
    The worst was this: my love was my decay.

Or I shall live your epitaph to make, 81
Or you survive when I in earth am rotten.
From hence your memory death cannot take,
Although in me each part will be forgotten. 4
Your name from hence immortal life shall have,
Though I, once gone, to all the world must die.
The earth can yield me but a common grave
When you entombèd in men's eyes shall lie. 8
Your monument shall be my gentle verse,
Which eyes not yet created shall o'erread;
And tongues to be your being shall rehearse
When all the breathers of this world are dead. 12
    You still shall live (such virtue hath my pen)
    Where breath most breathes, even in the mouths of men.

I grant thou wert not married to my Muse 82
And therefore mayst without attaint o'erlook
The dedicated words which writers use
Of their fair subject, blessing every book. 4
Thou art as fair in knowledge as in hue,
Finding thy worth a limit past my praise;
And therefore art enforced to seek anew
Some fresher stamp of the time-bettering days. 8
And do so, love; yet when they have devised
What strainèd touches rhetoric can lend,
Thou, truly fair, wert truly sympathized
In true plain words by thy true-telling friend: 12
    And their gross painting might be better used
    Where cheeks need blood; in thee it is abused.

77: 1 *glass* mirror; *wear* wear out 2 *dial* sun-dial 3 *vacant leaves* i.e. the blank leaves of a tablet (?) (cf. Sonnet 122); *mind's imprint* i.e. the reflections to be written in the tablet 4 *this learning* i.e. the wisdom brought by his own reflections 6 *mouthèd* devouring; *memory* reminder 8 *thievish* stealthy 9 *Look what* whatever 10 *waste blanks* blank pages 11 *nursed* preserved 13 *offices* regular duties; *look* i.e. at the glass, the dial, and what has been previously written in the book

78: 3 *As* that; *alien* i.e. belonging to outsiders; *got my use* followed my practise 4 *under thee* i.e. with you as their Muse 5 *on high* in exultation (like the lark) 7 *added feathers* i.e. imped their wings for still higher flights 8 *grace* (an attribute of majesty) 10 *Whose... thine* i.e. wholly inspired by you 11 *mend* i.e. merely improve

79: 4 *give another place* yield place to another 5 *thy lovely argument* the theme of your loveliness 11 *afford* offer 14 *owes* is obliged to give

80: 1 *faint* falter 2 *better spirit* i.e. more richly gifted poet 4 *tongue-tied* i.e. in comparison with the other 6 *as* as well as 8 *wilfully* i.e. boldly, in spite of all 10 *soundless* unfathomable 11 *wracked* wrecked; *boat* (any vessel less considerable than a ship) 12 *tall* sturdy; *pride* splendor 14 *decay* destruction

81: 1 *Or* either 3, 5 *hence* the present poems 4 *in... part* every part of me 8 *entombèd... lie* i.e. kept always before their eyes 11 *rehearse* recite 13 *virtue* power 14 *breath* speech (?), soul (?)

82: 2 *attaint* dishonor; *o'erlook* peruse 3 *dedicated* devoted; *writers* i.e. other writers 5 *hue* complexion 6 *Finding... past* i.e. knowing your worth to extend beyond 8 *stamp* imprint; *time-bettering* improving, progressing with the times 10 *strainèd* excessive 11 *sympathized* represented 14 *abused* i.e. an abuse

83 I never saw that you did painting need,
And therefore to your fair no painting set;
I found, or thought I found, you did exceed
4 The barren tender of a poet's debt:
And therefore have I slept in your report,
That you yourself, being extant, well might show
How far a modern quill doth come too short,
8 Speaking of worth, what worth in you doth grow.
This silence for my sin you did impute,
Which shall be most my glory, being dumb,
For I impair not beauty, being mute,
12 When others would give life and bring a tomb.
  There lives more life in one of your fair eyes
  Than both your poets can in praise devise.

84 Who is it that says most, which can say more
Than this rich praise, that you alone are you,
In whose confine immurèd is the store
4 Which should example where your equal grew?
Lean penury within that pen doth dwell
That to his subject lends not some small glory,
But he that writes of you, if he can tell
8 That you are you, so dignifies his story.
Let him but copy what in you is writ,
Not making worse what nature made so clear,
And such a counterpart shall fame his wit,
12 Making his style admirèd everywhere.
  You to your beauteous blessings add a curse,
  Being fond on praise, which makes your praises worse.

85 My tongue-tied Muse in manners holds her still
While comments of your praise, richly compiled,
Reserve their character with golden quill
And precious phrase by all the Muses filed.   4
I think good thoughts whilst other write good words,
And, like unlettered clerk, still cry 'Amen'
To every hymn that able spirit affords
In polished form of well-refinèd pen.   8
Hearing you praised, I say, ''Tis so, 'tis true,'
And to the most of praise add something more;
But that is in my thought, whose love to you,
Though words come hindmost, holds his rank before.   12
  Then others for the breath of words respect;
  Me for my dumb thoughts, speaking in effect.

86 Was it the proud full sail of his great verse,
Bound for the prize of all-too-precious you,
That did my ripe thoughts in my brain inhearse,
Making their tomb the womb wherein they grew?   4
Was it his spirit, by spirits taught to write
Above a mortal pitch, that struck me dead?
No, neither he, nor his compeers by night
Giving him aid, my verse astonishèd.   8
He, nor that affable familiar ghost
Which nightly gulls him with intelligence,
As victors, of my silence cannot boast;
I was not sick of any fear from thence: 12
  But when your countenance filled up his line,
  Then lacked I matter; that enfeebled mine.

87 Farewell: thou art too dear for my possessing,
And like enough thou know'st thy estimate.
The charter of thy worth gives thee releasing;
My bonds in thee are all determinate.   4
For how do I hold thee but by thy granting,
And for that riches where is my deserving?
The cause of this fair gift in me is wanting,
And so my patent back again is swerving.   8
Thyself thou gav'st, thy own worth then not knowing,
Or me, to whom thou gav'st it, else mistaking;
So thy great gift, upon misprision growing,
Comes home again, on better judgment making.   12
  Thus have I had thee as a dream doth flatter,
  In sleep a king, but waking no such matter.

88 When thou shalt be disposed to set me light
And place my merit in the eye of scorn,
Upon thy side against myself I'll fight
And prove thee virtuous, though thou art forsworn.   4
With mine own weakness being best acquainted,
Upon thy part I can set down a story
Of faults concealed wherein I am attainted,
That thou, in losing me, shall win much glory: 8
And I by this will be a gainer too;
For, bending all my loving thoughts on thee,
The injuries that to myself I do,
Doing thee vantage, double-vantage me.   12
  Such is my love, to thee I so belong,
  That for thy right myself will bear all wrong.

83: 2 *fair* beauty; *set* applied 4 *barren tender* worthless offering; *debt* payment 5 *slept . . . report* been inactive in writing of you 7 *modern* trite 8 *Speaking* in speaking; *what worth* i.e. to speak of such worth as 12 *bring a tomb* bring death (i.e. by reducing your living features to a dead image)

84: 1 *Who . . . more* i.e. who that says the utmost can say more 3–4 *In . . . grew* in whom are locked up all the qualities needed to provide an equal example 6 *his* its 8 *so* i.e. sufficiently 11 *counterpart* copy; *fame* bring fame to 14 *fond on* (probably a corruption: the *curse* would appear to be on poets, who fail because he is beyond their praise)

85: 1 *in . . . still* i.e. politely remains silent 2–3 *While . . . character* (an obscure passage. possibly corrupt) 2 *comments* expositions (?); *compiled* composed (?) 3 *Reserve* preserve (?); *character* writing (?) 4 *filed* polished 5 *other* others 6 *unlettered clerk* illiterate parish clerk; *still* always 6–7 *cry . . . affords* i.e. give approval to every poem offered by an able poet 10 *most* utmost 13 *the . . . words* i.e. actual speech 14 *speaking in effect* i.e. virtually speaking

86: 1 *his* i.e. an unidentified rival poet's 2 *Bound . . . of* i.e. designed to capture 3 *inhearse* coffin up 5 *spirits* divine inspirers 6 *dead* dead silent 7 *compeers by night* collaborators, spirit aids 8 *astonishèd* dumbfounded 10 *gulls . . . intelligence* tricks him with spying reports (allusion obscure) 13 *countenance filled up* approval repaired any defect in

87: 1 *dear* precious. costly 2 *estimate* value 3 *charter* privilege; *releasing* release from obligation 4 *bonds* claims; *determinate* ended 7 *cause* justification; *wanting* lacking 8 *patent* right; *swerving* turning away 10 *mistaking* i.e. overestimating 11 *upon misprision growing* based on error 12 *on . . . making* on your coming to a better judgment 13 *as . . . flatter* as in a flattering dream

88: 1 *set me light* make light of me 7 *attainted* dishonored 8 *losing* getting rid of 10 *bending* turning 12 *vantage* advantage

89 Say that thou didst forsake me for some fault,
And I will comment upon that offense;
Speak of my lameness, and I straight will halt,
4 Against thy reasons making no defense.
Thou canst not, love, disgrace me half so ill,
To set a form upon desirèd change,
As I'll myself disgrace; knowing thy will,
8 I will acquaintance strangle and look strange,
Be absent from thy walks, and in my tongue
Thy sweet belovèd name no more shall dwell,
Lest I, too much profane, should do it wrong
12 And haply of our old acquaintance tell.
  For thee, against myself I'll vow debate,
  For I must ne'er love him whom thou dost hate.

90 Then hate me when thou wilt; if ever, now;
Now, while the world is bent my deeds to cross,
Join with the spite of fortune, make me bow,
4 And do not drop in for an after-loss.
Ah, do not, when my heart hath scaped this sorrow,
Come in the rearward of a conquered woe;
Give not a windy night a rainy morrow,
8 To linger out a purposed overthrow.
If thou wilt leave me, do not leave me last,
When other petty griefs have done their spite,
But in the onset come: so shall I taste
12 At first the very worst of fortune's might;
  And other strains of woe, which now seem woe,
  Compared with loss of thee will not seem so.

91 Some glory in their birth, some in their skill,
Some in their wealth, some in their body's force,
Some in their garments, though newfangled ill,
4 Some in their hawks and hounds, some in their horse;
And every humor hath his adjunct pleasure,
Wherein it finds a joy above the rest,
But these particulars are not my measure;
8 All these I better in one general best.
Thy love is better than high birth to me,
Richer than wealth, prouder than garments' cost,
Of more delight than hawks or horses be;
12 And having thee, of all men's pride I boast:
  Wretched in this alone, that thou mayst take
  All this away and me most wretched make.

92 But do thy worst to steal thyself away,
For term of life thou art assurèd mine,
And life no longer than thy love will stay,
4 For it depends upon that love of thine.
Then need I not to fear the worst of wrongs
When in the least of them my life hath end;
I see a better state to me belongs
8 Than that which on thy humor doth depend.
Thou canst not vex me with inconstant mind,
Since that my life on thy revolt doth lie.
O, what a happy title do I find,
12 Happy to have thy love, happy to die!
  But what's so blessèd-fair that fears no blot?
  Thou mayst be false, and yet I know it not.

So shall I live, supposing thou art true, 93
Like a deceivèd husband; so love's face
May still seem love to me though altered new,
Thy looks with me, thy heart in other place. 4
For there can live no hatred in thine eye;
Therefore in that I cannot know thy change;
In many's looks the false heart's history
Is writ in moods and frowns and wrinkles strange: 8
But heaven in thy creation did decree
That in thy face sweet love should ever dwell;
Whate'er thy thoughts or thy heart's workings be,
Thy looks should nothing thence but sweetness tell. 12
  How like Eve's apple doth thy beauty grow
  If thy sweet virtue answer not thy show!

They that have pow'r to hurt and will do none, 94
That do not do the thing they most do show,
Who, moving others, are themselves as stone,
Unmovèd, cold, and to temptation slow; 4
They rightly do inherit heaven's graces
And husband nature's riches from expense;
They are the lords and owners of their faces,
Others but stewards of their excellence. 8
The summer's flow'r is to the summer sweet,
Though to itself it only live and die;
But if that flow'r with base infection meet,
The basest weed outbraves his dignity: 12
  For sweetest things turn sourest by their deeds;
  Lilies that fester smell far worse than weeds.

89 : 2 *comment* expatiate   3 *lameness* i.e. defect (metaphorical); *halt* limp   4 *reasons* charges   6 *To . . . change* i.e. to seem to justify the change you wish to make in our relationship   7 *disgrace* depreciate   8 *acquaintance* i.e. the fact of my being acquainted with you; *strange* as a stranger   12 *haply* accidentally   13 *vow debate* declare war

90 : 2 *bent* determined; *cross* thwart   4 *drop . . . after-loss* i.e. casually add to my griefs later on   5 *scaped* escaped   6 *Come . . . woe* i.e. attack after I have overcome my sorrow   8 *linger out* protract; *purposed* predestined   13 *strains* kinds

91 : 2 *force* strength   3 *newfangled ill* modishly ugly   4 *horse* horses   5 *humor* disposition; *his* its; *adjunct* corresponding   7 *particulars* i.e. various possessions; *measure* standard of happiness   8 *better* improve upon   12 *all men's pride* i.e. all the things that men take pride in

92 : 2 *term of life* my lifetime   5–6 *Then . . . end* i.e. there is no distinction in misfortunes since there is really only one – the loss of friendship, which ends life   8 *humor* whim   10 *on thy . . . lie* i.e. ends with your turning away from me   11 *happy title* title to happiness   14 *Thou . . . not* i.e. I may be denied the releasing death which certainty of your falsehood would bring

93 : 2 *face* appearance   8 *moods* looks of moodiness; *strange* unaccustomed   12 *thence* i.e. by themselves   13 *Eve's apple* i.e. fair only in appearance; *grow* become

94 : 1 *and . . . none* i.e. without actively trying to hurt   2 *show* i.e. seem to do, or seem capable of doing   5 *rightly* as a right, veritably   6 *expense* expenditure   7 *owners . . . faces* permanent possessors of the qualities that show in them   8 *stewards* dispensers   12 *outbraves his* outglories its   14 *Lilies . . . weeds* (this line also appears in the anonymous play *Edward III*, pub. 1596, ed. 1897, II, i, 451, in one of the scenes frequently attributed to Shakespeare)

95

How sweet and lovely dost thou make the shame
Which, like a canker in the fragrant rose,
Doth spot the beauty of thy budding name!
4 O, in what sweets dost thou thy sins enclose!
That tongue that tells the story of thy days,
Making lascivious comments on thy sport,
Cannot dispraise but in a kind of praise;
8 Naming thy name blesses an ill report.
O, what a mansion have those vices got
Which for their habitation chose out thee,
Where beauty's veil doth cover every blot
12 And all things turns to fair that eyes can see!
Take heed, dear heart, of this large privilege;
The hardest knife ill used doth lose his edge.

96

Some say thy fault is youth, some wantonness;
Some say thy grace is youth and gentle sport;
Both grace and faults are loved of more and less:
4 Thou mak'st faults graces that to thee resort.
As on the finger of a thronèd queen
The basest jewel will be well esteemed,
So are those errors that in thee are seen
8 To truths translated and for true things deemed.
How many lambs might the stern wolf betray
If like a lamb he could his looks translate!
How many gazers mightst thou lead away
12 If thou wouldst use the strength of all thy state!
But do not so; I love thee in such sort
As, thou being mine, mine is thy good report.

97

How like a winter hath my absence been
From thee, the pleasure of the fleeting year!
What freezings have I felt, what dark days seen!
4 What old December's bareness everywhere!
And yet this time removed was summer's time,
The teeming autumn, big with rich increase,
Bearing the wanton burden of the prime,
8 Like widowed wombs after their lords' decease:
Yet this abundant issue seemed to me
But hope of orphans and unfathered fruit;
For summer and his pleasures wait on thee,
12 And, thou away, the very birds are mute;
Or, if they sing, 'tis with so dull a cheer
That leaves look pale, dreading the winter's near.

98

From you have I been absent in the spring,
When proud-pied April, dressed in all his trim,
Hath put a spirit of youth in everything,
4 That heavy Saturn laughed and leapt with him;
Yet nor the lays of birds, nor the sweet smell
Of different flowers in odor and in hue,
Could make me any summer's story tell,
8 Or from their proud lap pluck them where they grew:
Nor did I wonder at the lily's white,
Nor praise the deep vermilion in the rose;
They were but sweet, but figures of delight,
12 Drawn after you, you pattern of all those.
Yet seemed it winter still, and you away,
As with your shadow I with these did play.

99

The forward violet thus did I chide:
Sweet thief, whence didst thou steal thy sweet that smells,
If not from my love's breath? The purple pride
4 Which on thy soft cheek for complexion dwells
In my love's veins thou hast too grossly dyed.
The lily I condemnèd for thy hand;
And buds of marjoram had stol'n thy hair;
8 The roses fearfully on thorns did stand,
One blushing shame, another white despair;
A third, nor red nor white, had stol'n of both,
And to his robb'ry had annexed thy breath;
12 But, for his theft, in pride of all his growth
A vengeful canker eat him up to death.
More flowers I noted, yet I none could see
But sweet or color it had stol'n from thee.

100

Where art thou, Muse, that thou forget'st so long
To speak of that which gives thee all thy might?
Spend'st thou thy fury on some worthless song,
4 Dark'ning thy pow'r to lend base subjects light?
Return, forgetful Muse, and straight redeem
In gentle numbers time so idly spent;
Sing to the ear that doth thy lays esteem
8 And gives thy pen both skill and argument.
Rise, resty Muse, my love's sweet face survey,
If Time have any wrinkle graven there;
If any, be a satire to decay
12 And make Time's spoils despisèd everywhere.
Give my love fame faster than Time wastes life;
So thou prevent'st his scythe and crooked knife.

95: **2** *canker* worm **3** *name* reputation **5** *thy days* i.e. how you spend
your days **6** *sport* amours **9** *mansion* dwelling **14** *his* its

96: **1** *wantonness* amorous dalliance (the *gentle sport* of l. 2) **3** *of more and
less* by great and small **8** *translated* transformed **9** *stern* cruel **12** *state*
power **13–14** *But . . . report* (the same couplet ends Sonnet 36)

97: **2** *pleasure* i.e. pleasant portion **5** *removed* i.e. when I was absent **6**
teeming fertile; *increase* harvest **7** *wanton burden* i.e. fruit of wantonness;
prime spring **9** *issue* progeny **10** *hope of orphans* orphaned hope **11**
his its

98: **2** *proud-pied* gloriously dappled; *trim* ornament **4** *heavy Saturn* (the
melancholy planet) **5** *nor . . . nor* neither . . . nor; *lays* songs **6** *different
flowers* flowers different **7** *summer's* summery, gay **8** *proud lap* i.e.
mother earth **11** *figures* emblems **14** *shadow* portrait

99: **1** *forward* early **3** *pride* splendor **5** *grossly* obviously **6** *condemnèd
for* i.e. found guilty of stealing the color of **11** *annexed* compounded the
theft of **13** *canker eat* worm ate **15** *sweet* scent

100: **3** *fury* poetic frenzy **4** *Dark'ning* diminishing **6** *gentle numbers*
noble verses **9** *resty* lazy **11** *be a satire to* satirize **14** *thou prevent'st*
you thwart

101 O truant Muse, what shall be thy amends
   For thy neglect of truth in beauty dyed?
   Both truth and beauty on my love depends;
 4 So dost thou too, and therein dignified.
   Make answer, Muse: wilt thou not haply say,
   'Truth needs no color with his color fixed,
   Beauty no pencil, beauty's truth to lay;
 8 But best is best, if never intermixed.'
   Because he needs no praise, wilt thou be dumb?
   Excuse not silence so, for 't lies in thee
   To make him much outlive a gilded tomb
12 And to be praised of ages yet to be.
      Then do thy office, Muse; I teach thee how
      To make him seem, long hence, as he shows now.

102 My love is strength'ned, though more weak in seeming;
   I love not less, though less the show appear:
   That love is merchandized whose rich esteeming
 4 The owner's tongue doth publish everywhere.
   Our love was new, and then but in the spring,
   When I was wont to greet it with my lays,
   As Philomel in summer's front doth sing
 8 And stops her pipe in growth of riper days;
   Not that the summer is less pleasant now
   Than when her mournful hymns did hush the night,
   But that wild music burdens every bough,
12 And sweets grown common lose their dear delight.
      Therefore, like her, I sometime hold my tongue,
      Because I would not dull you with my song.

103 Alack, what poverty my Muse brings forth,
   That, having such a scope to show her pride,
   The argument all bare is of more worth
 4 Than when it hath my added praise beside.
   O, blame me not if I no more can write!
   Look in your glass, and there appears a face
   That overgoes my blunt invention quite,
 8 Dulling my lines and doing me disgrace.
   Were it not sinful then, striving to mend,
   To mar the subject that before was well?
   For to no other pass my verses tend
12 Than of your graces and your gifts to tell;
      And more, much more, than in my verse can sit
      Your own glass shows you when you look in it.

104 To me, fair friend, you never can be old,
   For as you were when first your eye I eyed,
   Such seems your beauty still. Three winters cold
 4 Have from the forests shook three summers' pride,
   Three beauteous springs to yellow autumn turned
   In process of the seasons have I seen,
   Three April perfumes in three hot Junes burned,
 8 Since first I saw you fresh, which yet are green.
   Ah, yet doth beauty, like a dial hand,
   Steal from his figure, and no pace perceived;
   So your sweet hue, which methinks still doth stand,
12 Hath motion, and mine eye may be deceived;
      For fear of which, hear this, thou age unbred:
      Ere you were born was beauty's summer dead.

Let not my love be called idolatry,   105
   Nor my belovèd as an idol show,
   Since all alike my songs and praises be
   To one, of one, still such, and ever so.   4
   Kind is my love to-day, to-morrow kind,
   Still constant in a wondrous excellence;
   Therefore my verse, to constancy confined,
   One thing expressing, leaves out difference.   8
   'Fair, kind, and true' is all my argument,
   'Fair, kind, and true,' varying to other words;
   And in this change is my invention spent,
   Three themes in one, which wondrous scope affords.   12
      Fair, kind, and true have often lived alone,
      Which three till now never kept seat in one.

When in the chronicle of wasted time   106
   I see descriptions of the fairest wights,
   And beauty making beautiful old rime
   In praise of ladies dead and lovely knights;   4
   Then, in the blazon of sweet beauty's best,
   Of hand, of foot, of lip, of eye, of brow,
   I see their antique pen would have expressed
   Even such a beauty as you master now.   8
   So all their praises are but prophecies
   Of this our time, all you prefiguring;
   And, for they looked but with divining eyes,
   They had not skill enough your worth to sing: 12
      For we, which now behold these present days,
      Have eyes to wonder, but lack tongues to praise.

101: 2 *dyed* stamped 4 *thou* i.e. his Muse; *dignified* you are dignified 5
haply perchance 6 *no color* no artificial coloring; *his color fixed* its natural
and permanent color 7 *lay* lay on 8 *intermixed* i.e. with true and false
intermingled 13 *do thy office* perform your function

102: 1 *seeming* outward appearance 3 *merchandized* bartered; *esteeming*
valuation 7 *Philomel* the nightingale; *front* forefront. beginning 8 *riper*
later. more mature 11 *But . . . music* but because a wealth of bird-song
14 *dull* cloy, surfeit

103: 1 *poverty* inferior stuff 2 *pride* splendor 3 *argument* theme 7
overgoes outdoes; *blunt invention* crude creation 8 *Dulling* i.e. by comparison 11 *pass* purpose 13 *sit* reside

104: 6 *process* the progress 7 *burned* (as incense) 9 *dial* watch 10 *his
figure* (1) the dial's numeral. (2) the friend's form; *and . . . perceived* i.e. with
invisible movement 11 *sweet hue* fair aspect; *still* (1) motionless. unchanged, (2) always; *stand* remain constant 13 *unbred* unborn 14
summer i.e. peak (the friend)

105: 4 *one* (in contrast to the 'many' of idolatrous worship); *still* always 6
Still constant always the same 8 *difference* variety 9 *argument* theme
11 *in this change* i.e. in ringing these changes 14 *kept seat* lodged

106: 1 *wasted* past 2 *wights* persons 5 *blazon* commemorative record
8 *master* command 10 *prefiguring* picturing in advance 11 *for* because;
divining guessing 13 *we* i.e. even we

107
Not mine own fears, nor the prophetic soul
Of the wide world, dreaming on things to come,
Can yet the lease of my true love control,
4 Supposed as forfeit to a confined doom.
The mortal moon hath her eclipse endured,
And the sad augurs mock their own presage;
Incertainties now crown themselves assured,
8 And peace proclaims olives of endless age.
Now with the drops of this most balmy time
My love looks fresh, and Death to me subscribes,
Since, spite of him, I'll live in this poor rime,
12 While he insults o'er dull and speechless tribes:
    And thou in this shalt find thy monument
    When tyrants' crests and tombs of brass are spent.

108
What's in the brain that ink may character
Which hath not figured to thee my true spirit?
What's new to speak, what now to register,
4 That may express my love or thy dear merit?
Nothing, sweet boy; but yet, like prayers divine,
I must each day say o'er the very same;
Counting no old thing old, thou mine, I thine,
8 Even as when first I hallowed thy fair name.
So that eternal love in love's fresh case
Weighs not the dust and injury of age,
Nor gives to necessary wrinkles place,
12 But makes antiquity for aye his page,
    Finding the first conceit of love there bred
    Where time and outward form would show it dead.

O, never say that I was false of heart, **109**
Though absence seemed my flame to qualify;
As easy might I from myself depart
As from my soul, which in thy breast doth lie. 4
That is my home of love: if I have ranged,
Like him that travels I return again,
Just to the time, not with the time exchanged,
So that myself bring water for my stain. 8
Never believe, though in my nature reigned
All frailties that besiege all kinds of blood,
That it could so preposterously be stained
To leave for nothing all thy sum of good; 12
    For nothing this wide universe I call
    Save thou, my rose; in it thou art my all.

Alas, 'tis true I have gone here and there **110**
And made myself a motley to the view,
Gored mine own thoughts, sold cheap what is most dear,
Made old offenses of affections new. 4
Most true it is that I have looked on truth
Askance and strangely; but, by all above,
These blenches gave my heart another youth,
And worse essays proved thee my best of love. 8
Now all is done, have what shall have no end:
Mine appetite I never more will grind
On newer proof, to try an older friend,
A god in love, to whom I am confined. 12
    Then give me welcome, next my heaven the best,
    Even to thy pure and most most loving breast.

O, for my sake do you with Fortune chide, **111**
The guilty goddess of my harmful deeds,
That did not better for my life provide
Than public means which public manners breeds. 4
Thence comes it that my name receives a brand;
And almost thence my nature is subdued
To what it works in, like the dyer's hand:
Pity me then, and wish I were renewed, 8
Whilst, like a willing patient, I will drink
Potions of eisell 'gainst my strong infection;
No bitterness that I will bitter think,
Nor double penance, to correct correction. 12
    Pity me then, dear friend, and I assure ye
    Even that your pity is enough to cure me.

107: 3 *lease* term 4 *Supposed . . . doom* i.e. presumed to be subject to a limited duration 5 *mortal . . . endured* (an allusion variously interpreted, most plausibly related to the death in 1603 of Queen Elizabeth, 'Cynthia') 6 *sad augurs* foreboding prognosticators; *presage* predictions 7 *Incertainties . . . assured* i.e. uncertainty has triumphed as certainty 8 *olives . . . age* i.e. an eternal continuance of peace 10 *subscribes* surrenders 12 *insults* triumphs; *tribes* multitudes 14 *spent* wasted away

108: 1 *character* inscribe 2 *figured* revealed 3 *register* record 8 *hallowed* made sacred 9 *fresh case* youthful exterior 10 *Weighs not* cares not for 12 *page* i.e. to wait upon him 13 *conceit* conception

109: 2 *qualify* abate, cool 5 *ranged* wandered 7 *Just* punctual; *exchanged* changed 10 *blood* i.e. flesh 12 *for* in exchange for

110: 2 *motley* jester 3 *Gored* wounded 4 *offenses* trespasses; *affections* passions 6 *Askance and strangely* i.e. obliquely and at a distance 7 *blenches* turnings aside 8 *worse essays* trials of worse relationships 9 *shall . . . end* i.e. is eternal 10 *grind* whet 11 *proof* test 13 *my heaven* i.e. the Christian heaven

111: 1 *chide* quarrel 2 *guilty goddess* i.e. goddess responsible for 3 *life* livelihood 4 *public means* (probably an allusion to activity in the popular playhouses) 5 *brand* stigma 6–7 *subdued To* reduced to, made one with 8 *renewed* cleansed 10 *eisell* vinegar (used against the plague) 12 *Nor . . . correction* i.e. I will not consider the cure worse than the disease

112: 1 *th' impression fill* i.e. efface the scar 2 *vulgar scandal* i.e. notoriety (as a public performer?) 4 *o'ergreen* conceal with verdure; *allow* approve 6 *shames* faults 7–8 *None . . . wrong* (the sense of this obscure passage seems to be that no other human relationship affects his fixed sense of what is right and wrong) 9 *profound* deep 10 *adder's sense* i.e. deaf ears 12 *how . . . dispense* how I disregard public opinion 13 *so . . . bred* i.e. of such strong influence on my motives

Your love and pity doth th' impression fill **112**
Which vulgar scandal stamped upon my brow;
For what care I who calls me well or ill,
So you o'ergreen my bad, my good allow? 4
You are my all the world, and I must strive
To know my shames and praises from your tongue;
None else to me, nor I to none alive,
That my steeled sense or changes right or wrong. 8
In so profound abysm I throw all care
Of others' voices that my adder's sense
To critic and to flatterer stoppèd are;
Mark how with my neglect I do dispense: 12
    You are so strongly in my purpose bred
    That all the world besides methinks are dead.

113 Since I left you, mine eye is in my mind,
 And that which governs me to go about
 Doth part his function and is partly blind,
4 Seems seeing, but effectually is out;
 For it no form delivers to the heart
 Of bird, of flow'r, or shape which it doth latch;
 Of his quick objects hath the mind no part,
8 Nor his own vision holds what it doth catch;
 For if it see the rud'st or gentlest sight,
 The most sweet favor or deformèd'st creature,
 The mountain or the sea, the day or night,
12 The crow or dove, it shapes them to your feature.
  Incapable of more, replete with you,
  My most true mind thus maketh mine eye untrue.

114 Or whether doth my mind, being crowned with you,
 Drink up the monarch's plague, this flattery?
 Or whether shall I say mine eye saith true,
4 And that your love taught it this alchemy,
 To make of monsters and things indigest
 Such cherubins as your sweet self resemble,
 Creating every bad a perfect best
8 As fast as objects to his beams assemble?
 O, 'tis the first; 'tis flatt'ry in my seeing,
 And my great mind most kingly drinks it up:
 Mine eye well knows what with his gust is 'greeing,
12 And to his palate doth prepare the cup.
  If it be poisoned, 'tis the lesser sin
  That mine eye loves it and doth first begin.

115 Those lines that I before have writ do lie,
 Even those that said I could not love you dearer;
 Yet then my judgment knew no reason why
4 My most full flame should afterwards burn clearer.
 But reckoning Time, whose millioned accidents
 Creep in 'twixt vows and change decrees of kings,
 Tan sacred beauty, blunt the sharp'st intents,
8 Divert strong minds to th' course of alt'ring things!
 Alas, why, fearing of Time's tyranny,
 Might I not then say, 'Now I love you best'
 When I was certain o'er incertainty,
12 Crowning the present, doubting of the rest?
  Love is a babe; then might I not say so,
  To give full growth to that which still doth grow.

116 Let me not to the marriage of true minds
 Admit impediments; love is not love
 Which alters when it alteration finds
4 Or bends with the remover to remove.
 O, no, it is an ever-fixèd mark
 That looks on tempests and is never shaken;
 It is the star to every wand'ring bark,
8 Whose worth's unknown, although his height be taken.
 Love's not Time's fool, though rosy lips and cheeks
 Within his bending sickle's compass come;
 Love alters not with his brief hours and weeks,
12 But bears it out even to the edge of doom.
  If this be error, and upon me proved,
  I never writ, nor no man ever loved.

Accuse me thus, that I have scanted all   117
 Wherein I should your great deserts repay;
 Forgot upon your dearest love to call,
 Whereto all bonds do tie me day by day;   4
 That I have frequent been with unknown minds
 And given to time your own dear-purchased right;
 That I have hoisted sail to all the winds
 Which should transport me farthest from your sight.   8
 Book both my wilfulness and errors down,
 And on just proof surmise accumulate;
 Bring me within the level of your frown,
 But shoot not at me in your wakened hate: 12
  Since my appeal says I did strive to prove
  The constancy and virtue of your love.

113: 1 *mine ... mind* i.e. I am directed by inner sight 2 *governs ... about* i.e. directs my steps 3 *part* divide 3, 7, 8 *his* its (i.e. the physical eye's) 4 *effectually* in effect 6 *latch* catch sight of 7 *quick* fleeting 8 *Nor ... holds* i.e. nor does the eye itself retain 10 *favor* face 12 *feature* likeness 13 *replete* filled

114: 1, 3 *Or whether* (indicating alternative possibilities) 1 *being ... you* i.e. by being crowned by you 4 *alchemy* i.e. power to transform substances 5 *indigest* shapeless 6 *cherubins* angelic forms 8 *to ... assemble* i.e. are presented to the eye's gaze 11 *with ... 'greeing* is agreeable to the mind's taste 14 *That* since

115: 2 *dearer* more dearly 5 *reckoning ... accidents* i.e. time whose casual events are reckoned in the millions 7 *Tan* coarsen; *intents* intentions 8 *Divert* accommodate; *alt'ring things* things as they change 12 *Crowning* glorifying 13 *then* therefore; *so* i.e. 'Now I love you best'

116: 2 *impediments* (an echo of the marriage service) 4 *bends ... remove* i.e. agrees with the withdrawer to withdraw 5 *mark* sea-mark 8 *worth's unknown* i.e. value is incalculable; *his height* the star's altitude 9 *fool* plaything 10 *Within ... compass* i.e. within the range of Time's curving sickle 11 *his* Time's 12 *bears it out* persists 13 *upon* against

117: 1 *scanted* come short of 3 *Forgot ... call* have forgotten to invoke your most precious love 4 *bonds* obligations 5 *frequent* familiar; *unknown minds* i.e. negligible spirits 6 *given to time* i.e. wasted away 9 *Book ... down* i.e. record both my intentional and unintentional trespasses 10 *on ... accumulate* i.e. take account of valid circumstantial evidence 11 *level* range 13 *appeal* plea; *strive to prove* i.e. thus try to test

118 Like as to make our appetites more keen,
With eager compounds we our palate urge;
As to prevent our maladies unseen,
4 We sicken to shun sickness when we purge:
Even so, being full of your ne'er-cloying sweetness,
To bitter sauces did I frame my feeding;
And, sick of welfare, found a kind of meetness
8 To be diseased ere that there was true needing.
Thus policy in love, t' anticipate
The ills that were not, grew to faults assured,
And brought to medicine a healthful state
12 Which, rank of goodness, would by ill be cured.
     But thence I learn, and find the lesson true,
     Drugs poison him that so fell sick of you.

What potions have I drunk of Siren tears   119
Distilled from limbecks foul as hell within,
Applying fears to hopes and hopes to fears,
Still losing when I saw myself to win!   4
What wretched errors hath my heart committed
Whilst it hath thought itself so blessèd never!
How have mine eyes out of their spheres been fitted
In the distraction of this madding fever!   8
O benefit of ill: now I find true
That better is by evil still made better;
And ruined love, when it is built anew,
Grows fairer than at first, more strong, far greater. 12
     So I return rebuked to my content,
     And gain by ills thrice more than I have spent.

That you were once unkind befriends me now,   120
And for that sorrow which I then did feel
Needs must I under my transgression bow,
Unless my nerves were brass or hammered steel.   4
For if you were by my unkindness shaken,
As I by yours, you've passed a hell of time,
And I, a tyrant, have no leisure taken
To weigh how once I suffered in your crime.   8
O that our night of woe might have rememb'red
My deepest sense how hard true sorrow hits,
And soon to you, as you to me then, tend'red
The humble salve which wounded bosoms fits!   12
     But that your trespass now becomes a fee;
     Mine ransoms yours, and yours must ransom me.

'Tis better to be vile than vile esteemed   121
When not to be receives reproach of being,
And the just pleasure lost, which is so deemed
Not by our feeling but by others' seeing.   4
For why should others' false adulterate eyes
Give salutation to my sportive blood?
Or on my frailties why are frailer spies,
Which in their wills count bad what I think good?   8
No, I am that I am; and they that level
At my abuses reckon up their own:
I may be straight though they themselves be bevel;
By their rank thoughts my deeds must not be shown,   12
     Unless this general evil they maintain:
     All men are bad and in their badness reign.

Thy gift, thy tables, are within my brain   122
Full charactered with lasting memory,
Which shall above that idle rank remain
Beyond all date, even to eternity;   4
Or, at the least, so long as brain and heart
Have faculty by nature to subsist,
Till each to rased oblivion yield his part
Of thee, thy record never can be missed.   8
That poor retention could not so much hold,
Nor need I tallies thy dear love to score;
Therefore to give them from me was I bold,
To trust those tables that receive thee more.   12
     To keep an adjunct to remember thee
     Were to import forgetfulness in me.

118: **1** *Like as* just as **2** *eager compounds* sharp condiments; *urge* stimulate **3** *As* just as; *prevent* ward off, forestall **6** *bitter sauces* i.e. unsavory persons; *frame* direct **7** *meetness* appropriateness **9** *anticipate* forestall **10** *faults assured* actual faults **11** *medicine* i.e. medical treatment **12** *rank* too full **14** *so* thus

119: **1** *Siren tears* i.e. appeals of the temptress **2** *limbecks* alembics, stills (i.e. the person of the temptress) **3** *Applying* i.e. as a salve **4** *Still* always; *saw myself* expected **6** *so blessèd never* never so blessed **7** *spheres* sockets (?), orbits (?); *fitted* forced by fits **8** *madding* maddening, producing delirium

120: **2** *for* because of **3** *my transgression* i.e. my present unkindness to you **4** *nerves* sinews **7** *tyrant* oppressor; *no leisure taken* i.e. failed to take the time **8** *weigh* consider; *crime* i.e. unkindness to me **9** *night of woe* i.e. estrangement, for which you were responsible; *rememb'red* reminded **11** *tend'red* offered **12** *salve* apology; *fits* suits **13** *fee* payment **14** *ransoms* redeems, excuses

121: **1** *esteemed* considered **2** *not to be* i.e. not to be vile; *being* i.e. being vile **3** *just* right, proper; *so* i.e. vile **4** *Not . . . seeing* i.e. not in our own mind but in the view of others **5** *false adulterate* prurient **6** *Give salutation to* greet, i.e. meet more than halfway; *sportive* wanton **7** *frailties* faults; *frailer* faultier **8** *in their wills* i.e. wishfully **9** *that* what; *level* aim **10** *abuses* transgressions **11** *bevel* i.e. crooked

122: **1** *tables* writing-tablet **2** *charactered* inscribed **3** *that idle rank* the leaves of the tablet (?); *remain* endure **6** *faculty . . . subsist* natural power to survive **7** *rased* blank; *his* its **8** *missed* lost **9** *retention* retainer (i.e. the tablet) **10** *tallies* anything on which scores were kept **11** *to . . . from me* i.e. to give away that tablet **12** *those tables* i.e. the tablet of the memory **13** *adjunct* aid, implement **14** *import* imply

123 No, Time, thou shalt not boast that I do change :
    Thy pyramids built up with newer might
    To me are nothing novel, nothing strange ;
    4 They are but dressings of a former sight.
    Our dates are brief, and therefore we admire
    What thou dost foist upon us that is old,
    And rather make them born to our desire
    8 Than think that we before have heard them told.
    Thy registers and thee I both defy,
    Not wond'ring at the present nor the past ;
    For thy records and what we see doth lie,
    12 Made more or less by thy continual haste.
      This I do vow, and this shall ever be :
      I will be true, despite thy scythe and thee.

124 If my dear love were but the child of state,
    It might for Fortune's bastard be unfathered,
    As subject to Time's love or to Time's hate,
    4 Weeds among weeds, or flowers with flowers gathered.
    No, it was builded far from accident ;
    It suffers not in smiling pomp, nor falls
    Under the blow of thrallèd discontent,
    8 Whereto th' inviting time our fashion calls :
    It fears not Policy, that heretic
    Which works on leases of short-numb'red hours,
    But all alone stands hugely politic,
    12 That it nor grows with heat nor drowns with show'rs.
      To this I witness call the fools of Time,
      Which die for goodness, who have lived for crime.

125 Were't aught to me I bore the canopy,
    With my extern the outward honoring,
    Or laid great bases for eternity,
    4 Which proves more short than waste or ruining ?
    Have I not seen dwellers on form and favor
    Lose all and more by paying too much rent,
    For compound sweet forgoing simple savor,
    8 Pitiful thrivers, in their gazing spent ?
    No, let me be obsequious in thy heart,
    And take thou my oblation, poor but free,
    Which is not mixed with seconds, knows no art
    12 But mutual render, only me for thee.
      Hence, thou suborned informer ; a true soul
      When most impeached stands least in thy control.

126 O thou, my lovely boy, who in thy power
    Dost hold Time's fickle glass, his sickle hour ;
    Who hast by waning grown, and therein show'st
    4 Thy lovers withering as thy sweet self grow'st ;
    If Nature, sovereign mistress over wrack,
    As thou goest onwards, still will pluck thee back,
    She keeps thee to this purpose, that her skill
    8 May Time disgrace and wretched minutes kill.
    Yet fear her, O thou minion of her pleasure !
    She may detain, but not still keep, her treasure ;
    Her audit, though delayed, answered must be,
    12 And her quietus is to render thee.

In the old age black was not counted fair, 127
    Or, if it were, it bore not beauty's name ;
    But now is black beauty's successive heir,
    And beauty slandered with a bastard shame ;   4
    For since each hand hath put on nature's power,
    Fairing the foul with art's false borrowed face,
    Sweet beauty hath no name, no holy bower,
    But is profaned, if not lives in disgrace.   8
    Therefore my mistress' brows are raven black,
    Her eyes so suited, and they mourners seem
    At such who, not born fair, no beauty lack,
    Sland'ring creation with a false esteem :   12
      Yet so they mourn, becoming of their woe,
      That every tongue says beauty should look so.

123: 2 *pyramids . . . might* (perhaps a topical allusion, possibly to the pyramids erected on London streets as part of the pageant welcoming King James in 1603; cf. Sonnet 107) 4 *dressings* i.e. imitations 5 *dates* lifespans 7 *born . . . desire* i.e. created newly to our taste 8 *told* reckoned 9 *registers* records of time 11 *records . . . see* i.e. both past and present ; *lie* misrepresent

124: 1 *love* love of you ; *but* only ; *child of state* i.e. product of material circumstances 2 *for . . . unfathered* i.e. go unclaimed, as Fortune's bastard 5 *accident* chance occurrence 7 *thrallèd* oppressed 8 *Whereto . . . calls* to which condition our times invite us (?) 9 *Policy, that heretic* i.e. false practicality 10 *on . . . hours* i.e. on short-term leases 11 *all . . . politic* i.e. only love is truly practical 12 *That it nor* since it is neither 13 *fools* playthings 14 *Which . . . crime* i.e. eleventh-hour repenters (often dubiously associated with various Catholic or other martyrs of the time)

125: 1 *Were't aught* would it be anything ; *canopy* i.e. the covering with which the persons of the great are honored 2 *With . . . honoring* i.e. externally honoring the external 3 *bases* foundations (of monuments) 5 *dwellers on* i.e. those who dwell upon or overvalue (with pun on 'tenants') 8 *Pitiful thrivers* i.e. those who thrive pitifully since their gains are empty ; *in . . . spent* i.e. starved by mere looking 9 *be obsequious* have my devotion recognized 10 *oblation* offering 11 *seconds* i.e. second-best, inferior ; *art* artifice 12 *mutual . . . thee* i.e. surrender of my true self for your true self 13 *suborned informer* false witness 14 *impeached* accused

126: 2 *glass* mirror ; *hour* hourglass 3 *by waning grown* i.e. increased in loveliness with the passing of time ; *show'st* i.e. show in contrast 5 *wrack* wreckage, ruin 9 *minion* darling 11 *audit* final reckoning ; *answered* paid 12 *quietus* settlement ; *render* surrender

Number 126 is exceptional among the sonnets, since it is a poem of twelve lines rhyming in pairs.

127: 1 *old* former ; *black* i.e. brunette (equated with ugliness) ; *fair* beautiful (with play on 'blonde') 3 *successive heir* heir in line of succession 4 *slandered . . . shame* i.e. declared illegitimate 5 *put* taken 6 *Fairing* beautifying ; *art's . . . face* i.e. cosmetics 7 *Sweet beauty* i.e. natural blonde beauty ; *holy bower* i.e. shrine 8 *if . . . disgrace* (the sense seems to be that blonde beauty is so habitually enhanced or simulated with cosmetics that it is discredited in its natural form) 10 *so suited* i.e. also black 11 *At* for ; *no beauty lack* i.e. nevertheless possess the appearance of beauty 12 *Sland'ring . . . esteem* i.e. misrepresenting the natural process with counterfeit value 13 *becoming of* gracing

128 How oft, when thou, my music, music play'st
    Upon that blessèd wood whose motion sounds
    With thy sweet fingers when thou gently sway'st
4 The wiry concord that mine ear confounds,
    Do I envy those jacks that nimble leap
    To kiss the tender inward of thy hand,
    Whilst my poor lips, which should that harvest reap,
8 At the wood's boldness by thee blushing stand.
    To be so tickled they would change their state
    And situation with those dancing chips
    O'er whom thy fingers walk with gentle gait,
12 Making dead wood more blest than living lips.
      Since saucy jacks so happy are in this,
      Give them thy fingers, me thy lips to kiss.

Th' expense of spirit in a waste of shame   129
Is lust in action; and, till action, lust
Is perjured, murd'rous, bloody, full of blame,
Savage, extreme, rude, cruel, not to trust;   4
Enjoyed no sooner but despisèd straight;
Past reason hunted, and no sooner had,
Past reason hated as a swallowed bait
On purpose laid to make the taker mad: 8
Mad in pursuit, and in possession so;
Had, having, and in quest to have, extreme;
A bliss in proof, and proved, a very woe;
Before, a joy proposed; behind, a dream.   12
    All this the world well knows; yet none knows well
    To shun the heaven that leads men to this hell.

My mistress' eyes are nothing like the sun;   130
Coral is far more red than her lips' red;
If snow be white, why then her breasts are dun;
If hairs be wires, black wires grow on her head.   4
I have seen roses damasked, red and white,
But no such roses see I in her cheeks;
And in some perfumes is there more delight
Than in the breath that from my mistress reeks.   8
I love to hear her speak; yet well I know
That music hath a far more pleasing sound:
I grant I never saw a goddess go;
My mistress, when she walks, treads on the ground.   12
    And yet, by heaven, I think my love as rare
    As any she belied with false compare.

Thou art as tyrannous, so as thou art,   131
As those whose beauties proudly make them cruel;
For well thou know'st to my dear, doting heart
Thou art the fairest and most precious jewel.   4
Yet, in good faith, some say that thee behold,
Thy face hath not the power to make love groan;
To say they err I dare not be so bold,
Although I swear it to myself alone.   8
And, to be sure that is not false I swear,
A thousand groans, but thinking on thy face,
One on another's neck, do witness bear
Thy black is fairest in my judgment's place.   12
    In nothing art thou black save in thy deeds,
    And thence this slander, as I think, proceeds.

Thine eyes I love, and they, as pitying me,   132
Knowing thy heart torments me with disdain,
Have put on black and loving mourners be,
Looking with pretty ruth upon my pain.   4
And truly not the morning sun of heaven
Better becomes the gray cheeks of the east,
Nor that full star that ushers in the even
Doth half that glory to the sober west,   8
As those two mourning eyes become thy face.
O, let it then as well beseem thy heart
To mourn for me, since mourning doth thee grace,
And suit thy pity like in every part.   12
    Then will I swear beauty herself is black,
    And all they foul that thy complexion lack.

128: 2 *wood* keys of the spinet or virginal; *motion* mechanism 3 *thou* . . . *sway'st* you . . . control 4 *wiry concord* harmony of strings; *confounds* i.e. makes swoon 5 *jacks* (not the keys proper, which would be touched by the finger-tips, but the levers which on some virginals touched the *tender inward* of the hand when the instrument was played or tuned) 9 *they* i.e. the lips

129: 1 *Th' expense* . . . *shame* i.e. the expenditure of vital power in shameful waste 2 *action* consummation 4 *rude* brutal; *to trust* to be trusted 6 *Past reason hunted* i.e. madly sought 10 *quest* pursuit; *extreme* excessive, given to extremes 11 *in proof* in testing; *proved* tested 12 *dream* delusion 14 *heaven* i.e. promise of bliss

130: 5 *damasked* mingled red and white 8 *reeks* breathes forth 11 *go* walk 14 *compare* comparison (with sun, coral, snow, etc.)

131: 1 *so* . . . *art* even as you are (i.e. not a recognized beauty) 3 *dear* fond 8 *Although* (1) even providing that, (2) however (humorously ambiguous: it is not made certain whether the poet does or does not agree privately with her critics) 9 *to be sure* i.e. for proof 10 *but thinking* when I only think of 11 *One* . . . *neck* i.e. in quick succession 12 *in* . . . *place* where my judgment is 13 *black* i.e. not fair, foul

132: 4 *ruth* pity 6 *becomes* . . . *cheeks* i.e. adorns the early-morning sky 7 *even* evening 8 *Doth* i.e. renders 9 *mourning* (1) mourning, (2) morning 10 *beseem* i.e. be seemly to 12 *suit* . . . *like* dress your pity alike; *every part* i.e. heart as well as *eyes*

133 Beshrew that heart that makes my heart to groan
For that deep wound it gives my friend and me:
Is't not enough to torture me alone,
4 But slave to slavery my sweet'st friend must be?
Me from myself thy cruel eye hath taken,
And my next self thou harder hast engrossed;
Of him, myself, and thee I am forsaken,
8 A torment thrice threefold thus to be crossed.
Prison my heart in thy steel bosom's ward,
But then my friend's heart let my poor heart bail;
Whoe'er keeps me, let my heart be his guard:
12 Thou canst not then use rigor in my jail.
 And yet thou wilt; for I, being pent in thee,
 Perforce am thine, and all that is in me.

134 So, now I have confessed that he is thine
And I myself am mortgaged to thy will,
Myself I'll forfeit, so that other mine
4 Thou wilt restore to be my comfort still:
But thou wilt not, nor he will not be free,
For thou art covetous, and he is kind;
He learned but surety-like to write for me
8 Under that bond that him as fast doth bind.
The statute of thy beauty thou wilt take,
Thou usurer that put'st forth all to use,
And sue a friend came debtor for my sake;
12 So him I lose through my unkind abuse.
 Him have I lost, thou hast both him and me;
 He pays the whole, and yet am I not free.

135 Whoever hath her wish, thou hast thy Will,
And Will to boot, and Will in overplus.
More than enough am I that vex thee still,
4 To thy sweet will making addition thus.
Wilt thou, whose will is large and spacious,
Not once vouchsafe to hide my will in thine?
Shall will in others seem right gracious,
8 And in my will no fair acceptance shine?
The sea, all water, yet receives rain still
And in abundance addeth to his store;
So thou, being rich in Will, add to thy Will
12 One will of mine to make thy large Will more.
 Let no unkind, no fair beseechers kill;
 Think all but one, and me in that one Will.

136 If thy soul check thee that I come so near,
Swear to thy blind soul that I was thy Will,
And will, thy soul knows, is admitted there:
4 Thus far for love my love-suit, sweet, fulfil.
Will will fulfil the treasure of thy love
Ay, fill it full with wills, and my will one.
In things of great receipt with ease we prove
8 Among a number one is reckoned none.
Then in the number let me pass untold,
Though in thy store's account I one must be;
For nothing hold me, so it please thee hold
12 That nothing me, a something, sweet, to thee.
 Make but my name thy love, and love that still,
 And then thou lovest me, for my name is Will.

Thou blind fool, Love, what dost thou to mine eyes   137
That they behold and see not what they see?
They know what beauty is, see where it lies,
Yet what the best is take the worst to be.   4
If eyes, corrupt by over-partial looks,
Be anchored in the bay where all men ride,
Why of eyes' falsehood hast thou forgèd hooks,
Whereto the judgment of my heart is tied?   8
Why should my heart think that a several plot
Which my heart knows the wide world's common place?
Or mine eyes seeing this, say this is not,
To put fair truth upon so foul a face?   12
 In things right true my heart and eyes have erred,
 And to this false plague are they now transferred.

133: 1 *Beshrew* curse (mild in connotation) 2 *For* because of 4 *slave to slavery* i.e. sharer of my enslavement 5 *myself* i.e. my true self 6 *my . . . engrossed* i.e. you have placed my friend under even greater bondage 8 *crossed* afflicted 9 *ward* bondage 10 *bail* i.e. free by serving as substitute 11 *keeps* imprisons; *his guard* my friend's guardhouse 12 *rigor* cruelty; *jail* i.e. heart which holds the friend 13 *pent* pent up

134: 2 *mortgaged* held as security; *will* (1) purpose, (2) carnal desire 3 *other mine* i.e. alter ego 4 *restore* return; *still* always, in the future 5 *will not* (1) will not, (2) wills not to 6 *kind* compliant 7–8 *He . . . bind* i.e. it was as if to serve as security for me that he signed the bond that now binds us both (with a play on *learned . . . to write for me* in the sense of 'took my place with my mistress') 9 *take* invoke 10 *use* usury 11 *came* who became 12 *my unkind abuse* i.e. your deceiving me

135: 1 *Will* (1) one of various persons named 'Will,' including the poet and perhaps the friend and the husband, (2) carnal desire ('Will' is both capitalized and italicized in Q wherever capitalized here, in the present sonnet and Sonnet 136) 2 *to boot* i.e. in addition 3 *still* always 4 *will* (where so printed, here and in Q, the word seems usually to have the more neutral meaning of 'wish,' but it incorporates an indeterminable number of puns); *making addition thus* i.e. by adding myself 6 *vouchsafe* consent; *hide* shelter 8 *acceptance* acceptability 10 *his* its 13 *no unkind* i.e. no unkind word, no refusal; *no fair beseechers* i.e. no applicants for your favors (as punctuated, here and in Q, the line contains a double negative; some editors omit the comma and place the 'no' in quotation marks) 14 *and me* i.e. including me

136: 1 *check* rebuke; *come so near* (1) am so candid, (2) have access to you 2 *blind* obtuse 4 *fulfil* grant 5 *fulfil the treasure* fill the treasury 6 *one* among them 7 *receipt* capacity 8 *reckoned none* not counted (cf. an adage of the time, 'one is no number') 9 *untold* uncounted 10 *thy store's account* i.e. the inventory of your numerous lovers 13 *my name* i.e. 'will,' in the sense of 'carnal desire'

137: 3 *lies* resides 5 *corrupt* corrupted 6 *Be . . . ride* i.e. have brought me to anchor in a common roadway (with *double entendre* in 'ride') 7 *falsehood* deception; *forgèd* fashioned 9 *that . . . plot* i.e. that plot a private one 10 *knows* knows to be 11 *not* not so 13 *erred* gone astray 14 *false plague* (1) plague of falseness, (2) plaguey mistress

138
When my love swears that she is made of truth
I do believe her, though I know she lies,
That she might think me some untutored youth,
4 Unlearnèd in the world's false subtilties.
Thus vainly thinking that she thinks me young,
Although she knows my days are past the best,
Simply I credit her false-speaking tongue ;
8 On both sides thus is simple truth suppressed.
But wherefore says she not she is unjust ?
And wherefore say not I that I am old ?
O, love's best habit is in seeming trust,
12 And age in love loves not to have years told.
Therefore I lie with her and she with me,
And in our faults by lies we flattered be.

O, call not me to justify the wrong
That thy unkindness lays upon my heart ;
Wound me not with thine eye but with thy tongue ;
Use power with power, and slay me not by art. 4
Tell me thou lov'st elsewhere ; but in my sight,
Dear heart, forbear to glance thine eye aside ;
What need'st thou wound with cunning when thy might
Is more than my o'erpressed defense can bide ? 8
Let me excuse thee : ah, my love well knows
Her pretty looks have been mine enemies ;
And therefore from my face she turns my foes,
That they elsewhere might dart their injuries : 12
Yet do not so ; but since I am near slain,
Kill me outright with looks and rid my pain.
139

Be wise as thou art cruel : do not press
My tongue-tied patience with too much disdain,
Lest sorrow lend me words, and words express
The manner of my pity-wanting pain. 4
If I might teach thee wit, better it were,
Though not to love, yet, love, to tell me so ;
As testy sick men, when their deaths be near,
No news but health from their physicians know. 8
For if I should despair, I should grow mad,
And in my madness might speak ill of thee :
Now this ill-wresting world is grown so bad
Mad slanderers by mad ears believèd be. 12
That I may not be so, nor thou belied,
Bear thine eyes straight, though thy proud heart go wide.
140

138: 1 *truth* fidelity 2 *believe* seem to believe 5 *vainly thinking* i.e. acting as if I thought 7 *Simply* pretending to be simple ; *credit* give credence to 9 *unjust* unfaithful 11 *habit* dress, guise ; *seeming trust* apparent fidelity 12 *told* counted 13 *lie with* i.e. lie to (with *double entendre*)

In the version of the above sonnet printed in *The Passionate Pilgrim* (1st ed. 1599) the following variants appear : 4 *Unlearnèd* Unskillful *subtilties* forgeries 6 *she knows my days are* I know my years be 7 *Simply I* I smiling 8 *On both sides thus is simple truth suppressed* Outfacing faults in love, with love's ill rest 9 *she not she is unjust* my love that she is young 11 *habit is in seeming trust* habit's in a soothing tongue 12 *t'* to (the reading here adopted) 13 *I . . . her . . . she* I'll . . . love . . . love 14 *And in our faults by lies we flattered be* Since that our faults in love thus smothered be

139: 1 *call* call on, ask 2 *unkindness* i.e. infidelity 3 *not . . . tongue* i.e. not with roving looks but with actual words 4 *Use . . . power* i.e. use your power directly ; *art* artifice 5 *but* but while 8 *o'erpressed* i.e. attacked beyond its power to withstand ; *bide* stand 9 *excuse thee* i.e. excuse you thus 11 *foes* i.e. the pretty looks 14 *rid* dispatch

140: 1 *press* oppress 4 *manner* nature ; *pity-wanting* unpitied 5 *wit* wisdom 6 *so* i.e. that you do love me 7 *testy* peevish 8 *know* i.e. hear 11 *ill-wresting* i.e. that wrests things to an evil sense 13 *so* i.e. a 'mad slanderer' 14 *wide* astray

141: 4 *Who . . . view* i.e. which in spite of what is seen 6 *Nor . . . prone* i.e. nor does the delicate sense of feeling incline toward contact with you 8 *sensual feast* feast of the senses 9 *But* but neither ; *five wits* (the mental faculties, such as intelligence, imagination, memory, etc.) 11 *Who . . . man* i.e. which leaves ungoverned the outer man (i.e. the heart, which should be monarch of the body, has abdicated to become another's heart's slave) 13 *Only . . . gain* i.e. one thing certain, my suffering is to my advantage to the following extent 14 *That . . . pain* i.e. the sin is its own punishment

142: 2 *Hate . . . loving* i.e. hate of the adulterous character of my love 4 *it* i.e. my state 6 *scarlet ornaments* i.e. the lips (here equated with the seals of red wax authenticating documents) 7 *mine* i.e. mine have 8 *Robbed . . . rents* i.e. and stolen from wives the due of the marriage bed 9 *Be it lawful* i.e. consider it lawful that 12 *Thy . . . be* i.e. your pity will make you deserving of pity 13 *hide* withhold

In faith, I do not love thee with mine eyes,
For they in thee a thousand errors note ;
But 'tis my heart that loves what they despise,
Who in despite of view is pleased to dote. 4
Nor are mine ears with thy tongue's tune delighted,
Nor tender feeling to base touches prone,
Nor taste, nor smell, desire to be invited
To any sensual feast with thee alone ; 8
But my five wits nor my five senses can
Dissuade one foolish heart from serving thee,
Who leaves unswayed the likeness of a man,
Thy proud heart's slave and vassal wretch to be : 12
Only my plague thus far I count my gain,
That she that makes me sin awards me pain.
141

Love is my sin, and thy dear virtue hate,
Hate of my sin, grounded on sinful loving.
O, but with mine compare thou thine own state,
And thou shalt find it merits not reproving ; 4
Or if it do, not from those lips of thine,
That have profaned their scarlet ornaments
And sealed false bonds of love as oft as mine,
Robbed others' beds' revenues of their rents. 8
Be it lawful I love thee as thou lov'st those
Whom thine eyes woo as mine importune thee :
Root pity in thy heart, that, when it grows,
Thy pity may deserve to pitied be. 12
If thou dost seek to have what thou dost hide,
By self-example mayst thou be denied.
142

143 Lo, as a careful housewife runs to catch
One of her feathered creatures broke away,
Sets down her babe, and makes all swift dispatch
4 In pursuit of the thing she would have stay;
Whilst her neglected child holds her in chase,
Cries to catch her whose busy care is bent
To follow that which flies before her face,
8 Not prizing her poor infant's discontent:
So runn'st thou after that which flies from thee,
Whilst I, thy babe, chase thee afar behind;
But if thou catch thy hope, turn back to me
12 And play the mother's part, kiss me, be kind.
    So will I pray that thou mayst have thy Will,
    If thou turn back and my loud crying still.

144 Two loves I have, of comfort and despair,
Which like two spirits do suggest me still:
The better angel is a man right fair,
4 The worser spirit a woman colored ill.
To win me soon to hell, my female evil
Tempteth my better angel from my side,
And would corrupt my saint to be a devil,
8 Wooing his purity with her foul pride.
And whether that my angel be turned fiend
Suspect I may, yet not directly tell;
But being both from me, both to each friend,
12 I guess one angel in another's hell.
    Yet this shall I ne'er know, but live in doubt,
    Till my bad angel fire my good one out.

145 Those lips that Love's own hand did make
Breathed forth the sound that said 'I hate'
To me that languished for her sake;
4 But when she saw my woeful state,
Straight in her heart did mercy come,
Chiding that tongue that ever sweet
Was used in giving gentle doom,
8 And taught it thus anew to greet:
'I hate' she altered with an end
That followed it as gentle day
Doth follow night, who, like a fiend,
12 From heaven to hell is flown away.
    'I hate' from hate away she threw,
    And saved my life, saying 'not you.'

146 Poor soul, the center of my sinful earth,
[Fooled by] these rebel pow'rs that thee array,
Why dost thou pine within and suffer dearth,
4 Painting thy outward walls so costly gay?
Why so large cost, having so short a lease,
Dost thou upon thy fading mansion spend?
Shall worms, inheritors of this excess,
8 Eat up thy charge? Is this thy body's end?
Then, soul, live thou upon thy servant's loss,
And let that pine to aggravate thy store;
Buy terms divine in selling hours of dross;
12 Within be fed, without be rich no more:
    So shalt thou feed on Death, that feeds on men,
    And Death once dead, there's no more dying then.

147 My love is as a fever, longing still
For that which longer nurseth the disease,
Feeding on that which doth preserve the ill,
4 Th' uncertain sickly appetite to please.
My reason, the physician to my love,
Angry that his prescriptions are not kept,
Hath left me, and I desperate now approve
8 Desire is death, which physic did except.
Past cure I am, now reason is past care,
And frantic-mad with evermore unrest;
My thoughts and my discourse as madmen's are,
12 At randon from the truth vainly expressed:
    For I have sworn thee fair, and thought thee bright,
    Who art as black as hell, as dark as night.

148 O me, what eyes hath Love put in my head,
Which have no correspondence with true sight;
Or, if they have, where is my judgment fled,
4 That censures falsely what they see aright?
If that be fair whereon my false eyes dote,
What means the world to say it is not so?
If it be not, then love doth well denote
8 Love's eye is not so true as all men's no.
How can it? O, how can Love's eye be true,
That is so vexed with watching and with tears?
No marvel then though I mistake my view:
12 The sun itself sees not till heaven clears.
    O cunning Love, with tears thou keep'st me blind,
    Lest eyes well-seeing thy foul faults should find.

143: **3** *dispatch* haste **5** *holds ... chase* i.e. chases her in turn **8** *prizing* considering important **11** *hope* hoped-for object **13** *Will* (capitalized and italicized in Q; cf. Sonnets 135 and 136)

144: **1** *comfort and despair* i.e. mercy and despair (in Christian theology instrumental respectively in bringing the soul to salvation and damnation) **2** *suggest me still* always prompt me **4** *colored ill* i.e. dark **5** *evil* evil angel **8** *pride* sexual heat **11** *each* each other **12** *in another's hell* (a double entendre) **14** *fire ... out* i.e. infect with venereal disease

In the version of the above sonnet printed in *The Passionate Pilgrim* (1st ed. 1599) the following variants appear: **2** *Which* That **3** *The* My **4** *The* My **6** *sight* side (the reading here adopted) **8** *foul* fair **9** *find* fiend (the reading here adopted) **11** *But ... from* For ... to **13** *Yet this shall I ne'er* The truth I shall not

145: **7** *doom* sentence, judgment **8** *greet* i.e. accost me

The authenticity of this sonnet, in tetrameters and rudimentary diction, has been questioned, with considerable show of reason; in any case, it is not in context with the adjacent sonnets.

146: **1** *earth* i.e. body **2** *Fooled by* (Malone's conjecture; Q repeats 'My sinful earth'); *rebel pow'rs* rebellious flesh; *array* dress, enclose **4** *Painting* i.e. while ornamenting **5** *cost* sums **8** *charge* i.e. the costly body **9** *servant's* body's **10** *aggravate* increase **11** *terms divine* immortality in heaven; *hours of dross* wasteful hours

147: **1** *still* always **2** *longer nurseth* prolongs **4** *uncertain* fickle **6** *kept* followed **7** *approve* i.e. prove by my experience that **8** *Desire ... except* i.e. desire, which rejected reason's medicine, proves fatal **12** *At randon* at random, in deviation

148: **4** *censures* judges **7** *denote* indicate **8** *Love's eye* i.e. Love's 'ay' (punning with *men's no*) **10** *vexed* afflicted; *watching* lying awake **11** *my view* i.e. what I see **14** *find* discover

149 Canst thou, O cruel, say I love thee not
When I against myself with thee partake?
Do I not think on thee when I forgot
4 Am of myself, all tyrant for thy sake?
Who hateth thee that I do call my friend?
On whom frown'st thou that I do fawn upon?
Nay, if thou lour'st on me, do I not spend
8 Revenge upon myself with present moan?
What merit do I in myself respect
That is so proud thy service to despise,
When all my best doth worship thy defect,
12 Commanded by the motion of thine eyes?
   But, love, hate on, for now I know thy mind;
   Those that can see thou lov'st, and I am blind.

150 O, from what pow'r hast thou this pow'rful might
With insufficiency my heart to sway?
To make me give the lie to my true sight
4 And swear that brightness doth not grace the day?
Whence hast thou this becoming of things ill,
That in the very refuse of thy deeds
There is such strength and warrantise of skill
8 That in my mind thy worst all best exceeds?
Who taught thee how to make me love thee more,
The more I hear and see just cause of hate?
O, though I love what others do abhor,
12 With others thou shouldst not abhor my state:
   If thy unworthiness raised love in me,
   More worthy I to be beloved of thee.

151 Love is too young to know what conscience is;
Yet who knows not conscience is born of love?
Then, gentle cheater, urge not my amiss,
4 Lest guilty of my faults thy sweet self prove.
For, thou betraying me, I do betray
My nobler part to my gross body's treason;
My soul doth tell my body that he may
8 Triumph in love; flesh stays no farther reason,
But, rising at thy name, doth point out thee
As his triumphant prize. Proud of this pride,
He is contented thy poor drudge to be,
12 To stand in thy affairs, fall by thy side.
   No want of conscience hold it that I call
   Her 'love' for whose dear love I rise and fall.

152 In loving thee thou know'st I am forsworn,
But thou art twice forsworn, to me love swearing;
In act thy bed-vow broke, and new faith torn
4 In vowing new hate after new love bearing.
But why of two oaths' breach do I accuse thee
When I break twenty? I am perjured most,
For all my vows are oaths but to misuse thee,
8 And all my honest faith in thee is lost;
For I have sworn deep oaths of thy deep kindness,
Oaths of thy love, thy truth, thy constancy;
And, to enlighten thee, gave eyes to blindness,
12 Or made them swear against the thing they see;
   For I have sworn thee fair: more perjured eye,
   To swear against the truth so foul a lie.

153 Cupid laid by his brand and fell asleep:
A maid of Dian's this advantage found
And his love-kindling fire did quickly steep
4 In a cold valley-fountain of that ground;
Which borrowed from this holy fire of Love
A dateless lively heat, still to endure,
And grew a seething bath, which yet men prove
8 Against strange maladies a sovereign cure.
But at my mistress' eye Love's brand new-fired,
The boy for trial needs would touch my breast;
I, sick withal, the help of bath desired
12 And thither hied, a sad distempered guest,
   But found no cure: the bath for my help lies
   Where Cupid got new fire, my mistress' eyes.

154 The little Love-god, lying once asleep,
Laid by his side his heart-inflaming brand,
Whilst many nymphs that vowed chaste life to keep
4 Came tripping by; but in her maiden hand
The fairest votary took up that fire
Which many legions of true hearts had warmed;
And so the general of hot desire
8 Was, sleeping, by a virgin hand disarmed.
This brand she quenchèd in a cool well by,
Which from Love's fire took heat perpetual,
Growing a bath and healthful remedy
12 For men diseased; but I, my mistress' thrall,
   Came there for cure, and this by that I prove:
   Love's fire heats water, water cools not love.

149: 2 *partake* join 3–4 *I forgot . . . myself* i.e. I forget myself 4 *all tyrant* complete self-oppressor 7 *thou lour'st* you frown 8 *present moan* immediate suffering 10 *thy . . . despise* i.e. as to despise serving you 11 *defect* insufficiency (cf. Sonnet 150, l. 2) 14 *Those . . . lov'st* i.e. you love those who can see

150: 2 *sway* rule 4 *that . . . day* (the opposite, that darkness graces the day, is implied) 5 *becoming . . . ill* i.e. power to lend grace to evil things 6 *very . . . deeds* most worthless of your actions 7 *warrantise of skill* warranty of competence 12 *state* i.e. bemused condition

151: 1 *conscience* consciousness, awareness 3 *cheater* betrayer; *urge . . . amiss* i.e. do not press charges against me 8 *stays* awaits; *reason* reasoning 9 *rising* revolting (with *double entendre*) 10 *pride* i.e. heat 13 *want of conscience* lack of awareness

152: 1 *I am forsworn* i.e. have violated my marriage vows 3 *bed-vow* marriage vows; *new faith torn* i.e. a new contract of fidelity torn up 4 *bearing* i.e. professing 7 *but to misuse* i.e. merely to misrepresent 11 *enlighten* brighten; *gave . . . blindness* i.e. made the eyes swear to things they did not see 12 *swear against* i.e. falsely deny 13 *eye* eyes (with a pun on *I*, cf. ll. 11–12)

153: 1 *brand* torch 2 *Dian* Diana, goddess of chastity; *advantage* opportunity 4 *of that ground* i.e. nearby 6 *dateless* eternal; *still* always 7 *grew* became; *yet* to this day 10 *for . . . would* as an experiment had to 11 *withal* therefrom 12 *distempered* diseased

154: 5 *votary* votaress (nymph of Diana) 7 *general* commander (Cupid) 9 *by* nearby 12 *thrall* slave

The parts of Sonnets 153 and 154 having to do with the creation of a hot bath by means of the quenching of Cupid's torch are variations upon a theme treated in various earlier epigrams, including one in fifth-century Greek by Marianus Scholasticus. These sonnets seem detached from the rest of the sequence, and their authenticity has been questioned.

INDEX OF FIRST LINES

INDEX OF FIRST LINES

2. Gray Church S. Dunston in the East   J. Alhallows barking

Lyon kay Billings gate